A Catholic Commentary
on Holy Scripture

ACKNOWLEDGMENT

of the copy of the *Catholic Commentary* presented to Pope Pius XII

SEGRETERIA DI STATO
DI SUA SANTITA

No. 308185

Dal Vaticano, li
January 29, 1954

Dear Dom Orchard

I have the honour to acknowledge, at the august direction of the Holy Father, the copy of *A Catholic Commentary on Holy Scripture* which you in the name of the Editorial Committee presented to Him in the Audience of August 26th last, and also the specially bound copy of the same volume which was subsequently received by His Holiness.

The Sovereign Pontiff would have me convey to you and to all those associated with you in the preparation and publication of this volume, His sentiments of paternal gratification. In the accomplishment of the difficult task of editing a scientific commentary, in small compass, on the entire Bible, you have succeeded in producing a most useful work for all English-speaking countries. It is to be presumed that scholarly research and the zeal for accuracy of the Editorial Committee will further enhance this usefulness by the incorporation of necessary or opportune improvements in the future editions of so valuable a publication.

With the prayer that this Commentary may serve through its diffusion among English-speaking Catholics as an aid towards an increased knowledge and love of the Sacred Scriptures, the Sovereign Pontiff imparts to you, to the members of the Editorial Committee, and to all your associates, His special Apostolic Blessing.

With sentiments of esteem, I remain,
Devotedly yours in Christ,

J. B. MONTINI
Prosecr.

The Reverend
Dom Bernard Orchard, O.S.B.
Ealing Priory
London W. 5

A Catholic Commentary on Holy Scripture

✠

EDITORIAL COMMITTEE

Dom Bernard Orchard M.A. (Cantab.)
General Editor and New Testament Editor

Rev. Edmund F. Sutcliffe S.J., M.A. (Oxon.), L.S.S.
Old Testament Editor

Rev. Reginald C. Fuller D.D., L.S.S.
Secretary of the Catholic Biblical Association

Dom Ralph Russell D.D., M.A. (Oxon.)
Hon. Secretary and Treasurer

WITH A FOREWORD BY
THE CARDINAL ARCHBISHOP OF WESTMINSTER

דְּבַר־אֱלֹהֵינוּ יָקוּם לְעוֹלָם

The word of our God endureth for ever

Isaias 40:8

Thomas Nelson & Sons
TORONTO · NEW YORK · EDINBURGH

Nihil obstat : R. C. Fuller D.D., L.S.S.,
Censor Deputatus

Imprimatur : E. Morrogh Bernard,
Vic. Gen.

Westmonasterii, die 9 Aprilis 1951

FOREWORD

WHEN shortly after my appointment as Archbishop of Westminster at the end of 1943 I learned that some members of the Catholic Biblical Association were contemplating the preparation in one volume of a Catholic Commentary on Holy Scripture, I readily gave this ambitious venture my full approval and blessing. I was well aware of the need of such a work, and I was confident that those who proposed setting about this task were encouraged to do so largely by what our Holy Father, Pope Pius XII, had written earlier that year in his encyclical Divino afflante Spiritu. After dealing with the improved conditions for biblical study, His Holiness had written : ' Now, therefore, that textual criticism has attained such a high level of perfection, biblical scholars have the honourable though not always easy duty of using every endeavour to procure that, as soon as it is possible and opportune, editions of the Sacred Books and the ancient versions shall be prepared by Catholics in conformity with these critical standards ; editions, that is, in which a scrupulous observance of all the laws of criticism shall be combined with the deepest reverence for the sacred text '.

The editorial committee have laboured hard for nine years to produce this commentary. They have realized that their efforts will not produce a ' popular ' work, but all serious readers of the Bible will appreciate the immense value of this commentary. With new translations of Holy Scripture and with the improved presentation of texts which have come about by the devoted interest of publishers, more and more people are reading the Scriptures. There is a need for guidance in this matter and the appearance of this work is most opportune.

In his encyclical the Holy Father referred particularly to the serious obligation incumbent on the faithful to make use of the Scriptures and of the distilled wisdom of those who have endeavoured with great labour to interpret Holy Writ, for, writes the Pope, ' God did not grant the Sacred Books to men to satisfy their curiosity or to provide them with an object of study and research ; these divine oracles were bestowed as the Apostle tells us in order that they might " instruct to salvation by the Faith which is in Christ Jesus " and " that the man of God may be perfect, furnished to every good work " '.

There is no dearth of Catholic scriptural scholars and the committee has been fortunate in having so wide a field from which to select its commentators. Indeed, they are drawn from throughout the English-speaking world, from the secular clergy and the religious orders alike. I am confident that for many years the value of this commentary will be deeply appreciated by all English-speaking Catholics. I thank the Catholic Biblical Association and, in particular, the editorial committee for all they have done in so worthy a cause. Their work has borne great fruit, and I am confident that in welcoming the appearance of this commentary I am speaking for thousands who will appreciate its immense value and scholarship.

✝ Bernard Cardinal Griffin
Archbishop of Westminster

30 April 1952

PREFACE

A CATHOLIC COMMENTARY ON HOLY SCRIPTURE is the result of nine years' work by a group of scholars, who believe that biblical learning must be integrated with traditional Christianity if it is to bear any spiritual message or fruit for modern society. Their endeavour has been to sum up the results of international scholarship during the last fifty years, and put them at the disposal not only of Catholics but also of all those who respect and would be glad to know more of the Catholic Church's teaching on Scripture and of the way in which her members interpret it.

The Commentary thus fills a gap in English theological literature by providing a critical survey of modern biblical knowledge from the standpoint of all those, Catholic and non-Catholic alike, who accept the full doctrine of biblical inspiration. Those who deny in greater or lesser degree the objective truthfulness and the divine inspiration of the Bible have had ample opportunities for stating their views. It is desirable, bearing in mind the recent advances in biblical science, that there should be a more widespread knowledge and appreciation of the viewpoint of the religious body which gave us the Bible and claims it for her very own. Thus we venture to hope that the Commentary will help to restore the Bible to its true place in the culture and worship of the English-speaking nations.

The idea of a one-volume Commentary on Holy Scripture was first put forward at the 1942 meeting of the Catholic Biblical Association at Cambridge. Later on, in December 1943, a small group discussed the project in detail and decided to accept responsibility for it as the Editorial Committee. Archbishop (now Cardinal) Griffin gave his full approval. By a happy coincidence, when the scheme was taking shape, His Holiness Pope Pius XII published (30 September 1943) his encyclical Divino afflante Spiritu, in which he gave further encouragement to undertakings of this kind. The Committee was fortunate in securing the collaboration of Catholic scholars from Great Britain, Australia, Canada, Eire, Malta and the United States of America, as well as two from Austria and Germany.

The work is based on the full acceptance (1) of the divine Inspiration of Holy Scripture and of the teaching and discipline of the Catholic Church as a divine institution owing its origin to Christ himself, and (2) of the assured findings of modern research, in the conviction that there can be no clash between the Word of God and scientific truth. We claim that orthodoxy and freedom of spirit can and ought to go hand in hand to produce a satisfying synthesis. It should be added that this attempt to assess the present state of biblical knowledge from the Catholic standpoint is quite unofficial ; the official teaching of the Church on Holy Scripture is found in the decrees of the various Councils, and in the declarations made from time to time by the Holy See. There is no ' official ' view on any but a minute handful of biblical texts, and there is ample room for diversity of interpretation within the bounds of orthodoxy.

How wide those bounds are, and how effectively faith and learning combine to solve the problems which arise, will be shown, we think, by an unprejudiced reading of this work. We do not claim that all biblical problems are solved here, or solved correctly, but we claim that in principle we have the correct approach to them. It should not be forgotten that all scholars approach the Bible with certain preconceptions. Some of these are dangerous and the more so if unrecognized. Those critics, for example, who refuse to admit the possibility of miracles, automatically modify their interpretation of the texts and fail to account for all the facts. As long as they hold such presuppositions they cannot be expected to assent to the conclusions of this Commentary. Our work will be as unsatisfactory to them as theirs is to us. Yet we who interpret the Bible as children of the Church which possesses the living voice of Christ, have tried to ensure that our work is fully in accord with scientific investigation and right thinking. It has been well said that if Christianity is true, orthodox exegesis has all the advantages.

Contributors have freely stated their own views on their own responsibility. The Committee, however, has occasionally made a correction in a matter of fact and has offered many comments and suggestions, which for the most part have been adopted by the contributor. Any independent insertions of the editors have been initialled. Where there is more than one important and acceptable interpretation of a text, whether proposed by Catholic or non-Catholic, the alternatives have been stated, though the scope and character of the Commentary as well as considerations of space have precluded any extensive exposition of some of the more recently expressed views in Old Testament and New Testament criticism. Discussion of the main unorthodox positions has been relegated for the most part to the introductory articles. The preferences of individual contributors have naturally resulted in divergences on particular points of exegesis and on such matters as chronology, the interpretation of some Old Testament books, authorship in the Pentateuch, the synoptic problem and eschatology. Views not accepted by the contributor have been recorded with the respect required by the Holy Father in *Divino afflante Spiritu*.

Attention is drawn to the following points :

(1) The chief object of the Commentary is to open to the reader the true sense, the doctrinal import and, as far as may be, the spiritual value and marvellous beauty of the Word of God.

(2) The Douay Version of the Bible has been taken as basis ; it is the version still in widest circulation among Catholics. But the aim of every commentator has been to control it throughout by reference to the original text, and all important variations are noted. The Commentary assumes that the reader has a copy of this Version at hand, but it can easily be used in conjunction with the Authorized or Revised Version, or with more recent translations, such as the Westminster Version or Monsignor Knox's, to which many references are made.

(3) In the commentaries on individual Books a special endeavour is made to give adequate treatment to the doctrinal and spiritual content. Wherever possible the comment is so worded as to provide answers to current unorthodox views.

(4) The introductory articles, while preserving as far as possible the direct exposition of Catholic teaching, also take into consideration widely held unorthodox positions.

(5) Selected bibliographies are given for each Book and article. The mention of non-Catholic works in the bibliographies and elsewhere is not itself an indication that they are recommended to the Catholic public in general ; it means that scientific study must take account of them.

(6) The maps make full use of the modern Palestine Survey and of the researches of the Dominican School in Jerusalem.

(7) Each contributor has been responsible for checking his own references.

Acknowledgements. The grateful thanks of the Editorial Committee are due in the first place to His Eminence Cardinal Griffin for his patronage and warm support ; to the Right Reverend Abbot R. S. Trafford and the Very Reverend F. Mangan, S.J., then Jesuit Provincial, for the support and encouragement which made possible the inception of the project ; to the Abbot of Downside, the Prior of Ealing, the Rectors of Heythrop College and the President of St Edmund's College, Ware, for their hospitality to the Committee on many occasions ; to Mr Peter Morrison, the Managing Director of Messrs Thomas Nelson and Sons, for his belief in the enterprise, and for his unfailing patience, understanding and friendship, and to his Editorial Staff ; to Mr B. C. Widdowson, for supplying the materials for the maps, and to the Rev. H. Richards for helping to complete the topography ; to the Rev. E. Power, S.J. for his advice on topographical questions and for his unfailing support at all times ; to Mr Kenneth Thompson, for his devoted work in the compilation of the Index and for the valuable assistance he has rendered to the Editors in preparing the text for publication ; to the many friends, impossible to name, who have helped us from time to time ; and, certainly not least, to all our contributors, whose labours, often involving great sacrifice, have now borne fruit in a common work which we hope will stand the test of time.

We cannot conclude without asking our readers' prayers for the two contributors who did not live to see the completion of this work, the late Fr Hugh Pope, O.P., one of the pioneers of modern Catholic Biblical scholarship in this country, whose own contribution has since been expanded and revised by Fr Sebastian Bullough, O.P. ; and the late Rev. E. C. Messenger, Ph.D., who died last year after a long illness.

BERNARD ORCHARD, O.S.B.
EDMUND F. SUTCLIFFE, S.J.
R. C. FULLER
RALPH RUSSELL, O.S.B.

EALING PRIORY, W.5
30 September 1952

LIST OF CONTRIBUTORS

BARTON, Right Rev. Mgr J. M. T., D.D., L.S.S., F.S.A., Consultor of the Pontifical Biblical Commission, sometime Professor of Sacred Scripture, St Edmund's College, Ware, President (1952) of the Society for Old Testament Study

BÉVENOT, Rev. M., S.J., M.A., Professor of Fundamental Theology at Heythrop College, Oxon.

BIRD, Right Rev. Mgr T. E., D.D., Ph.D., sometime Professor of Sacred Scripture, Oscott College

BULLOUGH, Rev. S., O.P., M.A., S.T.Lect. & Lic., Scripture Master, Blackfriars School, Laxton

BUTLER, Right Rev. Dom B. Christopher, O.S.B., M.A., Abbot of Downside

CORBISHLEY, Rev. T., S.J., M.A., Master of Campion Hall, Oxford

CREHAN, Rev. Joseph H., S.J., M.A., Professor of Fundamental Theology, Heythrop College, Oxon.

DESSAIN, Rev. C. Stephen, M.A.

DeVINE, Rev. Charles F., C.SS.R., L.S.S., Professor of Sacred Scripture and Hebrew at St Alphonsus Seminary, Woodstock, Ontario

DYSON, Rev. R. A., S.J., S.T.D., L.S.S., Professor of Old Testament Exegesis at the Pontifical Biblical Institute, Rome

FOSTER, Rev. R. J., S.T.L., L.S.S., Professor of Sacred Scripture, Oscott College

FULLER, Rev. R. C., D.D., L.S.S., sometime Professor of Sacred Scripture, St Edmund's College, Ware, Editor of *Scripture*

GINNS, Rev. R., O.P., S.T.M., L.S.S., sometime Professor of Sacred Scripture, Lector Primarius at the Dominican House of Philosophy, Hawkesyard Priory

GRAF, Rev. Dom E., sometime Lecturer in Sacred Scripture, St Mary's Abbey, Buckfast

GRAHAM, Very Rev. Dom A., S.T.L., sometime Professor of Dogmatic Theology, Ampleforth Abbey

GUTWENGER, Rev. E., S.J., D.D., Ph.D., Professor at Innsbruck; sometime Professor of Fundamental Theology at Heythrop College

HODOUS, Rev. E. J., S.J., M.A., S.T.L., L.S.S., Professor of New Testament, West Baden College, Indiana, U.S.A.

JONES, Rev. A., S.T.L., L.S.S., Professor of Sacred Scripture and Hebrew, Upholland College, Wigan

KEARNS, Rev. C. J., O.P., D.S.S., Professor of Sacred Scripture, Dominican House of Studies, St Mary's, Tallaght, Co. Dublin

LATTEY, Rev. C., S.J., M.A., sometime Professor of Sacred Scripture, Heythrop College; President (1947) of the Society for Old Testament Study

LEAHY, Rev. D. J., D.D., Ph.D., L.S.S., Professor of Sacred Scripture, St John's Seminary, Wonersh

LEAHY, Rev. M., S.T.L., L.S.S., Old Testament Professor, St Patrick's College, Maynooth

LEONARD, Rev. W., D.D., Ph.D., D.S.S., sometime Professor of Sacred Scripture at St Patrick's Seminary, Manly, Sydney, N.S.W.

McKAY, Rev. Hugh, O.F.M., D.D., Professor of Sacred Scripture and Hebrew in the English Franciscan Province

McKENZIE, Rev. John L., S.J., M.A., S.T.D., Professor of Old Testament Exegesis and Hebrew, West Baden College, Indiana, U.S.A.

MACKENZIE, Rev. R. A. F., S.J., M.A., S.T.L., L.S.S., Professor of Old Testament Exegesis, Jesuit Seminary, Toronto, Canada

MARTINDALE, Rev. C. C., S.J., M.A.

† MESSENGER, Rev. E. C., Ph.D., sometime Professor of Philosophy, St Edmund's College, Ware

MORRIS, Rev. P. J., D.D., L.S.S., Professor of Sacred Scripture at St Joseph's College, Mill Hill

O'FLYNN, Rev. John A., L.S.S., New Testament Professor, St Patrick's College, Maynooth ; Lecturer in Biblical Theology, University College, Dublin

O'HERLIHY, Rev. D. J., Ph.D., D.D., L.S.S., Vice-Rector of the Irish College, Rome ; sometime Professor of Sacred Scripture, All Hallows College, Dublin

ORCHARD, Rev. Dom Bernard, M.A., sometime Lecturer in Sacred Scripture, Downside Abbey

† POPE, Rev. H., O.P., S.T.M., D.S.S., sometime Professor of Sacred Scripture in the English Dominican Province

POWER, Rev. E., S.J., Doct. Ling. Or., Professor of Sacred Scripture at Milltown Park, Dublin, sometime Professor of Biblical Archaeology and Geography, Arabic and Syriac at the Pontifical Biblical Institute, Rome

REES, Rev. W., M.A., B.Litt.

RUSSELL, Rev. Dom R., M.A., D.D., Professor of Dogmatic Theology, Downside Abbey

RYAN, Rev. C., D.D., L.S.S., Professor of Sacred Scripture, St Patrick's College, Thurles

SAYDON, Very Rev. Mgr P. P., D.D., L.S.S., Professor of Sacred Scripture at the Royal University, Valletta, Malta

SHEARER, Rev. S., C.P., sometime Lecturer in Sacred Scripture, St Anne's Retreat, Sutton, St Helens

SMYTH, Rev. K., S.J., M.A., Ph.D., Professor of Fundamental Theology, Milltown Park, Dublin

SUTCLIFFE, Rev. E. F., S.J., M.A., L.S.S., Professor of Old Testament Exegesis and Hebrew, Heythrop College, Oxon.

THEISSEN, Rev. A., D.D., sometime Professor of Sacred Scripture, Ushaw College, Durham ; Professor of Sacred Scripture, Priesterseminar, Cologne

WILLMERING, Rev. H., S.J., M.A., L.S.S., New Testament Professor, St Mary's College, St Mary's Kansas, U.S.A.

CONTENTS

ARTICLES OF GENERAL INTRODUCTION

ARTICLES OF INTRODUCTION TO THE OT

COMMENTARIES

CONTENTS

ARTICLES OF INTRODUCTION TO THE NT

COMMENTARIES

Maps (with Index of Place Names) based on material supplied by B. C. Widdowson Obl. O.S.B., B.A., F.R.G.S., completed by H. Richards S.T.L., L.S.S., and E. Power S.J.

Index (General) Kenneth C. Thompson M.A.

NOTES FOR THE READER

The Commentary is based on the current Douay Version of the Bible, but may be used with any other translation, such as the Westminster Version or Monsignor Knox's Version. The Douay Version is quoted between inverted commas and suggested emendations are printed in italics. Round brackets ( ) indicate omission to be made in the Douay Version.

Wherever possible, the commentary has been arranged according to the sense divisions of the text. Each such division has been given a brief heading indicating the subject-matter. Division of verses are indicated by one of the first letters of the alphabet.

Psalms are quoted according to the Vulgate enumeration, but that of the Revised Version is often added in brackets.

Cross-references and index references are given by section number and letter (and *not* by page numbers). Cross-references are not intended to take the place of the index, which is very full and will also be found a valuable guide to biblical theology.

A list of *abbreviations and transliterations* will be found on pages xiv–xvi.

The *bibliographies* are selective. The names of non-Catholic writers are marked with an asterisk. Their inclusion does not necessarily imply that they are recommended for general use. Index figures above dates in the bibliographies indicate the number of the edition.

Spelling of proper names. The Douay Version has been followed for names of persons except where some other form is universally accepted, as in the case of Assyrian kings. Similarly geographical names have been adapted as far as possible to conform to current usage.

Every effort has been made to ensure accuracy. But ' humanum est errare ', and the Committee would welcome notification of errors or misprints as well as suggestions for improvements. All such comments and suggestions should be forwarded to the General Editor, or to the Old Testament editor in matters concerning the Old Testament.

ABBREVIATIONS

★

BOOKS OF THE BIBLE

Old Testament : Gen Ex Lev Num Deut Jos Jg Ru Kg Par Esd Neh Tob Jdt Est Job Ps Prov Eccl Cant Wis Ecclus Is Jer Lam Bar Ez Dan Os Jl Am Abd Jon Mic Nah Hab Soph Agg Zach Mal Mac

New Testament : Mt Mk Lk Jn Ac Rom Cor Gal Eph Phil Col Thess Tim Tit Phm Heb Jas Pet Jn Jude Apoc

OTHER WORKS AND WRITERS

In all references to periodicals the number of the volume, the year of its publication and the page number are given in this form :

> RB 48 (1939) 181–206, which stands for *Revue Biblique*, volume 48, published in 1939, pages 181–206

Serial modern editions of ancient works and works in more than one volume are quoted by volume and column (or page, if the columns are not numbered), thus :

> PL 35, 420—which stands for *Patres Latini* (Migne), vol. 35, col. 420 ;
> and DBV(S) 3 (1936) 318–524 which stands for volume 3 of the Supplement
> to Vigouroux's *Dictionnaire de la Bible*, published in 1936, columns 318–524

AAS	Acta Apostolicae Sedis
AASOR	Annual of the American Schools of Oriental Research
AER	American Ecclesiastical Review
AJSLL	American Journal of Semitic Languages and Literature
Amb.	St Ambrose
AOT	H. Gressmann, *Altorientalische Texte*, Berlin und Leipzig, 1926²
Aquin.	St Thomas Aquinas
ASML	Abbott-Smith, *Manual Lexicon of the Greek New Testament*
ASS	Acta Sanctae Sedis
AtAb	*Alttestamentliche Abhandlungen*
ATAT	H. Gressmann, *Altorientalische Texte zum Alten Testament*, Berlin und Leipzig, 1926²
Ath.	St Athanasius
Aug.	St Augustine
BA	Biblical Archaeologist
BASOR	Bulletin of the American Schools of Oriental Research
BB	Bonn Bible Series
BBSAJ	Bulletin of the British School of Archaeology, Jerusalem
BDB	*Hebrew and English Lexicon*, ed. Brown, Driver and Briggs, Oxford, 1906
BEJC	Bonsirven, *Les Enseignements de Jésus-Christ*, 1946
BEP	Bonsirven, *L'Evangile de Paul*, 1948
BEREP	Bonsirven, *Exégèse Rabbinique et Exégèse Paulinienne*, 1939

Bfr	Blackfriars
BGDW	Bauer, *Griechisch-deutsches Wörterbuch*, Berlin, 1937³
Bi	Biblica
BJP	Bonsirven, *Le Judaïsme Palestinien*, 2 vols, 1935
BJRL	Bulletin of the John Rylands Library
Bs	Bibliotheca Sacra
BS	Biblische Studien
BZ	Biblische Zeitschrift
CAH	*Cambridge Ancient History*
CAP	Charles, *Apocrypha and Pseudepigrapha*, 2 vols, Oxford, 1913
CB	Corpus Berolinense (Die griechischen christlichen Schriftsteller der ersten drei Jahrhunderte, Leipzig, 1897–)
CBi	Century Bible
CBQ	Catholic Biblical Quarterly
CBSC	Cambridge Bible for Schools & Colleges
CE	Catholic Encyclopaedia
Chrys.	St John Chrysostom
CIC	Codex Iuris Canonici
CIS	Corpus Inscriptionum Semiticarum
Civ. Catt.	Civiltà Cattolica
CM	Cornely-Merk, *Compendium Introductionis*
CNT	Commentary on the *NT* (C.B.A. of America, 1942)
Coll. Brug.	Collationes Brugenses
CR	Clergy Review
CSAB	*Catholic Student's Aids to the Bible*, revised ed. 1926–37, by Rev. H. Pope, O.P.

CSEL	Corpus Scriptorum Ecclesiasticorum Latinorum, Vindobonae
CSS	Cursus Scripturae Sacrae, Paris, 1890–
CSSL	Cambridge Summer School Lectures
Cyr. Alex.	St Cyril of Alexandria
DAC	*Dictionnaire d'Archéologie Chrét. et de Liturgie* (Cabrol), 1907–
DAFC	*Dictionnaire Apologétique de la Foi Catholique*
DAS	Encyclical, *Divino afflante Spiritu* (1943)
DbR	Dublin Review
DBV	*Dictionnaire de la Bible* (Vigouroux) ; (S) = Supplement
DHPH	Desnoyers, *Histoire du peuple hébreu*
Dict. Spir.	*Dictionnaire de Spiritualité*
DR	Downside Review
DTC	*Dictionnaire de Théologie Catholique*
Dz	Denzinger-Bannwart, *Enchiridion Symbolorum*
EB	*Enchiridion Biblicum*
EBCB	*Encyclopaedia Biblica*, ed. Cheyne and Black
EcR	Ecclesiastical Review
Edersheim	Edersheim, *Jesus the Messiah*, 2 vols
EE	Estudios Eclesiasticos
EHAT	*Exegetisches Handbuch zum Alten Testament*
ER	Etudes Religieuses (Paris, 1856–)
EREH	*Encyclopaedia of Religion and Ethics*, ed. Hastings, 1908–21
ERS	Lagrange, *Etudes sur les Religions sémitiques*, Paris, 1905²
ET	Expository Times
ETL	Ephemerides Theologicae Lovanienses
Eus. HE	Eusebius, *Ecclesiastical History*
Exp	Expositor
FSAC	W. F. Albright, *From the Stone Age to Christianity*, Baltimore, 1940
Ges.	Gesenius' *Hebrew Dictionary*
GK	Gesenius' *Hebrew Grammar*, ed. E. Kautzsch. Eng. ed. revised by A. E. Cowley
Greg.	St Gregory the Great ; also = Gregorianum
GT	Gressmann, *Altorientalische Texte zum Alten Testament*, Berlin and Leipzig, 1926²
HAT	*Handkommentar zum Alten Testament*
HDB	Hastings' *Dictionary of the Bible*
HDT	Lebreton, *History of the Dogma of the Trinity*
HE	*Historia Ecclesiastica* (Eusebius)
H-G	Höpfl-Gut, *Compendium Introductionis*, Romae
Hier.	St Jerome
HJ	Hibbert Journal
Holz. Hist.	U. Holzmeister, S.J., *Historia Aetatis Novi Testamenti*, Romae, 1932
Holz. Chron.	Holzmeister, *Chronologia Vitae Christi*, Romae, 1933
HPR	American Homiletic and Pastoral Review
HRCS	Hatch and Redpath, *Concordance to the Septuagint*, 1897–1906
HTR	Harvard Theological Review
ICC	International Critical Commentary
IER	Irish Ecclesiastical Record
Ign. Ant.	St Ignatius of Antioch
ITQ	Irish Theological Quarterly
JAOS	Journal of the American Oriental Society
JBL	Journal of Biblical Literature (New York)
JE	*Jewish Encyclopedia*
Jer.	St Jerome
JNES	Journal of Near Eastern Studies
Jos. *Ant.*	Josephus, *Antiquities*
Jos. *B.J.*	Josephus, *De Bello Judaico*
Jos.*c.Ap.*	Josephus, *Contra Apionem*
JPOS	Journal of the Palestine Oriental Society
JRB	Bulletin of the John Rylands Library
JRel	Journal of Religion
JTS	Journal of Theological Studies (Oxford)

KAT	*Kommentar zum Alten Testament*
KHK	*Kurzer Handkommentar zum Alten Testament*
KIB	Keilinochriftliche Bibliothek
Knab.	J. Knabenbauer, S.J.
KNT	*New Testament in English*, trans. Knox, 1945
KTW	*Theologisches Wörterbuch zum NT* h. v. G. Kittel (1932–)
Lagr.	M.-J. Lagrange, O.P.
Lebr. ODT	J. Lebreton, S.J., *Les Origines du Dogme de la Trinité*, 1910
LERS	Lagrange, *Etudes sur les Religions sémitiques*, Paris, 1903²
LEJC	Lagrange, *L'Evangile de Jésus-Christ*
LGJC	Lagrange, *Gospel of Jesus Christ*, 1938 [Eng. ed. of above]
LOT	Driver, *Introduction to the Literature of the Old Testament*, Edinburgh, 1929⁹
LTK	*Lexikon für Theologie und Kirche* (Buchberger)
MCC	Encyclical, *Mystici Corporis Christi* (1943)
MGC	Moulton and Geden's *Concordance to Greek NT*
MMV	Moulton and Milligan's *Vocabulary of the Greek Testament*, 1930
Mn	The Month
NP	*Novum Psalterium* (Pontificii Instituti Biblici)
NRT	Nouvelle Revue Théologique (Tournai)
NtAb	*Neutestamentliche Abhandlungen*
ODT	Lebreton, *Origines du Dogme de la Trinité*
OLF	Oxford Library of the Fathers
Orig.	Origen
PCB	Peake's Commentary on the Bible
PD	Encyclical, *Providentissimus Deus* (1893)
PEF	Palestine Exploration Fund Quarterly Statement (1855–1937)
PEQ	Palestine Exploration Quarterly (1937–)
PG	Patrologia Graeca (Migne)
PJB	Palästina-Jahrbuch
PL	Patrologia Latina (Migne)
PW	Pauly-Wissowa, *Real-encyclopädie der classischen Altertumswissenschaft*, 1894–
RA	Revue Apologétique
RB	Revue Biblique
RBn	Revue Bénédictine (Maredsous)
RCF	Revue du Clergé français
RHE	Revue d'Histoire Ecclésiastique (Louvain)
RHPR	Revue d'Histoire et de Philosophie Religieuse
RSPT	Revue des Sciences Philosophiques et Théologiques
RSR	Recherches de Science Religieuse
RSRS	Robertson Smith, *Religion of the Semites*
RT	Revue Thomiste
SB	Strack und Billerbeck, *Kommentar zum N.T. aus Talmud und Midrasch*, 1922–8
SC	Studia Catholica (Nijmegen Univ.)
SCSS	Steinmueller's *Companion to Scripture Study*, 3 vols, New York, 1941–3
Sen.	Seneca
SHG	G. A. Smith, *Historical Geography of the Holy Land*
Simon-Prado	H. Simon and J. Prado, *Praelectiones Biblicae*
SP	Encyclical, *Spiritus Paraclitus* (1920)
SPIB	Scripta Pontificii Instituti Biblici
SSCC	Scripturae Sacrae Cursus Completus (Migne)
ST	*Summa Theologica* of St Thomas Aquinas
Std	Studies
StKr	*Theologische Studien und Kritiken*

ABBREVIATIONS

Tert. Tertullian
TG *Theologie und Glaube*
Th Rs (NF) Theologische Rundschau (Neue Folge)
TLZ Theologische Literaturzeitung
TPQ Theologische-praktische Quartalschrift (Linz)
TQ Theologische Quartalschrift (Tübingen)
TS Texts & Studies
TU Texte und Untersuchungen zur Geschichte der altchristlichen Literatur (3 series), ed. Harnack and others, Leipzig (1883–   )

VD Verbum Domini
Vg Vulgate (Sixtine-Clementine Edition)
VS 'Verbum Salutis' series

WC Westminster Commentaries
WH Westcott & Hort's ed. of NT
WV Westminster Version
WW Wordsworth & White's Vg NT
WZKM Wiener Zeitschrift für die Kunde des Morgenlandes

ZATW Zeitschrift für die alttestamentliche Wissenschaft
ZDPV Zeitschrift des deutschen Palästina-Vereins
ZKT Zeitschrift für katholische Theologie (Oen.)
ZLG *Novi Testamenti Lexicon Graecum*, auctore F. Zorell, S.J., 1931²
ZNTW Zeitschrift für die neutestamentliche Wissenschaft

OTHER ABBREVIATIONS USED

Aram. Aramaic
AV Authorized Version
Bab. Ba. Baba Bathra
Bab. Tal. Babylonian Talmud
Bk Book
c *circa*, about
cent. century
col, cc column, columns
ch, chh chapter, chapters
CTS Catholic Truth Society
d. or † died
DV Douay Version
E.Tr. English Translation
EVV English Versions (AV + RV)
f., ff. following verse(s), chapter(s), page(s), etc.
Gk Greek
Heb. Hebrew
HT Hebrew consonantal Text
ibid. in the same place
id. (idem), the same author (person)
Kh. Khirbet (ruins)
lit. literal, literally
loc. cit. in the place last quoted

LXX Septuagint : (A) Codex Alexandrinus ; (B) Codex Vaticanus
Mass. Massorah
MT Massoretic Text
NT New Testament
ob. *obiit*, died
obs. observe, observation
op. cit. in the work last cited, or in the bibliography above
OT Old Testament
Pent Pentateuch
RV Revised Version
RVm marginal reading of RV
Sam Samaritan Pentateuch
SL Sumerian Law
Syn. Synoptic(s)
Syr. Syriac Peshitta Version
s.v. *sub verbo* : under the heading
T. Tell
TB Babylonian Talmud
tr. translation, translated by
VSS Versions
W. West, or Wadi

*

TRANSLITERATION OF HEBREW LETTERS

א = '
ב בּ = b [with dageš] and b [without dageš]
ג גּ = g [with dageš] and g [without dageš]
ד דּ = d [with dageš] and d [without dageš]
ה = h
ו = w [consonantal] and u [vocalic]
ז = z
ח = ḥ
ט = ṭ
י = y
ךּ כ כּ = k [with dageš] and k [without dageš]
ל = l

מ, ם = m
נ, ן = n
ס = s
ע = ʻ
פ פּ ף = p [with dageš] and p [without dageš]
צ, ץ = ṣ
ק = q
ר = r
שׂ = ś
שׁ = š
ת תּ = t [with dageš] and t [without dageš]

Letters with a dageš forte are written twice. Vocal and haṭep šᵉwa (shewa) are written above the line, *e.g.* ḥᵃḵāmîm.
Vowels long by nature are written with a circumflex accent, those long by position with a horizontal line or bar, *e.g.* yôm, dāḇār.

xvi

THE PLACE OF THE BIBLE
IN THE CHURCH

By WILLIAM LEONARD and Dom BERNARD ORCHARD

1a Bibliography—*Concilium Tridentinum* (Görresgesellschaft Ed.) Tom. 5. Acta 1, 528–35; Tom. 12, Tractatus 1, 1–104; F. Cavallera, *La Bible en Langue Vulgaire au Concile de Trente* in *Mélanges Podechard*, 37–56 (1945); R. Bellarmino, *Controversiae : De Verbo Dei*, lib. 4; B. Malou, *La Lecture de la S. Bible en Langue Vulgaire* (2 vols, 1846); E. Mangenot, *Ecriture Sainte* in DTC 4, 2092–2101; J. Pérennès, *Tradition et Magistère* in DAFC; J. B. Franzelin, *De Traditione et Scriptura* (1870); C. Pesch, *De Inspiratione S. Scripturae*—cap. 6, De Perspicuitate et Sufficientia S. Scripturae (1906); H. von Noit, *Ueber Bibelkenntnis und Bibel* (1896); J. Hoffmann, *Die Heilige Schrift ein Volks—und Schulbuch* (1902); H. Höpfl, *Buch der Bücher* (1904); N. Peters, *Kirche und Bibel* (1908); id. *Unsere Bibel* (1929); H. G. Graham, *Where we got the Bible* (1911); A. Stonner, *Vom Sinn und Wert der Heiligen Schrift* (1927); H. Pope, *The Catholic Church and the Bible* (1928); Th. Soiron, *Das Heilige Buch* (1928); Th. Paffrath, *Gott Herr und Vater* (1930); A. d'Alès and P. Vigué, *La Bible et la Théologie* in *Initiation Biblique*, ch. 30, 751–774 (1939); *B. F. Westcott, *The Bible in the Church* (1864); *A. Harnack, *Bible Reading in the Early Church* (1912); *A. C. Paues, *A Fourteenth Century English Biblical Version* (1902); also *A Fourteenth Century Biblical Version* (1904) by the same authoress; *M. Deanesly, *The Lollard Bible and other Medieval English Versions* (1920); B. Smalley, *The Study of the Bible in the Middle Ages* (1941); J. F. H. Tregear, *The First English Bible*, CR, Jan.–Feb. (1946).

b Introductory—It may seem a little strange to begin a work on the Bible with a discussion of its place in the Church rather than with a formal account of its general character and history. But since the true position and authority of the Bible in Christian Society has been most unfortunately confused and obscured in the aftermath of the religious dissensions of the sixteenth century, it seems the most logical and candid thing to state unequivocally at the head of this Volume the conviction underlying the work of all the contributors to it, *viz.* that it is impossible to understand aright the Bible and its message unless the Bible itself be first viewed in its right setting, *i.e.* not merely as the eclectic product of certain outstanding members of that divine society that has existed in the world ever since God called Abram out of Ur of the Chaldees, but rather as the divinely inspired crystallization of the spirit and teaching of that society at times and places specially chosen by the Spirit of God dwelling within it.

It will therefore be well to state at the head of this article that both Church ('the Israel of God') and Bible belong to an order of providence which has destined man to a supernatural end. The divine decree, which elevated mankind from the beginning to fellowship in the divine nature, made necessary a supernatural revelation of God's purpose, of the secrets of his divinity, of the counsels of his wisdom and goodness. This communication of heavenly knowledge began to be made from the day of man's creation and, as God's purpose was not revoked after the fall, but more wonderfully embodied in a plan of redemption, supernatural revelation continued. The preparation of the Redeemer's coming was a progressive revelation, but the definitive manifestation of all God's

purpose on behalf of the human race was made by the **1b** Son of God Incarnate in the fullness of time, *cf.* Heb 1:1. **A living teaching authority is prior to every single c book of Divine Scripture**—There is no evidence for the existence (or destruction) of any divinely-inspired Scriptures of pre-mosaic date. Whatever divine revelation or communication there was in the early days of the human race probably took place by word of mouth only, and was handed on orally from generation to generation. God communicated his message to certain men and they in turn on his behalf transmitted it to their fellow-men in human language. This is what we mean by prophecy, which became a permanent—though variously distributed—institution in Israel, and produced all or nearly all of the forty-five books that form the Old Testament. From Moses onward God made provision that a part of what emanated 'from the chair of Moses' for the instruction of the people should under a charisma associated with and akin to prophetic inspiration be committed to writing. Thus the Bible grew.

We are here concerned, however, not with the Hebrew 'Church' and its Bible but with the Christian Church and the Bible which it partly inherited from Judaism and partly created out of the fund of Christian revelation and history. The same providence, indeed, obtains and is even more visibly in evidence when the Church of Christ begins to execute her divine commission to go out and teach all nations from Judaea to the ends of the earth. It is absurd, even psychologically, that the grace of Pentecost should be dominated by the letter of a book. The fact is that, while the Apostles looked upon themselves primarily as witnesses of Christ, the living organism ' which is the pillar and the ground of truth ' functioned as a *voice*, and its ministers were ' servants of the word ', the term ' word ' meaning the spoken word.

A living voice is not, however, incompatible with **d** a written source of revelation. A written fount of truth has its own special advantages. It is the fixation of a considerable part of the deposit entrusted to the Church. Thus Scripture becomes her patrimony, and is rightly reckoned amongst her greatest treasures. In preaching the living word she has the support of a fixed text. The **revelation** which she holds is, therefore, as the Council of Trent defined, ' **contained in written books and in traditions without writing**—traditions which were received from the mouth of Christ himself and from the Apostles under dictation of the Holy Spirit and have come down to us, delivered, as it were, from hand to hand ' (Sess. iv, EB 46).

We must not, however, imagine Scripture and **e** Tradition to be like two distinct reservoirs receiving the waters of divine truth from distinct and separate springs. There is in a sense but one source of revealed truth, *viz.* divine Tradition, by which is meant the body of revealed truth handed down from the Apostles through the ages and contained in the doctrine, teaching and practice of the Catholic Church. Yet since a large and important part of that revelation was committed to writing both before and after the time of Christ the Church is accustomed to speak of two sources of revelation, oral Tradition and Scripture. The peculiar character and importance of Scripture—the written part of this divine Tradition—derives solely from the

1e fact that it is the inspired word of God, ' a letter written by our heavenly father and transmitted by the sacred writers to the human race in its pilgrimage so far from its heavenly country ' (Chrys. *In Gen. hom.* 2.2).

The two streams of oral Tradition and Scripture happily mix, for in the living magisterium of the Church these are living waters springing together unto life everlasting. It is the Church, the holder of Tradition, that gives life to the dead letter of Scripture. Experience shows that it is only in the life of the Church, the Bride of Christ, that Scripture, divinely inspired as it is, becomes ' living and effectual, and more piercing than any two-edged sword ' (Heb 4:12).

f Since the Bible is not the only source from which the truths of revelation must be drawn, the Fathers of Trent expressly condemned the innovators who made the Bible the sole arbiter of doctrine, rejecting Tradition and substituting individual religious judgement for the judgement of a teaching Church. The things which the Church is commissioned to teach out of the Bible are matters of faith and morals pertinent to the building up of Christian doctrine. In regard to these truths the authority of Tradition and of the Bible is equal. Either one or the other will certify that a certain proposition is in the divine-apostolic deposit. Nevertheless, as we shall see later, the Church is superior to the Bible in the sense that she is the Living Voice of Christ, and therefore the sole infallible interpreter of the inspired Word, whenever an authoritative interpretation is required (§ 39*b*).

Moreover the inspiration of the whole Bible cannot be known from the Bible, but only through the Church. For the biblical Canon can only be established by the Church. Hence it is the Church alone that has made known which are the inspired books (*cf.* §§ 11–18). On the other hand the Church is not directly commissioned to teach everything narrated in the Bible, *e.g.* that Abraham lived in Hebron. Of itself the residence of a patriarch at Hebron does not enter into the edifice of Christian doctrine which guides souls by faith and good works to the bliss of eternity. The infallibility of the Church only pertains to all such necessary matters of faith and morality as lead men to heaven, while the infallibility of the Bible pertains to everything authentically contained in the biblical pages. It would be erroneous, however, to think that the Church has no interest in the fact of Abraham's residence at Hebron. It is asserted in Scripture and is therefore infallibly true. The Church, as the champion of the Bible's inerrancy, has the right to condemn any denial of an authentic biblical statement. At the same time, a secondary fact such as that mentioned from patriarchal history cannot itself directly be matter for a positive infallible definition.

Again the question is sometimes asked whether all revealed truth may not be found at least obscurely in Scripture. It is impossible, however, to make an absolute affirmation in the terms of the above question ; but, relatively speaking, so much is contained in the Bible that it is difficult to assert that certain particular truths of Christian faith and conduct are nowhere found in it. It is, for instance, said that the Bible nowhere teaches the distinction between mortal and venial sin. The distinction, it seems, is nowhere clearly enunciated, but it is hard to say that it cannot be gathered from the whole assemblage of passages where mention is made of great sins such as exclude from the kingdom of God and of other faults which do not seem to be regarded as seriously staining the honour of those who commit them.

g Since Scripture is a communication from an all-loving Providence for the purpose of guiding mankind in the path of perfection (*cf.* § 2), it is clear that it should be studied primarily with a view to one's own spiritual profit. That is, we should seek its spiritual message and apply it to ourselves. This is Bible study *par excellence*, which for its success always requires the help of God's grace. It is of course connected, to a greater or lesser degree, with what we may call scientific Bible study, which aims at elucidating the meaning of the text with the aid both of secular sciences such as philology and 1g archaeology, and of Church Tradition.

Purely scientific Bible study has its own place and h value in biblical matters, but its subordinate position should always be recognized. Such study is ultimately justified only if it helps to make the spiritual content clearer and more readily available. The philological elucidation or literary analysis of a passage may well be elevated to the spiritual plane by the motive of the one carrying it out, but in itself it has no spiritual value. For example, the study of the Synoptic Problem is in itself an exercise in literary criticism that has no more spiritual value for the student than the study of the Baconian theory of Shakespearean authorship, although the materials under discussion, the words of the Bible, are of course infinitely superior from the point of view of their origin.

We shall now proceed to study our subject under the following heads :

A. The Bible as the Book of Spiritual Perfection. i
B. The Church's Love of the Bible :
   1. Her use of the Bible :
      (*a*) In the time of Christ.
      (*b*) In the Apostolic Age.
      (*c*) In the Early Centuries.
      (*d*) In the Dark Ages.
      (*e*) In the Middle Ages.
      (*f*) In Modern Times.
   2. The History of Private Bible Reading.
   3. A Short History of Exegesis.
   4. Direction of Modern Biblical Study :
      (*a*) General Account.
      (*b*) Modern Catholic Biblical Activity.
      (*c*) Achievement of Non-Catholic Scholarship.
C. The Bible as the Church's Exclusive Possession.
D. Appendix on Bible Circulation.

A. THE BOOK OF SPIRITUAL PERFECTION AND SANCTIFICATION

The primary reason why all Catholics should know 2a the Bible well is (as above stated) the advancement of their own personal sanctification, for ' to be ignorant of the Scripture is not to know Christ ' (Jer. *De Stud. Script. ad Paulin., Ep.* 53, 3).

' All Scripture inspired of God is profitable to teach, to reprove, to correct, to instruct in justice : that the man of God may be perfect, furnished to every good work ', 2 Tim 3:16–17. These words of St Paul state clearly that God's purpose in giving the Scriptures to the Catholic Church was to make the man of God perfect. In order that we may ' be perfect as our heavenly Father is perfect ' we must study Jesus Christ, who is, as St John so finely says, ' the exegesis ' of the Father, 1:18. Prayer and good works without the proper direction of our spiritual effort resulting from earnest study of Our Blessed Lord (each according to his capacity) will be without fruit or use. This proper direction of our spiritual effort can result only from the continuous feeding, nay, saturation, of our minds with the teaching and atmosphere of Sacred Writ. For whosoever seeks true perfection by union with God and the perfect knitting of his soul and spirit with the Divinity must steadfastly aim to make himself like his Master Jesus Christ by imitating his virtues as they are depicted for us in the Gospels, Epistles and other New Testament writings (*cf.* § 10*b*).

Nor should we neglect the study of the OT where Christ is seen not so much in his own person but in his mysteries which are there prefigured. It was the Holy Spirit of Jesus, too, that inspired, for example, the writers of the Psalms, and the Books of Wisdom and Ecclesiasticus. What could be more profitable for a young man to meditate upon than Ps 118:33–40 ? Or, for an old man, Ps 70:5, 9–12, 17–19 ?

2a How can one meditate too long on Wis 6–8 describing the attractiveness of Wisdom, or fail to profit from a meditation on Ecclus 31, describing the danger of riches and of the just man's scorn of them ? ' Everything in the Sacred Book shines and glistens even in its outer shell : but the marrow of it is sweeter : if you want the kernel, you must break the shell ' (*Ep.* 69, 9). With these words St Jerome encourages us to persevere in meditating on the Scriptures for our own profit and that of others.

b The fruit and reward of Bible study is, as Pope Pius X tells us, threefold : Spiritual delight, love of Christ and zeal for his cause. St Jerome, writing to his disciple Paula (*Ep.* 30, 13) thus describes that interior satisfaction of spirit : ' Tell me whether you know of anything more sacred than this sacred mystery, anything more delightful than the pleasure found herein ? What food, what honey could be sweeter than to learn of God's Providence, to enter into his shrine and look into the mind of the Creator, to listen to the Lord's words at which the wise of this world laugh, but which are really full of spiritual teaching ? Others may have their wealth, may drink out of jewelled cups, be clad in silks, enjoy popular applause, find it impossible to exhaust their wealth by dissipating it in pleasures of all kinds ; but our delight is to meditate on the Law of the Lord day and night, to knock at his door when shut, to receive our food from the Trinity of Persons, and, under the guidance of the Lord, trample under foot the swelling tumults of this world.'

To know Christ is to love him. And how can our minds be fed with knowledge of his earthly life, save through the Scriptures that record it ?

c **How to study the Bible**—But though the Bible is the Book of Spiritual Perfection no spiritual profit can be derived from its study unless it be undertaken in a prayerful spirit, in piety and humility and in submission of the intellect to the Rule of Faith. We must in fact be prepared to study the Bible on our knees. Being written by the Holy Spirit we ' cannot otherwise read or understand it " than the Holy Spirit by whom it was written demands " ' (Jer. *In Gal*, 5:19). Hence to derive profit from Bible Study, in the true sense, we must live in a state of grace and be prepared like St Jerome to remove whatever in ourselves may prove a hindrance, *i.e.* detach ourselves from the love of the pleasures of this world and seek to form in ourselves ' the mind of Christ '. This latter involves our submission to the teaching authority of the Church of Christ, knowing that there can be nothing set down in the Bible by the Holy Spirit of Jesus that can in any way contradict the teaching of his Church, which is itself infallibly directed by the same Holy Spirit. We therefore follow in all our studies the Rule and Analogy of Faith. Lastly, to derive serious profit from our Bible study we must be as assiduously faithful to it as was Eustochium, the daughter of Paula, St Jerome's favourite disciple, to whom he wrote (*Ep.* 22, 17, 29) : ' Read assiduously and learn as much as you can. Let sleep find you holding your Bible, and when your head nods let it be resting on the sacred page ! '

B. THE CHURCH'S LOVE OF THE BIBLE

3a The love and veneration of the Church for the Bible can best be seen and appreciated by examining her use of it down the course of the centuries.

1. The Church's Use of the Bible—The use of the Bible for instruction is a practice which has descended from the one Master, Christ our Lord, through his Apostles to the Apostolic Church. Some of the Church's children may at times have neglected the Bible too much, but at no period of her history can it be said of her as a body that she kept the inspired writings closed and sealed.

b (*a*) **In the Time of Christ**—The example of our Lord is very striking. He came as one having authority, himself a fountain of wisdom and knowledge, speaking as no man ever spoke, and showing those potent motives of credibility which we call miracles. Yet he **3b** used the inspired Scriptures of the Hebrew people and appealed to them. He recognized them as writings that foretold him, Jn 5:39, as having irrefragable authority, 10:35, as writings of whose ordinances no jot or tittle should pass away, Mt 5:18. He solemnly read them and commented on them, Lk 4:16 ff. ; he made it clear that his life, death and resurrection would be fulfilment of the Scriptures. He pointed out how they testified to his mission and divinity, Mt 22:42 ; 26:64 ; with three texts of Deuteronomy he met the temptations of Satan, Mt 4:4, 7, 10 ; he employed the Scriptures in his instructions to his disciples, Mt 13:14 and to the crowds, Jn 6:45 ; he had recourse to them in rebuking and refuting Pharisees and Sadducees, Mt 8:13 ; 15:8 ; 22:32. The same Christ cites Moses, David, Isaias, Daniel by name, and touches the history of such biblical personages as the Queen of Sheba and Solomon, as Elias and the widow of Sarepta, Eliseus and Naaman the Syrian, Jonas and the Ninevites, Lot and his wife. Two of his seven words on the cross are Psalm passages, and a third contains an allusion to the words of a Psalm. Finally, after his resurrection Jesus explained the Scriptures— the Law, the Prophets and the Psalms, Lk 24:44—and opened the minds of his disciples to understand them.

c (*b*) **In the Apostolic Age**—It is no wonder, in view of this divine example, that the apostolic preaching of the Church's infancy is full of Holy Writ. St Peter's discourses at Jerusalem are mostly tissues of Scripture texts ; similarly the discourse of St James at the Council of Jerusalem and the sermon of St Paul in the synagogue of Pisidian Antioch. All the writings of the NT—Gospels, Acts and Epistles—either abound in scriptural arguments or are dyed with the colours of biblical language and biblical allusion.

St Paul is the Scripturist *par excellence*. It is not merely on account of the number of his citations and biblical arguments, but above all on account of his penetration of the Christian fecundity of the sacred page that we can truly call the Apostle of the Gentiles the great exponent of the Law and the Prophets, which he had learned at the feet of Gamaliel, even before he received the fullness of enlightenment from the Holy Spirit. We also know his view of the power and utility of the Bible as an apostolic instrument (*cf.* Heb 4:12). The same Apostle reminds Timothy that the Holy Scriptures which he had known from childhood were full of saving instruction by the faith which is in Christ Jesus, 2 Tim 3:15. Hence he says to Timothy : ' Attend to reading ', 1 Tim 4:13. Moreover, it is not merely as a Jewish patrimony to be used by Judaeo-Christians that he commends the use of the Bible. Writing to the predominantly Gentile community of Rome, after citing a text as an exhortation to patience and tolerance, he says : ' What things soever were written, were written for our learning : that through patience and the comfort of the Scriptures we might have hope, Rom 15:4. And only five verses further down, he cites no less than four passages from Ps, Deut and Is to show that ' the Gentiles are to glorify God for his mercy '.

d (*c*) **In the Early Centuries**—Those who exercised the office of teaching in the Church realized the cogency of this example of Christ and the Apostles as a law for their own lives. We need only cite two great ecclesiastical writers who sum up that law of Bible study. The beautiful code of priestly duty which St Jerome so elegantly penned to Nepotian contains these words : ' You should read the divine scriptures very frequently ; in fact, sacred reading should never be out of your hands. Learn what you must teach ; hold that genuine form of speech which accords with sound doctrine. . . . The words of a priest should be seasoned with the reading of the Scriptures ' (*Ep. ad Nepotianum*). Similarly that wise book, the *Regula Pastoralis* of St Gregory, which King Alfred translated into Anglo-Saxon, says : ' It is incumbent on those who attend to the office of preaching not to neglect the studious reading of the sacred volume ' (*Reg. Past* 2, 11).

3d Practice did not differ from precept. Certainly the pastors of the Church showed that they regarded the Bible as the indispensable 'sacerdotal book'. A cursory look through the **Apostolic Fathers** with the help of Funk's (or Bihlmeyer's) Scriptural indexes and of the Oxford Committee's *NT in the Apostolic Fathers* will show how permeated with biblical citation, allusion and colour these writings are.

e The earliest **Apologists** who wrote chiefly against paganism had less occasion to use Scripture (whose sacredness and antiquity, however, they do not omit to proclaim), but the vast array of biblical texts in Justin's *Dialogue* may be taken as representative of the Scriptural knowledge of these men (see Goodspeed's ed. with *Index locorum*). Certainly St Irenaeus exhibits an abundance (*cf.* Sanday-Turner *NT S. Irenaei*).

With the foundation of the **Catechetical School** (*Didaskaleion*) **of Alexandria,** a biblical centre in the strict sense of the term came into existence. Although its masters used Greek philosophy and science as a basic preparation, as Philo the Jew had done, their chief and almost exclusive occupation was the reading, exposition and defence of the written word of God. After producing an astounding mass of critical, expository, systematizing work, with Origen (†254) as its colossal genius, the *Didaskaleion* continued its work for a few centuries till after the death of Didymus the Blind (398), and then gradually foundered in the waves of the Origenistic controversies. We are not here concerned with the exaggerations of its allegorism. We should note, however, its strong influence over the East through Gregory Thaumaturgus (†270), through Eusebius of Caesarea (†339), through the Cappadocian Fathers, and also over the West through St Ambrose (†397). Alexandria had its last great exegete in Cyril (†444), the greatest theologian of the Oriental Church.

The rival **School of Antioch,** whose reputed founder was Lucian (†311), and which was, as it were, re-founded by Diodorus of Tarsus, produced a biblical movement which has few parallels in ecclesiastical history. St John Chrysostom (†407), disciple of Diodorus, is not only the prince of orators but the outstanding Catholic exegete of the Greek Church. The Antiochian method as represented by him is, in the main, the Catholic method of biblical exegesis. Syria had a similar master of genius in St Ephraem (†375). These are only a few names from Alexandria, Palestine, Antioch, Cappadocia, Syria, but they are names which show that the Bible was alive in the Catholic Church during that golden age.

f The **Latin Fathers** were not less assiduous and enthusiastic. If some measure of representative proof is required for the years that ended with the fall of the Roman Empire and the coming of a new age, it may suffice to refer to the *Testimonia ad Quirinum* of Cyprian (†258), and to the works of Hilary (†368), Ambrose, Leo and Gregory. **St Jerome** (†420) is the *Doctor Maximus* of Holy Writ, who regarded biblical learning as one of the Church's chief bulwarks (*In Is.* 54, 12). **St Augustine** (†430) left an immense harvest of scriptural discussion, exposition, and biblico-homiletic instruction. With his acute mind he contributed more than any other Father to the opening and exploitation of the theological riches which the Sacred Books contain.

(*d*) **In the Dark Ages.**—Golden ages do not last indefinitely. In a devastated Mediterranean world and in a Europe which had to be re-made and largely conquered for Christian civilization episcopal centres of learning and Bible knowledge could not easily flourish although, indeed, there were such bishops as Isidore of Seville (†636), who strove to be the scholarly educators of their countries.

g The **Monks** did their part valiantly to keep Bible learning alive from the 6th to the 11th cent. True, it was an age of copying manuscripts and exegetical compilation. Nevertheless Bede (†735), Alcuin, Walafrid Strabo, Anselm of Laon (†1109), Peter Damian (†1072) and Lanfranc (†1093) are names which **3g** remind us that the Bible was still a light in those so-called ages of darkness—a darkness out of which came the dawn of Christianity for Teutonic and Slavonic peoples. The splendid manuscripts of the Vulgate made in those centuries, the touching letter of St Boniface (†755) asking for a good copy of six Prophets as a consolation for his old age, the abundance of Scripture found in extant sermons, the wealth of patristic comment gathered into the *Glossa ordinaria* would rather suggest that the Bible was the one book that counted in that age. Moreover, all the sacred ministers of the Church and multitudes of religious were bound, then as now, to the daily recitation or chanting of the Divine Office. This involved not only constant familiarity with the Psalter, but also furnished them with a very considerable course of Scriptural reading (all the Books of the Bible being read through once a year) as well as of patristic lessons which were mostly comments on biblical texts.

(*e*) **In the Middle Ages**—In the 12th cent. the mellif- **h** luous language of **St Bernard** springs from the Bible source ; and in the great Scholastic century which followed, Holy Writ was (what it should be) the soul of theology, and consequently the life of Christian teaching. The greatest of medieval theologians, **St Thomas Aquinas,** was also the Prince of medieval exegetes.

From the Council of Vienne (1311), which introduced chairs of Hebrew and other oriental languages into the universities, to the Council of Trent (1545) the study of the Scriptures benefited from the new knowledge first of Hebrew and then of Greek antiquity, that led to the outstanding achievements of the following age. In 1546 the Council of Trent (Sess. 5 c. 1 *de ref.*) enacted that in cathedrals, monasteries, convents of friars and other religious houses, where study could conveniently flourish, exposition of Scripture should have its due place of honour and should be put in the hands of competent men. The same Council also strictly enacted that the preaching of the word of God should be a prime duty of pastors, so that on Sundays and solemn festivals the people should never be left without the food of God's word (*ibid.* c. 2).

The Bible in Art and Drama—Neither the use of the **i** written and printed page nor the more potent instrument of oral teaching exhausts the means which were employed by the Church to bring the word of salvation to the people. The renaissance of letters and the discovery of printing were great benefits in many ways, but they largely destroyed that visual kind of religious instruction which was so efficacious from the days of the catacombs to the days of Gothic cathedrals. The Bible in colour, chiefly as it appeared in the paintings of the catacombs and of Byzantine and Roman basilicas, the Bible in stone as it was given to the people by Gothic architects and sculptors, the Bible in stained glass in those same countries where Gothic art reigned—these were 'pedagogues to Christ' such as we can now appreciate only if we think back into the true historical atmosphere of the times. The parallel series of Old and New Testament scenes (representing type and antitype) painted on the walls of the parish churches filled the minds of the simplest folk with the truth of Christ, Saviour and Judge, as the real King and Centre of the ages of the world. The hand-drawn 'Bibles of the poor' with their scripts, and, after the invention of printing, the woodcuts with their scripts, continued this method of teaching, but later it was swamped in the prevalence of the printed page. The mystery-plays too of the Middle Ages were a potent factor in spreading knowledge of the Bible, especially among the unlettered.

(*f*) **In Modern Times**—The post-Tridentine period **j** (1560–1700) was like a return of the Age of the Fathers and is deservedly called the second Golden Age of biblical exegesis. Maldonatus and Cornelius a Lapide are but two of a whole host of scholars. There was no book of either Testament that did not find more than one able commentator, and no question of importance

3j at the time which did not exercise the minds of many scholars. The 18th cent. was much less brilliant, Calmet being perhaps the greatest commentator. Yet the biblical rationalism which had Semler for its father at the middle of this century did not find Catholic thought unprepared. On the eve of the 18th cent., **Richard Simon** had, in spite of many errors in his works, laid the foundations of Catholic critico-historical study of the Bible. However, new methods of meeting old and new difficulties do not come to maturity in a day. Simon was much ahead of his time, and it took more than a century for the seed which he cast to come to fruition, and this only after Catholic scholarship had battled with many winds of unorthodox temptation. Here the Holy See was a most beneficent lighthouse, as we shall see.

In the late 18th and early 19th cents., when the Church's enemies thought she was on her deathbed, scriptural activity was at a comparatively low ebb ; but a glance at §§ 29-31 will show that at that time even in Protestant England a great many Catholic editions of the Bible were being issued.

In the past hundred years (since 1858) there has been a tremendous resurgence of Catholic biblical activity in every country of the civilized world, about which more will be found in §§ 43-6.

4a **2. The History of Private Bible Reading**—The world which Christianity first entered was a Greco-Roman world. Greek first and then Latin were its languages. The providential spread of Common Greek made it possible for the Church to use practically one Bible, namely the Greek Bible, and one liturgical language throughout most of the Roman empire for nearly two centuries. From the first half of the 3rd cent. Latin began to prevail as the Christian language throughout the wide domain of the west. In the east Greek remained predominant, although locally Syriac and Coptic and, later, Ethiopic and Armenian and Georgian limited its range. Until the fateful year 410, which marks the success of Germanic irruptions, those who read the Bible read it in Greek or Latin. Private reading of Holy Writ in these languages must have been fairly common. History shows that those who could read and write were not a few, and copies of certain books were astonishingly cheap. Few, indeed, could possess a whole Bible, and parchments were mostly beyond ordinary purses, but ancient authors and papyrological discoveries show what extensive circulation papyrus rolls and even papyrus codices must have had. At the end of the 4th cent. St John Chrysostom suggests that every household in Constantinople, rich and poor, could well be expected to have a copy of the New Testament or a considerable part of it, and that not for show but for constant use.

b There is no evidence that the Church showed herself hostile to Bible reading in those centuries, and, if we speak particularly of vernacular versions, we have the striking fact that in Egypt between the second half of the 3rd and the end of the 6th cent. Holy Scripture was read in four or five different dialects of Coptic, namely, Sahidic, Bohairic, Fayumic, Achmimic and a Subachmimic, which is sometimes called Asyutic. Thus, before the end of the great patristic age (broadly A.D. 500–600) several versions had established themselves in the East. Travelling from Ethiopia to Georgia a man could come into contact with the Scriptures in some ten languages or dialects other than Greek. In the European territories of the patriarchate of Constantinople we know of only two early versions, the Gothic of Ulfilas (Wulfilas) in the 4th cent. and the Slavonic of SS. Cyril and Methodius in the 9th.

c In the patriarchate of the West, Latin was the sole literary language, and it was on the basis of the religion and culture which voiced itself in Latin that the Teutonic peoples were Christianized and civilized. Whoever in western Europe learned to read at all learned Latin. It is no wonder, therefore, that the Latin Bible remained untranslated, till neo-Latin and Teutonic tongues attained some literary development. Anglo-Saxon translators were first in the field (counting **4c** from Caedmon's paraphrase of combined parts of the Bible about 670 to Ven. Bede's translation of St John's Gospel, finished by the dying Saint on the eve of the Ascension 735, and thence to Aelfric's partial translation of the OT about 990). The Norman invasion came to interrupt this growth of an Anglo-Saxon Bible. Meanwhile, before the memorable year 1066, not a great deal had been done in the way of translation on the Continent either. As far as we are aware, no French version had appeared before two Norman-French Psalters came into use about 1100. In lands of German speech there was more activity, the Benedictine monastery of Mondsee being a pioneer with the translation of St Matthew's Gospel in 748. In monasteries like St Gall and Ebersberg we know of translations made in the 10th and 11th cents. by such scholars as Notker Labeo and Abbot Williram. Translation of the Bible into the vernacular had evidently established itself by that time in Germany. According to W. Walther (*Deutsche Bibelübersetzung des MA*) there were about 3,600 manuscripts of complete or partial German Bibles in circulation before printing was invented. Translation, according to needs, and manuscript circulation of translations evidently went on without let or hindrance.

The Carolingian renaissance in France stimulated **d** the use of the Latin language, but did not lead immediately to the upspringing of a French literature. This came only in the age of the Crusades and had its first centre in Normandy. In the course of the 13th cent., however, the stimulus of the University of Paris not only stirred men to revise the Vulgate, but to make a complete translation into French, the first complete French Bible. Things might have been the same in England, only that the English language had to await its victory over Norman French as the national language. The linguistic fusion in which the Anglo-Saxon element gained predominance was scarcely complete before the middle of the 13th cent. It has been said that the Psalter was the only part of the Bible to appear in English between 1250 and the days of the Black Death (the years before 1350). Just over 30 years later (1382) Wyclif's Bible appeared. This is the first Wycliffite Bible. A revised edition from the hand of the Wycliffite John Purvey appeared about 1388, some four years after Wyclif's death.

It may seem surprising that the first complete **Bible** **e** **in English** was produced by heretics, but the fact should be considered in the light of the circumstances. In the first place, at a time when a large part of the population was illiterate there could hardly be any very widespread demand for a version in English. For the educated classes, most of whom were French-speaking and understood Latin, there were versions in both Latin and French. Wyclif and his followers, however, like so many other innovators before and since, felt acutely the need for a vernacular version as a means of propagating their unorthodox opinions. It is not that the Wycliffite translation is in itself unorthodox, but that they could more easily put their private interpretation on a translation in English. It has been well said, however, that even if the Wycliffites had not made one, an English translation would almost certainly have been produced in the 14th cent., for English was by then an established language.

In the event, it was the Wycliffite Bible which became **f** generally used, not only by the common people, but also by the nobility and ecclesiastics. As a translation it was innocuous, as may be seen from extant copies, most of these being Purvey's revision, and once its heretical prologue had been removed there was no special reason why it should not be used by orthodox Catholics. The extant copies, once the property of kings, nobles and religious houses, testify that they were in fact so used. No doubt, a Bible produced by men notorious for unorthodox views was at first regarded with suspicion and even met with opposition. But as

4f time passed and it was seen to contain no erroneous doctrine, it circulated without let or hindrance.

g   This much should suffice against the charge that the Church kept the people in a state of Biblical starvation, and that this was especially the case before the Reformation. England, indeed, may have been slow in the sense explained above ; for historically speaking she has usually been a generation behind the Continent in her ideas. On the Continent vernacular versions had long had wide manuscript circulation, and had come from the printing presses in goodly numbers before Luther's Bible was published. It has been calculated that 104 editions of complete vernacular Bibles were printed before the first Protestant Bible : 20 Italian, 26 French, 19 Flemish, 2 Spanish, 6 Bohemian, 30 German, not to speak of portions of Scripture, especially New Testaments and the Book of Psalms. We may add that the first printed Bible in German appeared at Strassburg as early as 1466.

On Bible reading in England since the Reformation, see §§ 29-31.

h   In the midst of the modern inundation of the world with books whose spirit is earthly the Church has very decisively recommended to her children the pious use of the Bible, cf. the remarkable Brief of Pius VI to Monsignor Antonio Martini (16 Apr. 1778), and the Encyclical *Spiritus Paraclitus* of Benedict XV (5 Sept. 1920) ; cf. also the favour which the Holy See has shown, since its inception in Italy in 1902, to the Pious Society of St Jerome for the diffusion of the Gospels and Acts of the Apostles, and Pope Leo XIII's grant of spiritual favours in the form of Indulgences to spiritual reading made from the Bible : ' The faithful who spend at least a quarter of an hour in reading Holy Scripture with the great reverence due to the Word of God and after the manner of spiritual reading may gain an Indulgence of 300 days ', and a plenary indulgence may be gained monthly by those who make this reading a daily practice, 13 Dec. 1898.

5a 3. A Short History of Exegesis—In our Lord's time there existed in Palestine a rabbinical system of biblical interpretation, but it was in the more scientific atmosphere of the Hellenistic world that Christian biblical exegesis grew up. A beginning had been made amongst the Jews of Alexandria. Gradually, in the hands of several scholars and particularly in the hands of the philosopher Philo († A.D. 42), a system of allegorical interpretation was elaborated which was almost entirely psychological, ethical, metaphysical and un-Messianic. The allegorism of Philo was inherited by the Christian exegetical **School of Alexandria,** but the Messianic typology which was the theological core of Christian interpretation of the OT held its due place. The Christian allegorism, which was often pushed to excess by Origen and others, was rooted in the true principle that the Bible has a deeper meaning than the mere letter can reveal. The historical truth which the words yield, though not denied, was much neglected by Philo, but Christian exegesis, admitting the principle of typology, could never depart so far from the ground truth of history. In this way the Alexandrian school was substantially scientific. Moreover the philological training of its masters, the pioneer work of Origen in systematic theology, and especially the immense critical labour which he devoted to the text forbid us to dub the Alexandrian *didaskaleion* as just nebulous. In one of the Alexandrian Fathers we find the following sober and ' modern ' statement : ' Here (Heb 1:4) it is necessary (as indeed it is right and necessary in all Divine Scripture) to note the time at which the Apostle wrote, and the person about whom, and the point under consideration, lest the reader should from ignorance miss any of these or any like particular and thus be wide of the sense ' (Athanasius, *Contra Arianos* 1, 54). He adds that the eunuch of Queen

Candace was a truly scientific inquirer (φιλομαθής), **5a** when he asked whether Isaias in 53:7 was speaking of himself or of some other person. It should also be remarked that Eusebius, a follower of the Alexandrian School, laid the foundations of biblical ethnography and geography.

The truly scientific character of the **School of b Antioch** is seen both in its theory and its practice. The Antiochians were careful to avoid that play of the imagination which found such easy indulgence in allegorization. They adhered to the letter, while admitting that the Bible leads the mind from smaller to greater realities. This occurs chiefly in the typal relation of Israel to the Christian church. Thus Osee's ' Not-my-people ' becoming ' My people ' is realized only in a small way in Israel, but fully in the abundance of mercy given to the Church called from the Gentiles (cf. Rom 9:25). This perception of higher things through the medium of lower things they called by the technical term *theoria*. The limits of such intellectual perception were determined in a thoroughly scientific way, for the boundaries were the words of the sacred text themselves. The literal and historical sense was never abandoned or neglected ; see Bi (1920) 3-30.

St John Chrysostom, for example, a prominent repre- **c** sentative of this school, was careful to determine the scope of a book and its historical setting. He discusses the exact meaning of words, and considers the context ; he recognizes that divine books, being a mirror of the divine ' economy ', must show a linguistic ' condescension ' analogous to that of the Incarnation, while at the same time presenting *akribeia* or propriety of thought and expression ; he admits only the plain literal sense, an ordinary allegorical sense (as in the wolf at peace with the lamb in Is 11), and a typal sense which he calls a ' prophecy through figure'. The name which he gives to the ascent from the mere letter to the higher sense is *anagogē*.

In the Age of the Scholastics we find a strong **d** development of scientific and in some respects tediously scientific method in the scriptural field. Definition and division were the great instruments of those exact Doctors. They distinguished the various senses of the sacred words with a precision such as had never been attained before ; they estimated the theological weight of texts ; they divided and subdivided and defined the subject-matter of each part ; they investigated the purpose of the writer ; they explained the connexion of ideas. All this labour threw much new light on the meaning of obscure passages. Of scholastic commentaries, especially of those left by Aquinas, it may be said that patience is required to enter into sympathetic appreciation of their method, but once this is done, they richly repay the study of their thoughtful and powerful pages.

Of the **Post-Tridentine Period,** the second ' Golden **e** Age ' of Catholic exegesis (cf. 3j), we need say little here. Its close contact with patristic exposition was its main strength, but textual criticism, biblical geography and archaeology, and even metrology and numismatics received the attention of able scholars. It does not seem too bold to say that Lucas of Bruges deserves to stand amongst the greatest of textual critics, and that Agellius on the Psalms, Maldonatus on the Gospels, Estius on the Pauline Epistles (apart from his Bajanism) have never been surpassed.

Catholic Adoption of Modern Critical and Historical f Methods—During all those centuries Catholic scholarship had mainly concentrated on the doctrinal content of the Bible. This emphasis was undoubtedly right, but, owing to the undeveloped state of historical method, earlier exegesis considerably overlooked the concrete facts of literary origins, of oriental idiom, of the progress of OT revelation, of the ethnic and political environment of the Hebrews and other such philological and historical considerations. Consequently, the application of critical and historical

5f methods to the study of the Bible introduced a new phase of biblical science.

Because of the errors which disfigured the works of Richard Simon (*cf.* § 3j), and more especially because of the political turmoil that filled the second half of the 18th and the first half of the 19th cents., the foundations of critical method laid by this bold and acute pioneer did not quickly prove their utility. Meanwhile natural sciences had developed, history had come to be written according to more critical standards, the study of monuments and the excavation of ancient sites had brought new light from the East ; comparative philology and the scientific study of languages had made rapid progress, and the need had arisen to meet with new methods the rationalism which had invaded many centres of learning.

6a **4. The Direction of Modern Catholic Biblical Study**
(*a*) **General Account**—Owing to the defensive positions into which the Church had been forced after the Reformation, the lead in utilizing these new archaeological and scientific investigations and of the new critical and historical methods fell to the Protestant, and often rationalist, scholars of Holland, France, Germany and Great Britain. They fell not unnaturally into many excesses and absurdities in testing out the new methods and in applying the new knowledge to the study of the Bible. Nevertheless they succeeded in making a tremendous advance in the science of literary and textual criticism, in linguistics and in the knowledge of sacred antiquities, in all of which, for the reasons above stated, Catholics scholars had little share, though they were much impressed by some of the work done. There was in consequence from the beginning of the 19th cent. a tendency among some Catholic scholars to relax the rule of traditional interpretation. The Vatican Council curbed a general rationalistic tendency of this kind which had shown itself in a few authors like Jahn ; but a new crisis was soon to come, which we can only regard as a *felix culpa* in view of the magnificent measures then taken by the Holy See to guide Bible studies into the right path. A false view of inspiration, which allowed that the Bible did actually contain errors in matters of history and natural science, was the label of what came to be known as ' The Broad School '. The spread of this way of thinking from the publication of Lenormant's *Origines de l'histoire d'après la Bible et les traditions des peuples orientaux* (1880) to the appearance of Mgr d'Hulst's article *La Question Biblique* (*Correspondant*, 25 Jan. 1891) was the occasion of Pope Leo's celebrated Encyclical *Providentissimus Deus*. The document was published 18 Nov. 1893, and is justly called the *Magna Charta* of present day biblical studies. The teachings which it inculcated were further enforced and clarified by the Encyclical *Spiritus Paraclitus* of Benedict XV (15 Sept. 1920), and supplemented, as regards their application to present circumstances, by the Encyclical *Divino afflante Spiritu* of Pius XII (30 Sept. 1943). These great pronouncements and the practical provisions made by the Holy See for the promotion of biblical learning during the half century which they cover show where the Church now stands in regard to the scientific study of the Bible.

b The chief purpose of *Providentissimus Deus* was to set forth and defend the Church's doctrine on the absolute truth of the inspired Scriptures. There may be scribal errors in manuscripts, the meaning of a passage may be doubtful, a translator may be at fault ; but in an original Scripture, as it left the hand of the hagiographer, there can be no lapse from truth. The ancient and constant faith of the Church peremptorily disallows any restriction of inspiration to certain parts of the Bible, such, for instance, as doctrinal parts only, and equally forbids the concession that in some points—even a minor point or an *obiter dictum*—the sacred writer may have erred. The formula is that every Scripture is as necessarily inerrant

as it is necessarily impossible that God should be the **6b** Author of error.

After laying down the principles guiding the solution of the main difficulties Pope Leo went on to insist not only on close adherence to the Catholic tradition of interpretation, but also on the use of all modern helps, and especially on the utility of up-to-date introduction, of a knowledge of biblical and other oriental languages, of the critical establishment of the true text, of the rigorous application of sound hermeneutical rules, and of the external illustration of the Bible by apposite erudition—with the proviso that the doctrinal contents of the Bible be not swamped in a flood of philology, history, archaeology and the like.

The Encyclical of Pius XII, *Divino afflante Spiritu*, has, **c** like its predecessors, insisted on the doctrinal content of the Bible, and has supplemented Leo's great charter by commending the use of the scientific instruments and helps which the last half-century has placed at our disposal—helps which change the condition of biblical studies considerably. It has become increasingly easy to acquire a knowledge of oriental languages ; textual criticism has become an exact art, so that the best conditions for the preparation of critical editions of the biblical texts and ancient versions seem to have come in our day ; the means are at hand to bring out the literal sense with a fullness that will increasingly satisfy present-day hunger to know the word of God as it is ; knowledge of the biblical environment—literatures, events, customs, cults of ancient times—has grown in a surprising way ; the discovery of papyri has shed an abundance of light on the times of our Lord and the apostles ; greater attention has been given to the exegesis of the Fathers of the Church ; ancient oriental modes of speech, writing and narrative have been deeply studied.

In view of all this, it will be understood that the **d** time has arrived when the Catholic Church can draw more effectively on the wealth of its exegetical tradition and at the same time apply to the Bible all the varied erudition of the present age. Through modern methods and through the study of the Fathers Pope Pius XII hopes to see realized ' that happy and fruitful combination of the learning and spiritual unction of the ancients with the greater erudition and maturer skill of the moderns, which will bring forth new fruit in the field of Sacred Scripture, a field ever fertile and never sufficiently cultivated '.

Since the publication of *Providentissimus Deus* many **e** provisions have been made by ecclesiastical authority for the promotion of Bible Study. The Biblical School founded at Jerusalem by the Dominicans in 1889 has published the quarterly *Revue Biblique* since 1892 and has, especially through the fertile pens of the late Père J.-M. Lagrange and his colleagues, given the world the admirable series entitled *Études Bibliques*. The Pontifical Biblical Institute, since its foundation in 1909, has done splendid work in forming Professors ; also through its scientific quarterly *Biblica* (since 1920), through its less technical monthly (now bi-monthly) *Verbum Domini* (since 1921), and its numerous other publications. It has a house in Jerusalem, in which city there is (since 1924) also a Franciscan House of higher Biblical Studies to form lectors in Sacred Scripture for the Order.

The founding of the Biblical Commission in 1902 and the subsequent institution of biblical degrees, the programme of Bible studies ordered for Seminaries by Pius X in 1906, and the appointment of a special commission for the revision of the Vulgate (in 1914) are further evidence of the Church's solicitude for the good estate of biblical science.

(*b*) **Modern Catholic Biblical Activity**—This solici- **f** tude of the Church has not been slow in fructifying. The works and periodicals of the Pontifical Biblical Institute at Rome and of the École Biblique of Jerusalem, bear witness to the scholarly thoroughness of much recent Catholic biblical work. Pius XII takes note of this fact : ' It is not only to the regulations,

6f instructions and exhortations of Our Predecessors that we must ascribe the advance which has been made in the knowledge and use of the Sacred Scriptures amongst Catholics ; it is Our pleasing duty to attribute it also in no small measure to the work and labour of all those who have readily complied with these behests, by meditating on the Sacred Scriptures, by their research, writings, teaching and preaching, and by translating and circulating the Sacred Books. The higher schools of Theology and Sacred Scripture, and especially Our Pontifical Biblical Institute, have already produced and are daily producing many scriptural scholars animated by an intense enthusiasm for Holy Writ, who are enkindling the same ardent enthusiasm in the young clergy and diligently imparting to them the learning they have themselves acquired. Not a few of them have promoted and continue to promote biblical science in many ways by their writings also : publishing critical editions of the sacred texts, explaining and commenting upon them, translating them into the vernacular, making them accessible to the faithful for their devout reading and meditation, and studying and utilizing secular sciences which help the interpretation of the Scriptures ', DAS 14.

g Note should also be taken of the spread of biblical associations, of the biblical congresses and biblical weeks held in various places, of the efforts which are being made to propagate the reading and meditation of the Gospel. In the English-speaking world Catholic Biblical Associations have been founded both in the United States of America and in England ; and the example of these two countries is being followed in many other parts of the world. Much remains to be done, especially in elucidating the historical side of the Bible. The deeper study of the mode of inspiration has made it more and more clear not only that the Bible is an oriental book, but also that it must be read in the light of the personal characters, the social and cultural conditions, and the contemporary circumstances of the writers whom the Holy Ghost used as living instruments. The Encyclical *Divino afflante Spiritu* draws attention to these aspects of modern biblical study, and it should be read in its entirety, if a true estimate is to be formed of the freedom with which Catholics can face the many problems remaining to be solved in biblical science. (See also Letter of the Biblical Commission to Cardinal Suhard, § 53*i–m.*)

There can never be too much of the best scholarship dedicated to the study of the Bible, but the Bible can only be satisfactorily understood and expounded by those who bring to it not only adequate scholarship but also the standpoint of revelation and the tradition of its meaning. Without this Catholic requirement the most erudite exegesis will often be at fault.

h **(c) Achievement of non-Catholic Scholarship—** Many earnest religious men and highly competent scholars—who have not been Catholics—have been in the stream of Catholic exegetical tradition in a measure which does honour to their Christian character. Borrowing and applying the terms of a world broadcast by Pope Pius XII on 5 Sept. 1948, to the German Catholic Congress at Mainz, we can only avow the most sincere sympathy towards the quest of those men for the truth of God in the Scriptures, and we look forward, with hope in the power of the Almighty, to the day when we shall all ' be perfect in the same mind and in the same judgement ', holding the fullness of truth in the unity of that Church to which Christ entrusted his teaching, with the promise that he will be with it during all ages till the consummation of the world.

All modern Catholic exegetes are directly or indirectly indebted to the tremendous stream of non-Catholic works on biblical subjects, which flows universally over the western world, for their suggestive ideas, scholarly exegesis and broad and bold hypotheses. These when tested and examined by the touchstone of the Rule of Faith have yielded, and continue to yield, valuable lights and fresh illustration of the truth of God's Word. There is no doubt for instance that in retrospect the controversy over the Wellhausenian **6h** hypothesis (now seen to be false in its main elements) has had the good effect of giving us a deeper understanding of the composition of the Pentateuch. It is in fact one of the principal duties of the Catholic exegete to cull the good essence, like the bee, from every new hypothesis and exegetical suggestion and to incorporate it into the structure of Catholic hermeneutics.

C. THE BIBLE AS THE CHURCH'S EXCLUSIVE POSSESSION

It is the teaching of the Church that the Old **7a** Testament Scriptures were transferred to her ownership by Christ himself in view of her position as the new ' Israel of God ' and the heir of the OT promises ; and that the New Testament Scriptures being written within the Church by some of its members for the benefit of all (or more precisely, within the society of the Catholic Church by Catholics and for Catholics), are likewise her exclusive property, of which she is the absolute Owner, Guardian, Trustee and Interpreter. To those outside her Communion this may seem a fantastic claim, quite out of touch with reality. But as it determines the place of the Bible in the Church it is now time to examine it in some detail.

The Exclusive Owner and Trustee of Scripture—The **b** Church, being the divinely appointed trustee of the whole deposit of revelation, holds the Scriptures as her very own. They are part of the patrimony or dowry that she has received as the Bride of Christ. This truth was fully realized by Irenaeus and Tertullian, who both had to use their pens against the heretics of their time.

Irenaeus writes : ' The proofs being so great, we ought no more to look elsewhere for the truth which it is easy to get from the Church, the Apostles having therein deposited as in a rich storehouse whatsoever belongs to the truth, so that whosoever wishes can receive from her the draught of life. She is the entrance into life ; all the others are thieves and robbers. Therefore we ought to shun them and with all diligence to love what belongs to the Church and to lay hold of the tradition of truth. What then ? Even though a dispute on some small question were to arise, would it not be the proper thing to have recourse to the ancient churches, in which the Apostles lived, and from them to take concerning the present question what is certain and clear ? And even if no Scriptures had been left us by the Apostles themselves, should we not follow the order of tradition which they delivered to those whom they set in charge of the churches ? ' (*Adv. Haer.* 3, 4, 1, *Enchir. Patr.* 213). Tertullian, in a famous work (*De* **c** *praescriptione haereticorum* 37 ; *Enchir. Patr.* 298), argues that heretics should not even be allowed to use the Christian Scriptures, because they no longer belong to the society which has the right of possessing those same Scriptures. These words of Irenaeus and Tertullian **d** against heretics are exceedingly severe. They refer of course to Marcion and Valentine and to their contemporaries who were in the sin of formal heresy, and they are not strictly applicable to the ordinary non-Catholic of the present day. *Formal* heresy extinguishes supernatural faith and separates entirely from Christ. A *formal* heretic is not a Christian even though he may call himself a Christian. It is the legal aspect of this theological truth that Tertullian considers in this remarkable passage.

A phrase occurs in the dogmatic constitution *Dei Filius* of the Vatican Council (*Sess.* 3, Cap. 2. *De revelatione,* EB 62) which does not always receive sufficient attention : ' The Church holds (the books of the Bible) as sacred and canonical, not because, after having been composed by human industry, they afterwards received the approval of her authority, nor again because they contain revelation without error, but because having been written under the inspiration of the Holy Ghost they have God for their author and *as such have been handed to the Church herself* '. The italicized words bring out the point which we have been expounding. The

7d Church is, by God's donation, exclusive Owner and Trustee of the Scriptures. The Scriptures are a sacred trust in her hands. In the course of time she made a careful inventory of them, establishing from the earliest days by use and solemn declaration the full canon which was consecrated by solemn conciliar definition at the Council of Trent. She cannot and never did pretend to live her life without those divine volumes. They contain the written word of God and as such are precious letters from our Father in heaven graciously transmitted through sacred writers to his pilgrim children, providing a solace for their journey to their everlasting country (Chrys., Aug., Greg.) ; they are an immense treasure of heavenly teachings (Chrys., Aug.) ; they are perennial fountains of salvation (Athan.) ; they are rich meadows or delightful gardens in which the flock of Christ can find admirable pastures and delicious refreshment (Aug., Amb.). In affirming the primacy and dominion of the Church in regard to the Scriptures, we in no way detract from their unique value as a sacred patrimony of divine truth. Their singular value comes from the fact that they are not merely a source of revelation but the revealed word of God.

e **The Guardian and Defender**—Because the Bible ranks amongst the most precious jewels of her patrimony, the Church is the Bible's jealous guardian and defender. She exercises a wise vigilance over the purity of its text and sees that it does not circulate amongst her children except they take it from her hands.

8a **The Church's Care for the Purity of the Bible Text**—Since the Jews as a nation did not come into the Church founded by their Messias, the Hebrew Bible soon ceased to be the usual Bible of Christian teaching. Even the Apostles who were undoubtedly acquainted with the Hebrew text mostly cite from the Greek Alexandrian version the **Septuagint** (LXX), which was already, to a considerable extent, the Bible of the Jewish Diaspora. From the first days after Pentecost the Septuagint apparently became the Bible of the youthful Church. We therefore have no record of the solicitude of Christian pastors for the Hebrew and Aramaic texts of the OT. These remained in the hands of the Jews, and by the disposition of providence the Semitic conservatism and rabbinical scrupulosity of early Jewish scholars have secured for those Hebrew Scriptures—those of the Palestinian canon—a conservation which on the whole is singularly satisfying. These carefully copied synagogal manuscripts were the basis of the Latin translation of some forty Old Testament books made from the Hebrew texts by St Jerome.

b The Septuagint was surrounded by diligent ecclesiastical care. As far as we know, the first critical work carried out on this pre-Christian Greek Alexandrian version was due to Origen (†254). The immense work of the Hexapla would alone be sufficient to show that the desire for a pure biblical text was alive in the Church. Two other recensions also obtained currency, that by Hesychius, who is probably the same as a known martyr of the persecution of Diocletian (c 300), and that by Lucian a priest of Antioch martyred at Nicomedia in A.D. 311. Of these recensions St Jerome says : ' Alexandria and Egypt in their Septuagint give praise to the labours of Hesychius ; Constantinople even to Antioch approves the copies of Lucian ; the midway provinces between these read the Palestinian codices prepared by Origen and published by Eusebius and Pamphilus ', *Praef. in Paral.* It will be remembered, that the Hexapla, on which Origen worked for some twenty-eight years, were deposited at Caesarea of Palestine about the year 245. The ' threefold variety ' just mentioned was, no doubt, somewhat confusing, but each Church showed its solicitude to possess a pure form of biblical text. The western churches read the Scriptures in Greek till about the end of the 2nd cent. Two or more complete Latin versions seem to have been already in use by the middle of the 3rd cent. There were also innumerable versions of individual books. Their fidelity to the LXX was so great as to be almost servile, but from an exegetical point of view they were often very poor translations. To remedy this defect and the mistakes of copyists bishops were not inactive. Augustine was very concerned about choosing a version which adhered as closely as possible to the words of the LXX and, at the same time, gave a clear sense. His view of the necessity of emending current copies is expressed emphatically : ' The emendation of codices must be the first object of vigilant care on the part of those who desire to know the Scriptures, that those not emended should give place to emended copies ' (*De Doct. Christ.* 2, 21). **8b**

St Jerome (†420), commissioned and supported by **c** Pope Damasus, was the man of providence to give the Latin Church a splendid version of the Scriptures. Whatever defects the **Vulgate** may have, it is a masterly and majestic version. Its long use by the Roman Church, Mother and Mistress of all the churches, has given this translation a unique consecration. Care for the purity of its text has at intervals up to our own day given rise to critical revisions. There were almost unblemished copies of it in existence at the beginning of the 8th cent., as the great Codex Amiatinus shows, and in the 9th cent. the Alcuinian recension provided Charlemagne's empire with a very pure text. Less extensive emendation was carried out in the 11th cent. by Peter Damian and Lanfranc.

The Vulgate was the first book to be printed. It **d** came from Gutenberg's own press at Mainz about 1452, and about 100 editions had appeared before 1500. Critical endeavours, which properly began only with the **Complutensian Polyglot** and were continued in the Hittorpian editions at Cologne and the Stephanic at Paris, led to the making and multiplication of new Latin versions. Here the Council of Trent intervened, choosing the Vg as the official Latin version and proclaiming its juridical authenticity (*cf.* § 22*f*).

The official **Clementine edition** of 1592 being inadequate, the work of preparing a critical edition of the Vg has been in the hands of a special Benedictine Commission since 1907, and since 1933 has become the special work of the Monastery of St Jerome in Rome. The task of the monks is to restore the text of St Jerome, as far as that is possible. **e**

The foregoing summary, together with the fact that the excellent Sixtine edition of the LXX published in 1586 remained the received Septuagintal text for centuries, will show sufficiently the solicitude of the Church in providing correct copies of the Bible. Further critical work of the most modern kind has been encouraged by the Encyclical *Divino afflante Spiritu* of Sept. 30, 1943. In particular a new Latin translation of the Psalms and Canticles from the Hebrew for use in the Roman Breviary has been prepared by the Pontifical Biblical Institute (*Liber Psalmorum cum Canticis Romani Breviarii*, Rome 1945).

The Church the Sole Interpreter of the Bible—The **9a** Bible is a human book written by men according to current human modes of literary expression, and intended to be understood according to the rules of contemporary human language. Under this aspect the Bible is subject to all the laws of rational interpretation. There is, however, another aspect of the Bible. If it were merely a human book, philological and historical scholarship would suffice to discover and set forth its meaning. But the Bible is more than a human book ; it is a divine book having God for its author. God produced it by giving the supernatural charisma of inspiration to certain writers, and willed their inspired writings to belong to the deposit of truth which is the teaching Church's spiritual patrimony, to be administered by her for the religious enlightenment and eternal salvation of souls. The Church is, therefore, the supreme interpreter of the sacred volumes.

We must, however, understand this in its proper **b** sense. Some non-Catholic works convey the idea

9b that Catholic biblical scholars are entirely ruled by a teaching authority which is conceived as a sort of governmental machine for giving ready decisions and imposing them under threat of censure. The teaching Church—namely, the Pope and Bishops—is represented as holding the sense of every passage of the Bible ready, as it were, *in scrinio pectoris*, so that ecclesiastical interpretation is comparable to a ready-reckoner. According to this absurd view, in order to discover the meaning of a text all one need do is to find out how the local Ordinary, or the Bishops of a province, or the Pope or his representatives understand it ; and there can be no departure from the fixed formulae.

c Now it is quite true that the Church has occasionally forbidden all further controversy for a time on a disputed point, *e.g.* on the nature of efficacious grace in the 17th cent., when so much dust was raised and heat generated that the Church thought it necessary to allow the air to clear before permitting the resumption of the discussion. Similarly at the time of the Modernist Movement within the Church at the beginning of the 20th cent., the situation was so grave that the Biblical Commission, in the interests of Catholic scholars themselves as well as of the Church, had to undertake the delicate task of laying down the boundaries of biblical orthodoxy without killing the spirit of inquiry. Whatever some people may have felt at the time, the wisdom of their decisions has been proved beyond all doubt, (*a*) by the fact that the spirit of inquiry among Catholics after being warned off a false scent and momentarily checked, has resumed the main path with extraordinary success ; (*b*) by the fact that the extremist theories current fifty years ago have now become obsolete and that there has been a general return all along the line towards the Catholic and orthodox position, a movement that is still in full swing.

d An interesting example of how the decision of authority may fruitfully lead an open-minded scholar to change his views is provided by the late Abbot Chapman in his *Matthew, Mark and Luke*, London, 1937. He originally accepted the Two-document Hypothesis, but after its definite rejection by the Biblical Commission (26 June 1912), he determined to review the whole Synoptic problem anew, with the result that he came eventually to the full acceptance of the traditional view of the priority of the *Greek* Matthew over Mark. His scientific exposition of the old tradition is gradually winning its way to acceptance by scholars, and only one who never knew the Abbot would dare to assert that his change of view was lacking in sincerity or tinged by self-deception (*cf.* §§ 610–15).

People outside the Church forget that because she is ' the pillar and ground of truth ' she can afford to wait a few years or a few decades or even a few centuries in order to form an unbiased judgement. For she will never in any event relinquish the known truth for the sake of a passing fashion or some novelty. They also, quite naturally perhaps, fail to realize how fortunate Catholic scholars are in having an authority to point out the pitfalls of the fashionable folly of the moment, and to recommend suspension of judgement when the data are insufficient to justify a definite opinion.

We therefore see that the real purpose of the Biblical Commission is to afford true guidance to the scholar in doubt, without cramping the ardour of genuine scholarship, and Catholics are profoundly grateful to Pope Leo XIII for instituting it (*cf.* also §§ 47–53).

e Certainly the Church has no mechanical method of exegesis, and it would be wrong to regard her as a sort of studious professor of exegesis. She teaches faith and morals out of the two founts of revelation by acts of her ordinary every-day magisterium and sometimes by extraordinary acts of her solemn magisterium. Her judgement on the sense of scriptural texts relating to faith and morals has to mature under the guidance and working of the Holy Spirit, and this happens through the devout study which her Fathers and Doctors and theologians have given and give to the Sacred Page. Authoritative ecclesiastical judge- 9e ment is given only when the situation is clarified.

The teaching of the Church on her own scriptural f magisterium is clearly stated in the Encyclical *Providentissimus Deus* : ' It must be recognized that the sacred writings are wrapped in a certain religious obscurity, so that no one can enter their precincts without a guide. This is God's own arrangement (as the holy Fathers often tell us) in order to compel men to search the Scriptures with more ardent desire and with more earnest study. What is thus obtained from the Scriptures by laborious application will be more deeply impressed on the mind and heart. But God wills men above all to understand that he has delivered the Scriptures to the Church, so that in reading and using his sacred word they must follow the Church as their most certain guide and teacher. From early times St Irenaeus taught that where the charismata of the Lord are found, there the truth is to be learned ; and it is, he says, by those with whom apostolic succession resides that Scripture is expounded without fear of error. This teaching of Irenaeus and of the other Fathers the Vatican Council made its own, when, renewing the decree of Trent on the interpretation of the written word of God, it declared the following to be its mind : " In matters of faith and morals which belong to the building up of Christian doctrine, that sense is to be considered the true sense of Sacred Scripture which our Holy Mother the Church has held and holds. It is her prerogative to judge of the true sense and interpretation of the Holy Scriptures. Consequently no one is permitted to interpret Sacred Scripture contrary to this sense or contrary to the unanimous consent of the Fathers " ' (EB 93).

Pope Leo adds that this wise law of the Church puts g no trammels on biblical science. It is really to its advantage, for it preserves from error and helps it on the way of true progress. The field open before the private scholar is exceedingly wide. He has plenty of scope for his industry, and, while he himself is helped by the Church, he can help her. There are innumerable scriptural passages which have not yet received a certain and final exposition. Here private investigation may serve as an instrument of God's providence. It is in general only after long preparation of study on the part of her members that the judgement of the Church matures. Where the Church has already defined the sense of a passage, the private interpreter can employ himself with equal fruitfulness by setting the ecclesiastical exposition more clearly before the faithful, giving it the support of learning, or defending it from hostile attacks (EB 94).

Freedom of Research—There is no freedom to pursue h falsehood, but in devotedness to truth the liberty of Catholic exegesis is the full freedom of the children of God. Pope Pius XII made this admirably clear in the Encyclical *Divino afflante Spiritu*. His Holiness points out that biblical scholars must not be treated with suspicion when they face difficulties valiantly in their efforts to find interpretations consonant with the teachings of the Church and in harmony with the certain conclusions of the secular sciences. Indiscreetly zealous critics of those hard working labourers in the Vineyard should remember ' that the rules and laws laid down by the Church are concerned with the doctrine of faith and morals ; that among the many matters set forth in the legal, historical, sapiential and prophetic books of the Bible there are only a few whose sense has been declared by the authority of the Church, and equally few concerning which the opinion of the Holy Fathers is unanimous. There consequently remain important matters, in the explanation of which the sagacity and ingenuity of Catholic interpreters can and ought to be freely exercised, so that each in the measure of his powers may contribute to the common good, to the ever-greater advancement of sacred learning, and to the defence and honour of the Church ', AAS, xxxv (1943) 319.

D. APPENDIX ON BIBLE CIRCULATION

10a Vigilance over Bible Circulation—The guardianship of the Church also provides that the Bible shall circulate amongst her children only under her supervision. Her attitude is clearly discernible in her legislation. She has enacted in her canon law that books of Sacred Scripture or notes or commentaries on such books must not be published even by laymen without ecclesiastical permission. This prohibition refers also to books that have to do with Scripture or theology (*Codex Juris Canonici* can. 1385).

Translations of the Sacred Scriptures into vernacular languages may not be printed, unless they are approved by the Apostolic See, or published under the vigilance of the Bishops, and unless they carry notes taken from Catholic sources, especially from the Fathers of the Church and from learned Catholic writers (can. 1391).

Hence, editions of the original text and of the ancient Catholic versions, even those of the Oriental Church, if published by non-Catholics, are thereby forbidden ; likewise translations of Scripture into any language made or published by non-Catholics (can. 1399).

The use of non-Catholic editions of ancient Catholic versions and also of non-Catholic translations and of versions published without approval or notes is, however, permitted to those who devote themselves in any way to theological or biblical studies, provided that the said books are edited with fidelity and integrity, no dogma of Catholic faith being impugned either in their prolegomena or notes (can. 1400), *cf.* § 4*f*. Canon 2318, 2 subjects to the penalty of excommunication (not reserved) Catholic authors and publishers who cause books of the sacred Scriptures, or notes and commentaries on them to be printed without due licence.

In these days of armed neutrality and ideological propaganda there are few who doubt the wisdom of a wise censorship. And just as in the world of commerce big business enterprises employ trademarks and special signs to indicate the high quality of their goods, so for Catholics the *Imprimatur* of a bishop on the frontispiece of a Bible is a guarantee that the text provided is the official—and therefore the authentic —text.

b Is Bible Reading Necessary for Salvation ?—Undoubtedly the Divine Scriptures have been given to the whole Church and to all the children of the Church for their instruction. The Bible is certainly an ordinary and universal means of instruction, but at the same time there is no universal precept, either divine or apostolic, that all the faithful—every man, woman and child—should personally read the Bible. Heaven is open to illiterates. It is the doctrine of the Bible that matters, not knowledge of the letter. Those who teach religion—the pastors of the Church— should know the Book, but the faithful may, according to circumstances, know and live the faith which the Bible teaches without having spelled one sentence of its pages. Even in this present age of paper and of printing numberless Catholics live admirable and even sublime lives of faith, hope and charity without any direct reading of Holy Writ. They nourish their minds with the substance of the Bible through the liturgy of the Mass, through the mysteries of the Rosary, through the prayers which they know by heart, and through the sermons which they hear. Just as in countries which have an old traditional culture illiterate peasants can have an exquisite refinement of soul and manners, so also bookless peasants who have lived in the stream of Christian tradition can have all the grasp of faith and right living which are necessary for any, even the highest, degree of sanctity (*cf.* § 3*i*).

This is not a defence of illiteracy, but a warning against exaggerations. Self-instruction through reading must always be built on a basis of oral instruction received in the home, the school and the Church. The extent to which this supplementary aid can be used will depend on the available supply of books and on the ability of persons to read them fruitfully. Now

these two things have varied considerably at various **10b** times. Some knowledge of this variation of conditions— varying book facilities and varying spread of education —is necessary, in order to understand the wise providence of the Church in regard to the Bible at different times. We must also keep in mind that whenever or wherever reading endangers the purity of Christian thought and living—the *unum necessarium*—it has to be wisely restricted.

The foregoing considerations will help us to view **c** the Church's prohibition of non-Catholic Bibles not as obscurantist and tyrannical oppression, but as a reasonable measure justified by the circumstances.

The Church prevents any such circulation of the Bible amongst her children as is carried on under the pretence of false freedom and with the suggestion of the right of private interpretation. It was this duty of her guardianship that caused the Holy See to condemn the Bible Societies in the 19th cent., as she had condemned their forerunners since the end of the 12th.

The first known measure of this kind is found in two letters of Innocent III to the Church of Metz. They were written at the end of the 12th cent. with reference to a conventicle of men and women who (most probably under Albigensian or Waldensian influences) had several parts of the New Testament and the *Moralia* of St Gregory translated into French. In clandestine meetings these lay folk, men and women, read and discussed the said writings, and showed contempt for the reprimands of their pastors, who evidently regarded their practices as dangerous or schismatic. The Pope ordered a diligent inquiry to be made into the aims of the group, but gave instructions that kindness was to be used towards them in the meantime, in the hope of bringing them to a better mind.

We do not know the sequel of this case, but a Provincial Synod of Toulouse in 1229 prohibited the use of vernacular Scriptures to the laity. The motive of this enactment is plain enough considering that it was made, as it were, in the very heart of Albigensian territory. A very similar decree was issued in the 15th cent. (1408) by a Council of Oxford held under the presidency of Thomas Arundel, Archbishop of Canterbury. It was occasioned by the insubordinate Bible activities of Wyclif and his disciples, and prohibited vernacular translations of the Scriptures, except such as were approved by the diocesan Bishop or by a Provincial Council. There was no question of suppressing vernacular versions *as such*.

By their fruits they are known. Bible study which **d** produces or propagates heresy is a bad thing. In fact, as St Augustine noted, ' heresies have not arisen except when the good Scriptures were not well understood, and what was not well understood in them was rashly and boldly asserted ', *In Jo. Tr.* 18, 1. The circumstances of the times have always to be taken into account, and laws which today seem severe must be judged accordingly. Thus we find that the legislation which obtained under civil authority against vernacular Scriptures in Spain from James I of Aragon to Ferdinand and Isabella (1276–1516) served in no small measure to preserve a Catholic country from the ravages of heresy. Through Luther, although Calvin seems to have been the first to announce Monobiblicism clearly, the Bible became the arm of the Protestant revolt. A dumb and difficult book was substituted for the living voice of the Church, in order that each one should be able to make for himself the religion which suited his feelings. And the Bible open before every literate man and woman to interpret for themselves was the attractive bait used to win adherents. Not the solid rock of truth but the shifting sand of private interpretation is the foundation on which Protestantism was built. It is no wonder then that the Council of Trent drew up censorship regulations, later codified in the 3rd and 4th rules of the Index of 1564.

The utility and *necessity* of universal Bible-reading

10d was also advocated at the end of the 17th cent. by the Jansenist Paschase Quesnel, but his extreme views, in the sense in which he proposed them, were rejected in the condemnation of 101 of his propositions by the dogmatic constitution *Unigenitus* of Clement XI (8 Sept. 1713). Seven of these propositions (79–85 ; Dz 1429–35) refer to Bible reading. The views of Quesnel survived in Jansenistic circles and were again condemned, after they had been formulated by the Synod of Pistoia, in the Bull *Auctorem fidei* of Pius VI (28 Aug. 1794 ; Prop. 67, Dz 1567).

e Protestant Bible Societies—Within the past two hundred years the Church has from time to time had to take action to protect the faithful from the activities of certain Protestant societies publishing and disseminating indiscriminately copies of the Bible without note or comment. The dangerous fallacy underlying their activity is that of the ' private interpretation ' of the Scripture, a principle whose falsity is demonstrated by the infinite and absurd variety of doctrine and opinion wherever it has flourished. Not infrequently also the Sacred Book has been used as an instrument of proselytism against the Catholic Church in Catholic countries.

In condemning these Societies and the principles on which their activities are based the Church is not condemning Bible reading under proper conditions, as we have already noted above, §§ 2, 3, 5.

f The history of the Bible Societies, which is a long one, can only be lightly touched here, for we are only interested in the action of the Holy See in their regard. Before 1800 the Bibelanstalt founded in 1710 by Baron von Canstein at Halle had distributed 33,000,000 Bibles or parts of the Bible. Before the end of the 18th cent. the Society for Promoting Christian Knowledge (SPCK) and the Religious Tract Society were propagating the Bible from London. But the first Bible Society of world-wide scope and organization was the British and Foreign Bible Society (BFBS) founded at London, 7 March 1804. On its model and with its support a number of similar societies sprang into life in Germany, one of which (founded in 1813) is well known internationally, namely, the *Württemberg. Bibelanstalt* which in recent times has published the various editions of Nestle's NT, Kittel's Hebrew Bible, and Rahlf's Septuagint.

Between 1812 and 1815 two Bible enthusiasts, Paterson and Pinkerton, agents of the BFBS, had toured the whole of northern Europe, initiating the **10f** establishment of Bible centres in many cities of Scandinavia, Holland, Germany, Finland and Russia. It was after this invasion of Bible Society activities that the Holy See took action.

The first papal document is a letter of Pius VII to **g** Ignatius Raczynski, Archbishop of Gnesen in Poland, dated 29 June 1816. This prelate had denounced the work of the Bible sectaries who had been dishonestly disseminating the Polish Catholic version of the Jesuit, James Wujek, without note or comment. In praising the Archbishop the Pope recalls the abovementioned rules of the Index of 1564 and the decree of the Index issued under Benedict XIV, 13 June 1757, allowing to Catholics only the use of vernacular versions approved by the Holy See or published with notes taken from the Holy Fathers or learned Catholic interpreters.

On 3 Sept. of the same year, 1816, Pius VII sent a severe letter to Stanislaus Siestrzencewicz-Bohusz, Archbishop of Mohilev, who had approved the propagation of the forbidden versions in his diocese. The Archbishop was neither very Catholic nor very zealous, but a rather unripe convert from Calvinism and a creature of the Empress Catherine II. The Pope explained the Catholic position at considerable length and demanded that the Archbishop should repair the scandal which he had caused.

The other documents where the Bible Societies are mentioned in the same condemnatory terms are the Encyclicals of Leo XII *Ubi primum* (5 May 1824), of Pius VIII (24 May 1829), of Gregory XVI *Inter praecipuos* (6 May 1844), the *Syllabus* of Pius IX (8 Dec. 1864), and the Constitution *Officiorum et munerum* of Leo XIII (15 Jan. 1897).

Admiration for the beautiful and often very useful **h** publications of the Bible Societies must not prevent us from seeing the wisdom of this ecclesiastical attitude. Ancient versions faithfully edited and vernacular versions that are serviceable the Church freely allows to theological or biblical students, but she forbids the faithful generally to take, keep or use the versions of the Bible Societies, because their fundamental intention is to offer the Bible to all in disregard of the laws which the Church has made to keep her members from error. The Church is uncompromising in her guardianship of the truth and she wisely withholds from her children an excessive religious liberty which would lead them into unwholesome pastures.

THE FORMATION AND HISTORY OF THE CANON (OT AND NT)

By R. J. FOSTER

11a Bibliography—S. M. Zarb, O.P., *Historia Canonis Utriusque Testamenti*, Rome (Angelicum), 1934; M. J. Lagrange, O.P., *Histoire Ancienne du Canon du Nouveau Testament*, Paris, 1933; *Initiation Biblique* (ed. A. Robert and A. Tricot), Paris, 1939; H. Pope, O.P., CSAB, vols 1 and 4 London, 1926² and 1931; J. E. Steinmueller, *A Companion to Scripture Studies*, New York, vol. 1, 1941; J. H. Newman, *Development of Christian Doctrine*, London, 1897¹⁰; *B. F. Westcott, *A General Survey of the Canon N.T.*, London, 1896⁷; *H. E. Ryle, *The Canon of the Old Testament*, London, 1892; *A. Rahlfs, *Septuaginta*, Stuttgart, 1935; *F. Kenyon, *Our Bible and the Ancient MSS*, London, 1939⁴; Art. in DTC 2, 1550 ff., DBV 2, 134 ff., CE 3, 267 ff., HDB 3, 604 ff.

b Inspiration—Catholics have never admitted that the inspiration of a book can be judged by its effects upon the mind and heart of the reader. Inspiration is one thing, the power of inspiring is another, depending, as it must, upon the peculiar dispositions of the reader at the time of reading. We shall see later (§§ 34–38) that the inspired books are those which have God for their author. Before, however, we discuss the nature of Inspiration we will first consider the practical but kindred questions : which are the inspired books, what is their number, how do we know that they alone are inspired, why does the Catholic Bible differ from and contain more books than the Protestant Bible ? (*cf.* 13a ff. ; 15d). All these questions lie within the scope of the present article, for the *Canon* of Scripture is precisely the list or collection of books which are inspired.

c Meaning of Canon—The Greek word which gives us the word *Canon* primarily signified a rod or bar, and so came to mean a *measuring rod*. Then it was used metaphorically for any rule or standard of excellence in art or literature—thus the ancient Greek authors were called canons (Κανόνες)—or for a rule of conduct, as by St Paul, Gal 6:16. Similarly, the rules, decisions and decrees, enacted by the Church to be the standard of doctrine, discipline and worship, were called canons, and, for a like reason, men talked of the ' Canon of Scripture ' or of the ' Canonical Scriptures ', because they contained the rule or standard of faith and morals. But this is not the sense in which the phrase ' Canon of Scripture ' is commonly used. The word *Canon* was also used of lists or catalogues, of persons or objects to serve as a rule for distinguishing one from the other (*cf.* H. Stephanus, *Thesaurus Graecae Linguae*, London, 1823², 5, 4762). For example, Ptolemy's *Canon of Kings*, compiled in the 2nd cent. A.D., is a list of Babylonian, Persian, Greek and Roman kings with the length of their reigns (*cf. Cambridge Ancient History*, 1, 149 ; A. Deimel, S. J., *Veteris Testamenti Chronologia*, Rome, 1912, pp 25 ff.). The term ' Canon of Scripture ' might possibly have been used originally in this sense.

However the common understanding of the term is that it denotes *the collection or list of books acknowledged and accepted by the Church as inspired, i.e. Canon* is taken in the passive sense of the books conforming to the ' rule ' for their acceptance as inspired works. In which case the list or catalogue would serve to distinguish the sacred from the profane writings. Similarly books are said to be ' canonical ' or ' canonized ' when

they form part of the Canon. The earliest certain **11c** evidence of this usage is from the works of St Athanasius (*c* 350), although there are some who believe (from indications in Latin versions of his works) that it was used much earlier by Origen (†254). This scriptural Canon comprises the OT and NT, and it is the purpose of the present article to trace the formation and history of both.

THE OT CANON

Its Contents—Both for purpose of reference and the **d** sake of clarity it might be well at the outset to name the present Catholic Canon of the books of the OT. They are, in the order in which they occur in the Vulgate, Genesis, Exodus, Leviticus, Numbers, Deuteronomy, Josue, Judges, Ruth, four Books of Kings (the first two are also called 1 and 2 Samuel), 1 and 2 Paralipomenon (or Chronicles), 1 and 2 Esdras (the second also known as Nehemias), Tobias, Judith, Esther, Job, Psalms, Proverbs, Ecclesiastes, Canticle of Canticles, Wisdom, Ecclesiasticus (Sirach), Isaias, Jeremias, Lamentations, Baruch, Ezechiel, Daniel, 12 Minor Prophets, 1 and 2 Maccabees. To anyone comparing this list with the Protestant OT, it will be apparent that the latter is shorter and does not contain several books referred to as the Deuterocanonical Books, *viz.* Tob, Jdt, Wis, Ecclus, Bar, 1 & 2 Mac, and certain parts of Esther and Daniel, *viz.* Est 10:4–16:24 ; Dan 3:24–90 ; chh 13 & 14. These were found in the Greek Bible adopted by the Church but not in the Palestinian Canon as fixed in post-Christian times, which was the one eventually adopted by the Protestants. The Protocanonical Books, which form the Protestant Canon, therefore consist of the full list of the Catholic Canon given above, less the seven Deuterocanonical Books ; Esther and Daniel count as Protocanonical, though each has its deuterocanonical portion. But a further and fuller discussion of this important question can be given only in the light of the gradual formation and definition of the OT Canon.

FORMATION OF THE OT CANON

Esdras and the Great Synagogue—Nowhere in the **e** Bible do we find a description of the formation of the OT Canon, nor even a list of the books comprising it. The whole question is, therefore, largely one of inference from the evidence available, and the view adopted will depend inevitably upon the date and authorship assigned to the individual books of the Canon. Here we presuppose what is treated in the Special Introductions (*e.g.* the question of the Mosaic authorship of the Pentateuch). For a long time the opinion was current amongst the Jews that the formation and fixing of the Canon was the work of Esdras. It was supposed that Esdras gave it its final form and that no books written after his death were accepted as canonical. The origin of the ascription of this role to Esdras may be traced back to 4 Esd 14:42 ff. (*c* A.D. 95) where we are told that Esdras dictated ninety-four books (there are variant readings of the number), some of which were for the worthy and unworthy to read, and seventy for the wise only. This work is neither inspired nor authentic, and the story lacks foundation. It is

11e true that Esdras played a prominent part in the re-establishment of the observance of the law, but the formation of the Canon was not his work. A later form of the story was set forth in the 16th cent. by the Jewish scholar, Elias Levita, according to whom the Canon was completed by a body of men known as the Great Synagogue, over whom Esdras at one time presided. This suggestion also lacks any solid foundation in Jewish tradition, and to-day it is doubted whether there ever was such a body as the Great Synagogue, in the sense of a permanent body wielding authority. Everything seems to depend upon 2 Esd. 8–10, where, certainly, we read of a great meeting at Jerusalem, which subscribed to the covenant to observe the Law, but where there is nothing to show that it was an authoritative commission (*cf.* *W. Robertson Smith, *The OT in the Jewish Church*, 1892², pp 168 f.).

f **The Beginnings of a Canon**—The formation of the OT Canon must have been gradual, spread over the long course of Israel's history from the time of Moses until the Christian era. Several passages in the earlier OT books point to the beginning and gradual increase of a collection of books held in special esteem (*cf.* CSAB 1, 129 ff. ; 134 ff.). We read that Moses, at God's command, began to write and that he intended his writings to be a permanent record and guide to the Chosen People, *cf.* Deut 31:9–13, and Ex 17:14, where he is told to 'write this for a memorial in the book (bassēper)', its singular character being emphasized by Moses' command to 'put it in the side of the ark that it may be there for a testimony against thee', Deut 31:26. Inspiration did not cease with Moses, nor was it to be limited to his writings, but was to continue through the successive ages (*cf.* Heb 1:1). His successors in the leadership of Israel seem to have added to his work, and, as it were, continued it, *e.g.* Josue (Jos 24:26) and Samuel (1 Kgs 10:25).

Further Development—Later on, there is evidence of another collection of sacred writings, including those of David and Asaph, the Seer, in official use for the praise of God (2 Par 29:30) and of the industry of the scribes of Ezechias in preserving the proverbs of Solomon, Prov 25:1. Moreover, it was to be expected that the prophets, who were so largely responsible for the spiritual welfare and development of Israel, should leave some record of their teaching and prophecy ; and of this, too, there are several indications (Jer 36:4, 32 ; Zach 7:12). Already the nucleus of the later Jewish division of the OT, the Law, Prophets and Writings, is beginning to appear. By the time of the writing of the Prophecy of Daniel, some sort of recognized collection of sacred writings was in existence, for the writer referred to 'the books', Hassᵉpārîm (Dan 9:2), which was to become the most frequent designation for the whole collection of biblical writings (*cf.* JE 3, 140). This does not, however, mean that the collection was either complete or final.

12a **The Threefold Division of the OT**—A further indication of the tendency to group the sacred writings into some definite form is to be found in the threefold division of the Hebrew Bible, the Law, the Prophets and the Writings. The author of Ecclus seems to have known this division (*cf.* Ecclus 46–49 ; 44:5 ; 47:8–9, 17) and his grandson, who translated the book into Greek *c* 130 B.C., mentions it three times in his prologue. It may also be implied in our Lord's words after the Resurrection : 'All things must needs be fulfilled which are written in the Law of Moses and in the prophets and in the psalms, concerning me', Lk 24:44.

b **The Law**—The first collection comprised the five books of Moses or the Pentateuch ; it was certainly the oldest part of the Canon, and its sacred character and the high esteem in which it was held early in Jewish history is illustrated by its close association with the ark of the covenant (*cf. supra*). In 621, in the reign of Josias, an historic event of some importance

occurred, when the 'Book of the Law' was discovered **12b** in the house of God. Whether this was the whole Pentateuch or only Deuteronomy, it is clear that there was attached to it a special authority as containing God's law for Israel. During the exile the written word acquired a new significance and a more prominent place in the life of the nation. After their return its authority was still maintained, and it was solemnly and publicly read by Esdras to the people, who in turn pledged themselves to live up to its requirements (*cf.* 2 Esd 8 ff.). From then onwards it was read in the synagogues of Palestine and in the Diaspora, studied and copied by scribes, accepted by the Samaritans and, most important of all, translated into Greek for the benefit of the Jewish community at Alexandria.

The Prophets—This second section is divided into **c** the 'Earlier' Prophets (Jos, Jg, Kgs) and the 'Later' Prophets. The former are really historical books, and form a natural sequence to the Pentateuch, but the reason why they are grouped together with the Prophets is either because they relate the lives and teaching of several of the Prophets (Samuel, Nathan, Elias, Eliseus, Isaias and others), or because they were supposed to have been written by prophets (*cf.* Josephus *c Apion* 1:8). These books, together with those written by prophets, sometimes at God's express bidding (Is 30:8 ; 34:16 ; Jer 30:2), were probably recognized as sacred in character within a short space of time and quite independently of their being assigned to any particular collection of rolls.

The factor which shaped this collection was, according to some writers, the synagogue liturgy and worship (*cf.* S. M. Zarb, O.P., *De Historia Canonis Utriusque Testamenti*, 1934², pp 98 f.). The Pentateuch had been divided into sections so that the whole could be read publicly in a definite period of time. For some time the Pentateuch alone was used in this way, but later it was decided to illustrate the Pentateuch by passages selected from other sacred books. These in turn were, by this means, linked together and gradually formed the second collection of the Canon which was probably complete by 200 B.C.

The Writings—The third group is composite in **d** character and seems to have been made up of smaller collections. It is hard to discover any unifying principle. It was certainly in process of formation when the prologue of Ecclus was written (*c* 130 B.C.) and its limits remained undefined and uncertain even after the beginning of the Christian era.

While this threefold division cannot account for the formation of the OT Canon, since many of the books were recognized as sacred and canonical before they were assigned to any of the three groups, it does throw light on the clearer delineation of the extent of the Canon. Though we cannot decide too categorically in such a matter, the suggestion made by Steinmueller, *A Companion to Scripture Studies*, I p 68, may correspond to the facts : 'The threefold division is not based upon three different degrees of inspiration, nor upon a distinction between the prophetical office and the prophetical gifts, nor upon three stages in the religious development of the people (monotheism, prophetism and Judaism), but upon three different aspects in the evolution of synagogal liturgy'.

Summary of Process of Formation—The process of **e** formation, then, may have been somewhat as follows. The Law, the foundation of the Scriptures, would have been naturally recognized and declared sacred by the religious leaders of the people, by prophet and priest, though not necessarily by any formal process. Gradually other writings were accepted, under their guidance, because they assured the practice of the Law, were regarded almost as its continuance, or were written by men imbued with the Spirit of God. Later on this tradition, in process of formation, would crystallize under the influence of the synagogue liturgy and the scribes, until at last, towards the close of the pre-Christian era, the collection of sacred writings came to be regarded more and more as a perfect whole,

12e whose content should not be modified. After the fall of Jerusalem in A.D. 70 the Pharisees, anxious to preserve all they could of the past, and above all the sacred writings, affirmed their list of sacred writings at the Synod of Jamnia, c A.D. 90–100. Discussions regarding the canonicity of some books, however, continued even during the 2nd cent. (cf. infra §§ 13 f.).

OT CANON IN PALESTINE AND ALEXANDRIA

13a Protocanonical and Deuterocanonical Books—The picture is as yet by no means complete. We must remember that besides the Palestinian Jews, there was a large flourishing community of Greek-speaking Jews, whose principal centre was at Alexandria. These Jews played a most important and far-reaching part in the history of the Canon, because their practice differed from that of Palestine. It was for their benefit that the Greek translation of the Scriptures known as the Septuagint (LXX) was made, which contained together with the books found in the present Hebrew Bible additional books and passages now known as deuterocanonical books and passages.

b In view of the important place these parts of the Bible occupy in the succeeding pages and discussion, we ought to consider the meaning of the phrase a little more carefully before proceeding further. All the books found in the Hebrew Bible are called protocanonical, those found only in the Greek are called deuterocanonical. These phrases were first used by Sixtus of Siena, in 1566, protocanonical denoting those books whose inspired character had always been accepted, and deuterocanonical denoting those whose inspiration was recognized throughout the Universal Church after it had been doubted in some places, and which consequently came to occupy, in point of time, the second place in the Canon. Anglicans always refer to the deuterocanonical books as the Apocrypha, and in their Bibles they are printed separately under that heading, though nonconformist Bibles omit these altogether in accordance with the general Protestant rejection of them. Confusion may easily arise, unless it is borne in mind that for the Catholic apocryphal means that a work is neither inspired nor authentic, i.e. is not the work of the author to whom it is ascribed, or, if it is anonymous, does not belong to the date to which it is assigned. For the Protestant it might, according to context, have this meaning or it could refer to a deuterocanonical work. Because of the double use of the word apocryphal Catholics avoid applying it to the deuterocanonical books.

c Reason for Difference—What is the explanation of this discrepancy between the books accepted by the Palestinian and Hellenistic Jews? Some suppose that the facts prove the existence of two Canons, a shorter Palestinian one and a more extensive Alexandrian one. Others maintain that prior to the Christian era the limits of canonicity were more widely drawn, and embraced all the books of both Canons, and that later the deuterocanonical books were rejected by the application of narrow and rigid pharisaical criteria. The question is not an easy one to answer. First of all, it is unlikely that the Alexandrian Jews would go so far as to set up a different official Canon from that of Jerusalem, and, secondly, there is no trace of dissension between the communities upon this point. What is really more probable is that the Hellenistic Jews conceived a broader view of inspiration, not restricting it either to the Hebrew language or to the centuries preceding Esdras (cf. Wis 7:27), and that they used a larger number of books without troubling about whether they had received any formal sanction. In a word, then, the Alexandrians would accept books as inspired which might not be acceptable to the doctors in Jerusalem; but even in Palestine some of the deuterocanonical books seem to have been received and used before and after the Christian era, e.g. Baruch seems to have been used in the synagogues in

commemorating the fall of the Holy City (cf. Apostolic **13c** Constitutions; PG 1, 896), and, according to Irenaeus and Origen, appears at one time to have been united with Jer (cf. Adv Haer 5, 35; PG 7, 1219; Com in Ps I 12, 1084). Ecclus too was held in high esteem and was frequently quoted in rabbinical literature (cf. JE 3, 148). Similar evidence is available for the other **d** deuterocanonical writings. Doubts and differences were reduced for the Palestinian Jews towards the end of the first century A.D. when they seem to have accepted as sacred and canonical only those books distinguished by certain characteristics. It is suggested that these were : (i) Conformity with the Law of Moses (cf. Josephus c Apion 1:8), (ii) Antiquity, i.e. written not later than the time of Esdras (ibid.), (iii) Hebrew language (cf. *E. Schuerer, A History of the Jewish People, Eng. Tr. 1898, Div 2, vol 1, p 9 f.; Div 2, vol. 2, p 81 f.), (iv) Palestinian origin, as illustrated by the attempts to place the writing of Ezechiel in Palestine (cf. *H. E. Ryle, The Canon of the OT, 1892, p 263 f.). The deuterocanonical books did not meet these strict requirements, and despite the great spiritual value of some of them and the esteem in which they had been held, they were ultimately rejected. Wis and 2 Mac, for instance, were written in Greek, Ecclus and 1 Mac after the time of Esdras, Baruch outside Palestine, the rest probably in Aramaic, both of Palestinian and non-Palestinian origin. (On the whole question, cf. Zarb, op. cit. pp 71–78.)

Closing of Palestinian Canon—Josephus and 4 Esd, **e** towards the end of the 1st cent. A.D., give us the earliest estimates of the number of sacred books, but they do not actually name them. 4 Esd implies that the number is 24 (cf. § 11e supra, JE 3, 142); Josephus gives it as 22, which is probably an artificial modification suggested by the letters of the Hebrew alphabet and obtained by joining Ru to Jg and Lam to Jer (cf. JE 3, 151; c Apion 1:8). He appears to leave it an open question whether there might not also be other sacred writings besides these 22 : 'It is true, our history hath been written since Artaxerxes very particularly, but hath not been esteemed of the like authority with the former by our forefathers, because there hath not been an exact succession of prophets since that time', c Apion, 1:8.

At Jamnia—At the Synod held here decisions were **f** reached which greatly influenced the opinion of Palestinian Jewry, but in the light of the discussions which continued long after it, one would hardly be justified in holding that the Palestinian Canon was finally settled then. For various reasons objections continued to be raised against several of the protocanonical books, e.g. Prov, Ru, Est, Eccl and Cant (cf. HDB 1, 773; 3, 606 f.), which were not completely eliminated even at the end of the 2nd cent. At the same time there are signs that some at least of the deuterocanonical books found acceptance in Palestine (cf. supra, §13c and JE 3, 148). The available evidence points to the end of the 2nd cent. as the time when the shorter Canon was virtually settled. The earliest explicit testimony which is to be found in the Talmudic treatise Baba Bathra dates back to that time. 'In the course of the 2nd cent. of the common era a fixed group of hagiographa, to which a relatively less importance was ascribed than to the prophets, was constituted. The earliest testimony as to the contents of this group is B.B., 14b' (JE 3, 153). The Canon of Jewry, then, which finally excluded the deuterocanonical books, is later than the apostolic age, after which no Christian revelation was made, and during which, therefore, the Christian Canon must have been fixed in principle.

THE OT OF THE CHURCH

The First Three Centuries—Whatever the decisions **14a** of the Pharisees at Jamnia and of the later rabbinical writers, the Christian Church was not bound by them. The only source from which she could receive the OT

14a Canon was our Lord himself or the Holy Spirit through the Apostles. By their teaching and frequent appeal to the OT Scripture as the word of God, they, as it were, consecrated its authority and stressed once again its permanent and abiding value, Mk 7:13 ; Rom 3:2. But, which was the OT handed on to the Church ? Neither our Lord nor his Apostles have left us an explicit list of inspired OT writings, so that the answer is to be discovered by examining works of apostolic origin and tradition. From this combined evidence it may be shown that the Apostles recognized the Greek Bible, not indeed by any official decree, but rather by the use they made of it. The continuance of this same usage is witnessed in the apostolic and post-apostolic Fathers (*cf.* DTC 2, 1574 f.). We cannot know for certain exactly which books the Alexandrian Jews accepted, since we do not possess any Jewish MSS of the LXX, but, in view of the important part played by the OT in the conversion of the Hellenistic Jews, it is reasonable to suppose that they coincided, broadly speaking, with the books acknowledged by the Church and found in the earliest Christian MSS.

b In the NT itself there are no explicit, formal quotations from the deuterocanonical books—although one might almost claim Heb 1:3 (Wis 7:26) as an example. Referring to this passage one Protestant writer remarks : ' It is almost certain that the author of the Epistle to the Hebrews adapted the phrase ἀπαύγασμα τ. δόξης . . . αὐτοῦ in 1:3 from Wis 7:26 ; but such an adaptation, in view of the sacredness and importance of the subject—the Divine nature of the Son of God—would seem to imply a recognition of the authority of this book. Taken in connexion with the reference to 1 Mac in ch 11, it suggests that this Alexandrian writer accepted the whole collection of the Alexandrian LXX as Scripture ' (HDB 3, 609). But the absence of explicit quotation is not a conclusive argument against their acceptance, for the same also obtains in the case of several protocanonical books. There are, however, many passages which betray the influence of the disputed works : Mt 6:14 (Ecclus 28:2) ; Mt 27:39 ff. (Wis 2:13 ff.) ; Rom 1:20 ff. (Wis 13–14) ; Heb 11:35 (2 Mac 6:18–7:42) ; Jas 1:19 (Ecclus 5:13) ; 1 Pet 1:6 f. (Wis 3:3 ff.). Many other instances might be cited, though with less certainty. Moreover when the OT is quoted in the NT it usually agrees with the LXX : it is said that of about 300 quotations less than 50 disagree with it.

c Furthermore, the Greek Bible was, under Divine Providence, a most powerful factor in the conversion of the world to Christianity. Since knowledge of the Greek language was widely diffused, the Apostles, their helpers and successors, found in the LXX a ready point of contact wherever a knowledge of the OT had spread. In the synagogues they could prove to the Jews of the Dispersion and their adherents that Christ had fulfilled the OT prophecies, and, gaining some success, were usually able to gather together a number of people anxious to continue their instruction in the Christian religion. It was the success thus achieved that caused the Jews to become alienated from the LXX and eventually to repudiate it (*cf.* *A. Rahlfs, Septuaginta*, 1. p. xxiii ; *F. Kenyon, Our Bible and the Ancient MSS*, 1939⁴, pp 55 ff.).

d We must remember, as already stated, that it is only in the light of tradition that the evidence becomes conclusive, for the early Church would hardly have ventured to make use of the larger list of books and endorse it, unless this conformed to apostolic tradition and practice : yet this it has consistently done from the beginning, using all the books as equally the word of God and the source of doctrine. With the exception of Baruch which was usually added to Jer, and about the acceptance of which there can be little doubt, *all the deuterocanonical writings are quoted in the apostolic and early Fathers in the same way as the rest of the sacred books.* ' Thus ', writes Swete, ' Clement of Rome places the story of Judith side by side with that of Esther ; the Wisdom of Sirach (Ecclus) is cited by Barnabas and the Didache, and Tobit (Tobias) by **14d** Polycarp ; Clement of Alexandria and Origen appeal to Tobit and both the Wisdoms, to which Origen adds Judith. Our earliest MSS of the Greek Bible confirm the impression derived from the quotations of the earliest Christian writers '. *H. B. Swete, Introduction to OT in Greek*, 1900, p 224. The witness of Irenaeus, Hippolytus, Tertullian and Cyprian is the same.

The Earliest Lists—In view of all this evidence in **e** favour of the wider Canon in the early Church, it appears strange that the first lists of canonical books given by Christian writers should contain only the protocanonical books. The first is the one given by Melito of Sardis to Onesimus, to whom he writes : ' Having therefore gone up to the East and come to the place where these things were proclaimed and done, and having exactly learnt which are the books of the OT, I send you the list as given below '. Then follows his list, which does not include Est and the disputed books (Eus *H.E.* 4:26 ; PG 20, 395–398). The omission of Est may have been unintentional or it may be readily explained by the uncertainty felt by some Rabbis regarding its canonicity. Quite clearly, Melito is giving the Canon as he found it in Palestine, where by this time the deuterocanonical books had been rejected from the Canon. His purpose may have been polemical and his intention to give a list which the Jews would accept in controversy. It is, however, suggested by some that he himself did accept the shorter list on the authority of the Jews, and that, in so doing, he was departing from the established tradition of the Church. The second list is the one given by Origen ; in this case we naturally expect to find the deuterocanonical books excluded, for he tells us that he is giving the Jewish Canon. He begins with the words : ' But be it known that there are twenty-two books *according to the Hebrew tradition . . .* these are the twenty-two books *according to the Hebrews . . .*', *op. cit.* 6, 25 (PG 20, 579–582). Later writers used this passage as though it represented Origen's teaching on the Canon. The contrary is borne out by his constant **f** practice of quoting as Scripture passages found only in the Alexandrian Canon and also by his own words, when he refers to the question at issue. In his letter to Julius Africanus, for instance, he shows us the precise way in which he regarded the disputed books. Africanus had refused to accept the history of Susanna as canonical because, amongst other things, it was ' not contained in the Daniel received amongst the Jews '. The reply of Origen is interesting because he defends this and other deuterocanonical passages *on the ground that the Greek Bible had been received by the Church*, and adds the warning from Prov 22:28. ' It is well ', he says, ' to remember the words " Thou shalt not remove the ancient landmarks which thy Fathers have set " ', *Ep. Afric.* ; PG 11, 56–60. Summing up this period, a Protestant theologian writes : ' Once more we recall that the Christian theologians of this period knew the OT only in the Greek form (known as the Septuagint) and, consequently, made no further distinction between what we call canonical books (Hebrew) and apocryphal books (Greek). They quote the latter with the same confidence as the former, with the same titles of honour, and attribute to them an equal authority founded on an equal inspiration.' *E. Reuss, Histoire du Canon des Saintes Ecritures*, Strasbourg, 1863², p. 99.

The wide popularity the deuterocanonical books **g** enjoyed in the early Church is finally shown by their use in the liturgy and from the many illustrations taken from them found in the catacombs ; there are representations from Tob, Jdt, Bar, Mac and Dan 3:24 ff. (DBV 2, 155). They were made with the approval of the pastors of the Church who appreciated the value of pictures for instruction in the truths of religion. This would explain the presence of pictures from the deuterocanonical books and the absence of any from apocryphal works.

Rightly, then, it may be said that the practice of the early writers, together with the common use of the

14g books amongst the faithful, points back to a tradition coming from the Apostles themselves, who in turn received it from our Lord himself or through revelations of the Holy Spirit.

15a From the Beginning of the Fourth Century—This century introduces us to a period of confusion and uncertainty. Several factors seem to have been responsible. First of all, the appropriation of the Greek Bible by the Christians and the use made against the Jews of the Messianic prophecies as found in the LXX (especially Is 7:14) led the Jews to reject the Greek version (JE 3, 152). In consequence, the Christians in controversy were compelled to argue solely from books acknowledged as canonical by the Jews themselves (*cf.* St Justin Martyr, *Dial. Tryph*, 71 ; PG 6, 641-3). This in turn would lead to doubt about the divine authority of the books to be left aside.

b Secondly, the circulation of many apocryphal books (*cf.* §§ 92-4) bearing titles similar to genuine books of the Bible, tended to redound to the discredit of the deuterocanonical books. Sometimes these apocryphal works were quoted by the Fathers as Scripture, but at no time were any of them received by all the churches of the East and West and read with the canonical books in public services. There was a vast difference between the position enjoyed by the most favourably received apocryphal book and the deuterocanonicals, which explains why the former fell into oblivion, while the latter retained their position and continued to be used together with the protocanonical books. Nevertheless, this circulation of the apocryphal books led to a strict scrutiny of the claims of all inspired works. Many Fathers, owing to a too rigid conception of canonicity, were inclined to accept only those books recognized by the Jews, while setting aside the disputed books in a category of their own as ' useful for edification and instruction '.

c In Alexandria St Athanasius (295-373) drew up a Canon in which he recognizes only the Jewish canonical list, with the exception that he rejects Est and retains Bar, Ep. of Jer and the whole of Dan. St Cyril of Jerusalem, St Epiphanius and St Gregory Nazianzen also reject the deuterocanonical books, and Eusebius of Caesarea calls them ' antilegomena ' or disputed writings. The 60th Canon of the provincial Council of Laodicea (*c* 360) supports their view, and, even though its authenticity has been contested, it is an ancient witness to the opinions prevalent in Asia Minor in the 4th cent. Such was the general position in the East, and to deny it is to disregard the evidence. It is, however, remarkable that these same Fathers, who in theory confine inspiration and canonicity to the Palestinian Canon, in practice highly esteem and quote as Scripture all the books of the wider Canon. In this context one might well repeat Davidson's remark : ' Surely the practical use of writings is an evidence of their canonicity as strong as theoretical opinions '. (*S. Davidson, The Canon of the Bible*, 1878⁴, p 60 f.)

d Quite plainly in the case of the Eastern Fathers, however great may have been their hesitation, it did not greatly influence their practice, for in teaching the faithful and setting forth the proofs of revealed doctrine, they instinctively turned to the Greek Bible, and used indiscriminately all the books found there. They knew of a Jewish and Christian OT, and, while they had a bias towards the Jewish, they recognized the other as the one historically transmitted by the Church. Swete (*loc. cit.*) remarks : ' When Origen and the Greek Fathers who follow him fix the number of sacred books at twenty-two or twenty-four, they follow, not the earlier traditions of the Church, but the corrected estimate of Christian scholars who had learned it from their Jewish teachers '.

In the West the position was different and the rejection of the deuterocanonical books proved to be rather the exception. It was, of course, to be expected that the views so frequently expressed in the East should exercise some influence also in the West. Hilary of Poitiers (*c* 315-366), for instance, reproduces the Canon of Origen, and Rufinus (*c* 345-410) will allow **15d** the disputed books to be called ' ecclesiastical ' but not canonical.

St Jerome and the OT Canon—Most important of all **e** is the attitude of St Jerome (*c* 342-419), who, carried away by his long sojourn in Palestine and his Hebrew studies, threw the great weight of his authority against the canonicity of the deuterocanonical books. Frequently he repudiates any book not found in the Hebrew Bible ; and in the famous *Prologus Galeatus*, preface to his translation of Kings, he states that Wis, Ecclus, Tob and Jdt are ' not in the Canon '. Unlike the other Fathers, he carried his opposition even to the extent of sometimes quoting them with the caution ' that they are not canonical ' *in Jonam* 1, PL 25, 1119. But that is not all. His attitude is not consistent, for he does occasionally quote them as Scripture in accordance with the common practice, and so becomes an involuntary witness to their established position, Ep 65 ; PL 22, 624 ; *Com. in Eccl* 23, 1128 ; *Com. in Is* 24, 40. ' There is no book or fragment of the deuterocanon ', says Cornely, ' which he does not use with reverence and as a divine authority ', CSS 1, *Introd. Generalis*, Paris, 1885, p 107. Moreover towards the end of his life (*c* 402) he does try to justify himself to Rufinus regarding his rejection of the deuterocanonical portions of Dan and argues that he himself never really denied their inspiration, but was rather expressing ' what the Jews were accustomed to bring up against us '. *Apol. contra Ruf.* 11, 33 ; PL 23, 476. A further **f** illustration of the established position of the wider Canon in the Church is St Jerome's admission that he translated the deuterocanonical books into Latin as a concession to the authority of the bishops, and that the Church herself had them read for the edification of the faithful (*cf. Praef. in lib. Tob* ; PL 29, 24-25). Against those who put forward St Jerome's authority as decisive, it has been pointed out that after the decisions of the African Councils St Jerome seems to have changed his whole attitude to the deuterocanonical books : ' He would appear to have been influenced by the declarations of the Councils of Hippo and Carthage, and hence modified his opinion in his later works. In his later commentaries, for example, in that on *Isaias*, he quotes—as we have seen—the Deuterocanonical books as authorities, and that without hesitation. And it should be noted that his very wavering is the best proof of the Christian tradition in favour of the Deuterocanonical books ; the Church has never confined herself to the authority of one doctor, and it is at least remarkable that all through St Jerome's life we have repeated ecclesiastical and patristic testimonies in favour of the canonicity of the books of the second canon ', CSAB 1, 146 f.

St Augustine and the African Councils—St Augustine, **g** for instance, simply accepts the longer Canon and affirms its contents on the authority of the Church ; for him, this argument was paramount, *De Doct. Christ.* 8 ; PL 34, 41. Often he has to defend the disputed books and does so by recalling the Church's testimony. He defends the canonicity of Wis because ' it was found worthy of being read from the lector's pulpit in the Church of Christ for so long a course of years, and of being heard with the veneration due to divine authority by all Christians, from bishops even down to the lowest laity, the penitents and catechumens ', *Lib de Praedest. Sanctorum*, c. 14 ; PL 44, 980.

It is quite likely that the position taken up by St **h** Jerome was responsible for the earliest enactments of the Church which have come down to us. Reaction against his views was strong in Africa, where a list of canonical books, which included the deuterocanonicals, was drawn up at the Council of Hippo in 393, and subsequently repeated at the 3rd and 4th Councils of Carthage in 397 and 418. Appended to this decree on the contents of the Canon was a plea that their decision be sent to Rome for approval and confirmation : ' Let this also be made known to our brother and fellow priest, the holy Boniface, Bishop

15h of Rome, or to other priests of those parts, for the confirmation of this Canon ; for we have learned from the Fathers that we should read these in the Church '. The explanation of this request would appear to be the desire of the African bishops to counter the widespread views and influence of St Jerome. They reaffirm tradition regarding the Canon.

i Another official document was due to similar circumstances. St Exuperius, Bishop of Toulouse and friend of St Jerome, who had dedicated to him his commentary on Zacharias, wrote to Innocent I a formal letter asking him which were the canonical books, no doubt uneasy at his friend's defence of the shorter Canon. The Pope's reply, given in the letter *Consulenti Tibi* in A.D. 405 (EB 16) reaffirms the canonicity of the disputed books and the list given at Hippo a few years previously.

j Despite these decisions, opinion remained divided in the succeeding centuries. The majority of writers seem to have accepted the deuterocanonical books as part of the Canon, but a minority, including some important names, took up the position they thought was supported by the authority of St Jerome. Even Pope St Gregory the Great inclined to this view and speaks of the disputed books as ' books which, though not canonical, are received for the edification of the Church ', *Lib. Mor.* 19, 21 ; PL 76, 119. During the Middle Ages the divergence of opinion was even more pronounced, important ecclesiastical writers being found both for and against the complete authority of the full Canon. The *Prologus Galeatus* of St Jerome was widely known and those who accepted the views which are there expressed, reconciled their position with Church practice and Papal decrees by accepting a special dignity and authority for the deuterocanonical books and attributing to them great value for edification, though still refusing them full canonical status.

k **Decisions of the Councils**—The tradition of the Church was again proclaimed at the Council of Florence (1441) in the Decree for the Jacobites, Dz 703. The Council settled the question by issuing a list of books which were inspired writings, a list identical with that of the African Councils and Innocent I. Whether because the decision of the Council was not sufficiently widely known or fully appreciated, uncertainty was not altogether dissipated ; there were still some who hesitated and reserved the designation *canonical* for the Hebrew books alone, including the learned Cardinals Ximenes and Cajetan. In 1546 the Council of Trent repeated the decision of Florence and the books comprising the Canon were formally defined. Contrasted with this definition was the attitude of the Reformers, who, disapproving some of the doctrines which found support in the deuterocanonical books (*e.g.* purgatory in 2 Mac), were content to reject their authority in doctrinal matters. The Reformers were willing to admit their value as works of edification, and so they were included in many Protestant Bibles, but were placed apart under the heading ' Apocrypha '. This is practically the position adopted by the Anglican Church. The sixth of the Thirty-nine Articles reads : ' In the name of the holy Scriptures we do understand those canonical books of the Old and New Testament, of whose authority was never any doubt in the Church '. Then follows a list of the protocanonical books. It then adds ' and other books (as Hierome saith) the Church doth read for example of life and instruction of manners ; but yet it doth not apply them to establish any doctrine '. Though there is some discussion as to the meaning of the Article, the classic commentators regard it as equivalent to a rejection of the decision of Trent (*cf.* *E. J. Bicknell, *A Theological Introduction to the Thirty-nine Articles*, p 164 ; *E. C. S. Gibson, *The Thirty-nine Articles of the Church of England*, p 258). Nevertheless the Anglican Church legally requires these books to be present in her Bible, and, in fact, considerable use has been made of them in her liturgy.

l The Council of Trent formally discussed the position and status to be assigned to the disputed books. It finally decided that *all the books, deuterocanonical and* **15l** *protocanonical were inspired and were of equal authority.* ' This holy Synod receives and venerates with equal devotion and reverence all the books of both the OT and NT, since the One God is the Author of both. . . .' Then follows the list which is that of Florence and Hippo. All doubts were now set at rest by the decision of the Council. This decision was reaffirmed at the Council of the Vatican in 1870.

In the Greek Church similar fluctuations of opinion **m** prevailed. The position adopted by the Trullan Council is obscure ; it did not enumerate the separate books, but referred to older authorities, including the African Councils. It is maintained by some writers that it adopted the Roman Canon, but the evidence is not decisive. After the Reformation, the Patriarch, Cyril Lucar, favoured the doctrine of the Reformers, and upheld the old distinction between canonical and ecclesiastical books. The ' Confession of Cyril Lucar ' was rejected by his successors and by the Synod of Constantinople and Jerusalem in 1672, A. Fortescue, *The Orthodox Eastern Church*, pp 264 ff. Since the 18th cent. the shorter Canon has again found more and more acceptance, but the matter has not been settled for the Greeks by conciliar decision.

THE NT CANON

Its Formation—The formation of the NT Canon was, **16a** like that of the Old, a gradual process ; it was not produced all at one time as a completed whole. The writings of which it is made up were, in the first instance, separate, independent writings, called into being at different times, in different circumstances, to meet various needs. There was no intention on the part of the Apostles and their disciples of collaborating in the production of a common work to be left as a legacy. Our Lord and his Apostles were teachers rather than writers ; they taught and preached the word of God, for, in St Paul's words, ' Faith cometh by hearing ' (Rom 10:17). The written word was used as an additional means of spreading the gospel. We must remember that each book of the NT was issued separately and has its own history. St Paul, for instance, would write a letter to a community to meet some practical need, to give further instruction, to exhort or give warning against impending dangers. Such letters written to the different churches throughout the Empire would be interchanged between them, sometimes at the request of the Apostle himself (Col 4:16). The letters would increase in number and each community would acquire a collection of them ; we can already see how the germ of a Canon arose. This small collection of books would increase as further writings, which bore the unmistakable stamp or guarantee of apostolic origin, were added to it. In the NT itself there are clear signs of such a collection, in process of formation, taking its place alongside the OT Scriptures : ' As also our most dear brother Paul, according to the wisdom given him, hath written to you : as also *in all his epistles*, speaking in them of these things ; in which are certain things hard to be understood, which the unlearned and unstable wrest, as they do also *the other scriptures*, to their own destruction ', 2 Pet 3:15 f.

As the number of living witnesses gradually dwindled, **b** and as the number of communities increased through the rapid spread of the faith, it became more and more apparent how valuable it would be for the instruction of future generations if there were written records of the teaching, life, death and resurrection of our Lord. These written records, or Gospels, as they came to be called, would pass from one community to another in the same way as the letters, and each community would add the new writings to its collection as soon as they came to hand. Striking evidence regarding the early circulation of the Gospel of St John, for instance, has recently been produced by the discovery

16b of P 52, a papyrus fragment of Jn, which comes from Egypt and is dated as belonging to the first half of the 2nd cent. (*cf.* *C. H. Roberts, *An Unpublished Fragment of the Fourth Gospel*, 1935). Collections were not made rapidly, for progress would be impeded by slowness and difficulty of communication and limited means for the multiplication of copies of writings. In fact, a considerable period of time must have elapsed before the widely scattered churches possessed all the writings in circulation. There were other difficulties too : it was, for example, sometimes hard to tell if a smaller letter, more private in character and of less important doctrine, really emanated from genuine apostolic sources. In addition, the circulation of spurious and tendentious works, claiming apostolic origin, would tend to make people wary of accepting anything which was not of proven and undoubted apostolic authority. In these circumstances, then, it is not surprising that there were several books, genuine and inspired, whose full canonical status was

c not universally acknowledged for a long time. These have become known to us as the **deuterocanonical books of the NT** (*cf.* § 13*a*, *b*). They are Hebrews, James, Jude, 2 Peter, 2 and 3 John, and the Apocalypse. But there are no differences between Catholics and Protestants regarding the books which constitute the NT Canon : they are the four Gospels, the Acts of the Apostles, fourteen Epistles of Paul, the seven Catholic Epistles (James, 1 and 2 Peter, 1, 2 and 3 John, Jude), and the Apocalypse.

17a **History of the NT Canon**—It is reasonable to suppose that, quite early on, the more important churches, Rome, Alexandria, Corinth, Antioch and others, would possess apostolic writings which they regarded as authoritative, though at this stage their lists might vary. Already we have seen that there is evidence in the NT of a collection of Pauline writings received as Scripture. The Apostolic Fathers further illustrate the unique place occupied by the Gospels and the writings of the Apostles. The careful line of demarcation between these writings and their own is quite noticeable. St Clement of Rome, writing to the Corinthians (*c* A.D. 96), says : ' Take into your hands the epistle of the blessed Paul the Apostle. What did he write to you when the Gospel was first preached ? Truly, under divine inspiration (πνευματικῶς) he wrote to you concerning himself, and Cephas, and Apollo, because even then you had formed parties among yourselves ', *Ep. Cor* 47:1 ; PG 1, 305. St Ignatius of Antioch († *c* 117) remarks to the Ephes'ans that St Paul makes mention of them in ' every epistle ', a hyperbole which implies a collection of Pauline epistles of acknowledged authority, *Eph* 12:1 ; PG 5, 656. Eph 4:26 is quoted by St Polycarp (*c* 70–156), together with Ps 4:5, as in the ' Scriptures ', *Phil* 12:1 ; PG 5, 1014.

b Quite apart from these explicit passages, there are many incidental references and coincidences of thought and language which betray a remarkable acquaintance with the writings of St Paul, *cf.* F. X. Funk, *Patres Apostolici* (*Index Locorum SS*). ' Elsewhere in the Apostolic Fathers ', writes Westcott, ' there are clear traces of a knowledge of the Epistles of St Paul to the Romans, ·1 and 2 Corinthians, Galatians, Ephesians, Philippians, and 1 and 2 Timothy, of the Epistle to the Hebrews, of the Epistle of St James, the first Epistle of St Peter, and the first Epistle of St John. The allusions to the Epistles of St Paul to the Thessalonians, Colossians, to Titus and Philemon, and to 2 Peter are very uncertain ; and there are, I believe, no coincidences of language with the Epistle of Jude, and 2 and 3 John ', *History of Canon NT*, p 48. In fact, their familiarity with the epistles is so extensive that we can hardly doubt that a collection of them was in wide circulation and commonly known.

c There are allusions, too, to the written Gospels, although our Lord's life and teaching were still familiar from oral tradition (*cf.* Funk *loc. cit.*). Mt 22:14 is quoted by the Epistle of Barnabas (*c* 100) with the

Scriptural formula ὡς γέγραπται, ' as it is written ', **17c** 4:14 PG 2, 733. The judgement of the early writers is, therefore, clear, for they use the books as authoritative, accept them as apostolic and quote them as inspired.

The Apologists—During the succeeding period in the **d** life of the Church when she was faced by the persecution of the Roman Empire and the attacks of heretical false brethren, the Apologists came to her aid. In their works evidence for the canonical writings is abundant. St Justin Martyr describes them as resting upon apostolic authority : ' For the Apostles ', he writes, ' in the memoirs composed by them, which are called Gospels, have handed down to us what Jesus had thus enjoined upon them ', 1 *Apol* 1, 66 ; PG 6, 429. These ' memoirs ' were read together with the Prophets when the Christians met for worship on Sundays (1, 67), thus bearing witness to a Christian collection of writings which had taken its place alongside that of the OT. That Justin is speaking of the four Gospels which we possess today, seems to be confirmed by the work of his disciple, Tatian, who composed his *Diatessaron*, or harmony of the Gospels, exclusively from them. Justin also quotes the Apoc as by St John. St Denis of Corinth († *c* 176), in an interesting passage, complains of heretics corrupting his writings, but consoles himself with the thought that the same is done even to the Scriptures of the Lord, Euseb, *H.E.* 4, 23 ; PG 20, 389. The heretic Marcion (*c* 150) also gives direct testimony to the existence and authority of a NT Canon by drawing up one of his own, which included a mutilated Lk and ten Pauline epistles.

By the end of the 2nd cent. all the NT books were **e** generally known and the divine character of most of them universally admitted. Irenaeus (†202), familiar with the traditions of Asia Minor, Gaul and Rome, and connected through his teachers with the close of the apostolic age, explicitly names and accepts the four canonical Gospels, rejects the claims of others which are apocryphal, quotes twelve Epistles of St Paul as Scripture, accepts the Apoc as Johannine, and makes use of the Catholic epistles (CSAB 4, 84 ; *Adv. Haer.* 3, 11 ; PG 7, 885). He has no reference to Phm and does not think that Heb was written by St Paul.

The witness of Tertullian in North Africa and Clement **f** in Alexandria is the same. The former, writing against Marcion, reproves him for his treatment of the Gospels, and defends their authenticity and authority, *Adv. Marcion* 4, 2. He quotes all the NT books except 2 Pet, 2 and 3 Jn, but ascribes Heb to Barnabas and excludes it from Scripture. Clement quotes all the undisputed books of the NT, and, according to Eusebius, gave concise accounts of all the canonical Scriptures, not passing over the disputed books, *i.e.* Jude and the other Catholic Epistles, and also the Ep. Barn. and Apoc. Pet. He regarded Heb as Pauline, written in Hebrew for Hebrews, and translated into Greek by Luke, *H.E.* 6, 14 ; PG 20, 549.

The earliest *list* that has come down to us, though **g** it need be by no means the earliest written, is the Muratorian Fragment (*c* 200) discovered by Muratori in the Ambrosian Library, Milan, in 1740. It contains a catalogue of books which were recognized as authoritative at Rome at the end of the 2nd cent., *viz.* the four Gospels, the Epistles of St Paul (except Heb), two Epistles of Jn, Jude, Apoc. It omits, in addition to Heb, Jas, Epistles of Pet., and one Epistle of Jn. There also seems to be a reference to the Apoc. Pet. which ' some of us do not wish to be read in the Church '. The Pastor of Hermas is excluded because of its recent date. (Text CSAB 4, 90 ff.).

The NT part of the Chester Beatty papyri, dating back **h** to the first half of the 3rd cent. or earlier, comprises three codices which, when complete, would have covered the whole NT, except the Pastoral and Catholic Epistles. P 45 contains parts of the four Gospels and Ac ; P 46, most of the Pauline Epistles

17h with Heb in the second place ; P 47, part of the Apoc.

It is generally admitted from the evidence that, from the beginning of the 3rd cent., the NT was composed essentially of the same books as our present Canon. This does not mean that there was no hesitation, discussion or examination of the claims of the deuterocanonical books ; this there was, but the outcome of it all was that the writings, acknowledged as authoritative at the end of the 2nd cent., retained their status. Other writings which were held in high esteem, occasionally quoted as Scripture, and sometimes added to NT MSS., as, for instance, Ep. Clem., Pastor Herm., Ep. Barn., Didache, were excluded from the Canon. The pretensions of Marcion and the Edict of Diocletian (A.D. 303), which ordered the destruction of all sacred books, may have had some influence in furthering the final delimitation of the Canon.

i The Position of the Deuterocanonical Books—During the 3rd cent. some of the Fathers hesitated to accept some books because of doubts cast upon their authenticity. Some were short and not well known and, when their claims for full canonical status were considered, it is easy to understand that they might not be immediately conceded. Others, like the Apoc and Heb, were suspect for more positive reasons. The Apoc had been almost universally received from the earliest times but, during the 3rd cent., there was a reaction against it in the East. The occasion of the interruption of the long tradition seems to have been the use made of the Apoc to support the Millenarian heresy. It was this that led St Denis of Alexandria to examine again the claims of the book to be the work of an Apostle. He does not venture to deny its inspired character or canonicity—tradition was too strong—but the differences of style, thought and language led him to the conclusion that the fourth Gospel and the Apoc were not written by the same person. Almost inevitably doubts regarding the authorship resulted in hesitation as to its canonical authority. In the 4th cent. this hesitation is illustrated by Eusebius who strangely classes the Apoc both amongst the ' accepted ' books and amongst the ' spurious ' books, whereas in reality he calls in question only its authenticity. His writings are of interest because he actually undertakes to record any tradition which would throw light on the formation of the Canon (*H.E.* 3, 3 ; PG 20, 217), and gives a summary of his results **j** (*ibid.* 3, 25 ; Text CSAB 4, 77 f.). The books which he here enumerates are grouped into four classes : (i) The accepted writings, *viz.* four Gospels, Ac, fourteen Pauline Epistles, 1 Jn, 1 Pet, and Apoc ' if it seems right '. (ii) Disputed books, but accepted by the majority, Jas, Jude, 2 Pet, 2 and 3 Jn. (iii) Spurious writings, Ac of Pl, Shepherd Herm, Apoc Pet, Ep Barn, Didache and Apoc, ' if it seem right. This last, as I said, is rejected by some, others place it among the accepted writings '. (iv) Various heretical gospels and acts which are to be wholly rejected. In the first two classes, he has our present Canon, indicating, at the same time, the ' disputed ' character of the deuterocanonical books.

k The Apocalypse was not included amongst the canonical books by St Cyril of Jerusalem, the Council of Laodicea, St Gregory Nazianzen, Amphilochius and others in the East. In the West, however, the authority of the Apoc was upheld by St Jerome, St Augustine and the other great Latin Fathers. Finally, it was accepted in both East and West. St Athanasius mentions it and receives it along with other NT writings as one of the springs of salvation, Ep 39 ; PG 26, 1438.

l Hesitation in the acceptance of Heb was due to similar circumstances, but in this case, it was in the West and not in the East that it persisted for any length of time. In the West the epistle was not regarded as Pauline, and, in consequence, its canonical character was called in question. In the East it was

generally regarded as belonging to St Paul, either **171** directly or indirectly. Origen, for instance, suggested that the thought was the Apostle's but the style and composition were that of a disciple reproducing his master's teaching. Others followed this opinion and, though the immediate authorship of the book might be considered uncertain, it retained its traditional place amongst the canonical writings. Athanasius, who lists all our present canonical books, enumerates fourteen epistles of St Paul, including, of course, Heb. From the 4th cent., though its authorship might still be disputed, its canonical authority was recognized and acknowledged in the West as well as the East. It was included in the lists of the African Councils and that of Innocent I (*cf.* 15*h*). By the end of the 4th cent. the difficulties occasioned by certain books disappeared, and there was no further serious attempt to dispute the claims of accepted books. The Canon then received was the one finally defined at Trent and is the NT Canon universally accepted to-day.

CRITERION OF CANONICITY

Various Theories—We cannot conclude this survey **18a** without some reference, however brief, to the principle governing the formation of the Canon. As we have seen, the books comprising it are those which are inspired and are acknowledged as such by the Church. But since the inspiration or divine authorship of any particular work can be made known to us only by the Divine Author himself, any criterion or principle by which we can judge the inspired or canonical character of a book must include a divine witness. Such divine testimony is to be found solely in *tradition coming from Christ and his Apostles*, faithfully preserved in the Church and supported by her authoritative pronouncements. ' Let us omit ', writes Augustine, ' the fables of those scriptures which are called apocryphal, since their obscure origin was unknown to the Fathers from whom the authority of the true Scriptures has come down to us by a most certain and well ascertained succession ', *De Civ. Dei* 15, 23, 4 ; PL 41, 470. In the case of the NT Canon, a further question **b** arises : in what way did the Apostles make known the canonical books to the Church? Some are of opinion that the last surviving Apostle, St John, explicitly indicated them and formally made known the scriptural Canon. This hypothesis, however, could hardly be sustained in the light of later hesitation regarding the canonicity of some books and there is no confirmation of it from history.

Another suggestion has been put forward which **c** attempts a different answer (*cf.* Zarb, *op. cit.* pp 518 ff.). It is urged that, since the Apostles were sent to teach in the name of Christ and were his ambassadors, whatever they taught was to be received as the word of Christ, Rom 2:16 ; 16:25 ; 2 Cor 4:3. But why limit their teaching to the spoken word ? Were they not just as much the ambassadors of Christ when they wrote as when they spoke ? In this way, whatever was written by an Apostle was inspired and, on this understanding, was accepted by the faithful. The writings of Mk and Lk were received because they were considered as coming from Peter and Paul respectively. But, we may ask, is it right to make the transient charisma or gift of inspiration coextensive with the permanent office of apostleship, or to elevate Mk and Lk virtually to the status of Apostles ? In fact, it is possible to commit an Apostle's teaching to writing faithfully and yet not be inspired in the true sense of the word.

Other writers avoid these difficulties by maintaining **d** that the Apostles pointed out the NT scriptural books equivalently or implicitly in the way they treated and regarded them : by setting them apart, by putting them on a level with the OT books, by sanctioning their use in public worship. The Apostles, in the various regions where they preached the Gospel, would guide

18d the faithful in their acceptances, and apostolic tradition thus formed would be handed down in the great apostolic sees. This would leave room for the later hesitation, when smaller books, written to more isolated communities, became known, and for variations in the number of accepted books in different communities.

e The Catholic is free to take whatever view commends itself to him. The present state of our knowledge makes it impossible to be too definite. But in whatever way the apostolic teaching and guarantee regarding the Canon were conveyed to the Church, it was these which determined the acceptance of the books. The unerring precision of acceptance is remarkably demonstrated in the case of the small and almost private letter to Philemon which won universal recognition, while other writings, Ep. Clem., Ep. Barn., Pastor Herm., were rejected. In this regard, St Jerome writes in the Prologue to Phm, 'Those who uphold its genuine character urge that it would never have been received by all the churches throughout the whole world unless it had been believed to be the work of Paul, the Apostle', PL 26, 637.

The divine witness thus graciously given, was faithfully received, carefully handed down and, when occasion demanded, infallibly defined.

f Conclusion—On looking back over the history of the Canon, we see how different are God's ways from those which superficial minds expect of him. They would have him define everything from the outset. If he inspires a book, they would have him reveal to all mankind from the first moment of its production that he is the Author. They do not pause to think how **18f** God's providence always works through human minds, and does not spare them the anxieties and hesitations of struggle. An explicit grasp of much that was revealed is only reached after much labour.

If we turn our eyes back from the Canon, as defined in the 16th cent., to the writings of the early Fathers, we find a striking coincidence of range between their quotations and implicit references, and the limits of the present Canon. The reason is not far to seek. The scriptural Canon is a dogma, a revealed truth and as such has its history or development, not in the sense of addition or increase, for this is not possible after the death of the last Apostle, but in the sense of being more fully, more explicitly understood. Revealed truth is only gradually unfolded, and is not immediately understood in all its aspects, penetrated in all its depths, appreciated in all its richness and beauty, nor foreseen in all its implications. Newman, writing about the books of the NT Canon says, 'The fifth century acts as a comment on the obscure text of the centuries before it, and brings out a meaning, which with the help of the comment any candid person sees really to be theirs', *Development of Christian Doctrine*, 4:1, 3. The truth made known by our Lord and his apostles was received by the Church, was generally known in the 2nd cent., was made clearer by the opinions and controversies of the third and fourth, and when occasion demanded, was made explicit and final by definition. A later age holds more explicitly and, in this sense, more fully, what an earlier age accepted implicitly, but it does not possess a different doctrine or a new revelation.

THE LANGUAGES, TEXTS AND VERSIONS OF THE BIBLE

By E. POWER, S.J.

19a **Bibliography 1. Languages**—P. Dhorme, *Langues et écritures sémitiques*, Paris, 1930 ; P. Joüon, *Grammaire de l'hébreu biblique*, Rome, 1923 ; *A. B. Davidson, *An Introductory Hebrew Grammar*, Edinburgh, 1932²⁴ ; id., *Hebrew Syntax, ibid.*, 1924 ; C. F. Jean, *Inscriptions Sémitiques*, DBVS 4 (1943) 384–417 ; *G. A. Cooke, *North Semitic Inscriptions*, Oxford, 1909 ; *K. Marti, *Kurzgefasste Grammatik der bibl.—aram. Sprache*, Berlin, 1925³ ; G. Messina, *L'Arameo antico*, Miscell. Bibl. 2 (1934), 69–163 ; J. Linder, *Das Aramaeische im Buch Dan*, ZKT 59 (1935) 503–45 ; F. M. Abel, *Grammaire du Grec biblique*, Paris, 1927 ; *J. H. Moulton, *A Grammar of NT Greek*, London, 1920 ; *Moulton-Milligan, *The Vocabulary of the Greek Testament Illustrated from the Papyri*, London, 1930 ; J. Vergote, *Grec Biblique*,

b DBVS 3 (1938) 1330–69. **2. Hebrew OT Text**—*C. D. Ginsburg, *Introduction to the Massoretico—Critical Edition of the Hebrew Bible*, London, 1897 ; *A. S. Geden, *Outlines of Introduction to the Hebrew Bible*, Edinburgh, 1911 ; J. Vandervorst, *Introduction aux textes hébreu et grec de l'AT*, Malines, 1935 ; *F. C. Kenyon, *Our Bible and the Ancient MSS*, London, 1939⁴ ; *B. Kennicott, *VT hebraicum cum variis lectionibus*, Oxford, 1776–88 ; G. B. de Rossi, *Variae lectiones VT et Scholia critica in VT libros*, Parma, 1784–98 ; *H. L. Strack, *Prolegomena critica in VT hebr.*, Leipzig, 1873 ; *J. Kennedy, *An Aid to the Textual Emendment of the OT*, Edinburgh, 1928 ; L. Dennefeld, *Critique textuelle de l'AT*, DBVS 2 (1934) 240–56 ; J. Coppens, *La critique du texte hébreu de l'AT*, Bi 25 (1944), 9–49 ; *A. von Gall, *Der hebr. Pentateuch der Samaritaner*, Giessen, 1914–19 ; H. Hyvernat, *Petite introduction à l'étude de la Massora* in RB 11–14 (1902–05) ; *P. Kahle, *Massoreten des Ostens* (Leipzig, 1913), *des Westens* (Stuttgart, 1927).

c **3. Greek NT Text**—*Westcott-Hort, *The NT in the Original Greek. Introd.*, Oxford, 1881 ; *Scrivener-Miller, *A Plain Introduction to the Criticism of the NT*, London, 1894⁴ ; C. R. Gregory, *Prolegomena ad NT graece*, ed. Tischendorf, Leipzig, 1894 ; id., *Textkritik des NT, ibid.*, 1900–09 ; id., *Die griechischen Handschriften des NT, ibid.*, 1908 ; *H. von Soden, *Die Schriften des NT.*, I, Berlin, 1900–10 ; E. Jacquier, *Le NT dans l'Eglise chrétienne*, Paris, 1913 ; *E. Nestle, *Einfuehrung in das griech. NT.*, Goettingen, 1923⁴ ; H. J. Vogels, *Handbuch des neutest. Textkritik*, Muenster, 1923 ; *A. T. Robertson, *Introduction to the Textual Criticism of the NT*, New York, 1925 ; *K. Lake, *The Text of the NT*, London, 1928⁶ ; L. Vaganay, *Initiation à la critique textuelle néotestamentaire*, Paris, 1934 (trans. by B. Miller, London, 1937) ; M. J. Lagrange, *Critique Textuelle 2. Critique rationnelle*, Paris, 1935 ; *F. C. Kenyon, *The Text of the Greek Bible*, London, 1937 ; *K. Lake and *R. P. Blake, *The Caesarean Text of the Gospel of Mark*, HTR 21 (1928) 207–404 ; T. Ayuso, *Texto caesariense o precaesariense ?* Bi. 16 (1935) 369–415 ; *F. C. Kenyon, *The Western Text of the

d *Gospels and Acts*, London, 1939. **4. Septuagint**—*H. B. Swete, *An Introduction to the OT in Greek*, Cambridge, 1902 (revised by Ottley, New York, 1914) ; *P. de Lagarde, *Septuagintastudien*, Goettingen, 1892 ; *E. Nestle, *Septuagintastudien*, Stuttgart, 1899–1907 ; *A. Rahlfs, *Septuagintastudien*, Goettingen, 1904–11 ; id., *Verzeichnis der griech. Handschriften des OT*, Berlin, 1914 ; *O. Procksch, *Studien zur Geschichte der Septuaginta*, Leipzig, 1910 ; *R. R. Ottley, *A Handbook to

the Septuagint*, New York, 1920 ; A. Ceriani, *Le recensioni dei LXX*, Rendiconti R. Istit. Lombardo 19–21 (1883–84) ; *L. F. Schleusner, *Lexicon in LXX*, Leipzig, 1820–21 ; *Hatch and *Redpath, *A Concordance to the LXX*, Oxford, 1897 ; *H. Thackeray, *A Grammar of the OT in Greek*, Cambridge, 1909 ; F. Wutz, *Die Transkriptionen von der Sept. bis an Hieronymus*, Leipzig, 1925 (cf. A. Barrois, *Une nouvelle théorie de l'origine des LXX*, RB 39 (1930) 332–61) ; A. Venard, *Citations de l'AT dans le NT*, DBVS 2 (1934) 23–51. **5. Other Versions**—L. Haefeli, *Die Peschitta des AT*, Muenster, 1927 ; C. Peters, *Das Diatessaron Tatians*, Roma, 1939 ; H. J. Vogels, *Die altsyr. Evangelien in ihrem Verhaeltnis zu Tatians Diatessaron*, Freiburg, 1911 ; *G. Zuntz, *The Ancestry of the Heraklean NT*, London, 1945 ; *R. P. Blake, *Ancient Georgian Versions of the OT*, HTR 19 (1926) 271–97 ; S. Lyonnet, *Vestiges d'un Diatessaron arménien*, Bi 19 (1938) 121–50 ; id., *La première version arménienne des Évangiles*, RB 47 (1938) 355–82 ; *H. von Soden, *Das latein. NT in Afrika zur Zeit Cyprians*, Leipzig, 1909 ; A. d'Alès, *Vetus Romana*, Bi 4 (1923) 59–90 ; F. Stummer, *Einfuehrung in das latein. Bibel*, Paderborn, 1928 ; *A. V. Billen, *The Old Latin Texts of the Heptateuch*, Cambridge, 1927 ; A. Allgeier, *Die altlatein. Psalterien*, Freiburg, 1928 ; *A. Juelicher und *W. Matzkow, *Das NT in altlatein. Ueberlieferung Mt–Mk*, Berlin, 1938–40 ; A. Condamin, *Les caractères de la traduction de la Bible par Saint Jérôme*, RSR 1–4 (1911–14) ; *S. Berger, *Histoire de la Vulgate pendant les premiers siècles du moyen-âge*, Paris, 1893 ; C. Vercellone, *Variae lectiones vulgatae latinae Bibliorum editionis*, Roma, 1860–64 ; J. M. Vosté, *De latina Bibliorum versione quae dicitur Vulgata*, Roma, 1927 ; H. J. Vogels, *Vulgatastudien*, Muenster, 1928 ; H. Quentin, *Mémoire sur l'établissement du texte de la Vulgate*, Roma, 1922 ; P. Salmon, *La révision de la Vulgate*, Rome, 1937 ; J. M. Vosté, *La Volgata al Concilio di Trento*, Bi 27 (1946) 301–19 ; H. Hoepfl, *Beitraege zur Geschichte der Sixto-Klement-Vulgata*, Freiburg, 1913.

f **Languages of the Bible**—The protocanonical books of the OT, *i.e.* those contained in the Hebrew Bible, are all written in Hebrew except parts of Daniel (2:4–7:28) and Esdras (4:8–6:18, 7:12–26), and one verse of Jeremias (10:11, most probably a later insertion), which are written in Aramaic. Baruch, Judith, Tobit, 1 Mac and the deuterocanonical parts of Daniel and Esther are extant only in a Greek version. Ecclus also was only known in a Greek version until 1896, when about two-thirds of the Hebrew text was discovered. 2 Mac, Wis, and all the books of the NT except Mt were composed in Greek. Mt originally written in Aramaic, has only been preserved in a Greek version. Hebrew, Aramaic and Greek are thus the languages of the Bible. Greek belongs to the Aryan or Indo-European, Hebrew and Aramaic to the Semitic group of languages.

g **Semitic Languages**—The chief characteristics of this linguistic family are the following. The roots or ground forms from which the words are derived are usually composed of three consonants, though there are indications of biliteral roots in the earliest period. Vowels do not form part of the roots but merely help to express various modifications of the radical sense. They are

19g thus of much less importance than in Aryan languages and are usually not expressed in alphabetical writing since a reader, familiar with the structure of the language, can supply them from the context. The simple form of the verb is modified by added letters, lengthened vowels and reduplicated radicals to express intensive, causative, reciprocal and reflexive action. The passive is distinguished from the active by a change of vowels. Person and number are indicated by prefixes and affixes derived from the corresponding personal pronouns. Abbreviated forms of these pronouns are also affixed to verbs and nouns when **h** governed by them. The Semitic verb has no tenses in our sense of the word but modes of action. The perfect is the mode of completed, the imperfect of incompleted action, but both may express past, present and future time according to the context. The structure of the various nominal forms is in general similar to that of the verbal forms. Through the loss of short final vowels the cases of the nouns and the moods of the verbs, preserved in literary Arabic, have largely disappeared in Hebrew and Aramaic. In syntax the relation between the various parts of the sentence and in particular the exact character of dependent clauses are not as definitely expressed as in Aryan languages and must often be determined from the context. In general Semitic languages are defective in indicating delicate shades of meaning and are better adapted to narrative and poetry than to philosophical or scientific discussion. Finally they have some guttural sounds, not easily pronounced by non-Semites. When the Greeks borrowed the Phoenician alphabet they used these unfamiliar consonants to express vowels.

i The Semitic languages are usually divided into South-Semitic—Arabic, Ethiopic and Sabaean; East-Semitic—Assyro-Babylonian; and West-Semitic—Canaanite and Aramaic. Hebrew and biblical Aramaic are respectively dialects of Canaanite and Aramaic. Arabic is the most faithful to the ancient form of the original Semitic tongue, has an extensive literature and is still spoken in many parts of the East. Assyro-Babylonian lost the peculiar Semitic guttural sounds when adopted by non-Semites, but, like Babylonian civilization, was widely diffused in ancient times and appears as the diplomatic language of the Near East in the fourteenth cent. B.C. Canaanite and Aramaic as the languages of neighbouring regions, Canaan and the Syrian hinterland, are most closely allied. As languages of trade and commerce both were widely diffused at a later period. Canaanite was planted along the Mediterranean seaboard by the Phoenicians after 1200 B.C. Aramaean land traders made their language international over the Near East in the Persian period.

j **Hebrew**—The name is derived, through the Latin Hebraeus, Greek Ἑβραῖος, from the Aramaic 'eḇrāyā and primarily designates not the language but the people. Similarly ἑβραϊστί, lit. 'in Hebrew', in the NT usually indicates not Hebrew but Aramaic, the language then spoken by the Hebrew people. In the OT the language of the Hebrews is called 'the lip of Canaan' (Is 19:18) and y hûḏîṯ or Jewish (4 Kg 18:26, 28; 2 Esd 13:24). That Hebrew is the language of Canaan may also be inferred from the regular use of yâm, lit. 'sea', for west and neḡeḇ, lit. 'arid land', for south. Canaan is peculiar in having both desert for its southern and sea for its western boundary. The Hebrews therefore when they settled in Canaan adopted the language of the country, to which however their ancestral language, usually called West-Semitic and regarded by some as Canaanite, by others as Aramaic, was closely akin.

k For the study of the Hebrew language and script we have besides the biblical texts a number of inscriptions in Hebrew and other Canaanite dialects. The earliest Hebrew inscription is the agricultural calendar of Gezer, now dated about the tenth cent. B.C. It briefly enumerates the field labours associated with the different months of the year. Next come the **19k** seventy-five inscribed ostraca or potsherds, recording deliveries of oil and wine from various persons and places to the royal palace of Samaria in the early ninth cent. B.C. The Siloe inscription commemorates the building of a tunnel at Jerusalem in the reign of Ezechias, by which the waters of its only spring, Gihon, were conveyed into the city. The numerous but laconic inscriptions on jar-handles found in various cities of southern Palestine and most of the inscribed seals, whose owners can sometimes be identified with biblical personages, belong to the late monarchical period. Lastly the sixteen inscribed ostraca discovered at Tell ed-Duweir and commonly known as the Letters of Lachish were written shortly before the exile. These letters are invaluable for the information they give on the character of popular literary composition in the late pre-exilic period.

Ancient inscriptions in other Canaanite dialects **l** begin with the pre-Canaanite texts of the library recently discovered at Rās-Shamra (Ugarit) on the coast of northern Syria. They are dated c 1400 B.C. and are particularly important from their number and religious character. The Canaanite glosses of the Tell el-Amarna tablets belong to the fourteenth cent. B.C. The earliest Phoenician text is the sepulchral inscription of Ahiram of Byblos in the thirteenth cent. B.C. The Phoenician alphabet here fully developed, is used in all the Hebrew inscriptions mentioned above. Phoenician inscriptions are very numerous, cover a wide area and extend down to the second cent. A.D. They consist chiefly of dedications and memorials on tombs, are brief in content, and rarely antedate the Persian period. More closely akin to Hebrew is the long inscription of Meša (c 840 B.C.) discovered at Dibon in northern Moab.

Pre-exilic and Post-exilic Hebrew—Though every lan- **20a** guage evolves in the course of centuries there is little trace of evolution in biblical pre-exilic Hebrew. The canticle of Deborah alone informs us of dialectical peculiarities in the language of the northern tribes. The Shibboleth episode manifests diversity of pronunciation. Archaisms like ḥay⁵ṯô (Gen 1:25, etc.) are rare and not easily explained. In general the early books of the Bible exhibit the same stage of the language as the Lachish letters. It does not follow from this that all these books are of late pre-exilic origin. Writing was in common use among the Hebrews at a much earlier period. Moses and Josue were ordered to write. The copy of the Law discovered accidentally in the reign of Josias was of much earlier origin. Pre-exilic historical books attest the use of earlier written sources. The kings had their scribes. Ezechias collected the Proverbs of Solomon. Isaias and Jeremias were ordered to write some at least of their prophecies. The conclusion to be drawn from the linguistic uniformity of earlier and later texts is therefore that the language of the earlier writings was modernized in the later period.

The post-exilic Hebrew writers are markedly inferior **b** in literary genius to their pre-exilic predecessors. There is a corresponding deterioration in the language which manifests itself principally in two ways. The niceties of Hebrew idiom are often neglected and Aramaic forms of expression are adopted into the language. Some examples will show the character of these innovations. The first is exemplified by various irregularities in the use of the particle w, abbreviations of expression such as not repeating a preposition before a noun in apposition with its object or a governing noun before several succeeding genitives, double plurals in genitival combinations like 'men of names' for 'men of name', use of the article as a relative, frequent substitution of the infinitive absolute for a finite verb. The second is illustrated by new forms of the infinitive with m prefixed and of the pi'el of verbs with w as second radical, use of hēn 'behold' for 'im 'if', anticipation of noun object by a pronominal suffix, prefixion of l to noun object when

20b determined. The chief prose exponent of post-biblical Hebrew is the author of Chronicles, Esdras and Nehemias. Aramaisms in poetry are less remarkable as a form of poetical ornament. Their frequency in a prose writer like the Chronicler seems to indicate that Aramaic was the spoken language and Hebrew a dead language in his time.

c **Transition from Hebrew to Aramaic**—It is clear from 4 Kg 18:26 that the common people of Jerusalem did not understand Aramaic in 701 B.C. That the change of language was made in Palestine between this period and the exile is excluded by the testimony of the Lachish letters written in Hebrew. It was most probably during the exile when the Jews came into close contact with Aramaic-speaking peoples in southern Babylonia that they began to speak Aramaic. The objection made to this view that biblical Aramaic is not an eastern but a western dialect can no longer be sustained. The peculiarities of eastern Aramaic not found in biblical texts appear first in eastern Aramaic writings of the Christian era. Biblical Aramaic lacks no peculiarities of early eastern Aramaic texts discovered in Assyria and elsewhere. The passage of a people from one language to another is usually gradual. There is an indication that Hebrew was still spoken in the second half of the fifth cent. B.C. The Chronicler calls Hebrew *y'hûḍiṭ* (2 Par 32:18) and uses the same term for the language of the Jews in 2 Esd 13:44. The Aramaisms of the Chronicler and the use of Aramaic by Esdras not only in official documents but also in historical narrative make it very probable that the transition was completed in the fourth cent. B.C.

d **Aramaic**—This language, the rudest and simplest in syntactical structure of all the Semitic tongues, takes its name like Hebrew from the people who spoke it, the Aramaeans. They were nomads who spread from Arabia into Mesopotamia and thence crossing the Euphrates founded a number of city-states in the region extending from Armenia in the north to Transjordania in the south. Thus controlling the international highway of the Near East, for which empires had fought at an earlier period, they exercised a preponderating influence in international commerce in the early first millennium B.C. It is owing to this fact and the adventurous spirit of the Aramaean traders that Aramaic became so widely diffused as the language of trade and commerce.

e Our knowledge of ancient Aramaic is derived from recently discovered texts which range in time from the eighth cent. B.C. to well into the Christian era, and in space over all the countries of the Near East from Taxila on the Hydaspes to Elephantine on the Nile. The earliest and most important inscriptions discovered at Zingirli and in the neighbourhood of Aleppo in northern Syria belong to the eighth cent. B.C. Then too begin the Aramaic inscriptions on weights and Aramaic endorsements on Assyrian contracts. It was, however, in the Persian period that the language became most widely diffused, as the texts discovered in Iran, Mesopotamia, Asia Minor, Syria, Arabia and Egypt abundantly attest. The Aramaic documents of Esdras and narratives of Daniel belong to this period. For their better understanding and the solution of the vexed question of their date the considerable number of Aramaic papyri and ostraca discovered half a century ago at Elephantine are particularly important. These are dated in the fifth cent. B.C. The Aramaic texts of the Bible, if authentic, must exhibit, at least in their original form, the same stage of linguistic development.

f Languages develop in two ways, structurally and phonetically. Structural development is exhibited by the disappearance of old and the appearance of new forms in the structure of the language. As these forms are usually too firmly fixed to be much affected by textual transmission, the structural stage of a language is easily discerned. Phonetic development appears in sound changes and assimilation of sounds originally distinguished. When our knowledge of the

pronunciation of a language is derived from written **20f** texts its phonetic stage is often difficult to determine. Writing is orthographical as well as phonetical. It sometimes fails to register sound changes, as in modern English and French where spelling and pronunciation differ widely. There is a further difficulty in the case of biblical texts frequently copied. The original writing may have been modernized and systematized. We may conclude therefore that structural forms rather than alterations of letters, which may or may not attest phonetic development and in some cases can be definitely attributed to later copyists, are the best means of determining the original character of biblical Aramaic. Of these the causative forms of verbs, the prefix of the reflexive forms, the inner passives and the remains of the jussive attest a stage of the language at least as ancient as that of the Elephantine papyri. For the authenticity of the Esdras documents it is **g** important to note that they maintain the ancient final *m* of the 2 and 3 pl. pronominal suffixes. The Esdras narrative and Daniel have the later final *n* while the Elephantine papyri have both forms. The systematic use of *d* in biblical Aramaic to represent an ancient *z* has been interpreted as a sound change completed in the third cent. B.C. The sound in question, however, an aspirated *d*, which has no equivalent in the Phoenician alphabet, is expressed by *d* as well as *z* in Assyria in the eighth century. The omission or mode of expression of a final *a* is also a matter of orthography. These examples show that alterations of letters are less reliable indications of the date of biblical Aramaic than structural forms, even in the very improbable hypothesis that the biblical texts, repeatedly copied, are exact reproductions of the original.

Biblical Greek—The Greek of the original texts and **21a** of the LXX version of the Bible, recognized in the Renaissance period as a debased form of classical Greek, could not be satisfactorily explained as long as it remained an isolated phenomenon. The study of the numerous Greek papyri, discovered in Egypt during the last century, has finally revealed to us its origin and character. It is not a biblical or Jewish or Alexandrian dialect of Greek but the Koine or common Greek which supplanted the classical form of the language and became international in the Hellenistic period inaugurated by the African and Asiatic conquests of Alexander the Great. The zeal of Greek rulers for the Hellenization of their eastern subjects and still more the exigencies of trade and commerce account for its world-wide diffusion. Attic Greek had lost its purity even in Greece itself in the fourth cent. B.C. and was in any case, in its classical form, ill adapted to popular and international use. The Koine is the current Attic Greek modified and accommodated to a new and wider sphere of utility. It was naturally used by the sacred writers as the language understood by their contemporaries, providentially designed and admirably adapted for the preaching of the Gospel to all nations.

The Koine was not merely a spoken language. It **b** was taught in the schools and was the ordinary medium of literary expression. It thus preserved a general uniformity despite the variations resulting from the nationality or lack of education of the writer and the colloquial or literary character of his composition. It differed from Attic Greek mainly in aiming at a simpler and easier but at the same time clearer and more vigorous mode of expression. The vocabulary is less rich but more varied in its origin. In phonetics there is a tendency to reduce diphthongs to simple vowels. Declensions and conjugations are simplified and occasionally assimilated by analogy. There is a **c** preference for longer and composite rather than shorter and simple words. Co-ordination of dependent clauses is also preferred to subordination and direct speech to indirect. Prepositions are more frequently used not only in composition with verbs but also to strengthen the case endings of nouns and even pleonastically with adverbs. Pleonasm also appears in an

21c excessive repetition of personal pronouns. The vocative is often accompanied by the article for greater emphasis. The infinitive is used loosely with or without the article in final, consecutive or explanatory clauses, but is preferably replaced on the other hand by a ὅτι clause after verbs of saying and perceiving. The article is used more frequently and before clauses as well as nouns. Adjectives are often replaced by substantives in the genitive. The popular character of the Koine is manifested by sense constructions, anacolutha and other grammatical irregularities.

d The Greek of the Bible is distinguished from that of profane literature by the presence of semitisms, both hebraisms and aramaisms. The Septuagint interpreters of a Hebrew and sacred text reproduced in Greek some of the modes of expression and phraseology of the original Hebrew. These hebraisms vary in number according to the freedom or literalness of the different translators. They appear also in the NT owing to the influence exerted on the sacred writers by the language of the Septuagint which they consciously or unconsciously imitated. The aramaisms of the NT are explained by the fact that Aramaic was either the native language of the inspired writers or the language of sources which they used.

e The discovery in the Egyptian papyri of nearly all the words previously considered peculiar to Biblical Greek established the Koine origin of the NT vocabulary. The semitisms discovered in Egyptian Greek have been similarly interpreted as Koine idioms by many scholars. It should be noted, however, that semitisms in the Bible may appear as coptisms in the papyri. Coptic has many non-Greek idioms in common with Hebrew and Aramaic. Coptic writers would naturally reproduce their native modes of thought in their new medium of expression.

f **The Hebrew Text of the OT**—Under this heading the Aramaic texts are implicitly included. The deuterocanonical parts of the OT on the other hand, whether written originally in Greek or only extant in a Greek version, belong to the history of the Septuagint. By way of introduction to the history of the text some account must be given of the medium by which it was transmitted.

g Papyrus was the ordinary material used for writing in Palestine in biblical times. We learn from the narrative of Wen-Amon that it was imported in large quantities from Egypt to Canaan in the eleventh cent. B.C. Its rapid disintegration in a damp climate explains why so few literary remains and biblical texts have been discovered in Palestine. It was too fragile also to be a suitable material for Babylonian script, for which fine clay, not easily procurable in Palestine, was required. We may conclude therefore that the sacred text was not originally written in cuneiform characters but in alphabetic script, especially since the inscription of Aḥiram, discovered at Byblos in 1923, has shown that the Phoenician alphabet was fully developed before the time of Moses. From the use of this Phoenician script in ancient Hebrew inscriptions we may infer that it was the regular medium for the
h transmission of the Hebrew text of the OT. The Samaritan Pentateuch which retains the Phoenician script and may be approximately dated c 400 B.C. gives us a *terminus a quo* for the adoption of the Aramaic or square characters with which readers of the Hebrew Bible are familiar. The transition from Phoenician to Aramaic script was, however, very gradual and scarcely completed before the close of the third cent. B.C. The Nash papyrus variously dated (II cent. B.C.–I cent. A.D.) is written in Aramaic characters. Scribal errors in the Hebrew text, caused by the similarity of letters, attest the use of both forms of script.

i The form of the book in OT times was the roll or volume (*cf.* Jer 36). A long strip of papyrus was attached at one end to a support round which it was rolled. The writing was usually only on the inner side of the papyrus and began at the further end so that the volume would be gradually unrolled as it was **21i** read. Besides papyrus, leather or parchment was also used at least in the Greek period. The roll form of the book limited its dimensions, so that the Torah for instance filled five rolls or volumes and was therefore called Pentateuch by the Greeks. The codex form of the book was later admitted by the Jews for private copies of the sacred text but not for use in the synagogue.

The Phoenicians like the Greeks usually failed to **j** indicate the separation of words in their inscriptions. The Hebrews and Aramaeans on the other hand marked the end of each word by a point, like the Latins, in their inscriptions and by a short interval in their papyri. Errors in the division of words are of comparatively rare occurrence in the Hebrew text. Moreover the earliest specimens of the square script exhibit the peculiar final forms of the Hebrew letters. We may conclude, therefore, that the separate words were indicated, though perhaps not very clearly at times, certainly in the later and probably in the earlier period. Punctuation marks and vowel points are of later Massoretic origin.

History of the Hebrew Text—Our present Hebrew **k** text undoubtedly contains corruptions of various kinds —omissions attested by the LXX, incorrect readings, alterations of numbers and dates, errors in orthography and lexicography, interpolated glosses and marginal notes. There are many indications on the other hand that this text has remained practically unchanged from c A.D. 100 to the present day. The divergences from the archetype belong therefore almost entirely to the period of its gradual formation. This is not surprising since no special human safeguards would be devised for its preservation before its scattered parts were united and its sacred character was generally recognized. God undoubtedly watched over the text which he had inspired and preserved its substantial integrity, but he did not protect it from the minor alterations which all texts suffer in course of transmission.

Period of Formation—There are some means of establishing by comparison the state of the text in the later **l** part of this period. Passages repeated in different parts of the OT can be compared, *e.g.* Ps 14 and Ps 53 ; Ps 18 and 2 Kg 22 ; Is 36–39 and 4 Kg 18:13–20:19 ; Jer 52 and 4 Kg 24:18–25:30, etc. In all these cases we find substantial conformity of the texts compared, diversified by ordinary scribal errors. The Samaritan Pentateuch, when compared with MT, exhibits a few transpositions of short passages, a number of additions mostly superfluous and many unimportant variants chiefly orthographical and grammatical. The insertion of Deut 27:3-7 immediately after the decalogue in Ex and Deut and the alteration of Hebal to Garizim in this passage constitute the most interesting but least authentic peculiarity of this text. The comparison **m** of the MT with the LXX Greek version, dated c 250–100 B.C., covers a wider field and gives more important results. The LXX supplies short omissions in the MT, has occasionally better readings and is particularly remarkable for diversity in the order and extent of the matter contained in some books or parts of books. The chief instances of this diversity are Ex 36–39, where the order is different and the narrative shorter ; 1 Kg, where 17:12-31 and 17:55–18:5 are omitted ; 3 Kg, where the order is different in chh 4-7 ; 1 Par, where 1:10-23 are omitted ; 2 Esdr 11-12, where 23 verses are omitted ; Prov 24:23–31:10, where the order is different and there are short omissions and additions ; Jer, where the prophecies against the Gentiles are in the middle instead of at the end of the book and in a different order ; Lam, which has an introduction ; the deuterocanonical additions. From these peculiarities of the LXX we may conclude that the Hebrew text was not yet standardized when the Greek version was made. This conclusion is borne out by the Nash papyrus, recently assigned by Albright to the Maccabaean period, which exhibits a Hebrew text of the Decalogue and Deut 6:4

21m much closer to the LXX than to the MT. Josephus also sometimes differs from the MT in his citations from the Hebrew. On the other hand the recently published text of Isaias discovered in Palestine in 1947 and not later in date than the Nash papyrus is said to be practically identical with the MT (*cf.* §§ 80*l*, 422*g*). The study of the differences between the earlier LXX text and the later MT shows their substantial conformity but does not authorize an unreserved preference of one to the other. The individual cases of divergency must be judged according to their merits.

22a The History of the MT—Versions made from the Hebrew in the second cent., and later, exhibit a remarkable agreement with the MT against the LXX. This is the chief reason for assigning the unification of the Hebrew text to *c* A.D. 100. It was the work of the Hebrew Academy in Palestine, transferred to Jamnia after the fall of Jerusalem and thence later to Tiberias. A notice in the Talmud informs us that the single standard text was made by majority rule from three different texts preserved in the temple. All texts differing from the standard text were officially banned. Readings disagreeing with the MT may be found in Jewish and Christian works but are extremely rare.

b The Hebrew text received a further development in the period between its unification and our earliest extant MSS from the critical studies of the Scribes (I–VI cent.) and the Massoretes (VI–X cent.). The Scribes divided the text into verses, indicated the places where words should be altered or omitted or supplied by the reader, and marked with points doubtful or spurious readings. They are also supposed to have altered slightly some expressions which sounded irreverent. The euphemistic substitution of bless (God) for curse (God) may be cited as an instance. The Massoretes supplied the vowel points and the accents by which the pronunciation, the tone and the interconnection of the words were indicated. These innovations belong most probably to the seventh cent. and were only admitted in private copies of the text.

c Massora means tradition. The Massoretes also committed to writing traditions relating to the sacred text and handed down orally from the period of the Scribes. The Massora or textual tradition was usually written either on the lateral margins (*massora parva*) or at the top and bottom of the page (*massora magna*), or at the end of the papyrus roll (*massora finalis*). Such critical indications as the number of times a rare word occurred in the Bible, variations in the spelling of certain words, alterations of the written word to be made by the reader, were noted briefly in the *parva* but more fully in the *massora magna*. The *massora finalis* gave the number of verses in the different books or parts of books and other minute computations as well as various notes on peculiar words and expressions. The Massoretic schools of Palestine and Babylonia differed not only in their method of expressing the vowels but also to a less extent in the traditions which they

d recorded. In Palestine itself the rival schools of Ben Asher and Ben Nephtali flourished in the tenth cent. Later, however, the Tiberian vowel system was generally adopted and the Massora of Ben Asher prevailed over that of his rival. The present division of the text into chapters is of Christian origin. It was first introduced into the Latin Vulgate in the thirteenth cent. to facilitate references and later adopted by the Jews in private but not in liturgical copies of the sacred text.

e The earliest MSS of the Hebrew Bible, if we except that of Isaias mentioned above (§ 21*m*), belong to the tenth cent. The relatively few variants exhibited by the MSS have been collected by Kennicot and De Rossi. The first and less accurate editions of the printed Bible were superseded by that of Jacob ben Chaim (Venice 1525) which became the *textus receptus*. The third edition of Kittel's *Biblia Hebraica* (Stuttgart, 1937) is based on a Leningrad MS of the text of Ben Asher dated A.D. 1008. It gives also the *massora parva*

(edited by Kahle) on the outer margin of the page **22e** and a full critical apparatus underneath.

The critical authenticity, or conformity with the **f** originals of the MT may be inferred from its conformity with the ancient versions and from the scrupulous care of its custodians to preserve intact their sacred text. This authenticity is only substantial and does not exclude various corruptions which may often be corrected with the aid of the ancient versions, more especially the LXX. In such cases the authenticity of the rendering and its derivation from a different Hebrew text must be proved. Corruptions which occurred before any versions were made may also be corrected by conjectural emendation. These corrections presuppose grave doubt about the genuineness of the text, and may only be admitted when the recognized rules of textual emendation have been fully observed. From the dogmatic point of view the authenticity of the Latin Vulgate, decreed by the Council of Trent, presupposes the authenticity of the original Hebrew text which St Jerome translated.

The Greek Text of the NT—Some preliminary remarks **g** on the material and method of writing in early NT times will help us to understand the difficulties encountered in the transmission of the text. Papyrus was the fragile material on which it was written during the first three centuries. Only recently have valuable fragments of these early texts been discovered in Egypt. The use of the more durable parchment in the fourth cent. marks the beginning of manuscript tradition. In the early second cent. the codex form of book had supplanted the roll in papyrus copies of the sacred text. The writing in these copies was cursive, but the letters were neither connected by ligatures nor divided into separate words. The uncial script of the earlier MSS differs from the cursive in its large rounded letters written separately and continuously. There are no word intervals, no accents or breathings, no punctuation marks. The custom of assigning a separate line **h** to the individual members of parallelisms in the poetical books of the OT gave rise to a similar indication of the sense divisions in NT prose in the fourth cent. The minuscule script of the later MSS first appears in the ninth cent. and replaces the uncial or majuscule in the eleventh. This cursive writing is distinguished from that of the papyri by the ligatures with which the letters are connected. Only in these later MSS do we find small letters distinguished from capitals, intervals between the different words, breathings, accents and punctuation marks. As parchment was costly some old MSS were used a second time after the original writing had been obliterated. By deciphering the earlier script ancient biblical texts have been recovered from these MSS called palimpsests.

The Codices of the NT—The codices from which our **i** direct knowledge of the text is derived are estimated at about 210 uncials, 2,400 minuscules, 50 papyri and 1,610 lectionaries. Most of these are incomplete or fragmentary; the lectionaries are restricted to liturgical texts; 53 codices contain the whole NT. Individual codices in each of the four classes are now generally indicated by arabic numerals, according to the system introduced by C. R. Gregory, used alone for the minuscules but preceded by O, P and *l* respectively when designating uncials, papyri and lectionaries. The earlier method of indicating the 45 oldest uncials by Latin and Greek capitals is however generally retained and S usually replaces the Hebrew *aleph* for the cod. Sinaiticus. The oldest and most important **j** codices are the following: B = Vaticanus, fourth cent., probably of Egyptian origin, contains the whole Bible from Gen 46:28 to Heb 9:14; S = Sinaiticus, fourth–fifth cent., discovered in the monastery of Mt Sinai but now in the British Museum, contains the whole Bible with many OT omissions; A = Alexandrinus, fifth cent., belonged to the Patriarch of Alexandria, but is now in the British Museum and contains the whole Bible with occasional

22j omissions ; C = Codex Ephraemi rescriptus, fifth cent. palimpsest now in the Paris National Library, contains only fragments of the OT but nearly all the NT ; D = Codex Bezae, sixth cent., property of a Lyons monastery, presented by Beza to Cambridge University, contains Gospels and Acts in Greek and Latin ; D = Claromontanus, sixth cent , now in the Paris National Library, contains the Epistles of St Paul in Greek and Latin.

k Classification of the Codices—The critical investigations of numerous scholars during the last century have resulted in the division of the various witnesses to the NT text into families and groups and the recognition of three different types of text usually called Western, Eastern and Antiochian. These types are all recensions, *i.e.* deliberate revisions of earlier texts assumed to need correction and therefore amended according to the corrector's idea of the original text. The western recension of the Catholic Epistles and the Apocalypse is no longer extant. A fourth recension of the Gospels called Caesarean has been recently discovered.

l Character of the Recensions—The western recension is popular. It alters the text freely, clarifies obscurities by paraphrasing and eliminates difficulties by harmonizing. It has some peculiar additions adapted to popular taste and occasionally of a marvellous character. The eastern recension is critical and conservative. It has very few harmonizations. It avoids also linguistic alterations retaining the vulgar forms of Koine Greek and the stylistic peculiarities of the different sacred writers. It is remarkable for concision, and has some noteworthy omissions. The Antiochian recension is learned and ecclesiastical. It aims at elegance, clearness and fullness. The language is corrected by the substitution of classical for Koine forms. Obscurities are clarified, but more smoothly, and harmonizations appear, but less extensively than in the western recension. Variants derived from the two earlier recensions appear together in **m** conflated texts. The different method of the three revisers is illustrated by their treatment of the shorter Lucan form of the Lord's Prayer. The eastern preserves it unaltered, the western substitutes for it the Matthaean form, the Antiochian supplements it by appropriate additions from St Matthew. The Caesarean recension appears to be a reconstitution of the text based on the earlier eastern and western recensions.

23a History of the Recensions—The western recension is found in the Uncial D, Beza (Gospels and Ac) and Claromontanus (Pauline Epistles) and in the Old Latin and early Syriac versions. Fragments of Ac in P 38 (IV cent.) and P 48 (III cent.) and of Lk in O 171 (IV cent.) attest a Greek text of this recension in Egypt, where it very probably had its origin. It gives us the earliest known type of NT text which prevailed in the West and in Syria from the late second to the early fifth cent. and left traces in the Egyptian texts and versions of the third cent. The eastern recension is exhibited by the earliest uncials, A (except the Gospels which are Antiochian) SBC, by many other uncials and minuscules, by nearly all the papyri fragments and generally by the Latin Vulgate and by the Coptic, more especially the Bohairic, versions. Its use by Origen at one period of his critical emendation of the Gospels and in the Acts and Pauline Epistles of the Chester Beatty papyri establishes its existence in the early third cent. It prevailed in Egypt until the Arab conquest, and is still, substantially at least, the official text of the Latin Church. It is now generally recognized as **b** exhibiting the best form of the NT text. The Antiochian recension is contained mostly in late uncials, minuscules and lectionaries. The Gospels alone are early attested in A. It is universally attributed to Lucian, martyred at Antioch in 312 and author of a recension of the LXX which exhibits the same characteristics. The Syriac Peshitta version (V cent.)

is based on it. From Antioch and Constantinople **23c** it spread over the entire East after the Arab conquest of Egypt and Palestine and thence to the West after the fall of Constantinople where it became the text of the AV and was highly esteemed and the *textus receptus* until the critical studies of the nineteenth cent. revealed its defects. The Caesarean recension **d** appears in the eighth cent. uncial θ Koridethi of Palestinian origin, the minuscules fam. 1 and 13 and MSS 28.565.700, the Egyptian uncial W, P 45 and the Armenian and Georgian versions. It is attested in Palestine by Origen and Eusebius but seems to be of Egyptian origin. As a fusion of the earlier eastern and western recensions it offers a more mixed and less uniform type of text. In this sense the Latin Vulgate, predominantly eastern, may be called Caesarean.

Editions of the Greek NT—Critical editions of the **e** Greek NT begin in the nineteenth cent. when the Antiochian *textus receptus*, on which previous editions were based, was superseded by the better Eastern text. Noteworthy are those of C. Lachmann (Berlin, 1831), S. Tregelles (London, 1857–79), Westcott-Hort (Oxford, 1881), B. Weiss (Berlin, 1892), E. Nestle (Stuttgart, 1898–1941[17]) and the major editions with very full critical apparatus of C. Tischendorf (Leipzig, 1872[8]) and H. von Soden (Berlin, 1913). Mk and Mt (ed. S. E. F. Legg) have already appeared in an Oxford major edition of Westcott-Hort. Recent Catholic critical editions are those of H. J. Vogels (Duesseldorf, 1922), J. Bover (Madrid, 1943) and A. Merk (Rome, 1922[2]).

Authority of the NT Text—No classical text exhibits **f** claims to authenticity approaching those of the Greek NT, whether we consider the number and antiquity of its sources, all in substantial agreement, or the internal evidence of these sources, revealed by a century of critical investigation, or the unanimous verdict of critics of all schools of thought. The variant readings collected from so many codices are naturally very numerous but usually manifest unimportant differences in orthography, grammar, choice of synonyms and order of words. The sense is affected in about two hundred cases of which fifteen are important. The dogmatic teaching of the NT, derived from passages undoubtedly authentic, is independent of these variants.

Versions of the OT. The Septuagint—The ancient **g** versions of the Bible give us valuable information about the original text and its traditional interpretation. Of these the Greek version of the OT made at Alexandria and known as the Septuagint is by far the most important. It preserved for us the inspired deuterocanonical parts of the OT, was generally used in preference to the Hebrew text by the NT writers in their scriptural citations and was the Vulgate of the eastern and western Church for several centuries until it was superseded among the Latins by the Vulgate of St Jerome. The method of its transmission as regards writing, book-form, etc. was similar to that of the NT text, with which it is sometimes associated in the codices. The uncials and minuscules in which it is contained are 1534 in number but rarely exhibit the whole OT. The earliest and most important uncials are BSA already described. Still earlier fragments of the Septuagint have been recently discovered in Egypt, of which the Chester Beatty Papyri, Vol IV–VII of Kenyon's edition, are particularly important. Two short fragments of Deut, PRG 458, published by C. H. Roberts at the Manchester University Press in 1936, and P. Fouad 266, reproduced and studied by W. G. Waddell JTS 45 (1944) 158–61, may also be mentioned as our oldest Greek biblical texts belonging to the Maccabaean period.

Origin and Character of the Septuagint Version— **h** The Greek Letter of Aristeas to Philocrates, composed at latest in the second cent. B.C., informs us that Ptolemy II Philadelphos (285–247), a great bibliophile,

23h had the Hebrew Torah translated into Greek for his famous library by 72 Hebrew scholars summoned from Jerusalem and domiciled in the island of Pharos where they completed the version of the Pentateuch in 72 days. The segregation of the translators in different cells and the marvellous agreement of their different versions is a further embellishment of Philo. The later assumption that the whole OT was then translated explains the name Septuagint (LXX). Though the letter is a literary fiction and its author is not very trustworthy the version of the Pentateuch may be dated *c* 250 B.C. It seems to have been used by the Jewish historian, Demetrius, towards the close **i** of the third cent. B.C. The need felt by the hellenised Alexandrian Jews for a version of the sacred text is the most probable explanation of its origin and suggests also that the other sacred books were translated without much delay. The Prologue of Ecclus written in 132 B.C. records the translation into Greek of the Law, the Prophets and the Sacred Books as an accomplished fact. That the work was protracted over a considerable period may be concluded from the large number and different qualifications of the translators, revealed by internal evidence. It is generally supposed that the translators used texts written in Hebrew characters. The ancient theory of Tychsen, who supposed that the texts had been previously transliterated from Hebrew into Greek, has been recently revived by Wutz. This hypothesis, unsupported by solid arguments, is generally rejected.

j The character of the translation varies with the translators. It is literal in the Canticle, Ecclesiastes, the Psalms and the Prophets (except Daniel), faithful in the Pentateuch and the historical books, free in Job, Proverbs, Daniel and Esther. The Greek is good in the original works Wis and 2 Mach and in Job and Prov, fair in Pent., Jos, Is, 1 Mach but poor elsewhere. The sense of the Hebrew text is best indicated in the Pent., least well in Is, Minor Proph., Job, Prov. Important variations from the MT, due to the translators and to be distinguished from those already indicated as due to a different Hebrew text, are the following : frequent omissions in Job amounting to a sixth of the text, some additions and amplifications in Prov, a rendering of Dan so different from the original that it was rejected in the third or fourth cent., and replaced by the version of Theodotion.

k Later Greek Versions—For the better understanding of the history of LXX some account must be given here of the Greek versions made by Jews from the Hebrew text of the second cent. A.D. Disputes between Jews and Christians and the existence of a standard Hebrew text emphasized the differences between the text recognized by the Jews and the version to which the Christians appealed. The Hellenistic Jews in particular needed a Greek version of their official text for use in their synagogues and for polemical purposes. Three Greek versions of the whole Hebrew Bible were thus made in the second cent. by three Jews : Aquila (*c* 140), Symmachus (*c* 200) and Theodotion (*c* 180). According to St Jerome Aquila aimed at a word for word rendering, Symmachus sought to express the sense exactly, Theodotion reproduced with slight alterations the older LXX version. Three other anonymous translators of the poetical books are mentioned and cited by Origen. All these translations were utilized in his revision of the LXX.

l History of the Septuagint—The natural and well attested tendency of most ancient revisers of the LXX was to bring it into closer conformity with the Hebrew text. In the Greek OT as in the NT deliberate alterations are largely due to harmonization. Hence in cases of variant readings a free rendering which differs from the Hebrew is usually preferred to a slavish rendering in agreement with the Hebrew. This is the chief reason why the Vatican cod. B, though by no means free from errors, is generally held to be the best witness to the original form of the text in the Greek OT as well as in the NT. The

citations from LXX in Philo, Josephus and the NT **23l** rarely however exhibit B readings in disputed passages. NT citations from Dan agree with the later version of Theodotion against LXX. These OT citations in the NT may have been subsequently altered. It is more probable, however, that they are derived from a recension of LXX existing in the first cent. A.D. and later used by Theodotion.

Origen and the Hexapla—In compiling this monu- **m** mental work *c* A.D. 240 Origen's aim was twofold : to aid Christian apologists in their disputes with the Jews by indicating exactly what was and what was not contained in the Hebrew text and to provide the Church with a uniform text by removing the variants found in the codices. The Hexapla is so called from the six corresponding columns into which it was divided and which contained respectively : (1) the Hebrew text in Hebrew letters ; (2) the same in Greek letters ; (3) Aquila ; (4) Symmachus ; (5) LXX ; (6) Theodotion. An edition containing only the four Greek versions was called Tetrapla. The words Heptapla and Octopla are used to indicate the occasional addition of a seventh and eighth column containing extracts from the anonymous Greek versions mentioned above. The fifth column not only exhibited Origen's recension of the LXX text but also indicated how it differed from the Hebrew original. Words or **n** groups of words not in the Hebrew were marked by an *obelus* (÷ or ⸋) while the deficiencies of the LXX supplied from the other Greek versions were marked by an asterisk. The end of the LXX redundance or deficiency was also marked by a *metobelus* (: or / or ·/.). In establishing his LXX text Origen chose from the variant readings of the codices those which were supported by the later Greek versions. St Jerome rightly condemns this criterium as compromising the purity of the text. He also blames Origen for introducing into his fifth column passages from Theodotion's version (marked by asterisks). Origen followed the Hebrew order of the text in his Hexapla except in Prov, where however it was clearly indicated and Greek transpositions were marked by a combination of *obeli* and asterisks.

The Hexapla which must have numbered about **o** 12,000 pages was too vast to be ever copied in its entirety. But the recension of the LXX text in the fifth column was widely diffused and highly esteemed. The use made of the later Greek versions if critically questionable was practically advantageous for an ecclesiastical text thus brought into closer conformity with the inspired Hebrew original. The textual confusion resulting from Origen's recension must be attributed to the scribes who failed to reproduce the asterisks and *obeli* in their copies. Only two codices G = Colberto-Sarravianus (Gen–Jg) and 88 = Chisianus (Proph.) exhibit a marked text. The recension is found without the marks in 376 426 (Gen–Jg), A 247 (Kg), V 253 (Wisdom books), Q (Proph.). The marks have also been preserved in a Syriac version and in Jerome's Latin recension of Job, but are missing in the Armenian version and the Gallican Psalter. Fragments of the Hexapla and parts of Aquila's version were recovered half a century ago from two palimpsests found respectively in the Ambrosian library at Milan and the *geniza* or lumber-room of a synagogue at Cairo. Other additions made to Field's collection of citations from the Hexapla in 1879 are still dispersed in various publications.

Recensions of Hesychius and Lucian—St Jerome in- **24a** forms us (Praef. in Paralipom.) that three important recensions of the LXX were made respectively by Hesychius at Alexandria, Origen at Caesarea, and Lucian at Antioch, and were in general use, each in the country of its origin. We have no other direct information about Hesychius but he is generally identified with the Hesychius, martyred at Alexandria *c* A.D. 300. The character of his recension which became the Egyptian text of the fourth and fifth cent. can only be deduced from the citations of the Egyptian Fathers

24a and the Coptic versions. It was closer to the Hebrew than that of Origen, having been emended directly from the Hebrew text as well as from the later Greek versions in the columns of the Hexapla, and is found in MV 29 121 (histor. books) and Q 86 198 233 (Proph.). Some writers less probably find this recension in B which however is usually pre-Hexaplar and most probably contains the neutral text which Hesychius and Origen revised.

b Lucian and his recension are much better known. He was a priest of the Church of Antioch, where he died a martyr in A.D. 312. He is particularly noted for his knowledge of Hebrew and his extensive use of the original text in his emendation of the LXX. His renderings are sometimes peculiar, but scarcely imply, as some have held, that his Hebrew text differed much from the MT. His recension is used in the commentaries of the great Antiochian exegetes, Chrysostom and Theodoretus, and is sometimes explicitly indicated in the MSS. by a marginal l. It is found in K 54 59 75 (Gen–Jg) ; 19 82 93 108 (histor. books) ; VZ 22 36 48 51 281 (Proph.). It displays the same characteristics as have been already noted in the Antiochian recension of the NT : clearness and elegance of language, conflation of readings from different codices, additions chiefly from Theodotion, harmonizing corrections from the Hebrew. The text which he revised was different from that used by Origen and Hesychius and less close to B. This recension though most widely diffused in Byzantine times did not however supplant the others like Lucian's NT recension. The chief difficulty in reconstituting the original text is the mixture of the recensions in the different codices.

c **Editions of the LXX**—The Polyglot Bible of Cardinal Ximenes (Alcala, 1517) exhibits mainly a Lucianic text. The Aldine edition (Venice, 1518) is more doubtfully regarded as Hesychian. The Vatican edition of Sixtus V (Rome, 1587) is based on B, but other codices were also used to supply lacunae and correct errors. The resultant text was so highly esteemed and so frequently reproduced by various editors that it may be called *textus receptus*. Grabe's edition (Oxford, 1707–20) is based on A with various emendations always expressly indicated. The first really critical edition was that of Holmes and Parsons entitled *VT Graecum cum variis lectionibus* (Oxford, 1798–1827). Though not always accurate it is still useful as a **d** storehouse of materials. The edition of Tischendorf (Leipzig, 1869[4]) supervised by Nestle (*ib.* 1887[7]) has a revised Sixtine text with a critical apparatus derived from ASC. Lagarde's half-completed edition (Gen–Esth, Goettingen, 1883) is a reconstitution of Lucian's recension. Finally the Universities of Cambridge and Goettingen produced two minor editions of the LXX, Swete's in England (1894) and Rahlfs' in Germany (Stuttgart, 1935), and inaugurated two major editions of which the Pentateuch and the historical books (ed. Brooke and McClean) have already appeared in England and Ps (ed. Rahlfs), 1 Mac (ed. Kappler) and Is (ed. Ziegler) in Germany. The critical apparatus, generally restricted to the early uncials in the minor editions, is elaborate and carefully selected in the major editions. The printed text is traditional, that of B supplemented when necessary from S and A in the English editions, but critical as reconstituted by the editors in the German.

e **Authority of the LXX**—The substantial authenticity of our LXX text is critically established by the number and antiquity of the codices, all in substantial agreement, in which it is contained. Its authority as an authentic version of the inspired OT may be critically deduced from its substantial conformity with the MT and is dogmatically established by its exclusive use as the OT of the infallible Church for several centuries. The numerous critical studies of the codices during the last century, of which the fruits have now begun to appear, have for their object the restoration of the text to its original form. The older Hebrew text on which the LXX version is based can then be deter-mined with some degree of confidence and critically **24e** used to correct errors and clarify obscurities in the later MT.

The Targum—When Hebrew became a dead language, **f** unintelligible to the common people, the Palestinian Jews experienced the same need of an Aramaic version of the Bible as their Hellenistic brethren did of a Greek version. They preferred, however, to retain the sacred Hebrew text in their liturgy, but made it intelligible to all by adding an Aramaic version. Targum means ' version '. The Targums were *ex tempore* versions made by interpreters and preserved for centuries by oral tradition before they were committed to writing. They vary in origin, date, character and dialect. Three Targums of the Pentateuch are known, but only fragments of the earliest, called Jerusalemite or Palestinian, survive. The Targum of (Pseudo–) Jonathan derived from this renders the text freely and adds explanatory amplifications. The Targum of Onkelos (Aquila ?) is Babylonian and renders the text as literally as Aquila rendered it in Greek. This Targum came into general use after the fourth cent. A.D. and was so highly esteemed as to be provided with a Massora. The Targum of the Prophets **g** (histor. books and proph.) is attributed to Jonathan ben Uzziel, a disciple of Hillel, but belongs to the fifth cent. in its present form. It is not so literal as that of Onkelos especially in interpreting difficult passages. The Targums of the Sacred Writings show considerable variety. They are usually literal in Job, Ps, Prov, but very free and diffuse in the five Megilloth. In Job and Ps moreover double versions appear. In Prov the interpreter depends on the Syriac OT. Two Targums of Esther are extant but none of Dan and 1–2 Esdr. The Targums are less important for textual criticism than for the knowledge they give us of Jewish traditional interpretation. The principal ones will be found in the Polyglot Bibles and in the editions of A. Berliner (Onkelos ; Berlin, 1884) and P. de Lagarde (Prophetae, Hagiographa ; Leipzig, 1872–73).

Syriac Versions of the OT. The Peshitta—The word **h** *peshitta* literally means ' simple ' and, when applied to the Bible, indicates either the text of the simple and ordinary people as opposed to that of the learned or the simple text not marked with critical signs. The name first appears in the tenth cent. and distinguishes the Syriac version made from the Hebrew and in common use from later OT versions made from the Greek and of interest to scholars. The Peshitta OT, as attested by the early Syriac writers Aphraates and St Ephraem in the fourth cent., contained all the protocanonical books and Ecclus translated from the Hebrew and the remaining deuterocanonical books rendered from the Greek. The Hebrew text used differed little from the MT and the translators were apparently Jewish Christians. The Jewish element predominated in the early Syriac church and the Targums exercised a considerable influence especially on the version of the Pentateuch. The version is **i** usually dated in the second cent. A.D. Though more homogeneous than the LXX it gives indications of different translators and different periods. The rendering is, however, generally clear and elegant, neither too literal nor too free. The Peshitta has many readings, especially in Ps, Is and Minor Proph., in agreement with the Greek version where it differs from the MT. These might be due to the original translators or to later revisers. The two hypotheses are not mutually exclusive but the second is by far the more probable. Greek culture penetrated among the Syrians when they became subject to Rome in the third cent. and there is abundant evidence from the fifth cent. onwards of the efforts they made to conform their biblical texts to those of their highly esteemed Greek neighbours of the school of Antioch. The codices of the Peshitta are remarkable for their antiquity, as many belong to the fifth–sixth cent., and for their general uniformity. The chief editions are those of the Paris and London Polyglots (XVI cent.)

24i of Lee (London, 1823) and the missionaries of Urmiah (1852), both incomplete, and (latest and best) that of the Dominican Press (Mosul, 1888). Critical editions of a few books have appeared but none of the whole OT (*cf.* W. E. Barnes, *Peshitta Psalter*, Cambridge, 1904 ; *Pentateuchus syriace*. London, 1914).

25a Syriac Versions of the LXX. 1. The Philoxenian—This version of the whole Greek Bible takes its name from Philoxenus, the Monophysite Bishop of Mabbug, the Syrian Hierapolis, at whose bidding it was made by a certain Polycarp, c 508. Only fragments of Is and Ps are extant from the OT. They have been edited by Ceriani (*Monumenta sacra et profana* 5, 1, Milan, 1873) and Mingana (Exp 8, 19 [1920], 149–60).

b 2. The Syro-Hexaplar—Paul, Bishop of Tella, by order of the Patriarch of Antioch, Athanasius, translated into Syriac the Hexaplar text of Origen in 615-17. The version is very literal, reproduces exactly the critical signs of the original and gives a number of variants from the later Greek versions. It is thus of the greatest importance for the reconstitution of Origen's text. The first part of the eighth cent. codex of the Ambrosian Library of Milan in which it was preserved was lost in the sixteenth cent. The second part, containing the later Prophets and Sacred Writings, was published by Ceriani (*op. cit.* 7) in 1874. 4 Kg and other fragments from Paris and London MSS were edited by P. de Lagarde (Goettingen, 1886).

c 3. The Syro-Palestinian—This version of the Greek OT and NT was probably made in the fifth cent. for the use of the Melkite Syrians of Palestine. It is particularly remarkable for its west Syrian dialect, generally regarded as the best representative of the language used by Christ and his Apostles. It first became known from lectionaries of late date, but fragments were subsequently discovered in various codices, chiefly palimpsests, dating back to the sixth cent. and showing that the version was not restricted to merely liturgical texts. Of the deuterocanonical books Ecclus and Wis are represented. The text is hexaplaric and is entirely unaffected by eastern Syriac tradition. The most complete collection of the texts is that of H. Duensing, *Christlich-palaestinisch-aramaeische Texte und Fragmente*, Goettingen, 1906.

d Syriac Versions of the NT. 1. The Diatessaron—The first Syriac version of the Gospels was a harmonized narrative, called in Greek *Gospel by means of the Four* (*i.e.* Evangelists) and in Syriac *Gospel of the Mixed* (*i.e.* Evangelists). It is still disputed whether the original harmony was written in Greek or in Syriac, but the recent discovery of a Greek fragment at Dura-Europos in NE Syria dated c 225 shows that it was used in the east in Greek form at a very early period. Its author was Tatian, Syrian by birth but Greek by education. He was a disciple of St Justin, whom he accompanied to Rome and whose school he directed after his master's martyrdom, c 166. Later he returned to the east where he manifested heretical tendencies, condemning marriage and the use of wine and flesh meat, c 172. Traces of these tendencies in his work confirm its traditional authorship and indicate its approximate date. Tatian's object was to provide his countrymen with a popular life of Christ, compiled from its four authoritative sources after the fashion of oriental historians, and freed by harmonization from the difficulties encountered by ordinary readers in establishing the chronological order of events and reconciling the variations of the different evangelists. **e** His skill in arranging his materials and the charm of his presentation of the Gospel narratives are universally recognized and explain the success of his work. Our knowledge of it is chiefly derived from an Arabic eleventh cent. version of a Syriac Diatessaron, in which however the later Peshitta text had been generally substituted for that of Tatian, and from a fifth cent. Armenian version of St Ephraem's Syriac commentary. The later Latin harmony and its derivatives are also helpful. From these we conclude that the original order of the Diatessaron has been preserved in the

Arabic version and that it contained some important **25e** passages attested by the western and the Antiochian, but not by the eastern recension. The text and sources of Tatian remain uncertain. There is an English version of the Arabic Diatessaron by J. H. Hill (Edinburgh, 1910²). The most recent critical edition with French translation is that of A. S. Marmardji (Beirut, 1936). Moesinger published Ephraem's comm. in Latin (Venice 1876). A 13th cent. Persian translation of a very interesting Syriac Diatessaron is described by its discoverer, G. Messina, in Bi 24 (1943) 59–106.

2. Gospel of the Separate (Evangelists)—Two Syriac **f** codices of the separate Gospels were discovered within the last century, one, called Curetonian from its first editor, in a monastery of the Nitrian desert in Upper Egypt, the other, a palimpsest, called Sinaitic though of N. Syrian origin, in the monastery of St Catherine on Mt Sinai. They have approximately the same date (5th cent.) and the same type of text (western) and, though both incomplete, exhibit together nearly the whole four Gospels. This Syriac version, later than the Diatessaron but earlier than the Peshitta NT, was most probably made in the third–fourth cent. Under the title *Evangelion da Mepharreshe* F. C. Burkitt has edited the Curetonian text with the variants of Sin. (Cambridge, 1904) and A. S. Lewis the Sin. text, which she discovered, with the variants of Cur. (London, 1910). With these Gospels may be associated the first Syriac version of the Ac and the Pauline Epistles, attested by Armenian versions of Ephraem's commentaries and exhibiting undoubtedly in the Ac, but less markedly in the Epistles, the same western type of text. No trace remains of other books of the NT included doubtless in this early version.

3. The Peshitta NT—Rabbula, Metropolitan of Edessa **g** (411–35), according to his almost contemporary biographer, made a fresh translation of the NT from Greek into Syriac and ordered the separate Gospels to be read in the churches instead of the Diatessaron. This translation or recension is generally identified with the Peshitta NT, used by all Syriac writers, whether Jacobites, Nestorians or Catholics, after c 450. A new version universally received must have emanated from a source of outstanding authority and at a time prior to the disruption of the Syrian Church after the Council of Chalcedon. In Rabbula we have the time and the man. The Peshitta was probably a recension rather than a new translation and may be compared to the slightly earlier NT recension of St Jerome. It re- **h** sembles it in aiming at fidelity and correctness of language and retaining many expressions consecrated by usage, but differs from it in its type of text, not eastern but Antiochian. The original Peshitta omitted 2 Pet, 2-3 Jn, Jude and Apoc, added in the codices from later versions. As in the OT the codices are remarkable for their antiquity and their uniformity. G. H. Gwilliam's *Tetraevangelium Sanctum* (Oxford, 1901) is an excellent critical edition of the Gospels. His revision of Ac, Pauline Epistles, Jas, 1 Pet, 1 Jn and J. Gwynn's edition of 2 Pet, 2-3 Jn, Jude and Apoc are incorporated in the Bible Society's NT in Syriac (London, 1920).

4. The Heraklean NT—It is still disputed whether the **i** Heraklean version of Syriac tradition is identical or not with the NT of the Philoxenian Bible mentioned above, § 25a. The latter was intended for the Monophysites and rendered the Greek much more literally than the Peshitta. Thomas of Harkel, according to his own account, merely provided the Philoxenian NT text c 616 with critical signs (*obeli* and asterisks) and marginal notes derived from a collation of three Greek MSS. The *obeli* undoubtedly marked words or passages not in the Greek and to be omitted. The **j** asterisks must therefore have marked words and passages to be retained as attested in the Greek and consequently authentic. The marginal notes supplied variants from the Greek MSS consulted. It is more probable therefore that Thomas retained the Philoxenian text while providing materials for its revision.

25j Gwynn's edition of the lacunae in the Peshitta NT (Dublin, 1897 and 1909) exhibits a version undoubtedly different from the Heraklean and resembling the Peshitta in the freedom with which the Greek is rendered. It seems therefore that the missing books of the Peshitta were translated into Syriac before the Philoxenian version. The marginal variants of the Heraklean NT exhibit a western type of text. The only edition is that of J. White (Oxford, 1778–1803).

k 5. The Syro - Palestinian—To the remarks already made on the OT version it may be added that the NT exhibits a marked dependence on Origenian tradition in the place names and seems to be based on a Caesarean text.

l Coptic Versions of the Bible—Coptic is the language of the Egyptians, written in Greek letters with some supplementary characters, in the first cent. A.D. Though it is less well adapted than either Latin or Syriac to give an exact rendering of Greek texts the Coptic versions of the Greek Bible are nevertheless of great critical as well as historical importance owing to the types of text which they exhibit. They are written in five different dialects : Sahidic (S. or Upper Egypt), Bohairic (N. or Lower Egypt), Fayumic, Achmimic and Subachmimic or Assiutic (Middle Egypt). Of these Sahidic and Bohairic are the most important. All the NT except a few verses is extant in these two dialects and has been published with English translation and critical apparatus by G. Horner (*The Coptic Version of the NT in the Northern Dialect*, 4 vol., Oxford, 1898–1905, *in the Southern Dialect*, 7 vol., *ibid.* 1911–24).

m Only parts of the less complete OT have appeared in scattered publications. The Sahidic version is usually assigned to the third cent., the Bohairic to the fifth. The need of a vernacular rendering was felt earlier in S. Egypt and among the monks of the Thebaid than in N. Egypt where Greek was better known. The Bohairic exhibits moreover the greater precision and skill in translation which usually distinguishes later versions from earlier ones. A Sahidic Papyrus codex of OT fragments and Ac (Brit. Mus. Or. 7594) belongs to the very beginning of the fourth cent.

n Both Sahidic and Bohairic versions of the NT exhibit in the main an eastern type of text. The Sahidic has however many readings, but none of the manifestly spurious additions, of the western text. The Bohairic has a purer eastern text with some Antiochian contaminations. Thus the versions confirm the testimony of the papyri to the existence of a western type of text in Egypt in the second cent., gradually replaced by the better eastern type. The change, begun in the north, took some time to reach the south. The Sahidic has a mixed text in the Ac, the Bohairic and the Chester Beatty papyrus (early 3rd cent.) a relatively pure eastern text. The Coptic versions of the OT were made from the Greek, not the Hebrew, and include the deuterocanonical books. Though sometimes emended from other Greek codices they generally follow B. Fragments of the Sahidic Job in the Vatican library are uncontaminated by hexaplar additions.

26a Armenian and Georgian Versions—These versions may be considered together since it is now fairly certain that the Georgians derived their version from that of their Armenian neighbours. The latter, when converted to Christianity c 300, were analphabetic and seem to have first used the Syriac Scriptures. Traces of a Syriac Diatessaron have been discovered in their liturgy. The invention of their alphabet derived from the Greek is attributed to a certain Mesrop and was immediately followed by the translation of the Scriptures into Armenian undertaken by the Patriarch Isaac (390–440). There are independent reasons for dating the practically contemporary Georgian version before 450. The Armenian version of the separate Gospels was made directly from the Greek. Its many Syriacisms are best explained as due to the original translators who reproduced Syriac expressions from **b** their Diatessaron. The Armenian language is an excellent medium of translation and the version is

both faithful and elegant. The critical importance **26b** of the Armenian and Georgian versions is derived from the Origenian text of the OT and the Caesarean text of the Gospels which they exhibit. A plausible explanation of the existence of such a text at Constantinople is provided by the fifty Bibles copied in Palestine for the Emperor Constantine by Eusebius of Caesarea. The earliest codices of both versions belong to the eighth–ninth cent. The best edition of the Armenian Bible is that of J. Zohrab (Venice, 1805) which gives a collection of variant readings. Mt and Mk have already appeared in the excellent critical edition of the Georgian NT by R. P. Blake in *Patr. Orient.*, 20, 3 (Mk 1929) and 24, 1 (Mt 1933).

Gothic Version—According to the historian Philo- **c** storgius the Gothic Bishop Ulfilas (†383) translated the whole Bible except Kgs into Gothic. More than half the Gospel text is extant in the sixth cent. Codex Argenteus now at Uppsala but of North Italian origin. There are fragments of other books in various MSS. The type of text is Antiochian revised from the Old Latin. (*Cf.* W. Streitberg, *Die gothische Bibel*, 2 vol., Heidelberg, 1919–20, and W. S. Friedrichsen, *The Gothic Version of the Gospels*, Oxford, 1926.)

Arabic Versions—There is no definite indication of an **d** Arabic rendering of the Scriptures before the eighth cent. The Gospels and other books of the NT were then first translated from the Syriac Peshitta. The later version of the Syriac Diatessaron already mentioned is the only Arabic scriptural text of critical importance. The OT was translated from the Hebrew by Saadiya Gaon in the tenth cent. Other and probably earlier versions were made from the Syriac Peshitta and the Greek LXX. The Arabic text in the Paris and London Polyglots is partly from the MT (Pent.), partly from the Peshitta (Histor. Books and Job), and partly from the LXX (Prophets and Wisdom Books).

Ethiopic Version—As the Ethiopians or Abyssinians **e** were converted to Christianity in the fourth cent., the version of the Bible in their native language called Ge'ez must have been begun at latest in the fifth. It was most probably based on a Greek text of the B type and of Egyptian origin but not always correctly translated. This version was subsequently revised first from the Sahidic and later (c 13th cent.) from Arabic texts. The revision is occasionally manifested by double translations. The codices do not antedate the thirteenth cent. The only complete edition of the O and NT is that of the Italian Catholic Mission (Asmara, 1920–26). There are critical editions of parts of the OT by Dillmann (Leipzig, 1853–94), Bachmann (Berlin and Halle, 1893), Pereira (*Patr. Orient.*, 2.9.13) and Loefgren (Paris, 1927, and Uppsala, 1930).

Slavonic Version—This is the latest version made **f** directly from the Greek in the ninth cent. by the Slavonic Apostles, SS. Cyrillus and Methodius, who provided their converts with an alphabet derived from the Greek and a vernacular version of some of the sacred books. The version was generally believed to exhibit the Antiochian text then used in Constantinople. Of late, however, it is contended that the earlier codices (10th–11th cent.) differ from the later in presenting many Hesychian and Caesarean readings. The translators would then have derived their text from a codex of their monastery near Brussa. Gennadius of Novgorod completed the version from the Vg in the fifteenth cent.

The Old Latin Versions—The name indicates the **27a** versions of the Scriptures used in the Western Church before the introduction of the Vulgate of St Jerome. The need of a Latin version was felt earlier in the provinces than at Rome where Greek was better understood and more generally spoken. There is some indication of such a version in Gaul in 177 and the books and Pauline Epistles possessed by the martyrs of Scillum, who knew no Greek, attest the existence of a Latin version in Africa in 180. Tertullian confirms this attestation though he usually prefers his own render-

27a ings from the Greek. The numerous and consistent citations of St Cyprian indicate an African Latin version of the whole Bible and enable us to determine some of the codices in which it is found. The earliest indications of a Latin version at Rome belong to the middle of the third cent.

b St Augustine and St Jerome distinctly affirm the multiplicity of the Old Latin versions. Similarities of expression found in most codices are explained by the use made of earlier versions by later translators. It is now generally admitted that the older African is distinct from the later Italian version. The earlier version, as might be expected, is ruder and freer than the later. Hence St Augustine in a famous passage seems to prefer the Itala, which he discovered at Milan, to the African interpretations, which he previously used, as combining a more literal rendering of the Greek with a clear indication of the sense, *verborum tenacior cum perspicuitate sententiae*. This preference may have been particularly suggested by the version of the Pauline Epistles subsequently used by the Saint and partially extant in *r* (*Les fragments de Freising*, ed. De Bruyne, Rome, 1921). The vexed question of the Itala is discussed by B. Botte in DBVS 4 (1948) 777–82.

c The fragmentary remains of the Old Latin versions were collected and edited by P. Sabatier, *Bibliorum sacrorum latinae versiones*, 3 tom., Paris, 1751. A new edition is in preparation. *Old Latin Biblical Texts* (OLBT), Oxford, 1883- . . . and *Collectanea Biblica Latina* (CBL), Rome, 1912- . . . supplement Sabatier.

d Character and Value of the Old Latin Versions—All the versions are from the Greek and in popular Latin suited to the lower classes for whom they were intended. They are thus linguistically important for the study of the evolution of the Latin language. The early renderings, always literal but often mechanical and inexact, have little exegetical but much critical value as witnesses to the Greek text of the second cent. Unfortunately however the original versions are contaminated in the codices by the later Greek recensions. The NT exhibits predominantly a western type of text. Many codices have been revised from the Vulgate. The citations of the early Latin Fathers are the chief means of distinguishing in doubtful cases between Old Latin and Vulgate readings.

e The Latin Vulgate Version—The Latin Church owes its Bible to St Jerome (*c* 340–420), admirably fitted for his task by his learning and piety and the authority which he enjoyed among his contemporaries. He first in 383 ff. emended from the Greek the Old Latin versions of the NT. He next in 386 ff. emended the Old Latin versions of the protocanonical books of the OT from the Greek Hexapla. The Vulgate or Gallican Psalter belongs to this emendation. He finally in 390 ff. rendered the OT directly into Latin from the Hebrew and Aramaic. The NT emendation, undertaken at the bidding of Pope Damasus, was received with general applause and spread rapidly over the whole Latin Church. The OT version from the Hebrew, a private enterprise, encountered much initial opposition, but gradually imposed itself by its intrinsic merits and after two or three centuries secured universal recognition. Instead of the Hebrew Psalter, however, the Hexaplar version, called Gallican from its early popularity in Gaul, was used everywhere except at Rome and Milan.

f The Vulgate NT—St Jerome's object in emending the NT was to replace the discordant and corrupt Latin versions by a uniform and correct text. He selected therefore early Greek codices, free from harmonizations and later additions, and from them corrected the Latin codices. He improved the Latinity of previous translators but retained their diction when it rendered the sense correctly. As the Greek codices which he used were chiefly of the S and B types he thus endowed the Latin Church with a version revised from the more correct eastern text. St Jerome's revision of the NT is unduly restricted to the Gospels by a few critics. He

himself repeatedly affirms that he revised the NT. **27f** The other books of the Vg NT exhibit the same characteristics as the Gospels and are united with them in the codices. The Gospels, however, more deeply corrupted by harmonizations, were revised more carefully. An excellent critical text of the Vg NT has been published by Wordsworth and White in a complete minor (Oxford, 1911) and nearly complete major edition (*ib.* 1889- . . .).

The Vulgate OT—Much more difficult than the **g** emendation of the NT was the substitution for the Latin version of the LXX, sanctioned by ecclesiastical tradition, of a new version of the inspired Hebrew text used by Christ and his Apostles. Recognizing the impossibility of correctly interpreting a text not previously well understood, St Jerome first spent long years under Jewish instructors in acquiring a thorough knowledge of Hebrew and Aramaic. He did not aim at a literal rendering, but sought instead to reproduce the exact sense of the original in elegant Latin. His translation, though not free from defects, mostly inevitable in the time and circumstances, has been universally praised for its clearness, fidelity and elegance. Agreement with the Targum attests at times the influence of his Jewish preceptors. He also utilized the Greek versions of Aquila and Symmachus. Sometimes he retained the LXX interpretation either through haste or out of respect for tradition.

History of the Vulgate Text—From its origin until **h** the Council of Trent the text of the Vulgate suffered much from Old Latin interpolations, scribal errors and unskilled correctors. The MS tradition is chiefly represented by two families, the Italian and the Spanish. The Italian cod. Amiatinus is generally regarded as the best of all the surviving codices. It was copied *c* 700 in a Northumbrian monastery from an excellent ancient codex of Roman origin and contains the whole Bible. The early English Gospel codices Lindisfarnensis, Oxoniensis, Cantabrigiensis and the codices Karolinus, Rorigonis, Paulinus, Turicensis, Vallicellanus, which contain the recension of the whole Bible presented by Alcuin to Charlemagne in 801, are based on the Amiatinus. The early south Italian Fuldensis and Epternacensis and the north Italian Mediolanensis, Foroiulianus, Anconitanus and Sangallensis are closely akin to it. Except for the Amiatinus and its derivatives, the early Anglo-Saxon and Celtic Vulgate MSS have little critical but in some cases great artistic value (*cf.* S. Berger, *Histoire de la Vulgate*, ch 3). The oldest and best repre- **i** sentative of the Spanish family is the Pentateuchus Turonensis sixth–seventh cent. Later come the Cavensis (9th cent.) and the Toletanus, Legionensis, and Complutensis (10th cent.). The much interpolated recension of the Visigoth Theodulphus, Bishop of Orleans (†827), contained in the codd. Mesmianus, Sangermanensis parvus, Anicianus, Hubertianus, and less popular than the Alcuinian recension which it contaminated, is based on Spanish tradition. The next important stage in the history of the Vulgate is the establishment of a uniform text for the students of the University of Paris. The Paris Bible first exhibits the division into chapters introduced by Stephen Langton in 1214. Its corruptions produced many *correctoria*. The first printed Vulgate Bible, **j** produced by Gutenberg at Mainz in 1452, and those which immediately followed it exhibit the corrupt Parisian text. A better text based on Italian codices was edited by Leonardus Basileensis at Vicenza in 1476. Marginal corrections and variants first appear in the edition of Alb. Castellanus (Venice, 1511). Critical editions based on a collation of various codices followed, of which the Stephanian (Paris, 1528) and the Hitorpian Cologne, 1530) may be mentioned. The Stephanian edition of 1555 is memorable as the first to contain the division of the whole text into verses indicated by marginal numbers. Other critical editions either added to or substituted for the Vulgate in various places new interpretations. Finally entirely

27j new Latin versions like those of the NT by Erasmus (Basel, 1511) and the OT by Sebast. Munsterus (*ib.*, 1534) made their appearance. The confusion and uncertainty produced by the number and variety of the Latin biblical editions emphatically demanded a remedy from the Council of Trent. The Church required a trustworthy and uniform text.

28a The Vulgate and the Council of Trent—The corruption of the Vulgate text and the rejection of its authority were the evils to be remedied. The Council, therefore, in the second decree of its sixth session in 1546 proclaimed the juridical authenticity of the Vulgate and ordered the preparation and publication of a corrected edition of its text. *Eadem sacrosancta Synodus considerans non parum utilitatis accedere posse Ecclesiae Dei, si ex omnibus latinis editionibus quae circumferuntur sacrorum librorum, quaenam pro authentica habenda sit, innotescit, statuit et declarat, ut haec ipsa vetus et Vulgata editio, quae longo tot saeculorum usu in ipsa Ecclesia probata est, in publicis lectionibus, disputationibus, praedicationibus et expositionibus, pro authentica habeatur et ut nemo illam reiicere quovis praetextu audeat vel praesumat . . . Sed et impressoribus modum in hac parte, ut par est, imponere volens . . . decernit et statuit, ut posthac S. Scriptura, potissimum vero haec ipsa vetus et Vulgata editio quam emendatissime imprimatur.*

b Sense of the Decree—The decree is not concerned with the original texts or the various non-Latin versions but only with Latin editions of the sacred text. It does not judge or condemn any of these but prefers the Vulgate to the others and declares it the official Bible of the Latin Church. The essential requisite of an official Bible at all times and especially at the time of the decree was freedom from doctrinal error. The preference accorded to the Vulgate was based therefore not on its critical but on its doctrinal accuracy. Its long use and approbation in the Infallible Church guaranteed its substantial conformity with the original texts and its definite authority in matters of faith and morals. It was therefore declared authentic or authoritative in the sense that its testimony in doctrinal matters can never be legitimately rejected. Its accuracy in other respects is neither asserted nor implied. In his recent Encyclical *Divino Afflante Spiritu* Pius XII stresses the fact that the decree applies only to the Latin Church and the public use of the Scriptures and that it in no way diminishes the authority and value of the original texts in corroborating, confirming and elucidating Catholic doctrine (*cf.* AAS 35 (1943) 309).

c The Emendation of the Vulgate Text—A reconstitu-

tion of the text of St Jerome according to the modern **28c** canons of textual criticism could scarcely be expected at this period. Nevertheless the third Congregation of Cardinals appointed to prepare the new emended edition under the presidency of Cardinal Carafa in 1586, if we may judge from the record of their labours preserved in the Codex Carafianus, would have produced an excellent critical text had not Sixtus V rejected their corrections and himself prepared the Sixtine edition of the Vulgate, published at the new Vatican Press in 1590. This edition, recognized as needing correction even by Sixtus himself, was almost immediately withdrawn from circulation. The new and final edition of Clement VIII in 1592, prepared by Toletus, left much to be desired from the critical point of view. It was not until 1907 however that an official revision of the Vulgate text was undertaken by Pius X. The Benedictines to whom the work was assigned have already published an excellent text with a full critical apparatus of Gen–Kings. More recently Pius XII ordered the preparation of a new Latin version of the Psalter from the original texts, published in 1945, and permitted the use of this version in the daily recitation of the Breviary.

Vernacular Versions—Versions of the whole or of part **d** of the Bible in the language of the common people appear first in England and Germany in the eighth cent., in France and Hungary in the twelfth, in Italy, Spain, Holland, Poland and Bohemia in the thirteenth. The decree of the Council of Trent makes no reference to such versions, but the question was raised in the deliberations of the Council, and Cardinal Madruzzo emphatically declared that they should be not only permitted but encouraged. Subsequent Catholic vernacular versions were naturally from the official text of the Vulgate. The progress made in determining the original form of the Hebrew and Greek texts and the desire to provide the faithful with scriptural versions, not only doctrinally sound like the Vulgate, but also critically exact and accurately rendered, have produced in recent years numerous Catholic vernacular versions from the original texts. The use of these, previously restricted to private reading, has been extended by Pius XII, in a decree of the Biblical Commission in 1943, to public reading and instructions ; see § 53*b–d*. An authoritative interpretation of the decree by the Secretary of the Biblical Commission will be found in Bi 27 (1946) 319 ; see § 53*e*. The Church desires the faithful to be spiritually nourished from the best possible rendering and interpretation of the original inspired texts.

THE HISTORY OF THE
RHEIMS-DOUAY VERSION

By HUGH POPE, O.P.

(originally written by the late Fr Hugh Pope, O.P. (†1946), and since rewritten by Fr Sebastian Bullough, O.P.)

29a Bibliography—Preface to Rheims NT, 1582 ; Preface to Douay OT, 1609 ; N. Wiseman, *Catholic Versions of Scripture*, DR 2 (1837) 475 ff., repr. in *Essays on Various Subjects*, Vol. 1 ; *H. Cotton, *Rhemes and Doway*, 1855 (a work of bibliography and collation that no student of the subject can neglect, though the viewpoint is hostile, and details occasionally incomplete or in-accurate) ; J. H. Newman, *History of the Text of the Rheims and Douay Version of Holy Scripture*, in the *Rambler*, July 1859, repr. in *Tracts Theological and Ecclesiastical*, ed. 1895, p 403 (important) ; J. G. Shea, *A Bibliographical Account of Catholic Bibles and Testaments translated from the Latin Vulgate and printed in the United States*, 1859 ; E. B. O'Callaghan, *A List of the Editions of the Holy Scriptures printed in America previous to 1860*, 1861 ; J. Gillow, *Bibliographical Dictionary of the English Catholics*, art. Martin, Challoner, Pinkard, Haydock ; *J. G. Carleton, *The Part of Rheims in the Making of the English Bible*, 1902 ; E. H. Burton, *Life and Times of Bishop Challoner*, 1, 270–89, 1909 ; B. Ward, *The Eve of Catholic Emancipation*, 2, 189–204, 1911 ; J. S. Phillimore, *Scripture Versions and Variants*, DR 170 (1922) 20–46 (important judgement on DV style) ; H. Pope, O.P., CSAB 1, 246–73 ; Newton Thompson, *Verbal Concordance to the Rheims NT*, 1928 ; Newton Thompson and R. Stock, *Concordance to the Bible* (*DV*), 1942 ; R. A. Knox, ' Challoner and the DV ', in *Richard Challoner*, 33–6, 1946, repr. in *On Englishing the Bible*, 41–8, 1949 ; H. Pope, O.P., *The MacMahon Bibles*, IER 68 (1946), 1–11 ; T. Conneily, *The Haydock Bible*, in *Scripture* 1 (1946) 81–5 ; R. C. Fuller, *Bishop Challoner and the Douay Bible*, in *Scripture* 2 (1947) 8–18 ; W. J. Anderson, *A Note on the Challoner Revision*, in *Scripture* 2 (1947) 42 f. ; H. Pope, O.P., *English Versions of the Bible*, 1952.

In the standard histories of the English Bible Rheims-Douay is usually mentioned, but quite inadequately, *e.g.* in *J. Eadie, *The English Bible*, 1876 ; *W. F. Moulton, *The History of the English Bible*, 1878, 1911⁴ ; *J. H. Dore, *Old Bibles*, 1888² ; *B. F. Westcott, *A General View of the History of the English Bible*, 1905³ (good but brief) ; *J. Mombert, *The English Versions*, 1907³ ; *F. Kenyon, *Our Bible and the Ancient Manuscripts*, 1939⁴ (very inadequate) ; *I. M. Price (revised ed.), *The Ancestry of our English Bible*, 1949 ; *L. A. Weigle, *The English NT*, 1949.

b General Observations—The standard Catholic Bible in use for three and a half centuries has been the Douay Version, and the present commentary uses that text. The name comes from that of the OT volumes published at Douay in 1609–10. The NT had already been published, in 1582, at Rheims. The correct term for the NT is therefore the Rheims Version, with the name Douay for the OT, or by extension for the whole Bible, subsequent publications of the OT alone having been very rare. In the original editions the place-names were anglicized : Rhemes and Doway ; and it is worth noting that although the spelling now used is closer to the French, the old English pronunciation has always remained current among Catholics. Both the NT and OT were translated by **Gregory Martin** at Rheims, whither the English College of Douay removed for fifteen years, from 1578 to 1593, and where he was Professor of Theology, Scripture, Hebrew and Greek from 1578 until his death in 1582. The printing of the

OT was postponed until after the College had returned **29b** to Douay, where the President, Dr Worthington, saw it through the press in 1609–10.

Yet the Rheims-Douay version, as we know it now, **c** does not present the text as it left Dr Martin's hands : first of all **Dr Witham** published a revision of the Rheims NT in 1730, with new notes. This revision was, however, soon superseded by the several revisions made by **Dr Challoner** between the years 1749 and 1772, and it is on these that our current editions are based. Thus it is more exact to refer to our present texts as ' Rheims-Challoner ' or ' Douay-Challoner '. During the century following Challoner's death (1781) there was much confusion in the subsequent editing of the text, but during the last sixty years a fairly stable text has emerged, and the variants in current editions are in fact only in small details. In 1935 and 1941 fresh revisions were made in America. The history of the **d** Version is therefore somewhat complex, and is best divided as follows for more detailed study : I The Situation before Rheims, II The Original Rheims and Douay, III The work of Dr Challoner, IV Subsequent editions of Challoner's text, and V The Present State of the Text. An **Appendix** will mention modern revisions, and include a note on Catholic versions independent of the Rheims-Douay-Challoner tradition.

I The Situation before Rheims—The earlier history of **e** English vernacular versions is simply outlined in the Preface to Rheims (1582), where mention is made of Bede's translations, of versions ' extant in English even before the troubles that Wycliffe and his followers raised in our midst ', and of the ' provincial constitution of Thomas Arundel, Archbishop of Canterbury, in a Council holden at Oxford [1408], where strait provision was made that no heretical version . . . should be suffered nor . . . permitted to be read, being not approved and allowed by the Diocesan before. . . . So also it is there insinuated that . . . [no lawful translations] were ever in our country wholly forbidden '. The subject of the Pre-Wycliffite Bibles is a controversial one, and may here as well be left in Gregory Martin's terms.

With regard, however, to **printed texts,** we are on **f** more certain ground. The first printing of a biblical text in English was that of **John Fisher's** Penitential Psalms in 1505 (by Pynson), again printed in 1508, 1509, 1525 and 1529 by Wynken de Worde, and in 1510 again by Pynson. Most of these had appeared before **Tyndale's** NT of 1525, justly acclaimed as the first printed NT in English. Tyndale's Protestant text was soon followed by others, **Coverdale's** Bible 1535, ' **Matthew's** ' Bible (J. Rogers) 1537, the **Great Bible** 1539 (often known as Cranmer's because of his preface to the 2nd ed.), **Taverner's** 1539, the **Geneva** (Whittingham) 1560, and the ' **Bishops' Bible** ' 1568 ; to which should be added the English translations of **Erasmus'** Latin NT in 1540, and of **Beza's** in 1576, the latter, by Tomson, soon replacing the NT in the Geneva Bible (from 1603). (AV, 1611, of course came after both Rheims and Douay.)

The above were the texts of which Dr Allen, president **g** of Douay College, wrote in 1578 : ' Our adversaries, however, have at their finger tips from some heretical version all those passages of Scripture which seem to make for them, and by a certain deceptive adaptation

29g and alteration of the sacred words produce the effect of appearing to say nothing but what comes from the Bible. This evil might be remedied if we too had some Catholic version of the Bible, for all the English versions are most corrupt. . . . If his Holiness shall judge it expedient, we ourselves will endeavour to have the Bible faithfully, purely, and genuinely translated according to the edition approved by the Church, for we already have men most fitted for the work' (*Letters and Memorials of Cardinal Allen*, ed. Knox, pp 64 f., in Latin).

h **II The Original Rheims** (1582) **and Douay** (1609-10) —The task was entrusted to Gregory Martin, an illustrious scholar of St John's, Oxford, who had been compelled to flee to Douai in 1570. Dr William Allen, later Cardinal, and at the time President of Douay, was an Oxford man (Oriel), who had had to leave Oxford in 1561. The two others who were concerned were Richard Bristow and William Reynolds, both Oxford men (Exeter and New) and converts. The *Douay Diary* for 1578 has the entry : ' On Oct. 16 or thereabouts Mr Martin started translating the Bible into English in the hope of thus providing an antidote to the corrupt heretical versions which have been so long a misery to nearly everybody in our own land. With a view to the speedy production of what will, we trust, prove an exceedingly useful work, he will translate two chapters a day ; while to secure its exactitude, Drs Allen and Bristow will read them carefully and, if need be, make any corrections which prudence may demand'. Four years later (March 1582) : ' This month the final touches were given to the English version of the New Testament ' (*Records of the English Catholics* [= Douay Diaries I & II], pp 145, 186, in Latin). It is not now certain what share the others had beyond revision : the translation is entirely Martin's, Bristow perhaps wrote the notes (though he died already in 1581), Allen had worked in Rome on the preparation of the Sixtine Vulgate, and Reynolds it was who came in 1583 to write a refutation of the attacks upon Martin's work. It is very important to emphasize that these men were the very flower of Oxford scholarship, most learned men, and (as Dr Worthington put it in the Preface to Douay) ' well known to the world, to have been excellent in the tongues, sincere men, and great divines ', for these facts have been obscured by the obloquy that was poured on them from England at the time, and by the oblivion into which they fell in later years. If their version is considered to lack literary grace, it must be realized that this was done of set purpose.

i The NT was published at **Rheims in 1582** at a cost of 1,500 crowns, 1,000 of which had been collected by Fr Persons. The title page runs : *The New Testament of Jesus Christ, translated faithfully into English, out of the authentical Latin, according to the best corrected copies of the same, diligently conferred with the Greek and other editions in divers languages. With the Arguments of books and chapters, Annotations and other necessary helps for the better understanding of the text, and specially for the discovery of the corruptions of divers late translations, and for clearing the controversies in religion of these days. In the English College of Rhemes . . . Printed at Rhemes, by John Fogny, 1582.*

j The publication of the NT provoked an immediate **storm of abuse** from the Protestants. William Fulke of Cambridge had already in 1583 written a tract against one of Martin's on the corruption of Scripture by Protestants ; in 1583 William Whitaker attacked Martin's version, and similar attacks were launched by Thomas Bilson in 1585 and by George Wither and Edmund Bulkeley in 1588. In 1589 Fulke returned to the fray and published the Rheims text in parallel with the Bishops' Bible (at that time the official version of the Church of England), with the object of indicating the errors of Rheims, although this edition and its three reprints probably served to bring the Rheims version to the notice of many who might not otherwise have seen it, among whom were probably the framers **k** of the Authorized Version itself. But meanwhile

preparations continued and Dr Worthington published **29k** the first volume of the OT (Gen–Job) at **Douay in 1609,** and the second (Ps–Mac) in **1610**, the translation being Martin's, but the notes, preface, tables, etc., his own. The title page runs : *The Holy Bible, faithfully translated into English out of the authentical Latin. Diligently conferred with the Hebrew, Greek and other editions* [etc. as in Rheims]. *Printed at Doway by Laurence Kellam at the sign of the holy Lamb, MDCIX.* The principal cause of delay (the Preface says) was ' our poor estate in banishment ', but there was also, since 1582, the matter of the revision of the Vulgate text itself, the Sixtine edition appearing in 1590 and the definitive Clementine text in 1592. Dr Worthington in the preface says : ' we have again conferred this English translation, and conformed it to the most perfect Latin Edition '.

Both Rheims and Douay were provided with lengthy **l** **prefaces**, both of which are at pains to defend **three main contentions** : (1) That the Catholic Church has never forbidden vernacular versions—indeed many had appeared during the previous 300 years—but that she had expressly forbidden the use of heretical versions (' no other books in the world being so pernicious '), and always required the approval of lawful authority. At the present time a special necessity had arisen, which prompted the publication of this text. (2) That **m** the translation was deliberately made from the Latin Vulgate rather than from the original tongues principally because of the uncertainty of the existing Greek text compared with the considerable security of the existing Latin. Let us here add that subsequent studies of the Greek text, showing the corruption of the editions then current, have amply justified the wisdom of this move. One of the Protestant gibes at the time was this translation from the Latin, but we should observe that of all the Protestant versions that had by then appeared (*cf.* above *f*), only Tyndale's was truly a translation of the original : Coverdale's is from the Latin, and the others were all revisions of the preceding translations, ultimately Tyndale's or Coverdale's, though Taverner did consult the Greek, and Geneva both the Greek and the Hebrew ; yet the Rhemish translators made no less a claim when they ' diligently conferred ' their text with the original. (3) That the translation was deliberately **n** literal : ' following our copy . . . sometimes in the very words and phrases, which may seem to the vulgar reader and to common English ears not yet acquainted therewith, rudeness or ignorance : but to the discreet reader that deeply weigheth and considereth the importance of sacred words and speeches, and how easily the voluntary translator may miss the true sense of the Holy Ghost, we doubt not but our consideration and doing therein shall seem reasonable and necessary : yea, and that all sorts of Catholic readers will in short time think that familiar, which at first may seem strange, and will esteem it more when they shall otherwise be taught to understand it, than if it were the common known English ' (Rheims preface). Herein lies an important principle : that rather than bring down the sacred text to the level of ordinary language, everyday language must be enlarged to accommodate the language of Scripture. A **glossary** was therefore provided at the end of the NT, containing ' the explication of certain words in this translation, not familiar to the vulgar reader, which might not conveniently be uttered otherwise '. Some of these are purely biblical terms, such as Pasche, Azymes, Parasceve, etc., while others were regarded as theological technical terms which should be learned and understood (' far better to keep in the text and to tell their signification in the margent or in a table for that purpose, than to disgrace both the text and them with translating them '—Rheims preface), such are ' promerited ', Heb 13:16, and the famous ' exinanited himself ', Phil 2:7—a theological notion indeed, which has suffered mistranslation several times since, and notably in AV. Rheims preface adds, ' We cannot possibly attain to express these words fully in English, and we think much better that the reader staying at the difficulty of them, should take an occasion

29n to look in the table following, or otherwise to ask the full meaning of them, than by putting some usual English words that express them not, so to deceive the reader'. Other words again have passed from that glossary into current English, as Martin said they would, such as 'acquisition, advent, adulterating, allegory, character (= mark or stamp), co-operate, evangelize, gratis, issue (= good event), neophyte, prescience', cf. Phillimore, DR 170 [1922] 38).

o With these deliberate notions in mind we can approach the **criticism of the English style** of Rheims-Douay in a reasonable manner. It is probably true that the English language has been enriched by many words of Latin origin precisely through the influence of Rheims, perhaps by way of AV ; for the debt of AV to Rheims is now openly admitted, though of course Rheims was not specified for consultation by King James' revisers, and their sole reference to it is a contemptuous remark in their preface. Yet the revisers of 1881 allow that the AV ' shows evident traces of . . . the Rhemish, made from the Latin Vulgate, but by scholars conversant with the Greek Original ' (Preface to RV NT), and since Dr Carleton's book in 1902 (cf. above a) the matter is beyond question. It was Professor Phillimore (op. cit. p 36 ff.) who pointed out how in spite of its many Latinisms Rheims in fact often uses the everyday word rather than the consciously archaic as does AV (e.g. 'danger' in I Cor 15:30, for AV 'jeopardy'), producing in AV a 'biblical English ' more suited to the recitation of lessons in church than to everyday thought, for a Protestant version indeed sets out to provide a liturgy, while a Catholic version sets out to provide everyday instruction for simple folk whose daily liturgy is in Latin. Phillimore further (ibid. p 45) pleads for Rheims ' on its merits as a piece of English, to be read by those whose taste and training fit them to add the literary to the spiritual enjoyment ', and, adds Ronald Knox in this connection, ' he knew what style was ' (On Englishing the Bible, p 44).

Yet it must be admitted that the very literal rendering from the Latin presented frequent difficulties, and that the oft-repeated gibe ' It is a translation which needs a translation ' is not entirely without justification, though Martin would have been the first to agree that it needed a glossary. The translation of the Psalms is regarded as particularly deplorable, but it must be remembered that the Latin text as it stands is far from satisfactory, and that among Protestants the AV Psalms are equally deplored and compare unfavourably with those of the Prayer Book. Be that as it may, certain phrases of Rheims-Douay have been universally condemned as worthless translations, such as ' The voice of thy thunder in a wheel ', Ps 76:19, ' Deliver me from Bloods ', Ps 50:16, or 'sindon upon the bare ', Mk 14:51 ; though in fact contemporary Protestant texts are hardly less guilty, e.g. Geneva's 'harberous ' for Rheims ' given to hospitality ', Tit. 1:8, Coverdale's ' overbody coat ' for ' ephod ', Jg 17:5, or Tyndale's and Great Bible's 'linen upon the bare '. The call, however, for revision of Rheims-Douay was not long in coming, and this work is the subject of the succeeding sections of this article.

p **Subsequent Editions of the Rheims NT** were in 1600 (8vo Vervliet, Antwerp) and a 3rd in 1621 (16mo, Seldenslach, Antwerp). This 3rd edition was closely reproduced by the publisher in 1630, and is a rare book —the only copy known to Fr Hugh Pope was at Fort Augustus—and it is usually not listed. The next edition, that of 1633 (4to, Cousturier, Rouen) is therefore entitled the ' 4th '. The ' 5th ' edition, appearing in 1738 (fol., probably in London) was almost certainly the work of Dr Challoner, and the erratic spelling of 1582 was modernized and certain phrases were revised. The ' 6th ' edition appeared in 1788 (fol., Ferguson, Liverpool), and further copies were sold in Dublin in 1789 with a new title page bearing the name of Wogan (Cotton). This rare edition was printed after Dr Challoner's revisions had been made. Its text was printed again in Dr Troy's Bible of 1816. After this

some editions of the 1582 text were made for historical 29p interest only : a Protestant edition in 1834 (Leavitt, New York, modern spelling), 1841 (Bagster in the English Hexapla, original spelling), 1872 (Bagster—with Vulgate parallel, but by anachronism the Clementine Vulgate !—modern spelling), and lastly in 1926 the edition with modern spelling by Dom Roger Hudleston, O.S.B. (Burns, Oates & Washbourne). All other editions represent one or other of the revisions.

The only **Subsequent Edition of the Douay OT** was q that of 1635 (4to, Cousturier, Rouen), all other editions being later revisions.

It should be added that the three original 4to volumes of 1582, 1609 and 1610 far surpassed in type, paper and general appearance any previous English version.

The Authority of Rheims-Douay, or of its revisions, r has always been that of local episcopal approbation, and upon such approbation depends the authority of every vernacular version, and among Catholics it can hardly be said that a version is 'authorized' or ' appointed to be read in churches ' as the Bishops' Bible or the AV was among Protestants. It is only the Latin Vulgate that is in this sense declared ' authentic ' (Trent, sess. 4 [1546], EB 46). But Catholics are bound to use a vernacular text approved by ecclesiastical authority (Leo XIII Officiorum ac munerum § 7, EB 124–5), and may not, under pain of excommunication, print a text without this authorization (Canon Law, 1391, 2318). Thus the Catholics of these islands have always rightly refused to make use of heretical texts and have clung to the Catholic version. One of the earliest cases was the insistence of Mary Queen of Scots at her trial in 1587 on taking her oath upon the Rheims Testament (quoted by Eadie, 2, 136 ; Dore, 306 ; Mombert, 317). And in English courts of law a Catholic Bible has now to be provided for the oath of a Catholic witness. What is, however, probably the first public use of the words ' official version ' occurs in Cardinal Griffin's preface to Mgr Knox's NT of 1945, where both that version and Rheims receive this title. Mgr Knox's NT furthermore has the word ' authorized ' on the title page, which is explained by Mgr Knox himself (preface to OT) to mean ' authorized for use in church ', an authorization not yet granted to his OT. In 1934 the Biblical Commission decreed that for public reading in church an approved translation of the Vulgate must be used, though translations from the original may be approved and (according to the further decree of 1943) recommended to the faithful for private reading.

III Dr Challoner's Work—Richard Challoner (1691– 30a 1781) entered the college at Douay in 1704, and he became vice-president in 1720. The president at that time was **Dr Witham** who in 1730 published under the initials R. W. the first revision of Rheims NT, including new and admirable notes, with the title Annotations of the NT, in two volumes. A second edition appeared in 1733. Dr Challoner must have been in close contact with Dr Witham while the latter was preparing his text, and indeed Dr Challoner was called upon to give the nihil obstat, so that a certain influence of Witham's text upon the later work of Challoner may well be conjectured. **Challoner** left Douay for the mission in 1730. Evidently it was while he was working in London that he began to feel the pressing need of an adequate English Bible. In 1738, with the assistance of the Carmelite Fr Blyth, he issued the slightly revised text of Rheims already noted, though no name of a reviser appears on the volume itself.

In 1741 Challoner was consecrated a bishop and b became coadjutor to the Vicar Apostolic of the London district. In 1749 he brought out his **1st Revision** of the NT. The revision was far-reaching and marks a turning-point in the history of the version. The book was published in one volume in 12mo, without any indication of author or place of printing. Challoner himself would have been the first to admit that his work was not one of scholarship, though his ordinary Douay training would not have left him unfitted for such a work. But in his revision he had a purely

30b practical end in view, namely, of providing the faithful with a more portable and more readable edition of the Scriptures. His first preoccupation was therefore the modernization of the language and the presentation of the text in the attractive little volume that he produced, but at the same time he adjusted the text to that of the Clementine Vulgate, which had appeared since 1582 (*cf.* title page). The next year **1750** saw his **2nd Revision**, this time a five-volume set in the same format, the Douay OT being revised for the first time and the NT revised again to the extent (on Dr Cotton's estimate) of 124 new changes. These two revisions of the NT in 1749 and 1750 may be called the 'Early Challoner', and they are quite distinct from the later revisions, which involved much more drastic alterations. The distinction is important for the study of later and current editions. It is commonly stated (*e.g.* in Burton's *Life*, 1, 281) that in his revision Challoner had frequent recourse to AV, yet deliberately avoided a close reproduction. This is, however, more particularly true of the 'Late Challoner', the revisions from 1752. In all his revisions he altered the old translation of '*Dominus*' as 'Our Lord' to 'the Lord', and he also standardized the proper names in the Bible, using the Vulgate forms throughout, so that the same forms are found in both OT and NT, *e.g.* Elias and Isaias, which is not the case in AV. It is not now possible to ascertain what assistance, if any, Challoner had in his work : Fr Blyth is sometimes again mentioned, but since Fr Anderson's article in *Scripture* 2 (1947) 42 f. this seems no longer tenable, and it is likely that the work was largely shared by Fr Robert Pinkard (*cf.* also Gillow, art. Pinkard).

c In **1752** appeared the **3rd Revision** of the NT, still in the same size and type, but this time with (on Dr Cotton's estimate) over 2,000 alterations from 1750, mostly in the direction of AV. Certain omissions of 1749, such as 'And he commanded the people to sit down on the ground ' in Mk 8:6, and ' of promise, as in a strange country ' in Heb 11:9 were made good, but it is curious that the word ' counsel ', Ac 5:38, of 1582, 1749, 1750 and AV should appear in this and many later editions as ' council '. The style and syntax is considerably modernized, and in particular the inversions and participial constructions of the old version (*e.g.* Ac 21:12 ' Which when we had heard ') were altered (' And when we . . .'). In **1763-4** was published again the whole Bible, as before in five volumes in 12mo. This is the 2nd Revision of the OT with very few differences from 1750, and the **4th Revision** of the NT hardly differing from 1752. The edition of the NT in **1772** is the **5th Revision** with scarcely any further variations. This time the printer's name is given : J. Coghlan, of London. The identity of the printer of the earlier editions is disputed : Thomas Meighan, of London, is usually given, but Fr Anderson proposes Needham. The revisions of 1752-72 represent what may be called the 'Late Challoner'. All later editions were based on the earlier or later work of Challoner, but it is curious that all current editions have almost entirely rejected the later modernized text in favour of the earlier revisions. It should be observed that a revision of 1777 was mentioned by both Dr Milner and Charles Butler (*cf.* Cotton, pp 50, 118), but if it was ever made, no copy has come down to us.

d IV Subsequent Editions of Challoner's Text—During the first quarter century after Challoner's death in 1781 considerable confusion reigned with regard to the text of the NT, though Challoner's 1750 OT has remained almost unchanged to this day. It will only be possible here to notice the more important editions, and especially those which have had an effect on our current texts. In the first place we have the important editions of the **Rev. Bernard MacMahon** in Ireland, beginning with the NT commissioned by Abp Carpenter in 1783. (This text was only twice seen by Dr Cotton, and no known copy now exists ; it was called the ' 4th ' edition, *i.e.* the next after the 3rd revision of 1752.) The text is basically that of 1752, with many modifications, certain

of which have lasted to this day, notably ' What is that **30d** to me . . .' in Jn 2:4, where Challoner consistently had ' What is to me . . .' In 1791 MacMahon produced a complete Bible for Dr Troy, which was reprinted in 1794. This text of Dr Troy was that used in the famous **e Haydock Bibles**, the 1st edition of which appeared in weekly parts in 1811-14, printed in Manchester by Thomas Haydock, whose brother the Rev. George Leo Haydock composed new notes. The volumes were beautifully produced in folio, and came to be, in their several editions, the typical Catholic Family Bible of England. The most well-known is the 5th edition of 1853, known as Provost Husenbeth's from his abridgement of the notes. About the same time we have in **f** 1790 the **Philadelphia Bible** in 4to, in which the text is that of 1752, and the **Anonymous Edition of 1792,** probably printed at Edinburgh, the sole survivor of which is in the British Museum, and which again has basically the text of 1752, but with considerable alterations, notably ' What is it to me . . .' in Jn 2:4, which is still found in many editions. This text was reproduced in Fr Worswick's edition of 1812 at Newcastle, as far as Rom 3, after which he reverts to a pure 1752 (Cotton). The Bible authorized by **Dr Hay** in Edinburgh in 1796 follows mainly the text of the late revision of 1763-4 (Cotton). Thus most of the texts of this period represent the ' Late Challoner ' tradition, with notable changes introduced by MacMahon and the 1792. In 1813, however, **O. Syers**, a Manchester **g** publisher produced a Bible in parts (as Haydock had begun to do), reproducing the 1750 text in both OT and NT, together with Dr Witham's notes on the NT (Cotton). And thus began the return to the ' Early Challoner '.

In 1815 we find a NT that reverts to the 1749 re- **h** vision, though it incorporates many readings of 1750 and a few of 1752 (notably ' debased himself ' in Phil 2:7 for emptied himself ' of 1749-50). This was the famous edition of the ' **Catholic Board** ', a body founded in 1807 which in 1813 began to occupy itself with the production of a standard edition of the Catholic NT, edited by the Rev. Thomas Rigby for Dr Poynter (*cf.* Ward, *Eve of* . . ., 2, 189 ff.). This move was occasioned by the recent formation of the ' Catholic Fund ', a predominantly Protestant organization for the diffusion of a Rheims-Douay text (without notes) among Irish Catholics, which did in fact publish its noteless NT in 1820. It is here that we first find the misnomer ' Douay NT '. A reproduction of this Protestant edition was still on sale in Dublin in 1938. The ' Catholic Board ' edition was a handsome 8vo volume, which was reprinted seven times down to 1850. About the same time many other editions appeared in **i** England and Ireland, the most important of which were Dr Gibson's **Liverpool Edition** of 1816 in folio, following basically 1752 and reprinted in London for Dr Bramston in 1829 ; the ill-fated **Dr Troy's Bible** of 1816, which, owing to a misunderstanding between the archbishop and the printer, reproduced the NT text of 1582 (ed. 1788-9) with its controversial notes, which were regarded as unpropitious at a time when Catholic Emancipation was in near view (*cf.* Ward, *op. cit.*, p 201). During the first decades of the 19th cent., therefore, the dominant texts were MacMahon's of 1791 in Ireland, Haydock's of 1811-14 (which follows MacMahon) and the Catholic Board edition of 1815 in England, Dr Hay's of 1796 or Fr Worswick's of 1812 in Scotland and the north, and in America either Challoner's 1752 text of 1790 or an edition of MacMahon's of 1824. If the impression gained from the above sections is one of confusion, it is the right impression.

It was in 1825 that the Abp of Dublin, **Dr Murray, j** produced his **Stereotype Edition**, the NT of which, like the ' Catholic Board ' edition, was based on 1749, with some renderings of 1750, but hardly any of 1752. Dr Murray's Bible and his NT were reprinted many times, and especially notable is the long series of NTs that began in 1836 with the approbation of **Dr Denvir,** and is the basis of the current Irish editions. The texts

30j of Dr Murray and Dr Denvir became current in England in the mid-19th cent., and especially in their smaller format rivalled the large volumes of Haydock or the 'Catholic Board', for instance in 1851 we find Dr Denvir's text being issued in London, with many further editions later. Thus it happened that the Stereotype edition became the basis for the current 'English text'

k (see *l, n* below). One more special effort must, however, be chronicled : **Dr Wiseman's** NT published in 1847 by Richardson of Derby. This was a deliberate attempt at standardization, but its weakness was its dependence upon Haydock and therefore on MacMahon. One of the last editions of MacMahon's 1791 text was published by Sadlier of New York in 1852.

l **V Current Editions**—In more recent years a sort of '*textus receptus*' of the Rheims-Challoner NT has emerged. This text, which has become universal in modern editions, is mainly that of 1749-50, and 1752 has been almost entirely abandoned. It is derived from the Stereotype edition of Dr Murray, but small variations can be found, chiefly in the matter of adopting certain readings of 1752 or other later texts. These small variants can be grouped to form an '**English text**' on the one hand, or an '**American text**' on the other, where a few more readings of 1752 or MacMahon are adopted. The parentage of a current edition can only be determined by the observation of such variants, and sometimes by the inheritance of certain misprints. The title page seldom assists us, and sometimes, as in certain recent American editions claiming descent from 1752, positively misleads us. An interesting feature of nearly every modern edition is the abandonment of Challoner's reading in Jn 2:4 in favour of 1792 (English) or MacMahon (American).

m The table on this page lists the more interesting variants, their origin in Challoner's revisions being given with an abbreviated date.

correction to 'Nazarene' is made, the inferior reading **30n** 'council', Ac 5:38, is introduced, and 'put you', Col 3:8, from 1752. MacMahon is followed in 2 Pet 1:15. The omission of a line of print in 2 Tim 1:9 reduces the verse to nonsense, and the false reading 'therefore' for 'heretofore' in Gal 4:13 is found only here. This 574 pp edition was exactly reprinted in 1950 with merely reset title page and page-headings. The **CTS Gospels** of 1900 follow exactly the original 1896 text, but the reprint of 1920 deserves special mention for departing from all editions of the past 160 years and printing Challoner's reading in Jn 2:4, 'What is to me . . .', although unhappily the 1949 reprint has inserted the word 'that', which is quite alien to this type of text. Fr Hugh Pope's annotated **Layman's NT** (1928, 1934) follows the emended 448 pp edition, except for the reading 'the scribes' in Mt 7:29.

Meanwhile the important **Baltimore Bible** appeared **o** in 1899 with the approbation of **Cardinal Gibbons**. The NT of this Bible exhibits all the variants of the 'American text', showing traces of the 1752 and MacMahon persisting in America. This text was reproduced in **Washbourne's Bibles of 1900** and **1914**, the latter having a preface by **Cardinal Bourne** and being the most widely used Bible in England today. The same text appears in Washbourne's **707 pp** 16mo ('pocket') NT of 1909, which remained in print until 1939. The 1914 Bible was exactly reproduced in 16mo by Burns, Oates & Washbourne in **1931** (reprinted up to 1946 and 1947—the 1946 edition was actually printed in 1939 but lay in sheets in Belgium throughout the war), preserving faithfully even the amusing misprint proper to 1914 in Nah 2:10 'all the lions lose strength', for 'loins'. This standard English Bible, 1900, 1914 or 1931, is therefore in the 'American' tradition and not the 'English' as found in most NTs. The only peculiarity of the NT text is in 2 Tim 1:9 where in 1914 'our own works' appears for 'our

English Text		American Text	
Mt	2:23	Nazarite 49-50	Nazarene 52 (*correct*)
	7:29	their scribes 49-50 (*correct*)	the scribes 52
Mk	16:1	brought (Murray, *mispr.*)	bought (Chall., *correct*)
Jn	2:4	What is it (1792)	What is that (MacMahon)
Ac	5:38	counsel 49-50 (*correct*)	council 52
	11:29	proposed (1896 *mispr.*)	purposed 49-50
	14:16	with good (1896 *mispr.*)	with food (Chall., *correct*)
Gal	2:2	conferred with 49-50	communicated to 52
Col	3:8	lay you 49-50	put you 52
2 Pet	1:15	that after my decease also, you may often have 49-50	that you frequently have after my decease (MacMahon)

n A suitable starting point for the study of current editions is **Cardinal Vaughan's** NT of **448 pp** in 16mo ('pocket') published by Burns & Oates in 1896. This is a typical 'English text' and exhibits all the 'English' variants listed above, with its own peculiar misprints. This edition was reprinted by Burns, Oates & Washbourne about 1922 with a few alterations (the fresh type being clearly discernible), notably 'Nazarite' corrected to 'Nazarene', a confusion in 1 Tim 2:1-2 also corrected by 1752, and, a curious feature, in 2 Pet 1:15 the MacMahon rendering of the 'American text' was introduced. In this corrected form the text remained in print until 1937. In 1898 the 8vo 'pulpit edition' of **495 pp** was published, again with the approbation of Cardinal Vaughan. The text, reprinted in 1914 and 1934, is exactly that of 1896, except for the correction of 1 Tim 2:1-2. An exact reprint was published in America with Dr Corrigan's approbation of 1898, and this is still in print with Benziger with **Cardinal Hayes'** approbation of 1931. This is the only current example of an 'English text' in America. About the same time another 'pocket' 16mo edition of **574 pp** appeared with Cardinal Vaughan's approbation. This text generally follows the 448 pp edition, even including the misprint 'good' in Ac 14:16, but the

works' of all previous editions, while in the same verse in 1931 the same line of print is omitted as in the 574 pp NT.

The 'American text' was continued in the United **p** States by **Herders** in **Cardinal Farley's Bible** of 1911, in the well-known edition with an additional approbation of 1912, which includes many photographs of the Holy Land, and in **Cardinal Hayes'** Bibles of 1919 and 1929. More recently the **Douay Bible House** began to issue a very practical pocket NT in 1941. On the title page the text is stated to be that of 1752, but in fact it is the ordinary 'American text' with no more than the few readings of 1752 that are to be found in any edition. A merit, however, is that both Mk 8:6 and Heb 11:9 are completed from 1752, a rare enough feature in modern editions, which all follow basically 1749-50. **Benziger's** 'Red Letter Bible' of 1943 (with the words of Christ printed in red) has the usual text, but has its own special merit of at last correcting 'guard' in Neh 3:15 to 'garden', a misprint occurring in every edition after 1609, where the word stood at the end of a line, abbreviated 'gardē'.

The most recent fruit of the 'English' tradition is **q** the NT edited by **Dr Arendzen,** with new notes, and published by Sheed & Ward in 1947 as a handsomely

30q printed cr. 8vo volume. The text incorporates some of the best features of the 'English text' (based on 1749–50, not '1746' [*sic*] as stated in the introduction), including 'counsel', Acts 5:38, and 'their scribes', Mt 7:29; it corrects by 1752 to 'Nazarene', Mt 2:23, but also adopts the 'American' reading in Gal 2:2, Col 3:8 and 2 Pet 1:15; the misprint in Ac 14:16 is corrected, but unhappily not 'brought' in Mk 16:1; and Mk 8:6 and Heb 11:9 are not completed. A curious feature of all other current editions is the adoption of the false reading of 1750, which was correct in 1749 and again in 1752 and its dependents, in Rom 2:23, 'this uncircumcision' for 'his'. It is indeed praiseworthy that Dr Arendzen has 'his'.

31a **Appendix—I Revisions of Challoner's Text**—Since this commentary uses the Rheims-Douay-Challoner text, our concern is mainly with that text as various editions have presented it. Mention should, however, be made of two recent texts of the NT published in America, which set out to be revisions of Challoner. The first is that of **Fr Carey** in 1935. He expressly says that it is not a new version, but merely a text corrected 'where the existing English seems obviously wrong or meaningless'. A partial list of such corrections is given in the preface. The basic text is the usual 'American text', and not, as stated on the title page, that of 1752, and the revision of it is not nearly as extensive as was **b** Challoner's own in that year. The other work, *A revision of the Challoner-Rheims Version*, is a much more far-reaching venture: the **Confraternity Edition of the NT** of 1941. This is for practical purposes a new version, for although a distinct flavour of the original and the form 'thou' are retained, the diction and syntax have been modernized throughout and all archaic grammar ('goeth' etc.) has disappeared. The

latest editions of the Vulgate are taken into account, **31b** as well as modern editions of the Greek for purposes of comparison, and the notes often allude to the Greek text when it diverges.

II Independent Catholic Versions—The first Catholic **c** text independent of Rheims was the NT of **Dr Nary** of Dublin, 1719, translated from the Vulgate. **Dr Witham's** revision of Rheims, 1730, has already been mentioned. In 1836 we have the first translation from the Greek: **Dr Lingard's** version of the Gospels, published as 'by a Catholic'. In 1849 **Dr Kenrick,** then Bishop of Philadelphia, published the Gospels translated from the Vulgate, 'being a revision of the Rhemish translation', independent therefore of Challoner. In 1851 he published the rest of the NT, and in 1860–1 the three volumes of the OT, as a revision of Douay. In 1898 **Fr Aloysius Spencer, O.P.,** brought out in America a new translation of the Gospels from the Latin, and in 1901 from the Greek. His complete NT from the Greek did not appear until 1937 (long after his death in 1913), and it has been many times reprinted (latest 1946). The **Westminster Version,** under the general editorship of Fr Cuthbert Lattey, S.J., assisted at first by Fr J. Keating, S.J., is a translation of the Bible from the original tongues. The NT was begun in 1913 and finished in 1935, appearing in fascicules, and a fine four-volume edition appeared in 1921–36, and in 1948 an edition in one volume with abridged notes. The OT was begun in 1934 and is still in production, the latest volume being Fr Lattey's *Daniel* in 1949. The **Confraternity Edition of the OT,** translating from the Hebrew into entirely modern English, began with *Genesis* in 1948. Lastly we have the great work of **Mgr Knox,** who made a completely new translation from the Vulgate, publishing the NT in 1945 (after a 'trial edition' in 1944) and the OT in two volumes in 1949.

THE LITERARY CHARACTERISTICS
OF THE BIBLE

By D. J. LEAHY

32a Bibliography—A. Bea, S.J., *De Scripturae S. Inspiratione*, Rome 1935², 101–14 ; J. Chaine, art. *The OT—Semitism* in *P. Lagrange and the Scriptures*, Milwaukee 1946 ; *Le Livre de la Genèse*, Paris 1949 ; J. Coppens, *Les Harmonies des Deux Testaments*, Tournai-Paris 1949 ; A. Durand, S.J., art. *Inerrance Biblique* DAFC 2, 767–74 ; A. Fernández, S.J., art. *De Interpretatione* in *Institutiones Biblicae*, 1, Rome 1937 ; *J. Hempel, *The Contents of the Literature* in *Record and Revelation*, Oxford 1938 ; H. Höpfl, art. *Critique Biblique*, DBVS, 2, 202–12 ; F. von Hummelauer, S.J., *Exegetisches zur Inspirationsfrage*, BS 9 (1904) 58–73 ; *Sir F. G. Kenyon, *The Bible and Modern Criticism*, London, 1948 ; J. M. Lagrange O.P., *Historical Criticism and the OT*, London 1905 ; art. *L'Inspiration et les Exigences de la Critique* RB 5 (1896) 510–18 ; J. Levie, S.J., *L'Encyclique sur les Etudes Bibliques* NRT 68 (1946) 648–70 ; 766–98 ; *R. G. Moulton, *The Literary Study of the Bible*, London 1899² ; Pius XII *Divino afflante Spiritu* §§ 36–50 ; Pont. Biblical Comm., *Letter to Cardinal Suhard*, AAS (1948) 45–8, CR 29 (1948) 423 ff. ; HPR 48 (1948) 572 ff. ; *Scripture* 3 (1948) 65 ff. ; F. Prat, S.J., art. *Progrès et Tradition en Exégèse* in ER 93 (1902) 289 ff., 610 ff. ; A. Robert, art. *Historique (Genre)* DBVS 4, 7–23 ; A. Robert and A. Tricot, *Initiation Biblique*, Paris 1948², ch VI ; P. Synave and P. Benoit, O.P., *La Prophétie* (esp. Appendix II, 293–376) Paris 1947 ; P. Vincent O.P., *La Théorie des Genres Littéraires*, Paris 1934.

b Description—The Bible is a library. It has, it is true, an historical direction, but this is not so evident in the OT apart from the NT. We shall here concentrate on the OT, and at once observe that we do not read all the books of this library in the same way. The literary form of a book denotes that external pattern of writing which is regulated by custom in a certain epoch and region. At the same time it indicates the meaning of what the author has written ; for he chooses the pattern, *e.g.* of pure fiction (a parable) because he wants to reach his readers' imagination and will rather than instruct them on pure history. Like styles in architecture, the literary forms are expressions of a certain culture and period. It is claimed that Christianity made the Gothic style possible, and the Baroque is generally regarded as an expression of the Counter-Reformation, of ' the spirit of conquest which is the characteristic of that epoch, manifested both on the battle-field (*cf.* Lepanto) and in the field of the apostolate and of mystical devotion ', J. Duhr, S.J., *Le sens religieux dans l'architecture chrétienne*, NRT 69 (1947) 707. The Bible is sometimes described as a series of letters from God to man ; but they are addressed to men of a definite time and place, and they are couched in man-made language which can change its meaning in the course of time.

c The subject of the Literary Forms of the Bible has been studied carefully during the last sixty years. When critics declare that biblical judgements are contradicted by facts, historical or scientific, or when they point to alleged serious divergencies in the Bible, one of the keys which the student (*cf.* Inspiration and Inerrancy §§ 34–8) will use to open the way to a solution is that in different Books there are different literary forms, and forms different from those in use today. ' The literary form that the writer chooses **32c** indicates the character of his work ; it enables us to discover (*a*) the precise aspect of the object which he has in mind, (*b*) his fuller or less agreement with the statements he sets down, (*c*) whether he intends or does not intend to present what he writes as true teaching. The literary form of a work, then, is like the key to opening up the book's standpoint and interpretation ', Synave and Benoit, 367. These remarks reflect the words of Pius XII, DAS 38.

Everybody is agreed that the Bible contains various **d** literary forms, such as History, Poetry, Prophecy and Wisdom. Inside these forms there is ample scope for the individuality of each writer to express itself (*cf.* §§ 610–15). They are evident from even a cursory reading of the OT, and are not a subjective subterfuge for finding a way out of difficulties. ' Holy Scripture is the unchangeable word of God to which man must bend himself, and not something which he can bend to his own personal ideas ', J. Daniélou, *Les Divers Sens de l'Ecriture*, ETL 24 (1948) 120 (*cf.* Pesch, *De Inspiratione* (Freiburg im Breisgau 1925) n. 520). To claim that a book or passage has an unusual literary form, one must be able to produce evidence from the text or context ; in short, to produce cogent reasons (*cf. Prov. Deus*, EB, 97).

The Literary Form of History—The facts narrated **e** in the OT are not a tangle of incidents without purpose or direction. ' It must be emphasized that this Jewish and Christian attitude to Scripture does not . . . mean their treating of the OT merely as if it were a kind of Old Moore's Almanac. It means rather that they saw world history and God's purpose side by side, and were convinced that the two were connected ', *T. W. Manson, *The Argument from Prophecy*, JTS 46 (1945) 129. The OT is the record of events controlled by God's Providence and directed to a definite end, *viz.* to Christ and his reign (*cf.* 1 Cor 15:25 ; Col 1:16 ; Eph 1:10 ; Apoc 22:13). Though the writers of the OT historical books may not have perceived the full significance of the events they were inspired to record, they were well aware that history was under God's control. The unity of the Pentateuch, for example, is based on the belief that ' there exists a divine unchangeable plan continually developing despite all obstacles, the goal of which is the creation of the people of Israel as a theocratic nation, with Palestine as home, and the law of Moses as charter ', *Initiation Biblique*, 82. Not one of the sacred writers wanted to chronicle merely secular events without reference to God or religion (*cf.* J. Bonsirven, S.J., *Exégèse Rabbinique et Exégèse Paulinienne*, Paris 1939, 350 f. ; G. Courtade, S.J., *Le Sens de l'Histoire dans l'Ecriture*, RSR 36 (1949) 136 ff.). Though the teaching of historical fact and truth is not the only characteristic of the OT, it is its chief feature. Consequently, it is of the greatest importance to identify the kind of history the writers intended to present.

Pope Pius XII *invites* the interpreter to try to dis- **f** cern the literary forms used by the sacred writers, especially in history, DAS 38–42. The invitation marks a striking development in the history of interpretation. After the publication of *Prov. Deus* by Leo XIII in 1893 the question of the day was whether one could discern several kinds of literary forms in

32f the historical books of the Bible. In 1902 Père Lagrange, O.P., gave six conferences to the Catholic Institute at Toulouse, soon afterwards published in the book whose English translation is entitled *Historical Criticism and the OT*.

g He suggested three possibilities : (*a*) the sacred writer used history only as a literary dress to clothe some message of dogmatic or moral import. The persons and situations would then be merely the fruit of the writer's imagination, and the whole work could be labelled **Edifying History**. Tob, it is suggested, would be an example ; for it was not written to make formal assertions about persons and events, but to present Tobias as a model of ancient Jewish virtues. (*b*) **History Proper,** where the writer intends to write an official history. It is clear that the objective reality of the persons and facts reported must here be the writer's chief concern, 3 and 4 Kg would be an example. (*c*) **Primitive History,** which is intermediary between the two preceding, *op. cit.* 202. The early chapters of the Bible do not set out a complete history. But ' it was of importance to show by a continuous chain of evidence the unity of the history of salvation ', 206. In view of this end the Bible ' is taken up with tangible things, with discoveries which are still known ; it relates their origin and progress and leaves them in a hazy light, which has no outward semblance of actual history. If the personality of Lamech seems to stand out against this background, it is only in an elegy. Could the author have told us more clearly that there exists no history of these periods ? ' *ibid.*

h By 1904 F. von Hummelauer had developed these ideas into a system of eight categories. (*a*) **Fable,** in its etymological sense of something spoken about. It is not necessarily fictitious. There are two such fables in the OT, Jg 9:8–15 ; 4 Kg 14:9. They are used merely to illustrate. (*b*) **Parable** prescinds from historical fact and is used only as an envelope to deliver religious truth. (*c*) **Epic History** adorns some historical event with fanciful details aimed at arresting the reader's attention, *e.g.* the poetical description of the Plagues of Egypt, Wis 16–17. (*d*) **Religious History** selects or adapts situations and discourses in accordance with a religious goal. The writer gives the facts but does not record details with the care of a scientific historian. (*e*) **Ancient History,** like that of the ancient Greeks and Romans, sets out to record facts, but without critical work on the sources. For all the ancient peoples, history was an art ; for us it is a science. (*f*) **Popular Traditions,** where an historical core is enveloped by fabulous additions. The narratives of Gen 1–11 seem to belong to this class, the word *tôlⁱdôṯ* at the head of each part being a reference to the ancient popular traditions. Their value as history depends on the assertion of the inspired writer or the Church's tradition. Nobody today holds that the word *tôlⁱdôṯ* indicates a special literary form. In Gen it occurs regularly merely to introduce a summary of the history of certain families or tribes and their descendants (*cf.* Bea 113). (*g*) **Free Narrative** gives ' idealized history ', *i.e* real history mixed with fiction, *e.g.* Tob, Jdt, Est. It is closer to epic history than to Popular Tradition ; it adds fictitious ornament to real history. (*h*) **Haggadic Midrash** is a biblical narrative developed with great freedom to inculcate a moral truth. It resembles our historical novel. Perhaps Jdt is in this way an elaboration of some ancient story. True the word occurs in 2 Par 13:22 ; 24:27, but it is unlikely that it there denotes a literary form peculiar to the Jews, where objective truth is twisted to suit some ethical purpose. The Rabbinical use of Midrash appears only after the time of Christ (*cf.* SB *Einleitung in Talmud u. Midrasch*, 1925⁵, 195 ; Bea 113).

i These eight forms were suggested as eight different ways of extracting the objective truth from the narratives of the OT. At first they were warmly welcomed. They seemed to provide a ready reply to Rationalists who were protesting against the historical value of **32i** many narratives in the OT. Enthusiasm for these eight categories began to wane as men asked whether readers of the Bible could be left with the impression that historical narratives were only more or less true.

The fundamental error of the suggested catalogue was twofold. First, the author thought out these peculiar literary forms (not identified in other ancient histories), and then suggested that the basis of distinction one from another was the more or less distance from objective fact. The remark of J. Goettsberger holds good for at least many passages, ' That the narratives were not historical was a conclusion drawn not from some literary form discovered elsewhere ; rather it was because the narratives were considered to be unhistorical that the conclusion was drawn that they must belong to some peculiar literary forms. It is difficult to avoid in this matter the objection of a vicious circle ', BZ 3 (1905) 241.

In 1903 the Pontifical Biblical Commission, § 52*j*, stated that it is not legitimate to assert that narratives are historical only in appearance, or form, unless there are solid grounds for so interpreting them. This, of course, is a law of sound interpretation of any writings. Many people saw that the inerrancy of the Bible was called into question by the wild use of the principle of literary forms. Indeed, a certain reaction against the use of the principle at all set in ; *cf.* L. Billot, S.J., *De Inspiratione S. Scripturae* (Romae 1906² 143). But Rome had spoken not to condemn all use of the principle, but simply by arousing respect for the inerrancy of the Bible to declare that the questions of interpretation were not yet solved. What the Pontifical Biblical Commission wanted was the right use of the principle of literary forms.

j In 1920 Pope Benedict XV published his encyclical *Spiritus Paraclitus*. The principle of literary forms in history was accepted almost explicitly, but again with warnings against abuses, interpreters who too lightly adopt the hypothesis of implicit quotations or of narrative historical in appearance only, or who would use literary forms which compromise the truth of the Bible, Dz 2188 ; EB 474. This acceptance of principle was made fully explicit by the encyclical *Div. affl. Spir.* of Pope Pius XII : ' A knowledge and careful appreciation of ancient modes of expression and literary forms and styles will provide a solution to many of the objections made against the truth and historical accuracy of Holy Writ ', 42.

Since the days of Hummelauer the realization had grown that one could not regard a passage in a narrative as half historical merely because one could think out some literary form which had only that amount of historical truth in focus. The literary form of history is one, not a collection. At the same time it could be selective in the facts, incomplete, and have many manners of presenting the facts which are not like those we use today. The right use of the principle of literary forms is based on the distinction between objective facts and the manner of presenting them, between message and envelope. Semitic writers did not use the synthetic style of the Romans ; they reconstructed events in pieces, developing the narrative in concentric circles around a central nucleus. They kept repeating the central theme in order to add to the circumstances already alluded to, or omitted details already described but now considered irrelevant for the particular purpose they were pursuing. The early chapters of Gen are an example of this. They often prefer to group matters together in a logical, rather than a chronological, order ; they are content with quoting the sense, rather than the very words, of previous speakers or writers. Similar procedure can be identified in other ancient writings, but readers did not thereby accuse the authors of mixing error with truth.

k Sometimes the literary form can be ascertained from the text itself. For example, Gen 1, where the account

32k of the Creation is found to be arranged carefully in an artificial literary scheme, allied by the parallelism it employs to poetry rather than to historical record. The six days have opening and closing formulae which correspond, and the whole scheme divides into two symmetrical halves of three days and three days, each day of the first three being exactly parallel with the corresponding day of the second half. But it is not always easy to discern those features which mark off one form from another. If we are to read parables or allegories in the course of a book of narrative history, we need to have some indication either from the introduction (as in the Gospel and Prophetical Books), or from the nature of the argument, or, as we have seen in Gen 1, from the manner in which the narrative is set forth. And sometimes comparative study of other ancient modes of expression can guide us to identify a particular literary form in the Bible. ' Well understood, the principle can be light for interpreters ; badly understood, it can be the occasion for all sorts of fantasies and guesses. Doubtless, this disturbing alternative is the reason why there was so much delay on the part of ecclesiastical authority in the clear assertion of the principle, and even today in this, the oustanding page of the encyclical (*Div. affl. Spir.*) there is, probably by design, a certain obscurity. . . . We have to conclude, it seems, that while clearly approving the principle of distinguishing literary forms, the encyclical does not intend to give interpreters a free hand to decide how widely the principle may be applied. The task remains for Catholic interpreters to work out for themselves a way so true and exact that it will not have to be laid down all over again later ', J. Levie, 787–8.

l We may give the name **Primitive History** to the literary form employed in the first eleven chapters of Gen. They describe the origins of the human race and of the chosen people up to the call of Abraham. ' The events narrated in these two chapters, Gen. 10–11, have a place outside of known history. Languages are evidently not confused and multiplied from one day to the next ; comparative philology proves that variations in dialects are made slowly and constantly. Likewise the census of the peoples in the ethnographic table is limited to the Near East. The longevity of the patriarchs is contradicted by the teaching of palaeontology. . . . This entire period prior to Abraham is thus described with a mentality belonging to a period far later than the events recorded ', J. M. Vosté, O.P., art. *The Pontifical Biblical Commission on the Pentateuch*, HPR 48 (1948) 568. Perhaps the best commentary on the words of DAS and at the same time the best explanation of what is meant by the literary form, Primitive History, is to be read in the letter sent to Cardinal Suhard, for which see § 53*l*.

m A. Bea, S.J., in *La Civiltà Cattolica* (17 Apr. 1948) 122, has pointed out that the modern sciences of palaeontology, prehistory, archaeology and anthropology have presented so many serious difficulties against the ancient literal interpretation of the first eleven chapters of Gen, that it is no longer possible simply to keep the exegesis of our forefathers. If interpreters were to close their eyes to these facts, they would be seriously disloyal to the commission entrusted to them by Divine Providence for the good of the Church.

Job in so far as it is history stands in a class by itself. The hero was an historical person ; such at least is the impression gained from the prologue and epilogue (both written in prose). But the body of the book is poetical ; it is a didactic work about the problem of the just man under affliction. From the standpoint of its historical literary form we use here the term of P. Lagrange, **Edifying History.**

33a **The Literary Form of the Law**—The Pentateuch, and particularly the Books of Lev and Deut, indicated for an Israelite the way to obey the Covenant and to become holy. In the way the laws are presented we observe that they ' are not set out methodically ;

several are repeated ; some are related to a new **33a** historical context and their binding force is more or less adapted. These details indicate that Israel's legislation was closely bound to the life of the nation and to the Semitic world in general, and that consequently it evolved to a certain degree, the precise limit of which it is hard to determine ', A. Robert, *Initiation Biblique*, 164.

In Deut the writer aims at giving his reader intellectual conviction and resolute determination to carry out the prescriptions about worshipping God and living in his presence. Threats are comparatively few. But in Lev the laws are presented against a background of solemn warnings. In both works, and throughout the Pentateuch, the basic historical theological truth that the Israelites are bound by a Covenant with God, influences the manner of presentation of the laws. That characteristic serves to identify a particular literary form which can be called **Legal.**

The other books of the OT can from the point of **b** view of literary forms be classed as follows : **Lyric Poetry** (Pss ; portions of the Prophets, *e.g.* Is, Jer, and poems elsewhere) ; **Dramatic Poetry** (Cant) ; **Prophecy** (Is, Jer, Ez, the Twelve Minor Prophets) ; **Apocalypse** (Dan) ; **Wisdom Literature** (Prov, Eccl, Ecclus, Wis).

All these Books (with the exception of certain passages) were written in verse, and are cast in a poetical mould (the two are not the same ; for poetry can be expressed in prose ; *cf.* Moulton 76). The Hebrew poet was accorded a licence. He was not tied to the ordinary meanings of words or to the use of regular grammar. He could make comparatively free use of rhetoric, metaphor and anthropomorphisms when describing God, all of which would have a different sense in straight historical narrative. Thus, in interpreting, *e.g.* the Imprecatory Psalms, we must allow for their lyrical character, for the oriental exaggeration used in invective, and in this way reach the mind of the writer, whose basic teaching is that God is just, that the enemies of his people are his enemies, and that they must be crushed by his almighty power. The rest is secondary, ornamental.

The verses in **Biblical poetry** are based not on the **c** numbering of the syllables, but on a symmetry of clauses in a verse, which since the time of *R. Lowth (De Sacra Poesi Hebraeorum*, Oxford 1753) has come to be called Parallelism, for which see § 313*e*. Several rules for correct interpretation can be deduced from this fact of parallelism (*cf.* § 313*f*).

Sometimes, close attention to symmetry will reveal the author's plan of a book and its chapters, together with misplacements and additions by perhaps other writers ; *cf.* P. Gaechter, S.J., *Semitic Literary Forms in the Apocalypse and their Import* in *Theol. Studies* 8 (1947).

In **Dramatic Poetry** action predominates and the **d** author effaces his own personality in order to let his readers hear and see the characters taking part in the incident. The meaning of the writer has to be learned from the purpose of the book. It would be absurd to identify expressions and propositions taken at random from Shakespeare's characters with those of the author ; it would be equally absurd to take what Baldad the Suhite has to say in Job as the teaching of the author, as the teaching of God. The writer's contention there is to reject the theory of retribution expounded by the three friends, and he leaves the problem unsolved. Moreover, in a drama the author is not writing as an historian ; he is allowed to invent characters, and mix fiction with fact.

Prophecy—The Hebrew prophet (*Nābî*) had the **e** function to preach, and at times to foretell, what God revealed. He spoke under a special, divine, influence, like inspiration, but intended for the spoken, rather than the written word. Though foretelling was only a subordinate part of his office, it was important ; for one of the ways by which he could establish his

33e credentials was by pointing to the fulfilment of his predictions.

The prophets preached to men living in a certain place and time, and they used a language that would arrest, as well as inform, the minds of their audiences. Most of the prophecies were oral, though Jon, Dan 1–6, Is 36–39, Ez 40–47 are literary works. In the main, however, the prophecies belong to the literary form given to oratory, a form close to poetry (*cf.* A. Condamin, S.J., DAFC, 4 416 ff.). When we read what the prophet foretells we have to distinguish his message from the envelope. The latter is truly inspired as envelope, but its purpose is only to contain, protect and deliver the message ; it is determined by the conditions of the prophet's environment. When the fulfilment is reached, the envelope may be discarded (*cf.* A. Fernández, S.J., N. 64, *Scholion* 3).

f This distinction enables us to understand why secondary features were not fulfilled to the letter, *e.g.* the material and national restoration associated with the coming of the Messias in certain prophecies (Is 8:8 ff. ; 11:1 ff.). We, living in the time of the fulfilment, can see that the material hopes were secondary features—part of the envelope. It was only slowly, through the teaching of the Holy Spirit, that the Apostles themselves came to understand how completely Christ had fulfilled the ancient predictions (*cf.* Ac 1:6). Of course, not all the OT prophecies contained these secondary features about a temporal prosperity (*e.g.* Is 2:2–5 ; 9:1–6, and the Servant Oracles). The distinction holds ' nothing to alarm the student of Apologetics. On the contrary, he can win thereby a great advantage when confronting those who object the " prophecy after the event " theory. In fact, whilst the prophet was foretelling with certainty some future important event, he could suggest certain attendant circumstances as probable—in order to give his description life and concrete flavour. But it is obvious that if he were writing only *after* the event, he would have omitted every detail that did not correspond exactly with the details of the fulfilment. A prophecy about the fall of Babylon, uttered after 539, would be careful to avoid presenting the city as a deserted ruin ', A. Condamin, S.J., DAFC 4 419. There is sound historical evidence showing that when Cyrus conquered Babylon in 539 B.C., he did not destroy the city. The lesson we learn is that Isaias, 13 ; 47, and Jeremias, 50 ; 51, preached two primary facts : the fall of the Dynasty then in power in Babylon and the end of the Jewish captivity. The exact manner of the fall was secondary, part of the envelope inspired by God to give an arresting exposition of the certain primary facts (*cf.* Ez 9:1–10:8).

g A feature which sometimes causes difficulty for interpreters is the compenetration of time in the prophet's perspective, especially in apocalyptic passages. In history, chronological or logical order is demanded ; in prophecy this may be disregarded. For example, the term, the *Day of the Lord* in Is, Jer, Joel may have for its immediate subject some particular calamity regarded as God's chastisement, but along with this the prophet may combine characteristics of the Last Day (*cf.* R. Hull, S.J., *Compenetration in Prophecy* in *Medieval Theories of the Papacy*, London, 1934 ; C. Lattey, *Prophecy*, CTS, 1943).

h **Apocalypse** means ' removal of a veil ', *i.e.* a vision of the future. More precisely this literary form denotes eschatological events described in a didactic poem, the form of which is a series of revelations, represented dramatically and by symbols. When the voice of prophecy ceased in Israel this form of literature became common and continued until the 2nd cent. A.D. Its main purpose was to console and strengthen those who were called upon to witness to their faith in times of trial.

The apocryphal books written in this form when its appeal was greatest (from the 2nd cent. B.C. to the 2nd cent. A.D.) reveal a stereotyped general pattern. In the first part of his book the writer ' foretells '

events which have already been realized ; in the **33h** second part he expresses his hopes for the future in the light of events attendant on the Day of the Lord. Moreover, he uses conventional symbols as the vehicle of his thought, first to arouse his readers' curiosity, and secondly because he wants to conceal his teaching from hostile Gentiles.

This literary form is a special class of prophecy. **i** Like the prophets the apocalyptists were oral teachers as well as writers ; preachers who claimed that they wrote not only under the influence of inspiration but in ecstasy (*cf.* *W. O. E. Oesterley, *The Jews and Judaism during the Greek Period*, London 1941, 71). Daniel, among the Canonical Books, is acknowledged by all to be in some sense or other an apocalypse (*cf.* C. Lattey, S.J., *The Book of Daniel*, Dublin 1948, XXIII), and *Apoc* has obvious relations, though St John's theme and manner of presentation are not rigidly circumscribed by any borrowed pattern (*cf.* § 962 ff.).

The first appearances of apocalyptic literature were early (Deut 28:60–68) but it was in the period preceding and following the Exile that it became frequent in canonical literature (*cf.* Is 11:11–16 ; 34–35 ; Ps 47 ; Prov 1:20–23 ; Job 18:5 ff. ; Ez ; Jl ; Zach ; Mal). ' From the literary standpoint apocalyptic is artificial, cold, pedantic, moving with stereotyped catchwords, encompassed by subtlety and exaggerations, and consequently by the claim that it is trying to translate into human language the highest and most obscure facts ', A. Robert, *Initiation Biblique*, 187.

It would be a mistake to interpret an apocalyptic work as though the writer used historical narrative. It is possible that the writer used fiction, but ' there need have been no deceit on his part, either of himself or of his readers. Such works as apocalypses were not written for the common people, who would not be at all likely to read them, but for such as could appreciate their special conventions ', C. Lattey, S.J., *op. cit.*, XXVII (*cf.* P. Gaechter in § 33c).

The Literary Forms of the NT can very broadly **j** be grouped into three, the *Historical*, or *Documentary* (the Gospels and Ac), the *Epistles* (St Paul's and the Catholic epistles) and *Apocalypse*. The fourth Gospel is still a Gospel ; how it is included under the historical literary form can be read § 776 ff. Similarly the historicity of the other NT works is treated in the special introductions and in the general essays, §§ 60 ff., 610 ff., 661 ff.

We may mention here the theory of **Form Criticism. k** The name was borrowed from specialists in medieval German literature who classified and dated popular stories according to their contents and manner of presentation. Applied to the Synoptic Gospels the theory is really a development of Source Criticism. By 1919 non-Catholic critics had established to their own satisfaction the priority of Mk. But then they decided that literary criticism does not take us back far enough ; they wished to identify the material which Mk used. To meet this need the theory of Form Criticism was suggested by certain German scholars, and it is becoming increasingly popular in England. Cf. *M. Dibelius, *Die Formgeschichte des Evangeliums*, 1919, Eng. tr. *From Tradition to Gospel*, 1935 ; *F. J. Badcock, *Form Criticism*, ET 53 (1941) 16 ff. ; R. Bultmann, *Die Geschichte der Synoptischen Tradition*, 1931² ; F. M. Braun, O.P. *Où en est le Problème de Jésus ?* (Paris 1932) 215–65 ; J. J. Collins, S.J., *Form Criticism and the Synoptic Gospels* in *Theological Studies* (USA) Sept. 1941 ; S. E. Donlon, S.J., *The Form Critics, The Gospel and St Paul*, CBQ 6 (1944) 159–79 ; 306–25 ; *F. V. Filson, *Books on the Message* in *Journal of Bible and Religion* 10 (1942) 93–7 (a good bibliography) ; E. Florit, *La Storia delle Forme nei Vangeli*, Bi 14 (1933) 212–48 ; L. de Grandmaison, S.J., *Jésus-Christ* 1, 42 ff., London 1934² ; *R. H. Lightfoot, *Form Criticism and Gospel Study*, ET 53 (1941) 51 ff. ; *E. S. Redlich, *Form Criticism, its Value and Limitations*, London 1939 ; *K. L. Schmidt, *Der Rahmen der*

33k *Geschichte Jesu*, Berlin 1919 ; *V. Taylor, *The Formation of the Gospel Tradition*, London 1932.

l The Form Critics set themselves a twofold task. First they untie the strings with which the Evangelists are said to have bound together the individual stories of tradition. In other words, they set on one side the grouping, the chronology, the arrangement, the motives behind the writing of each passage. Then they classify the stories left over into *forms*. This is the essential characteristic of the whole theory. The Form Critics do not always agree on the labels to be attached to the forms, but the following represent those suggested by *Dibelius and *Bultmann : *Apophthegms* (practically the same as Dibelius's *Paradigms*), short illustrative stories of an event designed to fit the motive behind the writing. They are of three kinds, polemical, didactical, biographical. Then there are *Tales*, stories told for their own sake ; *Miracle stories ; Legends ; Myths ; Sayings ; Commentaries.*

m The second step is ' to relate the several stories to the life of the Church which cherished and preserved them, and made use of them to convey its message to the world ', Lightfoot. In other words, behind our Gospels lies the growth of the forms, the origins of which are to be discovered in the life of the early Christian community. ' The authors of the Gospels . . . are not " authors " in the literary sense, but collectors ', Dibelius, 60. R. Bultmann, an extreme Form Critic, declares ' We can know almost nothing concerning the early life and personality of Jesus, since the early Christian sources show no interest in either, are moreover fragmentary and often legendary ' (*Jesus*, 1934[2], American trans. *Jesus and the Word*, VIII–IX).

n There is both truth and error in the theories of the Form Critics. Certain observations therefore suggest themselves :—

(i) Their insistence on the importance of oral tradition is a corrective to the Two-Document Theory of the composition of the Synoptic Gospels (*cf.* § 610 ff.) ;

(ii) It is true that these Gospels ' inaugurate and form by themselves a new type in the field of doctrinal and apologetical biography ; a type which nothing else resembles, even among works which are equally intended to make known and to appraise a religious founder ', Grandmaison, 52 f. We may agree that they are not highly polished literary efforts, but simple, incomplete presentations of the Good Tidings, ' less apologies than epiphanies ', *ibid.*

But the fact that a story is told in popular manner, devoid of literary artifice, is no reason for saying it cannot be a true history of fact. There are popular stories which are fictitious ; there are also popular accounts of events by eyewitnesses. But the difference between the two is striking. The effacement of the **33n** Gospel-writers, their sober narrative even about awe-inspiring miracles, strike a marked contrast with, *e.g.* the apocryphal gospels.

The authors of the apocryphal Gospels ' do not speak with the voices of Paul or of John, or with the quiet simplicity of the three first Gospels ', *M. R. James, *The Apocryphal New Testament*, xii.

(iii) Thus when it is said that the Gospels were **o** written to portray the Christian belief in and worship of Christ as Lord, we may agree that they do indeed have such a religious goal, the portrayal of Christ as Messias, true God and true man, but that the sober character of the narrative points to its being a record of objective historical fact, as different as possible from the apocryphal writings of the second century.

(iv) Moreover, bearing in mind the dates of composition, is it reasonable to hold that a Christ-legend could have developed so soon ? Some generations ago, Rationalists, regarding the Gospels as unhistorical, rightly reasoned that a considerable length of time must be allowed for such a legend to take shape, and dated the Gospels in the second century. Today, it is no longer possible to maintain such late dates and serious scholars would allow a first century date for all four. Yet the Form Critics, while not disputing the dates, refuse to allow the historical character of the narrative. In short, they ask us to believe that in the space of thirty or forty years, at the end of which thousands of people who had seen Christ were still alive, fictitious accounts of ·his life and work were composed, widely circulated and accepted as fact. It was precisely to avoid such awkward witnesses that the older Rationalists proposed a second-century date (*cf.* § 609).

(v) We may classify the Gospel incidents, but ' Let us only remark that in judging a system which insists on classification by *form*, any considerable amount of formless matter possessing characteristics of several " forms " should raise definite uneasiness in our minds ', Donlon, 164.

(vi) The Form Critics have a strange notion of the early Christian community. Fr. Donlon has culled the following characteristics from the works of the leading exponents : ' The early Christian communities were (1) eschatological in thought and outlook, (2) uncontrolled and democratic, (3) in search of laws of living in the words and deeds of Jesus, (4) creative, (5) autonomous '.

This list will serve to indicate how far the mentality of the Form Critics is from that of the primitive Christians who formed the Body of Christ, which is his Church, Eph 1:23 (*cf.* article CHRISTIANITY IN APOSTOLIC TIMES).

THE INSPIRATION AND INERRANCY OF HOLY SCRIPTURE

By J. H. CREHAN, S.J.

34a **Bibliography**—Richard Fitzralph, *De erroribus Armenorum* (Paris 1512) lib. 1 cap. 1–6 ; Sixtus of Siena, *Bibliotheca sacra* (Frankfurt 1575) 672–8 ; Lessius, *Responsio ad censuram* (in Schneemann, *Controvers. de divina gratia*, Freiburg 1881) ; J.-B. Franzelin, *De divina traditione et scriptura* (Rome 1882³) ; M.-J. Lagrange, *L'inspiration et les exigences de la critique*, RB 5 (1896) 485–518 ; C. Pesch, S.J., *De sacrae scripturæ inspiratione* (Freiburg 1906 and suppl. 1926) ; H. Höpfl, O.S.B., *Tractatus de inspiratione* (Rome 1929²) ; J. Bainvel, S.J., *De scriptura sacra* (Paris 1910) ; R. Cornely and A. Merk, S.J., *Compendium introductionis* (CSS, Paris 1927⁹) ; A. Bea, S.J., *De sacrae scripturae inspiratione* (Rome 1935²) ; H. Lusseau et M. Collomb, *Manuel d'Etudes bibliques*, vol. 1 (Paris 1936) ; E. Dorsch, S.J., *Institutiones theologiae fundamentalis*, vol. 3 (Innsbruck 1927²) ; S. Tromp, S.J., *De sacrae scripturae inspiratione* (Rome 1945⁴) ; E. Mangenot, *Inspiration* (DTC) ; A. Durand, S.J., *Inerrance* (DAFC) ; G. Courtade, S.J., *Inspiration* (DBV[S]) ; F. Prat, S.J., *La bible et l'histoire* (Paris 1908⁵) ; J. Calès, S.J., *Le Père Fernand Prat* (Paris 1942) ; Various, *L'œuvre exégétique et historique du R. P. Lagrange* (Paris 1935) ; F. E. Gigot, *Biblical lectures* (New York 1901) ; J. Healy, *Papers and Addresses* (Dublin 1909) ; J. Arendzen, *Inspiration* (with Abp Downey, in *The Religion of the Scriptures*, Cambridge 1921²) ; F. Fabbi, *La condiscendenza divina nell' inspirazione biblica* Bi 14 (1933) 330–47 ; J. Duggan, S.J., *Num sententia Cardinalis Newman defendi possit?* VD 18 (1938) 219–24 ; K. Smyth, S.J., *The Criterion of NT Inspiration* CBQ 2 (1940) 229–44; A. Bea, S.J., *Deus auctor Scripturae* in *Angelicum* 20 (1943) 16–31 ; *W. Sanday, *Inspiration* (London 1893) ; *P. Thompson and *H. Symonds, *The inspiration and inerrancy of the Bible* (London 1939) ; *G. Bentley, *The resurrection of the Bible* (London 1940) ; *C. H. Dodd, *The authority of the Bible* (London 1928) ; H. Dutouquet, S.J., *La Psychologie de l'inspiration* ER 85 (1900) 158–71 ; H. Pope, O.P., *The Scholastic view of Inspiration* ITQ 6 (1911) 275–98 ; J. MacRory, *The Church and the Biblical Question* ITQ 1 (1906) 15–34 ; H. Lusseau, *Essai sur la nature de l'inspiration* (Paris 1930) with defence of same, Bi 13 (1932) 28–48 ; J. Garvin, *The morality of the Hebrews* (in *The Old Testament*, Cambridge summer school 1938). L. Billot, S.J., *De Inspiratione Sacrae Scripturae* (Rome 1906²) ; P. Synave and P. Benoit, O.P., Appendix on Inspiration and Inerrancy in *S. Thomas d'Aquin : Somme théologique : La Prophétie* (Paris 1947) 293–353. The encyclical *Divino afflante* of Pius XII is cited according to the official English translation : *Stand by the Bible*, 1944, which has paragraph numbers inserted.

b **Introductory**—In modern parlance an inspired statement is one which is probably untrue but which has been given out by some official source in the hope that it will be believed. This degradation of the word ' inspiration ' makes it necessary to state at once in general terms what Catholics understand by the inspiration of the Bible. The inspired books of the Bible are not merely the sacred books of Christianity, nor books which all generations of Christians have found to be redolent of God (whether because they found that their contents appealed to what was best in man or for any other reason), but these books have God for their author. Thus God is considered by

Catholics to have used the agency of men to produce **34b** books which he wished to have written, with such contents as he wished them to have. The difference will be noted at once of this view from modern Anglican ideas according to which it can be said that the writers of the inspired books are felt by us to have a quality sometimes more easy to recognize than to define, which makes what they wrote of unique and permanent religious value. The Catholic theology of inspiration will now be considered historically, according as it has developed, and thereafter some general account of the truth of the Bible and its freedom from error will be given.

Jewish Ideas on Inspiration—The Pentateuch was **c** commonly held by Jews to have come from God entire (TB *San.* 93a). Even Deut 34:5-12 was thought by some to have been dictated by Moses in prevision of his death, though generally (TB. *Baba Bathra* 14b) it was held that Josue wrote these verses. The prophets were thought to have undergone less complete control than Moses in their utterance, while the hagiographers were credited with a mere assistance from God. Certain books however were singled out from among the ' writings ' as being under the care of more favoured individuals. Thus Moses was credited with the writing of Job whether that means the composition or the copying of the work (TB. *Bab. B* 15a). Philo considered Scripture to have been written by men in ecstasy. It was ' a god-indwelt possession and madness ' (*Q. div. rer. her.* 249-58). The prophet ' uttereth nothing of his own, but entirely what belongs to another who prompts him the while '. Some think that Philo has contaminated Jewish ideas with Platonic thought here (*cf.* § 414e), but there is nothing in what he says that could not be matched from the OT. Philo has no trace of the Greek theory (visible in Plutarch, *de def. orac* 438a) that oracular speech was due to a fortunate conjunction of mephitic vapours, activated by the sun, with a person of the right temperament. ' The wise man ', Philo says, ' is a resonant instrument, struck and beaten by the unseen hand of God '. This inspiration was extended by him to the translators of LXX, in the well-known story of its origin which he recounts (*Vit. Mos* 2:37). The Targum, too, had its share of inspiration, for (TB *Meg* 3a) Jonathan ben Uzziel (disciple of Hillel) was said to have composed the Targum of the prophets with aid from Agg, Zach, and Mal, who cannot possibly have been regarded as his contemporaries. When it was finished, a voice from heaven asked : Who has revealed my secrets ? Josephus, interpreting Jewish beliefs for a pagan world, says (*contr. Ap* 1:8) that it is natural for all Jews from their youth up to look on the Bible as God's word, to cling to it and even to die for it.

Philo does use Plato's word ἐπίπνοια for ' inspiration ' **d** and speaks of prophets as θεόληπτοι or θεοφόρητοι, but apart from coining new words, what else could he have done ? It is perhaps significant that, when Christian sources are reached, a new term does appear. The Scriptures are θεόπνευστα (2 Tim 3:15), being thus called by a term which is unparalleled in earlier Greek writing. It is not used by LXX nor by Philo, and the one other usage cited as from a 1st cent. writer (Plutarch, *de plac. phil.* 904 f.) turns out to be from a work of the middle of the 2nd cent. which is printed with Plutarch's works.

34e **The OT itself** represents Moses as writing his canticle at God's dictation, Deut 31:19 : ' Now therefore write you this canticle . . . and this song may be unto me for a testimony amongst the children of Israel '. For other commands to write, see § 413c. David lays claim to inspiration in 2 Kg 23:2 : ' The spirit of the Lord hath spoken by me, and his word by my tongue .' In Mal 4:4 (3:24 LXX) the whole law is ascribed to God : ' Remember the law of Moses my servant which I commanded him in Horeb '. The text in Isaias, which is often used to show that he regarded his work as the book of Yahweh, Is 34:16, can no longer be taken to mean so much as that ; but the guarantee given by God to the prophet, Is 59:21, that his words shall not perish, though it does not mention writing, is perhaps an indication of belief in an inspired book. Jeremias is more clear, when he says : ' Baruch wrote from the mouth of Jeremias all the words of the Lord which he spoke to him, upon the roll of a book ', Jer 36:4. The evidence for the divine control of prophets in their utterance is given in §§ 410d and 414c–d. The foundation for the later Jewish theory of degrees of inspiration is in Num 12:6 : ' If there be among you a prophet of the Lord, I will appear to him in a vision, or I will speak to him in a dream. But it is not so with my servant Moses . . . for I speak to him mouth to mouth and plainly ; and not by riddles and figures. He hath seen the Lord '. No Christian writer took up this idea of degrees of inspiration before Theodore of Mopsuestia (PG 66, 697), who probably derived it from Jewish sources. The natural consequence of the divine inspiration of a prophet is that God sees to it that what has been foretold by his prophet comes to pass (cf. Jer 1:11 ; 28:15 ; 29:9). This is one way in which the inerrancy of Scripture comes to the notice of the Jews, and as they regarded most of the books in their canon as being prophetical (for Moses was the greatest prophet, the psalmist was the royal prophet and even the Books of Kings were called prophetical), it may be that from such a guarantee of the truth of prophecy the general truth of Scripture was supposed.

35a **NT Evidence for the Fact of Inspiration**—The Apostles reaffirm the idea that the Scriptures are inspired. St Paul, 2 Tim 3:16, says : ' All Scripture, inspired of God, is profitable to teach, to reprove, to correct, to instruct in justice '. (Here the qualification ' inspired of God ' is quite clearly meant to apply to every Scripture. Paul cannot have thought of a class of Scripture-writings which were *not* inspired. Whether he meant to include in Scripture any NT books such as Mt, must remain an open question.) St Peter, 2 Pet 1:21, agrees : ' Prophecy came not by the will of man at any time : but men spoke *on the part of God*, inspired by the Holy Ghost '. This is an echo of his sermon in Ac 3:21 : ' God hath spoken by the mouth of his holy prophets from the beginning of the world '. Mk 12:36 (which is also Peter's preaching) makes clear—as Mt and Lk do not at that place—that David was inspired by the Holy Spirit. It is in keeping with this emphasis on prophecy that Apoc gives fuller details of God's action upon man in the writing of a sacred book (cf. Apoc 1:17 ; 2:1–12 ; 14:13 ; 22:6). Apart from Apoc, no NT book makes open claim to be inspired, though Peter, 2 Pet 3:16, makes such a claim for ' the epistles of our dearest brother Paul ', when he says : ' The unlearned and unstable wrest *these epistles*, as they do also the other Scriptures, to their own destruction '. This verse is much challenged by those who have preconceived ideas about the inspiration of the NT, but if the rest of the epistle be authentic (cf. § 952b) there is no reason to refuse credence to this one verse.

b It can be sufficiently demonstrated, even from our Lord's own words by themselves, that the earliest Christians regarded the Bible as inspired. ' *You* search the Scriptures, for you think in them to have life everlasting ', Jn 5:39. Paul's words : ' Well did the Holy Ghost speak to our fathers by Isaias the prophet ', spoken to the Jewish elders at Rome, Ac 28:25, show that the doctrine of inspiration was common ground for

himself and his gainsayers. The property of freedom **35b** from error is also ascribed to the Bible : ' He called them gods to whom the word of God was spoken ; and the Scripture cannot be broken ', Jn 10:34 (cf. 1:45 ; Ac 1:20 ; Mt 5:18).

The Evidence of Tradition for Inspiration—It has **c** never been the practice of Catholic theologians to prove the inspiration of Scripture from the Bible alone. The logical shortcomings of such a method are so great as to make necessary the use of external testimony from the tradition of the Church. Of individual writers in the earliest age Pope Clement I may be cited as having in his letter to the Corinthians shown that he regarded Paul's letters to Corinth as inspired : ' In truth it was by the Spirit that he sent you a letter about himself and Kephas and Apollos ', 1 Clem 47:3. Harnack questioned whether Clement conceived Paul's gift of inspiration to be different from his gifts as Apostle, but the point is idle, since the early Church so often takes ' prophets and apostles ' as the equivalent of OT and NT. The *Epistle of Barnabas*, 4:14, quotes Mt 22:14 with the words : ' As it is written ', a formula usual with Scripture citation, and as the same unknown writer clearly regards the OT as inspired, 1:7, one might perhaps conclude that he regarded Mt as equally inspired. The nature of his argument precludes him from a direct examination of the gospels. The passage in Ignatius (*ad Phil.* 8:2), where he seems to be arguing with those who asked for scriptural proof of Christianity, is too ambiguous to be used here, but in *Smyr.* 5:1 he gives a clear sign that for him prophets, law, and ' gospel ' are on the same footing. (Whether gospel here means the written book or the spoken kerygma matters little, for if Peter's preaching is held to be inspired, a faithful written record such as Mark's would also be held to be inspired.) *Magn.* 8:2 shows that Ignatius regarded the prophets as inspired with a view to their preaching of Christ who was to come. The *a fortiori* that therefore the Apostles would also be regarded by him as inspired for the same purpose seems warranted. St Polycarp (*ep. ad Phil.* 7:1) declares that **d** he who shall be found to have twisted the oracles of the Lord to his own fancy and to have denied both resurrection and judgement is the first-born of Satan. This strong condemnation of tampering with at least some of the NT Scriptures, written c A.D. 115 by a disciple of John, shows that he certainly subscribed to their sacred and inspired character (cf. Apoc 22:18–19). That Polycarp deals with NT and not OT Scriptures may be concluded from the following points : the use of κυρίου, the fact that, Jn 5:22, all judgement is given to the Son and that the denial of it would therefore involve altering NT texts, while the evidence for the resurrection, whether of Christ or of all men, is primarily in the NT also. Irenaeus (*Adv. Haer.* pref.) echoes the phrase in a NT context. Denis of Corinth (*flor.* 170) re-echoes Polycarp, for he writes to Pope Soter (in Euseb. HE 4:23) that it is small wonder that the apostles of the devil tamper with his (Denis's) letters, seeing that they dare to do as much with the Scriptures of the Lord.

St Justin—The old man to whom (*Dial. Tryph* 3–7) **e** St Justin ascribes his conversion says : ' There were long ago men more ancient than any of the philosophers now in repute, men who were happy, upright, and beloved of God, who spoke by the divine Spirit and gave oracles of the future which are now coming to pass. These men are called prophets. They alone saw the truth and proclaimed it to men, not practising any restriction, not made shamefaced nor swayed by boastfulness, but proclaiming that and that alone which they heard and saw, being filled with Holy Spirit. Their writings are still extant '. This clearly shows that Christians of the time accepted all the OT as inspired, for the emphasis here placed on prophecy does not exclude from the scope of inspiration the law and the ' writings '. How Justin regarded the NT may be seen later in the same work (82). Here he has mentioned that ' John, one of the Apostles of Christ,

35e prophesied in a vision given to him ', and he continues : ' Amongst us even now there are prophetic graces, whence you [the Jews] ought to realize that those ancient gifts that were among you have been transferred to us. Just as in the times of the holy prophets among you false prophets arose, even so amongst us now [the ideal date of the dialogue is 132] there are many false teachers '. This equation of prophets and Apostles is again made by Justin (75) where he argues from Is 6:8 : ' Here I am, send me ', that it was proper for the real prophets of God to be Apostles, *i.e.* ' men sent ' (*cf.* also *Dial* 110).

f Marcion and the Manichees—Marcion's attack on the Scriptures (*c* 150) led to some further argument on the equal inspiration of OT and NT. Tertullian (*Adv. Mar.* 4:22) disputes Marcion's explanation of the Transfiguration. It was not true, as Marcion said, that : ' Hear ye him ' meant that Moses and Elias were not to be heard. If the two were alongside Christ as rejected figures, they would have been in rags and on the ground, not glorious and in friendly converse with Jesus, the one of them the *initiator veteris testamenti*, the other the *consummator novi*. *Cf.* also Marcion's omission of Lk 11:49–51, which tells its own tale.

Though Marcion had dealt roughly with the Scriptures, it was the rise of the Manichees which put the Church very strictly upon the defensive in this question of inspiration. The *Acta Archelai* (written before 350) show Mani on trial, proclaiming that Satan was responsible for the OT (*Acta Arch.* 15:10 = CB 16:24), and that the doctrine of Christ was renewed from day to day, since the Paraclete was said to receive of Christ's and to show it to Christians (*cf.* Jn 16:14). That Mani himself claimed to be the Paraclete is said by Titus of Bostra (*Adv. Manich.* 3 pref. = PG 18, 1209), writing about 363 : ' The gospels and the rest of the NT, Mani says, were given as lesson from the good principle, and he asserts that not even these are quite free from the element that is contrary to God. Thus he takes upon himself the correction of the Scriptures, and on this account he dares to suppose that he is the Holy Ghost, excising much of the Scriptures and leaving only a little, *i.e.* what seems to look forward to a harmony with the products of his own native wit '. Alexander of Lycopolis, an early opponent of the Manichees, writing *c* 300 (*cf.* JTS 39 [1938] 347) says : ' They use their own old and new scriptures, setting them up as inspired, and produce their own opinions as conclusions from them ', *De Plac. Man.* 5 = PG 18,

g 417. This clear acceptance, by Manichee and Christian, of the idea that genuine Scripture is inspired by the Holy Ghost, needs little emphasis. The addition of the words ' Who spoke by the prophets ' to the creed of Nicaea which expressed belief in the Holy Ghost is an obvious reply to the spread of Manichaean views that the devil had inspired the OT. This addition is known to Cyril of Jerusalem (in his *Catecheses*, preached 348–50) and to Epiphanius (in the *Ancoratus*, of 374) in a period when the Manichees were growing in importance. Further evidence of Mani's view on this can be obtained from hymn 223 in the newly discovered Coptic papyri, as also from Augustine (*contr. Ep. Fund.* 5 and 8 = CSEL 25:200–201). The Montanists differed from the Manichees. They were content to restore Christianity, as they said, while the Manichees ventured to reconstruct it. Tertullian in his Montanist days gives an indication of their attitude to the Scriptures. He is arguing against marriage, using 1 Cor 7, and he says : ' Olim sanctitati huic destinabamur. Nihil novi paracletus inducit. Quod praemonuit, definit ', *De Monog.* 3 = PL 2, 983. The Spirit is quite clearly thought of as inspiring Paul no less than the prophetesses of Montanus.

h Irenaeus (*c* 120–202) is the father of Christian theology and in his writings the work of the Holy Spirit in producing the Scriptures is fully attested. In a passage dealing with parables (*Adv. Haer.* 2:41, 1, Harvey) he says : ' If we cannot find explanations of all things which require investigation in the Scriptures, let us

not seek for a second god beyond the One who is, for **35h** that would be the height of impiety. We ought to leave such things to God who is after all our maker, and most justly to bear in mind that the Scriptures are perfect, being spoken by the Word of God and by his Spirit, while we, as lesser beings, and indeed as the least of all, in comparison with the Word of God and with his Spirit, in that proportion fall short of the understanding of God's mysteries '. (On the idea of Irenaeus that Word and Spirit are the two hands of God in creation of the world and of the Scriptures, *cf.* Armitage Robinson's introduction to *Irenaeus, the Apostolic Preaching*, p 51.) This *Demonstration of the apostolic preaching* (*ibid.* ch 49) declares : ' It is not David who speaks nor anyone of the prophets in his own person ; for it is not a man who speaks the prophecies, but the Spirit of God, assimilating and likening himself to the persons represented, speaks in the prophets, and utters the words, sometimes from Christ and sometimes from the Father '. **Athenagoras** (177), in putting the **i** same doctrine before the emperors M. Aurelius and L. Commodus (*Legat.* 9 = TU 4, 2 [1891] p 10), adopts the comparison of the player and the musical instrument which occurs in Philo : ' The words of the prophets guarantee our reasoning . . . for they, while the reasoning power within them was at a stand, under the motion of the divine Spirit, spoke forth what was being wrought in them, the Spirit working with them, as it were a piper who breathed into his pipe '. (The prophets mentioned are ' Moses, Isaias, Jeremias, and the rest '.) Theophilus of Antioch, a contemporary of Athenagoras, and like him an apologist, writes to Autolycus (2:9 = PG 6, 1064) : ' The men of God were spirit-borne and became prophets ; being breathed upon by God himself and made wise, they were taught of God, holy and just. Thus they were deemed fit to receive the name of the instruments of God, and were enabled to hold the wisdom of God by means of which they spoke about the creation of the world and all else. . . . And there were not one or two of them but many, and all spoke in harmony and accord with each other of those things which happened before their time, or during their time, and also of what is now coming to pass in our days '. Later (3:12 = PG 6, 1137) Theophilus declares that the NT is on the same level as the OT for inspiration : ' The statements of the prophets about justice and those of the gospels are found to be in harmony because their authors were all spirit-borne and spoke by the Spirit of God '.

The Official Teaching of the Catholic Church—In **36a** early creeds and Councils the Church is more concerned with the equal status of OT and NT and with the divine authorship of both than with theories of inspiration as such. The further elaboration of the idea was left to the theologians. Thus the creed of Toledo (Dz 28) of A.D. 400 anathematizes those who say there is one god of the OT and another of the NT. In 1053 St Leo IX requires Peter of Antioch (Dz 348) to profess the same faith in one divine author of OT and NT. The Waldensians are summoned in the same terms (Dz 421, *cf.* 426 : Omne quod legitur . . .). Michael Palaeologus at the Council of Lyons in 1274 encounters the same article (Dz 464). Lest anyone think (with Abbot Ford in his articles in *The Tablet* for 1905) that this talk of OT and NT envisaged merely the dispensations and not the books, it is made clear by the letter of Clement VI in 1351 to the Catholicos of Armenia (Dz 570r) that the books are meant : ' We ask if you believed and now believe that the NT and OT in all the books which the authority of the Roman Church has handed down to us contain unquestionable truth throughout '. It should be apparent from what is said above about the Manichees that it was always a question of books, and sometimes of the dispensations as well, but never of the dispensations alone. The Council of Florence in its decree for the Jacobites, (Dz 706) does but emphasize this when it declares that there is one God of the OT and NT, gives a list of the canonical books and then proceeds to anathematize

36a the Manichean view of the different gods of OT and NT. Trent and the Vatican (Dz 783 and 1787) are in this matter the echo of Florence.

b **The Elaborations of the Theologians**—St Thomas Aquinas did not discuss inspiration as such at any length. He devoted some *quaestiones* of his *Summa* (2a–2ae, 171–74) to a short treatise on prophecy while discussing the *charismata*. He there distinguishes *inspiratio*, which is needed for the raising of the mind above the disturbance of the passions and the onset of external cares, from *revelatio*, which puts the prophet in possession of divine truths. He is willing to admit that a prophet is sometimes instructed in these truths not by express revelation but by ' some subtle instinct ' which he may not recognize as a divine prompting. Richard Fitzralph (Archbishop of Armagh *c* 1356) in his dialogue with John the Armenian shows true critical ability when he begins his work by a discussion of the truth of Scripture and lays it down that the Holy Spirit is the *auctor primarius* of Scripture, while the human writer is *auctor immediatus*. But in general the Middle Ages took their Scripture for granted. After the Council of Trent a theory of ' subsequent inspiration ' began to be advanced for controversial ends. By this it was maintained that the approval of the Holy Ghost or of the Church, given after the event to a book which a man had written without any divine assistance,

c was sufficient to make a book inspired. In 1566 Sixtus of Siena, while defending the canonicity of 2 Mac, argued that its subsequent inspiration would be enough to make him accept the book although he dared not say whether it was by a sacred or a profane author in the first instance. Lessius in 1585 at Louvain gave out the same view in his lectures, with one modification. His enemies, some of them disciples of Baius, produced this proposition, which Lessius owned to be his : ' A book such as 2 Mac, written by human industry without the aid of the Holy Spirit, may afterwards, if the Holy Spirit give testimony that it contains nothing false, be ranked as holy Scripture '. Great heat was generated by the discussion of this and of several other propositions at Louvain and at Douai. Bellarmine did not like it but thought it tolerable. Lessius in his defence withdrew the reference to 2 Mac, and put his view forward as an hypothetical case. What the Vatican Council later came to deny (Dz 1787) was that it was the Church's approval that could make a book inspired. Lessius's theory was expressly excluded from the scope of the decree by speeches of the *relatores*, Mgri. Simor and Gasser, Mansi 51:47 and 283. Moreover Leo XIII was later to set aside this view by his teaching in *Providentissimus Deus*. It can be seen that in controversy with a Protestant it was tempting for a Catholic to envisage the idea that the Church not merely guarded the canon of Scripture but actually gave the book its inspired character. This latter view, upheld by Jahn of Vienna and Abbot Haneberg of Munich in the 19th cent., was condemned by the Vatican Council, which added a positive statement that it was because they had God for their (principal) author and as such were given to the Church that the books of the Bible were to be regarded as inspired. This was enough to show the difference between the Church's doctrine and all subjective criteria of inspiration.

d Lessius also rejected verbal inspiration (in its naïve form, which amounts to a theory of divine ventriloquism) and Bellarmine supported him. Cartwright, the Anglican critic of the Rheims translators, held verbal inspiration even to the exclusion of all textual corruption : ' Seeing the Scripture wholly both for matter and words is inspired of God, it must follow that the same words wherein the OT and NT were written and indited by the hand of God do remaine '. The Swiss *formula consensus* (1675) held that all vowel-points and accents were due to inspiration and that no barbarisms of language could occur in biblical Greek or Hebrew. Bañez' (*in 1am.* q. *1*, art 8, conc 2a) held this view, and the Vatican Council, Mansi 51:47, refrained

from pronouncing on the dispute between him and **36d** Lessius.

Modern Deepening of the Concept of Inspiration— **e** Leo XIII in 1893, in this as in much else completing the work of the Vatican Council, taught that inspiration included the arousing of the human author to write by the action of the Holy Spirit, and the assistance given by the Spirit in the work of composition, so that those things only and solely which he wished should be written down. All this was seen to be involved in the concept of the divine authorship of the Scriptures, a concept which was familiar to the tradition of the Church (Dz 1952, repeated in Dz 2186). Certainly that tradition abounds in evidence that the human authors were regarded as (musical) instruments in the hands of God.

The modern Thomist theory of Inspiration is based **f** upon the idea of an instrumental cause (though the latest Thomist to expound it [Benoit, 303] says that this notion of instrument must be taken in a wide and not a strict sense) and was originally formulated by Lagrange and Billot. An instrument is said to have no action at all except as moved or applied by some higher agent. Thus the biblical authors must be set in motion by God to produce even that effect which is within their natural powers. An inspired writer can indeed convey a message by his own power, but he can only convey a divine message as God's instrument, transmitting that power, which is communicated to him as a light illuminating his mind, to judge what to say and how to say it, and moving his will to write. It is not that God and man contribute each his own share to the inspired book ; there is not in the effect produced anything that belongs to the one cause and not to the other : the whole is due to each, but in different senses. Billot's extreme tidiness of mind made him **g** insist that Inspiration was everywhere in Scripture the same. The knowledge of what was to be written about might come by revelation or by natural investigation (divinely assisted) of the human author, but neither of these belonged to Inspiration. This was essentially a divine motion of the intellect under whose stress the human mind judged with divine clarity and certitude of what God wanted written, along with the necessary verbal expression, and then set in motion the task of writing these down. Thus for the old naïve verbal Inspiration was now substituted a ' total ' Inspiration whereby God was the total author (and not merely principal) of the book while man was to be regarded as the total author in his degree. [Some contemporary Thomists, however, deny that this doctrine of a ' total inspiration ' is a novelty, and claim that it has always been part of Thomist teaching.—Ed.] God was thought (Billot, 56) to sway the man's will in exactly the same way as when, on the theory of physical premotion (or predetermination), he gave him an efficacious actual grace. To the present writer and to others (Dorsch, 115, Lusseau Bi 13 [1932] 48) this view seems an oversimplification of the mystery. St Thomas distinguishes (1a–2ae, 111, 4c and ad 4) *charismata*, which are for the benefit of others, from graces which are only for our personal sanctification, and he would not expect their mechanism to be the same. Then the view that a man is the total author (albeit subordinate) of all that is in Scripture seems to the present writer to have been modified by the teaching of *Divino afflante* (par 31) that the spiritual significance of Scripture is due to God alone. David said : ' Thou wilt not give thy holy one to see corruption ' (Ps 15:10, *cf.* Dz 2133, 2272) ; the words refer to Christ's resurrection, but David hardly can be regarded as the author of that spiritual sense, which is God's very own.

The idea of instrumental cause does apply to Inspira- **h** tion, but as Pope Pius XII explains (*Divino afflante*, par. 37) : ' Catholic theologians, following the teaching of the holy fathers and especially of the Angelic and Common Doctor [St Thomas] have investigated and explained the nature and effects of divine inspiration better and more fully than was the custom in past

36h centuries. *Starting from* the principle that the sacred writer is the *organon*, or instrument, of the Holy Spirit, and *a living and rational instrument*, they rightly observe that under the influence of the divine motion he uses his own faculties and powers in such a way that from the book which is the fruit of his labour all may easily learn the distinctive genius and individual characteristics and features of each author'. St Thomas adumbrates this idea (*Comm. in ep. Hebr* 1:1) where he asks himself why it is said that God spoke *in* the prophets and not *through* the prophets, seeing that after all they were his instruments. He answers finally that this was done to exclude the error of those who say that the prophets did not understand what they said, and he quotes Agg 1:3 and 1 Cor 14:32. A mere instrument would be unintelligent and passive in the hands of God, but in the co-authorship of the Scriptures God acts *in and through* the human author, not merely *through him*, as through an instrument.

i The Divine Condescension—This development of the doctrine of inspiration which has come in the present day has allowed place to the idea that in spite of the inspiration of the Holy Ghost, or rather because of it, when it is rightly understood, a Catholic can expect to find in the different books of the Bible a difference of style and of literary genre which some theologians in Modernist times strictly refused to allow. (Thus that Wis 7:5-10 ; 8:14-15 and 9:7-10 should imply that Solomon wrote the book does not mean that the Holy Ghost is partner in a lie, but that he is allowing the human author to use the device of pseudepigraphy, on which *cf.* § 92*b*.) This divine condescension or συγκατάβασις (the Greek Fathers had a word for it) is accepted by such a judgement as that of Jerome (on Jer 6:1 = CSEL 59:368) that Jeremias writes like a man of poor education though he is most profound in the majesty of his thoughts. It is also the idea implied by the Muratori fragment (DAC *s.v.*) which says that though the gospels have different starting-points, this makes no difference to the faith of Catholics, seeing that all things in all of them are declared by one and the same Spirit. Denis of Alexandria (Feltoe, *Dionysius of Alexandria* [Cambridge 1904] 234) also echoes this : ' What the Holy Spirit imparted severally to the evangelists puts together the complete character of our Saviour from the utterance of each '. The principle that, where an event is recorded twice, an indication is given us that more than one source is being used by a compiler, may be valid for western historical documents, but has no application in the East. ' To express what they had in their minds the ancients of the East did not always use the same forms and expressions as we use today. They used those which were current among the people of their own time and place, and what these were the exegete cannot determine *a priori*, but only from a careful study of oriental literature ' (Pius XII, *Divino afflante*, par. 39). See further §§ 41*a-h*, 46*h*.

j There is one great limitation to be set upon the operation of the divine condescension in its allowing the human author his head ; it must always be without formal error (see § 37*a* on Inerrancy). This limitation leads Pius XII to point a comparison (found in Rabanus Maurus, PL 108, 248) between the Incarnate Word and the written word of God. ' Just as the substantial Word of God became like to men in all things, sin excepted, Heb 4:15, so the words of God, expressed in human language, became in all things like to human speech, error excepted ' (*Divino afflante*, par 41). This is certainly a principle of liberation for speculative theology, which in Modernist times faced an *impasse*. Some then said that all was divine in the Scriptures (just as the Monophysites had said that all was divine in Christ), and would not admit any literary genres but the historical, nor any concession to the humanity of the writer, not a literary device, not a mixed metaphor, not an uncouth word. Others by a ' vivisection ' divided the Scriptures into divine ideas and human words, just as the Nestorians had divided

Christ into two persons. The first group, making no **36j** allowance for the human work of the evangelist, heightened the difficulties of the exegete, already serious in days when the new discoveries of the remote past seemed to be telling against the truth of the Scriptures. The second, or Nestorian, group assumed that God could convey to a human mind ideas without imagery, a supposition which psychologists have not yet fully justified. Today all are encouraged to use the analogy of faith and to find new light on the mystery of Inspiration—for it is a mystery—by comparing it with the Incarnation. The acts of Christ on earth were some of them wholly divine, some merely human, and others mixed. Now with the human and mixed acts, the Divinity shared in the operation, while in such purely divine acts of the Word as creation the humanity did not share. Similarly in the production of the Scriptures, the literal sense (that which is expressed by the words themselves) was intended by God and by the human author, but there is sometimes to be found (*cf.* § 39*k*) a spiritual significance whose presence the human author did not even suspect. ' God alone was able to know this spiritual significance, and he alone could reveal it to us ' (*Divino afflante*, par 31). Thus while it is true that all in the Scriptures is from God, it is not true that all is from the human author.

The Psychology of Inspiration—God works through **37a** the human writer in producing the Scriptures as through his instrument (just as John Damascene can speak of the humanity of Christ being the instrument of the Divinity), but as the instrument is human, God works *in* him too, in his mind and will (just as St Paul can say, 2 Cor 5:19 : God was in Christ). The union of God and the writer is not hypostatic, for that is the greatest of all unions and is reserved for Christ, but somewhere not far below this mystery of hypostatic union comes the mystery of God's dealing with his evangelist. Analogies with mystical experience might help more in explaining it than speculation whether God illuminates the *intellectus agens* or only the *intellectus possibilis*. Undoubtedly modern interest in the psychology of authorship sets questionings astir about the psychology of Inspiration ; but if Inspiration is one of those mysteries which cannot be fully understood even when revealed to us (and to the present writer it seems so), then progress in psychological reconstruction must be slow.

St Thomas in his treatment of the degrees of pro- **b** phecy (2*a*-2*ae* 173, 3*c*) and in his statement (2*a*-2*ae* 174, 2 ad 3) that writers of the Hagiographa had usually only that aid of divine illumination which enabled them to know things naturally knowable but at present out of their ken, considers Inspiration to be not always the same. Here again the analogy with mystical experience will hold, and clearly the psychological account of one writer (such as John in Apoc) who was aware that he was being inspired must be different from that of one (such as the writer of 2 Mac) who was not. Theologians agree that the aid given to an inspired writer is greater than that enjoyed by a General Council—which yet does publish infallible decrees—and that a Council again has aid superior in kind to that given to each of the Fathers of the Church, who yet were left not without aid seeing that their united witness gives the true sense of Scripture and of Tradition.

When it is admitted that an inspired writer may have **c** used a secretary (*cf.* §§ 52*c*, 48*b*) it seems more reasonable to confine inspiration to the author (Paul or Moses) and to regard the secretary as uninspired. (If the secretary is the instrument of the author and the author is the instrument of God, one is well on the way to an infinite regress.) Some theologians consider the secretary as inspired too (*cf.* Bea, 66), but the principle invoked, that all who are intelligently concerned in the production of the inspired book are themselves inspired, would seem to include, if not the slaves who prepared the papyrus, at least an intelligent copying-slave. The use of a secretary may have been wider than is often

37c recognized. Jerome (*Ep.* 120:11 = CSEL 55:508) asking why Paul was unhappy, 2 Cor 7:5–6, until Titus came to him, remarks that Titus was Paul's *interpres*, and that Paul was sad, because he lacked at the moment that pipe or instrument of his preaching by which he used to sing to the Lord. He adds that Peter used secretaries too, and that the difference between the style and phrasing of 1 Pet and 2 Pet was due thereto.

The language of 2 Mac 2:24–32 ; 15:38–40, which shows the human author reflecting on his labours of composition, their difficulty, purpose, and method, is not really incompatible with the doctrine of inspiration. While God often gave the prophets their theme by direct revelation, so that they were aware they dealt with God, this was not at all necessary. God could with equal reason move a man to make an epitome of Jason's history, could guide him to take only what was true in it and could by condescension allow him to give vent to the weariness of the compiler who was unaware that he walked with God.

d **The Extent of Inspiration**—A theory first put out by Dr H. Holden, an English priest, in 1658 (*The Analysis of Divine Faith*, 61), limited the scope of inspiration. Holden said : ' The special and divine assistance which is given to the author of every such book as the Church receives for the Word of God doth only extend itself to those things which are doctrinal, or at least have some near or necessary relation unto them. But in those things which are written by the bye, or have reference to something else not concerning religion, I conceive the author had only such a divine assistance as other holy and saintly authors have '. Manning (*Temporal Mission of the Holy Ghost* [1865] 147–50) defended Holden as orthodox but muddled. Newman revived the theory of *obiter dicta* being uninspired (*The Nineteenth Century*, Feb. 1884) : ' *Obiter dictum* means, as I understand it, a phrase or sentence which, whether a statement of literal fact or not, is not from the circumstances binding upon our faith. . . . There does not seem to be any serious difficulty in admitting that they are found in Scripture. The Church has taught us in two councils that the divine inspiration of Scripture is to be assigned especially *rebus fidei et morum* '. This seems to be a plain confusion between what Trent and the Vatican had said about Vg's safety in faith and morals with what was said about inspiration. Dr Healy of Maynooth (later Archbishop of Tuam) attacked this view and Newman defended himself. After this, and in part too because of this, Leo XIII in 1893 wrote (Dz 1950) : ' The plan of those is not to be tolerated who, to rid themselves of these difficulties [of apparent error in the Bible] make no scruple to allow that divine inspiration reaches to matters of faith and morals and no farther '.

Diverging opinions are held by theologians on the inspiration of versions. Some of the Fathers shared Philo's view that LXX was inspired. On individual books such as 1 Mac and Mt, where the Hebrew original is lost, views have been expressed which range from affirmation (Lagrange, *Introd. to Mt*, p xxxiv) through qualified caution (Tromp, 103, who says that it is a pious belief that the Greek of Mt is inspired) to denial (Bea, 67) that versions are inspired as such, though they may be so equivalently, by being faithful renderings of an inspired text. (For further details *cf.* 226*a*–*b*.)

e **Inerrancy**—Truth and error in the Bible belong to statements, assertions and insinuations, but not to commands, advice, wishes or regrets. The claims made in the Scriptures themselves to freedom from error have been noticed above. The direct proof from tradition that the Church has ever regarded the Scriptures as free from error is simple. It is the application of the principle to individual texts which has provoked so much debate. The Fathers are quite overwhelming in their declarations of the principle. Routh (*Rel. Sac.* 1848², vol. 5, pp 335–53) collected a great list of passages, most of which can still be used. An attitude

of awe and reverence before the Scriptures is already **37e** present in Polycarp who writes (*Ad Phil.* 3) : ' It is not possible for anyone like myself to company with the wisdom of the blessed and renowned Paul . . . who wrote to you '. The care that the Spirit showed to keep corrupters of doctrine from the Scriptures is marked by Irenaeus (*Adv. Haer* 3:17, 1 H) : ' The Holy Spirit, foreseeing that there would be corrupters, guarded against their deceits and declared in Matthew " Now the manner of Christ's birth was thus " '. Theophilus of Antioch is sure that Law, prophets and gospels will all be found to agree, because all are spoken by the one Spirit (*Ad Autol.* 3:12 = PG 6, 1137), while Origen (*In Jn* 6:34 = CB 10:143) declares the principle formally : ' The evangelists neither lied nor made any mistake '. (That Origen should elsewhere (*In Mt* 27:9 = CB 38:249) ascribe the naming of Jeremias for Zachary to an *error scripturae* probably means that he saw in it a mistake of the copyist of the MS. The Greek of Origen is here lacking.) How completely the idea **f** of inerrancy held sway may be seen from the *Computus de Pascha* (CSEL 3, iii, p 258) which dates from A.D. 243 : ' From Josue to Samuel, according to the speech of St Paul, Ac 13:20, who was taught by the Spirit of God, there were completed 450 years '. Bishops such as Crescens of Cirta and Leucius of Theveste declare the Scriptures to be *deificae* and call those heretics blasphemers who dismember the holy and adorable Scriptures with deceitful words (*Sent. Episc.* ap. Cyprian, CSEL 3, 1:441 and 448), while Novatian (*De Trin.* 30 = PL 3, 948) says that it can never be by fault of the heavenly Scriptures (which never deceive us) that we should seem to give scandal, but only by the proud errors of men who are bent on being heretics. St Augustine's principle, which has guided western exegetes for many centuries, was thus expressed : ' If I come upon anything in the Scripture which seems contrary to the truth, I shall not hesitate to consider that it is no more than a faulty reading of the manuscript, or a failure of the translator to hit off what his text declared, or that I have not succeeded in understanding the passage ' (*Ep.* 82:1 = CSEL 34, 2:354). This principle is quoted with approval by Leo XIII (Dz 1952), for the Church has ever upheld the patristic tradition of biblical inerrancy. Benedict XV in 1920 summed up the tradition thus : ' The teaching of St Jerome is strikingly confirmed by what our predecessor Leo XIII declared to be the unbroken and ancient faith of the Church about the absolute immunity of the Scriptures from error of every kind '. Having cited the decrees of Florence and Trent which were confirmed at the Vatican, he adds : ' It makes no difference at all that the Holy Ghost should have taken men to be as it were his tools in writing, as if forsooth the men who were inspired, but not the divine author, might let fall some error. Not so, for he himself so stirred and roused them by his supernatural power to write, and was so present to them in their writing that they conceived correctly, and were minded to write faithfully, and expressed fittingly with unfailing truth, all those things and those only which he bade them write '.

Difficulties from Science and History—Leo XIII dealt **g** with the commonest 19th cent. objection to inerrancy, that it set the truth of the Bible in opposition to the truth of physical science. ' No error whatever exists in those cases in which the sacred writer, when treating of physical matters, followed sensible appearances (St Thomas, 1*a* q 70, art 1 ad 3), expressing himself either metaphorically or in the common manner of speaking current at the time, and current now also in many matters of daily experience, even amongst the most learned men. The sacred writers—or more properly the Holy Ghost who spoke through them—did not intend to teach men these matters (namely, the inner constitution of visible things) which are in no way profitable to salvation ' (Dz 1947 quoted *Divino afflante*, par 5). An instance might be the passage in 3 Kg 7:23 and the value of π which is there implied.

37g For the application of this principle to Galileo's case, see § 232i.

Pope Leo went on to indicate that this principle might well be used to deal with difficulties from cognate sciences, and especially from history. His words were the subject of many misunderstandings, and it is only now that these have been finally cleared up by the teaching of *Divino afflante* (*cf.* § 38a) on the importance of ascertaining the purpose of the scriptural writer (especially as shown in his choice of literary genre) before accusing him of errors. More recently the letter of the Biblical Commission of Jan 16, 1948, to Cardinal Suhard (*cf.* § 53k–m) applies this principle vigorously to the first eleven chapters of Gen. By reaction against the inconsistencies of documentary hypotheses—the Commission notes—some scholars are now, on critical and historical grounds alone, moved to see in the ill-fitting nature of the parts of the Pentateuch not so much a difference of documentary sources as an effect of the peculiarities of literary procedure, thought and expression in the ancient East. Catholic writers are invited to study these problems with patience, with charity to others and with an open mind.

Origen listed certain historical facts (*In Philem.*, PG 14, 1306) in Gen which must be believed ; Jerome copied his list (*In Philem.*, PL 26, 609), and it passed into tradition. The Biblical Commission used it in a decree of 1909 (Dz 2123), which is still in force, but the spirit of which has been changed by the new emphasis on wider research, an emphasis which could not have been contemplated in Modernist times. Now that the flight from the sources is ending in other departments of ancient history, and there is a return to a sane Herodotus and a real Homer, the danger of excesses in biblical criticism on the part of Catholic scholars is obviously lessened. (On the accuracy of OT dates and numbers *cf.* § 226c.)

h **The Use of Sources by Inspired Writers**—Another attempt to meet charges of error in Scripture was the theory of implicit citations, advanced by P. Prat and others in 1902–1907 (*cf.* § 225e). All ancient authors quoted freely and plagiarism was no offence ; might it not then be that the sacred writers when they seemed to be in error were really quoting from some profane author for whom they did not vouch, but whose words they did not display as a quotation. The scope of such a theory might be judged by a glance at 2 Mac 2:14, 24. If the author of Mac synopsized five books of Jason, might not the errors be put down to Jason ? The Biblical Commission did not condemn the theory, but urged restraint in its use (*cf.* § 52i). Benedict XV renewed this verdict (Dz 2188). The principle has been used by Catholics to account for some apparent discrepancies between texts (as 2 Kg 24:9 and 1 Par 21:5 ; also 2 Mac 1:11–17 and 2 Mac 9:1–29 ; 1 Mac 6:1–16). If Clement of Alexandria meant that the genealogies of Christ were written before the gospels of Mt and Lk, then discrepancies in the genealogies could be explained **i** on this principle too (CB 17, 197). A somewhat larger question of applying this principle is raised by the letter of the Biblical Commission to Cardinal Suhard (*cf.* § 53k–m). Recalling an earlier decision on the Pentateuch (Dz 1999), it states that no one can now call in question the use by Moses of earlier written documents and oral traditions—though these are not acknowledged by him in the text. What was Moses inspired to do in his selection or rejection of passages from earlier sources ? If he is thought to have made them his own and gone surety for their accuracy, then he must be held to have put them forward as true. If however he reports them as what was told to him, and does not vouch for them, then no question of the freedom from error of such citations could arise. The answer to this question depends on the view taken of the literary genre of the first eleven chapters of Gen, where most difficulties occur. Of these the Commission remarks that one can neither simply affirm nor deny that they are history without applying to them the standards of a literary genre which does not fit them.

They are not history in a classical or a modern sense, **37l** but the peoples of the Orient do seem to have had a special way of their own of recounting salient historical events which should be the subject of much patient and erudite investigation (*cf.* § 225c). It is open to no one, then, to say roundly that there is error in these chapters, but what the human author there seeks to affirm is not always clear, owing to our ignorance of his conventions.

Literary Genres and Inerrancy—Benedict XV (Dz **38a** 2188) spoke somewhat severely of scholars who too readily had recourse to literary genres incompatible with the full truth of the word of God. With due regard to this necessary warning, Pius XII (*Divino afflante*, par 39), no longer needing to check the vagaries of Catholic scholars, encourages the study of literary forms : ' It is absolutely necessary for the interpreter to go back in spirit to those remote centuries of the East, making proper use of the help afforded by history, archaeology, ethnology and other sciences, in order to discover what literary forms the writers of that early age intended to use and did in fact employ '. The coming of the Ras Shamra documents, the Lachish letters, the love-songs of Chester Beatty papyrus 1 (Bi 13 [1932] 209–27) and others, makes such research worth while. In the time of Benedict XV it would have been very much less possible to conduct such investigations and yet to avoid arbitrary conclusions. Pius XII notes that historians of the East (such as Eduard Meyer, *Ges. des Alter.* [1910] 1:227) allow that the people of Israel enjoyed a unique pre-eminence in historical writing among the ancient nations of the East. He urges (*ibid.* par 42) that use be made of this aid not only in exegesis but also in vindicating the immunity of the Scriptures from error. (Certain Catholics had allowed its first usefulness but condemned its use in the problem of inerrancy.) The Pope continues : The Catholic exegete must ask himself how far the form of expression or literary idiom employed by the sacred writer may contribute to the true and genuine interpretation ; and he may be sure that this part of his task cannot be neglected without great detriment to Catholic exegesis. For . . . in many cases in which the sacred authors are accused of some historical inaccuracy or of the inexact recording of some events, it is found to be a question of nothing more than those customary and characteristic forms of expression or styles of narrative which were current in human intercourse among the ancients, and which were in fact quite legitimately and commonly employed. A just impartiality therefore demands that when these are found in the word of God, which is expressed in human language for men's sake, they should be no more stigmatized as error than when similar expressions are employed in daily usage. Thus a knowledge and careful appreciation of ancient modes of expression and literary forms and styles will provide a solution to many of the objections made against the truth and historical accuracy of Holy Writ. (For examples of the application of this principle, *cf.* §§ 226i, 961b–c.) The **b** various genres which are to be found in Scripture are listed in the article on Literary Characteristics of the Bible, §§ 32–3. Here it may suffice to ask if the principle of inerrancy rules out any genre as incompatible with truth. It may be said at once that aetiological writing, such as the *Fasti* of Ovid, where the poet undertakes to give the reason (αἰτία) of some ritual practice by telling a legend of its origin, would be repugnant to the idea of inerrancy. Among the Jewish Midrashim, some were so far fictional as to use the names and known acts of scriptural characters to form the basis of imaginary narratives. The so-called *Biblical Antiquities* of Philo and the *Pirke* of R. Eliezer present enlargements upon the well-known themes of Scripture, some of them aetiological in style. Now it would certainly seem contrary to the idea of inspiration that the word of God should admit two contradictory versions of the same event, as may be found in these *apocrypha*. On the other hand the Jewish fondness for

38b telling a story by degrees in the course of two or more rehearsals must not be considered to be annihilated by the fact of inspiration. An obvious example is the treatment of Paul's conversion in Ac, while in the OT many parallel narratives in Kgs or 1 and 2 Par can be similarly explained (*e.g.* 1 Kg 21:8-9 with 1 Kg 22:9-14 and 2 Kg 3:9). For fiction in the OT see §§ 301*a-f*, 310*k-l*.

c **The Truth of Implications in Scripture**—Not only what the human writer states but also what he implies must be taken as true (*cf.* § 52*e*). This conclusion was not drawn by those who thought that Paul might have erred where he speaks in such a way as to imply (apparently) the nearness of Christ's second coming (*cf.* §§ 670-1, 914-5). They made a distinction, too fine to last, between the *veritas hominis* (which was not guaranteed) and the *veritas scriptoris*, which was. This theory was applied to such texts as 1 Thess 4:15. P. Prat had another way of dealing with the matter, a way which is set forth in his *Life* (Appendix II, pp 162-9, published from his papers by P. Calès). Prat notes how in some five epistles Paul has two passages, the one expressing expectancy of the second coming, the other envisaging the possibility of his death before it happens. (The list is : 1 Thess 4:15 and 5:10 ; 1 Cor 15:52 and 6:14 ; 2 Cor 5:3-4 and 5:1 ; Rom 13:11-12 and 14:7-8 ; Phil 3:21 and 1:20.) That Paul should thus express his ignorance of the date of the second coming by apparently opposed but in reality complementary texts is natural in a Jew. Semites had no half-tones in their register of vision, as Lawrence noted. They saw things as black and white where we see them as grey. Their thoughts were at ease only in extremes. To such minds approximation to a statement by opposed implications was not unnatural.

d **Moral Errors**—Inerrancy implies in Scripture an absence of immoral teaching, and it is therefore necessary to give some lines of explanation by which difficulties against the moral teaching of the Bible (the OT mainly) can be met. Stories of sin and crime can be related in the Bible, as in any book, without making it for that to be esteemed a bad book. The adultery of David is as relevant to history as that of Henry VIII. That the idolatry of Israel, the bride of Yahweh, should be described in terms of harlotry is not surprising, especially when it is remembered how often idolatry involved sacred prostitution at pagan temples. Sometimes commands may be given, such as the command to despoil the Egyptians (Ex 3:22 ; **38d** 11:2 ; 12:35-36), which at first sight seem to be immoral, but (as here) can be explained on moral grounds. The Israelites were entitled to some compensation for their labours in Egypt and God, as lord of all creation, could certainly tell them to take it where he willed. For the command to Osee to marry a wife of fornications, see § 514*c-f*.

Another common source of difficulty is caused by **e** the presence of glosses by later (uninspired) hands at certain points of the text. These are betrayed by their absence from some of the MSS or versions of the text, or from early patristic quotations of the passage. When Judith goes on her mission to the camp of Holofernes, the DV (at Jdt 10:4) makes God increase her beauty, but LXX merely says that she was exceedingly beautiful. Jerome remarks on the *varietas vitiosissima* of the *MSS* he had before him, and it is safe to say that God's action is inserted as a defence of Judith's conduct by some partisan.

Sometimes the faulty translation of a word will give rise to a doubt on the morality of an act. Thus in 1 Kg 15:33 Agag is said (DV) to have been hewed in pieces which looks like sadism. But the Hebrew word so rendered is never used elsewhere at all. LXX might be translated ' put to the sword ', and it is only with the Targum that the idea of intensive action comes in.

That God should have inspired even the writing down of the Jewish code of law may seem strange, but it is to be remembered that some of the laws are conditional, not absolute. If they have slaves, thus must they deal with them. If they are bent on putting away their wives, let it be overtly and for good (*cf.* Deut 24:1-4 and commentary). This is not perfect law but at least a deterrent to hasty action. A comparison of the Mosaic law with that of Hammurabi or with the Assyrian laws (*cf.* Condamin in DAFC 1, 360-7, and Driver and Miles, *The Assyrian Laws*, 1935) shows much advantage on the side of Moses for mildness and religious sanction. M. Cuq has tried to make out a case for Babylonian superiority (*Etudes sur le droit bab.*, 1929, p 35) but he is driven to using such texts as Ex 20:5 ; 34:7 as if they were Hebrew laws, when such blood feud is expressly forbidden by Deut 24:16. The Jews were still in a state of minority. That God should choose to leave them so, while providing the means of escape to higher ideals, is really his business and not ours.

THE INTERPRETATION OF
HOLY SCRIPTURE

By R. C. FULLER

39a Bibliography—Encyclical Letters : Leo XIII, *Prov. Deus* (1893) EB 66–119, Eng. tr. in Douay Bible (London 1914) ; Benedict XV, *Spiritus Paraclitus*, AAS 12 (1920) 385–422, EB 457–509 ; Pius XII, *Divino afflante Spiritu*, AAS 35 (1943) 297–325, Eng. tr. C. T. S. London (quoted here).
Dictionary Articles : P. Cruveilhier, *Herméneutique sacrée*, DBVS 3, 1482–1524 ; Vaganay, *Histoire de l'Interprétation*, DBVS 4, 561–646 ; H. Höpfl, *Critique Biblique*, DBVS 175–240 ; A. Durand, *Critique Biblique*, DAFC 1, 760–819 ; *Exégèse, ibid* 1811–41 ; Mangenot & Rivière, *Interprétation de l'Ecriture*, DTC 7, 2290–2343.
Manuals : *Traité d'Herméneutique Sacrée*, in H Lusseau-M. Collomb, *Manuel d'Etudes Bibliques*, 1, 485–573, Paris 1936 ; A. Vaccari, *De Interpretatione*, in *Institutiones Biblicae*, 1, 317–69 ; A. Fernandez, *Hermeneutica*, *ibid* 1, 371–509, Rome 1937 ; J. Renié, *Herméneutique*, in *Manuel d'Ecriture Sainte*, 1, 204–94 ; Cornely-Merk, *Compendium Introductionis in SS Libros, De Interpretatione SS* 233–300, Paris 1927 ; *L'Interprétation*, in Robert-Tricot, *Initiation Biblique*, 399–475, Paris 1948².
Monographs and Articles : F. Patrizi, *Institutio de interpretatione Bibliorum*, Rome 1876³ ; J. Corluy, *L'Interprétation de la Sainte Ecriture*, 1885 ; H. Höpfl, *Tractatus de inspiratione SS et compendium hermeneuticae Biblicae catholicae*, Rome 1923 ; *L'Œuvre exégétique et historique du R. P. Lagrange* O.P., Paris 1935 ; L. Bouyer, *Liturgie et exégèse spirituelle* in *La Maison Dieu* 7 (1946) 27 ; R. Bierberg, *Does Sacred Scripture have a Sensus Plenior ?* CBQ 10 (1948) 182–95 ; J. Coppens, *Les Harmonies des Deux Testaments*, Tournai 1949 ; J. Daniélou, *Sacramentum Futuri*, Etudes sur les origines de la typologie biblique, Paris 1950 ; *La Typologie d'Isaac dans le christianisme primitif*, Bi (1947) 363–406 ; *Les divers sens de l'Ecriture dans la tradition chrétienne primitive*, ETL 24 (1948) 119 ; *Déluge, Baptême, Jugement*, in *Dieu Vivant*, 8 (1947) 97–112 ; H. de Lubac, Introd. to *Origène, Homélies sur la Genèse* (Sources Chrétiennes, 7) Paris 1943 ; Introd. to *Origène, Hom. sur l'Exode* (Sources Chr. 16) Paris 1947 ; J. Gribomont, *Le lien des deux Testaments selon la théologie de St Thomas*, Notes sur le sens spirituel et implicite des Saintes Ecritures, ETL 22 (1946) 70–89 ; *A. G. Hebert, The Throne of David*, 1941 ; *The Authority of the Old Testament*, 1947 (*cf.* review of this book by Daniélou in *Dieu Vivant*, No. 11, 109 f.) ; De Vine, *The Consequent Sense*, CBQ 2 (1940) 145–55 ; R. Kehoe, *The Scriptures as Word of God*, Eastern Churches Quarterly, Suppl. no. 1947 Tradition and Scripture, 71–8 ; A. Vaccari, *La θεωρία nella scuola esegetica di Antiochia*, Bi 1 (1920) 3–36. M.-J. Lagrange, *L'Inspiration et les exigences de la critique*, RB 5 (1896) 498–578 ; *L'Interprétation de la sainte Ecriture*, RB 9 (1900) 135–42 ; I. Guidi, *L'Historiographie chez les Sémites*, RB 3 (1906), New Series, 509–19 ; *H. H. Rowley, The Authority of the Bible*, Birmingham 1950 ; A. Dubarle, *Le sens spirituel de l'Ecriture*, Revue Sc. Phil. Theol. 31 (1947) 41–72 ; St Thomas d'Aquin, *Somme Théologique, La Prophétie*, Fr. tr. by P. Synave and P. Benoît, Paris 1947 ; L. Cerfaux, J. Coppens, J. Gribomont, *Problèmes et Méthode d'Exégèse Théologique*, Louvain 1950 ; J. Bonsirven, *Exégèse rabbinique et exégèse paulinienne*, Paris 1939.
For the teaching of St Thomas, the reader may consult the various references given in the course of the article.

39b Introduction—'How can I understand (the Scriptures) ', said the eunuch of Queen Candace, ' unless some man show me ? ', Ac 8:31. The Bible consists of a collection of books, written over a long period of years by authors of widely different characters. All lived many centuries ago and in countries remote from us. We cannot therefore expect to understand their writings without preliminary study. No one would claim to understand, say, Virgil without a knowledge of his times ; but the books of the OT are all older than Virgil and those of the NT are almost contemporary. Far more important, however, than their human origin is the fact that these books have God for their Author and form a source of divine revelation. The interpreter will naturally look to the Church, guardian of that revelation, for guidance in discerning the various meanings in Scripture and drawing God's teaching therefrom. This does not imply, of course, that the Church is always ready with a definite interpretation of every text. Far from it. As will be seen later, § 42*b*, the Church pronounces on the meaning of a text only when it concerns matters of faith and morals, and even here she frequently gives no more than negative guidance, namely by warning against erroneous views, or by enabling us to ensure that the interpretation is in harmony with the general truths of faith. Where such negative guidance alone is given Catholics have often held, and hold, divergent views, just as there are also different schools of thought in theology. In other matters which do not concern faith or morals the Catholic is free to choose any interpretation which does not conflict with the inerrancy of Scripture (*cf.* §§ 37*e*–38*e*). The view chosen will naturally depend on the state of knowledge at the time. Until fairly recently, for example, it was commonly supposed that Gen 1 taught that the work of creation took place in six days (in the strict sense). Modern science has shown that this view is not tenable and many alternative views have been put forward. Any one of these might be the true one, but the Church has no direct authority to decide the matter, ' In those things which do not come under the obligation of faith the saints were at liberty to hold divergent opinions just as we ourselves are ', *Prov. Deus.* EB 107.

THE SENSES OF SCRIPTURE c

1. Literal Sense :

    (*a*) Nature
    (*b*) Kinds of Literal Sense
    (*c*) Every Part of Scripture has a literal sense
    (*d*) The Literal Sense is One
    (*e*) The Plenary Sense

2. Spiritual Sense :

    (*a*) Existence and Nature
    (*b*) Kinds of Spiritual Sense
    (*c*) Extent
    (*d*) Is the spiritual sense always Christological ?
    (*e*) Probative force

3. Accommodation of Scripture

39c PRINCIPLES OF INTERPRETATION

THE SENSES OF SCRIPTURE

In the composition of the books of Scripture God used men as his instruments (*cf.* § 36). These writers went through exactly the same process as would any other writer and they convey their meaning in the same way. But there is a difference. Since they were God's instruments, their meaning was also God's meaning. They could not write down anything not intended by him. ' The things which he ordered, and those only, they . . . expressed in apt words and with infallible truth ', EB 110. When we speak of the *sense* of Scripture we mean what God intended to convey by or through his written word. This may indeed involve more than the human author was conscious of. The Scriptures may have more than one meaning. The *literal sense* of Scripture is that which arises directly from the text and is intended by the inspired writer. There is also frequently in Scripture another sense which we call the *spiritual sense* (*cf.* § 40). This is a meaning authoritatively revealed by God to man. It is not however, strictly speaking, the meaning of the words. As St Thomas Aquinas says ' the *things* signified by the words (literal sense) may also signify other things (spiritual

d sense) '. This brings us at once to the central fact of the connection between the two Testaments, Old and New. The Old is a preparation for and foreshadows the New (*cf.* § 40*g*). It is a preparation not only in the theological but also in the historical order. Both must be kept in view. There is no sure road to the elucidation of the spiritual sense of Scripture save through the literal sense. There exists a tendency today to interpret the OT more from the standpoint of the Gospel than has hitherto been the case. It is a reaction to the somewhat exclusive preoccupation with the historical method which has been a feature of biblical exegesis during the past century, a preoccupation which can easily make one lose sight of the religious teaching of the Bible. There are of course dangers in the other direction (*cf.* § 39*i*). Sound exegesis will on the one hand take full account of the spiritual teaching of the Bible and yet at the same time require a solid foundation on the literal sense of Scripture for any spiritual meanings brought out. An investigation of the literal sense, keeping in view the unity of the Testaments and their common Divine Authorship, gives rise to the further question as to the existence of what is known as the *Plenary Sense* or *Sensus Plenior*. This is in effect an extension of the literal sense, for its existence is held by those who maintain that God may imply more in the words of Scripture than the human author is conscious of—a hidden meaning in fact which is revealed only later, whether by more explicit prophecy or by the fulfilment of it in events. This sense is also spiritual—but it differs from the spiritual sense referred to above in that it inheres in the words themselves and not in what is signified by those words, see § 40*a*.

e The Literal Sense :

(*a*) **Nature**—What we are seeking is the meaning which the writer intended to convey by the words he set down. A word taken by itself can evidently have many meanings, but in a given context it can have only one if the writer is keeping to the rules of

language—otherwise there would be ambiguity. **39e** ' The Word was made Flesh ' (Jn 1:14), describes the mystery of the Incarnation. ' Word ' and ' flesh ' can by themselves mean many things, but in this text ' word ' means the Son of God and ' flesh ' means the human nature assumed by him, as we may gather from the passage and indeed the Gospel as a whole.

(*b*) **Kinds of Literal Sense**—In the phrase already **f** quoted, ' the Word was made Flesh ' we have seen that the sense is : ' the Son of God became man '. This is the **explicit** sense. The phrase necessarily implies that Christ had a human soul, for without a soul a nature is not human. Other implications of this kind may be discerned. These **implicit** meanings are not different senses of Scripture for they are contained within the meaning of the terms used and do not go beyond the limits of the literal sense. For the same reason they are not to be regarded as separate literal senses.

A large number of truths may be described as deductions from the text rather than implications of it. Thus in Rom 1:21 St Paul rebukes the Gentiles because though they knew God they did not glorify him. But unless they were capable of morally good acts St Paul's rebuke would be unjust. We may therefore conclude that not all acts of unbelievers are necessarily sinful. This conclusion is certain but it cannot be said to be the inspired meaning of Scripture. It depends for its weight on the validity of the reasoning and is thus a **theological conclusion.** Such a conclusion is sometimes called the Consequent Sense—but it seems better not to use this term as it is not an inspired sense of Scripture. From the example given it is easy to see that there is an important difference between an implicit sense and a theological conclusion : the former is the inspired sense of Scripture, but the latter is not. The actual identification of each in practice however is often difficult and opinions will differ in many cases.

The sacred writer, like any other writer, used words, **g** sometimes in their ordinary sense, sometimes in their metaphorical sense. We usually call the former the literal sense, when dealing with writings other than Sacred Scripture. The sentence ' He sat at his host's right hand ' is to be taken literally, but ' Christ sits at the right hand of God the Father Almighty ' should be understood in a metaphorical sense. Thus we normally take ' literal ' and ' metaphorical ' as mutually exclusive. Indeed the definition of ' metaphor ' is : ' Application of name or descriptive term to an object to which it is not literally applicable '. But in interpreting Scripture we use these terms in a somewhat different way. We apply the term ' literal ' to the sense of Scripture intended by the sacred writer, whether the words are to be taken in the proper or ordinary sense (without metaphor) or metaphorically. Thus ' literal ' and ' metaphorical ' of common parlance are both included under the literal sense of Scripture. This difference of usage is made necessary by the fact that Scripture *is* different from other writings. Scripture differs because it is written by God and has a variety of meanings. Since there are often spiritual meanings besides the meaning which inheres directly in the words, it is necessary to distinguish one from another. Naturally the name ' literal ' is given to the meaning of the text as such. In the case of merely human writing this is, with certain rare exceptions, the only meaning. Hence there is no need to give it a special name, and the adjective ' literal ' may thus be reserved to describe words in their original, as distinct from their derived or metaphorical sense. In any given context the word will have one or the other, but not both simultaneously. In Scriptural terminology, however, the former is called the **literal proper** and the latter the **literal improper** sense.

In the historical parts of the Bible the narrative is **h** written largely without metaphor (literal proper sense). In the poetical books, on the other hand, imagery of all kinds abounds. The Psalms which contain some of the finest Hebrew poetry are full of words used in the metaphorical sense (literal improper), *e.g.* ' Thou art my

39h hiding-place and my shield ', Ps 119:114 (RV). But the authors of the historical books too used metaphor, in a way that would not be adopted by modern western historians, for example, certain features of the Garden of Eden ; though opinions may differ as to which are metaphorical. (For the ' plenary sense ', see § 39*k* below.)

i (*c*) **Every Part of Scripture has a Literal Sense**—Since the sacred writers composed their books in the same way as any other author there appears to be no reason to except any part of the text from the law that every passage has its own literal sense. In the early ages of Christianity some writers of the school of Alexandria, *e.g.* Origen, endeavouring to draw the fullest spiritual doctrine from the OT tended to do this in independence of the literal sense of the text and appeared at times even to deny the existence of the latter altogether. In modern times there has been a similar tendency. Such views have never been in accord with the tradition of the Church. Indeed in 1943 there appeared an able defence of Origen's exegetical views by H. de Lubac in which he attempts to show that the great Alexandrian has been misunderstood (*hom. sur la Genèse*). Origen's intense devotion to Christ, argues de Lubac, made him seek a spiritual and evangelical meaning in all Scripture. But he always admitted its historical character. If he said there were some purely spiritual episodes from which one cannot derive any literal sense, he probably meant only that one should take the passage as figurative or metaphorical. He confused the spiritual with the figurative. Or again, when Origen said that certain Bible episodes were not histories, what he meant was—they really happened, but if they had *only* their literal historical meaning there would be no sufficient reason for their happening at all, and we should be obliged to say that they never happened. In other words many events of the OT took place chiefly because they were intended by God to prefigure some mystery of the NT, *op. cit.* 51. Such are in brief the general lines of de Lubac's vindication.

j (*d*) **The Literal Sense is one**—A passage of Scripture (apart from the few which have been authoritatively interpreted by the Church) may be understood by different readers in different ways. Thus a text may have several possible meanings. ' The mighty ' spoken of in Is 49:24 are variously understood to be either the Babylonians or evil spirits. Again, many theological conclusions may be drawn from one text of Scripture, but they are not the inspired sense of the divine Author, though they may, of course, be truths revealed by God through Sacred Tradition, (*cf.* § 39*f*). But what we are here considering is whether one text of Scripture may have more than one inspired and certain literal meaning. Though the Fathers and Church writers are divided on the point it would seem to follow necessarily from the nature of inspiration that the literal sense can be only one. The sacred writer expresses himself in human fashion. To use words which in their context are capable of more than one literal meaning is to be ambiguous—and this, so far from conveying God's teaching, would only serve to obscure it. It is true that there are texts in the OT which are given different senses when quoted in the NT. Thus, according to many exegetes, Ps 2:7 is interpreted of the Resurrection in Ac 13:33 and of Our Lord's Divinity in Heb 1:5. But there is no need to assume that it is the literal sense which is being given in each case. Sometimes it is the spiritual sense which is being expounded, sometimes it is no more than an accommodation of the text, (*cf.* § 40*j*). Some writers, while admitting the unity of the literal sense, have nevertheless suggested that, at least in the poetical parts of the Bible, there may be varying shades of meaning according to the richness of content of the words and their associative background.

It might seem at first sight that to suppose the existence of the plenary sense (*cf.* § 39*k*) is to imply the multiplicity of the literal sense. This is not so however, for, as will be seen, the plenary sense is not a new and separate sense but rather an extension of the literal

sense. What we are excluding are separate and **39j** independent senses which imply equivocation ; but it is freely recognized that the Holy Spirit may go beyond the explicit thought of the human writer and, so far from obscuring it, add new depths and clarifications, Coppens, 54.

(*e*) **The Plenary Sense or Sensus Plenior**—Does God **k** at times intend a deeper or more abundant sense than that derivable from the text alone ? Many passages in the Bible suggest that this sense does exist. The prophets foretold one or other aspect of the Messias and his kingdom. No single prophet had before his eyes the whole picture. The view of the whole was possible only to later generations who had both prophecies and fulfilment before them. The literal sense of Gen 3:15 is of a struggle between mankind and Satan. The development of prophecy led men to see that it was in fact the Messias who would be victorious and this view was of course confirmed by the coming of Christ. It is the same God who both causes prophecy and effects its fulfilment. This would seem to be an example of the plenary sense—a sense of which the writer was not conscious. Let it be said at once that the concept of the plenary sense is still in process of elucidation and is far from being universally accepted. Yet the idea is surely very reasonable. We must remember that the OT with its very imperfect modes of expression is describing for us the sublime mysteries of the New ; that in fact the prophet had to use contemporary ways of thought and expression for he was, after all, speaking primarily for his contemporaries rather than for those later generations who saw his words fulfilled. Why should it surprise us if God put into his words a meaning which only later revelations would bring out ? The words of Leo XIII have their relevance here : ' In addition to the usual reasons which make ancient writings difficult to understand there are some which are peculiar to the Bible. For the language of the Sacred Books is employed to express, under the inspiration of the Holy Ghost, many things which are beyond the power and scope of the reason of man—that is to say, divine mysteries and many other things contained in them. There is sometimes in such passages a wealth of meaning more abundant and more profound than the letter of the text or the laws of interpretation seem to indicate ', *Prov. Deus* EB 93.

Some have thought of the OT as a collection of **l** separate pieces which, when finally fitted together, give us a picture of the New. Others, with a greater sense of historical development, realize that the OT is a record of a living and growing revelation. At each stage of the evolution we see the same features, the same religious themes, becoming steadily clearer until the Saviour comes. This means that at no stage of the process may we expect perfection until the NT is reached ; and we should accordingly be on our guard against the tendency to extract from the OT as clear, vivid and detailed a picture of Christ and his kingdom as we can obtain from the pages of the NT (*cf.* Cullmann, *Christ et le Temps*, Neuchâtel 1947).

There are those who say that the ' eyes of faith ' are needed to see this plenary sense : that only the believer has the vision to grasp the unity and collective significance of the two Testaments on which the plenary sense depends. But this needs qualification. It cannot be too often stressed that this sense is not something distinct from and independent of the literal sense. It is rather a deepening of that same literal sense. Thus one who applies the ordinary rules and principles of interpretation is on the right path to the elucidation of the plenary sense, though the interpreter who is also a believer has an advantage and is in a better condition to grasp the full connection between Old and New Testaments.

But if the sacred writer is ignorant of such a sense **m** or at least only very dimly aware of it, how can it be said to be an extension of the literal sense, which by definition is intended by the human author ? To answer

39m this, we must, with Coppens, distinguish between the mind of the sacred writer and that of the prophet. In so far as he is a sacred writer, the author must *necessarily* share in the sense which God communicates to the reader through the text. But the sacred writer is also sometimes a prophet, and it is in these conditions that the text of St Thomas concerning the mind of the prophet fully applies, ST II*a*–II*ae*, 173, 4, 'Because the mind of the prophet is a defective instrument . . . even true prophets do not know all that the Holy Ghost intends in the things seen, said or done by them'. It is in fact not only not required, it is even excluded that he should know all (Coppens 47), though it is possible that at times the prophet has an imperfect awareness of this plenary sense (*cf.* Gribomont 71).

It may be objected finally that such a sense implies an abuse of language, for the sacred writer's words are being made to mean several things. But, as Coppens points out, words and phrases are not wooden or merely mechanical. They have a certain elasticity. They have a margin of meaning which may or may not be drawn on in a particular case. The degree of meaning given to a word in a particular instance depends on the capacity, experience, emotions and knowledge of the user. The word has a wider meaning than that given to it at any particular time. This is more true of Hebrew than of our western languages. Hebrew idiom is dynamic not static. It need not therefore be a matter for surprise that the meaning attached to a phrase by the prophet uttering it does not exhaust the meaning attached to it by God and that the deeper meaning should become known to us only by degrees.

40a The Spiritual (Typological or Mystical) Sense :
(*a*) **Existence and Nature**—In Jn 19:33 it is related how the soldiers refrained from breaking the legs of our Lord because he was already dead. Jn adds (19:36), 'These things were done that the Scripture might be fulfilled : You shall not break a bone of him ', Ex 12:46. But the passage quoted apparently refers only to the paschal lamb eaten by the Israelites at the time of the Exodus. How can it be said to have been fulfilled in Christ ? Only on the supposition that there is another sense besides the literal. It is a meaning which, as will be apparent, arises directly, not from the words but from what is signified by the words. As the sacrifice of the lamb and the sprinkling of its blood saved the Israelites from the avenging angel, so Christ, by the shedding of his Blood on Calvary, saved mankind from a yet more terrible doom. Almighty God has thus willed that the persons, things and events described should often signify other persons, things and events. The former are called types and the latter antitypes. St Thomas puts this succinctly : ' In Sacra Scriptura manifestatur veritas dupliciter. Uno modo secundum quod res significantur per verba, et in hoc consistit sensus literalis : alio modo secundum quod res sunt figurae aliarum rerum, et in hoc consistit sensus spiritualis ', *Quaest. Quodlib.* VII, xiv, *in corp. Cf. ibid.* xv, ' resp. dicendum '. The sacred writer in fact has nothing to do with the production of the spiritual sense. It is put there by God and the human writer is unconscious of it. It is discovered only later.

b The full significance of the spiritual sense has not always been kept in sight. The NT writers were deeply impressed with a sense of the unity of the Testaments, the Old foreshadowing the New. St Paul's words referring to the Exodus are of moment in this connection : ' Now these things happened to them in figure and they are written for our correction ', 1 Cor 10:11. The truth is that the OT is full of types of various kinds, prefiguring the mysteries of the New Covenant. ' Christ is the Second Adam, head of redeemed humanity, Rom 5:12 ff. ; 1 Cor 15:21 ff., the new Noah, father of the rescued race who rise from the baptismal waters, 1 Pet 3:20 ff. ; 2 Pet 2:5. He is the prophet like to Moses, Deut 18:15, 18 ; Ac 3:22, who speaks to his people from the mountain and feeds them with heavenly manna, grace and truth coming through

him as the Law came through Moses ', Jn 1:17, 45 ; **40b** 6:14, 32 ; (*cf.* § 642*a*).

It is precisely this unity of the Testaments which, in **c** the opinion of certain modern writers, gives life to the OT and relevance to us today, ' the glory shines from Christ, but it shines back into the whole of Scripture, making it one glorious body, full of the Holy Spirit. Thus it is that the spiritual sense of Scripture is established ', R. Kehoe, *op. cit.* The fulfilment of OT in NT is, moreover, as Père Bouyer has noted, brought about largely by means of symbols. This fact has been scarcely noticed in modern times, in consequence of a very understandable reaction against the excesses of patristic and medieval interpretation, but also because of a certain unconscious rationalism, involving a fear of indulging in unfounded symbolism. But the liturgy which we use day by day is full of symbols, testifying that the OT is not a dead word buried in the past, but a living word addressed to man today. This is largely the usage of the Fathers too, and indeed of the early Christians as a whole. It was in the light of the NT that they looked at the Old and drew on its rich symbolism for their spiritual life in a way that we do not —and from which perhaps we have something to learn.

Some early writers, *e.g.* of the Alexandrian school (see § 39*i*) went too far ; and some medieval writers likewise seem to have put no limits to the wealth of imagery which they professed to see in the OT. They appear indeed to have found the whole cycle of Christian doctrine mirrored and prefigured in the pages of the OT. Père de Vaux has spoken of ' cette floraison d'allégories . . . qui peuvent aider la piété personnelle, mais qui sont artificielles et ne nous font pas pénétrer dans l'intelligence vraie de la Parole de Dieu ', RB 57 (1950) 141. Though this judgement may appear to some to do less than justice to the medievals, there can scarcely be any doubt that it was their exaggerations which chiefly led to the neglect of typological exegesis in later ages.

(*b*) **Kinds of Spiritual Sense**—There is no precise **d** limit to the variety of ways in which the OT can prefigure the NT and the life to come. As Père Daniélou has said in a remarkable article (*Les Divers Sens . . .*) it does not really matter what the number of ways is. What does matter is that one should not force texts into artificial moulds and thus exclude some aspect of their meaning and doctrine. Nevertheless, some division of senses is essential for the sake of clarity and it is possible to make use of a terminology in this matter which has achieved a large measure of agreement. In spite of all that has been written on the subject since the time of St Thomas Aquinas, it may be doubted whether any substantial improvement on the division and terminology adopted by him has been made. Since they are still in common use we propose to outline them here, always bearing in mind that no clear-cut division of this kind could do full justice to all the shades of meaning in the Scriptures.

Considering first *the manner of expression* we may say **e** that the spiritual sense is **metaphorical** if the literal sense on which it is based is metaphorical. In Ps 117:22 the people of Israel are described under the metaphor of a corner stone. In Mt 21:42 Christ applies this to himself—of course in the metaphorical sense also. On the other hand the Brazen Serpent, Num 21:6–9, is a signal instance of God's mercy described without metaphor, and consequently in Jn 3:14 it is applied to Christ on the Cross also in the **proper** sense. With regard to *the subject matter* : truth, says St Thomas, may be conveyed to us through Scripture with a view to (1) right belief, or (2) right conduct. If to right conduct, then it is the **moral** or tropological sense (τρόπος : a way of life). If to right belief, we must again distinguish : the Church is midway between the Jewish Synagogue and the Church triumphant. Hence there are types in the OT which prefigure the Church on earth and this sense we call the **allegorical** sense. Again there are types in both OT and NT which foreshadow the Church triumphant in heaven, and this sense we call

40e the **anagogical** sense (ἀνάγω : I lead or raise up) ; *cf. Quaest. Quodlib.* VII, xv, *in corp.*

f The following are examples of the above senses. The Paschal Lamb, Brazen Serpent and Corner Stone are familiar instances of the allegorical (also called the typical) sense. Others are the sacrifice of Isaac, a type of Christ's death ; the crossing of the Red Sea, a type of the freeing of mankind from the bondage of sin by Baptism. All these are fulfilled in the NT. For the anagogical sense we may cite St Paul's mention of Jerusalem as a type of the heavenly city which is our mother, Gal 4:26. The moral sense is conveyed to us in Wis 16:28 whence we learn that the manna which had to be collected before the sun rose, Ex 16, contains the lesson that we should rise early to praise and thank God, the author of all good.

It is not to be supposed that these senses are always found singly. Sometimes indeed, all three are found together. Thus the entry of the Hebrews into the Promised Land not only foreshadowed the entry of the Gentiles into the Church (allegorical sense) and the admittance of the elect into heaven (anagogical sense), but also teaches us the necessity of faith and the misery of unbelief (moral sense), Heb 4:1–11. Hence though the literal sense is one and the spiritual sense is always based on it, yet several spiritual senses may co-exist and be based on the one literal sense.

g *(c)* **Extent of the Spiritual Sense**—All are agreed that the OT as a whole prefigures the NT. We have already seen that some of the Fathers and early Church writers went further than this and interpreted everything in the OT, even every phrase and word, as typifying the NT. This means that they understood the spiritual sense as not merely based on the things, persons and events but overflowing, so to speak, into the text itself. While there may well be some basis for this principle, there can be none for the attempt to interpret everything and every phrase in a spiritual sense, for this would seem to imply that the private reader's judgement was equal to that of the Church. While therefore the OT as a whole prefigures the NT, and there are a number of types of great richness which are shown to be such by Scripture itself directly, the existence of other types and figures must be carefully investigated (*cf.* § 42*g*). Some deny the existence of types in the NT. They argue that the spiritual sense is inseparable from the time of preparation ; that it implies development and incompleteness, in so far as a type always falls short of the truth it prefigures. But the NT contains the fullness of revelation : nothing can surpass in value the Person of Christ, the Passion, Resurrection and Ascension. So Patrizi, *op. cit.* 203, 225. There is some truth in this. The fullness of revelation in the NT does seem to make it unlikely that there will be many types of future mysteries found therein. But surely no one would maintain that all the truths of revelation have already been unfolded to the full ? We have to admit that there are truths which still contain much mystery for us, especially perhaps that of the Church, the Kingdom of God, which passes from its earthly status to that of the Jerusalem which is above, Gal 4:26. This is the anagogical sense, see § 40*e*. 'Ipsa nova lex est figura futurae gloriae', ST I, i, 10.

h *(d)* **In what way is the Spiritual Sense Christological?** Père Daniélou has recently argued that the spiritual sense is christological in the widest sense of the term ; (*Les Divers Sens*). It always refers to the historical Christ, to Christ in the mysteries of his life, in the sacraments and in the church—lastly to Christ at his second coming and in his eternal kingdom. The typifying of Christ in the mysteries of his life, such as his death and Resurrection, is the category in which we must place the great types of the OT, such as the Paschal Lamb, the Brazen Serpent. This kind of typological exegesis is, in the opinion of Père Daniélou, the most important. Indeed he further maintains that we cannot even know Christ properly unless we are acquainted with the OT, for he is constantly described

(896)

in the NT as also in the Liturgy, in terms of the Old. **40h** There is, further, another group of types referring to the sacramental life of Christ's mystical Body, the Church. St John's Gospel is the one which enlarges on this sacramental exegesis. We need only think of the multiplication of the loaves (typifying the Eucharist) or the discourses with Nicodemus and the Samaritan woman (foreshadowing Baptism) which are to be seen in their turn against the background of the Exodus with its great ' sacraments ' : the paschal lamb, the manna, the living water. Lastly there is eschatological exegesis : types in OT and NT foreshadowing events to occur at Christ's second coming. Thus the imagery of the Exodus is applied to these events in Apoc ; it also refers to the sacraments, elsewhere in the NT. Again, the Flood which in 1 Pet 3:20 is quoted as a type of Baptism is also brought in as foreshadowing the Last Judgement (*cf.* Daniélou, *Déluge, Baptême, Jugement*).

Père Daniélou's study of patristic exegesis is illuminating in that it brings out the full significance of the symbolism of the OT. We may agree that it is centred on Christ. Yet the author seems to go too far in trying to reduce all the spiritual senses to a common christological interpretation. One may reasonably ask how the moral sense fits into this scheme ? It is true that Christ actively participates by his presence and by his grace in the spiritual life of the Christian and that the life of the true Christian is a faithful reflection of the life of Christ. But is this sufficient reason for asserting that here too, as in the other senses, Christ is the precise formal object of the typology ? (*cf.* Coppens, 88).

(e) **Probative Force of the Spiritual Sense**—St Thomas **i** appears to deny all probative force to the spiritual sense. He speaks of the literal sense ' from which alone an argument can be drawn ' ST I, 1, 10 ad 1. Elsewhere he refers to the difficulties in the way of using the spiritual sense, and hence, he says, it cannot be used in argument, *Quaest. Quodlib.* VII, 14 ad 4. He reminds us that we are not thereby deprived of any of the teaching of the Scripture, because there is nothing in the spiritual sense which is not also contained in the literal sense, ST, *loc. cit.* But since the NT writers used this sense to demonstrate truths we cannot doubt that it is a legitimate usage (*cf.* Bonsirven). St Paul by relating the story of Sara, and Agar, Gal 4, proves that the works of the Law do not of themselves effect justification. He is clearly referring to the spiritual sense of the passage to prove his point. If there were no spiritual sense there would be no proof. Moreover the fact that the spiritual sense is that of the Holy Ghost is sufficient to show that it must be of the highest value as a proof from authority. It goes without saying that it will be of value in argument only to those who are ready to accept that authority. St Paul could rightly use it to teach truths to his Galatian converts, but he did not use such arguments when addressing the pagan Athenians, Ac 17. It is not from any lack of authority in itself but because of the difficulty of always identifying it with certainty that the need arises for using the spiritual sense sparingly. Is, for example, St Paul's quotation of Deut 25:4 in 1 Cor 9:9, an indication of a spiritual sense or is it merely an accommodation ? Only if it is the former could it be a proof of his statement. If the latter, it would merely be a form of illustration. In so far therefore as the sense can be ascertained, to that extent may it be used in argument. Certainly the use of the OT by NT writers is often loose. Many of the texts which seem at first sight to give the spiritual sense contain in fact no more than an accommodation of the OT. There is no simple criterion which would enable us to distinguish the two rapidly and without difficulty whenever desired. It may seem strange that the meaning of the Holy Ghost is so often hard to discover. But this problem is not confined to the spiritual sense of Scripture.

Accommodation of the Text of Scripture—*(a)* A like- **j** ness may often be noticed between a Scripture text and

3a

40j a subject with which it has no strict connexion. One might say of St Francis of Assisi that he 'was a man sent by God ', Jn 1:6. The Gospel text of course refers to St John the Baptist. To apply it to St Francis is to adapt the text to a subject which God did not intend to signify by those words. Since this adaptation is not intended by God it is not a sense of Scripture at all. It is an accommodation of the text. We should avoid speaking of it as an accommodated sense, because this might lead to its being mistaken for a genuine sense of Scripture. Accommodation may be made in various ways. The idea contained in the text may be really applicable, as in the example given above. Many other instances are found in the Liturgy : *e.g.* Ecclus 44:17, which refers to Noah, is applied in the Breviary to any Confessor-Bishop. This is sometimes called accommodation **by extension.** On the other hand there may be no likeness of idea in the accommodation. Thus, in the Introit of the Mass within the octave of Christmas, Wis 18:14–15*a* is quoted to describe the Incarnation. The genuine sense of the passage however is a salutary reminder of God's avenging justice shown by the tenth plague of Egypt—as may be seen by the context of the quotation. In the application there is merely a verbal suitability. This is known as accommodation **by allusion.**

(*b*) Since authority uses both forms of accommodation there can be no doubt that it is a legitimate usage. But where there is genuine accommodation there can be no question of real proof of that to which the text is applied. Thus Ecclus 24:24 which refers to the Divine Wisdom may be applied to the Blessed Virgin as Universal Mediatrix of Graces, but it is not in any sense a proof of that doctrine.

k This application of Scripture may be easily abused. Preachers should use it sparingly to impress moral and dogmatic truths on their hearers. 'The faithful, and particularly those who are learned in both sacred and profane sciences, want to know what God himself means to say to us in the Scriptures rather than what some eloquent speaker or writer is expounding with a dexterous use of the words of the Bible ', DAS, 32–33. Hence : (1) An accommodation should never be put forward as the genuine sense of Scripture. (2) There should be some likeness to or analogy with the original text. The application should never contradict the literal sense. (3) An accommodation should not be put forward as proof of doctrine. (4) Scripture texts should not be applied to secular subjects. This caution against a too free use of accommodation must not be construed as a restriction on the right of the preacher to draw moral lessons from the text of Scripture. Such lessons drawn by legitimate argument from Scripture are inexhaustible. But these are quite distinct from this accommodation of Scripture texts. In the former case we have genuine deductions from the words of Scripture—in the latter, merely a loose form of illustration.

PRINCIPLES OF INTERPRETATION

41a The Scriptures may be regarded simply as ancient documents or as God's inspired word committed to his Church. There are thus two sets of principles, general and special, to be applied in their interpretation. Since God is the author of both the natural and the supernatural there can never be any real opposition between these sets of principles. Nor can we arrive at a true understanding of the Scriptures by a use of the former without the latter. At the same time whatever may be the spiritual meanings in any particular passage, the literal sense is always to be elucidated first as the correct basis for any further exegesis (*cf.* DAS, 28).

b **General Principles :**

(*a*) **The Background**—The utility and even necessity of an adequate knowledge of the historical and cultural background of the Bible in the ancient Near

East is amply demonstrated in §§ 76–81. Thus a **41b** knowledge of later Jewish history before Christ is necessary for an understanding of the parable of the Good Samaritan ; to understand the problem of St Paul's journeys through Galatia (*cf.* Ac 16:6) involves a knowledge of the Roman provinces of that time.

(*b*) **The Writer**—The Scriptures were written before **c** the rise of exact scientific and historical methods. We must not therefore expect the precision of statement characteristic of modern text-books. Again the writers were Orientals with their own modes of expression. Normally they prefer the concrete to the abstract, and they clothe their ideas in metaphor and imagery well suited to their vivid imagination (*cf.* § 39*h*). In genealogies, the Oriental is intent on the line of descent but is less concerned with the individuals in that line. Not infrequently names in the direct line are omitted and the words ' beget ' and ' son ' are used where a gap of perhaps several generations exists, *e.g.* see on Mt 1:8. This genealogy incidentally illustrates the tendency among the Semites to prefer round or symbolical numbers, see on Mt 1:17. One may recall also the frequent recurrence in the OT of the numbers seven and forty. Pharaoh dreamed of seven fat and seven lean kine. The Lord said to Moses that if Israel would obey him, their enemies would perish, ' One way shall they come out against thee, and seven ways shall they flee before thee ', Deut 28:7. The number seven was sacred among the Jews and entered into their religious rites, *cf.* the seven-branched candle-stick. Arising out of this religious significance was its symbolism of perfection and hence it came to indicate the whole of a thing. Multiples of seven were used in the same way. On the number forty, see § 124*l*. A curious feature of Semitic genealogies is the way in which races, tribes and towns are frequently personified and included in the list. In Gen 10:13 all the names are in the plural. Misraim, for example, means Egypt (lit. the two Masors). Many other instances are to be found in this genealogy.

Each writer has also his own particular circumstances and temperament and these are frequently mirrored in his work. The high degree of culture possessed by the prophet Isaias is clear from the elegance of his style. The shepherd Amos is naturally more rustic in expression, and the imagery of the countryside fills his pages. The burning zeal of St Paul may be contrasted with the calmer, though no less apostolic spirit of St John.

(*c*) **The Book**—' It is absolutely necessary for the inter- **d** preter to go back in spirit to those remote centuries of the past, and make proper use of the aids afforded by history, archaeology, ethnology and other sciences, in order to discover what literary forms the writers of that early age intended to use and did in fact employ ', DAS 39. Thus Pope Pius XII goes so far as to say that it is not merely desirable but absolutely necessary for the interpreter to possess this knowledge. These literary forms are discussed §§ 45, 46*h*. One must ascertain, *e.g.* whether the book in question is poetical or historical. In the OT, poetry is found, not only in the strictly poetical books, but also in the historical and prophetical. The imagery is not to be interpreted as if it were sober prose, ' Judah is a lion's whelp : to the prey my son, thou art gone up. Resting thou hast couched as a lion, and as a lioness who shall rouse him ? ' Gen 49:9. In the historical books one should not exclude the possibility of there being a certain dramatic element. Thus certain of the speeches in the Bible, *e.g.* that of Juda, Gen 44, may well be set down, not word for word as they were spoken, but in a way calculated to have the greatest effect on the readers. Set speeches like this are a familiar literary device, *cf.* Pericles' funeral oration in the History of Thucydides II, 35–46. In the NT one would naturally look for more exactness, but even here portions of different discourses are put together into one, *cf.* the Sermon on the Mount.

The prophetical books too have a character of their **e** own. In prophecy the essentials, which are fulfilled,

41e are to be distinguished from the accessory details which are not fulfilled and which are inserted only for the sake of the literary form. When spiritual truths are described in material terms this is inevitable. Some of the prophecies of the Restoration are of this kind, *e.g.* in Is 40 ff. Again when two events are foretold together the details of one are to be distinguished from those of the other, so far as possible. This is often difficult. Thus in Is 40 ff. it is not easy always to distinguish what refers only to the Return from Exile from what refers only to the foundation of the Church. Some parts of course refer to both. In unfulfilled prophecy much remains obscure, *e.g.* concerning the end of the world, the nature of Antichrist, and the mysterious prophecy in 2 Thess 2:6. It is apparently God's intention that many details shall be understood only when they have come to pass (*cf.* Jn 2:22).

The occasion and purpose of the book will have their part to play in determining its meaning. Thus the loose sequence of laws interspersed with historical matter in the Pentateuch is the result of the conditions in which Israel lived at the time of the Exodus and subsequently in the land of Promise. These conditions would also account for many differences in terminology. Thus the circumstances of their origin have to be borne in mind when interpreting the laws. The sacred writers kept in view those for whom they wrote. Both Mt and Mk use Jewish terms, but Mk writing for Gentiles adds a Greek translation (*e.g.* 5:41), or an explanation (*e.g.* 7:3). Mt, writing for Jews, makes statements which seem hard on Gentiles (*e.g.* 6:7 ; 15:26), while Lk is careful to avoid anything which might hurt their feelings.

f (*d*) **Vocabulary, Context and Parallel Passages**—The etymological meaning of words frequently differs from the meaning in actual use. Thus Areopagus (Hill of Ares) was originally the name of a hill in Athens. Then because the supreme Council of Athens had met there in early times the name was applied to the Council wherever it met, Ac 17:19. Again, the meaning of words changes from age to age. The mistake has often been made of interpreting the language of the NT as if it were classical Greek of the 5th cent. B.C. Modern discoveries of papyri in Greek of the time of Christ have gone far to rectify such misconceptions. A knowledge of the original languages is evidently necessary for an accurate study of the Bible. No one, says Pope Pius XII, can hope to be regarded seriously as an interpreter of Scripture, who is ignorant of these languages, DAS 20. Besides the original Hebrew, Greek and Aramaic, other languages such as Syriac, Arabic and Accadian contribute valuable aid to the elucidation of the text.

g The context too has its part to play in fixing the meaning of a passage. In Num 13:28 ' a land flowing with milk and honey ' is evidently according to the context a prosperous land. But in Is 7:15 ' he shall eat butter and honey ' seems from the context to indicate hardship. The meaning of the phrase in 7:22 will be determined by its meaning in 7:15 ; for the same word or words in the same context should, generally speaking, be interpreted in the same way. In a broader sense the whole book may be regarded as the context, and it should be read as a whole if a thorough understanding of a passage is desired. With due limitations there is much truth in the saying that the best interpreter of the Bible is the Bible itself. Too often a text or passage is examined as though it were isolated from the whole. The Sunday epistles and Gospels sometimes suffer this fate and in consequence are not always well understood. The epistles of St Paul, perhaps more than most other parts of the Bible, need to be read right through as whole letters in order to get the greatest benefit from them.

h Parallel passages, looked up in a concordance, are frequently of great help in elucidating a text. The word *almah* occurs in Is 7:14 (MT). In the other texts where it is found it seems to indicate an unmarried maiden. Though the word does not expressly indicate virginity it would naturally be presumed ; hence

virginity would be included in the meaning of **41h** Is 7:14. It may be noted also that in Is 7:14 both the LXX and Vg translate as ' virgin '. Parallel accounts of the same event can often throw much light on a text. Thus the faith of the bearers of the paralysed man in Mt 9:2 is explained in Mk 2:1–12, which describes how they made a hole in the roof of the house where Christ was and let down the sick man to his feet. In comparing parallel passages in the OT one must remember that it is the record of a developing revelation which reached its fullness in Christ. It is true that later prophecies throw much light on earlier ones, but it is necessary to resist the tendency to read more recent doctrines into the older statements. A study of the doctrine of the Divine Wisdom, for example, in Job, Prov, Ecclus and Wis would seem to show that only in the last named book does its personal character begin to appear. The full and definitive revelation was made at the time of the Incarnation. The parallelism of Hebrew poetry (*cf.* 313*e*–*f*) must also be taken into account in interpretation. Thus the ' sons of God ' in Ps 88:7 are angels and not men, as is seen from the reference to clouds in the first part of the verse.

Special Principles—Far more important than its value **42a** as ancient literature is the divine origin of Scripture. It follows that mere intelligence and hard work are not enough to discover its meaning. ' Wisdom will not enter a malicious soul nor dwell in a body subject to sins ', Wis 1:4. It is innocence of heart and the practice of virtue, which must come first. The obscurity of Scripture indeed is a direct test of our humility and patience (*cf.* DAS 47, *Imitation of Christ*, I, 5). To acquire such dispositions we need to pray. As St Augustine says of those who study the Scriptures ' Orent ut intelligant ', *De Doct. Christ*, III, 37. These Special Principles of Interpretation are of particular significance in ascertaining the spiritual sense of Scripture, which, as has been said, we can discover only through the sources of Revelation.

(*a*) The first consequence of the fact of Inspiration is that the Scriptures are without any formal error (*cf.* § 37*e*).

(*b*) Since Scripture is a source of Revelation, the **b** Church is the guardian and interpreter thereof and has authority to determine its meaning in all matters of faith and morals. This was defined by the Council of Trent (EB 47 ; Dz 786) and further explained by the Vatican Council (EB 63 ; Dz 1788). There are of course many other matters contained in the Bible, such as details of archaeology, geography and the like. Inspiration excludes formal error from these, but the Church has no authority to define their meaning except in so far as they have a connexion with doctrine. Thus the Church has, for example, no views on the vexed question of the chronology of the books of Kings. But in secular matters which affect truths of faith and morals the Church might condemn an erroneous view. Thus Evolution has a bearing on the doctrine of Original Sin, and an evolutionary theory which conflicted with that truth would be condemned by the Church. As regards the manner of interpretation, the Church sometimes **defines infallibly** the meaning of a text, *e.g.* Jn 3:5 (Dz 858) on the use of water in Baptism ; or condemns, a false interpretation, *e.g.* Deut 6:5, Mt 22:37 (Dz 1076). Again, Scripture texts are incorporated into dogmatic decrees in proof or illustration of particular doctrines. Gen 3:15 appears in the Bull *Ineffabilis Deus* defining the Immaculate Conception. Infallibility however applies only to the dogma defined and not to any particular argument adduced in support of it ; hence the interpretation of Gen 3:15, though of great weight, is not infallible by reason of its inclusion in this decree (*cf.* Durand, art. *Exégèse* DTC 1838). The number of texts infallibly interpreted by the Church is small : for further examples see Mangenot-Rivière, *art. cit.* 2317–9. It has been estimated indeed that the total of such texts is under twenty, though there are of course many others indirectly determined

42b (*cf.* Corluy, 426; Durand *art. cit.* 1838). It should also be observed that an infallible interpretation of a text does not necessarily exhaust its full meaning.

c Besides the solemn and infallible definitions of the Church there are many other **interpretations** of texts in the decrees **of Councils, Commissions and Congregations** which, though not infallible, **enjoy high authority.** In particular there are the Replies of the Biblical Commission designed to guide the Catholic along paths of prudent exegesis. In general it may be said that the Commission holds that the traditional interpretation should be adhered to unless and until, in some particular case and without prejudice to faith and morals, it has been shown that it is more reasonable to maintain some other view. This means therefore that acceptance of the Commission's conclusions does not preclude further investigation of the matter (*cf.* § 47*c*).

d The Council of Trent (EB 47; Dz 786) speaks of the **unanimous consent of the Fathers** as a norm of interpretation. This has always been the tradition of the Church. When the Fathers interpret a text pertaining to faith and morals in one and the same way they are of the highest authority ' because their unanimity clearly shows that such an interpretation has come down from the Apostles as a matter of Catholic Faith ', PD, EB 96, Dz 1944. Moral unanimity is sufficient, *i.e.* if a good number of Fathers in widely different parts of the Church, or of different ages agree on a point and no Father contradicts their teaching. Again the view must be given as certain and not as merely possible or probable. Lastly the doctrine must be put forward as revealed truth. Evidently these conditions are not often fulfilled simultaneously. The number of texts determined by the consent of the Fathers is even smaller than that of the texts determined by the decrees of the Church. We cite a few examples: the virginal conception of Christ, Is 7:14; the Passion of Christ, Is 53; existence of Purgatory, 2 Mac 12:43 (*cf.* Mangenot-Rivière, *art. cit.* 2328-30. For a discussion of the authority of commentators, see *ibid.* 2331.)

But even when there is not unanimity, a doctrine taught by many Fathers will be treated with the respect due to men of eminent theological learning and holiness. In matters other than those of faith and morals the Fathers have no special authority and their views are to be judged in the light of their arguments. Even if they all held, for example, that the world was made in six days of twenty-four hours we would not be bound to accept that view under authority because it is not a matter of faith and morals. When all is said, a large field is left to the interpreter. Very few texts have in fact been authoritatively determined and ' there consequently remain many important matters in the explanation of which the sagacity and ingenuity of Catholic interpreters can and should be freely exercised ', DAS 49.

e (*c*) The interpreter's guide in those parts not authoritatively determined, should be the faith which he professes and the harmony between its parts. No interpretation of a text can be adopted which conflicts with any point of revealed truth, ' for seeing that the same God is author of both the Sacred Books and the doctrine committed to the Church, it is clearly impossible that any teaching can by legitimate means be extracted from the former which shall in any respects be at variance with the latter ', PD, EB 94, Dz 1943. This norm of interpretation is called the **analogy of faith** (Rom 12:6), *cf.* Dz 2023. Pope Leo XIII here reminds us that besides the Written Word there is an unwritten Tradition of doctrine revealed by God. Indeed the books of the NT were not written in the first instance to impart the faith of Christ to infidels, but to instruct believers. The first readers of those books must therefore have been careful not to draw any meaning from them which would be at variance with the faith they had already been taught. Thus, Mt 19:9 cannot be interpreted as sanctioning divorce since this is explicitly forbidden a few lines higher up; Col 1:24 cannot mean that Christ's sufferings were not

adequate, since it is clear from many passages in the NT **42e** as well as Tradition that they were superabundant, *e.g.* Rom 5, Heb 7 ff.

(*d*) Positively, the interpreter will take as his guide **f** the general **harmony** existing **between the Testaments** which arises from their common divine origin. The plenary sense depends entirely on this underlying unity (*cf.* § 39*d*, *k-m*).

This unity of the Testaments has perhaps an even greater part to play in the discerning of the spiritual or typological sense (*cf.* 40*a-c*). For this sense, as Coppens observes, is simply the result of God operating in history. He it is who establishes outside the sacred writer's consciousness the mysterious but real harmonies between the Testaments. Since he alone put such meanings there, only he could reveal them to us. He discloses them to us in the ways outlined above. As already stated, comparatively few types have been solidly established in these ways. May we not look for more?

There are certain groups of types in the OT. For **g** example, the events of the Exodus, the conquest of Canaan. Are there further details to be interpreted of events in the NT? If this be easily granted in principle, it is more difficult to decide what criteria are to guide the interpreter here. The recognized sources must of course be scanned—the books of the NT, the writings of the Fathers, the declarations of the Church. The NT writers however need supplementing, for in the first place there are different kinds of typology to be found there (*e.g.* Matthaean, Johannine, Pauline) and in the second place it is often uncertain whether it is a question of a genuine typological sense or simply of an accommodation (*cf.* § 40*i*). Of patristic typology, while no doubt much must be discarded in the light of modern knowledge, nevertheless it may be used as a fruitful source of knowledge and vivid presentation of Biblical teaching. Within the framework of a recognized group of types, it is possible to proceed from the general to the particular, making use not only of patristic interpretation, but also of literary and historical principles. From a judicious combination of these, it may be hoped that the result will be a balanced one. On the one hand it is probable that many types familiar to us will ultimately disappear. On the other hand, new types may emerge. At the least there may well be a change of emphasis, some types emerging into prominence—others fading into the background.

Conclusion—From what has been said and from a **h** general consideration of God's purpose, it will be seen that the interpreter should aim above all at expounding the doctrinal content of Scripture. Matters of history, geography and the like have their importance ' but commentators must have as their chief object to show what is the theological doctrine concerning faith and morals of each book and text, so that their commentary may not only assist teachers of theology in expounding the dogmas of faith but also be useful to priests in their work of explaining Christian doctrine to the people and help all the faithful to lead a holy and Christian life ', DAS 29. This high ideal should be a constant stimulus to greater efforts in spite of the difficulties that remain. The number of problems solved is a pledge of further successful solutions while we remember that there may always be difficulties that escape our efforts to solve them.

The great freedom left to the interpreter should induce him to treat the views of others with tolerance. The attitude of mind which instinctively regards with suspicion an interpretation merely because it is new should be avoided. ' This true freedom of the sons of God, loyally maintaining the doctrine of the Church, and at the same time gratefully accepting as a gift from God and exploiting every contribution that profane knowledge may afford, must be vindicated and upheld by the zeal of all, for it is the condition and source of any real success, of any solid progress in Catholic science ', DAS 49.

HIGHER CRITICISM

With Special Reference to the Old Testament

BY R. A. DYSON AND R. A. F. MACKENZIE, S.J.

43a Bibliography—A. Bea, ' Der heutige Stand der Penta-teuchfrage ', Bi 16 (1935) 175–200 ; *id*., ' Il Problema del Pentateucho e della Storia Primordiale ', Civ Catt 99 (1948) 116–27 ; J. Coppens, *L'histoire critique de l'Ancien Testament*, Bruges, 1942, Eng. trans. *The Old Testament and the Critics*, Paterson, 1942 ; P. Cruveilhier, ' Herméneutique sacrée ', DBV (S) III, 1482–524 ; H. Hoepfl, ' Critique Biblique ', DBV (S) II, 175–240 ; M.-J. Lagrange, ' L'authenticité mosaïque de la Genèse et la théorie des documents ', RB 47 (1938) 163–83 ; V. Laridon, ' Novae encyclicae biblicae doctrina de generibus litterariis ', Coll Brug 42 (1946) 97–105 ; 127–34 ; A. Lemonnyer, ' Théorie des Apparences historiques ', DBV (S) I, 588–96 ; A. Robert, ' Genre Historique ', DBV (S) IV, 7–23 ; A. Robert-A. Tricot, *Initiation Biblique*, Paris, 1949 ; A. Vaccari, VD 17 (1937) 371–3 ; R. de Vaux, ' Les patriarches hébreux et les découvertes modernes ', RB 53 (1946) 321–48 ; *W. Baumgartner, ' Wellhausen und der heutige Stand der alttestamentlichen Wissen-schaft ', Th Rs N.F. 2 (1930) 287–307 ; *O. Eissfeldt, ' Die literarkritische Arbeit am A. T. in den letzten 12 Jahren ', Th Rs N.F. 10 (1938) 255–91 ; *H. H. Rowley, *The Re-Discovery of the Old Testament* (London, 1945) 24–58.

b Kinds of Criticism—Criticism may be defined as the art of distinguishing, in a literary work, what is genuine from what is false, what is authentic (due to the original author) from what is additional, and evaluat-ing the whole in terms of literary and other relevant standards. It is commonly distinguished into textual criticism, literary, *i.e.* ' higher ' criticism, and historical criticism, this last being understood in a broad sense, since its nature varies greatly according to the kind of matter dealt with—historical, theological, legal, etc.

c Of this art *textual* criticism is a fundamental branch. It is chiefly exercised on material transmitted through a manuscript tradition (as opposed to printed work in which it finds little scope). Its task is to eliminate accidental corruptions of the text (usually copyists' errors) and establish the *ipsissima verba*, in their original order, of the author or final editor. Given that text, as nearly as it can be established, ' higher ' or literary criticism then has the task of determining its origin and mode of composition, *i.e.* the author or authors, the materials used and to what extent they were recast, what kind of work the author intended to write, etc. After this analysis the *third* type of criticism (often grouped with the second as ' higher ') judges the value and significance of the work, its importance in history, and synthesizes the information that may be drawn from it.

d Criticism and Exegesis—As applied to the OT, textual and literary criticism are not essentially different from the same arts practised on profane literature (with one important qualification to be mentioned below). The third type of criticism, however, should be not only historical and sociological, but also theological, not merely compiling the religious history of Israel or describing its social development, but systematically analyzing the doctrine of the sacred books on God and religion, *i.e.* producing a biblical theology. Finally, given the divine character of the sacred text, all these critical arts must be handmaids to *exegesis*, *i.e.* the exposition of the meaning of the text, to which all **43d** biblical studies tend.

We may note here that criticism is not the same as **e** exegesis, although in practice, to some extent at least, criticism always accompanies exegesis ; more exactly, criticism leaves off where exegesis begins. The latter discipline has the task of expounding the divine message, and it is this which makes Scripture in the concrete ' profitable to teach, to reprove, to correct, to instruct in justice ', 2 Tim 3:16 ; it has its own rules which can only be a negative guide to the critic who approaches the material on a lower level, and from the human side. The confusion of criticism with exegesis may lead to a double error : the misconception of those who complain that biblical criticism is ' irreverent ' in treating the Bible as a human work, or disappointing because it contributes little to edification ; and the opposite error of deifying criticism and, for example, of producing commentaries in which the divine teaching in a given book is passed over in silence and only its human aspects considered. Both these attitudes mis-take the true function of biblical studies, which is, to serve and assist exegesis ; and it is precisely because modern criticism has made available such admirable new techniques for a deeper understanding of God's Word, that the Church encourages its development.

To the extent that it enters into even the simplest **f** exegesis, biblical criticism has been practised in the Church from the beginning ; but ' higher ' criticism, with its refined scientific methods, is chiefly a 19th cent. development. Hence we pass over the long and fruitful history of the Fathers of the Church, of the Schoolmen, of the post-Tridentine exegesis ; and the first name to be mentioned, as that of a critic in the modern sense of the word, is that of **Richard Simon** (1638–1712), the French Oratorian, justly called ' the father of biblical criticism '. He saw and formulated the major problems that have occupied criticism since his day, and boldly applied scientific methods for their solution. As a pioneer, it was inevitable that some of his solutions should be weak, and others too radical (his works were put on the Index) ; yet the ' orthodox ' exegetes (notably Bossuet) who so vigorously con-demned, not his errors alone, but his whole critical approach, had no idea of the importance of the work he was trying to do. In any event he founded no school, and further Catholic work on these lines was discouraged. The result was that the critical analysis of the Bible, when it came, was entirely non-Catholic—indeed anti-Catholic—and vastly more irresponsible and destructive than it need have been. Nearly the whole 19th cent. passed before Catholic exegetes took up the challenge seriously and began to demonstrate that ' criticism ' is not fatally destructive of Christian tradition—rather that the tools of criticism rightly used are a precious aid to the understanding and explaining of the Word of God. But Catholic scholarship in this matter has not yet made up for its late start.

Space forbids a review of the history of the higher **44a** criticism of the OT in the 19th cent., but the most famous name may be taken as summing up its tendencies and its findings. **J. Wellhausen** (1844–1918) taking up and developing earlier work, especially on the composition of the Pentateuch, set forth (1876 ff.) an elaborate reconstruction of the literary history of the

44a OT and the cultural and literary history of the Israelites, which until the end of World War I was the accepted framework for all non-Catholic study of the OT, and even today, though increasingly discarded, in part or in whole, has not been replaced by any synthesis of corresponding amplitude.

b Wellhausian Presuppositions—Wellhausen began his work with certain philosophical presuppositions which governed the whole of his thought. Schematically (and at the risk of over-simplification) we may reduce them to four : (1) exclusion of the supernatural, *i.e.* of any direct intervention of the deity in human history ; (2) the evolutionary scheme of unilinear progress in religious thought from animism or polydemonism through polytheism and henotheism to monotheism. He considered the fully developed religion of Israel to be latent in its earlier stages, spirit and law gradually replacing nature, all this development following strictly Hegelian dialectic : thesis (the preprophetic stage), antithesis (the prophetic reaction), synthesis (the monistic stage) ; (3) the presumption that Hebrew historiography is not to be relied on ; and (4) a conception of Israel living among its neighbours in splendid
c isolation. The first of these presuppositions needs no comment here, beyond pointing out the fact that it is scientifically unprovable, and, as an aprioristic contradiction of the viewpoint of almost every page of the OT, is hardly a good starting point for a sympathetic study of it. As for the second, Ethnology, Archaeology and the Philosophy of History have combined to declare such subjective reconstruction of Israelite religious history absolutely untenable. This reconstruction, however, naturally led to the third point, Wellhausen's scepticism about the truth of the picture given by Israelite writers of the people's early history. It was buttressed by the belief that writing was unknown to the Israelites of Moses' time. The fourth point was a curious carrying over from an earlier generation of OT scholars, which knew of no other source of world history, before the Greek period, than the OT. And this, even on scientific (as distinct from philosophic) grounds, was a grave defect in Wellhausen's method. Already in his time, Assyrian and Egyptian historical sources were beginning to be available, and in 1896 Winckler published the Amarna letters ; but even in the later editions of his work Wellhausen neglected to take this matter into account. Albright says of Wellhausen that ' he neglected the new material from the ancient Orient with a disdain as arrogant as it was complete ', JBL 59 (1940) 92. He conceived Israelite culture practically as a closed system, untouched by outside influences almost until the period of the Exile. And since supra-human influences were likewise excluded, the religion of the 6th cent. B.C. had to be shown as the term of an ' immanent ', self-explaining evolution from the presumed primitive cult of prehistoric origin.

d Wellhausian Sources of Pentateuch—Such were the principles which governed the investigation, but Wellhausen did not have to start from a *tabula rasa*. Much had already been accomplished. Four sources of the Pentateuch had already been distinguished : the ' Yahwist ' (J) and ' Elohist ' (E), *i.e.* two historical accounts of Hebrew origins, the latter including the Book of the Covenant ; the ' Deuteronomist ' (D) comprising chiefly the law code of Deuteronomy ; and the ' Priestly Code ' (P) containing mainly the legislation of Leviticus and Numbers (also Gen 1). Graf, in 1866, had given this theory almost its definitive form, in particular contending (after Reuss) that P, the document that served as the framework into which the others were inserted, was not the earliest, but the latest of all, a production of the Exile. Wellhausen, having minutely worked out the analysis of the documents, proposed the following chronology. J, the most ' primitive ' in style, was a history composed in Judah *c* 850–750 B.C. It contained an account (beginning in Gen 2:4) of human origins, of the patriarchs, of Israel down to the conquest of Canaan. E, of the 8th

cent. (before 721), was a product of the Northern **44d** Kingdom, a history covering the period from the call of Abraham to the Conquest. D, the law book, had been written shortly before it was ' found ' in the temple in 621 B.C. It contained the law code of Deut 12–26 and other fragments. J and E were woven into a united account (JE), containing naturally a certain amount of duplication, sometime between 721 and 621. Next, an editor of the Deuteronomic school revised JE and combined it with D, during or perhaps shortly before the Exile (586 B.C.). Finally, P was composed during the Exile, under the influence of Ezechiel, and into this new and rather theoretical legal work the already composite JED was inserted, probably by Esdras. Before 400 B.C. the Pentateuch, as we now know it, had reached its final form.

Supposed Religious Evolution of Israel—As with the **e** earlier critics, it was not literary criticism alone that led Wellhausen to come to these conclusions. Historical and literary criticism reacted on each other, both under the necessity of finding a solution consistent with his philosophic principles. The final effect of this emended order and late dating of the documents was the following reconstruction of Israelite religion. Presumably it began, as all primitive religion was supposed to begin, with animism, fetishism, or totemism ; but the earliest stage, of which considerable traces existed in the literature (in J), was polydemonism, the haphazard worship of a number of jinns and demons. This was the ' religion of the desert ' practised by the ancient ' Hebrew ' people, the common ancestor of Israelites, Moabites, Edomites, etc. (the only use Wellhausen made of the comparative method was in drawing on the cults of the pre-Islamic Arab Beduin to illustrate this supposed stage of Israelite religion). By the 13th cent. B.C. it was passing into real polytheism. It was the great political genius of Moses that welded several of these tribes into unity by binding them to the worship and service of a single deity, Yahweh. Their monolatrous Yahweh religion was not ethical, the Ten Commandments being a much later invention. This stage lasted through the Conquest and the period of the Judges, and began to be superseded only with the appearance of the prophets.

The next and decisive step was taken, in fact, by the **f** writing prophets, from Amos on (*c* 760 B.C.). They introduced morality into the idea of religion, presented Yahweh no longer as the god of armies, but as the god of justice, and insisted that he required of his people not ritual but righteousness—obedience rather than sacrifice. J was composed under the first dawning of this idea, E under its mature influence. The prophets and Deuteronomists rapidly developed this theology as the political collapse of their people drew nearer, and religion reached its peak in the great affliction of the Exile. Isaias, Jeremias, Ezechiel and, most of all, Deutero-Isaias were the great personalities that took the final steps from a god of justice to a god of love, almighty and supreme—the one god of monotheism.

The Law, far from being the foundation of the national **g** religion, was the product of it. Like other Semites, the Israelites originally were accustomed to submit cases for arbitration to the priests at a sanctuary where a body of traditional solutions and rules would exist ; but a written code was produced only under the stimulus of the ethical concept of the deity. P, the work of priestly scholars pining in exile for the glories of their lost temple and its ritual, was a retrojection into Moses' time of the cult they knew, combined with an exact programme of law for the future. But in their zeal they overshot the mark, and after the Exile, religion declined into a more and more formal and exterior religious observance, as far removed from the fervent and interior religion of the prophets as the earlier ritual observance—with this exception, that the strictest monotheism was scrupulously observed.

Triumph and Challenge of Wellhausian Synthesis— **h** Thus by a radical rearrangement, in the presumed

44h chronological order, of the material of the Pentateuch, and on the theory that its authors had presented as ancient history a great deal of their own experience—and even of their own invention—a strikingly consistent and plausible account could be given of Israelite history—in particular of the growth of monotheism—without admitting divine revelation or upsetting the process of evolution. Why Israel, rather than any other Semitic people, entered upon this monotheistic development, was left unexplained ; but after all, something had to be left for future critics to work on.

i The conclusions concerning the rest of the OT are of less importance for a history of the critical movement, being corollaries from the foregoing. Briefly, the older prophetical writings were thought to have undergone extensive editing and revision, especially in post-Exilic times ; originally they comprised only preachings on the justice of Yahweh, and prophecies of punishment for Israel's iniquity. Hence all eschatological, Messianic, and consolatory sections (and, of course, accurate prophecies) must date at the earliest from the Exile. The Psalter was judged to be post-Exilic and much of it was dated as late as the Maccabees.

j Wellhausen had a real genius for synthesis and exposition. His reconstruction had a triumph rarely won by scientific theories, and rapidly became—indeed it still remains—the 'classic' interpretation of OT history and literature. With minor reservations, it may be said that the great majority of non-Catholic OT critics speedily adopted it. It was readily welcomed in England where the philosophical temper of the age was powerfully influenced by the work of John Stuart Mill and Herbert Spencer, through whom the positivism of Comte passed into the history of religion and related fields. Thus it posed a challenge to Catholic scholarship that could not be evaded forever, nor dismissed as so much 'rationalism' and 'impiety'. The work was by no means merely negative ; a vast number of facts and some very real problems had been uncovered, for which older exegesis naturally had no explanation. Rationalistic criticism had given one, but it involved the negation of supernatural values and divine inspiration in the OT. Catholic exegetes had to do better.

45a **Slow Catholic Reaction against Wellhausen —** The two outstanding champions of Catholic tradition against Wellhausen were the German Jesuit Cornely and the French Abbé Vigouroux. The former drew attention to many details, especially in the Pentateuch, that told for the traditional date, but remained unexplained and inexplicable on the critical hypothesis. The latter called on the newly discovered Assyrian and Egyptian sources to illustrate how the cultural background of the Mosaic writings perfectly suited the 2nd millennium B.C., but could not be brought down into the first. Yet their works had not much to offer in the way of a positive solution of the problems ; they were negative and defensive in character and tone ; they might reassure the uneasy, they would never convert the erring. What was needed was a more progressive and positive approach, beginning with an attempt to distinguish what was possibly or probably true from what was false.

b For Wellhausen had succeeded in firmly uniting, in the minds of Catholics and non-Catholics alike, two things that should properly have been distinguished : the literary analysis and the historical criticism. The conclusions of the latter were undoubtedly to be rejected ; but there might still be truth in the former. After all, the Mosaic authorship was not an article of faith, and St Jerome, for one, had thought it of small importance whether Moses or Esdras was called the author of the Pentateuch. [But *cf.* § 134*b* for another interpretation of Jerome's words. — *Gen. Ed.*] Catholic tradition certainly held Moses to be the author of the Law ; but did that necessarily mean that he had written everything in the books that contained the Law ? At least, in the light of the grave problems raised by the new criticism, the question might well bear examination.

Such was the attitude of a few of the younger Catholic **45c** scholars of the time, among whom the outstanding figure was **M.-J. Lagrange, O.P.** At a famous congress at Fribourg (Switzerland) in 1897 he introduced a careful distinction between the literary tradition (Moses the author of the books) and the historical tradition (Moses the author of the Law). The latter, he suggested, was the substantial datum and could well stand without the former. He admitted the distinction of four documents in their main lines. In Gen he considered E as prior to Moses who availed himself of it. It was Moses who inspired the composition of J, tracing the broad outlines and ultimately giving it his approval. It was Moses also who gave the Israelites their law which, however, continued to be added to and developed in his spirit in the following centuries.

Effect of Modernist Crisis—Other exegetes, such as **d** Prat, Durand and von Hummelauer, showed a similar readiness to recognize post-Mosaic literary strata in the Pentateuch, while stressing the major role played by Moses as the fountain-head. But before they had done much work along these lines, the Modernist crisis developed, and, for a time, Catholic OT biblical studies came to a standstill. The chief battle-ground of the Modernists was the NT, but their complete surrender to the most radical doctrines of 'higher criticism' naturally involved the acceptance, in general, of Wellhausenism ; hence stringent measures of defence were adopted by the Church authorities, and for some years anything that savoured of 'novelty' in exegesis became suspect. Prat and Lagrange were directed into NT studies and the very term 'higher criticism' became synonymous with 'rationalistic criticism' (EB 276). The activity of the Pontifical Biblical Commission **e** (*cf.* § 47*b*) dates from this period, and has been of extreme importance in guiding all subsequent Catholic tradition. Its 'responses' were drafted with great prudence and moderation ; and since the motives of each decision were carefully listed, the possibility was never excluded that a change in the evidence might, later, occasion a change in the conclusion. In short, the burst of activity that had marked the last decade of Leo XIII's pontificate (1892–1902) was succeeded by twenty years of less sensational work, which, though it might seem to have been merely 'marking time', was really a necessary preparation for solid and well-tested progress.

Disintegration of the Wellhausian Hypothesis— f Meanwhile, a vast change was coming over non-Catholic criticism. The Wellhausen theory, which had seemed at one moment to be, in its main lines, a definitive solution of 'the critical problem', came to be called in question more and more. In the first decade of the 20th cent. the Pan-Babylonian school of Winckler and Jeremias claimed that Israelite culture and religion were nothing but a large-scale borrowing from the Babylonians. The absurd exaggerations of this theory prevented it from ever finding wide acceptance ; but it did at least make a breach in the magic circle of supposed Israelite 'isolation'. Then, the lengths to which some of Wellhausen's successors carried their analysis of the text, sometimes confidently dividing up a single verse among various authors and 'redactors', produced a reaction of healthy scepticism concerning the too arbitrary criteria adopted. Further, ethnologists and anthropologists questioned the soundness of the principle that every religion must necessarily have evolved from some 'primitive' form of animism to a 'higher' form of belief ; for evidence was accumulating that tended to show that polytheism, polydemonism, etc., were corruptions from a widespread 'primitive' monotheism. But the greatest single factor in undermining the Wellhausen structure was undoubtedly archaeology or the 'witness of the stones'.

The article on 'Archaeology and the Bible', §§ 76–81, **g** gives an account of the main discoveries which have a bearing on the Bible and its interpretation. Here we need only sum up its findings. Thanks to excavations conducted in Egypt, Assyria, Mesopotamia, Asia Minor,

45g Syria, and Palestine itself, and to an intense scientific study by hundreds of scholars of the material thus uncovered, two thousand years of history and dozens of nations and cultures have been brought to the light of day. The history of civilization now begins in the early 4th millennium B.C., and written documents are at hand from the late 3rd onwards. In the early 2nd millennium, before the Israelites existed as a people, when their patriarchal ancestors wandered about the pasture-lands of central Palestine, the Near East knew a flourishing and already ancient civilization, in which Egyptians, Hittites, Hurrians and Babylonians contended for dominance or balance of power. Israel was a late comer on the stage of history, taking advantage of a temporary lassitude among the great powers to establish itself in a corner which was also a crossroads of international relations. So far from being self-sufficient in culture, it borrowed from its neighbours and predecessors language, customs, arts and crafts—everything, in short, except its religion. And this strongly imitative and derivative character of Israelite culture in general throws the *unique* character of Israel's *religion* into still stronger relief. From these considerations a fact emerges as beyond dispute, namely, that the environment of the early Hebrews was culturally much more advanced than supposed by Wellhausen and his school and that the influence of these environmental factors upon them was more significant than factors drawn from the Beduin Arabs. So much for the myth of Israel's ' isolation '.

h Here it is worth noting that the older evolutionary idea has held on longest in England. It is surprising to read under the date of 1930 in Oesterley-Robinson's *Hebrew Religion*, 14 : ' These then are the three stages of belief (animatism—animism—polytheism) through which all races pass before they reach a higher form of religion ; and the Hebrew race was no exception as the evidence from the Old Testament shows ' ; or the statement by H. Wheeler Robinson in T. W. Manson's *A Companion to the Bible* (1946) 287 f. : ' From retrospective evidence of the Old Testament supplemented by what is known of Beduin Arabs in ancient and modern times, we can form a picture of this nomadic background . . . This type of religion is specially linked with natural objects concerning the life or welfare of the clan or tribe, namely, springs, trees, rocks, sun, moon and stars, together with flocks, herds and the wild creatures of the desert '. A much truer viewpoint is that expressed by S. H. Hooke in the same book, 273 : ' Modern research has shifted the emphasis formerly laid on the importance of the study of pre-Islamic Arab religion and social organization as the main source of light on the early religion of the Hebrews . . . It is equally true that when the first wave of Hebrew settlement, represented by the Abraham saga, entered Canaan, the original nomad element had already been largely transformed by the influence of Mesopotamian culture '. It is then rather against the background of the religious culture of the Fertile Crescent in the early 2nd millennium B.C. that we are to set the religion of the early Hebrews than in a pattern of the cult of trees, stones and sacred springs ; *cf.* also G. E. Wright, BA 10 (1947) 19 f., and W. F. Albright, JBL 65 (1946) 206.

i **American Leadership in OT Studies**—In recent years leadership in archaeological studies has passed to American scholars, of whom the most influential at present is W. F. Albright. He and his pupils have already defined the main outlines of a new synthesis of Israel's history, resting on a much broader factual basis than Wellhausen's and far more easily reconcilable with Christian tradition. Of the Wellhausen reconstruction of Israel's religious history G. E. Wright affirms that it is ' a vast over-simplification. In its circular reasoning, in its exclusive attention to the extreme simplification of the historical process along uni-lateral evolutionary lines, in its abnormal preoccupation with what is ' primitive ' and ' advanced ' according to an *a priori* scale of ethical judgements (under the guise of ' objectivity '), and in its inevitable naïveté regarding the conceptual life of the ancient world, it has been shown, **45i** and will be increasingly proved, to be utterly inadequate as a final interpretation of the religious data which the Old Testament presents ' (' The Present State of Biblical Archaeology ' in *The Study of the Bible Today and Tomorrow*, H. R. Willoughby [1947] 95). With regard to Yahweh : ' In our earliest, preprophetic sources . . . he is no personification of nature. He transcends nature and is nature's God ' (*ibid.*, 92).

Literary Genres—Literary criticism has developed **j** a new approach. Abundant materials are now available, from newly recovered literature in half a dozen languages, for a comparative study of ancient Israelite writings ; and they have made possible much sounder literary judgements, based on the recognition of literary *genres* unknown to our western tradition. This classification of *genera litteraria* (the unsatisfactory English phrase is ' literary forms ') is perhaps the greatest step forward taken by exegesis in our time, and *Divino afflante Spiritu* deals at length with its importance (*cf.* § 46*h–i*). The 19th cent. critics, relying on their achievements in Hebrew philology, did not realize the equal importance of competence in Hebrew literary psychology ; and there was a tendency to judge ancient Oriental writings almost as though they were the products of European culture and thought-patterns. Hence the arbitrary and extensive mutilations practised on OT books, on the presumption that only those sections could be genuine which the critic would have written had he been the author. Thus Duhm could reduce the ' authentic ' sections of Jeremias' prophecy to one-fifth of the present book ! Today, however, the study of the different categories of literary composition, practised by OT authors, each characterized by its own purpose, its own way of handling material, its own style and forms of expression has shown the inadequacy of such an approach to the OT.

Another development is the rise, in non-Catholic **k** circles, of the study of **Gattungen** or **categories** in the OT. A literary *Gattung* is a particular species of oral composition created by and for a certain situation and expressing certain more or less standard ideas, emotions or reflections. Examples are the song of triumph, the lament, the parable, the fable, the taunt-song, etc. All these constitute the raw material, so to speak, of a literature. They are folk-literature, learnt, repeated, modified, and handed down by tradition. They are born of the daily life of a people, and they change or disappear as those circumstances alter. Orally composed and orally preserved, they are comparatively brief ; above all, they tend to be rhythmic and formalized. Each *Gattung* develops its own rhetorical scheme, its own introductory formula, often its own vocabulary and metrical structure. Once recognized, they furnish the surest criterion for identifying recurrences of the type.

The relation of *Gattungsforschung* or **Form-Criticism l** to the Catholic study of *genera litteraria* is evidently close. Both techniques stress the significance of style, vocabulary and other formal elements, for the distinguishing of different classes of literary composition. They differ in that the *genera* are considered as norms of literary composition, followed by writers of books ; while the *Gattungen* are primarily oral patterns adopted by the nameless authors of folk-literature. The application of ' Form-Criticism ' is not new, for it was introduced by Gunkel in 1901, nor has it displaced literary analysis ; but it points out the insufficiency of the latter, and is increasingly used as a technique to detect earlier strata in the OT books and to determine the initial function of Biblical material and of the situation in the life of the people that evoked it. Instead of seeking the latest stage of redaction, it traces out the earliest composition of the materials, and thereby, as it were incidentally, establishes a much higher antiquity for their origin than the Wellhausen school was disposed to allow. It is vastly more respectful of the texts, and is rewarded by a deeper understanding of the meaning and intention of the author.

45m The translation, too, of the **law-codes of Israel's neighbours** (Sumerian *c* 1850 B.C. ; Babylonian *c* 1750 B.C. ; Hittite *c* 1300 B.C. ; Assyrian *c* 1100 B.C.) has given an impetus to a re-examination of the Pentateuchal laws. Jirku has shown that these laws are *culturally* more primitive even than the other known Oriental laws of earlier date. He and Alt recognize two principal types of law in Hebrew legislation : a ' casuistic type ' (' If a man . . .'), usually secular in type and patterned after neighbouring codes ; and an ' apodictic type ' (' Thou shalt not . . .'), which is more religious in nature. They argue that the casuistic type goes back to the Sumerian law of the 3rd millennium and was taken over by the Hebrews from the Canaanites during the period of the Judges and the reign of Saul. The ' apodictic ' type, however, cannot be paralleled outside Israel. Tradition traces such law to Moses, and Alt contends that nothing in these laws conflicts with conditions in Israel at the time of Moses. It is, we believe, a reasonable conclusion that the phrase ' Thou shalt not ' was the direct outcome of Moses' religious experience, and that his consciousness of the new *kind* of legal obligation which he had to transmit to the people inspired this new formula, as the construction by which the human language could best convey the urgency and transcendence of Yahweh's will.

n Fresh Analysis of Sources—Finally, even the documentary hypothesis, foundation and starting-point for all critical study of the Pentateuch, has been examined afresh. O. Eissfeldt sums up recent critical trends as three-fold : that of those who assume ' an indifferent attitude ' towards source analysis, or at least do not make it their primary aim, particularly A. Alt and his aetiological school ; that of those who use the analytic method to split the sources further, such as R. Smend, O. Eissfeldt and R. Pfeiffer ; and that of those who manifest ' an actual distrust of the analytic method ', among whom he mentions A. Bea, B. Jacob and U. Cassuto. To what ultimate positions these new directions will lead it is impossible to say. Up to the present the results produced, with the exception of those coming from Form-Criticism, have been negative rather than positive, perhaps because of the fact that no one has produced a synthesis comparable to Wellhausen's. At all events they have not been accepted by the majority of critics. The differences of style, the consistent variations in vocabulary, the doublets and repetitions, all these are facts that remain and require an explanation. Scholars like A. Klostermann and B. D. Eerdmans would solve these problems by the theory of ' supplementation ' of an existing principal document ; but the conception of supplementation is not far removed from the view that separate documents were used in the Pentateuch. In general, therefore, although classical Wellhausenism is no longer tenable, its basic scheme of four sources and their order of precedence continues to receive the endorsement of non-Catholic critics. In this sense, that it expresses a belief in multiple sources against the former concept of the unity of the Pentateuch, the documentary hypothesis still stands.

46a Growth of Catholic Critical Work—After World War I, when the alarm created by Modernism had spent itself, Catholic criticism knew a gradual revival. A place of honour belongs to the *Revue Biblique*, founded in 1893 by Fr. Lagrange, which had continued, ' through evil report and good report ', to publish the solid, scholarly research that has given it so high a place among Catholic Biblical periodicals. Another French publication, edited by Fr. D'Alès, S.J., also had a certain pioneering importance—the *Dictionnaire Apologétique de la Foi Catholique*, issued in parts from 1911–28. Its articles on Biblical subjects, from the standpoint of the Christian apologist, were mostly admirable in their scientific competence and firmly Catholic spirit. The article ' Moïse et Josué ', by J. Touzard (1919), was the first thorough examination of the Pentateuchal question by a Catholic since the decree of 1906 ; and though its conclusions were judged to be too radical, and the Holy Office declared that his theory ' cannot safely be taught '

(' tuto tradi non potest '), still the relative mildness of **46a** this censure showed that the decree was not supposed to have put an end to all discussion. And, in fact, there followed a number of treatments of the question by such scholars as J. Nikel (1924), P. Heinisch (1930), A. Vaccari (1937), M.-J. Lagrange (1938) and J. Coppens (1942), which in various ways combined a Mosaic origin of the materials with later and successive literary redactions.

An interesting theory is proposed by Fr. Vaccari, **b** VD 17 (1937) 371–3. Basing himself upon the view of Kittel and Albright regarding a single original document behind J and E, he suggests that this document, of Mosaic authorship, entered the phase of double transmission in Judah and Ephraim, perhaps after the fall of Shiloh. In the course of the transmission variations appeared, coming in part from local sources. After a period of oral transmission the two recensions were fixed in writing toward the end of the 8th cent. (J) and at the beginning of the 7th (E). They were united in the time of Josias, the redactor making use now of one recension, now of the other ; hence the difference in language and the divine names. At times both recensions were retained ; hence the presence of some doublets. More rarely, as in the account of the flood, they were woven into one narration. In any event, whatever be the true explanation of the phenomena of the Pentateuch, there are many hopeful signs to indicate that Catholic and non-Catholic criticisms, as they progress, tend more and more towards a *rapprochement*.

Space forbids a detailed presentation of current **c** Catholic activities in the OT field. In France, there is the *Revue Biblique* ; in the United States, *The Catholic Biblical Quarterly* ; in England, *Scripture* ; in Spain, *Estudios Biblicos* ; in Italy, *Biblica* and *Orientalia*, published by the Pontifical Biblical Institute ; in Germany, *Biblische Zeitschrift* and *Alttestamentliche Abhandlungen*, etc. Catholic commentaries on the OT are to be found in the collections ' Die Heilige Schrift des Alten Testamentes ', Bonn ; ' Exegetisches Handbuch zum Alten Testament ', Münster ; ' Echter Bibel ', Würzburg ; ' The Westminster Version ', London ; ' La Sacra Bibbia ', Rome ; and in the French Series ' Verbum Salutis ', ' Etudes Bibliques ' and ' Lectio Divina '. The Supplement to Vigouroux' *Dictionnaire de la Bible* offers some of the best work of Catholic scholarship. Today that scholarship is active in every area of OT study and the above list gives no idea of the voluminous production of advanced and highly technical studies. Yet it is only a beginning and much remains to be done, especially in the field of archaeology, linguistics and Biblical theology.

Era of Modernism ended—The great landmark in the **d** modern history of Catholic Biblical criticism was the publication (Sept. 30, 1943) of the Encyclical *Divino afflante Spiritu*, and it was generally hailed as a sign that the era of Modernism was officially closed, that the line between what was dangerous in doctrine and what was not had been clearly drawn, and that now the ' true freedom of the sons of God ' (to quote the Encyclical itself) had been restored to Catholic exegetes.

The Encyclical was prepared for, in a certain sense, by **e** an instructive incident in 1941, which attracted little notice at the time outside Italy. In that summer an anonymous Italian pamphlet was circulated to the Cardinals in Curia and the members of the Italian hierarchy, entitled ' A Grave Danger to the Church and to Souls : the Critico-Scientific System in the Study and Interpretation of Sacred Scripture, its Dangerous Tendencies and its Errors '. The author of this work condemns the scientific study of the Bible as so much ' rationalism, naturalism, modernism, scepticism and atheism '. The scientific spirit is ' a spirit of pride, of presumption, of shallowness '. Study of oriental languages is a mere show of learning, of questionable value ; textual criticism brings the sacred text down to the level of merely human writings ; to correct or criticize the text of the Vulgate is to reject the authority of the Church in proclaiming the Vulgate's authenticity. Rather, the Vulgate text *is* the

46e Bible, and no other need be taken into consideration ; in place of a pedantic exegesis of the literal sense, a meditative exegesis should be adopted ; all kinds of allegorical interpretations should be sought out, and these become the spiritual message of the Wisdom of God.

f The circulation of the pamphlet brought a prompt and vigorous reaction from the Pontifical Biblical Commission. In a letter addressed to the Archbishops and Bishops of Italy, AAS (1941) 465–72, the ' obscurantist ' tone of the pamphlet was censured, its notion of the ' authenticity ' of the Vulgate corrected, the subjectivism of such allegorical interpretation strongly condemned, and, above all, the fundamental importance, for exegesis, of scientific criticism was forcefully —one might almost say indignantly—vindicated. Two years later these points, among others, were stressed and developed in the stately language of the great Encyclical.

g Of the directives of *Divino afflante Spiritu*, which deserves the closest attention from every student or reader of the Bible, we mention here only those which concern our present subject. (References are to paragraph numbers in the translation by G. D. Smith, C.T.S., 1945.) In the first place there is a striking tribute to textual criticism (23) : ' It is true that a few decades ago this criticism was employed by many in a completely arbitrary manner, and frequently in such a way that one would have said that they were using it as a means of introducing their own preconceived opinions into the text. But today it has achieved such stability of principles that it has become an excellent instrument for producing a purer and more accurate edition of the Word of God ; and any abuse can now easily be detected '. Conscious of their human fallibility, probably few textual critics would venture to claim so much ; but it is reassuring to find it said for them by the highest authority.

h In the second place, prominence is given to the analysis of *genera litteraria*, ' literary forms ', as a key to the ' literal sense ' intended by the sacred authors. Fifty years ago this theory had a lukewarm reception in official circles, since it seemed at first a mere subterfuge to avoid having to take the Biblical narratives at their face value ; and von Hummelauer's *Exegetisches zur Inspirationsfrage* (1904), which imagined a large number of *genera* to which the narratives might be assigned, was undoubtedly arbitrary. Now the Encyclical very simply indicates the prime condition and safeguard of this investigation (39) : ' What these (literary forms) were, the exegete cannot determine *a priori*, but only from a careful study of ancient oriental literature '. Then it continues (40) : ' This study has been pursued during the past few decades with greater care and industry than formerly, and has made us better acquainted with the literary forms used in those ancient times . . ' ; therefore (39) ' it is absolutely necessary for the interpreter to go back in spirit to those remote centuries of the East, and to make proper use of the aids afforded by history, archaeology, ethnology and other sciences, in order to discover what literary forms the writers of that early age intended to use, and did in fact employ '. And, not satisfied with laying down **i** the general principle, the Encyclical proceeds to indicate how satisfactorily this method sheds light on the sacred author's meaning by obviating difficulties which have been raised only by an over-literal, ' Europeanized ', exegesis (42) ; ' In many cases in which the sacred authors are accused of some historical inaccuracy or of the inexact recording of some events, it is found to be a question of nothing more than those customary and characteristic forms of expression or styles of narrative which were current in human intercourse among the ancients, and which were in fact quite legitimately and commonly employed '. It is plain that this principle is of great importance in evaluating the ' historicity ' of such books as Tobias, Esther, Judith, or of the first eleven chapters of Genesis.

j Thirdly, while recognizing the due but subordinate place of spiritual or ' allegorical ' exegesis, the Holy Father speaks emphatically of the importance of Biblical theology ; it is this, and not far-fetched allegories, **46j** which makes the reading of Scripture spiritually profitable to a Christian (29) : ' Commentators must have as their chief object to show what is the theological doctrine of each book and text in matters of faith and morals, so that their commentary may not only assist teachers of theology in expounding and corroborating the dogmas of faith, but also be useful to priests in their work of explaining Christian doctrine to the people, and help all the faithful to lead a holy and Christian life.'

Conclusion : further Critical Research encouraged— k Finally here is the golden passage which dispelled the suspicion and misguided opposition which had so long overhung the work of many eminent Catholic scholars (49 f.) : ' Let all other children of the Church bear in mind that the efforts of these valiant labourers in the vineyard of the Lord are to be judged not only with fairness and justice, but also with the greatest charity ; they must avoid that somewhat indiscreet zeal which considers everything new for that very reason a fit object for attack or suspicion. Let them remember above all that the rules and laws laid down by the Church are concerned with the doctrine of faith and morals ; and that among the many matters set forth in the legal, historical, sapiential and prophetical books of the Bible there are only a few whose sense has been declared by the authority of the Church, and that there are equally few concerning which the opinion of the Holy Fathers is unanimous. There consequently remain many matters, and important matters, in the exposition and explanation of which the sagacity and ingenuity of Catholic interpreters can and ought to be freely exercised. . . . This true freedom of the sons of God, loyally maintaining the doctrine of the Church, and at the same time gratefully accepting as a gift of God, and exploiting every contribution that secular knowledge may afford, must be vindicated and upheld by the zeal of all, for it is the condition and source of any real success, of any solid progress in Catholic science '.

That this ' freedom ' is no dead letter was convincingly **l** shown by the latest document to emanate from the Pontifical Biblical Commission, the letter to Cardinal Suhard of Paris (*cf.* § 53*i–l*). The occasion of the letter was a request addressed to the Commission for a clarification of the old decisions on the sources of the Pentateuch and the historicity of the first eleven chapters of Genesis. The Commission expresses its intention of favouring freedom of investigation, citing the text of the Encyclical given above. Of the sources of the Pentateuch it says : ' Nowadays no one any longer questions the existence of these sources or refuses to admit a progressive growth of the Mosaic laws caused by the social and religious conditions of later times—a development which appears also in the historical narratives '. However, since at present, ' even among **m** non-Catholic exegetes there is great divergence of opinion concerning the nature and number of these documents, their distribution and their date ', the Commission prefers for the moment not to issue new decrees on these questions ; but it declares that the old decrees—on apparently historical narratives (*cf.* § 52*j*), on the Mosaic authorship of the Pentateuch (*cf.* § 48*a–d*), on the historicity of Gen 1–3 (*cf.* § 48*e–l*) —are to be liberally interpreted in the light of Pius XII's words on the liberty of the exegete, and that thus understood they will be seen to be ' by no means opposed to a further truly scientific study of these problems, in accordance with conclusions established in the last forty years '. Catholic scholars are formally invited to undertake this ' further study ', which will no doubt demonstrate in the Pentateuch ' the large contribution and profound influence of Moses as author and as legislator '. We think this last phrase is an indication of how ' Mosaic authenticity ' may now be understood. On the paragraph concerning Gen 1–11 (see § 53*l*), we quote the judgement of PEQ 81 (1949) 10 : ' It would be hard to state more explicitly the attitude of the best modern Old Testament scholarship towards the problems of the early chapters of Genesis '.

THE REPLIES
OF THE BIBLICAL COMMISSION

Translated with Introductory Note

By E. F. SUTCLIFFE, S.J.

47a **Bibliography**—Père L. Méchineau, S.J., himself a Consultor of the Biblical Commission, published several works on the Replies of the Commission. The following had all been printed first in the *Civiltà Cattolica*. *Gli Autori e il Tempo della Composizione dei Salmi secondo le Risposte della Commissione Biblica* (Roma, 1911) ; *Il Vangelo di S. Matteo . . .* (Roma, 1912) ; *I Vangeli di S. Marco e di S. Luca e la Questione Sinottica . . .* (Roma, 1913) ; *Gli Atti degli Apostoli e le Epistole Pastorali . . .* (Roma, 1914) ; *L'Epistola agli Ebrei . . .* (Roma, 1917) ; *La Parousia nelle Epistole di S. Paolo e degli altri Apostoli . . .* (Roma, 1921). See also Louis Pirot, *Les Actes des Apôtres et la Commission Biblique*, Paris, 1919 ; *Evangiles et Commission Biblique* in DBV(S) II, 1218-1297, on the Reply concerning the Epistle to the Hebrews, *ibid.* III, 1409-1440, and in collaboration with P. Cruveilhier on that about Genesis, *ibid.* 590-613. On implicit quotations see DBVS II 51-55 by A. Lemonnyer.

b **History and Purpose of the Commission**—The Biblical Commission, the official title of which, as commonly used, is ' Pontificia Commissio de Re Biblica ', was established by Pope Leo XIII when he issued the Apostolic Letter *Vigilantiae* of 30 Oct. 1902 (EB nn. 130 ff.). In this document the function of the Commission is stated to be to procure by all means within its power ' that Holy Writ should everywhere among us receive that more elaborate treatment which the times require and be preserved intact not only from any breath of error but also from all rash opinions '. The work of the Commission in securing the attainment of the first of the aims here put before it has been lightened by the creation of the Pontifical Biblical Institute. This was established by the Apostolic Letter *Vinea Electa*, dated 7 May 1909 (EB nn. 293 ff.). In pursuance of the second aim the Commission has issued positive and negative norms in its various decrees. The immense reverence due to the Bible as the Word of God demands unceasing vigilance in the pastors of the Church into whose keeping the Sacred Scriptures are entrusted, as it must be protected not only from erroneous interpretation but also from the disrespect and danger involved in rash suggestions put forward without solid ground and without regard to the mind of the Church and the analogy of the Faith. This watchful care is the more necessary, as Pope Leo wrote in his Letter *Vigilantiae*, on account of ' the religious obscurity in which Holy Writ is involved '. ' This obscurity,' he adds, ' cannot at times be dissipated by the laws of hermeneutics, but requires the guidance and teaching which God has given in the Church '. In the replies of the Biblical Commission we recognize, therefore, the love of the Church for Holy Scripture, and its wisdom in safeguarding by every means within its power the sacred treasure committed to its charge.

c **The Authority of the Replies of the Biblical Commission** —On this subject we have the explicit teaching of Pope Pius X in the *Motu Proprio Praestantia Scripturae*, 18 Nov. 1907 (ASS 40 [1907] 724 ff. ; EB nn. 278 f. ; Dz 2113 f.) : ' We now declare and expressly enjoin that all without exception are bound by an obligation of conscience to submit to the decisions of the Pontifical Biblical Commission, whether already issued or to be issued hereafter, exactly as to the decrees of the Sacred Congregations which are on matters of doctrine and **47c** approved by the Pope ; nor can anyone who by word or writing attacks the said decrees avoid the note both of disobedience and of rashness or be therefore without grave fault '. In the *Motu Proprio Illibatae custodiendae* of Pius X issued on 29 June 1910, the position of the words ' on matters of doctrine ' was altered so that the text runs ' to submit to the decisions of the Pontifical Biblical Commission on matters of doctrine [' ad doctrinam pertinentibus '] . . . exactly as to the decrees of the Sacred Congregations approved by the Pope ' (AAS 2 [1910] 470 ; EB 349). It is also to be noted that the word ' submit ' in this text is taken from the Letter *Tuas libenter* of Pius IX to the Archbishop of Munich, 21 Dec. 1863 : ' It does not suffice for wise Catholics to accept and revere the aforesaid dogmas of the Church, but it is further their duty to submit to the decisions on matters of doctrine issued by the Papal Congregations ' (Dz. 1684 ; EB 281).

It is the teaching of most theologians that this submis- **d** sion involves an internal assent. This cannot, however, be given in the spirit of divine faith, as the decrees of the Commission are not infallible, infallibility being a personal prerogative of the Holy Father which cannot be delegated. The assent is religious and is based on the very high authority entrusted by the Vicar of Christ to the Commission. In our daily lives we frequently give an internal assent to statements made to us by persons whom we know to be in a position to speak with knowledge on the subject in question, although we are of course aware that their utterances are anything but infallible. Theologians further recognize that as the decrees are not to be accepted with the assent that is due to matters defined as of faith, the case is not impossible in which some competent person may be conscientiously convinced that he has solid and satisfactory reasons for doubt. In such a case, they hold, assent may be legitimately withheld. The obligation of due respect, of avoiding scandal, of abstention from any form of attack on the decrees would remain. For a fuller discussion see *e.g.* C. Pesch, S.J., *Compendium Theologiae Dogmaticae* (1926³) 241 f. ; Lucien Choupin, S.J., *Valeur des Décisions Doctrinales et Disciplinaires du Saint-Siège* (Paris, 1913²), 82-94, 453-457. On p 84 Père Choupin writes as follows : ' By such decisions the Holy See wishes to provide for the *safety* of doctrine, to forestall dangers of the faith being perverted, rather than to pronounce a judgement *directly* on the *absolute truth* or *falsehood* of the proposition itself. . . . The meaning of a *doctrinal decision* issued by the supreme teaching authority but none the less not guaranteed by the gift of infallibility is this : Given the circumstances, the state of knowledge, it is prudent and *safe* to regard this proposition as true, in conformity to Holy Scripture . . . etc. Or, it is prudent and *safe* to regard this proposition as erroneous, rash, contrary to Holy Scripture, etc. ' (author's italics). See also the article *Commission Biblique* by L. Pirot in DBV(S) 2 (1934) 103-13.

Other theologians keep closer to the actual wording **e** adopted by Pius X. Thus the Abbé P. Cruveilhier writes as follows : ' The submission demanded by the Pope is obedience of the mind and will consisting at least " in not opposing by word or writing the decisions of the Biblical Commission ". In other words it is

47e formally forbidden to a Catholic exegete publicly to oppose the decisions of the Biblical Commission. The fact that this prohibition is directed against public manifestations hostile to the mind of the Commission makes it certain that some liberty is left to the exegete at least in regard to some decisions. If no one of them is without relation to the Faith, some concern dogma only more or less indirectly ', DBVS III (1938) 1520.

f In the letter by which he entrusted to the Benedictine Order the task of revising the text of the Vulgate Cardinal Rampolla, then President of the Biblical Commission, recalled that among the duties entrusted to the Commission was that of ' providing Catholic teaching with wise and safe norms ' (EB 178). And the introductory phrase to the Reply concerning implicit quotations speaks of giving ' a directive norm ' to students of Scripture. Is there a contradiction implied in calling a norm at one and the same time directive and obligatory ? Clearly there would be if the norm were intended as nothing more than advice which could be followed or not at will ; but there is none when the directive norm is intended to have binding force, is given with authority delegated by the Pope, and receives his sanction (*cf.* P. Castillon in NRT (1907) 245n).

g **The Interpretation of the Replies**—It must be borne in mind that the Replies are juridical documents and are intended to be interpreted as such. The wording is carefully chosen to convey a definite meaning and this meaning the interpretation should neither extend nor restrict. For instance the first question about the Mosaic authorship of the Pentateuch does not ask simply whether Moses was the author of the Pentateuch. It asks whether the arguments that have been adduced against the Mosaic authorship when pitted against all the evidence for that authorship justify the statement that Moses was not the author. As the answer is in the negative, the direction here given amounts to this that no known arguments avail to disprove the Mosaic authorship. It would be against the mind of the authors of this Reply to say that the Biblical Commission taught positively that Moses wrote the Pentateuch. This does not mean that the Commission (or for that matter the present writer) wishes to suggest the slightest doubt about the Mosaic authorship. The fact only emphasizes the extreme care with which these directions have been drawn up and the equal care that should be used in their interpretation (*cf.* §§ 45*e*, 46*m*).

h It is important, further, to remember that the Replies are not all of the same character. Pope Leo XIII in his Apostolic Letters *Vigilantiae* by which he instituted the Commission laid it down as part of its duty to exercise a proper control over the chief matters debated among Catholics and to bring both the guidance of its judgement and the weight of its authority to bear with a view to deciding them. This, the Pope adds, will give the Holy See suitable occasion ' for declaring what must be inviolably held by Catholics, what should be reserved for further investigation, and what should be left to the judgement of each one ' (EB 137). Several of the Replies treat only of what may be ' prudently ' affirmed or denied.

i **The Form of the Replies**—The Replies are couched in the form of question and answer. This form is due to the fact that among the duties entrusted to the Commission is that of ' giving replies when consulted and asked its opinion ' (EB 138), and also to the existing practice of the Roman Congregations. Actually the only published Replies addressed explicitly to an individual inquirer are those in § 53*a* and *i–m*. The rest have been addressed to the Church at large. Questions drawn up by the Commission itself are analogous to the inspired questions addressed to Cabinet Ministers in the House of Commons.

j **Note on the Following Translation**—The decrees are gathered here for the convenience of reference. With the same purpose in view the order given is not the chronological order of their appearance but that of the books of the Bible in the Vulgate and Douay Version,

so far as this is possible. The translator has not felt **47j** free to attempt to present the decrees in a form altogether corresponding to the character of our own language. This would have helped the cause of clarity, but there does not appear to be justification for breaking up the long sentences of juridical documents.

On the Mosaic Authorship of the Pentateuch, June 27, **48a** 1906 (ASS 39 [1906–07] 377 f. ; EB 174 ff. ; Dz 1997 ff.) :

I : Are the arguments gathered by critics to impugn the Mosaic authorship of the sacred books designated by the name of the Pentateuch of such weight in spite of the cumulative evidence of many passages of both Testaments, the unbroken unanimity of the Jewish people, and furthermore of the constant tradition of the Church besides the internal indications furnished by the text itself, as to justify the statement that these books are not of Mosaic authorship but were put together from sources mostly of post-Mosaic date ? Answer : In the negative.

II : Does the Mosaic authorship of the Pentateuch **b** necessarily imply a production of the whole work of such a character as to impose the belief that each and every word was written by Moses' own hand or was by him dictated to secretaries ; or is it a legitimate hypothesis that he conceived the work himself under the guidance of divine inspiration and then entrusted the writing of it to one or more persons, with the understanding that they reproduced his thoughts with fidelity and neither wrote nor omitted anything contrary to his will, and that finally the work composed after this fashion was approved by Moses, its principal and inspired author, and was published under his name ? Answer : In the negative to the first and in the affirmative to the second part.

III : Without prejudice to the Mosaic authorship of **c** the Pentateuch, may it be granted that in the composition of his work Moses used sources, written documents namely or oral traditions, from which in accordance with the special aim he entertained and under the guidance of divine inspiration he borrowed material and inserted it in his work either word for word or in substance, either abbreviated or amplified ? Answer : In the affirmative.

IV : Subject to the Mosaic authorship and the in- **d** tegrity of the Pentateuch being substantially safeguarded, may it be admitted that in the protracted course of centuries certain modifications befell it, such as : additions made after the death of Moses by an inspired writer, or glosses and explanations inserted in the text, certain words and forms changed from archaic into more recent speech, finally incorrect readings due to the fault of scribes which may be the subject of inquiry and judgement according to the laws of textual criticism ? Answer : In the affirmative, saving the judgement of the Church.

NOTE : see the later declaration on this subject, § 53*i–k*.

Concerning the Historical Character of the First Three **e** **Chapters of Genesis,** June 30, 1909 (AAS I [1909] 567 ff. ; EB 332 ff. ; Dz 2121 ff.).

I : Do the various exegetical systems excogitated and defended under the guise of science to exclude the literal historical sense of the first three chapters of Genesis rest on a solid foundation ? Answer : In the negative.

II : Notwithstanding the historical character and **f** form of Genesis, the special connection of the first three chapters with one another and with the following chapters, the manifold testimonies of the Scriptures both of the Old and of the New Testaments, the almost unanimous opinion of the holy Fathers and the traditional view which the people of Israel also has handed on and the Church has always held, may it be taught that : the aforesaid three chapters of Genesis contain not accounts of actual events, accounts, that is, which correspond to objective reality and historical truth, but either fables derived from the mythologies and

48f cosmogonies of ancient peoples and accommodated by the sacred writer to monotheistic doctrine after the expurgation of any polytheistic error ; or allegories and symbols without any foundation in objective reality proposed under the form of history to inculcate religious and philosophical truths ; or finally legends in part historical and in part fictitious freely composed with a view to instruction and edification ? Answer : In the negative to both parts.

g III : In particular may the literal historical sense be called in doubt in the case of facts narrated in the same chapters which touch the foundations of the Christian religion : as are, among others, the creation of all things by God in the beginning of time ; the special creation of man ; the formation of the first woman from the first man ; the unity of the human race ; the original felicity of our first parents in the state of justice, integrity, and immortality ; the command given by God to man to test his obedience ; the transgression of the divine command at the instigation of the devil under the form of a serpent ; the degradation of our first parents from that primeval state of innocence ; and the promise of a future Redeemer ? Answer : In the negative.

h IV : In the interpretation of those passages in these chapters which the Fathers and Doctors understood in different manners without proposing anything certain and definite, is it lawful, without prejudice to the judgement of the Church and with attention to the analogy of faith, to follow and defend the opinion that commends itself to each one ? Answer : In the affirmative.

i V : Must each and every word and phrase occurring in the aforesaid chapters always and necessarily be understood in its literal sense, so that it is never lawful to deviate from it, even when it appears obvious that the diction is employed in an applied sense, either metaphorical or anthropomorphical, and either reason forbids the retention or necessity imposes the abandonment of the literal sense ? Answer : In the negative. [The last clause from ' either reason ' is from St Augustine, *De Gen. ad litt.* Lib. VIII cap. 7, n. 13, EFS.]

j VI : Provided that the literal and historical sense is presupposed, may certain passages in the same chapters, in the light of the example of the holy Fathers and of the Church itself, be wisely and profitably interpreted in an allegorical and prophetic sense ? Answer : In the affirmative.

k VII : As it was not the mind of the sacred author in the composition of the first chapter of Genesis to give scientific teaching about the internal constitution of visible things and the entire order of creation, but rather to communicate to his people a popular notion in accord with the current speech of the time and suited to the understanding and capacity of men, must the exactness of scientific language be always meticulously sought for in the interpretation of these matters ? Answer : In the negative.

l VIII : In the designation and distinction of the six days mentioned in the first chapter of Genesis may the word *Yôm* (day) be taken either in the literal sense for the natural day or in an applied sense for a certain space of time, and may this question be the subject of free discussion among exegetes ? Answer : In the affirmative.

NOTE : See also the later declaration on this subject, § 53*ij–lm.*

49a **Concerning the Authors and Date of the Psalms,** May 1, 1910 (AAS II [1910] 354 f. ; EB 340 ff. ; Dz 2129 ff.) :

I : Have the titles *Psalms of David, Hymns of David, Book of the Psalms of David, Davidic Psalter,* employed in ancient collections and in the Councils themselves to designate the book of 150 psalms of the Old Testament ; and also the opinion of a number of Fathers and Doctors, who held that all the psalms of the Psalter without exception were to be ascribed to David alone, such weight that David should be held to be the only author of the whole Psalter ? Answer : In the negative.

II : Does the agreement of the Hebrew text with the **49b** Greek Alexandrine text and other ancient versions give ground for a valid argument that the titles of the psalms prefixed to the Hebrew text are more ancient than the Septuagint version ; and consequently, if not from the very authors of the psalms, at least derive from an ancient Jewish tradition ? Answer : In the affirmative.

III : Can the aforesaid titles of the psalms, witnesses **c** of Jewish tradition, be prudently called in doubt when there is no serious reason against their being genuine ? Answer : In the negative.

IV : In view of the not infrequent testimonies of sacred **d** Scripture to the natural talent, helped by a special gift of the Holy Ghost, which David had for the composition of religious songs, of his arrangements for the liturgical chant of the psalms, of the attribution of psalms to him both in the Old Testament and in the New as well as in the superscriptions prefixed of old to the psalms ; in view, moreover, of the agreement of the Jews, of the Fathers and Doctors of the Church, can it be prudently denied that David was the principal author of the songs of the Psalter, or on the contrary, affirmed that only a few songs are to be assigned to the royal psalmist ? Answer : In the negative to both parts.

V : In particular is it right to deny the Davidic origin **e** of those psalms which are explicitly cited under David's name in the Old or New Testament, among which are to be mentioned more especially psalm 2 *Quare fremuerunt gentes* ; psalm 15 *Conserva me, Domine* ; psalm 17 *Diligam te, Domine, fortitudo mea* ; psalm 31 *Beati quorum remissae sunt iniquitates* ; psalm 68 *Salvum me fac, Deus* ; psalm 109 *Dixit Dominus Domino meo* ? Answer : In the negative.

VI : May the opinion of those be admitted who hold **f** that among the psalms of the Psalter there are some, either of David's or of other authors, which on account of liturgical and musical reasons, the negligence of scribes, or other causes unknown have been divided into several or united into one ; also that there are other psalms, like the *Miserere mei, Deus,* which for the purpose of being better adapted to historical circumstances or solemnities of the Jewish people, were subjected to some slight rehandling or modification by the omission or addition of one or two verses, without prejudice however to the inspiration of the whole sacred text ? Answer : In the affirmative to both parts.

VII : Is it possible to maintain as probable the opinion **g** of those more recent writers who, relying on purely internal indications or an incorrect interpretation of the sacred text, have attempted to show that not a few psalms were composed after the times of Esdras and Nehemias and even in the Maccabean age ? Answer : In the negative.

VIII : On the authority of the manifold witness of the **h** sacred books of the New Testament and the unanimous agreement of the Fathers in harmony with the acknowledgement of Jewish writers, is it necessary to admit a number of prophetic and Messianic psalms, which foretold the future Saviour's coming, kingdom, priesthood, passion, death, and resurrection ; and consequently is it necessary to reject altogether the opinion of those who pervert the prophetic and Messianic character of the psalms and limit these oracles about Christ merely to the foretelling of the future lot of the chosen people ? Answer : In the affirmative to both parts.

Concerning the Character and Author of the Book of **i** **Isaias,** June 29, 1908 (ASS 41 [1908] 613 f. ; EB 287 ff. ; Dz 2115 ff.).

I : May it be taught that the predictions read in the Book of Isaias—and throughout the Scriptures—are not predictions properly so called, but either narrations put together after the event, or, if anything has to be acknowledged as foretold before the event, that the prophet foretold it not in accordance with a supernatural revelation of God who foreknows future events, but by conjectures formed felicitously and shrewdly by natural sharpness of mind on the basis of previous experience ? Answer : In the negative.

49j II : Can the opinion that Isaias and the other prophets did not put forth predictions except about events that were to happen in the immediate future or after no long space of time, be reconciled with the predictions, in particular Messianic and eschatological, certainly put forth by the same prophets concerning the distant future, and also with the common opinion of the holy Fathers who unanimously assert that the prophets also made prophecies that were to be fulfilled after many centuries ? Answer : In the negative.

k III : May it be admitted that the prophets, not only as correctors of human depravity and preachers of the divine word for the benefit of their hearers, but also as foretellers of future events, must consistently have addressed, not future, but present contemporary hearers in such a manner that they could be clearly understood by them ; and that in consequence the second part of the Book of Isaias (chapters 40–66), in which the prophet addresses and consoles, not the Jewish contemporaries of Isaias, but as if living among them, the Jews mourning in the Babylonian exile, could not have Isaias, long since dead, for its author, but must be ascribed to some unknown prophet living among the exiles ? Answer : In the negative.

l IV : Should the philological argument drawn from language and style to impugn identity of authorship throughout the Book of Isaias be deemed of such force as to compel a man of sound judgement with competent knowledge of Hebrew and of the art of criticism to recognize several authors in the same book ? Answer : In the negative.

m V : Do there exist arguments which even when taken together avail to demonstrate that the Book of Isaias must be attributed not to Isaias himself alone, but to two or even several authors ? Answer : In the negative.

50a Concerning the Author, the Date, and the Historical Truth of the Gospel according to Matthew, June 19, 1911 (AAS 3 [1911] 294 ff. ; EB 401 ff. ; Dz 2148 ff.).
I : Having regard to the universal and unwavering agreement of the Church ever since the first centuries, an agreement clearly attested by the express witness of the Fathers, by the titles of the Gospel manuscripts, the most ancient versions of the sacred books and the lists handed on by the holy Fathers, by ecclesiastical writers, by Popes and Councils, and finally by the liturgical use of the Church in the East and in the West, may and should it be affirmed as certain that Matthew, the Apostle of Christ, was in fact the author of the Gospel current under his name ? Answer : In the affirmative.

b II : Should the verdict of tradition be considered to give adequate support to the statement that Matthew wrote before the other Evangelists and wrote the first Gospel in the native language then used by the Jews of Palestine for whom the work was intended ? Answer : In the affirmative to both parts.

c III : Can the composition of this original text be postponed till after the time of the destruction of Jerusalem, so that the prophecies it contains about that destruction were written after the event ; or should the oft-quoted text of Irenaeus (*Adv. Haer.* Lib. 3, cap. 1, n. 2), of uncertain and controverted interpretation, be considered to have such weight as to impose the rejection of the opinion more in harmony with tradition according to which the composition of the Gospel was completed even before the arrival of Paul in Rome ? Answer : In the negative to both parts.
[In some editions of St Irenaeus this text is given in n. 1.]

d IV : Can even probable arguments be given in support of that opinion of certain recent writers according to which Matthew did not write a Gospel properly and strictly so-called, such as has been handed down to us, but merely a collection of the sayings or discourses of Christ which were drawn on by another anonymous author, whom they make the editor of the Gospel itself ? Answer : In the negative.

e V : Can the fact that all the Fathers and ecclesiastical writers and even the Church itself from its very cradle **50e** have used as canonical only the Greek text of the Gospel known under the name of Matthew, not even those being excepted who explicitly taught that the Apostle Matthew wrote in his native tongue, provide certain proof that the Greek Gospel is identical in substance with the Gospel written by that Apostle in his native tongue ? Answer : In the affirmative.

f VI : Do the facts that the aim of the author of the first Gospel is chiefly dogmatic and apologetic, namely, to prove to the Jews that Jesus was the Messias foretold by the prophets and born of the lineage of David, and that moreover in the arrangement of the facts and discourses which he narrates and reports, he does not always follow chronological order, justify the deduction that they ought not to be accepted as true ? Or may it also be affirmed that the accounts of the deeds and discourses of Christ, which are read in that Gospel, underwent a certain alteration and adaptation under the influence of the prophecies of the Old Testament and the more mature condition of the Church and are consequently not in conformity with historical truth ? Answer : In the negative to both parts.

g VII : In particular ought it to be held that there is no solid foundation to the opinions of those who call in doubt the historical authenticity of the first two chapters, in which an account is given of the genealogy and infancy of Christ, as also of certain passages of great dogmatic importance, such as are those which concern the primacy of Peter (16, 17–19), the form of baptism entrusted to the Apostles together with the mission of preaching everywhere (28, 19 f.), the Apostles' profession of faith in the divinity of Christ (14, 33), and other similar matters which are found in a special form in Matthew ? Answer : In the affirmative.

Concerning the Authors, Dates, and Historical Truth h of the Gospels according to Mark and Luke, June 26, 1912 (AAS 4 [1912] 463 ff. ; EB 408 ff. ; Dz 2155 ff.].
I : Does the clear verdict of tradition showing extraordinary unanimity from the beginnings of the Church and confirmed by manifold evidence, namely the explicit attestations of the holy Fathers and ecclesiastical writers, the quotations and allusions occurring in their writings, the use made by ancient heretics, the versions of the books of the New Testament, almost all the manuscripts including the most ancient, and also internal reasons drawn from the text of the sacred books impose the definite affirmation that Mark, the disciple and interpreter of Peter, and Luke, the doctor, the assistant (adiutorem) and companion of Paul, were really the authors of the Gospels that are attributed to them respectively ? Answer : In the affirmative.
[AAS and EB print *adiutorem*, Dz *auditorem*.]

i II : Are the reasons by which certain critics strive to prove that the last twelve verses of the Gospel of Mark (16, 9–20) were not written by Mark himself but were added by another hand, of such a character as to justify the statement that they are not to be accepted as inspired and canonical ? Or do they prove at least that Mark was not the author of the said verses ? Answer : In the negative to both parts.

j III : Similarly is it lawful to doubt the inspiration and canonicity of Luke's accounts of the infancy of Christ (chapters 1 and 2) ; or of the apparition of the Angel strengthening Jesus and the sweat of blood (22, 43 f.) ? Or can it at any rate be shown by solid reasons—a view preferred by ancient heretics and favoured also by certain modern critics—that the said accounts do not belong to the genuine Gospel of Luke ? Answer : In the negative to both parts.

k IV : Can and should those very few and altogether exceptional documents in which the Canticle *Magnificat* is attributed not to our Blessed Lady but to Elizabeth, in any way prevail against the unanimous testimony of almost all manuscripts both of the original Greek text and of the versions, and against the interpretation which is clearly demanded no less by the context than by the mind of our Lady herself and the constant tradition of the Church ? Answer : In the negative.

50 l **V** : As regards the chronological order of the Gospels is it right to depart from the opinion supported by the very ancient and constant testimony of tradition, which avers that after Matthew, who before all the others wrote his Gospel in his native tongue, Mark was the second in order, and Luke the third to write ? Or on the other hand is opposition to be found between this opinion and that which asserts the second and third Gospels to have been written before the Greek version of the first Gospel ? Answer : In the negative to both parts.

m **VI** : Is it lawful to postpone the date of composition of the Gospels of Mark and Luke till after the destruction of the city of Jerusalem ? Or, on the ground that our Lord's prophecy concerning the destruction of that city appears more detailed in Luke, can it be maintained that his Gospel at least was written after the siege had begun ? Answer : In the negative to both parts.

n **VII** : Should it be affirmed that the Gospel of Luke preceded the Acts of the Apostles ; and as this book, written by the same Luke (Acts 1, 1 f.), was finished at the close of the Apostle's imprisonment at Rome (Acts 28, 30 f.), that his Gospel was not composed after this time ? Answer : In the affirmative.

o **VIII** : In view both of the witness of tradition and the internal evidence concerning the sources used by each Evangelist in writing his Gospel, is it prudent to doubt the opinion that Mark wrote in accordance with the preaching of Peter and Luke in accordance with that of Paul, and also that these Evangelists had, besides, other trustworthy sources, whether oral or written ? Answer : In the negative.

p **IX** : Do the words and deeds which are reported by Mark accurately and almost in verbal agreement with Peter's preaching, and are faithfully set forth by Luke who had ' diligently attained to all things from the beginning ' through the help of entirely trustworthy witnesses ' who from the beginning were eye-witnesses and ministers of the word ' (Luke 1, 2 f.) rightly claim for themselves as historical that entire belief that the Church has always placed in them ? Or on the contrary ought the same facts and deeds to be regarded as in part at least destitute of historical truth, either on the ground that the writers were not eye-witnesses or that in the case of both Evangelists defects of order and disagreement in the succession of events are not seldom detected, or that, as they came on the scene and wrote rather late, they could not help recording ideas foreign to the mind of Christ and the Apostles or events already more or less distorted by popular imagination, or finally, that they indulged in preconceived dogmatic ideas, each one in accordance with his own aim ? Answer : In the affirmative to the first part, in the negative to the second.

51a **On the Synoptic Problem or the Mutual Relations of the First Three Gospels,** June 26, 1912 (AAS 4 [1912] 465 ; EB 117 f. ; Dz 2164 ff.).
I : Provided all is safeguarded that according to previous decisions must be safeguarded, especially concerning the authenticity and integrity of the three Gospels of Matthew, Mark, and Luke, the substantial identity of the Greek Gospel of Matthew with its original text, and the chronological order in which they were written, in order to explain their mutual similarities and dissimilarities, is it lawful for exegetes, given the many different and contradictory opinions proposed by writers, to discuss the question freely and to have recourse to the hypotheses of tradition, whether written or oral, or also of the dependence of one Gospel on another or on others that preceded it ? Answer : In the affirmative.

b **II** : Ought those to be considered faithful to the above prescriptions, who without the support of any traditional evidence or historical argument readily embrace what is commonly called ' the two-document hypothesis ', the purpose of which is to explain the composition of the Greek Gospel of Matthew and the Gospel of Luke chiefly by their dependence on the Gospel of Mark and a so-called collection of the dis-

courses of our Lord ; and are they consequently free to **51b** advocate it ? Answer : In the negative to both parts.
Concerning the Author and Historical Truth of the **c** **Fourth Gospel,** May 29, 1907 (ASS 40 [1907] 383 f. ; EB 180 ff. ; Dz 2110).
I : Does the constant, universal, and solemn tradition of the Church dating back to the second century and witnessed to principally : (a) by the holy Fathers, by ecclesiastical writers, and even by heretics, whose testimonies and allusions must have been derived from the disciples or first successors of the Apostles and so be linked with the very origin of the book ; (b) by the name of the author of the fourth Gospel having been at all times and places in the canon and lists of the sacred books ; (c) by the most ancient manuscripts of those books and the various versions ; (d) by public liturgical use in the whole world from the very beginnings of the Church ; prove that John the Apostle and no other is to be acknowledged as the author of the fourth Gospel, and that by an historical argument so firmly established (without reference to theological considerations) that the reasons adduced by critics to the contrary in no way weaken this tradition ? Answer : In the affirmative.

II : Should, further, internal reasons derived from the **d** text of the fourth Gospel considered by itself, from the witness of the writer and the manifest relationship of the Gospel itself to the first Epistle of John the Apostle, be judged to confirm the tradition that unhesitatingly attributes the fourth Gospel to the same Apostle ? And can the difficulties which arise from a comparison of the same Gospel with the other three, in view of the differences of time, aim, and hearers, for whom or against whom the author wrote, be given reasonable solutions, as has been done by the holy Fathers and Catholic exegetes in various works ? Answer : In the affirmative to both parts.

III : Notwithstanding the practice which has flourished **e** consistently in the whole Church from the earliest times, of arguing from the fourth Gospel as from a strictly historical document, and in consideration no less of the special character of the same Gospel and the manifest intention of the author to illustrate and vindicate the divinity of Christ from the very acts and discourses of our Lord, may it be said that the facts narrated in the fourth Gospel were invented wholly or in part, as allegories or doctrinal symbols and that the discourses of our Lord are not properly and truly the discourses of our Lord himself but the theological compositions of the writer though placed in the mouth of our Lord ? Answer : In the negative.

Concerning the Author, the Date, and the Historical **f** **Truth of the Acts of the Apostles,** June 12, 1913 (AAS 5 [1913] 291 f. ; EB 419 ff. ; Dz 2166 ff.).
I : In view especially of the tradition of the whole Church dating back to the earliest ecclesiastical writers, and in consideration of the internal characteristics of the book of Acts whether considered in itself or in its relation to the third Gospel, and especially of the mutual affinity and connection of both prologues (Luke 1, 1–4 ; Acts 1, 1 f.), should it be held as certain that the volume with the title *Actus Apostolorum* or Πράξεις Ἀποστόλων had the Evangelist Luke for its author ? Answer : In the affirmative.

II : Can critical reasons derived from language and **g** style, from the character of the narrative, and from the unity of aim and teaching, demonstrate that the Acts of the Apostles should be attributed to only one author ; and that consequently there is no foundation at all for the opinion of recent writers according to which Luke was not the only author of the book but different authors are recognized in the said book ? Answer : In the affirmative to both parts.

III : In particular, do those sections, so noticeable in **h** the Acts, in which the use of the third person is abandoned and the first person plural introduced (We-passages), weaken the unity of composition and the authenticity ; or, historically and philosophically considered, should they rather be said to confirm it ?

51h Answer : In the negative to the first part ; in the affirmative to the second.

i IV : Does the fact that the book hardly mentions the two years of Paul's first imprisonment at Rome and ends abruptly, warrant the inference that the author wrote a second but lost work or intended to write one, and consequently can the date of the composition of the Acts be postponed till long after the said captivity? Or rather is it legitimately and rightly to be maintained that Luke finished the book towards the close of the first imprisonment of the Apostle Paul at Rome? Answer : In the negative to the first part ; in the affirmative to the second.

j V : If consideration be given both to the frequent and easy intercourse that without doubt Luke had with the first and chief founders of the Church in Palestine and with Paul, the Apostle of the Gentiles, whom he helped in his preaching of the Gospel and accompanied on his journeys, and to his habitual industry and diligence in seeking witnesses and in personal observation of events, and finally to the frequently obvious and remarkable agreement of the Acts with Paul's own Epistles and with the more exact historical records, should it be held for certain that Luke had at his disposal entirely trustworthy sources and used them carefully, honestly, and faithfully, so that he rightly claims for himself full authority as an historian? Answer : In the affirmative.

k VI : Are the difficulties commonly raised both from the supernatural facts narrated by Luke, and from the report of certain discourses, which on account of their brevity are thought to be invented and adapted to circumstances, and from certain passages in at least apparent disagreement with history, whether profane or biblical, and finally from certain narrations in apparent conflict either with the author of Acts himself or with other sacred authors, of such a nature as to throw doubt on or at least in some measure to diminish the historical authority of Acts? Answer : In the negative.

l **Concerning the Author, the Integrity, and the Date of the Pastoral Epistles of St Paul,** June 12, 1913 (AAS 5 [1913] 292 f. ; EB 425 ff. ; EB 425 ff. ; Dz 2172 ff.).
I : In view of the tradition of the Church universally and firmly maintained from the beginning, as is witnessed in many ways by ancient ecclesiastical records, should it be held as certain that the Pastoral Epistles, the two, namely, to Timothy and another to Titus, notwithstanding the effrontery of certain heretics, who without giving any reason expunged them from the number of Pauline Epistles as being opposed to their tenets, were written by the Apostle Paul himself and were always listed among the genuine and canonical Epistles? Answer : In the affirmative.

m II : Can the so-called fragmentary hypothesis introduced and propounded in different ways by certain recent critics, who without any plausible reason and even at variance among themselves, maintain that the Pastoral Epistles were put together by unknown authors at a later date out of fragments of the Epistles or out of lost Pauline Epistles with notable additions, cause even any slight weakening of the clear and unshaken testimony of tradition? Answer : In the negative.

n III : Do the difficulties commonly alleged on many grounds, either on account of the style and language of the author, or of the errors, especially of the Gnostics, described as already then current, or of the presupposition that the ecclesiastical hierarchy was in an already developed state, and other similar arguments to the contrary, in any way weaken the opinion that holds the genuineness of the Pastoral Epistles to be established and certain? Answer : In the negative.

o IV : As the opinion that the Apostle Paul was twice imprisoned at Rome should be considered certain on account no less of historical reasons than of ecclesiastical tradition in harmony with the testimonies of the holy Fathers both in East and West, and also on account of the evidence readily available both in the abrupt conclusion of the Acts and in the Pauline Epistles **51o** written at Rome and especially in the second to Timothy ; can it be safely stated that the Pastoral Epistles were written in the interval between the liberation of the Apostle from the first imprisonment and his death? Answer : In the affirmative.

Concerning the Author and Manner of Composition 52a of the Epistle to the Hebrews, June 24, 1914 (AAS 6 [1914] 417 f. ; EB 429 ff. ; Dz 2176 ff.).
I : Are the doubts about the divine inspiration and Pauline origin of the Epistle to the Hebrews which influenced certain minds in the West in the first centuries, chiefly because of its abuse by heretics, of such importance that, bearing in mind the unbroken, unanimous, and unwavering affirmation of the eastern Fathers supported after the fourth century by the entire assent of the whole western Church, due weight also being given to the acts of the Popes and sacred Councils, especially that of Trent, and to the constant usage of the universal Church, it is lawful to hesitate about reckoning it definitively not only among the canonical Epistles—which has been defined as a matter of faith —but also among the genuine Epistles of the Apostle Paul? Answer : In the negative.

b II : Can the arguments commonly based either on the unusual absence of Paul's name and the omission of the customary introduction and salutation in the Epistle to the Hebrews—or on the purity of its Greek, the elegance and perfection of its diction and style—or on the character of its quotations and arguments from the Old Testament—or on certain differences alleged to exist between the doctrine of this and the other Pauline Epistles, in any way invalidate its Pauline origin? Or rather do the perfect unanimity in teaching and thought, the resemblance of the admonitions and exhortations, and the agreement in phrase and even in words pointed out also by some non-Catholics, which are seen to exist between it and the other writings of the Apostle of the Gentiles, clearly indicate and confirm the same Pauline origin? Answer : In the negative to the first part ; in the affirmative to the second.

c III : Should the Apostle Paul be considered the author of this Epistle after such manner that he must necessarily be said, not only to have conceived and expressed it all under the inspiration of the Holy Ghost, but also to have given it the form that it actually has? Answer : In the negative, saving the further judgement of the Church.

Concerning the Parousia or Second Coming of our d Lord Jesus Christ in the Epistles of the Apostle St Paul, June 18, 1915 (AAS 7 [1915] 357 f. ; EB 432 ff. ; Dz 2179 ff.).
I : In order to meet the difficulties occurring in the Epistles of St Paul and other Apostles in passages which treat of the ' Parousia ', as it is called, or second coming of our Lord Jesus Christ, is it allowed to a Catholic exegete to assert that, though the Apostles under the inspiration of the Holy Ghost teach nothing erroneous, they none the less express their own human opinions which may rest on error or misconception? Answer : In the negative.

e II : In view of the correct concept of the apostolic office and the undoubted fidelity of St Paul to the teaching of the Master ; in view also of the Catholic doctrine concerning the inspiration and inerrancy of Holy Scripture according to which whatever a sacred Writer asserts, declares, suggests, should be held to be asserted, declared, suggested by the Holy Ghost ; and after a careful examination on their own merits of the passages in the Epistles of St Paul which are in complete harmony with our Lord's own manner of speaking, should it be asserted that the Apostle Paul said nothing whatever in his writings which is not in complete harmony with that ignorance of the time of the Parousia which Christ himself proclaimed to belong to men? Answer : In the affirmative.

f III : After consideration of the Greek phrase ἡμεῖς οἱ ζῶντες οἱ περιλειπόμενοι ; and after careful examina-

52f tion of the exposition of the Fathers, above all of St John Chrysostom, who was completely at home both in his native language and in the Pauline Epistles, is it lawful to reject as far-fetched and destitute of any solid foundation the interpretation traditional in the Catholic schools (and retained even by the Reformers of the sixteenth century) that explains the words of St Paul in 1 Thessalonians 4, 15–17, without in any way involving the assertion that the Parousia was so near that the Apostle counted himself and his readers among the faithful who will be left alive and go to meet Christ ? Answer : In the negative.

g **Concerning the False Interpretation of Two Biblical Texts,** July 1, 1933 (AAS 25 [1933] 344) ; Dz 2272–3. I : Is it right for a Catholic, especially after the authentic interpretation given by the Princes of the Apostles (Acts 2, 24–33 ; 13, 35–37) to interpret the words of Psalm 15, 10 f. : ' Thou wilt not leave my soul in hell, nor wilt thou give thy holy one to see corruption. Thou hast made known to me the ways of life ', as if the sacred author did not speak of the resurrection of our Lord Jesus Christ ? Answer : In the negative.

h II : Is it licit to assert that the words of Jesus Christ, which are read in St Matthew 16, 26 : ' What doth it profit a man, if he gain the whole world and suffer the loss of his own soul ? ' and similarly those in St Luke 9, 25 : ' What is a man advantaged, if he gain the whole world and lose himself and cast away himself ? ' in the literal sense do not regard the eternal salvation of the soul, but only man's temporal life, notwithstanding the tenor of the words themselves and their context besides the unanimous interpretation of Catholics ? Answer : In the negative.

i **On Implicit Quotations in Holy Scripture,** Feb. 13, 1905 (ASS 37 [1904–05] 666 ; EB 153 ; Dz 1979).

To secure a directive norm for students of Holy Scripture the following question was proposed to the Pontifical Biblical Commission, namely :

To solve difficulties occurring in certain texts of Holy Scripture that appear to relate historical facts, may a Catholic exegete assert that the passage in question is a tacit or implicit quotation of a document written by a non-inspired author, all of whose assertions the inspired author does not mean to approve or make his own, and that these assertions cannot therefore be held immune from error ?

Answer : In the negative, except in a case where without prejudice to the mind and judgement of the Church it is proved by solid arguments : (1) that the sacred Writer does in fact cite the sayings or documents of another, and (2) neither approves nor makes the same his own, so that he is legitimately regarded as not speaking in his own name.

j **On Narratives Historical only in Appearance in Books of Holy Scripture Historical in Form,** June 23, 1905 (ASS 38 [1905–06] 124 f. ; EB 154 ; Dz 1980) :

Is it possible to admit as a principle of sound exegesis that books of sacred Scripture which are regarded as historical, at times do not relate, either wholly or in part, history properly so-called and objectively true, but present only the appearance of history with the purpose of expressing some meaning differing from the strictly literal or historical sense of the words ?

Answer : In the negative, except in a case neither easily nor rashly to be admitted, in which, the mind of the Church not being contrary and without prejudice to its judgement, it is proved by solid arguments that the sacred Writer intended not to recount true history, properly so-called, but under the guise and form of history to set forth a parable, an allegory, or some meaning distinct from the strictly literal or historical signification of the words.

NOTE : See further on this matter § 53*i*–*j*.

k **Concerning the Addition of Variant Readings in Editions of the Vulgate Version of the Old and New Testament,** Nov. 17, 1921 (AAS 14 [1922] 27 ; EB 509).

In the Preface to the Reader of the Clementine edition of the Vulgate version of the Sacred Scriptures **52k** it is said :

' Further in this edition there is nothing not canonical . . . no parallel passages in the margin (the addition of which in that position is not prohibited in the future), no notes, no variant readings, finally no prefaces. . . . But as the Apostolic See does not condemn the industry of those who have inserted in other editions parallel passages, variant readings, the prefaces of St Jerome, and similar matter, so neither does it forbid that with the use of different type such helps should be added in the future for the advantage and utility of students in this same Vatican edition ; with the exception, however, that variant readings may not be noted in the margin of the text '.

But as some are of opinion that these last words forbid the addition of variant readings not only in the margin at the side but also at the foot of the text, the question has been put to the Pontifical Biblical Commission : Is it lawful in editions of the Vulgate version both of the New and the Old Testaments to add variant readings and other similar helps for students at the foot of the text ?

After examination of the matter, the Pontifical Biblical Commission replied : In the affirmative.

Concerning the Use of Translations of Holy Scripture **53a** **in Churches,** April 30, 1934 (AAS 26 [1934] 315).

The following question was proposed by his Excellency the Bishop of S'Hertogenbosch [otherwise called Bois-le-Duc] in the name also of their Excellencies the other Bishops of the ecclesiastical province of Holland :

Can it be allowed to read to the people in Church the liturgical passages of the Epistles and Gospels in a translation not from ' the ancient Vulgate Latin version ', but from the original texts whether Greek or Hebrew ?

The Pontifical Biblical Commission decided that the following answer should be given : In the negative ; a translation should be publicly read to the Faithful made from the text approved by the Church for the sacred liturgy.

Concerning Translations of Holy Scripture in Modern **b** **Languages,** Aug. 22, 1943 (AAS 35 [1943] 270, CR 23 [1943] 524).

To answer a question proposed to it concerning the use and authority of biblical translations in modern languages, especially those made from the original texts, and to give further clarification to its decree *Concerning the Use of Translations of Holy Scripture in Churches* of April 30, 1934, the Pontifical Biblical Commission has considered it opportune to publish and commend the following norms :

Since Pope Leo XIII, of happy memory, in the Encyclical *Providentissimus Deus* (*Acta Leonis XIII*, Vol. 13, p 342 ; EB 91), for the more intimate knowledge and more fruitful explanation of the divine word recommended the use of the original texts of the Bible ; and since that recommendation, which clearly was not made for the exclusive advantage of exegetes and theologians, has seemed and seems almost to advise that the same texts, of course under the vigilant care of the competent ecclesiastical authorities, should be translated in accordance with the approved principles of sacred and indeed of profane science into the vernacular languages known to the mass of the people ;

Since, moreover, it is from the Vulgate translation, **c** which alone and exclusively among the Latin versions then in circulation the oecumenical Council of Trent declared authoritative (*Conc. Trid.*, sess. IV, decr. *De editione et usu Ss. Librorum* ; EB 46) that the biblical passages in the liturgical books of the Latin Church to be read publicly at the holy Sacrifice of the Mass and the Divine Office have for the most part been taken ; presupposing the observance of whatever should be observed :

1° Translations of Holy Scripture in modern languages **d** whether made from the Vulgate or from the original texts, provided they have been published with the per-

REPLIES OF THE BIBLICAL COMMISSION

53d mission of the competent ecclesiastical authority in accordance with canon 1391, may be duly used and read by the faithful for their private devotion ; moreover, if any translation, after a diligent examination both of the text and of the notes by men eminent in biblical and theological knowledge, is found to be more faithful and suitable, it may, if so desired, be especially recommended by the Bishops, either individually or in provincial or national meetings, to the faithful committed to their care.

2° The vernacular translation of the biblical passages which priests celebrating Mass are to read to the people, as custom or occasion demands, after the reading of the liturgical text, should, in accordance with the reply of the Pontifical Biblical Commission (*Acta Ap. Sedis*, 1934, p. 315), agree with the Latin liturgical text, though it remains permissible, if judged expedient, to give suitable explanation of the said translation by the help of the original text or of another clearer translation.

e *N.B.* G. M. Vosté, O. P., Secretary of the Biblical Commission, in Bi 27 (1946) 319 n. 2 writes of this last paragraph : ' Thus in fact will be read a version of the original text critically established. The scope and obligation, therefore, of the decree . . . of 30 April 1934 [here § 53a] should not be unduly pressed. . . . Finally . . . the Holy Father has authorized all who are obliged to recite the Breviary, to use for the Psalter " whether in private or in public " a new version made from the original texts (Motu Proprio *In cotidianis precibus*, AAS 1945, 65–7) '.

f Concerning the Work of R. D. Frederic Schmidtke entitled ' Die Einwanderung Israels in Kanaan ' Feb. 27, 1934 (AAS 26 [1934] 130 f.).

As the question has been addressed to this Pontifical Biblical Commission what is to be thought of the work entitled *Die Einwanderung Israels in Kanaan*, published at Breslau in the year 1933 by R. D. Frederic Schmidtke, it has decided that the following answer should be given :

R. D. Frederic Schmidtke, Professor Extraordinary of the Old Testament in the Theological Faculty of the University of Breslau in the volume mentioned above :

in his treatment of the Pentateuch follows the opinions of rationalistic criticism to the complete neglect of the decree of the Pontifical Biblical Commission of June 27, 1906 ;

g moreover, in the history of the Old Testament, without any attention to the decree of the same Pontifical Biblical Commission of June 23, 1905, he introduces a type of literature consisting of popular traditions mingling falsehood with truth ; contrary to the clear evidence of the sacred books he makes, among others, the assertions that the stories about the Patriarchs, at least in large part, give the history, not of individual men, but of tribes ; that Jacob was not the son of Isaac, but represents some Aramean tribe ; that the whole people of Israel did not enter Egypt but a part only, in particular the tribe of Joseph ;

also, doing violence to the sacred text, he explains many miracles of the Old Testament as purely natural events.

h The author, consequently, at least implicitly, denies the dogma of biblical inspiration and inerrancy ; he entirely neglects the norms of Catholic hermeneutics ; he contradicts the Catholic doctrine most clearly set forth in the Encyclicals *Providentissimus Deus* of Leo XIII and *Spiritus Paraclitus* of Benedict XV.

Hence the aforesaid work deserves reprobation on various grounds and should be kept out of Catholic schools.

The Pontifical Commission, moreover, takes this occasion to warn Catholic commentators to obey with due reverence the dogmatic Constitution of the Vatican Council, renewing the Decree of the sacred Council of Trent, by which it was solemnly ordained ' that in matters of faith and morals, appertaining to the building up of Christian doctrine, that is to be held as the true sense of sacred Scripture which was, and is, held by our holy mother the Church, to whom it belongs

to judge of the true sense and interpretation of the holy **53h** Scriptures, and therefore no one may interpret holy Scripture contrary to this sense or also against the unanimous consent of the Fathers '.

N.B. In a final paragraph here omitted the Commission recalls to the minds of all the faithful what is the authority of the Biblical Commission quoting the words of Pius X given above, § 47c.

Letter to Cardinal Suhard [on the Mosaic **i** authorship of the Pentateuch, and on the historical character of Gen 1–11] (AAS 40 [1948] 45–8).

' The Holy Father graciously entrusted to the Pontifical Biblical Commission the examination of two questions recently submitted to His Holiness concerning the sources of the Pentateuch and the historicity of the first eleven chapters of Genesis. . . . As the result of their deliberations His Holiness deigned to approve the following reply . . . on 16 January 1948.

' The Pontifical Biblical Commission . . . desires . . . to promote biblical studies by assuring to them the most complete liberty within the limits of the traditional teaching of the Church. This liberty has been proclaimed in explicit terms by the present Pope in his Encyclical *Divino afflante Spiritu* : " The Catholic exegete . . . ought not by any manner of means to debar himself from taking in hand, and that repeatedly, the difficult questions which have found no solution up to the present time . . . in an attempt to find a well-founded explanation in perfect harmony with the doctrine of the Church, in particular with that of biblical inerrancy, and at the same time capable of fully satisfying the certain conclusions of the secular sciences. The labours of these worthy workers in the vineyard of the Lord deserve to be judged not only with equity and justice, but with perfect charity ; and this is a point which all others sons of the Church should bear in mind. It is their duty to avoid that most imprudent zeal which considers it an obligation to attack or suspect whatever is new ", AAS (1943) 319.

' If this recommendation of the Pope's is borne in mind **j** in the interpretation of the three official replies given formerly by the Biblical Commission in connection with the above-mentioned questions, namely June 23, 1905, on narratives in the historical books of Holy Scripture which have only the appearance of history (EB 154), June 27, 1906, on the Mosaic authenticity of the Pentateuch (EB 174–7), and June 30, 1909, on the historical character of the first three chapters of Genesis (EB 332–9), it will be agreed that these replies are in no way a hindrance to further truly scientific examination of these problems in accordance with the results acquired in these last forty years. . . .

' As regards the composition of the Pentateuch, in the **k** above-mentioned decree of June 27, 1906, the Biblical Commission recognized already that it could be affirmed that Moses " in order to compose his work made use of written documents or of oral traditions " and that post-Mosaic modifications and additions could also be admitted (EB 176–7). No one today doubts the existence of these sources or rejects a gradual increase of Mosaic laws due to the social and religious conditions of later times, a process manifest also in the historical narratives. However, even among non-Catholic exegetes very diverse opinions are held today concerning the character and the number of these documents, their names and dates. There are even authors in different countries, who for purely critical and historical reasons quite unconnected with any religious purpose resolutely reject the theories most in favour up to the present, and seek the explanation of certain editorial peculiarities of the Pentateuch, not so much in the alleged diversity of documents as in the special psychology, the peculiar mental and literary processes of the ancient Orientals which are better known today, or again in the different literary forms which are required by the diversity of subject-matter. Hence we invite Catholic scholars to study these problems with an open mind in the light of sane

53k criticism and of the results of other sciences which have their part in these matters, and such study will without doubt establish the large share and the profound influence of Moses as author and as legislator.

l ' The question of the literary forms of the first eleven chapters of Genesis is far more obscure and complex. These literary forms do not correspond to any of our classical categories and cannot be judged in the light of the Greco-Latin or modern literary types. It is therefore impossible to deny or to affirm their historicity as a whole without unduly applying to them norms of a literary type under which they cannot be classed. If it is agreed not to see in these chapters history in the classical and modern sense, it must be admitted also that known scientific facts do not allow a *positive* solution of all the problems which they present. The first duty in this matter incumbent on scientific exegesis consists in the careful study of all the problems literary, scientific, historical, cultural, and religious connected with these chapters ; in the next place is required a close examination of the literary methods of the ancient oriental peoples, their psychology, their manner of expressing themselves and even their notion of historical truth ; the requisite, in a word, is to assemble without preformed judgements all the material of the palaeontological and historical, epigraphical and literary sciences.

It is only in this way that there is hope of attaining a **53 l** clearer view of the true nature of certain narratives in the first chapters of Genesis. To declare *a priori* that **m** these narratives do not contain history in the modern sense of the word might easily be understood to mean that they do not contain history in any sense, whereas they relate in simple and figurative language, adapted to the understanding of mankind at a lower stage of development, the fundamental truths underlying the divine scheme of salvation, as well as a popular description of the origins of the human race and of the chosen people. In the meantime it is necessary to practise patience which is part of prudence and the wisdom of life. This also is inculcated by the Holy Father in the Encyclical already quoted : " No one ", he says, " should be surprised that all the difficulties have not yet been clarified or solved. . . . But that is no reason for losing courage or forgetting that in the branches of human study it cannot be otherwise than in nature, where beginnings grow little by little, where the produce of the soil is not gathered except after prolonged labour. . . . There is ground, therefore, for hoping that (these difficulties) which today appear most complicated and arduous, will eventually, thanks to constant effort, admit of complete clarification " (AAS [1943] 318).'

THE PHYSICAL GEOGRAPHY OF THE
HOLY LAND

By Dom E. GRAF

54a **Bibliography**—F. M. Abel, O.P., *Géographie de la Palestine*, 2 vol., Paris, I 1933², II 1938 ; *idem, Les Guides Bleus : Syrie, Palestine*, Paris, 1932. L. Szczepanski, S.J., *Geographia Historica Palestinae Antiquae*, Romae 1928² ; Mgr Legendre, *The Cradle of the Bible* (Engl. transl.), London 1929 ; *G. A. Smith, *The Historical Geography of the Holy Land*, London, 1935²⁶ *idem, Historical Atlas of the Holy Land*, London, 1936² ; *G. E. Wright and F. V. Filson, *The Westminster Historical Atlas to the Bible*, London, 1947² (up-to-date, but not as full as Smith's). The two volumes of Abel's *Géographie* treat both the physical and the political geography of the Holy Land. The work is indispensable to the student of the Bible. The *Guide* is the most up-to-date work of the kind, and is the fruit of the author's long years of study and travel in Palestine.

b **Unique Situation**—The Israelites were a people with a mission. They were the depositaries of revealed religion, and alone among all the nations of the ancient world they knew and worshipped the true God. The strip of territory on the western edge of the Asiatic continent which, by divine command, they made their homeland, was admirably suited to the fulfilment of their destiny, for its physical and geographical conditions made it both a stronghold easy to defend and a bridge between two continents. ' Thus saith the Lord God : This is Jerusalem. I have set her in the midst of the nations and the countries round about her ' (Ez 5:5). The comparative isolation of the land should have kept its inhabitants immune from idolatry ; and since it was a thoroughfare between many peoples, it was surely in the designs of God that by this means these nations should become acquainted with the hope of Israel.

c **Palestine**—The name by which the land of Israel is generally known was given by the Greeks whose first contacts were with the Philistines on the sea coast. Palestine is literally Philistine land. It has long designated the land on both sides of the Jordan between the sea and the desert. Very recently, however, the name was politically restricted to the territory west of the Jordan and Eastern Palestine was called Transjordan.

d **Cisjordanic Palestine** is bounded on the north by the western bend of the river Litas (Litāni), now called Nahr el-Qāsimiye, which separates it from Mt Lebanon, and the 'Beqa' plain between Lebanon and Anti-Lebanon, on the west by the Mediterranean, on the east by the Jordan valley and the Dead Sea, and on the south by the Beersheba depression. **Political Palestine** restricts the northern limit in favour of Syria to a line running from the Ladder of Tyre to Lake Huleh, but extends the southern as far as Raphia on the west and the Gulf of 'Akaba on the east. The area is about 6,000 sq. m., *e.g.* less than that of Wales (7,446 sq. m.). The well-known biblical expression ' from Dan to Beersheba ' indicates the N. and S. limits and stands for a length of about 180 m. The breadth varies from 70 m. at the latitude of Beersheba to 25 m. between the Bay of Acre and the Lake of Galilee.

e **Transjordanic Palestine** extends geographically from Mt Hermon in the N. to the Gulf of 'Akaba in the S., and from the Jordan and 'Arābah valleys in the **54e** W. to the desert in the E. Its area is about 4,000 sq. m. and its length about 250 m. The breadth varies with the encroachment of the desert from about 60 m. in the Haurān region to a narrow mountain range in Edom.

The **Physical Configuration** of the land is remarkable, **f** and, indeed, unique, as the result of tremendous upheavals and fissures of the earth's crust in pre-historic times. The outstanding feature is the deep central valley running from north to south, from the base of Mt Hermon to the Gulf of 'Akaba. The northern part of the valley is divided into two roughly equal strips by the Jordan, which runs in a deep trench many feet below the level of the plain. On the east, the Jordan valley is bounded by the mountains of Moab, Galaad and Bashan, and on the west by the Judaean, Samaritan and Galilean hills. West of that central range, the coastal plain runs north and south. In the south, however, a considerable tract of foothills, the Shephēlah, separates the plain from the mountain range. It will be convenient to describe these several features of the country separately.

The **coastal plain** is the continuation of a level strip **g** which begins at the apex of the Gulf of Alexandretta and runs south in an almost straight line as far as the Wadi-el-Arish, where it bends to the west in the direction of the Nile delta. Its width varies considerably, in fact at the famous Ladder of Tyre the coastal road has had to be cut out of the mountain side. At Haifa, where the spur of Carmel juts out to seaward, the plain is only a few hundred yards wide, but from this point it broadens steadily, and at the latitude of Jaffa has a width of 20 m. This southern section of the coastal plain was known as the plain of Sharon (DV Saron, *cf.* Ac 9:35), whose beauty is described, or hinted at, in Is 35:2, 33:9. Underground water lies at no great depth, *viz.* at about 13 metres, in soft limestone, but as well-sinking is a costly undertaking with primitive tools, groups of families, or a whole community, may share the expense of drilling, and jointly own a well, as in OT days (*cf.* Jn 4:5, 6). The modern Jewish settlers do it cheaply with artesian borings.

The coastal belt south of Jaffa was occupied by the **h** Philistines. The ruins of once famous cities still bear witness to the power of a people with whom Israel warred almost continuously, but whom it never entirely conquered. The territory south of Philistia and the Wilderness of Judaea was known as the Negeb (South, lit. dry land). Tells and ruins show that it was not always the arid steppe it is now. Beersheba (DV, Bersabee), the southernmost town of Palestine, is also the most important inhabited place of a district populated chiefly by nomads who rear their flocks on the grazing grounds scattered here and there between vast stretches of sand and stone.

The maritime plain is intersected by a number of **i** wadis—river beds—most of them dry during the greater part of the year, but raging torrents after the heavy rainfalls of the winter. The chief rivers are, in the north, the Litas, which runs along the northern boundary of Palestine, and the Kishon (Cison), which, after meandering through the plain of Esdraelon which it drains, enters the sea at the foot of Mt Carmel. The

54i Kishon is a perennial stream only for a fraction of its course, but after rain, like all other Palestinian watercourses, it quickly swells to a considerable size. This was evidently the case on the occasion so vividly described in the song of Debbora (Jg 5:21).

j The principal river of the plain of Sharon is the Nahr el Auja, which rises at Ras-el-Ain (Antipatris) and enters the sea north of Jaffa. The head water of this river is now pumped up to Jerusalem, to supplement the scanty supply of the Holy City.

The most striking feature of the Palestinian coastline is the absence of indentations of any depth. With the exception of the Bay of Acre, no inlets break the long monotonous line, and the only good harbour is at Haifa (not mentioned in the Bible)—the roadstead at Jaffa can scarcely be described as a harbour. The absence of good harbours in their restricted coastline may have been a contributory cause of the Hebrews' lack of interest in the Mediterranean. Solomon however and later kings kept a fleet in the Gulf of 'Akaba for Red Sea trade.

55a **The Shephēlah**—This was a region of foothills, lit. lowland, which separated the mountains of Judah from the Philistine plain. It was fertile and contained many important cities. It was also a battleground where the men of Judah could meet the Philistines on fairly equal terms without encountering the war-chariots which made the plains inaccessible. Here north of Socho was the Vale of the Terebinth (Elah) where David slew Goliath.

b **Esdraelon**—The central mountain range of Palestine is broken by the historic plain of Esdraelon, which forms an irregular triangle of which the angles are Tabor, Carmel and Jenin (Engannim, Jos 15:34). In the Bible the plain is called 'The plain of Mageddo' (Biq'ath Megiddo), and the 'Valley of Jezreel' ('Emeq Yizre'el), Megiddo and Jezreel being its most important cities. Esdraelon is the Hellenized form of Jezreel and only occurs in the deuterocanonical books. The plain measures about 16 m. from N. to S. and a little over 20 from E. to W. (if we include the gap of Kishon which connects it with the plain of Acre). At its highest it lies some 260 ft above the Mediterranean. Its undulating surface is extremely fertile. It has been the theatre of many battles from the time when Gideon fought the Madianites and Saul the Philistines, up to the war of 1914–18. In the springtime the plain looks like a living carpet as the fields of growing wheat, studded with myriads of red anemones—the 'lilies of the field' of the Gospel —and other flowers of vivid hue, sway in the breeze : the sight is as enchanting as it is ephemeral. Today the land is being intensively cultivated by Jewish settlers.

c **Mountains**—The central range—the country's spinal column—is a prolongation of Lebanon running south in a continuous line all the way down to the Sinai peninsula. The mountains of Upper Galilee, as far south as the Lake of Galilee, rise to over 3,000 ft— the Jebel Jarmuk is nearly 4,000 ft. In Lower Galilee the range fans out into a number of lesser ridges, varying in height from 500 to 1,850 ft. Mount Tabor is unique. The site of the Transfiguration, according to a tradition dating at least from the 4th cent., is completely isolated from the surrounding hills and, like a mighty dome, rises solitary and majestic to a height of 1,843 ft. Its isolation conveys an impression of even greater height. Its flanks are clothed with large patches of brushwood and thickets of dwarf oaks, and from the oblong plateau on its summit the eye ranges over a large tract of Galilee, as far as Carmel and the silver line of the sea in the west, and in the east the blue waters of the Lake of Galilee, the Jordan Valley, and on the far N. horizon snow-capped Hermon. The north-western spur of Carmel, though only 550 ft above sea level, is most impressive by reason of its abruptness. The spur heads a range 17 m. long, with peaks of from 1,500 to 1,700 ft ; its southern section slopes down and gradually merges into the Samaritan

range. Some of the mountains of this and the Judaean **55c** range rise to over 2,000 ft—Garizim and Hebal to 2,849 and 3,077 respectively. The former is the mountain referred to by the woman of Samaria (Jn 4:20). Verdant Garizim and cactus-clad Hebal were the scene of the strange religious service described in Jos 8:30 ff.

Jerusalem stands on two mountains of 2,400 and 2,450 **d** ft respectively. The Tyropean Valley, now almost completely filled in with the rubble of the centuries, separated the western mountain from the eastern. The position of the unique spring Gihon determined the site of the ancient Jebusite stronghold on the southern projection of the eastern mountain. The city when captured by David formed a point of contact between Judah and the northern tribes, and became the natural capital of the united kingdom. Farther south, beyond Bethlehem and on the edge of the Judaean desert, Hebron, David's previous capital, one of the world's oldest cities and the burial place of Abraham, stands on a plateau 3,040 ft above the Mediterranean.

East and south of Jerusalem, as far as the Ghor (*i.e.* **e** the Jordan valley), the Dead Sea and Beersheba, there stretches a wild, mountainous region intersected by deep gorges, with hardly any perennial streams, and known as the **Desert of Judah.** This region has never been cultivated and cannot be reclaimed. From time immemorial it has been the home of robbers and outlaws or the refuge of the oppressed. David and his followers took to it in order to escape from Saul. In the Christian era it became a favourite retreat for monks and hermits, and Greek Orthodox monasteries still remind the pilgrim of a religious past whose glory is not wholly departed.

The Jordan—Of all the Palestinian watercourses, the **f** Jordan is the most important. Even as it traverses the whole length of the land, so may it be said to flow through the whole of Israel's history.

It has three sources of which the Ḥaṣbani, the most northerly, supplies an eighth, the Banyas, springing from the foot of Hermon at Caesarea Philippi, a fourth, and the Leddān, rising at Tell el-Qāḍi, the ancient Dan, five-eighths of its waters. These streams unite a few miles north of Lake Huleh. A unique feature of the Jordan is that most of its course runs several hundred feet below sea-level. At Banyas the stream is 1,000 ft above that level ; at Lake Huleh it is a couple of feet above, one foot at summer level ; at its exit from the Sea of Galilee it has dropped to 680 ft below, and when it finally mingles with the waters of the Dead Sea it has fallen to 1,291 ft below the Mediterranean. The deep valley (Ghor) through which the river winds its sinuous yet rapid course was an inland sea in diluvial times. The actual bed of the stream lies in a trench (Zor), many feet deep, which it has dug for itself out of the soft, calcareous soil of the Ghor. Here and there its banks rise as perpendicular cliffs from 20 to 100 ft or more ; elsewhere it winds itself round the bases of lofty knolls eroded by rain and storm, thrown together in wild confusion and looking like so many ruined forts and castles—the whole scene resembling a lunar landscape. There are not a few shallows where the stream may **g** be forded. Below the confluence of the Jabbok and the Jordan, at a spot still marked by the remains of the Roman bridge of Dāmiye, there is one such ford believed to have been the scene of the massacre of the Ephraimites (Jg 12:5, 6). From this point onwards the valley becomes wild and uncultivated and the water loses its clearness. In the spring, when the snows of Hermon melt and its own affluents are in spate, the Jordan overflows its banks ; the flood water may then spread over one or two miles. The distance from the southern end of the Lake of Galilee to the northern shore of the Dead Sea is less than 60 m. as the crow flies, but so numerous are the river's windings that its actual course covers some 200 m. Unlike the Nile and other famous rivers, the Jordan is not,

55g and never has been, a link between cities and peoples; on the contrary it is, and always has been, a line of cleavage. Towns and villages have never mirrored themselves in its water, nor has it carried the trade of nations, for its many rapids render navigation impossible—even a swim in the swift flowing stream is not without risk. Both banks are lined with trees—tamarisks, eucalyptuses, poplars. Nightingales sing in the thickets in which boars, hyenas and jackals lurk even today; kingfishers and other birds of bright plumage may be seen darting in and out of the bushes.

Its tributaries—The Yarmuk and the Jabbok are important affluents on its eastern bank; the Galud, believed to be the scene of the event recorded in Jg 7:4, 6, and the Wadi-el-Fara are perennial affluents on its right bank, as is the Wadi Kelt (identified by some with the brook Carith of 3 Kg 17:3), which flows through a deep, narrow fissure in the mountains.

h The Lake of Galilee—This lovely fresh-water lake was once part of the diluvial sea which covered the whole Jordan valley. The Hebrews called it *Kinnereth*, by reason of its harplike shape. It is 12½ m. long, 7½ m. wide at its broadest; its greatest depth is 126 ft and it lies 683 ft below the Mediterranean. Its waters teem with fish—twenty-two different species have been found—but only a few fishing-boats now ply on the lake. It is a safe conclusion, in view of the isolation of the valley and the oriental character which is averse to change, that the modern fisherfolk use the same methods as those once followed by Peter and Andrew and the sons of Zebedee. For centuries the shores of the lake have been desolate, especially on the eastern side, but broken columns and capitals, and mounds of dressed stones on the beaches and in the water, remind the visitor of the many pleasant little towns which centuries ago stood beside its clear waters. Of late the plain of Gennesareth on its NW shore has regained some of its pristine beauty and fertility. In this steaming valley every kind of cereal grows readily, and the vine, the olive tree and the date-palm also yield a rich harvest. Storms, which are both sudden and violent, are caused by currents of cold air rushing down from Mt Hermon. When these meet the hot air of the sub-tropical valley, they lash the quiet waters into fury. Almost more than anywhere else in Palestine the Christian visitor here feels himself close to the Master whose eyes rested on these hills, whose feet walked on these waves, who spoke his inspiring parables and wrought countless miracles amid this enchanting scenery.

56a The Dead Sea is another relic of the diluvial sea. Its length is 47 m., its greatest breadth 9½ m., the total area nearly 340 square miles, and since it lies nearly 1,300 ft below sea level, it has no outlet whatever. On the east a peninsula called the Lisân (Tongue) stretches half across the width of the sea. The greatest depths are found north of the Lisân, *viz.* 1,300 ft; south of the Lisân the depth decreases rapidly. Some 6,000,000 tons of fresh water pour daily into this strange sea both from the Jordan and from a number of streams, winter torrents for the most part, but some of them perennial, such as the Wadi el-Mōjib (the Arnon) which rushes down from the mountains of Moab between perpendicular walls of rock. For all that, the level of the Dead Sea varies but slightly, owing to the extraordinary evaporation which also accounts, in part, for the unusual mineral content of the water —23·4%—compared with approx. 4% in the ocean. Common table salt constitutes the largest part of this mineral content, the rest being magnesium chloride, calcium chloride, etc. Recently this chemical wealth has been systematically exploited, and the hundreds of workers thus employed have brought new life into a desolate region which in the summer, on account of the tremendous heat, makes great demands on human endurance. In the Bible the Dead Sea is called 'the Salt Sea'. The epithet 'dead' does not imply that its waters are motionless, but that no organic life can maintain itself in them. Fish coming down

from the Jordan or the Arnon die within seconds of **56a** entering these unpleasant waters.

Transjordanic Palestine—The various districts are **b** most conveniently grouped under the OT names: Bashan, Galaad, Moab and Edom. Bashan extended from Hermon to the river Yarmuk which enters the Jordan south of Lake Galilee, Galaad from the Yarmuk to the Wady Ḥesbān, another affluent of the Jordan near its mouth, Moab east of the Dead Sea from Wady Ḥesbān to Wady Ḥeṣa and Edom between Wady Ḥeṣa and the Gulf of 'Akaba. Galaad is divided into two fairly equal parts by the river Jabbok (Nahr ez-Zerka). Northern Galaad was originally part of Og's kingdom of Bashan. Moab is similarly divided by the river Arnon (Seil el-Mōjib). Northern Moab was part of Sehon's kingdom, then Israelitic territory and finally was conquered by Mesa and united with Southern Moab in the 9th cent. B.C. Neither Edom nor Southern Moab nor the small Ammonite kingdom east of Southern Galaad was ever inhabited by Israelites.

Bashan is a land of extinct volcanoes, fertile in the western districts of Gōlān and en-Nuḳra, where the lava is decomposed, but stony and barren in the eastern tract of el-Lejā, lit. the refuge (of robbers). South of this is the Ḥaurān, now called the Mountain of the Druses, with wooded slopes and a peak 6,000 ft high. The mountains of Gōlān do not reach 4,000 ft. Bashan was famous for its cattle. Eastern Bashan was also called Argob.

Galaad, also famous for flocks and herds, is an elevated **c** table-land, somewhat irregular on the western side where the symmetry is broken by steep valleys and lofty mountains reaching 4,000 ft. Northern Galaad now called 'Ajlūn was thickly wooded in OT times. Southern Galaad and Northern Moab are again united as in Sehon's time by a common name el-Belqa.

Moab like Galaad is a table-land, less elevated in the north (over 2,000 ft) than in the south (over 3,000 ft). It was famous for its wines, which were exported far and wide (Is 16:7-10). Southern Moab is now called Kerak. Its chief cities were 'Ar (er-Rabba) and Qir (el-Kerak).

Edom is a region of mountains reaching 5,000 ft and intersected by valleys whose waters either perish in the eastern desert or reach the Dead Sea and the Gulf of 'Akaba by the 'Arābah valley. Its capital Sela' (Gk Petra), in the south is 'the rose-red city half as old as time'. Fēnān in the north, famous for its copper mines, figures in the march to Canaan and in the Annals of the Martyrs.

Climate—Broadly speaking the climate of Palestine is **d** that of all Mediterranean countries, hot, dry summers, wet but mild winters, though in the Jordan valley it is tropical; in the maritime plain, though the heat is habitually tempered by cooling breezes, the atmosphere is moist and enervating. On the other hand in the hill country the heat is always bearable. At sunset there is a considerable drop in temperature and a cold night may succeed a day of torrid heat. On most days the country is swept by strong westerly winds which usually begin to blow about midday. This phenomenon is due to the fact that the limestone hills of the interior are more susceptible to heat and cold than the sea coast. The rush of the cold air into the region of the hot air is thus landwards by day and seawards by night. Deut 11:10-25 supplies us with an excellent picture of climatic conditions in the Holy Land. Moses warned the Israelites that ' the land which thou goest in to possess is not like the land of Egypt . . . where when the seed is sown waters are brought in to water it after the manner of gardens; but it is a land of hills and plains, expecting rain from heaven. And the Lord God doth always visit it . . . he will give to your land the early rain and the latter rain, that you may gather in your corn and your wine, and your oil, and your hay out of the fields. . . .'

Roughly speaking there are only two seasons, the hot **e**

56e and the cold, or the dry and the rainy season. The rainy season, or winter, begins in November with the fall of the early rain, but the coming of these first winter downpours is by no means regular and may be delayed until the early days of December and even later. Rain is invariably heralded by a few days of strong wind and a considerable drop in the temperature. 'The early rain' (Deut 11:14 ; Jer 5:24), which may be spread over a few days or even a week, is the signal for ploughing and sowing. Rainy days occur, of course, all through the winter months. 'The latter rain' may be expected in April : its failure spells disaster, for these last downpours of the rainy season assure 'the fullness of the yearly harvest' (Jer *ibid.*). As Palestine has always suffered from a shortage of water, necessity long ago taught the inhabitants to collect the precious rainfall. Large cisterns and smaller waterholes may be found all over the country ; the latter are mostly bottle-shaped cavities scooped out of the rock, the narrow neck being covered with a stone, often of a considerable weight and not easy to remove (*cf.* Gen 29:2, 8, 10). In this way water retains its freshness for a long time (Jer 6:7). The lack of rain is in some measure compensated for by the heavy dews of the night. All through the summer months, on cloudless nights the ground may be as wet as after a shower. This heavy dew suffices to bring to maturity the spring-sown grain, the grapes and other fruits. The Bible teems with allusions to this remarkable phenomenon, which was regarded as a symbol of God's goodness towards the dwellers in the Promised Land, whereas its failure was deemed a sign of displeasure ; in his lament for Saul and Jonathan, David could think of no heavier curse upon Gelboe, the scene of their death, than that 'neither dew nor rain' should come upon it (2 Kg 1:21).

f Fauna—There are 595 species of vertebrates ; the species of invertebrates cannot be calculated. Sheep and goats are the chief domestic animals, the former being remarkable for their long, glossy fleece, slender legs and fleshy tail. The black-haired goats provide the inhabitants with milk, and their hair provides the material from which the bedouins make their tents (Cant 1:4). Horses, mules and cows are of poor quality ; camels and donkeys still play their time-honoured role of beasts of burden. As for wild beasts : jackals, hyenas, foxes and wild boars are found in the Jordan valley and in the hilly districts ; packs of pariah dogs are also met with, but the numbers of these unofficial scavengers have been greatly reduced. In ancient times, before Palestine was stripped of its forests, lions (Jg 14:3 ; 1 Kg 13:14), leopards (Jer 5:6), bears (4 Kg 2:24) and other wild animals were not uncommon. Snakes, both poisonous and harmless, scorpions, poisonous centipedes and spiders may be found everywhere, also lizards, some of considerable size, and the ubiquitous gecko is not unwelcome even in the houses since he helps to keep down the plague of house flies. The bird population is both indigenous and migratory. Among the migrants is the stork ; in the spring huge swarms of these birds may be seen on the wing westward bound—it is a popular bird because of the war it makes on the locust whose depredations are greatly dreaded. There are also various species of vultures. Sparrows are very common.

g The **flora** of Palestine varies with the climate of the different regions. In the Jordan valley vegetation is **56g** tropical whereas in the maritime plain it resembles that of Mediterranean countries. Time was when the land was well wooded, but the cutting down of timber started centuries ago and no forests remain, with the result that wind and rain have washed away the good earth from the flanks of the hills which now stand gaunt and bare except where terraces have been laboriously rebuilt to contain the soil. Since the 1914–18 war a vigorous policy of afforestation has been pursued both by the government and by the Jewish settlers, and large copses of pines and cypresses are becoming a pleasing feature of a one-time desolate landscape. In the plain of Sharon vast orange groves make a beautiful sight, both in the spring when the trees are in flower, and in the autumn when the golden fruit glitters in its millions against a background of dark green foliage. Oranges and bananas are also grown in the plains of Jericho, but the bananas, though sweet, have neither the size nor the golden colour of the Jamaican and other varieties. Olive trees can be seen everywhere, but the Palestinian olive is of small size. Melons, figs and apricots abound, and the cultivation of the vine is rapidly becoming one of the country's major industries. The grape ripens according to climate : in the plain of Sharon this may be by the end of June or in the early days of July, whilst in the hill country the vintage only begins in August.

Roads—In OT times, when there was but little **h** vehicular traffic and goods were carried on the backs of beasts of burden, and travellers journeyed on foot or rode on donkeys or mules, the roads were merely rough tracks, although the great international trade routes between Egypt and Mesopotamia, between South Arabia and the Mediterranean passed through Palestine. It was only after the Jewish revolt of A.D. 66–70 that the Romans created a network of good roads with a view to the control of the country. Few of those enumerated in Eusebius' *Onomasticon* were in existence in the lifetime of our Lord. West of the Jordan there were three main roads, one running along the coast from Sidon to Gaza. At Tyre a branch road started eastward, in the direction of Caesarea Philippi, running across Galilee ; farther south, at Caesarea of Palestine, another road also led east, as far as Gabaa of Saul, where it joined the main road to Jerusalem. A section of this road, now but a rough track, may still be seen at Tell-el-Fûl, where it joins the modern road from Jerusalem to Haifa. Another road, starting at Damascus and crossing the Jordan south of the Lake of Galilee, passed through Scythopolis—the ancient Bethshan and modern Beisan—Nablus, Sichar, Bethel, Jerusalem and Hebron and thence to Gaza. Yet another road led from Beisan through the Jordan valley to Jericho, where it turned westwards towards Jerusalem. Some of the milestones which once marked the distances on these roads may be seen in the Palestine Museum at Jerusalem. These then are

'those holy fields
Over whose acres walked those blessed feet
Which fourteen hundred years ago were nailed
For our advantage on the bitter cross.'

(*Henry IV*, Pt I, Act I, Sc. i.)

THE POLITICAL GEOGRAPHY OF THE HOLY LAND

By E. POWER, S.J.

57a Bibliography—As in the preceding article and especially Abel, *Géographie de la Palestine*, Vol. 2.

N.B.—The bracketed name after the Biblical name in the text is the modern Arabic name of the place in question.

By way of introduction to the political geography of the land of Israel we shall first indicate the limits of the territory promised by God to the descendants of Abraham and give some account of its ancient names and early inhabitants.

b The Promised Land—The western boundary of the land of promise was the Mediterranean, the eastern the Jordan valley and the Dead Sea. Transjordania was not included. Its southern limit ran SW from the southern end of the Dead Sea through the desert of Sin to Qadeš, sixty miles south of Beersheba, and thence WNW to the River of Egypt (Wady el-'Ariš) and the Mediterranean. The northern limit is disputed and two views find support in the texts. The more probable of these makes Mt Lebanon, separated from Galilee by the Nahr el-Qāṣimiye, and the Beqaʻ plain north of Merǧ 'Ayyūn the northern boundary. This view is supported by the earliest texts and still more by the fact that no more northerly territory was assigned to any tribe. The other view includes all Lebanon and the Beqaʻ in the promised land. This limit, ideal rather than historical, is suggested by David's northern conquests. Ezechiel who supports it locates Dan in the extreme north, though that tribe only migrated northwards in the Judges' period and then settled south of the Beqaʻ. The Israelites occupied all the Promised Land except much of the sea coast held by the Philistines in the south and by the Phoenicians in the north.

c Ancient Names—The early Babylonians had no distinctive name for Palestine but included it with Syria in Amurru, 'Westland'. The later Assyrians named its political divisions Omri-land (the Northern Kingdom), Judah and Philistia. They also called Syria and Palestine the Land of the Hittites—an instructive example of oriental nomenclature. The Egyptians called both Syria and Palestine Reton and Hor. Originally Reton indicated a city state in Southern Palestine identified with Lydda since Egyptian *r* represents Semitic *r* and *l*. Upper Reton (= Palestine) was subsequently distinguished from Lower Reton (= the Syrian hinterland). The coast land of Phoenicia and perhaps also of Palestine was called Zahi. Hor or Huru, equated with the biblical Hor which designates the ancient inhabitants of Edom, was formerly understood to mean cave-dwellers but is now more commonly regarded as the Egyptian equivalent of Hurrites. This northern people seems to have ruled Palestine and Syria for three centuries before the conquest of Thuthmosis III in the early 15th cent. B.C. The name Canaan appears first in the el-Amarna Tablets of the 14th cent. B.C. It designated originally Phoenicia and Palestine, and there are traces of this wider sense in Phoenician inscriptions and in the OT. In the Bible, however, it more commonly indicates Cisjordanic Palestine.

d Early Inhabitants—At the time of the Hebrew invasion the land was inhabited mostly by Semites: Canaanites and Amorrhaeans. The former invaded Palestine

c 3000 B.C., the latter in the 19th cent. B.C. The names **57d** are sometimes used indiscriminately in the OT, sometimes with the difference that the Canaanites dwelt in the plains, the Amorrhaeans in the hilly country. The Hyksos invasion in the 18th cent. B.C. brought northern peoples into Palestine, certainly Hurrites and probably also Hittites. These two peoples were racially connected as both had an Aryan aristocracy. As Hurrites had disappeared in OT times while Hittites still survived, it is possible that both peoples are called Hittites. It is in and about Hebron, fortified by the Hyksos invaders, that Hittites are mentioned in Abraham's time. A third northern race, the Philistines, were one of the sea peoples pressed southwards towards the close of the 13th cent. B.C. Their origin is obscure as their undoubted connection with Crete may be political rather than racial. The other names of ancient inhabitants mentioned in the OT either indicate clans or subdivisions of these peoples or have no racial significance. The Pherezites were probably Hurrites, otherwise attested near Jerusalem. The Hevites are considered by some Amorrhaeans. Others regard Hevite as a scribal error for Hittite or Hurrite. The Jebusites of Jerusalem were probably Amorrhaeans. The Rephaim, shades of the dead or giants, are associated with regions containing megalithic monuments. The 'Anakim, long necks, were giants of Hebron and Philistia.

Tribal Organization—The Hebrews found Canaan **e** divided into numerous independent city states under native rulers only nominally subject to Egypt. Josue divided the land, still largely unconquered, into territories, assigned by lot to the different tribes and ruled by tribal chiefs usually called elders. These territories and the more important cities are here briefly indicated. In the identifications Tell means mound, Kh(irbet) ruin.

All Southern Palestine between the Mediterranean and the Dead Sea was allotted to **Judah** in whose territory **Simeon** received cities. The southern boundary was that of the Promised Land previously indicated. The northern boundary, separating Judah from Benjamin in the east and Dan in the west, ran from the northern end of the Dead Sea to Nahr Rubin near 'Eqron on the coast. The line is somewhat irregular. It bends south from Adummim near the modern Khan Khatrūr to 'Ain Rogel south of Jerusalem, then north to Qiryath-yearim, then south to Bethšemeš and then north to the sea-coast. Cities : (*a*) in the Shephelah : 'Eglon (Tell el-Ḥesi), Lakish (Tell ed-Duwēr), Maresha (Tell Sandahannah) southern forts, Adullam ('Idelmiye), Socho (Kh. 'Abbād near Kh. Šuweike) associated with David, 'Azeqa (Tell Zakariye) and Libna (Tell eṣ-Ṣafiye) northern forts, and Qiryath-yearim (Tell el-Azhar) abode of the Ark and point of contact of Judah, Dan and Benjamin ; (*b*) in the central mountain range : Qiryath-Sepher = Debir (Tell Beit-Mirsim) city of Othniel, Qiryath-Arbaʻ = Hebron (el-Khalīl the *friend* of God, Abraham), Beth Ṣūr or Bethsura (Beit Ṣūr) important stronghold, Bethlehem = Ephrat (Beit Laḥm) city of David. The five unconquered Philistine cities, Gaza, Ascalon, Ashdod, 'Eqron on or near the coast and Gath in the interior were in Judaean territory. Cities of Simeon in Southern Judah : Ṣiqlag (Tell el-Khuweilfe),

57e 'En Rimmon (Umm er-Rammāmin), Sharuḥen (Tell el-Fara') a Hyksos stronghold, Beersheba (Es-Seba') and Ṣefat renamed Ḥorma (Tell es-Seb'?).

f The tribes of **Dan** in the west and Benjamin in the east separated Judah from Ephraim. The line of demarcation between them ran from Judaean Qiryath-yearim in the south to Ephraimite Lower Bethoron in the north. As Ephraimites lived with Canaanites in Gezer, it is doubtful whether Dan ever reached the coast or occupied Jaffa. In his diminished portion Dan was so oppressed by Philistines and Amorrhaeans that six hundred Danite warriors migrated northwards in the Judges' period seeking a new home at Laiš, renamed Dan (Tell el-Qāḍi), in the fertile valley containing the principal source of the Jordan. Cities : = Bethšemeš (er-Rumeile) was a Danite city on the Judaean border. Nearby were Ṣor'a (Ṣar'a) and Eshtaol (Eshu') familiar from the history of Samson. In the north were Gibbeṭōn (Tell el-Melāt ?) and Aialon (Yālo).

Benjamin, younger son of Rachel, was usually reckoned with the House of Joseph, Ephraim and Manasses, who occupied all Central Palestine. The northern boundary passed south of Lower Bethoron and Bethel through the desert of Bethel to Deir Diwān and thence to Gebel Qaranṭal and the Jordan, leaving Jericho to Ephraim. Jerusalem, then occupying the southern part of the eastern hill, was allotted to Benjamin but was held by the Jebusites until David took it and made it his capital. In western Benjamin were Upper Bethoron (Beit 'Ur el-fōqā), Gibe'on (el-Gib), Kephira (Tell Kefire). North of Jerusalem were Gib'a (Tell el-Fūl) Saul's capital and the Gib'a of Benjamin, Rama (er-Rām), Miṣpeh (Tell en-Naṣbe) and Be'erōth (el-Bire). More easterly were Geba' (Geba') and Mikhmas (Mukhmas) facing each other across the Wady Suwēnit. Nob, an ancient sanctuary, was on Mt Scopus.

g The boundary between **Ephraim** and Manasses had its centre at Machmethath (el-Makhna just south of Shechem). On the east it inclined southwards to Ta'nath Šilo (Ta'na el-fōqā) and thence ran almost due south to Jericho and the Jordan. On the west it ran first south to Tappuaḥ, then nearly due west along the Wady Qāna to the river 'Augā and the sea. In the centre of Ephraim were Šilo (Kh. Seilūn), ancient sanctuary, and Timnathseraḥ (Kh. Tibne), city of Josue, in the south Lower Bethoron (Beit 'Ur et-taḥta), Bethel (Beitin) sanctuary of the Northern Kingdom, Yešana (Burg el-Isaneh), Jericho (Eriḥā) and Gilgal (Kh. el-Eṭele SE. of Jericho), first camp and headquarters of Josue.

The northern boundary of **Manasses** is indicated by the line of Canaanite strongholds from the Jordan to the coast Bethš'ān (Beisān), Yible'am (Bel'ame), Ta'anakh (Ta'anak), Megiddo (Tell el-Mutesellim), and Dōr (El-Burg near Ṭanṭūra). The western Jordan valley east of Ephraim seems also to have belonged to Manasses. Cities in the south : Shechem (el-Balāṭa), important trading centre, Samaria (Se-bastiye, NW. of Nablūs), Omri's capital, Tirṣa (near Tappuaḥ, perhaps Gemma'in), Jeroboam's capital, Pir'athōn (Far'ata), Ṣartān commanding the Jordan ford ed-Damiye ; in the north : Dōtain (Tell Dōtān), Tebes (Ṭūbas) and Abel-Meḥola (Gōr).

h To **Issachar** was allotted the rich but insecure plain of Esdraelon. The boundaries are only indicated by the cities mentioned of which Ḥapharaim (el-Farriye) is the most westerly, Kesulloth = Kisloth Thabor (Iksal) and Dāberat (Deburiye), west of Mt Thabor, the most northerly. In the eastern section between Wady Birē and Wady Maleḥ we find Manassites at 'Ophra (eṭ-Ṭaiyibe) in the Judges' period. Cities : Engannim (Genīn), Yizra'el (Zer'in) and Qedeš (Tell Abu Qedeis SE. of Megiddo) in the south, Šunam (Solem) and 'Endor ('Endūr) more central.

Zabulon occupied the centre of Southern Galilee between Asher on the west and Nephtali on the east and north. The boundary starting from Yoqne'am (Tell Qaimūn) runs first NNE. then due north to a **57h** little above Qabul, turns east to Ḥuqqoq (Yaqūq) in the latitude of Capharnaum, then south to Mt Thabor where it joins Issachar. Cities : Sarid or Šadīd (Tell eš-Šadūd), Šime'on or Šemeron (Es-Semuniye), Bethlehem (Beit Laḥm) and Ḥannaton (Tell el-Bedeiwiye).

Asher's portion, bounded by Nepthali, Zabulon, **i** Issachar and Manasses, lay along the coast from the Nahr el-Qāṣimiye to Shiḥor Libnath (Wady Zerka), south of Dor. The Tyrians, however, retained their territory in the north and received moreover from Solomon twenty cities in the region of Qabul. Cities from north to south : Aḥlab = Meḥebel (Kh. el-Maḥalib, NE. of Tyre), Qana (el-Qane), Qabul (Qabūl) in the interior, Akzib (ez-Zib) and 'Akkō (Acre) on the coast, Ḥaroseth (near Ḥariṭiye, perhaps Tell 'Amar), Sisera's capital, and Ḥelkath (el-Harbag ?) near Carmel.

Nephtali possessed all Eastern Galilee from the Nahr el-Qaṣimiye and the Beqa' to Wady Birē. The line of demarcation from Asher ran almost due north from the NW. extremity of Zabulon. Cities : Qedeš (Qades) NW. and Ḥaṣor (Tell el-Qēdah) SW. of Lake Ḥuleh, Merom (Meiron) and Beth 'Anath (Ba'ne) more to the west, Kinnereth (el-'Oreime) and Hammath by Lake Gennesareth, and in the south Ḥeleph ('Arbata near Mt Thabor), Adami ha-Neqeb (Damiye), Yabneel (Yemma) and Laqqum (Kh. el-Manṣūra).

Transjordania was divided by Moses before the conquest of Canaan between Ruben, Gad and half of Manasses. **Ruben** had disappeared in David's time. His territory, inhabited by Gadites, was added to Moab by Meša c 850 B.C. It lay between the Arnon (Wady Mōgib) and the Wady Ḥesbān, between the desert and the Dead Sea. Cities : Dībōn (Dībān), Qariathaim (el-Kureyyāt), 'Aṭārōth ('Aṭārūs), Nebō (en-Nebā), Mēdaba (Mādaba), Ḥešbōn (Ḥesbān), El'ālē (el-'Al) and Mepha'at (Neif'a).

Gad received the region between Ruben and the **j** Jabbok (Nahr ez-Zerka), between Ammon and the Jordan, i.e. Southern Gil'ad. Cities in the Jordan valley : Beth-Ḥaram (Tell er-Rame) Beth-Nimra (near Tell Nimrin), Sukkoth (Tell el-Akhṣās) and Saphon (Tell Sa'idiye) ; in the interior : Penuel (Tulūl ed-dahab) on the Jabbok, Miṣpeh (Kh. Gil'ad?), Ya'zer (Kh. Gazzir) and Yogbēha (Agbeihāt).

The **Manassites** in North Transjordania left the Aramaeans of Gešur and Beth-Ma'aka undisturbed but spread over a considerable territory in eastern Bashan and Northern Gil'ad. Cities : Maḥanaim (Kh. Maḥne), Jabeš-Gil'ad (on the Wady Yābis), Ramoth Gil'ad (Ḥoṣn 'Aglūn) and Edre'i (Der'a), Og's capital, in North Gil'ad ; Gōlān (Sahem el-Gōlān) and 'Aštarōth Qarnaim (Tell 'Astara) north of the Yarmuk, Boṣora (Buṣra eš-Šām) and Salcha (Salkhad) in the Ḥauran.

David's Kingdom—The census narrated in 2 Kg 25:5–8 **k** reveals to us the boundaries of the land inhabited by Israelites in the reign of David, practically identical with the region divided among the tribes. The census officials starting at Aroer on the Arnon passed through Gad, Jazer, Gilead, the land under *Hermon* and Dan, thence around the confines of Sidon and Tyre through the cities of the Canaanites and Hevites to the Negeb and Beersheba. Hermon is an easy correction, suggested by the context, of the unintelligible MT Hodši. Some read with Lucian for ' under Hodši ' *of the Hittites Qadeš* (on the Orontes), but subject peoples were excluded from this census. The nations subject to David were the Philistines in the SW, the Edomites in the SE., the Moabites and Ammonites in the east, and in the NE. the Aramaean city states of Ma'aka and Gešur in the Golan, Rehob in the southern Beqa', Ṭob (?), Damascus, Ṣōbah in the region of Homṣ, Anti-Lebanon and the northern Beqa'. As David was allied with Hiram of Tyre and Thou of Hamath, his kingdom was bounded by Tyre

57k and the Lebanon but included the Beqa', Anti-Lebanon and Damascus and reached the Orontes valley where Qadeš, Riblah and Šadūd mark the northern limit.

58a **Administrative Divisions of Solomon**—These divisions, made in view of taxation from which Judah was exempted, were: (1) The Mountain of Ephraim. (2) The ancient territory of Dan from Bethšemeš to Beth-Ḥanan (Beit 'Anan near el-Qubeibe). (3) Southern Sharon. (4) Northern Sharon from Wady Zerḳa to Carmel. (5) Cisjordanic Manasses including Megiddo, Taanach, Bethšean and the Jordan valley to Ṣartan. (6) Northern Transjordanic Manasses including Bashan and Argob. (7) Central Transjordanic Manasses. (8) Nephtali. (9) Asher and Zabulon. (10) Issachar. (11) Benjamin. (12) Gad (LXXB), Galaad (MT).

b **The Separate Kingdoms**—Solomon's oppression of the northern tribes was the chief cause of the schism which produced two separate kingdoms: Judah in the south and Israel, also called Ephraim, in the north. According to the texts Judah had one, Israel ten tribes. The numbers are verified if we understand tribes as separate tribal territories of which Ruben, Simeon and Levi had none and Manasses had two. Though Benjamin and Dan are reckoned with the northern tribes, much of their territories by force of circumstances was incorporated in Judah. The line of demarcation between the two kingdoms varied somewhat at different periods but originally and usually ran from the mouth of the Jordan south of Jericho, through the Wady Kelt and the Wady Suwēnit between Geba and Mikhmas, north of Rama and Gibeon, through the Wady Selmān north of Ayalon, and south of Gezer to the Nahr Rubin and the sea. Judah moreover had Edom and Israel Moab as vassal states.

c **Assyrian Administration**—The Assyrians, after deporting the principal inhabitants and installing foreigners in their place, established provinces under provincial governors in the countries which they added to their empire. Tiglathpileser III in 733 B.C. detached three such provinces from the Northern Kingdom: Gal'aza (Gilead), Du'uru (Dor or Sharon from the Nahr el-'Auga to Acre) and Magidu (Megiddo or Esdraelon with Zābulon and Nephtali). Subsequently Sargon II established the provinces of Samerina (Samaria or Ephraim and Manasses) in 721 and Ashdudu (Ashdod adjoining Du'uru in the north and controlling all Philistia) in 711. Judah was neither colonized nor made a province by the Babylonians but fell under the jurisdiction of the governor of Samaria. Many western cities had been given to Ashdudu by Sennacherib.

d **Palestine under the Persians**—The exiles returned to a much diminished Judah, surrounded by hostile peoples: in the north the Samaritans who claimed jurisdiction over them, in the east the Ammonites who had reached the Jordan, in the south the Arabians or Edomites who occupied most of their territory and in the west the Philistines or Azotians of the province of Ashdod. Their most southerly cities were Bethlehem and Netōpha (3 m. farther south), their most northerly Jericho, Bethel and the four cities of the Gibeonite confederacy. When Darius I divided the empire into satrapies, Judah became a province of the satrapy of Abar-Nahara, the lands beyond the river (Euphrates), under a pēḥa or provincial governor, but was not fully *sui iuris* until the time of Nehemias. Her southern boundary then extended to Zanoah (Kh. Zanuḥ) and Qeila (Kh. Qilā) in the Shephelah, Beth Ṣur and Thecua in the hilly country. Under the Persians the Phoenicians occupied all Sharon. Esdraelon belonged to the Samaritans who probably shared Galilee with the Phoenicians.

e **Palestine under the Greeks**—When the conquests of Alexander were finally divided between the Seleucids and the Lagids the Jews found themselves under the mild rule of the latter. Coelesyria, however, which then included all Syria and Palestine south of the

Orontes valley except the Phoenician coast land, was **58e** claimed by the Seleucids and finally conquered by Antiochus III in 198 B.C. The Jews thus became subject to the Seleucids. Satrap and satrapy were now superseded by Stratēgos and Stratēgia. The Stratēgia of Abar-Nahara contained in the north two Syrian regions, Seleucia and Coelesyria, and in the south Galaaditis (Northern Transjordania), Samaritis (Samaria and part of Galilee), Judaea, Idumaea (from Beth-Ṣur southwards), Paralia (the sea-coast from Ptolemais = Acre to the Egyptian frontier), Phoenicia. The Nabataeans spread northwards from Edom to Moab and Southern Galaad. City states were founded, the beginnings of the later Decapolis. Jonathan, the last of the Maccabees, extended considerably the northern boundary of Judah by annexing the Samaritan districts attached to Lydda, Ramathaim (Rentis), Aphairema (eṭ-Ṭaiyibe) and Acrabatta ('Aqrabe, 9 m. SE. of Nablus). The ephemeral conquests of the later Hasmonaean monarchs ended in internal dissensions and Roman intervention.

Palestine and Transjordania in NT Times—When **f** Christ was born nearly all the ancient land of Israel was a vassal kingdom of the Roman Empire ruled by Herod the Great. Northern Galilee, however, and the sea-coast as far as Dor belonged to the Phoenicians and Eastern Gilead to the city states of the Decapolis and the Nabataeans. After Herod's death (4 B.C.) his kingdom was divided between his three sons: Archelaus, ethnarch of Idumaea, Judaea and Samaria until A.D. 6, Herod Antipas, tetrarch of Galilaea and Peraea until A.D. 39, and Philip, tetrarch of Northern Transjordania and Ulatha-Paneas until A.D. 34. King Herod Agrippa I, grandson of Herod the Great, ruled over the tetrarchy of Philip from A.D. 37, that of Herod Antipas from A.D. 39, and the ethnarchy of Archelaus (governed by a Roman Procurator A.D. 6–41) from 41 until his death in A.D. 44 Idumaea, Judaea, Samaria, Galilaea and Peraea were then administered by a Roman Procurator subject to the governor of Syria until the Jewish revolt (A.D. 44–66), and after its suppression became the Roman province of Judaea (A.D. 70–135). The tetrarchy of Philip was directly attached to the province of Syria during all this period except A.D. 50–85 when it was ruled by King Herod Agrippa II. The following description of the regional divisions applies equally to kingdom and province.

Idumaea—Edomites, pressed westwards and north- **g** wards by the Nabataeans gave this region its name. At this period they had adopted the Jewish religion and institutions. Their southern boundary ran from a little above the end of the Dead Sea by Beersheba and Gaza to the Mediterranean. The northern limit is only vaguely determined by the location of Azotus (Esdūd), Bethgabris later Eleutheropolis (Beit Gibrīn) and Engaddi in Judaea, but of Ascalon, Beth-Ṣur and Masada (es-Sebbe) in Idumaea. Gaza is the only city mentioned in the NT.

Judaea—The name designates originally and strictly the land of post-exilic Judah between Idumaea and Samaria, but is used more widely to indicate Judaea and Idumaea, the kingdom of Herod and the Roman province. Its line of demarcation from Samaria, roughly from the Nahr el-'Auga above Jaffa to the Jordan above the Jabbok, lay north of Antipatris (Râs el-'Ain), Anuath Borcaeus (Ain Berḳīt), Acrabatta ('Akrabe) and Coreae (Karāwa). In Herod's time it was divided into eleven toparchies: Oreine (Montana, the Jerusalem district), Idumaea, Herodium (Fureidis near Thecua), Engaddi, Jericho, Pelle (Beit-Nettif), Emmaus, later Nicopolis ('Amwās), Lydda, Thamna (Tibne), Gophna (Gifne) and Acrabatta. Cities: Antipatris, Arimathaea (Rentis), Azotus, Bethania (el-'Azariyye), Bethlehem, Bethphage (Kefr eṭ-Tur), Emmaus (Qubeibe, 'Amwās?), Ephraim (eṭ-Ṭaiyibe), Jericho, Jerusalem, Joppe (Yāfā), Lydda, Rama, Siloam (Kefr-Silwān).

Samaria—We exclude Esdraelon which may have **h**

58h belonged to Samaria or Galilaea or been divided between them, Carmel which was Phoenician and Scythopolis (Beisān) part of the Decapolis. The northern boundary ran from the Wady Zerḳa above Caesarea by Jenin and Mt Gelboe to Wady Māliḥ and the Jordan. The Samaritans were hated and despised by the Jews as racially distinct and religiously unorthodox. Cities : Samaria, rebuilt by Herod and called Sebaste (Ṣebasṭiyye), Turris Stratonis, 8 m. S. of Dor, also rebuilt by Herod and called Caesarea, the capital and residence of the Procurator, Shechem (Balāṭa) and Sychar (village or suburb east of Shechem).

Galilaea—The boundary on the Phoenician frontier ran from the northern end of Lake Huleh or Semachonitis south of Cedeš and north of Gishcala (el-Gīš) to Baca (el-Buḳei'a), then southwards east of Qabūl to Gaba (Sheikh Abreik). The Scythopolis territory was south of Mt Moreh (ed-Daḥi) and the Sahel el-Aḥma. First Sepphoris (Saffūriya, 5 m. NNW. of Nazareth), then Tiberias (Ṭabariyya) was the capital. Galilaea included a narrow strip of land on the east side of the lake. Cities : Bethsaida (et-Tell and Kh. el-'Arag north of Lake Galilee), Cana (Kh. Qana, 9 m. N. of Nazareth), Capharnaum (Tell Ḥūm), Corozain (Kerāziye), Magdala (Megdel), Naim (Nein, 2 m. S. of Thabor), Nazareth (en-Nāṣire), Tiberias.

Peraea—The name is derived from the Greek πέραν beyond (the Jordan). Peraea with Galilee was ruled by Herod Antipas in Gospel times. It was a long narrow strip of land extending to Machaerus east of the Dead Sea (Mkāwer) where the Baptist was imprisoned and beheaded, and bounded by Pella (Fāḥil), refuge of the Christians of Jerusalem (A.D. 66), in the north, Gerasa and Philadelphia ('Ammān) in the east, and the Nabataean kingdom in the south-east and south. Its capital was Gadara (Tell Gadūr in South Gilead). The way from Galilee to Jerusalem passed through it. No cities are mentioned in the NT. **58h**

Ituraea and Trachonitis—The Ituraeans were Arabs who settled in NE. Palestine and South Syria in the 6th–5th cent. B.C. Lk 3:1 refers only to Palestinian Ituraea north of Lake Huleh consisting of Ulatha ('arḍ el-Hule) and Paneas (Banyās). Trachonitis is the stony region of the Legā but designates all the tetrarchy of Philip in Philo and Josephus, all except Ituraea in Lk, viz. Gaulanitis (Gōlān), most of the ancient Bashan, Batanea (en-Nuqra), a fertile region SE. of Gōlān, Trachonitis and Auranitis, the mountain of the Druses and the land watered by it.

Decapolis—These ten cities with their territories were autonomous states attached to the province of Syria. Two were isolated, Canatha in northern Auranitis and Damascus. The others were contiguous and occupied the region called Decapolis in the Gospels. They were Scythopolis in Cisjordania, Pella directly opposite in Transjordania, Hippos (Qala'at el-Ḥoṣn) in SW. Gaulanitis, Gadara (Mukeis) in NW. Gilead, Abila (Tell Abīl) east and Dion (Tell el-Ašari) farther east of Gadara, Gerasa (Geraš) SE. of Pella and Philadelphia ('Ammān). The Decapolis thus included ancient Gilead (except Peraea) and territories west and north of it. The coastal cities south of Joppe had a similar regime 4 B.C.–A.D. 41, but were incorporated in Judaea after the death of Herod Agrippa I in A.D. 44 These Hellenistic city states were a counterpoise to Jewish nationalism.

THE HISTORY OF ISRAEL

(to 130 B.C.)

By E. POWER, S.J.

59a Bibliography—Only recent and important works are indicated. Ricciotti (English tr. in preparation) is particularly recommended.
General History—*L. Albrecht, *Die Geschichte des Volkes Israel*, Gotha, 1926² ; *L. Browne, *The Story of the Jews from the Earliest Times to the Present Day*, London, 1926 ; *H. Gressmann, *E. Ebeling, *H. Ranke, *N. Rodokanakis, *Altorientalische Texte zum AT*, Berlin, 1926² ; *E. Montet, *Histoire du peuple d'Israël*, Paris, 1926 ; *N. H. Baynes, *Israel among the Nations*, London, 1927; *I. M. Price, *The Dramatic Story of OT History*, New York, 1927 ; L. C. Fillion, *Histoire d'Israël peuple de Dieu*, Paris, 1927–28 ; *G. A. Barton, *A History of the Hebrew People*, New York, 1930 ; L. Desnoyers, *Histoire du peuple hébreu* (Judges to Solomon), Paris, 1930 ; F. Feldmann, *Geschichte der Offenbarung des AT bis zum Exil*, Bonn, 1930³ ; *A. Lods, *Israël des origines au milieu du VIIIᵉ siècle*, Paris, 1930 (Tr. by S. H. Hooke, London, 1932) ; *A. Bentzen, *Israels Historie*, Copenhagen, 1931 ; *A. Jirku, *Geschichte des Volkes Israel*, Leipzig, 1931 ; *A. T. Olmstead, *History of Palestine and Syria*, New York, 1931 ; *R. Kittel, *Geschichte des Volkes Israel*, Stuttgart, I 1932⁷, II 1925⁶, III 1927–29 ; *T. H. Robinson and *W. O. E. Oesterley, *A History of Israel*, Oxford, 1932 ; *J. Hempel, *AT und Geschichte*, Guetersloh, 1932 ; A. Pohl, *Historia populi Israelis inde a divisione regni usque ad exilium*, Roma, 1933 ; G. Ricciotti, *Storia d'Israele*, Torino, 1932–34 ; L. Dennefeld, *Histoire d'Israël et de l'ancien Orient*, Paris, 1935 ; *E. Sellin, *Geschichte des isr.-jüd. Volkes*, Leipzig, I 1935², II 1932 ; *E. Auerbach, *Wueste und Gelobtes Land*, Berlin, 1932–36 ; J. Coppens, *Pour mieux comprendre et mieux enseigner l'histoire sainte de l'AT*, Paris, 1936 ; *T. G. Platten, *The Odyssey of Israel*, London, 1936 ; A. Allgeier, *Biblische Zeitgeschichte in den Grundlinien dargestellt*, Freiburg, 1937 ; J. Keulers, *Bijbelsche Geschiedenis*, Roermond, 1938² ; *H. W. Robinson (and others), *Record and Revelation*, Oxford, 1938 ; Pelt-Hennequin, *Histoire de l'Ancien Testament*, Paris, 1939 ;
b D. Rops, *Histoire Sainte*, Paris, 1943. **Patriarchial Period**—*K. Galling, *Die Erwaehlungstraditionen Israels*, Giessen, 1927 ; R. de Vaux, ' La Palestine et la Transjordanie au deuxième millénaire et les origines des Israélites ', ZATW 15 (1938) 225–38 ; P. Dhorme, ' Abraham dans le cadre de l'histoire ', RB 37 (1928) 367–85, 481–511 ; 40 (1931) 364–74, 503–18 ; *C. L. Woolley, *Abraham—Recent Discoveries and Hebrew Origins*, London, 1936 ; R. de Vaux, ' Les patriarches hébreux et les découvertes modernes ', RB 53 (1946) 321–48, 55 (1948) 321–47, 56 (1949) 5–36. **Egyptian, Desert, Conquest, and Judges Periods**—*Cf.* bibliographies to Comm. on Exodus, Josue and Judges. **United Monarchy**—*W. W. Cannon, ' The Reign of Saul ', *Theology* 25 (1932, 2) 326–35 ; L. Pirot, ' David ', DBVS 2 (1932) 287–330 ; R. de Vaux, ' Titres et fonctionnaires égyptiens à la cour de David et de Salomon ', RB 48 (1939) 394–405. **Divided Monarchy** —*J. Begrich, *Die Chronologie der Koenige von Israel und Juda*, Tuebingen, 1929 ; H. Haensler, ' Die biblische chronologie des 8. Jahrhunderts v. Christ ', Bi 10 (1929) 257–74, 377–93 ; 11 (1930) 63–80 ; P. Lemaire, ' Crise et effondrement de la monarchie davidique ', RB 45 (1936) 161–83 ; *W. W. Cannon, ' Israel and Moab ', *Theology* 20 (1930, 1) 184–96, 249–61 ; *O. Eissfeldt, ' Israelitisch-philistaeische Grenzverschie-

59b bungen von David bis auf die Assyrerzeit ', ZDPV 66 (1943) 115–28 ; R. de Vaux, ' Le schisme religieux de Jeroboam I ', *Angelicum* 20 (1943) 77–81 ; *H. Parzen, ' The Prophets and the Omri Dynasty ', HTR 33 (1940) 69–96 ; R. de Vaux, ' La chronologie de Hazaël et de Benhadad III rois de Damas ', RB 43 (1934) 512–18 ; *L. Honor, *Sennacherib's Invasion of Palestine*, New York, 1926. **Exilic Period**—A. Bea, ' Koenig Jojachin in Keilschrifturkunden ', Bi 23 (1942) 76–82 ; D. Sidersky, ' L'onomastique hébraïque des tablettes de Nippur ', Rev. Et. Juiv. 87 (1929, 1) 177–99. **Persian Period**—R. de Vaux, ' Les décrets de Cyrus et de Darius sur la reconstruction du Temple ', RB 46 (1937) 29–37 ; J. Touzard, ' Les Juifs au temps de la période persane ', RB 24 (1915) 59–133 ; *A. C. Welch, *Post-Exilic Judaism*, Edinburgh, 1935 ; J. Gabriel, *Zorobabel*, Wien, 1927 ; *H. H. Schaeder, *Esra der Schreiber*, Tuebingen, 1934 ; A. Van Hoonacker, ' La succession chronologique Néhémie-Esdras ', RB 32 (1932) 481–94 ; 33 (1924) 33–64 ; *M. Gaster, *The Samaritans*, Oxford, 1926. **Greek Period**—*E. R. Bevan, ' Syria and the Jews ', CAH 8 (1930) ch 16 ; F. M. Abel, ' Antiochus Epiphanes ', *Vivre et Penser* 1 (1941) 231–54 ; *A. Causse, *Les dispersés d'Israël*, Paris, 1929.

Introductory—The history of Israel begins with the **c** call of Abraham to the worship of the one true God and the revelations made to him which foretold the destiny of his race. His descendants, God's chosen people, should inhabit the land of Canaan and in his seed all the nations of the earth should be blessed. These fundamental facts cannot be ignored as they are the key to the correct interpretation of the sacred records. The inspired writers are chiefly concerned with setting forth the designs of God in his dealings with his chosen people and tracing the accomplishment of these designs in their history. They omit as irrelevant to their purpose much that we should like to know and often ignore the secondary causes and the concatenation of the events which they record. It is the task of the historian to supply as far as possible these omissions and to explain when necessary the circumstances, the sequence and the natural causes of the events. In this short sketch of the history of Israel many details and incidents of minor importance must be omitted. For these and for fuller information on other matters the reader is referred to the commentaries.
The Patriarchal Period—The children of Israel were **d** descended through Jacob and Isaac from Abraham, the son of Terah (Thare). Abraham first appears as a native of the Sumerian city of Ur in southern Babylonia. His name and the names of his clansmen, recorded in the sacred text, are Semitic and can be paralleled in the Babylonian records of the early second millenium. He belonged therefore to a branch of the Semites, nomadic peoples whose original home was Arabia and who migrated in considerable numbers about this period into the adjoining settled regions. Many writers attach Abraham, the Hebrew, to the Habiru immigrants since Hebrew and Habiru may be philologically akin and 'Eber (Heber), from whom Hebrew seems to be derived, was the common ancestor of Israelites and Arabs, Gen 10:25 f. Others prefer to associate him with the Aramaeans and Chaldaeans who however only appear in the texts under these names several

59d centuries later. Abraham's ancestors were polytheists, Jos 24:2 ; Jud 5:8, and very probably like most Semite nomads had a particular veneration for the Moon-god, the Babylonian Sin, who was the tutelary deity of Ur. The city moreover enjoyed great prosperity and ruled over all southern and central Mesopotamia at the close of the third millenium B.C. when Semites mingled with Sumerians in its streets. But it subsequently fell on evil days especially when its inhabitants were massacred by Sin-Muballit, the predecessor of Hammurabi. As Abraham was very probably a contemporary of Hammurabi the approach of this calamity to Ur may have been a factor in the migration of his clan to **Harran.** This city was a colony and, from the religious point of view, a replica of Ur, having the same tutelary deities, Sin and his consort, Ningal. It would thus be a natural place of refuge for fugitives from the mother-city. Its name, which means 'way', signalized its importance as the meeting-place of the two great routes to Syria from the south and east. It lay in the centre of the region circumscribed by the Euphrates and the Chabor, later called Aram Naharaim.

e Though Abraham received the first intimations of his mission in Ur it was in Harran that he was ordered by God to migrate to Canaan, Gen 12:1–5 ; Ac 7:2–4. We have an approximate indication of the date of this event in the synchronism of Gen 14:1. Abraham was in Canaan during the reign of Amraphel king of Senaar, the region which had Babylon for its capital, Gen 11:2, 9, and contained also the cities of Uruk (Arach) in southern and Agade (Akkad) in northern Babylonia, Gen 10:10. The only Babylonian monarch whose name resembles Amraphel is Hammurabi, also written Hammurapi. The Hebrew reproduction of the Babylonian name is sufficiently exact, except in the addition of a letter *l*, which is variously explained and does not materially affect the identification. The stratification of the finds made at Rās-Shamra, confirmed by other recent discoveries, places the reign of Hammurabi after the close of the twelfth Egyptian dynasty which can be dated absolutely, by our knowledge of the position of the seventh year of Senusret III in the corresponding Sothic period (*cf*. § 118*e*), *c* 1989–1776. Abraham may thus be assigned with much probability to the second half of the 18th cent. B.C. If however, with many recent historians, we reject the identification of Amraphel and Hammurabi, the patriarch's migration from Harran to Canaan may still be associated with the movement of nations from north to south in the early centuries of the second millenium B.C.

f **Canaan** is the region between the Mediterranean and the Jordan extending from Lebanon in the north to the Egyptian desert in the south. It was scantily inhabited in the fourth millenium B.C. by a non-Semitic people, probably of northern origin, who dwelt in caves and valleys, practised agriculture and did not fortify their cities. Semites invaded the land early in the third millenium. They settled especially in the plains and on the coast, built walled cities and developed the civilization of the Early Bronze Age. These are the Canaanites of the OT, often distinguished as plain dwellers from the Amorrhaeans in the hilly regions. Both names are however also used indiscriminately for

g the earlier inhabitants of Canaan. We have ample information on the invasion of the Amorrhaeans in the 19th cent. B.C, from the Egyptian Proscription texts (*cf*. § 118*h*) and archaeological investigations. The texts reveal to us a people recently settled in Palestine, whose names proclaim their kinship with the contemporary Amorrhaean invaders of Mesopotamia. Explorations in Transjordania show a change in the population from settlers to nomads at the same period. The invaders therefore overran Transjordania before they settled in Palestine. The earlier Proscription texts depict the nomadic invaders as still under tribal organization. The second collection, variously dated from a generation to a century later, manifests their political development into independent city states.

There are other indications that Egypt claimed and to **59g** some extent exercised a suzerainty over Palestine and Syria during the twelfth dynasty. The city of Megiddo, most important to the Egyptians as commanding the chief trade route to the north and not mentioned in the Proscription texts, had an Egyptian official resident. Another Egyptian official is attested at Ugarit in Syria. Canaan therefore at the period of Abraham's arrival was ruled by Amorrhaeans over whom Egypt claimed dominion. Egyptian interest was concentrated on the trade routes. The recent nomadic condition of the Amorrhaeans, still unchanged in Transjordania, forbids us to suppose that they had all become settled in Palestine. The city states had their territories but there remained considerable tracts of common land especially in the hill country at the disposal of nomads. Thus the Hebrew immigrants could lead there a nomadic or semi-nomadic life without being involved in political disturbances, except when, as in the case of Lot, they allied themselves with the city dwellers.

Recent discoveries have strikingly confirmed **the relia-** **h** **bility of the patriarchal traditions** recorded in Genesis. The names and customs of the patriarchs are those of the ancient period in which they lived, not of the later period in which the records were written. Abram, of which Abraham seems to be a dialectical variant, appears in Babylonia, only in the early second millennium, written Abaamrama, Abarama, Abaamraam. The name is Akkadian, meaning 'love the father', if the second element is the verb *ra'amu*, 'love', but Amorrhaean or west Semitic, meaning 'great as to the father' or 'well-born', if the second element is *râm*, 'be lofty'. Isaac and Jacob are apocopated theophoric names of which the complete forms are Yishaq-el, 'may God smile' or 'be favourable', and Ya'qob-el, most probably 'may God protect'. This form of name is west Semitic, common among the Amorrhaeans, rare among the Canaanites. Isaac is not attested outside the Bible but Jacob was recently discovered as a personal name Ya-ah-qu-ab-el at Shagar Bazar in northern Mesopotamia in the 18th cent. It appears also as a Palestinian place name in a 15th cent. Egyptian text (*cf*. Jephthah and Jephthahel). Thus the patriarchal names are undoubtedly personal names, in use among people to whom the patriarchs were akin and at the period to which they belong, but not attested at the later date when the records were written. Similarly the customs of the patriarchs, when they differ from those of the later Hebrews, indicate the land of their origin. With regard to marriage, for instance, the ornaments given by Eliezer to Rebecca, Gen 24:47, the dowry implied by the claims of Rachel and Lia, Gen 31:14 f., the gifts offered by Sichem to the father and brothers of Dina and the multiplication of the marriage price in atonement of his offence, Gen 34:12, are all in agreement with Babylonian law but are not attested in the law codes and later books of the OT.

The theory which makes the patriarchs not persons **i** but peoples and interprets the events recorded as tribal movements, alliances and contests, ignores entirely the religious character of the narratives and becomes ridiculous when consistently applied. An individual ancestor can represent a tribe, but such a use of a personal name cannot be supposed without proof. Israel is regularly used to represent the Israelites, but Jacob rarely as an equivalent of Israel and Abraham and Isaac only once or twice in poetic parallelism with Israel. The sacred writer clearly regards the patriarchs as individuals and since his description of them agrees with their historical milieu they were also individuals in his sources.

The Egyptian Period—Shortly after Abraham's arrival in Canaan northern peoples called **Hyksos** by the **60a** Egyptians and consisting chiefly of Hurrites and Semites invaded Palestine. Their superior armament, especially their horses and chariots, enabled them to conquer the Palestinians and subsequently the Egyptians

60a over whom they ruled *c* 1730-1580 B.C. It was apparently before the end of this period that the Israelites migrated to Egypt. Their arrival after the expulsion of the Hyksos seems improbable. The Egyptians were by no means inhospitable to Asiatic nomads, as their monuments attest, but were then so exasperated against all Asiatics that they would scarcely have elevated Joseph to his high dignity or accorded his kinsmen a favourable reception. The Israelites were assigned a district in Lower Egypt suitable for the raising of flocks and herds and called Goshen (LXX Gesem) and the land of Ramesses. The former identification of Goshen with one of the 'nomes' in the Delta was based on a false reading of Gesem for Sesem. The land of Ramesses means the land adjoining the city of Ramesses, very probably Tanis. The prodigies of the Exodus occurred in the land of Tanis, (Ps 77:12, 43). Even if Ramesses be located at the rival site of Qantir about fifteen miles south of Tanis the land of Ramesses could still be the land of Tanis.

b After the expulsion of the Hyksos in the eighteenth dynasty Egypt reached the height of its power in the reign of **Thuthmose III** (*c* 1485-1450 B.C.), the conqueror of Nubia, Palestine and Syria. From his fifteen Asiatic campaigns this Pharaoh undoubtedly brought back to Egypt many prisoners of war who became slaves and were employed in forced labours and military service. People called Aperu are mentioned in the Egyptian texts as thus employed during the whole period of Egyptian rule in Palestine and Syria (*c* 1500-1160 B.C.). It is natural to conclude that these were Asiatic slaves and to connect them with the Habiru of the Babylonian, Hittite, Ras-Shamra and Amarna texts. The connexion is suggested by the similarity of name, Asiatic origin, and social condition. The Israelites, known as Hebrews to foreigners, may have been akin to them. But they must not be identified with them since they were not slaves but alien residents. The forced labours to which slaves were subjected in Egypt were mostly building operations. The constructions of the Pharaohs of the eighteenth dynasty were, chiefly at least, in Upper Egypt where they resided. · With these the Israelites **c** in the Delta would have no concern. The situation was changed by **Ramesses II** (*c* 1298-1232) of the nineteenth dynasty who transferred the capital and royal residence from Thebes to the Delta and built especially, though not exclusively, in the region where he dwelt. He was the builder of Ramesses and Pithom, store cities commanding the two routes to Asia and natural bases of operation for his Asiatic campaigns. His close contact with the Israelites in the Delta made him realize their increase in number and his solicitude for the security of his empire made him regard them as a menace in the possible recurrence of an Asiatic invasion. By subjecting them to forced labours he hoped to diminish their numbers and break their spirit. From the peculiar circumstances of his reign we can easily understand the employment of the Israelites at the construction of Ramesses and Pithom, the record of the death of only one Pharaoh oppressor who had a very long reign and the residence of the Pharaoh in the immediate neighbourhood of the Israelites during the whole period of the oppression. It has been argued that earlier Pharaohs may also have built on the sites of Ramesses and Pithom and may have resided temporarily in the Delta. The first objection has considerable force. Ramesses II is known to have appropriated the labours of earlier Pharaohs and effaced their inscriptions from the monuments. The second scarcely takes sufficient account of the implications of the biblical narrative. On the whole the positive points of contact between the events recorded in Exodus and the historical situation of Egypt in the nineteenth dynasty are too strong to be ignored. They do not, however, justify an entirely definite conclusion. Archaeological discoveries in Transjordania and Palestine, more directly

concerned with the date of the Israelite occupation **60c** of Canaan, must also be considered.

The oppression of the Israelites by forced labours **d** under Ramesses II was aggravated by his son and successor, **Mernephtah** (1232-1224). It was in the first year of this Pharaoh's reign that the plagues and the exodus occurred. The cisterns dug for drinking water in the immediate neighbourhood of the Nile show that the river had not yet overflowed its banks at the time of the first plague towards the end of June. The institution of the Pasch fixes the tenth plague and the exodus about the beginning of the following April. All the plagues except the last were connected with natural phenomena which occur in Egypt. God's power over nature was thus attested in matters well known and of vital interest to the Egyptians. The miraculous character of the plagues was manifested by the abnormal intensity and effects of the phenomena and the preternatural determination of the time when they began and ended. If regarded merely as an exaggerated description of natural phenomena, they become ridiculous, since they cannot effect their avowed object of making the omnipotence of Yahweh known to the Egyptians. The tenth plague in particular defies all naturalistic explanations.

As the return to Sinai after **the exodus** had been **e** foretold to Moses, Ex 3:12, the immediate destination of the Israelites in their flight was not Canaan but Sinai. They followed therefore, not the way of the Philistines along the coast of the Mediterranean to Canaan, but the way of the desert to the Red Sea and Sinai. Marching from Ramesses in a southeasterly direction they made their first recorded halt at Succoth. The word means 'tents', *i.e.* 'encampment'. Its identification with Theku, Tell el-Maskhuta in the Wadi Tumilat, is not philologically assured but suits the direction of the march. They then proceeded to Etham, the Egyptian fortress (hetem) on the edge of the desert at the northern end of the Bitter Lakes. From Etham they turned back into Egypt and finally encamped on the Egyptian side of the Red Sea. At this period the Red Sea undoubtedly communicated with the Bitter Lakes but scarcely covered the more northerly Serapeum. There is one indication in the text that the camp of the Israelites was on the regular Egyptian route to Sinai. It lay between Migdol (DV Magdal) and the Red Sea. Migdol is a Semitic word borrowed by the Egyptians and meaning 'fort'. Several texts mention a Migdol of Seti I, predecessor of Ramesses II, guarding the northern route to Asia. In one however a Migdol of Seti is located by the context on the southern frontier. This Migdol, guarding the route to Sinai, seems to have been the fort discovered at Tell Abu Hasa about 5 m. SW. of the Bitter Lakes. It contained a temple dedicated to Hathor, the tutelary goddess of the mines at Sinai. The inscriptions commemorate Seti I and Ramesses II. The route to Sinai seems therefore to have crossed the Red Sea by a ford south of the Bitter Lakes. We can thus understand why the drying up of the shallow waters of the ford is described in the text as effected by a strong continuous hot wind sent by Yahweh to facilitate the crossing.

The Desert Period—Our information on the wander- **61a** ings of the Israelites during this period is practically restricted to their journeys from Egypt to Sinai, from Sinai to Cades and from Cades to the eastern border of Canaan. In their journey to Sinai they followed the ordinary Egyptian route to the mines in the north of the peninsula, branched off from it at Elim, proceeded southwards along the shore of the Red Sea and thence ascended by a lateral valley to the holy mountain in the south where God had appeared to Moses. After a stay of nearly a year at Sinai they marched NNE. to **Cades** about 60 m. south of Beersheba with the intention of invading Canaan from the south. Here the reports of a reconnoitring party so discouraged them that they planned to return to Egypt and revolted against Moses. Their punish-

61a ment was exclusion from the Promised Land and the consequent postponement of the invasion for a generation. Cades was the central point of their wanderings during the period which elapsed before the march to Canaan was resumed. The name is preserved in the modern diminutive form Qudeis. Three springs at some distance from one another provided a water supply and the desert was steppe land in which flocks **b** could subsist. The final stage of the journey was determined by the decision to invade Canaan from the east and by the refusal of the kings of Edom and Moab to grant the Israelites a passage through their dominions. Edom at this period lay west of the Arabah valley and only later included the mountainous district to the east of it. The Israelites therefore marched south-east to Ezion-geber at the southern end of the Arabah and thence north along the valley to stay southern confines of Moab, thus considerably lengthening their journey to avoid encroachment on Edomite territory. Moab originally included the whole region between the Dead Sea and the Arabah. At this period however the northern half and Southern Galaad were subject to the Amorrhaean king, **Sehon,** and were almost entirely peopled by nomads. The Israelites therefore, after making the circuit of Moab on the south and east, requested from Sehon, a peaceful passage to the banks of the Jordan. His refusal resulted in the conquest of his kingdom in which Ruben and Gad immediately settled. Unlike the tribes who occupied Canaan they had to build their own cities, Num 33:34-38, in this previously unsettled district. Recent discoveries have confirmed the accuracy of the biblical account of Sehon's kingdom and nomad subjects. The only traces of settlement during the Late Bronze Age in the whole region occupied by Ruben and Gad have been found in the neighbourhood of Sehon's capital Heshbon. Extensive settlement in the Early Iron Age dates the arrival of the Israelites *c* 1200 B.C.

c The desert period had for its object the preparation of the Israelites for the invasion of Canaan and still more their national and religious formation. The older generation, depressed and dispirited by slavery and unaccustomed to warfare, was replaced by a more vigorous race, hardened by the experience of desert life and trained to battle by encounters with desert tribes. The choice of Israel as God's first born among the nations was solemnly ratified by a special **covenant** between Yahweh and his chosen people amid the thunders of Sinai. Such a covenant would be incomplete and without practical value if unaccompanied by an account of the engagements of the contracting parties. The Israelites learned from the Decalogue, the Book of the Covenant and the ceremonial laws how they could become the holy people of Yahweh who would recompense their fidelity with special benevolence and constant assistance. As a stiff-necked people, prone to idolatry, they needed also a period of religious training in the desert before coming into close contact with Canaanite idol-worship. Six of the precepts of the **Decalogue** are found in more ancient Egyptian and Babylonian texts. Of the remaining four the prohibition of polytheism and the two prohibitions of evil desires show the incontestable religious and moral superiority of the Israelites over all other ancient peoples. The Sabbath observance is based on the ancient principle, exemplified also in the sacred character of first-fruits and first born, that a definite part of man's time must be denied to his own uses and dedicated to God in acknowledgement of his universal dominion. The application of this principle suggests a continuous division of time into seven-day periods, unknown to other ancient nations and first attested in Israel. There is thus nothing in the Decalogue at variance with its Mosaic origin.

d The discovery in the last half-century of ancient Sumerian, Babylonian, Assyrian and Hittite codes or fragments of codes has refuted the charge of anachronism brought against the **Mosaic code** and contributed

at the same time to its better understanding and more **61d** exact evaluation. It has much in common with the code of Hammurabi, as might be expected from the customs of the patriarchs and the diffusion of Babylonian institutions in the east. It is adapted however to a primitive people at a much lower stage of culture, but displays a more elevated morality especially in the consideration shown to slaves and solicitude for the weak and oppressed. There is no trace in the Mosaic code of the curious moral perversion by which the Babylonians sometimes punished the innocent for the sins of the guilty. It is often objected to the Mosaic origin of the Book of the Covenant that the agricultural legislation supposes the settlement in Canaan. It may be answered however that the Israelites had become familiar with agricultural labours in Egypt and that the legislator had chiefly in view, not the short stay in the desert, but the proximate settlement in Canaan.

The special care of God for his chosen people was **e** particularly manifested by the miraculous provision or **multiplication of manna** without which they could not have survived for a generation. The arid region of their sojourn supports today at most 10,000 nomads and cannot have been much more productive in ancient times. That they were many times more numerous may be concluded from their remarkable increase during their long stay in Egypt, Ex 1, and their successful invasion of Canaan. They were too few however to occupy immediately the whole region, where Canaanites survived for at least two centuries to save the land from the evils of depopulation, Ex 23:29 f. ; Deut 7:22. We must disregard therefore the 600,000 fighting men, suggested by a few misinterpreted or interpolated texts, but may accept the reckoning of the invading army at 40,000, Jos 4:13, which is confirmed by the 40,000 fighting men of Israel in Deborah's time, Jg 5:8. This text is particularly valuable as part of an ancient document contemporary with the events described. It takes no account of the southern tribes of Judah and Simeon and thus allows for a normal increase of the warriors in the interval between Josue and Deborah. The total population during the wanderings may thus be estimated as between 150,000 and 200,000. The description of the manna with which this multitude was nourished assimilates it to the sweet and nourishing substance exuded by insects which feed on the leaves of the tamarisk trees and called manna by the nomads of Sinai. This natural food is available however only in the months of June and July and in so small a quantity that the entire yearly product of the peninsula is about six cwt. God's provision for his people was more continuous and more abundant and lasted throughout the whole desert period, Jos 5:12. His choice of Israel for a most important mission is the only adequate explanation of so extraordinary a miracle.

The Conquest of Canaan—Canaan at this period was **62a** under Egyptian rule. That implied at most a regular payment of tribute by the Canaanite princes, but their subjection was often merely nominal unless enforced by military expeditions. Mernephtah boasts of his capture of the rebel cities of Ascalon, Gezer and Yenoam and of his defeat of Israel in the fifth year of his reign (*c* 1228 B.C.). The reference to Israel is regarded by some historians as a proof of the settlement of the Israelites in Canaan before the reign of that Pharaoh. It may equally well indicate an encounter with Israelites in the desert between Egypt and Canaan or even with a group of Israelites who settled in Canaan before the main body. No subsequent Egyptian expedition to Asia is recorded before the eighth year of Ramesses III who defeated and repulsed in that year (*c* 1193 B.C.) the land and sea forces of northern peoples driven southward by a European invasion of Asia Minor. These invaders were encamped in Syrian Amurru north of Qadesh and the combined land and sea battle was fought most probably on the Phoenician coast. Two of the five

62a peoples mentioned, the Philistines and the Zakkara, had invaded Egypt by sea three years previously. Repulsed by Ramesses III they had settled then or earlier on the southern coast of Canaan, the Philistines in Philistia, the Zakkara at Dor in Sharon. Pottery discoveries at Tell el-Fara' place the Philistine settlement before 1240 B.C.

b The political condition of Canaan presented by the book of Josue is very similar to that depicted in the **Amarna tablets** during the invasion of the Habiri. The Canaanites formed a large number of independent city states. The larger cities sought to extend their dominions and preside over coalitions in which their less powerful neighbours were grouped. Jerusalem headed such a coalition against the invaders under Arti-Khepa at the earlier and Adoni-Sedek at the later period. The Egyptians pursued the same policy of non-interference. The invaders however followed different modes of procedure. The Habiri took service under native leaders and were equally active in Canaan and Syria. The Israelites fought alone and only in Canaan. The invasions are further distinguished by the fact that the native princes of a number of cities bear entirely different names in the book of Josue and the Amarna tablets.

c God had promised possession of Canaan unconditionally to the descendants of Abraham. His chosen people were thus assured of his all-powerful assistance and the victories in Jos as well as in Jg are attributed entirely to Yahweh. This assistance was particularly needed and miraculously manifested at the siege of Jericho in the beginning of the campaign (*cf.* § 230*e, h*). **The army of Josue** was unskilled in the assault of fortified cities but well adapted for battle in the open field. His strategy was dictated by these circumstances. He showed his military superiority by signal defeats of Canaanite coalitions in pitched battles and established himself solidly in the centre of the land making Shiloh his first capital. Cities were captured in these campaigns by surprise or by stratagem or when denuded of their defenders, but Josue's forces were not sufficient to garrison them. They were therefore sometimes reoccupied by the Canaanites when the Israelite army moved elsewhere and had to be recaptured in the second phase of the conquest. The reduction of the Canaanite strongholds and the occupation of their entire territory was left to the individual tribes in their allotted territories. It was a lengthy operation requiring increase in numbers and advance in military skill and not completed before the reign of Solomon. The hill country was first occupied as war chariots debarred access to the plain lands.

The biblical attestation of two phases in the conquest of Canaan is consistent in itself and to be expected if Josue had a fairly large army at his disposal. Those historians who number the invaders at a few thousands exclude the first phase as a later invention. They have then to explain how the Israelites, so few originally, filled the whole land in two centuries, instead of being absorbed in the mass of the Canaanites like the 14th cent. Habiri.

d **The archaeological evidence** for the date of the conquest is as follows. The sites of the important cities of Jericho and Hasor were occupied in the Late Bronze Age, but abandoned in the Early Iron Age. The date of Josue's capture of the cities is disputed and their abandonment is definitely dated. The scriptural evidence, by associating the ban with the capture, dates the latter in the transition period from bronze to iron, *c* 1200 B.C. Excavations at Tell Beit-Mirsim (Debir) and Tell Duweir (Lachish), cities captured by the invading Israelites, manifest a change of inhabitants towards the close of the Late Bronze Age and a marked inferiority of culture in the newcomers who wrecked pagan sanctuaries on both sites. The date is determined by the pottery and still more precisely at Lachish by a hieroglyphic inscription on a bowl assigning it to the fourth year of some Pharaoh who cannot be earlier **62d** than Mernephtah. The pottery which dates the destruction of Bethel, recorded in Jg 1:22, is more commonly assigned to the same period. Shiloh, the first capital of the Israelites, was sparsely inhabited in the Late Bronze Age, but was walled and populous in the Early Iron Age. These discoveries attest a new period in the history of Canaan inaugurated by the arrival of the Israelites after 1229 B.C. The date agrees with the corresponding dates of the Exodus and the settlement in Transjordania.

The Judges' Period—This period (*c* 1200–1050 B.C.) **63a** corresponds with the second phase of the conquest. The empires of the Hurrites and the Hittites no longer existed. Assyrian expansion had not yet begun. Egypt became decadent after the reign of Ramesses III (*c* 1200–1163). The campaigns of that Pharaoh in Syria did not bring him into contact with the Israelites, still in the hill country, since his route northwards passed through the plain lands. The special providence which guided the destinies of the chosen people thus enabled them to develop in numbers and strength without major interference. Their only enemies were the small nations who were their immediate neighbours. These were allowed to oppress them in punishment of their infidelities that they might repent and return to Yahweh, their all-powerful protector.

The dispersion of the various tribes to the districts **b** allotted to them necessarily weakened the national unity. **The nation became divided into groups** with different interests and different problems. Judah, Simeon and Dan in the south had the Philistines in the plain and the Amorrhaeans in the hill country to contend with. Jerusalem in the east, Gezer in the west and the intervening cities of the Hevite confederacy, Gabaon, Caphira, Beroth and Cariathiarim, separated them from their northern brethren. Ephraim, Manasses and Benjamin formed a compact block in the centre of the land. Their problems were the deforestation of northern Samaria and the extirpation of the Canaanites in the plain of Esdraelon. The northern tribes of Asher, Nephtali and Zabulon had Sidonians and Canaanites to subdue and were cut off from their brethren in the south by a long line of Canaanite fortresses, Bethsan, Yebleam, Megiddo, Taanach and Dor. The lot of Issachar in Esdraelon long remained Canaanite territory. The major and the minor judge of that tribe resided respectively in Ephraim and Manasses. The transjordanic tribes of Ruben, Gad and half Manasses had Moabites, Ammonites and nomads for their neighbours and even appear in conflict with their western brethren. The force of circumstances did not however entirely obliterate the consciousness of national unity. The northern and central groups combine against the Canaanites in the days of Deborah. All worship the same God, Yahweh, and are prepared to act together in matters of supreme religious importance like the war of the tribes against Benjamin. **The great judges** moreover appear in all four groups, Othniel and Samson in the south, Aod (Ehud) and Gedeon in the centre, Deborah and Barac in the north and Jephte in Transjordania.

The equation of the Hebrew *šōpēt* with its philological **c** equivalent the Carthaginian *suffet* and the inference that the judges ruled over all Israel are erroneous. Only two judges, Deborah and Samuel, exercised authority outside the tribe or group to which they belonged and that in virtue of the prophetic charism with which they were endowed. Solicitude for the weak and the oppressed has been already noted as a distinctive characteristic of the Mosaic code. The chief function of a judge in Israel was to right the wrongs of the oppressed. Such is the judgement to be exercised by the future Messias (*cf.* Ps 71). Judge is thus the equivalent of deliverer. When the Israelites are oppressed by foreigners in punishment of their sins, and repenting appeal to Yahweh, he raises up a judge to deliver them. As the oppressors are different in the

63c different groups and the judge is always chosen from the oppressed group it follows that his mission and authority are restricted to that group. Oppressors and consequently judges may be contemporaneous, as the text insinuates in the case of the Ammonites and the Philistines. The sacred writer follows generally the chronological order of events, but the overlapping of the periods makes the lists of years recorded useless for chronological purposes.

d Lack of central authority and close contact with the idolatrous Canaanites had very injurious effects on **the religion and morality** of the Israelites during this period. The various oppressions and enslavements were the punishment of the abandonment of Yahweh and the worship of the local Baals and Asherahs or Ashtartes. We need not suppose, however, that the Israelites totally rejected Yahweh, but they violated the first commandment by worshipping Canaanite divinities as well. Even in the central region where Ark and Tabernacle had been installed at Shiloh there was a sanctuary of Baal at Ophra and Israelites and Canaanites lived together at Sichem (Shechem) and probably worshipped in the same sanctuary a god called El-berith (' God of the covenant ') by the former and Baal-berith (' Lord of the covenant ') by the latter. The Danites set up a tribal sanctuary in the north-east of Palestine where descendants of Moses officiated as idolatrous priests. In Transjordania religious ignorance was so great that Jephte considered himself obliged to offer a human sacrifice to Yahweh in fulfilment of a rash vow. Moral depravity is exemplified by the savagery of Abimelech, the *amours* of Samson and the gross violation of the rights of hospitality at Gabaa. There is however another side to the picture, represented by the religious fervour and whole-hearted devotion to Yahweh manifest in the canticle of Deborah, the zeal of Gedeon in the destruction of the sanctuary of Baal, the self-immolation of the blind Samson, the consultation of and recourse to Yahweh in national needs. It must be remembered too that the centralization of cult in force during the desert wandering was neither possible nor obligatory at this period as appears from Josue's erection of an altar at Sichem. Samuel, the last of the judges, sought to revive the relaxed religious spirit by organizing groups of religious enthusiasts at whose exercises he presided.

e **The United Monarchy**—The occupation of their lots by the various tribes when they had increased in number and in strength broke the barriers between the isolated groups and restored the national unity which had been temporarily disrupted. The southern group remained longest aloof and was only united with the main body when its special problem became a national problem. The Philistines were superior to the Israelites in military equipment and were thus enabled to hold Judah in subjection in the days of Samson. Later they extended their dominion over Benjamin and the plain of Esdraelon and became a menace to all Israel. This common danger consolidated the national unity and produced also a religious revival.

The Israelites were normally ruled in the Judges' period by the elders of the various tribes. Israel in Samuel's time was a theocracy ruled by God through his prophet. The reunited people, conscious of the need of centralized and stable authority, desired to be ruled by a king like the neighbouring nations. God ordered the reluctant Samuel to accede to their desire. The choice of Saul as the first king was probably motivated by the relative insignificance of his tribe. A monarch from the tribe of Judah would scarcely have been recognized by the haughty Ephraimites. David, the second king, ruled originally only over his own tribe of Judah with which Simeon was incorporated. His nobility of character and recognized capacity as a soldier and as a ruler secured him subsequently the voluntary adhesion of the northern tribes. His dynasty was established by the military successes and prosperity of his reign. The institution of the monarchy was a step towards the fulfilment of the second promise made to Abraham that

in his seed all the nations of the earth would be blessed. **63e** The future Messias was to spring from the line of David and the eternity promised by God through the prophet Nathan to the Davidic dynasty was to be realized in his eternal reign.

Saul was remarkable for personal bravery, simplicity **f** of manners and military capacity. Unable to meet the better armed Philistines in open battle he harassed them with guerilla warfare and organized a national army for more decisive combats. He forced the Ammonites to raise the siege of Jabes Galaad and extirpated the Amalecites, the hereditary enemies of Israel in the south. His slaughter of the Gabaonites, protected by their treaty with Josue, was a crime subsequently punished by a famine and expiated by the execution of his descendants. But the two sins for which he was rejected by Yahweh were his offering of sacrifice when the delay of Samuel seemed to deprive him of a favourable opportunity of joining battle with the Philistines and his violation of the ban imposed on the Amalecites by sparing their king Agag and the best of their flocks and herds. His fits of melancholy and jealousy, his persecution of David, consultation of the witch of Endor, and defeat and death on Mt Gelboe cast a shadow on the last part of his reign. He left the Philistines in possession of the plain of Esdraelon, a greater menace than ever to Israel.

David was the real founder of the monarchy. He had **g** distinguished himself in his youth by his exploits against the Philistines and excited the jealousy of Saul who sought his life. He thus became leader of a band of outlaws in the desert of Judah, but was obliged to take refuge with Achis, the Philistine king of Gath, who gave him Siceleg (Ziklag) for his residence. After the death of Saul he established himself in Hebron as king of Judah. Saul's son, Ishbaal (MT Ishbosheth), supported by Abner, ruled over the northern tribes. The slaughter of Abner by Joab and the assassination of Ishbaal by two of his officers resulted in the voluntary acceptance of David's rule by the elders of the northern tribes.

David (1012–972 B.C.) subdued all the neighbouring **h** nations, except the Phoenicians who were his allies, and extended the kingdom of Israel to its furthest limits, from the Egyptian desert to Syrian Hamath and from the Arabian desert to the Mediterranean. His rule was similar in many respects to that of other oriental monarchs. He was the vicegerent of Yahweh as other kings were assumed to be the vicegerents of their tutelary deities. Like them he had a harem and contracted at least one political alliance by marriage with the daughter of the Aramaean king of Gesur. As the Hittite monarchs had Habiri in their bodyguard he had foreign mercenaries attached to his person, Cretans and Philistines under Benaias and men of Gath under Ethai. He moved his capital from Hebron to a more central position in Jerusalem as the Assyrian kings moved theirs from Assur to Calah and Nineveh. His wars with neighbouring nations to extend his dominions and his alliance with Hiram of Tyre against a common enemy, the Philistines, are other points of resemblance. Solomon carried the likeness further and became a typical oriental monarch.

The profoundly religious spirit of David is manifested **i** in the Psalms and not least in his prompt and sincere repentance of his two great sins. He was punished by family troubles, so common in oriental monarchies, the slaughter of Amnon, the revolt and outrageous conduct of Absalom, the ambition of Adonias. He conceived the project, executed by Solomon, of a central sanctuary at Jerusalem and moved the ark of the covenant from Cariathiarim to the summit of Mt Moriah. Among his other projects of religious reform was a reorganization of the priests and Levites. His census of his people, regarded as an encroachment on the domain of Yahweh, was punished by a pestilence. There is no indication of pomp at his court. The court officials mentioned, a recorder, a scribe and a minister of public works, resemble those of the Pharaohs.

63j The fame of the ancient kings of the East was measured by their buildings as well as by their victories. In Israel David was the warrior, **Solomon** the builder, at peace with his neighbours during his whole reign (971–931 B.C.). He maintained his father's alliance with Hiram of Tyre whose assistance was indispensable in his new ventures. The Phoenicians not only aided him in building and equipping a fleet for Red Sea trade, but also supplied him with cedar and cypress wood from Lebanon for his edifices at Jerusalem and artificers for their adornment. As money was scarce their services were requited with the cession of twenty Galilaean towns. Solomon like other Eastern monarchs traded by sea and land to meet the expenses and supply the materials of his building operations. Among his numerous wives was a daughter of the Pharaoh Siamon, whose dowry was the city of Gezer taken by her father from the Canaanites. Solomon garrisoned certain key cities for the defence of his realm and supplemented David's infantry with horses and chariots. Magnificent stables for his horses were recently unearthed at Megiddo.

The chief buildings erected at Jerusalem were the Mello, the temple and the palace. The Mello (lit. 'filling') filled up the depression on the west between Moriah and Jebus. The magnificent temple, where alone Yahweh henceforth manifested himself to his worshippers, was built on the summit of Mt Moriah. The royal palace was south of it. Both were enclosed in an outer court. The inner court contained the temple and the altar of holocausts. Canaanite slaves were insufficient for the building operations. Solomon unwisely exempted Judah when imposing taxation and forced labours on the northern tribes. Still more fatal to the future prosperity of his kingdom was his worship of the false deities of his foreign wives. His reign, begun so splendidly on the foundations laid by David, ended in disaster.

64a **The Divided Monarchy**—The revolt of the ten tribes was the divine chastisement of Solomon's worship of false gods. Its chief natural cause was the old animosity between north and south, revived and inflamed by partiality to Judah and harsh treatment of the northern tribes. There were also contributory causes. The disproportion between the splendour of Solomon's court and the economic resources of his kingdom increased the misery of the poorer classes and provoked social unrest. His cult of false gods alienated worship-

pers of Yahweh and his establishment of a central **64a** sanctuary at Jerusalem offended those who were attached to the local sanctuaries and profited from their popularity. The schism which followed Roboam's contemptuous refusal to modify his father's policy was a political and religious disaster inferior only to the subsequent loss of national existence. The strength of the chosen people was weakened by division and internecine warfare. Each kingdom suffered from foreign alliances of its rival, often dearly bought. Religion was debased in the north by exclusion from the national centre of Yahweh worship and the establishment of rival sanctuaries at Bethel and Dan where Yahweh was worshipped under the form of a bull.

The history of the two kingdoms is naturally divided **b** into three periods, characterized respectively by hostility (931–885), alliance (885–841) and independent development (841–721). **A relative chronology** can be established from the lengths of the reigns of the various kings. Assyrian synchronisms make this chronology absolute and test its reliability. In the following table the kings of the sole kingdom of Judah and the contemporary monarchs of Damascus and Assyria have been included. It will be noted that the ninety years' period between the accession of Roboam (931) and the deaths of Ochozias of Judah and Joram of Israel (841) covers ninety-five years of six kings of Judah and ninety-eight years of nine kings of Israel. The apparent discrepancy is explained by the Hebrew custom of reckoning part of a year as a whole year and thus attributing the year of a king's death to him and to his successor. On the other hand the period of one hundred and thirty-four and a half years between the fall of Samaria (721 January) and the fall of Jerusalem (587 June) corresponds exactly with the sum of the years of the kings of Judah in the interval. It is clear that the Assyrian method of dating is adopted according to which a king's reign began on the New Year's day after his accession so that no year was counted twice. The intervening period of 120 years (841–721) is represented by 164 years in Judah and 144 in Israel. The chronological difficulties of this period have been **c** admirably solved by Dom B. Haensler in his articles in *Biblica* 1929–30. The co-reigns of Azarias with Amasias, deposed after his disastrous defeat by Joas of Israel, and of Joatham and Achaz with Azarias, incapacitated by leprosy, being reckoned twice, account for the superfluous years of the kings of Judah. In the

64d CHRONOLOGICAL TABLE OF THE DIVIDED MONARCHY PERIOD

Judah		Israel		Assyria		Aram
Roboam (17)	931–915	Jeroboam (22)	931–910			
Abia (3)	915–913					
Asa (41)	913–873	Nadab (2)	910–909			
		Baasa (24)	909–886			Benhadad I
		Ela (2)	886–885			
		Zambri (7 days)	885			
		Omri (12)	885–874			
Josaphat (25)	873–849	Achab (22)	874–853	Salmanasar III	859–824	Benhadad II
		Ochozias (2)	853–852			
Joram (8)	849–842	Joram (12)	852–841			
Ochozias (1)	841					
Athalia (6)	841–836	Jehu (28)	841–814	Samsi-Adad V	824–810	Hazael
Joas (40)	836–797	Joachaz (17)	814–798	Adadnirari III	810–782	
Amasias (29)	797–769	Joas (16)	798–783			Benhadad III
Azarias (52)	785–734	Jeroboam (41)	787–747	Salmanasar IV	782–772	Zakir (of Hamat)
Joatham (16)	757–742	Zacharias (1)	747	Assurdan III	772–753	
		Sellum (1 month)	746	Assurnirari V	753–745	
Achaz (16)	742–727	Menahem (10)	746–737	Tiglath-pileser III	745–727	Rasin
		Phaceia (2)	737–736			
		Phacee (20?)	736–732			
Ezechias (29)	726–697	Osee (9)	730–722	Salmanasar V	727–721	
				Sargon II	721–705	
Manasses (55)	696–642			Sennacherib	705–681	
Amon (2)	641–640			Asarhaddon	681–669	
Josias (31)	639–609			Assurbanipal	669–626	
Joachaz (3 mths)	609					
Joakim (11)	608–598			*Babylonia*		
Joachin (3 mths)	598			Nabupolassar	626–605	
Sedecias (11)	597–587			Nabuchodonosor	605–562	

64c Israelite list the length of Phacee's reign, obviously erroneous since he can only have reigned part of the time between Menahem's payment of tribute to Assyria in 738 and his own death in 732, is due to an interpolator who is also responsible for some incorrect synchronisms. Osee's reign is reckoned from his confirmation by Tiglath-pileser after payment of tribute. A co-reign of Jeroboam with Joas must be assumed if he reigned forty-one and not thirty-seven years (*cf.* §§ 123-5).

Judah had a much smaller and less fertile territory than Israel. She had the advantage of a stable dynasty, and was thus saved from the frequent revolutions which produced no less than ten dynasties in Israel. She was also less exposed than Israel to the attacks of powerful neighbours, the Aramaeans and the Assyrians.

e Hostility (931-885)—**Jeroboam,** an Ephraimite, had attracted Solomon's attention during the building of the Mello at Jerusalem and been appointed overseer of the Joseph tribes. Here he became the natural leader of the movement of revolt and had to flee to Egypt to escape the wrath of Solomon. After the latter's death he returned and became the first king of Israel. The schism may have inspired and certainly favoured the attempt made by the Pharaoh Sesac (Sheshonkh I), who had usurped the throne of Solomon's father-in-law Siamon, to restore Egyptian dominion in Palestine. He captured and sacked many cities, Jerusalem included, in Palestine and Transjordania and left a memorial of his conquests, recently discovered, in Megiddo. His death soon after however and the subsequent decadence of Egypt averted the threatened danger which Roboam forestalled by fortifying several important cities. Jeroboam fixed his capital at Sichem and also fortified Phanuel in Galaad against a possible Aramaean invasion. He was not successful in his wars with Judah and had to abandon to Roboam's son, Abia, the Ephraimite cities of Bethel, Jesana and Ephron. His dynasty terminated after the brief reign of his son, Nadab, slain in a military sedition. The usurper, Baasa, transferred his capital to a more northerly site at Thersa, still unidentified. He recovered the Ephraimite cities lost by Jeroboam and pressing southwards was fortifying Rama only six miles from Jerusalem when he was recalled to defend his northern territories invaded by the Aramaeans. **Asa** purchased with costly presents the aid of Benhadad I of Damascus against his rival, thus initiating a policy which was to prove fatal to both kingdoms. And yet Asa was the only pious monarch of this period. He solemnly renewed the covenant with Yahweh and abolished the worship of false gods and the practices of Canaanite cult which prevailed under his predecessors.

f Alliance (885-841)—When Zambri slew Baasa's son, Ela, at Thersa and usurped his throne, the army, then besieging Gibbethon, made their commander, **Omri,** king. Zambri perished after a seven days' reign but another pretender, Thebni, made a longer resistance. Thus Omri's chief exploits belong to the latter half of his reign. He built a new capital at Samaria, subdued the Moabites who had revolted after the death of Solomon and by a treaty with the Tyrians, from which he reaped great commercial advantages, inaugurated a system of alliances which made Israel materially prosperous but had disastrous religious effects on both kingdoms. He maintained peace with Judah but whether he or his successor made the alliance with that kingdom is uncertain. The alliances were cemented by marriages, Omri's son, Achab, espoused Jezabel, daughter of the king of Tyre, and Josaphat's son, Joram, wedded Athalia, daughter of Achab and Jezabel. The menace of Damascus, a very important trading centre which sought an outlet on the Mediterranean, was countered by these alliances. Judah was dependent on Israel during this whole period. She retained her autonomy and her northern boundary, fixed by Asa at Geba and Michmas, but her king and army had to accompany the northern monarchs in their military expedi-

tions against the Aramaeans and the Moabites. Omri **64f** was unsuccessful in his war with Benhadad I of Damascus to whom he surrendered many cities and granted trading posts in Samaria, his capital. His son, **Achab,** extended and adorned the royal residence **g** at Samaria. Recent excavations have revealed to us the splendour of his ' ivory house ' and the sumptuousness of his court. In the latter part of his reign he suffered much from Aramaean raids and was finally besieged in his capital by Benhadad II. Tardy repentance and divine aid turned defeat into victory. The cities lost by Omri were recovered and Israelite trading posts were set up in Damascus. The Assyrian menace now produced an alliance of all the smaller states against the dreaded invader Salmanasar III. Achab of Israel contributed 2,000 chariots and 10,000 foot-soldiers. The armies met at Karkar on the Orontes in 853. The Assyrian claimed victory but was checked in his advance. Later in the year war broke out again with Benhadad II who refused to give up Ramoth-Galaad. Achab besieged the city but was wounded by an arrow and died some hours later. Under his son and successor, Ochozias, Meša, king of Moab, revolted and annexed the Israelite territory between the Arnon and the Wady Hesban. An invasion of Moab from the south under Joram, brother of Ochozias and last of the Omrides, failed to recover the ancient lot of Ruben. The worship of Baal Melkart, promoted by Jezabel, largely replaced that of Yahweh during the reigns of the last three Omrides. Through the efforts of the great prophets, Elias and Eliseus, the national religion survived and finally prevailed when Jehu extirpated the Omrides and founded a new dynasty in 841.

Judah meanwhile prospered under Asa's son, **h Josaphat,** remarkable alike for religious zeal and civil reforms. He appointed catechists in the different cities to instruct his subjects in their religious duties, divided his kingdom into prefectures governed mostly by royal princes, built fortified cities and store cities, reorganized the standing army and established tribunals for the administration of justice in civil and religious matters. After quelling an Edomite revolt he built a fleet at Ezion-Geber to resume the profitable Red Sea trade. His one great error was his marriage with Athalia under whose evil influence his son, Joram, became a Baal worshipper. Joram's infidelity was punished by a successful Edomite revolt and devastating raids of Philistines and Arabs. His son Ochozias, also a Baal worshipper, was slain by Jehu when he visited the wounded Joram of Israel at Jezrael.

Independent Development (841-721)—Judah's pro- **65a** gress during this period contrasts with the decline of Israel interrupted by the prosperous reign of Jeroboam II. **Jehu** became king of Israel by divine appointment but was alone responsible for the ferocious cruelty with which he enforced his mandate. On the abrupt termination of the alliances with Judah and Tyre he applied to the Assyrians for aid and paid tribute in his first year to Shalmaneser (Salmanasar) III. After two expeditions against Damascus in 841 and 838 the Assyrians retired from the scene. Jehu was thus exposed to the vengeance of Hazael who reduced Israel to subjection and misery during his reign and that of Joachaz. The saviour sent by God to the latter towards the close of his reign was apparently Adadnirari III who in 802 subdued and received tributes from Sidon, Tyre, Israel, Philistia, Edom and Damascus. The king of Damascus was still Hazael according to the sacred writer but is called by the Assyrian chronicler Mari, an Aramaean royal title meaning lord and given to Hazael himself in a recently discovered inscription. Israel revived after the death of Hazael (*c* 797). Joas inflicted three defeats on Hazael's successor Benhadad III and expelled the Aramaeans from Cisjordania. Galaad was recovered by Jeroboam II under whom Israel reached its furthest limits and enjoyed peace and prosperity. This was a last divine favour and call to repentance.

65a The appeal was voiced by two great prophets, **Amos** and **Osee**, who, like Elias and Eliseus at an earlier period, preached a return to the pure worship of Yahweh towards the close of the reign of Jeroboam II.

b The natural causes of the recovery of Israel were the exhaustion of Damascus and the cessation of Assyrian intervention in Palestine from 802 to 738. There was an Assyrian expedition against Damascus in 783 and three against Hadrach in 774, 765 and 755. Hadrach was finally captured in 738. The powerful Aramaean kingdom the chief cities of which were Hadrach and Hamat blocked the Assyrian advance. The rejection of the prophets' appeal sealed the fate of Israel. The history of its remaining kings is a record of palace revolutions, short reigns, and violent deaths. Menahem alone died a natural death after paying tribute to Tiglath-pileser in 738. Phacee, a usurper, and Rasin of Damascus plotted a revolt from Assyria and tried to force Achaz of Judah to join the league. His refusal led to the Syro-Ephraimitic war in 735. Achaz, rejecting the inspired counsel of Isaias, purchased Assyrian aid. Tiglath-pileser, also called Phul (Pulu) as king of Babylonia, invaded Palestine in 734, subdued Philistia and devastated Galilee, deporting about 4,000 of its inhabitants. Phacee was slain in a popular uprising and succeeded by a usurper, Osee, subsequently recognized by the Assyrians on payment of a large tribute. Galilee and Galaad now became Assyrian provinces. When Osee refused tribute, relying on Egyptian aid, Samaria was attacked by Shalmaneser V and taken after a three years' siege by his successor, Sargon II, in January 721.

c In Judah after the death of Ochozias the queen mother Athalia usurped the throne, slew the males of the royal line and established official Baal worship in the holy city. **Joas,** the infant son of Ochozias, hidden in the temple by the wife of the high-priest Joiada, alone escaped the massacre. He became king and Athalia was slain when the country people and the priestly party organized a successful revolt in 836. He was a good king while Joiada lived and had the temple repaired from the contributions made by the people for that purpose which the priests had been appropriating. But instigated by the leading citizens who had previously supported Athalia he restored the pagan cult after the death of Joiada and silenced in blood the protests of the high-priest Zacharias. Defeated and wounded by Hazael of Damascus *c* 798, he only saved his capital from destruction by paying an enormous ransom. He was slain soon afterwards in an uprising probably provoked by this disaster. His son and successor, **Amasias,** reconquered the Edomites and reopened the Red Sea trade. He was less fortunate in his encounter with Joas of Israel, occasioned probably by a boundary dispute. Defeated and captured at Beth-Shemesh he was brought prisoner to Jerusalem whose walls were partially demolished for the triumphal entry of the king of Israel. This disastrous defeat may have caused the military revolt from which he fled to Lachish where he was captured and slain. There are some indications that his

d death did not immediately follow his deposition. His son and successor, **Azarias,** also called Ozias, was a capable ruler. He reorganized the army, repaired the fortifications of Jerusalem and other cities and promoted agriculture and viniculture. He subdued the Maonites who had seized Elath on the gulf of Akaba and thus interrupted the Red Sea trade, destroyed the Philistine cities of Gath, Jabne and Ashdod and subjugated some Arab tribes. When however he usurped the priestly function of offering incense and was struck with leprosy his son became regent. Joatham was a pious and successful monarch. He built the upper gate of the temple, increased the defences of his realm and reduced the Ammonites to tribute. **Achaz,** more exactly Joachaz, as we learn from an Assyrian tribute list, was perhaps the worst of the kings of Judah and gravely imperilled its national existence at a very critical period. He had no faith

in Yahweh but sought to propitiate the gods of his **65d** dangerous neighbours, the Damascenes and the Assyrians, and offered a holocaust of his son to the Canaanite god, Moloch. Judah had recovered from previous dangers without prophetic intervention. Now however two great prophets, Isaias and Micheas, were sent to her aid. By their ministry and the piety of Ezechias religious and political disaster was temporarily averted.

Last Years of Judah (721–587)—**Ezechias** had inau- **66a** gurated his reign by a great religious reform. He purified the temple, abolished all religious abuses, including the cult of Yahweh in the high places tolerated by his predecessors, and invited Ephraim and Manasses to a solemn celebration of the Pasch at Jerusalem. He also warred successfully against the Philistines and strengthened his capital by repairing the Mello and constructing an underground aqueduct by which the waters of Jerusalem's only spring, Gihon, were brought into the city. Other phases of his activity were the collection of the Proverbs of Solomon and the development of the musical accompaniment in the temple ritual. Judah as a vassal of Assyria was burdened with an annual tribute. The emergence of Egypt from a period of decadence revived hopes of independence in Ezechias. The embassy of the Babylonian king Merodach-Baladan in 713 to congratulate him on his recovery from a serious illness coincides remarkably with the revolt against Assyria then being plotted by Philistia, Moab and Edom. Ezechias was induced to take part in the rebellion but was saved from punishment by a timely submission when Philistia, the ringleader, was devastated by Sargon in 711. Judah played a leading part in the revolt of Phoenicia, Philistia, Judah, Ammon and Edom in 702 and suffered proportionately when Sennacherib invaded Palestine in 701. Forty-five cities were captured, some of which were transferred from Judah to Assyrian partisans in Philistia. Of their inhabitants 200,150 (probably a scribal error for 20,150) were deported. Jerusalem was closely invested. The retreat of his Egyptian allies left Ezechias without hope of human aid. He paid the heavy tribute demanded but refused to surrender his capital. The Assyrian chronicler, who does not record reverses, gives no explanation of the surprising retreat of Sennacherib at this juncture. From the Bible we learn of Yahweh's intervention and the destruction of the Assyrian host.

The pious Ezechias was succeeded by the impious **b** **Manasses** in whose reign all the abominations of Assyrian cult flourished in Judah. This was to some extent a consequence of subjection to the Assyrians who imposed the worship of their gods on subject states. Manasses appears twice in the tribute lists of Asarhaddon. Towards the end of his long reign he participated in a wide-spread revolt organized by the king of Babylon in 652. He was defeated and brought in chains to Nineveh where he repented his abandonment of Yahweh. Assurbanipal, the only Assyrian monarch who boasts of clemency to vanquished foes, pardoned and released him and restored him to his kingdom. There is no Assyrian record of this event as we have no information on the last years of Assurbanipal's reign, but the rebel Egyptian prince, Nechao, was similarly pardoned and reinstated by the same monarch at an earlier period. The disintegration of the Assyrian empire had now begun. The Pharaoh, Psammetichus I (663–610), after proclaiming his independence in 655 had invaded Palestine and besieged Ashdod. Manasses, fearing an Egyptian attack, organized his army and strengthened the defences of his capital. His son, Amon, restored Assyrian cult but was slain by his servants after a short reign. The pious king **Josias,** only eight years **c** old when he succeeded his father, abolished all religious abuses and restored the pure worship of Yahweh in Judah and Israel in the twelfth year of his reign. Six years later when the temple was being repaired the book of the law was discovered and read aloud to

66c the people. The discovery was followed by a renewal of the covenant with Yahweh and a very solemn celebration of the Pasch. After the fall of Nineveh in 612 the Assyrians under Assuruballit continued the struggle at Harran. A large Egyptian army marched to their aid in 609. Josias opposed its passage at Megiddo but was defeated and slain. The prevalence of Yahweh in the personal names of the recently discovered Lachish Letters attests the reality of his religious reforms.

d Josias was succeeded by a younger son, Sellum (Shallum), who took the name Joachaz and pursued his father's policy. He reigned only three months, being deposed and taken prisoner to Egypt by Nechao. Excluded from Mesopotamia by the Babylonians the Pharaoh had encamped at Riblah on the Orontes where he regulated the affairs and received the tribute of the western subject states. He made the eldest son of Josias, Eliakim, previously rejected by the people owing to his Egyptian sympathies, king of Judah and changed his name to **Joakim.** In the third year of Joakim (the fourth according to Hebrew reckoning, Sept. 606–605) the young Babylonian prince, Nabuchodonosor, defeated the Assyrians and their allies, at Carchemish on the Euphrates and pursued the Egyptians to the borders of Egypt whence he was recalled by the death of his father, Nabupolassar. The capture of Jerusalem in this expedition was the occasion of the first deportation in which Daniel and his three companions were included. A second deportation in 597, after Joachin, who reigned only three months, had succeeded his father, Joakim, was the punishment of a revolt instigated by the Pharaoh Nechao. The king and his household, the nobles and the treasures of the temple were taken to Babylon, where records of the provisions supplied to Joachin and his fellow captives were recently discovered in the storerooms of the royal palace. Matthanias, son of Josias, now became king and assumed the name of **Sedecias.** This weak monarch was induced by the Egyptian party to reject the inspired counsels of Jeremias and revolt against Nabuchodonosor, who captured Jerusalem after a two years' siege in June 587 and deported its inhabitants. Thus did Judah cease to exist through the impiety and folly of her kings and their refusal to hearken to the prophets sent to their aid.

e **The Exilic Period**—The exiles from the Northern Kingdom have left no trace in history except in the case of a single family whose fortunes are recorded in the book of Tobias. Their attachment to the worship of Yahweh, weakened by idolatry, scarcely survived the long period of nearly two centuries between the fall of Samaria and the Restoration. Much more favourable was the situation of the exiles of Judah. Their expatriation lasted only half a century (587–537), but covers approximately seventy years when reckoned from the first deportation in 605. Their worship of Yahweh was purer and had deeper roots. It was revived temporarily at least by the reforms of Ezechias and Josias. The preaching of the great prophets Isaias, Micheas and Jeremias might be unheeded during their lifetime but would be remembered later in the days of oppression and repentance. Another great prophet, **Ezechiel,** accompanied them into exile to keep alive their hope of restoration. Even the land of Judah seemed to await expectantly the return of its former inhabitants. Unlike Israel it had received no foreign colonists and had only to suffer the encroachments of the neighbouring nations, especially the Edomites.

f The Jews deported to southern Babylonia belonged chiefly to the upper classes of the urban population. Shepherds and agriculturists were left undisturbed since from them no political danger was feared. The exiles had much to suffer in the early days of their captivity, being employed as slaves in forced labours such as building cities, repairing canals and tilling the soil. Many of them lived together in settlements of which several are named in the Bible, but Tell Abib

on the Kabaru canal (very probably the modern Shatt **66f** en-Nil) in the neighbourhood of the ancient Nippur was particularly important. The excavators of Nippur unearthed 700 contract tablets recording the extensive banking operations of the sons and grandsons of a certain Murashu in the second half of the 5th cent. B.C. Many names of Jews appear in these tablets, some distinctively Jewish, containing the divine name Yahweh, others Babylonian like the biblical Zorobabel and Mardochai. These Jews included possessors of land and house property and holders of important official posts. We have thus a confirmation of the scriptural attestation of Jewish prosperity in Babylonia, and an explanation of the fact that many rich Jews did not return with the exiles but showed at the same time their religious sympathy by large contributions for the settlement of their brethren and the reconstruction of the temple.

The sufferings of the exiles at the hands of their oppressors, recognized as the just punishment of their infidelity, produced a religious revival as in the days of the Judges. They surrendered themselves to the guidance of Ezechiel who reminded them that they would not be held responsible for the sins of their fathers and would be pardoned for their own if they truly repented. His idealistic picture of the future state, guarded by laws more rigid than the Torah, manifests the legalistic trend of the reform. The order of scribes, devoted to the study of the law, now first appears. The legal observances, especially circumcision and the sabbath, were strictly enforced. Thus did the exiles prepare themselves for the day when Persian deliverers would replace Babylonian oppressors.

The Restoration—The origin of the Persians, their rise **67a** to power and the character of their rule are discussed in § 122*d–h*. Cyrus the Great, the founder of their empire, was the instrument of Yahweh in the execution of his merciful designs for his chosen people. In conformity with his conciliatory policy and respect for the religion of his subjects, he authorized the Jewish exiles to return to Judah and rebuild their temple and restored to them the sacred vessels plundered by the Babylonians. The rescripts of the Persian monarchs, Cyrus, Darius I, Artaxerxes I and Artaxerxes II, in favour of the Jews are recorded in Aramaic, the international language of the period, in the books of Esdras-Nehemias. To these we must now add a rescript of Darius II to the Jews of Elephantine in 419, which prescribed and regulated the celebration of the feast of Azymes. This recently discovered document shows that the Persian monarchs interested themselves in the religious observances of their subjects and thus refutes the objection so frequently made to the authenticity of the biblical rescripts. The Persians may have been predisposed in favour of the Jews by the resemblance between the Jewish worship of Yahweh and their own spiritual and not idolatrous cult of Ahuramazda, the god of heaven. Darius I declares himself in the inscription of Behistun a sincere worshipper of Ahuramazda. Cambyses, his predecessor, spared the Jewish temple of Yahweh when he demolished all the Egyptian sanctuaries at Elephantine. There is no direct evidence however that Cyrus and Cambyses worshipped Ahuramazda.

The returning exiles left Babylonia in the spring of 537. **b** Their caravan consisted of 42,360 Jews, 7,337 slaves and a considerable number of horses, mules, camels and asses. The various clans and families on their arrival sought their ancient homes in the lots of Judah and Benjamin. They were led by **Zorobabel,** also called Sheshbazzar, who as *pehah* represented the Persian monarch, and Joshua (Vg Jesus) the high-priest, grandson of the high-priest, Seraia, who had been slain at Riblah by Nabuchodonosor. They were fully occupied during the six months which followed their return in re-establishing themselves in their ancient homes. Ruined houses were laboriously rebuilt and inhabited ones were purchased from their occupants. Many had no doubt to be satisfied with tents

67b and temporary shelters. In the seventh month they began the rebuilding of the temple with the erection of an altar on which sacrifices could be offered. Building materials, including cedars from Lebanon, were then collected and the foundations of the temple **c** were laid. The fixed determination of the returned exiles to preserve the purity of their religion and their race was the chief cause of the difficulties which now almost overwhelmed them. Their exclusivism aroused the opposition and hostility of their neighbours and especially of the Samaritans. The mixed races of Samaria included the local god, Yahweh, in their Pantheon and probably regarded him as their principal deity. They offered their aid in the rebuilding of the temple and sought admission into the new community of Yahweh worshippers. The rejection of this offer made the Samaritans the bitterest enemies of the returned exiles. They sought by every means and especially by intrigues with the Persian officials to block all attempts at civil and religious restoration. As a result of this opposition and also through lack of resources and workers the exiles abandoned the rebuilding of the temple. The workers had to devote their immediate efforts to agriculture in order to provide the means of subsistence for themselves and their families. They then occupied themselves for fifteen years in building houses and improving their material conditions. Their religious enthusiasm had died away, but Yahweh, at length, raised up two prophets to revive it.

d In the second year of Darius (29 August 520) the prophet **Aggeus** reproached the people and their leaders with their lack of zeal for the house of God, and contrasted the ruins of the temple with the fine mansions of many citizens of Jerusalem. In a subsequent address he met the difficulty arising from lack of resources by declaring that the second temple would be rendered more glorious than the first by the presence of the Messias and by the rich gifts which would adorn it. The construction, of which the foundations had already been at least partially laid, was therefore resumed on the 21 September, and the builders were encouraged not only by Aggeus but by several addresses of another prophet **Zacharias.** The work was suspended for a brief period by Tattenai, the satrap of Abar-Nahara, the region beyond the Euphrates, who, instigated no doubt by the Samaritans, sent inspectors to Jerusalem. On being informed by the Jews of the authorization given by Cyrus the satrap referred the matter to Darius, who after inspecting the records not only authorized the Jews to rebuild their temple but ordered aid to be given them from the revenues of the satrapy and threatened with the direst penalties all who dared to oppose their project. The work of reconstruction was completed in March 515 and the pasch was celebrated, for the first time after the return, in the following month.

e Jerusalem was still an open city exposed to the attacks of hostile neighbours. Accusations made to the Persian monarchs, Xerxes and Artaxerxes I, against the Jews, imply in the first case and explicitly declare in the second that the walls of Jerusalem were being rebuilt. The fortification of the capital was interpreted as a preparation for revolt. We have no indication that Xerxes heeded the accusation. Artaxerxes however stopped the work and demolished the walls already erected. **Nehemias** at the Persian court in Susa received news of this calamity from Jews who arrived there in the twentieth year of Artaxerxes I (446–445). He was an able and zealous Jewish layman, born in exile, who held the important office of cup-bearer to the Persian monarch, Artaxerxes I. His affliction on hearing of the demolition of the walls of Jerusalem was increased by tidings, brought by his brother Hanani, of various social and religious abuses rampant in the holy city and vainly denounced a little earlier by Malachy, the last of the prophets. Using his influence at court for the good of his people he obtained from the Persian monarch permission to fortify the Jewish

capital, temporary leave of absence from court, and **67e** the office of *peḥah* to superintend the constructions and effect the necessary reforms. The exclusivism of the Jews had yielded to the pressure of their neighbours and Geshem the Arabian, Sanballat the Horonite (from Horonaim), who was *peḥah* of Samaria, and Tobias the Ammonite had free entry and influential partisans in the holy city. Nehemias therefore, to **f** forestall opposition, concealed his project until he had examined by night the state of the walls three days after his arrival in the summer of 445 (less probably 444). He then revealed his mission and his plans to the people. The builders were divided into parties of which each was charged with the immediate construction of a determined section of the wall. As the materials used in the previous attempt were still available and the wall then erected had not been entirely demolished, the work was completed, despite armed opposition, in the comparatively short space of fifty-two days. The city, already sparsely populated, was considerably enlarged on the north side and fresh dwellers from the neighbouring towns and country had to be introduced and provided for. This task and the still more difficult work of reform occupied twelve years. The greatest difficulty was presented by mixed marriages especially in the sacerdotal caste. The relatively small number of women among the exiles and the Pentateuchal toleration of marriages with all foreigners except Canaanites, Deut 7:3, seemed to justify the practice. But the exclusion of Moabites and Ammonites from the community, Deut 23:3, the oracles of the prophets of the restoration, and the evil results of these alliances necessitated their abolition. The economic crisis resulting from the cupidity and **g** rapacity of the rich and powerful was combated by Nehemias during the whole period of his rule. He succeeded in obtaining a promise from creditors to remit the debts with which many of the poor were burdened and, by renouncing the revenues of his office and relieving the needy from his private resources, gave his prosperous compatriots an outstanding example of the practice of charity. Every Jewish religious reform naturally included a renewal of the covenant with Yahweh. This took place on the 24 Tishri shortly after the completion of the walls, and was preceded by the public reading and explanation of the Torah during the earlier days of the month. The reader was the young priest and scribe, **Esdras.**

Some years later Nehemias again obtained leave of **h** absence from Artaxerxes and returned to Jerusalem to resume the work of reform. On this occasion he had to enforce the observance of the Sabbath, remove from the court of the Temple the bank which Tobias the Ammonite had erected there through the complaisance of the high-priest, with whom he was allied by marriage, and insist on the ban on mixed marriages. One of the delinquents was a grandson of the high-priest Eliashib who had married a daughter of Sanballat and now fled to his father-in-law in Samaria. Other priests subsequently followed his example. To those outcasts are generally attributed the Samaritan copy of the Pentateuch and the erection of a temple of Yahweh on Mt Garizim in the year 324. The aged Esdras who led a large caravan of returning exiles from Babylonia to Palestine probably in the seventh year of Artaxerxes II (398) also dissolved many mixed marriages.

From profane sources we learn that the Jews were involved in the revolt of the western satraps against Artaxerxes III, and that some of them were in consequence deported to Hyrcania on the shores of the Caspian Sea. The repression of this revolt seems to form the background of the Judith narrative. Holofernes was a general and Bagoas a cup-bearer of Artaxerxes III.

The Greek Period—The Jews most probably submitted **68a** voluntarily to Alexander the Great and enjoyed the benevolent tolerance which marked his relations with subject peoples. In the division of his empire after the

68a wars of the Diadochoi Palestine fell to Egypt. The Jews had to pay tribute to the Ptolemies but lived according to their religious and national customs under the rule of their high-priests. They helped to colonize the new Egyptian capital, where they had a Jewish quarter and were granted citizenship and other special privileges. Alexandria thus became the centre of Jewish Hellenism, which progressed so rapidly that the translation of the sacred books into Greek was begun about the middle of the 3rd cent. When however Antiochus the Great completely defeated the Egyptians at Baniyas in 198 B.C. the Seleucids, who reigned at Antioch in Syria, secured possession of Palestine. The new political situation, unwelcome to the Jews, was rendered more difficult by the interference of the Ammonite Tobiads in their affairs. Our information about these merchant princes is derived from Josephus, the Zeno papyri, and the excavations made at their stronghold 'Arak el-Amir in southern Transjordania. They were undoubtedly descendants of the Ammonite Tobias, encountered by Nehemias, and pursued more **b** successfully the same policy. Towards the middle of the 3rd cent. B.C. Joseph Tobias, in high favour with the Ptolemies, had married the daughter of the high-priest Onias II, established himself in the holy city and represented the Jews in all their dealings with Egypt. After the battle of Baniyas, Hyrcanus, son of Josephus, still supported the Egyptians from his stronghold in Transjordania. His brothers sided with the Seleucids and assumed the control of affairs in Jerusalem with the connivance of the high-priest, Simon II. Hyrcanus however intrigued with the Egyptian party in the city against his brothers and the Seleucids and found an ally in the next high-priest, Onias III, to whose care he committed a large sum of money deposited in the temple treasury. Seleucus IV was then in acute financial embarrassment owing to the crushing war indemnity imposed by the Romans after their victory at Magnesia in 190 B.C. Informed of the deposit of Hyrcanus and the other riches stored in the temple, he sent his minister Heliodorus to Jerusalem to seize the treasure for his own needs. The attempt was foiled by a supernatural intervention and soon afterwards the Tobiad brothers were expelled from Jerusalem. The city was thus controlled by the patriotic party when **Antiochus IV Epiphanes** (175–163), a fanatical Hellenist, became king. He deposed Onias III who was subsequently assassinated at Antioch and himself appointed high-priests from his partisans, first Jason brother of Onias and then Menelaus a Benjaminite, to establish Hellenism in Judaea.

c Dissatisfied with the results achieved by the Jerusalem Hellenists and regarding Jewish religion and national institutions as quite incompatible with Hellenism, Antiochus marched to Jerusalem in 167 after his campaign in Egypt had been interrupted by a Roman *veto*. He first plundered and profaned the temple, setting up in the Holy of Holies a statue of Olympian Jupiter, and then instituted a savage religious persecution continued after his departure by his general, Apollonius. Circumcision of infants, observance of the Sabbath, possession of the sacred books were punished with death. All were obliged under the same penalty to offer incense to the Greek gods and partake of the victims immolated to them. In this crisis, as in the days of Athalia, the country people upheld Yahwism.

d **The Maccabees,** so called from Judas Maccabaeus their first great leader, were the five sons of Mathathias, member of a priestly family of Modin or Moditha, the modern Mediye, about 8 m. E. of Lydda. Mathathias died after inaugurating the revolt and left it as a sacred inheritance to his sons. Their success in their heroic struggle under the leadership of Judas (165–160), Jonathan (160–143) and Simon (143–134) was due

above all to their faith and the determination inspired **68d** by the justice and sacredness of their cause. The Syrians, at first, underestimated the strength of the movement and were later prevented by dynastic rivalries from employing all the forces of their empire to quell it.

Judas, after defeating three Syrian armies, obtained a **e** truce from Lysias, regent of Antiochus Epiphanes, on conditions of mutual tolerance and liberty of cult. He then purified the temple, three years after its profanation, in December 164, fortified the temple area and the southern stronghold of Bethsur, campaigned in Idumaea, Transjordania and Galilee and besieged the Syrian garrison of the Acra, a fortress erected in Jerusalem on the southern or western hill opposite the temple. After being defeated however by Lysias, whom the Jerusalem Hellenists called to their aid in 163, he was besieged in the temple area and reduced to the last extremity when troubles at Antioch necessitating the immediate return of Lysias led to a renewal of the previous truce under the same conditions. Subsequently however Demetrius I, after defeating and slaying Lysias and the puppet king Antiochus V, sent two expeditions against Judas at the request of the Jerusalem Hellenists. The Jewish leader, victorious in the first encounter, was defeated and slain in the second owing to the desertion of his followers in 160.

Jonathan resorted to guerilla warfare until the death **f** of the high-priest, Alcimus, and the return of the Syrian general, Bacchides, to Antioch in 159. He was strong enough to come to terms with Bacchides when he returned to Jerusalem in 157. He then made Michmas his headquarters and ignoring Jerusalem extended his rule over Judaea. The rival claimants of the throne of Syria in 153, Alexander Balas and Demetrius I, outbid each other in their offers to secure his support. He sided with Balas who confirmed his authority in Judaea and appointed him to the office of high-priest, vacant since the death of Alcimus. When Balas was slain in battle with the Egyptians, Jonathan allied himself with Demetrius II, son of Demetrius I, from whom he received additional territory in Samaria. Demetrius also promised to withdraw the Syrian garrisons from the Acra and Bethsur in return for aid in quelling a rising in Antioch, but subsequently refused to fulfil his promise. Jonathan therefore went over to his rival, Antiochus VI, son of Balas, besieged and captured Bethsur, isolated the Acra with a high wall and proceeded to restore the fortifications of Jerusalem. In the height of his success in 143 he was treacherously captured and subsequently slain by Tryphon, the general of Antiochus VI.

Simon, the last of the Maccabees, completed the **g** fortification of Jerusalem and closely blockaded the Syrians in the Acra. He allied himself with Demetrius II when Tryphon slew his master, Antiochus, and proclaimed himself king. The concessions received from Demetrius were commemorated by the inauguration of a new era of independence, 142–141. The capture of Gezer in 141 secured communications with the seaport of Joppe. The Acra surrendered in the same year. The high-priesthood of Simon, a Syrian appointment, was confirmed by a decree of the people in 140. Like his predecessors he obtained from Rome in 139 diplomatic recognition but no military aid. He was now universally recognized as high-priest, general and ethnarch of the Jews. In 138 he supported Antiochus VII Sidetes in his campaign against Tryphon. He maintained his independence until his death in February 134 when he was treacherously slain at a banquet by his ambitious son-in-law, Ptolemy. But Simon's second son, John Hyrcanus, fortunately received warning in time to forestall his aggressors and to establish himself as head of the Hasmonaean house, and maintain its position.

THE HISTORY OF ISRAEL

(130 B.C.–A.D. 70)

By T. CORBISHLEY, S.J.

THE HASMONAEANS

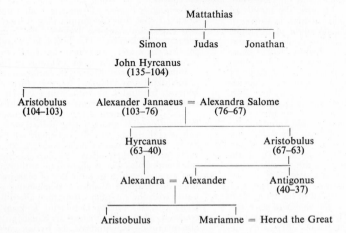

THE HERODIANS

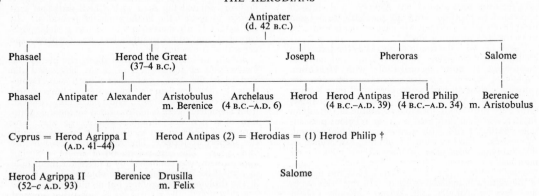

† According to Oesterley, *op. cit.*, Additional Note K, *The Family of Herod the Great* (cf. also pp 389–90), Herodias first married Herod, another son of Herod the Great, and not Herod Philip, who however later married Herodias' daughter Salome.

(N.B.—These tables are not complete but contain all the names appearing in the accompanying text.)

	JUDAEA + IDUMAEA	SAMARIA	GALILEE + PERAEA	ITURAEA, etc.
B.C.				
135		John Hyrcanus		
104		Aristobulus I		
103		Alexander Jannaeus		
76		Alexandra Salome		
67		Hyrcanus		
67		Aristobulus II		
63		Hyrcanus		
40		Antigonus		
37		Herod the Great		
4	Archelaus		Herod Antipas	Herod Philip
A.D.				
6	Coponius			
11	Ambivius			
14	Rufus			
16	Valerius Gratus			
27	Pontius Pilate			
34				(To Syria)
37	Marcellus			Herod Agrippa I
	Marullus			
39		Herod Agrippa I		
41	Herod Agrippa I			
44		Fadus		
46		Tib. Julius Alexander		
48		Cumanus		
52		Felix		Herod Agrippa II
59		Festus		
62		Albinus		
64		Gessius Florus		
66		Vespasian		
69		Titus		
70		Fall of Jerusalem		

70a **Bibliography**—Ancient Authorities : Josephus, *Antiquities of the Jews*, 13, 8–20, 11 ; *Wars of the Jews*, 1, 2–7, 11 ; *Life*. Tacitus, *Histories*, 5, 9–13 ; *Annals*, 2, 85 ; 12, 54. A full biography of modern authorities is to be found in Schürer (Eng. trans.) *A History of the Jewish People in the Time of Jesus-Christ* (1880, etc.), brought up-to-date in CAH, vol 9, ch 9 : vol 10, ch 11, ch 25. The following may be mentioned : M.-J. Lagrange, *Le Judaïsme avant Jésus-Christ*, 1931 ; J. Pickl, *Messias-könig Jesus* (Eng. trans. : *The Messias*, 1946) ; *A. H. M. Jones, *The Herods of Judaea* (1938) ; *W. Otto, *Herodes* in PW ; T. Corbishley, *The Chronology of the Reign of Herod the Great*, JTS, vol 36 ; *W. O. E. Oesterley, *A History of Israel*, vol II, 1932.

The political changes that occurred in Palestine during this period are complicated, but the following main lines of treatment suggest themselves.

I	The Hasmonaean dynasty	130–40 B.C.
II	Herod the Great	40–4 B.C.
III	Judaea under Archelaus and the Romans	4 B.C.–41 A.D.
IV	Galilee under Herod Antipas	4 B.C.–39 A.D.
V	Herod Agrippa I	37–44 A.D.
VI	Palestine under the Romans	44–66 A.D.
VII	The Rebellion	66–70 A.D.
VIII	The Jews of the Diaspora	

b **I The Hasmonaeans : 130-40 B.C.**—At the end of the story of the Maccabees we are left with the impression that the great national uprising associated with the name of Judas Maccabaeus and the Hasmonaean family (deriving its title from its founder Hashmon) had spent its force. **John Hyrcanus** had been compelled to pay tribute once more to Antiochus VII of Syria, and this would imply the end of the hard-won independence of the Jews. But with the death of Antiochus in 129, his kingdom began to break up. Ptolemy VII of Egypt fomented civil war in Syria and a succession of claimants fighting for the remnants of **70b** power in Antioch reduced the once great kingdom of the Seleucids to a condition of pathetic impotence. Small principalities were established in independence of the central authority and the Jews returned to complete autonomy. The bronze coinage of John Hyrcanus reappears, bearing a Hebrew legend : ' John the High-Priest and the Jewish Commonweal ', though the title of king does not yet occur. Not content with reasserting the independence of Judaea itself, John pushed forward the frontiers to the east, north and south. Beyond the Dead Sea, Madaba was annexed, whilst the power of Samaria was gradually worn down. The rival temple on Mt Gerizim was destroyed and later (108) the Greek city of Samaria was entirely obliterated, pits being dug so that water might undermine the foundations. The acquisition of Scythopolis (Beth-Shan), commanding the passage of the Jordan below the Sea of Galilee, paved the way for the annexation of Galilee itself. An event which was to be of unexpected significance was the conquest of Idumaea to the south. The inhabitants of the area were forcibly Judaized, being compelled to undergo circumcision, and it was from this half-Jewish, half-Gentile nation that the Herodian family sprang.

John Hyrcanus died in 104, being succeeded by his **c** son Judah (or Aristobulus), under whom the annexation and Judaization of Galilee were completed. After a brief reign, he was succeeded by his brother **Alexander Jannaeus** (103–76), who assumed the title of King and extended the frontiers of Israel, until it became practically co-terminous with the old kingdom of David. Campaigning beyond the Jordan, where he annexed Gadara and Amathus, he then turned south-west and after a year's siege reduced Gaza on the Hellenized Philistine coast (96). But a later expedition beyond Gadara into Gaulanitis brought him into conflict with the Nabataean Arabs, a powerful tribe which had also wrested its independence from Syria. He suffered **a**

70c severe reverse and almost lost his throne and life in a fierce popular revolt. But he succeeded in restoring his position and though he suffered further defeat at the hands of Aretas III, he made more conquests in Transjordania.

d At his death, the throne was occupied by his widow **Salome** (76–67). Her first step was to secure her position at home by allying herself with the growing power of the Pharisees. This group, apparently the successors of those Chasidim who had proved such valuable fighters under Mattathias, 1 Mac 2:42, had been at loggerheads with both John Hyrcanus and Alexander Jannaeus. They represented the stricter and more nationalistic element and were growing in importance ; over against them were the Hellenizing Sadducees, sceptical and worldly, including most of the priestly aristocracy. Salome, being a woman, could not hold the office of high-priest, so whilst she retained the royal title, her son Hyrcanus succeeded to the high-priesthood which had been held by his father. The Pharisees supported him against his brother Aristobulus, who was backed by the Sadducees. (In later times when the Pharisees were persecuted by Herod, the reign of Salome became for them a legendary golden age.) On her death, the quarrel between the brothers broke out into open strife and Aristobulus wrested kingship and high-priesthood from Hyrcanus.

e It is at this time that the power which was to grow into the Herodian monarchy first appears. An Idumaean, Antipater by name, son of one of the lieutenants of Jannaeus, espoused the cause of Hyrcanus, induced the Nabataeans to assist him and before long Aristobulus was besieged on the Temple site. But, more important still, Rome's power was now beginning to dominate the Levant. After the decline of Syria, the chief power in Asia Minor devolved upon Mithridates, king of Pontus. He soon tried conclusions with Rome and more than held his own until **Pompey** was sent by the Senate to end the threat to their interests in the Eastern Mediterranean. Having defeated Mithridates, Pompey resolved to settle the whole eastern question by a definitive arrangement. In addition to other annexations, the important province of Syria, with its capital at Antioch and stretching from the Mediterranean coast to the upper waters of the Euphrates, was added to the empire. This province, one of the most important of Rome's possessions, was destined to play a predominant part in the defence of the eastern frontier. In it were normally stationed three legions, which, in addition to warding off the menace of Parthia, could be employed to overawe the turbulent peoples to north and south, including the ever-troublesome Jews. It was necessary, at the same time, to make arrangements for the government of Palestine and in 63 Pompey was in Jerusalem. A couple of years earlier his lieutenants had made a temporary settlement by persuading the Nabataeans to withdraw their support from Hyrcanus and handing over the power in Palestine to Aristobulus. This decision was reversed by Pompey, who made Hyrcanus once more ruler and high-priest. Aristobulus himself saw the futility of resistance, but some of his followers held out, and could only be persuaded to yield by the arrival of Pompey in person at the head of an army. We are told that after reducing the citadel, Pompey made his way into the Holy of Holies itself, thereby shocking Jewish sentiment. Unlike other conquerors, however, he did not lay hands on the treasures of the Sanctuary. When Pompey returned to Rome to celebrate his triumph, Aristobulus was taken along with him.

f Though the Jews nominally retained their independence, henceforward they would always have to reckon with Rome. Their territory was reduced, the Greek cities and the seaboard being lost. Over Judaea, Idumaea, Galilee and Peraea reigned Hyrcanus, with the title of *tetrarch*, though he was also high-priest. He was in immediate subordination to the Roman governor of Syria and through him to the central authority in Rome. By way of controlling still more effectively this turbulent folk, Gabinius, governor of Syria (57–54) split up the Jewish territory for administrative purposes into five districts, each with its local συνέδριον, sitting at Jerusalem, Gaza, Amathus, Jericho and Sepphoris. The step was doubtless taken with a view to weakening the central government at Jerusalem, and preventing its becoming a threat to Syria as it had once been, but there were probably certain advantages to the Jews themselves in this devolution. At any rate we find traces of the survival of the local συνέδρια elsewhere than at Jerusalem, though of course in the NT it is only the Sanhedrin there that appears. **70f**

Theoretically then the destinies of the Jews at this **g** time were in the hands of Hyrcanus, high-priest and tetrarch. But the real power was wielded by **Antipater,** who was to play a role analogous to that of the Mayors of the Palace under the Merovingians. From now until the death of Herod the Great, the history of foreign affairs in Palestine is largely the story of the diplomatic relations between the Idumaean family and the successive claimants for supremacy at Rome. Pompey and Caesar, the 'liberators' and the triumvirs, Octavian and Mark Antony struggled in turn for the lordship of the world, and all the cunning of Antipater and Herod was needed to enable them to maintain their position.

In 54 B.C. Jerusalem received another visit from a **h** Roman army. Crassus, on his way to the Parthian war in which he was doomed to meet disaster and death, robbed the Temple of something like 10,000 talents. But this was but an isolated incident. In 49 war broke out between Pompey, defending the established government, and Julius Caesar, and in the circumstances there was only one possible choice for Antipater to make. Not only was Pompey the representative of lawful authority, but the eastern provinces were largely under his control, whilst Hyrcanus and Antipater owed their present positions to him. Naturally Caesar liberated Aristobulus to embarrass Hyrcanus, but fortunately for the latter his brother met his death at the hands of Pompeian troops whilst on his way to reclaim his kingdom. Pompey's death in Egypt created what might have been a very awkward situation for Antipater, but he won the favour of the dictator by assisting him with troops when fighting for his life at Alexandria (47). In the relieving force which marched to Caesar's rescue was a contingent of Jewish soldiers under the command of Antipater himself. By this means, he obtained from Caesar confirmation of Hyrcanus in his position and also the establishment of himself as administrator of Judaea, despite the protests and appeals of Antigonus, son of Aristobulus. Moreover, Joppa was restored to Judaea. On Caesar's assassination, Antipater characteristically transferred his allegiance to the party of Brutus and Cassius, who controlled the eastern provinces of the empire, but their defeat at Philippi raised no problems for him. He had already died of poison administered by a private enemy that same year (42).

II Herod the Great (i) **His Rise**—When Antipater **71a** died, his two eldest sons, Phasael and Herod, the latter a young man just over 30, were already prominent in public affairs. Phasael had acted as his father's lieutenant in Idumaea, whilst Herod had held a military command in Galilee. Here he had come into contact with one of those outbursts of violence characteristic of the period. Whether they were genuine nationalistic uprisings, on the model of the Maccabaean effort, or whether the 'zeal' of these men was little more than a cloak for personal aggrandisement and their activities not far removed from plain brigandage, we cannot decide. But we shall encounter a number of such incidents in the course of this review. The leader on this occasion was one Hezekiah. Herod suppressed the movement and killed the man himself, but he was summoned before the Sanhedrin at Jerusalem to stand his trial on a charge of killing a Jew unlawfully. The support of the Roman governor and his own high standing in the eyes of Hyrcanus resulted in his

71a acquittal (47 B.C.), but the incident rankled and he later exacted vengeance on those who had thus humiliated him.

b Mark Antony came to Palestine in 41 and, despite attempts on the part of the Jews to set him against the sons of Antipater, the Roman, appreciating Herod's capacity to control the Jews, showed favour to him and his brother and both were appointed tetrarchs. Antony's shrewdness was soon borne out by events. In 40 B.C., the Parthians, Rome's traditional enemy in that region, invaded Syria and the Jewish aristocracy saw in them a means to rid themselves of the Idumaean intruders. Jerusalem received a Parthian garrison, Phasael was killed, Herod fled. The high-priest, Hyrcanus, was mutilated and deported, and his brother's son, Mattathiah Antigonus, installed in his place, resuming the title of king. It was a repetition of the events of 67 B.C., with the Parthians playing the role assigned on that occasion to the Nabataeans.

c This Parthian invasion of Syria and Palestine meant, of course, that the cause of Herod was identified with the interests of Rome. He was formally recognized by the Triumvirs and the Senate as king of the Jews. The expulsion of the Parthians from Palestine, essential to the security of the Empire, was the necessary preliminary to Herod's assumption of power. Even after the Parthians had retreated, Rome co-operated with Herod in the military events leading up to the siege of Jerusalem, where Antigonus was resisting desperately. In 37 B.C., Herod entered into full possession of his kingdom, including Samaria once more. The last Hasmonaean king perished under a Roman axe.

(ii) Herod as King—Characteristically, Herod began
d his reign with a massacre. Of the members of the Sanhedrin who had brought him to trial ten years before, 45 were put to death, and the full quota of 71 was made up of Herod's own nominees. This broke the power of the aristocratic opposition, but at the same time left a rankling desire for vengeance. The situation was further complicated by domestic intrigue. Herod had married Mariamne, a member of the Hasmonaean family, whose mother Alexandra wanted her son Aristobulus to be made high-priest. For this purpose she intrigued with Cleopatra of Egypt, who was coveting some of Herod's territory. To placate her, Herod yielded. Soon afterwards, however, he solved the problem in his own way by having Aristobulus drowned. He escaped the effects of the anger of Cleopatra and therefore of Antony's displeasure because the latter could not afford an unstable Judaea at his back at a time when the final break with Octavian was looming ahead (c 34 B.C.). Henceforth Herod kept the appointment to the high-priesthood in his own hands, nominating only those who supported his policies. The break with the Hasmonaean family was completed by the execution of Hyrcanus, the old high-priest (30) and the murders of Mariamne (29) and her mother Alexandra (28 B.C.).

e Into all the details of the political and domestic intrigues that made up the background of Herod's reign, it is impossible for us to enter. It will suffice to say that it was only by the most ruthless measures and the employment of numbers of spies and informers that he could hope to maintain his throne. Parallel to this was his extensive work of fortification, beginning with the restoration of the walls of the capital and the fortress Hyrcania. Throughout his reign, we hear of cities founded or rebuilt and fortified, and the disposition of troops. Herod also established a string of colonies and fortified posts to protect his frontiers—we may mention Machaerus, the scene of John the Baptist's death—and apparently reorganized the local administration of the country. Of his army, we know that it was composed largely of mercenaries—Idumaeans, Thracians, Germans and Greeks (he received from Octavian Cleopatra's Celtic bodyguard)—though it included a number of Jews of the Diaspora, always more loyal to Herod than the Palestinians.

Many of Herod's measures were clearly directed to the repression of brigandage and other disturbances, **71e** and their success is proved by the almost complete absence of open rebellion during the reign. At the same time it should be said that his rule was manifestly efficient and prosperous, as is shown by the fact that he was able to make considerable reductions in taxation, even though his gifts were ostentatiously lavish.

Nor should it be thought that all his building was of a military nature. Outstanding was **his work on the f Temple.** Pagan and sceptical as he was, he was yet shrewd enough to appreciate his people's passionate concern for the worship of God, and vainglorious enough to desire the renown attaching to such a work. Side by side with an appreciation of his subjects' traditional religion went all those Hellenizing tendencies and practices by which he thought to assimilate himself to his fellow-princes and perhaps curry favour with Rome. The building of pagan temples and theatres, the establishment of games, in a word all those activities which had characterized the rule of Antiochus Epiphanes and led to the Maccabaean revolt, were repeated by Herod. But his knowledge of the Hebrew soul taught him where to halt.

The chief external events of the reign are naturally concerned with his **relations with Rome.** The enmity **g** of Cleopatra, due partly to her covetousness and partly to the intrigues of his household, turned out in the end to Herod's advantage. In the year before the battle of Actium, Herod had been on the point of associating himself with Antony's preparations against Octavian, when Cleopatra had him dispatched on a mission against the Arabs. This proved a more difficult task than he had expected and he did not complete his mission until after Antony had sailed to his disastrous defeat (31 B.C.). When therefore Octavian met Herod there was no reason why he should not confirm him in full possession of his dominion. In fact the Jewish king received from his Roman overlord certain territories (e.g. Jericho, Gaza, Azotus) which had been taken away from the Jewish kingdom either by Pompey or by Cleopatra. Later in the reign Augustus presented to Herod the districts of Trachonitis, Batanaea and Auronitis, and on the death of the tetrarch Zenodorus two years later (20 B.C.) the remainder of his former dominions, Ulatha and Paneas. This meant that the area of the kingdom ruled over by Herod was greater than it had ever been in the history of Israel, and though his brother Pheroras was nominated tetrarch of Peraea, Herod was his overlord.

According to Josephus, the relation between Augustus and Herod was that of intimate friends. This seems **h** hardly credible, but there is no doubt that Augustus took the greatest interest in the affairs of Palestine, which provides an excellent example of a ' client-kingdom '. Herod was nominally free, but all his policy was subordinate to the decision of the emperor. On one occasion we are told that, suspecting too great independence of action on the part of the Jewish king, the emperor wrote a sharp rebuke, saying that, whereas he had formerly treated Herod as a friend, henceforth he would deal with him as a subject. And in the closing years of the reign we are told of an occasion when the whole nation took an oath of loyalty to the emperor (the Pharisees manifesting their strong nationalistic feeling by refusing to take the oath).

Some account must be given of the **family quarrels i** which embittered the closing years of the king's life. The complete story is too involved owing to the complexity of interests causing the friction. Nor does the manifest bias of Josephus's sources help us to a clear picture. But in brief outline the facts seem to have been as follows. Alexander and Aristobulus, Herod's sons by Mariamme, stood high in their father's favour, a fact which aroused the jealousy of Antipater, a son by an earlier marriage, who hoped to succeed to the throne and now feared that he might be displaced. He alleged that he had discovered a plot of his two half-brothers to kill their father and usurp the throne. Whatever be the truth of the story, Herod was con-

71i vinced by the evidence adduced and had his sons put to death, only to discover that the informer was not less guilty than they. Antipater therefore met with the same fate, very shortly before Herod himself died in agony. (On hearing the story of these executions Augustus is said to have remarked : ' I'd rather be a sow of Herod's than his son '.)

There were other instances of intrigue, fostered by the women of the court—Herod was married at least ten times—and involving the opposition of the Pharisees, which still further clouded the mind of the king, and in the end he was almost insane with suspicion and fear. He had waded to the throne through blood, had maintained his position by assassination or judicial murder, and it is against such a background of ruthless and treacherous behaviour that we must read the story of the visit of the Magi and the massacre of the Innocents.

72a III Judaea under Archelaus and the Romans—On the death of Herod (4 B.C.) the kingdom was partitioned between three of his sons—Archelaus (who received Judaea, Samaria and Idumaea), Antipas (who held Galilee and Peraea) and Philip (to whom went the territory north-west of Galilee—Gaulanitis, Trachonitis, Ituraea, etc.). The settlement was not made without friction, as there had been some inconsistency in Herod's own arrangements. The Roman emperor, after appeals to him from the interested parties, decided on the division described above, conferring the title of tetrarch on the three rulers. This division of territory remained substantially unaltered until after the Crucifixion, the only alteration in status being that after ten years of rule, Archelaus was dispossessed and his tetrarchy incorporated into the full imperial system. In fact the chief importance of the reign of Archelaus is that it paved the way for this step. Even whilst the negotiations at Rome, following on the death of Herod, were still proceeding, various claimants to the title of **b** ' king ' made their appearance in Palestine. One of these was Judas or Theudas, son of that Hezekiah who had been put to death by Herod in 47 B.C. (perhaps to be identified with the Theudas of Ac 5:36). The Roman governor of Syria, Quintilius Varus, dispatched two legions to repress these movements, and an uneasy peace prevailed for a time in Judaea. But the efficiency and strength of Herod had not been inherited by Archelaus who became increasingly unpopular, and in A.D. 6 two separate embassies, one Jewish and one Samaritan, begged Augustus to abolish the monarchy. He decided that the only practicable solution was to make Archelaus's tetrarchy a Roman province and he accordingly instructed the governor of Syria, P. Sulpicius Quirinius (the ' Cyrinus ' of Lk 2:2) to make the necessary arrangements. A census of the district was initiated (cf. Ac 5:37) and a procurator, Coponius, was appointed. Another outburst of nationalistic feeling occurred, led by Judas the Galilean, who according to Josephus now founded the party of the ' Zealots '. If this last statement is true, he did little more than give formal character to a movement long in existence. Judas himself perished and his followers were disbanded, but he left sons who were to give trouble later. Archelaus retired into honourable exile in Southern Gaul.

c Judaea a Roman Province—A succession of procurators, nominated by the emperor for varying periods of office, now ruled Judaea, with their headquarters at Caesarea on the coast. Most of them have left little beyond their names on the page of history. The great exception is Pontius Pilate, the most famous governor in the history of the world. His governorship began in A.D. 27 and ended ten years later. During that period, apart from his share in the events culminating in the Crucifixion, he is known for his arrogance or, it may be, mere lack of tact in his handling of the Jews. Of the riots which his conduct occasioned, the most interesting for us is that which occurred when Pilate alienated some of the Temple funds to help to build an aqueduct to improve the Jerusalem water supply. It is probable **72c** that this incident is referred to in Lk 13:1, 2 ; and it is not at all unlikely that Barabbas took part in the movement. The final incident in Pilate's career was an unnecessarily brutal suppression of a Samaritan rising, leading to his removal from office by the governor of Syria, Vitellius.

IV Galilee under Herod Antipas—As we have seen, on **73a** Herod's death, a separate tetrarchy was constituted of Galilee and Peraea, ruled by Antipas. He took the name of Herod, as a sort of dynastic title and it is he who figures in various passages of the narrative of the Public Life. Apart from the building activities recorded of him by Josephus, we know little of the external events of his reign. It is of some interest to note that an unsuccessful expedition which he undertook against the king of Arabia Petraea is attributed by Josephus directly to his conduct in divorcing his wife, daughter of the Arabian king, in order to take his brother's wife, Herodias. There had been some previous friction about a disputed boundary, but the king made the treatment of his daughter a *casus belli* and fought a successful engagement against the troops of the ruler of Galilee. The people believed, we are told, that Herod's lack of success was due to his murder of John the Baptist. Like Archelaus in Judaea, Antipas was eventually deposed by Rome (at the instigation of his nephew, Herod Agrippa I, as we shall see later), and in the year A.D. 39 retired into exile in Gaul. His tetrarchy was for a time ruled by Agrippa.

Meanwhile, a word must be said of the remainder **b** of Herod the Great's kingdom, the region of Gaulanitis, etc. This passed into the hands of Philip, who also assumed the name of Herod. Like his father and his half-brother Antipas, he founded cities, notably Caesarea Philippi and Bethsaida Julias. He seems to have been an efficient and conscientious ruler and unlike most of the Herodians was universally regretted when the end came. He died in A.D. 34 and his tetrarchy was for a time attached to the province of Syria.

V Herod Agrippa I—When Aristobulus was executed **c** by his father, Herod the Great, he left two sons and several daughters. Of these Agrippa was to lead the most successful life and he laid the foundations of his future prosperity during the years of his sojourn at Rome. He was sent there (c 7 B.C.) when he was still quite a small boy by his mother Salome, whose own mother Berenice was a friend of the empress Livia. The boy, who was popular and attractive, was brought up in close association with the younger members of the imperial family circle, but after the deaths of Germanicus (A.D. 18) and Drusus (A.D. 23) his prospects seemed very gloomy and he returned to Palestine. At first he received a post at Tiberias, one of the new foundations made by his uncle, Herod Antipas, but after a time he attached himself to the governor of Syria, L. Pomponius Flaccus (32–35). (He was therefore almost certainly at Tiberias during the Public Life.) Eventually (A.D. 36) he returned to Rome, where he managed to curry favour with Gaius, shortly to become Emperor.

When Gaius (Caligula) ascended the throne, one **d** of his first acts was to make over to Agrippa the tetrarchy of Philip, who had died three years previously. Agrippa remained at Rome for the time being, setting sail for the East in the autumn of 38. His arrival at Alexandria, where he called on his way, began a disturbance which was to flare up into more serious riots, leading to the famous embassy to Caligula in which Philo took a leading part (cf. § 75b inf.).

Soon after Agrippa's arrival **in Palestine,** he managed by intrigue to obtain the deposition of his uncle, Herod Antipas, the tetrarch of Galilee. Antipas was exiled to Lyons, his dominions being added to the tetrarchy of Agrippa (A.D. 39). When, in 41, Claudius succeeded Caligula, he practically reconstituted the old Herodian

73d kingdom, conferring on Agrippa the title of king. In other words, a fresh attempt was to be made to restore the old position of client-kingdom. But the death of Agrippa within three years put an end to this solution and once again the kingdom came under direct Roman control. Agrippa left a son of the same name, but he was too young to be trusted with power and he was given the small kingdom of Chalcis to rule. In A.D. 53 a new arrangement was made, Chalcis reverting to the province of Syria and Agrippa receiving the territory that had constituted Philip's tetrarchy, with the addition of Abilene and some outlying districts. Little of this territory was in any sense Jewish, but Agrippa's own descent and the part he plays in the story of Acts make it necessary for some mention to be made here of his kingdom. Moreover, on the accession of Nero (54) some portions of Galilee were added to his dominions.

There is little to record of the reign. Styling himself Marcus Julius Agrippa, he manifested his desire to associate himself closely with the Roman aristocracy, and it is not surprising to find him consorting with the Roman governor of Judaea. In other respects, his reign recalls some of the features of his great-grand-father's, especially in the liberality of his benefactions, particularly to the Greek city of Berytus, but he seems to have been blest with a more placid disposition. At any rate, his long reign, which lasted until his death (probably in A.D. 93) was not marked by any serious internal or domestic troubles, despite the complexity of the matrimonial arrangements of the members of his family.

74a VI Palestine under the Romans—Tacitus's well-known sentence, *duravit patientia Judaeis usque ad Gessium Florum procuratorem*, aptly sums up the story of Israel between the death of Herod Agrippa I and the outbreak of the rebellion (A.D. 44–66). A succession of incompetent or rapacious governors inflamed the already irritated feelings of the Jews who, as a nation, never reconciled themselves to Roman rule.

It may be true that, as Josephus argues, the final breach was the work of a minority of extremists, but it is not less certain that those who were content with their position in the Roman system were still fewer. The story of Roman-Jewish relations is one of an irreconcilable cleavage of ideals. The Jewish tradition of an autonomous theocracy could not be squared with the cosmopolitanism of a regime in which everything, including religion, must be subordinated to the interests of a universal empire. Whilst the Romans did try to make all possible allowances for the idiosyncrasies of the people they governed, the peculiarity of the Jewish ethos was something they never understood. The Maccabees had carried the nation with them in their resistance to Hellenization by Syria ; we cannot doubt that the nation as a whole was behind the final attempt to win independence of Rome.

b The clash between **Fadus**, who took over the province on the death of Agrippa, and another Theudas, was followed by an outbreak, led by James and Simon, sons of that Judas who had raised the standard of revolt in A.D. 6. The governor of the time was an apostate Jew, Tiberius Julius Alexander—a tactless appointment though one which doubtless commended itself to the central government as providing a ruler who might be expected to understand this difficult race. The ring-leaders were crucified. We hear of further troubles under his successor Cumanus, due to the insolence of the occupying troops, though one serious outbreak occurred as the result of the chronic hostility of Jew and Samaritan.

c We come now to the governorships of **Felix and Festus**, known to us from the closing chapters of the *Acts*. The former is shown by Josephus to have been brutal and treacherous in his handling of the constant risings, and though his successor seems to have displayed more tact, the situation was getting rapidly out of control. Festus died in office and before his

successor arrived the Sanhedrin attempted to reassert **74c** its authority and independence by putting to death the Apostle James, bishop of Jerusalem. The high-priest was deposed for this, but no other punitive steps seem to have been taken. Albinus (62–64) appears to have been conciliatory in his treatment of the Jews, but his policy of appeasement received its inevitable reward. Mildness was mistaken for weakness.

VII The Rebellion—The anti-Roman element became **d** ever more violent, and when **Gessius Florus** arrived (64) he doubtless came with orders to spare no effort to retrieve the situation. The temper of the Jews was inflamed, and it was perhaps beyond human ingenuity to avert disaster. But in A.D. 66 Gessius Florus repeated the action of Pontius Pilate in sequestrating Temple funds for administrative purposes and this provoked a riot. The governor marched in person to Jerusalem with a large force, demanded the production of the ringleaders, and when he received no more than an apology from the Sanhedrin, ordered his troops to clear the Upper Market. Many casualties were inflicted on the people and much material damage done. The Sanhedrin seems to have been genuinely anxious to co-operate with the Romans in the preservation of order, but the conduct of the troops was too provocative. For a time Agrippa's intervention and appeals to the more responsible elements in the capital met with some success, but he could not persuade them to accept the rule of Florus and in the end he had to withdraw, baffled. The extremist Eleazar then precipitated a crisis by proposing the termination of the daily sacrifice which by custom had long been offered for the emperor. The pro-Roman party, or at least those who believed that their own interests and those of the nation would best be served by loyalty to Rome, resisted this proposal, but the majority sided with Eleazar. The sacrifice was suspended. The rebellion had begun.

The Sanhedrin appealed to Florus and to Agrippa **e** for military support, and though Florus did not think it prudent to risk his troops, a force was sent by Agrippa. Thus the rebellion began with a skirmish between the opposing parties amongst the Jews themselves. Passions rose higher, the whole city threw itself into the movement, the Roman garrison was besieged and when it surrendered on a promise that the lives of its members would be spared, they were all treacherously killed.

The inevitable sequel was an outbreak of anti-Semitism at Caesarea, where 20,000 Jews are said to have been massacred. The Jews in turn took reprisals and soon the whole country was aflame. The legate of Syria, Cestius Gallus, hastily led an army into Judaea, but after an unsuccessful siege of Jerusalem was compelled to withdraw to Caesarea.

The details of the story are inextricably confused, **f** partly because of the nature of the situation, partly because we have to rely on the rather disingenuous narrative of Josephus. Since he wrote his *Jewish War* chiefly with an eye to excusing his own conduct and that of his people, there are necessarily suppressions and evasions. Moreover, the Jews themselves were fiercely divided and much of the time were fighting amongst themselves. Nor do the details concern us here.

In the spring of 67, Nero sent out a new legate to conduct the operations—**Titus Flavius Vespasianus,** the future emperor. He set about reducing Galilee and the rebellious parts of Agrippa's kingdom. This occupied the whole of the campaigning season of that year and the following spring Vespasian began the task of methodically crushing the outposts of Peraea, Idumaea and Judaea, gradually closing in on the capital. But the death of Nero constitutionally terminated his commission and he waited for its renewal before laying siege to Jerusalem. Throughout the year of the Four Emperors operations were held up, and when Vespasian was himself proclaimed emperor by his troops, he left for Italy, leaving his son Titus to complete the task of suppressing the rebellion.

74g The story of **the siege of Jerusalem** is sufficiently well known. All that need be said here is that the Jews were already considerably weakened by their own internal dissensions. Neither fanaticism nor the fear of reprisals could resist the methodical onslaught of the Roman army. The Temple was taken in August and (apparently deliberately) given to the flames. By the end of September all resistance was at an end and the city reduced to a heap of rubble. The prophecy of the rejected Messias was terribly fulfilled. Judaea itself remained as a unit of the Roman Empire; but the Jewish national state came to an end with the destruction of Zion.

It seems likely that (as Eusebius tells us) the Christian community established at Jerusalem had withdrawn from the capital to Pella in Peraea before the siege operations began so that it was not involved in the common disaster. The final severance of Christianity from Judaism was achieved.

75a VIII The Jews of the Diaspora—No history of Israel is complete without some mention of those communities of Jews who lived scattered throughout the civilized world beyond the frontiers of Palestine. After the Babylonian captivity, a strong Jewish element remained in Mesopotamia, and we know that in Egypt also there were such large numbers of Jews as to constitute a special administrative problem. They had presumably made their way there originally for purposes of trading, as also they had established themselves in Asia Minor and Greece, and as far as Italy and Gaul. But many also, especially in Alexandria and the West, had come under compulsion, either as prisoners of war or deported by conquerors such as Ptolemy I of Egypt. It was reckoned that, at the beginning of the empire, there were in Egypt a million Jews to eight million Egyptians. We are told by Strabo that the Jews in Alexandria had their own national head, who apparently presided in certain legal and judicial processes. They also resided in special quarters of the city, as they seem to have done in most places (*e.g.* Antioch and Rome).

b One or two incidents may be singled out as exemplifying the nature of the problem created for the Jews themselves no less than for their rulers. Thus at Alexandria in A.D. 38 a fierce pogrom broke out, **75b** occasioned it would seem by the visit there of Agrippa I, on his way to Palestine. Jews were maltreated, their property destroyed. The situation deteriorated still further when the governor of Egypt, apparently in an attempt to curry favour with the emperor, ordered the statue of Gaius to be set up in the synagogues. In their distress and danger, the Jews appealed to Caesar. Two embassies, the Jewish one headed by the philosopher-exegete Philo, the Gentile one headed by Apion, dilettante and charlatan, appeared before Gaius. Needless to say, the emperor insisted on the carrying out of the prefect's orders, and went so far as to require the Jews at Jerusalem to set up a similar statue in the Temple. However, the intervention of Agrippa and the emperor's death relieved the situation. The incident is significant as indicating the **tension existing between Jew and non-Jew** in the empire, a tension liable to burst out into open rioting given the necessary occasion. At Rome itself, in A.D. 19, Tiberius expelled the Jewish community (though we are told that no less than 4,000 of them were drafted to Sardinia for police-work), ostensibly because of the trickery of four men, but we cannot doubt that the measure was taken as a means to keep the peace. Similarly we are told of constant riots in the capital, leading to a further expulsion in A.D. 49, an event having special interest for us because of the reference to it in Ac 18:2.

The surprising thing is that, so long as no popular **c** disturbance was caused, the Roman authorites as a whole seem to have treated the Jews with remarkable forbearance, granting them unusual immunities and dispensations. They were apparently exempt from military service, and their Sabbath law was respected. But with the growth and spread of Christianity, the occasions for disturbance in the empire multiplied, and there can be little doubt that this was one factor in the attitude of the government to the Christian body. How far the Jews were responsible, through Poppaea, for the turning of Nero's mind to the Christians after the fire of A.D. 64, we cannot be sure, but it is by no means an unlikely hypothesis. But this is a question beyond our present scope, as is the position of the Jews in the empire after the destruction of the Temple in A.D. 70.

ARCHAEOLOGY AND THE BIBLE

By E. POWER, S.J.

76a Bibliography—This list is necessarily limited but can be completed from the bibliographical indications in the books cited and the elenchus bibliographicus of Bi. **General information :** *G. A. Barton, *Archaeology and the Bible*, Philadelphia, 1933 ; *F. R. Kenyon, *Archaeology and the Bible*, London, 1940 ; *S. L. Caiger, *The OT and Modern Discoveries*, London, 1938 ; *H. Gressmann, *Altorientalische Texte und Bilder*, Berlin, 1926-7², 2 vol. ; *A. Jirku, *Altorientalischer Kommentar zum AT*, Leipzig, 1923 ; *C. M. Cobern, *The New Archaeological Discoveries and their Bearing on the NT*, New York, 1918 ; *W. Ramsay, *The Bearing of Recent Discovery on the Trustworthiness of the NT*, London, 1915 ; *A. Deissmann, *Licht vom Osten*, Tübingen, 1923 ; Id, *The NT in the Light of Modern Research*, London, 1929. **Egypt and the Bible :** H. J. Heyes, *Bibel und Aegypten*, Münster, 1904 ; *W. Spiegelberg, *Aegyptische Randglossen zum AT*, Strassburg, 1904 ; A. Mallon, *Les Hébreux en Egypte*, Rome, 1921 ; *A. Yahuda, *Die Sprache des Pentateuch in ihren Beziehungen zum Aegyptischen*, Berlin, 1929 ; *T. E. Peet, *A Comparative Study of the Literature of Egypt, Palestine and Mesopotamia*, London, 1931 ; L. Speelers, *Egypte*, DBVS 2 (1932) 756-919 ; *J. A. Knudtzon, *Die el-Amarna Tafeln*, Leipzig, 1915 ; P. Dhorme, *Amarna*, DBVS 1 (1928) 207-25 ; *A. Cowley, *Aramaic Papyri of the Fifth century B.C.*, Oxford, 1923 ; L. Hennequin, *Elephantine* DBVS 2 (1934) 962-1032 ; A. Vincent, *La religion des judéo-araméens d'Elephantine*, Paris, 1937. **Mesopotamia and the Bible :** *E. Schrader, *Die Keilinschriften und das AT*, 3. Aufl. von H. Winckler und H. Zimmern, Berlin, 1902 ; *A. Jeremias, *Das AT im Lichte des Alten Orients*, Leipzig, 1906 ; *H. Winckler, *Keilinschriftliches Textbuch zum AT*, Leipzig, 1909 ; A. Condamin, *Babylone et la Bible*, DAFC 1 (1911) 327-90 ; C. F. Jean, *Le milieu biblique*, Paris, 1923 ; J. Plessis, *Babylone et la Bible*, DBVS 1 (1928) 713-852. **Ras-Shamra :** Articles of R. de Langhe, ETL 16 (1939) 245-327 ; A. Bea, Bi 19 (1938) 435-53 and 20 (1939) 436-53 ; R. de Vaux, RB 46 (1937) 362-72 ; 526-55 ; *J. W. Jack, *The Ras-Shamra Tablets. Their Bearing on the OT*, London, 1935. **Palestine Explorations :** *W. F. Albright, *Archaeology of Palestine and the Bible*, New York, 1935 ; A. G. Barrois, *Manuel d'Archéologie Biblique*, Paris, 1939 ; *S. L. Caiger, *Bible and Spade, An Introduction to Biblical Archaeology*, London, 1936 ; *J. G. Duncan, *Digging up Biblical History. Recent Archaeology in Palestine and its Bearing on the OT*, London, 1931 ; L. Hennequin, *Fouilles en Palestine*, DBVS 3 (1936) 318-524 ; *R. A. S. Macalister, *A Century of Excavation in Palestine*, London, 1925 ; J. Simons, *Opgravingen in Palestine*, Roermond-Masseik, 1935 ; L. H. Vincent, *Canaan d'après l'exploration récente*, Paris, 1907 ; *C. Watzinger, *Denkmäler Palästinas*, Leipzig, 1935. **Lakish Letters :** Articles of A. Vaccari, Bi 20 (1939) 180-91 ; R. de Vaux, RB 48 (1939) 181-206 ; *J. W. Jack, PEQ 70 (1938) 165-87.

b Introductory—Archaeology has long been understood as a systematic presentation of the domestic, social, political, religious, literary, and artistic institutions of some ancient people, derived largely, or even exclusively, from the literary records of the past. Recently however it has come to be more generally regarded as the science of the monuments of antiquity

revealed to us by the eye of the explorer and the spade **76b** of the excavator. The importance of this comparatively new science for the scriptural student is indicated by Pope Pius XII in the following passage of his recent Encyclical on the most opportune way to promote biblical studies : ' All can easily perceive that the conditions of biblical studies and their subsidiary sciences have greatly changed within the last fifty years. For, apart from anything else, when Our Predecessor published the Encyclical Letter, *Providentissimus Deus*, hardly a single place in Palestine had begun to be explored by relevant excavations. Now however this kind of investigation is much more frequent and, since more precise methods and technical skill have been developed in the course of actual experience, it gives us information at once more abundant and more accurate. How much light has been derived from these explorations for the more correct and fuller understanding of the Sacred Books all experts know as well as those who devote themselves to these studies. The value of these excavations is enhanced by the discovery from time to time of written documents, which help much towards the knowledge of the languages, letters, events, customs, and forms of worship of most ancient times. And of no less importance are the discovery and investigation, so frequent in our times, of papyri which have contributed so much to the knowledge of letters and institutions, both public and private, especially of the time of our Saviour ', DAS, § 16.

The purpose of the following pages is to show how **c** much and in what different ways archaeological discoveries have contributed to the interpretation of the Bible. Excavations in Palestine provide only a small part of the immense material from which a selection must be made. The discoveries which receive the widest publicity, such as the treasures of the necropolis of Ur and of the tomb of Tut-Ankh-Amon are usually of the least importance for our purpose. Ancient documents merit particular attention since they offer the most valuable information. Very many of these have been unearthed in Mesopotamia and Egypt, but comparatively few in Syria and Palestine, chiefly because of the quality of the writing materials used in these different countries. In Mesopotamia the cuneiform characters were impressed on soft clay, which was dried and fired and could thus resist the ravages of weather and time. As an example of their abundance may be cited the discovery in 1933, at Tell el-Ḥarīri, the ancient Mari, on the Upper Euphrates, of a library of the 18th cent. B.C., containing over 20,000 clay tablets. In the western lands on the other hand papyrus leaves were the writing material usually employed, and these perished all too quickly in the damp climate of Syria and Palestine, but survived from very ancient times and in considerable number in the dry soil of Egypt. The very valuable library discovered at Rās-Shamra, the ancient Ugarīt, in the north-west corner of Syria, in 1929, owes its preservation to the fact that a cuneiform alphabet and clay tablets were used.

The geographical position of Palestine and the early **d** history of the Hebrews show clearly the necessity of archaeological research for the better understanding of the sacred text. Palestine was the bridge between

76d Asia and Africa, between the Indian Ocean and the Mediterranean, the meeting-place of the armies, the wares, and the cultures of the ancient world. The people who held this bridge could not fail to be influenced in many ways by the various ancient civilizations of the East. Their great ancestor, Abraham, was of Babylonian origin ; and Babylonian culture had spread to Canaan before they occupied it. Their great legislator, Moses, was learned in all the wisdom of the Egyptians ; and it was during their long sojourn in Egypt that they became a nation. Amorites, Hittites, Hurrites had penetrated into Palestine at an early period and contributed to the complex Canaanite culture from which they were to borrow. They subsequently experienced more than two centuries of Persian rule. And finally Hellenic culture and Roman government exercised a strong influence on them in late OT and NT times. It is clear therefore that a knowledge of the history, literature, and culture of these ancient nations is necessary to understand the milieu in which the sacred books were written. Thus only can the difficulties arising from ignorance of local circumstances and literary devices, of the customs of the land and the history of the period, be met and the errors caused by the use of alien literary criteria and subjective norms of interpretation be rectified.

77a **Egypt**—To Egypt above all we owe a number of biblical texts, older in date than any MSS we possess, of which four fragments : Papyrus Nash, Papyri Rylands Greek 457 and 458, Papyrus Fouad 266, and one large collection, Chester Beatty Papyri, are of special interest. **The Nash Papyrus**, discovered at Fayum in 1902 and previously dated *c* A.D. 100, but recently assigned by Albright for palaeographic reasons to 200–100 B.C., contains in Hebrew on a single page the decalogue and Deut 6:4. Its importance comes from its date, since we have no Hebrew MS of the MT earlier than A.D. 900, and especially from the character of its text, which is earlier than the MT and closer to the Greek and Samaritan texts. In particular it prefixes to the decalogue a descriptive title, absent from MT and Sam but found in LXX, and thus establishes the existence of a different type of Hebrew text prior to the MT and vindicates the authority of the Greek **b** translators who used it. PRG 457, discovered about 1920, probably at Fayum or Oxyrhynchus, and published by C. H. Roberts at the Manchester University Press in 1935, contained part of a sheet of a codex of St John's Gospel of which the fragments preserved belong to Jn 18:31–33, 37–38. Experts in palaeography assign the writing to the first half of the 2nd cent. It is truly remarkable, as a proof of the authenticity and early diffusion of the NT writings, to find a Gospel, written in Asia, already in public circulation in Egypt within less than half a century of its origin. **c** In 1936 appeared from the same press and editor PRG 458, the oldest Greek biblical text so far discovered, containing short fragments of Deut chh 23–28. This papyrus, which was found in the wrappings of a mummy, is assigned to the 2nd cent. B.C. and is thus only a century later than the original LXX. The fragmentary condition of the text makes the critical conclusions derived from it less decisive than its age might seem to warrant. It is generally good, though not free from scribal errors., and does not give exclusive support to any one of the later MS families against its rivals. **P.** Fouad 266, first published at Cairo in 1939 and studied by W. G. Waddell in JTS 45 (1944) 158–161, contains Deut 31:28–32:7. It is of the same date and uncertain origin as PRG 458 and, though better preserved, is too brief to warrant more definite critical conclusions. It vindicates St Jerome's statement, doubted by critics, that the divine name Yahweh was not rendered κύριος but was still written in ancient **d** Hebrew characters. The papyri, discovered in 1929 and called by the name of their original purchaser **Chester Beatty**, are Egypt's most important contribution to biblical study. They have all been published

by Sir Frederic Kenyon in seven volumes of Introduc- **77d** tion and Text and six volumes of Plates (London, Walker, 1933–7). The NT part (vol. II–III) contains considerable remains of two codices, one of the Gospels and Acts, the other of the Epistles of St Paul, both belonging to the early 3rd cent. and thus a century older than our earliest NT MSS, and some fragments of the Apocalypse (*c* A.D. 300). The critical study of these ancient documents has shown them to be, not indeed free from scribal errors or without unimportant variant readings, but nevertheless in such remarkable agreement with our best MSS as to prove conclusively that the text of the NT was fixed and certain at the end of the 2nd cent. The OT part (vol. IV–VII) comprises large extracts of Genesis in two codices of the 3rd and 4th cent., portions of Numbers and Deuteronomy from the beginning of the 2nd cent., passages of Isaias, Jeremias and Ecclesiasticus from the early 4th cent., and considerable sections of Ezechiel, Esther, and Daniel of the early 3rd cent. These documents, especially such as antedate the Hexapla of Origen, are of the greatest important for the study of the LXX text. So far the verdict seems to be that while they support a number of the supposed Hebrew corrections of A they are nevertheless in more general agreement with B.

The non-biblical papyri and ostraca or inscribed pot- **e** sherds have given us very valuable information on the language, the literary character and the historical background of the NT. We are not referring here to extracts from lost or extant literary works, though some of these have thrown fresh light on the religious history of the late Jewish and early Christian periods, but to the public and private original documents which have been discovered. The language of the NT is not classical but Hellenistic, the *Koine* or common Greek, which spread through the East after the conquests of Alexander. The *Koine* varies somewhat in character according as it is used for literary purposes or as the spoken and written language of the common people. The latter is the Greek of the Egyptian private letters and business documents, and also in general of the NT, though here there is a certain gradation from the more literary Epistle to the Hebrews at one end to Paul, John and Mark at the other. Biblical Greek thus appears for the first time in a historical linguistic setting. Most of the words formerly believed to be peculiar to it have been found in the papyri and ostraca. Its morphology and syntactical structure are illustrated and clarified. The accepted interpretation of certain expressions is more fully revealed, and a different interpretation of others is sometimes suggested by the new contexts in which they occur. Thus the difficulty of construing πλήρης as a genitive in Jn 1:14 disappears when we find that the adjective is not declined in the speech of the common people. The technical sense of ἐλλογεῖν ' set down to one's account ', βεβαιοῦν ' guarantee ', and ἀπέχειν ' receive full payment ', makes the force of these words clearer in several NT passages. The new meanings of πήρα ' begging-bag ', ἀπάρχη ' birth-certificate ', and ὑπόστασις ' title-deeds ', must be considered and may be found helpful in interpreting Lk 9:4, Rom 8:23, Heb 11:1. The use of ἀδελφός (lit. ' brother ') for ' kinsman ' in the recently published Adler papyri is an interesting linguistic confirmation of the traditional interpretation of the same word in the NT where it indicates not brother but kinsman of Our Lord.

St Paul tells us that the early Gentile converts be- **f** longed almost exclusively to the lower classes (1 Cor 1:26). It was for these that the NT was primarily intended, and it was written in language which they understood. It is not surprising therefore that the papyri and ostraca written by and for the common people offer many **literary parallels to** passages in the NT. Thus the plan of St Paul's letters : greeting, prayer, thanksgiving, subject-matter, salutations, farewell, is now revealed to us by Egyptian letters as the customary form of private correspondence. His method of

77f dictating his letters and inserting a passage of his own handwriting is abundantly illustrated in the papyri. His reference to those who have no hope (1 Thes 4:13) as opposed to the Christians who expect a better resurrection is exemplified by the conclusion of a letter of a certain Irene, written on the occasion of a death in the family : ' But still one can do nothing with regard to such matters. So console one another, and farewell '. St Paul concludes the passage, after describing the resurrection : ' So console one another with these words ' (18). The touching letter of the wretched Antonis Longus to his mother helps us to realize the state of mind of the prodigal son after he had spent his substance living riotously. The cases of conscience proposed by the Corinthians to St Paul in connection with the eating of flesh offered to idols are graphically illustrated by invitations to a banquet at the table of the Lord Serapis, sometimes in the temple of the god, sometimes in a private house.

g While Greek literary works are chiefly concerned with the upper grades of society the papyri and ostraca increase our knowledge of the **historical background of the NT** by revealing to us the lower classes in the Roman Empire. Their hopes and fears, their interests and occupations, their virtues and vices, their family relations and financial burdens are made known to us by public documents and private records. We find them more religiously minded than the higher classes, less acquainted with the pleasures than the hardships of life, and thus better disposed to accept the Gospel teaching. Our increased historical knowledge enables us to confirm suspected statements and elucidate obscure passages in the NT. Thus the release of an imprisoned malefactor by an Egyptian official at the request of the people on the occasion of a festival illustrates and confirms the episode of Barabbas

h narrated in the history of the Passion. The records of the census of Roman subjects taken regularly every fourteen years in view of taxation have made intelligible to us St Luke's indication of the occasion and date of Our Lord's birth. These records extend over a period of two and a half centuries. The earliest so far discovered is dated A.D 20. The census of A.D. 6 is attested by Luke and Josephus for Palestine and by CIL, III, 6687 for Apamea in Syria. Since our Lord was born sometime before the death of Herod in 4 B.C. St Luke must refer to the census of 9 B.C. as the first of the new fourteen-years system instituted by Augustus. This census was a house to house one ; absentees had to return to their place of origin for the enrolment ; the names of women also appear on the lists. The papyri have singularly vindicated St Luke's authority in the matter.

78a **The Egyptian historical records,** while attesting admissions into Egypt of emigrants from the east, make no mention of the arrival or departure of the Hebrews. But the Hyksos invasion explains the welcome they received and the position which Joseph attained. The store cities which they were forced to build, Pithom, the modern Tell el-Artabi (or less probably Tell el-Maskhūta), in the Wadi Tumilat, and Ramesses, probably the modern San el-Hagar and ancient Tanis, near the mouth of the Tanitic branch of the Nile, have been made known to us with their granaries and temples by recent excavations. The site of Ramesses, suggested indeed by the ' wonderful things . . . in the field of Tanis ' (Ps 77:12) which are obviously the prodigies of the Exodus, is still disputed, but P. Montet's discoveries in 1929 (R B 39 [1930] 5–28) have strengthened the claims of Tanis. Egyptian evidence strongly supports the view that Ramesses II was the Pharaoh of the oppression and that the Exodus took place in the beginning of the reign of his successor, Mernephtah (c 1232–1224). But it gives us also one of the strongest arguments for an earlier date in an inscription of the fifth year of the same Pharaoh where we read : ' Israel is destroyed ; it has no longer seed. Palestine is become as a widow for Egypt '. The argument is not conclusive but

cannot be discussed here. Finally may be mentioned **78a** the inscription of Sheshonk I, the biblical Sesac (3 Kg 14:25), at Karnak, which records his invasion of Palestine and gives the names of sixty cities which he pillaged c 930 B.C. A fragment of a stele, erected by this invader at Megiddo, was discovered in the recent excavation of that city.

Two very valuable collections of ancient documents, **b** written one in Babylonian and the other in Aramaic, have also been found in Egypt, the cuneiform tablets of Tell el-Amarna, and the Aramaic papyri of Elephantine. **The Letters of Tell el-Amarna,** 350 in number, were discovered accidentally in 1887 on the site of the ephemeral capital of Amenophis IV, about 200 m. S. of Cairo. They contain the foreign correspondence of Amenophis III (c 1413–1379) and Amenophis IV (c 1379–1362), mostly with their Syrian and Palestinian officials and vassals, but also with their ' brothers ', the kings of Assyria, Babylonia, Mitanni, Khatti, Cyprus and Arzawa. They give us invaluable information on the geography and history of Palestine in the first half of the 14th cent. B.C. The Ḥabīrī, who took a leading part in the struggle for independence which they record, were at first believed by many to be the Hebrew invaders, but are now better known as more ancient and more widespread than Israel. **The Elephantine Papyri,** about **c** 80 in number, of which nearly half are dated (495–400 B.C.), acquired partly by purchase but mostly by excavations in 1898–1908, are the records of a Jewish military colony, established at the southern outpost of Egypt most probably by Psammetichus I (663–609 B.C.). They contain official documents and family archives of especial interest. The language is closely akin to the Aramaic texts of the Bible and supports their traditional date. A Persian royal ordinance, minutely regulating the celebration of the feast of Azymes, refutes peremptorily the objection long urged by critics against the authenticity of the Persian royal decrees in the book of Esdras, namely that Persian monarchs did not interfere in the religious affairs of their foreign subjects.

Mesopotamia—Mesopotamia has given us no biblical **79a** texts, but its cuneiform tablets have provided a very instructive commentary to many parts of the OT. They have fixed the sense of numerous terms previously obscure, identified a number of cities and countries otherwise unknown, confirmed and supplemented the records of the historical books, dated definitely or approximately many important events, facilitated the understanding of the customs of the Patriarchs and the laws of the Mosaic code and shown by many parallels the superiority of the moral and religious ideas and institutions of Israel.

Babylonian parallels to the biblical narratives of **b** Gen 1–10, though hailed by many on their first discovery as sources of the first chapters of the Bible, have been shown by closer study to have no direct literary connection with them. There are undoubtedly points of contact, for instance, in the concept of the material world. But it is only in the story of the deluge that we find such similarities between the two accounts as suggest a common and more ancient source. The name of Noah, like that of the Babylonian hero of the deluge, Um (Ur ? Ut ?)—napištim seems to mean ' length of days ' ; and there is little doubt that the same individual is indicated under both names. The local floods, of which traces have been discovered in one layer at Ur and in three distinct layers at Kish are however too limited in extent and too recent in date to offer an adequate explanation of the deluge of the literary records. No genuine **c** parallels have been discovered to the description of Paradise and the temptation and fall of our first parents. Minor points however in the biblical narratives are usefully illustrated. The Cherubim at the gate of Paradise have their parallels in the genii that guarded the entrances of Babylonian temples and

79c palaces. The flame of the revolving sword (Gen 3:24) was probably a bronze thunderbolt like that erected by Tiglath-Pileser I on the ruins of a devastated city. The tree of life in Paradise has its counterpart in the plant of life sought by the hero Gilgamesh. The designation of the one God by a plural noun, Elohim, can no longer be regarded as a vestige of ancient polytheism, since a similar use of the plural to designate a single divinity is found in Babylonian, Hittite and Canaanite texts. Most of the peoples mentioned in the ethnographical table of Gen 10:1–32 are now known to us from the Assyrian and Babylonian documents.

d **The biblical chronology** of the monarchical period is based on the registration, in one of the Assyrian Canons giving the dates of the kings, of the solar eclipse, total at Nineveh, which occurred on the 15th June 763 B.C. This enables us to date exactly, for instance, the payment of tribute to Assyria by Jehu in 841 B.C. and by Menahem in 738 B.C., the fall of Samaria in 721 B.C., of Nineveh in 612 B.C. and Babylon in 587 B.C., the battles of Qarqar, where Israel led by Achab first met Assyria, in 853 B.C. and of Megiddo, where Josias was slain, in 609 B.C. We learn that the enigmatic Phul of 4 Kg 15:19 was the Assyrian Tiglath-pileser III, also called Pulu as king of Babylonia. We read the fulfilment of the prophecies of Isaias on the imminent Assyrian devastation of Samaria and Damascus (Is 7:16 ; 8:4) and on the weakness of Egypt as an ally against Assyria (Is 20:5–6) and of Ezechiel (29:19–20) on the invasion of Egypt by Nabuchodonosor II, which occurred in the 37th year of his reign (569 B.C.), The rebellion, deportation,

e and subsequent restoration of Manasses by Ashur-banipal (2 Par 33:11), not mentioned in Kings and regarded as a pure invention by the critics, is at least rendered credible by recent discoveries. That Manasses took part in the rebellion of the western subject peoples against Assyria in 652 B.C. is legitimately concluded from the discovery of two Assyrian contract tablets, dated 649 and 647, at Gezer, which attest Assyrian occupation of this Judaean city and thus presuppose a rebellion. His subsequent pardon and restoration is supported by an Assyrian record of the similar pardon and restoration of another of Ashurbanipal's royal

f prisoners, the Egyptian Nechao. Valuable information on the fortunes of the Jewish exiles is derived from the archives of a bank, discovered at Nippur in Southern Babylonia and published in 1896 and 1902 under the title *Business Documents of Murashi Sons*. In them we find the names of many Jews, descendants of those deported by Nabuchodonosor, enjoying full freedom, possessing lands and capital and engaged largely in commercial transactions. Several of them were tax-collectors and one, Hanani son of Menahem, had charge of the royal aviary. The condition of these Jews in the second half of the 5th cent. B.C. agrees with the indications of the sacred books ; and their prosperity explains the comparatively small number of the exiles who returned with Zorobabel and Esdras.

g The discovery in 1901 of the famous code of laws, drawn up by **Hammurabi** in the early 17th cent. B.C., was followed by the publication of fragments of a still earlier Sumerian code in 1916, of an Assyrian code of the 16th cent. B.C. in 1920 and of a Hittite code of the 13th cent. B.C. in 1921. These codes were all unknown when a Mosaic code was regarded in critical circles as an anachronism and the mass of Pentateuchal legislation was assigned to the exilic or post-exilic period. Their discovery makes it impossible to deny the existence of a Hebrew code of laws at a very early period, to which additions could have been made as occasion demanded. Hebrew and Babylonian laws have naturally much in common but are essentially different in character and spirit. The code of Ham-murabi supposes an advanced state of civilization, is based on principles of utility and aims at the protection of property. The law of Moses was enacted for a less civilized people, but has moral principles for

its base and the practice of justice and charity for its **79g** object.

A comparative study of **Hebrew and Babylonian h religion** reveals more contrasts than resemblances. The monotheism and supernatural prophecy, which are Israel's exclusive possession, are replaced in Babylon by numerous divinities and elaborate systems of divination. The Babylonians praise their gods, in psalms like those of the Hebrew Psalter, in order to assuage their anger and win their favour, but never with the *sole* object of religious worship. They beg for temporal favours and especially release from the chastisements which their sins have brought upon them, but never for release from the guilt of sin. They offer sacrifices like those of the Hebrews, but seem to have no conception of the need of moral dispositions for their efficacy. Attempts have been made to establish the Babylonian origin of the Hebrew feasts of Sabbath and Purim but without success. The Babylonian Sabbath, if it ever existed, was a monthly rather than a weekly religious celebration, not marked by abstention from servile work. Purim ('lots') has been definitely proved from the Kultepe texts to be a Hebrew loan-word of Babylonian origin (Bi 21 [1940] 198–9), but that only confirms the narrative of the book of Esther according to which the feast was instituted by Hebrew exiles in Babylonia. As an instance of ritual resemblances may be cited the twelve loaves of shewbread offered to Yahweh in the temple and the twelve cakes offered by the Babylonians to Ishtar. The prophet Jeremias in his protest against the introduction into Israel of the worship of Ishtar, the Queen of Heaven, twice refers to this rite (Jer 7:18 ; 44:19) and uses for cake the word *kawwān*, which is found in the Babylonian ritual texts, but nowhere else in the Hebrew Bible.

The antiquity and extensive character of Babylonian **i** ritual has revealed another error of the evolutionary theory which assigned the mass of Pentateuchal ritual to the exilic or post-exilic period. Quite recently the early origin of Hebrew ritual has been still more strikingly confirmed by the discovery of an extensive ritual, a little earlier than that of Moses, in the immediate neighbourhood of Palestine and in a language closely akin to Hebrew. The texts discovered at **Rās-Shamra** in the north-western corner of Syria and published in annual instalments 1930–39, are dated around 1400 B.C., written mainly in cuneiform alphabetic characters, and mostly of religious and mythological character. They exhibit extraordinary resemblances in language, style and ideological content to the poetical books of the OT. In them reappear the parallel members, emphatic repetitions and numerical gradations of Hebrew poetry and such expressions, literally reproduced, as ' the dew of heaven and the fat of earth ' (Gen 27:28), ' the hind longing for the springs of water ' (Ps 41:2), ' Leviathan the flying serpent and Leviathan the wounded serpent ' (Is 27:1), etc. Their full value for OT study cannot yet be realized. They must first be all published and their correct interpretation assured.

The biblical association of Abraham and his kins- **j** folk with Northern Mesopotamia calls for a brief mention here of the letters of Mari and the contract tablets of Nuzu, both written in Akkadian but not by Babylonians or Assyrians. **Mari,** the modern Tell-Ḥarīrī on the middle Euphrates, was the capital of a very prosperous and powerful Amorite state which dominated the whole upper Euphrates valley before it was subjugated by Hammurabi who subsequently dismantled the capital (1695 B.C.). The royal palace contained 200 apartments and covered 15 acres of ground. Its paintings and sculptures surpassed those of the Sumerians and Babylonians. The city had commercial relations with numerous states from Crete and Cyprus to Babylon and Susa. Of the 20,000 tablets unearthed about 5,000 are letters, the correspondence between the kings of Mari and subordinate officials or contemporary rulers. Those so far published

79j have considerably increased our historical and geographical knowledge. By the synchronisms which the letters provide the chronology of the 2nd and 3rd milleniums B.C. has been revolutionized and established on a solid basis. Personal names in the OT, Terah, Nachor, Sarug, reappear as city names in the Harran neighbourhood. The *dawidum* or leader of West-Semitic roving bands reveals the origin of the **k** name David. The **Nuzu** contract tablets, several thousand in number of which about 1,250 have been published, are private archives of families inhabiting the neighbouring towns of Nuzu (Yarghan Tepe) and Arrapkha (Kirkuk) near the little Zab, an eastern affluent of the middle Tigris. They were written in the 15th cent. B.C. largely by Hurrites, a people who had invaded Palestine in the 18th cent. B.C. The tablets reveal to us Hurrite customs and laws often in remarkable agreement with those of patriarchal times and early Hebrew legislation. We may instance the juridical condition of wives like Sarah and Hagar and of daughters like Leah and Rachel, the obligations of the Levirate, the right of daughters to inherit in default of male issue. These parallels are explained by the wide-spread diffusion of Mesopotamian civilization in the Near East and the Hurrite occupation of Palestine in the patriarchal period. They imply the antiquity and historical value of early Hebrew tradition.

80a **Palestine**—The method of excavation in Palestine has been considerably developed in recent times. The greatest attention is now paid to the collection of all available historical evidence. Digging of vertical shafts is being superseded, when possible, by surface stripping. The various layers, representing the different periods of occupation of the *tell* or mound are removed one by one, after they have been photographed and their contents carefully registered. The distinctive character of the various periods of occupation is thus revealed and their dates at least relatively determined. Layers of ash and other extensive traces of combustion, which indicate the capture and sack of a city, not only mark off different periods of occupation, but sometimes, especially if cultural changes manifest the predominance of occupants racially different in the later period, may be brought **b** into connexion with known historical events. Some objects discovered may be definitely dated and **pottery**, whether native or foreign, is always available for approximate dating. The fragility of pottery and its comparative worthlessness circumscribe narrowly the period at which vessels or pieces of vessels discovered were in use and thus make it an excellent material for this purpose. The various species, moreover, are so constantly changing and so easily distinguished from each other by peculiarities of technique, shape and ornamentation that comparative study of the finds made at different sites, scientifically excavated, has led to the determination of the century or so to which they belong. Already in 1937 could be seen in the new archaeological museum in Jerusalem a magnificent collection of Palestinian pottery from the earliest times to 1200 B.C., arranged in chronological order. In this necessarily brief account of the results of excavations made in Palestine we shall confine ourselves to the Hebrew period, beginning with the transition from the age of bronze to the age of iron *c* 1200 B.C., and to such discoveries as illustrate the contents of the sacred books and increase our knowledge of the historical milieu in which they were written.

c **The ancient cities** of the Israelites as revealed by the excavations were comparatively small, rarely more than ten or twelve acres in extent, were walled and fortified, though less strongly than those of the Canaanites, and had regular streets lined by moderate-sized houses. Many of the southern cities were more strongly fortified by Roboam (2 Par 11:5-11) and traces of his work have been found at Lakish, Azeca and Debir. The

similar work of the Maccabees is attested at several **80c** sites and even in writing at Gezer, where a discontented builder scribbled on a wall his wish ' that fire might descend from heaven and consume the palace of Simon '. The houses unearthed at Tell **d** Beit-Mirsim, the ancient Debir, consisted of a large central apartment, flanked by two or four small rooms, with an upper storey, supported on massive pillars, and reached by an outside staircase. The **palace of Achab,** an enlargement of Amri's, at Samaria, was naturally on a much grander scale. It occupied the north-east angle of a space of about 100 yards square enclosed by casemated walls. Here were found magnificent specimens of ivory work, representing cherubim, Egyptian divinities, plants and animals, some in Egyptian and some in Syrian style. These belong to the 9th cent. B.C. and consequently to the ivory house of Achab mentioned 3 Kg 22:29. In the centre of the enclosure were fifteen or more **e** chambers, apparently used for archives and storage, one of which contained seventy-five ostraca, bearing written records of contributions of wine and oil to the royal stores from various cities, and giving us much information on the language, geography, and economic and administrative organization of the Northern Kingdom. The counterparts of these ostraca in Judah were jar-handles, of which over 200 have been discovered at various sites, belonging to the last century of the monarchy and inscribed ' to the king ', followed by the name of one of the four southern cities : Hebron, Ziph, Socoh and Mamshat. These cities were apparently administrative centres holding a monopoly in the fabrication of jars of fixed measure for fiscal contributions. Among other buildings the elaborately **f** constructed stable with stalls for 120 horses found beside a military encampment at **Megiddo** is of particular interest. The stalls were separated by pillars, provided with rings for the attachment of the horses, and paved with rough stones to prevent them from slipping. This discovery led to the recognition of similar stables, previously excavated but not recognized, at Ta'anak near Megiddo, and at Gezer, Lakish, and Tell el-Ḥesy in the south. The three last mentioned are naturally ascribed to Solomon (3 Kg 10:26-29) to whom also the stables of Megiddo are definitely attributed by the excavators. Some important cities : Jerusalem, Gezer, Megiddo, Ammon **g** have elaborate tunnels, built with the bronze tools of the Canaanites, and designed to secure from an outside spring an adequate water-supply in time of siege. The tunnel at Jerusalem was supplemented by a new one, which brought the waters of Gihon into the city, under the menace of Sennacherib's invasion. This great work of Ezechias (4 Kg 20:20) is commemorated by a Hebrew inscription, recording the construction, and discovered with the tunnel in 1880. Canaanite sanctuaries also, such as the ' high place ' at Gezer and the temples at Beth-Shan, deserve at least a passing mention.

The occupations and interests of the people are indi- **h** cated by the objects discovered : cisterns for water-supply, silos for grain storage, wine-presses and oil-presses, smithies, ovens, dyeing vats, earthenware vessels of all kinds, seals, coins, lamps, scarabs, children's toys, perfume-boxes and combs of bone and ivory, sickles and ploughshares, arms and amulets, pearls, pendants, rings, bracelets, brooches, etc. The owners of three seals, found one at Maspha and two at Lakish, are most probably mentioned in the Bible : Ya'azinyahu servant of the king (Jezonias 4 Kg 25:23), Gedolyahu the major-domo (Godolias Jer 40-41) and Shebne [son of ?] Achab (Sobna, secretary of Ezechias 4 Kg 18:14, 18 ; Is 22:15 ; 36:3, 22). Eliacim servant of Jokhin, whose name appears on three jar-handles, is unknown to us, but his master is the penultimate king of Judah, Jechonias. Among religious objects discovered, numerous images of Astarte and even moulds for making them illustrate various references in the OT to the idolatrous worship of this

80h goddess. A small altar of incense with four horns, found at Tell Beit-Mirsim in Judah, refutes at once the critical theory which admits no pre-exilic altar of incense and confirms the authority of the much mis-judged Chronicler when he tells us that Achaz built altars to burn incense in all the cities of Judah (2 Par 28:25).

i The absence of all trace of writing in Canaan was once a stock objection to the early origin of the Pentateuch. Later on, the use of a cuneiform syllabary by the ancient Hebrew writers was seriously discussed. Now the question is rather which of the three **alphabets** existing before his time did Moses use? An ostracon, unearthed at Bethshemesh in 1930, bears an inscription of the 15th cent. B.C., written in characters resembling those of Rās-Shamra. The inscriptions, discovered in 1904–5 at Serābīṭ el-Khādem in the mines of Sinai and variously dated 1800–1500 B.C., are in an alphabetic linear script. Fragments of texts in similar alphabetic characters have been found more recently in Palestine, one at Gezer, one at Tell el-Ḥesy (Eglon?), one at Shechem and six at Tell ed-Duweir (Lakish). They are mostly assigned to the 13th or 14th cent. B.C., but one is of the Hyksos period (c 1730–1580 B.C.). The discovery of the royal necropolis at Byblos in 1922 revealed in the epitaph of Aḥiram of the 10th cent. B.C. the oldest inscription in the Phoenician alphabet, from which our own is derived. The finished form of the letters shows moreover that this alphabet was invented at a much earlier period.

j Three ancient records still remain to be mentioned, the agricultural calendar of Gezer, the inscription of Mesha of Moab and the Letters of Lakish. The first is a limestone tablet, engraved with cursive Hebrew characters, which may go back to the 11th cent. B.C., and acquainting us with the annual cycle of labours of the tillers of the soil. The Moabite Stone, discovered at Dibon in 1868, records, in a language closely akin to Hebrew, Mesha's successful revolt against Israel c 853 B.C. It supplements the Hebrew narrative and is besides of great linguistic and geographical import-**k** ance. The ostraca with writing on both sides, found at Tell ed-Duweir, the ancient Lakish, in 1935, and published by H. Torczyner (London, 1938) were at that time the most valuable discovery yet made in Palestine. The fragments of pottery when put together revealed eighteen separate written records, of which only six are so well preserved as to admit of interpretation. Nearly all are letters to a certain Yaʿōsh (abbreviated form of Josias), commander of the garrison of Lakish, and can be dated 587 B.C., shortly before the capture of Jerusalem by Nabuchodonosor. At this period only two fortified cities besides Jerusalem, namely Lakish and Azeca, still resisted, both of which are mentioned in the same order in the fourth letter and in Jer 34:7. The prophet, mentioned without name in the third letter, is very probably Jeremias. Most of the proper names occur also in the biblical records of the same period and are theophoric, having the divine name, Yahweh, fully written as the second element. This was probably a result of the religious reform of Josias. The most important conclusion to be deduced from these simple letters springs from their remarkable resemblance in language and style to our classical Hebrew texts. This suggests that these texts were carefully preserved and also supports their traditional pre-exilic date.

l **Palestinian Hebrew MSS**—A remarkable discovery of several ancient Hebrew MSS, as welcome as it was unexpected, was made in Palestine in 1947, not by excavators, but by Bedawin. The MSS are long rolls of skin not of parchment and were found in a cave near the northern end of the Dead Sea, wrapped in linen **m** and enclosed in jars sealed with pitch. Seven documents were first discovered, viz. (1) a complete text of Isaias, (2) an incomplete text of Isaias chh 42–66, (3) a commentary on Habacuc ch 1–2, (4) laws and institutions of a body of Jewish sectaries, (5) a collec-

tion of hymns of praise, (6) an account of the conflict **80m** between the sons of Light and the sons of Darkness, (7) an apocryphal work, probably the book of Lamech, of which only a few pages have been deciphered. All these works are in Hebrew except the last which is in Aramaic. An archaeological exploration of the cave in 1949 resulted in the further discovery of fragments of at least forty jars, similar to those containing the documents previously discovered, and various fragmentary texts some of which could be identified as parts of Genesis, Leviticus, Deuteronomy, Judges and Daniel. Of these the Leviticus texts were written in the early Phoenician script. All are agreed that the cave contained a considerable *cache* of sacred books made by Jewish sectaries and subsequently discovered and rifled. The discovery of such a *cache* in the neighbourhood of Jericho is recorded by Origen in the 3rd cent. A.D. and by Timotheus II, Syrian patriarch of Seleucia, in the 8th cent. A.D. As the jars were adjudged to the Hellenistic period the *cache* was first dated *c* 100 B.C. It is difficult to maintain this date as a *terminus ante quem* for all the documents discovered. Kahle suggests the 3rd cent. A.D. as the date not of the writings but of the *cache*. He notes that the later text of part of Isaias is closer to the MT than the earlier text of the whole book, while the latter exhibits later interlinear corrections which seem to be based on the MT. Both texts, therefore, one in its composition the other in its corrections, imply the existence and authority of the MT, usually dated *c* A.D. 100. The complete text of Isaias and the collection of laws and institutions are notably earlier than the five other documents. The lack of similar dated texts makes it practically impossible to date them palaeographically. It is noteworthy, however, that the use of special final forms of five Hebrew characters, fully developed in the MT and the Nash Papyrus, is still in an elementary stage in the complete Isaias text. Only *n* has the final form regularly, *k* and *m* occasionally, *p* and *ṣ* never. We can thus conclude that this text is earlier than the MT and the Nash Papyrus and must be dated in or before the 1st cent. A.D. When Hebrew as a spoken language was supplanted by Aramaic the vocalization of its consonantal script caused particular difficulty. This explains the chief peculiarity of the Isaias MS, which frequently inserts the semi-vocalic letters, a, h, w and y, to indicate vowel sounds and thus gives us valuable information on the pronunciation of Hebrew at this period. Variations from the MT in other respects are comparatively rare and unimportant. There are some useful corrections of the MT which, however, represents on the whole a better manuscript tradition.

NT Discoveries—To our previous remarks on the **81a** Egyptian papyri must be added here some instances of the contribution made to the text and interpretation of the NT by inscriptions and excavations. A fragment of Tatian's Diatessaron, consisting of 14 lines of Greek text written on one side of a parchment leaf was unearthed in 1933 by the excavators of Dura-Europos in north-eastern Syria and published by C. H. Kraeling (London, 1935). It contains the conclusion of the narrative of the passion, taken from all four Gospels, and is dated by the destruction of the city in 255 and the discovery of a neighbouring private house converted into a Christian oratory in 223 to the first quarter of the 3rd century or less than half a century after the composition of the Diatessaron. It is thus apparently our most ancient NT text after the fragment of St John's Gospel mentioned, § 77b. Ancient and **b** modern opponents of the perpetual virginity of the Mother of Christ have argued that the designation of Christ as 'her firstborn son' (Lk 2:7) implies that she had subsequently other children. St Jerome's reply, that 'firstborn' in this context, according to Jewish usage, only excludes an elder son and in no way implies future births, has been remarkably confirmed by a Greek funeral inscription, discovered at Tell el-Yehudieh in Egypt in 1922, which commemorates a

81b Jewish mother, Arsinoe, who died in the year 5 B.C. 'in the pangs of giving birth to her firstborn son'

c (*cf.* J. B. Frey Bi II [1930] 373–90). A dated letter of the Emperor Claudius, graven on a wall of the temple of Apollo at Delphi and published in 1905, mentions, as proconsul of Achaia, Gallio before whom Paul was arraigned by the Jews. From this we can date, at least very approximately, a central event in the life of St Paul and thus establish Pauline chronology on a solid basis.

d Other inscriptions found at Delphi record the freedom of slaves redeemed by the god Apollo. Slaves became free by paying their masters a fixed sum which they laboriously accumulated. But unscrupulous masters after receiving the ransom could retain the slave in bondage. Hence the practice of paying the money into the treasury of Apollo who purchased the slave from his master and secured him by his protection from further molestation. St Paul illustrates his teaching on the Redemption by frequent references to this form of contract, and a knowledge of the technical terms used is necessary for the full understanding of the texts. Christ purchased or redeemed us, the Gentiles from the slavery of sin, the Jews from the bondage of the Law. The completeness of this redemption is expressed by the prepositional prefix in ἀπελευθέρωσις and ἀπολύτρωσις. The Christian, whatever his condition in life, is no longer a slave, but the freed-man (ἀπελεύθερος) of the Lord. He differs however from the freed-man of Apollo in several respects which are emphasized by the Apostle. He cannot now 'do what he likes'—the privilege of the slave freed by Apollo according to the words of the contract—but must fulfil in all things the will of Christ to whom he entirely belongs. Christ has endowed him with a freedom which is not licence but holiness, and the first fruit of his redemption is eternal life. He has contributed nothing to the price of his freedom which has been freely and fully paid by Christ himself. The rendering of δοῦλος by 'servant' instead of 'slave' in some modern English versions here obscures the imagery of St Paul.

e **The meticulous accuracy of St Luke** as a historian is frequently attested by the new discoveries. According to him St Paul appeared before the supreme authorities in four Greek cities, the Strategoi at Philippi, the Politarchs at Thessalonica, the Areopagites at Athens, the Proconsul at Corinth. The local name is different in each case but is now known from inscriptions to be accurate in all. His location of Iconium in Phrygia and not in Lycaonia and his dating of the first Syrian government of Quirinius in the days of King Herod, though regarded half a century ago as manifest errors, have been shown to be correct by the Phrygian inscriptions of Iconium and the mentions of Quirinius in the Caristanii records of Pisidian Antioch and its neighbourhood.

f His account of St Paul's mission at Ephesus has been copiously illustrated and confirmed by the extensive excavations of the site made by the British Museum and the Austrian Archaeological Institute which culminated in the discovery of the empty tomb of the Apostle St John beneath the high altar of the later Byzantine Church. The Ephesian Artemis is now made known to us, not merely nor principally as the virgin huntress of the Greeks, but as the Asiatic goddess of fecundity, presiding over all manifestations of plant, animal and human life and fanatically worshipped as the mainstay of the material prosperity of the city and its inhabitants. Her temple, one of the seven wonders of the ancient world, the market-place where the

disturbance caused by the silversmiths occurred and **81f** the neighbouring theatre where the people assembled are all revealed to us. The title νεωκόρος or 'sacristan' (of Artemis) accorded to the city, the use of θεός and θεά to designate the goddess, the epithet of μεγάλη applied to her are paralleled in inscriptions there and elsewhere discovered. From them, too, we learn that the Asiarchs were members of a religious body elected, one each year, by each of the principal cities of the province, but retaining their honorific title after their period of office, that the town-clerk, his humble title notwithstanding, enjoyed all the authority attributed to him by St Luke, that Ephesus was conspicuous above other cities for magical and divinatory practices.

Excavations have considerably increased our know- **g** ledge of the **topography of Jerusalem** in NT times. The exact position of the enclosure of the second temple, constructed by Herod and frequented by our Lord, has been revealed to us. The sacred rock in the Mosque attributed to Omar, but built by Abd-el-Melek, locates the temple itself, at least approximately, since it is still disputed whether the rock occupies the site of the Altar of Holocausts or the Holy of Holies. One of the inscriptions, affixed to the gates of the Inner Temple and forbidding non-Jews under pain of death to penetrate beyond the Court of the Gentiles, has been unearthed, and illustrates the gravity of the false accusation brought by the Jews against St Paul (Ac 21:28 f.). The second wall of the city, which **h** determined its boundaries during our Lord's lifetime, has been traced and the traditional site of Calvary has been shown to be outside it. The site was providentially preserved by the erection thereon of temples of Jupiter, Juno and Venus when Jerusalem was made a Roman colony by Hadrian in A.D. 135. The stone which blocked the door of our Lord's sepulchre has been revealed to us by many parallels as having had the form of a large mill-stone fitted into a groove beside the opening and difficult to dislodge when it had been rolled into position. The extensive stone pavement or Lithostrotos in the Pretorium of Pilate, where Christ was condemned to death, has been discovered in the course of recent excavations on the site of the Herodian fortress of Antonia. Recent diggings have also more or less definitely established the location of other sites, such as Gethsemane, the house of Caiphas, and the Synagogue of the Libertini. Since early local tradition plays a considerable part in the identification of sacred sites, mention may here be made of the remarkable mosaic map of Palestine discovered in a church in the Moabite city of Madaba. Its graphic representation of the churches and monasteries of Jerusalem is a valuable record of Palestinian Christian tradition on this matter in and before the beginning of the 6th century.

Conclusion—Archaeological discoveries not only solve **i** old problems, but sometimes raise new ones. Caution is necessary in accepting conclusions derived from them and patience in awaiting new light on the problems they raise. But their cumulative effect is aptly indicated by the words of Pope Pius XII in his recent Encyclical : 'Thus has it come about that confidence in the authority and historical value of the Bible, somewhat shaken in the case of some by so many attacks, today among Catholics is completely restored ; moreover there are not wanting even non-Catholic writers, who by serious and calm inquiry have been led to abandon modern opinion and to return, at least in some points, to the more ancient ideas'.

MEASURES, WEIGHTS, MONEY AND TIME

By E. POWER, S.J.

82a Bibliography—A. Barrois, 'La Métrologie dans la Bible', RB 40 (1931) 185–213; 41 (1932) 50–76; *A. R. S. Kennedy, 'Some Problems of Herod's Temple (the Cubit)', ET 20 (1908–9) 14–17; *Id.*, Inscribed Hebrew Weights from Palestine, *ib.* 24 (1912–3) 488–91; 538–42; *O. Viedebant, *Antike Gewichtswesen und Muenzfuesse*, Berlin, 1924; *F. W. Madden, *Coins of the Jews*, London, 1903[2]; *J. G. Milne, *Greek Coinage*, Oxford, 1931; F. Prat, 'Les cours des monnaies en Palestine au temps de Jésus-Christ', RSR 15 (1925) 441–8; *id.* *Jésus-Christ* II, Paris, 1946, 487–500; U. Holzmeister, *Chronologia Vitae Christi*, Rome, 1933; *K. Schoch, *Planeten-Tafeln fuer jedermann*, Berlin, 1927; J. B. Schaumberger, 'Tabella Neomeniarum Vitae publicae Domini et Procurationis Pilati', VD 13 (1933) 104–8. Biblical Dictionaries and Manuals of Biblical Archaeology may also be consulted.

b Measures of Length—The Hebrew measures of length like all similar ancient measures are derived from the human body. They are the finger-breadth, the palm or hand-breadth, the span or open-hand breadth, from the tip of the thumb to the tip of the little finger, and the cubit or forearm, from the elbow to the tip of the middle finger. The cubit is that of a (full-grown) man, Deut 3:11. There was also a conventional measure of six cubits called a reed. All the names are Semitic.

The value of the chief unit of measure, the cubit, may have varied at different periods and can only be determined approximately. The only direct indication (c 700 B.C.) is the length of the Siloe canal, 1,749 ft. by modern measure and 1,200 cubits according to the inscription. This gives a cubit of 17·5 inches only in the very doubtful hypothesis that the ancient method of measuring agrees with the modern and that 1,200 is an exact rather than a round number. As the Hebrews are unlikely to have systematized their measures before the early monarchical period and were then closely associated with Egypt it is very probable that they adopted the Egyptian cubit. This was twofold: the common cubit of 24 finger-breadths = 17·7 inches and the royal cubit of 28 finger-breadths = 20·66 inches. The distinction made by Ezechiel, 40:5; 43:13, between the ordinary cubit of 6 palms = 24 finger-breadths and the temple cubit of 7 palms = 28 finger-breadths supports this view. The Chronicler also, 2 Par 3:3, suggests the royal Egyptian cubit of 7 palms when he mentions the cubit of ancient measure used in the building of Solomon's temple.

c In NT times it is very probable that the Greek cubit of almost exactly 18 inches was adopted. The only certain indication of the use of this cubit in Palestine belongs to the 4th cent. A.D. Kennedy's evaluation of the NT cubit at 17·6 inches, deduced from a comparative study of the dimensions of various parts of Herod's temple, seems less probable. The determination of the Sabbath journey of 2,000 cubits as 5 stadia according to Josephus and Epiphanius is of no value owing to the round numbers and the difficulty of defining the exact length of the stadium. The Alexandrian stadium was 202 yds., that of Delphi 194, that of Olympus 210. Besides the stadium (DV furlong) another Greek measure, the fathom or 'stretch' = 6 ft., and the Roman mile of 1,000 **82c** double-paces = 1,618 yds are mentioned in the NT.

TABLE OF LENGTH MEASURES

Names	Cubit		Span		Palm		Finger
Ratio	1	=	2	=	6	=	24
OT Value	17·7 in.		8·85		2·95		·74
NT Value	18 in.		9		3		·75

Measures of Capacity—The Hebrew measures of **d** capacity are naturally more disparate than the anatomical measures of length. They were originally utensils which became standards of measure. Some appear first in the monarchical period. Their names attest their different origin. Ephah and hin are Egyptian. Homer, lethekh and log appear in the Rās-Shamra tablets. Bath is Aramaean. Cor, seah and perhaps kab are Babylonian. The homer, lit. ass-load, was also used in Assyria. The 'omer (DV gomor) of Ex 16 is elsewhere replaced by the 'issaron or tenth of the ephah. Bath, hin, log and sometimes cor are liquid measures. Homer, ephah, seath and kab are dry measures.

The relative values of these measures are known to us partly from Scripture texts, partly from the Babylonian system and partly from Hebrew tradition. From Ezechiel we learn that homer = cor and ephah = bath and that the latter measure was a tenth of the former and from Ex 16:36 and Num 15:4 that the 'omer = 'issaron was a tenth of the ephah. St Jerome renders lethekh as half a cor, Os 3:2. The sutu = seah was a thirtieth of the gur = cor in the Babylonian system. Similarly Hebrew tradition makes the ephah = 3 seah. The kab corresponds to the Babylonian ka, a sixth of the sutu = seah. The relative values of the hin and the log are deduced from various texts of Josephus, St Jerome and the Talmud.

Our only information on the absolute value of these measures is derived from Josephus and later writers who equate the log with the Roman sextarius, the Hellenistic Xestes. This fixes the log at ·96 of a pint. It is estimated at a pint in the table to avoid complicated figures. These values possibly but not certainly go back to Ezechiel and the monarchical period. The Persian measure artabe, Dan 14:2, is estimated by Herodotus at a bushel.

In the NT period Hellenistic measures were in general **e** use. Hebrew measures: seah, bath, cor, appear only in Lucan parables, Lk 13:21; 16:6 f. The xestes, Mk 7:4, and the modios, Mt 5:15, are vessels rather than measures. But the metretes = 9 gal., Jn 2:6, and the choinix = 3 pecks, Apoc 4:6, are measures.

TABLE OF DRY MEASURE

Names	Homer		Lethekh		Ephah		Seah		'Omer		Kab
Ratio	1	=	2	=	10	=	30	=	100	=	180
Value	11¼ bush.		5⅝ bush.		4½ peck		1½ peck		⁹⁄₂₀ peck		¼ peck

TABLE OF LIQUID MEASURE

Names	Cor		Bath		Hin		Log
Ratio	1	=	10	=	60	=	720
Value	90 gal		9 gal		1½ gal		1 pint

82f **Weights**—The Hebrew system of weights is derived from the Babylonian. The talent (kikkar lit. round) contained 60 mines (maneh lit. part) and the mine or *mina* (Gk. *mna*) 60 sicles (shekel lit. weight) in Mesopotamia, but only 50 in Phoenicia.

The shekel contained 24 Babylonian giru, but 20 Hebrew gerah. According to Ex 38:25–27 (not Mosaic, *cf.* com.) the capitation tax of a half-shekel levied on 603,550 Israelites amounted to 100 talents and 1,775 shekels. A talent of 3,000 shekels based on the Phoenician mine of 50 shekels is implied. The mention of 100 shekels, Deut 22:19, and 50 shekels, Deut 22:29, suggests the same conclusion especially as the 50 shekels correspond to a mine in the code of Hammurabi. On the other hand, a half mine in the same code corresponds to 30 shekels in the earlier legislation of Ex 21:32 and thus suggests an earlier mine of 60 shekels. Ez 45:12, according to the more correct MT, fixes the mine at 20 + 25 + 15 = 60 shekels but implies at the same time an actual mine of 50 shekels by mentioning its parts. We may conclude therefore that the mine of the monarchical period was Phoenician and the earlier mine probably Babylonian.

g Theoretical evaluations of the shekel unit of weight, based on Babylonian and Phoenician values, have received no support from the stamped weights, about 50 in number, unearthed by recent excavators in Palestine. The more usual stamp is ☋, now generally interpreted shekel. All the weights so stamped, with one negligible exception, vary between 11 and 12 grammes and average approximately 11·5 grammes = ·4 oz. A gramme (gm.) is very nearly 15½ grains (gr.). Four weights marked *pym*, the dual of *peh* and thus meaning two-thirds, belong to the same standard. So also does a weight of 11·14 gms. inscribed in archaic letters *l^emelek* ' to the king '. Of the four weights marked *beqa'* or half-shekel two conform to the common standard but one is negligibly (12·2 gms.) and one appreciably (13·3) heavier. Finally nine weights marked *neṣef* and averaging 10 gms. (·35 oz.) indicate a lighter standard. It is still uncertain whether *neṣef* weights are shekels or half-shekels (according to the Arabic sense of *nṣf*), nor is it possible to establish a distinction in date between the periods at which the two standards were in use. The Persian mine, Esd 2:69, is practically equivalent to the common Hebrew mine. It contained 100 *sigloi* of 5·61 gms or 50 Hebrew shekels of 11·22 gms. The Jews of Elephantine had a shekel of similar weight at the same period since they evaluated the *kereš* or gold daric at 10 silver shekels. The Hebrew shekel cannot, however, be derived from the Persian. Several of the inscribed Hebrew weights belong palaeographically to the monarchical period.

h In the Hellenistic period the Greek system of weights was in general use. There were different standards of value of which the more common, Attic-Euboic and Aeginetan, are given in our table. An official market weight of 319 gms bearing a Greek inscription was discovered at Gezer. It is marked half and is dated probably in the year 84 of the Seleucid era, 229–228 B.C. It is apparently half of the Aeginetan mine of 630 gms. Another official market weight of 145 gms with a Greek inscription was found at Sandahannah. Though neither marked nor dated it seems to be a third of the Attic mina of 435 gms. The Seleucid monarchs adopted the Attic standard. Their coins show a debasement of the Attic drachm unit (4·35 gms) to 4·20 under Antiochus IV Epiphanes and 4 under Tryphon thirty years later. The weights mentioned in 1–2 Mac should be estimated at the Seleucid standard.

The Roman pound (5,050 grs) is twice mentioned in the NT, Jn 12:3 ; 19:39. The shekel was reckoned at four Phoenician drachms of 55 grs. Josephus equates the Hebrew mine with 2½ Roman pounds. He apparently reckons the mine at 50 shekels and the shekel at 4 Seleucid Attic drachms and thus makes the Hebrew mine = 2 Greek mines. However this may be, the talents, mines and drachms of the NT are Greek or Greco-Roman. The pre-monarchical weights and the original shekel of the sanctuary cannot be determined. 82h

TABLE OF HEBREW WEIGHTS i

Names	*Talent*		*Mine*		*Shekel*		*Gerah*
Ratio	1	=	60	=	3000	=	60,000
Values	75 lb		20 oz		·4 oz		9·6 grs

TABLE OF GREEK WEIGHTS

Names	*Talent*		*Mine*		*Drachm*		*Obol*
Ratio	1	=	60	=	6000	=	36,000
Att. Values	52 lb		13·85 oz		66·5 grs		11·09 grs
Aeg. Values	76 lb		20·25 oz		97 grs		16·2 grs

Money—The shekels, half-shekels, quarter-shekels of the OT were not coins but weights, usually of silver. The first coins used in Palestine were the gold and silver darics. The silver daric of 5·6 gms (87 grs) was ⅔ of the weight and $\frac{1}{20}$ of the value of the gold daric of 8·4 gms (130 grs). In the Hellenistic period Phoenician and Greek coins circulated in Palestine. Only copper coins were struck by Simon Maccabee and his successors. The silver shekels equivalent in weight to the Phoenician stater or tetradrachm and formerly attributed to the Maccabees are now generally ascribed to the Jewish rebels A.D. 66–70. Roman coins appear in the NT period. The coin most frequently mentioned is the denarius. Roman coinage was based on the aureus, a gold coin weighing $\frac{1}{42}$ of a Roman lb (120 grs). The silver denarius was half the weight and $\frac{1}{25}$ the value of the aureus. The as, reckoned as $\frac{1}{16}$ of the denarius, and its fractions were copper coins. The Asiatic and Phoenician coins still circulated. Beside the denarius of 60 grs were the Phoenician drachm of nearly 55 grs and the Asiatic drachm now reduced to 50 grs. Fiscal dues were paid in Roman weight, temple dues in Phoenician. In ordinary usage, however, denarius and drachm were regarded as equivalents, as were also shekel, stater, tetradrachm and argenteus. 83a

In turning ancient money into modern account must be taken of two important differences. Gold was rated at 12½ times the value of silver not 15½ as at present. Gold, moreover, was coined without alloy and the alloy in silver coins (·02) was practically negligible. It must be also noted that the purchase power of money was several times greater in biblical than in modern times. The values of the NT coins are determined according to the Roman gold standard of the period and the 1939 values of English money. b

SILVER COINS

Name	*Text*	*Weight*	*Value*
Roman denarius	passim	60 grs	10¼d
Phoenician drachm	Lk 15:8 ?	55 grs	9¼d
Asiatic drachm	Lk 15:8 ?	50 grs	8½d
Tyrian didrachm	Mt 17:24	110 grs	1s 6½d
Stater = tetradrachm	Mt 17:27	220 grs	3s 1d
Roman argenteus	Mt 26:15	240 grs	3s 5d

BRONZE COINS

Double as (dipondius)	Lk 12:6	1¼d
As (Gk. Assarion)	Mt 10:29	⅝d
Quadrans (fourth)	Mt 5:26	*c* ⅙d
Minutum (Gk lepton)	Mc 12:42	*c* $\frac{1}{12}$d

The mines and talents of the Gospels are weights of silver. Estimated at the drachm-denarius unit a mine = £4 5s 5d and a talent = £256 5s. The similar denominations of 1–2 Mac had practically the same value. The gold daric was worth about £1 2s 6d.

Time. 1. The Day—Day in Hebrew means either day and night or day as opposed to night. In the former sense it began originally at sunset but later as soon as three stars were visible. In the latter sense c

83c it was originally divided into three equal parts : morning, noontide and evening, and night similarly into three watches (*cf.* Jg 7:19 the middle watch). The Roman quadripartite division was however more commonly used in NT times (*cf.* Mt 14:25 ; Mk 6:48 the fourth watch). The division of the day into twelve hours was known, Jn 11:9, but St John is the only NT writer who uses it regularly (*cf.* Jn 1:39 ; 4:6 ; 4:52). The Synoptics use instead the four three-hour periods which they call morning, third hour, sixth hour, ninth hour. When therefore Mark puts the crucifixion at the third hour (9–12 a.m., 15:25), he agrees with John's 'about the sixth hour', (11–12 a.m., 19:14). The hour and three-hour periods naturally varied in length according to the time of year. Hour as a time measure was unknown to the Hebrews.

d 2. The Week—The continuous week of seven days, so intimately connected with the observance of the Sabbath, was long peculiar to the Hebrews. It existed before the Sinaitic legislation, Ex 16:22 ff., and has no parallel in Babylonian or Egyptian institutions. The days of the week except the Sabbath were indicated only by numbers. In the Hellenistic period the sixth day was called the eve of the Sabbath, Jud 8:6, and later the Parasceve or Preparation, Mk 15:42. The Greek pl. *sabbata* means week, Mk 16:2 ; Lk 24:1.

e 3. The Month—The Hebrew months were lunar months of 29 or 30 days since the period of the moon's revolution is roughly 29½ days. According to the Mishna (2nd cent. A.D.) the length of each month was determined not by calculation but by actual observation. If the New Moon was seen by three credible witnesses in the night following the twenty-ninth day of a month, that month had only twenty-nine days and the new month was announced by fire-signals all over Palestine. Otherwise the month had thirty days and the next month began automatically at the end of the thirtieth day. Party spirit and difference of opinion about the credibility of witnesses might thus produce two different computations of the days of a month. This is a common explanation of the discrepancy between John and the Synoptics on the date of Christ's last Pasch. The months are indicated by ancient Canaanite names, of which only four are mentioned, by numbers beginning with Nisan and by Babylonian names, of which seven appear in the sacred text. As the Macedonian names are used by Josephus and one is mentioned in 2 Mach 11:30, 33, 38, we include them in our table.

Babylonian	Canaanite	Macedonian	English Equivalent
Nisan	Abib	Xanthicos	March–April
Iyyar	Ziv	Artemisios	April–May
Sivan		Daisios	May–June
Tammuz		Panemos	June–July
Ab		Loios	July–Aug.
Elul		Gorpiaios	Aug.–Sept.
Tishri	Ethanim	Hyperberetaios	Sept.–Oct.
Marcheshvan	Bul	Dios	Oct.–Nov.
Kislev		Appellaios	Nov.–Dec.
Tebeth		Audynaios	Dec.–Jan.
Shebat		Perittos	Jan.–Feb.
Adar		Dystros	Feb.–March

4. The Year—The Hebrew year was not lunar but **g** lunisolar. This was necessitated by the harvest offerings at the annual feasts since harvest time is regulated by the sun. Another month, therefore, Adar II (Ve-Adar), was intercalated before Nisan if further time was needed for the ripening of the barley first-fruits to be offered during the feast of Pasch. It appears certain from the consistent evidence of the Mishna and Jewish tradition that the intercalation of Adar II was determined empirically and not according to a pre-arranged system by the Jewish authorities in NT times. Such systems, used earlier by the Greeks, were not adopted by the Jews before the 4th cent. A.D. The Elephantine papyri attest also an empirical Jewish calendar in the 5th cent. B.C. The date of the barley harvest in the warmest parts of Palestine warrants the conclusion that the Pasch was celebrated invariably in April. The various times of earliest visibility of the whole series of New Moons in ancient Palestine can be astronomically determined. In this reconstruction of the Hebrew calendar a possible error of a day must be reckoned with, as the New Moon may have been hidden by clouds. Such an error would not, however, affect subsequent observations.

The civil year began in the month of Tishri, Ex 23:16; **h** 34:22, the religious year in Nisan, Ex 12:2, 18, etc.). The redactor of Jer (*cf.* 29:1 and 46:2) assigns the battle of Carchemish and the accession of Nabucho-donosor to the fourth year of Joachim. As the battle took place before the accession but after Nisan 605, the Hebrew year of the redactor began not in Nisan but in Tishri. The occasional adoption of the Babylonian system of dating regnal years, which appears side by side with the Hebrew system, does not therefore prove that the Hebrew civil year began in Nisan.

Events are usually dated by the regnal years of the kings in the monarchical period, sometimes also by outstanding incidents. The Seleucid era which began in October 312 is used in 1–2 Mac. In 1 Mac, however, dates are reckoned from Spring 311. The only NT monarchical date is the fifteenth year of Tiberius.

OUR LADY IN THE SCRIPTURES

By E. C. MESSENGER, Ph.D.

84a **Bibliography**—In addition to the usual dogmatic treatises on Our Lady, see the following : A. d'Alès, ' Marie, Mère de Dieu, I, Marie dans l'Ecriture Sainte ', DAFC 3, 118–55 ; A. J. Maas, ' Virgin Mary ', CE 15, 464–70 ; J. P. Arendzen, ' Our Lady in the Old Testament ', in *Our Blessed Lady*, CSSL, 1933 ; *id.* ' The Virgin Mother ', in *The Gospels, Fact, Myth or Legend ?* pp 128–40 ; *id.* 'A Virgin shall conceive ', in *Prophets, Priests and Publicans*, pp 97–111 ; C. Lattey, S.J., ' Our Lady's Gospel ', in *Our Blessed Lady*, CSSL, 1933 ; R. A. Knox, ' Our Lady in the New Testament ', *ibid.*; Pohle-Preuss, *Mariology*; G. Smith, *Mary's Part in Our Redemption*; E. R. Hull, S.J., *First Book on Our Lady* ; E. F. Sutcliffe, S.J., ' Protoevangelium ', in CR, Aug. 1931 ; *cf.* CR, Jan. 1932 ; *id.* ' Our Lady and the Divinity of Christ ', Mn 180 (1944) 347–50 ; *id.* ' Scripture, Tradition and Mariology ', IER, Ser. 5, vol. 70 (1947) 807–14 ; F. M. Willam, *Mary the Mother of Jesus*, E. tr. by F. Eckhoff, St Louis and London, 1947[7]; P. F. Ceuppens, O.P., *De Mariologia Biblica*, Turin, 1949 ; Scheeben, *Mariology*, 2 vols (Engl. Trans. 1947–8, U.S.A.) ; J. Spencer Northcote, *Mary in the Gospels*, London, 1906 ; R. Garrigou-Lagrange, O.P., *The Mother of the Saviour* (Engl. Trans.), Dublin, 1948.

b **I. Introduction**—It is a defined point of Catholic Faith that our doctrines we depend not only upon the written Word of Divine Scripture, but also on Divine Tradition, which interprets, and in some cases, supplements it. In no subject is it more important to bear this in mind than in that of our Blessed Lady. For some of our knowledge concerning our Lady we are indebted to Tradition, and to that alone. By ' Tradition ' we here mean Dogmatic Tradition, *i.e.* the teaching and handing down of doctrines not expressly formulated in Scripture. This use of the term must be carefully distinguished from purely human tradition not guaranteed by divine authority, or by the Church, and from ' Tradition ' in the sense of legend or folklore. In some important matters, Scripture has various things to say about our Lady. But even here Tradition plays an important part in determining the meaning of the inspired text, and in clarifying it.

c In this connexion we must remember that much of the teaching contained in Scripture is implicit rather than explicit. The full meaning and implication of a text may not be obvious at a first reading. And further we must remember that a few pregnant words may imply a whole theology. We shall mention some instances of this in the course of our essay. But these principles enable us to answer the difficulty sometimes raised from the comparative silence of Scripture on our Lady. It is at most a *comparative* silence. And what Scripture does say about her is very important. In this connexion we must remember that the central doctrine of our Mariology is that Mary is the *Theotokos*, the Mother of God. It was as God's Mother that she was fore-ordained from the beginning of the world, immaculately conceived in the fullness of time, filled with all graces, and finally assumed bodily into heaven. It was as God's Mother that she was the Second Eve, co-operating in the work of our Redemption. Hence, if Scripture teaches this fundamental fact of the Motherhood of Mary, it gives us the most important fact.

Mary's prerogatives flow from and depend upon her **84c** divine Motherhood. Some of these prerogatives are hinted at in Scripture, but for the clear enunciation of others we have to depend upon Tradition illuminating and supplementing Scripture.

II. Mary in the Old Testament—In the preliminary **d** or expository part of the Bull *Ineffabilis Deus*, before the actual definition of the doctrine of the Immaculate Conception of our Lady, Pope Pius IX authoritatively stated in 1854 that God ' foresaw from all eternity the unhappy ruin of the whole human race of man through the sin of Adam ', and ' determined, by a mystery hidden from all ages, to accomplish the first work of his goodness in a secret dispensation, by the Incarnation of the Word '. Accordingly, God ' chose and ordained from the beginning and before all ages, a Mother for his only-begotten Son, that by taking flesh from her, he might be born in the blessed fulness of time '.

From the truth that God chose and ordained ' from **e** the beginning and before all ages ' a Mother for his Son, it does not follow that this divine intention was necessarily made plain to mankind from the first, in language admitting of no other interpretation. There was a very real development of doctrine in the Old Testament, and indeed a progressive series of *additions* to the Faith, as new doctrines were revealed by God to the patriarchs and prophets.

This being the case, we could hardly have been sur- **f** prised if there had been no reference at all in the books of the Old Testament to our Blessed Lady. Actually, however, there are some very significant references to her, and in particular we find the Blessed Virgin at least hinted at, and typically referred to, in the text rightly called the **Protoevangelium** or Original Gospel. This text is found in Gen 3:15. For details of its interpretation the reader is referred to the Commentary. We limit ourselves here to remarking that there is to be enmity between the Woman and the Serpent, as well as between the Seed of each. The victory is to be obtained by the Woman's Seed. In view of later prophecies such as those concerning Abraham's Seed, in which all the nations of the earth are to be blessed, it can hardly be doubted that, even though ' seed ' may have a collective sense, the Messias is included, *i.e.* Jesus Christ, in whom others are able to conquer the devil. Who, then, is the Woman ? Is it Eve herself, or Mary the Mother of Jesus ? Catholic scholars are not agreed as to the primary reference here. But even if the term refers in the first case to Eve, it can do so only because of her daughter Mary, the true and immediate Mother of the Seed which crushes the Serpent's head. Eve conquers through Mary, who is at once part of the (collective) Seed of the Woman, and at the same time the Mother of the Seed (in the singular).

Such is the meaning of this important text, when **g** viewed in the light of other texts of Scripture and Catholic Tradition. It does not, however, follow that its full meaning was understood from the first. We may hold, with Canon Arendzen, in CSSL (1933), pp 3 f., that the Woman ' is not *directly and exclusively* Mary the Mother of Christ ', and that when our first parents heard the promise of redemption, ' they only saw the direct reference to the guilty woman who stood

84g close by ', just as ' in her seed they may have seen the mass of the children descending from her . . . It is certain that in the Old Testament the Redeemer is gradually revealed as one individual Person, and thus as the seed of one individual Woman '. We now know that this individual Woman is Mary.

h We must carefully note that this first Scripture reference to the Blessed Virgin is one which mentions her enmity against the powers of evil, represented by the serpent, and her victory over those powers in and through her Seed. Rightly, then, does the Catholic Church see in this text a ' designation ' of the Blessed Virgin, and a foundation for the doctrine of her complete victory over sin, through her Son, in her Immaculate Conception, which preserved her from original sin, through the merits of Jesus Christ, applied beforehand to her soul. We say Mary is ' designated ' here because Pope Pius IX asserts that in this text, as interpreted by ' the Fathers and ecclesiastical writers ', the Redeemer is ' clare aperteque *demonstratum* ', and his Mother is ' designatam '. The ' designatio ' is obviously not so clear as the ' demonstratio '. But it is there.

After this first prophecy, Scripture is for a long time silent. The Messianic prophecies themselves were gradually added to and became clearer. Many of these were concerned less with the Messias himself than with the Kingdom which he was to inaugurate. We could hardly expect to find references to Mary in these prophecies concerning the Kingdom. But there are two significant references to her in prophets who also deal with the personal and individual Messias.

i The first we must mention is the famous prophecy in Is 7, concerning **the Virgin who is to conceive** and bear a son, who is to have the name ' Emmanuel ', meaning ' God with us '. Again we must leave to the Commentary a discussion of the many difficulties which this text involves. Suffice it to say that, even if a reference to some contemporary child need not be excluded, the final and definitive reference must be to the Messias. If this be so, Mary must here be indicated. It is true that the Hebrew word *'almāh* is not that technically used for a ' Virgin ', but denotes simply a ' Maiden '. Nevertheless this Hebrew word combines in itself the two ideas of youth and virginity and always means an unmarried young woman ; in fact, the LXX translates it by the Greek word ' parthenos ', which certainly means ' virgin '. Thus, the text ultimately implies the Virginal Conception, and is rightly quoted in Mt 1:23 with this meaning. Even so, we must make a reservation similar to that made in the case of the Protoevangelium. It by no means follows that the precise meaning of the prophecy of Isaias was fully understood at the time. Indeed, it seems clear that even our Lady herself, in spite of her undoubted knowledge of the Scriptures and her internal illumination by the Holy Ghost, did not realize the full implication of this text or the fact that Virginity was compatible with Motherhood. For when informed that her Son would be the Messias, and would occupy the throne of David, she at once interposed : ' How shall this be, for I know not man ? ' The answer of the angel reassured her, and doubtless opened the way to a fuller understanding of the text of Isaias.

85a The second reference among the prophets to our Lady is found in the work of Micheas, a prophet contemporary with Isaias. In 5:2–3 he tells us that out of Bethlehem is to come—

' He that is to be the Ruler of Israel,
   Whose origin is of old, and goes back to the days of yore.
   This is why God delivers them up,
   Till the day when She who will bear, shall bear ...'
Such is the translation given by Canon Arendzen (*Prophets, Priests and Publicans*, 102). Here the advent of the Ruler of Israel at Bethlehem is linked up with a reference to his Mother. It can hardly be doubted that ' She who will bear ' is the same person as ' the maiden who will conceive '. Thus the prophecy of Micheas confirms that of Isaias. It foretells the Motherhood of Mary, but throws no further light upon her.

There are other texts in the OT in which Catholic **85b** interpreters have found allusions or references to Mary. In some cases, however, the application to the Blessed Virgin may not be more than a typical one, and in others the meaning of the text is not clear. Thus we read in Jer 31:22 : ' A woman shall encompass a man ', and this has been taken to refer to Mary as the Mother of the Messias. But the original would seem to mean ' A woman shall woo a man ', which appears to have no reference to the Incarnation. Yet it is certainly curious that older Jewish commentators interpreted the text of the future Messias. All this would seem to show that the Mother of the Messias formed an integral, though subordinate, part of Jewish Tradition.

In the case of some texts ' applied ' to the Blessed Virgin **c** by Christian commentators, it must remain doubtful whether the application is more than an ' accommodation '. Thus Ez 44:1–2 speaks of the eastern gate of Jerusalem, through which God alone enters, and which is henceforth for ever shut. Catholic commentators have seen in this an allusion to the perpetual virginity of Mary. But it is doubtful whether that is its inspired meaning.

In any case, given the fact that the Messias was to have **d** a Mother who would be a person of great dignity and importance, it is not surprising that those acquainted with all the data of Tradition on the subject should apply to her texts which have a different primary significance. Ps 44, for example, gives us a picture of the Queen who stands on the right hand of the Messianic King. He is attracted by her beauty ; the daughters of Tyre and the rich seek her favour ; she is clothed in golden robes, and accompanied by virgins. This may certainly refer primarily to Israel, the Spouse of God, and to the Christian Church which is the spiritual Israel. But this collective meaning does not exclude the application of the text also to the King's Mother Mary.

Similarly, the Canticle of Canticles is full of praise of **e** the King's Spouse. This is variously interpreted of Israel and the human soul. But it may also be applied to the Mother of the Messias.

Again, pious writers, and even the Church herself in **f** her liturgy, have not hesitated to apply to the Blessed Virgin some passages of the OT which directly concern only Wisdom. Doubtless, as Cardinal Newman remarked in his *Development of Christian Doctrine*, ch 4, sect. 2, 8, this application to Mary arose in part from the Arian misuse of the texts in which wisdom is said to be ' created '. Even so, we must say with Pope Pius IX that the application of such texts to the Blessed Virgin is in the nature of a ' transference ', justified by the fact that ' the origin of the Virgin was decreed at one and the same time with the Incarnation of the Divine Wisdom ' (*Ineffabilis Deus*).

III. Mary in the New Testament—' When the fulness **g** of the time was come, God sent his Son, made of a woman, made under the Law '. This text (Gal 4:4) is the only one in which St Paul expressly refers to the Mother of Christ. But it is significant for two reasons. Firstly, in the context the phrase ' made of a woman ' is almost superfluous, and would seem to have been inserted expressly. Secondly, St Paul here avoids the usual word ' born ' and uses instead made ', the same verb as is used in Jn 1:14, ' The Word was made flesh '. St Paul thus, in his one reference to our Lady, stresses her Divine Motherhood, and seems by his unusual language to call our attention to the unusual birth of Our Lord.

St Luke and Our Lady—That birth is recorded for us **h** in two of the Gospels, Mt and Lk. In Mt the story is told mainly from the standpoint of St Joseph, whereas St Luke's informant must ultimately have been our Lady herself. It is St Luke who records the Annunciation. Notice the angel's words, which are translated ' Hail, full of grace ' in our version. Protestants prefer to translate ' highly favoured '. Lagrange concedes that the word might have this sense, though in any case the perfect participle signifies an eminent degree of beauty

85h or favour. Here the epithet takes the place of a proper name, ' as if it were especially suitable for the Virgin ' (Lagrange, *S. Luc, in loc.*). The text implies that Mary is the object of God's bounty, which theologians understand as a gift of sanctifying grace, extraordinary, though capable of increase. In other words, as interpreted by Tradition and Catholic Theology, this text implies that Mary is indeed ' full of grace ', and therefore all-holy. Reflection upon the implications of this

i text, taken in conjunction with the Protoevangelium, has contributed to the formulation of the doctrine of the Immaculate Conception, which declares that Mary was ' full of grace ' from the first moment of her existence, and therefore free from the stain of original sin. This gift is hers because of her Divine Motherhood, for all Mary's graces follow from her special office as Mother of God. (It is worth adding that the doctrine of the divine Maternity led logically to the doctrine of the Immaculate Conception, which has in turn thrown new light on many biblical passages referring to our Lady.) Well does her cousin Elizabeth greet her as ' Blessed among women ', and pronounce the same blessing upon her Child : ' Blessed is the Fruit of thy womb '. And well does Mary herself in her *Magnificat* prophesy that henceforth all generations will call her blessed, because God has done great things for her. Small wonder that Elizabeth should express her joy and astonishment at receiving a visit from the Blessed Virgin, whom she calls the ' Mother of her Lord ' : ' Whence is this to me, that the Mother of my Lord should visit me ? ' (Lk 1:43). Note too that the sanctification of John in his mother's womb is the first miracle performed by Our Lady, or, rather, by the Incarnate Word *through* Our Lady.

j Already we have an indication of the prominent position which Mary occupies in the Christian dispensation. God the Son derives from her his human nature. He will remain true man as well as true God for ever. He will therefore for ever be the Son of Mary, and Mary will for ever be the Mother of God.

Yet the fullness of her grace, and the exalted position to which she is raised by God, do not disturb her humility. She bows to God's will, and pronounces herself to be his handmaid. She keeps the great secret to herself, for she has not been authorized to communicate it as yet, and so she does not even tell her husband St Joseph, who has to be reassured by an angel.

k Although the Virginal Conception and Birth can have caused no stain, Mary fulfils the prescriptions of the Jewish Law, presents her Son in the temple, buys him back again, and offers a sin-offering, in a spirit of obedience to the divine ordinances. On this occasion she hears the fearful prophecy of her own future sorrows in the mysterious words : ' Thine own soul a sword shall pierce ' (Lk 2:35). Coming as they do after the prophecy that her Son is to be ' a sign which shall be contradicted ', these words insinuate the compassion of Mary (in the literal sense, com-passion).

l Then there is silence, until our Lord is twelve years of age, when we have the incident of his loss during a visit to Jerusalem. It is on this occasion that Mary said to Jesus : ' Son, why hast thou done so to us ? Behold thy father and I have sought thee sorrowing ' (Lk 2:48). Thereupon Jesus says : ' How is it that you sought me ? Did you not know that I must be about my Father's business ? ' (or possibly : ' in the house of my Father '). The inspired narrative adds, for our instruction, that neither our Lady nor St Joseph ' understood the words he had spoken to them ' (Lk 2:50). We must remember that, according to the doctrine of inspiration, the sacred writers wrote all those things and only those things which God willed them to write, and that accordingly the Holy Ghost deliberately willed these words to be written. Doubtless the Holy Ghost would have us realize that the fullness of grace which was our Lady's did not necessarily involve a corresponding fullness of knowledge of God's plans. Thus St Luke's words constitute a warning against unbridled *a priori* theological specula- **85l** tion concerning our Lady's gifts. Theological speculation there may and should be—for it is thus that doctrines develop—but in our reflections we are bound always to respect the formal statements of Scripture, and of course also the dogmatic Tradition of the Church. In virtue of this text of St Luke, we are not free to say that she knew all things, or understood all things. She had to walk by faith, as we do. For a fuller discussion of our Lady's knowledge, *cf.* articles by E. F. Sutcliffe, cited in the bibliography above. For a discussion of her other virtues, *cf.* Scheeben, *op. cit.* ; T. Livius, *The Blessed Virgin in the Fathers of the first six centuries*, London, 1893—uncritical, but a mine of information.

After this incident, the veil is dropped once more **86a** over both the Mother and her Son, and we hear nothing more until the opening of the Public Ministry. Significantly enough, however, at the commencement of this Ministry we get a surprising miracle, that of the turning of water into wine at Cana, recorded in Jn 2:1–11. Here we may well note that in spite of an apparent reluctance, Jesus performs the miracle at the suggestion of his Mother. Mary says to Jesus : ' Son, they have no wine '. Our Lord replies : ' What to me and to thee ? ' This is a Hebrew idiom, which as Lebreton says (*Life and Teaching of Jesus Christ*, Vol. 1, p 52, 1935) ' was everywhere employed to resist an interference or decline a request, and there is really no room for any other interpretation here '. Jesus adds : ' My hour is not yet come '. Yet Mary **b** is not dismayed by this apparent rebuff. She says to the waiters : ' Whatsoever he shall say to you, do ye '. Thereupon Jesus works the miracle. This is really quite in accordance with our Lord's way of acting. Over and over again in the Gospels we read how he apparently refuses requests, but only to grant them when they are repeated with greater faith and urgency Instances are : the healing of the ruler's son at Capharnaum (Jn 4:46–54), and the healing of the daughter of the Canaanite woman (Mt 15:21–28). Moreover, Jesus himself has given us the parable of the householder who, aroused at midnight and asked for bread for unexpected guests, at first refuses and then grants the request of his neighbour ' because of his importunity ', Lk 11:5–8. Hence in the incident at Cana our Lord's apparent reluctance to please his mother was meant only to evoke a greater act of faith and hope. [Others consider that our Lord aimed rather to show to posterity how powerful is Mary's intercession.—Gen. Ed.]

The event just referred to took place at the beginning **c** of the Ministry. Mary was to take no active part in the work of the Ministry itself, for that was not her vocation. It was hers to pray, to suffer, and to minister with the other holy women. Even so, we have two further references to her in the Gospels. One was the occasion when Jesus was told that his mother was waiting to see him. He replied : ' Whosoever shall do the will of my Father that is in heaven, he is my brother and sister and mother ', Mt 12:50. The other occasion was when a woman called out : ' Blessed is the womb that bare thee, and the paps that gave thee suck '. To this Jesus answered : ' Yea, rather, blessed are they that hear the Word of God and keep it ', Lk 11:28. The purpose of these two sayings of our Lord was certainly not to dishonour or disown his blessed Mother, but rather to point out the true source of her own blessedness. She was indeed blessed because she submitted to God's will : ' Behold the handmaid of the Lord '. She heard the Word of God and kept it : ' Mary kept all these things, pondering them in her heart ', Lk 2:19. As our own Venerable Bede says, ' the Mother of God is indeed blessed because she was the temporal minister of the Word Incarnate, but much more blessed because she remained the eternal keeper of his Love ', *Hom. in Luc, c.* 11.

At the close of our Lord's life, Mary was to be associated **d**

86d with him in his Passion. For, as St John tells us, ' there stood her by the Cross of Jesus, his Mother '. Jesus entrusted her to the care of St John : ' Woman, behold thy Son . . . Behold thy mother ', Jn 19:26–27. Christian tradition from the time of Origen (*Comm. in Joan.*, PG 14, 32) has seen in St John the representative of all Christians, of whom Mary is the spiritual Mother.

Finally, we find Mary at the birth of the Church. For when the disciples met together in the Upper Room to give themselves to prayers, awaiting the Holy Ghost, we read that Mary was there praying with them, Ac 1:14. Doubtless she received the Holy Ghost also on that occasion, though Scripture does not expressly say so.

e Catholic Tradition has consecrated a belief in our Lady's Assumption, and her Coronation as Queen of Heaven is commemorated in the Rosary, a belief that Pope Pius XII officially declared to be a dogma of the Church on 1 November 1950. There is no reference in Scripture to either of these events, whose historicity is a corollary of the doctrine of the Immaculate Conception, which is in turn based on the Motherhood of Mary as proclaimed in Scripture and Tradition, and on her position as the Second Eve. But it is significant that in the last book of the NT, St John, who had cared for our Lady during the remainder of her earthly life, describes a vision of ' a woman clothed with the sun, and the moon under her feet, and on her head a crown of twelve stars ', who ' brought forth a man child who was to rule all nations with an iron rod ' and who was **f** ' taken up to God and to his throne ', while the dragon made war upon the woman and ' with the rest of her seed ', Apoc 12. St John tells of the ' great battle ' between Michael together with his angels and the dragon with his angels, *ibid*. He says explicitly that the ' great dragon ' is ' that old serpent who is called the devil and Satan ', 12:9. The Son of the Woman, who is to rule all nations, is obviously Jesus Christ. Who, then, is the woman, and who are ' the rest of her seed ' ? As in the case of the OT prophecies, the seer may here be thinking of the Israel of God, continued in the Christian Church. But analogy surely suggests, to say the least, that together with this collective meaning the Woman has also a personal signification, and is none other than the Blessed Virgin, who is the Mother of Jesus and of all Christians. Pius X wrote, ' " A woman clothed with the sun ". . . . Everyone knows that that woman signified the Virgin Mary who, inviolate, brought forth our Head ' (Encyclical Letter *Ad diem illum*, 2 Feb. 1904). She, then, is ' the one clothed with the sun ', with ' the moon under her feet ', and ' on her head a crown of twelve stars '. Such is the picture of Mary in glory, painted for us by the inspired writer of the last book of the New Testament.

g IV. Conclusion. Catholic Doctrine in Relation to Scripture—Such are the scriptural *data* concerning our Lady. In one sense they amount to little. But what Scripture does tell us is of the utmost importance, and we may say with confidence that it contains in germ most if not all of the developed *doctrine* of the Church concerning her office. Her position as the Woman who is to be at enmity with the Serpent, and who through her Seed is to crush its head, coupled with the doctrine of St Paul that Jesus Christ is the Second Adam, easily lead us to the principle so strongly asserted in early Tradition, that Mary is the Second Eve. This is confirmed by the traditional interpretation that at the Cross St John represented all Christians in taking Mary for his Mother, as also by the picture he has painted in his *Apocalypse* of the Woman clothed with the sun, who has other seed besides the Son who is to rule all the nations.

h We have seen too that careful reflection upon the enmity between the Woman and the Serpent, and the **86h** angelical salutation, ' Hail, full of grace ', interpreted in the light of Catholic Tradition, has helped to illustrate the doctrine of the Immaculate Conception —a doctrine which in turn gives a full meaning to Mary's joy in God her Saviour in her *Magnificat*.

The statement of Simeon that a sword would pierce **i** Mary's soul, taken in conjunction with the statement of St John that Mary stood by the Cross, provides a basis for the doctrine of the compassion of Mary, which has won for her the title of Co-Redemptrix.

Mary exercised on earth her divine Motherhood by watching over her Son during his infancy, praying and ministering to him during the Ministry, and by standing by his Cross. She exercised her Motherhood of Christians by interceding at Cana in Galilee, where the first miracle was worked, and by praying with and for the Apostles and their followers, especially before Pentecost. St John's picture of our Lady in glory gives us a glimpse of her position in heaven.

There is, of course, much more that we should like to **j** know, especially concerning her earthly life. Scripture tells us practically nothing about Mary's parentage, her early years, or indeed her later life. It is silent about her Assumption. It was only natural that, where so much was left to our imagination or curiosity, pious Christian writers should have sought to supplement the data of Scripture. The Church has repudiated the Apocryphal Gospels, so full of details concerning our Lady. She does not deny, however, that they may contain some true traditions. Thus, the Church celebrates the feasts of Our Lady's parents, who are named in the Apocryphal Gospels as SS. Joachim and Anna (*e.g.* Gospel of James, Gospel of the Nativity of Mary). Similarly the Church celebrates Mary's Presentation in the Temple, an incident not mentioned in the canonical Gospels, but found in the same two apocryphal writings. The Church guarantees the occurrence of the events in question, but not the details found in these apocryphal works.

The above are instances of events outside Scripture. **k** In other cases Scripture and Tradition both combine and illustrate each other. An interesting example is to be found in the doctrine of our Lady's perpetual virginity. That our Lady was a virgin in her conception is definitely asserted by St Matthew and St Luke, and is also implied in her question : ' How shall this be, for I know not man ? ' Lk 1:34. That Mary was a virgin also in the actual birth of our Lord is not expressly asserted in Scripture, but it is formulated in the Apostles' Creed, in the words ' *born* of the *Virgin* Mary '. This is in harmony with the prophecy of Isaias, who says that the Virgin will not only conceive, but also bear a Son. Finally Christian **l** Tradition asserts that Mary remained ever a virgin. This, again, is not directly stated in Scripture. Indeed, Scripture uses language which at first sight seems to be contrary to this doctrine, for we read that ' Joseph knew not his wife till she brought forth her firstborn son ' (Mt 1:25), and again Scripture speaks of the ' brothers ' and ' sisters ' of Jesus. But the statement of St Matthew is an oriental expression which means precisely what it says and no more, *i.e.* that Joseph knew not Mary till the birth of Jesus. The ' brothers ' and ' sisters ' of Jesus are discussed in §§ 672–3.

This is an interesting example of the way in which **m** Tradition clarifies and to some extent supplements Scripture. Tradition gives us the key to the meaning of Scripture. But viewed apart from Tradition—so far as this may be possible—Scripture provides us with an adequate foundation for the Catholic doctrine concerning our Lady, and for our piety and devotion towards her.

THE MIRACULOUS ELEMENT IN THE BIBLE

By E. C. MESSENGER, Ph.D.

87a Bibliography—*H. S. Box, B.D., *Miracles and Critics*, London 1935 ; J. T. Driscoll, art. *Miracle*, CE ; L. de Grandmaison, S.J., *Jesus Christ*, Vol. 3 (Eng. trans.), London 1934 ; G. H. Joyce, S.J., *The Question of Miracles*, London 1914 ; R. A. Knox, *Miracles*, CTS, London 1927 ; H. Lesêtre, art. *Miracle* DBV ; *C. S. Lewis, *Miracles*, London 1947 ; J. H. Newman, *Essay on the Miracles of Scripture*, London 1870 ; J. de Tonquédec, art. *Miracle*, DAFC ; *R. H. Trench (Abp), *The Miracles of Our Lord*, London n.d. ; A. van Hove, *La Notion du Miracle chez Saint Thomas*, Paris 1927 ; also articles in *Religion and Science*, CSSL, 1939, by Rev. A. Manson, O.P., and Rev. C. Lattey, S.J. on *Miracles*, and by Canon Arendzen on *The Bible*.

b Ancient and Modern Attitude towards Miracles—The attentive reader of Holy Writ cannot but be struck by the prominent place which miracles occupy in the narratives. They are unhesitatingly presented as real historic events, and as certain signs of God's intervention in this world. More precisely, they are set forth as proofs that he is speaking and working through particular individuals. Thus, far from miracles needing to be proved, they are set forth in the Bible as undoubted facts which show that God is present and is speaking to us.

Modern incredulity and the rise of rationalistic exegesis, however, have radically changed this order of things, so that, far from biblical miracles being proofs of something else, it is held that they themselves are in considerable need of proof, and it is usually added that satisfactory proof of their reality is not available.

c The Supposed Impossibility of Miracles—There are two main lines of attack upon the reality of the miracles. The first is the philosophical approach. The Rationalists, for instance, insist for the most part that a miracle is an impossibility. Such a forthright statement, of course, calls for convincing proof. But the only argument which has been brought forward in support of it would seem to be that first advanced by Spinoza in his *Tractatus Theologico-Politicus* (1670). His argument is that the laws of nature are the expression of God's Decrees, which are based upon the Divine Nature itself. But the Divine Nature cannot change, and neither can the Divine Decrees based upon it. Hence natural laws are immutable, and miracles are impossible. The reasoning is obviously fallacious, for while we may rightly urge that God cannot act against the metaphysical laws of being, which indeed have their ultimate foundation in the unchangeable Divine Nature, no such necessity is inherent in the laws of physical nature, which are, in philosophical terminology, ' contingent ', and not ' necessary '. It is not possible to conceive that the laws of being, as expressed in the Principle of Contradiction, and the other first Principles, could be other than they are. But there is no such necessity inherent in physical or natural laws. Conceivably they might be different in a different order of things. Hence, as physical laws are contingent, and not metaphysically necessary, exceptions to them are not impossible.

d Another and more common argument against miracles is that they imply a change of mind in the Unchangeable God. This objection collapses if it be remembered that in our view, all miracles which have

ever happened were foreseen and intended by God **87d** from the first.

Again, it is urged that miracles, being derogations from or contradictions of laws of nature, imply that God's creation is imperfect, and needs to be supplemented or improved. The answer to this is that Nature is indeed perfect in its own sphere, and that miracles are primarily connected, not with the natural order, but with the supernatural order of grace. Grace perfects nature, but does not destroy it : rather, it presupposes it. The same is true of miracles and their relation to natural law.

There is thus no proof that miracles are impossible. On the contrary, we definitely assert that miracles are possible, precisely because natural laws are not in themselves absolutely necessary. The action of any one law is constantly being interfered with by the operation of some other law. *A fortiori*, the effect of a law in a particular case may be suspended through the special activity of the First Cause, who is the source of all Law. And that is what we mean by a miracle.

Can a miracle ever be proved ?—In more modern **e** times, the attempt to establish the impossibility of a miracle has been tacitly abandoned, and in its place we have various attempts to show that the reality of a miracle can never be established. Thus, Hume and Huxley have argued that the Principle of the Uniformity of Nature is established by universal experience. No supposed testimony to the reality of a miracle can prevail against this universal experience. But this statement obviously begs the question, because it assumes that there are not and indeed cannot be any exceptions to this general rule. In any case, human testimony which bears witness to the reality of a miracle is itself a part of universal experience. And there is no evident reason why the testimony in favour of uniformity should be accepted, while that in favour of a miraculous exception is rejected. Some modern writers object that to allow the reality of a miracle on human testimony would destroy the foundation of natural laws as such, for laws are but the expression or generalization of human experience. To that we reply that *normal* human testimony is quite able to provide a basis for the establishment of natural laws, and equally the *exceptional* human testimony to the reality of miracles establishes not only the fact of miracles, but also their miraculous character, *i.e.* the fact that they cannot be accounted for by the ordinary laws of nature.

Philosophical prejudices underlie rationalistic exegesis f —These philosophical considerations have in reality had a great influence even upon those who have professed to deal with miracles solely upon the grounds of evidence. Rationalists and others may indeed pretend to be impartial when they study the books of Sacred Scripture. But an attentive student cannot fail to notice that the rationalist rejection of miracles is usually based upon *a priori* philosophical considerations or prejudices such as those we have just mentioned, rather than upon an objective and impartial study of the evidence for the miracles themselves. The reasoning usually takes this form : This account of a particular miracle must be rejected and regarded as legendary, or as a misunderstanding of a merely natural event, or perhaps even of a coincidence. The reason for this attitude is not always expressed, but it is evidently

87f based upon the supposed impossibility or improbability of a miracle really happening. Accordingly, recourse is made to various alternative explanations of the narrative. Thus Strauss (1808–74) regarded miraculous events as mythical accretions to the original narrative, and as entirely unhistorical. The growth of a legend, or the development of a myth, requires a certain space of time, and therefore Strauss maintained that the books of Scripture, and especially those of the New Testament, must have been composed or given their present form long after the events narrated in them, and indeed long after the deaths of the writers to whom they have been attributed by tradition.

88a The late dating of the New Testament has had, however, to be abandoned, and it is now admitted that it was all written during the 1st cent. The critics have fared somewhat better with the Old Testament, for their comparatively late dates for the various books still meet with very wide acceptance. Accordingly, it is urged with plausibility that as some hundreds of years elapsed between the supposed events and our present records of them, there was ample time for legendary development. Even so, the critical position is by no means so strong as it was, and modern writers, while adhering to the late dates for the books, have been compelled to allow that the materials used in them were more or less contemporary with the events recorded. Thus, modern students of the Pentateuch are disposed to attribute a large part of the materials used in it to a time not much later than that of Moses himself.

Catholics for the most part adhere to the traditional early dates of the historical books of the Old Testament, which make the records contemporary with the events, though it is admitted that there may have been a certain amount of subsequent ' editing' of the books. But we maintain that such ' editing' could not consist in the subsequent incorporation of legends devoid of any historical basis. The reason is that, in general, the miracles narrated were *public events*, so intimately bound up with the course of history that they actually influenced it. Thus, the whole history of Israel during the Exodus from Egypt and after its subsequent settlement in Canaan supposes the historic reality of the miracles performed by Moses in Egypt and at the Red Sea. These produced such an impression upon the minds of the Israelites that subsequent Hebrew literature was full of repercussions and reflections of these great events, which formed part of the whole national tradition. To deny the historical reality of these miracles is to destroy the foundation of the history itself. Similar considerations apply to the miracles of Elias and Eliseus. (For further treatment of OT miracles see § 226 *f–h*.)

b **The supposed natural character of miraculous events** —Accordingly, some modern writers have suggested a more moderate theory. In their view, the miraculous events in the Bible had a real basis in fact. The underlying fact was some unusual event, probably due to natural causes, perhaps to unknown powers of nature, or again possibly due to the influence of mind upon matter. This is the basis of the ' faith-healing' view of miracles. Some non-Catholics accept the ' miracles of healing' narrated in the New Testament, but reject the ' cosmic miracles' in the world of inanimate nature. But there is no reasonable basis for such a distinction. Both are equally guaranteed by the records, and both are equally bound up with the history itself. Again, it is urged, especially against the New Testament, that many miracles consist in the expulsion of devils from those said to be possessed, and that the sacred writers, in accordance with the ideas of the time, attribute to diabolical possession many diseases which we now recognize to be quite normal, such as epilepsy or lunacy. But in point of fact, the New Testament writers clearly distinguish between cases of diabolical possession or obsession with their pathological accompaniments, and cases of diseases unaccompanied by any such diabolical possession, *cf.* Mt 4:24; 8:16; Mk 1:32, 34, etc. The existence of pathological symptoms in the case of those said to be possessed constitutes no special difficulty.

88b Why should not diabolical possession be a cause of disease in certain instances ? No one has ever proved that diabolical possession is impossible. Indeed, there are many facts in history both ancient and modern which point to its reality. In any case, the books of the New Testament assert, not only that the devil was expelled but that the pathological conditions were also suddenly remedied, so that the miracle remains to be explained.

c We conclude, then, that the rationalist attitude towards Scriptural miracles is unreasonable. It is based for the most part on *a priori* philosophical principles which are in fact false. Or else it involves an unjustifiable rejection of human testimony, or again a manipulation of the evidence for which prejudice alone can account.

89a **The Church's Teaching on Miracles**—What, then, is the Catholic attitude towards the miracles of the Bible ? The dogmatic position is set forth by the Vatican Council in its third Capitulum, *De Fide*, thus :

' In order that the service of our Faith should be agreeable to reason, God has willed to join to the internal helps of the Holy Spirit some external proofs of his revelation, namely, divine deeds, especially miracles and prophecies, which, inasmuch as they plainly show forth the omnipotence and infinite knowledge of God, are most certain signs of revelation and are suited to the intelligence of all. Wherefore, both Moses and the Prophets, and above all Christ the Lord himself, performed many and most manifest miracles and uttered prophecies ; and we read of the Apostles that " they, going forth, preached everywhere, the Lord working withal and confirming the word with signs that followed " '.

Also, we have the following canons of the same Vatican Council :

' If anyone shall say that divine revelation cannot be made credible by external signs, but that men must be moved to believe solely by the internal experience or private inspiration of each one, let him be anathema ' Dz 1812.

' If anyone shall say that no miracles can take place, and that in consequence all the accounts of them, even those contained in Holy Scripture, must be numbered amongst fables or myths, or that miracles can never be known for certain as such, or that the divine origin of the Christian revelation cannot properly be proved by them, let him be anathema ' Dz 1813.

b **Miracles and Revelation**—There are some points about these ecclesiastical definitions which must be noted carefully. First, we observe that miracles are considered by the Council in so far as they are ' external proofs of revelation '. It is not impossible that miracles might sometimes be worked for some other purpose, not immediately connected with divine revelation—for instance, to call men's attention to God's existence. But the Council is concerned with miracles only as proofs of revelation. Miracles prove a revelation, either by confirming the authority of a religious teacher, or by confirming the truth of a doctrine preached by him.

The Council does not say that God must work miracles to prove his revelation : it only says that God has willed to do so, in order that our faith should be reasonable. Such divine intervention is eminently suitable, because it gives convincing proof that God is present and is teaching us.

c **The Comparative Infrequency of Miracles**—This intimate connection with divine revelation explains the comparative infrequency of miracles in human history. The Vatican Council has nothing to say concerning miracles before the age of Moses : it neither affirms nor denies the existence of such divine interventions. It singles out for special mention the miracles of Moses and the Prophets in the Old Testament, and of our Lord and his Apostles in the New. This emphasizes the connexion between miracles and divine

89c revelation, for the foundation of the Mosaic religion, and the divine revelation on Mount Sinai were the occasion for an extraordinary number of miracles. There were some others, of course, which accompanied the establishment of the Chosen People in the land of Canaan, but they were less frequent and not so striking.

The next prominent group of miracles occurs in the vindication of the religion of Jahweh under the Monarchy—a vindication which was especially necessary in view of the tendency of the Chosen People to fall into idolatry and to adopt the pagan ideas of the peoples around them. There were few miracles during the Captivity : this catastrophe was in itself a manifest divine intervention and the fulfilment of prophecies. One might have expected a new outburst of miracles at the return from the Captivity. But miracles and prophecies almost ceased, and these special divine interventions were renewed only at the advent of Christ our Lord, when the divine revelation was given to us in its final form.

This intimate connexion between miracles and revelation enables us to see the reason for the miracles of Scripture. These are, as we have said, connected mainly with divine revelation. If the Mosaic religion was, as we hold, a special revelation from God—a fact which is confirmed by its transcendent character compared with the corrupt and immoral religions of the surrounding peoples—then it is not surprising that God should have confirmed his word by miracles. The same applies, of course, to the miracles of the New Testament.

d **Are we bound to believe in Particular Miracles ?**— Next, we must note that the Vatican Council, though mentioning groups of miracles, does not mention any particular one. Of course, the enumeration of two particular miracles in the Creeds—the Virginal Conception and Birth, and the Resurrection of our Lord—shows that these must specifically be accepted as of faith. Belief in other Scriptural miracles, taken individually, does not stand on the same footing. It is not precisely part of the defined Catholic Faith that every single marvellous event narrated in the Old and New Testaments was in fact a miracle. We are certainly bound to believe in the existence of groups of miracles, as we have already explained. But it would not be precisely heretical to say that some particular marvel narrated in the Old or New Testament was not in reality a true miracle. The Church leaves adequate room for discussion concerning the miraculous character of particular events. And the recent explicit approval by Pope Pius XII of the doctrine that there are varieties of literary form in the Bible emphasizes this freedom Thus, it is arguable that the common interpretation of the story of Jonas and the sea-monster is not necessarily the correct one. Again, there might be something to be said for the view that the Book of Tobias, with its strange miracles, is not really intended to be regarded as history but is a kind of pious romance. The majority of Catholic scholars will doubtless adhere to the conservative and traditional view, at least for the present. But we must not regard the more liberal view as heretical, or indeed as unsound, unless and until the Church officially declares it to be such.

90a Some will doubtless hold that, while other literary forms may exist in the Bible, the form of a ' pious romance ' is hardly compatible with the divine veracity. Leaving that question to be decided by the theologians and the exegetes, it is at least safe to call attention to the existence of the literary form of poetry, even in the historical books. That this has its bearing upon the study of some of the Scriptural miracles will be evident from the case of Josue's command that the sun should stand still. Poetry is the natural home of metaphor. It may be urged that the sacred writer himself says that the sun stood still and did not go down for a whole day, Jos 10:13. That is true. But Fr. Kugler, S.J., has shown that it was customary for ancient writers to call eclipses, thunder-storms and similar darknesses ' rests ' of the sun and moon. We have an example of this use of the term in Hab 3:11. In any case 90a the context in Josue shows that there was an unprecedented storm of hail, which dealt death at the opposing army. It was almost as dark as night, but after the storm, the sun reappeared, riding in the heavens as before. The divine intervention is still there. But as Canon Arendzen has put it, ' the miracle consisted, not in a useless standing still of sun and moon in the sky, but in the abnormal continuance of a storm which completely hid the sun during the day and the moon during the night ' (op. cit., p 218). [For other views on Jos 10:13 f. see the commentary in loc., § 232 f–i.]

Miracles and Natural Causes—This naturally leads us b to a more difficult and delicate question. How far did natural causes and powers contribute to the miraculous events in Scripture ? That these natural forces did play some part is evident at least in the case of the passage of the Red Sea, for Ex 14:21 says : ' When Moses had stretched forth his hand over the sea, the Lord took it away by a strong and burning wind blowing all the night, and turned it into dry ground, and the water was divided '. It is not impossible that natural phenomena also played some part in many of the Plagues of Egypt. As Canon Arendzen has written : ' The Nile waters turn red, breed frogs, mosquitoes, flies. Murrain attacks the cattle, ulcers come on man and beast, a hail-storm wrecks and destroys all on the fields, a cloud of locusts devours the crops, a darkness covers the land. These nine plagues are not infrequent disasters which afflict the land of Egypt. . . . The Catholic has no temptation to explain the miracles in Egypt away, but deeper scientific knowledge of the natural phenomena in Egypt has shown him that the miracles lay, not in their bizarre character, but in that a series of national calamities, of a kind not otherwise unknown, was *evoked* and *ceased* at the bidding of Moses '. He adds that ' obviously the exemption of the children of Israel from the effect of these plagues is of a miraculous kind, and cannot be explained by science ', and that ' the death of the firstborn of the Egyptians is manifestly an event which lies beyond the explanation of science ' (op. cit. pp 216–17). Similarly, it has been suggested that the miraculous crossing of the Jordan recorded in Jos 3–4 may have been due to a landslide or an earthquake such as has happened in those regions in comparatively recent times. But in this particular instance the crossing was prophesied beforehand. From the Jordan the Israelites proceeded to the siege of Jericho, where we are told that the walls fell down after seven days of procession round the city. Recent archaeological research has shown that the double east wall of the city did indeed collapse, and it has been suggested that either defective foundations or an earthquake may have been partial causes. But even if natural causes played their part, God's intervention is no less evident.

In this connexion it is interesting to note that, c according to Aquinas (ST I, 105, 8), a miracle may exceed the powers of nature either as regards the nature of the fact, in which case we have the highest kind of miracle ; or secondly, as regards not the fact itself but the subject in which the action takes place ; or thirdly, as regards the manner and order of the event. The first category would comprise events which nature could never bring about, *e.g.* the presence of two bodies in one and the same position in space. The second grade would consist in an event which nature can bring about, but not in that particular subject. It is interesting to note that St Thomas includes in this second category the giving of life to a dead body, for he argues that Nature can give life, but not to a corpse. The third and lowest category, which exceeds the powers of nature only in *mode* and *order*, includes the sudden bringing about of a cure which could be effected in a longer period by natural means, or the sudden production of a storm of rain, apart from the action of the ordinary natural causes. St Thomas thus seems to exclude any activity of these natural causes. But why should these not be present and active, God

90c supplementing their natural activity, so that they lead to a result which they could not produce by their ordinary power? Such an event would of course be a true miracle, for it could not take place without an exercise of special divine power. We could apply this to some of the physical cures recorded in the Bible, and to many which have happened since, down to our own day.

In any case St Thomas and all Catholic theologians after him hold that the raising of a dead person to life exceeds the powers of nature, and is definitely a true miracle, though of the second order. Such miracles occur both in the Old and New Testaments, the supreme example being the Resurrection of our Lord.

91a Diabolical and Other Marvels—The fact that natural causes may play some part in certain miracles enables us to understand the possibility of wonders being wrought by human means, with or without the aid either of devils or of angels. Both Old and New Testaments bear witness to the existence of such marvellous happenings. Thus, Pharaoh's 'magicians' were able to imitate the results of some of the plagues of Egypt. In the New Testament we have the case of Simon Magus, who deceived many by his 'sorceries'. Yet there are limits, and the magicians themselves were forced to recognize the power of God in the miracles of Moses. And Simon Magus 'wondered to see the signs and exceeding great miracles' done by the Apostles. There is plenty of room for speculation as to the means whereby Pharaoh's magicians and Simon Magus had worked their own marvels. Probably natural powers would account for much, if not all. But though natural powers may have played their part also in the divine miracles, God's intervention was quite manifest, because the effects produced transcended the powers of nature, either in the fact, or in the mode or circumstances of the fact.

[There is also a **Moral and Religious Quality** in the **Divine Miracles** (*cf.* their connexion with Revelation). It may of course be argued that no wonder worked by any created agent, whether angel, devil or wizard, could really be supernatural, since any power they had would be a natural power. This is no doubt true, though from the point of view of physical nature these powers might be of a higher order, and so if not supernatural, at least preter-natural. But however true this might be, from the standpoint of ordinary mortals it remains hard to tell the difference between them in fact. That is where the difference between the evidential character of Divine Miracles and their connexion with revelation is so important. One immediately senses that they are from God because of this. That is, perhaps, why our Lord refused to perform any miracle that did not bear on it the evident stamp of divine origin **91a** but might seem like a magical or diabolical wonder : as in the wilderness, or where faith was positively refused. St Paul also tells the Church to try the Spirits by their witness to the Truth, or denial of it.—Gen. Ed.]

The reality of the NT miracles—Abundant as the **b** evidence is for the reality of the Old Testament miracles, the evidence is still more cogent in the case of those recorded in the New. The books narrating them were written by eye-witnesses, or were based on the testimony of eye-witnesses. The miracles were many and varied. Thus, we have miracles wrought on irrational beings, such as the miraculous draughts of fishes, the stilling of storms, the multiplications of loaves and fishes, etc. ; the curing of innumerable physical maladies, some temporary, *e.g.* fever ; others chronic, *e.g.* paralysis ; and others organic, *e.g.* the man born blind. These are distinct from the exorcism of those possessed by devils. Finally we have the supreme **c** miracles of the raising of the dead to life. We have already pointed out that those miraculous events are bound up with the history itself, and that the one cannot be separated from the other. Most of these miracles were wrought in public and were well known, so that St Peter was able to say to the Jews that Jesus of Nazareth was 'a man approved of God among you by miracles and wonders and signs which God did by him in the midst of you, *as you do know*', Ac 2:22. Our Lord's bitterest opponents who disbelieved in his claims did not dare to deny the reality of his miracles. Indeed, they 'gathered a Council and said : "What do we, for this man doth many miracles?"', Jn 11:47. As they could not deny them, instead they attributed them to the use of diabolical power, Mk 3:22, Lk 11:15, or else they complained that they were worked on the Sabbath Day (Mk 3:23 f. and parallel passages). Quadratus, Bishop of Athens, writing at the beginning of the 2nd cent., was able to say that those whom Christ had cured were well known to many, long after Christ himself had died (in Eusebius, H.E. IV, *c* 3). Our Lord worked his miracles expressly in confirmation of his divine mission (*cf.* Mt 11:4–5 ; Jn 10:25, 37–38, etc.) or in proof of his teaching. This provides an explanation of the statement which has puzzled many, that at Nazareth Jesus could work no miracles 'because of their unbelief', Mt 13:58, Mk 6:5. It was not that the lack of faith in Christ's hearers made the working of a miracle physically impossible. Rather their obstinacy rendered the miracle useless in advance, for it would have failed in its primary purpose. It must never be forgotten that, while a miracle is a manifestation of God's Power, its performance is regulated by God's Wisdom.

THE APOCRYPHA

OF THE OLD TESTAMENT AND NEW TESTAMENT

By R. J. FOSTER

92a **Bibliography**—*R. H. Charles, *The Apocrypha and Pseudepigrapha of the OT in English*, Oxford, 1913, 2 vol.; *idem., Between the Old and New Testaments*, London, 1914; J. E. Steinmueller, *A Companion to Scripture Studies*, New York, 1941; *A Companion to the Bible*, ed. T. W. Manson, Edinburgh, 1943; *M. R. James, *Apocrypha Anecdota*, Cambridge, 1893–7 (= *Texts and Studies*, II (3) and V (1)); *ibid., The Lost Apocrypha of the Old Testament, their Titles and Fragments*, London, 1920'; *ibid., The Apocryphal New Testament*, Oxford, 1924; *E. Kautzsch, *Die Apokryphen und Pseudepigraphen des Alten Testamentes*, 2 vols, Tübingen, 1900; *C. Tischendorf, *Acta Apostolorum Apocrypha*, Leipzig, 1851; *ibid. Apocalypses Apocryphae*, Leipzig, 1866; DBV(S) *Apocryphes*; H. Pope, *The Apocryphal Books of NT*, in *The New Testament* (Papers read at the Cambridge Summer School), 1937. Ed. C. Lattey, S.J.; M.-J. Lagrange, *Le Messianisme chez les Juifs*, Paris, 1909; S. Székely, *Bibliotheca Apocrypha*, Freiburg i. Br., 1913; *E. Schürer, *The Jewish People in the Time of Jesus Christ*, Edinburgh, 1900; *Institutiones Biblicae*, I, 2, 73 ff.; DBV (S) 1, 354 ff.; CE 1, 601 ff.; HDB 1, 110 ff.; DTC 1, 1479 ff.; 1498 ff.

b The name *Apocrypha* is applied by Catholics to writings of a religious character, outside the scriptural Canon, which, though not inspired, made some pretensions to divine authority or were sometimes considered as sacred. To prevent possible misunderstanding it might be well to recall the different use of the word in Catholic and Protestant circles. By Protestants the term is applied to books which we hold to be inspired and canonical, *i.e.* the deuterocanonical books (*cf.* § 13*a–f*), and also to the Prayer of Manasses and 3 and 4 Esdras (*cf.* §§ 92*l*, 93*b*, *i*). Catholics reserve the name for those uncanonical writings, of uncertain or spurious origin, which appeared sometimes anonymously but usually under the assumed names of various patriarchs, prophets or apostles about the beginning of the Christian era. For these the Protestants introduced the name *Pseudepigrapha*.

This different usage of the term 'Apocrypha' in Catholic and Protestant circles is very confusing. In this article we use 'Apocrypha' and 'apocryphal' in the Catholic sense only, unless otherwise indicated. It is interesting to note that among the list of 'The Apocrypha' in the official AV and RV Anglican Bibles there are three items, viz., The Prayer of Manasses and 1 and 2 Esdras (in Catholic terminology, 3 and 4 Esdras) which Catholics regard as truly apocryphal, *i.e.* as being outside the Canon; the remaining items we regard as truly canonical (deuterocanonical as opposed to protocanonical, *cf.* § 13). The official view of the Church of England still is that its 'Apocrypha' are not fully inspired, so that while it reads them 'for example of life and instruction of manners, but yet doth it not apply them to establish any doctrine' (Art VI of the English Church [Lat. 1562, Eng. 1571]).

c **Meaning of the Name**—Etymologically the name is a neuter plural from the Greek ἀπόκρυφος, which means hidden or secret. When first applied to writings, it was used in a laudatory sense of books kept secret because they contained esoteric doctrine too sacred to be revealed to any save the initiated.

Thus the disciples of the Gnostic Prodicus boasted **92c** that they possessed the secret books, βίβλους ἀποκρύφους of Zoroaster, *Clement of Alexandria* Strom. 1, 15. P.G. 8, 773. In this way, too, St Gregory of Nyssa refers to the NT, speaking of Apoc as ἐν ἀποκρύφοις *In suam ordinationem*, P.G. 46, 549, *cf.* also JE 2, 1; 4 Esd 14:45 f. By degrees the original meaning became obscured, giving way to the unfavourable sense which it still retains, partly, no doubt, because esoteric literature flourished most amongst heretical sects and partly because the books themselves were pseudonymous.

Origen used it in a derogatory sense of questionable **d** works which contained 'much that is corrupt and contrary to the true faith', *Prol. Cant.* PG 13, 83. It eventually connoted writings which were false, spurious or heretical. St Augustine, for instance, writes, ' Let us omit, then, the fables of those scriptures which are called apocryphal, because their obscure origin was unknown to the fathers from whose authority the true Scripture has been transmitted to us . . .'; and again, ' Many writings are produced by heretics under the names both of other prophets and, more recently, under the names of apostles, all of which, after careful examination, have been set apart from canonical authority under the title of Apocrypha ', *The City of God*, Eng. trans., Edinburgh, 1934, 2, 95 f. And so the name came to be applied to certain Jewish and Christian writings, outside the Canon, composed about the beginning of the Christian era, of doubtful authority and ascribed to various patriarchs, prophets or apostles. In this way we understand the expression today. The Apocrypha are spoken of as OT or NT Apocrypha according as their subject matter refers to the OT or NT. The former are usually of Jewish, the latter of Christian origin, though many of the Jewish Apocrypha contain Christian interpolations.

It was not until Jerome's time that the word was used of the deuterocanonical books, and he was the first to do so (*cf.* PL 22, 877); his practice was followed by others, and in the sixteenth cent., when the Protestants adopted the Jewish Canon, they designated as Apocrypha the books they rejected.

THE APOCRYPHA OF THE OT

Their Origin and Purpose—Their origin was due to **e** the unfortunate plight of, and depressed state prevailing amongst, the chosen people just before and during the commencement of the Christian era. Despairing of the times in which they lived, conscious of their enslavement to the hard yoke of foreign domination, they felt keenly the disparity between their present state and the ideal future which was assuredly one day to be theirs. With no prophetic voice to guide, encourage and console them, the writers of the Apocrypha strove to turn the eyes of the nation to a time, not far distant, when Israel would realize its destiny as a nation chosen apart. They gloried in painting a vivid picture of the triumphant reign of the Messias, soon to come, in which all God's promises would be fulfilled and the triumph of the just would be evident to all. Hope is the keynote of the Apocrypha and, it has been well said, hope is the main underlying motive power which prompted the writing of many of

92e them. This apocryphal literature served, in various ways, to rekindle in the Jews their intense faith in their own inevitable glorious destiny. It thus afforded them comfort in their trials, satisfied the demand for prophetic guidance and helped to solve the perennial problems of the suffering of the just and the apparent hopelessness of any fulfilment of the prophetic utterances of the past. It also served to drive home the pre-eminence of the Law and the need for its strict observance, whilst throwing light on many of their theological questions, such as the prosperity of the wicked, the certainty of judgement and retribution, and the resurrection of the dead.

f To bring about this transformation of outlook various methods were adopted. At one time the writers would modify the sacred text of the Scriptures, as it were rewriting it to suit their purpose ; at another they would select one of the great characters of old and set him before their readers with added fictitious details and embellishments to inspire enthusiasm and provoke imitation (*cf.* Schürer, Div. 2, 3, p 133 f.). Most frequently they adopted the prophetic or apocalyptic method, peering into the hidden future and, in mysterious and enigmatic form, revealing its supposed secrets. To accomplish their purpose more surely, they chose to compel the attention of their contemporaries by assuming the names and guise of the men of the ancient and classic past. They wrote as though from the early days of Israel's history, but foretelling to their own generation what was shortly to come to pass. In this way they could effectively issue warnings and inspire hope. How well they succeeded has been summed up by Schürer, ' If we find that, from the date of the tax imposed by Quirinius, whereby Judaea was placed directly under Roman administration, revolutionary tendencies among the people grew stronger and stronger year by year till they led at last to the great insurrection of the year 66, then there cannot be a doubt that this process was essentially promoted if not exclusively caused by the apocalyptic literature ', *loc. cit.*, p 48.

g Division of Apocrypha—Although no division of the Apocrypha is entirely satisfactory nor completely free from criticism since many might be said to belong to more than one category, we might group them into three classes according to their character. This list is by no means exhaustive (*cf.* Charles, *op. cit.*).
Apocalyptic Apocrypha — Ethiopic and Slavonic Henoch, Assumption of Moses, 4 Esdras, Syriac and Greek Apocalypse of Baruch, Apocalypse of Abraham, Apocalypse of Elias, Testament of Abraham, Apocalypse of Sophonias, Sybilline Oracles.
Historical Apocrypha—Book of Jubilees, 3 Esdras, 3 Maccabees, Life of Adam and Eve (or Apocalypse of Moses), Ascension of Isaias, History of the Rechabites, Sadokite Fragment, Book of Aseneth, Testament of Job, Testament of Solomon.
Didactic Apocrypha—Testament of the Twelve Patriarchs, Psalm 151, Psalms of Solomon, Odes of Solomon, Prayer of Manasses, 4 Maccabees. Considerations of space preclude a detailed treatment, but it is possible to give a short description of some of the more important books.

1 APOCALYPTIC APOCRYPHA

h The Ethiopic Henoch, perhaps the most important of the Apocrypha, is an apocalyptic work, composite in character, whose various parts range from *c* 200 B.C. almost up to 1 B.C. It is known as 1 Henoch to distinguish it from the later Apocalypse, 2 Henoch ; or, alternatively, as Ethiopic Henoch to distinguish it from the Slavonic 2 Henoch after the earliest extant versions of each. The original language of both of them is thought to be Hebrew or Aramaic.
The book falls into 6 parts : 1–36, *The Angelic Book,* which recounts the judgement and punishment of the angelic ' watchers ' who fell on account of their love for the daughters of men, Gen 6:1–4, Henoch's inter-

cession for them, and finally his journeys through the **92h** earth and Sheol. It is an attempt to explain the origin of sin and evil in the world.

37–69 : *The Book of Parables* contains three parables **i** or similitudes : the first reveals the secrets of heaven, the second the Messias, the Elect One, the Son of Man, and the third tells of the Great Judgement and the happiness of the just. In a passage remarkable alike for its doctrine and beauty of expression, the second parable describes the Son of Man : ' And before the sun and the heavenly signs were created, before the stars of heaven were made, his name was named before the Lord of spirits. He shall be a staff for the just, that they may lean upon him and not fall ; he shall be the light of peoples, and he shall be the hope of those who suffer in their hearts. All those who dwell upon the dry land shall prostrate themselves and adore him, and they shall bless and sing praises to the Lord of spirits ' ; *cf.* L. de Grandmaison, *Jesus Christ* (London, 1932) 2, 27 f., where he discusses the phrase *Son of Man* and the use made of it by our Lord. 72–82 : *The Book of Astronomy* which comprises the revelations of the angel Uriel to Henoch concerning the heavenly bodies. 83–90 : *The Book of Visions,* which is Henoch's vision of the Flood and of Israel's history up to the establishment of the Messias' reign. 91–105 : *The Book of Exhortation,* a warning foretelling the doom of sinners and the blessings of the just. 93+91:12–17 : *Apocalypse of Weeks,* which stresses the final triumph of the just, their reward, and the final damnation of the wicked.
The Slavonic Henoch is an apocalypse which is some- **j** times known as the *Secrets of Henoch.* From its references to sacrifice it is concluded that the book was written before A.D. 70, and it probably belongs to the first cent. of the Christian era. Henoch in his 365th year is said to have been taken up by angels through the seven heavens to the throne of God. He sees the angels who rule the stars and keep the storehouses of snow and dew. The apostate angels ask him to pray for them. The main interest of the work is the light it throws on some scriptural allusions such as the seven heavens, the presence of evil spirits ' in heavenly places ', and Ezechiel's creatures ' full of eyes ' (*cf.* CE 1, 603).
The Assumption of Moses—This work typical of the **k** apocalyptic apocrypha was first edited in 1861 from a 6th cent. Latin MS found in the Ambrosian Library, Milan. The first few lines, which probably contained the title, and the end of the book are missing. It was written in Hebrew or Aramaic by a Palestinian Pharisee shortly after the deposition of Archelaus in A.D. 6. In character it is something like a *Testament* or *Farewell-speech.* Moses, after appointing Josue his successor, foretells the entry of the Israelites into Canaan, the subsequent schism of the ten tribes, the ever-increasing religious corruption, the Captivity, the impiety of priests and kings, but, in the end, the final heavenly judgement by which Israel would be raised to the stars. It is a good example of the attempts made to halt the growing secularization of religion and to inculcate strict obedience to the Law.
The Fourth Book of Esdras is one of the most widely **l** circulated, read and translated of the Apocrypha. It is a composite work : chh 3–14 were the Jewish original, to which the Christians added chh 1–2 ; 15–16. The Jewish part, written in Hebrew or Aramaic and dating back to the second half of the first cent. A.D. contains seven visions made to Esdras in Babylon during the Exile. The ever-present problems of human life form the subject of these visions : the trials of the just, the prosperity of the wicked, and the apparent greatness of the number of the damned.
The author finds his answer in the inability of the limited intellect of man fully to comprehend the plans of God, owing to the immensity of divine wisdom. In the last vision Esdras is bidden to write some books of instruction for future generations, because the Law had been burnt and the people had become ignorant

92 l of it. Esdras then dictated to five scribes twenty-four books which were to be for all, and, in addition, seventy which were esoteric or reserved for the wise.

Several antiphons and liturgical texts, including the famous Reproaches on Good Friday, the Easter antiphons for martyrs, and the *Requiem Aeternam* of the office of the Dead, may be traced to this book. Their presence in our liturgy may be due to Byzantine influence (*cf.* I. Schuster, *The Sacramentary* (London, 1924), I, 80 f., 405).

m **The Syriac Apocalypse of Baruch** is so called from the Syriac form in which it has come down to us. Though written towards the end of the first cent. A.D., it professes to describe revelations made to Baruch at the time of the destruction of Jerusalem by the Babylonians. Charles describes it as ' almost the last noble utterance of Judaism before it plunged into the dark and oppressive years that followed the destruction of Jerusalem ', CAP 2, 470. It is noteworthy for its treatment, from the point of view of the Pharisees, of such important doctrines as the Messias and his kingdom, original sin and free-will, the future judgement and the resurrection.

The Greek Apocalypse of Baruch is of Jewish origin, and relates the journey of Baruch through the five heavens. It belongs to the second cent., and shows signs of having been edited by a Christian writer.

n **The Apocalypse of Abraham** belongs to the end of the first or beginning of the second cent. A.D., and is of Jewish origin. It was originally written in Hebrew or Aramaic. Chh 1–8 tell of Abraham's conversion from idolatry to monotheism : the remaining chapters, which are apocalyptic, comprise visions concerning the future of the Jewish race.

o **The Sibylline Oracles** in their present form consist of twelve books numbered 1–8 ; 11–14 ; an enumeration which does not represent any single MS but is the result of the fusion of three different types of text (*cf.* *H. N. Bate, *The Sibylline Oracles* (London, 1918) 16). The oracles and predictions ascribed to the Sibyl, the oldest of the Greek prophets, enjoyed great popularity and veneration throughout the Graeco-Roman world. In the capital itself they were jealously guarded and consulted in times of serious crisis. Her prophecies, marked by no fixed sequence or form, spoke of doom and disaster. Because of their awe-inspiring influence in moulding the religious thought and outlook of the time, the Hellenistic Jews of Alexandria enlisted the support of this kind of literature during the second cent. B.C. as a powerful means of propagating Jewish doctrine and faith. This practice continued down to Christian times and was borrowed by Christians themselves who, in their turn, brought into existence Christian Sibylline oracles. In some cases Christians revised or interpolated the Jewish sibylline writings, and it is now almost impossible to determine exactly what is Christian and what Jewish. Arendzen writes, ' Probably a dozen different Jewish hands, if not more, worked at the Sibyllines from 160 B.C. to A.D. 240. The varying fortunes of the Jewish race for four hundred years are thus mirrored in this collection of oracles. They are mostly oracles of doom on Israel's foes, and rather poor copies of the *Burdens* against the nations of Isaias, Jeremias and Ezechiel. The destruction of the world by water, fire, war, pestilence, earthquake and famine, and the subsequent happiness of Israel in the Messianic kingdom are commonplaces which grow monotonous ', J. P. Arendzen, *Men and Manners in the Days of Christ* (London, 1928) 166. So it is that in the *Dies Irae* the Sibyl and David are quoted as testifying to the terrors of the judgement day, *Teste David cum Sibylla*, *cf.* *F. J. E. Raby, *A History of Christian-Latin Poetry* (Oxford, 1927) 446 f.

HISTORICAL APOCRYPHA

93a **The Book of Jubilees** derives its name from the fact that it divides the history of Israel, of which it treats,

from the Creation to the time of Moses and the giving **93a** of the Law on Sinai into jubilee periods of forty-nine years. It is really a free reproduction of the biblical narrative, interspersed with legendary additions, with special emphasis on the greatness of the Law and its abiding validity, and upon the divine origin of certain legal practices, the strict observance of which it is concerned to inculcate. The author was desirous of a reform in the rules concerning the regulation of the calendar and festivals. It is also known as the *Little Genesis* and the *Apocalypse of Moses*, to whom the revelation was supposed to have been made on Sinai by the Angel of the Presence, 1, 27. Its date and authorship are uncertain ; it may belong to the late second or first cent. B.C.

The Third Book of Esdras must be distinguished from **b** the canonical books of Esdras and Nehemias. Confusion is apt to arise since 3 Esd is sometimes called 1 Esd from its position in the LXX, the old Latin and Syriac versions, while Esd Neh which follow it are called 2 Esd. In the Vg it is set apart from the canonical books in an appendix under the name 3 Esd. For the most part the book corresponds with Esd Neh with the exception of the added section, 3:1–5:6, which is taken from elsewhere and describes an intellectual competition between three members of Darius' bodyguard in which Zorobabel, one of the three, was successful. 3 Esd seems to be independent of Esd Neh, and it is suggested that there are good grounds for maintaining that it is a direct translation of a Hebrew-Aramaic original, which differed in many ways, notably in the historical sequence of events, from the MT.

The Third Book of Maccabees—This is a strange title **c** for a book in which Maccabean history finds no place, but is due, no doubt, to its position in MSS after the first two Maccabean books. The author writes of events in Egypt during the reign of Ptolemy Philopater after his victory over Antiochus the Great at Raphia in 217 B.C. Enraged by the High Priest's refusal to allow him to enter the Holy of Holies, Ptolemy resolved to take his revenge on the Jews living in his domains. Ch 4 describes how they were brought to Alexandria and cruelly tormented. The king finally ordered that they should all be trampled to death in the hippodrome at Alexandria by infuriated elephants. At the prayer of Eleazar, a priest, angels sent from heaven rescue the Israelites by turning the elephants against their keepers. As a result of this Ptolemy becomes their friend and protector, issues a letter proclaiming their loyalty, grants them a seven days' feast, and allows them to return home and take vengeance upon apostates. The purpose behind the story is obviously to stimulate the enthusiasm of the Jews for their religion, to encourage them in adversity, to warn apostates, and to vindicate Jewish loyalty to civil authority. Events similar to those recounted in 3 Mac are to be found in Josephus *Contra Apionem*, 2, 5, but in a different context. Both accounts are based upon some historical events the time and circumstances of which cannot now be accurately determined. The book was written in Greek and belongs to the first cent. B.C. according to some scholars, but other prefer a later date, at the beginning of the first cent. A.D.

The Life of Adam and Eve, or Apocalypse of Moses— **d** The Latin *Life of Adam and Eve* and the Greek *Apocalypse of Moses* are both based upon the same Hebrew or Aramaic Jewish original. ' It is possible to prove that the apocryphas, *Apocalypsis Moysis* and *Vita Adae et Evae*, and to a certain degree even their Slavonic, Syriac, Ethiopic, and Arabic offshoots are of identical Jewish origin ', JE 1, 179. These works embody a mass of legend about the life of our first parents. They serve to show later Jewish teaching, especially on the resurrection and future life, at the end of the first cent. A.D. when they were written.

The Ascension of Isaias is a composite work comprising **e** three originally distinct writings, the *Martyrdom of Isaias*, 1:1–3:12 and 5:1*b*–14, which is of Jewish origin ;

93e a christian apocalypse, known as the *Testament of Ezechias*, 3:13–5:1a ; and the *Vision of Isaias*, also of Christian origin, 6:1–11:40.

In its present form it seems to date back to the second cent. A.D., but the first part is more likely to be earlier, probably belonging to the first cent., if not to pre-Christian times. We are introduced, in the earlier section, to Isaias the prophet foretelling his own death at the hands of Manasses, the king in ' whose heart Beliar dwelt '. He is later denounced to the king for his alleged prophecies against him and against Jerusalem. The outcome of it all is the martyrdom of Isaias, told in the story, so familiar to Jews and Christians, of his being sawn asunder with a wooden saw (*cf.* ch 5). But meanwhile the so-called *Testament of Ezechias* has explained the reason for Beliar's hatred of Isaias, namely because he had foretold the destruction of Satan's power by Christ. The third part, the *Vision*, describes the prophet's journeys through the seven heavens where he is allowed to contemplate many hidden secrets. The chief value of the work is the light it throws upon the life of the early Church.

f The Book of Aseneth is a romance woven round the references to Joseph's marriage to Aseneth in Gen 41:45 ff. It is Jewish in character, but has been subjected to Christian revision. Its date is probably second cent. A.D. Kohler says it belongs to ' the Hellenistic propaganda literature by which Jewish writers endeavoured to win the non-Jewish world for the Jewish faith, while at the same time representing their Hebrew ancestors as physical as well as moral heroes ', JE 2, 176.

DIDACTIC APOCRYPHA

g The Testament of the Twelve Patriarchs—The general theme of this work is ethical. The twelve sons of Jacob are represented as giving their last words to their children, as Jacob himself had done to his sons in Gen 49:1–27. Each discourse falls into three parts, a brief autobiographical sketch of the Patriarch with emphasis upon his characteristic vice or virtue, then a moral lesson and exhortation based upon it, and finally a prophecy regarding the future of his descendants. The original language was either Hebrew or Aramaic, and its date was the second half of the 2nd cent. B.C. The Greek text contains some Christian interpolations.

h The Psalms of Solomon—These Psalms, eighteen in number, were written at about the time when Pompey captured Jerusalem, 63 B.C. Their author, a Palestinian Pharisee, expresses his confidence in God and the future, his contempt for wrongdoers, his sorrow at his country's misfortunes, and his opposition to the Hasmonean dynasty. His hope is fixed on the coming glorious reign of the Messias. The reason for their ascription to Solomon is not clear ; the title may, of course, be a later scribal addition.

i The Prayer of Manasses owes its origin to 2 Par 33:11–13 ; 18 f. It is an attempt to supply the prayer to which the passage refers. Though short the prayer is beautiful : it opens with praise of God, vv 1–7 ; then follows an earnest prayer for pardon from sin, vv 8–18 ; it concludes with a short doxology. This prayer is found in the appendix to the Vg. The text of the prayer appears for the first time in the *Didascalia*, 2, 22, but its composition is much earlier, probably first cent. B.C.

j The Fourth Book of Maccabees is a Hellenistic work, written at the beginning of the Christian era, with the purpose of showing that right reason, under the guidance of the Law, was the complete master of all the passions—it is an attempt to blend orthodox Jewish faith and Stoic philosophy. The theme is illustrated from Jewish history, especially from the heroic sufferings of the Maccabean martyrs ; hence the title of the book. It has been argued that it was primarily a lecture or address for the synagogue.

Psalm 151 is found as an additional psalm in the LXX **93k** with the title : ' This psalm was written by David with his own hand, though it is outside the number, composed when he fought Goliad (*sic*) in single combat '. It is a short psalm of eight verses, in which David boasts that though the least of his brethren, he was chosen to fight and overcome Goliath. Its origin is uncertain, and it has no claim to be considered genuine. Part of it, however, is to be found in the second responsory of Matins for Sundays and Thursdays after Pentecost : ' He it was who sent his angel and took me from my father's sheep, and anointed me with the oil of his anointing '. The text of the psalm is to be found in HDB 4, 146.

THE APOCRYPHA OF THE NT

We do not include under this heading those **94a** books, produced during the 1st and 2nd cent., now grouped together under the name *Apostolic Fathers*, some of which, for a short time, seemed to linger on the edge of the Canon before being finally excluded, such as the Epistle of Clement to the Corinthians, the Epistles of Ignatius, the Epistle of Barnabas and the Pastor of Hermas. We intend to confine ourselves, rather, to those writings which seem to make a false claim to be considered canonical and part of the NT, and of which some were tendentious or heretical. They may be conveniently grouped, analogously to the NT, as Gospels, Acts, Epistles, and Apocalypses.

Apocryphal Gospels—The Gospels according to the **b** Hebrews, according to the Egyptians, of the Ebionites. The Protevangelium of James, the Gospels of Peter, Thomas, Bartholomew, Nicodemus, and Philip. The Arabic Gospel of the Infancy, the History of Joseph the Carpenter, and the Assumption of Mary.

Apocryphal Acts—Acts of Peter, John, Paul. The Preaching of Peter, Acts of Andrew, Thomas, Philip, Matthew, Barnabas.

Apocryphal Epistles—Letters of our Lord and Abgar ; Letters of Paul and Seneca ; Correspondence between Paul and the Corinthians, the Epistle to the Laodiceans, the Epistle of the Apostles or Discourses of our Lord with the Apostles.

Apocryphal Apocalypses—Apocalypses of Peter, Paul, Thomas, Stephen, John, Blessed Virgin Mary, and others.

In addition to these there are the **Agrapha**, *i.e.* deeds or sayings of our Lord which find no mention in the Gospels (*cf.* Jn 20:30 ; 21:25), but which have been preserved and handed down to us by tradition. They are to be found here and there in the writings of the Fathers, in some biblical MSS and a few papyri fragments, but not many of them are considered authentic (*cf.* Steinmueller, 1, 117).

The Origin of the NT Apocrypha—It may be said, **c** briefly, that the NT Apocrypha owe their existence to the fact that the narratives given to us in the canonical Scriptures are short and often undetailed. People were anxious to know more about our Lord's birth and early life. They wished for more details about his Mother and the other characters who played a part in the Gospel story. They wanted to know where those apostles, who are not mentioned in the Acts, exercised their missionary zeal. They were curious, too, about the future life and what happens after death. The Apocrypha set out to supply these apparent omissions and to supplement the knowledge of the faithful. Many legends were woven round the hidden life of our Lord, the life of Mary and the later activities of the Apostles, and more apocalypses appeared in order to satisfy popular desire. Most of this apocryphal literature is ill-founded, but some has been found worthy of credence and a small amount has been absorbed into the Church's liturgy and played its part in popular devotion and Christian art. We will now consider some of the more important works.

4d The Protevangelium of James is a very popular and widely read story of our Lady's life and the birth of her Son. It is based on the Gospel narrative which it fills out with many legendary and imaginative details, often of a puerile character. It tells how Mary was miraculously born to Joachim and Anna (incidentally, the first mention of the names of Mary's parents), and how, when three years old, she was presented in the Temple. Nine years later Joseph was miraculously singled out to be her spouse by a sign given to the High Priest—a dove coming forth from Joseph's rod and resting upon his head. The account of the birth of Christ is embellished with all kinds of unrestrained and unimpressive details. The book is of interest, however, as an indication of the early veneration for the Blessed Virgin and was written probably between A.D. 150 and 180.

e The Gospel of Thomas is another infancy gospel belonging to the 2nd cent. but of heterodox origin. It recounts extravagant youthful miracles of our Lord between the ages of five and twelve, as, for instance, when he formed clay birds on the Sabbath, and on being rebuked clapped his hands and caused them to fly away. The Child is represented as petulant, bringing sudden death to another child who collided with him, and when the bystanders blame him for such action, he strikes them with blindness. Such a picture stands in marked contrast to the quiet dignity of St Luke's story.

f The Assumption of Mary—The many translations and various forms of this work attest its wide popularity. In its Greek form it is introduced as ' The Narrative of St John the Theologian concerning the Falling Asleep of the Holy Mother of God ', but the Latin version ascribes it to Melito of Sardis. In all probability it belongs to the 4th cent. It tells of the death of Mary and how the apostles were summoned to mount upon the clouds and assemble from all parts of the earth round her deathbed. Those who had died were raised to life in order to be present. For three days after her death the ' voices of invisible angels were heard glorifying Christ our God which was born of her. And when the third day was fulfilled the voices were no more heard, and thereafter we all perceived that her spotless and precious body was translated into paradise ', James, *Apoc. NT*, 208. The interest which centred round the early tradition of Mary's Assumption is further illustrated by the added legendary details.

g The Letters of Our Lord and Abgar—The historian Eus., I, 13 (PG 20, 119 ff.) records the story of Abgar, king of Edessa, who wrote to our Lord asking him to come and cure him of the terrible disease with which he was afflicted. Jesus sends back a written reply, praising his faith and assuring him that although he could not come in person he would certainly send one of his apostles, after his Ascension, to heal him. This legend, which belongs to the first part of the 3rd cent., became popular during the Middle Ages and has left its mark on the Syrian and Celtic liturgies (*cf.* CE I, 43).

h The Letters of St Paul and Seneca—There are fourteen letters, written in Latin, which were known to Jerome and Augustine and were therefore in existence in the 4th cent. The contents of the letters are rather commonplace and the style is poor. Seneca tells Paul that he has been much refreshed by reading his epistles, but expresses his anxiety lest ' polish of style ' be wanting to his ' majesty of thought '. He mentions Nero's favourable reception of his views. In his reply the Apostle shows appreciation of the philosopher's goodwill, but warns him against bringing the Christian religion any more to the notice of Poppaea and Nero. Seneca then sends Paul a book on ' elegance of expression ', and sympathizes with the sufferings of the Christians. In conclusion Paul expresses the hope that he may become a ' new author, by showing forth with the graces of rhetoric the unblameable wisdom of Jesus Christ, which you, having wellnigh attained

it, will instil into the temporal monarch, his servants, **94h** and intimate friends ', James, *Apoc. NT*, 484.

The Acts of Peter were written in Greek *c* A.D. 200. **i** It is said that when Paul left Rome for Spain, Peter was summoned to the capital from Jerusalem to combat the errors of Simon Magus. It is these Acts which give us the famous and familiar ' Quo Vadis ' story and the description of Peter's being crucified head downwards. Traces of Gnostic influences are found here and there. One interesting example occurs quite early, in the description of the Eucharistic sacrifice offered by Paul before he sets out for Spain. We notice that bread and water are brought for the sacrifice in accordance with the Gnostic Encratite practice, for they regarded wine as evil, *cf.* Epiphanius, *Adv. Haer.*, 2, 1, 47 (PG 41, 853). ' Now they brought unto Paul bread and water for the sacrifice that he might make prayer and distribute it to every one. Among whom it befell that a woman named Rufina desired, she also, to receive the Eucharist at the hands of Paul ; to whom Paul, filled with the spirit of God, said as she drew near : Rufina, thou comest not worthily to the altar of God, arising from beside one that is not thine husband but an adulterer, and essayest to receive the Eucharist of God ', James, *Apoc. NT*, 304.

The Apocalypse of Paul—The author pretends that **j** this work was discovered in the foundations of St Paul's house at Tarsus. The Apostle is represented as urging the world to repent of its crimes because the forces of nature are crying out against the wickedness of the human race and calling for punishment of sinners. He witnesses the ultimate fate of just and unjust, and sees the torments of the wicked in Hell. The terrible scenes so vividly depicted were known to Dante, who made some use of them in his *Inferno*. Torments which surpass all others are reserved for those who confess not that ' Christ is come in the flesh and that the Virgin Mary bare him, and whosoever saith of the bread and the cup of blessing of the Eucharist that it is not the body and blood of Christ ', James, *Apoc. NT*, 547 (*cf.* DBV (S) I, 468). The work is generally assigned to the 4th cent. but some writers place it much earlier (*cf.* Pope, *op. cit.*, 293). The work was widely read in the Middle Ages, despite St Augustine's severe condemnation of it.

The Church and the Apocrypha—In the earliest period **k** little objection seems to have been made to the Apocrypha. The book of Henoch and the Assumption of Moses had been quoted in the canonical epistle of Jude, and there was in places a lingering hesitation about the inspired character of some of these books, such as the Esdras apocrypha. But with the rapid increase of Christian apocryphal literature and its widespread use by the heretical sects amongst whom some of it arose, the Fathers began to examine it more carefully. Their verdict was highly unfavourable, and they frequently warn the faithful against such writings. Irenaeus denounces the heretics because ' They adduce an unspeakable number of apocryphal and spurious writings, which they themselves have forged, to bewilder the minds of foolish men, and of such as are ignorant of the Scriptures of truth ', *Adv. Haer.*, I, 20. Origen was outspoken in his condemnation, and Eusebius no less severely writes, ' We have been compelled to make a catalogue . . . in order that we might know these same writings and those which have been put forward by the heretics in the name of the apostles, whether as containing Gospels of Peter, Thomas or Matthias or of some others besides these, or as containing Acts of Andrew and John and the other apostles. None of these has been thought worthy of any kind of mention in a treatise by any member of the successive generations of ecclesiastical writers. The character of their style, also, is far removed from that of the apostles, and the thought and tenor of their contents is so much out of harmony with true orthodoxy as to prove that they are certainly the forgeries of heretics. For this reason they ought not to be placed amongst the spurious writings, but

94k rejected as altogether monstrous and impious.', *Hist. Eccl.* 3, 25.

l The first official declaration about them comes from the Council of Hippo (A.D. 393) which said that apart from the canonical Scriptures nothing was to be read in the church under the heading 'Sacred Scripture'. This enactment was repeated at Carthage in 397, Dz 92. The so-called Decree of Gelasius, variously ascribed to Damasus, Gelasius, and Hormisdas, but, as now seems almost certain, of much later origin (*cf*. JTS 14 (1913) 321 ff. ; 469 ff.) contains a list of about forty books which it condemns as apocryphal. Innocent I in his letter to Exsuperius also condemns them, EB 17. In the course of time these condemnations were forgotten, the apocrypha came to enjoy once again great popularity, and in the Middle Ages exercised no small influence on devotion, art and literature.

m The Value of the Apocrypha—Their value, from the theological point of view, is small, for they contain little that could deepen our understanding of divine revelation. But both Jewish and Christian apocrypha serve to throw light on the times in which they were **94n** written. The former reveal the doctrines which were to the forefront and commonly accepted at the time of our Lord ; the latter make known to us what interested the early Christians. We learn what held their attention, what attracted their veneration and devotion, what ideals they cherished for this life and what they expected to find in the next. Nor must we overlook the part they have played in the liturgy and in the literature and art of the Middle Ages. To them we owe the feast of the Presentation of our Lady (*cf*. Schuster, *op. cit*., 5, 290) and the names of Joachim and Anna. Some of the masterpieces of art and literature drew their inspiration from them (*cf*. DBV (S) 1, 468 ; E. Male, *L'Art religieux en France* (Paris, 1923) ch 3). And finally, even where they fail, they are not without their value, for a mere cursory reading of the legends, marvels and aberrations of the Apocrypha intensifies our appreciation of the true Scriptures, setting in gratifying relief the quiet simplicity and unassuming majesty of the inspired Word of God.

(Sections 95 to 98 vacant)

THE MEANING OF THE OLD TESTAMENT

By E. F. SUTCLIFFE, S.J.

99a **The Non-Religious Interest of the OT**—Why do we still take an interest in the Old Testament? The OT has been replaced by the NT, and therefore why dissipate our energies which could be wholly and usefully devoted to the study of the NT and the effort to elucidate passages still obscure after all these centuries? Before answering these questions which raise a purely religious issue, it is well first to glance at the importance of the OT from the point of view of human interest and its place in various branches of study. In the history of world literature the books of the OT must always have an honoured place on account both of their antiquity and beauty as literary works of art. The literature of Rome is recent compared to that of Israel, and the most ancient monuments of Greek literature as handed down in the Homeric poems, even on the most generous estimate of their antiquity, were composed long after the time of Moses. The earliest Chinese songs and lyrics may antedate the oldest Hebrew literature, and as the Vedic hymns were already old and in part no longer understood when collected about 1000 B.C. their origin must go back several centuries earlier, probably into the first half **b** of the second millennium. Literature, it must be remembered, may be literature in fact before it can acquire the name in its etymological sense, before, that is, it is committed to writing. And the great stories of the patriarchs, at least in oral form, owe their origin to a time long preceding the age of Moses. Even in this form, however, they yield in antiquity to literary monuments of other Middle East races, the Sumerians, the Babylonians and the Egyptians. But inferior though they are in age, their literary merit far exceeds that of these other peoples. In the field of historical writing, in particular, as Pope Pius XII has recently reminded us, the discoveries of the last decades have shown the pre-eminence of the Hebrews in point both of antiquity and of accuracy, AAS 35 (1943) 315. Apart from divine inspiration this superiority is to be attributed to the religious character and aim of the historical records preserved in the Bible. This literary genius of the Hebrews is the more remarkable in view of their general artistic penury.

c These historical writings not only preserve the memory of the religious history of Israel but incidentally are valuable aids to the secular historian in reconstructing the partially known story of other ancient peoples. For the study of Semitic philology the OT is of prime importance as so few remains of ancient Hebrew exist outside its pages. The damp soil of Palestine has been unfavourable to the preservation of hand-written documents and the number of inscriptions cut on stone or rock is surprisingly small. Further, quite apart still from its religious values, the OT affords most interesting information concerning early 'scientific' beliefs, ancient customs, and legal practices. For us, however, the OT would always be of supreme importance even if it in no way served these secular branches of knowledge, and that on account of its religious character and divine origin. But before considering its importance for Christians we must first of all consider the purposes for which it was originally written.

d **The Meaning of the OT for the Israelites**—The OT was inspired and written primarily for the benefit of the Hebrew nation, which God had chosen to be his **99d** own special possession, Ex 19:5. For the members of that race it contained the history of the Covenant entered into with them by God, the divinely sanctioned code of law, both civil and religious, based upon the Covenant, and the history of the subsequent mutual relations of God and his people. It contained, in particular, the record of God's fulfilment of his promise, Deut 18:18, to send a line of prophets who should mediate between himself and the people, with a very full account of the messages delivered by them in God's name. And not only was it the devout Israelite's religious history and law-book, but also his prayer-book and practical guide to life with its collections of beautiful hymns of praise and thanksgiving and written storehouse of divinely sanctioned maxims of the wise handed on for the guidance of future generations.

In a word the OT was a divine library of books affording help and counsel, commands and prohibitions, **e** touching all aspects of life. But it was not a library of fixed extent and of definitely limited content. With the passing of the centuries the number of its scrolls grew as the Divine Wisdom extended the gift of inspiration to new writers and gradually too the extent of revelation expanded as God made known new truths, as about his own spiritual nature, the spiritual character of man's soul with its capacity for independent existence after severance from the body, the reward of the good and the punishment of the unrepentant wicked after death.

To what extent was this wonderful gift valued and **f** utilized by its recipients? With all its literary beauty the OT did not teach the highest form of religion, or the noblest norms of morality, or the most perfect system of law. But in all respects it offered what was most suitable to the mental and spiritual development attained by the Israelites. No doubt there were at all epochs devout souls whose delight it would have been to read and meditate on the holy books and strive to conform their lives to the ideals there presented. But to what extent did this divine library actually influence the people? The knowledge of letters seems to have been early diffused if we may judge by the example of the chance boy of Succoth who wrote down the names of seventy-seven men of the town, Jud 8:14. But were the scrolls of the law and other sacred books multiplied sufficiently to make them at all widely accessible? This seems improbable at the least. Moses ordered that his book should be laid up by the side of the ark of the covenant, Deut 31:26. On account of the sanctity of such a document laid **g** up in such a place it appears unlikely that copies would be made without express injunction given to that end, and the only injunction of the kind is that laid on the king at his accession to the throne, Deut 17:18. That this command was never obeyed cannot be affirmed, but the evidence afforded by the history of Israel up to the time of the Exile is that the law was not held in great honour and that the observance of the law, such as it was, was due rather to traditional knowledge than to study of its written prescriptions. The law according to Deut 31:10–13 was to be read every sabbatical year at the Feast of Tabernacles, but it is hard to believe that this was ever done during

99g the troubled period of the Judges, and what is recorded of the respect shown for the law after the building of the temple makes it doubtful whether the custom was then introduced. By the time of Josias the book of the law had been lost, though it was remembered that it had existed, 4 Kg 22:8. This suggests that the copy then found in the course of restoration work in the temple was the only one known to exist. After the exile the law came to be held in very high regard, but even then the knowledge and practice of it seem to have been of slow growth. In the time of Nehemias we are told that they ' discovered ' in reading the law how the Feast of Tabernacles was to be celebrated and then proceeded to keep it as it had not been kept since the days of Josue, Neh 8:14, 17. Later genuine religion reached in some the heroic heights exemplified by the sufferings cheerfully borne by the Maccabean Martyrs. With others religion degenerated into a legalistic idolatry of the law quite alien from its true spirit. This was one of the intensely hostile forces with which our Lord had to contend in his effort to establish the New Kingdom of God.

100a **Our Lord and the Old Testament**—Though our Lord repudiated the unbending and pitiless obedience to the letter of the law preached and practised by the Pharisees, Mt 12:1-7, 10-13, the law itself and the institutions of the OT were sacred. The temple was the house of God and must not be profaned by secular uses, Mt 21:12 f. ; the priests, whatever their personal shortcomings, were the accredited ministers of God to whom due deference must be paid, Mt 8:4. For him as for other Jews the books of the OT were inspired and sacred. Whatever was ' written ' was of unchallengeable authority, and if David wrote a psalm of the psalter it was written in the Spirit, Mt 4:4, 6, 7 ; 22:43. Still, early in his preaching career he indicated that sacred though it was, the validity of the OT was only for a time. Not the most insignificant portion of it would or could be set aside, he said, but with the added clause ' till all be fulfilled ', Mt 5:18 ; and he let it be known further that he himself had come to

b fulfil it, Mt 5:17. This same teaching he conveyed in different ways. He asserted his superiority to the temple, Mt 12:6, and his inherent authority over the God-given institution of the Sabbath. The Sabbath was made for the benefit of man, and as, he went on to imply, the Son of Man has full authority over man, so also has he authority over the Sabbath since it was instituted to serve man's needs, Mk 2:27 f. He set aside the Mosaic permission of divorce and recalled the law of marriage to its primitive strictness, Mt 19:8 f. He showed the imperfection of the moral law promulgated on Sinai, though written by God's own finger on the tablets of stone, and himself not only preached a higher norm of action but proclaimed its sanction in the life to come, Mt 5:21 f. In such various ways he made it clear that the Kingdom of God he preached and laboured to establish was to bring the old covenant to its fulfilment and by so doing to replace it. His culminating speech and act in this regard were reserved by him for the evening before he suffered, when he instituted the new covenant or testament and its central and most sacred rite, Mt 26:26-28.

101a **The Old Testament in Apostolic Times**—Though the Apostles followed, of course, in the footsteps of their Master, it did not become at once apparent to the early Church that the whole **ceremonial law of the OT** was **no longer binding** under the new covenant. In particular was this the case with regard to circumcision. It needed a vision and the outpouring of the Holy Ghost on uncircumcised Gentiles to teach this fundamentally important lesson to St Peter, and his witness and authority to have the matter definitively settled by the Council of Jerusalem, Act 10:1-48 ; 15:5-29. The Council decided the question of principle that the Mosaic law was not obligatory on Christians. Nonetheless the Council decreed that Christians should still observe certain prescriptions of the Mosaic law, as the prohibition of consuming blood, not, however,

in virtue of the old ordinance, but in virtue of the **101** authority of the Council, or because in its own words ' it has seemed good to the Holy Ghost and to us '. And the motive which prompted the Council to impose these restrictions, namely, the desire to avoid giving unnecessary scandal, 15:21, implied that the new law was a temporary measure designed to last only as long as the need. This Council, of course, did not itself abrogate the Mosaic law, but solemnly promulgated the fact that it had been already in fact abrogated by the new dispensation instituted by Christ. Together with the rest of the Mosaic ordinances the Council implicitly promulgated the freedom of Christians from the obligation of Sabbath observance. Already in the NT there are signs of Sunday observance, Ac 20:7 ; 1 Cor 16:2 ; Apoc 1:10 ; and cf. Rom 14:5. Later this practice of keeping the Sunday holy as a day of rest and worship attained the status of law and obligation, cf. DTC art. ' Dimanche ' 1309-12.

St Paul explained this Christian freedom to the **b** Galatians. He compared the law to a pedagogue or tutor, Gal 3:24, whose surveillance lasted only till his young charge was ripe enough in years and discretion to be allowed freedom from daily supervision. The law had acted as a tutor of the Jews until the time came when they could attain justification by faith in the living Christ. This time, St Paul pointed out, had come, and therefore ' we are no longer under a tutor ', Gal 3:23-25, for the state of sanctifying grace conferred by Christian faith and Baptism, as he implies, is a state of spiritual maturity compared to that attainable by virtue of the practices of the OT which were not instituted by God as channels of supernatural grace. The Apostle then uses another comparison to drive home this lesson of the freedom of Christians from servitude to the law. The spiritual state of people under the law was immature like the condition of a minor placed by his father's disposition under the control of guardians and stewards. And just as the ward attains his freedom and throws off this subjection on attaining the preordained age, so the Israelite people, now that the fullness of time ordained by God had come, were no longer bound by the material observances which had been imposed upon them during the long period of religious immaturity, Gal 4:1-5.

This preparatory character of the law is especially **c** manifest in its **incapacity to bestow true justification** in the sight of God or ' the righteousness of God ', Gal 3:11 ; Rom 10:3. The law could not offer the gifts of supernatural grace. Its promises of reward were confined to benefits of a purely temporal order. The recompense promised to legal righteousness, that is to strict observance of the law, was length of days and prosperity. ' Keep my statutes and my judgements : the man who does them, shall have life through them ', Lev 18:5 quoted Gal 3:12 and Rom 10:5. So the precept to pay due honour to father and mother, which St Paul calls ' the first commandment with a promise ', is followed by the words ' that thy days may be long and that it may be well with thee upon the land that Yahweh thy God is about to give thee ', Deut 5:16 quoted Eph 6:2 f.

What St Paul has to say of this immaturity and pre- **d** paratory character of the OT he sums up in the words **' the end of the law is Christ '** leading up to that righteousness of God which is bestowed as the reward of faith, Rom 10:4. The temporal end of the law as a valid dispensation came with the advent of Christ, but St Paul was not speaking chronologically. His meaning was that the purpose of the law and its scope was to lead on to Christ in whom it found its fulfilment. This beacon truth that the whole long course of OT history and development was on a road leading slowly but surely to Christ supposes and rests on the further truth that the hand of God was guiding the course of Israelite history as played out on the stage of human relationships and also the course of its literary record together with all the elements which went to produce it. This

01d means that we cannot reach the core of the OT if we conduct our study of it on the lines suitable to purely human history and purely human records. To hope for success we must attempt to read these sacred writings in the same spirit in which they were written.

e Otherwise we shall not see the New Testament fore-shadowed in the Old, despite the fact that as Augustine said, in the Old Testament the New is present though obscure and in the New the meaning of the Old is manifest (' In Vetere Testamento Novum latet et in Novo Vetus patet ', *Quaest. in Hept.* 2, 73, PL 34, 623). And Pope Leo XIII has warned us that as the Holy Ghost is the primary author of Holy Scripture, its words sometimes contain ' a fuller and more recondite sense than appears to be expressed by the letter or to be indicated by hermeneutical laws ', EB 93. St Augustine further says that our Saviour Jesus Christ ' spoke of himself in the prophets, for he is the Word of God, and if the prophets said aught of him, it was because they were full of the Word of God ; hence they announced Christ because they were full of Christ ', *Enarr. in Ps 142*, n. 2, PL 37, 1845. And St Jerome in the preface to his commentary on Isaias writes ' If according to the Apostle Paul Christ is the power of God and the wisdom of God and he who knows nothing of the Scriptures knows nothing of the power of God and his wisdom, ignorance of the Scriptures is ignorance of Christ ' (' ignoratio Scripturarum ignoratio Christi est ', PL 24, 17).

f Before we pass on to consider the meaning of the OT for our own age, it is worth mentioning one point of difference in the decades succeeding the Ascension. Then the books of the NT were either not written or not all written, or existed as yet in comparatively few copies. In other words the writings of the NT were not available even to the pastors of the Church at large for reading and meditation. The books of the Scriptures they had will have been those of the OT ; and for that reason they will probably have played a larger **part in the devotional life of the period** than at any subsequent time in the life of the Church. That St Paul carried copies of the OT Scriptures about with him, 2 Tim 4:13, is, I think, certain. He also exhorted St Timothy to be diligent in reading the Scriptures at the meetings of the faithful at which the reading was accompanied by a discourse, hortatory or doctrinal, 1 Tim 4:13. In this text the Gospels perhaps already included some of the Gospels ; *cf.* Justin, *Apol.* 1, 67, PG 6, 429B, in whose time likewise the sermon followed the reading of a portion of the Gospels or the prophets.

02a **The Meaning and Value of the Old Testament Today—** There can be no essential difference in the regard of the Church for the OT at different periods of her history, since its sacred character as the inspired word of God can never undergo modification. Hence, though it is profitable to consider it from the stand-point of our own times, we may be guided in our consideration by St Paul's teaching concerning it. Writing to the Romans, 15:4, he lays it down that whatever was written of old ' was written for our instruction that we might hold on to hope through the patience and consolation instilled by the Scriptures '. And to Timothy, who had been familiar with the books of the OT from childhood, he says that ' they are able to make you wise unto salvation through faith in Christ Jesus ; every Scripture being inspired of God is useful for teaching, for reproof, for correction, for training in justness, that the man of God may be perfect, equipped for every good work ', 2 Tim 3:15-17.

b The OT, therefore, was not intended by God for the exclusive benefit of those who lived under the old law. Not merely can Christians learn to bear the trials and sufferings of life and especially those endured for the sake of religion, from the examples and teaching of the OT, and from the same source derive **spiritual consolation** in times of affliction or persecution, but it was the positive purpose of God that they should. And this source of strength is by no means to be over-

looked even though more powerful motives for peace **102b** of mind and even cheerfulness in suffering are furnished by the words and deeds of the Son of God. The tense used by St Paul shows the meaning to be, not that we should win hope, but that we should be encouraged to persevere in hope through the consolation in endur-ance to be learnt from the Scriptures. So St John Chrysostom who paraphrases ' lest we be dejected ' and points out the interactions of patience and hope. Hope ministers strength to endure with fortitude, and patient endurance gives fresh ground for hope, PG 60, 646.

When St Paul further says that all Scripture is useful **c** for teaching, for rebuking and correction of moral faults and errors in doctrine, and for positive formation in right-doing, he is thinking of the benefit to be derived primarily by the student of Holy Writ him-self. Knowledge of the Scriptures is of the utmost importance for the preacher and moral reformer, but these will not achieve much unless they have first applied the lessons of the sacred books to themselves and the improvement of their own lives.

St Paul says that the OT is useful as a **source of teach- d ing,** but he would be the first to admit that it needs supplementing from the NT. The OT is definite from the beginning concerning man's survival after death, but for the greater part of its course it is vague con-cerning the constitution of man and what element of man actually survives. It is from the late book of Wisdom that we first learn that ' the souls ' of the departed just are in the hand of God, 3:1. Similarly it is only in the last centuries before Christ that the doctrine of future rewards and punishments is to be found. And it is only in 2 Macc 12:39-46 (2nd cent. B.C.) that we read of prayers and sacrifices for the dead with the implication that there is an intermediate state in which the departed are in a permanent state neither of rewards nor of punishment, and which we have come to call Purgatory. The doctrine of the Trinity remained to be revealed in the NT as also that of supernatural sanctifying grace. Still withal there is a large body of positive doctrine about God, his eternity, his ubiquity, his omnipotence, his justice, his mercy. But the OT has this in common with the NT, that it neither is nor contains a manual of theology. These theological teachings are consequently incidental. Moreover, on account of the development of doctrine over so many hundreds of years knowledge of a doctrine manifested in a later age must not be assumed to have existed in earlier times. It may be said that God reveals himself in the OT as much by action as by direct teaching. And this method of teaching is, of course, for most minds both more intelligible and more impressive than the enunciation of abstract truths.

As in the matter of theological doctrine, so also in that **e** of morality or right **standards of human conduct** the OT needs to be supplemented by the NT. It does not require to be corrected, as what it positively enjoins cannot be intrinsically evil, but, as our Lord taught in the Sermon on the Mount, it omitted positively to prohibit much that the fuller revelation of the NT shows to be sinful. In condescension to the less developed spiritual perceptions of the time only the broad outlines of morality, so to say, are dealt with. It has to be remembered, too, in regard to both positive and negative prescriptions of the old law, that not all rest on eternal and immutable principles of right and wrong. Some, like the strict prohibition to consume blood, were conditioned by the circumstances of the age, and were not, therefore, of permanent validity. Other teachings are not only of permanent, but also of the highest, value, as that of complete and confiding trust in God, a trust based on the conviction, which permeates the OT, that, despite appearances to the contrary, God guides and rules the universe. Nothing happens without his overruling providence : ' Lots are cast into the lap, but they are disposed by the Lord ', Prov. 16:33, which, of course, is far from

102e saying that the lot has been given to us as a means of discovering the secrets of God's omniscience.

f Though the abstract standard of moral rectitude put forward in the OT was so much inferior to that of the NT, nevertheless the ancient Scriptures record many instances of **heroic virtue**. It suffices to recall the faith of Abraham, ' who against hope believed in hope ', Rom 4:18, and his heroic obedience, Gen 22:16, the fearless chastity of Joseph, Gen 39:9, the humility and repentance of David, 2 Kg 12:13, the devouring zeal for God's honour of Elias, 3 Kg 19:14, the incomparable fortitude and fidelity of the Maccabean Martyrs, 2 Macc 7. One of the most moving chapters of the NT is in praise of these ancient Saints : ' They were stoned, they were cut asunder, they were tempted, they were put to death by the sword, they wandered about in sheepskins, in goatskins, being in want, distressed, afflicted, of whom the world was not worthy ', Heb 11:37 f. And this heroic virtue, be it remembered, without the help of the Sacraments, without, except for the Maccabees, the hope of eternal life, without,

g God, without the example of Christ. And if it be asked what especially distinguishes the perfection of Christian Saints from that of these Saints of the old law, I think we may answer that, apart from what was possible only after the Christian revelation such as personal love and devotion to Christ, God made Man, it is the realization of the nothingness of all temporal, earthly wealth. This was not taught in the OT, but is the fruit of the example and teaching of Christ : ' If thou wilt be perfect, go, sell what thou hast and give to the poor . . . and come, follow me ! ', Mt 19:21. It was from this teaching that the Christian world learnt that the goods of this world, beautiful though they are in themselves and the work of God's hands, nonetheless are as a veil that hides God from us, and tend to draw us from his complete service.

h And now it is time to go back to St Paul's teaching that the holy Scriptures of the OT can make wise ' unto salvation through faith in Christ Jesus ', 2 Tim 3:15, and that ' the end of the law is Christ ', Rom 10:4. Hence **the OT led up to Christ by prophecies**, or predictions in word, and by types or figures, or predictions in act and fact. The Jews knew well that their dispensation pointed to the Messias as its goal, as is manifest in the NT, but partly on account of the admitted obscurity of the prophecies, partly on account of the ambitious worldly mentality brought to the reading of the prophets, they had failed to interpret them aright. ' The end of the law is Christ ', writes St Ambrose, ' and his death gave the solution to the enigmas of the prophets, and what was unknown to the Jews when the prophecies were made, later became manifest as the effect of the Lord's passion ', *In Psalm 43 Enarr.* n. 57, PL 14, 1116B. Without this understanding of Christ the prophecies are insipid, says St Augustine : ' Prophecy without any understanding of Christ was only water. . . . Read all the prophetical books omitting Christ, what will you find so insipid and meaningless ? Understand Christ there and not only is your reading full of savour but also inebriating, diverting the mind from the body that forgetting the past you strain forward to the future ', *In Joan. Evang.* Tract. 9, 3, 2 (referring to Phil 3:13), PL 35, 1459. On the partial and apparently conflicting character of OT predictions see § 417e.

i This series of prophecies is scattered over the books of the OT. It begins with general predictions the reference of which to a **personal Messias** becomes intelligible only in the light of later prophecies. Once this central fact emerges that blessing and salvation are to come through one to whom above all others is to belong by special right the title of the Anointed of God, such being the meaning of the synonyms Messias and Christ derived respectively from Hebrew and Greek, then many individual traits of his person, character, kingdom and rule are successively revealed. But nowhere does the OT gather these various particular details

into one picture. Such a unifying delineation would **102** have manifested how apparently conflicting elements were to find their harmonious combination in one and the same person. As always God demands implicit trust and faith : ' Is anything too wonderful for God ? ', Gen 18:14. So often man falls short of this requirement and in his self-satisfaction thinks he can apply the foot-rule of his own limited ideas to the infinite wisdom and power of God. This unifying and harmonious correlation of the prophecies was not to be given till in the fullness of time Jesus Christ revealed it in the unfolding of his own life and death and in the kingdom which he lived and died to establish.

A sketch of **some outstanding prophecies** will serve to **j** illustrate these general and abstract remarks. After the wiles of the evil spirit symbolized by the serpent had robbed our first parents of their innocence and thereby also their descendants of the inheritance which would otherwise have been theirs, God promised the final victory to the human race, not indeed individually but collectively. The seed of the woman was to crush the serpent's head, Gen 3:15. But it could not have been yet understood that this victory was to be gained under the leadership and through the strength of one. In what has been called the second Messianic prophecy God takes the race of Sem under his special protection and promises to bestow especial favour upon it, Gen 9:26 f. Of the race of Sem Abraham then receives an individual call and the promise that through him and his seed all the nations of the earth shall be blessed, Gen 12:3 ; 18:18 ; 22:16–18. Of the issue of Abraham this promise is renewed to Isaac, the child of promise, Gen 26:4. And a further limitation is made when it is repeated to one of Isaac's sons, namely, to Jacob, Gen 28:14. The next limitation of the line of descent through which the blessing forecast was to be brought about, occurs in the blessing of Jacob. Here the patriarch predicts the right of the tribe of Judah to the sceptre which is to abide with it until he comes whose it is, Gen 49:10, a prediction to be echoed centuries later in the words spoken by the Angel of the Child to be born, ' He shall reign in the house of Jacob for ever ', Lk 1:32. The line of descent was still further defined **k** in the prophecy of Nathan, 2 Kg 7:14, in which God promises this honour to the posterity of David. This prediction made a deep impression in OT times. It is often referred to as in Ps 88 and in Ps 131, and gave rise to the designation of the coming King simply under the name of David, Os 3:5 ; Jer 30:9 ; Ez 34:23 f. No wonder the Pharisees knew that the Messias was to be David's son, Mt 22:41, and that the multitudes hailed him as the Son of David, Mt 21:9. With the Davidic ancestry of the Messias is aptly conjoined the prophecy of his birth at Bethlehem, the city of David, Mic 5:2, another prophecy well understood by the rulers of the Jews, Mt 2:5 f. That he was to be virginally conceived was also understood by the pre-Christian Jews, as is shown by the sense-translation of the LXX, ' Behold, a virgin shall conceive and bear a child ', Is 7:14. This, however, in the nature of things could not be a sign to mark him out to contemporaries.

Not only was the sceptre and royal dignity of the **l** Messias the subject of prophecy but also **the character of his rule**. His dominion was to be universal : ' Ask of me, and I will give thee the Gentiles for thy inheritance, and the utmost parts of the earth for thy possession ', Ps 2:8. And again : ' All kings of the earth shall adore him ; all nations shall serve him ', Ps 71:11. His rule was to be guided by justice. He was to judge the people with justice and the lowly with judgement and to secure their rights to the oppressed, Ps 71:2, 4. The consequence of such government would be a kingdom at peace without disturbance even in such dangerous regions as the mountains, *ibid.* 3. And so marked a characteristic was this tranquillity to be that the King would be called ' the Prince of Peace ', Is 9:6. Indeed, he would be the very embodiment of peace itself, Mic 5:5. The dominion being universal and peace reigning throughout its length and breadth

102 l there would be no need of warlike implements. 'They shall turn their swords into ploughshares and their spears into sickles ; nation shall not lift up sword against nation, neither shall they be exercised any more

m to war ', Is 2:4 = Mic 4:3. And if here it be asked how then does it come about that the Messias has come and yet the world is plagued with wars, the answer is simply that this picture of loving comradeship among the nations depicts the happy state that would flourish if the nations and their rulers submitted themselves to the sweet and light yoke of Christ. But despite its claim to universality Christ will not force his rule on unwilling peoples. His service must be free and willingly accepted. His purpose was not to deprive kings of their temporal rule to impose his own. In the beautiful language of the Church's hymn ' Non eripit mortalia qui regna dat coelestia '. For Christ's rule is a spiritual rule. Therefore the peoples of their own accord say ' Come and let us go up to the mountain of the Lord and to the house of the God of Jacob, and he will teach us his ways and we will walk in his paths ', Is 2:3 = Mic 4:2. There lies the root of the world's sorrows : they have not decided to put aside the lust for wealth and power and to learn the ways of Christ and walk in his paths.

n Into this canvas of a victorious king ruling in justice over a peaceful people it was difficult to fit the prophecies which foretold the humiliation, the rejection, the suffering and even the **violent death** of the Messias. Yet these are foretold in the OT with unusual wealth of detail. Read Ps 21 and Is 53. Of the psalm St Augustine says that to hear it sung one would almost think he was listening to the chanting of the Gospel, *Contra Faust. Man.* 12, 43, PL 42, 277. So clear was the evidence to many of the Jews that they bethought them of the solution of two persons to be named Messias, Messias ben David, the victorious king, and Messias ben Joseph, the sufferer, JE 8, 511. The Gospel story presents a more moving and a more beautiful solution.

o To other prophecies, though important, a brief reference must here suffice. The Messias was to be not only of kingly rank but also endowed with the **prophetic office, Deut** 18:18. It was this text that the priests and Levites had in mind when they asked John the Baptist whether he was ' the prophet ', whom they had not identified with the Messias, Jn 1:21. The Messias was further to combine with his royal dignity that of the **priestly order**. This was no projection into the future of the conditions of the past, as the Davidic origin of the Messias would appear incompatible with the priesthood, as among the Israelites only descendants of Aaron of the tribe of Levi could approach the altar. Even more surprising still, the Messianic priesthood is described in terms of a completely non-Israelite institution : ' Thou art a priest for ever according to the order of Melchisedech ', Ps 109:4. The sacrifice offered by this king-priest of Salem was one of bread and wine. Now the offering of sacrifice is the essential function of a priest and therefore the Messias King-Priest must have his sacrifice too. The prediction of this was reserved to Malachias, the last of the prophets. He foretold the rejection of the Jewish sacrifices and their substitution by ' a clean oblation ' offered among and by Gentiles from the rising of the sun even to the going down thereof, Mal 1:10 f.

p This outline will serve to give some idea of the rich content of the OT prophecies concerning Christ, of their completeness and their harmony. These predictions in word are supplemented by others in act which are called **types or figures**. The significance of these has become apparent in their fulfilment in the antitype. It is a moot question and one full of difficulty to know to what extent the OT was impregnated by divine disposition with the foreshadowing of Christ and his dispensation. St Paul's words, 1 Cor 10:11, ' all these things happened to them [the Israelites] in figure ' has been understood to refer to types, though the meaning is ' as (warning) examples ' to future

generations. Understanding the Apostle's saying in **102p** the former sense and giving an undue extension to his universal expression some have given the widest scope to this figurative significance of the OT. They found further motive in the consideration of the apparent inutility of the knowledge conveyed by many passages understood in the literal sense, as St Jerome asks what is the profit of knowing the age of Methusala at death or of Solomon at the time of his marriage, PL 26, 596BC, partly by the conviction that as divinely inspired the pages of Holy Writ must be replete with recondite meanings in accordance with the words of St Gregory the Great that the text of Scripture is ' exceedingly sublime and profound with a multiplicity of senses ', *In 1 Reg. Prooem.*, PL 79, 20. On this matter **q** the opinion expressed by St Augustine is, I think, in agreement with the mind of the Church : ' For my part I think those to be greatly in error who consider that no events (of the OT) have any other significance beyond their own historical truth, and equally those to be unduly rash who maintain that absolutely everything is wrapped up in allegorical allusions ', *De Civ. Dei* 17, 3, PL 41, 526. It is not a question of where we can detect some resemblance between the events of the OT on the one hand and on the other of the Kingdom of God either already glorious in heaven or yet engaged in the spiritual warfare of life on this earth. It is God only who can so dispose the events of life as to prefigure the future ; and the question is, therefore, in what events of the OT are we to see this purposeful guiding of the hand of God. Great stress is laid on this typological significance of the OT in the *Homily on the Passion* of St Melito of Sardis. In this venerable monument of the early Church dating from the second century and the earliest extant homily of the kind the Saint writes : ' The people became the pattern of the Church, and the Law the writing of a parable, and the Gospel the setting-forth and fulfilment of the Law . . . (Christ) is the Passover of our salvation; he it is who in many men suffered many things. This is he who in Abel was slain, in Isaac was bound, who in Jacob dwelt in a strange land, who in Joseph was sold, who in Moses was cast out, in the lamb was sacrificed, in David was hunted, in the prophets was dishonoured ' (edited by Campbell Bonner, 1940, nn. 40 and 69).

Our Lord himself pointed out the analogy of the **r** saving power of the brazen serpent lifted up by Moses in the desert and the salvation to be won through his own elevation upon the Cross. Indeed, Christ did more than indicate the analogy. By saying ' As Moses lifted up the serpent in the desert, so must the Son of Man be lifted up ', Jn 3:14 f. and Num 21:9, he showed that the analogy was divinely intended and that his own raising on the Cross was to be the fulfilment of the type. This figurative significance of the OT is, therefore, certain and should never be lost sight of in the reading of the Scriptures, though we may not always be sure whether the analogy we detect is one divinely intended. See further § 417g.

Knowledge of the OT indispensable for the Under- 103a standing of the NT—This interplay between the prophecies of the OT and their fulfilment in the NT, this delineation of types among the Israelites and their realization in the antitypes of the Christian dispensation, will have made it plain that there cannot be an adequate apprehension of the NT which is not based on a knowledge of the OT. But a knowledge of the OT is necessary in other ways besides. In the first place the NT taken in isolation is a torso, without foundations, and unable to explain itself. That this is so as regards the presentation of the new dispensation we have already seen, for the OT was the pedagogue or tutor leading the Israelites on to Christ. And it is also true as regards the whole Jewish background of the NT and in particular as regards the Jewish background of the life of Christ which in the main was that of a Jew among Jews led according to the traditional Jewish manner of life. A knowledge of its Roman

103a background is also obviously necessary, but that is not to our present purpose. The following are a few illustrations of the knowledge necessary for the due understanding of the NT : the law governing the purification of women after childbirth, that concerning leprosy, the annual visits to the temple at Jerusalem, the sacrifice of the Paschal Lamb and the Paschal Supper, the institution of the Sabbath, the Nazirite vow. Another important instance is the history of Samuel's birth and childhood which contributed so much as literary model to the manner of presentation of the infancy narratives in St Luke, *cf.* E. Burrows, S.J., *The Gospel of the Infancy*.

b Some reference should here be made to the question how far the language of the OT has influenced that of the NT. In the first place a distinction must be made between passages where the thought is expressed in language which though idiomatic Greek, is based upon the OT, and passages where the turn of language used is not idiomatic Greek but the reproduction of a Semitic original. In the latter case a further distinction must be made between texts in which the Semitic influence is that of the native Aramaic speech of the NT writer or of his source and texts in which the Semitism in question is a Hebraism mediated by the LXX translation of the original Hebrew. The subject is one of admitted difficulty and complexity in which expert opinion is frequently divided. Reference may be made to *J. H. Moulton and W. E. Howard, *A Grammar of NT Greek*, II (1929) 14–34, 413–85 ; *M. Black, *An Aramaic Approach to the Gospels and Acts*, Oxford, 1946. **103b**

THE RELIGION OF ISRAEL

By E. F. SUTCLIFFE, S.J.

104a Bibliography—M.-J. Lagrange, O.P., *Etudes sur les Religions sémitiques*, Paris, 1903 ; M. Hetzenauer, O.C., *Theologia Biblica*, I, Friburgi Brisgoviae, 1908 ; *G. F. Oehler, *Theology of the OT*, 2 vol., Edinburgh, 1874-5 ; *H. Ewald, *Old and New Testament Theology*, Edinburgh, 1888 ; *H. Schultz, *OT Theology*, 2 vol., Edinburgh, 1895 ; 1909² ; *W. H. Bennett, *The Theology of the OT*, London, 1896 ; *A. B. Davidson, *The Theology of the OT*, Edinburgh, 1904 ; *W. O. E. Oesterley and T. H. Robinson, *Hebrew Religion*, London, 1930 ; P. Heinisch, *Theologie des Alten Testamentes*, Bonn, 1940 ; *A. Edersheim, *The Temple, its Ministry and Services*, London, no date ; E. Mangenot, ' Dieu, sa Nature d'après la Bible ' in DTC 4, 948-1016 ; F. Prat, S.J., ' Jéhovah ' in DBV 3, 1220-41 ; F. X. Kortleitner, Ord. Praem., *De Hebraeorum ante Exsilium Babylonicum Monotheismo*, Innsbruck, 1910 ; J. Touzard, ' Le Monothéisme ' in DAFC 2, 1566-1614 ; A. Van Hoonacker, *Le Sacerdoce Lévitique dans la Loi et dans l'Histoire des Hébreux*, London and Louvain, 1899 ; ' La Date de l'Introduction de l'Encens dans le Culte de Jahwé' in RB (1914) 161-87 ; A. Médebielle, ' L'Expiation ' in DBV(S) 3, 1-112 ; *L'Expiation*, I, Rome, 1924 ; *J. H. Kurtz, *Sacrificial Worship of the Old Testament*, Edinburgh, 1863 ; *G. Buchanan Gray, *Sacrifice in the Old Testament*, Oxford, 1925 ; *W. O. E. Oesterley, *Sacrifices in Ancient Israel*, London, 1937 ; E. F. Sutcliffe, S.J., *The Old Testament and the Future Life*, London, 1947² ; *J. W. Jack, *The Ras Shamra Tablets : their Bearing on the Old Testament*, Edinburgh, 1935 ; in some respects now out of date ; *C. F. A. Schaeffer, *The Cuneiform Texts of Ras Shamra-Ugarit*, London, 1939 ; *R. Dussaud, *Les Découvertes de Ras Shamra (Ugarit) et l'Ancien Testament*, Paris, 1941².

b Introduction—By **religion** we mean a system of beliefs concerning the divinity and of man's duties in regard thereto. If such a system, whether practical or theoretical, is based merely on what the human reason can discover by its own powers, it is called natural religion. If it is based on knowledge communicated by God to man in some way outside the working of his ordinary providence, it is called revealed religion. Such was the religion of Israel, and it depended on divine revelation not only in its origin but also in the course of its development, for through the greater part of OT history God continued to speak to the people through the mouth of accredited messengers who delivered in his name and with his authority the **c** message which he wished (*cf.* § 409*e*). In this the religion of Israel differed sharply from Christianity, as the Christian revelation was completed by the death of the last of the Apostles. Since that time there has been no new revelation to the Church, though, under the guidance of the Holy Ghost, knowledge and understanding of the original revelation has deepened and widened. To say, however, that the religion of Israel was revealed does not mean that it was in all points revealed in the strict sense of that term. In this strict sense, only that is said to be revealed which man's natural powers are incapable of discovering. In a wider sense everything is said to be revealed which God makes known to man in a supernatural way. Again, the fact that Israel enjoyed a revealed religion does not preclude from it practices which grew up apart from revelation but received a subsequent divine sanction.

A systematized exposition of belief about God and his **104d** dealings with mankind is called **theology** and is distinguished into natural theology if based on the efforts of the human mind alone, and dogmatic theology if founded on the authority of revelation. But among the various kinds of literature in the Bible there is no such theological exposition. The ancient Hebrews were neither theologians nor philosophers. Their writers were deeply religious men whose minds were busy with the problems of life, but not in that coherent, logical and systematized manner characteristic of the theologian and the philosopher ; and the inspiration exercised on them by God was in harmony with their natural gifts and dispositions. As a result their writings contain the elements of a theology, not a theology itself. The correlative in religion to a system of beliefs about **e** God and his providence over man is a system of beliefs about the duties of man towards God. These duties may be summed up as the carrying out of his holy will, which is that we should do good and avoid evil. ' Hate evil and love good ' (Am 5:15). These duties in the first place regard God himself. And as man is an individual human being who is also a member of society, these God-regarding duties comprise both the individual relations of each to God, and the public manifestation of our relation to him by participation in public worship. Our duties in the second place concern our use of all creatures and especially our relations to our fellow-men. These various duties come under the heads of **ritual and liturgical obligations** in so far as they are concerned with the public worship of God, and all other obligations come under the head of **moral theology**. Ethics or deontology is concerned with our obligations in so far as these are known from reason alone, and moral theology in so far as they are known from revelation.

An exposition of the religion of Israel should therefore **f** set forth the beliefs of Israel concerning God as he is in himself and concerning his relations to men ; concerning man's worship of God ; and concerning man's relations to creatures, especially his fellow-men.

The religion of Israel, understood as the religion of the **g** people of Israel, began when Israel became a nation under the leadership of Moses. It was at one and the same time that the people was welded together into an independent, self-governing unit and received in a series of revelations at Sinai the main outlines of its religious life. But this religion was not something entirely new. It had its roots in the past, as the Israelites well knew. It was ' the God of Abraham, the God of Isaac and the God of Jacob ' (Ex 3:6), who appeared to Moses in the Burning Bush. Both the history of Israel and the history of its religion are unintelligible without the history of the Patriarchs and of their religion. An account of this, therefore, must stand at the head of our exposition. But it will be convenient to mention first a modern theory which would invalidate the history of Israelite religion as presented in the OT.

The Evolutionary Theory of Israelite Religion—The **h** evolutionary hypothesis, which came into such favour in the last decades of the 19th cent., was applied to all departments of life, including religion. According to this theory everything started in a lowly and undeveloped form and thereafter progressively evolved

104h into higher and more developed forms. In the sphere of religion this process was thought to necessitate initial stages of fetichism, totemism, animism and so up to polytheism, and then through monolatry to monotheism. The story of Hebrew religion, therefore, as recorded in the OT could not be historical, for in its pages monotheism is found in possession from the beginning. By a chronological rearrangement of the documents, however, it was found possible to date the introduction of this highest form of worship as late as the 8th cent. and to attribute its propagation to the great prophets. A brief discussion of this documentary theory has been given, §§ 44–5 and 135a–h. Apart from the difficulties there indicated that militate against its acceptance, it must be added here that exact researches into the religions of primitive peoples have established the contrary thesis to be the historical fact, namely that monotheism is not a higher development arisen from polytheism but that polytheism is a degradation of monotheism. See the monumental work of W. Schmidt, S.V.D., *Der Ursprung der Gottesidee*, Münster in W., I (1926²), II (1929)–IX (1949), also that of Mgr. Le **i** Roy, *La Religion des Primitifs* (Paris, 1909). Moreover, apart from this conflict with the conclusions of scientific research, this evolutionary theory of religion rests on the false assumption that in the investigation into the divine man must necessarily be left entirely to his own resources. This premise would be justified if it could be demonstrated that God, who created the universe, is nevertheless incapable of communicating directly with the rational creatures of his own making or, alternatively, had made it a condition of his government of the world never so to do. The first suggestion is not only incapable of proof, but it is actually a contradiction in terms to say that the omnipotent God has not the power to make any revelation to human beings. The second suggestion is not in itself impossible, but has against it an impressive weight of historical evidence and neither argument nor evidence in its favour.

Hence to such books as that by *Karl Marti, *The Religion of the Old Testament* (London, 1907, English trans.), must be applied the verdict passed by E. Kautzsch on works dealing with the same subject written before these new theories became fashionable : ' The view . . . held . . . gives so completely false a picture of the development of this religion, that in such works it is at most only the treatment of neutral points (where the question of gradual development does not occur) that can have any value ', HDB 5, 732.

105a **The Religion of the Patriarchs**—The historicity of the patriarchal narratives must be rejected by those who hold that God Almighty cannot intervene by miracle or revelation in the world he created. Its rejection is, of course, involved also by the theory, which has the same unsound philosophical basis, that religion is necessarily the product of natural evolution. There is, however, no serious difficulty against the historical character of these narratives ; see § 139.

b **Monotheism.**—Whether Abraham was ever an idolater is a question to which exegetes have given both a negative and an affirmative answer. Josue, speaking in the name of God to the Israelites, said : ' Your fathers dwelt of old on the other side of the river [Euphrates], Thare the father of Abraham and *the father of* Nachor ; and they served strange gods ' (Jos 24:2 ; *cf.* 24:14 f.). It is hard to see that Abraham is not included among those who served strange gods. And according to the tradition recounted by Achior Abraham and his family were converted to the worship of ' one God of heaven ' before settling in Haran (Jdt **c** 5:7–9, Gen 11:31). It is not explicitly stated that the Patriarchs, Abraham, Isaac and Jacob, recognized the existence of one and only one God, but there is no hint that they did not and the impression made by the whole story is that their religion was monotheistic. The God they worshipped was no territorial deity with power limited geographically. Yahweh's power and influence

extended wherever he willed. (It is disputed whether **105** God was known to the Patriarchs as Yahweh ; see § 165c. In any case when God spoke to Moses under this name, he said he was the God of the Patriarchs [Ex 3:6, 6:2 f.], and it will make for clearness to use it.) He brought Abraham from Ur of the Chaldees in Babylonia (Gen 15:7). He appears and speaks to the Patriarchs in various places in Canaan (Gen 12:7, 13:14, etc.), and promises the land to Abraham's seed (12:7, 13:15, etc.). He punishes the Pentapolis (chh 18 f.), chastises Pharaoh (12:17), promises to judge Egypt (15:14), threatens Abimelech, king of Gerara (20:3), gives victory to Abraham over the four invading kings north of Damascus (14:15, 20). He is ' the most high God ' (14:18, 19, 20, 22) ; ' *the possessor of* heaven and earth (14:22 and 19) ; ' the God of heaven and earth ' (24:3), the ' God of heaven ' (24:7), where LXX adds, probably rightly, ' and the God of earth '. In other words, his dominion is universal and absolute, and there is no god beside him. That the family of Abraham ' would not follow the gods of their fathers, who were in the land of the Chaldaeans, (but) forsaking the ceremonies of their fathers, which consisted in the worship of many gods, they worshipped one God of heaven ' (Jdt 5:7–9), most naturally means that they recognized the nothingness of those many gods and the existence of one only God. Moreover, there is no sign that Moses was introducing anything new in his monotheism. His system is proposed as a development of the worship of the great Patriarchs.

It has been asserted that Jacob chose his God. If this **d** were true, it would imply that his religion was not monotheistic but henotheistic, that is, a form of monolatry, by which, while acknowledging the existence of a plurality of divinities, he confined his worship to one only. It will be helpful first to recall the promise of Yahweh to Abraham : ' I will establish my covenant between me and thee and thy seed after thee . . . to be a God to thee and to thy seed after thee ; and I will give to thee and to thy seed the land of thy sojournment, all the land of Canaan for a perpetual possession, and I will be their God ' (Gen 17:7 f.). This does not mean **e** that if it were not for the covenant, Yahweh would not be the God of Abraham and of his posterity. It means that by his special providence and favour he would prove himself to be their divine protector. This same formula occurs in the late prophets whose pure monotheism is doubted by no one. Thus in Ez 34:24 : ' I the Lord will be their God ' ; similarly 11:20, 14:11, 37:23 ; Zach 8:8 : ' They shall be my people and I will be their God in truth and justice '. Jacob on his long and lonely journey to Haran made a vow saying, ' If God shall be with me and shall *protect me on this journey*, and shall give me bread to eat and raiment to put on and shall *bring me back in peace* to my father's *dwelling, and Yahweh shall be my God, then* this stone which I have set up as a title [a memorial pillar] shall be the house of God, and of all things that thou shalt give to me, I will offer *thee* tithes ' (Gen 28:20 ff.). That is, if Yahweh proves himself to be my protector, I will make special offerings in gratitude. Without any change of meaning, the HT allows the apodosis to begin earlier : ' then Yahweh will be my God and this stone . . . ' ; that is, if Yahweh's providence looks after me on my journey, he will have proved himself to be my divine protector and in gratitude I will offer tithes. On his return Jacob went to Bethel, where he had set up the stone, and there erected ' an altar to God, who heard me in the day of my affliction and accompanied me in my journey ' (Gen 35:3).

The Names of God—Both Elohim and El are used as **f** equivalents of our word ' God '. Both belong to the common Semitic stock and are of uncertain derivation. There is no perceptible difference of meaning between them. The former, though plural in form, is nearly always used with qualifying words in the singular. Its root meaning is possibly that of strength, and the form is probably that of the plural of majesty. El is qualified in various ways : El elyon ' The most high God '

05f (Gen 14:18) ; ' God eternal ' (DV), ' the Everlasting God ' (RV), Gen 21:33 ; ' God *of Vision* ', Agar in Gen 16:13 ; El shaddai occurs Gen 17:1, 28:3, 35:11, 43:14, 48:3, and, as a certain emendation, 49:25. The meaning of this last name is dubious and was already unknown to the LXX translators of Genesis, who substitute ' my God ' or ' thy God '. Vg in each case has ' Deus omnipotens ' in accordance with the translation used elsewhere by the LXX. ' The God of Bethel ' [Gen 31:13] (DV and RV) is a translation that sins against Hebrew usage, and in agreement with LXX and the Targums the text should read ' the God who appeared to thee at Bethel '.

g Attributes of God—He is eternal (Gen 21:33), though no doubt the full philosophical implications of eternity were not understood. He is just and will not inflict punishment unless it is fully deserved (Gen 15:16), but he abhors iniquity and metes out condign chastisement as in the case of Sodom and Gomorrha (Gen chh 18–19). He knows the future (Gen 15:13–16). That he can do his will with any nation (Gen 15:14) is a sign that his power was known to be unlimited.

06a Worship—Each of the three Patriarchs, Abraham, Isaac and Jacob is recorded to have offered sacrifice to God. Abraham built altars at Shechem (Gen 12:7) after a vision of Yahweh ; between Bethel and Ai (Gen 12:8, 13:4) ; at Hebron (Gen 13:18) ; ' in the land of *Moriah* ' (Gen 22:2, 9) [the Syriac has ' the land of the Amorite ']. Isaac built an altar at Beersheba after a vision of Yahweh (Gen 26:23–25), and Jacob at Salem near Shechem (Gen 33:18, 20), and at Bethel (Gen 35:1, 3, 7), where Yahweh had appeared to him on his journey to Haran. Altars, literally ' places of sacrifice ', were built both in spots sanctified by a divine vision and also where no such vision is recorded to have occurred. The nature of the victims is not mentioned except in the case of the ram offered instead of Isaac (Gen 22:13). And it is only in that story that we find details of the ritual. Abraham arranged wood on the altar, and then having bound Isaac placed him on the wood. Only then would he have killed him before igniting the whole had not the Angel of Yahweh intervened (Gen 22:9 f.). The ram substituted for Isaac was offered as an '*olāh*, *i.e.* a whole-burnt offering. It is curious that in the other passages only the building of the altar is mentioned and the sacrifices themselves are left to be understood. On the other hand sacrifices are said to have been offered by Jacob at Beersheba without mention of an altar (Gen 46:1), presumably because the erection of an altar there by Isaac had already been recorded (Gen 26:25). Prayer is sometimes mentioned in connexion with an altar (Gen 12:8, 26:25, 33:20), but the calling on the name of Yahweh, which is the vague phrase used, does not indicate whether it was a prayer of adoration, praise or petition.

b The purpose of these sacrifices is not mentioned, but we shall not be wrong in assuming that they were the expression of adoration and an acknowledgement of the supreme dominion of God. An element of thanksgiving and petition was no doubt also present. The acknowledgement of God's supreme dominion is clearly indicated in the sacrifice of Isaac. This was commanded by God as a sign that all things and persons are his and that man has no independent rights even over what is most dear to him. The command having taught this lesson and having met with absolute obedience from Abraham and from Isaac, whose resignation and obedience we are left to infer, was changed into a prohibition in order to show that God would never actually demand a human sacrifice. On Gen 15:9–21 and 31:54 see the commentary.

c Mention is made of an oak or oaks in the same context with an altar in Gen 12:6 and 13:18. In neither case is it explicitly said that the altar was erected under a tree, though very likely it was. In the second passage it is said, and in the former it is to be understood, that Abraham chose the spot for his own dwelling. He would wish to benefit by the shade against the heat of the Palestinian sun ; *cf*. Os 4:13 where sacrifice is said

to be offered under trees ' because the shade thereof **106c** was good '.

Moral Code—Besides acknowledgement of his supreme **d** rights God demanded of men also the avoidance of evil ; and the fear of God was a force to keep men from wrong-doing (Gen 20:11). The unnatural vices of the Amorites and other Canaanite nations (Gen 15:16 ; Lev 18:24–27), the cruelty of their human sacrifices (Deut 12:30 f.), their witchcraft and necromancy (Deut 18:10–12) were most displeasing to God. The abominations of Sodom and the neighbouring cities called for summary punishment (Gen chh 18–19). Adultery is sinful (Gen 12:17, 20:3, 39:9), as also the misuse of marriage rights (Gen 38:9). Jacob knew that deceit merited ' a curse instead of a blessing ' (Gen 27:12), though he allowed his mother to entice him into it ; and Judah knew that he had acted wrongly in withholding his son Sela from Thamar (Gen 38:26). Note that the punishments mentioned in 12:17 and 20:17 f. were not for adultery, which had it been committed would have been a material but not a formal sin as it was not known that Sara was married, but for the crime of her forceful seizure. A breach of an honourable covenant was known to be displeasing to God (Gen 31:44–54).

The Covenant with Abraham and his Seed—The ties **e** which bound the Patriarchs to God were strengthened by the privilege of a special covenant entered into by God with Abraham and his seed (Gen 15:18, 17:7). The covenant was ratified in the manner usual among the Semites at the time (Gen 15:8–18). On his side God promised the possession of the land of Canaan (Gen 15:18 ff.), the multiplication of Abraham's seed, the issue therefrom of kings (Gen 17:6), and that in his seed all the nations of the earth should be blessed (Gen 12:3, 22:18). From Abraham God demanded a blameless life, ' Walk before me and be perfect ' (Gen 17:1), and that all males should be circumcised as a sign of the covenant (Gen 17:11).

Circumcision—The rite of circumcision, which was **f** obligatory on the eighth day, became part of the Mosaic law (Gen 17:12 ; Lev 12:3), and was in force throughout OT times (Lk 2:21), though the practice was interrupted during the wanderings of the Exodus (Jos 5:5). As an initiation ceremony it is practised by tribes in Africa, Australia and America. That it was customary in Egypt is known both from Herodotus II 104 and from the ancient monuments. In Babylonia, whence Abraham came, the available evidence shows that the ceremony was not in use, B. Meissner, *Babylonien und Assyrien*, I (Heidelberg, 1920) 394. Its significance seems to lie in its connexion with the origin of life and in the shedding of blood which is entailed. God is the author of life, and ' the life of the flesh is in the blood ' and the blood of sacrifices was an expiation (Lev 17:11). Only the circumcised were allowed to eat the Pasch (Ex 12:44, 48). Indeed the uncircumcised, even of the descendants of Abraham, had no share in the privileges of the Hebrew people, because they were by the very fact unfaithful to the covenant (Gen 17:14).

Circumcision did not confer grace, for, as taught by **g** the Council of Florence, the rites of the OT were only figurative of the grace to be given through the Passion of Christ (Dz 695). It is the common opinion, however, that original sin was forgiven and sanctifying grace granted in, though, unlike baptism, not by, circumcision to infants and those properly disposed ; see St Thomas, *Sum. Theol.*, III, qu. 70, art. 4. This opinion is supported by the fact that the rite of circumcision signified aggregation to the holy people of God. And for the details of various theological views see *e.g.* V. Ermoni, art. ' Circoncision ' in DTC II 2523–7.

Infidelities—Scripture is not silent about the sins and **h** infidelities of those who figure in its pages. Here, however, as space is lacking for an enumeration of the virtues manifested by the Patriarchs like the faith of Abraham, the chastity and forgiveness of Joseph, so also for a detailed list of their shortcomings, like the

106h fornication of Judah, the hatred and cruelty of Joseph's brothers. Still special mention must be made of false
i worship. In flying with Jacob from Laban Rachel stole her father's *teraphim*, which he himself calls his 'gods' (Gen 31:19, 30). The exact nature of these objects and the derivation of the word are alike uncertain, but the DV is substantially correct in translating 'idols' in agreement with the Vg 'idola' and the LXX εἴδωλα. They seem to have varied in size, as Rachel was able to hide Laban's under a camel's trappings (Gen 31:34), whereas Michol put one in David's bed to simulate his presence (1 Kg 19:13, 16). They were used for divination (Ez 21:21 [MT 26], Zach 10:2). The influence of pagan worship affected others besides Rachel. When Jacob was commanded by God to offer sacrifice at Bethel, he '*said to his household and to all in his company : Put* away the strange gods that are among you', and after collecting these gods, probably *teraphim*, he buried them under a
j terebinth (Gen 35:2, 4). He also buried the earrings which had served as charms or amulets and perhaps bore pagan images. How long Jacob had tolerated these abuses is not clear. It may be that the pagan objects had been appropriated in the city recently plundered (Gen 34:27). A Lapide thought that Jacob first destroyed the images before burying them, as seems probable (*cf.* Ex 32:20 ; 4 Kg 18:4). If this tree near Shechem is the same as that at which Josue later persuaded the people again to put away 'strange gods' (though the vocalization of the MT is different), the probable explanation of Jacob's choice of the spot for the burial is that the sanctuary of Yahweh there (Jos 24:23, 26) already existed in his time and he wished to show the nothingness of the pagan images by contumeliously throwing them, as it were, under Yahweh's feet.

107 Religious Life in Egypt—Little is recorded of the religious life of this period. Josue speaks of pagan worship (24:14), and Ezechiel shows that the defection spread to many Israelites as God was minded to 'pour out (his) indignation upon them' (20:5-10). Others, however, were God-fearing, even to the braving of Pharaoh's anger (Ex 1:15-21). The practice of circumcision had not ceased (Jos 5:5), nor that of sacrifice (Ex 5:3, 20:24). It may be inferred from Ex 20:24 f. that the altars were of earth or unhewn stone, as Moses seems in this to have been sanctioning existing practice. Some have thought that the tabernacle of meeting (Ex 33:7-11), mentioned before the erection of the tabernacle of the testimony as ordered by God, was of pre-Mosaic origin ; *cf.* Hummelauer, *Comm. in Exod.* (1897) 178, 323. On this section see F. X. Kortleitner, *Israelitarum in Aegypto Commoratio* (Tongerloae, 1930) 92-6.

108a Mosaic Religion—Religion was organized and developed under the leadership of Moses. It was not a new creation. Its roots went back to the distant past. The God of the exodus and of Sinai was the God of the patriarchs (Ex 3:6, 6:2 f.). But the clan had become a people and the people was about to become a nation in possession of its own territory (Gen 15:18-21 ; Ex 3:8). With the people God renewed the covenant he had made with Abraham (Ex 24:6-8). And as a nation it was fitting that they should be ruled by divinely sanctioned law, and no longer by conscience and custom only. The legislation is based on the covenant by which the Israelites became God's 'peculiar possession above all people' though all the earth is his (Ex 19:5) and God would have them to be ' holy men ' (Ex 22:31). As they were to be ' a priestly kingdom and a holy nation ' (Ex 19:6) the whole of life was to come under the influence of religion and the whole was to be sanctified. In particular it was fitting that the outward expression of worship in cult and ritual should be regulated and should become richer and more elaborate. It must be borne in mind that the laws promulgated at Sinai had in view an imminent

entry into the Promised Land. It was only after the **108a** culminating sin of the people in murmuring against God when the messengers returned from spying out the land that God postponed the entry till all of twenty years old and upward had perished in the wilderness (Num 14:27-33).
Monotheism—The worship of other gods is strictly **b** forbidden (Ex 20:3, Deut 5:7). And (Deut 32:12) it is said of the people that Yahweh ' alone was his leader, and there was no strange god with him '. And again, Yahweh is ' the God of gods and the Lord of lords ' (Deut 10:17). Such texts taken alone would be consonant with a henotheistic religion. Actually they do not suppose the existence of other gods. Other gods among the nations ' were framed with men's hands ; wood and stone that neither see nor hear nor eat nor smell ' (Deut 4:27 f.). The idols of Egypt and the nations through which Israel passed are ' abominations and filth . . . wood and stone, silver and gold ' (Deut 29:17). The sun, moon and stars worshipped by other nations are creatures made by God (Ex 20:11 ; Deut 4:19). Yahweh has universal dominion : ' Behold heaven is the Lord's thy God, and the heaven of heaven, the earth and all things that are therein ' (Deut 10:14). Indeed ' the Lord made heaven and earth, and the sea, and all things that are in them ' (Ex 20:11) ; *cf.* Gen 1. As Yahweh made heaven and earth and all therein, there cannot be another god beside him. Whatever there is was made by him. Hence explicitly, ' The Lord he is God, and there is no other besides him ' (Deut 4:35) ; ' The Lord he is God in heaven above and in the earth beneath ; and there is no other ' (Deut 4:39). On Deut 6:4 see note and Hummelauer, *Comm. in Deut.* (1901) 243 f.

Certain texts, however, at first glance seem to approve **c** of the worship of other ' gods ' by pagan nations. ' They *have gone and* have served *other* gods and adored them, whom they *had not known* and for whom they had not been assigned ' or ' and who had not been assigned to them ' (Deut 29:26 [MT 25]). ' Lest perhaps lifting up thy eyes to heaven thou see the sun and the moon and the *stars, all the host of heaven, and be driven on to adore them* and serve them, which *Yahweh* thy God *assigned* to all the nations that are under heaven ' (Deut 4:19). St Jerome, as his version shows, understood this passage to say that God created the heavenly bodies to minister to all nations, but the use of the same word in both texts with their similar context is evidence of the correctness of the interpretation current in the 2nd cent. among both Christians and Jews as testified by their representatives St Justin Martyr and Trypho, who both say that the sun was given by God to be worshipped, *Dial. cum Tryph.*, 55, 121 (PG 6, 596, 757). All the passages which condemn pagan worship make it clear that the explanation lies in the difference between the permissive and the absolute will of God, a distinction which the ancient Hebrews did not make explicitly, though they knew that God neither causes nor approves the evil that he condemns and punishes. St Paul speaks in a similar way in Rom 1:24-26.

God's Works and Attributes—Yahweh is **the creator.** **109a** He ' made heaven and earth and the sea, and all things that are in them ' (Ex 20:11). He created the light and the heaven and the heavenly bodies out of nothing by his mere word (Gen 1:3, 6-8, 14-17). This is equivalent to saying that God is **omnipotent.** ' Is the hand of the Lord unable ? ' (Num 11:23).

The truth that God is the creator of all things has as its **b** correlative that he himself was made by none and that, therefore, he exists of himself and has the reason for his existence in himself. In other words he is **the one necessary being.** This truth is implicit in the doctrine of creation, and is the meaning of the divine name Yahweh. Yahweh is he who is ; he exists necessarily and of himself. A necessary consequence, which the Hebrews will not have consciously grasped, is that God is the fullness of all being, and is consequently infinitely perfect. Evil, it must be remembered in this con-

09b nection, is negative and consists in a lack of conformity to what is right and good. On the name Yahweh see § 165*a*–*c*. A further consequence of God's uncreated, necessary existence is his **eternity:** ' I live for ever ' (Deut 32:40).

c The spiritual **nature of God** was too refined a conception to be understood in the time of Moses and the idea of his nature remained vague. It contained, however, no gross or low element. Yahweh had no family and no consort, in this a great contrast to the gods of the pagan nations. That the nature of God was such as no form known to man could represent was strongly impressed on the Israelites by the repeated prohibition of fashioning any image whatsoever as a likeness of him (Ex 20:4 ; Lev 26:1 ; Deut 5:8). Moses strongly emphasizes this truth : ' You heard the *sound* of his words, but you saw not any form at all. . . . You saw not any similitude in the day that the Lord God spoke to you in Horeb from the midst of the fire, lest perhaps being deceived you might make you a graven similitude or image of male or female, the similitude of any beasts that are on the earth, or of birds that fly under heaven ', etc. (Deut 4:12, 15 ff.). This vague and negative conception was immensely superior to the ideas of the surrounding nations whose gods were conceived in human, zoomorphic and astral form. Though God did not allow the people to see him under any form whatever, he did appear in human form to Moses, Aaron and the elders, as A Lapide rightly says with Lyranus and Cajetan (Ex 24:9–11). (This last verse still speaks of the chosen group, and not of the children of Israel as in the DV.) In the case of these leaders there was not the same danger of misconception as in

d the case of the common people. Of Moses it is said that God spoke to him ' mouth to mouth ' and that ' he beheld the form [or, likeness] of Yahweh ' (Num 12:8). And with the same meaning of intimate communing it is said, ' The Lord spoke to Moses face to face, as a man is wont to speak to his friend ' (Ex 33:11). That these words are figurative is clear from Ex 33:20, ' Thou canst not see my face, for man shall not see me and live '. The face stands for the person, and is so translated in verse 15 in the Vg and DV. Anthropomorphisms are inevitable in speaking of God even among those fully conscious of his spiritual nature, as is evidenced by their frequent use even in the official documents of Christianity.

e Examples of **God's foreknowledge** of free human acts are given in Ex 3:19–22, 4:14, 14:4 ; Deut 31:16, 20 f. The last passage is a prophecy of the idolatry of the Israelites after their conquest of the Promised Land.

f Yahweh is ' great and mighty and terrible ', that is, to be feared (Deut 10:17), but above all his attributes is **his holiness.** Everything in any way connected with him is holy, a place in which he manifests himself (Ex 3:5), the sacerdotal vestments (Ex 28:2, 4), feast days (Ex 12:16, 31:15), meats from sacrifices (Ex 29:33). All such things have a mere extrinsic holiness, such as among us belongs to churches and chalices. It is based on their dedication to the service of him who is holy in himself and of his very nature : ' Be ye holy, because I the Lord your God am holy ' (Lev 19:2). The etymological meaning of the word *qādōš*, if it was that of ' separation ', is not helpful, partly because spiritual ideas have to be expressed by words of an originally material meaning, as the word ' spiritual ' itself, partly because words so applied come entirely to transcend their original connotation, and partly because the

g separation in question is of a unique kind. The word is sometimes used of legal holiness : ' I am the Lord your God ; be holy because I am holy ; defile not your souls by any creeping thing that moveth upon the earth ' (Lev 11:44). Here A Lapide says that the word is equivalent to ' clean ' as in Deut 23:14, ' Thou shalt cover that which thou art eased of, for the Lord thy God walketh in the midst of thy camp . . . and let thy camp be holy, and let *nothing indecent* appear therein'. But this does not do justice to the conception, which is

that uncleanness would be contrary to the holiness **109g** which belonged to the camp of the people of God, as with us uncleanness would be considered contrary to the holiness proper to a consecrated church. For the Hebrews the whole nation, the whole land and all that pertained thereto were holy because the Lord had chosen them ' to be his peculiar people ' (Deut 7:6). The concept, consequently, of extrinsic holiness was of far wider application with them than it is with us. In **h** the sphere of non-moral actions what offends against this extrinsic holiness depends largely on custom and common estimation as it does in the analogous matter of the exhibition of the reverence due to certain persons on account of their position and authority. In these regards God condescended to the received customs of his people, and for them there was something unclean, perhaps indecent, in eating and even touching certain animals. Of course, once such customs received the sanction of religious law, their violation became a transgression of that law and, therefore, took on a definitely moral character. The moral nature of Yahweh's holiness is shown by the moral nature of the holiness which he demanded of his people, and this is manifested in the decalogue ; see §§ 172*f*–173*c*.

Although in the time of Moses we do not expect to find **i** evidence of the abstract idea of **the omnipresence of God,** it was known that his presence was not confined to any one place. On the contrary, he manifested himself wherever he wished. He spoke to Abraham in Mesopotamia (Gen 12:1–4) ; he protected him in Canaan (Gen 14:20) ; he manifested his might by the plagues in Egypt, and his majesty by the theophany of Sinai. That his power was known to extend to the whole world is clear from Gen 1.

Secondly must be considered the divine attributes as **j** manifested in **God's government of the world.** He has supreme power over the universe. ' Heaven is the Lord's thy God, and the heaven of heaven, the earth and all things that are therein ' (Deut 10:14). He can ' shut up heaven that the rain come not down nor the earth yield her fruit ' (Deut 11:17). And all peoples who dwell on the earth are under his sway : ' This day will I begin to send the dread and fear of thee upon the nations that dwell under the whole heaven ' (Deut 2:25). This power was displayed in particular by the liberation of Israel against the will of the mighty people of Egypt and by giving the Israelites the land of ' great nations and stronger than they ' (Deut 4:37 f.).

It follows that man depends completely on God. All **k** he has comes from him. God said to Moses : ' Who made man's mouth ? or who made the dumb and the deaf, the seeing and the blind ? Did not I ? ' (Ex 4:11). So too, if men have any kind of skill, it is the gift of God. It was God who had ' filled with the spirit of wisdom ' all those who had the craftmanship to make the sacerdotal vestments (Ex 28:3).

So absolute is the divine power in the government of **l** the world that **everything is ascribed to God** whether in the realm of natural causes or in that of man's moral acts. ' God had not rained on the earth ' (Gen 2:5) ; and speaking of her sterility Sarah said, ' The Lord hath restrained me from bearing ' (Gen 16:2). As God is the author of nature and of its laws, this manner of speaking is quite exact, but is apt to mislead the unwary reader into thinking that the sacred writer is speaking of a miraculous intervention of God where nothing of the kind is intended. It is several times said that ' The Lord hardened Pharaoh's heart ' (Ex 9:12), etc., and no distinction is drawn between God's permissive will and his absolute will. In other words the text does not distinguish between God's taking positive action to harden Pharaoh's heart, and his permitting Pharaoh to harden his own heart. That the latter is the sense intended is shown by 1 Kg 6:6. ' Why do you harden your hearts as Egypt and Pharaoh hardened their hearts ? ' and by Deut 10:16 ' stiffen your neck no more '. It follows also from the sense of God's justice. Pharaoh's admission ' It is Yahweh who is just ' (Ex 9:27) certainly reflects the belief of the Israelites. The divine

109 l justice is also reflected in the law of Ex 23:7, 'The innocent and just person thou shalt not put to death'.

m **God's justice** is manifested by the punishments with which he visits iniquity. Mary's rebellious complaints against her brother Moses were punished by leprosy (Num 12:10), and the man who violated the Sabbath rest was ordered to be stoned (Num 15:35), and there are many other examples. If the punishments seem to be severe, it must be remembered that the doctrine of future retribution had not yet been revealed and that the people were spiritually crass and 'stiffnecked' (Ex 33:3, 5) and needed the help of a stern discipline.

n On the other hand **Yahweh is compassionate** and tender towards the weak : ' He doth judgement to the fatherless and the widow, loveth the stranger, and giveth him food and raiment' (Deut 10:18). He is 'merciful and gracious, patient and of much compassion, and true' (Ex 34:6) ; he is ' patient and full of mercy, taking away iniquity and wickedness' (Num 14:18). He is quick to forgive when man is worthy of forgiveness. Mary was quickly healed of her leprosy (Num 12:13 ff.). The idolatry of the people was foretold and their dispersal among the nations, but straightway was added the promise, ' When thou shalt seek there the Lord thy God, thou shalt find him ; yet so, if thou seek him with all thy heart and *with all thy soul*' (Deut 4:29). And see Deut 30:1-10.

110a **The Covenant between Yahweh and Israel**—That Yahweh was the Lord of all peoples we have seen in the above sketch of his nature and attributes as depicted in the Mosaic writings, but by a mysterious disposition of his providence he chose Israel out of all the peoples of the earth. ' The Lord thy God hath chosen thee to be his peculiar people of all peoples that are upon the earth, not because you surpass all nations in number is the Lord joined unto you, for you are the fewest of any people, but because the Lord hath loved you, and *because he* hath kept his oath which he swore to your fathers, *he* hath brought you out with a strong hand and redeemed you from the house of bondage, out of the hand of Pharaoh the king of Egypt' (Deut 7:6-8). ' Know that the Lord thy God giveth thee not this excellent land in possession for thy *justness*, for thou art a very stiffnecked people. Remember and forget not how thou provokedst the Lord thy God to wrath in the wilderness' (Deut 9:6 f.).

b With this stiffnecked race Yahweh renewed 'the covenant which he made with Abraham, Isaac and Jacob' (Ex 2:24). The solemn ceremony is described in Ex 24:4-8, and further detail, presumably derived from tradition, is given in Heb 9:19 f. The blood of the holocausts and peace offerings was divided into two equal parts, one half being poured upon the altar as representative of Yahweh and the other half sprinkled upon the people. This ritual of sprinkling the two parties to the covenant, or their representatives, with blood from a common source was symbolical of their entering into a living and lifelong partnership. See further § 111e. On his side God promised to fulfil the promise he had made to the patriarchs ' to give them the land of Canaan ' (Ex 6:4) and to protect and bless the people therein (Ex 23:23-31). On their side the people promised to observe all the obligations laid upon them in ' The Book of the Covenant ' (Ex chh 20-23) which Moses read out to them : ' All things that the Lord hath spoken we will do, we will be obedient ' (Ex 24:7). These precepts are partly moral, partly cultic, for the covenant was to make Israel ' a priestly kingdom and a holy nation ' (Ex 19:6). The religion of Israel was from the beginning an ethical monotheism. ' And now, Israel, what doth the Lord thy God require of thee but that thou fear the Lord thy God and walk in his ways and love him and serve the Lord thy God with all thy heart and with all thy soul, and keep the commandments of the Lord and his *precepts* which I command thee this day, that it may be well with thee ' (Deut 10:12 f.). ' The fear of God ' is practically the equivalent in Hebrew of the English word ' religion ', and the fear in question is filial fear

as shown by its conjunction with love, which is incompatible with servile fear.

As a consequence of the pact or covenant made with **c** the patriarchs and to be renewed with their descendants Yahweh regarded Israel as his son : ' Israel is my son, my firstborn ' (Ex 4:22). And the depth of **God's fatherly affection** is proclaimed by Moses : ' In the wilderness *thou hast seen how* the Lord thy God hath carried thee, as a man is wont to carry *his son*, all the way that you have come ' (Deut 1:31 ; *cf.* 8:5 ; 14:1 ; 32:6). And this relationship was conceived to exist not merely with the people as a whole but with its members separately : ' *Of* the *Rock who* begot thee *thou art unmindful* and hast forgotten *God who bare* thee ; the Lord saw *it with abhorrence* because his own sons and daughters provoked him ' (Deut 32:18 f.). Note that women are the children of God equally with men.

The Obligations of the Israelites—As their side of the **d** pact the Israelites bound themselves to be obedient to the law of God. Its contents were not all new. The supernatural builds on the natural, and many parts of the law will have been divine sanctions of existing custom and tradition. The wickedness of wilful murder will have been recognized by the popular conscience before the promulgation of the decalogue ; abstinence from the flesh of certain animals and birds considered unclean will have been a matter of ancient custom, and the texts unearthed at Rās-Shamra have shown that ritual practices of the Hebrews were also in vogue among the Canaanites, as would be expected from their proximity in race and territory. The two fundamental principles which underlie the law are that as God is holy, all that belongs to him is holy, and the people, as his special possession, should be holy ; and, secondly, that as the people belonged entirely to him, their land, their produce, their time, everything they had, were held in stewardship from him.

The **moral prescriptions** of the law are contained **e** chiefly in the decalogue, in the laws of the Book of the Covenant and in Lev 19. The commandments of the decalogue (*cf.* § 173*a-c*) are all precepts of the natural law, of their nature binding on all men, except for the obligation of Sabbath observance. This is a special definition of and application to the Hebrews of the principle that part of man's time should be set aside for divine worship. The Hebrews to whom the law was given were such as ' have need of milk and not of strong meat ' (Heb 5:12), and consequently the perfection of Christian morality must not be expected. It should be remembered, however, that sins of thought are already forbidden and not merely external acts (Ex 20:17 ; Deut 5:21). Faults of omission are taken account of as well as those of commission (Num 15:22). The sanctity of human life was safeguarded in the **f** decalogue itself. Yet the Hebrews, like the Assyrians, were merciless even in their official conduct of war. The wholesale slaughter, for instance, of Madianite men and women ordered by Moses (Num 31:1-19) was a ferocious act compared with the Christian (I cannot say, the modern) standard of warfare. To pass a just judgement on such conduct, it must be viewed in its historical context. The Israelites enjoyed a reputation for clemency among the Syrians (3 Kg 20:31). The particular case of the war against the Madianites must be seen in connection with the incidents of Num 25. And, in general, men had not yet had their ideals elevated and their innate brutality softened by the influence of Christianity. Moreover, the sense of corporate, collective responsibility was very strong, as it still is among the Arab tribes of today ; *cf.* A. Jaussen, O.P., *Coutumes des Arabes au Pays de Moab* (Paris, 1908) 436. The tribe or nation was guilty and all its members were liable to the penalty which could be justly inflicted for the crime committed. Christianity, by enhancing men's estimate of the worth of each individual man as created by God with an immortal soul and responsible by his own acts for his eternal welfare, has been instrumental in shifting the emphasis from collective to individual responsibility. The justice, however, of

110f collective responsibility and of collective retribution, unanimously admitted and acted on in OT times, has, of course, never been repudiated by Christian teaching, though Christianity has striven to make men forgiving, and, if justice demands retribution, more gentle in its

g execution. See also §§ 208f, 211g. The Mosaic code itself forbade the extension of the ancient concept of family solidarity to the execution of all the male members of a family for the crime of one. Such was the practice of the Persians and other ancient peoples ; cf. Herod. 3, 119, Quintus Curtius 6, 20. This prohibition is given in Deut 24:16, ' Fathers shall not be put to death together with their sons nor sons with their fathers '. The code also strove to mitigate man's natural harshness and selfishness. This can be illustrated by many prescriptions. The wickedness of abusing the weakness of the stranger, the widow and the orphan is stressed (Ex 22:21 f.). And in many ways the law strove to inculcate a positive spirit of humanity and kindliness. It is of obligation to help even a personal enemy among fellow-Israelites (Ex 23:4 f.). Help must be given when another man's animal has strayed or is in difficulties on a journey (Deut 22:1–4). Grapes may be eaten in another's vineyard and ears of corn in another's field, though grapes may not be carried away in a basket or a sickle be used in the field (Deut 23:24 f. [MT 25 f.]). The owner was not permitted to glean his own olive trees or vines. The gleanings were to be left for the stranger, the widow and the orphan (Deut 24:20 f.). The Hebrew must be kind to strangers and love them as God himself does (Lev 19:33 f. ; Deut 10:18 f.). Men were weaned from cruelty towards dumb animals by laws enjoining humanity and kindness in their use (Deut 22:6 f. ; 25:4).

h The ideal of monogamous marriage was proposed by the example of our first parents and was strongly recommended to the later Israelites by the prophets' habitual description of Yahweh's union with his people under the figure of a marital union (Is 1:2, Ez 16:8, etc.). But monogamy was not prescribed. The patriarchs Abraham and Jacob had each several wives. And the history of both shows that a sterile wife would invite her husband to take a handmaid as secondary wife in order to raise up issue. Following this precedent the Mosaic law recognized the practice of polygamy, stipulating only that the father may not substitute a son born to a specially loved wife for his firstborn, issue of a wife less esteemed (Deut 21:15–17). And kings were prohibited from multiplying their wives after the manner of oriental despots (Deut 17:17), a prohibition entirely disregarded by Solomon. Divorce also was not prohibited. Abraham dismissed Agar ; and the Mosaic law tolerated the practice on account of the hardness of men's hearts (Mt 19:8) but made repudiation more difficult by requiring legal formalities (Deut 24:1–4).

i Side by side with prescriptions relative to moral conduct are set down what today would be considered enactments of civil law (Ex 22–3 ; Deut 20). The civil law of Israel was thus a divinely sanctioned law in harmony with the character of Israel as God's ' peculiar possession ', every part of whose life came under the direction and protection of religion. Some of these laws are, as in all codes, a determination of the natural law. As an example may be cited the law regulating compensation when one man's ox gores and kills another's (Ex 21:35 f.). Such laws regulating the rights of property are fundamental, as all codes must endeavour to secure strict justice between the members of the commonwealth. This end of preventing the bounds of strict justice from being exceeded in a spirit of revenge was the purpose of the Lex Talionis, which allowed no greater injury in punishment than had been unjustly inflicted, ' an eye for an eye, a tooth for a tooth ' (Ex 21:24 f. ; Lev 24:19 f. ; Deut 19:19–21).

j Other laws are directly religious as regulating the outward forms of the worship of God and man's other duties in the direct service of God. Under the former

head come the laws and regulations concerning the **110j** Tabernacle, its ministers, sacrifices and feasts. Under the latter head are comprised tithes, firstfruits and vows. Lastly, there are religious observances connected with uncleanness, the avoidance of certain foods, the sabbatical year and the year of jubilee.

Divine Worship—The centre of the cult was the **111a** Tabernacle, which with its appurtenances is described in §§ 176f–178e. The Holy of Holies was entered by no one but the high-priest, who himself entered only on the day of atonement. The most important ceremony of this day was the sprinkling of the blood of the victims offered for sin on and in front of the propitiatory or mercy-seat. The purpose of the whole ceremony was not only to make atonement for the transgressions of the people but also to purify the sacred place from contamination caused by sin. And as it might be supposed that the Holy of Holies, to which there was no access except on this day, could not be contaminated, the ceremony was a striking witness to God's abhorrence of evil and demand for the most absolute sinlessness. Once in the year, on the same day, blood was to be sprinkled in atonement on the horns of the altar of incense (Ex 30:10) which stood in the Holy Place, the chamber immediately in front of the Holy of Holies. Otherwise this altar was reserved exclusively for the daily offering of incense, once in the morning and once in the evening(Ex 30:7 f. ; Lk 1:9 f.). This offering of incense was an act of adoration, and an atoning power is ascribed to the burning of incense in Num 16:46 f. (MT 17:11 f.), where DV has ' pray ' for ' atone '. The Psalmist compares it to prayer (Ps 140:2) ; cf. Apoc 5:8. The laying out of the twelve **loaves of b proposition** or shewbread on the table on the north side of the Holy Place was a cultic observance of which the Bible offers no explanation. The obvious symbolism was the recognition of the truth that man owes to God not only his existence but also his means of subsistence. The seven lamps on the lampstand (DV ' candlestick ', Num 8:2) were apparently to burn from evening to morning only. (They were trimmed at the time of the morning offering of incense [Ex 30:7] and were to be set up at the time of the evening offering of the same [v 8] ; Ex 27:21 and Lev 24:3 fix the time as ' from evening until morning ' [cf. 1 Kg 3:3] ; there were no windows in the Holy Place, but it would seem that the provision of artificial light was not deemed necessary between the two offerings of incense.) This suggests the symbolism that the burning lamps figure the worship of the sons of Israel during the hours of darkness when worshippers would not be present.

Hebrew cult had no feature more prominent or more **c** important than the frequent animal sacrifices. The altar of burnt offerings on which the victims were consumed by fire in whole or in part lay in the court before the Holy Place. See the description § 178d. The different types of sacrifice and offering are explained § 183a–e.

The supreme act of worship was the holocaust, in **d** which, as the name implies, the whole victim was consumed by fire on the altar and no part of it fell to the use of man. On its ritual see §184b–c. The actual slaying of the victim was a necessary preliminary but by no means the essential part of the ritual. The offering of sacrifice was a priestly act and only priests were allowed to minister at the altar of burnt offering (Ex 30:20) [where DV incorrectly ' offer incense '], but the duty of killing the animal fell to the offerer, who for the most part would be a layman (Lev 1:5, 3:2, etc.). The duty of the priests was to sprinkle the blood round about on the altar (Lev 1:5, 11, 3:2, etc.), and to arrange the portions of the victim on the altar to be burnt (Lev 1:9, 13). The consumption of blood was **e** prohibited to the Hebrews, whether priest or lay (Lev 3:17, 7:26 f.) ; and the reason is given in Deut 12:23, namely that the blood is the soul or life. The blood, that is to say, is the most obvious necessary condition of life ; an otherwise perfectly healthy body is dead when once drained of its blood. And in Lev 17:11 the

111e atoning power of blood is explicitly referred to this fact that it is the vehicle of life, though as the word *nepeš* is used both of the soul as spirit of life and of life itself, the exact translation is uncertain : ' The life of the flesh is in the blood, and I have given it to you that you may make atonement upon the altar for your souls, for it is the blood which makes atonement through the life '. This explains clearly the significance of the outpouring of the blood on the altar in the ritual of sacrifice. It was not the blood as such but the blood in its relation to life that had atoning power. God alone is the author of life, and the ritual act was a solemn confession of the supreme dominion of God the

f Creator over man as over all his creatures. The other part of the ritual, the burning of the victim upon the altar, had its own significance. The whole victim seemed to go up to heaven to God in the only way within the power of man as it rose in smoke from the altar ; and this rising up to God is expressed by *'ōlāh*, the Hebrew name for the holocaust. Man thus gave it back to God, from whom he had received it, in as absolute a manner as possible. And the complete destruction of the victim by fire was the means necessary to make possible this rising up to God, and at the same time entirely removed it from the ownership or use of man. The holocaust was thus the most solemn act of worship in Israel. In it alone was the whole victim burnt on the altar. In the case of sin-offerings made when the anointed priest had sinned and brought guilt on the people or when the people itself had sinned, the whole victim was burnt, but only part upon the altar and part without the camp (Lev 4:12, 21). In addition to being the supreme act of worship the holocaust had also expiatory value, as is explicitly noted Lev 1:4. Besides other occasions holocausts were ordered to be offered in perpetuity every morning and every evening (Ex 29:38–42).

g This atoning power of the holocaust was not held to suffice and was probably considered to apply only to sin of which the offerer was never fully conscious, as special sacrifices existed for the atonement of specific transgressions. These were **the sin-offering** and **trespass-offering** (RV ' guilt offering '). They are mentioned as different sacrifices (Lev 7:7). As the same word is used for ' sin ' and ' sin-offering ' and the same for ' trespass ' and ' trespass-offering ', there is in some passages room for different interpretations and the translations will accordingly be found at times to differ. It is a result of this double meaning that RV makes the sin-offering of Lev 5:6 also a ' guilt offering '. It is not easy to make a clear-cut distinction between the cases calling for atonement respectively by one or the other sacrifice : see § 183*c*. It may be noted here that the sprinkling of the blood of the victim on the altar either of incense or of burnt-offerings is characteristic of both offerings (Lev 4:7, 18, 25, 30, 34, 5:9 and Lev 7:2). On the other hand it is only in reference to the tresspass-offering that there is question of restitution, fine or money value of the victim (Lev 5:15 f., 18, 6:5 f.). (The absence of reference to the value of the trespass-offering to be made by lepers and Nazarites is due to the fact that the degree of legal uncleanness was not variable.) Both sacrifices were means of obtaining atonement and forgiveness (Lev 4:26, 31, 35, 5:10 and 5:16,18, 6:7), but the righting of a wrong done was proper to the trespass-offering.

h It is to be noted that all the faults calling for expiation by a sin-offering enumerated in Lev 4 and 5 are cases of inadvertence or complete ignorance (4:2, 13, 22, 27; 5:2, 3, 4) [DV incorrectly ' forget '], except 5:1 which is concerned with a sin of omission. Num 15:22–29 goes further and lays it down that sins such as the above could be atoned for, but not (22:30 f.) sins committed ' with a high hand ' (DV ' through pride '). Any committing such sins were to be cut off from the people with whom God had entered into a holy covenant. They had proved themselves unworthy of it. Grave sins were punished by death and there was no possibility of atonement (Ex 21:14–17, etc.). In

regard to the trespass-offering atonement is limited **111i** again among sins against God to those committed in inadvertence or ignorance (Lev 5:15, 17), whereas there is no such limitation as regards injustices against man. In these latter cases the emphasis is on righting the wrong done to another. The obligation to atone even for unwitting breaches of the divine law was a means aptly chosen to inculcate on Israel the absolute obedience and sinlessness required in the service of the all-holy God.

There remain the **peace offerings,** on which see § 183*b* ; **i** Lev 3, 7:11 ff. They might be offered either in thanksgiving for benefits received or in supplication for future divine favours. The sprinkling of the blood which formed part of this ritual also indicates a sense of the abiding need of sinful man for expiation. But the characteristic feature of this sacrifice, which was a joyful one, was the feast enjoyed by the offerer and his family or friends of those portions of the victim which belonged neither to God nor to the priests. The flesh could be eaten by all except those suffering from legal impurity. These peace offerings, as well as holocausts, were of pre-Mosaic origin (Ex 20:24).

A later Mosaic law turned all animals, whether ox, **j** sheep or goat, sacrificed for food into peace offerings (Lev 17:1–7). Moses found that his people, always so prone to idolatry, were killing these animals in honour of local desert spirits (DV ' devils '). In order to check this grave abuse God ordered that none of these animals should be killed anywhere, whether within or without the camp, except at the tabernacle. The animals which were then being killed ' in the field ' or open country, the Israelites are ordered in future to bring to the tabernacle, there to be slain and offered with the ritual of peace offerings. Thus every repast of flesh meat became a holy meal shared with the priests and sanctified by oblation to God. (The attempt to remove this law from its Sinaitic setting by excising ' the camp ' and ' the tent of meeting ' is quite arbitrary.) Moses foresaw the impossibility of this law once the tribes should have been dispersed over the Promised Land, and it was modified when the Israelites were about to cross the Jordan, to allow animals to be killed for food anywhere if the distance from the central place of sacrifice should be too great (Deut 12:20 f.).

The Israelites would always be exposed to the danger **11** of idolatry on account of their close contact with pagan nations ; and as worship entailed sacrifice, this danger would be mitigated by **the limitation of sacrifice to one shrine** erected in honour of Yahweh. In the earliest legislation there is no provision for such limitation. Sacrifice is allowed in every place which God has sanctified by some divine manifestation (DV ' where the memory of my name shall be ') [Ex 20:24]. But after the consecration of the ark and the tabernacle that shrine was the one and only such place always accessible to the Israelites during the period of the wanderings, and there they were commanded to bring their sacrifices (Lev 17:8 f.). Actually this law was not observed (Deut 12:8). This, however, is not surprising, as the Israelites fell into worse sins during the wanderings of the exodus. Despite the manifestations of divine power in their favour both in Egypt and at Sinai they fell into idolatry before entering Canaan (Lev 17:7; Num 25:2; Ez 20:16 f.). It is, therefore, to be expected that other less vital laws should have been violated. Moses could only hope that religious observance would improve when the people had come to rest in the possession that the Lord was to give them (Deut 12:9). With that end in view he insists upon the law with **b** emphasis and reiteration. In the place which the Lord should choose, there and there only was sacrifice to be offered (Deut 12:5, 11, 14, 18, 21, 26). This sixfold mention of the Lord's choice of a place is joined with the promise that God would give them peace from their enemies, and it is implied that this choice would not be made until peace had been granted (10). These conditions were not fulfilled until the time of

2b Solomon. The tabernacle and ark were long at Silo (Shiloh ; Jos 18:1 ; 1 Kg 1–4), and by the court of the tabernacle, and probably surrounding it, were buildings for the service of the ministers and for the needs of divine worship. These with the shrine itself were the *hêkāl* or temple mentioned in 1 Kg 3:3. (Compare the name ἱερόν ' temple ' given to the whole complex of buildings erected by Herod as opposed to the ναός ' shrine ' in which were the Holy Place and the Holy of Holies.) The evidence is against the idea that at Shiloh the ark was itself housed in a building. *Cf.* ' I chose no city . . . for a house to be built that my name might be there ' (3 Kg 8:16), and ' I have not dwelt in a house from the day that I brought the children of Israel out of the land of Egypt even to this day, but have *moved about* in a tabernacle and in a tent ' (2 Kg 7:6). In his message to David delivered through Nathan God said that he had never required any of the tribes (or, Judges) to build a temple, but David's son is to build a house to God's name, and ' my people . . . shall be disturbed no more, neither shall the children of iniquity afflict them any more as they did before from the day that I appointed Judges over my people Israel, and I will give them rest from all their enemies ' (2 Kg 7:7, 10 f., 13). And from the dedication of Solomon's temple Jerusalem is frequently spoken of as ' the city which the Lord chose out of all the tribes of Israel to put his name there ' (3 Kg 8:44, 48, 11:13, **c** 32, 36, 14:21 ; 4 Kg 21:7 ; 23:27). These considerations are supported by 3 Kg 3:2, ' the people sacrificed in the high places, for there was no temple built to the name of the Lord until that day ', and explain how it happened that during the period of the Judges sacrifices were legitimately offered in various places. After the dedication of Solomon's temple the conditions required for the law to come into force were fulfilled. The circumstances of the time, however, were most unfavourable for its observance or even for an attempt to enforce it. Solomon's own religious practice (*cf.* § 114i) was against the very purpose of the law, and the people had grown accustomed to the contrary practice during the **d** previous centuries. Then the revolt, which split the kingdom into two after Solomon's death, brought with it a religious schism. As a safeguard against attempts at reunion with the Southern Kingdom Jeroboam did everything in his power to prevent the people from making pilgrimage to Jerusalem. This was the object of his new shrines of Yahweh at Bethel and Dan where the God of Israel was to be worshipped under the image of a bull. And Baasa took measures to close the frontier to prevent all intercourse between the two kingdoms. In these circumstances the law of the one sanctuary became impossible of fulfilment in the Northern Kingdom, and altars were built to Yahweh to aid in the preservation of true religion. These altars were destroyed in the religious persecution of Baal-worshipping Achab and Jezabel, a destruction bemoaned by Elias, ' They have thrown down thy altars, they have slain thy prophets ' (3 Kg 18:32, 19:10, 14), and Elias himself built an altar on Mount Carmel. These altars are not in any way evidence that the law of the one sanctuary did not exist. What they do show is that the law did not demand a rigid observance to be urged even in circumstances when its purpose, which was to further the true worship of God, would not be furthered but rather hindered. That the altars promoted the worship of Yahweh is clear from the fact that their destruction sprang from the desire to uproot that worship altogether. Elias bewailed at the time that ' the children of Israel have forsaken thy covenant ' (3 Kg 19:14).

e **The Ministers of the Cult** from the time of Moses were divided into two grades. These were the priests for the sacerdotal work, and their assistants who came to have the exclusive designation of Levites. For **the priesthood** God appointed Aaron and his male descendants (Ex 28:1). The Hebrews, like the Arabs, attached particular importance to their line of ancestors, and the fact that the right to the priesthood depended on descent from Aaron was a strong added incentive to **112e** the maintenance of careful family tables. Accordingly after the exile we find that Esdras, priest and scribe, traced his descent through Sadoc and Eleazar to Aaron (Esd 7:1–5, 11), and those who could not establish their Aaronic descent by documentary evidence were expelled from the priesthood (Esd 2:62). There is no reason to doubt that in this matter the law was always adhered to rigidly. The priesthood was a vested interest and temporal advantage was a re-inforcement of the spiritual motive of obedience. At the same time the hereditary nature of the priesthood was unfortunately the cause of many entering its ranks for whom spiritual motives had small appeal. This was a recurring source of religious weakness and even indifference, and at least a contributory cause of many scandals in the national life. Aaron and his sons were initiated into their sacred office by a special form of consecration (Ex 29:1–37 ; Lev 8). And the future successors of Aaron as chief priest were also to be anointed and officially installed in office (Lev 16:32). There is no specific regulation about any ceremony by which the lesser priests were to be introduced to their work.

To the priests fell the most sacred functions, and, of **f** course, the sacerdotal act of offering sacrifice. It was their duty to offer the blood of the victims and to sprinkle it on the altar of burnt-offerings, to put part of it on the horns of the altar of incense or of burnt-offerings, or to pour it out at the base of the latter altar according to the nature of the sacrifice and its ritual (Lev 1:5, 4:7, 25). The actual killing of the victims and their division into parts were not sacerdotal acts (*cf.* §111d). It was further the duty of the priests to lay the portions of the victim on the altar and consume them with fire (Lev 1:8 f., 12 f., etc.). All the more sacred functions were performed exclusively by the priests. They performed all duties within the tabernacle. They offered incense on the altar of incense (Ex 30:7 f. ; Num 16:40), a duty which was reserved to the Aaronites under pain of death. In fact they alone were allowed within the Holy Place (Ex 30:19 f. ; Num 18:7) ; and consequently they had charge of the seven-branched lampstand and of the table of shewbread (Ex 27:20 f. ; Lev 24:5–9). Not only might no one but the priests enter the sanctuary, no one else was allowed even to touch the vessels and objects which belonged to it (Num 4:15). It was, therefore, the privilege of the priests to take down and wrap up all the appurtenances of the sanctuary when the Israelites were about to strike camp (Num 4:5–15). It was further the priestly office to bless the people (Num 6:23–27). The priests had also a teaching office entrusted to them. They were to instruct the people in the law of God (Lev 10:11 ; *cf.* Mal 2:7). Other duties, such as purification from the uncleanness of leprosy (Lev ch 13 f.) can only be alluded to here.

The name of **Levites** given to the second class of **g** ministers is not without ambiguity, as strictly it denotes all the members of the tribe of Levi to which the priestly family of Aaron also belonged. Thus Aaron himself is spoken of as ' Aaron the Levite ' (Ex 4:14) ; and the priests are included among the Levites of Num 35:2 ff. (*cf.* Jos 21:1–4). However, the name became the technical designation of the non-Aaronite male members of the tribe from the age at which they entered on office (Num 7:5–9). At the coming forth from Egypt God had claimed as his own all the firstborn males of Israel in memory of the manner in which the deliverance had been finally achieved. They were to be ' sanctified ' to God, that is, specially dedicated to his service, presumably as ministers of his worship (Ex 13:2), but another later law ordained that they should be ' redeemed ' or bought back (Ex 13:13, 34:20). Finally God chose the Levites to ' serve in his ministry ' in place of the firstborn (Num 8:11, 16–18). The age of service is laid down as ' twenty-five years old and upwards ' (Num 8:24), though those deputed to carry the tabernacle and its belongings on the march were only those between the ages of thirty and fifty

112h (Num 4:3 ff.). (Later the heavy work required during the wanderings being over, David lowered the age to twenty [1 Par 23:24–27], and in view of this passage the age of thirty given in 1 Par 23:3 must be a textual error based on Num 4:3. David's innovation is important as showing that the prescriptions of the law were not regarded as being immutable even when circumstances had completely altered.) Beyond the duty of carrying the tabernacle and its vessels on the march (Num 4) the office of the Levites is only vaguely indicated in the Pentateuch. They were to camp around the tabernacle and guard it (Num 1:53). For the rest it is laid down that they are to minister to Aaron and busy themselves with the work of the tabernacle, without, however, permission to touch the vessels of the sanctuary or the altar (Num 18:2–4). Later David organized them as porters, singers, musicians and so forth (1 Par 23–26).

i There is very little information about Levites in the early centuries after the occupation of Canaan. In the turbulent period of the Judges the law was honoured in the breach more than by observance : each did what seemed right in his own eyes (Jud 17:6, 21:24). In the days of Saul the ark was neglected (1 Par 13:3). For a period the ark and the tabernacle were even separated at different places (1 Par 16:39 ; 2 Par 1:3–5). This astonishing fact gives an idea of what the ritual observance must have been. Moreover, the authors of some of the early histories were not interested in or did not choose to give space to ritual matters. The Books of Paralipomenon, on the other hand, give abundant information on these topics drawn from ancient sources which the earlier histories had not utilized. It has even been suggested that the carrying of the ark by the priests on certain occasions is an indication that the Levites did not exist at the time, as this function is assigned to the latter in Num 4:5 f., 15. It must be remembered, however, that the Levites were to carry the ark when wrapped up for journeys in the wilderness. On solemn occasions when the ark would be carried uncovered, the Levites would not be permitted to touch it and the honour fell to the priests (Jos 4:9, 6:6). During times when the worship of God was neglected (4 Kg 23:5 ; 2 Par 28:24) and it was impossible for the Levites to gain their sustenance from service in the temple, many of them may have become merged in the people at large. Ezechiel (44:10–14) planned to recruit their ranks by the degradation of those priests who had fallen into idolatrous worship. Only ' the priests the Levites, the sons of Sadoc ' who had remained faithful, were to retain the sacerdotal office (44:15).

113a Feasts—As God created man and the whole of his life belongs to God, he is at all times to bear the law of God in mind faithfully to observe it (Deut 6:5–9), and every day public worship was offered especially by the morning and evening holocausts (Ex 29:38). In addition there were certain holy days and holy seasons. These came round every seven days, every month, every year, every seven years, and every seven times **b** seven years. The weekly feast was **the Sabbath** which fell on the last day of the week. (The first mention of it occurs Ex 16:23–30 ; on its origin see §172k and on the Sabbath precept of the decalogue §173b.) The day had its negative and positive observances. The name is taken from the negative element, as it was a day of strict rest or abstinence from all work (Ex 20:10). The special solemnity of the feast was marked by this complete prohibition of all work, whereas on other feasts only servile work is forbidden (Lev 23:7 and cf. Ex 12:16 ; Lev 23:8, 21, 25, 35 f.), with the exception of the day of atonement (Lev 23:28) [MT and LXX]. This complete rest incumbent on the whole household was a memorial of their liberation from the hard tasks of Egypt (Deut 5:15), and at the same time provided suitable rest and relaxation (Ex 23:12). The Sabbath was intended to be a day of gladness (Os 2:11), very different from the burdensome yoke it became in the time of Christ owing to the multiplication of Pharisaical **c** regulations. Every Sabbath the loaves of proposition

were changed (Lev 24:8), and special sacrifices were **11:** offered in addition to the daily holocausts (Num 28:9 f.). A ' holy convocation ' is prescribed (Lev 23:2 f.) [MT], but the exact meaning of this is nowhere explained. The term does not signify a meeting to be held at the sanctuary by all, as only thrice in the year were all males under an obligation to ' appear before the Lord ' (Ex 23:17) on the three chief feasts of the calendar. In later times these holy convocations were meetings in the synagogues for worship and preaching. So far as is known, there was nothing analogous to the Sabbath in the religions of neighbouring peoples.

As every week so every month was consecrated by a **d** feast, **the feast of the new moon** or first day of the month, as the Hebrew months were reckoned by the moon. Special holocausts were prescribed for this day, and a sin-offering in atonement for the wrong-doing of the previous month (Num 28:11–15). On this day the priests were to blow the silver trumpets at the time of the holocausts (Num 10:8, 10). Abstinence from work was not prescribed, nor a holy convocation. Custom, however, forbade trading on this day (Am 8:5), which was a holiday celebrated by a feast (1 Kg 20:5) and therefore unsuitable for fasting (Jdt 8:6).

The first day of Tishri (September–October) was a **e** feast of special solemnity (Lev 23:23 f. ; Num 29:1–6) commonly called **the Feast of Trumpets**. Whether this day owed its sacred character to its being the opening of the seventh month or the beginning of the civil year is not clear. It was to be celebrated by abstinence from servile work, by a holy convocation, special holocausts in addition to those belonging to the day as the first of the month and to the perpetual daily sacrifice, and by a sin-offering in atonement for the sins of the people. Further, as the name implies, there was a special blowing of trumpets, probably at intervals throughout the day, whereas on other feasts the silver trumpets were sounded only at the time of the sacrifices (Num 10:2, 10). As a distinguishing feature ram's horns seem to have been used on this day, and consequently the allusion in Ps 80(81)4 would be to this festival. See art. ' Trumpet ' in HDB.

As from the time of Moses the liturgical year began **f** with the month Abib, later called Nisan (March–April) [Ex 12:2], the first great festival was that of **the Pasch and feast of unleavened bread** (Lev 23:5 and 6 where they are spoken of separately). In practice the two coalesced into one, as no leaven was permitted from the evening of the 14th, when the Paschal supper was eaten, for the seven days to the evening of the 21st (Ex 12:18). The origin of the two feasts was probably different. That of the Pasch is given in Ex 12, §169e–f, and it is probable that the feast of unleavened bread was more ancient. It may have been the feast which Moses asked permission to go and celebrate in the desert (Ex 5:3, 10:24–26). The ancestors of the Israelites were not true nomads but remained long enough in one place to raise crops (Gen 26:12), and the agricultural feast of unleavened bread may have been celebrated by the patriarchs. Its essential feature was the consecration to God of the firstfruits of the new barley crop, the first of the year to mature. Before the new produce had been thus publicly acknowledged as the gift of God it was unlawful to partake of it in any form (Lev 23:6–14). The names Pasch and Phase (Ex 12:11 ; Deut 16:1) are synonyms, the former being derived from Aramaic and the latter from Hebrew. The equivalent English name is Passover, the feast commemorating the salvation of the Israelites when the avenging Angel passed over the dwellings of the Israelites to strike only all the firstborn of the Egyptians. On the whole feast see also Ex 13:3–10 ; Num 9:2–14, 28:16–25 ; Deut 16:1–8. The animal to be sacrificed **g** and eaten at the paschal supper was a lamb or a kid (Ex 12:5), and this animal is itself sometimes called the pasch or phase (Ex 12:21). In Deut 16:1–8 the feasts of the pasch and unleavened bread are so welded into one that victims for sacrificial meals on the days following the paschal supper are also called by the

3g name pasch or phase (Deut 16:2 f.). These could be sheep or oxen, and later received the name *chagîgah*, which originally denoted the celebration of a feast. This may be the meaning of pasch in Jn 18:28. It may further be noted here that in Ex 12:9 it is ordered that the pasch is to be eaten roasted, neither raw nor boiled. In Deut 16:7 cooking but not the manner of cooking is prescribed, the word used, *bāšal*, which originally meant ' to ripen ' (in the sun), being applied to the artificial ' ripening ' of food by cooking to make it fit for eating. At this feast all males were ' to appear before the Lord ', that is, to attend at the sanctuary (Ex 23:14–17). We have historical notices of the first pasch celebrated by Josue and the people after their entry into the Promised Land with which was connected the cessation of manna (Jos 5:10–12), of the pasch celebrated by Ezechias (2 Par 30), and also of that celebrated at the time of Josias' great reform (2 Par 35). The latter were celebrations such as had not been seen for centuries.

h As the feast of unleavened bread at the time of putting ' the sickle to the corn ' (Deut 16:9) sanctified the beginning of the barley harvest, so **the feast of weeks** (Ex 34:22) was that at which thanksgiving was made to God for the completion of the wheat harvest. Barley ripens several weeks before wheat in Palestine. The two feasts were thus complementary. And the initial and final character of the two festivals was appropriately symbolized by the waving before the Lord of a sheaf of barley at the former (Lev 23:11), and of two loaves made of fermented flour, such as the people were wont to eat, at the latter (Lev 23:17). The interval of time between the two offerings was to be seven weeks, so that the second offering took place fifty days after the first (Lev 23:15 f.), whence the NT **i** name of Pentecost (Ac 2:1). The exact day from which the count was to be made was disputed among the Jews themselves at the close of the OT period. The prevailing practice was to understand the Sabbath of Lev 23:11, 15, of the day of rest which opened the feast of unleavened bread (Lev 23:7), whereas the Sadducees claimed that the Sabbath in question was the weekly Sabbath which fell within the seven days of the feast ; see art. ' Pentecost ' HDB 740. The feast of weeks was the second of the three at which all male Hebrews were to ' appear before the Lord ' (Ex 23:14–17, 34:23). The legislation regarding the feast is given Lev 23:15–22; Num 28:26–31 ; Deut 16:9–12. (The difference in the number of victims read in Lev and Num respectively is probably due to textual corruption, Num 28:27 being correct in prescribing two young bulls and one ram in accordance with the practice at the new moon feasts and the seven days of the feast of unleavened bread [Num 28:11, 19, 24]. Josephus, however, records that in his time the two texts were taken to give two distinct prescriptions and two sets of victims were offered accordingly [*Ant.* 3, 10, 6], where, by another slip, the combined figure for the rams is given as two instead of three.)

j The third of the great feasts at which all male Israelites were required to repair to the sanctuary (Ex 23:14–17) was **the feast of tabernacles** (Lev 23:34), otherwise called the feast of ingathering (Ex 23:16 [where for ' corn ' read *produce*]). The feast proper lasted seven days from the 15th to the 21st day of the 7th month and was followed by one day of celebration on the 22nd, which brought the cycle of annual feasts to an end. This additional day tended inevitably to be identified with the feast proper ; contrast Lev 23:35 f., 39 and 2 Mac 10:6. In the agricultural calendar this festival celebrated the conclusion of the labours of the year when the crops had been gathered from field, vineyard and olive grove. This was the fundamental idea of the feast. It was a time of rejoicing and of thanksgiving when the good gifts of God had been gathered in from the land divinely given to the Hebrew people. For a comparatively primitive people an appropriate setting for such a festivity was in ' tabernacles ' or booths set up, for instance, in the vineyards. This gave the feast a further historical significance as a commemoration of

the long years the Hebrews had sojourned in tabernacles **113j** (Lev 23:43). Not all the Mosaic prescriptions were considered to bind for all time. Some were given for the preparatory period spent in the wanderings in the wilderness. And it is interesting that when the feast was celebrated in 444 under Esdras and Nehemias and the people made themselves tabernacles, it is recorded that the feast had not been kept in that manner since the days of Josue (Neh 8:17)—incidentally an illustration of the strict observance of the law which set in after the exile. The relevant legislation is given Lev 23:34–36, 39–43 ; Num 29:12–38 ; Deut 16:13–16, 31:10–13. This celebration as the final and greatest of the year is spoken of simply as ' the feast ', *e.g.* 3 Kg 8:2, 65 ; Neh 8:14.

Lastly must be mentioned **the day of atonement** (Lev **k** 25:9) in Ac 27:9 called ' the fast '. This fell on the 10th day of the 7th month between the feast of trumpets and the feast of tabernacles (Lev 23:27). Feasts and fasts were reckoned from evening to evening, and the 9th day of Lev 23:32 is a loose expression for the evening beginning the 10th day. The relevant passages are Ex 30:10; Lev 16, §191*d–k*, 23:27–32 ; Num 29:7–11, where the various sacrifices and special ceremonies of atonement are prescribed, and see § 111*a*. The day was one of fasting (the only one ordered in the law) called ' afflicting the soul ', and of abstinence from servile work. Thus, though the sacerdotal ceremonies of atonement took place in the tabernacle or temple, which there was no obligation to attend on this day, the whole nation had its part in the work of expiation by personal penance, and was encouraged to enter wholeheartedly into the spirit of repentance and purpose of amendment which were the natural fruits of such an observance. The atonement was for the wrong-doing of the whole nation including the priests and served also to purify the sanctuary from any defilement that the contact of sinful man might have brought upon it. In view of the paucity of the refer- **l** ences to the feasts in the OT it is not inexplicable that the only allusion to the day of atonement is in Ecclus 50:5 ff. (obscured in DV). It has, however, caused surprise that there is no mention of it in Neh 8–9, and the fact that a solemn day of atonement was celebrated on the 24th of the 7th month has been thought to imply a recent origin for the day of atonement on the 10th. Actually had the introduction of the day taken place, as is claimed, after the 7th month of Neh 8–9, the yearly day of atonement would have been fixed on the anniversary of that celebrated by Esdras (Neh 9:1). Moreover, it would not have been introduced in the form it has. The most solemn act of the whole year would not have been prescribed in a form incapable of fulfilment as the Holy of Holies was empty, the ark was not there nor the propitiatory. Actually, there is no valid argument from silence in the case. The feast **m** of trumpets is not named nor its ceremonies referred to. It is alluded to (Neh 8:1 ff.) merely on account of the reading of the law which took place that year on, though not prescribed for, that feast. Similarly, the feast of tabernacles is mentioned, not simply because it was kept, but because for many centuries it had not been kept as it was that year (Neh 8:17). There is thus no ground for saying that had the day of atonement been observed on the 10th, the fact would have been recorded. If it was kept in the ordinary way, there was no reason for recording it. The assumption of the argument used to prove the late introduction of the feast is that, had it been found in the book of the law, it would have been kept and the fact would have been recorded. Therefore, it is claimed, it was not in the law. But, if it was not in the law publicly read out on the feast of trumpets (Neh 8:2–9) and on each day of the feast of tabernacles (Neh 8:18), it could not have been subsequently introduced as of Mosaic origin. There was no reason to record the observance of the day on the 10th, and a special day of atonement was instituted that year on the 24th in preparation for the solemn covenant (Neh 10:29–31).

114a The Spirit of the Mosaic Religion—Mosaic religion inculcated the most **profound reverence for God,** whose majesty had been graphically symbolized by the terrifying theophany of Sinai. He had created the heavens and the earth and all that is in them (Ex 20:11). Everything in this world was subject to his dominion, as was manifested by the plagues of Egypt and the other miraculous events accompanying the liberation from Egypt. His dwelling was in heaven far exalted above the abode of men. In recognition of this supreme dominion of God the Israelites were under the obligation of offering sacrifices and of making pilgrimages to his shrine ; and as God had made all and all belonged by right to him, the Israelite was to recognize this divine ownership by ' redeeming ' or buying back his firstborn males, whether of his family, of his herd or his flock, by offering a tithe of the produce of his land, by setting aside part of his time, Sabbaths and other holy seasons, for the worship of God.

b Yet this God of supreme power and dominion did not wish to remain aloof from man as the remote object of worship. He was **the God of loving condescension.** He deigned to enter into a covenant with Israel, whom he chose as his own special possession (Ex 24:8, 34:10 ; Deut 5:2). And not merely that, he deigned to dwell in their midst and to manifest his presence in the Holy of Holies (Ex 25:22 ; Lev 16:2 ; Num 7:89). God was thus exalted above the earth in his heavenly dwelling and yet living in the midst of his people. They were his children, not merely his creatures ; Israel was his **c** firstborn (Ex 4:22). In answer to this love and favour God claimed not only exclusive adoration (Ex 20:1–5) but also an **absorbing love** : ' Thou shalt love Yahweh thy God with thy whole heart, and with thy whole soul, and with thy whole strength ' (Deut 6:5). And this exhortation not merely to reverence and obey God but to do so with wholehearted love is emphasized by repetition (Deut 10:12, 11:1, 13). The Hebrew words rendered in the received English form as ' with thy whole soul ' did not convey to the Hebrew mind quite what the English words signify to us, as the spiritual nature of the soul was a truth unknown in the time of Moses and for many centuries thereafter. The Hebrew word is *nepeš*, which has the same sense here as in Ps 40:3, ' Deliver him not up to the will (*nepeš*) of his enemies '. The word signifies that the Israelites were to love God with all the desire and longing of which they were capable, that is with an intense love. This precept, the noblest of the OT, alone raised the religion of Israel to heights undreamt of in the ancient pagan religions, and even the NT could offer no more exalted idea of the relation in which man should stand to God than this of wholehearted and intense love. To Christians the idea is so familiar that there is a danger of overlooking what would have appeared to non-Israelites as the revolutionary character of this religious precept.

d The God of majesty who thus manifested himself to Israel in loving condescension was also **the God of holiness** ; and this holiness of God was impressed on the people by emphasis on God's detestation of all evil and by the necessity of absolute ritual purity in his service. Our Lord's exhortation, ' Be ye perfect as also your heavenly father is perfect ' (Mt 5:48), is an echo, though with a higher connotation of perfection, of the ideal of Mosaic religion. One of Moses' last addresses to his people contains the appeal, ' Thou shalt be perfect and without spot before the Lord thy God ' (Deut 18:13) [where the words ' without spot ' are a doublet added by St Jerome to bring out the meaning of perfection]. What God asked of his people was obedience to his law (Deut 10:12). By correspondence to its just demands they would be what God desired above all ' a holy nation ' (Ex 19:6 ; Lev 20:7). This holiness would be manifested in just dealing and in respect for the rights of others. But the good Hebrew was not to be satisfied by conformity to the strict **e** demands of justice. His dealings were to be marked by kindness towards the weak and helpless. And the stranger, the fatherless and the widow are specially **114** singled out as requiring and deserving kindly help (Deut 14:29, 16:11, 14). Indeed the precept of charity extended to all fellow-Israelites : ' Thou shalt love thy *neighbour* as thyself ' (Lev 19:18). The Hebrew word *rēaʿ* here used does not warrant an extension of the precept to all men (Maldonatus, Knabenbauer ; it was allowed to exact usury from strangers though forbidden in the case of Israelites [Deut 23:19 f.]). It remained for our Lord, who came ' to fulfil the law ', to bring this precept to perfection by extension to the hated Samaritans, and by implication to all men (Lk 10:29–37). But even in its restricted sense the precept raised the religion of Israel above that of other ancient peoples, and represented the highest ideal the Israelites were capable of assimilating in their then stage of spiritual development.

Violations of God's commandments and precepts were, **f** of course, known to be offences against God the all-holy law-giver. The Israelite had a sense of sin. He did not think of it as a defilement of the soul, since not only the spiritual but also the substantial nature of the soul was not known till long after the Mosaic period. Sin was considered to make the whole man displeasing to God, which indeed it does. Neither was sin thought of as involving the loss of supernatural grace, as this too was unknown. The sense of sin shows that man was known to be free and responsible for his acts. And accordingly a clear distinction was drawn in the culpability incurred by different types of sin ; *cf.* § 111*h*. For grave offences no means of reconciliation was offered. Lesser offences were atoned for by sacrifices. Confession of guilt was explicitly ordered in the case of trespass-offerings (Lev 5:5 ; Num 5:7) and on the day of atonement (Lev 16:21). Penance was enjoined by the fast of the day of atonement (Lev 16:29) by the addition of a fifth of the value in the case of injured or usurped rights (Lev 5:16, 6:5, 22:14 ; Num 5:7). There was, besides, the pecuniary penance involved in providing the animals prescribed for sacrifice.

As no revelation had been made concerning rewards **g** and punishments after death, the sanctions proposed were all temporal (Ex 20:12 ; Lev 26 ; Deut 28). At its institution, therefore, the Mosaic religion could not be called either otherworldly or spiritual, the notion of spirit being too subtle to be grasped by a comparatively uncultured people. And such the religion remained for the greater part of OT history. Nonetheless it was the highest form of religion to which the people could attain at the time and was immeasurably superior to the religions of the surrounding nations. Faithful observance of Mosaic religion meant a profound sense of the majesty and holiness of God, of his right to the entire and pure service of man, and in daily life ensured a high standard of justice in all human relationships, of family morality and of kindliness to the weak and defenceless.

As regards the world at large, it remains to notice that **h** Hebrew religion was a national and not a universal religion. It was based on a covenant entered into by God with Abraham, the father of the race (Gen 15 and 17) and solemnly renewed with the people at Sinai (Ex 24). There is nowhere an exhortation to labour for the conversion of the pagan nations to the religion of Yahweh. Yet the religion was not on a narrowly racial basis. ' A mixed multitude without number ' came out of Egypt with the children of Israel (Ex 12:38). And any of these and any other strangers who were willing were free to become part of the people of the covenant. The one condition explicitly made was that all males were to undergo the rite of circumcision (Ex 12:48), which was the external sign of God's covenant (Gen 17:11). A later modification of this universal permission excluded Edomites and Egyptians to the third generation and Ammonites and Moabites to the tenth (Deut 23:3, 7 f.). This prohibition did not, of course, exclude any from the knowledge and worship of the true God. The exclusion was from the covenant and from participation in the temporal bless-

4h ings promised by God as reward for its faithful observance. To any believers thus shut out from membership of God's earthly kingdom, God would show his mercy in ways outside the covenant.

i Mosaic Religion in Practice—This sketch of Mosaic religion has attempted to set down in brief its beliefs, practices and ideals. These were, however, very imperfectly reflected in the history of the people. While the words of the decalogue were still ringing in their ears, they had violated one of its fundamental precepts by setting up the golden calf for worship and that with the connivance of Aaron himself (Ex 32). This was an evil presage for the future. Moses accused the people of being stiffnecked and of having striven against the Lord from the time of leaving Egypt (Deut 9:6 f., 31:27). Indeed it was not long before they fell into actual idolatry while Moses yet lived (Num 25:3 ; Ez 20:16, 24). And idolatry was to be rampant among them through the greater part of their history. In the time of Elias only seven thousand of all the population of the Northern Kingdom had not bowed the knee to Baal (3 Kg 19:18). Solomon himself not only worshipped false gods, like Astarte and Moloch, but actually built them temples near the holy city (3 Kg 11:5–8). Manasses even built idolatrous altars to the host of heaven in the very temple of God (4 Kg 21:4 f.). These are but a few examples. And where their leaders led the way, the people were not slow to follow. What such idolatry entailed in the neglect of God's law and

j its religious observances can be easily imagined. In the wilderness the rite of circumcision which impressed on man the outward and essential sign of his membership of the covenant race (Gen 17:14) was not observed (Jos 5:5 f.). Whatever the reason for this failure, the fact was not such as to train the people in an exact following of the ceremonial law. This tendency was accentuated by the turbulent conditions prevalent in Canaan during the period of the Judges when conditions made the due observance of the law impossible in many respects. Non-observance led to disregard, contempt, oblivion. In the days of Saul the ark, Israel's most sacred possession, was neglected (1 Par 13:3). Even among the pious the law seems to have been very imperfectly known. Elcana went once a year to offer sacrifice at Shilo (1 Kg 1:3, 7) [DV ' upon the appointed days ' is unwarranted], though the law ordered attendance at the three great festivals (Ex 34:23 ; Deut 16:16). After the time of the Judges when ' every one did that which seemed right to himself ' (Jg 21:24), and the general neglect of the days of Saul, it would not have been easy to institute a thorough reform in the nation even if such had been attempted. David, despite his zeal to honour the ark, violated the law of Num 4:15 and had the ark carried on a cart, an error which he

k subsequently avoided (1 Par 13:7, 15:13, 26). Things came to such a pass that the book of the law was actually lost until the only copy which apparently existed was found in the temple in the days of Josias (4 Kg 22:8). This gave new impetus to that king's reforms, which, though more thorough than that of Ezechias, did not produce lasting results. Of each of Josias's four successors, Joachaz, Joakim, Joachin and Sedecias, it is recorded that ' he did evil before the Lord according to all that his fathers had done ' (4 Kg 23:32, 37, 24:9, 19). It was only after the sufferings of the exile and the reform under Nehemias and Esdras when princes, priests, Levites and people made a solemn covenant to ' walk in the law of God ' (Neh 10:29) that the life of the nation was faithfully based on its observance.

l Apart from the constant danger of idolatry and consequent neglect of the worship of Yahweh, the other outstanding danger to which the Israelites were exposed was that of formalism and externalism. They were inclined to imagine that because God had chosen them and because his temple stood in their midst, he was certain to favour and protect them, forgetting that God is not pleased by the mere offering of sacrifice but requires the sacrifice to be offered with a pure heart

and with pure hands. The people needed constantly **114 l** to be reminded of the lesson given by Samuel to Saul, ' Doth the Lord desire holocausts and victims and not rather that the voice of the Lord should be obeyed ? ' (1 Kg 15:22). This is the meaning of the denunciation of feasts and sacrifices by prophets and psalmists (Is 1:13 f. ; Mic 6:6–8 ; Ps 49:9). These writers did not repudiate sacrifices as such any more than did Samuel who offered them himself ; *cf.* *H. H. Rowley, *The Unity of the Old Testament* reprinted from BJRL 29 (1946). Not all the efforts of the prophets were able to wean the Israelites from this formalism and externalism which, as the NT shows, became the besetting sin of a certain part of the population (Mt 23).

It would be an error, of course, to concentrate on the **m** gloomy side of the picture and to forget the faithful souls who in every age ' with zeal ' were ' zealous for the Lord God of hosts ' (3 Kg 19:10). Many suffered for their devotion, many like the prophets of Yahweh in the Northern Kingdom were ' slain with the sword ' (*ibid.*). And the Church has ever held in especial honour the seven brothers who with their mother suffered the glorious death of martyrs in the persecution of Antiochus (2 Mac 7). The faith and devotion of **n** these holy men, women and children were sustained and strengthened by the labours of **the prophets** whose preaching played a vital part in rebuking vice and in keeping alive the spirit of true religion. They did not form part of a regular organization like the priesthood with functions regulated by the law. But God had promised through Moses to raise up such a succession of men who would be his personal representatives and make his will known to the people (Deut 18:15), a succession which was to culminate in the person of Christ our Lord, king, priest, and prophet. See further § 409*e–j*.

Post-Mosaic Development—In the space remaining an **115a** attempt must be made to give some idea of the progress made in religious thought in the centuries subsequent to Moses. A more noble idea of **the nature of God** gradually developed. The idea of spiritual substance, so difficult for man to grasp, was evolved and it became known that God is a spirit : ' Egypt is man and not God, and their horses flesh and not spirit ' (Is 31:3). Useless to rely on man and flesh ; he only can give aid who is God and spirit. The omnipresence of God is clearly conceived and beautifully expressed : ' Whither shall I go from thy spirit ? and whither shall I flee from thy face ? ' etc. (Ps 138:7–10). The same psalm in unforgettable language tells of God's knowledge of the innermost thoughts of man : ' *When yet there is no word upon my tongue, thou, Yahweh, hast perfect knowledge thereof* ' (v 4 f.). God's foreknowledge was a thought familiar to Moses (Ex 3:12). In the time of David we find a realization of God's knowledge of what would happen if some condition never in fact to be fulfilled were actually fulfilled (1 Kg 23:10–13). Belief in **b** God's eternity is given utterance in Ps 89:2, 4 : ' Before the mountains were *given birth* and earth and world *begotten*, from eternity to eternity thou art God . . . for a thousand years in thy sight are as a by-gone yesterday and as a watch in the night '. And in Ps 101:26 ff. : ' The heavens are the work of thy hands. They shall perish but thou remainest. All of them shall grow old like a garment . . . but thou art the selfsame and thy years shall not fail '. God not only created the universe ; he created according to his good pleasure and his own free will : ' Whatsoever the Lord pleased he hath *made* in heaven, in earth, in the seas, and in all the deeps ' (Ps 134:6). This is a noble and elevated conception of the nature of God—spiritual in substance, eternal, omnipotent, omniscient, omnipresent, though, as the OT nowhere presents a theological treatise, these attributes are not expressed in this abstract language.

There was progress, too, in the knowledge of **the nature c of man,** though it appears only in the Greek-composed Book of Wisdom. The Hebrews had always known

115c that man is immortal, though they had no clear conception what part of man survived the corruption of the grave. In the older literature, when a man dies, ' he ' goes to Sheol ; it is never said that his soul or his spirit survives. It is God's breath breathed into man and beast that gives them life (Gen 2:7 ; Ps 103:29 f.). Ecclesiastes makes a distinction between the case of man and of beast despite the fact that to all appearance the life of man and the life of beast are the same. (The Hebrew ' Who knows ' means ' it is difficult to learn '.) He says literally ' Who knows whether the breath (*rûaḥ*) of the sons of man goes upward and the breath (*rûaḥ*) of the beasts goes downwards to the earth ? ' (3:21), and the meaning is ' It is difficult to learn whether the breath of man goes upwards, whereas the breath of beasts goes downwards to the earth ? ' For the construction, whereby a subordinate clause is expressed paratactically, *cf.* Mt 11:25 ; Rom 6:17 ; Is 12:1. (The *rûaḥ* in question cannot be other than the breath of life for it is said to be one and the same in man and beast 3:19.) Later Ecclesiastes expresses his faith clearly : ' The *breath* returned to God who gave it ' (12:7). The Book of Wisdom has advanced beyond this. After death ' the souls of the just are in the hands of God ' ; they seemed to die but in fact they are immortal (3:1-4).

d Towards the close of the OT period a development of fundamental importance, indeed a revolution, is to be noted in beliefs concerning **life after death.** Religion is no longer this-worldly looking for rewards and punishments on this earth alone. In life after death God will give to each according to his works, and man will live on not as a disembodied spirit but with soul and body reunited in the resurrection. These beliefs, however, did not become universal as the Sadducees persisted in the old ways and denied the resurrection and the existence of spirit (Mt 22:23-32 ; Ac 23:8). The first indication of belief in the resurrection and future retribution occurs in Dan 12:2. Belief in both was nobly professed by the Maccabean martyrs in presence of the tyrant king Antiochus : ' The King of the world will raise us up, who die for his laws, in the resurrection of eternal life ' (2 Mac 7:9, 10 f., 14, 23). This resurrection was not restricted to the just, though for the wicked like Antiochus himself there would be ' no resurrection unto life ' (14). This eternal life will be the reward of the just : ' My brethren . . . are under the covenant of eternal life, but thou by the judgement of God shalt receive just punishment for thy pride ' (36).

e The same faith in rewards and punishments for the good and wicked after death is found in the Book of Wisdom. Of the just it is said (3:1-4 and 5:16 f.), ' The just live for ever, and in the Lord is their reward and the care of them is with the Most High. Therefore they shall receive the kingdom of glory and the diadem of beauty from the hand of the Lord '. The chastisement of the wicked is implied in 3:1, ' the souls of the just are in the hands of God and torment shall not touch them ', and 3:10 reads, ' the impious . . . shall have chastisement who neglected the just and revolted from God '. And see 4:18-5:14.

f That there is further **an intermediate state after death** in which the departed have not received the final reward of the good and can still atone for sin was also known at this time. Judas Maccabeus collected and sent to Jerusalem a sum of money to have a sacrifice offered in atonement for the sin committed by men who had fallen in battle under his command (2 Mac 12:39-46). As the Greek reads, ' he made propitiation for the dead that they might be loosed from sin '.

g With a few restrictions Moses had allowed all foreigners who would to undergo the rite of circumcision and share in the privileges of the covenant people. But the OT records tell of few who embraced the worship of **11** Yahweh. There was Ruth the Moabitess (Ru 1:16) and Naaman the Syrian (4 Kg 5:15). And we read nothing of missionary effort to spread the faith. On the other hand there becomes manifest a generous attitude towards other nations and **a spirit of universalism.** ' O praise the Lord all ye nations ! Praise him all ye people ! ' (Ps 116), a passage quoted with others by St Paul to show that ' the Gentiles are to glorify God for his mercy ' (Rom 15:9-12). Isaias sees many peoples flocking to the mount of Yahweh (2:2-4 = Mic 4:1-3). Isaias even foresees the day when Gentiles shall become priests of God (66:21), and Malachy foretells the offering by Gentiles of a pure oblation from the rising of the sun to the going down thereof (1:11). Finally mention should be made of the passionate **love h of the law** and zeal for its strict observance which developed in Israel after the reform under Nehemias and the covenant then entered into to make it the rule of life (Neh 10). Unfortunately with many this love and zeal gradually took a wrong turning into the ways of external **formalism** without regard to the inner spirit. This became the outstanding characteristic of Pharisaism.

This outline of the growth of religious belief especially in the last centuries of the OT period gives also a general idea of the state of religion among the chosen people when Christ our Lord was born into the world. **Conclusion**—It is a remarkable fact that the people of **i** Israel, small in number and unimportant politically, should have been the only race in the ancient world among whom the worship of the one God, Creator and Lord of the world, should have been preached and practised. And the fact is not the less remarkable for the reason that Israel owed this unique honour not to any merit or exertion of its own but to divine election. It is an outstanding example of the divine policy so often manifested in history of choosing the weak things of the world to confound the strong (1 Cor 1:27). A study of the religious history of this chosen race makes its election even more remarkable still, for its record through the pages of the OT is largely one of backsliding and infidelity. Still with all its individual and even mass neglect of God the nation remained the one bright spot in the ancient religious world where pure and true worship was at least the ideal proposed to all and at all times found faithful followers.

Not only had Israel the glory of being the one centre **j** of monotheism, its beliefs about God were noble and pure. A glance at the zoomorphic gods of Egypt and at the fighting and ignoble conduct of the deities of Babylon brings into sharp relief the immeasurable superiority of the religion of Israel. And this nobler conception of the divinity is reflected in the far higher standard of conduct demanded of his people. Immorality and human sacrifice, which disgraced pagan cults, had no part in the worship of Israel ; necromancy and all forms of magic were forbidden. Above all else the religion of Israel owed its pre-eminence to the bond of strong personal love which it sought to establish between man and God. This was the tremendous truth revealed to Israel. The lord and master of the universe deigned to love Israel and to ask for the love of his people in return.

However, despite all the grandeur and nobility that elevated it above all the other religions of the world, the religion of Israel was not itself perfect either in its revelation of religious truth or in the standard of morality which it demanded of its adherents, for it was itself preparatory and destined to lead the people on to the spiritual and universal religion to be inaugurated by Christ our Lord. (On the Messianic prophecies and Israel as pedagogue to Christ see also §§ 102h-103a).

THE GENTILE NEIGHBOURS

By E. POWER, S.J.

a **Bibliography**—The Cambridge Ancient History, generally reliable, except in its very radical account of Israel, but occasionally antiquated by recent discoveries, must be consulted for older works, as only a selection from recent literature can be given here.

b **General History**—*W. F. Albright, ' How well can we know the Ancient Near East ? ' JAOS 56 (1936), 121–44 ; *F. Bilabel und *A. Grohmann, *Geschichte Vorderasiens und Aegyptens*, Heidelberg, 1927 ; B. Bonkamp, *Die Bibel im Lichte der Keilschriftforschung*, Recklinghausen, 1939 ; G. Capart et G. Contenau, *Histoire de l'Orient Ancien*, Paris, 1936 ; *V. G. Childe, *New Light on the Most Ancient East*, London, 1935² ; L. Delaporte, *Le Proche-Orient Asiatique*, Paris, 1938 ; L. Dennefeld, *Histoire d'Israel et de l'Ancient Orient*, Paris, 1935 ; *E. Ebeling, *Geschichte des alten Morgenlandes*, Berlin, 1929 ; *B. Hrozny, *Die aelteste Geschichte Vorderasiens*, Prague, 1939 ; H. Junker und L. Delaporte, *Die Aegypter, Babylonier, Assyrer, Perser, Phoeniker*, Freiburg, 1933 ; *E. Meyer und *H. L. Stier, *Geschichte des Altertums*, Leipzig, 1937² ; *A. Moret, *Histoire de l'Orient*, Paris, 1936 ; *M. Noth, *Die Welt des AT*, Berlin, 1940 ; J. Vandervost, *Israël et l'Ancien Orient*, Bruxelles, 1929².

c **Special Subjects**—*A. Alt, *Voelker und Staaten Syriens im fruehen Altertum*, Leipzig, 1936 ; *G. A. Barton, *Semitic and Hamitic Origins*, Philadelphia, 1934 ; A. Bea, ' La Palestina preisraelitica ', Bi 24 (1943), 231–60 ; G. Contenau, *La civilisation d'Assour et de Babylone*, Paris, 1937 ; E. Dhorme, ' Les Amorrhéens ', RB 37 (1928), 63–79, 161–80 ; 39 (1930), 161–78 ; 40 (1931), 161–84 ; C. F. Jean, ' Hammourapi ' DBVS 3 (1938), 1379–408 ; *A. Scharff, *Die Fruehkulturen Aegyptens und Mesopotamiens*, Leipzig, 1941 ; *S. Smith, *Alalakh and Chronology* (London, 1940) ; R. de Vaux, ' Les Patriarches hébreux et les découvertes modernes,' RB 53 (1946), 321–48 ; *E. Drioton et J. Vandier, *L'Egypte*, Paris, 1938 ; *K. Galling, ' Hyksosherrschaft und Hyksoskultur ', ZDPV 62 (1939), 89–115 ; * P. Montet, *Le drame d'Avaris*, Paris, 1939 ; *F. Petrie, *The Making of Egypt*, London, 1939 ; *H. Stock, *Studien zur Geschichte und Archaeologie der 13. bis 17. Dynastie Aegyptens*, Glueckstadt-Hamburg, 1942 ; L. H. Vincent, ' Les pays bibliques et l'Egypte à la fin de la XII dynastie ', RB 51 (1942), 187–212 ; G. Contenau, *La civilisation des Hittites et des Mitanniens*, Paris, 1934 ; *Id.*, ' Les Hourrites ', DBVS 4 (1941), 128–38 ;

d *A. Goetze, *Hethiter, Churriter und Assyrer*, Oslo, 1936 ; R. de Vaux, ' Etudes sur les Hurrites ', RB 50 (1941), 194–211 ; R. T. O'Callaghan, *Aram Naharaim (Upper Mesopotamia in the Second Millennium B.C.)*, Roma, 1948 ; L. Delaporte, *Les Hittites*, Paris, 1936 ; *Id.*, ' Les Hittites ', DBVS 4 (1941), 32–110 ; *J. Garstang, *The Hittite Empire*, London, 1929 ; E. Dhorme, ' La question des Habiri ', RHR 118 (1938) 170–87 ; *J. Lewy, ' Habiri and Hebrews ', Hebr. Union Coll. Ann. 14 (1938), 587–623 ; G. Contenau, *La Civilisation phénicienne*, Paris, 1939 ; *O. Eissfeldt, *Philister und Phoenizier*, Leipzig, 1936 ; *R. Weill, *La Phénicie et l'Asie Occidentale*, Paris, 1939 ; *G. Cameron, *History of Early Iran*, Chicago, 1935 ; E. Dhorme, ' Elam ', DBVS 2 (1932), 920–62 ; *K. Galling, *Syrien in der Politik der Achaemeniden bis 448 v. Chr.*, Leipzig, 1937 ; * F. W. Koenig, *Aelteste Geschichte der Meder und Perser*,

Leipzig, 1934 ; *E. Bickerman, *Institutions des Seleucides*, Paris, 1938. **116d**

Introduction—The most ancient civilizations revealed **e** to us by recent discoveries developed contemporaneously in Egypt and Mesopotamia. Between these two countries at their northern ends is a long, narrow strip of land lying between the Mediterranean sea and the Arabian desert. The northern and larger part of this bridge between east and west is Syria, the southern and smaller Palestine. Through these regions passed the chief trade routes of the ancient east. Their inhabitants had not politically developed beyond the stage of independent city states, constantly warring with one another. They were thus unprepared to resist the attacks of the more powerful and better organized neighbouring kingdoms which coveted their rich territory and lucrative trade routes. The ancient **f** history of the Near East is largely a record of the struggle for Syria and Palestine, in which the Babylonians, the Egyptians, the Hurrites, the Hittites, the Assyrians, the Chaldaeans, the Persians and the Greeks all took part at different periods. This history is further diversified by constant incursions into ' the fertile crescent ', formed by Egypt, Palestine, Syria and Mesopotamia, of fresh peoples seeking new homes, chiefly Aryans from the north and east, and Semites from the west and south. Of these the Hurrites, Hittites and Kassites were Aryanized Asianics ; the Medes, Persians and Greeks were Aryans ; the Assyrians, Amorrhaeans, Habiri, Aramaeans and Chaldaeans were Semites. Some knowledge of the history of these various peoples, who were the Gentile neighbours of the Palestinians before and after the Hebrew conquest of Canaan, is necessary for the biblical student. It enables him to locate the chosen people in their historical setting, to evaluate the foreign influences to which they were subjected, and to understand many obscure passages and incidental allusions in the sacred text.

The Babylonians—The ancient Babylonians inhabited **117a** the region between the Euphrates and Tigris from about 34° N. latitude to the Persian Gulf. These rivers then approached each other more nearly in their lower courses and entered the sea considerably higher up than they do at present, and Babylonia (OT Sennaar) was originally about the size of Belgium. Its alluvial soil was extraordinarily fertile and was irrigated by numerous canals, without which it would have suffered from drought in the dry season and annual devastation when its great rivers were flooded by the melting of the snows in the mountains of Armenia. Its southern and northern parts, later distinguished as Sumer and Akkad, were inhabited from the earliest known period by different races. The Akkadians were Semites of Arabian origin. The Sumerians were Asianics who had entered Babylonia from the north-east. Their earliest culture is an uninterrupted continuation of the still earlier culture of the Iranian plateau, which also appears with local variations in Northern Mesopotamia and Syria. Three stages in the development of this culture during the prehistoric period are named after the sites where they were first discovered : el-'Obeid near Ur (el-Mukeyir) and Uruk (Warka), both in Sumer, and Djemdet-Naṣr near Kish (el-Oḥeimir) in Akkad. After

117a el-'Obeid, when copper appears but is extremely rare, comes Uruk, memorable for the invention of writing.

b The earliest writing is pictographic. We can trace the development of the original pictograms into conventional phonetic signs with syllabic values in the following period at Djemdet-Naṣr. In hasty writing straight lines impressed with a stilus on clay tablets become wedge-shaped at one end. Hence the name cuneiform given to this script. The final stage appears in the inscriptions of Ur at the beginning of the historic period. The Elamites who first borrowed this script gave originally different syllabic values to the cuneiform characters, but later conformed entirely to the Babylonian system which was universally adopted in the Near East. The Djemdet-Naṣr culture had a very wide diffusion. We find undoubted traces of it at Mohenjo-daro in the Indus valley, at Megiddo, Jericho and Gezer in Palestine, and in Egypt during the late predynastic period and the early Thinite dynasties. The latest prehistoric cultural period at Kish is immediately preceded by an inundation of the Euphrates which destroyed the city. A similar inundation at Ur in the earlier el-'Obeid period is attested by a layer of silt ten feet deep. No other traces have been discovered of a Babylonian deluge. The distinction between postdiluvian and antediluvian kings, made by the later historians of Ur, seems therefore to be based on a local inundation. But an earlier deluge of much wider extension is presupposed by the Babylonian literary records as well as by the biblical narrative.

c The prehistoric period cannot be exactly dated, but most probably covered and overlapped the fourth millennium B.C. The historic period begins with the first dynasty of Ur. The earlier importance of Uruk and Kish is undoubted, but the records of their first dynasties are legendary. At Ur on the other hand the reigns of the kings are of normal length and A-anni-padda, son of the founder of the first dynasty Mes-anni-padda, appears in an inscription as the builder of a temple of Ninhursag at el-'Obeid. Recent discoveries which lower considerably the pivot date of the first Babylonian dynasty make it difficult to date the first dynasty of Ur earlier than c 2500 B.C. Of the subsequent monarchs Lugalzaggisi of Uruk is the first who claims to have extended his rule beyond Babylonia and to have reached the Mediterranean. He was dethroned by Sargon of Akkad or Agade (unidentified but near Kish), a Semite and founder of a dynasty which lasted nearly two centuries (c 2360–2180 B.C.). Akkad now first appears as the name of northern Babylonia and the struggle for dominion between Sumerians and Akkadians becomes pro-

d nounced. Sargon first subdued the Sumerian city states and then gradually extended his empire to the Lebanon and Amanus in the west, Cappadocia in the north, Elam in the east and parts of Arabia in the south-west. His empire was still intact and trade and commerce flourished under his third and most famous successor, Naram-Sin, but the last three kings were hard pressed by the Gutians who descended from the slopes of Mt Zagros into Babylonia and ruled the land for more than a century. The Sumerian states of Umma (Djoḥa), Lagash (Tello) and Ur apparently came to terms with the invaders and enjoyed a period

e of prosperity. The Gutians were finally expelled by Utu-Hegal of Uruk who, after a seven years' reign, was replaced by Ur-Nammu, founder of the third dynasty of Ur (c 2070–1960 B.C.). The first three kings of this dynasty were prosperous at home and abroad and extended their rule over most of northern Mesopotamia. The fourth, Gimil-Sin, had to build the Amurru wall, connecting the Euphrates with the Tigris in the region of Sippar, to avert a threatened Amorrhaean invasion from the west. The last, Ibi-Sin, succumbed finally after a long resistance to an invasion from the east and was dethroned and taken prisoner to Elam. The Sumerians are now politically unimportant. Originally mountaineers, they suffered

from the unhealthy climate and would in any case have **1** been overwhelmed by the constant inflow of Semites from the west. But the civilization which they created survived among their supplanters and exercised a profound influence over all the Near East, especially after the foundation of the Babylonian empire.

In the renewed struggle for dominion between the **f** city states, Isin (Bahriyat) in the north and Larsa (Senkereh) in the south play the leading parts for more than a century, after which a new claimant appears, the hitherto insignificant Akkadian city of Babylon (Hilleh). Sumu-Abum, an Amorrhaean or western Semite, founded the first Babylonian dynasty c 1830 B.C. His successor, Sumu-la-ilum, ruled over all Akkad and part of Sumer. It was not, however, until the defeat of Rim-Sin (very probably the Arioch or Riu-Aku of Gen 14:1) and the capture of Larsa by Hammurabi, the sixth and greatest of the Babylonian kings, that Sumer was completely subdued.

Hammurabi (c 1728–1686 B.C.), very probably the **g** Amraphel of Gen 14:1, is the most remarkable figure of all the ancient east. He reduced all Mesopotamia under his sway and as 'king of the west-land' seems to have claimed a suzerainty over Syria and Palestine. He is more famous, however, as a ruler and legislator than as a warrior. He was the first to establish a centralized administration in the home countries of Sumer and Akkad by substituting personally appointed governors for native princes and a single law-code for different local customs. In the outlying regions on the other hand vassal princes were confirmed in office and local usages were retained. He spent forty years **h** of his reign in preparing a most comprehensive code of laws which exercised a considerable influence, directly or indirectly, on all subsequent eastern legislation. He reformed religion by raising his city god, Marduk, to the head of the Pantheon and transferring to him the attributes of the other local gods and by conferring on his consort, the Semitic Ishtar, the same pre-eminence among the goddesses. In the ancient east religion was of first importance. Hittites and Assyrians as well as Babylonians regarded the ruler as the vicegerent of the principal divinity to whom the state belonged. Finally in his correspondence with his governors Hammurabi shows an admirable solicitude and personal interest in the administration of justice and of property, in works of piety and public utility and in everything which contributed to the welfare of his people.

Excavations have revealed the contacts existing be- **i** tween the remotest parts of the Near East at this period. It was by trade and commerce rather than by conquest that the civilization which the Babylonians borrowed from the Sumerians, script and legislation, cosmogony and natural science, religion and mythology, was so widely diffused. The OT commentaries will reveal how far the Hebrews surpassed the Babylonians in their religious ideas and how much they were indebted to them in almost every other department of knowledge.

Aryan peoples from the north-east invaded Cappa- **j** docia and northern Mesopotamia in the beginning of the second millennium B.C. and succeeded in establishing themselves as ruling classes over the Asiatic inhabitants among whom they settled. Their racial character is determined by their personal names and by the Aryan gods in their Pantheons. Of these were the Kassites, who made their first inroads into Babylonia under Hammurabi's successor, Shamsu-iluna. At the same time remnants of the Sumerians and other malcontents founded the second Babylonian dynasty in the maritime regions of the south. A disturbed period followed until a Hittite raid on Babylon put an end to the first Babylonian dynasty of the Amorrhaeans. It was succeeded by the partly contemporaneous third Babylonian dynasty of the Kassites (c 1600–1170 B.C.). Under these rulers Babylonia retained her independence and national existence, but never recovered her ancient pre-eminence. The second

j Babylonian dynasty maintained itself in the south for two and a half centuries while the first and third ruled in the north.

k **Chronological Note**—The reader may be surprised that the dates given in the preceding section are so much lower than those for instance of the Cambridge Ancient History. The reason is that the Babylonian chronology of the early historical period has been revolutionized by important discoveries. Babylonian inscriptions record various dynasties and regnal years of successive kings. They do not however inform us when these dynasties are contemporaneous or enable us to convert relative into absolute dates. Calculations based on the Venus tablets of Ammisaduga gave, at best, a choice of dates but no definite chronology. Assyrian inscriptions by recording an eclipse of the sun in 763 B.C. provide a solid foundation for an absolute chronology at a later period. A relatively complete list of regnal years of the Assyrian kings discovered at Khorsabad in 1933 extends this chronology, with due reservations, to the second millennium

l B.C. The most assured base of an absolute chronology is the Egyptian Sothic period (§ 118e). Synchronisms with Egypt and Assyria enable us to establish an approximate but reliable Babylonian chronology. Pottery and cylinder seals of the first Babylonian dynasty (now dated c 1830–1530) have been found at Ugarit above the layer containing finds of the XII Egyptian dynasty (c 1989–1776). More definite is the evidence derived from the letters discovered at Mari which establish beyond all doubt that Hammurabi (now dated 1728–1686) was a younger contemporary of Shamshi-Adad I of Assyria (c 1748–1716). This date is also archaeologically confirmed by the Khabur ware, unearthed at various sites in northern Mesopotamia, which covers a continuous period of about three centuries from the reign of Shamshi-Adad I (18th century) to the new ware of Nuzi (15th century). Finally the Byblian prince, Entin, attested by various scarabs and a hieroglyphic inscription as a contemporary of the Pharaoh Nefer-hotep I (XIII dynasty, c 1740–1730), appears in fuller form, Yantin-hamu, in a Mari document. He too was a contemporary of Hammurabi, who put an end to Mari's greatness in the thirty-second year of his reign. Earlier Babylonian periods, of which the length is known, are calculated backwards from the new date of Hammurabi.

a **The Egyptians**—Egypt is the long narrow strip of land extending from the Mediterranean in the north to Assuan in the south and bounded by deserts on either side. No larger than Belgium or ancient Babylonia, it owes its extraordinary fertility, and indeed its very existence, to the annual inundations of the Nile. Its original Hamitic inhabitants, dolichocephalic and small in stature, were racially akin to the Nubians in the south and the Libyans in the west. They had politically developed from city states into the two kingdoms of Upper and Lower Egypt and attained a high degree of civilization in the fourth millennium B.C. This civilization originated more probably in the Delta region, but it is still uncertain whether and how far

b Asiatic infiltrations contributed to it. The union of the two kingdoms seems to have been effected about 3000 B.C., when the historical and dynastic periods begin. The earliest inscriptions belong to the first dynasty, but the writing is then too developed for a recent invention. The script was and remained pictographic, but certain signs were conventionally used to express consonantal sounds so that the proper names and abstract ideas could be graphically indicated. The different materials used, papyrus in Egypt and clay tablets in Babylonia, largely explain the different developments of the Egyptian and Babylonian scripts, which seem to have originated independently and contemporaneously.

c The ancient historians reckoned thirty dynasties of Egyptian kings. Of these the best known and the most important are I–VI (Old Kingdom, c 3000–2350 B.C.), XI–XII (Middle Kingdom, c 2150–1776 B.C.) and

XVIII–XX (New Kingdom, c 1580–1090 B.C.). The **118c** dynasties of the disturbed intervening periods were less stable and to some extent contemporaneous. In the Old Kingdom period the union of North and South was consolidated by Khasekhem (II dynasty), who moved the capital from the south to Memphis at the apex of the Delta triangle. The erection of the pyramids was begun by his successor, Zoser (III dynasty). The three great pyramids at Ghizeh, however, belong to the IV dynasty and were built by Khufu (Cheops), Khufru and Menkaure (Mycerinus). A tomb and a chapel are the principal contents of these great funeral monuments, which still attest belief in and preparation for a life after death as a distinctive element of Egyptian religion. Contacts with Byblos **d** in Phoenicia are found throughout this whole period. It was not for conquest, but to secure materials for the building and adornment of temples and palaces, that expeditions were made by land and sea to distant regions. Granite was brought from Assuan, gold from Nubia, copper from Sinai and cedar-wood from Lebanon. Pottery and stone vases found in the royal tombs of the I dynasty at Abydos are of North Syrian origin. Conversely alabaster vases of the III dynasty were discovered at Hai in Palestine. The Old Kingdom reached its culminating point in art and organization in the IV dynasty under Snefru. Egypt was then divided into nomes or districts about forty in number. District rulers, judges and minor officials were royal nominees. Estates were settled on favourites by royal gift.

To this period at latest belongs the institution of the **e** calendar. The heliacal rising of Sothis or Sirius, the dog-star, at the beginning of the inundation of the Nile, introduced the first year of the new calendar. As the Egyptian year had invariably 365 days and was therefore nearly six hours shorter than the solar year, the next coincidence of the civil New Year and the heliacal rising of Sothis occurred after a period, roughly determined by the ancients as $365 \times 4 = 1460$, but more accurately by Schoch in 1928 as 1456 years. This is called a Sothic period. We know that the last Sothic period ended A.D. 140–43 and can thus fix the beginnings of two such periods at 2772–2769 and 1316–1313 B.C. A few events of which the relative date is recorded as coinciding with a rising of Sothis can thus be dated absolutely, since their position in a Sothic period is exactly determined.

Military expeditions to Palestine are recorded in **f** the last dynasties of the Old Kingdom. The capture of a walled town, probably Lydda, is represented on a fifth dynasty tomb. Uni, an officer of Pepi I of the sixth dynasty, boasts of five successful military expeditions against the neighbouring Asiatics. The fifth dynasty is remarkable for the elevation of Ra, the Sun-god, to the head of the Egyptian Pantheon. The sixth is a period of decentralization when authority passes over into the hands of noble families and local chiefs. Rival contemporary rulers now appear for a time at Heracleopolis in Middle Egypt and at Thebes in the south. The ultimate victory of the Thebans inaugurates the Middle Kingdom.

Little remarkable is recorded of the eleventh dynasty, **g** but the Amenemhets and Senusrets of the twelfth raised Egypt to the highest peak of power and prosperity yet attained. Amon, the human-headed Theban divinity, was particularly venerated by them. He was soon identified with Ra and under the name Amon-Ra became king of all the gods. They transferred the capital from Thebes to a more central position at Itht-toui south of Memphis, reintroduced centralization of government and reduced the power of the nobles. Magnificent buildings were erected and adorned. The arts were particularly cultivated. The twelfth dynasty is the classical age of the sculptor, the painter, the wood-carver and the jeweller. It is also the classical period of the Egyptian language. Trade and commerce flourished. The Kamares ware of Crete appears in Egypt in the reign of Senusret II.

118g Military expeditions are recorded. Senusret III (1876–1838), a great warrior, captured the town of Sichem in Palestine. His successor, Amenemhet III (1837–1789), the builder of the Labyrinth and the regulator of Lake Moeris, was a great and provident administrator, who devoted all his energies to increasing the prosperity of his people. He and Hammurabi are the best types of ancient rulers.

h Egyptian interest in Palestine and Syria at this period is strikingly illustrated by the ' Proscription Texts ' of the XII dynasty. They give lists of the enemies of Egypt, whose names and districts are inscribed either on buried clay statuettes or on shattered vases of earthenware or alabaster. The Asiatic districts are not all identified, but on the earlier statuettes we find Ascalon and Jerusalem in Palestine, Byblos, Arqatum, Ullaza and Yarimutu in Syria, and on the jar fragments, a generation later, also Sichem, Afek, Akko, Aksaph, Misael, Samkhuna, Cana, Pella, Rehob, Laiš, Iyyon. The personal names are all west Semitic like those of the first Babylonian dynasty. From the regional names we may conclude that Egyptian interest was concentrated on the plain land and trade routes, and from the personal ones that the Amorrhaeans or west Semites had recently invaded Palestine and Syria. The burying of the images and the shattering of the vases were intended to represent, if not magically effect, the destruction of Egypt's foes. Later, however, in the XIII dynasty, these hated Asiatics invaded Egypt and ruled over the land from 1730–1580 B.C.

i The Hurrites—Hurrite records are few and are written in a language of the agglutinative type still very imperfectly known. The Hurrites of Nuzi, east of the Middle Tigris, used the Babylonian tongue in their contract tablets, from which we obtain interesting information on their laws and customs. Our scant knowledge of their history is chiefly derived from excavated sites and from Babylonian, Egyptian and Hittite records. They were racially Asianics, most probably Armenoids, with an intermixture of

j Aryans who formed the ruling classes. Descending from the mountains in the north-east they settled in the basin of the Euphrates and Tigris, in the region subsequently known as Mitanni and called Khanigalbat by the later Assyrians. We find them also in outlying regions, Ugarit in western, Alalakh and Qatna in eastern Syria and Taanach in Palestine. Hurrite names first appear in the inscriptions of Naram-Sin and of the third dynasty of Ur and in the Cappadocian tablets of Kultepe. They are historically important as partakers in, and probably organizers of the Hyksos invasion of Egypt and as subsequent rulers of the great kingdom of Mitanni in Northern Mesopotamia, extending from Syrian Qadesh in the west to Mt Zagros in the east.

k The Hyksos—The word Hyksos, mistranslated Shepherd Kings by the ancients, literally means princes of the lands and was the ordinary Egyptian expression for the rulers of Asiatic districts. It gives no help therefore towards the racial identification of the invaders, most probably composed largely, if not entirely, of Hurrites and Semites. Some of the names of the Hyksos rulers are Semitic, but the majority appear to be Hurrite or Aryan. The invaders had superior military equipment, especially horses and chariots, then unknown to the Egyptians. The Hurrites were adepts in the rearing of horses. The invaders exhibit also a special technique in the fortification of cities by the use of glacis, fosse and counterscarp. This appears in the Hyksos stronghold of Tell el-Yehudieh in Egypt, in several Palestinian cities of the XVIII century B.C., Jericho, el-Fara' (most probably the Hyksos Sharuhen), Tell Beit-Mirsim, Lachish, Sichem, Haṣor and also at Qatna, a Hurrite outpost in Syria. The technique thus appears to be Hurrite and is certainly not Semitic. The fortifications show that a military occupation of

l the regions was intended. The era of Tanis, which began c 1730 B.C., seems to determine the date of the

invasion. Tanis was very probably the Hyksos capital, **1** Avaris. The statement in Num 13:22 that Hebron was built, *i.e.* fortified, seven years before Tanis refers to the same era in dating a Hyksos fortification in Palestine. The invaders seem to have penetrated beyond Thebes in the south. They introduced no new culture into Egypt, except in the matter of military equipment, and gradually became themselves Egyptianized. Resistance to their rule developed in the south and Ahmose I, the founder of the XVIII dynasty, at last succeeded in taking their capital and expelling , them from Egypt c 1580 B.C. He completed his victory by the capture of the strongly fortified Sharuhen in southern Palestine three years later. The Hyksos occupation inspired the Egyptian rulers with a great hatred of Asiatics and a strong determination to secure themselves against future invasion by the conquest of Palestine and Syria. The struggle between them and their northern rivals, the Hurrites of Mitanni and the Hittites of Asia Minor, for the possession of Syria, was to last for the next three centuries.

The Hittites—This ancient people (OT Hittim, DV **1** Hethites) takes its name from the city of Hattuš in the bend of the Halys in Cappadocia, about a hundred miles east of the Turkish capital, Angora. Their records, written mostly in the Hittite language but with Babylonian cuneiform characters, were discovered in the adjoining village of Boghazkeui and published at intervals during the last half-century. Originally Asianics like the Hurrites, they were to some extent Aryanized c 2000 B.C. by immigrants from the north-east, who became the ruling class and imposed their language on their subjects. The word Hittite is now specifically used of the empire founded by these Aryanized Asianics in the eighteenth century B.C. and destroyed by northern invaders c 1200 B.C. Hittites of earlier and later date are called respectively Proto-Hittites and Neo-Hittites. Little is known of the Proto-Hittites. **b** Their chief divinity was Wurušemu, the goddess of Arinna (unidentified), who remained, under the title Sun of Arinna, at the head of the Hittite pantheon. Her consort was the storm-god, the Hurrite Teshup and Syrian Haddad. Our first information on the foundation of the Hittite state is derived from the Cappadocian Tablets discovered at Kultepe, the ancient Ḳaneš, about a hundred miles south-east of Hattuš. One of them mentions the successful efforts of a certain Pithana, prince of Kussar, and his son, Anitta, to establish their dominion over the neighbouring city states. Their successors were Tudchaliya I and his two sons, whose names only are known to us. It is very probable that this Tudchaliya, a contemporary of Hammurabi, is the Tid'al of Gen 14:1.

The historical records of the ancient empire begin **c** with Labarna, usually regarded as its founder (c 1600 B.C.), who extended his conquests to the Mediterranean. His son, Hattušil I, invaded northern Syria, but failed to reduce Aleppo, captured eventually by his son and successor, Muršil I, who made Hattuš, his father's city, the capital of the empire. This monarch is also famous for his combats with the Hurrites and especially his raid into Babylonia, in which he captured and sacked Babylon and thus put an end to the first Babylonian dynasty c 1530 B.C. His assassination by his brother-in-law, Hantili, introduced a period of calamity under the usurpers Zidanta and Huzziya. Order was restored by Telepinu, who induced the assembly of the nobles to pass new laws regulating the succession to the throne and punishing crimes committed by members of the royal family. Hittite rule was less absolute than that of the Babylonians and Egyptians and the powers of the monarchy were constitutionally limited by those of the assembly of the nobles.

An obscure period follows the death of Telepinu **d** and marks the close of the old Hittite empire. Tudchaliya II inaugurated the new Hittite empire (c 1420 B.C.), checked at first in its expansion by the Hurrite kingdom of Mitanni in the east and the Egyptian

9d conquest of Syria in the south. His son and successor, Hattušil II, hard pressed by rebels in Asia Minor, was forced to yield Aleppo to the Hurrites. Under the next monarch, Tudchaliya III, the Hittites were beset by enemies on all sides. Kizwadna, the maritime region to which Tarsus and Adana belong, transferred its allegiance to Mitanni. Arzawa, west of Kizwadna in the south, Ashuwa, corresponding roughly to the later Roman province of Asia in the west, the Gasgas and Hiyasa in the Black Sea regions of the north revolted and ravaged the interior. At this dark period Šuppiluliuma became king (c 1375-1335 B.C.). The exploits of this great warrior, under whom the Hittites reached the height of their power and practically dominated the Near East, belong to the history of the Amarna period.

e **Egypt versus Mitanni**—We have no account of the expeditions of Ahmose I to Phoenicia and Thuthmose I to the Euphrates. The real conqueror of Palestine and Syria was Thuthmose III (c 1485-1450), who devoted to the task the campaigning seasons of at least fifteen years of his reign. The Egyptian inscriptions of the fifteenth century B.C. gave the name Huru, land of the Hurrites, to the conquered regions. The Hurrite kingdom of Mitanni in northern Mesopotamia (c 1500-1350 B.C.), which held the Assyrians in subjection and wrested territories from the Hittites, was then the most powerful state in the Near East. Its king bore the Aryan name of Šaušatar and organized the resistance to the Egyptians in the subject or allied states of the south. The Pharaoh confined his first campaigns to the subjugation and organization of Palestine. He surprised his foes—concentrated at Megiddo under the leadership of the prince of Qadesh on the Orontes—by the boldness of his advance, choosing the most direct but most difficult of the three

f passages across the mountain range. He then defeated them in pitched battle and after a siege of seven months captured the city. Little resistance was encountered elsewhere and an Egyptian fortress was erected at the entrance of the Beka' valley to secure Palestine against attacks from the north. The chiefs who submitted retained their authority, but rebels were replaced by loyal native rulers. The sons of these rulers were sent to Thebes and there educated after the Egyptian fashion to secure their future loyalty. A fixed annual tribute was the only burden imposed on the subject princes. Some Egyptian troops were left in the country and an Egyptian prefect or governor was appointed over the whole region. Sound strategy marked the Syrian campaigns. The Pharaoh perceived that the coast cities had to be first reduced and turned into bases of operation before the hinterland could be attacked with any hope of permanent success. A powerful fleet conveyed supplies and troops northwards and landed them in the neighbourhood of Arwad. The campaign by sea and by land quickly effected its object and subsequent expeditions, based not on distant Egypt but on neighbouring Phoenicia, easily reduced the Syrian cities. The Euphrates was crossed and a stele of victory erected, but no attempt was made to conquer Mesopotamia.

g The Assyrians, Hittites and Babylonians were deeply impressed by the victories of the Pharaoh and sent him valuable gifts, interpreted as tribute by the Egyptian. He extended his rule in Nubia to the fourth cataract of the Nile and reduced the oases of the Libyan desert. Egypt now overflowed with riches. Nubian and Asiatic captives were employed in the erection of magnificent monuments in Thebes and other cities of Upper Egypt. Thuthmose III was also an able and vigilant administrator. The Asiatic revolt which followed his death, according to the general custom of eastern subject peoples, was quickly repressed by his successor, Amenophis II, who made no further expedition into Asia. The next Pharaoh, Thuthmose IV, has also only one Asiatic campaign to his credit. He abandoned however the isolation policy of his predecessors and concluded alliances with

Mitanni and Babylonia. His son, Amenophis III **119h** (c 1405-1370), had a Mitanni princess for his mother, Mutemuya, daughter of Artatama I, the son and successor of Šaušatar. It was once very generally believed that Thuthmose III was the oppressor of the Hebrews and Amenophis II the Pharaoh of the Exodus. Both these Pharaohs, however, resided at Thebes and were chiefly occupied with building operations in Upper Egypt. They needed no Migdols on their eastern frontier to protect themselves from Asiatic inroads, since they were secure in the possession of Palestine and Syria. The Delta region on the other hand was the scene of the chief building operations of Ramesses II and it was there that he and Mernephtah resided.

The Amarna Age—We have abundant information on **i** the history of the Near East in the fourteenth century B.C. from the historical records of the Hittite monarchs and the diplomatic correspondence of the Egyptian Pharaohs, Amenophis III and Amenophis IV, discovered at Tell el-Amarna (cf. §78b). The Hittites now reached the height of their power. Assyria threw off the yoke of Mitanni and Babylonia and attained imperial status. The Hurrites lost their empire and the Egyptians their Asiatic dominions. The Hittite monarch, Šuppiluliuma, after establishing order provisionally in the interior, invaded Mitanni. A scission among the Hurrites had produced a second kingdom in the east, then ruled by Artatama II. By the neutrality or co-operation of this monarch Šuppiluliuma was enabled to overrun Mitanni from east to west and crossing the Euphrates near Carchemish to capture Aleppo and Qatna and reach Qadesh on the Orontes. He thus supplanted Mitanni and Egypt in northern Syria and, while avoiding open conflict with the Egyptians, extended his sphere of influence by intrigues with the native princes. Šutarna, king of Mitanni, whose daughter, Gilu-Khepa, became the wife of Amenophis III c 1400 B.C., was succeeded by his two sons, Artašumara, assassinated after a brief reign, and Tushratta (c 1385-1365). The latter, whose daughter, Tadu-Khepa, was married to Amenophis III and after his death to Amenophis IV, was also assassinated in a palace intrigue. The eastern Hurrite, Artatama II, **j** aided by the kings of Alshi and Assyria, then invaded Mitanni and installed his son, Šutarna II, as king under Assyrian protection. Tushratta's son, Muttiwaza, sought refuge in Babylonia, but when the Babylonian king, Burnaburiash II, became allied with Assyria and espoused the daughter of Aššuruballit, the dethroned monarch, fearing for his life, fled to his ancestral enemy, Šuppiluliuma. The Hittite received him graciously, gave him his daughter in marriage and a few years later expelled the Assyrians from Mitanni and restored him his kingdom. He had already enthroned his sons in northern Syria, Piyasili at Carchemish and Telepinu at Aleppo. Farther south Aziru, prince of Amurru, was his ally. His correspondence **k** with Naqamad, prince of Ugarit, enables us to date the cuneiform alphabet, invented during that monarch's reign. The Phoenician alphabet, still in use, was an earlier invention, though its earliest known occurrence is on a 10th cent. inscription at Byblos. The latter was intended for papyrus, the former for clay tablet writing. A presumed act of treachery on the part of the Egyptians provoked a declaration of war from the Hittites at the close of the Amarna period. Of its course we are only informed that Egyptians, made prisoners in the opening campaign, spread a pestilence among the Hittites, which raged twenty years, including among its victims Arnuwanda I, the son and successor of Šuppiluliuma.

Meanwhile in southern Syria and Palestine there was **l** a widespread revolt againt Egyptian rule, of which the successive phases are vividly depicted in the Amarna tablets. The loyal princes, among whom Rib-Addi of Byblos and Arti-Khepa of Jerusalem were the most conspicuous, described in their letters the progress of the movement and begged repeatedly for

119 l reinforcements. Foreign invaders, sometimes called Habiri, but more usually SA-GAZ, an ideogrammatic equivalent of the Akkadian *ḫabbatu* 'plunderer', devastated the land. Their most prominent leaders were native princes, Labaya in the south and Abd-Ashirti of Amurru in the north. When these leaders were slain their sons took their place. The rebel princes protested their loyalty to Egypt and their readiness to pay tribute, but at the same time supported the invaders and enlisted their aid to extend their own **m** dominions. The Egyptian officials temporized. A struggle for power between rival local potentates, all apparently loyal to their suzerain, may have appeared at first politically unimportant. Troops sent from Egypt were insufficient and sometimes failed to reach their objectives. Amenophis III lacked energy for a personal expedition and Amenophis IV was too absorbed by religious reforms to make any attempt to check the later stages of the revolt. Byblos finally joined the rebels and Rib-Addi was slain in exile at Sidon. Aziru, prince of Amurru, transferred his allegiance to the Hittites. Arti-Khepa's associates, according to his last letter, had all joined the Habiri and Jerusalem alone still acknowledged Egyptian rule.

120a **The Habiri**—Who were these foreign invaders of Syria and Palestine? Probably Bedawin from Arabia like the earlier Amorrhaeans. Habiri first appear as soldiers in the armies of Naram-Sin of Akkad, Rim-Sin of Larsa, Zimrilim of Mari and the Hittites of Asia Minor and subsequently *c* 1500 B.C. as immigrants from various Mesopotamian districts who have sold themselves into slavery at Nuzi, a south-eastern outpost of the Hurrite kingdom of Mitanni. They are called SA-GAZ as well as Habiri in the Hittite, Amarna and Rās-Shamra inscriptions. The alternative form of the name at Ras-Shamra 'apr(m) suggests also their identity with the Aperu, who appear as soldiers or slave-labourers in the Egyptian inscriptions from Thuthmose III to Ramesses IV (*c* 1500–1160 B.C.). From these texts it may be concluded that the Habiri were landless people or Bedawin who penetrated into various settled regions, where they were regarded as aliens, formed an inferior class of the population and were employed as mercenary troops or in servile works. **b** The Semitic word *ḫabiru* has been variously interpreted and may be either descriptive like *ḫabbatu* or racial. In the first alternative it has been derived from the root *ḫbr* 'bind', and understood either as confederates or as prisoners, deported persons. It seems more probable, however, from the evidence of the Rās-Shamra tablets, that the initial letter is 'ain rather than *ḫeth*. 'Hebrew' and 'Habiru' may thus be philologically akin. In the OT 'Hebrew' has a wider extension than 'Israelite' and is preferably used by foreigners such as Egyptians and Philistines to designate the chosen people. 'Eber moreover is the common ancestor of Israelites and Arabs (Gen 10:24 f.). Hebrews, who were not Israelites, may thus have invaded Palestine before the Exodus and remained in Egypt after it. Whatever be the origin of the name, it is certain at least that the people who bore it were more ancient and more wide-spread than the Israelites.

c **From Amarna to the Sea Peoples** (*c* 1350–1200 B.C.) —The Pharaohs of the eighteenth dynasty who succeeded Amenophis IV made no attempt to recover their Asiatic dominions. Their Hittite contemporary, Muršil II, campaigned chiefly in Asia Minor. He was obliged, however, to expel once more the Assyrians from Mitanni and to check their intrigues in northern Syria. Seti I of the XIX dynasty (*c* 1318–1298) restored Egyptian rule in Palestine in the first year of his reign and in a later campaign encountered the Hittites under Muwatalli, son and successor of Muršil II, at Qadesh on the Orontes. The only result of the battle was a brief Egyptian occupation of Qadesh. Seti also erected forts on the Asiatic border of Egypt, of which two are designated by the Semitic name Migdol, in Egyptian texts and in the OT, one in the north at

Tell el-Ḥer (Jer 44:1, 46:14; Ez 29:10, 30:6), the **120c** other in the south most probably at Abu Ḥasa southwest of the Bitter Lakes (Ex 14:2, *cf.* Mallon, *Les Hébreux en Egypte*, pp 167–71). Ramesses II, his successor, **d** the Pharaoh of the oppression (*c* 1298–1232), transferred the capital from Thebes to the Delta and inaugurated vast building operations in that region. He encountered the Hittites at Qadesh on the Orontes *c* 1294 B.C. and though victorious in battle failed to capture the city. His return to Egypt was followed by a widespread revolt in Palestine. Three years were spent in its reconquest. Syria was then invaded and cities north of Qadesh, Tunip and Qatna, were at least temporarily occupied. Meanwhile in the north the Assyrians had again invaded Mitanni and been expelled by Muwatalli. His brother Hattušil III, who had usurped the throne of his nephew, found increasing difficulty in resisting Assyrian pressure on Mitanni, now garrisoned by Hittite troops, and saw the expediency of peace and alliance with Egypt. We have Egyptian and Hittite copies of the treaty concluded between him and Ramesses II *c* 1278 B.C., which ended the long struggle of the two empires for the possession of Syria. The line of partition is not precisely defined in either document, but must have corresponded roughly with Qadesh and the Orontes valley, since Amurru remained a Hittite dependency. The alliance was offensive and defensive, and the delivery of fugitives to their overlords was expressly stipulated. The Hittite monarch visited the Pharaoh in 1265 B.C. when his daughter became the wife of **e** Ramesses II. Peace with Egypt was undisturbed under Ramesses' successor, Mernephtah. But the Assyrians again invaded Mitanni in the reign of Tudchaliya IV (*c* 1260–1230), defeated the allied forces of the Hittites and the Hurrites and deported the mass of the inhabitants. The Hurrites now disappear from history. Mitanni, repeopled by Aramaeans, becomes the Aram Naharaim of the OT.

The Sea Peoples—Our information on this movement **f** of peoples is chiefly derived from the inscriptions of the Pharaohs Mernephtah and Ramesses III, who record the repercussion in the Nile valley of a European invasion of the Near East. In the fifth year of Mernephtah, *c* 1228 B.C., an Aegean fleet, manned by Achaeans, Tyrrhenians, Lycians, Sardians and Sagalassians, entered the mouth of the Nile and co-operated with an army of Libyans who invaded the Delta region from the west. These sea peoples inhabited the coast of Asia Minor, where the Achaeans had settled more than a century earlier, as we learn from the Hittite inscriptions. Mernephtah succeeded in repelling the invaders. A second invasion of Libyans by land, Philistines and Zakkara by sea, was repelled by Ramesses III *c* 1196 B.C. These two sea peoples subsequently appear settled on the southern coast of Palestine. Three years later Ramesses had to equip **g** a fleet and lead a land army into Canaan to meet a third and more formidable group of immigrants seeking new homes. They were encamped in the land of Amurru and included Philistines, Zakkara, Sagalassians, Danaans and Wasasa. According to Ramesses no nation, not even the Hittites, had been able to resist them, but he defeated them with great slaughter in a combined land and sea engagement.

These invaders had apparently been pressed southward by Balkan peoples who had crossed the Hellespont and settled in Asia Minor. Of these the Phrygians and the Moschians now become known to us. The destruction of the empire of the Hittites may be attributed to their inveterate northern enemies, the Gasgas, aided by the Moschians, who had been pressed eastwards. Gasgas and Moschians subsequently fought against the Assyrians in the upper reaches of the Tigris and the Euphrates. Hittites in outlying regions who survived the disaster formed isolated city states like Malatya and Carchemish. The introduction of iron into Palestine is usually attributed to these northern invaders. Though mentioned earlier, especially in

0g Hittite inscriptions, it was not in general use in the Near East before 1200 B.C.

h **The Philistines**—Cretans and Philistines are associated in the OT, not only by parallelism (Soph 2:5 ; Ez 25:16), but also in the expression, Cerethi and Phelethi, by which David's bodyguard is designated. The absence of the sibilant in Phelethi may be due to assonance, but is more probably the result of assimilation (cf. LXX Pheletti = Pheletti = Phelešti). Their original home was Caphtor (Am 9:7), usually identified with Keftiu, the Egyptian name for Crete. It does not follow, however, that the Philistines came from the island of Crete, since Caphtor and Keftiu have a wider signification and include Cretan dependencies in the Aegean and on the coast of Asia Minor. Like the other sea peoples they came from the north, where they may have settled earlier like the Achaeans. The exact period of their arrival in Palestine is uncertain.

i The discovery of Philistine mercenaries in the army of Ramesses III and of so-called Philistine pottery at Tell el-Fara' in a stratum dated c 1250 B.C. has led some scholars to conclude that they were already in Palestine half a century before the northern invasion. The Caphtorites or Philistines (DV Cappadocians) mentioned in Deut 2:23 were not ancient inhabitants but late arrivals who dispossessed the Hevites. The word Philistine is sometimes used in the OT, not in a racial but in a local sense, of earlier inhabitants of the district subsequently occupied by the Philistines. These invaders were superior to the Israelites in culture and especially in military equipment, and held Judah in subjection until the period of the monarchy. Though of alien race and uncircumcised they soon became semitized in Palestine to which they gave their name, as the Assyrians gave theirs to Syria.

j **The Aramaeans**—The name first appears in an inscription of Tiglath-Pileser I, c 1100 B.C., who subdued Aḥlamu Aramaeans settled in the biblical Aram Naharaim. We meet the Aḥlamu, literally confederates, earlier, in the fourteenth century, and can locate them sometimes in the same region. This is very probably, but not quite certainly, the land of Aram, mentioned in a much earlier inscription of Naram-Sin. The Aramaeans were thus apparently nomads from the west, who got their distinctive name from the land in which they settled. They spread rapidly in Mesopotamia itself, and crossing the Euphrates from Aram Naharaim founded independent city states from Armenia in the north to Palestine in the south. Their states with which the Israelites had hostile or friendly relations were Damascus in the east, Soba and Beth-Reḥob in the north and south of the Beka', Gešur and Beth-Maacha east of the **k** upper Jordan. It was probably their ubiquity which gave their language its importance. There were Aramaean secretaries at the Assyrian court in the eighth century B.C., and Aramaic became the international language of the Near East two centuries later. It even supplanted Arabic in north Arabia and Hebrew in Palestine as the language of the people. In the OT Aramaean is used like Philistine in a local sense to designate earlier inhabitants of regions peopled by Aramaeans in biblical times. The geographical sense of the term is evident when Jacob is called an Aramaean (Deut 26:5) as long resident in Aram Naharaim. Abraham's brother, Nachor, was a Hebrew, but as he settled in Harran, a city of Aram Naharaim, his son, Bathuel, is called an Aramaean (Gen 25:20).

l **From the Sea Peoples to the Assyrian Invasion**—The fall of the Hurrite and Hittite empires, the decadence of Egypt after the reign of Ramesses III and internal disturbances in Mesopotamia gave the smaller nations of Syria and Palestine a providential breathing-space of nearly three centuries. The Israelites were thus enabled to complete the conquest of Canaan without serious external interference and under David's rule to throw off the Philistine yoke and reduce to subjection the Edomites, Moabites, Ammonites and Aramaeans.

120l The Phoenicians in the north, with whom they had friendly relations, had meantime monopolized the sea trade in the Mediterranean and established numerous colonies and trade centres at suitable positions on its islands and coasts. Their settlements at Gades and **m** Tharsis in Spain go back to the eleventh century after Tyre took the leadership from Sidon and became ' the mart of nations '. There was a Tyrian trading centre at Memphis in Egypt early in the twelfth century B.C. The Dorian invasion favoured Phoenician expansion by confining their Greek rivals to the Aegean. The only important Egyptian interference in Palestine during this period was a raid of Sheshonq I (Sesac), the founder of the twenty-second dynasty, c 927 B.C. The Pharaoh sacked Jerusalem and its temple and many other cities and erected a commemorative stele of victory at Megiddo of which a fragment has been discovered.

121a **The Assyrians**—They inhabited the region between $35°$ and $37°$ N. latitude bounded by the Middle Tigris on the west and the mountains of Kurdistan on the east. The old capital, Aššur, was the most southerly of their cities, and the only one on the west bank of the Tigris. It was superseded as capital, first by Kalḥu (Cale) on an affluent of the Upper Zab, c 1280 B.C., and two centuries later by Nineveh opposite the modern Mosul. The region had settled inhabitants before Babylonia and participated in the pre-Babylonian civilization of northern Mesopotamia. Its population was predominantly Semitic in the historic period and usually subject to Babylonia. The traders whose rights Naram-Sin enforced in north-eastern Asia Minor were probably Assyrians. In the nineteenth century B.C. Assyrian colonists had important and well-organized trading centres in this region, as we learn from the inscriptions of Kultepe, the ancient Ḳaneš. The geographical position of Assyria between Hurrites and Hittites in the north and the Babylonians in the south checked its expansion during the next four centuries. A vassal state of Hammurabi and later of the Kassites, it naturally welcomed the intervention of the Egyptians and was the first of the northern states to send presents and congratulations to the victorious Thuthmose III. Shortly afterwards, however, it was invaded by Saušatar and incorporated for a century in the empire of Mitanni. The Assyrians **b** recovered their independence under Aššur-uballit I (c 1380–1341) who aided the eastern Hurrite monarch, Artatama II, in invading Mitanni and assumed a protectorate over that kingdom. He also forced the Kassites to abandon their claim of suzerainty over Assyria, gave his daughter in marriage to the Kassite prince, Kurigalzu III, and secured the accession of his son-in-law, the future conqueror of Elam, to the throne of Babylon. Assyria was now a great power. Her monarchs during the next century fought against the Hittites in the north and the Babylonians in the south, without however materially extending their dominions. The first empire builder was Tukulti-Ninurta I (c 1255–1218) who finally drove the Hittites out of Mitanni and also subdued the Nairi region in the north, Gutium in the east and Babylon in the south. His successors however were unable to retain his conquests, but a century later Tiglath-pileser I (c 1116–1090) recovered and extended them. He wrested Commagene from the Moschians and Malatya from the Neo-Hittites, attacked the Aramaeans in Aram Naharaim and, crossing the Euphrates at Carchemish, reached the Mediterranean at Arwad on the Phoenician coast. But another period of weakness followed the conquest, and lasted for two centuries.

Assyrian expansion recommenced in the ninth **c** century B.C. Aššur-naṣir-pal II (884–860) crossed the Euphrates in 877 and received tribute from the Neo-Hittite states in the Syrian hinterland and the Phoenician cities on the coast. His successor, Shalmaneser III (859–824), pressed further south against the Aramaeans and was met at Qarqar on the Orontes in

121c 853 by a coalition of Aramaeans, Cilicians, Phoenicians, Israelites, Edomites and Arabians under the command of Adadidri (Ben Hadad) of Damascus. The Israelite contingent was led by Achab. The Assyrian claimed the victory but was checked in his advance. He returned to the attack in 848, 845 and 841, and on the last occasion devastated the territory of Damascus and received tribute, not only from Tyre and Sidon which had not joined the coalition, but also from Jehu of Israel. Besides their ancient enemies, the Aramaeans, Babylonians and Elamites, the Assyrians had now to contend with the Urartians, who appeared as powerful rivals in the regions about Lake Van and subsequently pressed southwards as far as Aleppo.

d They also met in battle for the first time their future conquerors, the Chaldaeans, nomads from the west who had settled in southern Babylonia, and the Medes, who had taken part in the great Aryan migration of c 2000 B.C. and found a home, at first in eastern, but later in western Iran. Shamshi-Adad V (824–810) lost the Syrian conquests of his predecessors and is best known as the husband of Sammuramat, the legendary Semiramis of the Greeks, who was regent during the first five years of the reign of her son Adad-nirari III (810–782). This monarch crossed the Euphrates in 802, conquered the Hittites and Phoenicians and reduced Damascus. Among his tributaries are mentioned Tyre, Sidon, Israel and Edom. The Syrian expeditions of Shalmaneser IV (782–772) and Assur-dan III (772–753) were directed almost exclusively against Hazrak. This was a powerful Aramaean state, extending from Hamath in the south to within twenty miles of Aleppo in the north, whose king, Zakir, was strong enough to defeat a coalition of Syrian states and check for a time the southern expansion of Assyria. Israel was thus unmolested during the prosperous reign of Jeroboam II.

e The fourth and last period of Assyrian expansion begins with Tiglath-pileser III (745–727), also called Pulu as king of Babylon (cf. 4 Kg 15:19, 29). He inaugurated the policy of deporting the inhabitants of devastated cities and replacing conquered rulers by Assyrian princes or governors. The Urartians were first expelled from north Syria in 744. Assyrian rule was then established in eastern Asia Minor. After a Syrian campaign in 738, Tiglath-pileser received tribute from Commagene, Malatya, Cue (Cilicia) and Tuwanawa (Tyana) in the north and from the kings of Tyre and Sidon, Menahem of Israel, and Rason of Damascus in the south. He invaded Philistia in 734 and sacked Gaza, whose king Hanun fled to

f Egypt. It was probably on this occasion that Achaz of Judah sent him presents and invoked his aid against Pekah (DV Phacee) of Israel and Rason of Damascus who were meditating a revolt against Assyria and sought to dethrone Achaz and set up a partisan monarch in Jerusalem. The result was the devastation of northern Israel, the sack of Damascus captured in 732, and the deportation of a large number of the inhabitants of both countries. A usurper, Osee, replaced Pekah in the diminished kingdom, obtaining Assyrian recognition by the payment of a heavy tribute. Assyrian provinces, Gal'azu, Magidu and Du'uru were established in Galaad, Galilee and Sharon. Under Shalmaneser V (727–721) Tyre and Israel revolted, relying on Egyptian aid. Tyre was soon reduced but Samaria was only captured after a three years' siege by Sargon II (721–705) in the winter of 722–721. Of its inhabitants 27,290 were then deported and the city was repeopled by colonists from Babylonia, Syria and Arabia.

g Sargon II, the son of Tiglath-pileser, was an indefatigable warrior, who pursued extensively his father's policy of transplanting conquered peoples and replacing native princes by Assyrian governors. His chief opponents in the north-west were Rusa of Urartu and Midas of Mushki, whose power he reduced by repeated campaigns. Assyrian rule was strengthened in eastern Asia Minor and extended to the island of Cyprus. An expedition to Syria in 720 was necessitated

by a revolt of Hamath, Arpad, Simirra, Damascus and **h** Samaria in the north and Gaza in the south. The northern rebels were defeated at Qarqar on the Orontes, and Hamath, whose prince Yaubidi organized and led the revolt, was repeopled by Assyrians. Hanun of Gaza, abandoned by his Egyptian allies, was conquered and made prisoner. Ezechias of Judah **h** is not included among the rebels, but later played a minor part with Moab and Edom in the Philistine revolt punished by the sack of Ashdod and Gath in 711. Three months after Sargon's accession to the throne Merodach-Baladan II, king of Bit-Yakin on the north-eastern coast of the Persian Gulf, proclaimed himself king of Babylon and, aided by the Elamites, defeated an Assyrian army sent against him. Sargon led another expedition into southern Babylonia, in 710 forced him to fly first to Bit-Yakin and then to Elam and repeopled Bit-Yakin with colonists from Commagene. Merodach-Baladan reappeared after Sargon's death but was defeated near Kish by Sennacherib (705–681). The embassy of Merodach-Baladan to Ezechias had no doubt a political object, the anti-Assyrian league of 713, but was not connected with the later revolt of Judah, Philistia and Phoenicia in 703. After two campaigns against the Kassites and **i** the Medes Sennacherib marched into Syria in 701 and quickly reduced the northern cities, most of which submitted without a battle. He then captured Ascalon in the south before the Egyptians arrived to relieve it. The relieving army was next routed at Eltekeh, but not pursued, Ekron (Accaron) was stormed and western Judah was devastated. Jerusalem was neither surrendered nor taken by assault, but Ezechias had to pay a heavy tribute and submit to the deportation of his people and the diminution of his territory. The disaster which closed the campaign is not recorded by the Assyrians. Sennacherib was troubled by Babylonian revolts during most of his reign. He finally destroyed the city itself and placed as governor over the district his son and successor, Esarhaddon (680–669).

Sennacherib had fallen victim to a conspiracy led **j** by his son, Arad-Malik (Vg Adramelech). Esarhaddon, a younger son, had first to quell the civil discord provoked by fraternal jealousy and to punish his father's murderers. He rebuilt Babylon, which his father had destroyed, and made some expeditions against the Medes and Scythians. But the chief event of his reign was the invasion of Egypt. The first campaigns were unsuccessful. Finally however in 671, after securing the co-operation of the Arabs whose camels were needed for desert transport, Esarhaddon subdued the land of the Nile. The native rulers of the various nomes were maintained in office but were assisted by Assyrian residents. There was a wide-spread revolt in 669 and Esarhaddon died on the march to repress it. Though the conquest of Egypt was desirable from the Assyrian point of view for the pacification of Palestine and Syria, it had the disadvantage of extending the empire unduly in the west when the real danger was in the east.

In the reign of Assurbanipal (669–626) Assyria **k** reached the height of its power and then hastened to its fall. Egypt was reconquered in 667 and Taharqa fled to Nubia. His nephew and successor, Tanut-Amon, again raised the standard of revolt in 663, but an Assyrian expedition restored order and sacked the southern capital, Thebes. Shamash-shum-ukin, Assurbanipal's jealous elder brother, had received from his father the kingdom of Babylonia. His constant intrigues culminated in 652 in the organization of a revolt extending from Elam to Egypt. Manasses of Judah seems to be included among the kings of Amurru who took part in it. The repression was severe. The Elamite capital, Susa, was sacked and Susiana became an Assyrian province. Shamash-shum-ukin perished in the flames of his palace at Babylon. Manasses was taken to Nineveh in chains, but was subsequently released and restored to his kingdom. About the same period Psammetichus threw off the Assyrian yoke in Egypt and Gyges of Lydia vainly invoked the aid of his suzerain against the invading Cimmerians.

Under the successors of Aššurbanipal, Aššur-etil-ilani (626–c 621) and Sin-shar-ishkun (c 620–612), three enemies gradually close in on Assyria, the Babylonians from the south and west, the Medes and Scythians from the north and east. The Babylonians under the Chaldaean general, Nabopolassar, founder of a dynasty called Chaldaean or Neo-Babylonian (626–605), had already reduced the chief cities in the south and west when the Medes under Cyaxares (633–584) captured Aššur in 614. A joint attack was then made on Nineveh which was taken and sacked in 612. In the subsequent division of the spoils the Medes received the northern and eastern provinces of the empire, the Babylonians the western and most of Mesopotamia. The Scythians settled in Aram Naharaim under the protection of the Medes. Another section of these European invaders pressed southward through Asia Minor, Syria and Palestine to the gates of Egypt. Scythopolis, the name given by the Greeks to Beth-Shan in Palestine, preserves the memory of this invasion. The marriage of Nabopolassar's son, Nabuchodonosor, to Cyaxares' daughter, Amytis, sealed the alliance between the Medes and the Babylonians.

The Assyrians are notorious among the peoples of the ancient east for their inhumanity, manifested in the severe penalties of their law code as well as in the harsh treatment of their vanquished foes. They were good soldiers but bad colonizers. Utterly indifferent to the welfare of the subject peoples, they squandered the resources of the provinces in the adornment of magnificent palaces and temples in the cities of Assyria, imposed on their inhabitants forced labours and military conscription and adopted extensively an inhuman and uneconomic deportation policy to lessen the danger of revolt. The sudden collapse of their hated empire was greeted with a universal outburst of joy and exultation.

The Chaldaeans—The nomads from the west who had attained power in Babylon, after the destruction of the remnants of the Assyrians under Aššur-uballit II in the region of Harran, had still to contend with the Egyptians for the possession of Syria and Palestine. Nechao II (609–594), who had succeeded his father, Psammetichus, on the throne of Egypt, marched at the head of an army to the aid of the Assyrians in 609 B.C. Josias, king of Judah, perished in the attempt to block his passage at Megiddo. Driven out of Mesopotamia, Nechao encamped at Riblah on the Orontes, where he received tribute from Phoenicia, Syria, Arabia and Edom. He deposed and imprisoned Joachaz of Judah and appointed in his stead his elder brother, Eliacim, whose name he changed to Joakim. His success was short-lived, for the Babylonians under the young prince Nabuchodonosor crossed the Euphrates in 606, defeated his army near Carchemish and pursued him to the Egyptian frontier. Egypt was only saved from invasion by the death of Nabopolassar which necessitated the return of the prince to Babylon. Secure in his western dominions, Nabuchodonosor II (605–562) devoted himself to the fortification and embellishment of his capital. He also reconstructed the Amurru wall of the third dynasty of Ur, now called the wall of the Medes. He repressed a revolt of Judah, Edom, Moab, Ammon, Tyre and Sidon, incited by Nechao, in 598, and taking Jerusalem, deported its principal inhabitants, including King Joachin, to Babylonia and placed Sedecias on the throne. Records of provisions supplied to Joachin and his more distinguished fellow-prisoners have been discovered in the royal palace in Babylon. A second revolt, provoked by the Pharaoh Apries, in which Judah and Tyre were particularly involved, was more severely punished. Jerusalem was captured after a long siege in 587. The city and temple were completely destroyed, the king Sedecias blinded and

imprisoned, the people deported. Nabuchodonosor invaded Egypt towards the close of his reign but achieved no permanent results. His three immediate successors, Evil-Merodach, Neriglissar and Lebashi-Marduk had short and inglorious reigns. A usurper, Nabu-na'id, the Nabuchodonosor of the book of Daniel (555–539), was the last king of Babylon. He repressed a revolt at Hamath in 553 and marched against Adummu and Tema' in Arabia the following year. He lived in retirement at Tema' for some years, leaving his son, Bel-shar-uṣur (Baltasar) as regent in Babylon. During his reign Cyrus II founded the Persian empire, subjugated the Medes and invaded Babylonia. His capture of Babylon in 539 put an end to the empire of the Chaldaeans.

The Persians—In the great Aryan migration (c 2000 B.C.) the Persians had settled beside the Medes in eastern Iran. Their kingdom of Anzan under Teispes (675–645), Cyrus I (644–588) and Cambyses I (587–558) acknowledged the suzerainty of the Medes. Cyrus II (557–529) proclaimed his independence and by his victories over the Medes in 549 and the Lydians in 546 had extended his empire from the Aegean to the Indus before he attacked and subjugated the Babylonians in 539. His mild and provident policy contrasts with that of his imperial predecessors. He sought to conciliate the subject peoples by honouring their gods and respecting their national customs. The Babylonian divinities, transported to the capital by Nabu-na'id, were restored to their respective cities where provision was made for their worship. The Jewish exiles in Babylonia were authorized to return to Jerusalem and to rebuild the temple of Yahweh. His son and successor, Cambyses (529–522), added Egypt to the empire. Faithful at first to his father's policy of religious toleration, he subsequently treated the Egyptian divinities with hostility and contempt. Thus at Elephantine, the southern outpost of Egypt, where Jews formed part of the Persian garrison, the Egyptian temples were all destroyed but the temple of Yahweh was not molested. The death of Cambyses, probably by suicide, in Syria coincided with a successful movement against a pretender in the east, organized by seven Persian nobles. One of these, Darius I, the greatest of the Persian monarchs, succeeded to the throne (529–485). Though himself a sincere worshipper of Ahura-Mazda, as we learn from the Behistun inscription which commemorates his exploits, he built temples to the Egyptian gods in Egypt, supported Greek worship in Asia Minor and forbade all opposition to the building of the temple of Yahweh in Jerusalem which was resumed and completed in the early years of his reign. The armies of Darius, though unsuccessful against the Greeks, extended his empire to Thrace, Macedonia and India. More famous as an administrator than as a warrior, he completed the political organization of his dominions begun by Cyrus. Now for the first time in the East the same administrative system was adopted for every part of a vast empire with equal rights and burdens for all. This unification admitted such exceptions as the exemption from tribute of the Medes and Persians and did not affect national religions and national customs and institutions. The empire was divided into twenty provinces, each governed by a satrap, though this title was also used to designate the rulers of smaller districts subject to the provincial governor. The latter had supreme civil, judicial and military authority in his province. His chief duties were to maintain order and security and to collect and transmit the tribute imposed. He was obliged to respect local forms of government like the regime of the high-priests in Judaea. His power was sometimes limited by royal appointments of military officers, directly responsible to the king, to special posts, and was to some extent controlled by a royal secretary in permanent residence and royal inspectors who paid unexpected visits. Darius used his enormous revenues for the public good. He connected the Nile with the Red Sea by a canal

122g and built roads to facilitate communications between Susa, the capital, and distant parts of the empire.

h Darius had no worthy successors. Xerxes I (485–464), portrayed in the book of Esther, is noteworthy for an attempt to impose the worship of Ahura-Mazda on his Babylonian subjects and for the disasters which followed his invasion of Greece. Artaxerxes I (464–424), who authorized his cup-bearer Nehemias to rebuild the walls of Jerusalem, quelled an Egyptian revolt, but was defied and twice defeated by Megabyzus, the satrap of Syria. Under Artaxerxes II (404–358) Egypt recovered its independence, several satraps refused obedience to their king and the defeat of a great Persian army by 10,000 Greeks at Cunaxa between Babylon and Baghdad in 401 showed the real weakness of the vast empire. Artaxerxes III (358–338) reconquered Egypt and, with the aid of the Greeks, overcame the rebellious satraps. Their repression is probably the background of the Judith narrative. He and his son died by poison and Darius III (335–330) had only begun to reign when Alexander embarked on his career of conquest in 334.

i The Lagids and the Seleucids. Hellenization.—The death of Alexander in 323 was followed by the wars of the Diadochi from which two of his generals, Ptolemy, son of Lagos (323–283), and Seleucus, son of Antiochus (312–280), ultimately emerged as the heirs of his African and Asiatic conquests. They founded the dynasties of the Lagids and the Seleucids, who reigned respectively at Alexandria in Egypt and at Antioch in Syria. Besides Egypt, Cyrenaica and Palestine the Lagids originally held some coastal regions in Asia Minor and Coelesyria, the Syrian depression. The latter district was, however, claimed by the Seleucids and remained a bone of contention during the third century B.C. Ptolemy II Philadelphos (283–246), Ptolemy III Euergetes (246–221), Ptolemy IV Philopator (221–203) were efficient rulers and held

j their own in the Syrian wars. But Ptolemy V Epiphanes (203–181) had to abandon all his Asiatic possessions, Palestine included, to the Seleucids. Egypt now fell under the protectorate of Rome and declined in power until it became a Roman province in 30 B.C. Seleucus, at first governor of Babylonia, then *protégé* of Ptolemy, finally extended his rule over the Asiatic provinces from Syria to India. His successors, Antiochus I Soter (280–261), Antiochus II Theos (261–247) and Seleucus II Callinicos (247–226) waged war on the Ptolemies for the possession of Coelesyria without decisive results. But Antiochus III, called the Great (223–187), by his victory at Banyas in 200 (or 198) expelled the Egyptians definitely from Asia. He also reduced to temporary obedience remote eastern provinces which had proclaimed their independence, but met disaster in a rash encounter with

the Romans. Defeated at Magnesia in 190, he was **122** forced to evacuate Asia Minor and pay a crushing war indemnity. Seleucus IV Eupator (187–175) is **k** noteworthy for his attempt to appropriate the treasures of the temple at Jerusalem. His brother, Antiochus IV Epiphanes (175–163), in his misguided zeal for Hellenism, sought by a cruel persecution to extirpate the religion and national institutions of the Jews. Checked in his designs on Egypt by a Roman veto, he died in Iran while endeavouring to consolidate his empire and restore Hellenism in the east. His puppet son only reigned a year when he and the real ruler, Lysias, were slain by Demetrius I Soter (162–150), son of Seleucus IV. Demetrius himself died fighting against a usurper, Alexander Balas (150–145), who was supported by the Romans and favoured by the Jews, but was opposed and slain in battle by the Egyptians. Syria had now two kings, Antiochus VI Dionysos, **l** son of Balas (145–142), later assassinated by his general Tryphon, and Demetrius II, son of Demetrius I (145–138). The Jews at first supported Antiochus, but after experiencing the treachery of Tryphon, embraced the cause of Demetrius, who subsequently lost his throne in an expedition against the Parthians, having been defeated and held prisoner by Mithridates I. His brother, Antiochus VII Sidetes (138–129), effected his liberation in 130, but was himself defeated and slain in 129. He was the last worthy successor of Seleucus. He forced the Jews to acknowledge his rule, but treated them kindly and respected their religion and national institutions. A period of confusion and rapid decline followed his reign. Syria was subject to Tigranes, king of Armenia, 95–69, and became a Roman province in 65 B.C.

The most important result of Alexander's conquests **m** was the Hellenization of the East, projected and inaugurated by the conqueror himself and energetically promoted by his successors. Thus the language and thought, the arts and sciences, the political and social institutions of the Greeks penetrated the vast Persian empire. Bactria on the confines of India is an example of an autonomous Hellenistic state in the middle of the third century B.C. The Jews were naturally affected by the movement and about the same period we find them at Alexandria, where they enjoyed a certain autonomy and filled a large quarter of the city, engaged in a Greek translation of their sacred books. The tolerance of the Lagids favoured the movement in Egypt as the intolerance of the Seleucids retarded it in Judaea and provoked the heroic and triumphant reaction of the Maccabees. But the language prevailed and 1 Mac. only survives in a Greek version while 2 Mac. like Wisdom is an original Greek work. Thus was a world tongue prepared to be the vehicle of Christ's message to all mankind.

THE CHRONOLOGY OF THE
OLD TESTAMENT

By E. F. SUTCLIFFE, S.J.

123a **Bibliography**—(1) *General :* *F. K. Ginzel, *Handbuch der mathemathischen und technischen Chronologie*, 3 vols, Leipzig 1906–14 ; *H. R. Hall, *Ancient History of the Near East*, London 1950[11] ; *D. D. Luckenbill, *Ancient Records of Assyria and Babylonia*, 2 vols, Chicago 1926–7 ; CAH I–VI, Cambridge 1925–7 ; A. Deimel, S.J., *Vet. Test. Chronologia Monumentis Bab.–Assyr. illustrata*, Romae 1912 ; F. X. Kugler, S.J., *Von Moses bis Paulus*, Münster in Westf. 1922 ; E. Ruffini, *Chronologia Vet, et Nov. Test.*, Romae 1924 ; E. Mangenot, DBV I (1895) 718–40 ; L. Pirot and V. Coucke DBV(S) I 1244–79 ; *E. L. Curtis, HDB I (1900) 397–403 ; I. G. Hagen, S.J. and J. Knabenbauer, S.J., in M. Hagen, S.J.'s *Lexicon Biblicum* I (CSS), Parisiis 1905, 882–910.

(2) *Maccabean Age :* J. Hontheim, S.J., ' Zur Chronologie der beiden Machabaerbüchen ' ZKT 43 (1919) 1–30.

(3) *Esdras-Nehemias :* A. Van Hoonacker, *Nouvelles Etudes sur la Restauration juive après l'Exil de Babylone*, Louvain 1896 ; RB 10 (1901) 5–26, 175–99 ; 32 (1923) 481–94 ; 33 (1924) 33–64 ; A. Fernandez, S.J., ' Epoca de la Actividad de Esdras ' Bi 2 (1921) 424–47 ; *W. M. F. Scott, 'Nehemiah-Ezra' ET 58 (1946–7) 263–7 ; *J. Stafford Wright, *The Date of Ezra's Coming to Jerusalem*, London 1947.

(4) *Period of the Kings :* J. Hontheim, S.J., ZKT 42 (1918) 463–82 ; 687–718 ; A. M. Kleber, O.S.B., Bi 2 (1921) 3–29 ; 170–205 ; H. Hänsler, O.S.B., Bi 10 (1929) 257–74 ; 377–93 ; 11 (1930) 63–80 ; *E. R. Thiele JNES 3 (1944) 137–86 ; *C. J. Gadd, *The Fall of Nineveh*, London 1923 ; B. Alfrink, ' Die Gadd'sche Chronik und die hl. Schrift ', Bi 8 (1927) 385–417 ; ' Die Schlacht bei Megiddo und der Tod des Josias (609) ' *Miscellanea Biblica* I, Roma 1935, 53–64 = Bi 15 (1934) 173–84.

(5) *Judges and Exodus :* J. Hontheim, S.J., ' Die Chronologie der Richterzeit in der Bibel und die ägyptische Chronologie' ZKT 37 (1913) 76–132. Supporting the earlier date for the Exodus : *J. W. Jack, *The Date of the Exodus*, Edinburgh 1925 ; L. Desnoyers, *Histoire du Peuple Hébreu* I, Paris 1922, 407–17 ; F. X. Kortleitner, Ord. Praem., *Israelitarum in Aegypto Commoratio*, Tongerloae 1930, 97–170 ; *J. Garrow Duncan, *Digging up Biblical History* I, London 1931, 232–8 ; *J. Garstang, *Joshua Judges*, London 1931, 51–66, 344–7. Favours the late date but leaves the question open : A. Fernandez, S.J., *Comm. in Lib. Josue* (CSS), Parisiis 1938, 16–22. Supporting the later date : L. R. de Vaux, O.P., ZAW 56 (1938) 225–38 ; L.-P. Vincent, O.P., RB 48 (1939) 579–83 ; *W. F. Albright, BASOR 74 (1939) 11–23 ; *H. H. Rowley, PEQ (1941) 152–7 ; *From Joseph to Joshua*, London 1950, gives an exhaustive bibliography. Favours the 14th cent. : *T. H. Robinson, ET 47 (1935–6) 53–5. See also references in the text.

b An adequate discussion of OT chronology would require, not an article, but a volume. Indeed the considerations relevant to the date of the Exodus alone have provided matter for a book. Hence the present treatment cannot be more than a bare summary. **The subject is complex and delicate** as the OT provides very imperfect information about relative chronology and none at all about absolute chronology. Though the broad sweep of the story is in chronological sequence **123b** this is not always the case with regard to particular events. In some cases events apparently successive in time were actually contemporaneous as in Judges ; the story itself is not complete, witness the gap of unspecified length between Esdras-Nehemias and Maccabees ; the numbers given are not always correct, they and proper names being most exposed to corruption in transmission ; numbers accurately transmitted are sometimes intentionally vague as in the frequent use of the number forty, and sometimes difficult of interpretation through ignorance of ancient methods of computation.

c Though the idea of an absolute chronology is foreign to the OT, it does contain information which renders possible the determination of definite dates for certain events around which others may be grouped with greater or less probability. **The history of the Maccabees** is reckoned by the Seleucid era, called in 1 Mac 1:11 ' of the kingdom of the Greeks '. This era was computed by the Greeks from 1 Oct. 312 B.C. There were, however, local variations, Ginzel 3, 41 f. The author of 2 Mac, writing in Greek, also begins the year in the autumn. 1 Mac, on the other hand, puts the beginning of the era in spring six months earlier, reckoning from 1 Nisan. The two systems thus overlap by half a year. This is the clue to apparently conflicting statements. In 1 Mac 6:16 Antiochus Epiphanes is said to have died in the year 149, whereas in 2 Mac 11:33 a letter of Antiochus Eupator, the son and successor of Antiochus Epiphanes, is dated the 15th of the month Xanthicus (§ 83f) in 148. The half-year Tishri to Nisan is the 2nd half of a year in 1 Mac and the 1st half of a year in 2 Mac. Thus Tishri to Nisan 148 is the 2nd half of that year in 1 Mac and the 1st half in 2 Mac. The following 6 months from Nisan to Tishri are the 1st half of 149 in 1 Mac and the 2nd half of 148 in 2 Mac.

d In order to convert a Seleucid year into the corresponding Julian year the number of the former is subtracted from 313. It should be remembered, moreover, that only the first 3 months of a Seleucid year beginning in Tishri fall in the corresponding Julian year and that the remainder fall in the following Julian year as the latter began on 1 Jan.

A discussion of the chronological order, Esdras–Nehemias or Nehemias–Esdras, will be found § 289i–q.

e The second great help in fixing the absolute chronology of the OT is **the Canon of Ptolemy**, a celebrated mathematician and astronomer who lived in Egypt in the 3rd cent. A.D. The Canon, which begins with the Babylonian king Nabû-nasir (Nabonassar), 747 B.C., after the Babylonian and Assyrian kings continues with the Persian and Greek monarchs, and ends with the Roman emperors in the Christian era. The year according to Egyptian custom is reckoned as beginning on the 1st day of the month Thoth. As the Egyptian year consisting of 365 days was a quarter of a day shorter than the solar year, the 1st Thoth moved through the course of the solar year returning to the same day of the solar year in a period of 1,460 years, the Sothic cycle. The regnal years are all given as full years. This method means that the year in which a king dies is reckoned wholly either to the deceased king or to his successor, *i.e.* either according to the

123e system of post-notation by which a king's regnal years were counted from the 1st Thoth following his accession, or the system of pre-notation according to which they were counted from the 1st Thoth preceding his accession. Calculation has shown that the Canon postdates up to Alexander exclusively and predates from his reign onwards, Hontheim ZKT 42 (1918) 465 f. For instance, the Emperor Titus is known to have commenced his rule on 23 June 79, whereas the accession year assigned to him in the Canon is that beginning 4 August 78, that year ending according to Egyptian reckoning on 3 August 79. The reliability of the Canon has been tested in various ways and is universally acknowledged. It may be consulted, *e.g.* in Ginzel I 139 or Ruffini opposite p 50.

f   The dates of this Canon partly coincide with those of a series of Assyrian documents which are of great importance for our purpose. These are **the Assyrian eponym lists,** the eponym being the official after whom each year was named. The lists are printed in Deimel 5 ff. and, with the results of later research, in Luckenbill II 427–9. In one form of these lists a brief historical note is attached recording some outstanding event of the year, generally a military campaign. For the eponymate of Bur-Sagale it is an eclipse of the sun, which astronomers have shown to have taken place in 763 B.C. By means of this entry the absolute date of all others can be fixed with the reservation made § 124e. The lists are thus found to extend from 893 (892) to 648, and in a partially fragmentary state from 1103 to 933. On the use of these Canons in fixing the dates of Assyrian monarchs see Deimel 19 and 32. In Assyria the kings reckoned their regnal years from 1 Nisan of the year following their accession. The period between the date of accession and the following 1 Nisan was called *rēš šarrūti* ' the beginning of my reign ' and is followed by ' the first regnal year '. For an example from the Obelisk of Shalmaneser III see Deimel 24, Luckenbill I, §§ 557 ff. Similarly Nabuchodonosor ascended the throne in the spring of 605, but counted his 1st regnal year from 1 Nisan 604.

124a   Fortunately for our chronology the contacts of the Hebrews with Assyria and Babylonia provide certain synchronisms which afford a sure basis for the determination of the absolute dates of many of **the kings of Israel and Judah.** It is convenient to begin with Josias. He fell in battle near Megiddo attempting to prevent the march north of Pharaoh Necho. The date of this encounter is fixed by the Babylonian chronicle which gives an account of the last years of the Assyrian empire and was published by C. J. Gadd, *The Fall of Nineveh* (London 1923). This shows that Necho's march to the Euphrates took place before Tammuz (the 4th month, June–July) in Nabopolassar's 17th year, which began Nisan 609. See B. Alfrink, Bi 8 (1927) 385–95. This fixes the 3 months reign of Joachaz from before the 4th month to before Tishri, the 7th month, 609. Hence Joakim, his successor, came to the throne before Tishri, and that month 609 began his 1st regnal year (post-dating, § 124h–i). This is supported by the addition in Jer 25:1 which equates the 4th year of Joakim with the accession year of Nabuchodonosor. This ended with Nisan 604, when his first regnal year began, whereas Joakim's 4th year ran from Tishri 606 to Tishri 605. Nabuchodonosor's *rēš šarrūti* or period of reign preceding his 1st complete year, thus overlapped with Joakim's 4th. Joakim died in the course of his 11th year, which began Tishri 599, and was followed by Joachin. His 3 months reign ended with his own captivity and that of many others including Ezechiel. This is dated in 4 Kg 24:12 in the 8th year of Nabuchodonosor, which (by pre-notation, the system followed for Nabuchodonosor elsewhere in Kg ; see below) began Nisan 598. In view of the synchronisms given in § 124b Sedecias's 1st regnal year began in Tishri of the same year 598 and his 11th and last in Tishri 588. Jerusalem fell in the 5th month of that regnal year, and the months being always calendar months this was Ab (July–Aug.) 587.

This month Ab 587 fell in the 18th year of Nabuchodonosor reckoned by post-notation and his 19th reckoned by pre-notation. This explains the different year assigned in different sources. The fall of Jerusalem is assigned to the 11th year of Sedecias in 4 Kg 25:2, Jer 39:2 and 52:5–6, and to the 19th year of Nabuchodonosor in 4 Kg 25:8 and Jer 52:12. With this agrees the equation of the 10th year of Sedecias to the 18th of the Babylonian in Jer 32:1. On the other hand, Jer 52:29, which is recognized to be from a different source, attributes the captivity following the siege of Jerusalem to the 18th year of Nabuchodonosor. Following the same system of post-notation Jer 52:28, from the same source as 52:29, assigns the captivity of Joachin to the Babylonian's 7th year, whereas in 4 Kg 24:12 it is assigned to his 8th. It is thus seen that for the Babylonian reign Kg + Jer follow pre-notation and Jer 52:28–30 post-notation.

Esarhaddon, 680–669, mentions Manasses among his c vassals, Luckenbill II, § 690 (*cf.* 2 Par 33:11). The year 701 saw Sennacherib's invasion of the kingdom of Ezechias ; see Luckenbill II, §§ 240, 312, and 4 Kg 18:13, where the 14th year should probably be reckoned from Ezechias' miraculous cure, Hänsler in Bi 10 (1929) 273 f. When this king celebrated his first Pasch, the Northern Kingdom is thought by some to have ceased to exist. Otherwise, it is stated, it would not have been possible to send his messengers as far as Dan and to invite the men of the northern tribes Ephraim, Manasses, Aser and Zabulon to celebrate the feast at his capital city, 2 Par 30:1, 5, 10 f., 18, nor for the men of Judah to march through the land destroying the altars and high places not only in the Southern Kingdom, but also in Ephraim and Manasses, 2 Par 31:1. But that the death of Achaz and the accession of Ezechias took place in 727, the year of Tiglath-pileser's death, is shown by Is 14:28 f., Coucke 1266 f., Hänsler in Bi 10 (1929) 269–72. And the happenings at the time of Ezechias' first Pasch are an indication of the weakness of the Northern Kingdom at the time. Moreover, Ezechias' accession year fell in the 3rd year of Osee, 4 Kg 18:1, and his 4th and 6th years in Osee's 7th and 9th respectively, 4 Kg 18:9 f. (Incidentally this shows that his accession year was not reckoned as one of his years of reign.)

The fall of Samaria marked the end of the Northern d Kingdom, 4 Kg 17:5 f. Shalmaneser is said to have begun the siege and taken the city, 4 Kg 18:9 f., but this may signify only that the credit of the capture was really his, as Sargon, 721–705, his successor, claimed to have captured the city himself before the second year of his reign, Luckenbill II, § 4. His accession took place at the death of Shalmaneser 10 Tebeth (= 20 Dec.) 722. This fixes the date within narrow limits, even if it is admitted with some that Sargon appropriated to himself a conquest which rightfully belonged to Shalmaneser. Further synchronisms are provided in the reign of Tiglath-pileser III, 745–727. Rasin, king of Damascus, and Phacee, king of Israel, attacked Achaz, king of Judah, who appealed for help to the Assyrian king, 4 Kg 16:5–7. Tiglath-pileser made a campaign against Philistia in 734, and against Damascus in 733 and 732 (eponym list ; tribute of Iauhazi of Judah, *i.e.* Achaz, Luckenbill I, § 801). He records that he set Ausi' (Osee) as king in Israel in place of Pakaha (Phacee), whom the people had deposed, Luckenbill I, § 816. Moreover, earlier in his reign Tiglath-pileser received tribute from Manahem, 4 Kg 15:19, where the Assyrian king is called by his Babylonian throne-name of Phul. The Assyrian monarch's mention of this tribute from Menihimmu in his annals (Luckenbill I, § 772) has led some to place this event in 738, Tiglath-pileser's 8th year, but without sufficient reason, and it can safely be dated several years earlier.

The two remaining synchronisms with Assyrian e history are the payment of tribute by Jehu to Shalmaneser III and the defeat inflicted by the latter at Qarqar on Achab and his confederates. These two events used to be dated with confidence in 842 and 854

e in reliance on what has been rashly styled 'the infallible Assyrian eponym-list'. But the fact is that above 786 dates will differ by one year according as Balatu who is given in one list as eponym for 787 is considered an erroneous insertion in that list or an accidental omission elsewhere. Here the shorter chronology is followed and the two events are dated 841 and 853 respectively. In either case the important fact remains that they are separated by an interval of just 12 years.

f Further help is provided by the synchronisms between the kings of Israel and of Judah. Jeroboam and Roboam, the first rulers of the divided kingdom, came to the throne almost at the same time. Jehu gave Joram of Israel and Ochozias of Judah their death-wound on the same day, 4 Kg 9:24-27. Moreover, the biblical story provides a whole series of cross-references between the reigns of the two kingdoms. These synchronisms of each kingdom in terms of the regnal years of the other fit into a consistent and harmonious scheme down to the death of Azarias in 740-739 if due account is taken of the time of year when the regnal years began in each kingdom and of their methods of treating a sovereign's accession year. Thiele's study has rendered invaluable service to chronology in these matters.

g To discover the method of computing regnal years it is necessary to bear in mind the Hebrew custom of counting a part of a year or a day as a whole year or day. Thus Abiam came to the throne of Judah in the 18th year of Jeroboam, and is said to have reigned 3 years though he died in the latter's 20th year, 3 Kg 15:1 f., 8 f. Similarly Nadab became king in the 2nd and was murdered in the 3rd year of Asa, but is said to have reigned 2 years, 3 Kg 15:25, 28.

h The method of computing regnal years was from Tishri in Judah and from Nisan in Israel. Solomon began the building of the temple in the 2nd month of his 4th year, and completed it in the 8th month of his 11th year, 3 Kg 6:1, 37 f. It would therefore seem that the building occupied $7\frac{1}{2}$ years. Actually it was $6\frac{1}{2}$ years recorded as 7 according to the custom of counting a part as a whole, 3 Kg 6:38. The months were counted from Nisan, Ex 12:2, and, if Solomon's regnal years had also been reckoned from Nisan, then the building would have taken $7\frac{1}{2}$ years. They must have been counted from Tishri, for in that case the building began in the 8th month (not calendar) reckoned from the beginning of his 4th regnal year, occupied the next 6 years reckoned from that month, and was concluded in the 2nd month reckoned from the beginning of his 11th year. Roboam and the other kings of Judah naturally followed the same system. Jeroboam and the other northern kings, on the other hand, reckoned their regnal years from Nisan, no doubt out of a desire to begin a new tradition and break away as far as possible from everything associated with the hated rule exercised from the southern capital. The proof of the change lies in the fact that on this basis of computation the synchronisms between the two kingdoms fit in harmoniously down to the death of Azarias.

i These synchronisms also reveal the method followed in the two kingdoms for dealing with the accession year of each sovereign. In Judah the accession year of a king was reckoned to his predecessor and the new king began the enumeration of his regnal years with the month Tishri following his accession. This is called post-notation or the accession-year system. The opposite system by which the accession year was counted as the 1st year of the new sovereign was adopted in Judah from 848 with the accession of Joram down to the accession of Amasias in 796. This would be explained by Athalia's desire to follow the custom of the northern court where she had been born, for there the system of pre-notation was followed. In this system the sovereign's accession year was reckoned both to himself and to his predecessor, and it was followed in Samaria from the dividing of the kingdom

down to the accession of Joas in 798. From this time **124i** the post-notation system was followed in both kingdoms to the end of their history, in this agreeing with the practice of Assyria and perhaps reflecting its influence.

As the beginning of the regnal year in the two king- **j** doms was separated by the six months between Nisan and Tishri, it may happen that the synchronisms fix the accession of a new ruler between either Nisan and Tishri or between Tishri and Nisan. In the former case the calendar year is fixed as both months fall in the same Julian year. In the latter case it remains uncertain whether the accession took place in the closing months of the preceding calendar year or the opening months of the following. Thus Joas of Judah came to the throne in 835 (between Nisan and Tishri) whereas Joachaz of Israel began his reign in 814-813 (between Tishri 814 and Nisan 813).

It will be seen that the chronological data are com- **k** plicated. Allowing for the different months in which the two kingdoms began their regnal years, for the systems of pre-notation and post-notation, and for certain co-regencies, all the regnal years fit in harmoniously except in the most difficult period 740-727. Here the years assigned to Phacee seem too long (20 in 4 Kg 15:27) and can only be accounted for on the very improbable supposition that he reckoned his years from the beginning of Manahem's reign, during a period when he was neither co-regent nor had any claim to the throne. So too there is no room for the 16 years assigned to Achaz, 4 Kg 16:2. His death appears to have fallen in the year of Ezechias' accession and he can hardly have been co-regent at the same time as his father. The possibility of two co-regents simultaneously may be ruled out.

The chronology of **the undivided kingdom** is vaguely **l** indicated. Solomon is said to have reigned 40 years, 3 Kg 11:42, so is David, 2 Kg 5:4, and so is Saul, Ac 13:21. This number 40 recurs in the history of the Judges (see §125a) and is used to indicate a period of long but uncertain duration. Still some events do actually occupy just or almost 40 years. David ruled 7 years and 6 months in Hebron, 2 Kg 2:11, and 33 years in Jerusalem, 3 Kg 2:11 ; 1 Par 29:27. And in the case of Solomon also the number 40 appears to be a close approximation. Synchronisms based on the reign of Hiram of Tyre lead to about 972 for the beginning of his reign, Jos. *C. Apion.* 1, 18 ; J. Hontheim, S.J., ZKT 36 (1912) 50-5 ; Kortleitner, 131 ff.

The length of **the period of the Judges** is variously **125a** estimated according as the Exodus from Egypt is dated in the 15th or in the 13th cent. The longer chronology squares with the 480 years said to have elapsed from the Exodus to Solomon's 4th year, in which he began the building of the temple, 3 Kg 6:1, and with the 300 years which Jephte averred to have elapsed from the occupation of the lands beyond the Jordan, *i.e.* from the end of the wandering in the wilderness, to the Ammonite oppression, Jg 11:26. But no accurate chronology is possible. As the rule of the Judges did not extend over the whole of Israel there is no reason to suppose that they were all successors in authority, but it is impossible to say how many of them may have been contemporaneous in whole or in part. Moreover the vague number 40 occurs five times. There were 40 years of rest under Othoniel, Jg 3:11 ; 40 more of rest after the victory of Debbora and Barac, 5:32 ; 40 of rest under Gedeon, 8:28. There were 40 years of oppression before Samson, 13:1, and Heli judged Israel for 40 years, 1 Kg 4:18. Further 80 (= 40 × 2) is the number of the years of rest recorded in Jg 3:30, and 20 years (= half 40) occurs 4:3 and 15:20.

The evidence for **the date of the Exodus** is conflicting **b** and diversely interpreted with the result that there is no unanimity on the matter. The two main views are that it occurred in the 15th cent. under the XVIII Egyptian dynasty and that it must be dated in the 13th cent. under the XIX dynasty. These may be called respectively the early and the late dating. For

125b the former, appeal is made to 3 Kg 6:1 where the 4th year of Solomon is equated with the 480th year after the Exodus. This equation carries less weight today when the artificial and schematic character of ancient numbers is widely recognized. The evidence of the Tell el-Amarna correspondence has also seemed to some to confirm the early dating. Letters from Palestinian princes to the Egyptian court in the early 14th cent. show that the country was being invaded by people called Habiru, a name which suggests the Hebrews under Josue. But it has become more and more widely admitted that the accounts in the Bible and in the letters do not really touch at any point. Both the names and the course of military operations are different. In Jos 10:31-32 it is recorded that Josue slew all the inhabitants of Lachish. In the correspondence, on the other hand, we read of help afforded to the invaders by this city, KIB V, p 306. The main support for the early date is that of the fall of Jericho, though this too is disputed. The city was destroyed by the Israelites, Jos 6, and thereafter remained practically in ruins till the time of Achab, 3 Kg 16:34. A. Rowe and J. Garstang, both distinguished Palestinian archaeologists and the latter excavator at Jericho, date its fall between 1400 and the accession of Akhenaton in 1380 (Hall) or 1375 (Breasted) : ' No other conclusion will satisfy the archaeological evidence as a whole ', PEF (1936) 170. Another leading authority, W. F. Albright, judged that ' the fall . . . took place somewhere between cir. 1375 and cir. 1300 B.C. in all probability ', BASOR 74 (1939) 20. In 1949, however, he favoured a date in the latter part of the 14th cent. or in the early 13th, *The Archaeology of Palestine* 109. Père Vincent puts the date lower still towards 1230, RB 48 (1939) 580, though Prof. G. E. Wright maintained that the publication of the pottery of the Lachish temple had given the final blow to this 13th cent. date, BASOR 86 (1942) 33. Later, while stating ' that it [Jericho] was abandoned by the 2nd or 3rd quarter of the 14th cent. seems certain ', he rallied to the 13th cent. for ' the main wave of the conquest ', BA 10 (1947) 14. This absence of decisive evidence is unfortunate, as the date of the fall of Jericho is crucial, since there is no question of its having been destroyed by anyone except the Israelites.

c A difficulty against the early dating is that little is known of building operations in the Delta by Pharaohs of the XVIII dynasty, whereas the late date is indicated by the many remains there of constructions of Ramses II in the 13th cent. The name of Ramesses (Raamses), where Israelites were set to forced labour, Ex 1:11, points to the Ramesside dynasty and the late date. The identification of the city, however, is still uncertain, and, as the name is compounded of that of the great god Ra, may be older than the XIX dynasty or may be the name later given to the place. Iron is mentioned as in use at the time of the conquest of Canaan, Jos 6:19, 24 ; 17:16, 18. But, though the beginning of the Iron Age in Palestine is dated about 1200 B.C., the use of iron is considerably older. As early as ' the 14th cent. B.C. . . . iron began to be used rather extensively for weapons ', W. F. Albright, *The Archaeology of Palestine* (1949) 110. The Israelites entered the country not as marauders in quest of booty but with the intention of permanent settlement to take possession of ' houses full of riches ', Deut 6:11, and theirs was no policy of indiscriminate ruin. The biblical account records their deliberate destruction only of Jericho, Jos 6:24, and Hasor, Jos 11:11. (On Jg 1:8, see note.) Lachish (identified on probable grounds with Tell ed-Duweir) they captured on the second day, Jos 10:32, and there is no mention of its destruction. This is dated on archaeological evidence late in the 13th cent. and is often ascribed to the Israelites as is that of other cities destroyed about the same time. The silence of the Bible, which is not a complete record, does not disprove this ascription. But neither is it proved correct by the fact that the destruction was soon followed by a new civilization which was of Israelite

stamp. J. W. Jack wrote on this question : ' The **125** destruction was undoubtedly due, as the excavators themselves prefer to believe, to Merenptah's Raid, which we know from this Pharaoh's Victory Stela occurred in 1230 B.C., and was more widespread and devastating than commonly supposed ', ET 52 (1940-1) 232. This supposes that the city was re-occupied by Canaanites after the slaughter of the original inhabitants by the Israelites, and that after the departure of the Egyptians the Israelites took the site for their own. The evidence of various short genealogies is also alleged, to show that the period in Egypt and the period from the Exodus to David were of no long duration. But the argument is not convincing. There is no evidence that the genealogies were meant to be complete. The writer may well have judged that a long list of unknown names would not be of interest to his readers. Moreover, it is reasonable to suppose that his purpose was not to establish but to indicate the line of descent, and it will be noticed that these genealogies lead back to some well-known or honoured figure as to Moses or to one of the twelve sons of Jacob. There could well be a firm and reliable tradition in a family that, say, Moses was their ancestor even though the names of many intervening progenitors had been forgotten. The reader will find the argument for a 13th date more fully discussed in §§ 163a-e, 228a-b. In view of the conflicting evidence it appears wiser to withhold judgement at present and to await a possible definitive solution of the problem as a result of further investigations.

The story of **the patriarchs** does not give time- **d** indications by which either the length or date of the period can be determined accurately. The figures by which the length of the period appears to be determined are : (1) Abraham was 75 years old at his entry into Canaan, Gen 12:4 ; (2) he was 100 at the time of Isaac's birth, 21:5 ; (3) Isaac was 60 at the birth of Jacob, 25:26 ; (4) Jacob was 130 years old when he left Canaan for Egypt, 47:9. This scheme gives 215 years as the period between Abraham's departure from Harran and Jacob's descent into Egypt. On the historical character of the figures see § 140b-f.

According to the Samaritan text of Ex 12:40 this **e** period of 215 years passed in Canaan is exactly equal to that of the sojourn in Egypt : ' The abode that the children of Israel and their fathers made in the land of Canaan and in Egypt was 430 years '. LXX, without the words ' and their fathers ' except in the Alexandrine codex, has the inverse order ' in Egypt and in the land of Canaan ', which cannot be judged original ; and MT mentions neither the fathers nor the land of Canaan. The mention of the sojourn in Canaan is not suitable in the context, but it is not easy to find a reason for the insertion of the words. On the other hand, a motive for their omission might be to give greater antiquity to the people, a motive which seems to have played its part in the manipulation of the numbers in Gen, chh 5 and 11. Ex 6:16-20 gives only two generations between Levi and Moses, who were respectively among those who entered and left Egypt. The list is : Levi, Caath, Amram, Moses. But arguments from the genealogies are apt to be misleading as intervening members are freely omitted as exemplified in Mt ch 1 and in Esd 7:1-5 compared with 1 Par 6:1-14.

That Joseph was elevated to high rank in Egypt and **f** his father and family so well received suggests that the Hyksos (§ 118k-l) were ruling at the beginning of the Israelite sojourn in that country. This would date the descent into Egypt in the period c 1720-1580. The Pharaoh who ' knew not Joseph ', Ex 1:8, no doubt belonged to a later dynasty of native Egyptian kings who would feel no gratitude for benefits conferred under the rule of the Asiatic invaders. On the other hand Gen 43:32 might suggest the opposite conclusion as the Hyksos would not be likely to share the Egyptian scruples of eating with foreigners. To this it may be answered that the Hyksos will have found it necessary

125f to accommodate themselves in many ways to the strong prejudices of the native population.

g The date of Abraham could be fixed by an external synchronism if Amraphel, Gen 14:1, could be proved to be Hammurabi of Babylon and the date of the latter were definitely known. We have certainty on neither point. Opinion is hardening against the identification since the allied kings cannot be fitted into this period.

The date of Hammurabi is much lower than used to be **125g** thought and is fixed with probability as 1728–1686, R. de Vaux, O.P., RB 53 (1946) 343, W. F. Albright, BASOR 88 (1942) 28 ff.; 106 (1947) 19. See also H. H. Rowley, *Recent Discovery and the Patriarchal Age*, reprint from BJRL 32 (1949); *From Joseph to Joshua*, 57 ff. On this as on other matters the future may set us in possession of fuller knowledge.

CHRONOLOGY OF THE OLD TESTAMENT
TABLE OF DATES

Egyptian Dynasties

THE XV AND XVI DYNASTIES (HYKSOS)

c 1720–1580	
c 1580	Expulsion of the Hyksos

THE XVIII DYNASTY

1580–1558	Amasis (Amosis)
1558–1545	Amenophis I
1545–1514	Thothmes I
1514–1501	Thothmes II
1501–1479	Hatshepsut
1479 (1501 –1447)	Thothmes III
1447–1420	Amenophis II
1420–1412	Thothmes IV
1412–1376	Amenophis III
1380–1362	Amenophis IV (Akhenaton)
1362–1360	Smenkhkara
1360–1350	Tutankhamen
1350–1346	Kheperkhepruarimaatra

THE XIX DYNASTY

1346–1322	Horemheb
1321	Ramses I
1321–1300	Seti I
1300–1233	Ramses II
1233–1223	Merenptah
1223–1220	Amenmeses (Amonmose)
1220–1214	Ramses–Siptah
1214–1210	Seti II

Hebrew History

c 1050–1012	Samuel ; Saul
c 1012–972	David
c 972 – 931	Solomon

Judah		Israel		Notable Events	
931–913	Roboam	931–910/9	Jeroboam	925	Shishak (Sheshonk I) invades Judah
913–911/10	Abiam			913	The 18th year of Jeroboam by Judahite reckoning, the 19th by Israelite
911/10–870/69	Asa	910/9–909/8	Nadab		
		909/8–886/5	Baasa		
		886/5–885	Ela		
		885	Zambri		
		885–874/3	Amri (Omri)		
		874/3–853	Achab		
				873	Asa's 38th year Josaphat becomes co-regent
870/69–848	Josaphat			858–824	Shalmaneser III
				854	Joram of Judah becomes co-regent
		853–852	Ochozias	853	Battle of Qarqar in Achab's last year
		852–841	Joram		
848–841	Joram				
841	Ochozias	841–814/3	Jehu	841	Jehu kills Joram of Israel and Ochozias of Judah on the same day ; he pays tribute to Shalmaneser III
841–835	Athalia				
835–796	Joas	814/3–798	Joachaz		
		798–782/1	Joas		

CHRONOLOGY OF THE OLD TESTAMENT

Judah	Israel	Notable Events
796–768 Amasias		793 Jeroboam II becomes co-regent
		791 Azarias becomes co-regent
	782/1–753 Jeroboam II	
768–740/39 Azarias		
	753–752 Zacharias	753 Joatham becomes co-regent
	752–752/1 Sellum	745–727 Tiglath-pileser (Phul)
	752/1–742/1 Manahem	743 (?) He receives tribute from Manahem
	742/1–740/39 Phaceia	
740/39–736/5 Joatham	740/39–730/29 Phacee	740/39 Death of Azarias (Ozias) ; call of Isaias
736/5–727 Achaz		735 Rasin of Damascus and Phacee attack Achaz
		734 Tiglath-pileser's expedition against Philistia
		733 and 732 His campaigns against Damascus
	730/29–721 Osee	
727–698/7 Ezechias		727–722 Shalmaneser V
		724 He begins the siege of Samaria
		722–705 Sargon II
	721 Destruction of Samaria ; end of the Northern Kingdom	
		714 The cure of Ezechias and mission of Merodachbaladan (Marduk-apal-iddin of Babylon, 722–711)
		705–681 Sennacherib
		701 He invades Judah
		680–669 Esarhaddon who names Manasses among his subject kings
698/7–643/2 Manasses		
643/2–641/0 Amon		628 Jeremias begins his mission
641/0–609 Josias		625–604 Nabopolassar
		623/2 The finding of the book of the Law
		612 Fall of Nineveh ; virtual end of the Assyrian Empire
609 Joachaz		609 Death of Josias defeated at Megiddo by Necho of Egypt (610–594)
609–598 Joakim		605–561 Nabuchodonosor
		604 Nabuchodonosor's 1st regnal year from 1 Nisan
598 Joachin		598 Captivity of Joachin
598–587 Sedecias		589 Jan. 15. Beginning of the siege of Jerusalem
		588 Imprisonment of Jeremias
587 End of the Kingdom of Judah ; deportation of Sedecias		587 Fall of Jerusalem ; Babylonian captivity
		574/3 The 25th year of Joachin's captivity and 14th from the fall of Jerusalem, Ez 40:1
		561–560 Evil-Merodach (Awel-Marduk)
		561 Joachin is released from prison
		560–556 Neriglissar (Nergal-shar-uṣur) of Babylon
		556 Labashi-Marduk
		556–539 Nabonidus ; Belshazzar

THE PERSIAN EMPIRE

Judah	Notable Events
	559–529 Cyrus
538/7 Decree of Cyrus permitting the return of the Jews	539 The beginning of the attack on Babylon
537/6 The foundations of the temple are laid	538 Cyrus captures Babylon
	529–522 Cambyses
	521–486 Darius I Hystaspes
520/19 Work is resumed on the temple	485–465 Xerxes I (Ahasuerus)
515 Dedication of the temple	464–424 Artaxerxes I Longimanus
458 Return under Esdras	
445 Return of Nehemias	
433 Nehemias goes back to Susa	
433/2 His second visit to Jerusalem	
	424 Xerxes II
	424 Sogdianus
	423–404 Darius II Nothus
	404–358 Artaxerxes II Mnemon
	358–338 Artaxerxes III Ochus
	338–336 Arses
	336–330 Darius III Codomannus
	333 His defeat by Alexander

CHRONOLOGY OF THE OLD TESTAMENT

The Earlier Seleucid Kings

312–280	Seleucus I Nicator		163–162	Antiochus V Eupator
280–262/1	Antiochus I Soter		162–150	Demetrius I Soter
261–247	Antiochus II Theos		150–145	Alexander Balas
247–226	Seleucus II Callinicus			
226–223	Seleucus III Soter		145–139/8	Demetrius II Nicator
223–187	Antiochus III the Great		145–142/1	Antiochus VI Epiphanes
187–175	Seleucus IV Philopator		139/8–129	Antiochus VII Sidetes
175–163	Antiochus IV Epiphanes			

The Earlier Ptolemies

323–283	Ptolemy I Soter
285–246	Ptolemy II Philadelphus (partly co-reign)
246–221	Ptolemy III Euergetes
221–203	Ptolemy IV Philopator
203–181/0	Ptolemy V Epiphanes
181/0–145	Ptolemy VI Philometor
145–116	Ptolemy VII Euergetes

NOTE 1—The first year given for the Hebrew kings is that of their accession, for the Persian kings that of their first regnal year. Two dates separated by a slanting line mean that the accession or other event occurred between Tishri of the first-named year and Nisan of the following year.

NOTE 2—For the chronology of the reign of Nabonidus and end of the Babylonian empire see *Babylonian Historical Texts*, by Sidney Smith, London 1924, esp. 107–10.

NOTE 3—For the detailed chronology of the Maccabean age see § 560a–b.

INTRODUCTION TO THE PENTATEUCH

By E. F. SUTCLIFFE, S.J.

with a section on

SOME RECENT CATHOLIC VIEWPOINTS

By R. A. DYSON, S.J.

126 Bibliography—R. Cornely, S.J., *Introd. in U.T. Libros Sacros* II i (Parisiis, 1887) 3–169 (CSS) ; *W. Möller, *Are the Critics Right ?* (London, 1903) ; G. Hoberg, *Moses und der Pentateuch* (Freiburg im Breisgau, 1905) = BS X iv ; L. Méchineau, S.J., *L'Origine mosaïque du Pentateuque* (Paris, 1905⁴) ; E. Mangenot, *L'Authenticité mosaïque du Pentateuque* (Paris, 1907) and ' Pentateuch ' DBV v 50–119 ; S.T.B., *Archbishop Smith and the Mosaic Authorship of the Pentateuch* (Aberdeen, 1911) ; *H. M. Wiener, *Essays in Pentateuchal Criticism* (London, 1910) ; and *Pentateuchal Studies* (London, 1912) ; *J. Dahse, *Is a Revolution in Pentateuchal Criticism at Hand ?* (London, 1912) ; F. E. Gigot, *The Message of Moses and Modern Higher Criticism* (New York, 1915) ; F. X. Kugler, S.J., ' Zum Alter der wichtigsten bürgerlichen und kultischen Gesetzesbestimmungen des Pentateuch, insbesondere des sog. Priesterkodex ' in *Von Moses bis Paulus* (Münster in Westf., 1922) 36–133 ; *E. Naville, *The Higher Criticism in relation to the Pentateuch* (Edinburgh, 1923) ; J. Goettsberger, *Einleitung in das Alte Testament* (Freiburg im Breisgau, 1928) 13–117 ; A. Bea, S.J., *De Pentateucho* (Romae, 1933²) = *Institutiones Biblicae* II i and ' Der heutige Stand der Pentateuchfrage ' *Bi* 16 (1935) 175–200 ; J. Coppens, *L'Histoire Critique de l'Ancien Testament* (Tournai-Paris, 1938)—English trans. with new material up to 1940, *The Old Testament and the Critics* trans. by E. A. Ryan, S.J. and E. W. Tribbe, S.J. (Paterson, N.J., 1943) ; H. Hoepfl, O.S.B., ' Pentateuque et Hexateuque ' DAFC III 1883–1920.

127 Names—The five books of Moses are commonly referred to as the Pentateuch, a word which signifies a book composed of five rolls. The second element of the word, *viz.* τεῦχος, originally meant a container or case for holding a manuscript roll and later came to stand for the roll which the case contained. It is used in this sense in *The Letter of Aristeas*, 179. In the *Letter to Flora* from Ptolemy, a Gnostic of the 2nd cent. A.D., is found the first occurrence of ' the Pentateuch of Moses ' (ἡ Μωσέως πεντάτευχος). The letter has been preserved by Epiphanius, *Adv. Haereses* 33, 4, 1, PG 41, 560. From the Greeks the name passed to the Latin writers and was used by Tertullian early in the 3rd cent., *Adv. Marcionem* 1, 10, PL 2, 257. The fivefold division itself is attested about two centuries earlier, as Philo, *De Abraham* 1, speaks of Genesis as the first of ' five books '.

In the NT the Pent. is called ' the book of the Law ' Gal 3:10 ; ' the Law ' Rom 3:21 ; ' the Law of Moses ' Lk 24:44. The expression ' the Law of the Lord ', Lk 2:23, may be, not the designation of the Pent., but a reference to the legislation it contains. As the Pent. contains much historical material, these appellations indicate which of the two elements, history and law, was most esteemed.

In the OT the Pent. is called ' the book of the Law of Yahweh ' 2 Par 17:9 ; ' the book of the Law of Moses ' Neh 8:1 ; ' the Law of Moses ' 2 Par 23:18 ; ' the book of Moses ' Neh 13:1, where the Lucianic recension of LXX has ' the book of the Law of Moses ' ; and in Neh 8:2 it is simply ' the Law '.

The names of the five books in DV, Genesis, Exodus, Leviticus, Numbers and Deuteronomy, are either adopted or adapted or translated from Vg, which itself acquired the names in the same way from the LXX ;

see §§ 136*c*, 162*c*, 182*b*, 196*b*, 210*b*. The Hebrew **127** names, which are taken from the opening words of the different books, are added in Vg as transcribed by St Jerome in his *Prologus Galeatus* or preface to the Books of Kings.

Contents—The Pent. contains the religious history of **128** the chosen people and of their ancestors traced from the creation of the first man to the death of Moses, and secondly, the laws, religious and social, of their theocratic system. Genesis indicates the line of descent from Adam to Abraham, and then narrates at length the history of this patriarch, of Isaac, of Jacob and his sons, and ends with the death of Joseph in Egypt. It is the necessary introduction to the other books, as it relates God's promise that Canaan was to be the possession of Abraham's descendants and explains how the Israelites came to be living in Egypt. Exodus continues the story with an account of the oppression of the Israelites in Egypt, the call of Moses, his liberation of the people, the Covenant at Sinai, and ends with the setting up of the Tabernacle in the first month of the second year after the departure from Egypt. Leviticus contains very little narrative and ends with the people still at Sinai. The Book of Numbers gives the remainder of the story up to the fortieth year. It opens with the numbering of the people preparatory to the departure from Sinai and ends with their encampment in the plain opposite Jericho. Deuteronomy like Leviticus has little narrative. The Covenant with God is renewed before the entry into Canaan, and the history ends with the death of Moses on Mount Nebo after he had seen the promised land he was not allowed to enter.

Of the legislation Genesis contains the law given to Noe after the Flood, ch 9, and the law of circumcision given to Abraham, ch 17. The laws in Ex, Lev and Num up to 10:10 were given at Mount Sinai, Lev 26:45; 27:34. Those in the rest of Num date from various times during the wandering in the desert, and the laws of Deut are a repetition and modification of previous legislation given by Moses in immediate preparation for the passage of the Jordan into the land of promise. This summary does not exclude the addition of laws in post-Mosaic times, *cf.* § 134*d–g*.

Certain collections of laws may be distinguished as the Decalogue, Ex 20:3–17, and its repetition, Deut 5:7–21. The initial legislation at Mount Sinai is given in the Book of the Covenant, Ex 24:7, from Ex 20:23 to 23:19. Collections of laws appertaining to the Sanctuary, the sacrifices and the priesthood are given in Ex 25–30; Lev 1–8, 10, 12–16, 21–24, 27 ; Num 15, 18–19, 28–9. The law of Deut. is given in chh 12–26.

Moses ; His Life and Achievements—As Moses was **129** the author of the Pent. (with due allowance for later additions and modifications ; see § 134), it will be convenient to gather here the main facts about his life, achievements and character. His birth fell during the period of oppression in Egypt. The fact that his life was saved through the pity of Pharaoh's daughter and that she adopted him as a son, Ex 2:1–10, ensured for him the best home and education possible in Egypt at the time and far superior to what would have been his, had he passed his youth among his own people. The Egyptians were a highly civilized nation. They had a keen eye for beauty and remarkable skill in the arts of

129a sculpture and architecture. They had an abundant literature and were famous in the Near East for their wisdom. It was in the highest circles of this refined society that Moses passed his youth. Thus alone of the Israelites he 'was instructed in all the wisdom of the Egyptians', Acts 7:22. This of itself must have won him pre-eminence among his countrymen, but he had it in him besides to become, as St Stephen put it, *ibid.*, 'mighty in his words and in his deeds'. Not that he had any natural gift of eloquence. On the contrary, as St Paul's speech was called 'contemptible', 2 Cor 10:10, so Moses described himself as '*heavy of mouth and heavy of tongue*', Ex 4:10. He suffered in fact from some impediment of speech, *cf.* Ex 6:12. Aaron, his brother, had to be his 'mouth' and 'speak in his stead to the people', Ex 4:16. But many years were to pass before he had to teach and guide his fellow-Israelites.

b His life falls into three periods, to each of which are assigned forty years. He was forty years old, Acts 7:23, 'when it came into his heart to visit his brethren'. He was 'eighty years old' when he went with Aaron to speak with Pharaoh, Ex 7:7. And he was 'a hundred and twenty years old' at the time of his death, Deut 31:2. According to these figures he spent forty years of private life, of which little is recorded, forty years as a fugitive in Madian, and forty years as leader of his people, all, except the period of struggle with Pharaoh, spent in the long wandering from Egypt to Canaan. This schematism combined with the Hebrew use of forty as a round and only approximate number shows that the figures are not meant to be exact. It will be recalled that in the same way forty years are assigned to the reigns of the three successive kings, Saul, David and Solomon ; see § 124*l*. It should be added that the records indicate that with all their culture and knowledge the Egyptians did not seem to have had a knowledge of their true ages ; see § 161*e*. The meaning of the figures, therefore, may be taken to be that Moses had reached an age at which he could be expected to act with authority when he attempted to intervene in the struggle between the Israelites, Ex 2:13, that he was long absent in Madian, and had reached an advanced age at the time of his death.

c **The second period** of Moses' life began with his flight from Egypt to Madian. This was necessitated by Pharaoh's determination to kill him for having slain an Egyptian in defence of one of his fellow-countrymen, Ex 2:11 f., 15. The personal courage he had shown on that occasion led him to defend the shepherd daughters of Jethro, the priest of Madian, against the violence of an unspecified number of men. The sequel of this bold act of kindness was his marriage with Sephora, who was one of the seven daughters. In appearance Moses was at this time an Egyptian and was taken to be such, Ex 2:19. Further, he was not true to the religious practices of his people, as an obscure narration makes it plain that he omitted the circumcision of one at least of his two sons, Ex 4:24–26, perhaps out of a fear of displeasing his wife. The fidelity of the story to fact is illustrated by the mention of Moses' marriage with a foreign woman and his neglect of circumcision. If the story had been written or edited in later ages with the purpose of edification at all costs, these facts, which did not make for the honour of the great lawgiver, would have been omitted. The same is true of his second marriage, which was with an Ethiopian (Cushite), Num 12:1, for this woman can hardly be identified with Sephora. This marriage was resented by Mary, Moses' sister, and by Aaron.

While living in Madian Moses took charge of his father-in-law's 'flock', Ex 3:1, which may have been of sheep or goats or, indeed, of both together. He thus belongs to the list of famous shepherds and goatherds, in which are the names of Jacob, David and Amos. Later, it was on Jethro's advice that Moses eased his burden of government by appointing rulers over sections of the people to judge the easier cases, Ex 18:13–26.

d **The third period** began with the divine mission to return to Egypt to free his people. This charge was **129d** given in the vision of the Burning Bush, Ex 3–4. There is still discussion whether God then revealed his sacred name of Yahweh for the first time, Ex 3:15. The text strongly suggests that Moses knew or suspected that God was known among his countrymen by a name that was unknown to him. He had lived all his life away from them, at the court of Pharaoh's daughter and in Madian. He seems to have foreseen incredulity if he could not tell his people the name of God who had sent him. 'Lo, I shall go to the children of Israel and say to them : The God of your fathers hath sent me to you. If they should say to me : What is his name ? what shall I say to them ?', Ex 3:13. If, in answer to this question, he had given a name that the Israelites had never heard before, it would have been an obstacle to the acceptance of his mission. If this is correct, it is evidence of what would be expected, *viz.* that Moses was not well-informed about the religion of his people. Apart from the liberation from Egypt, Ex 5–12, the **e** story of the remainder of Moses' life is that of the forty years' sojourn in the wilderness and its main outline is too well known to be summarized here. But something must be said of **his troubles**, his faults, and his virtues. His task was certainly a formidable one, for he had to bear the burden of a 'stiff-necked' people, Ex 32:9 ; 33:3, 5 ; 34:9 ; Deut 9:6, 13 ; 10:16. In spite of the miracles they had seen wrought on their behalf in Egypt they lacked trust in God and were constantly murmuring and complaining, for lack of water, Ex 15:24 ; 17:3 ; Num 20:5, of food, Ex 16:3 ; see also Num 11:1 ; 21:5. On one occasion the people so far forgot their indebtedness to Moses that he had reason to fear for his life : 'Yet a little more and they will stone me' Ex 17:4. And it was not only the common people who proved so ungrateful. Even those nearest and dearest to him, from whom he had the right to look for support and encouragement, found fault with and gave way to jealousy against him, as did Mary and Aaron, Num 12:1 f. On another occasion there was even open rebellion under the leadership of Core, Dathan and Abiron, Num 16. And although God vindicated his servant by the speedy punishment of the offenders, such ingratitude and opposition must have caused him great distress. Other instances of such opposition and murmuring are related Ex 2:14 ; 5:21 ; 6:9 ; 14:11 f. ; Num 14:2 f.

Even more distressing to Moses than these personal **f** affronts were the lack of trust in God and the grave breaches of his commandments. 'The Lord said to Moses : How long will this people *contemn* me ? how long will they not believe *in* me for all the signs that I have wrought *in the midst of* them ?', Num 14:11. Very soon after receiving the decalogue and with the portents of Egypt fresh in their minds, while Moses was yet in the mountain with God, they violated the precept never to make a graven image, and set up the golden calf : '*This is thy God,* O Israel, *who has* brought thee *up* out of the land of Israel', Ex 32:4 ; *cf.* 20:4. And not only did the people thus transgress, but even Aaron set up an altar before the image and proclaimed '*Tomorrow will be the feast in honour of Yahweh*', Ex 32:5. But far worse was to follow. When the people were shortly to enter the promised land, they took to fornication with the daughters of Moab, and when invited to the sacrifices of their gods '*the people did eat* and adored their gods ', Num 25:2. It cannot have been a surprise though it must have been heartbreaking to Moses, when shortly before his death and the end of the long pilgrimage in the desert God announced to him : 'Behold thou shalt sleep with thy fathers, and this people will rise up and go afornicating after strange gods in the land to which it goeth in to dwell : *they will* forsake me, and will make void the covenant, which I have made with them ', Deut 31:16.

No wonder that the burden on Moses' shoulders seemed **g** at times more than he could bear. He made his complaint to God : 'Why hast thou afflicted thy servant : wherefore do I not find favour before thee : and why

129g hast thou laid the weight of all this people upon me ? . . . I am not able alone to bear all this people, because it is too heavy for me ', Num 11:11, 14. So intense was his affliction that death seemed preferable : ' I beseech thee to kill me, and let me find grace in thy eyes, that I be not afflicted with so great evils ', Num 11:15. So to speak was no sign of virtue in Moses ; but the fault, if in the anguish of his soul fault there was, was slight and received no rebuke from God, who on the contrary arranged for the easing of Moses' burden, vv 16 f. On a previous occasion when Moses showed pusillanimity and lack of trust in God in almost refusing the mission to liberate Israel, God was angry with him, Ex 4:14.

h Here it may be remarked how frankly and humbly Moses relates his own **weaknesses and shortcomings**. In addition to the examples mentioned in the last paragraph there is the confession of his failure to circumcise his son, Ex 4:24 ff., and the offence which so displeased God as to merit Moses' exclusion from the land of promise. To this, allusion is made on several occasions, Num 20:12 ; 27:14 ; Deut 1:37 ; 3:27 ; 31:2 ; 32:52 ; 34:4 (probably post-Mosaic). From Num 20:12 ' Because you have not *trusted* me ' and Num 27:14 ' because you *were rebellious against my command* ' it appears that the fault of Moses was a failure to carry out the divine command just as it was given to him, the failure being due to a lack of trust based perhaps on the unworthiness of the people. Ps 105 (106) 33 in its allusion to this incident further charges Moses with having ' *spoken rashly* with his lips ', a reference to Moses' reprehension of the people, Num 20:10. God had ordered Moses to ' speak to the rock ', Num 20:8. This he did not do. Instead he struck the rock twice. Both in Deut 1:37 and 3:26 Moses tells the people that God was angry with him on their account. That is to say that it was the obstinacy and rebelliousness of the people which occasioned Moses' fault.

i This constant recurrence to his shortcomings is a sign of **great virtue** in Moses. He was completely devoid of the spirit of pride. His spirit of forgiveness is illustrated by his prayer to God to heal his sister Mary of leprosy although it was inflicted on her in punishment of her envy of him and evil talk against him, Num 12:13. This same forgiving spirit and at the same time unbounded devotion to his people is manifested in his petitions to God to spare them after some of their gravest transgressions. Thus after the worship of the golden calf he prayed : ' Either forgive them this trespass ; or if thou do not, strike me out of the book that thou hast written ', Ex 32:31 f. The doctrine of eternal bliss with God had not been revealed, and the book of which Moses speaks is ' the book of the living ' (*cf.* Ps 68 [69] 29), that is of those alive in this world. He prays to die if God will not spare his people. He had the same great spirit which led St Paul in the same sense to desire to be an anathema for his brethren, Rom 9:3. See St Jerome, *Ep. ad Algasiam* 121, qu. 9 (PL 22, 1028). Num 14:19 f. records another successful prayer of Moses for the forgiveness of his people.

j On the subject of Moses' virtues a word must be said of Num 12:3 : ' Moses was a man exceeding meek above all men that dwelt upon earth '. Accepting this to refer to ' meekness ' some have argued that Moses could have written so of himself ; others, as A Lapide, have considered the sentence a later addition. In subsequent usage the word combined the double notion of suffering affliction with patience, but here it seems to refer merely to the multitude of Moses' troubles and afflictions. This is favoured by the context which treats of the hostility of Mary and Aaron, those nearest and dearest to the great legislator. An allied word has the bare sense of ' affliction ' in Ex 3:7 and Deut 16:3, and another allied word has the meaning of ' in distressed circumstances ' ' needy ' in Deut 24:12, 14 f. This is not, of course, to say that Moses was not meek, as his ready forgiveness in this very instance shows that he was. Just anger is not opposed

to meekness and Moses often had occasion to manifest it, **129j** Ex 11:9 ; Lev 10:16 ; Ex 32:19.

Moses' **supernatural privileges** may be briefly referred **k** to. He was a prophet, that is, one commissioned to speak in the name of, and with the authority of God : ' I shall be in thy mouth ', Ex 4:15 ; see § 409e. And he speaks of himself as a prophet in the passage where he foretells that God will send Israel a succession of prophets to end with Christ : ' The Lord thy God will raise up to thee a prophet of thy nation and of thy brethren like unto me ', Deut 18:15. As a prophet God himself set Moses above all others : ' If there be among you a prophet of the Lord, I will appear to him in a vision, or I will speak to him in a dream. But it is not so with my servant Moses, who is most faithful in all my house ; for I speak to him mouth to mouth, and plainly and not by riddles, and figures doth he see the Lord ' (MT ' not by riddles, and the form of the Lord doth he see ') Num 12:6-8. So Ex 33:11 ' The Lord *used to speak* to Moses face to face, as a man is wont to speak to his friend '. Moses did not, of course, see God as he is in himself, but in some familiar apparition. When he came forth from these intimate colloquies with God, Moses' ' face was horned ', Ex 34:29-35. That is, the effulgence of God's presence caused the prophet's face to shine with beams or rays of light, which are metaphorically called horns. On two occasions Moses was forty days and forty nights alone with God in the mountain, and on neither occasion did he either eat or drink ; Ex 24:18 with Deut 9:9 describe the first occasion and Ex 34:28 the second. On Moses' office as a miracle-worker and as a lawgiver it is not necessary to dilate, as the last four books of the Pentateuch bear ample witness to his power and authority in both respects.

Such then was Moses—prophet, miracle-worker, **l** legislator, friend of God, leader of his people. He may justly be called the second father of his race and its founder as a nation. He freed them from the bondage of Egypt, ruled them in the wilderness, gave them a religious and social code that bound them in a close federal unity. But even he was not allowed to set foot on the soil of the promised land to which he led his nation. Such is God's displeasure at any breach of his holy law that this great and virtuous man was condemned to die in sight of the land he had so long desired.

Mosaic Authorship—It has long been recognized that **130a** the Pent. has not come down to us precisely as it left the hand of Moses and that apart from the errors of copyists it has received additions and modifications. For instance, Cornelius a Lapide, who died in 1637, wrote in his preface to the Pent. that ' Moses wrote the Pentateuch simply by way of a diary or annals, but Josue or someone similar put these annals of Moses into order, divided them up, and added and inserted some sentences '. So when the Mosaic authorship is spoken of, it must be borne in mind that the authorship meant is that of the work as a whole with allowance for subsequent modifications, for which see § 134.

There are **various references in the Pentateuch** to **b** Moses' literary activity. Moses is ordered by God to write down an account of the destruction of Amalec, Ex 17:14. This refers to Ex 17:8-13. ' Moses wrote down all the words of the Lord ', Ex 24:4, and what these were is made plain in 24:7 ' Taking the book of the covenant he read it in the hearing of the people '. The exact limits of this ' book ' or document are not easy to define and are variously set, by Hoberg 20-23, by Goettsberger 20:22-23:19, by Bea 20:23-23:33. After the defection of the people in worshipping the golden calf and the subsequent renewal of the covenant God again ordered Moses : ' Write thee these words by which I have made a covenant both with thee and with Israel ', Ex 34:27. This refers to 34:10-26. Num 33:2 records that Moses wrote down the places of encampment from the time of the departure from Egypt. The list follows in the same chapter. ' Moses wrote this law ', Deut 31:9, 24, and ordered it to be kept

130b with the Ark, v 26. The Canticle given in Deut 32 is said to have been written by Moses, 31:22, at the command of God, 31:19.

c What is to be concluded from these passages ? In the first place, Moses is shown to have been not only a legislator but also a writer. But the question is how much did he write ? A logical person may argue : as these texts explicitly testify that Moses wrote certain parts of the Pent., so they implicitly testify that he did not write those parts which are not attributed to him. This argument is guilty of the fallacy of interpreting these ancient oriental documents in accordance with our own modern western habits of mind. It is not probable that Moses wrote the whole Pent. in the plains of Moab shortly before his death. It is far more likely that he wrote different parts of it at different times during the course of the forty years' journeyings. In such protracted literary work it is in accordance with psychology that he should think at times of saying what at other times he did not think of saying. Moreover, it is one of the commonest literary devices in biblical style to use the *sensus praecisivus*, that is, a manner of writing which is concerned to express the truth of the statement in hand without any implication as to its being the whole truth or not. Thus it is said that Joseph 'knew her not till she brought forth her first-born son ', Mt 1:25, where nothing is implied as to their future relations ; *cf.* Ps 109 (110) 1 ' The Lord said to my Lord : Sit thou at my right hand, until I make thy enemies thy footstool ', where it is not implied that the place of honour accorded up to the time of victory is thereafter to be withdrawn. In accordance with this mode of expression the explicit attribution of certain passages to Moses does not deny him also the author-ship of others.

d As regards the Canticle of Deut 32 the previous chapter implies that Moses not only composed it but also inserted it in the book that contained ' the words of this law ', 31:24. It was to be a testimony against the children of Israel, who after entering into the promised land would despise God and make void his covenant, 31:19. Moses knew that he was soon to die and that Josue was to lead the people over Jordan, 31:23. Moses therefore completed the writing of his book and ordered it to be kept with the Ark, vv 24–26. This was not to be done immediately as Moses was first to read out to the people the words of the song he had composed, vv 27–30. The order of this narration shows that Moses set down his canticle in his book.

e The next question is **what was this book in which Moses wrote ' the words of this law ',** Deut 31:24. DV following Vg has ' volume ' here, that is, strictly speaking a roll, which is an undue narrowing of the meaning. *Meͨgillāh* is the Hebrew word for ' roll ', and, although the *sēper* or ' book ' had the form of a roll, the two words are not interchangeable, partly because the word *sēper* is used of any document, how-ever short, and partly because a long book had to be written in several rolls. The book is referred to also Deut 28:58 ' the words of this law that are written in this *book* ' ; and similar expressions occur 28:61 and 29:21 (MT 29:20). Moses commanded the priests to read ' the words of this law ' before the people every seven years ' in the year of remission ' at the feast of Tabernacles, 31:9–11. The observance of this law is recorded in the time of Nehemias, Neh 8:18 : ' He read in the book of the law of God day by day, from the first day till the last '. Was the reading merely from Deut, or was it from the Pent. as a whole ? There is no distinction of meaning between the two expressions ' the book of the law of God ' and ' the law ', which is used just before, Neh 8:14 : ' They found written in the law that the Lord had commanded *through* Moses that the children of Israel should dwell in tabernacles on the feast in the seventh month '. The feast of Tabernacles is mentioned in Deut 16:13–16 ; 31:10–12; but there is no mention in these texts of dwelling in tabernacles or booths. This is prescribed exclusively in Lev 23:42 f. In the time, therefore, of Esdras and

Nehemias ' this law ' and ' the words of this law in a **130e** *book* ', Deut 31:9, 24, were understood to refer to the legislation of the Pent. as a whole. In other words these texts were understood to record the writing by Moses of the legislation of the Pent. Moreover, the legislation and the narrative are so closely interwoven that to say Moses wrote the law is practically equivalent to saying that he wrote the Pent. as a whole. Indeed, the name of the Pent. in later times was simply the Law, the designation being taken from what was regarded as the most important element.

At the beginning of Deut it is said that ' Moses *took in* **f** *hand* to expound *this* law ', 1:5. ' This law ', or ' this Torah ', refers to the laws contained in the previous books, just as the opening words of Deut refer back to all the discourses pronounced by Moses during the previous forty years. The geographical expressions which follow the sentence ' These are the words which Moses spoke to all Israel ', 1:1, designate various places in the course of the forty years' wanderings. The word ' these ' is retrospective just as it is in Num 36:13 ; and the opening sentence of Deut in this way joins this book to its predecessors. And just as ' these words ' are those reported in the previous books, so ' this law ' refers to the legislation there recorded.

It is, perhaps, worth remarking in connection with the **g** meaning of ' this law ' that Goettsberger supposes Moses to have read the law to the people after he had finished writing it in a book, Deut 31:24. But what Moses read to the people was, not the law, but the Canticle of Deut 32 : ' I will speak these words in their hearing, and will call heaven and earth to witness against them ', 31:28. This alludes to the opening words of the Canticle, ' Hear, O ye heavens, the things I speak ; let the earth give ear to the words of my mouth ', 32:1. And the reason which Moses gives, **h** ' For I know that after my death you will do wickedly . . . and evils shall come upon you in the latter times ', 31:29, is amply illustrated in the Canticle, 32:5, 15 (on the prevarications) ; 32:20–25 (on the punish-ments). And finally, 31:30, ' Moses therefore spoke in the hearing of the whole assembly of Israel the words of this canticle ', records the carrying out of the purpose mentioned just before, 31:28

In the law of the kingdom the king is ordered to have **i** written out for him a copy of the law for his own use : ' After he is raised to the throne of his kingdom, he shall *write* out *for* himself *a copy* of this law in a volume *from that* of the priests of the Levitical tribe ', Deut 17:18. It would be arbitrary to limit this to Deut. The king's office would demand a knowledge of the whole legislation.

The prescription that ' the words of this law ' were to **j** be read publicly every seven years at the feast of Tabernacles, Deut 31:10 f., has been thought by some to imply the reading of something fairly short. But the limitation of the prescription to seven year intervals indicates that the obligation was an onerous one. The reading of the whole Pent. is not prescribed but only of the legislation. The purpose is stated explicitly, 31:12, ' that hearing they may learn, and fear the Lord your God, and keep and fulfil all the words of this law '. Only those parts, therefore, had to be read publicly which concerned the people. Those pre-scribing the duties of priests and Levites could be omitted. The rest could easily be read within the week of the feast. It is recorded of Esdras that he read before the people ' from *dawn* (Heb. ' from the light ') until midday ', Neh 8:3 ; and the expression ' he read *therein* ' implies that he read only selections. Compare the reading of the following day of fasting, Neh 9:3, when ' they read in the book of the law of the Lord their God '. This refers to the reading that took place on a single day.

In this connection reference should be made, lastly, **k** to the order given Deut 27:2 f. : ' When you are passed over the Jordan . . ., thou shalt set up great stones and shalt plaster them over with plaster, that thou mayst write on them all the words of this law ' ;

130k *cf.* v 8. The execution of this is recorded Jos 8:32–35. Note v 32 ' he [Josue] wrote *there* upon stones *a copy* of the law of Moses ' (*cf.* Deut 17:18), and v 34 ' after this he read all the words of the law, the blessing and the cursing, *according to all that was* written in the book of the law '. There are two questions here, (1) what was written on the stones, and (2) what did Josue read out to the people. The setting up of the stones was intended, not so much as a memorial of the law, as a public acknowledgement of its authority joined with an implicit undertaking to observe it. The injunction to set them up was given in an address of Moses and the elders of Israel to the people commencing with the admonition to ' keep every commandment that I command you this day ', Deut 27:1. There is no reason, therefore, to suppose that among the laws written on the stones were those that did not concern the conduct of the people directly. Neither is it probable that the many laws which are set down twice, and even oftener, like the law concerning the Pasch and the use of leaven, were written more than once on the stones. With these omissions there would be no great difficulty in writing the law of Moses on a number of great stones. The law of Hammurabi was carved on a stone, and as Goettsberger reminds us, ' this was not less extensive than the law of Moses '. The second question, what was read to the people at Josue's command, is secondary, partly because the biblical use of the word ' all ' is not so exact as in our usage, and partly because in spite of its obscurity the text seems only to mean that Josue had carried out the law or commandment of Moses recorded Deut 27:11–26, and had the cursings read in the words prescribed in the law there given. To these may have been added the blessings given in Deut 28, or perhaps with Fernandez ' it may be said that the blessings are implied in the curses as contraries ', *Comm. in Josue* (CSS, 1938) 126.

131a Jos and Kings speak of the law of Moses as written in a book—' The book of this law ', Jos 1:8, is spoken of as equivalent to ' all the law which Moses my servant hath commanded thee ' of the previous verse ; ' as . . . it is written in the book of the law of Moses ', 8:31 ; ' all things that are written in the book of the law of Moses ', 23:6. Also ' as it is written in the law of Moses ', 3 Kg 2:3 ; and Deut 24:16 is quoted 4 Kg 14:6 as ' written in the book of the law of Moses '. Such texts leave no doubt that Moses drew up a code of law which existed in writing, but they do not of themselves demonstrate that Moses was the author of the whole Pent. They do not amount to a demonstration, but in view of the evidence of the Pent. itself their natural meaning is that Moses was its author, a meaning which should not be rejected in the absence of convincing evidence to the contrary. The correctness of this interpretation is further evidenced by the close connection between the narrative and the legislative parts of the Pent. In a large measure the narrative prepares for the legislation and gives it its setting. The force of these allusions to the law of Moses, it may be added, is illustrated by the endeavour of those who deny the Mosaic authorship of the Pent. to treat them as glosses and later additions. If there had been an attempt to put back into a distant past a late belief in the Mosaic authorship, I think it is safe to say that it would have been carried through rather more energetically and above all in more explicit terms. The very fact that the allusions are not in themselves demonstrations goes to show that they were written by people with no ulterior motive.

b This brings us to **the witness of the NT.** Mk 12:26 attributes the words ' I am the God of Abraham, and the God of Isaac, and the God of Jacob ', to ' the book of Moses '. These occur in the narrative Ex 3:6. Various passages of Lev are ascribed to Moses, Lev 12 on the purification of women in Lk 2:22 ; Lev 12:3 on circumcision in Jn 7:22 ; Lev 14 concerning the cleansing of a leper in Mt 8:4 ; Lev 20:10 on the punishment of an adulteress in Jn 8:5 ; in Rom 10:5 it is said by Paul that ' Moses wrote ' a text of Lev 18:5.

St Stephen in Ac 7:37 attributes to Moses Deut 18:15 ; **131** the Jews in Mt 19:7 ascribe to Moses the legislation about divorce in Deut 24 and our Lord's answer, Mt 19:8 makes the same attribution. Deut 25:4 about muzzling the ox is ' written in the law of Moses ', 2 Cor 9:9. Deut 25:5, which gives the Levirate law, is said to have been written by Moses, Mk 12:19 ; Lk 20:28.

Philip, Jn 1:45, says that ' Moses in the law . . . did **c** write ' about the Messias ; and, more important, Christ himself, Jn 5:46, said to the Jews, ' If you did believe Moses, you would believe me also, for he wrote of me '. (The ' perhaps ' of DV in this text is due to a peculiarity of the Vg rendering of conditional sentences, and is best omitted in English.) According to the belief of the Jews, therefore, corroborated by our Lord, Moses was the writer of Messianic passages in the Pent. These are Gen 3:15 ; 12:3 and-parallels 18:18 ; 22.18 ; 26:4 ; 28:14 ; further Gen 49:10 ; Deut 18:15. Our Lord is here basing his claim to a supernatural mission on the witness borne to him by Moses, not merely, be it noted, on the witness in itself, but on the witness as being the witness of Moses. Christ would not base so important a dogmatic truth on a false premiss. First Christ appealed to the testimony of John the Baptist, vv 32–35, then to that of ' the Father himself ', v 37, and finally to that of Moses. He is speaking of the person Moses, in whom the Jews put their trust, v 45, and it is the person Moses who accuses them, *ibid*.

Among both Jews and Christians **tradition** has always **d** been in harmony with this testimony of Scripture. On the Jews see Bea 18 f., and on the Fathers Hoberg, 71 f. It must suffice here to mention two prominent Jewish writers of the first Christian century. Both Philo, *De Vita Mosis*, ed. Cohn 4 (1902) 267 f., and Josephus, *Ant.* 4, 8, 48, consider Moses to have written even the account of his own death. According to Josephus he was moved to write it out of fear lest the greatness of his fame might lead men rashly to say that he had departed to God.

The Pent. contains **internal evidence** that it was **e** composed at the time and under the conditions which Mosaic authorship postulates. This is only to be expected from the historical testimony examined above. It also presents not a few texts which taken alone would suggest a later date. Considered, however, in the light of all the evidence such texts show the presence of later additions and modifications.

The writer is more familiar with Egypt than with Canaan. Places in Egypt are mentioned without explanation, as the city of On (Heliopolis), Gen 41:45, the land of Gessen (Goshen), Gen 46:28, Socoth (Succoth), Ex 13:20, Phihahiroth, Ex 14:2. On the other hand, of Qiryath-arba it is added that it is ' in the land of Canaan ', Gen 23:2, and similarly of Mambre, where Abraham buried Sara, Gen 23:19. The same information is added about Shechem, Gen 33:18, and about Luza (Bethel), Gen 35:6. The situation of mounts Garizim (Gerizim) and Hebal (Ebal) is described in Deut 11:30. Again, to give an idea of the fertility of the country round about Jordan reference is made to Egypt as better known, Gen 13:10, and the date of the foundation of Hebron is fixed by that of Tanis (Zoan), Num 13:23. The prohibition to act ' according to the custom of the land of Egypt in which you dwelt ', Lev 18:3, is explicable only if it dates from a time not too distant from the delivery from that country. And the time is further fixed by the accompanying prohibition to act according to the customs of **f** Canaan ' into which I will bring you ', *ibid*. Similarly Ex 20:12 ; Deut 5:16 ; 17:14. Some laws are given explicitly to be observed after entry into the promised land, Num 15:2, 18. Other laws again clearly suppose that the people are living in camp. Lev 16:26 f. prescribes what is to be done to the scapegoat outside the camp and what are the conditions of re-entry into the camp. Then there are all the prescriptions laying down what is to be done in moving camp, Num 4:4 ff. The law ordering any ox, sheep or goat that was killed,

1f to be offered ' at the door of the tabernacle an oblation to the Lord ', Lev 17:3 f., could only be observed under the conditions of camp life. Once the people were scattered throught Canaan its observance would clearly be impossible. On the Egyptian colouring in the Pent. reference may be made to *A. S. Yahuda, *The Language of the Pentateuch in its relation to Egyptian* I (1933), and by the same author, *The Accuracy of the Bible* (1934).

2a Characteristics of the Pentateuch—Several important facts tend to be overlooked which are essential for the formation of a judgement of the Pent. as a piece of literature. In the first place, its composition extended over some forty years. Such a long period of time quite apart from differences of subject-matter could hardly fail to introduce differences of language, style and view-point. Then, Moses was not young when he led Israel to Sinai and he was a very old man when he arrived with the people in the country opposite Jericho. Repetition and fullness of style were characteristic of his people, and such characteristics would be emphasized in the style of an old man. Thirdly, not only is the Pent. an ancient and an oriental book, which it is quite unscientific to judge by the standards applicable to modern and western literature, it is further, in its own line, pioneer work. The marvel is that it is as perfect a production as we find it to be. No ancient literature has an historical work of similar compass which can be compared to it. And of course through divine inspiration God made use of human instruments as he found them. He did not interfere with their natural modes of thought, of speech, of style. Considered, therefore, simply on the plane of human achievement Moses wrote a truly remarkable work, which must take pride of place in any history of world literature.

b Perhaps the most striking feature of the Pent. is the **mixture of historical and legislative elements.** It contains the laws of Israel and yet cannot be called a legal handbook or code. The narrative gives the setting of the legislation and sometimes its historical occasion, Num 27:1 ff. ; 36:1 ff. But the narrative does not exist simply to illustrate the historical origin and growth of the legislation. It has, besides, its independent purpose to give a record of God's dealings with his people. The Pent., therefore, has a double thread, of historical narrative and of legal enactment.

c Whereas more often the legislation fits naturally into its historical setting as do the Sinaitic laws, and *cf.* Num 27 and 36, sometimes there is no apparent connexion and the transition from narrative to law is extremely abrupt ; *cf.* Num 15:1 ff. after 14:45, and 15:37-41 after 15:32-36. Contrary to the principle of grouping, such passages give the impression of having been slipped in without regard to the context. In the narrative portion such an abrupt insertion is found in Ex 9:30 f. This account of what the hail had or had not damaged in the fields of Egypt differs in spirit and style from the rest of the passage.

d In the narrative the primary purpose is not to record history as such. The record aims at giving **the religious history of Israel,** and there is consequently no mention of much that we moderns would like to know. The governing principle is the religious interest. One result of this is that the story is left with rough edges. For example, Sephora and her sons are with Moses in his journey from Madian to Egypt and are mentioned on account of the mysterious incident connected with the circumcision of one of them, Ex 4:20, 24-26. There is no mention of their having left Moses. This is learnt incidentally from Ex 18:2 ff. Another result is that chronological order is not rigidly adhered to. As in the case of Mt, within a broad framework which is definitely chronological, the details are sometimes arranged according to some other principle, for instance, common subject matter. Num 9:1 ff. is dated in the first month of the second year after the delivery from Egypt, whereas Num 1:1 is dated the first day of the second month of the same year. Num 7:1 ff. is dated to the day that Moses set up the Tabernacle ; according to Ex 40:2 this occurred on the first day of the first **132d** month, again of the same year. Ex 16:32-35 presents an example of the grouping of matter. First is recorded the command to lay up some manna for a memorial and secondly its execution by Aaron who put the required amount in the Tabernacle. This was in the second month of the first year after the delivery from Egypt, but the Tabernacle was not set up till the first month of the following year, Ex 40:2. Thirdly, it is added that the Israelites eat manna for forty years till they came to Canaan. But at this stage of their journey it was still anticipated that they were to enter almost at once on the conquest of that country.

There is no effort after brevity. On the contrary, **e repetition** would seem to have been a cause of pleasure. In the following examples it is sometimes part only of a verse that is repeated : Deut 7:5, 25 and 12:3 ; 8:3 and 16 ; 1:10 and 10:22 and 28:62 ; 6:7-9 and 11:18-20 ; 12:6 and 17 f. and 14:23 ; 12:16 and 23 f. and 15:23 ; 27:2 and 4 ; 28:4 and 11 ; 31:6 and 8 ; 31:30 and 32:44. An example on a large scale but of a slightly different character is provided by Ex 25-31 and 35-39 which in general treat of the same matters, the Ark, the Tabernacle and the like, the first section as a narration of the divine commands, the second of their execution. Some repetitions may be due to the conflation of two sources or may be later non-Mosaic additions. See the commentaries on the mission of Moses in Exodus and on the rebellion of Core in Numbers.

As an **illustration of the repetition and also of the f development of laws** may be taken those relative to the first-born males of beasts. Immediately after the deliverance from Egypt God claims as his own every firstborn, Ex 13:2. Moses then transmits the divine command to the people, 13:11-16. When they arrive in Canaan the firstborn of the male sex is to be consecrated to the Lord. The firstborn of an ass is to be changed for a lamb or a kid (the word *śeh* is applicable to both) ; otherwise it is to be killed. And the Israelites must hand on to their posterity the reason for this rite, namely that God delivered his people from Egypt by slaying all the firstborn of the land. The law is next included in the covenant legislation of Sinai with the explicit mention of oxen and the flock or herd. The word *ṣō'n* is applicable to both sheep and goats, and both DV and RV unduly limit the meaning by translating ' sheep '. New precision is given by the additional regulation that the animal is to be left with its dam for seven days and then to be given to God. In what manner the gift was to be made is not said. At the time this was general knowledge and did not need to be specified. Probably the owner himself killed it and consumed it at a sacrificial meal with his family. After the violation of the Covenant by the worship of the golden calf it was renewed and the law about the firstborn re-enacted, Ex 34:19. In place of the specification of the age at which the animal is to be given to God it is again laid down that the firstborn of an ass is to be redeemed by a lamb or kid. The next mention is in Lev 27:26. This chapter deals with free-will offerings and it is appropriately laid down that no one can make a free-will offering to God of the firstlings as they belong to God by right already. The subject comes up again in Num 18:15-18, this time from the point of view of the priest's rights. All firstlings which belong to God are assigned to the priest. Unclean beasts are to be bought back at the age of one month for five shekels of silver. Presumably the clean animals that could be legally sacrificed were still to be offered on the eighth day. The extension of the time to a month in the case of the unclean animals is probably a condescension to men's unwillingness to buy back very young animals with the greater uncertainty of their survival. If the animal was to die within the month the owner of its dam would be free of any obligation. The firstlings of cows, sheep, and goats may not be redeemed because they are holy to God. The priest is to sprinkle their blood on the altar and to burn their fat as a sweet odour to the Lord.

132f But the flesh is the priest's as is the breast of the wave-offering and the right shoulder ; on the breast and the shoulder see Lev 7:30–34, etc.

g The Deuteronomic legislation was given in immediate preparation for the new conditions of settled life after entry into Canaan. In Deut 12:6 it is prescribed that firstlings may be offered only in the central sanctuary, in the place that God should choose out of all their tribes. There the Israelites are to eat them with their families and servants and with the Levites who dwelt in their cities, 12:7, 17 f. ; 14:23. In these passages the firstlings are mentioned only incidentally to the law of the unity of the sanctuary. The matter is treated in its own right in Deut 15:19–23. As the offering was to be made only at the central sanctuary and some time might elapse between the birth and an opportunity to offer it there, it is enacted that no work might be done with the firstlings of cattle nor might the firstlings of sheep be shorn. They were entirely the property of God. It is again laid down that they are to be eaten by the Israelite and his household in the one sanctuary that God should choose. The concession is made that if the animal have any defect which renders it unfit to sacrifice to God, then it may be eaten anywhere, and by all, whether clean or unclean, under the one condition that its blood may not be consumed. The blood was to be poured out on the earth like water. The blood as typifying life was specially sacred to God. In Deut there seems to be a definite change in the previous legislation. In Num the flesh of the firstlings was assigned to the priest to be consumed under the same conditions as the breast and right shoulder, the priest's portion of peace-offerings. In Deut all Israelites (who are not labouring under a legal uncleanness) may join in the sacrificial meal provided by the flesh of the firstlings. It does not seem possible with A Lapide to understand the words of Deut as addressed to the priests. The language is quite general and the laws are addressed to all. Neither does it seem legitimate with Keil to suppose that a share of the sacrificial meal was dependent on the invitation of the priest to enjoy part of what legally belonged to him. The wording of the laws seems to make it plain that the flesh reverted of right to the offerer. Neither does it seem possible to understand Num 18:18 as granting the priest only the breast and the right shoulder. This was Hengstenberg's explanation. Nor again does *H. M. Wiener, *Pentateuchal Studies* (1912) 294 seem to be correct in saying that Num 18 applies only to heave-offerings and that usually the heave-offering consisted of one or more firstlings. Probably experience had shown that the priests did not require all that had been assigned to them and would stand in even less need of the firstlings in Canaan, as it was foreseen that the animals would be older and more fully grown before an opportunity occurred to bring them to the one central sanctuary.

133a A phenomenon that easily escapes attention in a translation is that connected with **the use of the divine names.** Sometimes we find Yahweh, the personal name by which God was known to the Israelites, and sometimes Elohim, the general name for God, used also of false gods. The former is rendered in DV by ' the Lord ' as Vg has ' Dominus ' (LXX κύριος), and the latter by

' God '. The first to comment on the varying usage **133a** of these designations seems to have been Tertullian, *Adv. Hermogenem* 3, PL 2, 199 f. The following table will give an idea of the distribution of the names. It is taken from Bea, 45, and R. Cornely, S.J., *Introd. in S. Script. Libr. Compend.*, edit. A. Merk, S.J. (1927⁹) 338 (= C-M).

In this list those instances are omitted in which Elohim is used in the construct state or with suffixes. As it is against Heb. usage to employ a proper name such as Yahweh either in the construct state or with personal suffixes, in certain cases the writer practically had no choice. The combination of the two names, Yahweh Elohim is found exclusively in Gen 2 and 3 except for Ex 9:30, where the equivalent of Elohim is not in LXX and is probably not original in HT. The probable explanation of this restricted use was the desire to stress the identity of Elohim, alone named in Gen 1, with Yahweh, named exclusively in Gen 4 except for v 25. It should further be noticed that in Ex up to 6:2 (exclusively) Yahweh occurs 23 times and Elohim 19 times. Thus in Gen and Ex up to this point the number of occurrences of the two names is approximately the same, thereafter Yahweh altogether predominates. This preference must be connected with the revelation of Ex 6:2 f. On this see the commentary and § 129*d*. If it is true that the name Yahweh was previously unknown, then it follows that its earlier occurrences in the text of the Pent. were not original in the stories of Gen as handed down to the time of Moses. And this would be true also of the proper names, such as Jochabed, that of Moses' mother, in which the Tetragrammaton forms an element ; *cf.* the case of Eliacim, whose name was changed to Joakim, 4 Kg 23:34. In any case some explanation is called for by the preference shown in different passages for one name or the other. Thus in Gen 10–16 Yahweh occurs 36 times, but Elohim not at all. On the other hand, in Gen 40–45 Elohim occurs 19 times, but Yahweh not at all.

A similar phenomenon occurs elsewhere. In Pss 1–40 **b** (41) Yahweh occurs 272 times (278 including titles and doxology), Elohim 15 times, of which 9 are required by the context. In Pss 41–82 (42–83) Elohim is used 200 times, Yahweh only 44 times including the doxology, Ps 71 (72) 18. Finally Pss 89 (90)–150 have the name of Yahweh 339 times, Elohim 6 times. Of these 6 occurrences 5 occur in Ps 107 (108) which is compiled from two Elohistic Pss, 56 (57) and 59 (60). The other is found in Ps 143 (144) 9. Then, that the present distribution of the divine names is at any rate sometimes due to an editor or editors, not to the original authors, is shown by the fact that though Ps 52 (53) is a rehandling of Ps 13 (14), the latter uses Yahweh where the former has Elohim. The same tendency is to be seen in Ps 69 (70) which is a rehandling of Ps 39 (40) 14–18. The explanation proposed by J. Calès, S.J., from whose work most of the above figures have been taken, is that the intention was to provide a collection of canticles for the use of the Jews dispersed in pagan lands, where it would have been a profanation to pronounce the sacred Tetragrammaton, *Le Livre des Psaumes* 1 (1936) 20 f.

These examples from the Pss make it clear that the use **c**

	Gen	Ex	Lev	Num	Deut	Total
Yahweh	145 (Bea) 143 (C-M)	393 (Bea) 394 (C-M)	310	387	547	⎧ 1782 (Bea) ⎩ 1781 (C-M)
Elohim	165	56	—	10	⎧ 10 (Bea) ⎩ 8 (C-M)	241 (Bea) 239 (C-M)
Yahweh Elohim	20	1	—	—	—	21

33c of the divine names in the existing HT is not always that of the original authors. This is further demonstrated as regards the Pent. by both external and internal evidence. Swete's edition of the LXX shows that in the four books Gen to Num the Greek text differs in the use of the divine names 180 times from the existing HT, Dahse, 9. In Gen 16:11 the reason given for the name Ishmael is that ' Yahweh has given ear '. It is difficult to escape the conclusion that Yahweh has been substituted in this sentence for an original El or Elohim, which latter is found in one Heb. MS.

d It is impossible to explain the choice of one name rather than the other in all cases, just as it is impossible always to assign a reason why we sometimes speak of Jesus, sometimes of Christ, sometimes of Jesus Christ, sometimes of our Lord. To some extent the matter is fixed by usage, as we speak of ' the blood royal ' but never of ' the throne royal '. So the Hebrews spoke of ' a man of God ' (Elohim), not of ' a man of Yahweh '. On the other hand ' Blessed be Yahweh ' is the regular expression (25 times), ' Blessed be Elohim ' occurring twice only, Ps 65 (66) 20 and Ps 67 (68) 36 both in the Elohistic section of the Psalter. In general it may be said that Elohim is used where there is question of God's omnipotence and transcendence, Yahweh where he appears as the guardian and protector of his people. In converse with non-Israelites the name Yahweh is as a rule avoided. The narratives of Gen were traditional in the time of Moses, and the name of God will have been left in the form handed down in the case of each story. It is possible that in pre-Mosaic times before special emphasis had been given to the name of Yahweh some tribes favoured the one name and others the other.

34a Post-Mosaic Elements—These may be either modifications or additions. The **modifications** may affect both common words and proper names. The remarkable stability of the language from the Mosaic age suggests that copyists may have changed obsolete forms and words for those used in later times. On the other hand, the Pent. presents some linguistic peculiarities which seem definitely archaic. If common significant words were changed in the course of transcription, the process was not carried through consistently. Dan is mentioned as a place-name in northern Canaan, Gen 14:14, Deut 34:1, but this name dates from the conquest of the country, Jos 19:47, Jg 18:29. Similarly the place-name Horma, Num 14:45, Deut 1:44, was given only at the conquest, Jg 1:17. Deut 1:1 speaks of discourses of Moses delivered ' beyond the Jordan '. This phrase suggests some writer other than Moses living on the western side of the Jordan, which Moses himself never crossed. A Lapide suggested long ago that Moses may have written ' on this side ' and that ' Josue or whoever edited Moses's diaries, as he was living in Canaan ' changed it to ' beyond the Jordan '. If such a change was made it was not made consistently. The expression is used of the country east of the Jordan, Num 22:1 ; 32:32 ; 34:15 ; 35:14 ; Deut 1:1, 5 ; 3:8 ; 4:41, 46, 47, 49. (In Gen 50:10 f. the topography is uncertain.) On the other hand ' beyond the Jordan ' signifies the country west of the river in Deut 3:20, 25 ; 11:30 ; and, be it noticed, in Jos 12:7, whereas in Jos 12:1 it signifies the country east of it. More remarkable still in Num 32:19 the phrase occurs twice and denotes first the western side and then the eastern side. DV has translated according to the sense ; but HT reads : ' We will not acquire a possession with them across the Jordan and beyond, for our possession has fallen to us across the Jordan eastwards '. The collation of these passages leads to the conclusion that the phrase could be used by a speaker or writer on either side of the Jordan with the sense of ' on this side of the Jordan ' or ' on the other side of the Jordan ' provided the context made the meaning intended plain.

b Additions to the text, as distinct from modifications of language or alterations of names, might be short glosses or the insertion of longer passages mostly historical or legal in character. Here some examples **134b** only can be given. Many consider as **glosses** the information given Gen 12:6 and 13:7 that the Canaanite and the Perizzite were living in Canaan in Abraham's time. However, such information is almost necessary to give the reader a correct setting for the narrative and to explain why there was not room for the flocks and herds of Abraham and Lot. Moreover, the wording prescinds altogether from the future state of the country, and, according to the Hebrew idiom, implies nothing as to whether those peoples were or were not there at the time of writing. On the apparent reference in Ex 15:17 to the temple on Mount Moriah see § 170h. The note that the gomer (omer) is the tenth part of an ephah, Ex 16:36, is a gloss, as the fact was known to contemporaries and Moses could hardly have foreseen that the note would be required by later generations. The measure is not mentioned elsewhere in the Bible. The note that the Arnon was the frontier of Moab, Num 21:13, has been considered a gloss ; but it seems gratuitous to suppose that this geographical fact must have been universally known to Moses' contemporaries considering that they had only just made acquaintance with those parts. A Lapide considered Num 21:14 f. to be a later addition, a view rejected by Hummelauer. Num 27:14 may well contain a gloss written originally in the margin. Deut 2:12 speaks of Israel as already ' in the land of his possession ', but this is not a certain sign of a later hand, as in the context it is reasonably taken to refer to the settlement of the two and a half tribes east of the Jordan. The note in Deut 3:9 giving the Sidonian and Amorite names for Hermon may well be a later gloss, and also that about Og in Deut 3:11. Of the phrase ' until this present day ' in the LXX of Gen 35:4 and in Deut 34:6 St Jerome wrote ' Certe hodiernus dies illius temporis aestimandus est quo historia ipsa contexta est, sive Moysen dicere volueris auctorem Pentateuchi, sive Ezram eiusdem instauratorem operis, non recuso ', PL 23, 190. In this passage which has been misunderstood, St Jerome expresses his belief that Moses was the author of the Pent., but says that the words ' up to the present day ' may apply not to his time but to that of Esdras as the restorer of the OT Canon after the troubles of the exile.

Among **historical additions** that which has attracted **c** most attention is perhaps the account of Moses' death in Deut 34. Alphonsus Tostatus, generally called Abulensis from his episcopal see of Avila (died 1455), restricted the addition to part of the chapter. Jacobus Bonfrerius, S.J., *Pentateuchus Moysis* (1625) 1062, rightly preferred to consider the whole chapter post-Mosaic, as it is not reasonable to ascribe historical narrative to prophecy in the absence of compelling cause. Another well-known addition is the list of Edomite kings in Gen 36:31-39. The note introducing them as reigning before an Israelite king ruled over Edom (cf. § 156f) takes the list down to the time of David, who subjugated the country, 2 Kg 8:14. This addition was recognized by Bonfrerius. Num 15:32-36, the account of the punishment of the man found collecting sticks on the Sabbath, is introduced by the remark that it occurred while the children of Israel were in the wilderness. No one would be likely to think of adding this information to the story as found in its present context. It suggests therefore that the whole story is an addition. Deut 10:6-9 is another probable example. Ex 16:35 suggests knowledge of the time when the manna ceased after the death of Moses. Num 32:41 narrates events which took place in the period of the Judges, Jg 10:3 f. There is a repetition of this in Deut 3:14. In Gen details about the ages of Abraham and the other patriarchs were not part of the original story ; see § 140b-f. On the blessings of Jacob see § 159b, and on Deut 32-33 § 222a and f. For other examples see §§ 162e-f, 181k.

That there are **legislative additions** is also not doubted. **d** The Pent. was the legal code of the nation and enactments required by changed conditions were naturally

134d inserted in it. See § 162*e–f* and on the law of the king, § 217*d*. The laws concerning tithe belong to different periods, Lev 27:30–33; Num 18:21–32; Deut 12:6, 11, 17–19; 14:22–29; 26:12–15. It may be doubted whether Hoberg, 66 f., is right in adducing Jos 24:26 as proof of such an insertion : Josue ' wrote all these things in the volume of the law of the Lord '. Hummelauer thought he discovered Josue's insertion in Deut 26:16–27:26, but he has found no adherents. The meaning probably is that Josue added his writing at the end of Deut. The reference seems to be to the contents of the Book of Josue as a whole ; so Cornely, II i 192. Nothing in the Pent. represents this writing of Josue, yet written as part of the law it seems extremely unlikely that it should have perished. Moreover, Jos is the natural and almost inevitable complement of the Pent. as it records the attainment of the promise made in the writings of Moses.

e Hoberg, 67, appeals also to 1 Kg 10:25, ' Samuel told the people the law of the kingdom and wrote it in a book, and laid it up before the Lord '. Hoberg himself thinks this law is that of Deut 17:14–20. But if Deut had been meant, it would have been said that Samuel wrote it in the book of the law, and not merely in a book. And the passage in Deut seems to reflect the abuses of Solomon's time.

f It is strange that both Hoberg, 68, and Goettsberger, 57, should lay down as a principle that those laws which suppose a settled population are post-Mosaic, *e.g.* Ex 23:10 ' Six years shalt thou sow thy ground '. When the Israelites left Egypt, it was confidently expected that they would soon take up their abode in the promised land, and all the Sinaitic legislation was enacted without any reason to doubt the speedy fulfilment of this expectation. It was only when Moses was on the point of leading the people into Canaan but met with murmuring and resistance due to their pusillanimity and lack of trust in God that that generation was condemned never to enter the holy land but to die in the wilderness. After forty years their children would see the fulfilment of the promise intended for them, Num 14:28–34. The Deuteronomic legislation also was given when the beginning of settled life was in sight just before the crossing of the Jordan.

g Lev 16:29–34 is perhaps post-Mosaic. This passage gives the law for the perpetual observance of the day of atonement. Hoberg, 48 f., considers it to be probably a later addition based on Lev 23:26–32. A case may be made for the post-Mosaic character of Lev 25:32–34. These laws about the right of redemption of houses in the cities of the Levites and about their fields presuppose Num 35, which contains the regulations about the granting of cities and fields to the Levites. The Levitical legislation is Sinaitic, that of Num 35 Moabitic, and belong therefore respectively to the beginning and the end of the forty years of life in the wilderness. Lev 25:32–34 therefore appears to be a later addition.

135a **Sources**—From the point of view of Moses' knowledge a distinction occurs at Ex 2:10. From this verse everything narrated fell within his own lifetime and within his own knowledge except for the historical additions, § 134*c*. The events narrated in the opening part of Ex were recent history when Moses came to years of discretion and will have been learnt by him partly from Pharaoh's daughter and partly from members of his own race. On the other hand the story of Gen refers to times long previous to his own and could have been learnt only from ' sources ' whether oral or written ; see § 137*g–i*. When writing is unknown or little used, the power of the human memory is such as to seem to us, the word is not too strong, prodigious. One has only to recall the oral tradition of the Veda and of the Homeric poems. There are references to such oral transmission in Ex 13:14. Moreover, not only is Gen comparatively a short composition, but its contents are for the most part vividly recounted stories which easily impress themselves even on indifferent memories. From constant repetition these stories would readily

acquire a comparatively fixed form, which would be **135a** handed on in the tents of Abraham, Isaac and Jacob from generation to generation. That the work of different minds is incorporated is clear from the difference not only of style but of outlook apparent in Gen, chh 1 and 2. The question is whether it is possible to dissect the Pent. into parts attributable to definite sources.

The sources together with the dates assigned to them, **b** which have won widest acceptance, have been those of **the Wellhausen School.** For a sketch of its history and of the variety of opinions maintained one of the books of introduction to the OT may be consulted or Coppens, 3–40, where a fairly exhaustive account will be found with ample bibliography. In particular may be mentioned here J. Wellhausen, *Die Composition des Hexateuchs* (1899³) and *The Composition of the Hexateuch* (1902) by J. Estlin Carpenter and G. Harford. In general the Pent. is traced to four sources designated respectively J, E, D and P. The origin of these designations being German, J stands for the Yahwist, E for the Elohist, D for Deut and Deuteronomical elements, and P for the Priestly Code. The first two names are derived from the view that the Yahwist writer thought the name of Yahweh to have been known from the beginning and made use of it accordingly, whereas the Elohist writer thought that the name was first made known to Moses, Ex 6:2, and therefore made no use of it in the previous narrative. The former is considered to have written in the kingdom of Judah about 850 B.C. and the latter in the Northern Kingdom about 750 B.C. These two were combined into a single narrative JE by about 650. Deut was written not so long after and hidden in the temple where it was discovered in the 18th year of Josias and being accepted as Mosaic became the starting-point of Josias' religious reformation. The incorporation of D with JE was accomplished by about the middle of the 6th cent. In the meantime the various elements of P came into existence in Babylonia and were finally worked into a unity with JED sometime before 450. This scheme involves much more than a denial of Mosaic authorship. It is designed to fit in with current evolutionary ideas according to which Israelite religion from animism and polytheism passed to monolatry and so finally in the age of the prophets to true monotheism. It supposes that the code of Deut was unknown until late in the 7th cent. and the priestly legislation till later still. It supposes further that the religious history was largely written without regard to historical fact in order to give a supposititious basis for the late priestly system. The Tabernacle, for instance, was an invention designed to throw back the origins of the temple worship into the days of Moses and so to win for it the authority of his name.

For the history of the period preceding his own time **c** Moses must, as already said, have made use of sources, and there is no reason to deny the possibility of his combining matter from different sources into one narrative. The question is whether there actually were two sources, **J and E,** which could be justly distinguished by the use of the divine names. In a number of passages where according to the criteria one or other source should be recognized actually the HT has the name that does not suit the theory. Such occurrences are explained as due to interpolations from the other source, or it is held that the two sources did not restrict themselves to Yahweh or Elohim respectively but only show a preference for the one name or the other. This latter suggestion, of course, renders the use of the divine names an uncertain basis for the distinction of the sources. Besides, the disagreement of the HT, the LXX and Sam. at times renders the correct reading uncertain. And as we have definite evidence that the divine names have been deliberately altered (see § 133*b–c*) there is considerable uncertainty what exactly was the use made of them in the original text. In the later parts of the Pent. also some Catholic writers have thought they detected the presence of the docu-

135c ments J and E. In this view the original Mosaic account had a double line of transmission, and in an editorial revision elements from both were incorporated in the Pent. as we know it. This distinction into sources leads at times to grave psychological difficulties. For example, the redactor of Num 22 is supposed to have preserved the same statement from both sources in v 3, ' And Moab was sore afraid of the people, because they were many ; and Moab was distressed because of the children of Israel ' (RV). Here the first half is said to be from E and the second from J. On the other hand when the whole story is split up into its two components, it is found that the redactor has omitted essential elements. He has preserved the unimportant and omitted the important. It is psychologically much more probable that the original writer indulged in repetition of a kind which the synonymous parallelism of the psalms shows to have been congenial to Hebrew writers. If it is contended that the original author could not have been guilty of tautological writing, then the question arises why should an editor have inserted what he could easily have omitted if it did not suit the genius of his language ? Another psychological diffi-culty arises over the supposed contradictions between the two sources. Balaam is said to have travelled according to E with the princes of Moab, 22:21, but according to J with two servants only, 22:22. Is it more likely that an editor should have inserted such contradictory facts in two consecutive verses or that the original writer with his mind concentrated on the religious side of the story should have left obscure to the reader what was plain to himself? Balaam will have desired to start the journey without the knowledge of his fellow-citizens and gone out with two servants to join the caravan somewhere outside the town. In some such way he will at first have been alone with the two servants ;. *cf.* Bi 18 (1937) 439 ff. This of course is only an illustration of the questions that arise when the matter is examined in detail. The small importance of such ' discrepancies ' may be shown from Jn 11:19 ' Many of the Jews were come to Martha and Mary ' and 11:45 ' Many of the Jews who were come to Mary '. (DV with Vg has here ' and Martha ', but these words are in neither the Gk nor Latin codices.) See *P. Volz u. W. Rudolph, *Der Elohist als Erzähler ein Irrweg der Pentateuchkritik*, Giessen, 1933.

d According to the Wellhausen reconstruction of history **Deuteronomy** was written in the 7th cent. and found in the temple, 4 Kg chh 22, 23. It purports to be Mosaic and was in fact accepted as such. That the book discovered was Deut has been held by many in the Church including St Jerome, PL 23, 217, and St John Chrystostom, PG 57, 181. Others, as Hoberg, 8 f., rightly hold that the book found was the Pent. ; *cf.* Bea, 98, Goettsberger, 86. However, for our present purpose the question may be discussed as if it were Deut alone. The first thought that strikes the enquirer is how could a book recently written have been taken for a long-lost document ? It is not easy to counterfeit antiquity and the very freshness of the roll and its writing would have aroused suspicion, for it is not easy to believe that the supposed fabricators of the document were so clever as in that age and that society to have given the script and the writing-material the appearance of antiquity, nor is it easy to believe that king Josias and his courtiers were so unsophisticated as to have been unable to distinguish new from old. It is more-over hard to believe that men should have accepted as of Mosaic authorship and of divine authority a series of new and burdensome laws if there was no tradition that Moses was the author of such a code—and the theory cannot admit such a tradition without destroy-ing itself. What was read, however, in the newly-found document did inspire salutary fear in king Josias and his counsellors who proceeded without delay to act upon the precepts they read. It is evident that they knew of the law of Moses though they had never seen it. The words of the high-priest Helcias show that the law he had found was known by repute though it had

been lost : ' I have found the book of the law in the **135d** house of the Lord ', 4 Kg 22:8. There is no parallel between a pseudepigraphical work such as Eccl is held to be and Deut. In the former, words of wisdom are put in the mouth of the wise king ; in the latter are numerous laws the binding force of which would not have been acknowledged except for the belief that they derived from Moses. Moreover Deut, if composed in the 7th cent., shows a remarkably consistent effort to reproduce the atmosphere and outlook of Mosaic times. The exhortation, 7:17-19, not to fear the inhabitants of the land was meaningless in the days of Josias. And so was the repeated injunction utterly to destroy them, 7:2 ; 20:13, 17. Certainly the supposed authors ' are credited with quite a fabulous refinement in their work ', Möller, 34, when they are imagined to have warned the Israelites that the extermination must be gradual ' lest perhaps the beasts of the earth should increase upon thee ', 7:22. The aim of the authors is said to have been the result which the reformation of Josias actually achieved, namely the centralization of worship at Jerusalem. But in the account of the reform this centralization is not stressed at all and appears only incidentally, 4 Kg chh 22 and 23. The whole emphasis is on the elimination of idolatry, which had defiled even the central sanctuary of Jeru-salem.

Evidence is not lacking that Deut is older. Ezechias **e** ' destroyed the high places and broke the statues in pieces, and . . . kept his commandments which the Lord commanded Moses ', 4 Kg 18:4, 6. And Rabshakeh, the Assyrian, who fancied this must be displeasing to Yahweh, tauntingly asked the Israelites how they could put their trust in Yahweh : ' Is it not he whose high places and altars Ezechias hath taken away, and hath commanded Judah, and Jerusalem : You shall worship before this altar in Jerusalem ? ' v 22. This is in virtue of the law of the unity of the sanctuary in Deut 12. If it is suggested that the passage is an insertion of a Deuteronomist editor, and, of course, in a case like this, an insertion means an invention, it may be replied that if Deuteronomist editors had undertaken the revision of ancient texts in the interest of their own views, they would surely have done the work more thoroughly by way of both excision and of addition.

Further it is difficult to believe that men of the high moral and religious standard betrayed by Deut were capable of the grave deception involved in passing off regulations of their own making as possessing the authority of Moses, and worse still, of securing their acceptance on the score of a feigned divine authority and sanction. Whoever wrote Deut, he or they possessed religious God-fearing dispositions and could not have been guilty of so heinous a crime against the reverence due to the Creator. For further evidence see *e.g.* Möller 44 ff., Bea 110 f.

The **Priestly Code** or P is said to have been of exilic and **f** post-exilic origin, and to have been either the law-book read by Esdras, Neh 8, or part of that book. Its principal parts are Ex 25-31:18*a* ; 35-40 ; Lev ; Num 1-10:28 ; 15 ; 17-19 ; 25:6-31 ; 33-36. The same difficulty meets us here. New and grave obligations are supposed to have been accepted as of Mosaic origin without the existence of a tradition attesting such origin. Yet the new code is said to have marked ' a reformation, one might almost say a revolution, in religious worship ', HDB ii 370*b*. On the other hand we are told that ' it is dealing with a dead past—a mere summary composed out of old written records ', *ibid.* It is certainly strange that a document composed to further a reformation or rather revolution in the life of the post-exilic community should be written in a style said to be marked by its ' stiffness, artificiality and con-ciseness of treatment '. It is also strange that given its alleged purpose, it should devote so much space to such antiquarian information as is found in Ex 25-31 and 35-40 concerning the Ark, the Tabernacle and its furniture. The Ark was lost at the time of the Baby-

135f Ionian exile ; and the Tabernacle is not admitted ever to have existed : ' The attitude . . . to the priestly legislation . . . and in particular to those sections of it which deal with the sanctuary and its worship, is patent on every page of this Dictionary, and is opposed to the historicity of P's tabernacle ', HDB iv 666*b*. This is not to attribute a lofty standard of honour to those circles anxious to produce a reformation in the service of God. And it is strange that this reforming legislation should make laws to centre round the Ark and the Tabernacle, as those of the Day of Atonement, Lev 16:2, 33, laws which accordingly could not be and never could have been observed. The same applies to the law, Lev 17:1-6, concerning the offering at the door of the Tabernacle of every ox, sheep or goat killed by any Israelite.

g ' All the people wept when they heard the words of the law ', Neh 8:9. They did not weep at the hearing of something new, for no man's conscience reproaches him with not observing obligations of which he has never heard ; nor did they weep for having violated precepts, the observance of which was impossible under changed conditions. They wept because it was brought home to them on hearing the law that they had not done what they well knew they could and should have done. The argument from the non-observance of a law to its non-existence is invalid. And the argument from silence may be quite misleading. There is no explicit reference to the celebration of the Day of Atonement anywhere in the OT ; but see Heb 9:7, 25, Ac 27:9. If P was written to effect the reformation it achieved, how is it that its prescriptions differ from post-exilic practice ? According to P, Ex 30:13-16, half a shekel was to be given for the use of the Tabernacle ; after the exile, presumably on account of the poverty of the people, the sum was fixed at the third of a shekel, Neh 10:32. After the exile the Levites began their service from the age of 20 years, Esd 3:8 ; how is it that in P it begins at 30, Num 4:3, and at 25, Num 8:24 ?

h The tenets of the Wellhausen school no longer hold the field as they once did. They have been attacked from many quarters and in many points, and various divergent views have been propounded to replace them. No one, however, of these new systems has achieved the popularity formerly enjoyed by the system it seeks to replace. *H. H. Rowley has sketched the situation in PEQ (1946) 52 f. : ' In recent years (the once normal critical views of the compilation of the Pent.) have been much attacked from many sides, and especially from two directly opposed sides. The one side has aimed to carry the sources back to an earlier date, while the other has aimed to carry them down to a later date. Again some scholars have questioned the existence of the once generally acknowledged sources, while others have attempted to carry the analysis further, and isolate still further sources. Never has there been so much fluidity in Pentateuchal criticism. Yet while many scholars would agree that the days of the Graf-Kuenen-Wellhausen theory are numbered, agreement ends as soon as the question what is to succeed is asked '.

*W. F. Albright : ' It is sheer hypercriticism to deny the substantial Mosaic character of the Mosaic tradition ', *The Archaeology of Palestine* (1949) 224. See also §§ 43-6. This article is supplemented by the following account of the opinions of Catholic writers.

SOME RECENT CATHOLIC VIEWPOINTS ON THE PENTATEUCHAL QUESTION

i The decrees of the Biblical Commission of June 27 1906 directed the adherence of Catholic scholars to the substantial (*quoad substantiam*) Mosaic authorship of the Pentateuch. It was, therefore, within this frame-

work that they approached the *literary* problems of the **135i** Pentateuch. J. Goettsberger in his *Einleitung in das Alte Testament*, 1928, while rejecting the Wellhausen hypothesis in its essence, distinguishes between the original Pentateuch and its present form, and admits the valuable contributions of the critical school. P. Heinisch in his commentary on Genesis, 1930, defends the theory of ' supplements ' ; *i.e.* the principal document is Mosaic, though it has been increased by inspired sizable additions (doublets) and undergone many alterations of a minor sort. We have already noted the solution suggested by Fr. Vaccari, S.J. (*cf.* § 46*b*). In a study of the same question Père Lagrange admits the existence of the documents E J P in Genesis. He believes that Moses either wrote E or put together its already existing material. He makes J also the work of Moses who inspired its composition, tracing out its broad lines to amanuenses and ultimately approving it. He considers P a later précis of the basic lines of the tradition.

A greater modification in the Catholic attitude is to **j** be noted in the recent work of J. Coppens, *The Old Testament and the Critics*, 1942. He tends to a broader interpretation of the Biblical Commission's *quoad substantiam* than it has hitherto received. Following a suggestion of Père Lagrange in his article in RB 47 (1938) 48 he feels that the words can be taken in a qualitative rather than quantitative sense. Such a view would see the Pentateuch as the outcome of a lengthy literary process initiated by Moses and continued in his spirit.

The most recent development in this question is the **k** letter of the Biblical Commission to Cardinal Suhard of Jan. 16, 1948 ; *cf.* AAS 40 (1948) 1, 2, pp 45-8. It declares that balanced criticism and the results of allied sciences will establish beyond doubt ' the large part and profound influence of Moses as author and legislator '—words that give an indication of how ' Mosaic authenticity ' may now be understood. The letter also points to the fact that no one today questions the existence of sources in the Pentateuch, the fact of progressive accretion to the Mosaic laws caused by the social and religious conditions of later times— a development which appears also in the historical narratives.

It is not then difficult to understand that some Catholic scholars believe that three distinct literary strands appear in Genesis, *i.e.* J E P, that seem to have the character of continuous narratives, although some hesitancy is felt that this can be fully verified in the case of E and, even more so, of P.

The problem of dating these sources is a vexing one, **l** but, in general, they would explain their origin and composition more or less in the following fashion. The narratives of Genesis existed, at least in oral form, long before the activity of Moses. They were handed on by rhapsodists in oral recitation which was the normal method of transmission. Albright says he is ' increasingly convinced that the narrative portions of the Pentateuch swarm with poetic phraseology and are strewn with reminiscences of the original verse form in which they were transmitted for centuries before being written down in prose ', JBL 62(1943) 359. Recited in the evenings before the tent-fires, any notable deviation in the well-known narrative would result in a popular outcry. ' As a rule, poetic sagas are preferable as historical sources to prose traditions concerning the same events, unless the latter are quite recent ' (*W. Albright, FSAC, 37), for both their external and internal forms are fixed.

Today competent historical and literary scholarship **m** places something more than half a millennium between the written record and the beginnings of that record ; it supports the essential reliability of oral transmission for the period preceding the written documents. Naturally however there would be some variations. According to some recent Catholic scholars (*cf.* DBV(S) II, 207, *Critique Biblique*) the patriarchal narratives give historical facts, but adorned here and there with additions serv-

35m ing a doctrinal purpose, written under Inspiration and possessing the truth of the didactic form of writing. In other words, Israelitic faith not only presupposed history but interpreted it, gave it its meaning and flavour, fixed its broad lines, thus favouring an extension to the point of mingling the historical with other genres (*ib.* p 8). Then, too, one should take into account the poetic modifications that would naturally occur during the long centuries of oral transmission in popular circles. For these reasons the same scholars speak of the literary genre of Genesis as a 'mixed genre', largely historical but partly didactic and poetic, rather than historical in our strict sense of the word. This, however, does not deny the fact that the patriarchal narratives have the character of historical records.

Such then would be the nature of the sources that Moses used for his written account of primeval history and the deeds of the patriarchs. His narrative, which may be dated about 1250 B.C., is the common source of J and E in Genesis. Of the other historical sections, of which Moses was an eyewitness (Ex, Num), he was the responsible author.

n But for the ordinary Hebrew the written document was of secondary importance ; oral recitation remained the norm of transmission. The fall of Shilo, however, Israel's central sanctuary, and, even more so, the division of the kingdom after the death of Solomon, undoubtedly affected the historical rhapsodists. Cut off to a large extent from one another, they gradually introduced into the Mosaic text adaptations which subtly reflected the partisan preferences of their audiences. Geographical influences also played a part. The narrative underwent certain modifications in Judah and Ephraim. The narrators of Ephraim speak not of God (Yahweh), but of the Divinity (Elohim), and retain or stress those details which glorify the house of Joseph and the northern sanctuaries, while the Judaean school retains the name of Yahweh and an interest in the sacred places of the Southern Kingdom. The suppression of unfavourable details is understandable. The rhapsodists, while preserving the sense, also substituted different literary conventions recognized as such and not touching the substance of the narrative.

o In the ninth and eighth centuries these diverging versions were given a definite written form, which superseded oral transmission as the authentic norm. In this fashion recent Catholic scholarship would explain the origin of J and E. But behind these two documents stands the one Mosaic narrative and unity of source, not multiplicity ; hence we have a twofold testimony to the truth of the narrative. They were joined together, in the fashion described in § 46*b*, after the collapse of the Northern Kingdom with the capture of Samaria by the Assyrians in 722 B.C., perhaps during the reign of Josias (638–609), whose efforts were directed towards both political and religious unity (*cf.* 4 Kg 23). After the finding of Deuteronomy (621 B.C.) there seems to have been a deuteronomistic revision of the sacred books then existing, which left Gen–Num almost intact, but joined Deuteronomy first with Jos– 4 Kg, then with the other books of the Pentateuch to form an account of sacred history from the creation of the world to the collapse of the kingdoms of Israel and Judah (Simon–Prado, 315).

p The question of Deuteronomy is a more delicate one. H. Junker rightly observes (*Das Buch Deuteronomium*, 1933, p 14) : ' We must agree with Goettsberger who believes that in view of the present state of investigation, one cannot ask a Catholic exegete to propose a definite theory of the origin and evolution of Deuteronomy. Such a theory would only have provisional value. He would do much better were he to point out the general lines that the evolution of the book seems to have followed. The laws given by Moses were the basis on which Israel's religious and social life developed. Moreover, in the OT religion, there existed from the beginning prophecy, which directed this development. No wonder then if there were an evolution of the law under prophetic authority '.

That much of the material in Deuteronomy is old, **135q** there can be no question (*cf.* W. Albright, FSAC, 241 ff. ; G. von Rad, *Deuteronomische Studien,* 1948 ; P. J. Hempel, *Die Schichten des Deut.*, 1914, 259 ff.). That there has been an introduction of new laws and a modification and abrogation of others is equally clear. Some Catholics speak of a long and complex evolution of Deuteronomy before it reached its final form. As an example we expound briefly the origin of Deuteronomy according to H. Cazelles in his book, *Le Deutéronome*, 1950, p 13 f. Moses himself wrote down a certain number of concrete applications of the Decalogue. This work was continued after his death, as he had foreseen, under the authority of the Levites, the guardians of his spirit and his law. In the Yahwistic sanctuaries practical solutions of difficult cases were given (*cf.* Deut 33:10). Thus the Mosaic law was continually applied to new economic and social conditions, and in certain cases there grew up the practice of setting down in writing the new solutions (*cf.* Os 8:12). After the fall of the Northern Kingdom in 722 B.C., its Levites fled to Jerusalem, 2 Par 11:14, bringing with them certain collections of this law (a number of laws found in the present Deuteronomy could have had their origin only in the Northern Kingdom). These legislative texts were, like the fifth group of Proverbs (chh 25–29), gathered and compiled in the time of Ezechias (*c* 700 B.C.), and a sort of theological commentary to them was placed in the mouth of Moses, the writer of the basic laws and the inspirer of all. In this way the first edition of the book came into being. This was the law found by Helcias during the repair of the temple in 621 B.C. Eventually there came the end of Jerusalem and the exile. The second edition of Deuteronomy was published in the days of Ezechiel. It possessed the same spirit as the first, but placed more emphasis on the exile, deliverance, and sapiential literature ; *cf.* ch 4. This edition added chh 1–4 which emphasize the conquest of Canaan, as symbol of the reconquest for which the exiles hoped. At the same time additions were made to the maledictions of 29, ch 31 was amplified, and 10:6-9 introduced into the text. Such is the solution proposed by Fr. Cazelles, *salvo meliori judicio.*

When we come to P (chiefly Leviticus) the problem **l** is even more complex. In view of certain critical arguments, some Catholic exegetes hold to a recent dating for its final composition ; nevertheless they consider it Mosaic either because it is only an application to new conditions of Mosaic principles or because its basic elements are Mosaic. They observe that laws in general can receive authoritative complements and modifications ; so too, they urge, for the Mosaic law under inspired prophetical or sacerdotal authority. In fact, no part of the Pentateuch was more liable to modification in the course of centuries than the ritual. It will, therefore, be of interest to see the attempt made by J. Nikel in *Die Pentateuchfrage*, 1921, pp 31–7, to reconcile the lawful demands of criticism with the traditional doctrine of Mosaic authorship of Leviticus.

The ' Code of Holiness ', Lev 17–26, he affirms, **s** comes from a time when Israel was already in peaceful possession of the promised land ; but it was a codification of an *older* law adapted to new circumstances. Because of certain points of contact it possesses with Ezechiel, it is possible that its final form was fixed during his lifetime or shortly after (p 48). In the matter of legislation on the tithes, a similar progressive adaptation occurred (p 41). If, however, some elements of the law are only mediately and indirectly Mosaic, they are, nevertheless, the applications to new conditions of the principles promulgated by Moses, and so the legislative evolution always remains organic (p 82). In his *Grundriss der Einleitung in das Alte Testament*, 1924, Nikel says of the sacerdotal law, Lev, in general that it presents itself ' as the condensation of the cultural life of Israel from Moses till the end of the exile ; this legislation, several times codified and revised according to need, was finally collected by the priesthood ' (p 55).

135s P. Heinisch, also, in his commentary on Leviticus, 1937, admits an evolution whose various steps he attempts to trace.

t In all this matter, the Catholic scholar must keep in mind the directives of the Encyclical *Humani Generis*. At the same time, there should be no biased censure of the exegete who, while conforming in all docility to the guidance of the ' magisterium ecclesiasticum ', abandons a purely defensive attitude to look squarely at the difficulties raised by the theory of Wellhausen. The progress of critical studies has clearly shown that certain conclusions of the new criticism, removed from all compromise with rationalistic evolution, can, without danger and even with profit, be incorporated into Catholic science. On the other hand, a good number of independent critics no longer assign a recent date for the composition of the whole *corpus* of legislation in the Pentateuch ; they admit the reality of the Sinaitic tradition and recognize in the law-code of the Pentateuch a Mosaic, or even pre-Mosaic, nucleus. On the one hand, one must admit that, without Moses, the law of Israel is inexplicable ; on the other, that no legislator would give a law that would remain unchangeable through the centuries ; *cf.* RB 45 (1936) 363-4.

GENESIS

By E. F. SUTCLIFFE, S.J.

136a Bibliography—T. J. Lamy, *Comm. in Librum Geneseos*, 2 vol. (Mechliniae, 1883-4) ; *A. Dillmann, *Die Genesis* (Leipzig, 1892⁶) ; F. de Hummelauer, *Comm. in Genesim* (CSS ; Parisiis, 1895) ; G. Hoberg, *Die Genesis* (Freiburg im Breisgau, 1908²) ; *J. Skinner, *Genesis* (ICC ; Edinburgh, 1912²) ; M. Hetzenauer, O.C., *Comm. in Librum Genesis* (Graecii et Viennae, 1910) ; P. Heinisch, *Das Buch Genesis* (BB ; Bonn, 1930) ; *S. R. Driver, *The Book of Genesis* (WC ; London, 1913⁹) ; *E. König, *Die Genesis* (Gütersloh, 1919) ; J. Chaine, *Le Livre de la Genèse* (Paris, 1948) ; H. Junker, *Genesis* (Echter Bibel ; Würzburg, 1949).

b P. F. Ceuppens, O.P., *Quaestiones selectae ex Historia Primaeva* (Torino-Roma, 1948²) ; *id.*, *Genèse* (no place, 1945) ; P. Heinisch, *Probleme der biblischen Urgeschichte* (Luzern, 1947) ; H. J. T. Johnson, *The Bible and the Early History of Mankind* (London, 1947²) ; C. Lattey, S.J., *Back to the Bible* (London, 1944) ; *W. F. Albright, *The Archaeology of Palestine and the Bible* (New York, 1932) ; R. T. O'Callaghan, S.J., *Aram Naharaim : a Contribution to the History of Upper Mesopotamia in the Second Millennium B.C.* (Rome, 1948) ; *E. A. Speiser, ' Ethnic Movements in the Near East in the second Millennium B.C.', AASOR 13 (1933) 13-54 ; R. de Vaux, O.P., ' Les patriarches hébreux et les découvertes modernes ', RB 53 (1946) 321-48 ; 55 (1948) 321-47; 56 (1949) 5-36 ; *H. H. Rowley, *Recent Discovery and the Patriarchal Age*, reprint from JRB 32 (1949).

c Name—Our English name is taken over from Vg, which itself owed it to LXX, and its meaning is accordingly that of Γένεσις ' becoming, beginning, coming into being '. The word was probably taken from 2:4, perhaps with an eye on 5:1. It is no objection to this origin of the title that it refers only to the beginning of the book. The book of Numbers is similarly named. The Hebrew title, indicated in Vg, is Bereshith, from the opening phrase of the book.

d Contents and Purpose—The book traces the descent of the ancestors of the people of Israel from the beginning of the world down to the twelve sons of Jacob who were the eponyms of the twelve tribes, and to their immediate descendants, ch 46. The story of these ancestors is carried down to the descent of Jacob and his family into Egypt, ch 46, and ends with the death of Joseph, 50:25.

e The main theme of the book is to narrate how the family of Jacob came to be the progenitors of the one race which God chose out of all the nations of the earth to be his own. Cain, the firstborn of Adam, was reprobated by God, 4:11, and the blessing of God then rested on Seth and his descendants, 5:1 ff. But they too corrupted their ways and were visited by the punishment of the Flood. Noe, the just man of his generation, was saved, but his descendants did not remain free from guilt, and the Semites were singled out by God for his especial favour, 9:26. But even among the Semites many fell away from God, 11:1–9, who finally chose Abraham and his line as the recipients of his favours, 12:1-3. With Abraham God entered into a covenant, 17:4, 7, which he renewed with Isaac, 26:2-5, and with Jacob, 28:13-15. The way is thus prepared for the central fact from which the

Old Testament takes its name, the covenant solemnly **136e** entered into with the people of Israel, Ex 24.

The Scheme of Genesis—It is important to notice the **f** process of elimination which accompanies the tracing of the descent of Jacob from Adam. Other descendants of the main figures in the line of descent are mentioned as the development of the story requires and are then cut out of the narrative. This process of elimination is at the same time a gradual narrowing of the theme. Thus the Cainites are eliminated, 4:24, and the story proceeds with the Sethites only. After the Flood the descendants of Noe are divided into Japhethites, Chamites and Semites. The two former are cut out of the story at 10:20 and it proceeds with the Semites alone. In 11:27 there is a sharp limitation to the family of Abraham. This patriarch begets Ishmael by Agar and various sons by Cetura (Keturah). Through these the Israelites, descendants of his son Isaac by Sara, are connected with the Ishmaelites, the Madianites, and other Arabian tribes, as through Abraham's nephew Lot they are blood relations of the Ammonites and Moabites. When these connections have been established, the story proceeds with Isaac, the inheritor of the promises. He in his turn is the father of two peoples, the Edomites through Esau and the Israelites through Jacob. The story proceeds exclusively with Jacob and his twelve sons.

All the many peoples mentioned are thus gradually **g** eliminated. None of them did God choose as his peculiar possession though many of them were more ancient, more powerful and more cultured than Israel. The wonder of God's favour and choice is thus strongly emphasized, but, as is the writer's way, such considerations are left to the reflexion of the reader.

This gradual narrowing of the theme and simul- **h** taneous elimination of elements foreign to it give important indications of whom the sacred writer is speaking at different stages of his narrative. These indications are the more valuable as the Hebrew habit of using universal expressions at times hyperbolically and at times with reference only to the matter in hand is apt to mislead modern western readers into thinking that the whole world and all mankind are the subject of discourse. Thus universal expressions are used in the narrative of the Flood, but the sacred writer having said all he had to say of the Cainites in ch 4 and then dismissing them from his story proceeds only with the Sethites, of whom these universal expressions are employed. So too in the case of the tower of Babel, 11:1–9, the Japhethites and Chamites having been eliminated from the story the narrative is concerned only with the Semites, and not with all of them ; *cf.* § 149*l*.

Another important feature in the scheme of the book is the interlocking of its various parts. This will be best explained together with the division of the book. **Division of the Book and Interlocking of its Parts**— **i** Considered from the point of view of the periods concerned the book falls into two parts. The first ends at 11:26 and the other occupies the rest of the book. The first deals with prehistory and protohistory whereas the second contains the narrative concerning the patriarchs who lived in historical times. Both parts, however, have fundamentally the same theme, which is that of the origins of the Chosen

136i People and the divine favours received by their ancestors. The story ends with the death of Joseph while his kinsfolk were still regarded with favour by the Egyptian court.

j The text itself gives no prominence to this division, the formula used to introduce 11:27 being only one of ten which stand at the head of as many sections of unequal length and importance. The characteristic word in these headings is *tôlᵉdôṯ* (always in the construct state). This word, derived from *yālaḏ* ' to give birth to ', means ' generations ' and so by passage from the cause to the effect ' the persons generated ' and finally the ' history ' of these persons. It consequently tends to introduce the story of the persons generated rather than that of their progenitor. It occurs in the following places : (1) 2:4*a*, the history of heaven and earth, *i.e.* of the inhabitants of the newly created world ; (2) 5:1, the book of the generations of Adam, his genealogical tree through Seth ; (3) 6:9, the story of Noe ; (4) 10:1, the generations of the sons of Noe ; (5) 11:10, the genealogy of Sem's descendants ; (6) 11:27, the generations of Thare (practically the history of Abraham) ; (7) 25:12, the generations of Ishmael ; (8) 25:19, the heading ' the generations of Isaac ' introduces the story of his son Jacob rather than of Isaac himself ; (9) 36:1, the generations of Esau ; (10) 37:2, here the chief figure in the generations of Jacob is his son Joseph.

k In the first instance, 2:4*a*, the word is used not metaphorically of the production of the world but in the developed sense of ' history '. That this is the meaning is shown by the analogy of the other occurrences in all of which the word is used in a title or introduction. This appears decisive against the view that it is here a subscription to the previous section referring to the creation of the universe.

l These ten sections, which are preceded by the account of God's creative work, 1:1–2:3, are not merely juxtaposed but are **interlocked**, the whole book being thus formed into a unity not only by its theme but by its form. Thus (1) is linked to the introduction by a brief reference to God's creation of earth and heaven, 2:4*b*. (2) is interlocked with both the introduction and (1) by the repetition that God made mankind in his image and made them male and female, 5:1 f. (3) resumes from the foregoing that Noe begot Sem, Cham and Japheth, 6:10. (4) links up with the previous narrative by a mention of the Flood, and that Sem, Cham and Japheth were Noe's sons, 10:1. The link in (5) is again the mention of the Flood, 11:10. (6) is interlocked by the repetition from the previous verse that Thare begot Abram, Nachor and Aran, 11:27. (7) repeats the detail of Ishmael's parentage, 25:12. (8) tells the reader what is now well known to him that Isaac was the son of Abraham and the husband of Rebecca, 25:19 f. (9) starts with a renewed account of Esau's marriages, 36:2 f., where, however, see note. Only in (10) is such repetitive interlocking entirely missing.

137a Doctrine—Our book manifests a **lofty conception of God**. He is one and there is no other beside him. This fundamental truth is taught not by abstract propositions but in more telling fashion. He it was who created the beings elevated by pagan nations to divine rank. As the Creator of all he is the supreme Lord and Master of the world. He is omnipotent : ' Is there anything hard to God ? ', 18:14. His mere word suffices to effect his will. ' He spoke and they were made ', Ps 148:5. These fundamental lessons are taught in ch 1, where the order and details, as of the days, serve only as a framework for the religious teaching ; see § 142*a*–*b*. As of the material universe, so also he is Creator and Lord of man. This truth is twice expressed, 1:27 and again, in anthropomorphic **b** language, in 2:7. In all this teaching the religious truth must be sharply distinguished from the setting in which it is conveyed. The Bible is not a handbook of physical science, which it was not God's purpose to teach as of itself of no avail for eternal salvation.

So Leo XIII in *Providentissimus Deus*, Dz 1947. As the **137** world owes its origin to God and the laws of nature are of his ordaining, the working out of these laws is in the Bible spoken of as God's act, as in 2:5. So in the case of the formation of man's body, 2:7, it cannot be concluded from the wording that it was fashioned immediately by God. The possibility of its having been gradually evolved by God's own laws from lower forms is not excluded by the teaching of Scripture ; see further § 143*k*.

God's power is not limited to any one region of the **c** earth as the pagans conceived the dominion of their deities to be confined to the territory of their own peoples. God's power extends to all peoples and countries, Mesopotamia, 12:1 ; 31:13, Egypt, 12:17 ; 50:20, the Pentapolis, chh 18–19, Gerar, 20:3. He guides events and draws good out of evil, a truth finely expressed in 50:20. But though the omnipotent Creator of man is able, if he wished, to impose absolute submission to his will as in the case of the lower creatures, he would not have of the human race a forced service. Man's obedience to God's law must be free. He is given a law, but he is left free to obey or to transgress, 2:17 and see on 4:7. But man is not left only to a sense of duty and of gratitude to God to help him to obey. Obedience is rewarded by happiness ; punishment is threatened for sin.

Some of these points of doctrine are more fully developed in the commentary on chh 1–3, where also others will be more conveniently dealt with. For a discussion of **the religion of the patriarchs** the reader is referred to §§ 105–6.

In the time of Moses neither revelation nor religious **d** philosophy had yet brought man to the highly refined and difficult **concept of spiritual substance**, and consequently there was only a vague idea of the nature of God, of angels, and of the human soul. The way to a higher conception was prepared by the prohibition to make any image of God in the likeness of anything whatsoever known to man, Ex 20:4 ; and the sublime concept of God's creative power producing its effects by his mere word cannot have rested on any but a vague, though lofty, conception of his nature. The first explicit expression of the belief that whereas man is flesh, God is spirit, occurs in Is 31:3.

It was known that the body does not live by any power **e** inherent in itself. For the body to live God breathes into it the breath of life, 2:7, but there was as yet no developed notion what this imports and the same is said of the life of animals, Ps 103:29 f. It was known however, from the earliest times that **man does not cease to exist at death**. His body is laid in the tomb or may be devoured by wild beasts, 23:19 ; 44:28, but he himself goes down to Sheol, the dwelling-place of all the dead deep in the earth, 37:35. Precisely what part of man survived is nowhere stated until the advanced doctrine of Wis 3:1, ' the souls of the just are in the hand of God '. It must be remembered that, though the Israelites were a religious people, they were little given to philosophic thought even on religious topics. For an understanding of the religious background of the time it must also be borne in mind that there was not yet knowledge of the existence of evil spirits. The tempter of our first parents, later known to have been the devil, Wis 2:24, is vaguely represented as a crafty serpent, 3:1. These various points illustrate the slow development of doctrine in OT times.

The **Messianic concept** has its roots in Genesis. In **f** 3:15 final victory over the powers of evil is promised to mankind, not indeed individually but collectively. But only in the light of later predictions does it become plain that this victory is to be won through the power and under the leadership of a single person, § 145*e*. Out of all the descendants of Adam God makes a covenant with Noe, ch 9, and of his offspring Sem is privileged to receive God's favour in a special degree, 9:26. Among the Semites Abraham is singled out by God as the recipient of the remarkable promise that

37f through him and his descendants all the nations of the earth are to be blessed, 12:3, and the religious ground for this promise, 18:18 f., shows that the blessing itself will carry with it spiritual benefits. This promise, confirmed to Abraham, 22:18, was not to be shared by all his descendants, for instance the Ishmaelites, but was renewed first to Isaac, 26:4, and then to Jacob, 28:14. Among his sons Judah is chosen out for leadership and promised a sceptre which will not be taken away till one come whose it is by special right, 49:10. And it is thus implied that when he comes, he shall retain it for ever. The previous promises show that the rule symbolized by this sceptre will be a source of blessing to mankind. For Melchisedech's prefiguring of the Christian sacrifice, see on 14:18–24.

g **Sources**—That Moses required sources for the compilation of Genesis is clear from the fact that the whole period treated was anterior to his time. And these sources can have been either oral or written. The possibility of written sources being available is demonstrated by what is now known of ancients scripts and their diffusion (*cf.* § 80*i*). The document quoted in ch 5 appears to be one such source. Written sources were not necessary for the transmission of most of the material of the book. Though writing was used, books were rare. They were days of hearing, not of reading ; and the stories of the patriarchs must have been repeated countless times round the camp fires and, during the years of servitude in Egypt, will have kept the hopes of the sufferers alive. The custom of such family history lessons long survived in Israel. ' How great things he commanded our fathers, that they should make the same known to their children ; that another generation might know them—the children that should be born and should rise up and declare them to their children ', Ps 77:5 f.

h That the whole book is not from the pen of one author is clear from the differences of style to be met in it. Were these confined to the treatment of different themes, the change of style might be explained as due to the requirements of the subject-matter. But in the sections 1:1–2:3 and 2:4–25, which provide a case of this kind, the former having the grandiose theme of the creative power of God and the latter the more personal theme of man's first earthly home, the difference of style is accompanied by the more subtle difference of mental outlook. In the second section this is more intimate, more personal, more simple. But even within this latter section there is one passage, 10–14, that describing the four rivers, which the reader feels to be out of harmony with the tone and spirit of the rest of the account and to be therefore from another mind.

i As yet there is no agreement about the division of the book as a whole, and we must agree with the verdict of Heinisch, *Genesis* 65, that ' much laborious and minute research is still required before we can form a clearer and more reliable picture ' of the sources which have contributed to its compilation. Further, it must not be forgotten that our effort is to understand the book in its final form, in that namely in which it was given to the Church. It is in this final form that the book has its inspired and sacred character. This is important but sometimes lost sight of. Even if it is possible to discern a more primitive form of a narrative behind that contained in the inspired text, this is a matter of only literary and perhaps historical interest. We have no right to read into the existing text what the compiler has carefully eliminated therefrom. And again we have no right to separate what he has combined. For instance, even if it were the case, as some have thought, that behind chh 2–3 are two narratives, one of which spoke only of the tree of life and the other only of the tree of knowledge, this would in no way alter the fact that the inspired text speaks of both as growing in the Garden of Eden. See further § 45*n*.

38a **Historical Character**—The narrative ending at 11:26 is concerned with the period of prehistory or proto-history, whereas the patriarchs who are the subjects of the rest of the book lived in the second millennium B.C.

in a period now well-known to history and reaching **138a** down almost to the time of Moses. A consideration of the historical character of the book falls naturally therefore into two parts.

The chapters on **the first ancestors of the Chosen** **b** **People** from Adam to Thare, namely, 2:4–11:26, carry the story back to the origins of the human race. The remoteness of this origin has become known only in modern times. In earlier ages when there was no reason to suppose the antiquity of the human race to exceed that apparently assigned in the Bible and nothing was known of the remote stone age, it appeared possible and credible that a tradition deriving from our first parents should have survived through the two thousand years which were thought to separate them from Abraham. Such faithful transmission seemed the more probable in that early men were credited with lives extending over hundreds of years. According to MT Adam died in the year of creation 930, when Mathusala was already 56 years old, and therefore of an age to be a reliable witness to the details of stories which would have fallen many times from the lips of Adam. When Mathusala came to die in the year of the world 1656, Noe was 600 years old ; and Noe survived the birth of Abraham by 60 years and died only 15 years before Abraham's departure from Harran for Canaan. Three lives, therefore, covered the whole of this period of proto-history, and there was no difficulty in accepting the faithful transmission of the scanty records preserved in the Bible. Now, how- **c** ever, the discovery of human bones and artefacts in strata the age of which can be determined with more or less accuracy has completely altered this simple presentment of human history. We do not yet know how long mankind has inhabited this globe, but it is now certain that the period is to be reckoned not in thousands, but in tens of thousands, if not in hundreds of thousands of years. Now it passes belief that detailed stories should have survived by mere human tradition through such immensely long periods of time. God could, of course, have provided miraculously for their preservation through countless generations or he could have revealed them to Moses. But the indications are against such a supposition. Cain and Abel, Adam's two first sons, are said to have been respectively an agriculturist and a shepherd, and there is nothing to suggest that the terms are not to be understood in the sense they bore in the time of Moses in the second millennium B.C. Now the first signs of agriculture discovered in archaeological research place its beginnings long after the first appearance of man, at the earliest in the mesolithic period ; and the animal remains found with the earliest beginnings of agriculture show that the domestication of animals was of later origin than the introduction of controlled crops. Similarly the statement that Cain built a city gives no hint that the word is not to be understood as it was in the time of Moses of a collection, however small, of dwellings built of stone or dried mud and mortar. See ' Le concordisme préhistorique ou la fin du concordisme,' by D. Buzy, S.C.J., in *Mélanges E. Podechard* (Faculté de Théologie de Lyon, 1945).

It is for such reasons that the Biblical Commission **d** wrote, ' It is impossible to deny or to affirm [the] historicity [of these chapters] as a whole without unduly applying to them norms of a literary type under which they cannot be classed '. And again, ' To declare *a priori* that these narratives do not contain history in the modern sense of the word might easily be understood to mean that they do not contain history in any sense, whereas they relate in simple and figurative language, adapted to the understanding of mankind at a lower stage of development, the fundamental truths underlying the divine scheme of salvation, as well as a popular description of the origins of the human race and of the Chosen People ', § 53*l–m*, where see the whole passage. Thus we conclude that the sacred author adopted a style of writing, recognizable as such by his contemporaries, by which he clothed

138d important religious truths in the form of a concrete graphic narrative. In a rude and uncultured people such vivid presentment was probably the only means possible for impressing these truths on their minds and hearts.

e These considerations do not mean that we are yet in a position to answer all the questions which these chapters present, and they do not apply with equal force to the whole of this proto-history of Israel. Certain incidents such as the Flood belong to times much nearer to those of the historical patriarchs and the memory of them had remained alive and vivid. The subject is delicate and complex. It is not yet possible to discriminate sharply between elements which are strictly historical and others which are symbolic or necessary for the completion of the picture as a whole. The Israelites knew that their people must be descended from the first human beings and also that their election by God to be what they were, his Chosen People, was no mere accident of time, but part of God's over-ruling Providence in the government of the world from the beginning of time. This is the lesson which lies behind the genealogies. We have an analogy to such quasi-historical records in the Babylonian tablets relating to prediluvian times, though without trace of the religious significance.

139a We now turn to **the stories of Abraham, Isaac and Jacob** who lived only some centuries before Moses in the second millennium B.C. Given the relatively small amount of material and its vivid, graphic character there is no difficulty in admitting its faithful oral transmission aided by constant repetition ; *cf.* § 135*a*. St Jerome records that the young Jews of his day could repeat from memory all the generations from Adam to Zorobabel with the same accuracy and fluency as they would give their own name, *In Ep. ad Tit.* 3:9 (PL 26, 595). On the power of memory see also G. Ricciotti, *Hist. d'Israël* I (1939) 200–3. That God could make the promises and prophecies recorded there is no doubt and no reference to them can be expected in any external source. And the fact of actions being attributed to God does not necessarily imply a direct divine intervention. The Israelites spoke of the effects of the **secondary causes** created by God as being the actions of God himself. This is not incorrect, but is apt to mislead us, with our different way of speaking, into supposing a miraculous intervention where none is intended. Thus 2:5 speaks of God raining on the earth. Similarly there is no adequate reason for thinking that the Lord's opening Lia's womb, 29:31, was a miraculous intervention ; *cf.* 30:22. So, too, the Lord's scourging of Pharaoh and his house, 12:17, was probably providential but not miraculous. Considered in the light of this usage the narrative is seen to be sober and free from any multiplication of the miraculous, such as would be alien to all we know of God's Providence.

b The veracity of the story is attested by the frank simplicity with which the wrong-doing of the patriarchs and others is set down—Jacob's inhumanity and covetousness in refusing food to his exhausted twin brother except at the price of his birthright, 25:29–34 ; the fraud and lies with which he extorted his father's dying blessing, ch 27 ; Rachel's theft of her father's teraphim, 31:19 ; the craft and savagery with which the sons of Jacob avenged the dishonour done to Dina, ch 34 ; their idolatry, 35:2 ; Ruben's sin of incest, 35:22 ; the hatred and cruelty Joseph met with from his brothers, ch 37 ; the wickedness of Judah's sons, Her and Onan, and their father's fornication with Thamar, ch 38. There is nothing here of which the Israelites would be proud, and the fidelity with which it is recorded is a guarantee of the endeavour of the human author to set down a veracious narrative.

c Mention of Abraham, Isaac and Jacob and of their experience is not to be looked for in contemporary records as they played no part in secular history. Joseph was an important personage in Egypt of whom archaeological discovery might have found a mention. But the period of the Hyksos (*c* 1720–*c* 1580), under

whom he most probably held office, is obscure and **13** little is known of it. The general setting of patriarchal times in the Near East, however, is now known from the abundant information revealed by extensive excavation carried on throughout this region. The more numerous the sites explored and the ancient tablets deciphered, the more evident it has become that the background of the lives of the patriarchs as set forth in Genesis is in full accord with the conditions prevailing in the first half of the second millennium B.C. Thus E. A. Speiser writes : ' There is today no reason to doubt the authenticity of the general background of the patriarchal narratives. In point of fact, recent discoveries have greatly increased our respect for their essential accuracy ', 43. And again, ' The minor incidents are demonstrably in keeping with the times, not to say conditioned by-them ', 45. So, too, W. F. Albright speaks of ' the extraordinary accuracy of the narratives of the patriarchs, when tested by our rapidly accumulating material ', *Archaeology*, 144, and see § 79*k*.

The patriarchs lived in tents, wandering from place to **d** place with their herds and flocks. They were not nomads in the strict sense ; they remained at times long enough in one place to grow corn. Now these wanderings are always in the mountain country and in the northern Negeb, not on the coastal plains. The country was already populated and had numerous towns, and the movements of the new-comers were conditioned by the geographical disposition of these existing inhabitants. And Albright has pointed out that this description of the lives of the patriarchs ' does not agree at all with conditions in any part of Palestine in the Iron Age ', *i.e.* from 1200 B.C., 131. ' In the Middle and Late Bronze Ages (2000–1600 and 1600–1200 B.C.) the hill-country was still but sparsely peopled, and almost the entire sedentary population occupied the coastal plains, Esdraelon and the Jordan Valley. The plains and broad valleys were dotted with towns. . . . Occupation in these regions was considerably denser than it was in the Iron Age ', whereas in the hill-country there was little hindrance to the movements of semi-nomads and their flocks, 131 f. Further, archaeology has established the age of many **e** inhabited sites, and of the towns mentioned in the patriarchal narratives it has been definitely proved that the following were in existence in the Middle Bronze Age, Shechem, Bethel, Ai, Gerar, Dothan, Beersheba. Circumstances have not allowed archaeological examination of Hebron, but there is ample reason to credit its equal antiquity. On the other hand, no one of the Israelite settlements, such as Mizpah and Gibeah, is mentioned, Albright, 133.

The Israelites could not fail to transmit faithfully the **f** names of their great patriarchs. For external evidence of the names Abraham and Jacob see § 59*h* and de Vaux (1946) 323 f. That of Isaac has not been found, but it is of regular formation and there is no reason to doubt its authenticity.

Much is now known of the legal codes of the ancient **g** Near East and in particular of those of the Babylonians, Assyrians and Hurrites roughly contemporary with the patriarchal age. A study of these shows how closely patriarchal customary law in the matters of marriage and inheritance agrees with that prevailing at the time in the neighbouring countries ; see C. H. Gordon in *The Biblical Archaeologist* III, 1 (Feb. 1940) 1–12 and de Vaux, 20–36. The latter writes : ' The Israelites of a later age had no knowledge of the documents we have been using ; they lived in another stage of civilization ; their customs were partly different. If, as has been said for long, they had reconstructed the past according to what they saw and what they imagined, the result would have been a picture different from that which we have, and it would have been incorrect ', 36.

In judging the reliability of the traditional text we must **h** remember that scribes sometimes feel justified in substituting better-known recent names for ancient as Dan

9h in 14:14. W. F. Albright writes of the Joseph narrative : ' Since the story was so popular, and dealt with Egypt, the temptation for Israelite scribes who were acquainted with the Egyptian language and with life in Egypt to revise the names and details was irresistible ', 143. The names may be anachronistic without detriment to the substantial historicity of the narrative.

i It must also be remembered that the narratives belong to the type of literature which may be called **popular tradition.** They do not belong to what would now be styled scientific history. In the case of the former, writer and reader are aware that absolute accuracy is not claimed for the details of dialogue. These may be such as the situation would naturally elicit. There is an analogy to this even in the professedly serious history of Thucydides, and, to touch a sacred theme, the words of Consecration pronounced by our Lord once at the Last Supper are differently recorded in various parts of the NT. The inerrancy attaching to any inspired book is that belonging to the type of literature to which it belongs. This has long been recognized, as J. Brucker, S.J., says in *L'Eglise et la Critique biblique* (1908) 222, ' Provided that the inspiration and historical character of Genesis is loyally maintained, Catholic tradition leaves us great liberty in the interpretation of this venerable document '. And he proceeds : ' In each of the little dramas presented by the stories of Genesis may be distinguished what constitutes their action strictly speaking, and the development of the incidents and the dialogue and even their embellishment. Ordinarily it is only the first of these elements which demands a strictly historical interpretation ', 223. Similarly Heinisch, 75, defines the aim of the ancient historian as ' agreement with fact in all essential points, freedom in the form of the presentation '.

10a A special feature of this ancient type of historical writing is **the use made of genealogies,** the outstanding example of which is given in the table of nations in ch 10. Of this use Heinisch writes : ' The genealogies, which enumerate peoples of regions as " sons " of a person or people or land, like . . . the lists of the posterity of Nachor in 22:20–24, of Abraham by Cetura in 25:1–6, of Ishmael in 25:12–16, also certain parts of the Edomite lists gathered in ch 36, are intended by the author to show that certain relations existed between the peoples named, not necessarily of blood-relationship in every case, but at least the relationship of neighbourhood in the present or the past and trade relations ', 83.

b A question which requires separate discussion is that of **the ages of the patriarchs.** The considerations mentioned (§ 138*b–d*) render it impossible to suppose that ch 5 presents a genuine historical tradition concerning the actual ages of the antediluvian patriarchs. The date of the postdiluvian patriarchs of ch 11 is in the main much more recent but still belongs to a past so remote that it would conflict with all our knowledge to suppose the figures to be accurate. Even in the second millennium B.C. men in general can have had little more than a rough idea of their age. Even where an era existed, as in Egypt, it would be beyond the ability of any but the learned to reckon by it. And an examination of the information afforded concerning the age of the historical patriarchs at various times in their lives reveals certain facts which strongly suggest that the figures given rest on an artificial scheme appropriate in prescientific history. A number of the figures give the impression of being round or approximate. Abraham is 75 when he travels to Canaan, 12:4. He is just 25 years older at Isaac's birth, 21:5, and 75 years older again at death, 25:7. The exact age of 99 given in 17:1, 24 clearly depends on his age of 100 at Isaac's birth, 21:5, preceded by the announcement of Isaac's coming conception in 18:10. Isaac is 60 years old at Jacob's birth, 25:26, and Esau is 40 at the time of his marriage, 26:34.

c Now Sara was 10 years younger than her husband, 17:17. So at the time of their arrival in Canaan she was 65. Yet some time later when they go down to Egypt, her beauty is so striking that she is taken to **140c** Pharaoh's court, 12:15. In 20:2 when she runs the same danger at the court of Abimelech, she appears to be over 90 (17:17). Isaac appears to be close to death when Jacob's ruse secures his blessing in ch 27. Actually according to the figures he was about 137, and survived some 43 years till his death at the age of 180 (35:28). (These ages are given by the following calculation. Joseph was 30 when put in control of Egypt, 41:46. After 7 years of plenty and 2 of famine, 45:11, he summoned Jacob to come to Egypt, 45:9. He was therefore about 39 at the time, and, as Jacob was then 130 [47:9], Jacob was about 91 at the time of Joseph's birth. And Joseph's birth occurred towards the end of Jacob's 14-year service with Laban, 30:25. Therefore when Jacob left Isaac and Rebecca to go to Mesopotamia, 27:43, he was about 77 ; and as his father Isaac was 60 at the time of Jacob's birth, he was then about 137 years old. And the last link in the argument is that Jacob's flight to his future father-in-law followed quickly after his outwitting Isaac and so gaining his blessing.)

The primary motive of Jacob's flight north was to **d** escape the vengeance of Esau, 27:42, 45. Rebecca preferred to put another reason before Isaac. She feared lest Jacob might follow the example of Esau and marry one of the women of Canaan and suggested that he should seek a wife among his cousins in Mesopotamia, 27:46–28:5. So according to the figures given Isaac and Rebecca become nervous about the danger of their son falling in love with a native woman of Canaan when he is not far from attaining the responsible age of nearly fourscore years. Furthermore, when he reached his uncle's home, he finds two of his female cousins both unmarried and both of marriageable age. In fact, they are both young enough for their father to postpone their marriages for another 7 years, 29:20. Rachel subsequently bore two children and Lia, the elder of the sisters, was still young enough to become the mother of six, 35:23 f.

These combined improbabilities force on the reader **e** the conviction that the figures are not intended to reflect the actual ages of the historical patriarchs but are schematic and to be considered in relation to those of the ante- and postdiluvian patriarchs. That these were known to be schematic only is indicated by the freedom with which they were altered in early times as is clear from a comparison of the Hebrew, Samaritan and LXX texts. The additions and subtractions are mostly of 100, 50 or 60 years, and the purpose, most apparent in LXX, was to increase the antiquity of the Israelite race. The original numbers are probably those of the Samaritan text, according to which the ages of the antediluvian patriarchs gradually diminished with almost complete regularity in each successive generation from Adam to Lamech : 930 ; 912 ; 905 ; 910 ; 895 ; 847 ; 365 (Enoch) ; 720 ; 653. This fits with the ancient conceptions that wisdom comes with years, that wisdom was the special prerogative of the ancients, and that its fountain-head was to be found in the first generation, Job 15:7. According to this scheme Noe, the second father of the stock whence sprang the Hebrew people, must have a life as long as the first father and indeed longer as Adam had incurred the divine displeasure whereas Noe had not. Accordingly Noe lived for 950 years, and after him the ages descend again, much more rapidly now that the list approaches historical times. The figures fall as follows : 600 ; 438 ; 433 ; 404 ; 239 ; 239 ; 230 ; 148 ; 145 (Thare). The numbers in MT and LXX are higher, but show in the main the same diminution.

It was fitting again that Abraham, the direct ancestor **f** of the Chosen People and recipient of the divine promises, should have a longer life than his father, but as a personage of historical times of relatively modest length. He lived to be 175, 25:7. Isaac lived to be 180, 35:28 ; Jacob 147, 47:28 ; and Joseph

140f 110, 50:25. (On Joseph see also § 161e.) And Moses, as the great law-giver and deliverer of the people, in his turn has a longer life, dying at the age of 120 years, Deut 34:7. The one disturbing feature in the scheme is the advanced age of Isaac, as there is no apparent reason why his span of life should exceed that of Abraham. It may well be that the number rests on an error in the textual transmission. Ch 27 which represents him as close to death suggests that the original figure was considerably smaller.

141a **I 1–II 3 God prepares a Home for Mankind**—When God first created the earth, it was without vegetation or animal life, as it was covered by water. Over the waters was only darkness, and the Spirit of God brooded over them preparing the earth and the waters for the production of life, 1-2. The universe was gradually brought into its present condition by successive divine operations extended over six days. The first three days saw the preparation of the fixed setting of the world, and the second three the adornment and peopling of its different regions by the creation of moving beings, inanimate and animate. The first day saw the creation of light and the consequent separation of light and darkness, 3-5. The work of the second day was the creation of the vault or firmament of heaven with the separation of the waters on the surface of the earth from those supported by the firmament which come down on the earth in due season in the form of rain, 6-8. On the third day God gathered the waters on the earth into one gathering which received the name of the seas. Thus a portion of the surface of the earth became visible and was then clothed with vegetation, 9-13. So far all was motionless or rooted in one spot. On the fourth day God created the sun, the moon and the stars, and placed them in the firmament of heaven, 14-19. On the fifth day God peopled the waters and the skies by the creation of the fish and other dwellers in the seas and of the birds, 20-23. On the sixth day God peopled the earth first by the creation of the terrestrial animals and secondly of man. God created man to his own image and decreed that he was to have dominion over the living creatures, whether in the air, in the waters or on the earth. To all the animals and birds as to man God gave the vegetable kingdom for their nourishment, 24-31. Having completed his work of creation God rested on the seventh day and sanctified it, 2:1-3.

b Various doctrinal and other questions are omitted from the following notes, which set down only such remarks as appear necessary on the separate verses; see §§ 137a–d, 142a–g. **1.** As the creation of the firmament is recorded in 7 f., 'heaven and earth' here stands for the universe, which Hebrew had no one word to express. The verse is thus a summary of what follows. For an alternative translation see § 142f. **2.** The earth was 'waste and empty', as it was without its vesture of vegetation and without any living creatures to move about on its surface. In the prescientific era the earth was naturally conceived to have been created in its solid mass and with its contours such as man has always known them. That this is the meaning is shown both by the fact that the earth presented a solid surface on which the waters rested and by Ps 103:6, where the Psalmist treating of the creation of the world says 'above the mountains stood the waters'. The darkness in which the world was created used to be described as 'chaos'. Thus in the breviary hymn for Sunday Vespers the oncoming of night is mentioned in the words 'illabitur tetrum chaos'. And this seems to have been the principal reason for the popularity of the idea that the world was created in a chaotic state. See Sutcliffe, 'Primeval Chaos not Scriptural' in *Miscellanea Biblica* II (1934) 203-15. The Spirit of God brooding over the waters depicts metaphorically God's loving care for the world and his preparation of it for the living creatures which were to come out of it. There appears to be no reason in the context for the 'powerful wind' which some would substitute as a translation for 'the Spirit of God'. **3.** In the form γενέσθω φῶς καὶ ἐγένετο this first divine command is quoted in illustration of its theme in the treatise of Longinus *On the Sublime*, 9, 9 (ed. W. R. Roberts, 1899, 64).

5. The Hebrew Sabbath began at evening on what **c** we call Friday and ended in the evening of what we call Saturday, and as God's rest on the seventh day after his six days of work is proposed as a model of the Sabbath rest, it seems clear that the days of creation are represented as beginning in the evening. With this agrees the fact that the first day begins with a period of darkness which is followed by a period of the newly created light. **7.** Omit the double 'that were', as there cannot have been waters above the firmament before its creation. **11.** Three kinds of plants are mentioned, those which appear to have no seed like grass, those which have seeds that may be called naked like wheat and barley, and those which produce fruit with the seed within itself like figs and apples. **14.** The heavenly bodies act as signs by aiding men to orientate themselves (the Hebrews fixed the points of the compass by facing the rising sun) and to find their direction when travelling. **20.** 'the *gliding* creature' is from LXX, and also the production of the birds from the waters; MT 'let the waters *swarm with swarms of living creatures, and let the birds* fly over the earth'. **24.** Cattle are domesticated from the beginning; 'the beasts of the earth' are the wild animals. **26.** For 'the beasts and the whole earth' read with Syr, 'the cattle and all the beasts of the earth.' 'Man' is used collectively, as is shown by the plural verb 'let *them* have dominion' (MT, LXX). Note the solemnity with which is introduced the crowning act of creation, namely that of man. All else was created for his benefit.

29. To man for food God gave all plants with naked **d** or covered seed (*cf.* on 11), but to the animal creation, **30,** except the fish which are not mentioned, 'all green herbs'. The suggestion is that peace and harmony reigned in the whole of creation. No animal was in danger from its fellows or from man. And the Messianic age is depicted in Is 11:6-9 as a return to this primitive condition of universal harmony. The underlying idea is to emphasize the state of innocence in which man was created and to prepare the reader for the disharmony which sin was later to introduce into the world. The creatures of the sea, mentioned before together with the birds in 20-22, could not be introduced here, and there is consequently no allusion to the food provided for them. **31.** After the various works of the previous days God saw that they were good, 4, 8 (LXX), 10, 12, 18, 21; and so also after the creation of the terrestrial animals on the sixth day, 25. Now when the creation of man had completed the execution of God's design, he saw that the world was 'very good'. This again prepares the reader's mind for the sad fact to become plain later in the story that everything evil which mars the perfection of the world, is due to the sin of man. **II:1.** 'The heavens and the earth' were completed in the work of the first three days. They provide the fixed setting of the theatre in which the drama of man's religious history is to be played out. The second three days witnessed the creation of their 'furniture' or adornment (LXX, Vg). MT (with 'aleph for yod) speaks of their 'host', the host of the firmament being the heavenly bodies, that of the seas the fish, and so forth. **2-3.** God finished his work on 'the *sixth* day' (Sam., LXX, Syr.). The seventh day (MT, Vg) was introduced here by an incautious copyist misled by its being mentioned later in the verse. DV 'rested' (Vg 'requievit') is a strong anthropomorphism. The word šābaṭ occurs twice in this passage, in both 2 and 3, and in both cases LXX translates by κατέπαυσεν ἀπό 'God desisted from all his works'; and the words are so quoted in Heb 4:4. But the idea of 'rest' is at least implicit in šābaṭ, and is quite explicit in Ex

141d 31:17 ' On the seventh day he rested and was refreshed ' (RV ; Vg and DV omit the second verb). Vg in 3 translates ' cessaverat ' though DV reverts to the word ' rested '. Such variety in the choice of expression is characteristic of St Jerome.

142a To understand this account aright it is important to bear in mind certain **theological principles of interpretation.** The Bible is not a handbook of physical science. Its purpose is religious truth. Consequently the sacred writers, or more correctly ' the Spirit of God who spoke through them, did not intend to teach men what would help no one to attain his salvation '. So taught St Augustine in words made his own by Leo XIII (Dz 1947 ; EB 106). The Pope goes on to say that the sacred writers consequently speak of the constitution of the visible world and of its phenomena as the men of their time spoke and in language intelligible to their contemporaries. Now it is clear that the account of the way the world was formed could depend only on either reason or revelation. The principle laid down by Leo XIII in *Providentissimus Deus* just quoted excludes the revelation of the truths of natural science. And it is not credible that in the early prescientific days of the Hebrew people human reason had reached that exact knowledge of the constitution of the universe which it has taken mankind at large some thousands of years to attain. It follows, therefore, that God did not intend to give us in Gen 1 an account of the world in full accord with the actual facts of physical science.

b What we have is **a popular account of the world** as conceived by the ancient Hebrews in accordance with appearances. This is borne out by an examination of the text. We have light even on dull days when the sun is completely obscured, and it consequently appears to be an independent entity. In accordance with this it existed for three days before the creation of the sun on the fourth day. The earth appears to be flat and to be surmounted by a celestial dome or vault, which we call the firmament, a name which, it may be recalled in passing, implies its solidity. Water descends from above in the form of rain, apparently from a celestial reservoir in which it is stored. This is naturally supposed to be supported by the solid firmament, 6 f. It falls when the apertures or ' flood gates ' are opened, 7:11. The plants and trees are created on the third day, 12, as part of the fixed scene, and so before the existence of the sun, without which they cannot flourish. The heavenly bodies appear to be set on the under surface of the firmament, 17, and the sun and moon seem to be of greater size than the stars, 16. That the days of creation are proposed as natural days seems evident from the following facts. They are set forth as a model of the Hebrew week which culminated in the Sabbath rest, 2:3. Each has an evening and a morning, and the day is ruled by the heavenly bodies, 16. These days are part of the popular account and not intended to specify the time actually occupied in the work of creation. St Athanasius, PG 26, 276, and St Augustine, PL 34, 231, understood this and taught that all things were created at one and the same time ; *cf.* Sutcliffe, *The Six Days of Creation* (CTS, 1945).

c This schematic and artistic presentation of the truth that the world belongs to God, that it was made by him and designed by him precisely as the home of man stands most suitably at the head of the OT, which in sum is the history of the covenant entered into by God with the people of Israel. From the first page the Israelite was reminded that the God whom he worshipped and who had condescended to make the children of Abraham his own chosen people out of all the nations of the earth was the one, true, only God, the Lord and Master of the whole world. The chapter contains besides other **important heads of doctrine.** This one, true God is depicted as alone creating and adorning the world. The sun and moon worshipped as divinities by the Babylonians are simply creatures, and so far from having any dominion over the human race were made by God for the service of man. So **142c** too the beasts and birds adored by the Egyptians are the work of God's hands and put by him under the control of man. This implicit **repudiation of polytheistic creeds** is more effective than any explicit denial of their validity. Moreover, everything being **d** made by God is good, even very good ; and this inherent goodness of all God's creatures serves to emphasize in the later development of the story the wicked use man so often makes of them, as of the power and rights of marriage here instituted and blessed by God. Man is the special object of God's care. All else is designed for him and he is made the lord of all ; *cf.* Ps 8. But though all else is subordinated to him, he is himself subordinated to his Maker and owes obedience to his commands. And this obedience is made the lighter by the loving condescension by which God deigned even to make man in his own image and likeness. It is to be noted that man as **e** such, composed of body and soul, is **made in the likeness of God,** not one part of him only, and the immediate context suggests that the likeness is to be found primarily in man's lordship of created things, which bear a relation of subordination to him analogous to that which he bears to his Creator. But this lordship is founded in man's exclusive possession of intellect and will without which this lordship would be impossible. And it is therefore in these faculties of the spiritual soul that man's likeness to God ultimately rests. This explanation goes beyond the meaning which the text would have conveyed to the early Israelites at a time when they had not yet arrived at the concept of spirituality. On this question see the full discussion in Petavius, *De Opificio Sex Dierum*, Lib. 2, cap. 2. (The angels too were created in the likeness of God, but Gen 1 treats only of the visible world.)

The **doctrine of creation** out of nothing is explicitly **f** stated in 2 Mac 7:28. Gen 1:1 speaks of ' creation ' but does not say in so many words that the creation was out of nothing. Hence the question arises whether the doctrine can be proved from these opening words of Scripture alone. The word *bārā'* ' create ' or ' make ', which is used exclusively of divine operations, does not of itself include the idea of making out of nothing. It is used three times in 1:27 of the making of man, whose body was formed out of pre-existing matter. If ' in the beginning ' is understood of the absolute beginning of time or of created things (both began together), then clearly, before God made the world, there was nothing out of which it could have been made. Petavius, however, *De Opificio Sex Dierum* I, i, 19 (Paris, ed., 1866) points out that the word ' beginning ' can be understood to include all the six days. These six days are the beginning in which God made the world and all that is in it. He therefore maintains that as far as the strict meaning and import of the words is concerned, it cannot be deduced from the opening sentence of Gen that God made all things out of nothing (*ibid.* n. 9). He adds, however, that the doctrine being known from other sources illustrates the full meaning of the words ' In the beginning God made heaven and earth '. This is the translation of LXX and Vg. The Hebrew even with massoretic vocalization (*cf.* GK 130d) can be rendered ' In the beginning when God created the heavens and the earth and the earth was desolate and void and darkness was on the face of the abyss and the Spirit of God was hovering over the face of the waters, then God said " Let there be light " '. According to this rendering of the text God's first recorded act was the creation of light, though, and this is important, it is not implied that God did not create the world out of nothing, and the statement sometimes made that an eternally existing mass is supposed, is incorrect. Hebrew style often emphasizes one truth without implying a denial of what is not explicitly stated.

The biblical account of creation is **independent of all g pagan cosmologies.** Not only is its religious outlook incomparably superior to the gross polytheism of

142g Israel's neighbours, the whole tone is far more lofty. The frame-work of six days followed by a day of rest is found nowhere else. There are, as would be expected, cosmological conceptions common to the Semitic world, such as the solid firmament and the waters above it, and *tᵉhôm*, the word used of the primeval ocean, recalls Tiamat, its personification in Babylonia. But speaking of *Enuma elish*, the Babylonian epic of creation, Sir Frederic Kenyon rightly says ' There is almost nothing to link the narrative to that of Genesis ', *Archaeology and the Bible* (1940) 47. The question is one of literary and historical, not of theological, interest. For the Babylonian accounts see Sir E. Wallis Budge, *Babylonian Legends of the Creation* (1931), R. Labat, *Le Poème babylonien de la Création* (1935).

143a **II 4-25 The Creation of the First Man and Woman—** With this section begins a narrative written in a simple homely style quite different from the elevated tone characteristic of ch 1. According to the plan of the book it is dove-tailed with the preceding section which leads up to the creation of mankind in general without reference to particular persons. The present section sets forth the creation and condition of the first human pair. It is not a second account of the creation of·the world, though the production of plants and animals is introduced at those points of the story where their relation to man requires it.

b In a certain region of the earth, probably Babylonia, there was as yet no vegetation of the smaller kinds which require surface water for growth as there was neither rain from heaven nor man to irrigate the soil, **5.** There was, however, a source of water which man would be able to turn to good account, **6.** God now formed the body of a man and made it to live, **7.** God then placed him in a lovely oasis in Eden, **8,** in which grew all manner of pleasant and fruitful trees, two in particular being the tree of life and the tree of knowledge of good and evil, **9.** The growth of these trees had been possible without the help of man as the undersoil received moisture from a river which ran through the oasis and on leaving it divided into four, **10-14.** This oasis, which we call Paradise, was to be man's home. He would have pleasant occupation in looking after it, **15,** and abundance of food from its variety of fruits, **16.** In these surroundings there was nothing to test his loyalty to God. So God made the continuance of his happy state, including the privilege of immortality, dependent on the observance of one command. Man must not eat of the fruit of the tree of the knowledge of good and of evil, **17.** Now the man was alone and God intended him to have a consort, but he must first understand his need, as he did when he came to see and know the animals in the oasis. No one of them was fit to be his companion, **18-20.** God then formed the first woman from his side, and in her the man recognized one of the same nature as himself and understood God's purpose in the institution of marriage, **21-24.** And having reason in complete control of their lower nature, although naked they had no cause for shame, **25.**

c **4.** ' *This is the history of the world* '. The word *tôlᵉdôt*, lit. ' begettings ' came to mean ' generations (of a family) ', ' genealogy ', and so ' history '. It is noteworthy that the history of a person is introduced as the history of his progenitor, as that of Abraham as ' the history of Thare ', 11:27. So here the story of the first human beings is introduced as the history of the world out of which they were formed, **7.** For the occurrences of the word, always as introduction to the following narrative, *cf.* § 136j-l. ' *When* the Lord God made heaven and earth, **5,** *there was as yet no herb of the field on the earth and no plant of the field had as yet sprung up*, for the Lord God had not rained upon the earth '. The actions of secondary causes tend to be ignored by biblical writers and their causality to be attributed directly to God who created them. This was in part due to ignorance of these causes, an ignorance which, indirectly, had the happy effect of putting into prominent relief the reality of God's

ever-continued government of the world. Note too **14** the Hebrew use of universal expressions limited only by the context. The writer has in mind not the whole earth, but the particular region of Babylonia, where the rainfall is negligible and the soil fruitful when irrigated by man from the rivers. ' and there was no man to till the *ground*, **3,** *and raise the flowing waters from the earth to irrigate the whole surface of the ground* '. The word *'ēd* is explained by the Sumerian *id* ' stream, canal ' and by extension is the water they contain; see further Bi 30 (1949) 77 f. **7.** God now formed the **d** body of man out of the *soil* and breathed into his *nostrils* the breath of life, and ' *the* man became a living *being* '. At the time of Moses it was not yet known that the body of man is animated by a spiritual soul; *cf.* Sutcliffe, *The Old Testament and the Future Life* (1947²) 152-9. The most obvious difference between a living and a dead body is that the latter has ceased to breathe. Accordingly life is spoken of as God's gift of breath, and death as his withdrawal of it as in Ps 103:29 f., where the phrase is used of the animals. There is consequently nothing in the expression to distinguish between the life of man and of brutes. **8.** Events are not all narrated in chronological order **e** but as the course of the story requires. God as a suitable home for man planted with trees ' *a garden in Eden* '. The familiar name ' Paradise ' is derived from LXX παράδεισος, itself of Persian origin and denoting originally an enclosed park. Eden may be Bit-Adini on the middle Euphrates or, perhaps more probably, may represent the Assyrian word *edinu* meaning an open plain or desert, as that is what the territory was in which the garden was situated. The word ' pleasure ' is due to the existence of a homonym with that meaning and the fact that the garden was a most delectable home. **9.** The trees had been able to **f** grow because the undersoil was moistened by the water which seeped through from the river, **10.** Some of the trees were purely ornamental, others also fruit-bearing. The tree of life is probably to be conceived as having fruit of preternatural power capable of entirely restoring human energy and vitality and so of preserving the strength of youth. By its means Adam and Eve, though mortal by nature, would have enjoyed the gift of immortality. Unlike this tree, the tree of knowledge of good and of evil would have no unusual powers in its fruit. But it was the subject of the one divine prohibition to which Adam was subjected, **17.** If he transgressed this prohibition and ate of its fruit, he would learn by bitter personal experience how transient is the enjoyment of sin and how bitter and enduring its consequences. He knew already the distinction between good and evil; unless he had known that it is sinful to disobey the commands of God, there could be nothing morally wrong in his disobedience. He was plainly warned of the unhappy consequences of transgression, but before his sin he did not know them by experience. At the same time, the name could be interpreted to mean omniscience according to the Hebrew idiom by which totality is expressed by means of the conjunction of opposites. Of this possibility the powers of evil were ready to take advantage, as the sequel shows, 3:5.

The passage, **10-14,** interrupts the narrative and is **g** marked by an entirely different style and outlook. Its purpose is to give a more exact geographical indication of the site of Paradise. This is done by the statement that a river watered the garden and after leaving it divided into four rivers, the names of which will have been well-known at the time when the narrative was written. As the Euphrates and the Tigris both gird Mesopotamia, various attempts have been made to identify the other two with confluents or canals in their upper, middle or lower courses. No such proposal bears the marks of probability. A more radical solution was current in the early Church. It must be remembered that geography is a science like astronomy, and, although scientific knowledge about the earth is more easily acquired than about

3g the stars, nonetheless its acquisition presented formidable difficulties which it took many generations to overcome. Exact statement of geographical fact must not be expected in the Bible any more than of astronomical ; *cf.* § 142a. Now according to St Augustine, whereas the Tigris and the Euphrates have retained their ancient names, the Phison and the Gehon have not, their new names being respectively the Ganges and the Nile, *De Gen. ad lit.*, Lib. 8, cap. 7 (PL 34, 378). These were the four great rivers known to the ancient world and the ideal site of the home of our first parents would be at the central point where these four rivers separate to water the four quarters of the earth. So too Josephus, *Ant. Jud.* 1, 1, 3, identifies the Phison with the Ganges and the Gehon with the Nile. This former identification is suggested by St Jerome, *Quaest. Hebr. in Gen.* (PL 23, 941) and the latter is made also in LXX Jer 2:18. The historian Arrian provides a good illustration of geographical knowledge as late as the 4th cent. B.C. When Alexander the Great reached the Indus, he thought he had found the source of the Nile, *Anabasis*, 6, 1, 2 f.

h The thread of the narrative is picked up again in **15** by the repetition from 8 that God placed man in this garden ' to dress it and keep it ', or ' tend it ' (not ' to guard it ' ; there was nothing and no one to guard it against). **16.** ' thou *mayest* eat '. **17** has been understood in two ways—as a threat either of immediate death which God did not carry out as the sinners were not obstinate, or of subjection to the law of death as they would no longer have access to the tree of life, 3:22. The Hebrew suggests the former. **19.** The animals in question are only those of Paradise ; see on 2:5. Being concerned with the story of Adam, and not with the creation of the world, this is the first time the writer has had occasion to mention them, and he does not mean that they were created now after man. The Hebrew mode of speaking does not warrant the idea that God miraculously brought all the animals before Adam ; see on 2:5. In the natural course of things Adam came to see and know the various kinds of animal in the garden and the adequacy of his knowledge is emphasized by the statement that he gave them names and did so correctly (' the same is its name '). The point of this is that for the Hebrews names were not thought of as mere labels but as denoting the nature, character or office of the thing

i or person named. **20.** It is thus brought home to Adam that surrounded as he is by living creatures, he is yet alone. **21.** God now proceeds to give him a consort. The ' deep sleep ' is expressed by the same word (*tardēmāh*) as is used for the natural slumber that overcame the weary Jonas, 1:5. There is no reason to doubt the translation ' rib ' which is supported both by the ancient versions and by the cognate word in Arabic. **23.** In the other living beings he had seen Adam had recognized no similarity of nature, but in the newly formed woman he recognized the very same nature as his own. This is an important point of doctrine against the view that woman is of a nature inferior to man. At the same time the manner in which her formation is described is designed to teach that in the institution of the family the husband and father is the natural and divinely instituted head to whom all the other members are subordinate as good order requires a central authority in every society. **24.** It is not clear whether these words are Adam's or the sacred writer's. In either case they can be attributed to God as our Lord appears to do, Mt 19:4 f. In the former case they are conceived as a divine prophecy put into the mouth of Adam and in the latter as due to the divine inspiration of the hagiographer. The Council of Trent attributes them to Adam, but does not pretend to settle a point of this kind, Dz 969. The words teach **the indissolubility of marriage** as one flesh cannot be divided. And that marriage by divine institution is between one man and one woman was made more plain by Christ when he referred to this passage and added, ' Therefore now they are not two

but one flesh ', Mt 19:6. **25** in the light of 3:7 signifies **143i** that in the state of innocence the lower powers of human nature were entirely subordinated to the rule of reason. Our first parents were thus placed in **conditions of j physical and spiritual felicity.** Their bodily needs were supplied by the trees of the garden, the care of which was designed to supply pleasant occupation. As they were created in adult life, God will have given them that knowledge which was necessary to their state, a knowledge that human beings have normally to acquire through the years of childhood and adolescence. Though by nature mortal, they had in the tree of life the means of preserving health and strength indefinitely. In other words, they had the gift of immortality. They had moreover the preternatural gift of integrity. That is, by a special privilege their nature was ' whole ' and without internal conflict, as their bodies with their physical powers were entirely under the control of reason, which had not therefore to control the spontaneous impulses of their lower nature. This gift of integrity is also called the absence of concupiscence, and is indicated by the fact that, though naked, they had no cause for any sense of shame. That they were created in the state of sanctifying grace and were destined for the beatific vision cannot be deduced from the OT, but is learnt from the NT.

The **theory of evolution** or transformism, which figures **k** so largely in modern text-books of biology, was unknown to the Hebrews and the animals are represented as created according to ' their kinds ' or their species, such as they were known to have at the time Genesis was written. What the book offers is a popular account suited to the mentality of the age, and directed to a purely religious purpose. It was not the wish of the Holy Ghost in inspiring the sacred writers to teach men· such matters of purely secular knowledge ; *cf.* § 142a. This applies also to the theory—it is nothing more than a theory lacking proof—that the human body has been evolved from lower forms. If it should ever be established, the religious teaching of Genesis would remain the same, namely, that the world was created for the sake of man, who is himself the work of God's hands no matter what path the divine wisdom chose to follow in the production of man's bodily frame. That man has a spiritual rational soul is established by philosophy as is also the fact that such a spiritual substance could not have its origin in anything material. And it is due to man's spiritual soul that his mental powers differ essentially from those of even the highest of the brute creation. The refined concept of spiritual being, however, was not attained till many centuries after the time of Moses.

Pius XII reminds us that the question does not **l** belong exclusively to the field of natural science and that the sources of revelation impose caution and moderation. It is one that may be freely discussed, provided we are prepared to accept the decision of the Church, to whom Christ committed the charge of interpreting Holy Scripture and of guarding the doctrines of the Faith (*Humani generis* AAS 42 (1950) 575 f.).

In the same Encyclical the Pope goes on to say that **m** as regards *polygenism* Catholics do not enjoy the same liberty. For the faithful cannot embrace the opinion that after Adam there lived on this earth true men not derived from him by natural generation, or that Adam signifies a plurality of first parents ' since it is not at all clear how such an opinion can be reconciled with what the sources of revelation and the acts of the Church's teaching authority put forward concerning original sin ' (*ibid.* 576).

III 1-24 The Temptation, Fall and Punishment of 144a Adam and Eve—1. Adam and Eve had no source of temptation in their own lower nature on account of the absence of concupiscence, and the incitement to evil came from without. At the time when Genesis was composed the existence of wicked spirits, angels fallen from their high estate, had not yet been revealed —the name Satan first occurs in the book of Job and

144a then not as that of a wicked spirit—and the power urging to evil is introduced under a symbolical form. The choice of **the serpent** was suitable for several reasons. The temptation to be proposed was subtle and the serpent was reputed to be crafty and cunning, Mt 10:16. As the narrative explains how the existing state of the world came to be, and God was to set enmity between the human race and the power that had incited to the first sin, 15, the animal chosen had to be one between whom and men hostility as a fact exists. This condition excluded all the domestic animals between which and Eve a friendly conversation might appear less surprising. But in Paradise peace and harmony existed between all creatures. The choice may also have been influenced by ideas current in the Semitic world. In the epic of Gilgamesh it was a serpent that deprived the hero of the precious plant of immortality. The choice may also have had a polemical purpose. Serpents were associated with Canaanite worship (J. Coppens, *La Connaissance du Bien et du Mal*, Louvain, 1948, 93 f., 123), and the part played by the serpent in procuring the downfall of mankind would tend to lessen the attractiveness of the cult. This supposition is strengthened by the consideration of the various polemical motives in ch 1. With the progress of revelation it came to be understood that the serpent is a symbol of the devil, Wis 2:24, Apoc 12:9

b The conversation starts with the untrue suggestion : '*Has God really commanded you not to eat of any of the trees in the garden ?* ' **3.** Omit ' perhaps ' which is due to the Latin idiom of Vg. **4.** Now the serpent boldly lies, and even, **5,** dares to attribute God's prohibition to a jealous desire to prevent his creatures from acquiring a knowledge which would make them like to himself. The serpent plays upon the name of the tree as suggesting omniscience ; *cf.* on 2:9. **6.** Thus ' the serpent seduced Eve by his subtlety ', 2 Cor 11:3, and she saw that the tree was ' *a delight to the eyes and desirable for the gaining of wisdom* '. **7.** The words of the serpent in 5 had been true but not in the sense it had insinuated. The knowledge immediately won was that of the power of their lower nature, now no longer under the complete control of reason, and their eyes were opened only to see their nakedness. **8.** They heard ' *the sound* ' of God's steps approaching. **10.** Again it is emphasized that the knowledge acquired was a knowledge of guilt and shame. **12.** Instead of humbly confessing his sin Adam attempts to throw the blame on his wife, who, in her turn, **13,** tries to make the serpent responsible. **14.** St Basil points out that a change is implied and that the serpent had previously walked on legs and feet, PG 30, 68. This, however, is dubious and in any case it is not intended that the change should be understood as an historical fact. The idea is probably polemical suggested by the pagan representation of the serpent standing erect. There is no evidence of an ancient popular belief that serpents do eat dirt (Is 65:25 is a reference to our passage) and the thought will have been suggested by the serpent's crawling gait and the metaphorical expression of abject humiliation as ' licking the dust ', Ps 71:9, Is 49:23.

c **15a.** The friendly terms that existed between Eve and the serpent are not to last. There will be hostility between them and between their respective descendants, signified by the word ' seed '. It is unusual that this should be used of a woman though it is also used of Rebecca, 24:60, with the same sense of ' posterity '. The hostility foretold is manifest in the relations normally existing between men and serpents. **15b.** It can hardly be doubted that the feminine pronoun had its origin in the error of an early copyist of Vg. In his *Lib. Quaest. Heb. in Gen.* St Jerome quotes the Old Latin version of this text with the masc. (*ipse*) and translates the Hebrew with the same, PL 23, 943, and *ipse* is the reading of various Vg MSS. It is therefore highly improbable that he translated *ipsa* here ; see Sutcliffe CR (1931) 151–3. As the word refers to the ' seed ', it may be replaced in

English by ' it '. The translation of the verbs requires **144** discussion. Both of the seed and of the serpent the word used is *šûp*. This occurs besides only Jb 9:17 ' he breaketh me with a tempest ' (RV) or ' he overwhelmeth me with a storm ', LXX ἐκτρίψῃ, Vg ' conteret ', and Ps 138 (139)11 ' darkness shall overwhelm me ' (RV), LXX καταπατήσει, Vg ' conculcabunt '. (To speak of darkness crushing or overwhelming is not out of keeping with Heb. diction, and there is no need to emend to *yᵉšûkkēnî* ' will cover me '.) In our passage LXX took the word as a parallel form of *šā'ap* and translated τηρήσει . . . τηρήσεις ' be on the watch for '. Syr. translates, first, *ndûš* ' crush ' and, secondly, *temhe* ' wound, strike '. Vg conjoins these two with ' conteret ' and ' insidiaberis '. AV RV have ' bruise ' in both places. This cannot be considered satisfactory. The word is unsuitable for the serpent, and is not in harmony either with the strength of the concept manifest in Jb 9:17 or with the antecedent probabilities of the outcome of an attack on the serpent's head. The outcome of enmity set by God between the two parties will not be a mere ' bruise ' on either side. The sense ' crush ' which the context suggests is supported by LXX, Syr. and Vg with the renderings quoted above. This meaning is clearly suitable to describe the action on the serpent but not that taken by it. That the word is used with this sense of the first action is not likely to have induced its use, though unsuitable, of the second. The most likely explanation is that the linguistic sense of the Hebrews, while rejoicing in the assonance, recognized that here the word is used in the other sense ' to be eager for ' attested by LXX and Vg. The allied form *šā'ap* has this sense, and that it is common to both is further suggested by the fact that both forms have in common the meaning ' crush '. Hence the translation : ' *It shall crush thy head and thou shalt lie in wait for its heel* '. On the meaning of the prophecy see § 145*d–e*.

16. ' I will multiply the sorrows *of* thy conceptions ' : **d** a hendiadys. ' *thy longing shall be to* thy husband '. The proper subordination of the wife to her husband (see on 2:23) is now changed, as often in the ancient Orient, to one of subjection. There is, of course, no moral objection to measures for the mitigation of the pains of childbirth any more than there is to facilitate, **17,** the labours of man in the production of food. In the garden no arduous toil was required to provide food. That is now changed. **18.** The word ' herbs ' is that used in 1:29 and includes those of which man eats only the seeds like wheat and barley. **19.** Note that the introduction, 7, and improvement, 21, of clothing is mentioned expressly, which shows that ' bread ' here does not denote baked flour. If this had been intended, there would have been a reference to its invention ; *cf.* 4:17–22. The word *leḥem* is used of food in general, both of man, Jg 13:15 f., and of beasts, Ps 146 (147) 9. From this verse come the words with which the Church reminds the faithful on Ash Wednesday of man's frail tenure of life adding the symbolic signing of the Cross with ashes on the forehead of each one. **20.** The name ' Adam ' means ' man ' and first occurs definitely as a proper name in 4:25. In all previous occurrences wherever Hebrew admits of the use of *hē'* (= the def. art.) it is found in MT ; and, against MT, was certainly intended with the preposition in 2:20 and 3:17. Thus here and elsewhere up to 4:25 Adam is spoken of simply as ' the man '. The name ' Eve ' denotes the source of (human) life. The position of this verse rather interrupts the easy flow of the narrative. **21.** On the omission of reference to secondary causes see on 2:5. The omission here, however, is probably due to the fact that life, which was created by God, is sacred to him. Man's diet is still spoken of as purely vegetable, 17–19, and permission to eat flesh is first given in 9:3. **22.** The construction of the sentence remains unfinished, but is readily understood. The foolish pride of the ambition to become like to God merited the severe irony of this sentence, which is in no way surprising in this strongly anthropo-

44d morphic passage. The irony is manifested by the context and not by any special form of speech. God determines that Adam shall not (again) eat of the tree of life. It is not implied that he had not previously done so. **23.** 'out of the *garden of Eden*'; *cf.* 2:8 'a garden in Eden'. **24.** The Cherubim are interpreted by Christian tradition as Angels. The word is of uncertain derivation; the Assyrian *karūbu* and *kurūbu* mean 'great, powerful'. A Mesopotamian analogy is provided by the twin figures of winged bulls guarding the entrance to temples.

45a The narrative is direct and objective and reflections such as the folly and ingratitude of Adam and Eve's conduct are left to the reader. Similarly there is no analysis of **the nature of the first sin**. It had various elements, but first and foremost it was **a sin of pride** by which they irrationally desired to rise above their nature and attain a divine prerogative, 5. 'Pride is the beginning of all sin', Ecclus 10:15. It was also a sin of disobedience, Rom 5:19, and a sin of grave irreverence against God in that they believed the serpent rather than God, and even its suggestion that God's prohibition was motivated by jealousy, 5. That Adam as well as Eve believed the serpent is implied in the statement made by God about his attainment of divine equality, 22.

b The further question now arises whether the sacred author under the symbol of **the tree of knowledge** and its fruit had some particular species of sin in mind. Such a possibility was indicated by St Augustine : ' If any wish to understand the tree not literally as a real tree having real fruit but figuratively, let the application be consonant with the faith and the demands of verisimilitude', *De Gen. ad lit.*, Lib. 11, cap. 41, n. 56 (PL 34, 452). The interpretation St Augustine had in mind is that which understood the eating of the fruit to signify the use of matrimonial rights. This was the teaching of Julius Cassianus, leader of the Docetae, who held such use to be sinful. He argued that the tree was the tree of knowledge and knowledge stands for sexual relations, 4:1, Clement of Alexandria, *Stromata*, 3, 14 (PG 8, 1193 f.). It was also the view of St Zeno, Bishop of Verona, though he does not explain wherein the malice of the act lay, *Tract.*, Lib. 1, 13, n. 5 (PL 11, 348). It is also urged that the close connexion established in the story between the eating of the fruit and the knowledge of concupiscence suggests a sexual interpretation. But the openness with which Scripture speaks of sexual relations is alone sufficient to show that if the sacred writer had had anything of the kind in mind he would not have hesitated to speak with some plainness. Moreover, the meaning attaching to the phrase ' to know ' a wife cannot be separated from the object of that knowledge and transferred to knowledge in general. The knowledge of concupiscence which followed the sin is adequately explained whatever the nature of the sin, for, on any hypothesis, it was an act of rebellion against the dominion of God, who in just punishment withdrew the gift of integrity and allowed our first parents to suffer the rebellion of their own lower nature and to know its influence anticipating the control of reason. God had blessed the union of the sexes ; he had created Eve precisely to be the necessary counterpart of Adam ; he wished the human race to increase and multiply. St Augustine pours scorn on the idea : ' ridiculum illud est ', *loc. cit.* The fact is that the story presents no satisfactory basis for any sexual interpretation. It is true that there are allusions to matters of sex just as there are to the procurement of food and eating. Both being fundamental in human life and both being adversely affected by the first sin, neither could be omitted from the account. The punishment of pain in childbirth affects the woman only whereas a sexual sin would have been common to both. These pains are the outstanding characteristic of woman's lot as the labour of procuring bodily nourishment in the sweat of his brow is characteristic of that of man. Each is punished according to natural disposition. As regards the trees, given the general inter-

pretation proposed, § 143*f*, there does not seem to be **145b** any cogent reason for looking beyond the surface suggestion of the narrative (see on 2:9) for any specific symbolism. It appears that the sacred writer had received no revelation as to the exact nature of the first sin, and, it being difficult to conceive to what but sin but pride and disobedience man in a state of innocence, with his lower nature entirely subject to reason, could be exposed, he represented the moral fall of man in a way suggested by the paradise in which he lived. The gravity of the sin lies in the fact that it is equivalent to the proud refusal ' I will not serve ', Jer 2:20.

In view of the apparent connection of the story with **c** Mesopotamia it might be expected that some similar account would be found in that region. Actually **no such story in Sumerian or Babylonian literature has** been found among the tens of thousands of tablets recovered. The story of Paradise and the Fall appears to have been unknown among those peoples. Certain elements of the story, however, are found among the Babylonians. This is not surprising as the sacred writer uses for his own sublime purpose symbols and ideas current in his time. The Babylonians were familiar with a tree or plant of life. There is, however, no moral purpose in Gilgamesh's being deprived of this plant by a serpent. A scene depicting Adam, Eve, a tree and the serpent was once supposed to be engraved on a certain cylinder seal. Such sensational interpretations are not uncommon when archaeological discoveries first become known. The scene probably represents two gods standing by the tree of life together with a serpent associated to their cult. See A. Condamin, S.J., DAFC I 339–42, esp. 341 ; also E. A. Wallis Budge, *The Babylonian Legends of the Creation* (1931) 74 ; A. Deimel, S.J., ' De Serpentibus in Religione Babyloniorum ' VD 4 (1924) 342 ff. ; J. de Fraine, S.J., ' Paradisus apud Sumeros ? ' VD 25 (1947) 161–71.

The punishment inflicted by God for the sin of Adam **d** and Eve was accompanied by a promise of victory over the powers of evil. This first announcement of good tidings to fallen man is commonly called **the Protoevangelium**, 15. The force of the prediction is not exhausted by the hostility foretold between mankind and the serpents. The serpent symbolized the power of evil (see on 3:1) and God promises that he will put enmity between it and the woman and their respective seeds. The initiative is therefore taken by God, which is itself a guarantee of continued divine help and of final victory. The words were spoken in the presence of Adam and Eve and were intended to be understood by them, though not necessarily in the fullness of their signification. In the circumstances as they knew of no other woman, they could not understand by ' the woman ' any other than Eve herself. Similarly the readers for whom Genesis was originally intended could have understood no one else, as no other woman is mentioned in the context either before or after. (It is true that Hebrew uses a definite form of speech, where we use the indef. art., as in Jg 4:21 where MT has ' the *peg* ', obviously not the only peg holding the tent but made definite as the peg used by Jahel ; but this construction is only possible where the context does not indicate exclusively one person or thing.) In the case of the devil ' seed ' is doubly metaphorical as his ' offspring ' are the spiritual beings who follow his leadership. Now as the seed of the serpent is collective, so also is the seed of the woman ; and Eve ' was the mother of all the living ', 3:20. God promises enmity, therefore, between the human race on the one hand and the devil and his spiritual accomplices on the other. God promises further that the seed (see on 3:15) shall crush the head of the serpent-devil, which denotes complete and final victory for the human race. The promise is made to the race collectively and not individually. It is for each one with the help of God and his own free will to ensure that he shares in the blessing promised to all. Then to the serpent God says that it will wound the heel of the seed or offspring of the woman. It will be able

145d to inflict minor but not fatal injury. This, therefore, is a most consoling promise of final victory for all unless they choose freely to rank themselves among the seed of the devil, Mt 3:7, Jn 8:44. But how and by what means and under whose leadership this victory was to be achieved was not yet revealed and became clear only with the gradual progress of revelation ; see J. Corluy, S.J., *Spicilegium Dogmatico-Biblicum* I (1884) 367.

e It is clear, however, in the full light of later revelation that what has been said does not exhaust the full meaning of the prophecy. For Jesus Christ was not only part of the human race to whom victory was thus promised, he was not only its leader in the victorious struggle, the victory was rendered possible solely by him. ' For this purpose the Son of God appeared that he might destroy the works of the devil ', 1 Jn 3:8. So too St Paul teaches that Christ became man that ' he might destroy him who had the empire of death, that is to say, the devil ', Heb 2:14. But the victory is ours with Christ. So St Paul alluding to the Protoevangelium : ' The God of peace crush Satan under your feet speedily ', Rom 16:20. But we are one with Christ, he the head and we the members. ' He saith not, And to his seeds, as of many, but as of one, And to thy seed, which is Christ ', Gal 3:16. Yet after this emphatic statement that the seed is one and is Christ, Paul goes on to say that if they are Christ's, the faithful are also the seed, 3:29 ; *cf.* Rom 9:7 f. This rests on the doctrine of the spiritual union of all in Christ's Mystical Body. In this true sense, as St Paul teaches, Christ is the seed. And from this it follows that the Woman is his Blessed Mother. This follows also from the typical relation existing between Eve and Mary, a relationship on which the Fathers loved to dwell and which is summed up in her title of the Second Eve. As Eve was the mother of all the living in the physical order, so Mary is the Mother of all the living in the spiritual order, just as Christ for an analogous reason is the Second Adam having in the first Adam ' a figure of him who was to come ', Rom 5:14. These considerations explain, as it seems, why the prophecy is addressed, not as we should have expected to Adam, the head of the race, but to Eve, and why use is made of the unusual expression of the seed of the woman. *Cf.* Sutcliffe, CR 2 (1931) 149–60.

146a IV 1–16 Cain's Murder of Abel—**1.** There are many popular etymologies of names in Gen. In the present instance the name seems rather to have been chosen as having a suitable assonance with Eve's utterance (*Qayin*, prob. ' smith ', *qānîtî*, ' I have got '). Eve sets an example to parents in gratefully acknowledging her indebtedness to God. **2.** Abel's name is the same in form as *hebel* ' breath ' and metaphorically ' what is evanescent, worthless ', but it is likely that this word was chosen to express the shortness of his life before it had acquired a disparaging sense. **4.** ' of their fat ' ; *cf.* Num 18:17. On similar occasions God showed his favour by consuming the offering by fire from heaven, Lev 9:24, Jg 6:21. **5.** We may deduce from God's displeasure that Cain had already been guilty of sin, as in fact St John teaches saying that Cain killed his brother ' because his own works were wicked and his brother's just ', 1 Jn 3:12 ; *cf.* Heb 11:4. **7.** ' If thou do well, *will there not be forgiveness ?* ' ; *cf.* 18:26 for the meaning of the verb. Sin is represented as an animal crouching at the door and ready to spring. ' *It shall lust after thee, but thou canst have the mastery over it* '. Note that man has free will and can overcome all appeals of evil ; also that one sin not repented prepares the way for other and greater sins, as actually happened in the case of Cain. **10.** For the other sins which cry to God for vengeance see 19:13, Ex 2:23, 3:9 ; Jas 5:4. **14.** Cain is driven forth from the area of cultivated ground. In biblical language when God is angry, he hides his face, Ps 29:8. Cain speaks as if he would no longer be under God's protecting care. The murder took place when there was already a large population. Seth was born after the murder, 25,

when Adam was 130 years old, 5:3. God had blessed **14** the race and commanded them to increase and multiply 1:28, and Adam begot unnamed and unnumbered sons and daughters, 5:4. As the story is told, therefore, in 130 years the number of men and women would have increased very considerably. **15.** ' sevenfold ' means ' severely '. The mark set on Cain showed that he belonged to God, was under his protection, and therefore could not be touched. It was an ancient custom for slaves attached to a temple to be marked with the emblem of their deity ; *cf.* Herod. 2, 113. **16.** ' and dwelt *in the land of Nod* ', which is otherwise unknown. The name suggests a land of wanderers or nomads.

This narrative shows how quickly after the first trans- **b** gression sin gained a hold in the world. It teaches how hateful to God the sin of murder and in particular of fratricide is ; how smaller sins, if neglected, lead on to greater ; that man is always master of and responsible for his actions ; that God is the just ruler of the world who cannot allow evil to go unpunished. On the historical character of the episode see §138c–d.

17–24 The Story of the Cainites—Biblical narratives **c** do not always follow chronological order. Matters are sometimes grouped according to subject, independently of whether they are in part earlier than events narrated earlier or later than others set forth subsequently. Thus the birth of Henoch, 17, will have occurred before the murder of Abel. Similarly, as the sacred writer wishes to put down here all he has to say about the Cainites and to leave them out of his story, part of the account may well refer to events after the Flood. This will be the case with the invention of metal-working.

17. ' As there were no human beings except those **d** born (of Adam and Eve) men took their sisters in marriage. This practice owes its early origin to necessity and its later culpability to the prohibition of religion ', St Augustine, *De Civ. Dei*, xv, 16. The ' city ' denotes a collection of dwellings surrrounded by some defensive work ; *cf.* § 138c. Cain was not accompanied in his banishment by his family and he feared that an attempt might be made to take revenge on them. **19.** The beginning of polygamy, a departure from strict morality on the part of the Cainites. **20.** Abel had been a shepherd ; Jabel introduced the nomadic life of herdsmen. His name in the older tradition of LXX was Jobel (Yobel) and denotes him as one leading his flocks in their migrations. **21.** ' *pipe* ' (DV ' organs '). The name Jubal (Yubal) is prob. connected with *yōbēl* ' ram's horn, cornet,' whence our ' jubilee '. **22.** Cain signifies ' smith ', the name again being chosen to suit the invention. The discovery of metal-working long antecedes the ' Ages ' named after them (Early Bronze ending *c* 2000 B.C., and the Iron Age beginning 1200 B.C.). According to Prof. Henry Louis, ' it appears to be generally held that iron was first produced in workable quantity on the southern flanks of the Caucasus, and the date assigned is usually somewhere about 3000 B.C.', *Nature* (18 May 1929) 762. But before the metal became available in any quantity the method of working it will for long have been preserved as a strict family or clan secret, as is implied in this story of Lamech. That with Lamech we reach proto-historical times after the Flood (see § 146c) is also indicated by the mention of Noema. The apparently pointless insertion of this name is explained if it rested on an ancient tradition which was set down as remembered. **23.** ' *Ada and Sella, hear my voice ; ye wives of Lamech, hearken to my speech ; for I kill the man who woundeth me and the youth who striketh me ; for sevenfold vengeance is taken for Cain but for Lamech seventy and sevenfold* '. This most ancient verse is already marked by the parallelism so characteristic of Heb. poetry. Lamech is in possession of new and formidable weapons far superior to the clubs and stones at the disposal of possible aggressors. As it was God himself who had promised vengeance

6d to Cain, Lamech's words are tinged with blasphemy, as well as a spirit of unbridled vengeance.

e Two characteristics stand out in the history of the Cainites. Nothing morally good is told of them, only evil—murder, polygamy, contempt of human life, the spirit of vengeance, irreverent speech about God. On the other hand, they excel in the arts of material human progress. To them is attributed the first ' city ', the craft of the herdsman leading a nomadic life, the invention of musical instruments, and the discovery of metal-working. These are not condemned ; they are good uses of the creatures put by God at man's disposal. But the lesson is clear. The more man gives himself to his material needs and temporal betterment, the greater the danger of his losing sight of his moral obligations. And in the extreme case, a life of luxury is unlikely to be one of virtue.

f 25-26 The History of Seth—25. The connection of this section with the preceding is that Seth was the first to be born to Adam after the murder of Abel. His name (Sheth) seems to be chosen to give the required assonance with *shath* (DV ' hath given '). In this verse ' Adam ' is used for the first time as a proper name. Previously he has been spoken of as ' the man ' = *hā-'ādām*. The massoretic vocalization is faulty in 2:20 and 3:17. **26.** ' Enosh ' means ' man '. ' Yahweh ' here has prob. supplanted original ' God ' : ' *then men began to be called by the name of God* '. So probably. This refers only to the Sethites whose genealogy is traced back to God in ch 5 and who in 6:2 are called ' the sons of God '. For the construction *cf.* Is 44:5.

g V 1-31 The Genealogy of the Sethites—The entirely new start which repeats even the creation of Adam shows that the Cainites are now dismissed from the story and that it is concerned now solely with the Sethites. On the numbers see § 140*b*–*e*. The Babylonians similarly listed ten antediluvian kings with immensely long reigns. The first, Alulim, is credited with 67,200 years, and his successor Alagar with 72,000 ; see B. Meissner, *Babylonien und Assyrien*, 2 (1925) 439. The names were chosen for reasons which escape us. The meaning of most is conjectural and the vocalization is sometimes uncertain. Malaleel means ' Praise of God '.

h 1. 'Document' or 'register' (DV 'book'). 'Adam' is here 'man, mankind', as is shown in 2 where it is said that God created them male and female and 'called their name *man*'. In 3 it again occurs as a proper name. The likeness to God which Adam himself received he passed on to Seth, who, it is implied, transmitted it to his descendants. This is not said of the race of the Cainites. **22.** Henoch was a man of markedly virtuous life, which is the meaning of ' he walked with God ' ; *cf.* 6:9. See Ecclus 44:16 ; 49:16 ; Wis 4:10–14. ' By faith Henoch was translated that he should not see death ', Heb 11:5. He and Elias are commonly understood to be the two witnesses of Apoc 11:3–14. **29.** ' This same shall *give us rest* ', so LXX in agreement with the name Noe ' rest ', prob. an allusion to Noe's cultivation of the vine, 9:20. **31.** Noe's three sons were not necessarily all born in the same year.

i VI 1-8 The Wickedness of the Sethites calls for Divine Chastisement—The narrative continues exclusively with the Sethites, whose genealogy has just been given, ch 5 ; *cf.* § 136*f*–*h*. As this traced their line back to God, whose likeness was transmitted by Adam to his offspring, Seth, this exclusive reference is indicated also by the title ' sons of God ' given to his descendants, 2. Universal expressions are here again, according to Heb. idiom, to be understood only of the subject-matter in hand.

j 1. ' after that ' is a conjunction. **2.** ' Sons of God ' is used of the Angels in Job, chh 1–2, but it is illegitimate to introduce this late use into this passage against the context both immediate and remote. Here it signifies the Sethites ; see just above. Women are styled ' the

daughters of man ', not because they do not figure in **146j** the genealogy but because the Sethites in their licentious polygamy took to wife whosoever pleased their fancy. **3.** The reference cannot be to the length of individual lives because the sentence of mortality had already been passed on man and many are reported later to have lived much longer than 120 years. The word ' man ' is here collective = ' mankind ', and the ' spirit of God ' = the breath of life, 2:7, Ps 103:29 f. The 120 years is the period allowed to man for repentance before the divine chastisement of the Flood is to come upon him ; *cf.* Jon 3:4. The number of 120 years as a respite for repentance is prob. to be explained as = 2 × 60, the Babylonian *soss* being = 60 (whence our 60 minutes and 60 seconds). **4.** ' *The* **k** *Nephilim* were upon the earth in those days, *and also after that*, when the sons of God. . . .' The Nephilim are mentioned Num 13:34 (MT 33) as a Canaanite race of giants in Moses' time ; hence the clause ' and also after that ', which is in origin a marginal gloss. The meaning and etymology of the name are unknown. They are referred to in Wis 14:6, Ecclus 16:8, Bar 3:26–8, etc. The term ' giants ' does not imply more than unusually tall stature, and its import is relative to the average height of the race using it. The Hebrews were not a tall nation. Tradition of old preserved stories of their exploits but these have long since perished. **6.** God does not change, Num 23:19, and the phrase is anthropomorphic. In like circumstances a man would regret what he had done. **7.** If men perish in a flood, the animal life of the region perishes also. **8.** Noe was the one man untouched by the corruption of the age.

VI 9-VIII 14 The Flood—9. ' perfect man *among his* **147a** *contemporaries* '. **11.** Men were corrupt in the sight of and in the judgement of God. **13.** ' with the earth ', with all that lives and grows on the earth, as in 11 ' the earth ' stands for the men living upon it. **14.** ' *of gopher wood* ', occurring only here. Pitch is still used in Iraq for making vessels water-tight, as of course elsewhere. **15.** The cubit is a natural measure of length = the forearm ; *cf.* foot. **16.** The opening for light and air was to be a cubit in height and to run round the sides of the ark (broken by the beams supporting the roof) high up under the projecting roof and so protected from the rain. So prob., though some for ' window ' translate ' roof '. **17.** ' *from* under heaven . . . *on* the earth '. **19.** ' *pairs* ' (DV ' two ') ; also in 20. VII:3. ' *pairs* ' (DV ' two and two '). The distinction between clean and unclean animals is of great antiquity and was incorporated into the Law as already sanctioned by custom, Lev 11:47, and *cf.* § 189*b*. **11.** LXX : ' 27th day '. The subterranean ocean broke through its vents and the upper waters, 1:7, were given free passage through the sluices in the firmament. There appears to be an ocean under the earth since water gushes out in many places as at the sources of the Jordan. This invasion of the land by subterranean waters implies not the inroad of the ocean, but the rising waters of the rivers, the Tigris and Euphrates, flooding the country. **12.** ' 40 ' is often used in the Bible for a large indefinite number ; see § 124*l*. **14.** ' all birds and all that fly ' is not in LXX and is prob. a marginal gloss. **17.** ' And the flood *broke upon* the earth '. ' forty days ' is another marginal gloss to which LXX add ' and forty nights '. **VIII:2.** Chronological order is not **b** always observed by Hebrew writers. The flood gates were shut up after forty days, 7:12. **3.** ' *Little by little* ' the waters diminished (DV ' coming and going '), ' and they *were* abated ' after 150 days, which counted from the 17th (LXX 27th) day of the 2nd month, 7:11, lead to the day, **4,** when the ark came to rest on the 17th (MT ; 27th Vg, LXX) day of the 7th month. MT ' the mountains of Ararat ', Accadian Urartu, a region corresponding to Armenia but extending further to the South. The reference is to the country and not to the mountain called Ararat today. ' Mountain ' is a relative term and varies in its application in different countries. In a flat country like Mesopotamia, the

147b word could be used in cases where it would be inadmissible in English just as most English mountains would not be so called by the French. The ark rested on top of a hill, as, **5**, the waters '*decreased gradually*' and allowed the tops of the hills to appear only in the 10th month. **6.** According to Heb. idiom the sense may be either the window' or 'a window' (= the window which he actually opened ; *cf.* § 145*d*). The word *ḥallôn* used here = 'window' is not subject to the doubt mentioned on 6:16. 'a raven *to see whether the waters were abated*'; with LXX. **7.** It 'went forth *to and fro*'. The negative, absent in MT, was added in Vg from the Old Latin. Ravens and crows were used by ancient mariners to find the direction of land in case they were driven out of their course. See H. Heras, S.J., '"The Crow" of Noe' CBQ 10 (1948) 131-9. **8.** The original text prob. stated that Noe waited first for 7 days, as is implied by 10. **11.** '*a twig*' of olive. Noe now knew that the waters had largely drained away. **13.** 'the waters were *dried up from off* the earth'. After the waters had disappeared from the surface of the earth, Noe had still to wait till, **14**, the earth itself had dried. Counting the day on which Noe entered the ark and the day he left it, the flood lasted a lunar year (= 354 days) + 11 days, which make a solar year of 365 days. **20.** In holocausts the whole victim was consumed by fire.

c **The Extent of the Flood**—The universal expressions used in the narrative referring alike to men, beasts, and sky, and even it was thought to the earth, long gave the impression that the flood covered the whole of the earth's surface and therefore necessarily involved the destruction of the entire human race and of the whole of the brute creation. This is called the theory of geographical universality. It arose at a time when the idiomatic usages of Hebrew speech were unfamiliar and the facts about the extent of the earth and the vast number of animal species were unknown. At the beginning of the 19th cent. it still held the field largely owing to the support of eminent geologists like Buckland who found in erratic blocks and striated rock-surfaces evidence of a worldwide deluge. Sea-shells high up on mountains, as on Moel Tryfaen in N. Wales, were also brought into the argument. But later the geologists, including Buckland, came to recognize that the boulder formation, the 'diluvium' as it was called, and the striated rocks were due to the action of glaciers. It was also recognized that no flood, however severe, but only changes in the level of the earth's surface could account for the deep deposits of marine shells found high on certain mountains. The idea of a world-wide deluge was then gradually abandoned by all. A series of unheard of miracles would have been required to bring the animals from all over the world, to house them, to keep them alive in a climate strange for most, to return them to their natural habitats. For such miracles the sacred text affords no evidence, as universal expressions in the Bible are used with reference to the subject matter in hand as in the case of 'all the beasts of the earth', 2:19, by which is meant all those in Paradise.

d A new theory then arose called that of mixed universality. According to this a limited region of the earth's surface was inundated but all mankind perished except those in the ark, as the race was supposed not yet to have spread beyond the boundaries of that region. The universal expressions were thus interpreted in a double sense. Those referring to the sky, the earth and the animal kingdom were taken to signify relative universality, whereas those referring to mankind were understood absolutely. As there is nothing in the text to warrant this distinction, it gradually became plain that the norm of relative universality must be applied in both cases.

e It has thus become ever more widely recognized that all the sacred writer's expressions in this narrative were intended in the sense of relative universality. Of this he has given some clear indications. 'Noe was a just and perfect man', but 'all flesh had corrupted its way', 6:9, 12 ; Noe and his family were safe, yet 'all

men' perished in the waters, 7:7, 21 ; even after 'the **14** tops of the mountains appeared', 'the waters were upon the whole earth', 8:5, 9. Moreover, from 5:1 the narrative is concerned with the Sethites alone (*cf.* §§ 136*f-h*, 146*g*) the Cainites having been dismissed from the story. And the attribution of certain inventions to the Cainites in ch 4 implies that these did not perish in the flood. Indeed, in the case of metal-working it is probable that the invention in the mind of the sacred writer dates from after the flood and that his mention of it before that event is due simply to the desire to group in one section all that he had to say about the Cainites and their eponym. In either case it follows that the Cainites did not perish in the flood. Further, in view of the insistence shown by the sacred writer on the multiplication of the race by the repeated declaration that each of the patriarchs begot 'sons and daughters', and that he allows so long a period between Adam and the flood (MT 1656 years, Samaritan text 1307, LXX 2256), it is hardly to be assumed that he thought all men could still be living in one region. In fact, the text indicates the contrary, for God not only gave the command to increase and multiply, but also to 'fill the earth', 1:28. This argument is not weakened by any theory about sources for the reason that we are concerned with the book as finished by its compiler and therefore with the sense which he has impressed on the whole. The mind of the sacred writer as thus manifested by himself is in agreement with discoveries in the field of anthropology as human remains have been discovered in various parts of the world, from China to South Africa, dating from times long anterior to any date which can be assigned to the flood.

See further Al. Motais, *Le Déluge biblique* (Paris, 1885), E. F. Sutcliffe, S.J., *Who perished in the Flood?* (CTS 1943, reprint 1947), Hummelauer, who gives a full historical account of the question, 223-56.

The Ark as Type of the Church—It was a common- **f** place among the Fathers that the ark was a type or figure of the Church ; and see 1 Pet 3:20. As the ark was the divinely appointed means of temporal salvation for Noe and his family, so the Church is the divinely appointed means of eternal salvation ; *cf.* St Cyprian, *De Unitate Ecclesiae* 6 (PL 4, 503), St Jerome, *Epist. 15 ad Damasum* 2 (PL 22, 355) ; St Augustine, *Contra Faust. Man.* 12, 14 (PL 42, 262). The fact that the Church is appointed by divine providence as the ordinary means of grace does not exclude God's extraordinary providence by which all who are not members of the visible Church but sincerely desire to do God's will as far as it is known to them also receive his grace and all that is necessary for salvation. This significance of the ark is not invalidated by the relative universality of the flood as in both figure and antitype the means of salvation have reference to all exposed to danger, in the one case physical and in the other spiritual. The outstanding difference between the type and the antitype is that in the type the means of salvation were offered only to a few, in the antitype they are offered to all.

The Purpose of the Flood—This was twofold. It was **14** the punishment of the wicked, 6:12 f., to whom a period of time had been allowed for repentance, 6:3 and 1 Pet 3:20 'when *the patience of God waited* in the days of Noe'. Unlike the Ninevites to whom also a time for repentance was allowed, Jon 3:4, the sinners of Noe's time paid no heed to the warning available to them at the sight of Noe's prolonged labour in the construction of the ark. The flood was likewise the means of freeing 'the sons of God' from the danger of the corruption which surrounded them. To apply the words of Wis 4:14, God 'hastened to bring (them) out of the midst of iniquities'. The ancestors of the Chosen People were thus given the opportunity to bring up a new generation in virtuous surroundings. With this we may compare God's order to Abraham to leave his home and restart life in a new land, 12:1.

Literary Criticism—The question whether the biblical **b**

48b narrative of the flood is conflated out of two separate accounts has been answered in the affirmative, *e.g.* by Heinisch, Ceuppens, Chaine, and in the negative by, *e.g.* Hummelauer, Hoberg, Bea. There are numerous repetitions which make it possible to disentangle at least the main outlines of two stories. At first sight this is itself convincing. But when it is noticed that even after the dissection has been carried through, the repetitions are still numerous, the conviction begins to grow that the repetitious style was deliberately chosen to heighten the dramatic effect. That the Hebrews had a predilection for repetition is clear from the parallelism characteristic of their poetry. In the parts assigned to P by Chaine it will be found that in 6:9–12 (after the heading of the section) each verse falls into two halves marked by parallelism, and that there are repetitions in 6:11 + 12 ; 13 + 17 ; 19 + 20 ; 7:18 + 19 + 24 ; 19 + 20 (the covering of the mountains) ; 8:17 + 9: 1 + 7 ; 9:9 + 11. Again though 7:13 seems to us to follow strangely on 7:12, neither does it follow easily on 7:11 (both P), nor does 8:2a on 8:1 (both P). Moreover, there are no contradictions. In 6:19 pairs of all animals are to be taken into the ark : in 7:2 this is made specific—there are to be 7 pairs of clean and one pair of unclean. The rain of 7:4 does not exclude the irruption of subterranean waters of 7:11. This mode of not excluding but of prescinding from some fact is distinctively Hebraic ; *cf.* the one and the two blind men at Jericho in the Gospels, where one does not exclude two. These ancient oriental writings have too often been judged by modern western ideas. ' It often happens that they do not at once set forth the whole of a narrative as the laws of logic and historical sequence would require, but they proceed with it as by stages, almost in the manner of concentric circles. Details which chronologically belong earlier, are " supplied " later in the narrative or another part or other circumstances of the same fact are added ', Bea 78. This trick of going back on the story to add new information is called by the Germans ' Nachholung ' and is acknowledged by Heinisch 176. The exact dating by years, months and days is probably due to the editor who added the years of the lives of the later patriarchs.

c **The Babylonian Flood and its Date**—In Babylonian tradition a great flood was recognized to have caused a break in the history of the country, and in the list of kings the first ten are recorded to have reigned before it. It is described in the 11th tablet of the Gilgamesh epic. See R. Campbell Thompson, *The Epic of Gilgamish* (1928) ; Brit. Mus., *The Babylonian Story of the Deluge* ; A. Deimel's Lat. trans. in VD 7 (1927) 186 ff. There are striking similarities and there is no doubt that the event is that of the biblical narrative. The boat is smeared with pitch and grounds on Mt Nizir. Birds are sent out, though in a different order, and after the flood the gods smell the sweet savour of the sacrifice offered. But there are also striking differences. The Babylonian story is crassly polytheistic and has no moral purpose. The gods are at variance among themselves ; they are stricken with terror at the deluge ; they assemble like flies round the sacrifice. The flood last for seven days only ; numerous persons are saved with the hero Utanapishtim. Neither account is dependent on the other, but both go back to a common source.

d Excavations in Mesopotamia have revealed the traces of several severe floods ; *cf.* H. Peake, *The Flood : New Light on an Old Story* (1930) ; E. Burrows, S.J., ' The Discovery of the Deluge ' in DbR 186 (1930) 1–20. At Kish S. Langdon discovered three dated provisionally 3400, 4000 and 4200 B.C. respectively. At Ur Sir Leonard Woolley found 11 feet of water-laid material, witness of a flood so prolonged that its identification with that of tradition at once suggested itself. Peake considered this flood to be identical with the most ancient found at Kish. E. Burrows dated it some 400 years later, *c* 3800. A date much more remote than this appears unlikely for the flood of biblical and Babylonian tradition, the memory of which remained

so fresh. The identification suggested, if correct, would **148d** provide the first, though only approximate date in biblical history. Opinion, however, has moved away from that first adopted. *J. Finegan, *Light from the Ancient Past* (Princeton, 1947) 24, speaks with reserve : ' It is difficult to say '. *Millar Burrows, *What Mean these Stones* (New Haven, 1941) 70 writes : ' The lower one [at Kish] is ascribed by Langdon to about 4000 B.C., and it is this one which he equates with the Ur inundation. None of the inundations at Kish, however, is contemporary with any at Ur, and none at either place marks a division between two different civilizations. . . In Woolley's own excavation at Tell Obeid, only four miles from Ur, there was no silt at the levels corresponding to those at which it was found at Ur '. The further argument that ' representations of Gilgamesh were found at a lower level than the " deluge " at Kish, showing that the Babylonian flood-story was of more ancient origin than this ', seems to overlook the fact that the two traditions may have become fused at a later date.

IX 1–17 God's Covenant with Noe—This covenant **149a** was followed by that with Abraham which again was succeeded by that with Moses and the people of Israel. These three covenants are three great landmarks in the history of God's providential preparation and election of Israel. Noe was saved out of a mass of corruption to raise up a new people pleasing to God. Abraham was taken from the pagan enticements of Mesopotamia to the isolation of nomadic life in Canaan. Moses with the people was delivered from Egypt to enter as a nation into the land destined to be their home. **3.** Now for the first time permission is explicitly given **b** to eat meat. The suggestion seems to be that as the thought of man's heart is prone to evil from his youth, 8:21, he would not acquiesce in that respect for the lives of brute creatures demanded by vegetarianism. **4.** An animal that loses its blood loses its life, ' for the life of all flesh is in the blood '. Lev 17:14 ; and life is made by God and is sacred to him. Therefore, although man may kill animals for his needs, he is to pay tribute to God's overlordship by abstaining from blood. This prohibition, re-enacted in the Mosaic law, was rigorously observed in NT times, Ac 15:20 f. **5.** The sanctity of human life is inculcated by the provision that any animal killing a man is itself to be destroyed, Ex 21:28. **6.** So, too, permission is given to take the life of a murderer : ' *by man* shall his blood be shed '. **13.** The rainbow is aptly chosen as sign of the covenant as rain from heaven had been one of the causes of the flood. It is now given a new significance.

18–29 The Blessing of Sem and the Curse on Canaan c **—21.** The Fathers excuse Noe on the ground of his ignorance of the effect of wine. **24.** The detail of the story seems to have been discreetly passed over in silence. ' his *youngest* son ' : from the order of the names Cham appears to be the second in age, and this ' son ' must be Noe's grandson, Canaan, who is the one actually cursed. **25.** ' a servant of servants ' = the lowliest of servants, according to this Heb. idiom for expressing the superlative ; *cf.* king of kings, canticle of canticles. (The origin of the papal title ' Servant of the servants of God ' is different, Sutcliffe CR 6 [1933] 378–86.) The curse figures the condition of the Canaanites on the completion of the Israelite conquest of their land. **26.** The second Messianic prophecy by which the line of Sem, as distinct from those of Cham and Japheth, is marked out for God's especial blessing and protection. ' Lord ' stands for ' Yahweh ' by which God was known only to the Israelites, the descendants of Sem, whereas in **27**, as the Japhethites had no part in the worship of Yahweh, the word used is ' God '. ' enlarge ' is in Heb. a play on the name of Japheth and refers to his prosperity in general just as ' straitened circumstances ' denotes the opposite. ' Dwelling in the tents of Sem ' denotes friendly relations and a willingness on Sem's part to share his privileges.

X 1–32 The Table of the Nations—The sons of Noe **d**

149d are enumerated in the order, Sem, Cham, Japheth, 5:31; 6:10; 7:13; 9:18; 10:1; but in this list of their 'descendants' the order is reversed, Japheth, Cham, Sem. The explanation is provided by the compiler's scheme of gradual elimination. The Japhethites and Chamites are to have no place in the main thread of the story which hereafter is to be narrowed down to the Semites only. These are therefore placed last in order to establish a connexion with the sequel of the narrative.

e The purpose of the list is to emphasize the privilege conferred on Israel in its election by God as his special people. Other nations might have been chosen. On any human estimate others had a far stronger claim in virtue of their greater antiquity, population, political power and more advanced culture. Israel was a newcomer among the nations. Jacob had gone down to Egypt with only a few score of his descendants when the civilization of that country was already ancient. Yet of all these peoples God cast his eyes on Israel. It is in the manner of Genesis to state the facts simply and to leave the reader to draw the conclusions which the story suggests.

f In the form of a genealogy the list contains the names of countries as Egypt (Misraim) and Canaan; of peoples as the Jebusites and the Amorites; and even of a city, Sidon, 15, 19, begotten by Canaan, the country in which it lay. Nations are not normally descended from a single ancestor, and even the Israelites, whose dominant stock rightly claimed Abraham as their ancestor, were of mixed race, for it is noted in Ex 12:38 that when they left Egypt there went with them 'a mixed multitude'.

g The principle of division is largely geographical. The Japhethites living in the farther north and west, the Chamites in the south including Canaan, and the Semites the intervening regions and the east. Some of the names cannot be identified with our present knowledge, others only conjecturally, and for a full discussion the reader is directed to one of the recent larger commentaries. The peoples of farther Asia and of America being unknown to the Israelites have no place in the list, nor have several peoples mentioned in Gen, as the Emim and Zuzim.

h 2-5 The Sons of Japheth—2. Cimmerians (Gomer), Medes (Madai), Ionians (Javan). **4.** Perhaps Cyprus (Elisa), Tarshish = Tartessus (in Spain), Dardanoi (MT Dodanim) or Rhodians (LXX, Sam, Rhodanim).

i 6-20 The Sons of Cham—6. Ethiopia (Kush), Egypt (Misraim), Canaan. **7.** Prob. all near the Red Sea and Gulf of Aden. **8.** Nemrod prob. = Nimurta, god of war and hunting, identified by Witzel with Gilgamesh, a deified king of the second postdiluvian dynasty, and by Deimel with Lugalbanda, another king of the same dynasty. **10.** Babylon was famous already in the time of Sargon I, c 2850 B.C. Uruk, today Warka, on the Euphrates. Akkad was the name of N. Mesopotamia (Sumerian, Agade) and also of the capital of Sargon I. Shinar (Sennaar) = Babylonia. **11.** Prob. ' out of that land *he went forth to Assyria* '; *cf.* Mic 5:6 where ' the land of Nemrod ' = Assyria. Nineveh, Rehoboth-Ir, and Calah which is now the ruined site called Nimrud at the confluence of the Upper Zab with the Tigris. **12.** Nineveh is ' the great city '. The gloss is misplaced. **8-12** is an insertion in the original text and also apparently misplaced, since, if Kush in 6 is territory S. of Egypt, as it seems to be, there can hardly be a connection with the origins of Babylonia and Assyria. And Kush (Chus) in 8 would rather refer to the Kashshu or Kassites who conquered and ruled Babylonia in the 2nd millennium

j B.C. **14.** The Philistines (§ 120*h–i*) came from Caphtor, Mic 9:7, which is Crete. The Chasluim are unknown, and if they were a larger unit of which the Caphtorim were a part, the mention of the Philistines in their present position would be explained. **15.** Canaan here in its wider sense embracing Phoenicia, the most important town of which in the earlier period was Sidon. The term Hittite is prob. used to signify also

the Hurrians (§ 118*i–j*). **16-17.** *Cf.* § 57*d*. Arka, Sin, **149** and **18**, Arvad and Semar on the Phoenician coast. Hamath on the Orontes. **19.** The W. boundary of Canaan ran from Sidon to Gaza, which the traveller would reach first as he went S. to Gerar, and the S. boundary from Gaza to Lesha in the direction of Sodom and Gomorrha (prob. at the S. end of the Dead Sea). *Cf.* 14:2.

21-31 The Sons of Sem—21. The expression ' all the **k** children of Heber ' suggests that the term ' Hebrews ' had a wider significance than ' Israelites ' and that the Israelites were part of a larger group of Hebrew peoples. **22.** Elam, in the earliest times inhabited by Semites, was later conquered by a non-Semitic people. Lud, uncertain, but not the Lydians. The Aramaeans were widely spread N. of Palestine. In the OT modern Syria is always called Aram. **15.** Phaleg denotes ' division '. The reference is to 11:8 f. **26-30** give the names of Arabian tribes and regions. Asarmoth, today Hadramaut. Solomon carried on a valuable trade with Ophir, 3 Kg 9:28; 10:11, 22.

XI 1-9 The Tower of Babel—In accordance with the **l** scheme of elimination already explained (§ 136*f–h*) this narrative is concerned only with Semites, and not with all of them as at the time (indicated vaguely in 10:25) of the dispersal there recorded there is no reason to doubt that the Semites were already widely distributed, and the universal expressions used must by Hebrew idiom be understood with the restrictions imposed by the narrative itself. See on 2:5, 19 and §§146*i*, 147*e*. S. H. Langdon wrote : ' The kings of Kish in the age of Mesilim left written records at Nippur, Lagash and Adab, which prove that these Sumerian cities belonged to a Semite kingdom in the north as early as 3650 B.C. ', CAH I 373. Meissner dated this 2nd dynasty of Kish about 3250. The age of Babylon itself can be estimated from its sacred character in the time of Sargon about 2850. He took soil from this holy city of Marduk therewith to consecrate his new capital city of Agade, CAH I 407. Such veneration shows that Babylon was already ancient in Sargon's time and points to a date well in the 4th millennium. There the inhabitants started to build a great stage-tower or ziggurat, which they raised to some considerable height and then were unable to complete. The massive remains were a visible reminder of the ineffectual attempt which tradition recorded to have been accompanied by discord and consequent migration of many of the population. This meagre historical record explains why the sacred writer did not mention the nature of the sin which led to the frustration of the grandiose design. But his deep conviction of God's overruling government of the world taught him that the attempt had been displeasing to God and the narrative suggests that the sin was one of overweening human pride and self-sufficiency.

The text does not say that the ziggurat was actually **m** in the city of Babylon and is probably that at Borsippa, today Birs-Nimrud, some 7 m. from the site of Babylon. Of this Nabuchodonosor (Nebuchadnezzar) records that an earlier king had raised it to the height of 42 cubits (about 60 ft.) without, however, having managed to complete it. In this state it had suffered great damage from the weather and water which had seeped through its cracked encasing bricks. His heart being moved by the great lord Marduk the king undertook and completed its restoration, KIB III ii 52 f.

The story has been widely understood to tell of a **n** miraculous intervention by which different languages were introduced and the population thus became unable to understand one another. But it must be noted that the different groups among not only the Japhethites and Chamites, 10:5, 20, but also among the Semites, 10:31, are already recorded to have had their various languages, and as the two former groups are already out of the story, the origin of languages is not recorded here. Moreover, the word for ' languages ' is *lāšōn* which is that used in 10:5, 20, 31. In our passage this word is not found. That used is *śāpāh* ' lip ', which also signifies ' utterance '. The natural meaning here is that the people at first in complete harmony ' all saying the same thing ' fell out among themselves and could not agree upon a common policy ; and as a result of the discord (and possibly of fighting) there was a migration. Already in the 4th cent. St Gregory of Nyssa was quite emphatic that God did not miraculously impose different languages on mankind, PG 45, 992 ff.

o 1. All lived together in harmony. Lit. ' all the earth was one lip and the same words '. 2. The Heb. is ambiguous and could mean ' to the east '. Sennaar = Babylonia. 3. Babylonia does not provide stone for building, and bitumen (DV ' slime ') was used for binding bricks together. 4. Babylonian inscriptions speak hyperbolically of buildings reaching to heaven ; *cf.* A. Pohl, S.J., Bi 12 (1931) 109 and our modern ' sky-scraper '. ' *lest* we be scattered ' : other peoples would be deterred from attacking them and trying to seize their lands when they learnt of their power. Incidentally this is another indication that ' all the earth ' in 1 is to be understood in a restricted sense. 7. ' *that they may not listen each to what the other says* '. Again secondary causes are neglected. 9. The Babylonians by another popular etymology said the name Babel (Babylon) = the Gate of God.

p 10-26 The Lineage of Sem—On the decreasing ages see § 140e. 10. In 5:31 Noe is 500 years old at the birth of Sem, in 7:6 600 at the beginning of the flood, which lasted one year (see on 8:14), and Sem is 100 here. The writer seems to have intended to give round numbers only. Arphaxad, 12, Sale, 14, Heber, and, 16, Phaleg are named also 10:22–25. 22. Nachor, the name of Abraham's grandfather, is also that of one of his brothers, 26.

q Harran in N. Mesopotamia, for a time the home of Abraham and his father, 31, remained the home of their relatives, 27:43, and in 24:10 it is called ' the city of Nachor '. Geographical names in the region of Harran closely resemble those of Abraham's three immediate ancestors : Til-Turahi, Til-Nahiri, Sarûgi ; *cf.* § 79j. It would be strange if this were accidental, but it would also be strange if Abraham and his family did not know the names of their immediate ancestors for some ten generations. Love of family genealogies is characteristic of the Semites. Arabs of today know by heart even the genealogy of their horses for as many generations.

0a XI 27-XXV 11 The History of Abraham
27-32 The Migration from Ur to Harran—27. Once more this section is linked to the preceding by a repetition from 26. 28. Ur, a famous and ancient city in S. Babylonia. 29. Jescha is not mentioned again and the insertion of her name points to a desire to preserve whatever was known of Abraham's family. 31. The first stage in the separation of the Chosen People is accomplished by the migration of Thare and his family from their kindred in Ur to Harran, the second by the migration of Abraham and Lot to Canaan, 12:4, and the final stage by the separation of these two, 13:11. The reason for Thare's journey is explained by St Stephen, Ac 7:2-4. The command to leave his home and go to a new land was given to Abraham while yet in Ur, though recorded in Gen 12:1 only after the arrival in Harran—another illustration of the important fact that biblical narratives do not always follow chronological order. No reason is given why the journey to Canaan was interrupted and a sojourn made in Harran. The death of Thare in that city suggests his failing health as the cause. Josue admitted as a well-known fact that the ancestors of the people had worshipped false gods when living beyond the Euphrates and includes Thare among the polytheists, Jos 24:2. We are left to infer that Abraham was the restorer of true religion in his family. It was to him that God appeared, Ac 7:2, and the migration to Canaan was to be the means of segregating him

and his from the pagan surroundings of their first **150a** home. See § 309f. Abraham may have been an Aramaean or a Babylonian. Laban, 28:5, and Jacob, Deut 26:5, are spoken of as Aramaeans, but the term may have been used on geographical grounds. The *Testament of Nephtali*, 1:10, calls Abraham a Chaldaean. 32. According to the Samaritan text Thare died aged 145. This is probably the age intended, as Abraham thus leaves Harran in the year of his father's death, 11:26 and 12:4 ; *cf.* Ac 7:4.

XII 1-12a Abram journeys to Canaan—1. The **b** language suits Ur better than Harran ; see on 11:31. 2. Abram's faith is already tested as Sarai was sterile, 11:30. 3. This great promise that a blessing is to come on all nations through Abram is repeated, 18:18, and in 22:18 it is added that the blessing is to be through his seed. History has shown that the source of the blessing was his descendant Christ. The prophecy is confirmed to Isaac and Jacob, 26:2–5; 28:14. 4. Lot's father was dead, 11:27 f. Abram's brother Nachor remained in Harran, 22:20 ; 24:10. 5. ' The souls ' are those in the service of Abram and Lot. Together they made a numerous caravan. Abram alone was able to muster 318 men of fighting age, 14:14. 6. Shechem lay between Ebal and Garizim ; today called Nablus. ' as far as *the Teacher's Terebinth* '; evidently a well-known tree (the species is not certain) where oracular answers were given to inquirers. ' The Canaanite was *already then* in the land '; so in our idiom. Hebrew prescinds from whether the Canaanite was also in the land later emphasizing only the point in hand. The remark indicates that it was a Canaanite oracle. The tree is mentioned again 35:4. 8. Bethel is proleptically so called. The name was changed from Luza only later, 28:19.

10b-20 Abram in Egypt—10b. He went down not **c** alone but with his followers. For a reproduction of the Egyptian picture at Beni Hasan of such a Semitic caravan entering the country, see DBV II opposite 1067. 13. Sarai was his half-sister, 20:12. In the circumstances he was not obliged to tell the whole truth as that would have meant his own death without saving Sarai. 16. Horses are not mentioned. These were introduced into Egypt by the Hyksos (§ 118k-l); *cf.* A. Mallon, S.J., *Les Hébreux en Égypte* (1921) 61, n. 4 ; 74. Camels were not in general use in Egypt before the Greco-Roman period, but were known there from predynastic times, before 3000 B.C. They were brought into Egypt by traders, 37:25, and were a suitable gift for a nomad sheikh such as Abram. See de Vaux, 7–10, with references, against *W. F. Albright, whose view may be read in *The Archaeology of Palestine* (1949) 206 f. 17. Sarai had not been molested, but the punishment was deserved, as it is right to infer, for the evil disposition that would not have stopped short of killing Abram to secure Sarai. 18. Pharaoh associated his calamity with his taking Sarai, made enquiries, and discovered the full facts. The incident illustrates the sanctity of marriage and God's providence in guarding Sarai to be the mother of Isaac the heir of the promises.

XIII 1-18 The Separation of Abram and Lot—2. **d** ' *in herds*, in silver and in gold '. 3. ' *He went by stages from the south* '. 7. Abram and Lot's great herds had not the whole country to themselves as it was *already* inhabited by others ; see on 12:6. 8. The word ' brother ' is used in Heb. to cover a wide range of relationships, here that of uncle and nephew, 11:27. 9. Abram, though the older, magnanimously leaves the choice to Lot. 10. ' *in the direction of Segor* ', one of the towns of the Pentapolis, 14:2. It is not implied that Lot could see as far as the S. of the Dead Sea from near Bethel. 11. ' *to* the east '. 12. ' *and pitched his tent as far as Sodom* '. 15. In Heb. ' for ever ', when used of human affairs, signifies a period of unforeseen and indefinite duration which may be no longer than a lifetime, Ex 21:6. Such divine promises and threats are always conditional on continuance in good or evil respectively even when pronounced

150d absolutely ; *cf.* § 417*d*. **18.** ' dwelt by the *terebinths* of Mambre *at* Hebron ', or oaks. Mambre is the LXX form, Heb. Mamre. Hebron, some 20 m. S. of Jerusalem, known to the Arabs as El-Khalîl, the town of Abraham, ' the friend ' of God, 2 Par 20:7.

e **XIV 1-16 Abram's Victory over the Invading Kings**—**1.** If it were possible to identify one of these kings of known date, we should have evidence from profane history by which to fix the time of Abram. Unfortunately even the immensely increased knowledge of the Near East in the 2nd millennium B.C. acquired of recent decades has not solved this question. And the opinion, once popular, that Amraphel is Hammurabi, the great law-giver of Babylon, is now abandoned by most scholars. The name Hammurâbi-ilu ' H. is my god ' has been found as that of a private citizen, but the king himself could not bear such a name. The LXX form Amarphal suggests an original Amar-pi-el ' The mouth of god has spoken ' or ' commanded '. Sennaar = Mesopotamia or Babylonia. Ariok of Ellasar has been identified on very doubtful grounds with Rim-Sin of Larsa. A prince of Mari bore the name Arriwuk, which is of Hurrian stamp. Kedorla'omer ' Servant (?) of Lagamar ', otherwise unattested, is of genuine Elamite formation ; *cf.* Kudur-Nankhundi ' Servant (?) of N. '. Lagamar was an Elamite divinity. Tid'al seems to be the Hittite name Tudchalia, perhaps called ' king of nations ' as leader of a band of international mercenaries. **3.** ' into the Vale of Siddim ', not mentioned elsewhere, apparently the shallow, southern part of the Dead Sea below the Lisan. There is some support for the idea that this was once dry in the fact that a ford existed in the early 19th cent. A.D. from the Lisan to the W. shore. This has long since ceased to be practicable. The Dead Sea existed long before the 2nd millennium B.C., and the reference here can be only to a part of it which was once dry. **4.** The Elamite king is leader of the expedition. There is evidence of Elamite power about this time. Mari texts speak of a strong Elamite force sent to Upper Mesopotamia in the time of Hammurabi, now commonly but not universally dated 1728–1686. And a little earlier Kudur-Mabuk ruled in Babylon and successively installed his two sons **f** as kings of Larsa. **5.** The line of march was S. through the country E. of Jordan to Edom, then W. towards the Wilderness of Paran, then NE. to Qadesh-barnea, and finally to the S. of the Dead Sea. At the time of this expedition there was a sedentary population in Transjordan. There was an abrupt break in the urban civilization of the country about 1800 and this may have been caused by the military operations of the Elamites and their confederates. Ashterothcarnaim, in the Hauran ; the Zuzim ' in Ham ', prob. modern Ham in 'Ajlûn ; Shave of Qiryathaim E. of the Dead Sea not far from Machaerus. **6.** The inhabitants of Seir at this time are now generally identified with the Hurrians, § 118*i–j*. Their country later fell to the Edomites. **7.** Hasason-tamar is identified with 'Ain Jidi (Engedi) on the W. shore of the Dead Sea in 2 Par 20:2. As this seems to indicate an impossible line of march previous to the encounter at the S. end of the Dead Sea, some have attempted to locate Hasason-tamar S. of the sea. But this overlooks the ancient method of grouping material. The writer has inserted the mention here in order not to interrupt afterwards his main theme which is the battle and Abram's **g** subsequent pursuit of the invading kings. **10.** In the Vale of Siddim there were many bitumen cavities, and bitumen still oozes out of the bed of the Dead Sea. The local kings chose this terrain for the battle as they were familiar with its dangers but were defeated in spite of this advantage. The kings of Sodom and Gomorrha, however, saved their lives by means of these bitumen pits : ' they fled and threw themselves in ' and so escaped the enemy. Thus the king of Sodom survived to congratulate Abram, 17. **13.** The designation of Abram as ' the Hebrew ' makes it prob. that this ancient document was taken over from a non-Israelite source. **14.** Originally prob. ' to Laish which is Dan ' ; *cf.* 2,

3, 7, 17 (the ancient names explained) and Jg 18:29. **15** Abram did not pursue alone with his own contingent of 318 men but aided by the forces of his three confederates, 24. **15.** ' on the *north* of Damascus ' ; the points of the compass being taken facing the E., the left hand stands for the N. **17.** The Vale of Shave is not mentioned elsewhere. Its later name ' the King's Vale ' occurs 2 Kg 18:18—in the neighbourhood of Jerusalem.

18-24 The Sacrifice of Melchisedech—Melchisedech **15** ' King of Justice ' is a remarkable figure. A non-Hebrew he is a worshipper of the true God whose service had been abandoned even by Abram's father, Jos 24:2. David proclaimed his priesthood as the type of that of the Messias, Ps 109:4. Given the nationalistic exclusiveness of the Hebrews, this was humanly speaking a most improbable, if not impossible, choice, but David spoke under divine inspiration (' in spirit ', Mt 22:43). And St Paul insists on the superiority of his priesthood to the Aaronic, for Abram was greater than his son Levi, but inferior to Melchisedech who blessed him, and ' that which is less is blessed by the better ', Heb 7:1-7. Instructed by these texts the Church has always recognized in his sacrifice of bread and wine a figure of the Christian sacrifice. So St Cyprian speaks of ' the image of (Christ's) sacrifice in bread and wine ', *Epist.* 63, n. 4. **18.** Salem was an ancient name of Jerusalem preserved **b** in poetry, Ps 75:3 ; *cf.* on 17. HT = ' and he was ' but DV rightly ' for he was ', this being a recognized value of the conjunction, BDB 253*b*. The essential function of the priestly office is to offer sacrifice, Heb 5:1, and in antiquity a similar meeting in celebration of such a victory would always be accompanied by a sacrifice of thanksgiving. **20.** Abraham gave tithes to the priest of all he had rescued from the invaders. **23.** Perhaps the reason for Abram's refusal was the disinclination to receive any benefit at the hands of the ruler of the wicked city of Sodom. **24.** The young men are the warriors who had taken part in the pursuit and victory.

XV 1-6 God's Promise to Abram of an Innumerable c Posterity—**1.** ' Thy *reward is* exceeding great '. So Abram understood the words as shown by his complaint in 2 that further riches are of no use to him : ' *for I go childless* '. Then prob. : ' *and the heir of my house is Eliezer the Damascene* ' ; *cf.* Syr. He is not named again. **4.** Adoption tablets found at Nuzu in NE. Iraq and dating from the 15th cent. B.C. show that an adopted son designated as heir lost his right to the chief inheritance should a son subsequently be born to the adopter, BA III i (1940) 2 f. **6.** Sara was sterile ; *cf.* Rom 4:3.

7-14 Further Promises : God's Covenant with Abram d—**8.** He does not doubt God's promise ; see 6. He asks what signs he may expect to show that the fulfilment of the promise is imminent. To this request he receives no direct answer but is instructed to prepare the ceremonial of a covenant. **9.** ' *a heifer . . . a turtle-dove* '. **10.** An ancient mode of making a covenant was for the parties to pass between the parts of a divided animal, the original symbolism being apparently that they called down on themselves a similar fate should they violate the treaty ; *cf.* Jer 34:18 f. and the similar symbolism of 1 Kg 11:7. The prevalence of this or similar rites is shown by the current expressions, *kāraṯ bᵉrîṯ*, ὅρκια τέμνειν, ' foedus ferire ', all meaning ' to make a covenant '. Such ceremonies survive after the thought which gave them origin has faded or been forgotten. And it is no objection to this interpretation that here the principal contracting party is God. In his condescension he would adopt the ritual usual among men. The act of passing between the pieces would be a solemn adjunct to the ceremony rather than essential to its significance. It is difficult to conceive the slaughtered animals to have represented the contracting parties or the standing between the pieces to have symbolized that they were taken within the mystical life of the victim. See further, *e.g.* *C. F. Keil on Gen 15:7-11, *W. Robertson Smith, *The Religion of the Semites* (1927³) 480 f. with S. A. Cook's note, 691 f.

d The birds were possibly for a sacrifice but this is not **e** mentioned. **11.** Abram's driving away the birds of prey symbolized the frustration of human attempts to hinder the fulfilment of the divine promises. **12.** The same word for ' deep sleep ' as in 2:21. 400 years : but in 16 the return is put in the 4th generation. Hence the 400 is prob. a gloss (so Heinisch) based on Ex 12:40, where MT gives 430 years as the period of the sojourn in Egypt whereas the Samaritan text gives it as the whole time elapsed between Abram's arrival in Canaan and the Exodus ; *cf*. LXX. **16.** Abram therefore learns that he is not to possess the land in his own person but in that of his descendants. **17.** A case of hendiadys : one object only passed through the divided parts. This was an oven from which issued flame and smoke. The ancients, and the Arabs today, prepare the portable oven for baking by first lighting a fire in it. Once it is well heated, the fire is removed and the dough inserted. The fire and smoke symbolized God, the flame as bright and almost immaterial and the smoke as impenetrable to the eye representing God's invisibility ; *cf*. Ex 3:2 ; 19:18 ; 24:17. **18.** The River of Egypt is prob. the Wady el-'Arîsh. All such promises are conditional, and that the territory of Israel reached the Euphrates only in the days of Solomon, 3 Kg 4:21, will have been due to the frequent infidelity of the **f** people. **19-21.** The **Qenites** (Kenites) seem to have had their principal seat in Sinai. They were kinsfolk of the Madianites, Num 10:29, Jg 4:11 ; and they or part of them associated themselves with the Israelites, Num 24:21, Jg 1:16. On the **Hittites** see § 119. The **Rephaim** (to be distinguished from the shades of the dead known by the same name) were an ancient people relatively of great stature who inhabited Transjordan and Canaan before the Semitic invasion, Gen 14:5, Deut 2:10 f. ; 3:11 (DV ' giants ' in both places), Jos 7:15. It is noteworthy that in the region where they dwelt are found numerous megalithic monuments. The territory of Amurru, the home of the **Amorites**, as so called by the Babylonians, comprised all the territory W. of the Euphrates, of which the chief part was Syria. The Amorites penetrated S. into Canaan, where they lived especially in the mountainous regions, Num 13:30 (MT 29). The **Jebusites** still dwelt in Jerusalem in the time of David, 2 Kg 5:6. For the Qenizzites, Qadmonites, Perizzites and Girgashites *cf*. F.-M. Abel, O.P., *Géographie de la Palestine* I (Paris, 1933) 274, 320–5.

g **XVI 1-16 The Birth of Ishmael**—**1.** St Jerome, like other Latin writers, sometimes omits the aspirate. Her name is Hagar. **2.** Secondary causes omitted ; see on 2:5. Sarai's offer was in accordance with the customs of the time ; *cf*. the Code of Hammurabi 144–6. **5.** Abram is reproached by Sarai for doing just what she had suggested. **7.** ' The Angel of Yahweh ' is identified in 13 with Yahweh himself ; so also 31:11 and 13. ' The Israelite did not ask himself how Yahweh can also be called the Messenger of Yahweh. It is one of the obscurities in which the OT abounds ', Heinisch. Rather Yahweh is said to speak because the Angel spoke in his name. Hagar fled towards her home in Egypt. **11.** Ishmael = ' God hears '. **12.** ' over against ' prob. = to the E. of Israel. **13.** ' *Thou art the God of Vision* ', who allows himself to be seen. Then perhaps : ' Have I even seen God and live after my vision ? ' **14.** Barad, unidentified.

h **XVII 1-27 Circumcision the Sign of the Covenant**— The removal of the foreskin is a ritual practised both in ancient and modern times by other peoples besides the Hebrews. The custom is in use among the Arabs, the Christian Abyssinians, American Indian tribes such as the Caribs, tribes of Central Australia, and others. The operation is commonly performed at puberty as a tribal initiation ceremony and as a preliminary to marriage. Among the Hebrews it was (and still is) performed on the eighth day after birth and has a definitely religious character as a mark of belonging to the people of God. By this mark the source of life, the natural means whereby the race was propagated, was consecrated to God.

1. ' Almighty God ' : El Shaddai, of uncertain mean- **151i** ing ; *cf*. Ex 6:3. **4.** Father of the Israelites through Isaac, of the Ishmaelites through Ishmael, of the Edomites through Esau, and *cf*. 25:2–4. **5.** The Arabic *ruhâm* means ' a large number '. **7.** ' to be a God to thee ' = to take them under my especial protection. **8.** ' perpetual ' : see on 13:15. **10.** Circumcision, here called the covenant, in 11 is more accurately called the sign of the covenant. The covenant itself was made earlier, 15:18. **14.** Any man violating the prescription will have no part in the blessings reserved for the people of God. **15.** The meaning of Sarai is uncertain : Sara signifies ' princess ', for she, **16**, is to be the mother of kings. Names were considered to denote character, function or nature ; *cf*. 5. **17.** Abraham's spirit of faith is praised, 15:6, Heb 11:8, and yet some strangely think that here he is represented as doubting. It is not true to his character to understand that he ' fell upon his face [before God] and laughed ' in derision at the divine promise. Nor would a play on his son's name (*cf*. § 139*f* ; ' he laughs ' = *yiṣḥaq* = Isaac) be here introduced as a perpetual memorial of a fault of his father's. To quote St Augustine, ' The laughter of Abraham was the exulting of joy, not the derision of disbelief', *De Civ. Dei* 16, 26. And if he had disbelieved, he would not at once, **18**, have expressed the hope that the birth of a son to Sara would not prejudice the fortunes of Ishmael. **20.** The exact mention of 12 chiefs is foreign to the style of prophecy (*cf*. § 418*b*) and is a later gloss inserted on the strength of 25:13–16.

XVIII 1-15 Abraham entertains Angels—**1.** See on **152a** 13:18. It is difficult to know whether Yahweh appeared in person or through the intermediary of an Angel ; see on 16:7. **2.** ' *he saw and lo !* three men '. This act of reverence was used to superiors in rank, as to Joseph by his brothers, 43:28, where the Heb. word is the same. **3.** He addresses directly only the one who was clearly the leader of the party. **8.** ' *curds* and milk '. **10.** ' I will return *when this season comes round again* ; and Sara thy wife shall have a son. *Now Sara was listening at the door of the tent which was standing behind him* '. **12.** Sara's laugh is again a play on the name of Isaac, but this time it is a laugh of disbelief. **14.** A profound truth simply expressed—God is omnipotent. See on 10.

16-33 Abraham intercedes for the Men of Sodom— **b** **18.** See on 12:3. **19.** ' *For my regard for him is to the end that he may* command his children '. God has a great design for Abraham. It is through him that a people is to arise who shall preserve the true worship of God. **20.** The cry is one that calls to heaven for vengeance ; see on 4:10. **22.** Two of the Angels go on to Sodom. **23-32** presents a wonderful scene—illustrating at once God's justice and his clemency. For the sake of ten just men he would spare a whole city whose iniquity cried aloud to heaven. **25.** ' *Shall he who ruleth all the world not act with justice ?* ' **28.** ' Wilt thou *for lack of five* destroy the whole city ? '

XIX 1-29 The Destruction of Sodom and the De- c liverance of Lot—**1.** It is now revealed that the two who had gone to Sodom, 18:22, were Angels. **2.** The proposal to sleep ' *in the square* ' or open space near the city gateway is prompted by courtesy. The visitors are unwilling to be a burden to Lot. **8.** Lot cannot be praised. He chose what he considered the less of two evils. **11.** They were struck not with total blindness but with inability to see the entrance to Lot's house ; see 4 Kg 6:18–20. The Sodomites have failed in the test, 18:21, and the doom of the city is sealed. **17.** He must not look back for there is not a moment to spare. **24.** On the direct attribution to divine action of the effects of natural causes see on 2:5. The cause of the disaster was probably the escape through earthquake action of compressed gases and petroleum from the subterranean deposits in the neighbourhood of the doomed cities. Spontaneous combustion is apt to occur in such circumstances and domestic fires would quickly ignite the escaping gases and oil. Such a fire would cause immense heavy clouds of smoke, **28**. The district is also rich in sulphur (brimstone) and I have picked

152c up pellets of it and pieces of bitumen lying on the shore of the Dead Sea. That the destruction of the cities was caused by these natural forces does not mean that it was not a divinely sent chastisement. God can obviously make use of the agencies he has created. **25.** An account of the widespread destruction to the countryside caused by such a disaster may be read in **d** *The Wide World Magazine* (Aug. 1932) 382–6. **26.** Lot's wife lingered to watch the spectacle. Her disobedience, 17, and recklessness, 19, cost her her life. She was overwhelmed probably by the fumes, and later her body became encrusted with salt. It is not true that everything in the neighbourhood of the Dead Sea is so encrusted. But the casts of human bodies preserved in the museum at Pompeii suggest what happened to Lot's wife. These casts preserve the exact form of the victims who were overwhelmed by the eruption and became encased in the falling ashes. **28.** ' *and lo the smoke rose up* '.

e For the results of archaeological exploration at the S. end of the Dead Sea *cf.* W. F. Albright AASOR 6 (1926) 54–62 and in popular form M. G. Kyle, *Explorations at Sodom* (1928) ; for some account of the sea and its surroundings E. F. Sutcliffe, ' A Week on the Dead Sea ' Mn (Aug. 1929) 108–16.

f **30-38 The Birth of Moab and Ammon—31.** All her acquaintances having been destroyed, she thought the future held no prospect of marriage. She cannot have thought that all mankind had perished as Segor was still standing undamaged, 23. **32.** The wickedness of the incest was mitigated by the intention, in itself excellent, of bearing children. This strong desire to have children is further exemplified in the lengths to which it led Thamar, ch 38.

g **XX 1-18 Sara saved from Danger in Gerar**—This incident is probably not recorded in its chronological place as in 18:11 Sara is already beyond the age of childbearing. It illustrates again like the similar story in ch 12 the sanctity of marriage and the importance of keeping the patriarchal line of descent free from contamination.

h **7.** The first mention of a prophet ; *cf.* § 409*e*. Note the value of intercessory prayer. In early times the sense of family and tribal solidarity was very strong. The individual tended to be regarded only as part of a larger unit ; and God Almighty accommodated himself to this strongly rooted sentiment. **8.** ' in the morning '. **10.** Prob. ' What didst thou *fear* '. **16.** The king gives 1,000 pieces of silver to Sara and puts them in Abraham's safe keeping. This generous gift will make her forget the dishonour of having been taken from her husband. Abimelech concludes : ' *and thy honour is vindicated before all* '. This present will show all that the king acknowledges that he did an injustice. **18.** This shows that Sara was in the royal harem some considerable time.

i **XXI 1-8 The Birth of Isaac—6.** For the play on Isaac's name *cf.* 17:17 ; 18:12. **8.** A child might not be weaned till the age of three, 2 Mac 7:27.

j **9-21 Dismissal of Hagar and Ishmael—9.** The sons of slave wives could be given the same rights as those of the first, chief wife as in the case of the sons of Jacob. No distinction was made between the sons of Bala and Zelpha and those of Rachel and Lia. Hence Sara feared that Isaac's interests might suffer. The conduct of Ishmael, apparently on the occasion of the weaning festival, aroused Sara and determined her to action. This cannot have been merely harmless play and St Paul, Gal 4:29, explains it as some form of persecution (ἐδίωκεν). The word *mᵉṣaḥēq* which is used of ' joking ', 19:14, ' playing ' and ' making sport ', Ex 32:6, Jg 16:25, *cf.* Gen 26:8, is also used of ' mocking ', 39:14, 17 (with a special application). The preposition (*bᵉ*) used in the last-mentioned passages may have stood in our text which in MT stops abruptly with *mᵉṣaḥēq* and the word ' with ' of LXX and Vg may be a translator's addition to an already mutilated text. **10.** According to an attractive suggestion of Junker's Sara's harsh words conceal the fact that technically her pro-

posal was to give Hagar her liberty. But this is hard **15** to accept in view of an adoption contract among the Nuzu tablets (15–14 cent. B.C.) which stipulates that the son of a slave wife shall not be sent away (edited by E. A. Speiser in AASOR 10 [1930] 31 f.). **12.** God knew that no harm would come to Hagar and Ishmael as the sequel shows and it was arranged by providence that the chosen people should have Isaac but not Ishmael among their ancestors. **14.** According to the schematic presentation of ages Ishmael was now over 14 years old, 16:16 and 21:5 ; but on this see § 140*b*–*f*. He was certainly older than Isaac and apparently capable of mischief, 9. ' a *skin* of water ', such as is still used by the Arabs. **15.** ' She cast ' just as the sick were ' cast ' at the feet of our Lord, Mt 15:30, clearly ' laid '. This does not necessarily imply that Hagar was carrying the boy. Indeed the contrary is implied by 18. **20.** ' and became an archer '.

22-24 Pact between Abraham and Abimelech—22. **k** Abraham was such a powerful sheikh and could put so many fighting men into the field, 14:14, that even the king of Gerar found it advantageous to make a treaty with him. **25.** Wells are so precious in dry regions that they have been the occasion of many strifes between Arab tribes. **26.** ' I *know* not '. **31.** Beersheba means lit. ' well of seven ', seven being a sacred number with the Hebrews. From it is derived the word for ' to swear ' used in 23 f. **33.** ' a *tamarisk tree* ', designed to serve as a memorial of the patriarch's rightful claim to the well. The Philistines, to whom Palestine owes its name, did not make their chief settlement in the country till *c* 1200 B.C., but from earlier times had smaller trading stations there.

XXII 1-19 The Sacrifice of Isaac—By his command **15** to sacrifice Isaac God Almighty proclaimed his absolute dominion over the lives of men who are the work of his hands. By the revocation of the order he manifested that he did not wish this dominion to be acknowledged by the actual sacrifice of human life. The double lesson was necessary as the Canaanites offered such sacrifices to their gods. On later idolatrous human sacrifice in Israel *cf.* Sutcliffe, *The OT and the Future Life*, 175 f. The command was a severe test of Abraham's obedience and also of his faith, since God had promised him posterity through Isaac. The Church has always seen in the sacrifice of Isaac a figure of the Eternal Father delivering his Incarnate Son to the Sacrifice of Calvary, Rom 8:32.

1. ' God *made trial of* Abraham '. **2.** ' into the land of **b** *the Amorites* ', so the Syr. ; MT ' of Moriah '. In 2 Par 3:1 the place is identified with the temple mount at Jerusalem, but this does not settle the original form of name. **3.** ' in the *morning* '. **4.** The distance from Beersheba to Jerusalem is 45 m. in a straight line, a journey which would be completed within 3 days. 5. Omit ' with speed '. **5.** Like Caiaphas Abraham uttered an unconscious prophecy. St Ambrose : ' prophetavit quod ignorabat ', PL 14, 447. **13.** In the royal cemetery at Ur dating from late in the 4th millennium B.C. were found two elaborately decorated figures of goats standing on their hind legs, each ' with a silver bond, apparently a chain, round his front fetlocks attaching him to the branches of a tree '. The two were supports for some lost object, possibly a tabletop. They are not caught by the horns and there is no apparent connection of symbolism with the story of Abraham. ' The " heraldic " composition of two animals facing each other and reared up on their hind legs against a bush of tree is a commonplace of Sumerian art at this period '. See C. L. Woolley, *Ur Excavations* II (1934) 264–6 and plates 87–90. **14.** ' The Lord *provideth* ', as in 8. Hence the proverb ' In the mountain the Lord will *provide* ' for the needs of his suppliants. **17.** The gates stand by synecdoche for the fortified towns, and so the power of their enemies as in Mt 16:18. **18.** See on 12:3.

20-24 The Family of Abraham's Brother Nachor— **c** The list provides an introduction to Isaac's marriage to Rebecca in ch 24. **20.** *Cf.* 11:29. The list is drawn

3c up on the same lines as the table of nations in ch 10 and stresses the relationship of various tribes to Israel. Elihu, Job 32:2 was a Buzite.

d XXIII 1-20 The Death and Burial of Sara—2. 'Abraham *went in* to mourn '. **3.** 'he rose *from the presence of his dead (wife)* '. In Palestine on account of the heat the obsequies generally take place the day of death. The Hittites, § 119*a–d*, were already widespread and had a colony in S. Canaan. **6.** ' *in the choicest of our* sepulchres '. Omit ' have power to '. **9.** ' the cave *of Machpelah* ', the name of the place in which the cave was, 17. The transaction took place according to custom in the open space near the city gate. This offered the publicity necessary to safeguard contracts. **11.** ' the children of my people ' = my compatriots. **15.** This is only oriental courtesy, as Abraham knew. **16.** Coined money was not introduced till after the exile. **17.** ' Ephron's *in Machpelah* '. **19.** ' *in the cave in the field of Machpelah* '.

e XXIV 1-67 A Bride for Isaac—2. This significance of this rite in the taking of an oath (again in 47:29) lay apparently in reverence for the source of life. For the euphemism see 46:26. **12.** ' *grant me good fortune* today '. **22.** ' *a golden ring half a shekel in weight and two golden bracelets* '. The ring was for the nose, see 47. **24.** *Cf.* 22:23. **25.** ' straw and *fodder* '. **27.** ' *his favour and his faithfulness* '. **28.** The part of her father's dwelling where the womenfolk lived apart from the men. **29***b* comes logically after 30*a*. **30.** ' the *ring* and the bracelets *on* his sister's *arms* '. **32.** ' straw and *fodder for the camels* '. **43.** ' *the maiden* '. **47.** ' So I put *a ring in her nose* '. **48.** ' my master's *kinsman* ' : Bathuel was Abraham's nephew. **50.** Bathuel has no part in the story outside this verse and here it is prob. a corruption of *bêtô* ' Laban and *his household* '. **51.** The Lord had manifested his will by the providential turn of events. **53.** Bathuel was evidently dead. ' brother ' ; in the singular. **60.** ' gates ' ; see on 22:17. **62.** *Cf.* 16:14. **65.** ' *to meet us* '. She covered herself with a *veil*, it being customary for the bride to be veiled in the presence of her betrothed till after the nuptial ceremony.

f XXV 1-6 Other Descendants of Abraham—This genealogical list is to be compared with those in ch 10 and 22:20–24. The names represent tribes with whom the Israelites claimed kinship. The best known are the Madianites, whose home was near the Gulf of Aqabah. To this tribe belonged Jethro, Moses' father-in-law, Ex 3:1. Bildad, Job's friend, was a Shuhite, Jb 2:11. The camels of Madian and Epha are mentioned together, Is 60:6. **6.** The two secondary wives were Hagar and Cetura.

g 7-11 The Death of Abraham—9. ' in the cave of Machpelah ' which he had bought of Ephron the Hittite, ch 23. **11.** The well is mentioned 16:14 ; 24 : 62. Isaac inherits the divine favour shown to Abraham.

h 12-18 Final Notice of Ishmael—13. Perhaps the Nabataeans. **15.** The city Teima is in NW. Arabia. Jetur and Naphish were tribes against whom the Israelites had later to fight, 1 Par 5:19. **16.** The Ishmaelites were partly nomadic and partly settled. They dwelt in ' *villages and encampments* '. **18.** Perhaps ' towards *Sur* '. Or the people named in 3 may be meant. ' He settled over against all his brethren ', as in 16:12.

i XXV 19-XXXV 29 The History of Isaac—As the history of Thare is almost entirely that of his son Abraham, so that of Isaac is principally concerned with his son Jacob.

j 19-26 The Birth of Esau and Jacob—22. The struggle portended the future hostility of Israel and Edom. ' *If things are so, what is to become of me ?* ' She went to a shrine, perhaps at Beersheba. **23.** Israel is to be a more mighty people than Edom. **25.** Perhaps the pronunciation originally intended was Eshau meaning ' hairy '. Jacob, the cunning, ' the overreacher ' even from the womb, tried to prevent Esau from being the firstborn and caught hold of ' his brother's *heel* '.

k 27-34 Esau sells his Birthright—27. ' hunter, *a man of the open spaces*, but Jacob a *quiet man, a stay-at-home* '. **30.**

Edom, a play on the name of the dish he asked for. **153k 31.** Jacob wrongfully takes advantage of Esau's exhaustion.

XXVI 1-5 The Promises renewed to Isaac—1. Prob. **l** another king of the same name as in 20:2. For the Philistines see on 21:33. **6-11 Rebecca escapes Danger in Gerar—7.** ' my **m** *kinswoman* ', the Heb. word covering a range of relationships ; see on 13:8 ; 24:48. Isaac followed the policy he had learnt from his father, 12:13 ; 20:2. **12-22 Trouble over Wells—**A recurring source of **n** quarrels among nomads ; *cf.* 21:25. **12.** Isaac was semi-nomad, semi-sedentary. The hundredfold stands for a very rich harvest. **14.** A great family of men in his service. **19.** ' *running* water '. **20.** He called the well ' *Contention* '. **23-33 The Covenant with Abimelech at Beersheba—** **o** Abraham had already made a covenant at Beersheba, prob. with a predecessor of this Abimelech, 21:27. **33.** This new well Isaac called ' Seven ' or ' Oath ', both of which names would have much the same meaning for a Hebrew ; see on 21:31. Just as the wells, 18, retained the names given them by Abraham, so also Beersheba (= Well of Seven, or, of the Oath) with a new confirmation from the name of the new well. **34-35 Esau's Wives—34.** Both his wives were of Hittite **p** stock according to MT, but the second according to the Samaritan text was a Hivite. **35.** Isaac's dislike of these women facilitated Jacob's departure for Harran, 27:46 f. **XXVII 1-40 Jacob by Fraud wins Isaac's Blessing—** **q** **19.** Jacob was guilty of false pretences and of several lies. This is in no way glossed over in the text. See H. Lillie, S.J., ' Did Jacob tell a Lie ? ' CR 10 (Aug. 1935) 97–108. There is no doubt what Isaac and Esau thought of the trick, 35 f. That Jacob knew of the prophecy, 25:23, that he, the younger, was to supplant his elder brother does not excuse his conduct. The proper course was to wait for Providence to bring the prophecy to fulfilment. For this wrongdoing Jacob had to pay heavily during his long years of hard toil with Laban, 31:40. **23.** ' *And he blessed him* '. The blessing comes only in 28 f. These anticipatory remarks are disconcerting to the modern reader, but are characteristic of Hebrew narrative ; *cf.* 31:46 ; 42:20, and *S. R. Driver, Hebrew Tenses* (1892³) § 75. By some they are considered a sign of the fusion of two documents. **28-29.** In Palestine where there is no rain **r** from April till November the heavy night dews are of the greatest importance. The blessing is stamped by the this-world outlook of Hebrew religion. They had no idea of rewards after death till the last centuries before the Christian era. **30.** ' abroad ' is an archaism for going out of a dwelling (here, a tent). **33.** Omit ' of all '. ' He shall be blessed ' : Isaac had pronounced his blessing under a misapprehension, but it did not occur to him that it could be invalid on that account. **34.** Esau ' *cried out with a great and very bitter cry and said . . .* ' **37.** Omit ' more '. **39.** Edom being regarded as less fertile than Canaan, the translation should prob. be : ' *Away from* the fat of the earth and *from* the dew of heaven above shall thy *dwelling* be '. The peaceful pursuit of agriculture is not suggested by 40, ' Thou shalt live by the sword '. The Edomites had the reputation of being a fierce race, Jos. *Bell. Jud.* 4, 4, 1. Edom revolted and obtained its independence under Joram, 4 Kg 8:20–22.

41-XXVIII 5 Jacob's Escape to Mesopotamia—Esau **154a** having been twice ' overreached ' by Jacob determined to kill him. Whereupon Rebecca counselled him to take refuge with her brother Laban in Mesopotamia. This reason she hid from Isaac and persuaded the old man to let him go to obtain a wife of their own kindred. **45.** She would lose both her sons, Jacob by death, and **b** Esau because he would be obliged to fly after the murder. **46.** *Cf.* 26:34 f. **XXVIII:1.** Isaac's speedy forgiveness of Jacob's misconduct will have been influenced by his recognition of the overruling provi-

154b dence of God. **2.** ' Mesopotamia of Syria '—so Vg and LXX for MT Paddan Aram, in which region lay Harran. Aramaeans dwelt not only in Syria but also E. of the Euphrates. **3.** ' God almighty ' = El Shaddai ; cf. 17:1.

c 6-9 Esau marries the Daughter of Ishmael—6. See on 2. **7.** ' to Paddan Aram '. **9.** Nabajoth ; cf. 25:13. Maheleth : only here ; see on 36:1-8.

d 10-22 Jacob's Journey : the Promises renewed—12. The vision of Angels, God's messengers as denoted by their name both in Heb. and Gk, is a reminder of God's constant care for his creatures. The Angels descend to earth bringing God's counsel and help ; they ascend to heaven carrying man's aspirations and prayers to the throne of God. The vision thus assured Jacob of divine help. The text is alluded to in Jn 1:51. **13.** See 12:7. The promise made to Abraham and confirmed to Jacob sets the divine seal on the blessing he had received from Isaac. **14.** See on 12:3. **16.** He knew that God had brought Abraham out of Mesopotamia and that his presence is not narrowly circumscribed. This was a specially holy place where God manifested his presence. **18.** ' title ' : a standing-stone, often trans. ' pillar ', but no English word exactly corresponds. Such sacred stones were prominent in Semitic cult. The Israelites were ordered to destroy those of the Canaanites, Ex 23:24. The unction was a form of consecration, used e.g. in the institution of kings, 1 Kg 10:1. **19.** Bethel = ' House of God '. **20.** ' and shall protect me on this journey '. **21-22.** Passages like ' I the Lord will be their God ', Ez 34:24, meaning ' will take them under my special divine protection ' show the meaning here. The apodosis begins with 22 : ' and Yahweh will have been my God, then . . . ' If Yahweh brings Jacob back safely, he will have proved himself to be his protector and Jacob will make the place a shrine and pay tithes there ; see § 105d-e. Omit ' called '. For the fulfilment of the vow see 35:6 f. The ark was at Bethel (today Beitin) for a time ; see on Jg 20:18.

e XXIX 1-11 Jacob meets Rachel—1. Actually NE. The ancients were not precise about the points of the compass. **7.** Jacob wants the shepherds to depart so that he can be alone with Rachel. **10.** Jacob manifested unusual strength in removing the stone which normally required the effort of several men. He wished Rachel to see and tell her father what a useful help he would be, for he wanted to take refuge for some time from Esau's anger. **11.** On western standards oriental weeping is loud and demonstrative. Jacob wept for joy at the happy ending of his journey and he had already fallen in love with Rachel, 18.

f 12-30 He serves Fourteen Years for Rachel and Lia —12. Jacob was Laban's nephew ; see on 13:8. **14.** A customary mode of expressing consanguinity ; cf. 2:23. **15.** True to his character Laban delayed a month before offering wages for Jacob's work. **17.** Rachel was ' beautiful in form and feature '. **18.** It was customary to make payment for a bride, 34:12 ; 1 Kg 18:25. Rich gifts had been paid for Rebecca, 24:53 ; but Jacob having been obliged to depart stealthily for fear of Esau had no such gifts. His toil is a further retribution for his deceit. **22.** ' made a feast '. **27.** The marriage celebrations lasted a week ; cf. Jg 14:12. **28.** This time he obtained his bride in advance of his seven years' service in payment for her.

g 31-35 Lia bears Four Sons—31. The Heb. word is ' hated ' used as in Lk 14:26 with the meaning ' loved less than another '. Each of the four names is linked by assonance to a word in Lia's utterances.

h XXX 1-13 Jacob's Sons by the Handmaids—For the custom see on 16:2. **2.** Jacob recognizes that God alone is the author of life. **3.** To receive a new-born child on one's knees was to acknowledge it as one's own ; cf. 50:22, Job 3:12. **8.** ' I have fought a mighty fight with my sister '.

i 14-24 Other Sons by Lia and Rachel—14. The mandrake or love-apple (Mandragora vernalis) is a comparatively rare plant believed by orientals, both

ancient and modern, to possess qualities favourable to **15** conception. Lia's new conception is nonetheless ascribed both by the sacred writer and by herself to God's favour, 17 f. **18.** There is a double play on the name Issachar, ' hired ' in 16 and ' reward ' here. **20.** ' now my husband will dwell with me ' ; so probably.

25-36 Jacob's New Contract with Laban—Jacob asks **j** for nothing except unusually coloured sheep and goats born of normal-coloured dams and sires. Abnormally coloured animals would be more likely to have such offspring, but as he does not ask for their young, the offer is at once accepted by Laban as highly advantageous to himself. The flocks are separated, the abnormally coloured being put in the charge of Laban's sons and the normal (white sheep and black goats) being left with Jacob. To make quite sure that Jacob is not dishonest Laban puts three days' journey between the two flocks. Then, as far as he is able, Jacob is to build up a flock of his own consisting only of dark-coloured sheep and variegated or speckled goats.

29. ' how thy cattle have fared at my hands '. **31.** ' But **k** he said " Thou wilt not have to give me anything " '. **32.** ' separate all the dark-coloured sheep and the variegated and spotted goats and [all such born thereafter of the remaining animals] shall be my wages '. Note the displacement in MT and LXX. **33.** Jacob's own flock, when he comes to own one, must not number a single white sheep or black goat. **35.** ' And the same day he separated the spotted and variegated he-goats and she-goats, all that showed any white, and all the dark-coloured sheep and put them in the charge of his sons '. Laban was making his position quite secure, and as a final measure he put a three days' journey ' between them and Jacob ' ; so Sam.

37-43 How Jacob grew Rich—Laban had outwitted **l** Jacob over his marriage. It is now Jacob's turn. On the method he used interesting information may be read in Bochart, Hierozoicon in Opera Omnia II (1692³) 543-7. St Jerome mentions that similar technique was said to be used in the Spanish horse-breeding industry, PL 23, 985A. **41 f.** Jacob made sure that his particoloured goats and black sheep should be conceived only when the flocks were most vigorous and healthy. At other times young could be born for Laban. **43** underlines the success that attended his manoeuvres.

XXXI 1-21 Jacob's Homeward Flight—1. Jacob had **m** not taken what was Laban's, but by his methods Laban's flocks had diminished and his own increased. **5.** God had been with Jacob giving success to his work. **7.** Nothing was said of this in the summary account of ch 30. **8.** LXX also has ' white ', but MT ' striped '. **19.** These idols (teraphim) are called his ' gods ' by Laban, 30. These were small, 34, whereas that mentioned 1 Kg 19:13, 16 was large and of human form. They were used for divining, Zach 10:2, and were perhaps household gods. It has been suggested on the evidence of the Nuzu tablets that Rachel in stealing the teraphim had an eye on a claim to Laban's property. In the circumstances it is more likely that she treasured them in the hope of thereby securing help and protection. **21.** The Euphrates was spoken of by the Hebrews as ' the river '.

22-43 Laban's Pursuit—22. The third day corresponds **n** to the three days' journey of 30:36. **23.** Jacob had seven days' start. ' He took his kinsfolk and set out in pursuit seven days march behind him '. Jacob lay nearer the Euphrates than Laban, and the seven days are accounted for by the 3 days of 22, the 3 others of 30:36, and 1 day of preparations. The distance to Galaad was about 350 m. **28.** Laban speaks of his grandsons as his sons. **42.** ' The fear of Isaac ' signifies God whom he reverenced. ' away empty-handed '. **43.** ' What can I do for my children ' ; cf. 50. It seems to be rather a way out of the awkward position in which he has involved himself than genuine solicitude for his daughters.

44-55 The Pact between Laban and Jacob—45. ' for **o** a memorial ' ; see on 28:18. **46.** This friendly meal sealing the pact is mentioned here by anticipation.

40 It followed the solemn oath, 54. See on 27:23. **47b** is an explanatory gloss of St Jerome's. In MT Laban names the mound in Aramaic, Jacob in Hebrew Gal'ed, which is a play on Galaad (Gilaad) the name of the region. **48.** ' The name thereof was called Galaad, **49**, and Mispah, because he said " May the Lord keep watch between us " '. Again a play on the name. Mispah means ' watch-place '. The place cannot be identified. **50.** ' besides them '. **51.** Though Jacob had set up the stone, 45, Laban had provided the occasion ; but the word is suspect also on philological grounds. **53.** ' fear ' : see on 42. **54.** They eat a sacrificial meal together. **55.** ' in the morning '. This verse is 32:1 in MT which consequently has its verse-numeration one higher than DV throughout ch 32.

p XXXII 1-2 Jacob is greeted by Angels—1. As Jacob had been comforted by a vision of Angels when he left the land of promise, 28:12, so now is he greeted on his return. He will not be deprived of God's protection. **2.** A play on the name of Mahanaim, later one of the Levitical cities in the territory of Gad, Jos 21:37. Perhaps = Khirbet Maḥneh.

q 3-23 His Preparations for the Meeting with Esau— 6. Omit ' with speed '. **10.** Omit ' of the least '. Jacob had had to escape to Harran and could say that he had set out with nothing but his staff. **11.** That is, ruthlessly slaughter us all ; cf. Os 10:14. **15.** ' ten bulls . . . and ten he-asses '. **16.** True to his character Jacob has calculated exactly what should be done. **21.** In one of the camps ; cf. 7 ; a Hebraism. **22.** ' And rising in the night '. This was part of his precautions. He did not wish Esau to come upon him while engaged in the difficult task of taking flocks and herds over the River Jabbok.

5a 24-32 Jacob wrestles with an Angel—This mysterious struggle took place on the S. side of the Jabbok, 22, during the later hours of the night after the whole caravan had passed over. It is possible that Jacob remained behind to show stragglers of his large company the way to follow. The ' man ' who wrestled with him was an Angel ; see on 28 and Os 12:4. It was only by divinely given strength that he could hold his own, and from this achievement he was to learn that God's blessing and protection would be with him in all the difficulties of the future. In particular it was a guarantee of a successful outcome of his meeting with the redoubtable Esau and his armed band. **b 24.** Jacob did not yet know that his assailant was not a man as he appeared to be ; cf. 18:2. **25.** ' and Jacob's thigh-bone was sprained as he wrestled with him '. He touched not the sinew but the curved part, generally understood to mean the socket. This was to prove to Jacob the reality of his experience. **26.** ' it is break of day '= We have struggled long enough and it is useless to continue, as neither can gain complete mastery. But Jacob will not let him go unless he first gives a sign that he departs without further evil intent. **27.** Jacob did not know that the ' man ' knew his name. **28.** A good example of a relative truth expressed in an absolute form. He is frequently called Jacob in later passages. Israel, like Ishmael, is compounded of a verb and El ' God '. The verb is of uncertain meaning, but in the light of the context and of Arabic most prob. = ' to contend ', the name being understood = ' Striver with God '. ' for thou hast striven with God and with men and hast prevailed '. ' God ' here is Elohim, a name applicable to any supernatural being, 1 Kg 28:13, but so frequently used of God himself that without contrary indication it cannot be otherwise understood. Prob. therefore = ' thou hast striven with God in the person of his representative, the Angel ' rather than ' with a supernatural being '. The new name with its explanation is a presage of future success. **30.** ' my life '. **31.** The halting is explained by 25. Its purpose being to assure him of the reality of the struggle, there is no reason to suppose that it was permanent. **32.** There is no legal prescription to this effect. Omit ' and it shrank '.

XXXIII 1-16 Meeting of Jacob and Esau—9. Oriental **155c** politeness imposes a preliminary refusal ; cf. 23:11. **10.** ' for I have been received into thy presence as into that of God, and thou hast been gracious to me '. ' God ' is in Heb. Elohim ; see on 32:28. For the phrase, to our ideas exaggerated, cf. 1 Kg 29:9. **11.** ' The blessing ' is the gift, the concrete expression of good wishes. **12.** Esau wished to provide an escort and was glad to be with his brother again. It is remarkable that he, the representative of Edom, hereditary foes of Israel, is depicted in so noble a light in this meeting. **13.** But Jacob is suspicious and would rather see his brother's back. He has not forgotten his fear of being attacked. **14.** ' the cattle and the children '. Whether he ever meant to go to Seir may be doubted. **17-20 Jacob reaches Shechem—17.** Jacob stayed some **d** years in Succoth, later in the territory of Gad, Jos 13:27, during which his children grew up to manhood, ch 34. **18.** There is a village called Salim N. of the plain E. of Shechem (= modern Nablus). But some, supported by Sam., take šālēm as an adj. ' unharmed ', which makes a suitable ending to the narrative of his long and dangerous journey. ' returned from Paddan Aram ' ; see on 28:2. **19.** ' lambs ' : so LXX, Vg ; Syr. ' sheep ' ; modern commentators, pieces of metal of unknown weight. The second plot of ground acquired in Canaan ; see 23:17 f. Here were buried the bones of Joseph, Jos 24:32. **20.** ' he named it " Mighty is the God of Israel " ' ; so prob., using the new name conferred upon him. Other names of altars, Ex 17:15, Jg 6:24. **XXXIV 1-31 Vengeance on the Shechemites—3. e** Omit ' whereas she was sad '. **10.** ' Remain, you may move around the country and settle in it '. **12.** ' Set the price of the bride high '. **21.** ' let them wander about in the land, which is large and wide enough to take them '. **25.** Simeon and Levi did not attack alone but at the head of their numerous followers. It is the wont of biblical writers to leave even important circumstances to be supplied by the reader's intelligence. Why Ruben, the firstborn, took no part it is impossible to say. The others may have been too young. **27.** The word ' other ' is an explanatory gloss of doubtful authenticity. **28.** Omit ' wasting '. The universal expression is to be understood with the qualification suggested by the context, viz. they took all they wished and could transport. **30.** Jacob here condemns only the imprudence of the slaughter. In 49:5-7 he condemns its immorality.

XXXV 1-15 Jacob again at Bethel—2. This prone- **f** ness to idolatry was to be Israel's curse for centuries. Rachel has the teraphim, 31:19, and see Jos 24:14. The cleansing through washing was a sign of reverence and a symbol of interior purity and perhaps had reference to the blood-shedding of ch 34. As a further sign of reverence they were to put on their best clothes, 27:15. **4.** The earrings, adorned with some pagan symbol, served as amulets or talismans. ' the terebinth by Shechem ' is prob. that of 12:6, Jg 9:37. **7.** Jacob confirms and publishes the name (Bethel = ' Habitation of God '), which he had previously given when alone, 28:19. Alternatively, it is possible that the name is mentioned in 28:19 by anticipation. **8.** Rebecca's nurse, who had accompanied her from Harran, 24:59, must have joined Jacob since his return. He had been back a considerable time (see on 33:17) and had certainly paid an unrecorded visit to his father. Possibly Debora joined Jacob on that occasion. She will have been about 80. **9-10.** It is not said that Jacob's name was changed at Bethel or that there the change made near the Jabbok, 32:28, was confirmed. It is said to have occurred ' after he returned from Paddan Aram '. This vague phrase would not have been used, had the intention been to relate an experience subsequent to that near the Jabbok. The present passage therefore seems to be a misplaced repetition of the incident related in ch 32. Possibly too **11-13** belong chronologically after 32:29, where the expected mention of the departure of Jacob's celestial visitant is

155f not found. 'God Almighty': see on 17:1. **14.** On the view of the passage here proposed, according to which 14 resumes the narrative of 6-8, the words 'where God had spoken to him' refer to the divine utterance of 28:13 f. The 'monument' set up by Jacob on his outward journey was a rough stone, 28:18, and was probably no longer standing. He therefore sets up another. A drink-offering or libation of wine became a regular part of the Mosaic liturgy. **15.** See on 7.

g **16-20 Birth of Benjamin and Death of Rachel—16.** '*After their departure from Bethel, when still at some distance from Ephrata*'. **18.** Omit 'for pain'. Jacob does not wish his son to have a name reminiscent of sorrow and calls him Benjamin 'Son of Good Fortune', the right hand (*yāmîn*) being associated with success and prosperity. **19.** Rachel's burial-place was some distance N. of Bethlehem, 16, and near the border of Benjamin, 1 Kg 10:2. This border touches Jerusalem, Jos 18:16, which is *c* 5 m. N. of Bethlehem. Jer 31:15 gives no indication of the site of the sepulchre. On the Tomb of Rachel situated on the Jerusalem road about a mile from Bethlehem see DBV v 926 f., HBD IV 193.

h **21-29 List of Jacob's Sons and Death of Isaac—21.** The Flock Tower seems to have stood between Bethlehem and Hebron. **22.** LXX has preserved the words 'and it was displeasing in his eyes'; *cf.* 49:4. **26.** Benjamin was born in Canaan, 17 f., yet it is said that all the sons were born in Mesopotamia. The difficulty is not removed by suggesting an incorrect gloss. No Hebrew scribe could have failed to know the circumstances of Benjamin's birth. The fact is that the ancient oriental did not set store on exactness as does the modern western mind; *cf.* the apparently exact enumeration of kings in Mt 1 although three are omitted. **29.** There was no occasion to mention Jacob's having greeted Isaac after his return and this is left to the intelligence of the reader to supply. His death is not necessarily recorded in strict chronological order. On his age see § 140*b-f*. As Isaac and Ishmael had met at the grave of Abraham, 25:9, so now Jacob and Esau at that of Isaac—a lesson in filial piety.

156a **XXXVI 1-43 Esau and the Edomites—**As after the death of Abraham Ishmael was to disappear from the story and an account of him and his family was inserted after the record of his father's burial, 25:12-18, so now after the mention of Isaac's death and burial there follows a notice devoted to Esau and the Edomites who looked to him as their forefather. The chapter is compiled from various documents. **1-8** Esau and his family; **9-14** clans descended from Esau; **15-19** governors of provinces; **20-28** and **29-30** the Horrites or Hurrians, who dwelt in the land before the Edomites, and their rulers; **31-39** list of the kings of Edom; **40-43** governors of Edom (after the conquest of Edom by David).

b **1-8.** This account of **Esau's family and fortunes** differs from that already given. It does not seem possible to reconcile the list of his wives with 26:34 and 28:9 or to account for the discrepancies by scribal errors. The account is introduced in 1 as a document and the explanation is probably that the compiler of Genesis, fully aware of the differences, preferred to set it down as he found it without making himself responsible for the accuracy of all its details. (In 2 read 'Ana, the *son* [Sam., LXX, Syr.] of Sebeon the *Horrite*'; *cf.* 24 f.) The same explanation seems to apply to **6-7** which suppose Esau to have left Canaan for Seir (= Edom) only after the return of Jacob from Mesopotamia whereas in 32:3 Esau is already established in Seir before Jacob's return. 7 is based on 13:6 and is prob. an addition to the document.

c **9-14.** This document repeats the names given in 1-8 and on the analogy of ch 10 adds the **names of clans** claiming descent from Esau. **11.** Theman was celebrated for wisdom, Jer 49:7, and Eliphaz, one of Job's wise friends, was a Themanite, Job 2:11. The Kenizzites (Cenezites) or a branch of them later became part of the tribe of Judah, Jos 14:6, 14. **12.** The Amalecite

clan here mentioned will have arisen through the **15** fusion of elements of the ancient people of that name, Num 24:20, with Edomite stock (Heinisch).

15-19. In this **list of Edomite princes** omit Core in 16 **d** with Sam. The names are the same as in 9-14. Note that in both 16 and 12 the son of the secondary wife Thamna is credited to Ada; *cf.* 16:2.

20-30. This **genealogical table of Horrites** (Hurrians) **e** **20-28**, and **list of their princes** or sheikhs, **29-30**, are inserted because the Horrites dwelt in the land before the Edomites and intermarried with them, 2, 14, 22. These princes will have been contemporary with the Edomites, 15-18. In 28 Vg with LXX has 'Aram', MT 'Aran'.

31-39. With the unification of the country Edom passed **f** under **the rule of kings.** The kingship was not hereditary; in no case is a king succeeded by his son. In 31 DV, in agreement with AV + RV, gives a possible translation, but the context requires '*before the kingship of the Israelites*', before the Israelites ruled over Edom, 2 Kg 8:14. **27.** 'Saul of Rehoboth *by the River*'; unidentified.

40-43. The kings were succeeded, 1 Par 1:51, by **g** **governors of provinces.** Those listed here, 40, '*by their clans, their provinces and names*', were probably of David's appointment.

XXXVII 1-11 Joseph's Dreams—2. MT, LXX and **h** Sam. have 'seventeen'. **3.** Benjamin is not taken into account as still too young. '*he used to make him [i.e.* have made for him] *a long sleeved tunic*'; so Vg in 23 'tunica talaris'. The ordinary working tunic was sleeveless and reached only to the knees. **5.** Omit the last clause with LXX. It has been inserted here from 8. **10.** '*bow down to the ground to honour thee?*'

12-36 Joseph is sold into Egypt—13. As indicated **i** already by his special tunic Joseph ordinarily stayed at home, though his first dream, 7, shows that he did join in the common tasks. The leading of the flocks to distant pastures combined with agriculture, 7, illustrates the semi-nomadic, semi-sedentary life led by the patriarchs; *cf.* 26:12. **14.** Hebron to Shechem is about 50 m. **15.** 'wandering in the *open country*'. **17.** Dothain is about 13 m. N. of Shechem. **20.** 'into *a cistern*'. So also in 22: '*but do not raise a hand against him*'. Ruben intends to rescue him from the cistern when the others are at a distance; they mean to leave him to die there. **23.** '*of the long sleeved tunic that he was wearing*'. Omit 'that . . . colours'. **26.** By letting Joseph die in the cistern they would kill him but with no trace of his blood to cry for vengeance, 4:10; Job 16:19. **28.** The traders, called Ishmaelites in 25, 27 and 39:1, are called Madianites. This is not a discrepancy or proof of diversity of sources. The names were used indifferently as may be seen in Jg 8:22, 24, 26. The two tribes were closely related, 25:2, 12, and intermingled. For the price *cf.* Lev 27:5. 'They drew him out', namely Joseph's brothers. Such changes of subject are characteristic of Hebrew. Of Joseph's agony at the brutal treatment we learn explicitly 42:21. **29.** When the others had moved camp, Ruben returned to the cistern in order to rescue Joseph, as he had planned. For this purpose he had found an excuse for absenting himself and so was not present at the time of the sale. **35.** 'into *Sheol*', the name given by the Hebrews to the subterranean abode whither all the dead were thought to go irrespective of the moral value of their lives; *cf.* Sutcliffe, *The Old Testament and the Future Life*, 1947². **30.** 'captain of the *guard*'.

XXXVIII 1-5 Judah's Marriage—1. This chapter inter- **j** rupts the story of Joseph with which it has no connection. The introductory phrase 'at that time' is a vague literary link with the preceding and affords no chronological information; *cf.* Mt 3:1. Adullam was a city of Judah, Jos 15:35. **2.** Unlike his father and grandfather Judah marries a Canaanite. **5b.** 'She was in Kezib [= Achzib, Jos 15:44] when she bore him'. So MT emended after LXX, but the sense renders this doubtful.

6-10 Death of Her and Onan—7. On account of his **k**

k wickedness Her died a premature death. On the omission of secondary causes see § 139a. **8.** ' and marry her *as her husband's brother* '. This custom of Levirate marriage was afterwards incorporated in the Mosaic law, Deut 25:5-10. **9.** According to Deut 25:6 the firstborn son took the dead brother's name and, it is clear, succeeded to his rights. Her was Judah's eldest son, and Onan wished to secure the right of inheritance for himself. ' He knowing that the *seed* '. **10.** It is explicitly said that Onan was punished for his wicked act. There was a strong social custom in favour of the Levirate marriage, but it was not a moral obligation, Deut 25:7-10.

l **11-30 Birth of Phares and Zara — 12.** Timnah (Thamnas), perhaps the town of that name near Hebron mentioned Jos 15:57. ' the Odollamite his *friend* '. **14.** ' *and covered herself with a veil and wrapped herself up. She then sat in the entrance to Enayim, which is on the way to Timnah* '. Thamar was now convinced that Judah did not mean to marry her to his third son Sela. **15.** Omit ' lest . . . known '. She had dressed herself to look like a harlot. **18.** ' *thy seal with its cord* ', by which it was worn hung round the neck. **20.** ' by his *friend* '. **21.** ' that sat *at Enayim by the wayside* '. **23.** ' *Let her keep them, lest we be put to shame* ', by its becoming known that the woman has played a successful trick. What she had was worth more than the promised kid. **24.** Thamar was betrothed to Sela. The later law was less severe, Deut 22:23 f., and the penalty of burning was reserved for the daughters of priests, Lev 21:9. **25.** ' whose *seal* and *cord* '. **26.** ' She is *more in the right* than I, because *this is the result of my not giving her* to Sela my son '. **28.** ' *came* forth '. **29.** Phares was an ancestor of David's, Ru 4:18-22. Hence through him Thamar has a place in the genealogy of Christ, Mt 1:3.

'a **XXXIX 1-23 Joseph is unjustly cast into Prison—1.** ' captain of the *guard* '. Some think that Putiphar is here called a eunuch in accordance with the extension of the term to men in high offices generally held by such. **5.** Yahweh (DV ' the Lord ') is no territorial god. His rule is exercised, as in Canaan, so in the land of the many gods of Egypt. **16.** Omit ' for . . . fidelity ' which is an explanatory gloss. **19.** Omit also ' and giving . . . words '.

b **XL 1-23 Joseph interprets the Dreams of Two Prisoners —1.** The butler and baker were two high court officials. They were probably arrested on suspicion of treason. **3.** ' the commander of the *guard* '. **7.** ' *Why do you look sad today ?* ' **8.** In the prison they could not consult a professional interpreter of dreams. Joseph replies that if God sends dreams they cannot be interpreted by human art but only by divine illumination. **13.** ' Pharaoh *will put an end to thy disgrace* ' ; lit. ' will lift up thy head ', a phrase used also 4 Kg 25:27. **15.** He was not stolen in the literal sense, but he was spirited away out of the country and the fact was kept secret from his father. Our word ' stealthily ' is akin to this Hebrew use of ' steal '. **16.** ' baskets of *white bread* '. On his head according to Egyptian custom. **19.** ' on a *tree* '. After execution he was to be suspended as prey for birds—for an Egyptian a most severe sentence on account of the national belief that the preservation of the body is essential to a happy existence after death. **22.** ' *according to the interpretation Joseph had given* '.

c **XLI 1-37 Joseph interprets Pharaoh's Two Dreams— 1.** The river is the Nile. **2.** ' and they *grazed among the rushes* '. **3b.** ' and *halted by the (other) kine* on the bank of the river '. **7.** ' Pharaoh *awoke and lo ! it was a dream* '. **8.** ' all the *diviners* of Egypt '. **10.** ' the captain of the *guard* '. **14.** Egyptians shaved the beard and some also the head. **16.** ' *Not I* '. **18.** ' And they grazed *among the rushes* '. **34.** As the years were to have extraordinary yields, there was no hardship in a tax of one-fifth to provide for the coming lean years. **37.** ' and all his *ministers* '.

d **38-46 Joseph appointed Viceroy of Egypt—42.** ' *and put it on Joseph's hand* '. **43.** Cf. the honour paid to Mardochai, Est 6:11. Heralds in advance of Joseph's chariot called out ' Abrek ', probably some Egyptian word but of uncertain meaning. **45.** His new Egyptian name Ṣāpᵉnaṭ-paʿnēaḥ has been variously interpreted. It would seem that it must have had a meaning like ' Feeder of the Land '. On = Heliopolis (= ' City of the Sun '), NW. of modern Cairo, had a great temple dedicated to the Sun-god. The priesthood was very influential and powerful. The marriage, arranged by Pharaoh himself, was one most honourable in Egyptian eyes. There was at this time no law forbidding the members of the patriarchal family from marrying foreigners ; cf. 26:34 (Esau), 38:2 (Judah), 38:6 (Thamar). (There was, however, a traditional feeling against so doing ; cf. 24:3 [Abraham], 26:35 and 28:1 [Isaac and Rebecca] ; and experience was already showing the evil effects that might be expected from such marriages, 38:7, 10.) **46.** ' To stand before the king ' = to be appointed a royal minister.

e **47-57 The Years of Abundance and of Famine : Joseph's Two Sons—51.** Joseph does not mean that he had lost all affection for or wished literally to forget his kindred. Cf. Ps 44 (45) 11 ' forget thy people and thy father's house '—an idiom expressing contentment and happiness in a new state of life. **52.** ' God hath made me *fruitful* in the land *where I suffered* '. **54.** Lit. ' in all lands '. The universal expression is to be understood, as always, in accord with the context, and here signifies all the neighbouring lands, the conditions prevailing in which could be known by report and by their people flocking to Egypt for corn.

f **XLII 1-5 Jacob sends his Sons to Egypt for Corn— 1.** ' Why are ye *so helpless* ? ' MT ' Why are ye gazing at one another ? ' **4.** ' Benjamin, *the brother of Joseph* ', by the same mother (Rachel).

g **6-25 Joseph's Treatment of his Brothers—11b.** ' We are *honest* men ; thy servants *have not been acting the spy* '. **14.** ' *It is as I* said '. **15.** Joseph had some ground to fear that they might have treated his brother german in some such way as they had treated him and wished to assure himself of Benjamin's safety. After his own experience his caution was fully justified and his treatment of his brothers in no way vindictive. **16.** ' till what you have said be *tested* '. **17.** According to idiom the ' three days ' comprised one full day and parts of two others. **18.** ' he brought them out of prison ' is an explanatory addition. **19.** ' *honest* men . . . and *take* corn *to relieve the need of your households* '. **20.** ' They did as he had said ', though the actual execution of Joseph's command is related only in 26 ; see on 27:23. **22.** Omit ' one of them '. **25.** Joseph retains not the oldest, for Ruben had striven to save him, but Simeon, the oldest of those who had treated him treacherously.

h **26-38 Nine Brothers return to Jacob—27.** ' *where they rested for the night* ' ; DV ' in the inn '. It was probably in the open. **30.** ' and *put us in prison as though we were spying out the land* ' ; cf. LXX. **31.** ' We are *honest* men and we *have not been playing the spy* '. **34d.** ' and afterwards you may *move freely about the country* '. **38.** ' *befall him on your journey* '. ' Hell ', see on 37:35.

i **XLIII 1-15 Jacob's Sons take Benjamin to Egypt—5.** ' as we have often said ' is an addition of Vg made to ease the style. **6.** ' *Why did you do me this wrong by telling him* '. **8.** ' both we *and thou* and our children '. **9.** I take responsibility for the boy. **11.** Storax is a resinous gum. The same word is translated ' spices ' in 37:25. The exact meaning is uncertain. In 35:4 ' the turpentine tree ' translates Vg ' terebintus ', the word which Vg has also here. This is the tree called by Linnaeus *Pistacia terebinthus*, and its product ' pistachio nuts ', said to be still a delicacy in Egypt, is that suggested here by Jacob. **12.** ' double money, *for you must take back what you found in your sacks* ', *i.e.* money for the new purchase as well as the price of the old. **14.** ' And *if I am to be bereaved of my children, well I shall be bereaved* '. Jacob is now resigned ; cf. 4 Kg 7:4.

j **16-34 Joseph, still unrecognized, gives a Feast to his Brothers—16.** Omit ' victims '. The steward was to provide fresh meat for the meal. Beef and goose were favourite dishes. **21.** ' *to where we spent the night.* '

157j **23.** '*The money you owed came into my keeping*'. **26.** ' the presents *they had brought*'. Again Joseph's dream came true. **30.** ' his brother, and *was on the verge of crying*'. **31.** ' he *restrained* himself'. **32.** The Hebrew guests have no difficulty in eating the Egyptian dishes. Contrast Dan 1:8, but the strict food regulations of later times did not yet exist. The Egyptians were extremely exclusive in regard of foreigners ; see Herod. 2, 41, Diod. Sic. 1, 67. **33.** By silently demonstrating that the details of their family history were known Joseph prepared his brothers for further developments.

k **XLIV 1-13 Benjamin is made to appear Guilty of Theft**—**2.** ' the sack of the *youngest*'. **5.** Joseph was thought by the Egyptians to use and to excel in such means of divination and he uses this reputation for his plan to test the dispositions of the others towards his own full brother Benjamin. In view of Joseph's virtue, 39:9, and his conscious reception of supernatural revelations from God, 40:8 and 41:16, it is not probable that he made use of a divining cup. On this method of divination see Varro in St Augustine, *De Civ. Dei* 7, 35. **6.** The first sentence is an addition of Vg to make the narrative run more smoothly. **12.** It is noteworthy that there is no word of accusation or explanation about the money which had been secretly placed in all the sacks, 1 f. Despite a certain diffusiveness of style these narratives leave much unsaid, and the reader is left to understand that the apparent theft of the cup showed all the baser in view of the generosity with which they had been treated.

l **14-34 The Subsequent Interview with Joseph**—**14.** Judah takes the lead as he had made himself responsible for Benjamin's safety, 43:8 f. Again Joseph's dream comes literally true. **15.** '*Do ye not know that a man like me practises divining ?*' See on 5. **16.** Judah, speaking in the name of all, accepts responsibility for all. There is no attempt to fix the blame on Benjamin. He must have known that Benjamin was not guilty, but he saw no means of proving him innocent. **18.** Omit ' boldly '. Judah recognizes that Joseph might resent his words '*for thy authority is that of Pharaoh himself*'. **21.** ' *that I may set my eyes on him*'. **22.** Jacob would die. **23.** 'You shall not *enter my presence again*'. **29.** On ' hell ' see on 37:35. **30.** Lit. ' his soul being bound up with his soul '.

m **XLV 1-15 Joseph reveals himself to his Brothers**— **1** gives a glimpse of Joseph's dignity and the number of his attendants. ' And no stranger *was* present *when he made himself known to his brothers*'. **4.** Omit ' mildly '. **5.** ' *Be not distressed*'. Joseph magnanimously recognizes the over-ruling providence of God in his being sold by his brothers into Egypt. **7.** ' *to give you posterity in the land and to preserve your lives by a wonderful deliverance*'. **8.** Joseph calls himself a father to Pharaoh as helping him by his counsel and by guarding his interests ; *cf.* Is 22:21. **10.** Goshen (Gessen) was the district lying nearest to Canaan on the NE. frontier of Egypt. Through it ran the fertile valley of the Wady Tumilat. This territory provided suitable pasture for Jacob's flocks and herds and also had the advantage of rendering departure comparatively easy should the need ever arise. **12.** ' My mouth ' : Joseph was now alone with his brothers and speaking in his native tongue, not as before, 42:23, through an interpreter.

n **16-28 Pharaoh invites Jacob to come to Egypt**—**16.** ' The brethren of Joseph ' : the Egyptians will have called Joseph by his Egyptian name. ' Pharaoh with all his *ministers*'. **20.** ' *Have no regret at leaving your belongings behind* ' : lit. ' Let not your eye take pity on your furniture '. **22.** ' *To each and all he gave festal garments . . . and five festal garments*'. **23.** ' *And to his father in like manner he sent ten he-asses to carry choice products of Egypt and as many she-asses with wheat, wine, and provisions for his journey*'. ' Bread ' (MT, Vg) would not have been a suitable provision for a journey which could not be begun for quite a time ; Syr. has ' wine '. **24.** Joseph foresees the danger of their falling to quarrelling about the guilt of having sold him into Egypt. They should let bygones be bygones. **26.** ' *But*

Jacob remained unmoved for he did not believe them '. Lit. ' his heart grew cold '. He did not become benumbed at news which he thought incredible. **28.** Jacob's love for Joseph had not dimmed with time.

XLVI 1-7 Jacob goes down into Egypt—**1.** ' with all *his dependants* came to *Beersheba* '. He started his journey from Hebron, 35:27. **3.** Isaac had built an altar at Beersheba, 26:23–5, and lived there, 28:10. ' I will make a great nation of thee there '. This promise is the culmination of the introductory character of Genesis and prepares the reader for the subsequent history narrated in Exodus. **5.** ' from *Beersheba* '. **6.** ' *And they took their cattle and all the substance which they had gained in the land of Canaan* '.

8-27 List of Jacob's Family—The list presents various **b** difficulties. It purports to give the names of those who entered Egypt with Jacob, 8, but includes Her and Onan, who died in Canaan, 12. It also gives the names of ten sons of Benjamin, 21, but he has just been described as a young boy, 44:20. The sum of the numbers given, $33 + 16 + 14 + 7$ (15, 18, 22, 25) add up to 70 (and if Jacob is added, the total is 71), but the total is given in 26 as 66. To this are added in 27 Joseph, his two sons, and Jacob, the sum being again 70. The wives of Jacob's sons are explicitly excluded, 26, and Jacob's own wives are not counted either. The total 66 in 26 is partially explained by the omission of Joseph and his two sons (mentioned in 20 and counted in the 14 of 22). This leaves one to account for. Dina is not counted in the total of 33 in 15 and her name, which fits awkwardly in MT, may be a later addition. Sara, another woman, 17, is included in the total of 16 in 18. A plausible explanation is that Her and Onan are also excluded as having died in Canaan, and that Dina is added. In 17 for ' Jesua and Jessuri ' MT has ' Yishwah and Yishwi ' but Yishwah is missing from the parallel list in Num 26:44–6, and it is perhaps a case of dittography. It is also possible that Ahod is an erroneous addition in 10. His name does not occur in the lists of Num 26:12 f. and 1 Par 4:24. A comparison of our list with those in Ex 6:14–6, Num 26 and 1 Par 2–8 presents further difficulties about the forms of names and the degrees of relationship. For instance, Jamuel's name occurs in the same form in Ex 6:15, but as Namuel (Nemuel) in Num 26:12 and 1 Par 4:24 both in MT and Vg. For a discussion the larger commentaries must be consulted, *e.g.* Hummelauer 570–4. The artificiality of the list recalls the remarks made on 35:26. Besides his family there went down also with Jacob the members of his large household. For the number *cf.* the total of Abraham's fighting-men, 14:14.

28-34 Meeting of Jacob and Joseph—**28.** Jacob sends **c** Judah, his fourth son. Ruben, Simeon and Levi had all incurred their father's displeasure, 35:22 ; 34:25–30. **34.** The Egyptians had flocks and herds of sheep and cattle, 47:17, Ex 9:3, and Pharaoh's own herds of cattle are mentioned in 47:6. They were tended by men of the lowest class who were despised apparently because the nature of their calling prevented that high standard of personal cleanliness cultivated in Egyptian society. Still greater would be the contempt for foreign shepherds and herdsmen.

XLVII 1-13 Jacob and his Family settle in Egypt— **d** **2.** Omit ' the last '. The number five seems to have been favoured by the Egyptians, 41:34 ; 43:34 ; 45:22. **6.** ' *able* men '. **7.** ' *Jacob blessed Pharaoh* ', *i.e.* saluted him with wishes for his welfare ; *cf.* 1 Kg 13:10, where the same Heb. word is translated ' salute '. So also twice in 4 Kg 4:29. **9.** ' The days of my *sojourning* '. The Heb. word does not convey the pious connotation of the English ' pilgrimage '. **10.** ' Blessing ' : see on 7. **11.** ' in the land *of* Ramesses ', that is, the territory of which the town of the same name, Ex 1:11, was the capital. This was in the eastern part of the Nile delta on the site known today as Ṣan el-Ḥagar. The territory will have been part of the land of Goshen (Gessen). On the city of Ramesses see § 163*b*. This was built by Ramses II, 1300–1233. The name is therefore pro-

3d leptic for the time of Joseph ; *cf.* the use of the name Dan in 14:14. Whether or not the name is anachronistic for the time of Moses depends on the further question whether the Exodus fell in the 15th or the 13th cent. ; *cf.* § 125*b–c*.

e 13-26 Political Effects of the Famine in Egypt—13. 'In the whole world there was want of bread, *for the famine was very grievous, and the land of Egypt and the land of Canaan were exhausted thereby*'. For the meaning of the universal expression ' the whole world ' see on 41:54. **22.** '*Except that the land of the priests he did not buy, for they had an allotted portion from Pharaoh and they ate the portion which Pharaoh gave them*'. **26.** The ordinance does not appear to have been wholly equitable. The people had first to surrender a fifth of their produce during the years of plenty, 41:34, and during the years of dearth were forced to buy it back until their resources were exhausted. On the other hand, in view of the fertility of Egypt the tax of one-fifth was not oppressive. Contrast the heavier taxes paid by the Jews, 1 Mac 10:29 f. The land of Egypt, according to Herod. II 109, 141, 168, Diod. Sic. I 54, 73 f., belonged to the king and the priests, and each of the military caste received his portion tax-free.

f 27-31 Jacob's End draws Near—27. 'Israel' is here used collectively of all Jacob's descendants. ' *they* grew and *were* multiplied '. **28.** ' And *Jacob* lived '. **29.** For the rite see on 24:2. ' this kindness and *fidelity* '. **30.** For the burial-place see 23:17–20 ; 25:9 ; 35:27–29. **31.** LXX has ' on the top of his staff ', implying the same consonants but different vocalization. This Greek reading is quoted Heb 11:21, where Vg omits the preposition. MT is supported by 48:2 ; and a different word is used for Jacob's staff in 32:10. Moreover, ' his ' is lacking in MT and, though not required with ' bed ', appears necessary with ' staff '.

g XLVIII 1-22 Jacob adopts Ephraim and Manasses, setting the Younger before the Elder—2. ' *gathering his strength together* '. **3.** Omit the stylistic gloss of Vg ' when . . . to him '. Luz = Bethel, 28:19. **4.** ' *a company of peoples* ', as in 28:3, referring to the twelve tribes. ' to thee and to thy seed ' : so LXX and Vg. MT only ' to thy seed '. But it was given to Jacob in the person of his descendants ; *cf.* 12:7 with 15:7. ' everlasting ' : see on 13:15. **5.** ' *And now* thy two sons '. Ephraim and Manasses were to become the heads of two tribes, taking the place of their father Joseph among Jacob's other sons. **6.** Joseph's other sons and their descendants were to be part of the tribes named after their two eldest brothers. **7.** ' Canaan *while I was on my way and yet at some distance from* Ephrata '. Rachel was the wife of Jacob's predilection and she had borne him two sons only, Joseph and Benjamin. To do her honour he adopts two of Joseph's sons as his own and secures a larger inheritance to her descendants. At the same time, the memory of his beloved wife leads him, as is natural in an old man, to a digression about the circumstances of her death and burial. **8.** Jacob will have seen them before but his eyes were dim with age, 10. According to 2 only Joseph had been announced. **11.** ' *I did not expect to see thy face again, and lo ! God hath granted me to see thy seed also* '. **12.** This act of deference to his father betokens real humility in one of Joseph's exalted rank. **13.** He thus put Ephraim, the younger, on Jacob's left, and Manasses, the elder, on his right. **15.** The metaphor in ' feedeth me ' is that of a shepherd ; *cf.* Ps 22:1 ' The Lord is my

h shepherd ' (the same word). **16.** The Angel, in whom God appeared to Jacob, stands for God himself, 31:11 ; 32:24–30. ' and let *them bear my name* '—they are to be reckoned as Jacob's own sons and so directly to inherit the blessings promised to him by God and before him to Isaac and Abraham. **18.** Joseph thought that his father's failing sight, 10, had misled him. ' *He too shall become a people* '. Manasses had territory both E. and W. of the Jordan and was a populous tribe. ' and his seed shall *be the most numerous in the nation* '; lit. ' the full one of the nations '. The word used, *gôyim*, became later a technical expression for Gentiles. Here it is used

as in 35:11, of the tribes of Israel. Ephraim became in **158h** fact the most powerful tribe in Israel and its name is used, as in Is 7:2, to signify the whole Northern Kingdom. **20.** ' *By you* shall *Israel utter a blessing* '. The prosperity of Ephraim and Manasses was to become proverbial and the ideal of happiness. *Cf.* the similar form of blessing in Ru 4:11 f. **22.** The firstborn had a **i** right to a double portion, Deut 21:17. Ruben had lost his right, 35:22, and Joseph as the saviour of his family merited it. Jacob by putting Joseph's two sons on a level with his own secured to Joseph a double portion, the territory, namely, of Ephraim and Manasses. At the same time he gave to Joseph personally the plot of ground which he had bought from the Canaanites for 100 *qesitas*, 33:19. This was near Shechem, and there Joseph was eventually buried, Jos 24:32. This seems to be the meaning and the text to have suffered early in the course of textual transmission. The corruption of *qesita* led to the introduction of the similar word for ' bow ', and the phrase was completed from Jos 24:12 (Hummelauer, Hoberg). There is probably corruption also in the first half of the verse, lit. ' I give thee one shoulder ', the Heb. word for which is the same as the name of the city Shechem.

XLIX 1-28 Jacob foretells the Future of his Sons— 159a The title ' Jacob's Blessings ', which is found already in the superscription added in Syr., is based on 28. But the words concerning Ruben, Simeon and Levi are an expression of displeasure and do not announce a happy future. As noted also in 28 the predictions concern not so much the sons in person as the tribes named after them. Nonetheless the twelve names are those of Jacob's twelve sons. Joseph is not replaced by Ephraim and Manasses. Contrast Num 1:5–15 ; 2:3–31.

The language of the blessings is elaborate and poetic, **b** and it is agreed that they cannot have been pronounced by the aged and dying Jacob in their present form. They must have been recast and embellished at some later time. Besides the elevated diction such an inspired poet may well have also been responsible for certain additions to the substance. God could, of course, reveal the future to Jacob in all its details, but it is not in accord with God's ordinary providence to reveal in advance the geographical location of the territory to be allotted to a tribe, as is the case here with Zabulon, 13. The date at which this editor did his work cannot now be fixed. The age of David has been suggested on account of the hegemony of Judah ; but against this may be urged the omission of a reference to the beginning of kingship in the tribe of Benjamin. Moreover, and this is a more weighty consideration, the utterances about Dan, Gad and Benjamin reflect a period when the tribes were still more or less independent units and there existed no central authority. The number of unusual expressions also points to an early date. That this editor worked on an existing source is shown by the reprobation of Levi which would have been unthinkable after the time of Moses, when this tribe received the honour of being entrusted with the care of the sanctuary and of liturgical worship.

The brothers are mentioned in the following order. **c** First are named the six sons of Lia, with Zabulon placed before Issachar. Then come the four sons of Bala and Zelpha with the two sons of the latter inserted between the two sons of the former. The list closes with the two sons of Rachel. The order is therefore that of age with the exceptions indicated.

Characteristic of the blessings are the plays upon the **d** names which were so favoured by the Hebrews. Some have found also allusions to the signs of the zodiac claimed to have been allotted to the twelve tribes. The fullest presentment of this theme is given by E. Burrows, S.J., *The Oracles of Jacob and Balaam* (London, 1939). It is founded on Joseph's dream in 37:9.

3-4 Ruben. 3. ' *Ruben, my firstborn art thou, my strength* **e** *and the firstfruit of my vigour, pre-eminent in majesty and pre-eminent in power, 4, uncontrollable like flowing water, thou*

159e *shalt not have pre-eminence, for thou didst go up on thy father's bed ; to my sorrow thou didst defile my couch '.* Ruben seems to have suggested *rab* ' captain, chief '—if so, a hidden allusion to the name. The reference to water is explained as an allusion to Aquarius. As the firstborn Ruben should have inherited the leadership, but this right he had forfeited by his disgraceful conduct, 35:22. For *'ālāh* read *'ālāy,* as in 48:7.

f **5-7 Simeon and Levi.** ' *Simeon and Levi are brethren ; tools of violence are their weapons.* **6.** *Into their council shall my soul not enter ; to their company my spirit shall not be united. For in their fury they slew a man, and in their wilfulness they lamed an ox.* **7.** *Accursed be their fury for its violence and their rage for its harshness. I will scatter them in Jacob and disperse them in Israel '.* **6.** All were brothers, and Simeon and Levi are here called brethren as being companions and partners in the deed of violence and cruelty so displeasing to their father, 34:25-30. ' Man ' and ' ox ' are singulars used collectively. The killing of the Shechemites, 34:25 ; the maiming of the oxen is not mentioned in the prose account, but may well have been part of their vengeance. **7.** The possessions of Simeon were scattered in the territory of Judah, Jos 19:1-9. The tribe of Levi was assigned cities and land in the territory of all the other tribes, Jos 21:1-40. This was not in fulfilment of this prediction but in honour of the priestly dignity. The Levites had merited a blessing at the time of the worship of the golden calf, Ex 32:26-29, and thus deserved to be released from Jacob's sentence.

g **8-12 Judah.** ' *Judah, thee shall thy brethren praise ; thy hand shall be against a fleeing foe ; the sons of thy father shall bow before thee.* **9.** *A lion's whelp is Judah ; from the prey, my son, thou goest up. He lies crouching like a lion ; who will dare to rouse him ?* **10.** *The sceptre shall not be taken from Judah nor the staff from between his feet till he comes to whom it belongs and his shall be the obedience of the peoples.* **11.** *He bindeth his ass to a vine and his ass's colt to a choice vine. He washeth his garment in wine and his vesture in the blood of grapes.* **12.** *His eyes are dark with wine and his teeth are white with milk '.* **8.** The Heb. opens with deliberate assonance, *yᵉhûdāh . . . yôdûkā.* **9.** On the zodiacal hypothesis the language describing Judah's strength and bravery is chosen with reference to the constellation Leo. **10.** The conduct of the three elder brothers had been gravely displeasing to their father. They are now passed over and supremacy is promised to Judah, the next in age. Most MSS of MT have *šîlōh* with the meaning ' till he comes to Shilo ' or ' till Shilo comes ', and the Rabbis saw in this latter a designation of the Messias as the one whose characteristic was to be a reign of peace. But this is unknown to the ancient versions, which nonetheless (except for the vocalic *yod*) represent the same Heb. text, *šlh* except Vg where ' mittendus est ' represents *šlḥ,* but this reading cannot be right against the other textual witnesses especially as the confusion between the two aspirates could easily occur. LXX MSS have both τὰ ἀποκείμενα αὐτῷ and ᾦ ἀπόκειται, to which correspond the translations of the Old Latin ' quae reposita sunt ei ' and ' cui reposita sunt '. Syriac has ' he whose it is ', and Targum Onkelos paraphrases ' till the Messias comes whose is the kingdom ' or ' the kingship ' (*malkûṭā'*). The Samaritan text supported by many Heb. codices also has *šlh* without the intrusive *yod.* This evidence leads us to *šellōh* for the original Heb. (the *h* representing the affixed pronoun as in 11) : ' till he comes whose it is '. And see the similar phrase in Ez 21:27 (MT 32). The parallelism suggests that sceptre and staff are two names for the same emblem of authority, the early sceptre being in the form of a staff, which is the original meaning of σκῆπτρον. Illustrations of such Assyrian sceptres may be seen in B. Meissner, *Babylonien und Assyrien* I (1920) plates 18, 19. **11 f.** describe the peace and prosperity that will mark Judah's supremacy—a land so bountifully covered with vines has not known the ravages of hostile armies ; *cf.* 4 Kg 3:19.

h The royal sceptre passed to the tribe of Judah in the person of David, and to him it was promised through **15** the prophet Nathan that ' Thy throne shall be firm for ever ', 2 Kg 7:16, a prophecy taken up in Ps 88 (89) 30-38 ' I will not lie unto David ; his seed shall endure for ever and his throne shall be as the sun before me '. His descendants lost the temporal throne at the Babylonian conquest in 587 through their manifold infidelities, Ps 131 (132) 12 f. ; 4 Kg 24:20. But the promise of an eternal kingdom remained, and its fulfilment was announced by the Angel Gabriel ' The Lord God shall give unto him the throne of David his father ; and he shall reign in the house of Jacob for ever and of his kingdom there shall be no end ', Lk 1:32 f. There is an echo of this prophecy in Apoc 5:5 with its mention of ' the lion of the tribe of Judah '. **11.** The parallelism indicates that two animals are not intended ; *cf.* sceptre and staff in 10.

13 Zabulon. Nothing is said of Zabulon except its **16** fortunate position in being able to draw on the wealth of the sea ; see also Deut 33:18 f. Josephus likewise mentions that the territory of the tribe touched the sea, *Ant.* 5, 5, 22. This maritime position does not appear in Jos 19:10-16, and the tribal boundaries must have varied at different periods.

14-15 Issachar. ' *Issachar is a strong-built ass lying* **b** *between the shelters. He saw that rest is sweet and the land delightful ; he bent his shoulder to the burden and became a band of labourers '.* The territory of Issachar, Jos 19:17-23, lay largely in the plain of Esdraelon noted for its fertility, Jos. *B.J.* 3, 3, 2. The ass was and is esteemed for its utility in the Near East. The hero Ajax is likened to an ass by Homer, *Iliad* 11, 557 f., and the Caliph Merwan II was called ' the ass of Mesopotamia ', König. On ' the shelters ' see Zorell's *Lex.* ; generally translated ' sheepfolds '. The idea is that of ease joined with security. Issachar is praised in Jg 5:15 for its warlike spirit and Josephus, *B.J.* 3, 3, 2, says that the Galileans were warriors from their youth. The word *mas* is normally used of a forced labour-gang, but here rather contemptuously of the lucrative service rendered largely by asses to the mercantile traffic which passed along the trade routes through the plain of Esdraelon.

16-18 Dan. ' *Dan shall vindicate the rights of his people* **c** *like the other tribes of Israel. He must be a snake by the way, a horned serpent by the path '.* The sentence begins with a play on the name, *dān yādîn.* The snake's power lies in the cunning suddenness of the attack rather than in open force. We are reminded of the strategems used in his exploits by Samson, who was of the tribe of Dan. The ancient chariots were open behind, and the rearing or shying of a terrified horse would easily throw the driver and warrior down backwards. 18, which makes a half-line only, may be a gloss.

19 Gad. ' *Gad raided by raiders himself raids their rear '.* **d** The Gadites dwelling in Galaad were exposed to the attacks of the Ammonites and of raiding Arab tribes, Jg chh 10-11 ; 1 Par 5:18-22, and inflicted heavy defeats on them. Here it is implied that they routed and pursued the retreating enemy.

20 Asher. ' *Asher, rich in food, provides the dainties of a* **e** *king '.* The territory of Asher (Aser) lying along the coast from Carmel northwards, Jos 19:24-31, was very fertile, Deut 33:24. The tribe owing to its proximity to Phoenicia will have had a large share of the trade with that country, Ez 27:17.

21 Nephtali. ' *Nephtali is a spreading terebinth ; he puts* **f** *forth boughs of beauty '.* So prob. after LXX ; perhaps ' oak '. Perhaps with MT : ' N. is a free-roaming hind ' with reference to branched antlers. The allusion would then be to Nephtali's spirit of freedom and eagerness to defend it.

22-26 Joseph. 22. ' *A young fruit-tree is Joseph, a young* **g** *fruit-tree by a spring, with tendrils climbing over the wall.* **23.** *In bitterness they shot at him and the archers persecuted him.* **24.** *But his bow remained firm, and supple were the muscles of his arms, through the help of the Mighty One of Jacob, through the power of the Shepherd of Israel,* **25,** *through the God of thy father, may he help thee ! and with the aid of Shaddai, may he bless thee ! with the blessings of the* heavens above, with the blessings of the deep beneath, with the blessings of breast and womb. **26.** *The blessings granted to thy father are mightier than the blessings of the eternal mountains, than the desire of the everlasting hills. May they come upon the head of Joseph, upon the crown of the head of the prince among his brethren*'. **22.** The allusion is to Joseph himself and his two tribes, Ephraim and Manasses. The vigorous vine, with all the advantages of abundant moisture and a protecting wall, is unhampered in its growth, and suggests the numerical strength of the two tribes. At the same time the pleasing picture presented recalls Joseph's comeliness of face and form, 39:6. **23.** Again a double allusion both to Joseph's persecution at the hands of his brothers and to attacks on the tribes. The Arabs were noted for their archery, 21:20, which suggests an allusion to their attacks on both sides of the Jordan, Jg 6:3 ff., 1 Par 5:18 ff. **24.** Both Joseph and his tribes triumphed through the help of God. Strong arms are needed for the handling of bows suitable for war. **25.** The blessings of the heavens are sunshine, rain and dew ; those of the great subterranean ocean are the springs and rivers which ancient thought conceived to be fed from it. To these blessings so necessary in Palestine is added the prayer for abundance of herds and flocks. **26.** The blessings of the eternal mountains and the ' desire ', the desirable things, the choice products, of the everlasting hills are described in Jl 3:18, Am 9:13, Ex 3:8, streams of sweet wine, milk and honey. The mountains are eternal because immovably fixed and existing from the beginning of the world ; see on 1:2. But Jacob had received blessings more wonderful than these, the promise of continual divine help, of the possession of the land of Canaan, of a multitude of descendants, that in him and his seed all the tribes of the earth should be blessed, 28:3-4, 13-15.

27 Benjamin. ' *Benjamin is a ravening wolf. In the morning he devoureth the prey and in the evening he divideth the spoil* '. He is at all times lustful of booty and ready for the attack. It is not meant that different activities are confined to special times. For an excellent example of this type of sentence see Prov 10:1. Benjamin, though small, was one of the most warlike tribes, Jg 5:14 ; 20:18 ff. ; 2 Kg 2:15. **28** shows that the pronouncements refer primarily to the tribes.

29-32 Jacob's Death—29. Omit ' double ' ; see ch 23. **30.** ' *in the cave which is in the field of Machpelah*, over against . . .' **31.** ' *and there I buried Lia* '. This verse is a parenthesis, 30 being continued in 32 : ' *the field and the cave therein bought from the Hittites* ', lit. ' the sons of Heth '. This is omitted in Vg + DV.

L 1-3 Mourning for Jacob—1. ' And when Joseph saw this ' is a stylistic addition of Jerome's. **2.** Embalming was an Egyptian, not an Israelite, custom, but it was necessary in the case of Jacob if he was to be honoured as the manners of the country required and his body to be transported for burial to Canaan. **3.** At a later date according to Herodotus II 86, 88 embalming took 70 days. According to Diodorus the Egyptian mourning for a king lasted 72 days, I 72. The honour paid to Jacob was for Joseph's sake. The Israelites mourned for Aaron and Moses for 30 days, Num 20:30, Deut 34:8.

4-13 The Burial of Jacob—4. Joseph asks for the intervention of Pharaoh's ' *household* '. For the chief minister of the crown to leave the country may well have required the assent of the other advisers of Pharaoh. **5.** Jacob may have prepared himself a resting-place in the cave of Machpelah, 49:29 f., before he left Canaan. It is also possible that Joseph expressed himself in accordance with Egyptian custom. The Pharaohs and other persons of high rank prepared themselves burial-places during their lifetime. **7.** A large number of the responsible officials of the royal court accompanied the funeral procession. This was primarily to do honour to Joseph. Universal expressions are used with latitude. **9.** A guard was necessary on such a long journey. **10.** The threshing-floor of Atad, or the bramble threshing-floor, is otherwise unknown. A threshing-floor is mentioned as a place of meeting in the MT of 3 Kg 22:10 (DV ' court '). The one here in question was east of the Jordan. Political reasons will have dictated the long march round the Dead Sea instead of the direct route through Beersheba. The mourning ceremonies there lasted 7 days in accordance with Hebrew custom, 1 Kg 31:13. **11.** The place was called (MT) Abel Misraim, ' Egyptian brook ' or ' meadow ', a name reminiscent of *'ēḇel* ' mourning '. The site is unknown. **12.** The Egyptian caravan did not cross into Canaan for the same reason that had imposed the easterly route, 10. **13.** ' *in the cave of the field of Machpelah* '.

14-21 Joseph's Magnanimity—15. Omit ' were afraid '. **19.** ' *Fear not. Am I in place of God ?* ' As 20 shows, the meaning is, can I take umbrage at what God's Providence manifestly has turned to the common good ? **20.** Omit ' exalt . . . see '.

22-25 Joseph's Last Days—22 (MT 23). Joseph saw the children of the third generation in descent from Ephraim, that is, his own great-grandsons, grandsons being the third generation, Ex 20:5. Machir was Manasses' eldest son, Jos 17:1. For ' to be born on the knees ' of someone, see on 30:3. **24** (MT 25). For the execution of this wish see Ex 13:19, Jos 24:32. **25** (MT 26). It is possible that the age of 110 assigned to Joseph is due to the Egyptians. A. Mallon, S.J., *Les Hébreux en Egypte* (Rome, 1921) 72 note, quotes with approval a remark of E. Naville's that it is not probable that the ancient Egyptians knew their true ages and that various inscriptions indicate that for them 110 was the extreme limit of old age. On this hypothesis the 110 years assigned to Joseph would mean that he had reached that advanced age.

EXODUS

By E. POWER, S.J.

162a Bibliography.

(A) Commentaries :

*Keil-Delitzsch, tr. J. P. Lange, Edinburgh 1868 ; *H. C. Strack (Strack-Zücklers Komm.), München 1894 ; *Dillmann-Ryssel, Leipzig 1897³ ; F. de Hummelauer (CSS), Paris 1897 ; *H. Holzinger (Marti's Handkomm.), Tübingen 1900 ; *B. Baentsch (Nowack's Hand-Komm.), Göttingen 1903 ; J. Weiss, Graz 1911 ; *S. R. Driver (CBSC), 1911, reprinted 1918 and 1929 ; *W. H. Bennett (CBi), Edinburgh undated ; *A. H. McNeile (WC), London 1918² ; H. J. Grimmelsman, Cincinnati 1927 ; B. Ubach, Monserrat 1927 ; *F. M. Th. Böhl, Groningen 1928 ; *J. H. Hertz, Pentateuch and Haftorahs II, Oxford 1930 ; F. Ceuppens, Bruges 1932 ; *W. H. Gispen, Kampen, chh 1–15, 1932, chh 16–40, 1939 ; P. Heinisch (BB), Bonn 1934 (most useful) ; *G. Beer, Tübingen 1939.

b (B) Special Subjects :

A. Mallon, *Les Hébreux en Egypte*, Rome 1921 ; F. X. Kortleitner, *Israelitarum in Aegypto Commoratio*, Tongerloo 1930 ; *H. H. Rowley, *Israel's Sojourn in Egypt*, Manchester 1938 ; P. Montet, ' Tanis, Avaris et Pi-Ramses ' RB 39 (1930) 5–28 ; B. Stein, ' Der Engel des Auszuges ' Bi 19 (1938) 286–97 ; *H. Bauer, ' Die Gottheiten von Ras-Schamra ' ZATW 51 (1933) 81–101 ; *O. Eissfeldt, ' Neue Zeugnisse für die Aussprache des Tetragramms als Jahwe ' ZATW 53 (1935) 59–77 ; A. Vaccari, ' Iahve e i nomi divini nelle religioni semitiche ' Bi 17 (1936) 1–10 ; C. Bourdon, ' La route de l'Exode de la terre de Gessé à Mara ' RB 41 (1932) 370–92, 538–49 ; A. Mallon, ' La mer rouge et l'Exode ' Bi 6 (1925) 396–400 ; *H. M. Wiener, ' The Date of the Exodus ' Bs 73 (1916) 454–80 ; *J. W. Jack, *The Date of the Exodus*, London 1925 ; A. Mallon, ' Exode ' DBV(S) 2 (1934) 1333–42 ; *T. H. Robinson, ' The Date of the Exodus ' ET 47 (1935–6) 53–5 ; *H. H. Scullard, ' The Passage of the Red Sea ' ET 42 (1930–1) 55–61 ; *T. H. Robinson, ' Der Durchzug durch das Rote Meer ' ZATW 51 (1933) 170–3 ; M.-J. Lagrange, ' Le Cantique de Moïse ' RB 8 (1899) 532–41 ; J. Linder, ' Das Siegeslied des Moses ' ZKT 44 (1920) 43–77 ; S. Garofalo, ' L'epinicio di Mose ' Bi 18 (1937) 1–22 ; *C. L. Woolley and *T. H. Lawrence, *The Wilderness of Zin*, London 1935 ; *R. Weill, *Le séjour des Israélites au désert et le Sinaï*, Paris 1909 ; L. Prévost, L. Dennefeld, M. David, D. Gorce, M. Lejeune, *Le Sinaï hier . . . aujourd'hui*, Paris 1937 ; *F. S. Bodenheimer und *O. Theodor, *Ergebnisse der Sinaiexpedition 1927*, Jerusalem 1929 ; K. Miketta, ' Wo lag der Berg Sinai ? ' in *Weidenauer Studien* 3 (1909) 77–123 ; 4 (1911) 47–145 ; J. Gabriel, ' Wo lag der biblische Sinai ? ' WZKM 39 (1932) 123–32 ; L. H. Vincent, ' Un nouveau Sinaï biblique ' RB 39 (1930) 73–83 ; *W. J. Phythian-Adams, ' The Mount of God ' PEF 62 (1930) 135–49, 192-202 ; P. Karge, *Geschichte des Bundesgedanken im AT* (AT Abhandlungen II 1-4), Münster 1910 ; *W. Staerk, ' Zum AT Erwählungsglauben ' ZATW 55 (1937) 1–36 ; A. Vaccari, ' De praeceptorum Decalogi distinctione et ordine ' VD 17 (1937) 317–20, 328–34 ; N. Peters, *Die älteste Abschrift der zehn Gebote*, Freiburg 1905 ; Anon, ' Le papyrus Nash ' RB 13 (1904) 242–50 ; *W. F. Albright, ' A Biblical Fragment from the Maccabaean Age : The Nash Papyrus ' JBL 56 (1937) 145–76 ; A. Eberharter, ' Décalogue ' DBV(S) 2 (1934) 341–51 ; K. Fruhstorfer, ' Der Dekalog ' TPQ 77 (1924) 92–101, 216–24 ; P. Heinisch, ' Alter und Eigenart des Dekalogs ' SC 10 (1933-4) 24–39 ; F. Feldmann, ' Das Alter des Dekalogs ' *Bonn Zts f. Th. und Seelsorge* 1 (1924) 213–31 ; I. Verquerre, ' Le Décalogue, code universel et éternel ' RA 63 (1936, 2) 149–66 ; *H. J. Flowers, *The Permanent Value of the Ten Commandments*, London 1927 ; J. Hehn, *Der Israelitische Sabbath* (Bibl. Zeitfragen 11, 12) Münster 1912 ; id. ' Zur Sabbathfrage ' BZ 14 (1917) 198–213 ; *J. Herrmann, ' Das Zehnte Gebot ' in *Sellin-Festschrift* 1927, 69–82 ; F. Prat, *Le Code de Sinaï : sa Genèse et son Evolution* (Science et Religion) Paris 1907 ; W. Stoderl, *Das Gesetz Israels nach Inhalt und Ursprung*, Marienbad 1933 ; *A. Jirku, *Das weltliche Recht im AT*, Gütersloh 1927 ; *A. Alt, *Der Ursprung des israelitischen Rechts*, Leipzig 1934 ; *W. Nowack, *Das Bundesbuch* (ZATW Beiheft 34) Berlin 1920 ; P. Cruveilhier, *Introduction au Code d'Hammourabi*, Paris 1937 ; id., *Commentaire du Code d'Hammourabi*, Paris 1938 ; id. ' Le Code d'Hammourabi et la législation civile des Hébreux ' RCF 69 (1912) 641–73 ; *S. A. Cook, *The Laws of Moses and the Code of Hammurabi*, London 1903 ; *G. R. Driver and *J. C. Miles, *The Assyrian Laws*, London 1935 ; M. Witzel, *Hethitische Keilschrifturkunden* (Keilinschr. Stud. 4), 1 (1924) 132–73 ; J. Nikel, *Das AT und die Nächstenliebe* (Bibl. Zeitfragen VI 11-12), Münster 1913 ; P. Heinisch, ' Das Sklavenrecht in Israel und im Alten Orient ' SC 11 (1934–5) 201–18 ; N. Peters, *Die soziale Fürsorge im AT*, Paderborn 1936 ; *C. Schick, *Der Stiftshütte, der Tempel in Jerusalem und der Tempelplatz der Jetztzeit*, Berlin 1896 ; *E. Sellin, ' Das Zelt Jahwes ' *Beiträge zur Wissenschaft des AT* 13 (1919) 168–92 ; G. Orfali, *De Arca Foederis*, Paris 1918 ; L. Dürr, ' Ursprung und Bedeutung der Bundeslade ' *Bonn. Zts. f. Th. und Seelsorge* 1 (1924) 17–32 ; *G. von Rad, ' Zelt und Lade ' *Neue Kirchl. Zts.* 42 (1931) 476–98 ; H. Lesêtre, ' Tabernacle ' DBV 5 (1912) 1951–61 ; *A. R. S. Kennedy, ' Tabernacle ' HDB 4 (1902) 653–68 ; P. Dhorme et L. H. Vincent, ' Les Chérubins ' RB 35 (1926) 328–58, 481–95 ; A. Eberharter, ' Das Horn im Kult des AT ' ZKT 51 (1927) 394–9 ; J. Gabriel, ' Untersuchungen über das AT Hohepriestertum mit besonderer Berücksichtigung des hohepriesterlichen Ornates ' (*Th. St. der österreichischer Leogesellschaft* 33), 1933 ; S. Landersdorfer, ' Das Problem der Priestersalbung im Gesetze ' TQ 107 (1926) 185–97 ; *M. Löhr, *Das Raucheropfer im AT*, Halle 1927 ; A. Eberharter, ' Das Weihrauchopfer im AT ' ZKT 50 (1926) 89–105 ; A. Van Hoonacker, ' La date de l'encens dans le culte de Jahve ' RB 23 (1914) 161–87 ; F. Steinmetzer, ' Das heilige Salböl des Alten Bundes ' Bz 7 (1909) 17–29 ; P. van Imschoot, ' Le veau d'or ' *Collationes Gandavenses* 14 (1927) 113–16 ; A. Eberharter, ' Die Verehrung des goldenen Kalbes ' *Pastor Bonus* 41 (1930) 109–3 ; *G. K. Berry, ' The Ritual Decalogue ' JBL 44 (1925) 38–43 ; A. Eberharter, ' Besitzen wir in Ex 23 und 34 zwei Rezensionen eines zweiten Dekalogs ? ' BZ 20 (1932) 157–67 ; F. Nötscher, *Das Angesicht Gottes schauen*, Würzburg 1924 ; J. Göttsberger, ' Die Hülle des Moses nach Ex 34 und 2 Kor 3 ' BZ 16

EXODUS

b (1924) 1–17; H. Cazelles, *Le Code de l'Alliance*, Paris 1946.

c Name—The Greek name of the book, Exodos, latinized Exodus, is generally derived from the LXX rendering of 19:1 : *In the third month of the Exodus of the children of Israel from the land of Egypt.* It refers directly only to the first part of the narrative, not to its climax, the Sinaitic Covenant, by which Israel became the chosen people of Yahweh. Typically, however, it indicates also the ultimate object of the Covenant, since the Exodus, by which Israel was delivered from the bondage of Egypt, is a type of the Redemption, by which mankind was freed from the slavery of sin. The Hebrew name of the book is W°ēlleh Š°mōt, the opening words of MT.

d Contents—Exodus is a religious history. It narrates the first and fundamental steps in the fulfilment of the promises made by God to Abraham that his descendants should become a great nation and that in his seed all the nations of the earth should be blessed. The opening chapter, which represents the Israelites as already a numerous people and cruelly oppressed by their Egyptian masters, shows that the time is ripe for the execution of God's designs in their regard. The call of Moses, the aggravated oppression of the people, the plagues of the Egyptians and the deliverance of the Israelites are first described. The march through the desert to Sinai follows, during which God miraculously provides for his people's bodily needs. Then comes the climax of the narrative, the Theophany and the Sinaitic Covenant with its necessary consequences, the Decalogue, the Book of the Covenant and the Ritual Legislation. The fall of the people into idolatry, necessitating the renewal of the Covenant, ends the narrative. The last six chapters are a kind of appendix, describing the execution of the directions already given for the organization of cult.

e Composition and Authorship—The remarkable unity of plan which characterizes the book is a strong confirmation of its substantial Mosaic authorship, already discussed. The principal narrative is interspersed, however, with passages, shown to be additions by their interruption of the context or their want of harmony with it in content or in date. Since the original narrative was not a diary, but received its literary form at a period subsequent to the events recorded, most of these additions are most probably Mosaic. Some, however, are of post-Mosaic origin and were inserted by an inspired editor who had other traditional sources at his disposal. There are, moreover, here as elsewhere, a few uninspired glosses and interpolations, introduced into the text in the course of transmission. As it is necessary for the better understanding of the narrative to determine these additions as far as possible, an attempt has been made to do so in the commentary, the results of which, summarized here, are not all equally well established and naturally make no claim to finality or completeness. The supplement to the ritual legislation (chh 30–1) and the appendix which supposes it (chh 35–40) as well as the homiletic additions to the decalogue (20:4–6 ; 9–11 ; 12*b* ; 17*b*) may be ascribed to Moses himself. Legislative additions (12:15–20 in whole or in part ; 12:43–51 ; 22:21*b* ; 27:20–21 ; 29:29–30 ; 34:20 ; 24) may be Mosaic or editorial. The historical additions, practically all editorial, are : the second account of the call of Moses with an insertion on the family history of Moses and Aaron (6:2–7:7), some elements in the plague narrative, in particular the third and sixth plagues (8:15–19 ; 9:8–12), some elements in the Manna narrative probably Mosaic (in particular 16:33–34), the second account of the Theophany (19:20–25), the second account of the ascent of Sinai (24:1–2 ; 9–11*b*), the tent of meeting (33:7–11). It will be noted that the historical additions refer to events of major importance about which various traditions would be current among the people. It is remarkable too that the later traditions, when properly interpreted, are not at variance

with the principal narrative. Glosses and interpolations **162f** are few (4:19 ; 11:3*b*, 10 ; 16:36 ; 19:13*a* ; 38:25–28). The attempt to distinguish definite sources JEDP throughout the entire book, which encumbers so many commentaries, is avoided here as conjectural and profitless, since our object is to explain the contents of the sacred text, all parts of which, except unauthorized glosses and interpolations, are equally inspired and authoritative.

Date—The numerical indications of the Bible are too **163a** uncertain in text and interpretation to determine the date of the Exodus either in the 15th cent. B.C., 480 years before the building of Solomon's temple (3 Kg 6:1), or in the 12–11th cent., 645 years after Abraham's arrival in Canaan (Gen 12:4 ; 17:17 ; 25:26 ; 47:9 ; Ex 12:40) according to the latest but still uncertain determination of Abraham's date. The contents of the sacred narrative and the historical data obtained from Egyptian texts and excavations offer more solid arguments for a solution of the problem. The Pharaoh of the oppression, very probably a single individual, had a long reign. He has therefore been identified with Thutmosis III of the XVIII dynasty (1484–1450) and Ramesses II of the XIX dynasty (1298–1232) and the Pharaoh of the Exodus with their respective successors, Amenophis II (1450–1421) and Mernephtah (1232–1224). The Pharaoh oppressor (the last, if there **b** was more than one) is distinguished as a builder of cities in the Delta region where the Hebrews dwelt. This characteristic is definitely verified in Ramesses II, but there is no trace of building in the Delta region on the part of Thutmosis III, since northern Egypt at that period was still insecure on the Asiatic side. The Pharaoh, builder and oppressor, had also his royal residence in the Delta near the Hebrews, a fact again definitely verified in Ramesses II, but not in the Pharaohs of the XVIII dynasty, residing at Thebes in Upper Egypt. Finally the cities built by the Hebrews, Ramesses and Pithom, and the site of their encampment in their flight, Migdōl, excavated and identified, still more definitely attach the Exodus to the Ramesses-Mernephtah period. Ramesses, the royal residence of Ramesses II, has been identified, more or less probably, by Montet's excavations in 1929 with the ancient Tanis on the Tanitic branch of the Nile, 4 m. S. of Lake Menzaleh. We find the same identification suggested in the Bible by juxtaposing the *field of Tanis*, scene of the plagues (Ps 77:12), *Ramesses*, starting-point of the Exodus (Ex 12:37) and *the land of Ramesses*, allotted to the Hebrews (Gen 47:11). Ramesses was a store city (Ex 1:11), provided with granaries for military expeditions and commanding the northern route to Asia. The name, Ramesses, first appears in the XIX dynasty and, if the Exodus occurred two centuries earlier, it would be strange to find only the later name of the city in the Mosaic narrative.

Pithom is either Tell el-Artabi or Tell el-Maskhuta, **c** neighbouring sites in the Wady Tumilat, excavated by Naville in 1883, both containing a *pi-thom*, temple of Thum, as well as granaries and commanding the southern route to Asia. The identification of Succoth (Ex 12:37) with Theku, ancient Egyptian name of Tell el-Maskhuta, is probable, but not definitely established. Migdōl (Ex 14:2), identified with Tell Abu-Hasa, excavated by Clédat in 1904, was the southern of two frontier forts, both called Migdōl (fort) of Mernephtah, another name of Seti I, predecessor of Ramesses II. It guarded the route to Sinai, had a temple of Hathor, patroness of the Sinai mines, and inscriptions of Seti I and Ramesses II. All the sites mentioned attest by their inscriptions building operations of Ramesses II. Against this accumulated evidence the stele of Mer- **d** nephtah has been objected as proof of an earlier date ; *cf.* § 78*a*. If Israel was already in Palestine in the fifth year of Mernephtah's reign, the Exodus must have occurred at least a generation earlier. Of the various explanations proposed it may be first noted that Israel is preceded in the text by the sign for *foreign people*, but not like the other names by the sign for *foreign land*. The

163d Israelites thus seem to be still nomads four years after the Exodus. The text may refer to the crossing of the Red Sea and may exemplify a well-known tendency of ancient recorders to register defeats as victories, with some show of reason in this case since the Hebrews fled from the Egyptians. Other explanations, not without support in this and other texts, interpret *Israel* either as Israelites detached from the main body, or as a tribe of similar name.

e The indirect evidence of Palestinian excavations is still disputed. As it refers directly to the date of the settlement in Canaan, it will be discussed more conveniently in the commentary on Josue. The Habiri of the Tell el-Amarna tablets, formerly identified with the Hebrews by upholders of the earlier date, are now better known as a people or class much more ancient and more widespread than Israel, *cf.* §§ 78*b* and 120*a–b*. We conclude, therefore, that the 13th cent. is the only date of the Exodus solidly, if not certainly, established by the existing evidence.

f Teaching—Exodus teaches us, in the first place, that God chose the Hebrew nation as his special instrument in the execution of his plan for the redemption of mankind. The freedom of this choice is clearly manifested. *I will show favour to whom I will show favour and I will show mercy to whom I will show mercy* (33:19). He first makes known to them his exalted nature by the revelation of the divine name, Yahweh. He then shows his goodness and his omnipotence by the prodigies through which he delivers them from the bondage of Egypt. The same attributes are manifested in his solicitude for their temporal needs by the miraculous provision of water, quails, and manna in the desert. He manifests to them his majesty at Sinai and makes a covenant with them, securing them his constant favour and protection and exacting from them special holiness of life and obedience to his commands. His wisdom and holiness appear in the ethical and religious precepts which he imposes on them, surpassing immeasurably the laws of other ancient peoples. When they revolt from him he manifests his detestation of their sin and threatens punishment, but finally, when they show repentance, yields to the intercession of Moses, admits them to pardon and renews his covenant with them. In all this the nature and attributes of God are abundantly revealed and our duties towards him are clearly manifested.

g Three undeniable historical facts narrated in Exodus prove that God's choice of Israel for the execution of his merciful design is not a patriotic fiction but a sublime reality : the divine name Yahweh, the miraculous provision of food in the desert, the unique character of the moral and religious laws. The nature of God, as revealed by the name Yahweh, implies the doctrine of Monotheism, a religious truth unknown to all ancient peoples and unattained even by such enlightened philosophers as Plato and Aristotle. The History of Religions thus supports the divine origin of the name, affirmed in the sacred text. The survival of the Hebrews for so many years in so destitute a region as the Sinaitic peninsula would have been impossible without divine intervention. The figure of the population given in 12:37 may be disputed, but the increase recorded in 1:7 ff. and the conquest of Canaan supposes a number many times superior to the 5,000 half-starved Bedouin whom Sinai supports with difficulty today. The prohibition of evil desires in the Decalogue, the special laws of charity and consideration for the poor and unprotected in the Book of the Covenant and the religious laws in general are unparalleled in antiquity and far surpass all that the lessons of history entitle us to expect from any ancient people. Their unique character can only be adequately explained by the divine origin which is claimed for them.

h St Augustine's pronouncement on the relation between the Old Testament and the New : *Novum in Vetere latet, Vetus in Novo patet*, the New is hidden in the Old, the Old is manifest in the New, is particularly true of Exodus. The Sinaitic Covenant or Testament is a **1** type of the New Testament. Its mediator, Moses, is a type of Christ. *The priestly people and holy nation* of Israel (19:6) is a type of the members of the Church, *the holy priesthood* (1 Pet 2:5), who enjoy the fulfilment of the promise. The sacrifice of the Pasch is a type of the sacrifice on Calvary. Its sacrificial commemoration is a type of the Eucharistic sacrifice. The Manna is a type of the sacrament of the Eucharist, also prefigured by God's visible presence among his chosen people. The typical character of the Tabernacle and the various ceremonies connected with it is developed in the Epistle to the Hebrews. The Church calls our Lady the Ark of the Covenant. Many rites of the old revealed religion are incorporated in our liturgy. The precepts of the Decalogue are still as actual as on the day when they were first promulgated. The principles of justice and charity inculcated in the Book of the Covenant still cry out for application to heal the wounds of the world of today. It may be said that the teaching of Exodus surpasses that of any other book of the OT in variety, extent and permanent value.

(A) Israel in Egypt (1:1-13:16)

I 1-22 Increase and Oppression of the Israelites— 1-5. All the sons of Jacob with their families descended into Egypt (Gen 35:23–25), seventy (MT) or seventy-five (LXX) in number. **6-7.** After their death their descendants increased mightily and spread over *the land*, the Delta region. **8-10.** A new Pharaoh, Ramesses II, or possibly one of his predecessors, *who knew not Joseph*, had no experience or appreciation of the services rendered by Joseph to the Egyptians and consequently no friendly regard for his kinsfolk, saw a danger to the nation in this rapidly increasing horde of foreigners and proposed to his people : ' *Let us deal craftily with them lest they increase and it come to pass, when a war breaks out, that they fight with our enemies against us and go up out of the land* '. **11-14.** The first measure of oppression was forced labour under Egyptian task-masters, more particularly the building of *store cities*, of which two, Pithom and Ramesses (*cf.* § 163*b–c*) are specified. The *corvée*, still in force at the time of the plagues, did not break the spirit of the Hebrews or lessen their increase. It included ' *hard service in mortar and in brick and all manner of service in the field, all their service wherein they made them serve with rigour* '. **15-21.** The second measure of oppression was the charge laid on the midwives to kill the male children at birth. MT has *Hebrew midwives*, the versions *midwives of the Hebrew women*—a better reading as the midwives were more probably Egyptians. Pharaoh would scarcely entrust Hebrews with the execution of such orders, and the midwives attended Egyptians as well as Hebrews (19). The Hebrew words : *Sephora* (*Šiprāh*) ' beauty ' and *Phua* ' brightness ' may be variations of Egyptian names. The second part of **16a** is rendered by some : *When you see* (*them*) *on the stones*, as Egyptian women knelt on flat stones in giving birth. But this does not agree with text or context, which require : *look to the sex*. The excuse given by the midwives to Pharaoh is that the Hebrew women, unlike the Egyptians, are *animals*, give birth quickly and easily like animals. God rewarded the midwives by *building them houses*, giving them husbands, children and descendants. **22.** Pharaoh now orders all his people to drown the male children of the Israelites in the Nile. Without excusing his ruthlessness we must not judge him by modern standards. Slave-labour and exposure of unwanted children were common enough in ancient times. The Egyptians in general were mild in character, not cruel like the Assyrians.

II 1-22 Moses' Birth, Upbringing and Sojourn in Madian—1-3. Moses was born soon after the edict of 1:22, which did not affect his three year old brother Aaron. His parents were both of the tribe of Levi. It is not implied that he was their eldest son. Aaron's birth is not mentioned because he has no part in the

4c narrative. His mother's love and faith (Heb 11:23) induced her to conceal him for three months when she saw that he was *vigorous* and likely to reach maturity. The canoe (DV basket, *cf.* Is 18:2) was a kind of chest, constructed of the pithy strips of the papyrus plant and made watertight by coats of asphalt, imported from the Dead Sea, and pitch. **4-7.** No doubt the mother knew where Pharaoh's daughter used to bathe and counted on her compassion to save the life of the child. The sister was left to watch and offer her services to provide a nurse. A Hebrew would naturally be sought since the edict of extermination made it easy to find one. **8-10.** After the child was weaned in his fourth year (*cf.* 2 Mac 7:27) he was taken to the royal palace and adopted as a son by the princess, who named him Moses and had him educated according to his position so that ' he was instructed in all the wisdom of the Egyptians ' (Act 7:22).

d Moses is an Egyptian word, as appears from such names as Thuthmosis, Ahmosis, Ramesses, where the first element is a divine name and the second a verb with an active or, more probably, passive meaning, ' gives a son ' or ' is born '. In the latter alternative Moses means ' child ' and Mes ' child ', without preformative, is attested in the monuments as a proper name. The derivation from the Hebrew *māšāh* ' draw ' is based on assonance and exemplifies popular as opposed to scientific etymology. The story of the birth of Moses only superficially resembles fabulous tales of the birth of great men like Sargon of Agade. It is not, like them, an isolated episode, but is firmly anchored in the account of the Egyptian captivity (Heinisch). It explains the origin of his undoubtedly Egyptian name and shows how he was providentially prepared to be the leader of his people. Hebrews would not invent so long and intimate an association of their deliverer with their oppressors.

e **11-14.** In Pharaoh's court Moses remained a Hebrew at heart and, on reaching man's estate, visited one of the labour gangs and, seeing a Hebrew workman beaten by an Egyptian taskmaster, slew the Egyptian. This act of reprisal, which its author no doubt considered justified, must not be judged by the standard of Christian morality. It is recorded, not for imitation, but to explain Moses' flight to Madian when he discovered that *surely the thing is known*. **15-22.** However highly placed, the slayer of an official could not remain unpunished. Canaan was under Egyptian rule. Hence Moses fled to Sinai where the Kenites, a Madianite tribe, then resided. Water-drawing in the East is a woman's task, and the first step to a marriage is often a meeting at a well (Gen 24:11 ; 29:9). Women too tend the flocks among the Bedouin. Moses met the daughters of a Madianite priest at a well, courteously defended them from bullying shepherds and watered their flock. He thus became their father's guest, *was content to dwell with the man*, and married his daughter, Sephora. The name (*Ṣippōrāh*) means ' little bird '. *Cf.* the names of the Madianite chiefs : Oreb ' raven ' and Zeb ' wolf ' (Jg 7:25). The explanation of *Gersham* (Vg Gershom) ' an alien there ' is suggested by assonance. The more probable derivation is from *gereš* ' sprout '. The new Vg edition, with MT and most Greek MSS, omits 22*b* as an interpolation from 18:4.

f **II 23-IV 17 Call of Moses—23-25.** *In those many days*, during the long period of oppression, the Pharaoh died and Moses could safely return. The protracted sufferings of the Israelites prepared them to welcome a liberator. God saw their sorrow and prayers and *made himself known to them* (LXX 25*b*). **III:1-16.** Moses herding the sheep of Jethro and seeking at a higher level the grass which had disappeared from the plain, *drove his flock to the back* (farther side) *of the desert* and on to the slopes of Mount Horeb. Horeb and Sinai, like Sarion and Sanir (Deut 3:9), are different names of the same mountain, called here by anticipation the mountain of God who would manifest himself thereon. The two names : **Jethro** ' excellence ' and **Raguel**

' friend of God ' probably represent a personal name **164f** and a by-name or official title.

The Angel of Yahweh designates Yahweh as manifest- **g** ing himself (*cf.* Gen 16:7) or less probably an angel sent by Yahweh. The substitution of an angel for Yahweh as the leader of the people is a threatened punishment of sin (32:34 ; 33:3). God, being a pure spirit, reveals himself by fire as the least material of the elements (*cf.* Gen 15:17). A thorn-bush attracts the attention of Moses by burning without being consumed. God speaks to him from it, ordering him to take off his shoes through reverence according to Eastern custom and declaring himself the God of his father, of Abraham, of Isaac, and of Jacob. Moses hides his face in fear lest he should see God and die (*cf.* Jg 13:22). **7-10.** God announces his intention to liberate his people and settle them in Canaan and appoints Moses their leader. A land flowing with milk and honey is an earthly paradise, producing abundantly all kinds of excellent food ; *cf.* VD 2 (1922) 52-5.

11-12. Moses, reluctant to accept the mission, raises **h** various difficulties. Firstly he humbly pleads his unfitness for so formidable a task. Moses has faith but needs encouragement. God replies therefore by promising him the aid of his Omnipotence and assuring him in advance of success. The sign is the proof of God's intervention but may be given before, or, as here, after the event (*cf.* 1 Kg 2:34 ; Is 7:14). **13-22.** Secondly Moses asks what he is to say to the Israelites when they ask him the name of the God of their fathers who sent him to them. The Israelites felt that the name *Elōhīm*, being generic, did not sufficiently distinguish their God from other gods. They desired a particular and distinctive name which would reveal his nature and by which they, his people, could more confidently invoke him. God replies by revealing his name, Yahweh (discussed in next paragraph), and then informs Moses how he is to execute his mission. He must first assemble the elders (heads of families and clans) who represent the people and tell them that God has appeared to him and declared that he has *taken notice* of their affliction and determined to deliver them. He must then go with the elders to Pharaoh, inform him that their God has *met* them and ask three days' leave of absence to offer him sacrifice in the desert. God's meeting with the people is his meeting with Moses, their representative. Three days is a conventional period. The demand is moderate and is to test the dispositions of Pharaoh, who will not let them go until forced by the plagues (**19-20**). *But* or *except* (LXX, Vg) is preferable to *no, not* (MT 19*b*). The Hebrews also who live among the Egyptians shall ask for *jewels* of silver and gold and raiment to take with them and so despoil the Egyptians. These objects, the wages of their labours (Wis 10:17), might also be regarded as the spoils of victory, assigned by God to the Hebrews. **IV:1-9.** Thirdly Moses objects that the **i** people will refuse to believe him. God replies by promising three signal miracles to prove his mission : change of his rod into a serpent and *vice versa*, production and removal of leprosy in his hand and conversion of Nile water into blood. Only by divine intervention can these prodigies be worked. The Egyptian magicians did not reproduce two of them (7:11, 22), but only deceitfully pretended to do so. **10-17.** Fourthly Moses represents to God his lack of oratory, needed by a prophet. God replies that he alone can and will make him eloquent. Moses, still reluctant, asks God to send someone else. God is offended and punishes him by leaving him without eloquence and appointing his brother Aaron to speak on his behalf. Moses remains God's envoy to whom the divine communications are made. He imparts them to Aaron, who announces them to the people. ' *Aaron is as mouth to Moses and Moses as God to Aaron* '. The same comparison is made 7:1, where *nābī'* ' prophet ' takes the place of ' mouth ' ; God speaks through his prophet to the people. The reluctance of Moses shows clearly that he became the leader and liberator of his people

164i not by personal initiative, but by divine appointment.

165a The Divine Name Yahweh (3:14-15)—The name has two forms : *Ehyeh* ' I am ' used by God or an envoy speaking in his name, and *Yahweh* ' He is ' used by his worshippers. It is therefore the impf. 1 sg and 3 sg of the Hebrew verb *hāyāh* or *hāwāh* ' to be ', and might grammatically be a present or a future. But the latter tense is excluded by the fact that absolute, not relative, being is expressed. God is, eternally and unchangeably, though his relations with his creatures may change. The name therefore expresses essential existence or aseity, the radical attribute of God by which he is most adequately distinguished from created beings. The fuller explanation of the name (14a) has been variously interpreted : (a) *I am who* (or what) *I am*, My being is mysterious and unutterable. This interpretation is incompatible with the fact that a name is actually given. (b) *I am because I am*, in me is the sole reason of my existence. This is a possible rendering and explanation of the name, but it interprets *'ăšer* in a less usual sense as a conjunction, not a relative. (c) *I am who am*, I am the existing one. I am therefore to be called Yahweh ' He is ', since that name best expresses my nature as essential existence. This rendering suits text and context best and is traditional, Ἐγώ εἰμι ὁ ὤν ' I am the existing one.' (LXX).

b It is objected that so exalted an idea of God, which none of the ancients attained, is incompatible with the stage of religious evolution in which the Hebrews then were. The objection by showing the difficulty of a human origin of the name only confirms its divine origin. It is based on a theory of religious evolution amply refuted by W. Schmidt's recent researches in the religion of primitive peoples. We need not suppose that all the Hebrews grasped immediately all the implications of the name. In the post-exilic period Adonai ' Lord ', or less frequently Elohim ' God ', was substituted through reverence for Yahweh, which was retained in the text but not read. Hence the LXX Κύριος, the Vg ' Dominus ' and the hybrid form Jehovah, an erroneous combination of the consonants of one word and the vowels of another. The name appears in the Bible in contracted forms : Yahu, Yau, Yo, Yah, always (except Yah) as an element of proper names. It is now admitted by sound philologists that the longer form is the original one, since the contractions are regular. The regularity of the contractions of Yahweh is evident. *Weh* becomes *u*, as *yištaḥ*ᵃ*weh* becomes *jištaḥû*. Yahu becomes Yau by omission of *h* as in the article combined with certain prepositions. Yau becomes Yô as *mauṭ* becomes *môṭ*. But there is no philological explanation of the derivation of Yahweh from Yah, Yau, etc. The name is almost as unique in form as in content. It is a purely verbal form. The hundreds of names of Semitic deities known to us are all nominal forms, except two Arabic names which occur in the Koran, Yaġûṭ (' he helps ') and Yanûḳ (' he hinders '). It is therefore quite improbable that the alleged Yau of the Rās-Shamra tablets, the Yau and Ya which appear as initial or final elements of geographical and personal names in the Tell el-Amarna tablets and similar forms in Babylonian personal names of the pre-Mosaic period, have any connection with Yahweh.

c Biblical evidence for a Hebrew pre-Mosaic Yahweh is not convincing. In Gen 4:26 the emphasis is on the cult rendered to God, not on the name Yahweh which appears earlier (chh 2-3), to show that Yahweh, the Hebrew God, is the world God. Aḥiyyah (1 Par 2:25) is probably a corruption of *ahaiu* ' his brothers '. The explanation of Bityah (1 Par 4:18) as daughter of Yahweh is very unlikely. In Abiyyah (1 Par 7:8) the Yah may be an exclamatory ending as in the Hittite name Uriyyah (2 Kg 11:3) or a later modification. The name of the mother of Moses, Yôkebed (6:20), may have been originally Elkebed, just as Yᵉhôyakîm was originally Elyakîm (4 Kg 23:34). It seems therefore most probable that the name Yahweh

was unknown before it was revealed to Moses on **16** Mount Sinai. If, however, it was previously known the new revelation would be made in view of the Sinaitic covenant. The theory that Yahweh was the god of the Kenites to whom Moses transferred his allegiance is expressly excluded by the sacred writer, who repeatedly identifies Yahweh with the God of Abraham, of Isaac and of Jacob.

IV 18-31 Return of Moses to Egypt—18-23. Moses, **d** warned by the anger of Yahweh, makes no further difficulties and immediately undertakes his mission of which the first step is to obtain Jethro's permission to return to Egypt. He does not reveal the principal object of his journey, as he would have done had Jethro been a worshipper of Yahweh, since no opposition from him could then be feared. The narrative is interrupted by **19**, originally connected with 3:22a (which LXX repeats here after 18). Against MT and the versions we must read *son* for ' sons ' (20), since only one son accompanied Moses and Sephora and the birth of the second son has not yet been narrated. *The rod of God* is the instrument by which God works wonders (2, 17, 30). God now gives a last instruction and assurance of success beginning : *When thou goest back into Egypt*. He foretells the effect of the wonders on Pharaoh and particularly mentions the last wonder which produces the desired result. The hardening of Pharaoh's heart is more usually attributed to God, the primary cause, because the sacred writer desires to emphasize the execution of God's designs. He does not, however, ignore the role of man's free-will and attributes the hardening also to Pharaoh himself, the secondary cause (8:15, 32 ; 9:34). The first-born son has a privileged position by right of birth. Israel, God's chosen people, has a similar position among the nations of the earth.

24-26. The general sense of the event narrated is clear. **e** The words of Sephora, however, are obscure as recorded in MT and Vg but intelligible in LXX : ' *Here is the blood of the circumcision of my son* ' (25b) and ' *Here is the blood of the circumcision* ' (26b). Youths were circumcised among the Arabs when they attained manhood and, originally at least, at the time of marriage, since the similar Arabic and Hebrew words for father-in-law and bridegroom mean literally circumciser and circumcised. Hebrew males on the other hand, according to the covenant made with Abraham, were circumcised on the eighth day after birth. Moses violated this law by conforming to the Arab custom at the instigation of his wife and father-in-law. For this he is threatened with death by Yahweh who appears to them in visible form at the *night-halt*. Moses can do nothing, but Sephora, aware of the cause of her husband's plight, quickly circumcises her son with a flint and prostrates herself at the feet of Yahweh saying : ' *Here is the blood of the circumcision* '. Yahweh on hearing her words desists from his attack on Moses. The whole event is a very emphatic warning to Moses at the beginning of his mission that he must not neglect any of the commands of Yahweh. **27-31.** Aaron is ordered by God to meet **f** Moses and the meeting takes place at Mount Sinai. It is not surprising that Jethro's residence was more than a day's journey from the mountain, since shepherds like Moses drive their sheep considerable distances in search of grass. Moses informs Aaron of the revelations he has received. The elders are assembled when Egypt is reached, are informed of everything by Aaron the spokesman, see the signs (2-9) worked by Moses and believe that God intends to deliver them. Sephora, after the meeting with Yahweh, must have been informed by Moses of the real object of his journey and returned with her son to Jethro.

V 1-VI 1 Unsuccessful Appeal to Pharaoh—1-4. **16**
Moses and Aaron appear before Pharaoh and announce the will of Yahweh : ' *Let my people go to hold a feast to me in the desert* '. Pharaoh refuses. *Who is Yahweh?* is an expression of contempt. The petitioners insist : ' *The God of the Hebrews has met us ; let us go three days' journey into the desert and offer sacrifice to Yahweh* '. Pharaoh

66a dismisses them after accusing them of encouraging idleness among the workers. **5-9.** Pharaoh's words (5) seem to be addressed to higher officials present at the interview. He reminds them that the people of the land—a contemptuous expression for the Hebrews—are too numerous and that forced labours are necessary to prevent their increase (cf. 1:9). Vg has two renderings of 5a. Pharaoh now increases the labours of the Hebrews. He orders the Egyptian taskmasters and the Hebrew foremen to let the workers find straw for themselves and yet exact from them the same *number* (DV

b 'task') of bricks. Nowadays as in antiquity bricks are made in Egypt of two different materials : reddish soil of the desert and black soil of the inundated regions. Sand in the former case, straw in the latter is needed for cohesion. The necessary quantity of prepared clay is rolled on a layer of sand or straw, sprinkled with water and thrown into the brick mould. This is a wooden frame, open at top and bottom, with a handle at one end. With the aid of the hand the brick takes the shape of the mould which is then removed and the operation recommences. The bricks are left undisturbed to dry and harden in the sun for about a week when they are fit for use. The bricks unearthed at the two suggested sites of Pithom are almost exclusively made of desert soil and sand. The bricks here mentioned were made in the vicinity of the royal residence at Tanis and thus in an inundated region where straw

c was absolutely necessary. **10-18.** The orders of Pharaoh are executed. Vg renders *taskmasters* by 'overseers' (6, 10, 13) and *foremen* by 'taskmasters' (6, 10). The foremen are beaten because the number of bricks is incomplete and complain to Pharaoh, but without result. In 16c MT reads : *thy people* (the workers, not the foremen) *is guilty*, but the reading of LXX and Vg is preferable. **19-VI:1.** The foremen now reproach Moses and Aaron. Moses appeals to Yahweh who reassures him. The *mighty hand* and the *strong hand* (6:1) indicate God's Omnipotence by which Pharaoh will be forced to yield.

d VI 2-VII 7 Mission and Family History of Moses and Aaron—This section is not a continuation but a repetition of the preceding narrative (3:1-6:1). It makes no mention of minor details, omits to indicate where the various events occurred and follows a logical rather than a chronological order. It is never in contradiction with the longer narrative, though apparently written by a later hand, and is interrupted in the middle by a piece of family history (6:13-28).

2-8. The events recorded are already known. Render : *And* (by) *my name Yahweh I was not made known to them* (**3b**) ; *whom the Egyptians keep in bondage* (**5b**) ; *from under the forced labours* (**6b**) and for Vg 'high' *outstretched* (**6a**). As the hand was lifted up in swearing, **8a** means : I solemnly promised. **9-12.** The apparent contradiction between the disbelief of the Israelites (**9**) and their belief (4:31) is explained by the fact that the summary omits all reference to the signs worked for the people and their favourable effect and only considers the final attitude of the people as manifested by the foremen (5:21). The mission to Pharaoh and the appointment of Aaron are located at Horeb in the longer narrative. Here there is no explicit indication of place. Similarly the statement that *the children of Israel have not hearkened to me* (**12b**) like the disbelief (9) supposes the situation indicated in 5:21. **29-VII:7.** After the interruption (13-28) the objection of Moses (**12c**) must be repeated to explain the appointment of Aaron. *Uncircumcised lips* does not imply a physical defect but unpreparedness to speak, since circumcision prepared people to belong to God. The *nābî'* or prophet is clearly defined as the spokesman of God. This is also the usual and etymological sense of προφήτης. The charge to Moses is similar to that of 3:18-20, but the order to ask leave to sacrifice in the desert (3:18)

e and its execution (5:1) are omitted. The age assigned to Moses is difficult. The number of years is schematic and apparently calculated on a lifetime of three generations passed one in Egypt, one in Madian and

one in the desert. It supposes (a) that the Pharaoh of **166e** the oppression reigned more than eighty years which is excluded by the records ; (b) that Moses, a Hebrew at heart, ignored his afflicted brethren until he was forty years old, which is improbable ; (c) that he spent forty years in Madian and yet left it before his second son Eliezer was born, which is still more improbable. As numbers are often altered and interpolated in the sacred text, it seems better to leave the age of Moses an open question.

The Genealogical List (6:14-28) is Levitical but **f** begins with Ruben and Simeon (14-15 = Gen 46:9-10) to introduce Levi as the third son of Jacob. *The heads of families*, literally heads of their fathers' houses, are referred exclusively to the descendants of Levi at the end of the list (**25**). For Vg 'kindreds' (15a, 17, 20b, 25b) read *families* and for 'kindreds' (16a) and 'families' (19b) read *generations*. On Levi's family tree cf. Gen 46:11 ; Num 3:17-20 ; 26 ; 57-61 ; 1 Par 6:1-38. Moses and Aaron belong to the fourth generation after Jacob here, but Aaron's wife, Elizabeth, was of the sixth generation (Ru 4:18-20 ; 1 Par 2:4-10). The stay in Egypt was still longer. Omissions, however, are common in such lists. Son may be used for grandson or descendant. Amram married his aunt (cousin LXX). Such marriages were subsequently forbidden (Lev 18:12). Elizabeth, Aaron's wife, was sister of Nahason, one of the princes of Judah (Num 1:7). The descendants of Aaron and Core are specially mentioned, the former by reason of their priestly character, the latter because of their part in the ritual of the temple. The progeny of Moses is not mentioned, perhaps because of their unworthiness (Jg 18:30). Note the contrast of the order of age, Aaron and Moses (**26**), with the order of dignity, Moses and Aaron (**27**). The list is preceded by an introduction or, more probably, marginal note (**13**) and is of later origin than the passage in which it is inserted, but the presence of Egyptian names like Phutiel and Phinees, guarantees the antiquity of its contents.

VII 8-13 Pharaoh sees a Wonder—This passage is **167a** best regarded not as part of the second tradition (Heinisch) but as the continuation of the principal narrative. It contains a new and essential element of the history and introduces the plagues. Pharaoh must have a proof of Yahweh's Omnipotence before he is punished for resistance to his will. His first words are : *Shew a wonder for yourselves*, to support your demand. **10b.** For Vg 'took' read *cast down*. Aaron turns his rod into a serpent, *tannîn*, a reptile of any size. **11b.** ' *And they also, the Egyptian magicians* [cf. Gen 41:8] *did in like manner with their enchantments.*' The fact that Aaron's rod swallowed their rods had no effect on the hardened heart of Pharaoh. He is therefore punished by plagues and gradually forced to yield. The modern Egyptian magicians also turn rods into snakes. This is sometimes done by pressing a certain part of the neck of a real snake which thus becomes cramped into rigidity and stretched out like a rod, but when thrown to the ground, after the pressure is removed, resumes its natural form and movements. At other times rods are substituted for snakes by the performer when he has distracted the attention of the spectators from his movements. Jewish tradition gives the names of the magicians as Jannes and Jambres (2 Tim 3:8).

VII 14-X 27 The Plagues of Egypt—The tenth **b** plague is not included in these general remarks. It differs from the others in its character and in its connection with the institution of the Pasch and the departure from Egypt. The plagues are obviously connected with natural phenomena occurring in Egypt between July and April either regularly each year or sporadically at longer intervals. The disappearance of grass in the plains (3:1) and the completion of the harvest when the Israelites collected the lower parts of the cornstalks left in the fields by the reapers (5:12) place the return of Moses in the month of April. The plagues could therefore have begun in July and occurred at the time of the natural phenomena. They were not,

167b however, merely natural phenomena since the effects produced were sometimes entirely new and always unusually intensive. Otherwise they would neither have impressed Pharaoh, nor manifested the Omnipotence of Yahweh. They were therefore miraculous, not in themselves since they did not surpass the powers of nature, but in the manner in which they occurred with unusual intensity and providential preordination

c of the circumstances of time and place. Their Egyptian character was not however a mere coincidence. God condescends in his manifestations to the customs and experiences of those to whom he manifests himself. It is for this reason that the rod is used in producing the plagues since every Egyptian magician had a magical rod. There is undoubtedly a *crescendo* movement in the narrative. The first four plagues produce annoyance and distress; the next four inflict serious damage to property and person; the ninth is mysterious and terrifying. Moses, at first courteous, becomes more and more outspoken; Pharaoh, at first indifferent, shows an increasing inclination to temporize and to yield; his magicians confess their impotence at the third plague and are unable to appear at the sixth;

d his courtiers advise surrender at the eighth. A study of the style and contents of the narrative suggests that the sacred writer had a second account of the plagues at his disposal which he partially incorporated in his text. The author of this account views the plagues, sent to manifest the Omnipotence of Yahweh, in the light of a contest between Yahweh and the Egyptian deities represented by the magicians. The third and sixth plagues, so distinctive in style and brevity and especially in their disregard for the human protagonists, Moses and Pharaoh, belong to this source. The principal narrator omitted them as hampering the dramatic movement of his narrative, but the final editor was inspired to include them in his work. Both are mentioned elsewhere in the poetical descriptions of the plagues, the third in Ps 104:31 and the sixth in Ps 77:50.

e VII 14-25 First Plague : Water turned into Blood— So extraordinary a miracle as the conversion of water into animal or human blood need not be supposed. Natural phenomena are described according to sensible appearances. The waters became red in colour and appeared to be blood. The Red Nile is the Egyptian counterpart of the plague. When the inundation is in full force in July the waters are reddened by the soil which they gather in their course. The colour which lasts during the inundation period varies with the impetus of the current and the turbulence of the stream but never attains the vivid hue of blood. The water remains potable, the fish uninjured. The plague therefore differs in two important respects from the phenomenon of the Red Nile. Elsewhere however waters have been found red in colour and lethal to fish owing to invading organisms (*cf.* Heinisch). **16.** Vg ' sacrifice to ' is literally *serve* or *worship*. **17.** The action of striking the waters with the rod is attributed directly to God to show that he is the real author of the prodigy. **18b.** '*The Egyptians shall loathe to drink*.' **19c.** '*And blood shall be in all the land of Egypt*' (in all the region near the capital). We are not informed how the magicians imitated the prodigy. Their audience was uncritical and favourably disposed. **23b.** Pharaoh remains unmoved. '*Neither did he lay even this to heart.*'

f VIII 1-15 Second Plague : Frogs—Frogs are numerous in Egypt, but cause no annoyance except by their croaking. We may conclude perhaps from the mention of fields and heaps (13-14) that the inundation was already on the wane and assign the plague to the second half of October. Its miraculous character is shown by the number and ubiquity of the frogs and especially by their simultaneous destruction at the precise time assigned beforehand by Pharaoh. Here too the magicians appeared after the cessation of the plague since they would hardly have pretended to increase the frogs when Pharoah only desired their disappearance. **3.** Read, *team with* for ' bring forth an

abundance of ' (Vg, LXX), *thy kneading-troughs* for ' remains of thy food '. **9.** Moses addresses Pharaoh : **16** *Assume the honour over me* to decide when the plague is to end. The courteousness is not merely assumed, but the real reason for leaving the decision to Pharaoh is to manifest more clearly the Omnipotence of Yahweh as appears from 10b. When the plague ceases Pharaoh hardens his heart and refuses to obey as Yahweh had *foretold* (4:21-23).

16-19 Third Plague : Mosquitoes—This plague **g** followed closely that of the frogs. Mosquitoes infest Egypt all the year round, but are most numerous and acitve after the inundation begins to decline since the quiet waters are their breeding ground. The ancients believed that they had their origin from the earth. The crust of the earth is therefore struck with the staff and thus commanded to produce them. Even allowing for rhetorical exaggeration in 17c, the mosquitoes must have been unusually numerous and troublesome to constitute a plague, since the natives are inured to their attacks. The only effect of the prodigy is the defeat of the magicians who recognized the finger of God. Pharaoh remains unmoved as Yahweh had *foretold*.

20-32 Fourth Plague : Flies—21. It is difficult to **h** determine what species of flies is meant since '*ārōb* literally means ' swarm ' (DV ' all kinds ', divers sorts of flies). Ordinary flies are so numerous in Egypt as to be a pest. But native indifference to them is incompatible with the effect produced on Pharaoh. It is stated moreover (Ps 77:45) that the swarm devoured the Egyptians. A more annoying species of flying insect such as the dog-fly seems indicated. The plague is miraculous in time, intensity, and restriction to Egyptian territory. **22a.** '*I will make a distinction as regards the land of Gessen.*' **23a.** *Redemption* (MT) by changing one letter becomes *distinction* in agreement with context and versions. **25-29.** Pharaoh asks Moses to offer sacrifice to Yahweh in order to end the plague. Moses replies, ' It is not fitting to do so ', because sacrifice to Yahweh in Egypt would be an abomination to the Egyptians and so endanger our lives or, less probably, understanding abomination as object of heathen cult, sacrifice of animals which Egyptians venerate would endanger our lives. He insists therefore on the three days' journey in the desert. Pharaoh agrees, but asks him not to go too far and to intercede for him with Yahweh. Moses assents, but reminds Pharaoh of his broken promise and warns him against further deceit. **30-31.** Moses prayed to Yahweh ' *and Yahweh did according to the word of Moses* '. **32.** But ' *Pharaoh made his heart heavy this time also and did not let the people go* '.

IX 1-7 Fifth Plague : Murrain—This plague is **16** called a *grievous pestilence* which destroys all kinds of domestic animals. Of these the horse was introduced in the Hyksos period and the camel was known, but not in use except in the outlying desert regions and in trading caravans which visited the country (*cf.* Gen 12:16). Cattle pests are rare in Egypt. **4.** Omit ' wonderful ' and read *beasts* for ' possessions '. The difficulty arising from the death of *all the beasts of the Egyptians*, since some were afterwards killed by hail, is usually solved by referring *all* to the classes enumerated, not to individuals. The pest, however, attacked the animals *in the field*, where they graze from January to April. If, therefore, it occurred in the beginning of January, the date suggested by its position in the narrative, animals not yet driven to pasture would be spared. The distinction assumed here between animals in the field and animals in the houses was in the author's mind since it is explicitly mentioned in the account of the hail plague.

8-12 Sixth Plague : Boils—Boils breaking out into **b** ulcers afflicted man and beast. It was not the bubonic pest, excluded by 9:15, nor the comparatively harmless Nile-scab, an irritating eruption occurring earlier at the beginning of the inundation period and unlikely to alarm Pharaoh or affect the movements of his magicians. Only by its effects do we know this ' Egyptian boil ' with which the Israelites themselves

8b are threatened if they violate the covenant (Deut 28:27). The ashes of the *furnace* or *kiln* are sprinkled towards heaven before Pharaoh, to show that the plague is sent by Yahweh. **8-9.** ' *And they shall become fine dust over all the land of Egypt, and the dust shall become a boil breaking out into ulcers on man and beast.*'

c 13-35 Seventh Plague : Hail—Hailstorms accompanied by thunder and lightning occur in Lower Egypt not every year but occasionally in January, February, March or April. Hailstones have been gathered as big as tennis balls. The indications given **(31-32)** assign the plague to February. It was miraculous in its intensity and in beginning and ending at an appointed time. The land of Gessen is again exempted, and Egyptians who believe in the Omnipotence of Yahweh may escape its effects. Pharaoh confesses his sinfulness, offers to let the people go without condition, but again breaks his promise when the plague ceases. **15-16.** ' *Had I put forth my hand and smitten thee . . . with pestilence, thou hadst been cut off from the earth ; but truly for this cause have I let thee live to show thee my power and that my name may be declared throughout all the earth.*' Pharaoh could be punished at once by death but is spared in view of prodigies which proclaim the Omnipotence of Yahweh. Vg and LXX, cited Rom 9:17, render : *have I raised thee up* (given thee life, 16*a*). This rendering does not affect the argument of St Paul since God's purpose is the same in giving Pharaoh life and in letting him continue to live. **17a.** For ' hold back ' read *exalt thyself against*. **19a.** For ' gather together ' read *bring to shelter*. **23b-24a.** ' *And the lightning* [lit. fire] *ran down to the earth. And there was hail and continually flashing fire in the midst of the hail.*' **27.** Omit ' also '. **28.** Pharaoh says : ' *Intercede with Yahweh ; there is enough voices of God* [thunder] *and hail ; and I will let you go and you shall stay no longer* '.

d X 1-20 Eighth Plague : Locusts—There is a most graphic description of the havoc wrought by locusts in Jl 1:2–2:17. They rarely appear in Egypt and at irregular intervals but cause enormous damage. The plague therefore in which the ordinary damage was greatly intensified (6, 14) was a terrible calamity. The time was in late February or early March. The exemption of Gessen may perhaps be assumed. Pharaoh, unmoved by the threat, is prevailed upon by his advisers to recall Moses and Aaron and make some concession to avert the calamity. He will let the men go to celebrate the feast, since men only were usually bound by such observances. Moses' answer reveals to him the full scope of the demand which he refuses to consider. The envoys are rudely expelled only to be recalled in haste after the locusts arrive, to intercede for Pharaoh.

e 1. Read *among them* for *in him*, a necessary textual correction. **5.** ' *And they shall so cover the face of the earth as to make the earth invisible ; and they shall eat the residue of that which is escaped, which remains to you from the hail.*' **7a.** ' *How long shall this man* [Moses] *be a snare to us ?* ' **10.** Pharaoh means : I swear by Yahweh that I will not let you go. ' *Look out for you are in danger of evil* ' (lit. for evil is before your faces). **13.** For ' burning ' read *east wind*, usually a hot wind. **15a.** ' *And the land was darkened* ' (MT), ravaged (LXX). **19a.** ' *And Yahweh made a very strong sea wind blow from the opposite direction.*' The sea wind is the west wind from the Mediterranean for a Palestinian but the north wind for an Egyptian. Here a north-west wind seems indicated, since the Red Sea was south-east of the infested region.

f 21-27 Ninth Plague : Darkness—The local element is the sandstorm, called Khamsîn or Khamassîn (Mallon), a hot and sometimes violent wind from the desert, which blows in March or April, lasts generally about three days and in its darkening effects resembles a London fog, but is much more oppressive owing to the sand and fine dust which it spreads everywhere. The staff or hand is raised towards heaven (10:22 ; 9:23) because the plagues come from above. **22b.**

Read *thick* for ' horrible '. **23-27.** That the Israelites **168f** are not affected by the darkness is obviously miraculous. Pharaoh now allows them to go and offer sacrifice with their children but without their flocks and herds. Moses replies that Pharaoh must let them take victims for slaughter-offerings and burnt-offerings ' *that we may sacrifice them to Yahweh our God* ', nay even that all the flocks and herds must accompany them since they do not yet know what Yahweh desires to be offered. Pharaoh again refuses to let them go.

X 28-XI 10 Tenth Plague announced : Death of the g Firstborn—The last two verses of ch 10 belong to the final interview between Moses and Pharaoh (11:4-8). They are needed after 8 to explain the anger of Moses. As the departure is to follow the plague immediately, *and after that he will let you go and when he lets you go altogether he will drive you out* (11:1*b*), preparations must be made quickly since the firstborn will be slain at midnight. **3b** is a marginal gloss suggested by 3*a*. **4.** ' *I will go through Egypt.*' **5.** The plague will smite the firstborn of *all the Egyptians* from the highest, the king on his throne, to the lowest, the maidservant behind the mill, and also of their domestic animals. **7a.** ' *But against the children of Israel not even a dog shall bark* [lit. whet his tongue] *against either man or beast.*' No alarm, not to say harm, will come to them. The Egyptians will then prostrate themselves before Moses and beg him to depart with his people and *after that I* (not we) *will depart*. **10:28-29.** Pharaoh now dismisses Moses rudely, forbidding his reappearance under pain of death. Moses replies that this is the last interview before the catastrophe (11:9-10) and leaves Pharaoh in anger at the rude dismissal and accompanying threat. Yahweh consoles him by explaining why Pharaoh never hears him. The summary of the plague narrative is probably an editorial insertion.

Pasch and Azymes : Introductory Remarks—The **169a** paschal sacrifice, which saved the Israelites from the exterminating angel of the tenth plague, and the unleavened bread, which they ate in the haste of their departure, are the essential elements of two annual religious observances by which the deliverance from the Egyptian captivity was to be perpetually commemorated. The Pasch and the Azymes have thus a definite historical origin and are of divine institution. They are inseparably united in Hebrew tradition as they were in the first paschal meal of which the flesh of the victim and the unleavened bread were the principal ingredients. An effort, however, has been **b** made to separate them, based on the observation that the Pasch is a nomadic, the Azymes an agricultural feast. It is supposed that the Israelites, when nomads, celebrated the Pasch in the spring and later, a settled people, borrowed the Azymes, an agricultural feast, from the Canaanites. The Israelites however were not originally nomads. It was a corn famine in Canaan which brought their ancestors to Egypt. There they at first tended flocks and herds but rapidly intermingled with the native agricultural population and shared their mode of life. They were employed during the period of the oppression in agricultural labours (1:14). The Sinaitic legislation inaugurated their brief nomadic existence in the desert, but naturally presupposed their proximate settlement in Canaan for which it provided them with agricultural feasts. The **c** institution of the feast would be accompanied by a description of the ritual to be observed at its first celebration, which however could be modified and supplemented at a future period. Thus, for instance, the offering of the first fruits of the barley harvest (Lev 23:10 f.) is not mentioned. Certain rites, revealed later, might also be included in the description, since the Hebrew historian does not always follow the chronological order of events. The words : ' *You shall observe the Azymes, for on this same day I brought forth your host out of the land of Egypt* ' (12:17) clearly indicate a subsequent revelation. We may assume therefore that such matters as the determination of the conditions under which non-Hebrew sojourners in the

169c land could participate in the feast and the obligation of repose on the first day of the Azymes, on which the departing Hebrews made their longest day's march, though narrated here, are subsequent developments of the original ritual.

d The name of the feast, *pesaḥ*, is derived in the text from a verb meaning ' pass over ', which is contrasted with another verb meaning ' pass through '. The destroyer passed over the houses of the Hebrews, sparing the inmates, but passed through the homes of the Egyptians, slaying the firstborn. The rite of smearing the lintel and doorposts of a house with sacrificial blood to avert evil from the inmates by divine protection is very ancient. It was practised by the Babylonians and is still in use among the Palestinian Arabs. Our use of holy water is a somewhat similar manifestation of the natural religious instinct to seek divine aid against manifold evils. The rite, however, was a particular observance of the first Pasch to avert a particular danger. Subsequently the blood of the victim, like all sacrificial blood, was poured on the altar. The Pasch in general by freeing the Israelites from slavery in Egypt and saving their firstborn from temporal death was a type of our liberation from the slavery of sin and salvation from eternal death. The Pasch as a sacrifice was a type of Christ's sacrifice on Calvary and his Eucharistic sacrifice. It belongs to the first class of the older division of sacrifice, slaughter-offerings and burnt-offerings, already mentioned (10:25). This class was subdivided into expiatory and pacific in the Sinaitic legislation.

e **XII 1-20 Institution of Pasch and Azymes**—The institution of the feast *in Egypt* is emphasized. The month Abib when the corn ripened, March–April, afterward called by its Babylonian name, Nisan, is to be the new beginning of the year which previously began in autumn. The selection of the lamb on the tenth day of the month was impossible at the first Pasch and was not observed for practical reasons in NT times. **3b.** Read : *by their households, a lamb for each household.* **4.** Render ' souls ' by ' *persons* '. ' *According to every man's eating you shall reckon the lamb.*' Remember that children and old men eat less than able-bodied men in reckoning the number required to eat the lamb. The minimum was later fixed at ten persons. **5b.** ' *You shall take it from the sheep or from the goats.*' Lamb or kid may be selected. As the day began in the evening the paschal meal was on the fifteenth of the month, the first day of the Azymes. The time of sacrifice was *at eventide* (6) or more precisely *in the evening at sunset* (Deut 16:6). A different vocalization of the Hebrew expression for *at eventide* gave rise to the later rendering ' between the two evenings ', either from 3 p.m. to sunset according to the Pharisees and Talmudists, or from sunset to darkness according to the Samaritans, Sadducees and Caraites. Roasting was prescribed as the quickest way of preparing a hasty meal. The *bitter herbs*, later identified as wild lettuce and wild endive, were in memory of the *bitter* oppression (1:14). The lamb was not to be eaten raw to avoid consumption of prohibited blood. Stewing was prohibited as a slower method of cooking though it seems prescribed in Deut 16:7, possibly by some new law later abrogated ; *cf.* §216d. **10b.** ' *And that which would otherwise be left*

f *until morning you shall burn with fire.*' **11.** The girding of the loins, the sandals on the feet and the staff in the hand indicate preparations for an immediate departure. **12.** The judgements executed against the Egyptian gods are the deaths of the firstborn whom they could not save. **15.** The feast of Azymes lasted seven days during which no leavened bread could be eaten, no leaven kept in the house. Whoever violated this law was cut off from Israel, originally put to death, later excommunicated. **16.** There was a *holy convocation*, religious gathering, on the first and last day on which also no work was allowed except cooking. **17.** Correct Vg ' I will bring forth ' to *I brought forth.* **19.** The prohibition of leaven affects the stranger as

well as the Israelite since there must be no leaven in **16** the land.

21-42 Tenth Plague and Exodus—21-28. The means **g** by which the Israelites will escape the plague are first indicated. The blood *in the basin* (Vg ' at the door ') is applied to the lintel and door-posts with hyssop, a herb frequently used in purification ceremonies. All must remain within the house. Yahweh seems to be identified with and yet distinguished from the destroyer owing to the custom of attributing directly to God what is done by his instrument. The Pasch is a perpetual institution and must be explained to children when they ask ' *What do you mean by this service ?* ' as ' *the sacrifice of Yahweh's passover* '. **29-33.** The death of the firstborn and its effect on the Egyptians are described. **29.** Omit ' woman '. Not only may the Hebrews depart with their flocks and herds but they are pressed to leave at once and thus unable to leaven their dough. **34b.** ' *Their kneading-troughs being bound up in their mantles on their shoulders.*' **35b.** The Egyptians ' *grant their request for jewels of silver and jewels of gold and raiment* '. The distance from Ramesses (Tanis) to Succoth (Theku ?) is about 30 miles. **37.** The 600,000 *gᵉbārîm* on foot are inter- **h** preted by some as *the fighting men*, which implies an absurd total number of about three millions, by others more correctly as *the vigorous people* strong enough to walk and contrasted with the *ṭap* infants in arms. Usually a group is described as consisting of men, women and *ṭap* ' children ' (Deut 2:34 ; 31:12 ; Jer 40:7 ; 43:6). We cannot suppose that the women and old men are tacitly included among the children. The infants in arms and *the mixed multitude* (omit ' without number ') would raise the total to practically the normal population of Palestine before the Jewish immigration of the present century, 757,182 according to the census of 1922. So large a number of persons with their cattle and belongings could scarcely cross the Red Sea by a ford in a single night (14:22, 27). Elsewhere moreover we are definitely informed that the Hebrews were too few to occupy the whole of Canaan and that some Canaanites would remain to prevent injury to the land from partial disoccupation until they became numerous enough to fill it (23:29–30). The number given is therefore doubtful and may be due to textual corruption. **40.** We find ' in Canaan ' interpolated before *in Egypt* (LXX), after *in Egypt* (Sam), apparently to abbreviate the stay in Egypt. **42a.** ' *This was a night of watching on the part of Yahweh to bring them forth* ', on which they in return must keep watch.

43-51 Additions to the Paschal Legislation—This new **i** *ordinance of the Pasch* determines more precisely who shall observe the feast. Aliens, temporary sojourners, hired servants presumed to be aliens and uncircumcised persons are excluded. The purchased slave, a member of the family, must be circumcised and take part in the feast. The resident alien who wishes to remain in the land and celebrate the Pasch must be circumcised with all the males of his family *and then let him approach and keep it.* The order not to break a bone of the lamb, here first recorded, was observed in the Antitype (Jn 19:36).

XIII 1-16 Azymes and Firstborn—1-10. The legis- **j** lation on the Azymes is similar to that of 12:15–20, but omits the special solemnity of the first day when recording that of the seventh. **2.** *Sanctify* means ' separate, dedicate '. **7b.** ' *No leavened bread shall be seen with thee, neither shall leaven be seen with thee in all thy borders.*' **11-16.** The law of the firstborn, attached to the Exodus by the tenth plague, ordains that every male firstborn of men or domestic animals *shall belong to Yahweh.* The male firstborn of men must be ransomed, those of clean animals sacrificed, that of the one unclean domestic animal, the ass, may be ransomed with a lamb or *have its neck broken.* **16.** The laws of Azymes and Firstborn must be perpetual reminders of the deliverance of Israel : *as a sign on thy hand and a memorial between thy eyes* (9). ' Memorial ' here becomes

169j 'bands,' intended figuratively in the same sense, but later literally interpreted as phylacteries.

B) From Egypt to Sinai (13:17-18:27)

170a XIII 17-XIV 31 The Crossing of the Red Sea— To understand the narrative and determine the site of the crossing a knowledge of the Egyptian boundary between Suez and Ismailia at the time of the Exodus is required. Before the construction of the Suez Canal there was between these two cities first a land barrier called Shaluf et-Terrabe immediately north of Suez, about 16 feet above sea-level at its highest point, then a long stretch of water called the Bitter Lakes, then a second land barrier called Serapeum, reaching a height of 26 feet above sea-level, and finally another lake, Timsah. At the time of the Exodus the Red Sea certainly extended northward to the Bitter Lakes, but it is almost certain that it did not reach Lake Timsah or cover the Serapeum. A caravan road passed by Theku in the Wady Tumilat and crossed the Serapeum into the desert. **17-22.** The Israelites were forbidden to take the more direct route, called the way of the Philistines, along the shore of the Mediterranean into Canaan, because they were too dispirited by long oppression to be ready as yet for hard battles with the Canaanites. Moses moreover had been already in-**b** formed that he was to return to Sinai (3:12). Accordingly the first stage of their journey as *free men* (read *ḥopšîm* instead of *ḥᵃmûšîm* 'armed' 13:20), not necessarily accomplished in a single day, was from Tanis to Succoth, probably Theku, whence they followed the caravan road to *Etham on the edge of the desert*. Etham was probably an Egyptian fortress (*hetem*) at the northern end of the Bitter Lakes. God manifested his presence by a pillar of cloud by day and pillar of fire by night, symbolizing respectively his mysterious and spiritual nature. **XIV:1-4.** The Israelites could now continue their march through the desert along the eastern shore of the Red Sea to Sinai, but God ordered them *to return* (into Egypt) or perhaps *to change the direction of their march* and, remaining in Egypt, to encamp between Migdōl (Vg Magdalum) and the Red Sea opposite Phihahiroth and Baalsaphon. God wished, by miraculously delivering them when their situation was desperate and by overthrowing their pursuers, to manifest his Omnipotence to both. Neither Phihahiroth nor Baalsaphon (Baal of the north) has been identified, but both were evidently near Migdōl which is most probably Tell Abu-Hasa, *c* 5 m. W. of the southern end of the Bitter Lakes where the route to Sinai crossed the Red Sea by a ford. The site was suited for a large encampment. The Israelites also crossed the Red Sea by a ford since the shallow waters were naturally divided by a particularly strong and **c** continuous east wind (21). **5-9.** Pharaoh, meanwhile, informed, probably by his official at Etham, that the fugitives had lost their way, determines to pursue them and bring them back. He sends chariots and charioteers, *picked men* (7b Vg 'captains') as the speediest and most effective force, who overtake the Israelites at their encampment by the sea, '*with all his* [Pharaoh's] *chariots* [MT chariot horses], *his charioteers and his host*'. **10-20.** The Israelites are dismayed and murmur against Moses who tells them to stand still and see the salvation of Yahweh. God orders them to advance to the Red Sea and promises deliverance and victory. The Angel of God and the pillar of cloud change their position from before to behind the Israelites to protect them. **20b.** '*And the cloud was darkness and the night passed without any contact between one party and the other during the whole night*.' **21.** Moses now stretches his hand over the sea (as ordered 16) '*and Yahweh made the sea go back by means of a strong east wind which blew the whole night so that the sea became dry ground and the waters were divided*'. **22a.** '*The Israelites passed through the sea* **d** *on dry ground*.' **23-25.** The Egyptians enter the sea in pursuit. But Yahweh observes them in the morning watch through the pillar of fire and cloud and *throws them into confusion*. Moreover '*he clogged the wheels of

their chariots so that they drove with difficulty'. **26-31. 170d** Moses now receives and executes the order to stretch his hand over the sea and bring back the waters to their *wonted flow*. '*The Egyptians fled against it* [the returning sea] *and Yahweh overthrew the Egyptians in the midst of the sea*' so that not one of them escaped. The effect produced on the Israelites by their marvellous deliverance is attested by many OT passages. The crossing was not miraculous in itself since the natural force of the wind divided the waters of the ford. Scipio's capture of New Carthage was similarly facilitated by a wind which drove back the waters of a lagoon. But it was miraculous in the intensity and continuity of the wind, in the circumstances of time and place and in the pillars of cloud and fire by which the Israelites were accompanied. There is no indication that Pharaoh himself perished or took part in the expedition. The poetical allusion (Ps 135:15) is not a historical statement to be strictly interpreted.

XV 1-21 Epinicia : The Canticle of Moses—This **e** magnificent paean celebrates two different victories : that over the Egyptians in the immediate past and that over the Canaanites and the surrounding nations in the future. Some maintain the unity of the Canticle considering the prophetic vision of future triumphs appropriately suggested by the glorious victory of the immediate past. Others regard 12-18 as a liturgical addition made by an inspired writer with the object of celebrating in a single ode the two paramount exploits of Yahweh. For the second view it is argued that 12-18 is less lyrical in tone and lacks the terseness of expression, vigour of thought and boldness of imagery so conspicuous in 1-11. It has however a beauty of its own and actual victory would naturally be celebrated more lyrically than prospective victory. The second view offers moreover no plausible interpretation of 12. We prefer therefore the first, as proposed in NP, in which 11-13 are satisfactorily explained as a middle or transition strophe. If, however, it were established that the Philistines did not settle in Canaan till after the Exodus, the second part, in which they are mentioned, would be a liturgical addition. That the canticle was sung by the men soon after the victory is indicated by the word *then* (1) and confirmed by other OT records of the immediate celebration of a victory by song and dance.

1-2. The introduction celebrates the majesty and the **f** power of God : '*I will sing to Yahweh because he is exalted, exalted ; the horse and the chariot* [LXX, driver MT] *he hath cast down into the sea. My strength and my force is Yahweh ; and he has become to me salvation. He is my God and I will praise him ; my father's God and I will exalt him*.' **3-5.** The first strophe summarily describes the destruction of the Egyptians : '*Yahweh is a warrior ; Yahweh is his name. Pharaoh's chariots and his host hath he cast into the sea ; and his chosen captains are sunk in the Red Sea. The deeps covered them ; they went down into the depths like a stone*' [quickly]. **6-8.** The second strophe shows more fully how the Omnipotence of Yahweh destroyed his foes : '*Thy right hand, Yahweh, excelleth in power ; thy right hand, Yahweh, dasheth into pieces the enemy. And in the greatness of thy exaltation thou overthrowest thy adversaries ; thou sendest forth thy wrath, it consumeth them like stubble. And with the breath of thy nostrils* [the east wind] *the waters were piled up ; the waves stood upright as in a heap ; the deeps were congealed in the midst of the sea*.' The figure of the *wall* (14:22, 29), here poetically developed, does not necessarily imply more than that the waters protected the Israelites like a wall on both sides. **9-10.** The third strophe depicts the Egyptians greedily expectant of carnage and booty as they are suddenly destroyed : '*The enemy said : I will pursue, I will overtake ; I will divide the spoil, my desire will be sated on them ; I will draw my sword, my hand will despoil them. Thou didst blow with thy wind, the sea covered them ; they sank like lead in the mighty waters*.' **11-13.** The transition strophe extols the Omnipotence **g** of Yahweh in its recent manifestation a pledge of future protection : '*Who is like thee, Yahweh, among the gods ?*

170g *Who is like thee, excelling in holiness? Fearful in praises, doing wonders? Thou stretchedst out thy right hand, the earth swallowed them. In thy mercy thou hast led the people whom thou hast redeemed; in thy power thou hast led them to thy holy habitation.'* *Gods* are the objects of heathen worship called gods by their worshippers. *Fearful in praises* means inspiring fear by the exploits for which thou art praised. *The earth* includes land and water and here indicates the latter element. It is impossible to refer 12 to the punishment of Dathan and Abiron (Num 16:32) and it is out of place here as a description of destruction in general. **14-16.** The next strophe describes the fear of the neighbouring peoples as the Israelites journey through the desert: ' *The peoples have heard, they have trembled, pangs have taken hold of the inhabitants of Philistia. Then were the princes of Edom terrified, trembling took hold of the leaders of Moab. All the inhabitants of Canaan melted away, terror and dread fell upon them. By the greatness of thy arm they have become still as a stone; until thy people, Yahweh, hath passed through; until thy people whom thou hast gotten hath passed through.'* The perfects are prophetic representing future events

h more vividly. **17-18.** The last strophe describes the settlement of the people in Canaan where Yahweh will be their eternal king: ' *Thou hast brought them in and planted them in the mountain of thy possession; in the place, Yahweh, which thou prepared for thy dwelling; in the sanctuary, Yahweh, which thy hands have founded. Yahweh shall reign for ever and ever.'* The *mountain* and the *sanctuary* refer to the mountainous region of Canaan, the holy land of Yahweh. **19a.** ' *The horses of Pharaoh and his chariots'* (mistranslated in Vg). The women now play their part led by Miriam, sister of Aaron (the elder brother) and a prophetess, divinely inspired. *And Miriam answered them* (the men, 21a) by singing either the paean which they had sung or its refrain.

171a **22-27 March to Mara and Elim**—The Israelites were now in the desert of Sur (' wall '), probably so called from the fortifications built on the eastern boundary of Egypt. They marched towards Sinai in a SSE. direction, and after three days reached Mara (' bitterness '), identified by some with the wells of Hawwāra, *c* 70 m. from the place of crossing, by others with 'Ain Mūsā (' Well of Moses ') only 24 m. from it. As the way was difficult and haste unnecessary the latter identification is more probable. The water at 'Ain Mūsā is abundant but bitter. The miraculous sweetening was temporary. The subject in **25b** is Yahweh and *him* is collective for the people. Elim (' terebinths ') is identified with the well-watered Wady Gharandel, over 50 m. from 'Ain Mūsā, a regular halting-place for caravans between Egypt and Sinai.

b **XVI 1-36 Food in the Desert: Quails and Manna**—The Sinaitic peninsula is a very barren region and supports with difficulty a nomadic population of about 5,000. The Hebrew immigrants could not therefore have subsisted on the natural resources of the country. A divine intervention was necessary and God fed his chosen people with quails and manna. The **quails** are mentioned only here and Num 11 (§ 201*d*). In the springtime quails from the interior of Africa fly over the Sinaitic peninsula in large numbers. Their first appearance to the Israelites in May was therefore later, their second in June considerably later, than the ordinary period of migration. They came at the moment willed by God and so numerous on the second occasion as to provide a month's food for all the people. The food was natural, the circumstances preternatural.

c The **manna** differed from the quails in being supplied constantly during the whole period of the wandering in the desert. This continuous and miraculous provision of food was a signal prodigy worked by Yahweh on behalf of his people. The bread from heaven was thus a most fitting type of the true bread from heaven, the sacrament of the Eucharist, our spiritual food during our journey to the promised land. The manna however was not entirely preternatural. A substance found beneath the tamarisk trees in Sinai in late May,

June and July is called manna by the natives. In an **1** expedition to Sinai in 1927 two professors of the Hebrew University of Jerusalem discovered that it was produced not by the tamarisk tree itself but by two species of cochineal which feed on its leaves. The viscous substance falls to the ground during the night and appears in the morning in the form of little balls never bigger than a hazel-nut and usually of a yellow-brown colour and transparent. It must be collected early since ants appear after 8.30 a.m. and devour or carry away what they find. Once hardened it neither melts under the heat of the sun or becomes in any way corrupt. As its content is mainly sugar it is very nourishing. The present annual output in Sinai is about 6 cwt., but the ancient yield was greater since there were more tamarisks. The biblical narrative here and Num 11:7-9 agrees with this description. The manna is food from heaven (**4**) as coming from **d** above and also miraculously multiplied since the natural supply was altogether insufficient. It fell by night around the camp and was gathered in the morning (**14**; Num 11:9). It is like hoar-frost in its white colour and fineness when it first exudes, like the coriander-seed in its clear brown colour and granular formation, like the bdellium gum in its colour, its viscous character and its pleasant odour (14, 31; Num 11:7). The corruption of the manna (**20**) was a miracle by which the people were warned to obey God and trust in him. Its melting when the sun grew hot cannot be explained by the ravages of the ants, since ' melt ' and ' disappear ' are not equivalent, but the drops which fell from the trees during the daytime would melt in the sun before they solidified (**21**). The manna was eaten either raw or cooked. In the latter case it was apparently mixed with meal and is thus compared in taste with honey-cakes (**30**) and oil-cakes (Num 11:8). An 'omer (Vg gomor) is *c* 6½ pints, an abundant daily ration. While the manna was certainly not the only food of the Israelites in the desert it is not stated whether it was provided all the year round or only during its season in May, June and July. The former view is more probable. A miracle is necessary to explain the extraordinarily large amount provided and also the double supply on the eve of the Sabbath. There is some confusion here as elsewhere **e** caused by the insertion in the text of traditional material, belonging to a later date. The order to place a pot of manna before Yahweh, that is, in the tabernacle, as Vg rightly interprets, and its execution (**33-34**) suppose the tabernacle, not yet built. The order to appear *before Yahweh* (9) is better referred to the Tent of Meeting (33:7-11). The narrative becomes more intelligible if 11-12 are read after 3.

Read *congregation* for ' multitude ', as the word has a **f** religious connotation. The desert of Sin is Debbet er-Ramle 50 m. NW. of Mt Sinai. **3.** For ' why ' read *because*. **5a.** ' *Let them order aright what they bring in.'* **7.** The *glory of the Lord* refers to the miraculous appearance of the manna but seems to be explained in **11** by the pillar of cloud in the desert. This verse however may have been altered by substituting *desert* for the original *tent* since the glory of the Lord appeared in a cloud at the Tent of Meeting (33:10). **14.** ' *And when the dew had lifted behold on the face of the desert was something fine, granular [?], fine as the hoar frost on the ground.'* *Mehuspās* only occurs here and is variously rendered *granular, round, scale-like*. **15.** The derivation of manna is popular but not scientific. **16b.** ' *Gather you of it, each according to his eating, an 'ōmer a head according to the number of persons, every man for those who are in his tent shall you take it.'* The words *according to his eating* imply, **g** as in the case of the paschal lamb, that some naturally eat more than others. The sense therefore of **18** is that this order was carried out, not that those who gathered more or less had ultimately the same amount. **22-30.** The observance of the Sabbath is here first imposed. The people collect a double quantity on the eve as ordered by Yahweh. The *rulers of the congregation* seek an explanation from Moses and are told to keep the

1g Sabbath. **23b**. ' *Bake what you will bake and stew what you will stew.*' **34**. The pot of manna was kept *before the testimony*, the Ark, which contained the tables of the Testimony (25:22). **36** is a gloss.

h **XVII 1-7 Water in the Desert : Massah and Meribah** —On reaching Raphidim, most probably the modern Wady Refāyid 8 m. NW. of Mt Sinai, the congregation of the Israelites suffering from thirst strove with Moses and tempted God. Moses at God's command struck a rock with his rod and the water gushed forth. The place is called *Massah* ' Temptation ', and *Meribah* ' Strife '. Vg omits Meribah. At another Meribah near Kadesh (Num 20:1–13) Moses sinned and was punished by exclusion from the promised land. **6**. Horeb is unintelligible and probably an interpolation.

i **8-16 Battle with the Amalekites**—The Amalekites were an ancient people (Gen 14:7 ; Num 24:20) residing in the south of Canaan and the north of the Sinaitic peninsula. Those who attacked the Israelites (Deut 25:17–18) had pushed farther to the south, whether permanently or temporarily, to find pasture for their flocks, and had very probably encamped in the Feiran oasis. By the prayer of Moses the Israelites triumph. An altar is built and called *Yahweh is my banner* and perpetual enmity between the people of Yahweh and the Amalekites is solemnly proclaimed. Here for the first time Moses is ordered to *write this for a memorial in a book*. This explains why Josue and Hur are mentioned incidentally since a short record would merely give their names and activities. **11**. Omit ' a little '. *Hands* should be read with Sam. and all versions, not ' hand ' (MT). Raising one hand would be here the gesture of command but raising the two hands is the gesture of prayer. **16**. The *hand (raised) up to the throne of Yahweh* indicates an oath or solemn declaration of perpetual war with Amalec (*cf*. Jg 6:3, 33 ; 1 Kg 15:2 ff. ; 30:1 ff.). For MT *kēs*e*yāh* read with the versions *kisse' Yah, throne of Yahweh, i.e.* heaven.

j **XVIII 1-27 Jethro visits Moses : Institution of Judges**—The events narrated in this chapter are not in chronological order. The visit of Jethro is located at Mount Sinai (6) but the Israelites are still at Raphidim (19:2). The judges were naturally instituted at Mount Sinai (Deut 1:6, 9 ff.), after the laws were revealed. Both events are narrated here by anticipation to avoid an interruption in the history of the Sinaitic legislation.

1-6. Jethro hearing of the return of Moses sets out with Sephora and her sons Gersam and Eliezer (born after the departure of Moses) and is met by his son-in-law to whom he has previously announced his visit. Moses' separation from Sephora was temporary for practical reasons, not a divorce. **7**. ' *And he* [Moses] *went out to meet his father-in-law and bowed down before him and kissed him ; and they inquired about each other's health and entered the tent.*' **8-11**. Moses relates the great deeds of Yahweh on behalf of his people. Jethro rejoices and recognizes that Yahweh is supreme : ' *Now I know that Yahweh is greater than all gods : yea in the very thing wherein they* [the gods of Egypt identified with the Egyptians] *dealt proudly against them* ' (the Hebrews). **12**. In thanksgiving he offers holocausts and victims for a sacrificial meal *before God* (*i.e.* given by God to his worshippers) to which Moses, Aaron and the elders of Israel are invited. As the sacrifices were offered to the true God the invited could partake of the sacrificial meal. Jethro now asks why Moses passes the whole **k** day in giving audience to the people. **15-16**. Moses replies : ' *The people come to me to inquire of God* [Moses is God's interpreter] *and in disputed matters I judge between a man and his neighbour and I make known to them the statutes of God and his laws* '. **19-23**. Jethro rejoins : ' *Hearken to my words, I will give thee counsel and may God be with thee : Represent thou the people with God and bring their disputes before God* ' and instruct them in their duties but appoint good men as judges in ordinary cases to share thy burden, and reserve only the more important cases to thyself. **23a**. ' *If thou shalt do this and God command thee so, then thou shalt be able to endure.*'

24-27. Moses therefore appoints judges. Jethro returns **171k** to his own land.

(C) Sinaitic Theophany, Covenant and Legislation 172a (19:1-40:36)

XIX 1-25 Theophany on Mount Sinai—Christian tradition from the end of the 4th cent. (Pilgrimage of Aetheria) has located **Mt Sinai in the Sinaitic peninsula**. Recently other sites have been proposed, but none of these is as well supported by the texts as the traditional Mt Sinai, the modern Gebel Mūsā or Mountain of Moses in the interior of the southern part of the peninsula. Those who seek Mt Sinai east instead of west of the Gulf of Aqabah rely mainly on three arguments : (*a*) Madian is in northern Arabia, not in the Sinaitic peninsula ; (*b*) Moses fled for safety from the lands subject to the Pharaoh of which Sinai was one ; (*c*) the theophany implies a volcanic eruption and there are volcanoes in Madian but not in Sinai. To (*a*) may be answered that Madian is a region of nomads, some of whom raided eastern Palestine for seven years (Jg 6:1) and that the Kenites with whom Moses took refuge (Jg 1:16) were living among the Amalekites in the Sinaitic peninsula in the time of Saul (1 Kg 15:6). To (*b*) one may reply that Egyptian influence in Sinai was confined to the region of the mines, considerably to the NW. of Gebel Mūsā, and that Egyptian troops only guarded the miners in their occasional expeditions but did not permanently occupy the district. As regards (*c*) a volcanic eruption is excluded by the fact that the people took up their position on the lower slope of the mountain while Moses ascended to its summit, that there is no mention of lava, and that the smoke (18) is only a figurative equivalent of the dark storm-cloud (16). In the description of a theophany in Ps 17 the smoke and fire of 9 are similarly identical with the dark stormclouds and lightning of 12 ff. Of **b** the other sites suggested Kadesh is excluded by the encampment at the Red Sea before reaching the desert of Sin (Num 33:10) ; Petra is an unsupported hypothesis arising out of Nielsen's moon-god speculations ; Serabit el-Chadem is most unlikely as an Egyptian outpost and sanctuary of the goddess Hathor, and Grimme's reading of Sinai on two ancient inscriptions there discovered has been shown to be erroneous by Ryckmans (Bi 9 [1928] 119 note) ; Gebel Serbal, NW. of Gebel Mūsā, is difficult to climb and has no open space beneath, where the Israelites could encamp in sight of it. The large plain of Er-Rāḥa north of Gebel Mūsā, on the other hand, formed a suitable encampment and water was provided by the four valleys which meet in the plain. The northern and lower peak of the mountain, Ras eṣ-Ṣafṣaf, 6,830 ft high, is reached in an hour and a half and is visible from every part of the plain underneath. The southern and more distant peak, 7,363 ft high, is hidden from the plain by the northern one on which the Decalogue was promulgated.

As the exact day of the arrival at Sinai is missing from **c** the text, we cannot definitely connect the Sinaitic legislation with the subsequent feast of Pentecost. Jewish tradition of such a connexion is not ancient but some of the Fathers, SS Augustine, Jerome and Leo, seem to suppose it when they compare the promulgation of the Old Law on Mt Sinai with that of the New Law on the first Christian Pentecost.

3-6. Moses first ascends the mountain and receives **d** the announcement of a solemn covenant to be made between God and Israel. The eagle metaphor is more fully developed in Deut 32:11. The covenant will make Israel God's chosen possession *above* (or *among*) *all peoples*, a specially favoured people. They on their part must heed his words and keep his laws, and be holy and a kingdom of priests, specially remarkable for piety and morality as nearer to God than other nations, just as priests, being nearer to God than laymen, should be distinguished by holiness of life. **7-8**. Moses makes the announcement to the people

172d who assent. He then *brings back* the answer of the people to Yahweh. As the ascent is made in an hour and a half, that of Gebel Serbal in five hours, two ascents in the same day confirm the traditional site. **9-12.** God then announces the theophany for the second next day with the object of convincing the people that Moses is his prophet. He will appear in a storm of thunder and lightning. The people must prepare themselves by sanctification keeping apart from anything that profanes and by washing **e** their garments, symbol of interior cleanliness. A limit must be assigned which the people may not pass, since to touch the holy mountain during the theophany is a profanation punished by death. **13.** Death in such a case would be an act of God, and **13a** is a gloss suggesting methods of execution by man without personal contact. Read : *no hands shall touch it* (the mountain, not 'him', the profaner, a false interpretation which gave rise to the gloss). A trumpet, lit. *ram's horn*, will summon the people to the lowest slope of the mountain (*cf.* 1 Thess 4:15 ; Apoc 8:8). **14-15.** Moses gives the message to the people and explains the sanctification order by the words : approach no woman. **16-19.** The theophany is described. The people are *on the lowest slope of the mount.* In their sight Moses speaks to God on the summit of the mount and God answers him *with voices* (loudly or amid thunderclaps). The tense of the verbs 'speak' and 'answer' implies a continued conversation. The law is, thus communicated to Moses in the sight and probably in the hearing of the people. *The people* (LXX) rather than *the mountain* (MT) *tremble.* **20-25.** We seem to have another traditional account of the facts narrated with some unimportant variations in the order of events and a new element in the mention of Aaron and the priests. The latter were apparently the sons of Aaron (*cf.* 24:1), called priests by anticipation, since their institution belongs to a later period. There is no mention of pre-Aaronic priests in the texts.

f **Introductory Remarks on the Decalogue**—The text is in Ex 20:1–17, Deut 5:6–21, and the Nash Papyrus (*cf.* § 77a and RB 13 [1904] 244 f.), which is certainly earlier than MT and assigned to the 2nd cent. B.C. by Albright (JBL 56 [1937] 145–76) ; *cf.* also Mt 19:18 f. ; Mk 10:19 ; Lk 18:20 ; Rom 13:9. It is certain that the decalogue contained ten distinct commandments (Ex 34:28 ; Deut 4:13 ; 10:4). It is generally believed that these were originally more lapidary in form, more similar in style and therefore in some cases briefer than they appear in the texts. The additions, chiefly concerned with the reason for a precept, the reward for observing it, and particular applications of it, may well have been made mostly or entirely by Moses himself when instructing the people on their observance. They are not always identical in Ex and Deut.

g **Two divisions of the commandments into ten** are still found among Christians, both derived from different Jewish divisions, one preferred by the Greeks and the other by the Latins. At the Reformation the Lutherans kept the Latin, the Calvinists adopted the Greek division. English Protestants took the Greek division from the Calvinists while Catholics retained the Latin one. The Hellenist Jews, Philo, Josephus, etc., so divided the commandments as to make the prohibition of images a distinct precept and combined the two prohibitions of evil desires into one precept. Origen who introduced this view into the Church attests the previous existence of a different one in which two precepts forbidding evil desires were recognized and one and the same precept forbade the worship of images and of strange gods. The Palestinian Jews, on the other hand, whose view is clearly defined in the Targum of Pseudo-Jonathan, regarded Ex 20:2 '*I am Yahweh thy God who brought thee out of the land of Egypt and out of the house of bondage*' as the first precept, the prohibition of the worship of strange gods and images as the second and the two prohibitions of evil desires as the tenth. The Christians therefore rightly rejected their first precept as an introduction to, not a part

of the decalogue, retained their second as the first and **17** divided their tenth into two forbidding two kinds of evil desires. St Augustine's exposition of this division secured its universal acceptance in the Latin Church.

The exegetical determination of the original division **h** is complicated by a problem in textual criticism. In Ex 20:17 we read : *Thou shalt not covet thy neighbour's house : Thou shalt not covet thy neighbour's wife ;* in Deut 5:21 : *Thou shalt not covet thy neighbour's wife : Thou shalt not desire thy neighbour's house.* Sam. has the reading of Ex, LXX that of Deut in both passages. But Pap. Nash, though generally agreeing with Ex against Deut, has the reading of Deut in this passage. The intrinsic reasons in favour of Deut and two precepts of desire are still stronger. As two acts of adultery and theft are forbidden in two separate precepts and as adultery precedes theft in all texts, versions and NT allusions, so we expect the two corresponding desires to be mentioned in the same order and to be forbidden in two distinct precepts. The argument is strengthened by the fact that the indulgence of two distinct evil passions, licentiousness and covetousness, is proscribed and that *thou shalt not covet* appears twice in both texts. The passage in Ex moreover contains further evidence of textual corruption in the omission of *his field*, found in Deut and Pap. Nash and required by the parallelism of pairs : house and field, manservant and maid-servant, ox and ass.

The case of **the first precept** is very different. Only **i** images of strange gods were prohibited as appears not only from the words : *Thou shalt not adore them ; thou shalt not serve them* (Ex 20:5a ; Deut 5:7) but also from the cherubim (Ex 25:18) and the brazen serpent (Num 21:8) which Yahweh ordered to be made and from the mural decorations of the Jewish synagogues in the early Christian period as excavations abundantly attest. There is question therefore not of a separate commandment which forbids the worship of all images but of an application of the precept forbidding the worship of strange gods. The prohibition of idols is found in the Book of the Covenant (20:23). It appears here in an amplified form (20:4–6) most probably as a later addition to the decalogue to illustrate and safeguard the first commandment. The Latin division of the commandments is thus the more reasonable one and the more likely to be original.

The antiquity and divine origin of the decalogue j are explicitly and repeatedly affirmed in the sacred text. The Mosaic legislation in general and the decalogue in particular are moreover the direct and necessary consequence of the Sinaitic covenant. The chosen people must be *a kingdom of priests and a holy nation* (19:6). The laws by the observance of which this holiness could be acquired must therefore be revealed to them. The prophet Osee recognizes the connexion between the covenant and the law when he says : *They have transgressed my covenant and violated my law* (Os 8:1). The prophets in general presuppose the law when they reproach the people for not observing it.

Six precepts of the decalogue are listed together in **k** ancient Babylonian, four in ancient Egyptian texts. Against the antiquity of these therefore no particular difficulty can be raised. The four peculiar to the Hebrews are the first, third, ninth and tenth. Of these **the Sabbath** has been particularly objected to by many critics as an exilic institution. It supposes the continuous division of time into weeks, unknown outside Israel. The Egyptians divided the month into ten-day periods, the Babylonians into irregular periods corresponding to the phases of the moon. Two theories of a foreign origin have been proposed. According to one it was originally a full moon feast, the Babylonian *šapattu*, and was so understood in pre-exilic texts when coupled with the new moon feast, but became a weekly feast during the exile. This theory ignores several pre-exilic texts which mention a weekly Sabbath, gives no indication of a full moon feast in Israel except the coupling of new moon and Sabbath, equally

2k natural in the sense of monthly feast and weekly feast, and has no plausible explanation of the change from full moon to seventh day. The second theory finds the origin of the Sabbath in the *dies nefasti* of the Assyrians, who regarded the 7th, 14th, 21st and 28th days of the month as days of ill-omen on which the gods should be propitiated and certain actions should not be done. But their 7th day was not marked by abstention from servile work, nor was the Hebrew Sabbath a *dies nefastus*. Neither theory explains the continuous time division into weeks essential to the **l** Sabbath. The chief objection to the first, ninth and tenth precepts is based on their exalted character at variance with the theory of religious evolution previously refuted (§ 163*g*). The monotheism of the first precept, already indicated by the divine name Yahweh, and the prohibition of evil desires in the two last show the definite religious and moral superiority of the Hebrew decalogue over the laws of all ancient peoples. This superiority cannot be explained away or adequately accounted for without divine intervention.

3a **XX 1-21 The Decalogue** (*cf.* Deut 5:6-22)—Though the decalogue sets forth the obligations imposed on Israel by the covenant, it is not nationalistic but universal in its outlook and expounds briefly and clearly the fundamental principles of all religious and moral obligation. The first three precepts prescribe man's duty to God, the last seven his duty to his neighbour. **3.** The first commandment forbids the worship of any other god but Yahweh. *Before me* means in my presence, not in preference to me. **4-6.** The prohibition of image worship, already discussed, (§ 172*i*), does not contemplate the case of an image of Yahweh, most probably forbidden in the Book of the Covenant (23). Deut 4:16 ff. insists, however, that he did not appear in material form lest the people should be led to make an image of him and misapprehend his spiritual nature. **b** **7.** The second commandment forbids all misuse of the divine name Yahweh, not only perjury but cursing, incantations, etc. The later Jews exaggerated this precept into a prohibition of even a reverent use of the sacred name. **8-11.** In the third commandment *Sabbath-day* instead of 'seventh day' and perhaps also *remember* (Deut, *observe*) imply that the Sabbath was already instituted and known (16:23 ff.). The fundamental object of the feast was to segregate a portion of man's time from his own uses and consecrate it to God as an acknowledgement that all his time belonged to God. The special reason for observing it given in Ex is that God rested on the seventh day after the creation. It is assumed that man's actions must be in harmony with God's. A different and more humanitarian reason is given in Deut, quite in accord with the general character of Deuteronomic legislation. The repose and religious observances on the Sabbath commemorate God's deliverance of the Hebrews from the hard labours of the Egyptian captivity. The fact that the two reasons are different, though not mutually exclusive, suggests that they are later additions. Pap. Nash agrees here with Ex. **c** **12.** The fourth commandment begins the second list of obligations, since the family comes before the state and parents have the first and strongest claim to their children's regard. The reward promised is probably a later addition. **13-15.** The fifth, sixth and seventh commandments safeguard the three main bulwarks of human society: the sacredness of life, the purity of marriage and the right of property. The distinction between the sixth and seventh commandments shows that the wife is not regarded as merely the property of her husband. **16.** The eighth commandment is directed against sins of the tongue and forbids all false testimony as to the neighbour's person, property or good name. **17.** Finally, licentious and covetous desires are prohibited as evil in themselves and leading to the actions already forbidden. The tenth commandment may have ended originally with *house* in the general sense of possessions. **18-19.** God himself announced the decalogue to the people (Deut 5:4;

22; 10:4 and probably Ex 19:19; 20:18 *voices*). **173c** This is clearly the chief reason of their terror and their request that Yahweh should not speak to them himself but through Moses, his interpreter.

XX 23-XXIII 19 The Book of the Covenant— **d** The first principles of religion and morality revealed in the decalogue did not sufficiently indicate the obligations of the Israelites as the holy people of Yahweh. They had to be developed into a code of laws, not exclusively cultual but ethical and religious like the decalogue, to attain their full object. These laws were not all new but combined approved customs already established with fresh legislation suited to the occasion. God's condescension to national customs and local circumstances, already exemplified in the plagues, is here abundantly manifested. His foresight also appears in adapting the legislation less to present nomadic conditions than to the proximate settlement in Canaan. The Israelites were in fact, as already remarked (§ 169*b*), familiar with agriculture and only temporarily nomads. The composition of the Book of the Covenant by Moses has recently been attached by H. Cazelles to the settlement of Reuben and Gad in Transjordania, RB 52 (1945) 173-91. This view finds an appropriate setting for the agricultural legislation at the cost of detaching the Mosaic code from the Sinaitic Covenant to which it naturally belongs.

The **original order of the text** seems to have been **e** disturbed. While the section on cult comes last, two cultual laws appear (20:23-26) before the introductory formula (21:1). Laws of religion and charity are intermingled (22:18-23:9), possibly because such precepts of charity, peculiar to the Hebrews, were regarded as religious obligations. Kidnapping intervenes between two offences against parents (21:15). The law of charity to one's enemy interrupts practical applications of the eighth commandment (23:4-5). In the law of first-fruits wine and oil (22:19*a*) are separated from corn (23:19*a*). The admonition not to appear empty-handed before Yahweh (23:15*c*) interrupts the context and naturally follows 23:17. The concluding formula (23:13*a*) appears earlier. As the examples show, these disarrangements are accidental and do not affect the character or interpretation of the code. A later addition (22:31*b*) incorporates the law of **f** Lev 17:15; Deut 14-21, excluded by 21:34-36. Legislation is never static and additions by which codes are brought up to date must be expected. The different forms in which the laws are expressed indicate according to some critics different strata of different date. But such diversities of expression are common to all classes of literature. Ancient laws moreover when codified would retain their original form. Heinisch compares the Salic Law which exhibits five different forms of expression in the five laws of its first title.

Much light has been thrown on the Mosaic Code **g** (MC) by the discovery in the last half-century of four more **ancient collections of laws**: the complete Babylonian Code of Hammurabi (CH), an Assyrian lawbook (AL), Sumerian laws (SL) and Hittite laws (HL). The antiquity of Eastern codes is thus established and a Hebrew code in the 13th cent. B.C. is no longer an apparent anachronism. A comparative study of the collections reveals in all a common element and a distinctive character. Babylonian law which spread early over the whole East was adopted by different peoples and modified according to their national customs and character. MC shows most contacts with CH but sometimes agrees with other collections against it and has naturally many distinctive features. Pre-Mosaic law in Genesis has a precisely similar character. There is no indication of literary dependence. The contacts are adequately explained by the origin of Abraham from Babylonia, the spread of Babylonian civilization, and the mixture of races in ancient Palestine. The main difference between MC and the **h** other collections is twofold. MC is more elementary and accommodated to a primitive state of society—

173h another indication of its antiquity. The other codes are more developed and suppose a more advanced stage of culture. MC has a higher standard of religion and morality, not precisely as including cultual laws, but because the religious spirit pervades the civil enactments, as appears in particular from the rights accorded to slaves and the special consideration shown to the poor and depressed. The other codes are chiefly concerned with the maintenance of property rights, show little regard for the poor, and favour the rich as the important members of the community. In the penalties imposed AL is the severest, HL the mildest and closest to MC. Illustrations of these remarks will be found in the commentary where the relations between the codes are studied in detail.

174a XX 22-26 Public Worship—23. Two distinct prohibitions are implied by the two verbs of which the second refers to idols, the first most probably to other gods suggested by *beside me* (MT). ' *You shall not make (other gods) beside me ; gods of silver and gods of gold you shall not make for yourselves.*' The second prohibition seems to include images of Yahweh. 24. ' *An altar of earth thou shalt make to me and thou shalt offer on it thy holocausts and thy peace-offerings, thy sheep and thy oxen, on every place* [or, *on all the place*] *where I cause my name to be remembered.*' *On all the place* is supported by the article with ' place ', *on every place* by LXX, Vg and Gen 20:13 where the article also appears but *every place* is meant. In the first view we have the law (Deut 12:5) allowing only one place of sacrifice but *all* is difficult to explain. According to some it implies permission for more than one altar only in the court of the tabernacle or temple. But such a permission is not supported by later usage or intelligible here before the tabernacle is mentioned. The legislation regards sacrifice in general, not exceptional cases. The same objections hold against the

b view that the law authorizes private altars at which animals can be ritually slaughtered, as opposed to the one altar of holocausts for public sacrifices. This interpretation moreover ignores the word *holocausts* and the need of special authorization for the erection of the altar. Thus the rendering *in every place* seems preferable. Altars may be erected only at such places as are duly authorized. This was the practice of divinely guided persons like Elias, Samuel and David. The law of Deut is of later, but not necessarily post-Mosaic origin, and visualizes the new situation created by the settlement in Canaan. 25-26. The altar was to be simple, made of earth or unhewn stones, and not reached by steps for the reason given which implies that the priest wore a single short garment. The legislation is primitive. Practical experience of a single altar in the desert would prepare the way for the subsequent legislation of Deut.

c XXI 1-11 Slaves—1-6. A Hebrew could be enslaved by a father's act (7) or through inability to pay a fine (22:3) or a debt (4 Kg 4:1). After six years he becomes free with his wife, if enslaved with him, and also receives raiment and other gifts (Deut 15:14). If he has taken a wife from his master's slaves, she and her children remain slaves. The slave may thus prefer to remain with his family. ' *In that case his master shall bring him before God* [the altar or sanctuary where he attests his decision, not the judges] *and he shall bring him to the door or door-post (of his house) and his master shall bore his ear through with an awl.*' The ear indicates obedience, the nailing to the door permanent attachment. 7-11. The case of a maiden sold into slavery to become the slave-wife of her master is considered. If she displease her master *who has determined her for himself*, he may not sell her to foreigners but must either let her be bought back by her father or, if he give her in marriage to his son, treat her as a daughter, or ' *if he take another slave-wife, her food, her raiment, her marriage intercourse he shall not diminish*'. Any infraction of these three rights sets her free. In CH and AL a free citizen enslaved served only three years, but had no rights and belonged entirely to his master. Even the milder HL imposes various forms of mutilation for offences punished by a fine

when committed by free citizens. The more humani- **17** tarian character of MC is evident.
12-32 Injuries to Person—12-14. As all life belongs **d** to God deliberate **shedding of blood** is an offence punished by shedding of blood (*cf.* Gen 9:5). The executioner was near kinsman of the slain (Num 35-19 ; Deut 19:12). In a more highly organized society public good requires that the state punish the murderer. Substitution of a member of the murderer's family or clan is not allowed in MC. It is not clear whether killing *which God brought about through his* (the slayer's) *instrumentality* includes manslaughter or refers only to inculpable homicide, but such killing was not punished and cities of refuge were subsequently appointed where the slayer might find asylum. Later legislation provides for hearing of witnesses and establishment of motive in doubtful cases (Num 25:20 ff. ; Deut 19:4 ff.). A case of extenuating circumstances where the blood-price is substituted for the death penalty is mentioned (31). The altar was a temporary place of refuge for the slayer, who, however, if found guilty, was removed and put to death. CH has no law on murder except that a wife who murdered her husband should be impaled. AL only mentions homicide resulting from wounds inflicted and punished by fines. HL distinguishes between wilful murder and killing like MC, but imposes only money fines in both cases.

15-17. Grave **offences against father or mother** by act **e** or word are punished with death (by stoning, Deut 21:18 ff.). The other codes ignore the mother and chiefly discuss offences of an adopted son. CH allows a father to cast out his son for a second grave offence and cut off his hand if struck by him. The greater severity of MC shows its higher estimate of the importance of obedience to parents. **16.** Death is the punishment of kidnapping, whether or not the person kidnapped be sold into slavery (*cf.* Gen 37:26 ff.). CH prescribes the same penalty. HL distinguishes various cases but never assigns the death penalty.

18-19. Injuries inflicted in a fight with a stone or club **f** (LXX fist ?), which, though not fatal, temporarily incapacitate the injured, entail compensation for time lost and payment of medical expenses. CH imposes only the second obligation, HL adds to both a pain-compensation of six silver half-shekels (7s 6d). **20-21.** A man who beats his slave to death with a rod is punished, not with death since the weapon is not lethal and homicide is presumably not intended, but apparently by a fine. If the slave survive two days, the connection of the death with the beating is not evident, and the loss of the master's *property* (DV ' money ') is considered sufficient punishment. CH also, by punishing a slave's disobedience with ear-mutilation, implies that a master could not put his slave to death at will. **22.** Injuries inflicted in a fight on a pregnant woman, resulting in the premature birth of a dead child, are punished by a fine, determined by the woman's husband. ' *And he shall pay for the miscarriage* ' (MT slightly corrected). The foetus is not regarded as a person, but if the woman dies the *lex talionis* is applied. The other codes agree with MC in imposing a fine but have a more developed legislation and distinguish different cases.

23-25. The **lex talionis** is a very ancient and widespread **g** law which makes the punishment agree with the offence. It checks passion and moderates the desire of vengeance. Except in the case of murder, the penalty was usually replaced among the Hebrews by a money compensation, more agreeable to the offender and profitable to the injured. The application of the penalty to innocent persons, like the son or wife of the offender, is a grave defect of justice in CH and AL, which also only impose a fine if the injured be inferior in rank. HL imposes a fine in all cases. The *lex talionis* holds only for freemen. **26-27.** Injury to a slave, even so slight as the loss of a tooth, sets him free. This humane law is peculiar to MC. Injury to a slave from an outsider was punished by a fine paid to his master in CH and HL. **28-32.** Death caused by an animal like the ox **h**

4h entails his slaughter (Gen 9:5), because he has failed in his end by being hurtful instead of useful to man. His flesh cannot be eaten because of the material blood-guilt attached to it. The owner, if culpably negligent, is subject to the *lex talionis*, usually commuted to a fine. Since the fine is substituted for the life of the offender the age or rank of the victim is irrelevant and the full blood-price, thirty silver shekels (nearly £4), must be paid if the victim be a slave. CH agrees with MC except in sparing the life of the ox and making the fine the blood-price of the victim, thirty shekels for a free man, twenty for a slave.

5a **XXI 33-XXII 17 Injuries to Property—33-36.** The loss of a domestic animal which falls into a neighbour's cistern or is gored by a neighbour's ox must be made good if the cistern was left uncovered or the ox was known to be ferocious. The owner receives the price of the animal, the neighbour retains the carcase. Cisterns for the preservation of rainwater are common in Palestine where springs are rare. If there was no culpable negligence, both persons share equally in the price of the ox which is sold and the carcase of the dead animal. Thus the flesh of an animal not ritually slaughtered was eaten at this period. Parallel cases of loss of property are similarly decided in CH and HL, though the latter once imposes double the restitution.

b **XXII:1.** The stealer of a domestic animal not recoverable must make fourfold or fivefold restitution, twofold if recoverable. **3b.** If insolvent he is sold as a slave. **2-3a.** A thief caught in the act may be slain with impunity by night, but not after sunrise. CH punishes similar offences with death in some cases and tenfold or thirtyfold restitution in others and allows a thief *in flagranti delicto* to be slain with impunity by day or by night. Death sometimes, but more commonly mutilation, is the punishment of theft in AL. HL is in almost complete agreement with MC, but exacts fuller restitution. **5-6.** Injury done to a neighbour's field or vineyard by letting one's beast loose on it must be made good. Injury caused by fire, catching in *brushwood* (Vg ' thorn ') and spreading to a neighbour's land, must also be made good. Negligence is presumed in both cases. CH and HL agree with MC, but are more precise in estimating damage and compensation in the first case.

c **7-8.** If a deposit be missing the thief must make twofold restitution. If he be not discovered the depositary must establish his innocence *before God*, possibly by an ordeal, more probably by an oath (LXX) which the guilty would fear to take. CH agrees with MC in imposing twofold restitution on the thief and making the depositary responsible if culpably negligent, but requires absolutely for the validity of the deposit a written contract attested by witnesses. Deposits were the usual means of safeguarding property during the absence of the owner. **9.** Cases of lost things alleged to be found in possession of another are to be decided *before God* as in 8. ' He whom God shall condemn shall pay double to his neighbour.' The fine is for theft in one case, for false accusation in the other. CH and HL also regard appropriation of things lost as theft and CH obliges the possessor to prove by witnesses that the object was honestly purchased.

d **10-13.** The case of an animal injured or lost in a neighbour's keeping is considered. If there are no witnesses to the death or injury or hostile seizure of the animal the neighbour must attest his innocence by oath ; if it was stolen from him he is bound to restitution ; if it was torn by a wild beast he must exhibit the torn carcase. CH also orders restitution if the animal was stolen, but not if it was seized by a wild beast or perished by lightning or pestilence when innocence can be established by oath. HL agrees with MC in the case of seizure by a wild beast. **14-15.** An animal may be lent to another *gratis* or for hire. In the first case injury to the animal must be made good, since neglect is presumed, unless the owner was present. In the second no compensation is exacted, since *if it was hired it came for its hire*. Others render : *If a hired servant*

(was present) *it comes on his hire* (is taken out of his **175d** wages). CH and HL only consider the case of an animal hired out to another, who must compensate the owner for damages, unless the beast perish by an act of God, when innocence must be established by oath. In the more primitive and humane MC such services were usually given *gratis*.

16-17. The seduction and violation of a virgin not **e** betrothed is considered here as affecting her father, who guards his daughter's interests and will find it difficult to get her a husband and thus lose the *mōhar*, purchase-money (DV ' dowry '). The seducer must pay the *mōhar* and also marry the maiden unless her father objects. It is uncertain whether the father at this period kept the *mōhar* or gave it in whole or in part as a dowry to the bride. AL has a similar enactment, but exacts a threefold *mōhar* from the seducer.

XXII 18-XXIII 9 Religion and Charity—18-21. **f** Sorcery, bestiality and worship of other gods are punished with death. Sorcery was similarly punished in CH and AL, not for a religious motive as in MC, but as causing injury to person and property. Bestiality was a capital offence in HL, but not in all cases. **21-24.** Oppression of resident aliens, widows, orphans and the poor is particularly prohibited. The poor and defenceless are under God's special care. **25-27.** The creditor must be considerate and merciful to his debtor. In particular the mantle of the debtor, if pledged as security, must be returned before nightfall, since it is the poor man's only coverlet. **25.** ' If thou lend money to any of my people with thee that is poor, thou shalt not be to him as a creditor, neither shall ye lay upon him interest.' Lending at interest to a poor Israelite is here forbidden as contrary to charity, but not as wrong in itself. Deut 23:20 expressly allows exaction of interest from foreign traders. CH allows interest in all cases of loan but seeks to regulate the rate and forbids exploitation of the temporary needs of a poor debtor. **28.** *Thou shalt* **g** *not curse God*, etc. Vg has ' gods ' understood as judges, but *'elōhîm* does not mean judges and Naboth was falsely accused of blaspheming God and the king (3 Kg 21:13). The mild HL punishes cursing the ruler with extermination of offender and family. **29-30.** The offering of the first-fruits of *thy fulness* (wine Num 28:27) *and thy tear* (oil) is prescribed. The first-born sons, originally consecrated by this law to the service of Yahweh, were subsequently ransomed when replaced by the Levites. The eighth day does not designate the exact time of the offering, but the beginning of a period in which it was made (Lev 22:27) as in Gen 2:17. **31.** This prohibition, as already explained (§ 173*f*), is a later insertion. **XXIII:1-9.** Practical applications **h** of the eighth commandment are considered. Strict adherence to truth is inculcated on witnesses, and judges are warned not to take bribes or pervert justice especially when the poor and resident aliens are concerned. Some correct ' poor man ' (3) to ' great man ', since false testimony on behalf of the poor is unexpected. No penalty is here imposed on offenders but the *lex talionis* is applied to false accusers and lying witnesses (Deut 19:16-21) as in CH and SL. **4-5.** Charity to one's enemy by helping him in difficulties is enjoined. This precept is not opposed to the words of Christ on the character of the Old Law (Mt 5:43). He refers to the general spirit of the legislation manifested by the *lex talionis* and contrasted with the New Law of universal charity and forgivingness.

XXIII 10-19 Public Worship—10-11. The Sabbath **i** year, more fully described (Lev 25:2-7 ; Deut 15:1-3), like the Sabbath day was the same for all. Its object was not economical, to increase the fertility of the soil, but religious, to acknowledge God's ownership of the land by renouncing its use every seventh year. Tillage and harvesting were forbidden and the spontaneous produce of the corn-land, the vines and the olive trees was assigned to the poor and after them to the beasts of the field. Lev, however, allows the proprietors a share of it and Deut prescribes a moratorium on debts, usually paid from harvest returns. **13b.**

175i This prohibition explains the substitution of *bōšeṯ*, 'shame' for *ba'al* 'master' in proper names. The originally inoffensive *ba'al* became notorious as the

j name of the chief Canaanite deity. **14–17.** The three annual feasts, usually called Pasch, Feast of Weeks (Pentecost in NT) and Feast of Tabernacles, are here named according to their agricultural character, Feast of Unleavened Bread, Feast of Harvest and Feast of Gathering. On the first *cf.* 12:15–20. The second was the feast of the wheat harvest and occurred seven weeks after the offering of the first-fruits of the barley harvest. The third began on the fifteenth of Tishri and lasted eight days. It celebrated the products of the fruit harvest, of which wine and oil were the most important. The corn, strangely associated with this feast in DV, is a mistranslation of Vg *fruges*. Read **15c** after 17. **18.** Nothing leavened could be offered on the altar, probably because changed from its natural condition ; *cf.* the similar prohibition of hewn stones (20:25). The fat, considered the most precious part of the victim, must be offered while still fresh and

k unspoiled. **19b.** The cooking of a kid in its mother's milk is forbidden, as a pagan sacrificial rite, according to an addition in Sam here and in some Greek MSS (Deut 14:20). The rite is now known from the Rās-Shamra tablets as pertaining to the cult of Asherah, the Canaanite goddess of fertility, and represents symbolically the nursing of a god by the mother goddess (*cf.* A. Casey VD 16 [1936] 142–8 ; 174–83). The legislation may have ended with 13a.

176a **20–33 Promises and Warnings for the March to Canaan**—This passage does not interrupt the history of the Covenant, but suitably precedes its ratification, as the similar discourse (34:11–16) subsequently precedes its renewal. Yahweh promises to guide, assist, nourish and multiply his people, to inspire fear and discouragement in their enemies, to make them victorious in battle and to give them possession of all Canaan, not immediately lest the land suffer from partial disoccupation, but gradually as they become numerous enough to fill ,it (*cf.* 12:37). He warns them on the other hand against all acts of disobedience, especially worshipping the gods of the Canaanites, imitating their evil actions, neglecting to destroy their *Massebas* and concluding alliances with them. The Massebas (DV 'statues') were idolatrous emblems of Baal, consisting of detached stone pillars erected in

b the Canaanite sanctuaries. **28.** The Hornets (*cf.* Deut 7:20 ; Jos 24:12 ; Wis 12:8) are usually interpreted figuratively in the sense of discouragement. Garstang sees in them the Egyptians whose destructive campaigns in Palestine in the 15th cent. B.C. made the land an easy prey to the invading Hebrews *c* 1406 B.C. (*Joshua Judges* [London 1931] 112–5 ; 258–60). But the symbol of Lower Egypt which he assumes to be the hornet is more usually regarded as the bee by Egyptologists, and his dating of the conquest and identification of the Habiri with the Hebrews are improbable. **31.** The boundaries of the promised land from the Gulf of Aqabah (Red Sea) to the Mediterranean (Sea of the Philistines) and from the desert of Sur to the river Euphrates are to some extent ideal and include subject nations.

c **XXIV 1–11 Ascent of the Mount and Ratification of the Covenant**—The order to ascend the mount (**1–2**) and its execution (**9–11b**) interrupt the context and register another tradition in which the accompaniment of Moses part of the way by the three future priests and seventy elders and the pediment on which Yahweh manifested himself were described. **3–8,11c.** The ratification of the Covenant immediately follows the Book of the Covenant. Moses first communicates to the people *all the words of Yahweh*, *viz.* the judicial decisions. The people undertake to observe them and Moses commits them to writing. Next morning an altar is built on the lower slope of the mount and twelve *Massebas* (DV 'titles') are erected, not as idolatrous emblems, but to commemorate the twelve tribes. Young men, probably first-born sons, slaughter

the victims, both holocausts and peace-offerings in **17** whose blood the Covenant will be ratified. Half of the blood is sprinkled on the altar and half is kept in sacrificial bowls and subsequently sprinkled on the people after Moses has solemnly read aloud the Book of the Covenant and they have again solemnly promised to observe it. The sacrificial banquet on the flesh of the peace-offerings given by Yahweh as host to his worshippers strengthens the bond between him and them and ends the ceremony of ratification. Since the **d** blood represented the life of the victim and the altar represented Yahweh, the pouring or sprinkling of the blood on the altar was the offering of the life of the victim to Yahweh, the essential element in every Hebrew sacrifice of a living victim. The sprinkling of part of the blood on the people was a special rite of the covenant sacrifice which expressed the special union between Yahweh and his people effected by the covenant. The sacrifice of Christ was also a covenant sacrifice by which the New Testament or Covenant was ratified. It is in the consecration of the chalice that this character is emphasized in its Eucharistic continuation.

12–18 Moses again ascends the Mount—The object **e** of this ascent is to receive from Yahweh firstly the two tables of stone containing the law commanded in the decalogue and secondly the instructions on the organization of cult recorded in chh 24–31. He is accompanied part of the way by his attendant Josue, the leader in the battle with the Amalekites (17:8 ff.). Aaron and Hur are given charge of the people during his absence. The mountain is covered by a cloud, visible sign of the presence of Yahweh, into which he is admitted on the seventh day and where he remains forty days. The numbers are symbolical, indicating more or less lengthy periods.

XXV–XXXI Introduction to the Ritual Legislation— **f** The ritual legislation was an essential element of the Sinaitic Covenant. Israel could not become God's holy people by mere observance of a legal code which made no provision for an organization of cult. To the ancients in particular religion without ritual was inconceivable. Excavations have revealed to us highly developed rituals in Egypt and Mesopotamia in the third millennium B.C. and in Syria in the middle of the second. The error of Wellhausen in regarding Hebrew ritual as almost entirely a post-exilic product is now generally recognized. The ritual law is still supposed by his followers to have been codified after the exile but is. conceded to incorporate much pre-exilic material. From historical parallels alone the conclusion is justified that the Hebrews had an organized cult at a very early period of their national existence. The text of Ex 25–31 contains moreover **g** indications of time and place in agreement with the origin claimed for it by the sacred writer. The use of bronze instead of iron for base metal work suggests a date in the age of bronze which ended in the Near East *c* 1200 B.C. The exclusive employment of the acacia tree for woodwork supposes Sinai, where it was abundant, rather than Palestine, where it was rare, as the place of construction of the tabernacle and its furniture. While the Cherubim of the time of Ezechiel recall Babylonian parallels, those of the ark reproduce exactly a representation in the temple of Dendera in Egypt and thus suggest an early date and an acquaintance with Egyptian art. Such indications assign chh 25–31 to the Mosaic rather than the post-exilic period. But where did the Hebrews **h** find the gold and silver and bronze, the linen and dyes and skins needed for their work ? In Egypt, undoubtedly a very rich country, especially prosperous during the period of their sojourn. They were from the beginning an acquisitive people and utilized the many years during which they enjoyed the favour of the Egyptians and lived among them to accumulate riches to which they added the spoils of victory secured before their departure. In Egypt too they acquired the skill needed for the work and from the trading

6h caravans which passed through Sinai to Egypt they could purchase perfumes and spices. Had they been a small number of poor ignorant nomads, as some critics have supposed, the tabernacle and the conquest of Canaan would be inexplicable. Objections made to the historicity of various parts of the narrative will be discussed more conveniently in the commentary.

7a XXV 1-9 Provision of Materials—The materials here registered were the voluntary *offerings* (DV 'first-fruits') of the people. The fine Egyptian linen was naturally white, but was also dyed dark blue, purple, and *bright* scarlet. Blue and purple dyes were got from shell-fish, the *murex trunculus* and the *murex brandaris*, scarlet from a species of cochineal, the *coccus ilicis*. Only the purple stuffs, not the scarlet, were twice dyed. Goats' hair is still woven into material for tent covering. The *taḥaš* was not a dye (Vg 'violet') but a marine animal, probably the sea-cow. *Šiṭṭîm* is the plural of an Egyptian word for acacia. The acacias of Sinai were probably larger in Mosaic times than they are today. *Onyx* is a conjectural rendering of the Hebrew *šōham*.

b 10-22 XXXVII 1-9 The Ark—The ark is described first as the most sacred instrument of cult. It was a chest made of acacia wood overlaid inside and outside with gold and measuring 2½ × 1½ × 1½ cubits (half yards). Its cover was a slab of pure gold, the propitiatory, place or instrument of propitiation, on which the blood of the victims was sprinkled on the Feast of the Atonement to expiate the sins of Israel. The word is used of Christ (Rom 3:25) who by offering satisfaction for our sins made God propitious to us. The top of the ark was adorned all round with a gold crown or moulding and on its four corners (*pinnôṯ* for MT 'feet') were four gold rings into which staves of acacia wood overlaid with gold were fitted on the shorter sides for the purpose of transportation. On the two ends of the propitiatory were two golden cherubim facing each other and spreading their wings over it. Their position on the ends excludes the view of Heinisch that they were worked in relief on the propitiatory so that their heads nearly met in the centre and suggests rather standing or kneeling figures of winged youths (since angels appear in human form in the Pentateuch). An Egyptian ark at Dendera is thus adorned.

c The ark served a two-fold purpose. It contained the Decalogue, a lasting testimony of the Sinaitic Covenant and was therefore called Ark of the Testimony (Ex) and Ark of the Covenant (Deut). It was the throne of Yahweh 'sitting on the Cherubim' (1 Kg 4:4, etc.) who there manifested himself to his people, received their prayers and offerings and led them in their expeditions and was therefore called Ark of God (1 Kg). The question, much debated by the critics, whether chest or throne was the original concept, is otiose for those who hold a divine institution with a two-fold purpose illustrated by the monuments and affirmed by the texts. All admit the antiquity of the ark, but not its Mosaic origin.

d 23-30 XXXVII 10-16 The Table—It also was made of acacia wood overlaid with gold and was of the same breadth and height as the ark but a half-cubit shorter in length. The legs were connected, about half-way up according to the representation on the Arch of Titus, by a golden rail or border, a handsbreadth in height, adorned with a crown or moulding. There was a similar moulding at the top. The rings and staves for transportation were like those of the ark, but the position of the rings is more clearly indicated as close to the rail or border. Salvers for loaves, cups for incense, flagons for wine and bowls for libations are also prescribed as the furniture of the table. Twelve loaves of unleavened bread were placed on the table as an offering to Yahweh on the eve of the Sabbath and after a week were replaced by fresh loaves and eaten by the priests. The incense was also renewed each week-end. The bread is called presence bread, holy bread, continual bread, bread

of proposition. Its ritual function is paralleled by the **177d** twelve cakes placed before Ishtar (Jer 7:18 ; 44:19). Its antiquity is attested by the episode of David and the high-priest (1 Kg 21:3–6).

31-40 XXXVII 17-24 The Lampstand—The lamp- **e** stand (DV candlestick) was a conventional representation of a flowering almond-tree, as appears from the *almond-blossoms* (DV 'cups as it were nuts', **33-34**). The *knop* (DV 'bowl') and the *flower* (DV 'lily') being in the singular do not indicate separate ornaments but the *calix* and the *corolla* or outer and inner parts of each blossom. The central shaft had four blossoms; the branches, three on each side, had three each. There were also knops but no flowers where the branches emerged from the central shaft. The seven blossoms on the top were the lamps. *Peraḥ* 'flower' denotes 'lamp-tray' in the Mishna. The lampstand was beaten-work of pure gold and weighed a talent (108 lb.). *The almond-tree* was called *šāqēḏ* 'vigilant' because it awoke so early in the spring from its winter sleep, and thus aptly symbolized the vigil kept by the lights before the ark. As this symbolism appears elsewhere (Jer 1:11 f. ; Eccl 12:5) and explains adequately the shape of the lampstand it is superfluous to connect it with the ancient veneration of sacred trees. The later tradition that some at least of the lamps burned also by day scarcely agrees with 1 Kg 3:3.

XXVI 1-37 XXXVI 8-38 The Tabernacle—The **f** coverings are first described, then the framework and lastly the internal arrangement. **1-14.** The **coverings** were four in number. The first (40 × 28 cubits) was of fine twisted linen of various colours, white, blue, purple, and scarlet, and adorned with figures of cherubim. Its two parts, each consisting of five curtains of the same dimensions (28 × 4 cubits), were united by means of fifty golden clasps fitted into corresponding blue loops in the curtains on either side. The second covering (44 × 30 cubits) was made of goats' hair like the Bedouin tent-covering. Its two parts, one of six and the other of five curtains measuring 30 × 4 cubits, were united like those of the first except that the colour of the loops is not given and the clasps were of bronze instead of gold. It is expressly stated that the excess in breadth of the second covering over the first overhung the tabernacle by one cubit on each side (13) and the excess in length by half a curtain or two cubits in the front (9) and at the back (12). It follows evidently from this, that the space covered on top was 40 cubits in length, not 30, as is generally assumed. Only the materials of the third and fourth coverings are given, skins of rams dyed red and skins of the sea-cow. **15-30.** The **g** **framework** consisted of boards of acacia wood overlaid with gold, measuring 10 × 1½ cubits, twenty on each side of the tabernacle, six at the back and two of special make at the corners between the sides and the back. **24.** The corner boards, variously explained, are thus described : '*And they shall be equal* [LXX ; *twins* MT vocalizing *tᵉʾōmîm*] *below and they shall be equal on the top of it* [the tent] *unto one ring so shall it be for both of them, at the two corners they shall be*'. Since the dimensions of the tabernacle like those of Solomon's temple were internal and did not include the thickness of the framework, if we assume this undefined thickness to be ¼ cubit, each corner board had a breadth of ¾ cubit or just half that of the other boards. This may explain the epithet twin. All the boards had two projections underneath inserted in silver sockets. The cohesion of the framework was secured by bars of acacia wood overlaid with gold, which passed through gold rings on the outside of the boards, five on each side. The central bar (omitted DV 28) is usually regarded as one of the five, but its special mention and its special fabrication after the others (36:33) exclude this hypothesis. **31-37.** The space **h** enclosed by the framework consisted of **the Holy Place** in front (20 × 10 cubits) and **the Holy of Holies** at the back (10 × 10 cubits). The Veil separating

177h them, like the first covering in material and ornamentation, was attached by golden hooks to four pillars of acacia wood overlaid with gold and resting on sockets of silver. The Ark alone was in the Holy of Holies, and the Table was on the right, the Lampstand on the left as one entered the Holy Place. ' Propitiatory' (*kappōreṭ*) is probably a misreading of ' veil ' (*pārōkeṭ*) (MT 34). Finally a **Screen** covered the entrance of the Tabernacle differing from the Veil in its adornment, devoid of figures of cherubim, and in its supports : five instead of four pillars and bronze instead of silver sockets.

i To verify these details we must assume that the tabernacle like all tents had not a flat but a sloping roof and that it was more like Solomon's temple (*cf.* Wis 9:8) than is generally supposed. The two parts of the temple which corresponded with the Holy Place and the Holy of Holies, the *hêḵāl* and the *dᵉḇîr* were respectively twice as long and twice as wide as their counterparts. They were also twice as high if the tabernacle had a sloping roof with a maximum height of 15 cubits. The lateral buildings on three sides of the temple and the atrium in front had their counterpart in an additional covered space of five cubits on all four sides of the tabernacle. Only in this hypothesis can the space covered have a length of 40 and a breadth of more than 10 cubits, suggested by the five pillars of the Screen as opposed to the four of the Veil. The sockets of the pillars supporting the Screen, being of bronze, must also have been at some distance from the framework, since all objects in immediate contact with the Holy Place were of gold or silver. The long centre pole at the top over which the coverings were laid was *the central bar* distinguished from the five lateral ones and described as being in the middle of or between the boards, since there were twenty-four on either side, and as extending from one extremity of the tent to the

j other. The centre pole would be supported by transverse beams two pairs of which would rest on the outer pillars upholding the veil and the screen and a third on similar pillars at the back not mentioned because they had no screen. The description of the corner boards seems to imply such transverse beams meeting at the top of the tent. The first covering was 28 cubits wide. It would thus occupy the seven cubits between the centre pole and the framework on either side, and thence descend in the same diagonal line for seven cubits to a point five cubits distant from the framework and the earth where it would be secured by ropes and pegs. This disposition of the covering avoids textual alterations and removes other difficulties in the common view. It makes the beautiful first covering everywhere visible, instead of being mostly concealed by the framework, and it prevents all the coverings from being soiled by contact with the earth. It provides also a sleeping-place for Samuel (1 Kg 3:3).

178a **The existence and sacred character of the tabernacle and the ark** during the whole period between the entry into Canaan and the building of the temple is clearly attested in the early historical books. Both appear at the army headquarters in Canaan, the ark at Gilgal (Jos 4:19), the tabernacle at Shiloh (Jos 18:1). The presence of the tabernacle implies that of the ark and *vice versa*. The ark moreover usually accompanied the army in battle and its presence is attested at the siege of Jericho (Jos 4:4 ff.) and in the Benjaminitic war (Jg 20:27). At Shiloh we subsequently find the house of God (Jg 18:31), an annual festival (Jg 21:19), the ark (1 Kg 3:3), the tabernacle (1 Kg 2:22), the house

b of God (1 Kg 3:15). It is objected that 1 Kg 2:22 is a later interpolation as it is omitted by LXX (B). But the omission is explained by the disedifying character of the verse and its presence in the text used by LXX is proved by the presence of the other not disedifying reference to the women watching at the entrance to the tabernacle (Ex 38:8). It is also objected that the house of God at Shiloh was not the tabernacle but a *hêḵāl* or sacred edifice of stone (1 Kg 1:7) with doorposts (1 Kg 1:9) and door (1 Kg 3:15). But this description

implies at most an edifice enclosing the tabernacle and certainly not replacing it, since it is repeatedly stated that Yahweh, regarded as seated on the cherubim of the ark, dwelt invariably, before the building of the temple, not in a house but in a tent (2 Kg 7:2, 6 ; 3 Kg 8:16). Recent excavations support this conclusion by showing that Shiloh, previously insignificant, enjoyed great prosperity in the early Israelitic period when it was the sacred city of Israel. The ark was captured by the **c** Philistines at the battle of Aphek (1 Kg 4:11) but restored to Israel seven months later and, after a brief stay at Beth-Shemesh, remained about eighty years at Kiryath-Yearim. After the capture of Jerusalem David had it removed to his new capital, where it remained for three months in the house of Obededom and subsequently in a special tent on Mt Sion until the temple was ready to receive it. The tabernacle on the other hand, when Shiloh was sacked by the Philistines, seems to have been removed to Nob, where we find, in the days of Saul, an important sanctuary, eighty-five priests including the high-priest Ahimelec, the Ephod containing the Urim and Thummim and the loaves of proposition (1 Kg 21:1–9). St Jerome is justified by these indications in rendering *before Yahweh* (7) by ' in the tabernacle of the Lord '. The destruction of Nob and the slaughter of its priests and people by Saul (1 Kg 22:9–19) offer a natural explanation of the transport of the tabernacle to Gabaon, where we find it in the beginning of Solomon's reign (2 Par 1:3–6). The separation of the ark from the tabernacle was a natural consequence of the historical vicissitudes of a disturbed period when restriction of public worship to a single sanctuary was practically impossible.

XXVII 1-8 XXXVIII 1-7 The Altar—It was made **d** of acacia wood overlaid with bronze and was five cubits in length and breadth and three in height. The lower half was surrounded by an ornamental grating of bronze network supporting a border required by the priests, owing to the height of the altar, for the performance of their functions. The interpretation (LXX, Josephus) of this grating as a hearth let down from the top into the interior of the altar is untenable. It was a *network*, not a hearth, and was *beneath the border* outside the altar. There were four horn-shaped projections at the corners, regarded as the most sacred parts of the altar, grasped by fugitives seeking asylum and smeared with sacrificial blood on certain occasions. Horns are found also on the altars of the Assyrians and other ancient peoples. They are symbols of strength. The altar was transported by means of staves of acacia wood overlaid with bronze which passed through rings attached to the upper extremities of the network grating. It was hollow and therefore useless unless filled with earth or stones (20:24–25) as is evidently implied. Some critics, who consider the narrative (chh 25–31) a post-exilic fiction, deny this implication and thus imagine the author so stupid as to invent a useless altar and yet so clever as to substitute bronze and acacia for iron and cedar in accordance with the requirements of time and place.

9-19 XXXVIII 9-20 The Court of the Tabernacle— **e** —It was 100 cubits long, from east to west, and 50 cubits wide and was enclosed by hangings supported on pillars, one for every 5 cubits and therefore 60 in all. The hangings were of fine twisted linen in its natural white colour except at the entrance in the middle of the east side. Here was a screen 20 cubits long of which the hangings were of various colours, white, blue, purple, and scarlet. The material of the pillars was acacia wood (not bronze Vg 38:10, 12) since they are not numbered among the bronze articles (38:30 f.). They had sockets of bronze, capitals of silver and fillets or neckings of silver at the base of the capitals. The hangings 5 cubits high were attached to the pillars by hooks. The altar was in the eastern half of the court, the tabernacle in the western, each probably in the centre of its respective square. God dwelt in the Holy of Holies, gave audience to his Ministers in the Holy Place, and received the homage of his people in the

8e Court. **20-21.** The command to provide oil for the Lampstand, out of place here, appears again in a more suitable context (Lev 24:2-4).

9a **XXVIII 1-5 Institution of the Aaronid Priesthood—** The priestly office in Israel is here assigned by Yahweh to Aaron and his descendants. The **high-priesthood** of Aaron is implicitly indicated by the distinction made between his vestments (6–39) and those of his sons, the priests (40–43). He is *sanctified* by the vestments, set apart and consecrated to the service of Yahweh. After the death without issue of Nadab and Abiu the high-priesthood was inherited by the Eleazer branch (Pinehas and later Sadoc) but was temporarily usurped by the line of Ithamar (Eli, Ahimelek, Abiathar).

b **6-30 XXXIX 1-21 Ephod and Ḥōšen—**They were united to form a single vestment, usually called **Ephod** and worn by the high-priest when he sought oracular responses from Yahweh by means of the Urim and Thummim contained in the *ḥōšen* or pouch (1 Kg 14:3 ; 18 [ephod LXX, ark MT, Vg] ; 23:9 ff. ; 30 :7 ff.). The full name *Ornament* (DV *rational*) *of Judgement* expresses the beauty and the function of the *ḥōšen*. Ephod designates a garment. A simple linen ephod was worn by priests (1 Kg 22:18) and the young Samuel (1 Kg 2:18), probably not very different from a loincloth since David could be called naked when wearing it (2 Kg 6:14, 20). The ephod of Gedeon (Jg 8:27) is not described and was probably similar to that of Micah (Jg 17:5 ; 18:14 ff.), which is clearly distinguished from his idol and appears from its association with the teraphim and its consultation by the Danites (Jg 18:5–6) to have been used for oracular purposes like the ephod of the high-priest. There is a similar association of ephod and teraphim in Os 3:4. The teraphim are consulted in Ez 21:21. It follows therefore that the critical theory, which regards the high-priests' ephod as a post-exilic invention, arising out of an erroneous identification of an ephod-idol with an ephod-garment,

c has no foundation in the texts. Both ephod and *ḥōšen* were made of linen of various colours interwoven with gold thread. The former was a single piece of brocade of indeterminate length, covering breast, back and sides from the armpits downwards and attached more closely to the body by a band of the same material and of one piece with it. It had two shoulder-straps, adorned each at the top with a *šōham* stone, inscribed with the names of six of the tribes of Israel. The brocade of the *ḥōšen* was doubled so as to form a pouch or burse, one handbreath in length and width, adorned on the outer side with twelve precious stones on which the names of the twelve tribes were engraved. It had two gold rings on the outside in its upper corners and two on the inside in its lower ones. The former were attached by gold chains to gold rosettes on the tops of the shoulder-straps, the latter by blue ribbons to gold rings on their ends. The gold chains were visible, the blue ribbons invisible. The *ḥōšen* rested on the band of the ephod and covered the upper part of the breast. The twelve precious stones have not been definitely identified. The inscriptions on them and on the two *šōham* stones of the shoulder-straps were to remind Yahweh of his people whom the high-priest represented.

d In ancient times the vestment was regularly worn in seeking oracular responses from Yahweh by means of the **Urim and Thummim** contained in the *ḥōšen*. These were lots of stone or wood, signifying conventionally one an affirmative, the other a negative reply to a question asked, or one approbation, the other disapprobation of a course of action proposed. The names of the lots according to the Masoretic vocalization, *lights and perfections*, have no bearing on their use. It is plausibly suggested that the original forms were *'ōrîm* from the root *'rr* ' curse ', and *tōmîm*, from the root *tmm* ' be innocent '. Sometimes no answer was given, a contingency usually provided for by a third lot, excluded here. It may be supposed that no lot or both lots together issued from the pouch in these cases. The reply given in the texts sometimes supposes several questions not recorded in detail. The oracle was con-

sulted only by the high-priest in presence of the ruler **179d** when he required divine guidance in matters of grave public importance. There is no recorded instance of such a consultation after the time of David. Prophets were approached instead.

31-43 XXXIX 22-31 Other Vestments of the High- **e** **priest and Priestly Vestments—**The high-priest wore also a blue linen robe, corresponding to the ordinary outer garment, called *the robe of the ephod*, a mitre or head-dress also of linen, a white linen tunic, corresponding to the ordinary inner garment, and a girdle or sash in linen of various colours by which the tunic was bound ; the priests had no outer robe but were otherwise similarly though less ornately vested. **31-35.** **f** The robe was of a single piece with apertures, one for the head, around which it was strengthened by a band, and two for the arms. It extended to the knees and was adorned at its extremities with pomegranates made of linen of various colours and little bells of gold arranged alternately. The object of the bells was later regarded as similar to that of the inscriptions on the precious stones (Ecclus 45:9), but the fact that they rang at the entrance to and exit from the Holy Place to protect the life of the high-priest implies that their ringing was originally intended to avert dangers from evil spirits. **36-38.** The mitre was a kind of turban, **g** similar to that worn by royalty, and specially adorned with a gold plate in front, attached by blue fillets and inscribed : ' Holy to Yahweh '. The inscription indicates that the high-priest is the offering of the people to Yahweh and thus atones in person for the offences committed by people and priests in making their offerings. **39.** The linen tunic is not described. **h** Probably it extended to the feet, was provided with sleeves and was elaborately adorned. The girdle, according to tradition, encircled the body several times and had lengthy extremities which were thrown over the shoulders during ceremonies. The Hebrew name *'abnēṭ* is of Egyptian origin. **40-41.** The vestments of the priests are not described, but were doubtless similar to the similarly named ones of the high-priest. As all served barefoot there is no mention of footgear. **42-43.** The linen ,breeches were not regarded as a priestly vestment.

XXIX 1-37 Consecration of Aaron and his Sons— 180a The actual consecration is narrated Lev 8:1–36. The offerings are first brought to the tabernacle. **3.** For ' offer ' read *bring in the basket*. The washing of Aaron and his sons which follows is an outward symbol of the internal purity required. **5-7.** Aaron is then clothed with the vestments of the high-priest and the oil of unction is poured on his head. For ' linen garment ' and ' tunick ' read *tunic and robe of the ephod*, for ' girdle ' *band of the ephod*. The plate is called *diadem* in MT. Render *7b and anoint him*. **8-9.** The sons of Aaron are also clothed with the priestly vestments and thus consecrated or *installed in office*. In Hebrew as in Assyro-Babylonian *to fill the hands* means ' to install in office '. The high-priest is specially designated as **the anointed** **b** **priest** (Lev 4:16 ; 21:10 ; Num 35:25). The anointing of other priests, not mentioned here or Lev 8, is clearly indicated (Ex 28:41 ; 30:30 ; 40:13 ; Lev 7:35 ; 10:7 ; Num 3:3). Some explain these texts as only implying that ordinary priests were radically anointed in their high-priest ancestor. Others suppose a modification in practice at a later period. This view is supported by the fact that some at least of the texts mentioned (Ex 28:41 ; 30:30) appear to be later additions. The sprinkling with blood and oil (21) may also have been regarded as a priestly anointing, though it was also enjoined for the recovered leper (Lev 14:14, 17). **10-14.** The young bullock, a sin-offering, was next **c** slain after Aaron and his sons had laid their hands on the victim's head in token of solidarity that it might be associated with them and expiate for them. The blood of the victim was first poured out on the horns and at the base of the altar to purify it ; the fatty parts were then burned on the altar and the rest burned outside the camp. The flesh of sin-offerings was usually eaten by

180c the priests, but not, as in this case, when their own sins
d were expiated. **15-18.** One of the rams is next offered as a holocaust. The ritual is the customary one : imposition of hands by those for whom the sacrifice is offered, slaughter of the victim, effusion of the blood round the altar, dissection, washing of entrails and feet and total
e destruction by fire on the altar. **19-28.** The second is then slain as a peace-offering but with certain rites peculiar to the occasion. Usually all the blood was poured on the altar. Here part of it is first smeared on the tip of the right ear, the right thumb, and the right big toe of Aaron and his sons to remind them that they must always listen to God's holy voice, do holy works and walk in holy ways. The blood is now poured on the altar as usual. Some of it is next taken and with some of the oil of unction sprinkled on the persons and vestments of Aaron and his sons to sanctify them (cf. 24:8) and unite them to God more closely than the people. The fatty parts of the peace-offering were consumed on the altar ; the breast and the right *thigh* (DV ' shoulder ') were usually assigned to the priest and the rest of the victim provided a sacrificial meal for the offerers. Here, however, Moses as priest receives the breast only ; the right thigh of *the ram of installation* is burned on the altar with the fatty parts and some of the bread offerings after they have been *waved* (DV ' elevated ') by Aaron and his sons. ' Wave ' has the general sense of ' offer ' but its special sense appears in the expression *breast of the wave offering* (27, DV ' consecrated breast ') as a movement of the offering towards God in the tabernacle and back again to the priestly offerer, signifying that it was God's gift to the priest ; cf. § 186k. The thigh is called the separation offering because separated from the people's
f part for the priest. **29-30.** The direction that Aaron's vestments are given to his sons or descendants at their installation in office is explained as referring to the son or descendant who becomes high-priest in his stead, but may be an interpolation as it interrupts the ritual. **31-32.** The sacrificial meal is cooked in a holy place and eaten at the entry of the tabernacle. **33.** ' Stranger ' means here not of a priestly or Levitical family. **34.** What is not eaten before morning must be burned. **36-37.** The sanctification of the altar by the sacrifice of a young steer is continued for seven days. The altar is most holy and cannot be touched with impunity.
g **38-42 The Daily Burnt-offering**—Morning and evening a lamb was offered as a holocaust accompanied by meal (nearly ½ peck) mingled with oil (nearly 3 pints) and a libation of wine (nearly 3 pints). A morning *minḥāh* is attested (4 Kg 3:20) and a morning holocaust and evening *minḥāh* (4 Kg 16:15). *Minḥāh* is always a meal offering in legal texts but sometimes denotes also an animal offering in historical ones (cf. Gen 4:4), so that entire agreement of legislation and pre-exilic practice cannot be affirmed or denied. Lack of materials (cf. Jl 1:13) might excuse non-observance of this law. **43-46.** The dwelling of Yahweh among his chosen people and the benefits which result from his presence form a fitting conclusion to the ritual laws and indicate the reward of their faithful observance.
h **XXX 1-XXXI 17 Supplement to the Ritual Legislation**—This section contains important additions to the directions given in chh 25-9. As it follows the conclusion (29:43-46) it is obviously an addition but not necessarily made by a different author.
i **XXX 1-10 XXXVII 25-28 The Altar of Incense**— It was made of the same materials as the Table, had a similar moulding on top and similar rings and staves for transport, was a cubit in length and breadth and two cubits in height. It was called the golden altar as distinguished from the bronze altar of holocausts, and like it had four horns. It was in the Holy Place before the veil and at its centre where it was in line with the Propitiatory. As the incense, offered morning and evening, was intended for the Holy of Holies, which it entered through the opening above the veil provided by the sloping roof, it belonged to the Holy of Holies (Heb 9:4) just as the incense-altar, in Solo-

mon's temple, belonged to the *Debir* (3 Kg 6:22). The order given (10) is ignored in the ritual of the Atonement-day (Lev 16). Offerings of incense, mentioned Lev 10:1 ; Num 16:6-7, were made with censers. It would seem therefore that an altar of incense was not prescribed in the original plan of the tabernacle. That does not mean however that it was not a Mosaic institution, much less that it is a post-exilic invention. Incense altars were used in Mesopotamia in the third millennium B.C. and have been found in Canaan at Megiddo and Ta'anak (8th cent. B.C.) and at Tell Beth Mirsim (10th cent. B.C.). There is no reason therefore to exclude even from Solomon's temple the incense-altar mentioned by the texts, notably 3 Kg 6:20 ; 7:48.
j **11-16 The Poll-tax**—The ancient Hebrews like the Romans considered a census an encroachment on God's domain (2 Kg 24:10). The poll-tax however of half a shekel (about 1s. 3d.), imposed alike on rich and poor and devoted to the upkeep of the sanctuary, would legitimate it. The narrative implies the Mosaic origin of the poll-tax, but was written after the construction of the tabernacle, since the census is that of Num 1:1 ff. The plague (DV ' scourge ', **12**) is not necessarily a reference to 2 Kg 24, but is based on the same belief.
k **17-21 XXXVIII 8 The Bronze Laver**—It is not described and is clearly a later institution since it was made from the bronze mirrors of the women who served at the entrance of the tabernacle and is not numbered among the bronze objects (38:29-31). A constant supply of water for the priests' ablutions would be difficult to procure in the desert.
l **22-38 XXXVII 29 Anointing Oil and Incense**— The holy oil consisted of pure olive oil, mixed in fixed proportions with four spices—myrrh, calamus, cinnamon and cassia. **Myrrh** was an Arabian gum exuding from the *balsamodendron myrrha* and is described as *flowing*, interpreted by some, spontaneously exuding, by others, of choicest quality. The three other spices were obtained from odoriferous shrubs indigenous to south-eastern Asia and imported by Sabaean merchants. The oil thus prepared was restricted in its use to the sacred persons and objects mentioned, but its ingredients could be used singly or mixed in different proportions for profane purposes. **The incense**, a gum imported by the Sabaeans, was also mixed with other ingredients, **stacte**, **onyx** and **galbanum**, and was seasoned with salt. The **stacte** and **galbanum** were gums exuding from trees indigenous to Palestine. The **onyx** was provided by a shell-fish found in the Red Sea. The mixture was reduced to powder, burned on the altar of incense, morning and evening, and only used for sacred purposes. The mention of the altar of incense and the laver shows that the passage is part of the later addition.
m **XXXI 1-11 Beseleel and Ooliab**—The chief constructors of the tabernacle and its furniture are here introduced. *Beṣal'ēl* means ' in the protection of God', *'Oh·liāḇ* ' father's tent'. This passage is also late since the sacred objects enumerated include those of ch 30. **5.** ' *And in the hewing of stone for setting and in the hewing of wood for construction—in all kinds of work.*' In **10**, ' *the finely wrought vestments, namely the holy vestments* ', the conjunction is explicative, not connective.
n **12-17 XXXV 1-3 The Sabbath**—Previous legislation on the Sabbath is here emphasized and amplified. As the passage has no connection with the tabernacle and its furniture it seems a later insertion. Originally therefore 18 followed 28:42, the conclusion of the directions given to Moses, after which he received the two tables of stone containing the decalogue.
18 **XXXII 1-35 XXXIII 1-6 The Golden Calf**—The sin of the people is shown by their demand : ' *Make us Elohim who shall go before us* '. Elohim means ' God ', when construed with a singular verb, but ' gods ' when the verb is plural, except in a few cases which may be textual errors. Here the meaning ' gods ' is determined by the plural verb and still more by

a the plural pronoun, *these* (**4b**), otherwise inexplicable. By asking for gods in the form of idols to lead them they show their abandonment of the leadership of Yahweh. Aaron weakly compromises. He makes an image of a young bull, like the Egyptian Apis and the Canaanite Baal, but by proclaiming a feast to Yahweh shows that he regards it as an image of Yahweh. Though he only made one image, *he* (LXX, not 'they' MT) said : *These are thy gods* (**4b**), meaning : this is my answer to your demand for gods. He remained loyal to Yahweh, but really debased him to the level of a pagan deity and led the people astray by violating the precept of 20:23.

b **1a.** Read *around* for 'against'. **4a.** Read *with a graving tool* for 'by founder's work'. God informs Moses on Sinai of the sin of the people. **8.** The action and words of Aaron are attributed to the people since he carried out their demand. **9b.** Read *I see* for 'see'. **10.** God proposes to destroy the people and make of Moses a great nation, but in a manner (*let me alone*) which invites the intercession of Moses on their behalf. **11-16.** Moses pleads for mercy to the people as required for the promotion of God's glory on earth and for the fulfilment of the promises made to the Patriarchs. Having obtained his request he descends from the mount with the two tables of stone, rejoins Josue and approaches the camp. **17-18.** The noise heard suggests fighting to Josue to whom Moses replies : ' *It is not the sound of the cry of might, and it is not the sound of the cry of defeat ; the sound of singing I hear* '. **19-24.** The anger of Moses on seeing the calf and the dancing is manifested by throwing down and breaking the two tables of stone and burning the calf which is ground into powder mixed with water to be drunk by the people. He reproaches Aaron, who pleads the wickedness of the people and repeats the facts narrated above. **25.** ' *And when Moses saw that the people had broken loose ; for Aaron had let them loose for a whispering among their enemies.* ' He realized that the issue was between the worship of Yahweh from whom they had revolted and the worship of strange gods and that immediate action and severe measures were necessary if the worship of Yahweh **c** was to prevail. **26-29.** The Levites show their zeal for Yahweh and execute the orders of Moses, who says : ' *You have consecrated yourselves* [LXX, not ' consecrate yourselves ' MT] *to-day to Yahweh, yea each man with his son and with his brother, that he may give you to-day a blessing* '. The subsequent choice of the Levites to minister in the sanctuary (Num 3:6 ff.) is here foreshadowed, and the victims of their zeal are likened to the sacrifices offered at their installation (Num 8:8).

d **30-35.** Next day Moses intercedes for the people with Yahweh and manifests his wish to die—not, however, to be anathema like St Paul (Rom 9:3)—if pardon be refused. Yahweh refuses to accept the offering of his life or to remit entirely the sin of the people, but shows at least that he still regards them as his people by ordering Moses to lead them to the land of promise. The punishment of their sin is not remitted but postponed ; not Yahweh himself but an angel will guide them. **XXXIII 1-6.** Yahweh reiterates his refusal. The people show their grief and repentance by ceasing to wear their ornaments from some of which the golden calf had been made. Yahweh still refuses to lead them on the march : ' *If I go up in the midst of you for one moment I shall destroy you* ', approves of their repentance and implies that its continued manifestation may render him more propitious towards them. The text of 33:1-6 is not in good order, but the general sense is clear.

e **XXXIII 7-11 The Tent of Meeting or Oracle Tent—** This tent was in constant use. *And Moses used to take the tent of meeting*, etc., where the tense of the verbs is frequentative. It is also mentioned Num 11:16 ff. ; 12:4 ff. and probably Deut 31:14 ff. It differs from the tabernacle or tent of testimony in its location outside, not in the centre of the camp ; in its minister Josue the Ephraimite, not the Levites ; in its small size since Moses, helped perhaps by Josue, carried **181e** and pitched it, while many Levites and wagons were required for the transport of the tabernacle ; in its use for meeting Yahweh and obtaining administrative and judicial decisions from him, not for ritual functions like the tabernacle. The tent was therefore not a ceremonial, but an oracle tent, where Yahweh manifested himself and gave his decisions to Moses. It must have preceded the erection of the tabernacle but was not immediately superseded by it, as its object was different and such changes are usually gradual. The early Christians frequented the Jewish temple even after they possessed meeting-places of their own. Verses 7-11 have no connection with the context, which they interrupt, and record an isolated tradition of no little interest and value.

12-23 Moses' Final Intercession and Request to see God **f** —Moses renews his request that Yahweh himself and not one of his angels accompany the people in their march. The last words of **5** left the matter doubtful, but gave an opening for further intercession. The words *Thy face* (**13**) mean ' thou thyself ' and are so rendered (**15**). Moses first pleads on his own behalf and then on behalf of the people that he and they may be *distinguished from* (DV ' glorified by ') *all the people on the face of the earth* by God's presence. The granting of his request emboldens him to a further demand to see the glory or the face of God. Such a vision, reserved for the future life, cannot be granted. But the figurative language of **21-23** indicates that a special knowledge of God was accorded to Moses superior to that given to other prophets, as we learn also from Num 12:7-8. **19b.** ' *I will be gracious to whom I will be gracious, and I will be merciful to whom I will be merciful* ' means that man has no claim to the gratuitous gifts of God, such as the favours accorded to Moses and the forgiveness accorded to the people, which he gives to whom he wills. St Paul cites this text to prove that the Jewish nation had no claim to the gratuitous gift of an efficacious call to the faith of Christ (Rom 9:15).

XXXIV 1-28 The Renewal of the Sinaitic Covenant— **g** Moses is ordered to ascend the mount for the last time bringing with him two tables of stone on which Yahweh will write the ten commandments to be preserved in the Ark of the Covenant. When Yahweh appears in a cloud it is Moses who invokes him by name (**5**), but it is Yahweh who passes before Moses and proclaims who he is in one of the finest passages of the OT (**6-7**). **9.** Moses makes three requests : reassurance of the favour already granted (33:14) that Yahweh will accompany the people notwithstanding their rebellious character, forgiveness of their sin, their reinstatement as the chosen people of Yahweh. Yahweh grants his requests by renewing the broken covenant. **10-11.** He states first his own engagements briefly but comprehensively. **12-26.** He then repeats the cultual obligations of the people taken from the Book of the Covenant, since it was in this matter they had sinned. **27-28.** Finally he orders Moses to write down the words of the renewed covenant and he himself similarly renews the legislation of the decalogue by writing the ten commandments on the tables of stone. The sequence of thought is clear and consistent **h** but the conclusion of the narrative is obscured by a gloss or corruption in the text. **28c.** MT reads : *And he wrote upon the tables the words of the covenant, the ten commandments.* *The tables* and *the ten commandments* naturally refer to the writing of Yahweh (**1**), *the words of the covenant* to the writing of Moses (**27**), but *he wrote* indicates only one writer, apparently Moses. The conclusion seems to be that either the original text, chronicling both writings, was abbreviated and obscured or that 28c is an unskilful gloss, since the execution of the promise (**1**) and the command (**27**) might well be taken for granted by the narrator. The critics have concluded from 28c, contrary to the manifest requirements of the context, that the laws of 12-26 were originally a cultual decalogue, the earliest form

181h of the Book of the Covenant. They are not agreed, however, as to the original form of this decalogue and cannot explain why the original book of the covenant, like the decalogue which it develops, should not contain both social and cultual laws.

i **12-16.** The law prohibiting the worship of strange gods or religious harlotry, since Israel was the bride of Yahweh, is especially inculcated. Canaanite altars and the stone pillars representing Baal as well as the wooden poles (DV 'groves') symbolizing his consort, Asherah, erected before them, must be destroyed and there must be no alliances or intermarriages with the Canaanites to avoid the danger of religious contamination. Asherah, the goddess of fecundity, mentioned 3 Kg 15:13 ; 18:19 ; 4 Kg 21:7 ; 23:4 (DV 'grove'), and supposed to be a textual error for Astarte by many critics, is now well known from the Rās-Shamra tablets. The development of the law of the firstborn (**20**), taken from 13:13 and not in the Book of the Covenant, and the homiletic comment on the law of the annual pilgrimages (**24**) seem to be later additions.

j **29-35 The Horns and the Veil**—Horns are lightning flashes which accompany a theophany (Hab 3:4) and similarly here indicate not excrescences but rays of light. St Paul explains the phenomenon as meaning that the brightness of the face of Moses, produced by his intimate and prolonged intercourse with Yahweh, was insupportable to the Israelites and had to be concealed by a veil which he only removed when he spoke with God (2 Cor 3:7). The religious lesson conveyed is that the greater our union with and

knowledge of God the more like to him we become 18 (2 Cor 3:18).

XXXV-XL Execution of the Ritual Precepts—This k section narrates the execution of the commands given in chh 25-31. The order is different and there are additions, discussed when important in the preceding commentary. LXX has an order of its own and some omissions of which only the incense-altar is noteworthy. As the version is by a new and perhaps less careful translator, these omissions may be accidental, but the different order suggests that there were different forms of the Hebrew text in the 3rd cent. B.C. Unsettlement in the order of a text does not affect its general authenticity but may expose it to minor interpolations. There seems to be one such in this section (**38:25-28**) which begins : *And the silver of them that were numbered of the congregation.* A voluntary contribution for the erection of the tabernacle (25:2 f.) is here identified with an obligatory poll-tax for the upkeep of the sanctuary (30:16) based on a census made after the tabernacle was erected (Num 1:1 ff.) and computed at a population figure several times greater than that of Ex 12:37. This evaluation of the silver is manifestly inaccurate and must have been substituted for the original one similar in character to the gold and bronze evaluations (38:24 ; 29-31).

The book concludes magnificently with the manifestation of the glory of Yahweh in the newly erected tabernacle where he dwells among his chosen people and directs them on their march to the promised land.

LEVITICUS

By P. P. SAYDON

2a Bibliography—A complete list of commentaries from the patristic age down to the 19th cent. is given by R. Cornely, *Historica et Critica Introductio in U. T. Libros sacros*, II i, Parisiis, 1897², 161-9 (CSS) ; A. Crampon, *La Sainte Bible*, I, *Pentateuque*, Paris, 1894 ; F. de Hummelauer, *Comm. in Exod. et Levit.*, Parisiis, 1897 (CSS)—abbreviated as Humm. ; *A. R. S. Kennedy, *Leviticus*, CB, 1911 ; *A. T. Chapman–A. B. Streane, *The Book of Leviticus*, CBSC, 1914 ; L. C. Fillion, *La Sainte Bible*, I, *Le Pentateuque*, Paris, 1925⁷ ; P. Heinisch, *Das Buch Leviticus*, BB, 1935 ; A. Clamer, art. *Lévitique* in DTC 9 (1926) 462-98 and *Lévitique, Nombres, Deutéronome* in *La Sainte Bible*, II, Paris, 1946 ; *La Bibbia tradotta dai testi originali : Il Pentateuco*, Milano, 1923 (the trans. of Leviticus is by A. Vaccari, S. J.).

On Sacrifice : F. X. Kortleitner, *Archaeologia Biblica*, Oeniponte, 1917, 291-354 ; A. Médebielle, *L'Expiation dans l'Ancien et le Nouveau Testament*, Rome, 1924 (on the cover but 1923 on the title-page) ; *G. B. Gray, *Sacrifice in the Old Testament*, Oxford, 1925.

For comparative purposes : M.-J. Lagrange, *Etudes sur les Religions Sémitiques*, Paris, 1903² ; *W. Robertson Smith, *The Religion of the Semites*, ed. by S. A. Cook, London, 1927³ ; E. Dhorme, *L'Evolution religieuse d'Israël*, Bruxelles, 1937.

Other subsidiary works : *S. R. Driver, *Introd. to the Literature of the Old Testament*, Edinburgh, 1913⁹ ; *A. Edersheim, *The Temple, its Ministry and Services*, London, no date².

b Title—Leviticus, the title of the third book of the Pentateuch, is derived through Vg from the LXX Λευειτικόν. Though the title may have been added by later editors, it is certainly very old and probably of pre-Christian origin (*H. B. Swete, *An Introduction to the Old Testament in Greek*, 215). In the Hebrew Bible it is called *wayyiqra* (St Jerome *Vaicra*) from its opening word. Leviticus is an appropriate title descriptive of the contents of the book which deals mainly with the Levites' duties in connection with the sacrificial worship. It was the liturgical book of the Israelites and may be compared to our Ritual.

c Contents—The contents of Leviticus fall into two main parts corresponding to the two aspects of God's relation to his people. Yahweh was the God of the Israelites whom he had called out of Egypt and adopted as his firstborn. He was a God infinitely holy, unapproachable by man (Ex 19:21 ; 24:2) and yet dwelling amidst his people (Lev 22:32 ; 26:12). As the supreme Lord of Israel he had the right to their obedience, reverence, love and worship, while his divine presence demanded of them such sanctity of life as would make them his worthy children (Lev 11:44 f. ; 19:2 ; 20:26). Sacrificial worship and sanctity of life are therefore the two leading motives of Leviticus and a general description of its contents which are exhibited more particularly in the following paragraphs.

d Analysis and Structure—The book of Exodus carries the history of Israel down to the erection of the Tabernacle. But there was yet no system of laws regulating divine worship, nor any body of ritual prescriptions expressive of that sanctity of life which was the indispensable condition for fellowship with God.

The liturgical and ceremonial legislation implement-ing the narrative of Exodus is contained in Leviticus **182d** which opens with a detailed description of all the forms of sacrifice (chh 1-7). Then follows an account of the priestly ordination of Aaron and his sons and their solemn entry upon office (chh 8 and 9). A short appendix stressing the necessity of sacerdotal sanctity is added (ch 10). Chh 11-15 deal with the distinction between cleanness and uncleanness and the ritual purification from uncleanness. Ch 16 describes the ceremonial of the Day of Atonement. Chh 17-26 **e** constitute a well-defined body of laws to which the title ' Law of Holiness ' has been appropriately given. Although the various groups of laws in this collection, and sometimes even the several laws, appear to be independent, their character is determined by the principle that holiness must be the distinguishing mark of Israel. They differ notably from the laws contained in the preceding chapters. Their outlook is broader, their range of application more extensive and more varied. Although the priesthood and the sacrificial worship are clearly in view, they do not occupy a central position as in chh 1-16. Ch 17 contains prescriptions on the slaughtering of animals for sacrifice and for food. Ch 18 deals with unlawful sexual intercourse. Ch 19 is a miscellaneous collection of ordinances of a religious, domestic, and social character. Ch 20 gives a punitive sanction for the offences specified in chh 18 and 19. Chh 21 and 22 extend the Law of Holiness to priests in their domestic life and in the performance of their sacerdotal duties. Ch 23 is a festal calendar indicating the days on which religious assemblies are to be held and prescribing the manner in which these days are to be observed. Ch 24 is an erratic block of miscellaneous ordinances interrupting the logical sequence of chh 23 and 25. Ch 25 relates the institution of the Sabbatical Year and of the Year of Jubilee. Apparently it is the sequel to ch 23 ; but on a closer examination the character of the institutions in the two chapters will be found to be completely different. The Sabbatical Year and the Jubilee Year are a social and an economic, rather than a liturgical, institution. No sacrificial offerings, no holy convocations, no abstention from work are enjoined. Ch 26 is a hortatory speech cast in the style of Deut 28, and concluding the section chh 17-26. Ch 27 contains two appendices on vows and tithes respectively.

It appears from a first reading that Lev is not a **f** complete and systematic exposition of the various laws regulating divine worship and the domestic and social life of Israel. It is rather the result of the combination of **various partial collections of laws.** The Law of Sacrifice (chh 1-7) formed certainly one collection with its proper superscription (1:1) and subscription (7:37). Chh 8-10 formed another collection. Chh 11-15 consist of minor collections logically, but not necessarily chronologically, related to each other. Ch 16 may have originally followed ch 10, but its position after chh 11-15 is more appropriate. Chh 17-26 formed one collection of laws made up of smaller groups characterized by a common style and phraseology and by the frequent insistence on holiness as the distinguishing mark of Israel. Ch 26 is probably the work of the compiler who closed the collection 17-25 with a hortatory discourse. The last

182f chapter was added when the rest of the book had already been completed.

183a **Sacrificial Terminology**—An explanation of the more frequent sacrificial terms is given here in order to relieve the commentary of useless repetitions. On the sacrifices see also § 111*d–j*.
(*a*) **The holocaust**; a word of Greek origin (ὁλόκαυστος; LXX ὁλοκαύτωμα) meaning literally 'a whole burnt-(offering)'. The corresponding Hebrew word, '*ōlāh*, is commonly derived from the verb '*ālāh*, ' to go up', hence 'that which goes up' (BDB *s.v.* '*ōlāh*), the victim being considered as going up in the flames of the altar to God and so expressing the ascent of the soul in worship (*ibid.*). The holocaust symbolized man's recognition of God's universal sovereignty and was therefore the noblest form of sacrifice (St Thom. 1, 2 q 102, a 3 ad 8 et 10). It had a great part in the Levitical liturgy. Besides the daily morning and evening holocaust (Ex 29:38–42 ; Num 28:3–8 ; etc.), others were offered on festal days and other specified occasions (Lev 12:6–8 ; 14:13 ; etc.).

b (*b*) **The peace-offering**; Heb. *šelāmîm* (Lev 3:1–17). It is difficult to say what the exact meaning of the Hebrew word is. Some link it with *šillēm* ' to requite ', hence *šelāmîm* is a sacrifice offered for favours bestowed by God (St Thom. *l.c.*). Others connect the word with the verb *šālēm* ' to be sound, safe ', and the noun *šālôm* ' peace, soundness '. Hence *šelāmîm* would denote peaceful, friendly relations with God. Though this meaning may not be the original one, it applies very well to all forms of peace-offerings, the distinguishing feature of which is the sacrificial meal of which the offerer has the right to partake. Peace-offerings were prescribed on the fulfilment of a Nazirite vow (Num 6:14) and on the Feast of Weeks (Lev 23:19).

c (*c*) **The sin-offering**; it is subdivided into two forms : the sin-offering (Vg ' pro peccato ') and the trespass-offering (Vg ' pro delicto '). Both were intended to expiate sin and to re-establish friendly relations with God, but the difference between them is not clear. It is commonly believed that ' trespass ' was an offence consisting in the unlawful withdrawal or retention of what was due to God or man, hence an offence involving material damage (Médebielle, 61 ; Kortleitner, 323 ; Gray, 58 ; and the dictionaries by BDB, Buhl, König, Zorell *s.v.* '*āšām*) and ' sin ' was any other ordinary sin. A slightly different distinction is proposed here. ' Sin ' was any ordinary offence committed through human frailty or passion. ' Trespass ' denotes fundamentally a state of culpability, imputability, indebtedness, *cf.* P. Joüon in Bi (1938) 454–9. The sense of indebtedness is evident in 6:4. The sense of culpability is also apparent as it is inseparable from sin, but it may not be so evident when the sin is said to have been committed through ignorance or inadvertence, as in the cases contemplated in 4:2, 3, 13, 22, 27 ; 5:2, 3. These unintentional sins constituted a real, though involuntary, transgression, and were therefore legally imputable and were to be expiated when the offender became conscious of his offence. ' Trespass ' was therefore a material sin or, in some cases, a formal sin involving material damage to one's neighbour. In both cases the offender is guilty. Sin-offerings were very common in the Levitical liturgy, *cf.* Lev 8:2 ; 12:6 ; 14:19 ; 16 ; 23:19 ; Num 6:11, 14 ; 28:15, 22, 30 ; 29:5, 16.

d (*d*) **Cereal-offerings**, Heb. *minḥāh*, originally ' a gift ', then a sacrificial term designating an oblation which consisted of uncooked flour, unleavened bread and parched grain.

e (*e*) **Libations** of wine, as a part of the sacrificial ritual, are mentioned only once in Leviticus (23:13), more frequently in Numbers (15:5, 7 ; 28:7 ; etc.).

f (*f*) ' **To expiate** ', Heb. *kippēr*. This verb, which occurs so frequently in the liturgical terminology, is inaccurately rendered by DV ' to pray ' (*cf.* 4:20, 26, 31, 35 ; 5:6, 13, 16, 18 ; etc.). Some interpreters, especially E. König, ET 22 (1910–11) 232–4, defend the meaning ' to cover ' on the grounds of biblical

usage and Arabic affinities. Expiation would then **182** mean a covering or a non-imputation of sins. Others, however, prefer to link up the verb *kippēr* with Assyrian *kapāru* ' to destroy, to wipe away '. An allied meaning is ' to be bright ', according to *C. F. Burney, JTS, 11 (1909–10) 437 footnote, brightness being the effect of wiping and polishing. According to this interpretation, which is preferable both philologically and exegetically, expiation implies the destruction of sin and the consequent cleansing of the soul. For a fuller discussion, see Médebielle, 69–83 ; Gray, 67–76.

Religious Value—As literature Leviticus is not one of **g** the more readable books of the Bible. The legal nature of its contents, the queerness of many of the liturgical regulations, the monotonous repetition of stereotyped forms and expressions combine to make the book unattractive to the average reader. But its apparent dullness is counterbalanced by the religious significance and the moral teaching which the book conveys and will ever retain throughout all ages. The following are some of the more important doctrinal points :
(*a*) **The importance and sanctity of the liturgical h service.** The law of sacrifice emphasizes the importance of the external cult based on the recognition of God's universal sovereignty and man's need of expiating his sins and thus re-establishing normal relations with God. The liturgy of the sacrifice is calculated to impress on us, as on the Israelites, the idea of the sanctity of God to whom alone sacrifice is offered. The sacrifice is offered through the ministry of a special caste—the priests ; the victim must be without blemish, and those who partake of the sacrificial meal must be free from any ceremonial uncleanness. Moreover, the sacrifice of the OT foreshadowed the sacrifice of Christ, and the sacrificial meal symbolized the sacramental communion of the New Law ; *cf.* St Paul's allegorical interpretation of the Aaronic priesthood and sacrifice in Hebrews.
(*b*) **The sanctity of priests.** The priests, God's ministers, **i** must be holy. Their duty of holiness is clearly expressed in Lev 21:6 : ' They shall be holy to their God. . . . For they offer the burnt offering of the Lord, and the bread of their God, and therefore they shall be holy.' The whole ceremonial of their consecration was expressive of the high degree of sanctity that was inherent in their office. See also ch 21.
(*c*) **Imitation of God.** The imitation of God's attri- **j** butes, especially his holiness, is an indispensable condition for fellowship with God. The Israelites must be holy because their God is holy (11:44 ; 19:2 ; 20:26). This is a fundamental principle of Christian life enunciated in the same words by Christ (Mt 5:48). Although the Levitical holiness was, to a large extent, external, it was by no means restricted to mere ceremonial cleanness irrespective of internal dispositions. In 19:2 the duty of holiness is further determined by such injunctions as respect towards one's parents, the worship of one God, which are religious and ethical precepts.
(*d*) **The observance of God's commandments and k temporal happiness.** The observance of God's commandments is a source of temporal happiness (26:3–13), while the transgression of his law carries with it severe punishment in this world itself (26:14–39). This is always true, provided, however, temporal happiness and calamities are viewed in their relation to eternal life.
(*e*) **Bodily cleanliness and religion.** Bodily cleanliness **l** is not without relation to religion. If life is the gift of God, all that contributes to its preservation may form the object of a divine enactment and thus become a religious practice. Thus the seclusion of lepers and certain ablutions were sanitary prescriptions with a religious significance.

A. Cult Institutions—Sacrifice and the Consecration of Priests (chh 1–10).

1 Various Kinds of Sacrifice and their Ritual (chh 1–7) **18**
The tabernacle having been erected (Ex 40), God

4a gives instructions regulating its service. Some general regulations had already been given (Ex 28;29), but in this book a fuller exposition of religious institutions and liturgical regulations is added. The Law of Sacrifice, on account of the central position which sacrifice holds in divine worship, heads the list of ritual prescriptions, although chronologically the institution of the priesthood may have preceded the sacrificial ritual.

All the Levitical laws are represented as communicated directly by God to Moses, but the expression ' the Lord spoke to Moses ' introducing the several ordinances must be understood in the sense of a divine assistance to Moses in the compilation and adaptation of existing laws and practices, though certain institutions must be referred directly to God (Humm., 356).

b **I 1-17 The Holocaust and its Ritual**—The first kind of sacrifice is the holocaust or whole burnt-offering (see § 183a). The victim could be of the bovine or ovine species, provided it was male and without blemish. Other domestic animals and wild animals could not be offered. For a list of disqualifying physical defects of the victims, see Lev 22:17-25 ; cf. also Deut 15:21, 22 ; 17:1 ; Mal 1:8. The offerer led the victim to the entrance of the tabernacle and there laid his hands on the head of the victim thus symbolically identifying himself with it and signifying his adoration, gratitude, etc., which made the sacrifice acceptable to God (4). The opinion held by St Thomas (1, 2, q. 102, a. 3 ad 5), Médebielle, 142, and others that the imposition of hands represented symbolically the transference of the offerer's sins to the victim which consequently incurred the death penalty (penal substitution), is less probable. Expiation was common to all forms of sacrifice (Lev 17:11), though it was more strongly felt in connexion

c with sin-offerings. After the imposition of hands the offerer himself *slays* the victim, *skins* it, *cuts* it into pieces, cleans the entrails and the legs, and hands it over to the priests who place it over the wood burning upon the altar after having poured the blood round over the altar. The victim is burnt entirely, except the hide which is assigned to the officiating priest (Lev 7:8). The sacrificial burning is expressed in Heb. by the verb *hiqṭîr* which, used in a liturgical sense, means ' to burn the victim in such a way as to make it exhale an odour of incense ' (C. Lattey, *The Book of Malachy*, in *WV*, xx f.). God's acceptance of the sacrifice is expressed anthropomorphically by the sweet agreeable odour rising up from the burnt victim ; cf. Gen 8:21. The expression ' a sweet savour ', originally ' a soothing odour ', has become a technical term denoting the divine pleasure or the divine acceptance.

If the victim is a sheep or goat the ritual is the same as for oxen, except that the northern side is chosen (11) for greater convenience. Of birds only turtle-doves and pigeons could be offered. The ritual, naturally, is slightly different. **15.** ' *The priest shall offer it at the altar, wring off its head and burn it upon the altar.*' **17.** ' *He shall break the pinions thereof without dividing it (into parts) and shall burn it upon the altar.*' The Levitical law allowed the offering of birds only in cases of poverty ; cf. 5:7-10 ; 12:6-8. Even a small offering is accepted by God when it comes from a sincere heart.

d **II 1-16 Bloodless Offerings and their Ritual**—These were brought as an accompaniment to animal sacrifice, cf. 8:26-28 ; 9:17 ; 23:13, 18 ; Num 6:15 ; 28:5 ; etc. They consisted of fine flour and oil prepared in different ways, and frankincense put on, but not mixed with, them. A portion of the offering and all the incense was burnt on the altar. This portion was called ' the memorial ' (2) because with its sweet odour it reminded God of the offerer. The rest which, after having been presented to God, had become most sacred, fell to the officiating priest. The sacredness of these offerings made it unlawful for laymen to partake of them (6:14-18). It is not without significance that bread was the commonest material of

bloodless offerings in the Hebrew ritual. Oil and salt **184d** were used as ingredients in the sacrificial offering, while wine was generally offered with an animal sacrifice or bread (Os 9:4). No other meal offerings were brought on the altar. The typical relation of the sacrificial meal of the OT to the Eucharistic meal of the New Law is obvious.

It was forbidden to make an offering of leavened **e** bread or of honey on the altar. Fermentation was associated with corruption and putrefaction, and honey is liable to ferment. In the NT leaven is the symbol of evil (Mt 16:6-12 ; Mk 8:15 ; Lk 12:1 ; 1 Cor 5:6-8 ; Gal 5:9). Leavened bread and honey could be presented to God only as offerings of firstfruits and, in the case of leavened bread, as a part of the sacrificial meal, but were never burnt on the altar, cf. 7:13 ; 23:17 ; 2 Par 31:5. Salt was an indispensable ingredient in all sacrificial offerings. It had a twofold use : it rendered the sacrificial meal, as any ordinary meal, more palatable, and it symbolized the inviolability of God's covenant with his people, hence the expression ' a covenant of salt ' to designate a permanent and inviolable bond, cf. 2 Par 13:5 and Num 18:19. The origin of the expression goes back to the nomadic custom which regarded those who have partaken of the same meal or taken salt together as united by a bond (W. R. Smith, 270 f.).

Cereal-offerings could be made not only as an accom- **f** paniment to an animal offering but also as an offering of firstfruits. This was their ritual. The ears of the new corn were dried at the fire and rubbed till the grain was separated from the husks. The grain was then ground and sifted, oil was poured upon it and frankincense added. The ' memorial ' was burnt upon the altar and the rest was eaten by the priests. Though the law here mentions only the firstfruits of corn, in Num 18:13 and Neh 10:37 it covers all the land produce. In the latter cases the ritual was different.

III 1-17 The Peace-offering and its Ritual—Of all **g** forms of sacrifice this bears the closest analogy to the Sacrament of the Eucharist. Its distinguishing feature was the sacrificial meal of which both the priest and the offerer partook after a portion of the victim had been burnt on the altar (Lev 7:11-21).

The victim could be of the ox, sheep or goat kind, male or female, but without blemish. The first part of the ceremonial is similar to that of the holocaust. The following fatty parts were burnt upon the altar : the fat covering the entrails and the fat connected therewith, the two kidneys, and the fat connected therewith near the loins, the caul of the liver *detached from above the kidneys*, and the whole tail if the victim was a sheep. These were burnt not as a separate holocaust, as Vg seems to imply (5), but with and upon the perpetual holocaust (6:12). The reason for the burning of these parts was either that they were regarded as a special delicacy and therefore to be reserved to God, or because the intestines, especially the kidneys and the liver, were considered by the Hebrews as the seat of life and emotion and therefore to be reserved to God like the blood. The first opinion is preferable. The Heb. *ḥēleb* ' fat ' is used not infrequently to designate the choicest part of the products of the land (Gen 45:18 ; Num 18:12, 29 ; Deut 32:14 ; etc.). Moreover although the kidneys and the liver are sometimes considered as the seats of emotion (Job 19:27 ; Ps 15:7 ; 72:21 ; Lam 2:11 ; cf. P. Dhorme, *L'emploi métaphorique des noms de parties du corps en Hébreu et en Akkadien* [Paris, 1923] 128-33), these internal organs become the symbol of an insensible and unresponsive heart when they are represented as enveloped by fat (Ps 16:10 ; 118:70). When the fat parts had been consumed by the priest and the offerer, the rest was eaten by the priest and the offerer (7:11-33).

IV 1-VI 7 Expiatory Sacrifices and their Ritual— **h** Sins are either expiable or inexpiable. Expiable sins are those committed through human frailty or through ignorance or inadvertence ; these are atoned for by a

184h sin-offering if they are sins of human frailty, and by a trespass-offering if they are sins of ignorance; *cf.* P. P. Saydon, *Sin-offering and trespass-offering*, CBQ (1946) 393–8. Inexpiable sins are punishable by death or excommunication (Lev 7:25; 17:9, 10; 19:8; 20:3; etc.). See also § 183c.

185a IV 1-12 Expiatory Offerings for the High-Priest—If the high-priest commits a sin through ignorance involving the whole people in his sin (A. Vaccari, *Il Pentateuco*, 153), he shall bring a young bull to the Lord for the expiation of his sin and slay it at the entrance of the tabernacle. The characteristic features of the ritual of this sacrifice are the disposal of the blood and the consumption by fire of the victim outside the camp. Since blood was regarded as the seat of life (Lev 17:11), the sprinkling of blood towards the veil, which concealed the inaccessible throne of God, and the smearing of the horns of the altar were a symbolical representation of the sinner crying before God for mercy and forgiveness and for the re-establishment of friendly relations with him. No part of the flesh could be eaten either by the priest or by the people, everyone being ceremonially unclean (2). Nor could the victim be burnt on the altar because it was not a holocaust. St Paul draws a parallel between the victim of the expiatory offering burnt outside the camp and Christ who suffered outside the gate of Jerusalem (Heb 13:12).

b 13-21 Expiatory Offering for the Community—13 f. are, for syntactical reasons, translated thus: '*If the whole community of Israel sins through ignorance by doing something which the Lord commanded not to be done, and the thing is concealed from the eyes of the assembly, they are guilty; and when the sin becomes known to them, the assembly shall bring....*' This is a material transgression of the law which must be expiated when it becomes known to the offender. The only difference in ritual from that described in 3–12 is that the rite of the imposition of hands is performed by the elders as representatives of the people. The identity of the ritual is a clear indication that the sin of the high-priest and that of the community were considered to be of equal gravity. **20b.** '*And the priest will expiate for them.*' Some sort of prayer may have formed part of the expiatory ritual.

c 22-26 Expiatory Offering for a Ruler—22 is translated on the same syntactical lines as 13 f.: '*If a prince sins by inadvertently doing something which the Lord, his God, commanded not to be done, he will incur guilt, and when he comes to know his sin, he shall bring....*' The sin of a chief of a tribe being considered to be of a lesser gravity than that of the whole people the expiation is obviously simpler. The victim is a he-goat without blemish. The ritual is like that in 13–21. But no blood is brought inside the sanctuary. The fat is burnt on the altar, and what remains of the victim is eaten by the priests (6:25 f.).

d 27-35 Expiatory Offering for an ordinary Israelite—27 is also translated according to the same syntactical rules implied in 13, 22: '*If a man of the land sins inadvertently by doing something that the Lord commanded not to be done, he will incur guilt, and when he comes to know his sin, he shall offer....*' The victim is either a she-goat or a ewe-lamb. The ritual is the same as that described in 24–26.

e V 1-13 Expiatory Sacrifices for Special Sins—This section specifies some particular offences for which an expiation is required. In ch 4 the expiation is considered in relation to the social condition of the offender; in 5:1–6:7 it is considered in relation to the offence. It is possible that all the sins enumerated in this section are sins of ignorance, though this is not expressly stated for all.

The first case (**1**) is that of a person who, having heard the curse uttered on an unknown offender, fails to reveal what he knows (*cf.* Humm. 383 who cites Jg 17:2 and Prov 29:24). He is guilty because he hinders the execution of justice. But as such reticence is generally due either to fear of vengeance or to an imperfect sense of duty, his sin is practically comparable to an unintentional sin.

The second case (**2, 3**) is that of a person who inadvertently touches the dead body of an unclean animal or an unclean person or something which man has rendered unclean. In all these cases such a person is really unclean. On unclean animals, see Lev 11 and on human uncleanness Lev 12–15.

The third case (**4**) is that of a person who swears rashly. A rash oath is a sin and needs expiation.

When a person, who has committed any one of the **f** sins mentioned above, becomes conscious of his sin, he must first *confess his sin* (**5**). Then he shall bring for his sin-offering a lamb or a goat as in the cases contemplated in 4:27–35. The ritual is the same as in similar expiatory sacrifices. If, however, the offender is not able to provide either a lamb or a goat, he shall offer two turtle-doves or two pigeons, one for a sin-offering and the other for a holocaust. But if he cannot provide even two turtle-doves or two pigeons, he shall bring as a sin-offering the tenth part of an ephah (*c* 7 pints; see § 82j and A.R.S. Kennedy, HDB, art. *Weights and Measures*, IV, 912) of fine flour without oil and frankincense which were excluded from all sin-offerings (Num 5:15). The ritual is that prescribed in 2:2, 3. A characteristic feature of the ritual of these expiatory sacrifices is the confession of the offender's sin accompanying the rite of imposition of hands. The confession of sins is expressly prescribed in this case (*cf.* Num 5:7) and in the ceremonial of the Day of Atonement (Lev 16:21), but very probably it was a feature common to all expiatory sacrifices; *cf.* F. Zorell in VD 1 (1921) 35.

V 14-VI 7 Expiatory Sacrifices for Sins of Fraud g against God and Man—When a person unlawfully retains or withholds what is due to God or to man, he shall offer an expiatory sacrifice, make good the damage caused to God or man and moreover pay a fine amounting to one-fifth of the value of the property unlawfully retained or withheld.

First case, **15-16.** A person who inadvertently fails to present such things as are claimed by Yahweh, such as tithes and firstfruits, shall offer a ram without blemish worth *as many shekels* (15) as the priest considers due by the standard shekel of the sanctuary (=2s 9d, *cf.* A. R. S. Kennedy, HDB, art. *Money*, III, 421–23). He shall also restore in full God's property and an additional fifth part of its value. These payments were made to the priests, God's representatives. On tithes and firstfruits, see Lev 27:30–33; Num 15:16–21; 18:8–24; 28:26; Deut 14:22–29; 15:19–23; 26:1–15.

Second case, **17-19.** It does not appear to what particular case of fraud this article of law refers. Humm. (p 387), following St Augustine, believes that the offences referred to in **17** are those made against the temple, the priests and the holy vessels, for which no restitution was required. One fails to see the reason for this distinction. A. Vaccari, 156, distinguishes between sins of omission (15) and sins of commission (17). But in this case the offering of a ram would hardly be enough. It is probable that 17–19 do not refer to any particular case, but contain a general statement which receives further determination in the cases contemplated in 6:1–7.

Third case **VI:1-7.** If a person withholds a deposit or a pledge or extorts something by force, or finds a thing that has been lost and denies it, and swears falsely that he has committed none of these acts of injustice, he has incurred guilt and shall give back in full to its rightful owner the thing itself together with one fifth of its value. And for his expiation he shall bring a ram without blemish of a certain value.

VI 8-VII 38 Supplementary Regulations concerning the Various Sacrifices.

8-13 The holocaust—Apart from private holocausts and those offered publicly on festivals, the law prescribed that two holocausts should be offered daily, one in the morning and the other in the evening

a (Ex 29:38–42 ; Num 28:3–8). It is the daily evening holocaust that the law refers to in 6:9. It was offered ' between the two evenings ' (Num 28:4), that is, according to later Jewish practice, between the afternoon and the evening (Jos. *Ant.* 14, 4, 3 ' about the ninth hour ', *i.e.* 3 pm ; *cf.* also Edersheim, 116). This holocaust is to be kept burning on a slow fire all night. As many sacrifices were offered during the day, the law, by this prescription of a night-long sacrifice, provided that there should not be a single moment in which a sacrifice was not offered to God, foreshadowing in this manner the sacrifice of the New Law which is offered at all times in all parts of the world. The fire on the altar must never be allowed to go out, and the priests must take care to put on fresh wood every morning. According to 9:24 this perpetual fire had a miraculous origin. It signifies God's perpetual presence among his people and has its Christian counterpart in the oil lamp continually burning in our Churches before the Blessed Sacrament.

b **14–18 Meal Offerings**—*Cf.* ch 2. They are presented through the ministry of the priests but not necessarily on their own account. The ritual is that prescribed in ch 2. They must be eaten in the tabernacle and cannot be taken away. As holiness is considered to be communicable through contact, any person or thing that touches the sacred oblations becomes holy and must have the holiness washed out by means of certain ablutions before returning to the ordinary business of life (*cf.* M.-J. Lagrange, 149 ; W. R. Smith, 446). Only the male descendants of Aaron could eat of them.

c **19–23 The High-Priest's Oblation**—According to later Jewish practice the high-priest, at his own expense, offered an oblation twice a day. It was made of flour mingled with oil and gently baked by the fire ; he brought the half of it to the fire in the morning, and the other half at night (Jos. *Ant.* 3, 10, 7). The words ' in the day of their anointing ' (**20**) very probably must be taken in the sense of ' On that day and onwards '. For a similar meaning of the expression ' in the day of ', *cf.* 7:35. Vaccari, 157, restricts the meaning of the word ' perpetual ' (Heb. *tāmîd*) to the seven days of the priestly ordination ceremony (Ex 29:35 ; Lev 8:33). But the word *tāmîd* is a technical term denoting the daily perpetual sacrifice. As this oblation was made by the high-priest, it could not be consumed either by himself or the priests, who were inferior to him, and therefore it had to be entirely burnt.

d **24–30 The Sin-offering**—It was a most holy offering and was therefore to be eaten in a holy place, *i.e.* in the court of the tabernacle. The officiating priest naturally called other priests to share in the sacred meal, as is implied in **29**, because it was impossible that any one man could consume such a quantity of meat in one meal. Its holiness could be communicated through contact ; see §186*b*. The regulation concerning the sacred meal did not apply to the cases when blood was brought inside the sanctuary (4:1–21) and to the expiatory sacrifice on the Day of Atonement.

e **VII 1–7 The Trespass-offering**—There is a close similarity between the ritual of the sin-offering and that of the trespass-offering. The words ' the same shall be the law of both these sacrifices ' (**7**) must be restricted to the concluding part of the verse, that is, in both sacrifices what remains of the victim belongs to the officiating priest.

f **8–10 Priests' Dues from Other Offerings**—The skin of the burnt-offering belonged to the ministrant. In the Carthaginian table of sacrificial fees the skin is also assigned to the priest (G. A. Cooke, *A Text-book of North Semitic Inscriptions*, Oxford, 1903, 123), but at Marseilles it went to the offerer (Cooke, 112). As regards the meal-offerings a distinction is made between cooked offerings, as those mentioned in 2:4–10, and uncooked offerings, whether mingled with oil or dry, as those specified in 2:14–17 and 5:11. The former went to the officiating priest, the latter were divided between all the sons of Aaron in equal portions. The **186f** reason for this different assignment was that the uncooked offerings were usually so abundant that they could not be consumed by one man (Crampon, 367).

g **11–21 The Peace-offering**—The Levitical liturgy distinguishes three kinds of peace-offerings, or rather three reasons for which peace-offerings are brought : (i) thank-offerings or ' sacrifices of praise ' (Ps 49:14, 23 ; Ps 106:22) ; (ii) vow-offerings made in fulfilment of a vow (Ps 60:9 ; 65:13,14) ; (iii) free-will offerings (Ps 53:8). There are some slight differences in the ritual of these various offerings. If it is a thank-offering, the offerer is to bring, *besides the victim* (omitted by Vg), unleavened cakes mingled with oil, unleavened wafers smeared with oil and fine flour well mixed and made into cakes mingled with oil. He shall also bring leavened bread which, however, is not presented on the altar (2:11), but is simply handed over to the priest and is intended for the sacrificial meal. The offerer presents one of each kind of cakes as a *contribution* (**14**) to Yahweh which goes to the priest who pours the blood of the victim. The remaining cakes go to the offerer. After the sacrifice has been offered, that is, after the portions reserved to the Lord have been burnt on the altar and the priest has taken his share of the flesh and the cakes, the offerer together with his relatives and friends sits at meal in the neighbourhood of the sanctuary. The whole of the flesh must be consumed on that day. In the case of vow- and free-will offerings the flesh may be eaten also on the following day. Only one day was allowed for the consumption of the thank-offering probably because the occasion being certainly a happy one, the offerer had to invite a number of guests such as would consume the whole of the flesh in one day and at the same time add to the festive character of the sacred meal. But **h** vow- and free-will offerings were more of a private matter ; there was no special reason for rejoicing and the flesh therefore could be consumed by fewer guests and in a longer time. But in no case was it permissible to eat the flesh on the third day. If any flesh was left over after the second day, it was to be burnt. Any eating on the third day rendered the sacrifice unacceptable, and in the case of a vow-offering the offerer would have to offer another sacrifice. Sacrificial meat could not be eaten after the second day because after the second day the flesh begins to go bad and becomes unfit for consumption. Such is the sanctity of the sacrificial meat that if it is brought into contact with anything that is unclean, it cannot be eaten but must be burnt ; and if it is eaten by an unclean person, that person shall be cut off from his people. The expression ' to be cut off from one's people ', used in a religious sense, is a technical expression for excommunication or exclusion from all the privileges and blessings granted by God to the Israelites. But in some cases the death penalty is meant.

i **22–27 The Use of the Fat and Blood of Animals**—This is an abridged repetition, with some new details, of the regulations in ch 3 concerning the use of fat and blood. In ch 3 it is laid down that specified fatty parts of the peace-offering are to be burnt upon the altar ; here it is forbidden to eat these parts, whether the animal (ox, sheep or goat) is killed as a sacrifice or for human consumption. They must always be brought before the Lord. In the case of other animals killed for human consumption it is not said what use the Israelites could make of the fat. As the Levitical legislator is concerned solely with the sacred offerings, this omission is easily accounted for. In the case of an animal, ox, sheep or goat, which dies of itself or is torn by some beast, it was allowed to make use of the fat but not to eat it. The prohibition of blood is more general. It extends to quadrupeds and fowls, and no distinction is made whether they are killed as sacrifice or for human consumption, or whether they die a natural death or are torn by a beast. Any person

186j who transgresses either of these laws shall be excommunicated ; *cf.* 21. See also Lev 17:10-14.

j **28-34 The Priests' Share of the Peace-offering**—It has been said above (12-14) that a portion of the oblation accompanying the peace-offering went to the priest. Now the law specifies which parts of the peace-offering itself fell to the priest. **29-32**. ' *He who offers to the Lord his peace-offering, shall bring an offering of his sacrifice to the Lord. His own hands shall bring the fire-offering of the Lord ; he shall bring the fat with the breast—the breast to be waved before the Lord. And the priest shall burn the fat upon the altar, but the breast shall be Aaron's and his sons. And you shall give the right thigh of your peace-offerings as a contribution to the priest.*' These verses supplement the ritual prescribed in ch 3. After having slain the victim, the offerer takes the fat and the breast upon his hands and carries them before the Lord, that is, to the altar. There the priest takes the fat to burn on the altar. Whether some ritual was prescribed for the presentation of the fat is not apparent, but in 8:26 f. the fat is said to be waved before the Lord.

k The **rite of waving**, which is certainly prescribed for the breast of the victim, consisted in swinging the offering towards the altar and back again with the hands of the offerer resting upon the hands of the priest. The forward motion was a symbolical declaration that those portions were given to God, while the backward motion signified that the gift was returned by God and assigned to his representative, the priest. This ceremony was so characteristic of certain offerings that the word *t^enûpāh* ' waving ' became a liturgical term denoting a wave-offering in general, or, in particular, the breast of the wave-offering (10:15). Another due of the priests was the right thigh of the victim, Heb. *t^erûmāh* ' a lifting up ', hence what is separated from the rest and raised up as a contribution. Probably the *t^erûmāh* was a liturgical rite with a religious significance analogous to that of the waving rite. Compare the analogous rite of the Offertory in the Mass.

l Although the Levitical law expressly assigned to the priests the breast and the right thigh of all peace-offerings, usage may have varied from time to time. The Deuteronomic law gives the priest ' the shoulder, the two cheeks and the stomach' (18:3). From 1 Kg 2:13 ff. it appears that priests claimed more than the shoulder and the right thigh.

m **35-36 Conclusion**—This is the conclusion of the section 6:8-7:34 dealing with the priestly dues. The Heb. word for ' anointing ' in 35 (AV and RV *anointing-portion*) should very probably be rendered ' fixed or measured portion ', the Heb. word *mišḥāh*, which literally means ' anointing ', being probably related to Assyrian *mašāḫu* ' to measure ', *mašīḫu* ' specific measure ' of grain, dates, etc. (Muss-Arnolt, *A Concise Dictionary of the Assyrian Language.*) The word occurs again with the same meaning in Num 18:8. For DV ' in the ceremonies ' read with Heb. ' *from the fire-offering* '. This right the priests begin to enjoy from the day of their priestly ordination, and they will continue to enjoy it for ever as the Lord has commanded ; see chh 8-10.

n **37-38 General Conclusion**—These verses are very probably a general conclusion of the whole section dealing with sacrifice (chh 1-7), though the order in which the various sacrifices are enumerated in **37**, holocaust, oblation, sin-offering, trespass-offering, consecration-offering and peace-offerings agrees with 6:8-7:34 more than with chh 1-6.

187a **2 Institution of the Aaronic Priesthood (chh 8-10)**—It is difficult to establish the chronological sequence of this section and the law of sacrifice (chh 1-7). The two are interrelated. The sacrificial legislation requires the priestly service and, on the other hand, the institution of the priesthood presupposes the existence of an organic body of sacrificial laws. The Israelites, even before the Sinaitic legislation, had their own sacrificial system (Ex 3:12, 18 ; 5:1, 3 ; etc.) which **18** was further developed when the priesthood became a permanent institution.

VIII 1-36 The Consecration of Aaron and his Sons b—The instructions given in Ex 29 are here carried into effect. As the account of the consecration agrees almost verbally with Ex 29, we shall limit ourselves to a brief exposition of the ceremony referring the reader to the commentary on Exodus for a fuller explanation.

1-4 Introduction = Ex 29:1-3—Moses, accompanied **c** by the congregation of Israel, leads Aaron and his sons to the entrance of the tabernacle carrying with him the sacred vestments, the anointing oil, the young bull for the sin-offering, the two rams and the basket of unleavened bread. The anointing oil is not mentioned in Ex 29:1-3 but in 7. The congregation has no part in Ex 29.

5-6 The Washing = Ex 29:4—Bodily cleanliness as a **d** sign of internal purity is an indispensable condition before approaching the altar.

7-9 The Vesting = Ex 29:5, 6—The Urim and **e** Thummim, DV ' Doctrine and Truth ', are not mentioned in Ex 29:5, 6 but in Ex 28:30.

10-12 The Anointing of the Tabernacle and Aaron— **f** The anointing of the tabernacle and the sacred vessels is prescribed in Ex 30:26-28 and 40:9-11, but not in Ex 29. There is hardly any reason for rejecting **10b**, **11** as an interpolation. The anointing of the tabernacle and that of Aaron are probably independent of each other and may have been prescribed on different occasions, but in point of fact they can hardly be separated as we cannot conceive of a consecrated tabernacle without consecrated priests and *vice versa*. For **12** *cf.* Ex 29:7.

13 The Vesting of Aaron's Sons = Ex 29:8, 9. **g**

14-17 The Sin-offering = Ex 29:10-14—The ritual **h** is that prescribed in Lev 4:4-12, with the omission of the sprinkling of blood against the veil and the smearing of the horns of the altar of incense. In **15b** it is expressly stated that the smearing of the horns of the altar of holocausts with blood had the effect of purifying, literally ' removing the sin from ', the altar and sanctifying it. This sin-offering, unlike that of Lev 4:1-12, is not intended to expiate any particular sin or sins of Aaron's, but only as an indispensable requisite of holiness demanded of all the ministers of the altar.

18-21 The Holocaust = Ex 29:15-18—The ritual is **i** that prescribed in Lev 1:10-13. After having purified and sanctified himself by the sin-offering, Aaron devotes himself entirely to God's service offering a holocaust.

22-32 The Ram of Consecration = Ex 29:19-34— **j** This sacrifice is called ' the consecration sacrifice ' (22, 28, 29) on account of the occasion on which it was offered. The Heb. word for consecration here is *millû'îm*, which is derived from the verb *millē* ' to fill ', which gave rise to the expression *millē' yād* lit. ' to fill the hand ' and as a liturgical expression ' to confer the power, to institute to a priestly office ' ; hence ' to consecrate '. Therefore *millû'îm* is ' institution to the priesthood, consecration '. But the fundamental idea conveyed by the word is the conferment of a certain power ; *cf.* P. Joüon in Bi (1922) 64-6. Though the occasion of the sacrifice gives it a special character, certain features, such as the apportionment of the priestly dues, make it resemble a peace-offering.

When Moses, who on that occasion held the office of **k** the officiating high-priest, had slain the second ram, he smeared with its blood the tip of Aaron's right ear, the thumb of his right hand and the great toe of his right foot, afterwards applying the blood to Aaron's sons in the same manner. The smearing of these organs with blood signified that ' the ear must be attentive to the commands of God, the hand ready to do his will, the foot prepared to walk in his ways ', Chapman-Streane, 48. Then Moses poured the rest of the blood round over the altar and took the fat, the right thigh, one unleavened cake, one cake of oiled

k bread and one wafer, putting the cakes upon the meat and placing everything on the hands of Aaron and his sons and then waving them before the Lord. Afterwards Moses took back all these things and burnt them on the altar, upon the burning holocaust as a sweet odour to the Lord. Then he waved the breast before the Lord and appropriated it as his priestly due. According to Lev 7:32 the right thigh too is reserved to the officiating priest, but Moses' portion was the breast only, the reason probably being that when priests were numerous it was but natural that they should have a more substantial share of the sacrifice, but when Moses alone could partake of the sacred meal a smaller portion may have been considered sufficient.

l The sacrifice being over, Moses sprinkled Aaron and his sons and their garments with oil and blood. The sprinkling with oil, though in strict conformity with the injunctions of Ex 29:21, raises some difficulties. There is no apparent reason why Aaron should be sprinkled with oil after having been anointed (12), nor is it clear whether there was only one sprinkling with blood and oil mingled together, or two separate sprinklings. The difficulty would disappear if we removed from the text of Ex 29:21 and Lev 8:30 the words ' the anointing oil ' as an interpolation, but the excision is hardly justified.

Aaron and his sons having thus received investiture as God's ministers, it was natural that they should rejoice before the Lord. Accordingly Moses ordered them to cook what remained of the second ram and to eat it together with the remaining bread.

m **33-36 Duration of the Consecration Ceremony**—Cf. Ex 29:35-37. The ceremony described above was to be repeated for seven consecutive days. During this time they were to abide at the entrance of the tabernacle performing the special service prescribed to them. It was only after seven days of uninterrupted preparations in the seclusion of the tabernacle that the priests were entirely purified and became fit to perform their priestly duties.

n **IX 1-24 The Inauguration of Aaron's Priestly Service**—The day after the seven days' consecratory ceremonies Aaron assisted by his sons solemnly offered his first sacrifices. From this time onward Moses no longer exercises any priestly function, all ecclesiastical powers being concentrated in Aaron and his successors. Aaron first offered his own expiatory sacrifice with the ritual prescribed in 4:4-12, with the exception of the imposition of hands and the sprinkling of the blood against the veil. It must be remarked that Aaron had not yet been solemnly introduced into the inner sanctuary. After the holocaust, offered with the same ritual as in 1:10-13, there followed the sacrifices of the people. Aaron brought first the he-goat (15), ' and offered it as a sin-offering, as the first one '. The oblation was burnt upon the altar (17), ' besides the morning holocaust '. The last words are an allusion either to the holocaust which had been burnt that very morning or to the daily perpetual holocaust (Ex 29:38-42 ; Num 28:3-8). In the latter case either the words are a later gloss or the account was written when the morning sacrifice had become a regular feature of the divine service.

o God's acceptance of the first sacrifices was manifested by a heavenly sign. Aaron, having performed all the sacrificial service, lifted up his hands and blessed the people, probably in the manner prescribed in Num 6:22-26, descended from the altar and went into the tabernacle with Moses. Probably Moses by introducing Aaron into the inner sanctuary, but not into the Holy of Holies, vested him with further priestly rights. This ceremony may be compared with the solemn entry of a new bishop into his Cathedral Church and his enthronement. It is not excluded that Moses and Aaron in the tabernacle prayed God that he might manifest his glory to the people. When they came out, they blessed the people and the glory of the Lord appeared in the sight of all in the form of a fire consuming all the offerings upon the altar. For a

similar manifestation of God's acceptance of a sacrifice **187o** cf. Jg 6:21 ; 3 Kg 18:38 ; 1 Par 21:26 ; 2 Par 7:1. As Aaron had already set fire to the several offerings, it is probable that the heavenly fire only accelerated the consumption of the victims.

X 1-7 The First Priestly Transgression and its Punish- 188a ment—It is not clear what the sin of Aaron's sons was. It was certainly irreverence connected with fire and incense-offering. It is commonly held that Nadab and Abiu made use of fire that was not taken from the altar. But the expression ' a strange fire ' probably means a fire-offering made against the regulations, therefore an irregular fire-offering, a fire-offering made not in the manner that was commanded. The irregularity may have been in the quality of the fire, the composition of the incense (Ex 30:9), the time and place of the offering. In any case it was irreverence which could not be left unpunished. The punishment was fatal. A fire like a flash of lightning struck them dead. For similar punishments cf. Num 11:1 ; 16:35 ; 4 Kg 1:12. The death penalty may have appeared disproportionate to the fault, but Moses justified the severity of the punishment on the ground of God's sanctity. God being holy, those who approach him must be holy. Any unholiness in his ministers would be reflected upon him and must therefore be punished with due severity in the presence of all the people. Moses here quoted God's words, but we cannot say on what occasion God pronounced them. The dead bodies of Nadab and Abiu were instantly removed and buried outside the camp. Aaron and his surviving sons, Eleazar and Ithamar, were strictly forbidden to show any sign of mourning, which, however, was allowed to other relatives and the whole people. The reason for this prohibition is given in Num 19:11-22. Later legislation was less strict as it permitted the priests, but not the high-priest, to mourn for their closest relatives ; cf. 21:1-6, 10-12.

8-11 The Priests forbidden to drink Wine—The close **b** connexion between this prohibition and the episode of Nadab and Abiu gave rise to the tradition that drunkenness during the divine service was the sin of the two priests. The priests, the only persons who could approach God and who were the recognized teachers in Israel, had to be perfectly sober both out of due reverence and in order that they might be able to discriminate between what was holy and what was not holy, between what was clean and what was unclean, and to teach the people all the laws given by God to Moses.

12-15 The Portions reserved to the Priests—This **c** passage is supplementary to the narrative relating the offering of Aaron's first sacrifice (ch 9). Aaron and his sons are commanded to eat the unleavened cakes left over from the oblation, and the breast and the right thigh of the peace-offerings. These oblations being most holy must be eaten in a holy place, beside the altar, while the other portions were to be eaten in a clean place. Only the sons of Aaron had a right to a portion of the oblation (6:18), his daughters being allowed to share in the peace-offerings only. For the persons who were entitled to a share in the priestly portions, see 22:11-13.

16-20 The Sin-offering not eaten by the Priests— **d** Besides his own sin-offering (9:8), Aaron offered also a he-goat as a sin-offering for the people (9:15). The first was entirely burnt as prescribed (4:4-12), of the other a portion was to be eaten by the priest (6:26). Contrary to the prescriptions of 6:26 the sin-offering of the people was completely burnt. Moses was angry with Eleazar and Ithamar and rebuked them because they had not eaten the holy portion in a holy place. He put forward two reasons : (i) God has given you a portion of the sin-offerings that you might, by eating it, expiate the sins of the people. The eating is a complementary part of the whole sacrificial ritual which is acceptable to God only if the several constituent actions are properly performed. (ii) No blood was brought into the sanctuary, a portion of the

188d victim was therefore to be reserved to the priest (6:26). Aaron answers for his sons as the only person responsible. He justifies his action by expressing his doubts about God's acceptance of his partaking of the sin-offering. His sons' sin-offering and their holocaust could not avert the calamity which had befallen him. How could he therefore hope that his eating the victim would propitiate God ? DV gives another meaning : ' How could I eat . . . having a sorrowful heart ? ' But the words ' having a sorrowful heart ' are not in Heb.

189a B. Laws of Purification and Atonement (chh 11-16).
1 Uncleanness and its Removal (chh 11-15)—In the Levitical legislation uncleanness denotes the state of a person who, on account of certain actions not necessarily sinful, cannot approach God. Both this person and the cause of his condition are said to be unclean. Uncleanness is generally external, not necessarily involving any transgression of the moral law, and therefore its removal too was an external ceremony reinstating the unclean person in his former condition. The study of anthropology has shown that the distinction between cleanness and uncleanness and the religious notions underlying the distinction are very widespread and far older than the Hebrew people. Some of these ideas and practices were taken over by the nomadic Israelites and were later sanctioned by God in so far as they were not inconsistent with monotheistic belief and as a means to train the Israelites to higher standards of moral cleanness. The moral and religious motive of the cleanness-laws is clearly stated in 11:44 : ' Be holy because I am holy.' On the subject of Cleanness and Uncleanness, see M.-J. Lagrange, 141-57 ; W. R. Smith, 446-56.

b XI 1-47 Clean and Unclean Food—The distinction between clean and unclean animals is based on sanitary grounds, on a sense of natural aversion and, to some extent, on religious considerations, certain animals having idolatrous and superstitious associations. A parallel list of unclean animals is given in Deut 14:3-20. For a comparison, see Driver, *Deuteronomy*, in ICC, 156-9.

c 1-8 Beasts = Deut 14:3-8—The criterion whereby animals are judged ' clean ' is that they must ' have the hoof divided and chew the cud '. According to this criterion the camel is pronounced unclean because it chews the cud but has not the hoof divided. For the same reason the rock-badger (DV cherogrillus) and the hare are unclean because they do not divide the hoof although they move the jaws like ruminants. The pig is unclean for the opposite reason. The swine was forbidden food to the Semites and an abomination to the Jews (2 Mac 6 :18 f.). Uncleanness, like holiness, could be transmitted by contact, and an unclean person had to be temporarily separated from all social intercourse until he was purified. Contact with a living unclean animal was not forbidden, otherwise the Israelites would have been deprived of their ordinary means of conveyance, the camel and the ass.

d 9-12 Fishes = Deut 14:11-18—The criterion of cleanness for aquatic animals is that they must have ' fins and scales '. No application of this general principle to particular cases is made either in Lev or in Deut.

e 13-19 Birds = Deut 14:9 f.—The principle underlying the classification of these birds as unclean is that they are mostly birds of prey feeding on carrion. Some of the birds enumerated are of doubtful identification.

f 20-23 Winged Insects = Deut 14:19, 20—All flying insects having four feet are classed with unclean animals except those that have two posterior legs of greater strength and length for leaping, such as certain kinds of locusts which may be eaten ; *cf.* Mt 3:4 ; Mk 1:6.

g 24-28 Uncleanness by Contact—As uncleanness is communicable by contact, whoever carries or touches, even inadvertently, the carcass of an unclean animal defiles himself and remains defiled till the evening. Contact with a dead unclean animal was believed to be dangerous whereas contact with a living unclean **18** animal was not ; *cf.* § 189c.

29-38 Uncleanness caused by Reptiles, etc.—The **h** uncleanness produced by reptiles is restricted to contact with their corpses as they were never used as food. Three ways of dealing with such uncleanness are here indicated. (i) The uncleanness adheres to the surface and can be washed away by water (**32**). (ii) The uncleanness penetrates into the thing itself which must therefore be destroyed (**33-35**). (iii) The uncleanness cannot be removed and may therefore be disregarded (**36, 37**).

39, 40 Contact with the Corpse of a Clean Animal— **i** This rule is meant to supplement the law concerning the contact with dead animals (24-28). By ' dead animal ' is meant an animal which dies a natural death.

41-47 Conclusion—This is a regulation supplementary **j** to 29-31 and the conclusion of the whole section on the prohibition of unclean food. The ultimate reason why the Israelites must guard themselves against any uncleanness is the Lord's holiness and his relation to the Israelites. Yahweh is the God of the Israelites, and the Israelites are his people. Fellowship with God implies a certain likeness to him, or imitation of his perfections. The Israelites must be holy because their God is holy. This is a fundamental principle of Christian life enunciated in almost the same terms by Jesus Christ : ' Be you therefore perfect, as also your heavenly Father is perfect ' (Mt 5:48).

XII 1-8 Purification after Childbirth—The origin of **k** life, which could not be explained naturally, was attributed by all primitive peoples to mysterious powers acting on woman. Generation was therefore always looked upon with superstitious awe, and women after childbirth were tabooed all the world over (*cf.* *J. C. Frazer, Taboo and the Perils of the Soul*, 1914³ [*The Golden Bough*, III] 147 ff. ; also Humm., 435). But the Levitical law has also a religious significance. God is the source of life, and a holocaust is accordingly offered him in recognition of the origin of a new life from him. The sin-offering (**6, 8**) does not imply that childbirth or conjugal intercourse were considered morally sinful. The only inference is that the mother after childbirth is ceremonially unclean, and atonement has to be made by a sin-offering (Humm., 437). Sin-offerings were also prescribed for other ceremonial uncleannesses ; *cf.* 14:19, 22 ; 15:15, 30.

1-4 The Birth of a Male—If a woman gives birth to **l** a male, she is unclean for seven days, as in her courses, and is therefore subject to the restrictions specified in 15:19-24. For the next thirty-three days she continues to purify herself, the only restriction being abstention from holy things and the sanctuary. The number thirty-three has no other value but that of a remainder of forty after subtracting seven. Seven and forty are two symbolical round numbers indicating two stages in the period of recovery from childbirth.

5 The Birth of a Female—In this case the two periods **m** of seven and thirty-three are doubled. The reason may be either the popular belief that the birth of a girl is physiologically more dangerous for her mother and therefore requires a longer period of convalescence, or the opinion that, as woman was the first to bring sin into the world, the birth of a female should impose on her mother a longer seclusion (Humm., 436 ; Crampon, 385).

6-8 The Purification—At the end of the purification **n** period the mother had to bring a lamb in its first year for a holocaust and a pigeon or a turtle-dove for a sin-offering. If she was poor, the law allowed her to bring two turtle-doves or two pigeons, one for the holocaust and the other for the sin-offering. The Virgin Mary offered the sacrifice allowed to a poor woman (Lk 2:24).

XIII-XIV Leprosy—Leprosy was a fairly common **1** disease in ancient times. References to it occur in both the OT and the NT, *cf.* Ex 4:6 ; Num 12:10 ; 2 Kg 3:29 ; 4 Kg 5:1, 27 ; 7:3 ; 15:5 ; Mt 10:8 ; 11:5 ; Lk 7:22 ; etc. But it is doubtful whether the

a Heb. word ṣāraʿat, LXX λέπρα, and Vg lepra denote always what is now known as leprosy, or are also applied to other skin diseases. In ch 13 various forms are described. The Hebrews always regarded leprosy as a contagious disease and perhaps as a punishment by God, and this explains both the isolation of the diseased and the necessity of ceremonial purification. On leprosy, see *A. R. Bennett, Diseases of the Bible (1887), 15–53 ; HDB, II, 95–9 ; DBV, IV, 175–87.

b XIII 2-8 First Form of Leprosy—Its symptoms are subcutaneous nodules, scabby patches on the skin, white shining spots. When these symptoms become visible the person affected must be brought before the priest who has to decide on the nature of the disease. If the priest observes that the hair in the affected part has turned white and the swelling has a depressed centre thus appearing deeper than the skin, he shall pronounce him unclean because it is leprosy. If these two distinctive marks are not present, the man is to be secluded for seven days and then examined again. If the disease has not spread, he is to be isolated for another week. If after the second week the symptoms have not spread, and on the contrary the white spots have faded, it is no leprosy, it is only scab or psoriasis, and the priest shall pronounce him clean. As a precautionary measure the man will have to wash his clothes. If however after being declared clean, the symptoms recur with increased intensity, he must appear again before the priest who shall pronounce him unclean.

c 9-17 Second Form—Its symptoms are a white tumour on the skin and the hair turned white, with raw flesh in the tumour or ulceration. This is a case of an inveterate leprosy, and the priest shall pronounce the person affected unclean without further examination. If there is only a white efflorescence covering the skin from head to foot, it is not leprosy but some form of psoriasis or scaly cutaneous disease which is neither contagious nor incurable, and the priest shall therefore pronounce him clean. But if there is an ulceration (' raw flesh '), which must be distinguished from a temporary sore, it is a case of leprosy, and the person affected must be declared unclean.

d 18-28 Third Form—This form of skin disease is characterized by white or reddish elevated patches with central depressions and hair turned white breaking out on the scar of a healed boil. It is a case of leprosy, and the person affected is unclean. But if the eruption is not deep-seated and the surrounding hair has not turned white, if the scar is dim-coloured, the suspected person shall be secluded for seven days, and if the symptoms do not spread, he shall be declared clean. If they spread, it is leprosy and he is unclean. The case of an eruption on the scar of a healed burn is treated in a similar manner.

e 29-37 Leprosy in the Hair—This is a skin disease affecting the hairy scalp and characterized by thin yellow hair. It is a contagious disease, and the person affected is unclean. Suspicious cases are to be re-examined after a week's quarantine. The patient must shave the hair of his head except that on the affected part. If the disease spreads, he is unclean ; otherwise, and especially if there is black hair, he must be declared clean.

f 38-39 White Spots on the Skin—The disease described here is a form of eczematous, cutaneous affection distinguished by spots of a dull white colour. It is not contagious and produces no uncleanness.

g 40-43 Baldness—Baldness is not infectious and produces no uncleanness except when it is complicated by the usual leprous symptoms. Such complicated cases are to be treated as the other cases of leprosy.

h 44-46 Seclusion of Lepers—A person pronounced unclean is excluded from the community. He must have his garments rent or open in front, his head unbound and the hair let loose, and the upper lip covered as in mourning, and must warn passers-by not to approach ; cf. 4 Kg 7:3 ; Lk 17:12.

i 47-59 Leprosy in Garments—What is meant by this form of leprosy is not clear. The opinion that leprous garments are those worn by lepers is not probable. It is commonly believed that the word ' leprosy ' is applied to certain greenish and reddish spots in garments caused by mildew on account of their similarity to the leprous symptoms and of their corrosive action and insanitary effects. The treatment is more or less the same as in the case of leprosy in man including isolation of the infected garment, washing and in some cases destruction.

190i

j XIV 1-32 The Purification of the Leper—Although true leprosy is an incurable disease and no purification will therefore be required, some of the varieties described in ch 13 can be cured. When a diseased person is cured, he must be formally readmitted into the community according to a prescribed ritual. The cleansing ceremony consists of two parts, the removal of the uncleanness (2-9) and the readmission to the community, and consequently to fellowship with God (10-20). When the leper is definitely cured he is brought before the priest. The priest goes to meet him outside the camp and on seeing that he is really healed orders two ' clean ' live birds, a piece of cedar wood, a scarlet band and a bunch of hyssop to be brought to him. One of the birds is killed over an earthen vessel filled with water from a spring. Then the other bird is dipped in the water mixed with blood together with the cedar wood to which the bunch of hyssop had been tied with the scarlet band. The priest sprinkles the leper seven times with blood and water, pronounces him clean and sets the bird free.

k The symbolism of this ceremony is obvious. The sprinkling cleanses ; the blood, and the water from a spring, not from a cistern, symbolize the new life which is being imparted to a person hitherto regarded as dead ; the setting of the bird free represents release from confinement and reinstatement in civil rights ; the cedar is noted for its soundness and medicinal powers ; the hyssop, not the hyssopus officinalis L. which does not grow in Palestine, but the caper (capparis spinosa L.) or a kind of marjoram (origanum marjorama L.) was selected for its cleansing properties ; the scarlet colour of the band represents the blood of a new life.

l When the first purificatory rite has been completed, the person to be cleansed washes his clothes, shaves all his hair and washes himself. He is then admitted into the camp, but must remain for seven days outside his dwelling. On the seventh day he repeats the same ablutions and thus the cleansing process is complete. The next day he shall bring his offerings consisting of two he-lambs, one ewe-lamb in its first year, three-tenths of an ephah of fine flour mingled with oil and one log (DV sextary) of oil. The first lamb is to be offered as a trespass-offering. The reason for such an offering is that the uncleanness of the leper is considered as an involuntary guilt which has to be atoned for as a sin of ignorance or inadvertence ; cf. Saydon, CBQ 8 (1946) 307.

m The guilt is of a lesser gravity in comparison with those specified in 5:14–6:7, and this is the reason why a lamb and not a ram is offered. The ritual of the sacrifice is substantially identical with that of other trespass-offerings, but is accompanied by additional ceremonies which give the sacrifice its distinguishing feature. The priest, not the offerer as in 7:29-34, waves the lamb together with the log of oil. It may be however that the waving ceremony is performed by the offerer himself assisted by the priest ; see note to 7:28-34. The lamb is then slain in the court of the sanctuary as the holocaust and the sin-offering. The smearing of the leper with blood has the same symbolical significance as in the consecration of priests (8:23), the purification of a leper being regarded as a reconsecration to the Lord's service. The priest next takes the log (c one pint) of oil pouring some of it on the palm of his left hand and with the forefinger of his right hand sprinkles it seven times before the Lord, and anoints the blood-smeared parts of the leper. The rest of the oil is poured over the leper's head. Finally the

190m priest offers the sin-offering and the holocaust according to the prescribed ritual, and the leper is declared clean and free to re-enter his house and to partake of the sacred offerings.

If the leper is poor and cannot provide all these offerings, he shall bring one lamb for the trespass-offering with one-tenth of an ephah of fine flour, tempered with oil, one log of oil, and two turtle-doves or two pigeons. The ritual is that prescribed for similar cases.

n **33-53 Leprosy in Houses**—Certain greenish and reddish patches in the inner walls of a house are called leprosy on account of their similarity to macular leprosy. Their natural cause is damp or decay, but they are represented as a plague inflicted by God. The infected house is examined by the priest who is to order the necessary repairs or its destruction or declare it clean according to the nature and gravity of the infection. It is a sanitary regulation with a religious significance.

o **33-42, 46-48 First Case**—When the symptoms first become visible, the owner of the house must inform the priest who will inspect the house after all the furniture has been removed. After seven days the priest inspects the house again, and if the spots have spread, the infected stones shall be removed and replaced by new ones, and the inner walls scraped and plastered again. If the infection is thus arrested, the house is clean, (48).

p **43-45 Second Case**—If after these repairs the discoloured spots reappear, the house shall be demolished.

q **49-53 Purification**—The rite of purification is similar to that prescribed for the leper (3-7). The setting of the bird free lends support to the opinion that this rite expresses symbolically the carrying away of the uncleanness by the fleeing bird (W. R. Smith, 422).

191a **XV 1-53 Sexual Uncleanness and its Purification**—Although hygienic considerations and the practice of many ancient peoples may lie at the root of these regulations, it cannot be reasonably doubted that their informing principle is eminently moral and religious. The immediate reason for such purifications is not the sinful character of the actions nor the pathological affections specified in this chapter, but the holiness of God which excludes from his service anything that offends decency.

b **1-18 Uncleanness in Men**—This is produced : (i) by abnormal seminal emission (2-3) ; (ii) by a normal emission as in the case of a nocturnal accident (16) [Deut 23:10] ; (iii) by lawful sexual intercourse (18).

c **19-30 Uncleanness in Women**—This is produced : (i) by normal periodical discharges. A woman during her courses is unclean and communicates her uncleanness by contact. The apparent contradiction between **24** and 20:18 is readily removed by supposing that the former deals with lawful conjugal relations and the latter with unlawful sexual relations during the prohibited time. Vg omits **23** (Heb) which reads thus : ' If it is the bed or anything on which she sits, he who touches it becomes unclean until the evening '. (ii) By abnormal discharges, that is, those occurring outside the ordinary course or lasting longer than usual. Purification is required on account of God's presence among his people. The tabernacle is his dwelling-place and anyone approaching the tabernacle with an uncleanness upon him defiles God's dwelling and deserves punishment.

d **2 Ritual of the Day of Atonement (ch 16)**—This day holds a prominent place in the Jewish calendar. Both its ritual and its religious significance mark it off from all other festival days and give it a special character which has earned for it, in later Judaism, the name *Yoma* ' the Day ', or *Yoma Rabba* ' the Great Day '. As regards its religious significance suffice it to remark that the public and solemn expiatory sacrifice is offered by, and for, the whole people collectively. The Israelites are considered as one moral person asking forgiveness for all past offences. And Yahweh thus propitiated continues to look upon his people favour-

ably, although he may be wrathful with individual persons for their private unexpiated sins. Additional regulations are laid down in 23:26-32 and Num 29:7-11. On the ritual and meaning of the festival see Médebielle, 89-114, and art. *Expiation* in DBV(S), especially the bibliography 259-62. The literary problems are discussed by S. Landersdorfer, *Studien zum bibl. Versöhnungstag*, Münster, 1924.

XVI 1 Historical Introduction—The institution is connected with the death of Aaron's sons, Nadab and Abiu. But it is difficult to see what this connexion really implies. **1** may be simply a chronological indication having no logical bearing on the narrative. Some non-Catholic critics believe that ch 16 deals ' in reality with two subjects, *viz.* (1) the conditions under which the high-priest might enter the Holy of Holies (see **2**), and (2) an atoning ceremony, to be enacted once annually, on behalf of the nation ' (*cf.* Driver, LOT, 47), and that the two ceremonials were imperfectly combined together when the entry into the Most Holy Place came gradually to be restricted to the single annual Day of Atonement. Some Catholic interpreters admit a development in the ritual of the Day of Atonement (Landersdorfer, 84 ; Heinisch, 77-79 ; Clamer, 122). Without denying the possibility of such development we prefer to consider that the entry into the Holy of Holies and the atoning ceremony were two complementary parts of a single institution. Now considering the close relation between these two actions and the expiatory virtue connected with the blood ritual performed within the Holy of Holies, one can easily understand why the legislator has combined together two apparently distinct ceremonials beginning with the more important one, namely, the entry into the Holy of Holies.

2-28 The Ritual—The high-priest is forbidden to enter freely at any time into the inner part of the sanctuary within the veil (Ex 26:31-33) lest he should die. It was only on the annual recurrence of this occasion that he was allowed to enter the Holy of Holies ; *cf.* the symbolical interpretation in Heb 9:6-12. Supplementing the biblical narrative by later traditions recorded in the Mishnah (tr. *Yoma*, English trans. by H. Danby) we can easily reconstruct the whole ceremony. After having offered the daily morning holocaust the high-priest put on the linen garments (**4**), laid his hands on the head of the young bull brought for his sin-offering and confessed his sins. Two buckgoats were then presented (**5**), one for a sin-offering on behalf of the people, the other for the atoning ceremony. Two lots bearing the inscriptions ' For Yahweh ' and ' For Azazel ' respectively were placed in a casket. The high-priest then shook the casket, drew the two lots, and bound a scarlet thread of wool on the head of the goat for Azazel and another thread about the throat of the goat for Yahweh. The true meaning of the word Azazel, which occurs nowhere else in the OT, is doubtful. Early Jewish tradition identified it with one of the fallen angels (*cf.* CAP II, 191 ff.). Christian writers protest against this interpretation on the ground that what has been presented to the Lord cannot belong to anyone else (see Humm., 461). LXX and Vg break the word up into two parts, *'ēz* ' goat ' and *'āzal* ' to go away ' and translate [Χίμαρος] ἀποπομπαῖος, ' caper emissarius ', whence DV ' emissary goat ' and AV ' [e]scapegoat '. But whatever the etymology, the symbolical meaning is clear ; see further on.

After the designation of the two goats (**11**), the high-priest killed the young bull of his sin-offering for himself and for his family. What follows is the most solemn part of the ceremony and one of its most distinctive features. **12-14.** The high-priest took the censer filled with burning coals from the altar and put a handful of frankincense in a cup and went into the sanctuary within the veil. There he burned the incense thus raising a cloud of smoke that concealed the majesty of God from human sight, ' for man shall not see the Lord and live ' (Ex 33:20). Then after a

g short prayer outside the veil he returned within the veil with a bowl of the slaughtered animal's blood and sprinkled it upon the propitiatory and in front of it once upwards and seven times downwards. This blood ritual is the essential part of the whole service. Blood has certainly a special expiatory virtue which becomes still greater when it is brought before the presence of God.

h 15. He then killed the goat set apart for Yahweh, brought the blood within the veil and sprinkled it as before. He again sprinkled first the blood of the young bull and afterwards the blood of the goat on the veil outside the Holy of Holies. 18-19. After these sprinklings the high-priest mixed the blood of the two animals and smeared the horns of the altar of incense and sprinkled the altar seven times, pouring out what was left of the blood at the base of the altar of holocaust. These blood aspersions had the effect of cleansing the sanctuary, the tabernacle and the altar from the defilement of the priests and the people. The sins of the people, their ceremonial uncleannesses, the transgressions of the priests themselves were considered as contaminating God's dwelling-place among his people and thus rendering the sacrificial worship unacceptable. A purification was necessary that would restore the temple to its sanctity and secure the forgiveness of sins and fellowship with God.

i After the expiatory and purificatory rites the forgiveness and complete destruction of sins was represented dramatically by a characteristic ceremonial. While the scapegoat stood before the people, the high-priest laid his hands on its head and confessed the sins of the people, thus laying them symbolically upon the goat. Then a man appointed for the purpose took the sin-laden goat to an uninhabited place in the wilderness and there let it go, or, according to the Mishnah, pushed it over the rocks from the top of a mountain. There is a similar symbolism in the purification of the leper (14:7). See the spiritual application to Christ made by St Paul in Heb 9.

j While the emissary goat was being taken into the wilderness, the high-priest put off his linen garments and arrayed himself in pontifical robes after having washed himself again. He then advanced to the altar and burned his holocaust and that of the people. No sacred meal followed, the young bull and the goat for the sin-offering being completely burnt outside the camp as their blood had been brought into the Holy of Holies (6:30). The man who led the scapegoat into the desert had to wash himself and his clothes, probably because the goat laden with sins was regarded as unclean and producing uncleanness by contact. For a complete description of the ceremonial at the time of Christ see A. Edersheim, 263–88.

k 29-34 Additional Ordinances and Annual Celebration —The ceremonial described above was instituted as an annual festival to be celebrated on the tenth day of Tishri, the seventh month (=Sept.–Oct.). The reason for this date is not stated. The two numbers ten and seven had a certain sanctity attached to them (*E. König in HDB, III, 565). Besides attending the service in the temple the Israelites and all resident foreigners had to ' afflict themselves ' and ' to abstain from work '. The expression ' to afflict oneself ' used in a liturgical sense, means ' to fast ' (Is 58:3–5). This is the only occasion for which **fasting** is prescribed, although fasting is a very ancient custom and is frequently referred to in the OT ; cf. 1 Kg 14:24 ; 2 Kg 1:12 ; 12:16 ; Jer 36:6,9 ; etc. An allusion to the fasting of the Day of Atonement is made in Ac 27:9. Abstention from work is not restricted to any particular kind of work. The prohibition is general, ' thou shalt do no work ' (cf. 23:28–30), and is emphatically expressed in 31 by the alliterative assonant expression šabbaṭ šabbāṭôn ' absolute rest '.

C. The Law of Holiness (chh 17-26).
XVII 1-16 Regulations concerning the Slaying of Animals for Food and for Sacrifice—These regulations are a fitting introduction to the collection of the laws **192a** of holiness. The underlying principle of the whole collection is that the people must be holy because their God is holy. Now the basis and root of holiness is the recognition and exclusive worship of the one true God, and therefore the avoidance of all practices that may lead to idolatry.

3-7 The Slaughter of Animals fit for Sacrifice—If an **b** Israelite wished to kill any such animal for domestic use, he had to bring it to the priest and present it before the Lord at the entrance of the tabernacle with certain religious rites. Private slaughter was therefore forbidden. This may point to a time when all slaughter of domestic animals was connected with sacrifice. Lagrange, 254, remarks that with the Arabs every immolation was in some way a sacrifice. The reason was that blood, considered as the source of life and as possessing a special atoning efficacy (11), belonged to God alone. Man therefore had no right over blood and consequently animal bloodshed was a crime, punishable by civil excommunication. The animal therefore must be killed at the tabernacle, the blood poured out at the base of the altar and the fat portions burnt on the altar. Another reason for the prohibition of domestic slaughter of animals was the danger of idolatrous and superstitious practices. If the Israelites had been allowed to kill their animals anywhere, they would hardly have resisted the inclination to offer sacrifices to the desert gods in the shape of goats (now called ' satyrs ', DV ' devils ') whom they worshipped so often. Idolatrous worship, generally involving prostitution, is called in the OT ' fornication ' ; cf. Ex 34:15, 16 ; Deut 31:16 ; Jg 2:17 ; 8:27, 33 ; etc. This was a temporary regulation meant for the time of the desert wanderings. When the people settled down in Canaan, it became impracticable and had to be modified, making the killing of an animal at home permissible (Deut 12:15). The words ' an ordinance for ever ' mean as long as possible and necessary.

8-9 The Place of the Sacrifice—All sacrifices, whether **c** holocausts or otherwise, must be made in the tabernacle, and transgressions are punishable by excommunication. This law, unlike the preceding one, binds resident foreigners also and was never abrogated nor modified, but was further developed in Deut 12:5–14.

10-12 The Use of Blood—The prohibition to eat flesh **d** with blood goes back to Noe's time (Gen 9:4), and is based on primitive physiological conceptions and on religious grounds. Blood is the seat of life, and as such is best suited for expiation. The relation between expiation and the blood or life of an animal is commonly explained by the substitution theory according to which the blood of an animal is accepted by God as a substitute for man's life. There is a penal substitution and a substitution which we may call simply symbolical. The supporters of the penal substitution theory explain the expiatory virtue of blood by the supposition that the animal is killed instead of the death-deserving sinner, and the blood of an animal is accepted by God for the blood of man (see Médebielle, 114–65, and more recently in DBV (S) art. Expiation). According to the non-penal or symbolical substitution theory the victim stands before God not as a substitute of a death-deserving man but as a concrete expression of the offerer's internal sentiments of repentance, love, adoration, etc., and the victim's blood or life is accepted by God as the expression of these sentiments. It is in view of these internal sentiments transferred symbolically to the victim by the imposition of hands that the blood or life becomes an efficacious means of re-establishing normal relations between God and man ; see A. Metzinger, Die Substitutionstheorie und das alttestamentliche Opfer in Bi (1940) 159–87, esp. 176 f., 247–72, 353–77. The latter theory seems to me preferable because it can be applied to all forms of sacrifice ; but it is by no means excluded that in particular cases an offerer may have expressed by his sacrifice and especially by the imposition of hands his

192d sense of death-guiltiness which he transferred to the victim.

e It should be remarked, however, that the theory of penal substitution has no support see **11** which in MT reads thus : ' Because the life of the flesh is in the blood, and I have given it to you (to be brought) upon the altar that you may make atonement (by it) for your lives, because the blood makes atonement by means of the life (which is in it) '. LXX has wrongly translated the phrase ' by means of the life ' as ' instead of life ', *i.e.* ' of your lives '. The offering of blood, therefore, represents the offering of life, and the offering of an animal's life symbolizes the offering of man's life. In this sense we may say that the blood of an animal is a substitute for human life.

f 13-14 Animals Caught by Hunting—A beast or a fowl that can be eaten but cannot be offered to the Lord, is not brought to the tabernacle, but its blood must be poured out and covered with dust before the flesh is eaten. But in no case is flesh to be eaten with blood.

g 15-16 The Eating of Dead Animals—Anyone eating of an animal which dies a natural death or has been torn by a beast becomes unclean and must wash himself and his clothes. As regards the blood, the disposition of 13, 14 must be applied. This law binds both the Israelite and the resident foreigner, but according to Deut 14:21 these foreigners are allowed to eat of an animal which dies a natural death.

h XVIII 1-5 Prohibition of Unlawful Marriages—On the whole subject see *E. Neufeld, *Ancient Hebrew Marriage Laws* (London, 1944) 191-212. The immoral practices of the Egyptians and the Canaanites are condemned, and God's will is to be Israel's only guide. Life and temporal prosperity (though spiritual rewards are not excluded) are promised to those who walk in the way of the Lord. **5b** is cited in Rom 10:5 and Gal 3:12. The expression ' I am the Lord your God ' at the beginning and at the end adds solemnity to the enactments which follow and may be compared with similar formulas in royal decrees.

i 6-18 Forbidden Degrees of Kinship—No man shall have sexual intercourse with a woman who is near of kin to him. This is a general prohibition specified by the following list of degrees of relationship : (i) a son and his mother (**7**) ; (ii) a son and his stepmother (**8**) ; this must have been a common case in polygamous families, *cf.* Gen 49:3 ; (iii) a brother and his paternal or maternal half-sister (**9**) ; the case of a marriage of a brother with his sister, though not expressly mentioned, is implied in this ; (iv) a father and his granddaughter (**10**) ; (v) a brother and his step-sister (**11**) ; this case is already contemplated in **9** unless we read there ' and ' instead of ' or ' thus making the half-sister a full sister and supplying the missing case ; (vi) a nephew and his paternal aunt (**12**) ; (vii) a nephew and his maternal aunt (**13**) ; (viii) a nephew and his uncle's wife (**14**) ; (ix) a father and his daughter-in-law (**15**) ; (x) a brother and his sister-in-law (**16**) ; see however the exception in Deut 25:5 ff. ; (xi) a father and his step-daughter (**17a**) ; (xii) a father and the daughter of his stepson or his stepdaughter (**17b**) ; (xii) a husband and his living wife's sister (**18**) ; but marriage with a deceased wife's sister was not prohibited. Jacob's marriages with the two sisters Lia and Rachel were not in conformity with this law. The words ' for a harlot ' in **18** have no equivalent in Heb. On the whole the Levitical marriage legislation is stricter than that of the patriarchal age, thus pointing to a more developed social organization.

j 19-23 Certain Cases of Unchastity and Moloch Worship—Sexual relations with one's lawful wife during the menstruation period are forbidden ; see also 15:24 ; 20:18. Moloch worship consisting in sacrificing children as burnt-offerings is severely condemned ; *cf.* 4 Kg 23:10 ; Ez 20:31 ; and E. Mader, *Die Menschenopfer der alten Hebräer*, in BS, XIV, 5, 6.

k 24-30 Parenetic Conclusion—In the introduction,

1-5, life and prosperity are promised to those who **1** keep God's commandments, the conclusion threatens transgressors with the loss of the land which God is about to give them.

XIX 1-37 A Miscellany of Laws—This is a hetero- **l** geneous collection of laws regulating the domestic and social life of the Israelites and inculcating the necessity of holiness as a condition of fellowship with God.

1-4 Introduction—Parental respect, the observance of the sabbath and prohibition of idolatry ; *cf.* the decalogue Ex 20:1-12.

5-8 Peace-offerings—*Cf.* 7:16-18.

9-10 Gleaning in the Cornfield and the Vineyard— **m** The corn was not to be reaped up to the corner of the field, but a strip was to be left for the poor, and the ears that slipped out of the reapers' hands were also to be left for them. *Cf.* the story of Ruth. Some bunches of grapes were also to be left to be gathered by the poor. *Cf.* 23:22 and Deut 24:19-21.

11-14 Duties of Justice towards One's Neighbours— **n** Unjust dealing is forbidden. The Heb. verbs rendered ' calumniate . . . oppress ' (**13**) mean ' to withhold what is due ' and ' to take away one's property ' ; *cf.* P. Joüon in Bi (1922) 445-7) The poor hireling must receive his wages daily. Unkind treatment of helpless persons is forbidden ; *cf.* Deut 24:14, 15.

15-18 Righteousness and Love for One's Neighbour— **o** Justice must be administered irrespective of social positions. One interpretation of **16b** is : You shall not stand by when your neighbour's life is in peril. Another : You shall not withhold your true witness against a murderer. Or : You shall not endanger your neighbour's life by slander. Mutual love and fraternal correction are commanded, and feelings of hatred and vengeance must be uprooted from the heart. **18** in Heb reads thus : ' Seek not revenge, nor bear rancour towards the children of thy people ; thou shalt love thy neighbour as thyself '. Note that the OT conception of ' neighbour ' was restricted to one's fellow-nationals. Love was first limited to fellow-Israelites, and then extended to the resident aliens (33,34). But the grand commandment of universal love was first proclaimed by our Lord ; *cf.* Mt 5:43, 44 and J. Dean in WV *ad loc.*

19 Unlawful Mixtures—The breeding together of **p** cattle of different species, the sowing of a field with two kinds of seed, the wearing of garments woven of two sorts, wool and linen, are forbidden. The prohibition in a slightly modified form occurs again in Deut 22:5, 9-11. ' The motive of the prohibition ', writes *S. R. Driver, ' appears to be the preservation of natural distinctions : species . . . are designed by God to be distinct (*cf.* Gen 1:11, 12, 21, 24, 25) ; each possesses its own characteristic features ; and a principle thus visibly impressed by the Creator upon nature is not to be interfered with by man ' (*Deuteronomy* in ICC, 252). This principle of individual existence applied to religion was meant to safeguard the integrity of the Israelite religion against any foreign heathenish infiltrations.

20-22 A Special Case of Adultery—Adultery with a bondmaid betrothed to a husband but not yet made free by her master is punishable though not by death as in the case of ordinary adultery (20:10.) The guilty man has to offer a trespass-offering.

23-25 Firstfruits—The fruit of trees newly planted in the land of Canaan shall *for the first three years* (**23**) be considered as uncircumcised infants and consequently unconsecrated, unclean, unfit to be offered to God. In the fourth year the fruit must be offered to God, and in the fifth the people are permitted to eat of it. The reason for this injunction is that fruit trees must be allowed to attain their full development before their fruit is offered to God or eaten by man. In **23** DV's ' firstfruits ' should with MT and Vg be *foreskins*.

26a Blood Eating again forbidden—See 17:10.

26b-31 Magic and Superstition—Divination and augury so very widely practised in the East are forbidden. The cutting off of the hair or a part of it was, with certain Arab tribes, a superstitious practice. Cuttings in the flesh or lacerations as a sign of mourning, and tattooing are condemned on account of their heathenish associations (W. R. Smith, 334). In **29** the reference is probably to sacred prostitution although the prohibition as worded comprehends all prostitution. The Israelites must not consult those who conjure *ghosts* (*cf.* 1 Kg 28), nor those who pretend to receive extraordinary knowledge from their 'familiar' spirit. Any connexion with diviners would be a source of moral defilement.

32-34 Rules of Behaviour—Old age deserves respect and resident foreigners must be treated with affection.

35-36 Righteousness in Judgements and Honesty in Trade—*Cf.* Deut 25:13-16. The bushel is the approximate equivalent of the Heb. *ephah*. The *hin* (DV 'sextary') is about 1½ gallons.

XX 1-21 Punitive Sanction of the Preceding Laws—This is a penal code supplementing the criminal code contained in ch 18. Certain penalties may appear disproportionate to the gravity of the offence, but they must be estimated according to the standards of the times. In the Code of Hammurabi many similar offences were punished by death (*C. H. W. Johns in HDB, V, 584-612).

2-5 Moloch Worship = 18:21—Stoning is the penalty inflicted on the offender. If the people take no heed of the offence, God himself will punish the offender by cutting him off from among his people. This divine punishment is not banishment from one's city, but death in some unspecified manner. Fornication in **5** and very often in the OT denotes unfaithfulness to God, idolatry.

6 Consulting Diviners = 19:31—Death is inflicted by God himself as above.

9 Cursing a Parent is punished by death ; *cf.* 19:3 ; Ex 21:17. And the offender is held responsible for his own death. In § 195 of the Code of Hammurabi a man who struck his father had his hands cut off.

10 Adultery—The penalty is the death of both parties. *Cf.* 18:20 ; Deut 22:22 and § 129 of the Code of Hammurabi.

11-21 The cases contemplated correspond to those in 18:8, 15, 22, 18, 23, 10, 19, 12, 14, 16 respectively.

22-26 Hortatory Conclusion—The ultimate reason for keeping these laws is God's holiness on which the writer insists so strongly and so often ; *cf.* 19:2 ; 20:7 f. If God is holy, his people must be holy. The holiness of the people demands their separation from other peoples considered as unholy. The discrimination between clean and unclean food was also meant to emphasize the idea of Israel's separateness from other nations.

27 Against Witchcraft—This precept is supplementary to 19:31 and 20:6, where the Israelites are forbidden to consult magicians.

XXI 1-XXII 16 The Holiness of Priests—(i) In their domestic life (21:1-15) and (ii) in the discharge of their priestly duties (21:16-22:16).

1-9 Regulations concerning Priests in general—As contact with a dead body produces uncleanness lasting seven days (Num 19:11), priests, who must always be ceremonially clean in order to be fit to offer the offerings of the Lord, are forbidden to mourn for any person except those who live in the same house. **4** is obscure in Heb and still more so in Vg. Probably the sense is : If he is married, he must not defile himself for his wife's relatives. The shaving of the head or, more precisely, of the forehead (Deut 14:1), the cutting of the corners of the beard, the scratching of the body were signs of mourning and superstitious practices ; *cf.* 19:27 f. The character of their wives must be above suspicion, because the priest is consecrated to God.

10-15 Analogous Regulations concerning the High-Priest—These were stricter and significant of the higher degree of sanctity inherent in the dignity of the high-priest. It was not permitted to him to mourn

even for his parents. He was not to depart from the **193k** sanctuary where he resided or where he was officiating, because on his return he would defile it. He must marry a virgin, otherwise his children would be unholy.

16-24 Physical Disqualifications for the Priesthood— **l** The following blemishes were considered as canonical irregularities : blindness, lameness, hare-lip (?), congenital malformation, leg or hand fracture, to be crook-backed, dwarfness (or perhaps, emaciation), defective sight (?), scab, scurvy, crushed testicles. The persons affected were not unclean and therefore were not excluded from a share of the sacred offerings.

XXII 1-9 Ceremonial Disqualifications in Priests to **m** **partake of a Sacrificial Meal**—The priests must be careful not to touch the holy offerings when they are in a condition of ceremonial impurity. Any transgression will be punished by degradation. On the impurities mentioned in **4-7** see chh 11 and 13-15 ; on **8** see 17:15.

10-16 Those Permitted to eat of the Priests' Portion— **n** The general rule is that only the members of a priests's family and those considered to belong thereto have the right to eat of the sacred offerings. Strangers have no right because they do not form part of the priest's household. A person living with a priest for a short time and a priest's hireling are not considered as members of his family. But a priest's slave and all those born in his house form part of his household. A priest's daughter married to one who is not a priest forfeits her right. But if she becomes a widow and, having no children, returns to her father's house, she becomes once more a member of the priestly family. Any unqualified person who inadvertently eats of the holy things, shall pay to the priest the price of the portion misappropriated and an additional fine equivalent to one-fifth of that price. No trespass-offerings are imposed.

17-25 Animals Disqualified for Sacrifice—Animals **o** offered for sacrifice must have no blemish in order that they may be acceptable to God. Victims that are blind or have a broken limb or are maimed, ulcerated, scabbed or scurvied shall not be offered to the Lord. A slight concession is made in the case of freewill offerings ; but in the case of vow-offerings when a benefit has been received from God the law admits of no exceptions. Such tainted victims are never accepted, not even if they are offered by a foreigner. On this general prohibition see Mal 1:8, 13.

26-30 Further Regulations concerning Sacrificial **p** **Victims**—These directions rest on humanitarian motives and are meant also to develop a stronger sense of parental affection.

31-33 Hortatory Conclusion. *Cf.* 20:22-26.

XXIII 1-44 A Festal Calendar—This is a popular **q** liturgical calendar regulating divine worship and prescribing the religious observances of each feast day ; *cf.* Num 28 and 29 ; Deut 16.

1-3 The Sabbath—The mention of the Sabbath is **r** very probably an insertion made by a reviser desiring to make a complete list. Note the repetition of the introductory formula : 'These are the feasts of the Lord' in 2 and 4 (Humm., 512) ; *cf.* §§ 172*k*, 173*b*.

4-14 The Passover (DV Phase)—For its institution **s** see Ex 12. The paschal observances were : attendance at the sanctuary on the first and the seventh day ; abstention from servile work, but not from ordinary domestic work, during these two days ; offering of sacrifices during the seven days of the festival. A ritual feature consisted in presenting a sheaf, the first-fruits of the harvest, to be waved by the priest before the Lord. On the waving ceremony see 7:30. This was done 'the next day after the sabbath' (**11**), the sabbath here denoting the first day of the paschal week, or, more probably, the sabbath falling during that week. The offering of the sheaf was a communal, not a private, offering. The consumption of the new crop became lawful only after the offering of the first sheaf. But bread could not be eaten before Pentecost (**17**).

193t 15-22 Pentecost or the Feast of Weeks—Its date fell seven weeks or fifty days after the offering of the first sheaf. This chronological relation between the Passover and Pentecost still survives in our liturgy. On this day a *new offering* is made by the whole community consisting of two leavened loaves, made of fine flour of that season, which are waved before the Lord. In addition to the loaves the following sacrifices are offered : seven lambs, a young bull and two rams for a holocaust with the usual oblation and libation ; a he-goat for a sin-offering and two lambs for a peace-offering. In Num 28:27 the victims are slightly different. This may be due to textual corruption in either text. Attendance at the sanctuary and abstention from servile work are obligatory. 22 is an insertion from 19:9.

u 23-25 New Year's Day—There were at least two ways of reckoning the year. The religious year, which regulated the annual cycle of festivals, commenced with Nisan (=March–Apr.) in the spring (Ex 12:2), and the civil year commenced with Tishri (=Sept.–Oct.) in the autumn, as is still the Jewish practice today (Mishnah, tr. *Rosh ha-shanah*). Therefore the first day of the seventh month was the beginning of the civil year. The religious observances were : blowing of trumpets (*cf*. Ps 80:4), attendance at the sanctuary, abstention from servile work and offerings as specified in Num 29:1-6.

v 26-32 The Day of Atonement—See ch 16, especially 29-34.

w 33-36 The Feast of Tabernacles—Its date is fixed for the full moon day of Tishri, the seventh month. The celebrations last seven days and include abstention from servile work, attendance at the sanctuary and sacrifices. The eighth day was a supernumerary day marked by an *ᵃṣereṭ* which is commonly taken to mean ' assembly ', but is probably a technical term denoting abstention from work. The expression ' you shall do no servile work ' would then be a popular way of expressing abstention from work. Supplementary instructions are given in 39-43. See also Num 29:7-11 ; Deut 16:13-15.

x 37-38 Subscription to the Calendar.

y 39-43 Supplementary Regulations concerning the Feast of Tabernacles—This seems to be an addition made when the calendar had already been closed. Here the festival is associated with the gathering of all the crops, though its historical origin is connected with the wanderings in the desert. Its characteristic feature was that during the seven days the Israelites were to dwell in booths. On the first day they carried in their hands fruits of beautiful trees, identified by a later tradition with the *ethrog* or citron, branches of palm trees, boughs of thick trees or, according to tradition, boughs of myrtle and willows of the brook. See Edersheim, 232-49.

44 is another conclusion which became necessary after the insertion of 39-43.

194a XXIV 1-9 Instructions respecting the Lamps of the Tabernacle and the Loaves of Proposition—This section forms an erratic block apparently detached from Ex 25-28. The reason for its actual position here and its relation to the law of holiness are matters of conjecture. **1-4** on the oil for the lamps are almost a verbal repetition of Ex 27:20 f.

b 5-9 The Loaves of Proposition—See Ex 25:30. Twelve cakes made of fine flour were to be placed in two symmetrical rows or piles on the golden table outside the veil of the sanctuary. Frankincense was put upon them in order with its sweet odour to remind God of the offering. They were a communal offering, not a sacrifice (9), and were most sacred. As they belonged to God, they could not be eaten except by the priests. Later references to the loaves of proposition or shewbread occur in 1 Kg 21:3-6 ; 3 Kg 7:48 ; *cf*. also Mt 12:3 f.

This practice of placing loaves upon a table before the deity was wide-spread and reflected the popular belief that gods, like men, needed daily nourishment

(W. R. Smith, 225 f.). But though the Israelitic practice may be a survival from an earlier stage of religious development, it acquired a higher significance. The bread was placed before God not for his nourishment but as a concrete expression of the nation's gratitude to God, the Giver of bread and all good things (Crampon on Ex 25:30).

10-23 The Punishment of a Blasphemer and the Law of Talion—It is not possible to determine either the historical context of this episode or its historical connexion with the penal laws apparently arising out of it. *Cf*. a similar incident in Num 15:32-36.

10-16, 23 The Blasphemer—Blasphemy was always regarded as one of the gravest offences. Later Judaism went so far as to forbid any mention of the Sacred Name substituting Adonai ' the Lord ' for Yahweh in the reading of the Scripture. There being as yet no punitive dispositions against blasphemy a divine ruling was given to the effect that a blasphemer should be put to death. The witnesses then laid their hands on the offender's head thus signifying that he must bear the burden of his sin, and the whole congregation stoned him to death.

17-22 The Law of Talion—The provisions here laid down are based on the principle of criminal law current among the Babylonians and the Arabs of the desert, namely, the law of retaliation (' lex talionis ') ; *cf*. Ex 21:23-25 and the Code of Hammurabi, §§ 116, 200, 210, 219, 229, 232, 245, 263.

XXV 1-55 The Sabbatical Year and the Year of Jubilee—Two different institutions, which at certain times coincided, form the object of the regulations in this chapter. For the sake of clarity we will deal with the two institutions separately.

1-7, 20-22 The Sabbatical Year—This law is parallel to the law of the Sabbath (Ex 20:8-11). As a period of six days is followed by a day of rest, so a period of six years is followed by a year of rest. The two laws have a religious and a humanitarian motive. After six days' work man must have a day's rest and turn his mind to God ; in the same manner the land, after having for six years exerted its full powers, must have a year's rest. Periodical fallow years were, and are still, normal in the agriculture of many countries, but the fixing of the fallow year permanently in the seventh year and the relation between the rest day and the rest year mark off the Hebrew institution from similar practices. In the seventh year it was not permitted to sow or to prune the vine. The spontaneous growth of the land could not be stored, but could only be gathered when needed for food by the owner of the field and his dependants (6) as well as by the poor people of the country (Ex 23:11). An assurance of divine providence in the shape of an abundant yield in the sixth year was intended to remove any apprehensiveness as to the sufficiency of the means of subsistence during the seventh year (20-22). The produce of the sixth year was to last not only for that year, but also for the following year and till the harvest time of the eighth year ; therefore practically for three years (21).

8-19, 23-55 The Year of Jubilee—This institution is but another form of the week-institution based on the same principle of a period of seven time-units the last one of which is consecrated to God, the time-unit in this case being a seven-year period and the day of rest being transferred to the year following the seven septennial periods. This year, which was the 50th year, was called the year of jubilee from Heb. *yōḇēl* which passed into our languages through Greek and Latin. The word *yōḇēl* means ' a ram's horn used as a cornet ' hence ' the blowing of cornets ' and metonymically ' a festival or an extraordinary occurrence announced by the blowing of cornets ' (BDB *s.v.*). The jubilee year was an institution of a social and economic character based on religious considerations. Its characteristic features were : (i) a fallow year ; (ii) the reverting of property to its former owners ; (iii) the emancipation of slaves ; (iv) the suspension or, perhaps, the remission of debts. The relation of meaning between the Hebrew jubilee and the Catholic jubilee is obvious ; *cf.* also Lk 4:19.

8-12 Institution of the Jubilee—The year of jubilee began on the tenth day of the seventh month (Tishri), that is, on the Day of Atonement and was announced by the blowing of trumpets. At the same time a proclamation went round that general release (DV 'remission') was granted, namely, that all landed property that had been sold, reverted to its original owners, and slaves were sent free to their families. It was also a fallow year, **11 f.**

13-19, 23-24 Alienation of Land—The law regulating the purchase of land was based on the fact that God was the sole owner and man had only the use thereof. Consequently no one could sell his property outright ; all he could do was to sell the usufruct, and even this sale was valid only to the next jubilee. In the jubilee year the usufruct thus acquired would expire and the land revert to its original owner. This law involves another social-economic principle, namely, that property is inseparably attached to the family.

25-28 Redemption of Land—This is a general provision of law based on the last-mentioned principle and contemplating, amongst other cases, one to which the jubilee concessions are applicable. If a person sells his field, his next-of-kin has the right to redeem it. If the vendor can afford it, he can buy it back himself. And if he cannot redeem it, and there is no kinsman to redeem it, he has to wait till the jubilee year when the land will be returned to him.

29-34 Redemption of Houses—**29-30.** A house in a walled city, if sold, may be redeemed within a year. If it is not redeemed within that period, it remains the permanent property of the buyer without enjoying the benefits of the jubilee law. But houses in a village or farmhouses are subject to the provisions of 14-28. **32.** The houses of the Levites are redeemable at any time. **33-34.** If they are *not* redeemed (the negative is to be retained with Vg against MT), they revert to their original owners in the jubilee year. But their 'suburbs', *i.e.* the farmland adjacent to their cities, are inalienable, because they are their only means of subsistence.

35-38 Prohibition of Usury—It was forbidden to receive any sort of interest on money or on food from an Israelite. An impoverished Israelite must be given such help as is accorded to anyone who receives hospitality at one's house.

39-55 Emancipation of Slaves—An Israelite who has sold himself to another Israelite is set free in the jubilee year. Permanent servitude and ill-treatment are forbidden. God is their only master. Slaves were to be bought from other nations, and these were to be bondservants for life. This different treatment was in accordance with the privileged position of Israel as God's chosen people.

The apparent discrepancy between the Levitical law on slavery and the parallel law in Ex 21:2 ff. and Deut 15:12 is easily explained. Slaves were to regain their liberty in the sabbatical year. As the interval between two consecutive sabbatical years was six years, a six-year service was the maximum period for which a Hebrew slave could be made to serve. The six-year servitude, therefore, of Ex and Deut is to be taken as a maximum period, not as an invariable duration. The sabbatical year being a year of release, and the jubilee year being for all legal purposes a sabbatical year, it is evident that the same concessions are accorded to both. If an Israelite is a slave of a resident foreigner he must be set free in the year of jubilee. But he may be redeemed before that year, the price of redemption being proportionate to the number of years intervening before the jubilee, as in the case of land (25-27).

XXVI 1-2 Prohibition of Idolatry—This is a repetition of precepts which are found in other parts of the law of holiness ; *cf.* 19:3 f.

3-46 Hortatory Conclusion—For similar exhortations see Ex 23:24-33 ; Lev 20:22-27 ; Deut 28.

3-13 The Blessings of Obedience—Blessings for this life are promised to those who obey God's law. They

are : rain in its proper season and abundant crops ; **194r** peace and security ; extermination of all enemies ; increase of offspring ; fulfilment of God's covenant ; familiarity with God. These blessings must be taken in their literal and proper sense in accordance with the spirit of the OT religion which had to be adapted to the mentality of a primitive people in order to train them up to higher ideals of an unseen world by means of promises of material blessings. Spiritual blessings, however, are not excluded.

14-39 The Curses of Disobedience—These are ar- **s** ranged in groups, each one being introduced by a statement of the people's obstinacy : (i) disease, terrible things such as consumption, fever and defeat in war ; (ii) drought will make the fertility of their land—the pride and the support of their *strength* (**19**) and the source of their prosperity—like a broken rod ; (iii) wild animals will ravage the country and devour the children ; (iv) siege and pestilence, the siege conditions being so severe that only a very scanty supply of bread will be available ; (v) famine, desolation, dispersion among the nations (*cf.* 4 Kg 6:28 f. and Lam 4:10), the places of worship will not escape the ravages of war, and sacrifices will no longer be acceptable to God. Then after the people's deportation the land will enjoy a rest, the sabbatical rest to which she is entitled and which she has not enjoyed on account of the people's disregard of the law. In this manner the land will pay back her due to God. And those who survive this terrible ordeal will drag on a miserable existence in the land of their enemies on account of their iniquities and those of their fathers.

40-46 Repentance and Restoration—God's temporal **t** punishments are corrective not vindictive. When their purpose is achieved forgiveness is granted. If the Israelites in the land of their exile confess their sins which have provoked God's anger, if they humble their insensible hearts acknowledging their punishment as an expiation for their sins, God will remember his covenant and will take them once more for his people. No mention of the return from the exile is made here as in Deut 30:3-5, the reason being that the restoration is represented as an accomplishment of God's promises to the patriarchs and not merely as a return to the land of their fathers.

D. Appendix. Commutation of Vows and Tithes 195a (ch 27).

XXVII 1-29 On Vows—The general law is that man is not obliged to make a vow ; but if he does, he is under an obligation to fulfil it (Deut 23:21-3). The Levitical legislation deals only with the commutation of vows and contemplates the cases of a person, cattle, houses and lands being offered to God by vow.

1-8 Persons—If anyone offers himself to God, he must **b** fulfil his vow by paying a sum of money corresponding to the estimated value of his person. The estimated value of male persons from the age of 20 years to 60 is 50 silver shekels. The estimate is different for different sexes and ages. In cases of poverty a reduction may be granted.

9-13 Cattle—No commutation is allowed for sacri- **c** ficial animals. If any commutation is attempted, both animals become consecrated to God. Unclean animals, if vowed, must be presented to the priest and sold at the price adjudged by him. The person who made the vow may redeem the votive animal paying its estimated price and one-fifth in addition.

14-15 Houses—The regulations for unclean animals **d** apply also to houses.

16-25 Fields—Two cases are contemplated. **16-21.** **e** If a field belongs to its owner by inheritance, the priest values it at the rate of 50 silver shekels for the amount of land that yields one homer (*c* 11 bushels) of barley. But as no inherited land can be alienated in perpetuity, the consecration of a field to God is only of temporary duration lasting till the next year of jubilee. Its price therefore will have to be lowered

195e according to the number of years since the last jubilee. The person consecrating a field has always the right of redemption as in the case of unclean animals and houses. If he fails to redeem it, his right will lapse, and in the jubilee year the field, instead of reverting to its original owner, will fall to the priests as sacred property. **22-25.** If a field belongs to its owner by purchase, as the purchase is only temporary (25:14-17), the consecration is also temporary, and in the year of jubilee the field will revert to the vendor. All these transactions must be made on the basis of the sacred shekel which is worth 20 *gerahs* or obols, the gerah or obol being equivalent to about 1¾d.

f 26-27 What may not be vowed—The firstlings of cattle, sheep and goats cannot be vowed to God because they are already his (Ex 13:2). The firstlings of unclean animals fall under the general provision for unclean animals (11-13). According to Ex 13:13 the firstling of an ass, a non-sacrificial animal, must be redeemed by a lamb.

g 28-29 Things interdicted—The technical Heb. word expressing religious interdict is *ḥerem*, Vg and DV *anathema*, EVV *ban*. The fundamental meaning of *ḥerem* is 'separation, seclusion' and, in a religious sense, the separation of a thing from ordinary use and its dedication to God. Hence the biblical notion of *ḥerem* is 'a thing or person irrevocably withdrawn from common use and entirely devoted to God'.

This general notion may be split up into two apparently opposite, though closely related, notions. A thing may be devoted to God either because it is agreeable to him, or because it is dangerous to the religious life of the people and therefore disagreeable to him. The first meaning naturally involves the idea of consecration the other that of destruction. What is irrevocably devoted to God, whether a man, animal or field, can neither be sold nor redeemed. If it is a thing consecrated to God, it goes to the priests for their maintenance or for the temple-service (Num 18:14; Ez 44:29); if it is harmful to the religious interests, it must be utterly destroyed (Ex 22:20; Num 21:2 f.; Deut 7:2; Jos 7; 1 Kg 15; etc.; *cf.* A. Fernandez, 'El ḥerem biblico' in Bi (1924) 3-25).

30-33 Tithes—One-tenth of all the agricultural produce went yearly to the Lord and was given to the Levites for their maintenance (Num 18:21). Tithes however were redeemable on payment of an additional fifth part of their estimated value. But the tithes of cattle were not redeemable nor commutable. Every tenth animal passing under the rod, while the flock or herd was being counted on entering or leaving the fold, was separated from the others and consecrated to God. Though the animals were counted daily, tithes were paid once a year only.

34 Conclusion—This is a conclusion not of the appendix only but of the whole book.

NUMBERS

By P. P. SAYDON

Bibliography—For a list of commentaries from the patristic age to the closing years of the 19th century see R. Cornely, *Historica et critica Intr. in U.T. libros sacros*, II, 161–9 (CSS).

The following may be added : L. Cl. Fillion, *La Sainte Bible commentée*, tome I, Paris, 1888, 1925 ; A. Crampon, *La Sainte Bible*, tome I, *Pentateuque*, Paris, 1894 ; F. de Hummelauer, *Commentarius in Numeros*, Paris, 1899 ; *G. B. Gray, *A critical and exegetical commentary on Numbers*, Edinburgh, 1903 ; *A. R. S. Kennedy, *Leviticus and Numbers* (CBi), London, 1910–11 ; *A. McNeile, *The Book of Numbers* (CBSC), 1911 ; *L. E. Binns, *The Book of Numbers* (WC), London, 1927 ; P. Heinisch, *Das Buch Numeri* (BB), 1936 ; A. Clamer, *Lévitique, Nombres, Deutéronome, La Sainte Bible* II, Paris, 1946.

For reference : F. M. Abel, *Géographie de la Palestine*, 2 vols, Paris, 1933–8 ; M. Hetzenauer, *Theologia biblica VT*, Freiburg i. B., 1908 ; Meignan, *L'Ancien Testament, de Moïse à David*, Paris, 1896 ; *W. R. Smith, *The Religion of the Semites*, London, 1927 ; *G. A. Smith, *The Historical Geography of the Holy Land*, London, 1935[26] ; A. Clamer, art. *Nombres* in DTC.

Title—Numbers, the title of the fourth book of the Pentateuch, is derived from the Greek 'Αριθμοί through the Latin *Numeri*. It occurs in our oldest MSS B and S and may probably be referred to a pre-Christian origin (*H. B. Swete, *An Introduction to the Old Testament in Greek*, Cambridge, 1914, 215). In our modern editions of the Hebrew Bible it is called *b⁼miḏbār* ' in the wilderness,' which is the fifth word of the book, but in older times it was called *way⁼dabbēr* ' and [Yahweh] spoke ', the opening words of the book (St Jerome, *Praef. in libros Sam. et Mal.*, PL 28, 552).

Contents—The Greek-Latin title fails to convey any idea of the contents of the book. The chapters relating the numbering of the people, occupy a very small and not very important part of the book. The Hebrew title is more indicative of the contents which relate the history of the wanderings of the Israelites in the wilderness from the Sinaitic region to the plains of Moab. The Israelites had been for about one year in the wilderness of Sinai. They had received a religious and a social constitution and a complete system of liturgical worship. After being thus socially and religiously organized they moved northwards in the direction of the land of Canaan. On arriving at Cades (Qadesh) they attempted to invade the country from the south, but were defeated and had to turn back. For many years they wandered in the wilderness marching down the Arabah and up the land of Edom to the plains of Moab. Balaam the magician was called by the king of Moab to curse the Israelites, but God turned the magician's words into a blessing and a promise of further conquests. The Madianites are conquered, the land east of the Jordan is allotted to the tribes of Ruben and Gad and the half-tribe of Manasses, and instructions are given for the division of the land of Canaan. Interspersed among the various episodes are a few groups of laws which are loosely connected with the narrative and can hardly be classified under headings.

Structure and Analysis—The Book of Numbers is made up of historical narratives and legislation. The

historical narrative covering a period of 38 years **196d** has many wide gaps which render the reconstruction of the history of the wanderings impossible. But this lack of unity and proportion is generally exaggerated. On closer examination it is not difficult to discover at least the main lines and the leading ideas of the whole narrative. The book falls into three main sections : the Sinai section (1:1–10:10) relating the last events in the Sinai region ; the desert section (10:11–22:1) relating some of the events which took place during the desert wanderings ; the Moab section (22:2–36:13) relating the events in Moab. The geographical connexion is obvious. Not less obvious is the logical sequence.

Part I is apparently an appendix to Exodus and **e** Leviticus, but it is also, at least in its general lines, an introduction to Part II. The establishment of the tribal divisions round the tabernacle was a practical means to ensure a regular march of that vast army (10:5 f.). Part II is the main part of the book and one expects there a fuller history of the journey. On the contrary only a few isolated events are picked out. There is however a slender thread linking together these seemingly disconnected events. The leading ideas are the people's lack of confidence in God and God's punitive justice and fidelity. The people murmured and were punished at *Qibrōṯ hatta'⁼wāh* (ch 11). Mary and Aaron murmured against Moses (ch 12). The people and the spies murmured again and God would have destroyed them had not Moses interceded (chh 13 and 14). Core, Dathan and Abiron rose up against Moses and were punished (ch 16). Once more the people murmured at Me Meribah (ch 20). Therefore rather than a history of the wanderings in the desert we have in Part II a few selected narratives illustrating the people's ingratitude and lack of faith and the justice and fidelity of God who punishes the ungrateful people, but in such a manner as not to render his promises void. Part III is an account of the end of the journey, the first conquests and the arrangements concerning the occupation and the division of the land of Canaan.

In each part there is a group of laws interrupting the **f** development of the narrative. Whether these laws have any chronological connexion with their historical context is not possible to determine. They are generally very loosely connected with the context and with each other. Some of them supplement previous laws, as 5:5–8 and Lev 6:1–7 ; 9:6–14 and Ex 12 ; 15:1–15 and Lev chh 1–5. Others introduce completely new matter as the Nazarite regulations in 6:1–21. The legal sections form a small part of the book and should not cause any serious difficulty in understanding the desert story.

Religious Value—Some of the religious truths of **g** Leviticus, such as the holiness and unapproachableness of God, the sanctity demanded of his worshippers and particularly of his ministers are common to Numbers. Among those characteristic of Numbers we may mention :

1. The institution of ecclesiastical hierarchy. The divine service was to be performed by one tribe alone chosen by God (1:51 ; 3:5–13 ; 16). Divine vocation was absolutely necessary, and any usurpation of rights was severely punished (1:51 ; 16 ; 18:7). The

196g hierarchy consisted of three grades : the high-priest, the ordinary priests and the Levites. They had different rights and different duties. As they served at the sanctuary, they derived their maintenance from the sanctuary.

2. God's presence with his people, his care of and love for, them. This is illustrated by the cloud ever present amidst the people (9:15-23) and God's explicit declaration (35:34) ; by his responsive attitude to the needs of the people (11:31 f. ; 20:2-13) ; by the assistance given to them to defeat their enemies and to conquer their lands (chh 21-31).

3. God's punitive justice and unchangeableness of purpose. Sin is always punished irrespective of the condition of the sinner. The people are punished (11:1-3, 33 ; 21:6 ; 25:1-5, 6-13) ; tribal chiefs are punished (14:36 f.) ; the Levites are punished (ch 16) ; Mary is punished (12:10) ; Moses and Aaron are punished (20:12). But the people is not totally exterminated, and so God's promises stand firm ; cf. Ez 20:18-22.

4. The power of intercession. ' The continual prayer of a just man availeth much ' (Jas 5:16). Moses, the faithful servant in the Lord's house (12:7 ; Heb 3:5) repeatedly and successfully interceded with God for his unfaithful people (12:11-14 ; 14:11-24).

197a A. I 10-X 10 The Last Events at Sinai.
I-IV Before the Departure from Sinai.
I The Census of the Twelve Tribes—The reason for this census is not stated. Allusions to a census in view of a religious tax occur in Ex 30:12 ; 38:25. The total number of the Israelites under the leadership of Moses is given on three most important occasions : when they set out from Egypt to Palestine (Ex 12:37), when they marched off from Sinai towards Palestine (Num 1), and when they were about to enter Palestine (Num 26). There appears therefore to be in the mind of the writer a relation between the number of the Israelites and the ultimate destination of their journey. This relation accounts for the numbering of the people better than any supposed motive of taxation and military service.

b 1-19 The Appointment of 12 Tribal Representatives— On the first of the second month of the second year after the departure from Egypt Moses was commanded to number all male Israelites from the age of 20 years and upwards. The census was to be carried out on the basis of military fitness or, better, on the principle that the age of 20 marked the beginning of manhood and that the real strength of a nation was represented by its fully-grown male members. Each tribe was to be numbered clan by clan and family by family. The tribe of Levi was not to be included (47).

c 20-46 The Numbers of the Several Tribes—The order of the tribes is slightly different in LXX. A more serious difficulty is raised by the numbers which seem exaggerated. Their historicity can hardly be maintained (Humm., 220-30, 321 ; Gray, 11-15). A total of 603,550 males from 20 years upwards represented a population of well over 2,000,000, including women and children. Now considering the size of the Sinaitic peninsula and the enormous provisions and supplies of water which this multitude and their cattle required, it is inconceivable how a population of two millions could live for over one year in the Sinaitic peninsula and travel in the wilderness for nearly forty years. But it is not easy to explain how these numbers arose. Humm. believes that a scribe (*inepte pius*) has multiplied each number a hundredfold, so that the total of 603,550 (**46**) is really 6,035 (**226**). There are other instances of similar numerical inflations (cf. 1 Kg 6:19), which are best explained sometimes as rhetorical devices and sometimes as textual corruptions.

d 47-54 The Levites not Numbered—The sacred duties of the Levites, as specified in 50 f., account for their not being numbered with the other tribes. They had no civil duties and therefore, constitutionally, they did not form part of the civil population, but were, so to say,

an independent unit, a religious group under ecclesiastical jurisdiction. No one but Levites had the right to approach the tabernacle. Intruders were punished by death. This unapproachableness of God symbolized the unbridgeable distance between God and man.

II The Arrangement of the Camp—This chapter embodies a description of the camp and the order of marching. The position of the priests and the Levites in the camp is given in the next chapter. The encampment was a vast quadrilateral with the central quadrangle occupied by the tabernacle. The Israelites were to pitch their tents on the four sides of the tabernacle, three tribes on each side, and everyone with his own company and under the ensign of his family. Judah was to encamp on the eastern side. This position of honour was a sign of the pre-eminence promised to Judah by his father (Gen 49:8 ff.). Next to them were Issachar and Zabulon. The three tribes formed one camp, the camp of Judah, and were to march first. Ruben was to encamp on the southern side with Simeon and Gad. They formed the camp of Ruben and were to march in the second place. Then followed the tabernacle, i.e. the camp of the Levites in the middle of the march. The western side was to be occupied by Ephraim with Manasses and Benjamin. They formed the camp of Ephraim and were to march in the third place or first after the Levites. The northern side was assigned to Dan with Nephtali and Aser. They formed the camp of Aser and were to march at the rear.

III-IV The Levites, their Numbers and Duties—The sacerdotal legislation of Leviticus makes no mention of the Levites, all priestly duties being performed by the sons of Aaron. The institution of the Levitical order is first narrated here. The genealogical relation between the priests and the Levites was as follows : the priests were the direct descendants of Aaron, the son of Amram, son of Caath, son of Levi (Ex 6:16-20) ; the Levites were the descendants of Levi by other branches. The priesthood was reserved to the sons of Aaron, who were assisted in their duties by the Levites.

III 1-4 The Priests—The Aaronitic priests were Eleazar and Ithamar and their offspring, Nadab and Abiu having died without issue (Lev 10:1 f.). Moses' name in 1 is unnecessary because his descendants had no right to the priesthood, but were simply Levites.

5-10 The Order of the Levites—The Levites are appointed to assist the priests in their service, such as the offering of sacrifices, and the community in their duties towards the sanctuary, to do all the work of the tabernacle and to take care of its furniture (cf. 1:50). They are given to Aaron and his descendants as a gift from the children of Israel, but the priesthood will be the exclusive right of the Aaronites, and any encroachment on their rights will be punished by death.

11-13 The Substitution of the Levites for the Firstborn —All the firstborn of Israel, representing as they do the first reproduction of life by a married couple, belong to God, the source of life. They became peculiarly his when he smote the firstborn of Egypt (Ex 13). They must therefore be devoted to his service. As this however was hardly practicable, God substituted the males of the tribe of Levi for the male firstborn of the other tribes. Thus the Levites became ' sanctified ', i.e. separated from the rest and dedicated to the divine service. The reason why the sons of Levi were elected as a substitute was perhaps the zeal shown by them in avenging the honour of God for the idolatrous worship of the golden calf (Ex 32:26-29).

14-39 The Census of the Levites, their Stations and Charges—The Levites were divided into three main divisions descending from the three sons of Levi, Gerson, Caath, and Merari respectively (Ex 6:16). They were to be numbered from the age of one month, because the firstborn were not redeemable before that age (Num 18:16). The Gerson division numbered 7,500. They were encamped on the western side of the tabernacle and were in charge of its hangings. The Caath division numbered 8,300 according to a generally adopted emendation of MT and Vg. They camped on the southern side and were entrusted with the care of the sacred furniture. The Merari division numbered 6,200. They camped on the northern side and had the care of the framework of the tabernacle. The eastern side was reserved to Moses and the priests. The camp of the Levites was between that of the Israelites and the tabernacle. The total number of the Levites was 22,000. The priests were not included. On the value of these numbers see note to 1:20–46.

40-51 The Substitution of the Levites—The substitution enjoined in 3:11–13 is carried into effect. The census of the redeemable firstborn yielded a total of 22,273 with an excess of 273 over the number of Levites. As there were no more Levites to substitute for the surplus firstborn, these were redeemed by the payment of 5 shekels (c 12s 6d) apiece. The proceeds were handed over to the priests.

IV 1-49 The Numbers of the Serving Levites and their Duties—In ch 3 the Levites were numbered in view of their substitution for the firstborn, here they are numbered in view of their special duties. In ch 3 their service is described in a general way, here it is defined more particularly. On account of the heavy work of transport they entered upon their service at the age of 30 and were released at 50. In 8:23–26 the period of Levitical service is from 25 to 50, and in 1 Par 23:24–27 from 20 and upwards; cf. also 2 Par 31:17; Esd 3:8. The difference may be easily explained by the nature of the duties they had to perform; see on 8:23–26.

The sons of Caath were entrusted with the transport of the ark, the table, the candlestick, the altar of incense, the altar of sacrifice and, according to LXX, the laver, and their vessels. As the Levites could not touch these sacred objects, the priests did all the preliminary work of wrapping them up, fitting them with staves and placing those which could not be so fitted upon a sort of wagon (DV ' bars ' **10, 12**). Then the sons of Caath would come and carry these objects. Eleazar exercised a general supervision over the tabernacle and had the immediate care of certain specified objects, **16**. The words ' and over them shall be Eleazar ' **16**, are not in MT, but they agree with 3:32; 4:28b, 33b. The sacredness of these objects was further emphasized by the death penalty with which any Levite imprudently looking at them was threatened (cf. 1 Kg 6:19).

The Gersonites were to carry the hangings of the tent and the court, and the curtain at the entrance of the court which was around the tabernacle and *around* the altar. They were under the supervision of Ithamar. The task of the Merarites was to carry the framework of the tabernacle, the pillars, boards, bars, sockets and cords. They too were under the supervision of Ithamar.

V 1-X 10 A Miscellany of Laws and Narratives—Some of these regulations and narratives, *e.g.* ch 7, would have had a better place in Exodus; others, as 5:5–6, 27, belong to the Levitical legislation; a few, as 5:1–4, 10:1–10, are supplemental to chh 1–4.

V 1-4 The Removal of Unclean Persons from the Camp—The camp, God's dwelling-place amidst his people, had to be kept clean by the removal of lepers (Lev 13), those who suffered from a discharge (Lev 15) and those who were defiled by contact with the dead (Num 19). Lepers were always excluded from cities (4 Kg 7:3; 15:5); natural discharges too involved exclusion from the military camp (Deut 23:9–11).

5-10 Reparation for Certain Offences, and Sacred Gifts—The regulation contained in **6-8** contemplates the case when the person to whom compensation for damages is due is dead and there is no relative to represent him. If a person commits a sin *that causes material damage to another person* (**6**), he will incur a guilt involving a duty of compensation; cf. Lev 6: 1–7. The words ' by negligence ' are not in MT, but have been improperly supplied by LXX and Vg from Lev 5:15; 6:2, etc. But if the wronged person is

dead and has no relative to receive the compensation, **198c** this shall be paid to the priest as God's representative. The offender shall moreover offer a ram for his expiation as prescribed in Lev 6:6.

9 f. are supplemental to Lev 7:28–38. The word **d** *t'rûmāh* (DV ' firstfruits ') is used in its liturgical sense of anything ' lifted off a larger mass, or separated from it, for sacred purposes ' (Driver, *Deuteronomy*, ICC, 142). This portion is assigned to the officiating priest, but the rest belongs to the offerer.

11-31 Trial by Ordeal—This was a widespread **e** practice in antiquity. It was known in Babylonia long before Moses (cf. *Code of Hammurabi* §§ 2 and 132; HDB, V, 599–608) and was common among many Semitic peoples (W. R. Smith, 179 ff.). It survived down to the Middle Ages, and the Church has repeatedly expressed her disapproval thereof. From the 14th and 15th cent. the practice was gradually discontinued (cf. J. P. Kirsch in CE art. Ordeal).

Although this practice rests on the universal belief **f** that no one guilty of any sin may appear before God with impunity, and that God will never permit an innocent person to be punished as guilty, with the Hebrews it had no superstitious associations nor any presumptuous call for a divine intervention. It does not subject the suspected person to any dreadful hazard such as walking over red-hot bars. An innocuous potion was the only means used as a test of innocence. Moreover, with other peoples this practice was intended to detect a secret sin; with the Hebrews, on the contrary, it was intended to prove one's innocence by washing away all suspicions of conjugal infidelity.

12 f. are a description of the sin which a woman is **g** suspected of having committed. When the suspicious husband has no legal proof against his wife, he has the right to bring her before the priest carrying with him an offering called ' the offering of jealousy ' or ' the offering of remembrance (of a real or supposed sin)' and consisting of one-tenth part of an ephah (7 pints) of barley meal without oil and without frankincense, as in the case of a poor man's offering (Lev 5:11). The priest then takes some water mixed with a small dose of dust from the floor of the sanctuary, leads the woman before the tabernacle, uncovers her head as a sign of distress and places the offering on her hands, while he holds the water which is ' holy ' (**17**) on account of the holiness of the place whence the dust has been taken, and ' bitter ' (**18**) on account either of its taste or of the harmful effect it was intended to produce in case of guilt. Then follows the most impressive part of the ceremony. The woman swears her innocence, calling down upon herself a divine punishment if she is really guilty. The punishment very probably was miscarriage or sterility or something similar. In order to express the entrance of the imprecations into the woman's bowels more forcibly, the curses were written down on a piece of skin or some other writing material and washed off into the bitter water which was then given to the woman to drink. Then the offering was brought to the altar. For the waving ceremony see Lev 7:30. It was not usual to wave cereal offerings. Although an instantaneous divine response was naturally expected, it appears that the result was not so speedy (**28**). Pregnancy and normal childbirth were infallible signs of innocence, but miscarriage would convict the unfortunate woman.

The concluding **29-31** must be interpreted in the same **h** sense as 12 f. *viz.* whether the woman is guilty or not, the husband has the right to bring her to the priest and call upon God to decide. If she is innocent, the husband is not to blame for having suspected his wife's fidelity; but if she is guilty, she will have to bear the consequences of her sin.

VI 1-21 The Nazarite Vow—A Nazarite is a person **i** who submits himself by vow to certain restrictions. The Hebrew word is *nāzîr* from the verb *nāzar* which implies the idea of a religious separation, hence

198i dedication to God (*cf.* BDB *s.v.*). The Nazarite vow was, as a rule, of temporary duration. Lifelong Nazarites were exceptional ; we know only of Samson (Jg 13:5) and Samuel (1 Kg 1:11), in both cases the vow being made by the mother. The institution survived into NT times. John the Baptist was probably a Nazarite (Lk 1:15) ; *cf.* also Ac 18:18 ; 21:23–25.

j The representation of a Nazarite as a person consecrated to God needs explanation. Considering the prominent part which hair plays in the Nazarite regulations, one feels inclined to consider the Nazarite vow as a hair-offering or as a consecration of one's hair to God. Hair is certainly an appreciable element of man's natural perfection, and its offering to God involves on the part of the offerer a loss which not many people may be willing to sustain. Hence the religious significance of the hair-offering does not lie in a symbolical union of the worshipper with the deity (W. R. Smith, 325–35), but rather in giving up to God, the Giver of all one has and is, a part of one's self. This consecration of one's hair renders the whole person in some way sacred, and it is in this sense that a Nazarite may be considered as a person consecrated to God.

k 2-8 Regulations to be Observed by the Nazarite—The Nazarite is to observe these regulations : (i) He shall abstain from all intoxicant liquors and from all the products of the vine. This may be considered as a secondary feature meant to render the consecration more agreeable to God ; (ii) The most important regulation is that the Nazarite must not cut his hair during the term of his vow. The reason is that his hair has already been promised to God and therefore cannot be cut until the day when it is actually offered on the altar. The period of the vow may therefore be regarded as a preparatory sanctification of one's hair before it is given to God. (iii) He must avoid any contact with a dead body. Not even for his closest relatives is he allowed to defile himself, because he has ' the consecration of his God upon his head ', *i.e.* he has on his head not only the mark of his consecration to God, but the thing itself that is consecrated to God.

l 9-12 Involuntary Violation of the Vow—These regulations were so stringent that if a Nazarite happened to defile himself unintentionally, his vow was considered violated and was therefore to be undertaken afresh. On the seventh day, when he purified himself, he shaved his head, his hair being no longer worthy to be offered to God, and the day after he brought to the priest two turtledoves or two pigeons for a sin-offering and a holocaust. He brought also a lamb for a *trespass* offering. The reason for this sacrifice was that the defilement of the Nazarite, though unintentional, constituted a real transgression which had to be expiated by a special sacrifice ; see P. P. Saydon, CBQ (1946) 397. On that day he recovered his sanctity and had to commence the period of his vow afresh.

m 13-21 The Conclusion of the Vow—On the expiration of the period of the vow the Nazarite was presented at the entrance of the tabernacle. Various sacrifices were offered with their accompaniments of cereal-offerings and libations. Then the Nazarite shaved off his hair and burned it over the fire on the altar. The ceremony might now be considered terminated ; what remained was the waving of the portions due to the priest and the sacred meal. On the waving ceremony see note to Lev 7:30. Although the law prescribed only three sacrifices, the Nazarite might bind himself to more (**21b**). The original significance of the ceremony, which was the offering of a part of one's self to God, was, to a great extent, obscured by the preponderant part played by the sacrifices which formed the central part of all the liturgical ceremonies.

n 22-27 The Form of the Priestly Blessing—This is obviously out of its context. Its original place was probably after Lev 9:22 where the first mention of Aaron's blessing occurs. It is a short poem of three verses with two members each : bless—keep ; shew

his face—have mercy ; turn his countenance—give **1** peace. It is a prayer for material prosperity and safety from enemies, divine pleasure symbolized by the brightness of the face and bestowal of divine favours, divine protection and security against all misfortunes. Thus the name of the Lord invoked upon the people will be for them a source of blessings. There is an echo of this form of blessing in Ps 66 ; *cf.* also Ecclus 50:22. The analogy of this triple benediction to the Christian form of benediction in the name of the Father and of the Son and of the Holy Ghost has already been noticed by the Fathers. *Cf.* also 2 Cor 13:13.

VII 1-89 The Gifts of the Princes—Chronologically **1** this chapter should come after Ex 40 or after Lev 8–9 where the consecration of the tabernacle is referred to (Lev 8:10 f.). Stylistically, however, it is related to chh 1–4, having in common with them the same love for classification, numbers, and names.

The heads of the twelve tribes made two offerings. The first consisted of six wagons and twelve oxen for the transport of the tabernacle. Moses received the gifts and assigned them to the Gersonites and to the Merarites who had to carry the tabernacle (4:21–33). To the Caathites he gave nothing as they had to carry the sacred objects on their shoulders (4:15).

The other offering (10–83) was a dedication gift of the same amount for the several tribes and was to be presented on separate days. Each gift consisted of one silver dish of *c* 60 oz. Troy, one silver bowl of *c* 33 oz., both full of fine flour tempered with oil, one golden mortar or saucer weighing *c* 4⅔ oz. full of frankincense, one bullock, one ram and one lamb for a holocaust, one he-goat for a sin-offering, and two oxen, five rams, five lambs for a peace-offering.

The concluding verse records the fulfilment of the divine promise contained in Ex 25:22, but it has hardly any relation to what precedes.

VIII 1-4 Instructions concerning the Setting of the b Lamps upon the Candlestick—For a detailed description of the candlestick and the manner in which the lamps were to be set up see Ex 25:31-39. **2** according to MT must read as follows : ' . . . When thou settest up the lamps, the seven lamps shall (be placed so as to) give light in front of the candlestick '.

5-22 The Institution of the Levites—This section **c** supplements the parallel passage in 3:5-13 where their institution is enjoined. The ritual comprehends two parts : purification and presentation, besides the usual sacrifices.

The Levites were first sprinkled with the water of purification, so called because it was intended to remove any ceremonial uncleanness (Num 19) ; *cf.* the rite of aspersion with holy water in the Catholic Church. Then they shaved themselves all over the body and washed their garments. This outward cleanness symbolized inward purity. They were not anointed like priests, hence their sanctity was merely negative.

When so cleansed, they were brought before the **d** tabernacle where the representatives of the people laid their hands on them. The imposition of hands, which in NT times became a rite of the ordination of presbyters and deacons, here meant that the Levites were set apart and appointed for a certain office ; *cf.* Ac 6:6 ; 13:3. Then followed the ' waving ceremony ' which consisted, probably, in a forward movement of the Levites towards the tabernacle and back again to their original position. The waving ceremony, which is expressed in Heb. by the verb *hēnîp*, is inadequately rendered by DV ' offered ' (Vg *oblatos*) **13,** and ' lifted ' (Vg *elevavit*) **21.** The offering of the sacrifices was the last part of the ceremonial, after which the Levites entered on their duties.

23-26 The Age Limits of the Levitical Service—The **e** period of Levitical service was from the age of twenty-five until fifty. This apparently contradicts 4:3, but **26** gives the clue to the solution. At the age of fifty the Levites were released from compulsory service, but were allowed to give voluntary assistance or to

9e do light work compatible with their age. We may therefore assume that the Levites entered upon their duties at the age of twenty-five, but the heavier work of transport was not compulsory before they were thirty (Humm., 68).

f **IX 1-14 The Institution of a Supplementary Passover** —This section may be divided into three parts: celebration of the Passover on the appointed day (**1-5**); a case arising out of the impossibility of unclean persons keeping the Passover (**6-8**); supplementary paschal regulations (**9-14**).

1-5. On the celebration of the Passover, see Ex 12:6 ff. On defilement through contact with a corpse, **6-8**, see Lev 21:1; Num 19:11. Implicitly these men asked for a modification of the existing law.

Supplementary regulations are given in **9-14**. The petition was granted and a new law was given providing also for the case of those who happened to be on a distant journey. The second Passover must be kept exactly according to all the prescriptions of the normal Passover; **11*b***=Ex 12:8; **12*a***=Ex 12:10, 46. Those who without any reason fail to keep the Passover on the appointed day are to be punished by civil excommunication or banishment. **14**=Ex 12:48, 49.

g **15-23 The Cloud Directing the Israelites**—This and the following section (10:1-10) close the Sinai period and are an introduction to another period of the history of the desert wanderings. The cloud has already been mentioned in Ex 40:34-38, but here a detailed description is given of its functions. It rested over the tabernacle all day and all night. It looked dark by day and bright by night. When it was lifted up, the people would march off, and where it stopped, they would halt and remain camped until it moved again. The cloud therefore served not only as a symbol of divine protection but also as a divine guidance through the desert. Despite a certain remote analogy with the smoking cresset mounted on a pole above Alexander's tent (Q. Curtius Rufus, *Hist. Alex. Magni*, 5, 2, 7), the cloud, both in its origin and movements, is represented as a miraculous phenomenon and for such it is generally held.

h **X 1-10 The Silver Trumpets**—The silver trumpet is described by *BDB* as 'a long, straight, slender metal tube, with a flaring end' like those that can still be seen represented on the Arch of Titus at Rome. Their purpose was to summon the community when the camp was to break up. They were also to be blown in battle and on all the festivals; *cf.* 31:6; Jos 6:4-20; 2 Par 13:12, 14; 2 Par 29:27; Ps 97:6.

0a **B. X 11-XX 21 From Sinai to Cades (Qadesh)**— This part covers a period of about thirty-eight years, which with the one-year sojourn in the Sinaitic wilderness and the three-month journey from Egypt to Sinai (Ex 19:1) make up the forty foretold (14:34). Although the number forty may not have an exact mathematical value, the time of the wanderings was certainly much longer than the events related suggest. Of the whole period very little is known, and all attempts to reconstruct the history must necessarily involve much guesswork.

X 11-XI 34*a* From Sinai to Qibrôt hatta'awāh.

X 11-36 The Departure from Sinai.

11-28 The Order of the March—On the twentieth of the second month of the second year, eleven months after their arrival in Sinai, the Israelites started again upon their journey towards the land of promise. The cloud of smoke rose up and the people marched out of Sinai by successive stages. After several days of journeying they reached the wilderness of Pharan which lay north of Sinai and south of the wilderness of Cades and is commonly identified with the eastern part of the desert of *et-Tih* (Abel, I, 434).

b The order of the march corresponds exactly with that described in ch 2. The order of the Levites is seemingly different. But in 2:17 the Levites are mentioned collectively as one body, while in 10:17 they are mentioned separately according to their various duties. It is but natural that those carrying **200b** the framework and the hangings of the tabernacle should march in front in order to have time to set up the tabernacle before the arrival of the ark and the sacred objects (Humm., 80).

29-32 Hobab requested to accompany the People— **c** Moses' father-in-law is called Hobab here and Jg 4:11, while in Ex 3:1 and 18:1 his name is Jethro. Moreover in 29 and Ex he is described as a Madianite, but in Jg he is called a Kenite. Finally Moses' request to Hobab is inconsistent with God's promise to lead the Israelites through the desert, Ex 32:34. Limiting ourselves to the exegetical aspect of the problem, we may say that Hobab was probably the real name of Moses' father-in-law, and Jethro an honorific title, while Raguel (Ex 2:18; Num 10:29) may have been the name of a remoter ancestor. It is possible that Hobab was Moses' brother-in-law, and Jethro his father-in-law (Humm., 81; Fillion, 463; Crampon, 486), but Heb. *hōtēn* denotes always the father-in-law. The Madianites and the Kenites were two racially related nomadic tribes whose centre of radiation was the eastern side of the Gulf of Aqabah and the rocky land SW. of the Dead Sea respectively. Lastly I am inclined to believe that Moses simply wished his kinsman to have a share of the good things which the Lord was about to give them (**29**). On Hobab's refusing this attractive promise, Moses urged his kinsman further alleging his own ignorance of the desert routes to Canaan (**31**). An alternative explanation of **31** is: You know well the places through which we shall have to travel under the direction of the cloud. It is not impossible, however, that Moses showed some lack of faith as on another occasion; *cf.* 20:10. We do not know Hobab's final reply.

33-34 The Departure from the Mount of the Lord— d They started on a three days' journey with the ark going before them. We are not to understand that they never halted during this time, but the halts were short. The position of the ark in front of the host contradicts v 21 which places the ark in the middle of the march. It may be that a detachment of Levites carrying the ark marched in front of the people while the other Levites carrying the sacred objects marched in the middle (Crampon, 486; Fillion, 464), or the words ' before them ' are to be taken in a wide sense denoting simply a prominent position of the ark in respect of the people (Humm., 84 f.). **33*b*** is perhaps a redactional addition made after Jos 3:11.

35-36 The Song of the Ark—These two verses are **e** probably the beginning of two songs composed after some victory; *cf.* 35 and Ps 67:1. Their martial tone hardly suits the conditions of the initial stages of the wanderings.

XI Incidents at Taberah and Qibrôt hatta'awāh— f The incidents related here are: the punishment of the murmurers; the lust for flesh and the quails; the appointment of the seventy elders.

1-3 The Murmurings at Taberah—Taberah is not **g** mentioned elsewhere in the OT except in Deut 9:22. The locality is unknown. After long months of sedentary life in the Sinaitic region the march through ' the terrible and vast wilderness ' (Deut 1:19) must have been far from pleasant, and soon produced an outburst of complaints. The Lord punished their lack of faith by fire, probably caused by lightning, which destroyed a part of the camp. Through Moses' intercession the fire was extinguished and the place was called *Tab'ērāh, i.e.* ' a burning.'

4-15 The Lust for Flesh—This incident seems to have **h** followed immediately upon the preceding, but no time indication is given. The people led by Moses were to some extent a mixed multitude (*cf.* Ex 12:38). There were some who had joined the Israelites without being particularly attached to the religion of Yahweh. As their chief interest was their material well-being, they asked for flesh as a change of diet. They were dissatisfied with the manna, and their dissatisfaction soon spread. The Israelites began to voice their dis-

200h content, remembering their varied diet in Egypt. In **6** Heb. *nepeš* (often ' soul ') means ' throat ' (P. Dhorme, *L'emploi métaphorique des noms de parties du corps en hébreu et en accadien*, 1923, Paris, 18 f.). The incident illustrates a fact of universal experience that bad company is a source of corruption ; *cf.* 1 Cor 5:6 ' A little leaven corrupteth the whole lump '. The mention of the manna has called for a parenthetic digression **(7–9)** supplementing the scanty information given in Ex 16:14, 31. The narrative then returns to v 6.

i Moses must have been sorely grieved at the people's insensibility and ingratitude, and his state of mind is clearly reflected in his expostulation with God which reaches its climax in his petition for a sudden death as a means of deliverance from a desperate situation. Moses' words, strong though they are, do not reveal any lack of confidence in God **(11–15)**. On the contrary they express an unshakeable conviction in God's power and a sense of filial attachment to him. Moses had accepted the task of leading the people through the desert, he had repeatedly warned them, he had wrought wonders before them, he had borne with their weaknesses, but their many infidelities were a burden too heavy for him to carry. He needed further assistance, but if he did not deserve it, then he was ready to give up his life to God rather than bear the responsibility of the people's offences. For similar outbursts of apparent despair *cf.* Ex 32:32 ; 3 Kg 19:4.

201a **16-17, 24-30 The Appointment of the Seventy Elders** —In his expostulation with God Moses raised two points : he was unable to carry the burden alone and he was unable to feed the people with meat. God's answer covers both points. For the sake of clarity however we separate the two, dealing first with the appointment of the elders and then with the feeding of the people.

b Moses was commanded to select seventy leading personalities of the people and bring them to the tent of meeting. There God would come down and communicate to them a portion of Moses' spirit in order that they might assist him in his difficult task. Though the spirit was conceived of materially as something that could be multiplied and divided (*cf.* 4 Kg 2:9 f.), the words ' taking away of the spirit that was in Moses' **(25)** must be taken in the sense of a communication of a divine spirit from the spirit that was in Moses, a communication which would involve no diminution of the spirit of Moses. Spirit here means a power enabling one to perform extraordinary deeds. On the appointed day a divine spirit descended upon the seventy elders who immediately began to prophesy. ' To prophesy ' does not mean ' to predict the future ', but ' to act and speak in the name of God, on his authority, as his delegate and spokesman ' (E. Tobac-J. Coppens, *Les Prophètes d'Israël*, I, Malines, 1932, 3–9). Therefore the seventy elders were to be God's representatives but subordinate to Moses. The exercise of the prophetic office may have involved the performance of certain actions which were intended to manifest the powers communicated to them by God and to enhance their authority over the people and thus to render their assistance to Moses more effective. The end of **25** should read : ' *and they ceased* '.

c Meanwhile two men, Eldad and Medad, received the gift of prophecy without going to the tent of meeting. Nothing is known of these two, not even whether they were two of the seventy prevented by some unknown reason from going to the tent or another two besides the seventy. On their manifesting by means of certain external actions the reception of the prophetic gift which was not a communication from the spirit of Moses, and which was therefore considered as placing them in a position of independence in regard to Moses, a young man brought him the news. ' To prophesy ' Josue, who from a youth had been his attendant, interfered asking that they should be stopped. Josue was too much concerned for Moses' honour and pre-eminence which, he thought, would be seriously jeopardized if similar prophetic outbreaks were permitted outside the control of his leader. But the latter was far more concerned for the **20** good of the people than for his own honour, and to his jealous attendant he replied expressing his desire that God would even bestow his spirit upon the whole people. The story besides illustrating the principle that the prophetic gift is not restricted to any class, reveals also a fine trait of Moses' character. *Cf.* Christ's reply to the sons of Zebedee, Lk 9:54–56. Nothing is known of the later history of this prophetic council.

18-23, 31-34a The Quails—God granted the second **d** request. The people were to be ceremonially clean on the following day when God would manifest his power before them. God's gifts are always generously given, and therefore the supply of meat would be so abundant as to satisfy the people's wish even for a month till at last the flesh became nauseous to them. Moses hardly believed this to be possible, or at least wondered how God could provide such an enormous quantity of flesh. But God removed all his doubts by asserting his unlimited power. God fulfilled his promise. A wind blowing in a NW. direction from the Gulf of Aqabah drove a huge flight of quails over the camp. It is a well-known fact that quails in springtime migrate in enormous flocks from the east, cross the Mediterranean and in autumn return to the south. In their long flights they are sometimes exhausted and fall to the ground so that they can easily be caught. See the chapter on ' Quail Netting ' in *Yesterday and To-day in Sinai*, by Major C. S. Jarvis (Edinburgh and London, 1933). The people soon began to catch the birds, and the quantity was so enormous that the least fortunate man caught as much as ten cores (=100 bushels). These were cured by drying and eaten without cooking. The people's lust for flesh was thus satisfied, but they had to pay a terrible penalty. They had not yet exhausted the whole supply of dried quails when an epidemic broke out. Intemperance may have been one of the causes of the mortality. Those who died were buried outside the camp, and the place was called *Qibrôt hatta'ªwāh* or ' the graves of lust '. The locality is generally identified with a site called *Rweis el-Ebeirig*, a ten hours' march from Jebel Musa (Abel, II, 214).

34b-XII 15 At Haseroth; Moses Vindicated—The **e** people moved from ' the graves of lust ' and camped at Haseroth, the modern 'Ain el-Hadra (Abel, II, 214). Whether this narrative relates a domestic incident originating in female jealousy (Binns, 75) or expresses a widespread feeling of opposition to marriages with foreigners (Humm., 98), such as we meet with in the time of Esdras, it is certainly intended to vindicate Moses' supreme authority and his lawful right to speak for Yahweh. Mary, Moses' sister, has the leading part. The motive of her murmuring was that Moses' wife was a *Cushite*. Cush, which usually denotes Ethiopia, is here probably the name of a N. Arabian tribe to which reference is made in 2 Par 14:9, 12 f. ; 16:8. According to Ex 2:15-21 Sephora, Moses' wife, was a Madianite, and Madian is in NW. Arabia. It is possible that Moses married another woman beside Sephora. Moses' wife may have enjoyed some special privileges on account of her husband's position. In any case the proud sister of the great leader would never tolerate that a man allied with a foreign woman should have pre-eminence over her and over her brother who had preserved unstained the purity of their race. She herself was a prophetess (Ex 15:20), and claimed equal authority and equal rights to leadership.

Mary's complaints were not unnoticed by Yahweh. **f** This anticipates the impending divine judgement. In a parenthetic remark Moses is said to be ' a man exceeding meek above all men '. Though he was attacked by his sister, he suffered silently and did not ask God to vindicate his honour. This laudatory statement is commonly toned down by modern commentators who give to the Heb. word translated ' meek ' the meaning ' afflicted, ill-treated, bowed down ' or

f 'humble, submissive' (E. König, *Hebr. und aram. Wörterbuch*, 338; Humm., 99 f.; Gray, 123). Yahweh himself took up the defence of his servant. Moses, Aaron, and Mary were summoned before him to the tabernacle where a statement of Moses' position was made. The ordinary mode of prophetic revelation is by means of visions and dreams (*cf.* Jl 2:28), but with Moses, who was Yahweh's most trusted servant (Heb 3:2), God dealt with greater intimacy speaking to him mouth to mouth or face to face (Ex 33:11; Deut 34:10), plainly and not enigmatically. Moreover Moses beheld the form of the Lord (DV 'not by riddles and figures doth he see the Lord'). It was a common belief in OT times that no one could see the deity and remain alive (Gen 32:30; Ex 33:20; Jg 6:22 f.; 13:22), but Moses was allowed to see the form of the Lord though not the Lord himself. The form of God was a human, though perhaps indistinct, appearance of God. It must be remarked, however, that the purpose of the writer is to illustrate the familiarity of intercourse between Yahweh and Moses, and consequently Moses' superiority over Mary and the other prophets rather than to express any definite theological conception of God.

g After this vindication of Moses' privileged position Yahweh punished Mary with leprosy, the white leprosy, which was a milder form of the disease. Aaron was not punished, either because of his dignity as high priest or because he had only an unimportant part in the complaint. But he fully acknowledged their fault and appealed to Moses to intercede with God for her expressing his fear that Mary *might become* half-consumed by leprosy. Yahweh acceded to Moses' intercession on condition however that she should be secluded for seven days. For if a father were to spit in his daughter's face, she would keep herself shut up for at least seven days in order to avoid the presence of her father and to hide her shame. We may assume that Mary too begged Moses to forgive her sin. This story is instructive as illustrating the necessity of repentance, confession, and satisfaction—the three elements of the sacramental confession of the New Law —for the forgiveness of sin.

a **XIII-XIV The Exploration of the Land of Canaan—** When the Israelites had reached the wilderness of Pharan, they proposed that, before attempting the invasion of Canaan, spies should be sent to reconnoitre the land and to report on the strength of its defences. The report had disastrous effects.

b **XIII 1-17 The Selection of the Spies—**When Moses' sister was healed from leprosy, the camp moved from Haseroth and halted in the wilderness of Pharan. This geographical indication is so wide that the locality of the halting-place cannot be determined. In **27** the general designation 'wilderness of Pharan' is further defined by the indication 'which is in Cades'. It is therefore legitimate to infer that the place reached by the Israelites was the northernmost part of the wilderness of Pharan. This bordered on the wilderness of Qadesh which lay south of Canaan. Twelve men, one from each tribe, were selected in order to spy out the land of Canaan. Although the mission is here referred to God, the first proposal was made by the people (Deut 1:22). At the end of the list it is added that Moses changed Osee's name, the representative of the tribe of Ephraim (**9**), into Josue. Osee, Heb. *hôšēaᶜ*, means 'salvation'; Josue, Heb. *yᵉhôšūaᶜ*, means 'Yahweh is salvation'. Jesus is a Greek form of Heb. *yᵉhôšūaᶜ*.

c **18-21 The Mission of the Spies—**The mission was both military and economic. They were to consider the fortifications of the land and its natural resources. They were directed to pass through the Negeb, the wilderness stretching along the southern boundary of Palestine, and to go up as far as the hill-country, which was later known as the mountains of Judah. There are many redundancies in these verses. On the Negeb see SHG, 278-86.

d **22-25 The Journey of the Spies—**Two narratives seem

to be here interwoven. In **22** the spies traverse the **202d** whole country from the wilderness of Sin, properly Ṣin, which lies NE. of Qadesh, up to Rohob in the north of Canaan, SW. of Mt Hermon. The wilderness of Sin (RV Zin) must be distinguished from the apparently homonymous place mentioned in Ex 17:1 and Num 33:11 f. The expression '*the entry of Emath*' is the name of a valley between Lebanon and Hermon, but as a topographical expression it denotes very often the northern boundary of Palestine (34:8; Jos 13:5; 1 Kg 8:65, etc.). But in **23** the spies come to Hebron which lies about 19 miles S. of Jerusalem and 70 miles N. of Qadesh. Thence they advance as far as the valley which was later called Wady Eshcol (**24 f.**) and which is generally identified with one of the valleys round Hebron (Abel, I, 404). The apparent inconsistency is easily removed if we assume that the spies were divided into two or more groups who were to explore different part of the country (Humm., 107). Their separate reports were then amalgamated into one. The Hebron group met three Enacite chieftains of gigantic stature. The writer adds parenthetically the historical remark that Hebron was built seven years before Tanis (Heb. *Ṣō'an*) of Egypt. Tanis was built probably before 2000 B.C. It is often mentioned in the OT (*cf.* Is 19:11, 13; Ez 30:14; Ps 77:12, 43). This is easily explained if Tanis is identified with the city of Ramesses where the Hebrews lived for many years. At a certain place, afterwards called Wady Eshcol or the valley of the cluster of grapes, the spies cut off a heavy bunch of grapes which they carried back home on a frame together with a quantity of pomegranates and figs.

26-34 Conflicting Reports—After 40 days the spies **e** were back at Qadesh to report. First a favourable report was given. It was a land flowing with milk and honey, a proverbial expression denoting great fertility of soil and exquisiteness of food; *cf.* Ex 3:8, 17; 13:5; 33:3, etc., and E. Power, VD, 2 (1922) 52–8. But the country was invincible. The report which promised to be very encouraging ended on a dismal note. The people began to murmur against Moses, but Caleb, one of the spies, tried to calm them by the assurance that they were strong enough to conquer the land. Although in **31** and in 14:24 Caleb alone is represented as opposing the majority report, in 14:5, 30, 38 he is supported by Josue. Considering that the 'Caleb sections' acknowledge Moses as the only leader, while the 'Caleb-Josue sections' associate Aaron with Moses, we do not hesitate to recognize another reason for the existence of two narratives and two reports combined into one story.

The majority report was alarmingly discouraging. The land did not produce enough to support its inhabitants. The people were stronger and taller. Although there may be some truth in this report (*cf.* Ez 36:13 f.; Am 2:9), one feels an exaggerated terror and a lack of confidence in God.

XIV 1-10 The Sedition—Terror soon spread like **f** wildfire and the people proposed to return to Egypt. They had completely forgotten the wonders wrought by God for them in the land of Egypt and how he had delivered them from the Egyptians, and now they dared to think that God was really leading them where they would certainly perish, as if he were unwilling or unable to protect them any longer.

On hearing this, Moses and Aaron fell on their faces, thus expressing their submission to God and humbly entreating him to forgive this incredulity of the people. Josue and Caleb, with their clothes rent as a sign of grief, came forward endeavouring to bring the people to their senses. They did not underestimate the strength of the Canaanitish peoples, but with the help of God they would be able to consume them as a morsel of bread. Their defensive forces and their protecting gods were as good as gone from them, and God being with the Israelites there was no need to fear. These words fell on deaf ears, and the people were about to stone the two men, when the glory of

202f Yahweh, *i.e.* the fiery cloud, appeared over the tabernacle.

g **11-25 The Punishment**—A voice came out of the cloud threatening the incredulous people with extermination and promising to make of Moses a greater and mightier nation. Moses very ably pleaded for his people in the same manner as in Ex 32:11-13. The sense of **13-15** is : The Egyptians know very well that you have brought out this people from their land and that you dwell among them. If therefore you destroy this people as one man, the Egyptians and all the peoples who may have heard of your fame will say that you destroyed them because you could not bring them into the land of Canaan. Let your power be manifested not by destroying this people but by showing forbearance and mercy, or by punishing them with leniency ; *cf.* Ex 34:6 f.

h After Moses' intercession God pardoned the people, but inflicted on them, as his justice demanded, the punishment of exclusion from the land of promise. By their persistent incredulity they had proved themselves unworthy. Caleb alone, in reward for his whole-hearted attachment to Yahweh, was to enter into the land and inherit his portion (Jos 14:12). Josue is not mentioned with Caleb as this passage is a Caleb-section.

i God immediately executed his sentence. You think, he says to the people, that you are unable to conquer the Amalecites and the Canaanites who dwell in the lowlands ; well, therefore, instead of proceeding any farther turn down southwards in the direction of the Red Sea, *i.e.* towards the Gulf of Aqabah which washes the right side of the Sinaitic peninsula.

j **26-38 The Forty Years' Wandering**—This is a duplicate account of the punishment of the people and is really the sequel to v 10. Josue is associated with Caleb, and Aaron with Moses. In 11–25 the punishment consists in the exclusion of the murmuring people from the land of Canaan ; in **26-38** it is described as a forty years' wandering in the desert until the death of all the living generation from the age of 20 years upwards. Their children under 20 years and, it may be reasonably assumed, the Levites together with Josue and Caleb will survive to enter the land of Canaan. Even these will share, to some extent, the lot which will befall the people. The number 40 is a round number. The spies who had spread a false report were struck by the Lord and died on the spot.

k **39-45 The Israelites defeated at Horma**—The people, repenting of their disobedience, changed their minds and prepared to enter the land of Canaan. But repentance, in order to be acceptable to God, must be accompanied by such satisfaction as the divine justice may demand. The seemingly repentant Israelites wishing to make up for their past lack of confidence presumptuously rushed into a military expedition in which they suffered a heavy defeat by the Amalecites and the Canaanites. Horma, so called on account of the facts related in 21:3, is generally placed in the vicinity of Beersheba (Abel, II, 350).

203a **XV A Miscellaneous Collection of Laws**—This chapter contains various disconnected regulations mostly concerning the sacrifices. No reason for their present position can be assigned.

1-15 The Quantities of Oblations and Libations accompanying the various Sacrifices—Every sacrifice was to be accompanied by an oblation and a libation according to the following table : for one lamb $\frac{1}{10}$ ephah (*c* 7 pints) of fine flour, $\frac{1}{4}$ hin (2$\frac{1}{2}$ pts) of oil and $\frac{1}{4}$ hin of wine. For a ram $\frac{2}{10}$ ephah of fine flour, $\frac{1}{3}$ hin of oil, $\frac{1}{3}$ hin of wine. For a bullock $\frac{3}{10}$ ephah of fine flour, $\frac{1}{2}$ hin of oil, $\frac{1}{2}$ hin of wine. If more than one victim was offered, these quantities were to be multiplied proportionally. A different scale is given in Ez 46:5–7, 11, 14. These are ritual oblations and libations prescribed for the public sacrifices. For private and voluntary oblations no fixed measure is prescribed.

b **16-21 The Dough-offering**—After their settlement in the land of Canaan the Israelites, before eating of the bread of the land, shall lift off a portion of the cereal produce, knead it into a cake and offer it to the Lord in the same manner as the contribution of the threshing-floor. **19.** The Heb. word *'arîsôt*, which may be approximately rendered ' dough ' is of uncertain meaning. DV ' firstfruits ' is not correct.

22-31 Unintentional and Intentional Sins—**22-29** are probably a more primitive form of the parallel legislation contained in Lev 4 and 5. The law here contemplates two cases only, a sin of ignorance committed by the community, and a sin of ignorance committed by an individual. In the first case expiation is made by a young bull offered for a holocaust and a he-goat for a sin-offering. The Levitical law requires one young bull only. In the second case a she-goat is to be offered as in Leviticus 30. Sins committed with *a high hand*, in defiance of the law, cannot be expiated, but the offender is to be punished with excommunication.

32-36 The Sabbath-breaker—Though Sabbath-breaking was a capital offence (Ex 31:14 ; 35:2), the present case may not have appeared of sufficient gravity to deserve the death penalty. A divine pronouncement was considered necessary.

37-41 The Tassels—The custom of attaching fringes or tassels to a garment is very old and probably connected with superstition (W. R. Smith, 437). The Israelites may have known and adopted this practice. Instead of rooting it up God impresses it with a new religious significance making it serve as a reminder of his commandments. The tassels were to be attached to the four corners of the mantle by a blue cord ; *cf.* Deut 22:12. References occur also in the NT ; *cf.* Mt 23:5. Christ himself wore a ' tasselled ' cloak (Mt 9:20 and parallel passages). This Jewish custom has survived down to modern times. For illustrations see DBV art. *Frange.*

XVI 1-XX 21 The Journey to Qadesh—The time and place of the events narrated in chh 16–19 are not indicated and cannot be determined with certainty. The incidents in ch 14 are localized in the wilderness of Qadesh whence the Israelites moved in a southerly direction. In 20:1 the Israelites are again in Qadesh. It is therefore probable that the events related in chh 16–19 took place during the journey from Qadesh to the Red Sea and back again.

XVI 1-40 The Rebellion of Core and its Punishment— —The narrative shows some signs of being composite. Moses addresses Core and his party, and Dathan and Abiron separately. Core was a Levite ; Dathan and Abiron were Rubenites. Core's grievance was that the Levites had not the same rights as the priests ; Dathan and Abiron complained that Moses and Aaron exercised full powers over the whole community. It is not improbable that two stories relating similar incidents have been amalgamated into one narrative. Core and his followers claimed the same priestly privileges as the sons of Aaron, while Dathan and Abiron, descendants of Ruben, Jacob's firstborn, may have claimed for themselves the primacy over the other tribes and consequently the leadership and supreme authority over the people. The sedition was therefore an attack on the religious rights of the priests and on the civil rights of Moses. The two attacks may or may not have been made at the same time. In Ecclus 45:22 the three rebels are mentioned together, but in Ps 105:17 Dathan and Abiron are mentioned alone, and in Jude 11 only Core.

A Levite and three Rubenites, one of whom however has no part in the narrative, rose up against Moses and Aaron challenging their authority. 250 of the leading personalities made common cause with the rebels. Their main grievance was that all the congregation being holy (Ex 19:6) Moses and Aaron should have no superior rights. Moses replied first to the Levites proposing to appeal to the tribunal of God. Election to the priesthood depended exclusively on divine vocation. It was a signal mark of honour to be separated from the rest of the people and assigned

3h to the service of the tabernacle, but any further pretensions to the priesthood were an act of revolt against God who had instituted the priesthood and not against Aaron against whom they were murmuring.

i Then Moses tried to appease the Rubenites (**12**). Their grievance was that Moses had brought them out from Egypt promising a land flowing with milk and honey without however being able to fulfil his promise. DV omits the negative in **14**, ' Thou hast *not* brought us '. On their refusing to appear before him, Moses requested God to disregard their *offerings* (**15**). Moses' request cannot be referred to any sacrifice being offered because the Rubenites were in their tents away from the tabernacle. Either something has fallen out of the text or Moses' words are to be taken in a general sense expressing a wish that God may never accept any offering made by the rebels.

j The narrative now reverts to Core (**16**) who is requested to appear together with his company before the Lord bringing their censers with them (6). Core accepted the proposal and on the appointed day he gathered his company round Moses and Aaron at the door of the tabernacle. Immediately the fiery cloud appeared to the whole congregation, and a voice came out of it threatening the rebels with destruction. Moses intervened in favour of the people praying God, the author of life, that he would not punish the people for the sin of a single man. For the doctrine of individual responsibility *cf.* Ez 18.

k There seems to be some inconsistency in **24**. Core is supposed to be in his tent as were Dathan and Abiron (so DV). But Core had come up to the tabernacle to burn the incense (**18**). But **24** is very probably corrupt. The Heb. *miškān* is always used of the Divine Tabernacle, never of human habitations, therefore the expression ' the tabernacle (DV ' the tents ') of Core ' can hardly be genuine. We can emend the text either by reading ' the tabernacle of Yahweh ' as in 17:13 (Heb 17:28) or by adopting the LXX reading ' the congregation of Core '. At any rate the sense of 24 requires simply a command to the people to separate themselves from Core and his followers. Dathan and Abiron cannot be joined in 24. After Moses' command to the people the narrative must originally have related the tragic end of Core and his adherents which in the present form of the text is put off to 32*b*, where Core is associated with Dathan and Abiron, and to 35, where the censer-bearers are said to have perished by fire (*cf.* 26:10). After the death of Core and his followers Moses went to the tents of Dathan and Abiron and requested God to declare by means of an extraordinary manifestation of his power who were his rightful representatives. Immediately the earth broke asunder swallowing men up with their households. The word ' hell ' (DV ; Vg ' infernum ') denotes here the underworld, the region of the departed.

l Eleazar was then commanded to remove the censers out of the burning and to beat them into plates wherewith to cover the altar of holocaust. The task of gathering the censers was entrusted to Eleazar because Aaron, the high-priest, was not allowed on any occasion to defile himself by contact with a dead body (Lev 21:11). Both the fire and the censers which had been brought before God had contracted holiness and had therefore to be removed from any profane use. **38a** should read : *the censers of the men who have sinned at the cost of their lives.*

m 41-50 Another Sedition—The following day the people murmured once more against Moses and Aaron laying upon them the responsibility for the death of so many of the people of the Lord. Immediately the fiery cloud overshadowed the tabernacle. On seeing this Moses and Aaron fled to the tent of meeting where the Lord threatened to destroy the whole people. Again Moses interceded for them and, at his command, Aaron took up the censer and rushed to the multitude among whom plague had already broken out. Aaron's propitiatory action (**48**) is expressed in Heb. by the

verb *kippēr* ' to expiate ' which, though generally used **203m** in connexion with sacrifice, is connected occasionally with other actions (*cf.* 8:19 ; 25:13 ; 31:50). DV as usual renders ' to pray ' ; see §183*f* for the meaning of *kippēr*. The expiatory smoke of the incense may be considered as symbolizing man's prayer rising up to God (Ps 140:2).

XVII 1-13 The Blossoming of Aaron's Rod—This **n** story is intended to vindicate the superiority of the tribe of Levi over the secular tribes and to quash their pretentious claims to the priesthood. The tribal representatives were commanded by Moses to bring each his own rod with his name carved on it. The tribe of Levi was represented by Aaron. The rods were to be brought before the ark where the Lord used to meet Moses (Ex 25:22). The election of the privileged tribe was to be demonstrated by the miraculous blossoming of the rod of the chosen one. On the following day Aaron's rod was found to have blossomed and borne fruit The superiority of the tribe of Levi being thus vindicated, Aaron's rod was kept in the tent of meeting as a permanent sign of pre-eminence.

12 f. are the introduction to ch 18 and a connecting link between chh 16 and 18.

XVIII The Duties and the Dues of the Priests and the 204a Levites—The sons of Aaron alone are authorized to approach the Lord, and they are assisted by the Levites in the performance of their duties. As the rightful representatives of God they have a share of all the offerings.

1-7 The Duties of the Priests and of the Levites—The **b** priests and the rest of the house of Levi shall be responsible for all the sins committed in connexion with the sanctuary, such as any unlawful approach thereto ; and the priests shall be responsible for all the offences committed by them and by others in connexion with the priestly functions. The tribe of Levi (' *the tribe* of thy father ' 2) is to assist the priests during the divine service and take care of the tabernacle and the sacred vessels (3:7 ; 4:15). No layman may interfere ; transgressions are to be punished by death. The Levites have been chosen from amongst the children of Israel as a gift to the Lord to serve in the tabernacle. But it is the exclusive right of the priests to serve at the altar and within the (outer) curtain of the tent. In the middle of **7** Vg and DV omit these words : ' as a service of gift I give you the priesthood ', the priesthood being considered, as it really is, a gift bestowed by God.

8-20 The Priestly Dues—As the priests possessed no **c** landed property, God assigned to them certain offerings made to himself. In a general way it is laid down that what is left over of all *the contributions* made to the Lord (*i.e.* those portions of the offerings which have not been burnt) belongs to the priests as a share perpetually assigned to them. These portions are then specifically enumerated : in every offering those portions of the meal-offering, of the sin-offering, and of the trespass-offering that are not burnt on the altar are most holy and belong to the priests (Lev 7:32-34). They must be eaten in the court of the tabernacle (Lev 10:12) by males only (Lev 6:18, 29). Likewise those parts of the peace-offering that are assigned to the priest (Lev 7:29, 34) may be eaten by all male and female members of his household, provided they are ceremonially clean. To the priests are assigned also the best of the oil, of the wine, and of the corn as new produce, and all the firstfruits which the Israelites bring to the Lord. Things devoted to God go to the priest (Lev 27:28). All the firstborn, whether of man or of animal, belong to the priest, who will receive the redemption price of five shekels for the firstborn of man, and an unfixed price (Lev 27:11) for the firstborn of an unclean animal. But the firstlings of cattle, sheep or goats, are to be offered for a peace-offering. The blood is poured round about the altar, the fat is burnt thereon, but *all* the flesh, not as in ordinary peace-offerings, falls to the priest. All these portions are assigned to the priests by an inviolable covenant.

253

204c For the meaning of 'covenant of salt' see note to Lev 1:13.

d 20 winds up the whole section on the Levitical and priestly dues. As the priests and the Levites were the only persons authorized to approach the sanctuary, they had to direct all their care to its service rather than to the cultivation of the land. They had to depend chiefly on the sanctuary for their means of subsistence. God was their possession in the sense that he gave them of the offerings made to him. A similar, though far loftier, idea is expressed by David in Ps 15:5 and applied by the Church to clerics on the reception of the tonsure.

e **21-24 The Levitical Dues**—The sons of Levi had no portion in the distribution of the land of Canaan, except some cities and the adjacent pasture-lands (35:3-8). In return for their service in the tabernacle on behalf of the people they were to receive a tithe of all agricultural produce. On tithes see Lev 27:30-33; Deut 14:22-29; 26:12-15.

f **25-32 A Tithe of the Tithes**—The tithes received by the Levites are themselves subject to a tithe payable to the priests (*cf.* Neh 10:38), all the Israelites, the Levites included, being obliged to offer to the Lord a contribution of their land produce. The tithe paid by the Levites must be the best of the tithes received from the people. What remains of the tithes may be eaten by them in any place, as the tithes are not holy things. By failing to pay the priests their due the Levites will incur guilt and became liable to the death penalty.

g **XIX The Water for Purification**—Many primitive peoples have considered contact with a dead body to be a source of uncleanness, and various purificatory rites have been practised to avert the dangerous influences which such contact was believed to exercise; see Gray, 243-44 and references. The Hebrew rite rests ultimately on this widespread belief, its scope however is not personal safety from dangerous influences, but the necessity of safeguarding the holiness of God's dwelling. In NT times it furnished ample matter for allegorizing, *cf.* Heb 9:13; Ep. Barn. 8, 1-7; Aug. *Quaest.* 33 *in Num.*, PL, 34, 732-7.

h **1-10 Preparation of the Water**—The preparatory ceremony is as follows: (i) a red, or rather a reddish brown, cow without blemish which has never borne the yoke, is brought to the priest Eleazar and slain by him outside the camp. As the cow is selected for a sacred purpose it must not have been put to ordinary uses. The officiating minister is Eleazar, not Aaron, as the ceremony involves a contamination of all who take part. The reason why the cow is, contrary to custom, slain away from the tabernacle is not apparent; (ii) the priest dips his finger in the blood and sprinkles it seven times in the direction of the tabernacle (*cf.* Heb 13:11), expressing thus the relation between the cow which has been slain and the Lord; (iii) the cow is entirely burnt, and while it burns the priest throws a piece of cedar wood and hyssop and a scarlet thread into the fire. As these ingredients are used in the purification of the leper (Lev 14:4), it is probable that they are used in this case with a similar, though perhaps weaker, symbolical meaning; (iv) when the cow has been burnt to ashes, the ashes are collected and deposited in a clean place outside the camp and kept there for the preparation of the water 'of impurity' (DV 'of aspersion'), *i.e.* destined to remove impurity, the cow being burnt for sin (DV), *i.e.* to remove sin.

i All who take part in the ceremony become unclean. The reason is either the similarity of the burning ceremony to the burning of the sin-offering outside the camp (Lev 4:12, 21), or the sanctity of the rite which is communicated to those who take part and who must therefore submit to an 'unsanctifying' action before entering again into intercourse with the rest of the people.

j **11-22 Cases requiring Purification**—Any person touching a dead body contracts uncleanness lasting seven days. He must be sprinkled on the third day and on the seventh with water mixed with the ashes **20** of the red cow. Failing to comply with this regulation he shall be cut off from the people in order not to defile God's dwelling. Defilement is produced also (i) by proximity to a dead body, therefore all those who happen to be in a tent when a person dies, become unclean; (ii) by walking over a grave, hence the need for whitewashing the graves as a warning to passers-by to keep away (Mt 23:27; Lk 11:44). When an unclean person is to be purified, some of the ashes of the cow are mixed with spring water and a clean person sprinkles him with a bunch of hyssop on the third day and on the seventh. On the seventh day the unclean person washes his clothes and bathes himself in water and at evening he is clean. The person performing the ceremony contracts uncleanness, and has to wash his clothes and remain unclean until the evening.

XX Events at Qadesh—The events related in this **k** section took place at the end of the forty years' wanderings, when the Israelites were about to march off for the definite conquest of the land of Canaan.

1 The Death of Mary—The Israelites arrived at the **l** desert of Sin (see note to 13:27) in the first month of an unspecified year. If this sojourn at Cades is identified with that related in 13:1, it took place in the third year of the journey; but if it is the return to a place whence the Israelites had previously departed, no conclusion for the determination of the year can be drawn. As the events related after Mary's death belong to the last period of the wanderings, it is probable that the year of her death was much nearer to the end than to the beginning of the desert wanderings. It is strange how briefly Mary's death is narrated. Neither her brother's grief nor the people's mourning is recorded.

2-13 The People's Murmuring for Lack of Water— **m** Shortage of water being an ordinary feature of the desert, no wonder that the Israelites with their large flocks suffered from it more than once. Unmindful of past benefits they assembled and expressed their complaints against Moses and Aaron in their usual aggressive manner (*cf.* Ex 16:2 f.; 17:3; Num 11:4, 6). Vg and DV have a long interpolation extending from 'and cried to the Lord' to 'cease to murmur', which is omitted in the revised edition of Vg (1936).

Moses is commanded to bring Aaron's rod (17:25), **n** from before the Lord (9). In Ex 17:6 he was commanded to strike the rock, and obviously a similar action was intended here. Moses obeying God's command summoned the people and addressed them with these words: 'Can we bring you forth water out of this rock?' These words have been interpreted as an expression of Moses' ill-temper (Corn. a Lap. *ad loc.*), or unbelief (Humm., 161), impatience and unbelief (Crampon, 520). The text is probably corrupt. In Ps 105:33 Moses is charged with uttering rash words while in a state of excitement. The charge of lack of faith is hardly admissible especially after the events of Ex 17. But Moses' unbelief may have been restricted to God's willingness to provide an ungrateful people with water, independently of any consideration of his power (Calmet, *ad loc.*; Humm., 161; Heinisch, 78; Clamer, 365; Fillion, 497). A certain degree of impatience, due to human imperfection, can hardly be excluded from Moses' words and action. In the same way is to be explained the double striking of the rock. Water soon gushed forth from the rock, but Moses and **o** Aaron were condemned, on account of their unbelief, not to enter into the land of promise. They thought, or may have thought, that God would no longer listen to their prayers. They believed in his punitive justice, not in his goodness, mercy, and fidelity. They expected a punishment rather than a manifestation of these attributes before the people. The place came to be called Mê mᵉrîbah or 'water of strife', because there the Israelites strove with words against the Lord, and he vindicated his holiness. On the name *meribah* see Ex 17:7.

14-21 The Embassy to the King of Edom—After the **p**

p failure of the attempted invasion of Canaan from the south (14:44 f.) the Israelites had to reach the land from the east. From Qadesh to the eastern side of the Dead Sea the way was through the land of Edom which stretched along the Arabah depression from the southern end of the Dead Sea down to the Gulf of Aqabah (SHG, 557-76).

Before crossing the land of Edom Moses sent messengers to the king requesting his permission and assuring him of his good intentions. In order to gain his favour he addressed him as ' brother '. The Edomites were in fact descendants of Esau, Jacob's brother, Gen 36:9-19. But mistrusting these assurances they refused the request, and the Israelites had therefore to make a detour to the south.

5a **C. XX 22-XXXVI 13 From Qadesh to the Plains of Moab XX 22-XXII 1 From Qadesh to Moab**—This section relates some military campaigns against peoples whose territory lay on the way of the Israelites towards the approaches to Canaan.

b **22-29 Death of Aaron and Investiture of Eleazar**—The site of Mt Hor is unknown. It was certainly on the borders of the land of Edom. In Deut 10:6 the place of Aaron's death is called *Mōsērāh*. This may be the name of a range of mountains one of whose peaks was Mt Hor. Moses accompanied by Aaron and Eleazar ascended the mountain and, as Aaron's end was approaching, divested his brother of his pontifical garments (see Lev 8·7-9) transferring them to Eleazar as prescribed in Ex 29:29. Thus Eleazar received the investiture of high-priest and on descending from the mountain was acknowledged by the people as the successor of Aaron.

c **XXI 1-3 The Victory of Horma**—The topographical names Arad, identified with Tell Arad some 50 miles N. of Cades and some 15 miles S. of Hebron, and Negeb, the wilderness in southern Palestine, take us to the southern borders of the land of Canaan, a position which is hardly consistent with the itinerary indicated in 14:25 and 20:21. Moreover it is not conceivable that the Israelites should not have exploited their victory (3) and developed their conquests from the south. The narrative is either out of its chronological context or relates a campaign led by a single tribe while the bulk of the Israelites marched in a southern direction. References to Horma occur in Jos 12:14 ; Jg 1:17. The expression ' the way of the spies ' (1) is scarcely helpful to determine the geographical position. Heb. *ʾaṭārîm* may be a place-name of impossible identification, or a common noun of doubtful meaning. DV (and Vg) rendering ' spies ', which is based on the reading *ṭārîm* for *ʾaṭārîm* must not be overlooked. In fulfilment of a vow the victorious Israelites placed the city under a ban, *i.e.* they utterly destroyed it and called the place Horma, which means, as St Jerome adds by way of explanation, ' anathema ' or destruction. On the *herem* or ban see Lev 27:28 f. and A. Fernandez in Bi (1924) 3-25.

d **4-9 The Bronze Serpent**—The people once more complained of the hardships of the journey. As a punishment they were attacked by venomous serpents, called ' fiery ' on account of the inflammation caused by their bites. On the people acknowledging their sin, Moses, by God's command, made a bronze serpent and raised it up on a pole so that anyone bitten could look at it and be healed. The story is an illustration of God's power, for he alone could heal a deadly bite by using means that were absolutely inadequate for the purpose. There is an echo of the serpent story in 4 Kg 18:4. See also Wis 16:6 f. In Jn 3:14 it is a type of Christ's elevation on the cross.

e **10-20 The Journey to the NE. of the Dead Sea**—In their detour round the territory of Edom the Israelites reached Oboth E. of Edom, and afterwards Jeabarim, SE. of the Dead Sea (Abel, II, 216) and E. of Moab. Then they camped in Wady Zared which flows into the southern end of the Dead Sea from the SE. Having

departed from W. Zared they halted at the northern **205e** side of the river Arnon (= Wady el-Mojib, SHG, 588), at a place in the wilderness to the E. of Moab and on the borders of the Amorrhites. A fragment of a popular song is cited from a collection of epic poems, called ' the Wars of Yahweh ', celebrating the victories of the Israelites over their enemies. The meaning of the fragmentary lines is obscure. This is a literal translation :

Waheb in Suphah and the valleys of Arnon,
And the slope of the valleys which stretches out to the site of Ar,
And leans on the border of Moab.

From Arnon they journeyed to Beer, a word meaning ' a well '. The site is unknown. The name is perhaps an abbreviation of an original form such as ' the well of God '. Another popular song is given here which was probably sung when water was being drawn :

> Spring up, O well ! Sing ye to it !
> The well which the princes dug,
> Which the chiefs of the people excavated
> With the sceptre, with their staffs.

Then following a NW. direction they came to a valley in the land of Moab, which is described by the appositional clause ' the top of Phasga ', NE. of the Dead Sea.

21-32 Defeat of King Sehon and the Occupation of his f Country—Before crossing the borders of the land of the Amorrhites, the Israelites sent messengers to their king, as they had done to the king of Edom (20:14-21), requesting permission to pass through his territory. Apparently the embassy was despatched from the place reached in 21:20. It is preferable however to make the mission of the messengers follow immediately after 13 as all the sites mentioned in 14-20 are in Sehon's territory. The Amorrhites refused the request and marched with arms to meet the Israelites at Jasa. They were defeated, and Israel occupied all their territory from the Arnon to the river Jabbok (Jeboc = *Nahr ez-Zerqa*) which flows into the Jordan from the east. The writer remarks that Jazer was on the borders of the Ammonites, and this statement would account for Sehon's limitation of territory. Hesebon (= the modern *Hesban*) was the capital of Sehon's kingdom and had been captured from the former king of Moab. A popular song is again cited celebrating the Israelites' **g** victory. Hesebon has been burnt down, who will build it up ? Moab, the former lord of Hesebon, has been forsaken by Chemosh (Chamos), their national god, and gone into captivity. The Israelites have conquered all the land.

33-35 Defeat of King Og and Occupation of his h Country—The Israelites continued their victorious march northwards, defeated Og, king of Bashan, at Edrai some 32 miles E. of the southern end of the Sea of Genesareth, and occupied all his territory.

XXII 1 Israel's Encampment in the Plains of Moab— **i** The plains of Moab, the scene of the last events before the crossing of the Jordan into Canaan, cover an area not more than 7 miles wide, N. of the Dead Sea and E. of the mouth of the Jordan.

XXII 2-XXXVI 13 Events in Moab—The contents **206a** of this section are the story of Balaam, a second census and a miscellaneous collection of laws and narratives.

XXII 2-XXIV 25 The Story of Balaam—The narra- **b** tive has formed the subject of important discussions and still engages the attention of scholars. Theologians are mainly concerned with the Messianic character of Balaam's predictions ; preachers moralize on his character ; critics analyse the narrative into sources ; interpreters aim at giving a clear and full exposition of facts.

Balaam's character is differently estimated. Jewish **c** tradition was always unfavourable, *cf.* 2 Pet 2:13 ff. ; Jude 11 ; Apoc 2:14. St Augustine calls him ' a very bad man ' (*Quaest. in Hept.*, q 47 in Num, PL 34, 740)

206c and St Thomas 'a prophet of the devil' (2, 2, q 172, a 6 ad 1). St Jerome is less hard upon him (*Quaest. in Gen.* 22, 20, PL 23, 971). Modern opinion is also divided. The question however is not one of great importance, because according to a universally admitted theological principle the gift of prophecy is bestowed in view of the good of others, irrespective of the merits of the prophet (St Thomas, *loc. cit.*).

d **2-14 The First Embassy to Balaam**—On receiving the news of the Israelites' conquests Balac, king of Moab, summoned his council in order to devise a plan of defence in case of invasion. One would expect ' Moab' instead of ' Madian' (4). But the Madianites are mentioned again together with the Moabites in 7. The presence of the Madianites in Moab may be due to the migratory movements of the nomadic tribes ; *cf.* Abel, RB (1931) 225. Balac first summoned his own council and then sought the advice of the Madianites who made common cause with him. Feeling themselves unable to resist the enemy the Moabites resort to a peculiar form of strategy, that of cursing the enemy in order to render them powerless. It was a common belief shared by the Israelites themselves (Gen 9:25-27 ; 27:27-40 ; 49:3-28) that the blessings and cursings of a person living in close relations with the deity were never ineffective. The king, accordingly, sends for Balaam, requesting him to curse the Israelites. Balaam lived at Pethor (DV ' soothsayer', **5**) which is commonly identified with *Pitru* of the Assyrian inscriptions, a city on the Euphrates some 400 miles from Moab. His country is called ' the land of the Ammonites' (Vg, DV), a description which suits the historical circumstances of Balaam's story, but not the location of Pethor on the Euphrates. MT, however, instead of ' the land of the Ammonites', has ' the land of his people', a reading preferred by many interpreters, E. Palis in DBV art. *Balaam* ; Fillion, 507 ; Crampon, 529 ; E. Sutcliffe in Bi (1926) 9-18, 31-9 and (1937) 439-42). This fits in with the preceding text which states that Balaam lived at Pethor.

e Balaam promised the messengers to give them an answer the following day according to the revelation which God would make to him that night. The use of the name Yahweh by Balaam has led interpreters to believe that Balaam was a worshipper of the true God whose advice he sought and acted upon. There is no *a priori* impossibility in this, but I am more inclined to believe that Balaam knew nothing of the true God and that the name of Yahweh has been put on his lips by later scribes, who on more than one occasion have interchanged the divine names, God and Yahweh. Most probably Balaam was a heathen magician who sought revelation from *his* own god, but the response was given by Yahweh himself.

f **15-20 The Second Embassy**—Balac, not at all discouraged by Balaam's refusal, sent another embassy with the promise of richer presents. Balaam, believing that his god might have changed his mind, sought his advice once more. This time God granted him the permission to accept Balac's invitation, on condition however that he would speak under his direction.

g **21-35 Balaam's Journey**—**21.** The next morning Balaam set out with the messengers. But the journey displeased Yahweh. **22** apparently contradicts **20b**, but it is generally agreed that God disapproved of Balaam's evil intention, not of the journey ; *cf.* Sutcliffe, Bi (1926) 23. Balaam's intention was certainly perverse (32) ; he believed that God had permitted him to curse the Israelites and that he would even suggest the words for the cursing, *cf.* ' do what I shall command thee' (20) *i.e.* ' speak what I shall command thee' (35). This however was not God's intention. God intended to turn evil into good, and it was in order to bring out the opposition between Balaam's intention and that of Yahweh that the episode has been recorded. **23-35.** The historical character of the episode of the angel obstructing the road and of the dialogue between Balaam and the ass is generally maintained. But it is not improbable that the dialogue

between Balaam and the ass is to some extent a dramatic **20** representation of an unusual incident which occurred in the journey, *cf.* Card. Meignan, *L'Ancien Testament, de Moïse à David* (Paris, 1896), 216, not. 1. The writer's main concern is made manifest from **35** : ' see that thou speak no other thing than what I shall command thee'. Balaam was to act as an instrument in the hands of God independently of Balac's instructions. The **story of the ass** is a source of trouble to com- **h** mentators. Non-Catholic interpreters consider it as folklore and endeavour to find parallels in ancient stories (Gray, 334 ; Binns, 157), but Catholic interpreters have always regarded the fact as historical and miraculous (St Aug. *Quaest in Num.*, 22, PL 34, 742 ; Humm., 275, etc.) and have tried to explain the way in which the miracle was wrought. As to its historical character reference is made to the principle laid down by the Pontifical Biblical Commission concerning narratives in a historical form ; see § 52*j*.

36-40 Balaam's Arrival at Moab—Balac went to meet **i** Balaam at Ir Moab which lay on the river Arnon, on the extreme border of his kingdom. After having explained to Balac the conditions of his mission, Balaam went with him to *Qiryat ḥuṣ̂ôt*, a place of unknown situation, where numerous sacrifices were offered and substantial portions were given to the honoured guest.

41-XXIII 12 Balaam's First Oracle—On the follow- **j** ing morning Balac took Balaam to Bamoth Baal, N. of the Arnon, whence he could see an extremity of the Israelite camp and so pronounce his curses in sight of the enemy. Preparatory to Balaam's receiving God's revelation seven bullocks and seven rams were offered on seven altars. Then Balaam went some distance away and there he was commanded by God to take back to Balac the following message.

Balaam's first parabolic utterance consists of seven **k** couplets cast in synonymous parallelism. The general thought is this : I have been called by Balac to curse this people ; but how can I curse a people which is not cursed by God ? There are unmistakable signs that this people is blessed by God. It is a people dwelling by itself, segregated from other nations. Who can count these descendants of Jacob who are innumerable as the dust of the earth ? (*cf.* Gen 13:16 ; 28:24). Who can count even a fourth part (or, according to LXX, the myriads) of the Israelites (10) ? At the end Balaam expresses the desire of a happy end like that of the Israelites. Some commentators have seen in these words an allusion to the belief in a future life which, for the righteous people, will be a life of happiness (Humm., 281). It is preferable however to interpret Balaam's words in the light of OT conceptions of future life as a desire of a happy end after a prosperous life.

XXIII 13-26 Balaam's Second Oracle—Balac, be- **l** lieving he could obtain a favourable response from God if the curses were pronounced in the presence of another part of Israel, took Balaam to the top of Mt Phasga (Pisgah) which commanded an extensive view of the Israelites' camp.

Balaam's second utterance is cast in the same poetical form as the first. Its general thought is the immutability of God's purpose and the irrevocability of his blessings. God will not change his mind like us mortals. I have been instructed by God to bless and I have no power to recall God's blessings. There are no evil-doers among the Israelites (or, there is no calamity in Israel). Yahweh is in their midst, and they proclaim him their king with joyful shouts. They are invincible because God who brought them out of Egypt is as strong as the wild ox (DV ' rhinoceros'). Living in such familiarity with God they need no divination, because God announces to them in due time what he intends to do. Balac seeing that all his endeavours to get a curse from Balaam had the contrary effect of stressing the privileged position of the Israelites stopped Balaam blessing.

27-XXIV 13 Balaam's Third Oracle—Balac tries **m**

6m once more to obtain a curse from Balaam. His persistence is easily explained by the analogous heathen custom of consulting the oracle repeatedly until a favourable response is obtained. Balac accordingly took Balaam to the top of Mt Phogor which overlooks the waste land stretching out E. of the mouth of the Jordan. Balaam inspired by God delivered his third oracle which differs from the others both in form and contents. It is introduced by the title : The oracle of Balaam, the oracle of a man whose eye is closed, of a man who hears the words of God, who sees the vision of the Almighty, whose eyes are opened when he falls down. The general sense of these words seems to be this : The seer, while receiving a divine communication, has his eyes closed ; after receiving the communication, he opens his eyes and falls down in a state of exhaustion (Humm., 289). The description of the seer with closed eyes has a parallel in the magical practices of the Arabs. The seer, while in communication with god, has his eyes covered, but after the divine communication the covering falls down and his eyes are opened to the reality of the world (see I. Guidi, in *Acts of the XIV Congress of Orientalists*, II, 8–12, Algiers, 1905).

n 5-9 form the body of the oracle. The tents of Israel and consequently the Israelites who dwell in them and the land in which they are to settle, are prosperous and beautiful as fertile valleys stretching far, as gardens near the river side, as aloe-trees planted by Yahweh, as cedars by the waterside. Their prosperity will be like water overflowing from a bucket, ' and his seed shall be in many waters'. These last words hardly make any sense. A slight emendation based on LXX gives this sense : his seed, *i.e.* Israel's posterity, will be spread among many nations. If we read *z⁻rō'ô* ' his arm ' for *zar'ô* ' his seed ' a still better sense is obtained : his arm, *i.e.* Israel's power, will be over many nations. Their king is mightier than Agag, king of the Amalecites (who was conquered by Saul, 1 Kg 15), and his kingdom will be exalted. King Balac, sorely disappointed, sends Balaam away.

o XXIV 14-25 Balaam's Last Oracles—Before leaving for home Balaam foretold what the Israelites would do to the Moabites in the future. The oracle contained in **15-19** is by far the most important on account of its reference to the Messias. For **15 f.** see note to 3 f. Balaam is contemplating, in an ecstatic vision, the Israel of the future. He beholds a star rising out of Jacob, and a sceptre coming out of Israel. ' Star ' and ' sceptre ' are used here metaphorically as symbols of royal power. For the use of the term ' star ' as a royal title in the Assyrian and Egyptian literatures, see L. Dürr, *Ursprung und Ausbau der israelitisch-jüdischen Heilandserwartung* (Berlin, 1925), 105–9 ; and for the metaphorical use of the word ' sceptre ' *cf.* Gen 49:10. This mighty king will smite the chiefs of Moab, or, generically, the inhabitants of Moab, the specific meaning of the Heb. word not being clear, and he will lay waste all the sons of *tumult*, this being a designation of the Moabites, *cf.* Is 16:6 ; Jer 48 :29, 39. He will conquer Edom and Seir, the land and its enemies. Edom and Seir are synonyms, *cf.* 36:8 ; Jg 5:4. Domination will come out, or will be exercised, from Jacob, and he will destroy all the survivors from the cities.

p Commentators have always endeavoured to identify this powerful king of Israel. David, naturally, was generally considered as possessing the strongest claims. He defeated the Moabites (2 Kg 8:2), the Edomites (2 Kg 8:13, 14 ; 3 Kg 11:15) and all the neighbouring hostile peoples. But from very early times Jewish and Christian interpreters have applied this prophecy to the Messias (Just., *Dial. cum Tryph.* 106, PG 4, 450 f. ; Iren., *Contra Haer.* III, 9, 2, PG 5, 782 ; Theodoretus, *Quaest. in Num.* 44, PG 80, 394 ; Hier., *Ep. ad Oceanum*, PL 22, 695) and the Messianic interpretation has remained general in the Christian Church. The Messias is represented here as a victorious king crushing all opposition and ruling over Israel and the conquered nations. The Moabites and the Edomites are, **206p** politically, the peoples conquered, though not permanently (*cf.* the Moabite stone, § 80*j*), by David, and are mentioned out of other nations conquered by David on account of the historical circumstances of the prophecy. But at the same time they represent all the nations that will have to submit to Christ. The prophecy, though applicable to David in a limited sense, had its complete fulfilment in Christ. It is interesting to note that the nativity of Christ was announced by a star (Mt 2:2) and Christ is called the morning star (Apoc 22:16). See F. Ceuppens, *De Prophetiis messianicis in Antiquo Testamento* (Rome, 1935), 84–101.

Three more oracles are added which have no con- **q** nexion with the Moabites. The first (20) refers to the Amalecites who are described as ' the beginning of the nations ', *i.e.* the first who fought against Israel (Ex 17:8 ff.) or, with a poetic exaggeration, the most powerful of the nations, but whose end was to be utter destruction (1 Kg 15). The second (**21 f.**) refers to the Kenites. The general sense is : though the Kenites dwell in rocky, inaccessible and therefore unassailable places (note the assonance of *qēn* ' nest ' and *qēnî* ' Kenite '), they will be led into captivity by the Assyrians. What particular deportation is here referred to we are unable to say. The last oracle (**23 f.**) is very obscure and seems to refer to the period of Greek domination. Ships will come from *Kittîm*, *i.e.* Cyprus, or, according to later usage, from the western maritime countries (Vg, Italy). The Kittim will conquer Assyria and Eber who will perish for ever. A detailed explanation is impossible.

XXV The Events at Beelphegor—After the events **207a** narrated in the last two chapters the Israelites were encamped in Shittim E. of the Jordan and not far from its mouth. There they mixed with the Moabites and had immoral intercourse with their women. As a result of this intimacy they partook of the sacrificial meals to which they were invited by the Moabite women. By this idolatrous worship the Israelites attached themselves to the Moabite deity Chemosh, called here Beelphegor or ' the Lord of Peor '. This idolatry provoked God's anger who commanded Moses to execute all the chiefs responsible for this act of infidelity. The execution of this order is not related. Very probably God commanded that all the offenders should be punished, but those who were responsible were to be punished in such a way as to serve as an example for others (St Thom, 2, 2, q 108, a 1 ad 5).

While the Israelites were mourning for the death of **b** their brethren, a chief of the tribe of Simeon publicly led a Madianite woman to the camp. This act suggests either a mixed marriage or immoral intercourse. The latter is the interpretation of Vg and DV (6 ' a harlot ', Heb. ' a Madianite '). On seeing this, Phinees, the grandson of Aaron, followed them to their tent and stabbed them with his dagger. Phinees' zeal became proverbial ; *cf.* Ps 105:30 ; Ecclus 45:28 ; 1 Mac. 2:26. Phinees was rewarded by the promise of the (high) priesthood which was to remain perpetually in his family. God had already chosen Eleazar for Aaron's successor (20:25), but now the right is given to Phinees' posterity to succeed their fathers as high-priests. The Ithamar line is therefore excluded from holding the office of high-priest, at least in perpetuity.

The Israelites were then commanded to avenge themselves on the Madianites for having seduced them into idolatry. The Madianites seem to have acted at the suggestion of Balaam ; *cf.* 31:16.

XXVI The Second Census—After so many disastrous **c** events during forty years' wanderings in the desert it was necessary to number the people again, now that they were about to enter the land of Promise (see note to 1:1).

1-51 The Census—It is taken according to the same **d** general directions as in ch 1. The order of the tribes is the same, except that Manasses and Ephraim change places. For each tribe the main clan divisions are given.

207d For the value of the numbers see the remarks on ch 1. ' Spoke to them ' (3) which is the reading of MT and Vg, should probably be corrected to *numbered them*.

e **52-56 General Directions concerning the Division of the Land**—The land was to be divided among the tribes according to their numerical strength, and each portion assigned by lot. In other words the extent of the several portions was determined by the size of the several tribes, but the situation of each portion was determined by lot. See Jos 13–19.
57-62 The Census of the Levites.
63-65 Conclusion.

f **XXVII 1-11 The Law of the Inheritance of Daughters** —Hebrew custom did not give women the right to inherit. Hence if a man died without male issue his property would go out of his family. The levirate marriage was an inadequate provision against this forced alienation of the family property (Deut 25:5–10 ; see also the Introduction to the Book of Ruth, xx–xxix by C. Lattey in WV). The present law gave daughters an equal share of their father's inheritance.

g The daughters of Salphaad, putting their case before Moses and the assembly, state that their father had no part in the revolt of Core, otherwise his property would probably have been confiscated, but died for his own personal sins. As one's name was inseparable from one's land-property, their father's name would die away if his property passed into other hands outside the family circle. Their claim was recognized and a general law promulgated giving daughters the right to inherit their father's property in default of male issue. A similar practice prevailed in the ancient Near East long before Moses ; *cf*. C. H. Gordon, ' *Parallèles Nouziens aux lois et coutumes de l'A. T.*' in RB (1935) 38. The law contemplates also other cases of succession to a father's property.

h **12-23 Josue Appointed Moses' Successor**—Moses' request to be allowed to enter the Promised Land (Deut 3:25 f.) was rejected for the reason stated in 14, but he was given, before his death, a view of the land from Mt Nebo, a peak of the range of Abarim, E. of the Dead Sea and the Jordan. The punishment may appear disproportionate to his fault, especially considering his faithful service for so many years. ' But the divine majesty had to be vindicated, and a public failure atoned for, by a striking and impressive punishment : moreover there was another Land of Promise from which Moses was not excluded by his offence ' (Binns, 189). It may be added that the divine punishments are proportionate not only to the gravity of the offence in itself but also to the position of the offender and to the degree of sanctity demanded of him.

i Moses humbly submitted to God's dispositions and asked him, the author of life (16:22), to appoint a successor who would lead the people into the Promised Land. Josue was chosen, a man endowed *with spirit*, *i.e.* the spirit of wisdom (Deut 34:9), or, in a general sense, ability for leadership. Moses was then commanded to lay his hands on Josue. The rite of imposition of hands in the O and NT has more than one significance ; *cf*. see J. Coppens, *L'Imposition des mains et les rites connexes dans le Nouveau Testament et dans l'Eglise ancienne* (Paris, 1925), esp. 162 f. Here it symbolizes the transference of power and may be compared with the analogous rite in the ordination of the Levites (8:10). Moses was further commanded to bestow upon Josue ' a part of his glory ', *i.e.* publicly to declare him to possess authority over the people and therefore to have the right to their obedience. Josue would stand before the priest, *i.e.* he would have an inferior position ; the priest would consult God for him by the use of the Urim (Ex 28:30), and both Josue and the people should abide by the instructions communicated to them by God through the priest. The secular authority was thus subordinated to the ecclesiastical authority.

208a **XXVIII-XXIX A Liturgical Calendar**—In Lev 23 a list of the yearly feast-days is given, here we have a table defining the sacrifices which are to be offered on **20** each festival.

1, 2 Introduction—The Israelites must regularly present to God the offerings due to him which are anthropomorphically represented as God's food.
3-8 The Daily Offerings—See Ex 29:38–42 ; Lev 6:8–13.
9, 10 The Sabbath-Offering—This was of equal value to the daily offering, and offered in addition to it.
11-15 The Offerings of the First Day of each Month—In 13 read : *one-tenth part of an ephah*.
16-25 The Offerings of Paschal Week—Liturgical prescriptions taken from Lev 23:5–8 with additional instructions.
26-31 The Offerings of the Day of the Firstfruits, called also the feast of Weeks (Lev 23:15–22).
XXIX 1-6 The Offerings for the Day of Trumpets— **b** See Lev 23:23–25. Since this festival fell on the first day of the month the offerings prescribed here were in addition to those prescribed in 28:11–15.
7-11 The Offerings for the Day of Atonement—See Lev 23:26–32 and Lev 16.
12-38 The Offerings for the Feast of Tabernacles—See Lev 23:33 ff.
39 Conclusion—These are public offerings made on behalf of the whole community. In addition any person may present freewill and vow-offerings on any of these festivals.
XXX On Vows especially those made by Women— **c** The following regulations are based on the principle that women are subject to their fathers or husbands, and therefore, without their approval, cannot promise to God anything that will interfere with the management of the house.
3 General Principle—If a man makes a vow to the Lord, or binds himself by oath to some abstinence, he shall keep his promise.
4-6 The Vows of an Unmarried Woman—If a marriageable girl makes a vow, the vow will be valid if the father, on becoming aware of it, does not express his disapproval. If he disapproves, her vow is annulled.
7-9, 11-16 The Vows of a Married Woman—A hus- **d** band has the right to veto his wife's vows, whether they were made before marriage or, inconsiderately, during marriage. God has no delight in hasty vows, Eccl 5:4. If a husband, after having tacitly approved his wife's vows, pretends to annul them, he will be guilty of a breach of promise, but his wife will be guiltless.

The vows of a widow and those of a divorced woman **e** are valid, **10**, as these women are no longer subject to their husbands. In **17** delete ' or ' (DV).
XXXI The Extermination of the Madianites—The **f** story is alleged to be an unhistorical account illustrating the way certain instructions such as those concerning total war, the removal of uncleanness through contact with the dead, and the distribution of the booty were to be carried out (Gray, 418). The reasons are not convincing. Certain apparent inconsistencies are due to rules of style and to the particular scope of the writer. Many important details are purposely left out and the whole campaign is represented as a single event of short duration. There may be rhetorical exaggeration in numbers as well as in the assertion that all the male Madianites were slain and their cities burnt down. See § 211*g*.
1-10 The Expedition—The incidents which caused **g** this war are related in ch 25. Moses organized an expedition of 12,000 men under the command of Phinees. The reason why Phinees, the priest, not Josue, the future leader of the people, is chosen as commander may be the zeal displayed by him for Yahweh's honour on another occasion (25:7 f.). He carried with him ' the holy vessels and the trumpets to sound '. On the trumpets see 10:1–10. What is meant by ' holy vessels ' is not clear. Humm. (345) takes them to mean the sacred vestments. The phrase ' the trumpets to sound ' must perhaps be read in apposition to ' the holy vessels '. The campaign was successful.

8h 11-18 Slaughter of Prisoners—When the warriors returned with prisoners and booty Moses disapproved of their sparing the women and the children and ordered that all the women who were either married or deflowered, and all the male children should be slain, the former for having seduced the Israelites into idolatry and immorality, the latter in order to ensure a total extinction of the Madianite race. The virgins alone were to be spared and given as a prize to the combatants (*cf.* Jg 21-11). The possibility of the girls seducing their husbands or masters was disregarded, but mixed marriages were, as a rule, prohibited; *cf.* Ex 34:16; 3 Kg 11:2.

i 19-24 Purification of the Warriors and the Spoil—The warriors owing to their state of defilement (Num 19:16-19) had to stay outside the camp until they purified themselves and the spoil according to the rite prescribed in Num 19:14-22. On this occasion Eleazar gave some further regulations. All objects of metal that could stand the fire were to be purified by fire and by the water of purification. All other objects were purified by water only.

j 25-47 The Division of the Spoil—The whole booty was to be divided into two equal parts between the combatants and those who remained in the camp. David acted in the same way (1 Kg 30 : 24, 25). Out of each moiety a tribute was to be paid to the Lord. The *contribution* of the warriors consisted of 1-500th of their entire portion and was handed over to Eleazar; that of the rest of the people was fixed at 1-50th of their share and was assigned to the Levites. Thus, although the booty was divided into two equal portions, the individual shares of those who fought were in reality greater than those of the non-combatants.

k 48-54 The Present of the Officers—The officers, of their own freewill and as a token of gratitude to Yahweh, made another offering to God consisting of various gold ornaments weighing 16,750 shekels, or *c* 5½ cwt.

l XXXII The Transjordanic Region is granted to the Tribes of Ruben and Gad and the half-tribe of Manasses —The tribes of Ruben and Gad, with whom the half-tribe of Manasses is later (33) associated, asked Moses to be allowed to settle down in the land E. of the Jordan. The request was granted under certain conditions.

m 1-5 The Request—Seeing that the land of Jazer and the land of Galaad were lands of pasture the Rubenites and the Gadites asked to settle there. The land of Jazer is the city of Jazer and its adjacent pasture-land. ' The land of Galaad ' sometimes denotes the whole region E. of the Jordan (Deut 3:12 f.); sometimes it is restricted to the country, S. of the river Jabbok, or N. of it, the river Jabbok being considered as dividing the land of Galaad into two halves (Jos 12:2). In this chapter it is used in both these restricted senses. As the places mentioned in **3** are all situated S. of the Jabbok, the land of Galaad in **1** designates southern Galaad (on Galaad, see SHG, ch 28).

n 6-32 The Request first Refused and then Granted—The request, if granted, would have encouraged the other tribes to stay where they were and give up all prospects of further conquests. This would frustrate God's promise and thus provoke his wrath, as on the occasion of the mission of the spies (chh 13 f.). In order to avert both consequences Moses strongly opposed their demands. The representatives of the two tribes explained to Moses that their request did not imply a refusal to take part in the conquest of the land W. of the Jordan. After assuring adequate protection for their wives, children, flocks and herds in the territory allotted to them, they would pass over the Jordan to fight together with the other tribes. Their explanation was accepted by Moses who directed that southern Galaad be assigned to them.

o 33-42 The Territory of the Rubenites, the Gadites and the half-tribe of Manasses—The 14 cities mentioned in **34-38** are all situated in a strip of land E. of the Dead Sea and the Jordan, measuring *c* 800 sq. miles. No

line of demarcation between the two groups of cities **208o** can be drawn. It appears that each city was provisionally assigned to either tribe, the definite demarcation being made later by Josue (Jos 13:8-28).

Of the tribe of Manasses some clans only had their **p** territory E. of the Jordan. The clan of Machir conquered northern Galaad. Jair, another Manassite clan, took the tent-villages (Heb. *ḥawwôt*) and called them after its name. This district was, very probably, in Galaad itself (Jg 10:3-5; 3 Kg 4:13; 1 Par 2:22) and SE. of the lake of Genesareth. Nobe, another clan, took the district of Canath, which was probably E. of Jair and on the western slopes of the Hauran.

XXXIII 1-49 The Itinerary from Egypt to Moab—This is **209a** a summary of the forty years' journeyings in the desert from Egypt to Moab through the various stages of the journey. The list of the stations is not complete. Many places cannot be identified with any degree of probability. Most of them have already been mentioned in Exodus or Numbers, but a few occur here for the first time. The description of the itinerary is said to have been written by Moses (2), valuable information for the determination of the authorship of this document. For the whole section see Abel, II, 208-17).

50-56 Directions respecting the Occupation of the b Land of Canaan—The Israelites are commanded : (i) to drive out and *dispossess* (**53**) all the inhabitants; a partial extermination will have for its effects retaliation by the Canaanites, seduction into idolatry, and punishment by God; (ii) to destroy all idolatrous representations carved on stone, and the molten images of their deities; (iii) to demolish all their high places, or places of worship (for a description of Canaanitish high places see *S. R. Driver, Modern Research as illustrating the Bible*, London, 1922, 60 f.); (iv) to divide the land by lot as prescribed in 26:55.

XXXIV The Boundaries of the Promised Land W. of c the Jordan—*Cf.* Ez 47:13-20. A distinction must be drawn between the boundaries promised by God and those actually possessed by the Israelites. The description given here is an ideal one representing the extension of the territory which the Israelites had the right to conquer, but which in point of fact they never completely conquered. Thus the western border, which is represented as running along the Mediterranean coast, was never in the hands of the Israelites, save for a small stretch in its central part, and even that for a short time only. The reason for this distinction is that God's promise was conditional, *i.e.* subject to the faithful observance of his law by the Israelites; *cf.* Jos 23:12 f.; Jg 3:1-4. The territory of Israel reached its greatest expansion during the reign of David.

3-5 The Southern Border—This is described in a **d** general way as running from the wilderness of Sin (13:21) along the side of Edom. More particularly the southern line started from the southernmost extremity of the Dead (or Salt) Sea on the east, turned to the south of the ascent or pass of *Aqrabbim*, passed through Sin, an unknown place, reached the south of Qadesh Barnea and followed its course to the Mediterranean Sea along the torrent of Egypt (=Wady el-'Arish) after passing through Hasar Addar and 'Asmon.

6 The Western Border ran along the coast of the **e** Mediterranean Sea.

7-9 The Northern Border extended from an undefined **f** point on the Mediterranean coast, reached *Mt Hor*, of uncertain identification but certainly different from that of Aaron's death (20:22), went to the pass of Emath (13:21) and ended at Ḥaṣar 'Enan, probably between Damascus and the Hauran, after passing through Sedada and Zephron.

10-12 The Eastern Border started from Ḥaṣar 'Enan **g** to Sepham, then it descended to Rebla east of an anonymous spring which an interpolation in the Vg arbitrarily calls ' Daphnis ', flanked the eastern side of the lake of Genesareth and followed the course of the Jordan down to the Dead Sea.

13-15 Conclusion.

209g 16-29 Appointment of Twelve Superintendents for the Division of the Land—*Cf.* Jos chh 14-19.

h XXXV 1-8 The Levitical Cities—As no territory was assigned to the Levites, provision was to be made whereby they could possess at least some cities to dwell in and the surrounding land for their flocks. The several tribes were therefore commanded to cede to the Levites some of their cities in proportion to the size of their respective territories. The execution of the command is related in Jos 21. The Levitical cities were 48 in all including the 6 cities of refuge (*cf.* 9-15). It is difficult to form a correct idea of the geometrical disposition of the Levitical possessions. In **4** the pasture-land extends 1,000 cubits, or 1,500 feet, from the wall of the city, and each side of the pasture-land is 2,000 cubits long (**5**). Some interpreters describe the Levitical possessions as consisting of a city and four square plots of ground, one on each side of the city and not adjoining each other (Humm., 373). But **5** implies that the whole space is a perfect square. But a square of 2,000 × 2,000 cubits and a width of 1,000 cubits from the outer line of the pasture-land to the inner wall of the city leaves no space for the city. Apart from the possibility of textual corruption (the LXX has 2,000 cubits in **4** instead of 1,000) there may be some artificiality in the numbers and in the description of the Levitical possessions.

i 9-34 The Cities of Refuge—Primitive social organization considered every individual as an inseparable part of his clan. Hence an offence against an individual was regarded as an offence against the whole clan and demanded adequate reparation. The Hebrew law modified this ancient custom by distinguishing between voluntary and involuntary manslaughter, and giving the right of blood-revenge to the next-of-kin only.

The right of sanctuary was common almost down to modern times when it had to be abolished on account of the abuses to which it led (see J. B. Sägmuller in CE art. *Privileges, in fin.*).

j 9-15 The Appointment of Six Cities of Refuge—If a man kills anyone he becomes liable to be slain by the nearest kinsman of the murdered person. Hebrew legislation modified this custom by establishing the principle that accidental killing cannot be punished by death. But the acquittal of an unintentional homicide is subject to certain conditions. He must appear before the assembly or popular council who will decide whether the killing was wilful or not, and, in case of an unintentional killing, the homicide will take refuge in an asylum where he will be safe from the blood-avenger. For the purpose of this law six cities were to be selected, the names of which are given in Jos 20:7 f.

k 16-23 Distinction between Wilful and Unintentional Killing—The killing was to be presumed wilful : (i) when the death was caused by an instrument the use of which was likely to be fatal, such as an instrument of iron, a heavy stone, a wooden instrument or staff ; (ii) when, failing this evidence, the relations between the homicide and the dead person were unfriendly, or when the death was premeditated. On the contrary the death was to be presumed to have been unintentional when, though it was caused by a murderous instrument, the relations between the two persons were friendly, and still more when the instrument was not in itself lethal. Therefore four cases may be distinguished : 1. Wilful murder : (i) death premeditated and caused by a murderous instrument ; (ii) death premeditated and caused by a non-murderous instrument. 2. Unintentional homicide : (i) unpremeditated death caused by a murderous instrument ; (ii) unpremeditated death caused by a non-murderous instrument.

l 24-32 Legal Procedure—All cases of killing must be decided according to these principles. If it is legally proved that the death was wilful, the murderer is delivered into the hands of the murdered person's relatives. But if the death was accidental, the innocent man-slayer is taken to his city of refuge where he must remain till the death of the high-priest. If during his period of detention the man-slayer leaves his asylum, he is no longer protected by the law. Only at the death of the high-priest is he allowed to return to his home.

m Further laws are added. In capital sentences at least two witnesses are required (*cf.* Deut 17:6 ; 19:15). It is forbidden to accept money as a ransom for the life of a wilful murderer and to allow the innocent man-slayer to return home before the death of the high-priest. Detention in a city of refuge was not only a deliverance from the hands of the blood-avenger, but also a sort of punishment for the shedding of human blood.

n 33-34 Hortatory Conclusion—The land of the Israelites is the habitation of Yahweh and therefore must be kept free from defilement. Bloodshed defiles the land, and this defilement cannot be expiated except by the blood of him that shed the blood.

o XXXVI The Marriage of Daughters possessing Landed Property—It had already been decided that daughters had the right to inherit their fathers' property when there was no male issue (27:1-11). This concession now raised an important case. If an heiress married outside her tribe, her property would go to another tribe which would consequently have its territory increased, while that of the wife's tribe would be diminished. Such a transference of property not being made by sale, was unaffected by the Jubilee concessions (Lev 25:13 ff.), and was therefore likely to produce a certain fluctuation and instability of the tribal possessions, and perhaps even an extensive absorption of one tribe by another. In order to prevent this inconvenience the principle was laid down that the tribe and its possessions were inseparable and therefore no property of one tribe could be transferred to another. According to this principle it was decided that the daughters of Salphaad should marry whom they pleased but within their own tribe.

DEUTERONOMY

By R. A. F. MACKENZIE, S.J.

0a Bibliography—F. de Hummelauer, S.J., *Deuteronomium*, CSS, 1901 ; A. Clamer, *Le Deutéronome*, in Pirot-Clamer, *La Sainte Bible*, II, Paris, 1940, reprinted 1946 (full and up-to-date) ; H. Junker, *Das Buch Deuteronomium*, BB, 1933 (briefer, more original work); *S. R. Driver, *Deuteronomy*, ICC, 1902³ ; *G. A. Smith *The Book of Deuteronomy*, CBSC, Cambridge, 1918 ; *H. Wheeler Robinson, *Deuteronomy and Joshua*, in CBi, London, n.d.

b Name—Deut is the last of the five books of which the Jewish *Tôrāh*, the Law, is composed. The name, meaning strictly ' a second law ', is taken from the LXX's faulty translation of a phrase in 17:18, properly ' a copy of this law ' ; but it is apt enough, since the book contains a later form, with some additional material, of much of the legislation of Ex and Num, presented as a second covenant, distinct from that of Sinai.

c Form and Contents—Unlike the other books of the Pentateuch, Deut is to be classified formally not as history or legislation but as oratory. It is a **homiletic exposition of law in an historical setting,** and in it both law and history are so treated as to produce the maximum of conviction and persuasion in the hearers. Hence the constant urging of motives, the impassioned tone of personal appeal, which make this ' book of the Law ' so very different from ordinary legal codes, whether ancient or modern. The greater part of the book is composed of three discourses, presented as spoken by Moses to the people of Israel in the land of Moab, shortly before his death. The second and longest speech contains the large body of legislation which is known as the Code of Deuteronomy. The last four chh of the book, distinct in composition from the speeches, form a conclusion to the Pentateuch as a whole. Neglecting some minor and transitional sections (1:1–5 ; 4:41–49 ; 32:44–52), the following scheme gives the outline of the book :

d I. 1:6-4:40 The First Discourse.
  1. 1:6–3:29 Historical section
  2. 4:1–40 Hortatory Section

II. 5:1-29:1 The Second Discourse.
  1. 5:1–11:32 Exhortation
    (*a*) 5:1–33 The Covenant of Sinai (the Decalogue)
    (*b*) 6:1–25 Duty of Faithfulness to Yahweh
    (*c*) 7:1–26 Duty of Exterminating the Canaanites
    (*d*) 8:1–20 Gratitude for God's Care in the Desert
    (*e*) 9:1–10:11 Past History as a Warning against Presumption
    (*f*) 10:12–11:32 Exhortation for the Future

  2. 12:1–26:19 **The Code of Deuteronomy.**
    (*a*) 12:2–16:17 ; 16:21–17:7 Religious Laws
    (*b*) 16:18–20 ; 17:8–18:22 Laws concerning Authorities
    (*c*) 19:1–25:19 Civil, Penal and Miscellaneous Laws
    (*d*) 26:1–15 Two Liturgical Ordinances

  3. 27:1–26 Directions for Memorial Ceremonies (an insertion, independent of the main discourse)

  4. 26:16–19 ; 28:1–29:1 Conclusion

III. 29:2-30:20 The Third Discourse. 210d

IV. 31:1-34:12 The Last Days of Moses.
  1. 31:1–21 Instructions to Josue
  2. 31:22–32:43 The Canticle
  3. 33:1–29 The Blessing of the Tribes
  4. 34:1–12 The Death of Moses

Style—Corresponding to the oratorical character of **e** Deut is its style of composition, unique among the books of the OT. Solemn, emphatic, repetitious, even tautologous, this style is a remarkable effort to expand the simple, limited syntax of classical Hebrew into sonorous and rhythmical oratorical periods. A number of phrases, such as ' Yahweh, your God ' or ' our God ', ' attach oneself to God ', ' with one's whole heart and one's whole soul ', etc., are so frequent here and so rare elsewhere as to form a distinct phraseology. And the fervent and reiterated exhortations to act in accordance with the doctrine taught are matched only by the equally passionate eloquence of some of the prophets.

Origin—Christian tradition has constantly held that **211a** Deut, as part of the Law, is to be attributed to Moses. Most non-Catholic scholars, however, in the last 100 years, have held that it is a 7th cent. composition, with nothing Mosaic about it. This ' liberal ' view, generally associated with the name of Wellhausen, was based chiefly on singularities of phraseology and diction (alluded to in § 210*e*) ; on inconsistencies and contradictions between the Code of Deut and the Book of the Covenant (Ex 20:23–23:19) and the Priestly Code (Lev) respectively ; on the remarkable correspondence between King Josias' religious reform (4 Kg 22 f., 2 Par 34) and the prescriptions of Deut ; on a conception of Israelite history as developing *in vacuo*, little touched by preceding or neighbouring cultures ; and, not least, on a philosophical concept of history as a unilinear evolution from less perfect to more perfect and from the simple to the complex. But greatly increased knowledge of the Ancient East and its literatures has occasioned, in the last 30 years, a growing tendency to reject W.'s conclusions as over-simplified, and to admit a more or less large proportion of ' Mosaic material ' in Deut. The philosophical bases of the theory are rejected, and more moderate and ' traditional ' explanations given of the other phenomena. Catholic writers, on the other hand, have steadily **b** maintained the ' substantial Mosaic authenticity ' of Deut (as of the rest of the Pentateuch), laid down by the 4th response of the Biblical Commission in 1906 (*cf.* § 48*d*) ; they have, however, varied considerably in their interpretations of this phrase, and there is as yet no general agreement on a satisfactory solution. The responses of the Commission itself make clear that it is not necessary to hold that Moses wrote or dictated every line of the book, nor even that its literary form is due to him—since it might be attributable to his ' secretaries '. He may also have used—with or without adaptations—earlier sources. Finally, an unspecified amount of additions may have accrued to the book after Moses' time. Some authors, inclining to a strict interpretation of these responses, have therefore held that Moses wrote a work substantially identical with our present Deut, to which was gradually added in succeeding centuries a small

211b quantity of notes, supplements, or glosses. Others, finding it difficult on these grounds to account for various characteristics which seemed to indicate a post-Mosaic date, have ventured on a broader interpretation, suggesting that the book contains the teaching and legislation of Moses—the latter in the form that it assumed after several centuries of evolution ; but that this material was composed into a book by a later writer, who was also inspired and to whom would be due its distinctive style and phraseology. It must be noted that in such a view there is no question of a belated adoption by Catholics of a position long taken for granted by those outside the Church. (The only such position so far has been that of Wellhausen, and its inadequacy has been abundantly demonstrated.) It is simply an effort at finding 'an explanation which will be faithfully consonant with the teaching of the Church, particularly with the traditional doctrine of the inerrancy of Scripture, while being at the same time in due conformity with the certain conclusions of profane sciences' (DAS §48).

The question has been put on a new footing by the recent (1948) letter of the Biblical Commission to Cardinal Suhard (cf. § 53k), which is a significant expression of the present mind of the Holy See on the subject. This letter lays down (not as an adventurous proposition that may be tolerated, but as a starting point, universally agreed to) that the Mosaic legislation, as well as the narrative sections of the Pentateuch, underwent a steady growth (un accroissement progressif) after Moses' time ; it further indicates that the responses of 1906 are not to be taken as settling the question once and for all, but are to be properly understood and interpreted in the light of certain paragraphs in the recent Encyclical. It is in the light of this letter, naturally, that the Commission's early decrees must henceforth be understood. In any view, then, a development of the Mosaic legislation, over a period of nearly a thousand years, must be allowed for. The Law was not from the first, what it had become by NT times, a sacrosanct formulary whose least phrase was sacred and untouchable. Rather it was something vital and growing, moulding the ethos of the people but also being itself moulded and developed in response to changing conditions and new situations. Its 'fossilization' probably did not occur before the time of Esdras. But it developed always from the principles and along the lines laid down by its first and principal author. Naturally those who committed to writing new laws or modified old ones, in so far as they contributed to the sacred text, enjoyed the charism of inspiration. In general, the form of the legislation in Deut seems to have been fixed at a stage midway between that of Ex and that of Lev.

The Law of the One Sanctuary—The principle set
c forth in the last paragraph is of some importance in considering the central law of the Deut Code in ch 12, which allows only one sanctuary in Palestine, where sacrifice may be offered to Yahweh. What relation has this prescription to the quite different laws regarding the place of sacrifice in Ex 20:22–26 and Lev 17:1–7 ? and further to the actual practice—also very different —followed by the Israelites in Palestine down to the time of Josias ? The following historical reconstruction may be proposed, but without any claim to be a definitive solution. At Sinai a cult law was promulgated, laying down that the worship of Yahweh must differ both in *manner* and in *place* from the cult of idols : in manner, by the abstention from images ; in place, by not sacrificing to him anywhere, but only at the spots that he should choose and indicate by a theophany or other sign. Sinai of course was the first of such sacred places ; cf. Ex 24:5. After the departure thence the Tabernacle, wherever it was, became the centre of the cult, and during the Wandering no other public sacrifices, at least, were allowed than those performed before the Tabernacle (Lev 17), though this law too may have allowed exceptions from time to time. Thus

a certain centralization of the cult was practised, which **21** Moses directed to be continued after the conquest of Palestine, as soon as settled conditions should allow the tribes to be periodically united in one place. But the conquest took so long, and the tribes were so scattered, that this command remained for centuries no more than a vague and vaguely-remembered ideal. The idea of a central sanctuary was kept alive—at first by the Ark at Shiloh and later by the temple in Jerusalem. We have striking evidence for a centralized worship at the latter (c 930 B.C.) in Jeroboam's action (3 Kg 12:26 ff.) in erecting sanctuaries at Dan and Bethel, expressly to prevent the Northerners from going to sacrifice at Jerusalem. This makes it clear that the law of one sanctuary, the temple, was well established and usually recognized by the orthodox, in spite of abuses. But the strict corollary, that *only* in this place should Yahweh be (sacrificially) worshipped, was in practice forgotten, or at least disregarded. Smaller Yahweh sanctuaries were in existence all over the country, often on the sites of Canaanite high places, and sacrifices were offered to him there, in all good faith, even by the prophets (see e.g. 1 Kg 9:12 f. ; 3 Kg 3:2–4 ; 1 Par 21:26 ff.). Nevertheless, in proportion as Israel learnt to adopt the Canaanite civilization (under the monarchy), the frequent contamination of these rites with pagan practices, and perhaps the identification, or at least association, of Yahweh with the local Ba'als in a syncretistic cult, became a scandal to all who had preserved a tradition of the Mosaic teaching on the transcendence and exclusiveness of the cult due to Yahweh. Partial measures of reform were undertaken by Ezechias (728–700 B.C.) ; and a thorough enforcement of the law in its strictest sense was made by Josias (641–609 B.C.). See also § 112a–d.

For the question of the 'book of the law of Moses' **d** found in the temple in 621 B.C. see on 4 Kg 22 and § 135d. The book was no doubt some edition of Deut ; but be it noted (against many critics) that the reform was at least started prior to, hence without dependence on, the discovery of the book. The chronological order of events is given in 2 Par 34, not in 4 Kg 22 ; and Josias feared the wrath of Yahweh for his fathers' infidelity, but had a clear conscience as to his own practice. Hence, even on the supposition of the late composition of Deut, it was not composed as the 'programme' for Josias' reform, but rather both it and the reform were products of the same movement. **Doctrine**—Deut is a treasure-house of practical theology, expounded with a warmth and eloquence **e** that touch the heart. The purpose of the discourses, never lost from sight, is to produce an unshakable fidelity to **God**, based on a realization of his transcendence and majesty, of his overflowing love for his Chosen People, of the kindness he has shown them and will yet show them in the future. For the Israelite this fidelity means observing the obligations of the Covenant : negatively, by having nothing to do with strange gods and their cult ; positively, by devotion to the cult of Yahweh and by keeping his commandments.

God is One, supreme ; sole Lord of man and of all that **f** is. ' I, I am the One ; and there is no other god but me' (32:39). In contrast to the 'gods' of the other nations, his relation to his people is not a natural one based on locality, function, or blood-relationship ; it is arbitrary and historical. He could have chosen any people : he did choose Israel—but out of sheer compassion, not for their importance or moral excellence. Israel has made a poor return for this astonishing kindness—Deut deals unsparingly with their obstinacy, infidelity, and ingratitude—but though he may punish for a time, they are still his people. Of all the divine attributes, Deut most stresses **Love**—the original free choice of an insignificant group, the granting of the Covenant, the fostering and protection against oppressors, the frequent—all too frequent !—forgiveness, the training in the Desert, the richness of the land

211f set aside for them, the desire to see them prospering and 'rejoicing before Yahweh'. The emphasis on joy, too (*cf.* 12:18 ; 16:14 f. ; etc.), is peculiar to Deut, as are also the kindness and thoughtful charity enjoined, towards one's neighbour, towards the helpless, and even towards dumb animals.

Israel's obligations arising from the above are clear. No temptation or weakness will excuse failure in this loyalty, based on every possible reason of obligation, of gratitude, of honour. And—not to omit any motive that may stimulate human weakness—the terrible results of God's displeasure, if they should still turn their backs on him, are eloquently set forth.

g A word must be said here about the **anathema** (2:34 ; 3:6 ; 7:2, etc.), a practice which is repugnant to the humane feelings inculcated by two thousand years of Christianity and seems to be inconsistent with the loving-kindness of God. But the difficulty will vanish once we replace this custom in its setting, and view it in the light of the religious and cultural conditions of the 13th cent. Israelites. Here, as in so many other points of primitive Israelite legislation—status of women, treatment of strangers, sexual morality, etc.— an intermediate stage of ethics, which seems so crude when we look back on it, represented in fact a considerable advance over what went before. The anathema, or ban (*herem*), meant originally that which is or must be separated and set aside, particularly that which, on account of some inherent evil, would be dangerous to the people ; in practice it meant killing living creatures and dedicating material things to use in the sanctuary or to destruction. The institution was not peculiar to Israel. Mesha, king of Moab in the 9th cent. B.C., records of his successful expedition against the Israelite city Nebo : ' I captured it and killed (them) all, 7,000 men and women, boys and girls, for I had made them anathema to Astarte-Chemosh'. For the ancient Semites war was a religious exercise, fought under their god's direction for the extension of his dominion, and captives and spoils were in the first place at the god's disposal ; if odious to him, they must be destroyed. This practice Moses regulated for the people of Yahweh ; it was to be strictly applied only to those who otherwise would be morally certain to corrupt Israel's faith. *Cf.* the distinction in 20:15 ff. between peoples in Palestine and elsewhere. In practice, the prescription was applied with varying degrees of severity or not at all, and Israelites and Canaanites intermingled to a large extent, with the inevitable results for the religion of the former. *Cf.* Jos 6:17 ff. ; 7:1 ff. ; 8:2 ; 11:8 ff. ; 1 Kg 15 ; Ps 105: 34 f. ; etc. With regard to the cruelty of the practice, according to Christian ideas, this may be said : (1) God, as Creator and sovereign Lord, may end the life he has given, as well by the agency of other men as by ' natural ' causes ; *cf.* the command to Abraham to sacrifice Isaac. (2) The Israelites—Moses included— were children of their time, and could rise only slowly to loftier conceptions of morality ; *cf.* the permission of divorce, expressly attributed by our Lord to ' the hardness of your heart ' (Mt 19:8 and par.). (3) By limiting the *herem* to those occasions when the people's fidelity to Yahweh was at stake, Moses did at least exclude the idea that God took any pleasure in the killing as such ; it was not on his account but on theirs. Contrast Mesha's remark on another Israelite city, ' I killed all its inhabitants, a (pleasing) sight for Chemosh', and the large-scale tortures and massacres by which the Assyrian kings rejoiced the heart of Aššur. The early Hebrew ethics, certainly, are inferior to those taught in the NT ; they are nonetheless in advance of those of contemporary and neighbouring peoples. See also §§ 110*f*, 208*f*.

h Christian Applications—The lessons of fidelity and gratitude so eloquently set forth in Deut sound with redoubled force in the ears of the Catholic. To every exhortation he can add, ' *A fortiori*, so should I '. To the choice of Israel, and the Covenant, he can add the Incarnation, his incorporation into Christ, and the history of the working of God's grace in his soul. And **211h** the fidelity which the inspired text preaches is for him not to the old Law and the worship of the temple, but to the teaching of the Gospel and the life of the Church.

I 1-5 Preliminary Verses—As **1** gives the conclusion **212a** of what precedes, it should really be attached to the book of Numbers. Deut is concerned only with the final lawgiving in Moab, not with the other places named, which are not only ' beyond the Jordan ' (from the Palestinian viewpoint) but far to the south. **2** as it stands seems to be a fragment out of place. **3** is a first introductory note ; ' fortieth year '—*scil.* after leaving Egypt ; forty is a round number, indicating the passing of one generation. **4 f.** is a second introduction ; in **5**, read a comma after ' Moab ' and omit ' And '. Note the word ' expound ' ; in Deut the Law is not simply announced but preached.

**I 6-IV 40 The First Discourse : the Lesson of History. b
I 6-III 29 Historical Section:
I 6-46 The First Approach to Palestine**—The orator recalls to the people their experiences since the revelation at Horeb (Deut's word for Sinai) ; Yahweh ordered them then, a generation earlier, to begin the conquest of Palestine from the south ; but it miscarried, through their want of trust in him. **7**. ' *Go up towards the hill country of the Amorites and all their neighbours, in the Jordan valley, in the highlands and in the Shephelah and in the Negeb and on the sea-coast.*' For the Shephelah *cf.* § 55*a*, for the Negeb § 54*h*. ' Euphrates ' is probably an erroneous gloss—the river referred to would be the Leontes. **9-17. Appointment of Subordinate Judges**—*Cf.* Ex 18:13-26. Jethro's part is here passed over, as not bearing on the orator's purpose. Moses chose suitable men, and (**15**) ' appointed them *rulers over thousands, and rulers over hundreds, and rulers over fifties, and rulers over tens*' —a civil organization based on military cadres. **19-46** summarizes the first, frustrated, attempt at the conquest of Palestine (see Num 13 f.). **19**. ' By the way of . . . ' : this idiom must not be understood like the Latin *viâ* ; it means ' *by the way that leads (eventually) to* '. So in 40 below, 2:1, 8, etc. The verse ends ' *And we arrived* at Kadesh-barnea ' ; the sending of the explorers *preceded* this arrival. **22 ff.** The brief account here stresses points that aggravated the people's guilt : they themselves had proposed the exploration (a detail omitted in Num 13:2 f. where it is given as a command of Yahweh), and they passed over the favourable account of the land to dwell on the discouraging news of its inhabitants. **28.** Enacims (Anakim) : see on 9:2. **41*b*.** ' *And everyone of you girded on his battle-array, and you thought it an easy thing to go up into the hill-country.*' The people passed abruptly from despair to presumption—both sins contrary to their due trust in Yahweh. **42.** Moses kept the ark, the sign of Yahweh's presence, in the camp, instead of letting it go in the van of the attack. **46.** ' A long time ' ; traditionally, one generation. Apparently in this period the Israelites led a semi-nomadic pastoral life, with the water-supply in the neighbourhood of Kadesh-barnea as their rallying-point.

II 1-15 The Second Approach to Palestine—not **c** directly from the south, but through Transjordan, from the east. (*Cf.* Num 20 f.) **2-8. The Transit through Edom**—According to Num 20:14 ff. Moses applied to the Edomites (in terms very similar to Yahweh's instructions here) for permission to cross their territory and was decisively refused. This necessitated a long detour to the south with eventually a march northward to Moab along the east side of Edom. This refusal is not mentioned in Deut ; and it becomes a question whether it should be understood here between **7** and **8** (so that Yahweh's instructions could not be put into practice), or in **1**, before the ' compassing of Mt Seir ' (which was Edomite territory). If the latter, then there were *two* applications to cross Edom, some 38 years apart, of which the later one was granted, and would be referred to here in 8 (reading with LXX ' passed *through* ') and in 29. **10-12** is an archaeological

212c note, awkwardly inserted in Yahweh's speech, giving popular traditions of the pre-Canaanite population of Palestine and Transjordan, who developed a flourishing chalcolithic culture 4000–3000 B.C. **13.** The first phrase is the conclusion of the speech in 9 : ' " *Now rise and cross the Wady Zared.*" *And we crossed the Wady Zared*'. This watercourse (modern W. el-Hesa) was evidently felt to mark the edge of the ' wilderness ' ; once it was crossed, the Wandering was over. **14** refers, not to the ' departure ' from Kadesh-barnea of 1, but to the ' going up ' (to attack Canaan) of 1:43, which occasioned the punishment of the long delay in the desert.

d **16-37 The Victory over Sehon**—**18.** ' Pass the border ', *i.e.* skirt the territory, not passing through. **20-23.** *Cf.* 10–12 above. **24.** If Yahweh's instructions really preceded Moses' message to Sehon (**26 ff.**), the latter has a strange air of insincerity ; yet there was really none, according to the Israelite conception of God's providence. Moses was making sure that his people would be blameless—and the fault fell only on Sehon, thanks to his ' hardened spirit '. On the other hand, since **31** repeats 24, the divine order may have come after Sehon's answer. In the concrete, this answer, in these circumstances, *was* the divine order—24 is how the Israelites would formulate it. **34.** For ' killing ' read ' *making anathema* ' ; see § 211*g*.

e **III 1-7 The Victory over Og**—Here again the anathema (**6**) was applied.

8-17 Division of Transjordan—A rather composite section : 8, 10, 12*a* give a summary of the successful outcome of these two campaigns, which was an impressive vindication of Moses' promise of God's assistance. 9, 11, 13*b*–14 are historical notes ; 12*b*–13*a* and 16–17 are duplicate accounts of the distribution of the land. **10.** The ' plain ' means the plateau of Moab, a high tableland which sinks abruptly to the Jordan valley. **11.** ' Bed of iron ' is thought to mean a basalt sarcophagus. **12.** ' And *this* land we *took possession of* at that time. From Aroer, which is beside the Wady Arnon, *half of the hill-country of Galaad with its towns* I gave to Ruben and to Gad.' **16 f.** repeat 12 more in detail : ' I gave *from Galaad* to the Arnon, *the torrent valley being the boundary*.' **17.** ' *And the Jordan valley, with the Jordan as the (western) boundary, from (the city) Cenereth to the Dead Sea.*' **18-20.** A brief account of the dispute in Num 32 (*cf.* Jos 1:12–18). **21 f.** anticipate the command of 28. **23-29 Moses' Petition Rejected**—*Cf.* Num 27:12 ff. and 32:48 ff. below. This prayer of Moses is not mentioned elsewhere. **25.** A petition : ' *Please let me pass over* and see. . . .' ' Mountain ' means hill-country or uplands. **27.** The fulfilment of the command is described in 34:1–4.

f **IV 1-40 Homiletic Section**—A reminder of the obligation they are under to be faithful to Yahweh and an exhortation to keep his Law. **1.** ' Commandments and judgements ' : these are the two main kinds of law represented in Deut, corresponding broadly to statute-law and case-law. A commandment (' statute ', ' testimony ' or ' ceremony ' : DV is unfortunately not consistent in its translations) is a precept, usually in the form ' Thou shalt (not) . . .' It is based on a categorical and ultimate authority— the Will of God, who is Justice and Holiness—and binds the individual's conscience before the act. A judgement is a legal principle, usually in the form ' If so-and-so has been done, such and such shall be the penalty or the result '. It is based on the authoritative or customary solution of previous cases, accepted as a precedent, and guides the judge's decision after the act. The Mosaic ' judgements ' are the Israelite form of Semitic ' common law ', and it is in them that are found the numerous parallels with the Babylonian, Assyrian and Hittite codes (which are all phrased in this conditional form). But it is in the ' commandments ' that the transcendence of the Israelite code and religion is seen, and these not only have Yahweh's authority but contain his revelation. The ' Ten Commandments ', however, are not so called in HT,

but usually ' The Ten Words ' ; also ' the Covenant ', **21** *par excellence*, or ' the Testimony '. **2.** ' Adding and taking away ' means altering without authority ; exact observance is enjoined, and three motives are added. **3.** The first, threat of annihilation. For Beelphegor see Num 25. **6.** Second motive : reputation with neighbours, who will say ' Surely a wise and prudent people *is* this great nation '. Other peoples will see ' greatness ' in the Israelites' military success ; but on examining their culture they will find also divine wisdom and prudence. **7** and **8** start each with the same phrase : ' *What great nation is there . . .?* ' Israel, though politically insignificant, is superior even to the ' great powers ', since they have not the protection and Law of Yahweh. **8** continues ' . . . that has (such) *righteous statutes and judgements as all this Law*, which I am going to set before you this day ? ' This is the third motive—the excellence of the Law in itself. **9.** ' *Only* take care and keep strict watch over thyself, *that* thou forget not the *things* . . .' *scil.* the favours received from Yahweh during the Wandering. **10.** Omit ' From ' ; that great day is one of the things to be remembered. **12.** Lit., ' *A sound of words you heard, but form you saw none ; only a sound* '. The doctrine that Yahweh has no visible or imitable form or shape is repeatedly emphasized in the Mosaic tradition, and is one of the points in which Israel's religion is unique among the religions of the Ancient East. In speech and writing the Israelites did not hesitate to use the most graphic anthropomorphisms ; they spoke of Yahweh's eyes, ears, nostrils, fingers, etc. But the attempt to represent him visibly, in clay, stone or metal, is in the canonical literature always unsparingly condemned. **13 f.** is a parenthesis ; 15 follows on 12. In **13**, omit ' and ' after ' do ' ; the Ten Words *were* the Covenant. The word ' covenant ', *bᵉrît*, may be used of any pact, alliance or agreement, between men or nations ; the Covenant between Yahweh and his people is so called only by analogy, since ordinarily a certain equality of the parties is presupposed. Here there was an act of unprecedented love and mercy on God's part, to which the acceptance and adherence of man were naturally due. Nevertheless, obligations arose on both sides : God chose Israel as his people, and thereby bound himself, as long as the Covenant stood, to protect them and advance their national prosperity ; on their side, Israel was bound to remain faithful to God by observing its terms —fidelity was the condition of its existence. **15-18. g** The prohibition is not directly against worship of other gods (idolatry in the NT sense) but against making representations of Yahweh, whether as man or woman, bird or beast or reptile—all forms under which the Egyptians represented their innumerable divinities. By multiplying images, this practice would have led to the worship of numerous ' Yahwehs ', and degraded him to the level of the multiple Ba'als of the Canaanites. See on 5:8. **19.** Prohibition of star-worship, which flourished especially in the Assyrian and Neo-Babylonian empires, and infiltrated into Palestine in the time of the monarchy. The heavenly bodies are only God's creatures, which he ' *has distributed* to all the peoples under every (part of the) heavens ', *scil.* to be worshipped by them. Some have suggested that this means that for other nations, not granted Israel's revelation, star-worship was approved by God as a means of leading them to a knowledge of himself. But no divine approval is implied here—Hebrew thought and expression ignore the distinction familiar to Christian theology, between willing (good) and permitting (moral evil). The idea is rather to answer the question (a difficult one according to the conceptions of the time), ' Why, if Yahweh is such a great God, the only God, is he known and worshipped only by one small people ? ' The answer is simply, that it pleased him to leave other nations to their own devices, while for himself he chose Israel as his people. **20.** HT emphasizes : ' But *you* Yahweh took and brought . . .' **21.** *Cf.* the end of ch 3. **25.** One of the great material

2g benefits that Yahweh bound himself by the Covenant to provide was the possession of their own land ; and their breaking of the Covenant would naturally be punished by its forfeiture. The books of Kings, and the Prophets, testify that Judah and Israel gave only too much cause for the Exile, threatened in **26-28. 28.** ' Serve gods ' : this does not here refer to formal idolatry, and hence apostasy from Yahweh ; that will have taken place already and been the cause of the Exile. A more material and unwilling servitude is meant : the mere working as captives, or state slaves, in a foreign land was itself a ' service ' to the divinities of that land—even apart from the specialized case, no doubt verified of many, of being slaves of some temple. **32-34.** This is the ' Deuteronomic style ' at its highest —a fervent and eloquent exclamation at the thought of a loving providence unique in history. **33.** ' *Has a people ever heard the voice of God . . . (34) or did God ever go and take . . .?* ' Here the First Discourse rises to its climax and summary in **39 f.**

h **41-43 The Cities of Refuge**—A note inserted between the Discourses. See on 19:1 ff. The cities cannot now be identified with certainty ; they are listed in order from south to north.

44-49 Introduction to the Second Discourse, either an editorial addition or an indication that at one time the book began here, and chh 1-4 were prefixed later. **45.** Omit ' And ' : ' *These are the edicts and the statutes and the judgements* which Moses *proclaimed. . .*' **45 ff.** is an expansion, or duplicate, of 44. **48.** ' Sion ' is not Jerusalem, but probably an error for ' Sirion '.

213a **V 1-XXIX 1 The Second Discourse.**
V 1-XI 32 Exhortation on Fidelity to Yahweh.
V 2-33 The Covenant of Sinai ; the Decalogue—
The original form of the ' Ten Words ' would be somewhat as follows :

> I, Yahweh, am thy God
> Thou shalt have no other gods than me
> Thou shalt not make thyself a graven image
> Thou shalt not swear by Yahweh falsely
> Take care to sanctify the Sabbath day
> Honour thy father and thy mother
> Thou shalt not murder
> Thou shalt not commit adultery
> Thou shalt not steal
> Thou shalt not testify falsely against thy neighbour
> Thou shalt not covet what belongs to thy neighbour

To these has been added, both here and in Ex 20:2-17, a certain amount of expansion and commentary, in oral tradition or by the inspired authors. **8.** Since the first commandment excludes other gods, the second prohibited originally images of Yahweh (see on 4:12, 15) ; but the explanation in **9** applies it to images of false gods, which were a prevalent temptation once the Israelites were settled in Palestine. **11.** This commandment might be rendered ' Thou shalt not *abuse* the Name of Yahweh ', excluding, besides perjury, its use for magic and superstitious purposes. One's name, in the mind of the ancient Semites, was one's very personality, one's essence ; to abuse Yahweh's Name was to abuse him. So penetrated were the Israelites by this idea that, to be on the safe side, they ceased using the Name at all. **12-15.** The Sabbath was evidently something already familiar, and so, like circumcision, a pre-Mosaic institution. Whatever its origin, it was consecrated at Sinai and given divine sanction. 15 gives for Sabbath observance a reason different from that in Ex 20:11. **16.** This is St Paul's ' commandment with a promise ' (Eph 6:2). **17.** ' Kill ' in English is too general a word ; Hebrew *rāṣaḥ* means the taking of human life, by a private person, unjustifiably. The commandment therefore did not abolish the obligation to avenge a kinsman's death by slaying his murderer (see on 19:1ff.), nor have any reference to warfare. **21.** Ex 20:17 has ' Thou shalt not covet thy neighbour's house ' (= property), and analyses the latter into wife,

slaves, cattle and ' anything he owns '. Deut, however, **213a** puts ' wife ' in a separate sentence, with a different verb : ' Thou shalt not *desire* thy neighbour's wife ; *and thou shalt not covet thy neighbour's property*'. The evident intention to safeguard the woman's dignity and avoid looking on her as merely one of the man's possessions marks an advance in civilization, and indicates that the editing of the Deut text is later than that of Ex. **22.** The Ten Words were spoken by **b** Yahweh himself, ' in a loud voice, adding nothing more ' ; hence they are more immediately from him than the rest of the ' commandments and judgements '. (The phrase ' And the Lord spoke to Moses, saying ', so frequent in the Pentateuch, is a conventional introduction to Israelite law ; it does not indicate innumerable divine revelations but merely that the prescription in question has God's authority behind it.) It is in the Decalogue that the Covenant consists ; hence the insistence of the prophets that the Covenant did not require sacrifices and ritual but justice and righteousness. See *e.g.* Jer 7:21 ff. ; Am 5:21 ff. **24-27.** *Cf.* Ex 20:18-21 ; it is an idea frequently expressed in the OT, that sinful man, if admitted to the presence of Yahweh, would shrivel up and die, in the blaze of his grandeur and purity—*e.g.* Jg 13:22 ; Is 6:5. The people had come before him once, and, contrary to expectation, had not died, but they would not risk it again.

VI 1-25 The Obligation of Faithfulness—**1.** ' *And this* **c** *is the Command, (consisting of) the statutes and judgements.*' **4.** The first word, *Sᵉma'*, ' Hear ! ', has given its name to the prayer, or profession of faith, of the devout Jew, recited morning and evening, from pre-Christian times to the present. It is made up of Deut 6:4-9, 11:13-21, and Num 15:37-41, introduced and concluded by various blessings. ' One Lord ' : the exact meaning of the phrase is doubtful ; either ' *Yahweh is our God, Yahweh alone* ', or, ' *Yahweh is our God, Yahweh is One* '. **5.** This is the commandment that our Lord declared to be the first and greatest (Mt 22:37 f. and par.). **6.** ' These words ' refers to 4 f. **7.** ' And thou shalt *talk about them*, sitting at home and walking abroad, *lying down* and rising up.' **8 f.**, probably meant only figuratively, were taken very literally indeed in later Judaism. The passages of the Torah thus distinguished (Deut 6:4-9 ; 11:13-21 ; Ex 13:1-10, 11-16) were written on parchment and enclosed in little leather pouches, worn on the left arm and the forehead. These were called (in Greek) phylacteries ; *cf.* Mt 23:5. **13.** ' Fear ' in Hebrew is a wider term than in English ; ' the fear of Yahweh ' practically = religion (*cf.* ' godfearing '), as comprised in internal dispositions : ' service ' refers to one's outward acts. ' Swear ' : the oath by a god played an important part in Semitic civil life, especially in connexion with law cases. To swear by a god was to acknowledge oneself subject to him ; hence the Israelites must swear only by Yahweh. **16.** To ' tempt God ' is to show a lack of due faith in him—to put him to the test, as it were, to see whether he is really able and willing to fulfil his promises. For the reference see Ex 17:1-7. **20-25.** Note the importance of family tradition. The knowledge of the Covenant, the marvellous fact of Yahweh's free choice of Israel, is a sacred trust that every Israelite must hand on to his sons. He must explain why this Law is the foundation and the condition of their liberty and prosperity. **24.** ' This day ' means the time of the successful occupation of Palestine. **25.** ' And *it will be (reckoned) justice* to us, if we take care to carry out all *this Command* in the sight of Yahweh, our God, according as he has commanded us.'

VII 1-26 Duty of Exterminating the Canaanites—**1.** **d** On the nations here listed see § 151*f* with references and § 57*d*. **2.** ' and Yahweh thy God shall have delivered them up to thee, and *thou shalt have defeated them, thou shalt make them strictly anathema* ' (*cf.* § 211*g*). **3 f.** are evidently a later addition to the text. If original, they would be not only an anticlimax but quite pointless after 2. They imply not only the survival

213d of the Canaanites but some social intercourse between them and the Hebrews. But this law too was much disregarded, and in the post-exilic community both Esdras and Nehemias had to struggle for its enforcement. **5** continues from **2**. 'Statues': *maṣṣēbôt* were large blocks of stone set upright in the ground and associated with the ritual of the high places. A *maṣṣēbāh* was not necessarily idolatrous; Jacob erected one (Gen 28:18), and Moses set up twelve on Mt Sinai (Ex 24:4). But those used by the Canaanites were to be destroyed. 'Groves': *'ašērîm*, wooden posts called after the goddess Astarte, and presumably carved in her image. 'Graven things': the idols, of Ba'al or Astarte. It is plain that the law was most imperfectly carried out; many of the Canaanite sanctuaries were used for the (illegitimate) cult of Yahweh down to the 7th cent. **10**. 'Forthwith', 'immediately': read, 'in person'. This is a qualification of the doctrine that sons suffer for their fathers' misdeeds. That is not denied, but it is stressed that the sinner himself will not escape punishment. **13-15**. A description, in rhetorical style, of the rewards they may expect for fidelity. **20**. If there is an historical allusion here it escapes us; whether 'hornets' be literal or figurative, the meaning is clear. **22**. Apparently a later writer, missing the conditional character of all these glowing promises—*if* Israel should be faithful to the Covenant—and finding that the Conquest turned out a much slower and more painful business than is here implied, inserted this 'explanation'. It is in marked opposition to the whole context—see *e.g.* 9:3. **23** follows on 21; for 'But' read '*And*'. **24**. To destroy a man's name included killing him, and much more besides—annihilating everything to which his personality, his 'soul', extended—his sons, his property, any memorials he might leave : to leave no trace that he had ever existed. **25**. '*The images of their gods* thou shalt burn with fire; thou shalt not covet the silver and gold (*which are*) *upon them*.' The idols, of wood or stone, had clothing or ornaments of precious metal; the latter would of course be melted to shapeless lumps in the fire, but even these the Israelites must not take into their own possession.

214a **VIII 1-20 Gratitude for God's Care in the Desert**—Here a new reason is given for the Wandering : it was not only a punishment for despair and presumption, it was also a time of testing, an education of the people to make them realize their utter dependence on Yahweh. Having been so looked after in the desert, where life was hard and provisions scarce, they should not forget, in easier circumstances, that it is still Yahweh who is caring and providing for them. *Cf.* 11:10 ff. **3**. 'Not in bread alone. . .' *Cf.* Ps 126 : 'Unless the Lord build the house. . .' God can provide for man, irrespective of the latter's co-operation. Manna was not produced by human means; ordinary bread is. Yet the one and the other are equally dependent on God's working, and the Israelites, when providing themselves with bread, must not forget that it is God's gift just as much as the manna 'which came down from heaven'. **4**. It is an example of God's providence that they have been able to clothe and otherwise provide for themselves during the long Wandering. We need not take this as literally as did some rabbinic commentators, who held that their clothes were miraculously renewed for forty years, and the children's clothing grew to keep pace with their growth ! **7**. 'For Yahweh thy God *is bringing thee* into a good land, *a land of running brooks, of springs and deep waters, welling up in its plains and hills*.' No single feature of the Land would sound more grateful to the ears of desert-dwellers than this. By European standards, Palestine is not particularly well-watered; but it is much better provided than the desert, and, under proper irrigation and cultivation, is really a fertile country, as has been often proved in its long history. In pre-Christian times, too, it was probably better afforested than it is today. **9**. Iron and copper are not found within the limits generally assigned to Palestine, but they are found,

and were mined, in Edom, which was under Israelite **214** control during the early monarchy. **15** recalls the perils of the desert : '*burning serpents* and scorpions, *and arid places without water*'. What 'burning' means is uncertain (*cf.* Num 21:6); the 'dipsas' is not a serpent but 'thirsty ground'. **16** ends with a purpose clause : '*in order to afflict thee and in order to test thee, to do thee good in the end*'.

IX 1-X 11 Past History as a Warning against Pre- **b** **sumption**—**2**. 'A people great and tall, sons *of Anak, as thou knowest ; and thou thyself hast heard (the saying) : Who can stand up to the sons of Anak ?*' 'Sons of Anak' or Anakim is not the name of any people then in Palestine; they were fabulous giants, and the phrase would be applied to any fierce warriors or very tall men. **3** gives an idealized description; see on 7:22. **7-24** recapitulate various infidelities of the Israelites in the desert, presenting them as so many motives for humility and gratitude. The chief, of course, is the breaking of the Covenant, almost as soon as made, at Horeb. The incident is recalled, in a summary of Ex 24, 32, 34. **9**. 'Forty days' is a conventional expression denoting a time of solemn preparation (*cf.* Gen 7:4; 3 Kg 19:8; Jon 3:4; Mt 4:2; Ac 1:3). **12**. 'For thy people, whom thou hast brought out of Egypt, *have acted corruptly*; they have quickly turned aside from the way which *I* commanded them.' Very striking is the change to the second person, 'thy people'; having broken Yahweh's Covenant, they are no longer his people. **13**. HT is more forceful : '*I have seen this people, and behold ! it is a stiff-necked people.*' **14**. 'Let me alone . . .' The implication is, that the 'prayer of a just man availeth much' (Jas 5:16). Yahweh wishes to destroy the people, but if Moses intercedes he will not be able to refuse him; and so of course it turned out (*cf.* 19 and Ex 32:11-14). 'Their name' : see on 7:24. **16**. The 'golden calf' was intended as an image of Yahweh (*cf.* Ex 32:4); but it was a grave and express violation of the second commandment and hence a breaking of the Covenant. **17**. '*I took hold of the two tablets and cast them down out of my hands and broke them to pieces before your eyes.*' This was not merely a display of holy anger on the part of Moses; it was a symbol of the broken covenant, to impress on the people what they had done. **21** for proper sequence should follow 17. **22 f.** mention other examples of the people's infidelity in the desert, at 'the Burning' (Num 11:1-3), 'the Place of Temptation' (Ex 17:7) and 'the Graves of Lust' (Num 11:4-34). These are proper names, artificially formed in memory of these incidents. **25-29**. As there is a decided break between 24 and 25, this section may have been displaced from between 18 and 19 (or between 19*a* and 19*b*). The motives urged by Moses why Yahweh should relent and forgive his people are drawn from his greatness and love, and his 'credit' in the eyes of the Egyptians; the merits of the patriarchs are also mentioned; but any merit or just claim on the part of contemporary Israelites is implicitly excluded. God merely owes it to himself, not to reject his unfaithful but chosen people.

X 1-9 contains various *notes*, presumably editorial **c** additions. The narrative of ch 9 is continued in 10:10 f. **1-5**. This section corresponds to the account of Ex 34:1-4, 28, 29, with the addition of the making of the ark, which, however, in Ex follows the inscribing of the tablets (Ex 25:10-21; 37:1). The two sets of instructions, given at different times, and their respective fulfilments, are here combined. **5** ends 'and there *they remained*, as Yahweh commanded me'. **6-7** is a fragment from the itinerary of the Wandering, long after the events at Horeb; see Num 33:31-33. Its insertion here is unexplained. **8-9** is inserted as a note to the mention of the ark (1-5) of which the tribe of Levi had charge. Three functions are mentioned as proper to the tribe of Levi as a whole; elsewhere (*e.g.* Num 3) the tribe is distinguished into priests and Levites, the latter caring for the ark, the former exercising the ministry and blessings.

10-11 give the conclusion of the incidents of ch 9.

214d **X 12-XI 32 Exhortation for the Future—12.** 'And now '—after the vivid review of their infidelity and God's love—' *what is Yahweh thy God asking of thee . . . ?* ' **14.** Yahweh is Lord of the whole universe ; nevertheless (**15**) ' *it was thy ancestors whom Yahweh took delight in, to make them an object of his love* '. **16.** Circumcision of the heart means the purifying of the will and affections, to make them receptive to Yahweh's will. **18.** ' Stranger ' or ' resident alien ' means a foreigner settled, for whatever reason, in an Israelite community. As having no blood-relationship with any Israelite family, and—according to the ideas of the Semites in general—no claim to the protection of the Israelite God, he would be quite defenceless against injustice ; but Yahweh is the God of justice, and has a special concern for the protection of the unprotected. **XI:2-7** is a long, complicated sentence, from which some words are missing in HT. Read prob. : ' And *bear in mind this day—for it is not with your children, who know not and who have not witnessed the teaching of Yahweh (that I speak)* —his great doings.' ' Chastisements ' : N. the Heb. means rather ' *instruction* ', ' *education* ', in the ethical sense. **4.** A rapid summary of Ex 14. **5.** ' To you ' : better, ' *for you* '. **6.** Cf. Num 16, where it seems that the stories of two rebellions are combined—that of Core, and that of Dathan and Abiron ; only the latter is mentioned here. **7** is better taken as the emphatic conclusion : ' *for it is your own eyes that have seen. . .*'

e **10-17** give an explanation why (according to Hebrew conceptions) their prosperity in Canaan will depend more immediately on God than does the success of Egyptian agriculture. In Egypt, where the overflow of the Nile is just as certain and regular as the seasons, man needs only to sow his seed in the soil thus unfailingly prepared ; but in Palestine he is dependent rather on the rains which come (within limits) irregularly, and vary greatly from year to year, and which he is quite helpless to control. Hence Yahweh, sending or withholding the rain, will seem to take a more active and significant part in their yearly well-being or otherwise. **10.** ' For the land into which thou art entering, in order to take possession of it, is not like the land of Egypt whence you [*sic*] have come, *where thou wert wont to sow thy seed and water it with thy foot, like a vegetable garden.*' ' Water with the foot ' is uncertain ; the most plausible explanation is that in ' vegetable gardens ' the water was distributed by shallow channels, whose entries could be opened or blocked by a little earth moved by the foot. **12.** The anthropomorphism is rather striking : the fertility of Palestine depends on Yahweh's constant supervision. **14.** ' He will send rain on your land *at the right time*, the early rains and the later rains . . . (**15**) and *he will give grass* in thy field for thy cattle ; *and thou shalt* eat and be filled '. **18-21.** Cf. 6:6-9. **24.** Read prob. : ' From the desert *to* Lebanon ', giving the extent from S. to N. **26-28.** This choice is developed at length in ch 28, which forms the conclusion of this speech. **29.** The Blessing and the Curse were thought of as material objects, to be set in prominent positions in the Land, ready to produce their effect as called for. *Cf.* ch 27 and Jos 8:33 f. **30** is a gloss, in the form of a question : ' *Are they not across the Jordan, beyond the western road, in the land of the Canaanites that live in the ʿArabah, in front of the galgala near the oak of Moreh ?* ' The ʿArabah is the Jordan valley. Galgala means ' a circle ' (of standing stones ?) and was the name of a well-known sanctuary near Jericho. But the latter is so far from the locality here described that possibly some other stone-circle, near Shechem, is meant. The oak of Moreh was an ancient landmark (*cf.* Gen 12:6 ; DV ' the noble vale ').

215a **XII 1-XXVI 15 The Deuteronomic Law-Code**—This section sets forth about eighty laws, with the amplification and emotional appeal proper to oratorical presentation. Many of the laws, as will be indicated in the notes, have parallels elsewhere, especially in the Book of the Covenant (Ex 20-23), along with some significant differences.

XII 1 Title to the Code. **215a**
XII 2-XVI 17 Laws on Religion.
XII 2-7 The Law of One Sanctuary : First Enunciation —This is the first and most characteristic law of Deut (see §§ 112*a-d*, 211*c*). In this one chapter it is enunciated four times, in slightly varying terms. **2f.** Read with LXX ' *You shall utterly* destroy all the places . . . ; *break in pieces their maṣṣebôt and cut down their ʾašêrîm and burn their idols in the fire* '. See on 7:5. **4.** ' You shall not do so ' ; this is vague, but explained in 5 and 30. The cult of Yahweh must differ both in place and in manner from the cults of the Baʿalim. Not in any ' natural ' place, like Baʿal and Astarte, but only in a place of his own choice would he accept man's worship. Thus is emphasized Yahweh's transcendence, as a God of revelation. The place— never named in Deut—is of course the temple in Jerusalem, which was ' chosen ' through David's capture of the city and Solomon's building there, of which God expressed his approval. ' To put his name there ' means that he would be present there, to receive his people's sacrifices and hear their prayers.•

8-12 Second Enunciation—8 f. The law is clearly **b** presented as an aspiration, a pious hope for the future, that could not be enforced in Moses' day nor for some time thereafter. Internal peace and security were not enjoyed by the Israelites in Palestine before David's reign, *c* 1000 B.C. **10** is a temporal clause : ' *When you shall have crossed the* Jordan and settled in the land . . . , *when you enjoy rest* from your enemies round about and *have settled down* in security, *then, to* the place that Yahweh chooses . . . you shall bring. . .'

13-19 Third Enunciation—13. ' Place ' has a technical **c** sense—the sacred places of the Canaanites. **15.** For the Semites generally, any slaughtering of cattle for food had originally a sacrificial character : the beast was first made sacred to the god, and then enjoyed by his worshippers. But meat, eaten by nomads only on rare occasions, would be available more frequently (though still not habitually) to sedentary farmers ; hence this important corollary is added to the law, that non-sacrificial meals are allowed, away from the temple. (Contrast Lev 17:1-7.) Beasts may be slaughtered at the homestead, without infringing the law reserving sacrifice to Jerusalem, and ' whether (*you are*) clean or unclean *you may eat it as you would gazelle or hart* '—i.e. game, which was not material for sacrifice. Ritual purity of course was necessary for those taking part in a sacrificial meal. **19.** The Levites, who theoretically were to live on the income of the central sanctuary, naturally suffered if the latter was neglected. See on 18:6 f. ; Jg 17:7 ff.

20-28 Fourth Enunciation—20. ' If Yahweh thy God **d** extends thy territory as he has *promised* thee, and *thou sayest* " *I would eat meat* ", because thou cravest to eat meat : *thou mayest eat meat as often as thou desirest.*' **23.** Although such a feast has no sacred character, God's rights to life (represented by the blood) must not be infringed : ' for the blood *is life* ; and thou must not eat *the life* along with the meat '. (*Cf.* Lev 17:10-14.)

29-31 Canaanite Practices forbidden—As the Canaanite places of cult are illicit, so is their manner of worship. It might lead even to child-sacrifice in honour of Yahweh. The section 16:21-17:7 may have originally followed these verses ; see below.

XII 32-XIII 18 Three Laws for the Punishment of e Apostates—32. Introduction—' *All the instruction that* I am commanding thee *thou shalt take care to observe* ; thou shalt neither add to nor take away from it.' **XIII 1-5 A Prophet**—In 18:22 unfulfilled prophecies are given as the indication of a false prophet. Here we see that the converse is not necessarily true : prophecies that come true are not an infallible sign of a true prophet. He must also be tested by his doctrine. (*Cf.* Gal 1:8.) **5.** HT is more forceful : ' because he *preached revolt against* Yahweh your God '. **6-11 Private Person—6.** ' If thy brother, *the son of thy father or* the son of thy mother,' i.e. half-brother or full brother. **9 f.** ' But thou shalt *forthwith denounce him* :

215e thy hand shall be on him first, then that of all the people, and (so) *thou shalt* stone him to death.' (*Cf.* note on 17:6 f.) **12-18 Israelite City—12 f.** ' If thou shalt hear that in one of thy cities . . . *worthless men* have gone forth from the midst of thee, *seducing* their fellow-citizens and saying . . .' ' Going forth' means abandoning the cult of Yahweh ; ' Belial ' is not a proper name, but ' *worthlessness* ', ' *iniquity* '. **16.** Not ' in the midst of the streets ' but ' *in the city-square* ', the open space inside the gate. The site shall be left as a ' heap ', i.e. a *tell*, the technical word for the mound covering the ruins of a city. The intensity of feeling expressed in the details of these three laws is remarkable. So grave a crime was it to reject the Covenant of God's love.

XIV 1-2 Pagan Mourning Rites—Incisions in the flesh and cutting off of hair were signs of mourning common to Israel and its pagan neighbours. They are referred to casually, and without rebuke, by the prophets (Is 22:12, Jer 16:6, Ez 7:18, etc.). Either this law remained a dead letter, or (more probably) it is a late (post-exilic) addition.

f **3-21 Unclean Foods**—*Cf.* Lev 11. That some beasts were ' clean ' for food, others not, was a rooted Semitic belief long before Moses. Given that distinction, the legislator imposes the natural conclusion that a holy people must eat only what is clean. Some of the creatures named cannot be identified with certainty. **4-8 Land Animals**—Two criteria are given—a clean animal must have divided hooves and be a ruminant (the latter not in the sense of modern zoology but according to appearances). The ' pygarg ' is a species of antelope, the ' camelopardalus ' probably a mountain-sheep, the ' cherogril ' a badger (?). **9 f. Aquatic Animals** ' without fins and scales ' are unclean, probably because of their resemblance to reptiles. **11-20. Winged Creatures**—No general criterion is given, but those forbidden all appear to be either birds of prey or scavengers. **15.** The ' larus ' is a gull, (**16**) the ' heron ', the ' swan ' and the ' stork ', three species of owl, (**17**) the ' porphirion ' an eagle, (**18**) the ' chara-drion ' a heron. **19 f.** Winged insects are unclean ; all clean flying things may be eaten. **21a.** A beast dying ' naturally ' is unclean ; this is not a hygienic precaution, but to avoid consuming the blood, which would remain in a carcass not ritually slaughtered. Hence the insistence of orthodox Jews, down to modern times, on slaughtering their own meat. **21b** forbids a Canaanite religious rite, to which reference is made in a mythological text from Rās-Shamra ; *cf.* A. Casey, S.J., in VD 16 (1936) 142-8 ; 174-83.

g **22-29 The Law of Tithes**—Different stages of this law are preserved in Lev 27:30-33 and Num 18:20-32. Deut supposes it as already in practice, and is concerned only with the modifications necessitated by the strict observance of the law of one sanctuary ; it insists that only there may the ritual tithe-banquet be enjoyed. **24.** Distance is no excuse—better to sell one's produce locally and then buy supplies in Jerusalem, than to have the tithe-banquet at any other place than the central sanctuary. (It was the abuses connected with the practice of this law that called for Our Lord's purifying of the temple, Mt 21:12 and par.) **28 f.** However, to compensate the former beneficiaries, the poor of one's own neighbourhood, every third year ' thou shalt *bring forth all the tithe of thy harvest of that year and shalt leave it* within thy gates ', instead of bringing it to the temple.

216a **XV 1-11 The Remission of Debts**—**1-3.** This appears to be not a law in the strict sense, for the regulation of commercial practice, but a pressing exhortation to fraternal charity. (*Cf.* in the NT the Sermon on the Mount, Mt 5:38-42, etc.) No sanction is suggested for its non-observance ; in fact there is no record of its ever being put in practice—unless it be Neh 5:7 ff., where however Nehemias does not invoke the authority of the Law. Attempts have been made to interpret it of remission of interest (but *cf.* 23:19 f.) or temporary suspension of claim to the principal ; but the text

almost certainly prescribes a simple extinction of the 216 debt. **4-6** seem to be a later insertion, protesting that if only they keep the Law, the question of borrowing will never arise : ' *Only* there will be no poor among thee, *for* Yahweh *will abundantly bless thee . . ., provided only that thou strictly obey the voice. . .*' **10.** ' Thou shalt give to him *generously, and not be grudging in thy giving ; because for this very thing* Yahweh will bless thee.'

12-18 The Freeing of Slaves—A man of little property, b if he fell hopelessly into debt, had often no option but to sell himself (or his children) to whoever would buy him, the price being the payment of his debts. Once a slave, he could be freed only if a kinsman bought him out or if he himself accumulated sufficient money ; but this law provides for automatic manumission after six years, and, with characteristic benevolence, insists that the slave is not to be turned out destitute. Jer 34:8-16 gives a repellent instance of how this law, generally disregarded, was temporarily put in force to avoid embarrassment, and later rescinded, by the slave-owners of Jerusalem. **17.** The ear was the ' organ ' of obedience ; hence the symbolism. **18.** ' *It shall not seem a burdensome thing to send him away free, for he has brought thee double the profit of a hired servant* for six years.' The owner, after all, has had more than his money's worth out of the slave, since he paid for his keep, but no salary.

19-23 Firstlings—*Cf.* Ex 22:29 f. ; Num 18:15-18 ; c §132 *f–g.* Another modification of law required by the insistence on the one sanctuary. Ex *loc. cit.* prescribes the offering within eight days, but Deut here allows firstlings to be kept until a yearly visit to the temple, when they shall (if unblemished) be duly sacrificed. In the meantime they must be set apart as belonging to Yahweh and no use be made of them. **20.** In Num *loc. cit.* the flesh of firstlings is the perquisite of the priests, and the offerer has no claim to share in it. Apparently we have in Ex, Deut, Num, three stages in the historic development of a Mosaic law.

XVI 1-17 The Three Yearly Feasts—Older customs d are here modified only in so far as concerns the obligation of celebrating these feasts in the place of Yahweh's choice, not ' in thy gates '. (*Cf.* Ex 23:15 f. ; 34:18, 22 f. ; Lev 23.) **1-8. The Pasch and Feast of Unleavened Bread**—(*Cf.* § 113 *f–g.*) Originally distinct, in the Mosaic legislation they are always associated, since the latter (the Azymes) began the day after the Paschal meal. (*Cf.* Lk 22:1.) ' Take care in the month *of Abib to celebrate a pasch* to Yahweh thy God.' Abib (later, Nisan) is the month of the ' new ears of corn ', March/April. **2.** ' Oxen ' : Ex 12:5 mentions only lambs and kids, but perhaps the larger beast is allowed for a more numerous party now that the feast is transferred to the temple. **3.** ' Leavened bread ' was considered unsuitable for cult purposes since the rising of the dough was regarded as a sort of corruption ; *cf.* St Paul's application (1 Cor 5:6-8). **7.** ' And thou shalt *boil* it ', which is forbidden in Ex 12:9 ; but this passage of Deut probably represents the original custom. **8.** Strictly, it is the Pasch and not the Azymes which must be celebrated at the sanctuary, since only that has the sacrificial meal ; hence Deut permits the return home for the celebration of the Azymes. ' And on the seventh day (*shall be held*) an *assembly in honour of* Yahweh thy God, when thou shalt do no work.' **9-12 The Feast of Weeks**—See § 113 *h–i.* **13-15 The Feast of Tabernacles**—See § 113 *j.* **16 f. Conclusion—16** is a quotation from Ex 23:17, 15*b*, with the Deuteronomic addition ' in the place which he shall choose '.

XVI 18-XVIII 22 Laws concerning Authorities. 217 **XVI 18-20 Judges**—Not only sacrificial worship was to be restricted to the temple, but also the other important function of a sanctuary, that of giving judicial decisions in God's name. **18** adds nothing to the practice observed by the tribes since leaving Sinai, but 17:8 states that the court of reference for difficult cases is to be ' the place which Yahweh thy God shall choose ', and, by implication, not any of the other

7a sanctuaries in the land. **19-20** succinctly outline the duties of a judge : ' *Thou shalt not pervert judgement, thou shalt not respect persons and thou shalt not take a bribe.*'

b **XVI 21-XVII 7 Crimes against Religion**—These three laws seem out of place, since they occur in the middle of the law on judges. They may have been transferred, accidentally or otherwise, from after 12:31. **21 f.** ' Thou shalt not plant *for thyself any tree-trunk as an* '*a*šērāh beside the altar of Yahweh . . . nor set up for thyself a *maṣṣēbāh* ' ; *cf.* on 7:5. **XVII:1.** From the context it would seem that Canaanite ritual permitted ' blemished ' victims. **2-5.** The case of individual apostasy—which probably introduced the other cases (13:1-17). **6 f.** *Cf.* 19:15-21. The witnesses are obliged to be the first to stone the culprit. This was intended as a check against malicious false witness ; the shedding of innocent blood was a crime crying to God for vengeance ; and the consciousness that he would be obliged to commit the crime might well deter a man from making the false accusation.

c **8-13 Continuation of the Law on Judges—8.** ' *If some matter of judgement be too intricate for thee, a question of homicide, a question of litigation, a question of wounding, matters of controversy in thy towns : thou shalt arise* and go up. . .' **9.** The court of reference consists of the priests of the temple and a lay judge ; *cf.* 2 Par 19:8, 11, where in the reign of Josaphat (870-847 B.C.) the same appointments are mentioned. Deut does not institute this tribunal but supposes it already existing.

d **14-20 The Law of the King**—It was almost inevitable that the Israelites, establishing themselves as a nation in the land of Canaan, should adopt the institution of monarchy, the universal form of government of the time. Hence there would be nothing surprising in Moses' having foreseen and provided for it. But the details of the present passage seem to contain obvious references to the career of Solomon, as recorded in 3 Kg 9-11. **16.** Solomon conducted a profitable trade in chariots and horses between Egypt and the Hittites ; whereas the king should not ' *cause the people to return* to Egypt, *in order to get many horses* '. The command (or prophecy ?) that there should be no return to Egypt is referred to again in 28:68, but is not found elsewhere. **17.** The reference must be to foreign wives who would be an occasion of apostasy from Yahweh. A frequent token of alliance between kings of the Amarna age (14th cent. B.C.) was the exchange of princesses for their harems. **18.** The king is to ' *have a copy* of this Law *written for himself, according to the book in the keeping of the Levite priests* '. The Law referred to would be Deut, at least the legislative part. **20.** He is not to ' *turn aside from the Command* to right or to left '.

e **XVIII 1-8 Law of the Priesthood**—This is not a code for the observance of the priests but instruction to the laity on what is due to the priests and Levites. Concerning the latter *cf.* § 112*g-i*. The distinction between the two classes is practically ignored in Deut ; yet this may be precisely because Deut is addressed to the laity. **1 f.** The tribe of Levi has a right to support from the offerings brought to the sanctuary. In 1 Kg 2:12-17, 29, the sons of Heli are severely blamed for demanding their share, contrary to custom, before the meat is cooked, and for ' getting fat ' on the choicest offerings. Deut here regulates the practice by determining the priests' portion and assigning to them all the firstfruits. **3.** ' Whether it be an ox or a smaller animal, he [the worshipper] shall give the priest the shoulder, *the jaws and the stomach.*' Still better and larger portions are assigned to the priests in Lev 7:31 ff. and Num 18:18. See on 15:20. **6 f.** ' *And if any Levite should wish to come from one of thy towns, from any part of Israel where he dwells as a stranger, and comes in the fullness of his desire* to the place which Yahweh shall choose, he shall serve in the name of Yahweh his God, like all his brethren (who are) ministering there before Yahweh.' This passage seems to ignore the ' Levitical cities ' (Num 35:1-8 ; Jos 21) ; but perhaps these never got beyond the ' planning ' stage. The meaning of **8b** is uncertain ; a suggested emendation would give

' except priests of idols and necromancers '. **6-8** has **217e** been interpreted by many of priests formerly officiating at the various local sanctuaries, which Deut desires to see abolished. By this law they would be permitted to migrate to Jerusalem and be on an equal footing there with the staff of the temple. But in view of Deut's attitude towards these illegitimate cult centres it is most improbable that their personnel should be welcomed to the One Sanctuary—even if the emendation of 8*b* (see above) be correct. And, in fact, in Josias' reform we see that the ' priests of the high places ' were excluded from the priestly ministry (4 Kg 23:8 f.). Rather, the law, like the many references to Levites in chh 12 f., aims at safeguarding the rights of a member of the tribe of Levi ; they do not lapse merely because he has lived long away from the temple.

9-22 Law of Prophets—When the Israelites desire to **f** know the divine will or purpose, they are not to have recourse to the magic and superstitious practices of the Gentiles. Nine different pagan modes of divination are specifically banned. **10.** None shall ' make his son or daughter pass through the fire ', *i.e.* immolate his children—a terrible rite thought to be of great magical efficacy by many of the ancient Semites. **12-14.** All these practices are abominable to Yahweh, and the destruction of the Canaanites is partly in punishment for this impiety. Yet the desire for superhuman guidance is itself not wrong ; and God has specially provided for the instruction of his people. **15.** ' A prophet *from among thy brethren*, like myself, will Yahweh raise up for thee ; him you shall obey.' The singular is collective, since 20-22 supposes a number of prophets, and the institution is to be a permanent one. Nevertheless it is also a prophecy of our Lord, the Prophet *par excellence*, foreshadowed in the OT by kings, priests and prophets alike (*cf.* Jn 6:14 ; 7:40 ; Ac 3:22 ff. ; and probably Jn 1:45). **16.** *Cf.* 5:25-28. **18-22.** The function of the prophet is not primarily to foretell the future, but to instruct and reprove the people in God's name. Predictions, and miracles in general, are intended as ' signs ' to establish his credentials (*cf.* § 415*c-f*).

XXI 1-XXV 19 Civil, Penal and Miscellaneous Laws. 218a
XIX 1-13 Cities of Refuge—*Cf.* 4:41 ff. ; Num 35:9-34 ; Ex 21:12-14 ; Jos 20. In the patriarchal society of Semitic nomads, an important institution for the protection of life was blood-vengeance : the obligation on members of a clan not to let the murder of a kinsman go unavenged. The execution of the murderer was a family responsibility, falling in the first place on the next-of-kin, like the lesser responsibilities of protecting kinsfolk against want, oppression, or the extinction of their name. (Hence the precarious and pitiable situation of the unprotected widow, orphan, and stranger.) But the lack of discrimination between voluntary and involuntary killing might lead to the ' execution ' in its turn being looked on as a murder ; then the resulting blood-feud might rage for generations. Hence any nascent civil authority among Semites had to come to grips with this practice and attempt to control its abuses. From their very first settlement in Transjordan, the Israelites had their ' cities ' of refuge, to which this law refers. **3-5.** ' *Thou shalt determine the distance* [*i.e.* to know where to set the division] *and divide in three the whole area of thy land*. . . . And this shall be the *test* of the slayer *taking refuge there, whether he shall be allowed to live : whether he struck his neighbour unintentionally*, not being previously his enemy. [For instance] *if he goes with another man to the woodland to cut timber, and as his hand is swinging the axe to cut down a tree the head flies off the handle and strikes the other man so that he dies* . . .' **6.** ' Grief ' : better, ' *in the heat of his anger* '. **10.** The purpose of this principle of asylum is only to allow a delay, in which the case may be examined coolly and responsibility determined. **12.** If the homicide was wilful, the ' elders ' from the slayer's city are to see that he is handed over to justice, *i.e.* execution by the next-of-kin. Unlike the Code of Hammurabi (and later Jewish practice) Deut makes

218a no provision for a commutation of the death penalty into monetary compensation made to the relatives of the slain.

b **14 Boundary Stones**—Since a man's inheritance from his fathers was his dearest possession, it was a shocking crime to encroach on a neighbour's land by secretly moving back ' *thy neighbour's border-stone, which the men of old set up* '. Thus far the verse quotes a law, drafted some time after the occupation of the Land ; ' *in thy possession* ', etc., is added to fit it into the framework of the discourse.

c **15-21 Law of Witnesses**—*Cf.* 17:6 ; Num 35:30. **15.** Not only for an accusation of apostasy, but ' whatsoever the sin or wickedness be ', at least two witnesses are required, and by their evidence ' *the matter shall be decided* ' (of course, the evidence must be concordant ; *cf.* Mk 14:56, 59). **16-21,** however, allow an exception to the foregoing, when a single ' malicious witness ', or rather accuser, persists in his accusation. The case must then be referred to God's decision, *i.e.* to the temple tribunal described in 17:9. But the law contains the presumption that the single witness, so persisting, is moved by malice and will be found to be a liar.

d **XX 1-20 Laws on War**—**1-4.** It is presumed that the war is religious in character and approved by Yahweh ; hence a priest is to exhort the army to remember that Yahweh fights on their side. ' Horsemen ' : rather, ' horses and chariots '. Cavalry as distinct from chariotry was introduced to the Near East only by the Persians in the 6th cent. B.C. **5-8.** These exemptions being ancient customs known to all, their proclamation on the eve of battle would be a formality, aimed rather at stimulating the whole-hearted courage of the warriors. In 1 Mac 3:56 the proclamation is recorded, but there is no suggestion that any took advantage of it. **10-20 Conduct of Sieges**—The bearing of this law is probably to mitigate earlier practice. The inhabitants of an enemy city must be given the chance of surrendering ; and if they do so, their lives are to be spared. **15-18** make clear that the rigour of the anathema was to be applied only to the cities in Palestine itself, at the time of the Conquest (see § 211*g*) ; hence this law belongs to an ' expansionist ' period in Israelite history, later than the period of the Judges. **19.** ' If *thou art besieging* a city for a long time, *assaulting it* in order to capture it, thou shalt not destroy its trees *by felling them with axes ; but thou mayest eat their fruit, without cutting them down*. For, *is a tree a man, that it should be besieged by thee ?* ' A sense of responsibility is enjoined and the duty of avoiding—what all armies are inclined to—purely wanton destruction. **20.** ' Only trees which *thou knowest* are not fruit-trees—those thou mayest destroy and cut down, and (*use to*) build siege-works.' This section supposes a technique of warfare far in advance of any that the Israelites possessed at the time of the Conquest. *Cf.* the need of a miracle for the capture of Jericho (Jos 6:2-5) and the stratagem by which they penetrated the defences of Hai (Jos ch 8).

e **XXI 1-9 Unsolved Cases of Murder**—Innocent blood involves a stain that must be expiated—if not by the guilty, then by his kin ; if not by them, then by the community in whose territory it has been shed. This law is not ' civil ', else it would specify, as does the Code of Hammurabi, compensation for the family of the slain. It is purely religious, to remove the blood-guilt that would otherwise rest upon the land. Hence it is curious that (2) ' thy elders and thy judges ' are to handle the matter, and the elders of the city concerned are to perform the ceremony. **4.** They are to bring an unbroken heifer to ' an uncultivated valley *with an ever-flowing stream, and there cut the heifer's throat into the stream* ', so that the blood is carried off by the water. Thus the act is not a sacrifice, but a symbolical removal of blood from the land. **5** has every appearance of being an addition to the text. **6.** ' And all the elders of that city, (*namely*) *the one nearest to where the corpse was found*, shall wash their hands over the heifer slain *into the stream*.'

10-14 Marriage with a Captive—This law is concerned **21** with humane treatment of the woman. Basically, she has the status of a slave, but, by becoming her master's concubine, she acquires a dignity and title to respect that can never be taken from her. As a slave she would be bound to the religion of Yahweh, so this custom is not to be confused with the marrying of free foreign women—which involved the peril of apostasy for the husband.

15-17 Right of Primogeniture—In patriarchal times **g** the father might convey the rights of head of the family to a younger son (*cf.* Gen 48:13 ff. ; 49:3 f., 8), but Deut excludes this, at least for the motive that the eldest son's mother is ' *not loved* ' (' hated ' is too strong). The eldest son had a right to twice as much of the father's goods as each of the other sons.

18-21 The Rebellious Son—While emphasizing the gravity of the offence, nevertheless this law, like the foregoing, restricts the old *patria potestas*, for the protection of the son. The father cannot inflict death at his discretion but must refer the case to the elders.

22-23 The Exposed Corpse—' *If a man has committed* **h** *a capital offence and been put to death, and thou hast hanged his body on a tree : thou shalt not leave his corpse on the tree (overnight) but bury it without fail that same day* ' (*cf.* Jos 10:26 f.). The exposure of the corpse was an additional infamy, for the criminal and for his family ; but it was also a sight which drew down God's curse, and it must not be allowed to infect the land (*cf.* Gal 3:13).

XXII 1-4 Helping One's Neighbour—' Brother ' **i** means any fellow-Israelite. Ex 23:4 f. stresses the obligation even towards a personal enemy. **4.** If a loaded animal fell down, one man unaided could not put it on its feet again without unpacking the load.

5-12 6. As in 20:19, a warning against wanton destruction. **5, 9-12.** These laws probably had some religious significance which now escapes us.

13-30 Offences concerned with Marriage—Hebrew **j** ' espousals ', at which the man paid the bride-price for the virgin, were a binding contract that constituted a legal marriage, even though months or years might pass before cohabitation began. Hence an ' espoused maiden ' is a wife, and her unchastity constitutes adultery. **13-21 Wife accused of Infidelity**—This law aims especially at protecting the innocent woman's reputation and the honour of her family. **15.** ' Tokens of her virginity ', *i.e.* a garment she wore at the time of the consummation of the marriage, which the husband had to hand over afterwards to her parents. It would bear traces of blood from the ruptured hymen, which were accepted as evidence of previous virginity. **20 f.** If guilty, however, the wife shall be brought ' *to the door of her father's house, and (there) the men of her city shall stone her to death* '. The penalty shows that the offence is presumed to have been committed since the espousals. This was more or less the case that presented itself to St Joseph in connection with the Blessed Virgin's pregnancy, and explains why he was unwilling ' publicly to expose her ' (Mt 1:19). **22-27 Adultery**—The general law (**22**) is qualified by **25-27,** which establishes a presumption in favour of the betrothed damsel, not yet under her husband's care, when the adultery took place out of reach of help. **28 f.** In a case of **rape** the girl's guilt or innocence is not considered, but the man's responsibilities are determined. **30.** ' His father's wife ' does not mean his own mother ; the law suppresses the practice of a son's inheriting his father's wives, along with the rest of his property. The custom is illustrated in 2 Kg 16:22 and 3 Kg 2:22. In both cases it is regarded as a claim to the father's position.

XXIII 1-8 Exclusions from the Israelite Community **k** —**1.** ' *A man* whose testicles are *crushed or penis amputated* shall not enter the assembly of Yahweh.' **2.** ' Mamzer ' is uncertain (' one born of a prostitute ' is the explanation St Jerome was given by the Rabbis of his time) ; it may mean the offspring of an incestuous union—or even be a general term for the Samaritans, the mixed

8k post-exilic population of the North. **7 f.** Such kindly feeling for Edom and Egypt would be surprising ; but the law refers not to the nations as such but to immigrants who settled down to live with the Israelites.

l 9-14 Purity in Time of War—Every war being a holy war, the soldiers must guard themselves against ritual impurity, of which nocturnal pollution is taken as an instance. More than that, respect for Yahweh's presence in the camp—at the Tabernacle of the Ark—requires that the necessities of nature be attended to outside it. The signs of parenthesis in **14** are unnecessary.

m 15-16 Fugitive Slaves, from neighbouring countries, are not to be arrested and sent back—nor are they to be enslaved by the Israelites. They are to have the status of ' resident aliens ', for whose considerate treatment the Law is frequently solicitous (10:18 f., etc.)

n 17-18 Sacred Prostitution—' There shall be no *sacred female prostitute . . . and no sacred male prostitute* ' ; another point in which Israel's religion is unique among ancient Semitic cults. **18.** ' Dog ' is an opprobrious term for the male hierodule.

o 19-20 Interest on Loans to Israelites forbidden—Cf. Ex 22:25 ; Lev 25:35 ff. It follows from the concept of blood-relationship that loans between Israelites, as between members of one family, should be charitable assistance, not commercial investments ; but the latter may be placed with the '*foreigner*' (*nokrî*, distinguished from *gēr* the 'resident alien'). **24-25** show a careful combination of charity to the wayfarer (or the poor) with justice to the owner of the land.

9a XXIV 1-4 No Remarriage with a Divorced Wife after her New Marriage—This law, which supposes divorce as already customary (but excluded in certain cases, 22:19, 29), aims at discouraging it by making it more formal, and irrevocable once the divorced wife has married again. The case is stated in **1-3**, the judgement only in **4**. ' If a man takes a wife and *marries her, and she does not please him because he has found in her something unseemly ; and he writes her a bill of divorce and gives it to her and sends her away ; and she leaves his house and goes and becomes another man's wife ; and the second man does not like her and writes her a bill of divorce and gives it to her and sends her away ; or else the second man who took her as his wife dies—her first husband, who sent her away, cannot again take her to be his wife, after she has been made unclean ; for that would be an abomination before Yahweh.*' The law is quoted in Jer 3:1. The nature of the woman's uncleanness is not clear. It is evidently relative only to her first husband, since it is not forbidden for a third man to marry her.

b XXIV 5-XXV 4 Miscellaneous Laws—**5.** Cf. 20:7. **7.** ' If a man is found *who has kidnapped one of his fellow-Israelites and has made him his slave or sold him, that kidnapper* shall be put to death.' **8.** On leprosy, cf. Lev 13 f. ; on Mary (Miriam), Num 12. **6, 10-13.** Pledges, as security for the loans of 23:19 f. The hand-mill, a necessity of life for the Israelite family, is excluded ; and if the borrower offers his only mantle, ' *thou shalt not sleep upon his pledge, but thou shalt return him his pledge without fail (each) evening, that he may sleep in his mantle and bless thee ; and it shall be (reckoned) justice to thee before Yahweh*'. **14 f.** ' Thou shalt not *oppress a poor and needy day-labourer* ' ; such were often paid not in money but in foodstuffs. **16.** Cf. §110g. **17-22. Justice and Charity towards the Unprotected** should be inspired by the hope of God's blessing, a sympathetic remembrance of their own unhappy condition in Egypt, and gratitude for their deliverance therefrom. **XXV 1-3 Corporal Punishment**—No passage in the Law determines for what offences the bastinado was to be inflicted. The present law aims at preventing its abuse. It may be inflicted only after trial, by due sentence, in presence of the judge, and to a limited number of strokes. **4.** Cf. 1 Cor 9:9 ; 1 Tim 5:18.

c XXV 5-10 Levirate Marriage—An old custom in Israel, but not mentioned elsewhere in the Law. Gen 38 and Ru 4:5 show that in default of a husband's brother the obligation rested on the next-of-kin. Deut limits it to brothers living on the same estate, one of **219c** whom dies ' without leaving *a son* ' (the law of Num 27:8 is ignored), and stresses the purpose of the law. A humiliating punishment is prescribed for the man who will not fulfil it ; the similar ceremony in Ru 4:7 is presented as merely a legal formality.

11-12 Indecent Assault—The barbarity of the punishment (the only instance of mutilation prescribed by Deut) marks this law as very old, probably pre-Mosaic. (The Middle Assyrian law-code, 1500–1250 B.C., had a similar clause.) It reflects not only the gravity of the injury likely to be suffered by the man, but also primitive reverence for the sexual organs as the source of life.

13-16 Commercial Honesty—**13-14** require only that **d** a man use the same standard for both buying and selling (*cf.* Am 8:5 ; Mt 7:2). **15,** however, evidently of later date, prescribes that the weight and measure be ' true ', conformed to some standard, presumably promulgated by the king.

17-19 The Amalekites were nomads who repeatedly harassed Israel during the Wandering and after (Ex 17:8 ff. ; Num 14:43 ; Jg 6:3, etc.). The barbarity here mentioned (not elsewhere recorded)—when they '*cut off all thy stragglers disorganized in thy rear, while thou wert weary and worn out*'—was particularly odious by the standards of desert warfare, and explains the severity of the condemnation. (*Cf.* 1 Kg 15:2 ff. ; 30:1 ff. ; 1 Par 4:41 ff.)

XXVI 1-15 Two Liturgical Ordinances—**1-11 Thanks-** **e** **giving**—At the offering of the firstfruits Israel shall publicly recall Yahweh's loving kindness, contrasting their original nomad condition with the present possession of their own fertile land. **3-4** seem to be an extract from a different version of the same ceremony. **5.** ' Thou shalt speak before Yahweh thy God : " *My ancestors were nomad Aramaeans, who went down into Egypt and dwelt there as aliens, few in numbers ; and there they became a people, great and strong and numerous* ".' **10.** ' And now, *behold, I bring the first-fruits.*' The essence of Deut's doctrine is in this fine prayer, stressing the gratitude due in return for so much love. Further, there is the intention to exclude any reference of the harvest blessings to the Canaanite fertility gods ; to Yahweh alone is due the increase.

12-15 The Triennial Tithe-Banquet, held at home for the benefit of the local poor (*cf.* 14:28 f.). **12 f.** ' When thou hast finished tithing . . . and *hast given it to the* Levite . . . (*then*) thou shalt speak in the sight of Yahweh . . .' Not less than the offerings in the temple, these foods belong to Yahweh and must not be profaned ; hence not partaken of by one in mourning, nor touched by one ritually unclean, nor used for an offering to the dead—*i.e.* food and drink set on a grave. **17-19.** Statement of the obligations mutually assumed by Yahweh and his people, in the making of the Covenant. ' This day ', in the context, is the day on which Moses is presented as making this speech, in Moab ; but also any day that a solemn renewal of the Covenant took place, when this formula might be used. This section continues in 28:1.

XXVII 1-26 Ceremonies to be performed on entering f the Promised Land—On crossing the Jordan the Israelites are to perform certain rites to signify that they take possession of the land on the terms laid down by Yahweh. The instruction is inserted here as a speech of Moses, independent of the main discourse (chh 5–28). For its fulfilment *cf.* Jos 8:30–35. **2.** An inscription painted on whitewashed stones would not survive long in the climate of Palestine ; but—evidence of the antiquity of this tradition—this was the technique used in Egypt. **5f.** For this occasion Mt Ebal would be a place chosen by Yahweh for sacrifice. **9-10** are out of place ; read as the introduction to ch 28. **14.** ' Levites ' are here distinguished, as functionaries, from the tribe of Levi, 12. **15-25.** The twelve curses listed are surprising ; one half of the crimes are not mentioned in the Deut Code, and some of Deut's gravest precepts are passed over. Hence this is

219f probably a selection, to fit the number of the tribes, from some much more elaborate ritual of anathemas.

g **XXVIII 1-68 Blessings and Curses**—The ratification of any covenant was accompanied by blessings for its fulfilment and curses for its infringement ; *cf.* the conclusion of the Book of the Covenant in Ex 23:20-33, of the Law of Holiness in Lev 26:3-45. This of Deut, in oratorical form, is the most tremendous of all. **3-14 Blessings**—**6.** An all-inclusive blessing, which ' signifies totality by the combination of opposites '. **10.** ' That the name . . . ' : freely, ' *that thou art the property and under the protection of Yahweh* '. **15-46 Curses** —Four short sections, rising each to its own climax in 19, 26, 34, 46. **15-19** correspond to 1-6. **25b.** ' and *thou shalt be an object of horror to* all the kingdoms of the earth.' **34.** ' And *thou shalt go mad by reason of* the things thine eyes shall see.' **36 f.** and **41** are out of context ; they probably go with the following section. **47-68 Additional Curses**—This section is of later composition than the rest. **58, 61** show that it is an addition, not to a speech but to a written book. **64.** *Cf.* note on 4:28. This stirring chapter, overwhelming in its vehement eloquence, shows us by implication how difficult in practice, and how imperfectly fulfilled, was the obligation of the Covenant. *Cf.* St Paul's comments (Rom 7:7 ff., etc.). We should not exaggerate the material character of the rewards and punishments so vividly pictured ; they are adduced only as the outward manifestations of the satisfaction or displeasure of Yahweh, whose sanctity and love are the norms to which his people must conform.

XXIX 1 Conclusion to the foregoing legislation (chh 12-26) constituting the Covenant of Moab, ' *as distinguished from* the covenant which he made with them at Horeb '.

220a **XXIX 2-XXX 20 Third Discourse**—**2-9 Motives for Gratitude** are briefly recalled, in historical summary. **4.** According to Heb. idiom this is not an excuse but an accusation ; it is equivalent to saying that they *would* not understand and obey. **6.** When the ordinary sustenance of bread and wine was lacking, Yahweh provided them with manna and with water from the rock.

b **10-29 The Covenant is for Future Generations ;** hence the responsibility of the whole community here present, when they (**12**) ' *agree to* the covenant of Yahweh thy God, *and his oath* ' or ' *malediction* '—the punishment for non-fulfilment of their contract. **16 f.** They know, from their own contact with idolatry, the need for such an agreement, to prevent there being among them now or later, anyone (**18**) ' who *secretly apostatizes* from Yahweh our God, to go and worship the gods of these peoples ', yet, (**19**) ' when he hears the words of this oath, *congratulates himself*, saying, " I shall have peace, *doing as I please* " ; and *so wet and dry shall be swept away together* '. The last phrase signifies the destruction of all the people, ' the green wood and the dry ', for the guilt of some. But in **23-28** the guilt is represented as having been universal. **28.** ' As it is seen this day ', even if it is part of the ' answer ', suggests that this chapter took its final form during the Exile. **29** is a gloss, of uncertain meaning ; presumably the ' secret things ' are future events, known only to God ; the ' manifest ' are those which have come to pass, which are a warning ' to us and to our children '.

c **XXX 1-10 Restoration promised even after Destruction** —*Cf.* 4:29-31. **1.** ' The blessing or the curse ' is probably a gloss ; ' all these things ' refers only to the chastisement, here presented as an historical fact. This section (1-10) is addressed directly to the exiles in Babylonia, 6th cent. B.C. **3.** ' Yahweh thy God will *restore* thee ', *i.e.* put an end to thy affliction. **5.** ' Thy fathers ', the generations from the time of Josue to the Exile. **6.** ' Circumcise ' : *cf.* 10:16.

d **11-14 No Excuse for Ignorance of the Law**—Yahweh has revealed his will clearly and unmistakably, so that they need not fear arbitrary and unpredictable punishments ; they know exactly what they have to do to please him.

15-20 Summary—**15.** *Cf.* 11:26 ff. **16.** LXX supplies **22...** a missing phrase : ' *If thou wilt obey the commands of Yahweh thy God, which I am commanding thee this day, to love Yahweh . . . thou shalt* live and multiply and *Yahweh thy God will* bless thee.' **20b.** ' *For that means life for thee*, and length of days.'

XXXI 1-XXXIV 12 Historical Appendix—These four **22...** chapters form a conclusion not so much to Deut as to the Pentateuch as a whole. They combine extracts from different sources, and the text is in some confusion.

XXXI 1-8 Appointment of Josue—This is an extract from a larger context. **1** seems to refer to some instruction just received from Yahweh. **2.** 120 is a round number, perhaps indicating a life-span of three generations. ' I can no longer go out ', *i.e.* ' I am not active as I used to be '—a different emphasis, at least, from that given in 34:7. **3b.** ' And this Josue . . . ' is out of place—should perhaps follow **6**.

9-13 Septennial Reading of the Law—This direction **b** represents an ideal, probably rarely put in practice before the era of Judaism. **9.** ' This law ' : there is no way of telling what is included in this expression— the Decalogue ? the Code of Deut ? or some other part of the Pentateuch ? *Cf.* 27:2 f. **12.** ' And *assemble* all the people.'

14-15, 23 Commission of Yahweh to Josue—*Cf.* the **c** parallel account in Num 27:18-23. This in Deut is fragmentary ; the ' charge ' of **14** comes only—and very briefly—in **23** ; the latter repeats the phrases of 7.

16-21 Instruction to Moses—A description of the conduct of the people, once settled in Palestine. Also fragmentary—*cf.* the sudden reference (**19**) to ' this canticle ', not mentioned before. **20.** ' *When I shall have brought them* into the land ' : there is a striking note of pathos in this reference to Yahweh's love.

22, 24-30 Introduction to the Canticle—As HT stands, **d** **24-27**, repeating 9, tell of the writing of a law and its delivery for safe-keeping to the Levites ; while **28-30** is a fragment, parallel to **22**, of an introduction to Moses' recitation of the canticle referred to in 19, 21 f. But a quite plausible correction of two letters —*haššîrāh* for *hattôrāh*—gives in **24** the reading ' words of this *canticle* ', adopted by most critics ; then the whole section is an introduction to the canticle.

XXXII 1-43 The Canticle of Moses—This majestic **22...** poem is a didactic psalm, recounting the familiar story of Yahweh's particular bounty to Israel and Israel's unfaithfulness to Yahweh. For this they have been severely punished, through foreign oppressors ; but in the end, since his own honour is at stake, Yahweh will rescue his people and turn his anger against their persecutors (*cf.* Ps 105). Not only the Wandering (10-12) but events in Palestine (13-18) are referred to as history, and ancient history at that (7), which is contrasted with Israel's triumphant vindication (35-43), still in the future. Hence this is a composition not of Moses' time but from some later period of unsuccessful war, following on a time of prosperity and corruption. Its ascription to Moses is an ordinary literary device, to indicate that this is the doctrine that he taught and the history that he foretold.

1-7 Announcement of the Theme : Yahweh's Good- b ness and Israel's Ingratitude—**1 f.** Invocation. **3 f.** Character of Yahweh. **4.** ' *The Rock, whose work is perfect* ' : a favourite term for God, here and in the earlier Psalms. **5 f.** Unreasonable ingratitude of Israel. **7.** Introduction to the main theme.

8-25 The History of God's Love and Israel's Ungrate- c fulness—**8-14 What Yahweh did for Israel**—**8 f.** In distributing territories (Gen 10:32) he set aside ample space for his people, ' For *Yahweh's own portion is Jacob —Israel is his allotted possession.*' **11** should be joined with the foregoing : ' *As an eagle, rousing his nestlings, Hovering over his fledglings, Spreads his wings and takes them, Bearing them on his pinions.*' **13.** ' *He let him ride on the heights of the land, And eat the produce of the hills* ' : the installation in Palestine. **14c.** ' *And the blood of the grape thou didst drink in foam ; Thou didst become fat and*

c *plump and sleek.*' The latter phrase has been displaced into 15. **15-18 How Israel abused his Kindness—15.** ' *But Jacob ate and was filled—And Jeshurun grew fat and kicked—And he abandoned God his Maker—And scorned the Rock his Saviour.*' ' Jeshurun ', a rare and poetical synonym for ' Israel ', is used here ironically ; it means ' the Righteous '. **18.** ' Thou hast abandoned *the Rock* who begot thee—And hast forgotten the God who *bore* thee.' **19-25 Just Anger of Yahweh—20.** Yahweh's speech, beginning here, goes to the end of 28. **24 f.** Famine, pestilence, and war are his instruments of chastisement.

d 26-42 Yahweh's Anger is diverted to Israel's Enemies —26-28. He will not let his people be utterly destroyed, lest their enemies take occasion to mock at him. **26 f.** ' *I would have said,* " *I will wipe them out,* I will abolish their memory among men* ", *But I dreaded the taunts* of the foe, Lest their enemies should *misunderstand.*' **28.** ' *For* they are a nation ', *scil.* the enemies. **29-31. Foolishness of the Enemies—**Here the poet speaks, interrupting Yahweh's soliloquy. The only reason for Israel's defeats—and by inferior numbers !—is that Yahweh so willed ; otherwise his people would naturally conquer, for, ' not like our *Rock* is their *rock*—Our enemies *can witness to that !*' **32-35a. Wickedness of the Enemies,** which is an offence to Yahweh. His speech continues. **35a.** ' Mine *shall* be the vengeance and the *requital, At the moment when their foot stumbles.*' **35b-42 Yahweh will destroy them—**The poet speaks again. **35b-36.** ' *For the day of their destruction is at hand, And their fate is overtaking them,* For Yahweh will *do justice to* his people, And will take pity on his servants.' But he will take care that they learn their lesson ; ironically, he will say **(37 f.)** ' Where are their gods, *The rock where they sought refuge ?* (*The gods*) *who ate the fat of their sacrifices—*And drank the wine of their libations ?—Let them rise up.' The speech continues to the end of 42. **39.** ' See now that *I, I am the One,* And there is no other god but me. It is I *who slay and who bring to life—I wound, and I give healing.*' **40 f.** Yahweh's solemn oath : ' *For I raise* my hand to heaven, *And I say,* " *As* I live for ever ; If I whet my sword . . ." '

e 43 Conclusion of the Canticle—' Exult loudly, ye nations, *for* his people, For he will avenge the blood of his servants, He will execute vengeance on *his* enemies, And *purify* his people's land.'

44-52 Conclusion ; Yahweh's Instructions to Moses —44 refers to the Canticle, **45 ff.** to the Law : ' *And when Moses finished speaking to all Israel,* he said to them, " *Set your hearts. . .*" ' **47.** ' *For this is not a trifling matter for you, but it means your life ;* (only) *in this way* will you live long.' **48-51** is a doublet of Num 27:12-14, with some editorial additions. **52** joins on to 34:1.

f XXXIII 1-29 The Blessing of Moses—This chapter contains (6-24) a series of oracular blessings, in poetic form, on eleven of the tribes (omitting Simeon) ; *cf.* the earlier Blessing of Jacob (Gen 49:2-27). The situation implied, the disappearance of Simeon, etc., suggest as a date of composition the late Judges period or the early monarchy. As introduction and conclusion to the blessings there are two parts (2-5, 26-29) of a ' national psalm ', glorifying the God of Israel in his leadership of the people. The text of the chapter is corrupt and uncertain in many places.

g 2-5 Psalm ; First Part—A theophany : Yahweh brings his people to Palestine. *Cf.* the same theme in Jg 5 : 4 f. ; Ps 17:7 ff. ; 77:13 ff. ; Hab 3:3 ff. Here the Wandering is outlined by the mention of four stages. **2b.** ' *He shone* from Mt Pharan ; *He came to Meribath-Kadesh. From his right hand, a burning fire.*' **3b-5.** ' *They received*

of his teaching, *The Law which he has commanded us.* The **222g** assembly of Jacob *is his possession,* And he became king in *Jeshurun,* When the heads of the people were assembled, *The tribes of Israel all together.*'

6-25 The Blessings—6 Ruben : ' *Let Ruben live,* **h** *though* his men are few in number.' **7 Judah :** ' *And* bring him *back* to his people. Let *thy* hands defend his cause ; Be *thou* his helper against his enemies.' **8-11 Levi :** ' *To Levi belong thy Thummim, And thy Urim, to the man of thy love.*' *Cf.* §179d. The tribe is praised for putting devotion to the cult and the Law above natural ties. **12 Benjamin :** ' *Benjamin is the beloved of Yahweh ; He abides in the security of the Most High, Who guards him all the day, And he reposes on his back* ', *i.e.* is carried like a child. **13-17 Ephraim and Manasses :** the two tribes are joined as one, Joseph. The blessing of fertility is a variant of Jacob's (Gen 49:25 f.). **13.** ' *Blessed of Yahweh be his land, By the excellence of the heavens above, And by the deep ocean lying below.*' **16.** ' *By the excellence of the earth and its fulness, May the favour of the Dweller in the bush Come upon the head of Joseph, Upon his head, who is the prince of his brethren.*' For the ' Dweller in the bush ' see Ex 3:2-4. **17.** ' His glory is that of *a first-born bull*—And the horns of *a wild ox* are his horns.' **18-19 Zabulon and Issachar : 19.** ' *They summon peoples to the mountain ; There they offer due sacrifice, For they suck the riches of the sea, And gather treasures from the sand.*' **20-21 Gad :** ' *Blessed be he that hath enlarged Gad ; Like a lion he crouches, Tearing the shoulder-blade and the head too.* And he saw that he got the best, For there is the allotment of the ruler ' ; not a reference to Moses (who was buried in Ruben's territory) but to the tribe's prosperity in Transjordan. **22 Dan :** ' Dan is a lion's cub ; *He springs out* from Bashan.' **23 Nephtali. 24-25 Aser :** ' *Let Aser be the most blessed of the sons, Favoured above his brothers* ', especially in possessing the luxuriant olive-groves of Galilee. ' Iron and bronze be *thy bars* ', *i.e.* gate-fastenings, as a symbol of security. **26-29 Psalm : Second Part—**Yahweh continually **i** protects his people. **26 f.** ' *There is none like the God of Jeshurun ; The Rider of the heavens is thy helper,* (*The Rider*) *of the clouds, in his majesty. On high is the God of ages,* And underneath are the everlasting arms ' : a beautiful figure for the protection he gives to Israel. **28.** ' *Israel shall dwell in security ; The fountain of Jacob be secluded, In a land of corn and wine ; Yea, his sky shall drop dew.*' **29c.** ' *Thy enemies shall submit to thee, And thou shalt march on the heights of their land.*'

XXXIV 1-12 The Death of Moses—The Pentateuch **j** closes solemnly with the death of the great Prophet and Legislator, who was God's instrument in forging a group of nomad tribes into a people, holy to the Lord, and so preparing the way for the far greater Prophet and Legislator whom he prefigured. **1-4 The View of the Promised Land—**' *The headland of Pisgah* ' (Phasga) runs out NNW. from Mt Nebo proper, and rises to a small promontory (modern Râs es-Siâghah) whence on a clear day there is a magnificent panorama of Palestine. Still, it does not include all the further limits here named, which define the land itself rather than Moses' view of it. **1b-3.** ' And Yahweh showed him all the land : Gilead as far as Dan ; all Nephtali ; the land of Ephraim and Manasses : all the land of Judah, to the *Western* Sea ; *the Negeb* ; and the *Dead Sea basin (that is, the Valley of Jericho,* the city of palms) as far [*south*] as Segor.' **5-12 Death of Moses and Succession of Josue—5 f.** ' And Moses . . . died there . . . *according to the word of Yahweh ;* and *he was buried in the valley* . . .' **7.** *Cf.* on 31:2 ; here, ' *his sight was not dimmed nor his vigour spent* '. **11-12,** awkwardly joined to **10,** are a later addition to the text.

THE HISTORICAL BOOKS

By E. POWER, S.J.

223a Names and Order of the Historical Books—The historical books are placed in the following order in our Bibles : Josue, Judges, Ruth, 1–4 Kings, 1–2 Paralipomenon, 1–2 Esdras (or Esdras and Nehemias), Tobias, Judith, Esther, and lastly, after a long interval, 1–2 Maccabees. It is generally admitted that Judith and 1 Maccabees were originally written in Hebrew. The primitive language of 2 Maccabees is Greek, that of Tobias is uncertain. In the Hebrew Bible 1–2 Kg is called Samuel, 3–4 Kg Kings, 1–2 Par Chronicles, and 1–2 Esd Ezra-Nehemiah. The word Paralipomenon means 'of things left out' and its substitution for ' Chronicles ' by the Greek translators shows that they regarded that book, not quite correctly, as a supplement to Kings. While we distinguish the books of the OT which follow the Pentateuch as historic, prophetic and didactic, according to their subject matter, the Hebrews had only two categories : Prophets, Former and Latter, and Writings or Sacred

b Writings. The Former Prophets comprised the four historical books : Josue, Judges, Samuel and Kings. Some scholars explain the honorific title given to these books as a consequence of their greater antiquity or earlier inclusion in the Canon. But the Rabbis are more correct in regarding it as an indication of the personal dignity of the authors. According to them Moses, author of the five books of the Torah, ranked highest (*cf.* Num 12:6–8), then the prophets, who wrote the eight prophetical books, and lastly the Wise Men, who composed the Sacred Writings. Grades of personal dignity do not imply grades of inspiration which are excluded by Catholic teaching. But the name of Prophets clearly indicates that the authors of the principal historical books were the exponents of a divine message, since a prophet was, according to the Hebrews, the mouth of God (*cf.* Ex 4:10–16 ; 7:1–2).

c Survey of the Contents of the Historical Books—The books called ' Former Prophets ' by the Hebrews give an outline of the history of the Chosen People from the invasion of Palestine to the Babylonian captivity. Josue describes the conquest and occupation of the Promised Land. Judges contains an episodic narrative of the disorderly period between the settlement in Palestine and the institution of the monarchy. Samuel (1–2 Kg) gives an account of the last of the judges and founder of the monarchy, Samuel, and of the reigns of the first two kings, Saul and David. Kings (3–4 Kg) continues the history of the monarchy through the reigns of Solomon and Roboam, the schism of the northern tribes and the separate kingdoms of Judah and Israel until their disappearance in the Assyrian and Babylonian captivities. There is no history of the captivity. But Esdras carries on the narrative with an account of the principal events of the first century of the restoration. In the Chronicles (1–2 Par) we have a kind of compendium of biblical history from Adam to the edict of Cyrus and additional information about the period of the monarchy, especially as regards the religious institutions of the Kingdom of Judah. There is a second lacuna of two centuries and a half between Esdras and Maccabees. 1 Mac relates the victorious wars of the family of the Maccabees against the Seleucid monarchs of Syria (177–136 B.C.). 2 Mac has the same theme, but only covers the first

d part of the period (177–161 B.C.). The four smaller

books are concerned, not with periods, but with single **2?** episodes. Ruth narrates the reception of a Moabitess among the Chosen People in the period of the Judges. Judith describes the deliverance of Israel from a foreign invasion, either of Assyrians in the 7th, or, more probably, of Persians in the 4th cent. B.C. In Esther we have a similar deliverance of Hebrews in exile from the extermination with which they are menaced by a decree of King Xerxes. The trials and rewards of a pious Hebrew family during the Assyrian captivity are the subject of the book of Tobias.

Purpose of the Historical Books—Though these books **e** narrate historical facts, it is evident from an examination of their contents that they have not been written from a merely historical standpoint. In such a hypothesis the historian of the period of the monarchy, for instance, would undoubtedly have informed us at some length of the exploits and fortunes of the various kings of Judah and Israel. The sacred writer, however, usually refers us to historical works, now no longer extant, for information on these matters. On the other hand he regularly points out the religious or irreligious character of the different monarchs and devotes considerable space to the activity of the two great prophets, Elias and Eliseus. The events of the life of King David are recounted at such length that they fill more than a fourth of the pages devoted to the whole history of Israel from the conquest of Canaan to the Babylonian captivity. The historical episodes related in the book of Judges depict, for the most part, recurring cycles of events : sin of Israel, punishment by foreign invasion, repentance of Israel, deliverance by Yahweh. This repeated sin of the Israelites is described in the prologue (Jg 2:20) as a violation of the covenant which God had made with their fathers. Thus we have here a clear indication that the main purpose of the sacred writer was to narrate the working out of the covenant made by God with his chosen people.

And the same idea of a history of the covenant offers **f** a satisfactory explanation of the choice of materials made by the authors of the other historical books. The parts played by Josue and David as God's instruments in the fulfilment of the two great promises made to Abraham (*cf.* Gen 12:7 and Jos 1:6 and the Messianic prophecies Gen 22:18 and 2 Kg 7:16) explain their predominant importance. Samuel among the judges, Elias and Eliseus among the prophets, Ezechias and Josias among the kings, receive particular attention as the great supporters and restorers of the national religion. The reigns of the most powerful and prosperous rulers of the kingdom of Israel are only briefly recorded. The impiety of Achab is depicted at length but it is only from Assyrian and Moabite inscriptions that we learn of such important historical facts as the first encounter between Israel and Assyria and the character of the revolt of Mesha, king of Moab. The final narrative of the restoration in Esdras completes the history of the covenant as a cycle of sin, punishment, repentance and deliverance, like the episodes of the book of Judges. In thus relating the fulfilment of the promises and threats attached to the observance and neglect of the covenant, the sacred writers had undoubtedly in mind the instruction of later generations in the religious teachings of their past history.

g We may thus define their purpose as religious and didactic rather than scientific and informative. The books are historical in the sense that the religious lessons are definitely based not on fictitious narratives but on the facts of history. But the history as such is incomplete, since only those facts are narrated which the authors found suitable to their purpose. The same conclusion may also be deduced from the general character of the Sacred Scriptures, which were given, not for the satisfaction of our intellectual curiosity, but in view of our eternal salvation. As St Paul tells us : ' All Scripture divinely inspired is profitable to teach, to reprove; to correct, to instruct in justice ' (2 Tim 3:16).

a Authorship and Date of Composition—1–2 Par and Esdras exhibit such striking similarities of language, style and method of composition that they are considered by all to have been written by the same hand. The unity of plan which appears in the other historical books suggests an individual author in each case, provided, of course, that we consider these books in their original extent and ignore the later division into two parts or books of Samuel, Kings, Chronicles and Esdras. But various diversities, not only of style and construction, but also of language and date, show that these authors are distinct from one another. Who they were cannot be definitely determined. Names like Josue, Samuel and Esdras do not refer to authorship, but to subject matter like Judges and Kings.

b Nor have we any reliable indications of the various dates of composition except such as can be deduced from the texts themselves. From these we conclude that Josue, Judges and Samuel are pre-exilic, since they make no allusion to the Babylonian exile. The mention of the captivity of the land in Jg 18:30, if authentic, must be referred evidently to the Assyrian captivity of the kingdom of Israel in 733 or 721 B.C. But even this date is uncertain, since a textual error, by which *land* has taken the place of an original *ark*, is suggested by the context. The citation from the *Book of the Just*, or of Yashar (Jos 10:13), which also contained David's elegy on Saul and Jonathan (2 Kg 1:18), shows that Josue was written after the death of Saul. But it would be unsafe to conclude from the reference to the Canaanite occupation of Gezer ' to the present day ' (Jos 16:10) that it was written at latest during the early part of Solomon's reign, since there may be question here, as in similar cases, of the citation of an ancient document. The author of Judges implies the existence of kings in Israel and must therefore have been written after the institution of the monarchy. The allusion in Samuel to the kings of Judah (1 Kg 27:6) shows that it was composed some time after the partition of the kingdom. The author of Kings undoubtedly writes in view of the exile, of which he sets forth the causes. He even mentions some events of the exilic period, but makes no mention of the restoration. The book may thus be assigned to the latter part of the exile. The language and contents of Esdras and Chronicles seem to exclude a date prior to the end of the 4th cent. B.C. Of the smaller books Ruth may be pre-exilic and Esther may belong to the Persian period, but both dates are disputed. The dates of Tobias and Judith cannot be even approximately determined. 1 Mac was probably written about 100 B.C., 2 Mac somewhat earlier, but not earlier than 124 B.C. if the first letter cited belonged to the original work.

c Literary Sources—The authority of a historian who had no direct contact with the events which he narrates depends mainly on the character of his sources. There are many indications that the Hebrew historians did not rely on oral tradition for their materials but had excellent contemporary documents at their disposal. References to writing in the earliest sacred books, which were regarded as anachronisms in some quarters not so very long ago, have been amply confirmed by archaeological proofs of its widespread diffusion in Palestine at a still earlier period, *cf.* § 80*i*.

That Josue left a written record of some events of his **224c** life and that this record was used by the sacred writer is an obvious conclusion from Jos 24:26. The lists of the cities of Palestine show their antiquity and documentary character by the use of ancient names, such as Baala, Cariath-Sepher, Hesron and Cariath-Arbe, which have to be supplemented by the author with their later equivalents. The statement at the end of the list of the cities of Judah that the Jebusites dwell in Jerusalem ' to this day ' (Jos 15:63) must be part of an ancient document, since David's capture of the fortress was a matter of general knowledge when the book was written. The author, however, does not explicitly mention his sources except in one case, the *Book of the Just* (Jos 10:13), which seems to have been a poetical collection of the exploits of the righteous men of Israel. In Jg 1 there are some statements, which figured already in Josue in identical terms, but in a different context. The language of the Canticle of Debbora proves that it is an ancient document and the intensity of feeling which it displays implies a very close contact with the events which it describes. The letter of Jephte to the king of the Ammonites (Jg 11:14–28) seems to have been known to the sacred writer, though this is not expressly stated.

We have much more direct and indirect evidence of **d** sources employed by the authors of Samuel, Kings and Chronicles. Only one source is explicitly mentioned in Samuel, the *Book of the Just*, from which David's elegy on Saul and Jonathan is taken (2 Kg 1:18). But we find a *mazkîr* or recorder included among the court officials of David and such abundant and detailed information on his life as to postulate the use of written documents. Here the Chronicler comes to our aid with a mention of the *Chronicles of King David* (1 Par 27:24) and of the *Acts of King David* written by the prophets, Samuel, Nathan and Gad (1 Par 29:29). Moreover, there are many passages, sometimes of considerable length, in Samuel and Kings on the one hand and Chronicles on the other, which are either literally or substantially identical and therefore suppose a literary borrowing either of the latest author from the two earlier ones or of all three from a common source. The latter alternative is the more probable. The Chronicler regularly indicates his sources and gives us at the same time much additional information, for which no sources would be indicated except Samuel and Kings, if he borrowed directly from them. It would seem, therefore, that the sources he indicates are different, since he could not cite from the earlier canonical books what they did not contain. It follows that the sources used by the author of Samuel are the same as those of the Chronicler, namely the *Chronicles of King David* and the written records of the contemporary prophets, Samuel, Nathan and Gad. The words ' to this day ' (3 Kg 8:8 ; 9:21 ; 12:19 ; 4 Kg 8:22) attest the use of documents in Kings, since they do not suit the time in which the book was composed. The author refers us, moreover, once to the *Annals of Solomon*, fifteen times to the *Annals of the Kings of Judah* and eighteen times to the *Annals of the Kings of Israel*. Though these works are directly indicated as sources of further information, there can be no doubt that the facts narrated were mainly derived from them.

A recorder is mentioned among the court officials of **e** the three kings, Solomon, Ezechias and Josias, whose reigns, owing to their religious importance, receive particular attention. We may, therefore, conclude that the other kings, about whom we are less fully informed, had also their recorders. It is most probable that this word designates an official historian, but it may possibly indicate also, or instead, one who had to remind the king of his duties and functions. If the recorders were historians, the annals of the kings of Judah and Israel would have been mainly derived from their records. Indeed the very mention of the annals seems to imply the existence of such officials. The singular omission of all reference to these annals in Kings and Chronicles for further information on

224e Sedecias, the last king of Judah whose death is mentioned, may be naturally explained by the fact that the tragic events of the period interrupted the work of the recorder.

f The Chronicler, who ignores the kingdom of Israel in his account of the monarchy, usually indicates his sources at the end of each reign. These are of two kinds : official chronicles and prophetic writings. Both are represented in the sources of the life of David already mentioned. The prophetic writings of Nathan, Ahias, Addo, Semeias, Jehu son of Hanani, Isaias son of Amos, and the official *Book of the Kings of Judah and Israel* are cited for the subsequent history of the monarchy, the prophets more usually in the earlier and the *Book of the Kings* in the later period. The special information on the religious institutions of the kingdom of Judah, in which the Chronicler was particularly interested, would naturally be mainly derived from the prophetic writings. . Esdras consists almost entirely of the personal narratives of Esdras and Nehemias, concerning events in which they took a leading part, official documents cited as such, and various lists of persons, derived apparently from public and private records. Only one of these records, a book of Chronicles which had a list of the children of Levi, is explicitly mentioned. The genealogies are mainly derived from the book of Genesis. The author of 1 Mac refers us to public records for the history of the last of the heroes whose exploits he chronicles (1 Mac 16:24), from which we may conclude that similar sources were at his disposal throughout his whole narrative. In 2 Mac we have a synopsis of a longer work of the Greek historian, Jason of Cyrene. There is no definite indication of the sources of Ruth, Tobias, Judith and Esther.

225a **Credibility of the Historical Books**—The ordinary reader cannot fail to be deeply impressed by the obvious sincerity of the Hebrew historians. This impression is mainly produced by two remarkable characteristics. The first is their special view of the function of history, which is quite different from that of the modern scientific historian. They see and trace in the facts of history the manifestations of an all-ruling Providence, rewarding good and punishing evil and directing all things according to a divine plan. The moderns, on the other hand, leave Providence aside and only seek to discover the natural causes of events. There is, of course, no conflict between these two different points of view, since each refers to a different order of causality and the Primary Cause concurs harmoniously with the secondary causes in producing the resultant effects. But the Hebrew view of history excludes all deliberate distortion of the facts, since such a mode of procedure would deprive it of its essential foundation and undermine its religious teaching. One might disagree with their interpretation of the facts in some cases, if one had not in the doctrine of inerrancy another and a higher motive for assenting to it, but one could scarcely believe that they knowingly substituted fiction for fact.

b The second important characteristic is their truly remarkable impartiality. They know that their people is the chosen people of God, charged with a special mission in the execution of the divine plan, and yet they narrate at length without dissimulation the various instances of their idolatry and moral obliquity, of their backsliding and ingratitude. The sins and scandals of national heroes like David and Solomon are frankly described. Jehu's ferocity and bloodthirstiness and Jephte's moral and religious deficiencies show us these two deliverers not as idealized figures but, as they really were, very imperfect human instruments of Yahweh. The error of the prophet Nathan in approving David's plan of building the temple is openly avowed, nor is there any concealment of the very human discouragement of Elias. This characteristic is a natural consequence of the elevated Hebrew concept of history. Alleged instances of partiality can be shown to be only apparent when the special purpose of

the sacred writer is considered. Thus the Chronicler's silence about the sins of David and Solomon is explained by the fact that his main interest was in the religious institutions of the kingdom of Judah on which they had no bearing.

Method of Composition : Oriental History—In his **c** Encyclical on Biblical Studies Pope Pius XII declares that the literal sense of a passage in Scripture, that is, the sense intended and expressed by the inspired writer, ' is not to be determined by the rules of grammar and philology alone, nor solely by the context ; the interpreter must, as it were, go back wholly in spirit to those remote centuries of the East, and with the aid of history, archaeology, ethnology and other sciences, accurately determine what modes of writing, so to speak, the authors of that ancient period would be likely to use, and in fact did use '. After remarking that this study of the past has more clearly shown the forms of expression used in recording the facts of history and ' the special pre-eminence of the people of Israel among all the other ancient nations of the East in their mode of compiling history, both by reason of its antiquity and by reason of the faithful record of the events ' he adds : ' Nevertheless no one, who has a correct idea of biblical inspiration, will be surprised to find, even in the sacred writers, as in other ancient authors, certain fixed ways of expounding and narrating, certain definite idioms, especially of a kind peculiar to the Semitic tongues, so-called approximations, and certain hyperbolical modes of expression, nay at times even paradoxical, which help to impress the ideas more clearly on the mind '. He then urges the Catholic exegete to make a prudent use of this means also in interpreting the sacred text, attributes to the neglect of it not a few accusations of historical error or inaccuracy made against the sacred writers in the past, and concludes with the words : ' By this knowledge and exact appreciation of the modes of speaking and writing in use among the ancients can be solved many difficulties, which are raised against the veracity and historical accuracy of the Divine Scripture ; and no less efficaciously does this study contribute to a fuller and more luminous understanding of the mind of the sacred writer '.

The ancient peoples of the East, Assyro-Babylonians, **d** Hittites, Egyptians, etc., have left us in their records historical materials, but no historical works. The Hebrews were the first to narrate the events of a period in a continuous narrative with a definite purpose and plan. Their materials were derived from the sources at their disposal, but the choice of the materials used, the ordering of the narrative and the interpretation of the facts were the task of the inspired writers. While, therefore, we derive much enlightenment on their language and customs, modes of expression and historical milieu from their eastern contemporaries, we obtain no direct information on their method of composition.

An effort, however, has been made to assimilate their **e** mode of procedure to the better-known methods of their earliest eastern counterparts, the much later Arab historians of the Mohammedan period. These were compilers rather than authors, who transcribed their sources or interwove them in their narrative, with or without explicit indication of their provenance, but with little or no attempt at a critical evaluation of their contents. When a modern historian incorporates in his narrative a passage from a literary source without explicitly indicating its author he makes it his own and assumes responsibility for it. Such a passage is an implicit citation. When on the contrary he indicates the author, he leaves the responsibility to him and it is only from the context that we can determine whether he accepts or rejects it in whole or in part. Here we have an explicit citation. The later Arab historians made no distinction between an explicit and an implicit citation. The assumption that the Hebrew historians like the Arab did not assume responsibility for implicit citations seemed to some Catholic exegetes

e to provide an easy means of solving historical difficulties against biblical inerrancy. But a decree of the Biblical Commission proscribed an indiscriminate use of the theory of implicit citations, authorizing it only in cases where it has been solidly proved that there is a citation and that the sacred writer does not approve it or make it his own; *cf.* § 52*i*. The reason of this decree is obvious. If the sacred writers did not guarantee the materials they have chosen from sources so extensively used, they would deprive their writings of historical value and would also undermine the religious lessons they intend to teach of an over-ruling Providence in the history of Israel, since these lessons are manifestly and necessarily based, not on dubious or fictitious narratives, but on definite historical facts. The exceptional cases referred to in the decree are not easily established owing to the difficulty of complying with the second condition laid down. One might suggest with all due reserve that the census lists of David provide an instance. It was just as manifest to contemporary readers of Samuel and Chronicles as it is to modern exegetes that these lists were derived from written sources. No prudent historian who knew how the census was made would regard the resultant figures as giving more than a good general idea of the population. The fact that different numbers, derived apparently from different sources, are given in 2 Kg 24:29 and 1 Par 21:5 seems to prove this point, since these numbers differ too much to be approximately exact in both cases.

f The evolutionary theory of Wellhausen, to which many modern critics still adhere, supposes a number of unhistorical post-exilic additions in Judges, Samuel and Kings and finds little historical value in the narratives of Josue and Chronicles. The arbitrary character of this theory has led to the modern reaction against it, even in critical circles, based on the results of recent archaeological discoveries; § 135*b–g*. As regards its special bearing on the value of the earlier historical books, two points may be noted here. Post-exilic additions made by inspired writers to these books are not excluded *a priori*, since they are found elsewhere in the Sacred Text, but cannot be determined as such by the mere requirements of the evolutionary theory. The special purpose of the authors of the different books provides the natural explanation of their choice of materials from their sources. The author of Kings, wishing to indicate the causes of the exile, brought about by the sins of the people, naturally concentrates on the history of the Northern Kingdom and has little to say about cult. The Chronicler, on the other hand, who is mainly interested in cult, confines himself to the Southern Kingdom, home of the ark and temple, and describes its religious institutions.

a **Texts and Versions**—We are concerned here only with the special character of texts and versions in the historical books of our Hebrew, Greek and Latin Bibles and its bearing on their historical accuracy and inerrancy. As inspiration is a personal attribute of the sacred writers, the inerrancy which it implies belongs primarily to the original autographs, which we do not possess, and can be attributed to our later texts and versions only in so far as they are in exact conformity with them. The inerrancy ascribed to the Latin Vulgate version by the Council of Trent is restricted to matters of faith and morals. We have therefore no guarantee that our present Hebrew, Greek and Latin texts, though substantially authentic, are free from historical errors, but know, on the contrary, from a study of their divergencies, that they all contain a number of them. This is not surprising since alterations invariably occur in literary texts during a long period of transmission and there was not the same reason for a special intervention of Divine Providence in safeguarding historical texts of minor importance as there was for the preservation of passages relating to faith and morals which Scripture is primarily intended to teach.

b The earlier Hebrew text used by the Septuagint

differed from the later text, translated by St Jerome, **226b** in the historical books by omitting 1 Kg 17:12–31; 17:55–18:5, showing a different order in 3 Kg 4–7, omitting 1 Par 1:10–23 and 23 verses of Neh 11–12 and adding 107 verses, more than a third of the whole book, to Esther. It also had a considerable number of similar but smaller variations. But it is not always easy to determine these accurately, since account must be taken of incorrect translations and of errors in the transmission of the Greek text. The Greek additions to Esther are inspired and canonical according to the decree of the Council of Trent. There is no rule of universal application with regard to the other variants which must be judged on their own merits. It is clear from a comparison of MT and LXX that the Hebrew text was neither so uniform nor so carefully preserved in earlier as in later times. The Greek version of the historical books is faithful on the whole, but not free from minor errors. We do not possess the original texts of Tobias and Judith and the Greek MSS in both cases present several types of texts, which differ considerably. The outstanding merit of St Jerome's version is universally recognized, but it must be remembered that Hebrew was less well known in his time than at present.

Numbers and Chronology—Some of the numbers **c** given in the historical books are incredible. The reason of this is twofold. Alterations in the text, both deliberate and accidental, are more frequent in the case of numbers and the Hebrew use and evaluation of numbers is often different from ours. Some examples of both sources of error may be given. The statement that Saul was one year old when he began to reign and that he reigned two years (1 Kg 13:1) is a clear case of textual corruption. Here, as in similar cases, the sacred writer intended to give and undoubtedly gave the length of the two periods of the monarch's life, and the numbers are from this point of view false and absurd, and therefore corrupt. Again Solomon had 40,000 chariot-horses according to 3 Kg 4:26 (= MT 5:6) but only 4,000, according to 2 Par 9:25. The first number is shown to be a textual corruption by the fact that the king had only 1,400 chariots (3 Kg 10:26; 2 Par 1:14) and only two or three horses, according to the Assyrian and Egyptian records, were yoked to a single chariot.

The interpretation of Hebrew numbers is not always **d** obvious. In 2 Kg 24:9 the results of the census of David are given as '800,000 fighting-men who drew the sword' for Israel and '500,000 men' for Judah. As the ratio of fighters to non-fighters is usually calculated as one to five, we should have in Palestine, according to the obvious interpretation, a population of 6½ millions, which is incredible as the land could not support them. Now the object of the census is twice expressly stated to be the numbering of the people, not of the fighting men only. This was probably done by counting the fighting men and calculating the whole population from the result. The numbers in the text give the whole population, practically the same as at the present day. The fighting men are mentioned to indicate the method of calculation. Some such expression as *l*ᵉ*pi* = ' according to ', must be understood before the fighting men. Often in the historical books the word *'elep* is used, not in its numerical sense as 1,000, but to designate a military division under an officer like a Roman centurion. The numerical interpretation of the word has resulted in quite absurd and incredible figures, such as a garrison of over 1,000,000 men in Jerusalem in the reign of Josaphat (2 Par 17:13–17) and armies of 400,000 men in Judah and 800,000 in Israel under Abia and Jeroboam (2 Par 13:3). The million men of Zara the Cushite in 2 Par 14:7 are simply a large indeterminate multitude, as in Gen 24:60, not of soldiers but of nomads seeking new homes. The rendering ' five thousand talents and ten thousand solids ' (1 Par 29:7) imputes a gross anachronism to the Chronicler through a misinterpretation of the Hebrew conjunction *w* which

226d here means not *and* but *or, equivalently*. The solids, literally darics, are contemporary gold coins of Persia and are mentioned to evaluate the weight *kikkār*, literally 'round', as equivalent to two of them and therefore containing about 17 grammes of gold. And thus the contributions of the people in gold seem no longer exaggerated when the text is exactly interpreted.

e Methods of computing numbers as well as textual errors make it impossible to build even a relative chronology on scriptural data. The practice of reckoning long periods by generations lessens considerably the value of the 480 years of 3 Kg 6:1 in determining the date of the Exodus. The Hebrew judges cannot be definitely assigned to successive periods. Even in the fuller indication of the length and succession of reigns in Kings cases of coreigns and regencies occur in which some years seem to have been reckoned twice. Sometimes the chronological order of events is not followed as in 1 Kg 16:14–23, since it was only after his victory over Goliath that David became a member of Saul's household.

f **Miracles**—The miracles in these books support rather than impair their historical character. The Hebrews were the chosen people of God, charged with a divine mission in view of the salvation of mankind. It is not surprising, therefore, especially to a believer in the miracles of the NT, to find recorded in their history instances of a special intervention of God for the preservation of their faith and their existence as a nation. These instances are fairly common because the people was stiff-necked and prone to idolatry, and miracles, like speaking with tongues, are for unbelievers rather than believers (1 Cor 14:22). The Hebrews who believed in an all-directing Providence and saw the hand of God in all the events of history had no special term for miracle in the strict sense of the word. Their 'signs', 'shining works', 'mighty works', 'wondrous works' can be and are all used to express natural as well as preternatural effects. But there is no doubt from the description of certain events that the sacred writers clearly recognized their preternatural character.

g These events are of two kinds : those which are preternatural in themselves and can only have God for their author and those which may in themselves be produced by natural causes, but actually occur in such a manner or in such circumstances as to postulate divine intervention. Examples of the first kind are the two resurrections from the dead narrated in the history of Elias and Eliseus (3 Kg 17:17–24 ; 4 Kg 4:18–37). It would be absurd to argue from the manner in which the miracles were performed that death was only apparent, since the sacred writer affirms that the child was dead in one case and that

the soul returned to the body in the other. The **22** means used by the prophets are merely the counterpart of the clay and spittle used by our Lord in restoring sight to the blind. Examples of the second kind are more common. The consumption of sacrificial offerings by fire from heaven is narrated several times. The drought, prophesied by Elias and recorded by Menander of Ephesus in his history of Tyre, may have been the result of entirely natural causes.

The teleological aspect of the miracles is particularly **h** important. Their object is to confirm the faith of the people in God's Omnipotence and Beneficence and to establish and uphold the authority of his envoys and interpreters, the prophets. The great miracles of the opening stages of the conquest of Canaan belong to a period when the assurance of divine assistance was particularly necessary. The miracle on the occasion of the sacrifice of Elias on Mount Carmel occurred at one of the greatest crises of religious history in Israel and secured the victory of the party of Yahweh. On the other hand the absurd and stereotyped prodigies, recorded by Greek and Roman historians as presages of remarkable events, are conspicuous by their absence from the historical books.

Historical Character of Ruth, Tobias, Judith and **i** **Esther**—These four historical books differ from the others in not indicating their literary sources and in not covering a period of history. They confine themselves to single episodes of an edifying character narrated at length with a didactic purpose. Such narratives lend themselves more easily to dramatization and the admission of fictitious elements. Hence the question has been raised whether they are strictly historical, like the other books, or rather, like our historical novels, based indeed on historical facts, but only historical in appearance, so far at least as some of their contents are concerned. There is no difficulty in the latter view from the side of inspiration, since inspired religious teaching, where the actual course of Divine Providence is not concerned, can be derived from fiction as well as from fact, as parables and allegories attest. There is, however, a decree of the Biblical Commission according to which the historical books must be considered strictly historical except in cases, not easily or lightly to be admitted, when the contrary is established by solid arguments, see § 52*j*. The final decision on the value of these arguments is, of course, reserved to the Church. Among Catholic scholars the historicity of the books of Ruth and Esther is generally admitted. There is less agreement about the deutero-canonical books, Tobias and Judith. Uncertainty regarding the exact contents of the original inspired text makes a definite solution of the problem in their case practically impossible.

JOSUE

(JOSHUA)

By E. POWER, S.J.

a **Bibliography—I Commentaries :** *K. F. Keil, Leipzig, 1874²; *A. Dillmann, Leipzig, 1886 ; *S. Oettli, München, 1893 ; *G. F. Maclear (CBSC), Cambridge, 1894 ; *W. H. Bennet, Leipzig, 1895 ; *H. Holzinger, Tübingen, 1901 ; F. de Hummelauer (CSS), Paris, 1903 ; *S. Friedeberg, London, 1913 ; *W. Schenz, Leipzig, 1914 ; *R. Breuer, Frankfurt a/M. 1915 ; *C. Steuernagel, Göttingen, 1923² ; A. Schulz, Bonn, 1924 ; *A. R. Whitham (School Com.), London, 1927 ; J. Keulers, Brugge, 1928 ; *J. de Groot, Groningen, 1931 ; *J. Garstang, London, 1931 ; *M. Noth, Tübingen, 1938 ; A. Fernandez (CSS), Paris, 1938 ; A. Gelin, Paris, 1949.

b **II Special Subjects :** *E. Meyer, ' Kritik der Berichte über die Eroberung Palästinas ', ZATW 1 (1881) 117–46 ; *C. Steuernagel, *Einwanderung der israelitischen Stämme in Kanaan*, Berlin, 1901 ; *C. F. Burney, *Israel's Settlement in Canaan*, London, 1921 ; *A. Alt, *Die Landnahme der Israeliten in Palaestina*, Leipzig, 1925 ; F. Schmidtke, *Die Einwanderung Israels in Kanaan*, Breslau, 1933 ; *M. Noth, ' Studien zu den historisch-geographischen Dokumenten des Josuabuches ', ZDPV 58 (1935) 185–255 ; *K Moehlenbrink, ' Die Landnahmesagen des Buches Josua ', ZATW 56 (1938) 238–68 ; H. Wiesmann, ' Israels Einzug in Kanaan (Jos 3:1–5:1) ', Bi 11 (1930) 216–30 ; A. Fernandez, ' Critica historico-literaria de Jos 3:1–5:1 ', Bi 12 (1931) 93–8 ; *C. M. Watson and *W. E. Stevenson, ' The Stoppage of the River Jordan in A.D. 1267 ', PEF (1895) 253–61, 334–8 ; R. M. Savignac, ' La conquête de Jéricho ', RB 19 (1910) 36–53 ; A. Fernandez, ' Fue Jerico tomada por Josue ? ', *Estudios Ecclesiasticos* 12 (1933) 100–13 ; *J. Garstang, ' Jericho ', *Annals of Archaeology and Anthropology*, Liverpool 19 (1932) 3–22, 35–54 ; 20 (1933) 3–42 ; 21 (1934) 99–136 ; 22 (1935) 143–84 ; 23 (1936) 67–100 and PEF 62 (1930) 123–32 ; 63 (1931) 105–7, 186–96 ; 67 (1935) 61–8 ; *Id.*, *The Story of Jericho*, London, 1940 ; L. H. Vincent, ' La chronologie des fouilles de Jéricho ', RB 39 (1930) 403–33 ; 41 (1932) 264–76 ; 44 (1935) 585–605 ;

c J. Doeller, ' Der Bann im AT und im späteren Judentum ', ZKT 37 (1913) 1–24 ; L. Delporte, ' L'Anathème de Jahweh ', RSR 5 (1914) 297–338 ; A. Fernandez, ' El Herem biblico ', Bi 5 (1924) 2–25 ; A. Tricot, ' La prise d'Ai (Jos 7:1–8:29) ', Bi 3 (1922) 273–300 ; A. Fernandez, ' La toma de Hai ', *Estudios Biblicos* 4 (1933–4) 407–14 ; *J. Krausse-Marquet, ' La deuxième campagne de fouilles à Ay (1934) ', *Syria* 16 (1935) 325–45 ; *R. Dussaud, ' Note additionnelle ', *ib.* 346–52 ; *A. Lods, ' Les fouilles d'Ai et l'époque de l'entrée des Israélites en Palestine ', *Mélanges F. Cumont* (Bruxelles, 1936) 842–57 ; *M. Noth, ' Bethel und Hai ', *Pal. Jahrbuch* 31 (1935) 7–29 ; L. H. Vincent, ' Les fouilles d'et-Tell = ' Ai ', RB 46 (1937) 231–66 ; R. Tonneau, ' Le sacrifice de Josué sur le mont Ebal ', RB 35 (1926) 98–109 ; J. Boulier, ' Josué a-t-il arrêté le soleil ? ' RCF 12 (1897 IV) 44–56 ; A. Véronnet, ' L'arrêt du soleil par Josué ', *ib.* 41 (1905 I) 585–603 ; *J. Reid, ' Did the Sun and Moon Stand Still ? ' ET 9 (1897–8) 151–4 ; *E. W. Maunder, ' A Misinterpreted Miracle ', Exp (Oct. 1910) 359–72 ; A. Van Hoonacker, ' Das Wunder Josuas ', TG (1913) 454–61 ; A. van Mierlo, ' Das Wunder Josuas ', ZKT 37 (1913) 895–911 ; *J. C. Matthes, ' Das Solstitium Jos 10, 12–14, ZATW 29 (1909) 259–67 ;

A. Kleber, ' Josue's Miracle. A Misunderstood Report **227c** of a Credible Event ', Ec R 54 (1917 I) 477–88 ; J. P. **d** van Kasteren, ' La frontière septentrionale de la Terre Promise ', RB 4 (1895) 23–36 ; R. de Vaux, ' Notes d'histoire et de topographie transjordanienne, *Vivre et Penser* (continuation de RB) 1 (1941) 16–47 ; *A. Alt, ' Das System der Staemmesgrenzen im Buche Josua ', *Sellin-Festschrift* (Leipzig, 1927) 13–24 ; *W. F. Albright, *Excavations at Tell Beit Mirsim, II The Bronze Age*, New Haven, 1938 (*cf.* L.-H. Vincent, RB 48 (1939) 486–9 ; *W. J. Phythian-Adams, ' The Boundary of Ephraim and Manasseh ', PEF 61 (1929) 228–41 ; *K. Elliger, ' Die Grenze zwischen Ephraim und Manasse ', ZDPV 53 (1930) 265–309 ; A. Fernandez, ' Los límites de Efraín y Manasés ', Bi 14 (1933) 22–40 ; *W. F. Albright, ' The Site of Tirzah and the Topography of Western Manasseh ', JPOS 11 (1931) 241–51 ; *H. Kjaer, ' The Excavation of Shiloh ', JPOS 10 (1930) 87–174, PEF 59 (1927) 202–13 ; 61 (1929) 71–80 ; A. Fernandez, ' El límite septentrional de Benjamín ', Bi 13 (1932) 49–60 ; *A. Alt, ' Eine galiläische Ortsliste in Jos 19 ', ZATW 45 (1927) 59–81 ; *W. F. Albright, ' The Topography of the Tribe of Issachar ', ZATW 44 (1926) 225–36 ; P. Auvray, ' Le livre de Josué ', DBV(S) 4 (1948) 1131–41.

Contents—The book of Josue narrates the fulfilment of **e** the promise made by God to Abraham that his descendants should possess the land of Canaan (Gen 12:7 ; 13:15 ; 15:7, 18 ; 17:8). Josue's campaigns of conquest are first related (chh 1–12), then his distribution of the land (chh 13–21), and finally, after the episode of the transjordanic altar of testimony, his last discourses and death (chh 22–24). The early events are described in detail : the crossing of the Jordan, the capture of Jericho, the capture of Hai, the treaty with the four Hevite cities, the relief of their capital, Gabaon, and the defeat and death of the five Amorite kings who besieged it. Only one subsequent campaign is recorded, the defeat of a great Canaanite coalition in Galilee. A list of the kings slain by Josue concludes the narrative. Its incompleteness is explained by the fact that the narrator restricts himself to those events in the conquest which attest most clearly the intervention of Yahweh. The second part is more complete **f** but not without omissions. The land to be divided and the land already divided are first described and the boundaries and chief cities of the transjordanic tribes are indicated. The allotment of Hebron to Caleb is then narrated. The first distribution at Gilgal follows, in which the most powerful tribes, Judah and the sons of Joseph, receive their lots. The remaining territory is next surveyed and divided into seven portions which are assigned by lot to the seven remaining tribes in a second distribution made at Shiloh, the new headquarters. Six cities are then appointed as places of refuge for involuntary homicides, and cities and pastures are assigned to priests and Levites in the lots of the various tribes. The boundaries and cities of the tribes are not given in the same order and detail in all cases, sometimes for practical reasons, as in the case of the northern boundary of Manasses, since much of the land was still unconquered or unsettled, sometimes owing to a lacuna in text or source as in the case of the western boundary of Zabulon. In the appendix,

227f the bond between the Israelites on both sides of the Jordan is manifested by the Altar of Testimony and Josue exhorts the people to complete the conquest of Canaan and persevere in their united allegiance to Yahweh.

g **Authorship and Composition**—The author of Josue, a prophet according to Jewish tradition, is unknown. From internal evidence we may conclude that the book was composed in the period of the monarchy and that ancient written sources were extensively used by its author. It contains only one explicit citation (10:12*b*–13*a*) taken from the *Book of the Just* which contained also the elegy of David on Saul and Jonathan (2 Kg 1:18). We are informed however that the survey of the land according to cities before the second distribution of territory was written in a book (18:9) and that the proceedings of the assembly at Shechem were written by Josue in the Book of the Law (24:26). It is remarkable that the boundaries of the tribes are more strictly according to cities and generally less orderly and less detailed in the second distribution than in the first, such in fact as we should naturally expect from a survey of territory still largely in Canaanite

h possession. There is thus justification for the assumption that this survey and other similar ancient records were utilized by the author, who finds himself obliged also to make some ancient city names intelligible by indicating their later equivalents (*cf.* 19:15 note) and some later elements in them do not affect their original date. The different sources more usually form constituent parts of the narrative (*cf.* chh 6, 9, 13, 16–17), but are sometimes added to it as in 15:63 ; 16:10, where we are incidentally informed that the Jebusites hold Jerusalem and the Canaanites Gezer *to the present day*. Two passages 15:13–19 and 24:28–31, also found in Judges 1:10–15 and 2:6–9, are most probably derived from a common source. The designation of Josue as the sixth book of the Hexateuch and the distribution of its contents to JEDP are beginning to be abandoned in critical circles. Noth emphatically affirms in his recent commentary that Josue has a literary history of its own, entirely different from that of the Pentateuch. There are occasional glosses and textual corruptions in the MT which are indicated, when important, in the commentary. The LXX is sometimes helpful in determining the original text (*cf.* especially chh 6–8).

228a **Date of the Conquest**—The date of the Hebrew conquest and occupation of Canaan can only be determined by a comparative study of scriptural and archaeological data. The use of bronze, not iron, in the construction of the tabernacle and its furniture and the reference to iron, a generation later, in Canaanite chariots (17:16, 18) and spoils of victory (6:24 ; 22:8) assign the conquest to the period of transition from bronze to iron, *c* 1200 B.C. Iron was probably introduced into Palestine by the northern invaders, beaten back from Egypt by Ramesses III *c* 1193 and 1190 B.C., of whom the Sakkala and the Philistines (who had iron chariots Jg 1:19) settled in the plains of Sharon and Philistia. The Philistines are attested earlier *c* 1230 B.C.

b Several cities, captured by the Israelites, have been recently excavated and the results of these excavations, however much disputed, generally favour the above date and never positively exclude it. Surface explorations recently made independently by Glueck and de Vaux in the region occupied by Ruben and Gad show that it was unsettled throughout the whole Late Bronze Age (1600–1200 B.C.), but settled in the Early Iron Age. Although a surface exploration is less reliable than a complete excavation, nevertheless the homogeneity of the results obtained from the investigation of many individual sites in a large area authorizes the conclusion that Ruben and Gad settled in Transjordania *c* 1200 B.C. The methodical excavations at Shiloh establish the same approximate date for the Hebrew occupation of Canaan. The first permanent civil and religious capital of the Israelites cannot have

long remained unwalled and sparsely populated. Yet **2** such was the condition of Shiloh in the Late Bronze Age, while it was walled and thickly populated in the Early Iron Age. The Canaanite city and temple at Tell ed-Duweir (Lachish) were destroyed by fire at the close of the Late Bronze Age. The date is clearly indicated by the associated pottery which includes a bowl assigned by a hieratic inscription to the fourth year (of Merneptah), *c* 1222 B.C. The demolition of a Canaanite sanctuary at Tell Beit Mirsim (Debir) and the destruction by fire of Beitin (Bethel) are both associated with the latest phase of Late Bronze Age pottery and may have occurred *c* 1200 B.C. but certainly not two centuries earlier. Hai, a ruin, as its name indicates, was uninhabited at both dates. In Jericho and Tell el-Qêda (most probably Hasor) pottery of the latest phase of the Late Bronze Age was discovered and both sites were uninhabited during the Early Iron Age. It is natural to associate this abandonment with the ban of Josue. Jericho and Hasor are the only cities which he completely banned and destroyed by fire. The fire at Hai was primarily a signal (8:21) not a ban which is excluded by other indications. The later date of the destruction of Jericho and Hasor seems therefore more probable and is alone in harmony with other archaeological evidence.

Extent of the Conquest—Josue's conquest of Canaan **c** appears at first sight inconsistent with Jg 1, where the task of subjugating the Canaanites seems to commence after his death. A closer study of the text reveals the incompleteness of his conquest and shows that both narratives are in perfect agreement. Josue overran the whole country, repeatedly defeated Canaanite coalitions against the invaders and thus established the Israelites in the land. He captured a number of cities by assault, put their inhabitants to the sword but did not burn them and render then uninhabitable (11:13), except Jericho and Hasor. He could not garrison them with an army of only 40,000 men, needed for his campaigns and for the protection of his headquarters, and they were consequently reoccupied by the enemy and had to be recaptured. The recapture of Hebron by Caleb and of Debir by Othoniel is related by anticipation (15:13–19) but reappears subsequently in its proper place as part of the narrative of Jg 1. Josue himself before his death speaks of many peoples still remaining to be conquered (23:4–5). The Hebrews were not **d** numerous enough to occupy all Canaan (Ex 23:29 ; Deut 7:22) and much of the territory remained in the hands of the Canaanites long after the period of Jg 1, especially walled cities like Yeblaam, Tanaach, Megiddo, Dor, Jerusalem and Gezer. The region occupied in Josue's time is only indicated by the mention of Shiloh and Shechem in Mt Ephraim and probably included also much of Benjamin and northern Judah. It was protected from the Canaanites, who were particularly strong in the north, by the barrier of northern Samaria then thickly wooded and practically uninhabited. As regards Galilee we are only informed that the mountainous region in the north was still unconquered (13:6). And so there was peace in the land, a breathing-space after the big campaigns, before the individual tribes undertook the task of completing the conquest of their lots. Subsequent consolidation of an initial conquest is a feature of all successful invasions. Remarkable confirmations of the biblical narrative from recent excavations are : agreement of the dates of the Exodus and the conquest determined independently, Madianite nomads in Transjordania unsettled in the Late Bronze Age, abandonment of Hai in the same period, prosperous condition of Shiloh, the first Hebrew capital, and abandonment of Jericho and Hasor, the only completely banned cities, in the Early Iron Age. Thus the historicity of Josue, denied by the critics, is vindicated by modern research.

Religious Teaching—The principal religious teaching of **e** Josue is the fidelity of God to his promises. He delivered the Israelites from the reproach of Egypt (5:9) and gave them possession of Canaan which he had promised to the seed of Abraham. It is repeatedly stated that Yahweh fought with and for Israel and only those events of the conquest are narrated which manifest most clearly divine intervention under the form of miraculous assistance or at least of supernatural guidance. In only one recorded instance, the first expedition against Hai, Yahweh withdraws his aid in consequence of the sin of Achan and disaster follows. This is a practical illustration of another lesson, frequently inculcated, that fidelity to the law of God is an essential contdition of divine aid and success. The absolute supremacy of religious values over all human considerations is taught clearly by the imposition of the ban on the Canaanites to avert religious contamination from a people prone to idolatry (24:14). The ban was not a moral instruction authorizing cruelty or savagery, but an inscrutable decree of God adapted to the execution of his mysterious designs.

f In Josue we have an example of a leader, chosen by God, in whom great natural qualities and fidelity to divine guidance are harmoniously united. His career is sketched and his exploits celebrated in Ecclus 46:1–10. No instance is recorded in which he showed unwillingness or hesitation in executing Yahweh's commands. His last words (chh 23–24) express eloquently his solicitude for his people and his earnest endeavours to keep them united in fidelity to their God. His name, originally *Hōšēa*' 'salvation' changed by Moses (Num 13:17) to *Yehōšūa*' ' Yahweh is salvation ' appears later (Neh 8:17) as *Yēšūa*', whence comes the Greek 'Ιησοῦς, our ' Jesus '. He is a type of the Saviour. Canaan is a type of the Messianic Kingdom (Rom 4:13). As Josue was the leader of the Israelites in the conquest of the promised land, so Jesus is our leader in the conquest of the kingdom of heaven.

The limits of this commentary exclude a discussion of the sites of the cities mentioned in the lists, for which we must refer the reader to standard works on Palestinian geography like those of Abel and Szczepanski.

a **A. I–XII Conquest of the Promised Land— I 1–9 Order to invade Canaan**—Josue, appointed by God successor to Moses (Num 27:17–23) and charged with the conquest of Canaan (Deut 3:28 ; 31:3), is now, after the death of Moses, commanded to lead the people across the Jordan into the promised land. God promises him success in his mission, exhorts him to be courageous and diligent in *securing possession* of the land for the people, and above all to be faithful in all points to the law of Moses since that is the condition on which God's help is given and success depends.

4. The boundaries of the promised land are briefly indicated : the desert region of Negeb in the south, the mountain of Lebanon in the north, the river Euphrates in the north-east and the Mediterranean Sea in the west. *The land of the Hittites*, not in LXX and probably a gloss, is an Assyrian designation of Syria and Palestine. These boundaries include subject nations, the Aramaeans, and thus differ in part from the boundaries of the land actually inhabited by the Israelites in which the sources of the Jordan and Mount Hermon take the place of the Euphrates. **7d.** ' *that thou mayest prosper whithersoever thou goest.*' **8a.** ' *Let not the book of the law depart from thy mouth* ' means speak frequently about the law. **8c.** ' *for then thou shalt make thy way prosperous and then thou shalt succeed.*'

b **10–18 Preparations for the Invasion**—Josue orders the people to collect supplies and be ready to cross the Jordan within three days. He reminds particularly those already in possession of their lots east of the Jordan (Ruben, Gad and half-Manasses) of the obligation imposed by Moses on their warriors to accompany their brethren in the invasion. All the people (not merely the transjordanic tribes) declare their willingness to obey Josue as they obeyed Moses in all things.

10. The order is communicated to the people by *šōṭᵉrîm*, lit. scribes but actually headmen (DV princes) as in Ex 5. **11.** The expression *beyond the Jordan* can

indicate either side of the river and is therefore some- **229b** times qualified as in **15** *towards sunrise*. **14.** The strong of hand or mighty in valour are the fighting men.

II 1–24 The Spies and Rahab—Josue sends two spies **c** to inspect Jericho, who are received by Rahab the harlot and safely concealed under flax-stalks on the roof of her house. She manifests her belief in the God of Israel (*cf.* Heb 11:31) and begs mercy for herself and her father's house in return for the mercy she has shown to the spies. They promise on oath to grant her request and admonish her to tie on her window a scarlet cord that her house may be known and her household spared ; she lets them down by a rope from the window of her house on the town-wall and warns them to flee to the hills for three days before recrossing the Jordan to avoid a meeting with their pursuers. The spies return safely and make their report to Josue.

1. Shittim, called Abel Shittim ' Acacia-meadow ' in Num 38:48, is the modern Tell Kefrēn, six m. E. of the Jordan. The conjunction after *land* is explanatory *namely* or *particularly*. Rahab seems also to have been an inn-keeper. **4–5a.** Correct ' I confess ' to *certainly* **d** and ' at the time ' to *about the time*, since the gate was shut later. **5c.** Read *surely* for ' and '. **6.** ' *had made . . . had covered . . . had laid in order on the roof.*' **12.** A true token is a reliable token. **14a.** ' *Our lives for yours to death if ye declare not this business of ours* ' means unless you betray us our lives are forfeit to God if any harm comes to you. **14b.** For ' truth ' read *fidelity*. **15b.** ' *For her house was against the inner surface of the wall, and she dwelt against the wall.*' The wall is the town-wall. The word *qîr* also means wall, regarded as a flat surface, here the inner surface of the town-wall to which the house of Rahab adhered (*cf.* 2 Cor 11:33). **16.** ' *lest the pursuers meet you and afterwards go your way.*' **18a.** ' *Behold when we come into the land thou shalt bind this twisting of scarlet thread.*' It is immaterial whether the conversation, mentioned first as most important, took place before or after the letting down of the spies. **21b.** For ' hung ' read *tied*. **23a.** Omit ' when they were gone back into the city '.

III 1–IV 18 Crossing of the Jordan—**1–6.** Directions **e** for the day's march from Shittim to the Jordan are first given. The priests carrying the ark lead the march ; the people follow at a thousand yards' distance ; the people must be sanctified for the crossing. **7–13.** Josue on reaching the Jordan is encouraged by Yahweh and receives instructions for the crossing on the morrow which he communicates to the people. The waters of the Jordan will be divided when the priests carrying the ark enter it, and they are to remain in the river bed until the people have crossed. **14–17.** The actual crossing is described. **IV:1–9.** Twelve men, one from each tribe, are to take each a heavy stone from the channel of the river to be kept as a memorial of the crossing. Twelve other stones are lodged in the channel where the priests halted with the ark. **10–14.** The halt of the priests in the river and the hasty crossing of the people are again narrated, then the ascent of the ark from the river and the march through the plains of Jericho. The confirmation of the authority of Josue by the miraculous crossing appropriately ends the narrative. **15–18.** It is followed however by an account of the ascent of the priests from the river and the return of the waters to their channel. The obvious interpolation (3:12) reappears in its proper place (4:2). The narrative is clear and consistent but contains many **f** repetitions which seem best explained by the use of different sources since there would naturally be several traditional accounts of so noteworthy an event. Vg misinterprets 3:1*c*–2*a* : ' *And they spent the night there before they passed over. And it came to pass after three days.*' The three days are those of 1:11. Preparations began 7 Nisan, march to the Jordan 9 Nisan, crossing 10 Nisan (4:19). The spies remained hid three days (2:22) : all 8 Nisan and parts of 7 and 9 Nisan. **3.** ' *follow it* [the ark] *as they go before.*' **4.** The people are to remain at a distance from the ark not through reverence but to discern the way more clearly. **5.** On the sanctifica-

229f tion *cf.* Ex 19:10, 15. **6-11.** Where DV has ' go ' (**6 ; 11**) MT has *cross* or *go across*, but only part of the crossing is meant, the entry into the river, since the people ascend from the river before the priests.

g The crossing of the Jordan will confirm the authority of Josue as the crossing of the Red Sea confirmed that of Moses (Ex 14:31) ; it is moreover an infallible sign of divine aid and final success in the invasion of Canaan, **13*b*,** ' *The waters of the Jordan shall be cut off, the waters from above, and they shall stand in a heap* ' ; *cf.* Ex 15:8*b*. Only the upper waters are mentioned in describing the prodigy since the lower waters flow naturally to the Dead Sea. **14-17.** ' *And it came to pass when the people left their tents to cross the Jordan that the priests bore the ark of the covenant before the people and as soon as the bearers of the ark reached the Jordan and the feet of the priests bearing the ark were dipped in the brim of the water—for the Jordan overflows all its banks during all the days of the harvest—the waters coming down from above stood and rose in a heap afar off by the city of Adam beside Sartan, but those coming down towards the Sea of the Arabah, the Salt Sea, were cut off altogether, and the people passed over right against Jericho. And the priests bearing the ark stood firm on dry ground in the middle of the Jordan while all Israel passed over on dry ground until all the people had completed the crossing of the Jordan.*' Adam is identified with ed-Damiye on the east bank of the Jordan about 16 m. N. of Shittim. The mention of this place where landslides occur as the site of the miracle raises the question whether the drying up of the Jordan was a natural phenomenon like the division of the waters of the Red Sea and thus only miraculous *quoad modum* in the providential circumstances of time and place. The landslides are caused by the waters themselves which undermine the high marl cliffs on the bank of the river. That of 1267, chronicled by the Arab historian Nuwairi, left the lower river bed waterless for sixteen hours ; that of 1927 (to which an earthquake contributed) for over twenty-one hours. The mention of Adam as the site of the stoppage and the analogy of the Red Sea crossing make this view more probable. **IV:3.** Read *stood firm* and omit ' very hard '. **10.** Omit with LXX ' and Moses had said to him '. **13.** The whole army, not merely the transjordanic forces, numbered 40,000 men ; *cf.* 1:16. Both number and interpretation are confirmed by Jg 5:8, a contemporary record, and agree with the indications of Ex 23:29 ; Deut 7:22. **18.** ' *And it came to pass when the priests bearing the ark of the covenant of Yahweh came from the middle of the Jordan the soles of the priests' feet were drawn out to the dry ground and the waters of the Jordan returned to their place and flowed as before over all its banks.*'

230a IV 19-V 1 Encampment at Gilgal and Result of the Crossing—The exact site of Gilgal between Jericho and the Jordan is disputed and uncertain. Garstang locates the camp on the north side of the Wady Kelt half-way between Jericho and the Jordan, Abel prefers Khirbet el-Ethele nearer Jericho. Gilgal remained the headquarters of Josue and site of the tabernacle until after the first distribution of the conquered territory five years later (14:10). The objection that this site was unsuitable as not sufficiently central ignores the fact that Josue had to keep in close contact with the transjordanic territory denuded of its warriors. It was only when these returned to their homes that headquarters and sanctuary were removed to a more central position at Shiloh (18:1) where ark and tabernacle are still found in the days of Samuel (1 Kg 1–3). The result of the miraculous crossing was to teach all peoples the omnipotence of Yahweh, inspire the Israelites with the fear of the Lord and the kings of Canaan with fear of the invaders.

b V 2-9 The Practice of Circumcision is resumed—Circumcision was obligatory on all male Israelites as a sign of the covenant made by God with Abraham and his descendants to whom the land of Canaan was promised (Gen 17:7–14). The practice was observed in Egypt but neglected in the desert. Since therefore those who came out of Egypt had died in the desert in punishment of their disobedience those who entered **23** Canaan were uncircumcised. Josue is now ordered, literally, *to return and circumcise them,* that is by circumcising them to return to the ancient practice. This he does with knives of flint according to custom. Vg abbreviates but gives the sense correctly. **2.** *The second time* is tautological, not in LXX and probably a marginal gloss. **9.** ' *This day have I rolled away from you the reproach of Egypt.*' Commentators of all schools refer these words of Yahweh to the rite of circumcision and consequently interpret the reproach of Egypt as uncircumcision. This is impossible if circumcision was practised in Egypt (**5**). We cannot assume with von Hummelauer that the Egyptian circumcision was material, not spiritual, and therefore equivalently uncircumcision or with Fernandez that Egypt is a time indication including the desert period of uncircumcision. Less conservative critics considerably alter the text, deny all previous practice of circumcision in Egypt or even in Canaan and find its earliest mention in this passage. All admit that the unexpected *gallōtî* **c** ' I have rolled ' is a play on the word Gilgal, but ignore the obvious conclusion that the explanation of the reproach of Egypt must be sought in Gilgal and more particularly in being encamped at Gilgal as indicated in the preceding and following verses. **The reproach of Egypt** was naturally the humiliating condition of the Hebrews there, slaves in a foreign land. This reproach was not removed while they were landless wanderers in the desert. It was only when Yahweh finally established them in their own land at Gilgal that he ' gilgalled ' away from them the reproach of Egypt. See ' Jos 5:9 and the Institution of Circumcision ', ITQ 18 (1951) 368–72.

10-16 Celebration of the Pasch and Apparition to d Josue—The Israelites celebrated the Pasch in Gilgal at the appointed time ; *cf.* Ex 12. **11.** ' *And they ate of the produce of the land* [' on the morrow of the pasch ', not in LXX, is probably a gloss], *unleavened cakes and roasted corn-ears on the same day.*' On the manna *cf.* Ex 16. It was not the only food of the Israelites, hence the preparation of supplies (1:11). **14.** It is not clear whether *the leader of the army of Yahweh* who appeared to Josue by Jericho was an angel (Michael ? *cf.* Dan 10:21) or Yahweh himself. His words rather suggest the latter alternative. The apparition was a guarantee of divine aid in the attack on Jericho. For ' no ' (MT) read *him* (LXX, Syr., some Heb. MSS) after ' answered '. As the Israelites had scarcely time to recover from the effects of circumcision in three days it is probable that here as elsewhere the chronological order of events is not strictly observed.

VI 1-47 Capture of Jericho—The interpretation of **e** ch 6 is complicated by the uncertainty of the text and the fusion into one narrative of two traditional accounts of the capture. MT seems to have received later additions, difficult to explain if authentic. LXX in 2-7 had a shorter and better text. According to one account the Israelites invest Jericho and when the trumpets are sounded raise a mighty shout on which the walls collapse and they enter the city. According to the other a processional march is made round the city once a day for six days and seven times on the seventh day after which at the order of Josue they raise a mighty shout with the same result. The traditions are not inconsistent since a march round a city does not exclude an investment and Josue's order would naturally be communicated by the trumpets. The miraculous character of the capture is emphasized in both. The marching and the blowing of trumpets were not perhaps intended to intimidate the besieged but may have been ancient ritual observances connected with the imposition of the ban. The trumpet announces the ban in Ex 19:13, 17 and even in the NT at the last judgement it introduces the final victory of the blessed and the eternal ban of the wicked.

1. For ' fenced ' read *remained shut up.* **3*a*.** ' *Place the* **f** *fighting men round in a circle.*' Omit 3*b*-4 (LXX). The trumpets are *made of rams' horns,* not ' used in the Jubilee '

¶ (Vg). **5a.** ' *And it shall come to pass when the ram's horn is sounded, when you hear the sound of the trumpet.*' **6-7.** After the words of Yahweh (2–5) Josue tells the priests to order the people to invest the city (LXX), but instructs first the priests, then the people, on the processional march round the city (MT). **8-9.** Instructions for the march are given (LXX), but the actual march is described (MT). **10.** ' And shout ' : ' *then shout* '. **11.** Omit ' a day '. **12-14.** The march of the second day is narrated. LXX erroneously puts the priests and the ark in the van instead of between vanguard and rearguard. **15-25.** The account of the seventh day's proceedings is interrupted between the order to shout (16) and its execution (20), by instructions concerning Rahab and the ban. Their execution is described. Rahab with her family, house and belongings was exempted from the ban. She dwelt among the chosen people and holds an honoured place in the ancestry of our Lord (Mt 1:5). She is praised for her faith (Heb 11:31) because she sided with Yahweh and his people.

g The *ḥērem* or **ban** was the prohibition of contact with certain persons or objects to avoid contamination of them, if sacred, or from them, if accursed. In war what was banned belonged to Yahweh, since he it was who gave victory to his people, in virtue not of a vow or a sacrifice but a right, the extent of which he alone determined. It was not the property of man or pleasing to God, two essential notes of sacrifice, with which it is contrasted (1 Kg 15). There was a ban on cities and a ban on persons. The banned city with its contents was destroyed by fire ; it was forbidden to rebuild it ; its inhabitants and their cattle were slain ; valuables not easily destroyed, gold, silver, vessels of bronze and iron, were reserved for religious uses. Only two cities, Jericho and Hasor, are said to have been thus banned, and both are now known to have been uninhabited, after their destruction, during the Early Iron Age. The ban on persons obliged the Israelites to slay all the Canaanites except those who voluntarily submitted like the Hevites (9:20 ; 11:20). Their slaughter is not fully accounted for by their iniquities, since the innocent children were included, nor by the barbarous customs of the age, since the Israelites had war laws of a more humane character, but by a special command of God to whom all lives belong (Deut 20:10–20). Its object was to preserve his chosen people from religious contamination that they might remain a fitting instrument for the execution of his merciful design to redeem mankind. **26.** Josue finally menaced prophetically the rebuilder of Jericho with the death of his eldest and youngest sons. The fulfilment of the prophecy is recorded (3 Kg 16:34). Some interpret the deaths of Hiel's sons as foundation sacrifices, but it is more probable that they were acts of God by which he punished the violation of his command. That Jericho was not inhabited between *c* 1200 and 870 B.C. is established by excavations on the site. Mentions of it in the interval (Jg 1:16 ; 3:13 ; 2 Kg 10:5) refer to temporary installations in its immediate vicinity.

h Garstang's recent excavations have illustrated and confirmed many details of the biblical narrative. The city captured by Josue was about five acres in extent and had a double wall of brick about 650 yards in circumference so that seven rounds of the walls could be made in a few hours. Many houses were observed built up against the city wall like Rahab's. This wall, 12 ft. thick, collapsed outwardly into the space between the two walls. The outer wall, 6 ft. thick, fell down the slope of the hill. The uncovering of the stone foundations showed that neither wall had been undermined. The walls wherever disclosed ' are found to be deeply fissured and as it were dislocated. The indications point to earthquake ' (Garstang). If God used this natural means, the providential determination of time and place would still be miraculous. The ruins show traces of deliberate incendiarism. Garstang dates the catastrophe 1400–1388, Vincent 1250–1200 B.C. The Late Bronze Age pottery discovered in both city and necropolis on which Vincent grounds his date is **230h** assigned by Garstang to subsequent partial occupation of the site.

VII 1-VIII 29 Capture of Hai—1-15. After mention- **231a** ing the violation of the *ḥērem* the narrator relates the first unsuccessful attack on Hai, then Josue's prayer to Yahweh, who reveals to him the cause of the defeat and the necessity and manner of expiating the sin committed. **16-26.** The culprit is discovered, avows his guilt and reveals where the spoils are concealed. They are restored to the sacred treasury, Achan is stoned to death and the anger of Yahweh is appeased. **VIII:1-9.** Yahweh orders a second attack on Hai now placed under a mild form of ban. Josue commands 3,000 men to ambush the city on the west side. They are to enter and set fire to the city when its defenders rush out to pursue the Israelites attacking on the east side and simulating flight. **10-29.** The attack is made on the morrow. The Canaanites are caught between the two parties and 12,000 are slain. The ban is executed on the occupants of the city, but the spoils and cattle fall to the victors. Here as in ch 6 LXX supposes a shorter and better Hebrew text than MT. *Hā-'ai* ' the Ruin ' is the modern et-Tell ' the heap of ruins ' over a mile east of Bethel. This identification agrees so well with the textual indications as to exclude all reasonable doubt. The easiest and most direct way to Hai from Jericho is up Mt Karantal between Wady Teisun and Wady Kelt, then by Wady Abu-Retme and straight on to the top of the mountain range. The distance is *c* 15 m.

2. Omit with LXX ' which is beside Bethaven ', a **b** MT gloss since Bethaven ' house of idolatry ' is most probably a later name for Bethel ' house of God ' ; *cf.* Am 5:5. **5.** *Sebarim*, lit. ' precipices ' or ' quarries ', rendered as a verb by LXX, is not identified. **6.** Omit with LXX ' the ark of ', a MT gloss. **14-18.** On the judgement by oracle *cf.* Ex 28:30 note. The casting of lots was a long process. Tribe, clan (DV kindred), house or family, individual was determined by elimination. **21.** For ' scarlet garment ' read *Babylonian mantle*, for ' golden rule ' *tongue* (tongue-shaped wedge) *of gold*, and for ' I covered with the earth which I dug up ' *was under them* (lit. *it* used collectively). **23-25.** According to LXX the stolen objects were not brought to the valley of Achor having been duly consigned to the sacred treasury (*cf.* 6:19) and only Achan was stoned. The burning and then stoning of *them* after the stoning of *him* is clearly a textual corruption in MT. It is therefore probable that the family of Achan was not slain (*cf.* Deut 24:16) and that *his sons and daughters* is an early interpolation. The name of the valley of Achor (' trouble ') is explained. Achan becomes Achor in LXX. The valley (*'ēmeq*) is not definitely identified. It may be the depression between the mountain range and the Jordan north or south of Jericho.

VIII:2. In the second attack an ambush is laid behind **c** (west of) the city. There is a suitable place behind a hill called Burgmus between Hai and Bethel which could be reached secretly by the Wady Zeitun and where a detachment though well concealed could observe the movements of friends and foes. **3.** Read *3,000* for 30,000, too many for an ambush. Omit with LXX 6*c* = DV 7*a*. **8.** ' *according to this word* [LXX ; ' the word of Yahweh ' MT] *you shall do. Take care ! I have commanded you.*' MT makes Josue's command more efficacious than Yahweh's. **9b.** Omit with LXX the pointless statement ' But Josue stayed that night in the midst of the people ', an explanatory gloss on 10*a*. **11b-13.** Omit with LXX except : ' *And the ambush for the city was on the west* '. According to MT Josue laid a second ambush of 5,000 men west of Hai, pitched his camp for a day and a night north of Hai, and during the night paid a purposeless visit to the valley between the camp and Hai. But a second ambush is out of the question, and the first would have been discovered during the day by the Bethelites if the attack was delayed. When the assailants appear (**11a**) the **d** king of Hai advances to meet them (**14a**). Omit with

231d LXX **14b** ' to the place appointed before the desert ' which is unintelligible. **15-16.** LXX continues : ' *And Josue saw and retreated with Israel before them, and they pursued the Israelites and were drawn away from the city* '— a better text than MT. **19.** The *javelin* (DV shield) is raised as a signal to those in ambush in LXX, where ' *and those in ambush will come forth quickly from their posts* ' appears between 18*a* and 18*b* of MT. LXX entirely omits **26** where Josue's extended javelin is strangely assimilated to the hands of Moses raised up in prayer (Ex 17:11 f.). **19-29.** The prearranged programme is carried out successfully. The king of Hai made prisoner is slain like the five Amorite kings (10:26) before being hung on a gibbet till sunset ; *cf.* Deut 21:22, where also death precedes suspension. He was buried in a pit (LXX) like Absalom (2 Kg 18:17) at the city gate (MT) probably in the unexcavated east wall.

e It is solidly established by the excavations at et-Tell (1933-5) that the site was uninhabited 2000-1200 B.C. It was partially occupied in the Early Iron Age (*c* 1200-1050) to which the alleged finds of Late Bronze pottery made earlier by Albright and Garstang really belong as Albright subsequently recognized. How can the inhabitants of an unoccupied city have repulsed the Israelites or been defeated by them ? The supposition that Hai had a different site or that a different city, Bethel, was attacked postulates a very improbable readaptation or a very arbitrary rewriting of the biblical narrative. Nor can it be expected that further excavations in the uninvestigated parts of the site will modify the conclusions reached since the separate attestations of walls, enclosure and necropolis are in **f** complete agreement. Vincent's solution of the problem still remains and is strongly supported by various indications in the text. The immediate need of the Israelites after the conquest of Jericho was a strong position on the central mountain range as a base of operations. Such bases in Josue's time were not Canaanite cities but unoccupied or sparsely occupied sites like Gilgal and Shiloh. *Ha-'ai* ' the Ruin ' by its nearness and accessibility, its natural defences and its fortifications only partially dismantled, was the most suitable objective. Its seizure seemed easy, since a reconnoitring party found it unoccupied, and 3,000 men were judged sufficient for the enterprise. So prudent a leader as Josue would undoubtedly have sent a much larger force, as he did in the second attack, if the post duly reconnoitred had then as later a garrison of 12,000 combatants (8:25). The repulse was a grievous surprise to Josue and, if the consequence of an error of judgement, could scarcely be attributed entirely to the sin of Achan. The object of the first attack is always (six times) called ' the Ruin ', but more frequently ' the City ' when known to be occupied. The Canaanites had seen the reconnoitring party, anticipated the move of Josue and garrisoned the post with contingents from the neighbouring cities. The Bethel contingent is actually mentioned (8:17). At Jericho, men and women, young and old were slain (6:21), at Hai only men and women (8:25) or combatants since women fought like men in those ancient times. Hai had no permanent residents. The ' king ' of Hai is the leader of the garrison in accordance with the stereotyped form of historical narrative. Similarly the pre-arranged fire-signal (8:8, 21) assumes the stereotyped form of the ban (8:28). Hai temporarily inhabited was really burned and made an uninhabited ruin by Josue, but it was not banned in the strict sense of the word like Jericho and Hasor for the spoils fell to the victors (8:2), and it was inhabited in the Early Iron Age. Similar occupations of ancient ruins occur in modern Arab warfare. The excavations, therefore, far from discrediting the biblical narrative of the conquest of Hai, have given us the key to its correct interpretation.

232a VIII 30-35 Altar and Religious Celebrations on Mt Hebal—Josue executes the commands of Moses (Deut 27) by erecting an altar on Mt Hebal, writing *a copy of the law* (not ' Deuteronomy ' DV) on stones, arranging the people half at the foot of Mt Hebal and half at the foot of Mt Garizim with the priests and the ark between them and having the law read aloud, particularly, though not exclusively, the blessings and curses assigned to its observance and non-observance, all in fact that Moses had ordered to be read. This passage appears after 9:2 in LXX and evidently registers an event which occurred at an indeterminate period after the conquest of southern Palestine. What Josue wrote on the stones is discussed in § 130*k*. Hebal and Garizim are not near Jericho, but respectively north and south of the modern Nablus, since Garizim is associated with Shechem explicitly (Jg 9:7) and implicitly by the terebinth (Deut 11:30). The Samaritan Pentateuch reads Garizim instead of Hebal (30), a deliberate falsification to give the halo of antiquity to their sacred mountain as is generally believed. **34.** ' *Josue read all the words of the law* ', had them read by the Levites (Deut 27:14).

IX 1-27 Covenant with the Gabaonites—1-5. A **b** confederation of four important cities in the centre of southern Palestine, terrified by the victories of Josue, send an embassy to his headquarters at Gilgal seeking an alliance. **7-15.** They obtain their request under the false pretence that they have come from a great distance and are not Canaanites. **16-27.** On the discovery of the fraud their lives are spared, but they are condemned to serve the Israelites for ever as hewers of wood and drawers of water. Of the four cities the most southerly is Kiriath-Yearim, Deir el-Azar, *c* 8 m. W. of Jerusalem on the southern road to Jaffa ; Caphira, Kefire, is 2 m. N. of it ; the most northerly is Beeroth, el-Bîreh, 10 m. N. of Jerusalem ; Gabaon, el-Gib, head of the confederacy, is 7 m. NNW. of Jerusalem. Some writers regard the narrative as a fiction to explain the subsequent condition of the Gabaonites as inferior temple servants, but the covenant is explicitly and implicitly attested in 2 Kg 21:1, since the famine which punished Saul's slaughter of the Gabaonites implies the violation of a special obligation. **1.** For ' plains ' read *foothills*, broken ground at the **c** foot of a mountain range, and for ' by Libanus ' *towards Libanus*, the northern boundary. **4b.** Read ' *and old sacks* (of fodder) *for their asses* '. **5b.** The bread was dry and *mouldy*. **6b.** Read after ' country ' ' *now therefore make a covenant with us* '. **6c.** For ' them ' read *the Hevite*. Some commentators read Hurrite (*ḥri*) for Hevite (*ḥwi*) here (with LXX) and also 11:3 and Jg 3:3. It seems preferable to retain Hevite with Abel and interpret the word as the name of an Amorite clan. **7a.** ' *Perhaps you dwell in the midst of us* ' is explained in Vg. The fact that the negotiations are conducted usually by Josue (8-13 ; 15*a* ; 22-27), sometimes by the Israelites (7) or the princes of the congregation (14 ; 15*b* ; 18-21) has suggested not improbably that two traditional accounts are fused into one narrative. The fusion appears where the ambassadors address Josue and the people first together (6) and then separately. The only difference is in the mode of expression and the additional but not contradictory details supplied. **9a.** ' *because of the name* '. **13.** Omit ' and burst . . . and almost consumed ' (Vg). **14a.** For ' they ' (Vg), ' the men ' (MT) read *the princes* (LXX). **15.** The oath of Josue is contained implicitly in the covenant. **17a.** *The third day* is not in LXX. Render ' multitude ' and ' (common) people ' by *congregation* (DV 18, 21, 27). **20.** *The wrath* is correctly interpreted of the Lord (Vg). **21c.** ' *As the princes had promised them.* ' **23.** The curse was : None of you shall be freed from bondage so that you will be hewers of wood, etc. **27.** ' *And Josue gave them that day as hewers of wood and drawers of water to the congregation . . . should choose.* ' The inferior temple servants, not all Gabaonites, are therefore usually called *N^eṯînîm* ' given '. As ' *unto this day* ' always ends an episode the last clause of 27 is probably a gloss.

X 1-15 Defeat of an Amorite Attack on Gabaon— d 1-5. Five Canaanite kings leagued under the leadership

of Adonisedec, king of Jerusalem, attack Gabaon,
stronghold of the Hevites, who had allied themselves
with the Hebrews. **6-10*b*.** The Gabaonites appeal for
aid to Josue, who marches by night from Gilgal to
Gabaon, surprises the besiegers and defeats them with
great slaughter. **10*c*-15.** During the pursuit of the
enemy God aids the Israelites by raining hailstones on
their foes and prolonging the daylight. The territory
of the five kings forms a rough quadrilateral. Jerusalem (Urusalim, ' city of peace ' or ' of Shalim ', in
the Amarna Tablets) was at the NE. angle, Hebron,
modern el-Khalil ' the friend (of God) ', *i.e.* Abraham,
19 m. S. of Jerusalem, at the SE., Jerimoth, el-Yarmuk,
16 m. WSW. of Jerusalem, at the NW., Lachish, the
recently excavated Tell ed-Duweir, 16 m. W. of Hebron
at the SW. The name and site of the fifth city is
uncertain, either Eglon (MT) probably Tell el-Hesy,
6 m. W. of Lachish, or, less probably, Adullam (LXX),
'Id-el-Ma, 4 m. SSE. of Jerimoth. The central and
most important part of southern Palestine is clearly
indicated. Adoni-sedec ' lord of justice ' recalls
Melchisedech ' king of justice ' (Gen 14:18 ; Heb 7:2).
The interpretation, ' Sedec is my lord ' (or ' king '),
supposes a divinity Sedec of which there is no proof.
The king of Jerusalem in the Amarna tablets had a
Hurrite name ' Servant of Khipa '.

e   **1.** ' And were in the midst of them ' (MT), ' and were
their confederates ' (DV), not in LXX, is probably
a gloss. **2.** For ' he ' read *they* (the king and his
subjects) and insert *as* before *one*. **5.** Omit with LXX
' being assembled together ' but read ' Amorite '
(MT, Vg) not ' Jebusite ' (LXX). Amorite is derived
from Amurru, ' Westland ' in Babylonian, with special
reference to the mountain regions. **7.** The conjunction
before *most valiant men* is not connective but explanatory.
Josue probably took the road to Hai turning to the left
at Mukhmas. The distance, *c* 16 m., could have been
covered in a night. **10.** ' He ' (DV) is Israel. The
enemy fled westward to the Vale of Aialon by the
northern route from Gabaon ascending to Upper
Bethhoron (House of the god Horon), Beit-'Ur el-fôqa,
5½ m. NW. of Gabaon, and descending thence to Lower
Bethhoron, Beit-'Ur et-taḥta, 2½ m. farther on. Azeca
and Makkeda are probably but uncertainly located
respectively at ez-Zakariyeh, 2 m. W. of Jerimoth, and
Khirbet el-Kheišum farther to the west. Makkeda
in the Shephelah (15:44) cannot be Moghār ' caves '
in the western plain, *c* 14 m. from Aialon.

f   **11.** The great stones were hailstones. **12-15.** The day
was rendered memorable and unique by a prayer of
Josue (12*a*), granted by Yahweh (14*b*), that the day
or light period should be prolonged to enable him to
complete his victory. The prayer is contained in an
explicit citation from the Book of the Just, a collection
of poems in praise of the great men of Israel, under the
poetical form of a command given by Josue to the
Sun and the Moon which they should execute.
12*b*-13*a*. ' *Stand still, Sun, in Gabaon and Moon in the
vale of Aialon. And the Sun stood still and the Moon halted
until the people avenged themselves on their enemies.*' As the
Sun rules the day and the Moon the night (Gen 1:16),
if the former halts to prolong the light period the latter
must also halt to arrest the darkness period. The
object of the halt is to give the people more time for
the pursuit which would have been checked by darkness. The sacred writer now gives us his authoritative
interpretation of the event. **13*c*-14.** '*And the Sun
stood still in the midst of the heavens and hasted not to set for
about a whole day. And there was no day like that before it or
after it for Yahweh hearkened to the voice of a man because
Yahweh fought for Israel.*' The explanation of *stood still*
as *hasted not to set* clearly indicates a stoppage in the
sun's normal course across the heavens to its setting.
He hastes or *runs his course* (Ps 18:6) as a good servant
executing with alacrity his master's behest. The verb
bō' ' enter ' always means ' set ' when used of the sun.
The sense of 13*c* is thus assured and with it the
meaning of the sun's stoppage intended by the sacred
writer and consequently by God himself. As the sun

stopped for a whole day or light period *one day became*
two (Ecclus 46:5, LXX, not fully extant in Heb.) and
was thus unique, not because God answered man's
prayers, but because, fighting for Israel, he answered
the particular prayer of the man Josue for the prolongation of the light period. Yahweh thus worked
a great and unique nature miracle for his people at
Josue's request.

It must not be supposed that the sacred writer is here   **g**
chronicling an astronomical observation or teaching
us astronomy. He is really recording an ancient
tradition at least two centuries after the event in
language suggested by the poetical citation from the
Book of Yashar and adapted to the comprehension of
his contemporaries who believed that the sun moved
daily across the heavens and that a prolongation of the
day or light period implied a temporary cessation of
that movement. He does not teach or affirm anything
about astronomy or other natural sciences but accommodates himself to the ideas and language of his time
in these matters. He does not err therefore by expressing his religious teaching in terms of an ancient
astronomical belief now known to be false. Nor does
his language authorize the conclusion of a disturbance
in the movements of the heavenly bodies since it is not
a description of an astronomical observation but an
accommodation to the ideas of his contemporaries.
He does not tell us how the miracle was worked. We
only know that *God said : Let there be light. And there
was light*, when naturally there would have been darkness. The miracle is not particularly commemorated
in the OT because it did not mark a stage in the history
of Israel like the miracles of the Exodus. The same is
true of other extraordinary miracles like the resurrections of the dead narrated in the history of Elias and
Eliseus.

A different interpretation of the event recorded in   **h**
Jos 10:12–14 has been proposed by some Catholic and
non-Catholic commentators. The stoppage of the sun
is explained as a cessation from his function of giving
light and/or heat by reason of the clouds accompanying
the hailstorm insinuated in 11. The meaning given
to the Hebrew verbs indicating the stoppage may be
admitted and it is possible, though not very natural,
to suppose that the narrator may be referring to the
same event in 11 and 12–14. There seems however
to be an insuperable objection to this interpretation in
13*c*. The mitigation of the sun's light and/or heat by
storm clouds does not impede or in any way affect his
hasting to his setting. The sacred writer moreover
clearly interprets the standing still of the sun as a
cessation of his normal course across the heavens and
his interpretation is authoritative. It might be added
that while the order given to the sun in the new interpretation is at least intelligible, the same order given
to the moon seems absurd, and that relief from the sun's
light and/or heat would be at least as advantageous
to the pursued as to the pursuers and thus ill adapted
to the avowed object of Josue's request. A hailstorm
moreover would scarcely be said to render a day unique.
In the case of Galileo the theologians consulted un-   **i**
doubtedly erred in their interpretation of this text and
showed a regrettable disregard for the principles laid
down by St Augustine and St Thomas (Dz 1947). The
decrees of the congregation however were not doctrinal
but disciplinary. They prohibited certain books and
condemned Galileo as suspected of heresy, but proposed
no teaching to the faithful.

16-43 Conquest of Southern Palestine—16-27. The   **233a**
five Amorite kings kept prisoners in a cave at Makkeda
are brought forth and put to death. **28-39.** Various
cities are now invested, captured and depopulated one
by one in the following order : Makkeda, Lebna,
Lachish, Eglon, Hebron, Debir. **40-43.** On the
completion of the campaign of conquest Josue returns
to Gilgal. The interval between this and the last
campaign was brief since the five Amorite kings have
still to be dealt with. They are brought forth and Josue
orders his captains to put their feet on the necks of their

233a foes (a common practice, Is 51:23 ; Ps 109:1) to increase their hope of future victories. The kings are then slain, suspended on gibbets till sunset and buried in their previous hiding-place which is blocked up with **b** great stones. The army moves southwards after taking Makkeda, first to Lebna, probably Tell es-Ṣafiyeh, Blanche Garde of the Crusaders, then to Lachish, the garrison of which had been strengthened by a contingent from Gezer. Two other cities of the League are next captured, Eglon to the west, and Hebron to the east, of Lachish. Debir, which is taken last, is most probably Tell Beit Mirsim, 12 m. WSW. of Hebron. The description of these captures is stereotyped as already noted in the case of Hai. The conquests are finally summed up by enumerating the various kinds of land in the region : mountain, southland, foothills, mountain slopes (40) and giving its boundaries : Qadesh-barnea ('Ain Qedeis), 50 m. S. of Beersheba, in the south, Gaza on the western seaboard and Goshen, not the Egyptian Goshen, but an undefined region in the north-east (*cf.* 11:16).

c XI 1-23 Defeat of a Northern Canaanite League and Completion of the Conquest of Canaan—**1-9.** Josue at the command of Yahweh, by a surprise attack, defeats a northern coalition under the leadership of Jabin, king of Hasor (Vg Asor) at the Waters of Merom. **10-15.** He then captures Hasor and the neighbouring cities, slays the inhabitants and destroys Hasor by fire. **16-23.** Finally, after a long war, he completes the conquest of Palestine.

1. The first places mentioned, Madon and Semeron in MT, Maron and Simoon (= Sim'on) in LXX, were most probably in eastern Galilee. The name Madon survives in Madin just south of Qarn Ḥattin, a strong position west of the Lake of Galilee. Sim'on is the Shamhuna of the Amarna Tablets, the modern Sem'uniye, west of Nazareth. **2.** Kinneroth (el-'Oreime), on the shore of the Lake of Galilee, is in the same region. Before ' Dor ' read *nāpaṭ* as in 12:23 ; 17:11 ; 3 Kg 4:7. The *district* of Dor was northern Sharon. The league extended from Dor, near Tantura, 15 m. S., and Achsaph (Tell Keisan), 8 m. NE. of Haifa on the western seaboard to Lake Galilee and the foot **d** of Mt Hermon in the east. **10.** The special importance of Hasor attested by Egyptian texts and the Amarna Tablets explains its position as head of the league and confirms its location by Garstang at Tell el-Qêda, about 5 m. SW. of Lake Huleh where there was a fortified camp, 1,200 yards long and 600 wide, on a level plateau, dominated by a city, sixteen acres in extent, at the SE. end. Hasor means ' enclosure '. The expression Waters of Merom implies a city, Merom, with an abundant water supply, hence Lake Huleh is not meant. Meiron, 11 m. WSW. of the lake, the ancient Merom, seems indicated. Josue was a day's journey to the south when he received the order for the attack and the promise of success. **2.** Read *over against* (LXX ; south of, MT) *Kinneroth*, in the valley of Gennesareth. **4.** The horses were not ridden but yoked two or three to each chariot. **8.** The fugitives scattered, some going north to Sidon, others NE. to Maspha, probably es-Subeibe above Baniyas, others west to Misrephoth-maim, el-Muṣeirefe on the coast just within the present northern boundary of Palestine. The date of the destruction of Hasor, where Garstang made extensive soundings in 1928, raises a problem like that of Jericho. ' The complete absence of Mykenaean specimens [in the camp], as at Jericho, suggests a date of destruction about 1400 B.C. . . . The occupation [of the city] seems to have continued, less intensively, until towards the end of Late Bronze Age III. Thereafter ensued a considerable gap in which specimens of Early Iron Age I were conspicuously absent ' (*Joshua Judges* 383). As Jericho and Hasor were the only cities completely banned and destroyed by fire it is surely more natural to regard the ' considerable gap ' in both cases as the immediate result **e** of the capture and ban. **13a.** ' But all the cities standing on the hills Israel did not burn.' **16.** Here as in 10:41 the

land of Goshen immediately follows the arid Negeb **2** (implicitly indicated by Qadesh-barnea in 10:41). LXX reads Gosom, and it seems probable that Goshem, lit. fertile (land), should be read. The Egyptian Goshen (LXX Gesem) might be similarly explained as the Hebrew allotment was very fertile. **17.** Baalgad is probably Baniyas at the foot of Hermon and the plain of Libanus at Merg 'Ayyun (*cf.* 13:5) ; Mt Ḥalaq, Gebel Halaq, 25 m. SW. of the Dead Sea, is the southern limit ; *cf.* 12:7. **20.** The hardening of the hearts of the Canaanites, a result of their own free-will, was permitted by God and formed part of the divine plan since their submission would hinder the Israelites in executing the ban and thus expose them to religious contamination. **21-22.** The Anakim, lit. long-necked, were a race of giants in the mountain range of southern Palestine and in the Philistine cities. Goliath was one of the Philistine Anakim who were not exterminated.

XII 1-24 Summary of Conquests—The conquests of **f** Moses in Transjordania are first indicated, then those of Josue in Cisjordania. **1.** Read after ' Hermon ' ' *and all the Arabah* [Jordan valley] *on the east side* '. **2-3.** Sehon ruled over half Galaad having the Arnon on the south, the lower Jabbok on the north, the Dead Sea and Jordan on the west and the Ammonite region bounded by the upper Jabbok on the east. Aroer is *in the middle of* (the line drawn by) *the torrent*. He possessed also all the eastern Arabah between Lake Gennesareth and the Dead Sea. This territory is further defined as extending at the south from Beth-Yeshimoth (Suweime) north-east of the Dead Sea, to underneath the slopes of Pisgah, Mt Nebo, since the Arabah widens considerably at this point. The *mîšōr*, plain between Madaba and Dibon, omitted here, appears in the similar description (13:9). **4-5.** Og **g** reigned over northern Transjordania from the Lower Jabbok in the south to Hermon in the north and from Salecha (Salkhad) in southern Hauran in the east to the Arabah and the regions of Geśur and Ma'aka, the modern Djōlān, in the west. His chief cities were Edrai, Dera'a, about 30 m. E. of the southern end of Lake Gennesareth and Astaroth (Tell el-Aš'ari) 11 m. NNW. of Dera'a. **7-8.** The description of Josue's conquests is that of 10:16 f. ' Part of ' (DV, **7**) is a proper name Ḥalaq ; *cf.* 11:17. **9b.** Hai alone is located by a neighbouring city, probably because it alone was not a city but a ruin. **9-23.** The district to which a city belongs is sometimes attached to it by a preposition ; *cf.* 22*b*. Hence we conclude that Sharon (**18**) is really the district containing Aphek, Nafat Dor that containing Dor (**23a**) and that Galil, Galilee (LXX) not Gilgal (MT) should be read in **23b**. The impossible *king of the nations of Galilee* could be rendered *king of the valley of the sea of Galilee*, probably a gloss localizing and then replacing the original *king of Kinneroth in Galilee*. It is not stated that Josue captured the cities mentioned but that he slew their kings.

B. XIII-XXI Division of the Land. **2?**
XIII 1-33 Land to be divided and Land already divided—**1-7.** The land to be divided among nine and a half tribes is specified. **8-14.** The territory already divided by Moses is defined and some provision is made for Levi. **15-33.** The boundaries and chief cities of the transjordanic tribes are indicated. The territories to be considered are three : Geshur, Philistia and Canaan. Geshur, the modern Djōlān, was an unconquered region in the NW. of Transjordania. It was not distributed or inhabited by Israelites (13).

2-3. *The districts* (DV Galilee) *of the Philistines*, extending from *Shiḥor* (DV troubled river) *in front of Egypt* to Accaron *are reckoned to the Canaanite* as original Canaanite territory and thus belong to Israel. They include five city states in the north and an Avite (DV Hevite) region conquered by the Philistines (Deut 2:23) in the south. Shihor ' Waters of Horus ' is the Egyptian name of the Pelusiac branch of the Nile ; *cf.* Is 23:3 ; Jer 2:18. LXX understands Rhino-

34a colura, the more northerly Wady el-'Arîsh, and this watercourse seems to be meant by the Torrent of Egypt (15:4). Between Shihor and Rhinocolura is a desert. Philistia fell to Judah but the city states retained their **b** independence. **4-5.** Finally Canaan is to be distributed and its northern boundary is indicated. The text is undoubtedly corrupt. Israelite territory, in the widest sense, including subject nations, extended ideally at least to the Euphrates in the NE., but it never included Lebanon, except implicitly in Ez 47:20, where the reference is however to the future Messianic Kingdom, not to the land distributed to Israel. Here Byblos, *the land of the Gebailite* (ungrammatically expressed), and *all Lebanon* is included in the land to be distributed. Lebanon moreover immediately reappears (6) again as the northern boundary. Buhl's correction, generally accepted, gives a consistent text. ' *And all the land of the Canaanite from* [MT, and] *Me'āra of the Sidonians to Aphek, to the boundary of the Amorite, and the land adjoining Lebanon* [MT, of the Gebailite and all Lebanon] *to the east from Baal-Gad under Mt Hermon to the Entry of Hamath.*' Me'āra, perhaps el-Mog̱eiriye, 6 m. NE. of Sidon, is in the west, Aphek, an unidentified city of Aser (19:30) in the centre, and the boundary of the Amorite, the spurs of Hermon, in the east of the northern limit. To this is added the region between Baal-Gad (Baniyas) and the Entry of Ḥamath, the northern extremity of Merg 'Ayyūn, whence the plain of the Beka' leads directly to distant Hamath. **6.** Yahweh promises to drive out the Sidonians from the mountainous region of northern Galilee. **8a.** *With whom* refers grammatically not to the transjordanic but **c** to the cisjordanic half-tribe of Manasses. Some omission after 7 must be supposed. The kingdom of Sihon, whose boundaries were indicated in 12:1-6, consisted originally of Heshbon and its immediate surroundings. Here alone in the whole region between the Jabbok and the Red Sea Late Bronze Age pottery has been discovered, at Galūl, 6 m. SE. of Heshbon— a valuable confirmation of the biblical narrative establishing the existence of Sihon's kingdom. By driving the Moabites south of the Arnon shortly before the arrival of the Hebrews the whole Mishor (northern Moab) was added to the original settlement. **21.** Thus Ruben received *all the kingdom* (DV kingdoms) *of Sihon*, the Mishor and the southern fringe of the Jordan valley, so that the Wady Ḥesbān roughly represents the boundary between Ruben and Gad. **24-28.** Since however the Madianite nomads in southern Galaad were under the suzerainty of Sihon (21), Gad also received part of Sihon's kingdom, Yazer (land of Yazer Num 32:1) most probably Gazzîr about 9 m. W. of Rabbath Ammon (Rabba, later Philadelphia, modern 'Amman), *all the cities of Galaad* (name originally indicating only southern Galaad but later extended to northern Galaad in the lot of Manasses) and the eastern Jordan valley as far as Lake Gennesareth. *Half the land of the Ammonites* most probably indicates an extension of the frontier in David's time since Israel was forbidden to occupy the land of the Ammonites (Deut 12:19, 37 ; Jg 11:18) and remains of Ammonite fortifications still indicate the original eastern boundary of Gad. Northern Galaad was then mostly thickly wooded and unsettled.

d XIV 1-15 Caleb asks for and receives Hebron—1-12. After an introduction in which the omission of Levi and the double representation of Joseph are indicated, Caleb interviews Josue, reminds him of the promises of Moses forty-five years earlier and asks for Hebron. **13-15.** Josue grants his request and the ancient name of Hebron is explained. **2a.** For ' dividing all by lot ' (DV) read *by lot for their possession.* **6-10.** Since Caleb was forty years old when sent to spy out the land in the second year of the desert period and was now eighty-five, the Israelites, still encamped at Gilgal, were seven years in Canaan when the distribution was made. **11.** *Go out* and *come in* (DV march) refer to non-military duties. **15.** MT interprets Cariath-Arbe, *city of Arbe* and adds : *He*

(Arbe) *was the greatest man of the Anakim.* LXX reads : **234d** *It* (Cariath-Arbe) *was the metropolis of the Anakim.* Adam ' man ' becomes a proper name in Vg.

XV 1-63 The Portion of Judah—The boundaries of **e** Judah are first described, then the special portion of Caleb and his younger brother Othoniel and lastly, the cities of Judah. **1.** ' *The boundary of Judah reaches the frontier of Edom, the desert of Sin in the south and is in the extreme south.*' This general description is amplified. **2-4.** The boundary goes from the southern end (lit. *tongue*, DV bay) of the Dead Sea to the Ascent of the Scorpions (Naqb eṣ-Ṣafa over 20 m. SW. of the Dead Sea), passes to Sin and ascends to the south of Qadesh-barnea ('Ain-Qedeis), reaches the Torrent of Egypt (Wady el-'Arish) and follows it to the Mediterranean. The other places mentioned are not definitely identified. **5.** The eastern boundary is the Dead Sea which probably extended more to the north in Josue's time. **6-8.** The northern boundary ascends to Beth Hogla (Qaṣr Hagle, SE. of Jericho) and through the Valley of Achor (7:24) to the Ascent of Adommim (Tal'at ed-Damm near Khan Khatrūr, midway between Jericho and Jerusalem), then southward to the Fountain of the Sun ('Ain el-Hôd, Fountain of the Apostles, near Bethany) and the Fountain of Rogel (Bir Ayyūb, Job's Well, SE. of Jerusalem). '*And the boundary ascends the Valley of the Son of Hinnom* [Wady er-Rabāby] *to the flank of the Jebusite on the south, that is Jerusalem, and ascends to the summit of the mountain* [Niqefuriyeh, W. of Jerusalem] *which is in front of the valley of Hinnom to the west and at the extremity of the Valley of Rephaim* [el-Beqa'a, SW. of Jerusalem] *to the north.*' Vincent renders *minne-geḇ* ' from the south ' instead of ' on the south ' and supposes the boundary after meeting Jerusalem to run north instead of west. He identifies the Valley of Hinnom with Tyropoeon (el-Wady) in the middle of later Jerusalem and the mountain with Râs Nādir = Baal-Peraṣim ' Baal of the Watershed ' (2 Kg 5:20), near Nephtõaḥ, the culminating point of the Palestinian watershed in the region. In both views ancient Jerusalem belonged to Benjamin. The statement that the Judaeans could not overcome the Jebusites in Jerusalem (63) seems to reflect the mentality of the period immediately preceding David's capture of the city. **9-11.** From the mountain the boundary inclines to the Waters of Nephtõaḥ ('Ain Lifta, NW. of Jerusalem) 'and thence to Cariathiarim (*cf.* 9:17), then southward to Chesalon (Kesla) and Bethshemesh ('Ain-Shems), westward to Timnah (Tibneh), northward to Accaron and Jebneel (later Jamnia, modern Yebnà) and thence westward to the sea.

13-14. Caleb takes Hebron, *the city of Arbe father of* **f** *Enac*, and slays three of the Anakim. **15-17.** He offers his daughter in marriage to the conqueror of Debir, formerly called Booktown. Othoniel takes Debir and marries his niece. Both cities were previously captured by Josue (10:36-9), but not being garrisoned were re-occupied by Canaanites. **18a.** The context requires not ' she incited him ' (MT) but *he incited her* (LXX). **18b.** Read *alighted from* for ' sighed on '. **19.** Read after ' blessing ' : ' *For thou hast given me* (in marriage) *to a dry land so give me a well* ' (LXX ; wells MT). Albright locates one well, 2 m. N., the other nearly 1 m. S. of Tell Beit Mirsim. The narrative (14-19) reappears in its proper place chronologically (Jg 1:10-15).

XVI 1-XVII 18 The Portion of the Sons of Joseph— **235a** There were two distributions, one to Joseph as a single tribe (16:1-4), the second to Ephraim and Manasses as separate tribes (16:5-10 ; 17:1-13). The reason of the second is given in 17:14-8. The southern boundary of the house of Joseph is subsequently only summarily indicated as the southern boundary of Ephraim, but the northern one is restated in practically identical terms as the dividing line between Ephraim and Manasses. Thus Ephraim retained the original lot of Joseph while Manasses received for his portion the extension subsequently granted in northern Samaria. No northern boundary of Manasses is indicated because the region was thickly wooded and its chief cities long

235a remained in the hands of the Canaanites. The eastern and western boundaries of both tribes were the Jordan and the Mediterranean.

1-3. ' *The lot of the sons of Joseph went from the Jordan in front of Jericho* [LXX ; from the Jordan of Jericho to the waters of Jericho, MT] *on the east. The boundary went up from Jericho to the mountain towards the desert of Bethel-Luza* [LXX ; Luza is an old name of Bethel ; MT is corrupt but in general agreement with LXX]. *And it went from Bethel-Luza and passed to the frontier of the Arkian at Aṭarōth* [Khirbet 'Aṭara, *c* 4 m. SSW. of Bethel] *and it descended westward to the frontier of the Yaphletian to the limit of Lower Bethhoron* [*cf.* 10:11] *and to Gezer* [Gazer ; *cf.* 10:32] *and ended at the sea.*' The same southern boundary of Ephraim in 5*b*–6*a* only mentions a different Aṭarōth in the east, Upper Bethhoron in the centre and the sea in the west. Addar is an interpolation. Arki and Yaphleti are clan names.

b **16:6-9-17:7-10.** The northern boundary of Ephraim begins in the middle at Machmethath (*in front of Sichem* 17:7, probably Khirbet Guleigil) *' inclines eastward to Thanathselo* [Ta'na el-fōqa, 8 m. SE. of Nablus], *passes it on the east side to Janoe* [Yanūn, south of Ta'na], *descends from Janoe to Aṭaroth* [mentioned 16:5 but unidentified] *and Naaratha* ['Ain Dūq, north of Jericho], *reaches Jericho and ends in the Jordan*'. On the western side only Taphua, south (DV on the right hand) of Machmethath (**17:7b**), probably Sheikh Abu Zarad, south of Yasūf, and the Torrent of Qāna (DV valley of Reeds, modern Wady Qana) are mentioned. Ephraim had also cities set apart in the territory of Manasses (**16:9**), of which Taphua alone is mentioned (**17:8**), since the statement : *These cities belong to Ephraim in the midst of the cities of Manasses* (**17:9b**) cannot refer to unmentioned cities in the Wady Qana and is probably a gloss. Gezer remained Canaanite until Solomon's time.

c In **17:1-6** we are informed that the descendants of six children of Manasses settled in Palestine while the rest remained in Transjordania. These children are not necessarily greatgrandsons of Manasses through Machir and Galaad (Num 26:30 f.,) since links in the chain of ancestry are frequently omitted. The portion of one, Hepher, whose son, Salphaad, had no male issue, fell to his five granddaughters. The warrior who received Galaad and Bashan, Machir, is not an individual but a clan, the Machirites, descended not from Galaad but from Machir's other sons (1 Par 7:15-17). **7a.** *From Aser*, not in LXX B, is probably a textual corruption by dittography. **11.** *Naphath* (DV Nopheth), of which Manasses possessed a third, was not a city but a large district attached to the city of Dor in the territory of Asher. Naphath Dor was one of the administrative districts of Solomon (3 Kg 4:11). From **14-18** we learn that the mountain land was first occupied by the Hebrews, then wooded regions were penetrated and lastly the plain land was secured. Iron-bound chariots are possible (*c* 1190) after the invasion of the Sea Peoples. **17b-18.** The Manassites had to work out their own salvation by enlarging their territory in Palestine to which no northern boundary is assigned, not by migrating to Transjordania, as some commentators hold, contrary to the direct evidence of the text : ' *You are a numerous people and you have great strength. You shall not have one portion only, for the mountain will be yours. If it be forest, cut it down and its outlets will be yours, for you must dispossess the Canaanite because he has iron chariots, because he is strong*'. The outlets to the plain of Esdraelon in Canaanite hands are clearly indicated.

d **XVIII 1-28 Second Distribution at Shiloh : The Portion of Benjamin**—In an assembly at Shiloh Josue orders the seven tribes who have not received portions to send each three men to survey the land still undistributed and divide it into seven lots. The first lot consisting of the territory between Judah and Ephraim falls to Benjamin. Its boundaries are described and its chief cities enumerated. The settlement of the tabernacle at Shiloh implies the permanent transfer thither of headquarters from Gilgal. The transfer **23** must have been recent, naturally coinciding with the return of the transjordanic warriors to their homes immediately after the distribution (22:1, 6). It is moreover unlikely that much time intervened between the first distribution at Gilgal and the second at Shiloh. The new and more central headquarters is identified with Khirbet Seilūn, 20 m. N. of Jerusalem. No structural and only sparse pottery remains of the Late Bronze Age (1600-1200) were there discovered, but in the Early Iron Age the city was walled and very prosperous owing no doubt to the civil and religious importance which it received from Josue. Its culture is markedly Palestinian. Here again as in Transjordania Israelite occupation long before 1200 B.C. is excluded.

1. Read *meeting* for ' testimony '. **4.** Read *according to* **e** *their inheritance* for ' number of each multitude '. **9.** Insert *by cities* after ' divided it '. The different lots were determined according to the number of cities which they contained. The boundaries of Benjamin are already known from those of Judah and Ephraim. **12.** The desert (16:1) is here the desert of Bethaven = Bethel. **13a.** Luz = Bethel is excluded by the boundary but included among the cities (**22**). The texts refer to different periods. **14a.** ' *And the boundary bends and turns to the south on the western side* [of the lot] *from the mountain in front of Bethhoron southwards.*' **15.** For ' part ' read *the end* (Cariathiarim is excluded) and omit ' towards the sea ', a textual corruption since the direction is eastward. **16.** ' *And the boundary descends to the extremity of the mountain, which is in front of the valley of Ben-Hinnom and by* [or, in] *the valley of Rephaim on its north side, and descends the valley of Hinnom to the flank of the Jebusite to the south and descends to the Fountain of Rogel* '; *cf.* 15:8. **17-18.** For ' Geliloth ' (DV hills) read *Gilgal* (15:7) unidentified but west of Khan Khatrur, and for 'Arabah (DV champaign countries) Beth-'Arabah (15:8), 'Ain Garba in the Wady Qelt.

XIX 1-9 Portion of Simeon—Simeon received seven- **23** teen cities in the southern part of the large territory of Judah. **2.** Sabee seems to be a dittography of (Beer)-sheba. Its omission verifies the number thirteen. No boundaries are given and the southern delimitation by means of a single city Ramoth (in the Negeb, 1 Kg 30:27) implies that there were none in the document utilized and refutes the conjectural theory that Simeon received originally a distinct territory, but was subsequently absorbed by Judah. The identified cities are all in the south.

10-16 Portion of Zabulon—Zabulon occupied the **b** centre of southern Galilee. The delimitation begins in the centre of the southern boundary (*cf.* 16:6 ; 17:7 ; 19:25), going first west and then east. Sarid (usually corrected to Sadid), Tell Shadūd, 6 m. SW. of Nazareth is the central point. Jeconam (Tell Qaimūn at the foot of Mt Carmel) marks the western, Mt Thabor the eastern end. Ceseleththabor is Iksāl at the foot of Thabor on the west and Dabereth is Deburiye or Dabura, NW. of Thabor ; Japhie is Yafa, SW. of Nazareth. **11a.** ' *And the lot ascended to the west and to Merala* '—probably Galta in the plain of the Qishon. Dabbesheth is Tell Shemmām, opposite Tell Qaimūn. **13.** ' *And thence it passes on the east side*.' The eastern boundary is meant. Gethhepher, birthplace of Jonas, is probably Khirbet ez-Zurra' near Meshed, 3 m. NE. of Nazareth, and Rammon is Rummāne farther north in the Baṭṭōf plain. Ne'a (DV Noa) is very probably Tell el-Wawiyat, and (**14**) Hannaton, the adjacent Tell el-Bedeiwiye. The valley of Yiphtah-el is most probably the Baṭṭōf plain called Asochis in NT times and drained by the Wady Melek at its western end. As the eastern boundary is not mentioned, we may perhaps assume a lacuna in text or source. The number of cities exceeds twelve, but such lists often receive additions (*cf.* Nephtali).

17-23 Portion of Issachar—Issachar received the rich **c** but insecure plain of Esdraelon (*cf.* Gen 49:14 f.)

3c between Zabulon-Nephtali on the north and Manasses on the south. The boundaries are not given and can only be deduced from the cities mentioned. They reached the Jordan on the east and the foot of Mt Carmel but not the Mediterranean on the west. The most westerly of the cities is Hapharaim (el-Farriye), 3 m. S. of Jeconam. **22.** Thabor does not indicate the mountain but a city upon it or at its foot as otherwise the total of cities would be incorrect. The southern boundary may have been omitted as still undefined since it was the same as the undetermined northern boundary of Manasses.

d 24-31 Portion of Aser—The coast land of northern Palestine from the confines of Sidon in the north to *Shihor Libnat* (Wady Zerqa just north of Caesarea), in the south fell to Aser. On the east were the portions of Manasses, Issachar, Zabulon and Nephtali. The boundary, indicated by cities, begins in the middle of the west side (**25-26a**), goes first south (**26b**), then east (**27a**), then north (**27b-28**) and finally returns south to its starting-point (**28**). Shihor is not the Nile, but nonetheless may mean Waters of Horus of Libnath. Crocodiles found in it may have suggested the Egyptian name. **27b.** For ' left ' read *north*, since Cabul (Qabūl, 9 m. NE. of Acco = Ptolemais, Acre, 'Akka) is in Aser. **28.** Cana is not the NT Cana but Qāna, 8 m. SE. of Tyre. **29.** ' The strong city of Tyre ' is the island fortress. Hosa is the continental part of the city. For ' from the portion of ' read Mahaleb (Mahalliba in Sennacherib's list, modern Mahalib, NE. of Tyre). **30.** Achzib, Ecdippa, modern ez-Zib, north of Acre, belongs to the last group of names where 'Umma is a misreading of 'Acco.

e 32-39 Portion of Nephtali—Nephtali inhabited the eastern side of Galilee. The southern and western boundaries are first indicated, then the cities. **33.** ' And their boundary was from Heleph [Arbaṭa at the foot of Thabor], from the terebinth of Bas'annim [Khan et-Tuggar ; *cf.* Jg 4:11] *and Adami-hanneceb and Yebnael* [probably ed-Damiye and Yemma, SW. of Lake Gennesareth] *as far as Lecum* [probably Aulam, south of Yemma] *and ended at the Jordan.*' The Jordan is of course the eastern boundary indicated here at its southern and later at its northern extremity. **34.** The western boundary runs north from Thabor to Hucuca (Yaquq, 5 m. W. of Capharnaum), ' *touches Zabulon in the south and Aser on the west and Judah of the Jordan in the east* '. Judah, not in LXX, is probably interpolated. The cities exceed nineteen if those of 33-34 are included.

f 40-48 Portion of Dan—The territory of Dan seems to have belonged originally, at least in part, to his more powerful neighbours, Ephraim in the north and Judah in the south. Accaron and Bethshemesh are on the southern, Mejarcon (Nahr el-'Audja) on the northern and Ayalon (Yalo, SE. of 'Amwas-Nicopolis) on the eastern boundary. **47a.** ' *And the territory of Dan went out from them* ', or (reading *yaṣṣēr*) ' *was too narrow for them.*' Unable to hold it against the Philistines they migrated to NE. Palestine where they captured Lešem (*sic* ? Laiš Jg 18:29) and called it Dan (modern Tell el-Qāḍi, Mound of the Judge—*i.e.* of Dan, site of the principal source of the Jordan). **49-51.** Josue himself received the city of Thamnath-Saraa in Mt Ephraim (probably Tibneh, 12 m. NE. of Lydda).

g XX 1-9 Cities of Refuge—God orders Josue to appoint six cities of refuge where whoever had unintentionally slain another might be protected from the vengeance of the relatives of the slain. The procedure in such cases is indicated. The cities are appointed and their object is defined. LXX(B) omits 4–6 probably because it is practically equivalent to 9 and consequently superfluous. The matter is more fully treated in Num 35:9–28 ; Deut 19:1–13.

3b. ' *And they shall be to you a refuge from the avenger of blood.*' **4.** Read ' *his business* ' instead of ' such things as prove him innocent '. **5.** Read ' *was not* ' instead of ' is not proved to have been '. **6.** The two periods during which the slayer remains in the city of refuge,

till his trial and till the death of the high-priest, must be **236g** distinguished. The former was appointed for all fugitives, the latter only for those who were subsequently judged innocent. The detention of the innocent was a safeguard rather than a punishment since the relatives of the slain would be eager for vengeance while the memory of their loss was recent. As this danger period could not be definitely fixed its end was vaguely determined by the death of the high-priest. **7-8.** The appointment of the six cities of refuge is the execution of the command given directly to Josue himself (1–2) and indirectly through Moses (Num 35:9 f.). The fact that Moses himself determined the three transjordanic cities of refuge (Deut 4:41–3) is no obstacle to their inclusion by Josue in the final execution of the mandate which he had received. In 7 Galil ' circle ' specifically designates Galilee, the northern part of Palestine.

XXI 1-42 Cities and Pasture-land for Priests and h Levites—The command given (Num 35:1–8) to provide cities of residence for priests and Levites and pastures for their flocks in the tribal territory of which they had received no separate portion is here executed. In the distribution of the land among the tribes the available territory was first divided into the requisite number of fairly equal parts and the part to be assigned to each tribe was then decided by lot. Similarly here the cities, forty-eight in all, including the six cities of refuge, seem to have been first determined, then divided into four parts and finally apportioned to the recipients as the lot decided. The Caath clan alone contained priests as well as Levites and thus received two portions : thirteen cities from Judah, Simeon and Benjamin for the Aaronite priests and ten cities from Ephraim, Dan and cisjordanic Manasses for the remaining Caathite Levites. The Gersonite Levites received thirteen cities from Issachar, Aser, Nephtali and transjordanic Manasses ; the Merarite Levites twelve from Ruben, Gad and Zabulon. The appropriate settlement of the priests near Jerusalem is thus determined by lot and an act of Divine Providence. The Levites had not exclusive possession of these cities but shared them with their tribal occupants. They had also certain township rights in the form of pasture-land consisting apparently of tracts located north, south, east and west of the city wall and each 2,000 by 1,000 cubits in extent. Similarly in modern Arabia ' there are circuits of the common soil about the desert village where no nomads may drive their cattle under pain of being accused to the Emir. Such township rights are called Hima ' (Doughty, *Travels in Arabia Deserta*, II, 245).

1. For ' families and kindreds ' read *clans*, *bēṭ 'ābôṭ*, **i** here abbreviated to *'ābôṭ*. The three sons of Levi, Caath, Gerson and Merari represent three clans. **2.** Read *pastures* for ' suburbs '. **4.** Render after ' Caath ' ' *and it was for the sons of Aaron, the Levitical priest* '. **5-6.** Read after ' remained ' and ' Gerson ' ' *according to their families* ' as in **7** where DV has ' kindreds ' for *families*. **11-12.** The first mention of the gift of Hebron is probably taken from a different source. **26.** For ' of the inferior degree ' read *remaining*. A few errors in the list of names can be corrected from the similar list in 1 Par 6:54–81 : Yeblaam for Gethremmon (**25**), Ashtaroth for Bosra (**27**), Hammon or Hammat (19:35), for Hammot-Dor (**32**). **36.** Mišor indicates not a city but the plateau south of Galaad between Wady Hesban and the Arnon where Bosor is located ; Yahsa and Qedemot should be read for Jaser and Jethson. LXX repeats 19:49 f. after 42, and adds that the flint knives mentioned 5:2 were kept at Thamnath-Saraa.

C. XXII-XXIV Appendix. **237a**
XXII 1-34 The Transjordanians return and erect an Altar—**1-8.** Josue dismisses the transjordanic warriors after commending their obedience, exhorting them to remain faithful to Yahweh, blessing them and enjoining them to share their spoils with their brethren.

237a 9-10. They depart and on reaching the Jordan erect an altar. **11-12.** The Cisjordanians hearing of this apparent violation of the law assemble in Shiloh for an expedition against them. **13-20.** First however the high-priest Eleazar and ten representatives of the ten tribes are sent to remonstrate with them for exposing all Israel to the wrath of Yahweh by erecting an altar of their own and abandoning his worship. **21-29.** The Transjordanians reply that the altar is not intended for the offering of sacrifices, but as a testimony to future generations that Yahweh is God of all the tribes of Israel. **30-34.** The ambassadors and subsequently the people accept this explanation of the altar of testimony.

b The address of Josue seems to end at **6.** Its resumption after the superfluous information in **7a-b** is probably from a different source. **8.** Note that iron is included in the spoils. **10-11.** The site of the altar was ' *on the Jordan, in the direction of the land of Canaan, at the tracts of the Jordan, over against* [or, *beyond*] *the Israelites* '. A transjordanic site is more probable especially as the altar is presumed in 19 to have been built to remove the uncleanness of Transjordania, not Yahwist territory. **14.** The ambassadors are called heads of clans, of whom one was selected from each of the ten tribes. **20b.** ' *And he alone* [lit. one man] *did not die for his sin*.' The people may also suffer for the sins of individuals. **29.** The law of unity of altar of sacrifice is here attested as obligatory, though not strictly observed. The altar on Mt Hebal (8:30) would be authorized, but an altar in Transjordania prohibited by the law of Ex 20:24. The half tribe of Manasses is mentioned with Ruben and Gad in 1, 9, 11, 15, 21, 30, but omitted in 25, 32, 33, 34. The text is uncertain. LXX differs from MT in omitting Ruben and Gad (**25**) and mentioning the half tribe of Manasses (**32, 33, 34**). It appears from Num 32 that Ruben and Gad received their lots before half Manasses received his from Moses, but no text suggests that Manassites did not settle in Transjordania before the distribution in Canaan.

c XXIII 1-16 Josue, near his End, exhorts Israel to be Faithful to Yahweh — 1-11. Josue summons the representatives of the people and after a general reference to the benefits received from Yahweh reminds them that enemies still remain to be subdued in the territory allotted to them and assures them that Yahweh will continue to give them victory in the future as in the past if they remain faithful to him and to his law and refrain from making alliances with the Canaanites or worshipping their gods. **12-16.** If they are unfaithful to Yahweh and accept Canaanite friendship and Canaanite worship he will destroy not their enemies but themselves.

d 2. Omit the first ' and ' not connective but explanatory. **3.** For ' round about ' read *before you*. **4.** MT is unintelligible owing to an interpolation ' and all the nations which I have destroyed ', rightly omitted in Vg since **5** shows that only enemies still to be conquered are indicated. **7.** ' *And cohabit not with the Gentiles who remain among you, and invoke not the name of their gods and swear not by them and worship them not and bow not down before them*.' **9.** ' *And the Lord God took away . . . nations that were . . . and no man resisted you to this day*.' **10.** Read *used to chase* and *fought*. **12a.** ' *But if you go back* [abandon Yahweh] *and adhere to the remnant of the Gentiles who remain among you*.' **13.** ' Not ' should be *no longer*, ' pit ' *trap*, ' stumbling-block ' *whip* and ' stakes ' *thorns*. **14b.** Read *know*. **16a.** For ' when '

read *if*. This speech of Josue shows clearly that his **23** conquest of Palestine was incomplete. Much of the territory distributed among the tribes was still in the possession of the Canaanites.

XXIV 1-33 Last Words and Death of Josue—1-13. e In an assembly at Shechem Josue reminds the Israelites of the many benefits received from Yahweh from Abraham's time to the present day. **14-18.** He then asks them to choose whom they will serve, Yahweh or strange gods, and they affirm their allegiance to Yahweh alone. **19-24.** He tests them by representing the difficulties of the service of Yahweh, but they repeatedly reaffirm that him only will they serve. **25-28.** He then makes a covenant with them, instructs them in their duties, registers the proceedings in the Book of the Law, sets a great stone under the terebinth in the sanctuary as a testimony and dismisses them to their homes. **29-33.** The death and burial of Josue and the last resting-places of Joseph and Phinees are briefly recorded.

1. LXX substitutes Shiloh, the capital, for Shechem **f** confirmed by the mention of the terebinth (26 ; *cf.* Gen 12:6 ; 35:4). Shechem was then the spot in Palestine most sacred to the Israelites because it was there that God first appeared to Abraham and promised Canaan to his descendants (Gen 12:7). It had a sanctuary implied (1, *before Yahweh*) and mentioned (26) and an altar (8:30) legitimately erected (Ex 20:24). The ark was probably transported thither and the events narrated 8:30–35 may have occurred on this occasion. **2.** *The river* is the Euphrates ; *your fathers* are generally, *Thare* particularly, indicated ; Abraham is not included among worshippers of false gods. **3.** Read after ' Abraham ' : ' *from the land beyond the River and I brought him through all the land of Canaan* '. **5b-6a.** ' *And I afflicted Egypt with what I did therein and I brought you forth*.' *Your fathers* here and in 17 is a gloss explaining that the preceding generation is meant. **9.** Read *was hostile to* for ' fought against '. There was no actual warfare (Num 22–24 ; Jg 11:25). **11.** The nations, probably interpolated, are those of Canaan, not of Jericho. **12.** After ' hornets ' (*cf.* Ex 23:28) read ' *to drive them out from before you, the kings of the Amorites* '. MT has *two* kings (Sihon and Og), LXX *twelve*, an incomplete correction since Canaanite kings are meant ; *cf.* ch 12. **15.** Apparently some Israelites then as later worshipped idols. **17a.** ' *Yahweh is our God* ' ; *cf.* 18b. **22a.** Insert *against yourselves* after ' witnesses '. **25.** Read after **g** ' covenant ' : ' *with the people and set before them* '. The covenant was with Josue not with God. **26.** *All these things* are the proceedings. The volume of the law is not the Pentateuch, since *all these things* are absent from it, but a lost record book. For ' oak ' read *terebinth*. **27.** Read for ' unto you ' *against you*, for ' that ' *because*, and for ' to you ' *to us*. **30.** A Moslem shrine, Neby Ghaith, on a mountain south of Tibneh (*cf.* 19:50) may preserve the Hebrew name *ga'aš*. **32.** The modern Tomb of Joseph east of Jacob's Well indicates approximately the ancient site. On the purchase of the land by Abraham *cf.* Gen 33:19. Qesiṭah (DV young ewe) is probably a fixed weight of silver. **33.** The Gabaath of Phinees is probably Gibya, NW. of Gifna and conveniently near Shiloh and Thamnath-Saraa. LXX has an addition to 30, again concerned with the knives of circumcision (*cf.* 21:42), and omits **31.** Jos 24:28–31 reappears in Jg 2:6–9 in a different order. Both authors probably used the same source.

JUDGES

By E. POWER, S.J.

8a Bibliography—I Commentaries—*K. F. Keil, Leipzig, 1874²; C. Clair, Paris, 1878; *E. Bertheau, Leipzig, 1883²; *P. Cassel, Bielefeld, 1887²; F. de Hummelauer (CSS), Paris, 1888; *J. S. Black, Cambridge, 1892; *S. Oettli, Muenchen, 1893; *G. F. Moore (ICC), Edinburgh, 1895; *K. Budde, Freiburg, 1897; *W. Nowack, Goettingen, 1900; B. Neteler, Muenster, 1900; M.-J. Lagrange, Paris, 1903; A. W. H. Sloet, s'Hertogenbosch, 1904; J. Sedlacek, Prag, 1910; *G. A. Cooke, Cambridge, 1913; *C. F. Burney, London, 1922²; *R. Breuer, Frankfurt a/M, 1922; V. Zapletal, Muenster, 1923; A. Schulz, Bonn, 1926; J. Keulers, Brugge, 1932; *C. J. Goslinga, Kampen, 1933-8; R. Tamisier, Paris, 1949.

b II Special Subjects—L. Desnoyers, *Histoire du peuple hébreu : La période des juges*, Paris, 1922; *O. Eissfeldt, *Die Quellen des Richterbuches*, Leipzig, 1925; *E. Auerbach, ' Die Einwanderung der Israeliten ', ZATW 48 (1930) 281–95; *H. W. Hertzberg, 'Adonibezeq', JPOS 6 (1926) 213-21; *T. K. Cheyne, ' Cushan-Rishathaim ', EB 1 (1899) 968–70; *J. W. Jack, ' Cushan-Rishataim ', ET 35 (1923-4) 426–8; H. Haensler, ' Der historische Hintergrund von Richter 3:8-10 ', Bi 11 (1930) 391–418, 12 (1931) 3–26, 276–96; *E. Auerbach, ' Ehud ', ZATW 51 (1933) 47–51; *E. G. Kraeling, ' Difficulties in the Story of Ehud ', JBL 54 (1935) 205–10; *B. Maisler, ' Shamgar Ben 'Anat ', PEF 66 (1934) 192–4; *W. F. Albright, ' Some additional notes on the Song of Deborah ', JPOS 2 (1922) 284 f.; *C. Bruston, ' Le Chant de Débora ', *Études Théol. et Relig.* (1927) 489–515; *E. Sellin, ' Das Deboralied ', *Procksch-Festschrift* (Leipzig) 1934, 149–66; *W. F. Albright, ' The Song of Deborah in the Light of Archaeology ', BASOR 62 (1936²) 26–31; A. Fernandez, ' La oda triunfal de Debora ', *Estudios Eclesiasticos* 15 (1936) 5–46; *S. Tolkowsky, ' Gedeon's Fleece ', JPOS 3 (1923) 197–99; *A. Mez, ' Jg 7:5 ', ZATW 21 (1901) 198–200; A. Condamin, ' Les 300 soldats de Gédéon qui ont lapé l'eau ', RSR 13 (1922) 218–20; *C. Weidenkaff, ' Ist 'en dschalud die AT Harodquelle ? ' *Pal. Jahrbuch* 17 (1921) 18–31; K. Fruhstorfer, ' Abimelechs Koenigtum ', TPQS 83 (1930) 87–106; A. Mallon, ' Chronique des fouilles : Sichem ', Bi 8 (1927) 377–81; L. H. Vincent, ' Fouilles allemandes à Balata-Sichem ', RB 36 (1927) 419–25; *G. Welter, ' Stand der Ausgrabungen in Sichem ', *Archaeologischer Anzeiger* (1932) 313 f.; A. Fernandez, ' Jephte ', VD 1 (1921) 77–81, 104–108, 299–304; A. van Hoonacker, *Le vœu de Jephté*, Louvain, 1903; V. Zapletal, *Der biblische Samson*, Freiburg (Schweiz), 1906; E. Kalt, *Samson*, Freiburg (Breisgau), 1912; *J. A. Bewer, ' The Composition of Judges, chh 17-18 ', AJSL 29 (1913–14) 261–83; A. Fernandez, ' El Santuario de Dan ', Bi 15 (1934) 237–64; id., ' El attentado de Gabaa ', *ibid.* 12 (1931) 297–315; *J. A. Bewer, ' The Composition of Judges, chh 19–21 ', AJSL 30 (1914–15) 81–93, 149–65; P. Joüon, ' Bélial ', Bi 5 (1924) 178–83; *W. F. Albright, ' Excavations and Results at Tell el-Ful (Gibeah of Saul) ', AASOR 4 (1924) 1–89; L. H. Vincent, ' Fouilles américaines à Tell el-Foul ', RB 32 (1923) 426–30.

d Name—The book of Judges is so called from the title given to the national heroes whose exploits are its main theme. Judge is not an equivalent of ruler. The **238d** Philistines were the rulers in Samson's time. Gedeon refused the rulership offered him after his victory. Jephte stipulates beforehand for rulership in Galaad as the reward of his conquest of Ammon. A judge is one who distributes justice to the people and in particular maintains the rights of the oppressed. The great judges were all raised up by God to defend the rights of the oppressed Israelites against foreign aggressors. Judge is thus equivalent to deliverer, and Samson is so called because he began to deliver Israel from the Philistines. Debora alone is a judge in the strict legal sense of the word before she becomes a deliverer. But no such office can be assigned for instance to Gedeon or Jephte before their call. The title of the five minor judges on the contrary seems to be understood in its strict legal sense. They are not recorded as deliverers or divinely appointed nor are their exploits mentioned.

Contents—The present book of Judges contains a **e** religious history of Israel from Josue to Samuel in the form of detached episodes. It begins with an account of the efforts of the tribes in Canaan to secure complete possession of their lots. Then comes an appropriate introduction to the narratives of the great judges raised up by God to deliver the people from their various oppressors. Israel's history throughout the period is depicted under the form of recurring cycles of sin, punishment, repentance, and deliverance. The victorious struggles of Othniel with the Edomites, Aod with the Moabites, Debora and Barac with the Canaanites, Gedeon with the Madianites, Jephte with the Ammonites, and Samson with the Philistines are then described. Between Aod and Debora is a brief reference to the exploits of ' Samgar ' against the Philistines. After Gedeon the episode of Abimelech and the Sichemites is related apparently by way of appendix. Immediately before and after Jephte the five minor judges are recorded. After Samson come the episodes of the origin and institution of the sanctuary of Dan and the outrage at Gabaa and war of the tribes against Benjamin.

Composition and Authorship—The book of Judges has **f** been twice edited. The first edition is indicated by the special introduction to the history of the great judges (2:6–3:6) and the attachment of this introduction to the close of the book of Josue by a textual citation (2:6–9=Jos 24:28–31). It contained the narratives of the six great judges. The second inspired editor added to these an account of the failures and successes in the wars of the tribes in Canaan at the beginning and the episodes of the Danite sanctuary and the outrage at Gabaa at the end. He evidently wished to inform his readers more fully of the anarchy and lawlessness of the period. We might perhaps assign to him the Abimelech episode, attributed usually to the first editor. The brief accounts of the minor judges, not agreeing in concept or treatment with the programme of the first editor, must also be adjudged to the second. Both editors seem to have used the same ancient sources. The critics assign the second edition to the post-exilic **g** period, the first, called deuteronomic or pre-deuteronomic, to the seventh century B.C. Their conclusions are based on the precarious literary criteria of the Wellhausen theory and disregard some facts. The second editor undoubtedly attributes the disorders of

238g the period to the non-existence of the monarchy. Would a post-exilic writer esteem the monarchy so highly after recent experience of the ruin of the state attributed for the most part to the impiety of its kings? It is also quite unlikely that a post-exilic editor would explicitly or implicitly approve infringements of the law of unity of sanctuary. The tacit approval of the ephod of Gedeon (8:28b, 33a) suggests an early monarchical date for the first edition. The ephod oracle seems to have fallen into disrepute after David's reign. The narratives are derived from ancient sources and in some cases at least, such as the story of Gedeon and the two final episodes, are composite. The Hebrew text is relatively well preserved. Several misplaced duplicates (2:11b; 5:11d, 16c; 17:3) and omissions supplied by LXX (after 4:8; 16:13; 18:8, 29; 21:11) are due to scribal negligence. There are some textual corruptions, interpolations and glosses, discussed when important in the commentary.

h Chronology of the Period—The chronology might be considered defined in the text by the years of oppression (8+18+20+7+18+40=111) and of rest (40+80+40+40+6+20=226) under the six great judges, the years (23+22+7+10+8=70) of the five minor judges and the years of Abimelech (3) which make a total of 410 years. We cannot assume, however, that these periods are successive. As they refer in all cases only to a part of Israel some of them may well have been contemporaneous. The numbers also are more commonly formulated in terms of a generation (40) or half a generation (20) or two generations (80), and thus useless for an exact chronology. The period of oppression in 10:8 is clearly a later addition. In 11:26 we are informed that the period between Moses' conquest of Sehon's kingdom and Jephte's victory over the Ammonites was 300 years. Here again we have apparently a later addition, artificially calculated, since the numbers previously recorded in Jg make a total of 301, and no account is taken of Josue's long leadership. The number given would, moreover, transfer Jephte to the period of the divided monarchy.

i We are thus forced to determine the chronology of the Judges' period by other data more solidly established, the invasion of Canaan c 1200 B.C. (cf. § 228 a, b), and the enthronement of Solomon c 970 B.C. Making due allowance for the reigns of David and Saul and the judgeship of Samuel we are left with about 150 years (c 1200–1050 B.C.) for the period covered by the book of Judges. The narratives of the six great judges seem to be arranged in chronological order. Othniel, a younger contemporary of Josue, is the first, and Samson, who began the deliverance from the Philistines completed by David, is the last. Debora is expressly indicated as the successor of Aod. It is very likely and suggested in 10:7 that the oppressions of the Ammonites in the east and Philistines in the south-west and consequently Jephte and Samson were more or less contemporaneous.

j Character of the Period—We have no information on the Judges' period from external sources. The empires of the Hittites and Hurrites no longer existed. Babylonians, Assyrians, and Egyptians had troubles of their own and were not interested in Palestine. The Israelites could thus increase and develop, if not without interference from neighbouring peoples, at least without danger of permanent subjection and deportation. The oppressions were temporary and local. The great judges, chosen naturally from the oppressed, all belonged to different tribes. As they were not always rulers the statement that they judged Israel implies at most that any Israelite might seek justice from **k** them. The first editor is chiefly concerned with the northern tribes. Judah engrossed in her struggle with the Philistines and separated from her brethren by the Hevite cities is rarely mentioned. Mt Ephraim is the centre of Israel as in the days of Josue. A great judge, Debora, and a minor judge, Thola, both Issacharites, reside there. Ephraim is the most powerful of the tribes, but his claim to leadership is resisted success-

fully by Jephte. The rival claims of Judah are set forth **23** by the second editor (1:2; 20:18). The tribes follow their own ways, but the consciousness of national and religious unity appears clearly in the Canticle of Debora and still more in the war against Benjamin. The Israelites readily desert Yahweh to worship idols. They live in harmony with the Canaanites at Sichem and elsewhere. The crimes of Abimelech, the human sacrifice of Jephte, the outrage at Gabaa are characteristic of a lawless period.

Religious Teaching—The book of Judges teaches in **l** particular the religious interpretation of the history of the chosen people. The facts are presented, not as the natural result of human causality, but as the execution of a divine plan. God uses the neighbouring nations to punish the sins of his people, and this punishment is an invitation to repentance, the indispensable condition of deliverance. His Wisdom is manifested in the plan, his Justice and Holiness in the punishment of sin, his Mercy in the pardon of the repentant sinner, and his Goodness and Omnipotence in the deliverance of the oppressed. That deliverance is the work, not of man, but of God, is particularly emphasized. The great judges are divinely appointed **m** and divinely inspired. Gedeon must diminish his forces, Barac must descend from Thabor to the plain that the real author of the victory may be known and glorified. Divine intervention is clearly manifested by the inadequacy of natural means. We thus learn that Divine Providence rules the world's history, that God interferes miraculously in human affairs, that national calamities are usually the punishment of sin, and that amendment of life is the best guarantee of the restoration of national prosperity. The religious teaching includes also the exemplary chastisement of grave crimes, such as idolatry and disobedience to God's commands in the dealings of the tribes with the Canaanites, lack of good faith in Abimelech and the Sichemites and flagrant violation of the sacred law of hospitality at Gabaa.

I 1-II 5 War of the Tribes in Canaan—Judges begins **2** with a summary account of the efforts of the individual tribes to complete the conquest of Canaan after the death of Josue. The exploits and failures of Juda and Simeon are first narrated (**1-21**), then the capture of Bethel by the house of Joseph (**22-26**), and finally the failures of Manasses (**27-28**), Ephraim (**29**), Zabulon (**30**), Aser (**31-32**), Nephtali (**33**) and Dan (**34-35**). Yahweh reproaches them and reminds them that their failures are the fulfilment of his threat not to drive out the Canaanites before them if they were unfaithful to his covenant (**2:1-5**).

I 1-3. The beginning of the campaign is assigned by **b** Yahweh, consulted through the Urim and Tummim (cf. Ex 28), to Judah (cf. 20:28), whom Simeon joins since his lot is within Judah's lot. **4. Go up against** means attack without necessarily implying an ascent. They defeat the Canaanites and the Pherezites, probably a Hurrite clan, at Bezec (unidentified but near Jerusalem) with great slaughter. **5-7.** Adonibezec, whose personal name is unknown since a title, Lord of Bezec, has been substituted for it, was King of Jerusalem. He is represented as a powerful ruler subsequently brought by his followers to that city. The Hebrews cut off his thumbs and his big toes (**6a**), not to incapacitate him for military service, but as a degrading mutilation in which the sufferer sees an application of the lex talionis. **8.** A scribe, incorrectly supposing that the Hebrews brought him to Jerusalem, interpolated in consequence an account of the capture and destruction of Jerusalem not realized before David's time (cf. 1:21; 19:12; Jos 15:63; 2 Kg 5:7). On **10-15** cf. Jos 15:13-19. The capture of Hebron is mentioned (**10**) as an episode of the tribal war and (**20**) as an exploit of Caleb. The Cinite nomads, kinsmen of the father-in-law of Moses, who had accompanied the Israelites as guides (Num 10:29-32) and fixed their tents temporarily near Jericho famous

9b for its palms, went with the invaders (**16**) into the wilderness of Judah in the Negeb of Arad, modern 'Arad seventeen miles south of Hebron, where they dwelt with the Amalecites (LXX, MT the people, **c** Vg him, *cf.* 1 Kg 15:6). **17.** Sephaath, renamed Horma (' anathema '), is the modern Sebaita nearly thirty miles south of Bersabee. Its capture is narrated proleptically Num 21:1-3. **18.** For ' took ' (MT **17**) read *did not take* (LXX), required by 3:3 and the context since exclusion from the maritime plain (**19**) implies exclusion from the cities. For ' armed with scythes ' DV (**19b**) read *of iron*. **21.** In Jos 15:63 Judah replaces Benjamin. The situation is different here where Benjamin is blamed for neglecting to capture her chief city. **22.** Bethel, recently excavated, was very prosperous and strongly fortified in the Late Bronze Age. This explains why it was not captured by Josue. Its destruction by fire towards the close of the Late Bronze Age is attested by the excavations. The success of the house of Joseph like that of Judah (2) is attributed to Yahweh. **23a.** *And the house of Joseph made a reconnaissance at Bethel.* **24b.** For ' the entrance ' read *the way to enter*, not the gate but the best point to attack. **26.** *The land of the Hittites* was north of Kadesh on the Orontes. On **27-29** *cf.* Jos 16:10 ; 17:11-13. The responsibility of the tribes is emphasized by changing ' could not destroy ' to *did not destroy*. **30-33.** **d** The three tribes of Galilee were particularly negligent and unsuccessful in extirpating the Canaanites. ' Made tributary ' (DV) is lit. *impressed for labour-gangs*. **34-35.** The Amorrhites after dispossessing Dan were themselves in course of time subjected to forced labour by the house of Joseph. The hill of Heres (' the sun ') most probably indicates Bethsames (' house of the sun ') elsewhere associated with Aialon and Salebim. **36.** ' Amorrhite ' is a corruption of *Edomite*. Since the Ascent of the Scorpion was at the eastern end of the boundary between Israel and Edom (Jos 15:1-3) the Rock indicates the western end at or near Kadesh. **II 1a.** The Angel of Yahweh is Yahweh himself, who reminds Israel of his past benefits, promise, and threat. For ' place of weepers ' read *Bethel* with LXX. The ascent is made from the eastern border at Galgal. In 5:4 Yahweh comes from the southern Edomite border. **3a.** *And I said : I will not*, etc. may be a past or a present threat. **5.** Bokim, lit. *Weepers*, is a place near Bethel probably identical with *the terebinth of weeping* (Gen 35:8). The sacrifice offered where Yahweh appeared attests repentance.

e **II 6-III 6 Introduction to the History of the Judges—** **II 6-9.** Judges is first attached to Josue by repeating the contents of Jos 24:28-31. **10-19.** Then the religious interpretation of the subsequent narratives is indicated. Israel's history appears as recurring cycles of sin, punishment, repentance, and deliverance. **II:20-III:6.** The domestic enemies are finally discussed : who they were, why they were left in the land, and how they led Israel astray. **f II 6.** *The Israelites went everyone to his inheritance to possess the land* by dispossessing the Canaanites. **7.** Omit ' a long time ' and read *saw* for ' knew '. **10b.** For ' others ' read *another generation after them* ; **knew not** means had no personal or experimental knowledge. **11b.** *And they served Baalim* belongs to **13** where the pl. Baalim should be read. They are the various local representatives of the chief Canaanite god Baal. For '*Aštārôt*, the 'Astarts, we should probably read '*Ašērôt*, the Ašerats, as in 3:7. Asherat is the ancient Canaanite consort of Baal in the Rās-Shamra Tablets. The regular plural form in 2 Par 19:3 ; 33:3 attests ancient sources. Ashtart, corresponding to the Babylonian Ishtar, was better known at a later date. **14b.** Read after ' plunderers ' *And they plundered them and he sold them*. **15a.** Insert *for evil* after ' them '. We should probably supply before **16** the third element of the cycle elsewhere regularly attested : And the children of Israel cried out to Yahweh. **20-23.** To punish violations of the covenant and to test Israel's fidelity

to Yahweh the Canaanites were not all extirpated. **239f** The trial motive and its result are indicated **3:4-6.** Benevolent motives are also attributed to Yahweh, that future generations of Israelites might be trained to fight (**3:2**) and that the land might not be injured by depopulation (Ex 23:29 ; Deut 7:22). Since God's Justice and Goodness work together harmoniously there is no difficulty in this multiplicity of motives. **III 1.** After ' left ' read : *to prove Israel by them, even all who had not experienced all the wars of Canaan, only on account of the generations of the children of Israel to teach them war, only such as formerly knew nothing of them* (the wars of Canaan). **3.** Mt Libanus here indicates the southern end of the range west of Merg 'Ayyūn called the plain of Lebanon Jos 11:17 (*cf.* Jos 13:4-5 note).

III 7-12 Othniel—As the oppressions are local and the **g** deliverer is usually one of the oppressed, it is improbable that Othniel, lord of Debir in southern Judah, would be chosen to repel invaders from Aram Naharaim, Aram of the two rivers (Euphrates and Chabor), in northern Mesopotamia. The second part of the oppressor's name, *Riš'ātayim*, ' of double wickedness ' (*cf.* double-dyed), is most probably a Hebrew qualification of the oppressor. Cushan has an Arabic termination and appears (Hab 3:7) in parallelism with Madian as an Arab tribe. There is question therefore of an Arab or Edomite invasion of southern Judah. The original ' Edom ' was read ' Aram '—a common error. As there were several Arams, Naharaim was inserted in **8**, but not in **10**, notwithstanding its remoteness from Palestine. The recent efforts of Jack and Haensler to introduce as the oppressor Tushratta (c 1390-1360 B.C.), king of Mitanni (geographically identical with Aram Naharaim), fail to identify the names and antedate the event by two centuries. **10a.** Read *came on him* for ' was in him '. **12-30 Aod**—Aod, Heb. Ehud, a Benjaminite, de- **h** livered his people from the Moabites and their allies, Ammon and Amalec. He seized the opportunity offered by the payment of tribute to slay Eglon, king of Moab, and raise the standard of revolt in Benjamin and Ephraim. **13b.** Eglon *took possession of the city of the palm-trees*, entrenched himself near Jericho to command the ford of the Jordan. **15.** Aod was left-handed, lit. *disabled in his right hand*. Presents is euphemistic for tribute, paid not in money but in kind, and thus requiring many bearers. **16.** The sword of Aod was a double-edged poniard with a short hilt so that its whole length was a short cubit (from elbow to knuckles). It was worn on the right thigh for a movement of the left hand towards the right would not arouse suspicion. **18.** Read *sent away* for ' followed '. **19.** Aod accompanied the departing bearers as far as *the graven images* near Gilgal. The reference is obscure. Thence he returns and announces a secret message for the king who dismisses his attendants with the word *silence* and receives Aod, sitting alone in his *cool upper chamber*. This was built on the flat roof of the house and had several windows to allow the free passage of air. When Aod declares that the message is from God the king rises out of reverence and Aod draws forth his poniard and thrusts it into him. **22-23.** *And the hilt went in after the blade and the fat closed over* **i** *the blade* (more probably *the hilt*, *cf.* Joüon Bi 21 [1940] 58 f.), *for he drew not the poniard out of his belly. And he went out into the vestibule. And Aod went out into the colonnade after shutting the doors of the upper chamber upon him and locking them.* The renderings vestibule and colonnade are not certain since the words are only found here. When Aod shot the bolt home he locked the door, for iron pins descended into holes in the bolt and held it fast. The wooden key was only used for opening. It was inserted in a groove in the bolt and had wooden pegs corresponding to the iron pins which pushed them back into their original position and thus allowed the bolt to be withdrawn. Aod's departure was not secret. He got time to escape by locking the door and delaying the discovery of the king's death. ' Till they were ashamed ' (**25**) means

239i till they were at their wit's end. For 'were in confusion' (**26a**) read *tarried*. The fords of the Jordan were seized to prevent escape of fugitives and arrival of reinforcements. Eglon's palace was east of the Jordan.

j 31 Shamgar son of Anat—This hero in the present text bears the name of an oppressor of Israel through a misunderstanding of 5:6. The verse moreover is a late insertion since 4:1 closely attaches the Debora to the Aod narrative. Its place is uncertain. Some Greek MSS attach it to the Samson narrative. Shamgar is a Hurrite name. Anat, a goddess, appears also as a man's name. For 'ploughshare' read *ox-goad*, a wooden pole nine feet long and sharply pointed.

240a IV 1-24 Debora and Barac—The two accounts of the deliverance from Canaanite oppression differ in one essential particular, the name of the oppressor. He is Shamgar son of Anat in the contemporary poem (ch 5) but Jabin king of Canaan reigning at Hasor in the later prose narrative (ch 4). Jabin was slain and his capital Hasor burnt by Josue (Jos 11). The city, moreover, if rightly identified with Tell el-Qêda, was uninhabited in the Judges' period. It follows that some of the contents of Jos 11 have been interpolated into Jg 4. There is one indication that the interpolation was made after the narrative was written, the description of Jabin as king of Canaan, since all scriptural writers agree with profane records in assigning not one but many kings to Canaan. A foreigner like Shamgar might vaunt this title but not the king of a Canaanite city. We exclude therefore from ch 4 Jabin and Hasor as interpolations.

b 1-3. Sisera, general of Shamgar, residing at Haroseth of the Gentiles at the western extremity of the plain of Esdraelon and possessing nine hundred iron chariots, oppresses Israel. 4-7. Debora, prophetess and judge, residing in Mt Ephraim, orders Barac, a Nephtalite, to assemble an army of 10,000 men on Mt Thabor ready to meet Sisera's army at the river Cison. 8-11. Barac obeys after stipulating that Debora must accompany him. 12-13. Sisera hearing of the revolt leads his army to the Cison in the centre of Esdraelon. 14-16. Barac, ordered by God through Debora, descends to meet him in the plain, but Yahweh throws the enemy into confusion and he gains a complete victory. 17-21. Sisera in his flight enters the tent of Jahel, wife of Heber the Cinite, who slays him as he sleeps by hammering a tent-peg into his brain. 22. Barac views the dead Sisera. 23-24. Israel gradually overpowers the oppressor.

c For 'Jabin' read *Shamgar* and omit 'who reigned in Hasor' (2). Haroseth is identified with Tell 'Amar, occupying a strategic position at the entrance to the plain of Esdraelon, near the village of Haritiye and inhabited in the Early Iron Age. 4. Debora was a prophetess in the strict sense of the word, as her communications to Barac show, and also a judge as the distributor of justice to the people.

d The palm-tree or possibly pillar (*cf.* Jer 10:5) of Debora between Bethel and Rama has no connexion with the terebinth of weeping (Gen 35:8), but merely indicates the site of her tribunal. Her residence in Mt Ephraim makes Barac's stipulation intelligible and explains the participation of Ephraim and Benjamin in the liberation of the northern tribes. Barac recalls the Punic Barca, 'lightning'. 6. Cedes in Nephtali, modern Kadis, is four miles WNW. of Lake Huleh. 7. Omit the gloss 'general of Jabin's army'. LXX has an addition probably authentic after 8. *For I know not on what day Yahweh will give me success.* 10. Vg omits 'to Cedes' after 'Nephtali'. MT supposes a muster at Cedes in Nephtali, but does not mention the subsequent march to Thabor. Some hold that Cedes in Issachar between Megiddo and Taanak, mentioned in 11, is meant, but that locality was most unsuitable for a muster of the forces of Nephtali and Zabulon confined to the highlands by the iron chariots of the Canaanites. 11. Heber is introduced before **e** the battle to explain the presence of Jahel. The

terebinth in Sa'annim was in the SW. of Nephtali **24** (Jos 19:33), and therefore near Thabor which is ten miles NE. of Cedes in Issachar, here indicated, but thirty miles south of Cedes in Nephtali. The battle was fought on the bank of the Cison between Megiddo and Taanak (5:19). Barac's descent into the plain to meet the chariots on their own ground was humanly unwise but ordered by God to show that he alone could turn defeat into victory. Omit 17b owing to the mention of Jabin and the fact that Sisera did not enter the tent spontaneously but by invitation (18). For 'cloak' read *fly-net*. 20. The giving of curdied milk instead of water was probably a Bedawin ruse perhaps to induce sleep. While Sisera sleeps Jahel takes a *tent-peg* (DV nail) and a mallet and drives the peg into his brain *and he moved convulsively between her knees* (LXX; for he was fast asleep MT), *fell back without force and died.* The reading of LXX is more natural. 23-24. Omit 'Jabin' and read *kings* for 'king'.

V The Triumph-Song—The victory was immediately **24** celebrated like that of Jephte (11:34) and of Moses (Ex 15). Fortunately the triumph-song has been preserved as is admitted by most critics who hold that the intensity of feeling displayed implies personal contact with the events described. Debora can hardly be the author since she is addressed in 7 where the ambiguous form *qamtî* appears from the context to mean *thou didst arise* rather than 'I arose'. The Aramaisms in the song are explained by poetical style, the peculiarities of the northern Hebrew dialect and the greater similarity between Hebrew and Aramaic in more ancient times. The interpretation is com- **b** plicated by textual corruptions which may be due to the partial illegibility of the ancient record. The versions give some aid, but the sequence of thought on which the strophic division depends and the parallelism which characterizes all Hebrew poetry are more helpful. We follow generally Burney's excellent rendering. The sequence of thought seems to be: Introduction (1-2), Coming of Yahweh to help his people (3-5), Oppression of Israel before the rising (6-8), Invitation to all to praise Yahweh (9-12), Praise of the patriotic tribes (13-15a), Reproach of the recreant tribes (15b-18), Battle (19-21), Flight (22-23), Exploit of Jahel (24-27), Anxiety and hopes of Sisera's mother (28-30), Conclusion (31a).

1-2 Introduction—*Then sang Debora and Barac, the son* **c** *of Abinoam, on that day saying* (*when long locks of hair were worn loose in Israel, when the people volunteered*), *Bless ye Yahweh!* The words in parenthesis indicate the occasion of the song, the rising of the volunteers, when warriors vowed not to shear their long locks until victory was won. The title of the song, *Bless ye Yahweh*, announces a hymn of thanksgiving.

3-5 Strophe 1—*Attend ye kings; give ear ye rulers: I— to Yahweh I will sing, will make melody to Yahweh, the God of Israel. Yahweh in thy progress from Seir, In thy march from the fields of Edom, Earth quaked, yea, heaven rocked, Yea, the clouds dropped water. The mountains shook before Yahweh, Before Yahweh, the God of Israel.* The renderings 'rocked' and 'shook', supported by LXX, suppose slight alterations of vowels or consonants in MT. Yahweh comes from Edom=Seir, the southern boundary of Palestine in the direction of Sinai (*cf.* 2:1). The natural phenomena are the regular accompaniments of a theophany. The storm made a swamp of the battlefield, preventing the use of the chariots. 'Sinai' in MT 5 is an incorrect gloss on 'mountains'.

6-8 Strophe 2—*In the days of Shamgar ben-Anath, In the* **e** *days of Jahel caravans ceased. And wayfarers used crooked paths. Villages ceased in Israel, ceased until thou didst arise Debora. Till thou didst arise a mother in Israel. Armourers had they none; armed men failed from the city, Was there seen a shield or a lance among forty thousand in Israel?* Failure to recognize that the oppression period described is called the days of the oppressor has changed Shamgar to a deliverer (3:31) and introduced Jahel here. For 'Jahel' read *Shamgar* (such repetitions are frequent in the song) or perhaps 'Sisera'. 6b. A e change of vowels transforms 'roads' (MT) into *caravans*, a good parallel to *wayfarers* (6c) who could only travel safely by roundabout paths. Canaanite mastery of the plain made undefended villages non-existent. The second *ceased* is unmetrical and may belong to a lost stich. 'One chooses new gods : then battling at the gates' (MT 8a) is intelligible in itself but out of harmony with the context. Burney's conjectural emendation adopted agrees well with 8b. The number 40,000 in a contemporary record confirms Jos 4:13.

f **9-12 Strophe 3**—*Come, ye commanders of Israel ! Ye that volunteered among the people bless ye Yahweh ! Let the riders on tawny she-asses review it. And let the wayfarers recall it to mind. Hark to the distributors of water at the wells ! There they recount the righteous acts of Yahweh. The righteous acts of his arm in Israel. Awake, awake, Debora ! Awake, awake, sing paean ! Rise up Barac and lead captive thy captors, O son of Abinoam !* 'Come ye' is a slight emendation of MT, 'My heart is with', suggested by parallelism and context. 'Let . . . review', pl. jussive, replaces sg. imperative in MT. 'Recall it to mind' is a tentative correction of an unintelligible text suggested by the context. Wayfarers and water-drawers represent the common people as opposed to the nobles riding on asses. All must praise Yahweh the deliverer. 'Arm' replaces a word of uncertain meaning. The special part of Debora in the celebration is to lead the women in song like Miriam (Ex 15:20), that of Barac is to marshal the prisoners in the triumphal procession. MT **11d** belongs to 13.

g **13-15a Strophe 4**—*Then down to the gates gat the nobles ; Yahweh's folk gat them down mid the heroes. From Ephraim they spread out on the vale.* 'After thee Benjamin' mid thy clansmen. *From Machir came down the commanders. And from Zabulon men wielding the truncheon. And the princes in Issachar were with Debora ; and Nephtali was leal to Barac : To the vale he was loosed at his heel.* The encomium on Ephraim, tentatively restored, is represented in MT by 'their root is in Amalec', apparently a vituperative gloss on Judah's later idolatrous rival, the kingdom of Ephraim. *After thee Benjamin* is the war-cry of Benjamin (Os 5:8). Machir as the eldest son of Manasses represents the western half-tribe. 'Of the scribe' (or, headman) after 'truncheon' (the staff of office) in MT disturbs the metre. **15b**. *Nephtali* replaces Issachar (MT), a scribal error. The inference that Debora was an Issacharite as Barac was a Nephtalite is quite consistent with her residence in Mt Ephraim, anciently the centre of Israel. *Cf.* also Thola (10:1).

h **15b-18 Strophe 5**—*Utterly reft into factions was Ruben : Great were his searchings of heart. Why sat'st thou still amid the folds, to hear the pastoral pipings ? Galaad beyond the Jordan dwelt, and Dan abideth by the ships. Asher are still by the shore of the seas, Dwelling beside his creeks. Zabulon is the folk that scorned its life to the death, and Nephtali in the heights of the field.* The first verse reappears by error in MT 16b, where *searchings* replaces the unintelligible 'statutes'. Searchings of heart here mean interchanges of opinion. The rendering *folds* is conjectural but the alternative 'ash-heaps' has no apparent connexion with pastoral life. Galaad, grandson of Manasses, most probably a tribal name as in Jos 17:1, designates the eastern half of Manasses. As a geographical term it would cover either Gad alone or Gad and eastern Manasses, but tribes, not districts, seem to be indicated. Dan may be still in his original coastal lot or already in northern Palestine engaged in sea-traffic with the Sidonians. His position in the list favours the latter view. The contrast with Zabulon and Nephtali sharpens the taunt of cowardice.

i **19-21 Strophe 6**—*On came the kings, they fought ; Then fought the kings of Canaan ; In Taanac by the rills of Megiddo ; the gain of money they took not. From heaven fought the stars, From their highways they fought with Sisera. The torrent Kishon swept them off ; The torrent of heroes is the torrent Kishon. Bless thou, my soul, the might of Yahweh !* The rills are small tributaries of the Kishon from the hills SE. of Megiddo. *The gain of money they took not* 241i means most probably that they fought whole-heartedly not like mercenaries. The fighting of the stars is a poetic figure. All nature sides with Yahweh. MT 21b reads : Thou treadest down, my soul, might.

22-23 Strophe 7—*Then loud beat the hoofs of the horses ;* j *off galloped, off galloped his chargers. Curse ye, curse ye Meroz ! Curse ye, curse ye her town-folk ! For they came not to the help of Yahweh, To the help of Yahweh mid the heroes.* In 22 slightly corrected after LXX the repetition is onomatopeic. **23**. MT reads 'Curse ye Meroz, said the Angel of Yahweh', but the Angel of Yahweh is unexpected and a second *curse ye* is suggested by the parallelism. Meroz is conjecturally identified with Kh. Mārūs 8 m. S. of Cedes in Nephtali.

24-27 Strophe 8—*Most blessed of women be Jael, Of* k *tent-dwelling women most blessed ! Water he asked ; milk she gave ; In a lordly dish she proffered curds. Her hand to the peg she put forth, And her right to the maul of the workman ; And she smote Sisera—destroyed his head, Shattered and pierced through his temples. 'Twixt her feet she bowed, he fell down, he lay prone ; 'Twixt her feet he bowed, he fell down. Where he bowed there he fell down undone.* Omit the prosaic gloss 'wife of Heber the Cinite ' after 'Jael' (MT 24). Some commentators object that Sisera is lying down in 4:21 but standing here when he receives the death-blow. In both cases however a wooden tent-peg is driven through his temples with a wooden hammer which could only be done when he lay prostrate. Nor could he fall between her feet if he received the blow standing. The description supposes not an erect posture but a convulsive movement before the final collapse. Jahel's weapons are naturally those of a tent-dweller. She is praised like Rahab for siding with Yahweh and his people. Her *ruse de guerre* would be considered legitimate by herself and her primitive contemporaries and is not to be judged by modern standards of morality.

28-30 Strophe 9—*And through the window she leaned and* l *exclaimed, The mother of Sisera out through the lattice :* 'Wherefore delayeth his car to come ? Wherefore tarrieth the clatter of his chariots ? ' Her wisest princesses make answer, Yea, she returneth her reply : ' Are they not finding —dividing the spoil ? A damsel—two damsels for every man : A spoil of dyed stuffs for Sisera, A spoil of dyed stuffs embroidered ; Two dyed embroideries for the neck of the queen. **29**. 'Princess', sg. for pl., is possible, but the reply given is that of Sisera's mother to herself. **30**. *Queen* is a plausible conjecture for ' spoil ' (MT) which ill suits the context. *Raham* 'damsel' elsewhere in Heb. means ' womb', but ' slave-girl', as here, in the Mesha inscription.

31-Conclusion—*So perish all thy foes Yahweh : But be thy friends like the sun going forth in his might.* **VI 1-VIII 35 Gedeon—VI 1-10.** The Israelites again 242a abandon Yahweh and are oppressed by the Madianites. **11-24.** Gedeon is called by God to deliver them. **25-32.** He destroys the altar of Baal at Ophra, erects an altar to Yahweh in its place and receives a new name Yerubbaal 'Baal-fighter'. **33-40.** He assembles an army and is assured of victory by a double sign. **VII 1-8.** Yahweh reduces the army to 300 men. **9-15.** Gedeon visits the hostile camp by night and hears a dream narrated. **16-22.** His men, armed with trumpets, torches, and pitchers, attack and rout the foe. **23-25.** The neighbouring Ephraimites intercept the fugitives at the ford of the Jordan and slay two of their leaders. **VIII 1-9.** Gedeon appeases the offended Ephraimites, continues his pursuit of the Madianite kings and is taunted and denied food for his hungry followers by the inhabitants of Succoth and Penuel. **10-21.** He captures the kings, slays the inhabitants, and burns the cities of Succoth and Penuel and finally slays the kings because they had slain his brothers. **22-27.** He refuses the rulership offered him, but accepts part of the spoils from which he makes an ephod. **28-35.** After a generation of peace he dies and the Israelites, forgetting Yahweh and Gedeon, again worship false gods. The narrative is clear and consistent, b

242b but evidently derived from more than one ancient source. This appears especially in the double account of the erection of the altar. In the second account the immediate occasion is narrated to illustrate the teaching that conversion must precede deliverance. The fact only is related in the first account (**VI:24**). The vague word *there* may have indicated in the source the place where Yahweh appeared, but the subsequent narrator must have referred it to *in Ophra* in the second part of the verse.

c VI 1-10 The Oppression—The Madianites, also called Ismaelites (8:24), joined by Amalecites and *the children of the east*, Arab tribes east of the Jordan, raided the land periodically. The verbs are frequentative, *used to come up*, etc. The *crevices* (DV dens, **2**) are lit. places hollowed out by water. Caves, natural and artificial, are common in the limestone hills of Palestine. The raids even reached Gaza, but would not always be equally extensive. The Israelites cry to Yahweh for deliverance and are reminded by a prophet of their sins and ingratitude.

d 11-24 Call of Gedeon—Gedeon was a Manassite of the clan of Abiezer (*cf.* Jos 17:2), dwelling in Ophra, eṭ-Ṭaiyibe five miles SE. of Endor. He was threshing corn, not with oxen on a threshing-floor, but *in a wine-press to save it from Madian*, when the Angel of Yahweh appeared to him under a terebinth and gave him his mission. He pleads incapacity, but is promised aid and success. Beginning to realize that his guest is no ordinary person he offers entertainment which is accepted. *Minḥāh*, entertainment, either a present or a sacred offering, seems to be intentionally ambiguous. The guest converts the loaves and flesh into a holocaust with his rod and then disappears. Gedeon now realizes who his visitor is and fears death. He is reassured by Yahweh, invisibly present. He erects there an altar called *Yahweh is Peace* (peaceful, or well disposed). **24b.** Render after ' peace ' : *Until this day it is still* (there) *in Ophra of the Abiezrites.*

e 25-32 He contends with Baal—*That night*, the night after the theophany, Gedeon receives the order : *Take ten men of thy servants and a bull seven years old and pull down the altar of Baal*, etc. The corrupt text is corrected from 26 and 28. For ' grove ' read *Ashēra* (sacred pole). **26.** The altar is built *upon the top of this stronghold* (probably an inaccessible crag) *in due form.* **31.** Joas refuses to surrender his son to his idolatrous townsmen, saying : *Will ye contend for Baal or will ye save him ? Whoever will contend for him will be put to death at morning ; if he be a god let him contend for himself, because he* (Gedeon) *has broken down his altar.* Gedeon's new name means therefore *let Baal contend* and thus implicitly designates him as a Baal-fighter.

f 33-VII 15 He prepares to Attack the Madianites—On the occasion of a Madianite raid into the plain of Esdraelon the spirit of the Lord entered into (lit. ' was clothed with ') Gedeon, who assembled a large army and received assurance of victory by a double sign. The threshing-floor, usually on a flat rocky hill-top, would not absorb the dew like the fleece, so that the first sign was inconclusive and consequently a second, undoubtedly miraculous, was asked and granted. Gedeon now pitched his camp at the foot of Mt Gilboa, having the fountain of Harod, the modern source and river Jalud, between his forces and the Madianite camp in the valley *beneath* (MT ' from ') Mt Moreh, the modern Neby Dahi opposite Gilboa on the north side of the plain. His forces, however, are too numerous for a God-given victory to be manifested by the in-

g adequacy of the natural means used. The departure of the timorous reduces the army from 32,000 to 10,000 men. The numbers are surprisingly large and may have been altered. **VII:3.** ' Galaad ' is perhaps a misreading of ' Galud ', ancient name of the hill from which the stream flows. A further reduction of the army to 300 men is effected by rejecting those who bend the knees in drinking and choosing those who drink like

a dog, conveying the water with the hand to the mouth. **24** No human drinker laps water with his tongue, but those who convey the water with the hand to the mouth resemble the dog by lapping the water with the hand, and thus satisfying their thirst slowly and unskilfully. The others who bend the knees so as to absorb the water directly and in large quantity with the mouth are more expeditious and resemble not the dog but the camel. The verb used of these drinkers is *kara'*, which means in Arabic to bend the knees in order to absorb water directly with the mouth. The less skilful drinkers are chosen to show that the victory is due not to man but to God. An interpretation **h** favoured by Lagrange and Burney distinguishes between the two classes of drinkers by their less or greater watchfulness in face of the enemy. Those who convey the water with the hand to the mouth are more watchful and therefore rejected. This method of drinking is supposed to have been originally attributed to the second class and erroneously transferred to the first class in the MT. The chosen drinkers resemble the dog by using their hands for support as the dog his forelegs but absorb the water directly. This interpretation is less natural, ignores the comparison between lapping and absorbing and gratuitously supposes an altered text. In **8a** we should probably replace ' victuals ', a useless encumbrance, by ' pitchers ' and render : *And they took the pitchers of the people in their hand and their trumpets.* Gedeon now, by order of God, reconnoitres the hostile camp, going down with Purah his servant *unto the outskirts of the armed men who were in the camp*, where he hears the Madianite's dream, a presage of victory.

VII 16-22 The Battle—Gedeon divided his forces into **i** three bands to assail the camp at three different points and make the enemy believe that they were surrounded. The Israelites had pitchers containing torches in their left hand and trumpets in their right. The din raised by the clashing of pitchers and sounding of trumpets in the dead of night on all sides of the camp threw the Madianites into confusion and panic so that they turned their swords against one another and sought safety in flight. **17b.** Read : *When I come into the outskirts of the camp do as I shall do.* Add after **18** : *And ye shall say, ' For Yahweh and for Gedeon '.* **19.** Omit ' three ', read *the outskirts* for ' part ' and *middle* for ' midnight '. The difficulty of carrying simultaneously trumpets, torches and pitchers is imaginary. By passing the handle of the torch through a hole in the bottom of the pitcher both could be carried in one hand. The trumpets could be inserted in bandoliers.

23-VIII 21 The Pursuit—Of the places mentioned in **j** **23a** only one, omitted in Vg, is known, Sereda = Saretan (*cf.* 3 Kg 7:46 and 2 Par 4:17), west of the Jordan near the ford at ed-Damiye (Jos 3:16). Here the Ephraimites intercepted some of the fugitives and Gedeon crossed the Jordan since Succoth, ' booths ', modern Tell el-Akhṣās, ' mound of booths ', commands the ford on the east side. The fords near Beisan would have been held by the neighbouring Nephtalites summoned to join in the pursuit (**23**). The Madianites therefore fled first eastward to the Jordan valley, then southward to cross the river at ed-Damiye. **VIII:1-4.** The haughtiness of the Ephraimites and the prudence of Gedeon are portrayed. The inference drawn from *the vintage of Abiezer* that Gedeon's 300 men were all Abiezrites is unjustified ; Gedeon refers to himself. **6.** The names of the Madianite kings Zebaḥ, ' sacrifice ', and Salmunna, ' shelter refused ', are probably altered. **7.** That fellow-Israelites should refuse food to the **k** famished warriors of Yahweh was a grievous crime. The punishment threatened and afterwards inflicted was to tear the flesh from the bones as the chaff is torn from the grain in threshing. **8.** Penuel is very probably Tulul eḍ-Ḍahab, NNE. of Succoth, commanding a ford of the Jabboc. **11.** From Penuel Gedeon went *towards the way of the tent-dwellers*, the modern pilgrimage route from Damascus to Ma'an, *east of Nobe and Jegbaa*, the modern Agbēhāt in SE. Galaad.

k 12b. He surprised the Madianites, captured the two kings, *and all the host he terrified.* **14.** For ' described ' read *wrote down.* Writing was then evidently in common use. **18-19.** *Where are the men whom ye slew at Thabor ? And they said, ' As thou art so were they : each resembled the children of a king '.* Gedeon asks the kings to produce his brothers. As they cannot do this and their doom is certain, they glory in their deed. **21.** For ' ornaments and bosses ' read *crescents.*

l VIII 22-35 Subsequent History of Gedeon—Having already erected by divine order a Yahweh-altar at Ophra, Gedeon now determines to establish there also a Yahweh-oracle, and uses for that purpose the golden earlets of the Madianites, his share of the spoils. All the gold, 1,700 shekels (42 lb.) was not expended on the ephod garment, and **27a** should be rendered : *And Gedeon used it for an ephod.* The reasons alleged for interpreting the ephod as an idol are well refuted by Burney. It may be added that establishment of idol worship would be inconsistent with peace in the land **(28)** and fidelity to Yahweh **(33)** during Gedeon's lifetime. These texts also imply that the institution of the Yahweh-oracle was not disapproved by the original writer. It follows that *27b* is a later addition since *whoring* (DV fornication) or infidelity to Yahweh, the true spouse of Israel, by worshipping other gods or using foreign religious rites, cannot be reconciled with the fidelity implied in **33.** Ephods like altars outside the sanctuary would be tolerated originally, but later condemned as a Canaanite cult incompatible with Yahweh worship. The ingratitude of the people to the house of Gedeon was shown in their toleration of the slaughter of his seventy sons by Abimelech.

a IX 1-57 Abimelech—Gedeon refused the rulership offered to him and his descendants after his victory, as being a usurpation of the rule of Yahweh (8:23, *cf.* 1 Kg 8:7). Abimelech, his son, abandoned Yahweh for Baal and secured kingship for himself through his kinsmen in Shechem, then inhabited by a mixed population of Israelites and Canaanites. He was the offspring of a *ṣadika* marriage between Gedeon and a Shechemite, whose nationality, Israelite or Canaanite, is not indicated. The female partner in this union lived with her own people, not in her husband's house, and the children were regarded as hers. Abimelech was therefore supported by the Shechemites against the Abiezrite sons of Gedeon. Shechem, the modern Balâṭa, about a mile east of Nablus, had very great importance in ancient Palestine owing to its central position and **b** command of all the trade routes. Recent excavations on the site have clarified the references to it in ch 9. There was a lower city on the east side and an upper on the west, each with its own gate. The upper city was artificially elevated above the plain and numbered among its edifices the palace of the ruler and the temple of Baal-Berith. It is twice called Beth-millo (6 ; 20). The Millo at Jerusalem, lit. ' filling ', was an earthwork strengthening a weak point in the fortifications, and had a *bêth,* fort or tower (4 Kg 12:28). The corresponding Assyrian *mulû* designates similarly a raised terrace on which a tower or fort was built. The lower city was first captured and those in the upper, informed by fugitives, took refuge in the fortified temple. Baal Berith ' Baal of the Alliance ' (8:33b, mistranslated in Vg:9:4), also called El Berith ' God of the Alliance ' (9:46), was the principal god of the Canaanites of Shechem. The Canaanite sanctuary on the side of Mt Garizim near Shechem cannot be the temple of El Berith in the Tower of Shechem, since it was destroyed by fire at the close of the Middle Bronze Age.

c The events narrated may be thus summarized : **1-6.** Abimelech is made king. **7-21.** Joatham's fable. **22-29.** Revolt of the Shechemites fomented by Gaal. **30-33.** Zebul's message to Abimelech. **34-49.** Abimelech's campaigns against the Shechemites ending in the destruction of the Lower and Upper city. **50-54.** Abimelech's death. **55-57.** Conclusion. A temple had always a treasury and was sometimes the repository of public treasure. **4.** Seventy silver shekels (half-

crowns) sufficed for the hiring of *worthless and reckless* **243c** followers. **5.** *Upon one stone* has no religious significance but indicates the slayer's ruthlessness. **6a.** After ' together ' read : *and all Beth-millo,* and after ' king ' (**6b** slightly corrected) : *by the terebinth of the Maṣṣēḇah,* probably the great stone of Jos 24:26. The parable of Joatham contrasts Gedeon and his sons who have worked for the common good with the selfish adventurer Abimelech and indicates the evil results to be expected from the foolish choice of the Shechemites. **7.** For ' the top ' read a *projection.* The summit was beyond earshot. Oil has various sacred uses, for temple lamps, bread-offerings, etc. The honour which it confers on man is illustrated by the anointing of distinguished guests. ' Be promoted among ' (9 DV) is lit. ' wave over '. Wine was a common drink-offering. The *buckthorn* (DV bramble, 14) is **d** a low and straggling bush. **15.** The invitation to its shelter shows the absurdity of the choice and the fire the misfortunes which will result from it. **16-20.** The application of the parable is indicated. The fundamental lack of good faith of the Shechemites in their dealings with Gedeon and his house will appear also in their dealings with Abimelech and result in the ruin of both parties. The city to which Joatham fled was the modern Bîra 6 m. N. of Beisân. **22.** ' Israel ' is a stereotyped expression. Abimelech ruled over a part of Israel. **23.** *And the citizens* (lit. owners) *of Shechem dealt treacherously with Abimelech.* The evil acts of men are often attributed to God, because, though forbidden by men they are part of the divine plan. **25.** Omit ' while they waited for his coming '. The ambushers sought to rob caravans which Abimelech owned or taxed. For ' wasting the vineyards ' read *gathering* (lit. cutting) *the vintage* and for ' singing and dancing ' *holding a praise-festival.* **28a.** *Who is Shechem ?* Shechem means Shechemites as Israel Israelites. **28b.** *Should not the son of Yerubbaal and Zebul his officer serve the men of Hamor, the father of Shechem ? but why should we serve him ?* The appeal of Gaal, a newcomer, is to the Canaanites of Shechem against the half-breed, Abimelech. **29.** *Oh, would that this people were under my hand ! then would I remove Abimelech and would say to Abimelech, ' Increase thy army and come out '.* **31.** For ' privately ' **e** read *to Aruma,* probably el-Ormeh, five miles SE. of Shechem. **34.** For ' places ' read *bands.* **37a.** *Middle,* lit. navel, indicates the central point of the Palestinian mountain range. **37b.** Render *by way of the soothsayers' terebinth.* **41a.** *And Abimelech dwelt in Aruma.* **44.** For ' besieging the city ' read *standing in the entry of the gate of the city.* The sowing of salt, also recorded in Assyrian inscriptions, was a symbolical act indicating a barren region. Here as frequently the account of one event is completed before that of a second is begun without regard to chronological sequence. **46a.** Read *They went into the crypt of the temple of El-Berith,* and omit the gloss (**46b**). The word rendered crypt etymologically indicates underground chamber. **49a.** Omit ' as fast as he could '. **49b.** Read after ' leader ' *and placed them* (the bundles of brushwood) *against the crypt and set fire to the crypt.* **50.** Thebes is probably the modern Tubas, twelve miles NE. of Shechem. **51.** For ' princes ' read *citizens.* **53.** *And a certain woman cast an upper millstone on the head of Abimelech and broke his skull.* The upper and revolving one of the two great stones of the handmill is indicated. It appears from **55** that Abimelech was supported by Israelites. The sacred writer concludes that Abimelech and the Shechemites were justly punished for their sins.

X 1-5 Thola and Jair—These were minor judges of **f** whom no achievements are related. **1.** For ' the uncle of Abimelech ' read *son of Dodo,* a proper name. Shamir may have been on the site of later Samaria. Thola, like Debora, was an Issacharite residing in Mt Ephraim. Jair was a Manassite. Camon is perhaps the modern Kumen near Pella. Havvoth means tent-villages. Their conquest by Jair is related Num 32:41.

X 6-XII 7 Jephte—The Jephte narrative contains a **g** few later additions and may be composite though

243g apparent discrepancies in the text are easily explained. The sins, oppression and repentance of Israel are first narrated (**X:6-16**), then the early history of Jephte (**X:17-XI:11**), his negotiations with the Ammonite king (**XI:12-28**), his war against Ammon and his vow (**XI:29-40**), and lastly his fight with the Ephraimites (**XII:1-7**).

h X 6-16 Sin, Oppression and Repentance—In this introduction to the narratives of Jephte and Samson the gods of Aram (*cf.* 3:8), Sidon, and Moab are out of place and probably a later addition. **8a.** *And they broke and crushed the children of Israel that year, eighteen years.* Eighteen years is clearly a later addition. **9.** After 'Ammon' read *passed over the Jordan to fight against.* There is no verb in **11** and the time of deliverance from Egypt is past, from Philistines and Ammonites future. Render *Have I not delivered you from the Egyptians and the Amorrhites?* (**11a**) and omit **11b**. Sidonian oppression is probable though not recorded. **12.** For Vg Canaan MT Ma'on read *Madian*.

i X 17-XI 11 Early History of Jephte—Maspha is most probably Ḥirbet Gele'ad, south of the Jabboc on the western border of Ammon. Jephte was the son of a harlot and a certain Galaad (or perhaps Galaadite). His brothers thrust him out as the son of *another mother*, and he went and dwelt in the land of Tob (Dubu, now eṭ-Ṭaiyibe, NE. of Galaad), where he collected a band of ne'er-do-wells who followed him on predatory expeditions. When the Ammonite war broke out the elders of Galaad offered to make him their captain. He first objects that it was they who drove him into exile (presumably by supporting his brothers), but subsequently accepts on condition that if victorious he shall be their ruler. **XI:10.** They reply, ' *Yahweh shall be hearer between us, surely according to thy word so shall we do* '. Jephte goes back with them to Maspha, where the agreement is ratified before Yahweh.

j XI 12-28 Negotiations with the Ammonite King—The territory in dispute was that between the Arnon and the Jabboc. The Ammonite was directly interested probably only in the northern part, but the argument used suggested a wider claim. He calls it his land, wrongfully seized by the Israelites during their journey from Egypt to Canaan. Jephte first defends his ancestors, alleging their forbearance towards Edom and Moab, and their petition for a mere passage through Sehon's land, the territory in dispute. Then he expounds Israel's right, the right of conquest in a war forced upon them. If the king of Ammon has a right to the conquests of his god has not Israel a right to the conquests of Yahweh? This *argumentum ad hominem* does not imply that Jephte put Yahweh on the same level as the Ammonite god as a merely national deity. He next argues that Balac, king of Moab, did not contest Israel's right even though the region between the Arnon and Heshbon was ancient Moabite territory, and concludes by asking why the Ammonite reclamation was so long delayed. In **26** read with LXX *Jazer* (MT Aroer) and *Jordan* (MT Arnon), and omit ' 300 years', a later addition. The references to Moab in the dispute are quite natural and do not suggest a quarrel with the Moabites. The only difficulty is the mention of the Moabite god Kamos (**24**) instead of the Ammonite Malik. This is probably due to an alteration of the text through a misinterpretation of Moloch as king.

k 29-40 Campaign and Vow of Jephte—Jephte, inspired by God, crossed from Maspha to *Ephraim* (MT Galaad, *cf.* 12:2) and Manasses to raise additional forces and returned to the camp at Maspha. Before the battle he vowed to offer to Yahweh as a holocaust whoever came forth from the door of his (recently acquired) house at Maspha to meet him on his victorious return. The terms used clearly indicate not an animal but a person, not a mere dedication but a sacrifice. Making a detour with his army he surprised and routed the Ammonites. The Ammonite Aroer was east of Rabbath-Ammon (Jos 13:25). Mannith and Abel-ceramim are unidentified. Jephte was met on his return by a band

of women celebrating the victory and led by his only **24** daughter. **35.** Mindful of his vow he says, ' *Alas, my daughter! thou hast indeed brought me low and art become the supreme cause of my trouble*', etc. **37.** The heroic daughter encourages her father to fulfil his vow, only requesting ' *Let me alone two months that I may go and wander free* (MT descend) *upon the mountains and weep my maidenhood—I and my companions*'. **39.** After two months Jephte fulfils his vow. *And she knew no man.* Lack of offspring made her death more tragic to the Israelites. Jephte's religious earnestness and religious ignorance in making and fulfilling his vow are equally apparent. The narrator informs us that he was inspired in his war measures but relates the other events of his career, including his early lapses and his barbarous vow, quite objectively without dissimulation and without comment.

XII 1-7 Jephte and the Ephraimites—The haughty **l** Ephraimites, again (*cf.* 8:1-3) offended at a victory won without their intervention, *were called to arms and passed over to Saphon.* Saphon associated with Succoth (Jos 13:27), is Tell Sa'îdiyye, guarding a Jordan ford near the mouth of W. Kafringi. Jephte's reasonable reply (*cf.* 11:29) to their challenge does not avert a conflict in which Ephraim is defeated. **4b.** Omit the reasons given, partly a misplaced dittography of **5b** and partly a gloss. **5.** Read after ' return ' *and whenever the fugitives of Ephraim said.* **6.** Shibboleth, glossed in Vg, also means ' stream '. A scribe has exaggerated the number of Ephraimites slain. In the World War 1914-18 Turks were similarly detected by Arabs at the crossing of the Jordan through their incorrect pronunciation of the emphatic ṣ in baṣal.

8-15 Ibsan, Elon, and Abdon—These are the last **m** minor judges. There was a Bethlehem in Judah and in Zabulon. The former is more probably intended as better known and elsewhere (19:1) explicitly indicated. **9.** ' And gave to husbands ' is a gloss in Vg explaining ' sent abroad '. **12.** For ' in Zabulon ' read *in Ayyalon in the land of Zabulon.* Pharathon is the modern Far'ata six miles WSW. of Shechem. **15.** The mount of Amalec is unknown.

XIII 1-XVI 31 Samson—Samson is portrayed as a **2** popular hero, dedicated to the service of Yahweh from his mother's womb and charged with the mission of beginning to deliver Israel from the oppression of the Philistines. As a Nazarite and a warrior (*cf.* 5:2) he may never shear his locks since his dedication and his warfare are lifelong. Victory over the Philistines was reserved to David. He has the three characteristics of the popular hero, bravery, weakness towards women, and mother-wit. His superhuman strength, naturally conditioned by the observance of the essential obligation of his state, is repeatedly attributed to the spirit of Yahweh, and Samson himself when he prays for its restoration recognizes it as a gift of Yahweh. His weakness towards women provides the opportunity for his exploits by bringing him into conflict with the Philistines. It has its place in God's designs but leads eventually to infidelity and betrayal. His mother-wit appears in his riddle and aphorisms and the humorous aspect of some of his exploits such as the destruction of the harvests of the Philistines. The historical and geographical situation is clear and consistent. The remnant of Dan, described as a clan, occupies the region of Saraa and Eshtaol as in 18:2 ff., the scene of the events narrated, and is subject to the Philistines. The neighbouring men of Juda, as elsewhere attested (1:19 ; 3:3), are under the same yoke and obediently hand over Samson to their oppressors.

The interpretation of the Samson narrative as a **b** solar myth is no longer proposed by critics. It is recognized that the Hebrew historians are not concerned with mythology, but with sacred history and that Samson is manifestly represented as a popular hero. Those who reject the sacred writer's explanation of his superhuman strength attribute his miraculous exploits to popular imagination working, according to some, on a substratum of solar mythology. Thus the solar myth reappears in a new form. Samson's long

4b locks are the rays of the sun in his strength, surely a fanciful hypothesis as compared with the historical explanation. His destruction of the harvests of the Philistines is the corn-blight popularly ascribed to the sun's rays. It is gratuitously assumed that this pseudo-scientific theory of later Latin writers was familiar to

c the Hebrews. A historical instance of scorched earth strategy by means of torches fastened to the tails of dogs and foxes is recorded in Syria in the fourteenth century Mongol invasion (*cf.* ZATW (1911) 71 f.). Dalila, 'servant' in Babylonian, designates Samson's betrayer as the servant of Ishtar, enemy of the sun-god. This is undoubtedly far-fetched, and if the name has a special significance, the Arabic sense 'informer' is suggested by the context. The pillars upset by Samson at Gaza are a reminiscence of the pillars of Herakles. The Greek solar hero travelled like the sun to the confines of the west. Samson was brought a prisoner to the chief city of his captors, where he performed his last exploit. The pillars are incidental and too ordinary a feature of an edifice to suggest the pillars of Herakles. These are the chief mythological parallels adduced, manifestly superficial and heterogeneous and more indicative of modern research than ancient folk-lore.

d **XIII 1-25 Vocation and Birth of Samson—1-5.** The Angel of Yahweh appears to Manue's wife in Saraa, announcing the birth of a son who shall begin to deliver Israel from the Philistines. **6-8.** She informs her husband, who begs Yahweh for a second apparition and instructions. **9-14.** His request is granted. **15-16.** Manue offers his guest a kid, refused as food but accepted as a holocaust to Yahweh. **17-20.** The guest reveals himself by ascending heavenwards in the flame of the holocaust. **21-23.** Manue fears death because he has seen Yahweh, but his wife reminds him of the gracious character of the visit. **24-25.** Birth and youth of Samson.

e Saraa is Sar'a on the north side of the Wady eṣ-Ṣarrār opposite Bethsames. Dan is a *clan* (DV race 2). The law of the Nazarite (Num 6) only considers a temporary dedication. Samson's was lifelong. Wearing the hair uncut was the essential obligation. Wine and strong drink were also forbidden. Unclean foods were prohibited to all. As Samson's dedication was pre-natal some privations were imposed on his mother lest he should be contaminated. **6a.** 'The man of God . . . the Angel of God' should probably be *a man . . . an angel*. **6b.** Read *I did not ask him and he did not tell me*. **12.** *Now let thy word come to pass what shall be the rule for the child and what shall he do?* **15.** Manue said, '*Prithee, let us detain thee*', since a guest had to be constrained to accept hospitality. **19.** For 'libations' read *meal-offering*. Manue knew Yahweh by his ascent in the flame of the holocaust, but the account of the apparition is concluded before the recognition is narrated. Eshtaol is Eshū', about two miles NE. of Saraa. The camp of Dan (not that of 18:12) is probably the long promontory between the two towns. **25.** The spirit of Yahweh is manifested apparently by feats of strength.

f **XIV 1-20 Samson marries a Philistine, slays a Lion and proposes a Riddle—1-4.** Samson wishes to marry a Philistine of Thimnah, but his parents refuse their consent, unaware that the marriage is designed by Yahweh as an occasion of conflict with the Philistines. **5-7.** On his way to Thimnah to arrange the marriage he meets a full-grown lion and tears it asunder with his bare hands. **8-9.** Going again to Thimnah for the wedding he finds a hive of bees and honey in the carcass of the lion. **10-14.** The marriage feast is prepared at Thimnah, and thirty Philistines are assigned to Samson, ostensibly as a guard of honour, but really through fear of him, to whom he proposes his riddle. **15-18.** They intimidate the bride, who finally receives the solution from Samson on the seventh day and reveals it to them. **19.** Samson procures the garments promised to the solvers by slaying and despoiling thirty Philistines of Ascalon. **20.** His wife is given to another.

g Thimnah is probably Ḥirbet Tibne, about four miles south of Saraa in the plain. The dissent of his parents, **244g** who object to Philistines as uncircumcised, obliges Samson to conduct the negotiations himself and to contract a *ṣadīka* marriage, the wife remaining with her people. ' His father and mother ' (5) and ' his father ' (10) seem to have been interpolated to regularize the marriage. If they had been with Samson they would have known that he slew the lion, and his father would have conducted the negotiations. **6.** Samson was inspired by Yahweh in his feat of strength, but not in his courtship. Returning to Thimnah for the wedding, he interrupted his journey to take back the honey to his parents, which is surprising though the way was short. The carcass of the lion would dry up quickly in the hot climate, and the jackals would pick the bones clean. For 'when they saw him' (MT 11) read *because they feared him*. **13.** The shirts are inner garments, lit. *linen wrappers*. The coats appear from **19** to have been outer garments. **15a.** For ' seventh ' read *fourth* (LXX). **18a.** ' Before the sun went down ' is generally rendered with a slight correction *before he (Samson) entered the bridal chamber*. **20.** As Samson departed in anger his bride was given to the best man, *his companion whom he had made his chief friend*. **19.** Yahweh again inspires him in his feats at Ascalon.

XV 1-20 Samson burns Harvests and slays Warriors h —1-3. Finding his wife given to another, Samson determines to avenge the wrong done him. **4-5.** He burns down the corn-fields, vineyards, and oliveyards of his enemies by letting loose into them torch-bearing jackals. **6-8.** The Philistines fail to appease him by putting his wife and father-in-law to death. **9-13.** They send an army to seize him at Etam in Judah, and the Judaeans deliver him to them. **14-17.** Samson bursts his bonds, seizes the jawbone of an ass, and slays with it a thousand Philistines at Ramathlechi. **18-20.** A spring of water gushes from the rock to assuage his thirst.

The husband usually brought a present when visit- **i** ing his *ṣadīka*-wife. **1b.** Omit ' as usual '. **2a.** *I verily thought thou didst truly hate her.* Both verbs are emphatic. **3a.** Samson said : *I am quits this time with the Philistines*. So sure is he of his future vengeance that he regards his obligation to avenge himself as already fulfilled. **3b.** The reason he gives, *for I am about to do them a mischief*, thus becomes intelligible. **4.** By foxes are probably meant jackals, which live in packs and are easily caught. Insert *the house of* before ' her father ' in **6b** (LXX and 14:15). **8a.** *And he smote them leg upon thigh.* This is most probably a wrestling term, corresponding to the English cross-buttock, ' when the party, advancing his right leg and thigh, closes with his antagonist, and catching him with his right arm, or giving a round blow, throws him over his right hip upon his head '. Etam is probably the rock, called 'Araq Samain, and **j** containing a cave, over two miles ESE. of Saraa. **9.** After ' Juda ' read *spread themselves abroad in Lechi* (probably Ḥirbet eṣ-Ṣiyyāj, SW. of 'Araq Samain). **14.** Read after ' fire ' *and his bonds melted from off his hands*. Note the inspiration for a feat of strength. **15.** Insert *fresh* before ' jawbone '. An old jawbone would be brittle. Samson said : *With the red ass's jawbone I have reddened them right red* (lit. I have thoroughly assed them) : *With the red ass's jawbone I have smitten a thousand men*. For the first verb MT has the meaningless ' of an ass of two asses ', but LXX has a verb as required. **17.** Ramathlechi certainly means the height or hill of the jawbone. If the name existed before Samson's exploit, as is suggested by its mention in **9** and **14** (which may however be proleptical), it would be derived from the shape of the hill like Golgotha ' skull ', or Luhith ' little jawbone ' (Is 15:5 and CIS Aram 196), and would be only punningly associated with his weapon by Samson. In the alternative hypothesis the name would be derived from the weapon. **19a.** *Then God clave the mortar that is in Lechi*. The mortar was a circular depression in the rock. The spring issued from the mortar, not from

244j the jawbone. It is named Spring of the Caller because Samson called to God who miraculously produced it. In a different context Caller would be interpreted Partridge, so named from the clear notes of its cry.

k **XVI 1-31 Samson at Gaza and with Dalila: his Capture and Death—1-3.** Samson escapes from the Philistines with the gate of Gaza on his shoulders. **4-5.** He becomes enamoured of Dalila, who is bribed by the lords of the Philistines to discover the secret of his strength. **6-14.** Her first attempts are unsuccessful. **15-22.** At the fourth attempt Samson reveals his secret, loses his strength when shorn of his locks, and is captured by his enemies. **23-30.** Brought to a feast in honour of the Philistine corn-god, Dagon (cf. Burney 384-7), after his hair has grown, he upsets the two pillars which support the edifice and slays more at his death than during his life. **31.** His burial.

l Samson's passion leads him into an ambuscade. **2.** The watch was by day while the gate was open, the silence by night. The gate was of one piece when locked. Hebron is thirty-eight miles from Gaza. The ancient name Sorec is preserved in Hirbet Sūrik, two miles west of Saraa. Dalila was a Philistine. The name may mean informer. **5.** She was to discover *by what means his strength is great* and inform the five lords of the Philistines, who agreed to pay her 1,100 silver shekels (half-crowns) each. **7.** The first binding was *with seven fresh bow-strings which have not been dried*. The Philistines lay in wait in another room. Omit ' twined with spittle ' (DV **9**). **11.** The second binding was with new ropes as in 15:13. **13.** For ' how long ' read *hitherto*. **13b-14a.** The third binding is complicated by an omission in MT, through homœoteleuton, supplied by LXX. Samson said: *If thou weave the seven locks of my head along with the web (and beat up with the pin, then shall I become weak and be like any other man. So when he slept Dalila took the seven locks of his head and wove them along with the web) and beat up with the pin.* **14b.** Samson on waking *plucked up the loom and the web* to which his hair was attached. The pin was a flat piece of wood by which the web was pressed together. It is rendered nail (DV) and interpolated ungrammatically before the loom in MT **14.** The mention of the hair marks an approach to the

m secret, revealed at the next attempt. Dalila sees that no test is necessary and summons the lords of the Philistines. **19.** *And she made him sleep on her knees, and called for a man, and he shaved off the seven locks of his head and he began to be reduced and his strength departed from him.* **20.** *Shake myself* means free myself from bonds. **21.** Grinding corn, the work of women, was an ignominious imposition. **24a.** *And when the people saw him* apparently refers to Samson and thus **25** originally preceded **24.** The scene suggested is a banqueting-hall opening on to a courtyard. Samson first disports himself before those in the court and on the roof, and is then led into the hall. The pillars in **26** and **29** are not those in **25** where Vg interpolates ' two '. Samson after his last prayer for the restoration of his strength, *strengthen me only this once*, bends the pillars so that the house collapses.

245a **XVII 1-XVIII 31 The Sanctuary of Dan**—The establishment of an idolatrous sanctuary at Dan in NE. Palestine is here narrated. The facts are objectively recorded, but the sacred writer evidently disapproves of the erection by private authority of a new religious centre in Israel. The sordid origin of the sanctuary, the high-handed usurpation of the Danites, the idolatrous form of worship speak for themselves. The sanctuary is contrasted with the House of God in Shiloh and its origin is explained by the general lawlessness of the period. It contained a molten image of Yahweh and an ephod like that of Gedeon. The image of molten work (cf. the calf of molten work Ex 32:4) became a (graven) image and a molten (image) by the insertion

b of ' and '. In a second source the image is called *teraphim*. This obscure word seems to designate an image substituted for the sleeping David (1 Kg 19:13).

It is associated with ephod in Os 3:4 and with divination **2** Ez 21:26. The multiplication of objects of cult in ch 18 is clearly due to interpolation, since it supposes the duplication of the Yahweh-image. The institution of the sanctuary of Micah on Mt Ephraim and his installation of a Levite as priest are first related (ch XVII) then the Danite discovery of a new home at Laiš, their seizure of Micah's sanctuary on their journey thither, their conquest of Laiš, renamed Dan, and their sanctuary and priest (ch XVIII).

Micah is an abbreviation of Micayᵉhu, ' who is like **c** Yahweh?' **XVII:2-3.** The text is disordered and contains a repetition of **4a.** Micah said: *The 1,100 shekels of silver which were taken from thee, concerning which thou didst take an oath and didst say also in my hearing ' I do surely consecrate the silver to Yahweh from my hand alone to make a molten image '—behold the silver is with me ; I took it ; and now I will restore it to thee. And his mother said ' Blessed of Yahweh be my son '.* The object of the oath was to bring a curse on the robber if he used the money. Its effect here was prompt restitution (**4a**). For *alone* MT reads ' for my son '. The mother had a molten image made from part of the silver and set it up in the house of Micah. To this he added an ephod for a Yahweh oracle (consulted by the Danites 18:6). **5.** *Fill the hand* means install in office. **7.** The Levite of the clan of Judah must have been adopted into that tribe. Micah's satisfaction in having a Levite for priest shows the antiquity of the levitical institution. **XVIII:1.** A territory was assigned to the Danites, but the Amorites and the Philistines restricted them to a small portion of it so that they did not actually receive their lot. **2a.** *And the children of Dan sent from their clan five men from their whole number* (lit. from their extremities) *men of valour.* **2b.** For ' rested ' read *passed the night*. **3.** The spies recognized the Levite by his voice already known to them. Their third question, lit. *What to thee here ?* means ' What interest hast thou in remaining here ? ' **6.** The oracle gives a favourable answer : *Go in peace : before Yahweh is your journey whereon ye go.* On Laiš cf. Jos 19:47. Render **7b**, emended from **10b**, after ' easy ' : *and there was no want of anything that is in the earth and they were far from the Sidonians and had no dealings with Aram* (MT adam, mankind). **8.** Render the query *What news have ye ?* **9.** The words *against* (DV to) them in the **d** answer imply an omission in MT supplied by LXX. *We entered and travelled through the land as far as Laiš and we saw the people in it dwelling in security after the manner of the Sidonians at a distance from the Sidonians and having no dealings with the Aramaeans.* Render after ' fruitful ' : *And will ye be still ? Be not slothful to go in to possess the land.* **14.** Laiš is a gloss. **16.** The *gate* (DV door) implies that Micah's house had a courtyard. The five spies entered the house and seized the image and the ephod while the priest was at the gate with the warriors. **22.** Micah's neighbours *were called to arms* and pursued the Danites, who say to Micah (**23b**), ' What aileth thee that thou art up in arms ? ' The pl. Elohim (**24**) indicates the Yahweh image (LXX), not a plurality of gods (Vg). **25.** *Enraged* is lit. bitter of soul. **27.** Read after ' took ' *that which Micah had made and the priest that had belonged to him*, and after ' Sidon ' (**28**) *and they had not dealings with Aram*. **30.** MT has a suspended ' n ' after the ' m ' of Moseh, thus reading Manasses through reverence for Moses without altering the text. **30b.** After ' day ' read *when the ark* (MT land) *went into captivity.* The emendation is based on the fact that **30** and **31** apparently indicate the same period of time. The capture of the ark and the destruction of Shiloh by the Philistines were practically contemporaneous, but the Assyrian captivity was several centuries later.

XIX-XXI Origin, History, and Consequence of the War e against Benjamin—The historicity of this narrative is wholly or partially denied by many critics. They argue that the united action of the tribes is out of harmony with the history of the period, and that the references to Jabes Galaad, with which Saul had

e friendly relations, manifest the intention of the narrator to denigrate the tribe and friends of Saul. Exaggeration of numbers and adaptation of the narratives of the crime of the Sodomites and the capture of Hai are also urged as suggestive of fiction. It may be answered that the disunited activity of the tribes in the Judges' period is explained by the fact that the troubles were local. The crime at Gabaa was a religious matter of universal importance, and particular measures were taken to secure the co-operation of all. There is no trace of special animosity to Saul or Benjamin in the other historical books. The disaffection of Jabes Galaad is paralleled by that of Meroz in Debora's **f** and Succoth and Penuel in Gedeon's time. Exaggeration in numbers, no greater here than in 12:6, is not uncommon in the present text of the OT and does not affect its historicity. The stereotyped character of OT historical narrative accounts for similarities in recording distinct occurrences. The crimes of the Sodomites and the Gabaites are different. The failures of the early attacks on Hai and Gabaa are not similarly explained. Osee on the other hand attests the outrage when he twice refers to ' the days of Gabaa ' as the depth of depravity (Os 9:9 ; 10:9). Recent excavations attest its punishment, the burning of the city in the period of the Judges. Saul attests its consequence when he calls Benjamin the least tribe of Israel (1 Kg 9:21). Note how Gedeon deprecating a similar honour does not belittle Manasses (Jg 6:15). Would a postexilic inventor attribute such depravity to the lack of a king or completely disregard the law of unity of sanctuary ?

g **XIX 1-30 The Crime at Gabaa**—A Levite, dwelling *in the furthermost parts* of Mt Ephraim, went to Bethlehem to recover his wife who *had been vexed with him* and returned to her parents. **3b.** *He came to her father's house* where he was warmly welcomed and received the customary three days' hospitality. **4.** For ' familiarly ' read *and they passed the night there*. Early on the fourth day he rose up to depart, but his host constrained him in eastern fashion (*cf.* Lk 24:29) to remain until the evening of the fifth day. The hospitable Bethlehemite is contrasted with the men of Gabaa whose crime, an abominable breach of the sacred law of hospitality, is thus foreshadowed. The guest refuses the last invitation and sets out in the afternoon. Unwilling to spend the night in Jebusite Jerusalem he presses on towards Gabaa. **13.** *Come, let us draw near to one of the places and stay the night in Gabaa or Rama*. Gabaa is Tell el-Ful, three miles north of Jerusalem, partly excavated by Albright 1922-3. The original fortress was ' built toward the end of the thirteenth century B.C., and burned near the end of the twelfth ' (Albright in AASOR 4 (1924) 8). It was subsequently rebuilt, and was fortified and prosperous as Saul's capital **h** 1050 B.C. Rama is er-Ram, five miles north of Jerusalem. The travellers at Gabaa vainly await an offer of hospitality in the *market-place* (DV street) near the gate. Finally an Ephraimite sojourner in the city discovers them and offers entertainment. **18.** The house of God is a copyist's error for *my house*. **19a.** Omit ' hay '. **22.** *Sons of Belial* are either worthless persons, interpreting Belial as ' without profit ' or abysmally wicked persons, from Belial ' abyss ' or ' underworld ', or fiends, from Belial the Archfiend. The talmudic derivation in Vg (DV without yoke) is incorrect. According to the present text the men of Belial are first Sodomites, later adulterers and murderers. The Levite however accuses them (20:5) of intentional murder, not sodomy, and actual murder and adultery. The reference to sodomy is an intrusion in the text from Gen. 19. **24.** The incorrect form of *concubine* and the twice repeated masculine instead of feminine pronoun *them* are evidences of interpolation. For ' the man ' (**24b**) read *the woman* and for ' him ' *her*. ' Crime against nature on the man ' (DV 24) is a mistranslation of *wantonness*. The men of Belial demand the concubine. To save his guest the host offers his daughter instead. The guest, ready to defend his concubine, nevertheless surrenders her to save his host's daughter. The men of Gabaa, unlike Bethlehemites and Ephraimites, refuse hospitality, and abuse and murder their city's sacred guest. An omission in MT after **29** through homœoteleuton is supplied by LXX. *And he commanded the men whom he sent saying*, ' *Thus shall ye say to all the sons of Israel* '.

245h

XX 1-48 The War against Benjamin — Maspha, **i** identified with modern Tell en-Naṣbe, was a border city of Benjamin, a mile south of the Ephraimite Bethel. **1.** *To Yahweh* implies the presence of the Ark. Dan and Bersabee are approximately the limits of the territory occupied by Israelites. *From Dan to Bersabee* (1) and *the corners* (DV chiefs) *of all the people* (2a) both mean all Israel (*cf.* 18:2). Most commentators interpret corners as chiefs. Vg unduly emphasizes the crime by adding ' with an incredible fury of lust ' (**5**), ' so great ' (**12**) and altering **6b** *because they had committed lewdness and wantonness in Israel*. Omit ' in common ' (DV **9**) and insert after ' Gabaa ' : *We shall go up* (accidentally omitted) *against it by lot*. The Benjaminites refuse to surrender the criminals and assemble in Gabaa to defend it. **16.** On *left-handed*, not ambidexter, *cf.* 3:15. **18.** The oracle was therefore consulted and declared ' *Let Judah be the first* '. St Jerome incorrectly renders *Bethel* as ' the house of God ', and adds the gloss ' in Shiloh ', thus vindicating the law of unity of sanctuary. This law was not observed in the period of Judges, and Bethel, sanctified by the apparitions of Yahweh to Jacob (Gen 35) and his descendants (Jg 2:1), was the temporary abode of the Ark, transferred thither from Shiloh for the campaign. **19.** For ' by ' read *against*. **22.** After ' Israel ' read *took courage and set their army*, etc. Read *And they went up* (**23a**). *And the children of Israel consulted Yahweh* (**27a**) . . . *saying*, etc. (**28b**). The mention of the Ark at Bethel **j** *in those days* and of Phinees *standing over it* in the omitted **27b-28a** is clearly a later interpolation interrupting the context. We cannot therefore conclude that the Ark was permanently located at Bethel or that the war was waged in the days of Phinees, a younger contemporary of Josue. The description of the battle is confused by the presence of two accounts and some textual corruptions, but the general sense is clear. The simulated retreat, the ambuscade, the fire-signal and the simultaneous attack on front and rear recall the capture of Hai. To draw the Benjaminites into the open country the retreat was made along two highways, the first to Bethel being the northern road from Jerusalem to Shechem, the second not to Gabaa (MT) but to Gabaon, branching off from this to the NW. half a mile from Gabaa. The ambuscade was posted on the (south)-*west of Geba* (LXX), three miles north of Gabaa, where there were caves and whence a secret approach could be made to Gabaa. The fire-signal indicated the capture of the city to both parties. The Benjaminites fled to the desert, but only six hundred reached Rimmon, the modern Ramman, three and a half miles east of Bethel, or the nearer and more suitable Mughāret Gela'y in the Wady Suwēnit. **48.** The execution of a ban, not explicitly mentioned, on the cities, inhabitants, and beasts of Benjamin is described. For ' the remains of the city ' read *the Benjaminites*.

XXI 1-24 The Survival of Benjamin—The Israelites **k** realizing that the tribe of Benjamin was doomed to extinction by their oath not to contract marriage alliances with its members and their slaughter of the women and children devise two expedients to avert this calamity. They slay all the inhabitants of Jabes Galaad, who had disobeyed the call to arms, except the virgins, four hundred in number, reserved for the Benjaminite survivors. They command the two hundred still unprovided to seize wives at Shiloh from among the unmarried maidens who danced there at an annual religious solemnity. **2.** Bethel becomes in Vg ' the house of God in Shiloh ' as in 20:18. **5.** The reference to the second oath perhaps originally belonged to **8**, where **5a** reappears more appropriately. **9.** And the **l**

245 1 *people were mustered and behold there was not there a man of the inhabitants of Jabes Galaad.* The city is not identified but the name is preserved in Wady Yabis in northern Galaad. **10.** For 'ten' read *twelve*. **11b.** *But the virgins ye shall save alive. And they did so* (LXX, not in MT) is required by the context. **12b.** *In Shiloh in the land of Canaan* is probably a gloss since the description is strange and the camp was elsewhere. **13.** Read after 'Rimmon' *and proclaimed peace to them.* **14a.** For 'came' read *returned.* **14b.** *And yet so they did not find enough for them.* **15.** *And the people were moved* to pity for Benjamin because Yahweh had made a breach in **24** the tribes of Israel. **17.** *And they said ' How shall a remnant be left to Benjamin, that a tribe be not blotted out from Israel ? '* **19.** The feast was one of the three great annual solemnities. Render **22b,** *Ye shall say ' Grant them graciously to us ; for we took not every man his wife in battle : for if ye had given them to us ye would now be guilty '.* The plea is that the middle course adopted avoids the two extremes of seizure in battle which would cause a blood feud and voluntary concession which would violate an oath.

RUTH

By W. LEONARD

246a **Bibliography**—Commentaries : Theodoretus (PG 80, 518–28) ; Bonfrère (SSCC, 1631) ; Calmet (1724) ; Hummelauer (CSS, 1888) ; Joüon (1924) ; Schulz (BB, 1925) ; Grimmelsman (1930) ; Lattey (WV, 1935) ; *Rudolph (KAT, 1939) ; *Haller (HAT, 1930) ; *Cooke (CBSC, 1913) ; *Thatcher (CBi). See also Zschokke, *Die biblischen Frauen des A.T.* (1882) ; *Neufeld, *Ancient Hebrew Marriage Laws* (1944).

b **Place and Subject**—In our Greek and Latin Bibles Ruth stands amongst the historical books, at the end of the so-called Octoteuch ; in Hebrew Bibles it takes its place first or second in the series of five Megilloth or Festal Rolls near the beginning of the *Kethubhim* or ' Writings '—that is, in the third part of the Bible. Josephus, Melito of Sardes, Origen, and Jerome seem to indicate that its primitive place is really after Judges, as in the Greek and Latin Bibles. Liturgical use may have transferred it to the festal groups consisting of the Canticle for the Pasch, Ruth for Pentecost, Lamentations for Mourning Day, Ecclesiastes for Tabernacles, Esther for Purim.

The **subject** of our book is an historical episode belonging to the age of Judges and concerning the ancestry of David. The Moabitess Ruth is its central personage. In consequence of misfortunes governed by the provident hand of God, devotedness to an Israelite mother-in-law brought her to the God of Israel and to Bethlehem-Ephrata. There by a marriage of the leviratical type (see § 246g) she entered the world's greatest ancestral line, that of David and the Divine Messias.

c **Purpose and Literary Character**—Ruth is a history which by its edifying examples of family devotedness or ' piety ' glorifies the ancestry of David. Admiration moved the writer, and the honour of David determined him to write. The closing genealogy should be regarded as an integral part of the Book. Because of David and, inspirationally, because of Christ our Lord, the Book of Ruth was written.

Ruth is a charming history charmingly told, an idyll of God-fearing domestic and agricultural life at Bethlehem. The style is simple, fresh, and abundant. The large place given to direct speech, the fascinating repetitions of phrase, and the finesse of the dialogue make it particularly pleasing. In reading it we feel that the eyes of God are on Bethlehem.

d **Date and Authorship**—On the origin of the Book nothing certain can be affirmed. Driver regarded the language as pre-exilic and equal to the best passages of Samuel. Neologisms and Aramaisms are few and uncertain, and the argument for late origin drawn from the author's reference to a custom ' of former times in Israel ' (4:7) can hardly be decisive. The Davidic purpose and the abruptly Davidic ending of the story would indicate that it was written by a contemporary of David.

e **Sacred Significance** — The Book breathes a deeply religious spirit. It is a mirror of Divine Providence, a writing of great moral edification, and it forecasts the calling of the Gentiles. Though not read in the Missal or the Breviary, the names of Booz and Ruth sound in the Roman Liturgy three times each year, when St Matthew's genealogy of Christ is read ; the ' Dominus vobiscum ' of Booz is heard eight times in the Latin Mass ; words of Noemi (1:20) express the **246f** sorrow of the Blessed Virgin in the first Responsory of 15 September ; and words of Ruth (2:13) voice sentiments of the Pure Heart of Mary in the third Responsory of that liturgical Office.

The Go'el Question—This term is important in con- **g** nexion with the relationship between Booz and Noemi and Ruth. *Gō'ēl* is the active participle and *gᵉ'ullāh* the abstract noun formed from the verb *gā'al*. ' Redeemer ' and ' Redemption ' are their most usual equivalents, but the biblical use of the terms and the notion behind them must be summarily examined here. In Ruth the verb *gā'al* (in its participle and other active parts only) occurs twenty times, and the noun *gᵉ'ullāh* twice. The words do not directly denote but rather connote ' kinship ', the idea inherent in the triliteral *g'l* being ' deliverance ' (Gen 48:16). The notion of kinship comes in, because when the ' delivering ' agent is not God but man, the deliverance is normally the act of a kinsman, generally the next of kin. This is in accordance with the primitive concept of family or tribal solidarity. In the Bible goelship is concerned with property, liberty and life only. The word is nowhere used of delivering a widow or her dead husband from childlessness, and consequently levirate marriage (Deut 25:5-10) is not conceived as a direct act of goelship. The vindication of the blood of a murdered relative, or of the liberty of an enslaved relative, or of the property of an expropriated relative are the objects envisaged. It is only in connexion with the liberation of property that levirate marriage, or more accurately marriage of a leviratical type, is regarded more or less as an act of goelship, and that only in the Book of Ruth. In fact, the law of levirate marriage in Deut 25:5-10 does not contain the verb *gā'al*, but the act of *levir* or brother-in-law (*yābām*) is designated by the denominative verb in Pi'el (*yibbēm*) : cf. Gen 38:8. We therefore conclude that the custom or law of levirate marriage was primarily concerned with the survival of families (' that the dead man's name might not be blotted out from Israel '), whereas the exercise of goelship was concerned with the vindication of a relative's blood by killing his murderer, or of a relative's liberty by buying him out of servitude, or of a relative's property by purchasing and saving it for him. (The case in Num 5:8 does not differ substantially.) It is as a vindicator of property that Booz contracts a marriage not strictly leviratical but of a leviratical type with Ruth.

Points of Law—Deut 23:3 excluded Moabites for ever **h** from the community of Israel. How then could Ruth have obtained the recognition of a religious man like Booz ? Undoubtedly it was as the widow of Mahalon and by reason of her own subsequent choice of the religion of Israel and—let us add—because of her virtue. Mahalon in exile did not marry Ruth in the face of any express legal prohibition, for the letter of the Mosaic law did not prohibit the taking of Moabite wives but of Canaanites only. Apart from positive law, there would be a natural objection to an Israelite-Moabite marriage, but Mahalon's long exile made marriage with a Moabitess more or less a matter of necessity.

Another question regards Elimelech's land. It is de- **i** scribed as the property of Noemi at her return from

303

246i Moab. How can this be, when Num 27:9-11 seems to exclude widows from inheritance? The silence of the law (apparently positive) would indeed seem to lead to that conclusion, but we know de facto that widows did inherit their husband's property in Israel. Prov 15:25 shows God as the guardian of the widow's boundary, and the widow Judith of Bethulia possessed her dead husband's moneys and cattle and lands (Jdt 8:7 LXX).

j It may also be asked : Does the Book of Ruth 4:10 represent Booz as purchasing his wife? The answer is *No*. The verb *qānāh* means to acquire on any other title as well as that of purchase. Booz purchased Elimelech's (now Noemi's) land and thereby had a right and even a pious obligation to marry Ruth, although he was not bound by the strict law of levirate. The Moabitess entered the house of Booz in place of Noemi, who was too old to have children. Hence the Bethlehemite women, with their instinct for the reality of the case, regarded Obed as a son of Noemi. The marriage of Ruth by Booz was what the Germans call an *Ersatzehe*—a substitute marriage.

247a **I 1-5 Emigration and Bereavement**—A severe famine in the land of Israel struck Ephrata ('the Fruitful'), in which was Bethlehem ('the Home of Bread'), and compelled a family of some standing to emigrate. Precise dating is not possible, but perhaps the second half of the age of Judges is the most plausible conjecture. The names are evidently real and not symbolic. Elimelech means 'God is King', Noemi (*No'omî*), 'my Sweetness' or 'Delight', but Mahalon and Chelion can suggest other things besides 'Sickness' and 'Consumption'. After Elimelech's death his sons, necessity excusing, took Moabite wives, Chelion marrying Orpha ('Rich-haired', rather than 'Stiff-necked'), and Mahalon Ruth ('Friendship', rather than 'Refreshment'). Before ten years were out both men were dead.

b **6-18 Ruth's Decision**—We note the disinterestedness of Noemi towards her daughters-in-law when they wished to accompany her on the way of return to the land of Judah. Their decision already reveals what a lovable mother-in-law she was. She bade them return each to her own mother's house—namely, to that portion of the women's quarters allotted to their respective mothers in their paternal homes. What Noemi wished for them was a divine requital of their kindness towards their dead husbands and herself and the 'rest' of new marriage settlements. In her second effort to dissuade them, she seems to have thought of levirate marriage (Deut 25:5) as their only hope of second wedlock in Israel. They could only expect husbands from Noemi's own body, a very forlorn hope indeed. The Vg and DV may be right in **13c**, but the connexion with **13d** (Heb *kî*) seems to suggest the translation : *No, my daughters, I am in much worse plight than you, for the hand of the Lord has gone out against me*. The alleged Aramaism *lāhēn* occurring twice in this verse probably represents an original *lahem* : '*For them would you wait. . . .?*'

Thereupon Orpha went back to her Moabite kin and to the Moabite Pantheon or simply to Chamos (Kemosh) the national god. Ruth's words of attachment to Noemi are as beautifully eloquent as they are sublimely heroic (**16, 17**). It was that cry of devotedness to the claims and pieties of her affinity that, under Providence, brought Ruth into the company of the θεοπροπάτορες, or progenitors of Christ.

c **19-22 Return to Bethlehem**—Bethlehem 'rang' (LXX) or 'was stirred' at the return of Noemi. The womenfolk voiced their surprise in the rhetorical question : 'Is this that Noemi?' 'Rather call me Mara', she said, that is '*Bitter*'. The word has an Aramaic ending in most MSS, but is this original or scribal? The beginning of the barley harvest was Psachal time in the month of April.

d **II 1-3 Ruth Gleaning**—Booz or Bō'az (etymologically, perhaps, 'Living vigour', but popularly='in him

strength') is introduced at once as a rich man related **2** by blood to Elimelech—a cousin, perhaps. Because of the poverty of Noemi, Ruth proposed to exercise her right of gleaning (Lev 19:9 ; 23:22 ; Deut 24:19) in some field where it would be accorded her with good grace. 3. *Her good fortune lighted on a field of Booz who was of the sept or gens of Elimelech* (Heb. *mišpāḥāh*).

4-17 Goodness and Kindness of Booz—Booz seems to **e** have arrived towards midday—a noble type of householder, religious, courteous, humane, generous. Note the exchange of religious salutations and his inquiry : '*To whom* does this young woman belong?' The end of the overseer's answer (**7c**) shows textual fluctuation (Heb, LXX, Vg ; Syr. omits). Joüon's emendation, though partly based on the LXX, is not entirely convincing. It reads : 'she has not rested even a little'. St Jerome's 'Not for a moment has she returned home' is unlikely. We can only guess that the overseer said : 'She has given herself little or no rest'. See also WV.

We note that Booz, an elderly man, addresses Ruth as **f** 'Daughter' (**8**), and the latter's humble reply receives in Hebrew (**10**) an elegant turn : an expression of gratitude for '*noticing an unknown* or foreign woman'— a play on the root *nkr*. The eulogy of Ruth by Booz (**11, 12**) ends poetically in the metaphor of the protecting wings of the God of Israel, and there is probably an allusion to them in the later words of Ruth to Booz (3:9) : 'Spread thy wing (or protecting cloak) over thy handmaid, for thou art a gō'ēl'. Ruth's reply here (**13**) to the kindness of the good man should begin : '*May I* (continue to) *find favour in your eyes !*' The simple finesse of the dialogue must be felt rather than expounded.

As Ruth obtained 'the freedom of the fields', her gleaning was very successful. Threshed with a stick, it amounted to an ephah of barley, about 8 gallons heaped measure or 1 bushel (not 3 bushels).

18-23 Return to Noemi—On receiving the news of **g** the day, Noemi spoke words (**20**) which should be rendered : 'Blessed is he by the Lord who (through the action of Booz) has not failed to continue his kindness towards the living (Ruth and Noemi) and the dead (Mahalon and Elimelech)'. She added : 'The man is nearly related to us, one of our gō'ªlîm'. This word, better left untranslated, has been explained in the introduction, and is the key to the rest of the Book. Ruth gleaned till the end of the wheat harvest, after Pentecost.

III 1-5 Noemi plans Marriage—Booz was no levir or **h** brother-in-law, but perhaps custom had extended the ancient (Gen 38:8) and Mosaic institution (Deut 25:5) of levirate marriage to more remote kinsmen, at least as a pious obligation, especially when such a marriage was associated with the vindication of a relative's inheritance. The appeal to the goelship of Booz planned by Noemi does not seem to be a direct marriage petition but undoubtedly she saw that if Booz were to act as gō'ēl, he would take Ruth in marriage. The mode of the petition involved moral risk, but the cause was good, the means merely dangerous—not bad—the persons concerned were virtuous, and Noemi's intention was entirely praiseworthy.

6-18 Ruth's Petition—The idea of lifting the covering **i** from the feet of Booz was that the cold should wake him. At midnight he awoke startled '*and turned this way and that* (to observe), *and behold, a woman was lying at his feet*'. To his question : '*Who art thou?*' she answered, '*I am Ruth, thy handmaid : spread thy wing over thy handmaid, for thou art a gō'ēl*'. In itself the gesture of spreading the skirt of the cloak over Ruth would only signify a kinsman's protection, but in the circumstances it was equivalent to a promise of marriage. Booz saw that it was devotedness to the obligations of kinship that prompted Ruth's petition, and he conceived his goelship as including the taking of Ruth as his wife. It is here (**12, 13**) that the vindication of a property (which Booz undoubtedly had in mind, as the sequel shows) becomes the vindication of a

i widow. Verse 13, in which the affixed pronoun is the object of *gā'al* three times over, may be translated : ' *If he* (who is a nearer *gō'ēl*) *claims thee, let him make his claim ; but if he does not claim thee, I will claim thee* '. (*Cf*. Joüon and his note ; Kennedy, *Gō'ēl* (HDB) cites Driver as making ' claim ' the basic meaning of *gā'al*. Our lexical knowledge of the word is not very perfect, since it does not occur in the cognate languages, except in Samaritan Aramaic—perhaps as a Hebrew loan-word.)

The ' six of barley ' which Ruth took home (**15**) should probably be computed as 6 *sᵉîm*, *i.e.* 16 gallons or 2 bushels.

j **IV 1-12 Transaction at the Gate**—At the gate, the place of legal business, Booz calls the *gō'ēl* by name, but the author of our book substitutes an indefinite *So-and-So*. In the presence of 10 ' aldermen ' witnesses, Booz announces as interpreter of Noemi's intention that she is selling a property of Elimelech's. First preference as buyer belonged to *So-and-So*, as next of kin. He was willing. Booz points out that in buying from Noemi, he must also take Ruth, Mahalon's widow, to provide an heir for the property. **5** should be rendered : ' *On the day thou takest* (by purchase) *the field from the hand of Noemi, Ruth also the Moabitess, the wife of the dead man, thou takest* (therewith), *to raise up the name of the dead on his inheritance* '. The *gō'ēl* then declined, because the transaction would involve loss of purchase money to himself and his family. The cession of right to Booz had to be ratified by the ceremonial handing of a shoe (**7**), the shoe being the symbol of possession (Ps 59:10), as a head-covering

is of authority. This ceremony, which had to some **247j** extent passed into desuetude when our book was written, is altogether distinct from the penal procedure of Deut 25:9.

Having solemnly witnessed the contract, both elders and people wished Booz all happiness with Ruth. Though only broadly equivalent to the Hebrew, St Jerome's version of their acclamation is very good. The Bethlehemite colour of the wish and its point in regard to the present event is heightened by evoking the memory of the house of Phares, for Phares was the son of levirate marriage, and the Bethlehemites were his descendants.

13-17 Birth of Obed—The marriage was blessed with **k** offspring. The congratulations of the women go to Noemi, for the son of Ruth is to secure the succession of Elimelech's family. The boy shall be the comfort of her old age, and Ruth has proved and shall prove better to her than seven sons (any number, *cf*. 1 Kg 1:8). Noemi took the child as her own and nursed him. At the suggestion of the neighbours (*cf*. Lk 1:59) his name was called Obed, ' One who serves ', *i.e.* ' Servant (of God) ' or ' Deicola ', rather than ' Servant of Noemi '. He was David's grandfather.

18-22 David's Genealogy—From Phares to David **l** inclusive there are only ten names, grouped apparently as 5 + 5. It is not a complete list. With special mention of the wives of Salmon and Booz, namely Rahab and Ruth, it has the signal honour of finding its place in the genealogy which ends with the words : ' Jacob begot Joseph the husband of Mary, and of her was born Jesus who is called Christ '.

1 and 2 KINGS

(1 and 2 SAMUEL)

By H. McKAY, O.F.M.

248a Bibliography—Commentaries. Claire, B., *Les Livres des Rois*, Paris, 1884²; Dhorme, P., *Les Livres de Samuel*, Paris, 1910; Leimbach, K., *Die Bücher Samuels*, Bonn, 1936; Schlögl, N., *Die Bücher Samuels*, Vienna, 1904; Schulz, A., *Die Bücher Samuel*, Münster, 1919; *Smith, H. P., *The Books of Samuel* (ICC), Edinburgh, 1912. Articles. *Batten, L. W., 'A Crisis in the History of Israel' JBL 49 (1930) 56–60; *Boyd, J. O., 'The Davidic Dynasty,' *Princeton Theol. Rev.* 25 (1927) 215–239; *Cornill, C. H., 'Noch einmal Sauls Königswahl u. Verwerfung' ZATW 10 (1890) 96–109; Desnoyers, L., 'L'établissement de la royauté en Israel', *Bulletin de Lit. ecclésiastique* (1927) 75–91; 'La politique et la religion dans l'établissement de la royauté en Israel', RA 45 (1927) 5–9; Lagrange, M.-J., 'Le Règne de Dieu dans le Judaïsme', RB (1908) 350–66; *North, C. R., 'The Religious Aspects of Hebrew Kingship', ZATW 9 (1932) 8–38; Schäfers, J.,' 1 Sm 1–15 literarkritisch untersucht', BZ 5 (1907) 1 ff., 126 ff., 235 ff., 359 ff.; Weismann, H., 'Die Einführung des Königtums in Israel, 1 Sam 8–12,' ZKT 34 (1910) II, 8.

b Title—It is clear from the writings of Origen, Eusebius, Cyril of Alexandria, and Jerome that the first two books of Kings were reckoned under the one title *Book of Samuel* in the Hebrew Canon. This agrees with the division adopted by the Talmud (*Baba Bathra*, 14a). The LXX translators of the Book of Samuel divided it and the following books of Kings into four books under the general title *Books of the Kingdom*. The Vg accepted this division, but substituted 'Books of Kings' for the LXX title. Eventually this division found its way into the Rabbinical Hebrew Bible of Bomberg published at Venice in 1516. By way of compromise with the Hebrew Canon, this edition retained the title Books of Samuel for 1 and 2 Kg. This title does not denote authorship, but focuses attention on one of the principal characters in the early chapters of the book.

c Contents—1 and 2 Kg are a continuation of the history of Israel described in the book of Judges and stand in an even closer connexion with the events narrated in 3 and 4 Kg. They cover a period of transition and development in which the common religion and the common race of Israel were welded into a single centralized State under the monarchy. This transition and development are crystallized round the persons of Samuel, Saul and David. In this way we are given a rough plan of the general contents of the books themselves. The following is a general analysis of the books, but we have adopted a more detailed subdivision in the actual text of the commentary: Samuel, 1 Kg 1–15; Saul and David, 1 Kg 16–2 Kg 1; David, 2 Kg 2–24.

d Composition—Literary criticism beginning with J. G. Eichorn (*Einl.* II. Teil, 450 ff.) has been engaged on the problem of the composition of these books since 1790. Yet there has been no solution to the problem of 'sources' such as might win the unanimous approval of Catholic and non-Catholic scholars alike. There has been the usual tendency to analyse these books into various literary strata, redactions, interpolations, duplicate accounts, and fragmentary sources. Their present unity is ascribed to the 'harmonizing' influence of subsequent editors. Following the lead given by *K. Budde (*Die Bücher Samuels*, Tübingen, 1902), many authors assume that the sources E and J

which they claim for the Pentateuch are continued in **2** Kg. An early editor is held to have combined these two sources into one book and later influences of a Deuteronomistic and Priestly-Codex group to have modified the whole work to a considerable extent. To these *O. Eissfeldt adds the source L. This is in keeping with his views on the composition of the Hexateuch; *cf. Die Komposition der Samuelisbücher*, Leipzig, 1931. Opposition to this claim for Pentateuchal sources comes not only from Catholic but also from non-Catholic authors such as H. Gressmann (*Die alttest. Geschichtsschreibung und Prophetie Israels*, Göttingen, 1921²); W. Caspari (*Kommentar z.A.T. herausg.* von Sellin, Leipzig, 1926); and J. O. Boyd, art. 'Monarchy in Israel' in the *Princeton Theol. Rev.* 26 (1928) 42 ff. Much of this literary criticism is of the highest value and can be utilized by the Catholic scholar as a permanent contribution to biblical science. However, a considerable part of it is vitiated by an arbitrary application of the analytical method, by prejudices against anything supernatural, and by a subjective approach to the problems that casts doubts on the truth of Scripture and is quite incompatible with Catholic teaching on the nature and effects of inspiration.

Most modern Catholic authorities admit that some **e** theory of sources must be adopted in solving the literary difficulties presented by 1 and 2 Kg. This is the conviction of writers like J. Schäfers, K. Leimbach, A. Schulz, N. Schlögl, and G. Ricciotti. They safeguard their historicity and for the most part admit that such sources were ultimately based upon the accounts provided by Samuel, Gad, Nathan, the Royal Archives and other documents indicated in the Scriptures themselves; *cf. § 224d.* According to Schäfers there are two independent sources in chh 8–12. These are called M(ispa), 8 and 10:17–27, and G(ilgal), 9 and 10:1–16; Chh 13–15 also belong to G. A later editor is considered responsible for 13:19–23; 14:47–51. Ch 13:7b–15b is thought to be an interpolated fragment from a traditional account of Saul's rejection. Schulz admits that it is extremely difficult to dissect the various sources incorporated in our present text, and still more difficult to determine their precise authorship and dating. M and G, he thinks, are found in a combined form in 7:2–12:25 and reappear in patches in other parts of the books. The G source originated in the last years of David's reign and the M source was composed during Solomon's time and both were welded into one about this same period. Then for many centuries interpolations, additions, and subsequent editing played their part in giving us our text in its present form. However, a careful reading of the many specialized and general studies published on this subject will reveal that no completely definitive solution has been made so far. In spite of this, it is well to remember that modern scholarship is practically unanimous in holding that these books provide us with contemporary material that is of the highest historical value. This is confirmed not only by the sincerity, perfect simplicity, and graphic minuteness of the accounts themselves, but also by extra-biblical sources which throw light on the social, political, and religious background of Palestine at the time of the early kings of Israel.

Date of Composition—These books were obviously **f**

written some time after the events they narrate. That is clear from the explanation of obsolete terms (1 Kg 9:9) and customs (2 Kg 13–18). There are also indications that the work was completed after the separation of the two kingdoms in the reign of Roboam. The expression 'kings of Juda' (1 Kg 27:6) presupposes this. It is impossible to say more than that these books were composed some time after the separation of the two kingdoms and some time before the end of the exile. The identity of the author is uncertain.

Text—Our modern MT leaves much to be desired, and the Hebrew MSS which give variant readings are not of much help in establishing a reliable critical text. Fortunately great assistance is given to the textual critic by the older versions, among which the LXX is *facile princeps*. The various recensions of this version are divided into two important groups—those based on the Codex Vaticanus (B) and those based on the Codex Alexandrinus (A). St Jerome's Vg follows the MT fairly closely. These together with a few readings from the Old Latin version are the chief materials at our service for the restoration of the text.

Religious Significance—Few books in the OT can rival 1 and 2 Kgs for strong emotion and dramatic action. The reader is almost compelled to see with his own eyes the more important scenes in this stirring epoch of Israel's history. Through vivid dialogues and graphic detail he is admitted into the counsels of kings, prophets, and warriors. Throughout the book he meets with saints, sinners, 'spoilt' sons, brave men, cripples, scheming women, devoted mothers, noble friends, and traitors. Life and human nature are presented with a realism which makes these narratives invaluable guides to all who would know the soul of man and the eternal background which is the horizon of life. The selection of the incidents and prominence given to the personal element reveal the religious and moral purpose which inspired the author of these early chronicles. The author is not merely writing history: he is interpreting it, so that the vital truths which it illustrates stand out in clear relief. In addition to this wealth of moral instruction these books are of great importance for the study of God's progressive revelation in the OT.

During the period of the Judges the religion and culture of the Canaanites, the internal discord among the scattered tribes, and external oppression and invasion had reduced the political and religious ideals of Israel to a very low level. At this juncture the cumulative effect of the events associated with the institution of the Hebrew monarchy caused a revival of Israel's national faith. In the first place religion profoundly influenced the whole character and institution of the monarchy itself. Secondly we can note the contemporary repercussions of this on the religious life of the nation, and lastly view its relation to the future and abiding Messianic Kingship of Christ.

(A) The old theocracy was still at work under a new form. This is seen in the divine sanction manifested in the method of election by lot, which left the designation of the candidate in the hands of God, and in the sacred rite of anointing. This rite was used under divine inspiration and administered by God's representative to inculcate the sacred character of the chosen king and to set the seal of divine blessing on his reign. It underlined the principle that this human deputy was to be king of God's grace and in some measure in God's stead, not as the rival but as the visible reflection of God's sovereignty. He must rule in God's name, by God's spirit, for God's purpose. Pagan kings were sometimes considered to sit on the throne of their deities, and were even regarded as incarnations of their gods. This was impossible in the real monotheistic theocracy; yet so closely was the Hebrew king united to Yahweh, that he bore the exalted title of 'son of God' (2 Kg 7:14) to signify God's fatherly care of him. The sacred sonship of the nation now culminated in the unique sonship of the king. It is worth remembering that the first personal confession of faith noted by

St John unites the dignity of sonship and royalty **248j** together : ' Rabbi Thou art the Son of God, Thou art the King of Israel ' Jn 1:49.

(B) It is not without significance that we know more of **k** David than of most other OT characters. His intense personality with all its faults has impressed the minds of Hebrews and Christians alike. But it is by his religious contribution to the world that his work has proved most enduring. His passionate loyalty to Yahweh and his zeal for Yahweh's glory revived the religious enthusiasm of his people. In making Jerusalem the city of David and dwelling-place of Yahweh's glory, in giving the riches of his psalms to his nation, in striving for the building of the Temple after the humiliations of previous centuries, he gave the Hebrews a new lease of religious fervour. Indeed some scholars like *Winckler (*Geschichte des Volkes Israel*, 1, 38), *Beer (*Saul, David, Salomo*, 1, 41), and *P. Haupt in his article ' Midian und Sinai ', ZDMG (1909) 506 ff., exaggerate this influence. They believe that until David's time, Yahweh had been nothing more than a local god of thunder worshipped in the north of Canaan. He became the national God of Israel only after David had the Ark brought to Mount Sion. Until that time there was religious disunion between the north and south with two rival centres of worship—the one in the north kept the Ark, while the south clung to the Tabernacle as its centre. This theory not only contradicts what we know of monotheism in Israel in pre-Davidic time (*cf.* *König, *Geschichte der Alttest. Religion*, Gütersloh, 1924, 335 f.), it fails to give convincing evidence of this religious disunion based on the distinction between Ark and Tabernacle. The fact is that the Tabernacle, from Josue to Saul, was first at Galgal in Ephraimitic territory (Jos 4:19 ; 9:6 ; 10:6 f.), then at Shiloh in a predominantly Canaanite region (Jos 18:1 ; Jg 18:31 ; 21:19). During Saul's reign it was kept in Nobe, a priestly city of the tribe of Benjamin, whereas under David it was at Gabaon until the building of the Temple (1 Par 16:39 ; 21:29 ; 2 Par 1:3). These changes from town to town up and down the country would hardly have been possible if Yahweh had not been recognized as the God of the whole of Israel before David's day. What we can say is that it was David's great achievement to have founded an earthly kingdom which won the support of both priest and prophet, and which was so suffused by his deep religious spirit that it was seen to be the earthly expression and willing instrument of Yahweh's kingdom. In a word, it was more than a preparation for, it was the imperfect embodiment of something that was destined to raise men's minds to thoughts of God's everlasting kingdom.

(C) Much of David's work was swept away by the **l** events of later history. The nation was split politically in two and at last even Judah lost her independence. But the abiding spiritual glory of his dynasty was part of Yahweh's sure mercies to David. From that Davidic line would arise the Great King, the Supreme High Priest, the greatest of the Prophets. After David's reign it is possible to draw a line through the Messianic teaching of the prophets and see that only a Davidic king in whom all the energies of Yahweh's transcendental kingship had become incarnate could be worthy of the everlasting kingdom of Yahweh's anointed ; *cf.* Is 9:6 ; 11:1 ff. ; Jer 23:5 ; Ez 34:4–26. When the prophets paint the picture of the future kingdom they are led by Gods' irrevocable oath to David to use the colours of the past. In the fullness of time what many kings and prophets desired to see came to pass. One whom David called his ' Lord ' was born in the city of David and of his kingdom there is no end.

THE FIRST BOOK OF KINGS

I–III Birth, Dedication, and Prophetic Call of Samuel— **249a** Anna, the Elizabeth of the OT, is the childless wife of Elcana. When her prayer for a son is heard, she dedicates him to the service of Yahweh in the sanctuary

249a at Shiloh. In contrast to the corrupt sons of the High Priest Heli, this boy Samuel grows in grace before God and man. God summons him to be his special prophet and gives him as the burden of his first prophecy the doom threatening the house of Heli.

b **I:1** The name Ramathaim means 'Two Heights'. The district of Sophim was probably called after Elcana's ancestors, *cf.* 1 Par 6:26. Mount Ephraim gives the impression of a single mountain. What is meant is the mountainous district of Ephraim. Probably the modern village of El Ram occupies the site of Ramatha. It lies about five miles north of Jerusalem, just east of the highroad to Ramallah, and it was at Ramatha that Samuel was born, lived and was buried. **2.** Elcana had two wives in accordance with the custom tolerated by the Mosaic law (Deut 21:15–17). Anna means 'Grace' and Phenenna means 'Pearl'—the equivalent of our 'Margaret'. **3.** 'Upon the appointed days': MT has 'year by year', or lit. 'from time to time'. The Law commanded every male to appear before the Lord three times in the year at the central **c** sanctuary (Ex 34:23; Deut 16:16). Shiloh: At this period there were some other minor sanctuaries, *e.g.* at Shechem, Galgala, Gabaon, Hebron, but Shiloh had a unique prestige. It was central and in the heart of the powerful tribe of Ephraim, and above all it had the Ark of Yahweh which implied the special presence of God. Thus it became the political and religious capital of the nation. Many obstacles stood in the way of the strict and literal observance of the Mosaic law (Deut 12:4–28) on the centralization of worship. The sporadic nature of the conquest, the dispersal of the tribes, and the lawless state of affairs during the period of the Judges, all militated against the ideal of a single centre of divine worship. But it is well to remember that the non-observance of a law does not mean its non-existence. Shiloh was the nearest practical approach to the ideal under the circumstances. It now corresponds to the site called Khirbet Seilun. **4.** 'the day came': the time for appearing at the sanctuary. **5.** 'One portion': part of the sacrifice consumed by the worshipper and his family. Like Sarah, Rebecca, and Rachel, Anna had to suffer the shame of being childless before she became the mother of an illustrious son. **6.** 'her rival': the cruel scorn of Phenenna ruined the happy atmosphere of the feast. **7.** Anna was so upset with grief that she refused to share in the sacrificial meal which was the climax of the religious celebration.

d **9-18 Anna's Prayer and Vow**—**9** 'Anna arose': LXX 'she rose after she had eaten and stood before Yahweh'. Heli sat watching her from his seat at the gateway of the sanctuary. He was a descendant of Ithamar, the younger of the two surviving sons of Aaron. Originally the high-priesthood was in the family of Eleazar, the elder of Aaron's two surviving sons. We are not told how this office was transferred to the family of Ithamar to which Heli belonged. Officially he was both High Priest and Judge, but he lacked the greatness of a Gedeon or a Deborah. We see him only in his old age, a man of mediocre ability and without any power of vigorous leadership. He was incapable of inspiring the fire of religious or political enthusiasm. Most of the active duties of his priestly office seem to have been handed over to his two sons with disastrous consequences. His affection and care for Samuel show that he was not without a spirit of benevolence and kindness, yet his whole character suffered from moral weakness. Hence his sinful leniency in dealing with the scandalous conduct of his two sons. On the whole, in his own passive and ineffectual way he was devoted to Yahweh. **11.** 'Look down on the affliction of thy *handmaid*': LXX has 'the lowliness of thy handmaid' —the words used by our Lady in her Magnificat. 'I will give him': like Samson her child would be a life-long Nazarite with the characteristic long, unshaven hair, symbolizing the complete dedication of the whole man with all his powers to Yahweh. **16.** 'daughters of Belial': no satisfactory Heb. derivation of the word

Belial has been found. It may have been a foreign importation and in NT times was used of Satan. Here the phrase means: I am not a disreputable woman. **19-28 Samuel's Birth and Consecration**—The child of **e** prayer was born and given the name Samuel. While still a child he was brought to the sanctuary of Shiloh in fulfilment of his mother's vow. **20.** 'Samuel': the Heb. name 'Shemuel' is connected here with the verb *šā'al* 'to ask' and according to this popular etymology his name means 'Asked of God'. This is grammatically untenable for it does not account for the *mem* in the middle of the name. Some authors suggest other possible meanings based upon the Heb. text—'Heard of God' and 'His name is God', *i.e.* 'Yahweh is God'. **21.** 'his vow': this assumes that Elcana had made some vow similar to that of Anna. **22.** 'till the child be weaned': in the east this might mean until the boy was two to three years old. Yahweh's sanctuary and its sacred associations were to be the earliest memories in the child's mind. **23.** 'his word': Elcana prays that Anna's hopes for Samuel's future may receive complete fulfilment. LXX, 'The Lord establish that which has gone forth from thy mouth'.

II:1-10 Anna's Hymn of Thanksgiving—This is some- **f** times called 'the Magnificat of the OT'. Both Mary's song and Anna's canticle are poetry and prophecy. St Luke's narrative (Lk 1:46–55) shows how deeply Anna's words had affected our Lady's mind. But when they pass through her soul, they catch something of the fragrance of her personality and are clothed with her own quiet restraint and selfless humility. In the present context, the leading idea seems to be the praise of Yahweh who has given deliverance to Anna. The proud and boastful must be silent before him, for he weighs all their thoughts and actions. In his sovereign government of the world he can reverse the positions of weak and strong, mighty and lowly. This great moral principle of his rule will receive its complete fulfilment in the judgement of the world and the exaltation of Yahweh's anointed King.

1. 'My horn is exalted': a symbol drawn from **g** animals tossing their heads in the air as if in pride. **2.** 'strong like our God': MT has 'there is no rock like our God'—a frequent metaphor describing the strength, solidity and unchangeableness of Yahweh's care which meets the needs of the weak and fickle souls of men. **3.** 'let old matters depart': better 'let not insolence or arrogance come forth from your mouth'; 'are thoughts prepared': the hidden springs of man's actions are weighed and estimated at their true worth. **4.** This knowledge and justice of God are often vindicated in the lives of individuals such as Anna, and receive their fullest justification in the ultimate triumph of Christ and his Church. **5.** 'the hungry are filled': by a slight alteration of the text we can read: 'have ceased to labour', and this gives us a perfect antithesis to the rich being forced to hire themselves for bread. **8.** 'dunghill': the mound of rubbish accumulating near an oriental town. Beggars often spend the night on it in default of a lodging. 'the poles of the earth... set the world': omitted by LXX which has 'granting his petition to him that prays and blesses the years of the just'. **9.** 'silent in darkness': perish. **10.** **h** 'exalt the horn of his Christ': the thought of God's judgement leads to the thought of the ministers and instruments of that judgement. It dwells first on its partial fulfilment in the future monarchy and its complete fulfilment in the Perfect Anointed One of Yahweh. This is the first time the word 'Messias' occurs in Scripture. There may be an allusion to this verse in the Benedictus of Zachary (Lk 1:69 f.). **11.** A study of the LXX readings will show that the original text had: 'She left him there before Yahweh and went to Ramatha; but the boy ministered to Yahweh in the presence of Heli the priest'.

12-26 The Unworthy Priests of Shiloh—The evil con- **i** duct of Heli's sons is set forth in vivid contrast to the faithful ministry of Samuel. As they fall into open profligacy, he grows in grace before God and man.

They are 'sons of Belial', *i.e.* degraded men. They
lack the basis of all true religion, knowledge of Yahweh
(*cf.* Os 4:1 ; 6:9), and being ignorant of his character,
they completely misunderstand
him and to his people. Their
They robbed the people by t
share of the sacrifice allotted
Between the offering and the
they intervened to procure '
rupting and profaning the offe
Their father rebuked their con
same sacred surroundings wl
degenerated into criminals we
Samuel's growth : his physica
mother must have observed
to Shiloh ; his moral growth,
the approval of Yahweh and l
growth, 3:19–21, when the re
him apart as God's prophet tc
ephod ' : there are three kin
in the OT. The special epl
priest (Ex 28:6 ff.), the garmc
occasionally by others taking
monies (22:18 ; 2 Kg 6:14)
which was some kind of litur
cover the divine will (Jg 8:2
the Heb. word *mᵉîl* is used of
worn by people of eminence.
. . . went ' : the Heb. sugg
peated or customary. 25. '
the crimes of Heli's sons wei
whom sacrifices were meant
outrage. 'the Lord would
ordinary graces would triur
positions, and their impeniter
them more and more unwo
the punishments God had
Rom 9:18.

27–36 Rejection of Heli's
God ' : a title given to m
Moses, Samuel, Elias. T
questions are merely empha
ments. 'in the house of Ph
to Pharaoh's house '. 29.
dishonour. Klostermann ai
reconstruction of the MT t
LXX, which has ' look upo
meaning is much the same.
Lord ' : God had promisec
all its branches that they sh
sanctuary ; but now the de
account of the outrageous
31. 'Cut off thy arm ' :
LXX applies the threat to
partial fulfilment of this w
slaughter of the priests at
rival ' : in the person of
would be most prosperous,
hood pass into another fa
deposition of Abiathar und
34. 'a sign to thee ' : the
prediction will be a terrible
of the remainder. 35. 'a
mentators see in this a
posterity remained in office
(1 Par 6:8), and the phi
evidently presupposes the
36. 'to somewhat of the
dants of Heli will be red
beggars, anxious to share
of the sanctuary to earn e
III:1–21 Call of Samuel
Heli's House—1. ' was p
significance of Samuel's
shows that in the degene
few revelations made to Is
3. ' Before the lamp of Gc
lit every night and burn
Samuel's vision must the

---

before daybreak. 'slept in the temple ' : the sanctuary **250a**
of Shiloh is called ' temple ' as in 1:9. Samuel did not
sleep literally inside the ' temple ' but in some room
k. 7. 'did not yet know the Lord ' : he
ike every pious Israelite, but not by any
elation. 11. 'both his ears shall tingle ' :
had been struck by a sudden blow. This
used by Jer 19:3, who also compares the
of Jerusalem to the destruction of Shiloh (Jer
' I will begin ' : not a single detail of God's
s will be omitted—his threats will be carried
ery end. 13. 'did not chastise them ' : he
them, but failed to remove them from those
actions which were the occasions of their
is he failed as father, high-priest, and Judge
17. 'May God do so and so ' : Samuel
n wounding one he loved and revered, and
es him by oath to tell everything. This
found only in the Books of Kings and Ruth.
me from the ceremony of slaying a victim
ath was taken, in which the parties prayed
te of the victim might be theirs, if their oath
n. 18. ' It is the Lord ' : when it is too late
s will, Heli at least loyally resigns himself to
Not one of his words fell ' : God ratified and
ted his prophetical mission to Israel, so that
were recognized to be true. 20. ' from Dan
e ' : from the most northerly town in Israel
e (Beersheba) in the extreme south, *i.e.* the
untry accepted Samuel as the accredited
f Yahweh.

War with the Philistines—This is the first **b**
of the Philistines in the Bks of Kg. They
ady well known in the Aegean world, includ-
asts of Asia Minor, and attempted a landing
yptian coast as early as 1190 B.C., at the time
es III. Some of them seem to have entered
ian imperial service and were used to garrison
points along the coast of Palestine, over which
ll claimed to exercise formal suzerainty. For
tailed information about their relation to
nd Palestine as well as the problem of their
gins, *cf.* *Garstang, *Joshua Judges* (London,
4, 311 ff.), and *W. J. Phythian-Adams,
he Origins ' in BBSAJ Bulletin No. 3 (1923)
n the small land of Palestine, it was almost
e that the two great waves of Philistine and
immigration should come into conflict.
t us fetch . . . the ark ' : In Num 10:35 we read **c**
Ark was carried in battle and the same was
he siege of Jericho (Jos 3:4). On this occasion
nd mechanical trust in the material presence
rk was disastrous. There was a similar false
the Temple in the days of Jeremias (Jer 7:4).
two sons of Heli ' : mentioned here because
e is involved in that of the Ark. 6. 'Hebrews ' :
e called Hebrews here as is generally the case
reigners speak of the Israelites (29:3) or when
s were contrasted with foreigners (13:7). 13.
at upon a stool ' : LXX 'Sat by the gate
g the road '—probably the gate of the sanc-
s in 1:9. 18. ' when he named the Ark of God ' :
slaughter, personal bereavement mounted up
e unbearable climax—the Ark of God is taken.
habod ' : ' Without glory ', for the visible sign
s presence in Israel had gone leaving them in
ss and despair—a fitting name for the son of the
hiefly responsible for the disaster.

The Ark among the Philistines—1. Azotus was **d**
the five cities of the Philistine confederation.
thers are mentioned later, Geth, 8, and Accaron,
. Dagon was the favourite Philistine god (Jg
. If the name has a Semitic root, it may mean
'. The fertile land of Philistia would fit the idea
rshipping a ' corn-god '. 6. ' afflicted Azotus ' :
nly was their national god humiliated before
eh, but the people also suffered from emerods or
and possibly from an outbreak of something like
ubonic plague. 8. 'lords of the Philistines ' : the

1 KINGS V

250d chiefs of the five Philistine cities, though enjoying independent authority over their own districts, were united in a defensive and offensive alliance. They set up a combined council of state to meet the emergency which had arisen. Their official title of 'Seren' is preserved in the MT.

e **VI:1-VII:1 Return of the Ark**—The epidemic of disease in the Philistine cities due to the presence of the Ark struck the Philistines with panic. At first they were determined to keep this great trophy of victory at all costs within their own territory, but the scourge of Yahweh's wrath impelled them to send it away with votive offerings of appeasement.

f 1. 'in the land of the Philistines': LXX adds 'their land swarmed with mice'. 3. 'empty': they must make some compensating offering for the infringement of Yahweh's rights. 5. 'golden mice': Hitzig, Wellhausen, and Dhorme agree against Smith that these golden mice were symbols of the pestilence. Smith says there is no analogous Hebrew case. But it is a question of finding analogies amongst other heathen people, and there is abundant evidence for this kind of practice (cf. Dhorme, 59). 7. 'shut up their calves': the natural instinct of cattle would make them stay with their calves. If they went away over the Israelite frontier, it would be a sign of some overriding divine compulsion. **12.** Bethsames: the site of Bethshemesh is now identified with the modern mound of Ain-Shems in the vale of Sorec, and as its name implies, it was a centre of sun-worship. **19.** 'he slew of the men of Bethsames': as it stands the text suggests that the mere looking at the Ark was a profanation punishable by death. Certainly all irreverent curiosity about the Ark was strictly forbidden (cf. Num 4:19 f.) More probably in this case the real reason is stated in the LXX text: 'The sons of Jeconias rejoiced not with the men of Bethshemesh when they saw the Ark'. Through lack of all religious feeling, they did not enter into the spirit of rejoicing which the Bethsamites displayed and were punished for their apathy. 'fifty thousand' obviously a gloss based on a corrupt text. LXX has 'seventy'. **20.** 'this holy God': different aspects of the divine nature are expressed in the Bible by the word 'holy'. Here it means that God's transcendent majesty and zeal for his honour are the objects of man's awestruck adoration, before which he is convicted of sin. **21.** Cariathiarim: 'city of forests'—a town some nine miles north of Bethshemesh, near the modern village of Qaryat el-Enab. Here the Ark remained for twenty years till removed to Jerusalem by David. The fact that no attempt was made to send it to Shiloh seems to imply that Shiloh had already been destroyed by the Philistines; cf. P. Nagle, 'De prima Siluntis destructione effossionibus recentibus illustrata' in *Antonianum* 6 (1931) 401-416. Cariathiarim had a large Canaanite population and could be regarded by the Philistines as neutral territory. The Philistines would be satisfied with preventing the rebuilding of Shiloh as a sanctuary for what they considered to be the symbol of their victory over the Israelites. In this way the Ark fell into comparative obscurity and explains why Saul and Samuel seem to have had little to do with it during this period. **VII:1.** 'they sanctified Eleazar': they set him apart to be keeper of the Ark.

251a **VII:2-17 Samuel as Reformer and Liberator**—During this period of national disgrace Samuel was not idle. He acted as Judge in the political sphere and as Levite in the work of religious reformation. By defeat and oppression Israel's self-confidence had been shattered and its trust in Yahweh was at a dangerously low ebb. The mass of the people were preoccupied with problems of personal security and the necessities of daily life. They began to turn to the local cults of Baal and Astaroth who were the heathen patrons of bountiful harvests and abundant flocks. Their allegiance to Yahweh became divided and debased by idolatrous practices and other forms of religious syncretism. To counteract this Samuel strove to promote the pure worship of Yahweh and build up the political reorganization of Israel. This work led to a religious revival and the defeat of the Philistines at Eben ha-ezer.

2. 'Israel rested': MT has: 'mourned after the Lord'. The idea may be that Israel, like some wilful child whom its father has punished, kept following after God with tears of repentance and a longing for reconciliation. **3.** 'Baalim and Astaroth': the principal heathen gods and goddesses worshipped in Canaan. **5.** Masphath (Mizpah): 'The Watch-Tower'. Its conjectured site is Nebi Samwîl, on a mountain some five miles north-west of Jerusalem. It was suitable for religious gatherings and concentration of troops. 'I may pray for you': Samuel was a child of prayer and a man of prayer. He is linked with Moses himself as an example of powerful intercessory prayer (cf. Ps 98:6; Jer 15:1). **6.** 'poured it out before the Lord': no exact parallel to this rite can be found in the OT; but it must have symbolized, as the Targum points out, the outpouring of their hearts in repentance (cf. Lam 2:19). 'judged': acted as chief religious and civil magistrate. **7.** 'Philistines heard': they suspected a rising and determined to crush it at once. This would be easy, because the Israelites at their religious gathering were probably unarmed. **10.** 'they were overthrown': the sequel to Samuel's prayer and sacrifice showed that it was Yahweh who overthrew them; the Israelites merely completed the rout. **13.** 'did not come any more': i.e. during Samuel's personal rule as Judge. It is not applicable to the period of the monarchy. **14.** Amorrhites were among the old native inhabitants of Canaan. **15.** 'all the days of his life': must be understood in a qualified sense, for he appointed his sons judges, and Saul was king before Samuel's death. It claims that he always enjoyed great influence and authority in all civil and religious matters affecting the nation. 'aforesaid places': they are all within a twenty-mile radius from Jerusalem.

VIII:1-22 The Demand for a King—Hitherto Israel had been a theocracy pure and simple. God was its Invisible King. Yet the idea of human kingship in some form was not excluded completely from divine revelation. In Deut 17:14-20 we have the Law of the King. Junker (*Das Buch Deuteronomium*, Bonn, 1933, 81) and others consider that this text in its present form has been re-edited by a later scribe in the light of the actual history of the monarchy, but some of its substantial features may belong to a much earlier period. However in actual practice God did not raise up kings but exceptional individuals called judges to act as his instruments of deliverance and administration in times of crisis. Meanwhile various political crises, and the silent social revolution which followed the conquest of Canaan, were straining the religious fabric of the theocracy. Until things reached their breaking point in Samuel's day, the national consciousness of Yahweh's immediate kingly sway neutralized the abortive attempt at human kingship which took place under Gedeon.

Samuel himself must have felt the need of stability and permanence, for his appointment of his sons as judges was a break with tradition. It was a semi-concession to the new ideas that were gaining ground amongst the people. Once that compromise broke down through his sons' venality, and the Philistine menace reappeared, something had to be done. The less conservative Israelites were convinced that the only alternative to political anarchy was to set up a properly constituted monarchy. In their eyes there could be no *via media*. Hence their demand for a king such as other nations had. The whole tone of their demand, the ideal they had formed of their type of king—like that of other nations—showed a purely earthly concept of the inner spirit and privileges of the theocracy. Those who made it implicitly voiced their weariness with theocratic government, as if the pressing calamities were the result not of their own faithlessness to God, but of some flaw in God's rule. Their attitude was a

310

c denial of all that their history should have taught them. They asked for a king like other nations, without reference to their unique religious vocation which alone constituted their true greatness for the history of mankind (*cf.* Leimbach, 43 ; Kittel, *Geschichte*, II, 80). **d** Apart from his own personal feelings in the matter, it was enough to fill Samuel's mind with forebodings, and many a far-sighted patriot must have shared his misgivings. Egypt, Edom, Moab, Assyria, and other nations round Israel had monarchic government. Their worldly prosperity and military efficiency were often the product of violence and despotism, which would be directly opposed to the sturdy independent spirit of the Israelite tribes. It seemed the height of imprudence and ingratitude to overthrow the traditional form of government and embark unreservedly upon a controvertible experiment at a critical moment in their history. If Moses could make them a great nation without becoming king, there was nothing to prevent Yahweh from renewing his past mercies to Israel, provided they sought the solution of their difficulties in loyalty to his rule instead of dabbling in new systems of government. Samuel therefore gave the people one last warning. A king would claim the rights of a typical oriental despot. He would dispose of their property, conscript them for forced labour, and levy excessive taxes (*cf.* I Kg 22:7, 17 ; 3 Kg 21:1-16 ; 5:13-18 ; 12:4 for instances where such abuses eventually happened). Political and social freedom could hardly survive in such an atmosphere.

This sombre account of the institution of the monarchy must have expressed the feelings of those Hebrews who viewed the kingship with disfavour. Probably later redactors who witnessed the melancholy tragedies of so many kings gave additional emphasis to the accounts, especially in 8:1-22 and 10:17-24. On the other hand chh 9-10:16 adopt a more favourable view of Israelite kingship. Naturally these political preferences are likely to have had a double repercussion on the sacred narratives. Yet it must not be forgotten that this double view of the monarchy expresses more than the respective preferences of later writers—it expresses something that was inherent in the historical situation itself (*cf.* Ricciotti, *Storia d'Israele* I, 320 f.). In the end God gave them a king, but not kingship incompatible with the very nature of the theocracy. The divine sanction is seen in the method of election by lot which left the designation of the candidate in the hands of God, and in the other sacred ceremonies, especially of anointing, which hallowed the kingdom as the medium through which the mercy-covenant of Yahweh could still attain its ends. **e** 2. Joel : ' Yahweh is God '. Abia : ' Yahweh is my father '. 4. ' elders ' : the official spokesmen of the people ; it was therefore an official deputation to Samuel, not simply a matter of popular outcry.

2a **IX:1-26 The Meeting of Saul and Samuel**—A providential meeting of the two men who held the key to the national crisis of their day. Saul, son of Cis, of the small and warlike tribe of Benjamin, was searching for some lost donkeys. Samuel who is mentally searching for the nation's future leader, meets him at a sacrificial meal at Ramatha and arouses Saul's mind to thoughts of a higher destiny. **b** 2. Saul : Heb. *Šā'ûl*—' Asked ', *i.e.* of God. Between Saul in the OT and Saul in the NT (Ac 7:57) this name became the most outstanding in the history of the tribe of Benjamin. Unlike Saul of the NT (*cf.* 2 Cor 10:10) the OT Saul had a very impressive presence—he looked every inch a king (*cf.* 9:2). 9. ' Prophet . . . Seer ' : for the meaning of these two terms, *cf.* § 409 *f*. 12. ' high place ' : *bāmāh* (plur. *bāmôt*) always denotes a place of worship. Originally this term may have been applied exclusively to a sanctuary built upon a hill or mountain, but it was applied to other places of sacrifice, *e.g.* in the valley of Hinnom, Jer 7:31. Generally speaking these high places are expressly condemned in the Bible as being places of idolatrous or illicit worship. Here the term is not used in this pejorative sense. There was no

central sanctuary for Israelite worship at the time and **252b** Samuel was simply carrying out the spirit of the Mosaic law, Ex 20:24. 15. ' revealed to the ear ' : lit. ' uncovered his ear '. A metaphor used to describe someone pulling aside the usual eastern headdress the better to whisper a secret into a person's ear. 20. ' as for the asses ' : *i.e.* why need you worry about three paltry asses, since the best of everything in Israel will be yours ? 21. ' a son of Jemini ', *i.e.* a Benjamite.

27-X 8 Saul is anointed King—The earliest mention **c** of anointing as a piece of court ceremonial occurs in Syrian territory about the sixteenth century B.C. during the period of Egyptian suzerainty over Syria. In Israel anointing had hitherto been reserved to priests. It should be noted that Saul is anointed privately in 10:1 as *Nâgîd* ' Prince '. In 10:24 he is publicly elected as King and then confirmed in his position after his Ammonite victory, 11:14 f. The history of the anointing of Israelite kings shows that it was a sacred rite used under divine inspiration and administered by God's representative to inculcate (*a*) the dedication of the king to Yahweh ; (*b*) the outpouring of Yahweh's Spirit upon him to fit him for his arduous duties ; (*c*) to set the seal of divine blessing upon his reign and mark his person as sacred. Although the sum total of Messianic hope is not limited to the picture of an ideal theocratic king, yet it is significant that in men's minds all such promises have entwined themselves round the title ' Messias '—' the Anointed '. With the unction of the Holy Ghost (Ac 10:38), he was fitted to rule the everlasting kingdom of Yahweh.

X 1. ' prince ' : Probably in Samuel's mind this was **d** not an unconditional anointing to kingly dignity. For the present Saul was made leader of the people in the struggle against the Philistines. ' shall be a sign ' : Samuel promised Saul three significant signs as confirmation of his new dignity : (*a*) the lost asses would be found ; (*b*) at Tabor men would offer him part of their sacrificial gifts to God ; (*c*) the spirit of prophecy would come upon him. The first sign was to convince him that he really was King by God's will, the second that as King it was partly as God's representative and subordinate to him, and the third that he must be King with the help of God's Spirit. 3. ' going up to God ' : to offer sacrifice. By giving Saul part of the sacrifice the men unconsciously paid tribute to the new dignity Yahweh had conferred on him. 6. ' thou shalt prophesy ' : not in the sense of predicting the future, but of giving enthusiastic expression to religious feelings in hymns and praises. 12. ' Who is their father ? ' : Saul's neighbours expressed surprise that he should now be numbered among the ' prophets ' ; on the nature of these prophets see § 410*c*. An onlooker rebukes them by asking who is the father of the other prophets, *i.e.* parentage and heredity have little to do with the free outpouring of God's gifts. The people of Nazareth were likewise surprised at the words and works of Christ, Mt 13:54-7.

X 17-27 Saul's Public Election—This account is a **e** continuation of 8:22. 25. ' law of the kingdom ' : Dhorme, 90, and Smith, 74, consider this to be ' the custom of the king ' already mentioned in 8:9-19. Leimbach, 52, thinks it was a legal document in the style of Deut 17:14-20, binding both king and people.

XI 1-15 Saul's Victory over Ammon : he is acclaimed f by the People—Probably the expedition against the Ammonites took place before Saul's election described in 10:17-25. For 12:12 presupposes an Ammonite invasion before Saul was made king. If this is so, then his success and popularity may have convinced Samuel that Saul had indeed won his spurs.

1. Jabes Galaad : the capital town of Gilead, east of **g** the Jordan. The Ammonites occupied territory north of Moab in Transjordania. This is the first mention of them since their defeat by Jephte Jg 11:21. 5. ' following oxen ' : so Cincinnatus was ploughing when messengers came to offer him the dictatorship, Livy III, 12. 7. ' sent them ' : he sent the bleeding remains of the oxen like a fiery cross to the chieftains of Israel

252g with the grim threat against all who failed to follow him in the fight for their countrymen. **8.** Bezec : on the hills west of the Jordan and practically opposite Jabes Galaad. 'three hundred thousand' : as figures of the actual available fighting men these numbers are highly improbable, and are in striking contrast with the numbers mentioned in 13:15. They seem to be an addition made to the text when the division between Israel and Judah was an accomplished fact. **14.** 'renew the kingdom' : it was time to proceed with what we should call the coronation service. Those who had questioned the ability of the tall enthusiast of Benjamin had been reduced to silence by his victory. We have then three stages in the development of Saul's full kingship. He is privately anointed as 'Prince' in Ramah ; elected by lot at Maspha, but only partially acknowledged and finally acclaimed by all the people at Galgal. There may have been a public anointing, for LXX has 'and Samuel anointed Saul there to be king'.

h XII 1-25 Samuel's Farewell Address and Resignation—Israel stood at the threshold of a new era. Samuel was the living link between the past and the future. At this moment the greatness of his character and importance of his work stand out in clear relief. Long years of devotion to Yahweh and the religious needs of his age had made him a venerable and awe-inspiring figure— the last and greatest of the Judges. There could be no doubt of the sheer force and scrupulous integrity of the man even in the minds of those who asked for a change of government. He was an Israelite in whom there was no guile. Whatever the cost in personal suffering, once God's will was known, he would carry it out with all the unwearied energy at his command. This unflinching devotion to God's will made him the counsellor and friend of Saul in his early years, until a new need arose and he was ready to give all his support to the rising power of David. In this way his work did not end with his death but culminated in the final establishment of monarchy described in 2 Kg. Before resigning Samuel solemnly reviewed the past with its gracious revelations of Yahweh's loving-kindness. If Israel had co-operated with them, human sovereignty would have been superfluous. Now that kingship was an accomplished fact, he outlined the religious principles which must guide both king and people in the future and assured them of the protection of his intercession.

i 2. 'goeth before you' : like a shepherd walking before his flock. **3.** 'Speak of me' : put my life on trial —you take the part of accusers—let Yahweh and his Anointed be the Judges. **6.** 'It is the Lord' : LXX 'Yahweh is Witness'.

j XIII-XIV Saul's Wars of Independence and Early Reign—The account of Saul's early campaigns against the Philistines ends with an episodic list of similar wars with the Edomites to the south and Moabites to the south-east, and with certain Aramaean tribes in the north. We must not forget, however, that Saul's victory over the Philistines was not completely decisive. Local border raids and reprisal counter-attacks continued intermittently throughout his reign. The digression wedged into the narrative in 7-15a is an account of the preliminary breach between Saul and Samuel. It prepares us for his final rejection in ch 15. Saul's lack of faith blinded him to the fact that his extremity was God's opportunity and his impatience must not set aside the supreme thing in life—God's will.

k XIII 1. 'a child of one year' : an obvious absurdity due to some copyist's error. We have no means of recovering the original number save by conjecture. The whole verse is lacking in the more important Gk MSS. **2.** Machmas : about 7 miles north-east of Jerusalem. **3.** 'smote the garrison' : the Heb. word *neṣîb* which DV translates 'garrison' is kept as a proper name in LXX as if it denoted the resident Philistine official of the fortress. 'Philistines had heard of it' : LXX gives grounds for reading 'the Philistines heard (the report), saying, the slaves (or, the Hebrews) have

revolted'. '**5.** 'thirty thousand' : the numbers need **2**revision. So many chariots in mountainous country would have been useless. Lucian's recension and the Gk codd. 83, 93, 108, give the number as 3,000. **7.** 'some of the Hebrews' : LXX 'they that went over crossed the Jordan to the land of Gad'. Many fled into Transjordania because they had lost all confidence. **8.** 'he waited' : Saul was chosen by God to free God's people, but not to act till duly commissioned by God's representative to do so. **13.** 'Thou hast done foolishly' : the penalty may seem excessive at first sight, but the whole principle of theocratic kingship was at stake. Saul in a moment of crisis chose to act *auto*cratically and not *theo*cratically. It was this inner weakness that led to the great tragedy of his life. **15.** 'Samuel arose' : a clause, fallen out of MT, should be restored from LXX : 'And Samuel arose and went up from Galgal and went his way, and the rest of the people went after Saul to meet the men of war and came from Galgal to Geba of Benjamin'. **17.** 'three companies' : the first group went north, the second west, and the third eastwards. Saul and Jonathan still barred the way to the south. The Philistines may have hoped to entice them out of their strongholds. **20.** 'down to the Philistines' : proof of the unarmed state of the Israelites. They could sharpen ordinary tools, but for any work which required a forge they had to apply to the Philistine authority.

XIV 4. 'The name of the one was Boses' : this means **l** 'shining' and refers to the gleaming chalky surface at the top of the cliff. *Sene* means 'the thorny' and may refer to the acacia trees in the district. **6.** 'It is easy for the Lord : *cf.* the noble words of Judas Maccabeus before the Battle of Beth-horon (1 Macc 3:16–21). **12.** 'will show you a thing' : a piece of provocative bantering. **18.** 'Ark' : read with LXX 'Ephod' instead of Ark. The Ark was still at Cariathiarim and was not used as an oracle of consultation. **19.** 'Draw in thy hand' : Saul characteristically interrupts the consultation, too impatient to wait for knowledge of the divine will. **21.** 'the Hebrews' are distinguished from the Israelites. Those who had been conscripted by the Philistines would be called Hebrews by their masters. **27.** 'eyes were enlightened' : lit. 'sparkled', *i.e.* shone as renewed strength spread through his exhausted body. **31.** 'from Machmas to Ailon' : gives the course of the battle—from Machmas in the north, then westwards to Bethaven, then down the pass of Bethhoron to Ailon in the plain of Philistia.

XV 1-35 Amalecite Campaign and Rejection of Saul— **2**For centuries there had been a legacy of hatred between Israel and Amalec. They had fought against Israel at Raphidim and God's judgement on them was recorded in Ex 17:14 : 'I will destroy the memory of Amalec from under heaven'. They were a rapacious and cruel people. **2 ff.** Samuel mentions some of their king Agag's recent brutalities. Ruthless severity was the only argument such a barbarous people could understand. It was a holy war and the *ḥerem* or sacred ban was to be applied in all its rigour. This meant that all living creatures were to be slain in honour of Yahweh as had been the fate of Jericho and Achan, Jos 6 ff. Here Saul was weighed in the balance and found wanting. At the beginning of his career he seemed to justify the hopes that had been placed in him. He was tall, endowed with manly strength, courageous, simple in his tastes and manner of life in contrast to the luxury and magnificence of later kings. He created the beginnings of a standing army and increased the sense of national unity. These were valuable foundations for the later achievements of David. In religion he was a rugged and simple-minded follower of Yahweh, and died in battle against the uncircumcised enemies of his people. At first his impassive, stolid, moody character must have left an unfavourable impression on some onlookers. 'How shall this man save us ?' (10:27). But the Spirit of God soon set his heart aflame with power and enthusiasm to fulfil his great destiny as first king of Israel. That new kingdom was the master-

3a ambition which gave meaning to his life. Yet his imperious self-will, his impetuous rashness, and wilful disobedience led him to grasp at the shadow of an earthly kingdom and miss the underlying principle of true theocratic rule. The threats of Samuel whom he loved, the rise of David, the misfortunes that were gathering around him gradually reduced his mind to a psychopathological state of remorse, fear, suspicion, obstinacy, excitability, and cruelty. The night before he died, in the witch's cave at Endor, he heard the sentence of his doom from the man who had anointed him king.

b 3. 'utterly destroy' : the Heb. means 'to devote', and what was devoted to Yahweh was withdrawn from common use and might not be taken as spoil. The same idea of exclusive dedication can be seen in the word 'harem'. 6. The Cinites (Kenites) belonged to the tribe of Moses' father-in-law and were old allies of Israel. 11. 'Samuel was grieved' : MT has 'he was angry'—deeply upset at the course of events. His sympathy was still with Saul and he cried to Yahweh with protests and intercession, but in vain. 16. 'Suffer me' : Heb. has 'stop'. Samuel cuts short his excuses. 22. 'Doth the Lord' : the whole of this rebuke is couched in poetical rhythm like a prophetical oracle. It summarizes much of the teaching of later prophets like Amos, Osee, Micheas, and Isaias, and is taken up by the greatest of the Prophets in Mt 9:13 ; 12:7. 28. 'The Lord has rent thy kingdom' : the accident was turned by Samuel into a parable ; cf. Ahias' symbolical action 3 Kg 11:30 ff. 29. 'the triumpher in Israel' : a title given to God in this passage only. 30. 'Honour me now' : he still clings to the external honours of his position. 35. 'Samuel mourned for Saul' : Saul must ever remain one of the greatest figures in human tragedy. There is pathos in his story as he is summoned to fill a position to which he proves unequal—a story of brilliant beginnings, failure, sudden outbursts of goodness and badness with utter desolation at the end.

c **XVI 1-XVIII 5 David's Introduction to Public Life**——Of David's Heb. name Dāwiḏ it is not possible to give a certain derivation. The principal sources for his history are to be found in 1 Kg 16–3, Kg 2. Further details are given in 1 Par 2–3 ; Ruth 4:17–22 and in some of the titles of the Psalms. Just as we have had two complementary accounts of the institution of the monarchy, so in the same way we seem to have a two-fold source for some of the facts of David's life, e.g. the killing of the giant Goliath and the apparently double account of David's introduction to public life. In ch 16 David is a shepherd lad specially skilled in music who is recommended to Saul and becomes his page. In ch 17 he is absent from court in time of war, and only accidently becomes known to Saul and Abner. To reconcile these differences it has been pointed out that (a) 17:15 implies that David went freely to and from his home, and therefore did not reside permanently at court. David may have been summoned at long intervals when the king was actually suffering from a fit of melancholy. If Saul was abstracted with his own gloomy thoughts, he might easily fail to recognize him at a later date ; (b) the fact that the sacred writer calls him 'armour-bearer' in 16:21 proves very little, because it is quite consistent with the style of a Hebrew historian to make this statement by way of anticipation ; (c) the questions in 17:55–58, it should be noted, concern David's parentage rather than David himself and Abner may not have previously troubled about the family history of a minstrel boy ; (d) LXX in Vatican Codex B differs from the present MT by omitting 17:12–31, 41, 50, 55–58 ; 18:1–5, 10 f., 17–19, and by itself forms a complete account without any of the difficulties implied in the MT. Yet the LXX itself may have resorted to a harmonistic treatment of the text precisely to remove these inconsistences. Ricciotti prefers to hold that the account comes from two complementary sources. The compiler of these two sources presupposes that his readers already know the full

details and makes a selection of the more important **253c** facts which unfortunately are insufficient for us to dogmatize on the exact relation between them.

16:1-13 David's Secret Anointing—Samuel is divinely **d** instructed to anoint one of Isai's sons as successor to the rejected Saul. To safeguard the secrecy of his errand, Yahweh tells Samuel to hold a religious gathering in the district. Contrary to all expectation Yahweh's choice falls on the youngest son David. He was the man according to God's heart, cf. 3 Kg 15:3, 11 ; 4 Kg 14:3 ; 18:3. His life as a whole can be said to justify such an epitaph. His magnetic personality and achievements bear the stamp of real greatness. He began life as a shepherd lad, and became musician, poet, hero of a hundred battles, outlaw, prophet, loyal friend, true patriot, devoted father, noble king, saint and sinner whose words and deeds have altered history. In spite of the obvious mistakes and failures of his life, Yahweh's honour and the glory of Israel are the real mainspring behind it all. He always understood the religious foundation of his kingly office, and was able to bring national and religious unity to Israel. In many incidents of courage, humility, unselfishness, wisdom, and tenderness he has won the affection and gratitude of men in a way that not even the shadows of sin can ever wholly destroy. His isolated unworthy deeds are forgotten and forgiven when we see him conscious of the greatness of Almighty God, thirsting after glimpses of his beauty, awe-struck before his inscrutable judgements and filled with gratitude at the immensity of his loving kindness. That, we feel, is the true David who won the heart of God.

1. 'Isai the Bethlehemite' : a grandson of Ruth the **e** Moabitess and a native of Bethlehem of the tribe of Judah, about six miles south of Jerusalem. 5. 'Be ye sanctified' : this involved purification from all ceremonial defilement. 7. 'man seeth' : while Samuel was musing within his own mind (wayyōmer is sometimes used in this sense of 'saying to oneself'), Yahweh warns him that the unseen qualities of the mind and heart rather than bodily appearance are the causes of the divine choice. 12. 'beautiful to behold and of a comely face' : lit. 'with beautiful eyes and good in appearance'. Fair skin and fine eyes are rare enough in hot countries of the East. 13. 'anointed him' : the full significance of this was hidden from his family. They may have imagined it meant that David was simply to be Samuel's closest friend at the sacrifice.

14-23 David at the Court of Saul—As Saul brooded **254a** over his broken life, his mistakes, and his loss of Samuel's friendship which had been the pledge of divine support, a sense of futility and helplessness plunged his mind into the depths of despair. Yahweh withdrew his grace and a melancholy akin to diabolic possession reduced him to fits of depression bordering on madness. David was chosen to soothe Saul by his music.

17. 'can play well' : the power of music to restore **b** the harmony of the mind is well known. 18. 'prudent in his words' : eloquent and tactful. These qualities and his attractive appearance and a certain invincible winning charm which God gave him, coupled with a unique spiritual force, are partly the foundations of his future greatness. 22. 'David stand before me' : as a court attendant. Here David would see the leaders who were determining the course of Israel's history, and gain an insight into the nation's needs.

XVII 1-58 David and Goliath—The Philistines in- **c** vaded Judah and marched in a north-west direction up the valley of Elah (i.e. 'the terebinth') to Socho, now Shuweikeh, W. of Bethlehem on the road to Gaza. The Israelites encamped on the eastern, the Philistines on the western slopes of the valley. As already noted 12–30 are not found in Codex B of the LXX and have the marks of an independent story.

4. 'Six cubits and a span' : about ten feet. This giant **d** may have been a descendant of the old race of Anakim (Jos 11:21, 22). 8. 'a Philistine' : lit. the Philistine— the official representative of my people. 17. 'fru-

254d menty ' : unripe ears of corn roasted. **20.** ' place of Magala ' : the Heb. root of this word suggests something round. It may refer to some kind of entrenchment or barricade round the camp. **28.** ' was angry with David ' : Eliab jealously accuses David of neglect of duty and arrogance. **29.** ' not cause to speak ? ' : LXX and Vg ' numquid non verbum est ? ' have given rise to two interpretations. Some take it to mean ' Can I not ask a harmless question ? ' Klostermann and Schlögl prefer ' was there not every reason for my conduct ? ' **32.** According to LXX this text stands in close connexion with v 11. **45.** ' in the name of the Lord ' : it was not only a question of skill against brute strength, but a struggle between the might of paganism and the absolute trust of the true worshipper of Yahweh. **47.** ' the Lord saveth ' : a lesson emphasized in both OT and NT ; Ps 43:6, 7 ; Os 1:7 ; 1 Cor 1:27. **51.** ' slew him ' : later (2 Kg 21:19) we shall deal with the account which seems to make Elhanan the killer of Goliath. **54.** ' brought it to Jerusalem ' : Jerusalem was still in the hands of the Jebusites. A little later we find Goliath's sword at Nobe, which was close to Jerusalem. It may be an anticipatory remark of a later redactor ; cf. 2 Kg 5:7. **55.** ' when Saul saw David ' : this whole section of Saul's inquiry is not in LXX (B).

e **XVIII 1-5 The Friendship of David and Jonathan**—Before the story of David's life darkens in an atmosphere of intrigue, rivalry, and bloodshed, we have a glimpse of an ennobling friendship between Jonathan, the heir-apparent, and David. These verses too are omitted by LXX (B).

f **1.** ' the soul of Jonathan ' : the same phrase is used of Jacob's love for Benjamin, Gen 44:30. **4.** ' Jonathan stripped himself ' : to ratify his bond of friendship and to show his public esteem for David.

g **6-30. Saul's Jealousy**—The main events of this later history of David's fortunes are preserved in LXX, though it omits 10–11, 17–19. MT tells how Saul's jealousy deepened into deadly hatred he tried himself to kill David and gave him promotion to expose him to new dangers. LXX continues and shows how Saul's daughter, Michol, being in love with David, Saul tried to use this love to ensure his death, but all in vain. 28b, 29b and 30 are not in LXX (B). **10.** ' Saul. . . prophesied ' : i.e. raved in a mad frenzy ; cf. § 410c. This incident may not give the psychological growth of Saul's enmity, but there is nothing incredible in this sudden outburst of passion in a man of Saul's character. **18.** ' what is my life ? ' : i.e. I am a poor man. What dowry can I offer for a princess ? **19.** ' Molathite ' : from Abel Mehola in the Jordan valley. **21.** ' In two things ' : the Heb. can only mean ' under two conditions ', but these are not specified. Klostermann and Schlögl emend MT and read ' in two years ', but this seems unwarranted. Others understand the phrase to have a caustic meaning, ' by the second ', i.e. by one at least of my daughters, thou shalt be my son-in-law.

h **XIX-XX Immediate Results of Saul's Jealousy**—These were open violence against David, a meeting with Samuel at Rama, and complete separation from his friend Jonathan. The kingship was not yet a well-established institution and each incident in David's career served as fuel for Saul's jealousy. David's victory over Goliath eclipsed Saul's own military prowess. His unique personal charm won the friendship of Saul's son, the love of his daughter, and the affection of his subjects. Many textual critics say that these chapters are late compilations by a redactor (R) from sources designated as E and J. No doubt such topics as Saul's jealousy, David's friendship with Jonathan, and Michol's love, were favourite themes of popular tradition and were incorporated by the redactor in different degrees into his book.

i **2.** ' Jonathan told David ' : it was difficult to know whether these outbursts of passion revealed Saul's true mind or were simply passing fits of madness. **11.** ' Saul sent his guards ' : we can join the phrase ' that night ' of

v 10, as LXX does, to 11, ' And it came to pass that **2a** night that Saul sent '. Smith, 178, conjectures that David's wedding night is intended, when he would be unsuspecting and his friends dispersed after the marriage feasting. In this way he accounts for the fact that in this section David seems unsuspicious of the king till warned by his wife. However, it may have been that David hoped to use Michol's influence with her father to calm his rage. The fragmentary condition of some of the accounts makes it difficult to assign the real chronological sequence of events. **13.** ' an image ' : MT has the plural ' Teraphim ', a kind of household charm in human shape, sometimes used for divination, Ez 21:19-22. Originally they were part of a fetish cult, but Michol may have regarded this image as nothing more than a household mascot, because she treated it with scant respect. **18.** ' Najoth ' : the word means ' dwellings ', a district near Rama, possibly the quarter of the town where the prophets lived in common to carry out their spiritual exercises under Samuel's direction. **24.** ' stripped himself also ' : the religious excitement of the prophets was contagious and affected Saul even more than it had affected his messengers so that he cast off his outer garments and lay helpless on the ground. This was to teach him that in contending against David he was contending against a Spirit that could override the petty schemes of men. The memory of this extraordinary event must have encouraged and convinced David that he was under divine protection. ' Is Saul ' : the old proverb about Saul 10:12 receives a new lease of life under circumstances which must have been a sad reminder to Saul of graces he had lost.

XX 1. ' came to Jonathan ' : if, as some commentators **j** think, 1a ' David fled from Najoth ' is only an editorial addition, this section may precede 19 chronologically. If not, then it shows David's unwillingness to give up hope till absolutely forced to do so and he may have thought Jonathan might effect a reconciliation. **5.** ' is the new moon ' : a religious festival ; cf. § 113d. **8.** ' covenant of the Lord ' : David's pact of friendship with Jonathan had been witnessed and ratified by Yahweh. **14.** ' If I live ' : the whole scene is full of the most noble-hearted friendship and there is pathos in the thought that Jonathan could foresee the downfall of his house and the rise of David. **19.** ' The stone called Ezel ' : the name ' Stone of Departure ' may have been given to it later. LXX ' Beside yonder heap of stones '. **23.** ' concerning the word ' : the pact of friendship we have just made. **26.** ' not clean ' : had incurred some ceremonial defilement. **30.** ' Saul being angry ' : Saul burst out into coarse abuse and the sting of the insult lay in the insinuation that Jonathan was no true son of his. **37.** ' is there further ' : Jonathan's loud cry to the boy who had actually reached the place of the arrow had no real reference to the exact position of the arrow. It was meant to make sure that David understood the significance of the sign they had agreed upon.

XXI-XXVII 32 David the Outlaw—Throughout this **2b** period David was not a rebel and never set himself up as a rival claimant to the throne. It was a time during which he grew to physical and spiritual maturity. Dangers, difficulties, and suffering taught him the great lesson of complete dependence on God—a lesson which Saul never learnt and which was essential to a ruler of a theocratic kingdom. Moreover his experience and training in military strategy and his leadership of armed men were invaluable preparations for future successes against the enemies of his kingdom. At first his band of followers numbered only 400. Two hundred more joined him when he returned to Judah from Moab. In 1 Par 12:1-22 we have a list of others who came later. David met with complete success in the end partly through his own daring exploits and shrewdness, but principally through the overruling Providence of God. It is quite possible that single stories of David's adventures as an outlaw existed in separate texts, and that these were threaded together in different ways, e.g. the

a flight to Nobe could be connected immediately with 19:17 or 19:18a.

b XXI David's Flight to Nobe and Geth—1. Nobe : a priestly town a little to the north of Jerusalem and the resting-place of the Tabernacle which has not been mentioned since Heli's days. David fled thither to obtain weapons and provisions and also to find out the divine will. Achimelech : the great-grandson of Heli. All the signs of hurried flight filled him with misgivings. 2. 'The King hath commanded me' : to allay suspicion, David pretends to be on a secret mission for Saul. 4. 'holy bread' : the Shewbread or the 'Presence-Bread' ; cf. § 194b. Only the priests are allowed to partake of it. Our Lord quoted this incident Mt 12:3 f. to show that ceremonial law must give way to man's necessity. 5. 'David answered the priest' : he settled the priest's scruples by assuring him that both the persons of his followers and their baggage for carrying the bread were in accord with liturgical law. 'this way is defiled' : the versions give us little help in solving the obscurities of this passage. The general sense seems to be : ' In all my expeditions (when there is danger of defilement) my followers observe ritual purity ; how much more so in carrying out this present business of the king '. 10. Achis : David hoped for safety in the territory of Israel's traditional enemy. It has been maintained that this first visit to Achis is a duplicate account of his second visit to the same prince. The two visits, however, are clearly distinct, and the treatment experienced on each occasion was quite different. A practically defenceless exile was a different person from the leader of a large band of reckless and well-armed adventurers offering their services in war. 11. ' king of the land ' : the courtiers repeat the exaggerated rumours which exalted David above Saul in popular estimation. 13. ' stumbled against the door ' : LXX has ' drummed on the doors of the gate '. He battered against the doors like a raving lunatic. As lunatics were held in special awe in the East, as being possessed by some powerful spirit, David was immune from attack.

c XXII 1-5 David at Odollam—David hurried farther south towards the home of his boyhood, to the stronghold of Odollam, some twelve miles SW. of Bethlehem. It was in Canaanite territory and within reach of his kinsmen in the south. He was joined by a mixed group of clansmen, malcontents, outcasts, and adventurers from neighbouring tribes and kingdoms. For safety's sake he placed his parents amongst the Moabites, because Jesse was the grandson of Ruth the Moabitess. Against David were the veteran troops of the royal army and the prestige of legal authority behind them, but probably the sympathies of the Judaean peasantry were with David, and as long as he acted on the defensive, the lives of his men were safe.

d 3. Maspha of Moab : mentioned here only. Jewish tradition claims that David's parents were murdered by the king of Moab and that David exacted signal vengeance on them in his later conquest of Moab, 2 Kg 8:2. 5. Gad : the first mention of this prophet who was to become the friend, counsellor, and chronicler of David's reign.

e 6-23 Saul's Vengeance on the Priests at Nobe— David's falsehood to the priests at Nobe had fatal consequences. Doeg, the Iago of Hebrew history, told Saul all he had seen there. Achimelech and his house were charged with high-treason and ordered to be slain. No one but the Syrian Doeg could be induced to carry out this sacrilegious murder ; cf. 9. Abiathar alone escaped and told David. The doom on Heli's house was being fulfilled, but in fulfilling it Saul was destroying his own. One by one the better elements of his court were being antagonized and forced to leave it. Shiloh had been destroyed, the Ark was at Cariathiarim, and as Abiathar fled with the Ephod, Saul had no legitimate means of communicating with God.

f 7. ' said to his servants ' : a sarcastic speech designed to arouse their tribal jealousy. ' You expect David, a hunted freebooter to give you more than I do, who am

your kinsman !'. 9. ' Doeg was chief ' : better with LXX, ' Doeg the Syrian who was set over Saul's mules ', **255f** which explains his presence at court. 15. ' Did I begin today ? ' : he pleaded that he was accustomed to act in this way for one whom he regarded as the king's favourite. 19. ' children and sucklings ' : a deed of cruel vengeance which he did not attempt to do against a heathen nation at God's command, 15:3, he now carries out against an innocent city of his own kingdom.

XXIII 1-28 Saul Seeks David's Life at Maon— Though technically a rebel, David was recognized as **g** loyal to the Hebrew cause. Ceila was raided by the Philistines and David went to the rescue. The ingratitude of the inhabitants forced him to flee from Saul to the wilderness of Ziph. During the period of pursuit Jonathan and David met for the last time.

1. Ceila : three miles south of Odollam. ' the barns ' : **h** these raids took place after the harvest when the corn was stacked ready for threshing. 11. ' Will the men of Ceila ' : it was ungrateful, but David's band of freebooters may have been a heavy burden on the resources of the citizens. Philistine pillage had been exchanged for exactions of another kind. Moreover, they probably feared to share the fate that had befallen the citizens of Nobe. 15. ' the desert of Ziph ' : the wild country between the mountains of Judah and the Dead Sea. 16. ' strengthened his hands in God ' : reminded him of God's promises and renewed his courage. 18. ' his house ' : at Gabaa. 19. Hachila : a hill in the wilderness of Ziph, lying to the south of Jeshimon, or ' the Waste '. 23. ' thousands ' : i.e. families. The term is used in this sense also in 10:19 ; Jg 6:15 ; Jos 22:14. 24. Maon : a district some seven miles south of Hebron. 28. ' Rock of Division ' : because there Saul was, as it were, torn away from David, through the intervention of Providence.

XXIV 1-23 David Spares Saul's Life at Engaddi— **i** Ch 26 gives a similar incident which some commentators believe to be the same. The differences of scene, conversation, and other circumstances make this unlikely. On both occasions Saul owed his life to the man whom he was hounding to death. David showed himself the true conqueror who could, by his self-evident moral greatness, wring recognition and friendship from his bitterest enemy. Assassination was a quick way to the throne ; David chose the longer and surer way. His restraint revealed an ever-deepening insight into the sacred character of ' Yahweh's Anointed ' which fitted him to become a type of that ideal in the future.

1. ' strongholds of Engaddi ' : on the western shores **j** of the Dead Sea. The district is honeycombed with caves. Coming in from the light into the intense darkness of the cave, Saul could be seen but could not see well himself. 6. ' David's heart struck him ' : even the slight indignity he had done to Saul caused him scruples of conscience. 8. ' stopped his men ' : lit. ' tore ' or ' lashed '—a strong expression to show that David restrained his men only with the greatest difficulty. 9. ' worshipped ' : made an act of reverence and homage in recognition of Saul's kingly dignity. 10. ' words of men ' : evidently David had enemies at court. Doeg was one. Chusi the Benjamite (Ps 7) was another. Such men inflamed Saul's already irritated mind by their baseless calumnies. 13. ' the Lord revenge me ' : David will not injure Saul, but if Saul persists in his persecution, then Yahweh will avenge such injustice. 14. A wicked heart produces evil. If my heart were evil, I should have killed you. 15. ' A dead dog ' : Saul brought out his army against an insignificant individual who could do him no harm. 17. ' my son David ' : a momentary gleam of the old affection for David broke through the cloud of suspicion. 21. ' now as I know ' : Samuel's words, 13:14, were still in his mind. He gives a practical proof that David will be king by exacting a promise that David would not kill Saul's family when the dynasty changed hands—a common practice of new oriental monarchs. 23. ' David and his men ' : that Saul

255j knew the divine will was no guarantee that he would not yet resist it.

k **XXV 1 Death of Samuel**—This has little connexion with what precedes or follows. The Israelites mourned for Samuel as they had mourned for Moses, Deut 34:8. He was the greatest figure since that time.

l **XXV 2-44 David, Nabal, and Abigail**—David's followers were largely dependent upon the hospitality of friendly clans, who in return were assured of protection against more dangerous marauders. Nabal, a mean boorish sheikh of the district of Carmel in Judah, refused to pay his tribute. The charm and wisdom of his beautiful wife saved David from murdering him. As a result of his debauched life and Abigail's account of David's intentions, Nabal had a fatal stroke and David married Abigail. In the course of the story we gain a valuable light on the way in which some sections of popular opinion regarded David's cause. Abigail's speech brings out the following facts. (*a*) Many Israelites knew that David was destined to be the future king of Israel. (*b*) His prudent and noble conduct had made a great impression on the people. (*c*) The people were convinced that he must wait God's own good time for the fulfilment of his promises.

m **2.** Maon : seven miles south of Hebron. Carmel : in the hill country of Judah, not that in north Palestine. **3.** Nabal : means 'fool' or 'reckless'. **15.** 'These men were very good': the justice of David's courteous demand is vouched for by Nabal's own men. **17.** 'no man can speak to him' : everyone was afraid of one of his ungovernable outbursts of rage. **18.** 'and took two hundred loaves' : great festivities usually marked these times of shearing and abundance of choice supplies would be at hand. **29.** 'as in the bundle of the living' : his life was like something precious carefully wrapped up and treasured by Yahweh. The lives of his enemies would be cast away like stones from a sling, signifying complete rejection. **31.** 'a scruple of heart' : restraint now will ensure the absence of remorse later, and David will come to the throne with no stain on his honour. **32.** David always had the power of recognizing and of profiting by his mistakes. **37.** 'his heart died' : probably an outburst of fear and rage brought on a stroke which was none the less a divine judgement on his folly. **43.** 'Moreover' : 43 f. are an appendix to the story of Abigail. From the reference to Achinoam in 27:3 and 30:5, it would seem that David had married her before meeting Abigail. Jezrahel : not the town of the tribe of Issachar in the north, but a town in the south in the territory of the tribe of Judah. **44.** 'Saul gave Michol' : he considered David's flight as the equivalent of desertion, but David never gave up his claim to Michol ; 2 Kg 3:13. Gallium : the only other reference shows that it was in the territory of Benjamin, Is 10:30.

256a **XXVI 1-25 David spares Saul's Life again**—We may note in passing some of the details which distinguish this incident from that related in ch 23. In the first case, Saul is alone, in a cave, where David is hidden with his men. Part of his robe is cut off and David makes himself known in a personal interview. In the second, Saul is in the midst of his camp surrounded by his men at night. David and Abisai steal their way alone to reach the sleeping king. This time David does not make himself known, till he is safely across the ravine to the opposite side of the hill. He does not trust himself to Saul and invites one of Saul's men to come and collect the king's property that he has stolen.

b **5.** 'in a tent' : LXX 'in a chariot' is a mistake, otherwise there could be no question of pinning him to the ground with one blow ; *cf.* 8. **6.** Achimelech : this man was a Hittite like Urias, 2 Kg 11:3. This is the only time he is mentioned in the Bible. Abisai : he and Joab were the sons of Sarvia, David's sister ; *cf.* 1 Par 2:16. He saved David's life in a campaign against the Philistines, 2 Kg 21:17, shared the command of the army with Joab, 2 Kg 10:10, joined in the murder of Abner, 2 Kg 3:30, and stood by David at the time of Absalom's rebellion. A brave man, but hardhearted like his brother Joab. **7.** 'his spear' : a symbol of his authority. He held it in his hand while he gave judgement ; *cf.* 22:6. **10.** 'unless the Lord' : Saul may die as a direct visitation of God, or by a natural death, or die in battle, but there must be no murder. **19.** 'If the Lord' : if Saul is simply Yahweh's instrument punishing David for his sins, David will seek to placate Yahweh by offering sacrifice. If, however, his persecution is due to the counsels of wicked men, they will be cursed by God. For they have cast him from among the people of God, from the land which Yahweh has chosen for his divinely revealed worship. Such banishment was equivalent to bidding him serve false gods. **20.** 'seek a flea' : a copyist's error which has crept into MT from 24:15. LXX has 'my life'.

c **XXVII 1-XXVIII 2 David Vassal of Achis, King of Geth**—Circumstances now forced David to guard against the insecurity of his present way of life. With the death of Samuel there was no power left in Israel strong enough to withstand the king. As chief of a large band of soldiers of fortune he entered the service of the Philistine king of Geth. But he had to reconcile two opposing loyalties. He must do nothing to alienate the goodwill of his Hebrew countrymen, and at the same time win the confidence of his Philistine overlord. At his own request David was made Achis' feudal vassal over the territory of Siceleg on the southern Philistine border. Here, with greater freedom and independence, he could build up his army and satisfy his Philistine masters with raids against the Amalecites who were ravaging their territory. Ostensibly these raids were against the Israelites. In reality they were directed against desert tribes who were in alliance with the Philistines. It was a dangerous game where one slip would spell disaster.

d **5.** 'why should thy servant' : it is too high an honour. David was angling for greater independence, away from the jealousy of Philistine courtiers where he could save his soldiers from being merged into the Philistine army. **6.** Siceleg : is mentioned in Jos 15:31, 19:5, but its exact site has not been identified. The compiler of this narrative regarded it as part of the crown estates of the kings of Judah, and therefore must have written this after Solomon and before the captivity. **7.** 'four months' : MT has 'a year and four months'. A longer period than four months is implied by 29:3. **8.** Gessuri and Gerzi : these were heathen tribes of southern Judah. Amalecite, *i.e.* such as had survived the attack by Saul, 15:8. 'These were of old' : with most commentators emend MT to 'For these nations dwelt in the land from Telam (a city in south Judah) until thou comest to Shur and to the land of Egypt' ; *cf.* 15:7. **10.** Jerameelites : descendants of Hesron who settled in south Judah (1 Par 2:9). Ceni : a clan in friendly relations with Israel. Jethro, the father-in-law of Moses, was a Kenite ; *cf.* 15:6. All these expeditions were in the south country and David led Achis to believe that they were directed against his own countrymen. To make sure that no one would live to tell the truth, he massacred those he had plundered and took no prisoners. We cannot justify every action of David by the standards of Christian morality. His dangerous position was only made bearable by falsehood and ruthless barbarity. **12.** 'Achis believed David' : Achis naturally thought that raids against David's own countrymen were the greatest proof of his loyalty. He promoted him to be the king's personal bodyguard and the next step involved David in an impossible dilemma. **XXVIII 2.** 'David said' : his answer was deliberately ambiguous, but Achis took it to be a fresh protestation of loyalty. Fortunately the suspicions of the Philistine commanders saved the situation, 29:3.

e **XXVIII 3-25 Saul and the Witch of Endor**—The incident related in this passage breaks the thread of the account of David's adventures amongst the Philistines. Its logical position is immediately before

e ch 31 on the eve of the battle of Gelboe. It has been borrowed probably from some old account of Samuel's life. Deprived of the counsel of Yahweh, Saul sought to know the outcome of the impending battle from an old heathen medium at Endor. In spite of his disguise, the medium recognized Saul as the destroyer of such forbidden arts in accordance with the Deuteronomic law 18:11. Some womanly instinct in the degraded witch was touched at the sight of the massive Saul lying prostrate with grief on the ground. She forced him to eat and rest before he walked out into the night to meet his doom.

f 3. This verse explains why Saul appealed to the witch at Endor. 4. 'camped at Sunam': opposite Gelboe. The armies were facing each other across the plain of Esdraelon. 7. 'hath a divining spirit': lit. 'that hath an *'ôḇ*'. This word often signifies the spirit speaking through the medium, or the possessor of such a spirit. It has been suggested that the *'ôḇ* may have been some part of the human body, *e.g.* a skull used for magical purposes. Endor: a little village on the north slope of Little Hermon, about ten miles from Gelboe, behind the Philistine army. 13. 'I saw gods ascending': supernatural beings from the region of Sheol. The witch describes the spirit, and Saul recognizes Samuel from the description. The weight of both Jewish and early Christian commentators seems to give an affirmative answer to the question: Did Samuel's spirit really appear? This interpretation agrees with the plain and natural meaning of the account; *cf.* Ecclus 46:23 and the LXX addition to 1 Par 10:13. It was God rather than the witch who summoned Samuel to make clear the connexion between Saul's present misfortunes and past sins. 14. 'with a mantle': such as Samuel used to wear when alive; *cf.* 15:27. 19. 'Israel with thee': the sins of the king involve the nation. 'with me': *i.e.* in Sheol, the abode of the dead.

g XXIX 1-11 **David's Dismissal from the Philistine Army**—In a general war of all the Philistine princes against Israel, the Philistine chiefs distrusted the presence of David in their ranks. His loyalty to Achis was never put to the test, as the Philistine king was forced to dismiss him and his mercenaries.

h 1. Aphec: unidentified, probably lying in the plain of Esdraelon. Jezrahel: an important strategic town linking the plain of Esdraelon with the Jordan valley. It was the scene of Naboth's murder and the killing of Jezabel; 3 Kg 21:13; 4 Kg 9:30. 2. 'marched': the Heb. participles used in this verse imply continuous action. The native army and the band of Hebrew mercenaries took part in a military parade past the five Philistine generals. 9. 'as an angel of the Lord': a comparison which occurs 2 Kg 14:17, 20; 19:27. The wording of this speech of Achis has been influenced by an editor of MT. It is unlikely that Achis used such a comparison and it has been omitted in LXX (B). 10. LXX adds 'and go to the place which I have appointed you (Siceleg) and put no evil design in thy heart for thou art good in my sight'. Achis tries to smooth the ruffled feelings and desire for revenge which he imagines a man like David must harbour in his mind because of his dismissal from the army.

i XXX 1-7 **Amalecites sack Siceleg in David's Absence**—On his return David found desolation and ruin. The Amalecites had raided the undefended town, burned its buildings, and carried off the women for spoil. This was a cruel shock to his men and there was danger of serious mutiny.

j 8-31 **The Pursuit and Division of Spoil**—David found an outlet for the mutinous feelings of his men in an annihilating raid on the retreating Amalecites. With characteristic foresight David sent a share of the spoils to various authorities in Judah. This was partly in gratitude for their former goodwill and partly to secure their support when his hour should come.

k 2. 'had not killed anyone': they would be more valuable if sold in the Egyptian slave-market. 9. Torrent Besor: unidentified. 13. 'left me': the heedless cruelty of his Amalecite master was to cost

the master dearly. 14. 'south side of the Cerethi': a **256k** tribe in the south country closely allied to the Philistines. 24. 'equal shall be the portion': the success of their efforts was due to God. Those who guard supplies play an essential part in military strategy and deserve a share in the spoils. 27. Bethel: not the Bethel in the territory of Benjamin, but Bethel near Siceleg in south Judah. Jether: a priestly town in the hill country of Judah. Aroer: also in south Judah and not to be confused with Aroer on the Arnon. Sephamoth: site unknown. Esthamo: about eight miles SSW. of Hebron. Rachal: not mentioned elsewhere. LXX has 'Carmel'. Jerameel . . . Ceni: these cities must have been in the Negeb or South Country. Arama: an ancient Canaanite city where the Israelites were defeated in the time of Moses (Num 14:45). Asan: in the extreme south of the Negeb, originally allotted to Judah and later to Simeon (Jos 15:42; 19:7). Athach: not mentioned elsewhere.

XXXI 1-13 **Battle of Gelboe and Death of Saul**—The **l** fortunes of Saul were now drawing to their fateful close. His army was routed and his sons lay dead. He himself was severely wounded and feared the mockery of his pitiless heathen foe, if taken alive. To avoid this he committed suicide. Next day the Philistines found and mutilated the body of the dead king. Only one touch of human feeling redeems the sordid scene. The men of Jabes Galaad who had not forgotten their debt to Saul, 11:1-11, rescued his body and buried it under a famous tree in their city.

4. 'fell on it': Saul died by his own hand. The **m** whole tragedy of his life is there. He himself was the instrument of his own ruin. 10. Bethsan: a city in the Jordan valley overlooking the modern village of Beisan. 12. 'burnt them there': though cremation was not a Hebrew practice, it was resorted to in this case to prevent the Philistines from inflicting any further indignities on the dead bodies, if they captured Jabes Galaad.

THE SECOND BOOK OF KINGS

I 1-16 **David learns of Saul's Death**—The division of **257a** the books is purely artificial and there is no break between the two. The Amalecite who claimed to have dealt the final blow which killed Saul and delivered David from his enemy was simply a liar. He was a typical oriental thief who plundered the dead. He miscalculated David's reactions to his tale, and paid for it with his life. There may have been a mixture of policy and impulse in David's act of vengeance. He might reap the advantages of Saul's death, but it must be made clear to the nation that he had in no way connived at it.

17-27 **David's Lament for Saul and Jonathan**—A poem **b** of great artistry and beauty revealing the innate nobility of David's mind. David invites the people to join with him in lamentation. He thinks with horror of the exultation of the Philistines, and the scene of the tragedy is cursed. He thinks of those he knew to be the great men of Israel. He bids the maidens remember what Saul had done for them and the nation. Then in one last passionate cry he voices his mighty love for Jonathan and his own bitter sorrow at his loss. This elegy was embodied in a national collection of poetry called the Book of Jasher, mentioned in Jos 10:13. The text has some obscurities which make the work of reconstructing the original extremely difficult.

18. 'the use of the bow': this cannot be right. The **c** bow was already widely used. LXX omits the word 'bow' and has 'he commanded to teach (it) to the children of Judah'. Some commentators consider 'the Bow' to have been the title of the elegy from the reference in 22 to Jonathan's bow. 21. 'fields of first fruits': Nature is summoned to sympathize by withholding its fertilizing dews, so that no fruitful field will be left from which first-fruit offerings can be made to Yahweh. 'not anointed with oil': in the Heb. not Saul but his shield is the subject of the anointing.

257c Dhorme renders, ' the shield of Saul was not anointed with oil, but with the blood of the wounded and the fat of heroes '. The Heb. (reading *mašû ḥ*) could mean, ' For there was the shield of heroes dishonoured, the shield of Saul, no more to be anointed with oil, for now (it is) without the blood of the slain '. In other words, it was the glory of a warrior's shield that it needed anointing to wipe away the blood of the slain ; but now the warrior himself lies dead and no such anointing will ever be needed again. **22.** ' The arrow of Jonathan . . . the sword of Saul ' are poetically described as devouring the bodies of their enemies. The bow was Jonathan's favourite weapon and the pledge of his friendship with David ; *cf.* 18:14. **26.** ' As the mother loveth ' : a marginal gloss introduced into the text.

d II 1-11 David King of Judah; Isboseth King of Israel —The disaster of Mt Gelboe left Palestine without a leader. In the south David occupied Hebron and was anointed king. Here he ruled for over seven years. In northern Palestine, Saul's able commander, Abner, succeeded in placing Isboseth on the throne. The internal condition of these respective kingdoms was very different. David's was compact, united, and externally secure, and his courteous message to the men of Jabes Galaad suggests that he was exploring the possibility of further dominion. Isboseth's position was weakened because there could be no real supreme direction from a king who was personally insignificant and completely dependent upon Abner who ruled the army. Furthermore the Philistines had no intention of allowing an effective revival of Saul's kingdom. They were masters of all western Palestine and the rivalry between the north and south would serve their interests and prevent any revolt on a large scale. It is significant of the dwindling prestige of the Northern Kingdom that the royal city was moved to Mahanaim on the Jabbok east of the Jordan. This fact is obscured by the DV which gives ' the camp ' for Mahanaim (8).

e 1. ' Shall I go up ? ' : Saul's death removed the chief obstacle to the throne which God had promised David. Before taking any decisive step in that direction, David asks for divine guidance. **6.** ' anointed him ' : David had already received royal anointing from Samuel. Here it was a question of public and official recognition by the people. Later he was again anointed as king over all Israel, 2 Kg 5:3. **8.** ' Abner . . . took Isboseth ' : Abner, son of Ner, the son of Abiel, was the great-uncle of Isboseth (*cf.* 1 Kg 14:50 f.). He was the real power behind his incompetent and jealous nephew. The name Isboseth (' man of shame ') was originally ' Ish-baal ' (1 Par 8:33), *i.e.* ' man of Baal '. As ' Baal ' means ' Lord ', it could be applied to Yahweh, but was usually applied to pagan gods. Hence to avoid even pronouncing the hated name of ' Baal ', the scribes substituted for it *bōšeṭ* ' shame '. **10a.** ' forty years old ' : this is a copyist's error or the writer has used the well-known round number 40. Isboseth's eldest brother Jonathan was probably about the same age as David, *i.e.* about thirty at the time of his death. **10b.** ' two years ' : his reign practically coincided with David's seven and a half years at Hebron, but it may have taken Abner five years to win recognition for his master over all Israel.

f 12-32 War between the Kingdoms—War broke out through the rivalry of the leaders Abner and Joab. David's men had marched northwards into the territory of Benjamin and were met by an Israelite force at Gabaon. In the encounter which followed Abner slew Joab's brother and thereby sealed his own fate. The whole chapter reveals that Joab was becoming indispensable to David, and that gratitude and self-interest prevented David from removing a man who was so unscrupulously devoted to his cause.

g 12. Gabaon : the site of this city is occupied by the modern village of El-Jib, five miles NW. of Jerusalem. **13.** Joab : the son of David's sister, Sarvia. His name means ' Yahweh is father '. He was a ruthless vindictive character whose one virtue was a passionate devotion to David. His services to David for good **2** (2 Kg 12:26 ; 18:2) and evil (2 Kg 11:14 ff.) made him more and more the king's master. **14.** ' play ' : a euphemism for a trial of arms in friendly rivalry. It soon developed into mutual slaughter. **16.** ' fellow ' : his antagonist. **18.** ' one of the roes ' : noted for their swiftness and grace. **22.** ' Go off ' : Abner was a seasoned warrior conscious of his superior skill, and had no wish to start a blood-feud between Joab and himself. **23.** ' stood still ' : grief-stricken and horrified at the sight of the young man's corpse.

III 1-22 Abner negotiates with David—1-5 are an **h** editorial note on David's family at Hebron. Three of the sons mentioned, Amnon, Absalom, and Adonias became notorious in various ways. The other three are not mentioned again. **6-12.** Isboseth had inherited the harem of his father. Abner, who regarded him as a mere puppet, took one of Saul's concubines for himself. According to Eastern ideas, this was equivalent to high-treason. Abner rejected Isboseth's expostulations with contempt and entered into negotiations with David to unite all Israel under him. **13-16.** David insisted on the return of his wife, Michol, as an essential condition. This public act was a blow to the prestige of Isboseth and a reminder to the northern tribes of David's connection with the house of Saul.

12. ' Whose is the land ? ' : is it not in my power to **i** make you king over all Israel ? Omitted by LXX. **16.** Bahurim : a Benjamite village on the road from Jerusalem to the Jordan fords. **19.** ' Abner spoke to Benjamin : while sounding the heads of the tribes on the change of allegiance to David, he would require special diplomacy to win over Saul's fellow-tribesmen. **21.** ' enter into a league ' : the heads of the clans would insist on some mutual agreement which safeguarded their interests in return for their loyalty. **22.** ' slain the robbers ' : lit. ' came from the troop ', *i.e.* from a raid or plundering expedition. There were no regular taxes and this was the only way of paying the army.

23-27 Joab murders Abner—24. ' Joab . . . said ' : **j** his masterful character stands out in this upbraiding of the king. He accuses David of failing to carry out the law of tribal blood-feud by leaving Abner alive and insists that he must be a deceiver.

28-39 David's Curse on Joab and Lament for Abner— k David denied any complicity in the crime, and the sincerity of his grief was accepted as proof of his innocence. He was not in a position to execute Joab, but Yahweh would chastise the guilty with fearful punishment. He gave Abner honourable burial and composed a special dirge for his funeral. **29.** ' come upon Joab ' : untimely death, venereal disease, and effeminacy will be the lot of the guilty house of Joab in each succeeding generation. ' holdeth the distaff ' : either effeminate or a cripple who supports himself with a crutch. Either of these would be curse in the warlike family of Joab. **33.** ' as cowards ' : lit. ' as dies a fool must Abner die ? '—an ignoble death for so brave a man ! **34.** ' hands were not bound ' : thou wert free to defend thyself. Only treachery could have killed thee.

IV 1-12 Assassination of Isboseth—Abner's death **2** deprived Isboseth of all real support for his kingdom. When Isboseth was murdered, the way was clear for David to ascend the throne Yahweh had destined for him. 4 is inserted to show that no direct representative of the house of Saul was left except Jonathan's cripple son Miphiboseth. Time had been on David's side against Isboseth and there was no need or justification for murder. Immediate execution of the assassins cleared David from any charge of complicity.

3. Berothites : the writer wishes to emphasize that the **b** murderers were of Isboseth's own tribe of Benjamin. He reminds the reader—without explanation—that the Gibeonite city of Beroth was regarded as belonging to the tribe of Benjamin ; *cf.* Jos 9:17. Its exact site is uncertain. Garstang, 362, locates it at Tell el Nasbeh some seven miles north of Jerusalem. **4.** Miphiboseth :

b his real name was Merib-baal ; *cf.* 1 Par 8:34. As is usual in the Bks of Kgs, *bōšĕṭ* 'shame' is a pious substitution for the hated name of *Baal*, and Merib has been corrupted into Miphi. **5.** 'house of Isboseth': at Mahanaim.

c V 1-5 David King of all Israel—David's hour had come. By his courage and nobility of character in trial and victory, he stood out as the one man able to govern and fight the battles of Israel against the Philistine. In offering him the throne of all Israel, the people were convinced that they were offering it to one whom Yahweh himself had chosen to be a man of destiny.

d **1.** 'We are thy bone': three reasons given for their choice—David-kinship, his military record, and the will of Yahweh. **2.** 'feed my people': like a shepherd feeding his flock. Kings were frequently described as shepherds of their people. It was especially appropriate in David's case ; *cf.* Ps 77:70-72. **3.** 'made a league with them': probably some charter defining the rights of king and people.

e **6-16 The Capture of Jerusalem**—This event probably took place after the war against the Philistines mentioned in 17-25 and 21:18-21, or during a propitious lull in one of the Philistine campaigns (*cf.* Ricciotti, *Storia d'Israele*, I. 342). It is introduced here to show the culmination of Israel's strength and unity under her one king. Certainly the new kingdom needed internal unity, for rivalry between the north and south might well come to a head over the question of a capital. David determined to chose a place that would be best from a political, civil, military, and religious point of view. Jerusalem was that place. It was midway between the southern and northern tribes and on neutral ground. If there was to be one sanctuary to which all were bound to come, Hebron was too far south. Jerusalem would serve well too for centralized civil administration, and as a fortress among the hills of the central plateau, it was magnificently situated.

f **6.** Jerusalem is mentioned as early as 2000 B.C. under the name of Ursalim in Egyptian texts found at Luxor in 1925. It is also mentioned in the Tell el Amarna letters *c* 1400-1370 B.C. It had never been captured permanently from the Jebusites. For details of topographical and archaeological interest, *cf.* H. Vincent in RB (1911) 566 ff. ; (1912) 86 f. ; Weill, *Revue des Etudes Juives* (1926) 103 f. ; J. W. Crowfoot, G. M. Fitzgerald, PEQ (1929) ; Krauss, 'Zion and Jerusalem', PEQ (1945) 15. **6.** 'shalt not come': read—'Thou shalt not come in hither unless thou take away the blind and the lame, saying (or meaning by that) David shall not come in hither'. The Jebusites thought Jerusalem so impregnable that a band of cripples and blind men could hold it. **7.** Sion : many authorities maintained that Sion occupied the south-western hill of Jerusalem. In more recent times all the evidence leads to the identification of Sion with the eastern hill upon which stood the Temple. By a gradual extension the names of Sion and City of David covered the whole of Jerusalem. **8.** 'David offered a reward': Vg is a paraphrase of this obscure and incomplete text. 'David said in that day : Whosoever smiteth the Jebusite (let him go up by the water-gully) and (smite) the blind and the lame, that are hated of David's soul ! Therefore it is said, the blind and the lame shall not come into the house.' 1 Par 11:6-9 may give a clue to what was the original text. LXX has 'house of the Lord'. David takes up the taunt of the Jebusites and in a spirit of contempt calls the garrison 'the blind and the lame'. Entry to the Temple was not forbidden to this class of persons, but they were forbidden to minister in the Temple, *cf.* Lev 21:18. Here it is not a question of the Temple but of the citadel. The proverb may have been something of an exclamation. 'Blind and lame ! he (an enemy) cannot come into the house !', *i.e.* the blind and lame are sufficient to defend it.

g **9.** Mello : part of the fortifications of Jerusalem. **11.** 'Hiram king of Tyre': 11-16 are probably not in their strict chronological order, and are meant to show how

10 was gradually fulfilled. According to Josephus' **258g** account in *C. Apionem* 1, 18 Hiram I of Tyre was king during the last 7 years of David's reign, whereas David's palace was built before his last 8 years. Abiba'al, the Tyrian king's father, seems like David to have been the founder of a dynasty, and was his contemporary, and the more familiar name of his son may have been substituted in the text. It is however possible that Abiba'al had been preceded by an earlier Hiram of whom we know nothing except what is here said, or the sacred writer may be using the name Hiram in a comprehensive and anticipatory sense, based on the fact that it was he who subsequently sent building materials to David for the construction of the temple. Tyre was one of the most important cities of Phoenicia, renowned for its art, wealth, and commerce. **14.** 'names': a list is given also in 1 Par 3 :5 ff. ; 14:4 ff. Nothing is known of any of them except Solomon and Nathan.

17-25 David at War with the Philistines—The Philis- **h** tine overlords quickly understood the menace behind David's growing power and independence. A concerted attack on a large scale was their answer. They spread out over the large fruitful valley of Rephaim ; *cf.* 18. David was forced to adopt the fighting tactics of his outlaw days in the cave of Odollam. At a moment announced by Yahweh, David's men broke through the Philistine ranks and partly avenged the battle of Gelboe. A second attempt by the Philistines in the same valley ended in their being completely routed and driven back to the coast.

17. 'a stronghold': probably a place he had learned **i** to use in his outlaw days, *e.g.* the cave at Odollam. **18.** Valley of Rephaim : stretching SW. from the neighbourhood of Jerusalem. **20.** 'divided my enemies': lit. 'The Lord hath broken down my enemies like the breaking of waters'—like a river in full flood sweeping through every obstacle. **21.** 'their idols' ; as Philistines had once captured the Ark, so now the Israelites capture the Philistine gods which had been carried into battle to ensure victory. **23.** 'fetch a compass behind them': go round behind them and attack them in the rear. **24.** 'peartree': the 'Baka-tree' was a kind of balsam tree. When they 'hear a rustling, it will be a sign that Yahweh is marching in front of their army.

VI 1-23 The Ark is brought to Jerusalem—To make **259a** his new capital a religious as well as a geographical centre, David transferred the Ark from the territory of Ephraim to Jerusalem. His design suffered a set-back in the death of Oza, but after the Ark had remained in the house of Obededom, David's project was crowned with success. Just as the Davidic kingdom was a visible monarchy with its centre in Jerusalem, so the inspired vision of the prophets foresaw a regenerated Sion, the City of the Great King, whither the nations would flock in vast numbers to walk in the paths of the God of Jacob ; *cf.* Ps 47:2 ; Am 9:11 ; Is 44. The NT writers likewise emphasize the One City which God himself frames and constructs on eternal foundations to be the new metropolis gathering men into unique fellowship before God. 'To this city you are come, to Mount Sion, and to the city of the living God, and to a heavenly Jerusalem . . . and to Jesus the mediator of the New Testament', Heb 12:22-24.

3. Gabaa : some hill near Cariathiarim. The writer **b** of 1 Par 13: 5 f. gives a more elaborate account of the whole incident. **7.** 'struck him': Num 4:5, 15, 19 forbade under pain of death any but priests to touch the Ark except with the staves provided for that purpose. The unapproachable holiness of Yahweh and the incomparable majesty of his Being placed a decisive gulf between Israel's God and the degraded deities of its neighbours. But it would take the wayward people of primitive Israel centuries to learn that most essential lesson thoroughly. It had to learn it the hard way, if divine revelation was to be preserved for mankind. No other way would impress a young nation surrounded by a world of licentious polytheism. The sudden death of Oza was a drastic reminder that the new era of

259b worship in the capital of the kingdom must keep in sight the overruling claims of the Holy One of Israel. By warding off even the slightest disregard or familiarity, God vindicated his unique greatness before men. **10.** ' Obededom the Gethite ' : a Levite from the Levitical city of Gath-rimmon. **16.** ' she despised him ' : she thought it a lack of all dignity for a king to lay aside his royal robes, and clothed only with a linen ephod to abandon himself to an outburst of religious fervour. **22.** ' little in my own eyes ' : David did not smoothe the queen's ruffled pride ; a king's true dignity comes from Yahweh who had rejected her father, and his subjects will understand the true motives of his actions. Michol's outburst of sarcastic temper ruined her relations with David for the rest of her life.

c VII 1-17 The Davidic Covenant—David proposed to build a temple for Yahweh. Yahweh rewarded this desire by promising rather to build him a royal house which would endure for ever. The force of this divine oracle was to bind his seed and house irrevocably to the kingly dignity of the future Messias. Most authors admit its great importance for the growth of the Messianic Hope in Israel. There are, however, two main modes of interpretation accepted by scholars. (1) The one applies part of the prophecy to Solomon and part of it to Christ, or accepts what is affirmed literally of Solomon as something to be applied typically to the Messias. In other words ' thy seed ' is understood in an individual sense. (2) More recent authors such as Dhorme, Ceuppens, Dennefeld, Leimbach, and Kittel understand the word ' seed ' in a collective sense, as embracing not only Solomon but the whole Davidic dynasty and including the culminating figure in that dynasty—the Messias. In their opinion the oracle does not deal exclusively with Solomon. 13 and 16 can hardly be true of Solomon's reign from 980–938 B.C. Secondly, 19 shows that David understood it to cover all his posterity, and the author of Ps 88:30–38 in his reference to this oracle obviously accepts it in a collective sense. Neither can this prophecy refer exclusively to the Messias for 14 cannot be applied to him, but is applicable to the

d dynasty of David as a whole. Hence according to this interpretation the prophecy is Messianic in the literal and not only in the typical sense, and promises that the posterity of David will reign forever, but certain things in it cannot be affirmed in the strict literal sense of each and every member of the royal line, *e.g.* 14 cannot be applied to the Messias, and of him only can be understood literally the king's divine sonship. The true fulfilment of the everlasting kingdom of David and the fullness of divine sonship are shown in Lk 1:32 f. and Heb 1:5. Père Desnoyers sums up the significance of this divine promise in these words : ' His (David's) whole mind is centred round the divine promise that his people are established as the people of Yahweh, and that his dynasty will reign forever over the people of his God. . . . Not only is the old covenant between Yahweh and Israel proclaimed anew, but the kingship itself, in spite of its newness, now shared in the solidity of that covenant : the work of Moses is completed by the work of David. Therefore the dynasty of David will have the duty of collaborating with the work of Yahweh on earth. Their destinies are linked together for all time ', *Peuple hébreu*, 3, 707 f.

e 1. ' when the king sat in his house ' : This ch is not in strict chronological relation with ch 6, but its subject-matter, the building of a temple for the Ark, does form a logical connexion. 1*b* would point to the later years of David's life. But 12 shows that Solomon was not yet born. We cannot deduce the exact date with any certainty. **2.** Nathan : one of the great religious leaders of David's reign. He rebuked David for his adultery (12:1), was tutor to Solomon (12:25), and wrote a history of the reign of David, and part at least of Solomon's reign (1 Par 29:29 ; 2 Par 9:29). **5.** ' Thus saith the Lord ' : the logical sequence of thought in 5–16 is fairly clear. Hitherto Yahweh had not

expressed any desire for such a house or temple as **2** David had in mind. David's kingdom was not completely established—wars had to go on—and the time was not yet ripe to build what was to be the temple of that kingdom. Nevertheless Yahweh's past mercies to him are to reach their culmination in a fresh covenant of grace with the house of David. The day will come when Yahweh shall build David a royal house that shall stand forever in his sight. **12.** ' thy seed ' : should be understood collectively, because it refers to a royal house that will endure forever. It includes Solomon, 3 Kg 8:15–20 ; then the line of kings who sat on the throne of Judah and finally Christ in whom it finds its highest fulfilment, Ac 2:29–30 ; 13:22 f. **13.** ' he shall build ' : explicitly this refers to David's dynasty in general, but implicitly it refers to Solomon who was one of its members. **14.** ' I will be to him a father ' : in view of Israel's special election by God, the theocratic people as a whole was the ' son of Yahweh ', Ex 4:22. In virtue of this special covenant, the sacred sonship of the nation culminated in the unique sonship of the king of Israel. Hence Christ, the Son of God, came in his Father's name, revealing His Father's mind, and speaking with his Father's authority, Jn 1:49 ; 5:43 ; 10:30 ; Heb 1:5.

18-29 David's Prayer of Thanksgiving—19. ' is the **f** law of Adam ' : lit. this is the instruction of man. Ewald compares this obscure phrase with the text of 1 Par 17:17 which he translates ' and thou allowest me to look on the succession of men upwards ', *i.e.* far into the future of my offspring. By changing the initial word *tôrāh* Dhorme reads ' and this thou hast announced to man '. Man is now made aware of the things God has destined for the future.

VIII 1-15 David's Conquest—The development of **g** David's kingdom is shown in this summary account of his victories over the Philistines, Moab, Soba, Damascus, and Edom. The power of the Philistines was broken along the Mediterranean sea-board, and by the conquest of Moab, and later, Ammon, David's kingdom became the dominant power of Syria, stretching from Lebanon to the Red Sea. These victories also opened on every side the highways for foreign trade which contributed so much to the opulence of Solomon's reign.

1. ' bridle of tribute ' : MT *meteg-hā-'ammāh*. The **h** Chronicler, 1 Par 18:1, read ' Gath ' for *meteg*, and understood *'ammah* in the sense of ' mother-city ' or metropolis. Sayce prefers to compare it with the Babylonian *meteg-ammati* which would signify ' the highroad of the mainland ' of Palestine, and would refer to the command of the highroad of trade which passed through Canaan from Asia to Egypt and Arabia. **3.** Soba : a small Aramaean kingdom north of Damascus. **7.** ' brought them to Jerusalem ' : LXX addition notes ' And Susakim [Sheshak], king of Egypt, took them when he went up to Jerusalem in the days of Roboam the son of Solomon '. **8.** Bete, Beroth : both unidentified. **9.** Emath : a town of considerable importance on the Orontes. **13.** Valley of the saltpits : on the borderline of Judah and Edom—the last place where we should expect to find Syrians. By reading *daleth* for *resh*, instead of Syrians, we can read ' Edom ', which lies to the south of the Dead Sea.

16-18 David's Officials and Administrators—This list **i** names the holders of the chief offices of State. Another list is given in 20:23–26. Joab was commander-in-chief of the army. Josaphat was something more than a recorder ; he was head of civil affairs. He kept the king informed of the business of state, and gave his counsel, like a Vizier of oriental courts. Saraias had the duty of drafting and keeping official documents, and perhaps of recording outstanding events of the reign. In religious affairs the chief priests were Sadoc and Abiathar whose name should be read second ; Achimelech had already been killed by Saul. Sadoc became the sole chief priest when Abiathar was deposed after Solomon's accession. In addition to the standing army the king had a personal bodyguard of foreign

9i troops, something like the Swiss Guard at the Vatican. These Cerethi (Cretans) and Phelethi (Philistines) could be depended upon in every crisis. In case of rebellion or disaffection among the people, they would have no scruple in fighting the king's fellow-country-men and at the same time the position of trust made them feel that they were as much the king's subjects as the Israelites themselves.

j 17. Sadoc belonged to the house of Eleazar, 1 Par 6:4–8. He joined David after Saul's death, 1 Par 12:28, and remained faithful to him all his life, and finally after sharing the priesthood with Abiathar was appointed the sole high priest, 3 Kg 2:35. 18. 'princes' : The Heb. word for priest, *kōhēn*, used here in MT, is derived from a root meaning ' to serve ' or ' to minister ', and is sometimes used of ministers at court, *cf.* 1 Par 18:17 which gives the paraphrase ' were chief about the king '.

0a IX 1-13 **David and Miphiboseth**—Chapters 9–20 are admitted by all to be a literary unit derived from a single document recording incidents of David's court life. They are of the utmost value as historical documents written close to the events they describe. Many a new dynasty has ensured its ultimate security by the complete destruction of every member of the house it has supplanted. In facing and in solving this question, David showed once more his noble generosity and political wisdom. He sought out Jonathan's lame son Miphiboseth, bestowed on him Saul's family estates and treated him like his own son. At the same time he kept him under his own eye at Jerusalem, and appointed Siba to act as bailiff of Miphiboseth's estates. The nobles of Benjamin would be less likely to think of the rights of Saul's house when Jonathan's son was out of the way.

b 3. ' the mercy of God ' : in fulfilment of his vow to Jonathan, 1 Kg 20:14–17, 42, David's kindness would be like God's kindness, enduring and bountiful. 4. Machir must have been an important personage in Lodabar, judging from his welcome to David when fleeing from Absalom, 17:27. Lodabar : a town E. of the Jordan, probably near Mahanaim. 10. ' may be maintained ' : though a guest of David, he needed the revenues from his estates to support his household. 11. ' And Siba said ' : the second half of this reply is out of place as the words of Siba. It is better to follow LXX which has ' So Miphiboseth ate at David's table, as one of the king's sons '.

c X-XII **War with the Ammonites**— On his accession to the throne of Ammon, Hanon (Hanun), the son of Naas, treated David's ambassadors in a most shameful fashion. This led immediately to war with Israel. The whole incident was intended to precipitate a crisis. David's growing power and undisputed independence aroused the suspicions of the neighbouring kingdoms. A settlement was becoming inevitable. A coalition of Aramaean kingdoms lying to the east and north-east joined with Ammon in opening hostilities. Joab, commander of David's army, met the united forces of the Ammonites and their Syrian allies. He divided his troops into two forces, one of which, under his brother Abisai, was to engage the Ammonites, while he countered any attack from the rear. The Ammonites fled to their city of Rabbath and the Syrians were routed, but the battle was not decisive. In a second campaign, 15–19, the Syrians were defeated by David, and the lesser kings in the neighbourhood also submitted. A year later Joab was sent to besiege the Ammonite capital.

d 2. ' shewed kindness to me ' : there is no express reference in Scripture to this kindness to David. Probably as an enemy of Saul he had sheltered David during his early wanderings. 4. ' shaved off the one half ' : the greatest of insults in a society where the beard was a symbol of manhood. They added to this by inflicting indecent exposure on the inviolable persons of ambassadors. 6. Rohob : a town in the Lebanon district near Dan. Maacha : a small kingdom in the same region as Soba. Istob : ' the men of Tob '—unidentified. The text of 1 Par 19, gives other

details, but the mention of 32,000 chariots must be due **260d** to a defective reading. 12. ' city of our God ' : an unusual phrase. Klostermann conjectures that the Ark of God must have been there. More probably it was simply equivalent to our expression ' For God and Fatherland '. 16. ' the river ' : the Euphrates. 17. Helam : unknown.

XI 2-27 David's Adultery—At the height of his **e** triumphs David fell into adultery with Bethsabee. To conceal his guilt he procured the death of the man he had wronged. Joab carried out David's orders, and Bethsabee married her seducer. Divine condemnation and punishment were announced by the prophet Nathan. David repented but the child of the union died. Saints and sinners have found in this story a lesson for all time, a warning of the power and consequence of sin, and a message of hope for the humble and contrite heart. Moreover the incident is important historically. It explains the sudden eclipse of the good fortune of David's prosperous reign. It also illustrates the great vigour and austerity of the moral standards of Israel which bound king and subject alike. ' To the ordinary eastern mind, for the king to take the wife of a subject is quite normal and natural, for the sovereign is well within his rights. Few men in David's position would have found it necessary either to conceal the act or get rid of the husband. But in Israel a man was a man, even though he were a subject and of foreign birth, and his property and rights must be respected. Characteristic, also, are the rebuke of Nathan and the repentance of the king. Neither would have been conceivable in any other nation of the ancient east ', *T. H. Robinson, A History of Israel*, I, 225.

1. Rabbath : twenty miles east of Jordan. 3. Urias **f** the Hethite : though a Hittite by race, his name, meaning ' light of Yahweh ', seems to show that he was a worshipper of Israel's God. 5. ' she told . . . David ' : the Mosaic law ordered the death penalty for adultery, Lev 20:10, but Bethsabee relied on David to find some way out of the difficulty. 6. ' David sent to Joab ' : 6–25 are a pitiless exposure of all the sinner's subterfuges. They show to what a grovelling level David's sin had reduced the once chivalrous idol of his people. 13. ' made him drunk ' : to make him forget his resolution not to go home to his wife. 14. ' by the hand of Urias ' : this brave officer was made to carry his own death-warrant. 21. ' who killed Abimelech ' : an interesting reference to Jg 9:50–4, which shows a familiarity with that period. 22. After this verse LXX adds that David was angry and spoke to the messenger in practically the same phrases as occur in 20 f. This addition may well be genuine, though it may seem strange that Joab should anticipate David's words so accurately. However it was probably an established maxim of Israelite warfare not to approach the walls of a besieged city too openly, and this was phrased proverbially by a reference to Abimelech's ignominious death. 24. ' king's servants ' : LXX gives the number as 18.

XII 1-31 Nathan's Parable—As if consulting David **g** about a case of heartless oppression of the poor by the rich, Nathan skilfully aroused the king's hatred of everything that was mean and cruel, until David seems the very embodiment of avenging justice. We can sense the dramatic pause after 6, and then like the thrust of a sword Nathan's ' Thou art the man ' tearing open David's inmost soul. Henceforth he is a changed man. He has tangled a coil of difficulties and sorrow around his life which will have terrible results in the future.

10. ' the sword shall never depart ' : an allusion to **h** the indirect consequences of David's sin in the deaths of Amnon, Absalom, and Adonias. 11. ' I will raise up evil ' : God would allow the same ungovernable passions that had mastered David, murder and lust, to be scourges of his sin. 23. ' I shall go to him ' : implies a belief that man lives on in Sheol after death. 24. Solomon : his name in Hebrew, *Šᵉlōmōh*, means ' Peaceful '. His other name Jedidiah, ' Beloved of Yahweh ', comes from a root cognate to that of David's

260h own name. **26.** ' Joab fought ' : the account of the siege of Rabbath is resumed. **30.** ' a talent of gold ' : about 100 lb.—too heavy to be worn, but the talent may refer to its great value rather than to its weight. **31.** ' sawed them ' : lit. he put them on the saw. Probably it means he made them his industrial slaves by employing them in sawmills and brickmills, etc.

261a XIII 1-38 The Sin of Amnon and its Consequences —The later years of David's life were clouded by the crimes of his own family. The dangers of his polygamous court now reveal themselves in the character and deeds of his sons, Amnon and Absalom. Amnon was tormented by the same passion that ruined his father. By the advice of the unscrupulous Jonadab, Amnon used trickery to commit a shameful outrage against his beautiful half-sister, Thamar—the full sister of Absalom. His crime and its brutality are described with a realism which is common to all these early denunciations of immorality. He was David's eldest son and his conduct was a cruel blow to his father ; yet David did not punish him, because he still loved him. David's weakness in the matter aroused Absalom to take the law into his own hands. He imitated his father's treachery in dealing with Urias, and where his father had been guilty of homicide, he became guilty of fratricide. To avoid the vengeance of Amnon's kinsmen, Absalom fled to his grandfather's court at Gessur.

b 6. ' two little messes ' : two little cakes suitable for an invalid. **13.** ' he will not deny me to thee ' : perhaps a last desperate expedient suggested by Thamar to gain time. Such marriages had been tolerated in patriarchal times, but were forbidden by the Mosaic law, Deut 27:22 ; Lev 18:9. **20.** ' hold thy peace ' : a public scandal must be avoided, and Absalom intended to take full vengeance for the crime. If nothing was said, Amnon's fears and suspicions would be allayed. **21.** ' exceedingly grieved ' : the rest of this verse is not in the MT. Many of the world's worst criminals are trained in homes where parents are too weak or selfish to insist on those vital lessons of discipline and justice which are the only bulwarks against the inevitable temptations of life. **27.** ' he let Amnon . . . go with him ' : even David is made an unconscious agent in the tragedy which followed. **32.** ' he was appointed by the mouth ' : Jonadab, the same man as in 3, sets aside the exaggerated rumours of wholesale slaughter. He tells David that the look on Absalom's face foretold who his victim was to be. **34.** ' young man that kept the watch ' : a sentinel on one of the towers of the city. LXX has an additional variation : ' And behold much people were coming in the way behind him by the side of the hill at the descent. And the watchman came and told the king and said : " I have seen men coming from the way of Oronen, by the side of the hill ". And Jonadab said ', etc. This Oronen probably represents Beth-horon, NW. of Jerusalem. **37.** Tholomai : the father of Absalom's mother. ' mourned for his son ' : Amnon, not Absalom. His first feelings towards Absalom were those of anger. **38.** ' ceased to pursue ' : in LXX the subject of ' pursue ' is not the king, but ' the spirit of the king '. AV describes the spirit of David as ' longing to go forth unto Absalom ', but the Heb. word does not bear that meaning here. The general sense required by the context is that David's active hostility to Absalom was dying away with the passing of the years.

c XIV 1-33 The Return of Absalom—After two years of exile Absalom enlisted the help of Joab to procure his return to his father's court. Joab sent a shrewd woman from Thecua near Bethlehem with a pathetic story which would appeal to David's sympathy. As in the case of Nathan, before he realized the drift of the appeal, he was committed to applying the principles of the story to his own case, and the old smouldering fire of affection for Absalom burst into flame. At first Absalom was not admitted into the king's presence, but with Joab's intervention the reconciliation was completed.

d 2. Thecua : 5 miles south of Bethlehem, the home of the shepherd prophet Amos. **7.** ' quench my spark ' : **26** if the demand for blood-revenge is carried out, it will mean the destruction forever of her family. **9.** ' may the king ' : she insinuates that the king is dismissing her with mere promises. This forces David to commit himself by oath that the woman's son shall be saved. **13.** ' Why hast thou ' : David had admitted there were possible exceptions to the general law of blood-revenge ; why did he not apply the same principle in the case of Absalom, his own son, where there was every reason for doing so ? His obstinacy in this matter was an injury done to God's people since it deprived them of an heir to the throne. He is acting against his own son like the blood-avengers in her own story. **14.** ' We all die ' : life is uncertain and no harshness to Absalom will bring back the dead Amnon. **19.** ' neither on the left hand ' : David's question had lighted on the exact truth. **26.** ' according to the common weight ' : rather ' according to the king's weight '. 200 ordinary shekels would mean about 61 lbs. Either the king's measure must have been much smaller, or as is often the case with numbers, some error has crept into the text. **27.** ' three sons ' : not named because none of them lived very long, *cf.* 18:18. **29.** ' he would not come ' : Joab was the soul of loyalty and hesitated to deal with one who was not yet a *persona grata* with David.

XV 1-XVI 23 Absalom's Rebellion—After four years **e** (the 40 of v 7 is a copyist's error), Absalom used the technique of a demagogue to win his father's throne. By his intrigues he implicated a great number of the nobility in the conspiracy at Hebron. David fled from Jerusalem, but the prominent men of his court remained faithful to him : Joab, the priests Sadoc and Abiathar, Chusai his counsellor, and his noble Philistine friend Ethai. David refused to take the Ark with him, and the two priests together with Chusai were sent back to Jerusalem to sabotage the enemy's plans. During his flight, Siba, who was Miphiboseth's estate-agent, met him with a welcome present of provisions. A second incident was humiliating to David. The resentment of those Benjamites who still remained faithful to Saul, found expression in the jeers and curses of a certain Semei (Shimei).

7. ' forty ' : this should be ' four ' according to the **f** Qeri of MT, Josephus, Syr. and Arabic versions. **9.** Hebron : the old capital of Judah which might still be jealous of the growing prestige of Jerusalem. **11.** ' two hundred men ' : these special guests were in a compromising situation. Their presence at the feast would seem to betoken complicity in Absalom's plot, and if they showed any lack of enthusiasm, they could easily be held as hostages. **12.** Achitophel : there is a strange parallel between this Judas of the OT and the Judas of NT times, *cf.* Jn 13:18 ff. Treachery and suicide are the marks of both. **18.** ' all his servants ' : the LXX rendering agrees with our MT with the addition of readings from a more primitive Hebrew text : ' And all his servants passed on beside him, and all the Cerethi and all the Phelethi, and halted at the olive tree in the wilderness. And all the people marched by close to him and all his attendants, and all the mighty men [Gibborim] and all the warriors, six hundred men, and were present by his side, and all the Cerethi and all the Phelethi, and all the Gethites, the six hundred men who came after him from Geth ', marched on before the king '. In this march-past of the troops, the general body of David's men come first, then the foreign mercenaries, and finally more recent reinforcements who were probably under the leadership of Ethai, mentioned in the next verse. **19.** ' said to Ethai ' : David suggests that this foreigner need not embroil himself in the king's misfortunes. He is free to enlist in the service of whatever king rules in Jerusalem. **23.** ' the brook Cedron ' : in the valley east of Jerusalem, mentioned in the NT when our Lord was leaving the city that had rejected him, Jn 18:1. **32.** Arachite : the Arachites are mentioned in Jos 16:2 between Luza and Ataroth.

1g **XVI 3.** 'Siba answered': he pretended that Jonathan's son was hoping that Absalom's revolt would benefit the house of Saul. David was hurt by this seeming ingratitude and without further inquiry made over Miphiboseth's estates to Siba. **10.** 'the king said': David refuses to adopt the feelings of these Sons of Thunder of the OT. In his old age he was not so magnanimous, *cf.* 3 Kg 2:8. The Kethib is to be translated, ' If he curseth, and if the Lord hath said to him, " Curse David ", then who shall say . . . ?' The Qeri makes better sense : ' So let him curse, for the Lord hath said . . . and who shall say . . .' Semei is only an instrument of Divine Providence permitted by God to make David suffer for his sins. **14.** ' came weary there ' : evidently some place-name has fallen out of the text. Lucian inserts ' beyond the Jordan '. **18.** ' Chusai answered ' : he pretends that ' vox populi, vox Dei ' has won him over to Absalom's cause. **21.** ' Achitophel said ' : Absalom must take possession of his father's harem. This act of royal authority would convince waverers in the party that nothing could now heal this final breach with his father. Otherwise they might well fear a possible reconciliation and then they would be left to face the consequences. **22.** ' spread a tent ' : the bridal tent of Semitic peoples, a relic of which may be seen in the Kuppah or canopy still used in the marriage ritual of modern Jews. **23.** ' as if a man : ' men listened to his advice as if they were listening to some divine oracle.

2a **XVII 1-29 Achitophel's Counsel Defeated by Chusai—** With great skill Chusai opposed Achitophel's proposal that David must be annihilated without the slightest delay. To give David time to rally stronger forces, he emphasized the need for the utmost caution in dealing with a man of David's reputation. He played upon Absalom's personal vanity by telling him that he must lead the army in person, and sent word to David telling him how to act. In the duel of wits, the crafty Chusai won the day. His rival Achitophel knew that his whole policy had received its death blow. When he committed suicide, Absalom's rebellion lost the brain which alone could have brought success.

b **3.** ' I will bring back ' : the copyist has obviously omitted some other words which are retained in the LXX. ' I will bring back all the people to thee as the bride returns to her husband ; only one man thou seekest—and all the people will be at peace ', *i.e.* there is no need for civil war, it is a question of one man disturbing the peace between Absalom and Israel. **8.** ' not lodge with people ' : either an experienced warrior like David will be hiding in some stronghold where he will not allow himself to be surprised by his enemies, or (if we take the verb as a *hiph'il*) he will not allow his men to rest, but will have them ready to ambush Absalom's men. **11.** ' thou shalt be ' : a flattering picture of Absalom leading an immense and victorious army. **17.** Rogel is probably Bir Ayyub near the junction of the valleys of Kidron and Hinnom. **22.** ' over the Jordan : he halted finally at ' the camp ', *i.e.* at Mahanaim as in 2:8. **25.** ' Jethra of Jezrael ' : MT has ' Ithra the Israelite ', but it would be superfluous to add his nationality, unless he were a foreigner. In 1 Par 2:17 he is called the Ishmaelite, and this seems more probable. Naas seems to be another name for Jesse in 1 Par 2:13, 16.

c **XVIII 1-33 Defeat and Death of Absalom—**When reviewing his troops before battle, David publicly commanded his three generals, Joab, Abisai, and Ethai to spare Absalom's life. Thousands of Absalom's men lost their lives in the thickets and bogs near the battlefield. Joab paid no attention to David's wishes, as often when they ran counter to his own. To him Absalom was a rebel and a serious threat to David's kingdom, and he made sure of his death. David's cry of heartbroken grief for his son remains one of the most moving passages in all literature.

d **3.** ' to succour us ' : by sending reinforcements, if need be. **8.** ' consumed ' : the pits, swamps, and trees so hindered those who fled that they were easily overtaken and slain. **9.** ' his head stuck ' : the mule riding at full speed left Absalom with his head wedged in the forked branch of an oak. **17.** ' great heap of stones ' : a monument of shame like that over the grave of Achan, Jos 7:26. This is in contrast with the splendid tomb Absalom had intended for himself, *cf.* next verse. **21.** ' Joab said ' : as his name implies, Chusai was probably an Egyptian or Nubian slave who, unlike Achimaas, had nothing to lose by being the bearer of bad news.

262d

XIX 1-40 David's Return to Jerusalem—At first, **e** David's outburst of grief for Absalom threatened to cause dismay and desertion among the troops. Once more Joab came to the rescue of his royal master. The good sense of this old soldier's gruff speech forced David to make a public appearance for the sake of the people who had indeed saved his throne. A general amnesty was granted to the rebels. On his way to Jerusalem he met the now obsequious Semei and Miphiboseth. His host Berzellai declined an invitation to come to court.

8. ' Israel fled ' : those of the people who had followed **f** Absalom, as contrasted with the rest of the nation. This prepares us for the account of the negotiations necessary for the full restoration of David to his throne. **10.** ' Absalom is dead ' : the people remembered the advantages of David's rule, now that Absalom was dead. The LXX ' And the word of all Israel came to the king ' implies that rumours in favour of his restoration had reached his ears. **11.** ' ancients of Judah ' : these elders hesitated about the king's return, because so many of their tribesmen had taken a prominent part in the rebellion. **13.** Amasa : David promised him Joab's post as head of the army. This was David's solitary attempt to curb his outspoken general. **21.** ' the Lord's anointed ' : to curse the king was to curse the representative of Yahweh himself and therefore akin to blasphemy. **20.** ' house of Joseph ' : the ten tribes of Israel as distinguished from Judah. **22.** ' a satan to me ' : an opponent of my true interests ; *cf.* Mt 16:23. Later by his command to Solomon, 3 Kg 2:8 ff., David broke the spirit, if not the letter, of his promise of clemency to Semei. **24.** ' had not washed ' : all these signs of neglect were marks of sorrow. **25.** ' at Jerusalem ' : should probably be emended to ' from Jerusalem '. A number of LXX MSS support this correction. **29.** ' divide ' : David insists on a compromise in order to placate both parties. **37.** ' Chamaam ' : Berzellai declines David's kind invitation because of his advanced age, but suggests that his son should take his place.

41-XX 22 Seba's Rebellion—The deep-rooted jealousy **g** between the tribes of the north and south was not destroyed by David's restoration. The men of Israel accused Judah of receiving preferential treatment from the king. Taking advantage of this quarrel, Seba, a Benjamite, raised a revolt. David commissioned Amasa to muster the army and deal with the rebellion, but Amasa lacked Joab's energy and prestige and was unable to carry out the king's orders. In desperation, David ordered Abisai to march against Seba. On this occasion Joab occupied a very subordinate position, and the murder of Abner with which Joab had begun his career, was repeated in the treacherous murder of Amasa at the close of it. Joab took command and the insurrection was soon at an end. He returned with his army to the capital to continue as the grim, invincible power behind the throne.

41. ' Stolen thee away ' : why have the men of Judah, **h** who were so slow in recognizing David as king again, been allowed to escort the king home, when only a fraction of the northern tribes were present ? The men of Judah are acting in this way to secure a monopoly of royal favours ! ' and all the men of David with him ' : this may mean, as Dhorme suggests, ' After all, all David's men are (equally) his people '—not merely the tribe of Judah. **42.** ' Have we eaten ' : they have not had any material benefit, if that is what these Israelites are insinuating. **XX 1.** ' there happened to be there ' :

262h in this tense atmosphere of sectional interests, Seba ambitiously asserted the rights of the tribe of Benjamin to the throne. His clan traced its descent back to **Bochri**, the second son of Benjamin, *cf*. Gen 46:21. **8.** ' great stone ': a well-known landmark; *cf*. 1 Kg 6:14 ff. **10.** ' Amasa did not notice ': LXX has " the sword came out and fell down ". He purposely let his ordinary sword fall down, as he approached Amasa, in order to disarm his suspicions, while he killed his rival with a dagger concealed beneath his military cloak. **15.** ' Abela and in Bethmaacha ': Abel-Beth-Macaacha is a place in the northern extremity of Israelite territory and is called Abel-Maim, ' Abel of the Waters ' in 2 Par 16:4. **19.** ' overthrow a mother ': this city is so renowned for its wisdom and traditions, that Joab should not destroy it, but pay it the veneration due to a mother. **22.** ' Joab returned to the king ': we are not told how David received him, but he must have realized that Joab was now indispensable.

i XX 23-26 David's Ministers—A list of people who held administrative posts at David's court concludes this account of his reign. The remaining chapters are in the nature of an appendix. An earlier list of officials has been given, 8:16-18. This second one must have been drawn up in the latter part of his reign. The material of these summaries is repeated by the Chronicler, who adds in 1 Par 27:25-34 a list of twelve officials who had charge of the royal estates and herds. David's reign had brought the country the benefits of organized administration and all the machinery of a civilized oriental state. Joab was head of the War Department. The names and offices of Josaphat, Sadoc, and Banaias occur again. Siva is apparently another name for Saraias of 8:17. Ira the Jairite's name is substituted in place of that of David's sons. A more important addition is the name of Aduram (LXX, Adoniram) who was head of the Royal Treasury, but his actual duties were more like those of the Ministry of Labour. One of Solomon's ministers called Adoniram was in charge of the labour gangs which were raised under a system of corvée. Probably he held a similar post in David's time.

263a XXI-XXIV Appendix—The four remaining chapters contain six appendices, derived from various sources and inserted here in order not to interrupt the narrative account of David's reign. The logical sequel to 20:26 is 3 Kgs 1:1.

b XXI 1-14 The Story of Respha and the Famine— A three years famine forced David to inquire of Yahweh why the land had suffered in this way. The answer was that it was due to Saul's breach of faith and slaughter of the Gabaonites in spite of their covenant with Israel. The Gabaonites demanded blood for blood. David shielded Miphiboseth, but two sons of Respha (Saul's concubine) and five sons of Merob were taken to be sacrificed. With the heroic devotion of motherhood Respha kept her terrible watch beside the dead. Day after day she beat off the vultures and birds of prey. Night after night she drove away the prowling beasts which came to feast among the dead. In the end when there was little left but bleached bones, David insisted on giving them honourable burial beside Saul and Jonathan.

c 1. ' in the days of David ': the literary style and primitive religious ideas of this narrative reveal its early date. It may be closely connected with the events of ch 9. ' his bloody house ': LXX seems to be nearer the Heb. original : ' Upon Saul and his house is blood-guiltiness '. Yahweh is represented as the avenger of the broken covenant between the Gabaonites and Israel (Jos 9:3 f.), though we are not told the exact details of Saul's crime. The sense of the rights and responsibilities of each individual was as yet undeveloped, and in these early days the sins of the heads of families were thought to involve all its members in their consequences. Later divine revelation made it clear that each individual conscience was responsible for its own guilt, Ez 18:2-4. Yet there is a deep psychological truth behind these primitive conceptions of family

unity. We are all bound to one another intellectually, **26** socially, and spiritually, each of us in some measure is a product of all that has gone before. This solidarity of mankind is raised to a divine unity in the doctrine of the Mystical Body of Christ. **2.** ' Now the Gabaonites ' : this is an explanatory gloss introduced into the text. **3.** ' the atonement ' : *i.e.* make some expiatory offering which will appease Yahweh's anger and bring a blessing upon Israel. **4.** ' any man ' : we have no quarrel with the Israelites in general, only with the house of Saul. **6.** ' crucify them ' : the exact meaning of the Heb. verb is uncertain. The general meaning of LXX suggests hanging. ' in *Gabaon* ' : this was to be the scene of the execution. Some MSS omit Saul's name. Then instead of *beḥîr Yahweh* (' the chosen of Yahweh ') we can read *behar Yahweh* (' in the mountain of Yahweh '). Thus the execution of vengeance would be a religious act done in the presence of Yahweh as in 1 Kg 15:33. We know from 3 Kg 3:4 that there was a special sanctuary at Gabaa in Solomon's time. **7.** ' Miphiboseth ' : not to be confused with Isboseth who was Saul's son. **8.** ' Michol ' : a copyist's mistake for Merob who was married to Hadriel. The Targum says these sons were adopted by Michol. **9.** ' barley began to be reaped ' : *i.e.* towards the end of April. **10.** ' water dropped ' : until October, unless the rainfall was earlier.

15-22 Exploits against the Philistines—All com- **d** mentators remark that the text here and in 23:8-39 is very uncertain. The main outline of the account seems to be that (*a*) David's life was in danger from a giant Philistine, but Abisai came to the rescue in the nick of time. (*b*) At Gob (unidentified) three more Philistines are slain. It is to be noted that 1 Par 20:47 gives a parallel account of the events narrated in 18-22 of this section. There seems no reason for doubting that the Goliath in 19 is the same person as in 1 Kg 17, and both David and Elhanan cannot have killed the same man. Hence many modern critics consider 1 Kg 17 embodies a later tradition in which the exploit of Elhanan was attributed to his royal master. This overlooks the fact that it must have been precisely some such astounding feat of arms which first brought David into public notice. Ewald suggests that the *name* of Goliath was borrowed from the conflict of the real Goliath with Elhanan to denote the Philistine giant slain by David. Jerome (*Quaest. Heb.*, *ad loc.*) makes David the same as Elhanan. Another solution put forward is based on the text of 1 Par 20:5. ' Elhanan (Adeodatus), son of Jair, slew Lahmi the brother of Goliath of Geth,' so that not Goliath, but Goliath's brother was Elhanan's victim. The Heb. letters of the word Bethlehemite (*bêṭ hallaḥmî 'ēṭ*) could easily be confused with *'eṭ-laḥmî 'aḥî* (' Lahmi the brother of ').

16. Arapha : the first vowel represents the Heb. **e** article in *Hā-Rāpāh*, a collective term for the prehistoric inhabitants of the land. **17.** ' put out the lamp ' : by losing his life the king would plunge the nation into the darkness of sorrow and disaster ; *cf*. Ps 131:17 ; 3 Kg 11:36 ; 4 Kg 8:19. **18.** Sobochai : one of David's generals ; *cf*. 1 Par 27:11. **21.** Jonathan: a nephew of David's. David's brother is called Semmaa in 13:3 ; Samma in 1 Kg 16:9 ; and Simmaa in 1 Par 2:13.

XXII 1-51 David's Song of Thanksgiving—This song **f** is repeated in the Psalter as Ps 17, where see commentary.

XXIII 1-7 David's Last Words—There is no way of **g** determining the exact date of this psalm of David's. Like Moses before his death (Deut 32) David is represented as giving his last will and testament in a prayer. It sums up David's confidence that Yahweh will keep his promise of an eternal covenant with the house of David. It is obviously poetic in structure.

> **1.** Oracle of David son of Jesse,
> Oracle of the man raised up on high,
> The Anointed of the God of Jacob,
> Sweet psalmist of Israel.

3g 2. The Spirit of Yahweh spoke by me,
And his word was on my tongue ;
3. The God of Jacob has spoken—
The Rock of Israel said to me—
He that ruleth over men justly,
Ruling in the fear of God ;
4. (He) is like the light of morning at sunrise,
The sun of a cloudless morning,
Making the green earth glisten after rain.
5. Yea, my house standeth firm with God,
For an everlasting covenant has he made with me ;
Firmly established in all things, and he will keep it,
For all my salvation and delight are in him.
6. But the wicked shall not flourish,
They are all like desert thorns,
They cannot be gathered by hand,
7. Nor can any man touch them,
Unless armed with iron and spear,
(Then) they shall be consumed with fire.

h There are many textual obscurities in this passage, but its general sense is quite clear. It should be considered as complementary to the divine promise made in 2 Kg 7. It celebrates the special glory of the Davidic dynasty, some features of which were partially realized in Solomon and the more noble of the kings of Judah, but completely so in Christ alone. As the Targum of Jonathan says : ' These are the words of the prophecy of David concerning the end of the age, concerning the days of consolation which are to come '. Many of its characteristic features are emphasized in the writings of later prophets. Ruler, *e.g.* Mic 5:2 ; Justice, Is 11:1–5 ; Jer 23:5 ; 33:15 ; Fear of the Lord, Is 11:3, and the closing words of the last prophet re-echo these last words of David, Mal 4:2.

i 1. ' said ' : lit. ' the utterance ', *neʾûm*, the technical Heb. word for a divinely inspired utterance ; *cf.* Num 24:3 ' The man . . . Christ ' : this follows LXX. The Old Latin has ' quem suscitavit Deus '. ' God of Jacob ' : the story of Jacob's wanderings, his trust in God's care, and God's covenant with him have their parallel in David's life. ' excellent psalmist ' : lit. ' delightful in Israel's psalms '. He educated and developed the religious life of the nation as much by his psalms as by his rule as king. 3. ' God of Israel ' : he claims divine inspiration for his oracle—the Ruling Force, the central Rock of the whole nation speaks in him. ' the ruler of men ' : in a few words he draws the portrait of the ideal king, completely under the guidance of the fear of God. 4. ' light of the morning ' : the blessings of his reign can only be compared to lifegiving sunshine and the fresh greenness that follows a springtide shower of rain. 5. ' Neither is my house ' : this negative seems to be the very opposite of what David wishes to say. For this reason some authors translate the Heb. particle *lōʾ* in a negative sense demanding an affirmative answer. ' firm in all things ' : carefully drawn up in every detail like a legal document. 6. ' as thorns ' : in contrast to the fresh green of the kingdom in its prosperity, there is the evil growth of thorns which cannot be touched with the naked hand ; they must be torn up with iron hooks.

4a 8-39 A List of David's Heroes and their Exploits—Under the warrior-king David both the army and methods of war were greatly improved. The Supreme Commander was Joab. As a rule the entire force was divided into three divisions and their leadership entrusted to chosen generals. A selected number called the Thirty, whose exploits and bravery were outstanding, provided the nucleus for a further corps of officers. In addition, a central mobile force of sixty picked men, called the Heroes (2 Kg 10:7) formed a body of household troops. Later in David's reign we meet with a special royal guard of professional soldiers of foreign extraction, but the Three divisional commanders and the Thirty Heroes formed the backbone of the army, Some of their deeds of bravery reveal a magnificent spirit of daring and chivalry. The parallel account in 1 Par 11:11–41 is put after David's election as King of Israel, and has a better preserved text. Logically **264a** this section seems to have been a continuation of 23:15–22, and must have become separated from it in the course of time.

8. ' Jesbaham, sitting in the chair ' : the text is better **b** preserved in 1 Par 11:11, and we should read : Jesbaham, a Hachmonite. ' chief among the three ' : 1 Par 11:11 has ' chief of the Thirty '. Confusion in the Heb. text of this section could easily arise, for the Heb. words for three, thirty, and aide-de-camp are very similar. ' tender little worm ' : MT is very corrupt ; lit. ' he is Adino the Eznite, over eight hundred slain at one time '. LXX also introduces ' Adino the Asonean is he who drew his sword against eight hundred warriors at once '. 1 Par. omits Adino and reads : ' Jesbaam . . . lifted up his spear against three hundred wounded by him at one time '. The reading usually adopted by commentators from this obscure collection of Heb. consonants is ' brandishing his spear '. ' three hundred ' : MT has eight hundred. In these exploits, he would probably be accompanied by his armour-bearers, 1 Kg 14:6. 9. Ahohite : a certain Ahoe is mentioned in 1 Par 8:4 as belonging to the Benjamite clan. ' were with David ' : the text does not say where, but it can be supplied from 1 Par 11:13, ' in Phesdomim ', the scene of the battle between David and Goliath. 13. ' three who were princes ' : not the three already mentioned, but belonging to the Thirty Group. It is hard to determine whether these Thirty mighty men numbered exactly thirty, or whether it was only an ideal number and actually more numerous, for this ch gives thirty-seven such heroes. But some of these may have been appointed to take the place of others who died in battle. To be allowed into this privileged body of men was equivalent to receiving the V.C. 15. ' drink of water ' : David was gazing at the scene of his childhood with all its happy memories crowding into his mind. 16. ' would not drink ' : the selfless bravery and deep affection of his men had changed the water of Bethlehem into the wine of sacrifice—something too precious for merely human use. 18. ' chief among three ' : there must have been a second trio of which only two names are given here. If we add these to the Three and Thirty and include Joab, we get 37, the number given in 39.

XXIV 1-25 David's Census of the Nation—Popular **c** feeling against David's census of the people was expressed by Joab, but we are not told why this normal act of administration was sinful. David may have intended merely compiling a register for the organization of military service, fresh taxation, and forced labour for his building schemes. However it was a common belief amongst ancient Semitic peoples that whoever knew the name of a person, the number of his possessions, herds, and household acquired a mysterious power over them ; *cf.* RB 53 (1946) 178. Hence David's action implied that he had absolute rights over his people, whereas he was merely Yahweh's representative in a strictly theocratic state.

1. ' again kindled ' : this must refer back to the **d** previous famine in ch 21. In the corresponding account of 1 Par 21, 1–27 Satan is the instigator of David's action. The case is like that of Job 1:12 ; 2:10 where we have both the permissive action of God and the malicious initiative of Satan. 3. Joab : Père Desnoyers, *op. cit.* 3, 351, n. 3 suggests that the league mentioned in 2 Kg 5:3 had as one of its clauses the prohibition of any census, to safeguard the rights of the nation against excessive demands by the king in matters of war and finance. A shrewd general like Joab would realize the danger of underrating this passion for freedom against external control which was strongly developed amongst the Israelites. It was part of the inheritance they had received from their forefathers and was ultimately based upon a religious conception of man. ' The ancient Semitic nomad would not have understood the term democracy, but he had deeply implanted within him an unconscious theory of life which corresponds to the attitude which that word

264d indicates in common speech. That which the free Athenian citizen of the fifth century B.C. boasted as his highest achievement was taken for granted by the ideal ancestors of Israel ' (T. Robinson, *A History of Israel*, I, 105). **5.** Aroer : probably identical with Kh. 'Arâ'ir which stood on the N. bank of the Arnon, some four miles SW. of Dibon (Dhiban), with which it is associated in Num 32:34. Joab's officials moved from SE. Palestine to the extreme N. ; then they turned W. and

e worked their way southwards. **6.** Hodsi : no certain locality has been found for this name. Some MSS of LXX give ' to the land of the Hittites to Qadesh ', on the Orontes. **9.** ' sum of the number ' : these numbers are clearly exaggerated, *cf.* Desnoyers, *op. cit.* 2, 266, and conflict with those of 1 Par 21:5. Apart from any question of textual corruption, the sacred writer reminds us that he is not accepting these numbers as the official statistics from authoritative national archives, *cf.* 1 Par 27:24. **13.** ' seven years ' : LXX and Chronicler's ' three years ' are more in accord with the symmetrical ' three ' in each punishment. **17.** ' It is I ' : David takes full responsibility. The ancient

world in the East had a strong sense of the social and **26** spiritual solidarity of men. This was particularly true of kings who represented their people before their gods ; *cf.* L. Dürr, *Ursprung und Ausbau der israelitisch-jüdischen Heilandserwartung* (Berlin 1925) 139 ff. The later disasters which followed in the wake of those kings of Israel whose hearts were not right with Yahweh were God's own commentary on the real vocation of the monarchy to represent Israel in his sight ; *cf.* 1 Par 10:13 ; 2 Par 12:2, 12. **18.** ' thrashing floor of Areuna ' : this was on Mt Moriah, the site of Solomon's temple, where now stands the Moslem Dome of the Rock. Areuna is called Ornan in 1 Par 21:15. **25.** ' offered holocausts ' : Mosaic legislation reserved to priests the right of offering sacrifice, Num 16:39, 40 ; 17:7. According to Van Hoonacker, Claire, and Kugler, this and similar passages are only apparent exceptions to the general rule, *i.e.* the king offered sacrifice through priests. Schulz, Schlögl, and Desnoyers prefer to consider such occasions as exceptions made by divine authority to the law of priestly sacrifice.

3 and 4 KINGS

(1 and 2 KINGS)

By K. SMYTH, S.J.

265a Bibliography—A. Šanda, *Die Bücher der Könige* (1911–1912) ; S. Landersdorfer, BB (1927) ; A. Médebielle, *La Sainte Bible*, ed. Pirot-Clamer, III (1949) ; *J. Skinner, 1 and 2 Kings (1904) ; *J. A. Montgomery, ICC (1951) ; *R. Kittel, *Die Bücher der Könige* (1900) ; F.-M. Abel, *Géographie de le Palestine*, I (1932), II (1938) ; L.-H. Vincent, *Jérusalem Antique* (1912) ; F. X. Kugler, *Von Moses bis Paulus* (1922) ; B. Bonkamp, *Die Bibel im Lichte der Keilschriftforschung* (1939) ; E. Schrader, *Keilinschriftliche Bibliothek* (1896 ff.) ; J. Breasted, *Ancient Records of Egypt* (1906 ff.) ; H. Gressmann, *Altorientalische Texte zum A. T.* (1927²) ; D. D. Luckenbill, *Ancient Records of Assyria and Babylonia*, I (1926) ; G. A. Cooke, *North-Semitic Inscriptions* (1903) ; *W. F. Albright, *Archaeology and the Religion of Israel* (1946²) ; L. Köhler, *Lexicon in Veteris Testamenti Libros* (1948 ff.). R. de Vaux, O.P., *Les Livres des Rois* (1949). Literature on particular points is noted in the course of the commentary.

b Title and Contents—3 and 4 Kg (Vg ; DV ; LXX, 3 and 4 Kingdoms) formed originally in the Hebrew one book. The division, which is artificial, appeared first in LXX and seems to have been occasioned by the normal size of the book-roll, too small to contain the whole in one roll. The Hebrew text was divided, into 1 and 2 Kg, only in the 15th cent. 3 and 4 Kg take up the narrative of 1 and 2 Kg (Hebrew, 1 and 2 Samuel) with an account of the last days of David and the accession of Solomon. Then comes the reign of Solomon, with the building of the temple. After the death of Solomon, the history falls readily into two divisions, the separate kingdoms of north and south, and the kingdom of Judah alone, till the destruction of the temple and the exile. This covers more than 400 years. For a general view of the events of this period, see §§ 63*d*–66*f*.

c Scope—The usual tripartite division (the united, divided and surviving monarchy) does not quite correspond to the author's view-point. For him the first part of the story ended with 3 Kg 10 : the Kingdom of David enjoying idyllic prosperity as the reward of faithful worship of Yahweh centred upon Solomon's temple. The second part of the story, running to the end of the book, was the decline and fall of the Kingdom of David, envisaged as the punishment of the worship of false gods introduced by Solomon. The fact that Israel in the north and Judah in the south went separate paths to their doom does not affect the unity of this conception. But in this second part, there is again a turning-point in the history of each kingdom. In the north, it was the worship of Yahweh under the form of a bull, 3 Kg 12. Up to this, Jeroboam, like Solomon before him, had enjoyed God's blessing. The illegitimate worship, to which was then added the cult of the Tyrian Baal, made Israel's destruction inevitable, though it was postponed as often as the northerners responded to the guidance of the prophets. In the south, the turning-point was delayed till the reign of Manasses, 4 Kg 20. The last chapters stand in the same relation to the idolatry of Manasses as the whole of the great second part to the idolatry of Solomon. The book is in fact composed for the specific purpose of religious edification. Like the other OT historians, the author's interest is not primarily political

narrative. His purpose is to show how Yahweh **265c** enforced his law of retribution in the course of history, rewarding obedience with prosperity, punishing sin with suffering.

Composition——This 'pragmatic' stand-point of the **d** author appears both in his personal contribution to the book and in his use of sources. He composed a frame-work within which the individual kings were dealt with, from the division of the kingdom onwards. For the kings of Israel, the introductory formula is : 'In the xth year of King N. of Judah, N., son of N., became King of Israel for x years'. For the kings of Judah : ' In the xth year of King N. of Israel, N., son of N., became King of Judah. He was x years old when he became King, and he reigned x years in Jerusalem. His mother's name was N.'. For Israel, the closing formula is : ' The rest of the history of N. and all his feats are available, as is well-known, in the Book of the History of the Kings of Israel. So N. was gathered to his fathers and was buried in Samaria, and his son N. reigned in his stead '. For Judah : ' The rest of the history of N. and all his feats, are available, as is well-known, in the Book of the History of the Kings of Judah. So N. was gathered to his fathers and was buried with his fathers in the city of David, and his son N. reigned in his stead '. These formulas may vary slightly, or be omitted in whole or part as circumstances demand, *e.g.* where a king died by violence, or in the case of the usurper Athalia. The order of the narrative is determined by the date of a king's accession. For instance, Achab of Israel and Josaphat of Judah were contemporaries. But since Achab, 3 Kg 16:29, became king a little earlier than Josaphat his whole reign is narrated, and then, 22:40, the writer turns back and narrates the reign of Josaphat to its close, though in the meantime two kings had succeeded Achab in Israel.

With the framework is linked the writer's verdict on **e** each king. For Israel it is invariably : ' And he did evil before the Lord ', the evil being ' the sin of Jeroboam '. This blame is accorded even to Zimri, 3 Kg 16:19, who reigned only a week. In Judah, eight kings are praised, Asa, Josaphat, Joas, Amasias, Azarias, Joatham, Ezechias and Josias. But the praise of the first six is restricted by a reference to their tolerating shrines of Yahweh outside Jerusalem. The remaining kings of Judah are condemned, the last six, significantly, in the terms applied to the kings of Israel : ' And he did evil before the Lord '. The sin of Jeroboam was the calf-worship, with the consequent organization of a non-Levitical priesthood at the illegitimate shrines, 3 Kg 12:26-31. These things were forbidden by Deut 4:15 ff. ; 9:8–21 ; 18:1 ff. Deut 12:2–18 is the source of the condemnation of the shrines of Yahweh in the south. Indeed, the constant recurrence of Deuteronomic phrases, *e.g.* 2 Kg 2:3 (*cf.* Deut 4:9) is characteristic of the author's work. A full list of parallels may be seen in Driver LOT, 200–2. The fullest formulation of his ' theology of history ' is given in the long comment on the fall of Samaria, 4 Kg 17:7–23. Within the setting of these synchronisms and moral judgements, the author incorporated his sources, sometimes almost unchanged, *e.g.* 3 Kg 17–19, sometimes interwoven with Deuteronomic considerations, *e.g.* 3 Kg 14, which appears in LXX 12:24*g–n* (Rahlfs) without the characteristic phrases.

265f Sources—The writer refers once to the 'Book of the Acts of Solomon', 3 Kg 11:41, 17 times to the 'Book of the History of the Kings of Israel', 15 times to the 'Book of the History of the Kings of Judah'. 'The Book of the History' is a technical term for official records; cf. Est 2:23; 6:1; 10:2; Neh 12:23; 1 Par 27:24. Possibly the Mazkîr 'Remembrancer', 3 Kg 4:3, was responsible for them. But what are cited in Kg were probably not the original state documents, but later compilations based on them, comparable to the prophetic writings of Nathan, Ahias, etc. cited in Par. The History of the Kings of Judah is cited for the last time for Joakim, 4 Kg 24:4, hence it was compiled under Sedecias, by someone who saw the coming peril and wished to save the substance of the threatened documents. The 'Histories', according to the allusions to them in Kg, described 'the activities', 'the victories', 'the wars', and 'the buildings' of the kings. By repeatedly referring the reader to these documents for information in these matters, the writer showed that his own object was not to give complete political narrative.

g Other material at the author's disposal, readily distinguishable from the Histories by its special contents and fullness of presentation, included accounts of Jeroboam, Achab and Jehu in the north, and of Joas, Ezechias and Josias in the south, and various histories of prophets. To these must be added the writer's own account of Joachin and Sedecias, 4 Kg 24:10–25:21. The high literary value of 3 Kg 1 (accession of Solomon), 3 Kg 17–19 (Stories of Elias) and 4 Kg 9–10 (Jehu) has often been remarked.

h His use of sources is influenced by his dominant idea, that Yahweh rewards obedience and punishes sin. The law of the one central sanctuary was particularly dear to him. Hence he gave special prominence to the building of the temple, and dwelt on incidents which touched its history, 3 Kg 14:26 ff., 15:18, 4 Kg 11–12. Fidelity to Yahweh demanded also obedience to the prophets, whose mission it was to proclaim the divine principle of retribution, 3 Kg 11:29, etc. Hence he retained the stirring details of the lives of Elias and Eliseus, and added accounts of false prophets, 3 Kg 20 and 22, to show the unhappy results of disregarding divine guidance. To illustrate his general principle, he could incorporate matter which had no direct relation either to the cult or the prophets. In the episode of Naboth's vineyard, for instance, 3 Kg 21, the lesson is the dire consequences of a 'divided heart' in the service of Yahweh.

i A result of the pragmatic stand-point is the omission, or compression into a passing reference, of much that must have been of great historical importance. This is most apparent in the treatment of Omri and Jeroboam II. They were the greatest of Israel's kings, but since the 'principle of retribution' could not be applied here immediately and in detail, the author confined himself to a reference to the 'History'. The same interest in the logical connexions of events led him at times to disregard the chronological order. For instance, 4 Kg 20 contains earlier matter than 18–19. But since Ezechias' fault illustrated the direction of history better than his triumph over Sennacherib, it was placed after the latter, as the real introduction to the decline which set in under Manasses.

j Historical Value—As the author's aim was not to be complete, but to expound the decisive factors in the period under review, the validity of his structure must be judged by the significance of his selected facts. Had they really the influence which he ascribed to them? A preliminary question is the historicity of the selected episodes. The usual criterions give a positive result. (1) Where the facts can be checked by 'profane' sources, they are found to be in accord with the general history of the period. See §§ 79d, 80c–k. Details are noticed in the Commentary. For the rest of the facts, the seriousness of the author and his constant appeals to documents by which his work could be checked, must be sufficient guarantees of his reliability. (2) The particular history of Israel, as **26** reflected in the prophetical books, Amos to Jeremias, shows the same situations as Kg. (3) He is objective and dispassionate. See especially the account of Solomon's accession. He does not hide the faults of his 'heroes', like Ezechias, nor the fine qualities of his 'villains', like Achab or even Jezabel, 4 Kg 10:30 ff. Prophecies too are kept in their authentic obscurity, **k** with no attempt to harmonize their terms with the details of their fulfilment; see especially 3 Kg 19:15. Again, though upholding the law of one sanctuary, he does not attempt to show that it always had the importance which he accorded to it. Thus Solomon's sacrifice at Gibeon, 3 Kg 3:4 ff., and Elias' on Carmel are recorded as acceptable. And in general, the attitude of the great northern prophets towards this law is left undefined. A less conscientious writer might have made them pronounce in its favour. (4) On the miraculous elements in general, see §§ 87–91. Here it must suffice to remark that the miracles have the same serious attestation as the rest of the book, and that the careers of the great prophets would be inexplicable without them. How indifferent the people was to the mere preaching and personality of the prophets may be seen from 3 Kg 18:21.

The accuracy of the author's interpretation of events **l** is guaranteed ultimately by the inspiration of the book, whose place in the Canon of Sacred Scripture has never been questioned. The rise and ruin of the Kingdom of David could indeed be traced to natural causes. But from the author we learn that God had a special purpose in raising up a David and a Solomon at the time when Assyria and Egypt were weak, and in depriving Judah of competent statesmen when the neo-Babylonian empire was most aggressive. Even from the merely historical view-point, however, the safety of the kingdom depended on its religion. The admission of idolatry set up divisions in the State between Yahwistic and anti-Yahwistic parties. It also led to a 'communio in sacris' with other countries, and so to political alliances which involved the two small states in great international conflicts. Had the reformation of Josias succeeded, Jeremias would not have preached submission in vain, and Judah might have survived Nabuchodonosor, a milder foe than Sennacherib. Thus the inequalities in the author's work—his brevity where we should expect fullness, his disproportionately long accounts of matters which history might ignore—are justified by the ultimate significance of his chosen events.

Date and Person of the Author—The book was finished **26** before 538, since there is no mention of the end of the exile, and cannot have been begun before the fall of Jerusalem, 587, since this dominates the conception of the history. If 4 Kg 25:27–30 belonged to the first draft, it must have been written after 561, 'the 37th year of the captivity of Joachin'. Šanda and others consider these verses an addition to the original, as being abrupt, isolated from any context, and betraying a mode of reckoning used only in Babylon. This last feature is explained by the author's habit of incorporating sources unchanged. The logical connexion with the foregoing is explained by the frequency with which God's promises to the house of David, 2 Kg 7:12–16, had been recalled, 3 Kg 2:4, 24; 3:6; 6:12; 8:25 f.; 9:5. The emphasis thus laid on the only trace of 'Messianism' in Kgs demanded the hopeful sign of 4 Kg 25:27–30.

Jeremias was named as author by the later Jews **b** (Talmud, *Baba Bathra* 15), a tradition accepted by A Lapide, Vigouroux, Cornely, Höpfl and others. The absence of the prophet from the history of Kg points in that direction, and the view-point of Kg agrees well with Jeremias. There are also similarities in phrasing; cf. Šanda I, xxxvii. More, however, cannot be proved than that the author was familiar and friendly with Jeremias. The prophet would have been nearly 100 in 561, before which the book cannot well have been written.

6c Text—MT preserves the original very well, better than in the prophetic books, but not so well as in the Pentateuch. LXX is important, not so much for the reading or explanation of difficult words in the Hebrew, as for the elimination of interpolated matter. The most remarkable features of LXX are its changes in the order of the text and the addition of some big sections. The chief variations are (1) 3 Kg 4:20–28 ; (2) 7 ; (3) 16:28a–h (LXX) where the reign of Josaphat appears before that of Achab, contrary to MT. In (1) LXX gives a better order of verses ; in (2) it describes the furniture of the temple before the palaces ; (3) results from a difference in chronology ; according to LXX Josaphat had come to the throne in the 11th year of Omri. The chief additions in LXX are (1) 3 Kg 2:35a–o ; (2) 2:46a–l ; (3) 12:24a–z. (1) and (2) contain practically nothing that does not occur somewhere in the Hebrew of 3–11. (3) seems to have come into LXX independently of the canonical Hebrew, from sources similar to those of Kg ; see Skinner, 443 ff. It contains matter which is historically helpful (see Commentary) but has itself been worked over and glossed according to MT. From this brief summary it will be seen that LXX interests textual criticism more than exegesis.

d Chronology—See § 124 for the general data of the chronological problem. The year 841, when Jehu paid tribute to Shalmaneser III provides a sure basis for the chronology between the division of Solomon's kingdom and the simultaneous accession of Jehu in Israel and of Athalia in Judah. As Achab was alive at Qarqar, 853, 12 years is the most that can be allowed for his successors, Ochozias and Joram. This suits the text of the Bible perfectly. Ochozias came to the throne in the 17th year of Josaphat, and reigned two years, 3 Kg 22:52. He died in the 18th of Josaphat, 4 Kg 3:1. The two years include the year of his accession and of his death, and are numerically one. Joram's reign is given as 12 years, and should be reckoned similarly as 11. Ochozias and Joram reigned 12 years altogether and Achab died in 853.

e The division of the kingdom was 37 years, 3 Kg 6:1 and 11:42, after the foundation of the temple (probably 968), therefore 931. Now Joram of Israel and Ochozias of Judah died the same year, 4 Kg 9. The totals of the reigns of the kings of Israel and Judah should be equal. In Israel, Jeroboam is given 22 years, Nadab 2, Baasa 24, Ela 2, Omri 12, Achab 22, Ochozias 2, Joram 12 : total, 98. In Judah Roboam is given 17, Abias 3, Asa 41, Josaphat 25, Joram 8, Ochozias 1 : total, 95. Subtract, however, from each total the number of years reckoned as 2 but really one, as above : 8 in Israel, 5 in Judah. The result is 90 in each case. It may be noted that this chronology is based on three independent sources : Josephus (for the temple ; see Kugler, 172–5), the Assyrian annals (for Qarqar and Jehu's tribute) and the Bible. If the battle of Qarqar is to be placed in 854 and Jehu's tribute in 842, as is done by many historians, the variation is insignificant.

f For the last period of the monarchy (Ezechias to the fall of Jerusalem) a start can be made, with some certainty, by dating the death of Achaz to spring 726. This date is indicated by Is 14:28 ff., as first suggested by H. Hänsler, Bi 10 (1929) 262–70 ; so too (independently) J. Begrich, *Die Chronologie der Könige von Israel und Juda*, 1929. It was soon after the death of Tiglath-pileser IV (Dec.–Jan., 727–726), to which the 'breaking of the rod' Is 14:29 refers. We assume that in this period the reigns in Judah are 'post-dated'. Note the synchronisms : '1st of Ezechias = 3rd of Osee, 4 Kg 18:1, 4th of Ezechias = 7th of Osee, 4 Kg 18:7. They differentiate between the year of Ezechias' succession, 726, 3rd Osee, and his first regnal year, 725, 4th Osee. Now Ezechias is given 29 years, Manasses 55, Amon 2, Josias 31, Joachaz 3 months, Joakim 11 years, Joachin 3 months, Sedecias 11 years : total, 139 years. Jerusalem fell in the 18th year of Nabuchodonosor (see on 4 Kg 24:12), 587. From 726 to 587 is 139 years, and so the chronology of Kg is exact, as in the period from **266f** 931–841.

In the present state of the text, the remaining period, **g** 841–726, causes difficulties. The reigns of the kings of Judah total 160 years, or 154 if allowance is made for ante-dating. This is at the least 38 years too much. The reigns of the kings of Israel total at least 138 years. And the last two kings, Peqah and Osee, are credited with a total of 29 years. That would put the accession of Peqah in 749, whereas it is certain that his predecessor but one, Menahem, was king in 738, when his tribute to Tiglath-pileser III is recorded. It is therefore imperative to reconstruct the chronology, correcting the corrupt text where necessary, but assuming that the chronology is fundamentally sound, as in the other two periods.

Some corruptions are obvious. 3 Kg 15:1 for **h** instance places the accession of Azarias of Judah in the 27th year of Jeroboam. But since the last 15 years of Amasias coincided with the first 15 of Jeroboam, 3 Kg 14:17, the accession of Azarias should be the 16th of Jeroboam. Another corruption is in 15:30, which speaks of the 20th year of Joatham, whereas 15:33 gives him 16 years all told.

The chronology adopted in the commentary is based **i** on the dates of the kings of Judah as given in Kg, with the corrections consequent on the assumption that Azarias, who is credited in the text with 52 years, reigned at most 13–14 years. The dates of the kings of Israel are brought into line with this, and it is supposed that Menahem was king some years before 738 (see above) and that Peqah lost the throne soon after Tiglath-pileser's action against Damascus and Syria (AOT 346–7), at the latest in 732. The figure 52 years for Azarias can be maintained only on the assumption of a co-regency with his father Amasias, dating from 785, and a co-regency with his son Joatham, extending over the whole reign of Joatham, and further, a co-regency of 8 years with his grandson Achaz. Now so far from the Bible's suggesting a co-regency of Azarias and Amasias, it states expressly that Azarias was enthroned, as a boy of sixteen, after his father's death, 4 Kg 14:19–21. Joatham was **j** undoubtedly co-regent with Azarias for some time, but reigned alone after Azarias' death, 4 Kg 15:6 f. There is no trace of a co-regency with Achaz. Since the co-regency with Joatham is expressly mentioned, the silence of the text with regard to others is equivalent to exclusion (*pace* § 64c). Relying then on all figures (for the kings of Judah) except the 52 years of Azarias, we arrive at the system : Athalia 841–836, Joas 836–797, Amasias 797–769, Azarias 769–756 (and some years co-regency), Joatham 756–741, Achaz 741–726, Ezechias 726–697. Some confirmation of this system may be found by working back from Achaz to Amasias, on the basis of the probable age of each king at the birth of the crown prince. Achaz was 20 at his accession in 741, 4 Kg 16:2. He was born in 761 when his father Joatham was *c* 20. Joatham was therefore born *c* 781, when his father Azarias was *c* 20. Azarias was born in 801, when Amasias was *c* 20. Amasias was therefore, on this rough average, 52 when he died in 769. Now 4 Kg 14:2 gives his age at his death as 53. The agreement shows that the system is probable, though of course a margin of error of one or two years must be allowed throughout.

THE THIRD BOOK OF KINGS

I 1–53 The Struggle for the Succession—David's **267a** debility explains how a crisis arose. **1–4.** He was bed-ridden, *cf.* 47 and 1 Kg 19:13, though only about 70 years of age, 2 Kg 5:4 ; 3 Kg 2:11. The method used to restore his circulation was recommended by ancient doctors (Galen etc.). The maid of Sunam (today Shôlem), on the northern rim of the plain of Jezreel, was regarded as a wife of David, see 2:22 ; her remaining a virgin is mentioned to excuse Adonias later. **5–7.** Adonias gave himself the royal privilege

267a of a bodyguard, like Absalom, 3 Kg 15. He was the eldest (surviving) son, personally attractive, and the general choice, 2:15. His chief supporters, the generalissimo Joab, 2 Kg 20:23, and Abiathar, 2 Kg 15:24-36, were devoted to David, but were ready to force his hand by presenting him with an accomplished fact ; his acquiescence in Adonias' conduct **b** led them to believe that he would welcome it. **8-10.** David, however, was engaged to Solomon by oath, ever since the divine predilection had been manifested through the prophet Nathan, 17, 30 ; see 2 Kg 12:24 f. This must have been public, at least at court, for Adonias excluded from his inaugural banquet Solomon and his friends. They included Banaias, the commander of the standing army, 2 Kg 20:23, and his soldiers ; Semei is perhaps the future minister of Solomon, 4:18. Rei, 'friend of', is probably not a proper name, but the title of David's aide-de-camp. Rogel, the 'Fuller's Well', is now Bir Ayub, 'Job's Well', SE. of Jerusalem ; Zoheleth· was the name of the smooth slope of rock which led down to it, today ez-Zahweileh, 'the Slide' (L.-H. Vincent, *Jérusalem Antique*, 139 f.). **11-31.** Nathan's approach to David had to be cautious, since the king knew exactly how things were shaping and was apparently satisfied. He worked on his pride and on his affections, by maintaining that his authority was being flouted, and that his best loved wife and her son were in danger of being treated as rebels. By pretending throughout that the king could not possibly have wavered, he **c** stung him to a belated sense of duty. **32-40.** The loyalty of the foreign mercenaries who formed the Palace Guard was a decisive factor ; see also 2 Kg 15:18 ; 4 Kg 11:4. Solomon was made co-regent. To explain the chronological data of 3 and 4 Kg, it may be assumed that other kings followed David's example in transferring the crown to their successors. Gihon, in the Cedron valley, is today the 'Spring of the Lady Mary'. **41-49.** Half a mile farther south, the old warrior Joab was the first to hear the sound of the trumpet. This life-like touch contributes to making the story of the succession one of the most picturesque in the Bible. David bowed like Jacob, ·Gen 47:31. **50-53.** The altar provided sanctuary ; its horns, upward projections of the four corners, were particularly sacred, Ex 29:12, etc. Adonias could wring from Solomon only a vague promise of safety ; the king reserved the right to take vengeance almost at will, and forbade Adonias to approach him ; *cf.* 2 Kg 14:24, 28.

d **II 1-11 David's Testament and Death—1-4.** Solomon needed courage, not to bear up under his father's death, but to observe the Law, for the good of the dynasty ; for the language, *cf.* Deut 31:7 etc., Jos 1:6 f. **5-6.** Joab had twice taken treacherous revenge for blood shed in fair fight ; thus, said David, ' staining the girdle upon *my* loins and the shoes upon *my* feet with *innocent* blood ' (LXX). David, who had given Joab the power which he had abused, felt responsible for the murders ; but unrequited murder brought evil on the land, 2 Kg 21 ; David's charge to Solomon must therefore be regarded as conscientious and public-spirited. He had not dared, or perhaps liked, to move himself against an old comrade-in-arms. **7-11.** The case of Semei is more difficult. David's humility had turned the curses into blessings, 2 Kg 16:12 ; his clemency had sufficiently upheld the royal dignity. But he could lawfully have punished any further misdemeanour. He could therefore urge Solomon to seek an occasion to exercise strict justice. David died *c* 971. The 'City of David' was on the SE. hill, running along the Cedron valley towards the pool of Siloah. Here David's descendants were also laid, at least till Achaz, 4 Kg 17:20.

e **12-45 Removal of the King's Opponents—12-21.** The Queen Mother, who had an official title (*geḇîrāh*, 15:13) was an important personage in the ancient east. Adonias asked her to obtain for him a poor substitute, as it were, for the kingdom which was rightly his.

Solomon treated the request as a renewal of his claim **26** to the kingship itself. To take over the women of a ruler was looked on as an exercise of the royal power, 2 Kg 16:21 ff ; *cf.* 3:7 ; 12:8. **26-27.** Anathoth, the home of the prophet Jeremias, today 'Anâta, was some 4 m. NE. of Jerusalem. Banishment excluded Abiathar from priestly functions. Here appears the Deuteronomic principle that worship could be offered only at one central shrine. The line of priests descending from Aaron's younger son, Ithamar, was closed. **28-35.** Solomon's plea, in killing Joab, was that **f** either the general or the royal house had to expiate his crimes. Sanctuary covered manslaughter, but not murder, Ex 21:14. There is no accusation of new treason ; 28 refers to the struggle for the succession. Thus the execution of Adonias remains questionable. Sadoc was descended from Aaron through Eleazar, 1 Par 6:8. **36-46.** The rashness of Semei, which had led him to curse David before his army, finally destroyed him. Solomon could claim that Semei's curses were no longer a menace to David's house, since they had exhausted their force upon their author. This idea of thwarting a curse by diverting it back upon the speaker, seems to lie behind the many attempts, in subsequent history, against the lives of the prophets who foretold evil.

III 1-28 Solomon's Piety and Wisdom—1. These **g** happy auguries were followed by a striking success in external affairs. By marrying the daughter of Pharaoh (? Siamon, of the 21st dynasty), he made his own the fruits of the Egyptian victory over the Philistines (*cf.* 9:16) and achieved the recognition of his empire as a great power. **2-4.** ' High places ' were shrines, mostly but not always on hill-tops, Jer 7:31 etc. ; for their prohibition, see on Deut 12. The ' Mosque of the Prophet Samuel ', on the top of the hill 5 m. NNW. of Jerusalem, probably corresponds to the ' high place ' of Gabaon, today el-Jib. **5-9.** Solomon's unselfish prayer was unique among those of ancient kings : *cf.* 11 and E. Dhorme, *La religion assyro-babylonienne*, 249-55. To ' walk before ', like ' stand before ' means to serve (Koehler). Solomon was about twenty years old ; *cf.* 14:21. **10-15.** In the answer, as in the prayer, conventional hyperbole is introduced, which asserts no more than a superlative. Solomon had everything but perseverance, a special gift of God which even the choicest graces do not guarantee. **16-28.** An instance of his judicial wisdom follows. Some hold it to be true merely in the sense that it evokes accurately the impression which Solomon made on history : the motif re-appears in other literatures. But essential traits of human nature, such as are at work here, can show themselves in many environments.

IV 1-19 Administration—1-2. The place of honour is **h** given to the high-priest. ' Son ' here is for grandson ; *cf.* 1 Par 6:8. The following list therefore refers to a late date in the reign ; 4 is an earlier fragment. **3.** Two Secretaries of State attended to official documents ; the Recorder was annalist, and in practice, Prime Minister. **5.** A son of Nathan was over the provincial *governors* (MT) ; another son (omit ' priest ' with LXX) was aide-de-camp ; *cf.* on 1:8. **6.** There was a chamberlain over the palace, and a minister for public works, over the *conscript labour* (Koehler). **7.** For taxation, **i** Israel, as distinct from Judah, was divided into 12 districts. The palaces and store-houses excavated at Lachish, Beth-Shemesh and Megiddo show how the provincial capitals were equipped. **8.** Part of the edge of the document here quoted was missing, as the absence of the proper names of the first four governors shows : *son of Hur* etc. The first district was based on Mount Ephraim, and ran from Joppa to the Jordan. **9.** The second, SW. of the first, comprised the hill-country of the southern settlement of Dan. **10.** The third, N. of the first, embraced the coastal plain of Sharon. **11.** The fourth ran NW. of the third to Carmel. **12.** The fifth ran in from Carmel across the plain of Esdraelon to the Jordan. **13.** The

671 sixth, N. and S. of the Yarmuk, was transjordanian Manasses. **14.** The seventh ran S. of the sixth to the Jabbok. **15.** The eighth was E. Galilee, along the lake and upper Jordan. **16.** W. Galilee, marching with the kingdom of Tyre, was the ninth. **17.** The tenth was S. of Galilee, around Mount Tabor. **18.** The eleventh was the eastern part of the territory S. of the province of Ephraim, to the NW. of Jerusalem. **19.** The twelfth was the most southerly of the three provinces E. of the Jordan, *Gad* (LXX), between the Jabbok and the Arnon. In 19*a* the reference to Sehon and Og seems to be a gloss ; in 19*b* read prob. ' a (chief) governor was over all (the governors) in the land ' ; *cf.* MT and 5. Districts eight to twelve followed old tribal divisions ; the rest natural boundaries. But the organization maintained fundamentally the dualism of N. and S., for Judah did not come under the general system : see A. Alt, *Israels Gaue unter Salomo* ; F.-M. Abel, *Géographie de la Palestine*, II, 79–83.

j 20-25 Extent and Riches of the Empire—**21.** Solomon may not have occupied much territory beyond David's conquests, which reached Riblah on the Orontes ; but his overlordship was acknowledged by tribute from as far N. as Thapsacus on ' the river ' Euphrates. **22-23.** 30 *cors = c* 340 bushels ; the quantities, enough for 14,000 persons, have probably been touched up by a scribe. **24.** ' Beyond the river ' is a term derived from Assyrian administration ; from the Jewish standpoint, the territory was the near side of the river. **25.** From the source of the Jordan to the edge of the southern desert, each Israelite had his own land and could live on its produce : proverbial felicity, Mic 4:4 ; Zach 3:10 etc. The revolt of Edom and Damascus late in the reign did not affect the general situation.

k 26-28 Armaments—**26a.** 4,000 is the original number of stalls according to LXX, 10:26 ; 2 Par 9:25 ; this corresponds well to the 1,400 chariots of 10:26, allowing two horses and a reserve to each chariot. **26b.** The strength of the cavalry is exceptional ; in 853, at the battle of Qarqar, Damascus had only 1,200 (inscription of Shalmaneser III, AOT 340 f.). Solomon's horse-trade perhaps explains it. Stables of Solomon's time excavated at Megiddo held at least 450 horses ; other depots have been found at Taʿanak, Gezer, Tell el-Hesy (? Aiglon), Haṣor. **28.** This provision was for the Palace Guard, which went on circuit with the king.

l 29-34 The Philosopher-King—**29.** Besides being a statesman of genius, Solomon was a sage, of penetrating and comprehensive insight, whose interests were so varied that they could be compared to the sands of the sea. **30.** The bent of the wisdom of the desert tribes and of the Egyptians was moralizing : Egyptian collections of maxims go back to 2000 B.C. **31.** Of the four sages only their fame is known. **32.** On Solomon's extant proverbs, *cf.* Prov 10:1–22:16 ; 25:1–29:27 ; (see § 364*d*, *e*, *i*) ; for his lyrics, see on Pss 71 ; 126. **33.** He was not a scientist, but drew on plant and animal life to illustrate his sayings ; *cf.* the imagery in Job 39–41 ; Prov 6.

m V 1-18 Preparations for the Temple—**1-3.** The embassy was to congratulate Solomon on his accession. Hiram had supplied materials and skilled workmen to David, 2 Kg 5:11. The historians Menander and Dios spoke of Hiram's great constructions at Tyre (Jos. *Ant.* 8, 5, 3 ; *C. Ap.* 1, 18). **4-5.** Settled conditions called for a temple to Yahweh, Deut 12:9. **6.** Sidon, the northern partner of Tyre, had lost the hegemony of the Phoenicians, but they were still called Sidonians (*cf.* 16:31) as late as Antiochus IV, 175–164 B.C. **7-8.** The famous voyage of the Egyptian Wen-Amon in 1100 B.C. was to obtain cedar-wood from Lebanon ; in spite of continual exploitation, it was still ' full of cedars, pine and cypress, marvellous in size and beauty ' when Diodorus was writing, 1st cent. B.C. Some of the few cedars still there today are 75 ft. high. *bᵉrôš* ' fir ' is often rendered ' cypress ', but though the use of the latter is not to be excluded,

' fir ' should be retained ; *cf.* Bi (1920) 496 ff. **9-11. 267n** The rafts were beached at Joppa, 2 Par 2:16. Wheat (20,000 *cors*, 230,000 bushels) and olive oil (20 *cors*, 1,800 gallons ; LXX 180,000) were articles of commerce, not the workmen's food. This ' purest ' oil was won by hand-pressure in a mortar. **12-14.** Work on sub-alpine Lebanon and raft-transport by sea were confined to the three summer months ; thus each draft had two of the working months free. **15-16.** The second group were Canaanites, 2 Par 2:17, and worked in the hills of Judaea, where there was excellent marble (*cf.* ' costly stones ' 17) and limestone, Abel I, 181 ff. Their lot was permanent slavery, 9:20 ff. **17-18.** The skilled foreign workmen included the Phoenicians of Gebal (Byblos), famous ship-wrights, Ez 27:9.

VI 1 The Foundation of the Temple—The original **268a** form of the record, placed here by LXX, may be seen at 37 : ' In the 4th year was the House of the Lord founded in the month (*yᵉraḥ*) Zio '. This was April–May *c* 968. ' The same is the second month ' (*ḥŏdeš*), seems to be a late gloss : the original writer would hardly use another word for month in the same verse ; and beginning the year in Nisan, March–April, seems to be late usage. See § 83*i-j*. For another view, see § 169*e*. No deduction as to the date of the Exodus can safely be based on this ' 480 years ', which attempts to date the temple midway between the Exodus and the return from the Babylonian exile. The figure was perhaps arrived at by counting 12 generations of 40 years, 12, a perfect number, symbolizing the stable possession of the Land ; *cf.* Deut 12:9. In the chronology as it stands, the reigns of the kings to the exile total 430 years ; with 50 years of exile, this gives a second period of 480 years. If the figure arose in this way, it is post-exilic, and so may be treated as a gloss, since the book was finished during the exile.

2-10 General Structure—*Cf.* L.-H. Vincent, *La Description* **b** *du Temple de Salomon*, RB, 16 (1907) 515 ff. (on which the following account is based) ; K. Möhlenbrink, *Der Tempel Salomos* (1932). Till the discovery of a 9th cent. temple at Tell Taïnât in N. Syria in 1936, the nearest analogy was in the classical Greek temple, with its pronaos, naos and adytos corresponding to the porch, nave and Holy of Holies of the Hebrew temple. This tripartite structure was a Syrian development which the Tyrians adopted and spread : see W. F. Albright, *Archaeology and the Religion of Israel²*, 142 ff. **2.** On the basis of the ' ancient ' cubit (see § 82*c*) the temple was approximately 103 ft. by 34 ft. by 51 ft. **3.** The porch was as wide as the main building, and was 17 ft. *deep*. **4.** The windows, *whose frames held trellises*, were high up in the walls. **5.** For built on to the outside was a cincture of rooms to serve as sacristies. **6.** This addition was 9 ft. wide on the ground-floor ; the floor-beams of the two upper storeys did not pierce the walls of the temple, but rested on the ledges formed by the walls where they were stepped in twice. **7.** The use of dressed stone did not exclude carpenter's work at the actual building. **8.** The entrance to the *ground-floor* of the side-buildings was on the south. **9.** The ceiling of the temple was of cedar, the joists and beams forming compartments (MT), visible from beneath. The roof was flat, since altars could be erected on it, 4 Kg 33:12. **10.** Cedar was used to roof the *side-buildings* also, each storey of which ' *round* all the House ' was 9 ft. high. The three ceilings *rested on* (the wall of) the House by means of cedar beams.

11-14 God's Promise—This was given, probably **c** through a prophet (*cf.* 11:9 with 3:5 and 9:2) to encourage Solomon in the difficulties of building. The meaning was : ' If you keep my commandments, I will keep my promises '.

15-22 Interior—The main features described are the **d** woodwork, the division into sanctuary and nave, the altar of incense, the decorations. **15.** The temple was lined with cedar and floored with fir (or cypress ; see on 5:8). **16.** The rear wall, to the height of 34 ft., formed the back of the innermost shrine, ' the oracle ' (*dᵉbîr*—from a root meaning hinder part ; St Jerome

268d connected it with *dabbēr* ' to speak '). It was a perfect cube, 20*a*, so there was a space of 17 ft. between its ceiling and the roof. **17.** The main hall, the nave, was 52 ft. long. **18.** There were carvings on the cedar walls : *colocynths and garlands of flowers* (MT). These probably linked the cherubs and palm-trees of 29. **20*b*-22.** To the cedar facings and the carvings a third element of decoration was added : gold-leaf, probably used only on the low relief of the carvings. So understand the generalization of 22, which says that ' everything ' was covered with gold. The text of these verses is badly confused, partly by the glosses of scribes who felt the urge to exaggerate the richness of the gilding. So too 30, where the interpolator is betrayed by the meaningless ' within and without '. From 21*b* it may be gathered that the doors of the Holy of Holies (*cf.* 31) had golden bolts (MT) ; and from 22, that there was an altar (for incense) in the nave, *in front of* the Holy of Holies, and that its cedar was embellished with gildings.

e **23-30 The Cherubim**—See P. Dhorme and L.-H. Vincent, *Les Chérubins*, RB 1926. Sentinel figures with wings outstretched to shelter it awaited the Ark, 19. The word *kᵉrûḇ* derives from the Babylonian, where *kâribu* ' intercessor ' was used anciently of minor gods who presented the prayers of suppliants. Later these *kâribu* appeared with human head on winged bodies of lions, etc., and were associated with the guardianship of temples and palaces from Mesopotamia to Egypt. The small figures which flanked the Ark in the Mosaic Tabernacle were in human form ; *cf.* § 177*b*. Reproduced here on a gigantic scale, they must also be supposed to be human in form. Hence Ezechiel's address to the king of Tyre, 28:14 : ' Thou, Cherub, anointed protector '. In 7:29 cherubs are distinguished from lions and oxen. Though they no longer formed the throne of Yahweh, as in the ancient Tabernacle, they still manifested his presence, and evoked reverence for his majesty ; *cf.* Gen 3:24 ; Ps 17:11. Since they were offered no cult and were not thought of as intercessors, they derive only in name and form from non-Israelite figures. On **29 f.**, see on 18 and 22.

f **31-35 The Doors of the Sanctuary and Nave**—**31.** ' *For the entrance of the Holy of Holies he made doors of olive wood. The frame was pentagonal* '. This means that the lintel was triangular. **32*a*** repeats 31*a* ; for **32*b*** see on 35*a*. **33.** On the door from the porch into the nave, the lintel was flat, so the ordinary rectangular opening resulted. Each of its two main leaves was of two sections, *turning upon pivots* (MT, *gᵉlîlîm*) ; the two centre pieces provided a convenient entrance for daily use. **35*a*.** The decorations are the same as those on the inner door ; the gilding was confined to the carvings, as elsewhere in the temple. **35*b*** shows how all the gold overlay is to be understood : ' *a thin layer applied with precision* ' (MT)—gold-leaf. The idea that the temple was walled and floored with plates of gold is a late fantasy.

g **36 The Inner Court**—The court in which the temple stood was within the great court, 7:12, which embraced all the king's buildings. Every three courses of stone were succeeded by one course of wood, a reinforcement once necessary in brick walls.

h **37-38 Duration of the Work**—This ancient record preserves two Canaanite names of months ; *cf.* Phoenician *Ƶib*, *B-l*. Bul was Oct.–Nov. The regnal year began in Tishri, Sept.–Oct. Thus the work lasted from the eighth month of Solomon's fourth year to the second month of his eleventh, six and a half years, roughly seven. In the parenthesis, the months are reckoned from Nisan, March–April ; see on 1.

i **VII 1-12 Palaces**—**1.** These were begun only when the temple was finished ; *cf.* 9:10. **2.** Furthest south from the temple was a great hall, intended for ceremonial occasions ; *cf.* 10:21. Larger than the temple, it was 172 ft. by 86 ft. by 52 ft. The *three* (LXX) *rows* of lofty pillars, fifteen to a row, gave the impression of a cedar forest, hence the name. **3-5.** It was not an open portico, for MT and LXX mention doors and windows ' facing

each other in sets of three '. Details are uncertain, **26** for the text is corrupt, especially in Vg. **6.** Next came a smaller hall of pillars, possibly the ante-chamber, **7,** to the Throne-room, where Solomon dispensed justice. **8.** Closest to the temple were the royal palaces : ' *his own dwelling-house was in another court, inwards* (towards the temple) *from the Throne-room* ' (MT). **9.** The stone was dressed on all faces, ' within and without '. **10-11 f.** 17 ft. blocks went into the lower courses : larger are still to be seen in the ' Wailing Wall ' of Jerusalem. **12.** The whole complex of buildings was enclosed in the ' Greater Court ', whose walls were of the type described 6:36.

The position of the Great Court was too well known **j** to be mentioned. Today it is the Haram esh-Sherîf, the ' Noble Sanctuary ' of the Mohammedans, an esplanade some 550 yards long and 320 yards wide, on the NE. hill. The site of the temple is occupied by the paved platform which surrounds the so-called Mosque of Omar, really the ' Dome of the Rock '. Inside this is a rock, some 60 ft. long and 40 ft. wide, rising nearly 6 ft. above floor level. On this was erected, as is generally agreed, the Altar of Holocausts ; *cf.* 2 Kg 24:25 ; 3 Kg 8:64. The temple was a little to the west, its façade looking east over the altar towards the Mount of Olives.

13-22 Jachin and Booz—Tyrian architects had built **k** the temple after their own models, and a Tyrian craftsman supplied the standard fittings. **15-16.** Standing free before the porch were two columns, 40 ft. high, 6 ft. in diameter, of hollow copper or bronze 3½ inches thick (4 fingerbreadths, LXX, Jer 52:21). Their capitals were crowned with *bowls* (41, ' cords '), upon which were *gratings* (' network, chainwork '—' seven ' comes from a scribal error). These features, and the ' lilywork ', when understood as knobs, 19, 22, suggest that the columns were stylized reproductions of the tall incense-stands or cressets (fire-altars) before many ancient temples. So W. F. Albright, 144 ff. ; usually they are compared with the stone columns or obelisks of Egypt etc. **18, 22.** Two necklaces of metal pomegranates decorated each capital ; *cf.* 42. **21.** The names suggest inscriptions like ' May Yahweh *establish* (*yāḵîn*) the temple ' or dynasty, and ' In the *strength* (*bᵉʿôz*) of Yahweh '.

23-26 ' The Sea '—From the 3rd millennium a **l** reservoir known as Apsu, the primeval fresh-water ocean, was usual in the temples of Lagash, Eridu, Ur, Babylon, etc. ; basins on stands of oxen are pictured on the reliefs of Nineveh. Such decorations became common in the early Iron Age. ' The Sea ' was at the SE. corner of the temple, 39, of metal nearly 4 inches thick, with castings of *open buds* ; to hold 2,000 *baths* (18,000 gallons) the sides must have curved outwards.

27-39 Water-wagons—Water for ablutions, 2 Par 4:6, **m** was carried from the ' Sea ' in wheeled *stands*, also common in ancient temples. The obscure and confused text has been illustrated by archaeological finds, such as the tiny model, probably an ex-voto, of the 2nd millennium, found in Cyprus, DBV IV fig. 260. The sides were panelled and decorated, and a small basin was set in a round opening in the top. **32-36** give a slightly varying account of the same things.

40-51 Other Furniture—**40** adds utensils used in **n** sacrifices, **41-45** recapitulate the objects described in 15-39. They were of *polished bronze*, an alloy of copper and tin, or pure copper ; brass, an alloy of copper and zinc, was not known. **46.** The foundries were near the mouth of the Jabbok. **47-51.** The Altar of Incense was of cedar, 6:20, but it was finished in gold-foil, like most of the larger objects ; see on 6:35. For the loaves of proposition, see § 177*d* ; for David's votive offerings, 2 Kg 8:11 f. ; for an Inerrancy problem, see § 37*g*.

VIII 1-11 Dedication—**1.** The entry of the Ark was the **26** central rite, by which Yahweh took possession of his temple, his presence being in a special manner attached to the Ark. **2.** It was ten months after the completion of the building. Ethanim (' perpetual streams ', the

a only ones flowing, the wadis having dried up) was the old name for Sept.–Oct., later Tishri, the first month in the old reckoning ; see on 6:1 and 37 f. **2b**, not in LXX (B, Lucian), reckons from Nisan. **3-9.** The precise details of the placing of the Ark suggest the record of an eye-witness, which was quoted literally (*cf.* ' unto this day ') though all had disappeared when the book was written. The staves by which it was carried ran out sideways from the Ark ; *cf.* § 177*b*. The door of the oracle being narrow, they were visible from the nave only when one stood close to the oracle. **10-11.** A dark storm-cloud (*cf.* 12) testified to Yahweh's acceptance of his new dwelling ; a similar miracle had sanctified the Mosaic Tabernacle, Ex 40:32 ff.

b **12-13 Solomon's Hymn**—With the help of LXX it may be thus restored : ' Yahweh has set the sun in the heavens. But he has decreed to dwell himself in great darkness. I have succeeded in building you a mansion, the fixed place of your abode for ever '. The abrupt change to direct address shows that this is only an excerpt from the whole psalm, which LXX says was preserved in a collection called ' The Book of the *Just* ' ; *cf.* Jos 10:12 ; 2 Kg 1:18. LXX here mistook *yāšār* ' just ' for *šîr* ' canticle '. The hymn is not merely to thank the creator for being content with the temple ; it rather marvels at Yahweh's deliberately choosing darkness as the mode of his presence : his mysterious nature is thus better expressed than even by the brightness of the heavens. Further, it sees in the temple a permanent bond between Yahweh and the dynasty.

c **14-61 Inaugural Address**—After dedicating the temple on his own behalf, the king spoke for all. He began with an address to the people, **15-21**, which proclaimed the temple the work of Providence, a sign of Yahweh's past and future faithfulness. A long prayer, **22-53**, recommends the people to Yahweh enthroned in the temple. An epilogue, **54-61**, blesses the people and exhorts them to perseverance.

14. The blessing was a greeting, as 4 Kg 4:29 ; the strict sense in 55 ; *cf.* 57. **15-21.** For the prehistory of the temple see 2 Kg 7 ; Deut 12. Since the name of Yahweh is attached to the temple (1) he watches over it as his property ; *cf.* Deut 28:10 ; Is 4:1, (2) his personal being is there, ruling and working ; *cf.* Is 30:27 ; 40:26. **22-26.** Solomon *placed himself* on his knees, 54, to pray for the complete fulfilment of the prophecies. **27-30.** According to 12 f. Yahweh dwelt in the temple. 27 does not deny this, but makes explicit the immensity of the Creator, already asserted in ' Yahweh has set the sun in the heavens '. The reminder that Yahweh watches from heaven, 29 f., guards against considering the ark as a fetich to which his presence was slavishly bound. **31.** The temple is to be the theatre of God's judgements ; *cf.* Num 5:21 f. **33-40.** Calamities are the punishment of sin ; the efficacy of prayer depends on sincere repentance. **41-43** refer to strangers' visits, like that of the Queen of Sheba (Saba) or Merodach Baladan's embassy, 4 Kg 20:12 ff. This is the climax of the prayer : the temple as the herald of God's glory to the ends of the earth. The systematic share of proselytes in the cult is not **d** envisaged. **44-50.** For prayer in the direction of the temple, *cf.* Dan 6:10 and the Mohammedans' turning to Mecca. **51.** The furnace is a metaphor for a dreadful fate, Deut 4:20, possibly because of its use as a death penalty ; *cf.* Dan 3. **54-61.** The king is ideally a ' Father Always ', Is 9:4 ; hence the paternal blessing, **57** ; *cf.* Ru 2:4. Praise of God precedes it ; *cf.* 15 ff. The bishop's blessing still begins with ' Sit nomen Domini benedictum '. The prayer for grace promises co-operation.

The prayer, 14-61, is hardly in its original tenor : note, *e.g.* the abrupt insertion of later theological precautions 27 ff. (KTW V 254 f.) ; 44 ff. are a variation on 33 ff. ; exile is vividly envisaged ; 52 f. are loosely attached to the preceding. In its present form the passage seems to date at least from the time of the first great deportations, 734-701, and interprets the

sentiments evoked by the dedication for the benefit of **269d** the readers.

62-66 Inaugural Celebrations—The numbers are not **e** correct : 1,800 an hour, 12 hours a day for 7 days ! **64.** On holocaust, *meal* and peace-offering see §§ 111*d-j*, 183*b*, 184*b-c*. **65.** The *seven* days coincided with Tabernacles, § 113*j*. The plain about Riblah and Kadesh on the Orontes was the ' Entrance of Hamath ', Abel II 78 ; the ' River of Egypt ' was the Wady el-'Arîsh, *c* 50 m. S. of Gaza.

IX 1-9 Concluding Vision—The substance of the **f** revelation has been elaborated by the inspired writer to meet a difficulty of the exiles. If the temple has perished, it is not because Yahweh was too weak to protect his own, but because he was too holy to tolerate evil in them. For ' example ' (MT *'elyôn* ' lofty ') read ' *ruins* ' (*'iyyîn*) with Old Latin, Syr. ; *cf.* Mic 3:12. **10-28 Finance and Public Works**—**10-14.** Solomon had to borrow to build, and ceded temporarily, 2 Par 8:2, part of E. Galilee with its revenues. Hiram's discontent was echoed in the name of the chief town, the most easterly of the tribe of Aser, Jos 19:27. Kabul perhaps suggested *Kᵉḇal*, ' like nothing at all '. **15.** A *record* follows of how *conscript labour* was used. **g** The Mello (*cf.* 11:27) seems to have been a massive fortification on the W., between Sion and the temple area ; *cf.* L.-H. Vincent, *Jérusalem* I 171-87. Haṣor (Heser ; prob. Tell el-Qedah, where great stables have been excavated ; *cf.* on 4:27) SW. of Lake Huleh, guarded the northern approaches. Megiddo, Tell el Mutesellim, commanded the plain of Esdraelon. **17.** The rebuilding of Gezer signified that Solomon was to be sole master in Palestine. Relations with Egypt were henceforth less friendly ; *cf.* 11:14 ff. The events of 16 were early in the reign. **18.** For ' Palmira ' read *Tamar* (MT), S. of the Dead Sea. **19.** Solomon fortified ' all the towns *where he stored provisions* ' and the cavalry depots ; *cf.* 4:7-26. There were iron mines as well as forests to be exploited on Lebanon. **20-22.** Only the remnants of the non-Israelite peoples were conscripted permanently ; *cf.* on 5:12 ff. **23-28.** David's conquest of Edom had given Solomon command of its copper and iron mines, as well as access to the Red Sea. Copper refineries of Solomon's time have been found at Tell el-Kheleifeh, the ancient Ezion-Geber, now ½ m. inland on the Gulf of Aqabah (Ailath). The site of Ophir is still debated : Somaliland, supposed to correspond to the Egyptian Punt, is credited with exports like those of 10:22, *cf.* W. F. Albright, 133 ; the most ancient tradition, LXX, Josephus etc., says India ; more probably S. Arabia, a gold-producing country (*cf.* Job 22:24) inhabited by the Jectanides ; *cf.* Gen 10:29. For 420 talents, LXX has 120.

X 1-29 Prestige and Wealth—Further proofs are **h** adduced to show how Yahweh fulfilled his promise to Solomon, 3:12 ff. **1.** The later Sabaean kingdom was in the Hadramaut, SW. Arabia. But the Sabaeans are constantly met with along the EW. trade route in N. Arabia before 700 B.C. See Tiglath-pileser's inscription of 728, Luckenbill I No. 799, and Gen 10:30 ; 25:3 ; Ez 38:13, etc. The name may still persist in the Wady esh-Shaba, near Medina, Abel I 293. Possibly the northern Sheba was a set of outposts of the southern. Tiglath-pileser mentions five Arab queens. The ' hard questions ' of the queen of Sheba were riddles and allegorical proverbs, of which Samson's, Jg 14:12-19, are examples. **2-10, 13.** Solomon's wisdom was proved as much by his riches as by his answers : poverty would have been no recommendation of his prudence. Our Lord made the generous admiration of the ' queen of the South ' a reproach to his incredulous hearers, Mt 12:42. **11-12.** The sources and display of Solomon's wealth **i** follow, in a series of disconnected notices. One great source was the joint naval expeditions with Hiram (*cf.* 22) exporting iron and copper, 9:26 ff. Thyine is citron-wood : MT *'almuggîm*, conjectured to be sandal-wood—impossible if found on Lebanon, 2 Par

269i 2:8. **14-15.** The figures have suffered. **16-17.** His guardsmen had ceremonial shields which, between parades, hung in the Lebanon Hall ; *cf.* 7:2. About 8 lb of gold (LXX) was used on each large shield, about 4 on the small : in 17 read '3 minas' (MT) for '300 lb'. **18-21.** Ebony thrones inlaid with gold and ivory were carried off from Megiddo by Thothmes III *c* 1480. **22.** The traders sailed in *Tarshish-ships* (MT), *i.e.* ocean-going vessels, such as those used by the Phoenicians sailing to Tarshish (in Spain and Sardinia). 'Peacocks' (*tukkî*, Malabar *togai*) is

j doubtful ; W. F. Albright, 212, 'monkeys'. **26.** See on 4:26. **28-29** give another source of wealth ; ' *The trade in horses, which was in Solomon's hands, between Egypt and Coa* (E. Cilicia) *was as follows : the kings' merchants procured them from Coa at the current price ; and a chariot was exported from Egypt at the rate of 600 silver shekels, a horse from Coa at 150 ; at this rate they delivered them to all the kings of the Hittites and of Syria'*. Cilicia was a great horse-breeding country ; Egypt manufactured chariots ; see Albright, 135. There is no need to substitute *Muṣri* (Cappadocia) for Egypt (*Miṣraîm*), as is often done ; besides, Solomon's middlemen could hardly have established a monopoly in a merely northern trade.

270a XI 1-8 Solomon's Sin—A final trait of Solomon's glory, the magnificence of his harem, links the sentence passed on his sin with the blessings bestowed on his piety. **1-3.** The spirit of Ex 34:16 and Deut 7:1-4, which forbade marriage with Canaanites, is here authentically interpreted to exclude all foreigners. Reasons of state, however, could have excused Solomon, like David, 2 Kg 3:3 ; 1 Par 3:2. It was customary for kings to send their daughters to one another's harems. Amenhotep III received from Naharina the princess Giluhipa with 317 ladies, Breasted, *Ancient Records* II 867. But Solomon surrendered himself completely to the will of his wives ; *cf.* Gen 3. **4-8.** Astarte was the fertility-goddess of the ancient east ; there were local Astartes like local Baals. *Milkom*, 5, 7, was the Ammonite form of Malik or Muluk (Moloch), a god common to the Semites. The shrines were S. of the Mount of Olives, 4 Kg 23:13.

b 9-13 Condemnation—Solomon, like Saul, 1 Kg 15:23, should hâve lost all. Judah, the one tribe left to his son, was to absorb Benjamin, perhaps by force ; *cf.* 2 Par 11:23. The enmity of foreigners, 15 ff., 25, was of long standing and the disaffection of subjects natural, 12:4. But since God did not intervene to check their course, or to remedy the defects of statesmanship, they appear in the following as the consequence of the sin which God had foreseen.

c 14-22, 25b Revolt of Edom—**15.** *lᵉqabbēr 'eṯ-haḥᵃlālîm*, ' to bury the slain ' is generally read *lᵉbaqqēr 'eṯ-haḥōrîm*, ' to search the caves '. **17-18.** The direct route being barred, the refugees gained Egypt by Madian, E. of the Gulf of Aqabah, and Pharan, N. of the Sinai peninsula. The young prince was of marriageable age : the same term was used by Solomon at his accession, 3:7. With Genubath, *cf.* Egyptian *genbt*, ' lock of hair ' : that of a crown prince was characteristic. As long as the Pharaoh was friendly to Solomon (see on 9:17) he detained Adad. **25b.** Later Adad set up an independent state in *Edom* (LXX), which in the end must have hampered Solomon's Red Sea trade.

d 23-25a Revolt of Razon—Solomon maintained his hold over Coele-Syria, 2 Par 8:3, but a new power arose in Damascus, which was to be the terrible enemy of Israel for 200 years.

e 26-40 Rebellion and Flight of Jeroboam—**26-28.** That the first sign of internal dissension came from an *Ephraimite* is significant. Jeroboam was in a position to share and exploit the resentment of the northerners under forced labour. For Sareda, *cf.* the valley of Serida, in the centre of the hill-country E. of Joppa, Abel II 457. For the Mello, see on 9:15. **29-31.** The prophet from Shiloh, long the resting-place of the Ark, supported Jeroboam, while affirming

the divine choice of Jerusalem, 32, and David, 34. **27** For the symbolic action *cf.* 1 Kg 15:27 ; Is 8:1-4 ; Jer 19:10. **32-35.** The count, *ten* tribes and one, disregards one tribe ; *cf.* 13. Jerusalem lay in Benjamin, and Judah was to include also Simeon and part of Dan. The prophet is not concerned with arithmetic. **36.** The lamp corresponds to ' hearth and home '. The metaphor means that the family of David would not become extinct. **37-38.** Jeroboam is placed on an equality with David, but with the same obligations. **39**, not in LXX, may be considered a gloss. **40.** *Shoshenq* (or Sheshonq), the founder of a new dynasty, had no ties with Solomon. At 12:24 LXX adds (24*a-z* in Rahlfs) a variant account of Jeroboam, from which may be retained the fact that he began his abortive rebellion by seizing the fortress which he had just constructed for Solomon at Sareda.

41-43 Death of Solomon—One of the author's sources **f** is given : ' the Annals of the Reign of Solomon '. For the compilers see 2 Par 9:29. He died *c* 931 ; LXX here adds that Jeroboam returned at once from Egypt to his native city. Under Solomon, Israel had advanced rapidly to its greatest power and prosperity. The international situation was favourable, with Assyria and Egypt passive, and the genius and energy of Solomon seized the opportunity to build up a great political and commercial empire. In the splendour of his royal dignity, which shone out in his wisdom and piety no less than in his buildings and armaments, he pre-figured the Messias and his spiritual kingdom. Initially, 8:66, south and north were united in enthusiastic loyalty towards his person. But he failed to weld them into an organic whole. Instead, he used his powers to submit his people, and not impartially, to oppressive taxation and conscription. Some of the fruits of empire went to strengthen its defences, but much went to maintain the magnificence of his court. Most of his subjects were ready to desert him by the time that he deserted his God.

XII 1-24 Secession of Israel—**1.** Shechem (near **g** Nablus) was central, and by reason of its religious associations, venerable, Gen 12:6 ; 33:18 ; Jos 24:32. But its choice for the national assembly shows that the northerners were insisting on consideration. In principle they all recognized the right of the heir of David to the throne. **2-3a** to ' came ' should be omitted with LXX (B, Lucian) ; *cf.* 20. **3b-14.** The delay in answering a reasonable demand must have caused resentment ; the answer was provocative in the extreme, because the whip was not just a metaphor. Forced labour was done under the lash ; the scorpion was a scourge fitted with hooks. **15.** The rashness of Roboam, a turning-point in the history of the people was *a disposition of Yahweh* (MT). Prudence could have saved Solomon's empire, but grace was withheld. **16.** The old cry˙ of the discontented northerners was revived ; *cf.* 2 Kg 20:1. Their land did not lie in Judah. Why then should they recognize David as king ? ' To your tents ' means ' Return home '. Here it was a refusal to remain under Roboam's orders. In future ' David ' must confine his attentions to his own tribe. **17-24.** The king's bodyguard failed to protect *Adoniram* (LXX, Syr. ; *cf.* 4:6), and it is doubtful if even the full muster of the South, though equipped with Solomon's armaments, could have imposed his will on the North.

25-32 Religious Schism—Jeroboam *fortified* Shechem **h** and made Phanuel, on the Jabbok, his base to protect the provinces E. of Jordan. **26-27.** Jerusalem still drew pilgrims, 2 Par 11:16. **28.** The ' *young bulls* ' were two images of the one Yahweh, as the appeal to Ex 32:4 shows ; the verb ' brought ' is in the plur. in MT, but was originally in the sing. ; *cf.* Neh 9:18. The Decalogue, Ex 20:4 etc., forbade images designed for worship, including in fact those of Yahweh (*cf.* Deut 4:15) but could possibly be interpreted as forbidding only images of false gods. The cult was not idolatrous, but the way was open for confusing Yahweh with his image, and his cult with that of the Phoenician and

h Canaanite Baals, also represented as bulls. The bull was the symbol of strength and life-giving force. It has been maintained (*cf.* W. F. Albright, *From the Stone Age to Christianity*[2], 229 f.) that the bull was merely the pedestal of Yahweh, like the cherubim of the Mosaic ark. But the Bible makes it clear that it was an image, and therefore the great sin and scandal of Jeroboam—not a mere 'rubrical' innovation. **29.** **i** Bethel (Beitîn) 10 m. N. of Jerusalem, was rich in memories of Abraham, Gen 12:8 ; 13:3, and of Jacob, Gen 28:10–22 ; 35:1–16. Dan (Tell el-Qâḍi) near the source of the Jordan, had been the shrine of a famous image, Jg 18:1–31. Thus the law of the one sanctuary was violated. **31–33.** But in restoring the ancient shrines, Jeroboam could present himself as the upholder of ancient traditions ; *cf.* 4 Kg 18:22. Priests were recruited *from all classes*, the Levites having migrated to Jerusalem, 2 Par 11:13. In 32 f. the text is disturbed by repetitions ; omit the first ' in Bethel '. The feast of Tabernacles was a month later than in Judah ; *cf.* 8:2, 65. Bethel became the Chapel Royal, Am 7:13.

j **XIII 1–10 Threat to Bethel**—Three prophets condemned the impiety of Jeroboam, first a Judaean, then a northerner, 32, then Ahias, 14:7 ff.—his former patron ; *cf.* 11:29. **1.** Jeroboam was pontificating *at* the altar. **2.** The gravest ritual impurity was from contact with corpses, Num 19:18. **3–10.** The prophet's aloofness marked the 'excommunication' of the cult.

k **11–34. The Northern Prophet**—**11–15.** His motives are obscure. Possibly he wished to gain popular credit by winning a special mark of favour from the wonder-worker. **16–19.** The Judaean, though he had had a revelation to the contrary, accepted his mere word without demanding a sign. **20–22.** Revelation was not confined to blameless characters ; *cf.* Balaam, Num 31:16, and Jonas. The Judaean had, publicly at least, disavowed the mandate of Yahweh ; the judgement on him had to be public (*cf.* 25) to restore the impression made by his sign. Burial among strangers was abhorrent ; *cf.* Gen 47:30 ; 50:25. **23–28.** Lions were native to Palestine, 1 Kg 17:34 etc., and, it is said, did not become extinct there till the 12th cent. A.D. **29–32.** Add with LXX ' that my bones may be undisturbed with his ', at 31*b*. For the fulfilment of his hopes see 4 Kg 23:18. ' Samaria ' is an anachronism, one of several signs of the late redaction of the story. ' To fill the hands ', a technical term, is to give the insignia or rights of priesthood ; *cf.* P. Joüon ', Bi 3 (1922) 64. **34.** ' *This was the sin of the house of Jeroboam* ' (LXX)—not merely the calf-worship but the non-Levitical priesthood.

l **XIV 1–20 Doom of Jeroboam's House**—**1.** The link with the foregoing is vague ; it was probably late in the reign ; *cf.* 10. **2.** Ahias was no longer friendly. The disguise sought to avert the worst. Jeroboam regarded the prophet as a magician who could sway the future, but could be tricked into giving a favourable verdict. **3.** The modest presents, which were in keeping with the disguise, included ' cracknels ', perhaps ' raisin bread ' (*niqqūḏîm* ' dotted '). **4–6.** The failing sight of Ahias heightens the miracle of his inspiration. **7.** This, with 12–14, is the original kernel of the sentence pronounced against Jeroboam's ingratitude. The rest, 8–11, 15 f., is an expansion of the theme in conventional terms. **8.** See 11:6, 31 ; Deut 12:25 ; 13:19 ; 21:9. **9.** ' Above all that were before ' can hardly refer to Solomon ; the phrase is part of the style ; *cf.* 16:25, 30, 33. **10** refers to all male descendants ; *cf.* 16:11 ; 21:21, etc. ' *The fettered and the free* ' means ' everybody ', Deut 32:36 etc., who supported him. **11** is again conventional ; *cf.* 16:4 ; 21:24. **m** **12–14.** Honourable burial was to be denied to the house of Jeroboam, but not to Jeroboam himself, 20, nor to the innocence of youth. The prophet looks beyond the brief reign of Nadab to Baasa, 15:27. **15–16.** The exile of 721, beyond the River, the Euphrates, was the last of a series of staggering blows. For ' groves ' see on 23 f. **17.** Read with LXX *Sareda* ; *cf.* 11:26. Baasa was to make Thersa his

capital. **18–20.** The wars of Jeroboam included (*a*) **270m** the defence of Transjordania, 12:25, possibly against the Ammonites ; (*b*) skirmishes with Roboam, 14:30 ; (*c*) open war with Abiam, 2 Par 13:2 ff. ; (*d*) possibly war with Damascus (*cf.* 15:19) ; (*e*) the invasion of Shishak ; *cf.* on 25 ff. These formed part of the Annals. He died *c* 909.

21–31 Roboam of Judah—21. He reigned *c* 931–915. **n** For the kings of Judah, the mother is regularly named ; *cf.* on 2:12 ; 15:9 f. Her influence no doubt furthered the idolatry which Solomon had favoured. **22–23.** In the Canaanite cults, stone pillars (DV ' statues ') and wooden posts (DV ' groves ') flanked the altars. The pillars represented Baal, the posts Ashera, his consort ; MT, *passim*, uses the proper name of the goddess, in the plur., *'ašērîm*, for the wooden posts. LXX, Vg render ' groves '. The Greeks used the name Hermes both for the god and for the pillar surmounted by his head. For the tree-trunk, supposed to be an ashera, excavated at Ai, see L.-H. Vincent, RB (1947) 248 f. Ashera, originally perhaps a sea-goddess (*cf.* Albright, 77 f.), was now more or less interchangeable with Astarte, goddess of fertility, of which green trees were the emblem. **24.** Sacred prostitution, involving **o** both sexes, was a permanent feature of these cults ; *cf.* Herodotus 1.199 ; Lucian, *de Dea Syra*. Not all the country shrines were idolatrous. The ' high places ' tolerated even by good kings (*cf.* 15:14 ; 22:44 etc.) were shrines of Yahweh. But they were against the law of one sanctuary, and their installations were apparently modelled on the Canaanite. Stone pillars could be legitimate (*cf.* Gen 28:17 f. with 35:7 and Ex 24:4) but their associations were pernicious. Hence the drastic action of Ezechias and Josias against them. **25–29.** Sixty northern towns are included in the inscription of Karnak which records the Palestine expedition of Shishak (Egyptian Shoshenq or Sheshonq) *c* 922. Possibly Jeroboam's neglect of promised tribute (*cf.* 11:40) was the cause of the raid ; it is placed here as the chastisement of Judah's impiety. **30–31.** Border skirmishes were frequent, the new boundaries still being fluid. Full-scale war had been averted, 12:19.

XV 1–8 Abiam of Judah—1–2. He reigned *c* 915–913. **271a** Daughter stands for grand-daughter here, as in 4 Kg 8:26. Maacha's father was Uriel of Gibea, 2 Par 13:2, husband of Absalom's daughter Tamar, 2 Kg 14:27. **3–7*a*.** With the continued religious decline, the dynasty would have gone the way of Jeroboam's, but for David's merits. **7*b*.** Abias even maintained the cult at Bethel, after capturing this and other towns from Jeroboam ; *cf.* 2 Par 13:9 ; 15:8.

9–24 Asa of Judah, 913–873—9–10. After the early **b** death of Abiam, Maacha, Asa's *grand*-mother, retained the dignity of queen mother ; *cf.* on 2:12 ; 14:21. In Babylon and Assyria also the king's mother received special honours, witness the legendary fame of Semiramis (Sammuramat, whose son, Adad-nirari III, called her ' Queen of the palace, his Lady ' ; *cf.* E. Schrader, KIB, 1,193). **13.** After some years, when the young king's piety would assert itself, ' he removed Maacha from being *queen mother, because she had made a hateful image* [Vg, in sacris Priapi] *of Ashera* [Vg, et in luco eius]. It was apparently not the plain wooden post, but probably an Astarte, usually represented naked and with obscene exaggerations. **14.** The country shrines of Yahweh were left undisturbed, in spite of the law of one sanctuary. They were not as yet contaminated with heathenism, hence Asa's heart could be said to be perfect. **15.** Abiam had won booty from Jeroboam, **c** and Asa from the Cushites ; *cf.* 2 Par 14:12. **16–17.** When the Israelites re-took Bethel, they advanced to within 5 m. of Jerusalem. **18–19.** The alliance between Tabrimmon and Abiam may explain Jeroboam's defeat ; *cf.* on 7*b*. **20.** Ahion (Tell Dibbin), Dan and Abel-beth-Maacha (Abil), lay round the source of the Jordan ; Cenneroth (Tell el-Oreimeh), from which the lake of Galilee took its ancient name, was the most southerly point of the Syrian invasion. The territory

271c was not permanently occupied (*cf.* 4 Kg 15:29) but Israel hardly regained it without making concessions of the type indicated in 20:34, as it covered the trade routes to Tyre and Egypt. All later wars had this prize in view. **21.** Baasa's capital, Thersa, possibly Gemmaîn, *c* 8 m. S. of Shechem, cannot be identified with certainty; *cf.* Abel II 485. **22-24.** Asa's new fortresses fixed the frontier a few miles N. of Ramah. At Mizpah (Maspha; Tell en-Nasbeh) walls of this era have been found up to 26 ft in width.

d 25-XVI 14 Dynastic Changes in Israel—25-26. During the long and happy reign of Asa in Judah, six kings, involving three dynasties, were to succeed each other in Israel. **27-28.** As Nadab (910-909) was with the army, his slayer must have been a general. Gibbethon (Tell el-Melāt, between Jerusalem and the coast) was left in Philistine hands; *cf.* 16:15. **29-XVI:6.** Baasa (909-886) disappointed the orthodox and led the people to defeat; *cf.* 15:21. The prophet's denunciation spurred the discontented to action. **7.** Jehu outlived Achab and Josaphat, 2 Par 19:2; 20:34. Omit the reference to his death (not in MT). **8-14.** With Ela (886-885) perished all the connexions who were bound to avenge him, his 'goëls'; *cf.* Num 35 : 19-27.

15-20 Death of Zambri—Though energetic and brave, he was not a good organizer, and had not time to muster his supporters. These were numerous, as the subsequent civil war shows, and probably represented the Ephraim-Manasses group of tribes, from which Jeroboam came. Omri (Amri) had land in Issachar (*cf.* ch 21) and so represented the more northerly group of tribes, like his patron Baasa, under whom he had conquered and governed Moab (Mesha Stone, § 80*j*). **17.** 'All Israel' is the army, 15. Contrast 'the people of Israel', 21, whose division later split the army.

e 21-28. Omri, 885-874—21-22. LXX (B, Lucian) shows that Joram, brother of Thebni, continued the civil war. **23.** It lasted four years, as Zambri died in Asa's 27th (15) and Omri's undisputed reign began in Asa's 31st. The twelve years are reckoned from Zambri's death (*cf.* 16) ending in Asa's 38th (29). **24.** Samaria (see § 80*d–e*, for fortifications, palaces and ivories), re-founded by Herod as Sebaste (now Sebastiyeh), was a central and strong position, on an almost isolated hill which dominated its neighbourhood by 300 ft. **25-26.** The severe blame (*cf.* Mic 6:16) is for introducing Phoenician worship and giving it state establishment, which he did when he married Achab to Jezabel. **27-28.** The marriage was one of his earliest political moves (Achab's grandson was 22 years old in 841, 4 Kg 8:26), and one of his ablest, since the Tyrian alliance kept Damascus in check. He was a great ruler, and the Assyrians knew Israel henceforth as 'the Land of the House of Omri'.

f 29-34 Achab, 874-853—Two enormities, the Baal temple and human sacrifice, heralded the religious crisis which Elias was to meet. **29-31.** Ethbaal had become king of Tyre and Sidon (*cf.* on 5:6) by killing his predecessor, according to Menander (in Josephus, *C. Ap.* 1, 18, 23). The new dynasties supported each other. Achab apparently paid a state visit to worship Melqart ('king of the city'), the Baal ('lord') of Tyre. He was however also a worshipper of Yahweh, as the names of his children show (Acha*zyah*; Joram, 'Yahweh is exalted'; Atal*yah*). Prophets of Yahweh will be found in his entourage. **32-33.** Beside the altar, *he set up an ashera* (*cf.* on 14:23) and naturally, other asheras and massebahs (pillars) throughout the land, 4 Kg 3:2. **34.** Excavations have shown that Jericho, deserted since *c* 1250, was re-built at this era; *cf.* L.-H. Vincent, RB (1909) 274; (1932) 268. The sacrifices, common at such undertakings (*cf.* L.-H. Vincent, *Canaan*, 199), were to avert calamity; the orthodox looked on them here as the fulfilment of the curse of Jos 6:26.

g XVII 1-9 Intervention of Elias—1. Eliyyāhû (Elijah), 'my God is Yahweh' fits the great fighter admirably. The name is preserved in the hill of Mar Elias, near el-Istib (Thisbeh). The drought, recorded also by **2** Menander for Phoenicia (Jos. *Ant.* 8, 13, 2) was at once the punishment of idolatry, Lev. 26:19 ff., Deut 28:23 ff., and a challenge to Baal, the sky-god, whose proper name was Hadad. It was the climax of a long struggle. The date will have been *c* 857, for Eliseus (*cf.* 19:19) cannot have been called much earlier, since he was still working under Joas, 798-783, 4 Kg 13. Elias appears suddenly and unannounced; this seems to be deliberate (*cf.* 13:1; 16:1; 21:7) to symbolize the sovereign and direct intervention of Yahweh into human history. **2-7.** The raven snatches eggs, chickens, etc. from farm-yards : there is the usual economy of means in the miracle. **8-9.** Sarephta, now Sarafand, on the sea till the time of the Crusades, is now 1 m. inland.

10-16 The Widow's Faith—Her blind obedience to **h** the movement of grace (*cf.* 9*b*) may be compared to Abraham's readiness to sacrifice his son. Her reward pre-figured the inexhaustible graces to be bestowed on the gentiles by Christ, Lk 6:38 ; 4:25. **17-24 Raising of the Dead Child**—18. The exclamation **i** of surprise, *mah lî wālāk*, has various nuances ; here : 'What does this mean?'; *cf.* Jn 2:4. The prophet's presence had seemed a blessing, but in the end only called Yahweh's attention to her sins. **19-23.** The rite which accompanied the prayer, (*cf.* 4 Kg 4:34, Ac 20:10) signified that the warmth of life should pass from the wonder-worker to the child. **24.** The mother re-affirms her faith in the divine mission of the prophet, and further, that Yahweh had been faithful all along to his first promise of blessing.

XVIII 1-15 Return of Elias—1-6. The new year had **j** come around twice in the drought, which lasted probably from after the March rains of one year till the November rains of the following year. The 3½ years of Lk 4:25, Jas 5:17 seems to be idiomatic, like the '3 days and 3 nights' of Mt 12:40. U. Holzmeister, VD (1939) 167 ff., takes it literally. But in such a spell, all vegetation and cattle would have been destroyed. The expeditions hoped to find wells and watered valleys where green fodder still grew. Achab does not seem to have been personally hostile to the true religion, since his chamberlain was a strict ' servant of Yahweh ', as his name implies ; the persecution is ascribed to Jezabel. **7-10.** Achab was on good terms with the neighbouring kings of Tyre, Syria, 20:34, Judah, 22:5 ; he was ruler of Moab ; hence he could make them swear *that* Elias was not to be found. **11-14.** The spirit of Yahweh is considered as an external force (*cf.* 46) whose plans the prophet cannot comprehend, 17:20, or guarantee. The contrast in our Lord's use of divine power is instructive. **15.** Elias was the servant of him who was about to reveal himself as ' Yahweh, (God) of hosts ' : i.e. lord of all earthly and heavenly forces ; *cf.* Gen 2:1 (nature), 1 Kg 4:4 (armies), Deut 4:19 (stars), Jos 5:14 (angels).

16-24 Challenge on Carmel—17. Achab's anger died **k** away with the prospect of relief. **19.** The majestic wooded range of Carmel was naturally sacred in the eyes of pagans (Tacitus, *Hist.* 2, 78 ; Suetonius, *Vespasian* 5 ; Iamblichus, *Pythagoras* 3:15) and was the site of a shrine of Yahweh, like Mt Nebo (Mesha Stone). Tradition placed the meeting at the height El-Muḥraqa ' Burnt Offering ', at the SE. end of the range, close to the Qishon, 40, and Jezreel, 46. A lower point near by, Bir el-Muḥraqa, with a spring, 34 f., suits the text better, as the sea was not visible without a climb, 43 f. Omit ' the prophets of the grove ' as an interpolation, not in LXX (Hexaplar) ; *cf.* 22, 40. **21.** The reproach, ' How long will you *limp from side to side* ? ' supposes that the people were already familiar with the exigencies of monotheism. It was not a novelty introduced by the great prophets, as so often said. The dilemma, ' Yahweh is all or nothing ', left no place for the henotheism which was content to worship one god while not denying the existence of others. The clear and peremptory message of Carmel ranks with that of Sinai in the history of revelation.

k 22-24. The ending of the drought might have been attributed to chance; lightning was decisive, especially as Baal, Hadad, 'Lord of Heaven', was the great storm-god.

l 25-49 Fire from Heaven—26. 'They *danced by* the altar': the Baal Marqod 'lord of the dance' had a shrine on Lebanon, and the ritual dances of Cybele and the Dea Syra were well known to antiquity. **27.** According to R. de Vaux (*Les prophètes de Baal sur le mont Carmel*, Bulletin du Musée de Beyrouth, 1943), Elias mocked four aspects of Baal : (1) the philosopher-inventor (' he is *meditating*'); (2) the patron of Phoenician merchants (' he is *busy*'); (3) the patron of his sailors ; (4) the winter-sleeper, for whose awakening a feast was held in Tyre and Carthage, Jos., *Ant.* 8, 5, 3. The last trait shows Baal as the vegetation-god. **28.** As a mourning-rite at least, self-wounding was prevalent, Deut 14:1, Jer 47:5. Originally based perhaps on the idea of blood-alliance with the god, it was here an intense mode of prayer. **29.** ' Prophesying' means ' in a frenzy' (*cf.* 1 Kg 19:23 f., 4 Kg 9:11) like dervishes, who also gash themselves. **29-31.** The time, 3 p.m., was fixed according to the temple ritual, and the twelve tribes were represented by the twelve stones of the altar. Elias seems to have wished for the united prayers of Judah and Israel, just as he acted in the interest of both. **32.** The narrow, shallow trench would hold ' two seahs of corn' (MT), *c* 3 pecks. **33-35.** The drenching was not to produce rain by ' sympathetic magic', but to heighten the effect of the miracle. **36-39.** As on Sinai, Yahweh revealed himself by fire, the one God who in the past had converted to himself the people's fathers. **40.** Elias used the enthusiasm of the people to eliminate the prophets who were outlaws in the realm of Yahweh.

m 41-46 Miracle of the Rain—41-42. Hearing its approach in spirit, Elias *crouched down* in an attitude of intense prayer. **43.** For ' foot' read ' hand' (MT). **44-46.** The prophet's solicitude for the king is friendly ; with the final demonstration of his superhuman power, *cf.* Ps 18:6. Jezreel (Zerîn) was *c* 15 m. away.

n XIX 1-8 Flight to Horeb—1-2. Jezabel did not dare to kill Elias, but, to uphold her authority, banished him by threats. **3.** He could not long rely on Achab and the fickle public : ' rising up, *he fled for his life* ', without pausing in Judah where since *c* 865 Josaphat's son Joram was married to Athalia, daughter of Achab and Jezabel. **4.** Under the shade of a *broom* (*rōṯem = genista*) the hardships and disappointments of his fugitive life wrung from him a plea for release, since his strength was but human. Prophetic energy and insight were transient, not permanent gifts ; *cf.* Jon 4:3. **5-8.** The 300 m. pilgrimage to Horeb (Sinai) was to seek counsel and to pray for the faithless people, 14. He may have had other food from traders making for Aqabah, 9:26. But his strength came fundamentally from the miraculous food. This is a figure of the Eucharist, ' strengthened by whose vigour', says the Council of Trent, ' Christians are enabled to travel this pilgrimage of misery, and come at last to their heavenly fatherland', Dz 882.

o 9-14 Theophany—9-12. Yahweh's coming was heralded by hurricane, earthquake and fire (lightning ?). But he was not therein—contrast Ex 19:18, Ps 17:12. His presence was felt only in the quiet of a gentle breeze, because his being is peace, his attributes wise counsel and calm constancy. As the zephyr contrasts with the hurricane, so the peaceful manifestation with the tempestuous zeal of Elias. **10-14.** Elias, depressed and bewildered, seems to ignore Carmel. But the miracle had not repaired the ravages of time. The revival of the threat to his life seemed to promise a revival of Baalism. The people who would not defend the wonder-worker were not likely to build well on the new foundation. He had come therefore to Horeb for help. Yahweh appeared in fact, but unmoved by the menace to his kingdom which racked the prophet. The reproof addressed to Elias in this striking revelation may perhaps be expressed in St Augustine's words :

' Thou regardest thy few days and in them thou dost **272b** wish all things to be fulfilled', PL 37, 1176.

15-18 The Divine Plan—Elias' life-work was nearly **c** over, but God had other instruments. **15.** The desert *of* Damascus is here probably the pasture-land E. of the Sea of Galilee, then held by Syria. Hazael was a dignitary of Benhadad III, 4 Kg 8:7 f., who was yet to succeed Benhadad II. **16.** Similarly, before Jehu, two kings were to succeed Achab. Thus, according to the immediate meaning of the text, Elias was to anoint Hazael and Jehu *c* 13 years before they came to the throne. In fact, it was only through Eliseus that Elias carried out his mandate. The prophecy was fulfilled substantially, but the terms were not modified to suit the event exactly. **18.** The ' Remnant' (this is the first instance of an idea common in the 8th cent. prophets), from which flourishing religious life was to grow, is given in a figurative number, the 7 suggesting health. Perhaps however the actual number of the orthodox in the North is indicated. For kissing as a religious rite, see Os 13:2, Job 31:27.

19-21 Vocation of Eliseus—19. The homeland of **d** Eliseus (*'elîšā' ' God has saved '*) was Abel-Meholah, 16, prob. Tell Abu Sifri, near the Jordan, S. of Beisan. The gesture with the distinctive mantle of the prophet (*cf.* 4 Kg 1:8, Zach 13:4, Mt 3:4) intimated the call. **20.** Elias' answer, ' *Go, return, for what have I done to (hinder) you ?* ' seems to be a concession. More probably it means ' Come, turn (after me), for (think) what I have done to you !' **21.** For Eliseus seems to have understood that Elias demanded an immediate break with the past ; *cf.* Lk 9:62. The anointing as prophet came later, probably just before the events of 4 Kg 2. Meanwhile Eliseus was considered merely the servant of Elias, 4 Kg 3:11.

XX 1-21 War with Syria—LXX (B, Lucian) puts ch 21 **e** before 20, leaving the connexion between 20 and 22 unbroken. **1.** It was probably *c* 858, before the drought ; for the causes see on 15:20. Benhadad II (*c* 875-845) put into the field at Qarqar, 853 B.C., 1,200 chariots, 1,200 horse, 20,000 foot, Luckenbill I no. 611. There, against Assyria, 11 kings were allied ; the 32 here must be chiefs of Syrian tribes. **2-9.** Achab was prepared to pay a certain contribution, but not to submit to an inspection in view of a general confiscation. **10.** Benhadad threatened to raze the city, claiming to have so many soldiers that its dust would not make a handful for each. **11.** Achab's reply was that a man putting on his armour should not boast like a victor laying it aside. **13.** Jezabel's persecution had not started. The prophet is not Elias, for tradition is inclined to ascribe rather more than less to an outstanding figure. **14-21.** Achab, a brave and devoted leader (*cf.* 18:6 ; 22:35) headed a sortie of picked troops, so few that the Syrians did not anticipate serious fighting. A full-scale attack routed them. The tactics are not made clear. The writer's intention was simply to show that victory came from Yahweh, 13.

22-34 Another Campaign—22-23. The heart of **f** Israel's territory was upland ; Yahweh was compared to the Baal Hermon or Baal Lebanon. The principle that chariots and cavalry could be better employed on plains than among hills was clothed in religious form. **24-26.** The undisciplined or untrustworthy sheikhs were replaced by regular officers, and Benhadad advanced along the E. of the Sea of Galilee (*cf.* on 19:15) basing his forces on Apheq (Fîq, a few miles N. of the Yarmuk). **27-30.** Yahweh was proved God of the *plains* as of the hills, therefore universal lord, since the battle was fought probably on the plateau SW. of Fîq. The numbers are not correctly transmitted ; *cf.* on 1. **30.** The walls were undermined, and house to house fighting followed. **31.** A burden on the back could be slung from a band round the forehead ; hence the rope on the head to signify submission. Josephus, *Ant.* 8, 14, 4, explains it as a custom of Syrian suppliants. **32.** ' Brother' was the normal form of address between kings of equal standing ; *cf.* 9:13. **33.** Vassals of Assyrian kings spoke of themselves as running beside

272f the chariot of their overlord ; *cf.* inscription of Bar-Rekub of Sam'al, Bonkamp, 402. **34.** Achab regained what Omri had lost in an otherwise unknown war, and his merchants set up their own bazaars in Damascus. Achab fought on the side of the Syrians at Qarqar ; *cf.* § 124*e*.

g **35-43 Condemnation of the Treaty**—In attacking twice against odds, Achab had obeyed Yahweh and been rewarded ; in making terms he had been guided only by politics and was punished. **35.** The ' sons of the prophets ' were disciples grouped round a recognized prophet ; *cf* .§ 410*e-f* and on 4 Kg 2:3. In 38 and 41 they are simply ' prophets '. **36.** One of them favoured Achab's policy to the extent of disregarding a ' word of the Lord '. **37-38.** The object of the wound, which presumably could be seen bleeding, was to distract attention from the *bandage* (MT, LXX) round his forehead, which merely concealed (tattoo-) markings by which a prophet could be known ; *cf.* Ez 9:4 ff. **39-41.** Like David before Nathan, 2 Kg 12:5, Achab passed sentence on himself. **42.** The captive was not his to dispose of, but Yahweh's—' *the man doomed to destruction by me* ' ; *cf.* Jos 6:17 etc. The misplaced clemency of Achab involved Israel in foreign commitments which in the end brought ruin. **43.** The true prophets aimed at preserving Israel as ' a people apart ', Deut 33:28 etc. It was possibly for their stand at this stage that Jezabel was allowed to proceed against them, 18:4.

h **XXI 1-16 Murder of Naboth**—After the Syrian wars, the events of chh 17-19 are probably to be inserted before this episode. **1.** The coveted vineyard was in Jezreel, as follows from 4 Kg 9:21-25 ; from 19 and 22:38 it might have been thought to be in Samaria. Hence the gloss ' who was in Samaria ', 18. **2-3.** Achab's request was not against Lev 25:23-28, for Naboth would not be left landless, nor against Num 36:7, since the land would not pass from the tribe of Issachar ; *cf.* on 16:16. Naboth was obstinately conservative. **4-8.** It was the sharpness of the refusal that angered Achab. · Hence the repetition in 4 and 6, to contrast the courtesy of the offer. But he was a constitutional monarch, educated to the Ten Commandments, and did not think of force. The pagan despot, Jezabel, was ruthless. Her irony stung Achab into delivering her the royal seal. The scene is characteristic for her power over Achab. **9.** The fast, suggesting impending calamity, Jl 1:14, Jg 20:26, built up an atmosphere of tension in which the people would be swift to punish an evil-doer. **10.** The two witnesses (*cf.* Deut 17:6 ; 19:15) were ' sons of *worthlessness* ' (*beliya'al*), scoundrels ; P. Joüon, Bi 5 (1924) 178 explains the term as ' devil ' ; *cf.* 2 Cor 6:15. The double blasphemy was against Lev 24:16, Ex 22:28. **11-13.** Naboth was stoned on his own land (*cf.* 19) property outside Jezreel, to which the kings rode out to meet Jehu, 4 Kg 9:21-26. The vineyard was in the town beside the palace. His sons were killed too, 4 Kg 9:26, to leave no heirs to dispute the confiscation of the property. There was no legal pretext for their death. But a king's enemies were always destroyed root and branch, 1:21 etc. **14-16.** Achab must have learned the details and certainly sanctioned the murders.

i **17-29 Condemnation and Repentance**—**19.** The prophecy was fulfilled vaguely in 22:38, but more precisely, as Jehu understood, in 4 Kg 9:25 f. Achab's blood flowed in Joram's veins. **20.** Achab confessed that he was caught in the act. His misgivings show that he had still a lively sense of justice. Elias' ' sold ' is apt ; Achab had sold himself to Jezabel for the price of a vineyard. **21, 22, 24** are a conventional interpretation of the prophecy by the writer ; *cf.* 14:10 f. ; 16:2 ff. **23** is original, but awkwardly placed ; a fuller form in 4 Kg 9:10, 36 f. In 24 read with MT ' Him that dieth of Achab ' etc. **25.** The mention of Jezabel's influence is not to excuse but to explain Achab's conduct ; a similar remark was made about Solomon, 11:3 f. **26.** The Amorites are a prototype of Canaanite

Baal-worshippers as in Am 2:9, Ez 16:3. Achab had **2** noble traits ; *cf.* 20 and on 20:14, which are faithfully recorded in spite of the writers unsympathetic attitude. There is an unmistakable ring of triumph in the pardon which reminds us of the parables of Lk 15 ; and perhaps the fiercely zealous Elias needed the lesson there taught by the father to the elder son. This episode is taken from a different source than that of chh 17-19 ; there the official cult of Baal is the chief factor in the downfall of the dynasty ; here, as in 2 Kg 2, the contribution of the king's personal sin is stressed.

XXII 1-28 Micheas and the False Prophets—1-3. 2 Israel probably regained territory E. of the Sea of Galilee after the victory of Apheq, 20:34, but Syria still held the border-town of Ramoth (Tell Ramîth), on the trade route from Damascus to N. Arabia. The battle of Qarqar (spring 853) had not appreciably weakened the Syrians, for the Assyrians had to return to the attack four times in the next 12 years. But Achab had been able to put 2,000 chariots into that battle, compared to Damascus' 1,200, Luckenbill I no. 611. He was therefore strong enough to take the offensive (autumn 853). **4-5.** Josaphat was allied both politically and by marriage to the house of Omri ; *cf.* on 19:3. **6.** The prophets who had survived persecution (18:4 ; 19:14) had ' bowed the knee to Baal ', 19:18, but still claimed to speak for Yahweh. **7.** Knowing their history Josaphat asked ' Is there not *some other* prophet of Yahweh ? ' (MT). **8.** This Micheas, who had kept up the menaces of 20:42, was confused with the eighth-century author of the prophetical book by the glossator of 28*b*. **9-14.** The false **b** prophets counted for little, since the verdict of Micheas could outweigh theirs. He had not as yet received a revelation ; it came while he was on his way ; *cf.* 17, ' I saw '. **15-17.** After echoing sarcastically the words of the false prophets, he foretold defeat, without stating clearly that Achab would die. The flight or capture of the king might have explained the leaderless state of the army. For the terms *cf.* Num 27:17 (Mt 9:36). **18.** The king sought to nullify the effect of his words by ascribing them to personal malice. **19.** Micheas therefore gave details of his revelation. **20.** ' Fall at ' (*nāpal b^e*) could be rendered ' fall upon ' ; *cf.* Jos 11:7, 2 Kg 17:9, Job 1:15. The reference to Achab's death is still veiled. **21** manifests belief in spiritual beings, distinct from God and closer to him than men. **22-23.** The false prophets are branded as conscious liars, though Micheas grants that Yahweh is in some way responsible ; *cf.* 2 Kg 24:1, 1 Kg 26:19, Ex 4:21, 2 Kg 16:10. No distinction was made between direct causality and mere permission. The Israelites were satisfied that Yahweh was the ultimate cause of every event and did not ask how precisely he was the cause both of good and evil. **24-28a.** Having warned the false prophets that they would have to fly for their lives one day (*cf.* 4 Kg 10:26) Micheas finally stated clearly that Achab would die in the battle. **28b.** *Cf.* Mic 1:2.

29-40 Achab's Last Campaign—29-30. Achab was **c** determined, if the end was come, to die among his soldiers, but he did not mean to make it easy for his destiny to overtake him. The Syrians were not to recognize him. He cannot have known their order of the day. Josaphat was in no special danger ; the silence of Micheas in his regard was reassuring. **31.** With possible future alliances against Assyria in view, the king of Syria planned to end the war with as little loss as possible on either side. **32.** Josaphat gave the Judaean war-cry to rally his men. **34.** The arrow struck *between the joints of the armour* (?)–MT. **35-37.** Achab did not allow himself to be taken to the rear, but, to avoid disheartening his troops, remained upright near the front (' against the Syrians ') till he bled to death. **38.** See on 21:19. **39.** Jericho was one of Achab's undertakings. For the fortifications and ivories of Samaria, see DBV (S) 3, 386-8 or W. F. Albright, *Archaeology of Palestine*, 137. His palace was

73c decorated with ivories, Am 3:15, Ps 44:9 ; they appear mostly as inlay for furniture. See § 80*d–e*.

d 41-51 Josaphat of Judah, 873-849—41-47. Continuing the reforms of Asa, he eliminated ritual prostitution ; *cf.* 15:12. **48.** Edom had been re-conquered ; *cf.* 11:14-25*b*. ' A *governor ruled* ' (LXX), who was a native sheikh, 4 Kg 3:9, probably with Jewish ministers. **49-50.** After a set-back, the Red Sea trade was apparently resumed. To bring 2 Par 20:35–37 into line with this passage, ' Achab ' may be read there for ' Ochozias ' ; the enterprise was hardly delayed till the end of Josaphat's long reign. **51.** Some idea of the importance of Josaphat as an administrator may be gathered from 2 Par 17-19. His measures included fortification of towns, re-organization of the army, re-distribution of provinces, provision of religious instruction and division of the judiciary.

THE FOURTH BOOK OF KINGS

e I 1-2 Ochozias of Israel, 853-852 : Invocation of Beelzebub—1. The loss of Moab (*cf.* Mesha Stone, § 80*j*) and the illness of the king are seen as chastisement for provoking Yahweh, 3 Kg 22:54. **2.** Baal Zebub (Beelzebub) means ' lord of flies ', *cf.* LXX and Jos., *Ant.* 9, 2, 1 ; he warded off the bearers of disease, like the Zeus Apomuios of Olympia. Zebub however is probably a contemptuous alteration of the original Zebul ' lofty mansion '. He was thus ' lord of the temple ' of Accaron (Eqrôn, a Philistine town). The true form and meaning survived in the NT, Mt 10:25 etc., though the later Jews associated it with *zibbul* ' dung '. The Rās-Shamra texts mention Z-b-l B-'-l, from which the sense of ' sublime, lordly ' cannot be excluded. Ochozias disavowed Yahweh as the true God and as the God of Israel.

f 3-18 Intervention of Elias—3-7. It is remarkable that he was not known to the soldiers. But he had always held aloof from the capital ; *cf.* 20:13 ; 22:8. **8.** His hairy mantle was distinctive ; *cf.* on 3 Kg 19:19. **9.** The command was to come down to Samaria ; *cf.* 15. Elias was not on an inaccessible crag. **10-12.** The answer involved a grim pun : not the man, *'îš*, of God, but fire, *'ēš*, of God (MT 12) was to come down. **11-16.** Why the destruction ? (1) Elias was defending his life ; *cf.* 15 and 3 Kg 19:2 f. (2) Disrespect for the prophetic office was visited with the extreme penalty ; *cf.* 2:23 ff. ; 3 Kg 20:36. The soldiers were executing an evidently sacrilegious order and the captain's ' man of God ' was sarcastic. (3) The people needed to be deterred from the sensual cult of Baal by the fear of God. Hence the prophet's appeal to motives of fear, 3 Kg 17:1 ; 21:21 ; 22:17. It was not a prophet's duty to preach, 3 Kg 20:42, or practise, 3 Kg 18:40, love of enemies. The perfection of charity was reserved for the NT ; *cf.* Lk 9:51-55. **17-18.** The dating has suffered from interpolation. Joram's accession was the 22nd year of Josaphat. They campaigned together, 3:6 ff.

g II 1-12 Assumption of Elias—1. The manner of his passing from this world is unique except for Henoch, Gen 5:22. It has been maintained, in view of Mal 4:5, that he is to return before the Second Coming ; but contrast Mk 9:10 ' Elias is already come ', in the person of the Baptist. There were several Gilgals, ' circle of stones ', the simplest type of shrine. This was probably the famous Gilgal between the Jordan and Jericho ; *cf.* 5:38 ; 6:3. **2-8.** They *went* (LXX) to Bethel, which was much higher. Elias paid a last visit of encouragement to the prophetic colleges (see § 410*e–f*) though he was not their head ; *cf.* ' *thy* master ', 3. They did not foresee his permanent disappearance (*cf.* 16) and they were not to witness his passing. Moses too had passed away alone, with no one to know his grave, Deut 34:6. Elias and Eliseus must have returned to the Jordan somewhere above Jericho, for there was a ford lower down, 2 Kg 19:40 f. The miracle (*cf.* Ex 14:21, Jos 3:13) prevented the others' following, and the bush then hid the pair from view. **9.** *Two-thirds* was the portion of the firstborn, Deut 21:17 ; Eliseus wished

to inherit, with the office, the miraculous power and **273g** the primacy of Elias. **10.** Elias doubted whether such extraordinary signs as he had wrought would be repeated in favour of an ungrateful people ; *cf.* 3 Kg 19:14 ff. **11.** The vision granted to Eliseus, however, was one withheld from ordinary men ; *cf.* 6:17. Elias ascended in a storm, like that in which Yahweh descended, Ez 1:4 ; Job 38:1. **12.** Elias, ' *Israel's chariots and cavalry* ' (MT), had been worth an army to his people. The event took place prob. in 851, after the death of Ochozias and before the Moabite campaign ; *cf.* 3:11, and 13:14 below. **13-18 The Mantle of Elias—13-15.** After repeating **h** Elias' miracle, the former servant was acknowledged as master. The text of 14 is disturbed ; omit ' and they were not divided ' with MT. **16-18.** The prophetic college had had only a vague idea of what was to happen to Elias. Apparently Eliseus did not enlighten them.

19-22 Healing of the Waters—19. The water at **i** Jericho was brackish and the land *caused miscarriages.* **20-22.** A new vessel was required for a sacred action, *cf.* 3 Kg 11:30 ; the salt signified preservation from foulness.

23-25 The Bears—23. The hostility at Bethel suggests **j** that the prophet inveighed against the calf-worship. ' Baldhead ' was probably a current sneer against the distinctive tonsure worn by the prophets, and familiar from the college at Bethel. For the Jewish idea of the collective responsibility of parents and children, see § 109*m* and § 110*e*. **24.** The children were *torn to pieces* ; *cf.* on 1:11 ff. **25.** Eliseus' own house was in Samaria, 5:9 ; 6:32. But he toured the country giving instruction. In the following he will be found at Carmel, Sunam, Gilgal, Jericho and Dothain.

III 1-3 Joram of Israel, 852-841—1. For the dating, **k** see on 1:17. **2.** Joram started well, impressed by the events of 1:2 ff. But he did not interfere with Jezabel's installations in the capital, and later there was a recrudescence of Baalism throughout the country ; *cf.* 10:21. Hence Eliseus' sharp reproof, 13, and his support of Jehu, 9:1 ff.

4-8 Campaign against Moab—4. Mesha recorded his **l** successful revolt on the memorial stone found at Dibon in 1869, now in the Louvre, § 80*j* ; see M.-J. Lagrange, RB 10 (1901) 522 ff. ; A. Vaccari, VD 2 (1922) 274 ff. The sheep-rearing is referred to on the stone, l. 30. It also speaks of ' 40 years' subjection ' ; see on 3 Kg 16:15-20. **5-8.** Mesha had seized the fortresses N. of the Arnon, Medeba, Qiryathayim, Ataroth, Nebo and Yahas. The attack was therefore launched from the SE., after a march round the S. of the Dead Sea and across the plateau of Edom.

9-20 Water in the Desert—9-10. For the vassal-king **m** of Edom, see on 3 Kg 22:48. On the border of Moab, 21, the army was exposed to attack when weakened by thirst. **11.** Eliseus was not well known. This places the campaign *c* 851. The Orientals did not dip their hands into a basin, when washing before and after meals : a servant poured for them. **13.** Joram's plea, ' *Say not so!* For it is indeed Yahweh ' etc., was a confession of faith. The true God alone could help. **14-15.** The ritual music (*cf.* § 414*b*) was to aid recollection. **16-17.** Rains over the plateau, too far away to be remarked, could fill the wadis lower down. Eliseus' foresight was supernatural. **18-20.** The order to devastate Moab was of exceptional severity ; *cf.* Deut 20:19 f.

21-27 Invasion of Moab—21-22. The rising sun **n** reddened the waters. ' Those who have visited the southern banks of the Dead Sea know what strange colours can change the look of things ', Lagrange, RB 10 (1901) 542. Older writers spoke of the red earth ; but the text is clear. **23-24.** The Moabites could easily suppose that the king of Edom had turned on the others. **25.** Only the capital, Qir Hareseth (DV ' brick walls ' ; *cf.* Is 16:7, 11) resisted the invaders. **26.** Mesha tried to break *through to* the Edomites, to make common cause with them. **27.** Then he had

273n recourse to human sacrifice, the Crown Prince probably offering himself freely, like Marcus Curtius in the Roman Forum or the Carthaginian general Hamilcar, who made himself a holocaust at Himera in 480 for the success of his army. Thus Mesha thought to avert the wrath of his god Kemosh (*cf.* Mesha Stone, lines 5, 6) and to render his ramparts inviolable. Then ' there came great indignation (of Yahweh) *upon* Israel ' ; *cf.* Jos 9:20 etc. Some calamity, probably a pestilence, forced the Israelites to retire. According to Stade, Šanda, Kittel, etc., the original narrative said ' the indignation of Kemosh '. But this would be at variance with ancient ways of thought, especially Israel's ; the Assyrians attributed a reverse to the anger of Nana, the Babylonians to the anger of Marduk. Mesha rebuilt his towns and remained unsubdued (Mesha Stone, lines 21–33).

274a **IV 1–7 Miraculous Multiplication of Oil**—This and the next three chapters are chiefly concerned with the miracles by which Eliseus continued the extraordinary mission of Elias. **1–2.** Insolvent debtors could be sold as slaves, Lev 25:39 ; Am 2:6 ; a father could sell his children, Ex 21:2–7. Loyalty to Yahweh had been costly under Achab. The widow had therefore special reasons for hope. **3–7.** The miracle was less lavish than that of Elias, 3 Kg 17, which was worked to avert the more enduring menace of famine.

b **8–10 Hospitality of the Lady of Shunem**—**8.** For Shunem (Sunam), see on 3 Kg 1:3. **9–10.** ' Holy ' here is not so much ' good ' as ' sacred ' ; hence Eliseus was lodged apart, in a ' *walled* chamber on the roof ' (MT). Such installations were sometimes only huts of leafy branches, 2 Kg 16:22 ; Neh 8:16. The furniture was a further mark of respect. Poor people sat and slept on the floor.

c **11–16 Promise of a Child**—**11–12.** The prophet holds himself notably aloof, treating with the lady only through his servant. This may be understood also in 16. **13.** His influence at court is understandable after the Moabite campaign. But the lady had clansmen to defend her interests. **16.** The promise was : ' In a year's time, at this very hour, you shall embrace a son ' (MT).

d **17–37 The Dead Child restored to Life**—**17–19.** The child died of sunstroke ; *cf.* Jdt 8:2 f. The translation misses some of the simple pathos of the original ' My head, my head ! ' (MT). **20–23.** It was evidently the custom to visit the prophet on holy days to seek instruction and counsel. This practice was perhaps the origin of the later Synagogues. The father's question was indifferent. He did not know that the boy was dead, and further discussion was cut off by a curt ' good-bye ' (MT). **24–28.** As the return journey was made the same day, 32, Eliseus may have been at El Muhraqa (*cf.* on 3 Kg 18:20), about 15 m. from Shunem. Out of politeness, he sent Giezi to meet the lady. She countered the conventional inquiry with an evasive answer. **29–31.** Two explanations of the mission of Giezi are possible. (1) Eliseus mistakenly thought that his staff would work a miracle, like Moses', Num 20:11. But earnest prayer was indispensable ; *cf.* Mk 9:28. (2) It was now evening, and the household at Shunem might have discovered the death. Eliseus therefore wished to take possession of the corpse, to prevent its being buried, or even mourned over, before his arrival next day. Giezi, however, who was crude and officious (*cf.* 27 ; 5:20 ff) presumed that he was to be the agent of a miracle, 31. The former explanation is simpler and perhaps preferable. **32–34.** Eliseus had thought to send the lady back with Giezi ; that he yielded to her insistence is perhaps a proof that he had not expected his staff to work a miracle. He followed the procedure of Elias, 3 Kg 17:21. **35.** The boy *sneezed* as life returned. **36–37.** The mother's gratitude is admirable ; she paused before the prophet before turning to her son.

e **38–41 ' Death in the Pot ! '**—**38.** The famine is perhaps that of 8:1 ff. Eliseus did not live in community with the prophetic guild, since he had to make special pro-

vision for entertaining them. Köhler suggests Dwarf **27** Mallow for ' wild herbs ' (*'ōrōṯ*). The creeping plant from which the gourds (*paqqū'ōṯ*) were gathered was probably the colocynth (Vg). It abounds in the Jordan valley (Hagen, *Lexicon Biblicum*), which suits the situation of Gilgal. **40.** The colocynth is still used in purgatives ; it is not poisonous, but it is very bitter. **41.** The meal would not make the dish edible without a miracle.

42–44 Multiplication of Bread—**42.** Baal-shalisha may **f** be Kefr Thilth on the coastal plain, Abel II 250 f. A hundred were fed by the miracle, more than ' the great pot ' could cater for. The scene is therefore different, in spite of the resemblance of ' the people ' in 41 and 42 f. The prophet perhaps took the place of the priests as recipients of the offerings of first-fruits, Lev 2:12 ff. ; 23:14–20. **44.** The fragments recall Mt 14:20.

V 1–14 Naaman the Leper—**1.** The king of Syria was **g** probably Benhadad II, whom the Assyrians attacked in vain ; *cf.* on 3 Kg 22:1. Yahweh is represented as universal Lord, even of the Syrians, as in 3 Kg 19:15–17. Naaman's disease was not real leprosy, for he remained at court, 18, whereas it was understood that lepers were segregated, 7:3. **2.** Syria, though at peace with Israel, 5–7, could not control all its restless frontier tribes. **4.** As a high official Naaman needed leave of absence. **5–6.** The courteous opening and ending of the letter have been omitted. The request was not so peremptory as it now reads. Naaman's gifts were princely, as befitted his state ; contrast 3 Kg 14:3. It was universally recognized that one should not approach a ' man of God ' with empty hands ; *cf.* 1 Kg 9:7. But the bulk of the presents was probably for the king, who was supposed to have the prophet at his beck and call like a court magician. **7.** The king was probably Joram—' **h** who had already received the rebuff from Eliseus—' Go to the prophets of thy father and thy mother ', 3:13. He had therefore no illusions as to his standing with Eliseus. But his demonstration of alarm was meant to reach the prophet's ears. **8–10.** Eliseus did not abate his customary reserve (*cf.* 4:12) even for the great lord. **11.** Naaman however expected personal attention from the prophet, and some familiar ceremony, such as ' *to wave his hand* '. Against LXX and St Jerome, some modern commentators translate further, ' towards the (Holy) Place '. But the hands were raised or outstretched in prayer, not waved ; *cf.* Ps 27:2. The adverbial phrase is perhaps to be omitted with LXX (Hexaplar). **12.** The Jordan is narrow and turbulent ; the great rivers of Syria, the present Nahr Barada and Nahr el-A'waj, are broad and clear. **13–14.** Naaman was loved and respected by his servants ; *cf.* 3. Like the favour bestowed on the Phoenician, 3 Kg 17:9 ff., the miracle was to have great significance in religious history, prefiguring the call of the Gentiles to the Messianic blessings, Lk 4:27.

15–19a Naaman's Faith—**15.** Naaman recognized in **i** Yahweh the one true God. He begged Eliseus to take a *farewell-present*. **16.** Eliseus refused. The holiness of Yahweh was reflected in his prophet's detachment from earthly things. The prophets took presents from Israelites (*cf.* on 5–6) ; but they were better instructed than this neophyte as to the nature of Yahweh. **17.** Naaman's desire to have Israelite earth for an altar does not mean that he had returned already to the pagan notion that gods were powerful only on their national territory. He recognized correctly that God is not indifferent to the way in which men worship him. **18.** The ancient Semitic storm-god, Hadad, became the ' Lord ' (Baal) *par excellence*. As national god of Syria he was known as Ramman. To refuse to conform, at least externally, to his worship would have been looked on as rebellion. **19a.** What Naaman proposed to do was unlawful. But Eliseus did not feel bound to enlighten him as to the full extent of his obligations. **19b–27 Punishment of Giezi**—**19b.** Naaman ' de- **j** parted from him *a certain distance* ' (MT). **20–21.** While Giezi thought with contempt of ' this Syrian ', Naaman was so respectful, even towards the servant, that he

74j alighted hastily (*wayyippōl*; *cf.* Gen 24:64). **22.** To show that the request was not unwelcome, he insisted on giving more than asked. With two talents of silver Omri had bought the site of Samaria, 3 Kg 16:24. **24.** ' When he was come *to the Hill* '. This was apparently a well-known part of Samaria. The term, which the versions confused with a similar word meaning darkness, is used elsewhere only of the SE. spur of the temple hill in Jerusalem ; but it is found on the Mesha Stone. **25-27.** Greed met with poetic justice ; but the story also inculcates reverence for the prophet (*cf.* 1:2 ff. ; 2:23 ff. ; 3 Kg 20:36 ff.), whose standing had been endangered by the abuse of his name. The leprosy was like Naaman's. Hence Giezi too could still move about freely, even at court, 8:4.

k VI 1-7 The Floating Axehead—1-2. The group from Jericho, 2:5, or Gilgal, 4:38, is involved in this homely incident, which shows the kindness and power of the prophet and the affectionate regard in which he was held. The richly-wooded banks of the Jordan supplied tamarisk, wild olive, poplar, etc., Abel I 213. **3-7.** What part the piece of wood played in the miracle is not clear ; perhaps it plunged into the axehead and floated it ashore.

l 8-23 ' There are more with us than with them '—8-10. This incident was perhaps part of the campaigns which led to the re-capture of Ramoth-Gilead, 9:1, some time before 841. The Syrians were harrying Israel by a series of raids, 23, possibly in the hope of seizing the king ; *cf.* 3 Kg 22:31. **12-14.** They knew of Eliseus since Naaman's cure ; if the incident is connected with 24-7:20, which was probably much later, he had also figured in the anointing of Hazael, ch 8. **13.** Dothan (Gen 37:17 Dothain) was *c* 12 m. N. of Samaria. **14.** It was illogical to hope to surprise the far-sighted prophet ; they did what they could. **15-17.** The fiery escort (*cf.* 2:11) did not intervene directly ; the vision was only for the believers. **18-20.** The Syrians did not lose their sight, but ' their eyes were held ' ; *cf.* Lk 24:16. **21-23.** Eliseus saved their lives, on the ground that they were not the king's prisoners. The custom of killing prisoners at will apparently extended to Israel. To avoid this implication, MT reads : ' Do you kill those whom you have captured ? '. Vg gives the original ; *cf.* LXX (Lucian). The ending of the raids was not a mark of gratitude towards Eliseus, but a recognition of his powers.

m 24-33 Siege and Starvation—24. The weakness of Israel, 7:13 (*cf.* 13:7) points to a date much later than 841 ; *cf.* on 8-10. After that date, Hazael reigned in Syria till *c* 800. The Benhadad is therefore the third of the name. The king of Israel was Joachaz, 814-798, rather than Joas, 798-783, who loved and respected Eliseus, 13:24 ; contrast 31 ff. **25.** The coarsest food reached fantastic prices. ' A pint of *earth-nuts* cost five silver shekels '. MT's *ḥᵃrê yônîm* ' pigeons' dung ', seems to be a scribal error for *ḥarṣônîm*, the edible tubers of the Star of Bethlehem, ornithogalum umbellatum ; so *I. Löw, Die Flora der Juden I 601, cf. Vaccari, Bi 19 (1938) 198 f. Among other conjectures are *ḥᵃrûbîm* ' carob-pods ' (*cf.* Lk 15:16) and *ḥarṣannîm* ' unripe grapes '. **26-29.** Cannibalism was not unheard-of ; see Deut 28:53-57, Lam 2:20, Ez 5:10 ; it is recorded of Ashurbanipal's siege of Babylon (Schrader KIB II, 190) and of Titus' siege of Jerusalem (Jos BJ, 6, 3, 4). **30-31.** Eliseus was held responsible. He must have encouraged resistance, when it was possible to come to terms, by holding out hopes of divine aid (*cf.* 33) ; the king's penitential garb suggests the influence of the prophet. **32-33.** The role of the messenger is not clear. The attempt on the life of Eliseus may be re-constructed as follows : the king first sent an executioner, then came himself when the officer returned to say that he could not enter. By this time the king's anger had died down and he (not the messenger ; *cf.* 7:2) made what was really a last plea for aid, though he professed to despair.

5a VII 1-20 Unexpected Deliverance—1. Sufficient though not superabundant relief was promised ; the prices are still high, at least according to later reckoning **275a** (Mishnah, '*Erubin* 8, 2). But a whole city had to be fed. **2.** The adjutant granted that Yahweh could send rain but doubted the food. In other words, Yahweh directed the ordinary course of nature, but could not or would not intervene miraculously. **3-4.** The lepers were allowed to live in the no-man's-land between the city and the besiegers. **5-7.** Hittite states, now mostly Aramaean in population, survived in N. Syria (Luckenbill I 595-611) ; they included Patin, Samal, Gurgum and Carchemish. Samal was allied later with Tiglath-pileser against Damascus, Bonkamp, 401 f. North of these states lay Musri, which figured at Qarqar (Luckenbill I no. 611) and this may be intended here by ' Egypt ' (*Miṣraîm*). Since it is a question of panic, there is no point in asking how these invaders could have traversed Syria, or how Egypt, if that be the original reading, could have put an army in the field, in view of her weakness at this period. The historical situation remains sufficiently thinkable. **7. b** The horses left behind were re-mounts ; the asses were pack-animals. **8-12.** The king was not over-cautious ; Ai had been captured by the stratagem which he feared, Jos 8:2-21. **13.** ' Five horses ' seems to be vague, like our ' half a dozen ' ; *cf.* 1 Kg 5:3, Is 30:17. **14.** If ' five ' is to be taken strictly, there was an outrider with the two *chariots*. **15.** It was about 30 m. to the Jordan near Bethshan, from which a highway ran E. of Lake Galilee to Damascus, Abel I 219. **16-17.** It is hardly likely that an officer was stationed at the gate merely to keep order while the people rushed out. Nor have the fixed prices much sense in a general pillage. Probably the king impounded the provisions while the people seized the rest of the booty. Then he set up a market in the usual place, the gate. The adjutant was knocked down accidentally ; he was weak from hunger. **19-20.** The moral of the story is again reverence for the prophet ; see on 5:25-27.

VIII 1-6 Power of the Prophet's Patronage—1. The **c** famine was due to a series of poor harvests ; the land still produced something ; *cf.* 6. **2.** The plain round Gaza was fruitful in corn. **3.** Some 14 years had passed since the miracle of 4:8-39. The lady had probably migrated under Joram, and returned under Jehu ; the tenant thought to profit by the revolution. Her family was no longer influential ; contrast 4:13. Her aged husband, 4:14, was dead. **4-6.** But Giezi had apparently prospered on Naaman's money and had a place at court, which his type of leprosy did not forbid ; see on 5:1, 25 ff. It is hardly likely that the healing of Naaman had not yet taken place. Jehu's contemporary in Syria was Hazael, and their relations with Eliseus would have been different from those described in ch 5 ; see the following. The lady had asked only for her property and rent ; she was granted her revenues in addition.

7-15 Eliseus in Damascus—7. Elias had left to Eliseus **d** the task of anointing Hazael, 3 Kg 19:15. Perhaps it was the report of Benhadad's illness that showed Eliseus that the time had come. His fame is easily explained if the healing of Naaman had already taken place. **8-10.** Wishing to spare a doomed man Eliseus told Hazael to soothe the king with a conventional re-assurance. A Lapide and others explain that as Eliseus had been asked only about Benhadad's illness, he answered that it was not mortal in the ordinary course of events. The *ketib* is : ' Say : thou shalt not recover '. This is to avoid the semblance of a lie in the prophet's mouth ; but then the Hebrew negative would not be in its normal place (P. Joüon, *Grammaire de l'hébreu biblique*, p 352) and one would expect ' for ' to introduce the next sentence. It is best to keep the more difficult reading, with the *qere*, 18 Heb. MSS. and the Versions. **11.** Then Eliseus ' *took on a fixed look and was deeply moved* ', as the prophetic vision rose up before him. **12.** Horrified, but not reproachful, war being what it was, Am 1:13, Ps 136:9 etc., he proclaimed Hazael as the scourge of God ; *cf.* Is 10:5 ; 45:1-7. ' Thy servant a dog ' is conventional humility,

275d 2 Kg 9:8, Lachish Letters RB 48 (1939) 250 ff. Some hold that the king died unexpectedly under a cold compress intended to ease the fever. But it was not the business of a great official like Hazael to nurse the king. Rather, the words of Eliseus worked on Hazael 'like the witches' prophecy in Macbeth' (Skinner). Shalmaneser, his contemporary, calls him 'the son of a nobody' (a usurper), Luckenbill I no. 681.

e 16-24 Joram of Judah, 849-842.—16-17. The meaningless 'and of Josaphat' etc., is a scribal error. **18-19.** It is generally assumed that his wife Athalia, 26, was the daughter of Jezabel. Under her influence Joram allowed a temple of Baal to be erected in Jerusalem, 11:18. There was a reaction which he suppressed bloodily, 2 Par 21:4, 13. **20.** See on 3 Kg 22:48. The success of Moab, ch 3, encouraged Edom; cf. 2 Par 20:1-10. **21-22a.** The text may be in disorder. The 'people' (army) which fled home must be the Judaeans. Apparently Joram was surrounded in Sa'ir, 5 m. NE. of Hebron, but cut his way out. **22b.** Libnah (Tell eṣ-Ṣafi), a Canaanite town not far from Geth, probably allied itself with the Philistines, who, with Arabians, Moabites and Edomites, formed a hostile block in the South, 2 Par 21:16. **23-24.** His defeats were attributed to his impiety, and he was denied burial in the royal tombs, 2 Par 21:20; see on 3 Kg 2:10. The second 'with his fathers' (MT) is to be taken vaguely or omitted.

f 25-29 Ochozias of Judah, 841—25-27. His reign actually lasted only 2 or 3 months. The youngest and only surviving son of Joram, 2 Par 21:17, he was dominated by his mother, the grand-daughter of Omri, 2 Par 22:3. The Baal-cult was maintained in Jerusalem, 11:18, and his political advisers were northerners, 2 Par 22:4. **28.** Ramoth-Gilead had been returned to Israel some time after 853 (cf. 3 Kg 23), probably as payment for help against Assyria. Hazael had been beaten off, but the army remained in the field to forestall any surprise attack. **29.** Joram's wound was slight (cf. 9:21); the kings had left the field because victory seemed secure. Relations between the two courts had perhaps never been closer; cf. 10:13. The destinies of the kings were linked together.

g IX 1-14 Anointing of Jehu—1-2. The work of Elias and Eliseus was about to bear fruit. The strict worshippers of Yahweh now formed a strong party (cf. 3 Kg 19:18), which was doubtless also opposed to the costly anti-Assyrian policy of the house of Omri; see on 3 Kg 20:34-43. One of Jehu's first moves was to send tribute to Shalmaneser III, Luckenbill I no. 590. **3-10.** As in the case of Hazael, 8:13, it was through Eliseus that Elias executed his mandate of anointing Jehu, 3 Kg 19:16. The secrecy left Jehu with the choice of the moment to strike. **11.** 'Madman' (meŝugga') was popularly applied to prophets, Os 9:7, Jer 29:26, with reference to their ecstasies; cf. 1 Kg 1:10 etc. Jehu was evasive—'It's all foolishness'—till he sensed that his fellow-generals had guessed the truth and were with him. **13.** With the laying of garments under his feet, on the [very = bare] steps, cf. Mt 21:8. It was in recognition of his kingship. The army was won over at once.

h 15-26 Death of Joram—15-19. Suspecting bad news from the front, Joram sent horsemen, who could arrive with tidings faster than the chariots. **20.** Jehu must have been known as a dashing leader of a division of chariots. **21.** The field of Naboth was not the vineyard, which was beside the palace, 3 Kg 21:1, but some land E. of Jezreel. The kings hurried out to hold a council of war at once if necessary. **22.** Jehu proclaimed himself as the champion of the religion of Yahweh. The fornications and sorceries of Jezabel were the idolatrous practices which she promoted. They were in fact often licentious. **23.** Joram himself was driving, in his haste he had not taken a charioteer nor put on armour. **24-26.** Jehu, as adjutant of Achab along with Bidkar, had been present at the meeting with Elias, 3 Kg 21:19-20. He made himself responsible for the fulfilment of the prophecy, which he knew had

been transferred to Joram, 3 Kg 21:29; cf. 10:10. **275i** Two striking details are added to the oracle as given in 3 Kg 21:19. (1) 'Yesterday': Achab had gone to claim the vineyard the very next day; (2) the death of Naboth's sons. The oracle was felt to justify Jehu's action and confirm his claims to the throne.

27-29 Murder of Ochozias—27. 'The garden house' **i** should be read as a proper name, Beth haggan, the En gannim of Jos 19:21 (modern Jenin). Ochozias had made about 7 m. when his pursuers came within bow-shot, at the rise of Gûr, near the modern Belameh; the Bileam of 2 Par 22:9 is another form of Yibleam. They gave up the pursuit after wounding him; they had already driven over 50 m. since leaving Ramoth. He was followed later and killed, according to 2 Par 22:9, where 'Samaria' may be understood as 'the land of Samaria'. Jehu's attack on Ochozias is explained by the closeness of his relations with Joram; see on 8:25-29. In the event of a war with Judah, the adherents of the house of Omri would have declared against Jehu. But after Ochozias' death, at the age of 22, there was no heir to the throne who could threaten Jehu.

30-37 Death of Jezabel—30. Jezabel did not lack **j** courage, and made no attempt to placate, but tried to charm Jehu. She was over sixty; cf. on 3 Kg 16:27 ff. Her attitude was: 'Show me, my women, like a **a** queen; go fetch my best attires' (Antony and Cleopatra, V, 2). Stibic stone (pûk 'antimony') was a cosmetic which made the eyes appear larger and more lustrous; cf. Jer 4:30. **31.** Her sarcastic 'Hail, Zambri, murderer of his master' branded Jehu as a treacherous upstart destined to perish quickly, 3 Kg 16:8-16. **32.** Jehu answered the taunt with contempt (Vg, LXX); according to MT, he cried out, 'Who is with me—who?'. The chamberlains declared for him at once. **33.** Jezabel's gruesome end was characteristic of Jehu's cruelty. **34.** He did not wish, however, to give extreme offence to her royal kinsmen of Tyre. **35-37.** But the scavengers of eastern cities had been at work (cf. Ps 58:7, 15) and the once feared and famous lady had been utterly disgraced.

X 1-10 Slaughter of the Israelite Princes—1. 'Sons' **276** stands here for all the male descendants of Achab; cf. 'daughter' 8:26. Not all were minors. **2.** The challenge was addressed to the civil and military governors, the elders (cf. 3 Kg 21:8) and the guardians of the young princes. They controlled the chariots and garrisons of the capital and other fortress-towns. **3.** But there was probably no competent leader in the royal family, and Jehu's combination of aggressiveness and sarcasm completely intimidated Samaria. **6.** The command was ambiguous. It might mean: 'Bring me the chief men among the king's sons'. **7-8.** The heads arrived in the dark, and were piled in a pyramid, Assyrian fashion. **9.** Jehu disowned the deed. He evidently could not claim that his call to the throne justified him. **10.** But he asserted that in overstepping his mandate, the responsible agents were Yahweh's instruments; cf. 3 Kg 21:29. The people dared not disagree, and Jehu, under the cloak of zeal, could go on to further enormities.

11 Massacre at Jezreel—The scene was the home-town **b** of the Omri family; see on 3 Kg 16:15. The object was to eliminate all possible avengers; see on 3 Kg 16:11. Read therefore 'his kinsmen' (gō'alāu) for 'his chief men' (gedōlāu) with LXX (Lucian) and Old Latin (Leg).

12-14 Murder of the Judaean Princes—12. Beth Eqed **c** of the Shepherds is generally identified with Beit Qad, 4 m. E. of Jenin. But it did not lie on Jehu's route. Kefr Qud W. of Jenin is more suitable. **13.** The brethren of Ochozias were distant relatives; see on 8:25; 2 Par 21:4. The sons of the queen are distinguished from the sons of the other ladies in the royal harem. It is surprising to find the princes N. of Samaria four or five days after the revolution. Possibly they had gone on to Megiddo and attended the dying Ochozias; cf. 9:27. On their way back they gave the

c original reason for their journey. **14.** Jehu killed them as a further measure of security.

d 15-17 Jonadab : Further Massacres in Samaria—15. The Rechabite clan, whose austere nomadic way of life is described in Jer 35, looked on Jonadab as their second founder. At a time when Baalism threatened the South as well as the North, he made the separatism of his clan the defence of monotheism. Jehu feared that he would see through his façade of zeal. Hence his distrustful question. But Jonadab pinned his faith in him, as Eliseus had done. The history of the North shows prophet after prophet entrusting the work of God to candidates who deceived them once they were helped to power. **16.** Jehu's language reminds us of what the historian von Pastor called ' Cromwell's revolting Puritan jargon '.

e 18-28 Elimination of the Cult of Baal—18-19. It seems that Jehu first gathered the official ministers who were in Samaria. They had to prepare the feast. **20-21.** Then he gathered the ministers from the country shrines. They feared the worst, but dared not refuse the invitation. The worshippers of Baal in general were too numerous to be summoned, unless perhaps there was question only of those who worshipped Baal exclusively. It is hardly possible to restrict the number to those whom fanaticism blinded to their danger (Médebielle). **22.** Special dress was often prescribed for religious ceremonies ; see Ex 19:10, Gen 35:2 ; M.-J. Lagrange, ERS 149. **23.** The main gathering was in the court of the temple. **24-25a.** Soldiers guarded the exits while Jehu and a bodyguard entered the temple proper. Jehu himself offered sacrifice (MT), then sent his guards back into the court. **25b-27.** The text has suffered. For *maṣṣēbôt* (DV ' statue ', 26), *'ašērāh* may be read ; *cf*. 3 Kg 16:33. The wooden upright could be burnt, but not a stone pillar. The destruction of the latter is mentioned in 27 : ' And they smashed the *maṣṣēbāh* of Baal ' (MT). ' Unto this day ' shows that the original account was written when the locality was still well known. **28.** It was the end of Baalism as an official cult, but remnants of it survived ; *cf*. 3 Kg 19:17.

f 29-36 Reign of Jehu—29-31. Jehu was praised for destroying the house of Achab, but the divine approval of his conduct ends there. Hence his dynasty was promised only a limited duration. Contrast the conditional promise of perpetuity made to Jeroboam, 3 Kg 11:38. His mass murders were not condoned. He himself recognized that he was going too far, 10:9 ; and a hundred years later, the memory of his crimes was still appalling : ' Thus saith the Lord : a little while yet, and I will visit the blood of Jezreel upon the house of Jehu, and I will make an end of the house of Israel ', Os 1:4. **32.** Meanwhile Israel was punished for its long apostasy ; *cf*. 3 Kg 19:17. Read perhaps : ' Yahweh began to cut away parts of Israel ' (MT). Jehu had estranged Judah and Tyre, and the Assyrians, in spite of his tribute, gave him no help. After attacking Damascus in 841 (Luckenbill I no. 672), they appeared in the west only once, in 838, in the next forty years. **33.** Eastern territory lost to Hazael included the northern part of Moab. Jehu had evidently driven the Moabites back S. of the Arnon once more. In 33*b* Galaad is taken in its strict sense, of the territory S. of the Yarmuk. **34-36.** Jehu died in 814.

g XI 1-3 Usurpation of Athalia—1. Joram, Athalia's late husband, had killed all his brothers, 2 Par 21:4. Ochozias was the only one of his sons to survive the Arab invasion, 2 Par 21:17, and he, with the forty-two princes, had been killed by Jehu, 9:27 ; 10:14. There was no one to oppose Athalia. What her intentions were with regard to the succession is it hard to say. Possibly, as grand-daughter of Ethbaal (*cf*. 3 Kg 16:31), she meant to hand over the kingdom of David to her kinsman Mettenos of Tyre. **2.** Josaba hid Joas *in the* bedchamber, probably that of the high-priest (her husband, 2 Par 22:11). **3** suggests that the high-priest had a house attached to the temple ; *cf*. 1 Kg 3:3 ff.

Priests had quarters E. of the Great Court of the temple **276g** at a later date, Neh 3:28.

4-12 Coronation of Joas—4. Joiada relied on ' *the* **h** *officers of the Carians and of the Guards* '. ' Carians ' (*cf*. 19) may be a scribal error for ' Cerethi ', 2 Kg 7:18 etc. The loyalty of these foreign mercenaries was traditional, 2 Kg 15:18 ff. ; 3 Kg 1:38. **5-6a.** The execution of the plot was planned for a Sabbath, when the changing of the guard took place. **6b** seems out of place, and is obscure ; perhaps it is a gloss, giving the ordinary stations of the temple guard. The gate of Sur was possibly the eastern or main entrance. The gate of the Guards (*cf*. 19) was on the south, since it led to the palace. The house of *Massah* is unknown. **7.** The finite verbs should be participles (MT) ; so too **6a.** The soldiers first receive their orders in **8.** The guards were in three battalions, two in the palace during the week and one in the temple. On the Sabbath it was the other way about. This particular Sabbath, the temple battalion was to stand firm, instead of retiring to the palace, when the other two marched in to relieve it. Thus the palace would be stripped of soldiers. **9-11.** The soldiers were already armed ; the officers, 2 Par 23:9, were given the venerable trophies of David, in honour of the occasion. **12.** The ceremony included a renewal of the covenant, which was both religious and political, 17 ; hence the imposition of the ' testimony ' (*'ēdût*), the Book of the Law ; *cf*. Deut 17:18 f. A common but unnecessary emendation for *'ēdût* is *ṣe'ādôt* ' bracelets ' ; *cf*. 2 Kg 1:10.

13-21 Death of Athalia—14. There was a special place **i** for the king (*cf*. 23:3), *by the pillar*, Jachin or Boaz ; *cf*. 3 Kg 7:21. His most enthusiastic supporters were ' the people of the land ', the common people or the countryfolk (*cf*. 18, 19, 20) ; they played an important part in a similar situation, 21:24. **16.** Athalia was brought back to the palace by an entrance on the East, corresponding to the Gate of the Horses ; *cf*. Jer 31:40. **18.** She and her Tyrian cult must have had followers among the city-folk. Hence the temple was guarded. **20.** If ' the people of the land ' means the country-folk, there is special point in the remark that the city was quiet ; it submitted. **21.** Joiada became regent, 12:3.

XII 1-5 Joas of Judah, 836-797—1-3. By the time the **j** king was about 25 years of age (*cf*. 6), the temple had been built for nearly 150 years and was in need of repairs. **4.** Read *'erek* ' assessment ' for *'ôbēr* ' those that pass by ' ; omit ' which is offered for the price of a soul ' as a gloss (*cf*. LXX B, Lucian ; Syr.), and translate : ' all the money brought to the temple as sacred gifts : the money prescribed for each man, and all money which of their own accord ' etc. Moneys prescribed were, *e.g.* the 5 shekels paid for each firstborn male, Num 18:16 ; payments on the occasion of certain vows, Lev 27:2-9 ; the poll-tax, Ex 30:13. **5.** Each priest was to take the money ' *from his acquaintance* ' (*makkār*) ; possibly each dealt with his clansmen, and the ' acquaintance ' would be his ' parishioner '.

6-16 Restoration of the Temple—6-8. The priests **k** were not conscientious ; perhaps they resented the king's interference. **9.** Their role was then confined to seeing that each man paid his due. **10.** The administration of the money was supervised by a high court official ; *cf*. 18:18 ; 3 Kg 4:3. **11-13.** Each contractor received a lump sum, and worked on an estimate, not on what we call a ' time and material ' basis. **13.** New utensils came later, 2 Par 24:14. **14-15.** The contractors gave satisfaction, and had not to give an account of their expenses and profits. **16.** Money accompanied or perhaps replaced certain sacrifices ; two are mentioned : ' trespass ' (*'āšām*), offered on the occasion of restitution for damage, Lev 5:14-16 ; 6:1-7 ; ' sin ' (*ḥaṭṭā't*), offered in reparation, Lev ch 4.

17-21 Troubles and Death of Joas—17. Joas may have **l** sent help to the Philistines, who interfered with the Egyptian trade of Damascus. **18.** The two preceding

276 kings had enriched the temple, in spite of their support of Baalism. **19-21.** According to 2 Par 24:17-25, there was a reaction against the priestly party after the death of Joiada ; cf. 2. Foreign cults were brought back, and Joiada's son was stoned. The king paid for it by defeat, illness and a violent death.

m XIII 1-9 Joachaz of Israel, 814-798—1. It was the *22nd* year of Joas ; cf. 10:36 ; 12:1. **2-4.** Syria had a free hand against Israel (see on 10:32) till Adad-nirari of Assyria attacked Damascus c 800. **5.** He may be ' the saviour ' ; some think of Jeroboam II, 14:25 ff. **6.** The ungrateful people re-introduced even an ashera ; see on 10:26. **7.** Achab had had 2,000 chariots at Qarqar ; Israel was brought very low.

n 10-19 Joas of Israel, 798-783 ; Last Prophecies of Eliseus—14. Eliseus was now nearly 90 ; see on 3 Kg 17:1. The king mourned the death of the champion who was worth an army ; see on 2:12 and 6:8-7:20. **15-16.** With the laying on of hands, to signify the passing of supernatural power from one to the other, cf. 4:34 f. Apheq was the scene of a former victory, 3 Kg 20:26-30. **18-19.** Eliseus' anger shows that the king was at fault ; he would be too negligent to press home his victories.

o 20-21 Death of Eliseus—20. He was buried with his fathers at Abel-Mehola in the Jordan valley ; cf. 3 Kg 19:19. With Israel so weak, the border foray is understandable. **21.** Cf. Ecclus 48:14 f. From Eliseus, the chain of prophets went back through Elias, Jehu and his father Hanani, 3 Kg 16:1, 2 Par 16:7, Ahias, 3 Kg 11:29, and Nathan to Samuel. Within 30 years, Osee was at work. The prophetic tradition was therefore unbroken in Israel till the Exile.

p 22-25 The Promised Victories—22. If this statement is pressed, Hazael survived Joachaz ; but 25 suggests that Benhadad III had succeeded him before the death of Joachaz ; see on 6:24. It is hardly possible to refer ' which he took ' to Hazael. **24.** Adad-nirari's inscriptions (Bonkamp 380 f.) call the king of Damascus in 802 ' Mari '. This is a title (' my lord '), not a proper name, R. de Vaux RB 43 (1934) 514-8 ; probably Benhadad is meant. **25.** The cities must have been W. of the Sea of Galilee, as the land E. of Jordan had been lost under Jehu, 10:33.

277a XIV 1-6 Amasias of Judah, 797-769—1-4. The verdict on Amasias is interrupted by an unusual restriction in 3*b* (' but yet ' etc.), which reads like a gloss based on 2 Par 24:15 (his idolatry). **5-6.** He could not condone the action which had given him the throne ; cf. 2 Kg 1:1-16 ; 4:1-12. The principle enunciated in Deut 24:16 was not always put into practice ; cf. 9:26, Ez 18:20.

b 7 War with Edom—The trade route to the Red Sea, closed since the revolt of Edom over 50 years before, 8:22, was at stake ; cf. 22. The Valley of Salt, E. of Beersheba, 2 Kg 8:13, may be the present Wady el Milḥ. ' He took Petra by storm '. This natural fortress, c 40 m. S. of the Dead Sea, became famous as the capital of the Nabataean kingdom, 100 B.C.-A.D. 100. Amasias made it a military outpost ; the new name, Yoqtᵉ'el ' Yahweh destroys ', refers to the slaughter of Edomites, 2 Par 25:12.

c 8-16 War with Israel—8. Joas probably demanded the return of territory annexed by Judah during Israel's decline. **7-10.** The fable pointed out the folly of Amasias' offer to fight it out. There does not seem to have been any request for the hand of an Israelite princess ; that could not have been treated as presumptuous. **11-12.** Bethshemesh, now 'Ain Shems, was c 25 m. W. of Jerusalem ; Joas took the initiative ; cf. on 8. **13.** According to Josephus, *Ant.* 9, 9, 3, the breach was made for the entry of the victors. It was in the northern wall, starting from the western corner, at the present Jaffa Gate.

d 17-22 End of Amasias—17-19. His apostasy was the cause of the revolt, 2 Par 25:14-27. The stronghold of Lachish (Tell ed-Duweir) was c 36 m. SW. of Jerusalem. **21.** Azarias was also known as Uzzias, the only name used of him in Par, Os, Am, Zach, Is. **2** According to Šanda, Azarias was used in the Annals of the kings of Judah, Uzzias was the popular name. **22.** He followed up Amasias' victory over Edom by fortifying the terminus of the trade-route, at the head of the Gulf of Aqabah.

23-29 Jeroboam II of Israel, 783-743—23. During **e** the long and prosperous reign of Jeroboam, Damascus, defeated by Zakir of Hamath c 785 and invaded by Shalmaneser IV in 772, was no longer a menace. **24.** The prophets Amos and Osee attest the decline of religion. **25.** For the ' Entrance of Hamath ', see on 3 Kg 8:65 ; the Sea of the Wilderness was the Dead Sea. Jeroboam attacked the Ammonites, Am 1:13, and as Azarias shared the spoils, 2 Par 26:8-10, it seems that Israel and Judah were allies again. The prophet who foretold Jeroboam's conquests has only the name in common with the author of the prophetic book ; the latter lived probably in the 7th cent., when Nineveh was capital of Assyria. Gath ha-Hepher, Jos 19:13 (now El-Meshed or Khirbet ez-Zurra) was a few miles N. of Nazareth. **26-28a.** For the last time, Israel was experiencing the divine favour, under perhaps the greatest of her kings. **28b.** Read possibly ' how he warred against Damascus and turned away the wrath of Yahweh ' ; MT is unintelligible.

XV 1-7 Azarias of Judah, 769-756—1. Read ' the *15th* **f** year of Jeroboam ' ; cf. 14:2, 23. The chronology in chh 15 and 16 has been systematically glossed ; for their basis, see § 266*d-j*. **2.** He must have been about 30 years of age ; his reign lasted 14 years. **5.** Read ' he dwelt in *his house free from duties* ' (MT). The regency did not last long, as Joatham was only 25 when Azarias died ; cf. 7, 33. **6.** His reign was prosperous, Is 2:7-16. 2 Par 26 recounts his organization of army, armaments and fortifications, his successful maintenance of the trade route to the Red Sea against Philistines and Arabs, his promotion of agriculture and sheep-rearing.

8-13 Zacharias of Israel, 743-8. Read ' the *14th year* **g** *of Joatham* '. **10.** Jabesh suggests Gilead, 1 Kg 11, where Syria must have gained partisans during her long occupation of the land. The dynasty of Jehu had probably remained pro-Assyrian ; see on 9:1 f. The revolt may have been a move in international politics ; but the social injustice described by Amos and Osee must have counted. Read ' in Yibleam ' (LXX, Lucian ; cf. 9:27) for ' publicly ' (*qobol-'ām*). **12.** The house of Jehu was being punished for the ' blood of Jezreel ', Os 1:4.

13-16 Shallum of Israel, 742—13. It was the 15th of **h** Joatham. Gilead belonged to transjordanian Manasses, Yibleam to cisjordanian, Jg 1:27. **14.** Possibly Menahem led an Ephraimite party ; he was pro-Assyrian ; cf. 19. Is 9:20 speaks of strife between Ephraim and Manasses. Menahem's base, Thersa, was in Ephraim ; see on 3 Kg 15:21. **16.** *Tappuah* (LXX, Lucian) was a few miles to the east.

17-22 Menahem of Israel, 742-737—17. It was **i** Joatham's 16th year. As the avenger of the dynasty of Jehu and upholder of its foreign policy, Menahem had a solid backing. Read ' 6 years '. **19.** Tiglath-pileser III (cf. 29) bore the name Pulu in his quality of king of Babylon. In 738 he marched against a league headed by Azriyau, king of Yaudi in Syria, and pressed on S. to Raspuna, probably the Hellenistic Apollonia, now Arsûf, c 12 m. N. of Joppa. Among the kings who paid him tribute were Rasin of Damascus (cf. 37) and Menahem, Luckenbill I no. 772. **20.** If the talent was 3,000 shekels, 60,000 rich men paid about 80 dollars each.

23-26 Pekahiah of Israel, 737-736—23. Read ' *the* **j** *5th year of Achaz* '. The new year occurred once in the reign. **25.** The dynasty supported by Assyria did not last long. The party which Shallum had represented was at work again, for Pekah had with him a picked force of 50 Gileadites ; hence the alliance with Syria. 37. Read ' *with* Argob and Arie ' ; these were perhaps faithful officers of Pekahiah. The treason and turbulence which heralded the ruin of Israel is vividly described by Osee, 7:3–7.

27-31 Pekah of Israel, 736-732—27. Read ' *the 6th year of Achaz* ' and ' *5 years* '. **29.** By 734 the king of Damascus, looking, like Israel (*cf.* Os 7:11) to Egypt, organized an anti-Assyrian league which included the Arabs and all the southern states of Palestine except Judah ; *cf.* 37. Tiglath-pileser's records of the ensuing war state that he annexed ' the city of Gal'aza, the city of Abillakka on the border of Bit-Humria [Israel = the land of Omri], the broad land of Naptali ', Bonkamp, 391. Gal'aza is Gilead (*z* for *d* as in the inscription of Zakir of Hamath, Bonkamp 395n) ; Abillakka is Abel Beth Maacha (*cf.* 3 Kg 15:20) ; Janoah was E. of Tyre ; Qedesh, N. of Lake Huleh ; for Hasor, see on 3 Kg 9:15. Israel thus lost all her western territory N. of Mt Tabor, and the whole of her transjordanian land. Of the deportations Tiglath-pileser writes : ' I carried away to Assur the people of Bit-Humria, all its inhabitants '. Deportation was standard Assyrian policy : ' Tiglath-pileser transported the peoples from the east to the west and from the west to the east ' (Inscription of Bar-Rekub, G. A. Cooke, no. 63). **30.** In 733 Tiglath-pileser attacked Damascus, and some time later a revolt in Samaria spared him another siege. ' They overthrew their king Paqaha ; I established Ausi [Osee] as king over them '. This inscription (Bonkamp, 392) connects the change of rulers with the fall of Damascus in 732. Another inscription (Bonkamp, 397) speaks of a further invasion of Israel, Is 8:23. Some time therefore elapsed again before Osee was installed (? 731). His official reign was dated from 730 ; *cf.* 17:1. It was the 11th or 12th year of Achaz.

32-38 Joatham of Judah, 756-741—32. Read ' *the 28th year of Jeroboam* '. They were contemporaries, 1 Par 5:17. **35.** Joatham was a great builder, 2 Par 27:1–9. He added a third entrance, from the north, Ez 9:2, to the inner court of the temple. There was already one on the east, Ez 11:1, and one on the south, 4 Kg 11:6, 19. 37 must be referred to the time of Achaz, 38. It is clearly out of its proper context. Even if it referred to Joatham's reign, it should be before 36.

XVI 1-4 Achaz of Judah, 741-726—1. Read ' *the second year of Menaham* '. **2.** For the decline in religion under Achaz, see Mic 5:9–13 ; 6:16. **3.** Child sacrifice, especially that of the first-born son, was always common among the neighbours of Israel, 3:27 ; 17:31. It was forbidden to Israel, Lev 18:21, Deut 12:31. **4.** See on 3 Kg 14:22 f.

5-9 Appeal to Assyria—5. Achaz, having refused to be drawn into the anti-Assyrian league (see on 15:29), was to be deposed, and a nominee of the league put in his place, Is 7:1–9. He was attacked from all sides, 2 Par 28:16 f. **6.** Troops from Syria restored Elath (' Aila ' ; see on 14:22) to *Edom*. **7-9.** In 734 Tiglath-pileser overran Galilee and Gilead, 15:29 ; then he marched south and plundered Gaza. Ascalon, Ammon, Edom and Moab paid tribute, and with them is named Yauhazi of Yauda, AOT 348. ' Achaz ' therefore was a popular form of the theophoric name ' Yahweh possesses '. Damascus was invested in 733 and fell in 732, Bonkamp, 400. The inhabitants were deported to *Qîr*, a region originally Aramaean, Am 1:5 ; 9:7, probably in S. Mesopotamia, near Elam, Is 22:6. Judah had lost an enemy, but the new friend was to prove a greater menace.

10-20 The New Altar—10. It was Tiglath-pileser's boast that ' in every country which I conquered, I set up a temple for the god Assur ; and in every country I made an image of my royalty, and set it up as a sign of victory, and of the dominion which I held over the nations, by the command of Assur, my god ', Bonkamp, 393 f. The altar which Achaz dutifully admired was therefore in several tiers, the ziggurat-form common in Assyria and Babylonia ; see on Ez 43:13–17. **12-13.** Inaugural ceremonies included all the types of sacrifice mentioned at Solomon's dedication, 3 Kg 8:64.

14-15. King Achaz ordered the ancient altar to be **278c** put aside ' *until I can attend to it* '. **17-18.** It probably shared the fate of the other bronze installations, 3 Kg 7:23–39, and of the Musach (' covered walk ' ?), and the royal door, which were *removed* at the same time. Their costly metals went towards paying the tribute to the king of Assyria. He was exigent, 2 Par 28:20. Achaz meant to convey to Tiglath-pileser that he acknowledged the gods of Assyria. But the actual introduction of Assyrian cults (*cf.* 21:3 ff. ; 23:4, 11 ; Jer 44:17 ; Ez 8) may also be ascribed to him, as well as the fostering of Baalism, 4. Neither Ezechias nor Josias could undo his work. See § 267d.

XVII 1-4 Osee of Israel, 731-722—1. The 12th year **d** of Achaz was 730 ; see on 15:30. **2.** The last king was not the worst. There was a strong party of Yahweh-worshippers in Samaria, 2 Par 28:9–15, and Osee favoured them. **3.** Shalmaneser V became king in Jan. 726. Menander (*cf.* Jos., *Ant.* 9, 14, 2) records a campaign against Phoenicia, which ended in Elulaeus of Tyre and his allies paying tribute. War was renewed when they fell away. This fits in with the Bible. **4.** Osee paid tribute in 725 (the Assyrian lists state that there was no campaign in 726, Bonkamp 412). He withheld it in 723, having paid it for two years what at the most. Sua (MT So', to be read Sēwe, *cf.* ketib) the Sib'e of Sargon's inscriptions (Bonkamp, 416–9), was commander-in-chief of Musri (Egypt) under its king Pir'u, possibly the Pharaoh Piankhi. As Sib'e had power to make war or peace, his popular designation as king is justified. Some hold that Musri here is an Arab state. But a king in the background with a viceroy in the Delta suits Egyptian conditions ; and Egypt was certainly involved, Os 7:11. Shalmaneser *held* Osee when he came to excuse himself. Josephus however, *Ant.* 9, 14, 1, says that Osee was taken when the city fell, and the long resistance certainly suggests the presence of the king during the siege. Thus 4*b* may anticipate events to round off the career of Osee. On the other hand, Sargon nowhere mentions Osee. Ordinarily the Assyrian annals mention the names of kings captured with their cities. It is best therefore to keep to the primary sense of the text and take it that Osee was captured before the siege. This would account for the 9 years' reign (*cf.* 1)—731–723.

5-6 Siege and Capture of Samaria—5. The only land **e** left to Israel lay between the northern rim of the plain of Jezreel and the boundary of Judah. The rest had been annexed 734–732. Samaria was well placed for a siege ; see on 3 Kg 16:24. The Assyrians could winter in their new province of Damascus. **6.** Shalmaneser died at the end of 722, before the end of the siege. His brother Sargon, who succeeded him in January 721, actually took Samaria, as he claims in four of his inscriptions, Bonkamp 414 f. It was in the interval before his official enthronement in Nisan. He states that he deported 27,290 captives, placed a governor over the land, and imposed on the inhabitants the same taxes as they had paid to their former kings. The city became the capital of an Assyrian province. Some of the deportees were settled at Halah, on the western slopes of the Zagros mountains ; others *in* Gozan, *by* the river Habor (Khabur), which flowed into the Euphrates near Carchemish ; others S. of the Caspian Sea.

7-23 Reflections on the Ruin of Israel—7-17. The **f** political process having been sufficiently explained, the deeper causes are recapitulated. One new grief is adduced, star-worship, 16 ; see on Amos 5:26. **18.** The long preparatory ' because ' culminates here in a ' therefore '. **19-20** repeat 18, inserting an anticipatory verdict on Judah, and give perhaps an afterthought. **21-23** retrace cause and effect for the third time. Read : ' *For* Israel was rent ' etc. The exile is the penalty of the calf-worship. The ' sin of Jeroboam ' dominated the author's thought throughout his history of Israel. 21–23 contain perhaps the original verdict, of which 7–18 is an elaboration.

24 New Settlers—The usual transfer of rebellious **g**

278g populations followed. It was not completed all at once. Cutha, the Sumerian Gudua, lay *c* 20 m. NE. of Babylon. Possibly the Cuthaites and Babylonians migrated freely. Sargon had no reason to deport them. But ' the king of the Assyrians ' may be taken as a general term. Sennacherib may have deported Babylonians to Israel after sacking Babylon in 689. They were among the strangers sent by his successors Esarhaddon and Ashurbanipal, Esd 4:2, 9 f. The deportations from Syria followed the defeat of Hamath in 720. Avah (MT *'Awwah*) is perhaps the Phoenician town called Ammia in the Tell el-Amarna letters ; Sepharvaim, the Syrian Shomeriya on Lake Homs (*cf.* 18:34 ; 19:13 ; Sanda II 224 f). In 715 Sargon settled Arabs in Israel, AOT 349. But Cuthaites predominated, for later Jews called the Samaritans simply Cuthaites, Jos., *Ant.* 9, 14, 3 etc.

h 25-28 The Cult of Yahweh—25. From 734 to 721 cultivation had suffered ; wild beasts could no longer be kept down. **26.** After Assyrian custom, Sargon had carried off the golden effigy from Bethel and abolished the cult ; Tiglath-pileser had done the same at Dan. **27-28.** Sargon's concession was based on the belief that each country was under the control of a national god, whose goodwill was essential to the country's well-being. The restored cult bound new and old inhabitants together, 32 ; it was still flourishing in the time of Josias, 23:15.

i 29-41 Samaritan Religion—29. Yahweh was of course not worshipped exclusively. And it must be supposed that most of the Israelites, to whom syncretism was no novelty, joined the new-comers in worshipping their gods. **30.** In Sochothbenoth may be recognized the Babylonian Sakkuth and Sarpanit ; *cf.* LXX Banit. Allowance must be made throughout for textual corruption of strange names. Nergal, god of the underworld, had a temple in Cutha. Ashima, probably the goddess-consort of Eshmun, was worshipped in Hamath; *cf.* M. Lidbarski, *Ephemeris* 2, 323 f. She occurs perhaps later in Ashim-Bethel ; see A. Vincent, *La religion des Judéo-Araméens d'Eléphantine*, 654–80. **31.** The Babylonian Nebo may be seen in Nebahaz ; he was worshipped in Syria ; *cf.* Šanda II 230. The Eblazer of LXX however suggests ' Baal the Helper '. Thartac is perhaps the Syrian Artagatis, the Atar (Astarte) of Attis. Adramelech identifies Milk (biblical Molech), the deity of child-sacrifice in Syria etc., with the storm-god Hadad. Anamelech may identify him with Anu, one of the supreme Babylonian triad, Anu, Marduk and Ea. Anu and Adad had a joint temple in Assur at this time, Albright, 163. But Anamelech may represent the goddess Anath, consort of Hadad. **32-41.** After this fusion of religions and races, Jerusalem came ultimately to disown the northerners, Esd 4:3. The kingdom of Israel had perished spiritually as well as politically.

279a XVIII **1-2 Ezechias of Judah, 726-697—**The third year of Osee agrees with 9, 10 if the reign of Ezechias is ' post-dated ' ; see § 124*i*. Then the year during which he came to the throne is not counted (*cf.* the Assyrian *rēš šarrūti*) and 3 Osee = 0 Ezechias, 7 Osee = 4 Ezechias etc. The speeches attributed to Ezechias in the beginning of his reign, 2 Par 29–30, suggest that Samaria had already fallen and that his accession be placed in 721 or later. But the references to defeat and exile can be explained by 15:29, 37 ; 16:5 f. ; 17:3. More probably, the speeches represent a comprehensive statement of the motives which sustained the reform throughout the reign.

b 3-12 Reforms—3. The prophets Isaias and Micheas found a strong and zealous champion. The fall of Samaria, recounted 9–12, re-inforced their message, Mic 1:9 ; 3:12 ; *cf.* Jer 26:18 f. **4.** Not only the pagan shrines of Achaz, 2 Par 28:25, but shrines of Yahweh outside Jerusalem were abolished. This follows (1), from the absence of the formula, ' but the high places he did not destroy ', used even of pious kings ; (2) from 22. Even the memorial of the miracle of Num 21:9 was destroyed. ' *It was called N^ehuštān* '. The name seems to express both the material (*n^ehōšet*

' bronze ') and the object (*nāḥāš* ' serpent '). For the **27** serpent as emblem of vegetation-deities, see J. Coppens, *La Connaissance du Bien et du Mal et le Péché du Paradis*. It is attested in Palestine, DBV(S) I 952 ; II 361 ; on the bronze serpent of Gezer, see L.-H. Vincent, *Canaan* 174 ff. Since Ezechias was combating fertility-cults, his action against the apparently harmless object is understandable. **7-8.** The campaign against the Philistines was probably connected with the revolt against Assyria after the death of Sargon in 705. Ashdod, Ekron, Ascalon and Gaza were then ruled by nominees of Assyria, Bonkamp 433 n. 4.

13-16 Invasion of Sennacherib—13. See § 66*b*. It **c** was the *26th* year of Ezechias. Sargon's son was detained in the East till 701. Then he turned against the West, where Phoenicia, Philistia, Edom, Moab and Judah were allied, with Egypt supporting them. **14-16.** The capture of the great fortress of Lachish is depicted on the famous bas-relief of Sennacherib in the British Museum. Ezechias pleaded for peace, and Sennacherib agreed to withdraw at the price of a crushing indemnity. Some of it no doubt was paid at once, but the rest was sent after Sennacherib to Nineveh ; see his own account, Luckenbill II no. 240, where the figures tally with the Bible, except that the silver is given as 800 talents. Probably the Hebrew text has suffered ; the cuneiform was never copied. Judah was almost beggared. Subsequently, it could pay only 10 silver minas yearly as tribute, while Ammon and Moab paid 2 and 1 gold minas respectively, R. H. Pfeiffer, JBL (1928) 185 f. A humiliated Judah barely escaped the fate of Samaria. Thus 13–16 summarize the campaign. The details of it, and the miracle which forced Sennacherib to be content with less than surrender, are told in 17–37 ; 19:1–36. The supplementary account is from another source whose style and interests are different ; the king's name is written Ḥizqiyyāhû throughout. Contrast Ḥizqiyyāh, 13–16.

17-37 First Summons to Surrender—17. The narrative **d** continues 13 ; *cf.* Is 36:1 ff. The besieging army surrounded Jerusalem, as Sennacherib relates, and the commander-in-chief (the Turtan or Tartān), the general (the Rab-šāqē) and the royal chamberlain (the Rab-sārîs) came to parley. At the SE. of the city, the aqueduct from the Upper Pool (Gihon, 3 Kg 1:33 = 'Ain Umm ed-Daraj or 'Ain Sitti Miryam) debouched into the Lower Pool (Siloah = Birket el-Ḥamrah). The ' Way of the Fuller's Field ' ran along a crest almost as high as Gihon. See Vincent, DBV(S), 942 ff. and Is 7:3 ; 22:9. **18.** For the Jewish delegates, see on Is 22:15–22. **19-20.** Ezechias, as a rebel, 20, is given no title. He had not yet humbled himself and paid tribute ; *cf.* 14 f. **21-25.** The prospect for Jerusalem was hopeless according to the Assyrians. Egypt was of no avail, 21, nor Yahweh, firstly, because he was angry with Ezechias, 22 ; then, because he had no natural resources to build on, 23 f. ; finally, he was on the side of Sennacherib, 25. This was based on Sennacherib's conquest of the country. **26-28.** Aramaic was then becoming the common language of business. The tactics of driving a wedge between king and people had been used successfully by Ashurnasirpal (Schrader, KIB 1, 64) and Tiglath-pileser, 15:30. The crude expression of 27 meant that the people faced starvation. **29-32.** The alternative was a truce for refreshment, **e** followed by the gift of goodly lands abroad. The fundamental object of the deportations was not so much to punish the common people, as to mingle the elements of the empire in a harmonious whole. In their own way, the Assyrians anticipated the policy of Alexander. **33-35.** The ultimatum culminated in the blasphemous statement that the real reason why Yahweh did not help, 22–24, was that he could not. Arpad, N. of Aleppo, is added to the states of 17:24. **36-37.** The actual terms of the military ultimatum are not given. But the fine rhetorical gradation of 19–34 does not alter the negotiations substantially. Assyrian soldiers chanted hymns to Ashur and Ishtar when marching to war ; the kings' inscriptions attri-

9e bute every victory to their gods. The analysis of the situation into confidence in Yahweh on one side, blasphemy on the other, prepares for the miraculous interventions of ch 19.

f **XIX 1-7 Anguish and Hope—1-2.** Isaias was another Eliseus ; *cf.* 13:14. He had constantly opposed Ezechias' policy. **3.** The king, through his own fault, was in a painful and dangerous situation. **4.** He based his hopes rather on Sennacherib's excesses than on his own merits. **5-6.** It was precisely the blasphemy that was answered. **7.** Yahweh was to induce a mood (of anxiety) in Sennacherib. Under its influence, disturbing news from home would decide him to return. The spirit was to be *put in him* (MT) ; it is a disposition (*cf.* Num 5:14, 30, Is 61:3, Os 4:12, Rom 8:15). The message cannot be news of the Egyptians, 9 ; that rather delayed his return. He did not meet his death till 681. But prophecy gives causal, not chronological connexions.

g **8-19 Second Summons to surrender—8.** The siege and the campaign continued. Perhaps the general took back with him an offer of tribute. For Libnah, see on 8:22. **9.** Tirhakah (Theraca), son of Piankhi (see on 17:4), last Pharaoh of the 25th (Ethiopian) dynasty, was the great power in the Delta since 715, under the Pharaohs Shabaka and Shabataqa. His title ' king ' may refer to this or anticipate his accession, *c* 690. According to Herodotus, 2:141, Sennacherib advanced to meet him, and Tirhakah did not venture across the border. However, the battle of Eltaqe, where Sennacherib states he routed the kings of Musri, may have taken place at this juncture. **9-11.** The new situation explains the second message. **12.** The countries, named from E. to W., lay around the Upper Euphrates. On Gozan, see 17:6 ; on Haran, Gen 11:31 ; Thelassar may represent Til-baseri in the Aramaean principality of Bit-Adini. **13.** See on 18:34. This is the real turning-point of the narrative : Sennacherib himself blasphemed, not merely his delegates. **14-19.** But instead of bringing up all his forces for a full-scale assault, he had merely sent a letter. Ezechias took it as the first sign of the promised relief. Hence he addressed Yahweh directly ; contrast the penitential approach to Isaias, 3-5.

h **20-34 Second Prophecy of Deliverance—20.** Before the message, 32 ff., is inserted a later poetic elaboration of it. **21-22.** The Assyrians are pictured as retreating. **23.** Sargon and Sennacherib used similar phrases, Schrader, KIB II, 40, 86. **24.** ' *I dug*, and drank of foreign waters ; and dried up . . . all *the waters of Egypt* '. The Assyrians invaded Egypt for the first time in 673. **25-28.** Yahweh had really performed the feats which Sennacherib ascribed to himself. The theme is Isaian ; *cf.* Is 10:6 ff. ; 45:1 ff. **29.** Ezechias would survive till better days. The promise would appear as a sign, or miracle, in the light of its unexpected fulfilment ; *cf.* Ex 3:12. **30-31.** The gaps made by the deportations would be repaired. **32-34.** The message makes explicit what was only implicit in 7. Sennacherib claimed that he threw up earthworks against Jerusalem. But apparently he never attacked it personally with his whole army.

i **35-37 Retreat of Sennacherib—35.** Some catastrophe struck the invaders. This is known also from Herodotus, whose version (2:141), suggests bubonic plague. The angel of the Lord struck through pestilence, 2 Kg 24:15 ff. 2 Par 32:31 gives no figures ; they have suffered from scribal exaggeration here. **36.** Sennacherib, already anxious to close the campaign, 7, gave up all idea of conquering Jerusalem and accepted tribute instead, 18:14-16. The miraculous deliverance is celebrated Pss 45-47 ; Is 31:8. Ezechias could not but send the tribute on to Nineveh. His losses had been severe, and Assyrian governors threatened him in Damascus and Samaria. To explain the payment of tribute and the double summons to surrender, it has often been assumed that we have here a conglomerate account of two or more expeditions of Sennacherib. But the analysis given above shows sufficiently that the

account is a self-consistent unity ; 19:9-34 is not a **279i** mere doublet of 18:17-19:8, but a progressive development of one situation, which fits into the framework of 18:13-16. Nor do the Assyrian annals give any grounds **j** for postulating further invasions. Another explanation of the course of events is that Sennacherib first accepted tribute, 18:13-16, and then demanded unconditional surrender. Treachery however was not an Assyrian trait. They made harsh demands but contented themselves with their fulfilment. Besides, this explanation does not take into account the difference of sources in 18:13-16, and 18:17-19:37, nor the statement of Sennacherib that the tribute was sent after him to Nineveh. See further Šanda II 242-96 ; Bonkamp 428-54. **37.** Nesroch is inexplicable, unless it is a corruption of (*mât*) *an-Assur-ki*, (the land) of the god Assur ; the consonants correspond, Bonkamp 457. Read probably ' Adramelech his son and Nabosarusur ' ; the latter was an officer of Sennacherib. The Assyrian and Babylonian accounts, AOT 359 f., then tally with the Bible.

XX 1-11 Illness and Miraculous Healing of Ezechias k —**1.** It was 15 years before his death, 6, therefore 712. The prophecy was comminatory, not irrevocable ; *cf.* 3 Kg 21:19 ff. **6.** About this time, Ezechias was threatened by Sargon, AOT, 351. **7a.** For the plaster, see Pliny, *Hist. Nat.* 23, 7 ; Jerome, PL 24, 396. **7b.** Read, with LXX (B, Lucian), Syr., ' *and lay it upon his boil and he shall live* '. **8-10.** Ezechias, naïvely enough, did not think that the acceleration of the sun's shadow, in its normal direction, was a sufficiently striking phenomenon. **11.** The symbolism (*cf.* Ps 101:12) has been often remarked—the shadow of death turned back from Ezechias. For solar miracles, see § 232*g*. Is 38:8 speaks of the shadow going down ; the ' dial ' may therefore have been in the form of steps.

12-19 Embassy from Babylon—12. Merodach-Baladan **l** (Marduk-aplu-iddin ' Marduk gave an heir '), ruler of the Aramaeans of Bit-Yakin on the Persian Gulf, was master of Babylon from 720-710, till he was driven out by Sargon. A tenacious enemy of Assyria, he returned in 703, to be driven out finally by Sennacherib in 702. The embassy was a move against Assyria. **13.** Ezechias' parade of his resources was both a promise of support and a boast of what he could do. **14-17.** Isaias, 7:4 ; 30:15, always insisted on neutrality ; to rely on foreigners was to doubt Yahweh ; *cf.* on 3 Kg 20:43. The prophecy was all the more striking since Babylon was then unimportant. **18.** The time of its fulfilment was not determined ; *cf.* 19:7. Sons could mean descendants in general. At the time, Ezechias had apparently no son ; *cf.* 21:1. **19.** A good example of ' Après moi, le déluge ' ; but the king knew that a prophecy could be revoked. See on 1.

20-21 Tunnel of Ezechias—20. From the time of **m** Solomon, a canal had brought the waters of Gihon, Jerusalem's one source, on the western slope of the Cedron valley, to the gardens in the SE. of the city. Achaz had turned the canal westward, at its southern end, and collected the waters at the base of the rampart across the Tyropoean valley ; *cf.* on 18:17. The canal remained within the reach of a besieging army. To remedy this Ezechias cut a tunnel, 560 yards long, under the ancient acropolis, which terminated in a great reservoir somewhat higher in the valley. In it the Siloah Inscription, § 80*g*, was found. When this aqueduct was completed, the source was covered in, and the older canal blocked ; *cf.* 2 Par 32:30 ; L.-H. Vincent, *Jérusalem*, DBV(S) 943-9 ; A.-G. Barrois, *Manuel d'Archéologie Biblique*, 228 ff. **21.** For Ezechias' other achievements, see 2 Par 29-32.

XXI 1-9 Paganism under Manasses, 697-642—1-2. **280a** The perennial tendency towards Baalism (see on 12:8 ; 13:18-21 ; 14:17 ff.), curbed by Ezechias, was now given free rein. Micheas, 6:6-8, had complained that the reform was only superficial. **3-5.** The predominance of the Assyrians explains the Jewish worship of their gods ; see on 16:10 ff. **6.** ' Pythons' (*'ôb*) were necromancers, 1 Kg 28:7 ff. Elsewhere in Vg (Deut

280a 18:11 ; Act 16:16) 'python' is used for the familiar spirit of a sorcerer. The name is derived from the Delphic oracle, whose original guardian was said to be a python ; the priestess was called the Pythia.

b **10-16 Opposition of the Prophets—13.** The measuring-line (cf. Lam 2:8) and the plummet (cf. Am 7:7) were builders' instruments. They refer here to demolition ; cf. Is 34:11. Read : 'and I will *wipe out* Jerusalem, *the way a dish is wiped, wiped and turned upside down*'. **16.** Reprisals followed protests. The later Jewish tradition (cf. Justin, *Dial. c. Tryph.*, 120) was that Isaias was sawn in two under Manasses ; cf. Heb. 11:37.

c **17-18 End of Manasses**—Esarhaddon names Manasses among the ' kings of the sea-coast ' who paid him tribute after the fall of Sidon, 677 ; Ashurbanipal names him among the vassals who supplied him with auxiliaries for his conquest of Egypt, 668 (Bonkamp, 462, 482). He fell foul of the Assyrians later ; see 2 Par 33:11-19. His subsequent conversion to Yahweh did not change the general trend of religion. Hence the verdict here ignores it.

d **19-26 Amon, 641-640—19-22.** He favoured the anti-Yahwistic party, re-introduced foreign cults into the temple, 23:6, 12, and thus undid the repentant efforts of Manasses ; cf. 2 Par 33:15. **23-24.** Still, the revolt was not the work of the Yahwistic party. But they seized the chance to stir up the people against the civil and military authorities and put their own candidate on the throne.

e **XXII 1-2 Josias, 639-609—1.** Read ' *18* years old ' ; cf. LXX. He was c 45 at his death (cf. 23:36), therefore at least 14 at his accession. **2.** Some efforts at reform in the first part of his reign were not very successful, Jer 2:1 ff. ; Soph 1:2 ff.

f **3-7 Repair of the Temple—3.** Thorough-going reform began in the winter of 622, to culminate in the Pasch, 23:23. **4-7.** The system was that of Joas, 12:10 ff.

g **8-11 Discovery of the Book of the Law**—Its substantial identity with Deuteronomy is probable. (1) The title is found exclusively in Deut 28:61 ; 29:30 ; 30:10 ; 31:2, 6. The 'Book of the Covenant', 23:2, is found only in Ex 24:7, but the Covenant is mentioned frequently in Deut. (2) It held threats of exile against king and people, 11, 16, 20 ; see Deut 4:25 f. ; 28:36 f., 63 ; 29:23-27 ; 30:3 ff. (3) The centralization of the cult, 23:8 f., corresponded to its prescriptions ; see Deut 12 etc. This holds good even if the events of 23:4-14 (whose ' statistical ' style indicates a new document) preceded the finding of the book ; cf. 2 Par 33:4 ff. Deut is the only book which could initiate or ratify the centralization. It was an ancient possession, rescued from oblivion, not a recent fiction, composed to justify the reform. (1) The name was familiar. Note the articles, pointing to a definite authority, which Helcias, Saphan and the king acknowledged at once. (2) All recognized that its prescriptions had bound their forefathers, 13. Even if the author invented the words attributed to Josias, he expressed his conviction that the book was available before Josias ; see further § 135*d-e*. (3) A recent invention would not have commanded universal acceptance, especially on the part of the country clergy, who suffered thereby ; see on 23:8 f. (4) The threats of the book moved everybody deeply. But contemporary prophets left the people cold. The book was known under Ezechias, 18:22 and perhaps Josaphat, 2 Par 17:9. The reigns of Manasses and Amon account for its neglect. It was the custom to deposit sacred documents in shrines, Deut 31:26 ; 1 Kg 10:25.

h **12-20 Consultation of the Prophetess Huldah—12-13.** The king feared that the end was near. The Scythians were then a menace, Herodotus 1:105 ; see Jer 1:13 etc. **14.** Huldah was asked if and how disaster could be averted. From their previous threats, the answer of the prophets Jeremias and Sophonias could be guessed. The Second (City), Soph 1:14, was the extension W. of the temple, which Ezechias had enclosed by a new outer wall, 2 Par 32:5. **15-17.** The fall of Jerusalem was only 35 years distant. **18-20.** **280** The king died in peace (cf. 23:29) in the sense given in 20*b*.

XXIII 1-3 Renewal of the Alliance—1. Like David **i** praying for his doomed child, 2 Kg 12:14-23, Josias stormed heaven. Huldah's prophecy could be revoked ; see on 21:1. **2.** Jer 11:1 ff. probably refer to this assembly. **3.** For the king's place by the pillar, see on 11:14. The people answered ' Amen ' ; cf. Jer 11:5.

4-14 Reform of the Cult—4. The work had been going **j** on for years, 2 Par 34:3. This section seems to catalogue the results without regard to chronological sequence ; hence it cannot be said that the whole reform was inspired by the newly-discovered book. ' Doorkeeper ' was the honorary title of a high order of priests, 12:10 ; 25:18. The actual duties of doorkeepers were performed by Levites, 1 Par 9:17 etc. **5.** ' He *abolished the idolatrous priests*' (*k^emārīm*) ; possibly they were killed, according to Deut 17:2 ff. Assyria was in decline. Hence Josias could proceed against Shamash (' the sun '), Sin (' the moon '), the Mazzaloth (*lit.* stations [of the sun] ; ' the twelve signs ' of the Zodiac, or perhaps the planets ; cf. Jer 7:8). **6.** For ' grove ' see on 3 Kg 14:23. The common cemetery was considered little better than a dung-heap, Jer 26:23. **7.** See on 3 Kg 14:24. Read perhaps ' wove *vestments* [LXX] *for Ashera*'. **8a.** These priests were orthodox, except that they functioned outside Jerusalem ; contrast 5 and 20. **8b.** Read ' the altars of the *goat-gods*' ; cf. Lev 17:7, 2 Par 11:15. Gabaa, 3 Kg 15:22, and Beersheba indicate the northern and southern limits of Judah. **9.** The priests transferred to Jerusalem were not admitted to the sacred ministry. It is not clear what provision was made for them. 9*b* can mean (1) they kept the Pasch, 21 ff., with their families (cf. Ex. 12:15, 18) ; (2) they lived on their portion of the sacrifices, like priests excluded from office by a legal blemish, Lev 21:21 ff. Eventually some at least were given minor functions ; see however on Deut 18:6-9. **10.** Topheth ' fire-place ' lay S. of **k** Jerusalem, at the junction of Ge-bene-Hinnom (the present Wady er-Rababi) and the Cedron valley. Gehenna, Mt 5:22 etc., corresponds to the short form Ge-Hinnom, Jos 15:8 etc. For child-sacrifice, see on 16:3 ; 17:31, Jer 7:31 f. ; 19:4 ff. ; 32:35. **11.** ' Horses and chariots of the sun ' were cult-objects of cosmic significance, lodged in a building or quarter called Pharurim. The name may be connected with E-Barbar (cf. 1 Par 28:18), the temple of the Sun-god in Babylonian Sippar. **12.** Roof-altars were for sacrifices to the heavenly bodies, Jer 19:13 ; 32:29 ; Soph 1:5. **13.** The pagan shrines, which had been restored each time after being suppressed by Josaphat, Ezechias etc., lay either on the southern shoulder of Mt Olivet, or on the Jebel baṭn el-Hawa, opposite the SE. hill of Jerusalem. As the common burial-place lay between the two, there were materials enough to defile the shrines ; cf. Num 5:2 f. ; 19:11.

15-20 In the North—15. With Assyria, hard pressed **l** by the Medes and Babylonians, losing her grip on the provinces, Josias could extend his zealous efforts beyond his own frontiers. Bethel was only a few hours to the N., but he reached even Nephthali, 2 Par 34:6 ; cf. 19. **16-18.** The prophecy of 3 Kg 13:31 f. was fulfilled. **20.** He followed the examples of Jehu, 10:18 ff. and Elias, 3 Kg 18:40 ; and see Deut 17:2 ff. ; these priests were treated as idolators. Contrast 8.

21-23 The Pasch—In addition to the ancient ritual **m** prescriptions of Ex 12, the precept of Deut 16:1 ff. was enforced. Never before had the Pasch been celebrated only in Jerusalem, and therefore never with such solemnity, 2 Par 35:1-19. This was the 14th Nisan, within a fortnight of the events of 22:3 ff., if the year began on the 1st Nisan. Either the year began with Tishri (see on 3 Kg 6:1), or the account of the reforms is not chronological.

24-28 Verdict on Josias and Judah—24. Josias tried to **n** stamp out even private superstitions. ' Figures of idols ' stands for teraphim, household gods, Gen 31:19

80n etc. **25.** His zeal for religion, like Ezechias' confidence in God, 18:5, was unrivalled. **26-28.** But idolatry had gone too deep to be eradicated by human efforts, as the next reigns showed ; cf. Jeremias, Ezechiel.

o 29-30 Death of Josias—Nineveh had fallen in 612, but the Assyrians fought on till 608 in the western province of Harran. See § 66d. Necho II ' went up to (aid) the king of Assyria ', AOT 362, Jos., *Ant.* 10, 5, 1 (reading '*el* ' to ' for '*al* ' against ' ; these Hebrew prepositions are constantly confused in MT). Megiddo commanded the passage from the coastal plain to the plain of Jezreel and the north. Josias was mortally wounded *as soon as he gave battle* (DV ' had seen him ' ; cf. 14:8, 11). His intervention in international conflicts was fatal, not only to himself, but to Judah.

p 31-35 Joachaz, 609—31-33. Necho's attitude shows that the popular movement, which placed Joachaz on the throne instead of his elder brother, was anti-Egyptian. Checked before Harran, Necho had returned to *Riblah* on the Orontes ' in the land of *Hamath* '. Joachaz, opposed by the upper classes at home, dared not disobey his summons. He must be the son of Josias, called Shallum, whose fate was more miserable than his father's, Jer 22:10–12. **34.** The change of name presented his successor as the creature of Necho, and possibly Necho as the instrument of Yahweh : *Y^ehô-yāqîm* ' Yahweh raises ' ; cf. 18:25. **35.** Joakim apparently paid for his throne out of the pockets of his opponents, not out of the treasury.

q 36-XXIV 7 Joakim, 609-598—36-XXIV:1a. In 605, the 4th year of Joakim (see Jer 25:1 ; 46:2), Necho suffered a crushing defeat, Jer 46:11 ff., at the hands of Nabuchodonosor, who became king of Babylon on the death of his father shortly after. Necho retired for good behind his frontiers, 7, and Nabuchodonosor annexed Syria and Palestine. He entered Jerusalem and carried off booty and captives, Dan 1:1 ; Jos., *Ant.* 10, 11, 1 (citing the historian Berossus). **1b-2.** Joakim kept up the friendly relations with Egypt, Jer 26:22 f., which were to be the ruin of Judah. As a result, he withheld tribute from Nabuchodonosor in 602, when some Syrian states revolted against their new master, Bonkamp 513. Nabuchodonosor marched against Syria, but sent only punitive expeditions, composed of troops of his loyal vassals, against Judah. Thus Joakim could hold out for five years. **3-5.** He was an impious and tyrannical ruler, the circumstances of whose death are mysterious. The omission of the usual notice of burial seems deliberate ; see Jer 22:13–19, 2 Par 36:6.

r 8-12 Joachin, 598—8. The new year occurred during his brief reign. Elnathan was a high official under Joakim, Jer 26:22 ; 36:12, 25. **9-10.** The siege was the outcome of the state of war which had lasted since 602. **11.** The arrival of Nabuchodonosor in person convinced Joachin that resistance was rash. **12.** His voluntary surrender spared Jerusalem the worst. According to Jer 52:28, it was the 7th year of Nabuchodonosor. This was the Babylonian reckoning, which did not count the *rēš šarrûti* (after Nisan 605 to Nisan 604 ; see § 279a) whereas the author of Kg, using the Jewish system, counted the *rēš šarrûti* as Nabuchodonosor's first year. So too in 25:8, where the 19th year corresponds to the 18th of Jer 52:29.

s 13-16 Pillage and Deportation—13. ' All the treasures ', and ' all Jerusalem ', 14, are wide terms indicating a general calamity. They are to be understood in the light of the more precise details which follow. The temple was only partially despoiled, 25:15 ; Jer 27:18. The gold and silver utensils were very numerous, Esd 1:11. Some had been carried off in 605, Dan 1:2, more were taken in 598, the rest in 587. Nabuchodonosor had as yet no intention of eliminating the Jewish king-ship and its official cult. **14-16.** The relation of the figures of 14 to those of 16 is not clear. The more general and acceptable view is that the total is given in 14, and some of the details in 16. The 10,000 was made up of 7,000 warriors (of the richer classes, 15:20), 1,000 skilled tradesmen, and 2,000 others (' princes ', 14, ' judges ', 15, ' ancients, priests and prophets ',

Jer 29:1 f.). Another view is that 14 gives the total of **280s** important persons, including the 7,000 warriors of 16, and that 1,000 skilled tradesmen must be added on, making 11,000 in all. 3,023 were deported from the countryside, Jer 52:28. Since wives and children went also, well over 30,000 persons must have been deported. Among them was the prophet Ezechiel, Ez 1:2. Joachin died in exile, Jer 22:20-30. Nabuchodonosor left the poorer classes to take over the property of the exiles, in the hope of creating a loyal population.

17-19 Sedecias, 598-587—17. Matthanias was a son **281a** of Josias, and brother of Joachaz, 23:31, and Joakim. For the change of name, see on 23:24. *Ṣidqîyāhû* ' justice of Yahweh ' was to recall the ' just ' punishment which Nabuchodonosor had inflicted on Jerusalem in 598 ; cf. Jer 40:2 f. Jeremias gave the name a different meaning, when he based on it the hope of a happier future, Jer 23:5 ff. **18.** The parallel accounts in Jer 52 begin here. Amital is the lioness of Ez 19. **19.** Idolatry in the temple is described vividly in Ez 8–11 ; and see Jer 23, 2 Par 36:14. Sedecias' guilt is compared with Joakim's (cf. 9), as Amon's with Manasses', 21:20. The fall of Jerusalem was, it is implied, due to the wickedness of her last kings, Josias excepted.

20 Last Revolt—Sedecias was a weak character and he **b** destroyed his people by wavering in his allegiance to Yahweh. Disregarding the warnings of Jeremias, the inspired spokesman of the orthodox, he threw himself into the arms of the anti-Yahwistic party, whose pro-Egyptian policy brought on the conflict with Babylon, Jer 27:2 ff. ; 37:2 ff. ; 38:17. Only the general trend of events is known. Sedecias had sworn allegiance to Nabuchodonosor, and sent two missions to Babylon to affirm his loyalty, Jer 29:3 ; 51:59. At the same time he was intriguing with the enemies of Babylon, especially Tyre and Egypt, Ez 26 ; 29:17 f., Jer 27:2 ff., Josephus, *C. Apion.* 1, 21. Psammetich II of Egypt visited Palestine in 592 (*A. Alt, ZATW 30 [1910] 288 ff.), and it was probably then that Sedecias committed himself to revolt, which began in 590 with an appeal for Egyptian aid, Ez 17:15.

XXV 1-3 Siege of Jerusalem—1. It began on 25 Jan. **c** 589. The Lachish Letters give an idea of the mounting pressure against Jerusalem, L.-H. Vincent, RB 48 (1939) 250 ff. Nabuchodonosor, who had to deal with the Phoenicians also, was not always present ; cf. Jer 38:17. The blockade wall, *dāyēq,* DV ' works ', is to be distinguished from the mounds, *sōl^elāh.* The former ran round the city at some distance from the walls (cf. Josephus, BJ 5, 12, 2), the latter, like the Roman *agger*, were built up against the walls where an assault could be launched. **2-3.** The siege lasted till the 9th day of the *fourth* month (June–July) 587, 30 months in all. The number of the month, missing in MT, can be supplied from Jer 39:2 ; 52:6. The siege however was not continuous. Psammetich died before he could attempt to relieve Jerusalem. But some time before Jan. 588, Ez 29:1-7, his son Hophra advanced and the Chaldaeans broke off the siege to meet him, Jer 37:4-10. He retired without effecting more and the siege was resumed. He attacked again in the course of 588 and 587, Ez 30:20 ff. ; 31:1 ff. ; 32:1 ff. ; but was no match for the Chaldaeans, Ez 17:7. Herodotus, 2:161, says that Apries (Hophra) sent an army against Sidon and a fleet against Tyre. They must in fact have operated against Nabuchodonosor, but they were too weak to impede him seriously, Ez 17:7. In Jerusalem, famine and pestilence, Jer 38:2, 9, weakened the defenders, and this time no ' angel of the Lord ', 18:35, came to the rescue.

4 Fall of Jerusalem—The breach was made prob. in **d** the N. wall (cf. 14:13) where the terrain was most suitable for attackers. Sedecias and the garrison escaped at the opposite end of the city. There an ancient wall enclosed the SE. hill, and the more recent wall of the SW. hill ran across the Tyropoean valley to join it. Jer 39:4 speaks of a gate and Is 22:11 of a pool ' between the two walls '. The latter would be

281d the lower pool of Siloah, the modern Birket el-ḥamra at the mouth of the central valley. The ' king's garden ' was to the SE., Neh 3:15. The refugees made for the Jordan valley, sometimes known as ' the Wilderness ', though the name is mostly given to the valley S. of the Dead Sea. They were making for Moab. The Chaldaeans (*Kaśdim*) were Aramaeans of the extreme S. of Babylonia, who, after many unsuccessful efforts, had succeeded in becoming masters of Babylon, under Nabopolassar (625–605). They formed the backbone of the Babylonian army.

e **5-7 Capture of Sedecias—5.** Controlling the good routes, the Chaldaeans soon came up with the king and his bodyguard. The rest of the army had already scattered and escaped, 23. Nabuchodonosor was at his headquarters at *Riblah* (see on 23:33) ; Jer 39:3 therefore speaks only of his officers at the fall of Jerusalem. **7.** According to Jer 52:10 f. Jewish princes were killed at the same time. These were probably the officers of the bodyguard. Sedecias was kept a captive till his death. The blinding of captives by a thrust of the lance is depicted on Assyrian monuments. Jer 34:3 prophesied that Sedecias would go to Babylon, Ez 12:13 that he would never see it.

f **8-10 Destruction of Jerusalem—8.** For the dating, see on 24:12. The day of the month is given as the 7th in MT, the 9th in Syr., LXX (Lucian), the 10th in Jer 52:12—July 26th to 28th. The fate of the city was decided after the trial of Sedecias. Nabuchodonosor then determined to replace the Jewish state by a province with its capital at Mizpah, 23. **9-10.** The walls were completely dismantled only in parts, Neh 4:1 ; hence they could be repaired in 52 days, Neh 6:15.

g **11-12 Deportations—**Read ' the remnant of the *artisans* ' (LXX, Jer 52:15). No doubt many of the poor, who had nothing to lose but their lives, fled after the fall of the city ; *cf.* Jer 40:11 f. Still the number of the deported, 832, as given in Jer 52:29 is remarkably small. It refers probably only to the upper classes, most of whom had been already deported in 598. **12.** Since the countryside was depopulated as well as the capital, the total must have been more like the 200,150 whom Sennacherib carried off in 701 ; see on 18:13 ff. Hence ' Judah went into exile ', 21*b*.

h **13-17 Stripping of the Temple—13.** ' bases ' : ' *cauldrons* ' ; *cf.* Syr. The stands had been removed by Achaz, 16:17. **14.** See on 3 Kg 7:50. The bronze altar of holocausts, 3 Kg 8:64, had been replaced by a stone structure (see on 16:17 f.) ; hence it is not mentioned here. Massive pieces were broken up for transport. The utensils were carried off intact ; *cf.* Jer 27:21 f. **16.** ' bases ' : ' *cauldrons* ', as in 13. **17.** Jer 52:21–23 gives a more complete description of the pillars (*cf.* 3 Kg 7:15 ff.) ; the text here has suffered.

i **18-21 Execution of the Ringleaders—18.** The Chaldaeans knew the inner history of the revolt, as their treatment of Jeremias shows, Jer 40. Seraias was grandson of Helcias, 22:4 ; his own son was not killed, **281** but deported ; *cf.* 1 Par 6:13 ff. Esdras was of this family, Esd 7:1. Sedecias had relied much on Sophonias, Jer 21:1 ; 37:3 ; 29:25, 29. The doorkeepers were ranked next to the high-priest and his vicegerent ; see on 23:4. Some of Jeremias' bitterest enemies were among the priesthood, Jer 20. **19.** ' Eunuch ' here, as very often means simply ' officer '. ' Sopher ' is not a proper name, but the secretary in charge of recruiting. The 72 were arrested in consequence of the enquiry held at Riblah, 6.

22-26 Fate of the Remainder—22. Jer 40-43 gives a **j** fuller account of what followed. Nabuchodonosor tried to conciliate the remaining Jews by giving them a fellow-countryman as provisional governor ; *cf.* Jer 40:10. Ahicam had been Josias' envoy to Huldah, 22:14, and the defender of Jeremias, Jer 26:24. The family was loyal to the policy of submission to Babylon which Jeremias had urged, Jer 27:6 ff. Godolias was entrusted with the command of a small detachment of Chaldaeans, 25 ; Jer 41:3. **23.** For Mizpah, see on 3 Kg 15:22. The generals had returned after the departure of the Chaldaean army and seized some towns, Jer 40:10. On promise of amnesty, they submitted to Godolias, and the rest of the army and many refugees returned, Jer 40:9-12. **25.** It was now autumn, for the fruits and grapes were being gathered, Jer 40:12. The king of Ammon planned the murder, Jer 40:14 ; it is not clear why. **26.** See Jer 41:10 ff. Ishmael tried to lead the Jews to Ammon, but was put to flight by the other leaders as soon as they learned of Godolias' death. Jeremias and Baruch, protesting against the migration to Egypt, were forced to go with the refugees. Few, if any, foreign settlers were transplanted to Judah ; the only opposition on the return of the exiles came from Samaria, Esd 4.

27-30 Hopeful Signs in Babylon—27. *Amel-Marduk* **k** (562–560) was son and successor of Nabuchodonosor. Evil-Merodach, suggesting ' a fool is Merodach ', is a tendentious alteration of a name meaning ' the man of Marduk '. Possibly he thought of making Judah a buffer-state against Egypt. The briefness of his reign prevented further developments. **28.** Joachin was given precedence over other vassals detained in Babylon. Many of the exiles were now prosperous business men ; no doubt their money had something to do with Joachin's honours. Nobles ate occasionally at the king's table, Schrader, KIB II 140. Joachin did not dine every day with the king ; but his needs were supplied by the court. The change of status was not unheard-of ; Ashurbanipal had restored the captive Necho of Egypt to a greater power and dignity than he had before his revolt. To the Jews it must have seemed that the wrath of Yahweh was at last appeased. Joachin's good fortune lasted ' till the day of his death ', Jer 52:34, which apparently took place before the end of Amel-Marduk's reign.

1 and 2 PARALIPOMENON

(CHRONICLES)

By E. F. SUTCLIFFE, S.J.

282a Bibliography—*Commentaries* : *C. F. Keil, *The Books of the Chronicles*, Eng. trans., Edinburgh 1872 ; *G. Rawlinson, in 'The Speaker's Bible', London 1873 ; B. Neteler, *Die Bücher der Chronik*, Münster i. W. 1899 ; *W. E. Barnes, *The Books of Chronicles*, Cambridge 1899 (CBSC) ; F. de Hummelauer, S.J., *Comm. in Lib. I Paralipomenon*, Parisiis 1905 (CSS) ; *E. L. Curtis and A. A. Madsen, *The Books of Chronicles*, Edinburgh 1910 (ICC) ; N. Schlögl, *Die Bücher der Chronik*, Wien 1911 ; *J. W. Rothstein und J. Hänel, *Komm. zum I Buch der Chronik*, Leipzig 1927 (KAT) ; J. Goettsberger, *Die Bücher der Chronik*, Bonn 1939 (BB) ; M. Rehm, *Die Bücher der Chronik*, Würzburg 1949 (Echter Bibel) ; L. Marchal, *Les Paralipomènes*, Paris 1949 (in L. Pirot-A. Clamer, *La Sainte Bible* IV).

b *Other* : P. Vannutelli, *Libri Synoptici Veteris Testamenti seu Librorum Regum et Chronicorum Loci Paralleli*, Romae 1931–4 ; Fr. von Hummelauer, S.J., *Das vormosaische Priesterthum in Israel, vergleichende Studie zu Exodus und I Chron. 2–8*, Freiburg im Breisgau 1899 ; M. Rehm, *Textkritische Untersuchungen zu den Parallelstellen der Samuel-Königsbücher und der Chronik*, Münster i. W. 1937 (Alttestamentliche Abhandlungen 13, 3) ; *A. C. Welch, *The Work of the Chronicler*, London 1939 (Schweich Lectures 1938) ; R. Cornely, S.J., *Introd. in U.T. Libros Sacros*, II 1, Parisiis 1887 (CSS) 311–50 ; F. X. Kugler, S.J., *Von Moses bis Paulus*, Münster i. W. 1922 ; *S. R. Driver, *LOT*, Edinburgh 1929⁹ ; *D. D. Luckenbill, *Ancient Records of Assyria and Babylonia*, Chicago 1926–7.

c *Articles* : *G. Buchanan Gray, ' The Title " King of Persia " ', ET 25 (1913–14) 245–51 ; E. Podechard, ' Les Références du Chroniqueur ', RB Nouv. Sér. 12 (1915) 236–47 ; ' Le premier chapitre des Paralipomènes ', RB Nouv. Sér. 13 (1916) 363–86 ; B. Alfrink, ' Die Gadd'sche Chronik und die Heilige Schrift ', Bi 8 (1927) 385–417 ; ' Die Schlacht bei Megiddo und der Tod des Josias (609) ', Bi 15 (1934) 173–84 ; P. Joüon, S.J., ' Notes philologiques sur le texte hébreu de 1 et 2 Chroniques ', Bi 13 (1932) 87–90 ; *A. Sperber, ' Hebrew based upon Biblical Passages in Parallel Transmission ', HUCA 14 (1939) 153–249 ; *A. Noordtzij, ' Les Intentions du Chroniste ', RB 49 (1940) 161–8 ; A. Bea, S.J., ' Neuere Arbeiten zum Problem der biblischen Chronikbücher ', Bi 22 (1941) 46–58 ; H. Van den Bussche, ' Le texte de la prophétie de Nathan sur la dynastie davidique ', ETL 24 (1948) 354–94 ; A. Clamer, DTC XI 1971–94 ; A Robert, DBV(S) iv 15–20.

d Name—The work is known by the two names of *Paralipomenon* and *Chronicles*. The former, that chiefly in use among Catholics, was taken over by the Latins (' Paralipomenon liber ', St Jerome, *Ep. 53 ad Paulinum* n. 8) from the Greeks (ἡ βίβλος τῶν παραλειπομένων, Theodoret, PG 80, 801). In origin, therefore, the name is the genitive plural of the Greek participle with the meaning ' the book of what was omitted '. As Theodoret explains, *ibid.*, the author of the book put together ' whatever the compiler of Kg had passed over ' (παρέλιπεν). The second title was given currency by St Jerome. After mentioning the Hebrew title *Dibrê hayyāmîm*, lit. ' events of the days ', he says ' quod significantius χρονικόν totius divinae historiae possumus appellare ', *Prol. Gal.*, PL 28, 554. The former

title is justified to the extent that the work does **282d** contain much that is not recorded in Kg, though supplements were not the main purpose of the author. Similarly the name ' Chronicles ' is apt in so far as the book is historical, but it does not take account of its special aim. These ancient writers did not give titles and still less sub-titles to their works. Otherwise our author might have chosen to write at its head ' The History of the Davidic Dynasty, the Recipient of a Divine Promise '.

Contents and Purpose—The work begins with Adam **e** and ends with the decree of Cyrus permitting the exiles to return from the Babylonian captivity. But the history is not treated in the same way throughout. The first nine chapters are given, for the most part, in the form of bare genealogical lists. The reader is supposed to be familiar with the story as set forth from the beginning of Genesis. Thus there is no word to explain who Adam was or why the book opens with his name. The chapters serve the purpose of briefly recalling to mind the whole early history of the Chosen Race and of the Providence of God which prepared for them through their ancestors from the very beginning. The author's predominant interest is shown from ch 2 where among the genealogies of the twelve sons of Jacob pride of place is given to that of Judah including the parentage of David, whose own posterity follows in ch 3. Then further information about the descendants of Judah is given in ch 4. Of the other tribes special prominence in point of length is given to that of Levi, chh 6 and 9. The death of Saul is narrated, ch 10, not for its own interest, but because the account of his rejection by the Lord was required to explain the divine choice of David to be the ruler of Israel. Here then in ch 11 the author enters on the real theme of his choice, the history of the divinely elected dynasty of David. This occupies the rest of the book, and is carried down to the conquest of Jerusalem by the Babylonians in 587 when the temporal rule of the dynasty came to an end.

This restriction of the theme explains the silence **f** about the history of the Northern Kingdom. This belongs to the history of Israel, but not to that of the dynasty of David and is consequently only recalled when it has bearings on the latter. Similarly, the reign of Athalia is hardly recognized because she was a usurper who was not of the line of David. The Davidic kings themselves, in whom interest centres, were heirs of the promise, not as individual persons, but in their official position as heirs of the Davidic throne. The Chronicler consequently omits incidents of their private lives. He omits the history of David's youth, of his exploits in the reign of Saul, the story of his adultery and its consequences. He thus omits both what was for the glory of his ideal of the theocratic king as well as what was for his shame. In any case there could be no question of the Chronicler's attempting to conceal the truth and falsify the picture. By the time his own history was written the books of Kings were well established in popular esteem and widely known, and he himself refers his readers for what he does not relate to accessible sources. The omission of direct reference to Solomon's idolatry is more striking, for this was punished by God by the rending of the kingdom and the removal of the greater

282f part from the rule of Solomon's successors, 3 Kg 11:29–36. The manner in which the Chronicler refers to the fulfilment of the prediction of the prophet Ahias recorded in this passage of Kg shows that in his opinion it was so familiar to his readers as not to require explicit repetition. The reference at any rate shows that there was no attempt to suppress the truth.

g The Davidic dynasty being the Chronicler's central theme, the divine promise to ' build David a house ', to grant him posterity, could not but be given prominence, ch 17. ' Thou hast spoken concerning the house of thy servant for the time to come ' ; ' O Lord, let the word which thou hast spoken to thy servant and concerning his house be established for ever, and do as thou hast said ' ; ' Let it be said : The Lord of hosts is God of Israel and the house of David his servant remaineth before him ' ; ' Thou hast *been pleased* to bless the house of thy servant that it may be always before thee ; for seeing thou blessest it, O Lord, it shall be blessed for ever '. Now, when the Chronicler wrote, these great promises seemed to have been rendered void. The Holy City with its temple had been destroyed ; the dynasty had been swept away ; the people lay in poverty and weakness under the rule of a foreign power. The Chronicler sets out to give the people new heart. The divine promises are not forgotten and God is not powerless to fulfil them :

h ' the word of the Lord endureth for ever '. He therefore shows how God in the history of the kingdom blessed right-doing with prosperity and punished evil with calamity. This is a recurrent theme of his work, 2 Par 12:1–2 ; 13:4–16 ; 14:11–13 ; 16:9 ; 19:2 ; 20:37 ; 21:10 ; 22:4–9, etc. In particular the final disaster of the destruction of Jerusalem is traced to the divine sentence provoked by the iniquities of kings and people, 2 Par 36:5, 8, 9, 12–16 : ' they mocked the messengers of God, and despised his words, and misused the prophets, until the wrath of the Lord arose against his people, and there was no remedy '. By such considerations the Chronicler attempted to move the people to a whole-hearted return to God. If that condition were fulfilled, they would again experience the happiness of the divine favour. The promise to David's dynasty might be in abeyance, might even seem to have lapsed, but the descendants of David through Zorobabel were still with them, 1 Par 3:19–24, and in God's good time the expected new David would arise among them.

i An essential part of loyalty to God and obedience to his law was the whole-hearted observance of the temple ritual and worship. Of this the post-exilic Jews were very negligent as is manifest from the reproaches of the prophets Aggeus and Malachy. The Chronicler, therefore, attempted to arouse their enthusiasm for this religious part of their national and individual responsibilities. Hence he wove into his story all that his sources recorded of the planning, building, inauguration, renovations, and general history of the temple, together with the arrangements prepared by David for the due and solemn celebration of the temple worship by the distribution of offices among the courses of priests and Levites, and the renewal of such arrangements by Joiada under Joas, by Ezechias, and by Josias. It was not merely the Chronicler's interest in these religious matters that prompted him to devote so large a part of his work to them, but his realization of their importance for the nation and of the need to arouse in the people a vivid sense of their obligations in this regard.

j **Position in the Canon**—In the printed editions of the Heb. Bible Par is placed last among the Hagiographa and so occupies the last place of all. And this position is sometimes said to have obtained in the time of Christ on the strength of Mt 23:35, ' from the blood of Abel even unto the blood of Zacharias '. As the murder of Zacharias by Joas took place as early as the 9th cent. and so was by no means the last in OT history, it is pointed out that, as the murder of Abel is recorded in the first book of the Bible, so that of

Zacharias must have been recorded in the last. On **2?** this basis is raised an argument as to the date of composition of Par or at least of its reception into the Canon. The history of the question is, however, more complex. St Melito, Bishop of Sardis in the late 2nd cent., in the Jewish Canon as learnt by him in Palestine (see JE III 151*a*) places Par after 1–4 Kg, and ends the list with Esdras (= Esd-Neh). The passage is preserved by Eusebius, *Hist. Eccl.* IV 26. Origen in his list of the 22 books received by the Jews, **k** PG 12, 1084, enumerates Par followed by 1–2 Esd after 1–4 Kg. Epiphanius, also in a list of the Heb. Canon, places Par before Kg and ends with 1–2 Esd and Esther, PG 43, 277. And St Jerome in his list of the same Canon in his *Prologus Galeatus*, PL 28, 554, gives the 7th place among the Hagiographa to Par, which is followed by 1–2 Esd, and ends the list with Esther. The Jewish evidence is also far from exhibiting unanimity. In the Babylonian Talmud, *Baba Bathra* 14*b*–15*a*, the list ends with Esd and Par. In the Heb. Bible contained in the St Petersburg codex dated A.D. 1009, Par appears first among the Kethubim or Hagiographa and Esd-Neh last. Moreover, the treatise *Adath Deborim* of A.D. 1207 pronounces this order, which was in accordance with western or Palestinian practice, to be correct as against the eastern or Babylonian custom of placing Par or Esther at the end. See C. D. Ginsburg, *Introd. to the Massoretico-Critical Edition of the Hebrew Bible* (London 1897) 1–8.

Relation to Esdras-Nehemias—The evidence for the **l** common authorship of Par and Esd-Neh is summarized, with many references, by Cornely, 328–30, 357 : the diction common to both books in regard of vocabulary, use of prepositions and other constructions ; the formula for quoting the Mosaic Law ; the functions of the Levites described with the same diffuse style and almost the same words ; the same frequency of genealogies and public lists ; both works centre on Jerusalem, the temple, and public worship ; in both there is the same solicitude for the divine Law and the same diligence in setting down information about the priests and Levites. The literary atmosphere of Esd-Neh, however, is very different from that of Par. Still the large number of common features proves at least that both works come from the same circle, if not from the same pen.

Identity of authorship, even if proved, does not, it **m** is plain, prove unity of composition. That Esd-Neh is the continuation of Par was affirmed by Alphonsus Tostatus, Bishop of Avila in the 15th cent., *Opera* XVI (Venetiis 1728) quaest. 5 *ad fin.*, and by many is considered certain at the present day. In favour of the unity of the two works it is pointed out that Esd-Neh begins precisely at the point where it is left by Par, and that Par ends with part of the decree with which Esd opens. These are weighty considerations, though on the supposition of one originally continuous work the decree will probably have been duplicated in part at the end of Par, when the works were separated, in order to indicate where its continuation was to be found. On the other hand, the verses could have been added to Par to ensure that book ending on a consoling note. We may compare the additions to certain Psalms. Both works would have been useful by way of information and of exhortation to the author's contemporaries, whenever he lived, and to subsequent generations. On the negative side it may be urged that the hypothesis has no historical support and that there is no trace in Esd-Neh of the Messianic hope although it would have been so easy to introduce it from the writings of the post-exilic prophets. Moreover, the presupposition of the identity of authorship is itself not quite certain. The evidence for unity, therefore, though strong, hardly amounts to a demonstration.

Date—That the work was not written till after the **n** return from the Babylonian captivity is indicated by the excerpt from the decree of Cyrus, 1 Par 36:22–23 ;

n and even with the possibility of this being a later addition the same conclusion follows from the mention of the establishment of the *kingdom* of Persia in 2 Par 36:20. If, as is probable, the Persian daric is the coin named in 1 Par 29:7, the date would be sufficiently long after its introduction by Darius I, 521–486, for its use and name to have become familiar in Palestine. The evidence of the list of Davidic descendants in 1 Par 3:19–24 is inconclusive partly because of the possibility of additions having been made to the text and partly because of its state and the difficulty of interpretation. Zorobabel was the first governor of the Jews after the return from the exile in 538, Agg 1:1. Various emendations and interpretations have been offered, but MT seems to give 6 generations after Zorobabel and LXX + Vg 11. If Hananias, the son of Zorobabel was already an adult at the time of the return and with the allowance of 20 years to a generation, MT would point to a date some century later. On the reading of LXX + Vg Semeia, the son of Sechenias, was in the 7th generation after Zorobabel, and he was one of those who assisted Nehemias in the rebuilding of the wall of Jerusalem in 445, Neh 3:29. If this is correct, each generation must have married very early as Zorobabel could not have been much more than 40 in 538, as his grandfather Joachin was 18 in 598. The remaining generations of LXX + Vg would carry the date down to about the middle of the 4th cent. Finally, if Par + Esd-Neh originally formed one work the date of the latter must be taken into account. See § 288*f*.

o Author—In the Babylonian Talmud, *Baba Bathra* 15*a*, Esdras is listed as the author of the book that bears his name (= Esd-Neh) and of the genealogies of Par. Nicolaus Lyranus extended this authorship to the whole of Par, and in this view found many adherents down into the 19th cent. But it is incompatible with the common authorship and the lower date of Esd-Neh advocated by many. The prevailing view is that no more can be said than that the interest manifest in the Levites including the singers and the doorkeepers suggests that the author was a Levite and probably one of the latter classes.

p Doctrine—The doctrine about God is mostly concerned with his relations with man, but has some important lessons about **God as he is in himself.** His universal presence is adumbrated in that ' heaven and the heaven of heavens cannot contain him ', 2 Par 2:6. Nothing escapes his knowledge because ' the eyes of the Lord *range* through all the earth ', 2 Par 16:9. In his hand is ' power and might ', 1 Par 29:12, and ' no one can resist ' him, 2 Par 20:6. ' All that is in heaven and on earth is ' his, 1 Par 29:11, so that man can give to God only what he has received from the divine bounty, 1 Par 29:14.

q But God does not live in glorious isolation in heaven ; he is **the omnipotent ruler of the world.** His rule is based on perfect knowledge, for ' the Lord searcheth all hearts and understandeth all the thoughts of minds ', 1 Par 28:9, and it extends to ' all the kingdoms and nations ', 2 Par 20:6. His will prevails ' for it belongeth to God both to help and to put to flight ', 2 Par 25:8. Theologically the doctrine of God's providential government of the world is inchoate, since the problem of the harmonious working of God's rule and man's free will had not yet presented itself and no distinction is made between God's absolute and his permissive will. Thus it was the will of God that Roboam should not condescend to the people's petition, 2 Par 10:15. So too of Ochozias's visit to Joram that resulted in his death, 2 Par 22:7, and of Amasias's disastrous decision to **r** make war on Joas of Israel, 2 Par 25:20. As the just ruler of the world and guardian of the moral order God must punish evil and reward good. But as the doctrine of retribution in the afterlife had not yet been revealed, this could be envisaged only in terms of prosperity and disaster in this world. In this Par merely reflects teaching that had been handed on from the Pentateuch, Jg, Kg, and various Psalms. The

doctrine has frequent application in our book, in the **282r** matter of punishment from the death of Saul for his iniquities, 1 Par 10:13–14, to the final destruction of Jerusalem and end of the kingdom, 2 Par 36:13–17, and in the matter of reward from the promise of David, 1 Par 12:13, to that of Ezechias, 2 Par 30:8 f. But, though God is just, ' his mercies are many ', 1 Par 21:13, and in his mercy he is always ready to forgive, 2 Par 30:9. He hears and answers the prayers of men, 2 Par 7:12–16, even to the extent of granting a miracle, 2 Par 32:24. Even one like Manasses, whose iniquities had provoked God to anger, is heard and forgiven in answer to repentant prayer, 2 Par 33:6, 12 f. For though the service of God is light compared to the service of earthly princes, 2 Par 12:8, man is very frail and ' there is no man that sinneth not ', 2 Par 6:36, and ' a perfect heart ' to keep God's commandments can come only from him, 1 Par 29:19 ; 2 Par 30:12.

Though God rules the whole world, yet he deigned **s** to establish an intimate **divine relationship to Israel.** He chose it out from all others and called it ' my people ', 1 Par 11:2. ' The covenant which he made with Abraham ' remained as ' an everlasting covenant ' with Israel, 1 Par 16:16 f. It was he who chose David to be king, 1 Par 11:2–3 ; 14:2 ; 17:7 ; 28:4 ; 2 Par 6:6. He chose Solomon to be his successor, 1 Par 17:11–12 ; 22:9 ; 28:5–7 ; 2 Par 1:8 ; 6:10. More than that, God promised David a dynasty that should rule for ever, 1 Par 17:17, 23–27. Sometimes this promise is accompanied by the condition of fidelity, 2 Par 6:16 ; 7:17–22. Sometimes it is unconditional, 2 Par 13:5 ; 21:7. The former referred to the temporal rule that came to an end through prolonged infidelity, 2 Par 36:13–17. The latter referred to the spiritual rule of Christ, the second David, of whom the Angel Gabriel foretold ' he shall reign in the house of Jacob for ever ', Lk 1:32. Herein lies the Messianic hope of our book.

Faithful to his promise, Deut 18:18–22, God raised **t** up a long **succession of prophets** to guide, warn and rebuke his people : Nathan, 1 Par 17:1, and Gad, 1 Par 21:9 (David) ; Ahias, 2 Par 10:15 (Solomon) ; Semeias, 11:2 ; 12:5 (Roboam) ; Addo, 13:22 (Abia) ; Azarias, 15:1, and Hanani, 16:7 (Asa) ; Micheas, the son of Jemla, 18:7 ff. (Achab and Josaphat) ; Jehu, the son of Hanani, 19:2, Jahazael, 20:14, and Eliezer, 20:37 (Josaphat) ; Elias, 21:12 (Joram) ; unnamed prophets, 24:19, and Zacharias, the son of Joiada, 24:20 (Joas) ; an unnamed man of God, 25:7, and a prophet, 25:15 (Amasias) ; Oded in Samaria, 28:9 (Achaz) ; seers, 33:18 (Manasses) ; messengers of God and prophets, 36:15–16 (Sedecias).

Despite the vivid consciousness of Israel's privileged **u** election our book betrays no narrow nationalism. The praise of God is put in the mouth of Hiram, king of Tyre, 2 Par 2:11–12, and of the queen of Sheba, 9:8. Appeal is made to the nations to come and adore God's presence symbolized by the ark, 1 Par 16:28–29. The renown of the temple is to spread to all nations, 1 Par 22:5. Solomon prays that the prayer of strangers who adore in the temple may be heard from heaven, ' that all the peoples of the earth may know ' the name of God and serve him, 2 Par 6:32–33.

Sources—At the end of his account of most reigns the **v** Chronicler names one or more works where further information may be obtained. The exceptions are the reigns of Joram, Ochozias, Amon, Joachaz, Joachin and Sedecias. For these Kg also omits to mention a source except for Joram and Amon, for the latter of whom the omission in Par may be explained by homoeoteleuton. The sources with historical titles are the following : (1) ' Book of the Kings of Israel and Judah ', 1 Par 9:1 (registration of the people) ; 2 Par 27:7 (Joatham) ; 35:27 (Josias) ; 36:8 (Joakim) ; (2) ' The Book of the Kings of Judah and Israel ', 2 Par 25:26 (Amasias) ; 28:26 (Achaz) ; 32:32 (Ezechias) ; (3) ' Book of the Kings of Judah and Israel ', 2 Par 16:11 (Asa), the title differing from (2) in grammatical construction only ; (4) ' Book of the

282v Kings of Israel', 2 Par 20:34 (Josaphat) ; (5) 'Acts of the Kings of Israel', 2 Par 33:18 ; (6) 'Study [Midrash] of the Book of Kings', 2 Par 24:27 (Joas). As books used not to have titles, a fixed and definite nomenclature is hardly to be expected, and there is no reason to doubt that (1), (2) and (3) represent the same work, and they are probably identical with (4) and (5). (6) appears to be a different work ; on the word 'midrash' see on 2 Par 13:22.

w   The sources named after prophets and seers are the following : (1) 'The Acts [or Words] of Samuel the Seer', 1 Par 29:29 (David) ; (2) 'The Acts of Nathan the Prophet', 1 Par 29:29 (David) ; 2 Par 9:29 (Solomon) ; (3) 'The Acts of Gad the Seer', 1 Par 29:29 (David) ; (4) 'The Prophecy of Ahias of Shilo', 2 Par 9:29 (Solomon) ; (5) 'The Vision of Addo the Seer concerning Jeroboam the Son of Nabat', 2 Par 9:29 (Solomon) ; 'The Acts of Addo the Seer', 12:15 (Roboam) ; 'The Study [Midrash ; or, Investigation] of the Prophet Addo', 13:22 (Abia) ; (6) 'The Acts of Semeias the Prophet', 12:15 (Roboam) ; (7) 'The Acts of Jehu, the Son of Hanani', 20:34 (Josaphat) ; (8) The history of Ozias was written by Isaias the prophet, the son of Amos, 26:22 ; 'The Vision of Isaias the Prophet, the Son of Amos', 32:32 (Ezechias) ; (9) 'The Acts of Hozai' or 'The Acts of the Seers', 33:19 (Manasses). Opinions differ considerably about the number and independent existence of these writings. Of (7) 'The Acts of Jehu' the text says explicitly that they were incorporated into 'The Book of the Kings of Israel', which, however, supposes at least their original independent existence. In the case of (8) 'The Vision of Isaias' the textual evidence is not unanimous and many think that it is not named as a part of a historical work ; see on 2 Par 32:32. The opinion that all these works were known to the Chronicler as parts of one large history seems to be definitely excluded by the separate mention in 2 Par 33:18–19 of both 'The Acts of the Kings of Israel' and of 'The Acts of Hozai' or 'of the Seers'.

x   The genealogies in 1 Par 1:1–9:44 are taken from unnamed sources. 1:1–2:5 is from Gen and the subsequent information could in part be derived from Ex, Num, Jos, Ru and Kg, but other parts, as 2:14–15, are from non-canonical sources.

y   The historical work called 'The Book of the Kings of Israel and Judah' etc. cannot be identified with our Kg as the former contained various facts not to be found in the latter : 1 Par 9:1, the genealogies ; 2 Par 27:7, victories of Joatham ; 33:18, the prayer of Manasses ; 36:8, the abominations of Manasses. Whether Kg was itself a source is controverted. The affirmative has been asserted on the ground of the close verbal resemblances, the grouping of facts, and the order followed. But all this is equally well explained by the use on the part of both works of a common source. Kg was without doubt a well-known book, and facts it narrates are supposed to be familiar to readers of Par, e.g. 2 Par 10:15, the prophecy of Ahias (3 Kg 11:29–39), 32:24, the sign given to Ezechias (4 Kg 20:8–11), 32:25, 31, the embassy from Babylon (4 Kg 20:12–19). On the other hand, Par adds many details not recorded in Kg as may be seen from the commentary. And on occasion Par makes the narrative of Kg intelligible. Compare, for instance, 2 Par 22:11 with 4 Kg 11:2 and 2 Par 24:14 with 4 Kg 12:13. These and similar cases show that Kg was not the source. The similarities and differences are best explained by the use of a common source from which each author chose what seemed to suit his purpose. So Rothstein-Hänel, Goettsberger, Rehm and others.

z   Reference is also made to genealogical registers drawn up in the time of Joatham and Jeroboam, 1 Par 5:17, to 'The Annals of King David', 27:24, and to a collection of Lamentations, 2 Par 35:25, different from that still extant.

aa   **Historical Trustworthiness**—The attack on the credibility of the Chronicler's narrative was launched by *W. L. M. de Wette, *Kritischer Versuch über die Glaub-*

würdigkeit der Bücher der Chronik (= *Beiträge zur Einleitung in d.A.T.* II), Halle 1807. His arguments, though previously refuted by F. C. Movers, *K. F. Keil and others, were taken up by J. Wellhausen, *Prolegomena to the History of Israel*, Eng. trans., Edinburgh 1885. This Wellhausen was forced to do by his theories of the composition of the Pentateuch as the evidence of Par shows that the Levitical Law was in force at the time of David and Solomon and was not, as Wellhausen maintained, a product of post-exilic times. A detailed examination of his chief arguments may be read in Cornely, 330–48, and in Kugler, 234–89. Many are met by a due appreciation of the mode of historical writing adopted by the ancient Hebrews and by a correct understanding of the text. Thus Par is accused of falsifying history by recording that immediately after the death of Saul David was chosen to be king of all Israel. The charge would be justified if Par had said that the one event followed at once on the other, which, however, is not the case. And just as the sacred writers frequently narrate events without regard to their chronological order, so the mere fact that the narration of one event follows immediately on that of another did not imply in the mind of the writer or in that of the Hebrew reader that the two events followed in immediate chronological succession. In the present instance Par so far from attempting to conceal the existence of Saul's son and successor, the rival of David, mentions him twice, 1 Par 8:33 and 9:39, by his true name of Eshbaal (also called Ishbosheth, 'man of shame' out of hatred for the name Baal on account of its idolatrous associations). Here, as in other cases (see § 282y), Par supposes a knowledge of facts narrated in Kg. Had the Chronicler wished, he could not have hoped to suppress knowledge of the history recorded in that popular book. As his purpose was not to set down all that was known of the history of Judah as is evidenced by his many references to further sources of information, from the mass of material available he chose what he judged suitable to his theme.

b   As another illustration of principle may be mentioned the further objection that according to 1 Par 11:1 'all Israel' gathered at Hebron to make David king over the whole nation. Wellhausen seems to have overlooked the fact that the parallel passage in 2 Kg 5:1 has a phrase of the same import narrating that 'all the tribes of Israel' came to Hebron for the same purpose. No one could suppose that either expression was intended in a strictly literal sense, and biblical usage shows the meaning to be that representatives of all the nation assembled or that those present represented the dominant will of the nation as a whole. Whatever there is in Par that modern historical sense finds exaggerated, is paralleled in Kg. Thus in the time of Joachin Nabuchodonosor 'carried away all Jerusalem and all the princes', 4 Kg 24:14, yet in the reign of Sedecias Jeremias has various references to 'the princes', 37:13–14 ; 38:4, 25, 27. St Augustine explained long ago that many apparent difficulties are solved if it is remembered that 'It is the custom of Scripture to speak of a part as if it were the whole', *Epist.* 149, ad Paulinum, PL 33, 638. On Wellhausen's treatment of the tribe of Levi reference may be made to C. Lattey, S.J., in CBQ 12 (1950) 277–91.

c   Wellhausen's whole-hearted condemnation of the historical veracity of the Chronicler was widely influential, and found many followers of the thesis that the Chronicler projected into the past the organization of the temple worship as existing in his own day and as set forth in the Priestly Code. He is said 'to have wished to draw the attention of his readers in the first place to the temple and its history and to bring out all that the pious kings of Israel-Judah had done for its glory and splendour' and 'to have sketched a picture of the past of his people with the colours of his time, to have idealized the past, so that, by and

354

large, his book cannot be considered worthy of credit ' ; so A. Noordtzij writing in 1940 of then prevalent non-Catholic opinion, 160. He goes on to show that the interest of the book is primarily in the house of David and its Messianic hope, not in matters of cult. In the genealogical tables Moses receives only one incidental mention, 1 Par 6:3, and it is the tribe of Judah with the house of David, not that of Levi, which is given prominence. Neither does the high-priest stand in the foreground of the narrative. He is subordinated to the king, who, and not the high-priest, renews the covenant with Yahweh, 2 Par 29:10 and 34:31. It is the king who presides at the great religious ceremonies, 1 Par 13:5 f., 2 Par 20:3 ff. ; 29:20 ff. ; 35:16 etc. It is the prophets and not the priests who play an important part in the religious history of the monarchy, § 282t, and who develop the work of Moses, 2 Par 29:25.

On other matters, which, it is allowed, were not affected by the Chronicler's special point of view and purposes, historical value is recognized in his traditions. Thus *M. Noth, *Überlieferungsgeschichtliche Studien* I (Halle 1943) is of opinion that Par had pre-exilic sources for the history of the kings only for Ezechias's tunnel, 2 Par 32:30, for the last battle and death of Josias, 35:20-24, and for various reports about the defensive works of the kings of Judah and their wars. But, as pointed out by A. Bea, S.J., in Bi 27 (1946) 145-6, if these reports are from ancient and reliable sources, there is every likelihood that other reports are similarly derived, and that the contrary must not be assumed but requires proof, which is not forthcoming.

Recent Catholic writers follow their predecessors in defending the historical character of our work. Thus L. Marchal : ' The type of literature adopted by the Chronicler is certainly historical ', 19 ; ' There is no serious reason to doubt the reality of the events vouched for by the author ', 20. M. Rehm : ' The author's purpose is to offer the truth and to find it by going back to older traditions ', 6. Similarly Goettsberger is at pains in his commentary to show how Par supplements and sometimes makes intelligible the narratives of Kg, and in general to defend it against charges of error. A. Clamer describes the book as ' a witness to the history of Israel, especially its religious history ', 1993. He admits, however, 1992, that there may be modifications of detail, adaptations, or the like. So too Goettsberger, 12, and Marchal, 17, admit a certain idealization of the past ; and the former, 13, says that where the Chronicler carries views of his own age back into the past, this is not very different from his giving his narrative in the speech and style of his own day.

The **numbers** given are sometimes incredibly high. Thus Abia had an army of 400,000 men and Jeroboam of 800,000, 2 Par 13:3. Taken alone this could mean the total number of men who could be called up. This would avoid the difficulty of such vast armies being engaged at one and the same time, but the difficulty would remain that the figures would suppose a total population larger than the small country of Palestine could support. Actually the explanation is ruled out by 13:17, which says that 500,000 of Jeroboam's army were victims of the battle. Another suggested explanation is that ' thousand ' stands for a fighting unit of that nominal number, though in fact it might be much under strength. But Josaphat is credited with 1,160,000 fighting men, or on this explanation 1,160 regiments of nominally 1,000 men, 2 Par 17:14-18. Even on the supposition that no unit was at more than half strength, the figures still leave an army of over 500,000 men. The problem is not confined to Par. There are very high numbers in Gen and Num. It seems, therefore, to be a characteristic of Hebrew historiography, a literary convention, understood and admitted as such by these ancient writers and their readers. Divine inspiration is incompatible only with those types of literary expression which admit not only material but also formal error.

The Chronicler as Author—A perusal of the work does **282gg** not leave the impression that it is by a literary artist. Both the language. which tends to be crabbed, and the manner of composition forbid such a favourable judgement of the author. He leaves from his sources elements which have no meaning in the new context. Thus the remark that David remained at Jerusalem, 1 Par 20:1, is pointless as the story of David's crime against Urias has been omitted. In 2 Par 20:35 the phrase ' after these things ' has no point of reference as the account of Josaphat's reign has been brought to a close. The ark is said to have been in the Holy of Holies ' unto this day ', 2 Par 5:9, a phrase in the source no longer true after the exile. There are similar remarks about Solomon's forced labour, 8:8, and the revolt of the northern tribes, 10:19.

There are curious repetitions, such as are not absent **hh** from Kg. Thus, *e.g.* Saul's genealogy is given both in 1 Par 8:29 ff. and 9:35 ff., and 2 Par 27:8 is repeated from 27:1. An association suggested by a word may occasion a long digression. 1 Par 23:1-2 begins the account of the great assembly in which David presented Solomon as his successor. Among those summoned were priests and Levites. This leads to long lists about them and the story of the assembly is taken up again only in 28:1. The mention of the gold given to Solomon by the queen of Sheba, 2 Par 9:9, occasions a digression about gold from Ophir, and the narrative about the queen is resumed again in 9:12. This instance was taken over from the source, and it appears also in 3 Kg 10:11 ff. Evidently such procedure was congenial to the ancient Hebrew writers. Despite these minor defects in execution the Chronicler had a definite plan in mind and succeeded in imprinting it on his work.

THE FIRST BOOK OF PARALIPOMENON

I 1-IX 44 Genealogies. **283a**
I 1-II 2 From Adam to Jacob—1-4. The antediluvian patriarchs. Gen 5:1-31. **5-23. The Table of the Nations** from Gen 10. **17.** After ' and Aram ' insert with one Heb. MS and LXX (A) ' and the sons of Aram ', Gen 10:23. The form ' Mosoch ', which may be due to a reminiscence of the name in 5, is replaced by *Mash* in some Heb. MSS and Syr in agreement with Gen 10:23. **24-27. The postdiluvian patriarchs** from Gen 11:10-26. **25.** ' Ragau ' and ' Reu ', Gen 11:18, are different transliterations of the Heb. *Re'û*. **27.** For the change of Abram's name see Gen 17:5. **28-34. The descendants of Abraham. 28.** For the birth of Isaac see Gen 21:1-4 and of Ishmael, the elder but named second as of less importance, Gen 16:15. The list of Ishmael's descendants, **29-31**, is from Gen 25:13-15. ' Hadad ' in 30 is the ' Hadar ' of Gen. These two final letters are often confused in Heb. and the textual evidence varies in both places. The names of the sons of Cetura in **32-33** are taken from Gen 25:1-4. She was a secondary wife, not concubine, of Abraham's. In Gen 25:1 she is called his wife. **34.** The sons of Isaac, unlike those of Abraham in 28, are given in the order of birth, Gen 25:25, and Jacob, Israel's original name, Gen 32:28, is not mentioned. **35-37. The sons of Esau,** from Gen 36:10-13. **38-42. The sons of Seir,** the aboriginal inhabitants of the land of Edom ; Gen 36:20-28. **39.** Homam is called Hemam in Gen, the divergence being due to the similarity of *yod* and *waw* in early Heb. script. The same remark applies in **40** to Alian and Sephi, who in Gen are Alvan and Sepho. Onam in some copies of DV is erroneously called Oman in Gen. Hamram, **41**, is Hamdan in Gen, where MT has Jethran with *n* as here. **42.** Jacan is named Acan in Gen. Aran is so spelt also in MT of Gen. **43-50. The kings of Edom,** Gen 36:31-39. The Heb. text is the same in 48 as in Gen. **50.** By a common confusion of consonants the name appears as Adad here and as Adar in Gen. **51-54. The ' dukes ' of Edom,** Gen 36:40-43. The mention of

283a the death of Adad II in **51**, which is absent from Gen, indicates that the rule of these governors was subsequent to the extinction of the kingship. The names may be partly personal and partly territorial.

b **II 3-VIII 40 The Twelve Tribes of Israel.**
II 3-IV 23 The Tribe of Judah—**3-4** come from Gen 38. **5.** Gen 46:12. **6.** Zamri's name appears as Zabdi in Jos 7:1, MT, Vg, but Zamri has there also the support of LXX. Ethan is mentioned among the wise men of 3 Kg 4:31 as an Ezrahite or descendant of Zera. After ' Ethan ' the words ' the sons of Hamul ', 5, have dropped out. In 3 Kg 4:31 Heman, Chalcol and Dorda appear as the sons of Mahol, which name, by inversion of letters, must disguise the name of Hamul. ' five in all ' is thus a gloss added after the disturbance of the text. **7.** As Charmi has not been mentioned previously the words ' and the son of Zamri: Charmi ' have prob. dropped out ; see Jos 7:1. For ' Achar ' read ' Achan ' with some MSS here and Jos 7:1, MT, Vg. **8.** Azarias, only here. **9.** Jerameel, only in this chapter. Ram (variant, Aram), Ru 4:19. Calubi appears in 18 as Caleb. **10-17. The sons of Ram. 10-12.** Ru 4:19–22. Isai, the father of David, is called Jesse in Is 11:1. **13 :** 1 Kg 17:13. **14-15 :** except David only here. **16.** Sarvia (Zeruiah) only here mentioned as sister of David ; her sons, 2 Kg 2:18. Abigail is called the daughter of Naas in 2 Kg 17:25 and will have been David's step-sister. **17 :** 2 Kg 17:25, where read with LXX (A) ' the Ishmaelite ', for ' of Jezrael '. **18-20. The sons of**

c **Caleb** ; *cf.* 9. This Caleb is a different person from the Caleb, son of Jephunneh, Num 13:7 (MT 6), one of those sent by Moses to ' spy out ' the promised land. The other names are otherwise unknown except Hur and Uri, Ex 31:2, and Ephrata, the daughter of Machir, 21, 24. The interest of the list for the Chronicler centres in Bezeleel, the craftsman responsible for the tabernacle and its furniture. **21-24. Further on Hesron**, 9. **21.** ' Afterwards ' refers to 9. The daughter of Machir was named Ephrata, 19, 24. Machir was a Manassite, Jos 17:1. This explains that Jair, who is here reckoned to Judah through Hesron, is also called a son of Manasses, Num 32:41, being connected with that tribe through his father Segub on the mother's side and living with the half-tribe of Manasses in Galaad. This Jair is prob. the Judge of Jg 10:3-5. The record of his exploits has been inserted in Num 32:41 and Deut 3:14 where note ' unto this present day '. The number 30 in Jg 10:4 is prob. a round one. **23.** ' *Geshur and Aram took* the towns of Jair '. Geshur : a territory in N. Transjordania ; Kenath (Canath) prob. the modern Qanawat west of the Hauran. **24.** ' Ephrata, the wife of Hesron his father ', a marriage forbidden by Lev 18:8. Ashhur = Hur, 19 ; 4:5. **25-41.** The descendants of Jerameel, 9 ; *cf.* 1 Kg 27:10 ; 30:29. **25.** Ram, 27. **26.** Onam, 28. **31.** As Sesan had no son, 34, Oholai will have been a daughter ; *cf.* 11:41. **32.** Jada, 28. **34-41** give the descendants of Sesan through a daughter. The Jerahmeelites lived in the Negeb and so in proximity to Egypt, 1 Kg

d 27:10. **36.** Zabad, 11:41. **42-55.** The sons of Caleb, 9, 18. **42.** For ' Mesa ' read with LXX *Maresa* (Maresha). Some of the descendants of Caleb are presented as the fathers or founders of towns in Judah. Ziph = modern Tell Zif, S. of Hebron. Some names seem to have fallen out after ' Maresa '. **43.** Tappuah, a town, Jos 15:34. **45.** Ma'on, Jos 15:55, today Tell Ma'in, S. of Hebron. Beth-sur, Jos 15:58, N. of Hebron. **47.** Jahaddai's name, which occurs here for the first time, must have dropped out from the previous list. **49.** Madmanna, Jos 15:31. A name has prob. fallen out before ' the father of Gabaa '. As only those women are included in genealogies who played some part in history, it is hard to resist the conclusion that this Achsa is the daughter of Caleb, the son of Jephunneh, Jos 15:16, Jg 1:12. Probably, therefore, the sentence is a misplaced interpolation here or ' daughter ' must signify ' descendant '. This suggestion is not without difficulty as Caleb, the son

of Jephunneh, is called a Qenizzite, Jos 14:6, 14, though closely connected with the tribe of Judah, Jg 1:10-12. **50.** After ' Caleb ' there should be a full stop, the sentence referring to 42-49. ' The *sons* of ' Hur, 2:19, were Sobal, Salma and Hariph. **51.** Bethgader, perhaps Khirbet Jedûr, NW. of Hebron. **52.** Proper names have been translated : Re'aya (Raia, 4:2), the half of Manahath ; see 54. **53.** Of the *clans* of Kiriathjearim the Jethrites (Ithrites) are mentioned 2 Kg 23:38. Şor'a, now Şar'a, near Beth-Shemesh ; Eshtaol, Jos 15:33. The clans are the inhabitants of the neighbouring localities. **54.** Again as in 52 proper names have been treated as common nouns : ' and *the Netophathites, Atroth-beth-Joab, and half the Manahathites, the Sorites* '. Netopha, SW. of Bethlehem. Manahath and Şor'a had mixed populations, 52, 53. **55.** ' that dwell in Jabes, *Tir'athites, Shim'athites, Sukathites. These are the Kenites who came in from Ḥammath, the father of Beth-rekab* '. Shema', Jos 15:26 ; Socoh, Jos 15:35. Kain was a town of Judah, Jos 15:57. The Kenites were a non-Israelite tribe that came to be closely associated with Judah. As ' the father of ' in this ch is followed by a local name, a reference to the Rechabites, Jer 35:2, is doubtful.

David was introduced in 2:15. **III 1-4. The sons of David born in Hebron**, 2 Kg 3:2-5. The second son is called Daniel in Par, supported by LXX in Kg, and Cheleab in Kg supported by Syr in Par. Possibly he had two names. **5-8. David's sons born in Jerusalem**, 2 Kg 5:14-16 and repeated in 1 Par 14:4-7. **5.** Simmaa, differently vocalized in Kg and 14:4. Ammiel is called Eliam in 2 Kg 11:3, with inversion of the two elements of the name ; *cf.* the inversion in Ahazias (Ochozias), 3:11, and Joachaz, 2 Par 21:17. **6.** Elisama is the name of a brother, 8, and is here a scribal error for Elisua, the form given in the other lists. **7.** Eliphaleth appears here by dittography from 8 as in 14:5, but not in Kg. Noge also is given in 14:6, but not in Kg. Two of the letters are the same as in Nepheg, of which it is prob. a duplicate. **8.** Eliada, which corresponds to Baaliada in 14:7, is an altered form with elimination of Baal which came to be associated with pagan worship. The number ' 9 ' which is additional to the ' 4 ' in 5, was added after the list had received accretions. **9 :** 2 Kg 5:13. Thamar : 2 Kg 13:1. **10-24. The descendants of David. 10** picks up the thread from 5. **15.** Johanan does not occur in Kg and prob. died before or with his father. Sellum, Jer 22:11, was also called Joachaz, prob. as a throne-name. On the evidence of the ages and length of Joakim's reign given in 4 Kg 23:31, 36 ; 24:18, Sellum was born before Sedecias, and is mentioned last here perhaps as a sign of degradation, Jer 22:10:12, Ez 19:3 f. **16.** Sedecias, otherwise unknown. **17.** As Salathiel (Shealtiel) was born after the deportation of Jechonias to Babylon, Mt 1:12, ' Asir ' is prob. a common noun : ' The sons of Jechonias *the captive* were. . . .' **19.** Zorobabel is styled the son of Shealtiel, 17, in Esd 3:2 etc. Prob. Phadaia was his true father and Shealtiel only in the legal sense, Deut 25:5 f. **20.** Either the number ' 5 ' has been wrongly copied or names have been erroneously added to the text. **21-22.** Zorobabel returned from Babylon shortly after the decree of Cyrus, 538 B.C., and Semeia, the son of Sechenias, worked on the building of the wall of Jerusalem, Neh 3:29, with Nehemias, who returned from exile in 445 B.C. In this interval of time it is difficult to fit all the generations supposed by Vg + DV. However the text is uncertain and is understood by some in the sense that Hananias was the father of all named in 21. Semeia should thus be in the third generation from Zorobabel. Hattus seems to be called the son of Secenias, Esd 8:2 f. This and the statement that the sons were six, renders it prob. that the words ' whose sons were ' should be omitted. **23.** Elioenai returned with Esdras, Esd 8:4, where read ' the son

Naaria'. **24.** According to the suggestions made on 21-22 it is not certain that this list allows more than six generations inclusive of Zorobabel. **IV 1-23. Further Judaite genealogies—1.** Charmi, 2:7. If this name is changed from Calubi = Caleb we have a list of descendants in the direct line, 2:4, 5, 9, 19, 50. **2.** Raia : see on 2:52. 'families of *the Saraites*', as 2:53, where the Heb. is the same. **3-4.** Etam, 2 Par 11:6, Jezreel, Jos 15:56, Gedor, Jos 15:58, are towns in Judah. Ephrata, 2:19. In 2:51 Salma, the son of Hur, is called father of Bethlehem. Such a metaphorical fatherhood could well be predicted of this father and son. **5-7.** Ashhur ; see on 2:24. **9-10.** Jabes in 2:55 a local, is here a personal name. The prayer forms an incomplete sentence. Jabes must have been known in the time of the Chronicler. **11-12.** The identification of this Caleb as the brother of Sua seems to distinguish him from Caleb the brother of Jerameel, 2:42. Paseaḥ, Esd 2:49. **13-14.** Othoniel, Jg 1:13 ; 3:9. Ophra was a city of Benjamin, Jos 18:23, to which tribe belonged also the valley of artificers, Neh 11:35. 'For they were *artificers*', or 'craftsmen'. **15.** This Caleb, son of Jephunneh, may be the same as the Caleb of 11. **17.** Eshtemoh : a city of Judah, Jos 15:50. MT has 'she begot Mariam', suggesting that a mention of the Egyptian wife, 18, has fallen out. This explains also in 18 the distinction made : 'his *Jewish* wife'. Gedor ; see on 4. There were two places named Socoh in Judah, Jos 15:35, 48, also two called Zanoah, Jos 15:34, 56. **18b** seems to be a misplaced note with an uncertain text. **19** opens with an uncertain text. Keilah, Jos 15:44 ; Maachah, a region SW. of Mt Hermon. **20.** Another unconnected fragment. 'Rinna, *Ben-Hanan*', four sons in all. **21.** Shelah (Sela), 2:3. Mareshah, Jos 15:44. 'fine linen in *Beth-Ashbea*', otherwise unknown. **22.** Other sons of Shelah : '*and Yokim and the men of Cozeba and Joash and Saraph who became masters in Moab and returned to (Beth)lehem. These are events of old time*', of which this is the only record. **23.** 'These are the potters, *who dwelt in Neta'im and Gederah ; they dwelt there in the king's service*'. Gederah : a city of Judah, Jos 15:36. The names have been lost from this fragment. On jars made in Hebron, Socoh and Ziph has been found the imprint 'For the King'; see D. Diringer, BA XII (1949) 70 ff. **IV 24-43 The Tribe of Simeon—24:** Gen 46:10 = Ex 6:15 ; Num 26:12 f. Namuel : in Gen + Ex Jamuel. Jarib : Jachin in the other lists. Zeraḥ, also in Num : in Gen + Ex Sôḥar. **28-33. The territory of Simeon,** Jos 19:1-9. Bethberai in 31 is prob. corrupted from Bethlebaoth in Jos. On Siceleg in David's time see 1 Kg 27:5 f. Etam : in the territory of Judah as noted Jos 19:9. **34-38. Leading men of Simeon.** The tribes were divided, 38, into clans and the clans into families. **39-43. Territorial conquests. 39.** 'And they went *to the confines of Gerara*', LXX. As the former inhabitants were non-Israelite, they felt justified in seizing their lands, Deut 7:2. **41.** 'and slew the *Maonites* that were found there'. Ma'on was the place SE. of Petra whence they had wandered. The time indicated, 'unto this day', is that of the Chronicler's source which cannot be fixed. So too in 43. **42-43.** The mountainous country of Seir (Edom) extended S. of the Dead Sea. Saul's war against Amalec, 1 Kg 15:7 f., and David's, 2 Kg 8:12. The names of the captains occur only here and do not help to fix the date of this event.

V 1-10 The Tribe of Ruben—1. Ruben's crime, Gen 35:22. **2.** Joseph, reckoned as the firstborn, had the privilege of a double portion of the inheritance, Deut 21:17. Hence the double territory of Ephraim and Manasses, the two tribes descended from him. **3.** Gen 46:9. **6.** Tiglath-pileser's expedition against Galaad, 4 Kg 15:29, prob. 734 B.C. **8.** Aroer, Jos 13:16, Nebo and Baalmeon, Num 32:38, fell to Ruben. **10.** The Hagrites, called in the Assyrian inscriptions Hagaranu, lived in NE. Arabia. In Syriac the name

came to be used as a designation of Arabs in general, **283i** Curtis 120. **11-17 The Tribe of Gad—11.** The Gadites' territory **j** ran north from that of Ruben. Bashan had been given originally to Manasses, Jos 13:30. **12-13.** These are not the immediate descendants of Gad, Gen 46:16 ; Num 26:15-17, but leading men of a later time. **14.** The sons of Abihail are missing. **15.** 'their brethren' is a doubtful emendation. **16.** 'in all the *pasture-lands of Sharon*', or, as Sharon E. of the Jordan is unknown, perhaps 'of all the upland pastures', reading *mîšôr*. **17.** Jeroboam II 782/1-753 and Joatham 740/739-736/5 ; but the numbering will have been made while Joatham was acting as regent for his father Azarias. Shortly after this the history of the transjordanic tribes came to an end with the invasion and deportation carried out by Tiglath-pileser, 734 B.C. **19-22 War against the Hagrites and their Allies— k** This is a fuller account of the war briefly noticed in 10 as waged in the time of Saul. **19-20.** '*They went to war against the Hagrites and the Ituraeans and Naphish and Nodab, 20, and they were given help against them*'. For the Hagrites see on 10. In Gen Jetur and Naphish are the eponyms of Arab tribes. Nodab : only here. It is explained that God helped them because of their prayer and trust. **21-22.** 'of men a hundred thousand souls, *for* many fell down slain '. These men were not taken captive, and are loosely attached to the main verb. That this is the meaning is shown by the particle 'for'. The deportation of the Israelite tribes : see on 17. **23-24 The Half-Tribe of Manasses—23.** Bashan was **l** inhabited by Gad ; see on 11. The Manassites had the land on its northern boundary. Baal-Hermon : perhaps modern Baneas. Senir was the Amorite name for Hermon, Deut 3:9, but in Heb. usage was distinguished as part of the range ; so also Cant 4:8. **24.** Nothing more is known of these men. **25-26 The Transjordanic Tribes are punished for m Idolatry—**Tiglath-pileser, king of Assyria 745-727, effected the union of Babylonia with Assyria by setting himself on the throne of the former country under the name of Pulu. Both names occur separately in 4 Kg 15:19, 29. In the existing text here the two names occur as if of two different persons. The name of Pulu is not mentioned in Syr and is prob. a gloss. This is confirmed by the fact that the invasion here spoken of, 734 B.C., is that of 4 Kg 15:29 where the king of Assyria is named Tiglath-pileser. Read prob. : 'and brought *them to Halah and Habor the river of Gozan and the mountains of Media*' ; see on 4 Kg 17:6. **VI 1-81 The Tribe of Levi (MT 5:27-6:66)—1.** Ex **n** 6:16. **2-15. The descendants of Caath, chiefly of Aaron. 2.** Ex 6:18. **3a.** Par adds Mary to the children of Amram, Ex 6:20. **3b.** Ex 6:23. **4a.** Ex 6:25. The genealogy of Esdras, Esd 7:1-5, is the same as far as Sadoc, 8, except that an Azarias is inserted between Maraioth and Amarias, 7. From Sadoc, 8, the Esdras list passes to the son of Sadoc, 12. Names were traditional in families and there is nothing surprising in various generations having the same name. **8.** Sadoc, high-priest under Solomon, 3 Kg 2:35. Achimaas, 2 Kg 15:27. **9.** Azarias, high-priest under Solomon, 3 Kg 4:2. **11.** Amarias, high-priest under Josaphat, 2 Par 19:11. **13.** Helcias, high-priest under Josias, 2 Par 34:9. **14.** Saraias, high-priest at the fall of Jerusalem, 4 Kg 25:18. **15.** Josedec, Agg 1:1, Esd 3:2.

The list is given as that of the descendants of Aaron, **o** not as that of high-priests, though some in the list are known to have held that office. Others known to have done so are not mentioned, Joiada, 2 Par 22:11, Azarias under Ozias, 2 Par 26:20, and the number of generations given could not cover the interval of time between Aaron and the 6th cent. B.C. Josephus, *Ant*. 5, 11, 5, states that the line of Eleazar retained the high-priesthood till Ozi, 6:5, after whom it passed to Eli of the line of Ithamar to return to the line of Eleazar under Solomon. It is probable that the office

283o did not always pass in the direct line of descent. It is remarkable that the Chronicler with his interest in the temple and public worship nowhere gives a list of high-priests as such.

p **The sons of Levi, 16-19,** repeat 1 in 16 and 2 in 18. **17.** Ex 6:17, Num 3:18. **19.** Ex 6:19. **20-21. The sons of Gerson,** 1, 17. **22-28. The sons of Caath** (Kohath). **22-23.** Aminadab is not mentioned above, and the father of Core, according to 37 f. and Num 16:1 is Isaar. This passage clarifies Ex 6:24 where Asir, Elcana and Abisaph might be taken for brothers. **24.** Uriel, of David's time, 15:5. **15.** Elcana, 23. **26-28.** ' Elcana : the sons of Elcana ' ; there is no copula in MT. This list of Samuel's ancestors gives the same names as in 33-35 and 1 Kg 1:1, but in altered forms. The sons of Samuel were Joel and Abia, 1 Kg 8:2. The first name has fallen out here both in MT and LXX, and the Heb. expression for ' and the second ' appears as a proper name ' Vasseni '. **29-30. The sons of Merari,** 1, 19. There is nothing surprising in the names Lobni and Semei appearing in a different generation as those of sons of Gerson, 17.

q **31-32. David's arrangement of liturgical singing.** His removal of the ark, 2 Kg 6 ; his establishment of the three guilds of Levitical singers under Heman, Asaph and Ethan = Iduthun, 1 Par 25. **33-38. The genealogy of Heman.** The list runs parallel to 22-28, but with omissions, scribal deformations (Johel, 36 = Saul, 24), and different names of the same person (Azarias, 36 = Ozias, 24). Samuel's Levitical origin, 28, 33, shows that the designation of Ephraimite given to his father, 1 Kg 1:1, has a local sense. He was a Levite dwelling in Ephraimite territory. **39-43. The genealogy of Asaph.** Asaph was related to his ' brother ' Heman through their common descent from Levi, being descended from Levi's sons Gerson and Caath respectively. The position of Asaph's choir was ' at the right hand ' of Heman's in the temple services. From Zara, **41,** the names begin to agree with those in 20-21, with discrepancies usual in these ancient and imperfectly copied lists. **44-47. The genealogy of Ethan.** It is not stated that Ethan changed his name or had two, but after 15:19 he is called Idithun (Jeduthun), 16:42 etc. Other OT personages with two names are Abraham, Sara, Jacob, Joakim, Sedecias, and in the NT St Paul. Ethan's choir stood on the left of Heman's during service in the temple. **47** agrees with 19. **48-49. The duties of the other Levites and of the priests.** In 48 omit ' who '. **49.** ' to pray for ' : ' to atone for ' by the sacrifices and purificatory rites of the Law. Not only sin- and trespass-offerings but also holocausts availed for expiation, Lev 1:4. **50-53. The list of Aaron's descendants** is repeated as far as Achimaas, 3-8, as

r he was of the time of David, 2 Kg 15:27. **54-60. The cities allotted to the priests,** Jos 21:1-4 ; 10-19. **54.** ' their dwelling-places *according to their districts* '. **55.** ' and the *pasture-lands* thereof '. **57.** According to Jos 20, of these cities only Hebron was a city of refuge. **59.** Ashan, mentioned as a city of Juda in 4:32, appears as Ain in Jos. Before ' Beth-shemesh ' insert ' *Jutta* ' with LXX, Syr. **60.** Read ' *Gibeon and Geba* ', the former having fallen out by haplography. **61-81. The cities of the Levites. 61-65.** A summary, Jos 21:4-8. **61.** Those descendants of Caath are meant who were not of the priestly order. Complete the sentence by the addition from Jos of Ephraim and Dan. Here the cisjordanic half of Manasses is meant. **65** mentions the three remaining tribes in whose territory cities were given to the Aaronites as recounted in 55-60. **66-70. The cities of the Caathites,** Jos 21:20-26. **66.** ' And the kindred of the sons of Caath *had their cities by lot* in the tribe of Ephraim '. **68.** Jokmeam : in Jos Kibzaim. **69.** Elteke and Gibbethon, Jos 21:23, have fallen out of Par. These were both in Dan, as were *Aijalon* and Gath-rimmon. **70.** *Taanach*, Jos, and *Ibleam*. **71-76. The cities of the Gersonites,** Jos 21:27-33. **71.** Ashtaroth : altered in Jos to a Heb. form interpreted as ' Bosra '. **72.** Kedesh :

prob. read Kishion, Jos. **73.** ' Anem ' has arisen out of *En-gannim*, Jos, today Jenîn. **75.** Hukok : Jos, Helkath. **76.** Hammon : today el-Ḥammi, S. of Tiberias. **77-81.** The Merarite cities, Jos 21:34-38. **77.** Jokmeam and Kartah, Jos, must have fallen out as 63 reckons 12 cities to Merari. Thabor : in Jos, Nahalal. It is prob. that in some at least of these cases of divergency Par gives the actual practice as opposed to the original intention registered in Jos. **80.** *Mahanaim.*

VII 1-5 The Tribe of Issachar—1. Gen 46:13 and Num 26:23 f. have Puwwah for Pu'ah ; and in Gen read *Yashub* (Jasub) for ' Job '. **2.** The numbering, 21:5. This number excludes the descendants of Ozi, 3 f. **5.** Previous numbers : Num 1:29 = 54,400 ; 26:25 = 64,300. **6-12a The Tribe of Benjamin—**Benjamin occurs again in ch 8 whereas there is no account of Zabulon, to which tribe it is therefore prob. that the following list should really belong. But it cannot be simply transferred to Zabulon as a comparison of 6 with Gen 46:14 and 21 indicates. See also the very different list in Num 26:38-41. **12b The Tribe of Dan—**It is probable that this halfverse is a remnant of the lost Danite list. 12b is not linked with 12a and Husim is the one Danite name in Gen 36:23. It appears with inversion of consonants as Suham in Num 26:42. **13 The Tribe of Nephtali—**Gen 46:24 ; Num 24:48 f. **14-19 The Tribe of Manasses—**Num 26:29-34 ; Jos 17:1-3. The text has suffered considerably. **14.** Ezriel (Asriel) was the son of Manasses' grandson Galaad, Num. **15.** Maacha was the name of Machir's wife, 16. The true text is lost. Salphaad (Zelophahad) was the son of Hepher, Num. Par speaks of him as ' the second (son) ' and therefore had an independent source. **16-17.** The names of these descendants are not in Num. **18.** ' Goodlyman ' : Jerome translated the proper name Ishhod as ' Virusdecorus ', a practice he occasionally follows elsewhere. **20-27 The Tribe of Ephraim—**Num 26:35-37, where the names as elsewhere do not exactly agree, does not make it plain that the names form a line of descent. **21.** The names of ancestors were often given to children of the same family. As the Philistine city of Gath was not captured by Josue, Jos 11:22, the Hebrews would be likely to make a raid ' *to take their cattle* '. That the men of Gath are said to have been born in the land suggests that the Hebrew invaders had not. Ephraim was born in Egypt, Gen 41:52, and raiders from Egypt would not be said to ' come down ' to Canaan. The difficulty of placing the raid in or after the time of Josue is its connexion with the genealogical table. But this is also a difficulty against putting it in the lifetime of Ephraim on account of various intervening generations. The difficulty is not removed by the suggestion that Ephraim in 22 is used figuratively as is Rachel in Jer 31:15. A fragment of history seems to have become connected with the genealogy, but out of its chronological setting. **24.** Beth-horon : see on Jos 10:10. Uzzen-sheerah : today Beit Sira, W. of the Beth-horons. **28-29 The Territory of Ephraim and Manasses—**The ' daughters ' are the dependent villages. **28.** Ephraim. Naaran : see Naaratha § 235b. Gazer and Shechem : both Levite cities, 6:67. **29.** Jos 17:11. **30-40 The Tribe of Aser—30.** Gen 46:17 ; Num 26:44. **31.** Num 26:45. Birzaith : a place-name, today Birzeit, NW. of Beitin = Bethel. **32.** Heber's genealogy is given only in Par. **33.** Chamaam : *Bimhal.* **35.** Helem ; the name appears as Hotham in 32. **38.** Jether is called Jethran in 37. **39.** Olla is prob. the same person as Ara, 38. **40.** Num 1:41 the total given is 41,500 and 26:47 53,400. **VIII 1-40 The Tribe of Benjamin—**7:6-12a ; Gen 46:21 ; Num 26:38-41. **1.** In Gen 46:21 read ' Bela, *his firstborn* and Ashbel '. Gera and Naaman, sons of Bela, are there given as ' sons ' of Benjamin in the sense of descendants. In Num 26:38-40 Ahara is called Ahiram, and Sephuphan is Supham. In **3** read 'Gera *the father of Aod*' (or, Ehud), Jg 3:15. The repetition of Gera, 3 and 5, must be a slip. **6.** The names of the sons of Ahod (Aod, Ehud; see on 3) have fallen out, also the name of the enemies who took these Benjaminites captive to Manahath, a place of uncertain identification. In **7** the leader who deported them is not named. The words about deportation may be corruptions of proper names, though the deportation is supported by the otherwise unexplained sojourn in Moab, 8. **8.** Saharim is mentioned abruptly without introduction. **11.** '*Of Husim* [his wife, 8] he begot Abitob'. **12.** Ono: today Kefr 'Anā; Lod: today Ludd (Lydda) SE. of Jaffa. **16.** Baria, 13. **17-18.** The sons of Elphaal, 11 f. Here from another source. **19-21.** The sons of Semei = Sama, 13. **22-25.** The sons of Sesac, 11. **26-27.** The sons of Jeroham = Jerimoth, 14. Zechri was a name popular in the family, belonging to sons of Semei, 19, Sesac, 23, and Jeroham, 27. **28.** Jerusalem allotted to Benjamin, Jos 18:28, was a border city and was shared with Judah, Jos 15:63, Jg 1:21. **29-40. The family of Saul** = 9:35-44. **29.** 'At Gabaon [Jos 18:25, a city of Benjamin] dwelt *Jehiel* [9:35] *the father of Gabaon*', not its founder but principal citizen. Saul's own home was in Gibeah (Gabaa), 1 Kg 10:26. **30.** After 'Baal' supply *Ner* from 9:36. **33.** In Mt 1 the use of the word 'begot' does not exclude the omission of intervening generations and by analogy the ancestors of Cis (Kish) listed in 1 Kg 9:1 might here have been omitted between Ner and Cis. But this is excluded by 1 Kg 14:50 where Abner, the son of Ner, is called Saul's uncle (DV 'cousin german'), and therefore was brother or half-brother to Cis. Those named in 30 will not all have been sons of the first generation, and Cis' known ancestors will have been (among) the intervening links. Thus Ner's name should be supplied in Kg 9:1. Josephus's opinion, *Ant.* 6, 6, 5, that Ner and Cis were brothers and Ner Saul's uncle (the opinion followed by Vg + DV in 1 Kg 14:50) is against the present passage. See also 1 Kg 10:21 for another ancestor. All Saul's sons figure in his history. Esbaal = Ishbosheth 'man of shame', 2 Kg 2:8. The name of Baal was replaced by an opprobrious word to signify hatred of pagan cults. Par alone uses the form Esbaal, evidently reproducing an ancient source. The same holds, **34,** of Meribbaal, elsewhere always called Mephibosheth, 2 Kg 4:4. Micha, 2 Kg 9:12. **35-40.** Micha's posterity: only in Par. **40.** The names of Ulam's sons are missing.

IX 1a Appendix—The author indicates his source for the preceding genealogies which was not the canonical books of Samuel and Kings, as much of the information given is not to be found there.

IX 1b-34 List of Dwellers in Jerusalem—The list gives laymen, 3-9, priests, 10-13, Levites, 14-34, among whom are porters, 17-27, and other officials, 28-34. The insertion of the list may have been suggested by 8:28 'the families who dwelt in Jerusalem'. The period to which the list belongs is controverted. Kugler, 289 ff., assigns it to 621-597; Goettsberger considers it to be post-exilic and substantially identical with that in Neh 11, which Kugler dates in the reign of Sedecias.

2. The Israelites here are the laymen. The Nethinim were persons dedicated to the service of the Levites in the time of David, Esd 8:20. **5.** Sela, the half-brother, 2:3 f., of Phares, 4, and Zara, 5, was the eponym of the Silonites. Read with Neh 'Asaia [Maasia], *the son of Baruch*, and his sons'. 6 is not in Neh. **10-13. The Priests. 10.** These three stand here perhaps for the respective 'courses' of which they were the heads in the time of David, 24:7, 17. **11.** *Cf.* 6:12 f. 'Achitob, the *prince* of the house of God'. **12.** Melchias was the head of the fifth course, 24:9. **14-16. Levites. 15.** 'Bacbacar, *Heresh*, and Galal'. Mathania is mentioned among the singers, Neh 11:17. **16.** These Levites dwelt 'in the Netophatite villages'; so Neh 12:28 and see on 2:54. **17-27. The door-keepers,**

a separate group of Levites. **17-18.** Esd 2:42; Neh 7:46; 11:19; 12:25. 'Sellum was the *chief*, 18, *and until now at the king's gate on the east. They are the porters of the Levites' quarters*'. **19-20.** They had this office under Phinees, Num 25:7, in the days of the wanderings. He succeeded his father, Eleazar, in the office, Num 3:32. **22.** They lived in Jerusalem when on duty. Samuel's regulations are mentioned only here, David's in ch 26. **25.** They 'came *for seven days*' when their turn came round. **26.** The four are named in 17. **28-34. Other officials. 30.** '*And some of the priests' sons compounded the mixture of the spices*'; see Ex 30:34-38. **32.** For the shew-bread see Lev 24:5-9. **33.** The expected list of singers is not given, either here or Neh 11:22 f. **35-44.** The family of Saul. See 8:29-38.

X 1-XXIX 30 The Reign of David.

X 1-14 Saul's Kingdom transferred to David— 1 Kg 31:1-13. The account serves the purpose both of introducing David's succession to the throne and of illustrating the theme that neglect of God's service is punished by adversity. **1-5.** = Kg 1-5. **6** compresses 'his armourbearer and all his men' to 'all his *household*'. This does not, however, include Ishbosheth who survived. He is mentioned in 8:33 with his three brothers, whose death with Saul is recorded in 2. **7.** 'saw *that they had fled and that* Saul and his sons *were dead*'. **8-10.** Kg is precise in recording that the weapons were laid up in the temple of Astarte, Par in recording that the skull was put in the temple of Dagon, 1 Kg 5:2. **12.** They took the bodies from the wall of Beth-shan where the Philistines had exposed them, Kg. 12 omits the burning of the bodies, which is mentioned in Kg, but supposes it by saying that they buried the bones. Kg says the spot was under an '*ešel* = tamarisk, Par under an '*ēlāh*, a tree of uncertain identification. In LXX and Vg it is called an oak and a terebinth, and according to Gesenius-Buhl it signifies any large tree. The similarity of the words may indicate a textual error. The bones were finally laid to rest in the sepulchre of Saul's father, 2 Kg 21:12-14. **13-14.** These moral reflections repeat those of 1 Kg 28:17 f. For Saul's transgression, see 1 Kg 15:1-11; his consulting the witch 1 Kg 28.

XI 1-3 David is anointed King over all Israel— 2 Kg 5:1-3. The immediate sequence in the narrative of David's accession to the throne of all Israel does not of itself indicate that it followed immediately in time. The methods of ancient oriental historians, even though inspired, must not be judged by modern western standards. The readers of Par were well acquainted with the long war between David and the house of Saul, and the fact that it was the murder of Ishbosheth which gave him control over all Israel, 2 Kg chh 3-4. Par supposes and does not disguise these facts, 3:4. Par adds in 3 'according to the word of the Lord'; see 1 Kg 16:1-13.

4-9 David makes Jerusalem the Capital—2 Kg 5:6-10. Hebron was too southerly to be suitable as capital city. Jebus, on the SE. hill of present Jerusalem, had also the advantage of being almost impregnable. **4.** Kg: 'the king and all *his followers* went to Jerusalem'. 'all Israel' went in the same sense as 'all Israel', 1, had assembled at Hebron, *viz.* in the persons of their representatives. **6** adds the promise to Kg's account. Joab was David's nephew by his sister Sarvia, 2:16. Abner had been in command of David's forces, 1 Kg 26:5, but was treacherously slain by Joab to David's sorrow and indignation, 2 Kg 3:27-39. The king now found himself obliged by his promise to promote the murderer to the chief command. **8.** Par adds that 'Joab *repaired* the rest of the city'. David's first thought was to strengthen the fortifications of his new capital.

10-46 David's Chief Supporters—2 Kg 23:8-39. Exploits of 'the three' are recounted, 10-14, then those of three other heroes, 15-25. There follow two lists of valiant men, 26-41a and 41b-46. **10-14. The**

284d **Three. 10,** not in Kg. **11** introduces the *list* of the heroes. Jesbaam (see also 27:2) *killed* three hundred at one time. **12-13a.** Eleazar was the son of *Dodo* or Dodai ; see 27:4. For the occasion of his exploit at Ephes-dammim, see 1 Kg 17:1 ff. ; for the exploit itself, 2 Kg 23:10. It has been lost here by homoeoteleuton, the scribe's eye passing from one mention of the Philistines gathering for battle to another. Both mentions are preserved in 2 Kg 23:9 and 11. **13b-14.** The same scribal error has caused the omission of the name of the third hero, given in 2 Kg 23:11 as Semma (Samma). He was the hero who defended a field of barley, Par, or lentils, Kg. The consonants of the two words are similar in Heb., and it is impossible to say which is original, *śĕʿōrîm* or *ʿᵃḏāšîm*. Read : ' but *he* stood . . . and defended it '. **15-19. An exploit of three valiant men,** not those just mentioned. The text says merely ' three of the thirty '. Two are afterwards named, Abisai, 20, and Banaias, 22. That they are not mentioned in 15 is due to the author's habit of juxtaposing his excerpts from his sources without weaving them into a consecutive narrative. **15.** ' *At the beginning of harvest time* three of the thirty went down to David at the cave of Adullam '—*haṣûr* ' the rock ' is a corruption of *qāṣîr*, the word in 2 Kg 23:13. The season explains David's unusual thirst. **18.** ' but *poured it out as an offering* to the Lord ' ; for a similar libation of water, see 1 Kg 7:6. **19.** ' These *were the exploits of the three heroes* ', mentioned in 15. No doubt they had slipped away unknown to David to fulfil what he had uttered as an idle wish. **20-25. Abisai**
e **and Banaias,** heroes of the exploit, 15-19. The name of the third is not preserved. **20.** Abisai, 2:16. ' He was chief of *the three* '. **21.** ' and *more* illustrious *than the thirty* and their captain '. ' Thirty ' as in 25. In Heb. idiom this can mean ' than the rest of the thirty '. In Kg v 19, which corresponds to this verse, *hᵃḳî* is certainly a corruption of *hinnô* ' lo he ' the word which occurs in the similarly worded 25. This shows that it is the original reading replaced by ' second '. ' First ' is not in MT or LXX but correctly gives the sense. Jesbaam, Eleazar and Semma were ' the three ' without further qualification, 11-14. Those of 15-19 were ' the three ' engaged in that famous adventure. **22-25.** Banaias, captain of the army and son of Joiada the priest, 27:5 f. **22.** ' He slew the two *sons of* Ariel of Moab ' ; so with Kg (LXX). Ariel ; otherwise unknown. **25.** ' And David *set him over his personal bodyguard* ' ; 18:17. **26-41a. A list of valiant men** = 2 Kg 23:24-39. Both lists have suffered textually. Many are mentioned as high officers of the army : Asahel, 26, Sammoth (?) and Helles, 27, Ira and Abiezer, 28, Sobbochai, 29, Marharai and Heled, 30, Banai, 31 ; see 27:7, 8, 10, 9, 12, 11, 13, 15, 14. **26.** Elchanan was the son of *Dodo*. **27.** Helles was a Paltite from Beth-pelet. **32.** Hurai came from the *ravines* of Mt Gaash, Jos 24:30. Azmoth of Bahurim was David's treasurer, 27:25. **38.** Nathan, evidently a well-known man, perhaps the prophet of that name. 2 Kg 23:39 gives the total as 37. The list in Par = 31 + ' the three ' + Abisai and Banaias, 20, 22, + Elica the Harodite, 2 Kg 23:25, omitted in Par, = 37. **41b-46. A further list of valiant men.** Not in Kg. If Zabad is the same person as in 2:36, he was a descendant of Oholi (Ahlai), for whom see 2:31. **44.** Hotham was from Aroer, just N. of the Arnon.
f **XII 1-22 David's Supporters at Ziklag**—Only in Par. **1-7. Men of Benjamin** abandoned their fellow-tribesman, Saul, and espoused the cause of David. It was two of the tribe who even murdered Saul's son Ishbosheth, 2 Kg 4:2. The insertion of the passage here implies that many at least of these supporters later helped David to win the kingship over all Israel. **1.** David's retirement at Ziklag, 1 Kg 27:6, a town presented to him by the Philistine king Achis. The Benjaminites were famous for ambidexterity, Jg 3:15 ; and 20:16 where their skill with the sling is also lauded. Their skill with the bow, 8:40 ; 2 Par 14:8 ; 1 Kg

20:20 ; 2 Kg 1:22. **3.** Azmoth, 11:32, of Bahurim **28** in Benjamin. **4.** For ' the thirty ', see 11:15. Of these Samaias was one of the bravest and he had under him a group of thirty warriors. Gedera was a city of Judah, Jos 16:36, where a Benjaminite might be living. However, some Judaites came to David with men of Benjamin, 16. **5.** The Haruphite was a man of some unknown locality. **6.** Perhaps members of the clan of Core (Korah) of 2:43. **7.** Gedor, 4:4, a town in Judah. **8-15. Supporters from the tribe** **g** **of Gad. 8.** At this time David was at Adullam, 11:15 ; 1 Kg 22:1. **14.** It is not said that they brought such large contingents of men with them ; *cf.* 20. **15.** They were not deterred by the fact that the Jordan ' *had overflowed* its banks '. This was caused by the melting of the snow on Hermon in March–April and by unusually heavy rains. They put to flight all Saul's adherents who sought to oppose them on their way through the valleys to join David. **16-18. An episode.** **18.** Had Amasai been the same person as Amasa, David's nephew, 2:17, the fact would prob. have been mentioned. The inspiration that came to him is not said to have been supernatural. Natural events are attributed to God as the Creator and Ruler of the universe. **19-20. Support from Manasses. 19.** See 1 Kg 28:1-2 ; 29:1-11. The Philistine lords suspected that David would use treachery against them as a means of reconciliation with Saul, 1 Kg 29:4. **20.** Omit the second mention of Ednas, not in MT or LXX, though two Jozabads are listed. **21-22. Conclusion.** The *raiders* were Amalecites ; see 1 Kg ch 30. ' They became a great *camp*, like a *camp of God* '. This is a superlative expression ; *cf.* Ps 35:7 ; 79:11.
23-40 David's Supporters at Hebron—23. The **h** numbers given are those of the total contingents from each tribe. That from Judah is surprisingly small and the figure for Zabulon seems to have fallen out. **27.** Joiada, 11:22 ; 27:5. He was present as representative of his tribe. **28.** Sadoc, 6:8 ; 18:16. **32.** ' men *with good judgement of the times* to know what Israel should do '. **36.** ' And of Aser forty thousand *used to war and pitched battle* '. **40.** Among the provisions were *fig-cakes* (DV ' figs ').
XIII 1-14 David's Attempt to bring the Ark to Sion— **i** **1-4. Consultation** thereupon ; not in Kg. **1.** David was now dwelling in Jerusalem, 13. **2** introduces a general assembly after the private consultation with the leaders. ' and if *the plan be* from the Lord our God, let us send *everywhere* to the rest of our brethren in all the *territories* of Israel '. The priests and Levites especially are to be summoned who ' dwell in the cities *by their pastures* '. **3.** ' for in the days of Saul *we had no (due) regard for it* '. **5-14. The abortive attempt,** 2 Kg 6:1-11. The limits of Israel are indicated by the southern and northern boundaries, the Shihor or Nile standing loosely for the former and ' the *approach to Hamath* ' in Syria for the latter. **6.** ' David went up . . . *to Baalah* to Kiriath-jearim . . . to bring thence *the Ark of God, Yahweh enthroned on the Cherubim, as his name is called* '. How the ark came there, 1 Kg 7:1. Baalah, so called after a shrine of Baal, was the older name of the city, Jos 15:9. The appellation of Yahweh, 1 Kg 4:4, Is 37:16. **7.** ' Oza and *Ahio* led the cart ', which was newly made so that nothing profane had touched it. **8.** ' before God ', the ark being the symbol of his presence, 6. **9.** ' to the *threshing-floor* . . . for the oxen stumbled ' ; the exact sense is uncertain. **10.** The **j** ark should by law have been carried on its bars, Ex 25:12-14 ; the right to touch it was allowed only to the priests, Num 4:5, and explicitly forbidden under pain of death to the Levites whose exclusive privilege it was to carry it, Num 4:15. During the troublous times of the Judges the Law was in general neglected, Jg 21:24, and so largely forgotten. David did not make the same mistake a second time, but insisted on the ark being carried by Levites, 15:2, which shows that Oza and Ahio were not Levites. Although Oza acted in good faith, the Israelites, so prone to idolatry through failure to understand the unique majesty of

4j God, had to be taught the reverence due to him and his Law. **11.** 'the Lord had *broken out* on Oza . . . to this day', *viz.* when Par's source was written. **13-14.** Obededom, a man of Gath, and not an Israelite, was blessed by God for his care of the ark. When David heard this, he took heart, 2 Kg 6:12, and brought the ark into his own city, 1 Par 15.

k **XIV 1-17 David's Palace ; his Sons ; Trouble with the Philistines**—The interval between chh 13 and 15 was three months, 13:14 ; and the events here narrated occurred partly earlier (the legation from Tyre and the building of a palace, 1, trouble with the Philistines, 8-16) and partly later (the birth of David's sons, 3-7). **1-2.** 2 Kg 5:11-12. The ambassadors will have brought congratulations on David's elevation to the throne of all Israel. According to Kg the Tyrian craftsmen actually built the palace. ' and [that the Lord] had exalted his kingdom *for the sake of* his people Israel '. **3-7. David's sons ;** see on 3:5-8. **8-16. Encounters with the Philistines.** 2 Kg 5:17-25. **12.** David took the idols away, Kg, and burnt them, Par, in accordance with Deut 7:5, 25. **13.** In the valley of Rephaim, Kg. **14.** Perhaps balsam trees. **15.** ' the sound of marching ' : suggestive of the aid from God approaching. **16.** Gabaon : Geba, Kg. **17** is not in Kg. The fear of David's power extended ' to ' all nations ' near which heard of his exploits—a case of relative universality. Here the divine name ' Yahweh ' is used. In 8-16 it is used only in 10*b* = Kg, whereas in 10*a*, 11, 14, 15, 16 ' Elohim ' is used where Kg has ' Yahweh '.

l **XV 1-24 Introduction to the Procession with the Ark** **—1.** David will have started this building soon after capturing the city from the Jebusites, 11:7 f. ; 14:1. The place for the ark will have been prepared before the first procession to bring it to Jerusalem, ch 13. It is a question why a new tabernacle was constructed instead of bringing the Mosaic tabernacle from Gibeon, where it now was, 2 Par 1:3. Possibly the priests and population there opposed the removal. **2-24. The priests and Levites ;** not in Kg. **2.** See on 13:10. David had now discovered his error. **5-7.** Caath, Merari, Gerson, 6:1. Uriel, 6:24. Asaia, 6:30. **8.** Elisaphan was also a Caathite, Ex 6:18, 22, but his clan had become independent. **9.** Hebron, also a Caathite, Ex 6:18. **10.** Oziel, another son of Caath, 6:2. Aminadab, 6:22. **11.** Sadoc of the line of Eleazar, 6:8. Abiathar of the line of Ithamar, 6:3. The Levites are those of 5-10. **12.** For various means of Levitical purification, see Ex 19:10, 15 ; 30:19 ; Lev 10:9. **13.** ' *Because on the first occasion* [ch 13] *you* (*did*) *not* (*carry the ark*), *the Lord broke out against us, because we did not show due reverence for it* '. **15** is anticipatory ; see 25. See on 13:10. **17.** See 6:33, 39, 44. **18.** ' and Ben ' : ' and son ', inserted by error, as the name does not occur in the repetition, 20, and the word is never used as a proper name. Obededom is a different person from the Gathite of 13:13. Only he and Jehiel (= Jehias, 24) were porters or gate-keepers, but they were also singers, 21. **20-21** give names repeated from 18, where that of Ozaziu has prob. fallen out. ' sung mysteries upon psalteries ' : prob. ' *with high-pitched* psalteries '. ' sung a song ' etc. : perhaps ' *with deep-toned harps to lead* (*the music*) '. **22.** ' presided . . . tunes ' : uncertain. The reference to his skill makes the suggestion improbable that he was in charge of carrying the ark, as does also the context. Prob. : he ' *was in charge of the singing* (*and*) *directed the singing* '. **24.** Trumpets were priestly instruments, Num 10:2, 8. Obededom and Jehias, 18.

m **25-XVI 3 The Procession with the Ark to the City of David**—2 Kg 6:13-19 in substance. Par omits that David learnt that the anger of God had ceased by the divine blessing given to the house of Obededom, v 12 of Kg. He left readers to infer it from 13:14. **26.** Even so after the sudden death of Oza the Levite carriers of the ark felt considerable anxiety. When they had safely traversed a short distance and felt assured of God's help, they offered a sacrifice of

thanksgiving, the victims being of the traditionally **284m** sacred number, Gen 21:29. **27.** ' Chonenias *the director of the singing* '. **29.** Par omits the sequel given 2 Kg 6:20-23, which is surprising as the punishment which befell Michol would have illustrated his doctrine of retribution. **XVI : 2.** Blessing was not an exclusively priestly function any more than it is today. **3.** ' a loaf of bread, a *date-cake and a raisin-cake* ' ; see L. Koehler TZ 4 (1948) 397 f.

XVI 4-6 Fresh Ordinances of Levitical Service— **n** Only in Par. **5.** ' . . . and Obededom and Jehiel *with instruments of psaltery* '.

7-12 The Hymn of Praise—7. ' *Then on that day at* **o** *the beginning* [of the new Levitical choral service] *David appointed* [the following hymn] *wherewith Asaph and his brethren should praise the Lord* '. **8-22. The hymn** = Ps 104:1-15. **10.** ' *Glory in* his holy name '. **13.** Isaac : Ps, Abraham. **15.** ' *He has remembered* ' ; so Ps correctly.

23-36 Later Additions to the Hymn—23-33 = Ps **p** 95:1-13, without 1*a*, 2*a*, 10*c*, 13*c*-*d*. **24.** ' Declare . . . his wonders *among all the peoples* '. **29.** ' Come ye into his sight ' : this represents the original wording. 8*b* of the Ps ' into his courts ' dates from after the building of the temple. ' adore the Lord in holy *attire* '. It was becoming to wear festal garments in public worship. **34-36** = Ps 105:1 and 47. These, the first and last verses, seem to be set down as an indication that the whole Ps was to be sung. **36** is the doxology at the end of the 4th book of Psalms. As this Ps is post-exilic (see 35) and therefore a later liturgical addition to David's ordinance, it is prob. that 22-33 is a similar addition.

37-42 Arrangement for Divine Service with the Ark **q** **and the Tabernacle**—Only in Par. **37-38. Service with the ark.** Singers and porters are appointed ; there is no mention of sacrifice. ' day . . . courses ' : ' *according to the task of each day* '. Obededom, 15:18. Hosa, 26:10 f., 16. **39-42. Service at the tabernacle at Gibeon ;** 6:32 ; 2 Par 1:3. **40.** The morning and evening sacrifices, Ex 29:38-42.

43 Conclusion of the Transference of the Ark—2 Kg **r** 6:19*b*-20*a*. David returned to *greet* his *household* ; see on Gen 47:7. The religious ceremony was no doubt followed by a domestic feast. This verse is the immediate continuation of 16:3, from which Par has separated it by the long insertion about David's cultic arrangements.

XVII 1-6 David's Desire to build a Temple is not **s** **accepted**—2 Kg 7:1-7. **5.** ' I brought up Israel ' out of Egypt. **6.** ' *Wherever I went* with all Israel, did I ever . . . '. ' Judges ' : Kg by scribal error ' tribes '. **7-15 Glorious Promises to David : his Throne to stand** **t** **for ever**—2 Kg 7:8-17. **8.** ' and *shall make . . .*, **9,** and I *shall give . . .*, **10,** and *shall humble* '. **13** omits words of 14*b*-*c* in Kg. David's royal descendants will be punished if they commit iniquity, but David's line will never be wholly cast off. The prophecy received its full explanation from the Angel Gabriel in his words concerning Jesus Christ : ' He shall reign in the house of Jacob for ever and of his kingdom there shall be no end ', Lk 1:32 f.

16-17 David's Prayer of Thanksgiving—2 Kg 7:18-29. **u** **16.** David ' sat before the Lord ' : in the tabernacle in presence of the ark, which symbolized God's presence. **17.** The last sentence represents a corrupt Heb. text. **18.** ' seeing . . . servant ' : uncertain. ' known him ' : with favour, a pregnant sense as in Ps 1:6. **22.** Yahweh was necessarily the God of Israel and of the world, but he had taken Israel under his especial protection.

XVIII 1-13 David's Successful Wars—2 Kg 8:1-14. **v** The reason for the insertion of this account at this point seems to have been that it illustrates the divine favour enjoyed by David and also explains the source of much of the wealth used in the preparation of the temple. **1.** The ' daughters ' of Gath are the villages dependent on it. Conquered kings were often left in office as vassals and Gath had a king in the time

284v of Solomon, 3 Kg 2:39 ; *cf.* 2 Par 9:26 = 3 Kg 4:21. **2.** ' gifts ' : ' *tribute* '. Par omits 2*b*–*e* of Kg. **3.** Hadarezer is a late and incorrect form of Hadadezer ' Hadad [the supreme god of Syria] (gives) help '. David defeated him ' *towards the land of Hamath* ' between which and Damascus lay the kingdom of Soba. **4.** The figures here given are supported by LXX both for Par and Kg. David ' houghed all the chariot horses *and reserved only a hundred* for himself '; *cf.* Deut 17:16 ; Jos 11:9. **6.** The kingdom of Syria, of which Damascus was capital, paid *tribute*. **7.** ' quivers ' ; uncertain ; perhaps shields. **8.** The use made by Solomon of the *bronze* is recorded by LXX also in Kg. **9.** The name of Thou's son, Hadoram, supported by LXX both here and in Kg, is prob. a corruption of Hadadram ' Hadad is exalted '. **12.** Abishai, 2:17. As he won this victory for the king, it is in Kg attributed to David. The valley, today Wady el-Milḥ, runs SW. from the Dead Sea.

w **14-17 David's Officials**—2 Kg 8:15–18 ; *cf.* 2 Kg 20:23–26. **16.** ' *Abiathar the son of Achimelech* ' ; see 1 Kg 22:20 ; 23:6 ; 30:7, where Achimelech is father of Abiathar, who appears as the peer of Sadoc in the priesthood under David, 15:11 and 2 Kg 20:25, and up till the accession of Solomon, 3 Kg 1:7–8 ; 2:26, but 3 Kg 2:35 indicates his superiority. The name of Susa, the Secretary of State, occurs in various forms : Sisa, 3 Kg 4:3 (in certain Heb. MSS these two forms would be indistinguishable) ; Siva, 2 Kg 20:25 ; in view of these the form Seraias, 2 Kg 8:17, must be a scribal error. **17.** ' and the eldest sons of David were in the King's service '. Par's source may have had that they were *kōhᵃnîm* or ' ministers ' (of the Crown) as in Kg. By the time of Par this word had only the sense of ' priests ' and would be changed to a contemporary equivalent. The etymological meaning seems to be ' seer ' and persons credited with the powers of such would tend to be used as counsellors in early times. It thus appears that the semantic development to ' minister ' in the secular sense became obsolete, and that to ' priest ' or minister in the religious sense became permanent.

x **XIX 1-19 David's Defeat of the Ammonites and their Confederates**—2 Kg 10:1–19. **3.** ' his servants are come to thee to *explore and to overthrow* and to spy out the land '. The order in Kg is more logical. **4.** Kg : ' he shaved off the one half of their beards ' ; Par, he ' shaved them ', DV adding the incorrect explanation that he shaved their ' heads and beards '. The indecent cutting short of their garments suggests that the hair was shaved off one-half of their bodies. For a similar incident, see Herod. II 121. **6.** ' the children of Ammon saw that they had *made themselves most offensive* to David '. Par adds ' a thousand talents of silver '. Mesopotamia : Aram Naharaim, prob. the land on both sides of the Euphrates where it flows nearest to the Orontes. Soba : see on 18:3. **7.** Kg gives a total of 33,000 men in agreement with the 32,000 of Par + 1,000 from Maacha (numbered in Kg but not in Par). But in Par by a textual error the number has become attached to ' chariots ', to which it cannot refer. Medaba : a city E. of the northern end of the Dead Sea. The city is not named in Kg leaving the geographical situation obscure. **16.** The general in command was named either Sophach (Par) or Sobach (Kg)—a textual error. Hadadezer : see on 18:3. **18.** Kg with more probability has 700 chariots. **19.** ' they *made peace with David* '.

y **XX 1-3 Capture of the Ammonite Capital**—2 Kg 11:1 ; 12:30–31. **1.** ' Joab . . . besieged Rabba, but David stayed at Jerusalem. And Joab smote Rabba and destroyed it '. It is strange that Par has kept the remark that David remained at Jerusalem. In his source, as in Kg, it introduced the story of David's adultery with Bethsabee. With this omitted it has no purpose ; and David was present at the final capture of Rabba, today Amman, 2 Kg 12:27 ff., though the victory was really that of Joab, his com-

mander-in-chief. **2.** Milcom, the chief god of the Ammonites, was represented by a large image capable of bearing a golden crown weighing *c* 100 lb. The name of this divinity has been erroneously vocalized in MT as *malkām* ' their king '. From this crown ' *a precious stone* ', and no doubt part of the gold were utilized to make a diadem for David. **3.** David ' *put them (to work) with saws and iron picks and axes* '. This is widely recognized to be the true meaning here and in 2 Kg 12:31. The instruments named suggest task work, not torture ; and had David been guilty of unmitigated cruelty Par would have omitted the passage as it omitted 2 Kg 8:2 and the account of David's deliberately procuring the death of Urias. For task-work, see Jos 9:21–22 ; 2 Par 2:17 f.

4-7 Exploits against the Philistines—2 Kg 21:18–22. **4.** Kg has ' at Gob ' : otherwise unknown ; a scribal error. **5.** St Jerome has translated the names : ' *Elhanan, the son of Jair*, a Bethlehemite, slew the brother of Goliath '. For the death of Goliath at the hand of David, see 1 Kg 17:49 ; 19:5 ; 21:9 ; 22:10. Textual corruption has occurred in both Par and Kg. ' the Bethlehemite ' of Kg (*bēṯ-hallaḥmî*) has become ' Lahmi ' in Par (MT) (*'eṯ-laḥmî*), thus providing a name for Goliath's brother. Vg + DV have kept the true text. And *'ᵃḥî* (Par) ' the brother of ' has become in Kg *'ēṯ* (sign of the definite object) with the result that Elhanan has been credited in this text with killing Goliath. The name of Goliath's brother was either not known or not considered worth preserving, as was the case also with the Philistine of **6-7**. He, like the other two, was of the ancient race of the Rephaim, famous for their stature.

XXI 1-XXII 1 The Census and its Punishment lead to the Choice of a Site for the Temple—2 Kg 24:1–25. Par and Kg cover the same ground but the differences, especially in language, are marked ; and the two accounts are prob. not from the same immediate source. Par may well depend on ' the book of Gad the seer ', 29:29. Par omits of Kg's matter 4*d*–7 and adds 6, 16, 26*b*–22:1. Par normally omits what is not to the honour of David but has included this account of David's census, though displeasing to God, because its sequel was the choice of the site for the temple, the building and arrangements of which occupied so prominent a place in the Chronicler's interests. The purpose of the census is indicated in 5 ; those numbered were only the fighting men. The time must have been early in David's reign over the united kingdom as the numbers were assessed separately for Judah, the kingdom over which he ruled from Hebron, and Israel, the rest of the tribes which had been under the rule of Ishbosheth. The sinfulness of the census is indicated, 3, 7, but not the ground thereof. It was known to readers that according to the conscience of Israel to number the people was to trespass on the supreme rights of God ; see Ex 30:12.

1 reflects the more developed theology of Par. In Kg it is God who stirs up David to number Israel in accordance with the broad concept that whatever happens in the world is attributable to the divine power that rules the universe. In this simple stage of theological development no explicit distinction was made between God's absolute and permissive will. The elements of the distinction were, however, already present, as God was known to be holy and to hate evil, of which he could not therefore be the true cause whether physical or moral. There is thus no contradiction but only clearer statement when Par represents David as yielding to the instigation of a created cause. Later ' Satan ' came to designate an evil spirit, Mk 3:23, and often, and it may well already have that sense here. In itself it means ' an adversary '. See also § 320*e* and Jas 1:13 f. **4.** The census took 9 months and 20 days, Kg. **5.** The figures in Kg are 800,000 and 500,000. Either set of numbers give a surprisingly high total population of about 6,000,000, and neither is likely to be correct. The textual tradition may be at fault. 7*b* is said by anticipation ; see

10-14. **23.** 'drays': '*threshing-sledges*'. **25.** Kg seems to say that the price of threshing-floor and oxen was 50 silver shekels, Par that of the site alone 600 gold shekels. The former seems unduly low, as Abraham paid 400 shekels of silver for a plot of ground with its trees and burial-place, Gen 23:16 ; the latter seems unduly high even for a royal and penitent purchaser. Barnes gives a good solution : 'The text of [2 Kg] is probably corrupt, and should perhaps run, *bought the threshing-floor for money, even six hundred shekels, and the oxen for money, even fifty shekels*'. This means that the words 'for money, even six hundred shekels' were accidentally omitted by an early copyist, and the word 'gold' would be an erroneous addition in Par. **28.** David's sacrifice : see on 2 Kg 24:25. **29-30** form a parenthesis separating 28 and 22:1. The tabernacle at Gibeon ; 16:39 f. ; 2 Par 1:3-5.

XXII 2-19 Preparations for building the Temple— 2-5. Material Preparations. 2. David first took a census, 2 Par 2:17, of the *resident aliens*, the survivors of the conquered inhabitants. **3.** The word 'brass' was used in older English to signify *copper*, which was mined in the Sinaitic peninsula ; and David obtained large supplies in his wars, 18:8. Bronze may be meant but brass was little known. **5.** Solomon was 'young and *inexperienced*'. **6-16 David's charge to Solomon. 8.** The shedding of blood as a ground for David's unsuitability to build the temple has not been previously mentioned in ch 17 or 2 Kg 7. It was not in harmony with the complete Levitical purity required in everything closely connected with the divine cult. **9.** Peace in Solomon's days, 3 Kg 4:24 ; 5:4. **12.** Solomon's gift of wisdom, 3 Kg 3:11 f. **14.** 'Timber also and stones I have prepared, and *thou shalt increase the amount*'. No ancient reader would have thought of taking literally the amount of treasure here mentioned. The hyperbolic character of the statement is more obvious in the Heb. : a hundred thousand talents of gold and a thousand thousand talents of silver. It recalls the statement that silver was as plentiful as stones in Jerusalem, 3 Kg 10:27. **17-19.** The princes are charged to assist Solomon in the work.

XXIII 1-32 The Courses and Offices of the Levites—1-2 anticipate ch 28. The mention of the Levites is the only link with what follows. **3-5 The numbers and offices of the Levites. 3.** From the age of 30 as in Num 4:3, 23. But this is perhaps a scribal error, as when more help was required this age limit had been reduced to 25, Num 8:24, and David reduced it still further to 20, 23:27. 38,000 equals the total of the numbers given in 4 f. **4.** As three were 24 courses of priests, ch 24, and 24 of the musicians, ch 25, and 24,000 Levites are here allotted to the general work of the cult, it seems clear that they too were divided into 24 courses. As the names in 6-23 do not yield this number, we may suspect some defect in the text. The Levites as judges, 26:29 and 2 Par 19:8-10. **5.** David's musical instruments, Am 6:5 ; 2 Par 29:26 ; Neh 12:35. **6-24 The distribution by courses. 7.** Leedan will have been a descendant of Gerson ; see 6:17, Ex 6:17. **8.** Again 'sons' is used in a broad sense. Zethan and Joel were sons of Jahiel, 26:21 f. **9a**, as the text stands, must be read after **9b**. **12**=6:2. **13.** It was a priestly function 'to bless *in* his [God's] name', Num 6:23-27 ; but see on 16:2. **15.** Moses' sons, Ex 18:3 f. **17.** Rohobia, 26:25. **20.** The sons of Oziel, but not of the first generation, Ex 6:22. **21.** See 6:19, 47. **25-32. Further Levitical ordinances. 25.** 'and *he dwells* now in Jerusalem for ever'. So it would no longer fall to the Levites to transport the ark. **28.** 'in the *courts* and in the chambers, and *for the purification of whatever is holy*'. **29.** The Levites had charge also (omit 'the priests') of 'the fine flour *for the meal-offering*'. **31.** Omit 'ceremonies'. **32.** 'And let them *attend to* the tabernacle of the covenant and to the sanctuary and to the sons of Aaron'.

XXIV 1-19 The Twenty-four Courses of the Priests— 1-6. Preliminary explanations. 1. 6:3. **2.** Lev 10:1 f.;

Num 3:4. **3.** Ahimelech ; see on 18:16. **6.** See on 3. 285e The priestly families were chosen by lot, '*one family of the line of Eleazar and one of the line of Ithamar*' alternately. **7-19. The heads of the twenty-four priestly courses. 7.** Names were traditional in families ; hence these names recur, 9:10. Josephus, *Life* 1, belonged to the first priestly course. **9.** A descendant of Melchia in 9:12. **10.** The course of Abia, Lk 1:5. **14.** Emmer, 9:12. **19.** '*This is the order of their coming* to the house of the Lord *for their ministry (to be performed) according to the ordinance concerning them given through* Aaron their father'.

20-31 The Heads of the Levitical Families—This list f refers to a later time than that of 23:6-24. Some of the sons of Amram were the priestly descendants of Aaron, and these have already been dealt with, 1-19. The list begins with the Caathites ; see 23:15 f. ; 6:2 f., and proceeds with the Merarites, 26-30. The Gersonites have fallen out. **21.** Rohobia, 23:17. **22.** See 23:12, 18. **23.** The text is defective. These are the sons of Hebron ; see 23:12, 19. **24.** See 23:12, 20. **26.** See 23:21. **28-29.** See 23:21 f. **30.** See 23:23.

XXV 1-31 The Twenty-four Courses of the Musicians— g **1.** The three families represented respectively, Asaph the Gersonites, 6:39-43, Heman the Caathites, 6:33, and Idithun (= Ethan), the Merarites, 6:44. That their function was to 'prophesy' to the sound of music is explained in 3 as singing the praises of God. The music and singing was in general loud and enthusiastic ; see Ps 32:3 and § 410c. **2.** 'under the *direction* of Asaph *who prophesied according to the ordinance* of the king'. **3.** Supply the missing name from 17. **4.** The form and order of the last nine names suggest, with certain changes, a prayer which Curtis translates thus : 'Be gracious unto me, Oh Yah, be gracious unto me, Thou art my God whom I magnify and exalt. Oh my help [or : Thou art my help] when in trouble, I say, He giveth [or : Give] an abundance of visions'. **5.** Heman had this numerous progeny '*according to the* h *promise of God to raise up (his) horn*'. His large family would win him great respect among the Israelites who would see in it a signal blessing of God ; See Ps 127:3. **7.** The number of those '*instructed in the songs of the Lord , each one an expert*' was 24 × 12, as enumerated 9-31. **8.** The phrase 'the expert and the pupil' is not happily chosen in this connexion. It is an example of the Hebrew idiom by which a totality is expressed by the conjunction of opposites, and does not imply against 7 that any were not expert. **9-31** gives the order in which the names of 2-4 came out by lot. It illustrates the difficulty of the accurate literary transmission of names. Although both lists occur in the same chapter, 10 differ more or less in MT including 2 cases of *scriptio plena et defectiva*, 6 in Vg, and 7 in a modern edition of DV (partly in dependence on Vg). 9, 10, 12, 14 give the courses that fell to Asaph ; 9, 11, 15, 17, 19, 21 those of Idithun, and the rest those of Heman. These highly trained singers and musicians were assisted by the 4,000 of 23:5.

XXVI 1-19 The Courses of the Porters—These were i a special section of the Levites as were the musicians ; and they will have taken their turn of office in the same way as the courses of priests. As with the other groups only the heads of families are named here. They were assisted by the 4,000 of 23:5. There were two main groups only among them, Caathites represented by the sons of Core, 6:22, and the Merarites, 10. The Gersonites had other functions, 26:21.

1. Selemia : the name occurs in various forms, j 26:14 ; 9:21 ; 9:17, 19, 31. Asaph : '*Abiasaph*' ; see 9:19, and here LXX (B). **4.** Obededom : 15:18, 24 ; 16:38 (not 13:14). **10.** Hosa : 16:38. Semri's eldest brother must have died childless 'for *though he was not the* firstborn, his father made him chief'. **12.** '*These, the courses of the gate-keepers, under their chiefs, had their charges*, as well as their brethren, *in the ministry* of the house of the Lord'. The other Levites had other functions. **15.** 'to Obededom that [the gate]

285j towards the south, *and to his sons the storehouse*'. **16.** Omit 'Sephim' (dittography). 'To Hosa (the gate) towards the west *together with the gate of Shalleketh* [otherwise unknown] *by the rising causeway*'. This may reflect a time later than David's. The temple-hill was on a higher level than the ground to S. and W. The remains of two causeways have been discovered on the W. named Wilson's Arch and Robinson's Arch. **17.** ' towards the east were six (*guards*) *a day* . . . and *for the storehouse* two and two ' : two for each entrance, unless it is meant that there were two storehouses. **18.** '*For the Parbar on the west, four for the causeway, two for the Parbar*'. The nature of the Parbar is uncertain, the name being derived from a Persian word denoting some structure admitting light, perhaps colonnade.

k 20-32 Other Functions of the Levites—20-28. Guardianship of the treasuries. 20. '*And the Levites, their brethren, were over the treasuries* of the house of God and the treasuries of the sacred offerings'. They had charge both of the valuable properties required for divine worship, 9:26-29, and over what the faithful had dedicated to the sanctuary, 26:26-28. **21-22.** ' The sons of Ledan, *the Gersonites* [6:1] : of Ledan were heads of families ; of Ledan *the Gersonite* : Jehieli'. See 23:7 f. with note. **23.** See 6:2. The text is incomplete. Those in 24-25 are Amramites ; the Isaarites and Hebronites are mentioned 29-31, but the Ozielites are omitted. **24-25.** See 23:14-17. Isaias = Jesias, 24:21. **28.** There was a treasury attached to the tabernacle already in the time of Josue, Jos 6:24. **29-32. Secular functions. 29.** These Isaarites were employed in the capacity of civil servants ' as officials and judges'. **31.** Jeria : 23:19 ; 24:23. ' An enquiry was made' by David concerning these Hebronites with favourable results. Jazer : 6:81 ; Jos 21:37.

l XXVII 1-15 The Captains of the Army—The list dates at least in part from an early period of David's reign ; see on 7. Nearly all the commanders were heroes of David's early days, ch 11. **1.** ' who came on duty and went off duty month by month, every month of the year, each company of 24,000'. **2.** 11:11. **3.** He owed his position in part to his descent from Judah through Phares, 2:4. **4.** ' Eleazar, the son of Dodai ' ; see on 11-12. For 'after him . . . the army' read ' under him were '. **5-6.** 11:22-25. See on 11:25 the explanation why his son was commander in his stead. **7.** Asael, 11:26, was killed while David was still at Hebron, 2 Kg 2:18-23, and was succeeded by his son. **8.** 11:27. **9.** 11:28. **10.** See on 11:27 ; also 2 Kg 23:26. **11.** 11:29. **12.** Abiezer was *a Benjaminite* from Anathoth. **13.** 11:30. **14.** 11:31. **15.** Holdai, 11:30, was a descendant of *Othoniel*, 4:13.

m 16-22 The Chiefs of the Tribes—The text is incomplete, Gad and Asher being wanting. **18.** David's eldest brother was Eliab, 2:13 ; 1 Kg 16:6 ; 17:13, 28. **21.** Abner, prob. the celebrated commander of the army.

n 23-24 A Fragment on the Census—This seems to take up the reference to a census in 1. **23.** The census being a measure of preparation in case of war, according to Num 1:3 David *did not* number those under the conscript age of 20. The point of the reference to the prophecy of Gen 22:17 may have been clear in Par's source. It cannot give the reason for the omission to count the younger members of the community, as this is sufficiently explained by Num 1.3 ; and if it was a valid reason for the young, it would be equally so for all. In the original context it prob. gave a reason for the census as a whole, not to test but to illustrate the fulfilment of the divine promise. **24.** Joab was opposed to the census from the beginning, 21:3. He reported the result to the king, 21:5, but when David realized his error, he forbade it to be entered in the official chronicle.

o 25-31 The Stewards over David's Property—25. Azmoth was over the treasury in the capital, Jonathan over those *in the countryside*, in the other cities, villages and *towers*. These last, 2 Par 26:10, were for the use

of those guarding the herds. **27.** Semeias was from Rama, 3 Kg 15:17. **28.** Baalhanan was over the oliveyards and *sycomore-trees*, which bear fruit and are allied to the fig. He was from Gedera, Jos 15:36. **31.** For the Hagrites, see on 5:10.

32-34 David's Ministers—The only officials in common with the earlier list in 18:15-17 are Joab and Abiathar. **32.** David had also a nephew named Jonathan, 20:7. The uncle and Jahiel, son of Hachamoni, 11:11, were guardians of the king's numerous sons, 3:1-9. **33.** ' The king's friend ' seems to have been an official title. **34.** Achitophel killed himself in Absalom's rebellion, 2 Kg 17:23. He was replaced by Joiada, the son of Banaias. Joiada named his own son Banaias after the boy's grandfather, 18:17. It is possible, however, that the names have been here accidentally inverted.

XXVIII 1-XXIX 20 David in Solemn Assembly proclaims Solomon King—The Chronicler's interest in the temple has led him to give such prominence to the plans for its construction as rather to obscure the main purpose of the assembly which was to proclaim Solomon as David's successor. The assembly has been already introduced, 23:1 f. The enumeration of those summoned led to the long digression, 23:3-27:34, with its lists of the important persons belonging to the various classes. **1** gives a further list of those summoned with the omission of the leading priests and Levites already mentioned in 23:2. **2-10. First part of David's speech.** This is in substance a repetition of 22:7-16, a passage which belongs to this assembly. **2.** For David's desire to build a temple and God's refusal, see ch 17. Omit ' all things '. **4.** The choice of Judah, Gen 49:8-10 ; the choice of David's house, 1 Kg 16:1 ; of David, 1 Kg 16:13. **9.** ' Know God ' in the pregnant sense of knowing with veneration and love ; cf. Ps 1:6. **11-19. A digression on plans for the temple. 11.** The house for the mercy-seat is the Holy of Holies. **14.** For gold objects the pattern was given by weight of gold, for silver objects by weight of silver. **16.** 3 Kg 7:48 mentions only one table of shew-bread, but Solomon made 10, 2 Par 4:8, 19, though the others will have been used, *e.g.* as stands for lights. **17.** ' censers ' : ' beakers ' ; cf. Num 4:7. ' little lions ' (*kᵉpîrê*) : ' basins ' (*kᵉpôrê*). **18.** God is poetically spoken of as riding on the cherubim, Ps 17:11 ; 98:1. **19.** ' Everything he explained in writing, according to the guidance of the Lord, all the works of the pattern'. This does not mean that David received revelations about all the details, but that he worked them out under the guiding Providence of God. **20-XXIX : 5. Continuation of David's address. 20** repeats the exhortation of 10, where the speech was interrupted. **29:1.** Solomon was yet ' young and inexperienced' (repeated from 22:5). **2.** ' onyx stones with (their) settings, carbuncles [? ; reading *nōpek*] and stones of variegated colour . . . and alabaster in abundance'. **4.** The mention here of gold of Ophir, prob. in southern Arabia, is not an anachronism. The expeditions which Solomon sent to obtain gold from there, 2 Par 8:18 ; 9:10, show that Ophir was already known as an important source of supply, and David will have obtained his gold from intermediaries. Three thousand talents of gold would exceed 300,000 lb. in weight. The walls of the temple are recorded to have been overlaid with gold, 2 Par 3:4 f., but overlaying with silver is mentioned only here. It may be that Solomon found his supply of gold to be ample and used only the more precious metal for the purpose. **6-9. Offerings for the Temple. 7.** ' solids ' ; in MT '*ᵃdarkōnîm*, by some identified with the Persian daric, a coin first struck by Darius I, 521-486, but a coin called the *dariku* occurs already in an inscription of Nabonidus, the last Babylonian king, 555-539 (W. Muss-Arnolt, *A Concise Dict. of the Assyrian Language, s.v.*). Others connect the word with the Greek drachma. Whatever its derivation, it is used here to denote the smaller offerings. Note that the numbers are all round ; the precise figures were unknown. **8.** The precious stones were confided directly to Jehiel, who was in charge of the sacred treasury, 26:21 f. **10-19. David's beautiful prayer. 11.** 'Thine is . . . glory and *splendour*'. **15.** Men on earth are like strangers sojourning in a foreign land only for a short time. **17.** God loves *uprightness* and David makes his offering in the *uprightness* of his heart. **20-22a. Sacrifices and a sacrificial banquet.** In addition to holocausts they sacrificed also peace-offerings of which the offerers partook in a sacred meal, Lev 7:11-16. These were offered in such abundance as to suffice for all the Israelites present. **22b-25. The inauguration of Solomon's reign.** The turbulent background to this peaceful scene is given in 3 Kg 1. **22b.** 'They *made* Solomon *king*', not 'the second time' (wanting in LXX [B]) as added by a glossator with an eye on the anticipatory statement of 23:1. It was Sadoc who anointed Solomon, 3 Kg 1:39, and when the new sovereign banished Abiathar, 3 Kg 2:27, Sadoc remained as high-priest, *ib.* 35. **26-30. The Death of David. 27** is less exact than 3:4, omitting the six odd months of David's reign in Hebron. **28** with its mention of Solomon's reign shows that this section and the preceding are from different sources. **29** offers another example of totality being expressed by the conjunction of opposites, 'the first and last acts of David' signifying all his history. On the three titles applied to the writers referred to see § 409*f.* The Chronicler did not wish to set down all he knew about David but he had no desire to conceal other facts, including the less honourable, and he tells his readers where they can find them. These writings are unfortunately lost. All three were personally acquainted with David, Samuel, 1 Kg 16:13, Nathan, 1 Par 17:2, Gad, 21:9.

THE SECOND BOOK OF PARALIPOMENON

I 1-IX 31 The Reign of Solomon—3 Kg 2:12-11:43. **I 1-6 Solomon's Sacrifices at Gibeon**—3 Kg 3:4. The ark of the covenant was now in the city of David, 1 Par ch 15, but the tabernacle, which had housed it from the time of Moses till its capture and return by the Philistines, 1 Kg 7:2, together with the altar of holocausts was at Gibeon. They had previously been at Nob till Saul massacred the priests there, 1 Kg 21:1 ff. ; 22:19. David had appointed Sadoc and his brethren priests at Gibeon, 1 Par 16:39 f. Through their ministry Solomon offered his numerous holocausts in thanksgiving for his elevation to the throne. **7-13 Solomon's Vision at Gibeon**—3 Kg 3:5-15. Par omits the conditional promise of length of days, 3 Kg 3:14, perhaps because Solomon fell away and did not fulfil the condition, 3 Kg 11:4. **13.** Read '*from before the tabernacle of the covenant*' which was at Gibeon. **14-17 Solomon's Military Power and Wealth** — 3 Kg 10:26-29. **15.** Gold is not mentioned in Kg. **17.** Omit 'of four horses'. 'And in this manner *they were instrumental in exporting to all the kings of the Hittites and of Syria*'. Solomon's wealth was greatly increased by this trade in horses and chariots. **II 1-18 Preparations for the Temple ; Hiram's Promise of Help ; Forced Labour—1.** The completion of Solomon's own palace is mentioned in 7:11. **2** is repeated but more fully in 17 f. **3-16. Negotiations with Hiram.** 3 Kg 5:1-14. **5.** The exaltation of Yahweh above all gods would not be diplomatic in an appeal for help to a pagan king and suggests that the Chronicler did not have the actual wording of Solomon's missive ; so also Rehm. **8.** ' pine trees ' : algum trees, in 1 Kg 10:11 (AV) called almug ; by some thought to be sandal wood, which does not grow on Lebanon. The mercantile Phoenicians, however, may well have traded in it. T. K. Cheyne suggested a species of cypress, ET 9 (1897/98) 470-3. **10.** Solomon offered pay for Hiram's workmen and it was at the latter's request that he sent supplies of food, 3 Kg 5:6,

9, 11. Par for brevity combines two of Solomon's **286d** letters into one. He offered 20,000 *baths* of wine and the same number of oil. For the cor and the bath, see § 82*k.* Kg mentions only 20 cors of fine oil according to MT and Vg, but the LXX gives the same measure as Par. **13.** The craftsman's true name **e** seems to have been Hiramabi or Huramabi. See 4:16 where it is deformed to 'Hiram his father'. 'my father' here is a translation of the second element of the name. It is not against this that his name is elsewhere abbreviated as in 4:11. **14.** He was Hebrew on his mother's side. She was of the tribe of Dan, Par here, a widow of the tribe of Nephtali, 3 Kg 7:13 f. That is, born into the tribe of Dan, she married into that of Nephtali, and after her husband's death married a Tyrian. **17-18. The labour gangs.** 3 Kg 5:15-16. **17.** Solomon took a census of all the *non-Hebrews resident* in Israel, that is the remnants of the conquered inhabitants, whom his father had already numbered, 1 Par 22:2. As the total equals the sum of the separate gangs spoken of in **18**, it is evidently that of the able-bodied only. Kg in MT + Vg, prob. through the accidental addition of one letter, has 3,300 overseers, but LXX(B) in agreement with Par has 3,600. If the 30,000 sent by Solomon to help on Lebanon are added to the 150,000 mentioned here, we have the proportion of 180,000 workmen to 3,600 overseers, that is 1 to every 50.

III 1-17 Measurements and Adornments of the Temple f —1. Mount Moriah was the scene of Abraham's sacrifice of Isaac ; see on Gen 22:2. The threshing-floor of Ornan, 1 Par 21:15 ff. **2-4. Time and Measurements.** 3 Kg 6:1-3. **2.** On the relation of months to regnal years, see § 124*h.* **3.** The length of the sanctuary (Holy Place and Holy of Holies) was 60 cubits *by the ancient measure*, cubits, that is, of 7 handbreadths ; see § 82*c.* **4.** The porch or vestibule was 10 cubits deep, Kg, and 20 cubits, the same as the Holy Place behind it, in width. This width is here called its 'length' as being its longer measure. **5-7. The Holy Place.** 3 Kg 6:15-18. **5.** The Holy Place is 'the greater house' as being 40 cubits long, whereas the Holy of Holies was 20. **6.** The floor was made of planks of fir, overlaid with gold, 3 Kg 6:15, 30, and is not mentioned here. '*He ornamented the house with precious stones*'. In many respects Par and Kg mutually supplement each other. **7.** The gold was 'of the finest' : '*of Parwayim*', perhaps from Parwa in the Yemen. **8. The Holy of Holies.** 3 Kg 6:19-20. **g** Par adds the weight of gold used. **9.** Prob. only the heads of the nails, 3 Kg 6:21, were covered with gold. 50 shekels = c 20 oz. The upper chambers, 3 Kg 6:10. **10-13. The cherubim.** 3 Kg 6:23-28. **13.** They faced towards the Holy Place. **14.** The veil, not mentioned in Kg, will have been hung against the partition separating the Holy Place from the Holy of Holies, 3 Kg 6:16. The material was *fine linen*. **15-17. The two pillars.** 3 Kg 7:15-22. Hiram made the pillars, Kg ; here the work is attributed to Solomon who had commissioned it. They were 18 cubits high, Kg, Jer 52:21 ; and so Syr here also. **16.** 'He made also *garlands in a chain*' surrounding each pillar (*rābîd* misread as *d^ebîr*). **IV 1-22 Other Appurtenances of the Temple—1 h** supplies the dimensions of the bronze altar, mentioned 3 Kg 8:64. The height of the altar implies an approach to it by steps. This deviation from the prescription of Ex 20:26 may be explained by a change in the form of the dress worn. **2-5. The molten sea.** 3 Kg 7:23-26. **3.** The word 'oxen' here is a slip due to the oxen, 4, on which the sea rested. What are here described are knops or gourd-shaped ornaments under the brim, Kg, '*compassing it, ten to a cubit, surrounding the sea, the knops being in two rows, cast together with the sea*'. **5.** The divergence as to its capacity, here 3,000 baths, in Kg 2,000, is prob. to be explained by the accidental omission of ' three ' in Kg, the Heb. consonants for ' thousands ' and ' two thousand ' being the same. **6.** 3 Kg 7:38 f.

286h Par adds the purpose of the lavers (' to wash in them ; *what appertained to the holocaust they rinsed in them* ') and of the sea. **7.** Ex 25:31–40 speaks of one ' candlestick '

i only. 3 Kg 7:49 has ten, as here. **9.** ' a great hall ' : ' *the great court* ' outside the court of the priests. **10.** The position of the sea, 3 Kg 7:39, was at the NE. of the sanctuary. **11-22.** 3 Kg 7:40–51. **11.** ' flesh-hooks ' : ' *shovels* ' ; also in 16 ; where ' Hiram his father ' = Hiramabi ; see on 2:13. ' finest brass ' : ' *polished bronze* '. **17.** ' in a clay ground ' : some emend to ' at the ford of Adamah '. Par puts the place between Succoth and Zereda, Kg between the former and Zarethan, the similarity showing that there is a clerical error. **19.** 2 Par 13:11 and 29:18 speak of only one table of shew-bread. One of the ten, 8, therefore was for this purpose ; the others perhaps supported the golden and silver, 1 Par 28:15, candlesticks. The parallel passage, 3 Kg 7:48, has one table of shew-bread only. **20.** A light was to burn before the Holy of Holies according to the *ordinance* of Ex 27:20 f. **22.** ' *And the snuffers and the bowls and the censers and the fire-pans*, of pure gold '.

j V **1-14 Transference of the Ark to the Temple—1.** 3 Kg 7:51. ' David . . . had *dedicated* '. **2-11a.** 3 Kg 8:1–10a. **3.** ' The solemn day ' was the Feast of Tabernacles, § 113j. **4.** The priests, Kg, and the Levites, Par, both had their share in the work. It was the duty of the former to wrap up the ark and then for the latter to carry it, Num 4:5, 15 ; and see on 7. **5.** They brought the ark ' *together with the tabernacle and all its holy furniture ; the priests and the Levites brought them up* ' from the lower-lying city of David. **7.** The Levites could not enter the Holy of Holies, and therefore the priests carried the ark on this last stage of its journey. 11b–13g is not in Kg. **11.** ' all the priests present *had purified themselves ; the courses were not observed* ' that day, as all the priests were expected to take part in the great ceremonial. **13h-14.** Kg 10b–11. This is an anticipation of 7:1 f.

k VI **1-42 Solomon's Address and Prayer at the Dedication of the Temple—1-11. The address.** 3 Kg 8:12–21. **5f-6b.** Not in Kg but clearly part of the common source. **12-42. The prayer.** 3 Kg 8:22–50a. **13.** Solomon had had a ' *bronze stand* ' made ' in the midst of the *court* ' ; not in Kg which, however, mentions that he prayed kneeling, 8:54. **20.** ' where thou hast promised *to set thy name* ', which practically means to manifest thy presence. **21.** Solomon prayed turned ' *towards* it ' (the sanctuary), that whosoever should pray ' *towards* this place ' should be heard in heaven. So also in 26, 29, 32. This applied whether the suppliant was in the temple precincts or even in a distant country ; see Ps 5:8 ; 137:2 ; Dan 6:10. **22.** ' If any man sins against his neighbour, *who takes an oath upon himself and gives occasion to* (the *offender*) *to do likewise and he does take an oath upon himself before thy* altar in this house, **23**, then do thou hear from heaven '. If an oath of accusation is met by an oath of denial, God Almighty is begged to judge between the two parties. **24.** Omit ' and do penance ' ; also in 37. The case contemplates the defeat of Israel ' *by reason of their sinning* ' against God. **40-42**, which are not in Kg, closely resemble Ps 131:8–10 in 41–42. If, as seems to be the case, the psalm celebrates David's transference of the ark to Sion, the borrowing is on the part of Par. **40.** ' *Now, O my God, let thy eyes* ' etc. **42.** To turn away the face of a suppliant is to reject his petition, 3 Kg 2:16. Solomon prays that God will remember the *favours* he showered on David and treat his posterity with the same love.

l VII **1-22 God's Sign of Acceptance of the Temple ; Other Details ; God's Assurance to Solomon—1-3. Fire from heaven and a cloud filling the temple.** Not in Kg except 1a = 3 Kg 8:54a ; but see on 5:13 f. **1.** The same miracle occurred after Aaron's consecration and sacrifices, Lev 9:24. **2.** Similarly at the dedication of the tabernacle, Ex 40:32 f. **3** quotes the words of the antiphon chanted by the people which occurs in Ps 135:1 and elsewhere. **4-7. The sacrifices.**

3 Kg 8:62–64. Rawlinson points out on 3 Kg 8:63 that ' profusion was a usual feature of the sacrifices of antiquity. Three hundred oxen formed a common sacrifice at Athens. Five hundred kids were offered annually at the Marathonia. (Böckh's *Athens* I 283, E.T.) Sacrifices of a thousand oxen were not infrequent. According to an Arabian historian (Kotibeddyn) the Caliph Moktader sacrificed during his pilgrimage to Mecca in the year of the Hegira 350, 40,000 camels and cows, and 50,000 sheep. Tavernier speaks of 100,000 victims as offered by the King of Tonquin. (See Milman's ' Gibbon ', IV 96, note) '. **6,** not in Kg, repeats part of the antiphon from 3. Trumpets : see on 1 Par 15:24. **7.** ' the sacrifices ' : ' *the meal-offering* ' ; see § 183d. **8-11. The Feast of Tabernacles ; conclusion.** 3 Kg 8:65–66. **8.** ' the solemnity ' : the Feast of Tabernacles was distinguished by being called simply ' the feast '. For ' *the approach to Hamath* ', see on 1 Par 13:5. **9.** On the solemn assembly following the feast, see § 113j. ' Because ' begins a new sentence. Because the dedication had lasted 7 days and the feast 7 days, followed by the solemn assembly on the 8th day, the people could be dismissed, 10, on the 23rd. The feast began on the 15th. **11.** Solomon *successfully accomplished* all that he had designed ' to do. **12-22. God's assurance to Solomon.** 3 Kg 9:1–9. **13-15.** Not in Kg. **14.** To ' seek out God's *presence* ' is to visit the temple. **17.** ' *my statutes and my ordinances* '. **21.** ' This house shall *become a ruin* ; all that pass by shall be *awestruck* ' ; *cf.* Syr.

VIII **1-18 Various Activities of Solomon's—1-6. Building operations.** See 3 Kg 9:10–19. **1.** The time indicated is ' at the end of *the* twenty years *in which* Solomon had built ' the temple and his palace. **2.** Hiram gave these cities *back* to Solomon. For the prehistory of this event, see 3 Kg 9:11–13. Hiram had been disappointed with the cities. **3.** For Hamath and Soba, see on 1 Par 18:3. **4.** In the region of Hamath he built *store-cities*. **7-10. Labour gangs.** 3 Kg 9:20–23. **8.** He ' *raised a levy for forced labour* '. **10.** ' *And these* [the officers of 9] *were Solomon's chief overseers* ' of his labour gangs. The subordinate overseers were chosen from among the non-Israelites forced to work. In number they were 250, Par, 550, Kg. The discrepancy may be due to a copyist's error or to a difference in the basis of the computation. **11. Pharaoh's daughter.** *Cf.* 3 Kg 9:24. It was not merely because she was a foreigner that she could not live in the royal palace : ' *No wife of mine* shall dwell. . . .' Par presupposes the reader's knowledge of the marriage, 3 Kg 3:1 ; 7:8. 11b is not in Kg. **12-16. Solomon's care for the cult.** 3 Kg 9:25. **13.** On these feasts, see § 113a-j. **14.** He maintained David's arrangements : ' the courses of the priests ', 1 Par 24 ; ' the Levites in their *charges* ', 1 Par 25:1–6 ; 26:20–28 ; the porters, 1 Par 26:1–19. **16.** ' *Thus all Solomon's work was accomplished . . . he finished it. The house of the Lord was completed* '. **17-18. Expedition to Ophir.** 3 Kg 9:26–28. Solomon went to Ezion-geber to supervise the construction of his ships there, Kg. In this work he was no doubt assisted by Hiram, who sent his experienced seafaring men with Solomon's in these ships, Kg. The text of Par has been understood by many, as in DV, to state that Hiram sent Solomon ships for the expedition, which could only be explained if the Phoenicians already had in the Persian gulf the trading stations mentioned by Strabo, 16, 3, 4 (ed. I. Casaubon, 1587, 527). But it is more likely that the text says that Hiram sent ships not ' to him ' but ' for him ' : ' and Hiram *assisted by sending ships* [those built by Solomon at Ezion-geber] *manned by his men, men familiar with seafaring* '. Hiram's men were helped by Solomon's, who were only novices in the art of navigation. The amount of gold obtained was 450 talents, MT, 400, Syr, 420 Kg, MT, 120, Kg, LXX(B). The last figure is the most probable.

IX **1-31 Solomon's Wisdom and Wealth ; his Death —1-9 and 12. The Visit of the Queen of Sheba.**

o 3 Kg 10:1-10 and 13. **4.** Literally, she was ' out of breath ' with astonishment. **5.** There is no mention of Solomon's virtues : ' thy *accomplishments* and wisdom '. **9.** Josephus, *Ant.* 8, 6, 6, states that she gave 20 talents of gold, which prob. preserves the true reading. **12.** Solomon showed his munificence by giving her all that she asked ' *without any regard to (the value of) what she had brought to him* '.

p **10-11 ; 13-28 Solomon's Wealth and Glory**—3 Kg 10:11-12 ; 14-26. **15.** ' spears ' : ' *bucklers* ', shields to cover the body, larger than those of **16**, where omit ' the covering of '. They were put in ' *the house of the forest of Lebanon* '. **21.** The destination of this expedition cannot have been Tarshish (Tartessus) in Spain both because of the products acquired and because in the similar passage, 20:36-37, the vessels were constructed at Ezion-geber at the head of the Gulf of Aqaba on the E. side of the Sinaitic peninsula. These were damaged (in a storm) and ' could not go to Tarshish '. Moreover, in the parallel passage in 3 Kg 22:49 these ships were destined for Ophir, prob. on the S. coast of Arabia or the E. coast of Africa. It therefore appears that the Phoenicians will have given the name Tarshish to some distant trading-place perhaps on the Persian Gulf. There Strabo (see on 8:17-18) reports the existence of such stations adding that the Phoenicians gave their familiar names to new localities. **25.** ' Solomon had *4,000 stalls for horses and chariots* '. So MT, which agrees in form with 3 Kg 4:26 (MT 5:6), where, however, the number is erroneously 40,000. LXX(B) here has ' 4,000 horses for chariots '. And see 2 Par 1:14. **26** = 3 Kg 4:21*a*. **27** repeats 2 Par 1:15. **28** repeats in part 2 Par 1:16. For the other countries, see 14, 23 f. **29-31. Conclusion on Solomon.** 3 Kg 11:41-43, which as source names only Solomon's chronicles. Nathan, 1 Par 17:1 ; Ahias, 2 Par 10:15 ; Addo, 12:15, who wrote *concerning* Jeroboam.

q **X 1-XXXVI 21 The History of Judah from Roboam to the Fall of Jerusalem.**
X I-XII 16 Roboam 931-913.
X I-19 Secession of the Northern Tribes—3 Kg 12:1-20. **10.** Omit ' in pleasure '. **15** supposes knowledge of the event described in 3 Kg 11:26-40. **16.** The king is spoken of as a shepherd who ' feeds ' or pastures his flock. **18.** Adoniram (so LXX[B] and Syr ; and see 3 Kg 4:6) was over *the forced labour*.

r **XI 1-4 War against the Northern Tribes forbidden**—3 Kg 12:21-24.
5-12 Fortifications—Not in Kg. Following close upon the threat of war with the newly established Northern Kingdom this account might suggest that the fortifications were a defence measure against that state. But the cities best situated for that purpose as those in the northerly lying Benjamin are not named. The position of the towns fortified in the south and west shows that they were directed against a threat from Egypt. The account thus prepares for the invasion of the Pharaoh in ch 12 and underlines the lesson that no human efforts can avert punishment designed by God, 12:5. **10.** As no towns in Benjamin are listed, the expression ' Judah and Benjamin ' designates the Southern Kingdom. **11.** Roboam arranged for ' *stores* of provisions, oil and wine ' against possible siege.

s **13-17 Refugees from the Northern Kingdom**—**13.** Not in Kg. The Levites were living scattered throughout Israel in the cities assigned to them according to the law, Num 35:2-8 ; Jos ch 21. **14.** They left their *pastures* and possessions. Jeroboam's high places and calf-worship, 3 Kg 12:26-31. **15.** ' devils ' : lit. ' he-goats ', a contemptuous appellation based on mythology. Jeroboam himself introduced an illegitimate cult of Yahweh under the image of calves, Ex 20:4, but under his ' sons ', 14, or successors the cult became debased to idolatry.

t **18-23 Roboam's Family**—Not in Kg. **18.** Jeromoth : otherwise unknown, prob. the son of a secondary wife.

Abihail, introduced without adequate connexion, was **286t** prob. the mother of Mahalath and daughter of Eliab, 1 Par 2:13, in the first generation. **19.** ' *she* bore him sons ', MT, LXX, namely Mahalath. **20.** Maacha will have been the grand-daughter of Absalom, whose only daughter was Thamar, 2 Kg 14:27. **22.** As Abia was not the eldest, who was prob. Jehus, this preference of him was against Deut 21:15-17. **23.** ' *He prudently dispersed some of his sons in all the territories of Judah . . . and he took wives for them* '. His motives will have been further to guard against the threat of invasion and to diminish the possibility of the brothers taking action against the elevation of Abia.

XII 1-12 The Invasion of Sheshenk—3 Kg 14:25-28. **u** Sheshenk I, *c* 945-*c* 924, founded the XXII (Bubastite) dynasty. He has left a record of this Palestinian expedition on the walls of Karnak. **1.** The name ' Israel ' is used of the Southern Kingdom alone. The details of the idolatry are given 3 Kg 14:22-24. **3.** Troglodites : so LXX ; MT Sukkiyim, not mentioned elsewhere. **5.** Semeias, 11:2. **6.** The princes and the king *humbled themselves*. **7.** ' I will *soon grant them deliverance* '. As the wrath of God was not poured out on Jerusalem, the city was not captured by storm ; and, **8**, the treasure carried away by the Pharaoh will have been voluntarily surrendered to save the city. Solomon's golden shields, 9:15 f.

13-16 Conclusion—3 Kg 14:21-22, 29-31. **13** repeats **v** from another source the strengthening of the king's position, 1, and does not refer to the time after Sheshenk's invasion. **15.** ' and diligently recorded ' : perhaps ' *concerning genealogies* ' was the title of the book taken from its opening phrase (Barnes).

XIII 1-XIV 1*a* Abia (Abiam) 913-911/910. **w**
XXX 1-2*a* Introductory—3 Kg 15:1 f. **1.** This is the only case in which Par indicates a synchronism between the two kingdoms, prob. as leading up to the war with Jeroboam, 2*b*. That Roboam reigned 17 years and yet his son succeeded to the throne in the 18th year of Jeroboam, although the two kingdoms both began after the death of Solomon, is explained by the different systems of calculating regnal years followed in the two. Roboam's 1st regnal year began Tishri 930, his first post-accession year ; Jeroboam's 1st year was reckoned from Nisan 931, which was his accession year. See § 124*h-j*. **2.** For the explanation of the 3 years, see § 124*g*. Michaia is a deformation of Maacha, 11:20, whose father was Uriel and whose grandfather was Absalom, 11:20. Her mother will have been Thamar, 2 Kg 14:27, and she herself received the name of her great-grandmother, 2 Kg 3:3.

2*b*-20 War with Jeroboam—3 Kg 15:7*c*. **3.** When **x** Abia *began the war*, he had a fighting force of 400,000 and Jeroboam of 800,000, the numbers being about those of David's census, 2 Kg 24:9. **4.** It need not be supposed that Par had an exact record of Abia's speech. After the manner of ancient historians like Thucydides he will have set down the substance of what the occasion demanded. **5.** Salt being incorruptible, ' a covenant of salt ' is a perpetual covenant, Num 18:19. **7.** To call the adherents of Jeroboam ' *irresponsible and worthless men* ' is special pleading in view of the account in ch 10. Roboam was inexperienced, lit. ' a youth ', much as we sometimes speak of a grown man as a child. He was 41 years old at his accession, 12:13. **9.** See 11:13-15. **11.** ' *sweet-smelling* incense '. **14.** For the priests with their trumpets in war, see Num 10:8 f. **19.** The ' daughters ' are the dependencies of these towns. **20.** The circumstances of Jeroboam's death are unknown.

21-XIV 1*a* Conclusion—3 Kg 15:7-8. **22.** For **y** further information about Abia Par refers to ' the *Midrash* of Addo the prophet ' (omit ' diligently '). A Midrash is an enquiry or study, and so a commentary. Centuries later the rabbinic commentaries treated their material with great freedom and the word took on a corresponding shade of meaning, but

286y there is no ground for reading that meaning back into earlier centuries. Par omits an animadversion on Abia's sins such as is given 3 Kg 15:3, but indications that 'his heart was not perfect with the Lord' are not wanting. His son Asa had to abolish the idolatrous altars, 14:2, and the false worship of Maacha is mentioned in 15:16. But Abia did not wholly abandon the worship of Yahweh. On the contrary, he made offerings to the temple, 3 Kg 15:15.

z **XIV 1b–XVI 14 Asa** 911/910–870/869.
XIV 1b–5 Religious Reform—3 Kg 15:11 f. **1b.** The 10 years of peace are generally understood to be the opening years of the reign before the invasion of Zara. The war waged with Baasa all their days, 3 Kg 15:16, 32, must have been intermittent. **3.** On the *maṣṣēbôṭ* and the *'aṣērîm*, see on Deut 7:5. **5.** 'temples': perhaps *sun-pillars* erected in honour of Baal as the solar deity, or *incense-stands*.

aa **6–8 Military Preparations**—3 Kg 15:23 ; Jer 41:9. **6.** There were no wars *in those years*. **8.** These are the numbers of fighting men who could be called on, not the numbers of a standing army.

bb **9–15 The Invasion of Zara**—Not in Kg. Zara has been identified with Osorkon I of Egypt, but he is called a Kushite, which normally means an Ethiopian, and the XXII dynasty, to which Osorkon belonged, was Libyan (Champollion ; accepted by H. R. Hall, *The Ancient History of the Near East* [1950¹¹] 439). Goettsberger thinks he was a general in command of auxiliary Egyptian troops. F. Hommel, ET 8 (1896/7) 378, considers Zara to be a Kushite of Central Arabia. The narrative suggests an invading horde of would-be settlers in the Fertile Crescent rather than an organized army. LXX(B) gives his host as ' thousands with 300 chariots ', which may be correct. **10.** Asa set his army in array ' in the vale to the north of Mareshah ', LXX. No valley of Sephata is known. **13.** Gerar : modern Umm Jerar, S. of Gaza. **14.** Asa took advantage of the alarm aroused by his complete rout of Zara to attack the Philistines.

cc **XV 1–7 Warning of the Prophet Azarias**—Not in Kg. **1.** Azarias is otherwise unknown. **2.** The occasion was the return of Asa from the defeat of Zara. **3–6** should have past tenses, the reference being to the lawless period of the Judges ; see Jg 2:10–20. It was a time of repeated cycles of idolatry, affliction, repentance and forgiveness. In **5–6** the reference is to the tribes and cities of Israel. The war against Benjamin, Jg chh 20 f. ; the destruction of Shechem, Jg 9:45.

dd **8–18 Religious Reform**—**8.** See 3 Kg 15:12. The reform in 14:2–5 is an anticipatory mention of that recorded here but from another source. Here too the statement that he removed the idols (lit. abominations) out of the cities of Ephraim he had taken (see 17:2) seems to be an anticipation as till now Asa seems to have had no war with the Northern Kingdom. He also *renovated* the altar before the vestibule of the sanctuary. **12.** 'And *they entered into a* covenant to seek the Lord'. A similar renewal under Ezechias, 29:10, and Josias 34:31. **15.** ' *All Judah rejoiced at the oath* '. **16–18.** 3 Kg 15:13–15. **16.** Maacha was Asa's grandmother, 11:20. Alternatively Maacha was also the name of Asa's mother. ' She had made *a disgraceful thing in honour of Asherah* ', the Canaanite goddess. **17.** These high places were not for idolatrous cults but for the illegitimate worship of Yahweh. **18.** Abia had prob. made these offerings at such illegal high places. **19 Reward for Fidelity**—This period of peace was a reward for the return to true religion, 15. As Baasa interrupted this peace, 16:1, and he died in the 26th year of Asa, 3 Kg 16:8, the number here and in 16:1 seems to be erroneous. Basaa came to the throne in the 3rd year of Asa, 3 Kg 15:33, and according to 3 Kg 15:16 ' there was war between Asa and Baasa . . . all their days '. But this does not mean that there was war from the time of Baasa's accession but that from the time the war started it lasted as long as both were reigning together. With this agrees Hanani's

prophecy of continual wars from this time, 16:9. That **28** the report of the war in 16:1–5 is very incomplete is shown by the reference in 15:8 to the cities of Ephraim captured by Asa.
XVI 1–6 War with Israel—3 Kg 15:17–22. **4.** ' all **ee** the *store*-cities ' provided with war materials.
7–10 Reproof and Prophecy of the Seer Hanani—Not in Kg. **7.** Hanani, 19:2. Had Asa put his trust in God, he could have defeated the combined forces of Baasa and Benhadad. **8.** The Libyans were not mentioned in 14:9–13. **10.** Asa *treated cruelly* many who had presumably sided with Hanani against him.
11–14 Asa's Death and Burial—3 Kg 15:23 f. **12.** The **ff** ' *very grievous disease* in his feet ' may have been mortification due to a defect in the circulation. **14.** ' And *an immense fire was burnt in his honour* ', prob. with odoriferous shrubs. This mark of respect was customary, 21:19 ; Jer 34:5.
Appendix on the Chronology of Asa's Reign—The **g** problem of fitting the information given into a satisfactory pattern has not found a convincing solution. The fortifications are likely to have been undertaken early in the reign, and they were carried out in a time of peace, 14:6–7. The 10 years of quiet, 14:1, therefore seem to have initiated the reign. This would place Zara's invasion in Asa's 11th year. But the sacrifice of the spoils in the 15th year, 15:10–11, seems in the context to refer to that event. As the defeat of Zara can hardly have taken some 4 years, his invasion was prob. preceded by an unrecorded conflict. The defeat of Zara, therefore, prob. fell in the 14th year, and was followed by the religious reform, 14:2–5 and 15:8–16. This had as sequel and reward a period of peace broken eventually by war with Baasa, 16:1. The suggestion that this time of quiet lasted the 10 years of 14:1, would put the outbreak of war with Baasa in Asa's 24th year, but as Baasa died in Asa's 26th year, 3 Kg 16:8, this would not leave long enough to do justice to the statement of 3 Kg 15:16 that there was a war between the two monarchs all their days, as this implies a prolonged conflict.

XVII 1–XXI 1a Josaphat 870/869–848. **h**
XVII 1–19 His Care for Religion ; Success ; Military Preparations—Not in Kg except 1a = 3 Kg 15:24b. **1b–2.** Military preparations necessitated by the late war with Israel. **3–5.** Religious spirit and consequent divine blessing. In 3 omit ' David ' with Heb. MSS and LXX. **6–9. Religious reform and instruction of the people. 6.** The people were so prone to idolatry that fresh measures were already necessary after the action of Asa, 14:3, which see for ' groves '. But like his father, 15:17, he did not remove the high places dedicated to the unlawful worship of Yahweh, 20:33. In **8** omit ' Thobadonias ', a dittography compounded of the two previous names. In **9** note the book of Mosaic law. **10–11.** Salutary respect of the neighbouring nations. **12–19.** Military strength. **12.** In Judah he built ' *forts and store-cities* '. **17.** ' After him ': ' *From Benjamin* ' (*min-Binyāmîn*). The Benjaminites were celebrated for their skill with the bow ; see on 1 Par 12:1 f. Each archer, whose two hands were required to shoot with the bow, was protected by a companion holding a shield ; see illustrations in DBV I 905.
XVIII 1–34 War with Achab against Syria—**1a ii** repeats verbally 17:5b. **1b.** Josaphat's son Joram married Athalia the daughter of Achab, 21:6 ; 22:2. **2–34. Consultation and War.** 3 Kg 22:2b–35. **25.** Joas ' *the king's son* ' : only here. 27d is a marginal gloss from Mic 1:2. **30–31.** ' cavalry ' : ' *chariots* '. ' to the Lord ' is an explanatory addition. ' and *the Lord* helped him ' etc. is not in Kg. **33.** The arrow struck Achab ' between the *breastplate and its appendages* ', prob. a leather protective covering hanging from the breastplate. **34.** Achab ' *remained propped up* in his chariot '.
XIX 1–3 Jehu's Rebuke to Josaphat—Not in Kg. **jj** **2.** Jehu : see 20:34 ; 3 Kg 16:1. It is not indicated

that any punishment followed. **3.** ' groves ' : *'ašĕrîm* ;
see on Deut 7:5.

4-11 Religious and Legal Reform—Not in Kg. The
legal reform was itself religious in that Israel was a
theocratic state, and its law was enshrined with divine
sanction in the sacred books. **5.** Deut 16:18 ordered
the appointment of judges in all the cities. David
had already appointed judges, 1 Par 23:4, but the
system required reorganizing and may have fallen
partly into desuetude. **6.** The law they had to
administer was the law of God. And, therefore, 6*d*,
' he is with you in delivering judgement '. **10.** This court
at Jerusalem was to be a court of appeal to which
cases would be sent from the provinces. It was to
decide ' between blood and blood ', *i.e.* in cases of
homicide to adjudicate whether there was accident
or guilt, Ex 21:12-23. And its functions were concerned with ' the law, the commandments, *the statutes
and the judgements* ', or legal decisions of the courts.
Unwitting transgressions of the law had to be atoned
for, Lev ch 4. **11.** The court had two departments,
the strictly religious and the civil, and the secular
judges, 8, had the help of Levites as *assessors*, who
would be experts in the law. The King ends with the
prayer : ' *May the Lord be with the good* '.

XX 1-30 God grants Victory over Invaders—Not in
Kg. **1.** The Moabites and Ammonites were accompanied by *Maonites*, whose name seems to be preserved
in El-Ma'an, SE. of Petra ; see 10 and on 1 Par 4:41.
2. The Moabites were from E. of the Dead Sea and
the Maonites from *Edom* (elsewhere also misread as
Aram = Syria). Engaddi is the modern 'Ain Jidi on
the W. coast of the Dead Sea. **3.** Previous general
fasts, Jg 20:26 ; 1 Kg 7:6. **5.** As Josaphat stood in
the midst of the people ' before the new court ', the
court in question would be that of the priests, 4:9,
but unless some unrecorded renovation had taken
place, it would hardly be called the new court. Some
think that the Chronicler is using a term current in
his own day. **7.** God *dispossessed* the earlier inhabitants
in favour of Israel. **9** recalls the answer given to
Solomon's prayer, 6:24-35 and 7:12-16. **10.** Deut
2:4, 9, 19. **11.** ' *Behold, they are requiting us by coming
to cast us out* '. **16.** The *gully* would be dry in summer.
Jeruel, only here, but part of the wilderness of Judah.
19. The sons of Core were also sons of Caath, 1 Par
6:22, but for some reason it was wished here to give
them special prominence. They praised God ' with
voices loud and strong '. **20.** Tekoa : S. by E. of Bethlehem. **21.** The singers were clad ' *in holy attire* ', see
on 1 Par 16:29. **22-23.** No miracle is implied in the
defeat of the invaders. They destroyed themselves.
' The Lord *set an ambush against* ' the invaders, by
inspiring Josaphat to do so. In the confusion that
ensued in the early morning light the Moabites and
Ammonites suspected the Edomites of treachery and
the final result was mutual massacre. **24.** ' When
Judah came to a *spot with a view towards the desert, they
turned towards the host (of invaders) and saw their corpses
lying on the ground without a survivor* '. **25.** ' they found
cattle in abundance, baggage and garments '.

31-XXI 1*a* Conclusion ; Death of Josaphat—3 Kg
22:41-51*a*. **33.** He did not abolish the high places
where sacrifice was offered to God against the prescription of Deut 12 as he had those established for
idolatrous worship, 17:6. The people were not fully
loyal. **34.** The *chronicles* of Jehu, 19:2, *were incorporated
into the book* giving the history of the kings of Israel,
the name standing for Judah as in 21:4, or for both
the kingdoms together. The account in **35-37** of the
proposed mercantile expedition to Ophir and Tarshish
supplements and is supplemented by that in Kg. See
on 9:21. The rebuke of the prophet Eliezer (otherwise unknown) explains Josaphat's refusal of further
aid from Ochozias, Kg v. 50.

XXI 1*b*-20 Joram 848-841.

2-4 Slaughter of his brothers. Not in Kg. **3.** Josaphat
in putting his sons in command of fortified cities had

followed the policy of Roboam, 11:23. In addition **287a**
to gold and silver he had given them *rich presents* of
unspecified nature (DV ' pensions '). **4** suggests that
so far from Joram's rule being accepted by all, his
brothers aided by some of the leading men had con-
spired against him, and 13 indicates that their opposition was due to his idolatrous practices. **5-7. Summary
of the reign**=4 Kg 8:17-19. **8-10*b* Revolt of Edom
and Libnah.** 4 Kg 8:20-22. **9.** The local name
' Seira ' in Kg is a corruption of the phrase ' with his
princes '. He took with him *chariots*. He was unable
to crush the revolt, but though surrounded by the
Edomites he managed to break through and escape.
Kg adds that his men fled. **10*c*-20*c*.** Not in Kg.
10*c*-11. His evil-doing. Idolatry was called fornication as Israel was considered to be the spouse of God.
12-15. Epistle from Elias. The order of the narrative **b**
in Kg might suggest that Elias had already been rapt
into the skies, 4 Kg ch 2, but the Hebrew historians
often do not follow the chronological sequence of
events, and this passage shows that he was still working in the Northern Kingdom. Hence he communicates
with Joram by letter. **16-17. Invasion of Judah.** It
is unlikely that the Ethiopians across the Red Sea
would here be styled neighbours of the Arabs, and
there were prob. *Cushites* in S. Arabia. His sons had
promoted the worship of Baal, 24:7. Joachaz is another
form of the name Ochozias, that of the next king, 22:1.
19. For the ceremonial fire, see on 16:14. **20*a*** repeats
5. **20*d*. His burial.** 4 Kg 8:24*b*. He was buried in
the city of David, where his fathers were buried, Kg,
but not in the royal sepulchres, Par.

XXII 1-9*d* Ochozias (Ahaziah) 841. **c**
1-2 Introductory. 4 Kg 8:24*b*-26. The invasion in
which his brothers were killed, 21:17. His father was
40 at the time of his death, 21:20, and Ochozias was
twenty-two years old at his accession, Kg. Athalia was
the daughter of Achab, 21:6, and the grand-daughter
of Amri (Omri). **3-4. His wickedness.** 4 Kg 8:27.
5-6. Expedition with Joram. 4 Kg 8:28 f. **7-9*c*.
His death.** 4 Kg 9:21-27. **7.** He went out with
Joram ' to meet Jehu '. **8.** Ochozias may have had
nephews old enough to be his pages, but perhaps
LXX is right reading ' brothers ', *i.e.* ' *relatives* of
Ochozias '. **9.** When Ochozias was brought to Jehu
' *they* [Jehu's men] killed him '. Par and Kg supplement each other, but the succinctness of the accounts
does not permit certainty as to the course of events.
Ochozias, seeing that Jehu had killed Joram, fled by
way of Beth haggan (Jenin), pursued by Jehu, Kg.
[Ochozias, however, succeeded in escaping], whereupon Jehu caused him to be searched for, and his
men captured him in Samaria, where he was in hiding
and brought him to Jehu, Par. (The verb may be
conative. In this case, he never reached Samaria, as
his attempt to take refuge there was frustrated.) Then
Par's terse statement that they killed him is amplified
in Kg. When Jehu saw him, he ordered his men to
kill him in his chariot. They struck and wounded
him at the ascent of Gur near Ibleam, but he managed
to escape to Megiddo, where he died of his injuries.
See also § 275*i*.

XXII 9*e*-XXIII 15 Athalia 841-835. **d**
The memory of Athalia as a usurper who was not of
Davidic descent was so hateful to the Chronicler that
he contents himself with a bare mention of her six
years' reign. Nothing is recorded of it except the
bloody measure by which she secured the throne, 10,
the means by which the future king was secured
from her murderous purpose, 11-12, his eventual
coronation, 23:1-11, and her ignominious death,
12-15.

9*e*-10 Athalia seizes the throne. 4 Kg 11:1. ' *There* **e**
was no one of the house of Ochozias strong enough to reign '.
His brothers had been killed, 21:1 ; he himself died
in his 23rd year (see on 21:2) and his offspring were
children. In 10 omit ' for '. **11-12. Joas is saved.**

287e 4 Kg 11:2 f. Par adds that Josabeth was married to the high-priest. This enabled the boy to be concealed in the priest's quarters in the temple ; and the danger of discovery was the less that Athalia, as a worshipper of Baal, would not frequent the temple. **23:1-11. The conspiracy and coronation of Joas.** 4 Kg 11:4-12. **2.** The name 'Israel' is used of Judah as in 21:4. **3.** God's promise to David, 2 Kg 7:16. **5.** The priestly and Levitical courses, 1 Par chh 23-26, changed offices on the Sabbath. That day was suitable for the conspirators as larger numbers would not attract attention. The 1st division of Par corresponds to the 3rd of Kg, and the 2nd and 3rd to the 1st and 2nd of Kg. The 'foundation' gate is called 'the gate of Sur' in Kg, the similarity of the two names in Heb. being evidence of textual corruption. **11.** The addition in Vg + DV 'and gave him the law to hold in his hand' is to explain that 'the testimony' is a name given to the law as God's witness of his holy will ; so in Ps 18:8. **12-15. Death of Athalia.** 4 Kg 11:13-16. **12.** An attractive emendation of Goettsberger's reads : 'when Athalia heard the sound of the trumpets and the acclamations of the king' ; see 13. **13.** The king 'was standing *by his pillar*' ; see on 4 Kg 11:14. 'at the entrance' : '*as the manner was*' ; so in Kg. **14.** Joiada '*gave orders to the captains in charge of the soldiery saying "Take her forth between the files and whoever follows her is to be slain with the sword"*'. **15.** '*they made way for her*' ; so LXX and Syr.

f XXIII 16-XXIV 27 Joas 835-796.
16-19. The covenant of Sinai renewed. 4 Kg 11:17-18. **20-21. Enthronement of Joas.** 4 Kg 11:19 f. This will have taken place before the religious reforms of 16-19. The mention of Athalia's death is repeated from 15. **XXIV 1-3 Introductory.** 4 Kg 12:1-3. **3.** Joadan, one of his wives, is mentioned in 25:1. **4-14. Repair of the temple.** 4 Kg 12:4-16. The two accounts supplement each other on various points. **6.** The contribution appointed by Moses, Ex 30:11-16 and 38:25. The negligence had been not merely in collecting the money but in applying it to the repairs. It had gone into the common temple treasury and been applied to the ordinary expenses, Kg 8 f. **8.** The chest will have been placed on the outside of the gate leading into the inner court. The text in Kg, 9, which says the chest was placed 'by the altar' must be understood in a wide sense, since the people had no access to the court of the priests ; but the words are prob. corrupt. **14.** No money was spent on utensils for the temple while the work of repair was in progress, Kg 13, but when it was finished it was found that there was a considerable sum still in hand and this was used for the provision of precious vessels **g** for use in divine worship. **15-16. Death of Joiada.** Not in Kg. He lived to a very advanced age. If the figures are correctly transmitted, he must have been in his eighties when he married Josabeth, the daughter of Joram, 22:11, who died at the age of 40, 21:20 ; and consequently the marriage could not have taken place many years before. 'He had done good to Israel, *for God* and for his house', the temple. **17-22. Idolatry and consequent murder of Zacharias.** Not in Kg. The religious reform after the death of Athalia had not been whole-hearted. **18.** 'groves' ; see on Deut 7:5. **21.** If the Syrian invasion was already threatening, the king may have considered that the prophet's announcement that the people could not prosper after forsaking God, would discourage them. St Matthew, in possession of a more detailed tradition, knew that Zacharias was killed between the sanctuary and the altar, 23:35. As he calls him the son of Barachias, it may be that tradition had preserved his father's name and that Joiada, 20, was his grandfather. Par had, as Mt had not, every reason for mentioning his descent from Joiada, 22, and Joiada lived long enough to see several generations of descendants. **23-24. Invasion of Syrians.** 4 Kg 12:17 f. They did not capture Jerusalem, as Joas bought them off with

valuable treasure, Kg. Omit 'shameful'. **25-27. 28 Death of Joas.** 4 Kg 12:19-21. **25.** The time-link with the invasion suggests that Joas' sickness was due to wounds. He was buried where his fathers were buried, Kg, in the city of David, Kg + Par, but not in the royal sepulchre, Par. **26.** Zabad : Jozachar, Kg, perhaps rightly. **27.** Further information was to be found 'written *in the commentary of* the book of the kings'. For the commentary or midrash see on 13:22.

XXV 1-28 Amasias 796-768. **h**
1-2. Introductory. 4 Kg 14:1-4. He did not abolish the high places, Kg, and later fell into idolatry, 14. **3-4. Punishment of his father's murderers.** 4 Kg 14:5 f. They were *his courtiers*. **5-10. Preparations for war.** Not in Kg. **7.** A similar reprimand for partnership with idolatrous Israel, 20:35-37. **10.** The anger of the hired Israelites will have been due in part to the loss of the expected booty. Their reprisals are related in 13. **11-12. War with Edom.** 4 Kg 14:7. He cast his prisoners down from *a mountain-peak in Sela*, later named Petra 'the rose-red city half as old as time'. **13. Revenge of the Israelite mercenaries.** Not in Kg. They took advantage of Amasias' absence during the Edomite campaign, and, starting from Samaria, made *a raid against* the cities of Judah *as far as Bethhoron*, a border town at this time belonging to Judah. **14-16. Amasias is reprimanded for idolatry.** Not in Kg. **17-24. War with Israel.** 4 Kg 14:8-14. **20.** The mention of the gods of Edom refers to 14. **24.** The house of Obededom had retained the charge of the treasury since the time of David ; see 1 Par 26:15 with note. Omit 'the sons of'. **25-28. Conclusion and death of Amasias.** 4 Kg 14:17-20. **27.** The remark that the conspiracy occurred after his idolatry (not in Kg) marks, not a temporal, but **a** moral connection between the two events.

XXVI 1-23 Ozias (Azarias) 768-740/739. **i**
1-4 Introductory. 4 Kg 14:21-22 ; 15:2 f. **1.** That the people made him king does not signify their choice of a younger in preference to an elder brother, but that the unpopularity incurred by his father on account of the foolish and ruinous war undertaken against Israel led to his deposition. Otherwise the remark in 2 that his reconquest of the Red Sea port of Ailath took place after his father's death would be meaningless. **4.** He acted rightly as Amasias had done in the first part of his reign before he fell into idolatry. **5. His goodness not lasting.** Not in Kg. Zacharias, who '*taught him the fear of God*' or true religion, is otherwise unknown. **6-15. Military preparations and successful wars.** Not in Kg. **6.** Jabnia or Jabne was later called Jamnia, 1 Mac 4:15. **7.** For the Maonites (Vg + DV 'Ammonites'), see on 1 Par 4:41. **7.** Gurbaal is otherwise unknown. **9.** The corner-gate, also 25:23, at the NW. of the city ; the valley-gate, prob. at the SW. leading from the valley of Ge-hinnom. The third was *by the angle*, of uncertain location. Omit 'and the rest . . . wall'. **10.** He had herds in *the Shephelah*, § 55a, *and on the* **j** *tableland*, prob. that N. of the Arnon. He had also *husbandmen* and vine-dressers both in the mountains and in (more) fertile districts. 'Carmel' cannot here be the name of the mountain range which was in the territory of the Northern Kingdom ; the word is also a common noun signifying land suitable for orchards and gardens ; see David's possessions, 1 Par 27:26-31. **11.** The census of the fighting men was in the hands of Jehiel and an official (the title occurs Jos 1:10 etc.) named Maasias, and the commanding officer was Hananias. **16-21. Usurpation of sacerdotal functions and chastisement.** 4 Kg 15:5 records that God struck the king, but omits the reason. **16.** He *acted faithlessly towards* God by disobeying his law, Num 16:1-40 ; 18:1-7 ; 1 Kg 2:28. **20.** A leper was levitically unclean, Lev 13:11. **21.** Lev 13:46 gives the law of isolation. **22-23. Conclusion.** 4 Kg 15:6 f. Isaias'

7j call to the prophetic office fell in the last year of Ozias, Is 6:1.

k XXVII 1-9 Joatham 740/739-736/735. **1-2. Introductory.** 4 Kg 15:32-35*b*. The transgression of the people, Par, was prob. the frequenting of the illegitimate high places, Kg. **3-4. His buildings.** 4 Kg 15:35*c*. Ophel : the southern projection of the hill on which stood the temple. **5-6. Successful war against the Ammonites ; piety rewarded.** Not in Kg. The Ammonites had paid tribute to Ozias, 26:8, but now again asserted their independence. The subjugation by Joatham was also temporary as tribute was paid for only three years. The Ammonites prob. took advantage of the Syro-Israelite invasion, 4 Kg 15:37. The measure or *kor* equalled about 11 bushels, HDB IV 912. **7-9. Conclusion.** 4 Kg 15:36-38.

l XXVIII 1-27 Achaz 736/735-727. **1-4. Introductory ; idolatry.** 4 Kg 16:2-4. **1.** Ezechias is said to have been 25 when he succeeded his father Achaz, 29:1. Either this number is corrupt, or Achaz must have been over 20 at his accession. According to the existing figures he died aged 36. **2.** The Baalim (plur. of Baal) are the various divinities known as ' Lord ' in their respective localities. **3.** The valley of Bene-hinnom is that now called Wady er-Rababi S. and W. of Jerusalem. He ' *burnt* his sons according to the *abominations* of the nations whom the Lord *dispossessed* '. Elsewhere the consonants of the word ' burnt ' are inverted, as here in Kg, to mean ' made to pass through ' the fire. **5-7. Punishment by invasion.** 4 Kg 16:5 f. ; Is 7:1. **5.** Rasin, king of Syria, took many *captives*. **8-15. Israel returns the captives.** Not in Kg. **10.** It was forbidden to make bondservants of fellow-Israelites, Lev 25:39-43. **15.** Jericho belonged to the Northern Kingdom already in the time of Achab, 3 Kg 16:34. **16-21. Appeal to Tiglath-pileser for help.** 4 Kg 16:7-9. **17.** The Edomites, ruthless enemies of the Israelites, took many *captives*. **19.** Achaz ' had *acted wantonly in Judah* and had *acted faithlessly towards the Lord* '. **21.** Here again Par supposes knowledge of Kg. The statement that the appeal to the Assyrian availed him nothing is based on the long view that in the end Achaz was no better off for it. Kg records the immediate relief afforded by Tiglath-pileser's attack on Damascus in the years **m** 733-732. **22-25. Achaz gives himself entirely to idolatry.** 4 Kg 16:10-18. The two accounts differ in their selection of material from the common source. **23.** The gods of Damascus ' struck ' Achaz. The sacred writer accommodates his words to the impious king's belief instead of saying ' whom he believed to strike him '. This resolve of the king's will have been formed before the conquest of Damascus by the Assyrian army. **24.** The closing of the temple may have taken place some time after the innovations in worship recorded in Kg. The meaning, however, may be that the king prevented the access of the people to the temple lest they should insist on the worship of Yahweh, but carried on his own idolatrous worship within its precincts ; see 29:3-5. **26-27. Conclusion.** 4 Kg 16:19-20. Achaz was buried with his fathers in Jerusalem, Par, in the city of David, Kg, but not in the royal sepulchres, Par.

n XXIX 1-XXXII 33 Ezechias 727-698/697. **XXIX 1-2. Introductory.** 4 Kg 18:1-3. **3-19. The purification of the temple.** Not in Kg. **3.** Achaz had closed the temple, 28:24 ; it was reopened on 1st Nisan 726 ; see 17. Ezechias fastened plates of gold on the doors, 4 Kg 18:16. **4.** The assembly was held in the *open space* on the east, no doubt within the temple. **5.** The priests and Levites were to make sure that they were in a state of Levitical purity. Then they were to remove all the ' filth ' of idolatry from the temple. **12.** For the triple division of the Levites, see 1 Par 23:6. Mahath, 1 Par 6:35 ; Joel, 1 Par

6:36 ; Cis, 1 Par 6:44 ; Joah, 1 Par 6:20 f. **13-14. 287n** Elisaphan ; see on 1 Par 15:8. The triple division of the Levite musicians, 1 Par 25:1-6. **20-30. Inauguration of the renewed temple-worship.** Not in Kg. **21.** The he-goats were for sin-offerings, 23, the other victims for holocausts. They were offered for *the royal house*, for the ministers of the temple, and for the people. **22.** For the sprinkling of the blood round about the altar, see Lev 1:5, 11. **23.** Laying the hand on the victim, Lev 1:4 ; 4:4. **24.** Again Israel stands for the Southern Kingdom, which Par considered the true Israel as ruled by the divinely appointed Davidic dynasty. **25.** The regulation of David, 1 Par 23:5 f. Priests with trumpets ; see on 1 Par 15:24. **27.** The holocausts followed the sin-offerings, 23 f.

31-36. Further celebration of the reopening of the o temple. Not in Kg. **31.** The king said ' You have *consecrated yourselves to the Lord* '. After the long neglect of the temple the sacrifices offered had been equivalent to a re-consecration to God's services. To ' fill the hand ' is a technical term for consecration. In holocausts, as in sin-offerings, no part of the victim was returned for the use of the offerer. So it was *those of generous heart* who offered holocausts. **33.** The number of other victims was nearly ten times as large. On the sacrificial meal following peace-offerings, Lev 7:11-17. **34.** The priests were inadequate in number, in part at least because comparatively few were in a state of Levitical cleanness ' for the Levites *were more earnest in purifying themselves* than the priests '. MT of Lev 1:6 with sing. verb assigns the task of flaying the victim to the offerer, but Sam., LXX (and Vg) to the priests. It would certainly expedite matters that the ceremonial act should be entrusted to men skilled by long practice. **35.** Thus the temple services were *re-established*. **36.** And all rejoiced ' *that God had re-established it for the people, for it had been effected in a surprisingly short time* '.

XXX 1-27 Solemn celebration of the Pasch. Not in p Kg. **1** is an anticipatory statement explaining the theme of the chapter. ' Phase ' (two syllables) is a name of the Passover derived from Heb. as ' Pasch ' is from Aramaic. The date is in the 1st year of Ezechias' reign and the Northern Kingdom had not yet fallen to the Assyrians. That he was able to send his messengers north is explained by its weakness at this time. **2.** The celebration of the Pasch in the 2nd month is an extension of the permission given Num 9:10 f. **6.** Tiglath-pileser had carried many into captivity in 734, 4 Kg 15:29. **13.** On the relation of the Pasch and the feast of unleavened bread, see § 113*f*. **14.** Jerusalem where the feast was to be celebrated was first purified by the destruction of idolatrous shrines ; see 28:24. After the feast the good work was extended throughout the land, 31:1. **15.** Priests and Levites *were shamed* (DV ' at length ') by the spontaneous zeal of the people into putting off their ceremonial uncleanness. **17.** Normally it was the duty of the heads of families to kill the paschal victim, Ex 12:3-6. On this occasion the duty was undertaken by Levites ' for *all who by reason of legal uncleanness could not make an offering to Yahweh* '. **20. q** To such the Lord was merciful and did not punish, Lev 15:31 ; 26:14-16. **21.** The Levites and the priests praised the Lord ' with *all their strength* '. **22.** Thus ' they *concluded* [LXX] the seven days of the solemnity '. **25.** The multitude comprised inhabitants of Judah, visitors from the northern tribes, and ' *strangers* ' of the land of Israel ' who had settled in Judah, 9:9. **26.** Since the division of the kingdom after Solomon no such festival attended by visitors from all Israel had been possible. **27.** ' The priests the Levites ' (so MT ; all the priests were of the tribe of Levi) blessed the people. The liturgical blessing was a function reserved to the priesthood, Num 6:23-27. **XXXI 1. Destruction of idolatrous shrines.** 4 Kg 18:4. At the end of the Paschal festival by a spontaneous movement ' all *the Israelites present went forth* [from Jerusalem] *to* the cities of Judah ', and destroyed the *maṣṣēbôṯ* and

287q the *'ašērîm* (DV ' idols ', ' groves ') ; see § 213*d*. **2-3. The king's care for the temple worship.** Not in Kg. The neglect of the days of Achaz will have rendered necessary a fresh assignment of duties to the members **r** of the different courses. **4-19. Provision for the needs of priests and Levites.** Not in Kg. **5.** They offered ' the firstfruits of . . . honey *and of all the products of the fields, and they brought the tithes of everything in abundance* '. **7.** The harvest began in the 3rd month and the fruits were gathered in the 7th. **10.** ' firstfruits ' : ' *offerings*'. **14.** It was Core's office to take charge of the free-will offerings ' and *to distribute the offerings of the Lord and the most holy portions* '. The title ' most holy ' is used, *e.g.* of the priestly perquisites of sin-offerings and trespass-offerings, Lev 6:25 ; 7:1, 6. **16-19.** The sequence of thought is not clear and seems to have been disturbed by the insertion of clauses regarding conditions for participating in the distributions. **16.** ' *provided they were registered among* the males from three years old and upwards '. **17.** ' *This is the registration of* the priests . . . and *of* the Levites '. **18.** ' *The registration comprised the whole family, their young ones, wives, sons, and daughters, because their office sanctified them to partake of the holy gifts* '. **19.** ' The priests, the sons of Aaron, *in the pastures of their various cities had men appointed by name* to distribute portions to all males among the priests and *to all the Levites who were registered* '. **20-21. Praise of Ezechias' religious zeal.** Not in Kg.

s XXXII 1-22 Sennacherib invades Judah. 4 Kg 18:13-19 :37 ; Is 36:1-37:38 ; Ecclus 48:19-24. **1.** That the invasion occurred ' after these *events* and this *manifestation of fidelity* ' to God prepares the reader for the providential deliverance. **2-8. Defensive measures.** Not in Kg. **4.** The brook that flowed in the open was fed by Gihon, now 'Aïn Sitti Mariam, and ran originally down the Kidron valley. The immense labour of cutting the underground tunnel which later brought its waters within the city of David to the Pool of Siloam, 30, could not have been accomplished in the time allowed by war conditions. **5.** Mello ; see on 3 Kg 9:15. **6.** The address was given in the *open space* near one of the city gates. **8.** God's spiritual aid is vaguely indicated. **9-16. Sennacherib's officers call for surrender.** 4 Kg 18:17-37. **12.** The incidental and unexpected mention of Ezechias' efforts to put an end to sacrificial worship outside the temple shows conclusively that the law of the unity of the sanctuary, Deut 12, was not something new in the time of Josias. **17-20. The blasphemies of the Assyrian move Ezechias and Isaias to prayer.** 4 Kg 18:28 ff. ; 19:15-19. **17.** The reception, but not the writing of this letter, is mentioned in 4 Kg 19:14. **21. Rout of the Assyrian army.** 4 Kg 19:35-37. Peculiar to Par is the mention of the death of the officers. Unlike Kg, Par gives no estimate of the number of the slain. **22-23. Subsequent international fame of Ezechias.** Not in Kg. **22.** The Lord ' gave **t** them *rest* on every side '. **24-31. Various supplementary information. 24.** This very succinct account supposes in the reader a knowledge of 4 Kg 20:1-11, where 6 shows that, although Par mentions the king's sickness after the Assyrian invasion, in time it preceded it. **25-26** allude to the display of self-satisfaction and pride manifested 4 Kg 20:12-19, a passage which is rendered more intelligible by the mention of the king's humbling himself and the postponement of punishment. **27-29.** The king's riches. *Cf.* 4 Kg 20:13. **28.** He had ' stalls for *many cattle* and folds for *flocks* '. **29.** ' And he *acquired flocks* ' ('*ădārîm* for '*ārîm* ' cities ') ; but the word is prob. to be omitted as due to dittography. **30.** See on 4 and 4 Kg 20:20. The king blocked up access to the spring from without the city, and from this *higher* level led the water *underground* to the Pool of Siloam. **31.** 4 Kg 20:12-19 ; also 25-26 above. **32-33. Conclusion.** 4 Kg 20:20 f. For the other acts and *pious deeds* of the king reference is first made to ' the vision of Iasias, the son of Amos ', which without ' the prophet ' is the title of the canonical

book ; see Is 36-39. MT and Syr by omitting the **28** following ' and ', which is found in LXX and Vg, imply that this section of Isaias as found embodied in a chronicle of the Israelite kings was used as source by Par, since without the copula only one source is named. But Par has information not to be found in Isaias. **33.** Ezechias was buried ' *in the ascent to* ' the royal sepulchres. He seems to have been honoured by a special sepulchre.

XXXIII 1-20 Manasses 698/697-643/642. **u 1-9. Introduction ; Manasses' wickedness.** 4 Kg 21:1-9. **3.** Omit ' he turned and '. ' groves ' ; see on 19:3. **6.** Par adds ' in the valley of Ben-hinnom ' ; see on 28:3. **7.** ' *The sculptured image he had made* ', which he set up in the temple, was of Ashera (Kg) ; see on 3 Kg 15:13. **10. Warning.** 4 Kg 21:10-15. **11-13. Punishment and pardon.** Not in Kg. **11.** ' They *seized* Manasses *in his hiding-place* ' : the same word as in 1 Kg 13:6 (DV ' thickets ') ; see *L. Koehler TZ 5 (1949) 314. Omit ' chains and '. **12.** In his tribulation ' he *humbled himself* exceedingly ' before God. Manasses is known from the Assyrian inscriptions to have been a vassal of both Esarhaddon, 681-669, and of Ashurbanipal, 669-626 ; see Luckenbill II nos. 690, 876. His recorded tribute to the former was paid in 676/675, and the revolt prob. took place after this, followed by captivity at Babylon, of which city Shamash-shum-ukin, one of Esarhaddon's sons, was prince-regent. The return was prob. under Ashurbanipal, who is known to have restored conquered kings in the hope of securing their continued allegiance. **14-17. Fortifications ; rejection of idols.** Not in Kg. **14.** The **v** wall ran from the Fish Gate, prob. in the N. wall, along the W. slope of the Kidron valley down to the hill of Ophel at the SE. corner of the city. Gihon ; see on 32:4. **15.** ' the idol ' ; see on 7. **17.** ' The people still sacrificed in the high places *but only* to the Lord '. The conversion of the king and people can have been neither deep-rooted nor long continued. Amon, 22, must have learnt his idolatry during his father's lifetime, and the final destruction of Jerusalem is attributed to the wickedness of Manasses' reign, 4 Kg 23:26, Jer 15:4. **18-20. Conclusion.** 4 Kg 21:17-18. **18.** The prayer of Manasses, which was recorded in the *chronicles* of the kings, has been lost. An apocryphal prayer is printed at the end of editions of Vg. **19.** Hozai ; perhaps not a proper name, but to be emended and read as ' his seers '. ' did penance ' : ' *humbled himself* '. **20.** That Manasses was not buried with his fathers is thought by some to indicate his relapse into idolatry. On the other hand, that would not have displeased his idolatrous successor.

XXXIII 21-25 Amon 643/642-641/640. **w 21-25. Introduction ; idolatry, conspiracy and death.** 4 Kg 21:19-26, where mention is made further of the source for his reign and of his burial.

XXXIV 1-XXXV 27 Josias 641/640-609. **x XXXIV 1-2. Introductory.** 4 Kg 22:1 f. **3-7. Destruction of idolatrous shrines.** Not in Kg, but with 4, 5 and 7 *cf.* respectively 4 Kg 23:6, 16, 19 f. Par is more exact chronologically in setting part of Josias' reforming activity before the finding of the book of the law in his 18th year of reign. The order of narrative in the Bible is frequently not the chronological order. **3.** The beginning of the reform in Josias' 12th year may have been due to the influence of Jeremias. The 13th year of Josias in which Jeremias received his mission, Jer 1:2, reckoned by the pre-notation system would be the same as the 12th reckoned by the post-notation system ; see § 124*i*. ' groves ' : see on 19:3. He destroyed ' the idols and *molten images* '. **4.** He ' demolished the *sun-pillars* ' set up as emblems of sun-worship. **6.** These cities were nominally in the Assyrian province of Samaria, but the Assyrian empire was no longer able to exercise effective control so far

7x from the capital. In these northern cities too he
y ' demolished all the *sun-pillars* ', as in 4. **8-19. The**
finding of the book of the Law. 4 Kg 22:3-11. See
also §§ 135*d*, 211*d*. **9.** The ' *Levite* porters ' gathered
the money. **13.** These scribes were those charged
with the clerical work required by the extensive
repairs. **18.** He read passages before the king (lit.
' read in it '). **20-28. God's answer through the
prophetess.** 4 Kg 22:12-20. **21.** The king ordered
the party to ' go and *enquire of* the Lord '. **22.** They
went to Olda (Huldah) who was living in the second
quarter of Jerusalem ; see on Soph 1:10. The mention of her being available on the spot perhaps indirectly explains by his absence why Jeremias was
not consulted. **24.** Omit ' and ' ; the evils were those
threatened in the curses. **28.** The word ' now ' is
here consequential, not temporal. Josias died on the
field of battle at Megiddo in 609, but the words of the
prophetess had a restricted meaning. The king's
peace was not to be disturbed by the final catastrophe
of the destruction of Jerusalem. It is, however, a
testimony to Par's fidelity to its sources that the
passage has been reproduced without alteration to
make it more obviously fit the king's end. **29-32.
Renewal of the covenant.** 4 Kg 23:1-3. **30.** ' And
the king read in their hearing all the words of the
book *of the covenant which had been found* in thé house
of the Lord '. This was not the whole book of the
Law that had been found. The king's purpose was to
renew the covenant of Sinai, Ex 24:4-8. The suitable
procedure was consequently to read ' the book of the
covenant ', which Moses had read when the people
had first entered into the solemn pact with God,
Ex 24:7. This suggests that the book found was the
Pentateuch. The loss of the book was due to the
idolatry that reigned even in the temple under kings
z like Amon, Manasses and Achaz. **33. Abolition of
idolatry.** 4 Kg 23:4-20, which in part belongs chronologically to the period before the finding of the book
of the Law = 2 Par 34:3-7. **XXXV 1-19. Solemn
celebration of the Pasch.** 4 Kg 23:21-23. **1.** Phase ;
see on 30:1. **3.** He ordered ' the Levites, *who instructed
all Israel and were consecrated to the Lord* ' to ' put the
holy ark in the temple '. The teaching office of the
Levites, also 17:8 f. The removal of the ark from
the Holy of Holies has not been mentioned. Some
think it was removed during the repairs to the temple
fabric ; others that the profanations of Josias' predecessors had not spared the most holy spot of all.
Once the ark was restored to its proper place in the
Debir, the Levites would not again have to carry it
as they had done during the wanderings in the wilderness. **6.** The Levites were ordered to kill the paschal
victims ; see on 30:17. **7.** The lambs and kids, Ex
12:5, were to be killed as paschal victims (omit ' and
of other small cattle '), the oxen as peace-offerings,
Deut 16:2. **11.** The sprinkling of the blood, also
30:16. ' The Levites flayed *them* ' ; see on 29:34.
13. For this preparation of a sacrificial meal, see
1 Kg 2:13 f. **15.** The three leaders of the Levitical
musicians (see 1 Par 25:1-6) are here called ' the
king's *seers* ' ; see 29:30 ; 1 Par 25:5. **17.** On the
relation between the Pasch and the feast of unleavened
bread, see § 113*f*. **18.** See on 30:26. The Pasch of
Josias was made the more solemn and memorable by
aa the discovery of the book of the law. **20-24e. Death
of Josias in battle.** 4 Kg 23:29 f. **20.** In 609, the year
of his accession, Necho marched to the Euphrates to
fight against the Medes and Babylonians, Jos., *Ant.*
10, 5, 1, who had practically destroyed the Assyrian
empire, the capital having been lost in 612. Necho
wished to secure at least Syria and Palestine for himself. Signs of the Egyptian occupation of Carchemish
at this period have been discovered there. The
Babylonians, however, under Nabuchodonosor put an
end to the Asian dominion of Egypt in the expedition
of 606-605. Josias, now free from the fear of Assyrian
domination and misjudging the rising strength of
Babylon, thought that the only danger to his inde-

pendence lay with Egypt. **21.** ' but to fight against **287aa**
another house ' : ' but *to my war quarters* ' ; see
B. Alfrink, Bi 15 (1934) 173-9. Necho claimed to
have received divine commands, probably from Ra,
the sun-god and head of the Egyptian pantheon.
22. The phrase ' the words of Necho from the mouth
of God ' do not imply that the Chronicler believed
him actually to have received a divine revelation. In
the nature of things, Josias could not be asked to take
the word of a potential aggressor on such a question.
God had promised to give his revelations to his own
people by means of men of their own race, not through
foreigners, Deut 18:18. Josias was under no obligation
to believe the Pharaoh. Par does not blame him.
He speaks here in the same spirit as in 28:23, where
it is said that Achaz sacrificed to the gods of Damascus
' that struck him '. B. Alfrink, Bi 15 (1934) 180,
suggests that just as the Egyptian Pharaoh was styled
ilâni ' god ' by vassal princes in the Amarna correspondence, so now Necho spoke of his Assyrian liege-
lord by the same title. Megiddo : in the great plain
of Esdraelon, which Necho reached after following the
coastal route from Egypt. **24.** They moved him from
his war-chariot into one more comfortable built for
civilian use. **24f-25. Mourning for Josias.** Not in
Kg. These lamentations of Jeremias for Josias have
perished. It became a law or custom to sing these
dirges every year on the anniversary of his death.
' Behold, *they are* written in the Lamentations '. There
used to be other collections besides that still extant.
26-27. Conclusion. 4 Kg 23:28. The source is
indicated where might be found his other acts ' and
good deeds '.

XXXVI 1-3 + 4b Joachaz 609. **bb**
The story is told rather more fully in 4 Kg 23:30*d*-
33 + 34*c-d*. Kg adds that he did evil before the
Lord ; misreads ' he deposed him ', Par 3, as ' he
bound him ', Kg 33 ; adds that Joachaz died in
Egypt. The deposition took place at Riblah on the
Orontes, Kg 33. Par 3 reads lit. ' and the king of
Egypt deposed him in Jerusalem ' (paraphrased in
Vg + DV), but a word has been omitted and the
true text would be ' deposed him from reigning in
Jerusalem ' ; see Kg 33.

XXXVI 4a + 5-8 Joakim 609-598. **cc**
Par adds to 4 Kg 23:34-24:5 the information of
6*b*-7. The text does not say that he was actually
carried away to Babylon, but he ' bound *him in chains
to take him* to Babylon '. In Kg this incident would
come after 24:1*a*. Nabuchodonosor satisfied himself
that he would be a loyal vassal if treated generously
and reinstated him on the throne, but he again rebelled
after three years. The Babylonian showed his magnanimity also in carrying away only *part* of the temple
treasures. Further details are given in Dan 1:1-2.
Jerusalem was besieged and Daniel with others was
taken captive to Babylon. The date will have been
not long before the 3rd year of Joakim ended with
Tishri 606 in the 20th year of Nabopolassar. Nabuchodonosor was on his way to the invasion of Egypt from
which he was recalled by the news of his father's
death. See B. Alfrink, Bi 8 (1927) 395-408, who
shows the fragile foundation on which rests the theory
of a battle at Carchemish in 605.

XXXVI 9-10b Joachin 598. **dd**
Par is much more summary than 4 Kg 24:8-16.
Joachin was *eighteen* when he began to reign, Kg, and
was married, Kg 15. Par adds that his reign lasted
10 days over the 3 months. His deportation occurred
at ' the return of the year ', *i.e.* in the spring when
kings went forth to war.

XXXVI 10c-20a Sedecias 598-587. **ee**
10c-13a. Introductory ; revolt. 4 Kg 24:17-20.
12. For a list of the chapters of Jeremias dealing with
this reign, see § 452*b*. **13a.** Ezechiel dilates on the

287ee sinfulness of violating this oath, 17:18-19. **13b-16. Wickedness of king and people. 15.** The Hebraism 'rising early' signifies earnestness in pursuing a course of action. **17-19. The destruction of Jerusalem.** 4 Kg 25:1-21; Jer 39:1-9; 52:4-27. **20-21. The Babylonian captivity a fulfilment of prophecy.** Not in Kg. Jer 25:9-12. The law had been persistently neglected and among its other provisions that of the rest of the land every seventh year, Lev 25:4. The Chronicler recalls that an enforced sabbath of the land should come when the people were scattered **28** among the nations, Lev 26:33-35.

22-23 Decree of Cyrus permitting Return from Exile ff —This passage is verbally the same as Esd 1:1-3b. A possible explanation of the double occurrence is that, when Esd-Neh was separated from Par, the passage was left at the end of Par as well as at the beginning of Esd to indicate that the books in fact belonged together. But see § 282m.

ESDRAS-NEHEMIAS

(EZRA-NEHEMIAH)

By R. A. DYSON, S.J.

288a Bibliography—M. Seisenberger, *Die Bücher Esdras, Nehemias und Esther*, Vienna, 1901 ; C. Holzhey, *Die Bücher Esdras und Nehemias*, Munich, 1902 ; Lusseau-Collomb II, Paris, 1934 ; A. Vaccari, S.J., *Esdra, Neemia, La Sacra Bibbia*, III, Florence, 1948 ; *D. C. Siegfried, HAT, Göttingen, 1901 ; *A. Bertholet, *Esra und Nehemias*, KHK, Freiburg-Tübingen, 1902 ; *H. E. Ryle, *Ezra and Nehemiah*, CBSC, 1907 ; *T. Witton-Davies, CBi, London ; *L. W. Batten, *Ezra and Nehemiah*, ICC, 1913 ; *R. Breuer, *Die Bücher Esra und Nehemia übersetzt und erläutert*, Frankfurt, 1933.

Special works : A. Van Hoonacker, ' Néhémie et Esdras. Une nouvelle hypothèse', *Muséon* 9 (1890) 151–84 ; 317–51 ; 389–401 ; *id.*, RB 10 (1901) 5–26 ; 175–99 ; *id.*, ' La succession chronologique Néhémie-Esdras ', RB 32 (1923) 481–94 ; 33 (1924) 33–64 ; J. Nikel, *Die Wiederherstellung des jüdischen Gemeinwesens nach dem babyl. Exil*, BS 5, 1900 ; J. Theis, *Geschichtliche u. literarkritische Fragen in Esra*, At Ab 2–5, 1910 ; J. Touzard, ' Les Juifs au temps de la période persane ', RB 12 (1915) 59–133 ; A. Fernandez, ' Epoca de la actividad de Esdras ', Bi 2 (1921) 424–47 ; J. Gabriel, *Zorobabel*, Vienna, 1927 ; A. Clamer, ' Esdras et Néhémie ', DTC, 5, 625 ; R. de Vaux, ' Les décrets de Cyrus et de Darius sur la reconstruction du Temple ', RB 46 (1937) 29–57 ; *E. Meyer, *Die Entstehung des Judenthums*, Halle, 1896 ; *C. C. Torrey, *Esra Studies*, Chicago, 1910 ; *id.*, *The Apocryphal Literature*, 1946, 45–8 ; *L. E. Brown, *Early Judaism*, Cambridge, 1920 ; *H. H. Schaeder, *Esra der Schreiber*, 1930 ; *id.*, ' Esra', *Iran. Beit.* I, 212 ff. ; *W. M. F. Scott, ' Nehemiah-Ezra ', ET 58 (1947) 263–67 ; *J. Stafford Wright, *The Date of Ezra's Coming to Jerusalem*, London, 1947.

b Name and Place in the Canon—In the early Hebrew Bible Esd and Neh formed one book entitled ' The Book of Esdras ' (*cf.* Jos. *c. Ap.*, I, 8 ; *Baba bathra*, 15a ; Melito Sard. in Euseb., *Eccl. Hist.* IV, 26 ; Origenes, *ibid.* VI, 25 and St Jerome, *Ep.* 53 ad Paulinum, n.7, PL 28, 1403). The Massoretes considered the middle verse of ' The Book of Esdras ' to be Neh 3:32. The division into two books is first found in a Heb. MS of 1448, and the modern Heb. Bibles refer to them as the Books of Ezra and Nehemiah. In LXX MSS they also formed one book with the title Esdras B and were placed immediately after the apocryphal book called Esd A. Origen, in the beginning of the 3rd cent., is the first to attest to a division in the LXX version ; *cf.* Euseb., *Eccl. Hist.*, 6, 25, PG 20, 581. In Vg they are known as 1 and 2 Esdras, though the title of the second book is ' L. Nehemiae, qui et Esdras secundus dicitur '. The second book we shall refer to as the book of Neh purely for the advantage of citations.

In HT the two books are found among the Kethubim or Hagiographa, immediately before 1 and 2 Par ; in LXX and Vg they are placed among the historical writings after the books of Par.

c Contents and Division—Esd-Neh deal with the period from the return of the exiles after the Decree of Cyrus, 538 B.C., to the second mission of Neh in the 32nd year of Artaxerxes I, 433 B.C., but the history of this period is by no means complete. There are comparatively long periods of which nothing is related,

e.g. between 536 and 520 ; between 515 and 458, and **288c** between the first and second mission of Neh. The books actually deal with a few episodes, and may be divided into four parts :

Part I : The Return of the Jews under Sheshbazzar (Sassabasar : 538) and its immediate sequel (Esd 1 : 1–6:22) :
- (*a*) The edict of Cyrus and return under Sheshbazzar with the sacred vessels belonging to the temple, 1:1–11.
- (*b*) A list of the exiles who returned and of the cities they occupied, 2:1–70.
- (*c*) The building of the altar of holocausts, 3:1–7.
- (*d*) The laying of the foundations of the temple, 3:8–13.
- (*e*) Opposition from the Samaritans until 520 B.C., 4:1–24.
- (*f*) The completion of the temple under Zorobabel and Josue, 5:1–6:15.
- (*g*) The dedication of the temple and the celebration of the Passover, 6:16–22.

Part II. The Return under Esdras (Esd 7:1–10:44):
- (*a*) The return of the exiles, 7:1–8:36.
- (*b*) The dissolution of mixed marriages, 9:1–10:44.

Part III. The Rebuilding of the Walls by Nehemias (Neh 1:1–7:73) :
- (*a*) In the 20th year of Artaxerxes I (445) Neh. asks permission to return to Jerusalem, 1:1–2:8.
- (*b*) Neh. returns and inspects the walls by night, 2:9–20.
- (*c*) The rebuilding of the walls under difficult conditions, 3:1–6:19.
- (*d*) The appointment of watchmen, 7:1–3, and a census of the people, 7:4–73.

Part IV. Religious Reforms and Political Organization (8:1–13:31) :
- (*a*) The Renewal of the Covenant, 8:1–10:39.
- (*b*) The population of Jerusalem is augmented ; various lists, 11:1–12:26.
- (*c*) The dedication of the walls, 12:27–42.
- (*d*) Provision for the support of priests and Levites, 12:43–46.
- (*e*) Neh. returns to Jerusalem a second time and corrects various abuses, 13:1–31.

Purpose—It is clear from the fragmentary character **d** of the books that the aim of the writer was not to give a complete history of the period, but rather to describe the religious and political reorganization of the community after the Return. At the same time the author intends to show forth God's providence and faithfulness in the fulfilment of all that he had promised through his prophets (Esd 1:1).

Origin of the Books : their Literary Character, Date e and Author—That the author made use of a variety of sources is evident. Some parts are in Hebrew, some in Aramaic ; some parts use the first person, some the third ; the style changes abruptly from one passage to another. The number of sources is uncertain, but the following can be detected without difficulty : (1) the Memoirs of Esdras, Esd 7:27–9:15 ; (2) the Memoirs of Nehemias, Neh 1:1–7:73 ; 12:27–13:31 ; (*a*) Aramaic documents, Esd 4:7 (8)–6:18 and 7:12–26. The

375

288e first contains the protest of Rehum to Artaxerxes I against the rebuilding of the walls, 4:7(8)–16 ; the king's reply, 4:18–22 ; the letter of Thathanai to Darius concerning the reconstruction of the temple, 5:7–17, and Darius' answer, 6:1–12 ; the dedication of the temple, 6:13–18. The second has the edict of Artaxerxes to Esdras, Esd 7:12–26 ; (4) Hebrew documents from the state archives : the decree of Cyrus, 1:2–4 ; the lists of those who first returned, Esd 2:1–70 = Neh 7:6–72 ; who returned with Esdras, Esd 8:1–14 ; who contracted mixed marriages, Esd 10:18–44 ; who helped in the building of the walls, Neh 3 ; who signed the covenant, Neh 10 ; who inhabited Jerusalem, etc., Neh 11:3–35, and who as priests or Levites returned with Zorobabel, 12:1–26. These are first-class sources that give to the books a character of historical credibility.

f Although the documents which compose the books of Esd and Neh are, in part, the work of these persons, our canonical books are later than both. The **date** of their compilation was probably during the period of Greek domination, *i.e.* in the latter part of the 4th cent. B.C. ; for the list of high-priests (Neh 12:11) stops with Jeddoa, a contemporary of Darius (12:22), who was, according to Jos. (*Ant.* 11, 7, 2 and 8, 2 ff.) Darius III Codomannus (336–331). Other indications reinforce this conclusion. Esdras and Nehemias are spoken of as persons who have long since disappeared from the historical scene, Neh 12:26, 46. The frequent use of the expression ' the King of the Persians ', Esd 1:1, 2, 8 ; 3:7 ; 4:3, 5, 7, 24 ; 7:1, insinuates that the Persians were no longer masters of Palestine. There are many Aramaisms as in the books of Par.

g It is very likely that the same person was the **author** or compiler of Esd, Neh and 1 and 2 Par. Many authorities maintain that these four books originally formed one work ; for the last 3 vv of 2 Par are identical with the first 3 of Esd ; there is the same predilection for statistical and genealogical lists ; a common sympathy for liturgical matters, and a common use of the same Aramaic and late Hebrew languages.

h Text and Versions—Apart from the two Aramaic fragments, the books were written in Hebrew, but the language is shot through with Aramaisms. One also finds expressions of Persian origin. The Aramaic is that spoken in the 5th cent. B.C., as is evident from comparison with the Elephantine papyri written in the same language. The HT on the whole is in a poor state, especially in the genealogical lists the transcription of which is always subject to errors.

i In LXX there are two **Greek Versions**. These are the two texts, Esdras A and B. Esd B corresponds to the canonical Esd-Neh, while Esd A is the apocryphal 3 Esd to be found in the Vg Appendix. Consisting of 9 chh it is another version of the last 2 chh of 2 Par, of all of Esd (with the transposition of Esd 4:7–24 to the end of ch 2) and of Neh 8:1–12. It has proper to itself a long account of a literary contest between three pages of the court of Darius I, the third of whom, Zorobabel, was victorious and obtained from the king permission and help to bring back to Jerusalem his co-nationalists, the Jews, 3:1–5:6.

j According to some modern writers (Torrey, Howarth) 3 Esd is a fragment of the LXX version of the original Semitic text, while Esd B (*i.e.* the Greek version of our canonical books) is the version of Theodotion. Most scholars are, however, against this view. The book is rather due to a compiler who wished to describe the history of the temple and divine worship from the Passover of Josias to the full restoration at the time of Esdras, Neh 8 ; since, however, in this work Zorobabel played an important part, his story was adorned with the fable of the three youths (probably from an Aramaic original). 3 Esd seems to have been compiled before the LXX version, Esd B, was made. It was used by Josephus and was cited by not a few Fathers as inspired, but from the 5th cent. it was considered by all as apocryphal.

For the **Syriac** version *cf.* Walton, *Biblia Polyglotta*, **2** Ldn. IV 1–29 and C. A. Howley, *A critical examination of the Peshitto version of the book of Ezra*, N.Y., 1922.

The **Vg** in general renders the HT faithfully enough.

Historical Background—**1.** Israel in exile. The exiles, **2** whose number is estimated at 60,000–80,000, were settled in various districts near Babylon, *e.g.* Tell Abib, Ez 3:15, Tell Charsa, Tell Melach, Esd 2:59, and Casiphia, Esd 8:17. In their new home they came to enjoy considerable freedom. Many continued to lead an agricultural life, others followed commercial pursuits and gradually acquired wealth, Esd 2 ; Zach 6:10 ff. Excavations at Nippur have unearthed ledgers of the Jewish banking family of ' Murashu and Sons ', 450–400 B.C. The ancient position of the elders of the people seems to have been recognized by the Babylonians, Ez 8:1 ; 14:1 ; 20:1. They resisted religious apostasy, Ez 14:1–11, despite the temptation in the popular mind to feel that Yahweh was presumably showing himself less powerful than the Babylonian Marduk.

2. Israel in Judah. Of the life of those who remained **b** in Judah (30,000–40,000) little is known. As a Babylonian province the land must have been placed under the charge of a governor. It is difficult to determine the boundaries, but the province was a small one from Bethel to Bethzur. Lam describes the distress of those left behind, and Jer 44, Ez 33:23–26 show that religious syncretism, idolatry and immorality increased, furthered, no doubt, by infiltration into the empty land from Moab, Ammon, and particularly from Edom.

3. The Return. The Jews owed their liberation to **c** one of those recurring surprises which make the course of history, humanly speaking, unpredictable. Cyrus the Great (559–529), son of Cambyses of the Achaemenid family, was a member of a Persian tribe —the Pasagardae. The little kingdom of the Achaemenids, in the district of Susa, placed itself at the head of a coalition of Persian tribes. By 549 Ecbatana, the capital of the Median overlords, had fallen and Cyrus declared himself ' king of Persia '. The attention of the world was now focussed on this extraordinary individual in whom the prophets had already seen an anointed of the Lord who ' shall give the nations before him ' (Cyrus) and he shall rule over kings ', Is 41:2 ; 44:28 ; 45:1. With the collapse of its Median partner, Babylonia took fright and its king Nabonidus (556–539) made league with Lydia and with Egypt. By 546 Sardis, the capital of Lydia, had fallen to Cyrus. He was then ready to strike at Babylonia, and in 539 he defeated the Chaldaean army and entered Babylon without opposition. In 525 Egypt was added to the Persian Empire by Cyrus' son Cambyses. Later repeated attempts were made to conquer Greece. One expedition sent by Darius I was defeated at Marathon, 490 B.C. ; another, in 480, was led by Xerxes I who was defeated in the naval battle of Salamis. Unable to subdue Greece, the Persians nevertheless kept a firm hold over the interior of Asia for about two centuries.

Cyrus the Persian had none of the ruthlessness of **d** Semitic conquerors. His faith (Zoroastrianism) and his political foresight made him broadminded, and he came to exiled Judah as a liberator rather than a conqueror. Within a short time of his occupation of Babylon, Cyrus issued the edict, Esd 1:2–4, which was to restore the fortunes of Israel.

The first group of returning exiles was led by **e** Sheshbazzar who immediately laid the foundations for a new temple on the site of the one destroyed, Esd 5:16, but the Jews were unable to complete it because of opposition from hostile neighbours and it was not until 515 B.C. that Zorobabel as governor of the province with the help of the high-priest Josue and the encouragement of the prophets Aggeus and Zacharias finally finished the building.

During the reign of Artaxerxes I (465–424) two other **f** groups of exiles returned. The first was led by Esdras

(458 B.C.) who brought with him a letter from the king authorizing him to take the leadership in the reform of the religious life of the community. In 445 B.C. another group returned under the leadership of Nehemias who had been made governor with permission to rebuild the walls of Jerusalem, Neh 1–6. The nation of Israel, dedicated to the Law, isolated from foreign influence, and localized about Jerusalem, is henceforth the people of Judah, or the ' Jews '.

For a list of the Persian kings, see § 125e.

Historical Value—Non-Catholic higher criticism in general acknowledges as historical the ' Memoirs ' of Esdras and Nehemias, but does not place much faith in the other parts of the books. Some critics accuse the chronicler of having falsified the documents and even of having invented them with a tendentious motive. The more moderate reproach him with an ignorance of Persian history. The answer to these charges is given in the text ; meanwhile, it may be noted : (1) that while the sacred writer wrote religious history, religious history is not to be equated with tendentious history ; (2) archaeological discoveries confirm the picture of Cyrus drawn by the chronicler. They show him as a monarch very tolerant in religious matters, who allowed all deported people to return to their native lands, and who showed respect for their local sanctuaries, restoring, e.g., the temple of Marduk in Babylon ; (3) the Elephantine papyri, discovered at the beginning of this century, confirm the historical framework of the books. From them we learn, e.g., that Samaria was the governor's seat, that his name was Sanballat who was in all likelihood the bitter enemy of Nehemias, Neh 2, etc. ; that there was in Judah a twofold authority, civil and religious ; that the high-priest of 408–407 was Johanan, Neh 12:11 ; (4) the activity of the returned exiles is confirmed by the prophetic books of Aggeus and Zacharias.

Critical Problems—1. The identity of, or distinction between, Sheshbazzar and Zorobabel : cf. § 290d. 2. The authenticity and original place in the narrative of the list of returned exiles, Esd 2 and Neh 7 : cf. § 290f. 3. The laying of the foundations of the temple in the second year of the return, Esd 3:8, appears to conflict with the statements in the Aramaic document, Esd 5:2, and in Agg 2:1, which seem to imply that work on the temple was not begun until the second year of Darius, 520 : cf. § 291d. 4. The passage Esd 4:6–23 appears to be misplaced. It deals with the reign of Xerxes I, Artaxerxes I and the rebuilding of the walls, while the context deals with the reign of Cyrus, Darius and the rebuilding of the temple : cf. § 291f–h. 5. The story of the reading of the Law in Neh 8–10 is considered by many to belong to the Esdras narrative. It interrupts the account of the peopling of the city and fills a gap in the story of Esdras : cf. §§ 294a, 297a–d.

Chronology—Who came first to Jerusalem, Esdras or Nehemias ? Some scholars believe that the Artaxerxes of Esd is not Art. I (465–424), but Art. II (404–358) ; therefore the date of Esdras' arrival ' in the 7th year of Artaxerxes ', Esd 7:7, is held to be 398 instead of 458, while Nehemias' arrival ' in the 20th year of Artaxerxes ', Neh 2:1, is still dated at 445. The majority of those who defend this opinion also make Neh 8–10 a part of the Esdras narrative and consider that the mention of Nehemias in Neh 8:9 and 10:1 is a gloss added after those chapters were transposed to their present place in the Nehemias story. Van Hoonacker, however, believing that Neh 8–10 is in its proper place, holds that Esdras first came as a young man with Nehemias in 445, then returned 47 years later as head of the caravan described in Esd 7 ff. ; cf. § 297a–d.

In the first place it is certain that Nehemias came to Jerusalem c 445, for he is found there together with Eliasib, the high-priest, Neh 3:1, and Joiada his son, Neh 13:28 ; moreover his Samaritan contemporary was Sanballat, Neh 2:19, etc. Now from the Ele-

phantine papyri (Sachau I) we know that the sons **289j** of Sanballat and Johanan, the son and successor of Joiada in the office of high-priest, were living in 408–407 B.C. This fixes decisively the activity of Nehemias during the reign of Art. I (465–424).

Objections to the view that Esdras came in 458, i.e. **k** 13 years before Nehemias are : (1) The condition of Jerusalem at the time of Nehemias' arrival cannot be reconciled with an earlier activity of Esdras ; for (a) ' the people were few therein ', Neh 7:4, whereas Esdras found ' a very great congregation ' gathered together, Esd 10:1 ; (b) the walls were broken down, Neh 1:3 ; (c) influential Jews lived on intimate terms with non-Jews and mixed marriages were rife, Neh 6:17–19, a condition of things which precludes their previous dissolution by Esdras, Esd 9 ff. ; (d) in Neh 1–6 there is no mention of any previous activity on the part of Esdras.

In reply it may be observed : (a) the question of **l** population is relative ; moreover, the congregation attracted by Esdras was not confined to Jerusalem, but came ' out of Israel ', Esd 10:1 ; (b) the attack on Jerusalem recorded ' in the days of Art. I ', Esd 4:7–23, was probably due to an attempt by Esdras to rebuild the walls and was the event which prompted Nehemias to go to Jerusalem in 445 (cf. Neh 1:3) ; (c) our knowledge of the result of Esdras' reformation is meagre ; the book ends abruptly and it appears that his mission met with failure. No doubt every difficulty was put in his way over the question of mixed marriages and, while his drastic measures in this matter did not succeed, they would account for the opposition that Nehemias encountered from the very beginning (cf. infra, n) ; (d) the argument from silence in the OT is precarious ; e.g. neither Aggeus nor Zacharias speak of each other although they were contemporaries ; the same is true of Isaias and Micheas, etc. ; moreover, the work of Esdras was essentially religious, while that of Nehemias was chiefly political.

(2) On his arrival Esdras found the city walls rebuilt, **m** Esd 9:9. But the word here translated ' wall ' (gāḏēr) does not occur again in the whole of Esd-Neh though the wall is one of its chief topics. In fact the word means a ' low wall ', e.g. the fence of vineyard, and is here, as in Ps 79:13, Is 5:5, used figuratively in the sense of ' protection '. Moreover it is ' a wall in Judah and Jerusalem ' where the wall in the case of Judah must be figurative ; hence Batten, 334, is forced to delete ' Judah ' from the text, or read ' around ' instead of ' and '.

(3) Esdras' reforms were more radical than those of **n** Nehemias, for while Esdras dissolved all marriages with foreign wives, Nehemias merely required parents to take an oath not to allow their children to contract such unions. The work of Nehemias has, therefore, the appearance of being tentative and introductory to that of Esdras. Briefly it may be replied that the drastic reforms attempted by Esdras broke down and in their place Nehemias put a more reasonable scheme that aimed at prevention more than cure. ' Politica est ars possibilium '.

(4) At the time when Nehemias rebuilt the walls, **o** Eliasib was high-priest, Neh 3:1 ; 13:4, but according to Esd 10:6, Esdras ' went into the chamber of Johanan ' who was the son, Esd 10:6, i.e. the grandson, Neh 12:11, of Eliasib. Now we know from the Elephantine papyri that Johanan was high-priest in 407. Hence Esdras must have come to Jerusalem in 398, not 458. The objection may be met in several ways : (a) the Johanan of Esd 10:6 is not the same person as Johanan the high-priest of Neh 12:11 ; the former was a son, the latter a grandson of Eliasib ; (b) Eliasib, Esd 10:6, is not Eliasib the high-priest of Neh 3:1, for whenever Eliasib the high-priest comes into this story the sacred writer is careful to mention that he is the high-priest, Neh 3:1, 20 ; 13:28. Perhaps Johanan was the son of the priest Eliasib who

289o was prefect of the treasury, Neh 13:4 ; (c) the words ' the chamber of Johanan son of Eliasib ' refer to the high-priest's son, but are used proleptically, *i.e.* the writer gives to the room the name by which it was known in his own day. The last solution is the most likely one.

p According to Van Hoonacker confusion arose owing to the fact that there were two kings with the name of Artaxerxes. Nehemias came in the 20th year of Art. I, while Esdras came in the 7th year of Art. II. A reader, assuming that the references were to the same Art., and considering that an event which took place in the 7th year should precede one which happened in the 20th year, made the transposition which we find in our present text. But it is unlikely that any reader would deal so drastically with the text, and, if he did, it is very unlikely that it would have been accepted by others without question.

q There is then no valid reason for abandoning the traditional chronology, and today there is a marked reaction in its favour ; *cf.* ET 58 (1947) 263. In any event, to hold that the sacred writer erroneously believed that Esdras preceded Nehemias is incompatible with the fundamental principles of inspiration.

r **The Significance of Esd-Neh**—With the return from exile there began a new phase in the history of Israel. It was no more an independent nation, but a Persian province. From the political standpoint all was lost. One thing alone remained, its religious patrimony. Israel was still the Chosen People. The repatriates were still that ' remnant ' out of which would rise the new and glorious Israel. The old Israel had been destroyed because it had forsaken Yahweh ; the new Israel must therefore rededicate itself to him. At the same time the purity and exclusiveness of its religion would preserve its national life. Hence the Jews were to be separated from the pagan influences about them. This was effected by Esdras and Nehemias. Esdras belonged to the class of ' scribes ' (*sopherim*) which had worked so assiduously on the literary legacy of Israel, the only consolation of the faithful in exile. This was the inspired *Torah* (Law) or Pentateuch, Neh 8:1, 2, 18 ; 9:3, 13–14, 29, 34, which Esdras brought with him to Jerusalem, Esd 7, where it was publicly read and proclaimed as the charter of post-exilic Israel. The wall which Nehemias built around the city was a symbol of his work for the racial and, therefore, religious purity of his people. Both fought unceasingly against marriage with non-Israelites.

s From this time on, the influence of the priesthood so grew that when, for a period under the Maccabees, the Jews won their political liberty, both spiritual and temporal power were in its hands. The Mosaic institutions, too, received several additions : (1) the ' scribes ', many of them laymen, devoted to the study and explanation of the Law ; (2) the Sanhedrin or council of elders, which during the Greek domination was the chief administrative authority in matters both spiritual and temporal ; (3) the synagogue. Thus arose Judaism with its advantages and defects, which, in the fullness of time, its mission completed, was to give place to the universalism of Christ.

t **Canonicity**—The books of Esd-Neh are not quoted either in the OT or the NT. The passage about Nehemias in 2 Mac 1:18–2:13 is drawn from another source. But Jewish tradition has always inscribed them among the canonical writings and, apart from some hesitation on the part of the Antiochean school, Christian tradition sanctioned this verdict. The Council of Trent has defined them as canonical.

ESDRAS

290a **Section I : Esd I-VI : The Return of the Jewish Exiles to Jerusalem : the Re-establishment of Worship and Rebuilding of the Temple.**
I 1 The Edict of Cyrus—The book begins with the last words of 2 Par, vv 1, 2, 3*a* occurring in 2 Par 36:22, 23. Very likely 1 and 2 Par, Esd and Neh

originally constituted one work, but subsequently the **29** arrangement in MT was altered to Esd, Neh, 1 and 2 Par in order to complete the history narrated in 4 Kg by an account of the Return from Captivity. The opening verses of Esd were then made to serve as the conclusion of 2 Par. ' first year ' : *i.e.* of Cyrus' reign over the conquered Babylonian empire (538 B.C.). As king of Persia (Anshan) he had ruled since 559 ; *cf.* 5:13 and § 289*c*. ' Cyrus ' : Accadian, Kurush ; in MT *Kōreš*. ' the word of the Lord ' : *cf.* Jer 25:12 ; 29:10 where the period of captivity was predicted as 70 years. Its actual duration from the Fall of Jerusalem in 586 was about 50 years but the first deportation seems to have taken place in 606, the third year of the reign of Joakim, king of Judah (608–596) ; *cf.* Dan 1:1 ; 4 Kg 24:1 ; 2 Par 36:6 ; Jos. *Ant.* 10, 11 ; *c. Ap.* 1:19. This would give almost 70 years ; *cf.* Bi 8 (1927) 408. The sacred writer makes clear that the religious purpose of the book is to demonstrate the fulfilment of prophecy ; *cf.* Jer 29:10–14 ; Is 44:28 ; 45:1–4. ' the Lord stirred up . . . Cyrus ' ; *cf.* Is 45:1 where Cyrus is styled ' Yahweh's anointed '. He was the instrument chosen for the fulfilment of the divine plan. ' proclamation ' : the Cyrus cylinder in the Brit. Museum shows that Cyrus gave similar permission to all subject and deported peoples. The announcement would be in a special form (and language) for promulgation to each separate group. The writer gives the particular form in which it was announced to the Jewish people. This was not the decree cited 6:2 ff. but the ' proclamation ' by which heralds made that decree known. ' in writing ' ; *cf.* 6:2 ff.

2-4 The Proclamation—**2.** ' the Lord God of Heaven **b** hath given me ' : ' the Lord ' represents, as always, the divine name ' Yahweh '. Although not a monotheist, Cyrus had great regard for the religious beliefs of his subjects, and claimed the patronage of each local divinity ; *e.g.* his capture of Babylon is ascribed to the favour of Marduk. So here his success is attributed to Yahweh. **3.** If the permission to rebuild the temple was an act of political insight, it was also a fulfilment of the divine plan for the restoration of Israel. ' Whosoever there is among you of all his people, his God [*i.e.* Yahweh] be with him '. The words are a common form of greeting. ' among you ' : all the subjects of the Persian empire. ' of all his people ' : the proclamation has in view the Jews of the Southern Kingdom who had been deported by Nabuchodonosor. It is not likely that Cyrus would have known of the deportation of the Northern Kingdom to Assyria in 721 B.C. ' All the rest ', etc. : ' *whosoever is left* ' ; in any place where the survivors of the Jewish captivity are to be found, let the people of that place, apparently non-Israelites (6) as well as those Jews who would not wish to return themselves, render him all assistance. **4.** ' besides . . . freely ' : gifts of money, etc., towards the expenses of rebuilding the temple.

5-11 The Return of the Jews.—**5.** The Effect. ' chief **c** of the fathers ' : elliptical for ' the heads of the families or clans '. ' and every one ' : ' *even all* ', etc., implying that many did not avail themselves of the opportunity of returning. The lot of many of the exiles was not unhappy. **6.** ' all they that were round about ' : their pagan neighbours and those Jews who preferred to remain. ' helped their hands ' : furnished them with whatever was necessary for their return and settlement in the fatherland. ' furniture ' : ' *precious things* '. ' besides . . . accord ' : the free-will offerings for the temple (*cf.* 4). The other gifts were personal to the travellers.

7-8. Cyrus restores the vessels taken from the Temple. **d** **7.** ' vessels ' : Cyrus was sending back to the various cities of Babylon the deities, *i.e.* statues of idols, carried off by his predecessor Nabonidus to Babylon, and rebuilding temples for them where necessary. The God of the Jews had no image that could be returned, but his temple could be rebuilt and some of its furniture restored. ' Nabuchodonosor had taken ' ; *cf.* 4 Kg 24:13 ; 25:13–17. **8.** ' Mitredath '—' dedicated to

90d Mithra' the Persian god. 'the son of Gazabar': '*the treasurer*', Persian 'gangewar'. 'Sassabasar': Sheshbazzar (Shamash-abu-uṣur 'Shamash, protect the father' [?]). His identity is puzzling, as he is named only here and in 5:14, 15, whereas throughout the rest of this section Zorobabel appears as the leader. Some scholars think that Sheshbazzar and Zorobabel are two names for the same individual. In favour of this view are the facts that. (*a*) the foundation of the temple is ascribed to both, 3:8 ; 5:16 ; (*b*) Sheshbazzar is a 'prince (*nāśī*') of Judah', and Zorobabel is of the Davidic line, 1 Par 3:18 ; (*c*) the title of governor (*peḥāh*) is given to both, 5:11 and Agg 1:1. Yet (*a*) it is strange to find the same person, a Jew, called by two *Babylonian* names ; (*b*) in Esd 5:14 f., the Persian Satrap quotes the statement of the Jewish leaders, Zorobabel and Josue, who seem to refer to Sheshbazzar as a different individual. More probably then, Sheshbazzar was the *predecessor* of Zorobabel. Some identify him with Shenassar, the uncle of Zorobabel, 1 Par 3:18, but the evidence is not convincing. It is more likely that he was a Persian official.

e 9-11. The number of the vessels. 9. 'knives': probably '*censers*' or '*liturgical knives*' (Zorell) ; Torrey suggests 'snuffers'. 10. 'second sort': of inferior quality or for inferior purposes ; the Heb. word, however, seems to be a corruption of the numeral 'two thousand' ; read with 3 Esd 2:13, 'Silver cups 2410'. 11. 'five thousand and four hundred': the vessels enumerated make up only 2,499. 3 Esd has '1000 bowls of gold' and '2410 silver cups', giving a total of 5,469. Either MT is corrupt or only the larger vessels are enumerated and the full number was made up of smaller utensils.

f II 1-70 The Register of the Jews who returned—The list is repeated in Neh 7:6-73 and 3 Esd 5:7-45 with some differences in names and numbers due to the mistakes of copyists. Its original place is disputed. It certainly existed in the Memoirs of Neh, but whether the author of Esd took it over from this source or from the archives of Jerusalem, is difficult to decide. In any event, it is not, as some critics contend, a list of inhabitants at the time of Esd and Neh (after 458 B.C.). The Tirshatha (governor) in 63 is Sheshbazzar. The title (1), the mention of Babylonian localities from which certain families came (59), the need of establishing one's genealogy (62 f.), the numbering of the singing men and women (65) and the mention of transport animals only (66 f.), are all undesigned confirmations that the document was composed shortly after the Return.

g 1-2a Introduction. 1. 'children of the province': the Jews inhabiting the Persian subprovince of Judaea, the district of which Jerusalem was the centre and of which Zorobabel was governor after Sheshbazzar. 'returned': the return was chiefly a migration to the land of their fathers by Jews born in Babylonia. The majority of Nabuchodonosor's deportees would have died during the intervening years. 'every man to his city': to the city to which his clan belonged, in so far as this was practicable. The Persian province of Judaea was smaller in area than the kingdom of 50 years before. Zorobabel : the name means 'seed of Babel'. The descendant of Jechonias (Jehoiachin), he was of royal blood ; *cf.* 1:8 and 3:2. Josue (MT *Yēšúa‘*) was the high-priest of the Return, Agg 1:1-12 ; Zach 3:1, the son of Josedec and grandson of the high-priest Seraias whom Nabuchodonosor put to death at Riblah (Reblatha) after the destruction of Jerusalem ; *cf.* 1 Par 6:1-15 ; 4 Kg 25:18-21. 'Nehemia': not to be confused with Nehemias, the son of Helchias, Neh 1:1. The names number 11, but the list in Neh 7:7 has 12, naming also, after Raheleia, a certain Nahamani, omitted here by an error in transcription. They are probably intended to be symbolic of the 12 tribes of Israel.

h 2b-19. A list of 'the men of Israel', the laity as distinct from the priests and Levites. The names are those of *families* or clans. 3. Pharos (Parosh) is a strange proper name meaning a 'flea'. Though a 'new'

family it is placed first in all the lists. 6. 'Phahath **290h** Moab': '*governor of* Moab'. Probably the founder of this family had exercised rule over some portion of Moab ; *cf.* 1 Par 4:22. 'Josua : Joab': *Jeshua* (and) Joab were special branches of the main family, otherwise unknown. 14. Beguai (*Biguai*) : this family seems to have adopted a Persian name. 16. 'of Ather who were of Ezechias': the descendants of Ather through the branch of Ezechias.

20-35. Another list according to localities (except **i** 30-32) which are all within a radius of 25 m. from Jerusalem. MT has '*sons of*' (Bethlehem, etc.), but in Heb. 'son' has a much wider sense than in English. The numbers are much smaller than those of the families in 3-19. 20. Gebbar : Neh 7:25 has 'Gabaon, a well-known city (*cf.* Jos 9 ; 3 Kg 3:4, etc.). 22. Netupha : probably Beit Nettif, 20 m. W. of Bethlehem, a Levitical city, 1 Par 9:16. 23. Anathoth : the home of Jeremias, Jer 1:1. 24. Azmaveth, elsewhere called Beth-Azmot (LXX and Neh 7:28), is thought to be the modern el-Hizma, 5 m. N. of Jerusalem, 2 m. from Anathoth. 29. Nebo : identified by some with Nob in Judaea (Is 10:32), by others with the modern Nuba near Qeila, S. of Jerusalem. 30-32. Megbis (*Magbish*) does not occur in the parallel lists ; 'the other Elam' (in contrast to 7) and Harim are names of peoples, not of towns. 35. Senaa was, from the number of its inhabitants, an important city. It was identified by Eusebius and Jerome with Magdalsenna ('tower of Senna'), about 5 m. N. of Jericho. Today there remain only a few ruins.

36-39. Of the four priestly houses mentioned here, one, **j** Peshur (Pashur) is not among the 24 enumerated in 1 Par 24:7-18 ; it was probably a branch of the house of Melchia (*cf.* 1 Par 9:12 ; 24:9 ; Neh 10:3).

40-42. The families of the Levites. These include the **k** Levites proper, 1 Par 24:20-31, the singers, 1 Par 25:1-7, 9-31, and the doorkeepers, 1 Par 26:1-19. The number of Levites (74) is surprisingly small. 40. 'the *sons* of Josue, of Kadmiel, *of Binnui*, of Hodaviah', reading *binnûi* for *b[e]nê* with Neh 12:8 and 3 Esd.

43-54. 'The Nathinites': *Nethinim*. The name means **l** 'given' to the temple service ; *cf.* 1 Par 9:2. They formed a distinct class and assisted the Levites in the discharge of the more menial tasks, and were originally captives of war, Jos 9:23 ; on the return from exile they were reckoned as members of the Israelite community, Neh 10:29. 50. Munim (*Me‘unim*), inhabitants of Maon, were an Arab people subjugated by Ozias, king of Judah, 2 Par 26:7. Nephusim (*Nephisim*) : an Ishmaelite tribe, Gen 25:15 ; hence also Arab (*cf.* 1 Par 5:18-22).

55-58. 'Solomon's servants': the descendants of the **m** native Canaanites conquered by Solomon and employed on his buildings, 3 Kg 9:21. They formed a subdivision of the Nethinim, Neh 7:28 ; *cf.* 7:60 ; 11:3.

59-63. Israelites and priests of uncertain origin. 59. Thelmela, etc. : localities in Babylonia. 61. *Barzillai*, the Galaadite, benefactor and then favourite of David, 2 Kg 17:27. His estates were inherited by his daughters, one of whom was married to a priest who thereupon received the family name ; hence, probably, the difficulty about his genealogy. 62 bears witness to the care taken of family registers and to the importance attached to the genealogical lists in the sacred writings. 63. Athersatha : *Tirshatha*, Persian *tarshata*, 'he who is feared', is here applied to Sheshbazzar. It is roughly equivalent to 'His Excellency'. 'holy of holies': 'holy *things*', the priest's portion of the sacrificial meat, Lev 7:31-34. 'learned and perfect': '*with Urim and Thummim*'; *cf.* Ex 28:30. Probably at the time of Esdras the stones (?) were lost together with the high-priest's apparel.

64-67 A Summary—The total of the returned exiles **n** (42,360) agrees with that given in Neh 7:66 and 3 Esd 5:41. The items, however, in all three lists fail to produce the sum, Esd 29, 818 ; Neh 31,089 ;

290n 3 Esd 30,143). Perhaps the 12,000 persons unaccounted for were the women (only the more wealthy would be accompanied by their wives), or Israelite elements of the old kingdom of Samaria who, during the exile, came into contact with the deportees from Judaea. It is not necessary to conclude that there were 42,360 in the first caravan. The list, probably compiled about 520 B.C., includes all those who returned at various times up to that date, considering them as parts of one migration. Neh 7:5 testifies to the authenticity of the list.

o **65.** ' singing men . . . women ' : not the temple singers of 41, but those employed to sing at feasts and funerals, etc., 2 Sam 19:35 ; Eccl 2:7. Evidently there were several wealthy Jews in the caravan. Some commentators liken the singers to camp-followers (*cf.* Ex 12:30 ; Num 11:4).

66-67. The animals enumerated are beasts of burden, an argument for the contemporaneity of the list with the migration. The horses and mules would be ridden by the wealthier, the asses by the poorer classes. The camels and asses would carry the baggage.

p **68-69.** The gifts for the construction of the temple. **68.** ' chief of the fathers ' ; *cf.* 1:5. **69.** ' solids ' : *dark^emônîm*, probably not the Persian daric (*cf.* 8:27, *'adarkōnîm*), but the drachma, itself of foreign origin (BDB, 204). If we accept the drachma instead of the daric, the total sum given is about $300,000 ; or taking the daric, about $450,000 ; *cf.* §83*d–f*. The daric was worth about 5 dollars ; a ' pound ' (*maneh*) of silver about 30 dollars. Neh 7:10 ff. breaks these totals down into contributions from ' His Excellency ', from the chiefs of the clans, and from the people.

70. The verse sums up the whole list. ' So the priests, the Levites, the singers, the porters and, *of the laymen*, the Nethinim were dwelling in their cities and (so) all Israel in their cities.' *Cf.* Neh 7, 73 and 3 Esd 5, 46.

291a **III 1-13 The Renewal of Worship and the Beginning of the New Temple.**
1-3 The Building of the Altar—1. ' the seventh month ' of the religious year (Tishri, presumably Sept.–Oct. 537 B.C.), the first of the civil. **2.** Jesua ; *cf.* 2:2. Zorobabel's ' brethren ' are the heads of the families (2:2). ' son of Salathiel ' : in 1 Par 3:19 Zorobabel is called the son of Phadaia (Pedaiah), the brother of Salathiel (Shealtiel). The discrepancy may be explained by the suppositions (*a*) that he was the real son of Pedaiah and the legal son of Shealtiel (Pedaiah having married Shealtiel's childless widow, according to the law of Deut 25:5 f.), or (*b*) (following some MSS), the son of Pedaiah and the grandson of Shealtiel. ' built the altar ' : the chief purpose of the return was to restore to Yahweh his due cult in Sion ' which he had chosen '. Both love and duty to God required the exiles to make the venture. Ps 125 (126) pictures the desolation of Israel in its inability to perform the temple liturgy. Ezechiel and other prophets had, during the Exile, filled them with longing enthusiasm for the day of Yahweh, associated often with the Messianic coming, when a purified remnant of God's people should rebuild the temple more glorious than before ; and though in face of innumerable obstacles their fervour slackened (as Aggeus trenchantly reminded them) we see here the first enthusiasm of the Return, when they were able to renew the sacrifice on Mt Sion, the symbol of a reunited people, and make plans for the re-erection of the temple. **3.** ' upon its bases ' : *i.e.* of the former altar or, by a slight emendation ' *in its place* ', where it had formerly stood. An effort seems to have been made to continue the worship on the site of the temple after its destruction, Jer 41:5, but the present situation demanded a new altar. ' put them in fear ' : ' in fear *upon them from* the people of the lands ', but the phrase is awkward and the text corrupt. A slight change (from *b^e'ēmāh* ' in fear ' to *bāmāh*) gives ' upon its bases, *for there was a high place upon them* (made by) the people of the land '. For ' *high place* ' *cf.* § 252*b*. As it stands, the text alludes

to the opposition mentioned in 4:1–5 and may be a **291** note that has fallen out of its proper place.

4-6 The Feast of Tabernacles ; *cf.* Num 29:12–39 **b** and § 113*j*. **5.** ' and afterwards ' : after the celebration of this feast, the use of the prescribed daily sacrifice (a lamb every morning and evening) as well as the offerings of the first of the month (new-moon) and of all the set feasts, were resumed, together with the sacrifices dictated by private devotion ; *cf.* Num 28:11–15 ; Lev 23:1–44.

7-13 The Laying of the Temple Foundation—7. ' *to* **c** *the sea, to Joppe* '. The operation, as in the case of the first temple, 3 Kg 5:6–11, involved hauling timber from Lebanon down to the coast, then floating it in rafts to Joppe, whence the Jews undertook its further transport to Jerusalem. ' orders ' : ' *permit* '. **8.** ' the second month ' : Apr.–May, 536 B.C. **8b.** ' began. And they appointed ' : ' *made a beginning by appointing* '. ' hasten forward ' : ' *direct* '. **9.** Josue : not the Josue of 8 (who was high-priest), but a Levite, 2:40. ' Cedmihel, and his sons, and the children of Judah ' : read with Esd 2:40 ; Neh 12:8, ' *Kadmiel, Binnui and Hodaviah* ', *i.e.* the heads of the Levites. ' Henadad-Levites ' seems to be a marginal gloss for Hodaviah which crept into the text. **10.** ' by the hands of ' : *i.e.* according to the norms outlined by David, 1 Par 16, or ' chanting Psalms composed and ordered by David '. **11.** ' together ' : antiphonally. The words of praise which follow are the refrain of Ps 135 (136). ' foundations ' : this was a promising beginning but the work was shortly abandoned to be resumed again only after 16 years. Aggeus blames their inertness and lack of zeal ; the present book speaks only of vague ' hindrance ', 4:4–5, but it is easy to fill in the details. The population already inhabiting Judaea, consisting partly of the descendants of the Jews who were never deported, but mostly of neighbouring peoples, their traditional enemies who had drifted in to occupy the abandoned countryside, would naturally resent the sudden irruption of an organized and active band of settlers, fiercely exclusive in their Law and religion, claiming rightful ownership of the territory and bent on rebuilding Jerusalem into a powerful and prosperous state. Hence the struggle, a life-and-death matter for the Jewish community, to make good their claim to practise their own way of life in the midst of the nations—a struggle not finally won until the completion of Nehemias' work, a hundred years later.

Some critics have questioned whether the foundations **d** of the temple were really laid in the 2nd year of the Return on the ground that Agg 2:1 and Zach 8:9 seem to imply that it was not begun until the 2nd year of Darius Hystaspes (520 B.C.). But the statements of the prophets are sufficiently explained if it is assumed that a commencement was made in 536, that the progress of the work was suspended because of opposition, and that the renewal of it in 520 was practically a fresh start, as indeed the book of Esdras itself declares it to have been, 5:2. ' wept ' : there is no suggestion here (as there is in Agg 2:3) of a contrast between the appearance of the old temple and the new—which did not exist. The old people were simply overcome with emotion at what must have been, for them, a deeply moving ceremony. **13.** ' one with another ' : omit.

IV 1-24 The Record of Opposition—(1) from the reign **e** of Cyrus to the reign of Darius, 4:1–5 ; (2) during the reign of Xerxes, 4:6 ; (3) during the reign of Artaxerxes I, 4:7–23. **1.** ' the enemies ' : the descendants of the immigrants, who, to replace the Israelite population that had been deported after the fall of Samaria (721 B.C.), had been introduced, first of all by Sargon from Babylon and the East, 4 Kg 17:24, then by Esarhaddon (2) and Ashurbanipal (10). **2.** ' we seek your God ' : the claim to co-operate in the work of building the temple is based upon common worship. An Israelite priest had been brought back from captivity to teach them the worship of Yahweh, 4 Kg 17:28. Esarhaddon (681–668), the successor

1e of Sennacherib. **3.** 'nothing to do with us': the Samaritans had made of their own pagan religion and of the Israelite worship a hybrid syncretism which was the principal reason for their repulse by the Jews; the official reason offered was the fact that the Exiles were not authorized to extend to others the privileges conferred upon them by Cyrus. **4.** 'Then': 'and'. 'the people of the land': the non-Israelites (not only Samaritans) who had settled in Palestine as well as the Jews who had never been in exile. 'weakened' the hands: disheartened. The Heb. construction gives the idea of a continuous policy of hindering, terrifying and bribing. **5.** 'hired': 'were bribing' the local Persian officials. The effect of this opposition was the interruption of the building of the temple up to the 2nd year of Darius Hystaspes, from 536 to 520.

f **6-23** deal with much later history. Having mentioned that the opposition of hostile neighbours prevented the Jews from speedily building the temple, the sacred writer apparently collects from his sources three *later* instances of similar opposition in which recourse was had to the Persian court. **6.** Of the first, to Xerxes (Assuerus) in 485, we know neither the authors nor the object. **7.** Of the second, to Artaxerxes I, the authors are named but not the object, perhaps because the accusation was without effect. 'the rest *of their associates*'. 'written in *the* Syrian *character* and *set forth* in the Syrian tongue': i.e. in Aramaic, the language of Syria and N. Palestine at this time, and soon to be adopted by the Jews themselves. It was the *lingua franca* of the Fertile Crescent and regularly used in Persian administrative documents dealing with lands west of the Euphrates. This verse, like the preceding, is apparently a citation from a larger context.

g **8-23.** The third recourse (also to Artaxerxes I) is reported extensively (11-16) and is followed by the reply of the king (17-22). The writer probably drew from an Aramaic source, since the text continues in Aramaic till 6:19 where Hebrew is abruptly resumed. Since both Xerxes and Artaxerxes lived after Darius to whom 24 refers and to whose reign the events of ch 5 belong, the section, 4:6-23, departs from chronological order, because the writer wished to give a comprehensive summary of the several occasions when opposition was offered to the Jews by their enemies. The charge made in this section is not the building of the temple (the subject of which is resumed in 24 and ch 5), but the fortification of Jerusalem (12), very probably by the group which returned with Esdras (458 B.C.); cf. ch 7.

h Some modern commentators think that the Aramaic document 4:8-6:18 was a Memorandum written by the Jews to Artaxerxes I in which was first quoted the denunciation by Rehum and the reply of Art. forbidding the construction of the walls, then the very different conduct of Darius I on the occasion of the building of the temple. They contend that 7 is also Aramaic and to be read: 'And in the days of Art., in *harmony with* [*biše lōm*: cf. 3 Esd] Mithridates [a Persian governor], Tabe'el [a Jew] wrote', etc. In this solution, 4:24 is either a gloss due to a misunderstanding of the context, or the conclusion of a summary of events from the time of Cyrus to that of Art., of which the author cites only the concluding lines. 6 (Xerxes) is also held to be a gloss, so that there is only one accusation (Rehum's); cf. Schaeder, *Iran. Beitr.* I 212 ff.

i **8.** Beeltem is not a proper name, but a title, 'chief officer', i.e. governor of the province. 'scribe': the governor's secretary. The greater part of 9-11 is a parenthesis to explain who the colleagues were that associated themselves to Rehum in the accusation. The names of the nationalities to which the Samaritans belonged, show their non-Jewish origin; the identification of most of them is uncertain. The Apharsites were Persian, the Erchuites, natives of Erech, and the Susanechites, colonists from Susa, the Elamite capital. Perhaps Apharsathacites and Apharsites are different

transcriptions of the same name. **10a.** Asenaphar: **291i** *Ashurbanipal* (668-626), successor of Esarhaddon. Following the Assyrian practice of transferring captured populations, he used central Palestine as a convenient dumping-ground for the peoples mentioned—who were from widely different localities. It is curious that the petitioners should qualify an Assyrian king as 'great and glorious' when writing to a Persian monarch. 'this side of the river': the regions west of the Euphrates which formed the Syrian satrapy of Abar-Nahara ('beyond the river'). 'In peace': '*and now*'. As in 11 and 17, it is an epistolary form, marking a transition.

11-16 The Letter—11. 'send greeting': '*And now*', **j** be it known, etc. **12.** The reference is probably to the caravan led by Esdras (458); cf. § 289f. 'which . . . walls': 'which they are *rebuilding and are finishing* [*yešaklelûn*] *the walls and repairing the foundations*'. The text is obscure. **13.** 'repaired': '*finished*'. **13b.** 'and this loss', etc.: '*and in the end it* will *damage the kings*': affect the revenue injuriously. **4.** '*But* because we eat the salt of the palace': because we are in the king's pay; cf. *salarium*, money given to provide salt. 'and because it *is not right* for us to *witness* the king's *dishonour*'. **15.** 'histories': records kept by Artaxerxes' predecessors. **16.** 'repaired': '*finished*'. **16b.** The Syrian province will be lost to Persia.

17-22 Artaxerxes' Reply—17b. 'sending', etc.: **k** '*Peace to you. And now*'. **18.** 'plainly': the allusions, etc., of the letter had been faithfully explained. **20.** 'powerful kings': as David, Solomon, Menahem, etc. **21.** '*Now give command that these men cease* and that this city be not built until *a decree* [further permission to build] *is issued* from me'. **22b.** 'lest *damage should increase to the kings' hurt*'. **23.** 'with *an army* and troops': i.e. an armed force. **24.** 'the second year of Darius': 520 B.C. The narrative of Neh shows how utterly the attempt to restore Jerusalem had failed. We may infer that the enemy destroyed what work had been accomplished; for it seems to have been on this occasion that 'its walls were broken down, and its gates burned with fire', Neh 1:4. With 24 the writer returns to the history of the previous century, repeating 5b. 'Then': '*thus*', i.e. by this sort of thing.

V 1-17 The Building of the Temple recommended— 292a 1-2. The narrative of 4:5 is resumed. There is silence regarding the period 536-520 B.C. The hostility of their neighbours had so discouraged the Jews that they said: 'The time is not come for Yahweh's house to be built', Agg 1:2. Out of this despondency they were roused by two prophets, Aggeus and Zacharias; cf. §§ 543b, 545b. **1.** 'in the name of the God of Israel which was upon them': i.e. inspired them; cf. Deut 28:10; Jer 7:10, etc. **2.** 'began to build': i.e. recommenced; cf. 3:18 f The earlier attempt had failed so completely that the resumption of the work could be considered a new undertaking.

3-5 The Complaint against the Jews—3. Thathanai: **b** he is named in a Babylonian document of 502 as governor 'beyond the river', i.e. satrap of Abar-Nahara; cf. JNES 3 (1944) 46. In this document Ta-at-'tan-ni' is clearly distinguished from Ushtani his superior with whom previous commentators have identified him. Stharbuzanai: Shethar is the name, Boznai perhaps an official title of unknown meaning. 'counsellors': '*associates*'. 'counsel': '*a permit*'. We may assume that complaints from the Samaritans led the satrap to inquire what authority the Jews had received to undertake the work. That authorization was required to rebuild a temple under Persian rule is evidenced by the Elephantine papyri; cf. § 289g. 'wall': the sense of the Aram. word is uncertain; probably the *plinth* of the old temple on which they planned to construct the new. Joüon, Bi 22 (1941) 38 reads 'wainscoting'. **4.** The text is corrupt. Read with a correction from 3 Esd 6:4: 'Then we spoke to them as follows: *What are* the names of the men

292b *who are building this house?'* **3** and **4** contain two separate questions asked by the satrap. The Jews' replies are given at length in the following letter. **5.** The eye (favour) of God is shown in the fact that Thathanai allowed the work to go on until he had learned the decision of Darius. **5b.** '*so that* they did not hinder them *until a report* should be *sent* to Darius and a *written reply returned about this affair*'.

c 6-17 The Letter of Thathanai to Darius—Thathanai could not venture to arrest a work which was alleged to have the sanction of Cyrus (**13**), but cautiously decided to refer the whole matter to Darius. The tone and contents of his report are studiously fair and dispassionate. **6.** 'his counsellors', etc.: '*his Persian associates*'. **8.** 'we went': the satrap's residence was in Samaria. 'house': '*temple*'. 'unpolished': '*massive*', lit. '*stones of rolling*', so large that they had to be moved on rollers. **9.** 'repair these walls': '*finish this sanctuary*' (?). **10b.** 'and *that we might write*'. 'chief among them': those who would be held responsible. **11.** 'a great king': Solomon, 'the great king', 3 Kg 6:8. **12** gives the reason why the temple had been destroyed. **13.** 'Cyrus the king of Babylon': the king of Persia was also master of the great Chaldaean capital. **14.** 'governor': of the district of Judaea, under the authority of the satrap of 'Beyond-the-River'. **15.** 'the temple that is in Jerusalem': this phrase is frequently used, even of the time when the temple lay in ruins. **16.** 'since that time': from 536 to 520 B.C. **17.** '*let search be made*'. 'library': '*house . of treasures*', which was apparently the repository of important documents as well as of treasure.

d VI 1-22 The Persian King approves the Rebuilding of the Temple: its Completion and Dedication.
1-5 The Finding of the Decree of Cyrus—**1.** 'library', etc.: '*in the house of the archives where the treasures were stored* in Babylon' (*cf.* 5:17). 'Babylon': as in 5:17 the word is used loosely by the Jewish writer as meaning not the city alone, but the kingdom of Babylonia, including Persia. **2.** 'Ecbatana': the capital of Media and the summer residence of the Persian kings. It is the modern Hamadan in Iran. Cyrus had remained in Babylon, after its capture, from Dec. 539 to March 538. In the summer of 538 he was in Ecbatana, and a decree of his 'first year' would naturally be dated there and preserved there. (This detail is interesting evidence of the reliability of the writer's sources: Ecbatana was deserted after Alexander's conquests, and a Jewish writer of the Greek period would never think of locating Cyrus' archives there.) **2.** '*in the* castle [*i.e.* royal palace] that is in the province of Media'. 'a book': '*roll*' of leather or parchment. The use of these materials, rather than clay tablets, was favoured by the adoption of the Aramaic script in the Persian chancellery. Cuneiform could not well be written on parchment. 'in which this record,' etc.: '*and in it was thus written: Memorandum*. In the first year' etc. It refers to the 'minute' of an oral decision taken by Cyrus. There is no need to suppose that this and 1:2-4 are different versions of a single document. The 'proclamation' was public; the 'record' here given is a memorandum notifying the royal pleasure to the officials whose duty it was to put it into force. Its curt and business-like **e** style is natural to such a document. **3.** The 'Memorandum' of Cyrus is now quoted. 'and that they lay the foundations that may support'. The text is corrupt, perhaps (with 3 Esd): '*and where they offer sacrifices by fire*'. '*It's* height', etc. The length of the temple is not given, and the other dimensions are twice those of Solomon's temple; *cf.* 3 Kg 6:2. The figures seem wrong, for the new temple was inferior to the old one; *cf.* Agg 2:4. **4.** 'Three rows of *massive* stones and *a row* of new timber': the meaning is not clear: perhaps (*a*) three *storeys* of stone surmounted by one of wood; (*b*) each three *layers* of stone was followed by one of wood (*cf.* 3 Kg 6:36). The 'charges' (expenses) were to be defrayed from

the royal revenue. **5.** 'which also were placed': **292** '*and place them*'. For the fulfilment of this decree, *cf.* 1:7-11.
6-12 The Decree of Darius to Thathanai—**6.** 'Now **f** therefore': an abrupt transition to the decree of Darius to which there is no introduction. Probably the sacred writer had before him the complete text of Darius' reply to Thathanai in which the rediscovered edict of Cyrus was quoted. The first part of the reply he merely summarized (**1, 2**); the Cyrus Memorandum he quoted in full (**3-5**); then he continued copying in full the last part of Darius' letter. 'depart from them': do not interfere with the work. **8.** 'I also', etc.: '*From me comes the order what he shall do for the elders . . . that expenses* be diligently given to these men, *and that without delay*'. The abrupt closing clause stresses the urgency of the royal rescript. **9.** 'And *whatever is* necessary, *young bullocks, rams and lambs*'. 'that there be no complaint in anything': MT more trenchantly '*without fail*'. **10.** 'oblations': '*sacrifices of sweet odour*'; *cf.* Jer 29:7 and Bar 1:10-12, where the Jews are bidden to pray for the welfare of their Neo-Babylonian rulers. There is no indication, however, that the Persian kings had a special reverence for the God of the Jews. Similar directions for prayers and sacrifices for the king were issued to the Babylonian and Egyptian polytheists. **11.** 'and set up', etc.: '*let him be lifted up*, and *fastened* upon it' by impalement or crucifixion. 'confiscated': '*made a dunghill*'. **12.** 'resist': '*alter*' (the decree).

In view of the detailed knowledge of the requirements **g** for Jewish ritual (**9**), it has been questioned whether this is a copy of a Persian decree, and not rather a digest of it by the Jewish writer in his own words. It seems likely that the decree was drafted by a Jewish secretary, for we know from the narratives of Neh and Dan that Jews did occupy posts of importance at the Persian court. And if such friendly intervention was possible, it would be highly desirable for Zorobabel and his companions to get as detailed a commission as possible, which would leave little scope for restrictive interpretations of the king's will by local officials.
13-18 The Completion and Dedication of the Temple —**14.** 'according to': '*thanks to*' the prophetic ministry, *i.e.* strengthened by the inspired words of Agg. and Zach. **14.** Artaxerxes: the temple was really completed in the reign of Darius (*cf.* **15**). The name is mentioned either in anticipation of his contributions (*cf.* 7:1) or is a gloss added through misunderstanding of the documents in 4:7-23. **15.** 'the third of Adar' which fell between Feb. and March. 'the sixth year': 515 B.C. The work, resumed in the 2nd year of Darius, 5:2, had taken more than four years to finish. **17.** The modest number of the sacrificial beasts speaks eloquently of the poverty of the community, at least in livestock. Contrast the numbers given in 3 Kg 8:5-63. 'all Israel': the 'remnant' that returned is conscious of representing the whole people of God. Hence the sin-offering for the twelve tribes, although ten had been swallowed up in the Assyrian empire. **19.** Here the narrative is resumed in Hebrew and a new section begins.
19-22 The Celebration of the Pasch—**19.** 'phase': **i** '*Pasch*'. **20.** 'as one man': *i.e.* '*together*'. 'all were clean': '*purified themselves*'. Originally the paschal lamb was immolated by the head of each household, Ex 12:3-7; here, as in the days of Josias, 2 Par 35:14, by the Levites. **21.** 'all that had separated themselves': Israelites left in the country when the rest were deported, who having mixed with the surrounding pagans, now threw in their lot with the new community. **22.** 'the king of Assyria': the Persian empire included the former one of Assyria.

Section II The Work of Esdras, VII-X. **29**
VII 1-10 Introduction—**1a.** 'Now after': there is an interval of about 57 years. Artaxerxes is Artaxerxes I whose 7th year (**7**) corresponds to 458 B.C. If it were Artaxerxes II, as some modern scholars contend,

93a Esdras would have gone to Jerusalem in 398 B.C., some 50 years after Nehemias (445 B.C.); cf. § 289i. In the early years of Artaxerxes I an effort was made to surround Jerusalem with a wall (4:12), though with no success. Probably to the same period should be assigned the ministry of the prophet Malachias; cf. § 555c. **1b-5.** For the genealogy of Esdras, cf. I Par 6:4-14. In 1-5 it is schematic; only 16 generations are given for a period of 800 years. Possibly it is arranged to give prominence to the three leading figures, Aaron, Azarias (Solomon's high-priest), and Esdras, with seven generations between each pair. **6.** 'a ready scribe': in later Judaism and in NT 'scribe' has the technical sense of an official interpreter of the Law. Before the Exile it meant a writer or copyist, and in particular a royal secretary, 2 Kg 8:17; 3 Kg 4:3, etc. The change in meaning dates from this application of the term to Esdras. We cannot tell whether he began as a scribe for the Persian government (which is likely, in view of his favour with the king), or as a copyist (of the sacred Books) for the Jewish community. In any event he devoted himself to the study of the Law, and his authority is based largely on his intimate acquaintance with its prescriptions. 'his request': i.e. as contained in the **b** letter in 12-26. **8.** 'fifth month': Ab July-Aug. 458 B.C. **9.** 'first month': Nisan (Mar.-Apr.), 'he began to go up': i.e. 'he fixed the departure' for the first day. Because of difficulties, the actual journey was not begun till the twelfth day, 8:31. The journey occupied nearly four months and the distance travelled was about 900 miles. **10.** Though Esdras led a body of settlers his mission appears to have had purely religious ends in view; he was sent to inquire into the religious condition of Jerusalem, to correct abuses, and to enforce the observance of the Law (14, 26). His purpose 'to search for' truth, to live by it, and to teach it to his countrymen is an epitome of the ideal scribe's career; cf. Ac 1:1. **11.** 'of the edict': omit. 'ceremonies': 'precepts'. **c** **12-26 The Letter of Artaxerxes**—It is written in Aramaic. On account of the acquaintance with the Jewish ritual and the temple personnel which it displays, some commentators have thought that it is not the original document, but a version composed by the sacred writer, giving its substance in Jewish terms. Against this view are, (a) the explicit introduction, 'this is a copy of the letter'; (b) other Persian documents show equal familiarity with the cults of subject peoples; e.g. among the Elephantine papyri is a letter from a Jewish official in the Persian service, relaying explicit instructions from Darius II about the celebration of the Pasch (419 B.C.). It is likely then that Artaxerxes' letter either was drafted by a Jewish secretary, or is in response to a petition by Esdras, in which these details would naturally occur. **12.** 'king of kings' and 'god of heaven' are authentic Persian phrases. 'greeting': thus LXX and Vg interpret the Aram. $g^emîr$ ('perfect', 'accomplished'). Many scholars consider it as the equivalent of our 'etc.', replacing the long titulary and greeting of the ceremonious East. **14.** 'seven counsellors': cf. Est 1:14. 'visit': 'investigate' (with authority to correct abuses). The norm of the investigation is to be 'the law of thy God with the interpretation of which you are charged' (lit. 'is in thy hand'). **15.** 'tabernacle': 'dwelling'. **16.** 'all the silver and gold': Esdras has a roving commission to raise money. In 15-16 three kinds of offerings are mentioned: (1) from the king and his counsellors; (2) from the people of Babylonia (cf. 1:4, 6); (3) from priests and people—free-will offerings. **17.** 'Take freely and buy': 'Therefore thou shalt solicitously buy'. 'with the sacrifices and oblations': 'and their meal-offerings and libations' that accompanied the animal sacrifices; cf. Lev 2. **19.** 'in the sight of': 'before'. **20.** 'and by me': these words should go with the following v. 'And by me, Artaxerxes the king, a decree is made to **d** all the treasurers'. **22.** 'talents . . . cores . . . bates':

this weight of silver would be equal in modern values **293d** to £200,000. In 701 B.C., the Assyrians claim to have received 800 talents as only part of the ransom paid by Ezechias. For the cor and bath, see §82k. **23.** 'why should there be wrath against the realm?' Some have thought that the Persians identified the Jewish 'god of heaven' with Ahura-Mazda whom they worshipped without temple or priesthood. But this passage tells strongly against this theory, at least for the time of Artaxerxes, and also against the monotheism which the Zoroastrians theoretically held. We have here rather the familiar oriental conception of a local divinity who will be offended if his rites are not duly performed in a given place; and who, if offended, is capable of punishing the offenders in that same place. Palestine, which guarded the route to Egypt, was of great importance for the Persian control of that country; and by these measures Artaxerxes meant to win the goodwill of the local divinity as well as of the inhabitants. **24.** All persons connected with the service of the temple are to be exempt from taxation. **25.** 'the ignorant': this phrase like the preceding 'them who know' is restricted to those of Jewish origin. 'law of thy God and the law of the king': the Mosaic law, as interpreted by the scribes, is made the law of the Jews of 'Beyond the river' and is supported by royal sanction; cf. Darius I's codification of Egyptian law in AJSL 51 (1935) 247.

27. Here begins in Hebrew a verbatim extract from **e** the personal Memoirs of Esdras, extending to the end of ch 9. 'Blessed be the Lord': Esdras appreciates perfectly well the interested motives of the Persian, but he understands that God is using Artaxerxes, as he had used Cyrus earlier, to further his plans for Israel. Nor should we underestimate the providential character of the Return. The stubborn resistance of the Jews to assimilation during the Captivity, their mass remigration to their ancestral land against every worldly advantage, and the astonishing co-operation given them by the Persians, are without parallel in the history of the East.

VIII 1-36 The Journey to Jerusalem—1-14. A List **f** of those who accompanied Esdras. **1.** 'The "heads"' of the families': i.e. of the clans. The number given, of men only, is 1,496. With women, children and a small number of slaves, the caravan comprised about 6,000–8,000 persons. **2.** Gersom and Daniel represent respectively the senior and cadet lines of the Aaronic priesthood; Hattus, the line of David. These have the place of honour. **2-3.** 'Of the descendants of David, Hattus, son of Sechenias. Of the descendants of Pharos, Zacharias'. **5.** 'Of the descendants of Zattu, Sechenias, son of Jahaziel', I Par 3:22. **10.** 'Of the descendants of Bani, Selomith'. Most of these families appear (with some variations) in Esd 2 as having contributed members to the first group of immigrants under Cyrus. **15-20 The Rendezvous at Ahava—15.** Ahava is the **g** name of a canal (cf. 21, 31). Esdras ordered the clans to gather near its confluence with another 'canal'. 'And I inspected the people and the priests and found none there of the sons of Levi.' 'sons of Levi': only 74 Levites had accompanied the first expedition, 2:40. They were indispensable for the revival of the temple worship. **16.** There seems to be some duplication of names, and perhaps the last part should read 'Meshullam, leaders of discretion' (cf. 3 Esd). **17.** Casiphia: unidentified, but presumably near Babylon. There appears to have been a colony of Levites and Nethinim there. **18.** 'by the good hand of God upon us': by Divine Providence. 'and Sarabias': 'namely' Sarabias who seems to have been the 'learned man'; cf. Neh 8:7; 9:4, etc. **20.** 'called by their names': i.e. their genealogies were verified, or it may simply mean that a list was made. **21-23 The Fast at Ahava—21.** 'a right way': 'a **h** prosperous journey'. Apart from the ordinary difficulties of organization, there was real danger of attack from brigands or Bedouin. A large caravan, including women and children, and bringing treasure, would be

293h a tempting prey without the protection of a military escort. **22.** To seek protection by human means seemed to Esdras a sign of little faith in the power and goodness of God ; *cf.* Ps 117 (118) 8–9 ; 146:2–6.

i **24-30 The Offerings**—**24.** Esdras appoints 12 priests and 12 Levites to take charge of the treasure. **25.** ' that were found ' : all Israel ' *there present* '. **26.** ' 650 silver talents ' : about £1,250,000 ; *100 gold talents* : about $2,800,000. The surprisingly large amount suggests textual corruption or exaggeration by copyists. ' solids ' : ' *darics* ' ; *cf.* 2:69. **27.** ' two ' : 3 Esd ' 12 ' ; LXX with a change of vowels, ' *diverse* ', which is a better reading. **28.** ' You are *holy* [*i.e.* consecrated] *unto Yahweh.* **29.** ' into the treasure ' : ' *in the rooms* ' adjacent to the temple where the objects and treasures needed for worship were kept.

j **31-36 The Arrival in Jerusalem**—**31.** ' twelfth day ' : they had set out from Babylon on the 1st day and assembled at Ahava on the 9th. **32.** The journey lasted about 110 days. ' stayed ' : ' *rested* '. **33.** The vessels were counted and the bullion weighed. ' *into the hand of* ' the two priests charged with receiving gifts made to the temple. **34.** ' at that time ' should be joined with **35.** **36.** ' And they delivered the king's edicts to the king's *satraps* '. The satrap ruled a province ; the governor administered a small district. ' they ' : the last two vv summarize this part of Esdras' ' Memoirs '.

294a **IX 1-15 The Question of ' Mixed Marriages '**—According to Torrey, Neh 7:70–73 ; 8:1–18 joins immediately on to Esd 8. He holds that Neh 7:70–73 does not belong to the list of those who returned under Cyrus, but deals with money and vestments brought by Esdras' caravan ; hence this section (together with Neh 8:1–18) originally followed Esd 8. Because, however, of its similarity to the end of the list in Esd 2:68 ff., a copyist thought that in it he had found the end of the list in Neh 7 ; so he transferred 7:70–8:18 from Esd to its present place in Neh. The original order would then be : (1) the arrival in Jerusalem, Esd 7:31–36 ; (2) the donation to the treasury, Neh 7:70–73 ; (3) the public reading of the Law, Neh 8:1–12 ; (4) the feast of Tabernacles, Neh 8:13–18 ; (5) Esdras' crusade against mixed marriages, Esd 9–10, (plus Neh 9–10). Against this view it is sufficient to state that (1) Neh 7:70–73 does not deal with the period of Esdras ; (2) this arrangement does violence to the literary unity of Neh 8–10 ; (3) Esd 9 logically follows Esd 8. The bewilderment of Esdras when he discovered the scandal of mixed marriages, Esd 9:1–12, is hardly compatible with a previous solemn convocation of the people and public reading of the Law, Neh 8:1–18 ; for after these events his ignorance of the existence of the evil would be inexplicable. *Cf.* Neh 8.

b **1-5 The Sin of the People**—Reason and experience had shown that marriages with idolatrous people were a grave danger for the religion of Israel, because the pagan consort, especially the woman who is more inclined to be tenacious in the practice of religion, could draw the Israelite partner to pagan superstitions (' *abominations* ') ; hence the rigorous measures adopted : *cf.* Ex 34:15 ; Deut 7:1 ff. ; 3 Kg 11:7–13. **1.** ' princes ' : heads of the clans. ' people of the lands ' : non-Jews, not only the communities bordering on Jewish territory. At this time a proportion of the inhabitants of Judaea itself must have been Gentiles. The list combines names familiar in the older writings, with those of countries which were the chief source of more recent corruption (Ammon, Moab, Egypt). **2.** ' holy seed ' : a people set apart and consecrated to God ; *cf.* Is 6:13. **3.** Oriental demonstrations of great sorrow ; *cf.* Lev 10:6 ; Jos 7:6 ; Job 2:13 ff. ' mantle and coat ' : ' *tunic* and mantle '. The former was the undergarment, worn close to the body, the latter was the flowing cloak that covered it. ' I sat down *bewildered* '. **4.** ' feared ' : ' *dreaded the words of the God of Israel* ', *i.e.* the divine punishments threatened in the Law. **5.** Esdras stood before the people

assembled in the temple at the time of the evening **2?** oblation (*cf.* 10:1) and united them with him in his confession.

6-15 Esdras' Prayer—**6.** ' sins ' : ' *guilt* ' ; also in **c** 7, 13. **7.** ' From the days of our fathers we *have been greatly guilty* unto this day '. **8.** ' And now *for a little moment* [from the time of the edict of Cyrus, about 80 years] there hath been *grace from Yahweh* our God '. ' remnant ' : thus were called the returning exiles, the survivors of the nation's shipwreck ; *cf.* Ez 14:22. ' pin ' : ' *a nail* ' driven into the wall or a ' *tent-peg* ' which holds up or supports. Perhaps the English equivalent would be ' foothold '. ' enlighten our eyes ' : grant well-being ; *cf.* 1 Kg 14:29.

9. ' are bondmen ' : subjects of the Persian king. **d** ' king ' : ' *kings* '. ' fence ' : Heb. *gāḏēr*. If meant literally it would refer to the city wall, and so the mission of Esdras would have followed that of Nehemias ; but it should be interpreted figuratively in the sense of ' divine protection ' (*cf.* Ps 79 [80] 13) or as referring to the royal edict forbidding interference with the Jews in Jerusalem ; *cf.* § 289m. **11.** ' prophets ' : principally Moses in the Pentateuch ; Deut 7:1–3 and Lev 18:24 ff. are cited according to sense. ' according to ', etc. : ' *with the filthiness of* the people of *the lands* '. ' mouth to mouth ' : *i.e.* end to end ; *cf.* 4 Kg 10:21 ; 21:16. **12.** ' nor seek their peace ' ; *cf.* Deut 23:6 ; Ex 23:32. **12b.** ' *and leave it for an inheritance to* your children forever '. **13.** ' seeing that ' : ' *truly our God has reckoned our sins downwards* [chastised us less than we deserved] and has given us *such* deliverance as this ' (the return of the ' remnant '). **14.** ' *Shall* we *again* turn and break '. **15.** ' for we *are* left (*but*) a remnant today '. ' no standing before thee ' : their guilt is inexcusable. With this humble confession, full of trust in the goodness of God, Esdras ends and crowns his prayer.

X 1-44 The Expulsion of the Foreign Wives—**1-5.** **e** **The People's Confession and Pledge.** The narrative is resumed in the third person ; from now on the sacred writer presents the ' Memoirs ' of Esdras in a summary form. **1.** ' thus ' : omit. ' beseeching ' : ' *making confession* '. ' lying ' : prostrating himself. ' assembly ' : presumably the same group as in 9:4, but increased in numbers. **2.** ' Sechenias ' : his own father, Jehiel, had married a foreign wife ; *cf.* 26 (if it is the same Jehiel). **2b.** ' *But* now there is (still) *hope for* Israel *in this matter* '. Stern measures may appease the divine wrath. **3.** ' the will of the Lord ' : ' *the counsel of my lord* ' (*i.e.* Esdras). This is the first time we have heard of Esdras' ' counsel ' to expel the foreign wives ; 2–4 appear to summarize a debate in which various speakers, including Esdras, had taken part. Sechenias' argument would have particular effect if his own family (step-mother ?) were affected. ' according to the law ' : either (*a*) the general law forbidding such marriages is now to be enforced ; or (*b*) the ' putting away ' is to be performed in accordance with the regulations for divorce contained in the law, Deut 24:1–2. **4.** ' *on thee is the affair* ' ; Esdras has, by his commission from the king, both power and responsibility to enforce the law. ' we *are* with thee ' : an assurance of support against anticipated opposition.

6-8 The Proclamation—**6.** ' chamber ' : one of the **f** rooms adjacent to the temple. ' Johanan ' : if the Eliasib meant is the high-priest who was contemporary with Nehemias, Neh 13:4, 7, and Johanan was really his grandson (not his son, *cf.* Neh 12:23), then Johanan must have lived a long time *after* Esdras, and consequently the writer is giving to the room the name by which it was known in his own day. But it is possible that another Johanan was intended ; *cf.* § 289o. ' entered in thither ' : ' *spent the night there* ', reading with 3 Esd *wayyālen*. **7.** The men alone were summoned ; *cf.* 9. **8.** ' taken away ' : ' *devoted* ', *i.e.* put under a religious ban. Property so ' devoted ' was to be destroyed or confiscated to sacred uses : *cf.* § 230g. ' cast out ' : excommunicated.

9-14 The Assembly—**9.** ' the ninth month ' of the **g**

94g religious year began towards the end of Nov. and hence fell in the rainy season. 'sat in the street': waited in the 'open space' or square. 'because of this matter and from (the discomfort of) the rain'. The first half of the phrase may be a gloss. **11.** 'make confession': 'give glory'. It was used as an invitation to a culprit to speak the truth and acknowledge his fault; cf. Jos 7:19 and Jn 9:24. **12.** 'so be it done': 'so it behoveth us to do'. **13.** Time was needed to straighten out the involved question of mixed marriages; meanwhile the people who had come in from a distance could not, in the rainy weather, live and sleep in the open air. **14a.** 'Let our leaders represent all the people'; let a committee of the leading men handle the matter. 'in all our cities' should follow 'wives'. The 'divorce court' sat in Jerusalem. The elders and judges would be required to give evidence concerning the marriages and afterwards to see that the decision was carried out.

h 15-17 The Commission—**15** should stand in parentheses since it breaks the connection between 14 and 16. 'However, Jonathan . . . and Jaasia opposed this; and Mesollam and Sebethai the Levite helped them'. They were opponents of Esdras' admittedly drastic measures. **16.** Read with 3 Esd and some LXX MSS: 'And Esdras the priest chose [wayyaḅdēl lô] heads of families, according to their fathers' houses, and all of them by name; and they began their sittings on the first day'. 'tenth month': Tebeth (Dec.-Jan.). This first sitting was held 13 days after the announcement of 9:1 and the hearings were terminated within 90 days, i.e. by the first day of Nisan (Mar.-Apr.). The harsh measures here described were adopted by Esdras in order to keep the worship of God from being contaminated by, and finally lost in, the surrounding paganism. A small and feeble community was peculiarly exposed to external influences, and Esdras might well fear the results, if marriage alliances were permitted with the neighbouring peoples, whose women were 'the daughters of a strange god', Mal 2:11.

i 18-44 The List of the Offenders—It falls into five groups of 17 priests, 6 Levites, 1 singer, 3 porters and 86 laymen—113 in all. The Nethinim alone are not named, probably because, as slaves of alien origin, they were not at that time looked on as part of the Jewish community. **19.** 'gave their hands': swore. **25.** 'of Israel': as distinct from the preceding, who were dedicated to the temple service. The list that follows goes by the names of the heads of families mentioned in 2:3-20, but in a different order. The text, especially towards the end, is badly copied and uncertain. **44.** 'there were among them', etc.: the clause in MT is beset with difficulties. 3 Esd 9:36 reads 'and they put them away along with their children' which may represent the original text.

j With the list of 18-43 the activity of Esdras comes abruptly to an end, to be resumed in an unexpected fashion in Neh 8:1 ff., where he appears as a co-worker with Nehemias, who, however, is only mentioned casually in two places; hence several commentators believe that Neh 8-10 should follow immediately Esd 10 and that Nehemias' name occurring in Neh 8:9; 10, 22 is a later gloss. Cf. § 297a–d.

NEHEMIAS

5a I-VI The Governorship of Nehemias and the Rebuilding of the Walls.
I 1a. Introduction: 'The words': as originally compiled, the 'Memoirs' of Nehemias followed Esdras without a break; this introduction was inserted by the sacred writer to indicate that now another source (the 'Memoirs' of Neh.) is being quoted. The abruptness of the second sentence shows that the extract does not start with the beginning of Nehemias' story.
b 1b-4a Evil Tidings from Jerusalem—1b. 'Casleu': the ninth month, Nov.-Dec. 'twentieth year': of the reign of Artaxerxes I, 445 B.C. This phrase is probably a later insertion taken from 2:1, but really

contradicting it, for the 20th year of Artaxerxes began, **295b** 2:1; with Nisan (Mar.-Apr.), 445 B.C., and Casleu was the 9th month of that year. Yet the events of ch 1 obviously preceded the interview with the king in ch 2. Susa was the winter residence of the Persian kings; Ecbatana, the summer; cf. Esd 6:2. **2.** 'brethren': 'kinsmen'. Hanani introduced to Nehemias some new arrivals from Jerusalem, with their sad story, very likely in the hope that Nehemias would use his influence with the king; in fact, this may have been the purpose of the Judaeans' long journey. 'that remained', etc.: 'the survivors who were left'; so too in 3. The reference is to those descendants of the exiles who had migrated to Palestine. **3.** 'the wall . . . the gates': very likely this destruction occurred on the receipt of Artaxerxes' letter (cf. Esd 4:7-23), which had not ordered the destruction of the work done, but that would almost inevitably follow. Some authors suppose the allusion to be to the destruction of the walls by Nabuchodonosor in 586, some 140 years before, but that would hardly be news.

5-11 Nehemias' Prayer—It consists of a confession **c** of sin (5-7), an appeal to God's promise (8-9), and an entreaty for help in the undertaking he contemplated (10-11). The stereotyped form, the striking resemblance to other OT prayers, Esd 9:5-18; Dan 9:4-19, and the liberal use of Deuteronomic passages, have led many scholars to conclude that the prayer is the composition of the sacred writer, not of Nehemias. These characteristics, however, may be explained on the assumption that it is a compendium of the many prayers that Nehemias uttered during the four months that intervened before his approach to the king, and that, in composing it for his 'Memoirs' he followed the norms of literary composition that prevailed in OT prayers.
5. 'covenant': promises made to Israel. **7.** 'We have been seduced by vanity': 'we have acted very corruptly'. 'ceremonies': 'commandments'. **8-9.** Cf. Lev 26:27-45; Deut 4:25-31; 30:1-5. **11.** 'Now I was the king's cupbearer': this is added to show that the words 'of this man' refer to Artaxerxes, and that this prayer was in the heart of Nehemias while serving the king, 2:4. 'a cupbearer': therefore, not the only one nor the chief one. The cupbearers of the Persian court were generally non-Persian eunuchs. It was their duty to pour out and taste some of the wine as a precaution against an attempt to poison the king.

II 1-20 Nehemias' Appointment as Governor and d Arrival in Jerusalem.
1-8 The Commission of Nehemias—1. Nisan (Mar.-Apr.), 445 B.C. 'before him': LXX has 'wine before me', implying that it was Nehemias' turn to act as cupbearer. 'languishing': HT is uncertain —perhaps, 'I had not been out of favour with him', i.e. Nehemias regarded himself, with some reason, as the king's favourite, and hoped, therefore, that his petition would be granted. **2.** MT is shorter and simpler: 'Why is thy countenance sad? Thou art not ill, (therefore) this can only be sadness of heart. And I was sore afraid'. Since sadness was a breach of court etiquette (cf. Est 4:2) and Nehemias' petition would be for the exact opposite of the king's recent decision (cf. Esd 4:7-23), he had reason enough to be apprehensive. **3.** 'of the place': omit 'of'. Nehemias makes his appeal on the ground of filial piety, saying nothing about building fortifications which would have an ominous sound to an eastern ruler, only too accustomed to periodical revolts in outlying provinces. **4.** 'I prayed': in my heart, secretly. **5.** This is the crucial request, and the double introduction conveys the intense earnestness with which Nehemias made it. 'sepulchres of my fathers'. 'build it': the request implied authority over the people, independence of local Persian officials, a certain financial control—in short, the office of governor. **6.** 'the queen': the Heb. implies 'a favourite member of the harem.'

295d 'I fixed him a time': Nehemias was governor for 12 years, 5:14. **7.** 'governors': besides the satrap who governed all the province of 'Beyond-the-River', there were Persian governors of its various districts. It was such an appointment that Nehemias now received in Jerusalem. **8.** 'forest': the Persian word is *pardes* from which is derived the English 'paradise'. 'The royal park' is the nearest equivalent. It is identified by some with Etham, 4 m. S. of Bethlehem, 2 Par 11:6, where (according to Jos. *Ant.* 8, 7, 3) Solomon built pleasant gardens. **8.** 'that I may cover', etc.: '*place beams for* the gates of the *citadel* of the house'. The citadel (*cf.* 7:2 in HT) seems to have been intended as a defence for the temple ('the house'). 'the house that I shall enter': the governor's palace.

e **9-10 The Journey to Jerusalem—9.** 'captains of soldiers': Nehemias as Tirshatha or governor, 8:9 ; 10:1, was invested with civil and not, like Esdras, ecclesiastical authority; and consequently was attended by a bodyguard ; contrast Esd 8:22. 'the letters': of safe-conduct (7). **10.** 'Sanballat': an Assyrian name meaning 'Sin [the lunar god] gives life.' He is named *the Horonite* either because he was from Beth-Horon or, more probably, from Horonaim in Moab (*cf.* Is 15:5). He was governor of Samaria. In a document among the papyri fragments of Elephantine, dated the 17th year of Darius II (407 B.C.) we read that the sons of 'Sanballat governor of Samaria' have great authority ; hence the proof that the Artaxerxes of Nehemias is the *first* of that name, not the *second* ; *cf.* § 289g. 'Tobias the Ammonite' was in all likelihood of the lineage (perhaps the head) of the family of the Tobiads, which as we know from Josephus (*Ant.* 12, 5, 1) and from recently discovered papyri was famous about 300 B.C. for its wealth and power in the region of Ammon. 'the servant': the word means 'slave', Ex 21:1-7, but it is also an honorary title, 1 Kg 29:3 ; 4 Kg 22:12. Here Tobias certainly has a part in the government of the province. 'heard it': of his arrival, not of his purpose. It was a sufficiently disturbing idea that a strict and zealous Jew, backed by the king's authority, should be governor in Jerusalem.

f **13-16 The Inspection of the City Walls by Night—13.** 'in the night': to avoid rousing the suspicion of his foes and the intemperate enthusiasm of the people. 'no beast': a cavalcade would have attracted notice. **13-14.** The topography of ancient Jerusalem is too obscure to admit of the various parts of its walls being identified with certainty, but Nehemias began his tour from the SW. and pursued his course, first along the S. wall, then along the E. wall up the side of the 'torrent', *i.e.* 'the Kidron'. The first gate was probably named from the valley of Hinnom ; some scholars, believing that the western hill was not then occupied, think it was the Tyropoeon valley which ran between the eastern and western hills. 'before the dragon fountain': '*in the direction of*'. This fountain, not mentioned elsewhere, is perhaps to be identified with the well of Rogel which was near the 'serpent's stone', 3 Kg 1:9. 'the dung gate', out of which the town refuse was carried, stood where the Tyropoeon valley met the valley of Hinnom. **g** **14.** 'the gate of the fountain' (of Siloe) was at the SE. corner of the city. 'the king's aqueduct': '*the royal pool*', perhaps the lower pool of Siloe (mentioned in 3:15 as near the royal gardens), the overflow of which irrigated the lower part of the Kidron valley where the kings of Judaea had gardens, 4 Kg 25:4 ; or perhaps the (now) lost pool of Solomon farther up the Kidron valley. 'no place to pass': the ground was so encumbered by fallen masonry that Nehemias could not follow the line of the wall closely ; so he descended into the valley and followed the Kidron 'torrent'. **15.** 'and turned back': retraced his steps. Others think that he turned back along the N. wall, thus completing the circuit of the city.

h **17-20 Nehemias' Appeal : the Derision of his Enemies**

—Nehemias, having satisfied himself as to the practi- **29** cability of his plan, called an assembly. The sacred writer is utilizing, not transcribing, Nehemias' Memoirs. **17.** 'a reproach': an object of derision, by reason of our inability to defend ourselves. **18.** 'the hand of God': the divine blessing which had so far favoured him. 'strengthened *for* the good (work)'. **19.** To the two adversaries already mentioned is added Geshem the Arab, also coming from Transjordan. '*will* you rebel?': the same construction had been put upon the undertaking of Esd 4:7-23. **20b.** 'You have no *portion*, nor *right*, nor *memorial* [*i.e.* nothing by which to remember you] in Jerusalem'. These words resemble the declaration in Esd 4:3 and imply a claim on the part of the Samaritans to share in the fortunes of Jerusalem.

III 1-31 A List of the Builders of the Wall—This **i** chapter was taken from some official record of the repairing of the wall and inserted in Nehemias' narrative. The workers were organized according to families, localities, or professions, into 42 groups, each headed by one or two men. Those dwelling in nearby villages—Jericho, Tekoa (Thecua), etc.—were also summoned. Each group was assigned a certain gateway or section of wall—the lengths of the latter varying considerably, according as the need of repair was greater or less. The Heb. text is in a poor state and many of the plentiful topographical details are quite obscure. It is clear, however, that the description starts at the east end of the north wall and proceeds counterclockwise. See Map C, page 1311.

1. 'Eliasib': *cf.* Esd 3:2 ; Neh 12:10 and 13:4, **j** where his close connexion with Tobias shows that he did not sympathize with the policy of Nehemias. 'built': '*repaired*'. 'the *sheep* gate': in the NE. section of the wall. Through it the sacrificial animals were led to the temple ; *cf.* Jn 5:2. 'sanctified it': *qidde̊šûhû* has been substituted out of respect for the priesthood for *qērûhû* 'laid its beams' of the other gate-building accounts (*cf.* 3, 6). 'the tower of *Hammeah*' (*i.e.* 'The Hundred'): the origin of the name is unknown. 'sanctified': '*repaired*' the wall. Hananel: *cf.* Jer 31:38 ; Zach 14:10. **3.** 'the fish gate': about the middle of the northern wall. 'covered it': '*laid its beams*'. 'built': '*repaired*' is to be read throughout, except in 13, 14, 15. The work consisted in repairing the wall and filling. in the breaches. **5.** 'necks': the metaphor is taken from the ox ploughing with its neck in the yoke. 'their lord': *i.e.* Nehemias ; the chiefs of Tekoa refused to join in the work.

6. 'old gate': probably so called either because it **k** gave access to the old part of the city or because it belonged to a part of the wall older than the repaired wall of Ezechias, 2 Par 32:5. It was probably on the northern side of the city to the west of the fish gate. **7.** 'for the governor': HT is obscure ; perhaps it denotes the limit of the restoration undertaken by the men of Gabaon and Mizpah : *i.e.* 'up to' the place where the satrap of 'Beyond-the-River' held court on his visits to Jerusalem. **8.** 'left' ; 'girded' is a probable rare sense of the Heb. word ; *cf.* 4:2. Some authors read *yᵉʿazzᵉzû* ('strengthened') for *yaʿazᵉ̄bû*. 'unto the broad wall' : the portion between the gate of Ephraim, 12:38, and the tower of the furnaces, 11, on the western (?) side of the city. **9.** 'lord of the street' : '*prefect of half the district*' ; the province, ruled by a governor was divided into districts, and these often into two parts, each of which was ruled by a 'prefect'. So also in 12, 14, 15, 16, 17. **11.** 'built half the street' : '*repaired a second portion*', either 'a further portion' of the same section or, more probably, 'undertook another piece of restoration work'. Some, more zealous than others, repaired two sections : compare 3:21, 27 with 3:3, 5 ; 18 with 24. 'the tower of the furnaces' : between the gate of Ephraim and the valley gate. **12.** Sellum : *Shallum* shared with Rephaia (9) the prefecture 'of the *district* of Jerusalem'. 'he and his daughters' : perhaps '*it* [the half district]

k and *its villages*'; cf. 11:25, 27 Heb. **13.** 'the valley gate': cf. 2:13. This was the main entrance on the western side. 'a thousand cubits' (about 500 yards) is a doubtful reading; the distance seems to be too great. 'the dung gate': cf. 2:13. The wall, having passed due east from the valley gate to the dung gate, then turned in a northerly direction.

l **15.** 'guard': '*garden*'; cf. 2:14. 'the steps': at the southern extremity of the eastern hill. A similar flight of steps was unearthed in 1895 near the pool of Siloe and another in 1913–14 at the southern point of Ophel. 'the city of David': the Jerusalem that David captured from the Jebusites. It embraced the eastern hill, known as Ophel. **16.** 'the *sepulchres*': according to this text they should be on the SE. slope of Ophel, 2 Par 32:3, where, in fact they were found (1913–14). 'pool': 'the *artificial* pool and the house of the *warriors*'. The 'pool': distinct from the lower pool of Siloe is probably the pool of Solomon mentioned above under 2:14; cf. Is 22:11. 'the house of the warriors': probably barracks for the royal bodyguard. **17.** 'street': '*district*'.

m **19-24.** 'another measure'; a second piece of the wall; cf. 11. The places here indicated cannot be exactly identified, but we find ourselves on the eastern wall, approaching the temple and so we meet the houses of the 'priests' (21 ff.). **22.** HT reads simply 'the men *of the Oval*', the technical name given to the oval plain of the Jordan valley near Jericho; cf. Gen 13:10. **26.** The verse is a parenthesis, probably a later addition to be read after 27. The Nathinites' quarters adjoined the temple on the south. 'temple': '*Ophel*' 'protuberance': the southern section of the temple hill. 'the water gate': leading to the spring of Gihon in the ravine of the Kidron (?). **28.** 'the horse gate'; cf. Jer 31:40; 4 Kg 11:16. **30b.** 'opposite the *reviewing* gate and *up to* the *upper* chamber of the corner'. 'the reviewing gate': perhaps where the army was mustered. 'upper chamber': apparently a well known *solarium* above the NE. angle of the wall. **32.** With the *sheep* gate the circuit is complete.

a **IV 1-23 Opposition**—This ch in the HT does not begin until v 7.

1-6 The Samaritans ridicule the Work—1. Here Nehemias' 'Memoirs' are resumed; 1–3 narrate an incident similar to that of 2:19–20. Sanballat: his irritation at Nehemias' arrival, 2:10, increased after work on the wall was begun. 'moved': '*vexed*'. **2.** 'silly': '*feeble*'. 'Will the Gentiles [*i.e.* Persian authorities] let them alone?': read probably, 'Will they build an encirclement for themselves?' Cf. however 3:8. By changing *lāhem* ('for themselves') to *lē'lōhîm* we may read: 'Will they leave (the matter) to God?' The rest of the passage is obscure and Vg offers perhaps as good a version as any. '*sacrifice*', etc.: do they think that they have only to sacrifice to their God and the work will be done? **3.** '*Even what they are building*—if a jackal go up, he shall *break down* their wall *of stones*'; it will crumble under a jackal's weight. 'their wall *of stones*' is a phrase of contempt; the building of a wall, adequate for defence, is a laborious task. **4-5.** This is the first of the parenthetical prayers, which characterize Nehemias' writings; cf. 5:19; 6:9; 13:14, 22. **4.** 'to be despised': HT, '*up to spoiling*', i.e. may they experience the fate of Judah. The consonants of both words are the same in Heb. **5.** 'they have mocked *the* builders'. **6.** As the different parties worked simultaneously on the wall, it was quickly restored up to one half of its height, and this success was a stimulus to greater effort.

b **7-12 Threats—7.** An early inspection had satisfied the foe that nothing effective would be accomplished by the Jews; now they hear that an essential part has been done. 'Azotians': the people of Ashdod, one of the principal Philistine cities. 'made up': '*went forward*'. **8.** 'to prepare ambushes: '*to make confusion therein*'. **10.** A rhythmic song; similar popular refrains are not uncommon in the historical

books; cf. 1 Kg 18:7; 2 Kg 20:1; 3 Kg 12:16; **296b** 2 Par 18:16. Besides the hostility of the Samaritans, the Jews themselves were becoming overwhelmed by fatigue. **12.** Read with LXX 'And when the Jews that dwelt *beside* them came (to Jerusalem) they told us: *They are coming up against* us from all places (*where they live* [Syr])'. Jews living in Samaritan cities heard of the plot and came to warn Nehemias.

13-23 Measures for Defence—13-15. The text is very **c** difficult. **13.** Vg compresses 13a and b (Heb.) into a single sentence. Read with a correction (from good LXX codices and Syr) of the first Heb. verb: '*And they have taken their stand at the lowest part of the space behind* [*i.e.* outside] *the wall in the open. Then* I set the people', etc. The sense is now clear. The enemy had prepared an assault in strength (13a), but Nehemias took countermeasures (13b), and the Samaritans lost courage when they saw themselves discovered. **15.** 'counsel': '*plot*'. **16.** 'From that day half of my young men [his personal bodyguard] did the work, and half *of them held* the spears and the shields and the bows and the coats of mail; and the *chiefs stood behind* (to direct) each house [clan group] of Judah (**17**) *that was building* the wall. They that carried burdens were armed; each worked with one hand, and with the other held a *missile*' (javelin?). **18.** 'And the builders had each one his sword girded upon his loins while *he built. Now the trumpeter was by my side*'. **19-20.** Because of the great extent of the wall, the defenders were scattered; hence the need of collecting all available forces quickly to any threatened point. **21.** '*So we wrought* in the work; and one half of them held the spears', etc. Perhaps 'and one half ... spears' is a copyist's repetition from 10 and to be omitted. **22.** The Jews dwelling in the suburbs used to return home for the night. Because they were needed for defence, Nehemias made them lodge in the city. 'And let us take', etc.: '*and they shall be a guard for us* by night and a *working force* by day'. **13.** 'watchmen': 'men *of the guard*'. 'only every man', etc. HT is hopeless; Vg is at least clear.

V 1-19 Difficulties within the City: Nehemias' **d** **Governorship**—This ch can hardly be in its right place; there was neither occasion nor leisure for such complaints and proceedings during the 52 days of feverish activity that marked the rebuilding of the wall. Moreover the date in 5:14 shows that we are at the end of Nehemias' rule. The ch appears to belong to a later period and describes later acts of Nehemias' administration.

1-13 Social Abuses—1. 'against their (own) Jewish **e** brethren': *i.e.* the rich and the nobles (7). The story of the oppression of the poor by the rich is a familiar one with the prophets. It is distressing to see how quickly in a poor and struggling community avaricious 'capitalism' had revived. **2.** 'Some *were saying*: "*We are giving in pledge* our sons and daughters, *in order to get* corn *to* eat and live"'. **3.** *Others were saying*: "*We are giving in pledge* our *fields* and our vineyards and our houses *that we may get* corn *in the famine*". **4.** And others *were saying*: "*We have* borrowed money for the king's *tax* (*with* our fields and vineyards *as security*)"'. The parenthesis is a repetition from 3. This social-economic crisis was due to a bad harvest and consequent famine. The poor had no resource but to borrow from wealthy money-lenders, and, as security, to give either their property, when they had any, or their children. Deprived of the profits from their holdings and the labour of their children, there was little hope of ever paying off the debt; hence their children would remain slaves and their vineyards be seized. 'the king's *tax*': the royal tax was one that Nehemias dared not fail to collect, although he did his best to lighten the burden (14). The last part of this verse is probably a gloss. **5.** 'our flesh', etc.: we and our children are Jews just as they are; such oppression should have no place among brethren of the same blood. The selling of children into bondage to defray a debt was recognized in the Law,

296e Ex 21:2-6 ; Deut 15:12. The complaint is that the creditors are making unfair use of the crisis.

f 7. 'You exact usury every one of *his* brethren' : loans at interest to fellow-Israelites were prohibited, Ex 22:25 ; Deut 13:19 ; Lev 26:35-37, but the prohibition seems to have been interpreted as applying only to charitable loans. Usury as a financial transaction between Jews was apparently recognized (*cf.* Lk 6:35). 8. Nehemias and other pious men had, out of their purses, redeemed Jews who had been enslaved for debt by their pagan creditors. 9. 're-proaches' : such cruel treatment of fellow-Jews makes the nation and its religion a byword to the pagans. 10. 'lent' : the Heb. word always means 'lend at interest' ; but in view of Nehemias' generosity in other respects we cannot suppose that he treated his debtors as the nobles treated theirs. His proposal is probably an appeal to his hearers to follow the example he has already been setting. 'Let us . . . to us' : the Heb. reads simply : 'Let us *relinquish this interest*'. 11. 'the hundredth part' : read *maššaʾṭ* : the interest on' for *meʿaṭ*. 'give it rather for them' : omit. 12. 'The priests' were called not to take the oath but to adminʾster it. 13. 'lap' : 'the *fold of my garment*' : the action was symbolic.

g 14-19 Nehemias' Governorship—This is Nehemias' *apologia* for his administration, particularly on the financial side. In the East high political office has been fatally accompanied by corruption, oppression, and self-enrichment ; from all these evils Nehemias refrained 'for love of God'. More than that, out of pity for his people's poverty, he waived his own salary as governor and bore the expenses of the office out of his own pocket. Evidently he was rich enough to afford it ; but such generosity is no less remarkable in the rich than in the poor. 14. His governorship lasted from 445-433 B.C. It is to be assumed that his leave of absence, 2:6, was extended by the king. 'yearly allowance . . . governors' : lit. 'the bread of the governor'. A proportion of the taxes was allotted to the governor and his establishment for their maintenance. This allowance Nehemias forewent. 15. 'forty shekels' : about $30—with much greater purchasing power. 16. 'Moreover I was occupied in the work of *this* wall, *although* I (had) *acquired* no land'. Only those who possessed land had the strict duty of co-operating in the work ; at the same time there is an allusion to 10 ; Nehemias had refrained from enriching himself by buying up the land of the poor. 17. He regularly entertained 150 officials and welcomed Jews from the Dispersion to his table. 18. 'I gave store', etc. : '*every ten days all wine in abundance*'. 'for the people', etc. : 'for *the bondage* [tribute exacted by the Persian government] *was heavy upon the people*'.

h VI 1-19 The Wall completed—The narrative about the rebuilding of the walls, which was broken by ch 5, is here resumed.

1-9 Opposition from without—2. The wall proper was now finished, therefore the opportunity for attack had gone by ; so Sanballat and his conferates seek to allure Nehemias to a conference in order to get him into their power. Ono : now Kefr Ana, some 7 m. E. by SE. of Jaffa. Perhaps under the Heb. word for 'the villages' is concealed the proper name 'Kefira'. At all events, the article indicates a definite place. 3*b*. 'lest', etc. : '*Why should the work cease*, while *I leave it* and go down to you ?' Nehemias refuses to go on the ground that he is too busy with the work on hand. 5. 'according to the former word' : in like manner. 'an *open* letter' : that its content might reach and intimidate others. 6-7. In the letter Sanballat pretends to give friendly information of the dangerous gossip which is so widespread that the Persian king is sure to hear of it, and suggests a conference that they may find a way of extricating Nehemias from his perilous situation. 6. 'For which end' : join with 7. 9. 'thinking', etc. : '*saying* : " *Their* hands *will* cease from the work and *it will not*

be done ". And now strengthen my hand' (an ejacu- **2** latory prayer).

10-14 A Further Attempt to entrap Nehemias—This **i** section is very compressed and the text corrupt. The general sense is that Sanballat had hired a false prophet to persuade Nehemias that his life was in danger and to induce him to seek safety in the inner sanctuary of the temple, where no layman was permitted to enter. Such an impious act would have gravely discredited him in the eyes of the people. 10. Samaia : not otherwise known. 'privately' : MT *ʾaṣûr* '*and he was shut up* ' : obscure. Vaccari reads 'and it [the house] was shut up ', i.e. bolted, and for 'and he said : " Let us consult " ' (*niwwāʿēd*) he suggests 'And said Noadias (*nôʿadyāh*) : " Go into " ' ; *cf.* 14. 'in the midst of the temple' : in the Holy Place, which corresponded to our modern nave. 11. 'to save his life' : '*and live*'. It was forbidden to a layman to enter the inner sanctuary under pain of death ; *cf.* Num 18:7. 12. 'Then I understood, *and lo*, God had not sent him ; but he had spoken the (pretended) prophecy *about me, because* Tobias and Sanballat had hired him '. 13. 'He *was bribed in order that I should be* afraid and do *so* [as he advised] and sin ; *so that I might be to them for an evil name that they might discredit me*'. Vg gives the general sense. 14. 'Remember, O my God, *Tobias*', etc. 'Noadias the prophet' : the name is not found elsewhere. HT reads 'the prophetess' ; LXX agrees with Vg.

15-16 Completion of the Work—15. 'Elul' : the sixth month, Aug.-Sept. of 444. For another instance of the rapid erection of walls under patriotic impulse, *cf.* the action of Themistocles and the Athenians.

17-19 Enemies within—During the whole of this period a treasonable correspondence was carried on between Tobias and the disaffected Jewish nobles. 18. 'were sworn to him', etc. : Tobias' connexion by marriage ensured him the support of many leading Jews. He was the son-in-law of Sechenias (probably distinct, as a noble of the house of Arah, Esd 2:5, from the Sechenias of 3:29, and the father-in-law of the daughter of Mosollam, 3-4. Tobias was also related by marriage to the high-priest Eliasib, 13:4.

VII 1-73 Arrangements for the Protection of the **J** City : A List of the Returned Exiles.

1-4 Nehemias' Precautions—1. 'numbered' : 'appointed'. 2. 'ruler of the house' : '*captain of the fortress*' (probably connected with the temple and doubtless the military headquarters as well as the seat of government). 'the rest' : 'many'. 3. City gates were usually opened at sunrise and closed at sunset. 'yet standing' : i.e. before they went to bed. Every precaution was taken lest the citizens be surprised by an assault at a time when they could not promptly defend themselves. 4. 'the houses were not built' could also mean that the offspring of the returned exiles was not yet numerous ; *cf.* Ex 1:21.

5. As a preliminary step to increasing the population **l** of Jerusalem, Nehemias proposed to take a census of all persons of Jewish descent. 'found a book' : the genealogical record 'of them who came up at first', during the reign of Cyrus. This record must have been found in the archives of Jerusalem. It is identical with the list in Esd 2:3-58, but with variants in the names and sometimes in the numbers.

6-73 The List—15. Bannui : in Esd 2:10 *Bani* with 642 descendants. In both places read *Bennui*. 21. 'of Hezechias' : i.e. of the subdivision which took its name from Hezechias, probably not the king of that name. 61-73. This section is found almost identically in Esd 2:59-70. 68 is omitted in some of the oldest Hebrew MSS, probably through an oversight, but found in Esd 2:66. 70. '530 garments' : read with LXX *30* and *cf.* Esd 2:69.

VIII-X Religious Reform—Some modern scholars, Catholics and non-Catholics, believe that this section originally belonged to the Esdras narrative, although they vary in assigning its proper place in that book. Some place it after Esd 8 or 10. Batten, 352, leaves

a only Neh 8 as part of the Esdras story, finds it impossible to trace the origin of ch 9, and places Neh 10 after Neh 13. Torrey proposes the order Esd 7, Neh 7:70–8:18 ; Esd 9–10 ; Neh 9–10.

The arguments of Batten and Torrey against the literary unity of Neh 8–10 are ill-founded. Neh 10 does not follow Neh 13 but is presupposed by it (*cf. e.g.* 13:10 and 10:38). Torrey's view that Neh 7:70–73 does not belong to the list of those who first returned, but refers to money, etc., brought to Jerusalem by Esdras' caravan, is unjustifiable.

b The literary unity of Neh 8–10 being granted, the reasons offered for transferring it to the book of Esd are : (1) chh 8–10 interrupt the story of Nehemias' plan to find inhabitants for Jerusalem, Neh 7:4, which is resumed only in 11:1 ; 2) the unexpected re-appearance of Esdras in this section ; (3) Esdras came to Jerusalem to teach and establish the Law, Esd 7:5–26, but it is only thirteen years after his arrival that he first presents it to the people, Neh 8–10 ; (4) the change in the narrative of Neh 8–10 from the first to the third person.

By inserting Neh 8–10 after Esd 8 we have a natural sequence of events : the arrival of Esdras on the 1st day of the 5th month, 458 B.C., Esd 7:9 ; the reading of the Law on the 1st day of the 7th month, Neh 8:2 ; the signing of the covenant on the 24th day of the 7th month, Neh 9:1–28 ; the question of mixed marriages raised in the 9th month, Esd 10:9 ; the end of the commission on the 1st day of the 1st month (457 B.C.). A serious objection, however, to this arrangement is that it does not explain Esdras' ignorance about mixed marriages, Esd 9:13, *after* the assembly of the people in which the scandalous state of things is indicated, Neh 10:30. To defend this view (as well as that which places Neh 8–10 after Esd 10) it is also necessary to strike out, as a gloss, the mention of Nehemias in 8:10 and 10:1.

c Those who hold that Neh 8–10 is in its proper place explain the change from the first to the third person and the impression of an interpolation, by affirming that Nehemias wrote in his Memoirs the facts contained in Neh 8–10, but in a brief fashion, since they dealt solely with religious matters ; hence the sacred writer, leaving for a time the text of Nehemias' Memoirs, describes these events in greater detail, relying both on the Memoirs and other sources. Thus the whole section appears out of place.

The present writer is inclined to the view that Neh 8–10 originally followed Esd 10. This arrangement fills out a gap in the Esdras narrative, and removes the difficulty caused in the present text by the presence of Neh 8–10 between 7:4 and 11:1. Perhaps the transfer was due to the fact that the opening lines of Neh 8 are identical with the lines following the register in Esd 2, and so the entire section was placed after the register in Neh 7. Perhaps, however, it is only enriching Esdras at the expense of Nehemias.

VIII 1–18 The Reading of the Law and the Feast of Tabernacles.
1–12 The Reading of the Law by Esdras—1. ' the seventh month ' : Tishri. That the events described in ch 8 followed immediately upon the completion of the wall seems to be suggested by the sacred writer, for the mention of the 25th of the 6th month, 6:15, is followed by the mention of the 1st of the 7th month, 8:1, 2. The opening words of ch 8 are very similar to those in Esd 3:1 after the list of names. Apparently the close of the list and the mention of the 7th month in Esd contained suitable words with which to resume the narrative here ; but *cf.* § 297*d*. ' street ' : ' *the broad place* ' ; so also in 3, 16. ' watergate ' : SE. of the temple area ; *cf.* 3:26. **2.** This is the first time that Esdras is mentioned in Nehemias ; if Neh 8–10 belongs to the book of Neh then Esdras either returned to Babylon after effecting the reforms described in Esd 9 and 10, and only revisited Jerusalem after Nehemias' arrival there, or the failure of his

efforts to fortify Jerusalem, Esd 4:6–23, and the **297e** opposition of unpatriotic Jews may have led him to go into retirement until the coming of Nehemias. He is not mentioned among those who helped to build the walls (ch 3), but even if he were present, there would be little to distinguish his co-operation from that of the other priests, 3:1. ' the first day of the 7th month ' of Tishri : the Feast of Trumpets ; *cf.* § 113*e*. **4.** ' step ' : ' *tower* ', a raised wooden platform. **6.** ' lifting up their hands ' : in token of approval and solidarity. **7.** ' made silence ' : the Levites, scattered through the throng, kept the people quiet and attentive. **8.** ' and plainly ', etc. : ' and with attention to the *sense* and they [the people] understood *the reading* '. This is the simplest version. **9.** ' Athersatha ' : *i.e.* governor. Omit ' Nehemias ' with 3 Esd. LXX omits the word for ' governor '. The same title was borne by Sheshbazzar (*cf.* Esd 2:63). ' who interpreted ' : ' *kept the attention* ' of the people (*cf.* 7, 11). ' wept ' : when they saw how they had broken the Law. **10.** ' Eat *the* fat and drink *the* sweet ', a proverbial expression ; remorse should not impede the holy joy proper to a festal day. **12.** ' the words that he had taught them ' : ' that had *been made known* to them '.

13–18 The Feast of Tabernacles—13. ' the second **f** day ' : of the 7th month, Tishri (Sept.–Oct.). ' that he should interpret ' : ' *to give* (further) *attention to* '. **14.** ' written in the Law ' : on the feast *cf.* § 113*j*. **15.** ' mount ' : ' *hill country* '. ' of beautiful wood ' : probably ' *of oleaster* '. **16.** ' street ' : ' *open space* '. ' gate of Ephraim ' : *cf.* 12:39. **17.** ' since the days of Josue the son of Nun ' they had not celebrated the feast with such joy and festal pomp ; for previous celebrations, however, *cf.* Os 12:9 and Esd 3:4. The emphasis is on ' so ', *i.e.* in such a manner. Some exegetes think that the reference is to the high-priest Josue (Esd 3:1) and that ' the son of Nun ' is an interpolation. **18.** ' the 8th day ' ; *cf.* Num 29:35, Lev 23:36 and § 113*j*. ' manner ' : *i.e.* the regulations prescribed by the Law.

IX 1–38 The Renewal of the Covenant—1–5 A Day g of Fasting and Sackcloth—1. ' four and twentieth day ' : the second day after the solemn closing of the feast of tabernacles. **2.** ' confessed their sins ' : as a nation in the manner described in 6–37. **3.** ' rose up *in their place* '. ' they read ' : the Levites, while the people listened. ' four times ' : ' *a fourth part of* the day ', *i.e.* 3 hours. **4.** ' step ' : ' *platform* ' ; *cf.* 8:4. **6.** At the invitation of the Levites : ' Bless the Lord ', etc., the people (though it is not expressly stated) responded, joining in the divine praise and in the confession which followed.

6–37 The National Confession—After an act of faith **h** in one God, the creator of heaven and earth, it first recalls God's early mercies to Israel, the nation's unworthy return, the divine forbearance, the people's renewed disobedience, and their consequent punishment ; it then acknowledges the justice of their chastisement and concludes abruptly with a picture of Israel's present plight, which is, in itself, an appeal. It was recited by the Levites with whom the people associated themselves. There are no compelling reasons for asserting that it is a later insertion. Its ' vagueness ' can well be explained by its liturgical character common to so many OT prayers.

6. ' Thou *art Yahweh, even thou* alone.' ' host ' : the stars ; *cf.* Gen 2:1. ' host of heaven ' : probably the angels ; *cf.* Ps 102 (103) 21. **7.** ' Abram . . . Abraham ' : *cf.* Gen 17:5. ' fire ' : ' *Ur* '. **8.** *Cf.* Gen 15:18–21. ' just ' : therefore faithful to thy promises. **9.** *Cf.* Ex 3:7 ; 14:10. **10.** ' against them ' : the Israelites. ' name ' : reputation ; *cf.* Ex 9:16. **11.** *Cf.* Ex 14:21 ; 15:4, 5, 19. **12.** *Cf.* Ex 13:21. ' that they might see ' : ' *to give them light in* '. **13.** ' ceremonies ' : ' *statutes* '. **15.** *Cf.* Ex 16:4 ff. ; 17:6. ' lifted up thy hand ' : the gesture accompanying an oath. **16.** ' dealt proudly ' : acted presumptuously. **17.** ' gave the head . . . contention ' : ' *set the head*

297h to return to their bondage *in Egypt*'; *cf.* Num 14:4. 'in Egypt': thus some MSS and LXX. **18.** *Cf.* Ex 32:1-4. 'blasphemies': words and acts contemptuous of God. **20.** 'thy good spirit': 'thy *favourable breath*', *i.e.* thy help; perhaps the figure contains an allusion to the sending of quails carried by the wind (Num 11:31). 'to teach them': '*to make them prosper*'. **21.** 'worn': '*blistered*'; *cf.* Deut. 8:4; 29:5. **22.** 'divided lots': '*allot as a surplus*'. The kingdoms of Transjordan were not included, in the strict sense, in the land promised to their fathers, Gen 12:7; Num 32:7; Deut 2:30-3:20. **25.** 'made by others': **i** '*hewn out*'. **27.** The period of the Judges. 'saviours': this title is given to the 'judges'; *cf.* Jg 2:16, etc. **29a.** 'And thou didst *testify against* them *to bring* them *back* to thy law'; *cf.* 4 Kg 17:13. *b.* 'which if a man do', etc., is parenthetical; *cf.* Lk 10:28, 'This do and thou shalt live.' 'withdrew the shoulder': like an ox that refuses the yoke. **30.** *Cf.* Zach 7:12. 'spirit': divine revelation made to the prophets. 'people of the lands': *cf.* 3:2. **32b.** 'turn not . . . labour': '*let not all the hardship seem little before thee*'. Assur: the domination by Assyria had been succeeded by that of Babylon and Persia. **33b.** 'done truth': *i.e.* fulfilled thy word in sending both weal and woe. **34b.** 'testified *against* them'. **35.** 'kingdoms' should be singular. **36b.** 'behold we this day are bondmen': subjects of Persia. **37.** The taxes were excessive. **38.** 'because of all this': *i.e.* in view of a *sure* covenant. The covenant is the conclusion of the whole religious reform initiated by Esdras and Nehemias. It is connected with the previous confession in general subject-matter, though it was probably not signed on the same day. It is a promise, signed and sealed, to observe the divine Law in the future. Its substance is outlined in 10:30-39 and the signatories given in 10:1-28. **38b.** 'and *sign* it . . . and our princes . . . (are enrolled) *upon the sealed deed*'. The signatures were written on the outside; *cf.* Jer 32:14. This verse is 10:1 in MT.

j **X 1-29 The List of Signatories—1.** 'the subscribers': '(enrolled) *upon the sealed acts*': the plural is used to show that several copies were made. The names include priests, Levites and the families whose heads signed on behalf of their houses. Those who hold that chh 8-10 belong to the book of Esdras consider 'Nehemias' to be a late insertion in 8:9.

k **30-39 The Obligations of the Covenant—30.** No intermarriage with non-Israelites: *cf.* Ex 34:16; Deut 7:3. **31.** No trading on the Sabbath day, Ex 31:12-14; 23-12; Deut 5:12; Lev 19:3; and the observance of the sabbatical year by allowing the land to lie fallow, Ex 23:10 f.; Lev 25:2-7, and by not exacting the payment of debts, Deut 15:1-6. 'exaction of every hand' is literal. **32-33.** Payment of the temple tax. This is a modification of the half shekel prescribed in Ex 30:11-16 (*cf.* Mt 17:24). Perhaps the change was due to the straitened circumstances of the community. **33.** 'loaves of proposition': '*bread of the setting forth*'; *cf.* §§ 177*d*, 194*b*. **34.** Provision of wood for the altar. 'cast lots': to determine the time and order in which each family was to supply wood. 'as it is written' refers to the burning, not the fetching of the wood; *cf.* Lev 6:12. **35-37.** The offering of first-fruits, Ex 23:19; Deut 26:2-10, first-born, Ex 13:13; Num 18:16-19, and of tithes, Lev 27:30; Num 18;21-32; Deut 14:22-29. **37.** 'meats': '*coarse meal*' in the form of a paste, Num 15:21. 'libations': '*offerings*', lit. 'something separated', *i.e.* the portion of first-fruits and of sacrifices set apart for the priests; *cf.* Lev 7:14, 32, 34. 'receive', etc.: 'receive tithes out of all the cities of our *tillage*'. **38.** A priest was present when the tithes were collected. The Levites received a tenth from the people and gave to the priests a tenth of all they received; *cf.* Num 18:25-28. This was placed in the storerooms that stood around the temple. **-39.** 'forsake': '*neglect*'; *cf.* however, 13:10-13, where they failed to keep this promise.

XI 1-XII 26 The City peopled—This section takes **2** up the thread that had been dropped at 7:4. The inhabitants of Jerusalem were few in proportion to the area of the city, 7:4. Chiefly the official classes dwelt in Jerusalem; the mass of the people lived in the surrounding villages, 11:1. Nehemias decided to select by lot one man in ten to reside in the city. For this purpose a census was required, and Nehemias was about to undertake this task when he discovered a list of the returned exiles already drawn up, 7:5-73. His 'Memoirs' were then interrupted by a description of the feast of tabernacles and the covenant (chh 8-10). The text now returns to the subject of repopulating Jerusalem and briefly describes the method adopted. **2.** Some apparently, over and above the tenth selected by lot, volunteered to dwell in Jerusalem. 11:3-12:26 contains lists taken from the state archives with abridgments and necessary adaptations.

3-24 The List of the Residents of Jerusalem—The same **b** list is found in 1 Par 9:2-19 with variations. **3-9.** The chief laymen. **3b.** Read: '*But in the cities of Judah everyone dwelt in his possession*', etc. The whole sentence is parenthetical. Nathanites: *cf.* 7:47. 'children of the servants of Solomon': *cf.* 7:57. **8.** The text seems corrupt. A suggested emendation is w^e*eḥā(y)u gibbôrê ḥayil*, 'And *his kinsmen were mighty warriors*'. **9.** 'their ruler': of the Benjamites. 'second over the city': second in charge. **10-14 The List of the Priests—14b.** 'the son of the **c** mighty': '*of the great ones*'. The better Gk codices omit the phrase. We should expect a proper name. **15-18.** The Levites. **19.** The Porters. **20** interrupts the account of the residents of Jerusalem; it would be more appropriate before 25. **22-24.** Notes about various officers and the singers. **23.** 'an order', etc.: '*a fixed provision for the singers*'. The king is Artaxerxes; *cf.* 24. **24.** 'Phathalia' seems to have been an official representative of Jewish interests at the Persian court. **25-36.** The towns and villages occupied by the Jews. **25-30.** The Judaean towns. **25.** 'And *as to* the villages *with* their fields [the unwalled towns], *some* of the *sons* of Judah dwelt', etc. **30.** The 'valley of *Gehinnom*' ran along the SW. wall of Jerusalem. **31-36.** The Benjamite towns.

XII 1-26 A List of Priests and Levites arranged by periods; it carries us down to the times of the sacred writer. **1-9.** A list of priests and Levites who came with Zorobabel and Josue, the high-priest. The names in 1-7 also appear with some variations in 10:3-8; 12:12-21; see also Esd 2:36-39. 'everyone in his office': '*were opposite them for the functions*', for antiphonal singing. **10-11.** The succession of high-priests is carried down from Josue (c 538) to Jeddoa, who was contemporary with Alexander the Great (c 333). Eliasib was high-priest at the time of Nehemias. **12-21.** The list in 1-7 was of the contemporaries of Zorobabel; this list gives the heads of those same families 'in the days of Joacim', the successor of Josue as high-priest. **17.** Miamin: the name of the representative of this family has fallen out. **22-26.** Further Lists. **22.** 'Darius the Persian': Darius III (Codomannus), defeated by Alexander. In his day Jeddoa was high-priest; *cf.* 11. **23.** 'the book of Chronicles': not the Chronicles (Par) of the OT. **24.** 'Josue, *Binnui*, Cadmiel: *cf.* 8; 10:9. 'by their courses': '*opposite them*' in the choir. 'to wait equally in order': lit. '*watch over against watch*' for antiphonal chant.

27-43 The Dedication of the Walls—One would naturally expect this event to follow closely upon their completion on the 25th of Elul (*cf.* 6:15). This section, therefore, may be out of place; on the other hand, the dedication may have been delayed because of the approaching feast of tabernacles (chh 8-9). The description is taken in the main from the 'Memoirs' of Nehemias (*cf.* the use of the first person), but for 33-36 and 40-43 the sacred writer probably had recourse to a temple or a priestly document. The dedication was a symbolic handing over of the walls to the possession and guardianship of Yahweh. The high-priest is not mentioned as taking part in the procession because he awaited its arrival at the temple.

f 27-30 The Preparation—27. ' out of all their places ' : the cities in which they dwelt. ' psalteries ' : Heb. ' *nebel* ', a kind of harp. **28.** ' sons of the singing men ' : merely ' *singers* '. ' the plain country ' : ' *the circle* ', here the environs of Jerusalem. Nethuphati : ' of the Netophathites '. Netophah was about 15 m. S. of Jerusalem. **29.** ' the house of Gilgal ' : ' *Beth-Gilgal* '. **30.** ' were purified ' : ' *purified themselves* ' for the solemnity by ceremonial purification ; *cf.* Esd 6:20.

g 31-39 The Procession—It was marshalled in two great choirs ; starting from the western side of the city, one choir went round the southern half of the wall, and the other round the northern half. They joined in the open space before the temple. **31.** ' two great choirs to give praise. And they went ' : the Heb. ' *two great thanksgivings and processions* ' is doubtful. For *weṭah͞a-lukôṯ*, ' processions ', read ' *weh͞ā'aḥaṯ*. ' *And one* went '. One group went ' on the right hand ' ; *i.e.* of one facing eastwards towards the temple. The choir on the right moved along the southern wall, that on the left along the northern. **32-33.** Behind the singers and musicians came one half of the chiefs of Judaea with Osias, otherwise unknown, at their head. **34-35.** They were followed by seven heads of the priestly families with clarions, and eight of the Levitical with accompanying instruments, while Esdras walked at the head of the priests. **34.** ' sons of the priests ' = priests ; *cf.* 28. The critics who place the activity of Esdras in 398 after Nehemias (445) believe his presence here to be an interpolation of the Chronicler ; on the other hand, his presence supposed, we have a perfect correspondence in the arrangement of the two columns : (*a*) Oasis, seven priests, eight Levites, Esdras, 32-35 ; (*b*) Nehemias, seven priests, eight Levites, Jezraia, 39-41. Esdras is not the leader of the first column, but he is at the head of the sacred ministers. Catholic scholars who follow the same late dating for Esdras but admit his presence as a young man on this occasion (as well as in chh 8-10), are embarrassed by his eminent place at the head of the priests. Those who hold that chh 8-10 are a part of Esd consider that the mention of Esdras here is a later insertion.

h The Route of the Procession—From the Gate of the Valley the two columns moved in opposite directions. Along the southern route of the first column were the Dung Gate, the Fountain Gate, the Stairs of David and the Water Gate at the east of the temple ; along the northern course of the second column, the tower of the Furnaces, the Broad Wall, the Gate of Ephraim, the Gate *of Jeshanah* (Old Gate ?), the Fish Gate, the tower of Hananeel, the tower of *Meah*, the Sheep Gate, and the *Prison* Gate (the Gate Miphkad of 3:31 [?]). **35b-36.** ' And Esdras the scribe was before them. *And at the gate of the fountain, going straight on*, they went up by the stairs of the city of David [*i.e.* Ophel] *where the wall climbed from the house* [tomb (?)] of David '. If the Gate of the Valley be either the Gate of the Essenes or that found in the Tyropoeon Valley, the distance travelled by each column was about the same (*c* 1600 and *c* 1300 yards). **42.** The two columns met in the open space before the temple and songs of rejoicing were sung and sacrifices of thanksgiving offered. See Map C, page 1311.

i 43-46. Officers are appointed to supervise the collection of the revenues for the temple and its ministers. **43.** ' in that day ' : at that time. The particular time intended is uncertain. ' libations ' : *cf.* 10:37. ' that the rulers . . . thanksgiving ' : ' *to gather into them* [the storehouses] *out of the fields of the cities the legal portions for* the priests ', etc. **44.** HT is obscure. ' and they kept the *charge* of their God and the observance of *purification as* did the singers and the porters, according to the command of David and of Solomon his son '. The priests, Levites, singers and porters discharged

the duties of their office. **46.** ' sanctified : ' *Thus they* **298i** *set apart for* ' : the people ' set apart ' a tenth portion for the Levites (who were the singers and porters) who in turn gave a part to the priests according to Num 18:25-32.

XIII 1-31 Nehemias' Second Mission—Nehemias re- **299a** mained in Jerusalem for twelve years (445-433 B.C.) and then returned to Susa. He followed anxiously the life of the people of Jerusalem, and when informed of alarming symptoms in their spiritual state, once more obtained permission to visit the city. The date of this second mission is uncertain ; probably shortly before the death of Artaxerxes (424 B.C.). It concerns abuses that had arisen in Judaea during Nehemias' absence.

1-3 Excommunication of Foreigners—1. ' on that **b** day ' ; ' *at that time* '. The particular time intended is uncertain, but the event seems to have been introduced here to prepare the reader for the expulsion of Tobias from the temple precincts, 4-9, and belongs, therefore, to Nehemias' second mission (7). ' was found written ' : the rest of this verse and 2 is an almost integral citation of Deut 23:3-5. ' church ' : ' *assembly* '. **3.** ' stranger ' : all those not of purely Israelite blood were expelled from the religious body of Israel.

4-9 The Expulsion of Tobias from the Sacred Precincts c —4. ' And over this ' : ' *Now before* this ', before the excommunication of the non-Israelites and before Nehemias' return. Eliasib : the high-priest of 3:1. ' treasury ' : ' *rooms* '. ' Tobias ' : one of Nehemias' chief enemies, 2:10, and a relative of Eliasib. He persuaded the high-priest to give him a room inside the temple precincts, doubtless offering Eliasib some percentage. This room became a branch office of the Bank of Tobias whose head office was in Ammon. **5.** ' before him ' : ' *formerly* '. In the rooms about the temple courtyard were stored whatever was needed for divine worship and for the maintenance of the sacred ministers ; *cf.* 12:46. **6.** ' because in the 32nd year of Artaxerxes I *returned* to the king '. Neh. returned to Babylon at the end of the period for which he had asked leave of the king, 2:6. **6b-7.** ' And after certain days, I asked (leave of) the king, and I came (a second time) to Jerusalem ', after an interval perhaps of some years. Tobias was an Ammonite, 2:10 ; 4:3, and, as such, his presence in the temple precincts, apart from his business, was an affront to the holiness of the place. **8.** ' vessels of the house ' : ' *household furniture* '.

10-14. Nehemias, finding that the contribution for **d** the support of the Levites had been neglected with the result that they had to seek a livelihood in the country to the detriment of the temple service, brought them back to Jerusalem, insisted on the payment of tithes, and appointed a commission of two priests and two Levites to supervise the distribution. **14.** One of the parenthetic prayers of Nehemias ; he prays that he may be remembered for his zeal on behalf of the temple.

15-22 The Observance of the Sabbath—15. He found **e** men treading grapes, harvesting, bringing produce into the city and (according to Vg) selling it on the Sabbath day. MT reads 15*b* : ' And I protested on the day they sold provisions ' as if they were sold during the week. The difficulty is solved by placing this section after 16. The Vg reading is an attempt to clarify the difficulty in the HT. **16.** The Tyrians, sailors and fishermen, as pagans were not interested in the Mosaic Law. **17-19.** Nehemias rebuked the leading citizens and ordered the gates to be shut on the eve of the Sabbath and the law of rest to be observed. **19.** ' when the gates of Jerusalem *grew dark before* the Sabbath, I commanded that the gates be shut '. The Sabbath began at sunset. **20.** The merchants, for a week or two, set up a market outside the walls. **21.** Nehemias promptly used his authority as governor to put down this evasion of his regulations.

23-29 Measures against Mixed Marriages—The old **f** question of mixed marriages was again giving trouble.

299f Nehemias found Judaeans married to Philistines, Ammonites and Moabites, and their children unable to speak Hebrew. The guilty were punished and an oath exacted against the repetition of the offence. Even the high-priest's family was involved in guilt. **23.** *Cf.* Esd 9:1-3. **24.** '*half of their children spoke Ashdodite*'. **25.** 'shaved': '*plucked out*'. **26.** *Cf.* 3 Kg 11:3. **28.** One violation of the law gave particular offence; a grandson of the high-priest had married the daughter of Sanballat (*cf.* 2:10). The offender was banished and, according to Jewish legend, he set **29** up a schismatic priesthood in Samaria, and later had a temple built on Mt Gerizim. **29.** 'defiled the priesthood': the family of the high-priest was contaminated by the incident of 29.

30-31 A Brief Recapitulation—31. 'the offering of **g** wood'; *cf.* 10:34. The book ends with the words: 'Remember me, O my God, for good. Amen.' We do not know when Nehemias died. He is lauded in Ecclus 49:15.

THE BOOK OF TOBIAS

(TOBIT)

By C. F. DeVine

a **Bibliography**—St Ambrose, *De Tobia*, CSEL 32, 11, 517 ; Ven. Bede, *In Librum B. Patris Tobiae allegorica interpretatio*, PL 91, 923 ff. ; Cornelius à Lapide, *Commentaria in Tobiam* (Paris, 1878) ; E. Cosquin, *Le livre de Tobie et l'histoire du Sage Ahikar*, RB 8 (1899) 50 ff., 510 ff. ; P. Vetter, *Das Buch Tobias und die Achikar-Sage*, TQ, 86 (1904) 321 ff., 512 ff., 87 (1905) 321 ff., 497 ff. ; J. O'Carroll, *Tobias and Achikar*, DbR 93 (1929) 252 ff. ; R. Galdos, *Commentarius in librum Tobit*, CSS, 1930 ; M. M. Schumpp, *Das Buch Tobias* (München, 1933) ; A. Miller & J. Schilden-berger, *Die Bücher Tobias, Judith und Esther* (Bonn, 1940) ; *D. C. Simpson, *Tobit*, in CAP I.

b **The Text**—It is generally acknowledged that the primitive text has not been preserved. It is important, then to bear this well in mind in any discussion of the Book of Tobias, for many of the difficulties encountered therein are fundamentally textual difficulties. At the present stage of our knowledge it is impossible to determine with certainty the language of the original form of our book. Eminent authorities have proposed in turn that it was Hebrew, Aramaic or Greek. It seems probable at least that the original language was Semitic, whether Hebrew or Aramaic cannot at present be decided.

c The book has been transmitted to us in several noticeably divergent forms. The Greek form of the text is represented by : (*a*) the Codex Sinaiticus ; (*b*) Codices B and A ; and (*c*) the minuscules 44, 106, 107. The Hebrew, which is certainly not primitive in its present form, is found in the edition of *S. Munster (1542), which may represent a 5th cent. text ; in that of *P. Fagius, which offers perhaps a text of the 12th cent. ; and in the London Hebrew MS (Brit. Mus. Add. 11639) and the Hebrew of *M. Gaster. The date of the London and Gaster Hebrew is uncertain. An Aramaic form (possibly 7th cent.) of the text was discovered at Oxford in the Bodleian Library and has been edited (1878) by *A. Neubauer. The Old Latin Version, preserved in three forms, follows quite closely the Greek recension exhibited in the Codex Sinaiticus. Most of the Greek minuscules follow the B A form of the text, as do also the Armenian and Ethiopic Versions, and the Syriac in part. Vg is the work of St Jerome who tells us that, ' Since the Chaldean speech is allied to the Hebrew, I found someone who spoke both languages readily, and, taking a day's work, what he said to me in Hebrew that I rendered into Latin to a notary whom I had engaged ' (*Praef. in librum Tobiae*, PL 29, 25 f.). The Aramaic text used by Jerome has not come down to us. The Neubauer Aramaic referred to above, although it manifests some affinity with Vg, is not its source. Jerome's work, produced in his early days as a translator, shows that he rendered his original with considerable freedom. Frequently it is clear that he has translated the sense of a passage rather than its exact literal meaning. In general, it can be said that Tobias is less carefully done than most of his other work.

d Although it is true that the various forms of the book just mentioned differ noticeably one from the other, still substantially the book is the same in all forms. They all show the same simple story throughout, the **same** characters, the same events in the same order.

The differences, though striking at times, are mainly **300d** in unimportant details, proper names, discourses, and the like. Nevertheless, the work of the text-critic who seeks to restore the original form of the book is not easy. He will sense at once that the present Hebrew and Aramaic forms, although worthy of consideration, cannot be looked upon as primitive. Approaching the Greek, he will notice that B and its affiliates present a shorter text of Hellenistic character, while Sinaiticus is Hebraistic and longer. He will remark the striking similarity between the Old Latin and Sinaiticus, and will not overlook the influence of the Old Latin on Vg. What then should be his choice of method ? Various replies would undoubtedly be given to this question. Without being dogmatic we would suggest cautiously that the primitive text could best be restored by taking Sinaiticus, rigorously compared with the Old Latin, as a groundwork, and collating this basic text with the other known forms of the book. In this task a careful workman will not overlook the ancient Vg, for even though it was done in a day by St Jerome, it does not follow, as suggested in some circles, that it is altogether devoid of critical value. In the commentary to follow, the Bible-text to be used is the current DV ; however the preferences just indicated will exercise some influence, especially in passages where the difficulty is mainly textual.

Title and Author of the Book—In Vg and DV both **e** father and son are called Tobias (1:9). However, in the other forms of the book the father's name is *Tobit* and his son's *Tobias*. This latter designation is the correct one. However, both names are of Hebrew derivation and are closely related. They have the meaning, ' Yahweh is my good ', or ' my good is Yahweh '. The ancient forms of the book bear a variety of titles. It is probable that the most ancient title was simply, ' The Words of Tobit '. If the words ' publish (other texts, " write ") all his wonderful works ' (12:20) are authentic, the title would indicate that Tobit and Tobias were the authors of the book. It is quite possible that these main characters were the first to put the narrative in form and that the original story stems from them. It could easily have been handed down orally or in a very simple written form, until at a much later date it was composed under inspiration by the actual author who would have used the earlier written or oral sources. Nothing, however, has come down to us concerning the actual author of the book.

Date of the Book—From several indications in the **f** book itself, as well as from a comparison of the various forms in which it appears at present, it seems fairly certain that the narrative went through several stages over a fairly long period of time. There is a marked personal tone throughout, and so, it is quite possible that the story was first related in a simple form by the principal characters, Tobias and his son, and was then handed down orally in the family. Later this simple outline would have been transferred to writing, and at some still later date it would have received substantially the common form in which we read it today. At best, however, this viewpoint is conjectural, since, as already stated, the original text of the work has not been preserved. At any rate it is beyond question that one or all of the unnamed authors of the

300f written work wrote the story down under divine Inspiration.

g In view of the uncertainty surrounding the history of the text of Tobias it is not strange that we find wide disagreement among authorities as to the actual time of composition of the written work. Some non-Catholic authors (*v.g.* *Schürer, *Lohr) assign the book to the 2nd cent. and Simpson to a date nearer 170 than 350 B.C. ; while others put it as late as the 2nd cent. A.D. Several Catholic scholars (*v.g.* Vetter), influenced by the fact that certain customs are alluded to in some forms of the book (the threefold tithes, the levirate duty, etc.) have argued that this definitely assigns the book to a period roughly from 250 B.C. to 150 B.C. Although these reasons are not altogether convincing, it seems clear, on the one hand, that the book was composed after Assyrian times. Otherwise it is difficult to see why it was not accepted into the Palestinian Canon. Furthermore, intrinsic reasons point to an author who held views on the future life prevalent in the post-exilic period. Much of the doctrine and counsel of Tobias would sound well on the lips of a contemporary of the author of Ecclus. On the other hand, the author gives no sign that he knows of the great national upheavals of Maccabean times nor is he aware of the penetrating influence of Pharisaism. Convincing arguments have not yet been advanced to date the written composition of Tobias.

h Uncertainty also surrounds the question as to the country of composition. Several have been suggested with some probability—Palestine, Egypt, Babylonia and Persia. Palestine has been excluded since, it is alleged, it is difficult to see why the book was not added to the Palestinian Canon if composed in that country. However, this reasoning is not convincing. The work is thoroughly Palestinian in its whole conception, and its origin in Palestine is a possibility. Some scholars favour Egypt, but if the book originated in the Jewish colony there, we should expect to find traces of Hellenistic influence. Further, it is unlikely that an author writing in Egypt would relegate the demon to his own country (8:3). Both Babylonia and Persia are attractive suggestions, but there is no conclusive evidence that the author of the written work resided in those countries. It is prudent to withhold judgement until more convincing evidence has been adduced.

301a Literary Character of the Book—The delicate and vexatious problem here treated is concerned with the question : What type of literature are we dealing with in this book ? Is the story of Tobias to be viewed as strict history or not ? For, although the work is in every sense a fully inspired and canonical book, this is not the same thing as saying that it relates strict history, since any type of literature is compatible with biblical Inspiration so long as it is not by its very nature unworthy of God. St Thomas Aquinas pointed out centuries ago that, ' In Scripture divine things are presented to us in the manner which is in common use amongst men '. The determination of the type of literature, however, is not a mere literary problem for it must greatly influence the subsequent interpretation of the book. Hence this whole question must be handled with prudence and caution. Moreover, the ultimate decision must necessarily rest with the Church since she alone is the infallible interpreter of all inspired Scripture. Thus far the Church has not expressed her mind in this matter specifically. She has given general directions, but no decision. Quite recently, new impetus has been given to the study of the problem by the clear and precise directives of the Encyclical *Divino Afflante Spiritu*, which has an extremely valuable section on the importance of the ' mode of writing ' or ' literary forms ' in Sacred Scripture. These directives of Pius XII, as well as those of his Predecessors and the Fathers and Doctors of the Church, must be borne in mind by the investigator who seeks to attain the true sense of any inspired literature.

A brief glance at the **history of interpretation** of our **30** book suffices to show that a definite judgement on its literary character is not easily formed. The Fathers and ancient writers have scattered references to the Book of Tobias in their works, but they have left us no full commentary. Ambrose on Tobias is really a treatise against usury. Bede's work can scarcely be called a strict commentary, being but a brief allegorical outline. Strabo is merely a repetition of Bede. None of the ancients has left us a definite treatment of the literary character of Tobias or questioned its historicity. In a sense, then, it may be said that they presumed that the book is strictly historical since no other consideration had arisen for them. *M. Luther was one of the first to deny its historical character. For him it was a devout drama, a legend with a didactic purpose. Non-Catholic authors, for the most part, deny altogether the historicity of Tobias, viewing it as a poetic fiction, a pure fable or a fantastic fairy-tale. A few Catholic writers expressed much the same views, *v.g.* J. Jahn and C. Movers. Most Catholic scholars, however, consider the book historical, at least to some extent ; although A. Scholz proposed the peculiar subjective theory that Tobias is an allegorical prophecy describing Israel's return to the Church at the end of time. Among Catholic scholars who have treated the problem expressly, Gutberlet, Reusch, Vigouroux, Cornely-Merk, Galdos and others defend a strictly historical conception of the book in all its details ; others, as Hummelauer, N. Peters, P. Vetter and A. Miller prefer to view the book as historical in a broader sense : there is a definite historical foundation or nucleus, but the author's principal purpose is didactic. Vetter was one of the earliest to propose this opinion with considered argumentation ; Miller has recently attracted attention by presenting the theory in a new way. Thus it can be seen that even amongst Catholic scholars there has not been uniformity of viewpoint regarding the literary form of the Book of Tobias.

It is apparent at once that there are two radically **c** opposed views in this matter. (1) There is the opinion of those who hold that the book is strictly historical in every detail. Their reasons : the tradition of the Church ; the fact that the book has every appearance of intending to relate history and nothing else—it gives us an account of real persons, in real geographical and historical circumstances. (2) Those who assert that the story of Tobias is pure fiction, and who defend their position with the following reasons : there are historical and geographical errors in the book sufficient to destroy its historicity ; a good part of the narrative presumes the intervention of supernatural forces or is clearly intended to imply the working of miracles ; there are several references in the book to the fables of the Grateful Dead and to the legend of Achikar.

If a solution can be given in the present state of our **d** knowledge, it probably lies somewhere between these two extreme positions. It is quite true that an unbiased reading of the book leads one to conclude that the author's obvious intention was to relate historical happenings, at least in a general way. This point of evidence is capital and must enter into any solution of the problem. Whether an appeal to tradition yields the conclusion that the book must be considered strict history in every detail, is questionable. As has already been pointed out, the ancients did not pose our specific problem. The fact that the Councils of Trent and the Vatican list Tobias among historical books scarcely proves that our book must be viewed in the strictest historical sense. Nor is an appeal to the Decree of Gelasius (EB 19) conclusive. True, this document lists Tobias under the heading, *Item ordo historiarum* ; but it also includes the Book of Job in the same list, and yet scarcely anyone would consider Job an historical work in all its details. A decree of the Consistorial Congregation (29 June, 1912) excluded a work of C. Holzhey from use in Seminaries for its very audacious opinions. That concerning Tobias, which holds it to be pure, poetic fiction, is mentioned among others. Still, it does not follow from this decree that Tobias must be viewed as a work strictly historical in the sense, say, of St Luke's Gospel. It would follow, though, that to consider Tobias as altogether un-historical and as pure fiction would be presumptuous. This is the tendency of writers of the other extreme ; and their arguments are even less probative. Thus, for example, to assert that there are geographical and historical errors in Tobias and that therefore its historicity is destroyed, is to misread the evidence badly. There are historical and geographical diffi-culties in the current forms of the book, but these can be solved adequately as purely textual problems. Hence they need not be imputed to the original author and do not affect the literary character of the book one way or the other. Nor does the fact of supernatural intervention, or of the miraculous, in the narrative destroy its historicity. This is a purely rationalistic conception. If the fact of a miracle is firmly established exegetically it must be accepted ; to reject it solely because miraculous is to proceed unscientifically. The bearing of the Achikar legend on the Book of Tobias will be discussed § 301*h-i*.

By way of summary, the following points can be made. The Church has not yet given a definite decision con-cerning the literary form of the Book of Tobias. How-ever, since traditionally the book has always been considered historical in some way, and since the author's obvious intention is to give a real, historical setting to his story, the exegete should consider that at least the substantial framework is historical. Since, on the other hand, the story is related with perceptible artistry and to inculcate a moral, its didactic purpose must be considered the principal intention of the author. This didactic purpose does not destroy the historical founda-tion of the book. The decree of the Biblical Com-mission (June 23, 1905) concerning those books of Holy Scripture which are regarded as historical, either wholly or in part, should be recalled here ; *cf.* § 52*j*. If such books are to be considered to give at times only the *appearance of history*, then this viewpoint must be proven by solid arguments and subject to the ultimate decision of the Church. The view, then, that the story of Tobias relates real historical facts is in possession, and the opposite must be proved in each case. On account of the doubtful state of the text of this book it is next to impossible at the present time to be more determinate or to say with certainty that this or that section of the narrative is, or is not, strict history.

The connexion of several widely-known **legends** or fables with the Tobias story is a question of some importance since it has a bearing on the literary character of our book. Some of these, such as the legend of the Grateful Dead and the Egyptian Khonsu legend, can be dismissed almost at once. The Grateful Dead story has a rather grotesque similarity to Tobias, but since it does not pre-date Christian times there can be no question of literary relationship to our book unless, perhaps, it is a pure distortion of Tobias. The Khonsu fable (*cf.* *J. H. Breasted, *Ancient Records of Egypt*, 3 (1906) 188 ff.) was composed earlier, but its only similarity to Tobias is in the account of the king's daughter who was tormented by a spirit or demon—a very narrow basis on which to establish any sort of dependence.

The story of **Achikar** deserves more attention. This tale, widely read in antiquity, was certainly known to the Jews and apparently treasured by them even though its setting was pagan. It has come down to us in a great variety of forms in many languages ; *cf.* *F. C. Cony-beare, Harris, Lewis, *The Story of Aḥiḳar* (1913²). In brief, it relates the story of Achikar, the grand chan-cellor of king Sennacherib of Assyria, and his wicked nephew, Nadan. Achikar had brought up the nephew as his own son, and yet the ungrateful youth, who had not absorbed the piety and wisdom of the uncle, managed successfully, by very devious methods, to have the aged Achikar accused before the king of treason and condemned to prison. Later the evil was discovered and Nadan paid for his treachery with his life. The tale is embellished with a host of proverbs or maxims of Achikar, but the most surprising thing about it al! is that the story of Achikar is quoted in the present form of the Book of Tobias. For some this fact alone has been sufficient proof that Tobias is not intended as history in any sense. It clearly shows, they claim, that the story of Tobias is a legend or fable similar to that of Achikar, and that the author of Tobias simply incorporated parts of the Achikar legend in his own fictitious narrative. The whole question is involved and is beset with many uncertainties.

Vg and DV have only one citation (11:20) from Achikar ; in this passage Achikar and Nadan are found rejoicing with Tobias and his son over their good fortune. The other forms of the Book of Tobias give also at least three further citations from Achikar ; 1:21, 22 ; 2:10 ; 14:10. These places are so well attested by textual evidence that (except perhaps for the citation in 14:10) they must be considered as probably part of the text of Tobias. Furthermore, on account of recent findings in connexion with the Achikar story, it is now generally admitted that the story of Achikar was in existence before the com-position of the Book of Tobias. This is not enough in itself, however, to establish a certain literary depen-dence of Tobias on Achikar. The two narratives are quite dissimilar and independent, although both have an obvious didactic purpose. Moreover, the brief sections cited in Tobias are so very loosely bound in with the Tobias story that they can be omitted without affecting it in the least. The Achikar text like that of Tobias has been only imperfectly transmitted, and we are no more certain of the original form and language of the Achikar legend than we are of the Tobias story. Some evidence has been produced to show that Achikar was a real, historical personage, and that at least the outline of his story is historical, but it is not altogether conclusive. At any rate, before making definite judgements on the relation of Achikar, and his story and sayings, to Tobias, we need much more evidence than we now possess. It would seem best to conclude at the present time that even if the Achikar citations in Tobias are certainly authentic, and this can still be questioned, we can deduce nothing from this to prove or reject the historicity of the Book of Tobias.

Theme and Analysis of the Book—With spontaneous 302a artistry and naturalness the author of this book gives us the very beautiful and highly edifying life-stories of the pious Israelite Tobias and of his son, also called Tobias. It pictures a family living in captivity amongst a pagan people, far from its homeland, yet fully observant of the Law of Moses and trusting in God amidst many trials and difficulties. The theme of the book, then, is the inculcation of the truth that the most important thing in this life is to put full confidence in God, seeing in all things his benevolent Providence, and accepting from his hand with trusting resignation both prosperity and misfortune.

The story opens with Tobias, the elder, a captive of **b** the Assyrians in the city of Nineveh. With a quick, retrospective glance, 1:4–10, the author then shows us that even as a boy Tobias walked always in the way of the Lord. Among those in captivity his conduct was most exemplary, for, fearing God rather than men, he was careful to give alms and to bury the bodies of the dead, even though this incurred the anger of the king. When afflicted with blindness he did not blame God for this misfortune but bore it patiently even in the face of the upbraidings of his own wife, 1:11–3:6. While these events were taking place, the scene changes with gentle, dramatic effect to Sara a young maiden of Ecbatana, who would one day be the wife of Tobias' son. We find her pouring out a touching prayer to God for help in her great misery, 3:7–23. The story then returns to Tobias, who had prayed to

302b be allowed to die if God so willed. Expecting that God might take him from this world, Tobias admonishes his son to lead a virtuous life, 4:1–20, and tells him to seek out Gabelus, a fellow-tribesman living in Rages, to whom he had given a sum of money, 4:21–23. The young Tobias is fearful of setting out on so long a journey into unknown country, but he is unexpectedly assisted by the Angel Raphael in the guise of a young man who offers to guide him to Gabelus, 5:1–28. This offer is accepted and the two set out on their journey. After an exciting adventure with a large fish, 6:1–9, they seek lodging at the home of a kinsman who is Raguel, the father of Sara, the maiden already

c mentioned. The Angel counsels Tobias to seek the hand of Sara in marriage, but he is reluctant as he had heard that Sara had already had seven husbands who were killed by a devil. The Angel reassures the young man and instructs him how to overcome the power of the demon, 6:10–22. So they go to Raguel and are received with joy. When Tobias asks for the hand of Sara, her parents express great fear lest if they consent Tobias, too, will be killed. However, Raguel finally yields to the young man's entreaties, and Tobias is betrothed to Sara, 7:1–20. Things turn out well as the Angel had predicted, for on the marriage night Sara and Tobias pray together, the power of the demon is broken, and no harm ensues 8:1–24. Tobias then remains with Raguel while the Angel journeys on to meet Gabelus and redeem Tobias' note, 9:1–12. Meanwhile, at home the elder Tobias and his wife, Anna, become solicitous for their son since he has not returned at the appointed time; the mother, especially, is disconsolate, 10:1–7. However, Tobias as a good son takes leave of Raguel, despite his pressing invitation to remain, and begins the homeward journey with his bride, 10:8–13. The homecoming is a joyful one indeed, and it is further gladdened when Tobias at the Angel's bidding anoints his father's eyes with the gall of the fish and the old man's blindness leaves him, 11:1–21. When Tobias seeks to repay the Angel for all he had done, not knowing, of course, that this kind stranger was really an Angel of God, Raphael makes himself known. He tells Tobias and his son that their afflictions were permitted by God to try them; and as they are thunderstruck at this revelation, the Angel disappears from their sight, 12:1–22. The final chapters, in the form of a sort of epilogue, contain the blessing of Tobias the elder, prophecies of the future of the Holy City, ch 13, and an account of the later happy life and holy death of Tobias, father and son, ch 14.

d Doctrinal Content—The book is a veritable treasure-house of doctrine, both speculative and practical. It teaches by both word and example: the history of Tobias and his family inculcates particularly the moral virtues and the happy result, in general, of remaining faithful to God and his commandments. The various prayers and admonitions and counsels contain admirable expositions of doctrine.

e The existence of a **personal God** is both presumed and mentioned directly; his **perfections** are referred to frequently. Especially in the prayers and admonitions the God addressed, or referred to, is the one God of Israel, the Creator of all things. The book is thoroughly monotheistic: Yahweh is God; he is omnipotent, eternal, no one can escape his hand, 13:1–4. His benign Providence watches over all things and guides the destinies of all men: events are arranged according to his will, 3:19; 7:14. He certainly sends us trials and permits temptations to prove us, 3:21; 12:13; but just as surely, if we are faithful, he will deliver us from the trials and reward our fidelity, 13:2; 3:22. This God, though eminently just, 3:2, is yet filled with mercy and fatherly solicitude for his children, 3:21 f.; 'he hath chastised us for our iniquities: and he will save us for his own mercy', 13:5. In a word, the God of the Book of Tobias is the one, true God, who rules all things wisely; the God of Israel, who is omnipotent, just and merciful, who

will reward the good and punish the wicked; 'Thou art **302** great, O Lord, for ever, and thy kingdom is unto all ages', 13:1.

The teaching on the angels and demons is almost **f** all found in the explanations of the Angel Raphael himself. Raphael is an angel (*mal'āk*) sent by God, 12:14, 20. He is incorporeal, 12:19; 'one of the seven, who stand before the Lord', 12:15. His duties are to carry out the commands of God who sent him, and to intercede for men before the face of God, 12:12. Angels guard and protect men, 5:21, 27; 10:11. They also have power from God over the demons, 8:3; 12:14. The book tells us a number of things about these demons, although it is by no means a treatise on demonology, and much less is it to be considered a reflection of the beliefs of the Persians or Babylonians on this subject. Here, one devil, Asmodeus, plays the chief role. He has killed the husbands of Sara, 3:10; he torments her household, 8:18; but he remains subject to God's power and to the Angel sent by God, 8:3; 12:14. Nor has he power over all men but only over those who leave themselves open to his machinations, 6:16, 17.

Man is a creature of God and therefore should not **g** live like the heathens 'that know not God', 6:17; 8:5, 8. He has a higher destiny, 4:11, 23; 12:9, and should by his good works make himself worthy of it. Whether the author of the book had a clear concept of the future life can be questioned. Several allusions would lead us to think that at least he knew that man would live after death and would then receive the reward for his good deeds which he could not expect in this life. We cannot anticipate, of course, at this period, the clarity of NT teaching on the future life.

Tobias has always been a favourite source of instruction on the sanctity of **marriage**. In it the state of matrimony is very clearly regarded as a holy union, 8:5. It is to be entered upon with a clean and upright conscience, 4:13; 3:16, 18; its use is to be held sacred, 6:17, 22, and approached with prayer, 6:18. Its main purpose is not sensual gratification, but the procreation of children, 'for the love of posterity, in which thy name (O Lord) may be blessed for ever and ever', 8:9; 6:21 f. Those who profane this sacred state deserve punishment and lay themselves open to the power of the demons, 'they who in such manner receive matrimony, as to shut out God from themselves, and from their mind, and to give themselves to their lust, as the horse and mule, which have not understanding: over them the devil hath power', 6:17. Cf. the Commentary on 3:8 and 6:16 ff. The spouses should be a mutual support to each other; they should be faithful, 4:13; the husband should respect his wife, and the wife should love her husband, 10:13.

Good works are counselled on almost every page of **i** the book. Since the author's chief aim is to inculcate the advantages of an upright, moral life, this is not surprising. He teaches this lesson mainly by the example of the true Israelite, Tobias, and by that of his family. Tobias, even as a boy, observes the Law strictly, 1:4, 8. Later he performs many good deeds, 1:11–20; and he admonishes his son to do likewise, 4:2–20. He had no human respect in all this, for he feared God more than the king, and more than his mocking relatives, 2:9, 18. Nor did he work and hope in vain, for his fidelity to God was rewarded, 12:12 ff.

Four types of good works are especially practised and inculcated: prayer, the burial of the dead, fasting and alms-giving. All the principal characters of the book practise **prayer** with confidence: Tobias, 3:1 ff.; Sara, 3:10 ff.; Raguel and Anna, 8:6, 16; Tobias, the son, and Sara, 8:4, 6. They pray frequently, 2:14; they pray publicly, 1:6, and privately. They pray alone and with others. They also pray with great fervor, 3:1, 11; 8:6; 12:22. Moreover, their prayers were heard by God, thus testifying to the efficacy of trustful prayer, 12:8, 12.

There is frequent mention of Tobias' zeal in **burying the dead.** With great danger to himself and heroic sacrifice, he hid the bodies of those slain by the king and buried them carefully by night, 1:20 f. ; 2:4, 9 f. ; 12:12.

Fasting and alms-giving are both commended and practised : Tobias, according to the Law, kept himself from the defilement of pagan foods, 1:12. Sara fasted to make her prayer more worthy, 3:10 ; and the Angel Raphael gave the valuable counsel : ' Prayer is good with fasting and alms : more than to lay up treasures of gold '. It is often related of Tobias that he helped the needy with his alms, 1:17, 19 ; 2:16 ; and he also counsels his son to give generously, 4:9 ff. Besides these good works, others are mentioned, *e.g.* feeding the hungry and clothing the naked, 1:20. All these good deeds please God and merit a reward, 4:10 ; 12:8 f.

I 1 The Prologue—In most forms of the book the story opens with a brief genealogical preface. This has been abbreviated in Vg, either because St Jerome did not find it in his Aramaic text or because he deliberately shortened it to essentials, perhaps because of his distaste for extended genealogies ; *cf.* PL 26, 594 f. A tendency to abbreviate or summarize on the part of Jerome is noticeable throughout the Vg of Tobias, and particularly in this first chapter. It is difficult to determine just how much of the various forms of the genealogy here should be considered primitive. The same holds for the succeeding geographical designation. It is probable that the following elements are original : ' Tobias, *of the seed of Asiel,* of the tribe of Nephtali, of a *certain* city of that tribe *which was situated* in upper Galilee, *being on the south of Qadesh* [of Nephtali] *and to the north of Safed, and with Aser* [Hazor] *to the West,* was made captive . . .'

2-10 Early Piety of Tobias—The general historical setting is given in this first chapter. The scene is laid ' in the days of Salmanasar king of the Assyrians '. In view of 1:18, especially, it is quite clear that this cannot have been Shalmaneser V (727–722), but must have been Sargon II (721–705). This is sometimes urged as a clinching proof of the historical inaccuracy of the book. However, the difficulty is not serious. ' Salmanasar ' is either a pure textual error, or a scribal correction influenced by the name, *Enemessar,* found in the various Greek forms of the book. *Enemessar* is an unknown name, but it may be explained as the result of an inversion of the compound Assyrian form (*Šarru-ukîn*) of the name ' Sargon '. Hence the correct reading here is *Enemessar, i.e. Sargon.* We are, then, in the days of Isaias the Prophet, in the 8th cent. B.C., when the kingdoms of Judah and Israel were divided, and Assyria the predominant world-power. The principal character in the story is Tobias, a pious inhabitant of the Northern Kingdom, who was carried into captivity by the Assyrian invaders. Such deportations were the common method of keeping the conquered peoples in subjugation. There is no difficulty in admitting that Tobias of Nephtali was carried off in the deportation of Sargon in 721, just after the capture of Samaria. For although there was an earlier deportation of Nephtali, certainly not all the citizens were carried off at that time, and Sargon can easily be presumed to have deported some of the inhabitants of the other cities of Israel on his return from the capture of Samaria. Although the exiles were usually treated well by the conquerors, there was always danger of a lapse in their religious observance due to the pagan influences to which they were necessarily exposed. Tobias, however, is pictured as a faithful observer of the law. **4.** ' And when he (*I*) *was still quite young all the tribe of Nephtali fell away from the house of David* . . .'. **5.** Nephtali had followed the idolatrous practices of the other tribes of the Northern Kingdom, instituted back in the early days of the division of the people of God under Jeroboam, 3 Kg 12:19 ff. Tobias (one need not

take *alone* too strictly ; not everyone in Israel aposta-**303c** tized) remained faithful to God. **6.** The journey to the Temple at Jerusalem was prescribed three times a year, Ex 23:17, for the Feasts of the Pasch, Pentecost, and Tabernacles. Tobias made the journeys required by the Law and moreover offered the prescribed first-fruits and tithes. The argument advanced by some for the late composition of the book from the fact that the Greek mentions three classes of tithes is not wholly convincing. **9.** Tobias took a wife of his own nation, Ex 34:11 f., and perhaps also of his own tribe and family. *Tobit,* the father, called his son Tobias, a name similar to his own, *cf.* § 300e.

11-17 Charity of Tobias towards his Fellow-Captives d —11. From the available evidence, it is very difficult to establish a complete chronology for the Book of Tobias. Vg would suggest here that Tobias was married and had a son at the time of his deportation. However, the greater number of important textual witnesses do not suggest this, and permit the conclusion that Tobias was married and begot his son during the captivity. This latter seems much the better view and fits in quite well with the whole narrative. Tobias was carried to Nineveh, which was the most flourishing city of the Assyrian Empire and became the capital city soon afterwards, under Sennacherib (705–681). **14.** The other forms of the text indicate that Sargon, the king, was impressed by the attractive appearance of Tobias and appointed him his steward, or purchasing-agent, *cf.* Gen 41:40 ff. ; Dan 1:1 ff. The great liberty accorded to Tobias by the king is not to be considered as altogether unusual, for the Assyrians allowed the exiles a fair measure of freedom in the hope that they would forget the home-land. **16.** The pious youth made good use of his favour with the king, and, while keeping the prescriptions of the Law of Moses, managed to be of great service to his fellow-captives. One example of his charity and generosity is given here which will later have an important bearing on the story. Rages (Rhey or Rai, ruins near Teheran ?) was a city of the Medes, far distant from Nineveh, but it can be supposed that Tobias was on one of his purchasing trips for the king. **17.** His loan to Gabelus was a very large one, probably amounting to more than three thousand pounds.

18-25 Corporal Works of Mercy—18. Since Senna- **e** cherib was the son, not of Shalmaneser but of Sargon, the name ' Salmanasar ' must be emended here, as in 2 and 13, to *Enemessar, i.e.* ' Sargon '. In Scripture mediate as well as immediate successors are often called ' sons ', but that does not appear to be the solution of the difficulty here. It is more likely to be a question of a faulty text. The facts related in this and the following verses correspond with the data found in the Assyrian records of the time of Sennacherib as well as with the historical references of the Bible ; *cf.* 4 Kg 18:17 ff. ; Is 36 f. **21-25.** In almost all forms of the text except Vg this section is more detailed : Tobias' good deeds are recounted in much the same form, but Vg omits entirely any reference to Achikar, *cf.* § 301*h-i.* In the other forms of the text Achikar is described as the administrator, or overseer, of the Assyrian king. He is called the cousin german of Tobias, and by his intercession with the king Tobias was permitted to return to Nineveh. It is clear that the time interval mentioned in 24 must refer to Tobias' flight (23) and should, therefore, be understood of the period just preceding the assassination of Sennacherib ; hence it has no connexion with Sennacherib's retreat from Jerusalem (21) which took place some twenty years earlier.

II 1-18 The Blindness of Tobias—1. Notwithstand- **304a** ing his many charitable works and his strict observance of the Law, the pious Israelite, Tobias, was soon to be afflicted with grave personal sufferings. Even in the ancient dispensation, God permitted his saints to be overwhelmed with afflictions that they might be more and more purified in the fire of suffering. In the Greek, the circumstances of the ' festival ' are

304a more detailed : Esarhaddon (681–669) is the Assyrian king, and the festival is the Feast of Pentecost. Such details fill out the narrative, but at least some of them are surely later additions. **4.** Tobias acted with great caution lest he should again attract the unfavourable attention of the public authorities. **6.** Amos, who prophesied some twenty-five years before the time of Tobias, is here cited freely. More literally the prophecy (Am 8:10) reads : ' And I will turn your feasts into mourning and all your songs into lamentation '. **10-11.** The Greek indicates that Tobias was blinded on the very night of the Feast ; it also mentions sparrows rather than swallows, a very unimportant detail.

b **12-18.** Of greater importance and interest is the fact that this brief passage is found only in Vg. The Greek has details of its own, for example, it relates Tobias' unsuccessful visits to the physicians, and a further mention of Achikar, who ' nourished me two years until he went to Elymais ' (*cf.* § 301*h–i*). It is extremely difficult to determine the exact form of the original text for this section. The differences in the Greek form are shared substantially by the other forms of the text now extant, and there is no exact agreement. As for the longer form of Vg, it is hard to believe that St Jerome simply added his own spiritual reflexions to the text he was translating. He must have had some basis for his rendering, even though it must be admitted that he translated freely. The Vg fragment, at any rate, offers a precious spiritual lesson : the sufferings of Tobias were permitted by God, and this fact was clearly appreciated by the pious Israelite who looked towards a heavenly reward for his fidelity.

c **19-23 Tobias upbraided by his Wife**—The Greek makes it clearer why Tobias was worried : the kid was given to Anna by her employer over and above her wages. Hence Tobias, knowing that such a thing was not her ordinary wage, and realizing that it was beyond her simple means to purchase, feared that it had been stolen. **22.** The domestic altercation that followed is delightful in its realism : the husband reasonably suspicious ; the wife in perfectly good faith, and in no mood for argument after a hard day's work ; both quite blameless ; and the wife very angry.

d **III 1-6 Tobias trusts in God**—This passage contains one of the five strikingly beautiful prayers quoted in the book : 3:1-6 ; 3:13-23 ; 8:7-9 ; 8:17-19 ; 13:1-23. These prayers are noticeably similar in form, and they contain several common elements : (1) praise of God ; (2) confession ; (3) petition ; (4) doxology. The doxology is omitted in the first and fourth prayers, and the petitions vary in circumstance, but otherwise the similarity is remarkable. This similarity could easily be due to the fact that the Hebrews of the time used a uniform general formula in their prayers, as well as to the personal touch of a redactor. It is quite probable that the substantial elements of the prayers are due to the original characters themselves, although it is not necessary to attribute to them the exact verbal form. Perhaps the most striking doctrinal note in this first prayer is Tobias' full submission to the will of God. **4.** Just as God had so often promised : If Israel would not remain faithful she would certainly be punished, see 2 Kg 7:14, and *passim* in the Prophets.

e **7-10a Sara is rebuked by a Maidservant**—Previous to this section, in most forms of the book, Tobias has related the story in the first person : 'I Tobias. . . .'. Henceforward, as in Vg, the narrative is in the third person. **7.** At the same time that Tobias was being upbraided by his wife, Sara was reproached by one of her father's maidservants. The city of Sara and Raguel is *Ecbatana*, not Rages of Vg and DV. **8.** This is the first mention of an episode (*cf.* 6:14 ; 7:11 ; 8:12) which appears altogether incredible to many authors ; some even viewing it as absolutely conclusive evidence that the whole book is a fantastic fairy-tale, with certain borrowings from pagan demonology. A more exhaustive study of the question, however, shows

that the evidence for such views is far from conclusive. It should be noted in regard to the derivation of the name Asmodeus, that this is quite adequately explained by the Hebrew root *šāmaḏ*, hence ' the Destroyer '. Recourse to Persian derivation, *v.g. aešma daēva*, should be had only when the word cannot be explained through Semitic etymology. It should also be noted that the references to Asmodeus in Tobias are quite different from those on the same subject found in later Jewish extrabiblical literature. These fabulous accounts cannot be used in explanation of our book. Moreover, even if a Persian derivation of the name be granted, a dependence of Tobias on Iranian demonology would not be proved. Asmodeus could have been a name commonly in use in Semitic circles for the devil, somewhat as *Beelzebub* at the time of Christ, and without any doctrinal implications.

Nor is there sufficient reason to believe that Sara was a subject of diabolic possession, *cf.* 6:15. It has been urged, nevertheless, that it is quite incredible that Sara should have had seven successive husbands, and that all these men should have been killed by Asmodeus at the time of their first marital relations with her. Regarding the number seven, it is recognized Hebrew usage (*cf.* Gen 4:15 ; Lev 26:28 ; Deut 28:7 ; Prov 6:31 ; Ecclus 35:13 ; Lk 17:4 ; etc.) that this number often means ' several ', ' a number ', or that it stands for the perfect number, or fullness, without specific designation. So, Sara could easily have had several husbands, not necessarily seven. But were they all killed at the time of their first relations with her ? The text does not indicate this with certainty, either here or elsewhere in the book. True, Vg implies it, but the better textual witnesses have simply : ' *before they had been with her as it is appointed for women* ', hence *before* marital congress. So, Sara's husbands were killed by the devil, with God's permission, before they had intercourse with her, and due to some guilt on their part. Though extraordinary, such an account is not incredible. Some have seen in this text an argument against the sin of Birth Prevention. The argument, based mainly on the assumption that the husbands were killed ' at their first going in unto her ', is not well-founded in the light of the better reading of the text. If the reasons given for the death of the husbands of Sara in Vg are authentic (see 6:17 ; 7:12, 14), one might argue thus, *a fortiori*, against the crime of Birth Prevention : since the husbands were punished by God on account of their lustful approach to matrimony, then the abuse of marriage by the direct interference of contraception would deserve even greater punishment. **9.** The rejoinder of the servant is bitter and calumnious, for Sara had no guilt in the matter. The accusation, ' thou murderer of thy husbands ', is either a gossip report or a purely mischievous invention of the maid.

10b-23 Sara's Confidence in God—**10b.** The bitterness of the accusation, coupled, no doubt, with the memory of the facts, caused Sara to become greatly upset. Her emotions were in turmoil, she wished to be alone, she would neither eat nor drink. It is even likely that the Greek is correct here in its addition, ' and (she) desired to hang herself ', for such a temptation could easily arise under great emotional stress. Sara, however, turned to God for help, and the prayer which follows is a model for those in great affliction. It is more extensive, more reasoned, in Vg than in the Greek. The latter seems more primitive. **16.** She never desired a husband lustfully. **17.** ' Play ', in the sense of sensual levity. **19.** See 7:12, 14. The Greek indicates that Sara was the only heir of Raguel.

III 24-IV 23 Tobias instructs his Son—**24-25.** At *about* the same time the prayers of Tobias and Sara were heard by God, who sent the Angel Raphael to help them. These two verses act as a sort of summary introduction to the second part of the book, which deals chiefly with the intervention of the Archangel Raphael. **IV:1.** Tobias senior felt that his prayer (3:6) had been heard and that he would soon die. As

5a a true Israelite (*cf.* Gen 49:1 ; Deut 33:1 ; 1 Mac 2:49, etc.) he called his son to give him a father's parting counsel. His words of paternal advice are exemplary in every way. Vg, again, is freer than the Greek ; and this is probably due to St Jerome. **6.** Splendid counsel for a young man. **7-12.** The truly religious man cannot turn away his face from the poor, and God in turn will look kindly on him. All should help the needy in so far as they can. **13.** Tobias junior is instructed to keep from all impurity, and further (Greek) ' to take first a wife of the seed of thy fathers, take not a strange wife, who is not of the tribe of thy father'. **14.** The different codices show a variety of readings with regard to the evils of pride. Vg and DV give a sufficiently adequate summary of the sense of the passage. **16.** This verse states negatively what our Lord later prescribed in positive form as the teaching of the Law and the Prophets, *cf.* Mt 7:12. It is also the equivalent of the Saviour's command : ' Thou shalt love thy neighbour as thyself', Mt 22:39, from Lev 19:18.

b **18.** The unusual character of this verse, which in the Greek reads : ' Pour out thy bread and wine on the tomb of the just . . .', has given rise to much speculation. Some have at once jumped to the conclusion that this is a reference to sacrifice to the dead, or ancestor worship, or to pagan funeral rites. There is absolutely no evidence for this view. In fact it is incredible and incompatible with the context, that a pious Hebrew parent who thought he was about to die should recommend such practices to his son. Practices and rites of this nature were common amongst the gentiles, but were forbidden by the Law and altogether abhorrent to the fervent Israelite. The same holds for the rather common pagan practice of burying food with the dead or leaving it in their tombs, presumably for their needs in the after-life. On account of the difficulties involved, some authors recommend an emendation of the text : as if some scribe had written in Hebrew ' tomb ' or ' burial ' for ' in the midst of ' ; or ' bread ' in place of ' mercy '. These textual corrections do solve the difficulties fairly well, but they are not sufficiently supported by the evidence to be admitted. Many older commentators suggested that the reference was to the practice of bringing food to the cemeteries as a sort of alms on behalf of the dead, the food being distributed to the surviving relatives or to the poor. It cannot be proven, however, that this practice was in use in OT times.

c A much better proposal is the one which considers this verse as a recommendation to take part, according to custom, in the so-called ' death banquets ' or funeral feasts, held as a means of dispensing consolation to the mourners at the funeral, somewhat after the fashion of the modern wake. The further recommendation of Tobias ' do not eat and drink thereof with sinners ', fits in well with this explanation. Then the youth, Tobias, would be instructed not to fraternize with the gentiles in their funeral feasts. There is good evidence that such customs did exist among the Hebrews, see Jer 16:7 ; Ez 24:17 ; also Josephus, *Bell. Jud.* 2, 1, 1. As for the alleged connexion between this verse and the Achikar story (*cf.* § 301*h–i*) the evidence is very tenuous. It should be noted, too, that any evidence there is depends on a general similarity between our verse and a passage found in the later, but not in the earlier, forms of the Achikar story. **21-23.** This piece follows easily on the preceding section. The father, after having given several spiritual counsels, now thinks of the temporal care of his son and widow, *cf.* 1:16. He concludes his recommendations with a fitting exhortation to serve God faithfully above all things.

V 1-9 Tobias meets the Archangel Raphael—1-2. Tobias junior is quite ready to obey, but he foresees two difficulties : he is unknown to Gabelus, and he is ignorant of the way leading to Rages of Media. Tobias senior gives a satisfactory answer to both objections. **5.** The Angel had taken human form in order to carry

out the mission given to him by God. The description **305d** of the Angel here is found only in Vg.

10-22. They set out on their Journey—16. The **e** prudent father wishes to know something more of the stranger before committing his son to his care. **18.** Some have wondered that the Angel should apparently tell a lie. In reality there is no question of a lie. The heavenly messenger had every right to conceal the truth of his identity, which he does by playing on the Hebrew names ' Azarias ' (Heb. ' The Lord has given aid ') and ' Ananias ' (Heb. ' The Lord is clement '), which truthfully describe his particular mission. Admittedly, there is always something mysterious from our viewpoint about the appearances in human form of the Angels, as they are described in Sacred Scripture. Such phenomena have no analogy in the natural order, and so, human terminology is usually inadequate to describe them. In this case it could well be that the Angel is expressing, by approximation, a twofold reality : his angelic nature and his appearance in human form. Thus when he says that he is ' of the children of Israel ' (5:7), and that he is a ' kinsman ' of Tobias senior (5:14, Gk) he means : ' I, though an angel of God, have taken, at God's command, the human form of the individual Israelite Azarias'. The language is vague and involved, but it is not false. That Tobias senior was deceived does not enter into the question of the veracity of the Angel's statement. He had no obligation to make known his full identity. **19.** At this stage Vg is briefer than the other forms of the text, which add various details : Tobias senior remarks that he knew ' Ananias and Nathan, the two sons of Semelias the great ' ; he offers the Angel ' a drachma a day as wages', etc. **21.** A typically Israelitic farewell. ' His angel accompany you ', is particularly apt in the circumstances, although the father did not realize the full implication of his words.

23-28 A Mother's Tears—23. Anna, the mother, as **f** mothers do, wept at the departure of her son on a long journey to a far country. **24.** She was much more ready to give up the money than to lose her son. The Greek is more pointed : ' let the money perish, rather than our son '. **26-27.** The father, more confident, offers a good reason for his assurance. His words, once again, were more filled with meaning than he knew.

VI 1-9 Tobias' Adventure with the Fish—1. The **g** reference to the dog adds a note of simple authenticity to the narrative. The author of our book has been accused of being ignorant of his geography : Nineveh, the city of Tobias, was situated on the river Tigris, and now, after a full day's journey they reach this river. However, the text does not say that, but only ' they lodged by the river Tigris the first night '. In other words, Tobias and the Angel, after a day's walking along the river valley, rested the first night by the river. **2-4.** It is possible to view this passage as altogether miraculous and to explain all the details as so many different miracles. Still, miracles are not to be multiplied without necessity, and the text does not demand a miracle in every detail. First of all, the extant forms of the text, although in agreement about the substance of the event, vary considerably regarding the details. In some, the fish is not qualified by any adjective such as ' monstrous' as in Vg and DV. In one form, at least, the fish attacks the youth's foot ; in another, the fish tries to devour the youth's bread. It is a question of what exactly in these accounts should be retained as primitive. It would seem quite probable that the integrity of the text is adequately preserved as follows : ' *and the youth went down to wash himself* (' *his feet* ' ?) *and a fish leaped out of the river seeking to devour the youth*'. There is no need to presume that the fish was capable of swallowing the youth ; it is sufficient to see here the snapping attack of some large river fish (some think a species of pike) which would easily frighten the youth by its suddenness and ferocity. Most forms of the text then have the Angel simply telling the youth to seize the fish, which he does, hauling it up on land.

305h **5.** The internal organs of certain species of fish are still considered valuable medicaments. **6.** '*The youth did as the Angel told him, and having roasted the fish they ate it. And they journeyed both of them together until they came to Ecbatana*'. **8.** It is clear that burning parts of the fish could have no direct physical effect on incorporeal demons. The effect actually produced on Asmodeus, 8:3, is due to the power of God and his Angel. However, there is nothing against viewing this effect as produced in connexion with some religious symbolism attached to the action. The effect would then be attained indirectly through the material object, much as the effect of sacramentals approved by the Church— holy water, the sign of the cross, etc. In Vg the heart of the fish is mentioned in this verse, and the liver in 6:19 and 8:2. Other forms of the text mention both the heart and the liver in all three passages. The omission of one or the other word in Vg derives, perhaps, from the custom of classing heart and liver together ; so, if one only is mentioned the other is to be presumed.

i **9.** Many older Catholic commentators considered the cure of Tobias' blindness, through the application of the gall of the fish, a natural process. The gall of various species of fish was considered in antiquity to have valuable curative powers in diseases and irritations of the eyes. Ointments made of this substance were highly prized for their stimulating and cleansing properties. Hence, the effect of the application of the gall (11:13 ff.) may have been a purely natural one, produced by a natural agent. However, the author of the book in his whole context seems to attribute the effect to God's intervention on behalf of Tobias, *cf.* 12:14, even though he does not say precisely whether the healing was miraculous or natural. It would be well to bear in mind that it is an angel who prescribes a remedy apparently unknown to Tobias, and that the particular material used is an instrument for the operation of the power of God. This incident recalls the cure of the blind man by our Lord, Jn 9:6.

j **10-22 The Angel counsels Marriage with Sara—10-13.** Sara, the sole heir to the property and wealth of her parents, was obliged to marry one of her own tribe, Num 36:6 ff. Since Tobias, as it appears, was the only one who fulfilled this requirement, he alone was a suitable husband for Sara. The purpose of the Law was to keep tribal and family possessions from passing to strangers. For this reason, then, the Angel recommends marriage with Sara. **14.** See above, 3:7. Note that Tobias' objection is based on hearsay evidence and is not a statement of the author of the book. **15.** The Vatican Codex and the Old Latin and Syriac Versions are the principal witnesses to an odd addition to this verse : they give as the reason why the devil killed the seven husbands, 'because a devil loves (or 'is fond of') her'. Even with these witnesses the authenticity of the addition may be questioned. If the statement is genuine, it should not be attributed to the sacred author, since it forms part of the hearsay popular opinion quoted by Tobias. Nor, on the same presumption, would it follow that the devil sought Sara with a carnal love, for at least in the Greek the verb used ordinarily indicates 'to like' or 'to cherish'.

k **17.** Although the doctrine in this verse, so beautifully as well as realistically expressed, is both beyond question as well as in agreement with Jewish ideas on the sanctity of marriage, it can hardly be proved that the verse as it stands is authentic. Since it is found only in Vg it is probably due to the influence of St Jerome or some previous redactor. Part of it is undoubtedly a borrowing from Ps 31:9. **18-22.** Similar recommendations are ascribed to the Angel in all forms of the text. They recommend prayer as a preparation for the marital union, although the three-day period of continence is not found in all. In 22 Vg alone has the counsel, 'moved rather for love of children than for lust'. This is quite in line with the general context,

but the actual expressions used are probably the result **30** of Jerome's free translation.

VII 1-10 The Welcome of Raguel—This section is **30** clear, and substantially the same in all forms. There is some variation in the details : Raguel's wife in Vg and Old Latin is 'Anna', while the Greek reads 'Edna' ; the questions of Raguel in 3 and 5 are asked by his wife in most forms of the text ; while the response of the Angel (Vg 6) is attributed to Tobias himself by all but Vg. The Latin rendering is simpler and more connected. The sincere and ready hospitality extended to the visitors, especially as they were both considered kinsmen, is typically Semitic. Tobias loses no time in requesting the hand of Sara.

11-20 Marriage Negotiations—11. The thoughtful sus- **b** pense of Raguel in Vg and DV is put into words by the Greek, for Raguel there replies at length. **14.** Gentile marriages were not altogether forbidden by Law to the Hebrews, although they were commanded not to intermarry with certain Canaanite tribes, Ex 34:11 ff. ; Deut 7:1 ff. ; *cf.* also Num 36:1-10. Since, however, marriages with pagans always carried with them a danger to the faith, they were never fully approved ; hence, the chaste Sara would be much more appropriately betrothed to the God-fearing youth, Tobias, than to her previous pagan consorts. **15.** Describes the actual betrothal ceremony of Tobias and Sara. The giving of the right hand as a sign or pledge of faith was used in antiquity much as it is today, although this is the only scriptural example of its use in a betrothal ceremony. The signing of a marriage document is not described elsewhere in Scripture, but scarcely anywhere else do we find so detailed and intimate an account of a marriage ceremony. **19.** The Greek suggests that both mother and daughter wept ; nor is this unlikely on so solemn an occasion.

VIII 1-10 A Chaste Marriage—The delicate artistry **c** of the author is much in evidence throughout this chapter. **1.** The simple dinner of welcome had turned into a happy marriage-banquet. **2.** See 6:8. It is clearer here that the chief efficacy of the burning heart and liver of the fish is due to the power of God and his Angel over the demon. **3.** There is no question of the demon being bound in chains, or otherwise made captive materially ; it is a moral restraint, exercised by one spirit on another. The 'desert of Upper Egypt ', a place far distant from Nineveh and Ecbatana, is used figuratively of the complete removal of Asmodeus' harmful influence over Sara. The desert was popularly considered the normal abode of demons, *cf.* Mt 12:43. **4-6.** While Vg continues the idea of the three nights, *cf.* 6:18, the Greek implies that the events take place during one night. All forms narrate the prayers of Tobias and Sara for God's help. **7-10.** The third prayer ; *cf.* 3:1. The main doctrinal elements are : the recognition of God as creator of all things, 7 ; and the confession of sincerity in 9, which shows the upright purpose with which Tobias entered matrimony.

11-20 Thanksgiving for the Safety of Tobias and Sara **d** **—11.** Apparently Raguel was not fully reassured by the Angel ; he hoped, but he wondered ; and he feared lest the fate of the former husbands of Sara should befall Tobias. The time indicated, 'about the cock-crowing', is a Vg reading ; the other forms of the text have the equivalent of 'by night' or 'during the night'. **14.** The Greek assigns the reason for Raguel's stealth : 'and if he is dead that we may bury him, so that no one know it '. **17-19.** The theme of this, the fourth prayer, *cf.* 3:1, is clearly thanksgiving to God for the favour received.

21-24 A Joyful Feast—21. Only Vg suggests that the **e** preparations are for a journey. It is more likely that Raguel gave orders to prepare the nuptial banquet, which now could be fully celebrated ; this would be the banquet described in the following verse. The preparation for a journey would not fit well with Raguel's invitation, **23**, to remain. **24.** This is

96e substantially the same in all forms, except that Vg alone relates that the promise was put in writing.

f **IX 1-12 The Angel Raphael visits Gabelus**—**2** is a Vg reading. **3.** In the Greek, Tobias tells Raphael to take four servants and two camels, *cf.* Vg 6. **6.** Raphael made the journey, as requested, from Ecbatana to Rages, and redeemed the money deposited with Gabelus, see 1:17; 4:21. **8.** Owing to the Semitic colouring of the passage it would seem that Raphael is still the subject, whereas it is really Gabelus, as Vg indicates, who enters, weeps and blesses. **11.** A truly Hebrew blessing, both polite and religious.

g **X 1-7 Anxiety of the Parents of Tobias**—**1-2.** While these events were taking place in Ecbatana and Rages, Tobias, the father, was counting the days in Nineveh. No doubt he had often made this journey himself and knew exactly how long it should take. Since his son did not return on schedule he became anxious, and, as a father would, began to consider the possibility of misfortune. **3.** In the Greek, although Tobias begins to grieve, there is more than a suggestion that he hides his sorrow in attempting to console his wife. The domestic scene is both beautifully related and very touching. **4-7.** The mother is not so easily comforted: 'And she said to him (Tobias): *Hold thy peace and do not deceive me; my child has perished*'.

h **8-13 Tobias sets out for Home**—**8-10.** Raguel invites Tobias junior to stay on with him, possibly to continue the wedding festivities; but Tobias, knowing that his parents will be anxious for his return, feels bound to refuse. Raguel then hands over half of his possessions, as he had promised to do, *cf.* 8:24. **11.** Raguel speaks more truly than he knows when he mentions the Angel of the Lord; however, in the other forms of the text, the blessing is invoked in the name of 'the Lord of heaven'. **13.** The admonitions in Vg are most likely a summarization and adaptation of St Jerome's. In the Greek, Raguel tells Sara to go to her father-in-law and to look upon him and his wife as her own parents; then he bids her farewell, saying: '*May I hear a good report of thee as long as I shall live!* Then Anna (Edna), the wife, addresses Tobias: '*Beloved child and brother, may the Lord bring thee back, and may I see children of thee while I live, and of Sara my daughter before I die. I commit my daughter to thee in trust before the Lord. Grieve her not all the days of thy life*'.

i **XI 1-12 The Home-coming**—**1.** The place-name seems to have been *Akram* or *Charam*, but its exact location cannot be determined. It is certainly not Haran, Abraham's city, of Gen 11:31. The further determinations, 'midway to Nineveh, the eleventh day', are found only in Vg. **2-3.** The caravan was moving too slowly, whereas Raphael and Tobias, travelling alone, could quickly reach Nineveh. **4.** The Greek suggests that the fish-gall, through its astringent qualities, will scale off the films from the eyes of the elder Tobias. However, here (*cf.* 6:9) there is also a hint that the effect is due to some higher power. The Angel is more certain of the effect being produced than the use of an ordinary medicine would warrant, see 8; 12:14. **9.** The reference to the celebrated dog of Tobias is surely an authentic part of the narrative here as in 6:1; although most of the dog's antics are related only in Vg, and are likely to be an addition. **10.** The picture of the blind old father stumbling out to meet his son is very affecting; it is also surely authentic.

j **13-17 Tobias recovers his Sight**—**13-15.** All the textual witnesses report the healing of Tobias' blindness in substantially the same way. The variants to be found are mostly verbal: Vg alone has the time interval, 'about half an hour', as also the description, 'like the skin of an egg'. Other forms indicate a peeling of 'white films' or 'white scales'. **16.** 'All that knew him', is more detailed in the Greek, which pictures the men of Nineveh marvelling that Tobias was cured and able to walk without anyone to lead him. **17.** The Scriptures frequently relate similar

praises or blessings, see Deut 32:39; 1 Kg 2:6; Wis 16:13. **306j**

18-21. The Arrival of Sara—**18-19.** Once again Vg **k** and the London Hebrew alone have the time interval, 'after seven days'; also the mention of the family and the cattle and the abundance of money is proper to these two texts which are curiously interrelated throughout the whole story. **20.** This is the only reference in Vg to the Achikar story, see § 301*h–i*. Although the names are slightly different here, it is clear that the same persons are intended; 'Achior' is simply a Latin transcription of *Achikar*, and 'Nabath' the equivalent of the nephew's name, *i.e.* *Nadan*.

XII 1-5 Raphael is offered a Reward—There is a **307a** remarkable agreement among the textual witnesses, including Vg, in this little section. Except for the Aramaic, which goes its own strange way, all forms of the story which have come down to us are very similar in content and order. **3.** 'Devoured by the fish', is probably an addition. **4-5.** If the Greek, 5:19, was correct in recording that the proffered wages amounted to 'a drachma a day', the father and son are now exceedingly more generous.

6-22 Raphael reveals his Identity—**6.** The Angel **b** probably took them aside into an inner room of the house to reveal his secret. The first point of his revelation was the mercy of God; in fact, this is the core of Raphael's whole message. **7.** What the king deigns to reveal to his subjects should be treated confidentially; still, in the case of God, whose works are always eminently just and good, there is no need of secrecy. **8.** Raphael proceeds somewhat obliquely: first, he shows the value of good works, works which Tobias and his son had done; then he will explain why, despite these good deeds, they had to suffer. It is here, particularly, that the Angel stresses the value of almsgiving. Some forms read: 'Prayer is good with *truth*'. **9.** Clearly states the value of good works. **10.** As good deeds lead to eternal life, wicked deeds lead to death. 'Enemies of their own *life*', *i.e.* those who do evil, kill themselves. Some argue that since this is not necessarily true of mortal life, the reference must be to eternal life and death.

11-13. The revelation of the secret proper. The whole **c** life of Tobias was mysterious, enigmatic: although from his youth he had been faithful to God, he seemed to gain no reward but rather more and greater afflictions. Now all is made clear: God permitted Tobias to suffer in order to try him. While he was suffering, Raphael was interceding for him before the throne of God. **15.** Previously the Angel had opened out to Tobias the secret of the forces at work in the life of the pious Israelite, now Raphael reveals the secret of his own person. He is an Angel, and amongst these heavenly spirits one of a special order who assist at the throne of God, *i.e.* who constantly see God face to face and receive from him special revelations. He is 'one of the seven': the number 'seven' probably refers to a special group holding a particularly important office, rather than to an exact number. It is not unlikely that the term 'seven' is an allusion to Median court terminology, because at that time among the Medes the celebrated 'seven counsellors' were familiar to everyone, *cf.* Esd 7:14. There is no evidence, however, to support the view of some scholars who profess to see here a reference to the Zoroastrian teaching on the spirits who stand about the throne of Ahura-Mazda. There is nothing but a very superficial similarity between the spirits of Parseeism and the Angels of the Bible; the basic doctrines of each are poles apart.

16-17. There was a belief among the Hebrews that **d** whoever looked upon an angel would die at once, see Jg 6:22; 13:21 f. Hence Tobias and his son were greatly frightened when Raphael revealed his identity. This circumstance as well as the consoling words of the Angel recall other similar angelic appearances in Scripture, *v.g.* Dan 10:12; Lk 1:13, 30. **18.** There is no need of fear, because the Angel has been with them

307d at God's command. Angels are *sent* to men by the will of God. **19.** The second part of this verse, in most forms of the text, declares, ' *and I did neither eat nor drink* '. St Jerome probably attempted to clarify this by showing that the Angel was sustained otherwise than by natural food. **20.** Raphael's special mission from God was now finished. Many forms have ' *write down all these things . . .* ', *cf.* § 300e. **21-22.** Only Vg extends their prayer, ' for three hours '.

e XIII 1-10 The Canticle of Tobias : First Part— This section contains the fifth prayer of the book. Although longer, in general form it is similar to the others already mentioned, *cf.* 3:1. These two final chapters form a sort of epilogue. **2.** See above, 11:17. By the ' hand of God ' is usually meant his Power, or his Providence guiding all things. **5.** The children of Israel had brought chastisement on themselves by their own sins ; they will be saved solely through God's mercy. **7.** What he recommends to others, Tobias will do himself. The poetic parallelism noticeable throughout this passage is more striking here if the Old Latin form is followed : ' *I confess him in the land of my captivity, and I show forth his power and majesty before a sinful nation* '.

f 11-23 Canticle : Second Part— Whereas the first part of Tobias' prayer, or canticle, was almost wholly taken up with praise of God, this second part is principally prophetical. The entire canticle is poetical in form, and for the most part in synonymous parallelism. Vg in some instances seems to have connected the verses poorly, and several are apparently out of their proper order. On the whole, the various forms of the text are in fair agreement.

g 12. Vg seems to intimate that Jerusalem and the temple have been already destroyed, whereas these calamities did not come to pass until after the death of Tobias. It is possible that Tobias, in a prophetic vision, saw both the destruction and restoration of the Holy City. However, the reference to the temple is not textually certain, for the text could read : ' let new *homes* be built ' ; and so, the destruction of the city would not necessarily be implied. Besides, Jerusalem often stood as a symbol of the lot of the People of Israel. Thus, when Jerusalem was said to flourish, Israel's lot was a happy one ; when Jerusalem suffered, the nation

was in peril, *cf.* Is 60. Hence Tobias may have been **307** praying for, or even predicting, the return of the captives to their homeland and the future happier lot of the Children of Israel. If such a general interpretation be decided upon, the particular verses in Vg and DV hardly require comment. **21-22.** In the Greek, the towers are built with gold, and the streets are paved with carbuncles and stones from Ophir. These precious minerals and gems are used figuratively to signify the prosperity of the New Jerusalem. According to some interpreters, all the references to Jerusalem have, besides their literal meaning, a typical sense. Then, the earthly Jerusalem would be a type of the heavenly Jerusalem, much as in the strikingly similar passage of Apoc 21:2, 18 ff.

XIV 1-17 The Last Days of Tobias and his Son—1-4. h The chronological data of this final chapter seem to have suffered greatly at the hands of copyists or redactors. It is next to impossible, in view of the great variation among textual witnesses, to reconstruct any satisfactory chronology of the history of Tobias. Nor is it surprising that the figures should vary so greatly in the different recensions and versions. As all who have worked with ancient documents know, numbers easily suffer corruption as they are transcribed. This fact is observable in many books of the OT which have been transmitted to us in a far better state than the Book of Tobias. It would be beyond the scope of this commentary to attempt to estimate the value of the divergent chronological tables found in the different forms of the book. Suffice it to say that Vg and DV, as they stand, must be revised ; and that no single form of the book as we have it today is certainly accurate in this connexion. **5-9.** Tobias, **i** the elder, foretells the destruction of Nineveh (612 B.C.) and Jerusalem (587), as well as the restoration of Israel. **10-13.** The Greek, Syriac and Old Latin contain a rather lengthy reference to the story of Achikar (*cf.* § 301h–i). This is less likely to be an authentic part of the narrative than were the previous allusions to the Achikar story. **14-17.** After the death of Tobias senior his son leaves Nineveh as he had been counselled to do, and with his family goes to live with Raguel and Anna in Ecbatana. There he had the happiness of seeing many descendants before dying in the Lord.

JUDITH

By M. LEAHY

Bibliography—*C. J. Ball, *The Book of Judith*, in *Apocrypha*, ed. H. Wace ; M. Sales, *La Sacra Bibbia*, Torino, 1925 ; A. Miller and J. Schildenberger, *Die Bücher Tobias, Judith und Esther*, Bonn, 1940 ; F. Stummer, *Geographie des Buches Judith*, Stuttgart, 1947 ; A. Condamin, art. ' Judith ', DAFC ; F. Prat, art. ' Judith ', DBV ; L. Soubigou in *La Sainte Bible*, Tome IV.

Text and Versions—Owing to the fact that the Greek text which we possess contains so many Hebraisms, modern critics generally maintain that the original text of Judith, of which no manuscripts survive, was written in Hebrew. The Greek is preserved in three recensions, *viz.* (i) that contained in codices S, B, A, and in the majority of the cursive MSS, (ii) the form found in codex 58 from which are derived the Syr. and one of the two recensions of the Old Latin ; and (iii) the form found in codices 19 and 108. Vg was made by Jerome from an Aramaic text. In the preface to the translation he tells us that he did the work in haste, devoting to it but ' una lucubratiuncula ', not attempting word-for-word exactness so long as he gave the sense, not considering the variant readings of the Greek and Latin manuscripts and giving only those particulars of the story for which he was able to find clear warrant in his Aramaic text. He had before him a copy of the Old Latin because we find that on occasions he reproduces the identical phraseology of this older version. Vg, while agreeing substantially with the Greek, differs from it not a little in accidentals, *viz.* in the form of proper names, in figures, in the omission of various incidents and geographical place names, and in the insertion of homiletic remarks. In addition to the above-mentioned versions there are also extant some late Hebrew recensions mostly of a midrashic character.

Contents—Nabuchodonosor, king of the Assyrians, defeated Arphaxad, king of the Medes, and then demanded the submission of the western nations. They, however, refused to submit and he dispatched his general Holofernes to wreak vengeance upon them. He overran much territory and so terrified many lands that they hastened to submit to him. Even these latter he treated as enemies and destroyed their sanctuaries and their gods. The Israelites feared for Jerusalem and the temple, and at the instigation of the high priest Eliachim prepared to resist the invader. They fortified certain mountain towns (among them Bethulia), which commanded the passes leading through the mountains of Ephraim, and then they suppliantly committed their cause to God. Holofernes, who had seemingly never heard of this nation, learned its wonderful history from Achior, the leader of the Ammonites, who urged him not to attack them unless he were assured that they had offended against their God. Holofernes and his chief officers were so enraged at Achior's words that they handed him over to the Jews that he might die with them when Bethulia fell to the Assyrian hosts. Instead of making a direct assault on the town of Bethulia, Holofernes cut off its external water supply and soon reduced the inhabitants to such a plight·that the governor decided under pressure to surrender the town unless relieved within five days.

Judith, a noble, chaste and beautiful widow, heard **308d** of the governor's decision and upbraided those in authority for their want of trust in God. She exhorted them to pray and sought to inspire confidence by reminding them of what God had done for his people in the past. Finally she declared that God would by her hand liberate Bethulia. Fortified by prayer and beautifully attired she left the town by night and with her maid went towards the Assyrian camp ; admiring sentries conducted her to the tent of their chief. Holofernes was beguiled by her beauty and she deceived him by pretending to be a deserter and by predicting the speedy destruction of her people because she saw that they would offend God by partaking of forbidden food ; she herself would advise Holofernes when the Hebrews having offended against their God might be subdued. Judith was permitted to live according to the regulations of the Jewish law ; she partook only of the food which she had taken with her and used to go outside the camp every night to perform the customary ablutions before prayer (*cf.* Ex 30:17 ff) and to communicate with God. On the fourth day she consented to attend a banquet at which Holofernes, goaded by lust, drank to excess. As he lay on his bed in a drunken stupor Judith cut off his head, and going out as usual under the pretence of devotion escaped with the head to Bethulia. At Bethulia she was enthusiastically received by the admiring citizens. Achior, having seen what the God of Israel had done, believed in him as the only true God. The besieged acting on Judith's advice feigned an attack on the camp of the Assyrians who, terrified at discovering that their leader was dead, became panic-stricken and fled. Joachim (Eliachim) and the ancients came from Jerusalem to honour Judith and Judith returned thanks to God for the victory. The book ends with a brief account of the remainder of Judith's life.

Historical Inaccuracies—(i) Nabuchodonosor bears the **e** title ' king of the Assyrians ' and is said to reign in Nineveh. But the historical Nabuchodonosor was king of the Neo-babylonian empire from 604 to 562 B.C. The Assyrian empire had then ceased to exist and so also had Nineveh which was destroyed in 612 B.C. (ii) The Assyrian monarchy is assumed to be still in existence, yet the following passages seem to assign the events narrated to the period following the Babylonian captivity—4:3 (LXX) reads, ' For they were lately come up from the captivity . . . and the vessels, the altar and the house were sanctified after their profanation ' ; 5:18 f.(LXX) reads, ' They were led captive into a land that was not theirs, and the temple of their God was cast to the ground ($\epsilon\gamma\epsilon\nu\eta\theta\eta$ ϵὶs $\epsilon\delta\alpha\phi$os) . . . and now they are returned to their God, and are come up from the dispersion where they were dispersed, and have possessed Jerusalem where their sanctuary is ' ; 5:22 f.(Vg) reads, ' many of them were led away captive into a strange land. But of late returning . . . they are come together . . . and possess Jerusalem again, where their sanctuary is '. Moreover other passages (*e.g.* 4:5) imply that there was no king reigning, for the supreme authority, even over the Northern Kingdom, was vested in the high-priest assisted by the Sanhedrin ($\dot{\eta}$ $\gamma\epsilon\rho o\upsilon\sigma\dot{\iota}a$ *cf.* LXX 4:8 ; 15:8). (iii) None of the known Median kings

308e was named Arphaxad. (iv) Holofernes was a Persian as his name implies, and we should not expect a Persian in command of the Assyrian armies.

f Literary Form—The opinions of modern critics with regard to the literary form of the book may be reduced to three, viz. (i) a fictitious narrative, (ii) an historical nucleus surrounded with unhistorical additions, (iii) a purely historical narrative.

The first opinion, held principally by non-Catholics, is that the story is not a sober chronicle of past events but was concocted, perhaps during the Maccabean fight for religious and political freedom, to encourage the Jews to resist and to remain faithful to the law of Moses ; the purpose of the book is to show that as long as God's people do not offend against him, no matter in what danger they may temporarily be placed, he will not permit their enemies to triumph over them. In proof of the theory that the book is a fictitious narrative with a didactic purpose, the following arguments are advanced : (*a*) the above-mentioned historical inaccuracies show that the author did not intend to write history ; (*b*) the author is ever pointing out that Judith was punctilious in the observance of one or other regulation of the law ; (*c*) Judith in her main discourse quotes from Israel's past history examples where God's all-powerful help was never wanting to those who kept his law (*cf*. 8:22 f.) ; (*d*) the setting seems arranged for Achior, a non-Jew, to deliver before other non-Jews a discourse which emphasizes the fact that Israel from the time of Abraham was unconquerable as long as it remained faithful to God (*cf*. ch 5). All this gives the impression of a certain artificiality and points to the conclusion that the author had no intention of recording actual events. We gather from a Reply of the Biblical Commission on parts of Scripture historical in appearance only (*cf*. § 52*j*) that Catholics might hold this theory provided it could be proved by solid arguments that the sacred author was not intending to write history.

g The second opinion which has found some advocates (*e.g.* a recent Catholic commentator, Miller) is that the author made an historical event the basis of his story, but that he embellished the record of that event. He thus meant his work to be read as a free description of the past.

h The vast majority of Catholic critics regard the book as a record of fact and they endeavour to answer the difficulties urged in the name of history against its accuracy. The arguments which they advance are the following : (*a*) Jewish and Christian tradition and all commentators prior to the sixteenth century regarded the book as historical ; (*b*) the minute historical, geographical, chronological and genealogical details indicate a straightforward narrative of real events ; (*c*) the author speaks of descendants of Achior being alive in his time (14:6), and of a festival celebrated annually up to his day in commemoration of Judith's victory (16:31). Those who uphold the historicity (or, at least, a historical nucleus) of the narration take the view that 'Nabuchodonosor' and 'Arphaxad' are pseudonyms disguising historical persons whose identity cannot be ascertained with certainty. There are many different opinions as to the identity of the king covered by the name 'Nabuchodonosor', the most widely-held opinion being that according to which the name stands for the Persian king Artaxerxes III Ochus (359–336). We know from extra-biblical sources that Artaxerxes campaigned against Asia Minor, Phoenicia and Egypt. According to Diodorus Siculus (*Hist*. 31, 19, 2–3) one of his generals was named Holofernes, the brother of a Cappadocian king, and the same authority informs us (*Hist*. 16, 47, 4) that another of his generals was called Bagoas (Vagao of Vg 14:13). Moreover Eusebius (*Chron*. 1, 11) states that Artaxerxes deported some Jews to Hyrcania near the Caspian Sea. Furthermore, Nabuchodonosor's demand of 'earth and water' in token of submission (*cf*. Gk 2:7) is reminiscent of a Persian custom (*cf*. Herodotus 6, 48 f.). Again the

mention of Persians in 16:12 seems to show that the author was really thinking of the campaign of a Persian king. We should also note that Persian kings were sometimes called kings of Assyria (*cf*. 1 Esd 6:22). The war against the Medes led by the unknown 'Arphaxad' may well have been waged to crush an attempted revolt by them against their over-lords, the Persians. Finally the word γερουσία does not here mean the actual Sanhedrin, an institution which is not earlier than the Maccabean age ; the Greek translator of the original used a word common in his day to designate the council of the ancients of the people.

Another opinion which still finds some supporters holds that Nabuchodonosor is the Assyrian king Ashurbanipal (669–626) and that Arphaxad is either the Median king Deioces or his son Phraortes. The high-priest was in charge of political affairs because the victorious advance of Holofernes (who was probably a tributary king) coincided with the period when Manasses of Judah was held captive in Babylon (*cf*. 2 Par 33:11 ff.). The return from captivity refers not to the whole people but rather to some isolated group, and the casting down of the temple refers to its profanation in the days of Manasses (4 Kg 21:7 ; 2 Par 33:7).

The chief argument against the historical character of the book of Judith is admittedly to be found in the many historical difficulties contained therein. Many Catholic scholars believe that all the difficulties have met with plausible answers (*cf*. § 308*h, i* above). The present commentator thinks that the opinion mentioned in § 308*g* above is the most probable. In narrating the adventures of Judith whom God used as his instrument to save his people from an imminent disaster the author's aim seems to be to encourage his contemporaries who are faced with some similar calamity to have absolute confidence in that same God. This aim would not be served so effectively by an episode which was purely imaginary. We cannot say with any certainty when Judith performed her heroic deed, but it was probably in the reign of Artaxerxes III.

Author and Date of Composition— The intimate knowledge of the topography of Canaan and the fact that the book was probably written in Hebrew point to a Palestinian Jew as the author. As regards the date of writing it was certainly much later than the date of the events recorded because there is mention of the death of Judith and the descendants of Achior (14:6 ; 16:30). Nothing further can be deduced with any certainty.

Canonicity—Although the book did not form part of the Hebrew Canon, the Church considered it from the beginning as divinely inspired, having received it together with the other sacred books contained in the LXX. It was quoted with approbation by Clement of Rome (1 Cor 55) and cited on an equality with other Scripture by Clement of Alexandria (*Strom*. 2, 7), Origen (*De Orat*. 13, 29 ; *Hom*. 9 *on Jg* ; *Hom*. 19 *on Jer*.) and Ambrose (*De Off. Min*. 3, 13). The Councils of Hippo (A.D. 393) and Carthage (A.D. 397 and 419) enumerated it among the canonical books. St Augustine (*De Doctrina Christiana* 2, 8) had it on his list of sacred books.

The Moral Conduct of Judith—She lied to the sentries and to Holofernes ; her personal attractions to which she gave such attention excited his base passions ; she acted imprudently by remaining alone in the tent of one who was inordinately attracted towards her ; her killing of Holofernes was an act of treachery. Yet notwithstanding all this Judith is praised by the Sacred Writer (and later by the Fathers of the Church). The following remarks will help to solve the difficulty. (i) The mention by the inspired writer of Judith's actions does not necessarily imply approval. (ii) If one is praised because of one or many noble deed one is not thereby declared immune from every fault or lauded for all one's deeds ; the heroism of Judith is eulogized because of the motives which animated her and the patriotism which she showed, ' Judith laudatur, non quia mentita est Holoferni, sed propter affectum quem habuit ad salutem populi, pro qua periculis se exposuit ' (St Thomas 11–11, q. 110, a. 3 ad 3). (iii) While the lies she told are not excusable in themselves, her good faith seems incontestable. (iv) In those pre-Christian days when the ideal of sanctity was less sublime, many things were considered lawful in a war against the enemies of Israel. (v) Judith's purpose in decorating herself was not to seduce Holofernes but rather to ingratiate herself with him so as to be allowed to come and go to his tent without hindrance until the opportunity presented itself of slaying him. (vi) As regards the suggestion that she was imprudent, we may take it that Judith had implicit confidence that God would safeguard her chastity ; did she not pray to him before setting out on her perilous self-imposed mission ?

Doctrine—God is the Creator and Lord of the visible universe (9:17 ; 13:24 ; 16:17). He is a merciful and a just God for he chastises the enemies of his people (13:18, 21 ; 16:4, 6, 20 f.). He never fails in the hour of danger to help those who remain faithful to the law of Moses (chh 5, 8). The efficacy of prayer and mortification is specially emphasized.

I Nabuchodonosor's Victory over Arphaxad and his Demand for the Submission of the Western States—**1.** The word ' built' corresponds to the Heb. *bānāh*, which may also have the meaning of repairing with the added notion of enlarging, *cf.* Jos 19:50 ; Jg 21:23, etc. Ecbatana (*cf.* 1 Esd 6:2 ; Tob 3:7) was the capital of Media Magna ; it was founded about 700 B.C. by the Median King Deioces (*cf.* Herod 1, 98) and was located near where today is Hamadan. **2 f.** The walls, according to the true reading of Vg, were 70 cubits high and 30 broad. The square towers were broader by 40 feet, for they jutted out 20 feet from each side of the wall. Arphaxad made the gates *proportionate* to the height of the towers. **5 ff.** Vg says that Nabuchodonosor overcame Arphaxad in the plain of Ragau about the Euphrates, etc. (6), and then sought the submission of the western states. But the corresponding verses in LXX state that the two kings made war in the plain of Ragau and that there came unto him (*i.e.* Arphaxad the Mede, very probably, and not Nabuchodonosor) they who dwelt in the hill country, and about the Euphrates, and the Tigris, and the Hydaspes, and the plain of Arioch, king of the Elymeans, and that there came together many nations to the array of the sons of Cheleoud. The Gk goes on to say that Nabuchodonosor sent unto all that dwelt in Persia, and in Cilicia, etc. demanding, it seems, military help in his war against Arphaxad, but that his ambassadors found them unwilling and, therefore, Nabuchodonosor threatened vengeance. The latter then, according to the Gk, defeated Arphaxad and prepared to carry out his threat. Vg incorrectly puts the plain of Ragau near the Euphrates, for Ragau is the Rages of the Book of Tobias, and its ruins (called Rai) are not far to the SE. of Teheran, the Persian capital.

The Jadason may be the Dijala which joins the Tigris six miles below Baghdad (*cf.* Stummer) ; Syr. has Ulai (*cf.* Dan 8:2) which is the Eulaeus of Pliny (*Hist. Nat.* 6, 31) and flowed near Susa. The Elymeans (Vg Elicians) were the inhabitants of Elymais, meaning here Elam (*cf.* Syr.), north of the Persian Gulf. The identity of Arioch (Vg Erioch) has not been established but the name occurs in Gen 14 where the one referred to is probably Arriwuk, the son of Zimri-Lim king of Mari (Tell-Hariri) in Northern Mesopotamia (*cf.* F. M. Th. Böhl in *Bibliotheca Orientalis*, 11/4, 1945, 66). Cheleoud of Gk may be Chilmad (the hill-country of Iran) above Baghdad (*cf.* Ball) ; the sons of Cheleoud are Medes, not followers of Nabuchodonosor.

8. Cedar was a tribe descended from Ismael (*cf.* Gen

25:13) ; its territory lay in the Syro-Arabian desert, to the NW. of Teima. The Gk has ' Galaad '. **9.** The land of Jesse (Gk Gesem) is the Egyptian district of Goshen in the Delta. In addition to the places mentioned in Vg the Gk has Persia, Antilibanus, the sea coast, Betane (Beth 'Enun, N. of Hebron), Chelous (El-Chalassa in Idumaea), Kades (*cf.* Gen 14:7), the River of Egypt (Wady el-'Arish), Taphnas (Tell ed-Dafenne in the Delta, Ramesse (*cf.* Ex 1:11), Tanis and Memphis (both in Egypt). **309b**

II–III The March of Holofernes—**12 f.** Ange may be **c** either the Argaeus in Cappadocia mentioned in the classics, or a spur of the Taurus. The mountains lay north (lit. on the left) of (upper, so Gk) Cilicia. Melothus is probably Melitene, the present-day Malatia in eastern Cappadocia. The Gk has Bektileth and the Syr. Bêth-qṭilath which means ' House of slaughter '. For ' Tharsis ' we should read with Gk ' Rassis ', *i.e.* Arsûs on the Gulf of Issus. The children of *Ishmael* (*cf.* Gen 25:13, 18) were nomad peoples and those against whom Holofernes marched were S. of the land of Cellon (Gk Chellians), *i.e.* Cholle (el-Challe) between the Euphrates and Palmyra (*cf.* Ball). **14.** Mambre (Gk Abrona, *i.e.* Chaboras of the ancients, the present-day Chabur flowing into the Euphrates) is to be located where stood the later Mambri, ' a fortress built by Diocletian near Roman m. S. of Zenobia, which may have stood on a watercourse of the same name ' (so Wolff quoted by Ball). The sea is perhaps the Persian Gulf. **15.** The Gk reads ' And he took the borders (*i.e.* territories) *of Cilicia* ', etc. This reading is to be accepted. Japheth is 'Ephah (*cf.* Is 60:6) according to Stummer. **16 f.** In the previous verse the author gave the two extreme limits of this particular campaign of Holofernes and he now goes on to mention the country in between. The tribe of Madian (*cf.* Gen 25:2) first established itself E. of the Gulf of Aqaba and later inhabited the country E. of Moab and Ammon. **18.** Vg here omits the proper names found in Gk, *viz.* Sidon, Tyre, Sur (which is the Hebrew name of Tyre, here accidentally repeated), Ocina ('Acco), Jemnaan (Jamnia), Azotus and Ascalon.

III 1.—*Mesopotamian Syria* (Heb ' Aram Naharaim ') **d** was in north-west Mesopotamia ; DV ' Syria, Mesopotamia ' is incorrect. Syria *of Ṣôbāh* lay between Hamath and Damascus in the region of Baalbek. Libya points to Egypt (*i.e.* its western border ; *cf.* 1:9, where Ethiopia is referred to as the southern border). **12b.** The ancient Semites erected near their altars a sacred pole to represent the goddess 'Ashērāh. In MT the one word 'ashērāh is either the sacred pole (the ' grove ' of LXX and Vg) or is an epithet of the goddess Ashtoreth (Astarte). **14.** Apamea was a district NW. of Hamath. The march through the land E. of Jordan to the Idumaeans is not mentioned in the corresponding passage in Gk, but it is implied in other passages (*cf* Gk 5:2, 5 ; 6:2, 5 ; 7:8). On the other hand the Gk reading here is implied by Vg (*cf.* 4:5). The Gk has ' And he (Holofernes) came over against Esdraelon (=Jezreel=Zerin) near unto Dotaia (*i.e.* Dothan ; Vg 4:5 Dothain) which is opposite the great serrated mountain of Judaea : and he pitched between Gaibai (probably Jelâmet el-Mansurah, NW. of Tell Qaimūn) and Scythopolis (Beisan) '. It seems, therefore, that the original text contained more than either Vg or Gk has preserved. Jerome's abridged account incorrectly puts the Idumaeans in Gabaa (Gk Gaibai) ; it has confused and joined together two distinct operations, one against the Idumaeans and the other which brought the army of Holofernes between Gaibai (Vg Gabaa) and Scythopolis.

IV The Determination of the Israelites to resist—**3 f.** **e** The Israelites of Judah sent word to the towns of Samaria *to occupy* the mountain-tops and *to fortify* the towns, etc. **5.** Eliachim (Gk Joachim) is the same person as the Joachim of 15:9 ; it is a name not uncommon in the OT. **12.** For the defeat of Amalec *cf.* Ex 17:8 ff. **15.** Hair-cloth (*i.e.* sackcloth), the garment of humiliation and mourning, was made

309e from goat's or camel's hair. The Gk mentions three classes of sacrifices, the daily (morning and evening) holocaust, the vow-offering and the voluntary offering.

f V 1-25 The History of the Israelites as given by Achior—4. The other versions read 'west' instead of 'east'. **6 f.** Abraham, the father of the Hebrew nation, was born at Ur of the Chaldees (Gen 11:28) ; ancient Chaldaea lay in the lower basin of the Tigris and the Euphrates, and extended to the Persian Gulf. **9.** Instead of 'Charan' (Haran) we should read with Gk and Syr. 'Canaan', because Gen 12:10 relates that the famine raged in Canaan. Abraham did sojourn in Haran, a city due E. of Carchemish and SSE. of Edessa, but that was when in Mesopotamia (*cf.* 5:7). Ex 12:40 gives the number of years as 430 ; 400 is a round number. **20.** The peoples mentioned were the pre-Israelite inhabitants of cisjordanic and transjordanic Palestine. Heshbon lay ENE. of the Jordan mouth. **22.** The principal nations were the Egyptians, the Philistines, the Syrians, the Assyrians and the Neo-babylonians. **23.** Of the exiles who returned from Babylonia, not all came back during the reign of Cyrus. A group, for example, returned with Esdras.

g V 26-VI 21 The Fate of Achior—7. This is the first mention of Bethulia in Vg. The Gk, however, mentions it earlier, for it states that Joachim charged the citizens of Bethulia and Betomesthaim (*i.e.* Misilya SE. of Dothan according to Abel in *Géographie de la Palestine*, II, 283) to keep the passes of the hill country, etc. (*cf.* Gk 4:6). Bethulia is probably to be located on Sheikh Shibel, above Kafr Kūd in Northern Samaria. There was a city called Bethul in the territory of Simeon in SW. Judaea (*cf.* Jos 19:4) and this name was given to the place where Judith, who came of Simeonite stock (*cf.* 9:2), performed her heroic deed (*cf.* Stummer). **11.** According to 8:9 the governors of Bethulia were Ozias, Chabri and Charmi. Here, however, Charmi is confused with Gothoniel (who was the father of Chabri ; *cf.* Gk 6:15) and all mention of Chabri is omitted.

h VII The Siege of Bethulia—2. Holofernes had in his mighty army conscripts from the various provinces which he had subjected ; for 'preparations' write 'baggage'. **3.** Holofernes had given orders to break up camp and march against Bethulia. Then, according to the Gk, the army camped in the valley near Bethulia, and spread itself in breadth in the direction over against Dothan and on to Belbaim (Balamon of Gk 8:3, Belma of Vg, Jible'am of Jos 17:11, the modern Khirbet Bel'ame), and in length from Bethulia to Kyamon (Chelmon of Vg, Jokne'am of Jos 12:22, the modern Tell Qaimūn). The Gk later states that when the city's external water-supply had been cut off the Edomite and Ammonite contingents in the army of Holofernes camped in the hill country over against Dothan and a part was sent to take up positions towards the south, and towards the east, over against Ekrebel (*i.e.* Aqrabeh, 10 m. SE. of Nablus). Thus we get a picture of the final positions taken up by the Assyrian army. **11.** Instead of attempting a direct assault the Assyrians blockaded the city and sealed off its external water supplies ; after 20 days of siege the water in the underground cisterns, which are a feature of all oriental cities, was almost exhausted and was severely rationed.

i VIII Judith and her Discourse to the Governors—1. Instead of 'Ruben' read 'Israel' (Jacob), *cf.* Syr. **6.** The usual period of mourning was seven days, (*cf.* 16:29). **15.** God remains always the merciful and benign father who forgives his disloyal children when they return to him with a contrite heart. **22.** Abraham was *tried* by God when commanded to immolate his son Isaac (*cf.* Gen 22). **29.** The Gk states that Judith was requested to pray for water to replenish the water cisterns.

j IX Judith's Prayer for God's Protection—2-5. She prayed to the God of her fathers for courage and zeal such as he gave to Simeon to slay the Shechemites

because Shechem violated his sister Dina (*cf.* Gen 34). She based her request upon the fact that all events happen in accordance with God's all-wise providence. **10.** 'destroyest' means 'putest an end to'. **11b.** The horns of the altar were curved projections at the four corners. The oblation of a victim which was the specific act of the priest consisted in touching those horns with his finger dipped in the blood of the animal, and in pouring the remainder at the foot of the altar (Lev 4:17 f.). The intention of Holofernes was to suppress the worship of the God of the Israelites ; *cf.* 3:13. **13.** To succeed in her enterprise Judith had first to fascinate Holofernes.

X Judith's Arrival at the Tent of Holofernes—3. The bonnet was some kind of tiara, the garments of gladness her festal garments, and the lilies may have been a scarf embroidered with lilies. **5.** *Roasted* corn (Heb. *qālî*) was a common article of food. Judith brought provisions so as not to be obliged to use heathen food which might have been offered to idols (*cf.* Ex 34:15), or might be meat of animals not slaughtered in the proper manner (*cf.* Lev 17:15), or of animals prohibited to the Israelites as food (*cf.* Lev 11:4 ff. ; 2 Mac 6:18 ff.). **18b.** According to Gk they said that not one man of the Hebrews must be left because the Hebrews would cajole the world with the beauty of their women folk.

XI Judith in the Presence of Holofernes—4. The last clause is intentionally ambiguous : Holofernes thinks of victory for his arms, Judith of the death of the enemy of her people. **11.** The drinking of the blood of animals was a primeval prohibition (Gen 9:4) which was re-enacted in the Mosaic law (Lev 17:10-14). **12.** Every Hebrew was bound to offer to God the first-fruits of his vineyard, of his trees, and of his corn and these were to be eaten by the priests only (*cf.* Num 18:11). The loaves of proposition likewise belonged to the priests (Lev 24:9). Everyone was forbidden to eat the fat covering the intestines, the great lobe of the liver, the kidneys and the fat adhering to them (Ex 29:13 ; Lev 3:4, 10, 15, etc.). **14.** It was necessary, Judith declared, that she should remain in communication with her God and that this could take place only outside the camp and (adds LXX) by night. The liberty to go and come was essential for the execution of Judith's plan. **19b.** For 'sense of words' Gk reads 'understanding of things'.

XII-XIII The Killing of Holofernes—1. Judith was led into the dining-hall where his *silver-plate* (ἀργυρώματα) was set. **7.** The Hebrews were accustomed to perform a ceremonial washing before prayer (*cf.* Ex 30:17 ff. ; Ps 25:6). **13-14.** The opportunity to put her plan into execution is now come, and Judith answers in a tone of feigned humility and eagerness. **18.** She wishes to drink her own wine. **XIII:5.** Judith had made this arrangement with her maid before the banquet. **10.** The canopy was probably the mosquito-net which she took as a trophy. **19.** The wallet was the bag which had contained the provisions (*cf.* 10:5). **28b** together with 15:10b is read in the Gradual of the Mass for the Feast of the Immaculate Conception. The words are used in the accommodated sense of our Blessed Lady.

XIV-XV The Rout of the Terrified Assyrians—2. Judith advises the besieged to feign an attack on the Assyrian outposts. Every man is to arm himself and rush out as if intending to go down the hillside, he is not actually to do so. **3 f.** The watchmen will be alarmed by this show of attack and will hasten to arouse their general ; on finding him dead the Assyrians will flee in panic. **5.** They are to follow their enemies without apprehension (DV 'securely') for God will destroy them. **12.** For 'mice' (Heb. *'akbārîm*) Gk has 'slaves' (Heb. *'abādîm*). **XV:11** Judith's abstinence from second marriage is also mentioned in 16:26. Since every woman in ancient Israel desired a numerous progeny (*cf.* Gen 24:60) and regarded childlessness as a dire misfortune (*cf.* Gen 30:1 ; 1 Kg 1:6), we may conclude that voluntary celibacy was rare among

9n them, and also that second marriages after widowhood were not infrequent among those who were still young. Judith according to Gk 16:22 had many suitors, but nevertheless did not remarry from (the text suggests) a religious motive. The Mosaic laws say nothing of remarriage after the death of one of the parties except in the case of Levirate marriage (*cf.* Deut 25:5).

o XVI 1-21 The Canticle of Judith—2. 'Begin' means 'lead off the canticle'. **8.** Holofernes was struck down not by men of huge physique, but, to his eternal disgrace, by a mere woman. The word 'tall giants' corresponds to Heb. *gibbôrîm*, while the sons of Titan were probably the Rephaim of Gen 14:5; Deut 2:20, etc. The valley 'of Rephaim' (near Jerusalem) mentioned in 2 Kg 5:18 is called in LXX the 'valley of the Titans'. **14.** The weak (lit. 'sons of the damsels') overthrew the fainthearted (Gk 'sons of deserters'). **18.** The waters are those of the Great Abyss which according to popular conception lay below the flat earth; *cf.* Ps 23:2. **19.** We have here a striking case of haplography. It is due to the copyist of the Gk text upon which the Old Latin is based and entered Vg through the Old Latin. The eye of the Gk copyist leaped from φοβουμένοις in 15*c* to φοβούμενος in 16*c*. The complete text reads : ' But to them that fear thee, thou art propitious, because a small thing is every sacrifice for a sweet savour, and a very small thing is all fat for a holocaust unto thee, but he that fears the Lord is great continually '. **20 f.** The day of judgement corresponds to the 'day of Yahweh', referred to frequently by the **309o** prophets (*cf.* § 527*i*) as the day when God will intervene to punish iniquity and to reward righteousness. Their dead bodies will lie unburied, a prey to worms ; they will be got rid of by burning instead of by burial ; ' *and they will weep* (LXX κλαύσονται) *feeling pain unceasingly* '. The words ' for ever ' (Gk ἕως αἰῶνος) mean here, as frequently in OT (*cf.* Ex 19:9), ' while they last '. Our Lord (Mt 13:42, 50) mentions fire when speaking of eternal woes, and, if he is alluding to this passage, he is but extending the words to describe the torments of Gehenna. The words of Jesus in Mk 9:47 allude to Is 66:24 and are likewise used in the accommodated sense.

22-31 The Remainder of Judith's Life-Story—22. Purification was necessary because of the legal uncleanness contracted in killing the Assyrians (*cf.* Num 19:11 ; 31:19). **23.** An offering for an anathema of oblivion meant an offering for total destruction (Heb. *ḥērem*). **29.** Seven days was the ordinary period of mourning among the Israelites (1 Kg 31:13 ; Ecclus 22:13). This custom technically known as *Šiḇᶜāh* (*i.e.* ' seven ') is a very ancient one (*cf.* Gen 50:10) and is still observed by all orthodox Jews. **30.** She lived to be 105 years old (*cf.* 28) and the peace she procured lasted a long time. It seems, therefore, that Judith's glorious deed cannot have taken place in the reign of Ashurbanipal, because Josias of Judah was defeated and slain at Megiddo in 609. **31.** Vg alone mentions this festival and nothing further is known about it.

ESTHER

By C. RYAN

310a Bibliography—F. E. Gigot, *Special Introduction to the Study of the OT*, I (New York, 1903³) 355–63 ; F. X. Roiron, *Les Parties Deutérocanoniques du Livre d'Esther*, RSR 6 (1916) 1–16 ; M. Sales, *La Sacra Bibbia* (Turin, 1926) ; Cornely-Merk, CSS (Paris, 1933¹¹); Lusseau et Collomb, *Manuel d'Etudes Bibliques* (Paris, 1934²) ; *C. F. Keil, *The Book of Esther* (Edinburgh, 1888) ; *L. B. Paton, *The Book of Esther*, ICC (1908) ; *A. W. Streane, *The Book of Esther* (Cambridge, 1922).

b Theme and Contents of the Book—The theme of the book is God's providential care of Israel manifested in his saving the nation from a grave danger that threatened it while still in exile, in the reign of Assuerus, king of Persia. God visited Aman and the enemies of Israel with the evils they had designed for the Jews. So evident was God's guiding hand to the chief characters of the story, two exiled Jews, Mardochai and his foster-child Esther, that Mardochai, who at the beginning ' was thinking what God would do ' (11:12), at the end understood that ' **God hath done these things** ' (10:4), that ' **the Lord remembered his people, and had mercy on his inheritance** ' (10:12).

c The story opens in the second year of the reign of Assuerus with Mardochai's dream, foreshadowing the future danger and the deliverance from it. The danger arose in the following manner. In the third year of his reign Assuerus deposed Queen Vasthi and, in the seventh year, set Esther in her place. Mardochai discovered, and revealed to the king through Esther, a conspiracy of two eunuchs against the king's life. He thereby incurred the enmity of Aman, chief minister of the king, not only for himself, but for his whole nation. When he refused to bow the knee in worship of Aman this enmity came to a climax, and Aman decided that there must be a general massacre of the Jews. He succeeded in obtaining from the king a decree to this effect. Mardochai asked Esther to intercede with the king, and she agreed to do so provided that the people first prayed and fasted for three days. She then approached the king and asked him to a banquet, at which Aman was also a guest. At the banquet she invited them to another on the following day. During the night, the king, unable to sleep, ordered the chronicles of the kingdom to be read to him. He was thus reminded of the loyal service of Mardochai, to whom the next day he ordered Aman to do special honour. At the banquet on that day Esther accused Aman before the king. The result was that Aman was hanged on the gibbet which he had prepared for Mardochai, who was made chief minister in his place. Since the decree ordering the massacre of the Jews was irrevocable, a new decree was obtained by Mardochai enabling the Jews to defend themselves. They gained a great victory on the day appointed for their destruction, and to commemorate their deliverance the feast of Purim (Phurim : ' lots ') was instituted. The story ends with the interpretation of the dream with which it began.

d Text and Versions—There are two widely differing editions of the book of Esther, the Greek and the Hebrew. They differ frequently in detail, and notably in length, the Greek containing a number of passages lacking in the Hebrew. In Vg St Jerome gathered all these passages and placed them, freely translated into

Latin, at the end (after 10:3) of his word-for-word **310** translation of the Hebrew, indicating the places in the book where they were found. DV follows St Jerome's order, but gives no indication of the place of the passages in the Greek. The passages, seven in number, are as follows in the order of the Greek : (1) Prologue, the dream of Mardochai, and his discovery of the conspiracy, 11:2–12:6, before 1:1. (2) Decree of Assuerus ordering the massacre of the Jews, 13:1–7, after 3:13. (3) Mardochai's exhortation to Esther, 15:1–3, after 4:8. (4) Prayers of Mardochai and Esther, 13:8–14:19, after 4:17. (5) Visit of Esther to Assuerus, 15:4–19, after 5:2. (6) Decree of Assuerus in favour of the Jews, 16:1–24, after 8:12. (7) Interpretation of the dream, 10:4–13, after 10:3. A note on the introduction of the book into Egypt is added in 11:1.

The Greek version exists in two recensions : the LXX text, found in the uncial manuscripts Sin., A, B, and the text found in the codices 19, 93, 108, which is shorter and probably later than the other. The Syriac version derives from the Hebrew ; the Old Latin from the Greek.

Canonicity—The canonicity of the book in its Hebrew **e** form, questioned among the Jews of the 1st cent. A.D., was upheld by the Jewish councils of Jerusalem and Jamnia. The Church, however, has from the beginning recognized the book in its Greek form as sacred Scripture. The consent of the great majority of the Fathers testifies to this tradition. St Clement of Rome (1st cent. ; 1 *ad Cor.*, ch 55, PG 1, 32), Clement of Alexandria (2nd cent., *Strom.* 4, 19, PG 8, 1328 f.), and Origen (3rd cent. ; *De Oratione*, 14, PG 11, 452 ; *Hom. 27 in Num.*, PG 12, 780) accept as Scripture the passages not found in the Hebrew. Some few Fathers doubted the canonicity of the book. St Jerome in theory rejected but in practice used the Greek additions. The canonicity of the whole book, Hebrew and Greek parts, has been defined by the Councils of Florence and Trent ; *cf.* H. Pope, *Why does the Protestant Church read the book of Esther*, DbR July (1905) 77–98.

The Original Form of the Book—Various hypotheses **f** are advanced on the original form of the book which exists in two so widely differing editions. Apart from the Protestant theory declaring the Hebrew edition to be the original and rejecting as spurious the Greek ' additions ', the history of the problem among Catholic scholars shows four different viewpoints and consequently four different solutions.

(1) Some of the older exegetes held that there were two authors, equally and independently inspired, one the author of the Greek book, the other of the Hebrew. This theory had the approval of St Robert Bellarmine and it has recently been revived ; *cf.* A. Miller, O.S.B. and J. Schildenberger, O.S.B., *Tobias, Judith und Esther* (BB, 1940).

(2) Some few modern Catholic scholars assert that the Greek additions are a later inspired composition, originally written in Greek and added to the Greek version of the Hebrew book. As we shall see presently, the arguments in favour of Greek as the original language of these additions are by no means convincing.

(3) Most modern Catholic writers hold that the **g** original form of the book was **a Hebrew text substantially the same as the LXX.** They adduce the

g following reasons pointing to such a text : (i) Both Greek recensions contain the additions ; (ii) these additions were used by Josephus, *Ant.* 11, 6 ; (iii) there existed an Aramaic version of them amongst the Jews, *cf.* J. B. De Rossi, *Chald. Estheris Additamenta*, Rome, 1782 ; (iv) the note at the end of LXX and DV, 11:1, reads : ' In the fourth year of the reign of Ptolemy and Cleopatra, Dositheus, who said he was a priest, and of the Levitical race, and Ptolemy his son brought this epistle of Purim, which they said Lysimachus, the son of Ptolemy, had interpreted in Jerusalem ' ; the words ' this epistle of Purim ', since they immediately follow the interpretation of the dream of Mardochai, and thus suppose the dream to have been related in the beginning, must designate the whole book including the Greek additions ; (v) without these additions the book is incomplete and almost non-religious, for in the whole Hebrew text the name of God does not once occur : his help is not sought, his providence is not mentioned, he is not thanked for his assistance ; with the additions, and with others of a minor nature which occur throughout LXX, the religious character of the book is apparent.

h Difficulties : the more important arguments in favour of a Greek original for the additions may be reduced to : **(a) the language,** which lacks the characteristics of a version and shows literary superiority to the rest of the Greek book ; **(b) the repetitions of LXX,** which are due to the additions and are inexplicable in an original text, *viz.* the genealogy of Mardochai, 2:5-6 and 11:2-4 ; the conspiracy against the king, 2:21-23 and 12:1-3 ; the king's two decrees, each given first in summary and immediately afterwards in full, 3:12-13 ; 13:1-7 and 8:9-12 ; 16:1-24. **Answer to (a) :** the argument from the language is not convincing. Hebraisms, explained as arguments for Jewish authorship, may point just as strongly to a Hebrew original. Interesting evidence on the alleged literary superiority is to be seen in the verdict of a non-Catholic writer : ' a comparison between the Greek rendering of the Hebrew and the Greek of the additions does not seem to justify us in differentiating with any degree of confidence the authorship of the two parts, or in assuming the existence of an otherwise unknown Greek version corresponding to the Hebrew form of the book ', A. W. Streane, p xxx. A ready explanation of the purer Greek of the royal decrees is found in the very probable existence of an official Greek version of these, *cf.* 3:12, which the LXX translator could have used. **Answer to (b) :** the argument based on the repetitions is of more weight. An answer to it depends on the further question of **how and why the shorter MT came into existence.** J. B. De Rossi gives, and most Catholic scholars accept, the following hypothesis. The book of Esther was read at the Feast of Purim. When this feast degenerated into a purely profane festival the Sanhedrin made a compendium of the book appropriate for public reading. To save the name of God from insult and religion from dishonour, the more religious parts and the divine name were omitted ; other parts were summarized. The result was the present Hebrew text. From this abridgment there passed into the original text, through the carelessness of copyists, passages which in the fuller text were superfluous. The LXX translation was made from a text thus corrupted.

i (4) An hypothesis worthy of consideration has been put forward by F. X. Roiron, S.J., in RSR 6 (1916) 1–16, based on the references, in MT and LXX, to the two letters of Mardochai to the Jews. Disagreeing with the common interpretation of ' this epistle of Purim ' (11:1), he identifies it with the first letter of Mardochai (9:20), in the Greek **' the epistle of Purim '** LXX 8:64 (*cf.* LXX 8:61), which he tentatively re-constructs from 9:23–25 and from among the Greek additions. The second letter of Mardochai and Esther (9:29), in the Hebrew **' this second epistle of Purim '**, in the Greek ' the confirmation of the epistle of Purim ' (LXX 8:64), he identifies substantially with the present

MT which, for the same reason as De Rossi, he holds **310i** to be a text deliberately excised of its more religious features. This second letter is the original book of Esther. The contents of the first letter were : the dream at the beginning, its interpretation at the end, and in between a summary account of what justified that interpretation, *viz.* the conspiracy of the eunuchs, the hatred, intrigues, and fall of Aman, *cf.* 9:23–25 ; LXX 8:58–60.

According to this theory the LXX translator under **j** divine inspiration was the first to combine these two letters by substituting the second—a long detailed history—at a place in the first where a shorter account of the same history had appeared. Except for this substitution and the insertion of the decrees the LXX translator reproduced faithfully both letters, hence the repetitions of LXX. Since the royal decrees were already known to the Jews they may never have been fully in either letter. They would then be documentary additions in LXX. This hypothesis offers a satisfactory explanation not only of the repetitions but also of the different, though not contradictory, viewpoints of the Hebrew book and of the Greek additions.

The Historical Value of the Book—The book of Esther **k** is subject to the same criticisms as those of Tobias and Judith. Some non-Catholic critics regard it as completely devoid of historical value. A more conservative opinion is sponsored by other Protestant scholars who hold that ' there is at bottom a veritable historical basis, though we may admit that the element of romance has its share in the general result ', *cf.* Streane, p xiv. This latter opinion has found a measure of support from some modern Catholic scholars, *cf.* F. Prat, ER 18 (1902) 298–312 ; 610–33, but while in theory it is consonant with the Catholic doctrine of inspiration and interpretation, in fact it does not seem to have in its favour the solid arguments necessary to warrant a departure from the traditional view of the book as **a true historical document**, *cf.* P. Höpfl, DBV(S) 207–8. Until the end of the 18th cent. no doubt was voiced on the historical nature of the book. The following are the chief arguments in favour of the **l** traditional view : (1) the insistence on topographical and chronological details ; the great number of proper names ; the reference to the annals of the Medes and Persians ; (2) the existence and observance of the Feast of Purim, which in the 2nd cent. B.C. was already known as Mardochai's day (2 Mac 15:37). The feast of Purim is celebrated to the present day by Jews on the 14th Adar (Feb.–March). Proof of the biblical meaning ' lot ' given to the word ' pur ' (3:7, 9:24, etc.) has recently been found, *cf.* A. Bea, Bi 21 (1940) 198–9. ' Pur ' is originally a Babylonian word *puru* from the root *parū* ' to cut ' (*praecidere*) and therefore ' to allot by cutting ' (*praecidendo attribuere*). This fact justifies us in concluding that the feast of Purim was instituted in Babylonia during the Exile as is declared in the book of Esther since the name is the Babylonian not the Hebrew word for ' lot '—*gōrāl*. (3) Remarkable archaeological corroboration of the book's description of the acropolis of Susa was found in the excavations of M. Dieulafoy and J. de Morgan. Though the remains are not those of the palace of Xerxes and Esther, which was burned in 440 B.C., it is very probable that the later buildings of Artaxerxes II, 404–359 B.C., followed the general plan of the former ; *cf.* Dhorme DBV(S) *Elam*, 948 ff. ; 960 ; Vigouroux, *La Bible et les Découvertes Modernes* 4 (Paris, 1896⁶) 621–70.

The Persian king is **Xerxes,** 486–465 B.C. Different **m** names, Assuerus from the Hebrew and Artaxerxes from LXX, appear in the respective parts of Vg and DV. Herodotus informs us that Xerxes, in the 3rd year of his reign, gathered the princes in Susa to consult on making war against Greece. That occasion fits the feasting at which Assuerus deposed Vasthi (1:3). Xerxes in his 6th year, 480 B.C., undertook the unsuccessful expedition against Greece and returned the following year. Preparation for war and the war itself excellently

310m explain the delay between the deposing of Vasthi and the election of Esther.

n Date and Author—The author is unknown. Clement of Alexandria and many early commentators ascribed the book to Mardochai. Many modern Catholic scholars hold that the author was a later Jew living in Persia whose sources of information were the memoirs of Mardochai : some attribute to Mardochai the greater part of the book (1:1–9:22), and to a later writer (9:23–32). The date of the book is therefore not certain, but it was probably written in Persia very soon after the events narrated.

N.B.—The commentary follows the Greek order, the order in which the DV should be read.

311a XI 2-12 Mardochai's Dream—3. 'Among the first' is said by anticipation. LXX has 'who served in the king's court. **4.** Jechonias was made captive in 597 B.C. It is not necessary to suppose that Mardochai was as old as this. He was a descendant of exiled Jews and thus '*he was of the captivity which Nabuchodonosor*', etc. **12.** He knew the divine origin but not the meaning of his dream.

b XII 1-6 Mardochai reveals the Conspiracy of Two Eunuchs—1. 'At that time' is not the time of the dream, the 2nd year, but the time when Esther was already queen (2:21 ff.). 'In the king's court' is a general indication of the place more particularly defined by 'at the king's gate' (2:19, 21). **2.** 'He told the king thereof', indirectly through Esther (2:22). **5.** The 'command' in 5a may indicate that he was not previously employed in the palace, that 12:1 refers to his 'care for Esther's welfare' (2:11, 19 f.), and that now part of his reward is employment in the palace. There may perhaps be question of better employment. There is an apparent contradiction between 5*b* and 'he hath received no reward' (6:3). The difficulty is solved either by referring 5*b* to the reward given later or since no mention of the reward was made in the chronicles (6:3), it was so small as to be reckoned, by the servants, no reward. **6.** The Greek has Bugite here and in 3:1, while MT and DV (3:1 and 9:24) have Agag. The Greek is the better reading. The Greek word means 'bully, braggart' but probably here it is a transliteration of a Babylonian tribal or place name. Agag of MT is a deliberate corruption of the text to brand Aman as an Amalecite, the accursed enemy of Israel, *cf.* 1 Kg 15. Aman was probably in the conspiracy. The hatred begotten here matured in 3:1 ff.

c I 1-22 The Feast and Deposition of Queen Vasthi—2. '*When he sat on the throne of his kingdom which was in Susa the fortress.*' In the HT there is a distinction between the '*fortress*' (*bîrāh*) of Susa and the city of Susa (*Šûšān* alone or *hā'îr Šûšān*) *cf.* MT 8:15. The *bîrāh* is the Acropolis, *cf.* Neh 1:1. **4.** 180 days during which guests were entertained in relays. **6.** The beds are sofas used for the reclining position at meals. **7.** HT and Greek refer only to drinking. For 'one after another' read '*the vessels differing one from another*'. Such a quantity of vessels stresses the wealth of the king. **8.** Persian custom seems ordinarily to have imposed the drinking of a definite amount, *cf.* Josephus, *Ant.* 11, 6. **9.** The historical accuracy of the account is impugned because the queen at this time according to Herodotus was Amestris. Herodotus, however, does not call Amestris queen but only the wife of Xerxes, and moreover the royal harem had often simultaneously many queens of different rank and dignity. **14.** On the seven counsellors, *cf.* Esd. 7:14. **19.** The laws of the Medes and Persians were in theory irrevocable (8:8, Dan 6:8), in practice the absolute power of the king found a way out, *cf.* Herodotus 3, 31.

d II 1-23 Esther, chosen Queen, reveals the Conspiracy to the King—1 implies remorse on the part of the king. LXX gives the opposite meaning 'he no longer remembered Vasthi'. **2.** Fear of the vengeance of Vasthi, if reinstated, made the servants seek to render

her return impossible. **5-6.** The genealogy of Mar- **3** dochai is here repeated, *cf.* 11:2 ff. **7.** Vg and DV read 'his brother's daughter', the Greek 'the daughter of the brother of his father', and MT 'the daughter of his uncle'. Edissa 'myrtle' is Hebrew ; Esther 'star' is Persian. The Greek adds that Mardochai intended to marry her. Perhaps as the sole heir of her parents she had to marry one of her own tribe, *cf.* Num 36:6–12. **10.** Mardochai forbade Esther to reveal her nationality lest it might ruin her chance of becoming queen. With a Persian name and in the surroundings of the harem she could pass as Persian. Possibly Persian law required that the queen be of the Achaemenid family (Herodotus 3, 84) but as already stated (1:19), the king could do as he pleased.

15. Note the modesty and simplicity of Esther. **16. e** Tebeth is Dec.–Jan. LXX has the 12th month Adar, Feb.–March. The 7th year is 479–478 B.C. The battle of Salamis (480 B.C.) was in September. The battles of Plataea in Greece and Mycale in Asia Minor (479 B.C.) were a little earlier in the season than that. The fugitives from Mycale reached Sardis while Xerxes was still there. After their arrival he returned to Susa. Xerxes could therefore have been back in Susa before the end of Tebeth (Dec.–Jan.) 479–478 B.C. LXX giving the 12th month extends the time to the middle of March. This supposes the gathering of the virgins during his absence. **17.** The law forbidding Jewish-pagan marriages (*cf.* § 557*c*) did not bind Esther in these extraordinary circumstances. Since she was brought to the harem by force she was almost certainly advised by Mardochai on the lawfulness of her marriage with the king ; *cf.* 14:15 f. Polygamy was tolerated in the Old Law. **19.** It is not certain whether a second gathering of maidens or a continuation of the first is meant here. The whole phrase 19*a* is omitted in LXX. **20.** '*Neither had Esther as yet declared her country and people, for thus Mardochai ordered her, to fear God and to observe his commandments as when she was with him. And Esther did not change her way of life*', LXX. **21-23.** The conspiracy is here repeated, *cf.* 12:1 ff. Conspiracies in the palace were not rare in Persia and Xerxes himself was later the victim of one.

III 1-13 XIII 1-7 III 14-15 The Royal Decree f for the Extermination of the Jews—1-6. The events here described took place between the 7th (*cf.* 2:16) and the 12th years. Aman already angered by Mardochai's discovery of the conspiracy (12:6) took further offence at the Jew's refusal to prostrate himself before him. This act in itself was not forbidden, *cf.* Gen 23:7–12 ; 33:3 ; Ex 18:7. In Persia however it seems to have been a species of idolatry. For this reason the Spartan ambassadors refused a like homage to Xerxes, *cf.* Herodotus 7:136. It is possible that we have here something analogous to Dan 6:5 ff., or to the over-scrupulosity in Tob 2:21. It is certain that Mardochai's refusal proceeded from a religious motive (13:12–14). The excessive vengeance of Aman against the whole Jewish nation is paralleled in other instances from eastern history, *cf.* Herodotus, 1:106 ; 3:79. **7.** Vg with DV gives an inexact translation of MT which is itself corrupt. LXX gives a better reading though it has 14th instead of the correct 13th day, *cf.* 13:6. '*In the first month, which is the month Nisan, in the twelfth year of king Assuerus, Pur, that is the lot, was cast, before Aman from day to day and from month to month, and the lot fell on the thirteenth day of the twelfth month that is the month Adar.*' On Pur see §310*l*. **10-13.** The injustice of the king's action is marked by his taking no counsel ; *cf.* 1:13. The summary of the decree is given in **13. XIII:1-7.** The decree follows in LXX. The publication of this decree eleven months before its execution is intelligible in view of the superstitious faith in 'lots' and the impossibility of a Jewish flight from the vast Persian empire. The 14th day is a slip of the copyists here and elsewhere in LXX for the correct 13th. The name Jew is not mentioned in 8 nor in the decree itself.

IV 1-8 XV 1-3 IV 9-17 Mardochai's Mourning g and Petition to Esther to intercede for her People—4.

g The friendship between Esther and Mardochai was well known to her maids and the eunuchs. They may also at this time have known their kinship and the Jewish nationality of both. That the king and Aman did not know of Esther's nationality is explained by the customs and circumstances of the Persian court. **XV:1-3.** In LXX these verses are contained in one verse, namely 8. The religious characteristic of the Greek is evident in the mention of God. **IV:9-11.** Esther could have sought an audience but thinking herself not in favour she saw little hope of its being granted. **16.** LXX and MT have 'fast' not 'pray'.

a **XIII 8-18 Mardochai's Prayer—13-14.** He explains the reason for his not prostrating himself before Aman. His willingness to do so in other circumstances shows that the acts were not intrinsically evil, but were considered by him unlawful in this case. It is never lawful to give to another the honour due to God, and on the other hand it is necessary to avoid scandal and all that in given circumstances would be considered a denial of the true faith; cf. 2 Mac 6:21 ff. **15-17.** Israel is the people of God, his inheritance, his portion, his lot—titles frequent in Scripture. 'Shut not the mouths', i.e. in death.

b **XIV 1-19 Esther's Prayer—4.** Her danger is so imminent that it is said to be in her hands, cf. Job 13:14. **7.** There is no suggestion that she herself was guilty of idolatry. **11.** The promises include those concerning the Messias; cf. Gen 12:3. 'Thy sceptre' is either God's kingly power (Gen 49:10; Num 24:17) or Israel (Num 18:2; Jer 10:16). 'Them that are not' are idols; cf. 1 Cor 8:4, 10. **13.** The lion is the king. **14-19.** Esther proclaims her fidelity to God and her abhorrence of her marriage which is so repugnant to her religious sentiments. For the wine of the drink-offerings to false gods, cf. Deut 32:38.

c **V 1-2 XV 4-19 V 3-14 Esther's Interview with the King and the Banquet—1-2.** There is great variation between the MT and the Greek accounts of Esther's visit. Here we have an obvious instance of deliberate interference with the original HT. The original, as in the Greek, attributed the change in the king to the intervention of God. In suppressing the name of God the originators of MT suppressed also all that had direct relation with God's name, i.e. the anger of the king and the fainting of Esther. **XV:11.** God was the principal cause of the king's changed sentiments, his affection for Esther the instrument God used for his purpose. **12.** 'Thy brother' is an expression of tenderness, protection and equality. **13.** The law is that which punished with death uninvited visitors to the king.

d **VI 1-14 Aman is commanded to honour Mardochai—1.** 'The Lord withheld sleep from the king', LXX—another example of deliberate interference with the text. **3.** See note on 12:5. **8.** The honour rendered was common in the East; cf. Gen 41:42 ff.; 1 Kg 18:4; 3 Kg 1:38. In LXX and in 10-11 the royal crown is not mentioned. **9-11.** It can justly be presumed that the chronicles mentioned the nationality of Mardochai. The king however seems to have forgotten the decree against the Jews. The capricious character of the tyrant king and the careless indifference in issuing the decree explain this forgetfulness; cf. 3:11. **13.** Even among the pagans many were convinced that the Jews had special divine protection. Add: 'because the living God is with him' (Greek).

e **VII 1-10 Execution of Aman—4.** In MT 4c is probably corrupt and its meaning certainly obscure. DV gives a good sense: the cruelty of Aman could be imputed to the king because the plan had royal sanction. RV reads 'although the adversary could not have compensated for the king's damage'. The general sense of MT is that Aman in his action against the Jews would damage more than benefit the king. LXX reads 'for the slanderer is not worthy of the king's court'. **8.** The covering of the face of a condemned man was a custom in Rome and Greece; however a slight consonantal change in MT would give the LXX reading 'his face grew red', i.e. with confusion. **9-10.** The gibbet was brought before the city gates for the execution; cf. 16:18.

312e

f **VIII 1-12 XVI 1-24 VIII 13-17 Mardochai as Chief Minister: the Royal Decree in favour of the Jews—2.** Her house is the house of Aman (MT). **3-4.** Esther again entered the king's presence, apparently uninvited. **7-8.** In MT the king speaks throughout 8. The meaning of the king's reply is that, since he cannot revoke the former decree he grants another enabling the Jews to defend themselves. **9.** Read with LXX 'the twenty-third of the first month, that is Nisan, of the same year'. On this reading there were only 10 days between the two decrees, instead of two months according to MT and DV. **11-12.** The phrase 'and to stand for their lives' gives the essential feature of the faculty granted to the Jews. It is not then a case of unlawful revenge on the part of Esther and Mardochai, rather it is the only way open to them and the Jews, granted the unwillingness of the king directly to revoke the former decree. It is not stated that the Jews made **g** use of the permission to kill the women and children; it is stated that they did not avail themselves of the permission to take the spoils; cf. 9:10. **XVI:1-9.** A thinly veiled apology for the former decree is made here. **10-14.** The hatred of Aman for the Jews is said to be part of his treasonable activity against the king and the Persian Empire; cf. 12:6. 'Macedonian', if authentic, means traitor. It may be a later corruption for Bugite; cf. 12:6. **15-16.** The innocence of the Jews is affirmed in words that contain a reference to Cyrus, Xerxes' predecessor, who admitted having received the kingdom from the God of the Jews, Esd 1:2; 6:10; 7:23. **17.** The first decree is implicitly revoked. In this sense we must understand the words of Vg and DV. The Greek reads 'wherefore you shall do well not to put in execution the letters sent you by Aman', etc. **18.** All his kindred (Greek household) did not include his ten sons who probably lived apart from Aman; cf. 9:13 f. **VIII:13-17.** Some conversions were sincere, others were not.

h **IX 1-16 The Jews' Victory over their Enemies—2.** Withstand successfully; cf. Jos 10:8; 21:42. **5.** This action of the Jews must not be judged by the standard of the New Law, but by that of the Old Law with its lex talionis; cf. Ex 21:23; Lev 24:20. **13.** Esther asks only the same permission as on the previous day. This supposes that the enemies intended a further attack the following day. The special reasons for this in Susa are not stated. Possibly Aman's partisans were here more numerous and more determined in their opposition. The accusation that Esther here manifests vengeful cruelty is answered by the intended attack, and cruelty is foreign to the character of Esther as portrayed in the whole book. The hanging of bodies on a gibbet was customary in Persia as a warning to others. **16.** LXX gives 15,000, a reading preferred by many.

i **IX 17-32 Institution and Observance of the Feast of Purim—26.** Omit 'because Pur, that is the lot, was cast into the urn'. The remaining words and the initial words of the following verse are obscure in Vg and DV. Read 26b as in RV, 'Therefore because of all the words of this letter and of that which they had seen concerning this matter and that which had come unto them (27) the Jews ordained and took', etc. **32.** 'And the commandment of Esther confirmed these matters of Purim and it was written in the book', possibly the book of Esther.

j **X 1 - XI 1 Assuerus' Greatness: Mardochai's Dignity: Interpretation of the Dream—1.** The exact meaning of this verse is not clear. Probably it merely proclaims the wealth and power of Assuerus. 'Islands of the sea' are the islands and coastlands of the eastern Mediterranean. 'Tributary': MT mas, 'forced labourers', probably means tribute in kind. **XI:1.** Four Ptolemies had wives named Cleopatra. Commentators favour Philometor, 181–146 B.C.

THE POETICAL AND WISDOM LITERATURE

By R. A. DYSON, S.J.

I OLD TESTAMENT POETRY

313a Bibliography—A. Vaccari, S.J., *De libris didacticis*, Romae, 1935 ; A. Condamin, S.J., *Poèmes de la Bible*, Paris, 1933 ; F. Zorell, S.J., ' De forma quadam carminum hebraeorum frequenter adhibita parum explorata', *Misc. Bibl.* II (Romae, 1934) 297–310 ; W. H. McClellan, S.J., 'The Elements of OT Poetry', CBQ 3 (1941) 203 ff. ; J. E. Steinmüller, *A Companion to the OT*, New York, 1945, 276–300 ; *G. B. Gray, *The Forms of Hebrew Poetry*, London, 1915 ; *T. J. Meek, ' The Structure of Hebrew Poetry', J Rel 9 (1929) 523–50 ; *T. H. Robinson, *Poetry and Poets of the OT*, London, 1947.

b The Poetic Books—The OT contains all that we know of the poetry of Israel. As with other peoples, poetry seems to have been the earliest form of literary expression in Hebrew. Several fragments and some complete poems are embodied in the narrative books, all of them very old. The more notable are : the sword-song of Lamech (Gen 4:23 f.) ; the blessings of Isaac (27:27–29, 39–40) ; the blessings of Jacob (49:1–27) ; Moses' song of triumph (Ex 1:1–18) ; the song of the well (Num 21:17–18) ; the prophecies of Balaam (Num 23:7–10, 18–24 ; 24:3–9, 15–24) ; the song of Moses (Deut 32:1–43) ; the death-bed blessings of Moses (Deut 33:2–29) ; Josue's command to the sun and moon, taken from the book of Jasher (Jos 10:12–13) ; the song of Debbora (Jg 5:2–31) ; Samson's proverbs (Jg 14:14, 16). Specimens from the later books are : Anna's prayer (often compared with the Magnificat) 1 Kg 2:1–10 ; the maidens' acclamation of David (1 Kg 18:7) ; David's lament over Saul and Jonathan (2 Kg 1:19–27), and Abner (2 Kg 3:33–34) ; the song of David (2 Kg 22:2–51) ; David's last words (2 Kg 23:1–7) ; and the song of David when the ark was placed in the tent (1 Par 16:8–36).

c Of the prophetic writings some books or portions of books are in prose, *e.g.* Agg, Jon (except ch 2), much of Jer, chh 40–8 of Ez, and parts of Is, Os and Zach. Others (Jl, Abd, Mic, Hab, Soph, Mal) are definitely poetic, with the same kind of metrical structure which is used in Pss and the other poetical books.

d The didactic books which are wholly versified form a consecutive group of seven. The book of Job is a didactic poem arranged in the dramatic scheme of a dialogue ; the Psalms are devotional lyrics ; Prov and Ecclus may be called didactic lyrics and Eccles a reflective lyric ; Cant is a nuptial hymn with the dramatic form of a dialogue ; Wis is a reflective, and Ecclus, like Prov, a didactic lyric.

e External Form—The technique of Hebrew poetry is by no means fully understood, but some things seem to be clear. Thought and, therefore, sentences are the basis of its external form. The line or stich is the fundamental unit. The second unit is the verse, usually consisting of two lines (distich), but occasionally of three (tristich). The lines are united by **parallelism,** *i.e.* by an equal distribution or balance of thought so that the individual lines correspond with one another. This parallelism is called synonymous when the second line merely echoes the first with some modification (*e.g.* Ps 2:4 ; 36:1–2 ; 50:9 ; 69:2 ; 75:3 ; Prov 3:13–18) ; antithetic when it is in sharp contrast with

the first line (*e.g.* Ps 1:6 ; 19:8 9 ; Prov 10:1–4, 16, 28 ; 13:9) ; synthetic or progressive, when the idea expressed in the first line is developed and completed in the following lines (*e.g.* Ps 1:1 ; 3:5, 6 ; 18:8–10 ; Prov 26:3). Sometimes, too, we find four lines so connected that the first corresponds to the third and the second to the fourth (*e.g.* Ps 126:1), or the first with the fourth and the second with the third (*e.g.* Ps 136:5–6).

This pairing of similar thoughts is often an aid to the **f** correct exegesis of an ambiguous word or phrase : *e.g.* ' the *breath* of his mouth ' in Ps 32:6*b* is simply the ' word ' of line *a* by which the heavens were made : *cf.* also Ps 87:11. It should also be noted that in a couplet the phrasing is often so distributed that only from both lines do we get the adequate subject and predicate ; *e.g.* Ps 91:3 means ' to praise thy mercy and fidelity day and night ' ; *cf.* also Ps 18:1–2 ; 41:9 ; Gen 49:27.

Rhythm—Hebrew poetry is rhythmical, *i.e.* there is a **g** recurrence of stressed and unstressed syllables in a relatively regular succession. This rhythm is due to the rising (arsis) or falling (thesis) of the voice in the intonation of words. To obtain this effect some of the monosyllabic particles lose their accent to the next word, and the construct state forms one unit with its following noun. These and other peculiarities help to determine the number of accents or beats within each verse. The Hebrew verse usually has three or four accents to a line, but the rhythmic unit is not rigid or uniform. As an example we cite Jg 5:4 :

> *Yahwéh, b^eṣē'ṭ^eḳá miś-śē'îr,*
> *b^eṣa'd^eḳá miś-s^edēh '^edóm,*
> *'éreṣ rā'ášâh, gam-šāmáyîm nāṭápû,*
> *gam-'ăbîm nâṭ^epû máyim.*

> ' Yáhweh, at thy márch from Sé'ir,
>   thine attáck from the field of Édom,
>   éarth was sháken and héaven collápsed,
>   and the clóuds póured down wáter.'

Sometimes we find parallelism and rhythm in perfect agreement, each word having a stress :

> *ya'^aróp kammáṭár liqhí,*
> *tizzál kaṭṭál 'imráṭí.*

> ' May my dóctrine dróp as the ráin,
>   may my spéech distíl as the déw ' (Deut 32:2*a*).

A line of five accents regularly has a caesura or pause after the third ; this type of verse is called the *qinah* because it is used in the *qinoth* or Lamentations of Jeremias to produce a plaintive melancholy cadence. It is also found in the Psalms, *e.g.* Ps 18:10 :

> The féar of Yáhweh is púre, endúring foréver
>   the júdgements of Yáhweh are trúe, júst altogéther.

Metre—The line itself is not governed by a fixed number of long and short syllables as in our western poetry, but by a determined number of stresses or accents (beats), and the number of unstressed syllables between any two beats seems to be governed only by the possibilities of pronunciation and the laws of euphony. The expression 'metrical structure' is, therefore, analogous rather than precise.

Strophe or Stanza—The sense itself often demands the division of the poem into strophes : *cf. e.g.* the arrangement of Ps 2 in the new Latin Psalter. As the lines are related to each other within a verse by parallelism, so the strophes themselves are often connected by a higher echo of the same. Synonymous strophic parallelism is the repetition of the thought expressed in a previous strophe by further amplification (Ps 21:2–12 and 13–22) ; antithetic strophic parallelism expresses the contrast between various parts of a poem (Is 14:4*b*–8 and 9–11) ; synthetic strophic parallelism develops and completes the thought expressed in the first strophe (Ps 103).

The strophic arrangement of a poem may also be identified by various stylistic devices used in the construction of a strophe : *e.g.* the refrain or intercalary verse : *cf.* Ps 41:6, 12 and 42:5 which form one poem ; 45 ; 48 ; 91 ; the anaphora or the repetition of a word or expression at the beginning of several successive verses : *cf.* Ps 12:2–4 ; the epiphora or repetition of the same words at the end of successive lines : *cf.* Ps 117:10–12 ; the symploce or repetition of one word or expression at the beginning and of another at the end of successive verses : *cf.* Ps 117:2–4.

The acrostic or alphabetical poem may also help in the reconstruction of the strophic unit : *cf.* Ps 9:24:33 ; 36:118:144 ; Prov 31:10–31 ; Ecclus 51:13–29 ; Lam 1–4. On the Hebrew word *selāh cf.* § 335*e*.

Some scholars believe that nearly all Hebrew poems can be divided into strophes in such a way that the second (antistrophe) corresponds to the first, the third (epode or alternative strophe) differing from the first two both in matter and form. If the poem has a number of strophes, the fourth and the fifth will correspond with each other and also with the first and second, while the sixth (or epode) is either independent or corresponds to the third : *cf.* Ps 38 as explained by J. K. Zenner, S.J., *Chorgesänge* (1896) 28. It is worth noting that the Rās-Shamra poetry comes from a cultural and literary setting more closely allied to Hebrew poetry than either the Babylonian or Egyptian, and that there are points of contact in their structural forms, *e.g.* in Ps 28 and 69 ; *cf.* Bs 103 (1946) 283.

Internal Qualities—These are determined by the age, condition of life and environment in which the writers lived. Although the OT is of divine authorship, it comes also within the scope of literature, and is to be appreciated as such. For the Holy Spirit in 'Inspiration' poured the flood of his exalted message into the mould of oriental minds, leaving clearly impressed upon it the peculiarities of style of each writer and his time. The substance of the message remains unchanged, but its shapes are various. Using a simple but vigorous diction, profuse figures of speech and rhetorical devices the sacred writers left as a heritage a sublime imagery of religious thought and a great wealth of deep feeling. Thus we find :

(*a*) simile, *i.e.* an expressed resemblance between two objects of unlike classes : *e.g.* man's transient existence (Ps 102:15 ; 128:6 ; Job 7:6 ; 9:25, 26 ; 14:2, 11) ; (*b*) metaphor, *i.e.* an implied comparison (Ps 17:3 ; 70:3 ; Gen 49:3–27) ; (*c*) allegory, *i.e.* a developed and continued metaphor (Ps 79 ; Is 5:1–7 ; Ez 17:1–10 ; Prov 24:30–34) ; (*d*) personification (Ps 18:6 ; Is 44:23 ; 49:13 ; Prov 8:12–36 ; Wis 8:2 ; Job 28:14, 22) ; (*e*) hyperbole (Ps 108:6–15) where the author prays for retribution upon his enemies in the 'fine frenzy' of the poet ; (*f*) irony (Is 5:22 ; 47:1, 5, 8–9, 13–14 ; 14:9–20 ; Am 4:4–5) ; (*g*) word-play (*cf.* the Heb. of Mic 1:8–16 ; Am 5:5 ; 6:13 ; Os 6:8–10 ; 12:12 ; Is 10:28–29). An example from Is 5:7 will illustrate its effectiveness :

'And he looked for judgement (*mišpāṭ*) ; but, lo !
  bloodshed (*mišpāḥ*),
for justice (*ṣedāqāh*) ; but, lo ! a cry (*ṣeʿāqāh*) '.

In this article we have endeavoured to explain only **313n** the rudiments of Hebrew poetry. It is, however, essential to keep in mind that the poet was not bound to absolute regularity either in parallelism or rhythm or in strophic construction. He wrote because of the divine inspiration within him and in its expression he was fettered by no poetic structure that was meticulously exact or regular in form.

II THE WISDOM LITERATURE

Bibliography—H. Pope, O.P., CSAB, 1930, II 188– **314a** 268 ; A. Vaccari, S.J., *De libris didacticis*, Romae, 1935 ; *id.* ' Sapientiaux (Livres) ', DAFC, IV, 1182–1214 ; H. Duesberg, *Les Scribes inspirés*, Paris, 1938 ; J. M. McGlinchey, *The Teaching of Amen-em-ope and the Book of Proverbs*, Washington, D.C., 1938 ; M. P. Stapleton, ' Ancient Wisdom and Modern Times ' CBQ 4 (1942), 311–22 ; 5 (1943) 47–62 ; L. Pirot– A. Clamer, *La Sainte Bible*, Tome VI, Paris, 1946 ; Höpfl-Miller-Metzinger, *Introd. Spec. in UT*, Romae, 1946, 253–381 ; A. M. Dubarle, *Les Sages d'Israël*, Paris, 1946 ; *W. O. E. Oesterley, *The Wisdom of Egypt and the OT*, London, 1927 ; *O. S. Rankin, *Israel's Wisdom Literature*, Edinburgh, 1936.

The Wisdom Books—Wisdom literature is the general **b** name given to those books of the OT whose main theme is wisdom. They are written, for the most part, in a proverbial or aphoristic style which today we call gnomic, and in form and subject-matter they find a parallel in the gnomic poetry of classical literature. These books are Prov, Job, Eccles, Ecclus (Ben Sirach) and Wis, to which are sometimes added Cant and Ps. Yet the last two books are not, strictly speaking, Wisdom literature. The former is a lyrical poem, and most of the Psalms are not, in the precise sense of the word, sapiential, although Ps 1, 36, 38, 48, 72, 111, 138 and portions of other Psalms belong to this class. Job, though not gnomic in form, merits a place among the sapiential books because of its speculative discussions on the origin and moral value of suffering and its hymn to Wisdom (ch 28). Typical of wisdom literature are Prov, Ecclus and, to a lesser degree, Eccles. They consist of sententious sayings that are independent, or, at most, grouped about a definite subject. The book of Wisdom, written in Greek, is more philosophical and less gnomic.

These seven books, both in the Hebrew Bible and in Vg, where they are placed in the middle, form a special group, to which we may add the eulogy of Wisdom in Bar 3:9–4:4. In the Roman Missal they have, with the exception of Ps, the collective title of ' Liber Sapientiae ', when read as Epistles in the Mass.

Origin—The proverb is the standard form of folk **c** wisdom. Every people has its own collection and proverbial style of utterance is popular among Orientals. These proverbs pass from lip to lip and embody the wisdom gained by experience. They express, in short pithy sayings, something that common experience has shown to be true. A proverb is ' the wisdom of many and the wit of one '. Among the Hebrews such popular sayings often took a religious form, and a number of proverbs, both secular and religious, are found in the early literature of Israel : *e.g.* ' Is Saul also among the prophets ? ' (1 Kg 10:12 and 19:24) ; ' From the wicked shall wickedness come forth ' (1 Kg 24:13) ; ' the strength of a man is according to his age ' (Jg 8:21). Other early forms of wisdom are the riddle (*e.g.* Jg 14:14) ; the fable (*e.g.* Jg 9:8–15) and the parable (*e.g.* 2 Kg 12:1–6).

In the OT the golden age of proverbial utterance is **d** associated with the name of Solomon, the wise king *par excellence*. 3 Kg 4:29–30 states that ' God gave to Solomon wisdom and understanding exceeding much and largeness of *mind* as the sand that is on the seashore '. According to 3 Kg 4:32 he ' spoke three thousand proverbs '. There is no reason to deny that

314d he possessed an acute power of observation, a shrewd insight into human nature and the faculty of expressing himself in pointed sayings, a number of which are preserved in the older portions of ' Proverbs ' (10:1–22: 16 ; 25:1–29:27).

e The Hebrew word for proverb is *māšāl*. Originally it seems to have meant ' likeness ', then a short saying containing a comparison. Eventually however the word acquired an extended sense and became an expression for a sententious saying or authoritative utterance in figurative and poetic form (Num 23:7, 18 ; Is 14:4–6). It was in this popular form of expression that the Wisdom literature was chiefly written.

f The Wise Men—A number of proverbial sayings in the Wisdom literature of the OT may have come at first from the lips of the people, but if so, they have been altered and modified so that the stamp of the professional teacher is upon them. The prophets speak of the existence of ' wise men '. In Jer 18:18 they are clearly marked off from the other two great classes of religious teachers : ' the law shall not perish from the priest, nor counsel from the wise, nor the word from the prophet '. The wise men, therefore, occupied a definite position in the religious community and the study and teaching of wisdom was a recognized pursuit. It is frequently stated that the prophets often condemn wise men and wisdom (Is 5:21 ; 29:14 ; 44:25 ; Jer 4:22 ; 8:9 ; 9:23), but a study of these texts shows that the abuse, not the use of wisdom, is the object of the prophets' invective. Moreover it is clear from other texts that they greatly valued true wisdom. For Isaias it is a gift of God (33:6), and upon the Messias shall rest the spirit of wisdom (11:2). In fact it is a prophet who calls God himself for the first time by the name of Wisdom (Is 31:2 ; *cf.* 28:23–29), and Jeremias, in full agreement with the sapiential books, proclaims in a formula dogmatically significant, that God in his wisdom created the universe (10:12 ; 51:15). The wise men base their teaching on revelation and human experience, the one illuminating the other, but they regard revelation as the ultimate foundation of wisdom and the fear of God as its beginning and characteristic quality.

g Wisdom in the Historical Books—In the earlier OT writings wisdom generally means the professional skill of craftsmen or administrative ability. The makers of the tabernacle (Ex 35:31–35) and of the priestly garments (Ex 28:3) received the gift of wisdom. Joseph possessed such political foresight as to win from Pharaoh the encomium of ' the wisest man ' (Gen 41:39) ; Josue, Moses' successor, was divinely filled with the spirit of wisdom (Deut 34:9) and Solomon's wisdom ranged from political acumen (3 Kg 5:12) and keen jurisprudence (3 Kg 3:28) to the solution of riddles (3 Kg 10:1–4) and knowledge of natural history (3 Kg 4:33). This wisdom, however, is an intellectual, not a moral quality ; it is practical ability, not a religious virtue.

h Wisdom in the Sapiential Books—Among these books, Prov, Ecclus and Wis are of chief importance. Of lesser value for our study are Job, Eccles and Bar (3:9–4:4). Prov hold perhaps the highest place among the sapiential books. It is a composite work that gets its name from the two oldest and longest portions (chh 10–22:16 and chh 25–9) which are entitled ' The Proverbs (*mišlê*) of Solomon ', and in it we may trace the development of wisdom literature from its earliest forms to the most evolved. Ecclus was written, like Prov, in Hebrew *māšāls*. It was composed about 180 B.C. and translated into Greek by Ben Sirach's grandson shortly after 132 B.C. It is a practical moral guide and praises particularly the divine wisdom manifested in the Law. Although written in the heyday of Hellenism, its author remained uninfluenced by Grecian culture and exhorted his readers to remain faithful to the Law and true wisdom (24:1–47 ; 36:1–19 ; 44:1–50:31). Wis was written in Egypt, probably at Alexandria, 150–50 B.C. It praises the divine wisdom as manifested in the history of Israel. In the clarity of its doctrine on immortality (chh 3–5) it far excels other OT writings. Its language is Greek like certain of its ideas, but its doctrine is Jewish. Its purpose was to console the Jews in Egypt and to put them on their guard against the false wisdom of Hellenism.

Job is a book apart. Its author is a Hebrew, but the **i** characters of the drama, even Job himself, are not ; *cf.* §318a. Wisdom, then, in the mind of the Jews, though bound up with religion, can be independent of revelation ; but its principles, drawn from reason and experience, shine forth in greater relief beneath the light of revelation. Eccles is a difficult book. Whatever be the solution to the problem of its literary composition (§ 376m–n), it teaches the vanity of earthly things and the value of true wisdom. It condemns the search for pleasure when it is absorbing and divorced from the fear of God (2:1 ; 7:14–15), and its final conclusion is ' Fear God and keep his commandments, for this is the whole duty of man ' (12:13). The alleged influence of Greek philosophy has been much exaggerated. By showing the insufficiency of earthly joys, Ecclesiastes prepared the Jewish mind for a fuller revelation of the future life.

The Notion of Wisdom—It is from the above mentioned **3** writings that we gather the Hebrew notion of wisdom. In order to arrange this matter more conveniently we propose, with Fr. A. Vaccari, S.J., *Greg* 1 (1920) 218, the following division :

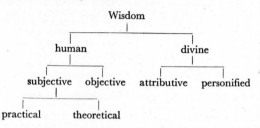

Human Wisdom—In the older portions of Prov that **b** elementary *practical* wisdom which consists in knowing how to live rightly plays a notable part. It has a special name, '*ormāh* (' discernment ', ' shrewd insight ') and its contrary is *petî* or *p^etayyût* (' simplicity ', ' inexperience ') ; *cf.* Prov 14:15 ; 22:3 ; 27:12. But this prudence, at first sight worldly and self-interested, is not without a religious content. There is a God-ward thought at the back of the writers' minds that hallowed what we call worldly wisdom, sanctified common sense, and brought religion into every nook and cranny of daily life. If, then, this human prudence is to be penetrated with religion, it is not surprising that religious wisdom itself (*ḥokmāh*) is constantly stressed. It is to this form of wisdom that the first nine chapters of Prov exhort us and their doctrine is epitomized in the axiom that is the key-note of the book : ' the fear of God is the beginning of wisdom ' (Prov 1:7 ; *cf.* 9:10 ; 15:33 ; 30:3 ; Job 28:28 ; Ecclus 1:16). This fear is synonymous with reverence and filial devotion. It is ' the fullness of wisdom ' (Ecclus 1:20) ; ' the crown of wisdom ' (1:22) ; ' the root of wisdom ' (1:25). In the concrete it is the practice of religion.

Theoretical Wisdom—The intellectual curiosity which **c** gave rise to speculations about nature, man and God, is not characteristic of Hebrew wisdom. Hence it is that speculative wisdom has little place in the sacred books. Eccles, which so highly stresses and recommends practical wisdom, declares vain that wisdom which would know the ultimate reason of things, especially in the divine government of the world (1:12–18). The author of Job proposes a profound theological problem, the divine Providence in the government of the world (28:12–14), to which, however, no one but God can give an adequate answer

(28:23). As far as man is concerned, he concludes tersely :

' Behold the fear of the Lord, that is wisdom ;
And to *shun* evil, that is understanding ' (28:28).

The starting point, then, of the Hebrew sage is not a question but a creed. Given that there is a Supreme Being, Creator, Sustainer, Ruler, Judge of all, then wisdom is to understand, so far as may be, God's words and ways and to turn that knowledge to practical account. Wisdom is, in all the complex relations of life and conduct, to do the will of God.

Objective Wisdom—Since the practice of religion is essential to true wisdom, it follows that the observance of the revealed Mosaic Law is a prominent element of objective wisdom. Actually the sapiential literature, especially the older part, does not seek either the basis or the formulas of morality in the letter of the Law, *i.e.* in something that is specifically Hebrew. It transcends all that is local and temporary, giving to its teaching an absolute, rational foundation based on the psychological observation of the human heart and human life. Cradled in the stronghold of exclusiveness, it overleaps the barriers and reaches forth to the whole family of man. Hence its precepts have a universal application. They are the patrimony of all mankind.

Still, revealed Law is a manifestation of divine wisdom; hence the two, the Law and Wisdom came to be identified. This identification is emphasized in Baruch (3:10–4:1) and Ben Sirach expresses the same idea in a more dramatic and poetical fashion when he pictures wisdom as proceeding out of the mouth of the Most High, seeking a dwelling-place among the nations (Ecclus 24:7–12) and receiving an abode in Sion, where she found her full expression in the Book of the Law (24:23–24). In thus identifying the Law with wisdom, Baruch and Ben Sirach only gave greater relief to the idea already expressed in Deut 4:5–8 : ' I [Moses] have taught you *laws* and statutes as the Lord my God hath commanded me . . . observe and fulfil them ; for this is your *wisdom* ', etc. It is not difficult, therefore, to understand how the Hebrews came to give the name of Wisdom to the revealed Law.

Wisdom as a Divine Attribute—To the writers of the sapiential books ' all wisdom is from God ' (Ecclus 1:1). He is its source and he alone can give it to man (Prov 2:6). Wisdom then is an attribute of God whose clear reflection is seen in the never-ending marvels of nature (Ps 103:24 ; Prov 3:19–20 ; Wis 13:1–9), and in the ordering of human events (Ecclus 17:14–15 ; 18:12–14). God therefore is all-wise ; in fact he is Wisdom personified. Conversely Wisdom is God himself.

Personified Wisdom—Wisdom as a principle of moral life regulating human actions is personified in Prov 1:20–28 ; 8:1–3, 12–15 and 9:1–5. But in the mind of the poet wisdom is more than a practical virtue. In Prov 8:22–31 he places on her lips those sublime and familiar words (*cf.* § 368*m–n*) :

' God possessed me as (in) the beginning of his ways,
    before *his works, of old* ;
I was set up from *everlasting,*
    from the beginning, before the earth was.
When there were no *primeval waters,* I was conceived, . . .
When he *established* the heavens, I was present, . . .
I was by him *as a master-workman,*
    and I *was daily his delight,*
    exulting always before him,
Exulting in *his habitable earth,*
    and my *delight was* with the *sons* of men '.

The Wisdom that speaks here is in God, as the idea of a masterpiece in the mind of the artist ; but it is also conceived as distinct from God, proceeding from him by way of generation, and subsistent. It seems to be more than a poetical personification, though not yet a clearly defined personality. Meanwhile it **316b** prepares the way for and prefigures the doctrine of the distinction of persons in God.

In Ecclus 24:1–16, Wisdom, again speaking in the **c** first person, presents herself under another aspect. In this passage Wisdom is a personification of the Law. The truth revealed by God and the Law imposed by him are properly conceived as outward manifestations of the eternal divine Wisdom, as the word (*logos*) of God, as something that goes forth from God and comes to man, and on the journey takes on, as it were, a personality all its own ; then, deposited in writing, is concretized in the books of the Law. The same mental process may be observed in Baruch.

If, lastly, we turn to Wis, its abstract thought and **d** philosophical speculation tell us that, without having left Israel, we are on the terrain of Hellenism. In his description of Wisdom the author exhausts the rich philosophical dictionary of Greece. For him, too, as in Prov, Wisdom is the artificer of all, but he prefers to describe her, not in the act of creating the universe, but as continually active in penetrating (7:24), ordering (8:1) and renewing (7:27) all things. Yet though she fills the universe, she is intrinsic to God ; for ' she is a *breath* of the power of God, an emanation all pure of the glory of the *Omnipotent* ; the *splendour* of eternal light and the unspotted mirror of God's *activity* and the image of his goodness ' (7:25–27) ; words so sublime and profound that St Paul appropriated them to describe in human language the ineffable mystery of the divine generation of the Word (*cf.* Heb 1:3 ; also Col 1:15, 17). From this portrayal of Wisdom to the definitely Personal Wisdom (*Logos*) of the NT was but a step.

Foreign Influence—Analogous collections of gnomic **e** poetry were in existence in Babylonia and Egypt before the Hebrew sapiential books were composed. Of special interest is the Egyptian hieratic text of ' The Teaching of Amenemope ' published by Sir Wallis Budge in 1923–4. There is a curious resemblance between the thirty chapters of this work and the thirty quatrains (read *šelôšîm* = 30 in Prov 22:20) which compose Prov 22:17–24:22, as well as between the thought-content and verbal expression as far as Prov 23:11. The relation between them is more than fortuitous, but scholars differ in determining it. P. Mallon (Bi 8 [1927] 3–30) admits the dependence of Prov upon the Egyptian sapiential book ; others affirm a common dependence upon an older Egyptian or Hebrew source.

Since the ' Teaching of Amenemope ' is variously **f** dated between 1000 and 600 B.C., chronology cannot settle the question of dependence. It is to be noted, however, that the thirty quatrains in Prov run consecutively, but in Amenemope they are scattered throughout the work. This would be difficult to understand in the case of a direct dependence of the Hebrew work on the Egyptian, but is intelligible if the compiler of Proverbs made, more or less, a copy of an older Hebrew writing, while Amenemope took a number of its ideas and elaborated them in his own way, inserting them in his text wherever he thought it suitable. In any event, wherever the inspired authors have made use of the wisdom literature of other nations, they have put their own impress upon it and carefully left out all that might savour of polytheism or offend the majesty of God.

It is often stated that the personification of wisdom in **g** the later sapiential literature is due to the impact of Greek thought. It is, however, a canon of sound criticism not to explain by foreign influence what may well be accounted for by indigenous factors. Actually, personification of the divine attributes is not at all alien to the Hebrew mind (*cf.* Ps 84:14 ; 88:14–15 ; 93:15) ; and it was quite natural that the revealed word (*logos*) of God should be graphically personified (Ecclus 24:1–16). There is no doubt that the author of Wis was acquainted with Greek philosophy and adopted in part its logical classifications. Deeply

316g versed in the OT doctrine, his aim was to prove to his fellow-Jews the superiority of Hebrew wisdom and to win the gentile reader to his view. To this end he clothed old truths in new formulas that were understood and appreciated by those familiar with Greek philosophy. Hellenism, however, does not enter into the texture of his thought. The closest resemblance is found in 7:22–24, but the ' spirit of understanding ' that ' *pervades and penetrates all things* ' (24*b*) is not the world-soul (*logos*) of the Stoics, immanent in all things, the active principle of a pantheistic all, but is as distinct from the world as a workman from his work, intrinsic to God and transcendent.

h In a word, the speculations of Hellas had a purely metaphysical origin and were born from the search for **3** a rational explanation of the world and its phenomena. The wisdom of the Hebrew sages springs from morality and religion. It is a divine plant with its roots in the rich soil of revelation. It is offered, not as the scientific explanation of the essence of things, but as a guide to virtue. Its personification played a great part in evolving and formulating the NT doctrine of the Word of God. In the OT all the essential elements were there. St John supplied that when, in his prologue, he proclaimed to the world the Word as the only begotten Son of God, the second Person of the Blessed Trinity.

JOB

By E. F. SUTCLIFFE, S.J.

317a **Bibliography**—*Commentaries :* G. Sanctius, S.J. [Sanchez], *In Libr. Iob Comm.* (Lugduni, 1625) ; J. de Pineda, S.J., *Comm. in Iob*, 2 vol. (Coloniae Agrippinae, 1701) ; C. F. Houbigant, *Not. Crit. in Vet. Test. Libr.* (Francofurti ad Moenum, 1777) ; *E. F. C. Rosenmüller, *Schol. in Vet. Test.* V (Lipsiae, 1806) ; J. Knabenbauer, S.J., *Comm. in Libr. Iob* (CSS, Parisiis, 1886) ; *K. Budde, *Das Buch Hiob* (HAT, Göttingen, 1896, 1913²) ; J. Hontheim, S.J., *Das Buch Job* (BS 9, 1–3, Freiburg im Breisgau, 1904) ; *A. B. Ehrlich, *Randglossen* VI (Leipzig, 1918) ; *H. Torczyner, *Das Buch Hiob* (Wien und Berlin, 1920) ; *S. R. Driver and G. R. Gray, *The Book of Job* (ICC, Edinburgh, 1921 ; the parts due to each are indicated p viii) ; *M. Buttenwieser, *The Book of Job* (London, 1922) ; *C. J. Ball, *The Book of Job* (Oxford, 1922) ; G. Ricciotti, *Il Libro di Giobbe* (Torino-Roma, 1924) ; P. Dhorme, *Le Livre de Job* (Paris, 1926) ; N. Peters, *Das Buch Job* (EHAT, Münster in Westf., 1928) ; *E. König, *Das Buch Hiob* (Gütersloh, 1929) ; P. Szczygiel, M.S.C., *Das Buch Job* (BB, Bonn, 1931) ; *G. Hölscher, *Das Buch Hiob* (Tübingen, 1937) ; E. J. Kissane, *The Book of Job* (Dublin, 1939) ; Mgr P. P. Saydon, *Ktieb Ġob* (Malta, 1947) ; *W. B. Stevenson, *The Poem of Job* (London, 1947).

Articles on the text : *N. Herz, ZATW 20 (1900) 160–3 ; *G. R. Driver, JTS 34 (1933) 380 ; AJSLL 52 (1936) 160–70 ; ET 57 (1945–6) 192 f. ; 249 ; *D. Winton Thomas, JTS 36 (1935) 411 f. ; *R. Gordis, JTS 41 (1940) 40–2 ; *J. J. Stamm, TZ 4 (1948) 331–8 ; E. F. Sutcliffe, Bi 30 (1949) 66–90 ; 31 (1950) 365–78.

Other : A. Vaccari, S.J., ' Il Concetto della Sapienza nell' Antico Testamento ', *Gregorianum* 1 (1920) 218–51 ; S. Landersdorfer, O.S.B., *Eine babylonische Quelle für das Buch Iob* (BS 16, 2 ; 1911) ; J. Royer, *Die Eschatologie des Buches Job* (BS 6, 5 ; 1901) ; G. Schiaparelli, *Astronomy in the Old Test.* (Oxford, 1905) ; *W. M. Flinders Petrie, *Researches in Sinai* (London, 1906).

b **Contents**—In the land of Hus there lived a God-fearing man named Job, rich in flocks, herds and the produce of the land, and blessed with a numerous progeny. According to current notions of God's government of the world his virtuous life and prosperity were thought to be interrelated, the latter being the God-given reward for the former, and this belief was shared by the wealthy man himself. In a council held in heaven it was urged that Job's virtue was purely self-seeking and would vanish with his wealth. With the sanction of God he was quickly despoiled of all his children and of all his belongings, but his virtue proved to be deep-rooted in a profound conviction of man's due relation to the godhead, which he expressed in the famous words ' The Lord hath given, the Lord hath taken away ; blessed be the name of the Lord ', words redolent of perfect resignation to the divine will. A second and more violent temptation was unable to weaken his faith and trust in God. This time his whole body was smitten with a loathsome disease, so loathsome that he was deprived of the moral support of his wife, who lost her faith in the justice of the divine government of the world and urged him to show his anger by cursing God and then to die. But Job's faith was stronger than his wife's. He rejected the invitation to put an end to his life and again showed complete resignation : ' If we have received good things at the hand of God, why should we not receive evil ? '

317b

c Three friends belonging to different tribes and localities now heard of Job's calamitous change of fortune and arranged to come together to comfort him. When these three, Eliphaz, Bildad and Sophar, arrived and saw Job in his appalling state, reduced to sitting on a refuse-heap, their pity evaporated as they were at once convinced that they were in the presence of one cursed by God. They shared the current view that prosperity is the divine reward of virtue and calamity the divinely sent punishment of iniquity ; and in view of the extreme severity of Job's losses and bodily disease it was clear to them that Job's iniquity, though concealed from men, had been very great. Silence seemed the only course ; and they feared even to enter into relations with one so obviously under God's curse.

d Job had now been suffering for months. It had taken that time for the news to reach the friends, for them to arrange and then to accomplish their journey in common. Job was now reduced to skin and bones (19:20). The obvious hardness of the friends' attitude and Job's bitter disappointment at the lack of all sympathy coming after the wearing experience of prolonged mental anguish and physical suffering at last proved too strong for even his heroic patience, and he broke the silence with the utterance of bitter regret that God had ever let him see the light of day.

e This outburst aroused the friends who proceeded to justify God's treatment of Job according to their own theological preconceptions. Job is guilty and has merited his lot. This is insinuated at first, but later boldly stated. If Job will repent and turn to God, all will yet be well with him. God's chastisement is a blessing in disguise (5:17). God wounds but he is ready to heal. Their diagnosis of the case is based upon and defended by appeal to experience, to traditional lore and to the justice of God. Knowing nothing of rewards and punishments after death or of what had happened at the council in heaven it seemed to them that there could not be any other explanation of what had befallen Job. The sufferer on his side vehemently repelled this interpretation. He knew he was innocent and could not in conscience admit himself to have been guilty. He admits those smaller transgressions of which all men are guilty (13:26 ; 14:4), but nothing that could account for the sufferings he had to endure. Hence a terrible struggle in Job's soul. He knew God to be just ; yet everything seemed to point to injustice on the part of God. He too had always shared the common conviction that God's treatment of man was in proportion to man's merit or demerit. How could God's justice be reconciled with his own crushing experience ? The friends had an answer, but his conscience gave him complete assurance that it was false. These two apparently irreconcilable convictions, God's absolute justice and his own innocence, caused him mental anguish as painful as his bodily affliction and wrung from his tortured soul irreconcilable declarations. He accused God of treating him unjustly (27:2), and yet was firmly convinced that if only he could meet God and lay his case before the divine majesty all would be well (23:3–7). It seemed as if God did not know the true facts. If only Job could bring these to his notice, justice would be done. But all the time

317e Job knew that nothing in the world he had made escaped the notice of its Creator (16:20). These shiftings of view reflect the bewilderment begotten in Job's soul by the apparently insoluble problem of reconciling God's known justice with the hard facts of experience. But in spite of all waverings he held to his belief that justice would be done him by God in the end (19:23–27), and the final words of his last long speech express his conviction both of his own innocence and of God's justice (31:35–37).

f At this point the argument is taken up by a young man named Elihu who has been in the circle of listeners following the debate. He is angered that his elders have been unable to vindicate God's justice and convince Job of his guilt. He is self-confident and verbose but capable of real poetic expression. Though he does not substantially further the debate, he does give emphasis to one important point which the friends had merely touched on, namely that suffering and calamity are not only vindictive but also medicinal. By them God opens the ear of the sufferer to withdraw him from his evil ways (36:7–12 ; 33:14–28). By his final description of the power and majesty of God manifested in storm, lightning and thunder, which he depicts as actually raging as he speaks, Elihu prepares for the coming of God himself.

g The Almighty himself appears in a storm to end the debate. It might have been expected that he would reveal to Job, who is directly addressed, the decision taken in the heavenly council to try his virtue, and so by this revelation place his problem in an entirely new light. But it is not for man to know the secrets of God's plans. It is for man to acknowledge not only the power but above all the wisdom of God, and therefore humbly to accept his government of the world and to submit trustingly to his providence even though it surpasses his puny understanding. The divine discourse is devoted accordingly to driving home the lesson of God's power and wisdom as manifested in the creation of the world, in the marvels of light, rain, snow and the rest, and of the animal kingdom. Again and again it is brought home to Job that he understands none of these things. How can he, who has not the understanding to explain any of the daily events of nature, expect to understand God's moral government of the world and how dare he set himself up as judge of the rightness or wrongness of that government?

These sobering thoughts restore its equilibrium to Job's fundamentally upright and God-fearing nature. He answers humbly that he has spoken inconsiderately and has no word to add.

h God now resumes his discourse this time to insist on his power and man's impotence. God made the mighty beasts like the hippopotamus and the crocodile, before which man is impotent. It is clear then that God has power to punish the wicked among men even though they appear powerful ; and, if he does not, it is not through lack of strength but for reasons known to himself.

Job thereupon submits, acknowledging God's omnipotence and his own feeble understanding. He repudiates his utterances and declares his repentance.

God finally rebukes the friends for their foolish sayings concerning him but forgives them at Job's intercession. He restores to Job in double measure all that he had. Job is again blessed with a numerous offspring and dies at length in a prosperous and advanced old age.

i Unity and Consistency of the Book—Two questions now arise : (1) whether the book has reached us in the form left by its author, and (2) whether there are inconsistencies between its different elements. The former question is one of literary investigation and does not touch the inspired character of the book as a whole. Any substantial additions, as distinct from insignificant glosses, made to biblical books after they had left the hands of their original authors were made by inspired writers (Dz 784).

If **the prologue** were omitted the dialogue would be in **31** the air and unintelligible. It is clearly necessary for the understanding of the subsequent psychological drama. Whether it was found and taken over by the author is a different question. Its artistic finish as a gem of clear, concise narrative appears decisive against the suggestion that it was a popular tale that passed from mouth to mouth. It has been urged, however, that the problem posed in the prologue is not that dealt with in the dialogue. In the prologue the question is whether the virtue even of the most God-fearing man can be purely disinterested, whereas the problem of the dialogue is whether God's providence can allow an innocent man to suffer. But this dichotomy is unwarranted. The course of the dialogue shows Job's virtue, in spite of outbursts of impatience, to stand the test, and he does not, as the Satan had foretold (2:5), abandon his religion and curse God. The question of the prologue is thus answered in the dialogue. On the other hand the problem of the dialogue is conditioned by the question of the prologue and arises out of it. It is the testing of Job's virtue by unmerited affliction which raises the problem of the suffering of the innocent.

The organic unity of the prologue and the dialogue is **k** further shown by the references in the latter to the former. Reference to the loss of Job's children (1:19) occurs in 5:25 ; 8:4 ; (on 19:17 see comment) ; to his disease (2:7 f.) in 7:5 ; 19:17, 20 ; 30:17, 30 ; to Job's arable land (1:14) in 31:38–40 ; to lightning as instrument of his loss (1:16) in 20:26. Mention of the Satan after the prologue is not to be expected, for he is nothing more than the instrument of God, the supreme ruler of the world. The praise of Job's virtue (1:8 ; 2:3) is not in conflict with Job's admission of such smaller moral failings as are found in all (13:26), and he himself maintains his essential innocence to the last (27:5 ; 31:35–8). The breakdown in his high standard of patience and resignation manifest in the dialogue is not to be wondered at in view of the prolongation of his sufferings, the heartlessness of those from whom solace was to be expected, and the mental torture arising from his inability to comprehend God's dealings with him, running counter as they did to all he had been brought up to believe. The reader must also bear in mind the poet's free use of metaphor in the allusions to Job's calamities. God has removed the crown from his head and his troops had encamped round about Job's tent (19:9–12). See also 16:10–15 ; 22:10 f. ; 30:12–14. The poet must be allowed his traditional licence and not be accused of inconsistency for his use of it.

Job's last speech contains a **poem in praise of wisdom, l ch 28.** This is very loosely attached to its context and as an independent unit can be removed without the creation of an apparent gap. Moreover the last line (28:28), though an integral part of the poem, unduly anticipates Job's final submission to God's providence. It has therefore the definite appearance of an interpolation by a later hand. The poetic artistry of the author of Job would not have allowed the insertion of the poem except as an organic member of the whole work. Every sign of a later addition is presented also by **the m speech of Elihu, chh 32-7.** This too can be excised without leaving a trace of the operation. Elihu is mentioned neither before nor after. No notice is taken of his utterance by Job, who had answered each of the friends, nor by God in his speech, nor in the epilogue. The divine discourse with its address to Job (38:2 ff.) would follow naturally and admirably after the latter's final assertion of his innocence (31:37). The author of Job would have integrated the young man's utterance into his work and not inserted it without adequate connexion. It is true that the description of God's power manifested in the storm (ch 37) prepares the way for the theophany of ch 38, but the conception of this link would not exceed the inventiveness of an interpolator. His purpose seems to have been to emphasize the medicinal function of deserved calamity m as a means of bringing a man back to God. Budde and Peters understand this of the purpose of unmerited suffering to warn a man against the roots of evil within him. They consequently see in Elihu's teaching on suffering a definite advance on that of the dialogue and the high-point of the original author's own doctrine. But in view of passages like 33:17, 27 ; 36:9, it seems clear that Elihu shared the friends' view that all suffering is deserved, and they had at least admitted its correctional value (5:17). The linguistic argument is developed in the larger commentaries.

n The argument is not quite so strong with regard to the poetic **descriptions of the hippotamus and the crocodile** (40:10–41:25). They have the appearance of an addition. God's case is amply expounded and convincingly established without them, and the whole, but especially the conclusion, lacks that application to Job's attitude which the poet's style gives warrant for expecting.

o Without **the epilogue** the work would be incomplete, which must be judged not in the light of Christian ideas about suffering but of those prevalent for so many centuries in Israel. The author of Job and his contemporaries had no thought of rewards and punishments after death (see Sutcliffe, *The OT and the Future Life*). They had a deep conviction however that God as the just ruler of the world must requite men according to their deeds. So far as they knew, this could only be done in this life ; and, therefore, although the author of Job rose to the conception of suffering being inflicted on a just man as a trial, he could not envisage this as a lifelong state. Job had to be restored to prosperity. Indeed the unmerited suffering endured itself called for compensation in order to restore the balance. Hence Job received back his former possessions even in double measure.

p Strange little interpolations are found in 42:3a, 4, words which Job could not possibly address to the Almighty in his now submissive frame of mind and which are taken from God's address to him (38:2, 3b) with parts of 33:1, 31.

a **The Setting of the Story in Place and Time**—It is a remarkable fact that all the persons who take part in the story of Job are non-Israelites. Job's own parentage and tribe are not mentioned. The locality of his home is, however, given as in the land of Hus (*'ûs*), which LXX 42:17b under the name of Ausitis assigns, it seems correctly, to the borders of Idumaea (= Edom) and Arabia. The name of Eliphaz of Teman, the more influential and probably the oldest of the three friends, is Edomite (*cf.* Gen 36:4, 11). Teman was situated in Edom (Am 1:11 f.) and was famous for its wisdom (Jer 49:7), a reputation which suits Eliphaz as Job's principal interlocutor. Bildad of Shuah (the Shuhite) probably came from Edom or Arabia. Sophar's name may mean ' Little Bird ', and Naamah, his homeland, has been plausibly identified with the Arabian Gebel el-Na'âmeh.

b Yahweh, the specifically Israelite name of God, is accordingly avoided in the dialogue as foreign to the speakers. The exception in 12:9 may be due to a copyist's reminiscence of Is 41:20. The other exception in 1:21 is not so easily explained but is possibly due to the words having a fixed form in common use. On the other hand the narrator uses this divine name freely as in 1:6–9 ; 38:1, etc.

c The general setting reflects that of patriarchal times. Sacrifice is offered not by priests, though they are mentioned in 12:19, but by the head of the family. Only the holocaust is spoken of and is offered, contrary to Israelite practice, in atonement for sin (1:5). Vows, known also in patriarchal times (Gen 28:20), are referred to (22:27) here of sacrifices of thanksgiving. And Elihu speaks of seeing the face of God, an expression which implies worship of God at a sanctuary (33:26). So also Job's husbandry, both pastoral and agricultural, recalls that of Genesis (Job 1:3, 14 ; Gen 26:12–4).

d **Historical Nucleus**—Much in the book is clearly not intended to be taken as corresponding closely to **318d** historical fact. The poetic form of the speeches excludes the idea that the reader is given a transcript of the dialogue that passed between Job and the friends. The double scene in heaven with the consultation between God and the Satan is a device to admit the reader to the secret which lies at the root of Job's troubles. The arrangement by which the news of the multiple calamities pours in on the sufferer in quick successive blows is artificially planned to heighten the impression produced by his catastrophic change of fortune. But these elements are not adequate to justify the opinion that Job never existed and is presented merely as a type. The reasons which led the unnamed Rabbi to hold this view are not recorded (TB *Baba Bathra* 15a). The ancients were wont to weave their stories about real personages ; and had Job and his story been the product of imagination, would a non-Israelite have been chosen as the hero ? Moreover, Job is introduced in Ez 14:14, 20 as a man renowned for his uprightness side by side with Noe ; *cf.* Jas 5:11. Even a nursery rhyme like ' Little John Horner ' has its historical basis. And the tradition of the Church has always regarded Job as an historical personage.

The Type of Literature—The prose introduction and e epilogue cannot be used to decide the literary type of the book as a whole. In the form of a story they provide the necessary framework without which the book is not intelligible. The substance of the book is in poetry and comprises the monologues and dialogues devoted to threshing out the fundamental question whether a man may be innocent and yet the victim of calamity. The book, therefore, belongs to the Wisdom Literature characterized, as this is, by the use of human wisdom based on religion, reason, and experience. The book, moreover, is didactic in the sense that the great lesson is meant to be learnt from it, that even great suffering is no proof of antecedent iniquity, but it is not openly didactic in formally propounding the intended lesson. In the same indirect way the book may be said to be hortatory in that it proposes an example, if not of consistent patience, at least of final resignation and humble submission to the divine will.

The adjectives epic and dramatic are sometimes f applied to the book, but it lacks the continuous narrative found in epic poetry, and drama is normally understood to imply not only dialogue but also action, which is lacking outside prologue and epilogue. Neither is the book just a philosophical dialogue. It is a poem, mainly in the form of dialogue, predominantly reflective but with outbursts of passion, set in the frame of a prose narrative. In so far as this study of human suffering establishes the fact of innocent suffering but provides no intellectual explanation beyond the inscrutable will of God, it may be called a problem book.

The Author of Job—According to an opinion recorded g in TB *Baba Bathra* 14b, to St Methodius (PL 103, 1145) and others, the book was written by Moses. Mosaic authorship may have been suggested by the fact that the story recalls the time of the patriarchs and that no one was known as the chronicler of that period except the author of the Pentateuch. There is no plausible case for any other suggested authorship, and we must confess our complete ignorance, strange though it be that the author of this masterpiece of literature should have become completely forgotten.

The wide knowledge manifested in the book and in h particular the deep knowledge of human nature suggest that the writer was at least middle-aged, and his intense sympathy with the sufferings of his hero joined to his interest in the problem they raise was probably won by personal experience of such misfortunes. He was an Israelite and clearly a devout servant of God. The number of Arabisms in the book, commented on already by St Jerome (PL 28, 1081), suggests a home not far removed from the Arabic-speaking world where Hebrew would be likely to make borrowings from that language. This home may therefore have been in

318h Transjordan, not far from the desert with which the poet shows himself familiar. His date will be discussed more conveniently after a consideration of the doctrine embodied in the work.

i Canonicity and Authority—The **canonicity** of Job, which occurs in the Jewish list of sacred books attributed to the 2nd or 3rd cent. A.D. (*Baba Bathra* 14*b*), has never been questioned in the Church except that Theodore of Mopsuestia added an attack on the book to his other errors. His assertions on the matter were condemned by the 2nd Council of Constantinople in A.D. 553 (Mansi 9, 223–5, PG 66, 697 f.). Just before this condemnation, probably in 551, his error was repeated by his admirer Junilius Africanus (PL 68, 17).

j The canonicity of the book, however, does not confer **divine authority** on all that is said in the course of it. What the inspired writer himself asserts is true in the sense intended as is all to which he gives his approval, and he certainly approves of whatever utterance is attributed to God. But the same whole-hearted approval does not extend to all that is said by Job and the other human speakers. Job admits indiscreet talk (39:34) and for this he is rebuked by God (38:2). The friends too are rebuked by God for not having ' spoken the thing that is right before me as my servant Job hath ' (42:7). This neither approves all Job's utterances nor condemns everything said by the friends. The approval and disapproval seem therefore to fall on the views expressed by them respectively on the main topic of discussion. Great caution is consequently required in using the sayings of the human participants in the discussion as dogmatic proofs. That such use is not necessarily excluded however is shown by St Paul's introducing words of Eliphaz with the solemn formula ' It is written ' which is used only of the inspired utterances of Scripture. In the discussion of his problem the author is willing to put into the mouths of the disputants opinions with which he disagrees. By these he intends to emphasize by contrast the truth which he means finally to teach. But no such purpose would be served by the expression of false doctrines on other matters when nothing is said by way of correction. The theologian has therefore good ground for the opinion that other doctrines expressed by the disputants have the silent approbation of the inspired writer.

k Doctrine—As is manifest from the analysis of the book (§ 317*e*), the problem debated is **the suffering of the just,** the friends maintaining the traditional view (15:18) that suffering is always the punishment of guilt and Job asserting that this is not so in his own case. The old simple view dominates Ps 36 (37), which the title assigns to David. Ps 57 depicts the wicked as powerful and prosperous, but its last verse conveys the suggestion that the continuation of such conditions would provoke doubts as to God's government of the world. The psalm may be of the 8th cent. The problem was keenly felt by Jeremias (12:1–4) towards the close of the 7th cent., but he attempts no solution. The doctrine of individual responsibility and retribution is strongly urged by Ezechiel, 6th cent., together with insistence on God's willingness to forgive and forget the iniquity of the repentant (ch 18 ; 33:12–20). The complaints of the people in Mal 3:13–5, 5th cent., though based on mistaken self-righteousness, reveal the continued pressure of the apparent inequality of God's dealings with men. The acute anguish and even religious doubt that this could cause is to be seen in Pss 48 and 72. What is the contribution of our book towards a solution ? It is that suffering and calamity are not necessarily and always the punishment of sin. The upright, God-fearing man may be sorely afflicted as a means of testing his virtue. If his virtue is purely selfish, seeking only God's rewards of piety, it will not stand the strain. Such a man will abandon his service of God as not worth while. The book also emphasizes, as we have seen § 317*f*, the salutary nature of condign punishment as a means of bringing a sinner to a better frame of mind, and thereby emphasizes also God's

willingness to forgive. But it does not abandon the **31** principle of retribution. This could not be, as it is founded on the conviction that God is the guardian of the moral order and the just ruler of the world he has made. And as retribution beyond the grave was as yet unknown to the Israelites, it could only be conceived in terms of this life. Hence Job's prosperity had to be restored and even in greater measure to atone for his unmerited affliction. The progress therefore, though real, is partial. Fuller understanding had to wait for the revelation of the rewards and punishments of the life to come and still more for the example of God Incarnate suffering on earth, himself led as a sheep to the slaughter.

Among **the divine attributes** that which lies at the **l** root of this problem is God's absolute justice. This is the presupposition of the book, though questioned by Job in moments of anguish. God's power is extolled (5:9–14 ; 40:10–41:25) for the lesson to be derived from this account is that of God's absolute control (42:2). Similarly the divine power and wisdom contrasted with man's ignorance and impotence is the theme of chh 38–9. God's mercy in willingness to forgive has been touched on above.

Chief among **the duties of man** on the negative side **m** is the obligation to avoid evil, the sense of which obligation permeates the book. The duty of resignation to God's will and the humble acceptance of his government even when it transcends the comprehension of our puny minds is the lesson inculcated in chh 38–9. A detailed catalogue of man's moral obligations is given in Job's ' negative confession ' in ch 31. Kindness to the weak and the fatherless is stressed and especially noteworthy is the recognition of sins of desire (31:1).

Prominent in the book is the doctrine that **no man is n entirely innocent** before God (4:17 ; 15:14 ; 25:4). This belief could be founded not only on experience but also on the doctrine of retribution. All men suffer in some degree, even the youngest, and therefore all must be in some measure guilty. 14:4 as paraphrased by LXX reflects such a conception : ' Who shall be pure from defilement ? Nay, not one though his life on earth be of a single day.' This is not the developed doctrine of original sin but has in common with it the fundamental element that all mankind lies in some degree under the displeasure of its Creator. Yet from this displeasure our first parents were excluded for they are recorded to have been pleasing to God (Gen 1:31). This same doctrine inspires also Ps 50:7. *Cf.* §§ 321*c*, 324*e*.

The author of Job shares with all OT writers belief **o** in **the survival of man** after death. But beyond this bare fact all knowledge of man's future state was negative ; *cf.* Sutcliffe, *The OT and the Future Life* (59–69). Experience taught that once a man had passed to Sheol, the common abode of the dead (14:13), there was no hope of his returning to this life. This Job recognized (14:12, 14) ; but to read into his statement of this fact a denial of the final resurrection is to make him deny what had never occurred to his mind ; *cf.* § 115*d*.

An argument *a fortiori* to demonstrate the guilt of **p** man at large is based in 4:18 and 15:15 on the fact that God had reason to distrust even his **Angels** and found in them ' folly ' or ' error ' ; see on 4:18 and Knabenbauer. Before they could earn their reward the Angels like man were subjected to a state of probation and not all stood up to the test. Sanchez supposes this to have been a revelation made to the patriarchs, but of this there is no evidence. He also writes on 4:18 that Gentile nations came to know that there are good and evil Angels ' whom they called good and evil *genii* ' from the daily experience of being violently impelled to evil and contrariwise recalled from evil to good. The same experience would be clarified for the Israelites by the story of Gen ch 3. As a sharp distinction is made in Gen 1 and 2 between man and the animals and God created all things good, the Israelites would understand that behind this serpent instigator

9p to evil there lurked as principal agent some other
q unseen and wicked power. Some, as Knabenbauer, have recognized in **the Satan** of Job 1:6 the chief of these evil spirits. But, as pointed out by Ricciotti and Kissane, in Job the name is accompanied by the definite article. It is not yet a proper name but a common noun signifying ' adversary ' or ' opposer ', a sense that it still bears in Mt 16:23. It is in 1 Par 21:1 that the noun first appears without the article as the proper name of one instigating to evil. In Job the Satan does not instigate to evil. He had his place in the court of heaven with the other Angels, and his function, which is analogous to that of our *advocatus diaboli* in processes of canonization, is to test the reality of men's virtue. The good Angels are called ' the Holy Ones ' (5:1 ; 15:15, as in Ps 88:6, 8 and Zach 14:5). Their power of intercession is recognized in 5:1.

r Date of the Poem—In the course of the centuries the date has been assigned to various periods from that of Moses (§ 318*g*) to early Ptolemaic times, as by Peters. Recent opinions range from this latter date to the 7th cent. as upper limit. To cite a few examples, Budde and Buttenwieser give *c* 400, Dhorme 500–450, Kissane between 538 and the formation of LXX with preference for a higher date within these limits, König soon after 597, Ricciotti the reign of Manasses. The argument from literary borrowings is uncertain as apt to be coloured by subjective impressions ; and different minds come to contradictory conclusions as to who is source and who is borrower. The allusion to the captivity of kings and priests (12:18 f.) brings us down at least to the capture of Samaria, 721. Priests and others were then transported to Assyria (4 Kg 17:6, 28), but the king may have been killed in the siege. And the allusion suggests rather the triple deportation of Joachaz, Joachin and Sedecias (4 Kg 23:33 ; 24:15 ; 25:7). This gives a date after 587. The nature of the problem discussed leads to a date at least as late (*cf.* § 318*k*) as do the mention of ' the Satan ' and the designation of the Angels as ' the Holy Ones ' (*cf.* § 318*q*). The allusion to the danger of worshipping the sun and moon (31:26–28) does not favour a date long after the return from the Babylonian exile in 538, and the merit of the work as a masterpiece of Hebrew poetry suggests that it is unlikely to date from the later period of literary decadence.

9a Ancient Near Eastern Parallels—Suffering is too universal an experience not to have presented a problem to the reflective minds of other nations, and wherever literature flourished it was inevitable that this theme of the misery of man should attract the attention of writers. From the theological point of view there is no reason why the sacred writers of Israel should not derive certain of their thoughts and expressions from pagan models. As a question of literary criticism more is required to prove dependence than community of theme if this is one common to mankind the world over, and, in this case, even identity of certain thoughts and expressions is not conclusive. The nearest ancient parallels to the book of Job are the Egyptian *Colloquy of a World-weary Man with his Soul* and the Babylonian poem *I will praise the Lord of Wisdom*. The latter describes the misery of an innocent sufferer and his eventual restoration to health by Marduk. Both may be read in H. Gressmann ATAT 25 ff. and 273 ff. The contents of neither work suffice to prove dependence but, as Peters 55* points out, the probability that the Egyptian poem was known to the author of Job is suggested by the similarity of Job's ' Negative Confession ' in ch 31 to the famous document in *The Book of the Dead* 125 and the author's familiarity with Egypt. The study of the Babylonian work by S. Landersdorfer, O.S.B., *Eine babylonische Quelle für das Buch Job*, 1911 (= BS 16, 2) leads to the conclusion that there is no evidence even of indirect dependence.

b Text and Versions—The book employs many words which occur nowhere else in the OT. Many are explicable only by reference to Accadian, Aramaic or Arabic. This difficult vocabulary was not favourable

to the accurate transmission of the text, which contains **319b** a number of erroneous readings. Some have rated **the value of the traditional text** unduly low, and it has been calculated that only about a third of the verses have escaped the attention of ' correctors '. It is now recognized that most of these emendations rested on a misunderstanding of the sense due to a lack of appreciation of the author's style or to a rejection of words which subsequent investigation has shown to be original. Peters' verdict in agreement with Budde's is that the state of the text is fairly good, but he rightly adds that the emphasis should be laid on the adjective. My own study of the text has led me to the conclusion that many of the erroneous readings are due not to copyists but to the labour of some early editor or editors. The original text made little or no use of *matres lectionis* and omitted *aleph* when silent. Early attempts to clarify the text by the addition of these elements were sometimes based on unlucky guesses as to the meaning with the result that the author's thought was quite distorted.

As to **the order of the text** an extreme view was taken **c** by Buttenwieser and Torczyner, who worked on the assumption that an editor had composed the book as best he might from torn fragments. All, however, are in agreement that there are certain dislocations. Some smaller examples may be explained as accidental omissions inserted in the margin and then later transferred to a wrong position in the text. Thus it seems certain that Job's final speech ends with 31:37 and that vv 38–40 should come after v 32. Another cause of dislocation appears to have been the desire of an early editor to put more ' orthodox ' sentiments into the mouth of Job. Thus 27:13–23 now occurs as part of Job's discourse, but its tenor is the reverse of all that Job has been maintaining and represents the attitude of the friends. The passage is probably part of Sophar's third speech, which is entirely absent from the received text.

Defective readings of MT may be remedied by the help **d** of the ancient versions, the evidence of which however demands cautious handling. **LXX** is free in its treatment of the text. It is often paraphrastic and abbreviates liberally. It is reckoned to be shorter than MT by about one-fifth. In general the omissions become more numerous as the book proceeds ; and the explanation seems certainly to be that the translator judged the book to be unduly diffuse and shortened to his own taste.

Caution is also needed in the use of **the Latin Vulgate** **e** for textual emendation. St Jerome himself warns his reader that he is at times paraphrastic (' Haec translatio . . . nunc verba, nunc sensus, nunc simul utrumque resonabit ', PL 28, 1081). He took particular pains over the task on account of the recognized difficulty of the book (' Obliquus etiam apud Hebraeos totus liber fertur et lubricus ', *ibid.*) and even incurred considerable expense in hiring the services of the foremost Palestinian Rabbi of the day. Peters thinks that Jerome doubted whether this teaching had been of any help (p 89). But Jerome's words are only a modest refusal to praise himself—' It is not for me to say how much I profited by his instruction ' (' cujus doctrina an aliquid profecerim, nescio ; hoc unum scio, non potuisse me interpretari nisi quod antea intellexeram ', *ibid.*).

Poetic Form—The verses composing the dialogue are **f** normally composed of two members and are called distichs. Not a few, however, are tristichs and have three members. It is the modern custom to print the two halves of a verse on the same line, with the result that the tristichs appear to upset the balance and have consequently been unwarrantably questioned or rejected by some critics. With the separate members of each verse written in a column each under the preceding this apparent lack of balance disappears.

The principle governing the verses is not metre but **g** **rhythm,** and St Jerome's statement that the verses are written in hexameters is correct only in the sense that

319g the normal number of stressed syllables in each distich is six. These stresses are usually divided equally over the two halves of each verse. The number of unstressed syllables is unimportant provided it does not interfere with the movement of the verse ; and the number of beats may depart from the norm and fall to two or rise to four. There is no fixed law and the arbiter is the ear. This may be illustrated in a lower plane of composition by the unstudied rhythm of the English lines : ' So they húnted and they hóllo'd till the sétting of the sún ; And they'd nóught to bring away at lást when the húnting day was dóne.' Some maintain that the individual discourses, at least in part, were written as strophes, but the case is not yet demonstrated.

h Structure of the Book :

Prologue chh 1-2.

Job's monologue ch 3.

First round of the debate : Eliphaz chh 4-5 ; Job chh 6-7 ; Bildad ch 8 ; Job chh 9-10 ; Sophar ch 11 ; Job chh 12-14.

Second round of the debate : Eliphaz ch 15 ; Job chh 16-17 ; Bildad ch 18 ; Job ch 19 ; Sophar ch 20 ; Job ch 21.

Third round of the debate : Eliphaz ch 22 ; Job ch 23-24:17, 25 ; Bildad 25:1-6 ; 26:5-14 ; Job 26:1-4 ; 27:1-6, 12 ; Sophar 27:7-11, 13 ; 24:18-24 ; 27:14-23 ; Job chh 29-31.

Hymn in praise of Wisdom : ch 28.

Interlude introducing Elihu : 32:1-6a ; his address : 32:6b-37:24.

God's first speech : 38:1-39:32 followed by Job's confession 39:33-35.

God's second speech : chh 40-41 followed by Job's submission 42:1-6.

Epilogue : 42:7-16.

i Note on Translations and Commentary—On account of the state of the Hebrew text and the number of emendations required it would be beyond the scope of this volume to indicate in every case the reading adopted. The reader will be able to supply these for himself or from the references given. Not all the readings followed or explanations given are certain, but reasons of space, as a rule, preclude the discussion of other views. It is hoped that the analysis of the speeches will facilitate the understanding of the debate.

320a I 1-5 Job's Uprightness and Corresponding Prosperity —Job is introduced as someone previously unknown to the reader, as in our way of beginning a story with ' Once upon a time '. He was a man of a profoundly religious character, whose reverence for God influenced all the actions of his life. His fear of any offence against God was such that he even offered expiatory sacrifices for the sins his children might have committed. The measure of his virtue is indicated by the vastness of his wealth in accordance with the prevalent idea that virtue and vice met with fitting retribution in this life.

b 1. The land of Hus is mentioned also in Lam 4:21 and Jer 25:20 (here with the article, hence the form ' Ausitis '). It lay to the east of Palestine (3), contained land suitable for pasture (3) and for agriculture (14). Job's property lay near a town (29:7) but near enough to the desert to be a prey to raiders (15, 17). Job himself was ' *faultless* and upright, *a religious man* and *averse to* evil '. The Heb. expression for ' religion ' is ' the fear of God '. 2. His virtue was rewarded by a numerous offspring (*cf.* Ps 126:3 ; 127:3), the number of his 7 sons being the ideal (1 Kg 2:5 [MT ' seven ', DV ' many '], Ru 4:15). 3. The number of those in his service (DV ' family ') corresponded to the vastness of his possessions. 4. On suitable occasions, as after sheep-shearing (2 Kg 13:23-27), Job's sons held a round of feasts for 7 days, each day in the house of one of the brothers. This is mentioned to illustrate their father's extreme abhorrence of evil, to heighten the idea of his prosperity, and to fill in the background **c** for the impending calamity. 5. For fear that his children might have sinned by unworthy thoughts of God (' blessing God ' is a euphemism) Job offered an

expiatory sacrifice for each of them. The previous day **32** he sent and prepared them for the solemnity (in what way is not clear) and early next day offered the holocausts. As head of the family Job was its priest and himself offered sacrifice as did Abraham. In expiation he offered holocausts, for he was not an Israelite. For expiation the Mosaic law prescribed sin-offerings and trespass-offerings (Lev 4-6), but even in that code the expiatory value of the holocaust is expressly mentioned (Lev 1:4). Such God-fearing conduct was nothing unusual in Job's life : ' *Such was Job's regular practice* '. The scene is now set. It was on such a blameless man as this that the most appalling calamities were to fall.

6-12 The Accusing Angel receives Divine Authority d to test Job—The reader is now transported in thought to the divine abode, where God is represented as holding a court surrounded by his Angels as in the vision of Micheas, the son of Jemla (3 Kg 22:19). Job's virtue is of course known to God, but one of the Angels, whose function was to watch the conduct of men and accuse them before God, suggests that Job's good life is based on self-interest. The temporal prosperity God has showered upon him has made it worth his while to be good. God thereupon grants permission to test Job's virtue by destroying his possessions.

6. Just as ' the sons of man ' (Gen 11:5) are men, and **e** ' the sons of the prophets ' are prophets (1 Kg 10:10 ; 4 Kg 2:3, etc.), so ' the sons of Elohim ' are themselves Elohim or supernatural beings (1 Kg 28:13, Ps 81:6). They are not, however, gods but Angels, though the word Elohim came to signify principally God himself. One among them bore the name of the Satan or ' the opponent '. The word was originally a common noun which could be used of any adversary (1 Kg 29:4 ; 3 Kg 5:4 [MT 5:18]). Here it is the appellation of one of the heavenly court whose duty it was to watch men and report to God on their delinquencies and weaknesses. Later it became the name of one who instigates men to commit evil (1 Par 21:1). 7. That God should be said to have enquired of him where he had been is due only to the dramatic necessity of eliciting his reply (*cf.* the divine question in Ex 4:2). 9. ' *The Satan answered Yahweh : " Is it for nothing that Job is religious ? "* ' Job's wealth, he suggests, makes it well worth his while to be good.

13-19 Calamity after Calamity is reported to Job— f The Satan quickly puts Job's virtue to the test, and makes his blows the more stunning by ensuring that they are all reported to Job within the selfsame hour. He chose moreover some festive occasion when Job's children had begun a new round of feasts.

13. The banquets would begin in the house of the eldest brother. If these Sabaean raiders belonged to Sheba in southern Arabia, it would be surprising to find them so far north, but there was an homonymous place in the region of Teyma. 16. ' The fire of God ' was probably a large thunderbolt to judge by the devastation caused. 17. The Chaldaeans or Kasdim were an Aramaean tribe whose eponym Kesed is mentioned in Gen 22:22. They were probably widespread, and Nabopolassar, who made himself master of Babylon in 625, belonged to this people. 19. The destructive wind ' from *across* the desert ' was a whirlwind involving the whole house in disaster.

20-23 Job's Resignation to God's Will—This is one of **g** the most elevated and moving passages in the OT and has inspired countless generations of readers to strive to imitate the patience and resignation of holy Job.

20. That Job is said to have arisen is no indication that he had received the tragic news seated. It is the Heb. mode of introducing decided or energetic action (*cf.* Lk 1:39). In rending his garment Job gave the customary manifestation of profound sorrow (*cf.* Esd 9:3). To pluck out the hair of the beard and head, as did Esdras (9:3), was a sign of uncontrolled grief. To shave the head (*cf.* Jer 7:29) was a more deliberate proceeding, which shows that Job did not fall but

20g ' *prostrated himself* on the ground ' in worship. **21.** When men die, they can take nothing away (Ps 48:18). God, Job implies, has deprived him of his property and family a little sooner than he would have done in any case. The word ' thither ' is difficult, but does not warrant understanding either clause of mother earth. No one reading of ' my mother's womb ' could understand the words except in the literal sense. Contrast ' from the day of their coming out of their mother's womb unto the day of their burial into the mother of all ' (Ecclus 40:1). The phrase is perhaps a loosely conceived paraphrase of ' Dust thou art and unto dust thou shalt return ' (Gen 3:19). **22.** Probably, as in Is 9:20, where the same phrase occurs, ' *Despite all that had happened* ' Job spoke no sinful word.

h II 1-8 Job's Fresh Trial—In a renewed session of the court of heaven the Satan suggests that at least Job's virtue will not be strong enough to endure an attack on his bodily health. He uses the divine permission to strike Job's whole body with a loathsome disease.

2. The Satan's failure to mention Job suggests an unwillingness to acknowledge the falsity of his prediction. **4.** The origin and exact meaning of the proverb ' skin for skin ' is unknown to us. From the context, however, the general sense is clear. A man will sacrifice anything for the integrity of his skin and his life. He would give his skin, if that were possible, to save his skin. **7.** The nature of the disease designated ' a very grievous ulcer ' has been widely discussed. The term *šᵉḥin* connotes inflammation. ' The discharge and the subsequent crusting over of these eruptions are referred to in 7:5. Other symptoms . . . are the maggots bred in the ulcers (7:5), the fetid breath (19:17), the corrosion of the bones (30:17), the blackening and falling off of the skin (30:30), feelings of terror (3:25 ; 6:4c), and by night terrifying dreams and nightmares (7:14 ; *cf.* 7:4)', Gray 23. Dr E. W. G. Masterman writes : ' The type of disease in the writer's mind may have been true leprosy (*Elephantiasis Graecorum*), smallpox (*variola*) or, perhaps more probably, a very extensive *erythema* ' (PEF [1918] 168). **8.** ' scraped the corrupt matter ' : so also LXX. It is not clear whether the word had this pregnant sense, or whether the literal translation should be only ' scraped himself '. The ' dunghill ', lit. ' ashes ', is the *mezbaleh*, as the Arabs call it, to be seen outside oriental villages. The mixture of ashes and burnt dung coalesces into a compact mass, sometimes of considerable dimensions. The suggestion is that Job's state was so appalling that he was unfit to dwell with his fellow-men.

i 9-10 Job's Patience unmoved—That Job is represented as a monogamist is perhaps intended as a further indication of his virtue. He is tempted to evil by his wife as Adam was by Eve.

j 11-13 The Arrival of Job's Three Friends—Some time was required for the news of Job's calamities to reach his friends, for them to arrange a meeting-place, and to travel to Job's home. By the time of their arrival, therefore, the dread effects of the disease had had time to develop. **11.** See § 318a. They came to ' condole with him and comfort him '. **12.** Even from a distance they could see Job on the *mezbaleh*. Among the exuberant oriental manifestations of grief was also the strewing of dust on the head (1 Kg 4:12). **13.** See § 317c. Seven days was the period allotted to mourning for the dead (Gen 50:10 ; Ecclus 22:13).

k III 1-26 Job's First Speech—Job senses a lack of sympathy on the part of the friends, and this bitter disappointment added to his calamities makes him break out into words which manifest the depth of his suffering and misery. After cursing the day of his birth (**3-12** and **16**) he depicts the state of the dead as preferable to that of the living (**13-15, 17-19**). He then poses the question why life is given to the miserable (**20-23**) and suggests the application of the question to himself by describing his own misery, though only in vague terms. The depth of his present suffering causes him to pass over the years of prosperity and happiness as if they had never been. He paints his life as if it had **320k** never been lit up by a ray of joy. This shows how the prolongation of his afflictions had worn down his spirit and made him forget the sublime resignation to God's holy will which at first inspired the memorable words ' As it hath pleased the Lord, so is it done ' (1:21).

1-12 Job curses the Day of His Birth—1. ' his day ' is **l** his existence. His cursing falls more on the night of his conception than on the day of his birth. The words ' opened his mouth ' introduce a pronouncement of importance. So before the Sermon on the Mount (Mat 5:2). **3.** ' the night *which said* ' : the night is credited with a knowledge no man could have shared. **5.** ' Let darkness and *gloom disfigure* it ; let a *cloud* overspread it ; let *day-dark be its terror* '. Eclipses cause great alarm to peoples ignorant of their explanation. **6.** ' Let *pitch dark* seize upon that night ' : that night is to be relieved by no light from moon or star. **7.** ' be *sterile ; let no joyful cry break in upon it* ' : no human being is to be conceived therein and it is not to hear the joyful welcome of a new-born babe. **8.** ' to raise up leviathan ' : best explained as an allusion to the supposed powers of magicians to render a day unlucky and even to cause a celestial monster to devour the sun and bring about the calamity of an eclipse. **9.** ' Let the stars *of its dusk* be darkened ; let it expect the light *in vain, and let it not gaze upon the eyelashes of the dawn* ' : it is to be an unending night, never to see the rays (eyelashes) of the rising sun. **11.** ' Why did I not *issue from the womb to die, come forth from the belly to expire ?* ' **12.** The father received the new-born child on his knees in recognition of paternity.

13-19 The State of the Dead would be Preferable !— m 13. ' For now I *had lain me down in stillness.*' The conception of death as sleep survives in our word ' cemetery '. **14.** ' With kings and *counsellors of the land.*' The solitudes of DV may well be right. The pyramids built in the desert waste were famous. **15.** The treasure is probably that stored up in their sepulchral homes, here called ' houses ' or dwelling-places as in Is 14:18. **16.** ' untimely birth *that was not* '. **17.** The rest of the weary is conceived as due to the enforced cessation of the activity of the wicked. **18.** ' *So too captives are at ease ; they hear not the cry of the task-master.*' **19.** ' Small and great are there *the same.*' Social distinctions are obliterated in the grave.

20-26 Why is Life given to Sufferers like Job ?—21. n ' *and search for it more eagerly than hidden treasure* '. **22.** ' *who are gladdened by the tomb* [lit. ' cairn '] *and rejoice when they have found the grave* '. **23** is a continuation of the question asked in 20. ' *and whom God has fenced about* '. For the thought *cf.* 19:8. Job's way is hidden in darkness and perplexity and he can find no issue. **24.** ' *Because as food I have my sighing ;* and as overflowing waters so is *my groaning.*' Lit. ' like my food ', for which meaning of the Heb. word *cf.* 4:19 and 1 Kg 1:16. **25.** ' *cometh upon me . . . befalleth me* '. There seems to be no end to his miseries. **26.** ' *I have no peace and no quiet ; I have no rest, but what comes is trouble.*'

IV 1-V 27 The First Speech of Eliphaz—After excusing **321a** his intervention (2) Eliphaz points out that though Job had comforted many in their distress he seems to think that his own case is beyond comfort or remedy (**3-5**). As Job's trust was in religion, he should remember that no upright man ever perished altogether and that such complete and final disaster was always the fruit of previous evil-living (**6-11**). Eliphaz had learnt in a mysterious vision that no man is completely just before God. The inference implied is that all men must expect their share of suffering (**12-21**). Job will find no advocate in his plaint against God (**V:1**) ; it is only the morally insensate who foster irritation at God's dealings (**2-5**). Trouble does not arise outside of man ; it is involved in his very being (**6-7**). The wise man will have recourse to God who is benevolent and all-powerful (**8-16**). Happy the man who submits to God's chastisements as Job would find to his own benefit (**17-27**).

2-11 Job should not despair—3. ' *fortified* many . . . **b**

321b feeble hands '; see G. R. Driver JTS 36 (1935) 295.
5. Not a reproach, but a reminder that affliction is not beyond the reach of consolation. **6.** ' Is not thy religion thy confidence, thy hope the perfection of thy ways ? ' Religion, generally called the fear of God, is here called simply fear. The innocence of Job judged by normal human standards is admitted, and, as God is just, he need not therefore fear the worst outcome of his afflictions. **8.** ' As I have seen, they who cultivate iniquity and sow mischief, do reap them ', i.e. their fruits ; but such Job has not been. **10 f.** Merciless oppressive men, who devour the substance of the weak, are spoken of under the figure of lions. ' Lioness ': in the Heb. another word for ' lion ', perhaps ' adult lion '. **11.** ' The old lion ' . . . the young of the lioness ', the former unable through feebleness to catch its prey.

c 12-21 No Man is really Innocent before God—**12.** ' in secret, and my ear caught its whisper '. **13.** ' in the thoughts caused by visions of the night . . . fall on men '. **14.** ' the quaking of my bones affrighted me '. Cf. Assyrian rābu ' to tremble ' and 33:19. **15.** ' a breath passed '. **16.** ' It stood but I could not discern its appearance . . . I heard a voice in the stillness.' **17.** ' Can a man be just in the eyes of God or pure in the judgement of his Maker ? ' For this use of min cf. 32:2, Num 32:22, and for the doctrine Ps 142:2. As no man is completely just and pure, all men must expect a mead of suffering. The doctrine is based on a conviction of God's absolute justice and of the connexion between suffering and moral evil. Experience shows that all mankind suffers, even babes. Therefore mankind cannot be wholly right before God. Experience showed that the sentence pronounced by God on Adam (Gen 3:17–19) falls on all men. All must therefore be guilty ; cf. § 318n. The words spoken by the voice probably do not extend beyond this verse. There follows a confirmation by an argument a fortiori—even the Angels were not steadfast **d** in goodness. **18.** ' If in his servants he cannot trust and lays wickedness to the charge of his angels.' God's servants are his Angels, whose name both in Heb. and in Gk means ' messengers '. The general sense of the word translated ' wickedness ' is clear from the purpose of the argument to prove that man is not just nor pure ; its exact sense is conjectural. The reference is to the fall of the Angels. As the words are those of a non-Israelite, Sanchez suggests that the existence of good and wicked Angels could become known through the daily experience of impulses to evil and of contrary impulses to turn from evil to good. The author, however, was an Israelite. **19.** ' be crushed like the moth **(20)** between morning and evening '. Man is said hyperbolically to be as perishable and ephemeral as the moth. ' They are broken because . . . ' Eliphaz speaks of premature deaths caused by man's moral foolishness ; cf. 5:2. So in **21** : ' and not through wisdom ', but through folly. **21a** is quite uncertain.

e V 1-5 The Lot of the morally Foolish—**1.** ' to whom of the Holy Ones wilt thou turn ? ' i.e. of the Angels, prayer to whom is attested by this verse. But it is useless to appeal to them with a plaint against God. **2.** ' Vexation . . . indignation slayeth the silly ' : a reference to irrational repining against God's government of men, a fault Eliphaz silently imputes to Job. **3.** A moral fool prospering but only temporarily. ' but suddenly his habitation was cursed ', i.e. by God. So probably ; and in **4-5** which depict the result of the curse, read the present tense. **5b** quite uncertain.

f 6-7 Why Trouble is Man's Lot—**6.** For iniquity does not issue from the soil. Trouble and travail (DV ' sorrow ') are the fruit of iniquity and do not come without cause. The cause is man, who **(7)** is born ' for travail as the sons of the lightning to fly aloft '. ' The bird ' alluded to is the vulture in LXX or the eagle (Dhorme).

g 8-16 Appeal should be addressed to God : his Power and Benevolence—**8.** ' But for my part I should seek after the Lord and lay my cause before God ', in contrast to the suggestion of 1. **10b.** ' sendeth forth water on the face of the fields ', gushing forth from springs in the earth. **11.** ' and the downcast are raised aloft to safety ', in a

metaphorical sense. **12.** ' of the crafty . . . accomplish **3** their purpose '. **13.** ' so that the counsel of intriguers fails through haste '. **15.** ' He saves the ruined man from their jaws.' Oppressors are conceived as beasts of prey ; ' ruined ' is an emendation (Dhorme). **16.** ' The weak recover hope, and iniquity stops her mouth.'

17-27 The Happy Effects of Loyal Submission to God's h Visitation—**17** is an important verse. God's chastisements are for the correction of the evil-doer. **18.** ' He bindeth up the wound he caused.' **19** gives an instance of the common figure of arithmetical progression, here denoting the unlimited extent of divine succour ; cf. A. Bea, S.J., ' Der Zahlenspruch im Hebräischen und Ugaritischen ' Bi 21 (1940) 196 ff. and § 364h. The six evils are enumerated in **20-22**, ' calamity ' and ' destruction ' in 21 f. translating the same Heb. word. **22.** ' At destruction . . . and shalt have no cause to fear the beasts of the field ', which were one of the terrors of the ancients ; cf. Ez 14:21. So far from being in danger of dearth Job, if he is submissive, will find his fields fruitful in virtue of a pact **(23)** with the stones of **i** the field that they will not invade his land. One of the great obstacles to agriculture in Palestine is the stony nature of the ground, not to speak of frequent outcrops of rock ; cf. Mat 13:5 ; 4 Kg 3:19, 25. The wild beasts will respect Job's flocks and will not trample down his crops. **24b.** ' When thou visitest thy pastures, thou shalt find nothing missing.' **25.** This is cold-hearted comfort for a father afflicted by the loss of all his children. **26.** Job shall not die till his life reaches its natural term, when the full tale of his years is completed, just as it is only in the proper season that the shocks of corn are taken up to the threshing floor. **27b.** ' This have we heard [LXX, Syr.] and do thou make the knowledge thine own.' Eliphaz speaks more in the tone of a schoolmaster than of a comforter.

VI 1-VII 21 Job's Second Speech—His vexation of **j** spirit is fully justified by his sufferings **(2-7)**. His only hope now is in death **(8-10)**. He has not the strength to wait for future relief **(11-13)**. His comforters have been as disappointing to him as a dried-up stream to thirsty travellers **(14-21)**. He had not asked for any material aid **(22 f.)** Their reprovings are vain and hard-hearted **(24-30)**. Man's life is a weary bondage and his own a constant torment **(VII:1-6)**. Soon he will be in Sheol, whence there is no return **(7-10)**. He addresses reproaches to God : why does he behave as a warder, as a tormentor, to him **(11-16)** ? Man is so insignificant ; why does not God leave Job alone and overlook whatever he may have done wrong ; he will soon be in the grave **(17-21)**.

2-7 Job's Anguish of Spirit is Fully justified—**2.** **k** ' O that my anguish could be weighed and my calamity be put therewith on a balance ! ' **3.** ' They would outweigh the sands of the sea-shore ! Therefore is it that my words are charged with grief.' **4b-c.** ' the venom whereof my spirit drinketh in ; the terrors of the Lord are ranged against me '. **5.** ' low over his fodder '. Contented animals are quiet ; Job's friends should understand how terrible are the sufferings which wring from him cries of distress. **6.** ' or is there flavour in the white of an egg ? ' : lit. ' in the slimy liquid of the yolk '. So probably. Proverbial expressions meaning that men cannot eat what gives no satisfaction. How much less can Job endure his lot ! **7.** ' My soul refuseth to be quiet ; it is troubled by the sickness of my flesh.' So emended by Kissane.

8-10 Death is his only Hope—**9.** ' May God be pleased **l** to crush me ! ' **10b-c.** ' I should be steadfast in anguish that spareth not, for I have not disregarded the decrees of the Holy One.' In death, which however painful will be a release, Job will have the comfort of knowing that he has been faithful to God's will. In Job's miserable condition and without thought of reward after death this is a sign of profound devotion to God, the Holy One.

11-13 Job has no Strength to wait for a Change in his Condition—Eliphaz had held out the hope of a happy future (5:19–26), but Job's resources of resistance to calamity are exhausted. **11.** ' end that I should prolong

JOB VIII

desire ?' **13.** '*What source of help have I within myself, when care for the morrow is banished from me ?*'

14-23 He is Disappointed of Help from his Friends—14. '*To one in misfortune is due loyal kindness from his friend, even to one who neglects the fear of God.*' Though he were guilty, Job would have his claims ; but these are disregarded by his friends, whom he calls his brethren. **15.** '*My brethren are treacherous as a brook, as the channel of the brooks that pass by.*' They are changeable and not to be relied on. **16.** '*They are darkened by a pall of ice ; the snow heaps up upon them.*' The happy dashing waters are stilled by the frost. **17.** '*When they are heated, they perish ; when the season is warm, they are extinguished out of their place.*' **18.** '*They follow their meandering course ; they make their way into the waste and perish.*' After the description of the streams in winter and summer, this verse gives a general statement. The streams die away in the desert sands (Bi 30 [1949] 68-70). **19.** '*The caravans of Tema are on the watch ; the companies of Saba look for them with hope.*' But when they at last reach what they thought to be a source of water (20), '*Their confidence is confounded ; they arrive thereat and their hopes are dashed*'. **21.** '*Such now have you been to me*' (reading *kēn* for *kî*). And he had not expected from them material aid or physical effort —only sympathy and understanding ! **22.** '*Make me a present, or of your substance make a gift on my behalf*' (23) '*or . . . out of the hands of tyrants*'.

24-30 The Friends' Reproofs are Vain—24. '*and instruct me wherein I have erred*'. **25.** '*How weighty are upright words ! But what avails reproof from you ?*' **26.** '*Is it your mind to find fault with words, or to take the speeches of one in despair as empty air ?*' Let them show sin in his conduct and not just carp at what he says as if there were no meaning in the words of a soul in anguish ! It is clear that their hearts are hard (27) ; '*Even on the fatherless you would cast lots and make profit out of a friend*'. Children were taken as slaves in payment of a father's debts. **28.** '*And now be pleased to turn to me ! I shall not lie to your face !*' Apparently during Job's rebuke the friends had averted their faces. **29.** '*Begin again, pray ! Let there be no unfairness ! Begin again ! My righteousness yet stands !*' **30.** '*Is there unfairness on my tongue, or cannot my palate discern what is pernicious ?*' What he expresses by his tongue is a fair account of the impression received by his palate, the organ of taste being used metaphorically for the power of mental discernment.

VII 1-5 The Life of Man is Hard and the Life of Job Calamitous—1. '*Is not the life of man on earth a soldier's service ?*' The point is not that an army has to fight but that it has to submit to all the hardships of military life. **2.** '*for his wages*'. **4.** '*If I lie down to sleep, I say : When will the day come ? and when I rise, again : When will the evening come ? And I am sated with restlessness till the dusk*' (so after LXX). **5.** '*Rottenness*' of DV may be right, the Heb. '*worms*' (collective singular) being used metaphorically. For actual worms *cf.* 2 Mac 9:9, Antiochus Epiphanes, Ac 12:23, Herod Agrippa : '*filth of dust*' : '*dirty crusts*' referring to the state of his skin produced by his malady. 5*b* is uncertain. '*My skin has cracked and run*' (Dhorme) ; '*my skin hardens, and then runneth (again)*' (Driver). **6.** '*My days have sped quicker than the shuttle.*'

7-10 Job's Life is near its End—7. '*My eye will not again see prosperity*', i.e. he will not again experience it. **8.** '*The eye of him that seeth me will not behold me more ;* thy eyes *will be* upon me, *but* I shall *not be.*' **9.** '*to hell*' : in Heb. '*to Sheol*', the home of all the dead deep under the earth. It is the land from which there is no return.

11-21 Job complains : Why does God torment him ? —Job now (according to some from 7) addresses God directly. **11.** '*withhold my words*', lit. '*restrain my mouth*' ; '*I will utter my complaint in the bitterness of my soul*'. **12.** '*Am I the sea or a monster of the deep that thou dost set a guard upon me ?*' God set limits to the domain of the sea (Gen 1:9). If these limits were overpassed, it would be a disaster for the earth (Ps 103:9).

13. '*My couch will alleviate my complaining*', the effect **322c** standing for the cause. **14.** '*Thou dost.*' **15.** '*strangling ; death rather than my sufferings*', reading *beth* for *mem*. **16.** '*I would not live on*', the word '*ōlām* denoting a future of indefinite length. '*Leave me to myself, for my days are but a breath*' ; lit. '*cease from me*'. **17.** '*dost treat him as something great* and dost set thy *thoughts* upon him ?' The heart in Heb. diction is the seat of understanding rather than of the emotions, and Job is not thinking here of divine love. Job suggests that man is too insignificant for God, as it were, to trouble to keep a watch on his actions. Similarly Ps 8 expresses wonder that God should take thought of man and make him the lord of the visible creation. **18.** '*so that thou dost visit him every morning and test him* **d** *every moment*', i.e. constantly visit and test him. **19.** '*For how long* wilt thou not *turn away thy gaze from me* nor *leave me in peace even for* an instant ?' lit. '*till I swallow down my spittle*', a proverbial phrase used also in Arabic. **20.** '*Had I sinned, what could I do in thy regard ? . . . Why hast thou set me up as thy target ? And why am I become a burden to thee ?*' The Scribes changed '*thee*' to '*me*' to avoid the appearance of irreverence. The actions of puny man cannot harm God ; but in his prosperity Job had offered holocausts in atonement even for possible sins (1:5). In his heart Job knew that God is the just guardian of the moral order. **21.** What good can it do God that I continue to suffer ? Heb. uses the same word for iniquity and its punishment. Both would be removed together ; but Job has no thought of further happiness. He is soon to die, and why cannot he have peace for the brief interval before he goes down to Sheol.

VIII 1-22 Bildad's First Speech—He rebukes Job for **e** casting aspersions on the justice of God (2 f.). If Job is upright and turns to God, his future prosperity will excel that of the past (4-7). This is the wisdom to be learnt from the ancients (8-10). As plants cannot live without water, neither can man without God (11-13). The godless man has nothing substantial on which to rely (14 f.). He may flourish for a time but is like a plant of luxuriant growth that is soon plucked up and forgotten (16-19). As God does not reject the innocent, Job [if he is really such] will again know happy times (20-22).

2-7 Job is Rebuked : the Great Reward of turning **f** **to God in Innocence—2.** Job's language is vehement but idle as the wind. **3.** '*Doth the Almighty distort justice ?*' **4.** '*If thy children have sinned against him, he hath delivered them into the power of their iniquity*', which brings its own retribution : a reference to 1:19. **5.** '*If thou wilt seek earnestly after God. . . .* **6.** if thou art . . . assuredly he will presently bestir himself in thy behalf and restore the dwelling of thy righteousness*' : the home where Job lived in righteousness will be restored to him. Bildad does not believe that Job is innocent, as according to his religious philosophy sin brings suffering and suffering presupposes sin, and he politely hints at his doubt. **7.** '*And thy former estate will have been a small affair and thy later will be magnified exceedingly*' : an unconscious prophecy of the actual outcome.

8-10 Appeal to the Wisdom of the Ancients—8. '*and* **g** *be attentive to what the fathers have searched out*'. Wisdom was known to be matured by long experience, and therefore both age and traditional lore were held in veneration. Our use of proverbs which enshrine '*the wisdom of many and the wit of one*', is an acknowledgement of the same truth. **9.** '*and have no knowledge ; for our days. . . .*'. The shadow is the type of what is fleeting.

11-19 The Fate of the Godless illustrated from Nature **h** **—11.** '*Can the papyrus grow up without moist soil ?*' **12.** '*and not ready to be plucked*' : it provided writing material for the ancients (*cf.* also Ex 2:3, Is 18:2). **13.** The meaning '*hypocrite*' is unsuitable here— '*the godless*'. **14.** '*His reliance is on gossamer and his trust is a spider's web.*' The sense demands something like gossamer. If the godless man has wealth, it is ephemeral and no ground for confidence. **15b.** '*but*

322h *it will not hold firm*'. His house is not the material structure, but his household and property—all that he so confidently relies upon. **16.** '*He is a luxuriant plant in the warmth of the sun, which spreadeth its shoots over its garden-home.*' **17.** '*About a spring are its roots entwined ; on a bed of stones it rejoiceth.*' The plant is one like the vine or gourd with fruit to ripen. Stones placed beneath for the purpose reflect the rays of the sun, increase the warmth and retain it longer at night. So the plant has every advantage, warmth, water, room to grow in a garden. Such happy circumstances may be enjoyed by the godless, but not for long, for (**18**) '*If it is plucked up out of its place, it disowns it, " I never saw thee "*'. **19.** '*Lo, such is the joy of its career, and from the soil another springs up.*' After a brief period of well-being it perishes and is forgotten.

i **20-22 As God's Retribution is Just, Job will yet know Happiness—20.** '*God does not reject the innocent nor strengthen the hands of the wicked.*' Bildad pretends to suppose that Job belongs to the former class ; therefore (**21**) '*Laughter will yet fill thy mouth and cries of joy be on thy lips*'. Read '*ōd* for '*ad*. **22.** The parallelism shows that they who hate Job are synonymous with the wicked. They are not enemies on private grounds, but men who abhor virtue. It is not implied that Job actually had enemies. The sense is hypothetical : ' if any hate thee '.

j **IX 1-X 22 Job's Third Speech**—Job speaks again in the bitterness of his soul. It is useless for man to contend with God for justice ; he is too powerful. This theme Job illustrates by examples of the divine control over nature (**2-13**). [Eliphaz had also given instances but drawn from God's beneficent action (5:9-15).] It would be futile for Job to cite God to show cause for his treatment of him (**14-21**). God treats good and bad alike, or rather favours the wicked (**22-24**). His days have sped by without happiness (**25 f.**). Now it is impossible to put his unhappiness aside, for whatever happens, he will be put in the wrong (**27-32**). If only there were one to arbitrate between him and God, he would speak out fearlessly (**33-X:1**). He would demand to know the ground of the conflict and put forward many considerations against the treatment he experiences, as that he was himself the work of God's hands and loving care (**2-12**). In spite of that God had secret designs against him (**13-17**). Why had he not been allowed to die in the womb ? (**18 f.**) In the little of life that remains to him, let him have peace before he goes down to the land of darkness (**20-22**).

k **2-13 Man cannot maintain his Right against Almighty God!**—2a if it refers to Bildad's statements is ironical. **2b.** '*How can a man be acquitted in conflict with God ?*' **3.** '*If God consents to argue with him,* man cannot answer him one *word in* a thousand.' **5.** The mountains personified are overthrown with such speed and ease that they know nothing of it. **8b.** ' And walketh upon the *high places* of the sea ', when it is beaten up into towering billows. **9.** ' He *made*.' The first three constellations are probably the Hyades (or the Great Bear), Orion and the Pleiades. ' The Chambers of the South ' may be identified with the ' imposing constellation, more brilliant than any other, not excepting Orion, (which) on the charts of today is distributed between Argo, the Southern Cross and the Centaur ' (Schiaparelli 66). This was visible from Palestine in the first millennium B.C., though no longer to be seen from that latitude owing to the fact of precession. **10.** '*His mighty works are beyond comprehension, and his marvels beyond numbering.*' **11.** '*If he moveth by me, I see him not ; if he passeth on, I discern him not.*' God's invisibility is also an obstacle, according to Job's reasoning, in the way of a mortal man's obtaining justice against him. **12.** '*If he seizeth violently, who shall repulse him ?*' (taking away, *e.g.* a man's family and property). **13.** '*God doth not revoke his anger ; under him bow down the helpers of Rahab*', an allusion to the mythological sea-monster or personification of the sea which was supposed to have rebelled to its cost against God (*cf.* 26:12, Ps 88:11,

Is 51:9, where in each case DV has ' the proud one ').
14-21 Futility of Job's attempting to dispute his Case with God—14. ' *How much less can I answer him and make choice of my words in dispute with him.*' **15.** '*So that even with right on my side* I should not answer ; I should make supplication *to my opponent.*' In all this section God is considered not as judge but as the other party to a suit. **16.** '*If I cited him and he answered me, I do* not believe that he *would give ear to* my voice.' Job knows that there is no tribunal before which he can cite God ; but if he could, it would be the worse for him. **17.** ' For he *would* crush me *with ease* ', lit. ' for (the price of) a hair '. This rendering is suggested by the parallelism ' without cause ' ; also where ' whirlwind ' occurs in this book it is spelt with *samech* and not with *śin*. **18.** '*He would not allow me to take breath but would sate me with bitterness.*' **20.** '*If my plea be just, he would condemn me ; if I am innocent, he would prove me crooked.*' **21.** '*I am innocent ; I care not for my life ; I reject it.*' The first clause is probably an accidental repetition of the same words in the previous verse. ' To know ' in Heb. has the pregnant sense of ' know with favour, be kindly disposed to ' (*cf.* Ps 1:6, Mat 25:12 ' I know you not ').

22-24 God seems even to favour the Wicked—22a. ' There is no difference ; therefore I say . . .' **23.** ' If a *scourge bring sudden death, he mocketh at the despair* of the innocent ' ; or perhaps ' at the trial of '. Pestilence, famine and war are scourges which do not discriminate. **24.** Bribes blind judges to the claims of justice. This God allows ; and as it is God who governs the world, Job says that he does it, making no distinction between what God tolerates and what he positively wills.

25-31 Job's Brief Days filled with Unhappiness which he cannot ignore—25. The ' post ' is a runner bearing a message. ' Good ' meaning happiness and prosperity. Job's months of weary suffering (7:3) have made him forget his earlier days blessed with wealth and peace. **26.** ' as reed-built boats ', light and swift which were used on the Nile. ' as an eagle *swooping on the prey* ', lit. on food. **27.** ' If I say : " I will *forget my complaining, I will* change to a smiling face ", (**28**) *I dread all my pains, I know that thou wilt not* hold me innocent.' He addresses God directly. For the change of expression *cf.* 1 Kg 1:11. **29.** ' *I shall be held guilty ; why then do I weary myself in vain ?*' **30.** ' *If I washed myself with snow and cleansed my hands with lye,* (**31**) *thou wouldst* plunge me in filth and my very garments *would* abhor me.' Snow, a symbol of whiteness and purity, was supposed to have special cleansing powers. By a striking figure his very garments are personified.

32-X 12 Were there an Arbitrator Job would speak out —32. ' *Indeed he is not a man like me that I can answer him, that we can come together* in judgement.' **33.** ' *Would that there were one to make award between us, to impose his authority on us both* (**34**), *to take his rod from on me that the fear of him might not terrify me.* **35.** *I would speak out and would* not fear him, *for that is not my way* . . . **X:1** . . . *I would give free vent to my complaining ; I would* . . .' As he is weary of life, in any case he would have no cause to fear. **2.** ' *I would say* . . . " *Let me know wherefore thou strivest against me.* **3.** *Is it any benefit to thee that thou oppressest me and spurnest the work of thy hands and lookest benignly on the counsel of the wicked ?*"' **4.** A suggested but confessedly impossible explanation of God's conduct. Man with eyes of flesh sees only the exterior and may judge amiss. **5.** The meaning may be either ' Are thy days short like those of man that thou must act precipitately for fear of being unable to act at all ? ', or, ' days ' being used as in 7:1 for what fills up the days, ' Dost thou spend thy days in the petty spitefulness which so often occupies the time of men ? ' **6.** ' that thou shouldst inquire after iniquity *in me* and search after sin *in me ?* ' (**7**), *although thou knowest* . . . ?' **8.** ' Thy hands have *formed* me and made me ; *and dost thou after turn and consume me ?* ' (so probably to be emended). He finds this change in God's attitude incomprehensible. **9.** ' Thou hast made **b** me as *of* clay.' An appeal to God to remember the

23b frailty of man, no fit object of sustained persecution. **10.** ' *Didst thou not pour me out like milk ?* ' The verse refers to the formation of the embryo in the womb. **11b.** ' Thou *didst weave* me together with ' ; so in Ps 138:13. **12.** God's visitation may be in love or in anger ; here it is beneficent, preserving Job's life. The most obvious sign of life is respiration ; and accordingly man was said to live by the ' spirit ' or spiration, that is breath, which God breathed into his nostrils (Gen 2:7 ; Ps 103:29). Yet, Job now goes on to say, under these marks of apparent love, there lurked some sinister design.

c **13-17 God seems to harbour a Design against Job**— **13.** ' *Yet these thoughts* thou didst conceal in thy heart ; I know that *this is thy mind.*' This refers to what follows. **14.** ' If I sinned, thou *wouldst set a watch upon me and wouldst not acquit me of my iniquity.*' **15c.** ' *being sated with dishonour and having drunk my fill of affliction* '. **16.** ' *In my weariness thou wouldst hunt me as a lion and again show thy prowess against me* ' (reading *yāgîa*'). **17.** ' Thou wouldst renew thy *enmity* against me (reading '*edyᵉḳā*) . . . and *warlike reinforcements against me.*'

d **18-22 Job again laments his Birth but reflects that soon he will go to Sheol**—**18b.** ' *Why did I not expire* ', adding the negative with LXX. **20.** ' *Are not the days of my existence few ?* ' (reading *ḥeldî*). ' *Let him leave me alone that I may have a little solace.*' **21b.** ' *to the land of darkness and gloom* ', to Sheol, the abode of the dead. **22.** ' *to the land of obscurity and disorder, where the very light is darkness* ' (omitting three words as erroneous repetitions).

e **XI 1-20 Sophar's First Speech**—A flow of language does not establish Job's innocence and must be answered (**2 f.**). If only God would himself speak and put Job to the question (**4-6**). Does Job imagine that he can comprehend the perfection of God (**7-9**) ? He is irresistible and knows iniquity and its workers (**10 f.**). But there is hope for Job. If he will turn to God and put away iniquity, his future will be bright and he will have no cause at all for fear (**12-19**). For the wicked, however, there is no hope (**20**). Sophar, like his friends, assumes Job's guilt, because he sees his suffering and suffering is the chastisement of sin.

f **2-3 Job's Foolish Talk must be answered**—**2.** ' *Is a master of words not to be answered ? Or is a man right because he is eloquent ?* ' **3.** ' *Is thy empty talk to silence men ? And when thou mockest, is none to put thee to shame ?* ' Sophar means that he has been mocking the justice of God.

g **4-6 He wishes that God would himself answer Job**—**4.** ' in thy sight ', in the sight of God. **5.** ' open his lips in conflict with thee '. **6b.** ' his *providence* is manifold ' ; uncertain and by many emended. *Tūšîyāh* seems to mean ' wisdom in planning, prevision, providence, purpose '.

h **7-11 God's Perfection, Omnipotence and Justice**—**7.** ' *Canst thou discover the mystery* [lit. the searching out] *of God ? or reach to the perfection of the Almighty ?* ' **8.** ' *It* is higher ' : the subject is God's perfection. ' Hell ' stands for Sheol (*cf.* § 322b). **9.** ' The measure *thereof.*' **10.** ' *If he seizeth and imprisoneth or bringeth to public trial, who shall repulse him ?* ' (reading *yaḥṭōp* ; *cf.* 9:12 and 11:10b). The meaning is that God is perfectly right when he administers justice whether he chooses to manifest the reasons for his action or not. Job claimed to be innocent, but Sophar is convinced that he is not, though he himself does not know wherein Job's wickedness lay. But God is under no obligation to manifest to all what is the reason for the chastisement he inflicts. This is supported by **11** : ' For he knoweth *men of empty show*, and when he seeth iniquity, *is he not to take cognisance thereof ?* ' The implication is that men may not have seen Job's wickedness, but God has. .

i **12-20 Job's Return to God will spell Prosperity and Happiness**—**12.** ' *A witless wight may get wit when a mule is bred a stallion.*' Neither is naturally possible ; but Job's case is not so hopeless if he will turn to God, as is developed in the following lines. (MT reads : ' a wild-ass colt may be born a man ' ; *cf.* Bi 30 [1949]

70 f.). **13.** ' *If thou dost set thy heart aright* (*cf.* Ps 77:8) and *stretch out thy hands to him.*' **17.** ' *Brighter than noontide shall thy life endure ; the very darkness shall be as the morn.*' Job will have no dark and gloomy periods at all. **18b.** ' *and well protected shalt lie down to* sleep secure ', without anxiety (*sine cura = securus*). The book being distinguished by the number of Arabic words justifies reading the *puʿal* with the meaning the word has in that language. **19b.** ' entreat thy face ' : seek thy favour. **20** is a warning to Job of worse to come if he remains unrepentant. ' and their *one hope shall be to breathe forth the ghost* '. Life will offer no inducement to live.

XII 1-XIV 22 Job's Fourth Speech—Job's friends are **j** no wiser than he and the first-comer could discourse as well as they have done (**2-3**). The just man is mocked and oppressed by the care-free wicked (**4-6**). Even brute creatures know that the strong prey on the weak (**7-8**) and that all this lies in the hand of God (**9-10**). The thing is obvious (**11**). Useless to say that wisdom belongs to the aged, and as for God's wisdom Job suggests that it does not control his power. He gives illustrations of the divine power to humiliate and destroy but says no word to indicate that God has good reason for so acting. The implication is that God's punitive action is unaccountable, and that, therefore, Job's sufferings are no proof of his guilt. **12-25.** Job knows all that the friends know. It is not with them he wishes to plead, but with God. They invent falsehoods in defence of God's action, which the fear of the divine anger should prevent them from doing (**XIII 1-12**). Come what may, Job will plead his cause with God. Indeed, the very fact that he dares to do so is proof of his innocence (**13-19**). Job now addresses God directly. On condition that God refrains from using his overwhelming power against him Job is prepared to be either defendant or accuser (**20-22**). Let God tell him of his iniquity ! And how can God bring his terrors to bear on Job, who is as powerless as a fallen leaf driven before the wind (**23-27**) ? Is a creature so frail as man worthy of God's indignation (**XIV 1-3**) ? How can the defiled be made pure (**4**) ? Let man have peace in his brief life (**5-6**). If a tree is cut down, it may yet flourish again ; but man when dead can never rise again (**7-12**). Job would gladly be hidden in Sheol as a temporary refuge from God's wrath, but God has allowed no hope of new life for man (**13-19**). When God overpowers man by death, he knows no more what was dear to him in life (**20-22**).

XII 2-3 Job laughs at the Friends' Wisdom—**1.** ' *Of a* **k** *truth you are the men who know and with you wisdom will die* ' : MT ' you are the people '. **3.** For the heart as seat of intelligence *cf.* 7:17 ; 10:13.

4-6 The Just are mocked, the Wicked prosper—**4.** **l** ' *A laughing-stock to his friend is he who calls on God and is answered.*' To Job the friends' lack of understanding and pitiless words are no better than mockery. **5.** ' *Misfortune is despised in the thought of men at ease ; for those who stumble there's a blow.*' Job's sad experience has taught him that human nature has little fellow-feeling for the failure and the outcast. **6.** ' *The tents of brigands are at peace and free from care are men who provoke God and think themselves almighty.*' This is perhaps the sense of the last clause, lit. ' and to him who brings God in his hand '. ' Hand ' stands for ' power ' (*cf.* 1:12 ; 2:6). God does not seem to regard men according to their deserts.

7-11 The very Beasts know the Law of the Strong— **m** If the friends doubt the truth of his assertions, let them learn of the beasts. They know that the strong are rapacious and prey on the weak. **8.** ' The earth ' coming between the beasts, the birds and the fishes points to a corruption of the text, which is plausibly emended to ' the reptiles of the earth '. **9.** ' *Who among them all doth not know that the hand of the Lord hath done this ?* ' The knowledge which experience gives them of the fact is hyperbolically extended to include the Creator. On the occurrence of the name Yahweh see § 318b. **11** is a proverbial saying signifying that

323m some things are obvious and patent to all. Job implies that the prosperity of the wicked and misery of the just should be as clear to all as the taste of food, and therefore his own sufferings are no indication of guilt on his part.

n 12-13 The Appeal to Age is Useless—Bildad had appealed to the authority of tradition (8:8-9) as had Eliphaz before him (5:27) on the ground that only time can beget wisdom. In 12 Job ironically quotes a proverb to this effect. He has just shown that some facts are obvious and are known even to the beasts. Wisdom and knowledge, it is clear, are not the exclusive property of old men like Eliphaz. Men attribute wisdom also to God, who certainly ·has power which Job proceeds to illustrate in a way which suggests that it is exercised harshly and not necessarily according to wisdom.

o 14-25 Illustrations of God's Absolute Power over Creatures—14 has no reference to the beneficent action of rain, but only to the consequences of defect and excess, drought and flood. This is in accordance with Job's theme, which is the overruling power of God, not his paternal government. **16b.** ' to him belong both he that goes, and he that leads, astray ', *i.e.* all men according to the Heb. idiom whereby the conjunction of two opposites signifies totality. All are in God's power ; the DV reference to knowledge is out of place. **18.** ' He looseneth the *bond* of kings.' The kings, whose captives he frees, he reduces to servitude. **19.** ' He leadeth priests *barefoot* ', and so in ignominy. This, the only mention of priests in Job, is general in tenor but will have been suggested by the domestic experience of Israel ; *cf.* § 318r. **20.** ' *He turneth aside* the speech of the *trusty* and *depriveth* the aged *of judgement*.' **21b.** ' *and looseneth the girdle of the strong* '. For vigorous action the Orientals must gird up their flowing robes. **22.** ' He discovereth deep things out of *obscurity* and bringeth *forth darkness* into light.' This enigmatic statement interrupts the easy sequence of the passage and probably belonged originally to another context. **23b.** ' *He enlargeth peoples and blotteth them out*.' The last verb is an emendation, with *mem* for *nun*, demanded by the parallelism with 'destroyeth'. **24b.** ' *and causeth them to wander in a pathless waste* '.

324a XIII 1-12 With God Job would speak : the Friends are inventing Falsehoods—3. ' *Howbeit, it is to the Almighty that I would speak ; and it is to God that I desire to address my case.* ' **4b.** ' *and worthless healers, all of you !* ' *i.e.* in their defence, probably, of God's action by the assumption that all who suffer are guilty. **5.** *Cf.* ' Si tacuisses, philosophus mansisses '. **6b.** ' to the *contention* of my lips ', which he forthwith proceeds to utter. **7a.** ' *Is it in God's cause that you speak falsely, and do you . . . ?* ' **8.** ' *Is your motive regard for him, and is it for God you plead ?* ' Lit. ' Is it his face you are lifting up ? ' the idiom meaning to help and comfort a person in distress with bowed head, and so to act out of regard for one, to show partiality. Job means that their line of conduct cannot be pleasing to God. **9.** ' *Will it be well for you when he examineth you ?* ' As they cannot deceive God, they are exposing themselves to an investigation which they would regret. **10b.** ' *if you are secretly partial* ' ; *cf.* 8. **11.** ' *Does not his excellence terrify you ?* ' Lit. exaltation, so majesty, excellence. **12.** ' *Your maxims are proverbs of dust and your answers answers of clay*.' Their sententious sayings are no more weighty than the dust blown away by the first gust of wind, and their replies are moulded as arbitrarily as a potter chooses the form to give to his clay.

b 13-19 Whatever the Outcome, Job will speak out : his Plea is Ready—13b. ' *that I may speak, come what may upon me* '. He has nothing more to lose. **14.** ' *I will take up my flesh in my teeth and lay my life in my hand*.' The first metaphor, which occurs nowhere else (but see on 19:20), signifies the greatest danger, possibly referring to the peril of a body carried by a lion in its jaws. **15.** ' *Although he would kill me, I would not tremble, but would plead my ways in his sight*.' ' tremble ', an emendation by changing the order of *yod* and *heth*,

He would not desist from presenting his cause though **324** he knew that the outcome would be his death. **16.** ' *Rather that would be for my salvation*, for no hypocrite *dare* come before his presence.' The fact that Job wishes to have his case tried before God is itself an indication of his innocence. **17b.** ' *my declaration* ' ; DV ' hidden truths '. **18a.** ' *See now, I have arranged my pleas*.' His case is ready to be heard. **19.** ' *Would anyone contend against me now that I am about to hold my peace and expire ?* ' He has already announced his impending demise (7:21). It would be cruel now to contest his case. Still he is ready to face the issue if God will meet him fairly, as he goes on to explain.

20-28 Job addresses God—20b. ' I shall not *hide* **c** *myself*.' Not that he thought that he could hide himself. The sense is : then will I gladly come before thee. The two conditions follow in **21**. **25** is a question in MT. **26.** As a judge puts his verdict in writing. **26b.** ' and *imputest to me* ', lit. ' makest me to inherit '. He admits some guilt in youth, but this was venial on the ground of age, and the sins of youth are not punished in adult life. **27.** Better in the present tense with MT. **28** is in the 3rd person in MT and does not fit well in this position. It fits better after 14:3. *a* is lit. ' who is like a worn-out water-skin '.

XIV 1-3 Man, Frail and Ephemeral, seems Unworthy d of God's Anger—1c. ' *sated with anxious care* '.

4 Man is by Nature Defiled—' *Who can make pure out* **e** *of defiled ? No one at all.*' According as the preposition is understood as introducing the material out of which the pure is to be made or the source whence it is to be derived, the question means ' Who can make pure man who is defiled ? ' or ' How can man be pure seeing that he is born of an impure source ? ' In either case the underlying idea is that man deserves divine commiseration and forbearance not only because he is physically frail (**1-3**) but also in his nature morally defiled or impure. In the second interpretation this moral defect is explicitly traced to its source in human generation, and in the first implicitly, as the defect is common to all. The root of the doctrine is to be found in the universality of human suffering, even in those who by reason of age or undeveloped reason are incapable of wrong-doing. This universality shows that human nature has somehow been perverted from that rectitude which God intended. This is the doctrine of original sin in germ. The idea may have been fostered by the laws concerning the purification of mothers after childbirth (Lev 12). And there may be allusion here to ' man born of woman ' in 1, where the phrase is used only to stress the frailty of man's origin. For the moral use of the two words (*cf.* 17:9 ; Is 6:5). DV with Vg paraphrases and takes ' one ' to refer to God. The negative answer of MT refers only to men. *Cf.* § 318n.

5-6 Man's Brief Life calls for Peace—5a. ' The days **f** of man are *decreed*.' Their number has been appointed by God. **6.** ' *Take thy gaze from off him and forbear, till like a hireling he acquit himself of his day's task*.' God's gaze in anger is thought of as a burden on man. For the meaning of *rāṣāh* see Dhorme. The commoner meaning followed by Driver-Gray ' till he can enjoy, as an hireling, his day ' is against the concept of the hireling given by Job 7:1, and the day is the labour of the day, figurative of the life of man.

7-12 A Felled Tree has Hope, but not a Dead Man— g 8b. ' its stock is *dying in the soil* '. **10.** ' *But a man at death wastes away ; he expires and is no more*.' MT and Vg ' where is he ? ' by change of *waw* to *nun* gives ' is no more ', which better suits the context and poetic style of the passage. *Water may fail from the sea and a river become arid and dry* (**12**), *yet man . . .* '. Even if the impossible should come to pass in nature, for man once dead there is no rising again to this life.

13-19 Job would take Refuge in Sheol, could it be for h a Time only—13. ' *O that thou wouldst lay me by in Sheol*.' **14.** ' *If a man could die and live again, all the days of my service I would wait* until my *relief should come*.' On the impossible supposition considered Job would patiently bear his lot, which is expressed in terms of

24h military service. **15.** Still conditional : ' thou *wouldst call* ', etc. **16.** ' *For then* [on this supposition] *thou wouldst count my steps* [with loving care] *and wouldst not keep watch for my sin* ', *i.e.* to catch me in sin, as he accuses God of now doing. **17.** Still conditional : ' *My transgression would be* sealed up ', etc. Job does not claim to be entirely innocent, but denies that his wrongdoing has been such as to merit his present affliction. But whatever his sin, it would then be hidden away, forgotten and forgiven. **18-19.** But all this is on the supposition of the impossible. Unlikely things can come to pass over the ages, but no matter what the space of time allowed man once dead can never return to life. ' A mountain *may fall and crumble and a rock be* removed out of its place.' These are conceivable happenings. A rock may slowly wear away and cease to be where it was. ' *But the hope of man thou hast destroyed.*' **20.** ' *Thou overpowerest him for ever and he passeth away* ' in death.

i 21-22 Sad State of the Dead—The Hebrews had received no revelation about the condition of the dead, and their conceptions about it were negative. They knew that after death men are deprived of all that belongs to the state of the living ; and what is said of the dead is to be understood of this condition of deprivation of the enjoyment and knowledge of the living. Positive knowledge of the state of the dead was not conceded to the Hebrews till the last centuries before the Christian era ; *cf.* Sutcliffe, *The Old Testament and the Future Life*, ch 7. **21.** ' *His sons are in honour but he knows it not ; they become of no account, but he perceives it not.*' **22.** ' *Only for himself is his flesh afflicted ; only for himself doth his soul grieve.*' The thought is expressed with poetic licence. It was not imagined that the body in the grave had the power of feeling. The personal part of man, that which enables a man to speak of himself as ' I ', is described as going down to Sheol (Gen 37:35). On this sad note Job ends his speech. He knows of no hope for man once death has separated soul and flesh. This is important for the right understanding of the subsequent development of the discussion.

25a XV 1-35 The Second Speech of Eliphaz—Job is not as wise as he thinks, for wise men do not use empty language (1f.). Indeed, his words are blasphemous (4). They are inspired by his guilt and are a self-condemnation (5 f.). He has no monopoly of wisdom (7-10). Pride incites him to speak against God (11-13). No man is innocent—least of all one as corrupt as Job (14-16). Eliphaz, from his personal experience (17) and from traditional lore (18 f.) sets forth the retribution which wickedness brings on men (20-35). He leaves it to be understood that Job is reaping the harvest sown by his own wickedness. His tone is far more severe than in his first speech, in which he had held out the hope of recovery if Job would turn to God.

b 1-10 Job has no Monopoly of Wisdom : in fact his Words are Foolish and Blasphemous—**2.** ' *answer with windy knowledge and fill his belly with the east wind ?* ' The windy knowledge is contemptuously described as conceived in the belly, not in the heart, the seat of understanding. The east wind is chosen in parallelism as being oppressive and noxious. **3.** ' *Arguing with profitless words and speeches which avail him not ?* ' **4.** ' *Moreover, thou makest religion void and doest away with pious consideration* ', lit. ' with consideration before God '. Job is not considering his calamities in a proper religious spirit. ' Fear ' stands for ' religion ' as in Eliphaz's first speech (4:6). **5b.** ' *and thou choosest the tongue of the crafty* '. **6.** ' mouth *condemneth* . . . lips *testify against thee* '. **7.** ' *wast thou brought forth* '. Wisdom is conceived as belonging to the ancients, and the first man was nearest to the Wisdom that was with the Lord in the work of creation and was brought forth before the hills and the mountains (Prov 8:25). **8b.** ' *dost thou confine wisdom to thyself ?* ' **10b.** ' than thy *father* '.

c 11-13 Job's Words instigated by Pride—**11.** ' *Are divine consolations too meagre for thee, and words spoken gently with thee ?* ' Eliphaz refers to the consolation **325c** offered by himself, as based on his knowledge of divine things and as the privileged recipient of the mysterious message (4:12 ff.). **12.** ' Why doth thy heart *carry thee away, and why are thine eyes exalted ?* ' ' Exalted ' with LXX ' as if . . . things ' is an epexegetic addition. **13a.** ' that thou *dost turn thine indignation against God ?* '

14-16 No Man is Innocent, certainly not Job—Eliphaz **d** repeats the thought he had expressed before (4:17-19), but adds a bitter attack on Job. **15.** ' *Lo ! in his Holy Ones he putteth not trust.*' The parallelism suggests that the heavens stand metonymically for the Angels who dwell there. However, the material heavens themselves are a symbol of purity in Ex 24:10. For the doctrine see on 4:18. **16a.** ' How much more *one* abominable *and corrupt !* ' He means Job.

17-35 The Normal Lot of the Wicked—By describing **e** the misery of the wicked Eliphaz leaves it to be understood that as Job is suffering great misery, he must be wicked. **17.** What he has to say is the fruit of his experience, and also traditional lore, for it is (18) ' *what the wise profess and proclaim as the teaching of their fathers* '. **19** carries the tradition back to Abraham, Isaac and Jacob, to whom ' *the land* ' was given (Gen 12:7 ; 26:3 ; 28:4). They lived a nomadic life removed from possible contamination by foreign people. **20.** ' The wicked man is *tormented* all his days and *few* [*cf.* Eccles 2:3] *are the years allotted to the tyrant*.' **21b.** ' *the destroyer will come upon him* '. **22.** ' *He has no confidence that he will escape from darkness but (feels himself) marked out for the sword.*' Darkness, a metaphor for calamity (*cf.* Is 9:2). After death by the sword (23) ' *He is cast away as food for the vulture ; he knoweth that his calamity is determined.*' Read *nōdād*, *'ayyāh*, *pîdô*. **24.** ' *The day of darkness terrifies him ; tribulation and distress encompass him.*' So with different verse-division. **26.** ' *He charges against him like a foe armed with his thick-bossed buckler.*' **27.** Corpulence among some nations as among the Chinese is considered a sign of prosperity. In the Hebrew view it makes the mind gross (Ps 118:70 MT) and inclines man to neglect God (Deut 32:15). **28.** To make them his own he is ready to ravage and destroy the land of others. **29c** is quite uncertain. **30c.** Probably to be emended : ' his buds shall be carried away by the storm ' (*cf.* Dhorme). **31.** ' *Let him not be led astray and trust in delusion for delusion shall be his gain.*' **32.** ' *His shoots shall wither before their time and his fronds shall not flourish* ' (*cf.* LXX, Syr.). **33.** ' *He shall drop his grapes unripe like a vine and cast his blossom like an olive tree.*' Lit. ' treat with violence ' and so drop prematurely. **34.** ' the *ungodly* ', DV ' the hypocrite '.

XVI 1-XVII 16 Job's Fifth Speech—All that he has **f** heard is empty talk signifying nothing. Were their positions reversed, he could have said it all himself (1-5). On his side neither speech nor silence gives relief (6). Eliphaz and the others have treated him cruelly. He turns on them and calls them wicked (7-10). When he was at peace, God crushed him, made him a target for his arrows, though there was no wrong in his dealings (11-17). His case calls for vengeance ; and God in heaven, though his persecutor, is his witness. If only there were a court where man's case against God could be tried ! But Job's days are nearly at an end (18-XVII:1). Job then proceeds, in loosely connected and often highly obscure sentences, to dwell upon his unhappy state (2, 6 f., 11) and the folly of his friends (4, 10). Again he ends on a note of hopelessness : nothing awaits him but the corruption of the grave and descent to Sheol. No hope or prosperity can accompany him there (13-16).

2-5 The Friends are Troublesome Comforters—**3b.** **g** ' *or what ails thee that thou must speak ?* ' : as if Eliphaz suffered from some disease that caused a flow of words. **4.** ' I also could speak like you, *were you in my condition.*' This verse and 5 in DV correspond to 4 in MT with the result that all subsequent verses of this chapter in DV are numbered one higher than in MT. **5.** ' *I could join words together against you and could* . . . (6), *I could* . . . *and not withhold the solace of my lips* ' (*cf.* LXX,

325g Syr.). Were the situations reversed, Job could treat them to the same sort of talk he had had to endure from them.

h **7-10 Violence of the Attack on Job**—It is disputed who is the author of the attack. Driver-Gray attributes the hostility to God, Dhorme says vaguely ' an enemy '. Job appears to speak of Eliphaz and his friends, which would explain the passage from singular to plural. **7.** ' But . . . do ? ' is added by Vg–DV to ease the transition. **8.** ' But now an envious man has exhausted me ; all his band seizes upon me ' : Dhorme's conjecture. **9.** ' *He has become a witness and stood against me ; my calumniator deposes against me* ' : cf. Dhorme. **10.** ' *His wrath hath rent and treated me with hatred ; he hath gnashed his teeth against me ; my enemy whets his eyes against me.*' **11c.** ' *united they have their way against me* '.

i **12-16 God's Attack on Innocent Job**—**12a.** ' hath *handed me over to* '. Job does not spare his words against the friends. Eliphaz, the last speaker, is the unjust man, and the other two are the wicked. **13.** Job's metaphors here and in 14 f. are strongly worded. **14.** ' *His archers have* compassed me around . . . poured out my *gall* ' ; cf. Lam 2:11. **15.** ' *He hath* breached me with breach upon breach ; he rusheth against me like a warrior '. **16b.** ' *I have plunged my horn in the dust.*' A metaphor for complete powerlessness and prostration as the elevation of the horn is of power and victory (cf. Ps 148:14). **17a.** ' *is reddened* '. **18.** ' though there is no injustice in my hands and my prayer is pure '. Sacrifices and prayers are impure and unacceptable to God when offered by persons whose hands are stained by blood or who are guilty of other crimes. The hands were intimately connected in thought with prayer on account of the practice of praying with outstretched hands (3 Kg 8:22).

j **19-XVII 1 Job is Innocent and soon to die**—**19.** Omit ' in thee '. Another strong metaphor—Job speaks as if his death were by murder. Blood unjustly shed on the ground cried to God for vengeance (Gen 4:10). If covered over its voice is poetically conceived as stifled. Job's cry is to go straight to God and not find a lurking-place on the way. In spite of all he has said of God's attacks upon him, Job knows in his heart that God is both faithful and just. His mind is torn between his experience and his faith. The latter now prevails and he thinks of God as his vindicator and faithful witness. **20b.** ' he that *can depose for me* is on high '. **21a.** ' *May my wish come to pass.*' So with LXX. He longs for his innocence to be vindicated by God. **22.** ' *O that mortals could try their case with God, even as a man does with his neighbour !* ' So with Syr. **23.** ' For short years *are to come and I shall go by a road whence there is no return.*' **XVII:1.** ' *His indignation has destroyed* my days and only the grave remaineth for me.' Read *rûḥô*, pi'el for pu'al, and *ne'ezbû*. MT ' graves for me ' is not an expression that a Hebrew would have used to express the thought, and MT ' my days are extinguished ' not only is in conflict with 16:23 but uses a verb the authenticity of which is doubtful.

k **XVII 2-12 Various Reflections on his State**—**2a.** ' *Of a truth I am the object of mockery.*' **3.** ' *Lay by, pray, my pledge with thee, for no man will go surety far me.*' No man will go bail for Job's innocence and his only hope is in the sure knowledge of God which can give a pledge in his favour. Again the appeal from God whom he thinks to persecute him to God whom he knows to be the faithful guardian of men. **4.** If the friends had an understanding heart, they would not doubt of his uprightness. They shall not be victorious in their attack upon him. **5.** ' *For a portion one denounces friends* and the eyes of his children fail.' Apparently a proverb about the retribution which falls on infidelity and treachery. The sense of the solidarity of the family was strong among the Hebrews. The friends are left to take the lesson to heart. **6.** Omit ' as it were ' and read ' peoples '. The knowledge of Job's case has spread beyond the confines of his country. ' *Men even spit in my face* ' ; probably another strongly-worded

metaphor. **7b.** ' *my limbs are wasting away like a* **325** *shadow* ' ; read *kālim*. **8b.** ' the innocent *moved to indignation against the godless* ', i.e. seeing the unmerited suffering of the guiltless and the contrasted state of the wicked. **9.** ' but the just man . . .' There is no contrast between the classes mentioned in 8 and 9, the synonyms being chosen for variety. The upright are astounded but not scandalized. **10.** ' *Howbeit, do ye all turn and come, pray.*' **11.** ' My days have passed away *in loathsomeness ; the desires of* my heart are dissipated.' So a conjecture of Beer's ; MT seems certainly corrupt. **12.** ' They *turn night into day—light is near to darkness* ', reading *minni*, an Arabic use of the preposition justified by the Arabisms which characterize this book. The allusion appears to be to Sophar's prediction in 11:17, the thought of which is paraphrased in 12b with the meaning that Job's present gloom will soon give place to light.

13-16 Death excludes all Hope—**13.** ' If I await *Sheol* **l** *as my dwelling*, if in the darkness I *spread my couch* (**14**), *to corruption I call* " Thou art my father " and to maggots " My mother " and " My sister " (**15**), where is then my *hope* and who *shall see my prosperity* [with LXX] ? **16.** *Will they descend with me* into Sheol or shall we go down together to the dust ? ' The parallelism to ' maggots ' is a sure guarantee of the meaning ' corruption '. In 16 read *habbᵉyāḏî* and *nēḥāṯ*. This is Job's answer to what he considers Sophar's facile promise. He has no hope and will never see prosperity again.

XVIII 1-21 Bildad's Second Speech—Job misuses **32** words (2). He even likens the friends to dumb beasts (3). Job must not expect to be treated differently from the rest of the world (4). What befalls men who act wrongly is described at length (5-21). The sufferer is tacitly invited to draw the conclusion that he falls under the same condemnation.

2-4 Introductory Remarks—**2.** ' How long will you **b** *put fetters on* words ? ' ' Fetters ' as the Assyrian *qinṣu*. Job is guilty of misusing language. If he will be sensible, further discussion will be possible. **3** refers to 16:10. The friends cannot be expected to carry on the exchange of ideas if Job is to treat them in this fashion. **4a** is taken by DV as a vocative, but this is not the natural meaning of the words, which read like an incomplete sentence. **14a** seems out of its context and probably belongs here : ' *he who rends himself in his fury has his assurance torn from his tent* '. For the proverbial form cf. Prov 17:5. Job had accused Eliphaz of rending him (16:10), but Bildad suggests that it is Job whose fury resembles that of a maddened beast. The ' assurance ' is all that in which a man trusted, all that gave him security. He finds himself ruined. **4b-c.** Job seems to expect treatment different from that common to mankind at large. But he falls under the same law of retribution.

5-21 The Law of Retribution for the Wicked—**7.** The **c** firm rapid stride congenial to his strength shall become cautious and hesitating on account of the pitfalls and snares which beset him. **8.** ' *shall* thrust . . . and walk onto *a pitfall* ', covered over by earth on crossed sticks, such as are used for entrapping animals. **9.** ' His heel shall be caught in a snare ; *a gin shall seize upon him.*' **11b.** ' and shall drive him at the heels '. **12b.** ' and let disaster be ready for his stumbling '. **13.** ' *His skin shall be consumed by malady ; the firstborn of death shall devour his limbs* (**14b**) *and shall conduct him to the king of terrors.*' In *a* read niph'al and *biḏway* (Dhorme) ; others, however, perhaps rightly, omit as dittography. The firstborn of death is pestilence or the like ; and the king of terrors is a mythological allusion to the ruler of the underworld. **14a** after 4a. **15a.** ' *They who are none of his shall dwell in his tabernacle.*' **16b.** ' *and above his branches shall be withered* '. **18.** The subject is indefinite ' they shall ', equivalent to the passive. **20.** ' They that went before ' would be the departed in Sheol ; but this would conflict with the common conception expressed in 14:21. ' *They of the west . . . they of the east* ', that is, all mankind (cf. 23:8). The points of the compass were taken facing the rising sun ; hence the east is in front and the west behind.

XIX 1-29 Job's Sixth Speech—He again rebukes the friends for their heartlessness (2-3). If he had been guilty of some fault, it would, after all, be his own affair ; but they should know that all his trouble has come from God (4-6). He again describes his pitiable condition (7-20). Then his tone changes and for the first time he appeals for compassion and sympathy, for he has been struck by the hand of God (21 f.). He would fain have his words inscribed for a perpetual memorial (23 f.). Again he forgets what he has said of God as his persecutor and speaks of him as the just vindicator of men. He has certain assurance that the living God will make manifest the justice of his cause and that he himself will live to see this vindication (25-27). He closes with a reminder to the friends of the retribution which awaits unjust conduct such as theirs (28 f.).

2-3 Rebuke of the Comforters—3. ' *humiliate* ', DV ' confound '. ' oppress ' : the exact meaning is uncertain.

4-6 His State is due to Divine Action—4. ' *And even had I erred indeed, my error would abide with me.*' It would be his own affair ; but he does not suggest that he could have committed any sin which would merit his actual sufferings. **5.** DV ' reproaches ' means ground for reproach—' my *humiliation* '. **6.** ' *Know ye then that God hath dealt perversely with me and encompassed me with his net* '. **7.** ' there is no *justice* '. **10b.** ' and he hath *plucked up my hope like a tree* '. **12.** ' His troops *come on together . . . against* me.' **13b.** ' and my acquaintances have *become estranged* from me '. **14.** ' My kinsmen and my *intimates have failed* ; they that *sojourn* in my house have forgotten me.' The first words of 15 belong here as is shown by the respective length of the lines and by the gender of the verbs. **17b.** ' *and I am become loathsome to* '. This meaning is required by the parallelism and is supported by Arabic usage. Job's children had all perished (1:19). Some therefore regard this sentence as a mere poetical amplification in Job's description of his misery, but this view implies too flagrant a disregard of paternal psychology. It is more natural to understand ' my womb ' as in 3:10 where it is the Hebrew expression for ' the womb that bore me '. By ' the children of my womb ' Job accordingly means his brothers and sisters. In both passages the usage is strange to us. **18.** ' *Even children spurn me ; when I rise up, they speak* against me.' When children are rude, they normally run away at a sign of possible action against them, but Job's condition is such that they know he cannot chase and punish them. 19b should be in the plural. **20.** DV represents conjectural restoration. Better : ' *My bone cleaveth to my skin and there is no soundness in my body* ', lit. ' I have escaped with the skin of my teeth '. The gums, which are the skin of the teeth, may remain undamaged when all the external surface of the body is one wound. Hence the proverbial expression.

21-22 Appeal for Commiseration—21. The tenderness of this appeal has made it one of the best-known lines in the whole Bible. **22b.** DV gives the sense well. MT ' and cannot be sated with my flesh ', cannot feel that you have had enough of it. This comparison of the friends to wild beasts attacking prey renders almost certain the restoration of *yod*, giving '*ayyāl* (for '*ēl* ' God ') : ' Why must you pursue me like a hart ? '

23-24 Job's Wish for a Perpetual Memorial of his Protestation of Innocence—23. ' Who will grant ' is the Hebrew idiom for expressing a wish. As the Hebrew word translated ' marked down ' signifies ' to incise, engrave ', the suggestion may well be correct that *seper* here, and in Is 30:8, has the meaning not ' book ' but ' copper ' corresponding to the Assyrian *sipparu*. Ordinary writing-material, moreover, would be too perishable for Job's purpose. **24.** ' *that with an iron graver and with lead they might be inscribed for ever on a rock* '. Many ancient rock-inscriptions survive to the present day including the famous Siloam inscription at

Jerusalem. There is nothing in MT corresponding to **326l** ' or else ' and therefore the ' plate of lead ' can hardly be defended. The lead was used apparently for filling in the letters cut in the rock, but there is no independent evidence of this.

25-27 Job's Complete Confidence of his Vindication by j God—These verses as Dhorme puts it ' have caused floods of ink to flow '. Several words are capable of more than one meaning and the text is not free from corruption. Hence in the detail of interpretation it may be said that opinions and writers are equal in number. St Jerome has treated the text with some freedom and has made it express belief in physical resurrection at the end of the world. St John Chrysostom, on the other hand, says explicitly of Job that ' Since he was just and knew nothing of the resurrection, this was the chief cause of his perturbation that he did not know the cause of his sufferings ' (*Epist.* 2, 8, PG 52, 565). Peters 206, 208 has well explained how Jerome reached his paraphrase. Understanding 25b of Job himself, ' and last [= at the last] he will arise on the dust ', he reworded the sentence after his manner to make the eschatological meaning plain. And 26a he took to mean literally ' and after with my skin they shall encompass this ', and again clothed the thought so won in clearer and more harmonious language. The verb ' shall rise ' of 25b is in the 3rd person in MT and all other ancient versions and has for its subject ' my redeemer ' or ' my vindicator ' of 25a. Had Job spoken of the resurrection it would have introduced an entirely new element into the discussion, which up to this point has been carried on by both sides on the supposition that all divine rewards and punishments for good and evil living are confined to this life. Had Job now asserted his belief in resurrection after death to be followed by a blessed union with God, the basis of the discussion would have been altered and the problem of the sufferings of the innocent in this life would have been on a fair way to its solution. But in fact the exchange of speeches continues after as before on the ground of the same postulate that all retribution is confined to this side of the grave. The solemnity of the passage, which must have contributed to its eschatological interpretation, is due to the earnestness with which Job is fighting for the recognition of his innocence against the assumption of his friends that the very violence of his sufferings is proof patent of his wickedness, hidden though that may have been. A fuller discussion may be found in Sutcliffe, *The Old Testament and the Future Life*, 131-7.

25. ' *For I on my side know, my redeemer liveth, and as* **k** *vindicator will take his stand upon the earth.*' The conjunction ' for ' indicates that Job is about to utter the substance, though not the form, of what he desired to be put on permanent record. The insertion of the personal pronoun, being neither required to indicate the speaker nor normal, is emphatic. Job's knowledge based on his conviction of his own innocence and of God's justice was not shared by the friends. The redeemer is God, as the sequel here shows. On the word see § 246g. The significance of ' liveth ' is that he is a person conscious and active, who will not remain a merely passive spectator. ' vindicator ' is based on post-biblical Hebrew (' surety, guarantee ') and on the indication of the parallelism. Alternatively the word means ' last ', the one whose word would finally settle the dispute. ' on the earth ' in contrast to 16:20 where Job spoke of God as his witness in heaven. In other words, God will guarantee Job's innocence to men, for he esteems that it would be an injustice permanently to let men think him guilty of such iniquity as to merit his present distress. As the epilogue of the book shows, God did finally vindicate the moral integrity of his servant. **26.** There is no approach to agreement as to **l** the meaning of this verse which all admit to be partially corrupt. With various emendations the following versions have been proposed. Dhorme : ' And behind my skin I shall stand erect and from my flesh I shall see God '. Peters : ' And behind my skin thus flayed,

326 l from out of my body I shall see God'. König: 'And after the loss of my skin which has been mangled to that there, and even robbed of my flesh I shall see God'. These are quite unconvincing. Apart from the general consideration outlined above, it does not follow from the fact that a language can say 'after the rain' to signify 'after the rain has ceased' that it can also say 'after my skin' to mean 'after my skin has ceased to exist'. The dislocation of words in 20 suggests that here too they need only to be re-arranged as follows : '*Should my skin be flayed from my flesh, even after this I shall see God*'. Such an emphatic expression of his invincible confidence in his ultimate vindication by God is what the context demands, and its form is suggested to Job by the state of his disease (2:7 f.). **27**. 'This my hope', etc., expresses the sense well.

m **28-29 Warning to the Friends—28**. '*If you say, " How shall we persecute him and find a pretext for action against him "* ', (29) '*Have a fear for yourselves of the sword, for wrath is kindled against iniquities.*' Read *tiḥar* (tau omitted by haplography) and transpose *beth* before iniquities.

327a **XX 1-29 Sophar's Second Speech**—He must answer Job's insulting language (**2-3**). The prosperity of the wicked is illusory and transitory (**4-29**).

b **2-3 Job's Words are Insulting**—There is agreement as to the meaning of 3*a* only. **2**. '*Therefore my thoughts make me answer even by reason of my eagerness within me.*' 'Therefore': because Job has just insisted that there is a judgement ruling the world, Sophar is eager to set forth what he conceives to be its true nature. **3**. '*A reproof that would put me to shame I hear, and wind without understanding answers me*', omitting the possessive suffix after 'understanding'.

c **4-29 The Prosperity of the Wicked is Brief and Illusory**—**4**. Insert colon after 'know', and in **5** omit 'that'. '*triumph*' (DV 'praise') ; '*godless*' (DV 'hypocrite'). **7**. '*like his own dung*'. **10***b*. 'and his hands shall *restore his wealth*', which was ill-gotten. The logical order would not be restored by the removal of this verse, as 12 returns to the lifetime of the impious after his death in **11**, where omit erroneous explanatory addition 'the vices of', and in *b* read 'it'. He dies prematurely. **12-13** form a protasis to which **14** gives the apodosis, the enjoyment of evil being compared to the holding of a delicious morsel in the mouth and its turning to poison in the bowels. **13**. 'and will not let it go and holds it back on his palate'. **14**. 'His food' (DV 'his bread'). **16**. '*poison*' (DV 'head'). **17**. Probably 'streams of *oil*' (*cf*. 29:6). 'see' in the sense of 'have the use and enjoyment of'. **18**. '*He restores the fruit of his labour and cannot swallow it down ; in the product of his commerce he has no enjoyment.*' So probably ; his labour, as the whole context indicates, has been for

d dishonest ends. **19**. '*Because with his might he crushed the weak . . . and shall not build it up*', probably in the sense of leaving posterity (*cf*. Ex 1:21 ; 2 Kg 7:11). These are not intended to be utterances of mere general import. Sophar is hinting here that he believes Job's wealth to have been unjustly acquired. **20**. '*Because he has not known contentment in his belly, his prized possessions shall not enable him to escape.*' Gluttony is here a figure for rapacity (*cf*. 15). **21**. '*No one survived his devouring, therefore his wealth shall not be abiding.*' **22**. '*In the fulness of his sufficiency straits come upon him.*' **23**. '*When he is about to* fill his belly, (God) *sends . . .*' **24***b*. 'and a bow of brass shall *pierce* him', with its arrows. **25**. '*The missile cometh out at his back and the bright point from his gall*', reading *šelaḥ* (LXX). 25*c* with **26**. '*Terrors are stored up for him ; all darkness is laid up for him . . . it consumes what is left in his tent*' (*cf*. Kissane). The fire is lightning from heaven, a clear indication that Sophar has Job himself in mind. Darkness is a synonym of Sheol (*cf*. 10:21 f.). **28**. '*A flood shall roll away his house, streams of water* in the day of wrath.' Read *yāgōl*, or perhaps *yābāl*. 29*b*. '*and his inheritance decreed* by God '.

e **XXI 1-34 Job's Seventh Speech**—His friends must listen. That is the only comfort he wants from them

(**2 f.**). His complaint is not against man, and what they will hear should astound them (**4 f.**). On their theory why should the wicked prosper ? In fact they do (**8-13**), even though they impiously deny their need of God (**14 f.**) on account of their self-sufficiency (**16**). How often do they meet with retribution ? (**17 f.**) It is no answer to say that they are punished in their children, for after death they have no further interest in their families (**19-21**) and God is well aware of this (**22**). All men are alike in death, whatever their lives have been (**23-26**). Job knows their thoughts about him : his house and household have perished, and therefore he must be wicked (**27 f.**). But any passer-by could tell them (**29**) that in life the wicked are powerful and protected from harm, and in death receive an honourable interment (**30-33**). So their proferred consolations are based on misrepresentations (**34**).

2-5 Introductory—**2b**. ' and let this be your way of consoling ! ' **3**. ' if you please ' is an addition, but the sense suggests rather ' if you can '. **5b**. A gesture of silent amazement (29:9) or merely of silence (Jg 18:19).

6-13 The Disturbing Fact—the Prosperity of the Wicked—**6a**. ' I am *disturbed*.' **8**. Omit ' a multitude of kinsmen '. **10**. ' *Their bull is fertile.*' **12**. ' *They lift up their voices with . . . the sound of the pipe.*' **13**. ' in a moment ' : in the midst of their prosperity. No calamity intervenes before they join the dead in Sheol.

14-18 Their Godless Self-sufficiency—Without approving the blasphemous deduction drawn by the wicked, Job, nonetheless, confirms the fact of their self-sufficiency. **16**. ' Lo ! *Their prosperity is in their own power* ; the counsel of the wicked is far from *him*.' Omit negative with LXX ; ' power ', lit. ' hand ' ; ' him ' with LXX. A much-disputed verse. They have acquired their wealth and keep it by their own exertions. God in no way interferes with them nor does he appear to concern himself with their projects. Calamity (**17 f.**) comes upon them so seldom that it does not seem to be due to divine retribution. ' How often *doth calamity* come upon them, *and how often does* he distribute sorrows *in his wrath* ? ' **18**. ' *How often are they as straw before the wind and as chaff swept away by the whirlwind ?* ' Contrast Ps 1:4.

19-22 Punishment of Offspring is not Punishment of the Guilty—**19a** quotes an objection. God punishes the wicked at least in their children—this is in accord with the strong Semitic conviction of the solidarity of the family : ' God lays up the *iniquity* for his children '. This is answered in *b* : ' *Let him requite it to the man himself that he may know of it* '. **20**. ' *Let* his own eyes see his own *misfortune*, and let him . . .' **21b**. ' when the number of his *allotted* months *is finished ?* ' *Cf*. 14:21. **22**. ' *those who* are on high ', *i.e.* the Angels (*cf*. 4:18 ; 15:15). If we know that a man is not punished by what befalls his children after him, quite obviously God knows it too, and therefore this cannot be his way of chastising the wicked.

23-26 No Difference between the Deaths of the Prosperous and the Unfortunate—**23**. ' *happy and peaceful* '. **25**. ' without *having tasted prosperity* '. The suggestion is that the prosperous have acquired their wealth unjustly or misused it ; and according to the friends' theory there should not be this equality in death. Job will presently go on to show that the wicked are honoured in death.

27-33 Falsity of the Insinuation against him : the Wicked are Powerful in Life and Honoured in Death—**28**. This question is directed against Job, whose household had been destroyed in the midst of his prosperity. **29**. ' *and do you not give heed to the examples they can give ?* ' The matter is common knowledge ; any passer-by can confirm it from his own experience. The sense is weakened by the translation ' widely-travelled ', which, moreover, is against the usage of ' they that pass by the way ' (*cf*. Ps 79:13 ; 88:42 ; Lam 1:12 ; 2:15). **30**. ' *On* the day of destruction the wicked man *is spared* and *on* the day of wrath he *is delivered*.' **32**. ' *He is carried to the graveyard and watch is*

j *kept over his tomb.'* The wicked man receives every mark of honour after death. 33. ' *The clods of the valley he finds pleasant.'* He rests peacefully in the earth used in the construction of his grave. St Jerome strangely took the reference to be to a stream in the underworld and introduced Cocytus, the classical name of such a river. ' *After him all men march and before him they are without number* '—a description of the crowd at the obsequies.

k 34. Emptiness of the Proffered Consolation—'*How then can you offer me empty comfort when your answers remain a deception?*'—because contrary to the facts of experience.

l XXII 1-30 Eliphaz's Third Speech—The virtue of man can confer no benefit on God (2-3), but as God does not call man to book for leading a good life, it is clear that Job's iniquity is very great (4-5). As Job's wealth had been exceptionally great, Eliphaz draws the conclusion that he must have acquired and increased it by harsh and unjust dealings (6-9). This has brought on his present distress (10-11). Job is accused of saying that as God's dwelling is far aloft in the high heavens he can know nothing of what happens here below (12-14). Job appears to be following the example of the godless men who were destroyed by the Flood, a catastrophe which proves that God is not disinterested in human conduct (15-18). And good men rejoice at such condign punishment (19-20). If only Job will be reconciled to God and put away his iniquity (21-23), he shall have boundless wealth (24-25), and all will be according to his heart's desire (26-28), for God humbles the proud and heaps his blessings on innocent lives (29-30).

m 2-11 The Immensity of Job's Wickedness—2. ' *Can man confer a benefit on God ? It is the prudent who benefit by their prudence !* ' 3. ' *Does the Almighty find pleasure in your being just ?* ' ' Way ' as often means ' the way one behaves '. 4. ' *Is it because you are God-fearing that he reproves you ?* ' ' The fear of God ', here ' fear ' alone, is the Hebrew expression for ' religion, a life religiously spent '. The argument is still the same : Job suffers greatly, therefore, though his iniquity has not been manifest, he must have been guilty of enormous wickedness. 6. The scantily clothed poor are hyperbolically called naked. 7. Not ' withdrawn ', but ' withheld '. 11. This wickedness is the reason further why ' *Light has become darkness so that thou canst not see and an inundation of waters overwhelms thee* '. Light is a symbol of prosperous times, darkness and inundation stand for calamity.

n 12-20 The Flood a Proof that God is not Inactive in High Heaven—12. ' *Is not God on high in heaven and doth he not look upon the stars aloft ?* ' This is the basis of the following assertion in the sense that God is too elevated above the dwellings of men to be concerned in their conduct. Hence (13), ' *So thou sayest . . . Can he judge behind a dark cloud ?* ' 14. ' *Clouds conceal him and he cannot see ;* he walketh in the *vault* of heaven.' But the thought is that the clouds conceal the world from him. 15-17. Job appears to be following in the footsteps of the corrupt generation swept away by the Flood, Eliphaz cleverly turns the argument by putting into their mouths the impious words attributed by Job to the wicked (21:14 f.). 18*b*. ' *Yet the counsel of the wicked was far from him* '; with LXX. Again cleverly, Eliphaz quotes and gives a new meaning to 21:16*b*. Though God had heaped benefits upon them, their whole way of life disregarded him. 19-20. In mentioning the rejoicing of the just Eliphaz hints at other famous examples of the punishment of the wicked, as that of Sodom and Gomorrha (Gen 19), of Core, Dathan and Abiron (Num 16:35), in which fire was a means of destruction.

o 23-30 Job's Repentance would be blessed by Wonderful Prosperity—23. ' and *humble thyself* and put away ': so LXX. DV ' be built up ' (so MT) interrupts the condition of restoration, of which the putting away of iniquity is part. 24. ' *Then shalt thou hold gold as dust and the fine gold of Ophir as the pebbles of the wadies.'* A hyperbolic description of the reward of virtue ; *cf.* 5:19-26, esp. 25. To understand the line as expressing

contempt for wealth is to neglect the this-worldly outlook of the friends and their thesis that virtue meets with material reward. The words could signify the worthlessness of gold if it were a question of Job's parting with affection for his own lost wealth considered to have been the fruit of wickedness. 25. ' And the Almighty shall be *thy gold* and silver heaped up for thee.' Job later declares that his wealth had not been the source of his joy (31:25). 27*b*. Vows of thank-offerings were made in petitions for benefits. So, to say that Job will pay his vows implies that his petitions will have been answered. 29. ' *For he humbles the exalted and the proud* '; so probably with Beer. **327o**

a XXIII 1-XXIV 17, 25 Job's Eighth Speech—If only he could find God and put his case before him, he is confident that his innocence would be established, but do what he will, he cannot make contact with God (2-12). God has his own ways, which no man can thwart. And that is why Job is filled with fear. God is the cause of this distress and not his misfortunes as such (13-17). Why does God not visit his wrath on the wicked (XXIV:1-3) ? They oppress the weak and the poor in every conceivable way, but God disregards it (4-12). The murderer, the thief and the adulterer carry on their evil course (13-17). [18-24 after 27:13] Who can belie Job's words ? (25) **328a**

b 2-12 If Job could meet God his Innocence would be established—2*b*. ' *His hand is heavy despite my groaning.*' ' His ' with LXX. 3. ' Who will grant ' is a Hebrew expression to introduce a wish. ' know and find ' means ' know how to find '. 4. ' I would set *my case* before him . . . with *pleadings*.' 6. ' *Would he contend . . . No ! Surely he would heed me !* ' 7. ' *He would listen to a just man pleading with him and I should free myself with victory from my judge* '; reading *yišma*'. 8. But Job's trouble is that he cannot enter into direct relations with God. ' if to the west I *perceive* him not '. 9. ' *In the north I seek him but see him not ; I turn to the south but discern him not* '; reading *qoph* for '*ain in a.* 10. ' *my way* ': lit. with Syr. ' my going and my standing still ', *i.e.* he knows all about me, Heb. idiom expressing totality by the conjunction of two opposites. ' *after he had tested me, I should go forth like gold* ', pure as gold from the crucible.

c 13-17 God's Ways are Inscrutable and the Cause of Job's Fears—God has chosen a line of action and he cannot be turned from it. He will not let Job plead his case before him, and it is this attitude of God's that fills Job with forebodings and fear, not his calamities merely in themselves. This is in answer to Eliphaz (22:10 f.). 13. ' *When he has made his choice, who can turn him back ?* ' 14. ' *He will fulfil.*' Job hints that it is not only in his regard that God's actions are arbitrary. 15. ' Therefore *it is, on account of him, that I am troubled ; of him my thoughts put me in fear.*' Not ' at his presence ', which is precisely what Job longed for. If he could come into God's presence, he could settle the issue of his innocence. Eliphaz had said (22:10 f.) that on account of his wickedness Job was troubled by snares, fear and darkness. Here (15-17) Job answers that it is the attitude of God that causes his trouble and fear. 17. ' . . . darkness, nor *of the gloom that encompasses me* '.

d XXIV 1-3 God seems to disregard Iniquity—1. ' *Why are* the times hidden from the Almighty and *why do* they that know him, not *see his day ?* ' Omit the first ' not ' with LXX. ' Times ' implying ' happenings ' as in our ' What terrible times !' ' Know ' with pregnant meaning ' know with favour, love ' as in Ps 1:6. God's day is the day of his vengeance on the sinner. 2. ' *with the shepherd* ' with LXX ; DV ' and fed them '. Not content with stealing the flock they enslave the shepherd.

e 4-12 The Wretched State of the Defenceless—4. *They turn aside the poor from the way ; humble folk are all forced to hide.'* For fear of maltreatment they dare not be seen on the public ways. 5. ' *Lo ! As* wild asses in the wilderness they go forth in their toil, searching for food in the desert, there is nothing to nourish their children.'* 6. ' *They reap in fields not their own and gather the vintage for the wicked.'* In Job's present frame of mind the wicked and

328e the rich are synonymous. **7.** '*Naked they pass the night without clothing and* have no covering in the cold.' For '*naked*' *cf.* 22:6. **8.** '*press close to the rock*' to get what little shelter it can afford. **9.** *They rob the orphan from the breast and take in pledge the infant of the needy.*' Later they will grow up as useful slave-workers. This verse introduces a new unnamed subject and interrupts the description of the misery of the common folk. It probably belongs after 3. **10.** '*Naked they go about without clothing and in hunger they carry the sheaves.*' **11.** '*Bereft of song they press out the oil. They tread the vine-vats and thirst*'; *cf.* Sutcliffe, JTS 50 (1949) 174–6. They are incapable of the glad songs which normally accompanied such work. **12.** '*From the cities come the groans of the dying* and the soul of the wounded *cries out, but God regardeth not the scandal.*'

f **13–17 Murderers, Adulterers, Burglars**—Job now leaves those who practised open oppression and turns to crimes committed under the shelter of darkness. Common to them all is that they shun the light. Hence in 14 for *lā'ôr* read *lō' 'ôr*, 'The murderer riseth *in the dark to* kill'. 14c after 15. **15.** The adulterer waits for night saying, '*It will provide concealment for my face*'. **14c.** '*By night the burglar stalks abroad*' (*yᵉhallēk*). **16a.** It was the burglar, not the adulterer, who dug his way through the wall of sun-dried mud to effect an easy entrance; *cf.* Mt 24:43. **16b–c.** '*By day they shut themselves up ; they are strangers to the light.*' 17 is uncertain in detail. They sleep when others work. 'To them all daytime is night-time.' **18–24.** after 27:13. **25b.** '*and set my words at nought*'.

g **XXV 1–6 XXVI 5–14 Bildad's Third Speech : The Power of God and the Vileness of Man**—As it stands now in MT Bildad's third speech consists of five verses only, which is against the analogy of all the other speeches. Moreover, these five verses are a doxology but have the appearance of a mere torso, and as the attribution of the speeches in this part has become confused in other respects (*cf.* 24:18–24 ; 27:13–23) and the doxology of 26:5–14 forms the natural complement of 25:1–6, there is little doubt but that the two passages belong together.

Bildad praises the power of God on high (**1–2**) and points out the impossibility of man being just or pure in his sight (**3–6**). He then lauds the omniscience and power of God in regard of the underworld, the earth, the clouds, the pillars of heaven, the sea (**XXVI:5–13**). And all that man has heard of his doings is but as a whisper (**14**).

h **2.** God's power gives reason to man to fear. His rule is the source of peace in heaven. 3 is a picturesque description of God's might. The parallelism favours LXX : 'And *against* whom doth not his *ambush* arise ?' **4.** '*How can man be just before God ?*' Job had said this himself (9:2). **XXVI:5.** '*The shades below are made to tremble ; the waters and they that dwell therein feel awe.*' 'giants' is due to a confusion of Rephaim, the name of the shades of the dead, with its homonym, the name of an early race of great stature (Deut 2:11, etc.). The waters are those under the earth (Deut 4:18, etc.) which themselves were over Sheol, the abode of the dead. 'awe' inserting with Dhorme *yᵉhattû* omitted by haplography. **6.** 'Hell' stands for Sheol ; *cf.* comm. on 5. 'destruction' is a translation of the proper name Abaddon, a synonym for Sheol. **7.** The north, the part in parallelism with the whole, is mentioned perhaps as being unknown and mysterious to the ancients and in mythology even regarded as the **i** home of the gods. **8b.** '*they are not split open under their weight*', lit. 'under them'. **9.** God's throne is the firmament (Is 66:1), the undersurface of which is its face for man. This God '*covereth*' by his clouds. **10.** The flat earth was conceived as surrounded by an ocean which itself was bounded by the fixed horizon. '*he appointed the boundary between light and darkness*', reading *yā'ad*. Light and darkness, both conceived as positive realities with independent existences, had their home, at least for the poet, at the confines of the earth. There they retired when their period of service in the

world was over ; *cf.* 38:19. **11.** The supports of the **32** firmament rest on the utmost boundary of the earth. **12.** Omit 'suddenly' ; '. . . *smote through Rahab*'. God showed his dominion over the ocean by confining its primeval waters and allowing the dry land to appear (Gen 1:9 ; Ps 103:6–9). Rahab is the personification of the sea in revolt. **13b.** '*his hand hath pierced the coiling serpent*', which is mentioned also in Is 27:1 and in the Rās-Shamra literature ; *cf. Syria* 15 (1934) 305,*W. F. Albright in CBQ 7 (1945) 30,* C. Rabin in JTS 47 (1946) 38–41. The parallelism shows the serpent to be a celestial constellation, probably Draco. This is probably leviathan of 3:8 mythologically conceived as a monster capable of attacking the sun and obscuring its light. See Ball on 3:8. **14.** '*Lo, these are the fringes of his ways and what a feeble whisper thereof do we catch, and the thunder of his prowess who can understand ?*' Ball's suggestion, *rō'š* for *ra'am*, is attractive : 'the sum of his exploits'.

XXVI 1–4 XXVII 1–6, 12 Job's Ninth Speech— **j** This speech as it stands has extraneous elements inserted in it. For 26:5–14 see after 25:6, § 328g–h. 27:7–11 treat of God's anger with the wicked, which is the theme, not of Job, but of his friends. Job maintains in his bitterness of soul that the prosperity of the wicked seems rather to indicate God's favour (9:22–24 ; 21:7–33). And as in the existing arrangement the third cycle of speeches is incomplete and Sophar has no speech at all, it seems that his third speech has been broken up into 27:7–11, 13 ; 24:18–24 ; 27:14–23, passages which in MT are attributed to Job but, as setting forth the sad state of the wicked, could not have been spoken by him. Note also the curious introductory formula of 27:1 which differs from all that precede and comes in the middle of words attributed to Job. What remains of Job's speech is incomplete.

Bildad has given neither help nor counsel (**2–4**). God **k** has deprived Job of justice (**XXVII:2**). As long as he lives Job will not admit the accusations levelled by the friends against him, but will stoutly maintain his innocence (**3–6, 12**).

2–4 Job taunts Bildad—2. '*What help thou hast given to* **l** *one bereft of strength and help to the powerless arm !*' **3.** '*What counsel thou hast given where wisdom is needed and what an abundance of sanity thou hast shown !*' **4.** '*To whom hast thou been declaring mere words ? And whose is the spirit that has issued from thy mouth ?*' For the construction of *a cf.* 31:37, and for 'words' in the sense of 'mere words' 15:13. Job stands on his dignity ; he does not wish to be treated as an ignoramus. *b* is ironical. Bildad has shown such marvellous wisdom that someone must have prompted him ! **5–14.** See after 25:4.

XXVII 2–6, 12 Job will maintain his Innocence to his **m** **Last Breath—3.** As in Gen 2:7 ; Ps 103 (104) 29 f. **4.** '*what is false*' (DV 'iniquity') by admitting guilt. **5.** '*to be right*' (DV 'to be just') in asserting his guilt. **XXVII 7–11, 13 XXIV 18–24, XXVII 14–23 Sophar's** **n** **Third Speech**—On the reconstruction of this speech see § 328j. God will not hear the prayers of the godless man (**27:7–11**). This means as long as he remains wedded to his evil life, and does not contradict the friends' advice to Job, whom they suppose to be wicked, to turn to God, for this advice is joined to the exhortation to put away his wickedness (5:17 ; 11:14 ; 22:23). In 13 Sophar announces his intention of describing the lot of the wicked. This he does in 24:13–24 and 27:14–23 insisting on the fallaciousness of riches and the rich man's uncertain hold on life.

XXVII 7–11, 13 God does not hear the Prayers of the **o** **Impious—7.** 'be as' means 'share the lot of' as in 1 Kg 25:26. **8.** '*For what hope has the impious when he intercedes* [*yipga'*], *when he lifts up his soul to God ?*' A metaphor for prayer as in Ps 24 (25) 1. **11.** 'I will teach *thee what* [with LXX] *is in* the hand of God and the *dispensation* of the Almighty I will not conceal', namely the lot reserved by God for the wicked. 13 puts this in plainer words.

XXIV 18–24 XXVII 14–23 The Lot of the Impious— **3** **18a.** He is tossed about and has no stability. **18c.**

a Perhaps : ' *The wine-presser turns not to their vineyards* ' (*dōrēḵ karmām*, Dhorme) because there is no work to be done there. **19.** ' *The heat dries up the snow-waters and Sheol snatcheth away the sinner.* ' So perhaps (*cf.* Ball). **20.** ' *The womb that formed him* [*pᵉṭāqô*, Dhorme] shall forget him ; *his name* [*šᵉmô*] shall be remembered no more.' **21.** ' *He hath dealt evilly* [*hēraʿ*, with LXX] with the barren.' The barren woman has no children and the widow no husband to defend her. **22a** : with LXX ' *He drags off the poor by his might* '. **22b–23.** ' *He may stand erect* [*i.e.* seems prosperous] *but cannot* trust to his life [it may end at any time] ; *God may grant him to dwell in security*, but his eyes are upon his ways ' ; reading *yiškōn.* **24.** ' *He is* lifted up for a little while and *is no more ; he wilts like a plucked* mallow [*cf.* LXX] and *withers* like an ear of corn.'

b XXVII 14-23 The Unhappy Fate of the Impious continued—14b. ' *offspring* '. **15a.** ' *brought to the grave through pestilence* '; for this pregnant meaning of ' death ', suggested already by Sanchez, *cf.* Jer 15:2. **18.** ' *like a bird's nest and like a booth made by a watchman* ', in a vineyard or plantation ; both frail and unenduring. **19.** ' *He lies down rich and it seemed secure ; he opens his eyes and it is no more.* ' He loses his wealth (figured by his unsubstantial house in 18) in a single night. **20.** ' *Terrors overtake it like waters ; in the night a storm-wind spirits it away* ', namely his household and fortune. So in **21.** ' *The east wind carries it away and it vanishes ; it sweeps it out of its place.* ' **22.** ' *God hurleth at him without mercy ; he would fain flee from his hand.* ' In 13 Sophar set out to depict God's treatment of the wicked and so the subject of the sentence could be left implicit here. **23.** ' *He claps his hands against him and hisses at him from his dwelling* ' in Heaven. With this strong anthropomorphism *cf.* Ps 77 (78) 65. For the signs of triumphant contempt *cf.* Lam 2:15.

c XXVIII 1-28 Hymn in Praise of Wisdom—This is an insertion in the dialogue (see § 317*l*). Man has marvellous knowledge. He has explored uninhabited regions, even the bowels of the earth. He knows where the metals may be found, disguised though they are in the form of ore (**1-11**). But the home of wisdom he does not know (**12-14**). No gold nor precious stones are comparable in value (**15-19**). But the source of wisdom man does not know (**20-22**). This God alone knows (**23**). When he fashioned the universe, wisdom was with him (**24-27**). Wisdom for man is the service of God (**28**).

d 1-11 Man's Marvellous Knowledge—1. ' Silver hath its *source* and the gold men *refine hath its home.*' **2.** ' *copper* '. **3.** ' *Man setteth a limit to darkness and with all exactness searcheth out stone that lay in pitchy gloom.*' Man conquers darkness in the mines by light-shafts (see Petrie 60 f., 156) and by the use of artificial light. **4.** ' *A sojourning people breaketh through wadies forgotten by human foot ; they are exiles and wanderers from mankind.*' The poet stresses the remoteness of the mines, perhaps those in Sinai of which Flinders Petrie, without any thought of Job, wrote that they ' have been the only cause of man ever visiting this region ' (59). Even in these uninhabited valleys man had discovered the presence of precious stones and metals, which could be worked only by people who had come from their distant homes. The mines of Sinai were horizontal shafts cut through the sides of the wadies (*cf.* Flinders Petrie, 59–61, 154–9). **5.** ' *Out of the earth comes forth bread, but underneath it is overturned as by fire* ', by the labours of the miners. For the expression *cf.* Gen 19:24 f. about Sodom and Gomorrha. **6.** ' *and gold-dust too is there* '. **8.** Lit. ' sons of pride ', lions. Yet man has discovered this untrodden spot. **10.** Rivers is used with poetic licence either for the wet galleries of the workings or for channels to carry off the water. **11** gives a different example of man's ingenuity in finding what is precious, namely by securing gold from the beds of streams.

e 12-22 But the Home of Wisdom Man does not know ; its Incomparable Value—13. ' Man knoweth not *the way thereto* ', with LXX. ' the land of the living ' is this world ; omit ' in delights '. **15.** ' neither *can*

silver ', etc. **16a.** ' with the gold of Ophir ', which **329e** was probably in S. Arabia. **18a.** ' *Coral and crystal.* ' **18b.** ' *a casket of wisdom is above one of pearls* ' ; lit. ' bag '. **19b.** ' *pure gold* '.

23-28 God Alone knows Wisdom : its Meaning for f Man—23. ' the way of it ' is the way that leads to it. **24.** ' *When he beheld.* ' Wisdom was with God in the creation and regulation of the world. See Ps 103 (104) 24 ; Prov 8:12–31.

XXIX 1-XXXI 40 Job's Last Speech to the Friends— g The three main themes of this long speech occupy each one of the three chapters into which it is divided. In ch 29 Job wistfully recalls the days of his greatness and happiness with some account of the protection and solace which his position of power and influence enabled him to afford to the weak and needy (**12-17**). Ch 30 describes plaintively the contrast to this lost glory offered by his present sad condition. He has become an object of scorn and abhorrence to the meanest (**1-12**). He depicts his troubles, especially under warlike metaphors, and with allusion to pains in his bones (**13-17**). He complains that God has become cruel to him (**18-23**). Though he had been kind to the poor he has become sorely afflicted and an outcast (**24-31**). Ch 31, which is only loosely joined to the preceding, contains his ' negative confession '. He pleads his innocence of the many forms of wrong-doing which might have justified his sufferings and calamities. He has never been guilty of adultery, of injustice to his servants, of idolatry, of robbery. He still has complete confidence in the case he would like to put before the Almighty (**33-37**). He thus maintains to the end that his sufferings are entirely unmerited and are therefore inexplicable.

XXIX 1-25 Job recalls the Days of his Felicity and h Power—1. ' *Job resumed his utterance.* ' **3.** The lamp hanging in the living-room was the symbol of domestic peace. There was no darkness then in Job's life, always illuminated, as it was, by the light of God's favour. **4.** HT ' in the days of my autumn ', the time when fruits ripen, the time of maturity. ' when God *protected* my tabernacle ', lit. ' put a screen over ' reading *kaph* for *daleth.* **5b.** ' my servants *stood* [from HT of 6*b*] round about me '. **6.** ' with *curds* ', a sign of luxury. The rock stands for the olive-presses which were often hewn out of the rock. **7.** ' *and in the square set up my seat* '. Within the city-gate was an open space, the regular meeting-place of the citizens. Here business was transacted and justice administered. **8.** ' hid themselves ' is a hyperbole for ' made way for me ' or ' effaced themselves ' (Kissane). **21-25** belong here after **10**. They continue the theme of the preceding verses and in their present position the verbs lack a subject. **21.** Omit ' being attentive '. **22.** ' dropped upon them ' like a beneficent shower of rain. **23.** The latter rains are the spring rains which are necessary for the growth of the crops. For these rains the earth eagerly opens its mouth and the figure is transferred to Job's listeners. **24.** ' *when I smiled at them, they could not* **i** *believe it* '. They looked on it as remarkable condescension on the part of so great a man. ' and the light of my countenance *they did not diminish* ', lit. ' let fall '. They were unwilling in any way to displease Job. ' The light of the countenance ' signifies benevolence and favour (*cf.* Ps 4:7). **25.** Job was always a welcome and highly honoured guest. Omit ' when '. For the last clause read perhaps with Ball ' like a captain of thousands in the host '. **14.** ' *I put on justice as a garment and it was my covering ; my judgement was like a mantle and a turban.*' **16.** ' the cause *of him whom* I knew not '. **18.** ' *I thought : I shall perish with my nest, I shall multiply my days like the phoenix.*' DV ' palm tree ', Gk φοῖνξ, points back to the ancient Jewish tradition that the allusion here is to the fabulously long life of the phoenix, which was supposed to perish with its nest. Possible is ' I shall die with my nestlings [*cf.* Deut 32:11], I shall multiply my days like the sand '. This would be a reference to the prologue. On the phoenix, see H. Heras, S.J., in CBQ 11 (1949) 263–79. **19b.** ' *and the dew*

329i *shall abide in my branches'*. 19 and 20 continue the reflection begun in 18. **20.** 'My glory *untarnished in my keeping* and my bow *prospering* in my hand'. The bow is introduced here as a symbol of power (*cf.* Jer 49:35).

330a **XXX 1-31 The Sad Contrast of Job's Present State—** The contrast is emphasized by the repetition of 'but now' (1, 9, 16). **2b-3a.** '*Their vigour was perished within them through want and harsh dearth.*' **3b-c.** '*who gnawed roots* [*cf.* Ball] *in the wilderness, in the land* (?) *of devastation and desolation*'. So with Vg 'gnawed', but more probably with LXX 'who fled into the wilderness'. Other short stichs are found in 5a and 19a, and the description of their rough food comes in 4. '*who plucked purslane leaves from the shrubs and whose food was the root* of the broom' called by the Arabs *retem* (see Flinders Petrie, 29). To use these roots for fuel is normal with the Bedouin, and, as Dhorme remarks, such use would not be a sign of special hardship. They are not normally eaten, and the indigence of these miserable folk is shown by their being driven to use them for food. **5.** '*They were driven forth from the community, while men set up a cry at them as at thieves* (6) *to take up their abode on the side of the wadies, in holes in the earth and among the rocks.*' **7.** '*Among the shrubs they uttered their raucous cries, and under the thistles they huddled together.*' Perhaps 'they brayed', as if they were wild asses. For an interesting account of an Arab who preferred sleeping in the open whatever the weather, see Flinders Petrie, 30. **8.** '*The sons of fools, the sons of nameless men, they were scourged out of the land*'—a strong expression, but the passage is strongly worded. **11.** '*When (God) loosened my bowstring and humbled me, they cast off the halter before me.*' God as in 3:20 ; 30:18 is spoken of though not named. For the metaphor of the bow *cf.* 29:20. The unworthy men of 30:1 ff. took advantage of God's afflicting Job to throw off all restraint. The figure is that of a horse out of control. 12 is corrupt and may perhaps be emended to '*Against me his troops arise ; they mound up their paths of destruction*'. Job's calamities are the forces sent against him by God. Preparations for the siege alluded to in 14 are mentioned here. The causeways are mounded up with the **b** purpose of procuring Job's destruction. **13.** 'They have destroyed my *path for my undoing ; they mount up with none to restrain them.*' **14.** '*As through a wide breach they come on ; in the din and crashing they roll on.*' The noise (one word in HT) is the din of battle heightened by the falling masonry of the ramparts. **15a-b.** '*Overwhelming terrors came upon me ; as by the wind my noble estate is chased away.*' **17b.** '*my wasted skeleton doth not rest* ' ; lit. 'bones with the flesh removed' as in Arabic —a different word from that used in 30:3. **18** is of doubtful meaning : 'With mighty power he seizeth [so LXX] my garment ; he bindeth me as with the collar of my tunic.' The general sense is that God took violent hold of Job and bound him preparatory to **19** : '*He cast me into the mire ; and I am become like to dust and ashes*', something to be disregarded and cast away. **22b.** '*and tossest me in the roaring storm*'. **23b.** '*and to the dwelling appointed*'. 24 is corrupt and uncertain. '*Assuredly against the lowly I did not put forth my hand, if in his calamity he called to me* (25), *but I wept for him whose fate was hard.*' **27.** DV 'have prevented me' is an archaic Latinism for 'have come to meet me'. **28.** 'without *comfort*', adding *nun*. 'I arose crying *aloud*', reading b⁽ᵉ⁾qôlî. This is almost necessary to explain in **29** the resemblance of Job's mournful cries to those of *jackals* and ostriches (Mic 1:8).

c **XXXI 1-40 Job's Solemn Protestation of Innocence—** **2.** ' *For what is the award of God above and the heritage of the Almighty in the heights ?* ' This introduces **3**, which gives the principle of retribution Job had always believed to hold good till his unmerited calamity came upon him. **6** is a parenthesis. ' *my innocence* '. **8.** ' *my produce* ', or crops, as shown by the parallelism. **12b.** ' *and would burn* (*tišrōp*) *all my increase*'. **14.** ' *what should* ', etc. ; conditional, in the hypothesis that Job had committed this heinous sin. **15b.** ' *form us* '.

16b. ' *of the widow languish* '. **18.** ' *No, from his youth* **3** *I brought him up* [*ᵃgadd⁽ᵉ⁾lennū*] *like a father* and from *his mother's womb I guided him* ', namely the orphan of 17. The quite improbable hyperbole of MT requires the change of the suffixes. **19.** ' *If I saw one perishing*'. **20.** ' *his loins* '. These are mentioned as the parts most in need of the warm clothing Job provided. **21b.** ' *when I saw my supporters at the gate* ' of the city, the meeting-place for all forms of business. **22b.** ' *let my arm be broken from its socket* '. **23.** ' *For the fear of God was heavy upon me, and by reason of his majesty I was powerless* ' ; reading *yā⁽ʾ⁾îd* with Driver. **24a.** ' *my trust* '. **27a.** ' *and my heart in secret was seduced* ' to worship sun and moon as did the Babylonians. For kissing as an expression of worship *cf.* 3 Kg 19:18, Os 13:2. **28.** ' *That too would be a grievous crime, for I had been false to God above* '. **30b.** ' *by demanding his life with a curse* '. **31b.** ' *Who has not had his fill of flesh from his table* ', lit. ' *of his flesh* ', of flesh from his flocks and herds. **33.** Job has not been guilty of manifest sin, **d** neither had he occasion like Adam to try to conceal wrong-doing (Gen 3:8) (**34**) ' *because I dreaded a great clamour* and the contempt of kinsmen terrified me and *I remained quiet not going out of doors* '. **35.** ' *Would that God would hear me ; this is my desire that the Almighty would answer me and that mine adversary had written a scroll* ' ; *cf.* Bi 30 (1949) 71 f. God is Job's adversary, or rather Job so conceives him, and it is still the sufferer's complaint that, though God's hand is heavy against him, no charge has been formulated, and he is left in ignorance of the accusation against him. If only, therefore, God would commit his case against Job to writing in a scroll. The meaning ' scroll ', for which see Is 34:4, is indicated by 36b. So confident is Job of his innocence that any formulation of accusations against him would be an instrument redounding to his honour to be worn as an ornament. **37.** ' *The tale of my steps I would relate to him ; as a prince I would present myself before him.*' In 14:16 Job said that God was observing all his steps, *i.e.* his every action. A close scrutiny would reveal nothing amiss, and therefore he would come before God not with the shamefaced look of a criminal but with confidence marking his bearing. For the intransitive use of *qᵉrēḇ cf.* Ez 36:8. **38 f.** ' the *owners* thereof '. Job has not robbed weaker men either of their hire, their land or its produce. **40.** ' *thorns . . . noxious weeds* '. This is an unlikely ending to Job's final solemn protestation of innocence and it is probable that 38-40 are misplaced and should be read before 33. **XXXII 1-5 Introduction to Elihu's Discourse—**This **e** is an addition to the original poem (see § 317m). **1.** That Job was just in his own eyes does not adequately explain why the friends should give no further answer, for he had maintained his innocence from the beginning. According to LXX, Sym. Syr., Job had now convinced them : ' for *they deemed him to be just* '. **2.** Omit ' was angry and '. The town of Buz (Jer 25:23) appears to have lain in NW. Arabia near to Idumaea. **3.** Omit ' reasonable '. ' had condemned Job ' : an ancient tradition of the Jews records that this is a correction of the Scribes (*tiqqun sopherim*) introduced as certain others to avoid apparent irreverence, and that the original text was ' had condemned *God* ', that is, were convinced that he was punishing Job without cause (*cf.* comm. on 1). **4.** ' while *they spoke with* Job '. Omit ' that were speaking '.

6-XXXVII 24 Elihu's Speech—Out of respect for age **f** he, as the younger man, has remained silent (**6-7**), but in fact mere years do not impart wisdom, but the spirit of God, and therefore he too will speak (**8-10**). No satisfactory answer has been given to Job (**11-13**). Now they are silent, he will give voice to his wisdom and will certainly not use arguments like theirs (**14-17**). He feels an irresistible urge to speak and will do so without fear or favour (**18-22**). With solemnity he appeals to Job to listen to his words full of wisdom which comes to him from the Almighty. Let Job answer if he can (**XXXIII:1-5**). Job need not be afraid, as he is only a man like himself (**6-7**). He has heard Job protest his innocence and assert that God nonetheless reckons him as an enemy (**8-12**). Why does he strive with God, who will answer never a word (**13-14**)? It is in dreams of the night that God makes his revelations to withdraw man from his evil way and so save him from the grave (**15-18**). Or God uses sickness to try to bring man back to a better mind (**19-22**). Then with the aid of a wise counsellor he can be saved, entirely rejuvenated, and received back into God's favour (**23-26**). And he confesses before men that he had sinned and that God had saved him from death (**27-28**). All this God is ready to do for man to save him from death (**29-30**). Job should listen and answer if he can (**31-32**). Let them listen and test the truth of his words (**XXXIV:1-4**). Job has asserted that he is innocent and that God has perverted judgement (**5-6**). Does any man but Job indulge in such mockery, Job who associates with the wicked and claims that man gains nothing by seeking good-will with God (**7-9**)? The Almighty is incapable of wickedness and he requites man according to his works (**10-12**). He is supreme and all life depends utterly on him (**13-15**). It is impossible that the ruler of the world should hate justice, he who reproves kings, gives no favour to princes and strikes the mighty. He watches all man's ways, and the wicked cannot hide from his gaze (**16-22**). He does not enter into controversy with men, but crushes the mighty for their wickedness in rejecting his allegiance and causing the cry of the weak to rise up to him (**23-28**). He is beyond the reach of any action of man's, and watches over nations and individuals alike (**29-30**). If a man confesses his sin and promises amendment, does Job think that God will punish? (**31-33**) Job does not speak with knowledge, but adds to his sin in multiplying words against God (**34-37**). God must take cognizance of evil. It is true that the good-living of man confers no benefit, as his evil deeds inflict no harm, on God. But man's acts do affect other men, and that God cannot be indifferent (**XXXV:1-8**). Still God does not always intervene. Men cry out in affliction, but without thought of God (**9-10**). This is to cry out like animals, and men should know better. In these circumstances God cannot be expected to pay heed (**11-12**). Neither will God regard a foolish cry like Job's, who wants to dictate to God when to act and what to do (**13-14**). So Job's complaint that God does not punish the wicked is baseless (**15-16**). But Elihu finds that he has more to say in defence of God, who guards the rights of the weak and the just (**XXXVI:1-7a**). If kings whom he has set on their thrones grow proud, and he sets them in bondage, he makes them know their iniquity. If they give ear, they complete their days in prosperity; if not, they meet their end through lack of knowledge (**7b-12**). The impious do not cry for help, and they die in youth. The lowly God saves (**13-15**). These principles are applied to Job; only let him beware of returning to evil, which has been the cause of his affliction (**16-21**). Elihu breaks out into the praise of God. He is exalted, beyond the control of any power and beyond the comprehension of man (**22-26**). It is his power that is manifested alike in destructive flood and beneficent rain, in the poising of the clouds and in the lightning that proceeds from them (**27-33**). The terrors of thunder and of lightning are from him (**XXXVII:1-5**). Snow, rain, frost and lightning are all his ministers to carry out his will in missions whether of punishment or of mercy (**6-13**). What does Job understand of the marvels of God's creation? And what part has he in God's works? (**14-18**) **19-22a**; see comm. Elihu ends with a doxology (**22b-24**).

XXXII 6-XXXIII 7 Elihu's Apology and Reasons for his Intervention—6. ' therefore *out of respect* I was afraid '. **8.** ' *Howbeit, the* spirit *of God is* in men.' He insinuates that youth may be wiser than age, for, after all, wisdom comes from God, and his spirit is in young as well as old. In Gen 2:7 and Ps 103:30 the spirit or breath of God is the source of life. Elihu points out

that it is also the source of wisdom. **9.** Elihu does not **331a** mean that the aged are never wise, but that age alone does not confer wisdom—a polite hint that he does not find wisdom in the friends. **10.** ' Therefore I *say* . . . I also will *declare what I know*.' **11b-c.** ' *I listened for your reasons while you sought out words*.' **12.** ' *I gave you my attention,* but . . .' **13.** ' Do not say, " We have discovered wisdom; God may rout him, but not man ".' This agrees with 1 and 3; see comm. The friends had discovered unexpected wisdom in Job's answers and had been convinced. But they had not reckoned with Elihu's powers of argument. He will show them how it should be done. **14.** ' *I will not marshal talk like yours* '; so with Syr., but lit. ' like these '. **16.** ' *And I waited because they speak not, because they stopped and have answered no more*.' He waited patiently not only while they spoke, but even when they ceased to speak, he did not hold forth at once. He gave time for them to begin again. **17b.** ' *I too will declare what I know*.' **b** **19b.** ' *like skins of new wine it is ready to burst* '. He gives the same excuse for speaking as Eliphaz (4:2). **20a.** ' *Let me speak and have relief*.' **21.** ' *It is not for me to show favour or to flatter any man*.' **22.** ' *For I know not how to flatter; for a little may my Maker bear with me*.' The last clause is commonly taken to mean that God would soon take me away in punishment, but it is unlikely that Elihu would think such a penalty proportionate to yielding to human respect. The words betray a knowledge on the author's part that God is soon to intervene himself. **XXXIII 4** is not out of place. The thought is the same as that of 32:8. God in making man gave him of his own spirit and thereby not only life but also wisdom. **5b.** ' *marshal thy reasons before me; take thy stand*'. **6.** ' Behold *I am like thee, not God; I too was made of a bit of clay*.' ' not God ', *aleph* omitted by haplography. This introduces 7 giving the reason why Job has no ground for fear. Before moulding his product the potter first squeezes a portion of clay from the lump. **7.** ' *Lo, fear of me shall not terrify thee, and my hand shall not be heavy upon thee*.' The reference is to Job's words (9:34; 13:21).

XXXIII 8-13 Ground for Criticism of Job—9 is not **c** a quotation of Job's words. The same accusation had been made against him by Sophar (11:4). He had admitted ordinary human sinfulness (7:21; 13:26). He denied wickedness which would merit his sufferings (9:20; 10:7; 13:18; 16:18). **10.** Omit ' because ' and ' therefore '. **10b** reproduces Job's words in 13:24b and **11**, others in 13:27. **12.** ' *because* God '. Read prob. with LXX and Ball : ' How canst thou say " Right is with me but I am not answered "'? Will God strive with man?' This well introduces **13**: ' *Why* dost thou strive against him, because he *will* not answer all thy words?'

14-30 How God speaks and works Man's Conversion d —14. God will not debate with man; his word is final; *cf.* 12 f., and see 40:5. **16b.** ' *and by admonition inspireth fear* '; *cf.* LXX. **18.** ' *Holding his soul back from the pit and his life from passing to the grave*.' For the rare word *šelah*, which recurs 36:12, *cf.* Dhorme. God does not desire man's death; *cf.* 2 Kg 14:14; Ez 18:32; 33:11. The second method used by God for bringing men to a better frame of mind is introduced in **19**, ' by *suffering* '. The particular form indicated is fever: ' *when his limbs* [lit. bones] *tremble continuously* '. **20.** Omit ' in his life '. **21.** ' is consumed away . . . *are* made bare '; present tense describing the course of the illness. **22.** Better ' to the *grave* '. ' The destroyers ' are otherwise unknown in this connexion. Perhaps we should emend to ' the home of the dead '. **23.** The word *mal'āk* in Job occurs elsewhere only 4:18 **e** where it means ' Angels ', who are God's messengers, and (1:14) of a human messenger. This latter is the meaning here, as ' one among a thousand ' signifies rarity (9:3, Eccles 7:29) and all Angels are competent to interpret God's purpose to man, but among men the gift is rare. ' an *interpreter*, one among a thousand '. This messenger-interpreter of God is a holy man, possibly a prophet. ' to declare to man his *duty* ';

331e what he should do to be upright. **24.** The holy man finds in the sinner signs of repentance, and prays for his recovery. This prayer is continued in **25** : ' Let *his flesh become fresher than in childhood ; let him return to the days of his youth* '. **26.** ' To see the face of God ' is the Heb. expression for approaching God's presence in his sanctuary (Ex 23:15 ; 34:20) [DV ' appear before me ']. The verse is a good example of the Heb. habit of leaving a change of subject to be divined from the context. The sinner prays ; God is gracious. The sinner approaches the divine presence ; God forgives his sin. **27.** ' look upon ' : perhaps ' he returns to ' men from his bed of sickness. ' offended ' : ' I have *perverted the right* '. **29.** ' Behold, all this God worketh *twice and thrice with man.*' God's patience and love are not exhausted by one effort ; he makes many attempts to save man. For the arithmetical progression, see 5:19 comm. **30.** ' from the *grave* '.

f 31-33 Job must listen or answer—Elihu is afraid neither of repetition (32:10 ; 33:1, 5) nor of proclaiming his knowledge and wisdom (32:10, 17 ; 33:3).

g XXXIV 1-37 Elihu refutes Job's Accusation that God perverts Justice—**3.** ' trieth ' : tests, examines ; ' as the mouth '. A comparison already used by Job (12:11). **4.** ' Let us *examine* [an Aramaism, *cf.* Is 48:10] *for ourselves what is right . . . what is good.*' **5.** Elihu repeats Job's words from 27:2. See 33:9 comm. **6b.** ' my *wound* [prefixing *mem* ; DV ' arrow '] *is sore though transgression there was none* '. **9.** ' *What doth man profit by his good will with God ?* ' *Cf.* 9:22-24 ; 21:7-15. **12.** Omit ' in very deed ' and read *ḥinnām* for *'omnām*. **13.** ' *Who hath given him charge of his earth or entrusted to him the whole world ?* ' As supreme lord of the world it is not possible that he should be swayed by any unworthy motive to act unjustly. **14.** ' *If he take back his spirit to himself and gather his breath to him* (**15**), *all flesh alike expires and man returns to dust.*' Read *yāśîb* and omit ' his heart ' introduced to make some sense after the misreading of *yāśîm*. For God's breath giving life and its withdrawal bringing death see Gen 2:7, Ps 103:29 f.

h 17. ' *Can he restore to health a hater of justice ? And darest thou condemn the Mighty, the Just One ?* ' (Bi 30 [1949] 73-5). This alludes to Job's repudiation of God's justice in governing the world (34:5). The absolute impartiality of God stressed in **18-19** shows that he cannot act against equity. And **20** emphasizes his power over potentates : ' In a moment they die and in the middle of the night they expire ' (add *yigwā'û* omitted by haplography ; Bi 30 [1949] 75-7). This is an allusion to the fate of the firstborn of Pharaoh at the hand of the destroying Angel who passed through Egypt at midnight (Ex 11:4 f.). ' *He strikes nobles and they pass away ; he removes the mighty by power unseen.*' For this meaning of ' not by hand ' *cf.* Lam 4:6, Dan 2:34 ; 8:25 ; divide *yigga' šō'îm.* **22.** ' and there is no obscurity '. Read **23-24** after **25** : ' But he observes *their doings ; he overthrows them in the night and they are crushed.*' The explanation of such sudden retribution is given in **23** : ' *For he does not appoint man a time to enter into judgement with God ;* (**24**) *He breaketh the mighty without trial and makes others to stand in their stead.*' For '*ōd* read *mō'ēd* (mem omitted by haplography). **25** after **22**. **27.** ' *Because they failed to follow him.*' **29a-b.** However, God does not always take action against the wicked as described in 24-28. He is the supreme Lord : ' *If he remains inactive, who can condemn him ? And if he hides his face, who can spy him out ?* ' God's hiding his face is his not showing himself by

i intervention. **29c-30.** The sense is uncertain and there is no agreement among commentators. Perhaps : ' He watcheth [*yāḥaz*] over nation and individual that there may not reign a man perverting [*me'aqqēš*] the people.' Read ' godless ', which prolongs this verse unduly, as subject of **31** : ' *When a godless man saith to God* " *I have been beguiled* [*niśśē'tî*] *; no more* ['*ōd*] *will I act corruptly* (**32**), *I have sinned, do thou teach me ; if I have worked iniquity, I will do so no more* ". **33.** *Do you think he will requite it, seeing that you reject* (*the teaching of our fathers*) *?* ' *Cf.* Dhorme. Both the length of the verse

and the sense seem to show that some similar words **3** have been accidentally omitted. ' *For thou must test* [Aramaism as 34:4 comm.] *the matter and not I ; and what thou knowest, speak.*' **34.** ' Men of understanding *will say* to me and wise man *who hear me* : (**35**) " Job speaketh without knowledge and his words *are without understanding* ".' **36.** ' *Howbeit* ['*ǎbāl*] let Job be tested to the end *for his answers in the manner of wicked men.*' **37.** ' *For he addeth to his iniquity ; he mocketh rebelliously* [*pōša'*] *in our presence ; he multiplieth his words against God.*'

XXXV 1-8 Refutation of Job's Assertion that Human 3 Conduct does not concern God—**2.** ' Hast thou devised *this as a plea and said* " *Right is with me* [*ṣādaqtî* with LXX, Vg] *rather than with God* ", (**3**) *as thou sayest* " *How does it concern thee and what do I if I sin ?* " ' Read with LXX *'ep'al 'im.* Elihu now takes up Job's plea in 7:20 that even if he were guilty his acts could in no way affect God. **4.** ' *It is left to me to answer thee.*' Lit. ' I, I will answer.' The friends had failed to do so. **5.** ' what *dost* thou give him or what *doth* he receive of thy hand ? ' Elihu agrees that man's acts can neither harm nor benefit God, but goes on to point out the fallacy of Job's deduction that therefore God need not concern himself with human conduct. It affects other human beings and God's paternal care extends to all. **8b.** ' thy just-*doing* may help *a fellow mortal* '.

9-16 Why God at times seems Deaf—**9.** ' *The weight* **b** *of oppression makes men cry out.*' Elihu now answers Job's allegation made in 24:12. He admits the fact, but denies that it tells against God's moral government of the world, for men's cry is not a cry to God for help : (**10**) ' But *they do not say,* " *Where is God who made us ?* " ' Read the plural with Syr. This form of words, which appears strange to us as an appeal to God for help, occurs 4 Kg 2:14 ; Jer 2:6, 8. ' who giveth *succour* in the night ' of affliction. ' Succour ' as in Ex 15:2, Is 12:2. Night as figure of calamity as in Is 21:11. **11.** An allusion to 12:7 f. and 18:3. The beasts can cry out in suffering, but have not the intelligence required to turn to God for help. **12.** ' So it is they cry out unanswered.' ' So it is ', in these circumstances. God does not answer the cries evoked by the cruelty of proud men because they are uttered without thought of him.

13-16 And God will not listen to Foolish Cries—**13.** **c** ' *Howbeit,* God will not *hear an empty plea and the Almighty will not regard it.*' Not only must the cry for help be directed to God but it must be a plea founded in reason. **14.** ' *Much less when thou sayest thou canst not see him ; the case is before him, and thou dost wait for him.*' A reference to 23:8-10 ; 13:18. Attempts to dictate the manner and time of God's action are, of course, rebuffed. **15** is a further allusion to Job's accusations (21:7 ff.) and is taken up (36:7b-15). ' *And now because he doth not make visitation in his wrath.*'

XXXVI 2-15 Corrective Value of God's Visitations—**3.** ' *I will take up my theme.*' **4b.** ' *One perfect in knowledge is with thee.*' Elihu is not modest, though the faultless knowledge he claims is limited to the subject in hand. **5.** ' *Lo, God is mighty and fainteth not, mighty in strength and wise of heart !* ' Read *yimmā'ēs* (*cf.* 7:5 ; Ps 58:8), the root being parallel to mss. *waḥ"kam* omitted by haplography. **6a.** ' *He doth not suffer the wicked to live.*' **7b.** ' Doth he place kings on the throne *and establish them for ever but they become exalted* (**8**), *then he putteth* (*śām*) *them bound in chains, caught in the bonds of affliction* (**9**), *and sheweth them their works and their transgressions in that they have acted proudly* (**10**), *and openeth their ear to correct them and biddeth them to return from iniquity.*' **11.** ' *If they listen and submit,* **d** they accomplish their days in *prosperity* and their years in *delights*.' **12.** ' But if they *listen* not, they pass away *to the grave* [*cf.* on 33:18] *and expire through lack of knowledge.*' 7b-c forms the protasis, 8-10 the apodosis and 11-12 give the consequence. The poet refers to the exile and restoration of Manasses (2 Par 33:6, 11-13) and to the fate of Joakim (2 Par 36:5 f.), of Joachin (4 Kg 24:9, 15 ; 2 Par 36:9 f.) and of Sedecias

d (4 Kg 24:19 ; 25:7 ; Jer 52:11). **13.** ' *The godless of heart cherish wrath.*' Instead of benefiting by God's chastisement they are embittered against divine providence. **14.** ' in youth '. As soul and life are synonymous, the meaning is that the godless die young and unregretted. There is no need to press the parallelism in the sense that the male temple prostitutes proverbially died young. These adjuncts of pagan worship were held in contempt by decent Israelites ; *cf.* Deut 23:17 (18) ; 3 Kg 14:24 ; 15:12 ; 22:47 ; 4 Kg 23:7. **15.** ' *He delivers the afflicted through their affliction and opens their ear by means of distress.*' Again the valuable lesson of the divinely intended medicinal efficacy of suffering.

e **16-21 Application of this Teaching to Job**—The following lines have been imperfectly transmitted, but may be emended as follows. **16.** ' *Yea, he enticeth thee out of affliction into broad unstraitened spaces and to repose with thy table laden with good things.*' For the Hebrew wide spaces symbolized freedom and well-being as for us straits symbolize trouble and distress. **17.** ' *Thou shalt judge the cause of the wicked and thy hands shall uphold justice.*' **18.** ' *Watch lest thou be seduced by wealth and let not great ransom turn thee aside.*' This exhortation insinuates the wrongs Elihu thinks Job must have committed in the administration of justice. **19.** ' *Is thy welfare to be compared to gold and the power of riches ?* ' This consideration reinforces the foregoing exhortation. Mere riches do not spell happiness. **20.** ' *Crush not strangers that thy kinsfolk may mount up in their place.*' So Kissane, Saydon. **21.** ' *Beware lest thou turn to iniquity for on that account thou hast been tested by calamity.*'

f **22-XXXVII 24 Elihu's Doxology—22b.** ' *There is no teacher his equal.*' Vg adopted the specialized sense of teacher of the Torah ; hence ' law-giver '. But the reference is to the admonition God gives by tribulation (7-15). **23a.** ' *Who shall call him to account for his actions ?* ' **24.** ' *Remember that thou shouldst extol his work which men have made the theme of song.*' **25.** ' *All mankind doth gaze thereon ;* every one beholdeth *from afar.*' For the wonders of God's works Elihu has in mind are those of the skies. **27.** ' *When he releaseth* [*yiḡra'*] *the drops of water, they pour forth as destructive rain* (28) *and what the clouds send down falls on the land in showers.*' Water released directly from the celestial ocean (Gen 1:7 ; Ps 148:4) comes down with destructive force as at the time of the Flood ; dropped from the clouds it is beneficent rain. **29-30** after 31, which according to the sense follows 28. **31.** ' *For by these* [destructive downpours and beneficent rain] *he executeth judgement* on the peoples and giveth food *in abundance* '. **29.** ' *Yea who* [so Syr] *understandeth the poising of the clouds, the elevation* of his *pavilion.*' The suspension of the heavy, water-laden clouds in the air was mysterious to the ancients. The heavenly firmament is God's pavilion. Some exegetes introduce thunder here, but this is the subject of 37:1 ff. where it **g** has its own solemn introduction. **30.** ' *Lo, he spreads his light thereon and covers its roots with the sea.*' Light is one of God's marvellous creatures. As man looks up, he sees its brightness on the whole firmament. This was thought to be solid (Gen 1:6 f. ; Job 37:18). Its supporting walls resting on the horizon had their ' roots ' (*cf.* the roots of the mountains, 28:9) down in the ocean. Similarly of the mountains in Jon 2:7. **32.** ' *He covereth his hands with light and giveth it command against the mark.*' God at his will sends forth lightning conceived as a condensed and, of course, destructive form of light. **33.** Elihu now alludes, I think, to the destruction of Job's shepherds and flocks by lightning, Read, with redivision of the consonants : *yeḡaddēa lerō'îm miqneh pā'al 'ōlāh.* ' *It cutteth down the shepherds ; of the flock it maketh a holocaust.*' See 1:16, and for reason. supporting the translation of 27-33 Bi 30 (1949) 77-89. **XXXVII** begins with the fear and wonder inspired by thunder which were the greater the less its physical cause was understood. **2.** ' the *rumbling* of his voice '. Thunder is spoken of as the voice of God. **3.** ' *He sendeth it forth* under all the heavens and his *lightning to*

the ends of the earth.' **4.** ' After it *his* voice doth **332g** roar . . . *he doth not hold back the flashes* when his voice is heard.' Supply *beräqîm* omitted by haplography. **6b** suffers from dittography : ' and the *downpour of rain to be violent* ' (*'ozzû*). **7.** Omit ' hand ' and read *be'aḏ.* By severe weather God keeps men at home and puts a stop to their work abroad. **8** gives a further effect **h** of the storm. **9.** ' Out of *its store-chamber* ' (*cf.* Ps 134:7) in the South, whence came heat (37:17) and storms (Is 21:1 ; Zach 9:14). **10b.** ' and the broad waters are *frozen* '. **11.** ' Yea, the clouds hurl flashes [*beräqîm*]. ' light ' here is ' lightning '. **12.** ' *And all around it* [the lightning] *turneth and followeth the course* [*yithallēk* omitted by haplography] *of his direction.*' **13.** ' *If it be for a scourge, it fulfils his pleasure* [*yemallē' reṣōnô*] ; *if for mercy, it attains its goal.*' **15.** ' *Dost thou know of God's laying his charge upon them* [the elements mentioned above] *and how his clouds flash forth the light ?* ' **16.** ' *Hast thou knowledge of the poising of the clouds, of the marvels of the All-knowing ?* ' **17b.** ' *when the south wind turns all sultry ?* ' The unpleasant heat is a sign of man's impotence against the powers of nature. **19b.** ' in the darkness of ignorance *we cannot marshal speech* '. LXX : ' and we will cease from marshalling words '. **20.** ' *Must it be told him that I speak ? Or can one say that he must be informed ?* ' God is omniscient. The words seem to reflect confidence that God will act on what is said and intervene. **21-22a.** ' *Just now the light could not be seen ; it was obscured by the clouds. But a wind hath passed and cleared the sky ; from the north cometh a golden sheen.*' The brightness heralds the approach of God. The springing of the light from the north is no reflection of meteorological fact or fancy but a poetic allusion to the ancient idea that the seat of divinity was in that far unknown region ; *cf.* Is 14:13. **22b-23.** ' *About the godhead is awe and majesty ; Shaddai we have not found. Manifold in power and judgement and a righteous cause he will not pervert.*' God is about to manifest himself, but human attempts to come into direct contact with him are vain. **24.** ' *Therefore men should reverence* him ; *he will not regard those wise in their own esteem.*'

XXXVIII 1-XXXIX 32 Yahweh's First Discourse— **333a** God does not explain the reasons why he allows the innocent to suffer. The approach to the problem is indirect. By repeated examples God brings home to Job the lesson of divine omnipotence and omniscience and by contrast man's puny strength and feeble intellect. Who then is Job or any man that he should presume to sit in judgement on God's government of the world ? It is for man humbly to acknowledge God's wisdom and to submit to his providence trusting, though he may not understand, that all is for the best. The questions addressed to Job are of those unanswerable by the science of the day. In our time a different series would be substituted, but with the same result. Who can say what is the electricity which warms and lights our homes ? Who can say what is gravity which makes the apple fall to the ground ? And who can explain the simple fact that damp cold is felt more keenly than dry ? Where was Job when God established the world and its laws ? (**4-11**) What power has he over the dawn and what does he know of the ocean depths, of the abode of the dead, even of the wide earth (**12-18**) ? Of the mysteries of light and darkness, of snow and hail, of rain, lightning and thunder, frost and ice (**19-30**) ? What power has Job over the constellations, lightning, clouds (**31-38**) ? And can Job provide food for lion and raven (**39-41**) ? What does he know of the life-story of the mountain-goat (**XXXIX:1-4**) ? Can he control the wild ass (**5-8**) or the wild ox (**9-12**) ? The wonders of God's creation are illustrated by the ostrich (**13-18**), the horse (**19-25**), the hawk and the eagle (**26-30**). The whole ends with God's challenge to Job (**31** f.).

XXXVIII 1-38 The Contrast between Divine and **b** **Human Power and Knowledge**—**1.** The storm or storm-wind is symbolic of God's majesty. So also Ez 1:4, and *cf.* the thunder and lightning of Sinai (Ex 19:16, 18). The golden splendour heralding the

333b divine approach was only momentary. **2.** ' *Who is this that darkeneth counsel with wordy ignorance ?* ' **7.** The stars of morning occur only here. Night was symbolic of sorrow and disaster and therefore a time unsuitable for the joyous ceremony of laying the foundation-stone of the earth (*cf.* Esd 3:10). For the personification *cf.* Ps 18 (19) 2 f. ; 95 (96) 11 f. ; 97 (98) 7 f. The sons of God are the angels as 1:6, etc. Note that here the stars have been created before the earth exists. The chronological sequence of Gen 1 was understood to be schematic and artistic only. **13.** It is the light of dawn arising in the distant east that takes hold of the extremities of the earth ; and thereupon the wicked, who have plied their trade by night, must retire to their lairs (*cf.* 24:15-17). **14.** With the coming of light the earth ' *is transformed as clay under the seal* '. All the fair colours of which night had robbed it, are restored.

c Not only are the trees, shrubs and plants ' the garment ' of the earth, but like a garment they are of beautiful hues. **15.** By ' their light ', it seems, must be understood the night which the wicked have turned into their day. And with the coming of dawn the arm of the wicked loses its power. Grave sins, conscious and defiant, are said to be committed with ' a high hand ' (*cf.* § 203*c*). **16.** ' Hast thou *gone* to the *sources* of the sea ? ' where it wells up from the subterranean ocean, referred to in 8. **17.** The entrance to Sheol, the realm of the dead. **18.** ' tell me, if thou knowest *it all* '. **19.** Light and darkness were conceived as two beings succeeding each other over the surface of the earth. But where did the absent one go ? To this question Job must know the answer (**20**), God implies ironically, ' *for thou canst take them to their bounds and discernest the paths to their dwelling* '. **21.** ' *Thou knowest, for then wert thou born and the tale of thy days is long.* ' Crushing irony ! As if Job were as old as the first day of creation when the world was planned and measured and every creature was assigned its place (4-11). **22.** Where the *storehouses* of hail and those of snow lay the primitive science of the day did not even attempt to define. It was not suspected that they are forms of frozen ' rain '. These, God says (**23**), ' *I hold in reserve for times of trouble* '. By heavy hail God aided Josue's defeat of the five kings (Jos 10:11 ; *cf.* Ps 17:14 ; Is 30:30). **24.** Probably ' mist ' (DV ' light ') with LXX. The heat is that

d brought and spread by the sultry east wind. **26.** The purpose of rain was conceived as either beneficent or destructive (37:27 f., 31) and therefore rain on the uninhabited desert was mysterious. **27b.** Add ' *from arid ground* ' (*missiyyāh for mōṣā'*). **30a.** ' They are hidden as with stone.' **31b.** ' *or canst thou loosen the bonds of Orion ?* ' The three stars at his waist were judged to bind him to the sky. **32.** Mazzaroth, a conspicuous star or constellation noted for its rising and setting, is probably Venus (so Vg ' Lucifer ' and DV ' the day star '), Schiaparelli 74 ff. There is doubt about the last constellation (DV ' evening star '). If ' *and guide the Bear with her children* ', the latter will be the three stars appended to the quadrilateral. If it is the Hyades, then the children are the minor stars which surround Aldebaran. **33b.** ' *Or dost thou establish its rule over the earth ?* ' as exercised by sun and moon (Gen 1:16-18). **34.** Job cannot issue orders to the clouds ' that *they answer* thee with abundance of water ' (with LXX). In 35 omit ' will they return '. ' Here we are ', thy servants ready to do thy bidding. **36.** Prob. the ibis (DV ' the heart of man ') is intended ; so Dhorme. It was credited with wisdom as able to foretell the Nile floods, and was sacred to Thoth, the god of wisdom and of writing. The wisdom of the cock is shown by its skill in forecasting the coming of dawn. **37.** ' *Whose is the wisdom to spread out the clouds and who pours out the waterskins of heaven* (**38**) *when the soil is hard and caked and the clods cleave together ?* ' ' spread out ', *i.e. yiprōs = yiprōṣ.*

e **39-XXXIX 32 The Ignorance and Feebleness of Man illustrated from the Animal World—39-41.** It is God alone who can and does feed all the multitude of the beasts and birds (Ps 146:9), a simple but telling thought to which man seldom adverts. **XXXIX:1.** A coloured 33 illustration of the mountain-goat or ibex, which chooses for its dwelling remote rocky regions seldom visited by man, may be seen in H. B. Tristram, *The Flora and Fauna of Palestine* (1884) 6. **3b.** ' they cast *their little ones* ' (lit. ' they put forth their conceptions '). The emphasis is on the ease and speed of the delivery. **9-12** treat of **the wild ox** or buffalo which is still found in Palestine. **12.** Couldst thou trust him *to return and gather thy seed* into thy barnfloor ? ' **13-18. The Ostrich** —**13.** ' There is joy in the wing of the ostrich, gracious in feather and plumage.' MT may be so translated with '*ēm* for '*im.* But the ostrich has rudimentary wings which could not be singled out for praise. But emended with Kissane in the light of Vg : ' *Is the wing of the ostrich like the pinion of the stork or the hawk ?* ' This gives the reason for **14** : ' *For she must leave her eggs on the ground and hatches them on the soil.*' It is stated sometimes that the ostrich leaves the incubation of the eggs entirely to the warmth of the sun. In fact, the task is shared by the hen with the cock bird. **16b.** ' *She has no concern for the frustration of her labour.*' **18.** Though the presence of an unknown word in *a* makes the exact sense doubtful, *b* shows the sense to be that in flight she easily outstrips pursuers.

19-25 The Horse—19b. ' Canst thou clothe his neck with *its* mane? ' Dhorme has pointed out that the root meaning of *r'm* is ' commotion ', ' trembling ', and that its application to thunder with its noise is secondary. Hence here prob. ' (quivering) mane '. **20.** ' *Canst thou make him leap like the locust ? His majestic snorting inspireth terror.*' **21.** ' *He paweth the ground in his might ; he rejoiceth in his strength as he goeth forth to meet the weaponed host.*' ' Might ' is a meaning recovered from Ugaritic. **22a.** ' *He laugheth at fear and is not dismayed.*' **23.** ' On him.' **24b.** ' *nor will he stand quiet* when the trumpet soundeth '. `26-30. Birds of prey. **27.** Sennacherib describes an inaccessible fortress as ' the nest of an eagle, the prince among birds '. **28.** The eagle dwells ' *in the crags and fastnesses* '. **29-30** speak of the marvellous speed with which birds of prey alight from out of sight on fallen bodies ; *cf.* Mt 24:28.

XXXIX 33-35 Job's Submission (= MT 40:1-5) f —**35.** ' Once have I spoken, but I *will not answer* [*cf.* 32*b*], and *twice* but I will add no more.'

XL 1-XLI 25 God's Second Discourse—(MT 40:6- 33 41:26). God first reproaches Job with making light of the divine justice in order to maintain his own innocence (**3**) and then reminds him in various ways of his impotence (**4-9**). God's wisdom and power, on the one hand, and man's weakness on the other are then illustrated by the wonderful qualities of and man's inferior strength compared to the hippopotamus (**10-19**) and the crocodile (**20-41:25**).

1-9 Job's Weakness—2 is repeated from 38:3. **4.** ' like b *God's* . . . like *his* '. Thunder coming from the heavens was thought of as the voice of God (37:2, 4). **5b.** ' *and clothe thyself with glory and splendour* '. **7b.** ' *where they stand* '—on the spot. All this is irony. Job knows that these feats surpass his strength, but are easy to the power of God. **8b.** ' *imprison them in gaol* '. **9.** ' Then [if Job prove equal to the tasks proposed] *I also will praise thee, for....* '

10-19 The Hippopotamus—Ancient accounts may be c read in Herodotus 2, 71 and Pliny *Hist. Nat.* 8, 25 f. **11b.** ' his force in the *thews* of his belly '. **12b.** ' the *sinews of his thighs are close-knit* '. **13b.** ' his frame like *bars of iron* '. **14b.** ' he *was made the leader of his fellows* ' (with consonantal change into *nōgēś*). **15.** ' *The mountain beasts stare at him* [in fear and wonder] ; *he laughs at the beasts of the field* [in scorn] '. *Cf.* Assyrian *būlu* ' quadruped, wild animal ' and read *l^e kol . . . yiṣḥaq.* **16a.** ' He reclineth under the lotus.' **17a.** ' The *shadow of the lotus trees screeneth him.*' **18.** ' *If the river overwhelms him, he has no care, nor fear at a stream in spate.*' **19.** Ball and Dhorme suggest a reference to the method which Herodotus (2, 70) records to have been used in Egypt, of easily overpowering a crocodile's resistance by first smearing its eyes with mud. But this was done

c only after the capture. Read prob. *l^e* for *b^e*: ' *Who can catch him when he is on the watch ?* ' The ' stakes ' refer to some method either of capture or of keeping an animal under control like our ring in a bull's nostrils.

d **20–XLI 25 The Crocodile (Leviathan)** (MT 25–41:26)—Ancient accounts in Herodotus 2, 68–70 and Pliny, *Hist. Nat.* 8, 25 f. **21.** ' ring ' : so also Theodotion ; others ' cord '. ' buckle ' : hook or fetter. **25a.** ' *Can the dealers make trade with it ?* ' **26.** ' *Canst thou fill his hide with barbs or his head with fish-spears ?* ' **27c.** ' *Thou wilt not do it again.*' Read **28** (= MT 41:1) after **XLI:1** : ' *Is he not fierce when aroused ? Who dare stand before him ?* ' **40:28.** ' *even at the sight of it he is* cast down ' : his courage will fail him. **41:2.** ' *Who hath faced him and been scatheless ? Under the wide heavens there is none.*' **3.** ' *I will not be silent about his members and will tell of his unequalled strength.*' **4.** ' *Who can strip off his garment or penetrate his double mail ?* ' **5.** The portals of his face stand for his jaws. No need for emendation. **6.** ' *His back is of channelled shields, shut in by a wall of flint* ' (read *ḥōmaṭ* for *ḥōṭām*). **9.** ' *His snorting flasheth light*', the spray cast up glittering in the bright sunlight. ' The reddish eyes of the crocodile appear gleaming through the water before the head appears above the surface. In the Egyptian hieroglyphics the dawn is denoted by the crocodile's eyes ' (Driver). **10–12** give a poetic picture of the shining spray thrown up as the animal rises to the surface. **13b.** *Dismay* spreads at his approach. **14.** ' *The folds of his flesh are solid : firm-set upon him, it shaketh not* ' (Ball). **15b.** ' firm as the *nether millstone* '. **16.** ' *the billows are in dread, the breakers of the sea take to flight* ' (so prob.). **17b.** ' *the spear glanceth from* his breast-plate '. **19.** *Arrow* (DV ' archer '). **20.** ' Hammer ' : uncertain, perhaps ' club '. ' to scorn the *hurtling javelin* '. **21.** ' *Under him are the sharpest of potsherds ; he stretcheth himself like a threshing-sledge on the mire.*' His sharp scales are compared to the pointed pieces of basalt or other hard stone fixed under a wooden sledge and drawn by oxen over the corn to break up the straw and thresh out the grain—an instrument still in use among the Arabs. **22b.** ' *and maketh the sea like an ointment-pot* ' as the water is lashed into foam at his passage. **23b.** ' *The deep has the look of a hoary head.*' **25a** means as it stands that he is unconcerned no matter what he sees, but prob. ' *all that is mighty feareth him* ' (*'ōṭō . . . yîrā* ').

e **XLII 1–6 Job's Submission**—*3a* is taken with some variation from 38:2 and **4b** from 38:3*b*. They could not possibly be uttered by Job in the present context as expressing his own mind, and there is no point in Job's repeating them as quotations of God's words. Moreover **4a** is composed of fragments of Elihu's speech (33:1, 31) and is also quite out of place. *3a* and 4 are therefore seen to be interpolations. God did not convict Job of sin nor assert that his calamities were merited. He demonstrated the weakness and ignorance of man and of Job in particular and at the same time the power and wisdom of the godhead. It is useless for man to fight against God, and whatever God does is wisely done. Job humbly confesses that he has learnt both lessons, the omnipotence of God (2) and that his

failure, *his inability* to understand the wisdom of God's **334e** government is due to the limitation of his own powers (3).

7–9 The Friends do Penance—**7.** The rebuke is **f** addressed to Eliphaz as the oldest and the leader of the three. Elihu is disregarded—a further indication that his discourse was not part of the original composition (*cf.* § 317*m*). The whole burden of their speeches has been that suffering is always the punishment of wrongdoing and that therefore Job has been guilty. They are told that they have not spoken aright and their theology of suffering is repudiated. From this it does not follow that sin is never punished by suffering in this world ; but it is wrong for man to sit in judgement on his neighbour and condemn him as guilty on the ground of his afflictions. **8.** ' *I will pay regard to him and not treat you severely.*' Moral wrongness not only in act but in thought and speech does merit chastisement, and the friends have done wrongly in obstinately maintaining their view against the evidence, but the intercession of a just (and maligned but forgiving) man has great power with God. Note the number 7, especially sacred among the Hebrews (*cf.* Gen 21:30, etc.).

10–16 Job's Reward and Subsequent Prosperity—10. **g** ' *Yahweh restored the fortunes of Job* when he prayed for his friends.' Not only did Job's prayer avail to avert God's indignation from the friends, but brought a great reward to himself. His prayer was an act of selfless forgiveness, by which he put away all rancour from his heart at a time when he did not yet know how God was about to restore his fortunes. **11.** Job's relations recover their affection as he recovered his prosperity. ' ewe ' : LXX ' lamb ' and so Ibn Ezra, but most understand of metal means of payment (elsewhere only Gen 33:19 = Jos 24:32). **13.** Prob. ' fourteen ' sons (a dual form = ' twice-seven '). Everything was doubled except the number of daughters. ' For the oriental it is the sons who count : daughters are not wealth ' (Dhorme). **14.** The daughters were named Yemîma (Jemima), Qeṣî'a and Qerenhappûk, equivalent to Dove, Fragrance (from cassia, *cf.* Ps 44:9), Beauty (lit. horn of antimony, used for beautifying the eyes ; see on Jer 4:30). **15.** According **h** to Hebrew law a daughter had a right to her father's inheritance only in the absence of sons (Num 27:8), but Job was not a Hebrew. His wealth was so great that his daughters could be admitted to a share without detracting from the shares due to the sons. **16.** If LXX is right here is assigning the age of 70 to Job at the time of his visitation, he lived to enjoy the doubled fortune granted to him by God thereafter for twice as long as he had enjoyed prosperity before calamity came upon him. The principle of retribution is shown in action and is thereby re-affirmed. But the story of Job has modified the accepted principle in one important respect—all suffering is not punishment of sin. A just man may be visited by grievous misfortune as a divinely intended test of his virtue ; and if the sufferer's virtue emerges purified from the crucible—Job never lost his inmost conviction of God's justice (23:7 ; 31:35)—his endurance of calamity and suffering is itself rewarded generously.

THE PSALMS

By T. E. BIRD

334 Bibliography—Migne, *Patrologia Graeca et Latina*; St Thomas Aquinas, *In Davidem* (Rome, 1570); A. Agelli, *Commentarius in Psalmos* (Rome, 1606); St Robert Bellarmine, *Explanatio in Psalmos* (1542–1621; Eng. Tr. 1866); A. Calmet, *Commentaire sur la Bible*, t. 4 (Paris, 1724); De Muis-Bossuet, *Commentarius in Psalmos* (Louvain, 1770); J. A. Van Steenkiste, *Commentarius in Librum Psalmorum* (Bruges, 1870); D. Schilling, *Vaticinia Messiana Libri Psalmorum* (Paris, 1884); J. M'Swiney, S.J., *Translation of the Psalms and Canticles* (St Louis, 1901); M.-B. d'Eyragues *Les Psaumes* (Paris, 1904); M.-J. Lagrange, O.P., *Notes sur le Messianisme dans les Psaumes* (RB, 1905); L. Méchineau, S.J., *Gli Autori e il Tempo della Composizione dei Salmi* (Rome, 1911); V. Zapletal, O.P., *De Poesi Hebraeorum* (Fribourg, 1911); J. Knabenbauer, S.J., *Commentarius in Psalmos* (Paris, 1912); E. Pannier, *Psalterium iuxta hebraicam veritatem* (Lille, 1913); P. Boylan, *The Psalms* (Dublin, 1920, 1924); T. E. Bird, *Commentary on the Psalms* (London, 1927); F. Zorell, S.J., *Psalterium ex Hebraeo Latinum* (Rome, 1928); C. J. Callan and J. A. McHugh, O.P., *The Psalms Explained* (New York, 1929); H. Herkenne, *Das Buch der Psalmen* (Bonn, 1936); J. Calès, S.J., *Le Livre des Psaumes* (Paris, 1936); C. Lattey, S.J., *The First Book of Psalms* (London, 1939); W. H. McClellan, S.J., *Obscurities in the Latin Psalter* (CBQ, Washington, 1939–44); C. J. Callan, O.P., *The Psalms translated from the Latin Psalter* (New York, 1944); C. Lattey, S.J., *The Psalter in the Westminster Version* (London, 1945); Professors of the Biblical Institute, *Liber Psalmorum cum Canticis Breviarii Romani* (Rome, 1945); R. J. Foster, *Psalms and Canticles of the Breviary* (Cork, 1947); R. A. Knox, *The Book of Psalms* (new Latin version translated into English), (London, 1947); E. Lussier, *The New Latin Psalter: An Exegetical Commentary* (CBQ, Washington, April 1947 ff.); Dom Savin Ely, *Le Psautier Romain* (St Maurice, Suisse, 1948); *F. Bäthgen, *Die Psalmen* (Göttingen, 1897); *B. Duhm, *Die Psalmen* (Freiburg, 1899); *A. F. Kirkpatrick, *The Book of Psalms* (Cambridge, 1902, frequently reprinted); *S. R. Driver, *The Parallel Psalter* (Oxford, 1904²); *W. Emery Barnes, *Lex in Corde* (London, 1910); *C. A. Briggs, *Psalms* (ICC, Edinburgh, 1916); *E. G. King, *Early Religious Poetry of the Hebrews* (Cambridge, 1911); *D. C. Simpson, *The Psalmists* (Oxford, 1926); *A. C. Welch, *The Psalter* (Oxford, 1926); *H. Gunkel, *Die Psalmen* (Göttingen, 1926⁴); *C. C. Keet, *Liturgical Study of the Psalter* (London, 1928); *W. E. Barnes, *The Psalms* (W.C.; London, 1931); *A. Rahlfs, *Septuaginta : Psalmi cum Odis* (Göttingen, 1931); *W. O. Oesterley, *The Psalms, Bk III; The Psalms, Bk IV* (London, 1933, 1936), *A Fresh Approach to the Psalms* (London, 1937), *The Psalms* (London, 1939); *B. D. Eerdmans, *The Hebrew Book of Psalms* (Leiden, 1947).

335a Introduction—The inspired hymnal of the OT, known as the Psalter, was taken over by the Christian Church not only as part of the sacred Scriptures but also as her hymn-book. Her divine Founder had made quotations from it, had used it in prayer, and had explained it to his disciples, Mt 5:4; 7:23; 21:16, 42; 26:30; 27:46; Lk 24:44. His followers imitated his

example, Ac 1:20; 2:25–28, 30, 34 f.; 4:11, 25 f. **3** SS. Paul and James both advised the faithful to use the psalms in community worship, Eph 5:19; Col 3:16; Jas 5:13. From that time onward the inspired hymns became an important part of the Church's prayers. Describing the funeral of St Paula, St Jerome tells us how the psalms were chanted by the clergy, 'now in Greek, now in Latin, and now in Syriac; and this not only during the three days that elapsed before she was buried beneath the church and close to the cave of our Lord, but throughout the remainder of the week' (*Letter* 108:30). From the same writer we learn that the psalms chanted in the churches were also sung in the fields : 'the toiling reaper sings psalms as he works, and the vine-dresser, as he prunes his vines, sings one of David's songs' (*Letter* 46:12). Before long, not only the clergy but the laity also could recite the Psalter by heart. When the times of persecution were passed away, the Church at Rome instituted the public recitation of the psalms at the canonical hours of prayer. St Benedict (†547) founded his monastic office on the Roman usage; and these two offices—the Roman and the Benedictine—became the sources of the breviary which every cleric in major orders is now bound by law to recite (*Codex Juris Canonici*, can 135).

Hebrew Poetry—For the proper understanding of the **b** psalms something must be known about the principles and structure of Hebrew poetry. Like all other peoples the Hebrews had their poets—profane and religious. Quotations from the profane poetry crept into the sacred writings; *cf.* Gen 4:23 f.; Num 21:17 f., 27–30; Is 23:16. The psalms are religious poems of the character of lyrics. As the Greek title of the whole collection indicates, they were sung with musical accompaniment—ψάλλειν means to play on a stringed instrument. Many of them were, in the first instance, private prayers; some were composed for public worship; others were votive offerings—hymns of thanksgiving sung at the sanctuary or temple after escape from danger or persecution. Eventually all became liturgical hymns. See my article in DbR (July 1928) 95 ff.

The distinctive feature of Hebrew poetry is **c** **parallelism**, that is, the repetition of the same thought in different words. It is not peculiar to Hebrew verse since it is found in Babylonian and Egyptian poems. See further § 313e–f.

Hebrew poetry has no **metre** (see § 313g–h) in the **d** classical sense of the term. See Castellino, *Il Ritmo ebraico nel Pensiero degli Antichi*, Bi 15 (1934) 505–16. The *qinah* or 'dirge' measure occurs in the Psalter only in 18:8 ff.; 83, which two psalms, curiously enough, are not dirges at all. Often there is a lack of uniformity in the same poem, so much so that some writers come to the conclusion that the Hebrew poets delighted in irregular metre, while others distort the text in order to force it into regular metre, with the result that they 'merely render hideous that which is beautiful' (*Margoliouth, *Relations between Arabs and Israelites*, 43). 'We are still far from fully understanding the rules of Hebrew accentuation', wrote *George Adam Smith in 1910 (*The Early Poetry of Israel*, 12)—words that still hold good. All that we know for certain is that there is a rhythmic accentuation

442

in the poetry. Eerdmans, 13, is right when he says : ' Metric studies do not give a reliable foundation for text-emendations '.

e Were the original psalms divided into **strophes** ? This question cannot be answered with certainty. An affirmative answer is suggested by the occurrence of refrains in some of the hymns (41, 42, 45, 48, 55, 56, 58, 79, 98, 106, 143), yet a refrain does not necessarily indicate the end of a strophe. Modern translators usually divide the psalms into strophes or stanzas ; but it has yet to be demonstrated that all Hebrew poetry was originally strophic. For a criticism of Condamin's *Poèmes de la Bible, avec une introduction sur la strophique hébraïque* (1933), see M.-J. Lagrange in RB 43 (1934) 128–32. The presence of *Sela* at the end of a line has been regarded by some writers as indicating the end of a strophe, but its meaning and purpose are quite uncertain. St Marcella wrote to St Jerome to inquire the meaning of the word. In his reply, St Jerome enumerated the explanations given by commentators— change of metre, pause for breath, change of meaning, a musical direction, and gave his own preference for Aquila's ἀεί ' for ever ' (*Letter* 28). Thus it would be a kind of ejaculation, like *Amen*, with which, indeed, it is coupled in a synagogue inscription of the 4th or early 5th cent. A.D. (*Sukenik, The Ancient Synagogue of El-Hammeh, 41). From the root-meaning of the word, ' lift up ', some modern writers favour one of the explanations mentioned by St Jerome, *viz.* a musical direction, indicating either that the music is to become *forte*, or that the voice is to be raised for the blessing ; *cf.* Dom Hugh Bévenot, RB 42 (1933) 510 f. Proof that the term was not used to mark the end of a stanza is found in the fact that although it occurs in thirty-nine psalms and three times in Hab 3 it is nowhere else found in the Bible. See further § 313*i–l*.

There is no evidence to show that the Hebrew poets intentionally used **rhyme**. In the few instances to be found it is accidental rather than deliberate. On the other hand, some psalms are deliberately **alphabetical** : either each line begins with a successive letter of the alphabet (110, 111), or each distich (24, 33, 144), or each quatrain (9, 36), while in 118 the eight lines of each section have the same letter and the whole alphabet runs down the entire psalm. See also § 313*k*.

f Numbering of Psalms—In MT and Vg there are 150 psalms. The LXX and Syr. versions add a 151st, telling of the victory of David over Goliath. The numbering of the psalms in MT does not tally with that in LXX ; hence the disagreement between the Catholic versions (which follow LXX) and the Protestant versions (which follow MT). The following table indicates the discrepancies :

LXX, Vg, DV	MT, AV, RV
1–8	1–8
9	9, 10
10–112	11–113
113	114, 115
114, 115	116
116–145	117–146
146, 147	147
148–150	148–150

MT and the versions dependent upon it are wrong in dividing 9 (Vg), for, although some of the initial letters have been lost through textual corruption, the psalm was originally alphabetical. Both traditions are wrong in reading 41, 42 (Vg) as two psalms, for the common refrain indicates a unity. External evidence favours the unity of 113 (Vg), but internal evidence suggests the division. MT is probably correct in reading one psalm for Vg 114, 115 ; on the other hand it is preferable to read two psalms 146, 147 (Vg) instead of one 147 (MT). The Jews divided the Psalter into five books, probably in imitation of the Pentateuch, Vg 1–40 ; 41–71 ; 72–88 ; 89–105 ; 106–150. Each book closes with a doxology, ending

with *So be it, so be it*, except the fifth book, where some **335f** commentators regard the last psalm as itself the doxology ; more probably, however, none was added because it was not known whether the canon of Scripture (at least as far as inspired hymns were concerned) was closed. At the end of the second book a colophon was added : ' The praises (or, prayers) of David, son of Jesse, are ended '. This shows that the present arrangement is not original, since other psalms, attributed to David, are found in later books. Further evidence of re-arrangement is seen in the repetition of psalms ; thus 13 re-occurs as 52 in the second book ; 39:14–18 is reproduced as 69 ; 56 : 8–12 reappears as 107:2–6 ; and 59:7–14 is found again as 107:7–14. All this points to editorial manipulation. An editor also seems to have altered the divine names : for example, when 13 reappears as 52 the name *Elohim* is substituted for *Yahweh*. In the first book *Yahweh* occurs 272 times (MT) and *Elohim* 15 times (exclusive of titles) ; in the second book *Elohim* predominates— 164 times against 30 ; in the third book the names are almost equally distributed—44 and 43 ; the fourth and fifth books employ *Yahweh* exclusively, except when 56 and 59 are repeated, and in 143:9.

Titles—Most of the psalms have titles or superscrip- **336** tions. The meaning of many of these is far from certain. What is surprising is that, as far back as the 2nd cent. B.C., the Jews translating the Psalter into Greek at Alexandria faced the same difficulty over the titles as we do today, and, presumably, the rabbis at Jerusalem were unable to shed any light on the problems. As obscurity had enveloped many of these titles at so early a date, they must have represented a tradition of venerable antiquity. On this score they deserve our respectful attention and should not lightly be set aside as valueless ; *cf.* § 49*b–c*.

The meaning of some of the title-words is known. They are as follows. *Mizmor* (57 times) means a hymn sung to the accompaniment of a stringed instrument. Hence it is the proper word for *a psalm*, indicating more than *šîr* or *šîrāh* (18 times), which simply means *a song*. Five times we meet *tᵉpillāh*, which is rightly translated *a prayer*, but only once *tᵉhillāh*, meaning *praise*, although the plural of this word gives the Hebrew title of the whole Psalter. *Nᵉgînôt* (7 times) means *stringed instruments*. So much for titles the meanings of which are not in doubt ; but the following are all disputed.

Above no less than 55 psalms is the word *lamnaṣṣeaḥ*, found nowhere else in the Bible except Hab 3:19. Vg, following LXX εἰς τὸ τέλος, translates *in finem*, but Aquila, Symmachus, Theodotion and St Jerome adopt the Aramaic meaning of the word—*victory* or *victor*. Several modern writers, relying on the use of the verb in 1 Par 23:4 ; 2 Par 2:2, 18 ; 34:12 ; Esd 3:8, think that the reference is to the *overseer* of the music—the choirmaster or conductor or band-master or soloist. BDB's interpretation, *viz.* that psalms with this title were taken over by an editor from an older Psalter known as the ' Director's Collection ' is not more than a conjecture. How could Hab 3 belong to this Psalter ?

Maśkîl, Vg *intellectus* or *ad intellectum* (13 times) ; *miktām*, Vg *tituli inscriptio* (6 times) ; *'el-hannᵉḥîlôt*, DV ' for her that obtaineth the inheritance ', Ps 5 ; *šiggāyôn*, DV ' a psalm ' (Ps 7 ; *cf.* § 540*r*) ; *'al mût labbēn*, DV ' for the hidden things of the Son ', Ps 9 ; *'al-maḥᵃlat*, DV ' For Maeleth ', St Jer. *per chorum* (Ps 52, followed by *lᵉᵉannôt*, DV ' to answer ', St Jer. *ad praecinendum* at the head of 87) all await solution ; so also does the long expression ' For a people that is removed at a distance from the sanctuary ' (LXX, Vg, DV), for which St Jerome has ' For the dumb dove because it (or, David) may have gone far away ', Ps 55 ; Eerdman's' idea that it refers to a carrier-pigeon, sent to the temple, is unlikely.

Other terms are not quite so inexplicable. Some modern commentators, depending on a statement in the Targum, suppose that *'al-haggittît* (3 times) has reference to a musical instrument invented in the

336 town of Gath ; but the ancient versions are probably right in reading ' for the presses ' or ' winepresses ' (DV 8, 80, 83), associating the psalm with the vintage. There is reason to suppose that '*al-ʿalāmôt*, DV ' for the hidden ', Ps 45, means ' for boys' soprano voices '. In what sense Ps 59 was *to teach* (DV ' for doctrine ') is not clear ; *cf.* 2 Kg 1:18. Nowadays it is generally agreed that what are called *Gradual psalms* (DV 119-133) were pilgrimage psalms, *songs of ascents*, because they were sung by the pilgrims ' going up ' to Jerusalem for the great festivals ; *cf.* 1 Kg 1:3 ; Is 30:29 ; Ps 121:4. When we recite St Ambrose's homily on a feast of many martyrs we say : ' Pro octava enim multi inscribuntur psalmi '. Actually *for the octave* is only found above Pss 6, 11. Some commentators think that the reference is to the scale of an octave, but it is very doubtful whether Hebrew music used the octave, since the primitive type of Arabian music known to us is not based on eight tones ; there were, however, eight-stringed instruments (*cf.* 1 Par 15:21), and to these the term in the title may refer.

Some modern writers think that they can detect names of popular **melodies** in the superscriptions. Above 21 (DV) we read ' for the morning protection ', but St Jerome translated correctly from the Hebrew : *the hind of the morning*, which, according to some, including NP (2nd edit.), was the tune to which the psalm was sung. This, however, is not more than a conjecture ; by a slight correction Agelli renders the phrase ' at break of day ' (*cf.* Gen 32:24 (25) ; Jg 19:25; 1 Kg 9:26). Another tune is supposed in the titles of 44, 59, 68, 79, where, in DV, we read ' For them that shall be changed ', but in St Jer. : *For the lilies*, and NP : *Secundum ' Lilia '*. The reference, however, may be not to a tune, but to lily-shaped instruments ; or the word may be of Babylonian origin and mean, according to Professor S. Langdon, an instrument of three notes, ' probably the curious pipe fashioned in the form of an ox head and found at Babylon ' (*Journal of Royal Asiatic Society*, 1921, 180). ' Destroy not ' is also supposed to be the tune for 56-58, 74 (DV), but it seems strange that this same melody should suit these dissimilar psalms ; perhaps Eerdmans solution ' thou shalt not curtail (the text of the psalm) ' is correct.

Some titles contain **liturgical notes :** 91 is for *the sabbath day* ; 23 for *the first day of the week* ; 47 for *the second day* ; 93 for *the fourth* and 92 for *the day before the sabbath* ; but all these, with the exception of 91, are taken from LXX. The Old Latin version, supported by the Mishnah, assigns 80 to *the fifth day of the week*, while the Mishnah alone gives us a Ps for *the third day*, viz. 81. The meaning of *for a remembrance* or *to bring to remembrance* (37 and 69) — εἰς ἀνάμνησιν—is probably that these psalms were to be sung during the offering of the *minḥāh* sacrifice, for the same expression is found in Lev 24:7 ; *cf.* Lk 22:19 ; 1 Cor 11:25. Ps 99 may have been sung during sacrifices of thanksgiving, Lev 7:12, for its title is rightly translated by St Jerome *in gratiarum actione*. At the great festivals the Jews sang or recited Pss 112-117 (Vg), a group known as the *Hallel* or *Hymns of Praise* (*cf.* Mt 26:30)— each psalm bearing the title *Alleluia*, i.e. ' Praise ye Yah '.

A wide field of exploration is open to a student who would search out the original meanings of many of the terms in the superscriptions ; but he will have to solve enigmas which, as we have already remarked, baffled the Greek translators of the 2nd cent. B.C. Bearing in mind that the titles represent a very ancient tradition, it would be rash to disregard their evidence when they give **the names of the composers of the hymns.** Psalms are attributed to Moses (89), Solomon (71, 126), the sons of Core (41-48, 83, 84, 86), Eman (87), Ethan (88), Asaph (49, 72-82) and, probably, Idithun (38, 61, 76) ; but by far the largest attribution is to David (73 times in MT, 84 in LXX). Prefixed to these names is the preposition '*lamed*, which the older

grammarians named *lamed auctoris*, and rightly so. **3** Some writers today interpret the preposition to mean ' belonging to a collection known as (David's) '. But is it likely that Moses, Eman, Ethan and Solomon all had their collections, from which only one or two hymns came into the Psalter ? And are we to suppose that Hab 3:1 bears this strange meaning ? The title-writers clearly had authorship in mind, for often they mention the occasion on which David vowed that he would compose a hymn of thanksgiving should he escape from peril : ' when he fled from the face of his son Absalom ' (3) ; ' which he sang to the Lord, for the words of Chusi the son of Jemini ' (7) ; ' when he changed his countenance before Achimelech ' (33) ; ' when Doeg the Edomite came and told Saul ' (51) ; ' when the men of Ziph had come and said to Saul : Is not David hidden with us ? ' (53) ; ' when the Philistines held him in Geth ' (55) ; ' when Saul sent and watched his house to kill him ' (58) ; ' when he was in the cave ' (141). It is idle to suppose that these incidents were chosen haphazard from the Books of Samuel.

Authorship and Date—Modern criticism has called **3** the Psalter ' the hymn-book of the second temple '. But did the great temple of Solomon never resound with the chanting of hymns ? What religion has ever been without its sacred music ? Are we to suppose that at the Tabernacle, at the sanctuary at Shiloh and at Solomon's temple the voices of hymn-singers were never heard, that the sacrifices were offered and the altar encompassed without chant, or that, if they were, Jewish tradition lost all memory of the pre-exilic hymns ? No, the ' songs of Sion ', ' Yahweh's songs ', were sung before the captivity, Ps 136:3 f. ; pilgrimage psalms were known in the 8th cent. B.C. Is 30:29, and, at this same time, sacred songs, with musical accompaniment, associated with the name of David, formed part of the divine worship, Am 5:21-23 ; 6:5. David was both poet and musician, 1 Kg 16:14-23 ; 2 Kg 1:17-27 ; 3:33 f. ; 22. Traditionally he is the national poet of the Hebrews, ' Israel's beautiful psalmist ', 2 Kg 23:1. He was able to conduct an orchestra of ' harps, lutes, timbrels, cornets and cymbals ', Kg 6:5. Throughout the latter part of the OT he was recognized as the promoter of Israel's liturgical chant ; 1 Par 16:7-36 ; 23:5 ; 25:1-7 ; 2 Par 23:18 ; 29:25-27, 30 ; 35:15 ; Esd 3:10 f. ; Neh 12 : 24, 35, 44-46 ; Ecclus 47:9-12. In the NT Christ attributes 109 to David ; St Peter quotes David as the author of 2 and 15, and St Paul ascribes 31 and 68 to him, Mt 22:43 ; Ac 4:25 ; 2:25-28 ; 13:35 f. ; Rom 4:6 ; 11:9. For the teaching of the Fathers and ecclesiastical writers, see my *Commentary* i, 30 f.

David, therefore, was Israel's best-known hymn-writer. It is not improbable that besides composing psalms he also re-edited ancient liturgical hymns ; a clear example of editing is 67, where we have a combination of at least three sacred songs. A cursory examination of the Psalter shows that before the Greek translation was made in the 2nd cent. B.C. much re-editing had taken place. Hymns were combined (*e.g.* 107 ; 1 Par 16), or wrongly divided (*e.g.* 41 and 42), or combined with an alteration of the divine Name (see § 335*b*), or modified (13 and 52 ; 39:14-18 and 69 ; 17 and 2 Kg 22) ; liturgical additions were made at the end of psalms ; and into the Greek text of 13 an extraordinary insertion was introduced. *Cf.* § 49*f.*

Now that the Graf-Wellhausen theory of OT history is gradually losing favour (the supposed ' P ' document written, it is contended, during or after the Exile, has not a word to say about liturgical chant !) the way is being opened for a broader view of development of Jewish worship ; and it is not too much to expect that eventually the Psalter may be shown to be a magnificent collection of poems reaching from the time of the Exodus right up to the Maccabean period.

Latin Versions—In the 2nd cent. B.C., if not earlier, **3**

a the Greek-speaking Jews resident in Egypt felt the need of a hymn-book in their every-day language ; and the result was the Alexandrian version (LXX). This was to have far-reaching influence in the Christian Church. From it, with few exceptions, the quotations in the NT were taken, and the Latin versions (except one of St Jerome's translations and the New Psalter, see § 338*b*) were made. Before the introduction of the New Psalter, the only breviary version of the psalms was the Alexandrian version in its Latin dress.

The first Latin translation was probably made at Carthage in the 2nd cent. A.D. Whether this was the parent of all subsequent Latin versions or there were other independent African and European (Rome, Milan, Spain) translations has yet to be decided. What we know is that by the middle of the 4th cent. there were so many divergent Latin versions that Pope Damasus (366–84) decided to authorize a uniform text. He turned to the greatest scholar in Rome at the time, Eusebius Hieronymus Sophronius. After completing a correction of the Gospels (383), Jerome turned to the Old Latin versions of the Psalter. For his revision he studied the LXX (known as the ' koine ' or ' vulgate '), using, in all probability, the Antiochian edition, which, from the name of its reputed writer, the martyr St Lucian, became known as the Lucian text. This first of Jerome's works on the Psalter is usually identified with the **Roman Psalter**, recited in the churches at Rome and in Italy up to the pontificate of Pope St Pius V, and still used in St Peter's, Rome ; but, of recent years, this identification has been assailed. In our present breviary the *Invitatorium*, antiphons, versicles and responsories are all taken from the Roman Psalter.

b St Jerome was dissatisfied with his first work ; he complained also of copyists' mistakes. So, after he had settled at Bethlehem in the autumn of 386, he decided to write a new edition. As an aid, he borrowed Origen's *Hexapla* from the library at Caesarea (*Letter* 106.2). This recension became known as the **Gallican Psalter.** because of its use in the churches of Gaul, into which country it was introduced by St Gregory of Tours, and later established by Charlemagne, probably on the advice of Alcuin. It is this recension that we all recited at the divine office before the authorization of the New Psalter, and it is that printed in the Vulgate Bible. The Anglican Prayer Book Psalter also is taken from it and consequently differs from the Psalter of the Authorized Version, which was made from a Hebrew text. The older version was retained in the Prayer Book because of its popularity.

By the year 405 St Jerome had translated the OT from Hebrew into Latin, which work included a translation of the Psalter (389–92). This third translation, known as the **Hebrew Psalter** and written to help Christians in their controversies with the Jews, was never officially adopted by the Church ; again popular attachment favoured the Roman and Gallican versions. In *Die Psalmen der Vulgata* (1940) A. Allgeier maintains that the Gallican Psalter was the third of St Jerome's versions—written for liturgical use in the Church.

On March 24, 1945, Pope Pius XII, by Motu Proprio *In cotidianis precibus*, gave permission to all who recite the divine office to use **the New Psalter.** For an account of its making see *Il Nuovo Salterio Latino* (1946²), or the French translation *Le Nouveau Psautier Latin* (1947), written by Fr Augustine Bea, S.J., rector of the Biblical Institute at Rome, and Chairman of the Committee chosen to compose the new version. An article in English by the same writer appeared in CBQ 8 (1946) 4–35.

The Supreme Pontiff had commissioned the Biblical Institute (January 19, 1941) to prepare a new Psalter which should combine a faithful rendering of the original text with a careful regard, as far as feasible, for the venerable Vulgate and for the other ancient versions. Associated with Fr Bea were five other professors of the Institute : Fathers Vaccari, Zorell,

Merk, Semkowski and Köbert. Translations prepared **338b** by members of this committee were discussed in plenary sessions, revisions and corrections were considered, until agreement was reached. After three and a half years the new translation was submitted to the Pope (August 1944), who then authorized the printing of two editions, one containing the psalms in their biblical order, the other in the order of the Psalter of the divine office.

There can be no doubt that the new Psalter (hereafter referred to as NP) is far superior to any Latin version heretofore made. Its basis is the Massoretic Hebrew, often corrected (but not so often as some may wish) by LXX or another of the ancient versions. Less of the Gallican Vulgate remains than one would have supposed ; thus out of about 350 verses that make up the first 25 psalms, only 14 are unchanged. Moreover some 150 corrections, not based on any external authority, have been introduced. Many of these are of minor, but others of greater consequence, bringing in, as they do, words or phrases hitherto never recited in the Christian Church. These emendations are delicate ; we want good reason for regarding them as original and inspired. We doubt whether every one of them will stand the test of time.

The Committee wisely refrained from following any metrical theory. ' All corrections were barred which depended on certain metrical systems, such as have been proposed and defended by some specialists, not because they are unwarranted but because none of them is at present generally admitted ', Bea, CBQ 8 (1946) 12.

The Alexandrians were afraid of the anthropomorphisms and of some of the concrete expressions of the Hebrew original, so they toned them down to satisfy Hellenistic mood. From LXX these weaker renderings found their way into Vg. NP has rightly restored these hardy and vivid similes and metaphors. The best example is 17:2 f., where David's God is no longer his *firmament, refuge, helper, protector, horn* and *support*, but his *rampart, stronghold, rock, shield, horn* and *fortress.*

The Latinity of the Psalter has been greatly improved by the new version. Hebrew ' tenses ' have been given their proper significance, and strange and unsuitable words have been eliminated. On the other hand, certain liberties have been taken with Hebrew words, *e.g.* ḥeṣed is ' gratia ' or ' bonitas ' or ' misericordia ' ; *yāḍa*ʻ (even in the same *Qal* form) is translated by ' curo ' or ' nosco ' or ' cognosco ' or ' scio ' or ' contueor ' ; the *Hiphil* form of *yāḍāh* is frequently rendered by ' celebro ', but as some of the psalms are *ex-votos*, one might prefer ' gratias ago '. At times the arrangement of the lines and division of stanzas seem open to question. In a few cases the Latin is not clear, *e.g.* 67:19*c* : ' vel eos qui nolunt habitare apud Dominum Deum ', or, in the same Ps, verse 24*b* : ' ut linguis canum tuorum sit portio ex inimicis '. Seldom does the new translation seem inferior to the old ; but we may question whether, *e.g.* ' Extollunt flumina, Domine, extollunt flumina vocem suam ', 92:3, really does express the figure of ' the mighty waves of the sea, which break in greatest tumult on the shore ' (Bea) better than : ' Elevaverunt flumina, Domine, elevaverunt flumina vocem suam '—where the swell of the rolling breakers is distinctly felt.

A second edition of NP, introducing half a dozen alterations, was published in 1945. Invitations are given to readers to propose further improvements.

Translations of NP into English have already been attempted. Comments on these by Mgr J. M. T. Barton may be read in CR 30 (1948) 10–21. Criticism of Mgr R. A. Knox's translation was made in CBQ 10 (1948) 42–54 ; *The Tablet*, March 6, 1948 ; CR 29 (1948) 305–18 (Mgr Knox's reply) ; CR 30 (1948) 69–72 (my reply to Mgr Knox). Although not a translation of NP, Fr R. J. Foster's *Psalms and Canticles of the Breviary*, an excellent ' aid ' to the devout recitation of the Breviary, mirrors the new version by

338b reflexions and explanations, here and there translating individual verses.

339a **Messianic Psalms**—An exalted and mysterious person appears in some of the psalms. He is the anointed Son of Yahweh, who will rule over the whole world, Ps 2. His throne is to remain for ever ; he is addressed as 'God', Ps 44. He is a king ; on earth he rules from Sion, in heaven he shares Yahweh's throne. Moreover he is a priest, not however, in the Levitical line, but a priest-king like Melchisedech, Ps 109. Again he is introduced as a king and the son of a king ; his reign will bring peace and justice, all kings and nations are to worship him, and all the tribes of the earth are to be blessed by him ; he shall reign until the sun and moon are no more, Ps 71. Yet this One, the ruler of nations, whom all tribes must worship, will undergo terrible sufferings, becoming a worm rather than a man, enduring insults from a pack of evil-doers who will strip him of his clothes, dig nails into his hands and feet, and stand staring at his bones protruding from his emaciated body ; howbeit when he shall have established his kingdom, a world-wide assembly, including rich and poor alike, will pay homage to him, and will partake of a sacrificial meal in his honour, Ps 21. An anointed priest, an anointed king, far superior to any merely human priest or king, this is *The Anointed One*, the Messias. These five psalms, 2, 21, 44, 71, 109 are Messianic ; they are to be recognized as 'prophetic and Messianic psalms, foretelling the coming, kingdom, priesthood, passion, death and resurrection of the future Liberator', § 49h.

b We must never lose sight of the fact that when the risen Christ interpreted the Psalter to his disciples, they learnt that its content was far deeper than Jewish readers had suspected, Lk 24:27, 32, 44-46. It follows that when St Peter, St John and St Paul expound passages that were not recognized by the rabbis as Messianic, we may take it that this Messianic sense was taught by the divine Master. Not that all the texts are as strictly Messianic as are the psalms mentioned above ; rather their complete meaning is understood—they are 'fulfilled'—only when applied to Christ. Examples are 8:5-7 ; 15:8-11 ; 117:22 f. Psalms that are *new songs* ('canticum novum') should be accounted as Messianic, for they foretell Messianic times when the Gentiles will be converted to worship the one true God ; cf. Eusebius of Caesarea, *Demonstratio Evangelica*, 1, 4 ; St Augustine, *De Civ. Dei*, viii, 24. No one who reads the commentaries of the Fathers can fail to notice how much Christianity they found in the Psalter. St Augustine may exaggerate when he says : ' Vix est ut in psalmis invenias voces nisi Christi et Ecclesiae, aut Christi tantum, aut Ecclesiae tantum, quod utique ex parte et nos sumus ' (*In Ps 59*) ; but in our days there is a tendency to exaggerate in the opposite direction ; to find little more than the rabbis found in the Psalter ; to exclude from interpretation anything that might be unintelligible to the crowds that frequented the post-exilic temple ; in brief, to forget that Christ enlightening the minds of his disciples made them understand what the holy Spirit meant in the Psalter, that was to become the hymn-book of the Christian Church. Wisely does the reigning Pontiff warn interpreters of Holy Writ that after discovering the literal sense of the words of the Bible, they ' must take into equally careful consideration the explanations and declarations of the teaching authority of the Church, the interpretation given by the holy Fathers, and also the " analogy of faith ", as Leo XIII wisely enjoins in his Encyclical *Providentissimus Deus.* . . . It is therefore the duty of the exegete to discover and expound not only the proper or " literal " meaning of the words which the sacred writer intended and expressed, but also their spiritual significance, on condition of its being established that such meaning has been given to them by God ' (*Divino afflante Spiritu*). And the Holy Father goes on to say that this sense is taught by the divine Saviour in the Gospels, is indicated by the **3** Apostles both in speech and writing, is found in the perpetual teaching of the Church, as well as in the most ancient liturgical usage. In the commentary we will follow the apostolic and patristic rather than the rabbinical method of interpretation.

Penitential Psalms—This is a Christian designation of **c** seven psalms which awaken sorrow for sin : 6, 31, 37, 50, 101, 129, 142. They are enumerated by Cassiodorus (†583), but they seem to have been well known before his time : ' Remember ', he says, ' that this psalm (6) is the first of the Penitentials ' (PL 70, 60). It is probable that Possidius is referring to these psalms when, recording St Augustine's last illness, he tells us that the saint requested that the ' psalmos davidicos . . . de paenitentia ' should be copied out and put on the wall beside his bed. He goes on to say that the dying saint read them continually, shedding copious tears (PL 32, 63).

Imprecatory Psalms—In some psalms we meet passages that appear to invoke curses and revengeful punishments on enemies. During the First World War (1914-18) it was thought that these offensive passages encouraged the plea for ' reprisals ', and Anglicans proposed to delete them from the Psalter of the Book of Common Prayer. It was argued that these comminatory passages owed their origin to the imperfect morality of the OT. Examples are 39:15 f. ; 68:23-29 ; 69:3-5 ; 108:6-19 ; 128:5-8 ; 136:7-9.

True it is that under the old dispensation the Christian law of love was unknown, and that the *lex talionis*, the bill of divorce, blood vengeance, etc., were in vogue. But when St Thomas Aquinas deals with the question (*Summa*, 2a, 2ae, q. 25, a. 6) he does not solve it by appealing to the imperfect morality of the OT. In the body of the article he teaches that we must distinguish in sinners their nature and their guilt. Their nature, he says, is from God, and is capable of everlasting happiness ; hence, according to their nature, sinners must be loved. But their guilt is something opposed to God and is an obstacle to everlasting happiness ; hence, inasmuch as he is guilty and opposed to God, a sinner is to be hated—even if father or mother or relative. He concludes : ' Debemus in peccatoribus odire quod peccatores sunt, et diligere quod homines sunt beatitudinis capaces ; et hoc est eos vere ex charitate diligere propter Deum '. In reply to the third objection of the article, he explains the imprecations in Sacred Scripture. ' These imprecations ', he says, ' can be taken in three ways. First as *predictions*, and not as wishes, so that the meaning of " convertantur peccatores in infernum " is " convertentur ". Secondly, as *wishes*, but in the sense that what is desired is not the punishment of men, but the justice of the One who punishes ; so in Ps 57 : " The just shall rejoice when he shall see the vengeance " ; for even when God punishes he " hath not pleasure in the destruction " of the wicked, Wis 1, but in his own justice, for " the Lord is just and hath loved justice ", Ps 10. Thirdly, the desire may be for *the removal of the guilt* and not the infliction of punishment, that is, that sin may be destroyed while man remains '.

The underlying idea of most of these imprecations is expressed in 138:21 : ' Have I not hated them, O Lord, that hated thee ? ' Those who hated the Chosen People were enemies of Yahweh ; and even an individual might hate a pious Israelite simply because the latter was serving Yahweh. Holy Church prays : ' Ut inimicos Ecclesiae humiliare digneris ', and when consecrating a bishop she says : ' qui maledixerit ei sit ille maledictus '. Finally, when reciting the imprecatory passages of the OT we must not forget oriental modes of expression—vivid and vehement, but not to be interpreted too literally. *Cf.* Merk, 'De Inspiratione', *Institutiones Biblicae*, I, 64 f.

The Doctrine of the Psalter—The dominant theme is **e** **the greatness of the one and only God,** the creator of all things, the ruler of the world, the King of kings, the Lord and Defender of Israel his chosen race. He is the supreme Law-giver and Judge, the Vindicator of the oppressed, the Saviour of all who have recourse to him, the great Wonder-worker. Many of the hymns speak of his power and glory; his mercy, justice and love are extolled; his wonderful knowledge and his omnipresence are described in 138. He is the most Holy One, to whom are due worship and reverence from all men. He rewards the just; he punishes the wicked. His throne is in heaven, where he dwells surrounded by a court of angels; in a peculiar manner he is present in his people's sanctuary at Shiloh or Sion. *Cf.* 8; 10:5; 18:2; 32; 46; 94:3 f.; etc.

It is **man's duty to worship God** by loving him, by praying to him, by observing his law and by taking part in the liturgical services. In sickness and in health, in sorrow and in joy, in youth and age, in times of peace and in times of war man must pray. He must also observe the Law given to Moses and meditate on it; he must seek his friends among the God-fearing, avoiding evil-doers; he must be kind, faithful to his word, immune from bribery, innocent in hands and clean of heart. He must offer sacrifices in praise, thanksgiving and adoration of the God of Israel, taking care that this external cultus is accompanied by internal dispositions. This liturgical worship is most important; the true Israelite should love to frequent the sanctuary and take part in the services. He must also confess and beg pardon for his sins. *Cf.* 14; 23; 25:6–12; 26:4 f.; 31; 41:5; etc.

f The faithful Israelite's belief in **God's retributive justice** was troubled by the prosperity of wicked men. The psalmists solved the problem by saying that God hates the wicked; that their families become extinct; that they die miserable deaths, and in Sheol come under the dominion of the just. On the other hand, the just are loved by God; they experience delight in worshipping him, especially at his sanctuary; they live on in this world through their descendants, who carry on the family name; in the next life they will not be left abandoned in Sheol, but will awake from the sleep of death, to behold the 'form' of God, to see his face, and to be taken to glory—flashes of truths that were to be revealed fully in the NT. *Cf.* 1:6; 5:6–8; 15:11; 16:15; 33:17; 36; 48:16; 72; 74:5–11; etc.

It must be admitted, however, that this interpretation does not commend itself to all scholars. There are those (of whom Fr E. F. Sutcliffe, S.J., in his treatise, *The Old Testament and the Future Life*, is the best exponent) who find in the Psalter very little trace of reward for the just after death. Much depends on the interpretation of individual passages and words (*e.g. tᵉmûnāh*, 'awaken', 'in the morning'), but discussion of these must be left to the commentary. In general we may state here that in this matter as in other OT teachings (*e.g.* Messianic prophecies) we must not expect to find a trend of doctrine gradually evolving from the indistinct to the distinct, nor must we expect inspired writers to be conditioned by the stage of belief of the ordinary people of their times. In the history of religion, as in the lives of mystics, revelation sometimes comes like a flash, rather than by transition from twilight to dawn. And the flash may pass unnoticed by others, and even be forgotten by the recipient. (Compare Simon Peter at Caesarea Philippi and in the courtyard of Caiaphas' house.) All Hebrews from Abraham onwards (except the Sadducees) believed in survival after death. In general their ideas were vague. The good and the wicked all went to Sheol. On earth the latter had a far better time, materially, than the former; hence the flashes of the truth (in the psalms mentioned above) that there is a reward for the just *hereafter*. Compare the Messianic Ps 15 in which ' *the sacred writer speaks of the resurrection of our Lord* ' (Biblical Commission; *cf.* § 52g). Danger of imitation of Egyptian cult of

the dead may account for the paucity of Hebrew **339f** revelation on the after-life.

The Psalter and History—The whole history of the **g** OT, from the creation up to (at least) the Babylonian exile, is put into poetry by the psalmists: the creation, 8 and 103; the deluge, 28:10; Sodom and Gomorrha, 10:7; from the patriarchs to David, 77; Solomon, 71; the destruction of Jerusalem (the Pss are disputed); the exile, 136.

Christ and the Psalter—The Psalter was Jesus' prayer- **h** book. He learnt it at home; he used it in synagogue and temple; he recited the 'Gradual Psalms' when going up to Jerusalem for the festivals, the *Hallel* after the Last Supper, Ps 21 when hanging on the cross, and 30:6 when he breathed his last. No wonder Holy Church bids us pray ' in unione illius divinae intentionis qua ipse in terris laudes Deo persolvisti '; no wonder she has made the Psalter her prayer-book from earliest times. In our days it is generally recited in its entirety every week by all clerics in major orders throughout the world.

During Holy Mass psalms or parts of psalms come to the lips of the celebrant. At the foot of the altar he recites Ps 42; while he incenses the altar he uses verses of Ps 140; he washes his hands praying Ps 25. In the earliest missals the Introit, Gradual, Tract, Offertory and Communion prayer were all taken from the Psalter, a feature largely preserved in our Lenten Masses. *Cf.* R. Galdos in VD 14 (1934) 71–80.

The prayer-book of Christ and of his Church—such is the Psalter. Within the limits of space allowed to us we offer the reader the following notes to elucidate some of its difficult passages.

BOOK I

I—The Ps bears no title. Is it the preface to the **340a** Psalter, as some commentators have thought? This is unlikely, because it resembles 111. St Justin (PG 6, 389) and other early Christian writers, with Codex Bezae, Ac 13:33, wrongly combine 1 and 2 into one Ps. On the point see E. F. Sutcliffe, S.J. in VD 5 (1925) 372.

The way of life of the just man is contrasted with that of the wicked. The one is like a majestic tree in foliage, growing by the side of a running stream; the other is like chaff blown about by every wind. Sinners will be condemned at God's tribunal, for he observes the just man's way of life, while the wicked walk to their ruin. See Arbez in CBQ 7 (1945) 398–404. **1.** ' Blessed ': Heb. is an exclamation: ' *O the happiness of!* ' **2.** The law is probably the written Pentateuch, *cf.* Deut 17:18 f.; Jos 1:8. **3.** *Cf.* Jer 17:8; Ez 47:12, but all three are probably independent. **4.** ' the dust ': ' *the chaff* '. ' After the corn had been threshed to loosen the grain from the husks, it was winnowed by throwing up the mingled stalks and chaff and grain with a fork or shovel against the wind, when the grain would fall to the ground and the rest be blown away ' (Lattey). *Cf.* John the Baptist's words, Mt 3:12. **5.** ' rise again ': ' *stand up* ' to justify their conduct. Some think the reference is to the ordinary Jewish court, but more probably the eschatological Judgement is meant, *cf.* Eccl 12:14; Wis 5:1–5; Nah 1:6. **6.** The supreme Judge takes note of the behaviour of the good and of the wicked. The end of the way of sinners is ruin.

II—1 and 111 are companion psalms; so are 2 and **b** 109; they should be read together. Both are Messianic. The theme of 2 is the conflict between the forces of evil and God, with his anointed King. Hence the frequent use of the Ps by the author of the Apocalypse, 2:26–28; 11:15, 18; 12:5; 19:15, 19. There are four parts. (i) The scene on earth—nations with their rulers attempting by rebellion to break the bonds of religion (**1–3**). (ii) The scene in heaven—God laughing at the rebels (oriental expression) and bringing terror upon them by the appointment of his own

340b Son as King (4-6). (iii) The royal Son, begotten of God, proclaims his sway over all nations and his irresistible power over them (7-9). (iv) The psalmist advises kings and rulers to serve and reverence Yahweh and his Son lest they perish in a blaze of divine anger (10-13).

The Jews of old recognized the Ps as Messianic ; *cf. Psalms of Solomon* 17, 23, and the passages quoted by *Edersheim, *Life and Times of Jesus the Messiah*, 2, 716 ff. In the NT Jesus is called ' my beloved Son ' by his Father at the Baptism and the Transfiguration. The early Christians numbered the Jews and Gentiles who had put Christ to death, together with Herod and Pontius Pilate, among the enemies of God foretold in this Ps. St Paul regarded the Ps as Messianic, Ac 4:25 f. ; Rom 1:4 ; 1 Cor 15:24 ; Heb 1:5 ; 5:5. The early Christians attributed the Ps to David, Ac 4:25 ; *cf.* § 49*e*.

3. The cry of the rebels. 'yoke': 'cords'. 'Let us endeavour that the Christian religion does not bind or be imposed upon us ' (St Augustine, PL 36, 70). **6.** '*I myself have set up my king upon Sion, my holy mountain*'. Then the king speaks : ' *I will promulgate Yahweh's decree*'. **7.** The solemn Introit of Christmas' midnight Mass. ' this day ' corresponds to ' before the day-star ' in 109:3, both signifying, as St Augustine points out, the eternal generation of the Son. Such an explicit affirmation of divine sonship is nowhere else found in the OT ; it rules out any reference to King David ; *cf.* VD 15 (1935) 79. Neither can 8 and 9 be applied to any Hebrew king. **9.** The breaking of jars symbolized the crushing of one's enemies ; *cf.* Kleber in CBQ 5 (1943) 63-7. **12.** 'Embrace discipline ': MT 'Kiss the Son', which may be correct (*cf.* 1 Kg 10:1 ; 3 Kg 19:18) ; so St Jerome at first, but, later, following Aquila and Symmachus, he read 'purely' (*bar* or *bōr*), PL 23, 432. 'Kiss purely ', however, in the sense of paying homage, has no parallel in the OT. For a plausible emendation ' Kiss his feet ', see RB 32 (1923) 207 ; so NP paraphrases, after joining to 11 : ' cum tremore praestate obsequium illi, Ne irascatur et pereatis de via '. Here ' illi ' must refer to Yahweh ; but the anthropomorphism of kissing Yahweh's feet is without parallel and very unlikely. **13.** Again the eschatological Judgement is probably meant ; *cf.* 1:6.

c III—A morning prayer (6). Threatened by an insurrection (2-3) David places his trust in God (4-5). His sleep is not disturbed ; he rises in the morning, sure that victory will be his (6-8). The occasion is Absalom's rebellion, as the title states, and this is confirmed by 7 ; but the actual composition was probably later—a votive offering in thanksgiving for success. The Ps ends with a blessing (9), probably added when it was made a liturgical hymn.

3. ' my soul ': Heb. *nepeš* often means ' self ', here *me*. ' salvation ' (also 9) means *deliverance* or *victory*. ' in his God ': the sacred name Yahweh is not put on the lips of evil-doers (*cf. e.g.* Gen 3, where it is excluded from the conversation between Eve and the Serpent, although it is the divine name in the rest of the chapter). **4.** ' protector ': Heb ' *shield* ', a frequent metaphor in Davidic Pss. ' the lifter up of my head ', the one who takes away my humiliation ; *cf.* 23:7 ; 26:6 ; Gen 40:13 ; 4 Kg 25:27 ; Ecclus 11:1. **5.** ' his holy hill ' is Sion ; *cf.* 2:6 ; 13:7 ; 19:3. **6.** An Easter antiphon ; the whole Ps can be applied to Christ humiliated and exalted. **8.** ' without cause ': Heb ' *on the cheek* '. Oriental poetry is vividly expressive.

d IV—A companion to Ps 3 ; but now the danger is well nigh over (7-9). The psalmist, obviously a man of dignity (David, according to the title), prays that God may hear his prayer and deliver him from enemies (2-3). He is sure that his prayer will be answered, because God has always treated him in a wonderful manner (4). He advises his enemies to think out matters quietly at night ; then offer sacrifices with a right spirit (5-6). Many, weary of the strife, sigh for

peace and God's favour (7). The joy of a rich harvest **3** cannot compare with the psalmist's spiritual joy (8). So sure is he of God's protection that he can go to a peaceful bed (9). A Compline Ps ; *cf.* 5, 9. **2.** ' enlarged me ': brought me relief, taken a load off my mind. **3.** ' dull (*hard*) of heart '; *cf.* Ex 7:14. The text of LXX, Vg, NP is preferable to MT ; *cf.* Bi 16 (1935) 335. **5.** ' Be ye angry ' with yourselves ; so LXX, Syr, St Jer., Eph 4:26, against MT, NP : ' tremble ' in awe of Yahweh. ' the things you say ', etc. ' *Commune with your heart, when on your bed, and be silent* ' (MT, NP) ; let them examine their consciences at night and resolve to cease complaining ; *cf.* Zach 8:16 f. **8.** Spiritual joy is deeper than harvest rejoicing. **9.** ' As soon as I lie down I fall asleep—so tranquil is David, even in the midst of tribulations that sleep escapes him not for a moment', Kroon in VD 8 (1928) 210. **10.** ' singularly ': NP ' *in security* ', unmolested by enemies ; *cf.* Deut 33:28. **V**—Beset by boastful, lying and murderous enemies **e** (who are also rebelling against God), the psalmist prays that he may be protected and allowed to return to the sanctuary. The situation is that of the two previous Pss, the time of Absalom's rebellion. In the Breviary the Ps retains its time-honoured place as the second Ps at Lauds on Monday ; 4, 5 make it a morning hymn.

5. ' will stand ': Heb. ' set in order ' ; the vb is used of preparing an *altar* for sacrifice, of drawing up a *speech*, or of arranging *forces* for battle. NP supposes the arranging of words in prayer, ' propono tibi preces meas ', but there is no ' preces meas ' in MT. Probably the meaning is ' I will prepare for battle '. Knox : ' I will present myself before thee ' can hardly be got out of the Hebrew. ' see ': keep a sharp look out. **8.** ' temple ': the sanctuary set up by David on Sion, *hêkāl* is used of God's residence in heaven, 10:5 ; 17:7 ; Is 6:1, his sanctuary at Shiloh, 1 Kg 1:9 ; 3:3, or on Sion, 2 Kg 12:20, or at Solomon's temple, 3 Kg 6, or at the second temple, Agg 2:19. **12-13** contain the thanksgiving part of this votive Ps. ' shall dwell in them ': better ' *shall protect them* ' (NP). Knox : ' wilt dwell among them ' reverts to the Gallican text.

VI—The first of the penitential psalms. Physically **f** exhausted (3) and mentally depressed (4) because of persecution (8-9), the psalmist feels that his life is ebbing away (6-7) ; but, after prayer (2, 5), he gains radiant hope that his enemies will be confounded (9-11). The historical occasion is probably that of Pss 3-5. Because of 7 it is a Compline Ps (Monday). It can also be used in preparation for confession. **6.** ' hell ': *Sheol*, the Heb. name for the abode of the dead. OT ideas on the future life were vague and sometimes dismal ; here the lament seems to be that in the underworld there is no liturgical worship, no ' remembrance ' or ' praise '. We shall find brighter hopes in Pss 16, 48, 72. **VII**—Against enemies who are bent on ruining his **34** character by bringing false charges against him, the psalmist prays for protection (2-6). That his innocence may be vindicated, he appeals to God to hold an assize (7-11). God's punishments, which the wicked bring upon themselves, are described by vivid metaphors (12-17). **18** may have been added when, the danger over, the psalmist presented his composition as a votive offering for liturgical singing. The Ps is recited at Compline on Monday ; in part it implies an examination of conscience, and so is suitable for night prayers. The title is probably original ; Kush (Chusi) the Benjamite is otherwise unknown ; a late editor would have chosen a familiar name for the adversary.

5b. NP ' qui salvavi adversantes mihi iniuste ' seems unlikely. See note in my commentary, and read with St Jer. : ' *and sent away mine adversaries empty-handed* '. **7b.** ' *Lift thyself up against the fury of mine adversaries* ' (with NP). **8.** ' return thou on high ': take thy throne on high, and there give judgement in my favour. **9.** David, as a suppliant, pleads his innocence before the Judge. **14.** ' for them that burn ' refers to *fiery* arrows. **15.** The enemy is compared to (1) a woman in travail, the child being all manner of iniquity ; (2) a man digging a pitfall to entrap an animal, then falling into it himself ; (3) a man throwing a missile that rebounds on his own head—a boomerang.

VIII—God the Creator, and man the lord of Creation. *The* Son of Man is Jesus Christ ; hence the application of the Ps in 1 Cor 15:26 ; Eph 1:22 ; Heb 2:6–8. Meditating, probably on Gen 1:14–30, the psalmist breaks out into admiration of God's work (**2**). Arguments of godless men are silenced by delightful cries of little children gazing at the sky (**3**). And when the psalmist himself looks up at the starry heavens he is led to wonder why the great Creator should care for puny man (**4-5**), whom he has made almost divine, giving him glory and honour and subjecting all other creatures on earth to his dominion (**6-9**). A renewed exclamation of wonder brings the poem to an end (**10**). For a thorough treatment of the Ps, see Conrad Louis, O.S.B. *The Theology of Psalm VIII* (Cath. University of America Press, 1946).
2b. ' *Thou hast set thy majesty upon the heavens* '. **3.** *Cf.* Mt 21:15 f. **6.** ' angels ': so Vg, LXX, Syr., NP ; but Aq., Theod., Quinta, Sexta, St Jer. all give ' Elohim ' here its primary sense, ' God ', and, in view of Gen 1:26 f. they are correct.

IX (IX–X)—MT, AV, RV wrongly divide this Ps into two. It is an acrostic, the letters of the Hebrew alphabet running down the Ps in order, although some letters have been lost through textual corruption. The first part (**2-21**) is an act of thanksgiving for victory over foreign foes. God has favoured Israel ; the enemy is vanquished ; his cities are in ruins ; he has been punished for forgetting that there is a God ; now let him realize that man is but man. The second part (**22-34**) is concerned with another enemy—the godless Israelites. Puffed up by pride, convinced of his own security, and denying divine providence, he persecutes the faithful Israelite. May God rise up against this loud-mouthed blasphemer. The conclusion (**35-39**) sounds a note of triumph : God *does* see the mischief wrought by the wicked ; he *does* hear the prayers of the afflicted ; he will bring to nought the power of both foreign and domestic foes, and will reign supreme, King for evermore. For textual study, consult *G. R. Driver, *Semitic Writing* (1948) 200 ff. (Schweich Lectures 1944).
7a. ' *The enemy are stilled, uprooted for ever* '. **9.** To be fulfilled by Christ, Ac 17:31. **13.** ' requiring their blood ' : Yahweh is likened to a ' goel ', a blood avenger. A kinsman was bound to avenge the blood of a murdered relative ; Yahweh was united to Israel by ties of relationship ; *cf.* § 246*g*. **15f.** He is raised ' from the gates of death ', from imminent danger of death, to celebrate victory over God's foes (' thy salvation ') by singing psalms (' thy praises ') ' at the gates of the daughter of Sion '—a poetical personification of the city and its inhabitants ; *cf.* Is 1:8 ; 10:32 ; Lam 2:15, etc. **18.** ' shall be turned into hell ' : lit. ' *return to Sheol* '—not as though the wicked have come from the underworld ; the meaning is that their progress in life will be cut short by death ; *cf.* Gen 3:19 ; Pss 54:16 ; 62:10 ; 89:3. **21.** ' a lawgiver ' : so LXX, Vg. NP follows Aq., Theod., St Jer. in reading Heb. as ' terror ' ; but Sym. νόμου, in the sense of ' lesson ', seems best ; see Driver 204.
22 (MT X:1). ' retired afar off ' : stood aloof, not manifesting his power. **23.** ' *Through the wicked man's pride the afflicted is burning* ' (with anxiety). **25 ff.** ' hath provoked the Lord ', hath contemned Yahweh. The impious man says : ' He (Yahweh) will not seek ', *i.e.* God does not concern himself with what happens on earth. He goes on to say (Heb.) : ' There is no God '—not that he is an atheist ; he is godless inasmuch as he holds that God does not interfere in human affairs ; *cf.* Is 29:15 ; Ez 9:9. To his mind God is too

far away to bother with mankind ; divine chastise- **341c** ments do not fall upon a sinner, they are ' removed ' from him ; he has no fear of being ' moved ' by threats of punishments ; he boasts that he will live on ' without evil '. **29.** ' *He sitteth in ambush in villages* ; *in secret spots he doth murder the innocent* '. **30.** The figure of a brigand lurking in out-of-the-way places changes to that of a lion ready to pounce from his lair. **36.** ' arm ' : power ; *cf.* Lk 1:51. **38.** NP follows MT and gives : ' Thou hast strengthened their heart, thou hast given thine ear ', but LXX, Vg : ' Thine ear is attentive to the disposition of their heart ' may be correct ; Driver : ' Thine ear inclines to hear the purpose of his heart '.

X (XI)—To friends advising him to escape to the **d** hills from enemies who are seeking his life, the psalmist replies by expressing complete confidence in God, who, from his throne in heaven, carefully observes everything that happens on earth (**2-5**). He sees the deeds of the good and of the wicked, and will reward the former and punish the latter.
2b-4. Words of the faint-hearted friends. **4.** ' *Since the foundations* (of social order) *are being subverted, what can the just man do ?* '. **5.** ' the poor man ', or (Theod., LXX U) ' the world '. One or other of these has fallen out of MT, and NP also omits. **6b.** ' *But the lover of violence his* [God's] *soul doth hate* ' ; *cf.* Is 1:14. **7.** ' snares '. Read with Symmachus, NP : ' *coals of fire* '—an allusion to the punishment on Sodom and Gomorrha, Gen 19:24. **8b.** ' *The upright shall behold his face* '(NP). Used of earthly kings the expression signifies favourable regard of a person, 2 Kg 14:24, 28, 32, but, in relation to God, it has deeper meaning, 15:11 ; 16:15 ; *cf.* 48:16 ; 72:24–27, until, in the NT, it refers to the beatific vision, 1 Jn 3:2 ; Apoc 22:4.

XI (XII)—The mischief done by unbridled and sinful **e** tongues. The psalmist complains of the dearth of godly men and of the influence exercised by loud-mouthed hypocrites (**2-5**). In **6** God speaks, assuring protection for the afflicted and the poor. **7** is either a continuation of God's words or the comment of the psalmist. The hymn concludes with confidence in divine aid (**8-9**). Reciting the Ps at Compline (Tuesday) we may examine our conscience in the matter of unbridled speech.
2. ' truths ' : parallelism favours St Jerome's ' fideles ' (also Lattey) against NP ' fidelitas '. **3.** ' double heart ' ; *cf.* 1 Par 12:33 ; Jas 1:8. **7.** G. R. Driver sees here a conflation of alternative readings and reduces the words to : ' Like silver refined in the crucible, like gold purified sevenfold ', JTS 36 (1935) 147. **9b.** St Jer. : ' *since the vilest of the sons of men are being promoted* '.

XII (XIII)—The psalmist is afraid that God is aban- **f** doning him to his enemies (**1-3**). He begs for help, lest he be done to death (**4-5**). The hymn ends on a note of joyful confidence (**6**). A Compline Ps (Tuesday) because of **4**.
2. ' counsels ' : plans to evade the schemes of his enemies ; but NP, Zorell, Lattey, after Syr, read ' sorrows ', which has parallelism in its favour. **4.** Death is spoken of as sleep, as in 1 Cor 15:51, and at the *Memento* at Mass. **6.** NP, following MT, omits the last line of LXX, Vg.

XIII (XIV)—The moral corruption of a group of **342a** persons, apparently under the leadership of a man, *the fool*, whose slogan is ' There is no God ', in the sense that God does not interfere in human affairs (**1**). But all the time Yahweh is looking down from heaven upon these senseless men, who are attempting to devour Israel (**3a-b, 4, 5a**). **7** was probably added when the Ps was chosen for liturgical use.

It may be that we have here an ancient hymn telling of the oppression in Egypt, and re-edited by David. It was re-edited again—Ps 52. Another manipulation is found in Vg. After quoting **2b**, **3a**, St Paul, in Rom 3:13–18, adds a string of quotations, Pss 5:11 ; 139:4*b* ; 9:28*a* ; Is 59:7 f. ; Ps 35:2*b*. It would seem that a Christian interpolated the passages in LXX.

342a They are not found, however, in LXX A, MT, St Jerome's Hebrew psalter, and have been omitted in NP. Peculiarly enough they occur *in Hebrew* in a Hebrew-Latin Psalter at Leyden (Kennicott 649).

1. ' The fool '—not in the sense of a stupid person, but an impious man who denies that Yahweh is God. (The sacred name is not put on his lips ; see on 3:3.) If, as we have suggested, the original Ps spoke of the oppression in Egypt, the fool will be Pharaoh ; *cf.* Ex 5:2. The plural ' They ' will then refer to the Egyptians, the subjects of the fool. **4.** Yahweh is probably the speaker. ' devour my people as they eat bread ', figurative of slandering ; *cf.* 26:2 ; 78:7 ; Job 19:22 ; Mic 3:3 ; Hab 3:14 ; Is 3:15 ; Jer 30:16 ; and contrast this metaphorical with the literal sense in Jn 6 ; see also Wiseman's *Lectures on the . . . Blessed Eucharist* and my article in *St Paul and His Teaching*. 95. In Ex 3-10 Israel is frequently called ' my people '. **5.** ' there ' : NP ' then '. The psalmist has in mind some occasion when Yahweh's enemies were stricken with fear. The reference may be to the plagues of Egypt ; but when the Ps was re-edited (52) the allusion was to the annihilation of Sennacherib's army, for there we read ' God hath scattered the bones of those who besieged thee '. ' where there was no fear ' : NP, following MT, omits, probably wrongly ; *cf.* 52:6. **6.** ' you have confounded the counsel of the poor man ' becomes in 52 ' they have been confounded, because God hath despised them '. In the original, the poor man may have been Moses, advising Pharaoh to ' let my people go '. **7.** A Messianic addition. ' *O that from Sion would come the salvation of Israel* ' ; *cf.* 84.10 ; Lk 2:30 f. ' turned away the captivity ' means restored the prosperity of Israel ; it does not refer to the Babylonian captivity.

b XIV (XV)—The virtues required of a worthy citizen of Sion, living in close proximity to the sanctuary. These virtues are uprightness, honesty, truthfulness, brotherly love, friendship with good men but not with evil-doers, faithfulness to the pledged word, immunity from usury and bribery. The Ps is a companion to 23, and was probably composed for the same occasion, the bringing of the Ark to Sion. Is 33:15 seems to know the Ps. Reciting it in the breviary, the priest may let his mind dwell on the virtues required of one who lives close to the Tabernacle.

1. ' tabernacle ' : the sacred tent which David set up on the holy hill of Sion ; *cf.* 2 Kg 6:12, 17. **3.** ' used deceit ' : NP ' calumniatur ' seems inferior to St Jer. ' est facilis (in lingua sua) '. **4.** ' to his neighbour ', as Vg, LXX, Syr. seems preferable to MT ' to his hurt ' and NP ' cum damno suo '.

c XV (XVI)—This Ps was written by David (*cf.* § 49*e*), but he was speaking not of himself but of Christ, as St Peter, Ac 2:24-33, explained to the people but a few days after he himself had learnt from the Master what passages in the psalms referred to him, Lk 24:44. St Paul gave the same interpretation at Antioch, Ac 13:34-37. The Biblical Commission replied in the negative to the question whether a Catholic is free to deny that the sacred writer was speaking of the resurrection of our Lord Jesus Christ ; *cf.* § 52*g*. For the force of this decision consult Vaccari in Bi 14 (1933) 408-34, VD 13 (1933) 321-32 ; but see especially *Conserva Me Domine* by Rudolph P. Bierberg (Cath. University of America, 1945) where every detail of the Ps is thoroughly examined. In the divine Office the Ps is recited at Compline on Tuesday. 8-11 account for its place at Tenebrae before Holy Saturday. 5 forms part of the ceremony of the First Tonsure, the candidate repeating the words after the bishop.

1-3. While his body rests in the tomb, Christ prays to his Father, who is his sole goodness (MT ' my goodness is not beyond thee '), and has given him the saints on earth for his delight. **4.** A difficult verse, see Bierberg for various solutions. The general sense is that he will have nothing to do with those who adopt false cults ; he will have no part in their sacrifices ;

he will not take their names upon his lips ; *cf.* Is 65:13- **342** 15 ; Mt 7:23. **6.** ' The lines ' are the measuring-lines wherewith a portion of land was assigned to a person. (Christ's inheritance is the Catholic Church, *cf.* 2:8 ; 21:28). **9-10.** Because Yahweh is with him, his heart is glad and his soul rejoices ; his very body also (' my flesh ') will rest securely, because it will not be left in Sheol, there to suffer decay. **11.** Yahweh will lead him into eternal life, where, in his presence, he will enjoy gladness and delight for ever. Such, in outline, is the Messianic interpretation of the whole Ps. It is fair to state that many exegetes refer only 8-11 to Christ, and some only in the full sense of the words. One must not, however, lose sight of the Biblical Commission's decision that *the sacred writer* of 10, 11 was himself speaking of Christ's resurrection.

XVI (XVII)—In peril because impious enemies (one **d** of whom is conspicuous, **13**) are closing in about him, the psalmist, pleading his innocence, appeals to God for help. His enemies are worldly men, seeking only this life's enjoyments. He, on the contrary, desires something far more satisfying—the beholding of Yahweh's face, the seeing, ' on awakening ' of Yahweh's *t*e*mûnâh*, God's likeness.

4. Obscure. NP ' the ways of *the law* ' depends on Accadian and Arabic ; see Zorell, VD 1 (1921) 232, Kissane Bi 9 (1928) 90. The word is not yet catalogued in Hebrew dictionaries. St Jer. ' I have kept the ways of a robber ' would refer to David's life as an outlaw. **8.** The apple of the eye is so delicate and precious that nature protects it very carefully. **10.** ' their fat ' (of the intestines) means their heart ; they are without pity. **11.** The distich probably contained four verbs, the first being *šûr* : ' they lie in wait '. ' bowing down to the earth '. What is the object—the psalmist or the eyes of his enemies (scouring the land) ? The latter seems preferable. **14-15.** Difficult. The main idea is that he may be delivered from men who seek after this world's goods, who fill their bellies with choicest foods, and who have many children to whom they bequeath their wealth ; *cf.* 48:11. He, on the contrary, seeks to behold Yahweh's face and (parallel) his *t*e*mûnâh* ' likeness ', which LXX understood to mean the very ' glory ' of God. He prays, in other words, for a privilege granted to Moses, Num 12:8, but denied to other mortals, Deut 4:12 ; he prays that he may receive it ' on awaking '. Does this merely mean that he hopes to see the *t*e*mûnâh* of Yahweh next morning when he goes to the sanctuary ? An impossible supposition. No, but as the note in NP correctly has it, he ' speaks of a hope of seeing God, after he has *awakened*, namely from the sleep of death '. For this idea of awakening from death, ' in the morning ' of another life, see 48:15 ; 72:20 ; Job 19:26 (' see Eloah ') ; Is 26:19 ; Dan 12:2 ; 2 Mac 12:45 ; Apoc 22:4. In this Ps the antithesis is between men ' whose portion is in (this) life ', and the pious who look for satisfaction beyond this life. *Oesterley comments : ' Taken in contrast with what is said in 14, there is some justification for the view that the psalmist envisages, though it be vaguely, awaking from the sleep of death ; this would be prompted by his sense of close communion with God as exhibited in the opening verses of the Ps ; his unexpressed thought may well have been : How can communion with the ever-living God be broken by death ? ' There are commentators, however, who do not hold this interpretation, *e.g.* E. F. Sutcliffe, S.J. (*The Old Testament and the Future Life*, 70-5), but in our view, the inspired writer had a sudden and passing flash of the truth that full satisfaction, with the vision of God, awaits the pious beyond the grave.

XVII (XVIII)—David's hymn of thanksgiving, repro- **e** duced, with slight alterations, from 2 Kg 22. He begins with an outburst of love ; then likens Yahweh, his protector, to concrete means of defence ; he has been (MT, NP) David's ' rampart ', ' stronghold ', ' rock ' of refuge, ' shield ', ' horn ' for attack, and ' high fortress ' (**2-4**). In times of danger of death he prayed to God, and his prayer was heard in heaven (5-7). There follows a magnificent description of God's power, as shown in earthquake, volcanic eruption, thunderstorm and tidal wave. Heaven's clouds are bowed down, as he seems to descend, the lowest clouds serving as a cushion for his feet. The rushing winds are his chariot, driven by the powerful cherubim (for which see Dhorme and Vincent, RB 35 [1926] 328 ff., 481 ff.), like those in Ezechiel's storm, 1:4 ff.; 9:3; 11:22, and in Ps 103:3. Dense clouds charged with rain conceal his presence; clouds, hail and lightning hide the brightness of his glory; thunder is his voice, flashes of lightning are his arrows (8-15). This same mighty God of the storm has rescued David from many a danger, because he has kept the moral law—God's *ways, judgements* and *justices* (16-23). In 24 there may be an allusion to the king's sin of adultery —*mine iniquity*—which he is resolved never again to commit. God favours men according to their works, so that the pious, the perfect and the pure find help in their spiritual lives; the perverse, however, look on him as a harsh judge; he brings down their pride by punishing them (25-28). For David, Yahweh is his guiding lamp, his leader in attack, his shield in defence. All his victories came by the help of the one God, who trained him in the art of warfare and gave him strength to conquer all his enemies, both rebellious Israelites and foreign foes (29-46). So this Hebrew *Te Deum* ends with jubilant praise of the great God who has given salvation to the House of David. 50 is quoted in Rom 15:9 as foretelling the conversion of the Gentiles. David's 'seed for ever' is Christ, who obtained from Yahweh the throne of David, Lk 1:32 (47-51).

a **XVIII** (XIX)—Hebrew poets were fond, as in this Ps, of putting in juxtaposition the physical and the moral orders—God the Creator and God the Lawgiver. In 2-7 the heavens declare the work of the Creator; in 8-14 the excellence of the moral Law is proclaimed. 15 is a conclusion. The Ps is recited as a morning prayer (Prime on Monday) because of 6, 7; it has its place in the *Common of Apostles* because of St Paul's use of 5 in Rom 10:18, and on feasts of the Blessed Virgin because Christ the 'bridegroom', Mt 9:15; 25:1, issued from Mary's womb. 3. 'The psalmist most beautifully and poetically imagines how one day, having performed its course and spent it in announcing the glory of God, hands over this duty to the next day; the night also, after doing its part, gives charge to the following night to do the same' (St Robert Bellarmine). 6. The sun comes out in the morning, like a bridegroom setting forth from the bridal canopy, whence he races, like a strong runner, across the sky. 13. '*Who knows his own mistakes?*' Transgressions of the Law are meant, those committed through error or inadvertence; for these he asks forgiveness. 14. 'from those of others': 'alienis' Vg after LXX supposes *zārîm*, in which case he prays that he may be withheld from serving false gods; *cf.* Deut 32:16. MT has *zēdîm* 'from proud ones'. LXX, Vg may be correct.

b **XIX** (XX)—This and the next Ps are companions. Here we have a prayer offered by a king before battle; his thanksgiving for victory is the theme of the next Ps. The people ask God to grant protection to their king from the sanctuary at Sion, where sacrifices for victory have been offered (2-7a). Then the king speaks, full of confidence that God will grant him success; his enemies are relying on their superior military strength, but he and his men put their trust in the name of Yahweh (7b-9). The people (at the sanctuary) cry 'God save the king' (10). The Ps may be used as a priest's prayer for his anointed brethren; 4 may be applied to their Masses. 4. 'be made fat', *i.e.* acceptable. 6. 'we shall be exalted'. NP, following MT, gives 'extollamus vexilla'; but parallelism suggests that *nāgîl* 'we shall exult' or 'delight' is better than *nidgōl*. 10 is recited after the principal Mass on Sunday as a prayer for the king.

XX (XXI)—The people thank God for blessings **343c** bestowed on their king (2-8). God's punishments of Israel's enemies are described (9-13). 14 is the people's conclusion. In its full sense the Ps is Messianic —Christ is God's King who lives for ever and ever; *cf.* 2 Kg 7:13; Ps 88:5, 30, 38. 5. Agelli comments: 'This can only be understood as referring to Christ, who lives for ever, and by whom David lives and reigns, fulfilling the oracle which God spoke of him through Nathan'. 9-14. Addressed to God rather than to the king; so Agelli, Zorell and others. 11. 'Their fruit': their children. 13. 'in thy remnants thou shalt prepare their face'. St Jer.: 'funes tuos firmabis contra facies eorum', in the sense of fixing tent-cords in front of them, is probably correct. NP and others: 'thou shalt shoot (from) thy bowstring against them' seems less probable; see my *Commentary* 1, 192-3.

XXI (XXII)—Is 52:13-53:12 is the Passion Prophecy; **d** Ps 21 is the Passion Psalm. Neither David nor any other person in the OT (the Ps clearly speaks of the sufferings of an *individual*, not a community; *cf.* Lagrange, RB 14 [1905] 51) suffered as does the character of this Ps; and no single Israelite could have expected, as the outcome of his sufferings, the conversion of the Gentiles. Christ, hanging on the Cross, uttered aloud the opening words of this Ps, and probably recited it through to the end. That this scripture 'might be fulfilled', his garments were divided among his executioners (19). He experienced the parching thirst (16); his bones were disjointed (15, 18); his hands and feet were dug into by nails (17). His enemies mocked at him, using the very words of 9; they stood staring at him (18). St Paul quotes 23 as spoken by Jesus who tasted death on behalf of us all, Heb 2:9, 12. St Thomas Aquinas writes: 'Among other matters this psalm has as its special theme the Passion of Christ; hence this is its literal sense'. The 'other matters' are the Resurrection, the conversion of the Gentiles, etc. He continues: 'And so, although in a figurative sense the psalm speaks of David, yet especially it refers literally to Christ', and he draws attention to the condemnation of Theodore of Mopsuestia at the fifth oecumenical Council for interpreting the Ps literally of David, to the exclusion of Christ (*In David, ad loc.*). For St Thomas' teaching on the literal sense of Scripture, see *Summa* 1a q1 art 10.

The Ps is divided into two parts, 2-22 and 23-32. The first describes the grief and afflictions of the sufferer; the second tells of his passion's mediatorial value. The rhythm is purposely changed, to give one note for grief and another for triumph—a minor and major key, as Lagrange points out. Naturally it is a Good Friday Ps. In the weekly office it is recited at Prime on Friday. Pss 21-24 are traditionally Prime psalms. 2. Quoted in Aramaic by Christ on the cross, Mk 15:34. Read with MT '*the words of my groaning*'; NP 'verbis clamoris mei'. 3. 'and it shall not be reputed as folly in me'. NP 'et non attendis ad me' follows Vaccari 'non est auscultatio mihi', VD 7 (1927) 298. 7. *Cf.* Is 53:3. 8. Mt 27:39; Mk 15:29; Lk 23:35. 9. Mt 27:43. 'Wonderful prophecy, predicting not only the facts, but the very words used!' (St Robert Bellarmine). 10. Christ's Virgin Mother has a place in the Ps. 'In a particular manner Christ is said to have been drawn forth from his mother's womb, because he was conceived in a wonderful manner, and born without a human father, while his mother remained a virgin' (St Thomas Aquinas, *ad loc.*). 11. After the maternity, the divine paternity. When a Hebrew child was born, he was placed on his father's knees, who thereby recognized him as his own son; Gen 30:3; 50:22; Job 3:12. 13. He likens his enemies to wild beasts. 15. 'scattered': '*are out of joint*'. 16. Jn 19:28. 17. His cruel enemies are likened to a pack of savage dogs. They have dug (MT 'like a lion' is impossible) into his hands and feet; they stare and gloat over his emaciated and

343d naked body. **19.** Jn 19:24 ; Mt 27:35. **21.** ' my only one ', my life, parallel with ' my soul '. **22** is alluded to in 2 Tim 4:17. ' my lowness ' : ' *my afflicted soul* '.

23-25. The preaching first to the Jews ; *cf.* Heb 2:12. Then, **26-27**, the praise ' in a great church ' (assembly)—the Church Catholic—in which he will pay his vows. ' What are " his vows " '? The sacrifice which he offered to God. Do you know what that sacrifice was ? The faithful know what vows he paid in the sight of them that fear him, for the text continues : ' " The poor shall eat and be filled ! " . . . The faithful know the sacrifice of peace, the sacrifice of love, the sacrifice of his Body ' (*cf.* St Augustine, PL 36, 178). **28-29.** The great assembly becomes worldwide ; all nations worship the true God ; his Kingdom is established on earth. **30.** Rich and poor alike— ' fat ones of the earth ' and ' they that go down to the earth '—shall partake of a sacrificial meal. Making three corrections in MT, and following recent commentators, NP renders **30a** ' All those who sleep in the earth shall worship him alone '. As Calès remarks : ' Le changement est séduisant, mais ne s'impose pas '. **31.** ' my seed ', according to the Targum, is the seed of Abraham, which, in the NT, is the Christian Church ; Gal 3:16, 19, 29 ; Rom 9:7 f. **32.** ' a generation to come . . . a people that shall be born ' : the future Christian people.

e **XXII** (XXIII)—Two exquisite representations of God : the Good Shepherd (**1-4**) and the Kind Host (**5-6**). The Good Shepherd leads his sheep to rich pastures beside running waters, where they rest without fear, for he is close to them, ready to defend them against attack. The Kind Host invites his guests to his table ; he anoints their hair ; he fills their cup to the brim ; throughout their stay at his house goodness and kindness are lavished upon them. This delicious poem was written by the shepherd-poet who became a guest at Saul's table. It is probably one of his earliest compositions. When recited at Prime on Thursday it can be read as a eucharistic prayer. It may also be interpreted as a hymn on the Sacraments : ' water of refreshment ' (Baptism), ' led me on the paths of justice ' (Confirmation), ' thy rod and thy staff ' (Penance), ' prepared a table ' (Eucharist), ' though I should walk in the midst of the shadow of death ' (Extreme Unction), ' anointed my head with oil, and my chalice ', etc. (Holy Orders), ' goodness and kindness all the days of my life ' (Matrimony).

1. ' ruleth me ' : ' *is my shepherd* '. **3.** ' converted my soul ' : ' *revived me* '. ' paths of justice ' are *right paths*. **4.** ' The club for defending the flock, and the crook for guiding it ; *cf.* VD 1 (1921) 23 f.' (note in NP). **5.** ' against them that afflict me ', *i.e.* while my adversaries look on, astonished that the host should be favouring him. ' anointed my head '—a sign of his host's respect ; *cf.* Am 6:6 ; Lk 7:46. **5b-6a.** ' *My cup overflows. Naught but goodness and kindness shall follow me* '.

344a **XXIII** (XXIV)—A processional hymn, written, perhaps, to celebrate the bringing of the Ark to Sion (2 Kg 6). Originally **1-6** may have been a separate Ps, a companion to Ps 14, enumerating the qualities required of a worthy visitor to the sanctuary at Sion. **7-10** may have been added for the procession of the Ark to Sion. One group of singers calls upon the gates of the old city of the Jebusites to lift up their heads in honour, because the King of Glory is to pass through them to his new sanctuary. Another group asks : ' Who is this King of Glory ? ' The reply is given : ' Yahweh, strong and mighty, Yahweh mighty in battle '. The question is repeated, and the answer rings out : ' Yahweh of hosts, he is the King of Glory '.

1 is quoted by St Paul in 1 Cor 10:26 in support of his teaching that Christians may lawfully eat all foods. **2.** ' He is not using scientific language but speaking according to common opinion, or, rather, according to appearances ' (Agelli, on Ps 17:16). **4.** ' *who hath not lifted up his soul to falsehood* ', the reference being

mainly to false religion. **7.** Read with NP : ' *Lift* **3** *up your heads, O ye portals* '. The ancient (' eternal ') gates of the old city of the Jebusites are told to lift up their heads, that is, to become honourable and proud (*cf.* on 3:4), that, no longer debased by idolatrous worship, they may enclose the sanctuary of the King of Glory symbolically present over the Ark (1 Kg 4:21). **10.** The Lord of hosts, sometimes denoting the hosts of *angels*, Ps 102:21, etc. ; sometimes the hosts of heaven—*sun, moon* and *stars*, 32:6, etc. ; at other times the *armies* of Israel, 43:10, etc. Here the reference may be to armies, but more probably to angelic hosts.

XXIV (XXV)—An alphabetical Ps. As usual with **b** these Pss, the ideas are loosely strung together ; hence, in recitation, each verse should be considered by itself. Nevertheless the main thought is contrition and forgiveness of sins. Trusting in God, the psalmist prays that he may not be put to shame before his enemies (**1-3**). He asks for instruction, guidance and mercy (**4-5**). May the sins of his youth not be remembered by God, who is always ready to teach and guide the meek in the right way of life (**6-10**). Again he asks for pardon, for his sin has been very great (**11**). He considers the blessings that accrue to a just man—prosperity, children and intimacy with Yahweh (**12-14**). (Contrast this with what is said in 16:14, 15.) So he turns his eyes towards God, that he may have mercy on him, free him from anxiety, and forgive him all his sins (**15-18**). His unjust enemies are many ; may he be safeguarded because of his trust in God (**19-21**). **22** is probably a liturgical addition.

XXV (XXVI)—Examining his conscience, the psalmist **c** does not find himself guilty of sinful ways, yet he is not thereby justified ; he asks God to examine him (**1-5**). He desires to lead a blameless life, praising God at the altar of the sanctuary which he loves so well (**6-8**). May he never consort with sinners—men of blood and bribery, but keep on the right path, blessing God with the crowds at the sanctuary (**9-12**). It is a companion to 100, and can serve as a model for priestly life—meditation, examination, unworldliness, purity, love of the altar and of the sacred ceremonies. When the celebrant washes his hands at Mass he recites **6-12**. St Thomas Aquinas (quoting Dionysius) observes that the *extremities* of the fingers are washed to remind the priest that he should be free from the slightest stains of sin (*Summa* p 3 q 83, art 5 ad 1 um).

4-5. *Cf.* 1:1. **6.** Priests washed their hands and feet before approaching the altar in the Tabernacle, Ex 30:17-21. Hand-washing also as a sign of innocence, Deut 21:6 ; Ps 72:13 ; Mt 27:24. ' compass ' : ' It was the custom to walk around the altar while the sacrifices were being offered ' (Agelli). **8.** ' beauty ' : so Vg, LXX (*cf.* 26:4), which seems more probable than MT, where, by the transposition of the initial and final letters the word becomes ' habitation '.

XXVI (XXVII)—Hostilities have broken out, but the **d** psalmist is not afraid ; he has not sought the fight ; his only desire is to serve God at the sanctuary (**1-4**). Recalling former occasions when God protected him, he is confident that he will celebrate victory by offering sacrifices of thanksgiving at the Tabernacle with the music of psalms (**5-6**). Then the tone changes entirely. Aware of the danger before him, he begs God for help (**7-12**). But stout confidence ends the prayer (**13-14**). Several commentators are of opinion that two distinct psalms have been combined ; this may be so, but we must not forget the Hebrew love of antithesis—here, confidence and anxiety.

2. ' eat my flesh ' : see on 13:4. **3.** ' in this ' : in what follows in **4.** ' see the delight ' : ' *enjoy the sweetness* ', NP. **6.** ' I have gone round ' : see on 25:6. Here we have probably a conflation of alternative readings ; see G. R. Driver in JTS 36 (1935) 147. **10a.** A proverbial expression, meaning that one is bereft of nearest and dearest friends. A similar expression is found in a Babylonian poem, RB 32

d (1923) 9. **13.** 'in the land of the living'—opposed to Sheol ; *cf.* 51:7 ; 55:13 ; 141:6. He believes that he will receive blessings (including peaceful worship at the sanctuary) during the remainder of his life.

e **XXVII** (XXVIII)—An urgent prayer (**1-2**) that God will not allow 'his anointed' and 'his people' (**8**), to fall into the hands of evil-doers (**3**). May these wicked men be punished, because they have no regard for Yahweh's works (**5**). As in other psalms, anxiety is balanced by joyful confidence : Yahweh is the psalmist's helper, shield and protection (**6-7**). **9** may have been added when the Ps was chosen for public worship.

1. 'the pit' : Sheol. **2.** 'thy holy temple' : the shrine in the innermost part of the sanctuary, also called the Holy of Holies. **3.** 'Draw me not'—like a criminal led to death. **4.** 'Give thou to them', etc. 'This is not said in a malevolent spirit, but as approving of what God does' (Agelli). **7.** 'And my flesh hath flourished again', etc. So LXX, Vg, Syr. ; but read with MT, St Jer., NP : *'my heart exulteth, and with my song I praise him'.* **9** is quoted in the *Te Deum.* 'rule them' : '*shepherd them*' (*cf.* 22:1) ; 'exalt' : carry (the lambs) in the arms (*cf.* Is 40:11) ; so Knox, beautifully translating NP, 'evermore in thy arms upholding them'.

f **XXVIII** (XXIX)—God's power and majesty are seen in a mighty thunderstorm. Seven times the thunder crashes with *Qôl Yahweh—Voice of Yahweh.* From the north the storm sweeps down upon the Lebanon range of mountains, smashing great cedars to pieces (**3-5**). Mountains leap, earth quakes, lightning flashes forth (**6-7**). The gale races southward, reaching down to the desert of Kadesh, where the sand rises up in a mad dance (**8**). Peal follows peal of thunder ; the affrighted hinds give premature birth (but see below) ; the forests are stripped bare. The angels (see below) witnessing the storm, sing out praise in heaven to the glory of God (**9**). He who presided at the greatest of all storms, the Deluge, presides as King for ever. He will give strength and peace to his people (**10-11**).

1. 'ye children of God'. Angels ? *Cf.* 88:7 ; Job 1:6 ; 2:1 ; 38:7 ; so Targum, Zorell, Boylan and NP (both 'probably'). Men (especially priests) ? *Cf.* 81:6 ; Deut 14:1 ; so Ogara in VD 17 (1937) 142, Lattey and others. When the verse is repeated in 95:7 all texts read 'ye kindreds of the people', also 1 Par 16:28. 'the offspring of rams' : not in MT nor 95:7, and probably due to a conflation of readings, *'ēlîm* 'mighty' (for LXX *Elohim* 'God') and *'ēlîm* 'rams'. St Jer., seems to read only one line : 'Afferte Domino filios arietum'. **2.** 'in his holy court' : MT, St Jer., NP : 'in holy attire'. In 95:9 we find both 'courts' and 'attire'. Whether the 'courts' are those of heaven or those of the sanctuary on earth depends on the reading 'angels' or 'priests' in 1 ; so with 'attire'—either vestments of angels or of priests ; *cf.* Ex 28:2. **3.** 'upon the waters'. Generally understood of the Mediterranean Sea, north of the Lebanon range ; so Lattey, Oesterley, NP and others. Possibly, however, the waters of the clouds are meant, as in 17:12. **6.** MT reads : 'He maketh them to leap up like a calf, Lebanon and Siryon like a young wild-ox'. NP, with recent commentators, puts 'Lebanon' in the first line, and 'Sarion' in the second. Siryon is the Sidonian name for Mt Hermon. 'Lebanon and Hermon are mentioned as being the noblest mountains familiar to the Hebrews, and as being to the north of Palestine, while Kadesh (**8**) is to the south' (Lattey). **8.** 'divideth the flame of fire' : '*heweth out flames of fire*'—lightning flashing from the sky, as if cut out by the divine axe. **9.** 'prepareth the stags' : 'bringeth the birth-pangs on hinds' (St Jerome) ; hinds are known to drop their young prematurely, when frightened by thunder. Omitting one letter, NP reads : 'oaks' instead of 'hinds' ; parallelism may be said to favour the correction, but MT can be retained : it describes the effect of the

storm on beasts and trees' (Zorell). 'discover', in **344f** the sense of stripping the forests bare. 'in his temple' : either the angels in heaven or the priests at the sanctuary, according to the interpretation given to verse 1. 'While the storm is raging on earth, all in heaven are praising God', NP. **10.** 'maketh the flood to dwell' : '*presided* [as King] *at the Flood*', the first great storm recorded in OT history. He presides over all storms ; yet his people have nothing to fear from the mighty Storm-King.

XXIX (XXX)—Thanksgiving after recovery from **345a** illness (**2-6**). The psalmist describes his state of mind before and during his sickness (**7-11**) ; then expresses gratitude for restoration to health (**12-13**). Originally the Ps was personal ; later, after the plague mentioned in 1 Par 21, it was used for public recitation ; *cf.* Porporato in VD 9 (1929) 236–40. Calmet refers the title, 'dedication of the house', to the dedication of Ornan's threshing-floor (1 Par 21:28–22:1) ; but perhaps it refers to David's own house or palace (2 Kg 5:11).

4b. *Cf.* 27:1. MT is incorrect against LXX, Vg, Syr, NP. He was nigh unto death, but just as he felt that he was descending to the underworld, Yahweh raised him up. **5.** 'memory' : name ; *cf.* 134:13. **6.** '*For a moment lasts his anger, while his favour is life-long*' (MT) ; but see G. R. Driver in JTS 36 (July 1935) 299. **7.** Like many others, when in good health he thought that he was proof against illness. 'my abundance': '*prosperity*' or '*ease*'. **10.** A gloomy prospect of life after death ; *cf.* 6:6 ; Is 38:18 ; no further opportunity of praising God. **12.** 'joy' : '*dancing*', NP. **13.** 'glory', *i.e.* soul.

XXX (XXXI)—Committing himself to God, the **b** psalmist relies on divine protection against enemies, men who were following a false religion (**2-9**). He is worn out in body and mind and deserted even by his friends (**10-14**). But his confidence is unshaken (**15-19**) ; and he knows that his prayer is answered (**20-23**). He exhorts the faithful to love God and be of good cheer, for God protects the good and punishes the proud (**24-25**). Christ uttered **6** when dying on the Cross (Lk 23:46). We may read the whole Ps as a prayer of the suffering Redeemer.

4a. *Cf.* 17:3. **6.** Fittingly recited at Compline. **7.** 'vanities to no purpose' : '*vain idols*', NP ; *cf.* Deut 32:21 ; Jer 8:19 ; Jon 2:9. **13a.** '*I am forgotten from mind, like a dead man*', NP. **17.** 'Make thy face to shine' : smile with approval. **22.** 'in a fortified city' : 'perhaps metaphorical for pressing difficulties' (Lattey).

XXXI (XXXII)—The second of the penitential psalms. **c** It tells of the happiness of the man whose sins are forgiven (**1-2**), the torture of conscience he suffered while refusing to confess (**3-4**), his resolve to confess, and the forgiveness granted by God (**5**). He urges every pious man to pray that thereby he may be preserved from dangers (**6**). God is indeed a refuge for those who are in distress (**7**). God then speaks, promising instruction and guidance, provided that one is not obstinate like a mule or horse (**8-9**). In conclusion, the troubles of the wicked are contrasted with the blessings of the upright of heart (**10-11**).

The textual difficulties are considerable. For these we must refer the reader to the commentaries ; also to Arconada in VD 9 (1929) 171–8 ; 193–201, and G. R. Driver in JTS 32 (1931) 256. The title ascribes the Ps to David, so does St Paul in Rom 4:6 ; see § 49e. He may have composed it after his confession of adultery and murder, 2 Kg 12:13.

1-2 are quoted in Rom 4:6–8. Sins that are covered and not imputed are taken away altogether and treated as non-existent. **3.** Remorse of conscience affects bodily health ; confession is good for the body as well as for the soul. **4b.** 'whilst the thorn is fastened' : possibly *by the pricking of a thorn, i.e.* the pricking of conscience ; see my *Commentary*, and *cf.* Ez 28:24 ; Ac 9:5 ; 26:14. 'My strength was consumed as if by summer droughts', NP. **6.** 'a flood of many waters'

345c —a frequent metaphor for distress and danger; *cf.* 17:17, etc. **8-9.** God is the speaker.

d XXXII (XXXIII)—A hymn of praise, probably composed after a victory. It is ' a new song ' (**3**), hence we may expect a reference to the conversion of the Gentiles (§ 339*b*), and this we find in **8**, where all mankind are called upon to reverence Yahweh, the maker of the heavens, earth and seas (**6, 7, 9**). From heaven he looks down upon all the inhabitants of the earth; he sees their works, he knows their thoughts, for he fashioned every heart (**13-15**). Happy is Israel whose God is Yahweh; unhappy the Gentiles whose designs he will thwart (**10-12**). Military force is of no avail without reliance on him (**16-19**). A prayer from his trustful servants concludes the Ps (**20-22**).

6, 7, 9. A summary of Gen 1. We may see here a foreshadowing of the doctrine of the Blessed Trinity— ' word ', ' Yahweh ', ' spirit of his mouth '. ' There is no doubt but that the Holy Ghost meant to glance at the mystery of the Holy Trinity, to be revealed in the New Testament ' (St Robert Bellarmine).

e XXXIII (XXXIV)—Another alphabetical Ps, but letter *waw* is missing, and 23 is additional. The title states that it was written by David when he feigned madness at Geth (1 Kg 21:11–14). As there is nothing in the Ps itself to suggest this incident, the writer must have had some reason for the ascription. Probably David wrote it, in thanksgiving for his escape, when he returned to Jerusalem; thus it is a votive psalm. The ideas are loosely strung together, but the main theme is God's saving power and his watchful care over those who take refuge in him. Nowadays the Ps is recited at Compline on Wednesday. In the early Church it was said or sung at Mass, during the distribution of Holy Communion; *cf. Apostolic Constitutions* 8, 13; *Catechism of St Cyril of Jerusalem* 23. In the Stowe (Celtic) and Mozarabic missals **9** is found as a Communion prayer.

6. ' As he was mounting the stairs (of the scaffold on the Tower Hill), the south-east sun shined very bright in his face, whereupon he said to himself these words, lifting up his hands: "Accedite ad eum, et illumina-mini, et facies vestrae non confundentur "' (Dr Hall, *Life of St John Fisher*). **9.** Quoted in 1 Pet 2:3. The same epistle, 3:10–12, quotes **13-17a.** Lucinius, a wealthy Spaniard of Baetica, wrote to St Jerome asking whether he should go to Holy Communion every day, as was customary in the churches of Rome and Spain. This verse is cited in the reply, advising him to go to Communion daily (*Letter* 71, 6).

f XXXIV (XXXV)—A prayer for deliverance from cruel and treacherous enemies. There are three parts, **1-10, 11-18, 19-28**, each beginning with a request and ending with a promise of thanksgiving (Duhm). (i) The singer calls on God to come forth as an armed warrior and fight for him against his foes; when these are vanquished, he will rejoice and say: ' Yahweh, who is like unto thee !' (ii) He describes the base ingratitude of the enemies: they have requited good with evil; when they were sick he fasted and prayed for their recovery as if they were his nearest relatives and friends; but now that he is in trouble they are his bitterest foes. He vows to thank God in a great assembly if his life is spared. (iii) He prays that the treachery, cunning and insolence of his opponents may not prevail, and that all good men may join with him in praise of Yahweh who has vindicated the cause of his servant. With the Fathers of the Church we may read the Ps as descriptive of the sufferings of Christ. His enemies ' fulfilled ' **19** by hating him without cause, Jn 15:25; his scourging may be seen in **15**, and the false witnesses of **11** will recall Mt 26:60.

5. *Cf.* 1:4. **7.** ' they have upbraided my soul ': ' *they have dug a pit for me* ', NP. ' The figure is taken from hunting ' (Lattey). **11.** ' things I knew not ': crimes unknown to my conscience. **12.** ' to the depriving me of my soul ': lit. ' sterility for my soul ', *i.e.* they denied him the fruit of his good works. **13.** Prayer, fasting and almsdeeds were practised by the

Hebrews to implore the mercy of God. ' my prayer **3** shall be turned into my bosom '; either his head, bent in sorrow, uttered the prayer on to his breast (*cf.* Lam 2:10; Bar 2:18), or the prayer, bringing no blessing on his enemies, returned as a blessing upon himself. **14.** ' so did I please ': ' *I walked about* ', MT, NP. ' as one mourning '. St Jer : ' as a mother in mourning '; NP : ' as one that mourns his mother '. The *maqqeph* in MT may be a relic of *k*; this would give : ' as a friend, as a brother . . . as a mourner, as a mother '. **15.** ' *yet upon my stumbling they were glad; they gathered together to scourge me, and I knew not why* '. **16.** ' *They tore me and did not cease* ' (St Jer., NP). **20.** A difficult verse; see Commentaries, also Kroon in VD 8 (1928) 204.

XXXV (XXXVI)—The wickedness wrought by a god- **3** less man (**2-5**) is contrasted with God's goodness and kindness (**6-10**). The psalmist prays that he may be protected from evil-doers, who ride for a fall (**11-13**).

2-3. Obscure. In MT ' Transgression ' is personified; it is an evil oracle whispering temptation to a reprobate man, telling him that God never seeks out a sinner's iniquity, and does not hate him; *cf.* 9:25, 34. Another interpretation is that the wicked man flatters himself at finding that his iniquity is an object of hatred. **4.** ' understand '; ' *consider* '. He ceases to think of doing good, like the fool in 13:2 f. **7.** ' mountains of God '; the loftiest and most majestic mountains. God's justice is as high and as mighty as these; his judgements have unfathomed depth. All living creatures depend on his providence. **9.** God is likened to a kind host, as in 22:5 f. **13.** There seems to be a reference to some occasion unknown to us, but the meaning may be general. NP ' Behold, they have fallen, the workers of iniquity '.

XXXVI (XXXVII)—Not knowing the full truth about **b** the hereafter, the pious Hebrew was often perplexed at seeing wicked men prosperous and good men in affliction. Here the psalmist attempts an answer to the problem. His solution is that a good Hebrew lives on after death through his ' seed ', his ' posterity ', his ' name ', his ' house ' (**3, 9b, 11, 18, 22a, 23, 28b, 29, 34b, 37**), while the wicked man is cut off with no earthly future (**2, 9a, 10, 13, 15, 17a, 20, 22b, 28d, 34c-36, 38**). The Ps is alphabetical.

3. The land is Canaan. Throughout the Ps insistence is laid on inheriting the land given by God to his Chosen People. A godly man lives on through his descendants carrying on the family name. Hence one of the reasons why the Hebrews attached importance to genealogical tables. **11a.** One of the Beatitudes, Mt 5:4, but Christ gave a higher meaning to ' the land '; *cf.* the concluding line of the ' O Salutaris Hostia '. **13.** ' his day '; the sinner's. **17.** ' the arms ' of the body, not military weapons. **20b.** Difficult; see Commentaries. NP follows MT : ' as the splendour of the meadows ', implying, presumably, that as flowers in Palestinian meadows are quickly burnt up by the sun, so do the wicked perish. For the idea in LXX, Vg, *cf.* Job 24:24. **22.** ' as bless him . . . as curse him ': ' *blessed by him* [Yahweh] . . . *cursed by him* '. **37.** ' remnants ': posterity, also **38**.

XXXVII (XXXVIII)—The third penitential psalm. **c** Afflicted in body and mind, because of sin, abandoned by his friends and persecuted by enemies, the psalmist implores God's help. By confession of sin he hopes that God will succour him. We may read the Ps as a description of Christ's sufferings, who became sin for us. In his second homily on this Ps, Origen has a long passage on Confession (PG 12, 1386). For fuller explanation of the text see Arconada in VD 10 (1930) 48–56 and G. R. Driver in JTS 35 (1934) 386.

2. Almost word for word in 6:2. **5.** ' Like rushing waters that reach over my head and submerge me ' (Agelli). **12.** ' *My friends and my companions stand aloof from my plague, and my neighbours stand afar off* ', NP. He is regarded as a leper; *cf.* Is 53:4; Lk 23:49. **14-15.** *Cf.* Is 53:7.

XXXVIII (XXXIX)—' Here too, as in the last psalm, **d**

d the psalmist is conscious he is being chastised for sin ; but the interest is not primarily either in the sin or in the chastisement, but in his own mental attitude' (Lattey). With wicked men, the psalmist will not discuss his physical and mental sufferings (**2-4**). He will address himself to God, to learn something about the brevity and emptiness of human existence (**5-7**). He comes to realize that man's only hope is in God, and that chastisement is because of transgression (**8-12**). With tears he asks for two favours before his sojourn on earth is finished, forgiveness and restoration of health (**13-14**).

3. 'from good things'. 'I kept absolute silence, speaking neither good nor bad' (Kirkpatrick) ; cf. Gen 31:24. **4.** '*In my musing the fire kindled*', MT, NP. Silence only made his feelings more bitter. He must speak to somebody ; he will speak to God. **6.** 'my substance' : Heb. lit. 'duration' (of life) ; NP 'my life'. **8.** 'substance : '*hope*' or '*confidence*' (MT, NP, St Jer.). **11b.** '*By the blow of thy hand I am come to an end. With chastisement dost thou correct man's iniquity ; like a moth thou dost consume his loveliness*'. **13cd.** Cf. Gen 23:4 ; 1 Par 29:15 ; Heb 11:13. For the Christian interpretation see Eph 2:19 ; 1 Pet 2:11. **14.** Cf. Job 10:20 f. 'He does not speak about a future life, but he does not deny it' (note in NP).

e **XXXIX** (XL)—A 'new song' (**4**) ; hence it has Messianic import. NP remarks : 'Ps 39 (40) is Messianic (*cf.* 7–9), and according to many, especially the older commentators, it is Messianic in a direct sense '. We may connect it with the preceding Ps. There the psalmist put his trust in God alone. This confidence has not been misplaced. God has heard his cry ; has lifted him out of the slough of despondency ; has put a new song into his mouth, has shown him that many will be brought to put their trust in God, turning away from idolatry (**2-6**). Then he foretells the end of Jewish sacrifices, and the coming of One whose delight it will be to do God's will. In a great assembly this One will proclaim good tidings of God's justice, truth, mercy and salvation (**7-11**). So completely does the tone then change that some commentators think that **12-18** is a separate Ps ; and, indeed, 15–18 were detached to form a hymn for the memorial part of the sacrifice, Ps 69. Yet, on reading **12-18** attentively, we see that they tally with the description of the Sufferer in Ps 21. Encompassed by evils and laden with sin, he prays that God may hasten to help him, and that his mocking enemies may be brought to confusion. **7-9** are put into the mouth of Christ in Heb 10:1–10.

4. Many hearing the new canticle will come to worship God. **5.** 'vanities and lying follies' ; idolatry, with its lying oracles. **7.** 'thou hast pierced ears for me'. MT : 'ears hast thou dug for me' ('an extraordinary mode of expression', Oesterley), which is generally explained in the sense that God made the cavity of the psalmist's ear, and that he is always ready to hear and obey God's will. LXX : 'a body hast thou fashioned for me', quoted in Heb 10:5. **8.** 'In the head of the book' ; '*In the book-roll*', *i.e.* the book itself ; the parchment was wound round rollers. What book is meant ? The OT in general (Didymus, Bellarmine, Boylan, NP) ? The Mosaic Law (Targum, Calès, Oesterley) ? 'Perhaps the passage in 1 Kg 15:22' (Boylan) ? **10.** Cf. 21:28. **13.** 'my iniquities': Christ became sin for us.

f **XL** (XLI)—'The inspired prophet sings this psalm in the person of Christ. In the first part he speaks of Christ ; then follow the words of the Mediator speaking to his Father' (*Breviarium in Psalmos*, PL 26, 1003). St Cyril of Alexandria, St Augustine, Cassiodorus and many others interpret the Ps in a Messianic sense (PG 69, 991 ; PL 36, 452 ; 70, 294).

2. 'the needy and the poor' (one) : *cf.* 39:18. None so lowly and poor as Christ our Lord, 2 Cor 8:9. **4b.** 'thou hast turned all his couch in his sickness' : probably in the sense of helping him almost as a nurse ; see parallel. **5.** 'Is this said by Christ ? Is this said

by our Head, who is sinless ? Can it be he ? Yes, **346f** indeed, he is speaking for his members ; for the cry of his members is his own cry . . . In him, then, we find our cry : *Heal my soul, for I have sinned against thee* ', St Augustine, who quotes 21:2 ; Rom 6:6. **9.** 'an unjust word' : MT 'a word of Belial', which St Jerome renders : 'verbum diaboli'. It would seem that this *base* (the probable meaning of 'Belial') *word* or resolution is given in the next line : '*He that is lying down shall never get up again*'. NP puts the first line also into the mouths of the enemies : 'A malign disease is put into him', changing *deḇār* to *deḇer* ; yet notice the same expression in 100:3 and Deut 15:9. **10.** Christ teaches us that this was fulfilled by Judas' treachery, Jn 13:18. See Porporato in VD 12 (1932) 70–5. **14.** A doxology closing the first book of the Psalter.

BOOK II

XLI (XLII)—The second book of the Psalter com- **347a** prises Pss 41–71. The first two should be read as one, as the recurring refrain indicates ; 41:6, 12 ; 42:5. We begin the hymns written by 'the sons of Core (Qorah)', men appointed by David to direct liturgical music, 1 Par 25:4–8 ; 6:33–37. Notice the difference of tone and style between these Pss and those ascribed to David.

The singer is an exile from Jerusalem, living near the Jordan (**7**). Probably he is a Levite, a companion of David in his flight across the Jordan at the time of Absalom's revolt, 2 Kg 15:16 ff. His one desire is to return to the sanctuary (**3**). Enemies tell him that he is abandoned by God (**4, 11**) ; but he takes heart, confident that God will again allow him to take part in the festivals at the sanctuary (**5, 6, 9, 10, 12**).

3. 'appear before the face of God' : come on pilgrimage to Jerusalem, Ex 23:17, etc. **5.** 'poured out my soul', in earnest prayer, 1 Kg 1:15 ; Lam 2:19. 'I shall go over into the place of the wonderful tabernacle'. It is not clear whether he is recalling past pilgrimages or looking forward to one in the future. NP follows MT *sāḵ* 'throng', but the word is very dubious and only found here. Adding one letter we get *māsāḵ*, the term in Exodus and Numbers for the *curtain* at the entrance of the Tabernacle. What more likely than that a Qorahite exile should sigh to be back at the entrance of the sanctuary ? The Qorahites had charge of the outer curtain, Num 3:31. **7.** 'Hermoniim from the little hill' : the Hermon range of mountains and the hill called 'Misar'. The note in NP places Misar 3 kilometres S. of Banyas : see Bechtel in Bi 6 (1925) 405 ; McClellan in CBQ 2 (1940) 68. **8-9.** The waters roaring over the falls remind him of dangers threatening to engulf him ; but Bechtel suggests that the torrents, calling one to another, say to the psalmist : 'Day and night Yahweh sends his mercy ; sing with me a hymn to the living God'. Agelli, however, thinks that the psalmist consoles himself with the thought that God sends his mercy, like an angel, to protect him by day, while at night he consoles himself by singing psalms.

XLII (XLIII)—A continuation of the previous Ps, **b** unfortunately separated from it in the divine office. The singer asks God to champion his cause against an ungodly nation (**1**). Why has God cast him off ? (**2**). May light and truth bring him back to Jerusalem, where, at the altar, he will make thanksgiving with harp and hymn (**3-5a**). The refrain concludes the psalm (**5b-6**). This Ps is recited at the beginning of Mass, the words 'Introibo ad altare Dei' making it appropriate.

1. 'the unjust and deceitful man' : probably Achitophel, 2 Kg 15:31. **3.** God's light and truth are represented as angels. With the whole verse, *cf.* 2 Kg 15:25.

XLIII (XLIV)—The singer recalls the tradition that **c** the conquest of Canaan, under Josue, was not due to

347c force of arms but to divine aid (**2-4**). Now, in a present emergency, he exhorts his people to rely on the name of God, not on bows and swords (**5-9**), and this, in spite of a recent defeat with terrible slaughter (**10-22**). A passionate cry for help closes the Ps (**23-26**).

Almost every date when Israel suffered defeat has been suggested for this Ps. St John Chrysostom thought that it *predicted* the trials of the Maccabean age (see Lesson IV in the breviary for the 4th Sunday of October), an opinion followed by Theodoret and Euthymius (PG 80, 1177 ; 128, 477). Kirkpatrick assigns it to the period of the monarchy ; Delitzsch to David's campaign against the Ammonites and Syrians ; so also Vigouroux and Fillion. Calès thinks that the original Ps was written during the Persian period, then adapted in Maccabean times. The note in NP states that a Maccabean date is not necessarily indicated, and that the occasion may be in Ezechias' reign (*cf.* 4 Kg 18:13, 22-27 ; 19:4, 14-19) or the troublesome times that followed the death of Josias, 4 Kg 23:25-30, or the persecution in the Persian period.

2. OT tradition ; *cf.* Ex 10:2 ; 12:26, etc. **3.** 'thou plantedst them'—the Chosen People, like a vine on new soil ; *cf.* Ex 15:17 ; Ps 79:9 ff. 'cast them out' : prob. '*spread them out*' (*cf.* 79:12), *i.e.* the Israelites, like a spreading vine (Agelli). **4d.** 'the light of thy countenance'—God's encouraging smile. **6b.** 'despise' : MT, NP '*trample down*'. **13b.** '*and thou hast made no profit out of the sale*', MT, NP. **20a.** 'in the place of affliction' : so NP ; but MT : 'place of jackals'. Some moderns prefer St Jer. 'in loco draconum' ; the dragons may be the Egyptians, *cf.* 73:14 ; Ez 29:3 ; 32:2. **22.** Quoted by St Paul to encourage Roman Christians to face persecution, Rom 8:36. **25.** 'our soul', *i.e.* person ; see Joüon in Bi 11 (1930) 82 f.

d XLIV (XLV)—'The poem is a marriage ode delivered on the occasion of a king's wedding. Apart from the introduction (**2**) and conclusion (**17-18**) it has two parts, the first dedicated to the king, and the second to the queen. The actual wedding ceremony is the setting for the expression of the poet's thoughts : he follows the bridegroom's procession to the bride's house, assists at the meeting of the two groups and at the return to the royal palace, and expresses the sentiments which the magnificent spectacle suggests to him', Podechard in RB 32 (1923) 28.

But although the poem may have been written in honour of a royal wedding (probably Solomon's), the inspired writer's thoughts reach beyond the actual event ; he sees a king fairer than an ordinary man (**3**), one whom he addresses as 'God' (**7, 8**), one whose throne is to remain for ever (**7**), whose rule is to extend over the world, and whose name is to be remembered through all generations (**17, 18**). It is not surprising, therefore, that Jews and Christians have seen here the espousals between the Messias and his people. The Targum treats the Ps as strictly Messianic ; St John Chrysostom could say that on this point Jews and Christians were agreed (PG 55, 183) ; St Thomas Aquinas gives the Catholic interpretation : 'The subject-matter of this psalm is the espousals between Christ and the Church'. On feasts of the Blessed Virgin, the Ps is recited at Matins ; **10-16** are applied to her as the Spouse of the Holy Ghost and the Queen of Heaven. **3.** In reference to Christ, *cf.* Lk 4:22 ; Jn 7:46. **4.** The mighty one (*cf.* Is 9:6) goes forth like the Messianic warrior in Apoc 6:2. **6.** 'under thee shall people fall' should be read as a parenthesis. **7.** 'So clearly does this verse speak of the divinity that no other exposition is possible' (Agelli). 'The poet now addresses the king directly as *God*. . . . The context which says, *therefore hath God anointed thee*, shows that in 6 the words, *thy throne, O God*, are addressed to the king' (Oesterley). 'In the OT princes and judges are also called by the title *Elohim*, as taking the place of God (*cf.* Ps 81:1 f.) ; but the psalmist, writing under the influence of inspiration, must here be deemed to

be indicating the divinity of the Messias' (note in NP). **3** See also Ogara in VD 14 (1934) 81. St Paul quotes 7, 8 in proof of Christ's divinity, Heb 1:8 ; *cf.* Lk 1:32 f. For the anointing of King Messias *cf.* 2:2. **8.** St Augustine regards the first 'God' as a vocative, addressed to the Messias : 'O tu Deus, unxit te Deus tuus' (PL 36, 505). 'God has anointed (his Son) with the oil of gladness, an oil of coronation that will bring more gladness than it usually brings to kings anointed' (Boylan, WV Heb 1:8). See also Arconada in Bi 17 (1936) 323 note ; and *cf.* Is 61:1 ; Lk 4:18. **9.** Put full stop after 'garments', and continue : '*From ivory palaces* [*cf.* 3 Kg 22:39 ; Am 3:15] *stringed music gladdens thee. Kings' daughters come to meet thee*' (so NP after Podechard ; but, possibly, *are among thy maids of honour*'). **10.** The queen-bride, in the Messianic sense, is the Church. She takes her place on the right of the bridegroom. Her dress of cloth-of-gold is made of '*gold of Ophir*' (Heb.), the finest gold then known, obtained at a place 'on the sea coast of southern Arabia or of east Africa' (note in NP) ; *cf.* Is 13:12 ; Ez 16:13 ; 1 Par 29:4. St Thomas remarks : 'The whole of this can be interpreted of the Blessed Virgin Mary, who is queen and mother of the king, and who stands above all the choirs of angels in her golden dress, gilded by the divinity ; not that she is God, but because she is the mother of God'.

11. Address to the queen. In her love of the king, she is to forget those dear to her before her marriage. (Jews must forget the old dispensation, and Gentiles their pagan worship.) In return, rich nations (symbolized by the Tyrians) will pay her homage ; *cf.* 21:30 ; 71:10 f. ; Is 60:4-6. **14.** A stop should be put after 'within'. Within what ? Some say 'within the palace' ; but the queen has not yet entered the palace (16). NP changes the adverb into a verb ('Tota decora *ingreditur* filia regis'), but this is without warrant. St Jer : 'intrinsecus' is nearer the meaning. The poet is interested in the bride's wedding-dress ; 'within' refers to the *lining* of the dress ; even that is beautiful. The second line should read : '*Inwrought with gold is her robe of check with diamond pattern*' ; *cf.* Is 61:10 ; Apoc 21:2. **15b.** The bridesmaids ; *cf.* Mt 25:1 ; Apoc 14:4. Applying this to the Blessed Virgin, St Thomas remarks that her virgins are led to Christ by the observance of chastity and other virtues. **17.** A new generation. We can apply 'princes over all the earth' to the Apostles and their successors.

XLV (XLVI)—A severe earthquake has shaken Gentile **3** territory (**3, 4, 7, 9**), but, because of God's presence in her midst, Sion has escaped (**5, 6**). Gentile power will eventually be overthrown, and God will be exalted among the nations (**9-12**). We may read the Ps as descriptive of the Catholic Church, firm as a rock amid the turmoils of history. Because God is in her midst, she cannot be overthrown.

2b. '*a fully proven* [*lit.* 'to be much found'] *help in troubles*', MT. **4b.** MT : '*Mountains shake at the swelling thereof*'. **5.** Perhaps a reference to the waters of Siloe (Siloam) ; *cf.* the Ps with Is 8, esp. v 6. Others understand the river as metaphorical for the temple or God himself, *cf.* Is 33:16-21 ; Jl 3:18. **9.** Possibly a reference to the defeat of Sennacherib (Is 37:36), but symbolical of a greater peace.

XLVI (XLVII)—In the Messianic age all nations will **b** give praise to the God of Israel (**2-5**). He will be enthroned as King amid jubilation (**6-7**). Gentile rulers will unite with the children of Abraham in worshipping the true God (**8-10**). 'The Ps, as the Fathers saw, is a sublime presage of the future', Lagrange in RB 14 (1905) 196. It is obviously a Lauds' Ps (Monday), and one for Ascension Day.

5. *Cf.* Ex 15:17 ; Am 8:7. **6.** 'is ascended'—as king on his throne. **10b.** '*Because the shield of the earth*' [powerful rulers, protectors of their peoples] *belong to God, he is greatly exalted*' ; *cf.* 88:19.

XLVII (XLVIII)—A eulogy of Sion, the city of God **c** (**2-4**), protected from attack, because of the presence of God. The invading kings became dismayed and took to flight (**5-8**). Thanksgiving is made at the sanctuary (**9-12**) ; then the city's fortresses are inspected (**13-15**). The Ps is a companion to 45. Again we may apply it to the invincibility of the Catholic Church. **3.** '*A beautiful height, the joy of all the earth, is mount Sion*', MT. ' on the sides of the north ' : the extreme north was regarded as the assembly place of pagan gods ; see Jack, *The Ras Shamra Tablets*, 20, and *cf.* Is 14:13 ff. ; Ez 1:4 ; *Book of Enoch* 24, 25. The psalmist seems to be saying that the only God resides at Sion. *Cf.* Mt 5:35. **4.** ' houses ' : Heb. ' *towers* ' or ' *palaces* '. **6.** ' wondered, troubled, were moved ' : Heb, ' *amazed, dismayed, hurried away in alarm* '. **8.** ' ships of Tharsis ' : Tarshish was the Phoenician colony in Spain. Large ships were required for the long voyage, and the expression became indicative of great merchantmen (Is 2:16). As these mighty vessels are powerless against a strong east wind, so were Sion's enemies powerless against God. **12.** ' daughters of Sion ' : the villages near Jerusalem. **14.** ' distribute her houses ' : Heb. ' *count her forts* '.

d **XLVIII (XLIX)**—Again the problem of the prosperity of wicked men. In Ps 36 the solution was found in the possessing of the land by the good Hebrew and his posterity, and the cutting off of the evil-doer. Nevertheless the pious saw around them godless men not only growing rich and prosperous but acquiring land and giving their names to properties. Was there a further solution ? Here the Korahite poet invites all men to give ear to his teaching (**2-5**). Rich men must die, and they cannot take their wealth with them (**6-10**). They go down to Sheol, where the upright gain dominion over them (**11-15**). And God will take the pious from the grasp of Sheol (**16**). So good men need not be anxious at seeing wicked men becoming rich, because their wealth will be of no advantage to them in a land where they will never see the light (**17-21**).

3. ' earthborn and sons of men ' : men of humble birth and men of high degree. **5.** ' a parable ' : possibly in the sense of ' a mystery ' (Lattey), but it may refer to the refrain, 13, 21. **6.** ' my heel ' : NP ' insidiantium ', ' my treacherous foes ' (Boylan). **8-10.** Difficult ; see commentaries and McClellan in CBQ 2 (1940) 176–8. The general sense is that money cannot purchase prolongation of life from God. By the Mosaic Law, Ex 21:30, a homicide could, in certain circumstances, escape capital punishment by the payment of compensation. **11.** ' He shall not see destruction ' : his money will not save him from ' the pit ' of Sheol. Full stop after ' destruction '. ' leave their riches to strangers ' ; *cf.* 16:14. **12.** Men who proudly gave their names to towns or districts possess, after death, only the space of their tombs. Agelli instances Caesarea, Alexandria, Antioch, Seleucia. **13.** ' and is become like to them ' : MT, NP ' *that perish* '. Podechard suggests that there is a comparison between the wealthy ' swell ' and the fat beast ready for slaughter. **14.** ' afterwards ' : NP ' and this is the end of them ' seems inferior to Symmachus ' they who come after them ' (their posterity). **15.** ' death shall feed upon them ' : ' Death *becomes their shepherd* ', MT. In Sheol ' the just shall have dominion over (the wicked) in the morning '. What is meant by ' the morning ' ? (So Heb. against NP which interprets : ' Cito ', and attaches the word to the next line.) For the correct meaning see on 16:15. The reference is to the *awaking from the night of death*. The just, after death, shall have dominion over the wicked. *Cf.* Wis 3:8. ' and their help ', etc. : the meaning of the Heb. is that the forms, or shades, of the wicked will wear out in Sheol. **16.** ' receive me ' : Heb. ' *take me* '. The truth flashes across the mind of the inspired writer : while the wicked go down to Sheol, like a flock of sheep, there, in darkness, and under the dominion of the just, to waste away, God ' redeems ' (*pādāh*, as in 8) the lives of the just, taking them from the grasp (lit.

hand) of Sheol, as he took Enoch and Elias from **348d** death, Gen 5:24 ; 4 Kg 2:1–11. A later psalmist will tell us that they are taken ' into glory ', 72:24. See also note in NP. **19.** ' his soul will be blessed ' : Heb. means that ' the rich man congratulates himself on his happy life ' (Zorell). The second member is better taken as a parenthesis : ' And men praise thee when all goes well with thee ', referring to ' the popular esteem of success and wealth ' (Sutcliffe).

XLIX (L)—A theophany. With lightning and storm, **e** Yahweh, summoning all the inhabitants of the earth, comes from Sion to hold an assize. First he judges those who mean to serve him well—' his pious ones ', ' my people '. Their external worship is satisfactory, but he is not honoured by this alone. All creatures offered in sacrifice—private herds, wild animals, birds and reptiles—are his already, for ' the world is mine and the fulness thereof ' ; over and above these material offerings he requires the spiritual worship of the heart (**1-15**). Then he judges Israelites who break his commandments, thinking that because they are children of the covenant all is well with them. He warns them that he will punish them (**16-22**). Again he insists on thanksgiving from the heart (**23**). See Rinaldi in VD 18 (1938) 43–6, 109–14.

2. ' the loveliness of his beauty ' : ' *cf.* Lam 2:15. **7.** God is the speaker. **11.** ' the beauty of the field '. The Heb. probably means ' reptiles ' ; ' whatever moves in the field is mine ' (Rinaldi). **14.** He does not condemn sacrifices as such, but sacrifices offered without proper dispositions of heart ; *cf.* 1 Kg 15:22 ; Os 6:6 ; etc. **17.** ' my words ' : the ten commandments. He speaks of three of these, against stealing, adultery and bearing false witness. **23b.** '*And he that walketh uprightly, I will show him the salvation of God* ', NP. We may read a Messianic interpretation into ' the salvation of God ' ; *cf.* Simeon's *Nunc Dimittis*.

L (LI)—The Miserere. In the old Roman and **349a** Benedictine Offices it was recited every day at Lauds. Pope Pius X partially restored this custom by placing it in the second scheme for Lauds. In the general arrangement it is recited at Matins on Wednesday.

An act of contrition, confession and supplication uttered by a repentant sinner. According to the title he is David, who had committed adultery with Bethsabee. As satisfaction for his sin he promises to strive to lead sinners back to God, by preaching divine justice. Instead of a merely external sacrifice, he offers the tribute of a contrite and humble heart. Besides the Commentaries, consult Galdos in VD 10 (1930) 67–79 and Arconada in VD 11 (1931) 197–206.

3-5. There are three terms in MT, ' iniquity ', ' sin ', ' transgression '. The first refers to the state of the soul, which needs washing, the second to the evil, which is to be cleansed away, and the third to the violation of God's commandment, which violation must be blotted out. **6c-d.** Various interpretations are offered ; see Commentaries. NP : ' that thou mayest be seen to be just in thy sentence, right in thy judgement '. St Paul quotes the text to teach that God will always prevail in judgement over man's iniquities, Rom 3:4. **7.** ' Catholic tradition rightly sees here an indication of the doctrine of original sin ' (NP)—not, however, that the psalmist understood the doctrine in the full sense. See § 324*e*. **9.** Hyssop is a caperplant, 3 Kg 4:33, the sprigs of which were tied into a bunch and used for sprinkling, Ex 12:22 ; Lev 14:4 ; Num 19:6. **10.** ' bones that have been humbled ' : crushed by God. **12.** ' a right spirit ' : ' the spirit of a steadfast man ', G. R. Driver in JTS 43 (1942) 156. The ' perfect spirit ' (**14**) is a ' *generous* ' (NP) or noble spirit. **16.** ' Deliver me from blood ', from the guilt of having shed blood—the blood of Urias. **18.** External ritual without inward contrition will not satisfy God ; see § 348*e*. **20-21.** Probably liturgical additions made after the destruction of Jerusalem, 586 B.C. ; see § 49*f*. Mgr Knox refers to the fortifications mentioned in 2 Kg 5:9.

LI (LII)—A warning to a powerful mischief-maker **b**

349b and tale-bearer, who, according to the title, is Doeg, 1 Kg 21:7; 22:9 ff. God will bring him to ruin (**3-7**). Good men will be glad to see him punished (**8-9**). The Ps was probably written as a votive offering, when David was able to revisit the house of God, there to give thanks for his escape (**10-11**).

3-4. The Vg reading and division seem best. Doeg's tongue, like a sharp razor, brought about a bloody massacre, 1 Kg 22:18 f. **8.** Not with malicious gloating, but with reverential awe will good men witness the retribution. **9.** 'prevailed in his vanity'. The true reading is found in Targum and Syr. '*in his wealth*', parallel to 'his riches'. The wicked man regarded wealth as power.

c **LII (LIII)**—A second edition of Ps 13. The chief variants are 'iniquities' instead of 'ways' (**2**); 'God' instead of 'the Lord' (**3, 6**); the omission of the passage that crept into 13 (LXX, Vg) from Rom 3:13-18, and a different text in **6c-d**: 'For God hath scattered the bones of them that please men [MT, NP: 'of those encamped against thee']: they have been confounded [MT: 'Thou hast confounded them'] because God hath despised them'. This variation is deliberate. We suggested that Ps 13 was originally a poem on Pharaoh and the Egyptians at the time of the Exodus. This new edition probably celebrates the failure of Sennacherib to capture Jerusalem.

d **LIII (LIV)**—A prayer for help against impious enemies (**3-5**). The psalmist is confident that God will help him (**6-7**). He promises to offer sacrifice in thanksgiving (**8-9**). Reciting the Ps at Prime, we may connect it with the sacrifice of the Mass and thank God for victory over temptations.

8. 'I will freely sacrifice to thee'. The freewill-offering was not an obligatory sacrifice, but one offered in gratitude to God, Ex 35:29. **9.** 'my eye hath looked down upon my enemies'. Complete victory. The expression probably originated from the custom of treading on the neck of a vanquished foe. *Cf.* the inscription on Mesha's stele (Moabite Stone); also 58:12; 90:8; 111:8; 117:7.

e **LIV (LV)**—Physically and mentally distressed by evils brought upon the city at a time of rebellion, the psalmist would fain escape into solitude, there to rest with God (**2-9**). May God bring the designs of the rebels to confusion. At their head is a once trusted friend, now turned traitor (**10-16**). The psalmist is sure that his prayer will be heard because these men are God's enemies (**17-20**). The duplicity of the traitor is described (**21-22**). A miserable fate awaits these bloody and deceitful men (**23-24**).

The Ps was probably written at the time of Absalom's rebellion. The treacherous friend may well be Achitophel. But, as Christians and following the example of the Fathers, we may read it as descriptive of the sufferings of the Son of David. See Eusebius of Caesarea, Origen, St Athanasius, St Hilary, St Augustine (PG 23, 473; 12, 1463; 27, 249; PL 9, 347; 36, 628). Kirkpatrick quotes the heading of a MS of St Jerome's Latin Version: 'The voice of Christ against the Jewish rulers and the traitor Judas'.

3. 'in my exercise' of mind: anxiety. **5.** 'My soul is sorrowful even unto death', Mt 26:38. **9.** 'from pusillanimity of spirit and a storm'; MT, NP '*from the stormy wind and tempest*'. **10a.** Allusion to punishments that befell former enemies of God—Dathan, Abiron and the builders of Babel, Num 16:30-34; Gen 11:7-9. **13.** We may apply this to Christ's grief at the fall of Judas. **14.** 'a man of one mind, my guide, and my familiar': MT '*mine equal, my companion, and my friend*'. **15.** Heb. has 'with whom I took sweet counsel, we walked together in the house of God with the throng (of worshippers)'; but LXX, Syr, Sym, Vg: 'in concord' gives better parallelism. **16.** Again an allusion to the fate of Dathan and Abiron. **19b.** '*for many were against me*' (so St Jer.). **20.** 'no change'. 'The context suggests the sense of moral change—amendment'

(Calès). Full stop after 'God'; then (**21**): 'He hath stretched forth his hand against those who were at peace with him: he hath profaned the pact (of friendship)'. **22.** 'they are divided', etc.: '*Smoother than butter was his face, but war was in his heart. Softer than oil were his words, yet they were drawn swords*' (MT, NP). He was a smirking hypocrite. **23.** 'care'. The Heb. word occurs only here; St Jer. 'caritatem tuam'. *Cf.* 1 Pet 5:7. **24.** 'shall not live out half their days'. Premature death will come upon them; *cf.* Is 38:10; Jer 17:11; Ps 101:25. Judas ended his life by suicide.

LV (LVI)—A prayer for help against enemies who are **f** trampling on the psalmist, spying on him, and lying in wait to kill him (**2, 3, 6-9**). He trusts in God, knowing that God will protect him (**4, 5, 10-12**). The danger over, he comes to the sanctuary to make the thank-offering he had vowed (**13-14**).

4. 'From the height of the day'. The best rendering is that of St Jer., NP: '*O Most High*'. **6.** 'detested': '*distort*'. **7.** 'They will dwell': '*They gather together*' (MT, NP). **8.** 'for nothing shalt thou save them': '*Let there be no escape for them*'; *cf.* St Jer. '*Quia nullus est salus in eis*'. **9c.** 'As also in thy promise'. '*Are they not in thy record book?*' (MT, St Jer., NP)—referring to the tears. **12-13.** The psalmist had vowed that if his life was spared, he would offer thanksgiving at the sanctuary. He fulfils his vow by composing this Ps. **14.** 'please': '*walk*', MT, NP.

LVI (LVII)—Although beset by enemies (**4, 5, 7**) the **g** psalmist is confident that God will help him (**2-3**). With a joyful heart he promises to sing to the Gentiles a hymn of God's mercy and truth (**8-11**). A refrain occurs in **6, 12**.

2. 'the shadow of thy wings'. Like a nestling under the mother bird; *cf.* Mt 23:37. Reference to the wings of the cherubs over the Ark is less likely. **5c.** 'I slept troubled'. No text is satisfactory. Probably: '*My soul is among lions: I must lie down among men blazing (with hate)—the sons of men; whose teeth are spears and arrows, and whose tongue is a sharp sword*'. **9.** 'my glory': my soul, *cf.* 7:6.

LVII (LVIII)—An indictment of corrupt judges— **h** their disregard of justice, their lying, their deafness to the pleadings of the innocent, their maladministration of the law (**2-6**). In a series of vivid images, the psalmist describes the awful punishments that await these judges (**7-10**). Good men, witnessing the retribution, will rejoice (**11-12**). The text is very obscure in parts.

4. 'are alienated from the womb': become estranged from the moral law in their earliest years; *cf.* Gen 8:21; Is 48:8. **5.** 'madness': Heb '*poison*'. 'The Arabs distinguish the "deaf" serpent from that which answers the call of the charmer by hissing' (Kirkpatrick). **6.** 'the wizard that charmeth wisely': Heb. '*the skilful spell-binder*'. **7-10.** Vivid oriental poetry. **9** and **10** 'are a famous *crux interpretum*, and no satisfactory sense has yet been made of them', G. R. Driver in JTS 34 (1933) 41. NP gives 9*b* correctly: 'Like a woman's abortion', but instead of 'which does not see the sun', we prefer: '*let them not see the sun*' (*cf.* LXX). NP is doubtful in 10: 'Before your pots feel the thorn, while it is green, a whirlwind will sweep it away', for the Heb. word here translated 'whirlwind' always means *God's anger*. For the idea of God's sweeping anger, see Jer 30:23 f. Just as a violent storm uproots and sweeps away young thorn-bushes (*cf.* LXX, St Jer.) before they grow thick and hard, so will God in his anger sweep these wicked judges from the earth. 'as alive', may be an oath, *as God lives!* **11.** 'hands': Heb '*feet*'. The picture is that of a field of slaughter through which the just wade in the blood of the wicked, happy to know that there is a Judge who avenges injustice.

LVIII (LIX)—A prayer for deliverance from enemies **3** who lie in wait to take the psalmist's life (**2-6**). They curse, they lie, they blaspheme divine providence; but God laughs at these dogs (**8, 9, 11b-14, 16**). In thanksgiving for his escape the psalmist sings of God's

a might and kindness (17). A double refrain occurs in 7, 15 and 10-11*a*, 18. This 'exceedingly difficult Ps' (Briggs) seems to be composite : 9 is borrowed from 2:4 ; 5*b* and 6 are foreign to the context, and 14 is awkward. Perhaps a Ps, written when Saul sent men to kill David (see title) was adapted as a national prayer when hostile nations threatened the existence of Israel.

4. ' they have caught my soul ' : ' *they lie in wait for my life* ', MT, NP. 7. ' *growl like dogs and prowl around the city* ', MT, NP. The spies, lurking at night near David's house, are likened to wild dogs, which keep out of the way in the day-time, but come into the town at night to prowl for food. 8. ' Who hath heard us ? ' They deny that God cares about what happens on earth ; *cf.* 9:25, 32, 34 ; 63:6. 10. ' *O my strength to thee will I sing* ' ; *cf.* 18. Syr. has ' sing ' in both places. 12. ' slay them not '. Perhaps ' the psalmist wants them to be a lesson to his people, seeing them unable to brew mischief ' (Eerdmans). 14. ' *Consume them in wrath, consume them, that they may cease to be* ', NP. 17. ' in the morning ' : poetically, after a night of distress (BDB), rather than at the morning sacrifice.

b LIX (LX)—During a military campaign, the situation has become so serious that defeat seems inevitable (3-6) ; but recollection of a divine promise brings confidence (7-10). God will again lead his people to victory (11-12). Human endeavours may fail, but with God's help success is certain (13-14).

3. ' *thou hast been angry, O turn back to us !* ' ; but the second clause may mean ' thou hast turned hostile towards us ' ; *cf.* Jos 24:20. 4. The disaster threatening Israel is likened to an earthquake. 6. ' thy beloved ', a name of Israel, God's darling children. 8*b*. It is uncertain whether this and what follows to 10 give the divine oracle or are spoken by David. Agelli thinks that the oracle is that of 2 Kg 3:18. The places mentioned are E. and W. of the Jordan. ' The vale of tabernacles ' is Succoth, E. of Jordan, in the territory of Gad, Jos 13:27. 9. ' the strength of my head '. Ephraim, a warrior tribe, provided military forces (Agelli), while Judah was the political centre, Gen 49:10. 10. Moab, the pagan territory E. of the Dead Sea, was subject to David ; no honorific title is given to it, it is his ' *washing-basin* ' (MT, NP), perhaps for washing the feet of the victorious warrior. Edom, the extensive tract of country S. of the Dead Sea, has also a menial role—to pick up the master's sandals, unless it means that David will take possession of that land, Ru 4:7. The foreigners are the Philistines. 11. ' the strong city '. ' Probably Bosra, Gen 36:33 ; Is 34:6 ; Am 1:12, etc., the capital of Edom, a city highly fortified and difficult of access ', NP, note.

c LX (LXI)—A fugitive from enemies, the psalmist prays for aid and protection (2-4). He is confident that he will return to the sanctuary (5-6). 7-9 are the fulfilment of his vow ; he prays for undisturbed possession of his throne for many years. The Targum interprets the king (7) as the Messias. David's throne was to remain for ever because of his Messianic Son ; Lk 1:32 f.

3. ' the ends of the earth ' : the confines of the land whither David has gone to escape from Absalom ; *cf.* 2 Kg 15:22-26. 5. ' the covert of thy wings '. Here the reference is probably to the wings of the cherubs over the Ark, for the parallel line speaks of the tabernacle. 6. The inheritance is Canaan. 7. *Cf.* 2 Kg 7:12-17.

d LXI (LXII)—Only in God does the singer trust for deliverance from enemies (2-5). The people are exhorted to have the same confidence as their leader (6-9). Man is nothing compared with God ; extortion and theft avail for naught (10-11). The singer ends by reminding the people of God's power and mercy revealed at Sinai (12-13). ' The different ways in which this psalm is interpreted is the measure of the difficulties presented by it ; difficulties which are increased by the uncertainty of the text in several of the verses ' (Oesterley).

2. ' *Only in God is my soul at rest* ', NP. The key- **350d** word of the Ps is *Only* 2, 3, 5, 6, 7, 10. 5. ' I ran in thirst ' is from LXX ἐν δίψει, which is a corruption of ἐν ψεύδει (Agelli), and ἔδραμον is mistaken by Vg as 1st person sing., whereas it is 3rd plur. Read, therefore, with NP : ' *they delight in falsehood* '. 6. ' my patience ' ; ' *my trust* '. 10. ' Truly nothing are sons of men ; in the scales they would rise up by their nothingness, all together ', McClellan in *CBQ* 3 (1941) 55. NP : ' Only breath are sons of men, delusive are sons of men ; in the scales they rise, altogether they are lighter than breath '. 12. God spoke on one solemn occasion, at Sinai, when he uttered two truths, namely that power and mercy belong to him; *cf.* Ex 20:5 f. 13*b*. Quoted in Rom 2:6. On the day of judgement God will render to every man according to the good or evil he has done during life.

e LXII (LXIII)—A morning prayer (2) of a king (12) who is hiding from his foes (3, 10, 11). He expresses his love for God's sanctuary, his delight in prayer and his reliance on divine aid (3-9). His enemies will be punished and reduced to silence (10-12). The Ps, one of the most beautiful in the Psalter, has been part of the Church's morning prayers from early times ; *cf. Apost. Constit.*, PG 1, 744. Nowadays it is recited at Lauds on Sundays and proper feasts.

2. ' Soul ' and ' flesh ' make up the whole man. 3. ' *I contemplate thee* ', MT, NP. 5. ' lift up my hands ' : in prayer ; *cf.* 27:2. 6. By prayer the soul is nourished as if with marrow and fatness. 7. ' in the morning ' : Heb. ' watches '—the night-watches, as parallelism shows. 11. ' foxes ' : ' *jackals* ', animals that devour carcasses.

f LXIII (LXIV)—A prayer for protection from slanderers, who, disbelieving in divine intervention, conspire against the psalmist (2-7). God will punish them suddenly ; the upright of heart will rejoice in awe (8-11). 4*b*. ' *They discharge bitter words like arrows* ', G. R. Driver in JTS 43 (1942) 158. 7. ' Man shall come to a deep heart '. MT has literally : ' And the inward part of each and a deep heart ', rendered by NP : ' And the mind and heart of each are deep '. LXX has ' Each one approaches (to attack) with a deep heart ' ; *cf.* Is 29:15. Kroon declaims against preachers who use this text in sermons on the Sacred Heart, VD 9 (1929) 164. 8-9*a*. Prob. : ' *God will shoot at them with an arrow ; suddenly they shall be wounded ; and their tongues shall fail them* ', i.e. their plans will fall into confusion. NP : ' their tongue shall prepare ruin for them '. 9*b*. ' were troubled ' : NP ' wag their heads ', but St Jer. ' shall flee away ' (in terror) may be correct.

g LXIV (LXV)—Praise to God in Sion (2-3). After confessing their sins (4), the people express delight at being present at the sanctuary (5), worshipping God who made the mountains and the seas (6-9), and gives to men the fruits of the earth (10). A parenthetic blessing is invoked on the soil (11). From God come all good things—pastures and wooded hills, flocks of sheep, valleys golden with corn—and all join in the hymn of joy (12-14). Obviously a harvest hymn, sung probably at the feast of Firstfruits (Pentecost).

2-3. Fittingly chosen as the Introit of a Requiem Mass. NP, with LXX B and St Jer. omit ' in Jerusalem ', but parallelism seems to favour its insertion, and haplography would easily explain the omission, the verb being y^ešullām. ' all flesh ' includes Gentiles with Jews. 9. ' the outgoings of the morning and of the evening ', where the sun rises and sets, which together indicate the whole earth. Hence the meaning is : Thou dost fill the whole world with joy. 10. ' The river of God ' is the rainfall. The *preparation* of the ground is described in 11 : ' *Drenching its furrows, levelling its ridges : thou softenest it with showers, thou blessest its young shoots* '. 12*b*. NP : ' Thy tracks drip fatness ', usually explained as the fattening showers of the latter rains before harvest ; but the tracks may be those of the laden waggons bringing in the harvest.

350g Oesterley renders : 'and thy waggons drip with fatness'.

351a LXV (LXVI)—All nations are called upon to worship God because of his mighty works (**1-4**). The miraculous crossing of the Red Sea and of the Jordan were instances of his power over his enemies. (**5-7**). He established Israel as a nation after many tribulations (**8-12**). In gratitude for his blessings, the nation, represented by one person, offers sacrifice (**13-20**). Some commentators are of opinion that two psalms are here united, the first (**1-12**) being a national hymn of praise, and the second (**13-20**) a thanksgiving prayer of an individual who has escaped from persecution.

3b. ' *Because of the greatness of that might of thine, thine enemies cringe before thee* ' (NP) ; *cf.* 17:45 ; 80:16. **6.** Ex 14 ; Jos 3:14-16. ' There ' : NP gives a logical sense ' So let us rejoice in him ! ', but the local sense may be correct. **9.** Establishment in Canaan gave Israel a new and permanent life. **10.** Reference to the sufferings in Egypt ; *cf.* 3 Kg 8:51. **12a.** Heb : ' *thou hast made men ride over our heads* '. Egyptian monuments show conquerors riding in chariots over their prostrate foes. **13-14.** Here is an example of a Ps being part of a votive offering ; see my article in DbR (July 1928) 95 ff.

b LXVI (LXVII)—A prayer that God may bless Israel, so that the Gentiles may be led to recognize him and praise him as their leader (**2-6**). It is a harvest hymn (**7**), but a Messianic harvest may be implied, when the whole world may pay reverence to him as the one true God (**8**). How admirably this was fulfilled at the first Christian Pentecost !
2. *Cf.* the priestly blessing in Num 6:23-27, and notice the change of the divine name. **5.** ' judgest ', in the sense of *rule*, *cf.* parallelism. **7.** ' the earth hath yielded her fruit ' : for a Messianic sense, *cf.* 84:12, 13 ; Is 4:2 ; Jl 3:18.

c LXVII (LXVIII)—' Every conceivable occasion and date have been suggested for this psalm, from the age of Joshua to that of the Maccabees ' (Kirkpatrick). To us it seems to be a compilation of three sacred songs. The first may date from the time of the Exodus : Num 10:12-35 should be read in conjunction with **2-11** ; **16-28**. Here we have the old marching-song, the manifestation at Sinai, and the gift of the manna (**2-11**). The giving of the Law, and the order of the march through the desert are commemorated in **16-18**. But another hymn was inserted in **12-15**, where we meet with words, thoughts and phrases that can be read in Jg 4-5. The theme is the call to arms proclaimed by Debbora. A third Ps seems to begin at **29** and continues to the end. Here the existence of the sanctuary at Jerusalem is supposed, and prayer is made to God that enemies may be conquered and foreign nations pay tribute to him, until all the kingdoms of the earth join in acknowledging the power of the God of Israel. As the Ps celebrates the giving of the Law and looks forward to the conversion of the Gentiles, it is recited throughout the octave of Pentecost—when the promulgation of the New Law is commemorated.
2. *Cf.* Num 10:35. **5.** ' who ascendeth upon the west ' : ' *who rideth through the deserts* ' (MT, NP). **7.** ' men of one manner ' : ' *solitary ones* ', *i.e.* men with no fixed home, as were the Israelites in the wilderness. They ' were bound ', *i.e.* were bondmen in Egypt, but were brought forth ' *to prosperity* ' (instead of ' in strength '). **7c.** Prob. : ' *But the rebellious abide in a scorched land* '. Antithetical parallelism suggests an opposition to ' prosperity '. **8.** The reference is to the marching in the wilderness, Ex 13:21. **9.** Ex 19:16; Jg 5:4. **10.** The manna, which God freely rained down, Ex 16:4, for his ' inheritance ', *i.e.* Israel (Deut 4:20 ; etc.) when the people were ' weakened ', Ex 16:3. **11.** ' thy animals ' : Israel, God's flock in the wilderness.
12. Yahweh commands by an oracle. His message is published by female heralds (Heb.), probably Debbora and her associates. ' great power ' is usually

attached to the women heralds ; they are ' a mighty host ' ; we prefer to regard it as their call to arms : ' *Let the army be a mighty one !* ' **13.** Difficult. Instead of ' the beloved ', read with MT, NP : ' *they flee ! they flee !* ' The women are cheering the men on to put the enemy to rout. ' the beauty of the house ' : the wives and maidens, who will divide the spoils of war among themselves. *Cf.* Jg 5:30 ; 1 Kg 18:6 ; Is 9:3 ; Ps 118:162. **14** is also difficult. If the women are still speaking, they are saying : ' *If you lie asleep among your borders* [*cf.* LXX, Vg, St Jer., Sym.] *shall the Dove's wings be covered with silver, and her pinions with sheen of gold ?* ' They are upbraiding slackers, like the Reubenites, Jg 5:16. The ' dove ' is Israel, Os 7:11; 9:11. If her wings are to shine with silver and gold, that is, if she is to win the spoils of victory, her children must fight for her cause. **15.** MT reads : ' While the Almighty scattereth kings on her, it snoweth on Salmon '. The last phrase may be interrogative : *Will you (slackers) lie still like snow on Salmon ?* Other interpretations are (1) a snowfall helped the Israelites to conquer ; (2) the snow represents the whitened bones of the slain kings ; (3) the enemy fell as numerous as snow-flakes (note in NP). Salmon is mentioned elsewhere only in Jg 9:48.
16. Join on to **11**. We understand ' the mountain of God ' as Sinai, not Sion or Hermon. Instead of MT, NP *bāšān*, we read, with LXX, Vg, Syr., St Jer., Theod, *dāšēn*. ' curdled ' comes from reading a verb, from which the noun in Job 10:10 is derived. The meaning of the passage, we suggest, is that the abodes of the pagan gods may well envy Sinai, the luxuriant and creamy mountain of God (*cf.* 9), to which he was pleased to come, attended by myriads of angels. (The pagans believed that their gods fed on cream.) Arguing, however, from the Canaanite language as revealed in the Amarna letters, *Prof. Albright renders **17** : ' Why do you dance, ye doméd mountains, mountains God coveted for his abode ? ' CBQ 7 (1945) 24. **19.** The general sense is that Yahweh, who is God, received tribute, yea, even from those who had rebelled against him. (In Heb. the word for ' those that do not believe ' is the same as that for ' them that provoke ' in **7**.) The situation may still be the giving of the Law at Sinai, the offering of sacrifices, and the conversion of those who had worshipped the golden calf, Ex 24:6 ; 33:4 f. For the Christian application see Eph 4:8. **21.** ' issues from death ' : escapes from death. **23.** Again the meaning is obscure : either God will bring back his enemies as captives, even if they try to escape to the high hills of Bashan or to the depths of the western sea ; or, he will repeat what he did to Og of Bashan (Num 21:33-35) and to the Egyptians at the Red Sea (Ex 14). **24.** ' *That thy feet may be reddened with blood, and thy dogs' tongues with the same (blood) of enemies* '. **25.** The nations through whose territories Israel marched saw the procession of the Ark, Num 10:12-28. **27.** ' In the churches ' : the companies on the march. ' the fountains of Israel ' means the true stock of Jacob. **28.** ' in ecstasy of mind ' : Heb ' *in command of them* ', or ' *leading them* ' (NP). Judah marched in the van, Num 2:9 ; 10:14.
29. Here begins the third part, distinctly later, in our opinion, than the other sections of the Ps. May God show his strength at Jerusalem, as he did at Sinai and during the march to Canaan. **31.** May Egypt, symbolized by ' the beasts of the reed ' (the crocodile and hippopotamus) be kept in check ; may her leaders, symbolized by bulls, and the people who follow them (' kine ') be overthrown. **33.** The outlook becomes Catholic : all nations unite in worshipping Yahweh. **34.** ' heavens, to the east ' : ' *the ancient heavens* '. **36.** LXX reads ' among his saints ', for which *cf.* 15:3 ; 33:10 ; Deut 33:3.

LXVIII (LXIX)—A sufferer in distress prays to God for help against unjust enemies (**2-5**). He is suffering because of sin, and in God's cause, for which reason he is subjected to jibes (**6-13**). His prayer becomes more intense (**14-19**), for God alone understands him (**20-22**). He foretells the punishments which his enemies will receive (**23-30**). **31-37** seem to have been added later, probably to encourage the captives in Babylonia. These would see their own miseries reflected in the original hymn ; but with Cyrus' conquests hope revived, and this appendix was added.

There is an over-anxiety even with some Catholic writers to limit themselves to what we might call the OT interpretation of the Pss. The writers of the NT and the Fathers had not this scruple. Why ? Because Christ gave his Apostles a new insight into the Psalter, Lk 24:44. So here, the NT gives an interpretation unknown before Christ's teaching : *cf.* **5***b* with Jn 15:25 **10***a* with Jn 2:17 ; **10***b* with Rom 15:3 ; **23-24** with Rom 11:9, 10 ; **26** with Ac 1:20 ; **22** with Mt 27:34, 48 ; Jn 19:29, 30. See Porporato in VD 10 (1930) 36–42.

5. ' then did I pay ' : prob. a proverbial saying. **6.** ' What was more like foolishness than that having in his power to overthrow his persecutors by a single word, Christ allowed himself to be arrested, scourged, spat upon, flogged, crowned with thorns, nailed to a cross ? It looked like imprudence ; but this foolishness overcame the wise. . . . Christ committed no offences ; he bore offences but committed none ', St Augustine (PL 36, 849). **13.** ' They that sat in the gate ' : loafers and gossipers who met together at the city's gates. **14.** ' for the time of thy good pleasure ' : Heb. ' *at an acceptable time* ' ; *cf.* Is 49:8. **16.** ' the pit ' : Sheol. **23-30.** Terrible imprecations ; but it must be remembered that the enemies are opposed to God's designs. St Paul regarded them as prophetic, intended for the Jews who persecuted and rejected Christ, Rom 11:9 f. ; also Ac 1:20. **31.** Here begins the appendix ; *cf.* 50:20 f.

LXIX (LXX)—A re-edition of Ps 39:14-18, with slight alterations. The divine name *Yahweh* is changed to *Elohim* in **2***a*, **5***c*, **6***b* (MT).

LXX (LXXI)—The psalmist, an old man (**18**), persecuted by enemies, seeks help from God, who has protected him from infancy and made him a portent to many men (**1-8**). Now that his strength is failing, may God be close to him, and may his enemies be covered with reproach and shame (**9-13**). Remembrance of blessings during his long life brings him hope and comfort (**14-21**). Singing on the harp to the Holy One of Israel, he brings the Ps to an end (**22-24**).

1-3. From 30:2-4. **7.** ' as a wonder '—because God has favoured him so signally. **21.** ' thy magnificence ' : so LXX, against MT, St Jer., NP ' *my* magnificence '. ' Except in the Book of Esther the word for greatness is used of *God's* greatness ' (Kirkpatrick).

LXXI (LXXII)—A Messianic Ps. ' It is the manner of sacred Scripture to present the truth of future things by types, as, for example, in Ps 71, which is entitled *of Solomon*, but which contains many statements which cannot be applied to Solomon. For he did not *continue with the sun, and before the moon, throughout all generations*, neither did he *rule from sea to sea, and from the river unto the ends of the earth*, nor did *all nations serve him*, nor did *his name continue before the sun*, nor were *all the tribes of the earth blessed by him*, nor did *all nations magnify him*. Only in part, and as if in the shadow and image of truth are these statements made first about Solomon (' in Salomone praemissa sunt ') that they may be completely fulfilled in the Lord our Saviour ' (St Jerome, *Com. on Daniel* c. xi ; PL 25, 565). See also St Thomas Aquinas's *Proemium in David* ; Lagrange in RB 14 (1905) 45 ; Ab Alpe in VD 13 (1933) 271 ff., 302 ff.

The ideal King will bring justice and fair judgement ; he will succour the poor and the oppressed ; nature will welcome his coming (**1-4**). His reign will go on from generation to generation, bringing peace and justice ; it will extend all over the world, for all kings will worship him (**5-11**). The poor, the weak,

the needy and the oppressed will be under his special **352d** care (**12-14**). Gold will be presented to him, prayer will be offered to him, a wondrous growth of wheat will spring up, and his name will be blessed by all tribes and nations (**15-17**). An outburst of praise to Yahweh because of this wonderful king brings the Ps to a close (**18-19**). A note (**20**) was appended by an editor saying that the Davidic Pss are here ended. Apparently he was unaware of other Pss ascribed to David not included in his collection. For a detailed examination, consult *A Study of Psalm 72 (71)*, by R. E. Murphy, O. Carm. (Cath. University of America Press, 1948).

2. The king is the Messias, as the Targum rightly states ; the king's son is the same person, *the* Son of David, of whom Solomon, King David's son, was a type. **3.** ' the mountains . . . the hills ' : nature takes her part in the Messianic blessedness ; *cf.* Is 32:15-20 ; 52:7 ; Ez 36:8. **5.** ' before the moon ' : either : ' in the presence of the moon ', or (St Jer.) ' beyond (the age of) the moon '. In either case the sense is that he will reign as long as sun and moon are in the heavens ; *cf.* 88:37 f. **6.** ' He shall come down like rain upon the fleece '. This may be the true meaning. Moderns render : ' upon the mown grass ' ; but the usual meaning of the Heb. word is ' fleece '. There may be a reference to Gedeon's fleece, Jg 6:37 f. ; the Messias's coming will be mysterious and quiet ; *cf.* Os 6:3 ; Is 55:10, 11 ; Wis 18:15. **8.** He will rule over the entire world, which, as known to the psalmist, stretched from the Mediterranean to the Indian Ocean, and from the river Euphrates to the farthest parts of the west. **9.** ' the Ethiopians '. The Heb. means ' *beasts of the desert* '. Moderns alter the word to ' his foes ', but without textual authority. See the inscription of Ouni. **10.** Tharsis. See on 47:8. The islands are those of the Mediterranean—the extreme west ; the south is represented by the kings of the Arabians and of Saba ; *cf.* Is 60:6. **14.** ' names ' : ' *blood* ', MT, NP. **16.** On the earth there shall be abundance of wheat ; its fruit shall rustle (or ' rise up ') like Libanus ; see NP. In Messianic times wheat will be so plentiful that it will grow even on mountain-tops, rustling like the trees of Lebanon (or growing as tall as mount Lebanon) ; *cf.* Am 9:13. We may apply this to the Eucharistic Bread which the Messias has given to us. ' And they of the city ' : the population will increase and flourish under Messianic rule.

BOOK III

LXXII (LXXIII)—Again the vexed question : why **353a** do the wicked prosper while good men suffer tribulations ? In Ps 36 the psalmist told us that the godfearing will possess the land, while the families of the wicked will be cut off. In 16:14 f., comparing his lot with that of irreligious men having good food, children and money saved up, the psalmist found consolation in looking forward to seeing the form or image of God on awakening from death. Further light on the problem was given to the Korahite psalmist (**48**) : good and bad men die alike ; the latter go to Sheol, where they have a dismal existence in darkness ; but the upright awake in the morning after death, are taken by God from the grasp of Sheol, live in light, and have dominion over the wicked. Now Asaph seeks a solution. In our opinion he finds it in rewards and punishments after this life. For another view, however, see Sutcliffe, *OT and the Future Life*, 102–8. Originally the Ps was probably a private meditation.

The first verse is introductory, based on the solution of the problem. Then he tells how he nearly gave up his religion because of the prosperity of the irreligious, who have no anxiety about death, who escape the trials of good men. They are proud, violent, defiant of authority, and yet they prosper (**2-9**). Friends of the psalmist are equally perturbed. Does God really concern himself with human affairs ? Is a moral and

353a mortified life to no purpose? The psalmist rejects the thought; to entertain it would make him a faithless Israelite (**10-15**). So he determines to find a solution. This he discovers in the final lot of the wicked—ruin, desolation, terrors. (Again we meet with the *awaking* of 16:15.) Spurned by God, they will exist as figures in a dream (**16-20**). The solution found, the psalmist reproaches himself for his former ignorance and stupidity (**21-22**). What then is the just man's reward? God is always close to him, guiding him through life's ways, until, hereafter, he takes him into glory (**23-24**). So the psalmist chooses God as his portion for ever, knowing that they who do otherwise are lost (**25-28**). **3.** ' I had a zeal ': ' *I was envious* '. **4.** ' no regard to their death ': either that they never let death worry them, or that they die easy deaths. MT and all versions read ' death '; NP follows moderns in altering the text. For a similar association of death and physical health see Job 21:23 f. **6.** ' *Therefore pride is their necklace* '. **7.** ' *their hearts' desires pass all bounds* '. **9.** They blaspheme God, and their wicked tongues spare nobody. **10.** ' It is said that few verses of the Bible have been more variously translated ' (Rickaby, *The Psalms made Easy*). With LXX, Vg, Syr., NP read ' *my people* ' instead of MT ' his people '. The psalmist's friends look at prosperous sinners; then, with tears in their eyes, they say ' Does God really know what passes on earth ? ' Or ' abundant waters ' (MT, NP)—instead of ' full days '—may signify sorrow and distress. **17.** The problem was a sore puzzle until he went ' into the sanctuary '. But the Heb. word is plural and the context shows that mental contemplation is meant; hence, with Sym. τὰ ἁγιάσματα, we read *mysteries*; *cf.* Wis 2:22 ; 6:24 and note in NP. ' their last ends ': their deaths; *cf.* Num 23:10 ; Prov 5:11, etc. **18.** Here begins the psalmist's solution, arrived at after his meditation ; it envisages the plight of the wicked after death (**19**). There would be no solution if he meant that wicked men all die terribly. He must have seen, as we do today, many prosperous worldlings die without terror or desolation. ' *Yea, in slippery places thou dost set them, thou dost hurl them down to ruin. How are they become a waste* [better perhaps, ' to appalment ', parallel to ' terrors '] *in a moment. Consumed with terror they come to an end* '. **20.** Variously interpreted ; the ' awaking ' is after the sleep of death ; see on 16:15. Life in Sheol will be gloomy for the wicked ; their image ', *i.e.* their shades or phantoms, will be held in contempt by God ; *cf.* Wis 4:18 ; Dan 12:2, and perhaps the obscure line in 89:5. **23-24.** The psalmist (and all faithful Israelites) has God at his side, leading him through life by his counsel ; then, after this life, he is ' taken ' (as in 48:16) to God in ' glory '. Read with St Jerome : ' et postea in gloria suscipies me '. **25.** So, in heaven as on earth, God alone is his delight. **26.** His mortal body may ' *waste away* ' (*cf.* Job 33:21), but ' *the rock* ' of his heart and his portion for ever is God.

b LXXIII (LXXIV)—An enemy, intent on destroying the religion of Israel, has wrought havoc in the sanctuary (**3-9**). God has not intervened ; he seems to have abandoned his sheep (**1, 10, 11**). Meditating on God's power against Egypt in the past, the psalmist asks for like help in the present emergency (**2, 12-17**). Are not Israel's enemies God's enemies ? Are not those who are being afflicted the children of the Covenant (**18-21**) ? An appeal to God to vindicate his cause closes the Ps. With many commentators NP refers the Ps to the destruction of the temple, 586 B.C. Others favour the profanation in the Maccabean age, 167 B.C. We prefer a much earlier date, *viz.* the plundering of the temple by Sheshenk (Sesac), king of Egypt, *c* 935 B.C. **3a.** MT : ' *Lift up thy feet to the everlasting ruins* ', *i.e.* run in haste to see the ruins wrought by the enemy. **4.** ' made their boasts ': Heb. ' have roared '. **5b.** MT, NP : ' *They were like men brandishing axes in a forest-thicket ; with hatchet and hammer they have smashed down all its carved work* ' (NP ' doors '). **9.** Words of

the afflicted Israelites. **9c.** Prob. : ' *and there is no one among us who knoweth how long* ' the defeat will last. **11b.** NP : ' *Why keepest thou thy right hand in thy bosom ?* ', failing to stretch it out to protect Israel. **13.** The crossing of the Red Sea and the drowning of the Egyptians. **14.** ' the dragon ': Heb. Leviathan, the Lôtan of the Ugarit tablets ; see J. W. Jack, *The Ras Shamra Tablets*, 46 and RB 46 (1937) 545 ; here probably symbolical of Egypt. ' the people of the Ethiopians ': usually and probably rightly explained as ' desert-yelpers ', *i.e.* jackals. **15a.** *Cf.* Ex 17:6 ; Num 20:8. ' the Ethan rivers ': ' *perennial rivers* ', the reference being to the Jordan, Jos 3:13-16 ; 4:23. **16.** ' the morning light and the sun ': LXX ' *sun and moon* '; see Dumaine in RB 46 (1937) 174-7. **17.** ' summer and the spring ': MT, St Jer., NP ' *summer and winter* '. **10.** MT : ' *the dark places of the land are full of the haunts of violence* '.

LXXIV (LXXV)—God addresses the people after they have given thanks, declaring that he will judge mankind at the end of the world (**2-4**). The proud are warned that, failing to find help on the Judgement Day, they will drink the cup of divine wrath (**5-9**). **11** seems to be a divine sentence. **4.** *Cf.* St Peter's description of the end of the world, 2 Pet 3:10-12. ' Lift not up the horn ': do not proudly toss your heads. **7.** Something must be supplied to complete the sense, *e.g. shall help come* ; NP alters the second member to read : ' neither from the desert nor from the mountains '. **9.** For the cup of wrath, see Is 51:17 ; Jer 25:15-33 ; Hab 2:16. ' Though many sinners have drunk of the cup, it is not empty. The lees are reserved for the present enemies of Yahweh ' (Boylan).

LXXV (LXXVI)—The mighty God, whose abode is at Sion, has destroyed an army attacking Israel (**2-7**). (LXX and Vg state in the title that Assyria was the enemy). No one can withstand God's anger ; the very earth quakes at his presence (**8-10**). Pagans as well as Israelites will pay homage to him whom all the kings of the earth must fear (**11-13**). **2.** ' Judaea ': ' *Judah* ', MT, NP. **3.** ' in peace ': ' *Salem* ', *i.e.* Jerusalem ; *cf.* Gen 14:18. **5.** ' everlasting hills ': so LXX, Vg, NP, which is preferable to MT ' hills of prey '. The reference is to the hills about Jerusalem. **6.** ' The stout-hearted are spoiled ', MT, NP ; but LXX, Vg, Syr. ' lie prostrate ' gives better parallel to ' they slept ' ; see obs. in my *Commentary*. The sleep is death. ' the men of riches ' are ' *the mighty men* ' of Sennacherib's army. **11.** The meaning is obscure. NP emends to read : ' For the wrath of Edom will glorify thee, and the remnant of Emath will keep festival for thee '. If we keep MT, ' the wrath of man ' means God's enemies, and ' the remnant of wraths ' the last of the pagan nations ; the words would then have Messianic meaning ; all nations will one day ' keep holiday ', hold festival in honour of the true and terrible God.

LXXVI (LXXVII)—In anguish of mind the psalmist prayed earnestly to God, but without consolation (**2-4**). During sleepless nights he wondered whether God had rejected Israel (**5-10**) ; but pondering over divine actions in the past (those commemorated in the Canticle of Moses), his soul found relief and comfort (**11-21**). The reference to prayer at night makes the Ps suitable for Compline ; it is assigned to Friday. **3.** ' I was not deceived '. MT : ' *without growing numb* '. **4.** ' was delighted ': MT, St Jer. ' *was troubled* '. **5.** ' My eyes prevented the watches ': so LXX, which may be preferable to MT, NP : ' Thou holdest mine eyes awake ', for *cf.* 118:148. **11.** ' Now I have begun '. According to LXX, Vg, the psalmist indicates his change from despondency to confidence, a change brought about by his meditation on ' the works of Yah ', as recounted in the Canticle of Moses, Ex 15. NP follows Aquila and St Jer. and renders : ' This is my grief, that the right hand of the Almighty hath changed ', meaning that God no longer helps Israel. **13.** ' inventions ': deeds.

a **14a.** ' *Thy way, O God, is holy* ' (or, ' in holiness ').
19. ' in a wheel ' : prob. ' *in a whirlwind* ', but perhaps the rolling of the wheels of God's thunder-chariot is meant. **20.** The crossing of the Red Sea, Ex 15:8. The divided waters returned, leaving no trace of the passage made by God for the Israelites, Ex 14:28. **21.** The subject-matter of the meditation has been the Exodus.

b **LXXVII** (LXXVIII)—The history of Israel given in a poem, from the time of the Egyptian enslavement up to the appointment of David as king. Emphasis is laid on rebellions against God's rule and subsequent punishments. The writer's object is to give a warning against disloyalty to Yahweh. An early date is suggested by the closing of the Ps with David's accession.
2. Quoted in Mt 13:35 ' from the beginning ' : from the past. **3.** The Jews valued patristic tradition. **9.** No historical reference can be found in the OT ; probably the event was handed down by oral tradition. **12.** Tanis : Heb. Zoan, a city on the eastern bank of the Tanitic arm of the Nile. There Rameses II held his court, and from there the Israelites marched out of Egypt. *Cf.* Ex 13:21–17:6 ; Num 11:1, 4 ; 20:8–11. **25.** ' bread of angels ' : lit. ' bread of strong ones '. The manna came by the ministration of angels ; *cf.* Wis 16:20. **33.** Num 14:22 f. **44.** The plagues of Egypt, Ex 7–12. ' showers ' : ' *streams* '. **46.** ' the blast ' : Heb. ' *the caterpillar* ', Ex 10:12–20. **51.** Cham was the ancestor of Egypt, Gen 10:6. **54.** ' the mountain of his sanctuary ' : Heb. ' *his holy boundary* ', the border of the Promised Land, Ex 15:13, 17. **57.** ' they were turned aside as a crooked bow ' : Heb. ' *they recoiled like a deceitful bow* ' ; *cf.* Os 7:16. **60.** ' put away ' : ' *forsook* '. Shiloh was north of Bethel. There the Tabernacle and Ark were set up ; Jg 18:31 ; 1 Kg 1:3. **61.** ' strength . . . beauty ', descriptive of the Ark, 1 Kg 4:11–21. The Ark was captured by the Philistines. **63.** ' were not lamented ' : *cf.* Jg 11:38. The Heb. word read by LXX, St Jer. is preferable to MT : ' were not praised ', generally understood as ' had no marriage song ' (RV). **64.** ' priests ', including Ophni and Phinees, 1 Kg 4:11. ' did not mourn ' : Vg ' non plorabantur '. as LXX, Syr, St Jer. (' non sunt fletae ') reading *niph'al* instead of *qal* (MT, Sym, NP) ; the former is preferable. **66.** The Philistines were afflicted with boils, 1 Kg 5:6, 9. **67-68.** When the Ark returned it no longer found its place at Shiloh in Ephraim ; eventually it was brought to Mount Sion of the tribe of Judah, 2 Kg 6:2. **69.** ' as of unicorns ' : MT ' as the heights ', which NP renders : ' as the heaven ', explaining this as ' an hyperbole expressive of the height of the temple '. **70.** *Cf.* 1 Kg 16:11–13.

c **LXXVIII** (LXXIX)—Gentiles have invaded Jerusalem, sacked the temple and slain many of God's servants, making Israel an object of scorn to neighbouring nations (**1-4**). God has been angry with his people ; the psalmist implores him to forget past transgressions and show compassion (**5-8**). He renews his appeal, pleading that the enemy will deny Yahweh's existence (**9-11**). May sevenfold punishment be meted out to foes who insult God, while his people, the sheep of his pasture, render him thanks (**12-13**).
NP follows many commentators who think that the Ps was composed at the time when Jerusalem was destroyed by Nabuchodonosor. Others prefer a Maccabean date. But it is not improbable that it was written (like 73) after the mighty army of Sheshenq (Sesac) the Egyptian had attacked the city, polluted the temple and carried away much treasure, ' because Israel had sinned against Yahweh ', 3 Kg 14:25 f. ; 2 Par 12:2–9.
1. ' a place to keep fruit ' : ' *a heap of ruins* '. **2.** Quoted in 1 Mac 7:17, apparently as ancient Scripture. **6-7.** *Cf.* Jer 10:25 ; also 2 Par 12:7. **11.** Prayer for prisoners of war. **12.** ' sevenfold ' : completely ; *cf.* Gen 4:15, 24 ; Prov 6:31 ; Ps 11:7.

d **LXXIX** (LXXX)—An appeal to the Shepherd of

Israel to come to the aid of his flock (**2-4**). Enemies **354d** are humiliating Israel ; how long will God's wrath last ? (**5-8**). His luxuriant vine, which he planted in the Promised Land is now being trampled down and eaten up (**9-14**). May the vine be revived ; may God's people be delivered (**15-20**).
A refrain occurs in **4, 8, 20** ; originally it may have come also after **12**. LXX refers the Ps to the Assyrian invasion. Cardinal Wiseman chose the Ps as a prayer for the conversion of England : may the Good Shepherd look kindly upon a country afflicted by heresy and unbelief, and bring it back to unity of faith, under his vicar-shepherd.
2. ' thou that rulest Israel ' : Heb. ' *Shepherd of Israel* '. **3.** Ephraim, Benjamin and Manasses—neighbouring tribes in the Northern Kingdom. It would seem that these territories were being overrun. **4.** ' show us thy face ', in loving smile ; *cf.* RB 30 (1921) 386. **9.** ' vineyard ' : Heb. ' *a vine* ' ; *cf.* Is 3:14 ; 5:1–7 ; etc. **11.** ' cedars of God ' : tall and mighty cedars, such as grew on Lebanon. **12.** The sea is the Mediterranean ; the river is the Euphrates. **14.** ' a singular wild beast ' is a mistranslation of the Latin ' singularis ', which is a noun, meaning ' boar ' or ' wild ass ' (French ' sanglier '). **16b** is probably out of place, see **18b.** **17.** It is the vine that is set on fire and ' *cut down* ' (not ' dug down '). They that ' perish at the rebuke of thy countenance ' are ' the people of Israel typified by the vine ' (Boylan). **18.** The Targum interprets the son of man as the Messias ; also the Fathers, St Robert Bellarmine, Agelli and others ; see also 109:1. But modern writers (also NP) refer it to the vine planted at God's right hand, that is, the Hebrew nation.

e **LXXX** (LXXXI)—A Ps for the Feast of Tabernacles, celebrated on the 15th day of the 7th month, at the time of the full moon (**4b**). On the 1st day of the same month the trumpets were blown (**4a**). The fruits were gathered in during this festival, hence the title ' for the wine-presses ' and **17.** It was the most joyous of Hebrew feasts (**2-4**) ; it commemorated the Exodus (**5-13**). Israel is exhorted to listen to the true God ; failure to do this in the past has led to wars and defeat (**14-16**).
4. ' on the noted day of your solemnity ' : ' *at the full moon, our festival day* ' ; *cf.* Lev 23:24 ; Num 29:12 ff. **5.** ' an ordinance of Jacob's God '. **6b.** Joseph represents Israel coming out (so LXX, Vg, Lattey, Oesterley against MT, NP ' against the land ') of Egypt. **6c.** NP begins a new stanza, introducing the priest or prophet who utters the words of God that occupy the rest of the Ps ; but LXX, Syr, Vg, with verbs in 3rd person may be correct : *Joseph* heard a tongue which he knew not, that is, the voice of God speaking as a Saviour who would remove the burdens from the backs of the Hebrew slaves carrying bricks in baskets. **8.** ' the secret place of tempest ' : the thunder-cloud. ' waters of contradiction : ' *waters of Meriba* ', Ex 17:1–7 ; Num 20:1–13. *Cf.* Ex 20:2 ; Deut 5:6. **11.** ' Open thy mouth wide and I will fill it ' : God will give a plentiful harvest ; no foreign god can do this. **12.** The disobediences during the wanderings. **16.** ' have lied ' : MT, NP ' *come cringing* '. **16b** is difficult. Whose time is meant ? NP translates ' their lot ', and suggests that the lot of Israel's enemies will be irreparable and perpetual. Others think that the ' time ' is that of Israel, whose good fortune will last for ever. But parallelism makes it possible that the conversion of the Gentiles who have submitted to Yahweh is meant. **17.** ' them ' (bis) : we prefer this, with LXX, Vg, St Jer., to ' him ', MT, NP ; also the 3rd pers. for verbs. Who is to be fed ? Either Israel or the converted Gentiles, according to the interpretation adopted in 16b. ' the fat of wheat ' is the choicest wheat, and ' honey out of the rock ' signifies abundance of honey, Jl 3:18. In the Corpus Christi Office, the Church uses the verse to express the sweetness of the Bread from heaven.

LXXXI (LXXXII)—God, the supreme Judge, up- **355a**

355a braids earthly judges for their favouritism and their injustice to the poor (**2-4**). These men are undermining the moral and civil life of the nation (**5**). God reminds them that although, because of their high office, they are entitled to be called ' gods ' and ' sons of the Most High ', yet they are but mortal men who will die like Adam or ' one of the princes ' (**6-7**). The Ps ends with an appeal to the universal Judge. Similar denunciations are found in Is 1:23 ; 3:13-16 ; 5:23 f. **1.** See *Wheeler Robinson in JTS 45 (1944) 155 ; but the usual interpretation of ' gods ' is judges ; *cf.* Ex 21:6 ; 22:8 f., 28 ; Deut 19:17. **6.** Christ used these words, Jn 10:34-38, when accused of blasphemy. **7.** ' like men ' : Heb. *'āḏām* might mean ' Adam ' (so St Jer.) or ' mankind '. The parallel ' one of the princes ' favours the singular, which expression the older commentators (Eusebius Caesar., Theodoret, Origen, Hesychius, St Augustine and others) referred to the fall of Satan. Moderns, however, think that it means simply ' like any prince '. Zorell explains this by saying that ' in every age some princes die a sad and violent death ', but this fails to account for *kᵉaḥaḏ*, which supposes an individual.

b **LXXXII** (LXXXIII)—Enumerating the nations hostile to Israel (**6-9**) the psalmist prays that they may be overthrown, for they are God's enemies also (**2-5**). Past victories are recalled (**10-12**). May present foes be defeated ; may they recognize that Yahweh alone is the Most High God (**13-19**). **2.** ' who shall be like to thee ? ' Read with MT, St Jer., NP : ' *be not silent* '. **7-9.** Apparently an idealistic rather than a factual confederation. For the occasions when Israel was in conflict with any of these nations see my *Commentary*, II, 87 f. **10-13.** *Cf.* Jg 4-5 ; 7:25 ; 8:3. **14.** ' like a wheel ' : either whirling dust, or a wild artichoke with wheel-shaped top, which, when detached, is driven by the wind across the Palestinian plains.

c **LXXXIII** (LXXXIV)—This Ps has affinity with Pss 41-42, and seems to be a sequel, thereby confirming the title : ' for the sons of Core '. The singer has returned to the sanctuary, like a bird flown back to its nest (**2-5**). Happy is he to make this pilgrimage to Sion, in spite of the difficulties that came his way (**6-8**). At the sanctuary he prays for the king (**9-10**) ; he declares that one day at God's house is worth a thousand spent elsewhere (**11**) ; and he thanks God for blessings bestowed on those who lead innocent lives (**12-13**). This is the first of the psalms in the priest's Preparation for Mass. It has a natural place in the Corpus Christi Office.

6b-8. Difficult. ' the vale of tears ' may be his place of exile ; *cf.* 41:4. Many moderns regard it as a proper name ' Balsam-vale ', but such a place is not mentioned elsewhere. NP renders : ' dry valley ', referring to Arabic *baka'a*, meaning ' having little moisture '. **10.** ' our protector ' : Heb. ' *our shield* ', *i.e.* the king, parallel with ' Christ ', *i.e.* anointed one. **11.** ' be an abject in ' : MT, NP : ' *be at the threshold of* ' ; the sons of Core were the *ostiarii* of the OT, 1 Par 9:19 ; 26:19.

d **LXXXIV** (LXXXV)—Using the prophetic perfect tense the psalmist foresees a golden age when God will no longer be angry with his people (**2-4**). At the present moment, however, God's wrath hangs over the nation (**5-8**). Let the people take heart : a reign of peace, security and glory is to come, wherein mercy, truth, peace and prosperity will be established on earth (**9-14**). Thus the main theme is the Messianic age. This is the second Ps of the Preparation for Mass. **2.** ' turned away the captivity of Jacob ' : not a reference to the Babylonian Captivity, for the expression is found in pre-exilic writings ; it means restoration of Israel's fortunes. **10.** ' glory ' : the divine presence. (When reciting this Ps before Mass, we may think of the graces that come from Christ's Presence on our altars.) **11.** ' Mercy and truth ' came with the Incarnation, Jn 1:17. It also brought justice

and peace, Rom 5:1 f. **13.** Spiritual blessings are meant rather than fertility of the soil. The Church uses the verse in its Messianic sense at the Communion on the 1st Sunday of Advent. **14.** *Cf.* the Corpus Christi hymn : ' Per tuas semitas duc nos quo tendimus, ad lucem quam inhabitas '.

LXXXV (LXXXVI)—Reciting this Ps as the third in the Preparation for Mass we may hear Christ, ' the servant ' of Yahweh (**2, 16**), praying to his Father, who is so kind to all who invoke his aid (**1-7**). May all nations come to worship the one and only God (**8-10**). The servant rejoices, and will praise Yahweh's name for ever, because he has delivered him from the underworld (**11-13**). He asks for strength against his insolent and godless enemies ; he begs for a sign that those who hate him may be abashed when they see Yahweh helping and comforting him (**14-17**). The Ps is largely composed of passages from other Pss. **9.** Messianic universalism ; *cf.* 21:28 ; Apoc 15:4. **13.** ' lower hell ' : perhaps poetical for the depths of hell ; *cf.* Deut 32:22. **16.** ' the son of thy handmaid ' : ' Whose handmaid ? She who replied when his birth was announced : Behold the handmaid of the Lord ' (St Augustine).

LXXXVI (LXXXVII)—' I think this is the most difficult of all the psalms ', Mgr Knox (*Tablet*, June 23rd 1945). The main idea is that glorious Sion, beloved of God, is the spiritual mother of all nations. NP speaks of the psalmist ' lyrically binding together the prophecies concerning Sion, Is 2:2-4 ; 54:1-3 ; 60:3-9 ; Ez 37:28 ; Am 9:11 ff. ; Mich 4:1-3 ; Gal 4:26 '. **1.** MT : ' His (God's) foundations are on holy mountains '—Sion and Moriah upon which the Holy City was built. **4.** Who is the speaker ? Commentators are not agreed. Some say God, others Sion, others the psalmist. Rahab is Egypt ; the foreigners are the Philistines. ' these were there ' : MT, St Jer. : ' *this man was born there* '. **5.** Heb. : ' *Yea, of Sion it shall be said : Every man* (lit. ' man and man ') *was born in her. Yea, the Most High doth establish her. Yahweh doth record in the peoples' register : This one was born there* '. For God's record-book, see 68:29 ; 138:16 ; Ex 32:32 ; Is 4:3. **7** in our opinion is a kind of colophon, a tribute to the temple choir —every one of the singers and pipers was born at Sion. The word translated ' rejoicing ' comes from a Hebrew root meaning ' play on the pipe ' or from a similar root meaning ' dance '. Then ' princes ' (**6**) is in Heb. ' *singers* '. The singers and the pipers (or dancers) are all natives of Jerusalem. *Cf.* 67:27.

LXXXVII (LXXXVIII)—Day and night the psalmist prays, for he is exceedingly depressed and feels like a man dead and buried (**2-7**). God's wrath lies heavily upon him ; all his friends have forsaken him (**8-10a**). With outstretched hands he prays that he be not sent to Sheol (**10b-13**). Still he prays, asking why has he been rejected, why have so many troubles come upon him, for what reason has he incurred the divine displeasure, and why have his dearest friends deserted him ? (**14-19**). Such is the ordinary interpretation of the Ps, but another is very probable, *viz.* : the sufferer is meditating on death, and pictures himself as *already in Sheol* (**5-7**) ; the questions he asks (**11-13**) are genuine : contrary to common belief, he asks, may there not be room in Sheol for God's wonders ? may it not be that the dead *can* praise God, and recount his mercy, truth and justice ? May not his prayer greet Yahweh when he (the psalmist) awakes from death ?

5. ' the pit ' : ' *Sheol* '. **6.** ' free ' : see Job 3:19 ; all are equal in Sheol. But NP, detecting a similar word, found only in Ez 27:20, meaning ' saddlecloths ', renders ' Among the dead is my bed '. We regard it as uncertain. **9c.** Heb. ' *I am under restraint and cannot come forth* '. **10.** ' poverty ' : Heb. ' *affliction* '. **11.** ' physicians ' : ' *the shades* ' of the dead. In the Rās-Shamra tablets the ' rephaim ' (the Heb. word here) are the dead. **12.** ' destruction ' : ' *Abaddon* ', proper name, meaning ' place of destruction'; a synonym for Sheol. **14.** If the second interpretation (above) is correct, ' in the morning ' means the same as in 48:15, *i.e.* after death ; see on 16:15. **16b.** MT ' I have carried thy terrors, I am distracted', but the meaning of the last verb (found only here) is uncertain. It is generally emended to mean ' I grow faint ' ; so NP.

b LXXXVIII (LXXXIX)—Inasmuch as the main argument is that the throne of David is guaranteed by divine promise to remain for ever, the Ps is Messianic. It begins by stating that God's mercy and truth cannot fail, his promise to the House of David can never become void (**2-5**). Who can compare with God, all powerful in heaven and on earth, kind, just and faithful to his people and to their king ? (**6-19**). Then the psalmist recalls the promise made to David (2 Kg 7), whereby an everlasting covenant was established and the throne secured (**20-30**). Even if Israel should prove faithless and have to be punished, the promise to David's House will never be annulled (**31-38**). But now the promise seems to have failed. David's kingdom is in a desperate condition ; its enemies are triumphant ; its fortifications are destroyed ; its throne is overturned (**39-46**). May God remember his great promise, otherwise the House of David will suffer everlasting reproach (**47-52**). **53** is a doxology closing Book III of the Psalter. The title attributes the Ps to Ethan the Ezrahite. As this man lived in the reign of Solomon, 3 Kg 4:31, it is not unreasonable to suppose that he witnessed the sack of Jerusalem by Sheshenq (Sesac) of Egypt, 3 Kg 14:25 f. For the first time since the great promise was uttered by Nathan, the House of David had suffered a violent shock. The Ps was written, in our opinion, not in Exilic or Maccabean times but in the 5th year of the reign of Roboam.

6. ' the church of the saints ' : Heb. ' *the assembly of holy ones* ', the angels ; also **8.** ' the sons of God ' in **7** are also the angels. *Cf.* Job 1:6, etc. **11.** ' the proud one ' : Heb. ' *Rahab* ', a primeval monster of the sea (*cf.* Job 9:13, etc.). In 86:4 it was used as an emblematical name for Egypt (because the Nile was supposed to rise from the subterranean ocean), also Is 30:7. **13b.** Thabor and Hermon—the chief mountains of Palestine—here represent all mountains. **18.** ' our horn ', *i.e.* power, also **25. 19.** ' our protection ', *i.e.* the king (see parallelism) ; Heb. ' shield ', who is our king, ' belongeth to Yahweh '. **20.** ' thy saints '—Nathan and David, 2 Kg 7:8-16. **21.** *Cf.* 1 Kg 13:14 ; 16:1-13 ; 2 Kg 12:7. **26.** ' set his hand ' : give him dominion over the sea (the Mediterranean) and the rivers (prob. the Euphrates and Tigris) The prophecy foretells the universal reign of the Son of David, the Messias. **30.** ' as the days of heaven ' : ' as long as this world lasts ' (note in NP). **38.** ' a faithful witness ' : either the moon (so note in NP), or the rainbow (St Robert Bellarmine and others) or God himself, Job 16:20.

39. Here begins the psalmist's complaint. If the disaster refers to Sheshonq's sack of Jerusalem, ' thy anointed ' is Roboam. **45.** ' made his purification to cease ' : Heb. ' *put an end to his lustre* '. **46.** ' shortened the days of his time ' : ' *of his youth* '. The House of David has become prematurely old. This suggests that the disaster has followed soon after the promise to David. **48.** ' Remember what my substance is ' : Heb. ' *Remember how short is my time* '. **52.** ' the change ' : MT, St Jer., NP ' *the footsteps* '. The Targum applies this to the delay in the coming of the Messias.

BOOK IV

a LXXXIX (XC)—This is one of the most beautiful of the Pss. The eternity of God is contrasted with the brevity of human life (**1-6**). Man may make his short life miserable by committing sin, thereby living under God's displeasure (**7-10**). May men be given the spirit of wisdom that they may enjoy years of happiness

under divine direction, instead of years of affliction **357a** (**11-17**). The title attributes the Ps to ' Moses, the man of God '. On this, Mgr Knox remarks : ' Not that Moses necessarily wrote it, but that it refers throughout to the Mosaic situation ; *i.e.* to the divine sentence which condemned the first generation of Israelites to perish, for their infidelity, in the wilderness. Re-read the poem with that in view, and the whole falls into place ' (*Tablet*, July 14th 1945).

3. ' Turn not man away to be brought low ' : Heb. ' *Thou turnest man back to dust* '. ' Be converted, O ye sons of men ' : Heb. ' *Return, ye children of Adam* '. The reference is to Gen 3:19. **5-6a.** Obscure. Perhaps : ' *Thou dost sweep them away ; they become (like) sleep, as grass that fadeth in the morning* '. The underlying notion may be that of 72:20, life after death is like living in dreamland. **9c.** ' *We bring our years to a close as a sigh* ' (NP)—a passing sound full of sorrow. **10.** ' For mildness is come upon us : and we shall be corrected ' : ' *It* [life] *is soon over, and we take our flight* ' (MT). **12.** ' and men ... in wisdom ' : ' *that we may acquire a heart of wisdom* ' (MT, NP). See McClellan in CBQ 4 (1942) 256. May knowledge of the brevity of life lead men to spend it wisely. **15.** ' *Make us glad as many days as thou hast afflicted us* ' (MT, NP).

XC (XCI)—An act of calm confidence in God. The **b** soul that shelters under God's protection shall be shielded from all dangers—especially from the plague ; the guardian angel shall keep it from all harm and lead it through all perils into safety (**1-13**). Then God speaks : he will indeed protect the soul that trusts in him ; he will give it long life and salvation (**14-16**). It is a Compline Ps (Sundays and special feasts). During the Second World War many recited it during air-raids.

3. ' sharp word ' : ' *pernicious pestilence* ' (MT, NP). **6b.** ' business ' : ' *pestilence* '. **6c.** ' *the destruction that wasteth at noonday* ' (MT, NP). This is the fourth mention of time : he that trusts in God will escape evil at whatever time of the day it is abroad. **11.** Guardian angels ; *cf.* Gen 24:7 ; Ex 23:20 ; Ps 33:8. This verse and **12** were uttered by Satan when he tempted Christ, Matt 4:6 ; Lk 4:10 f. **13.** Figurative expressions ; *cf.* Mk 16:18 ; Lk 10:19.

XCI (XCII)—It is good to sing the praises of God to **c** the accompaniment of the harp, to tell of his mercy, fidelity and creative works (**2-5**). Godless men flourish but for a time ; their end is destruction (**6-10**). God-fearing men live on to old age, and witness the downfall of the wicked (**11-12**). The final stanza describes, under the figure of a majestic tree, the spiritual growth of holy men (**13-16**).

7. The senseless man and the fool is the person who denies that there is a divine Providence ; *cf.* 13:1 ; Rom 1:21. **8c.** ' The destruction of evil-doers is eternal ; it is not a question of merely temporal punishment ' (NP note). **10.** *Cf.* Rās-Shamra text in RB 46 (1937) 534. **11.** ' the unicorn ' : Heb. ' *wild-ox* ' ; *cf.* 21:22 ; Deut 33:17—a symbol of strength. ' in plentiful mercy ' : ' *oil* ' (MT, Sym.). Rubbed into the limbs, oil gives suppleness and a feeling of youthful vigour ; hence a symbol of well-being.

XCII (XCIII)—God, the eternal King, reigns over the **d** world he has made (**1-2**). He is Lord also of the rushing waters and the breaking waves (**3-4**). The moral order was established by him ; holiness becometh his house (**5**). The Ps keeps its traditional place at Lauds on Sunday.

1. God's creative work is like a beautiful robe. **5.** The juxtaposition of the physical and moral orders is not uncommon in the OT.

XCIII (XCIV)—May God punish those who ignore **e** the moral law : the vices and blasphemies of these sinners are enumerated (**1-7**). Addressing these senseless men the psalmist asks whether the designer of the ear and eye cannot hear and see ? Cannot he who punishes pagan nations punish individual sinners ? Does not he from whom all knowledge comes know the vain thoughts of men ? (**8-11**) It is well for a man

357e to live under God's rule ; he will enjoy peace and protection, while the wicked go to their doom (**12-15**). God's kindness and consolations have sustained the psalmist's hope (**16-19**). He is the refuge of those persecuted by sinners, and he will bring iniquity to an end (**20-23**).

1. 'hath acted freely': '*shine forth*' (MT, St Jer., NP). **10a.** 'This assumption that there is a divine education of the Gentiles, as of Israel, is practically unique in the Old Testament ; the Targum substitutes the Jews for the Gentiles' (Lattey). **10b.** The original probably read : *He that teacheth man, hath he no knowledge ?* **11.** Quoted in 1 Cor 3:20. **15.** '*For judgement shall come back to justice, and all the upright of heart shall follow it*' ; the administration of justice will cease to be corrupt. **17.** 'hell': Heb. '*silence*', or, probably '*darkness*' of Sheol. **20.** 'seat of iniquity' : the bench of unjust judges. Can this be allied to the divine law so long as it frames mischief against innocent men by distortion of the law ?

f XCIV (XCV)—The invitatory psalm of the Divine Office. Let Israel worship Yahweh the great God and King, Creator and Lord of earth and seas (**1-5**). Let the people kneel down and worship him as the Shepherd of Israel (**6-7**). Speaking in the person of God, a cantor warns the worshippers against falling into disobedience, thereby incurring God's wrath and rejection, as did their fathers in the wilderness (**8-11**).

1. 'God our saviour': Heb. '*Rock of our salvation*'. **3.** 'above all gods' : not that these had any real existence in the psalmist's thought. **6.** 'weep': MT, St Jer., NP '*bend the knee*' ; but see Emery Barnes in JTS 36 (1935) 127. **9.** 'in the provocation': Heb. proper name '*Meriba*', and 'temptation' is '*Massa*' ; *cf.* Ex 17:7 ; Num 20:2-13. 'they proved me, and saw my works' : they tried to put me to the test, by demanding further miracles after seeing all the signs I did in Egypt and in the wilderness ; *cf.* Num 14:22. **11.** Num 14:23-33. For St Paul's application see Heb 3 and 4.

g XCV (XCVI)—A 'New Song'—Messianic in the sense that it foresees the Kingdom of Yahweh extended over the whole world. Jews and Gentiles acclaim his glorious name. Yea, the whole of nature rejoices and makes merry at the coming of Yahweh as King. All nations are called upon to proclaim Yahweh's glory (**1-3**) ; for he alone is the true God, who made the heavens, where honour and glory are given to his excellent majesty (**4-6**). All peoples are summoned to take part in worshipping him and acclaiming him as king (**7-10**). Nature participates in the universal rejoicings (**11-13**). Rightly does St Augustine refer the Ps to the establishment of the City of God, the Catholic Church, all the world over (*De Civ. Dei* 8:24). One edition of the Ps was sung by Asaph and his brethren when the Ark was brought to Sion, 1 Par 16:23-33.

5. 'devils': Heb. '*things of nought*', NP 'figmenta'. **6.** 'his sanctuary' : the context suggests heaven. **9.** 'his holy court': Heb. '*in holy attire*' ; see on 28:2. **10.** Some Gk, OL and Roman copies have 'reigned from the tree' ; hence the line in the hymn *Vexilla Regis* 'Regnavit a ligno Deus', where the 'tree' or 'wood' is that of the Cross ; but the addition is unauthentic.

h XCVI (XCVII)—A companion to the preceding Ps. Yahweh is King. Nature rejoices as he comes in stormy theophany to judge mankind (**1-6**). Sion is glad, and those who adore idols are confounded (**7-9**). The final stanza exhorts just men to hate evil and to rejoice in him who guards their lives and gives them light and gladness (**10-12**).

2. *Cf.* 17:8-16. **7.** 'his angels': Heb. '*all ye gods*' ; *cf.* 95:5. **8.** 'The daughters of Judah' are Sion's neighbouring towns ; *cf.* 47:12.

358a XCVII (XCVIII)—Another 'New Song', closely allied to 95 and 96. Again the theme is the acclamation of Yahweh by the whole world. He has done a marvellous thing inasmuch as the ends of the earth recognize that he has kept faith with the House of Israel (**1-3**). All nations join in orchestral tribute to the King (**4-6**). Nature also plays her part ; seas, rivers and mountains shout for joy together (**7-9**).

1. '*His right hand and his holy arm have wrought victory for him*' (MT, NP). Messianic triumph seems to be in the singer's mind.

XCVIII (XCIX)—Yahweh, enthroned at Sion, is King **b** of all nations. Let people praise his great and terrible name, for it is holy (**1-3**). Justice marks his reign : let Israel worship him before the Ark, for it is holy (**4-5**). Let prayer be made to him, prayer such as Moses, Aaron and Samuel offered, for he answered their prayers, even though their misdeeds had to be punished (**6-8**). Let Israel worship towards his holy mountain of Sion, for he is holy (**9**).

1. 'be angry': Heb. '*tremble* (in awe)'. 'the cherubims': over the Ark ; *cf.* 79:2 ; Ex 25:22 ; 1 Kg 4:4. **4.** 'Thou hast prepared directions': Heb. '*Thou hast established rightfulness*'. **5.** 'adore his footstool' : '*before his footstool*', the Ark ; *cf.* 1 Par 28:2 ; Ex 25:22 ; Lam 2:1 ; Ps 131:7. **6.** *Cf.* Ex 17:10-16 ; Num 14:13-19 ; 16:46 ; 1 Kg 7:5, 8 f. ; 12:18.

XCIX (C)—All nations are invited to unite with Israel **c** in worshipping the one true God, maker and shepherd of all men (**2-3**). May they praise and bless his holy name, for he is good, kind and ever faithful (**4, 5**).

3. 'and not we ourselves' : '*and we are his*' (Qeri, St Jer., NP).

C (CI)—David's resolutions for leading a perfect life **d** worthy of a god-fearing man (**1-2**). He will not look at anything vile ; he will have no friendship with apostates and sinners (**3-4**). No slanderer or proud man shall sit at his table ; honest men alone shall be his ministers (**5-6**). Deceivers and liars need expect no favours from him ; daily he will bring the force of the law against evil-doers, until he has thoroughly purged the city of Yahweh (**7-8**).

2. 'when . . . to me' : an aspiration '*Ah, when wilt thou come to me !*' **8.** 'In the morning' : MT 'Morning after morning', *i.e.* '*daily*' (NP). The courts of justice were held in the morning, 2 Kg 15:2 ; Jer 21:12.

CI (CII)—The fifth of the penitential psalms. Afflicted **e** in mind and body, mocked by enemies and cast off by God, the psalmist implores him to hear his prayer (**2-13**). Then the tone changes : May Yahweh have pity on ruined Sion, rebuild the city, and bring Gentile nations there to worship him (**14-23**). The original theme is resumed at **24**. The singer complains that his strength is exhausted and begs to be saved from premature death. God's eternity is contrasted with the transitoriness of heaven and earth ; his changelessness assures the permanence of the race of Israel (**24-29**). It seems clear that **14-23** refer to the time of the Babylonian Exile. The question is whether these verses were inserted into an earlier Ps describing the sufferings of an individual, or whether, in the first and third parts, the individual represents the misery of the nation during the Exile ? We prefer the former of these alternatives.

5. Illness has robbed him of his appetite. **6.** He is reduced to skin and bones. **7.** The pelican is a bird that seeks solitude ; the 'night raven' (*i.e.* the owl) makes its home among dismal ruins. **9b.** Those that used to praise him now swear against him. This reading of Vg, LXX, Syr. seems preferable to MT, NP : 'those mad against me'. **10.** 'ashes': a symbol of mourning ; *cf.* Job 2:12 ; Lam 3:16. **11.** Like Job, blessed by prosperity, then reduced to ruin. **12.** As the sun sets, the shadows lengthen ; so his life is drawing to a close. **13.** 'memorial', *i.e.* name ; *cf.* 29:5 ; 96:12. **21.** '*children doomed to death*' (MT, NP), probably referring to the exiles in Babylonia. **24.** '*He hath brought low my strength in the way ; he hath shortened my days*' (MT, NP) ; the 'way' is life's journey. **25.** 'in the midst of my days' : in middle age ; *cf.* Ezechias' prayer in Is 38:10. **26-28.** A beautiful description of God's eternity and immutability. See the application in Heb 1:10–12. 29 may be an addition. God does not change ; hence his promises to Israel cannot fail.

CII (CIII)—Thanksgiving to the good God who has pardoned the psalmist's sins and restored health to his body (**1-5**). How compassionate and forgiving is God, who has made his ways known to Moses and Israel ! (**6-10**). His kindness is that of a father, who, knowing the frailty of his children, is ever ready to forgive (**11-14**). Man's life is brief, but God's mercy is unfailing towards those mindful of his commandments (**15-18**). The angels in heaven and God's works on earth are invited to join in his praise (**19-22**). The recitation of the Ps at Compline on Saturdays gives us an opportunity of expressing our gratitude to God for all the blessings of the past week.

5. There was an ancient belief that the eagle renewed its youth by soaring up to the sun and then diving into the sea. But some think that the reference here is to the yearly renewal of the eagle's plumage, while others say that the poet has in mind the long age of the griffon-vulture. **8**. Cf. Ex 34:6 ; Ps 144:8 ; Jl 2:13 ; Jon 4:2. **13**. Such fatherly love of God for his faithful children is almost unique in the OT. **16**. ' the spirit ' ; the *wind*, that passes over the flowers of the field.

CIII (CIV)—A magnificent hymn of the Creation. God created light ; then the heavens above (**1-4**). He separated the waters from the land ; he formed mountains and valleys (**5-9**). He made rivers and rainfalls, that give drink to beasts and birds ; grass for cattle and corn for man's bread (**10-15**) ; tall trees and mountain heights which are the habitats of birds and beasts (**16-18**) ; the sun and moon ; night-time, during which beasts prowl about, day-time for man to do his work (**19-23**). The inhabitants of earth and seas all depend on divine Providence (**24-30**). Glory be to Yahweh, who can cause earthquakes and volcanic eruptions ! May he accept this hymn of praise ; may sinners cease to exist ! (**31-35**). There are striking parallels between this Ps and the Egyptian hymn composed by Akhenaton (Amenophis IV) in honour of the Sun as supreme god. The psalmist, however, makes Yahweh the one and only God and the maker of the sun. See Oesterley, *A Fresh Approach to the Psalms*, 15–18.

1. ' put on *splendour* and beauty '—by his wonderful work of creation. **2**. ' like a pavilion ' : a tent-curtain. **3**. The waters above the firmament are regarded as the floor of ' the higher rooms ' in which God dwells ; cf. Gen 1:17 ; Am 9:6. The clouds are the divine chariot, as in the Rās-Shamra texts ; cf. RB 46 (1937) 548. **4** is capable of various renderings ; see my Commentary. NP chooses : ' Thou makest winds thy messengers, a flaming fire thy ministers ', referring to Heb 1:7 and explaining St Paul as follows : ' As far as the angels are concerned, their dignity is less that the dignity of the Son ; for God uses even winds for the office (of messengers), and flames of fire for the office of ministration '. But we prefer Mgr Knox's translation : ' Thou wilt have thy angels be like the winds, the servants that wait on thee like a flame of fire '. **6**. ' The deep ' : same word in Gen 1:2. **7**. Cf. Gen 1–9. **11**. ' As a specimen of the wild beasts provided for, the psalmist mentions the wildest and least partial to men—the wild ass ' (Boylan). **16**. ' The trees of the field ' : originally ' trees of the Almighty ', which was changed to ' Yahweh's trees ', meaning gigantic trees. But *Sparks suggests that the original was ' trees of Sirion ', parallel to ' trees of Lebanon ', JTS 48 (1947) 58. **17**. ' the highest of them ' : MT, NP ' the fir trees ', but if the psalmist has Lebanon in mind, fir trees are not found there. The stork (' heron ') makes its nest on the top of trees ; so LXX may have the true text. **18**. ' irchins ' : conies ; see photograph and article in RB 44 (1935) 581. **19**. Gen 1:14. **25**. Gen 1:20–22. **26**. ' sea dragon ' : Heb. ' Leviathan ', originally a mythical monster, but here representing all sea monsters that

besport themselves in God's oceans ; see RB 46 (1937) **358g** 545. **30**. Heb. ' *Thou sendest forth thy spirit (i.e. ' breath '), they are created ; and thou renewest the face of the earth* '. See Porporato VD 12 (1932) 140–7. **35**. The only blot on God's creation is man's sin ; sinners must be converted or perish. At the close of the Ps in MT, NP we find the first occurrence of *Hallelu-Yah*, a liturgical call for praise of Yahweh. LXX, Vg place it at the head of the next Ps, where it is more suitable. The same applies to the three following Pss.

CIV (CV)—The psalmist invites Israel to sing and **359a** make music in praise of Yahweh (**1-7**), who made a covenant with Abraham, renewed it with Isaac and Jacob, promising them the land of Canaan, and protecting the tribe during its nomadic infancy (**8-15**). Joseph became a slave in Egypt, but later was released, whereby Jacob and his family came to reside in Egypt (**16-23**). When the Chosen People were suffering persecution, Moses and Aaron were sent to deliver them (**24-26**). As a result of plagues inflicted on the Egyptians, Israel was allowed to depart with much treasure (**27-38**). During the wanderings God manifested his presence in wonderful ways—the cloud and the fire, the quails, the manna, the water from the rock (**39-41**). He kept his word to Abraham, by giving the people Canaan, where they were to live and to observe laws (**42-45**).

1. Quoted in Is 12:4. **8**. Cf. Lk 1:72. **9**. Cf. Gen 12:7 ; 13:14–17 ; 15:18–21 ; 22:16–18 ; 26:2–5. **15**. ' my anointed . . . my prophets ' : the patriarchs ; cf. Gen 12:11–20 ; 20:1–18 ; 26:7–11. **18**. ' the iron pierced his soul ' : NP follows Calès : ' his neck was bound by an iron (collar) ' ; but the Hebrew word is the ordinary one for ' soul '. **19**. ' until his word came ', *viz.* to fulfilment. Some think that the ' word ' is God's, but it may be Joseph's interpretation of Pharaoh's dream ; Gen 41:39. **20**. Gen 41:14. **23**. ' land of Cham ' : Egypt, Gen 10:6. **28**. ' grieved not his words ' : ' *they resisted his words* ' (LXX, Syr., NP). For the plagues, see Ex 7–12, but the order is different. **31**. ' sciniphs ' : gnats. **34**. The ' bruchus ' is the cankerworm, locusts in the larva state. **40**. ' the bread of heaven ' is the manna, Ex 16:4. **44**. ' the labours of the people ' : the cities built by the Canaanites and their cultivated lands.

CV (CVI)—A companion to the preceding ; but here, **b** in contrast to God's faithfulness to the covenant, we have Israel's repeated infidelity. Both Pss were sung when the Ark was brought by David to Sion and were probably composed for that occasion, 1 Par 16. After the invitation to praise the greatness of Yahweh and to ask his favour (**1-5**) the poet enters upon his theme —Israel's ingratitude. The people sinned in Egypt and at the Red Sea (**6-12**). They sinned during the wanderings—at the graves of lust, at the time of the rebellion of Dathan and Abiram, and in making the golden calf (**13-20**). But for the intercession of Moses, God would have made an end of them, yet disaffection again broke out at the return of the spies (**21-27**). Another relapse occurred at Baal-Peor ; it was punished by a pestilence, and only the conduct of Phinees prevented extermination. At Meriba even Moses fell into sin and had to be punished (**28-33**). Settled in Canaan they disregarded the divine injunctions, so God allowed enemies to oppress them (**34-42**). Again and again in their history God forgave them, for he would not break the covenant (**34-42**). **46** may be a later addition ; **47** is post-exilic ; **48** is a doxology closing the fourth book of the Psalter. The last line is a liturgical direction.

6. Cf. 3 Kg 8:47. The solidarity of the nation. Sins of Israel's ancestors must be confessed by succeeding generations ; cf. Lev 26:39 f. ; Ps 108:14. **7**. Cf. Ex 14:11 f. **14**. Num 11:4–7 ; Ps 77:29–31. **15**. ' fulness ' : LXX and Syr prob. read *zārā* ' a loathsome thing ' ; cf. Num 11:20. MT, St Jer. ' leanness ' seems less probable. **16-18**. Cf. Num 16. **20**. ' their glory ' : God manifesting himself by what was later called the

359b *Shekina*. **23.** ' in the breach '—a military metaphor of an heroic soldier defending the wall. **24.** *Cf.* Num 13-14. The desirable land is Canaan, Jer 3:19 ; Zach 7:14. **26.** ' lifted up his hand ' in solemn oath. **28.** Beelphegor—the Baal of Peor, *i.e.* Chemosh, the god of the Moabites. ' sacrifices of the dead ' : sacrifices to dead idols. **30.** Num 25:7-15. **32-33.** *Cf.* Num 20:1-13. Moses was punished by not being allowed to enter the Promised Land. ' He distinguished with his lips ' means that he spoke rashly with his lips. **34.** *Cf.* Jg 1:21, 27, 29 ; 2:2, 11 ; 3:5-7. **39.** ' went aside ' : Heb. ' *went a-whoring* '. Israel was Yahweh's spouse ; by unfaithfulness to him the nation committed spiritual adultery ; *cf.* Ex 34:15 f. ; Deut 31:16 ; Os 2:2.

BOOK V

360a **CVI** (CVII)—Men rescued from perils by God's kindness are called upon to give thanks to him (**1-3**). Four classes are mentioned : (i) travellers who had lost their way in the desert (**4-9**) ; (ii) prisoners released from misery and hard labour (**10-16**) ; (iii) sick men restored to health (**17-22**) ; (iv) shipwrecked sailors brought safely to harbour (**23-32**). At **33** the structure and tone change so abruptly that some are of opinion that two distinct Pss have been joined together. The poet draws two pictures : the first of a fertile land (Sodom and Gomorrha ?) made barren because of the sins of its inhabitants ; the second of a wilderness made fertile and populous (**32-42**). The conclusion (**43**) exhorts wise men to take note of God's mercies. A refrain is found in **8, 15, 21, 31**. NP says that the liberation of Israel from the Babylonian Exile is clearly indicated in **2**. But *the redeemed of Yahweh* are not necessarily the exiles ; they are those mentioned in the subsequent verses, men rescued from divers disasters ; we do not hear of Babylonian exiles returning by sea (23-32).

8. The refrain : ' *Let these thank Yahweh for his mercy, and for his wondrous dealings with the children of men* '. **9b.** Quoted in the *Magnificat*, Lk 1:53. **17a.** Read, either MT : ' Fools because of their way of transgressions ', or NP : ' They were sick because of their transgression '. **20.** ' sent his word ', like an angel ; *cf.* Wis 16:12 ; 18:15. **32.** Let them praise him at the city's gate, where crowds gather and elders sit in council ; *cf.* Ruth 4:2. **34.** *Cf.* Deut 29:23 ; Gen 19:24. **37.** ' fruit of birth ' : Heb. ' *fruitful produce* ', good harvests. **40.** Apparently a quotation from Job 12:21. **42.** *Cf.* Job 22:19. **43.** A quotation from Os 14:10.

b **CVII** (CVIII)—This Ps is made up of two fragments, borrowed from 56:8-12 and 59:6c-14.

c **CVIII** (CIX)—An appeal for divine aid against enemies who have repaid the singer's love with calumny and treachery (**2-5**). Terrible curses are invoked upon their leader, because he is merciless, has persecuted ' the afflicted and poor one ', and despises blessings (**6-19**). The psalmist renews his appeal for help ; his strength is failing, while his enemies are wagging their heads at him (**20-25**). A third time he prays, asking that his enemies be covered with shame, while he gives thanks to Yahweh in the midst of many people (**26-31**).

The imprecations in **6-19** are dreadful. Traditional interpretation frankly admits that they come from the lips of the psalmist himself ; but some modern writers, including Boylan, Rickaby and Barnes, would say that the curses are invoked on the psalmist by his enemies. This solution, however, is not without difficulty, for in the OT we have similar, if not such awful, imprecations. Regarding them as uttered by the psalmist we must bear in mind (1) that he lived under the old Law which included the *lex talionis* ; (2) that oriental poetry is vividly expressed ; (3) that he would rather that his sinful enemies were converted than punished. St Peter applies **8** to Judas, Ac 1:20.

Reading these verses in the Divine Office we cannot do better than follow the mind of the Fathers, who regarded them as prophetic of punishments on Christ's enemies. **1.** ' in my praise ' : ' *O God whom I praise* ' (MT, NP). **6.** ' the devil ' : Heb. ' satan ', here a human ' accuser ' ; *cf.* Zach 3:1 f. **7b.** ' May his prayer be inefficacious ' (Zorell). **8.** ' bishopric ' : the Heb. word means ' *office* ' ; see Ac 1:20. **12-16.** The solidarity of the Hebrew family is in the writer's mind. **23.** Tossed about by a strong wind, locusts become helpless ; so the psalmist feels that his staying-power has gone. **24.** His flesh is reduced from fatness to thinness through lack of nourishing oil. **25.** See the description of the Messianic sufferer in 21:8.

CIX (CX)—' The principle key to the interpretation of Ps 110 (109) is Ps 2. The two Pss have the same subject—enthronement or appointment of a king ; both mention a divine decree or oracle addressed to or concerning the king ; both allude to hostile nations and kings ; both mention the anger of Yahweh ; both allude to Sion as the theocratic capital ; both allude to the king's rod of iron or might ' (E. Burrows, *The Gospel of the Infancy and other Biblical Essays*, 81).

The psalmist has in mind the ideal Priest-king of the House of David. The Talmud interprets the Ps in a Messianic sense. Christ himself, SS Peter, Paul and Stephen all bear witness to its Messianic character. ' The text itself, the testimony of the NT, the unanimous consent of the Fathers and of Catholic commentators all show that this Ps treats of the Messias. Christ, our Lord, himself interpreted the Ps of the Messias, Mt 22:42-46 ', NP. The author is David ; see title and § 49*e*.

David's Lord, his enemies vanquished, is summoned by Yahweh, to sit enthroned at his right hand (**1**). Messianic rule will originate from Sion (**2**). **3** is obscure ; the text of LXX seems best—the Messias, who was begotten before the creation of the stars, will one day manifest his power and glory. By solemn oath Yahweh has appointed the Messias a priest for ever after the order of Melchisedech (**4**). He shall overthrow all foes, even kings, and gain complete victory (**5-7**). In addition to the commentaries, consult Sisto VD 10 (1930) 169-75, 201-10 ; Ogara VD 13 (1933) 209-14 ; Herkenne Bi 11 (1930) 450-7. With 109 the Vesper psalms commence.

1. The Heb. is : ' *Oracle of Yahweh to my Lord* ' (' *ādôn* ') ; *cf.* Num 36:2. Here the ' Adon ' is the anointed son of Yahweh. *Cf.* 2:2, 7 and Mk 16:19 ; Ac 7:55. On the footstool of Tutankhamen's throne are representations of defeated enemies. **2.** The Lord here is Yahweh. He addresses David's Lord, the Messias. ' Rule thou ', etc. : *cf.* 2:6 ; Is 2:3. **3.** See McClellan CBQ 5 (1943) 207 ; Bea CBQ 8 (1946) 8 f. Challoner's translation comes close to the original ; but ' principality ' should be *power* or *nobility*, and ' in the brightness of the saints ' should be *in holy adornment* (*cf.* MT 29:2 ; 96:9 ; 1 Par 16:29), referring to the holy adornment of the Priest-king. ' from the womb before the day star I begot thee ' : hence ' before the day star ' (or ' dawn ') is parallel to ' today ' in 2:7 ; both refer to the eternal generation of the Son. Reference to 2:7 also shows that there is no need to correct (as some Catholic commentators do) ' I begot thee '. NP happily retains ' genui te ', but its omission of ' ex utero ' and reading ' tanquam rorem ' is perhaps less felicitous. The LXX is clearly superior to MT, which reads, word for word : ' Thy people are freewill offerings in the day of thy might, in the majesties of holiness ; from the womb from dawn for thee dew of thy youth '. For the Hebrew underlying LXX see my Commentary II, 243. Consult also G. R. Driver in JTS 32 (1931) 46. **4.** By an irrevocable decree Yahweh ordains his Son a priest (*cf.* Zac 6:13) after the manner of Melchisedech, the Priest-king of Salem who offered a sacrifice of bread and wine, Gen 14:18. The Levitical priesthood is thus set aside ; *cf.* Heb 7:11-28. **5.** ' The Lord ' is again David's Lord, the

Messias, who, with Yahweh's help, will overthrow his enemies. ' in the day of his wrath ' refers especially to the Messianic judgement at the end of time; *cf.* 2:13. **6.** ' fill ruins ' : ' *heap up corpses* ' (NP). ' in the land of many ' : ' *over a wide country* ' (MT). **7.** Many interpretations are given : (i) he will relentlessly pursue his enemies, halting, but for a moment, to quench his thirst at a wayside brook, then, on again, until he lifts his head high as a victor, so NP. (2) Like Samson, worn out by the slaughter, he needs refreshment to raise himself revived ; *cf.* Jg 15:18. (3) The heads of his slain enemies will lie in ditches as if drinking the water there (Boylan). (4) Many of the Fathers see in *a* the humiliation of Christ, and in *b* his exaltation. This seems the best interpretation. ' lift up the head ' signifies exaltation after humiliation (see on 3:4) ; the drinking ' of the torrent in the way ' shows that the fight is over.

CX (CXI)—An alphabetical Ps extolling the omnipotence, majesty, mercy and fidelity of Yahweh. He has kept the covenant he made with Israel, giving the lands of the Canaanite nations to his people. His laws are stable ; his name is holy and awe-inspiring ; reverence of God is the zenith of wisdom. **2b.** Heb. means : ' *to be studied by all who delight in them* '. **4.** The remembrance is the paschal meal ; *cf.* Ex 12:14, 24. The Church applies the verse to the Eucharist. **9.** The redemption is the release from Egypt ; *cf.* Deut 7:8 ; 2 Kg 7:23.

CXI (CXII)—Another alphabetical Ps and twin to 110. What was said of Yahweh there is here said of the godly man. Happy is the man who reflects God in his life. The blessings that will be his are enumerated. **3b.** *Cf.* 110:3*b*. **4b.** *Cf.* 110:4*b*. The exemplary life of a religious man is a light in this world's darkness. Christ is the Light of the world. **5a.** ' From this we gather that rich men are not sole owners of their wealth, but stewards and dispensers ' (Agelli). **5b.** *Cf.* 110:7*b*. **6.** He will never come to ruin. **8.** ' *look down* ' on his enemies reduced to shame. **9.** Applied to the abundance of grace given by God, 2 Cor 9:9. The horn here means dignity or power. **10c.** *Cf.* 1:6*b*.

CXII (CXIII)—The group 112–117 form the *Hallel* or Hymn of Praise, which was embodied in the Hebrew liturgy for the great festivals. At the paschal meal 112–113:8 were sung before, and 113:9–117 after the supper. For the latter see Mt 26:30 ; Mk 14:26. The singer invites the servants of Yahweh to praise his name day by day (**1-3**) ; for no being can be likened to him who dwells in heaven and condescends to look down to earth in order to lift up the poor and the lowly and to make a barren wife a happy mother (**4-9**). **1.** ' *ye servants* '. **7-8b.** Taken from 1 Kg 2:8. The dunghill signifies extreme degradation ; outcasts and lepers sat by the *mazbala* to get warmth from the smouldering rubbish ; *cf.* Job 2:8. **9.** *Cf.* 1 Kg 2:5.

CXIII (CXIV–CXV)—At **9** MT begins another Ps, and Vg, DV number the verses afresh. The first part tells of the share nature took in the story of the Exodus —the Red Sea, the river Jordan, the trembling mountains of Sinai, the quaking earth (**1-7**). **8** seems to be an afterthought—the striking of the rock. The second part (or next Ps) compares Yahweh the living God with the lifeless idols of the heathens. Priests, people and proselytes of Israel, trusting in Yahweh, find that he is their help and shield. May he bless them all, increase their numbers and give them life, that they may bless him henceforth and for ever (**9-18**). **1.** ' a barbarous people ' : Heb. : ' *a people of strange speech* ' ; *cf.* Gen 42:23. **3.** Ex 15:8 ; Jos 3:17. **4.** Ex 19:16-19 ; Jg 5:5 ; Ps 67:9. **8.** Ex 17:6 ; Num 20:11.

CXIV–CXV (CXVI)—In MT these two psalms are one. The first is an act of the love of God recited by one who has been rescued from death. The second is an act of hope in God recited by one who has lost confidence in men ; to God he will make an *ex-voto* offering as an act of public thanksgiving. These two Pss are recited at Vespers on Monday. Ps 115 is part of the priest's Preparation for Mass ; reciting it, we may refer it to Christ, ' the servant of Yahweh ', offering the ' chalice of salvation ' in the presence of all nations, as a memorial of his death, so precious in the sight of his Father. **1.** Heb. should probably be rendered : ' *I love !* [a fervent ejaculation] *because Yahweh hath heard* '. **2.** ' in my days ' : all my life, now that I am restored to health. **3.** ' sorrows ' : ' *cords* ' (MT, NP). ' hell ' : Heb. ' *Sheol* ' ; *cf.* 17:5-7. **6.** The little ones are those who depend on God as their father ; *cf.* 18:8 ; Mt 11:25. **9.** See on 26:13. **10.** NP : ' *I was confident, even when I said : I am exceedingly afflicted* '. **11.** ' in my excess ' : the Heb. root means ' haste ' ; here we suggest *in my emotion*. **13.** A reference to the drink-offering that accompanied the thanksgiving sacrifice. *Cf.* Mt 26:27. **15.** The meaning is that the life of a saint is so precious in the sight of God that he will preserve it from violent death. When we use the verse on the feast of martyrs, the sense is that their heroic deaths are precious in God's sight.

CXVI (CXVII)—All nations are invited to praise Yahweh because of his kindness and fidelity. The psalmist, as a prophet, foresees the conversion of the Gentiles. **2** may be understood as their own prayer (*cf.* Rom 15:11) ; and in this sense we sing the Ps at the close of Benediction.

CXVIII (CXVIII)—The last Ps of the Hallel. Assuming that this was the ' hymn ' mentioned in Mt 26:30, Christ recited it when, rejected by the Jews, he was about to become the corner-stone of the Church (**22**). Originally a processional hymn, it was sung antiphonally by people, priests and proselytes entering into the temple to thank Yahweh for victory and renewal of national life (**1-18**). The thanksgiving is repeated and a day of rejoicing is proclaimed at Yahweh's altar (**19-29**). **1.** ' *Give thanks* '. *Cf.* 105:1 ; 106:1 ; 135:1. **5.** ' enlarged me ' : ' *gave me relief* '. **14.** Based on Ex 15:2 ; *cf.* Is 12:2. **15.** The Ps was sung on the Feast of Tabernacles (Succoth). **22.** The stone is the Hebrew nation, regarded as useless by Gentile nations, but now raised by God to a conspicuous position, made the important corner-stone that binds the walls together ; *cf.* Is 28:16. Our Lord, as the Jewish Messias, applied this verse to his own rejection and exaltation ; Mt 21:42 ; etc. **25.** ' save ' : omit ' me '. Heb. *hôšî'a-nā* ' becomes ' Hosanna ' in Aramaic—a liturgical cry ; *cf.* Mt 21:8 f. **27.** ' Appoint . . . the altar '. NP : ' Arrange a procession with thickly woven boughs ' may be correct, but an alternative is : ' Bind the festal sacrifices (or ' victim ') to the horns of the altar with cords ' ; in favour of ' thickly woven boughs ' see 2 Mac 10:7. ' horn ' should be *horns* ; the corners of the altar of holocausts were shaped like horns, Ex 27:2. See McClellan in CBQ 5 (1943) 211–3.

CXVIII (CXIX)—An alphabetical Ps, in which the initial letter of each set of eight consecutive verses is the same, until the alphabet is exhausted. The subject is the observance of the Mosaic Law with its eight divisions : laws, judgements, precepts, statutes, commandments, judgements, words and sayings. The artificial arrangement is at the expense of consecutive thought ; hence, at the divine Office, each verse should be read as a separate entity. Consult Bi 4 (1923) 375 ; RB 46 (1937) 182–206 ; 48 (1939) 5–20 ; CBQ 5 (1943) 345–7. **5.** ' justifications ' : ' *statutes* ' (NP). So elsewhere in the Ps. **11.** ' words ' : ' *sayings* ', and so throughout. **27.** ' *I will meditate on thy wonderful deeds* ' (MT, NP). **28.** ' *My soul melteth* [or ' sheds tears ', NP] *through grief* ' (MT). **39.** ' reproach *whereof I am afraid* ' (MT, NP). He fears the contempt and insults of his enemies. **48.** ' lifted up my hands '—venerating the commandments, as if in prayer. **67.** ' *Before I was afflicted* ' (MT, NP) ; suffering brought his soul to God. **69.** The Heb. is : ' *The proud have besmeared me with lies* ' ; NP renders ' Machinantur fraudes '. **70.**

360i

361a

b

c

361c 'curdled like milk' : 'gross as fat' ; a heart wedded to sin becomes insensible to spiritual impressions ; cf. 16:10 ; Mt 13:15. **73.** A beautiful thought : God makes and moulds the soul, and will give it spiritual understanding : cf. Deut 32:6 ; Job 10:8. **83.** 'a bottle in the frost' : NP with MT 'a bottle in the smoke' ; but LXX, Vg, St Jer., Syr., Sym. may well be right in reading 'frost' : a wine-skin bottle lying in the frost becomes shrivelled up and needs warmth ; so does the psalmist need the warmth of divine comfort. If we read 'smoke' we must suppose that the wine-skin is shrivelled up and blackened by the smoke of the fire in the house. **91.** The Hebrew means that the permanence of heaven and earth is a symbol of the Law that does not change. **96.** 'What men call "perfect" is limited, but the divine Law has no limits' (NP ,note). **103.** Cf. 18:10 f. **109.** He is continually exposed to death ; cf. Jg 12:3 ; 1 Kg 19:5 ; 28:21. **120.** MT, NP : 'My flesh shudders for fear of thee'. 'A profound religious awe is meant' (Lattey). **131.** Like a thirsty deer panting for water, he longs for the spiritual refreshment of the Law ; cf. 41:2. **140.** 'refined' : like gold or silver in fire ; cf. 11:7. **148.** He forestalls the dawn to meditate on the Law. **160.** Cf. Jn 17:17. **164.** 'Seven times a day' : throughout the whole day—seven denoting completion ; cf. 11:7 ; 78:12 ; Prov 24:16. The division of the Church's prayer into seven canonical hours may have been derived from this text.

d CXIX (CXX)—The first of the fifteen 'Gradual' Pss, Pss appointed to be sung by pilgrims 'going up' to Jerusalem. Here the pilgrim prays for deliverance from treacherous enemies who use their tongues against him (**1-4**) ; and he laments that he has to live amongst godless barbarians who give him no peace (**5-7**). **3.** A form of oath. May God curse thee, thou deceitful tongue ! Cf. 1 Kg 3:17 ; 14:44 ; 25:22. **4.** Often understood as the punishments of the curse invoked in 3 (so NP), but in the light of other OT passages (63:4-6, 8 f. ; Prov 25:18 ; Jer 9:3, 8) it would seem to be descriptive of the treacherous tongue. The evil tongue is likened to 'a fighter's sharpened arrows' and 'hot charcoal of broom-wood' (MT). Cf. Jas 3:6 ; Prov 16:27. **5.** 'is prolonged' : 'is in Mesech' (so MT ; NP 'Mosoch'). The Moschi were a barbarian tribe dwelling between the mountains of Armenia and the Black Sea, Gen 10:2 ; 1 Par 1:5 ; Ez 27:13 ; 38:3 ; 39:1. The tribesmen of Kedar dwelt in the Syro-Arabian desert, Gen 25:13 ; Is 21:16 f. ; 60:7 ; Jer 49:28. The two names are representative of hostile tribes through whose territories pilgrims had to pass on their way up to Jerusalem.

e CXX (CXXI)—A beautiful hymn sung by the pilgrims as they made their way over rough roads (**3**) in the heat of the day or during night-time (**6**) towards the hills of Judah, on which Sion was built (**1**). Yahweh, Maker of heaven and earth and Guardian of Israel is their Guide on the journey (**2, 4, 5, 7, 8**). **5.** 'protection' : Heb. 'shade' ; cf. 90:1 f. **6.** The moon is really dangerous in oriental countries, where it produces, in those exposed too long to its rays, painful ophthalmia and cerebral inflammation, which sometimes proves fatal (Fillion). **8.** 'coming in and going out' is an expression denoting all one's activities ; cf. Deut 28:6 ; 31:2, etc.

f CXXI (CXXII)—Joy at the prospect of making the pilgrimage (**1**). Arrival at the city, which is the seat of government (**2-5**). Prayer that Jerusalem and its temple may enjoy peace and prosperity (**6-9**). **4.** 'the testimony of Israel' ; cf. Ex 23:17 ; 34:23 ; Deut 16:16. **5.** 'Yea, there the seats of judgement are set, the seats of David's house' (MT, NP), i.e. the law courts.

g CXXII (CXXIII)—It is not easy to find a pilgrimage motif in this Ps. The singers are being persecuted. Perhaps the proud (**4**) are the heathens who attack the pilgrims, or, possibly, they are godless Israelites who pour scorn on the pilgrimage. As slaves keep their eyes fixed on the hands of their masters or mistresses for signals, so do the pilgrims lift up their eyes to **g** Yahweh, waiting for him to show them pity in the distress they are suffering from their enemies.

CXXIII (CXXIV)—Thanksgiving to God who has **h** intervened in defence of Israel when enemies (perhaps those mentioned in the previous Ps) would have overwhelmed them like a rushing torrent. The pilgrims were like a bird caught in a trap ; the snare is broken and the pilgrims are safe.

8. Frequently used in the Church's liturgy. In the Ps it means that the pilgrims obtained help by invoking the name of Yahweh, who, as Maker of heaven and earth, has illimitable power.

CXXIV (CXXV)—The girdle of hills around Jerusalem **i** reminds the pilgrims of God's protection of his people (**1-2**). He will not allow pagans to hold sway over the land of Canaan, lest his people be contaminated by their evil manners (**3**). Prayer is offered for blessings on the upright of heart, for chastisement of those who follow pagan ways, and for peace upon Israel (**4-5**). **3.** 'the sceptre of the wicked' (LXX, Syr., Sym.), 'the lot of the just' is Canaan, the land assigned by God to Israel. **5.** 'bonds' : Heb. 'crooked ways', i.e. pagan practices.

CXXV (CXXVI)—The singer looks forward to Messianic days, when, as in dreamland, the people will be **j** exceedingly happy. Then, also, will the Gentiles recognize what great things Yahweh has done for Jews and Gentiles (**1-3**). But these happy days are in the future ; at the moment the people are sowing seed with tears. May God bring prosperity, as water brings fertility to the parched Negeb (**4-6**). The Ps regards the future and the present in much the same way as Ps 84. It is taken for granted by some commentators (including NP) that this is a hymn of the exiles returning from Babylonia ; rather it is a 'pilgrim psalm', supposing the existence of the temple. **1.** 'brought back the captivity of Sion' : restored prosperity to Sion. There is no allusion to the Babylonian exile ; cf. 13:7 ; 84:2 ; Job 42:10. 'like men comforted' : Heb. 'like men in a dream', i.e. enjoying happiness that seems too good to be true. **2.** 'shall be'. **4.** The Negeb, or southern desert of Judah, was parched in the summer, but its stream ran with copious water when the autumn rains fell. So Israel, now dry and fruitless, will gain prosperity in the Messianic days to come.

CXXVI (CXXVII)—The blessing of having a large **k** family. Children are God's gift ; without them the labours of the present generation are in vain, and the security of the state is imperilled (**1-3**). Children are like arrows in a warrior's quiver ; with weapons like these a man can defy his adversaries (**4-5**). **1.** 'build the house', i.e. give offspring, so that the family line may continue ; cf. Ex 1:21 ; Deut 25:9, etc. **2.** 'and take rest late, eating bread of toil' (MT). Vain for men to get up early and work till late at night if there is no family to benefit by this. 'When he shall give sleep to his beloved' : differently interpreted. It would seem that the 'beloved' are the Chosen People, Deut 33:12 ; Is 5:1 ; Jer 11:15 ; Ps 59:6. As they 'sleep' in death, Job 14:12, they need sons to follow after them. Another interpretation is that God gives children, forming them in the womb during sleep ; cf. Wis 7:2. See also Joüon in Bi 11 (1930) 84 ; Kroon in VD 11 (1931) 38 ; McClellan in CBQ 5 (1943) 348. **4.** 'children of youth' (MT, NP), children born when their parents are young ; these sons will grow up to defend their parents before the latter come to die. **5.** 'the desire' : 'his quiver' (MT, NP) 'Obviously a strong bodyguard of sturdy sons would help to secure for their father fair play when he had trouble with rivals at the gate of the city' (Boylan).

CXXVII (CXXVIII)—A sequel to the previous Ps. **l** Here are described the blessings of religious home-life. The good father provides for the needs of his family ; his wife attends to the household duties, and, like a fruitful vine, bears healthy children, who sit round the family board like so many olive-shoots from the parent l stem (**1-3**). God bless this good father, giving him long life, while peace and prosperity reign in Jerusalem! (**4-6**).

3. ' *in the inner parts of thy house* ' (MT, NP). She does not gossip on the door-step, like the foolish woman of Prov 9:13 f. The olive is a symbol of health and vigour; as the parent tree grows old, young shoots spring up around it.

l **CXXVIII** (CXXIX)—From the time of her youth (in Egypt) Israel has suffered many persecutions, but has never been exterminated. Her foes have cut long furrows into her back, but Yahweh has always come to her aid (**1-4**). May Sion's enemies be confounded; may they be as short-lived as grass that grows on a house-top and is never reaped with a harvest blessing (**5-8**).

3. ' *Upon my back ploughmen have ploughed : long were the furrows they made* ' (St Jer.) ; *cf.* Is 51:23 ; Mic 3:12. **4.** ' necks ', as LXX, may be correct ; MT, NP ' ropes ' may refer to the ropes of the yoke (3). **6.** ' On the flat and mud-plastered roofs of Palestinian houses of yore grass sprang up after the rains, but it quickly withered away in the heat of the sun ' (NP). **8.** The greeting of the reapers ; *cf.* Ru 2:4.

a **CXXIX** (CXXX)—The sixth penitential and the final Ps in the Preparation for Mass is an act of contrition. The Church has adopted it as an official prayer for the holy souls in Purgatory. From the depths of depression, due to a sense of sin, the psalmist cries out to God to hear his prayer. Should strict justice be demanded no man would be acquitted ; but God is forgiving (**1-4**). So, with hope and patience, the singer (representing Israel) waits for redemption from all iniquities (**5-8**).

4b. NP ' that thou mayest be served with reverence ' follows MT ; but LXX, Vg ' by reason of thy law I wait for thee ' deserves attention. The law contained the ' word ', *i.e.* the promise of forgiveness ; *cf.* 118:74, 81. See Arconada in VD 12 (1932) 213-9. **6.** ' From the morning watch even until night ', as LXX (Sin.), Vg, may be preferable to MT ' more than watchers for the morning, watchers for the morning ' where dittography may reasonably be suspected. NP follows MT but makes the second phrase the opening of a new stanza.

b **CXXX** (CXXXI)—As a baby reposes untroubled in its mother's lap, so does the singer, disdaining high and mighty thoughts, commit himself entirely to God. 3 may be an addition. With the Ps *cf.* Mt 18:3 ; 1 Pet 5:7. Here the ' Little Way ' of St Teresa of Lisieux is found in a nutshell ; see my article in *Sicut Parvuli* 8 (1946) 134 ff.

c **CXXXI** (CXXXII)—The first part tells of David's ardent desire to build a temple for the God of Jacob (**1-5**). The second part expresses the enthusiasm of the people and their eagerness to bring the Ark to Sion (**6-10**). The third part speaks of the establishment of the Davidic throne (**11-12**). God's promise of blessings on Sion is given in the fourth part : he will provision the city, feed its poor, sanctify its priests ; and from the House of David shall come forth the Messias, whose enemies shall be brought to shame (**13-18**). *Cf.* Ps 88.

2. ' God ' : Heb. ' *Mighty One* ' (also **5**). *Cf.* Gen 49:24 ; etc. **6.** Ephrata is probably another name for Bethlehem, David's native town, Gen 35:19 etc. ' the fields of the wood ' : Heb. ' *fields of Ya'ar* ' is Qiryathyearim where the Ark remained for some years, 1 Kg 7:1 f. **7.** ' the place where his feet stood ' is the Ark, upon which the divine Presence was enthroned ; *cf.* 98:5 ; 1 Par 28:2 ; Lam 2:1. **8.** ' thy resting place ' is the permanent sanctuary at Sion, 1 Par 28:2 ; 2 Par 6:41 f. **9.** *Cf.* David's command in 1 Par 15:12, 14, 27 ; 2 Kg 6:12, 15. **10.** ' thy anointed ' is Solomon. **11.** ' Of the fruit of thy womb ' ; see 2 Kg 7:12. **14.** See David's words in 1 Par 28:2. **15.** ' *I will indeed bless her supply of food* ' (MT, NP) ; but see Joüon in Bi 11 (1930) 85. **17.** ' bring forth a horn ' : the Heb. means ' *cause to sprout* ', whence Messianic name *ṣemaḥ* ' the sprout ' ; *cf.* Jer 23:5, etc.

The horn, *par excellence* is the Messias ; *cf.* Lk 1:69. 362c The ever-burning lamp is the permanence of the Davidic line : *cf.* 2 Kg 21:17, etc. The Jews understood that the verse referred to the Messias ; doubtless this was also the meaning in the psalmist's mind.

CXXXII (CXXXIII)—How good and pleasant for d pilgrims to be gathered together at Sion ! As the sacred oil of consecration, poured upon Aaron's head, trickled down to his beard and then to the collar of his robe, and as the dew of Hermon may be said to descend on Sion's hill, so do God's blessings flow from Sion, the capital city, and extend over the whole land, giving life to its people for evermore.

3. For the many interpretations of this verse see my *Commentary* II, 350 f. If the text is left unaltered we have the choice of taking ' the dew of Hermon ' proverbially or literally. NP prefers the former : dew, as abundant as that on Hermon, represents the crowds of pilgrims to Jerusalem. But the literal meaning is more in keeping with 2. As the sacred oil falls first on Aaron's head and then comes right down to his collar, and as dew falls first on Canaan's most conspicuous mountain and later reaches the hill of Sion, so do God's blessings fall first on the capital city and from there extend over the whole land.

CXXXIII (CXXXIV)—Priests and Levites are sum- e moned to praise God at night service in the temple. Or the ' servants of the Lord ' may be pilgrims who are worshipping at the sanctuary during the night. 3 gives the priestly blessing (Num 6:24). Obviously a Compline Ps (Sunday).

CXXXIV (CXXXV)—God's servants, gathered to- f gether in the temple, are called upon to praise Yahweh for choosing out Israel as his special possession (**1-4**). Yahweh alone is God, Lord of heaven and earth ; it is he who causes mists, lightnings and rain (**5-7**). He brought Israel out of Egypt and gave Canaan to his people, after smiting kings—Og, Sehon and the kings of Canaan (**8-12**). Idols are fashioned by men's hands (**13-18**). May all classes of Israelites bless Yahweh, whose dwelling-place is at Sion (**19-21**).

4. Based on Deut 7:6 ; *cf.* Ex 19:5 ; Deut 14:2 ; 26:18. ' Though Israel was God's special possession, to the Word made Flesh it was said : Ask of me and I will give thee the Gentiles for thine inheritance ' (Agelli). **5.** ' gods ' ; see on 94:3. **11.** Sehon and Og seem to have been regarded in early Hebrew history as the most formidable opponents of Israel's entry into the Promised Land ; Num 21:21 ff. ; Deut 2:30 ff., etc.

CXXXV (CXXXVI)—The theme is similar to that g of Ps 134 ; but here the matter is arranged in litany form for antiphonal chanting. Praise and thanksgiving are offered to Yahweh, Maker of heaven and earth, who brought Israel out of Egypt, smote Pharaoh's army, led the people through the wilderness, slew their enemies and gave them possession of Canaan. The good God feeds all his living creatures ; his kindness never fails. In the Talmud the Ps is known as the Great Hallel. It was sung on the seventh day of the passover feast. See *Slotki in JTS 29 (1928) 255 ff.

5. ' in understanding ' : in an orderly manner, not haphazard ; *cf.* 103:24 ; Prov 3:19.

CXXXVI (CXXXVII)—The only Ps that *unmistakably* h speaks of the Babylonian Exile. It was composed during or soon after the Captivity. Gathered together on the banks of Babylon's streams (probably for ceremonial ablutions) the captives, with tears in their eyes, remember Sion. Their musical instruments, that once accompanied Pss in the temple, now hang silent on the poplar trees (**1-2**). How impossible to sing a hymn to Yahweh on a foreign soil ! (**3-4**). Cursed be the hand and tongue of any exile who should forget Sion ! (**5-6**). May God bear in mind the savage cruelty of the Edomites on the day of Jerusalem's downfall ; may vengeance come upon the Babylonians who have taken Israel into captivity (**7-9**).

5. ' my right hand be forgotten ' : become paralysed and unable to play on the harp. **6.** ' cleave to my

362h palate ', and so be unable to sing Pss any more. **7.** For the hostility of the Edomites towards their Hebrew kinsmen see Is 34:5-15 ; Jer 49:7-22, etc. **9.** ' The cruelty mentioned in the text was common in wars of those times. It was not regarded as unjust. It was a right, or rather an intolerable abuse, authorized by custom and recognized by either side of the combatants. We find it in Os 14:1 and in Homer, *Iliad*, XXII ' (Calmet).

i **CXXXVII** (CXXXVIII)—Thanksgiving to God for his kindness and faithfulness and because he has heard the psalmist's prayer (**1-3**). May all the kings of the world sing his praises, for great is his glory (**4-6**). He will surely protect the singer from his adversaries ; he never forsakes the works of his hands (**7-8**).
1. ' angels ' : so LXX, Vg, NP. Heb. ' elohim ' may mean ' gods ', so St Jer., Aq., Quinta, EVV. If ' gods ' is the meaning, the psalmist is, as it were, challenging them, without, however, implying their existence. **2.** ' temple ' : prob. heaven. **4.** ' the words of thy mouth ' : perhaps God's Messianic revelation ; cf. 2:10-13 ; 71:11. **5.** ' sing *of* thy ways ' (MT, NP). **8a.** ' will repay for me ' : LXX ' dealeth well with me ' seems correct against MT ' will bring to an end on my behalf ', which NP renders ' but perfect for me what is begun '.

j **CXXXVIII** (CXXXIX)—A beautiful Ps, but textually difficult. It describes God's omniscience (**1-6**), omnipresence (**7-12**), and his marvellous formation of the human frame (**13-16**). Beyond reckoning are his plans ; wickedness alone mars his work ; may sinners be slain ; the psalmist hates them because they hate God (**17-22**). Should he be going astray, may God lead him back to the right way (**23-24**).
3. ' my line ' : besides meaning ' line ' or ' rope ' the word in LXX means a ' rush-bed ', which agrees with Heb. ' my lying down '. God knows every act of our lives. **4b-5a.** ' *For ere a word is on my tongue, lo, Yahweh, thou knowest it thoroughly* ' (MT, NP) ; cf. Mt 6:8. **5b.** ' the last and those of old ' : ' *Back and front thou hast fashioned me* ' (St Jer.) ; cf. 118:73. **11b.** Probably : ' *Night shall be (as) light about me* '. **13.** ' possessed my reins ' : formed the internal parts of my body. ' protected me ' : Heb. ' *knit me together* '. **15.** The foetus hidden in the mother's womb developed under God's watchful eye. **16.** ' my imperfect being ' : my embryo state. A modern emendation ' my acts ' is adopted by NP. ' *And in thy book all (my life) was written ; days were fixed, although not one of them as yet had come* '. Our lives are foreseen by God, and all our actions are recorded, as it were, in his book, even before we are born. See CBQ 6 (1944) 99 ; VD 11 (1931) 243. **17.** ' *How precious* [perhaps in the sense of ' inscrutable ' ; but NP reads ' arduous ' following some moderns] *are thy thoughts unto me, O God ! How great the sum of them !* ' (MT). **18.** ' I rose up ' : Heb. ' *I awake* '. Some say, to consciousness at birth ; others that he awakes to find himself doing what he did before he went to sleep, namely meditating on God's works. NP reads ' if I finish ' (also Gunkel, Oesterley). The awakening may be from death ; cf. 16:15 ; 72:20. Death does not separate the singer from God : ' I am still with thee '. **19.** ' O that thou wouldst ' **20.** The text is corrupt. With Boylan and Oesterley we prefer to read : ' *They take thy name in vain* '. NP has ' Thine enemies are puffed up perfidiously '. **21b.** ' *and loathe those who rise up against thee* ' (MT). **24.** ' the eternal way ' : NP has ' the ancient way ', *i.e.* the way in which the pious men of old walked, Noe, Abraham and others ; cf. Jer 6:16 ; 18:15.

k **CXXXIX** (CXL)—Prayer for deliverance from enemies who, by poisonous words and plotting, seek to ensnare the psalmist (**2-6**). May God thwart their designs and punish them (**7-12**). May pious men thank Yahweh, who maintains the cause of the oppressed (**13-14**). This and the next three Pss are in the style of the Davidic hymns of the first book of the Psalter.
8. ' overshadowed my head '—as a helmet. **9a.** ' *Grant not, O Yahweh, the desires of the wicked* ' (MT, NP).

10. A difficult verse ; see commentaries. We prefer (with Oesterley) : ' *May they who surround me not lift up their heads* ', but be humiliated. **b.** ' *may the mischief of their lips overwhelm them* ' (NP). **11.** Punishment such as fell on the Sodomites. **11b.** Probably : ' *may they fall into pits whence they shall not rise* '. **12.** ' A man full of tongue ' is a slanderer.

CXL (CXLI)—After a petition that his prayer may be heard, the singer asks that he may be kept from associating with men whose speech is evil and whose deeds are iniquitous (**1-4**). He welcomes correction from pious men, but has no desire to consort with sinners ; rather he wishes to see them destroyed (**5-7**). Lifting up his eyes to God, he prays that he may escape traps set to catch him. May the wicked fall into their own traps, while he passes on his way safely (**8-10**). In the early Church the Ps was known as the *epiluchnios* because it was recited at evening (**2**), when the lamps were lit (*Apost. Constit.* 2, 59 ; 8, 35). 2-4b are recited at Mass, when the altar is being incensed at the offertory.
2. Incense was offered morning and evening at the altar, Ex 30:7, 34, 37. The lifting up of hands signifies prayer, 27:2. **4.** ' to make excuses in sins ' : ' *to commit wicked deeds* ' (NP). ' I will not . . . of them ' : ' *Let me not eat of their dainties* ' (MT). Agelli sees a reference to fornication, Prov 9:17 ; 30:20 ; others say that he refuses invitations to banquets given by worldly men. **5.** We prefer LXX, Vg ; the double *rō's* in MT is suspicious. Oil was poured on the head of guests ; the psalmist does not want this oil from sinners. **6-7.** Very difficult ; see commentaries. The ' judges ' are probably the leaders of the psalmist's adversaries. In vivid language he asks that they be hurled down a cliff, that their bodies may burst open, and that their bones be strewn before the mouth of devouring Sheol. *Cf.* 2 Par 25:12 ; Ac 1:18. **10.** Heb. ' *while I pass on (unharmed)* '.

CXLI (CXLII)—In utter distress because he is caught in an ambush, the psalmist cries out to God, his only hope, for release and restoration to his friends. The title says that the Ps was composed by David ' when he was in the cave ', 1 Kg 22 or 24. We need not suppose that it was written in the cave ; rather it is a thanksgiving hymn (**8**) commemorating the occasion. Internal evidence supports the Davidic authorship. We may apply it (Vespers on Friday) to the sufferings of the Son of David.
5. ' my soul ' : my life. **6.** ' the land of the living ' ; see on 26:13. **8.** ' prison ' : probably figurative of David's distress.

CXLII (CXLIII)—The last of the penitential psalms. The singer prays for clemency, for, in God's sight, no living man is perfect (**1-2**). Persecuted by an enemy and sick at heart, he recalls God's former mercies, ardently desiring his aid (**3-6**). May his prayer be speedily answered ; may he be granted deliverance and guidance (**7-8**). He repeats his request and asks for the destruction of his enemies, for he is the servant of Yahweh (**9-12**).
2. Should God judge men according to strict justice, no one would be acquitted ; cf. 50:6 ; 129:3, etc. The verse is recited at the Burial Service. **3c-d.** Quoted in Lam 3:6. ' darkness ' : Heb. ' *dark places* ', either figuratively or referring to the dark cave in which David was forced to hide, places where ' those that have been dead of old ' were buried. **8.** To say that when he worships the next morning (the morning being one of the times of prayer) he hopes to hear God's mercy, seems too banal an interpretation. Hardly satisfactory is the suggestion that the morning will bring hope after a dark night. NP interprets ' in the morning ' by ' cito '. Possibly the phrase may refer to the morning after the night of death (cf. 16:15 ; 48:15) ; the psalmist has just spoken of those who ' go down to the pit ' of Sheol. **10.** He prays that the holy spirit of God (cf. 2 Esd 9:20) may lead him in (or ' into ') a ' right land '. The mention of ' land ' is strange. May he be thinking of life hereafter ?

d CXLIII (CXLIV)—The first part of the Ps, in which the singer thanks God for military victories, asks for a theophany and for protection against foreign foes, is made up of passages taken from other Davidic Pss (**1-8**). In the second part (or is it a separate hymn ?) it becomes Messianic—' a new song '. It foresees victory for the House of David and happy times for the people : fine sons and daughters, storehouses full, thousands of flocks, an end of wars and civic strife. Happy the people who shall live in this golden age ! (**9-15**).

1. ' my God ' : Heb. ' *my rock* ' ; *cf.* 17:3. **3.** ' that thou . . . to him ' : ' *that thou takest knowledge of him* ' (MT) ; *cf.* 8:5. **4.** ' vanity ' : the Heb. also means ' breath ', ' vapour ' ; NP ' *a breath of air* '. **7.** ' strange children ' : foreigners. **8b.** The right hand was uplifted when taking an oath ; hence NP ' their right hand swears a lie '. **12.** NP ' sculptured as columns of a temple ' ; but a slight change in the Heb. gives the meaning that the maidens were clothed in dark-hued dresses, such as were worn in palaces. See Agelli, and *cf.* 2 Kg 1:24 ; Ps 44:15.

e CXLIV (CXLV)—An alphabetical Ps. Letter *n* is missing in MT but preserved in LXX, Vg. As usual the flow of thought is hampered by this artificial setting, but the keynote is in **13** ; God's kingdom shall last for ever. The hymn opens with praise to God, the great King, whose wonderful deeds are to be proclaimed throughout all generations (**1-7**). He is patient and good to all men ; may his pious servants extol the splendour of his kingdom (**8-13**). He is faithful ; he is holy ; he lifts up the fallen ; all creatures depend on his providence (**14-16**). He is just ; he listens to the prayers of those who revere him ; he watches over those who love him, but he destroys wicked men (**17-20**). May all mankind bless his holy name (**21**). Part of our Grace after Meals is taken from **15-16**, verses which occur in the Gradual for the Feast of Corpus Christi ; from early times they have been used as an Eucharistic prayer ; see St John Chrysostom, PG 55, 464.

5. The text in LXX, Vg is better than that in MT. **8.** *Cf.* 102:8 ; Ex 34:6.

f CXLV (CXLVI)—Instead of relying on human potentates, let faithful Israelites trust in Yahweh ; for whereas princes die, he who made heaven and earth remains for ever (**2-6**). It is he who gives just judgements, feeds the hungry, releases prisoners from captivity, gives sight to the blind, lifts up the downtrodden, loves the upright, watches over travellers, helps widows and orphans, but punishes the wicked (**7-9**). Sion's God reigns for ever (**10**).

4a. An allusion to Gen 3:19 ; see also 1 Mac 2:63.

g CXLVI (CXLVII 1-11)—Praise to Yahweh who has built up Jerusalem and gathered together the dispersed of Israel, healing the broken-hearted and binding the wounds of those who have been hurt (**1-3**). He who can count the stars and whose knowledge is infinite upholds the afflicted and brings down the wicked (**4-6**). What follows is probably an attachment ; for whereas the first part seems to celebrate the dedication of the walls of the City after the return from Captivity (2 Esd 12:27 ff.), at **7** there begins a hymn of thanksgiving to God, by whose providence beasts and birds are fed. He delights not in physical strength but in the love of those who revere

him (**7-11**). MT continues with what in LXX, Vg is Ps 147. Originally there may have been three Pss. **363g**

8. *Cf.* 103:13 f. **9.** Young ravens are mentioned because, left at an early age to fend for themselves, they require special protection from the Lord (Boylan). **10.** ' the legs of a man '—upon which he depends for flight from danger ; *cf.* 17:34 ; Am 2:14 f.

CXLVII (CXLVII 12-20)—Let Jerusalem praise **h** Yahweh, because he has made it secure, blessed its inhabitants, established peace on the borders of Israel, and given a good harvest (**1-3**). He is Lord of all nature ; at his bidding fleecy snowflakes fall, frost lies like powder on the ground, layers of ice appear on the waters (**4-6**). Again, at his command, the thaw sets in and the waters flow again (**7**). Nature's Lord is also the great Lawgiver ; he has revealed himself to Israel as his chosen race (**8-9**).

5. ' mists ' : ' *hoarfrost* '. ' ashes ' : white ash or powder. **6.** ' crystal ' : ice. ' morsels ' : the ice on the water resembles thin layers of bread ; but if, with NP, the former word is translated ' hailstones ', the meaning will be that these come down like ' crumbs ' of bread. **8.** *Cf.* Deut 4:8.

CXLVIII—All creatures are summoned to praise God. **i** First, those in heaven and the sky—the angelic host, the sun, moon, stars and clouds : they must praise God because, at his word, they came into being (**1-6**). Then, the creatures below the heavens—the great deep and its monsters, all kinds of severe weather, mountains and hills, vegetative life, sensitive life, intellectual life from kings to babies (**7-12**). He is worthy of all praise, for he reigns in majesty above earth and heaven. He has given strength to his people, in thanksgiving for which this hymn is written (**13-14**).

2. ' hosts ' : here angelic armies, as the parallelism shows ; *cf.* Jos 5:14 ; 3 Kg 22:19. **4.** ' heavens of heavens ' : the highest heavens ; *cf.* Deut 10:14 ; 3 Kg 8:27. ' waters above the heavens ' : *cf.* Gen 1:6 f. ; Ps 103:3. **7.** ' dragons ' : sea-monsters, Gen 1:21. **14.** ' the horn of his people ' may mean strength and dignity as in 17:3, or may have Messianic significance as in 131:17 ; Lk 1:69.

CXLIX—A ' new song ' celebrating the triumph of **j** the people of God over Gentile nations. The singer pictures the victory celebrations—singing, dancing, cheering, with swords ready for any emergency. The Christian counterpart is the ' new song ' of Apoc 5:9, the Messianic triumph over every tribe and nation and race.

3. ' choir ' : Vg ' choro ' here means ' *dance* '. For religious dances see Ex 15:20 ; 1 Kg 18:6 ; 2 Kg 6:16 ; Jer 31:4 ; Ps 150:4. The timbrel is the tambourine ; the psaltery is a kind of lyre. **5.** ' in their beds '—resting after victory ; *cf.* Os 2:18. **7-8.** *Cf.* Messianic Ps 2:6-9 ; Is 45:14. **9.** ' the judgement that is written ', the prophecies foretelling victory over the Gentiles, *e.g.* Ps 2. The subjection of the Gentiles will redound to the glory of pious Israelites.

CL—The full orchestra—horns, harps, lyres, tam- **k** bourines, stringed instruments, castanets and cymbals —bursts forth in a magnificent *finale*, calling upon the angels in heaven and every living creature to praise God because of his mighty deeds and his abundant greatness. It is part of the priest's Thanksgiving after Mass. The angelic orchestra accompany him in thanking God for the adorable mystery of the altar ! Alleluia !

PROVERBS

By R. A. DYSON, S.J.

364a **Bibliography**—J. Knabenbauer, S.J., *Commentarius in Proverbia*, Paris, 1910 ; H. Wiesmann, S.J., *Das Buch der Sprüche*, Bonn, 1923 ; A. Vaccari, S.J., *Libri Poetici della Bibbia*, Rome, 1925 ; H. Duesberg, *Les Scribes inspirés*, Paris, 1938 ; L. Pirot-A. Clamer, *La Sainte Bible*, Tome VI, *Le Livre des Proverbes*, par H. Renard, Paris, 1946 ; *T. T. Perowne, *The Proverbs*, CBSC, 1899 ; *C. H. Toy, *Proverbs*, ICC, 1904 ; *R. T. Horton, *The Book of Proverbs*, 1920 ; *W. O. E. Oesterley, *The Book of Proverbs*, WC, 1929 ; *B. Gemser, *Sprüche Salomons*, HAT, 1937 ; *A. D. Power, *The Proverbs of Solomon*, London, 1949.

b **Title**—In MT the title is ' Mishle Shelomoh '. The word *māšāl* seems originally to have signified ' likeness ', ' resemblance ' (*e.g.* 26:1 f.), then a short comparison (*e.g.* 25:25 f.), and eventually a sententious saying in general. In the oldest texts in which the word *māšāl* is found (Num 23:7, 18 ; 24:3, 15), it designates the revelation granted by God to Balaam as expressed by him in a figurative and poetic form, and in the Psalms (*e.g.* MT, 49:5 and 78:2) it is again the vehicle of divinely inspired instruction. The ' three thousand proverbs ' (*māšāl*) pronounced by Solomon were the results of the ' wisdom given by God to the king ' (3 Kg 4:29, 32). Every *māšāl* of the Prov is also regarded as a divinely inspired teaching, often enclosed in an expressed or hidden comparison which demands from the reader the effort of penetration necessary to grasp its meaning and import. LXX bears the title παροιμίαι Σαλωμῶντος which can mean either the ' Proverbs ' or ' Parables ' of Solomon. Vg has translated the word *māšāl* by ' parable ' in 1:1. The book was also known to the Fathers of the Church as the ' Wisdom of Solomon '.

c **Division**—The book may be divided according to author, matter, and literary form, into nine sections with a short introduction (1:1–7) containing the title and purpose.

Section

1. A general invitation to acquire Wisdom   1:8–9:18
2. A first collection of Solomon's proverbs   10:1–22:16
3. A collection of sayings of the wise men   22:17–24:22
4. Another small collection of sayings of the wise men   24:23–34
5. A collection of ' Proverbs of Solomon gathered together by the people of Ezechias '   25:1–29:27
6. The ' Sayings of Agur, son of Jakeh '   30:1–14
7. Numerical sayings   30:15–33
8. The ' Sayings of King Lemuel '   31:1–9
9. A portrait of the virtuous wife   31:10–31

In LXX, these sections follow in the order 1, 2, 3, 6, 4, 7, 8, 9, 5. It also has quantitative difference, *i.e.* longer or shorter verses, an indication that two different recensions of the book were once in circulation.

d **Authorship, Date, and Method of Composition**—The authors (with the exception of the anonymous sections

1, 7 and 9) are named in the text. The body of the book consists of two collections of proverbs attributed to Solomon (10:1–22:16 and 25:1–29:27), to which section 1 (1:1–9:18) serves as an introduction, and the smaller sections 6–9 form an appendix. This is why the book itself, taking the name of the principal author, is called in the title and in ecclesiastical usage ' Proverbs of Solomon '.

That the aphorisms of sections 2 and 5 go back to the **e** initiative of Solomon is beyond reasonable doubt. 3 Kg 4:30–32 tells us that the wisdom of Solomon surpassed the wisdom of all the Orientals and that ' he pronounced about three thousand parables ' (*mešālîm*). From the use of the word, ' pronounced ' however, we may gather that the wise maxims uttered by Solomon in his discourses were first handed on orally, and were only later put into writing. One confirmation of this is found in the text itself (25:1), where it is stated that the second series of Solomon's proverbs was collected by King Ezechias (721–693) ; another in the fact that the second series repeats several proverbs of the first, and that there are repetitions in the first series itself (*cf.* 14:12 and 16:25 ; 16:2 and 21:2). The proverbs attributed to Solomon in our book number about 510.

The ' wise men ', authors of sections 3 and 4, are **f** unknown. They treat of social duties and of man's relations with his neighbour, in quatrains of synonymous parallelism.

The sayings of Agur (section 6) extol the divine **g** wisdom and the ' golden mean ' in the possession of earthly goods ; those of Lemuel (section 8) give advice to kings in quatrains. For these two persons, otherwise unknown, *cf.* § 375*a*.

The anonymous author of section 7 presents his **h** observations in a literary form relished by the ancient Hebrews and recently found among the writings of Rās-Shamra : ' Three things have a certain characteristic and a fourth more so ', followed by their enumeration (*cf.* also 6:16–19, Am 1:2, and note on Job 5:19).

Section 9 is one of the finest examples of an alphabetic poem in the OT in the form of synthetic parallelism.

The present arrangement of the book may with **i** good likelihood be explained in this fashion. About 800 B.C., of the many sayings of Solomon, about 375 were collected in a book and given the title ' The Proverbs of Solomon ' (section 2). Shortly afterwards ' the sayings of the wise men ' (section 3) were added to this collection. The initiative of King Ezechias was responsible for the editing of a second series of Solomon's proverbs (section 5). Other maxims (sections 4, 6–8), composed or collected somewhat later (perhaps after the exile) were then added to the Solomonic collections, and in a different manner in different editions (*cf.* the arrangement in LXX). Finally in the 4th cent. B.C., a last editor added the appendix on the worthy wife (section 9) and the general introduction (section 1).

Content—The sayings of ' Proverbs ' deal with the **j** art of right living. They deal with a great variety of subjects, but handle certain points with special emphasis and detail. Thus Wisdom and Folly, Justice and Injustice, Piety and Impiety, Pride and Humility,

Honesty and Dishonesty, Love and Hate, Anger and Meekness, Wealth and Poverty, Industry and Idleness, hold a prominent place. Emphasis is laid on the relations between God and man, parents and children, kings and subjects, man and woman, master and servant, friend and enemy. There are warnings against debauchery, hard-heartedness and cruelty, unrighteousness and dishonesty, corruption and evildoing, avarice and greed, hypocrisy and flattery, anger and quarrelsomeness. Unwearyingly recommended are the fear of God, love of one's neighbour, charity, truthfulness, temperance, sagacity, careful speech and prudent silence. The law of retribution receives special stress, cf. § 365f.

Purpose—The purpose of the book is to enable the reader, especially the young, to live rightly. For the attainment of this goal, it offers to the understanding wholesome teaching about true Wisdom, and to the will powerful incentives for the ordering of life according to the knowledge acquired. For the adequate management of life, however, there is required not only a knowledge of important philosophical and religious truths and a way of life in harmony therewith, but also the possession of a certain measure of practical sagacity in the conduct of everyday affairs. Hence its counsels are not restricted to fundamental beliefs and moral teachings but embrace all human activity. The book also aims at furthering OT piety. It would win the reader to the Wisdom contained in revealed religion and impress its principles upon every aspect of his life ; so it presents them in a variety of forms and displays their excellence in a manner calculated to woo and inspire. It endeavours, by earnest warning and by stressing the advantages of virtue, to shape the reader's life in accordance with its teaching.

Moral and Religious Instruction—Wisdom is the central theme of Proverbs. It is, by definition, knowledge and understanding of words and things, reflection and insight in the realm of thought and action (1:2-7) ; but its special interest lies in practical life which it aims to direct in conformity with the laws of religion and morality. He, therefore, alone is 'wise' who knows and fears Yahweh (2:1-5), who understands and puts into practice uprightness and equity (2:9). The ungodly and the sinner are 'foolish' (5:23 ; 9:13, etc.). The fear of Yahweh (i.e. true worship of God) is the beginning of wisdom (1:7 ; 9:10) and it goes hand in hand with confidence in him (3:5 ; 29:25), having the same prerogatives and producing the same effects (16:20 ; 28:25). Fear of God and confidence in him are thus the basis of religion and morality.

In the course of the book all Israelite society is passed in review and judged according to a norm of morality the sources of which are human experience and religion. From experience, the teacher of life, the sages draw practical lessons. Religion, although not systematically expounded, either in its dogmatic foundations or in its liturgical practices (since the purpose of the book is rather to offer maxims of right conduct), is, however, always presupposed and, in fact, regarded as the basis of all morality (1:7 ; 9:10 ; 14:2, etc.) and declared the source of all true happiness (14:26 ; 15:16). Stress is often laid upon the essential truths that God sees all things (5:21 ; 15:3, 11), takes account of everything, even the heart's most hidden thought (16:2 ; 17:3), governs all (20:12, 24 ; 22:2 ; 29:13), and can do all (19:21 ; 21:30) ; that apart from God there can be no good (15:29) ; that to submit to him is to find strength, contentment and joy (3:5 ; 16:20 ; 18:10, etc.). Most effective in its simplicity of expression is the oft-repeated motive for avoiding sin, ' it displeaseth God ', ' God abominateth ', etc. (3:32 ; 11:1, 20 ; 12:22).

Man and his Destiny—(a) Man is endowed with a life principle (n˙šāmāh, 'vital breath'). This is compared to a 'lamp' which is lighted by Yahweh himself and illumines man's whole ' interior ' (20:27).

This life-principle is in a body (20:27b), also made by Yahweh (20:12).

(b) In his moral existence man is free. He can resist the call of Wisdom and neglect her counsels (1:24 f.). By nature, therefore, he is not immune from sin and cannot be certain that he has never sinned (20:9).

(c) Immortality. That man in some way lives on after death is the constant teaching of the OT. According to Proverbs the dead ' descend ' (1:12 ; 5:5 ; 7:27) to Sheol, the abode of all the departed. There they form a sort of ' assembly ' (2:18 ; 9:18 ; 21:16) and are called Repha'im (feeble ones, shades), but the ontological reason for their continued existence, i.e the possession of an immortal soul, is nowhere given.

(d) Retribution. The book accepts the prevailing OT view that the just are rewarded and the wicked punished in this life. It is generally denied that there is mention of a sanction beyond the grave. The pertinent texts are 10:25 ; 11:4 ; 12:28 ; 14:32 ; 15:24 ; 23:18 (cf. 24:14) ; 24:20. Of these 10:25 ; 11:4 need only mean that the just live out their full life's span while the wicked die prematurely. 14:32 ' the just hath hope in his death ' seems decisive in MT, but LXX and Syr. read ' in his integrity '. The probative value of 23:18 and 24:20 depends upon the meaning there of 'aḥᵃrît. Elsewhere it means ' consequence ' (5:4, 11) ; ' the end or final outcome of a course of action ' (14:12) ; ' a future ', i.e. a happy close of life (19:20). This latter appears to be its meaning in 23:18 and 24:14, i.e. the just will experience that mellow period of peaceful decline denied to the evil-doer. Perhaps, too, in these texts, the word contains a suggestion of ' posterity ' ; cf. Ps 37:37 (MT). In MT 12:28 there seems to be a clear enough statement of a blessed life after death, but the reading is doubtful (cf. comm.). 15:24, ' The path of life (goeth) upward for the wise, so that he turneth from Sheol beneath ', may only have in view the reward of a long life for the just. It must be observed however that, according to more than one exegete, the statement in both 12:28 and 15:24 that virtue leads to life, is expressed in such a manner that it is difficult to avoid the conclusion of a blessed hereafter for the just. But if the sages had attained to the notion of a blessed immortality, they would have made more use of a doctrine which would have solved an urgent problem and have provided them with another strong motive for right living.

Sources of Proverbs—The proverbial style of utterance is a favourite form of oriental literature. Israel, too, had its own popular proverbs which passed from lip to lip and embodied much current wisdom. Such may have been the source of a number of the sayings in the book, but if they came from the lips of the people, they have been polished into epigrammatic form by reflexion and literary skill, and written down under divine inspiration. The consideration of the already existing OT books could also have inspired the writers of the later collections to present their reflexions upon them in gnomic form. Nor is there any reason why they should not have availed themselves of non-Israelite material. Recent discoveries have brought to light Egyptian gnomic writings older than Prov and their resemblance suggests an influence upon it. This resemblance is most marked between the ' Teaching of Amen-em-ope ' (Amenophis) and Prov 22:17-13:11 ; see § 316e.

Text and Versions—Prov was written in Hebrew, but MT is not in good condition, chiefly because of the mistakes of copyists. The principal versions are LXX (from which were made the Coptic, the Hexaplar Syriac and the Old Latin), the Peshitta Syriac, the Targum, fragments of the later Greek translations (Symmachus, Aquila, Theodotion), and the Latin of St Jerome.

The value of LXX is limited : sometimes the translator misunderstood the Hebrew prototype ; at other times the translation is more elegant than literal ;

365c

d

e

f

g

h

365h the text is often paraphrased and contains additions (*e.g.* 4:27 ; 9:12 ; 24:22, etc.), some of which may come from a Hebrew text older and better than MT (*e.g.* 11:16 ; 27:20, 21). Omissions also are to be observed (*e.g.* 1:16 ; 4:7 ; 8:29, etc.) : *cf.* Vaccari, *De Libris didacticis*, nr. 57. Vg, translated from the Heb. about A.D. 398, was hastily made (*cf.* Praef. in libros Salomonis, PL 28, 1307), but does not differ much from MT. In the course of time a number of additions from LXX (Old Latin) were introduced into the text and of these about twenty remain in the Clementine Bible ; this however does not exclude the study of other texts to determine their authenticity.

i Canonicity—The Jewish synagogue considered the book canonical and ranked it among the ' Sacred Writings '. The Greek translator of Ecclus appears to allude to it in Ecclus 47, 18 (Vg), while Talmudic difficulties caused by certain inconsistencies in MT (*e.g.* 26:4–5) and by the realistic description of the adulterous woman (7:10–22) were settled by the Council of Jamnia, *c* A.D. 100.

The Christian Church has always acknowledged Prov as canonical. The NT has citations from it (*cf.* Jas 4:6 with Prov 3:34 ; Heb 12:5 with Prov 3:11 ; Rom 3:15 with Prov 1:16 and 12:20 with 25:21–22), and allusions to it (1 P 2:17 ; 4:8, 18 ; 5:5 ; 2 P 2:22). Our Lord himself seems to have illustrated some of its maxims (*cf.* Lk 14:10 with Prov 25:7).

The Fathers of the Church found in Prov abundant matter for the instruction and edification of the faithful, and today it holds an important place among the sapiential books in the lessons of the Greek and Latin liturgies. The Second Council of Constantinople (553) condemned Theodore of Mopsuestia for denying its inspired character.

366a I–IX Section 1 The Praise of Wisdom.
I 1–7 Introduction—**1.** The title refers especially to 10:1–22:16 and 25:1–29:27 (*cf.* § 364*d*) which form the greater part of the book. ' parables ' : *cf.* § 364*b*. 2–6 state the purpose of Prov, (*a*) theoretical : to instruct the reader in true Wisdom ; (*b*) practical : to have its principles accepted as the rule of life and basis of conduct. It is primarily intended for the instruction of the young (4), but it will also enrich the store of those who are already wise (5). 1–4 form a single sentence : ' Proverbs (given) *that a man may* know wisdom ', etc. The motto (7) is the key-note of all the teaching that is to follow, and an epitome of its spirit.

b **2a.** Wisdom is the central theme of Prov and in the following verses its scope and functions are variously expressed. It is ' instruction ', or rather ' *discipline* ', not only intellectual, but also corrective. **3a.** It is intelligent, understanding ' words of prudence ', *i.e.* instructive discourse. **3b.** It is practical, for it educates in ' doctrine ' (' *wise dealing* '). It trains in ' justice and judgement (' *probity* ') and equity '.— **4.** It matures the judgement, for it imparts ' subtlety ' or ' *shrewdness* ' (in a good sense) to ' little ones ' (' *the inexperienced* '). **5.** It makes ' wiser ' those already wise, and gives ' governments ' (' *steerings* '), *i.e.* skill and facility in the management of life. **6.** It enables one to understand a ' parable ' (*i.e.* a ' *proverb* '), and whatever needs interpretation ; ' the words of the wise, and their mysterious sayings ' (the figurative language in which a proverb is often clothed) ; *cf.* Perowne, 40. **7.** ' The fear of the Lord [*i.e.* religion] is the beginning of wisdom ' : the first of the virtues and the foundation of right living. MT can also be rendered ' the *chief part* of wisdom '.

c 8–19 A Warning against Evil Companions—**8a.** ' My son '. Throughout this section of Proverbs (chh 1–9) the sage addresses himself to the young with the affection and solicitude of a father. **8b.** ' law ' : ' *teaching* ' or ' *admonition* '. **9a.** ' *For they shall be a graceful chaplet unto* thy head '. **11a.** ' If they shall say ' : governs 11–14 ; the apodosis is found in 15. **11b.** ' for blood ' : *i.e.* to shed blood. The phrase signifies robbery with

violence. **11c.** ' hide snares ' : ' *lurk* '. **12a.** ' hell ' : 3 Sheol, to which ' the pit ' of 12*b* is a parallel. The thought is that of a sudden murderous assault. **13–14** state the inducement that the robbers hold out to induce their recruit to join their ranks. **15–19.** The reason for avoiding such companions. **17.** ' *Surely* in vain the net is spread *in the sight of any bird* '. If it sees the net, it takes alarm. In like manner, for youth to be forewarned is to be forearmed. **18.** Evil-doers really prepare destruction for themselves. **18b.** ' *and lurk for their own lives* ' (*cf.* 11). **19.** Read with LXX '*aḥ*ᵃ*rît* (fate) for '*orḥôt* (ways). ' *Such is the fate* of every covetous man ; *it taketh away the life of its possessors* '. Those who plot against others dig their own graves.

20–33 The Invitation of Wisdom—Objective Wisdom, **d** *i.e.* the moral law which is an emanation of the essential holiness and justice of God, and which makes itself heard by the voice of conscience, the preaching of God's ministers, etc., is here personified, and speaks and acts with divine authority. **20.** ' Wisdom *crieth aloud in the streets, in the broad places* she uttereth her voice ', *i.e.* in the places of assembly before the city gates. **21a.** ' She *calleth out on the top of the walls* ' (LXX). **22a.** ' children ' : *i.e.* without proper training or virtue. **22b.** ' *and scoffers delight in scoffing, and fools* hate knowledge ? ' The ' *scoffers* ' are defiant and cynical despisers of religion and morality ; the ' fool ' is ' one who is insensible to moral truth and acts without regard to it ' (Toy). **23a.** ' Turn ye ' : listen to my reproof. This reproof is contained in the verses which follow. **24a.** ' Because ' governs the verbs of 24 and 25 ; the apodosis is 26. **26a.** ' destruction ' : ' *calamity* '. Wisdom will justly rejoice that their obstinate perversity has been punished. **27.** ' *When your (ground for) fear cometh as a storm ; when distress and anguish befalleth you* '. **28.** Those who have deliberately rejected the counsels and appeals of Wisdom, will cry out to her in the day of distress, but solely to escape punishment ; then, however, it will be too late ; *cf.* Jn 7:34 ; 8:21. **29b.** ' received not ' : ' *chose not* '. **31.** As they sowed, so they shall reap. Punishment is, in the just ordination of God, the natural ' fruit ' of sin. **32.** ' The turning away ' from Wisdom and right living will prove the undoing ' of little ones ', the ' *inexperienced* ' who are easily led into temptation, and the ' *careless ease* of fools shall destroy them '. **33b.** ' enjoy abundance ' : ' *be secure* '.

II 1–22 The Blessings conferred by Wisdom—This **e** section is divided into two parts of similar construction, 1–9 and 10–22. Part 1 : Diligent application to the study of Wisdom (**1–4**) will result in the fear and knowledge of God (**5**), the divine protection (**6–8**), and right understanding (**9**). Part 2 : Wisdom, indwelling in the soul (**10**), will be a guide (**11**), which will save the young from evil men (**12–15**) and evil women (**16–19**), and so lead to the reward of the just (**20–21**) in contrast with the fate of the wicked (**22**).

1–9. The speaker is now the sage. **1b.** ' hide ' as a **f** treasure carefully stored. **2.** ' *So that thou incline* thine ear unto wisdom, and *apply* thy heart to prudence '. **3.** ' *Yea, if thou criest unto understanding, and liftest up thy voice* to prudence '. Wisdom, prudence and understanding are different aspects of the same virtue. **4a.** ' money ' : ' *silver* '. **5.** The fear of the Lord (*cf.* 1:7) and the knowledge of God are the essence of true Wisdom. Only the virtuous can grasp and appreciate it. This and the following verses reveal the deeply religious conception of Wisdom. **6.** As God is the author of Wisdom, he must also be the goal of every human search of it. **7.** ' He *layeth up* salvation *for* the righteous, *is a shield to them that walk uprightly* '. **8a.** ' justice ' : or ' *probity* '. **8b.** ' saints ' : God's devoted followers. The verse emphasizes the divine protection of searchers after true Wisdom. **9.** It is assumed that he who knows the good path will follow it.

10–22. 11. ' *Reflection shall watch over thee, discernment* **g** *shall guard thee* '. The transforming effect upon the character of the young of these companion gifts of wisdom is presented in a striking personification. **12.**

'That thou mayest be delivered' may be read : 'She (Wisdom) will save thee': so also 16. **16.** 'Strange women' and 'stranger' are the author's words for the dissolute woman, either because she is not the wife of the person addressed or because women of this class were often non-Israelites. It is difficult to see in the 'strange woman' a personification of Greek culture against which the Maccabees were later to rise. **16b.** 'softeneth': uses cajoling words. **17.** The first line of 18 should be joined with this verse. The woman who by her evil arts seeks to seduce the young, betrays not only her husband but also God, who was called to witness her fidelity to the marriage contract, which is of divine origin and sanction (cf. Mal 2:14). 'guide': 'associate' or 'companion' (cf. Jer 3:4; Prov 5:18). **18.** 'hell': 'the dead'. 'Her house': association with her leads to ruin and death. **19.** The harlot is like a whirlpool that engulfs its victims and from which there is no return. **20a.** 'That thou mayest walk', etc., may be read : 'Thus thou shalt walk in the way of the good'. **21a.** 'earth': land of Israel. **21b.** 'simple': 'perfect'. **22.** The happiness promised in the OT to the Chosen People consisted above all in the long and peaceful enjoyment of the Promised Land. Expulsion from it by exile or death was the principal sanction of the old economy : cf. Ex 20:12; Deut 5:16; Ps 36 (37):9, 22, 29. **22a.** 'destroyed': 'cut off'. The unrighteous shall have no place in Israel. How this was to be effected is not stated here.

III 1-10 The Blessings of Obedience and Trust in God —The sage exhorts the young man to heed his instructions; the reward will be a long and happy life, and the favour of God and man (**1-4**). He is to trust in God (**5-6**), fear him and avoid sin (**7-8**), and render him his due (**9-10**). **1a.** 'my law': my precepts for right living. **3a.** 'mercy and truth': the Heb. words are better expressed by 'goodness' of heart towards God and one's neighbour, and 'faithfulness' or fidelity to one's word and social obligations. These two virtues are often recommended, 14:22; 20:28, etc. **3b.** 'put': 'bind'. **4a.** 'grace': 'favour'. **6b.** 'direct': 'make smooth thy paths'. **7a.** 'conceit': 'eyes'. **8a.** 'navel': the addition of a single letter gives the Heb. word for 'body' (bāśār). **8b.** 'moistening': refreshment. The practice of religion and morality will also promote bodily health. **9.** 'substance': riches. **10.** With this promise cf. Deut 28:8. 'abundance': read with LXX 'corn'.

11-20 The Excellence of Wisdom—Even if you suffer in the pursuit of Wisdom, do not be downcast (**11-12**); for it is well worth the cost (**13-20**). **11b.** 'faint': 'feel not loathing'. **12b.** Read with a correction from LXX (cf. Heb 12:6): 'and afflicteth the son that he holdeth dear'. The quatrain (**11-12**) anticipates an objection against the rich promise of the preceding verses; the apparent exceptions in the sufferings of the just are divinely given for their correction and instruction; cf. Job 5:17 f. **13b.** 'is rich in': 'obtaineth'. **14.** 'Her acquisition is better than the acquisition of silver, and her revenue than fine gold'. **15.** 'She is more precious than pearls; no treasures are to be compared with her'. **16.** Wisdom confers a long and honoured life upon those who are attached to her. **16b.** 'glory': 'honour'. **18.** The practice of Wisdom will result in advantages analogous to the beneficent effects of the tree of life, Gen 2:9. **19-20.** Wisdom is a source of blessing because it has its origin in God who manifested it in the creation of the world and still manifests it in the physical order of the universe. **20.** When 'the fountains of the deep burst forth' (cf. Gen 7:11), and when 'the clouds drop dew', the Wisdom of God is working; cf. 8:22 ff.

21-26 The Security given by Wisdom—It confers both strength and beauty (**22**); it preserves alike in action and repose (**23-24**); it is equal to any emergency (**25-26**). **21b.** 'prudence and discretion' (or 'reflection'). **22.** 'They shall be life unto thy soul and grace to thy neck'. They will be as attractive on your person as a gracious ornament on a woman's neck. **25b.** 'nor of the storm of the wicked when it cometh'. **26a.** 'For the Lord will be thy confidence, and will keep thy feet from capture' by the snares of deceit and misfortune.

27-35. A series of short, detached maxims enjoining Kindness to one's Neighbour, differing from the rest of chh 1-9 and more closely resembling the aphorisms of Solomon, especially 16:1-22. **27.** 'Withhold not good from the needy, when it is thy power to do it' (LXX). **28b.** 'when thou hast it by thee'. **29a.** 'Practice': rather 'Devise'. **29b.** 'while he dwelleth trustfully by thee'. **31a.** 'the unjust man': 'the man of violence' who oppresses his neighbour. **31b.** 'nor be incensed because of' (LXX). **32a.** 'mocker': 'the perverse man'. **32b.** 'communication': his intimate converse is with the upright. **33.** 'The curse of the Lord is on the house of the wicked; but the habitation of the just he blesseth'. **35a.** 'possess glory': 'inherit honour'. **35b.** 'promotion' is the Heb. verb 'to exalt'. 'Shame exalteth fools' is possible, but forced. The parallel suggests an easy emendation : 'fools shall gain shame'.

IV 1-9 The Paternal Lesson—In a tender passage the sage repeats to his young disciple the lesson he himself had learned at the feet of his parents. It gives a charming picture of a pious Jewish household; cf. Wordsworth's 'Wisdom doth live with children round her knees'. **2.** 'For good counsel I give you : forsake not my teaching'. **3a.** 'tender': i.e. of youthful age. **6.** Both sense and grammar demand that 6 be placed after 7. **7a.** 'The beginning of wisdom (is) get wisdom'. A suggested emendation is : 'In the beginning of thy strength, get wisdom'. **7b.** 'with all thy possession': at all cost. **8a.** 'Take hold on her': 'prize her'. **8b.** 'she shall bring thee honour, if thou embrace her'. **9.** 'She shall give to thy head a chaplet of beauty, bestow on thee a crown of glory'; cf. 1:9.

10-19 The Two Ways—It is difficult to decide whether these are the words of the sage or of the father. The contrasted fortunes of the wicked and the just are presented as motives for right living.

12. 'When thou walkest, thy steps shall not be straitened [hampered], and when thou runnest, thou shalt not stumble'. In a virtuous life there will be no narrow or difficult ways. **13.** 'instruction': 'discipline', a virtue which demands a strict control of self. **13b.** 'Note the gradual deepening of the sense of 'life', beginning with prolonging of days, as in Deut 32:47, and gaining in spiritual content until it comes to mean the knowledge of God and communion with him (Jn 17:3; 1 Tim 6:19)! (S. H. Hooke in Peake's Comm. on the Bible, 399). **14a.** 'Be not delighted': 'Enter not'. **14b.** 'and go not in the way of evil men'. **16b.** The wicked are unable to sleep unless they have done some evil deed; cf. Juv. Sat. III 281 f. **17b.** 'iniquity': 'violence'. This verse may mean either, wickedness and violence are to them as meat and drink, or, they get their living by fraud and violence. **18.** 'The path of the just is like the light of dawn that shineth (ever) brighter till the full day cometh'. **19a.** 'darkness': 'like darkness'.

20-27 Exhortation to Constancy—All man's faculties must co-operate in the moral life; this whole-hearted striving for virtue will also bring material blessings.

22b. 'flesh': i.e. to 'their' whole being. **23b.** 'for out from it are the issues [origins] of life'. The heart is the inward source of spiritual life; to keep it pure, great diligence is needed. **24b.** 'detracting': 'perverse'. **25b.** 'and let thy eyelids be straight before thee'. The virtuous man fixes his eyelids (metaphorically for 'gaze') upon the goal and lets nothing turn them aside. **26a.** 'Make straight': rather 'weigh', 'ponder'. **26b.** 'established': ordered aright. Take care that the way along which you wish to walk be the right way of virtue. **27.** One can deviate to the right by an excess of zeal or to the left by lack of it. Virtus stat in mediis. After 27, LXX, Vg insert two verses. It is difficult to decide whether these lines ever had any Heb. original or are the work of a scribe.

367g **V 1-23 The Sixth Commandment**—After the usual exhortation to give heed to Wisdom (**1-2**), the sage describes the deadly influence of the wanton woman (**3-6**), cautions the disciple to avoid her lest dishonour, destitution, physical deterioration and the pangs of remorse come upon him (**7-14**), urges him to conjugal fidelity (**15-20**), the motive presented being the fate of the wicked (**21-22**).

h **2.** A suggested emendation reads : ' That thou mayest keep *the counsel of my mouth* and preserve the *knowledge of my lips* '. The last line is an addition from LXX. **3a.** ' For the lips of a harlot *drop honey* '. On ' harlot ', *cf.* 2:16, note. **3b.** ' throat ' : ' *palate* ' used figuratively for ' speech '. Mistress of cajolery (7:14-18), she invites to sin. **4a.** ' her end ' : the final outcome of relations with her. Line *a* may be read : ' But *at the last* she is bitter as wormwood '. **5.** ' Her feet go down *to* Death and her steps *lead down to Sheol* ' ; to associate with her is to go the way that shortens life and leads to spiritual death. **6.** Read perhaps : ' *She treadeth not* (reading *bal* or *lô* for *pen*) the path of life ; her steps *stray*, she knoweth not (whither) '. ' life ' : in the moral as well as in the physical sense.

i **7-14.** The folly of sexual licentiousness. **9a.** ' Give not ' : ' *lest thou give* '. ' thy honour ' : the freshness and grace of youth. **9b.** ' the cruel ' : refers apparently to the outraged husband ; *cf.* 6:34 f. **10a.** ' strength ' : ' *wealth* '. The victim of lust is like the prodigal son who ' devoured his substance with harlots ' (Lk 16:30) and was forced to become a hired servant. **11.** The physical results of sexual indulgence. **12-14.** The pangs of remorse and upbraidings of conscience form the terrible climax to the loss of honour and health and substance (Perowne). **14.** ' *I had almost fallen into* all evil in the midst of the *congregation* and *assembly* ' ; *i.e.* into condemnation to death by the judicial court according to the law against adulterers (Lev 20:10 ; Deut 22:22).

j **15-20** The remedy is to be found in the divinely ordained intercourse of marriage. In figurative and decorous language the disciple is exhorted to be content with his lawful wife and to give her all his affection. **15.** For the wife as a ' cistern ' or spring, *cf.* Cant 4:15. **16.** ' *Should thy spring be scattered abroad ?* Thy *streams of water* in the streets ? ' **17a.** ' *Do not squander thy virile strength* '. **18a.** ' vein ' : rather ' *fountain* '. ' blessed ' : LXX reads ' *thine own* ' which agrees well with the preceding context. **19.** The ' hind ' and the ' graceful fawn ' (' doe ') are, for the oriental poet, symbols of grace and feminine beauty. **19c.** ' delighted ' : ' *ravished* '. **20a.** ' art thou seduced ' : ' *dost thou go astray with* '. **20b.** ' art cherished ' : ' *embrace* '.

k **21-23.** A final motive for conjugal fidelity. **21b.** ' considereth ' : ' *weigheth carefully* '. **23a.** ' He shall die *for want of discipline* ', for lack of the corrective influence of Wisdom. **23b.** ' be deceived ' : ' *go astray* '. A slight change from *yiśgeh* to *yissāp̄eh* gives ' he shall *perish* '.

l **VI 1-15** contains three illustrations of Folly written in the style of the ' Sayings of the wise men ' (22:17-24:34) : *cf.* 6:6-11 and 24:30-34. They are followed by a numerical saying (16-19), resembling in form 30:15-33 ; then the subject of sexual immorality is continued from ch 5. The section 1-19 thus breaks the connexion and was probably inserted after the compilation of chh 1-9 as an exemplification of the principle announced in 5:23b.

m **1-5 The Danger of Suretyship**—The practice of being surety for a friend, and the folly entailed by that risk is a frequent subject of warning in Prov. (11:15 ; 17:18 ; 20:16 ; 22:26 ; 27:13). **1b.** ' *If thou hast stricken the hand for another* ', pledged thyself for thy friend ; ' friend ' and ' another ' are synonymous, not contrasted. Striking hands was a way of sealing a bargain ; *cf.* 4 Kg 10:15. **3-5.** The endangered surety should take strong measures to force his friend either to meet his liabilities or to set him free from his bond. **3.** ' *Then do this*, my son, *to* deliver thyself,

because thou art fallen into the hand of thy neighbour ; go, *bestir thyself and storm* thy friend '. **5a.** ' from the hand ' : the addition of a consonant to the Heb. word for ' hand ' (*yād*) gives ' hunter ' (*ṣayyād*).

6-11 The Sluggard—The ant is often mentioned n in ancient folklore as an example of thrift and industry (*cf.* 24:30-34). LXX adds a parallel passage on the bee, quoted in several patristic writings, *e.g.* Clement Alex., *Strom.* 1.6. **10.** ' A little sleep, a little slumber, a little *folding of* the hands *to* rest '. These lines continue the remonstrance of the sage. **11a.** ' traveller ' : in the sense of ' highwayman '. Want and poverty are dangerous assailants who will make away with the sluggard's substance. The last distich is from LXX.

12-15 The Mischief-Maker—**12.** ' A man of *Belial* ' o (Heb. *bᵉliyaʿal* a worthless, good-for-nothing person), a man *of iniquity*, walketh with *crookedness of* mouth ' (*i.e.* deals in lying speech). **13-14** describe the underhand methods, the veiled suggestions of mischief-makers. **15a.** ' To such a one ' : ' *Therefore* '. **15b.** ' and shall no longer have any remedy ' : ' and no *healing* '.

16-19 Seven Things Hateful to God (*cf.* 30:15-33). p **16a.** ' *Yea*, seven *are an abomination to him* '. Six things . . . seven is a rhetorical way of expressing an approximate number without implying that the list is complete. The seven sins are then enumerated.

20-35 Warning against the Adulteress—This section q is a continuation of ch 5, having the same general theme. Obedience to parental instruction is invoked (**20-23**), ' to give weight to another earnest warning against the sin which destroys purity and saps the foundations of family life ' (**24-35**), Perowne, 69. **20a.** ' commandments ' : ' *precept* '. **20b.** ' law ' : ' *instruction* '. **21.** *Cf.* 3:3. **22-23.** Sense and syntax demand the inversion of these two verses. **23a.** ' commandment and law ' : ' *precept and instruction* '. **23b.** ' reproofs of instruction ' : moral admonitions. Parental teaching will, like a lighthouse, guide the young man embarking on the sea of life. **22.** ' *When thou goest, it shall lead thee ; . . . it shall talk with thee* '. **24a.** ' to keep thee ', etc. ' evil woman ' : a slight alteration of MT from *rā* to *rēa* gives the meaning ' wife *of another* '. **25b.** ' winks ' : ' *eye-lids* ' with allusion to seductive glances. **26.** MT is obscure. There is a contrast between the harlot and the adulteress ; the latter commits the graver sin. **26b.** ' the woman ' ; the adulteress. A change in the Heb. of the first line (*bᵉʿad* to *tāṣûd*) gives the same verb in each line : ' A harlot *hunteth for a piece of bread* [*i.e.* a livelihood], but the *adulteress hunteth* the precious *life* '. **27a.** ' hide ' : ' *take* '. **29b.** ' *whoever toucheth her shall not go unpunished* '. **30.** ' *Do not men despise a thief if* he stealeth to *satisfy his appetite ?* (*i.e.* his greed). **31a.** ' sevenfold ' : according to Ex 22:1, fivefold was the legal limit of restitution ; ' sevenfold ' is here a general term meaning ' in full measure ' (*cf.* Mt 18:22). **32.** ' But he that is an adulterer *is void of sense* ; he destroyeth *himself who so acteth* '. **33-35.** An allusion to the penalty and shame that both the law and public opinion inflict upon the adulterer. **34a.** ' Because jealousy is *fury in a man* ' ; it enrages the husband. **35.** ' nor will he *regard any ransom nor be content, though thou givest* many gifts '. The adulterer cannot escape the penalty of the law by any private arrangement with the jealous husband.

VII 1-27 The Adulteress—After an earnest plea for 3 obedience to his words (**1-3**), *i.e.* to Wisdom (**4**), that the pupil may avoid the adulteress (**5**), the sage describes her fatal wiles (**6-23**) and the fate of her victim (**24-27**). The chapter has high dramatic merit. **2a.** ' thou shalt live ' : the practice of Wisdom will b ensure a happy life and save from premature death. **4b.** ' friend ' : ' one well known ', here as in Ruth 2:1, ' kinswoman '. The writer wishes to inculcate deep affection for, and familiarity with, virtue.

6. ' For at the window of my house, through my c lattice, *I looked* forth '. The sage begins the description c of a scene that he had more than once observed from behind an oriental window with its elaborate lattice work which forms an effective screen from the street, though permitting the watcher within to observe all that goes on without. **7.** The transposition of *na'ar* to line *a* gives : ' And I *beheld among the simple ones* [the thoughtless] *a youth, and I discerned among the youths one void of understanding* '. **8a.** ' by the corner ' : ' *near* '. The young man is pictured as taking the road where the house of the adulteress stood.

d **10-12 Description of the Adulteress.—10b.** For the harlots dress *cf.* Gen 38:14. ' prepared to deceive souls ' : MT is obscure ; Vaccari renders ' *with secret intent* '. Line *c* should be transferred to **11.** ' wandering ' : ' *wilful* ', though *sôbābet* for *sôrāret* gives the Vg reading. **11b.** ' *Her feet rest not in her house* '. **12.** ' Now in the streets, now in the *broad places* [squares], *now at every corner she lurketh* '.

e **13-20 Her Invitation—13b.** ' flattereth ' : not in MT. **14.** ' *A sacrifice was due from me* : this day I *pay my vows* '. She has promised a sacrifice of thanksgiving for a favour received. Such sacrifices ended in a sacred banquet to which friends were invited to consume the meats offered at the altar (Lev 3:16 f. ; 7:15). **14b.** ' this day ' : the meat had to be eaten the same day or burnt. **15a.** ' Therefore ' : since I am able to provide a banquet. **16.** ' I have *spread my couch with coverlets, with striped cloths of Egyptian yarn* '. **18.** ' *Come let us take our fill of love till morning, let us solace ourselves with loves* '.

f **21-23 The Youth yields—22-23** must be taken together. The text is extremely difficult. With corrections from LXX we may render : ' *He goeth after her stupidly, as an ox goeth to the slaughter, as a stag fastened to a chain until an arrow strike through its liver ; as a bird hasteneth to a snare, and knoweth not that it concerneth his life* '. The verses describe the brute-like stupidity with which the youth goes to his doom.

g **24-27 The Fate of her Victims—25a.** ' be drawn away in ' : ' *turn aside to* '. **25b.** ' *and go not astray in* '. **26.** ' For many are the *dead* she hath cast down, and *numerous are her slain* ' ; *i.e.* materially and morally ruined. **27a.** ' hell ' : ' *Sheol* '. **27b.** ' reaching ' : ' *going* '. Though said of temporal death it is not less true of eternal death, of hell in the Christian sense.

h **VIII 1-36 The Appeal of Wisdom—**This chapter forms the climax of the first section. Wisdom is personified as in 1:20-33, but with greater relief and richness. After an appeal to be heard attentively (**1-11**), she proclaims her salutary efficaciousness in human society (**12-21**), and her activity in the creation of the universe (**22-31**), concluding with yet another plea to seek blessedness in following her (**32-36**).

i **1-11 The Call of Wisdom—3.** ' Beside the gates, *at the entry of the city, at the entrance of the gates she crieth aloud* '. ' gates ' : *cf.* 1:21, note. **5.** ' *Learn, O ye simple, sagacity, and ye fools, learn understanding* '. The simple fools are those who do not lead a ' *wise* ' life : *cf.* 1:22, note. Sagacity means true knowlege of the principles of life. **6a.** ' great ' : ' *princely* ' or ' *noble* '. **6b.** ' *and the utterance of my lips shall be* right things '. **7a.** ' meditate ' : ' *uttereth* ' ; present tense. **8.** The Wisdom that speaks here is neither deceived nor wishes to deceive. She speaks with divine authority. **10a.** ' money ' : ' *silver* '. **10b.** ' *and knowledge* [doctrine] rather than *fine* gold '. **11.** *Cf.* 3:15.

j **12-14 The Attributes of Wisdom—12.** ' I, Wisdom, dwell *with sagacity, I possess knowledge and insight* '. **13a** is to be omitted because of metre and context. **13c.** ' double ' : ' *perverse* '. **14.** ' *With me is* counsel and *skill* : *I am prudence* ; strength is mine '. Wisdom alone can give these gifts to her friends. Here Wisdom identifies herself with God, the source of all good ; in fact, what Wisdom claims for herself here, is attributed directly to God in Job 12:13-16.

k **15-16.** Rulers discharge their duties through the guidance of Wisdom. **15b.** ' and *magistrates administer justice* '. **16b.** MT : ' and nobles, (yea), all the

rulers of the earth ' ; LXX better : ' and *nobles* **368k** *govern the earth* '.

17-21 The rewards of Wisdom. Those who seek her l not only find her, but gain riches, honour, and blessings more valuable than gold. **17b.** ' and they that *seek me*, find me '. **18a.** ' glory ' : ' *honour* '. **18b.** ' glorious ' : ' *ancient* ' and so ' *durable* '. The idea is that of a patrimony built up for many years. **20-21.** Wisdom concludes her promises by affirming that she deals equitably with her friends.

22-31 Wisdom in the Creation and Ordering of the m Universe—Here the eulogy of Wisdom touches the sublime. God himself made use of Wisdom as a ' master-workman ' in the construction of the marvellous universe, as well as in the establishment of the wondrous order that rules it. The picture is similar to that of 3:19-20, but is more detailed and striking. Wisdom is presented as a concrete being, living and operating at the side of God. It is not, however, a creature, but a divine being, for it existed before the creation of anything (**22-26**), and concurred in the creation of all things (**27-31**). On the one hand, it is intrinsic to God, his essential Wisdom ; on the other, it is represented as something distinct from God and coming from him by way of generation (**24-25**). It is not yet a distinctly defined personality, but it is so vividly personified that from this description to the distinction of more than one person in God was only a step. That step was manifest when the divine Wisdom was made incarnate in Christ Jesus. See § 316b.

22-26. Wisdom was with God at the beginning of n creation. **22a.** ' possessed ' : the Heb. word *qānāh* means ' to acquire ' without defining the method of acquisition. In Gen 14:19, 22, it is by ' creation ' ; here, however, it is by ' generation ' (*cf.* 24 where Wisdom is portrayed as the possession of God by the title of ' generation ', not ' creation '). Perhaps the most satisfactory rendering of *qānānî* is ' *begat me* '. For the meaning ' possessed ', *cf.* Prov 1:5 ; 4:5, 7 ; 15:32 ; 16:16 ; Deut 32:6 ; Pss 74:2 (H) ; 139:13 (H) ; Is 1:3. **22b.** ' in the beginning ' : ' *(as) the beginning* ' or ' *principle* ' of the divine activity, either because Wisdom was conceived before all divine works in regard of creatures, or because she concurred in the creation of everything (30). Wisdom was before the universe was made ; she is placed outside the works of creation. **24.** ' *When there were no* depths, I was *born, when there were no* fountains *rich* in waters '. **25a.** ' *Before* the mountains *were sunk* ' in their fixed places. **26b.** ' rivers ', etc. : ' *fields*, nor the *first* [or, mass of] *dust of the world* '. **27-31.** Wisdom was present at, and rejoiced in, the works of creation. **27b.** ' when he *set a vault upon the face of the deep* ' : the vault of the firmament whose rim seems to rest upon the surface of the ocean. **28a.** ' When he *made firm* the *skies* above '. **28b.** ' poised ' : ' *fixed fast* '(LXX). **29a.** ' When he *set bounds to the sea* '. **29c.** ' balanced ' : ' *laid* '. **30a.** ' I was *at his side* (as) *a master workman* ', giving him, so to speak, the design of the things to be made. Wisdom found intense joy in the task assigned to her by God and in the contemplation of the works of creation ; above all she rejoiced in man, the most perfect creature of the visible world. **30-31** is a poetical description of Gen 1:31.

32-36 Closing Exhortation—32a. ' Now therefore ', o because I give, and am, all this. **32b.** ' children ' : ' *sons* '. **35b.** ' salvation ' : ' *favour* '. **36a.** ' shall sin against ' : ' *misseth* ', which preserves the contrast with ' findeth ' in the previous verse. ' soul ' : ' *life* ' or ' *self* '.

IX 1-18 The Choice between Wisdom and Folly— p The chapter contains contrasted pictures of Wisdom (**1-6**) and Folly (**13-18**). Between them is inserted a section of general teaching (**7-12**).

1-6 The feast which Wisdom offers. Wisdom is here q presented as the rich and virtuous mistress of a palace who invites her followers to a sumptuous feast. The exquisite viands are the sublime doctrine and noble virtues inculcated by the divine law. **1b.** ' seven

368q pillars ': 'the number invites mystical treatment (*e.g.* seven gifts of the Holy Spirit, seven Sacraments), but probably originally it signified completeness' (A. E. Morris in *A New Comm. on Holy Scripture*, 388). **2b**. 'mingled her wine': with spices. **3b**. 'to the tower' etc.: '*from the high places* of the city'. The maidens are in fact the preachers of the divine word; *f.* 1:20, note. **4a**. 'a little one': 'simple'. It is in parallelism with the 'unwise' of **4b**. **6a**. The fruit of Wisdom is life in the deepest sense of the word: *cf.* 3:18 ; 4:13 ; Jn 17:3.

r 7-12 contain short aphorisms drawn from some other source and introduced here by a later editor. 7–9 are in the style of 22:17–24 and deal with the opportuneness of correction, and 10–12 are isolated couplets. **7a**. 'He that *correcteth* a *scoffer*, *getteth* to himself *ignominy*' (or 'insult'). **7b**. 'blot': the blemish of a useless reprehension. **9**. 'Give (*counsel*) to a wise man, and *he will be yet wiser*': teach a just man, and he *shall increase in learning*'. **10a**. Cf. 1:7. **10b**. 'and *to know the Holy One is understanding*': 'holy': the parallel shows almost certainly that God is meant. The knowledge of God is the 'beginning' or 'chief part' of Wisdom, and the recognition of him in a practical way by the fulfilment of religious duties is true Wisdom. **12**. The individual both reaps the benefit of his wisdom and pays the penalty of his contempt for the moral law.

s 13-18 The Character of Dame Folly—This section is in sharp contrast to the picture of Wisdom given in 1–6. Folly, represented by a woman of vicious life, has, like Wisdom, her own house (**14**), where she spreads her feast (**15**), and then issues her invitation (**16**), couched, in part at least, in identical terms. This description has something in common with that of the wanton woman in 2:18 and 7:11–19. Here she represents vice in general, but in the mind of the sage impurity stands first among the vices.

t **13a**. 'and full': 'is full'. 'allurements': MT reads '*simplicity*' but a slight alteration from *peṭayyûṭ* to *mepattāh* gives the meaning 'enticing' adopted by Vg. **14a**. 'sat': 'sitteth'. **15b**. 'to call *to them that are going their ways*'. **16**. Cf. 9:4. **17b**. 'hidden bread': bread eaten in secret. The sage has sexual immorality in mind. **18**. '*But he knoweth not* that *the dead* are there, that her guests are in the depths of *Sheol*'. The acceptance of her invitation leads to physical and spiritual death: *cf.* 5:8–10 ; 7:21–27. The house of Folly is, so to speak, a grave that holds entombed all who enter: *cf.* 7:27.

369a X 1-XXII 16 Section 2 The First Collection of the Proverbs of Solomon—This is the central part of the book and the oldest portion: *cf.* § 364*e*. It consists of 375 proverbs, each of two lines formed strictly on the model of Hebrew parallelism. The parallelism from ch 10 to ch 15 is, as a rule, antithetical; from 16:1 to 22:16 synthetic or progressive. There is but little attempt at subject-grouping and no indication of the way in which the collection came to be made. **X 1-10—2**. *Cf.* 11:4. Only good works (here perhaps 'justice' = '*almsgiving*') merit a long life ; *cf.* 11:19 ; 12:28. **3b**. 'deceitful practices': 'desire'. This verse, like 2, is in harmony with the OT doctrine of temporal reward and punishment. **4**. The additional couplet is found only in LXX and Syr. after 9:12. **5**. 'He that *gathereth* in *summer* is a wise son ; but he that *sleepeth* in *harvest* the son of confusion'. **6a**. 'blessings'. **6b** does not fit here. It is also found in 11 where it is evidently in place. Perhaps the original half-verse was lost. MT : 'the mouth of the wicked *hideth violence*'. **7a**. 'with praises': '*is blessed*'. **7b**. 'shall rot': an emendation of MT gives '*is cursed*'. **8b**. 'a fool is beaten with lips': '*a prating fool shall fall*'. **9b**. 'shall be manifest' destroys the antithesis. A slight change in MT (*yērôaʿ* for *yiwwāḏēaʿ*) gives '*shall suffer hurt*'. **10b** has come in by mistake from **8b**. LXX and Syr. have apparently preserved the right reading, '*he that reproveth frankly maketh*

peace'. To close the eye to wrongdoing is mistaken **3** kindness.

11-20 Proper Speech—11. 'vein': 'fountain'. The **b** utterance of the just man is a source of wisdom and inspiration to others. **11b**. 'covereth iniquity': conceals his wicked purpose. **12b**. 'charity' which forgives the transgressions of others ; *cf.* 17:9 ; 1 Cor 13:17 ; 1 P 4:8. **14a**. 'lay up knowledge': '*conceal their knowledge*'. **14b**. 'next to confusion': '*impending destruction*'. At times silence is golden ; he who senselessly blurts out all he knows, only does mischief ; *cf.* 12:23. **15**. 'The rich man's *wealth is his strong city* ; *the terror* of the poor is their poverty'. Wealth is a protection against the vicissitudes of life. **16a**. 'work': 'earnings'. For the good riches may lead to long life and happiness ; for the wicked they only multiply sin. **17**. '*He is on* the way *of* life *that heedeth instruction* ; but he that *neglecteth admonition* goeth astray'. **18b**. 'uttereth reproach': '*spreadeth calumny*'. **19**. The wise man controls his tongue. **20b**. 'nothing': 'little'.

21-XI 8 The Happiness of a Virtuous Life—21. The **c** just man not only walks in the right way himself, but guides others along it. **22b**. 'neither to them': '*and toil addeth nothing thereto*'. God's blessing is the chief reason for prosperity ; human effort counts for little : *cf.* Ecclus 11:23 ; Ps 127 (128). **23**. '*It is as a sport for a fool* to work mischief *and for a man of sense to act wisely*'. The latter practises virtue with the same ease that the fool commits evil. **24**. God will, in his own good time, mete out the requital that the wicked fear and the good desire ; *cf.* 1:26. **25b**. The tempest of divine retribution will sweep away the wicked (*cf.* 1:27), but the just will stand like a house on the rock, unshaken by the storm : *cf.* Mt 7:24–27. **26**. A shiftless messenger gives more trouble than real service. **27**. Cf. 3:2 ; 4:10 ; Ex 20:12 ; Ps 54 (55):24. A long peaceful life is normally the reward of piety. This belief was later challenged in Job. **28**. 'is joy': will end in gladness. **29**. '*God is a stronghold to* the upright *in* way, *but the terror of evil-doers*'. **30**. Cf. note to 2:21 f.

XI 1 'deceitful': 'false'. **1b**. 'will': 'delight'. **d** **2**. '*When* pride *cometh, then cometh shame, but with the lowly* is wisdom'. Pride ends in failure and disgrace ; humility is a wise counsellor, bringing wisdom and honour. **3a**. 'simplicity': 'integrity'. **4a**. 'revenge': 'wrath'. The words refer to any divine judgement. When God decides upon the chastisement of the wicked, riches are powerless to avert it. **5**. 'make his way prosperous': 'make *smooth* his way': *cf.* 3:6. **6b**. snares': 'calamity'. **7** is difficult. MT with '*ewilîm* (ungodly) for '*ônîm* (strength) may be rendered : 'When the wicked man *dieth*, hope *perisheth*, and the expectation of the *ungodly* perisheth', *i.e.* the hope of the evildoer to escape retribution is frustrated by the divine punishment of death. But there is no satisfactory antithesis in the second half of the verse. LXX remedies this defect : 'When the *just man dieth*, hope *perisheth not*, but the boast *of the ungodly perisheth*', a reference to the happy lot of the just after death. **8**. 'shall be given up for him': '*taketh his place*'. The wicked fall into the peril in which they had plotted to involve the just, *cf.* Mardochai and Aman, Daniel, Susanna. This concept is founded on the justice of God who governs the world.

9-16 The Public Good—9b. '*but through* the knowledge **e** of the just they [the 'friend' of *a*] are rescued'. **10b**. 'praise': 'jubilation'. Upright citizens are true promoters of the public good. **11a**. 'by the blessing of the just' either by their prosperity, as in 10, or the blessing conferred on a city by their presence and beneficent words (involving deeds). **12**. '*The senseless man sheweth contempt for his neighbour, but the man of discretion keepeth silent*'. The discreet man, whatever he thinks, keeps his thoughts to himself. **13**. '*a tale-bearer* revealeth secrets, but *a trustworthy man* concealeth *the matter*', keeps a confidence. **14b**. 'much counsel': '*a wealth of counsellors*': *cf.* 15:22 ; 20:18 ; 24:6. **15b**. 'he that *hateth suretyship* is secure': *cf.* 6:1–5. **16a**. 'glory': 'honour'. **16b**. 'the strong': '*ruthless*

9e men'. The grace of true womanhood wins honour as surely as the ruthless acquire riches.

f **17-23 Rewards and Punishments—17b.** 'casteth off his own kindred': '*doeth harm to himself*'. **18.** 'The wicked *earn delusive wages*, but he that soweth justice a *sure reward*'. The apparent prosperity of the wicked is illusory. **19.** MT is uncertain; perhaps: '*He that followeth justice taketh the road to life ; he that pursueth evil the road to* death'. **21a.** 'Hand in hand': a Heb. expression meaning perhaps '*of a truth*' or '*sooner or later*'. '*shall not be innocent*': '*shall not go unpunished*'. **22b.** '*is a fair woman lacking in taste*'. The nose ring was a regular ornament of the oriental woman; cf. Is 3:21. **23.** 'The desire of the just *endeth only in good* ; the expectation of the wicked *in wrath*'. The desires of the just are satisfied, but divine wrath prepares chastisement for the wicked.

g **XI 24-XII 12 Beneficence—25b.** 'he that *watereth* shall be *watered* himself'; an agricultural metaphor, expressing the same thought as Lk 6:38 'Give and it shall be given unto you'. **27.** MT: '*He that* seeketh *good winneth favour*, but he that seeketh after evil, *it shall come unto him*'. The good seek (and find) God's favour ; the wicked only bring upon themselves the evil they pursue. **28.** The man who trusts in riches without regard for virtue will wither and fall like a leaf without sap. **29.** 'inherit the winds.': he who manages his household stupidly will find his substance reduced to nothing and will become the slave of a more prudent man. **30.** The sense of 30b is uncertain in MT ; following LXX we may read : 'The fruit of *justice* is a tree of life, but *violence destroyeth men's lives*'. **31.** If the just will not escape the consequences of their faults '*on* the earth', how much less the wicked. **XII:2.** '*A good man findeth favour with Yahweh but the wicked man he condemneth*'; cf. Wis 2:14-16 ; 4:16. **4.** 'A *worthy wife* is a crown to her husband, *but a shameful one* is (like) *rot in his bones*'. 'The Heb. phrase is 'a woman of power', *i.e.* the capable mother of a family who knows how to manage her household ; cf. 31:10 ff. **5a.** 'judgements': *i.e.* right. **6.** Slander, false testimony, etc., are like assassins lying in wait for victims. **7a.** 'The wicked turn *about* and *are not*', *i.e.* they will 'vanish in the twinkling of an eye' ; cf. 10:25 ; 12:3. **10.** The good man treats animals with kindness ; the wicked is cruel even to his fellow-men. **11.** LXX and Vg add another couplet to this verse, not found in MT. **12.** With an emendation of MT (*lehem* for *lēḇ*), 11 and 12 may be read : 'He that tilleth his land *shall have plenty of* bread, but he that *followeth idle pursuits shall have none*. Wickedness is a net of evils, but the root of the just *yieldeth* (*fruit*)'. Evil men are caught by their own bad conduct.

h **13-23 Use of the Tongue—13a.** '*By* the sin of the lips the *sinner falleth into snares*' (LXX), which the sincere and candid in speech escape. **14a.** 'with good things' is probably a gloss. A man reaps what he sows. **18.** '*There is* (one) *that speaketh rashly like sword-thrusts ;* but the tongue of the wise man *bringeth healing*' by pouring the balm of kindly words into the wounds opened by ill-considered speech. **19b.** 'but *for an eyewink* [for a moment only] a lying tongue'. **20b.** 'take': '*give*'. **21a.** '*No mischief* befalleth the just, but the wicked *are full of misfortune*'.

i **24-XIII 6 Labour—24a.** 'valiant': '*diligent*'. **26.** MT : '*The just man surpasseth his neighbour, but the way of the wicked leadeth them astray*', *i.e.* virtue gives its possessor an advantage over other men. The text, however, may be corrupt. **27a** appears to be a hunting metaphor and may be read : '*The slothful man roasteth* (*starteth*) *not his prey*' ; and **27b**, by the transposition of one word, gives 'but *plenteous* is the substance of the *diligent* man'. **28b** is a *crux interpretum*. MT may be read : 'and walking in its pathway—not death' (Zorell, *Heb. Lex.*). From this reading one would conclude to eternal life for the just. A slight correction of the text gives with Vg and DV, 'the by-way (or '*the way of the wicked*') leadeth to death'. Amid a variety of readings it seems best to retain Vg and DV, in which, however, 'life' of the first line, according to some commentators, is used in a sense so wide and embracing that it is not to be restricted to long life on this earth ; cf. § 365.f. **369i**

XIII 1 The addition of the letter *h* to the Heb. for **j** 'father' gives : 'The wise son *loveth instruction*, but *the petulant* heareth not *rebuke*'. **2b.** ' the *desire of the treacherous is* (*for*) *violence*'. He whose counsels help others will share in the blessing he bestows ; but the perverse will seek only their own advantage in the harm they do their fellow-men. **3a.** 'soul': '*life*'. **4.** 'The sluggard *desireth but* (*getteth*) *nothing* ; the *desire of the diligent is richly supplied*' (lit. 'made fat'). **5b.** 'but the wicked *acteth odiously and shamefully*'. **6a.** ' the way of the innocent': '*the man of integrity*'. Goodness is the best guarantee of a proper life ; cf. 11:5.

7-12 Poverty and Riches—7. 'One *feigneth to be* rich, **k** *yet* hath nothing ; another *feigneth to be* poor, *yet* great riches'. **8b.** 'beareth': '*heareth*'. The wealthy can buy their way out of any peril. The last part of *b* seems to be an erroneous repetition of MT from the end of 1b. The thought is not characteristic of Prov and gives no contrast to *a*. The original reading has been lost. **9a.** 'giveth joy': an emendation of the Heb. verb (*yiśmaḥ* to *yizrāḥ*) gives the preferable reading '*shineth brightly*'. 'Light' and 'lamp' are symbols of life and prosperity ; cf. 4:18 ; 24:20. **10b.** '*with them that take* counsel, *is* wisdom'. **11b.** 'but *he that little by little amasseth*, increaseth'. **12.** 'Hope deferred *maketh the heart sick ; but desire fulfilled is a tree of life*' ; it gladdens and gives refreshment.

13-20 Docility—13. A small change in MT gives : **l** ' He that *despiseth an order shall perish*, but he that feareth the *command* shall be required'. Observance of law, both human and divine, is recommended. Vg and DV add a couplet found in LXX after 9. **14b.** 'ruin': '*snares*' ; cf. 10:11 ; 14:27. **15** is obscure, but MT may be read : '*Fine perception winneth favour*, but the *behaviour of the treacherous is hard*' (or by reading '*êḏām* for '*êṯān* ' *is their ruin*'). Gentle and considerate treatment of others wins their esteem. **16b.** 'layeth open his folly': '*maketh a display of folly*'. **17a.** 'An *incompetent messenger maketh* (his sender) *to fall*'. The contrast is between the mischief caused by an unreliable messenger and the success insured by a competent envoy. **19.** 'Desire *fulfilled is sweet to the* soul ; *but fools hate to turn from* evil'. The two lines appear to be unrelated. **20b.** 'become like to them': ' *shall become evil*': cf. Ecclus 22:14 and 13:11.

21-XIV 14 Rewards of the Just—21. Cf. 10:24 ; **m** 11:21, 27. **23.** The wide variety of renderings in the versions shows the obscurity of this verse. MT, slightly modified, may be read : 'The *great man devoureth the land of the poor*, but *such is swept away without judicial process*', *i.e.* he is punished by divine judgement. **24.** 'Spare the rod and spoil the child' ; cf. 3:12. **25.** 'and filleth his soul': '*to his heart's content*' ; cf. 10:3.

XIV 1. Read perhaps : 'A wise woman buildeth **370a** *up* her house, but *folly teareth it down*'. The well-being of a household depends chiefly on maternal solicitude. **2.** 'He that walketh *uprightly* feareth *the Lord*, but he *whose ways are crooked, despiseth him*'. **3a.** 'rod': '*shoot*'. 'The branch of pride springs from its stem in the fool's mouth' (Toy) ; cf. Apoc 1:16. Some suggest 'the rod *for his pride*', *i.e.* his words will be a scourge to the fool himself. **4.** An emendation ('*ēḇûs* to '*epes*) gives : 'Where there are no oxen, *there is no corn ; an abundant crop* is in the strength of the ox'. **6b.** ' but *to the man of understanding, knowledge* is easy'. Wisdom is readily found by the sincere seeker ; cf. 2:1-6. **7.** 'Go *from the presence of a foolish man, for thou hast not discerned* (there) *lips of prudence*'. Perhaps MT is corrupt. **8.** Foresight and a capacity to choose the proper course of action are characteristic of the prudent man. **9** makes good sense, but differs from MT, in itself obscure. By adding ' among ' to *a* and by a change of one letter in the verb (*ṣ* to *n*), we may read : '*Among fools guilt abideth*, but among the just *favour*', *i.e.* of God. Fools always have a conscience burdened

370a with guilt ; only on the upright does God's favour rest. **10.** 'The heart knoweth *its own* bitterness *and* in its joy *no stranger* shareth '. **11.** *Cf.* 12:7. **13.** ' *Even in* laughter *the heart is sad*, and the end of joy *is* mourning '. *Cf.* Shelley's Ode to a Skylark : ' Our sincerest laughter with some pain is fraught, our sweetest songs are those that tell of saddest thoughts '. **14.** ' *The recreant shall reap the fruit of* his ways, and the good man *of his deeds* '.

b **15-25 Prudence—15.** ' innocent ' : inexperienced. The second couplet is found in LXX. **17b.** ' but the prudent man *endureth* ' (LXX), is patient. **18a.** ' childish ' : inexperienced. **18b.** ' look ' : ' embrace '. **19.** Moral goodness will triumph ; the wicked will ' bow ' as suppliants at the gates of the just. **22.** ' Do they *not* err that *devise* evil ? but *benevolence* and *fidelity* [God's constant favour] *shall be to them that devise good* '. **23.** ' In *all* labour *there is profit*, but mere talk tendeth to *penury* '. **24.** ' The crown of the wise is *wisdom*, the *chaplet* of fools is *their* folly ' (LXX). **25b.** ' he that uttereth lies *is a cheat* '.

c **26-35 Religion and the State—26.** ' In the fear of the Lord is *the hope of the strong man*, and *to* his children *it shall be a refuge* '. Even the strong man must not rely on his strength, but on the practice of religion. **27b.** ' ruin ' : ' snares '. Religion gives strength to avoid sin which draws down divine chastisement ; *cf.* 13:14. **29.** ' He that is slow to anger showeth much wisdom ; *the short-tempered showeth great folly* '. **30a.** ' A tranquil mind is the life *of the body* '. **32b.** ' death ' : read, by transposing two letters, *be̔tummô* (innocence) ; ' but the just *findeth refuge* in his *innocence* '. **33b.** ' and *even among fools it is made known* '. Wisdom also makes itself heard in the remorseful conscience of the wicked.

d **XV 1-12 Gentleness—1a.** ' breaketh ' : ' *turneth away* ', ' *sootheth* '. **2.** The urbanity of the wise makes knowledge pleasing and acceptable ; *cf.* 15:7. **3b.** ' behold ' : ' *keeping watch upon* '. Nothing escapes the eye of God ; *cf.* 5:21. **4.** A gentle tongue has the power to heal and lift up the spirit ; *cf.* 12:18. **5b.** ' shall become prudent ' : ' *acteth wisely* '. The second couplet comes from LXX. **6.** ' *In the house of the just there is ample wealth ;* the *revenue* of the wicked is (only) trouble ' ; *cf.* 10:16. **7b.** ' *the mind of the foolish is not right* '. The wise man knows how to communicate wisdom ; the fool is himself too confused to be of assistance to others. **8.** ' The *sacrifice* of the wicked *is an abomination* to the Lord, but the *prayer* of the *upright is his delight* '. External worship without interior holiness is not pleasing to God. **10a.** ' There is stern *correction for* him that forsaketh the way '. **11.** ' Hell and destruction ' : ' *Sheol* and *Abaddon* lie open before the Lord '. Abaddon is a synonym for Sheol ; *cf.* 27:20. If the profound and mysterious abode of the dead lies open before God, how much more the thoughts and motives of men. **12b.** ' nor will he *walk with* the wise '.

e **13-24 Happiness of Heart—15.** ' All the days of the poor are *sad*, but a joyous heart is a continual feast '. True happiness is found in contentment and joy of heart. **16.** *Cf.* Amenophis : ' Better is poverty at the hand of God than riches in the storehouse. Better is bread with happy heart than riches with vexation '. **17.** ' Better *a dish of herbs where love is* than a fatted *ox and* hatred *with it* '. **19.** ' The way of the slothful is *hedged with* thorns, but the *path* of the *diligent* is *a highway* ' (LXX) ; *cf.* Is 57:14. **22b.** ' are established ' : ' *stand* ', succeed ; *cf.* 11:14 ; 20:18. **23.** ' An apt utterance is a joy to a man ; and a word in *season, how good it is !* ' **24.** ' The path of life *(goeth) upward* to the wise, *so that he turneth from Sheol beneath* ' : another form of the proverb that virtue leads to life (*cf.* 10:17 ; 13:14) and sin to death ; but here expressed in a manner that makes it difficult to avoid the impression of a blessed hereafter for the just ; *cf.* however §365b.

f **25-33 Enemies and Friends of God—25b.** ' widow ' : as typical of the poor and oppressed. God will not permit the removal of the boundary stone marking the limits of her land ; *cf.* Deut 19:14. **26b.** Perhaps the original reading was ' and *gracious* words *are pleasing*

to him '. **27.** Inordinate desire of wealth leads to bribery and acts of injustice that eventually bring ruin ; but the man of incorruptible honour will be rewarded with a happy life. **28a.** ' obedience ' : ' to answer ', the prudent man weighs his words before giving answer. **30a.** ' The light of the eyes ' : a radiant countenance. **30b.** ' good *news* maketh the bones fat ', a figure for physical well-being. **31a.** ' of life ' : salutary. **32a.** ' soul ' : ' *life* '. **33a.** ' lesson ' : ' *guidance to* wisdom '. Religion is the basis of right living. Humble submission to God is the way to ' honour ' ; *cf.* 18:12 ; 22:4.

XVI 1-9 Divine Providence—1. ' *To* man *belongeth* **g** *the preparations of the mind, but from* the Lord *cometh the answer of* the tongue '. Man's words, like his deeds, are subject to divine control ; *cf.* Mt 10:19. **2a.** ' open ' : ' *pure* [right] *in his own eyes* ' ; yet the final verdict comes from God. **3a.** ' lay open ' : ' *commit* '. **4a.** ' The Lord hath made *everything for its own end* '. MT, however, permits the translation ' for *his* own end '. By making a thing to serve its own purpose, God makes it serve his purpose. **4b.** The wicked, by a deliberate choice of evil, fall under the divine law of chastisement. **6.** ' redeemed ' : rather ' *expiated* '. Kindness towards our neighbour can repay our debt to God ; *cf.* Lk 11:41. **9.** Man proposes and God disposes : *cf.* 1.

10-15 The Ideal King—10a. ' Divination ' : ' *an* **h** *oracle* '. The king's decisions are divinely guided. **11.** The reading : ' *Balance and scales are set by the king* ; all the *stones* in the bag are *his concern* ', seems preferable in the context. ' the bag ', in which sellers kept their weights ; *cf.* 11:1 ; 20:10. **13b.** ' *they love him* that speaketh right things '. A ruler needs honest counsellors. **14.** It is perilous to antagonize a monarch ; this was especially true of the Ancient East. **15b.** ' latter rain ' : ' *like a spring rain-cloud* ', necessary for the ripening of the corn.

16-22 Wisdom and Humility—16. The omission of **i** *mah* in the Heb. (dittography) gives : ' The getting of wisdom is better than gold, and *the getting* of understanding more precious than silver '. **17b.** ' he that *guardeth* his way [conduct] keepeth his *life* '. **18b.** ' and a *haughty* spirit before a fall ' ; *cf.* Lk 14:11. **20a.** ' He that giveth heed to the *word* shall find good '. The ' word ' refers to the divine admonitions contained in the Mosaic Law ; *cf.* 13:13. **21b.** ' and *sweetness of speech increaseth persuasiveness* '. A pleasant manner of imparting wisdom will make teaching more effective.

23-33 The Gift of Speech—23b. ' grace ' : ' *persuasiveness* ' ; *cf.* 21. **24a.** ' Well ordered ' : ' *gracious* '. **25b.** ' but the end thereof *(is) the way* to death ' : a repetition of 14:12. **26.** ' *The appetite of the labourer*, laboureth for *him* ; because his mouth [hunger] *impelleth him* '. Man is driven to work to provide himself with food ; *cf.* Gen 3:19. **27-30.** Slander. **27b.** The tongue of the slanderer is like a devastating fire ; *cf.* Jas 3:5-6. **28b.** ' and a *whisperer* separeth *friends* '. **30.** ' He that *winketh* his eyes deviseth *falsehoods* ; he that *compresseth* his lips *hath* brought evil to pass '. The outward expression betrays the inner thought ; *cf.* 6:13. **31b.** ' when ' : ' *and* '. The practice of virtue will lead to a venerable old age ; *cf.* 3:2 ; 4:10 ; 10:27. **32.** It is more glorious to control one's passions than to win battles ; *cf.* Ovid (*Epist. ex Pont. II.* 75) : ' Fortior est qui se quam qui fortissima vincit moenia '. **33.** The favourable or unfavourable decision of the lot depends on God. In OT the use of the lot to decide public and private affairs, to resolve doubts, etc., was accepted ; *cf.* 1 Kg 10:20 ff ; Jos 7:14 ; Lev 16:8 ; and in NT Acts 1:26.

XVII 1-14 Kindness to Others—1. ' Better a **k** morsel and *peace with it*, than a house full of *feasting* and strife ' ; *cf.* 15:16 f. **2a.** ' foolish ' : ' *shameful* '. An intelligent servant may be raised to the position of son. **3.** ' *The crucible is for* silver, *and* the furnace *for* gold, *but* the Lord is the *trier* of hearts '. **4a.** ' obeyeth ' : ' *giveth heed to malicious lips* '. **7.** ' Eloquent words ' : ' *sublime speech* '. A proposed correction of MT (*yeṭer* to *yōṣer*) gives '*upright speech*'. **7b.** ' *how much less do* lying lips a prince '. **8.** A difficult verse. ' *A bribe is a precious* jewel *to its possessor; wherever he* turneth, *he prospereth* '. The glitter of gold is a strong temptation and often the means of success in a dishonest undertaking. **9.** ' He that seeketh *friendship* concealeth a transgression; but that repeateth a matter separateth friends '. A true friend will overlook the faults of another; cf. 1 Cor 13:7. **11.** ' evil ' : ' *rebellious* '. **11b.** ' angel ' : ' *messenger* '; he will receive a sharp lesson. **12.** ' Meet a bear robbed of her whelps, *but not a fool in his folly* '. **14.** A difficult verse. MT may be rendered : ' The beginning of *strife* (is as) when one *setteth* water *free* : *and before there be quarrelling, cease* '. A small fissure in a dam may open the way to an overwhelming flood; so contention to a passionate outburst.

l 15-26 Justice—16. ' *Of* what avail *is* money in the hand of a fool to buy wisdom, if he hath no sense ' ? The second couplet is found in LXX. **17b.** ' and a brother *is born for adversity* '. A friend is friendly at all times, but the specific function of a brother is for the hour when friendship is most severely tested. **18.** ' *Void of sense* is he that *pledgeth* himself [lit. striketh hands], *and becometh* surety for his *neighbour* '; cf. 6:1-6; 11:15. **19.** ' He *loveth* sin that loveth *strife*; he that raiseth *high* his door, seeketh ruin '. Sin is the ordinary sequel to strife: ostentation, exemplified in the building of a pretentious house-door, can dissipate a fortune. **21.** ' *He that begetteth a fool, doth it to his sorrow* '; and the father of *a fool hath no joy* '. **22a.** ' *A joyful heart* maketh *for sound health*. **23a.** ' taketh ' : ' *receiveth* ' a bribe from the fold of the garment in which it is concealed. **24a.** ' Wisdom *is before* the face of the wise ', as the object of his contemplation and the norm of his conduct, whereas the fool is incapable of fixing his mind on anything. **26a.** ' to do hurt ' : ' *to fine* '. **26b.** ' nor to *scourge the noble against equity* ', *i.e.* unjustly. The verse deprecates injustice in the law-courts.

m 27-XVIII 5 Practical Wisdom—27b. ' precious ' : ' *calm* '. **28.** The value of silence. **XVIII : 1.** An obscure verse. Vg and DV state that a man, wishing to alienate himself from his friends, seeks pretexts, but is always liable to reproach. MT may be emended to read : ' *The unsocial man seeketh pretexts* (for *quarrel*); *he quarreleth with all* (sound) *wisdom* '. **2.** ' A fool *hath no delight in understanding, but only in revealing* his heart ', in blurting out his own ideas and opinions. **3.** ' *When wickedness cometh, there cometh contempt, and with dishonour cometh* reproach '. **4.** The words of the wise are profound, beneficent and instructive. **5.** As in 17:26 the reference is to the perversion of justice in the law-courts.

n 6-15 Foolish Talk—6a. ' intermeddle with ' : ' *enter into* ' or ' *bring* '. **6b.** ' quarrels ' : ' *stripes* '. The fool's thoughtless words involve him in disputes that call for punishment. **7b.** ' soul ' : ' *life* '; cf. 10:14; 12:13; 13:3. **8.** ' The words of the *whisperer* are like *dainty morsels, that go down to the inner parts of the belly* '. Malicious gossip is eagerly welcomed and deeply affects men's thoughts and actions; cf. 26:22. The second couplet is from LXX. **9.** The slothful and the spendthrift make a well-matched pair. **10a.** ' The name of the Lord ' : all that which the ineffable name of Yahweh connotes. In true religion man finds a sure bulwark against the vicissitudes of life. **10b.** ' exalted ' : ' *safe* '. **11.** The wealthy, by contrast, place their hopes in riches; cf. 10:15. **12.** Cf. 15:33; 16:18; Lk 14:11. **14.** ' *A brave* spirit upholdeth *a man in* his infirmity, but a *broken* spirit who can bear ? ' When the spirit, which is the source of strength, is itself crushed, what hope is there ?

o 16-23 Litigation—16. ' A gift maketh room *for* a man, and *bringeth him before* the great '. The reference is to the oriental custom of making presents to influential men to gain their favour and patronage; cf. Gen 33. **17.** ' *He appeareth right who pleadeth first in his own cuase* ;

then cometh *the other* and *testeth* him '. An admonition **370o** that both parties to a dispute must be heard. **18.** A doubtful case was settled by the lot, thus preventing recourse to violence. **19.** MT is untranslatable : ' A brother *offended* (?) is (more than ?) a strong city, and *contentions* are like the bars of a *castle* '; they form an impassable barrier to reconciliation. *a* of Vg and DV follows LXX and is a praise of brotherly help. **20b.** ' offspring ' : ' *outcome* '. Prudence is required in speech, for a man must take the consequences of his words; cf. 12:14; 13:2. **21** is a development of the preceding verse. **22b.** ' *and obtaineth favour* from the Lord '; cf. 12:4; 19:14; 31:10. The second couplet is an addition from LXX. **23.** ' The poor man *useth entreaties; but* the rich *answereth* roughly.

24-XIX 7 The True Friend—24. ' *There are friends for* **371a** *society, and there is a friend that clingeth closer* than a brother '. This reading, however, is somewhat doubtful. **XIX : 1a.** ' simplicity ' : ' *integrity* '. **1b.** The contrast and the parallel in 28:6 suggest the reading ' than he that is perverse in his lips and *rich* '. **2.** MT reads : ' *Zeal, too, without reflection is not* good; he that hasteth with his feet *misseth* (*his way*) '. A warning not to follow impetuously the blind impulse of passion. **3.** ' The folly of a man *subverteth* his way; and his mind fretteth against God '. How often we blame God for our misfortune, though the fault is with ourselves. **4b.** ' but the poor man *is forsaken by his friend* '; cf. 14:20; 19:7. **6a.** ' honour ' : ' *smooth the face of* ', flatter. **7b.** Read : ' *how much more do* his friends *stand aloof* from him '. In MT a single defective line follows this couplet. The DV rendering of it is conjectural.

8-15 The Man of Sense and the Fool—8a. ' He that **b** *acquireth understanding wisheth well to himself* '. **9.** Cf. 19:5. **11.** ' *It is good sense in a man to restrain his anger, and it is his glory to pass over an offence* '. This maxim approaches the NT precept of the forgiveness of injuries. **12b.** ' cheerfulness ' : ' *favour* '. A king's anger is a fearful thing, but his favour is refreshing. **13b.** ' *the contentions of a wife, a continual dripping* '. The incessant wrangling of a wife becomes as intolerable as the steady dripping of water from the roof. **14.** Cf. 18:22; 31:10. ' True marriages are made in heaven '. **15a.** ' He who will not work reaches a state in which he cannot work ' (Oesterley).

16-23 Respect for God—16. ' soul ' : ' *life* '. It is **c** probable that ' his ' in *b* represents an original abbreviation of the name ' Yahweh '. **17.** Cf. Mt 25:40. **18a.** ' despair not ' : ' *seeing there is hope* ', of emendation. **18b** might be a warning against either excessive correction or over-indulgence, both of which may prove fatal. **19.** MT is corrupt. Perhaps : ' He that *giveth way to anger shall pay the fine; and if he sheweth contempt* (of court) *he hath to pay more* '. **20b.** ' in thy latter end ' : in the future. **21a.** ' thoughts ', projects, schemes. **21b.** ' *but the plan* [design] *of God will succeed* '; cf. 16:1, 9, 33. **22.** Another *crux interpretum*. Perhaps : ' *The ornament of a man is his kindness, and better a poor man than a liar* '. **23.** Long life and prosperity are the normal rewards of the God-fearing; cf. 14:27.

24-XX 6 Correction and Laziness—24a. ' The slothful **d** *burieth* his hand *in the dish* ', after the oriental fashion of eating. **25a.** ' wicked man ' : ' *scoffer* '. ' fool ' : ' *simple* '. The chastisement of the irreligious will afford an object lesson to the merely ignorant. A simple admonition is sufficient for the man of sense. **26b.** ' *acteth shamefully and disgracefully* '. **27.** ' Cease, my son, to hear instruction, *if it be only to wander* from words of knowledge '. It is useless to hear advice without desire to put it into practice. **28a.** ' An unjust witness *scoffeth at justice* '; cf. 15:28. **29a.** ' judgements ' : MT *šᵉpāṭîm* (judgements) is a textual error for *šᵉbāṭîm* (strokes) which offers a better parallel to ' *stripes* ' (not ' striking hammers ') of *b*. **XX 1.** ' Wine is a *mocker, strong drink a brawler; he that is intoxicated* therewith *is not wise* '. ' *mocker* ' : scoffing at all things good and holy. **2a.** ' *dread* ', inspired by the fury of a king : a suggested change in MT gives ' *wrath* ' (*ḥᵃmaṭ*). **2b.** He who provokes a king to anger

371d may forfeit his *life* (DV ' soul ') ; *cf.* 16:14. **4.** ' The sluggard *will* not plough *in autumn* ; (then) *he seeketh in the harvest, and there is nought* '. The word rendered ' autumn ' is a general one for the colder half of the year when ploughing is done. **5.** A clever man by shrewd inquiries can draw out of others their secret thoughts. **6a.** ' are called merciful ' : ' *profess kindness* ', *i.e.* to be well disposed. ' Fair promises are common, but faithful performance of them is rare ' (Perowne).

e XX 7-15 Right Conduct—**7a.** ' simplicity ' : ' *integrity* '. The virtuous life of a father also ensures the future for his children : *cf.* 14:26. **8b.** scattereth : ' *winnoweth* ', *i.e.* he quickly perceives evil and applies a remedy. **9.** Man cannot be absolutely certain that he is free from sin : *cf.* 3 Kg 8:46 ; Job 14:4 ; 15:14 ; Ps 18 (19), 13 ; Eccl 7:21 ; Ecclus 5:5 ; Rom 3:23 ; 1 Jn 1:8. **10.** *Cf.* 11:1 ; 16:11 ; 20:23. **11a.** ' inclinations ' : ' *actions* '. Children show their character by their conduct ; hence the training of the young must begin early. **12.** All man's faculties are the gift of God. The suggestion is that they must be used in obedience to him. **13.** *Cf.* 6:9-11 ; 12:11 ; 19:15. **14a.** ' *Bad, bad*, saith the buyer '. The buyer, in order to get an article cheaply, depreciates it, and then goes his way, boasting of his cleverness.

f 16-25 Just and Unjust Acquisition—**16b.** ' and *hold him in* pledge [as security] *for* strangers '. If a man has been foolish enough to go surety for another, the creditor is to hold him to strict account. According to Ex 22:26 ; Deut 24:10-13, a man's garment could be taken as security. **18.** By reading *t'ḵōn* for *tikkōn* we get ' *Regulate thy plans* by counsel, *and make war* (only) *under wise guidance* ' : *cf.* 15:22 ; 24:6. **19.** ' *A talebearer* revealeth secrets ; meddle not with him that openeth wide his lips ', with a gossip. **20b.** ' in the midst of darkness ' : ' in *deepest* darkness '. ' his lamp ': a figure for prosperity ; *cf.* 13:9. **21.** *Cf.* the prodigal son, Lk 15:13. **24b.** ' how then [or, *how little*] can a man understand his way '. Man's intellect cannot comprehend the Providence which guides him. He must learn to trust God ; then his life will be properly directed. **25.** ' It is *a snare* for a man *rashly to say* : *It is holy* ; and *to reflect* (only) *after his* vows '. By pronouncing the word ' Holy ! ' over an object it was removed from profane use (*cf.* Mk 7:11 ff.) and reserved for God and sacred purposes. A warning against binding oneself by vow without due reflection.

g 26-XXI 5 King and Government—**26a.** ' A wise king *winnoweth* the wicked, and bringeth over them the wheel ', *i.e.* of the threshing cart that separates the wheat from the chaff ; *cf.* Is 28:27. **27a.** ' The spirit of man ', which is infused by God. *Cf.* Gen 2:7 where the same Heb. word is employed to designate the vital principle or soul. Here, however, it rather means ' conscience ' ; *cf.* 1 Cor 2:11. **30.** ' *Wounds from stripes cleanse* away evil ; *and strokes*, the inward parts of the belly '. Chastisement effects moral improvement. **XXI 1.** ' The heart of a king is *like channels* of water in the hand of the Lord ; he turneth it whithersoever he will '. The irrigator has full control over the water supply ; so also God over his earthly representative. **2.** *Cf.* 16:2. **3b.** ' victims ': sacrifices. The outer act without the observance of the moral precepts, is but an empty form ; *cf.* 15:8 ; 21:27 ; Am 5:22 ; Is 1:11. **4.** ' *Haughty look and proud heart*'—the lamp of the wicked is sin '. The wicked place their happiness in self-exaltation and pride of place (*cf.* 13:9 for the ' lamp ' as a symbol of prosperity), but precisely in this consists their sin. Some commentators read *nîr* ' *tillage* ' for *nēr* ' *lamp* '. **5.** ' The *plans* of the industrious (tend) *to profit*, but every one *that hasteth*, (cometh) *to want* '. The Vg and DV reading, however, supplies a better antithesis.

h XXI 6-12 Malice—**6b.** ' is vain and foolish ' : by emending *niddāp* to *rōḏēp* MT reads : ' *pursueth after* a *vapour and the* snares of death '. **7a.** ' robberies ' : ' *violence* '. **7b.** ' do judgement ' : act justly. **8.** ' *Crooked* is the way of the *vicious* man ; but *the doing of the* pure

is right '. **9b.** ' common ' : a house shared in common with her. A transposition of the Heb. letters gives the reading ' *wide* ' (*rāḥāḇ*) ; *cf.* 25:24. **11.** ' When *the scoffer* is punished the simple *becometh wise* ; when the wise *man is instructed, he gaineth* knowledge ' ; *cf.* 19:25. **12.** ' The Just *One* considereth the house of the wicked ; *he overthroweth* the wicked *to their ruin* '. God observes and punishes the actions of the wicked.

13-29 Charity and Justice—**14.** *Cf.* 17:23 ; 18:16 ; 19:6. **15a.** ' do judgement ' : act justly. **16.** ' A man that *wandereth* from the *path* of *wisdom* shall abide in the *assembly* of the *Shades* ' ; *cf.* 2:18 ; 5:5 ; 7:27. Most commentators understand the verse to mean that evil men die prematurely ; on the other hand, the assertion that the penalty of evil conduct is to dwell always among the dead, may imply that perpetual life in Sheol will not be the fate of the just. The Vg and DV rendering of ' giants ' is due to a mistaken reading of MT. **18.** ' The wicked man *is a ransom* for the just ; and the *faithless taketh the place of the upright* '. The chastisement of the wicked is, so to speak, the price paid for the immunity of the just. **20a.** ' to be desired ': precious. The wise man is thrifty ; the fool wasteful. **22b.** ' hath cast '. Knowledge and skill are superior to brute strength. **23b.** ' his soul ' : ' *himself* ' ; *cf.* 13:3 ; 18:21. **24.** ' The proud and arrogant *man, scoffer is his name !* He worketh *in unbridled* pride '. **25-26.** He whose desires never materialize into action ruins himself, but the just man is ceaseless in his works of charity. **27b.** ' *How much more when he bringeth it with evil intention* ', *e.g.* to save himself from the consequences of evil-doing without inner repentance ; *cf.* 15:8 ; 21:3. **28b.** MT reads : ' the man *that heareth, speaketh constantly* '. A lying witness forfeits the right to be heard, but he who speaks only after careful consideration will always be heard. Neither the text nor sense is certain. **29b.** ' correcteth ' : ' *maketh firm* '. The comparison is between firmness of conduct and hardness of face.

30-XXII 16 Divine Sovereignty—**30.** *Cf.* 1 Cor 1:19 ; 3:19. **31b.** ' safety ' ; ' victory ' or ' deliverance '. Human effort is required but the final outcome of everything depends on God. **XXII : 2.** ' have met ' : ' meet one another ', stand side by side in the present order. ' The true remedy for social inequalities is to recognize who it is that has appointed them and the obligations of mutual consideration and respect which they involve ' (Perowne) ; *cf.* 29:13. **3.** ' The prudent man *forseeth danger* and *hideth* himself : the simple *go on* and *pay the penalty* ' ; *cf.* 27:12. **4a.** ' is ' : ' *and* '. Worship of God in true humility will win the divine blessing. **5.** ' *Thorns and snares are on the path of the wicked* ; he that *watcheth over himself* departeth far from them ' ; *cf.* 16:17. **6a.** MT reads : ' *Train up a child* according to his way ', in the way he is to go. The child is father to the man. **8b.** A slight alteration of MT gives ' and the produce of his tillage (*šeḇer 'aḇōḏāṯô*) shall fail '. **9.** *Cf.* 14:21 ; 19:17. The additional couplet is from LXX. **11.** ' *The Lord* loveth cleanness of heart : grace of lips *pleaseth* the king ' (LXX). Purity of heart pleases God ; graciousness in speech, earthly monarchs. **12.** God, who sees all, protects ' knowledge ', *i.e.* the wise man, and brings to nought the subterfuges of the wicked. **13.** Humorous sarcasm to show how the indolent exaggerate difficulties ; *cf.* 26:13. **14.** The seductive mouth of the adulteress is like a deep pit dug by the hunter for his prey. **15a.** ' bound up ' : folly is part and parcel of his life. The discipline of the rod is the best remedy ; *cf.* 13:24 ; 19:18 ; 23:13 ; 29:15. **16.** Perhaps the best reading is : ' He that oppresseth the poor (only) *enricheth him* ; he that giveth *to* the rich *doeth it* (only) *to his want* '. Evil done to the poor does not profit the oppressor, but rather, by the disposition of divine Providence, the poor themselves.

XXII 17-XXIV 22 Section 3 The Sayings of the Wise—This section is marked off from Part II

2a by the introduction (17–21), its hortatory tone, and by the strophic arrangement (usually four lines to a strophe) instead of couplets. The first half of the quatrain generally contains a prohibition, for which the second half gives the reason. This collection contains several striking similarities with the Teaching of Amenophis (*cf.* §316*e*).

b **17-21 Introduction**—The unknown author speaks to the reader as to a son, after the fashion of chh 1–7, exhorting him to study the maxims and to make them his spiritual possession. Through them he will acquire trust in God and an adequate answer for all who question him. MT is poorly preserved. **17.** ' Apply thy heart to *knowledge* '. **18.** ' *For* it shall be *pleasant* to keep them in thy breast, *and to have them ready on thy* lips. **19.** That thy trust may be in the Lord, I have *made known* to thee this day *his ways*. **20.** Behold ! I have *written for thee thirty sayings, wherein are counsels* and knowledge. **21.** *To make thee know the truth, sincere words, that thou mayest answer him that questioneth thee*'. **20.** ' three ' : ' *thirty* ', the number of maxims contained in this collection. The Heb. *šālîšîm* should be *šᵉlōšîm*.

c **22-29 22*b*.** in the gate : at the city entrance, where the court of law was held (Deut 21:19). **23*b*.** ' and will *despoil of life* them that *despoil them* '. **25*b*.** ' *and get a snare* to thy *life* '. **26*a*.** ' fasten down ' : ' *strike* '; *cf.* 6:1 note. **27*b*.** Omit ' what cause is there ' and read ' *they will take away thy bed from under thee* '. The usual warning against suretyship ; the creditors, in compensation, will seize even necessary furniture. **28*a*.** ' bounds ' : ' *landmark* ' designating the limits of one's property. The land of the poor was often encroached upon by the powerful ; *cf.* Deut 19:14 ; 27:17. **29*a*.** ' swift ' : ' *deft* ' or ' *diligent* '.

d **XXIII 1-3 At Table**—This saying inculcates respect and circumspection when dining with the great. **2*a*.** ' put a knife to thy throat ' : probably a proverbial expression of self-restraint. **2*b*.** ' *if thou be a man of keen appetite* '. **3*a*.** ' meats ' : ' *dainties* '. **3*b*.** His hospitality may be only to cloak some ulterior purpose.

e **4-5 Against Anxiety for Wealth**—**4*b*.** ' *desist* from thy *wisdom* ', from such a thought. **5.** Read with correction of MT ' *When thou settest thine eyes upon it* [wealth], *it is gone ; for it maketh itself* wings like an eagle that flieth towards heaven'. Riches can vanish in a moment.

f **6-8 The Niggardly Host**—**6*a*.** ' envious ' : ' *avaricious* ' or ' *grudging* '. **7*a*.** Lit. ' *As he thinketh within himself, so is he* ', an obscure line which may, perhaps, be emended to ' *He thinketh only of himself* '. **8*b*.** ' and thou shalt *waste thy goodly words* '. The feast will be a failure. The food will nauseate and any attempt at agreeable conversation will be thrown away.

g **9 The Fool. 10-11 The Land of the Poor**—**10*a*.** ' *Remove not the landmark of the widow* '; *cf.* 22:28. **11*a*.** ' near kinsman ' : lit. ' *redeemer* ', *i.e.* the next of kin who was bound by law to redeem his kinsman's land ; *cf.* Lev 25:25. Here it is God himself who will protect the widow and the orphan.

h **12-14 Training of Children**—**13*b*.** Death here is the consequence of the sin, into which the pampered child will fall, rather than the effect of corporal punishment. This view is borne out by the next verse. **14*b*.** ' hell ' : ' *Sheol* '.

i **15-18 Reward of the God-Fearing**—**16.** The heart and the kidneys were regarded as the seats of intellectual and emotional life. **18.** ' *If thou keepest it* [fear of the Lord], *it shall be well with thee* in the end, and thy *hope shall not fail* ' (LXX): thy last days shall be blessed ; *cf.* 24:14.

j **19-21 Warning against Drunkenness and Gluttony**—**20-21.** ' Be not *thou among wine-bibbers, among gluttonous eaters* of flesh, *for the drunkard and the glutton shall come to poverty*, and drowsiness *shall clothe a man* in rags '. ' drowsiness ' : the torpor occasioned by excessive eating and drinking.

22-25 Value of Parental Instruction.

k **26-28 Warning against the Harlot**—**26.** The sage identifies himself with Wisdom (*cf.* chh 1–9). **27.** *Cf.*

22:14. **28*b*.** ' and *increaseth the faithless among men* '. She seduces men to betray the faith pledged to their consorts and to God ; *cf.* 2:17.

29-35 Against Intemperance—**29*a*.** ' Who *crieth* **l** ' woe ' ? *who* ' alas ' ? who hath contentions ? who *complains* ' ? **30*b*.** ' *and go to test mixed wine* ', mixed with spices. **31*a*.** ' yellow ' : ' ruddy '; **31*b*.** ' when it *giveth its eye* [gleameth] in the *cup* '. **31*c*** should be transferred to 32. **32*b*.** ' basilisk ' : a fabulous creature. The species of snake meant is unknown ; one common rendering is ' *adder* '. **33-34.** The physiological effects of drunkenness. **33*a*.** ' women ' : ' *things* '. **33*b*.** ' perverse ' : distorted. A reference to the distorted fancies and irresponsible speech of the drunkard. **34** is difficult. ' Thou shalt be as one *that lieth down at sea, as one that sleepeth upon the top of a mast* (?) ' ; the ground will seem to rise and fall as though he were on board ship or at the mast-head in a rough sea. **34*b*** is translated by LXX : ' as a pilot *in a violent storm* '. **35.** The half-stupid utterances of returning consciousness. The drunkard's first thought is to get back to his debauch. **35*b*.** ' they drew ' : ' they *have smitten* '.

XXIV 1-6 Diverse Utterances—**1*a*.** ' Seek not ' : **m** ' *Do not envy* '. **2*a*.** ' robberies ' : ' *violence* '; *cf.* 3:31 ; 23:17. **3-4.** Practical utility of Wisdom. The reference is to the literal building and furnishing of the home. **5-6.** Value of Wisdom in military strategy. **5.** ' A wise man is *better than a warrior*, and a man *of knowledge than he that hath strength* ' (Toy). **6.** ' For war is managed by *wise guidance*, and *victory lieth in counsellors* '. *Cf.* 11:14 ; 20:18.

7-10 contain couplets in the style of the ' Proverbs of **n** Solomon '. **7*a*.** ' Wisdom is *corals* to a fool '. Vg gives the best sense possible of an obscure line. **7*b*.** ' in the gate ' : in the place of public deliberation the fool will have no authority. **8*b*.** ' *Men call him a master of* (evil) *plans* '. **9*a*.** Sin is the aim and object of the fool's planning. **9*b*.** ' detractor ' : ' *scoffer* ' at religion and morality. **10.** MT is incomplete. ' *If thou art slack in the day of prosperity* (?), *in the day of adversity thy strength shall be little* '.

11-22 Duties towards One's Neighbour—**11-12** deal **o** with the same subject. **11*b*.** ' drawn to death ' : ' *tottering to the slaughter* '. **12.** ' If thou sayest ' *Behold I knew not this* ' (reading *yāḏaʿtî* for *yāḏaʿnû*), he that *weigheth hearts, doth he not take note ? He that observeth thy life, doth he not know ? And shall he not render to every man according to his work ? *' He who is able to prevent another's death and, on a weak pretext, fails to do so, will be held guilty by divine justice. **13-14.** Wisdom (virtue) is to the soul what honey is to the ' *palate* '. **14*b*.** ' If thou *findest it, it shall be well with thee in the future* ', etc. ; *cf.* 23:18 note. **15-16.** A warning against violence to the just. **15.** ' Lie not in wait, *O wicked man*, for the house of the just, *and lay not waste his dwelling-place* '. **16*a*.** ' seven ' is a round number ; *cf.* Lk 17:4 ; Mt 18:21. The just man, no matter how often he is struck down by misfortune, will, with God's help, rise again, but the wicked ' *are made to stumble* ', succumb to calamity. **17-18.** To rejoice in the misfortune of enemies displeases God ; perhaps his anger will turn from thy neighbour to thee. **19-20.** The wicked are not to be envied. **19.** ' *Be not wrathful over the wicked, and envy not the ungodly* '. **20*a*.** The prosperity of the wicked will not last. **20*b*.** *Cf.* 13:9, note. **21-22.** Disobedience to authority is dangerous. **21*b*.** ' detractors ', lit. ' *those who change* ', *i.e.* the factious. **22*b*.** ' the ruin of both ', inflicted by God and king.

XXIV 23-34 Section 4 Further Sayings of the Wise 373a Men—This small, independent collection of proverbs, forms a second appendix to the first collection of the Proverbs of Solomon (10:1–22:16).

23*a*. ' *These also are the sayings of the wise men* '. **23*b*-25.** Partiality in judicial decisions invokes the curse of God and man ; justice brings rich blessing ; *cf.* 17:15 ; 28:21. **25*b*.** ' a blessing ' : MT adds ' rich '. **26.** Straightforward speech is a mark of true friendship. The kissing of lips is nowhere else mentioned in the OT.

373a 27. An exhortation to get the land well in order and have a definite source of income before setting up a home and family. **27c.** ' that ' : ' then '. **29.** Cf. Mt 7:12. **30-34.** The sluggard's vineyard. **32b.** ' I *saw and I learned a lesson* '. **33-34.** Cf. 6:10-11.

b XXV-XXIX. Section 5 Proverbs of Solomon. Second Series (cf. § 364e)—**1.** The title informs us that, in addition to the proverbs of 10:1-22:16, other collections of Solomon's sayings were in existence, probably in written form, and that these were edited by scribes of the court of Ezechias, king of Judah (721-693).

c 2-7 On Kings—**2a** ' the word ' : ' *a thing* '. **2b.** ' the speech ' : ' *a thing* ' or ' *a matter* '. The inscrutability of God's designs in the government of the world (cf. Rom 11:33 f. ; 1 Tim 6:16) is both a proof and the glory of his transcendental Sovereignty over creation. Earthly rulers ought not to decide affairs without examination and discussion. **3.** At times, however, in the purposes of kings, there must necessarily be an element of secrecy. **4-5** form a comparison. **4a.** ' rust ' : ' *dross* '. **5a.** ' wickedness ' : ' *the wicked* '. As silver must be freed from dross, so the ruler from evil counsellors. **6-7** also form one quatrain. **6a.** ' Appear not glorious ' : do not put on airs. **7b.** ' be humbled ' : be put lower (at table) ; cf. Lk 14:8-11.

d 8-15 The Contentious Spirit—**8b.** ' *for what wilt thou do hereafter when thy neighbour putteth thee to shame ?* ' The forced withdrawal of a rash charge will only fill one with confusion. **9a.** ' friend ' : ' *neighbour* '. **10.** ' *Lest he that heareth, reproach thee, and thine ill-repute pass not away* ' ; i.e. ' Do not talk about your neighbour's affairs lest you become known as a gossip '. The second couplet is from LXX. **11-12** : a quatrain on the value of wise advice. MT is obscure ; a probable rendering is : ' *Golden fruit on silver platters is a word fitly spoken*. A golden earring and a *necklace of gold, is a wise reprover* to an obedient ear '. An emendation of the Heb. word for ' time ' ($b^e y \hat{o}m$ to $b^e h \hat{o}m$) gives the reading ' heat '. **13b.** ' *for* ', etc., is a gloss. **14.** The original is more forceful. ' Clouds and wind and no rain—so is the man that boasteth *of a false gift* ', one he does not give. The rising wind and gathering clouds unaccompanied by rain are an apt symbol of empty promises. **15b.** ' hardness ' : ' *the bone* '. Forbearance and mildness overcome the greatest obstacles.

e 16-28 Moderation—**16a.** ' *If thou findest* honey '. Self-control is recommended even in pleasant things. **17a.** ' *Let thy foot be seldom in* '. **18b.** ' dart ' : ' *hammer* '. **19b.** ' weary ' : read $m \hat{o}^c a \underline{d} e \underline{t}$ ' *tottering* '. One cannot rely on a bad tooth or a tottering foot ; nor can a disloyal friend be trusted in time of trouble. **20** should begin with ' Vinegar '. The preceding line is probably due to the mistake of a scribe who inadvertently copied the Heb. consonants of 19b twice over. ' As vinegar on a wound, so is *the singing of* songs to a *troubled* heart ' (LXX) ; both give an added pang. **22.** A quatrain on kindness to enemies. **22a.** ' *coals of fire* ' : the burning pangs of shame which may lead to repentance and charity ; cf. Rom 12:20. **23.** ' The north wind *bringeth* rain, and the backbiting tongue an *angry* countenance ', to the right-minded hearer. **24.** Cf. 21:9. **25.** Cf. 15:30. **26.** ' falling down ' : ' *wavering* ' in the practice of virtue out of human respect. ' troubled ' : ' *trampled* '. His weakness of character ruins his other good qualities. **27b.** MT reads ' *and the investigation of their glory is glory* '. Vaccari suggests ' It is not good to eat much honey, *and to search into* majesty *is no* glory ' ; too much curiosity about the divine Majesty brings neither glory nor profit to man. **28.** ' A *breached* city *without a* wall—such is a man *without self-control* '. He is easily conquered by his passions.

f XXVI 1-12 The Fool—**1b.** ' glory ' : ' *honour* ', high position. **2.** ' *Like the sparrow in its flitting, like the swallow in its flying, so a curse that is groundless : it cometh* [striketh] *not* '. A protest against the popular

superstition that gave magical power to a curse. **37** **4-5.** Do not descend to the level of a fool unless it be to make him conscious of his folly. **6b.** ' *cutteth off* (his own) feet, drinketh *violence* '. An incompetent envoy is harmful to the sender. **7a.** The verb is not clear. A probable reading is : ' The legs *of the* lame *hang loose* ; so *doth a proverb* in the mouth of fools '. A fool can make no better use of a wise saying than a lame man of his limbs. **8.** The least improbable translation of MT is : ' As *one that bindeth* a stone *in a sling*, so is he that giveth honour to a fool '. In each case the act is absurd, for a sling is meant to discharge stones, not to hold them. In Vg the reference is to a casting of stones on the cairns sacred to Mercury and the comparison is with the folly of pagan superstitions. **9.** Obscure. ' A thorn*stick that cometh into* the hand of a drunkard, so is a *proverb* in the mouth of fools '. A wise saying may be misused. **10** is perhaps the most obscure and difficult in the book. The following translation seems preferable : ' *As an archer that woundeth every passer-by, so is he that hireth a fool and a drunkard* ' (Bickell) ; i.e. both acts are foolish. Vaccari renders : ' *The litigant setteth everything in motion ; he hireth the foolish and the passer-by* '. **11.** Cf. 2 Pet 2:22. **12.** Presumption and self-conceit are worse than ignorance.

13-16 The Sluggard—**13.** Cf. 22:13. **14.** ' Move- **g** ment, without progress '. **15.** Cf. 19:24. **16b.** ' that speak sentences ' : ' that (know how to) *answer discreetly* '. Ignorance, the daughter of slothfulness, is the mother of presumption.

17-22 The Busybody—**17.** ' He taketh a dog by the **h** ears (LXX : ' *tail* ') who meddleth with a quarrel *not his own* '. Both acts invite trouble. **18-19.** ' As a *madman* that *casteth* brands and arrows, so is he that *deceiveth* his *neighbour*, and saith : ' I did it in jest ! ' A condemnation of malicious cleverness. **20b.** ' and *where there is no talebearer* ', etc. **21b.** ' coals ' : ' *bellows* ' (LXX). **21b.** ' so a *quarrelsome* man to *inflame* strife '. **22a.** ' simple ' : ' *dainty morsels* ' ; cf. 18:8. **23-28 The Hypocrite**—**23.** ' Swelling ' : read with **i** LXX $h^a l \bar{a} q \hat{i} m$ ' *smooth* ' or ' *flattering* ' for $d \bar{o} l^e q \hat{i} m$. A fair exterior hides the inner falseness of the flatterer. **24a.** ' *He that hateth, dissembleth* with his lips, but in his heart he *layeth up* deceit. **25a.** ' When he *maketh gracious his voice* '. **25b.** ' seven ' : cf. 24:16, note. **26.** Though one may with guile conceal his hatred for another, sooner or later it will be made public, perhaps in a judicial assembly. **27.** Mischief recoils on the perpetrator. **28a.** ' loveth not truth ' : ' *hateth the oppressed* ', a corrupt text. Read perhaps *yasgî*, ' *multiplieth the oppressed* ' (Zorell).

XXVII 1-22 A Collection of Aphorisms on Various **37** **Subjects**—**1-2.** On boasting. **1a.** ' for ' : ' *of* ' : cf. Jas 4:13 f. **3b.** Some suggest that ' anger ' is an addition ; it is the fool himself who is a burden ; cf. Ecclus 22:18. **4.** ' *Wrath is ruthless, anger a torrent ; but before jealousy who can stand ?* ' It is the most tenacious and terrible of the passions : cf. 6:34. **5-6.** Salutary rebuke. **5a.** ' *love that conceals* ' : that fears to rebuke. **6.** ' *Faithful* [well meant] are the wounds of *him that loveth*, deceitful the kisses *of him that hateth* '. **7.** Hunger is the best sauce. ' *He that is full trampleth upon* [rejecteth] the honeycomb ; *but to the hungry every* bitter thing *is* sweet '. Cf. Horace, Sat. II, 2, 38. **8.** There is no place like home. **9b.** MT is untranslatable ; Vg, by inversion, has an appropriate parallel. **10.** Hold fast to old friendships. In the day of trouble a tried friend of the family, if he be near at hand, is of more worth than a kinsman who dwells far off. **11b.** ' that *I may* answer him that reproacheth *me* '. The good conduct of the pupil will be the best proof of the character of the master's teaching. **12.** Cf. 22:3. **13.** A repetition of 20:16. **14a.** ' in the night ' : ' *morning* '. **14b.** ' *it shall be reckoned a curse* to him ', the neighbour. Excessive demonstrations of affection are suspect. **15.** Cf. 19:13. **16.** MT is corrupt ; ' *The north wind is a severe wind, but by its name is termed auspicious* ' (LXX). Vg connects the verse with the

4a preceding, but 16b should be read : ' and whose right hand *encountereth* oil ' ; it is as difficult to restrain a contentious woman as to restrain the winds or grasp oil. **17b.** ' countenance ' : the person. Social intercourse sharpens the wits. ' Confeience maketh a ready man '. **18b.** ' *honoured* '. Duty well done brings its own reward. **19.** MT runs : ' As (*in*) water *face* (*answereth*) *to face*, so the heart of man *to man* '. As the face seen in water resembles the face of which it is a reflection, so do the hearts of men resemble one another in the essential features of their common nature. ' As water ', however, is probably a mistaken translation of the Heb. *kᵉmô* = ' as ' ; hence the original text would read ' *As face to face, so the heart of man to man* ' ; as human countenances show differences, so too, there is diversity in the inner, moral being of men. **20a.** ' *Sheol and Abaddon* are never filled '. *Abaddon* : *cf.* 15:11, note. The desires of men are as insatiable as Sheol. **21.** Praise tests a man's virtue as fire tests metal. The second couplet is from LXX. **22b.** ' sodden barley ' : ' *grain* ', but the clause reads like a gloss and should be omitted. The proverb states graphically that the fool's folly is his nature.

b 23-28 Care of the Flock—23a. ' countenance ' : ' *state* ' or ' *appearance* '. **24a.** ' power ' : ' *riches* '. **24b.** For *wᵉ'im nēzer* (' and doth a crown ? ') read ' *wᵉ'ên 'ôṣār*, *nor wealth from generation to generation* '. The continual effort of the farmer is necessary against the day of want. **25.** ' *When the hay is removed, the tender grass* (of the second crop) *appeareth, and the herbs* of the mountains [the upland pastures which are mown later] *are* gathered *in* '. **26b.** The sale of flocks will purchase more land. **27a.** ' *There shall be* goat's milk enough ', etc.

c XXVIII 1-XXIX 1—1. The courage of a good conscience ; *cf.* Hamlet : ' Conscience doth make cowards of us all '. **2.** The text is uncertain. ' For the *transgressions* of a land *its* tyrants are many ; *but by a* man of intelligence *and insight right order is prolonged* ' (Vaccari). **3.** ' A *wicked* man [or ' *ruler* '] that oppresseth the poor is a *beating rain—and no bread* ' (LXX) ; he is like a rain which takes away man's food by flattening the grain and washing the seed out of the earth. **4a.** ' that forsake the law ', divine or moral. **5.** ' Evil men *do not understand justice*, but they that seek the Lord *understand all* '. Vice destroys the moral sense in man ; but the sincerely religious man has a mind exquisitely attuned to the perception of all things, *cf.* 1 Cor 2:14 f. **6a.** ' in his simplicity ' : ' *uprightly* '. **6b.** ' than *one perverse in his ways. though he be* rich ' ; *cf.* 19:1. **7b.** ' he that *consorteth with profligates* '. **8a.** ' loan ' : ' *interest* '. Money wrongfully acquired (*cf.* Ex 22:25 ; Deut 23:19 f.) will finally fall into the hand of the charitable man ; *cf.* 13:22. **9.** Prayer made with an obstinate affection for sin is an insult to God. **10a.** ' deceiveth ' : ' *causeth to go astray* '. ' destruction ' : ' *pit* '. **11.** The ability to amass wealth is no sure sign of wisdom ; a poor man who has discernment is able to see through the rich. **12.** ' *When* the just *triumph*, there is great glory ; when the wicked *rise*, men *hide themselves* ' [lit. ' must be searched for ']. When evil men are in power, the people suffer. **13.** *Cf.* Ps 31 (32) 5 f. **16a.** ' A prince that is void of *understanding multiplieth extortions* '. **17.** ' A man *oppressed by* [laden with] blood *guilt runneth* to the grave ; no one succoureth him '. There is no sympathy for a murderer. **20.** ' A *trustworthy* man shall be *richly blessed* ; but he that hasteneth to enrich himself shall not *go unpunished* '. A commendation of honest dealing. **21.** ' To have respect of persons *is not good*—for a morsel of bread a man *sinneth* ! ' To pervert justice by showing partiality in the law-court is a grave sin ; yet how many are tempted even by a small bribe ! **22.** ' An *avaricious* man [lit. ' a man of evil eye ', *i.e.* selfseeking] hasteneth to be rich, and *knoweth* not that *want shall come upon* him '. **24.** He who steals from his parents is ready for any crime. **25.** ' A *greedy* man stirreth up quarrels ; he that trusteth in the Lord shall be *made fat* '. A man of grasping

disposition rouses antagonism, but he who trusts in **374c** God and not in riches will prosper. **26.** ' He that trusteth in himself is entrusted to a great fool ' (St Augustine). **27b.** ' *He that hideth his eyes* ,' who takes no notice. **XXIX:1.** ' *He that being often reproved hardeneth his neck* (like an obstinate ox), *shall suddenly be destroyed, and that without remedy* '.

XXIX 2-14 Good Government—2a. ' increase ' : a **d** slight emendation of the Heb. word *birḥôt* to *birḏôt* gives ' are in authority ', a change demanded by the parallel in 2b. **3b.** ' maintaineth ' : ' *consorteth with* ' ; *cf.* the prodigal son (Lk 15:30). **4b.** ' covetous ' : lit. ' a man of contributions ', whose exactions are excessive. **5.** ' A man *that flattereth his neighbour* spreadeth a net for his *steps* '. **6.** ' *In the path of* the wicked man is a snare, but the just shall *sing* and rejoice '. The path of the wicked seems enviable, but, in reality, it leads to perdition. **7b.** ' is void of knowledge ' : does not bother to look into the case. **8a.** ' *Scoffers* [at moral obligations] set a city on fire ', by fanning the passions of men. Prudent men, on the other hand, bring calm. **9b.** There is no coming to an understanding with a fool, either by severity or by banter. **10b.** ' soul ' : ' life ', *i.e.* the just seek his well-being. **11.** ' A fool uttereth all his *anger*, but a wise man *stilleth it in the end* '. **12.** If a ruler listens to falsehood, the entire court becomes corrupt. **13.** ' The poor and the *oppressor meet together* [*e.g.* in the market-place], and the Lord *giveth light to the eyes of both* '. Although it takes all sorts to make up a world, it is God, who gives to all the ' light ' of life and keeps them in existence ; *cf.* 22:2.

15-21 Education—15. *Cf.* 10:1 ; 13:24 ; 17:21 ; **e** 19:18 ; 22:15 ; 23:13. **17a.** ' refresh ' : ' *give rest* ' from anxiety. **18a.** Without divine ' revelation ' the bonds which hold society together are relaxed and broken. The salvation of a people and the individual stands in the observance of a divinely given law. **19.** The servant, like the son, must be corrected by the rod. **20.** ' *Seest* thou a man hasty *in his words* ? There is more hope for a fool than for him '. **21b.** MT is uncertain, the last word never occurring elsewhere. The Vg reading makes good sense.

22-27 Mildness and Humility—22a. ' passionate ' : **f** ' *irascible* '. **22b.** prone to : ' *abounding in* '. **23b.** ' but he who is humble of spirit *shall obtain honour* ', *cf.* 16:18. **24a.** ' *hateth himself* ', by incurring the guilt and penalty of a thief. **24b.** As a partner in crime he is like one who, having been put on oath in a law-court to reveal what he knows, conceals the perpetrator of a crime (Lev 5:1). **25a.** ' *The fear of man layeth a snare* ', *i.e.* by yielding to human respect one may easily be led to do something wrong, or to refrain from doing what is right. **25b.** ' on high ' : in a safe place. **26.** It is the favour of God and not of men that one must seek, for the destiny of men depends on God alone. **27.** MT is more trenchant : ' The *abomination of* the just is the wicked man ; and the *abomination of* the wicked *is he of upright* way '.

XXX 1-14 Section 6 The Sayings of Agur—A short **375 a** collection of miscellaneous proverbs. **1** is enigmatic. **1a** constitutes a title ; **1b** is to be joined with 2-4. **1a.** ' *The sayings of Agur, the son of Jakeh, the Massaïte* '. DV gives the signification of the names, ' Gatherer ' and ' Vomiter ', not the names themselves. *Agur*, like Lemuel with whom he is to be ethnologically connected (31:1), came from Massa (if, as is probable, *maśśā'* is a place name), a region in Transjordan originally inhabited by the Ishmaelites (Gen 25:14). In the course of time, however, Israelite families must have settled there, bringing with them their religion, for Agur is a worshipper of Yahweh (30:9) and both he and Lemuel have merited a place among the inspired writers. *Maśśā'*, however, could also be read as a noun signifying ' oracle ' (*cf.* Is 13:1 ; Nah 1:1). The more commonly accepted reading of 1b is : ' *The inspired utterance of that man :* " *I have wearied myself, O God. I have wearied myself, and I am faint* " '.

375a **2-4.** The divine nature and its attributes transcend human intelligence. A proof of this is to be found in the marvels of creation (*cf.* Job 38:4-11). **2a.** ' For I am *more brutish* [stupid] *than* men (in general) '. **3b.** ' saints ' : ' *of holy things* ' or ' *of the Holy One* ' ; *cf.* 9:10, note. **4c.** ' as in a garment ' : *i.e.* in the clouds. **4d.** ' raised up ' : ' *fixed* '. **4e.** To know a man's name or his son's name, is to be well acquainted with him. The meaning of the verse is that no man is responsible for the magnificence of the universe but God, who is beyond the feebleness of human comprehension. **5.** Revealed doctrine is true and trustworthy like metal that has passed through the refining pot, *cf.* Ps 11 (12) 7 ; like a shield it wards off error. **6.** Do not give out your own thoughts as divine revelation ; *cf.* Deut 4:2 ; Apoc 22:18. **7-9.** A prayer to be kept from insincerity and from the evils of excessive wealth and poverty. **8a.** ' vanity ' : ' *falsehood* ' on account of the parallel. **9b.** ' forswear ' : blaspheme or charge God foolishly. **10a.** ' Accuse ' : ' *Defame* '. **10b.** ' and thou *pay the penalty* '. **11-14.** Four odious types : despisers of parents, self-righteous, proud, and extortionate. **13.** ' Men of haughty looks and supercilious bearing ' (Toy). **14b.** Lit. ' and their jaw-teeth *as knives* '.

b **XXX 15-33 Section 7 Numerical Sayings**—The fact that in LXX these verses stand after 24:34, indicates that they once formed a separate collection. MT is poorly preserved.

c **15-16.** Four insatiable things. Sheol (*cf.* 1:2 ; 2:18 ; 27:20), the barren womb, earth, and fire. **15a** is probably corrupt, and may be a gloss. In view of what follows, the original thought seems to have been that the leech is never sated with blood. **15b.** ' three . . . fourth ' : a rhetorical figure. **16a.** ' *the closing* of the womb '. The reference is to the desire of a childless wife for children. **17.** Punishment of filial disobedience. **17a.** ' labour ' : ' *old age* ' (LXX). ' in bearing him ' : omit.

d **18-20.** Four wondrous things. **18b.** ' *yea, four which I know not* '. **19d.** ' in youth ' : ' in *a young woman* ' or ' *with a maid* '. The soaring flight of a bird, the mysterious movement of a serpent, the path of a ship through the sea, the procreation and growth of a human being in the womb (*cf.* Ps 138 (139) 13-18 ; Job 10:11)—or perhaps the birth in the heart of a youth of that affection by which he is drawn to a maid—all excite admiration. In the first explanation *'almāh* means a young woman of marriageable age, presumably a virgin, who in lawful matrimony will realize the mysterious designs of Providence in the procreation of life. **20** is only loosely connected with 19 and is probably a gloss. Presumably it was thought to be an appropriate explanation of the last line of 19 where however there is no question of an immoral act ; nor is the point of 19 their tracelessness but the wonder they excite.

e **21-23.** Four unbearable things. **23a.** ' odious ' : not beloved. **23b.** ' is heir to ' : supplants.

f **24-28** Four things small but wise. **25b.** ' *summer* '. **26a.** ' *rock-badger* '. **28a.** ' *The lizard can be taken hold of with the hands, yet* ', etc.

g **29-31** Four majestic things. **29.** Lit. ' *are stately in step* ' and ' *stately in going* '. **30b.** ' *and turneth not back before anything* '. **31a.** ' cock ' : thus all the ancient versions, but some moderns suggest ' *the war-horse* ' accoutred for battle (*cf.* Job 39:19-25). **31b.** ' whom none can resist ' : MT is corrupt. Vaccari reads ' *at the head of his people* ' (*cf.* Zorell under the word *'alqûm*).

h **32-33** MT is uncertain. Perhaps : ' *If thou hast done foolishly in exalting thyself, reflect—hand to mouth* ' ; *i.e.*

learn to keep a modest silence. ' *For pressing milk* **3?** *bringeth forth curd, and pressing the* nose bringeth *forth* blood, and *pressing* wrath bringeth forth strife '. Self-glorification (*cf.* 32) only rouses wrath that ends in strife.

XXXI 1-9 Section 8 The Sayings of Lemuel—This **i** short collection consists of four quatrains containing counsels of moderation and generosity, given to the king by his mother. In terms of ardent affection (2), she warns him again impurity (3), inebriety (4-7), and urges him to befriend the helpless and judge with equity (8-9). MT is in a very poor state. **1.** Superscription. ' The *sayings* of Lemuel, king *of* **j** *Massa which* his mother *taught him* '. ' Lemuel ' : *cf.* 30:1. ' vision ' : ' *of Massa* '. **2.** ' What ' : thrice repeated, it expresses earnestness. ' beloved ' : ' son '. ' of my vows ' : given as a result of vows ; *cf.* 1 Kg 1:11. **3a.** ' substance ' : ' *virile strength* '. **3b.** ' *and thy ways* (of life) *to them that destroy kings* ', *i.e.* evil women. **4.** ' *It is not for* kings, O Lemuel, *it is not for* kings *to drink* wine, *nor for rulers to desire strong drink* '. **5a.** ' Lest they drink and forget *that which is decreed* ', the laws. **6-7.** Two proper occasions for the use of wine, bodily suffering and mental distress ; *cf.* Ps 103 (104) 15. **6a.** ' sad ' : ' *perishing* ' from hunger and want. **8a.** ' dumb ' : defend those who have no one to plead for them. **8b.** ' children that pass ' : (read *ḥōlî* for *ḥ^alôp*) ' the sons of sickness ', *i.e* all who suffer.

XXXI 10-31 Section 9 The Virtuous Wife—An **k** anonymous, alphabetical poem, the ' ABC ' of the ideal wife. **10a.** ' valiant woman ' : lit. ' woman of strength ' or ' capacity '. The best English rendering is ' a worthy wife '. **10b.** ' far above *pearls* is *her worth* '. **11b.** ' and he shall have no *lack of gain* ', *i.e.* income. Her husband confides to her the management of the household, certain that all will go well. **13a.** ' She *seeketh* wool ' for the weaving of garments. **13b.** ' counsel ' : ' *alacrity* '. **14.** From all quarters she provides maintenance for the household. **15a.** ' a prey ' : ' *food* '. **15c.** ' victuals ' : ' *tasks* '. **16b.** ' with the fruit of her hands ' : with her earnings. **18a.** ' She hath tasted ' : she perceives with relish that her commerce is profitable. **18b.** ' her lamp *goeth not out by* night ' : either she works indefatigably, or, because the lamp is the symbol of prosperity (13:9 ; 24:20), her house is prosperous even in distressing times. **19a.** ' to strong things ' : ' *to the distaff* ', but this meaning is not certain. **20.** Economy does not forbid charity. **22a.** ' clothing of tapestry ' : ' *coverlets* '. **23a.** ' honourable ' : ' *known* ', *i.e.* honoured. ' gates ' : the assembly place of the city's ' *elders* ' ; *cf.* 24:7. **24b.** ' Chanaanite ' : the word came to be synonymous with ' *trader* ' to whom she ' *gives* ' the girdles she has woven in exchange for money, etc. The Canaanites or Phoenicians were the great mercantile people of the period. **25a.** ' beauty ' : ' dignity '. **25b.** ' in the latter day ' : ' *at the future* '. Her foresight has enabled her to face the future without anxiety. **26a.** ' *with wisdom* '. **26b.** ' law of clemency ' : kindly counsel. **27.** She keeps diligent watch over the conduct of her family and domestics. **28.** Peace and harmony reign in the household ; she is appreciated and praised by husband and children. **29.** The encomium of her husband. ' Many daughters [*i.e.* women] *have done well* '. **30-31.** ' Favour ' (or ' *grace* ') and beauty are prized in a woman, but they will pass away. Of how much more value is virtue founded on the ' fear of the Lord ', *i.e.* on religion. ' Thus does Wisdom return in her last utterance to her first (1:7), and place once again the crown on the head of the godly ' (Perowne).

ECCLESIASTES

By M. LEAHY

376a Bibliography—*E. H. Plumptre, *Ecclesiastes* (CBSC), Cambridge, 1881 ; G. Gietmann, *Commentarius in Eccli. et Cant.* (CSS), Parisiis, 1890 ; *A. H. McNeile, *Introduction to Ecclesiastes*, Cambridge, 1904 ; *G. A. Barton, *Ecclesiastes* (ICC), Edinburgh, 1908 ; V. Zapletal, *Das Buch Kohelet*, Freiburg in B., 1911² ; E. Podechard, *L'Ecclésiaste*, Paris, 1912 ; *A. L. Williams, *Ecclesiastes* (CBSC), Cambridge, 1922 ; A. Allgeier, *Das Buch des Predigers oder Koheleth*, Bonn, 1925 ; E. Tobac, *Les cinq Livres de Salomon*, Bruxelles, 1926 ; *H. Odeberg, *Qohaelaeth*, Upsala, 1929 ; RB 8 (1899), 9 (1900), 31 (1934) ; Bi 2 (1921), 3 (1922) ; RA 49 (1929) ; IER 20 (1922), 64 (1944) ; JTS 23 (1921-2) ; *Miscellanea Biblica*, II, Romae, 1934 ; A. Bea, S.J., *Liber Ecclesiastae* (Romae, 1950).

b Name—The Hebrew title is *Qōhelet* which in LXX is rendered by Ἐκκλησιαστής. The Vg ' Ecclesiastes ' is but a transcription of the title in LXX. The Hebrew form is the active participle in the feminine singular of the *Qal* conjugation, from a verb *qāhal* found elsewhere only in *niph'al* and *hiph'il* and meaning ' to assemble '. The precise meaning of the form here is uncertain. The principal renderings put forward by commentators are : one who convenes an assembly ; member of an assembly ; official speaker in an assembly ; head of an assembly of wise men ; preacher ; debater ; the great collector of sayings. The feminine form may be explained either (*a*) as arising from the abstract conception of an office, *e.g.* Podestà, the Italian designation for Mayor, means literally ' power ', or (*b*) as in Arabic, denoting an individual as one who realizes in its completeness the idea expressed in the root.

c Canonicity—The canonicity of Eccles. was doubted by none of the early Fathers or ecclesiastical writers, not even by Theodore of Mopsuestia who, however, attributed to it a minor degree of inspiration. In the Jewish world a discussion arose between the disciples of Hillel and those of Shammai as to its admission into the Canon of Sacred Books. Eccles., however, was accepted as canonical at the Jewish Council of Jamnia (about A.D. 95), although echoes of the former discussion lingered on even to the time of Jerome.

d Authorship and Date—Scholars generally up to the 19th century held that Solomon was the author of the book. They argued from Jewish and Christian tradition, from their interpretation of 1:1, 12, and from the mention, especially in ch 2, of the great wisdom and opulence which the writer says he acquired. Critics today, with perhaps some exceptions, are agreed that the book is pseudepigraphal, and that the authorship of Solomon—who was for the Hebrews the ideal wise man—is a literary artifice. The Book of Wisdom is another instance, admitted by all, of this not uncommon literary device. The arguments put forward against Solomonic authorship seem convincing : (*a*) The book contains many words and constructions which elsewhere are found only in the latest parts of the Hebrew OT, and some others used elsewhere only in the Mishnah. The latter book received its present form about A.D. 230 but contains much older elements. (*b*) The social state described in the book is unlike what we know to have been the condition of the Israelites in Solomon's day. The author deplores the greed and cruel tyranny of corrupt officials and the consequent misery of the rank and file. He speaks of disorders in the state due to incompetent rulers. It is, moreover, unlikely that Solomon would have given this picture of moral and social evils the responsibility for which would in great part be his. It seems then that the writer, part of whose purpose was to point out that earthly goods are unsatisfying, chose to impersonate Solomon, since he above all others was noted for all those possessions which seem to make for happiness. The words of such a one as Solomon would enforce most effectively the teaching that material prosperity is unsatisfying. We notice that the claim to personate Solomon is more in evidence in the earlier part of the book.

376d appears in margin.

While critics are agreed that the book is post-exilic, **e** they disagree as to the precise period to which it should be ascribed. From the contents of the book we may conclude that it is earlier than Ecclesiasticus (written 190 B.C.) which seems to have been acquainted with its teaching, and that it is later than Proverbs and Job since the old doctrine of earthly retribution is definitely abandoned. It holds, therefore, a central position in the Wisdom literature and belongs to a transitional period when the currents of thought which gave rise to the Sadducees, Pharisees and Essenes were already in existence and when Jewish writers began to be acquainted with Greek philosophy. From these considerations we may fix the date somewhere towards the close of the 3rd century B.C.

Argument and Theme—When Ecclesiastes wrote, the **f** dogma of retribution in a life hereafter had not yet been definitely accepted in the Hebrew creed. Rewards and chastisements were therefore considered in terms of this life. An infinitely just God rewarded obedience to his laws by the bestowal of temporal goods, and punished disobedience by their deprivation. Interest was thus riveted on life on earth and men's ambition was a long and prosperous one. But this doctrine of earthly retribution as applied to the individual caused perplexity, for the experiences of life contradicted it. Those experiences taught Ecclesiastes that temporal goods, wisdom, pleasures, power, riches, were inadequate as a reward for the observance of the Law.

Ecclesiastes firmly believes that God created the **g** world and man (7:14, 30*a* ; 12:1), that he still orders their affairs (8:17 ; 9:1), and that being infinitely just he will reward the good and punish the wicked (3:17 ; 8:12 f. ; 11:9*b*). His problem is to reconcile with God's creative and administrative power and his retributive justice the following facts drawn from experience and observation. Man's labour is profitless and meaningless. Those things which man acquires by his labour and which—according to the received doctrine—constitute the rewards of a virtuous life are transitory and unsatisfying. Moreover, the distribution of those goods—such as they are—is sometimes made without regard to merits or demerits ; the wicked man is sometimes seen to flourish and the just man to suffer. And, what is more, man is crushed by his fellow-man ; oppression and tyranny caused by despotic officials and corrupt judges are rife in the state. And because judgement is not speedily pronounced against these evil-doers they continue in their evil ways. Belief and experience, then, are in conflict. Experience

376g points to seeming inconsistencies in the divine moral government of the universe. In the days of Ecclesiastes thinking people, no doubt, began to ask : why all the feverish activity, why the varying fortunes of individuals ? There was a tendency to abandon the effort of living a moral life, for doubts would have arisen as to the existence of a divine administration of the affairs of men. Some must have finally given way to religious and moral laxity, for the accepted doctrine lacked the efficacious sanction of the Law. The thoughts of those people would not have been unlike those expressed by St Paul : ' If (according to man) I fought with beasts at Ephesus, what doth it profit me if the dead rise not again ? ' (1 Cor 15:32).

h Ecclesiastes' problem is, then, to reconcile with the creative and administrative power of an infinitely just God the facts of human life. He declares that the reason why human endeavour seems profitless and aimless is that the circumstances and events of life form part of a divine plan which for man is unsearchable. Man cannot discover the divine purpose, and so fails to comprehend the importance of his labours in the whole scheme of God's administration and to know why the just man sometimes suffers while the wicked man prospers (cf. 3:1–8, 11 ; 7:28–30a ; 8:17 ; 11:5). Ecclesiastes furthermore declares that the received doctrine of temporal retribution finds no justification in fact (cf. 7:16 ; 8:14 ; 9:2 f.). He does not, however, deny the justice of God. On the contrary, he insists that God will intervene in judgement to redress injustice and reward righteousness (cf. 3:17 ; 8:12 f. ; 11:9b). When and how this will happen Ecclesiastes does not say. The fuller revelation of the true nature of the hereafter had yet to come, and his teaching is in consequence necessarily negative.

i Ecclesiastes is not wholly concerned with giving the facts of human life drawn from experience and observation, and with making the above-mentioned declarations. In addition, he proffers positive advice to the people of his day how best to live their lives. This advice scattered here and there, frequently repeated and often enforced by the insertion of maxims, may be summarized as having reference to man's private, social and religious life.

j **Private Life**—(i) Every man can and should find real happiness, fleeting though it be, in and through his daily labour. A discreet and temperate enjoyment of the fruits of labour is to be indulged in, for this is man's portion given to him by God and is a means of soothing the sorrows of life. A day-to-day enjoyment is counselled and man is not to trouble himself with speculations about what the future may bring by way of happiness. This advice, which connects ' eating and drinking ' with ' labour ' and speaks of the enjoyment as the gift of God, is very different from the Epicurean doctrine which makes a slothful self-indulgence the *summum bonum*. The advice of Ecclesiastes is found in 2:24 f. ; 3:12 f., 22 ; 5:17 ff. ; 7:15 ; 8:15 ; 9:7 ff. ; 11:7 ff. (ii) Gravity rather than frivolity is to be cultivated (7:3–7). (iii) Hasty anger and foolish talk are to be avoided (7:9–11). (iv) **Man** should engage in prudent enterprise (11:1–6).

k **Social Life**—(i) Companionship and a spirit of co-operation are advantageous (4:9–12). (ii) Silent submission in face of despotism and the capriciousness of rulers is best (7:30b–8:8 ; 10:4–7, 20).

l **Religious Life**—(i) Proper worship is to be practised (4:17–5:6). (ii) God is to be feared (7:19b ; 8:12). Note that the expression ' to fear God ' means generally in the OT to be pious, to recognize in practice God's claim to the homage of his creatures. Finally, Ecclesiastes urges that man be guided in all the activities of his private, social and religious life by wisdom. While wisdom from the point of view of making one happy is a vanity, yet as a guiding principle of life's activities it is to be sought after.

m **Unity**—The reader of Eccles. in its present form will notice, firstly, the lack of any systematic development of the theme, and, secondly, the presence of statements

and passages some of which apparently interrupt, and **37** others contradict, the context. The lack of logical development may be explained by the supposition that the book is in the nature of a diary written up over a period by the author. The presence of statements and passages which apparently interrupt or contradict the context has led to various explanations. Certain critics advance a theory of multiple authorship, although there is some disagreement among them as to the number of authors who contributed and as to the extent of the individual contributions. The view most common among them, however, is in its main outlines that first put forward by McNeile. It is substantially as follows. Four successive authors thus contributed :

(i) A pessimist who is responsible for the original core of the work.

(ii) A wise man—the ḥāḳām glossator—who sought to emphasize the importance of wisdom as he believed it to be unfairly depreciated. To him are assigned 4:5, 9–12 ; 6:7, 9a ; 7:2a, 5–13, 20, 30b ; 8:1 ; 9:17 f. ; 10:1–3, 8–14a, 15, 18 f. ; 12:11 f. These passages are alleged to interrupt the context.

(iii) A pious Jew—the ḥāsîd glossator—who, believing that the work was unsafe for the orthodox ' gave a religious impress to the book by adding sentences which centre round two chief thoughts : (a) the paramount duty of fearing God, and (b) the certainty of God's judgement on those who do not fear and please him ', so Oesterley and Robinson, *Introd. to the Books of the OT* (London, 1934), 212. These sentences are : 2:26 (except the last clause) ; 3:14b, 17 ; 4:17–5:6 ; 7:19b, 27b, 30a ; 8:2b, 3a, 5, 6a, 11–13 ; 11:9b ; 12:1a, 13 f. These passages are said to contradict the general argument.

(iv) An editor who is responsible for the passages in which Ecclesiastes is spoken of in the third person, viz. 1:1 f. ; 7:28 ; 12:8–10.

Many exegetes especially among Catholics maintain, **n** however, that a solution may be found within the framework of unity of authorship, although they too advance various theories. They all seem to agree in denying that the context is frequently interrupted, while admitting that the connexion of thought is often difficult to grasp. They disagree in their explanations of the apparent contradictions of context. The enumeration of the theories put forward would here serve no useful purpose. The theory which we favour is this : with the exception of the passages 1:1 f. ; 7:28 ; 12:8–14 which were probably inserted by a later inspired editor, the book is a unity and was composed by the so-called ' pessimist '. It is unnecessary to postulate the existence of the two glossators of the multiple-authorship theory, because (a) as will be seen from the commentary the passages given above under (ii), with the exception of 7:20, do not, when rightly understood, break up their context, and (b) it will be seen from a correct understanding of the argument of Ecclesiastes that the sentences given under (iii) above do not contradict the context. Ecclesiastes denies that a divine retribution of the kind taught by the traditional or received Jewish doctrine exists. But his belief in God postulates a divine retribution, for God's justice demands that he intervene in judgement. And if, as Ecclesiastes is convinced, this judgement is a certainty, it is hard to see why he should not have warned his readers to fear God.

The book of Eccles. marks a step forward in the de- **o** velopment of the doctrine of retribution ; the traditional theory of earthly rewards and punishments is weighed and found wanting, and men's minds are thereby directed away from transitory and unsatisfying goods to the expectation of more lasting and more substantial rewards. It points to the need of a fuller revelation of God's will and purpose for man. We who, though participants of that fuller revelation, are sometimes perplexed by the many anomalies and inconsistencies of life here below may well sympathize with those early Hebrews who in their sorrows and privations had no bright hope of a blissful immortality to sustain them.

a **I 1 Title**—See § 376*b*.

b **2-11 Preface**—The feverish activity of all creation, especially of man, is profitless and meaningless. Even granting that something tangible does result from all the labour of life, it is ' vanity '.—Vanity (Heb. *heḇel*) means ' a breath ' or ' a vapour ', and ' vanity of vanities ' is the Hebrew way of saying ' the merest breath '. **3.** Under the sun : in the visible universe. **4.** The earth remains unaffected by the labours of succeeding generations of inhabitants. **5.** Returneth : *panteth* to his place where he ariseth. **6.** *The wind goes to the south and circles to the north, it circles, circles on its course, and on its circuits the wind returns.* In 5-7 the writer, according to an ancient conception, views the earth as a flat disc resting on the waters of the Great Abyss, and crowned by the arched canopy of the sky. He pictures the sun as moving across the sky from east to west by day, and returning hurriedly eastwards beneath the earth by night. The wind he conceives as ever gyrating, presenting a series of endless repetitions. Finally, he represents the rivers as coming from the Great Abyss through fissures in the earth's surface and flowing into the sea, which in turn has an outlet to the Great Abyss, the source of all. **8.** All things are toiling to weariness ; no tongue can describe nor can eye or ear grasp all this wearisome toil. **9 ff.** All activity has accomplished nothing new. One may, by way of challenge, point to some new phenomenon or some new gain, but all to no purpose. It has been before in past ages. It seems new to men because former things are soon buried in oblivion. So also the future shall not be remembered by still later generations.

c **12-II 26 Lessons from Experience in the Pursuit of Wisdom and Pleasure**—Ecclesiastes speaks in the person of Solomon, who for the Hebrews was the ideal wise man and was, moreover, noted for his wealth and for his pleasure-seeking. He sets his mind (Heb. ' heart ' ; in Hebrew psychology the word ' heart ' embraces the whole mind, feelings, will, and especially the intellect) to investigate the results of human activity, being guided in his investigations by the wisdom which he has. It is God who placed in man the desire to search out everything, but it is a painful pursuit because the desire cannot be satisfied. All the works of man are vanity and *striving after wind* (DV ' vexation of spirit '). Much knowledge, sense pleasures, and worldly goods are shortlived and empty. **14.** ' Vanity ' indicates the brevity and transitory character of earthly things, while ' striving after wind ' indicates the fruitlessness of effort. **15.** *What is bent cannot be straightened, and a deficit cannot be counted as a whole.* One cannot rectify the essential positive and negative defects of created beings. This is the first of many aphorisms quoted by the writer as already current. **16 ff.** To acquire wisdom, he expends much labour, even toiling to study folly and madness (DV ' errors ') in order to grasp more clearly their opposite, *viz.* wisdom. He arrives at the conclusion that no happiness results from wisdom. We should note that in later passages the writer praises wisdom. There is no real contradiction, however, for, while denying that wisdom is a real gain in itself, Ecclesiastes recommends it as a guiding principle of life's activities.

d **II:1-11.** He tries the more material pleasures of life and finds that they likewise are vanity and a striving after wind. He gives way to merriment and indulges in the pleasures of the table. To satisfy every wish, he has new and costly palaces built, vineyards and orchards planted, and reservoirs dug. He surrounds himself with a retinue of servants ; raises fine herds and flocks ; gets tribute from subject kings ; amasses great wealth ; employs the best musicians ; keeps in his harem many concubines. When, however, he turns to contemplate his delights and the toil they cost him, he finds nothing solid, nothing by way of profit. **2.** *I said of laughter, it is mad : and of mirth, what does it do ?* (*i.e.* what use is it). **3.** *I sought in my heart to pamper my flesh with wine, and, while guiding my heart with*

wisdom, to lay hold on folly till I could see what was good for **377d** the children of men to do*, etc. Folly is practised not for its own sake but under the guidance of wisdom in order to learn its value from experience. **7a.** *And had home-born slaves* (DV ' a great family ') : there were two classes of slaves, *viz.* those born and reared in the master's house, and those bought or taken captive in war. **8.** The words rendered ' cups and vessels ', etc. in DV are obscure and probably indicate concubines. The DV (following Vg) derives the two words of the Hebrew text from the Aramaic root *šᵉḏā* ' to pour out '. **12-17.** Ecclesiastes pauses here to compare wisdom and folly on their practical side. Wisdom has a superiority over folly, because it is a light which enables man to see not only the vanity of folly but also the insufficiency of wisdom itself. Yet what use is this when the same fate, *viz.* death and oblivion, overtakes both the wise man and the fool ? Life with its toils seems to no purpose. **12b** is out of place and should follow 18 below. **14b.** *And I learned that one fate befalls them all.* **15b.** *And why was I then over-wise ?* (DV ' what doth it avail me ', etc.). **18, 12b, 19 ff.** Ecclesiastes recounts another reason why he hates his labours. There is no guarantee that improvements made by a wise man will last, since his successor is likely to act like previous less wise rulers. From the thought expressed in 16, *viz.* that because the wise man must die his toil is vain, Ecclesiastes goes on to say that even the good he has done may not last but be undone by his successor. This shows the vanity of labour. **12b.** *For what will the man do who comes after the king ? what they have done formerly* (*i.e.* that which men have done before). **19.** At death the fruits of his toil will pass to an heir who has not laboured for them, and who, moreover, may be a fool and riotously squander them. **20.** *Therefore I abandoned my heart to despair for all* **e** *the labours in which I had toiled under the sun.* He looks back despairingly at the absence of any satisfying gain from his labours. **24-26.** Practical advice (see § 376*j*). Enjoyment, fleeting and incapable of satisfying all man's desires though it be, may be experienced both in labour itself and in the fruits of labour. This present enjoyment men should take, for it is God's gift to man. The writer connects ' eating and drinking ' with ' labour ', and speaks of enjoyment as the gift of God. His advice is thereby far removed from that of epicureans, for whom a slothful self-indulgence is the *summum bonum*. We are not, however, to expect from Ecclesiastes the perfect morality of the New Dispensation. **25.** Who can eat or have delight *apart from him* ? (DV ' as I '). This reading is that of LXX, Syr. and Jer. **26.** There is no reference here to the old Jewish doctrine of temporal retribution. It is simply the general law of God's giving that the morally good man is enriched still more with God's gifts of wisdom, knowledge and peace of mind. The sinner, on the contrary, loses God's favours, and is frequently given worldly cares the fruit of which will eventually be inherited by the good man. This (*viz.* the labour of the sinner) also is vanity and *a striving after wind* (DV ' a fruitless solicitude of mind ').

III 1-17 The Divine Plan and Man's Inability to **f** **comprehend it**—The circumstances and events of life form part of a divine plan, but since this plan is for man inscrutable he rarely orders his life in conformity with its ordinances. Each event is appropriate in its season (DV ' good in its time ' **11a**), but man cannot be sure that he has found the right season, ignorant as he is of the divine purpose. Moreover God has placed in man's heart the desire to grasp as one whole the successive and varying events of life (DV ' the world ' ; Heb. *'ōlām*) which form part of God's plan. Man, however, can see them only according as they appear, and hence disjointed and unconnected. The only course is to follow the practical advice given above in 2:24-26. The works of God are permanent (in the sense that each obeys fixed laws) and complete. God made them so, that man, contemplating the immutable ordinances of the Governor of the universe, should

377f reverence him. And, a further point, there are corruptions in civil administration and men thereby suffer. But God, in his own good time, will right all wrongs, for he has fixed a time for every concern and for every work. **12.** The words ' to do well ' have not the ethical sense that they have in 7:21. They are to be understood rather as a synonym of rejoicing, *i.e. to do oneself well* ; we find a similar use of *ṭôḇ*, ' good ', in the same context in the following verse and elsewhere. **14.** Man cannot alter the arrangements of Divine Providence with reference to human actions (*cf.* 3:1-8). **15.** God's works are of an everlasting sameness. **17b.** *for he has fixed* (reading *šām* for *šăm* which means ' there ') *a time for every concern and for every work.*

378a **18-23 Man compared with the Beasts**—God wishes to convince man of his insignificance. Human observation shows that man is similar to the beast. What happens to man happens likewise to the beast, each dies. Man and beast have one spirit. At death the bodies of both man and beast return to dust. What of the spirit after death ? **21.** Who knows whether man's spirit goes up and the beast's spirit goes down ? The writer sees that there is another view but does not accept it. This statement is sometimes taken to be a denial of the spirituality and immortality of the human soul. Many commentators explain it as follows. Man, according to the Semitic notion, was composed of three elements (trichotomy), body, soul, and breath of life (Heb. *bāśār, nepeš,* and *rûaḥ*). In the statement under consideration there is question not of the soul but rather of the breath of life. Against this view, however, there seems to be no clear evidence in the Bible for the existence of a trichotomy. There is no real distinction between soul and breath of life. The two words are interchanged in the same passage, correspond to each other in parallel passages, and receive the same attributes. Hence both words indicate one and the same soul as opposed to the body (*cf.* Prat, *St Paul,* 1913⁴, II 73-9). The words themselves differ not really but conceptually, the word *rûaḥ* being used to emphasize the immaterial, spiritual aspect of the soul, while *nepeš* is used of the soul as united with the body. Thus *nepeš* suggests the soul regarded as sentient, *rûaḥ* the soul regarded as intellectual. If Ecclesiastes held the theory of trichotomy we should not expect him to use *rûaḥ* but *nepeš* of the soul of the beast. In the above statement, therefore, *rûaḥ* means the soul as opposed to the body. The true interpretation of the passage depends on the time and circumstances of the author which have been discussed in the Introduction.

b The accepted Jewish teaching of the time spoke of the souls of the dead as going down to Sheol, which was conceived as located in the bowels of the earth. Ecclesiastes has heard of the view held by a sect called the Essenes who, following the Greek teaching of Plato and others, maintained that souls ' when they are set free from the bonds of the flesh, then, as released from a long bondage, rejoice and mount upwards ' (Jos BJ 2, 8, 11, ed. Whiston). They held, therefore, that the souls of men go upwards to God after death. But Jewish religious authorities have not yet accepted the new doctrine, and so Ecclesiastes does not admit it. At the same time he does not call it a false doctrine, and later on (12:7) he seems to accept it. There is no reason to deny a progress in his thought on this matter. There is, therefore, no direct reference to the immortality of the human soul, which in both views, *viz.* that of the accepted Jewish teaching and that of the new doctrine, survives after death ; the reference is rather to the destination of the human soul. **22.** The result of the writer's meditations—present enjoyment is best ; for man, being ignorant of the principles of the divine administration, cannot know the order in which future events will unfold themselves.

c **IV 1-16 Reflections on Oppression, Envy, Miserliness, High Position**—In all four sections of this passage the writer includes a contrast, the oppressed and the unborn (**1-3**), the striver and the idler (**4-6**), the

solitary miser and two or three in co-operation (**7-12**), the old foolish king and the young wise king (**13-16**).

1-3. Ecclesiastes states that inhumanity and oppression make 'life not worth living. **4-6.** The striver and the idler are compared to the advantage of the idler. The striver's efforts are spoiled by the jealousy of his neighbour. The expression ' he eateth his own flesh ' means that he becomes thin through not having sufficient food. One sees especially in eastern towns idlers who loll about in indolence content with a little food. (The word ' saying ' of 5 is to be omitted with the MT and LXX.) The vanity of life is shown by the fact that the strivers who should fare better than the idlers often fare worse relatively, in the sense that their efforts remain barren and unrewarded by happiness while idlers make no efforts. Hence, *one handful of rest is better than two handfuls of toil and fruitless effort* (**6**). Ecclesiastes does not recommend idleness but merely shows the vanity of toil when as often labour is without its reward. **7-12.** The writer contemplates the insatiable striving of the lone and kinless miser to amass wealth, and turns to show by illustrations the advantages of pulling harmoniously together in a spirit of companionship and co-operation. **13-16.** Better than an old but foolish king who will no longer accept advice is the youthful but wise man who, with wisdom as his sole advantage, overcame the initial disadvantages of youthfulness, poverty and imprisonment—evidence of his intrinsic worth—and rose to the highest position in the land. This wise young man began to reign as the popular hero, but, in a very short time, even he—a wise king—lost his popularity. The lesson of the whole passage is that wisdom even when it obtains the greatest success is still vanity and a striving after wind because its fruits do not last. **13b.** *Who knows not to accept advice any more.* **14.** *For out of prison he* (the youth of 13) *came forth to reign ; yea, even in his kingdom he was born poor.* **15.** *I saw all the living that walk under the sun with the second* (namely) *the youth that stood up in his stead.* **16.** ' *All that were before him* ' : *all in front of whom he was.* He is pictured as marching at their head.

17-V 6 Counsels concerning Proper Worship—Reference **d** is made to worship in general (**4:17**), prayer (**5:1 f.**), and the fulfilment of vows (**5:3 ff.**).

17a. *Watch thy step* (DV ' Keep thy foot') when thou goest to the Temple. The words have a moral sense. **17b.** Obedience is more acceptable to God than the sacrifice of evil-doers. Ecclesiastes condemns not sacrifice nor ritual but sacrifice offered without the proper dispositions (*cf.* Ps 49). **5:1.** Undue haste and excess in words at prayer are condemned. The great gulf which separates us from God should inspire us with reverence. **2.** As a mind much occupied with business cares occasions dreams, so a thoughtless fool utters verbal prayers lacking in sincerity and reality. **3 ff.** The writer warns the reader that vows, once they are uttered, are to be performed without delay (*cf.* Deut 23:21-23). He also warns the reader against uttering a vow which he will not duly perform, for he thereby deliberately sins (*cf.* Deut 23:21-23). We should note that, generally speaking, a vow had to be supplemented in due time by the presentation of a thank-offering in the Temple. This involved great expense and, it seems, some of the contemporaries of Ecclesiastes sought to evade the offering of the sacrifice. Ecclesiastes warns them, in particular, against representing the *priest* (DV ' angel ') who offers sacrifices that the vow was inadvertently uttered. A vow uttered without advertence constituted, indeed, *a sin of inadvertence* (DV ' there is no providence '), but the sacrifice required to expiate it was not costly (*cf.* Num 15:27 ff.). Ecclesiastes declares that God will be angry with him who utters a vow in connexion with his service and then lies saying that the vow was inadvertently made. **6.** *For in a multitude of dreams and of words there are many vanities : fear God !*

V 7-VII 1 The Greed of State Officials and the Vanity of Wealth—**5:7.** One is not to wonder at the oppression

9a of the poor, for there are many officials, high and low, who seek to enrich themselves. **8.** *And the profit of the land is for all* (*i.e.* the avaricious officials of 7), *a king is served in view of land.* Service is given not out of loyalty but solely in the hope of aggrandizement. **9.** Wealth is unsatisfying. **10.** With the increase of a man's riches comes an increase in the number of retainers whom he must support, and the rich man's only advantage is the sight of his riches. **11.** Anxiety to increase wealth and worry lest it be diminished cause sleeplessness. **12 ff.** Suppose furthermore that through a reverse of fortune he loses his money, his heir is left destitute, and at death he has not even the satisfaction of having done well in life. He has stinted himself to amass riches, lived in misery, and gained nothing save mere wind. **17 ff.** The writer, as before (*cf.* 2:24; 3:12 f., 22), counsels present enjoyment—such as it is —of the fruits of labour, such enjoyment and the capacity to enjoy being God's gifts to man. He who takes the joys of each day as they come will not worry himself with speculations as to what the future has in store for him. **6:1 ff.** A rich man may lack the ability to enjoy what life offers; he may be denied by God the capacity to enjoy; he may not have even the satisfaction of leaving his possessions to children of his own. Even though he should have a numerous progeny and attain to a ripe old age, yet if he lacks the capacity to experience enjoyment, feels dissatisfaction, and receives no burial, he is worse off than the premature, still-born child. **4.** *For it* (*i.e.* the untimely born) *comes in vanity and departs in darkness, and its name is covered in darkness* (*i.e.* is not announced). **5a.** *Moreover, it* (the untimely born) *has not seen the sun,* and thereby has escaped all the trials which are the normal experience of life on earth. **6.** Yea, if the rich man has lived very many years and has not enjoyed his life, what advantage is there in a long life? There is but one end to all men, *i.e.* Sheol, whence they **b** do not return. **7.** Man labours to get enjoyment but he is never satisfied. **8.** The wise man together with the fool, the poor man who knows how to live prudently (lit. ' to walk before his fellow-men '; DV ' to go thither where there is life '), all find life's enjoyment unsatisfying. **9.** Present enjoyment, fleeting and unsubstantial though it be, is better than yearning after the unattainable. **10.** *Whatsoever is, its name has been already called* (*i.e.* it already existed, *cf.* 1:10) *and that which is man is known : he cannot contend,* etc. The first clause states that the world in general does not change. The second clause means that what man was yesterday he still is and always will be. Man is powerless to foresee or modify the course of events; he can never alter the ordinances of the divine government of the universe, and thus is unable to attain all his desires. **11.** Expostulation with God is worse than useless. *To multiply words is to multiply vanities and brings no advantage to man.* Vg misinterprets the last member of this verse and attaches it incorrectly to the first member of the next verse (7:1a). **7:1.** This verse gives an added reason why it is futile to dispute with God. Man knows not what is best for him to do during the days of his life which flits like a shadow. For this a knowledge of the future would be necessary.

c VII 2-23 Rules of Right Conduct and Practical Aphorisms—**2.** A good name (Heb. *šēm*) is better than precious ointment (Heb. *šemen*). Note the play on words. The day of death which brings relief from life's sufferings (*cf.* 4:2) is better than the day of birth. **3 ff.** Seriousness rather than frivolity should be cultivated. Serious thought on life's trials and sorrows builds up character. A deathbed scene reminds man that he too must die. Trouble purifies the heart. **4a.** Sorrow (not ' anger ') *is better than laughter.* **7b-8.** *And this also is vanity, that exactions turn a wise man into a fool, and presents corrupt the heart.* Extortion drives a man to do foolish things through indignation. **9 ff.** Hasty anger and foolish talk are condemned. We should be exceedingly cautious in speech; we should be patient, not hasty and arrogant. **12 f.** Wisdom together with

a patrimony is good; they are an especially profitable **379c** combination. Both are a defence against life's ills, but the excellency of wisdom is that it preserves the life of him who possesses it. **14 f.** Man's attempts to change God's handiwork are futile, so he is to enjoy the prosperity God gives, and in the day of adversity consider that God's method with regard to the distribution of adversity and prosperity is to balance one against the other, so that man may find no fault with him. **14.** *Consider the work of God : for who can make straight what He has made crooked ?* **15.** *In the day of prosperity be glad, and in the day of adversity consider : God has even made the one side by side with the other, to the end that man should not find out anything after him.* **16.** The observations of Ecclesiastes contradict the accepted Jewish doctrine that a just man may hope for length of days (*cf.* Ps 90:16) and that a wicked man will be cut off prematurely (*cf.* Ps 36:10). **17 f.** In interpreting these **d** two verses we should note that the currents of ideas from which the Pharisaic rigorists and the Sadducean libertines sprang existed already in the time of Ecclesiastes, and that righteousness consisted in the observance of the Law. In 17 the writer warns against the excessive legalism of those early Pharisees, and in 18 he issues a warning against people who go to the other extreme and reject regulations of the Mosaic legislation. In 16* above Ecclesiastes remarks that the wicked man lives on. Here he states that excess in wickedness will probably shorten life. **19.** Do whatever your hand findeth to do without being overscrupulous, for if you fear God you will succeed in everything. *It is good that thou shouldst take hold of this* (DV ' the just ' is incorrect); *yea, also from that withdraw not thy hand : for he that fears God shall come successfully out of everything.* **20.** Real strength and support in life is found in wisdom rather than in power and influence. This verse interrupts its context and originally may have followed 13. **21.** *Verily, there is not a righteous man upon earth, that does good and sins not.* No man, however pious, is entirely righteous (*cf.* 3 Kg 8:46; Job 15:14 f.; 25:5 f.). **22 f.** These verses give a new rule of conduct suggested by 21. Don't be too curious to know everything that is said, lest you hear your servant cursing you. Your conscience knows that you have spoken ill of others. Not being perfect yourself, you are not to expect perfection from others.

24-30a Intense Search after Wisdom in its Fullness brings Disappointment—**24a.** *All this I have tried by* **e** *wisdom;* all his experiences above related he subjected to an examination, using whatever wisdom he had, for he sought to increase his natural wisdom by understanding the scheme of the universe and the divine government thereof. **25.** *The real nature of things escapes us : it is profound, exceedingly profound ; who shall find it ?* **26.** *I applied myself earnestly to know and to search out, and to seek wisdom and the reason for things, and to know that wickedness is folly, and that foolishness is madness.* **27.** The problem which especially exercised the attention of Ecclesiastes was the existence of such wickedness in the universe which God created and governs. *And I find a thing more bitter than death, the woman who is a snare, her heart nets and her hands fetters.* Seeing that the writer is here using the terms (*viz.* snare, nets, fetters) of the descriptions of the harlot given in Prov 5 and 7, he must be referring to this one class of women only. *He who is good before God shall escape from her, but the sinner shall be taken by her.* The escape is attributed not to God's action, ' but to the legitimate and, so to say, natural result of the man's previous life. And so in the contrary case of the sinner ' (Williams, 87). **28-30a.** His diligent search after a reasonable explanation (DV ' the account ') of things in general is a failure. As regards human beings, the appalling conditions of the period and place of his investigations led him to observe that perfect men are few, while perfect women are still fewer. But—this much he knows—the degeneracy is not to be attributed to God; the fault lies with man who uses his free-will to introduce into life corrupting complications (DV

379e 'he hath entangled himself with an infinity of questions'), and so mars the divine plan.

380a **30b–VIII 8 The Wise Man and a Despotic Ruler**—The wise man will submit to the wrongs which spring from the tyranny of the king and confidently await the execution of justice.

7:30b. Who is as the wise man? and who knows the solution of any question? This verse belongs more correctly, as in MT, to the first verse of ch 8. *8:1. A man's wisdom causes his face to shine, and the hardness of his face is changed.* **2.** *Obey the king's command and that on account of the oath of God* (*i.e.* the oath of fealty exacted by the king). **3 f.** Do not rashly resign office ; do not be disloyal by engaging in a conspiracy. The king will tolerate no opposition ; his word is final. **5.** He who keeps the command of the king (or, according to some commentators, the commandments of God) shall experience no ill. The wise man knows to bide his time and await judgement (DV 'answer'). **6 f.** There is a time and judgement (DV 'opportunity') for every business. Truly, the misery of man is great upon him *because he knows not that which shall be, because how it shall be, who can tell him?* The nature and manner of the judgement in which justice will be done are unknown to him ; that justice will be executed he knows. **8.** In the meantime it is consoling to know that the tyrant cannot live always. He must die ; no discharge from the obligation of fighting is possible (DV 'neither is he suffered to rest') in the war against death ; the wickedness of the tyrant will not save him.

b **VIII 9–15 Contrast of Doctrine and Fact**—Ecclesiastes declares that the received Jewish doctrine that the righteous man prospers and the wicked man suffers is contradicted by the stern facts of life. He firmly believes that God will punish wickedness and reward righteousness, but beyond asserting that the received doctrine of retribution does not correspond with facts he does not proceed to the obvious conclusion. The doctrine of retribution hereafter had not yet been revealed. It often happens that a just man suffers and a wicked man prospers. Such being the case, all that is left for man is to take what pleasure is given by God, who has so arranged the world. *This enjoyment should accompany him in his labour all the days of his life.* **9.** Ecclesiastes, when considering life, has seen a man using his power to hurt his fellow-man (DV 'to his own hurt' is incorrect). **10.** *And then I saw the wicked buried ; they had frequented the holy place, and they were praised in the city who had acted thus.* Ecclesiastes has seen the wicked receive decent burial (*cf.* 6:3), the wicked who during their lifetime did not hesitate to enter the Temple to worship God. Those ungodly people were even praised. **12.** *Insomuch as a sinner does evil a hundred times, and prolongs his days, surely also I know that it shall be well with those who fear God, who fear before Him.* **13.** *But it shall not be well with the wicked—neither shall he prolong his days which are as a shadow—because he does not fear before God.* The clause 'neither . . . shadow' is to be treated as a parenthesis which refers back to the clause 'and prolongs his days' of the previous verse, to which it seems at first sight in direct contradiction. The parenthesis, however, means that the wicked man shall not in reality prolong his days, for they still flit away, as do the days of all men (*cf.* 7:1), like a shadow.

c **16–IX 10 God's Providence is Inscrutable**—When Ecclesiastes sought to understand the travail of daily life—for man works incessantly—he saw that no one, however wise, can give a satisfactory explanation of what is happening 'under the sun'. The righteous and the wise and their works are in God's hands for him to deal with at his sole discretion. But no one knows whether God loves him or hates him, because happiness and adversity, coming as they do to the righteous and the wicked alike, are no indication of how a man stands with God. *Everything* (whether adversity or prosperity) *in front of man* (*i.e.* which man will experience) *is vanity* (DV 9:2a, 'are kept uncertain'). That things happen alike to both good and **3** bad has the effect of favouring the development of evil and misconduct (DV 'contempt') in men while they live, and afterwards they go to Sheol, where they will no more participate in the activities that make up life on earth. Man is here and now to take enjoyment in and by his labour and to manifest exteriorly his interior contentment, for such is God's will. Moreover he is to engage in physical and mental activities while life lasts, for the activities of earth are absent from the abode of the dead. **9:2a.** The reading given above involves a slight change in the Hebrew (*cf.* Barton, p 158). **7b.** Thy works—with special reference to eating and drinking—have God's approval, for he has so arranged the world that this is the only thing you can do.

IX 11–17 Reward for Work is not guaranteed and the **d** **Value of Wisdom is not recognized**—**11 f.** Given the apparent conditions for success, good results do not necessarily follow ; there are still the elements of time (*cf.* 3:1–8) and chance (*e.g.* accident, misfortune, luck) to be considered ; death may come unexpectedly and spoil a well-laid plan. **13 ff.** Ecclesiastes gives a concrete example. A poor but wise man delivered a city by his wisdom but went unrewarded. All the apparent conditions for the gaining of a reward were present, yet his request for recognition (DV 9:16 'his words') went unheeded.

17–X:3 Proverbial Sayings about Wisdom—The insertion of these sayings was suggested by 9:15a. **17.** *The words of the wise* (uttered) *in quietness are heard more than the cry of a leader among fools.* **18b.** *But one fault will ruin much good.* **10:1.** This verse illustrates 9:18b. *Dying flies cause the ointment of the apothecary to putrify and ferment ; so a litile folly outweighs* (Heb. *yāqār*, but here given the meaning it has in Aramaic) *wisdom and honour.* **2.** The intelligence of a wise man is on the side of the most important of his endeavours, that of a fool on the side of the less important. **3.** *Yea even when a fool walks on the way his intelligence fails him, and he declares to every man his folly.*

X 4–7 The Cultivation of Meekness—These verses **f** counsel meekness in face of the capriciousness of rulers which leads them to promote the wrong people. **4b.** *Because meekness leaves great offences undone :* both parties will be saved from serious faults.

8–15 The Advantage of Wisdom and some of the **3** **Results of Folly**—**8–11.** Many activities involve risk and it is only wisdom to be prepared for contingencies. **10.** *If the axe becomes blunt and one does not whet the edge, then must one use more strength, but wisdom is advantageous for success.* A wise man would sharpen the axe, thus saving himself much physical effort and accomplishing his task more successfully. **11.** Mere proficiency brings no advantage to a man unless he uses it in good time. *If the serpent bite before it is charmed, then there is no advantage for the charmer.* 'Charmer': lit. 'the owner of the tongue', which the Syr. and LXX rightly render by 'the charmer'—the snake-charmer uses his voice to effect the charm. Vg understood the word to mean 'one who backbites'. **12a.** *Win favour* (DV 'are grace'). **12b.** *Shall ruin him* (DV 'shall throw him down headlong'). **13b.** *Madness* (DV 'error'). **14.** A fool talks fluently of the future as though it could be foreseen by man. **15.** *The labour of the fool wearies him, for he had not the understanding to migrate to a city.* The true interpretation of this verse seems to lie in the distinction between the country people and some of the city people. In Palestine all the former have to labour for their daily bread, while in the cities there are always some who do no work but still manage to live (*cf.* 4:5). The country fool has to work for a living, the city fool gets it without working.

16–20 Reflexions on Rulers—**16.** *Woe to thee, O land,* **b** *when thy king is a slave* (DV 'a child') *and thy princes eat in the morning.* The morning is a most valuable time for the eastern, who rises early to get work done before the intense heat from noon till evening. The

b state is in an evil plight when its princes feast so unseasonably. **17a.** *Happy art thou, O land, when thy king is a noble by birth* (DV ' noble '). **18 f.** When the rafters supporting the roof are neglected they give way and cause leakage (DV ' drop through '). So shall the fabric of the state crumble because of the sloth and dissipation of its rulers who are wealthy enough to indulge in all sorts of pleasure. **20.** The subject's safety lies, however, in silent submission to authority.

c XI 1-6 Encouragement of Prudent Enterprise—1-2. Ecclesiastes commends a spirit of commercial enterprise like that of exporting corn, for no loss will be incurred by the venture. Man is to be prudent, however, and divide the venture between several ships, for it is unwise to put all one's eggs in one basket ; one does not know what evil may happen upon earth. **3.** The thought of this verse is joined to that which precedes it by the mention of ' evil ' in 2*b*. There will inevitably be some evils (*i.e.* calamities) upon the earth, for natural causes produce natural effects and man is powerless to control them. **4.** Man, nevertheless, is not to stand hesitant waiting until success is absolutely assured. He who waits for ideal conditions will get nothing done. **5.** God's works are known to man as little as the way of the *wind* (DV ' spirit '), or the formation of the bones in the womb of the pregnant (*cf.* Ps 138:15). **6.** Man is, therefore, to use every opportunity, for he cannot know which effort will turn out well.

d 7-XII 1 Man is to enjoy Life while Youth lasts, being Mindful, however, of God and his Judgement—7 f. ' The light is sweet and the sun *is pleasant to behold.* If man *should* live many years *let him rejoice* in them all ', and the more so for remembering that many darksome days are to follow in the evening of life. All the days of life are vanity (*i.e.* a mere breath). **9.** Let youth be cheerful, but let there be present that which shall check excess, *viz.* the knowledge that one's deeds will be weighed in the balance of divine justice. **10.** Let man shun all trouble (DV ' anger ') and bodily ill (DV ' evil ') for the heyday of life is soon past (lit. ' is vanity '). **12:1.** Finally let man reverence his Creator in the days of youthful vigour before advancing years bring bodily and mental inactivity.

e XII 2-7 A Figurative and somewhat Enigmatical Description of Old Age—The most widely held opinion among critics maintains that in 2–5*a* we have figurative descriptions of the failing bodily members of the old man. There is, however, wide divergence among these critics in the application of these figures to definite parts of the body. We shall give what we consider the most representative applications.

2. With advancing and clouding old age life loses its brightness (*i.e.* its charm). **3.** Hands (' keepers of the house ') tremble, legs (' strong men ') become bent, teeth (' grinders ') are few and feeble, eyes (' those that look through the *latticed windows* ') lose their sight. **4.** Ears (' doors in the street ') fail to catch the sounds of others' voices (*the sound of the grinding*), the song of the bird (' the voice of the bird ') or the sound of music (' the daughters of music '). **5.** The old man suffers from giddiness (' he fears high things ') and from timidity (' he is afraid in the way ') ; he has white hair (' the almond tree in blossom '), a halting gait (*the grasshopper drags itself along*), a languid palate (*the caper berry is made ineffectual*). This explanation of the passage requires the following readings : the clause ' one shall rise up at the voice of the bird '

in 4 is to be emended to read ' the voice of the bird is **381e** silent ', changing *weyāqûm le*, ' rises up at ', to *weyiddōm*, ' is silent '. In 5 the reading ' the almond tree blossoms ' is that of the versions, while that of MT, with the verb pointed as impf., *niph'al*, is ' the almond tree is cast aside '. The reading ' the caper berry is made ineffectual ' is got by reading the passive form of the verb. Read thus, the clause may also mean ' the caper shrub is broken '.

The whole passage 2-5*a* may also be interpreted as an **f** allegory of a thunderstorm, a terrifying phenomenon in the east, to express the alarm, desolation and gloom that follow the death of a member of a household. The gathering, bursting and wake of destruction are described. As the storm gathers over an eastern city the light is darkened, the thick clouds pile up and cut off brightness. **3.** The lightning flashes and the thunder peals, sending terror into the hearts of all, of the police who guard the mansions of the wealthy, of the strong men of the city, of the women whose hands have forgotten their task of grinding, and into the darkened faces of those who peep timidly through their latticed windows. **4.** When the storm breaks, doors are shut against the wind and rain, the sound of the grinding is hardly heard, the birds are silent, and merry-makers are terrorized into silence. **5a.** Men are afraid of the awful majesty of the storm (*of that which is high*) and there are terrors in the street. In the wake of the storm lies the battered, torn earth ; the almond tree is cast aside, the caper shrub is broken, and even the least thing that moves, the tiny grasshopper, has felt the power of the storm. The sequence of thought in the whole passage, *viz.* 2-8, is : Remember thy Creator (understood from 12:1) before old age or death (2–5*a*) ; because man is going to his eternal home (5*b*) ; before the silver cord be *snapped*, etc.

6. The broken vessels refer to the dissolution of the body regarded as the container of the soul. ' Before the silver cord [from which the bowl was suspended] be snapped (emend Heb. root to *ntq*), *and the golden bowl be broken, and the pitcher* ', etc. **7.** The soul goes back to God (*cf.* note on 3:21).

8-14 Epilogue eulogizing Ecclesiastes and summarizing g his Teaching—This passage is probably an addition made by the editor (*cf.* § 376*n*). **9.** *And further, because Ecclesiastes was wise, he still taught the people knowledge* (*i.e.* he was not satisfied with having written this book), *and he tested, investigated, and arranged many proverbs.* **10.** Ecclesiastes sought to give his work an attractive form, and to write with sincerity words of truth. **11.** Podechard, 477, translates : *The words of the wise are as goads, and as nails firmly fixed holders of provisions ; they* (*i.e.* the words of the wise) *are given from one shepherd.* The nails are those fixed in a wall on which are hung baskets containing food. The words of the wise stimulate to action, and they sustain ; all wisdom comes ultimately from one shepherd, God. **12.** One is to be contented with the words of the wise—*as for more than these, my son, be warned.* One can save oneself the weariness of much reading. **13 f.** The editor sums up the teaching of the book : Fear God and keep his commandments, *for this is every man* (DV ' all man '), *i.e.* ' this is expected of, and can be accomplished in, every man ' (so Williams, 163). **14.** This verse gives the reason for fearing God : *For God shall bring every work into judgement, concerning every hidden thing* (DV ' every error '), *whether it be good or whether it be evil.*

THE CANTICLE OF CANTICLES

(THE SONG OF SONGS)

By P. P. SAYDON

382a **Bibliography**—Origen, PG 13, 37–58, 61–216 ; 17, 253–88 ; St Ambrose, *Comm. in Cant.*, PL 15, 1851–1962 ; St Gregory the Great, *Testimonia in Cant.*, PL 79, 905–16 ; Rupert of Deutz, *In Cant. Libri vii*, PL 168, 839–962 ; St Bernard, *Sermones in Cant.*, PL 183, 799–1198 ; G. Gietmann, S.J., *Comm. in Ecclesiasten et Canticum Canticorum* (CSS), Paris, 1890 ; Card. Meignan, *Salomon, son règne, ses écrits*, Paris, 1890 ; *K. Budde, *Das Hohelied erklärt*, Freiburg i. B., 1898 ; *C. Siegfried, *Das Hohelied*, Göttingen, 1898 ; *A. Harper, *The Song of Solomon* (CBSC), 1907 ; V. Zapletal, *Das Hohelied kritisch und metrisch untersucht*, Freiburg i. Sch., 1907 ; J. Hontheim, S.J., *Das Hohelied* (BS), Freiburg i. B., 1908 ; P. Joüon, S.J., *Le Cantique des Cantiques*, Paris, 1909 ; A. Miller, O.S.B., *Das Hohelied* (BB), Bonn, 1927 ; G. Ricciotti, *Il Cantico dei Cantici*, Turin, 1928 ; G. Pouget-G. Guitton, *Le Cantique des Cantiques*, Paris, 1934 ; Card. Lépicier, *In Cant. Canticorum commentarius*, Rome, 1936 ; G. Girotti, O.P., *Il Cantico dei Cantici* in M. Sales *La Sacra Bibbia commentata*, Turin, 1938, Vol. VI ; A. Geslin, *Le Cantique des Cantiques*, Sées (Orne), 1938 ; *M. Haller, *Das Hohelied* (HAT), Tübingen, 1940 ; D. Buzy, *Cantique des Cantiques* in Pirot-Clamer *La Sainte Bible*, Paris, 1946, Vol. VI ; R. Rios O.S.B., *El Cantar de los Cantares*, Málaga, 1928. For a fuller and critical bibliography down to the year 1924 see Ricciotti, 172–92.

b The following articles deserve to be mentioned : E. Tobac, *Une page d'histoire de l'exégèse* in Rev. d'hist. eccl. 21 (1925) 510 ff., reprinted in *Les cinq Livres de Salomon*, Bruxelles, 1926, 76–110 ; A. Vaccari, S.J., *Il Cantico dei Cantici nelle recenti pubblicazioni*, Bi 9 (1928) 443–57 ; D. Buzy, *La composition littéraire du Cantique des Cantiques*, RB 49 (1940) 169–94 ; Id., *Un chef-d'œuvre de poésie pure : Le Cantique des Cantiques*, in *Mémorial Lagrange*, Paris, 1940, 147–62 ; P. P. Parente, *The Canticle of Canticles in Mystical Theology*, CBQ 6 (1944) 142–58 ; D. Buzy, *L'Allégorie Matrimoniale de Jahvé et d'Israël et le Cantique des Cantiques*, Vivre et Penser, III, 1945, 77–90 ; A. Robert, *Le genre littéraire du Cantique des Cantiques, ibid.*, 192–213.

c **Title**—The full Hebrew title is ' The Song of Songs, which is Solomon's '. The first half is a periphrastic Hebrew way of expressing the superlative, hence the meaning is ' the best of songs ' ; *cf.* ' holy of holies ' = most holy. It is indeed a most beautiful poem both for its lyrical inspiration and rich imagery as well as for the loftiness of its meaning. The second half of the title is generally considered by modern scholars as a literary device whereby the poem is attributed to Solomon in the same manner as the book of Wisdom is attributed to him, though written at a much later date.

d **Canonicity and Place in the Canon**—The canonicity of Cant has always been recognized by the Church. Theodore of Mopsuestia, who rejected its spiritual meaning and probably also its inspiration, had no followers (L. Dennefeld, *Der alttestamentliche Kanon der Antiochenischen Schule* (BS), xiv, 1909, 47). Among the Jews there were some doubts in the 1st cent. A.D., but these were dispelled in the Synod of Jabne (c A.D. 100), chiefly by the authority of R. Aqiba who said : ' All the Hagiographa are holy, but the Canticle is most holy ' (*cf. Mishna, Yadayim* 3, 5).

e In the Hebrew Canon it forms part of the Hagio-grapha, the third division of the canonical books. In our printed editions of MT it is the first of the 5 Megilloth **382** or ' Scrolls ', *i.e.* Canticle, Ruth, Ecclesiastes, Lamentations, Esther. The Alexandrine translators, however, arranged the books according to their literary character and so included Cant among the poetical books. In Vg too it is reckoned with the poetical books.

Contents and Analysis—Canticle is a love-song in **f** which two young shepherds praise each other's beauty and express their mutual love and desire for an indissoluble union. The analysis is difficult because the sense of certain passages and the nexus between the several parts are not always apparent. Those who hold that Cant is a drama divide the poem into acts and scenes according to their way of representing the development of the action. On the contrary, those who reject the unity of the poem make of it a collection of songs varying in number according to their subjective criteria.

Some sections are easily distinguishable by the recur- **g** rence of the refrain or by their opening words. On the grounds of these criteria we propose the following division :

1:1–2:7, the bride's yearning for the beloved ; mutual praises ; their meeting.

2:8–3:5, the bride is invited to the fields ; in the evening they return to their homes ; the bride is restless until she again finds her beloved.

3:6–5:1, the pomp of a royal pageant ; the bridegroom is enraptured by his bride's graceful charm and beauty and rejoices in her company.

5:2–6:2, while the bride is on her bed, the bridegroom comes unexpectedly ; when she rises to open he has vanished ; she goes out in search of him ; description of the bridegroom ; the joy of their union.

6:3–8:4, the bridegroom's admiration of his bride's beauty ; mutual praises ; the bride declares her unswerving attachment to her lover.

8:5–7, the two lovers are inseparably united.

8:8–14, appendix.

Literary Form—Although it is universally admitted **h** that Cant is a love poem, there is no agreement as to the manner in which the subject is treated. This is a brief exposition of the different views :

(1) Cant is a collection of separate love-songs having **i** no other link but the common subject, so *J. G. Herder, *Lieder der Liebe, die ältesten und schönsten aus dem Morgen-lande*, Leipzig, 1778, 89–106 ; *M. Jastrow, *The Song of Songs, being a collection of love lyrics of Ancient Palestine*, London, 1922 ; *H. W. Robinson, *The Old Testament : its making and meaning*, London, 1937, 161 f. ; *H. H. Rowley, *The Interpretation of the Song of Songs*, JTS 38 (1937) 358.

(2) Cant is a collection of popular nuptial songs that **j** were sung during the nuptial week, so J. B. Bossuet, A. Calmet. *J. G. Wetzstein tried to find a support for this explanation in the marriage customs of Hauran in Syria. This theory was further developed by *K. Budde.

(3) Cant is a drama. The dramatic theory has been **k** proposed in two forms : (i) A shepherd girl is taken away from her home by Solomon and made his wife, so *Frz Delitzsch (1875), F. Kaulen (1899). (ii) The shepherd girl is taken away by the king, but she remains faithful to her shepherd lover to whom she

k had pledged her heart, so *Ewald (1826), *Harper (1907), Pouget-Guitton (1934), A. Geslin (1938).

l (4) Cant is made up of lyrical dialogues alternating with monologues, with a slight dramatic movement, so the majority of Catholic interpreters.

m (5) Cant consists of seven short poems running parallel to each other. There is no development of action, but only a progressive movement within the several poems. The general plan of each poem is : the yearning of one part for the other, mutual praises and the joy of their union. They are like seven penitential Psalms which, with a variety of literary devices, develop the same ideas of sin, repentance and pardon, D. Buzy in RB, 49 (1940) 161–94 and in his commentary on Cant in Pirot-Clamer *La Sainte Bible*, 1946, 290.

n The first of these theories, in the form proposed by Herder, Jastrow and Robinson is certainly untenable. Throughout the whole poem there is unity of style and purpose, and this points to unity of authorship. But there is nothing against Rowley's explanation in so far as he admits unity of authorship and a certain development of the theme. (2) has no sufficient basis. Though love is considered in relation to marriage, there is nothing suggesting that we are assisting at a wedding. The dramatic theory is losing favour with critics. There is hardly any action in Cant, the dialogues and the change of scene are not enough to give it a dramatic movement. (4), though entirely acceptable, is rather vague and does not convey an adequate idea of the structure of the poem. The dialogue form is secondary. Even the development of the plot seems to be somewhat exaggerated. There is much to be said in favour of Buzy's theory, but the textual excisions and transpositions to which he has to resort have no justification except his own theory.

o Cant is a collection of love-songs composed by one writer with one definite purpose. Love is represented with a view to marriage. The several songs are as many tableaux or episodes in the story of two lovers. A certain development corresponding to the development of their love may be admitted, but whether the poem describes all the stages of love from its inception to its culmination in marriage remains undecided. The dialogue, monologues and the part played by the daughters of Jerusalem are poetical devices meant to give life to the descriptions and to the sentiments of the two lovers.

a **Systems of Interpretation**—The most important problem in Cant is its meaning and interpretation. Apparently Cant is an erotic poem with or without a higher aim of describing love in its purest form or of extolling the excellence of monogamy and conjugal fidelity. This is the view prevailing among non-Catholic interpreters and we have no right to introduce any other sense unless we have solid reasons, and these reasons must be sought for not in the book itself but in other biblical books and in Tradition.

The Fathers of the Church were so strongly convinced of the spiritual meaning of Cant that they ignored the literal sense. The heterodox view of Theodore of Mopsuestia, who maintained that Cant celebrated Solomon's marriage with the Egyptian Princess, was condemned by the II Council of Constantinople (553) ; Mansi, *Sacrorum Conc. Coll.*, ix, 225-7. The scriptural proof is provided by the writings of the prophets who very often represent the relation between Yahweh and Israel as that of husband and wife. Yahweh chose Israel for his Spouse, arrayed her with gold and silver and rich garments and made her renowned among the nations for her beauty and splendour (Ez. 16:3–14 ; cf. also Is 54:6 ff. ; 62:4 f. ; Jer 2:2 ' the love of thy betrothal ' ; Os 2:19 f.).

b There existed therefore a tradition representing Yahweh's relation to Israel as a marriage. This tradition is the strongest argument for admitting a higher and spiritual sense in Cant. In order to give a clear idea of the manner in which this higher sense is expressed and should be understood, a few preliminary remarks are necessary.

The literal proper sense, or the naturalistic inter- 383c pretation, being excluded as contrary to the prophetic teaching and Tradition, there remain the allegorical, the typical and the parabolic interpretations. An **allegory** is a sustained metaphor or series of metaphors about the same subject, cf. Is. 5:1–6. All the details of the allegory have their own meaning. The **parable** is a fictitious but lifelike narrative composed to illustrate a fact or truth. The doctrine of the parable emerges from the narrative as a whole, not from its constituent parts, some of which may be mere embellishments without symbolical meaning. The essential difference between parable and allegory is that in the parable the two objects, the one illustrating and the other illustrated, are kept distinct and placed side by side, while in the allegory they are blended together and are represented as a single object. Sometimes parable and allegory run into each other and give rise to a mixed form, the parable mixed with allegoric elements. The **typical sense** differs widely from the allegorical. The latter is a sense understood and intended by the writer ; the former is an additional sense intended by God and unknown to the writer except by revelation. The typical sense is always based upon the literal sense, proper or improper.

Of these, **the typical interpretation** does not seem to d have a sound basis. A type may be a historical fact or person or an ideal one. The historical type of Cant is generally considered to be Solomon's marriage with Pharaoh's daughter (3 Kg 3:1) ; so Honorius of Autun (*Expos. in Cant.* PL 172, 347–494), Bossuet, Calmet. But there is no evidence in Scripture or Tradition that a marriage of a polygamous king is a type of the essentially monogamous union of Yahweh with Israel or of Christ with the Church. The ideal type is the conjugal union in its ideal form, as instituted by God (Gen 2:24), represented in a concrete form but without any reference to historical persons (Miller, 6 f.). It is a fictitious marriage, described as a real one and representing God's union with man. A similar view has been propounded by Pouget-Guitton (146 f.), Geslin (38–105), Chaine (in A. Robert–A. Tricot, *Initiation biblique* [1948] 175), who maintain that the sacred writer intended only to describe conjugal love and to inculcate the sanctity of marriage as instituted by God. Cant is, therefore, a moral lesson on the sanctity and indissolubility of marriage, and conjugal fidelity. Nothing more than that was meant by the writer. But in the mind of God, the primary author of Scripture, the conjugal union was to serve as a type of Christ's union with his Church and of his immense love for her. Cant represents in a parabolic form an ideal marriage foreshadowing Christ's union with the Church. The ideal-typical interpretation may be accepted, but it is doubtful whether the text provides solid ground for it. The writer indulges in his description of the two shepherds' love, their mutual yearning and admiration, but their union is passed over almost in silence. Although love is admittedly represented in view to marriage, and the two lovers are certainly married, the writer concentrates upon their love rather than on their marriage. If this is true, we can hardly understand how marriage can be the main object of Cant. But we can easily understand the writer's unwillingness to describe the happiness of married life if his object was really to symbolize God's love for man under the figure of human conjugal love.

In **the parabolic interpretation** Cant describes, in its e literal sense, the love between two imaginary shepherds with a view to illustrating God's love for man (Tobac, 110). Its meaning must be sought in the book as a whole, not in the several details, some of which serve only to render the picture more lifelike.

In its strictest form generally adopted by the Fathers, f **the allegorical interpretation** applies the whole description of the marriage to Christ and the Church, and tries to find a meaning for all such details as the hair, eyes, lips, etc., of the bride. This system has led

383f to the most varied, and sometimes fanciful, interpretations which are nothing else but pious accommodations. Some allegorical elements must, however, be recognized. The appellation of God as a shepherd is a familiar OT metaphor ; *cf*. Ps 23:1 ; 80:1 ; Jer 31:10 ; Ez 34:11, 19 ; Zach 11:17. The designation of the shepherd-lover as *dôḏî* ' my beloved ', which occurs thirty times in Cant, recalls Is 5:1–6, an allegory in which the same word *dôḏî* is used of Yahweh.

g As neither the parabolic nor the purely allegorical interpretation fully satisfies the exegetical requirements of the text, modern interpreters mostly prefer the mixed or **parabolic-allegorical interpretation.** Cant is essentially a parable placing side by side, as the Gospel parables, two facts, an imaginary and a real one, and illustrating the one by the other. It follows, according to the hermeneutical rules of parables, that many details must be considered as mere literary embellishments having no historical reality corresponding to them. It must be remarked also that although the parabolic-allegorical interpretation has been preferred to the typical-ideal, we do not deny that Cant teaches, at least implicitly, a moral lesson on the sanctity of marriage which was later raised to the dignity of a sacrament by Christ.

h We pass now to define the object and limits of this allegorical parable. Some interpreters as Nicholas de Lyra (†1340) and in recent times Joüon and Ricciotti, following in the steps of Jewish interpreters, explain Cant as an allegorical representation of Yahweh's dealings with Israel from the Exodus to the return from the Exile. Although a ' Judaic sense ' must absolutely be admitted, the historico-allegorical interpretation has never been popular in Christian exegesis. In fact, it requires a great power of imagination to find a correspondence between the several literary features of Cant and Jewish history.

i Other interpreters, from Hippolytus to modern times, have applied the allegory to the union of Christ with the Church. The basis for such an interpretation is provided by the NT which describes the foundation of the Church as a nuptial feast (Mt 22:1–14) and Christ as the Bridegroom (Mt 9:15 ; *cf*. also Jn 3:29 ; 2 Cor 11:2 ; Eph 5:23–32 ; Apoc 21:9).

j This interpretation, which is called ' the Christian interpretation ', must be taken as a development of the Judaic sense in order to be fully acceptable. In the plan of divine providence the election of Israel was a preparation for the establishment of the Church by Christ. The foundation of the Israelitic theocracy and that of the Church were not two independent events, but two successive stages in God's work of redemption. God's love for Israel foreshadowed Christ's love for his Church. If Cant, therefore, symbolizes Yahweh's love for Israel, it must necessarily symbolize also Christ's love for his Church. This is the fuller sense of Cant which, though not perceived by the Jewish reader, is certainly contained in it and intended by God. The two senses—Judaic and Christian—are two complementary senses forming together one sense and one interpretation which is that followed by the majority of Catholic exegetes.

k The Judaic aspect of this interpretation, however, requires to be defined more accurately. It is universally recognized that in the prophetic books Yahweh's relations to Israel are those of husband and wife. But in the earlier books Yahweh is represented as Israel's father and Israel as Yahweh's firstborn (Ex 4:22 f.). This image is further developed in Deut where Yahweh is described as a father carrying his son in his arms (1:31), educating him (8:5), and as the author of his existence (32:18) ; *cf*. also Os 11:1–14, etc. The marriage-figure originated with the prophets who, however, always represent Israel as a faithless wife divorced by her husband (Is 50:1; Jer 3:8 ; Ez 16:1–58 ; Os 2). There is not the slightest allusion to the first happy days of their marriage ; Israel proved faithless from the very first day of her marriage (Ez 16:15 ; Os 9:10). There is no time from the Sinaitic alliance

to the return from the Exile in which Israel could say **8** of Yahweh ' He is mine and I am his '.

But Israel's infidelity and her repudiation by Yahweh **l** were not to last for ever. After having atoned for her misbehaviour she would be taken up again by Yahweh and re-united with him by an eternal bond of love. This re-instatement of Israel is clearly foretold by the prophets (Is 49:14 f. ; 54:6 ff. ; Ez 16:59–63 ; Os 2:19 f.). It is this reconciliation or re-marriage of Yahweh to Israel, which is the object of Cant. (Buzy, *Vivre et Penser*, III, 1945, 77–90.)

An extension, or what may be called a consequential **m** sense, of the allegorical interpretation is the ascetico-mystical interpretation which identifies the bridegroom as Christ and the bride as the faithful soul. This interpretation first proposed by Origen, became common in the Middle Ages with St Bernard as its chief representative. Closely related to it is the Mariological interpretation. Not only is the Virgin Mary the holiest of all the members of the Church, but she also concurred in the accomplishment of the mystical union of the Son of God with humanity. Special prominence to the Mariological interpretation is given by Cardinal Lépicier and Girotti in their respective commentaries. Of mediaeval expositors Rupert of Deutz is one of the best.

Author and Date—Tradition has always attributed **n** Cant to Solomon. The authority of the title, however, is not decisive as it is either a later addition or a literary artifice. The language bears marks of a later origin. But the strongest argument against Solomonic authorship is the marriage allegory which originated with Osee. Cant is therefore later than the 8th cent. B.C. If the subject of Cant is Israel's reconciliation with Yahweh, its date must be fixed at the end of the Exile or a little later. This is also confirmed by the anthological character of the poem (A. Robert, *Vivre et Penser*, III [1945] 192–213). There are no reasons for placing its composition as late as the Greek period.

I The Title—See § 382c. As the title forms part of **3** ch 1 in MT, the numeration of verses is one verse in advance in respect to Vg and DV. For practical reasons we follow the latter.

I 1–II 7 First Song—The Bride longs for her Bride-**b** groom, admires her beauty and rejoices at his presence. **1–3 The Bride yearning for her Beloved—1.** The bride yearns for her beloved's *caresses* (DV breasts) which she values more than aught else. Wine here denotes all earthly pleasures, *cf*. Eccles 2:3. **2.** Her lover is as attractive as the sweetest perfume ; his name, *i.e.* all his person, is like a bottle of scented ointment which, when poured out, spreads its sweet fragrance abroad. His charms are irresistible. **3.** Punctuate : Draw me after thee : let us run. The words : ' to the odour of thy ointments ' are wanting in MT and have probably crept in from 2*a*. Enraptured by his loveliness she is resolved to follow him everywhere. The nexus between 3*a* and 3*b* is not apparent. Her lover was not a king. Was she abducted by the king ? Is ' king ' a nuptial title of the bridegroom ? Some interpreters read an imperative : ' Take me, O king '. An excellent sense is obtained if MT is translated thus : ' If the king were to take me into his inner apartments, I should be glad and rejoice in thee and praise thy love more than the (royal) banquet '. In other words, she will never give her love to another, not even to the king himself ; she is happy with her beloved ; it is *delightful* to love him. **4 f. The Bride's Humble Condition—4.** The bride is **c** not praising herself ; she is declaring her condition in life. She was not a negress ; the Heb. adjective for ' black ' here means ' of a swarthy complexion, sunburnt '. But she was not ugly. The tents of Cedar (Kedar) were the goatshair tents of the Cedarenes, a nomadic tribe dwelling in the N. Arabian desert (Gen 25:13). The curtains of Solomon are said to be the magnificent hangings of Solomon's temple (Joüon) or those of his palace (Siegfried, Budde). But according to the rules of Hebrew poetry it is preferable to make ' Solomon's curtains ' parallel to the ' tents of Cedar '

c and to read instead of Solomon the name of a place or tribe such as Salma, near Cedar (Miller, Ricciotti), or Salom (Pouget-Guitton), or Salem for Jerusalem (Buzy). **5.** She gives the cause of her dark complexion. She had to pass the long summer days guarding the vineyards, a hard task assigned to her by her malevolent brothers. Why she abandoned her work is not stated. Perhaps she sought a better opportunity of meeting her lover ; see 6 f.

d **6-7 The Bride in search of her Lover**—The bride desires to meet her lover. She is represented here as a shepherdess tending her flock in the vicinity of her beloved without knowing precisely the place where he grazes his flock or where he rests and waters it at noon. The dialogue expresses the intense passion of the shepherdess.

e **8-10 The Bridegroom's Praise of his Bride**—The bride has found her lover who is fascinated by her beauty. **8.** He compares her to a *mare* in Pharaoh's chariot. The point of comparison is the gorgeousness of the trappings of the royal mare, not the mare itself. **9.** Her cheeks are beautiful *with ear-rings*, her neck *with* jewels. **10.** He promises to make her more beautiful with gold *ear-rings* and silver *necklaces*. Some interpreters believe that these are the words of a seducer trying to divert the guileless heart of the shepherdess from the simplicity of pastoral life to the pomp and splendour of the court. But there is nothing in the text suggesting this sense. For the mention of the king see 11.

f **11-13 The Bride's Praise of her Bridegroom**—The bride very courteously returns her bridegroom's compliments. **11.** The scene is, apparently, in the king's palace. But the king has no part in the dialogue, nor is he addressed in the 2nd person or as ' my king '. We have here probably a tacit comparison. She will pour her odorous perfumes upon the head of her beloved, thus showing her immense love for him, just as the king's attendants and courtiers pay homage to him while he is sitting on his couch. The scene is reminiscent of Lk 7:37 f. and Jn 12:3. **12.** The bridegroom is compared to a *sachet* full of myrrh which she always carries on her breast as her favourite scent. The subject of ' shall abide ' is the sachet. Myrrh is a fragrant resinous gum which exudes from the *Balsamodendron Myrrha* ; *cf.* Ps 44:9 ; Prov 7:17 ; Eccles 24:20. **13.** He is also compared to a bunch of henna which grows in the plains of Engaddi, on the west shore of the Dead Sea. Henna was used by the Arabs for tinting the nails with a red hue and for its smell.

g **14-II 3 Expressions of Mutual Love**—The dialogue reaches its climax. Unable to repress their emotions the two lovers express their affection and mutual admiration with tender words and exquisite images. **14.** The bride's eyes are *like doves.* Her looks are full of candour reminiscent of a dove, the symbol of innocence and simplicity (Mt 10:16). **15.** Her reply almost repeats her lover's words but adds : ' *our tent is green* '. The reference is to the shepherd's hut of green branches and leaves where the two lovers had met. **16.** Mark the contrast between the bride's words and the more elevated tone of the bridegroom's expressions of praise. She had said : our dwelling is a poor shepherd's hut. He replies : our habitation, adorned with our love, is like a royal palace with cedar beams and cypress ceiling. **II 1.** The bride with her characteristic modesty describes herself as a *narcissus* which grows in the plains or more particularly in the plain of Sharon, and to a lily of the valley. In other words, she is as humble as a little meadow flower. **2.** The bridegroom turns this declaration of modesty into a flattering compliment. Your beauty among other maidens is that of a lily among thorns. **3.** Sensible of the compliment she replies in the same strain. You excel all other men in beauty and goodness as much as an apple-tree, or in a general sense a fruit-tree, excels all the trees of the forest. The image of the fruit-tree naturally evokes that of shade and fruit. She longs for, and sits down in, the shade of the tree enjoying its delicious fruit.

4-7 The Union of the two Lovers—From the leafy hut **384h** we are taken to a banqueting-hall to assist at the wedding of the two lovers. **4.** The bridegroom takes his bride into the *banqueting-hall* or, as we should say, the reception hall. As the marriage ceremony consisted in the introduction of the bride into the bridegroom's home, we have here an allusion to the marriage feast. But the poet is more interested in their mutual love than in their wedding ; he therefore omits all details to concentrate on the intensity of their love. In fact the bridegroom's affection for his bride is described as an attack by a powerful army ; *he arrayed against me his army of love, 4b*. **5.** Unable to resist the attack she falls like a wounded soldier. Vg-DV ' I languish ' renders the idea well, and we need not suppose that she was ill as Heb. *hôlaṭ* seems to suggest. She asks for assistance : Stay me up with *raisin-cakes, refresh* me with apples. **6.** The bridegroom runs to her side supporting her head with his left hand and embracing her with his right arm. **7.** These words are spoken by the bridegroom. The bride, overwhelmed by the power of love, has fallen asleep in his arms, and he entreats her friends not to disturb her rest. The gazelles are either a symbol of feminine grace or a mere poetical figure.

Allegorical interpretation. Israel, reborn after the **i** Exile, desires to be re-united with Yahweh whose love she knows so well. She will never let herself be led astray by the fascinating splendour of other religions. Yahweh will be her only God, her only happiness. Though few in number and unimpressive in their external appearance the Israelites were beautiful in the sight of God as they were faithful to him (Is 54:6-8). The Church too rejoices in Christ, her Founder and the source of all her prosperity. ' Thy name ' is the name of Jesus (*cf.* St Bernard, *Serm. 15 in Cant.* PL 183, 846). Though humble in her origin, the Church stands high in God's favour who loves and adorns her with supernatural gifts. The life of the just is a continual aspiration for mystical union with God.

8-III 5 Second Song—It develops the same theme **j** on the same lines, but with different descriptions. The bridegroom comes to meet his bride ; they spend a happy day in the fields ; during the night she becomes restless until she finds him again.

8-9 An Unexpected Visit from the Bridegroom—8. k She is still in her house when she suddenly hears her lover's footsteps approaching. With a bold poetical figure he is described as a gazelle or a young hart running and leaping over hills and mountains to arrive more quickly near his bride. **9.** He has arrived, and now he stands by the wall of her house looking through the latticed window to assure her of his coming.

10-17 The Bridegroom's Invitation—10-13. The **l** bridegroom calls his bride with the most affectionate terms ' my love ', ' my beautiful one ' (omit ' my dove '). He invites her to come out because winter has passed ; flowers are in bloom ; the time of *singing* has arrived ; all nature has awakened to new life after the long deathlike sleep of winter. **14.** He repeats his invitation making a strong appeal to her sensitive feminine nature. You are like a dove in the crevices of rocks and old walls. Let me hear your sweet voice and see your fair face. We must not imagine the bride staying in her house and quietly listening to her friend's serenade before she rises to open. As remarked above, the dialogue form is a literary device to give life to the scene. **15** is considered to be a popular song sung by the bride **m** in response to her lover's invitation. Buzy rejects 15-17 as a later addition. Joüon makes 15 the beginning of another scene. But 15-17 may also be regarded as a dramatic description of the way the two lovers spent the day in the fields. Although it is not expressly stated that the bride accepted the invitation, this is at least implied in 17. We are then naturally led to imagine the two lovers running through the fields, enjoying the beautiful scenery and chasing the little foxes that ravage the flourishing vines. **16.** Before

384m parting she once more professes her unchangeable love. He is mine and I am his. The words 'who feedeth (his flock) among the lilies' do not imply that the bridegroom was actually tending his flock (Buzy). They simply denote his ordinary work, hinting at the same time at a higher meaning, namely, his predilection for fragrant flowers, the symbol of virtue. **17.** As night approaches they part. *Before the day breathes* (*i.e.* 'before the cool evening breeze begins to breathe') and the shadows *stretch out*, he goes back to the mountains of Bether with the same swiftness with which he had come. Thus 17 links up with 8 and cannot be regarded as a later addition. The name 'Bether' creates a difficulty. Many interpreters, on the ground of analogy (*cf.* 4:6), take it as the name of an aromatic plant which they identify with the *malabathron* which passed into Hebrew in a syncopated form [*mala*] *bathr*[*on*] = *bether*.

n **III 1-5 Seeking the Bridegroom—1.** It was late in the evening when the two lovers returned to their homes (2:17). Now with her heart and mind still full of the emotions of the day she imagines herself to be still with her beloved. There is nothing to suggest that she is relating a dream. **2 f.** Unable to repress her emotions she hastens out in search of her beloved. Nothing is impossible to love, still less to a poet. **4.** No sooner has she passed the night patrol than she finds her beloved, lays hold on him and takes him to her mother's home. Where and how she found him at that time of night, the words they exchanged, are matters that fall outside the poet's interest. **5.** The refrain, which recurs in 2:7 and 8:3, describes the quiet joy of the union of the two lovers. Once she has found the object of her love she falls into an ecstatic sleep which her beloved does not wish to disturb.

o Allegorical interpretation. In 2:8-14 it is the bridegroom who seeks his bride; in 3:1-4 it is the bride who goes in search of her beloved. The two scenes represent their yearning for each other. Yahweh called Israel and Israel responded, and though for some time she turned her back on him, she returned once more to him, was received and made again the object of his love. The Fathers explain the bridegroom's leaping over the mountains as God's approach to man by way of the Virgin's womb, the manger, the Cross, the tomb and heaven (St Greg. the Great *In expos. Evang. hom.* 29, PL 79, 907). The description of spring means that God's appeal to man is made at a time when response is more likely to follow. Spring in fact is the time for love. But such details as the latticed window, winter, rain, figs, etc. are mere parabolic elements.

385a **III 6-V 1 Third Song—**A contrast between the pomp of a royal marriage and the simple unconventional manifestations of love between the two shepherds. Buzy thinks 3:6-11 to be interpolated. Probably the poet by describing Solomon's marriage intended to give a stronger relief to the simple way of living of the countryfolk.

b **III 6-8 The Royal Procession—6.** The people are astonished on seeing a cloud of dust in the desert approaching the city and ask : *What* is *this?* The point of comparison is the rising cloud of the smoke not its fragrance. This is mentioned only in view of what is to follow. **7 f.** When the procession comes nearer, they can see Solomon's *litter* escorted by sixty of the most valiant men of Israel, all well-trained in the use of arms and carrying their swords against some possible night attack.

c **9-11 The Royal Pavilion—9.** When the procession arrives in the city, the king sits down on his throne under a pavilion that had been erected for the occasion. Heb. '*appiryôn*, translated by Vg-DV 'ferculum-litter', is now rendered 'pavilion' (Joüon, Buzy) or 'throne' (Miller). **10.** The pavilion had silver pillars, a golden *ceiling*, and the *seat* upholstered with purple embroidery and *inlaid with ebony* (Siegfried, Miller, Ricciotti). **11.** The maidens of Jerusalem are invited to admire the magnificence of the king crowned by his mother. The mention of the king's mother is embarrassing.

There is no evidence of a king being crowned by his **3** mother. Moreover, if the king is Yahweh and his bride is Israel, who is the king's mother? But both the crown and the king's mother may be a mere literary development of the nuptial comparison.

IV 1-7 The Bride's Beauty—From Solomon's mar- **d** riage-feast we are taken back to the fields to admire once more the bride's beauty. **1.** The opening words are identical with 1:14. For DV 'besides what is hid within' read 'through the veil' or 'amidst your locks'. Her dove-like eyes can be seen through the thin, transparent veil which covers her face. Her long, wavy locks are like a flock of goats streaming down from Mount Galaad. **2.** Her teeth are as white as a flock of sheep coming up from the washing before being shorn. They are also paired, and there is none *missing*. Whiteness and symmetry of teeth are meant. **3.** Her lips are like a red thread and her mouth, or speech, is graceful. 'Besides that which lieth hid within', see 1. **4.** Her neck is erect and stately as a tower built *for the trophies*, or *as a fortress* ; the mention of David adds nothing to the image. If the neck is a tower, the bucklers and the armour of the warriors are the necklaces and pendants. **5.** 'Which feed among the lilies', these words serve only to add gracefulness to the description ; see 2:16. **6** is repeated with slight modifications from 2:17 and is the conclusion of the first part of the song, though perhaps loosely connected with the context.

7-9 The Bridegroom fascinated by his Bride's Beauty **e** —7 is similar to 4:1. The Heb. word for 'spot' means 'a physical defect', *cf.* 2 Kg 14:25. *7b* is applied by the Church in an accommodated sense to the Immaculate Conception : 'et macula originalis non est in te'. Hence the appellation 'Immaculate'. **8.** MT has 'with me' for the first two 'come' of DV. The reading of Vg, which is that of LXX and the Syriac version, is preferred by many modern interpreters (Miller, Buzy). By changing a vowel or two in MT this sense is obtained : 'Me from Lebanon, my Spouse, me from Lebanon thou dost bring back'. This sense is preferable because it is the bridegroom, not the bride, that is represented coming from the mountains, *cf.* 2:8, 17 ; 4:6. Vg-DV 'thou shalt be crowned' is a misinterpretation of MT which is usually rendered : 'advance, come forth'. But as the person coming from the mountains is the bridegroom, we translate : 'induce me to come' (A. Vaccari, Bi [1947] 395). Amana, Sanir, Hermon are peaks in the Antilebanon range. The bridegroom is drawn by his bride's beauty from the most distant and inaccessible places. **9.** The power of the bride's fascinating beauty is now explicitly asserted. One glance from her charming eyes, one *bead* of her necklaces is enough to make his heart burn with love. For 'wounded' read '*ravished*'.

10-15 Other Praises of the Bride's Beauty—10 recalls **f** 1:2 f. The bride's *caresses*, the expression of her love, are sweeter than wine, the symbol of joy and pleasure. **11.** Milk mixed with honey was, and still is, a favourite drink in the East (Power, VD [1922] 54 f.). Here it symbolizes sweetness of speech. Even the perfumes of the bride's garments contribute to make her more lovely. **12.** MT reads : 'a garden enclosed . . . a spring shut up' ; but probably we must read 'a spring' twice, the two Heb. words *gan* and *gal* being easily interchangeable (Joüon, Buzy). Springs of water were sometimes enclosed by a wall with a locked entrance in order to make them inaccessible to intruders. The metaphor is obvious. **13.** The *conduits* conveying water from the enclosed spring irrigate an orchard of pomegranates and trees of exquisite fruits, henna and spikenard. The unusual plural *nerādîm* 'spikenards' and the repetition of the same word in the singular in 14 have led some interpreters to read *werādîm* 'roses', a word which occurs in Mishnaic Hebrew. **14.** A list of aromatic plants irrigated by the invisible spring. Instead of 'Libanus' read 'incense' and 'balm-trees' for 'perfumes'. **15.** The poet reverts to the image of the spring. The bride is compared to a spring, which

5f is not only inaccessible but also yields streams of water all the year round. Two qualities of the bride's love are here signified : it is unalterable and beneficent.

g **16–V 1 The Union—16.** The bridegroom requests the winds to blow and to saturate the air with the fragrance of the flowers that he may enjoy the aromatic perfume of the garden. The garden is another metaphor for the bride. The bridegroom wishes to enjoy the delightful presence of his bride. **V 1a.** The bride manifests the same desire. Let him come near and enjoy the pleasure of his bride's love. Both garden and fruit are *his*, the bridegroom's, because the bride has given her heart to him alone. **1b.** The bridegroom is now with his bride. Read : '*I gather. . . I eat . . . I drink*'. **1c.** The lovers' meeting is represented as a marriage feast at which friends are necessarily present.

h Allegorical interpretation. The meaning of 3:6–11 must be considered in relation to the whole song. If this relation is one of contrast and if 4:1–5:1 describes the pure love of two shepherds unaffected by the conventionalism of a more refined society, then 6–11 represent all that can defile or frustrate that love. But if there is no opposition between 3:6–11 and 4:1–5:1, the king's marriage may be taken to represent Christ's union with the Church, or his assumption of human nature in the Incarnation, or Yahweh's installation in the temple of Jerusalem.

i The beautiful bride is Israel cleansed from her sins and arrayed with her finest garments (Is 52:1), or the Church purified by the blood of Christ, ' cleansed by the laver of water in the word of life : . . . a glorious church not having spot or wrinkle . . . but holy and without blemish' (Eph 5:26 f.). The several parts of the body— eyes, hair, teeth, etc.—are parabolic elements. God's love for man knows no obstacles. He so loved the world as to give his only-begotten Son (Jn 3:16) ; and this immense love is vividly described as drawing him near to mankind from distant and inaccessible places, *i.e.* from heaven. Man is beautiful in the sight of God because he is made in the divine image, but still more beautiful does he become when he is adorned with sanctifying grace. The figure of the sealed fountain represents the inalienable love of the Church whose heart is shut to all affections but that for her divine Bridegroom. The Fathers have applied the figure to the virginity of Mary. In this song, and throughout the whole poem, love is represented in its purest form. The bride is called ' sister-bride ' and the union of the two lovers is a spiritual one.

j **V 2–VI 3 Fourth Song—**Here too we have the usual theme : the bridegroom's yearning for his bride, the bride's description of her bridegroom's beauty, and the joy of their union. A new feature is the painful proof to which the bridegroom subjects his bride.

k **V 2–5 A Night Visit.—2.** She is sleeping, but her mind is wakeful. Of a sudden she hears a knock. Her beloved has come and calls her insistently in the most endearing terms and asks her to open. **3.** Apparently she refuses to open for a trifling pretext (Calmet, Joüon, Ricciotti). But this is hardly compatible with the statement that even during sleep her mind is absorbed by her beloved. It is preferable to regard her words as a poetic device meant to account for the sudden disappearance of the bridegroom (Miller, Buzy). **4.** The bridegroom tries to open by passing his hand or finger through the keyhole and removing the bolt. On hearing the sound and perhaps on seeing his hand through the hole, she is seized by violent emotion. For ' at his touch ' read ' on account of him ' or ' of this '. **5.** She rises up to open, and as soon as she touches the bolt her hands become moist with myrrh. Probably the bridegroom had bathed his hands in myrrh and so left its perfume upon the bolt.

l **6–8 In search of the Bridegroom—6.** Unable to open the door the bridegroom departs. The words ' my soul melted when he spoke ' are out of place, because as he had already gone, she could not hear him speaking. Some interpreters transpose these words after 4 (Miller,

Buzy). If we read '*br* ' to pass away, to depart ' for **385l** MT *dbr* ' to speak ', the consonants ' and *d* being easily interchangeable in the old Heb. script, we obtain this sense : I fainted when he went away. No transposition is necessary. Immediately she hurries out looking for him and calling for him in vain. **7.** This ill-treatment is another poetical fiction meant to heighten her distress. **8.** As has been often remarked, the dialogue is sometimes intended to give a dramatic effect to the internal feelings of the actor. So we need not ask how the daughters of Jerusalem happened to be outdoors at that time of night.

9–16 Description of the Bridegroom—9. The question **m** of the maidens serves to introduce the following description. **10.** My beloved is white and ruddy, distinguished out of thousands. **11.** His head is finest gold ; his locks are like palms and black as a raven. **12.** His eyes are like doves beside the water-brooks. In 12*b* read : ' His teeth are bathed in milk, ensconced in their setting ' (A. Vaccari, Bi [1947] 399 f.). **13.** His cheeks are beds of balsam shrubs, *rich in* perfume ; his lips are like lilies, dropping choice myrrh. **14.** His *arms* are *rods* of gold, *set with topaz* ; his *breast* is ivory set with sapphires. **15.** His legs are pillars of *alabaster*, set upon *sockets of fine* gold. His aspect is like that of (the trees of) Lebanon, stately as the cedars. **16.** His mouth is full of sweetness ; he is all lovely. **17.** After this panegyric on the bridegroom's beauty, the maidens show themselves ready to help her.

VI 1 f. The Meeting—1. The scene changes ; the **n** maidens have disappeared ; it is daylight ; the bride and the bridegroom are together in the garden. We are not told how the bride found her bridegroom. The poet depicts the amorous scenes by a few strokes and leaves it to the imagination to fill up the gaps. The bridegroom is in his garden planted with *balsam shrubs*, feeding his flock and gathering lilies. The two details of feeding the flock in the garden and gathering lilies, unlikely though they are, are two delicate touches which render the picture more attractive. **2.** The joy of their union is expressed with the same words as in 2:16.

Allegorical interpretation. The most salient traits of **o** this song are : The bridegroom's unexpected visit, the bride's apparent indifference, the bridegroom's disappearance, the bride's night search and description of the bridegroom, their union. Applied to the history of Israel these may refer to Israel's infidelity, punishment and conversion. The Church too sometimes seems to be deserted by her divine Spouse. She is persecuted by her enemies who try to strip her of her bridal raiment, which is her sanctity. But she remains faithful to Christ, the most beautiful of the sons of man. In the Liturgy the description of the bridegroom is applied to Christ. Everlasting happiness is the reward for her fidelity. The song is particularly rich in ascetic applications. God knocks at the door of our heart in the quiet of the night, far from the distractions of the world, in solitude (Os 2:14) ; he comes unexpectedly, and we must be ever ready to respond. Those who are neglectful will miss the benefits of God's grace, and it is through penance that they may regain them. Sometimes God seems to abandon the faithful soul but it is only to test her attachment. The soul that comes out victorious is rewarded with more abundant graces and with the spiritual joy of a closer union with God.

VI 3–VIII 4 Fifth Song—The analysis is difficult. **386a** The beginning and the end are in the style of the other songs, but the connexion and internal development of the ideas are not always clear.

3–8 Praises of the Bride—3. She is as beautiful *as* **b** *Tirsah*, the old capital of the Northern Kingdom (3 Kg 15:33). Tirsah, not Samaria, has been chosen as a term of comparison both for its connexion with the verb *rāṣāh* ' to be pleased with ', as well as for Samaria's association with heathen cult. Her beauty could conquer all hearts as a powerful army ready for the attack. **4a.** Her eyes are *fascinating*. The words ' turn

386b away thy eyes from me ' express the marvellous beauty of the bride's eyes. **4b-6.** See on 4:*1b-3*. **7 f.** A contrast between the polygamy of oriental rulers and the monogamous union of the two shepherd-lovers. The sense is : Let a king have as many as sixty wives having legal rights (queens), and as many as eighty other secondary wives (concubines) and a host of maidens attending upon his wives, or, more probably, awaiting their turn to be introduced to the king (Est 2:9–14), I have only one, who is the only, and therefore most beloved, daughter of her mother and the object of universal praise and admiration.

c 9-11 The Bride's Sudden Appearance—9. The bride, whose extraordinary beauty has just been described, now makes a sudden appearance, exciting admiration in the spectators. Her charming beauty and stately aspect are compared to the splendour of *dawn*, the moon and the sun, and to the imposing march of an army. The verse is a familiar antiphon in the Office of our Lady's Assumption. **10.** The subject is probably the bridegroom who alone is represented as going to his garden (4:16 ; 5:1 ; 6:1). **11.** While he is in the garden, something, that it is difficult to determine, happens to him. The source of the difficulty is the Heb. expression '*ammî nāḏîḇ* which is taken as a proper noun by LXX and Vg, while modern interpreters generally translate ' noble people ' (Joüon), ' prince of my people ' (Pouget-Guitton), ' princely cortège ' (Miller). As the word *nāḏîḇ* recurs in 7:1 in an analogous phrase ' noble daughter ', it seems that we should retain the same meaning here and translate ' noble people ', the final *i* in '*ammî* being a paragogic *i*. But ' the chariots of a noble people ' hardly makes sense and the context requires the name of some well-known personage whose chariots were renowned for their speed. Buzy's reference to the chariot carrying the ark from Abinadab's house (2 Kg 6:3) is far-fetched. The general sense of 11 seems to be : The bridegroom was so struck by the unexpected appearance of his beautiful bride that he ran out of his garden with all possible speed.

d 12-VII 5 Other Praises by the Chorus—12. The bride is requested to return that the maidens may admire her beauty once more. This is another poetic device meant to bring the bride into the scene as the object of the praises that are to follow. She is described here as ' the Shulamite ', a native of Shulam, a village in the plain of Esdraelon ; the word may be a variant of Shunamite (3 Kg 1:3). This appellation occurs here and in 7:1 only, and seems to be chosen for some literary motive rather than for historical reasons. **VII 1a.** *Why would you gaze at the Shulamite, as upon a chorus in two bands ?* This difficult verse has received many different interpretations. As *meḥōlaṭ hammaḥ*ᵃ*nayim* is generally translated ' dance of two companies ', the bride's words are taken as a refusal of the maidens' invitation to dance (Vaccari, *I Libri Poetici della Bibbia*, Rome, 1925), or as an acceptance (Miller, Ricciotti, Pouget-Guitton). Joüon, followed by Buzy, thinks that these words were spoken by the bridegroom, who modestly agrees that his bride should come before the maidens. The reference to dancing seems to be excluded by the shyness and modesty of the bride and by the general tone of Cant. *Meḥōlaṭ hammaḥ*ᵃ*nayim* may also be rendered ' a chorus in two bands '. The bride is supposed to be advancing between two rows of girls singing alternately and accompanying their singing with a rhythmical movement of their bodies

e (Buzy). **1b.** How *graceful* are thy steps in *sandals*, O prince's daughter ! The praises of the bride are sung by the two halves of the chorus alternately. **1c.** The *roundings* of thy thighs (or, *the pillars of thy legs*) are like *the links of a chain, the work of an artist's hand*. They are perfectly rounded. **2a.** Thy navel is like a *rounded goblet, wherein wine is not wanting*. The literary taste of oriental poets differs from ours. The image of wine has been called forth by that of the goblet. **2b.** Palestinian farmers heap up the corn on the threshing-floor and surround it with thorns to protect it from

animals before carrying it to their barns. But the **3** image represents the heap of wheat surrounded with lilies, the symbol of purity. **3** is repeated from 4:5. **4a.** Her neck is compared to a tower for its erectness, and to ivory for its whiteness. **4b.** Thine eyes are like **f** the *pools* of Heshbon, by the gate of *Bath-Rabbim*. Heshbon was the ancient capital of the Amorites in Transjordania (Num 21:25). Probably it had some water reservoirs. Bath-Rabbim is an unknown locality, perhaps in the land of the Ammonites, *cf.* Rabbath Ammon, the capital of the Ammonites (Jer 48:3). But the geography of the author is more poetical than scientific. **4c.** Her nose is compared to an imaginary tower built on Lebanon guarding the way to Damascus. Here again we have no right to impose our aesthetic rules upon the oriental poet. **5.** Her head is erect and majestic as Mount Carmel ; the tresses of her head are like purple ; in 4:1 they are black, but the poet has the right to vary the comparisons. *A king is held captive in the locks thereof.* The king is not Solomon, the supposed rival of the shepherd-lover, but the shepherd himself who is called king according to the nuptial language. The sense may be also : Thy tresses are so beautiful as to captivate even a king. The captivating power of the bride is also recorded in 4:9 ; 6:5.

6-9 Other Praises by the Bridegroom—6. The ex- **g** clamation ' How beautiful art thou ! ' which recurs in 1:13 ; 4:1, 7 ; and 6:4 suggests that it is the bridegroom who is speaking. Instead of ' in delights ' read with the Syriac and many modern interpreters ' daughter of delights ', *i.e.* exceedingly delightful. **7.** The palmtree is a favourite figure in oriental poetry to describe the stateliness of a slender and graceful body. Tamar (= palm-tree) was also a frequent name for women, *cf.* Gen 38:6 ; 4 Kg 13:1. **8.** The bridegroom is not content with admiring the bride's bodily perfections, he is also anxious to enjoy them. He is longing for the complete possession of his bride. **9.** In MT and Vg these words are spoken by the bride. But, as the context shows, they are the continuation of the bridegroom's praise of his bride's beauty. A slight modification of MT would give this sense : Thy mouth, *i.e.* thy speech, is like the choicest wine dropping gently on my palate, gliding over my lips and teeth.

10-VIII 4 The Joy of their Union—10. The bride **h** gives herself up entirely to her beloved who is irresistibly drawn towards her. **11.** She invites him to go for a walk through the fields. **12.** It is spring-time, and she now invites him to the vineyards, where she will give him her *love, i.e.* she will offer herself to him. **13.** The images are all expressive of love. The mandrakes are a fruit of the size and colour of a small apple. They ripen in May. Their flowers have a pleasant smell, and the fruit was believed to possess aphrodisiac properties (Gen 30:14), hence called also ' love-apples '. **VIII 1.** In her ecstasy of love the bride expresses the desire to become the sister of her bridegroom without, however, renouncing her condition of bride. She had already expressed her self-surrender to her bridegroom in the solitary vineyard, far from the sight of men. She now desires to show her love for him anywhere without shame or fear. **2** emended reads thus : I would bring you into my mother's house, into the chamber of her who bare me ; I will give you to drink spiced wine, my wine of pomegranates. **3 f.** See on 2:6 f.

Allegorical interpretation. In general it is identical **i** with that of the other songs, particularly the third which describes the incomparable beauty of the bride and her irresistible attractiveness. Points of special interest are : the uniqueness of the bride. As God has selected only one people in the OT, so Christ founded only one Church, whom he loved so much as to shed his blood for her (Eph 2:16). The heap of corn surrounded by lilies suggests the virginal fecundity of the Church. The image of the corn and the goblet of wine is, according to the Fathers, an allusion to the Eucharist. The bridegroom gathering the fruits of his palm-like bride is Christ rejoicing in the children of the Church

31 and their virtues. The intimacy between Christ and his Church is as chaste as that existing between a brother and a sister. The Fathers agree in explaining 8:1 as the Synagogue's ardent desire for the Incarnation of the Son of God. Through his human nature Christ became like men (Phil 2:7 ; Heb 2:17) and their brother (Rom 8:29 ; Heb 2:11).

a **VIII 5-7 Sixth Song**—The Triumph of Love. In this short song, which may be considered as the conclusion of that preceding, the two lovers are represented in the fullness of their joy, united for ever with an indissoluble bond of love. **5a.** Omit ' flowing with delights '. The poet is describing the nuptial cortège proceeding to the bridegroom's house. **5b.** Read : ' Under the apple-tree I raised thee up, where thy mother brought thee forth, where she that bare thee brought thee forth '. These words are spoken by the bridegroom probably in the first days of their love. The beginning of their mutual affection is poetically associated with the apple-tree and the maternal house, which are, in a different **b** way, symbols of love. **6 f.** A hymn to love. The bride begs to remain inseparably united with her bridegroom, as a signet ring which is usually bound round the neck with a cord or fastened to the arm (Gen 38:18 ; Jer 22:24). Her love for him is as strong as death which none can escape, and her *passion* is as *inexorable* as *Sheol*, which never gives back any who come under its sway. Its flashes are flashes of fire, which warms, burns and consumes ; and its flames *are flames of Yahweh* ; Yahweh is added to denote the intensity of the flames of love. *Love* is so strong and intense that it can neither be extinguished by flooding waters nor swept away by impetuous rivers ; *cf.* Rom 8:35 ff. Love is more precious than riches, and whoever attempts to bargain for love deserves the utmost contempt. The sense of DV is slightly different : If love could be bought for money, man would give all his possessions to acquire it ; *cf.* the parable of the pearl, Mt 13:45 f. **c** Allegorical interpretation. Both Israel after the exile and the Church declare their inseparable attachment to God. More particularly, Israel is described, according to some interpreters, returning from the exile accompanied by Yahweh (Is 52:12) who recalls to her memory her humble origin (Ricciotti). The Fathers generally refer the whole scene to Christ's marriage with the triumphant Church, Apoc 19:7 f. **d** **VIII 8-15 Appendix**—After this magnificent apotheosis of love one feels reluctant to assist at a marriage contract such as is described in 8-12. This section is

therefore rejected as an interpolation by Meignan (545) **387d** and Buzy (360). Joüon with greater probability believes that it was added by the poet himself sometime after he had finished the poem. Other interpreters, however, consider it to be the conclusion of the book. **8-10 The Marriage Bargain**—**8.** We have a young **e** sister who is not yet of marriageable age, what shall we do when she is asked in marriage ? The elder brothers, the guardians of their younger sister ask themselves what sum will they ask from the prospective suitor of their sister. In those times the prospective bridegroom had to pay a sum of money ; *cf.* Gen 24:25 ; 34:11. **9.** If she is comparable to a wall, *i.e.* a walled city, let us make it impregnable by constructing silver bulwarks ; if she is a gate, or the city gate, we will bar it with cedar planks. In other words, the brothers are unwilling to give her away unless for a very high price. **10.** The sister proudly claims that she is fully mature and that she has found peace since she has found the man of her heart.

11-12 Solomon's Vineyard—**11.** Solomon had a vine- **f** yard at *Baal-Hamon*, which he gave in charge to keepers for the sum of one thousand shekels. Baal-Hamon is an unknown place. It is not clear by whom these words were spoken. **12.** The bridegroom steps in. My vineyard, *i.e.* my bride, is here before me. I am ready to pay the sum you asked and an additional remuneration to you, the keepers of the vineyard. Solomon is the type of the wealthy man.

13-14 Conclusion—**13.** The price has been agreed **g** upon and paid by the bridegroom who now addresses his bride : O thou that dwellest in the gardens, let me hear in the presence of friends thy consent to my demand. **14.** She replies asking him to take her away with him wherever he pleases. She now belongs to him and will live with him for ever.

Allegorical interpretation. It depends on the literal **h** sense which is not clear. Supposing the appendix to be written by the same author, we can easily trace the main lines of interpretation. Bride and bridegroom are, in a particular way, the Church and Christ. The price which Christ had to pay for his bride was far in excess of what any man could offer ; in fact, it was Christ's own blood (1 Pet 1:19). The bride's brothers, trying to frustrate her marriage, are the heathen peoples and all the persecutors of the Church. The vineyard is a familiar metaphor for Israel (Is 5:1) and the Church (Mt 20:1 ff. ; 21:33 ff.). The bride's last words to the bridegroom express a desire for the consummation of their union in heaven.

THE BOOK OF WISDOM

(THE WISDOM OF SOLOMON)

By C. LATTEY, S.J.

388a Bibliography—St Jerome, as is well known, followed his Jewish teachers in Hebrew in rejecting the deutero-canonical books, including Wisdom, the text of which in Vg (translated in DV) consequently does not go back to him, but to an earlier African translation. For the original Greek text *Swete's edition (Cambridge, 1930³) has been followed. Upon the whole the book has fared well at the hands of English commentators, the chief being *Deane (Oxford, 1881) ; *Goodrick (Rivingtons, 1913) ; *Holmes (in CAP, I) ; *Oester-ley (mainly translation : S.P.C.K., 1917) ; *Gregg (Cambridge, 1922). The chief Catholic commentaries are those by Fr Cornely, S.J., in CSS, edited after his death by Fr Zorell, S.J. (1910) and Dr Feldmann's *Das Buch der Weisheit* in BB (1926). Two useful books of more general scope are *Swete's *Introduction to the OT in Greek* (ed. 2 by R. R. Ottley, Cambridge, 1914) and *Introductionis in S. Scripturae Libros Compendium* by Fr Cornely, S.J., in CSS (ed. 9 by Fr Merk, S.J., 1927).

b Title and Language—' The Book of Wisdom ' is the title of the work in the Latin Bible, but the Greek and Syriac Bibles entitle it ' the Wisdom of Solomon '. St Jerome in his preface to the Wisdom books expressly affirms that it was written in Greek, an opinion now generally admitted, which of course rules out Solomon as author. St Augustine (*De Civ. Dei*, XVII. 20, 1) remarks that the more learned have no doubt that the work is not Solomon's. Swete (268) writes that ' no other book in the Greek Bible is so manifestly Alexandrian in tone and style '. The proof that it was written in Greek rests chiefly upon the fact that ' throughout the book compound words abound—a mark of Alexandrian Greek ' (Holmes, 525 : *cf*. Swete, 311), upon the use of alliteration and assonances and philosophical terms, all pointing to a Greek original, and to the impossibility of translating the book adequately into Hebrew. It is an example of ' pseudepigraphy ', the text of the work indicating verbally Solomon as author (especially in 9:7–8, 12) though he did not really write it.

c Date of Composition—It appears to have been written in the first half of the 2nd cent. B.C. The hostile attitude adopted towards the ancient Egyptians indicates a period when they were still quite distinct from the Greek immigrants. A fair interval of time would probably be required for a work written in Greek to be recognized as Holy Scripture ; yet there is no sign that there was any difficulty about receiving it into the Greek OT, nor does the employment of it in the NT suggest that there was any controversy or doubt about its authority. The Alexandrian Jews were not likely to recognize a book as canonical that would be repudiated in Jerusalem, nor were the NT writers likely to appeal to it. The true reason for the ultimate exclusion of the Book of Wisdom from the Jewish canon is doubtless that given by Dr Ginzberg in JE, I, 305–6, in the article *Akiba ben Joseph* : Rabbi Akiba was the one who definitely fixed the Jewish canon, and in rejecting Wisdom and some other books he was guided by the desire to disarm Christians—especially Jewish Christians—who drew their arguments from them. The exclusion was also doubtless part of a reaction towards the exclusive use of Hebrew.

d The use of Wisdom is most conspicuous in St Paul,

who bases his exposition in Rom 1:18–32 on Wis **3** 13:1–10. In Rom 9:19–23 we may trace the influence of Wis 11:22 ; 12:12 ; 15:7 ; and there are reminiscences in other passages of his epistles, and in other NT works. Very significant is Mt 27:43, where (for example) *Nestle in his small NT rightly marks a reference to Wis 2:13, 18–20, for his reference to Ps 22:9 does not exhaust the citation. When we consider St Matthew's constant insistence on the fulfilment of the OT, it is clear that he found it here also. In general, ' of the deutero-canonical books of the OT there is none that the apostles and early Church used oftener ' (Cornely-Merk, 512).

Considerations such as the above put out of court any **e** attempt to date the book to the reign of the Roman Emperor Gaius (Caligula). It is astonishing to find Goodrick (15 f.), for example, suggesting A.D. 41–4 ; though it is in part accounted for by his still more surprising statement (16) that the deification of the Ptolemies ' seems certain in very few cases, possibly only in that of Ptolemy I '. Mahaffy, to whom he refers, has made the matter sufficiently clear in his *Empire of the Ptolemies* (MacMillan, 1895), and it is now certain that their worship was a permanent part of their royal style, as it was afterwards in that of the Roman emperors. The temporary disturbance under Gaius would not explain Pseudo-Solomon's explicit (yet cautious) attack on ruler-worship in 14:12–21, nearly so well as the steady pressure of the earlier cult centred at Alexandria itself, and in its essence inherited through Alexander the Great from the Pharaohs.

Literary Type—The element of historical fiction con- **f** tained in Wisdom may go beyond pseudepigraphy, and make of it a ' midrash ' treatise. This is a convenient technical term, founded on the Hebrew word ' midrash ', and implies a pious but imaginative meditation upon sacred history, of a kind still to some extent in use. Not only is the work ascribed verbally to Solomon, but he is represented as writing for the benefit of other kings (6:2, etc.) ; and the description of OT events appears to be heightened for the author's special purposes. The question arises mainly in regard to Part V (chh 16–19) ; *cf*. § 394*a*. The need of a careful investigation of literary form in biblical studies has been stressed by His Holiness Pope Pius XII in his encyclical, *Divino afflante Spiritu* (30 Sept., 1943).

Doctrine—The Book of Wisdom has a strong personi- **g** fying tendency, which prepares the way for the doctrine of the Blessed Trinity, without explicitly affirming Wisdom to be more than a divine attribute. Thus in regard of Wisdom itself we may compare 9:4 with St Paul's declaring Christ ' the Wisdom of God ' (1 Cor 1:24), and Wis 7:25 with all Col 1:15–19. In Wis 18:15 we even read of the ' almighty word ' or *Logos* of God, which prepares us for St John's gospel. The term had a philosophical past, and was to become even more prominent between the dates of Wisdom and the fourth gospel in the writings of the Jewish Alexandrian Philo, but still without definitely signifying a distinct person. It is a question whether at the time of the composition of Wisdom the rabbis had already begun in the targums (the Aramaic paraphrases for public reading of the Hebrew OT) to write ' the Word of the Lord ' in place of ' Yahweh '. This use of the ' Word ' (*Memra*), like the *Logos* of Philo tended to exclude the mention of God himself; but there is nothing of this tendency appearing in the Book of Wisdom.

Somewhat similarly we read that 'the spirit of the Lord filleth the inhabited earth' (Wis 1:7; *cf.* 9:17, etc.), with which we may compare 1 Cor 2:10-16, etc. At the beginning of the development we may put Gen 1:2, and at the end Ac 5:3-4.

The Book of Wisdom is largely concerned with **rewards and punishments after death**, to which we get the first rather vague reference in Dan 12:2. The doctrines of the immortality and immateriality of the soul find here their first certain expression. The lot of the just hereafter (3:1-9) is contrasted with that of the wicked (5:1-15): the Lord shall reward the former (5:16-17), but overwhelm the latter (5:18-24). The problem of evil is thus settled by reference to the next world, in the sense that men are ultimately requited according to their deserts. Indeed, the merit of suffering well borne is so stressed in the first part (chh 1-5) as to present an other-worldly outlook. On the other hand the last part (chh 16-19) lays hardly less emphasis on God's especial favour to the Israelites in this world; nor does the writer envisage clearly the possibility of Israelites being lost or Egyptians saved. He is at pains to say that God was giving the Egyptians the chance of repentance, but with the evident implication that the grace was not taken (11:24-12:2; 12:8-10, etc.). In one place (19:4) he writes that 'a necessity well deserved' was drawing the Egyptians on to their destruction, much as in Ex 7:3; 9:12; 10:1, God is said to have hardened the heart of Pharaoh. Thus the author does not appear to have found a perfect synthesis of individual and collective salvation, or of this-world and other-worldly retribution, or of grace and free will; rather he opens up problems which had not yet presented themselves in all their force, and which it was to be the task of Christianity to solve, so far as it is given to man here below to solve them at all.

There is no hint of a Messias in the book; in spite of the questions of which the author shows himself aware, he does not contemplate any radical change in the Jewish theocratic ideal. Neither is there any apocalyptic feature, a fact which in a work of this particular kind makes for a date before the period of the Jewish apocalypses, to which he must have stood very close. On the other hand there is no trace of the narrow rabbinical reaction which prevented Judaism from blossoming gently and naturally into Christianity. The Jewish professor, Dr Joseph Klausner, has written in his work, *From Jesus to Paul* (Engl. transl., 1943: 136) ' Truly, therefore, the Wisdom of Solomon as a syncretistic book, a mixture of Judaism and Hellenism, had no equal for purposes of Christian propaganda'. But it is 'syncretistic' only to one who, like himself, looks upon rabbinical Judaism as the only legitimate development of the OT. In reality the book is genuinely and intensely Jewish, but it does not altogether ignore the universalism in the OT, which so clearly demanded fuller expression. The absence of Messianism prevented it from being at all equal to the prophets 'for the purposes of Christian propaganda'.

The Book of Wisdom certainly found an attentive reader in St Paul; but, like most, if not all, pious Jews of his time, he was steeped in the Messianic hope. The book would chiefly serve to reconcile him to a Messias who must suffer, to give him a definitely other-worldly outlook, to strengthen the universalism which he would draw from the OT itself, and even to prepare his mind for the mystery of the Blessed Trinity.

Plan of the Book—This appears to be as follows. Part I (chh 1-5) is in the nature of a general introduction. Part II (chh 6-9) contains the positive exposition of Wisdom, which Part III (chh 10-12) illustrates from history. Part IV (chh 13-15) contains an attack upon idolatry, the negative or polemical justification of Wisdom, which Part V (chh 16-19) once more illustrates from history.

PART I chh 1-5. The Righteous and the Wicked— 389a This introductory part reminds us somewhat of Ps 1, the introduction to the whole Psalter, which sets forth the two opposed ways of virtue and vice.

I 1-16 Wisdom is only for the Righteous—The opening appeal is to 'ye that judge the earth', in the sense of ruling it, as in Jg 6:2 'judges' is parallel to 'kings'. In the main, however, the book is of universal application. **1.** Man must have holy thoughts about God and make it his single purpose to do his will. Already in **4-6** Wisdom is personified and is identified in the parallelism with God himself (**6a, c**). He is witness of man's 'reins', *i.e.* kidneys, where we should say 'heart'. ('Heart' itself comes nearer to our 'mind'.) **6-11.** God's knowledge is urged as an incentive to virtue, his 'spirit' being likewise personified in a way that prepares the definite revelation of the Third Person of the Blessed Trinity, to whom it is applied in the Whitsuntide liturgy, though the literal sense does not refer to the Pentecostal gift of tongues: God's spirit is everywhere, filling the whole world, ' and that which *holdeth all things together* hath knowledge ' of all that the voice of man utters. **10.** God is a jealous God (*cf.* Ex 20:5; 34:14, etc.) and will not suffer murmurings against his government of the world. **11.** ' The mouth that lieth killeth the soul '; with that the argument passes to external works (**12-16**).

The transition to works introduces a new theme of life **c** and death. In **15** 'perpetual and' should probably be omitted, and the words, 'but wickedness is the attainment of death', be added: they furnish the necessary parallel line to what precedes, and also the mention of ' death ' which is necessary to make sense of the next line, supplying the reference to the pronoun ' it '. They have some Latin support. In view of the emphasis on immortality here and elsewhere, ' death ' is best understood to include spiritual death and the loss of a happy eternity. But the word for ' hell ' (**14**) is the Greek ' Hades ', which of itself signifies no more than the abode of the dead in general, as when we say that Christ ' descended into hell '. The writer denies that God delights in death: ' He created all things that they might have being ', so we should perhaps translate the difficult words that follow, ' *and all things that are produced upon the earth are helpful* '. Only ' the wicked . . . call it [death] to them, and esteeming it a friend *pine away* ' for love of it. They have covenanted with it and deserve it.

II 1-25 The Thoughts of the Wicked—(i) (**1-5**) They **d** reject the idea of immortality: (ii) (**6-9**) abandon themselves to pleasure: (iii) (**10-20**) persecute the ' poor just man ': (iv) (**21-25**) the author himself condemns these thoughts. In spite of the disedifying sentiments expressed, the vigorous and poetical style of this chapter makes it one of the finest in the book. **2.** ' We were born *by mere chance* . . . and *reason is* **e** *but a spark kindled by the beating of our hearts* '. **5.** ' No one reverseth ' our last end. **8.** And so to the reckless pursuit of pleasure! ' Let no meadow escape our riot ': this is not in the Greek, but ' is almost certainly genuine ' (Goodrick: similarly Oesterley): it is required for parallelism and on other grounds. **10.** ' The poor just man ' is the '*anî* of the OT, the ' poor in spirit ' of Mt 5:3, who bears oppression in meek submission to the Divine Will. The type finds its supreme expression in Christ (*cf.* Mt 11:28-30) like the OT institution of prophecy (*cf.* Deut 18:15-19; Ac 3: 22-23; 7:37). In **12** lax or apostate Jews must be speaking, since ' the poor just man ' reproaches them with breaches both of the Mosaic Law and of the unwritten and traditional law (' sins against our discipline ' or way of life); such mention of wicked Jews is unique in the book, and gives the more point to the reference to Wis 2:13, 18-20 in Mt 27:43, already mentioned as marked by Nestle (§ 388*d*). But the general tenor of the book forbids us to think that such alone are envisaged; there is question of the Gentiles (*e.g.*) in 4:14, and with these the bad Jews are presumably to be reckoned.

389f In **16** the poor just man's expectation of immortality is derided, and a shameful death is suggested for him in **20a**. The following words seem to be ironical : **20.** ' *To judge from his words, there will be divine protection for him* '. **21-25.** The author himself condemns these thoughts of the wicked ; (**21-22**) they are blinded by malice from perceiving the mysteries of God, of which several are at once set forth, concluding with the entry of death into the world through the devil's jealousy, and the fact that (**25**) ' *they who are of his party experience it* '. The word for ' experience ' has this sense also in 12:26. Spiritual death is meant, as in 1:15, where see the commentary ; for physical death is common to all. See also 5:16, etc. The Fall is referred to in **24-25** ; the doctrine is more fully developed in Rom 5 :12–21, which (like so much else in that epistle) is partly based on Wisdom.

g III 1-9 The Righteous Hereafter—This section would more logically furnish a triumphant finale to Part I, where but little (5:16–17) is left to be said of the reward of the righteous, and the emphasis is on the punishment of the wicked.

The emphasis on immortality continues, though ' of death ' in **1** should be omitted. **4-6.** A value is laid upon suffering which to a large extent is a novelty in the OT, and prepares the way for the doctrine of the Cross, especially in St Paul. The glory of the reward is described without direct mention of the beatific vision : (**7**) ' as sparks *among stubble* they shall run to and fro ', bright, swift, triumphant **9.** They shall judge the Gentiles, and the Lord shall be their King, in a kingdom of truth and love and grace and mercy. There is strong evidence for adding, ' and he will have regard to his holy ones ' ; on the other hand doubts are cast on these and the preceding words from the fact that they practically duplicate 4:15.

390a 10-IV 6 The Present Punishment of the Wicked—Their punishment in the *next* life is reserved for ch 5. **11.** In spite of their brave words in ch 2, they are miserable and hopeless and ineffective, (**12**) their wives are foolish, their children wicked. **13.** On the other hand the chaste but barren wife shall have fruit (*i.e.* in merit and reward) ' *at the examination of souls* ' after death ; (**14**) and to the virtuous eunuch also shall be given ' *peculiar favour for his faithfulness* ' : not of course ' the gift of faith ' which he is supposed to have had already in life. **16-19.** The children of adulterers will lead frustrated lives, unhonoured if they be long-lived, without hope against God's judgement if they die young. Such must be understood to be the natural, but not necessarily universal, effect of the parents' bad example. **IV:1**—*Better childlessness with virtue*, he repeats, with an appeal now to the immortal memory of it with both God and man ; (**2**) virtue wins the tribute of imitation when present, of regret after death, of everlasting and undefiled rewards. And then again, with a lack of orderly construction in the book that reminds us once again of St Paul's epistles, the author turns to pronounce the numerous progeny of the impious a failure : without deep root or firm foundation, trees torn up by the wind, with branches broken and fruit unripe, (**6**) they bear witness against their parents when the latter are put by God upon their trial.

b The stern judgement passed upon the children of unlawful unions may perhaps be explained in part by the peculiar circumstances of Egypt. The Ptolemies, who ruled there from Alexander the Great to Augustus, adopted the ancient practice of the Pharaohs of marrying their sisters, and each succeeding couple was deified even in life. This encouraged sister-marriage generally, which also obviated the necessity of dividing the inheritance, otherwise demanded by the equal rights enjoyed by brothers and sisters in matters of inheritance (*cf.* *Bouché-Leclercq, Histoire des Lagides*, IV, 80 : Paris, 1907). Such an incestuous practice called for strong reprobation.

c IV 7-14b The Blessedness of the Righteous even in

Premature Death—7-9. The author turns back for a moment to the righteous, to say that even if their life be short, it is honourable, (**7, 14**) making also an implicit appeal to immortality. He takes the patriarch Henoch as a typical case (*cf.* Gen 5:24 ; Ecclus 44:16 ; Heb 11:5), though (after his wont) without mentioning his name. A considerable apocryphal literature was soon to gather about it, to some of which there is probably a reference in Jude 14–15 ; Henoch and Elias, too, are doubtless the ' two witnesses ' of Apoc 11:1–13. **12.** Henoch was taken away because ' *the fascination of badness obscureth good things, and restless lust perverteth the guileless mind* '. **13.** He was perfected in a short space, the most short-lived of the ante-diluvian patriarchs.

14c-20 The Wicked do not understand until they die— There still seems to be question of Henoch in **14c-18**, though even more than before as a typical case, so that **18-20** applies to the wicked in general, and 5:1 to the righteous in general. The two parallel condemnations in **16** (the second by ' youth soon *perfected* ' : *cf.* 4:13) are factual, by contrasting conduct, rather than verbal. In **17-18** the wicked have not yet realized the truth ; (**19**) ' *but after this they shall become dishonoured carcases, and be a mockery* among the dead for ever. He shall dash them headlong, speechless '. Their ignorance is blameworthy : (**20**) ' They shall come *to the reckoning up of their sins* in cowardly fear, and their lawless deeds [personified after the author's manner] shall convict them to their face '.

V 1-15 Remorse of the Wicked at the Judgement— The judgement spoken of in this book is collective, at the end of time, but is not said to be impending. **1.** The wicked are to understand something of the happiness of the just : *cf.* Lk 16:19–31. ' The righteous man shall stand with much *boldness* before the face of those who afflicted him, and *reckoned his troubles* [lit. labours] *of no account* . . . (**2**) they shall be amazed at the *unexpectedness of his deliverance* '. Their remorse is not true contrition. ' The post ' in **9** (Greek, ' message ' ; Latin, ' messenger ') may be understood of the official couriers. For the similes in **10-11**, *cf.* Prov 30:19 ; in **11**, ' *but the light wind, lashed by the stroke of her pinions, and divided by the force of her flight, is traversed as her wings move, after which no sign of her passage is found therein* '. **13.** ' So we also . . . have been utterly squandered [have squandered our lives away] in our wickedness '. **14.** (Vg) is not found in any other text, and was perhaps originally a marginal note.

16-24 God rewards the Righteous, and assails the Wicked—Once more we have a strong assertion of immortality (**16**), before the author goes on to depict with rich imagery the rewards and punishments of the next life. With **18-21** should be compared Eph 6:11–17, which (in view of the knowledge which St Paul shows elsewhere of this book) has doubtless been influenced by it, though both may well go back to Is 59:17. **18.** ' *He shall take his zeal for his panoply, and make the creation his weapon for vengeance upon his enemies* ', as is set forth in **21-24**, and more at large in Part V : the picture here may be based partly on Ps 17:12–16 (=2 Kg 22:12–16). **22.** ' *Well-aimed* shafts of lightning . . . *hailstones full of wrath as from a sling* ', sea, rivers, wind, shall all fight with God ' against the *madmen* ' (**21**). Part I concludes with the general truth that ' *lawlessness* shall make a desert of the whole earth, and evil-doing shall overthrow the thrones of potentates ' (**24**). These last words prepare the way for the address to kings which follows.

PART II chh 6-9. The Nature of Wisdom—This is the core of the work, in which the nature of Wisdom is set forth (chh 7–8), preceded by an exhortation (ch 6), and followed by a prayer to obtain it (ch 9).

VI 1-27 An Exhortation to Rulers—The first verse in the Latin text is not found elsewhere, and was probably inserted later as a heading, without being inspired. The address to rulers is, in the main, part of the literary form of the book, no less than the presenta-

1b tion of Solomon as speaking (*e.g.* in 9:7–8, 12). Although they appear to be charged with not having observed the Mosaic Law (**5** : omit ' of justice '), this is best interpreted, as in Rom 2:14–15, of the Mosaic Law as representing not merely the ideal code, but to a large extent what we should call the natural law. Terrible judgement awaits them (**8**) for God is no respecter of persons.

c **13.** Wisdom ' is easily beheld by those who love her ' : the theme is developed with strong and characteristic personification, until in ch 8 Solomon desires to have her for bride. Rather, (**17**) Wisdom herself ' goeth about seeking such as are worthy of her, and *in their paths she showeth herself graciously to them, and meeteth their every purpose*'. There follows a rather loose chain-argument or ' sorites ', which may be summed up thus : (**18-20**) the beginning of Wisdom=love of instruction=keeping of her laws=assurance of immortality=nearness to God. **21.** ' So then ', runs the conclusion, ' the desire for wisdom leadeth to a kingdom ', which means that Wisdom will make the reign of rulers (here nominally addressed) firm and enduring. **23** in Vg and DV is not found elsewhere, and once more is probably an uninspired heading like 6:1. Solomon accordingly undertakes to expound Wisdom to rulers : (**26**) ' a wise king is the stay of his people '. These peoples in turn should profit the whole world.

d **VII 1-VIII 1 Solomon received Wisdom from God—1-3.** Solomon, like other men, was descended from Adam, and was born after ten (perhaps lunar) months, wailing out his first cry as do all. **10.** Realizing his helplessness, he prayed for Wisdom and obtained her, and esteemed and loved her before all. **11.** All good things came to him along with her ; this inexhaustible treasure of Wisdom he is ready to share with others. This Wisdom has a wide sweep, (**17-20**) embracing knowledge of the constitution of the world and of the elements, chronology and astronomy, ' *the turns of the solstices*' and the changes of the seasons, zoology, psychology, botany. The passage is doubtless founded on 3 Kings 4:29–34.

e There follows a highly poetical description of Wisdom, opening with twenty isolated epithets of the spirit which is in her, and concluding with a twenty-first to which other words are attached ; the number 21 (3×7) may be intentional, 3 and 7 being sacred numbers, as for example in St Matthew's gospel. **22-23.** She is ' *only-begotten* ' (rather than ' one ') as the unique offspring of God ; yet ' manifold ' as containing in her own infinite perfection the possibility of innumerable finite perfections, ' subtle, *mobile*, piercing, undefiled, sure, *impassible*, loving the good, keen to discern, irresistible, beneficent, loving man, steadfast, secure, free from care, all-powerful, all-surveying, and *pervading all spirits that are understanding* : pure and most subtle ' or spiritual. Wisdom is a breath (lit. vapour) of God's power, an effluence of his glory, and therefore utterly undefiled : one herself, she can do all things : ever the same in herself, she reneweth all things. **27.** ' *From generation to generation* ' she passes into holy souls, making friends of God and prophets. **29.** She is beautiful beyond compare, and evil is powerless against her : (**VIII:1**) she reaches everywhere and orders all things well.

f **VIII 2-21 Solomon's Praise of Wisdom, his Bride—** In spite of the preceding exaltation of Wisdom, Solomon goes on to speak of her as a lover of his bride ; for it is no longer the divine attribute that is primarily in question, but created wisdom as a virtue of men, a finite reflection or communication of the infinite perfection of God. Not that the distinction between the two is very sharply drawn. **2.** After remarking that from his youth he sought to win her, he launches out once again into her praises. It seems best to explain (**3**) of her glorifying man's nobility rather than her own ; when a man shows himself noble by the practice of virtue, she will make this nobility of his far more glorious by giving her help in virtue and much else, as is explained in what follows. God himself loves

her : (**4**) ' *she is an initiate in the knowledge of God* ', and **391f** decides what God shall do. Thus we are back at increate Wisdom, but the writer quickly returns to the advantages of Wisdom to man, yet without forgetting her divine origin. **5.** She is rich, because she can make all things, (**6**) and fashion them more skilfully than any merely human cunning ; (**7**) if righteousness be desired, the very efforts prescribed by Wisdom are acts of virtue. Wisdom, it is said, teaches the four cardinal virtues, prudence, justice, fortitude and temperance. Plato first enumerated them as the chief virtues, but the name ' cardinal ' may come from St Ambrose. **8.** If experience be desired, Wisdom knows the past and can foretell the future ; she understands arguments and riddles, and foresees signs and wonders, and the turn that events will take.

9. Solomon therefore determined to have her for bride, **g** knowing that she would be a wise counsellor, and a comforter in care and grief : (**10**) that she would bring him praise and honour, (**11**) a keenness of judgement that would excite admiration among the powerful and make them listen to him, (**13**) an ' immortality ' that seems best explained here by the parallel expression, an ' everlasting memory ', undying fame. **14-15.** He would govern peoples well and be feared by dreaded tyrants ; he would prove his worth in peace and war. **16.** At home he would find her company a joy. **18.** Realizing that in union with her was immortality, and delight in her friendship, riches in her labours and prudence in assiduous conference with her, and renown in her conversation, he went about seeking how to win her. **19-20.** Not only was he blessed with a good soul but it came into a flawless body ; he guards the reader against inferring from his words the pre-existence of the body, but still less is there question of pre-existence of the soul. **21.** Yet, knowing that even when so gifted he could not come to possess Wisdom except by the gift of God, and that to be aware of this was itself the fruit of understanding, he prayed for her with his whole heart.

IX 1-19 Solomon's Prayer for Wisdom—This prayer, **h** more than the rest of the book, follows the literary device of presenting the author as Solomon, chosen to be king of Israel (**7**), and to build the temple (**8**). **1-3.** God is invoked by his mercy, as having set man over his creation to order the world and judge aright : this with evident reference to Solomon's own kingship as an especial example of it. **4.** He prays for Wisdom, ' that sitteth *by thee upon thy throne* ' : (**5-6**) he is but a weak and short-lived man, lacking in understanding of judgement and laws : indeed, without Wisdom from God man is worth nothing. **7-8.** God has chosen Solomon to be king of Israel and to build the temple, a copy upon a more magnificent scale of the Mosaic tabernacle with its covering tent (*cf.* Ex 26, etc.) which was intended to lead up to it. **9-11** May God communicate that Wisdom which is ever with him, and knows what is pleasing to him, to Solomon, that she may teach him likewise what is pleasing to God, and guide his actions, guarding him with her ' glorious light,' (an uncertain translation, lit. ' glory ', but some means of ' guiding ', and of ' guarding ' against false steps, seems required).

12. Thus Solomon's works will be acceptable, his **i** government just, himself worthy of David's throne. **13-17.** Otherwise how can a man know God's plan ? Man is only too well justified in fearing mistakes ; the body weighs down the soul, and with difficulty we understand even the things of earth ; how then are we to search out things heavenly, unless God give us wisdom, and send his holy Spirit from on high ? Here again we have a strong personification of God's ' holy Spirit ', which yet does not amount to declaring him a distinct Person within the Blessed Trinity, though it prepares the way for this.

A textual question here arises. In the first place we **j** must translate in **18** ' *were* corrected ' and ' *were* taught ', not ' may be ' ; the writer is leading up to Part III, which is mainly historical. We must also

391j render, ' they were *saved* ' rather than ' healed '. And what follows after ' saved ' (or ' healed ') can hardly have been part of the original text, not being found (apart from the Latin) in the MSS or versions. Still, this addition must be fairly old, as it can be traced in some of the early Christian liturgies.

392a **PART III chh 10-12. Wisdom in History**—Divine Wisdom is seen in the story of the great men of old (ch 10), and especially in its contrasted treatment of the Israelites and Egyptians (11:1–12:2), and of the Canaanites and Israelites (12:3–27) ; but in this last section the main emphasis is soon laid upon God's forbearance.

b **X 1-21 Wisdom's Dealings with the Holy Men of Old** —**1-2.** The list begins with Adam, who was preserved and forgiven and left as lord of creation ; (**3-4**) but Cain, who deserted Wisdom in his anger, perished also in his fratricidal rage. The meaning appears to be that he perished no less than Abel ; Cain's whole life became one long punishment, and perhaps punishment in the next world also is to be understood. The Flood is also ascribed to him, doubtless as having started a tradition of wickedness, but Wisdom preserved Noe by means of wood of little price (not needing more elaborate means), and the earth with him. Just as the enumeration jumps from Cain to the Flood, so it passes at once (**5-8**) from the Tower of Babel to Abraham, and to the deliverance of Lot from the fire which came upon the five cities of Gen 14:2, of which destruction the memorials are Dead Sea fruit and a pillar of salt. **9-12.** Wisdom protected Jacob from Esau (*cf.* Gen 27:41–45), showed him the kingdom of God (by which is probably meant the vision of Gen 28:10–17), (**11**) *made him rich* at the expense of Laban, who was warned to leave him alone (Gen 31:24 : for ' seducers ' in **12** read rather ' liers in wait '), and gave him victory over the angel (Gen 32:24–30). **13-14.** The story of Joseph is easily followed, and (**15-21**) brings us to Moses and the Exodus. In **19** read ' from the depth *of the abyss* ', *i.e.* of the Red Sea. Cornely-Zorell understand **21** as a poetical hyperbole, claiming this as the commoner and correct view : we may compare the singing of the babies to the mountains skipping like rams in Ps 113:4. Such imagery is common in poetical and rhetorical styles.

c **XI 1-XII 2 The Contrasted Treatment of Israelites and Egyptians**—Although the theme is still Divine Wisdom, the writer addresses all this section directly to God without mention of it, showing more clearly than ever that he looks upon it simply as a divine attribute. Two features are pointed out in the working of the Divine Wisdom : (i) the Israelites were benefited by those very things whereby their foes were punished (**5** : *cf.* 13–14) : and (ii) in general, ' by what things a man sinneth, by these he is *punished* ' (**17**). God, however, did not exclude the Egyptians from his love : ' Thou hast mercy upon all ' (**24**). This thought is further developed in the following section.

d Moses led the Israelites through the desert, and gave them water from the rock (Ex 17:1–7 ; Num 20:1–13). In **4**, as in some other places, the conduct of the ' *holy* people ' (10:15) is to some extent idealized, for they were rebellious. **5-6.** But while they were benefited by water, their foes were punished by it : ' For through those things whereby their foes were punished, by these they in their need were benefited '. The Latin has some extra words which are not in the other versions or in the Greek text. **7-8.** The waters of Egypt were turned to blood (Ex 7:19–25) : ' instead of a river's ever-flowing fountain ', which was now ' *turbid with clotted blood* ', a punishment for the decree to kill the babes of the Hebrews, ' thou gavest to them ', *i.e.* the Hebrews, ' abundant water, unlooked for '. **9-10.** By the thirst wherewith they were tried in the desert, the Israelites understood how God had punished their enemies. **15.** Moses the Egyptians had wickedly exposed to perish along with the other babes, but through him they were punished, and they learnt to

respect him when suffering from a thirst more terrible **3** than that of the righteous Israelites. In the same way as a punishment for the Egyptian worship of animals, God, whose almighty hand ' *had created the world out of formless matter* '—a compressed summary of its beginnings from lifeless mass—was well able to send upon them bears and lions or horrible and unheard of monsters ; but in fact he ordered all things (**21**) ' by measure and number and weight ', by which expression are indicated the careful workings of divine providence and mercy.

21-22. For instead of gloating over the workings of **e** divine wrath and power, the author, at a moment when we least expect it, proclaims magnificently God's universal love : (**27-XII:1**) ' Thou hast mercy upon all men . . . and overlookest the sins of men, that they may repent : thou lovest all things . . . Thou sparest all things, because they are thine, O Lord, lover of souls ; *for thine imperishable spirit is in all things* '. **2.** The example of the Egyptians shows how God admonishes sinners little by little (as he did through the plagues), ' and dost admonish them *by reminding them* [in their very punishment, as explained above (*cf.* 17)] of the things wherein they sin, that [in this way] they may escape from their wickedness and believe in thee, O Lord '.

XII 2-27 The Canaanites : God's Forbearance— **f** God was minded to destroy the previous inhabitants of Palestine in order to settle the Hebrews there ; yet he did so only little by little, in order to bring them to repentance. His forbearance is expounded at some length. In regard of the crimes imputed to the Canaanites in **3-6**, Oesterley remarks in his note on the cannibalism that ' recent excavations on the site of ancient Gezer by the Palestine Exploration Fund prove this to have been literally true ', but I have not been able to find evidence for it in the official account of the excavations (*The Excavation of Gezer*, by *R.A.S. Macalister, London, 1912 : 3 vols.). In general, *cf.* Deut 18:9–12 ; Ez 16:20–21, etc. Archaeology affords adequate proof of infant sacrifices at Gezer and elsewhere : *cf. Modern Research as illustrating the Bible*, by *S. R. Driver (London, 1909) 50, 67–73. The last words of **5** (DV ' from the midst of thy consecration ') are not clear : perhaps the most likely rendering is ' and initiates from the midst of a frenzied troop ', *e.g.* of Bacchants : so Cornely-Zorell, supplying the ' and '. **6.** But although God ' was minded ' to destroy the **g** previous inhabitants, and was ' not unable ' to do so, he sent hornets in advance of the Hebrews, and in general executed his judgements by degrees, so as to give them an opportunity of repentance, having regard to the inborn wickedness (**11**) of a seed accursed from the beginning. Who can accuse him in regard of the nations destroyed ? He orders all things rightly, and does not punish unjustly : ' Thy being Lord of all maketh thee to spare all '. He shows the fullness of his power upon those who believe him not, and convicts those who do know him (omit ' no ' in DV) of their presumption : nevertheless (**18**) ' *thou dost govern us with much forbearance* ', for God's power is always there if he choose to use it. **19.** And this forbearance was intended as an example for his chosen people, teaching ' *that the righteous man must be a lover of men* ', and filling them with hope by the way in which he offers repentance to those who have sinned ; for if he took vengeance upon their enemies, who deserved death, with so much deliberation ' *and indulgence* ' (the probable reading and meaning : the word is omitted in Vg), with what circumspection has he judged his own children ! **22.** While chastising these latter, he scourges their enemies ten thousandfold, that when judging others they may be mindful of his goodness and forbearance, and when judged themselves may be sure of his mercy.

In the last verses of the chapter the writer harks back **h** to the Egyptians, and completes his discussion of them by the mention of their final destruction in the Red Sea. Still insisting that ' by what things a man sinneth,

h by these he is punished' (11:17 ; see above), he points out (23) that they were tormented ' *through their own abominations*'. 24. 'They wandered *very far* in the ways of error, taking as gods *beasts despised even among our enemies*', *i.e.* crocodiles, etc., despised even among the Gentiles, ' *being deceived like silly children*'. And so the earlier plagues were sent to them as though in mockery, as fit only for children. But they that are not corrected by such lighter chastisements (26) ' *shall experience a judgement worthy of God.*' in its severity, such as befell the Egyptians. They were vexed at their own sufferings, being punished where they had sinned, by means of the very creatures which they thought to be gods. 27. Thus they came to recognize him for the true God whom they had of old denied to be such : ' wherefore final condemnation came upon them'. God manifested himself ever more clearly unto them by his increasing punishments. When they crowned their iniquity by refusing to submit to him even after they had been brought to recognize him clearly, their punishment also culminated in their utter destruction.

a PART IV chh 13-15. Against Idolatry—Idolatry is the very opposite of Wisdom, and is attacked in its three chief manifestations, with emphasis upon its folly and its consequences.

b XIII 1-9 The Worship of Natural Objects—The Greek text asserts that ' all men are vain *by nature*', where the Latin omits ' by nature', perhaps owing to the difficulty of the sense. In 12:10 the Canaanites are said to have a nature evil by birth, and inborn wickedness, wherefore God in his mercy punished them little by little, to give them a chance of repentance. Those therefore who are ' vain by nature' have remained so through their own fault, and chiefly because they have blinded themselves voluntarily to the evident existence of ' him that is', a title taken from Ex 3:14, ' I am who am'. First of all those are considered who think the forces of nature or the like to be ' the gods that rule the world '; whereas they ought to have been able to reason from them ' analogously' to their Creator. 5. ' Is beheld *analogously*' means by an argument from the less to the greater ; and the author appears to be coining two words in 3 and 5 in order to bring out the full sense of ' Creator '.

And now he brushes aside an excuse : ' perhaps but little blame' attaches to this category : such men were anxious to find God, and were dazzled by the beauty of what they saw. 8. But no, he answers, even men of this category are not to be excused ; for if they were able to find out so much about the world (which seems to show that he has the ancient philosophers and other students of nature especially in view), how was it that they did not find out all the sooner the Lord of all these things ?

c 10-XIV 11 The Worship of Men's Handiwork—Those in the next category are in a far worse way, and are in a condition as hopeless as that of corpses. These are they who make gods of gold or silver or stone or wood. And the author goes on to elaborate Is 44:9-20 with bitter irony. Out of the remains of a piece of wood, of which he can make nothing further of any use, he takes a bit, (13) ' crooked and full of knots ', and proceeds in his leisure moments to carve it into the shape of a man, ' or likens it to some *paltry beast*', making a little shrine for it, which he fastens on the wall with a nail (16) for fear it should fall, ' knowing that it is unable to help itself'. And *then* he is not ashamed to pray for life to that which is dead—and so forth. Again (XIV:1), another, ' about to journey through the raging waves, calleth upon a piece of wood more *rotten* than the *vessel* which carrieth him '.

d No, it is Divine Providence that is really watching over the ship ; for our author even in all his bitterness never quite lets go of his principle : (11:24, 27) ' Thou hast mercy upon all men . . . and overlookest the sins of men, that they may repent. . . . Thou sparest all things, because they are thine, O Lord, lover of souls '. Human wisdom built the ship for gain, but God's

providence guides it through the waves, so that (5) **393d** ' men entrust their lives even to a very small piece of wood, and *passing through the surge on a raft* reach safety '. The reference is probably to some practice of the Egyptian sailors or fishermen. The word ' raft' seems to be used depreciatingly of the frailty of the boat compared to the force of the sea ; it is used again at once (6) of Noe's ark, the supreme and blessed example of God's providence in this kind. 7-10. But the wood fashioned to be a god is accursed, as well as he who so fashioned it ; both shall have their punishment. The idols appear to be identified with the devils who have, so to speak, identified themselves with the idols : *cf.* Jer 10:14-15, which may well have been in the author's mind, and Deut 32:17, this latter quoted in 1 Cor 10:20. 11. ' For this reason *there shall be a visitation* of the idols of the gentiles, *because they have become an abomination in the guise of God's creatures*', *i.e.* the devils have misused God's creatures and made abominations of them by taking possession of them and causing them to be worshipped. The ' no' in Vg should be omitted.

XIV 12-21 The Worship of Rulers—Egypt was the **e** chief source and centre of ruler-worship in the Mediterranean world. The Pharaohs had been gods to their subjects, and it was chiefly in order to step into their shoes that Alexander the Great came to claim divinity and worship. His successors followed his example, especially (as was to be expected) the Ptolemies in Egypt. From these Hellenistic kings it passed to the Roman Emperors. The author was familiar with the Egyptian worship, and attacks this species of idolatry also. 12. ' The devising of idols was the beginning of fornication '. This last word was itself understood in Holy Scripture to signify idolatry, partly because Israel was Yahweh's chosen bride, partly because of the impurity usually connected with idolatry. But here it probably has simply its frequent sense of impurity in general. It was the ' vanity of men' (*i.e.* of rulers) that brought this third kind of idolatry into the world ; (14) ' *and it was devised on account of their abrupt end* '. This last clause presupposes an ancient and simple emendation of the text, fitting well into what follows, in place of a text otherwise hardly intelligible. 15. The abuse began with such cases as that of an afflicted father, mourning for a son prematurely lost to him ; he would make an image of his son, and proceed to honour him as a god, and enjoin such rites upon his dependents. (Such, it may be remarked, was Cicero's purpose in regard of his daughter Tullia.) 16-17. And thus in course of time by order of the rulers their images came to be worshipped, so that when they were far off they were still flattered as present. In fact worship went further still : (19-20) for the artist, ' wishing perhaps to please the *ruler, forced by his art the likeness to greater beauty*' than the ruler really possessed, and the multitude were allured by the grace of the work to worship him. 21. And this became ' *a snare*' for men, who under the pressure ' *either of misfortune or tyranny*' invested stones or wood with ' the incommunicable name', by which is not meant the name ' Yahweh', which the Jews never pronounced, but probably the title ' God' itself, which can never be shared by creatures.

22-31 The Fruits of Idolatry—Having thus enumerated **f** the three chief kinds of idolatry current in his time, the writer dwells upon its evil consequences : (27) it is ' *the beginning and cause and extreme of every evil*', and (30) ' a just doom shall pursue' idolaters. With this section may be compared Rom 1:24-32, a passage doubtless based in part upon this one ; but it is peculiar to St Paul to assert that God delivered up to these vices those who refused to recognize him (Rom 1:24, 26, 28).

22. Living in a great war produced by their ignorance (by which appears to be meant the wild and disturbed manner of life described in what follows), they call such great evils peace : (23) the ritual murder of children (such as we read of in the OT), secret rites, ' *the frantic revels of strange ordinances*' in the Greek or Asiatic mysteries, murder, adultery, robbery and the

393f rest. **26.** 'Forgetfulness of God' implies a wrong reading and should rather be 'forgetfulness of benefits received' : 'disorder in marriage' may refer to marriage of sisters ; *cf.* § 390*b*. **29.** Trusting lifeless idols, men anticipate no punishment for perjury ; but punishment will come, both for the idolatry and the perjury. **31.** Not the power of their false gods, but due justice will follow them.

g XV 1-19 The Making of Idols—1-6. After touching briefly upon the freedom of Israel from idolatry (7-13) the writer dwells upon the wickedness of making idols (14-17) and the folly of those who believe in them.

1-3. God is 'our God . . . even if we sin, we are thine . . . *but we shall not sin, knowing that we are reckoned thine.* For to know thee is perfect righteousness '. Israel has not been led astray by idols ; **(6)** they who make them and they who desire them and they who worship them are all 'lovers of evil things'. **7-8.** Such a one is the potter, who among other things makes a god out of earth, even as he himself was made out of earth and shall return thither. What he is anxious about is not his toil or his short life, but the fact that he is competing with workers in gold and silver and bronze, and he thinks it to his credit to be making ' counterfeits '. **10-11.** ' *His hope is more worthless than earth* ', his material, because he knows not his Maker. **12.** He reckons life a mere plaything, a fair at which to make profit, ' *for, saith he, one must get rich as best one can, even by evil means* '. **13.** ' *This man beyond all others knoweth that he sinneth* '.

h **14-15.** ' But *the enemies* [*i.e.* the Egyptians] *of thy people, who oppress them are more foolish than all, and miserable beyond the soul of a babe,* because they regard all the idols of the gentiles as gods ' ; and the writer inserts an obvious reference to Ps 113 (2nd part) : 4-7 ; 134:15-17. **16.** ' No man can make *an image* like to himself ', **(17)** being in fact better than the objects of his worship ; for he is alive, which they can never be. **18.** Moreover the Egyptians worship the most hateful creatures, ' *for compared in brutishness they are worse than the other* ' animals, **(19)** *nor are they by any chance beautiful, so as (viewed as beasts) to be desired ; but they have eluded* [apparently an ironical word] both the praise of God [for any beauty they might have possessed] and his blessing,' because they serve as idols.

394a PART V chh 16-19. The Egyptians and Israelites—A contrast is worked out in various ways between God's treatment of the Egyptians and of the Israelites. It is not clear that what is related need always be taken as absolute historical fact. There is in any case admitted to be a considerable amount of fiction in the book, which in outward expression is written by Solomon for other kings. The narrative itself is so strange as naturally to provoke the suspicion that here too there is some fiction ; and Catholic historians of the OT and commentators on the Pentateuch do not appear to feel bound to incorporate the details from this book. It may be conforming to a well-known type of Jewish literature known by the Hebrew name of ' midrash '. The substantial reasons required by the Biblical Commission for such an interpretation (23 June, 1905) may well seem fulfilled.

b XVI 1-29 The Contrast in Divine Punishments—**1-3.** It was right that worshippers of the contemptible animals indicated in 15:18-19 should be ' *tormented* ' by a multitude of such beasts so disgusting as to turn them even from necessary food, while the Israelites were regaled with a pleasant diet of quails (*cf.* Ex 16:13 ; Num 11:31-35). **5-8.** Even when the serpents came among them, ' they were troubled but a short time for their correction ', for those who looked upon the brazen serpent were saved (Num 21:9), not through any virtue of its own, but by God, the Saviour of all, who thus showed the Egyptians that it is he who delivers from every evil. The Egyptians died from the bites of locusts and flies (*cf.* Ex 8:24 ; 10:4) ; **(10-11)** but even venomous serpents did not overcome the Israelites, ' *for they were bitten to remind them of divine oracles* ', and were quickly healed. **12-13.** ' For it was neither herb

nor ointment that healed them, but thy word, O Lord, **3** which healeth all things ; for thou hast power over life and death '. The bites were sufficient to kill the Israelites, but God saved them ; **(14)** when man deals a mortal stroke (lit. ' kills ') he cannot call back the soul. There does not seem to be a reference to God raising the dead ; the context does not demand it, and the author would speak clearly if he meant to propound so great a truth.

Not only animals, but also fire and water punished the Egyptians, but had no power against the Israelites. **16.** The former were ' pursued by strange rains and **c** fire ' (*cf.* Ex 9:24), **(17-18)** which latter even prevailed over the waters, only refraining from the animals sent against the Egyptians (probably based partly on Ex 9:26), **(19)** while burning up the products of their land in spite of all the water (*cf.* Ex 9:25). **20.** The Israelites on the other hand were fed miraculously with the manna, which (though more or less of the nature of ice : *cf.* 19:20) did not melt. It is called ' the food of angels ' either as being ministered by them (Cornely-Zorell), or as supporting human life without human effort in the same way that Almighty God maintains the angels in being without labour on their part. In this way it is a type of the Holy Eucharist, which is freely bestowed to maintain our supernatural life (*cf.* Jn 6:49 f.). **22-24.** Thus snow and ice and fire showed in a like miraculous way how ' creation, serving thee its Maker, straineth itself to punish the unrighteous, and restrains itself for the benefit of those who trust in thee '. **28.** The author returns to the topic of the manna, which was to teach the Israelites not to trust in crops, but in God's word, and to rise before the sun to thank and petition him.

XVII 1-XVIII 4 Darkness and Light—The horrors **d** of the Egyptian darkness are vividly depicted ; it was the ninth plague (Ex 10:21-23). **3.** The Egyptians, ' *thinking to escape notice with their secret sins under the dark curtain of forgetfulness, were plunged in darkness* '. This last verb seems a better reading than ' were scattered ', because in the preceding verse they were ' shut in under their roofs '. **4-5.** They were ' troubled by *spectres* ' and strange noises and gloomy phantoms ; no fire nor stars could give them light. **6** perhaps refers to flashes of lightning, so terrifying that they exaggerated in the darkness the things which they had for an instant beheld, ' *being terrified by that sight when they saw it not* '. Their magic was of no avail, and their vaunted wisdom was put to shame ; **(9)** even when there was nothing to affright them, they perished with fear of the passing beasts and of the hissing reptiles. **11.** ' For fear is nothing else but a yielding up of the succours of thought '. **12.** The hope from within, founded upon reason, being all too slight, a man is more alarmed by his own ignorance than by the cause of his trouble, as when the Egyptians were alarmed at a powerless night which came from an equally powerless Hades. **13.** That they should further be described as ' sleeping the same sleep ' is puzzling, but seems to refer to their enforced rest during the three days of Ex 10:22. **14-15.** They were molested by portentous apparitions, and ' *were paralysed by the soul's surrender* ' to panic, **(18)** and collapsed (wherever they happened to be) into a very prison of darkness, swooning for fear at any and every noise. **19.** For the whole world was lit up clearly, and engaged in unhindered labours ; **(20)** the Egyptians alone were in heavy night, an image of the darkness awaiting them in the next world, and in their terror they were more grievous to themselves even than the darkness.

XVIII 1-2. But the Israelites enjoyed bright light ; **e** and the Egyptians, who heard but did not see them, counted them happy, and were grateful that the Israelites did not take revenge upon them, ' *and because they had been at variance with them, supplicated them* ' to depart (Ex 11:8 ; this translation ' been at variance ' is not certain). **3.** The Israelites on their side had a burning pillar of fire as a guide (Ex 13:21, etc.), and a ' harmless sun *in their honourable exile* ' in the wilderness. **4.** The Egyptians deserved to be imprisoned in darkness for having kept the Israelites shut up, '*through* whom the *incorruptible* light of the Law was to be given to the world'.

XVIII 5-25 Retributive Justice—The theme of this section is shortly announced in **5**: the Egyptians planned to kill the Israelite babies, but God, having saved Moses, destroyed the firstborn of the Egyptians in the last plague, and all the host of the Egyptians in the Red Sea. This last destruction may also be intended to be taken as a fitting punishment, on the supposition that the Hebrew babies were being killed in the way intended in the case of Moses. **6-7.** The Hebrews had 'received' the news beforehand of the impending salvation of the righteous and destruction of the wicked. **9.** They gathered secretly to offer the passover, '*and with one accord set forth what the divine law required*', sharing blessings and dangers together, '*while the fathers were already intoning praises*'. **10-11.** In contrast they heard the shouting of the Egyptians, and their lamentations for their firstborn. Master suffered with servant, and the king with the common people. **12.** The corpses were without number, too many to be buried, and included the sons of the noblest families. **13.** The magicians had made them disbelieve, but the destruction of the firstborn caused them to confess Israel for God's son, *cf.* Ex 4:22.

14-16. There follows a passage of great poetical beauty, telling how in the silence of midnight, 'thine almighty Word leapt down from thy royal throne in heaven, a stern warrior into the midst of the doomed land . . . and he filled all things with death'. This passage has often been applied to the Incarnation, for which so strong a personification of the Word of God certainly prepared the way; but Christ came to save, not to destroy. **17-19.** Then the Egyptians with evil dreams and unlooked-for fears, thrown down half dead, manifested the cause of their death, which had been revealed to them in the dreams.

20-21. It is true that the Israelites also had some experience of the punishment of death from the plague (Num 16:44-50), and a multitude were killed; but God's anger did not last for long, for Aaron hastened to pray for the people, and to propitiate the Lord with the burning of incense, 'showing that he was thy servant'. **22.** The Greek continues, 'He overcame the multitude', which hardly makes sense, but we should probably read, by a mere transposition of two letters, 'he overcame *the wrath*', much as in **23** ('beat back the wrath'), 'the wrath' being thus almost personified (after the manner of the author) and identified with 'the punisher' (22) and 'the destroyer' (25), evidently to be understood as an angel. Aaron 'stood between the dead and the living' (Num 16:48), and blocked the further progress of the plague by means of prayer and incensation (21); also, it is implied (24), by the majesty of his vestments and mitre (or turban), for which see Ex 28. The writer finds a typical meaning in robe and mitre different from that of Josephus (*Ant.* 3, 7, 7) and Philo (*Life of Moses*, 3, 11-14: and elsewhere), who interpret the high-priest's garments to represent the several parts of nature. **25.** To all these 'the destroyer yielded', and the Israelites '*regarded them with awe*'; a mere trial of God's wrath was enough for them, though not for the Egyptians.

XIX 1-20 The Crossing of the Red Sea—Upon the Egyptians came pitiless wrath, until they were finally drowned in the Red Sea. **2.** For God knew before- **395d** hand how, '*having changed their mind about the departure*' of the Israelites (this translation is somewhat uncertain), they would pursue those whom they had sped on their way. **4.** For a fate (lit. 'necessity') well deserved drew them on to this end, and made them forget what had already befallen them, in order that they might have their full punishment. **6.** 'For *the whole creation* in its several kinds was fashioned again from above', displaying miraculous activities in obedience to the divine command: (7) a cloud overshadowed the Hebrew camp, a clear way appeared through the Red Sea, a grassy plain was seen in place of the raging waves. **8-10.** The Israelites crossed with wonder and joy, remembering also how Egypt had brought forth *lice* in place of cattle (*cf.* Ex 8:17), and the Nile, frogs instead of fish; (11-12) for their own comfort a little later there came quails from the sea (*cf.* 16:1-3).

The guilt of the Egyptians is further brought out by **e** comparison with that of the men of Sodom, whom however the author (after his wont) does not actually name; *cf.* Gen 19. **13.** The Sodomites were inhospitable to strangers (*i.e.* to the two angels), but the Egyptians enslaved benefactors (the reference is especially to Joseph). **14-15.** 'And not only so, but the visitation', *i.e.* punishment, of the Egyptians, 'shall be of another sort', *i.e.* much severer (such seems the best reading and sense), since the Sodomites received as enemies those who were strangers, whereas the Egyptians, '*having welcomed with feastings those who already shared the same rights as themselves*' thereupon '*vexed them with grievous labours*'. **16.** Just as the Sodomites were stricken with blindness at Lot's door, so the Egyptians, unable to see in the immense darkness which encompassed them ('immense' is an uncertain rendering) sought a way through their own doors. The writer, as is his way, presents one side of the picture, even putting forward the Sodomites as in some way superior to the Egyptians, and saying nothing of their sin, any more than he tells the full story of the quails in 19:12; 16:1-3; *cf.* Ps 77:30-31, etc.

17. The author now appears to hark back to the **f** thought of 6, but sense and grammar are alike difficult. A comparison is made to a psaltery, probably a triangular stringed instrument with base and sounding-board above, struck downwards with a plectrum. Each string keeps its own sound, but the tune is determined by the various combinations of notes. Even so (it appears to be meant) the different elements changed their mutual relations. **18.** 'For land-creatures became water-creatures', apparently referring to the Israelites and their cattle crossing the Red Sea, 'and swimming creatures passed on to the earth', meaning the frogs (Ex 8:3): (19) 'fire retained *its own power* in water, and water forgot its power to quench', as set forth in 16:17, 19. **20.** 'Contrariwise, the flames did not waste the flesh of easily corruptible animals that walked in them'; this harks back to 16:18. 'Nor did they melt the easily melted ice-like grains of ambrosial food', the manna, already by implication compared to ice in 16:22; *cf.* Ex 16:14.

The author concludes with the thought which has dominated the book as a whole, and especially the third and fourth parts: 'For in all things, O Lord, thou didst magnify and glorify thy people, and didst not *overlook* them, standing by them at every time and place'.

ECCLESIASTICUS

(THE WISDOM OF JESUS, THE SON OF SIRACH)

By C. J. KEARNS, O.P.

396a Bibliography—*G. H. Box and *W. O. E. Oesterley, *Book of Sirach*, CAP vol I, 1913 (quoted ' Box ') ; G. Girotti, O.P., *I Sapienziali* (Sales-Girotti, *Sacra Bibbia Commentata*, VT vol VI, 1939) ; A. Eberharter, *Das Buch Jesus Sirach*, BB, 1925 ; *J. H. A. Hart, *Ecclesiasticus, Greek Text of Codex 248*, 1909 ; J. Knabenbauer, S.J., *Ecclesiasticus*, CSS 1902 ; H. Lesêtre, *L'Ecclésiastique*, 1884 ; *W. O. E. Oesterley, *Ecclesiasticus*, CBSC, 1912 (quoted ' Oesterley ') ; N. Peters, *Das Buch Jesus Sirach* (*Exeg. Handbuch zum AT*, ed. Nikel), 1913 ; *id. Ecclesiasticus Hebraice*, 1905 ; *S. Schechter and *C. Taylor, *Wisdom of Ben Sira . . . from Heb. MSS*, 1899 ; *R. Smend, *Weisheit des Jesus Sirach erklärt*, 1906 ; *id., Weisheit des JS, hebräisch und deutsch*, 1906.

b Title and Canonicity—The evidence of the Heb. subscription to ch 51, of the rabbinical citations, and of the Gk and Syr. versions suggests that Ecclus early bore the title *The Wisdom-Book of Ben Sirach*. In Latin the title *Ecclesiasticus* is found already in St Cyprian, *Testim.* II. 1, PL 4, 696, etc. Rufinus, who excluded it from the canon, explains this as meaning of *ecclesiastical* authority only, not canonical. It was a *church book* also in the sense that it was used with others as a handbook of moral training for catechumens (Athanas. *Ep. fest.* 39, PG 26, 1177 ; 1437 ; Orig. *In Num., Hom.* 27, PG 12, 780). In liturgical use it has, in common with Prov, Eccl, Cant, Wis, the generic title *Liber Sapientiae*. As regards **Canonicity** Ecclus has the same history as the other deuterocanonical books of OT. See §§ 14, 15.

c Text and Versions—The **original Heb. text** grew rare once Ecclus was excluded from the Jewish canon. It was still known in Jerome's time and not unknown even in the 11th cent. A.D. It then disappeared and was not again available until the discovery of about two-thirds of it in one form or another amongst the MSS of the Cairo Geniza in 1896 and following years ; *cf.* *P. E. Kahle, *Cairo Geniza* (1947) 1-11. For nomenclature of these MSS—A, B, C, D—and details of the portions of the text they offer, see Oesterley, lxxxix f. For MS E, covering 32:16 (Vg 18)–34:1, see *Marcus, *Newly discovered Original of Ben Sira*, Philadelphia, 1931. Critical study of the MSS and of quotations in rabbinical literature shows that already before 132 B.C. the Heb. text existed in at least two recensions. The evidence of Gk, Syr. and Latin versions strongly confirms this conclusion. These recensions are here called Primary and Secondary Text. See § 396g.

d All MSS of the **Greek Version**, through a misplacement in their archetype, follow a wrong order in chh 30:26–36:18. The Latin, followed by DV, AV, RV, preserves the true order, as do Heb., Syr. and Armenian (Swete, *OT in Gk*, II, 1907[3], p vi f.). Following the cleavage in the Heb. MS tradition, there are two recensions of Gk. The Primary Gk, made by the author's grandson (see Prologue), represents Primary Heb. It is found in the main uncial MSS of LXX, such as A, B, Sin, and in nearly all printed editions of LXX, and underlies RV. The Secondary Gk, made as early as 80 B.C. (?) from Secondary Heb. is found in cursive MS 248 (ed. by Hart with apparatus from supporting MSS 55, 70, 106, 253, 254), and in the Complutensian Polyglot, and underlies AV and Latin with DV.

The **Latin Version,** here called Vg, is in fact the Old **e** Latin, originating in N. Africa early in 3rd cent. A.D., and left untouched by St Jerome. See § 27a–d. It was made from a MS of Primary Gk which had been emended to agree with a MS of Secondary Heb. In many passages Vg offers evidence, not now available in any Gk MS, for characteristic readings of Secondary Gk.

There are two **Syriac Versions.** The **Peshitta** Syriac **f** (see § 24h–i) was made c A.D. 200, probably by a Christian. It was made from a Heb. text of a purer form than any now known, but was subsequently altered to agree with a Gk MS of Secondary type. It contains large portions insufficiently represented in Gk and Latin, and missing from Heb. The **Syro-Hexaplar** (see § 25b) probably represents Origen's critical work on the Gk text. (Collation by Hart, 73 ff.)

Secondary Text : Character and Inspiration—A **g** rough idea of the differences between the Primary and Secondary Texts can be had by comparing RV (substantially Primary) with AV or DV (substantially Secondary). A number of the differences are purely *scribal* : marginal glosses, explanatory expansions, alternative readings or renderings (technically called ' doublets ') of one original text. But there are also many *editorial additions* incorporated in the Secondary Text. A small number of these are *Christian glosses*, adapting Ecclus to its function as a church handbook. But the greater number are *pre-Christian supplements*, intended to emphasize a certain theological outlook which the editor or editors thought insufficiently represented in the Primary Text. They stress in particular the spiritual nature of creatures ; the value of the individual soul and the human person ; the part repentance can play in undoing sin, God's appreciation of such repentance, and his part in bringing it about. Above all they supplement the rudimentary eschatology of the Primary Text by stressing the ideas of judgement at or after death, of conscious survival in the next world, of the moral aspects of human immortality, of lasting punishment and reward beyond the grave. (*E.g.* 6:23 ; 15:8 ; 16:22 ; 17:25 ; 18:22 ; 20:4 ; 24:46.)

That these secondary additions, whilst not the work of the original writer, are nevertheless inspired is the view taken in the present commentary. (Compare the view taken by many of Jn 7:53–8:11.) Ecclus is thus equated with the Pentateuch, concerning which it may (theologically speaking) be freely held that in the form in which it has come down to us it contains not only glosses and explanatory notes inserted in the text, but also *additions by an inspired author* made after the time of Moses, § 48d. The Western Church has received Ecclus in a form which exhibits most of the characteristic Secondary features, *viz.* the Vg (or Old Latin, as it really is), so there is good ground for maintaining their canonicity. The Council of Trent has declared canonical all the ' parts ' of the Vg (EB 45). And it would be hard to deny to many of the additions the right to be called parts—*integral* parts—of Ecclus *as we have it in the Vg*, since it would be doctrinally the poorer if these passages were shorn away.

Authorship and Date—The data of the Prologue, of **h** 50:29 and 51:1 in Vg, of 50:27 in LXX, and of 50:27

6h and colophon after ch 51 in Heb. (in the last two of which the name 'Simeon' is critically suspect), show that the author's name was *Yešuaʿ* (Gk 'Jesus'), his father's name Eleazer, and his grandfather's Sirach. In Heb. idiom he is often called *Yešuaʿ ben Sirach* 'Jesus son of Sirach'; or simply Ben Sirach. The Prologue, and various passages of his book (34:9–13; 38:25; 39:1–5; 50:29; 51:3–5, 18, 31, 37), show him as an inhabitant of Jerusalem, a member of the scribal class, with the necessary wealth and leisure to devote himself in his youth entirely to the study of the Scriptures which he loved; as one who in his maturity travelled abroad, mixed with high society, found employment with some foreign potentate (in the course of which he escaped providentially from a mortal danger which a slanderous conspiracy had raised against him); as one, finally, who in later years settled in Jerusalem and opened a school for the scriptural and moral instruction of his younger fellow-countrymen, and composed the present work. For his doctrinal purpose and outlook see §§ 396*i*, 397. As to the date at which he wrote, the Prologue shows his grandson to have been of mature age 'in the 38th year when (Ptolemy) Euergetes was king'. This is best taken as meaning the 38th year of Euergetes II, 132 B.C. The grandfather, Ben Sirach, would have flourished 60 or 50 years previously, *i.e.* 190–180 B.C. This fits in with his ref. in 50:1 ff. to 'Simon the son of Onias (*al.* Ionias)' in such a way as to show he had known him and that he was dead when this was written. The high-priest referred to was Simeon II, son of Jochanan II. He held office *c* 219–196 B.C. This confirms 190–180 B.C. as the date of writing. For the historical background this date implies see § 68*b*–*c*, and *cf.* on 35:22 ff.

i **Scope, Procedure and Contents**—The author touches on his purpose and procedure in 24:40–49; 33:16–19; 39:16–20, 38 f.: 50:29–31; 51:31–38. Having been given by the Lord a store of divine wisdom through study of the Scriptures and reflexion on life, he proposes to put it into writing, following at a distance the wise men who have gone before (Prov was especially his model). He calls on thoughtful men to ponder on his teaching and put it into practice. By doing so they will find the same wisdom he has found himself, and the same spiritual riches. The translator in the Prologue emphasizes the practical scope of the work, with its insistence on the Law as the divine guide to human life. This end is served by weaving together whole series of pithy sayings about life, summing up the fruits of study of the Scriptures, experience and mature reflection.

At intervals, however, there occur meditative passages of a more abstract character, where the nature of wisdom itself and its theological relations with God are expounded. The recurrence of such passages enables us to separate the strata which went to the building up of the book and make the following **Outline of Contents:** Part One—1:1–43:37, Wisdom considered in its ethical bearings on human life, and in its higher aspects and its relationship to God. Sub-divisions, on the basis just indicated, begin respectively at 1:1; 4:12; 6:18; 14:22; 16:24; 24:1; 33:7; 39:16. Part Two—44:1–50:31, Praises of the Ancients of Israel. Appendix—51:1–17, Prayer of Thanksgiving for Deliverance. Conclusion—51:18–38, Acrostic Poem showing the spirit in which wisdom is acquired and imparted.

7a **Doctrinal Content**—Dogmatic truths are pre-supposed rather than expounded. **The Messianic Hope** as embodying an explicit reference to an individual Messias is found in 24:34, but only in Vg and without supporting context. But in the sense of a reliance on the promises made to Abraham, David and his successors, and an explicit recalling of the terms of these promises, it is found wherever the context calls for an expression of it. (See 36:10, 17, 18; 44:20–23; 45:31; 47:13, 24; 48:17.) The second coming of Elias as prophesied by Mal 4:5 is referred to in 48:10; and the everlasting glory destined for the temple of

Zorobabel in 36:16 and 49:14. It is in his **moral 397a teaching,** understood as including also those dogmatic truths which underlie God's guidance of the universe and his shaping of the moral life of man, that all that is deepest in the message of Ben Sirach is to be looked for. A convenient series of headings under which to summarize it is suggested by the arrangement of ch 24, the climax of his thought—here followed in reverse order (see commentary on 24). In this summary the wording of some verses is slightly modified to facilitate their being woven together effectively, and the distinction between Primary and Secondary readings is noted only where they are in doctrinal contrast.

Wisdom comes to Israel through the Law——All **b** wisdom originates with God; but before he can impart it to men he must externalize it for them in his revealing word. This **word of revelation** is for men the fountain-head of wisdom (1:1–7). Its waters flow perennially in the Book of the Law, which bears within it vitalizing forces like the four rivers of Eden. Every moral precept and every ritual ordinance is a channel branching off from this great stream; and every faithful scribe is a cultivator bringing to mankind its life-giving waters (24:32–47; also 6:37; 15:1).

Wisdom and the Temple Worship—When it is said that **c** the fear of the Lord is the beginning and the fullness of wisdom (1:16, 20) and conversely that the perfection of the fear of God is wisdom (21:13), the fear spoken of is the religious fear fundamental in the OT. It is that reverential awe of the divinity which brings home to man that God is the one supreme and worshipful being, and which expresses this conviction both by rendering him the worship he requires (a worship which for the Israelite is that prescribed in the Law), and by doing his will in the sphere of moral conduct. This fear is **the beginning of wisdom** in a twofold sense. First, this religious attitude itself is the soil in which wisdom *takes root* within the soul. And secondly, the observance of the ritual law, in the proper spirit (including therefore worthy moral dispositions), is the *choicest fruit* of that wisdom whose possession ensures man's enlightened co-operation with all God's plans. Hence Ben Sirach's eulogy of Aaron and his divinely bestowed priesthood (45:7–27; see 33:12). Hence, too, the transport with which he describes Simon the high-priest as he had often seen him, offering the sacrifice in full solemnity (50:12–23; see 47:9–12). The possession of this incomparable Service makes of Israel a priestly people, set apart among mankind for purposes of worship, like the oil of priestly consecration and the incense of the sanctuary (24:20 f.). And it is against this background that every Israelite is exhorted to 'fear' the Lord and reverence his priests, giving them their sacred dues (7:31–35).

Wisdom and Moral Conduct—Fundamental though **d** worship is, right conduct is more fundamental still. **The Law is essentially a moral law.** Ritual observances which are not accompanied in the worshipper by a virtuous life and fitting inward dispositions are roundly denounced (2:18–23; 7:8–11; 34:21–35:22). From this root-principle stems that foliage of proverbial lore which bulks so large throughout the book. Its author enriches every portion of the vast field of the moral commonplace in which 'the ancients', especially the compiler of Prov, had already so shrewdly toiled (33:16–19; 39:1–3). (For lists of references under appropriate headings see Knabenbauer, 4; Lesètre, 26–30.)

Wisdom and the Inner Life—Wise conduct in the **e** broader fields of morality is within the reach of every prudent man, Israelite or not. But there is a choicer fruit of wisdom proper to the chosen people amongst whom wisdom dwells at home (24:12–16). This is **the special favour of God** bestowed on those he makes his friends (33:12); the special intimacy with him which they enjoy; the special sensitivity to what he desires and the will to fulfil it, cost what it may of hardship, which they study to perfect. This wisdom of the inner life is drawn first from the sacred books (38:39*b*–39:1;

397e see 24:32–47 and § 397*b*). Nor is it only as a record of God's words that Holy Writ inspires and instructs, but also as a record of his dealings with the Fathers, and of their surrender of themselves to be moulded to his purposes. This thought dominates chh 44–50.

The profound **study of the Scriptures** which this implies demands to a great extent renunciation of other occupations (38:25). But there is a higher step than mere professional devotion to scholarship and reflection. Wisdom comes in the long run only by the **communion of mind with Mind.** The thinker must grow into the contemplative. The spirit of man must immerse itself in the Spirit of God and commune with him in the give and take of loving conversation. He must give his heart to resort early to the Lord that made him and must pray in the sight of the Most High. For if the great Lord please he will fill him with the spirit of understanding and will direct his counsel and his knowledge : ' Come to me all ye that desire me, and be filled with my fruits ; for my spirit is sweet above honey, and the possession of me above honey and the honeycomb. They that eat me shall hunger still, and they that drink me shall yet have thirst ' (39:6–10 ; 24:26–29 ; see 51:18–27).

f This sweet familiarity is not bestowed until the seeker has been **purified by trial** in sense and in spirit. His quest involves a wrestling of the soul and a torment of the heart (51:25, 29) : within, a sense of frailty and sin (22:23–23:6) ; without, a struggle against abandonment by friends and the treachery and violence of foes (51:3–10). ' When thou comest to the service of God prepare thy soul for trial. Take all that shall be brought upon thee, and in thy pain endure and in humiliation keep thy patience : for gold is tried in the fire and acceptable men in the furnace of humiliation ' (2:1–5). ' For wisdom walks with a man by trials when she chooses him at first. She brings upon him fear and dread ; she scourges him with the affliction of her discipline, until she tries him by her laws and trusts his soul. Then she strengthens him and gives him joy, and discloses her secrets to him and heaps upon him treasures of knowledge and of understanding ' (4:18–21; see 6:25–32).

But ' her bonds are a healthful binding ' (6:31), for they bind the soul to **God, its Father and its Friend.** He is the Father of every soul that rises to him in prayer (23:1, 4 ; 51:14). He also is its Friend, giving and inviting the love of friend for friend. This concept, based on Deut 6:5, is brought out clearly in the Primary Text, and repeatedly emphasized in the Secondary. (Primary : 1:10 ; 2:18, 19 ; 4:15 ; 7:32 ; 47:10. Secondary : 1:14 ; 2:10 ; 3:4 ; 13:18 ; 24:24 ; 25:16 ; 34:15.)

g Wisdom and Mankind at large—Wisdom, whilst dwelling in Israel as in its proper home (24:12 f.), was yet, in a measure fixed by God, poured out from the beginning upon all mankind (1:10 ; 24:9–11). Man was created in the image of God, a spiritual being endowed with intellect and will, holding the supremacy among created things, and bearing in his conscience the moral law which God had given him to guide his conduct (17:1–12). The moral responsibility thus imposed was matched by the endowment of free will. ' When God made man from the beginning he put him in the hand of his own counsel : If thou wilt thou shalt keep the commandments. Death and life are before a man ; that which he wills shall be given him ' (15:14–18 after Heb.). The object here is to prove that God is not responsible for sin. Man is responsible, by abusing his free will. What then is responsible for man's abuse of this divine endowment ? Ben Sirach does not say it is the Fall of man. His paraphrase (17:1–12) of Gen 2 stops short of the Fall. In 25:33 he says ' From a woman was the beginning of sin, and because of her we all die '. But *beginning* here is taken numerically : the first recorded sin is that of Eve. It is not said to have a *causal influence* on the sins of her posterity. As regards the **consequences of the Fall,** Ben Sirach does not go beyond the data of Gen 2:16–19, *viz.* it results

in the yoke of affliction which is laid upon the children **39?** of Adam, and results eventually in death (40:1–8).

As to sin, Ben Sirach traces it to a twofold root within **h** the human soul. (1) The inherent defectibility of every man by the very fact of his creaturehood. ' All things cannot be in men, because the son of man is not immortal ; all men are earth and ashes. What is man and what good is he ? A drop of water in the sea or a pebble on the sand, so are his few days in the day of eternity ' (17:29, 31 ; 18:7, 8). (2) But there is a more sinister element in man : an inherent **propensity to moral evil.** ' He that keepeth the Law subdueth his impulse ' (21:12, Syr.) ; ' The sun faileth, and how much more man, who hath the inclination of flesh and blood ' (17:30) ; ' God sees the presumption of men's heart, that it is wicked ' (18:10 Vg) ; ' O wicked propensity, wherefore wast thou formed, to fill the face of the world with deceit ? ' (37:3, Heb. emended). The Heb. here underlying *impulse, inclination, presumption, propensity,* is *yēṣer,* the word translated ' counsel ', *i.e. free will,* in 15:14 above. In the abstract, the *yēṣer* is free will, regarded as something ontologically good and morally indifferent. In the concrete, however, experience shows that man habitually misuses his free will; it shows itself in practice as impaired. This misuse of it so predominates that Rabbinism eventually came to use the term *yēṣer* exclusively in a pejorative sense, to describe that strong inclination to evil which St Paul later traced to original sin. Ben Sirach does not trace it back so far. He is satisfied to explain sin as due, not to God, but to man's misuse of a good thing God has given him ; and to explain that misuse itself as arising from a moral defectibility, and still more from a moral disorder, in the sinner's own make-up. Why this is found in *every* man, he leaves unexplained. The sad fact remains : ' We all of us are guilty ' (8:6) ; ' as a lion lies in wait for prey, so does sin for workers of wickedness ' (27:11 ; see 21:3). Every man is thus a Satan to himself, and ' when the wrongdoer curses the Adversary it is himself he curses ' (21:30). No man therefore can say ' My transgression is from God ', for God hates sin and did not make it (15:11). He made, however, the power of free will, and made the very action whose concomitant defect is sin. For he is the cause of everything that is ; and everything that is, is good (18:1 ; 39:21, 39). He even made those things which scourge sinners for their wickedness, for the punishment of sin is good (11:11–30 ; 33:7–15).

Sin is evil. But **out of evil God draws good** in many **i** ways. (1) The sinner's frailty is of itself a claim on **God's compassion.** ' God is patient with men and pours forth his mercy upon them. He compassionates and teaches and corrects, as a shepherd does his flock ' (18:8–14). (2) In the Law he gives **guidance to avoid sin,** and the practice of the Law gives moral stamina to keep sin's stirrings in control (11:15, 17 ; 15:15 f. ; 21:12). (3) Consciousness of propensity to sin is an occasion of prayer, and **prayer wins grace** to overcome it, so that with God's help a man can ' flee from sin as from the face of a serpent ' (22:33–23:6 ; 21:2). (4) Thus it is **an occasion of merit** also. ' Blessed is the man that is found without blemish. Tried and found perfect, he shall have glory. Able to transgress and not transgressing, able to do evil and doing it not, his good is established and all the congregation shall declare his praise ' (31:8–11). (5) And even when sin has been yielded to, **repentance** for it draws men closer to God, **and amendment** cancels its effects (17:20–28 ; 34:30 f. ; 35:5).

But evil not repented of, God sees and punishes. ' **He judges everyone according to his works ;** the **j** sinner shall not escape with his plunder, and whoever does righteousness shall have his reward. Their iniquities are not hid from him, and their sins are in his sight ; and afterwards he shall rise up and render them their recompense ' (16:16–20 ; 23:25–29 ; 17:13–19 ; 42:18–20).

What is the nature of that recompense ? The Primary Text expresses **the older view** that the wrongdoer is punished in this life. After death he is punished only in the sense of leaving no children, or only such as are to his discredit, so that his name is blotted out (40:15 ; 41:8-10). In the same way the just man will be rewarded by prosperity here below, even should he first have to undergo a period of purifying trial (1:13). And after his death worthy children and a name long held in honour will carry on his reputation and be a permanent reward (30:4-6 ; 37:28 f. ; 41:14-16 ; 44:13-15). In the Secondary Text, however, **sanctions after death** of a truly personal and lasting kind are clearly spoken of. 'The examination of all is in the end' (16:22). 'The gathering together of sinners is like tow gathered together, and the end of them is a flame of fire. The way of sinners is made smooth from stones, but the end thereof is the pit of Hades, *and darkness and pains*' (21:10 f.). The underlined phrase, which is Secondary, changes the complexion of what precedes ; as does the Secondary addition to 7:19 (see comm.). The righteous man, likewise, is rewarded after death. He shall enter the world of the Holy Ones (the 'holy age' of 17:25 ; 24:46 ; see in comm. Syr additions to 1:22 and 18:8). There he shall enjoy 'the reward of God which continues for ever' (18:22) : life everlasting (24:31) ; a life whose delight is drawn from gazing upon God (6:23 ; 15:8).

k **Wisdom in the Universe**—Man is made in God's image, and has dominion over other living things (17:1-4). The larger world of nature has a meaning as a parable and an instrument of God's dealings with mankind (33:7-15 ; 39:26-37). But the world has also **a value apart from man** (17:31). The sweep of God's power through the firmament, the penetration of his glance to the heart of the Deep, the reflexion of his beauty and the imprint of his skill in the innumerable armies of being that fill earth and sky and sea, the resistless energy with which he holds all these together and draws them forward to their goal—these are manifestations of the Lord which man in his littleness cannot convey nor even comprehend. It is fitting, therefore, that God should from the beginning 'pour out his wisdom upon *all* his works' (1:10).

Wisdom, thus, can speak of itself as the medium of his creating, sustaining and energizing power throughout the universe. 'Like a cloud I hung above the earth ; I circled round the vault of heaven, my path lay in the depth of the abyss, upon the waves of ocean did I walk' (24:6-9*a*). Ordered variety, purposive and unfailing energy are the characteristics wisdom stamps upon the works of God. 'In making them he gave to each its part. He set an everlasting order on his works. They hunger not nor tire, and cease not from their operations, nor does any of them cross his fellow or ever disobey the Lord's command' (16:25-29). To grasp something of what God's revelation of himself in nature meant to Israel's sages, the **Hymn to the Creator** (42:15-43:37) must be read and pondered, alive as it is with spiritual and aesthetic sensitivity, vibrant with awe and adoration, aglow with love that strives for utterance, groping for the Word as yet ungiven. 'Even his Holy Ones have not power to recount his wondrous works. All his works are truly lovely, and all that we can see is but a spark. And he himself surpasses all his works. Exalt him all you can, yet will he overtop your utmost praise. Set to and grow not weary, and yet he will outstrip you. Who can see him, who can express him, who can sound his praises as he is ?' (42:17, 23 ; 43:29-35).

l **Wisdom and God**—'The Lord upon his throne alone is wise' (1:8, Gk) ; wise of his very nature. Wisdom is *with* him (1:1), and when regarded as distinct from him, originates within him and from him comes forth (1:1 ; 24:5). It is with him from eternity (1:1). Its eternity, however, is of that purely relative kind which the Heb. *'ōlām* frequently expresses—pre-existence as compared with other things (1:4 ; 24:14). For, in fact, **wisdom was created** (1:4, 9 ; 24:12, 14). But once created it is to last for ever. 'From the beginning was I created, and unto the world to come I shall not cease

to be' (24:14 ; *cf.* 1:5). This creation of wisdom as **397l** something distinct from God was effected by his utterance of a word. **The creative word** which brought all other creatures into being, which first ' came forth from the mouth of the Most High ' (24:5), was itself the externalizing of that wisdom which had hitherto been identical with God himself. Henceforth wisdom as distinct from God exists, and is the medium of his dealings with the world (42:15 and 43:28 as in comm. See 39:37).

Besides being just a ' word ', the medium of God's **m** external operations, **is wisdom a person?** The texts show a gradation in this respect. In 6:25-32 wisdom is personified purely as a figure of speech, as the concluding phrases show. In 14:23-27 no advance on this is perceptible. The passage merges into 15:1-8 where, whilst ' her ' personality takes on more concrete attributes, the note of metaphor is still predominant. It is an advance on this to present wisdom speaking of herself, as in 4:16-22 (Heb). But it is of what happens in and to wisdom's votary that the passage speaks, not of wisdom's personality itself. The crucial passage is 24:1-31, where wisdom speaks in her own name, describing what she is and what she does. We have here a unity of concept, not merely of image. It is the concept of God's giving of himself in and to the world which he has made. Wisdom is presented as **God's revelation of himself** in nature his handiwork, and in man his image. It is his revelation of himself also in the teaching which he gives in the sacred writings, and in the moral law which he implants in every heart. It is **his inward giving of himself,** too, to those he loves : in the form of the light which makes them know him as a friend, and in the form of the impulse from on high which makes them respond in prayer to his advances, rendering him their service and giving him their friendship in return. Wisdom is thus neither an abstraction nor just a single attribute of God. It is his many-sided self-bestowing, **personified** to make it comprehensible. But it is **not personalized.** It is not here presented as an hypostasis of God, coming to men to bring them the divine. Not yet. But in the growing light of revelation these inspired reflexions on what God has begun to do for men, and on what he is calling them to, will soon be seen to adumbrate an ineffable fulfilment. One short step and the Wise Men of the Old Testament will stand upon the threshold of the New. The Son of Sirach will pass the pen to the Son of Thunder.

N.B.—Round brackets ( ) in the commentary signify an omission to be made in DV.

Prologue—A spurious prologue of little value ' by an **398a** uncertain author ' is given by AV and by some ed. of Vg, *e.g.* SSCC, 17, 681. It comes from the Gk of Pseudo-Athanasius, *Synop. Scrip. Sac.* (PG 28, 376 f. ; Hart, p xviii). The genuine prologue, though not canonical, is the authentic work of the grandson of Ben Sirach. It falls into four paragraphs. (1) 'The knowledge . . . wisdom, *and since they that read them must not only become adept themselves, but in their learning should also by speech and writing be of use to those outside.'* Israel has received a treasure in the Scriptures. Her learned men have a corresponding duty to pass on the knowledge of them to the less favoured, the Jews of the Dispersion. (2) ' (*Therefore*) my grandfather . . . learn, *being instructed in these things, may progress more and more by living according to the Law.'* In fulfilling the duty outlined in (1), ' Jesus ', *i.e.* Ben Sirach, composed his work on a scriptural basis, treating of wisdom with the practical aim of helping his readers to live according to the Law of Moses. (3) ' I entreat . . .' The translator asks his readers to remember the practical aim of the book, and to be indulgent to the imperfections which any Gk translation of a Heb. original must exhibit. For the significance of the references here and in (1) and (2) to ' the Law, the prophets, and the rest of the books ', and to the existence of Gk translations of them, see §§ 12*a*-*d* and 23*g*-*k*. (4) ' For

398a in the eighth and thirtieth year . . . time, *I found a copy of no small instruction . . .*'. When and where the Gk version originated. See § 396*h*. The word 'copy' is uncertain; perhaps '*a copy of a notable (book of) Instruction (-literature)*', which book included Ben Sirach's work. The translator's aim is, like the author's, to help his readers ' to live according to the Law '. They are dwellers in ' *a land of sojourning* ' (Gk), *i.e.* they are members of the Dispersion.

b **I 1-IV 11 Eulogy of Wisdom ; Man's Duties** to God, his parents, his neighbour.

I 1-10 Wisdom's Origin from God—(Heb. text is not available before 3:10.) For the doctrine of the passage see § 397*l*, where 1, 4, 9 are explained. **2.** '*Who shall number . . . and the days of eternity ? . . .*' Only God can do these things, for he alone possesses wisdom in its fullness. See 8, 9. Heaven, earth, abyss, are divisions of the universe according to Heb. cosmogony (Gen 1). 3 is a doublet of 2*b*, 4*a*. **5.** The fountain-head from which wisdom comes to men is the word by which God creates the world and reveals himself. The ' ways ' or channels through which its life-giving waters flow down to men are God's commandments, especially in the Law of Moses. (See 24:32 ff. ; 33:3, Heb. ; § 397*b*). This verse is Secondary, but its doctrine is that of 42:15 ; 43:26. **6.** To whom has God's self-manifestation in nature and revelation been granted ? 8–10 give the answer. **7.** Doublet of 6. **8.** '*There is one wise, greatly to be feared, sitting upon his throne, the Lord.*' He alone is wise in himself, but he has communicated his wisdom to creatures. **9.** 'He created her ( ) and saw her and numbered her ( ).' He externalized his wisdom in the word which was his creative medium ; in that word he ' saw ' or possessed all his wisdom in so far as it was to be imparted to creatures ; he then portioned it out to different branches of creation. ' In the holy ghost ' is Secondary, after Wis 1:4-7. **10.** ' According to his gift ' ; in measured quantity, to the material universe and to mankind in general ; but ' to them that love him ', *i.e.* to Israel, he gave unstintedly (Gk).

c **I 11-II 23 Wisdom and the Fear of the Lord**—Wisdom taking root in men, and their response to it, are now described ; chiefly applicable to the Chosen People. The fear of the Lord by which they respond is explained in § 397*c*. **14, 15.** Secondary. **16*a*.** ' Beginning ' : its root and choicest fruit. See §397*c*. **16*b*.** ' The faithful ' are the Israelites, whose patrimony wisdom is. **16*c*.** '*Among faithful men she hath been established from of old.*' Meaning as 16*b*. **18, 19, 23,** doublets of 12, 13, 9, 10. **22.** After this verse Syr. adds 12 vv describing the future reward of the wise or virtuous man. It is said to be ' *an eternal crown and eternal righteousness among the holy ones* ' ; ' *life as an eternal heritage* ' ; ' *being inscribed in the book of life.*' See § 397*j*. **24-26.** Fear of the Lord brings wisdom, honour and long life. **27-30.** It brings patience and self-control. **31-33.** It accompanies the true worship of God. **34, 35.** It ensures fidelity to his Law, and meekness towards fellow-men.

1:36-2:23. To fear the Lord means to serve him ; dispositions necessary for this. **36-40.** Hypocrisy is ruled out. **36.** ' Be not *disobedient* '. . .' **II 1-6.** To serve the Lord brings trials, which call for constancy. **1.** ' Prepare *thyself to be tested*.' ' Soul ' is a Hebraism for ' self '. ' Temptation ' : test or trial. **2.** ' *Control thy heart . . . and run not when calamity comes.*' **7-13.** Faith, hope and love, towards God, are necessary, based on his fidelity and compassionate forgiveness of sins. **10.** Secondary, completing the triad of virtues. **14-17.** Woe to the heart that is insincere or fickle. **14.** See 1:36. **18-23.** True fear and love of God do his will and trust his mercy. **18.** ' . . . will not be *disobedient* to his *words* . . .' **22.** ' If we do not penance . . .' : Secondary addition. See § 396*g*.

d **III 1-IV 11 Fear of God expressed in Acts of Virtue**—**III 1-18.** Filial piety. **1.** Vg only. **4.** Secondary. **10.** (Heb. text begins to be available.) **16.** ' Repaid thee for *thy* sins ' : filial piety will merit forgiveness

of sin. Doublet of 17*a*. **19-26.** A due sense of one's **3** limitations. **24*b*.** Doublet of 22*d*. **26.** ' *For many are the speculations of the sons of men, and ill imaginings lead astray.*' A rebuke to Greek philosophizing. **27-32.** The stubborn heart and the wise heart : a contrast. **27*a*.** ' *Fare evil.*' ' Fear evil ' is a misprint in some edd. of DV. **27*b*.** ' *But* he that loveth *good things* shall *be led by them.*' **3:33-4:11. Kindness to the poor** and afflicted. **33.** ' *expiates* sins '. See 7:36 ; 29:15-17 ; Dan 4:24 ; Tob 4:7-12. **IV 6.** ' For the *plaint* of him that *crieth* in bitterness of soul.' **9*b*, 10.** ' and be not *harshminded in judgement. Be a father to* the fatherless '. **11*b*.** ' And he will have mercy on thee *and save thee from the grave* ' : will reward thee with long life.

IV 12-VI 17 Wisdom's Hardships and Rewards ; 3 Thoughts on Conduct. IV 12-22. Wisdom's Good Things, and her severe training. **12.** A heading for what follows. ' Wisdom *instructs* her children and *exhorts all those who give her heed*.' **13-15.** Wisdom and the inner life : a bond between the soul and God, bringing life, glory, blessing and love. **13.** ' *They that love* her *love* life, and they that *seek* her *find grace from the Lord*.' **14.** ' They that hold her fast *find glory from the Lord, and abide in the blessing of the Lord*.' **15.** ' They that serve her *serve* the Holy One, and God loveth them that love her.' **16-22.** How wisdom trains her clients. In Heb. wisdom speaks in the first person : for *her* read *me*, for *she* read *I*. For the doctrine see § 397*f*. **21, 22.** A reference to Solomon's defection. See 47:15-23.

23-31 Sincerity in Speech—**27.** ' thy neighbour *to thine own detriment* ' : undue servility. **32-36. Contrasts in conduct. 31*a*** goes with **32*b*** : the facts will sweep away our words if we deny that we are sinners. **31*b*, 32*a*** go together : ' *Prostrate* not thyself *for a fool to tread on, and accept not the person* of the mighty.' Sense as 27. **33*a*.** ' *Strive for justice with* thy soul ' : doublet of **33*b*.** ' And even until death fight for justice ' : constantly, all your life long, let principle not partiality be your guide.

V 1-10 Against presuming on God's Forbearance—**1. b** ' *Trust not in thy wealth and say not* " I have power ".' 1*b* is a doublet of 10. **5.** ' *About forgiveness be not confident, adding sin upon sin.*' Do not go on sinning, presuming on eventual forgiveness by God. Future forgiveness is spoken of, not past. **8-10.** Against presumptuous delay in turning to God. **5:11-6:4. Wise self-control** in speech and conduct. **11, 12.** Against being guided by expediency rather than truth. **VI 1** continues 5:18. ' *Deal justly alike* with the small and the great, *and* instead of . . .' **2.** Control of passion. ' *Yield* not thyself *to the power of passsion, lest it eat up thy strength* like a bull.' ' Passion ' : Heb. *nepeš* lit. *soul* (2, 4) means the soul as the seat of *bodily* appetites.

6:5-17. Friendship, false and true. **5-7.** Care in choosing friends. **8-13.** False friendship. **9*b*.** He will betray your confidences (see 6). **11.** ' *In thy prosperity he shall be* as thyself, *but in thy misfortune he shall desert thee*.' **12.** ' *When misfortune comes he shall turn againt thee and hide himself from thee*.' **13.** Pseudo-friends are meant. **14-17.** True friendship.

VI 18-XIV 21 The Quest of Wisdom ; cautions about **4** social relationships—**18-32. Its Hardships and Rewards —21.** ' How *repellent is she to a fool*.' ' The " fool ", as usually in wisdom literature, is the man culpably devoid of religious insight and moral feeling. **23*a*.** ' *Discipline* is according to her name, and *comes not easy* to many.' Possibly a play on the words *mûsār* ' discipline ' and *môsēr* ' fetter ' (see 25, 30). **23*b*.** ' *She continueth even to the sight of God*.' Secondary, reflecting an advanced idea of next-world happiness (see 15:8 and § 397*j*). **26.** Wisdom's discipline is a yoke (see 51:34). **29-32.** The seeker's toil rewarded by a deeper spiritual life, and success as a teacher (see 51:18-38). **33-37.** Frequent the company of the wise. **35.** ' *and let no proverb of wisdom escape thee* '. **37*d*.** ' *And the wisdom thou desirest* shall be given thee.' The verse shows the Law (' precepts ') and the ' commandments ' as a source of wisdom (see 24:32 ff. and § 397*b*).

VII 1-IX 23 Social Relationships—**1-11.** On avoiding **5**

b ambition and presumption. **2.** 'Depart from *iniquity* and *it* shall . . .' **7b.** 'And *do not ruin thyself with* the people' : by corrupt use of power. **8-11.** Presuming on God's forgiveness without amendment of life. **11.** See 34:23 and § 397*d*. **12-20.** Some social virtues. **15b.** See Mt 6:7 with 26:44. **16.** 'Ordained' : see Gen 2:5, 15 ; 3:17. **17-19.** Act virtuously, for God punishes vice. **19b.** 'For *the expectation of man is worms*' : a motive for humility is the thought that the body is destined to corruption. The Secondary Text expands to '*punishment* (on the flesh) *of the wicked is fire and worm*', referring to punishment in the next life. **20.** 'for gold *of Ophir*' see 3 Kg 9:28 ; Job 22:24 (Heb.) ; 28:16 ; BDB *s.v.* **21-30.** Household and family virtues. **21.** Deprecates divorce ; see 28 ; contrast 25:36. **22, 23.** Servants. Refers to Ex 21:2 ; Lev 25:39-43 ; Deut 15:12-15. **25.** 'Hast thou *sons? Train* them and *give them wives in their youth*' (see 27). **26 f.** Unmarried daughters, by oriental social custom, are to be strictly treated, and husbands are chosen by the father. **28.** See 21. **29.** 'the *pangs of thy* mother'. **31-40.** Duties of religion. **31-35.** To reverence and support Levites and priests is an act of the fear and love of God, and is commanded by the Law. **34, 35.** The sacrificial portions prescribed for their support. **36-39.** Works of mercy : to give alms, respect the dead, comfort mourners, visit the sick. **36.** See Deut 14:28, 29 ; 26:11, 12, etc. **37b.** 'And *deny* not *respect* to the dead.' 'Respect' was shown by mourning for them and burying them fittingly (38:16-18), by showing solicitude for their dependants and their good name, and—as revelation progressed (see 2 Mac 12:43)—by offering prayer and sacrifice on their behalf (see Tob 1:19 ff.). **40.** 'Thy last end.' For Primary Text, the punishment which would overtake the sinner before death ; for Secondary, death and subsequent judgement (see Eccl 11:9-12:7 and § 397*j*).

c **VIII 1-22 On dealing with Various Classes** of men—**20.** 'for they cannot *keep thy secret*'. **IX 1-23. Cautions**, mainly about women. **12.** 'Sit not *at table* . . . nor *recline* upon the *elbow* with her.' Refers to reclining at table ; DV mistranslates as 'bed' Vg *cubitum* which means 'elbow'. **13.** 'And *revel* not with her . . . *in thy blood thou go down to the grave*' : blood vengeance by the injured husband (see Lev 20:10 ; Deut 22:22). **14-23.** Various social relationships. **17.** 'Knowing that *unto the grave he shall not go unpunished*' : the older view, retribution before death. **20.** 'walking upon *nets*'. **21.** '*cherish* thy neighbour'.

d **IX 24-XI 6 Human Greatness,** false and true. **24 ff.** Good government. **X 5.** 'the person of the *leader*'. **6-22.** Pride goes before a fall. **7b.** 'And all *oppression is offensive to both*'. **8.** The fate of Babylonia, Persia, Macedonia, etc. (see 17-21). **11, 12.** Heb. probably means 'A *little* sickness *mocks* the physician' : a king today and tomorrow *a corpse*.' **13.** 'inherit *corruption and worms, vermin and creeping things*' (see 7:19, Primary Text). **14, 15a.** The temptation of rulers is to forget that they have a Ruler. To turn from God belongs essentially to pride, whilst in other sins it follows as a consequence. **15b.** '*For the reservoir of pride is sin, and its well-head gushes forth wickedness*.' From the reservoir which pride brings into being in the soul, all kinds of sin flow out. Vg is true to this sense : 'Pride is the beginning of all sin.' **16-21.** God's dealings with the proud peoples of biblical history ; a commentary on 8, parallel to 16:7-10. Sodom and Gomorrha, and the Canaanites, are in mind. **22.** The moral : pride ill befits man's lowly origin. **23-27.** True greatness is based on the fear of God, here taken in its broadest sense (see § 397*c*). **10:28-11:6.** True greatness and false. **28.** To be wise (god-fearing) is true nobility, 'and a prudent man will not murmur (*at this*)'. **29b.** 'And *boast* not in the time of distress', about what might have been ; the facts, as **30** adds, show the hollowness of such boasting. **33.** 'glorified *for his wisdom*'. **34b.** 'And he that is *inglorious* in wealth, *how much more in* poverty!' **XI :1.** See 39:4. **2-4a.** Judge not by appearances : **2** whether 'looks', **3** or

size (see 1 Kg 16:7), **4a** or apparel. **4b-6.** For God **400d** can in an instant reverse the externals on which men's estimates are based. **5.** 'Many *downtrodden* have sat' (see Ps 104:17-22 ; 1 Kg 9:21). **6.** See 1 Kg 15:28, 35.

XI 7-XIV 21 Miscellaneous Cautions—discretion in **e** conduct, the poor and the rich, the certainty of death. **7-10.** Meddlesomeness. **10.** 'And if thou *dost*, thou shalt not *escape the penalty*.' **11-30.** The possession of good things depends ultimately on God ; he gives them in the long run only to the just. **11.** 'There is *a* man that . . .' **12.** 'Again there is *a destitute* man.' **13, 14.** Man's lot in this life does not ultimately depend on his own ability or efforts, but on the overruling providence of God. (**15, 16.** Secondary ; see after 24.) **17.** But in point of fact it is God's will to give them in stable fashion only to the just : 'and his *good-pleasure grants lasting* success'. **18-20.** A little parable. Lk 12:16-21 is closely parallel. **21-24** draw the conclusion from 17, *viz.* **21,** 'Be steadfast in *thy task*', *i.e.* of doing right, even in distress ; **22** '*marvel* not' that sinners seem to prosper ; 'but trust *in the Lord and wait for his light*', **23, 24** for he will redress the balance in the long run. **15, 16.** Secondary addition, giving a deeper meaning to the traditional teaching on God's reward of the just as contained in the Primary Text. The addition is found in Heb. Vg Syr., and in Secondary Gk MSS. **15b.** 'Love and *upright* ways are with him.' **16.** '*Folly* and darkness are *formed for* sinners.' Besides outward things like fortune, life, etc. (13, 14), there is an inward and spiritual 'gift' (17), which makes man what he truly is and gives him value in God's sight. This gift includes wisdom, moral training and character, knowledge of the Law, love of God, and 'upright ways' of conduct (15). *These* are not withdrawn irrespective of man's conduct and for inscrutable reasons, as material good things are. Their possession is related to man's conduct and character. From sinners, they are withdrawn, leaving them to folly, darkness, evil (16). When men use them well they abide with them and give them that success that is everlasting (17). **25-30.** The thought of the Primary Text continued : good fortune and bad are essentially transient. **30.** '*Call* not any man *happy* before death, for a man is known by his *end*.' **31-36.** Beware of strangers. **33b.** 'And on *what is praiseworthy* he will lay a blot.'

XII 1-7 Discretion in Almsgiving. 8-19. False friend- f ship—10b. 'For as *brass* his wickedness rusteth.' **13.** 'Who will pity a (*snake-*) *charmer* struck . . .' **14b.** 'If thou *go down* he will not *last*.' **18b.** 'Will *trip up* thy feet.' **19.** '*Wag* his head' : a gesture of derisive triumph (see 13:8 ; Ps 21:8 ; Mt 27:39). 'Whisper', conspiring against thee. **XIII 1-30. The poor and the rich:** fellowship between them is ill-advised, as liable to be unequal and insincere. The 'rich' spoken of are the worldly-minded rich. **3.** 'Kettle' : a *brass* cauldron (see Ez 24:3, 6) ; hence the saying explains itself. **8.** 'When he seeth thee he will *pass thee by* and *wag* his head at thee' (see on 12:19). **22.** 'What fellowship hath a *hyena* with a dog?' There is a natural enmity between the shepherd's dog and the hyena that skulks about the flocks, on the watch for a straying sheep (see Job 30:1 ; Is 56:10). **26.** 'When a rich man *speaketh*.' **27.** 'The poor man *speaketh*.' **30b.** 'And poverty is evil *which is the consequence of impiety*.' **31 ff.** Sayings on joy and sadness. **XIV 3-10 The miseries of the niggard—8, 10.** 'Evil **g** eye' is Heb. idiom for envy (see Mt 20:15) ; here it is the miser's envy of others' wealth. **11-21.** 'Death is not slow', therefore let us do good while we have time. **12b.** 'And that the covenant of *Sheol* hath *not* been shown to thee.' You have not come to terms with Sheol (the grave, death ; see on 17*b*) and it will inevitably claim you for its own. Contrast Is 28:15. **12c.** '*And the everlasting decree is* "*Thou shalt* surely die".' **16.** 'And *indulge* thy soul' : *carpe diem*. **17a.** '*Before thy death do good*' ; doublet of 13*a*. **17b.** 'For in *Sheol* there is no *delight*.' Sheol is the underworld of OT eschatology. According to the

400g older view here presented (but transcended in Secondary Text throughout), it was a place where all souls went after death, and remained in a state of suspended animation, unaffected by pleasure or pain (see § 397j).

401a XIV 22-XVI 23 **The Pursuit of Wisdom**; principles of moral conduct—14:22-27. The eagerness and perseverance demanded of the seeker after wisdom : a series of metaphors. **26.** 'He sets his nest in her foliage and lodges in her branches.' **27.** ' and dwells in her habitation'. **XV 1-10.** The benefits which wisdom will bestow on her follower. **1.** 'He that feareth the Lord will do this, and he that holdeth fast the Law shall lay hold on her.' **2b.** 'As a wife married of a virgin.' Some edd. of DV read 'from a virgin'. The expression corresponds to ' the wife of thy youth' in Prov 5:18 ; Is 54:6 ; Mal 2:14, 15 : the wife whom a man marries in early manhood and with whom mutual attachment grows stronger as life advances. Such is the attachment between wisdom and her followers, resembling, too, the understanding guidance and support of ' an honoured mother'. **3c, 4a.** 'And he shall be made strong by her . . . and he shall hold her fast . . .' **7-10.** Sinners and ' fools' (see on 6:21) shall not possess wisdom. **8.** 'But men that speak truth . . .' to end of the verse is Secondary, with its exalted view of the ultimate reward of wisdom, ' the sight of God' (see 6:23 and § 397j). **10a.** 'Wisdom came not forth to him from God ', i.e. was not imparted to the sinner, who therefore gives no true praise to God. **10b-c.** 'By the mouth of the wise man praise is uttered, and he who masters (wisdom) shall teach her.'

b XV 11-21 **Free Will and Responsibility for Sin**—In not imparting wisdom to the sinner, is God responsible for sin ? The answer follows, logically developed. Some of the points it presupposes are more fully indicated in 17:1-12—man's spiritual nature and faculties, God's making known to him of the moral law with its sanctions. **11a.** The blame for sin is not to be thrown on God. ' Say not " From God is my transgression ".' **11b.** For God hates sin, ' and he doth not the thing he hateth '. **12.** His hatred of sin is not ineffective, as if he were constrained to cause or permit sin for providential purposes. ' Say not " It is he that caused me to fall ", for he hath no need of wicked men.' **13.** On the contrary, he gives men help to keep clear of sin, and they who fear him can and do avoid it. ' The Lord hateth evil and abomination ( ), and to them that fear him he lets it not draw nigh.' **14.** Nor can it be argued that God is responsible in that he created man with a nature already flawed. As he left the hand of God man was endowed with the good gift of free will. ' God created man from the beginning ( ), and set him in the power of his free will.' After beginning Heb. inserts ' and placed him in the power of that which carries him away (lit. his snatcher away) '. This is not found in Vg Gk Syr., and is apparently a gloss explanatory of the phrase which follows and from which it does not differ in meaning. ' Free will ' is in Heb. yēṣer. The root verb means ' to form, devise, plan ' or ' purpose '; cf. BDB s.v. The noun elsewhere in the Bible means the form or framing of a thing ; and that which is devised or determined on by the mind. In New Heb. it ' is common in sense of impulse : . . . of good and bad tendency in man ' (BDB 428). In rabbinical writings it usually means an inherent propensity to evil. But in the present context it has a ' neutral sense ' (Box), best rendered by ' free will '. This translation is supported by Gk διαβούλιον ' deliberation, determination ', and Vg consilium ' counsel '. As 16-18 show, this endowment places it in man's power to choose moral good or evil, and their consequences ; and here lies the answer to the question posed. See more fully in § 397h. **15.** In Vg only.

16. God gave man helps to use his free will to choose the morally good ; he embodied it in commandments, which he made known to man. ' If thou wilt, thou shalt keep the commandments, and the practice of fidelity

is his good pleasure.' For ' commandments' see on **40** 17:9-12 ; 21:12. **17.** As further God added sanctions to his moral law, rewards for observing it, punishments for breaking it. ' Water and fire are set before thee, stretch forth thy hand to which thou wilt.' Water and fire are figures of reward and punishment. Possibly Deut 28-30 was in mind. Cf. Deut 28:11, 12, 21, 24. The outlook is the older one, of material rewards and punishments. ' Fire ' here has no eschatological significance. **18** continues the thought of 17 : ' Before man is life and death ( ), that which he wills shall be given him.' The phrase ' good and evil ' is a gloss ; it refers to good and evil fortune as moral sanctions. Man is free to make his choice ; but now, in choosing sin he also chooses its punishment, and in choosing good he chooses its reward. **19, 20.** And these sanctions will inevitably follow, for God is wise to see ' every work of man ' (20), and ' strong in power ' (19) to requite. **21.** Conclusion : the sinner's accusation of God (11 f.) is unfounded. God makes no one sin, commands no one to sin, gives leave or power to no one to sin. ' He commanded no man to sin, and he gave not strength to men for falsehood.' ' Falsehood ' here is infidelity to the moral law, the opposite of the ' fidelity ' of 16b.

15:22-16:6. The misfortune of having ungodly **c** children. **XVI 5.** See Gen 15:5 ; Is 51:2. **16:7-23. The certainty of the punishment of sin. 7-11.** Illustrated from biblical history (see 10:16-21). **7.** 'And in a disobedient nation wrath flamed out ' (see Num 16:35 ; Ps 2:12, 13). **8.** The Flood (see Gen 6:4 ; Wis 14:6). **9.** Sodom and Gomorrha (Gen 19:24 ff. ; Ez 16:49 [their pride]). **10.** 'He had not pity on the accursed nation ' : extirpation of the Canaanites. **11a.** The murmurers during the Exodus (Num 14). On the figure 600,000 see §197c, and cf. Num 1:45 f. ; 11:21 ; 14:22 ff. ; Ecclus 46:10. **11b.** Individuals too are punished. ' And if only one be stiffnecked, it is a wonder if he escape unpunished.' **15.** 'Everyone that does rightly shall receive his reward, and every man shall receive from him according to his works.' **16-23.** Folly of the sinner in thinking to elude judgement. Parallel to 23:25-29. **21** continues the thoughts of the fool : ' If I sin no eye beholds it, if I secretly deal falsely, who will know it ? ' **22.** Still the reasonings of the sinner : requital is doubtful, or so far off as to be negligible. ' My works of justice who shall declare ? What is there to expect ? The sentence is far off.' Last phrase of this verse is Secondary : there is a final divine judgement (see § 397j). **23.** All such reasoning is folly. ' He . . . thinketh these things, and the foolish . . . thinketh thus.'

XVI 24-XXIII 38 **On Creation, and the Moral Nature** **4C** **of Man ;** admonitions—16:24-17:20. Creation of the world, and of man as a moral being. (Heb. is missing from 16:27 to 30:10, except for occasional fragments.) **24, 25.** Prefatory. What follows is based on Gen chh 1, 2. **26-29.** Creation of inanimate nature. **29.** ' Or disobey his word.' **31.** Creation of living things. ' Every living thing hath covered . . .' **XVII 1-4.** Creation of man. **5b, 6a-b.** Man's intellectual nature. Free will was probably spoken of in Heb. where Vg has consilium ' counsel ' and Gk διαβούλιον, the words which translate yēṣer in 15:14, where see note. **6c.** Man's moral nature. ' Both good and evil ' : referring to Gen 2:17. **7, 8.** Man's power to know the Creator from his handiwork. **9-12.** The moral law imposed on man. **10.** Perhaps a reference to the promulgation of the Law on Sinai ; but it can well refer to Gen 2:17. **11.** The familiarity between God and man before the Fall (see Gen 2:16-22 ; 3:8). **12.** The natural law which (as Gen 3:8 implies) man was aware of from the beginning. **13-20.** Man's (and especially Israel's) moral responsibility to God, enforced by God's scrutiny of his conduct. **17.** ' Their sins are not hid from him.' **18b.** ' and he preserves the bounteous deed of a man '. **20.** Repentance turns aside punishment. ' To the repentant he gives a return to justice and strengthens them that are losing hope.'

XVII 21-31 **Exhortation to turn to God**—on the value **b**

2b of repentance and of prayer as connected with it. **21-23.** Repent, pray for forgiveness, and amend. **24.** Secondary. (**25, 26a-b.** See after 27.) **26c.** Since a dead man is ' *as one that is not* ', **27** the time to repent and to praise God is before death. **25, 26a-b.** Secondary addition, giving a loftier view of the state of the just after death. There is a ' holy age ' or *world* (*saeculum*) after death, where men who have turned from ' the error of the ungodly ' will ' live and give praise to God '. This interpretation of ' holy age ' is supported by other Secondary Texts : 24:46 ; Syr. additions to 1:22 and 18:8. See § 397*j*. **28-31.** God condescends to man. **30b-c.** ' Yet it *faileth; and how much more man who hath the inclination* of flesh and blood ! ' (Box). The ' inclination ' is the *yēṣer* in its bad sense of propensity to evil. *Cf.* § 397*h*.

c XVIII 1-14 Mighty and Majestic as the Creator is, he is tender and merciful to man—**1-6.** The greatness of the Creator. **1a.** Vg ' *Qui vivit in aeternum creavit omnia simul* ', partly underlies the profession of faith of the 4th Lateran Council, repeated by the Vatican Council : *Creator omnium . . . sua omnipotenti virtute simul ab initio temporis utramque de nihilo condidit creaturam, spiritualem et corporalem* (Dz 428, 1783). St Augustine took *simul* to mean *simultaneously* (*De Gen ad litt.*, 4:33, 34 ; 5:23 ; 6:3 ; *cf.* Knabenbauer, 205). But the Gk is κοινῇ, and the Heb. must be a construction of *yaḥaḍ* ; the meaning is therefore *equally, all alike* ; God created all things without exception (see Jn 1:3). **1b.** ' *The Lord alone* shall be justified ', *i.e.*, as Syr. implies, recognized as triumphantly supreme. **3 ff.** See 43:29-37. **7, 8.** Man's insignificance and transitoriness in comparison with the Eternal. **7.** ' and what is his *profit* ? ' **8.** Syr. adds ' So a thousand years of this world are not even as one day in the world of the Righteous '. **9-14.** And yet God regards him with tender compassion. The first half of **10** is in Vg only ; but probably from a Heb. original which mentioned man's evil ' proclivity ' (*yēṣer*). The context is the same as 17:30 ; and in 37:3 Vg *praesumptio* represents *yēṣer*.

d XVIII 15-XXIII 38 Advice, chiefly on bridling the tongue—**15-18.** Graciousness in giving. **18:19-19:6.** On taking thought beforehand. **22b.** ' *Delay not until death to be justified.*' **22c.** Secondary : the everlasting reward of the just man. **23.** ' *Before thou vowest prepare thy vows* ' : against rash vows. **24.** Death and judgement. **29.** ' Words ' : wise sayings, proverbs. **XIX 1.** Heb. connects with 18:33, ' *Be not a squanderer and a drunkard, or there will be* nothing in thy purse. *He that doth this* shall not be rich, and he that contemneth small things shall *become altogether naked*'. The wage-earner, making little of his small daily earnings by squandering them in drink, will soon be in beggary. **7-12.** Control of the tongue. **13-17.** On administering reproof. **18-27.** Wisdom and craft contrasted. **21** is notable in laying down that even ' understanding ' does not of itself lead to fulfilling the Law. **24,** last phrase : ' *but when not observed he will outwit thee* '. **26.** ' when *he meets* him *knows him* by his countenance '. **28** belongs to what follows. **XX : 1-29.** Use and abuse of the tongue. **30-33.** Miscellaneous proverbs. (32 f. recur in 41:17 f.)

e XXI 1-11 Thoughts on Sin and Sinners—2-4. Three figures of the ever-impending and mortal danger of sin. **2.** ' *Flee from sin . . . near it*, it will *bite* thee.' **3.** ' *Killing the souls of men* ', lit. ' destroying the lives of men '. **4.** ' There is no remedy ', *i.e.* humanly speaking ; but 1 shows that by repentance, amendment and prayer, sin's effects may be undone. This verse, with 2, 3, may be an expression of the older view that sin is punished by temporal misfortune, sickness and death. But Catholic commentators tend to see in the passage a reference to the spiritual damage and death inflicted on the *soul* by sin. Perhaps we see here a dawning consciousness of the existence of a spiritual life in the soul which is destroyed by ' mortal ' sin. Other points to note are : (1) Sin is personified ; *cf.* Rom chh 5-7. (2) It lurks serpent-like within the

soul in the form of a propensity to evil. (3) But it can **402e** be avoided or ' fled ' from. (4) And its evil effects can be undone by God, through the sinner's repentance and prayer. On all this see § 397*h-i*. **6.** See 35:16-21. **7b.** ' will turn to *him with all* his heart '. **9a.** Building up a fortune dishonestly. **9b.** ' Is as he that gathereth stones *for his tomb* ' : is preparing his own destruction. **10, 11a-b.** Primary text. Let sinners prosper as they may, their end will be disgraceful ; their corpses are likely to be burnt as those of reprobates, and the oblivion of Sheol will engulf them. **11c.** ' and darkness and pains ' : Secondary addition, showing the concept of Sheol as not a place of mere oblivion but of punishment. See § 397*j*.

12-31 The wise man and the fool—See on 6:21. **12.** ' He that keepeth *the law subdues his impulse.*' Rendering based on Syr. ; the reference is to the *yēṣer* as the evil tendency (§ 397*h*). To keep the Law is the way to control it. St Paul will show later that keeping the Law in the face of concupiscence is precisely the difficulty (*cf.* Rom 7). See § 397*i*. **16.** See 24:40-47. **19.** ' like a burden *on a journey* '. **23.** Omit ' scarce '. **30.** ' *When* the ungodly curseth the *Adversary*,' he curseth his own *self*.' ' Adversary ', lit. ' the Satan '. The sinner cannot blame an adversary outside himself for his sin ; by his evil impulse he is his own Satan. *Cf.* § 397*h*.

XXII 1-5 Sluggards ; and discreditable children. **6-23.** Thoughts on fools. **12.** Omit ' wicked ' each time. **24-32.** Friends and how to treat them.

XXII 33-XXIII 6 A prayer for God's help against f evil tendencies. **22:33 f.** For help against sins of the tongue. **33.** ' *O for a guard upon* my mouth and a *cunning* seal upon my lips.' The seal on the lips must not be the mere mechanical one of perpetual silence, but a deliberate ' cunning ' control, knowing when to speak and when to be silent. **XXIII 1.** ' O Lord, father, and . . . ruler of my life ( ), suffer me *not* to fall by them.' The phrase ' leave me not . . .' belongs to 4*b* only. ' Father ' implies a tender interest in the individual soul's problems, going beyond even that of the ' shepherd ' of 18:13. ' Ruler of my life ' assumes a lofty theology in which grace, free will and the supremacy of God's providence fall into their proper places. **2-4.** For help against darkness of the understanding, weakness of the will, and the propensity to evil which infects the higher parts of the soul. **2.** ' *O for* scourges over my *thought* and a *rod of correction* over my heart, *to* spare not their *ignorant doings* and *to let not pass* their sins.' ' Heart ' in Heb. often stands for the higher part of the soul, including both mind and will ; when distinguished from ' thought ' as here, it represents the will, and ' thought ' the intellect. The prayer is that these faculties, infected by the tendency to sin, be both checked and purified by the rod of God. ' Ignorant doings ' are sins into which a man is betrayed without obstinate malice. Contrast Num 15:22-29 with Num 15:30 f. **3.** In the light of 4*b* the ' enemy ' may be the ' Adversary ' of 21:30, the personified ' sin ' of 21:2-5, the evil impulse in man which inclines him to sin. **4a.** See on 1. **4b.** ' Devices ' probably represents Heb. *yēṣer* as in 15:14. But here it is the evil *yēṣer*, sinful propensity. See § 397*h*. **5, 6.** For help against pride and passion. **6.** First phrase is a doublet of second. ' ( ) Let not the *lust* of the flesh *and impurity* take hold of me, and give me not over to a shameless ( ) mind.' **7-20.** Control of the tongue. **15.** ' *comparable* to death '. **17.** ' to *unclean* speech, for *that is a sinful thing* '. **21-38.** Sinners against purity. **21.** The three ' sorts ' follow, *viz.* solitary sinners, fornicators, adulterers. **22 f.** Solitary sin. **23.** ' in the *body* of his flesh '. **24.** The fornicator. **25-31.** The adulterer. **27.** ' and the eyes of men *are his* (only) *fear* '. See 16:16-23. **30b.** Added by Vg. **32-38.** The adulteress. **34.** ' Inquisition ' as to paternity. See Lev 20:10 ; Deut 22:22 ; Jn 7:53 ff.

XXIV 1-XXXIII 6 Wisdom coming forth from God 403a and imparted to Man—Various practical counsels. **XXIV 1-31 Wisdom praises Herself—1-4.** Intro-

403a ductory. Wisdom, personified, is about to speak in her own name. For the personification of wisdom see § 397m. **1.** 'Wisdom praises herself and *speaks her glory in the midst of her people*', *i.e.* as pre-eminent in the midst of Israel, she makes known her glory. **2.** 'She *opens* her mouth in the *assembly* of the Most High, and *is honoured* in the sight of his *hosts*.' Her glory is manifest also amidst the angels in the heavenly court (see Job 1:6 ; 2:1 ; 3 Kg 22:19 ff.), and throughout the 'hosts' or armies of being which fill the material creation (see Gen 2:1). **3, 4.** Vg only ; doublets of 1, 2. **5-11a.** Wisdom's origin from God and her presence throughout creation. The passage is strongly influenced by Prov 8:22–31. **5a.** Wisdom, originating within God, was externalized by his spoken word, *i.e.* his creative command and his revealed will. See on 1:5 ff. and § 397l. **5b.** 'The firstborn before all creatures', Vg only ; perhaps a Christian gloss from Col 1:15. **6a.** 'I made . . . faileth.' Secondary ; but keeping close to Prov *loc. cit.* and Gen 1:1–4. **6b.** 'and as a *mist* I covered ( ) the earth'. 'Earth' here and 'heaven', 'abyss', 'sea' of 8, name all the departments of the visible universe. The 'mist' to which wisdom is compared may be that of Gen 2:6 (meaning uncertain) ; but more probably wisdom is identified with the 'spirit of God' of Gen 1:2, hovering cloudlike over chaos. **7.** 'and my throne *was on* a pillar of cloud'. Wisdom was enthroned alongside of God himself (as in Wis 9:4, 10), 'in the *high* places', *i.e.* heaven, above the clouds, here pictured as the supports of God's throne (see Ps 96:2 ; 103:3). **8.** 'Circuit' : the 'firmament' of Gen 1:6–8. **9a.** Omit 'have stood'. **9b-10.** New sentence : 'And in every people and in every nation . . .' Wisdom dominates the conscious creation also. See on 1:10. **11a.** 'And by my power . . . high and low' : Secondary.

b **11b-15.** Wisdom commanded by God to dwell permanently in Israel. **11b.** 'And in all these I sought a *resting-place*, and (asked) "*In whose possession shall I settle ?*"' **12.** 'Then the creator . . . commanded ( ) me, and he that *created* me *made my tent to rest*.' In the last phrase Vg takes transitive as intransitive ; see on 24 f. The sense is as in 1:10c, 16. **13-15.** Wisdom obeys God's command to dwell in Israel : God entrusts his revelation of himself to Israel. See Rom 9:4. **14b.** On wisdom's 'eternity' see § 397l. **14c, 15.** Wisdom's part in Israel's worship, first in the tabernacle, then in the temple. 'In the holy *tabernacle* I ministered before him ; moreover I was established in Sion . . .' An allusion to the pillar of cloud of Ex 33:9, 10 ; in 21 wisdom is compared to the cloud of incense-smoke in the tabernacle. 'Ministered' : the Mosaic worship was the gift of God's revelation ('wisdom') to Israel. See 20, 21. **15b.** 'And my *authority* was in Jerusalem.' Besides the laws of worship, moral and civil laws were contained in the revelation for which 'wisdom' stands. The 'authority' to interpret and apply it was in the hands of the priesthood in Jerusalem with the king's co-operation. See 17–19. **17-19.** Wisdom's beneficent operation in and through Israel, described under the figure of flourishing and graceful trees ; an expansion of 14, 15, which shows wisdom bringing true worship and moral law to Israel. The trees figure the moral excellence which indwelling wisdom gives to Israel among the nations. See Ps 1:3. **16.** Omit 'and my abode', etc. **17a.** The cedars of Lebanon are proverbial for their majestic growth, and the beauty and durability of their wood. **17b.** 'And as a cypress on *the range of Hermon*.' The qualities of the cypress parallel those of the cedar, as the Hermon range parallels the Lebanon. **18.** 'Like a palm tree in *Engaddi*', on the west shore of the Dead Sea, celebrated for its palm groves. The 'rose plant' is the oleander, which is especially abundant about Jericho. **19.** Omit 'in the streets'.

c **20, 21.** By imagery based on the description of the sacred anointing oil and the incense (Ex 30:22-36) it is shown that wisdom, by revealing to Israel the accept-

able way of worship, marks it out as a sacred and priestly nation. **20.** 'Aromatical balm', lit. *aspalathus*. **21.** '( ) like galbanum and onyx and *stacte*, and as frankincense *smoke in the tabernacle*'. This last phrase gives the key to the imagery ; see 14c. **22, 23.** Wisdom's influence spreads out from Israel to other nations : the religious and moral influence especially of the Dispersion. **22.** 'The turpentine tree' is remarkable for its far-spreading branches. **23.** 'As the vine I *put* forth *shoots of beauty*, and my flowers *became* fruit of honour and riches.' See Ps 79:9–12 ; and especially Ez 17:5–15, where Judah *in her relations with the Nations* (Babylonia, Egypt) is figured as 'a spreading vine which grew into branches and shot forth sprigs'. The 'beauty, honour, riches' which these bear are the same as in 22. See 51:19, 36. **24** is Secondary, making clear the spiritual meaning of the fruit of wisdom. For wisdom as a mother see 15:2 ; Wis 7:12. 'Fear' is the characteristic fruit of wisdom ; love, knowledge (faith ?), hope, are the Christian triad. See 2:8–10. **25.** In Vg only ; a Christian gloss based on Jn 14:6. 24, 25, with Vg of 12, opened the way for the liturgical accommodation of this ch to our Lady. **26-31.** Wisdom's invitation to all to gather and enjoy her fruits. Gentiles are not excluded. See on 22 f. **27.** 'For *to be mindful of me* is sweet above honey, and *to possess me is sweet* above ( ) the honeycomb.' See Ps 18:11, referring to the Law. **28.** A doublet of 14b. **29.** The appetite for wisdom grows by what it feeds on. Contrast Jn 6:35. **30.** To 'hearken to' is to obey ; 30a and 30b are synonymous. **31** is Secondary, stressing the reward of the *teacher* of wisdom. See Dan 12:3. The reward is, characteristically, 'life everlasting' ; see § 397j.

XXIV 32-39 Wisdom in her Plenitude is contained **d** in the Law. See § 397b. **32.** 'All these things are the book of ( ) the covenant.' **33.** '*The Law which* Moses commanded.' **34.** Vg addition, belonging rather to context of 45:3 or 47:11. **35 ff.** For 'who' read 'which'. The reference is to the Law. **37.** '*Which poureth forth* knowledge as the *Nile*' : to the four rivers of Eden (Gen 2:11–14), the Jordan and the Nile are added to fill in the picture of the Law's abundance of wisdom. **38.** '*The* first *had not* perfect knowledge of it, and *the last* shall not search *it* out.' The students of the Law from the first to the last, will never fathom the fullness of its doctrine.

XXIV 40-47 The author spreads abroad the knowledge of wisdom like a channel branching off from a river. **40.** Secondary. Omit 'wisdom' ; the author is speaking in person. **41a.** Doublet of 41b. 'like an aqueduct came *forth into a garden*', to bring the waters of the Law to his own disciples (42). **43.** But his work grew under his hand to unexpected proportions. **44.** 'Afar off' ; the Dispersion. **45.** Vg only. Generally taken as a Christian gloss, based on Eph 4:9 ; 1 Pet 3:19 f., implying that Christ is the wisdom spoken of, but Smend (Comm. CXVII f.) argues for a Heb. original. **46.** Inspiration wells up within him as in a prophet ; see 39:16 ; Am 3:8 ; Jer 20:9. 'Even to the holy age' : Secondary ; see on 17:25. **47.** Also found (better) in 33:18.

XXV 1-16 Miscellaneous Counsels—4. 'And an old **e** man that is *an adulterer and lacking sense*.' **16.** Secondary. **XXV 17-XXVI 24. On women, bad and good.** **22.** 'There is no *poison* worse than the *poison* of a serpent.' **33.** The first recorded sin is that of Eve ; the punishment that came on our first parents meant the exclusion of themselves and their posterity from access to the tree of life (Gen 3:22–24) ; therefore 'we all die'. See § 397g. **36.** Divorce her. 'Flesh' means family ; before divorce they had been 'in one flesh' (Gen 2:24). **XXVI 4.** Omit 'if'. **13.** 'On a *headstrong* daughter set . . . she *use it for herself*.' **16b.** 'and shall fat his bones *with her intelligence*'. **17.** '*A* gift of God (18) is a wise . . .' **22a.** 'The holy candlestick' : the seven-branched lampstand of the temple. **22b.** 'So is the beauty of the face *upon a stately figure*.' After **24** a passage (found in AV 24:19-27) is added in Gk MSS 70, 248, Syr., Arabic; it comes from a Secondary Heb.

XXVI 25–XXVIII 14 Miscellaneous Counsels—XXVII 2. 'As a *nail*.' **17–24.** Against disclosing secrets. **XXVIII:1–9.** Forgive and God will forgive you. See Mt 6:14 f.; 18:21–35. **7.** '(*Remember*) corruption and death; *abide* in his commandments.' See on 7:40. **10–14.** Against quarrelling. **15–30.** The mischief of a wicked tongue (from which Ben Sirach himself had suffered, *cf.* 51:3–7). **16.** The 'third person' is the slanderer, the other two being the one slandered and the listener. **19.** His tongue 'hath cast out *good wives*' by causing divorce. **22.** 'By *the* tongue.' **25.** Subjection to slander is a living death; it is better to die outright and go down to the Underworld. **26a.** 'Its *power* shall not be *on the godly*.' **28.** 'Hedge in thy *vineyard* with thorns ( ), and make doors and bars to thy mouth.' **29.** '*Lock up* thy gold and silver, and make a balance *and weight* for thy words.'

XXIX 1–26. On lending, borrowing, giving, and standing surety. **1.** 'and he that *upholds him with his* hand'. **8.** 'But if not (*able to repay*).' **12.** 'The commandment': Deut 15:7–11. **14.** '*Lay out* thy treasure *according to* the commandments . . .' See 12. The text of **16–17**, being merely a repetition of 17:18 f., is omitted in official Vg. DV, however, assigns the Nos. 16, 17 to what Vg calls 18; thus 19–35 of Vg correspond to 18–34 of DV. **18–26.** Suretyship. An advance on Prov 6:1–5; 17:18. **25** refers to those who go surety for the sake of usury. **27–34.** Poverty, but not dependence.

XXX 1–13 On bringing up Children—1. 'that he may rejoice': that *the father* may have a happy old age. **7.** '*He that pampers his son* shall bind.' He fusses over the scratches of his darling. **11.** (Heb. is available until 34:1.) **14–21.** On health and sickness. **17.** 'Everlasting rest': the older view of the Underworld, as a place of surcease. *Cf.* 28:25 and § 397j. The *requies aeterna* of Vg, understood in the higher sense, supplies the Christian term for happiness in the next world. **18.** 'Good things *poured out for* a mouth.' Good food is useless for the invalid who cannot take it. The next verses illustrate the same point. **22–27.** Sadness shortens life, joy prolongs it. **24.** '*Comfort* thy own soul ( ) *and rest* thy heart, ( ) and drive away . . .' **26.** At this point begins the displacement in Gk MSS which affects 30:26–36:18. See § 396d.

XXXI 1–11 The right attitude towards wealth—2. Heb. repeats the thought of 1. **4.** 'The poor man *labours for lack of substance, and when he rests he suffers want*': antithesis of 3. **8–11.** How rare is the rich man who does not succumb to the temptations of wealth. See Mt 19:23–26. **8b.** 'And that hath not gone *astray* after *wealth*.' 'Gold' of DV is *māmôn* in Heb. It is a loan-word from Aramaic, frequent in rabbinical Heb., but only here in biblical. See on Mt 6:24; Lk 16:9, 11, 13. **10.** Interrogative. 'Who hath been . . . *so that* he shall have glory ( )? *Who is* he that could have transgressed . . .?'

31:12–42 Temperance in food and drink—27. 'In all thy works *show restraint*.' In **28** for 'faithful' and in **29** for 'true' read *lasting*. **30–42.** Wine in moderation. **30a.** '*At wine be not a champion*.' **31b.** 'So wine ( ) *proves* the hearts of *mockers*': *in vino veritas*. **32.** 'is *a water of* life to men'. **33.** 'who is *without* wine?' **34.** Mistaken doublet of 33. **42b.** 'And quarrel not with him in company.'

XXXII 1–17 Manners at a Banquet—1–3. The one who presides. **1.** 'Ruler (*of a banquet*)?' See Jn 2:8, 9. **3.** 'That thou mayest *enjoy honour from* them, and receive *the* crown *due to good manners*.' **4–9.** Etiquette for elders. Music and song have their place at a banquet, as well as words of wisdom. **10–17.** For younger guests. **18–28.** The provident and godfearing man contrasted with the sinner. **18.** 'Early': diligently. **23.** Doublet of 22. **27.** 'In every work of thine *watch thyself constantly*.'

XXXIII 1–3. Keep the Law and it will keep thee.

1. 'Temptation': trial. **3b.** 'And the Law is **403h** faithful to him *as the Urim*': it guides his life as surely as would a direct answer from the oracle of God. On Urim and Thummim see Ex 28:30; 1 Kg 14:41 f. **4–6.** Steadfastness of mind. **6.** '*The friendship of a fool* is like a *saddled* horse.' As a horse just saddled, eager to be off, neighs happily no matter who mounts him, so a fool bestows his shallow 'friendship' on any chance acquaintance that suits his whim.

XXXIII 7–XXXIX 15 God's Wisdom in governing the 404a World; the writer's purpose in studying it; guidance on many subjects.—**33:7–15.** Unity and diversity in creation. **7–10b.** The calendar is ruled by one and the same sun, yet God wills that some days and seasons should excel others. **10c.** So, too, all men are made of the same clay (**11**), yet God in his wisdom has '*distinguished* them and diversified . . .' **12a.** The race of Israel 'he has blessed and exalted', to be his Chosen People. **12b.** And even within Israel some groups are honoured above others. The priestly family he sanctified in a special manner, and 'brought nigh' to himself. (See Num 16:5, 10.) **12c–d.** Other nations he treated as aliens. The terminology is that of Gen 9:25–27, where Canaan is made inferior to Sem. The vigorous contrast between *blessing* and *cursing* is purely literary, not theological. (See on Gen 25:23; Mal 1:2; Rom 9:6–13.) The theological contrast is between a Chosen People and others *not specially chosen*. **13–15.** And as with nations, so with individuals. All come equally from God's hand, but the lot assigned by him to each is different. (See Is 45:9; Jer 18:1–6; Rom 9:21.) **14a.** 'All . . . ordering' ('offering' by misprint in some DV ed.) is a doublet of **14c**: 'And he will *allot* to him according to his *own decision*.' It is not a question of final requital, but of the whole course of a man's life; God is the 'ruler' of it all, as in 23:1. **15.** Good and bad *fortune* in the affairs of men, life and death *in the physical universe*, are needed in the world and arranged for by its Creator. Even the sinner has a place in it besides the good man. This must be read in the light of 15:11–21.

16–19. The author's work is based on that of earlier sages, and is destined for the teachers who will succeed him. **18.** Same as 24:47. **19.** 'ye great men *of the* people': it is instructors of Israelites he has in mind, in such schools as his own (see on 51:31, 37), and in those operated by the 'rulers of the *congregation*' in the synagogues which already at this date existed in the Dispersion.

20–33. Advice to the head of a house. **20–24.** During **b** life not to surrender property and independence. **25–30.** Strict treatment for a lazy slave. **31–33.** Kind treatment for a good one. **XXXIV 1–8.** The vanity of dreams and omens. **2.** (Heb. is missing till 35:11.) **6.** Allowance is made for God-given dreams, of which Scripture records many. **9–20.** Experience is a good teacher, the fear of the Lord a better. **11.** Doublet of 10. **12.** Ben Sirach's own experience, enlarged by travel. See 39:5; 51:8. **13.** '*and by* these things I have been delivered'. His experience and wisdom helped to save his life. 'By the grace of God' is a Vg addition, expressing a true sense, as 51:1–17 testifies. **14–20.** The fear of the Lord, even more than experience and skill, brings protection. **14.** 'The spirit of those that fear God *shall live*': God will save them in danger. **19c.** 'A defence from the *burning wind*' or simoom. See Is 25:4. **34:21–35:15.** Sacrifice: **c** when displeasing and when pleasing. The teaching is that emphasized by the prophets from Amos onwards. (Am 5:11–27; 8:4–10); ritual sacrifice pleases God only when it comes from one moved inwardly by the spirit of true religion, and doing the will of God by keeping his moral law. **21–31.** Unacceptable sacrifice. **XXXV 1–15.** Acceptable sacrifice. **11.** (Heb. becomes available till 38:28, with some lacunae.)

16–21. God hears the prayer of the distressed. **20.** 'He that adoreth God *in the way that pleases him* shall be accepted.' **21.** It is humility, the sense of

404c dependence on God, that gives wings to prayer : ' and till it come *unto God* it will not *rest* ; and *it* will not depart till the Most High behold '. **22-26.** God will therefore hear the prayer of distressed Israel. The oppression of the Jews alluded to here and in the prayer which follows (36:1 ff.) refers to a general situation, not to a particular tyrant. Ptolemy IV of Egypt (*d.* 205 B.C.) personally rode roughshod over Jewish susceptibilities, but Jews in his dominions were well treated. Antiochus III of Syria (223-187 B.C.), ruler of Palestine when Ben Sirach wrote, was favourable to them (Jos. *Ant.* 12, 3, 3). Two things, nevertheless, made even the kindest of Gentile rulers tyrants in Jewish eyes : (1) the fact that they *were* Gentiles, ruling, by right of force only, over the theocratic people ; (2) the Hellenistic and therefore paganizing culture which was the inevitable concomitant of their rule everywhere it was exercised. The conditions which led up to the crisis of the Maccabean period were already perceptible in Ben Sirach's time. **24.** ' according to their deeds, and ( ) the works of *man* according to his presumption '. **25b.** ' And ( ) delight *them* with his mercy '.

d XXXVI 1-19 A Prayer for Israel—It contains many expressions which are found in the *Eighteen Blessings* of the Synagogue liturgy. **1, 2.** Theme of the prayer : salvation for Israel, fear of God on the Nations. This ' fear ' is not exclusively dread, but includes recognition of the truth about God, leading to worship of him. See § 397c. **3-7.** Enlightenment for the Gentiles through chastisement. **3.** ' Lift up thy hand ', to chastise them. **4.** As thou hast shown the Gentiles how holy thou art by thy treatment of us—punishing our sins by subjecting us to the nations—so now show us how holy thou art by punishing the sins and tyranny of the Gentiles. See Is 10:5-21. **5.** The happy result of the chastisement of the Gentiles. **6, 7.** Renew the wonders wrought at Israel's deliverance from Egypt. A favourite theme in Is 40-66. **8-12.** The crushing of Israel's particular enemies. **10.** ' *Hasten the end and take thought for the time, for who shall say to thee :* " *What doest thou ?* " ' The reference is to the ' last time ' or Messianic era, which God is asked to bring quickly, with its fulfilment of Israel's hopes. See 17, 18. **11.** Not in Heb. If he escapes vengeance in one form, let him find it in another. See 3 Kg 19:17. **12.** ' The head of the princes of the *enemy* ' : perhaps Antiochus III (see on 35:22-26). For ' enemy ' Heb. reads *Moab* (traditional figure of Israel's enemies), but this may be a copyist's mistake. **13-14.** Gather together as freemen in their homeland the scattered tribes of the chosen people. **13b.** ' That they may ( ) *hold their inheritance as in the olden days.*' **15-18.** Glorify Jerusalem and the temple on Mount Sion, by fulfilling the Messianic promises. **16.** ' Fill Sion with thy praise and *the temple* with thy glory ' : an allusion (as in 49:14) to the Messianic prophecy of Agg 2:7-9, which includes the conversion of the Gentiles. **17.** ' *Testify in favour of the first of thy works,* and *verify the prophecy spoken* in thy name.' Vindicate Israel's position as thy firstborn and favoured son (see 14) by fulfilling thy promise made to him. **18.** ' for thee, *in* that thy prophets be found faithful ' : reward the hopes of those who trust in thy promise by verifying it as thy prophets foretold. Last phrase in Vg belongs to what follows. **18c, 19.** Conclusion of the prayer. ' according to *thy goodwill towards* thy people ( ), and let *all the ends of* the earth know that thou art God *from eternity* ': *i.e.* the same God who *of old* chose Israel and gave him the promises.

e XXXVI 20-XXXVII 34 Discrimination — **20-22.** Discrimination in general. **23-28.** Discrimination in choosing a wife. **25.** ' a *soothing* tongue '. **26a.** ' *obtaineth* a *choice* possession '. **26b.** See Gen 2:18, 20. **28.** A roving bachelor, ' that hath no *nest* ', *i.e.* home of his own, with a wife. ' Rest ', DV, is a misprint (Vg *nidum*). **XXXVII 1-6.** Discrimination in choice of friends. **2.** Omit ' but ' and ' shall be '. It continues the question of 1. **3.** ' O wicked *propensity wherefore*

wast thou formed' : the evil inclination (*yēṣer*) that turns friendship awry. See § 397h. **5** refers to a true friend ; ' for his belly's sake ' belongs to 4. **7-19.** Discrimination in choosing counsellors. **12** at end : ' nor with *a grudging* man about *benevolence* '. **18.** ' Watchmen ' : astrologers. **19.** God is the best counsellor. **20-21d.** Deliberation in plan, action and speech. **21c-29.** False wisdom and true. **28.** As long as Israel lasts, *viz.* for ever, the name of its sages will be kept alive. See 44:13-15. **30-34.** Discretion in eating. **30.** Learn by experience, ' and *what is bad for thee, permit thyself not* '. See 31:19-24.

XXXVIII 1-15 Physicians and Medical Care—1-3. f The physician is to be treated with deference even by kings, because he is a minister of God, ' created ', *i.e. appointed* by him for human needs. **4-8.** The healing power of medicines is also from God. **5.** The reference is to Ex 15:23-26. **6a** continues **5** : ' *that he might make his power known to all men* '. **7.** ' He ' : *the physician* (Heb.). ' The apothecary ' was by trade a perfumer (Ex 30:25 ; 37:29 ; 2 Par 16:14 ; Ecclus 49:1) who also stocked salves and ointments. **7d, 8.** ' *That* of his works there *may not be an end, and health from God may* be over all ' : apothecary and physician are providential instruments for carrying on God's healing work. **9-11b.** In time of sickness turn first to God, by **9** prayer, **10** repentance and **11** sacrifice (Lev 2:1-3). See 2 Par 16:12, where Asa's fault is that he neglected this. **11c-15.** The physician must also be consulted, as God's appointed means of cure. But he himself depends on God and must pray to him. **13.** ' For there is a time when *success lies in his hand* (**14**), *since he also beseeches God to prosper his study and his healing treatment.*' **15.** Sin leads to sickness, either as a direct result or as a punishment sent by God. That it *always* does so, or that all sickness results from personal sin, is not asserted. **16-24.** Mourning for the dead : it is a good work in itself, and convention demands it ; but when unduly prolonged it is harmful to the living. **16.** ' According to *his due*.' **19.** ' Of sadness cometh *harm*, ( ) and sorrow of heart boweth down the *strength* '. **20.** Gk (emended) : ' In *misfortune sadness* remaineth and *sorrow* (lit. ' a curse ') *of heart is a life of affliction*'. Heb. omits. Possibly a gloss on 19. **23.** ' Remember his *lot* . . . so : " Yesterday for me, and today for thee." ' It is the common lot, and mourning will not change it ; so, **24b** ' comfort *thee when* his spirit *departs* '.

XXXVIII 25-XXXIX 15 Contrasting Pictures of the **g** manual worker and the student of wisdom. **25.** Introductory : opportunity for study and reflection is necessary for the acquisition of wisdom. **26-34.** The manual worker's occupations, demanding concentration for their proper performance, do not allow him this opportunity. Examples follow. **26, 27.** The farmer. **28.** The engraver. **29-31.** The metalworker. (Heb. is lacking till 39:20.) **32-34.** The potter. **33b.** ' And *treads* down *its substance beneath his feet* ' : kneading the wet clay by trampling ; see Is 41:25. **35-39b.** Such manual workers are essential to the well-being of the state, although not fitted for the higher public offices. **37.** ' And *where they* dwell *the people hunger not. Yet* they shall not . . . ' **37b, 38.** The tasks proper to the learned. **39b.** ' And their *mind is on* the work of their craft.' **39c** belongs to what follows.

XXXIX 1 (with 38:39c)-15 Picture of the Student of h Wisdom—38:39c. ' *Not so he that applies his* soul *to* searching in the Law of the Most High.' **XXXIX 1.** ' *He* will seek out.' With preceding verse, enumerates the three divisions of the Heb. canon : Law, Prophets, ' wisdom of the ancients '. **2, 3.** ' The sayings ' are the oral wisdom of the Sages, passed on in schools such as Ben Sirach himself conducted (51:31, 37). **4.** Actual service as councillor to some magnate is another school of wisdom. **5.** So is the school of experience and travel. See 34:9-13 ; 51:1-17, 18. **6-8.** Nevertheless, the scribe's wisdom is fundamentally religious, its source is the one true God of Israel, and prayer is its surest channel. **9-11.** By this contact with God, he himself will become a living well of wisdom. **12-15.** The reward of the scribe : honour during life, lasting fame after death. See 37:26–29 ; 44:1–15. **13b.** ' And his name shall *live*.' **14.** The ' church ' is the Hebrew community. See 33:18. **15.** ' *As long as he lives his name shall be honoured* above a thousand, and *when he dies it suffices for him* ' : his name survives him and takes his place when he is dead.

XXXIX 16-XLIII 37 Eulogy of God's Wisdom in his governance of the Universe—with practical reflexions, and a hymn to the Creator. **39:16-20.** Invitation to join with him in praising the Creator. **16b.** ' I am filled as *the moon at the full* ' : full of the light of wisdom. Compare 24:41 ; 33:17. **17-20.** Omit first phrase. He invites his fellow-Israelites to join him in his hymn. The imagery is that of 24:17–23. **20.** (Heb. is in the main available for the rest of the book.) **21-41.** ' All the works of the Lord are good.' **21-26.** They all show forth his power and wisdom. After **21** Gk inserts the refrain which we have in 26, 40. **22** refers to Gen 1:6–10 ; see Ps 32:6, 7. **23.** Paraphrase : By a word from him his will is done, and nothing can limit the good he wills. **24, 25.** His eye is all-seeing and his wisdom all-pervading. See 16:16–22 ; 17:13–17 ; 23:26–29. **26.** See on 21. Each work is good in relation to God's purpose for it. **27-29.** Both his benignity and his severity manifest his goodness. **27, 28a.** ' overflowed like *the Nile*, and *like the River* hath watered . . .' The Nile and the River (*i.e.* Euphrates), on which whole peoples depend, are figures of God's goodness to the world. **28b, 29a.** His punishment of sinners is equally effective. ' So *doth his wrath disinherit nations* . . . *he turned a watered land* into *salt* ' : Sodom and Gomorrha. **30-32a.** Good things were created for the good. **32b-37.** Punitive agencies were created for evil-doers. **33.** ' Spirits ' : winds. **37.** They obey God's will in punishing the wicked. **38-41.** Conclusion echoing 16–21.

XL 1-10 The Hardships of Human Life : reflexions on Gen 3:17–19. Though all God's works are good, man's Fall has brought suffering on himself. **1.** ' *hath God appointed* for all men '. It is God's sentence on fallen men, Gen *lòc. cit.* ' The mother of all ' : mother earth, from which man is formed. See 16:31 f. ; 33:10. **8.** ' Such things ' refers to what follows, in **9** (omit ' moreover '). **10.** ' *Calamity* is created . . . came *destruction* ' : an echo of 39:33 ff.

11-17. What passes and what abides. **15b.** ' and *are as unclean roots* ' : fated to wither. **17.** ' Grace ', *i.e.* generous kindness. **18-28.** Series of comparisons, with a refrain, exalting the fear of the Lord. **23.** ' a wife *of discretion*.' **24.** ' *A brother and a helper* in time of trouble, but *righteousness is a deliverer above them both.*' **28b.** ' and *its canopy is above every* glory ' : the divine protection which the fear of God wins. See Is 4:5. **29-30.** ' My son, lead not a life of beggary.' **31.** ' *Which to a man . . . is inner torment.*'

XLI 1-XLII 8 A Series of Contrasts—XLI 1-7. Death, welcome and unwelcome. **5-7.** The older, naturalistic view of death, as in 38:21–24. **7.** ' For *in Sheol there* is no *inquiring concerning* (*length of*) life ' : the older view—the Underworld is the end of all. See § 397j. On Sheol see note on 14:17. **8-16.** The memorials left by the wicked and the just : their children and their reputation after death. For the wicked, these decay ; for the just, they prosper. **12.** ' If you *increase it will be for harm, if you have children it shall be for sighing* ; *if you stumble—a lasting joy, if you die—an execration.*' **16.** See 37:28 f. ; 39:12–15. **41:17-42:1c.** Things to be ashamed of. **17b-18.** Same as 20:32, 33. **20b.** ' to keep *every kind of* shamefacedness '. **23b.** ' And of (*joining with*) *the foreigner* in the place where thou *sojournest.*' Recommends exclusivism to Jews who dwell amongst Gentiles. **24a.** ' *Of breaking an oath or a* covenant.' **24b.** See 31:16–21. **XLII 1c.** ' So shalt thou be *rightly shamefaced* ', refers back to all that precedes, from 41:19. To be ashamed of doing the disgraceful things mentioned is to be rightly ashamed.

XLII 1d-8 Things not to be ashamed of—1d. ' These things ' which follow. **4b, 5.** ' Of much or little **405d** *profit, and of gain from the wares of* merchants.' **9-14.** The care of daughters. **12.** ' *Let her not show her beauty to a man, nor* tarry *in converse* among (*married*) women ' : the seclusion of well-bred oriental young women. It is married women of disedifying life and conversation who are warned against, as the sequel shows. **13b.** ' And from *one* woman the *wickedness of another.*' **14a.** The wickedness of men (which the daughter will be on her guard against and shielded from) is not so dangerous for her as the corrupting friendship of the type of woman spoken of. **14b.** ' And a *shameful daughter is a source of* reproach.'

XLII 15-XLIII 37 Hymn to God the Creator, con- e cluding Part One of the book.—**42:15-26.** God's greatness in his works in general : his unique glory, his omniscience, his omnipotence. **15c-d.** ' By the *word* of the Lord his works *were done, and his will was accomplished by his decree.*' See 1:5 ; 43:28 ; and § 397l. **16.** As the sun gives light to all things, God gives being, and all things reflect his glory. **17.** ' *The Holy Ones of God have not the power* to declare all his wonderful works. *It is God who gives strength to his hosts to stand in his glorious presence.*' ' The Holy Ones ' are the angels (Deut 33:2 f. ; Job 5:1 ; 15:15 ; Ps 88:6–9, etc.). Even they could not endure to look upon the unveiled glory of God, did he not strengthen them to do so. *Cf.* Job 4:17, 18 ; 15:15 f. ; Is 6:2. **18.** He fathoms the unfathomable. See 24:8–11. **19.** Past and future to him are present. **20.** ' Word ', *i.e.* thing. **21b-c, 22.** ' And he is *one* from eternity.' He is one, eternal, self-existing, self-sufficient. **23.** ' O how *lovely* ' : lovable as are his created works, they are but a spark compared with the blaze of his own lovableness. **24.** All that he created is sustained and ruled by him. **25.** ' All things are *different*, one *from* another ; *yet* he hath made *none of them without its purpose.*' **26.** ' One thing excels another in goodness, and who shall be filled with beholding *their beauty* ? '

XLIII 1-28 God's Greatness in his Works in particular f —**1.** The firmament, or visible vault of heaven. See Ex 24:10. **2-5.** The sun. See Ps 18:6, 7. **6-9.** The moon. The Hebrew calendar, year, months, and festivals were ruled by the moon. **6,** end : ' And *an everlasting* sign '—as long as the world lasts. See Ps 71:5. **7b.** Her light wanes after the full. **8b.** ' *How awe-inspiring in her changes !* ' **9.** ' *The signal* of the *cloud-army* on high, *she shineth* gloriously ' : rallying the hosts of the clouds (lit. water-vessels, see Job 38:37 Heb.). **10-11..** The stars. ' By the *word* of the Holy One they stand *at their post* ' : like sentinels on high. See Bar 3:34 f. ' Word ' : see 42:15 ; 43:28. **12, 13.** The rainbow. **14-18.** The storm. **14.** ' *His power writes the lightning* (*in the sky*) *and sets ablaze the flashes of his vengeance* (**15**) *for the sake of which his treasuries are* opened.' ' Vengeance ', see 39:33–37. ' Treasuries ' : see Deut 28:12 ; Job 38:22 ; Jer 51:16. **18a, 17, 18b.** Read in that order. **19-24.** The snow, frost and dew. **21b.** ' And makes its flowers to flash like sapphires.' **24.** ' A ( ) remedy of all *this* is the *dropping* of a cloud, and *the dew which alights for refreshment after drought.*' **25-27.** The sea. **25a.** Doublet. **25b.** See Gen 1:2, 6–10. **28.** ' By reason of *him his work succeeds*, and by his *word his will is accomplished.*' ' By his word ', see 1:5 ; 42:15 ; and § 397l. **29-37.** Conclusion of the hymn : ' The Almighty himself is above all his works.' **33.** Paraphrased by Aquinas in his *Quantum potes tantum aude quia maior omni laude.* **35.** ' Who *has seen* him *that he may* declare him ? And who shall magnify him as he is ( ) ? ' The answer was yet future (Jn 1:18).

XLIV 1-L 31 The Praise of the Ancients of Israel— 406a The Ancients are praised ' in their generations ', *i.e.* in chronological order, beginning with Henoch and ending with Simon the high-priest, the author's contemporary. God's dealings with the Fathers and their response to his special providence are hymned as examples of that divine wisdom to whose exposition the book is devoted.

XLIV 1-15 Introduction—1. ' Let us now praise men

406a of *piety*.' *Cf.* 10. **2.** 'The Lord hath *allotted them* great glory, *and* his magnificence.' The various categories now to be mentioned won honour *in their own day.* **3a-b.** Warriors and rulers, like Josue and David. **3c-d.** 'Counsellors by their wisdom, *and seers of all things by their prophetic skill*', *e.g.* Elias, Isaias. **4a-b.** 'Ruling over the *Gentiles by their counsels* and *leaders by reason of their shrewdness*', *e.g.* Joseph. **4c-d.** Not in Vg : '*Wise in thought through their book-learning, and exercising rule through their functions*'. The 'functions' are probably those of the priesthood (Peters) ; the 'book-learning' would be that of Scribes. **5a.** Inspired psalmists. **5b.** 'And *set forth proverbs in writing*' : like Solomon. **6.** '*Men well-off in wealth and strong in substance, living at peace*' : like the Patriarchs. **7.** Conclusion of the sentence begun in 3. The honour some had *after* their own times he now goes on to speak of. **8.** '*There are some* of them *who* have left' : some of the great men honoured in their own days left an honoured memory ever after ; **(9)** others did not. The reason for the difference is given in ff. vv. Those who were not remembered after death were men prominent in their day by position and influence, but not by *piety*. *Cf.* 47:27-31 ; 48:18 ; 49:5-7. **10.** 'But these were men of *piety* . . . *will* not *fail*.' 'Piety', Heb. *hesed.* Here and in 1 this word of many meanings (*cf.* BDB) is connected, by the examples given, with the idea of *duteous love* of God and *devotion to his service.* The great men of the past who excelled in this will never be forgotten. Three things keep their memory alive : (1) **11-13,** their posterity flourishes, generation after generation, worthy of their forbears ; (2) **14a,** the honourable graves in which they were buried, after a blessed death ; (3) **14b, 15,** their reputation for 'wisdom' as well as piety, which shall continue as long as Israel lasts. See 37:28, 29 ; 39:14.

b **16.** Henoch. See Gen 5:22-24 ; Heb 11:5. **16b.** '*a marvel of knowledge to all generations*' : *i.e.* a marvellous example of the high destiny to which perfect knowledge can serve to raise one. The unfinished notes on Adam, Seth, Enos, Sem, Joseph, grouped with another mention of Henoch in 49:16-19, suggest that Ben Sirach intended to fit in these other Ancients too, had his work received the final touches he had in mind. **17-19.** Noe. **17.** 'was made a *renewal*' : from him, after the Flood, humanity was renewed. **19.** '*An everlasting covenant was* made.' See Gen 8:21 ; 9:9-17. **20-26.** Abraham, Isaac and Jacob. **20b.** 'And there was not found *a stain* in *his* glory.' See Gen 17:4-6. **21.** 'In his flesh', by circumcision. See Gen 17:9-11 ; 24. 'In *trial* he was found faithful' : Gen 22:1-12. **22, 23.** See Gen 22:15-18. 'The River' is the Euphrates, as in 39:28 ; see Gen 15:18 ; Ex 23:31 ; Deut 11:24 ; Ps 71:8. **24.** See Gen 26:3-5. **25, 26a.** The blessings passed on to Jacob ; Gen 27:27-29. **26b.** See Gen 49. **27.** Belongs to what follows (Moses) : 'And he *brought forth from him a righteous man*, that found . . .'

c **XLV 1-6 (with 44:27).** Moses.—**2a.** 'The saints.' Heb. is '*elōhîm*, which may mean *angels* (also called 'saints' or 'holy ones' in 42 :17 ; the reference would be to Ex 34:29-35), or *God* (referring to Ex 4:16 [MT] ; 7:1). **2c.** 'He made prodigies *come to pass*' ; the plagues of Egypt. **3c.** 'His glory' : Ex 33:18-34:8. **4.** '( ) *For* his faithfulness and meekness *he* chose him' : Num 12:3, 7. **5.** Ex 20:21 ; 24:18. **6.** 'Commandments *face to* face' : Secondary, from Ex 33:11 ; Deut 34:10. 'Law of life and *understanding*' : the Law whose observance brings life and wisdom ; see Deut 30:15 ; 32:47 ; 4:6. **7-27.** Aaron. For Ben Sirach's appreciation of the Aaronic priesthood see § 397c. **7, 8.** Aaron chosen as priest by 'an everlasting *ordinance*'. See Ex 29:9. **9-14.** The priestly garments and adornments. See Ex 28. **12.** 'Judgement and truth', *i.e.* Urim and Thummim ; see on 33:3. **15-21.** To Aaron and his descendants alone was given the power to offer sacrifice, to bless the people in God's name, and to teach and apply the Law. See Lev 10:10f.; Deut 17:8 ff. **22-24.** The rejection of rival claimants. See Num 16. **25-27.** Provision for the support of the

priests. See Num 18. **28-31.** The promise to Phinees. See Num 25. **31.** Text corrupt. After 'seed' add : '*so the inheritance of Aaron is also unto his seed*' : the high-priesthood is as assured in the line of Aaron as the kingship in the line of David. See Jer 33:14-26. There follows an address to the living representatives of the Aaronic priesthood : '*And now bless the Lord who has crowned you with honour, giving* wisdom into *your* heart . . . that *your* good things *may* not be abolished, and *your* glory *for* everlasting *generations.*'

XLVI 1-12. Josue and Caleb—**1.** 'Jesus the son of Nave' : Gk form of *Yešua' ben Nun*, as in Jos 1:1, etc. 'According to his name', which signifies *the Lord is salvation.* **2-8.** Josue's leadership in the conquest of Canaan ; see Jos 6-11. **9-12.** The 'work of *piety*' of Josue and Caleb, and its reward. See Num 14:6-38. **10.** 'Six hundred thousand' : see on 16:11. **11.** See Jos 14:6-14. **13-15. The Judges. 14b.** 'May their bones *sprout forth* out of their place.' The same expression occurs in 49:12. It has not been satisfactorily explained. It is not a reference to the resurrection of the body, but a prayer that the merits of the Judges may be rewarded by an enduring spiritual posterity. See Is 58:11 ; 66:14. **16-23. Samuel. 16.** 'Anointed princes' : Saul and David, 1 Kg 10:1 ; 16:13. **17b.** Text uncertain ; perhaps : 'and *the Lord visited* Jacob', *i.e.* sent them a leader ; see Ex 4:31. **18.** 'And he was faithful in his words *as a seer*.' See 1 Kg 3:19 ff. ; 9:6 ff. **19-21.** See 1 Kg 7. **21a.** 'And he crushed the princes of the *enemy*.' **22.** See 1 Kg 12:1-5. **23.** See 1 Kg 28:8-20.

XLVII 1-13 David—**2.** 'The fat' : the portion not to be eaten but reserved for sacrifice ; see Lev 3:3-5 ; 4:8-10. In the same way David was singled out as sacred. **3-6.** See 1 Kg 17:34-54. 'Set up the horn' : the common figure for triumphant prowess ; see vv. 8, 13. **7.** See 1 Kg 18:6 f. **8.** See 2 Kg 8. **9.** David as psalmist. 2 Kg 22 (Ps 17) would be a case in point. **10.** The emphasis on his *love* of God is noteworthy ; the terms are those of Deut 6:5. **11, 12.** See 1 Par 16:4 ; 25:1 ff. **13.** See 2 Kg 12:13 ; 7:12-16. **14-20.** Solomon's glory. **14.** 'For his sake', *i.e.* David's, as 2 Kg 7:12. **15.** See 3 Kg 3:1. **16.** 'Thou wast filled *like the Nile*.' See on 24:37 ; 39:27. **17, 18.** See 3 Kg 4:29-34 ; 10:1-13. **19.** 'And thou wast called *by the glorious name by which Israel is called*', *i.e.* the name of Yahweh. Solomon's name originally was Yedidiah, *beloved of Yahweh* (2 Kg 12:25). **20.** See 3 Kg 10:14-27. **21-25.** Solomon's defection. See 3 Kg 11:1-13, 31-39. **24, 25.** A firm assertion of the Messianic hope, 'He *will give* a remnant to Jacob, and to David *a shoot*' : see Is 11:1, 10. **26-31.** Denunciation of Roboam and Jeroboam. See 3 Kg 12 ; 13 ; 4 Kg 17:20-23.

XLVIII 1-12 Elias—**1.** 'Burnt like a *furnace*' : prophesying the drought (3 Kg 17) and bringing down fire (3). **2, 3.** See 3 Kg 17 ; 18:37 f. ; 4 Kg 1:10, 12. **5.** See 3 Kg 17:21, 22. **6.** His prophecies of doom : 3 Kg 21:21-24 ; 4 Kg 1:4 ; 2 Par 21:12 ff. **7.** See 3 Kg 19:15-17. **8.** 'Who anointedst kings *for retribution*' : 3 Kg *loc. cit.* 'And *a prophet as a successor*' : Eliseus, 3 Kg 19:16. **9.** See 4 Kg 2:11. **10.** 'Who art *written down as ready for the time appointed*, to appease . . .' : *i.e.* in Mal 4 :5, 6. **11.** 'Blessed is he who sees thee and *dies*.' The reference seems to be to Elias's return as precursor of the Messias : blessed is he who will see thee thus before he dies. Text uncertain ; probably 'And *blessed art thou, for thou livest on*' : Elias never died.

13-18. Eliseus, and subsequent generations. **13a-b.** See 4 Kg 2:9-15. **13c-d.** Earthly power did not overawe him. See 4 Kg 3:13 ff. ; 6:16. **14a.** 'Nothing was too *wonderful for him* (to do).' **14b.** 'Prophesied', *i.e.* exercised the miraculous powers with which prophets sometimes authenticated their mission. See 4 Kg 13:21. **16.** The destruction of Israel. **17, 18.** The survival of Judah as a kingdom for some time still. Those in it who 'did that which pleased God' will be noted in the verses which follow. **17.** 'There was left but a small people *unto Judah, but still* a prince *to* the house of

David.' The Messianic promise still in process of fulfilment. **19-28.** Ezechias and Isaias. **19.** See 2 Par 32:5, 30 ; 4 Kg 20:20. **20-24.** See 4 Kg 18 ; Is 36 ; 37. **26.** See 4 Kg 20:1-11 ; Is 38:1-8. **27, 28.** The reference is to the message and the prophecies of Is 40-66. It is clear that Ben Sirach attributes these chh to Isaias. See Is 40:1-11 ; 41:21-29 ; 42:9 ; 46:9-12 ; 61:1-7.

XLIX 1-9 Josias and Jeremias, with a reference to Judah's evil kings.—**1.** As in 24:20, 21, the figure expresses chiefly zeal for the worship of God according to the Mosaic regulations. See 4 Kg 23:1-25 ; 2 Par 34 ; 35. **2.** See 32:5-8. **5.** Besides these three kings, Asa, Josaphat and Joas are also praised in Kg and Par, but with reserve. See 3 Kg 15:11-15 ; 22:43-47 ; 4 Kg 12:2, 3 ; 2 Par 19:2, 3 ; 20:37. **6, 7.** The complement of 48:17. See 4 Kg 23:25-27. **8.** See 4 Kg 25 ; Jer 36:29, etc ; 39. **9.** See Jer 1:5-10 ; 37:38.

10-19. Brief notices of some other famous men. **10.** Ezechiel. See Ez 1. **11.** Job. 'And he made mention of *Job, who kept* right ways.' See Ez 14:14, 20. **12.** The Twelve Prophets, the so-called ' minor prophets '. ' Their bones ' : see on 46:14. **13.** Zorobabel. See Agg 2:24. **14.** Josue (' Jesus '), son of Josedec. See Agg 1:12 ; 2:3 ; Esd 3:2. ' Everlasting glory' : the reference is to Agg 2:7-10 ; see on 36:16. **15.** Nehemias. See Neh 3-6. **16-19.** Returns to the ancestors of the human race, with Joseph. See on 44:16. **16.** ' *Few men were* born upon earth ' : Heb. thus leaves place for Elias, who was also ' taken up '. **17.** See Gen 37:5-10 ; 42-47. **18a.** ' Visited ', *i.e.* providentially cared for, in accordance with prophecy. See Gen 50:23 f. ; Ex 13:19 ; Jos 24:32. **18b.** A gloss added from 48:14. **19.** ' Seth and Sem *and Enos* obtained glory, *but* above every *living thing* Adam.' Seth's glory was to be ancestor of the virtuous part of mankind before the Flood (Gen 4:25) ; Sem's, to be ancestor of the Chosen People after the Flood (Gen 10) ; Enos's, to have initiated ' calling upon the name of the Lord ' (Gen 4:26). Adam's glory surpassed all these in that he was created directly by God without human parents ; he was glorious ' *by his origin* ' as Gk and Latin add.

L 1-26 The High-Priest Simeon son of Jochanan (' Simon son of Onias '). See § 396h. He was a contemporary of Ben Sirach and held office *c* 219-196 B.C. **1.** ' *Great among his brethren and the glory of his people was* Simon the high-priest.' This phrase is misplaced in 49:17 by Vg and Gk. ' In his life ' : he was dead when this was written. **1b-3.** The renovations carried out in the temple. Their exact nature is not clear. That Antiochus the Great supported them is asserted by Josephus in *Ant.* 12, 3, 3. **3.** The water-supply he provided is compared to ' the Sea ', *i.e.* the great laver of Solomon's temple (3 Kg 7:23 ff.). **4.** ' Delivered it from destruction ' : by his prayers when Ptolemy IV threatened destruction in 217 B.C. (see 3 Macc 2) ; and later by winning the friendship of Antiochus the Great (Jos. *loc. cit.*). **5a** continues 4 : ' *He fortified his city against the enemy*.' **5b-23.** Description of the high-priest offering the burnt-offering on the Day of Atonement. The ceremonial is that of Lev 16, and *Mishnah, Yoma* 3 ff. ; *Tamid* 7 (Danby's Eng. trans., 164 ff., 588 f.). **5b.** ' How glorious was he when he looked forth from the *tabernacle, and when he came forth from the holy place* ' : after the ritual bath, vested for the sacrifice. **6-11.** Eleven comparisons describing the impression of awe-inspiring majesty and the ecstatic thrill of worship which the high-priest's appearance produced. The figures are those used in 43:1-13 and 24:17-23 to convey the same ideas. **11c-d-12.** ' when he went up to the *lofty* altar and *made glorious the holy precincts*'. **13-15b.** His offering of the sacrificial portions, surrounded by the assistant-priests. **15c-17.** The sacrifice completed by the libation of wine. See Num 28:7-10 ; Phil 2:17. **18-21.** Trumpet-sound and choral song as the people bow down in prayer. See Num 10: 2, 10; 2 Par 29:27-30. (In v **20** some edd. of DV misprint ' sinners ' for ' singers '.) **22, 23.** The

high-priest's final blessing. The formula was that of **406h** Num 6:24-27. **22c-d.** ' *And the blessing of the Lord was upon his lips and he glorified himself with the name of Yahweh*.' The high-priest alone, on occasion of this blessing once a year, had the privilege of pronouncing the ineffable name ' Yahweh '. **23.** ' *And again they prostrated, to receive from him the blessing*.'

24-26. Ben Sirach's prayer that God may continue to **i** bless Simon in his priestly successors. **25a.** ' May he grant *you* wisdom of heart ' : the leading idea of the whole work comes out strongly as it draws near its close. **26.** ' *May his love abide upon Simeon, may he keep in him his covenant with Phinees ; may it never fail unto him and his offspring whilst the heavens endure*.' **27, 28.** In contrast with what precedes comes this reprobation of the Edomites, Philistines and Samaritans. **27.** Omit ' which I hate '. Samaria ' is no *people* ', *i.e.* no people *of God* ; it has apostatized. See Deut 32:21 ; Os 1:9 f. ; 2:24. **28.** ' Mount Seir ', the centre of Edom's power, south of the Dead Sea. The traditional enmity of the Edomites for Israel was particularly bitter at and after the Exile. See Abd 11-14 ; Mal 1:2-5 ; Ps 136:7 ; 1 Macc 5:65. ' The Philistines ', another traditional enemy. In Ben Sirach's time their cities were strongholds of Hellenistic paganism. Shechem, the modern Nablus, in the centre of Samaria.

29-31. The author's subscription to his book. **29.** His name in Heb. text is given as ' *Simeon son of Yešua' son of Eleazar son of Sirach* '. But critics, with reason (Oesterley, xv) emend to ' Yešua' son of Eleazar son of Sirach ', omitting mention of Simeon, as they do in colophon to ch 51. See § 396h.

LI 1-17 Appendix : a Prayer of Thanksgiving for 407 Deliverance—Knabenbauer, after Rabanus, interprets it collectively, as spoken in the name of the Hebrew people. The common view is that it expresses Ben Sirach's own gratitude for deliverance from personal dangers. What the circumstances were is not clear. It seems that (probably during his period of service abroad, see 34:12, 13 ; 39:4, 5 ; 51:18) a slanderous conspiracy against him had put him in danger of his life ; he turned to God in prayer and was delivered. **1.** ' O King.' See Ps 144:1 ; Ex 15:2. **2.** ' Name ' stands for *person* as known and revered. Heb. continues ' *sustainer of my life*, for thou hast *saved my soul from death* '. **3a.** Parallel to preceding. ' Destruction ' : the grave. **3b-c.** Specifies the danger : deadly slander. See 28:15-27. **3d.** In the *face* of them that stood *against me*, thou hast . . .' **4b.** ' From *the snare of* them that *lay in wait* to devour ' : his enemies planned to trap him like an animal for food. See Job 19:22. **5b.** ' And from *many* afflictions *thou didst save me*.' **6b.** ' And in the midst of the fire *which I had not fanned* ' : figurative ; he had done nothing culpable to draw the attack upon himself. **7a.** ' Hell ', *i.e.* Sheol ; God delivered him from going down in death. See Jon 2:3. **7d-e.** ' From an unclean tongue, and from *concocters of lies* and *the arrows of a deceitful* tongue.' See Ps 51:2. **8.** ' My soul *drew nigh* even to death.' **9.** ' Hell ' ; Sheol, as 7. **10 ff.** See Ps 21:5-22. **12.** ' And savest them out of *all evil*.' **13.** ' *I sent up* my supplication *from* the earth, and *cried out from the gates of Sheol* ' : when on the point of going to his grave, and figuratively standing on the threshold of the Underworld. **14-15b.** He quotes the prayer he uttered in his anguish : ' *And I cried " O Lord, thou art my father, for thou art the mighty one of my salvation. Do* not leave me in the day of trouble "*.' ' My father ' : see 23:1, 5. **15c, 16.** Result of his appeal. ' And my prayer *the Lord* heard, *and he gave ear to my appeal* ', etc. in third person. **17.** After this verse Heb. inserts a hymn of praise, of 16 verses. Its authenticity is generally rejected. (English translation in Oesterley, 349 f. ; Box, 514 f.)

LI 18-38 Poem concluding the Whole Book—It serves **408a** the purpose of a modern preface. It was originally an acrostic, the verses beginning with successive letters of the Heb. alphabet, but the surviving Heb. is defective. **18-24.** The writer's zeal in seeking wisdom, praying for it, and practising it when found. **25-30.**

408a His success in finding it. **26.** Heb. adds ' *My hand un-latched her door and I entered in and gazed upon her*'. See 14:24–27. **30.** With wisdom the Lord has given him a gift of self-expression, both in prayer and in teaching. **31-38.** Hence his readiness to teach all who seek wisdom as he himself had sought it. **31, 32.** An invitation to learners to frequent his *beth midrash* or ' house of *instruction*'. This is the earliest mention of the practice, which developed after the Exile, of experts in the Scriptures giving lessons in their own houses to groups of disciples. **32b.** ' *How long will ye lack these things* ? ' **33.** In his school they will find wisdom, not for money but for earnest application—a reference to the Scribes' custom of not charging for their lessons on the sacred text. **34.** ' The yoke ' : see 6:25–32. **35, 36.** The gains he himself has made : peace of soul (' *peace* to myself ', 35), and abundant spiritual riches. **4** These are figuratively described as ' money ' and ' gold ' in 36. See Prov 3:13–15 ; 8:10–21 ; Wis 7:7–12. **37.** ' Let your soul rejoice in *my place of teaching* ' : Heb. *yᵉšîḇāh*, lit. *chair*. From meaning the *chair* from which the teacher lectured it came to have the technical meaning of *the class* which he taught, and also the *lecture-hall* where it assembled.

After 38 Heb adds a colophon, which in all probability **b** is a scribal addition. In it, the name Simeon is regarded as an unauthentic interpolation, as in 50:29. It runs : ' *Blessed be the Lord for ever, and praised be his name for all generations. Thus far are the words of Simeon son of Yešuaʿ called Ben Sirach. The wisdom of Simeon son of Yešuaʿ son of Eleazar son of Sirach. Blessed be the name of the Lord from now and unto eternity.*'

PROPHETICAL LITERATURE

By E. F. SUTCLIFFE, S.J.

Bibliography—C. à Lapide, S.J., ' In Prophetas Prooemium : Canones Prophetis Facem Praeferentes' (printed as introduction to his commentary on the major prophets) ; *G. F. Oehler, *Theology of the OT* 2 (Edinburgh 1875) 139–49, 192–7, 313–62 ; H. Zschokke, *Theologie der Propheten* (Freiburg 1877) ; R. Cornely, S.J., *Hist. et Crit. Introd. in utriusque Test. Libros Sacros*, ii 2 (Parisiis 1887) 267–305 ; *H. Schultz, *OT Theology*, Engl. trans., i (Edinburgh 1895) 235–300 ; F. Leitner, *Die prophetische Inspiration* (Freiburg im Breis. 1896) =BS I 4, 5 ; *A .F. Kirkpatrick, *The Doctrine of the Prophets* (London 1915³) ; E. Tobac, *Les Prophètes d'Israël*, 2 vols (Lierre 1919 ; Malines 1921) ; D. Buzy, *Les Symboles de l'Ancien Testament* (Paris 1923) ; M. A. Van den Oudenrijn, O.P., *De Prophetiae Charismate in Populo Israelitico* (Romae 1926), and ' De Vocabulis quibusdam termino nabi' synonymis' Bi 6 (1925) 294–311, 406–17 ; J. Chaine, *Introduction à la Lecture des Prophètes* (Paris 1932) ; C. Lattey, S.J., *Prophecy* (CTS 1942) ; E. Walter, ' Das Prophetenthum des Alten Bundes in seinem sozialen Berufe,' ZKT 23 (1899) 385–422, 577–604 ; A. Condamin, S.J., ' La Mission surnaturelle des Prophètes d'Israël ' ER 118 (1909) 5–32 ; P. Synave, O.P., ' La Causalité de l'intelligence humaine dans la révélation prophétique ' RSPT 8 (1914) 218–35 ; N. Peters, ' Sache und Bild in den messianischen Weissagungen ' TQ 112 (1931) 451–89 ; A. Meli, ' I beni temporali nelle profezie messianiche ' Bi 16 (1935) 307–29 ; *H. H. Rowley, ' The Nature of Prophecy in the Light of Recent Study ', HTR 38 (1945) 1–38 ; E. Mangenot, ' Prophètes ', ' Prophétie ', ' Prophétisme ' DBV ; H. Lesêtre, ' Ravissement ', ' Vision ' DBV.

Minor Prophets—F. Ribera, S.J., *In Librum Duodecim Prophetarum Commentarii* (Coloniae Agrippinae 1599, etc.) ; G. Sanctius, S.J., *In Duodecim Prophetas Minores et Baruch Commentarii* (Lugduni 1621, etc.) ; B. Neteler, *Gliederung des Buches der Zwölf Propheten* (Münster i. Westf. 1871) ; J. Knabenbauer, S.J., *Commentarius in Prophetas Minores*, 2 vols (CSS) 1886 ; *idem edidit* M. Hagen, S.J., 1924 ; A. Van Hoonacker, *Les Douze petits Prophètes*, Paris 1908 ; P. Riessler, *Die kleinen Propheten . . . nach dem Urtext übersetzt und erklärt* (Rottenburg 1911) ; J. Lippl–J. Theis, *Die zwölf kleinen Propheten* (BB) 1937 ; *C. R. Keil, *The Twelve Minor Prophets*, 2 vols, English trans., Edinburgh 1874 ; T. H. Robinson–F. Horst, *Die zwölf kleinen Propheten*, Tübingen 1938 ; F. Nötscher, *Zwölfprophetenbuch*, Echter Bibel, Würzburg 1948.

The Prophetical Literature—This section of the Bible comprises the four major and the twelve minor prophets together with Baruch and Lamentations as an appendix to the book of Jeremias. The order of the four major prophets is chronological and that of the minor prophets was intended to be so, but the dates of some are uncertain. The writing of Baruch owes its place to the fact that he was secretary to Jeremias, Jer 36:4, the author of Lamentations as of the book which bears his name. The prose book of Jonas differs so widely from the other prophetic writings that at first sight it appears to be out of place among them. As a prophet, however, is one who announces to the people the message which God puts into his mouth (§ 409*e*), Jonas

was a true prophet and his book in the right series. **409c** On the other hand, the book of Daniel as well as Lam. has its place in the Hebrew Bible, not among the prophets but in the third division among the Hagiographa. (The Hebrew canon does not acknowledge the sacred character of Baruch.) This is not unreasonable as, though Daniel received divine revelations, he lived his life at a foreign court and was not charged with a divine mission to preach.

The Hebrew Bible, moreover, classes all those whom **d** we call prophets, with the exceptions of Baruch and Daniel, as ' the later prophets ' and under the title of ' the former prophets ' includes Jos, Jud, 1 and 2 Samuel, and 1 and 2 Kg (the last four being our 1–4 Kg). The explanation is that the history of the Chosen People was viewed as the story of God's relations with them through the intermediary of the series of prophets whom he had promised to raise up after Moses as his divinely authorized spokesmen, *cf.* § 409*i*. The distinction of the prophets into major and minor refers only to the length of their compositions, and has nothing to do with their authority, which is the same for all. The terms were used already by St Augustine : ' Propterea dicuntur minores quia sermones eorum sunt breves in eorum comparatione qui maiores ideo vocantur quia prolixa volumina condiderunt ', *De Civ. Dei* 18, 29.

The Essence of the Prophetic Office — The OT **e** prophet was an intermediary between God and the people. He received from God the message which God wished to be communicated, and then himself handed it on. He was God's mouth. This essential function of the prophet is clearly shown in the relation which God established between Moses and Aaron. When the former protested his inability to carry out the mission God was imposing upon him, on the ground of the defect of speech which afflicted him, God ordered Moses to put the divine words into Aaron's mouth for him to speak to the people in Moses' stead : ' He shall be thy mouth and thou shalt be *for him a god*', Ex 4:16. And that the function here assigned to Aaron is that of the prophet as between God and the people is shown by the parallel passage, Ex 7:1 f., where God says to Moses : ' Behold I have appointed thee the God of Pharaoh, and Aaron thy brother shall be thy prophet ; thou shalt speak to him all that I command thee and he shall speak to Pharaoh '. As the function of Aaron was to deliver to Pharaoh the message Moses put into his mouth, so the function of the prophet was to deliver the message put into his mouth by God. This is the account which the prophets give of themselves. Jeremias says of his own appointment as prophet : ' The Lord put forth his hand and touched my mouth ; and the Lord said to me : Behold I have *put* my words in thy mouth', 1:9. So Zach 7:12, ' They made their heart as the adamant stone lest they should hear the law and the words which the Lord of hosts sent in his spirit by the hand of the former prophets ' ; *cf.* Ez 3:17. The prediction of the future was a frequent but not a necessary part of a prophet's work. This was understood long ago by St Augustine, ' A prophet is just this, an announcer of the words of God to men ', *Quaest. 17 in Exod.*, PL34, 601. Similarly St John Chrysostom, ' The mouth of the prophets is the mouth

409e of God' and ' A prophet is God's interpreter ', PG 60, 156 and 61, 311.

f Names used for a Prophet—In 1 Kg 9:9 it is said, ' He that is now called a prophet, in time past was called a seer '. The former name in Hebrew is the common word *nābî'*, the etymological examination of which is not helpful. The root does not occur in Hebrew except in connexion with prophecy, and the word itself does not occur in the kindred languages. In accordance with the Assyrian *nabū* ' to call ' a *nābî* could mean ' one called ' as *māšîaḥ* means ' one anointed '. The Hebrew word *rō'eh*, translated ' seer ', is the present participle of the common word for ' to see ' and takes its rise from the prophet's knowledge of distant or hidden events as of the fate of the lost asses sought by Saul, 1 Kg 10:2. A synonym of this word is another present participle *ḥōzeh*. It is not possible to establish diversity of meaning between the two. The three words occur in the order given above in 1 Par 29:29, ' Samuel the seer ', ' Nathan the prophet ', and ' Gad the seer '. Samuel and Gad are elsewhere styled prophets, 1 Kg 3:20, and 2 Kg 24:11. Hanani is called a prophet in 3 Kg 16:7, and is also designated by both the words for seer, 2 Par 16:7, 10 and 19:2.

g In the LXX *nābî'* is always translated by προφήτης except where understood of a false prophet. This word well represents the Hebrew as it also signifies one who speaks in place of another as interpreter. In particular it was used of the interpreter of the oracles given by the μάντις at Delphi, Plato *Timaeus* 72a, Herodotus, 8, 36 f.

h As the prophets were charged to deliver the word of God they are aptly called his messengers, Is 44:26, Agg 1:13, Mal 3:1. By reason of his union with God a prophet is designated ' a man of God ', Jos 14:6 (of Moses), 1 Kg 2:27 (unnamed), 9:6 (of Samuel), etc., and as doing his will they are his ' servants ', Am 3:7, Jer 7:25 ; 25:4. As it was in virtue of ' the spirit of the Lord ' which came upon him that a prophet uttered his prophecy, 2 Par 20:14, a prophet was ' *a man of the spirit* ', Os 9:7. In the only passage where this phrase occurs it is actually used collectively of false prophets as is the word ' prophet ' in the same place, so that the sense is ' he who is reputed by the people to be a prophet, a man of the spirit '. In virtue of his office a prophet is a watchman set upon the walls to warn of danger, Jer 6:17, Ez 3:17, etc.

i God's Promise of Prophets—God's promise to raise up a succession of prophets among his people is given in Deut 18:9-19. At Sinai the Hebrews were overwhelmed by the majesty of the theophany and implored God not to let them hear his voice again or witness the manifestations of the theophany. In answer God promised to deal with his people through the intermediary of prophets : ' I will raise them up a prophet out of the midst of their brethren like to thee, and I will put my words in his mouth and he shall speak to them all that I shall command him ', v 18. The future prophets were not to be like Moses in all respects, for ' there arose no more a prophet in Israel like unto Moses whom the Lord knew face to face ', Deut 34:10. They were to be like Moses in their essential function of being intermediaries between God and his people and of communicating to them the divine commands. They were to be Israelites but not of any particular family like the priests, Ex 28:1, 43, nor of a particular tribe like the Levites, Num 3:6 f., 45. God would appoint whomsoever he chose. By the presence in their midst of this succession of prophets the people would be safeguarded against the danger of imitating the evil practices of the Canaanites whose land they were to dwell in. Those pagan peoples had wizards, soothsayers and necromancers—all an abomination to the Lord and the Israelites were forbidden to have any dealings with them. They should consult God's own chosen representatives.

j Although the divine promise speaks in the singular of a prophet, it is clear from the whole context that this, in accordance with Hebrew idiom, is a collective singular and refers not merely to Christ himself but to the whole succession of prophets, which was to culminate in the king of prophets, Christ our Lord. As the immediately foregoing passages deal with judges, 16:18-17:13, with the institution of the kingship, 17:14-20, with the priests and Levites, 18:1-8, so our passage deals with prophets. The institution of prophets was promised to guard the people from imminent dangers, 14 f. ; these dangers would not be met by the sending of a great prophet after many hundreds of years. Again, the promise was made in answer to the petition of the people for an intermediary, a petition which would not be met by the raising up of one in the distant future. Finally, the passage closes with a warning against false prophets, which would be unnecessary if the coming of only one great prophet were foretold. The patristic evidence is adequately dealt with by Cornely, 279. The passage makes it clear that the succession of prophets was not to be an organized institution. It was not to be hereditary like the priesthood. No one could make himself a prophet nor could one train another and induct him into the office. God himself would ' raise up ', 18, as prophets those whom he should choose.

Historical—The passage we have been considering as well as Moses' whole career show that he was himself a prophet ; *cf.* Os 12:13. His sister Mary is called a prophetess, Ex 15:20, for God spoke also by or through her, Num 12:2. Among the patriarchs Abraham is called a prophet and indeed by God himself, Gen 20:7, for Abraham had been made the intermediary of the divine revelation concerning the covenant with himself and his seed and concerning its outward sign, the sign of circumcision, Gen 17:10 f. The word *nābî'*, used in the Pentateuch for prophet was not that in current use among the people in the days of Samuel, 1 Kg 9:9, and only became popular later, but that, of course, does not mean that the word was previously unknown and never used.

From the time of Moses to the cessation of prophecy the history of the prophets falls into two periods, **the period preceding the reign of Jeroboam II,** *c* 800 B.C., and that beginning with it. The distinction is based partly on the fact that the prophets of the second period produced a more abundant and still extant prophetical literature, and partly on a development of prophecy characteristic of the later period. At the beginning of the first period between Moses and Samuel little is heard of prophets. In the Gk and Latin texts of Ecclus 46:1 Josue is said to have been the successor of Moses in the prophetical office, but according to the original Hebrew text he was ' the minister of Moses ' in that office in accordance with Ex 33:11. Deborah, who was also one of the Judges, was a prophetess, Jud 4:4 ; *cf.* 4:6, 14. Jud 6:8-10 narrates how a prophet in the name of God let the people know that the sufferings inflicted on them by the Madianites were a punishment for their worship of local Amorite gods. This infidelity of the people was perhaps the reason why God did not send more prophets during this period, the divine promise to help the Chosen People with a succession of prophets being like all such promises accompanied by the tacit condition that the people do not make themselves unworthy of the favour. The only other prophet mentioned before Samuel is the ' man of God ' who announced the divine sentence of reprobation against Heli and his house, 1 Kg 2:27-36. And it is explicitly remarked that ' the word of the Lord was *rare* in those days ; there was no *public* vision ', that is, revelation intended for the people at large, 1 Kg 3:1. There is some legitimate hyperbole in Jer 7:25 according to which God had sent prophets without intermission from the time of the Exodus.

It is in the time of Samuel that we twice read of **' a company of prophets '**, the one at Saul's home town of Gibeah, 1 Kg 10:5, and the other at Naioth in Ramah, 1 Kg 19:20. These men do not seem to have

0c been prophets in the strict sense which we have been considering hitherto. The first company was 'prophesying' to the accompaniment of various musical instruments, of which, however, there is no mention in connexion with the prophesying of the second group. The text does not indicate in what this 'prophesying' consisted. In 1 Par 25:1-7, however, where it is narrated how David set aside the families of Asaph, Heman and Idithun for the ministry of music and song at the tabernacle, their chants of praise and thanksgiving to God are called 'prophesying'. No doubt the prophesying of the companies of prophets also consisted in singing the praises of the God of Israel, but accompanied in these cases by some extraordinary psychic manifestations, some superexcitation of the faculties bordering on frenzy. It was owing to 'the spirit of the Lord' coming upon them that Saul and his messengers joined the bands in prophesying, 1 Kg 10:10 ; 19:20, 23. At Ramah, it should be noted, the spirit came upon Saul before he actually met the company. Something similar had happened when God took of the spirit which was in Moses and set it on the seventy elders, the newly appointed assistants of Moses. Not only those who had gone out with Moses to the tent of meeting, began to 'prophesy', but also two who, though nominated, had not gone out with the others, Num 11:25-27. These two examples show that the prophesying was not due to any contagious psychic influence. The extraordinary

d nature of the manifestations at Ramah is shown by what is said of Saul that '*he also*,' he like the others, 'stripped himself of his garments and prophesied before Samuel and lay naked all that day and night', 1 Kg 19:24. That Saul stripped off his garments points to literal nakedness and not merely to the removal of his outer clothing. The frenzied character of this 'prophesying' is further indicated by the fact that the same form of the same verb is used when an evil spirit came upon Saul and he cast his spear at David with the intention of killing him. Here the meaning is that Saul 'raved' in his house, 1 Kg 10:10. (The passages where prophets are called 'mad' are sometimes quoted in this connexion, but their context makes such an inference from them precarious ; 4 Kg 9:11 army officers speaking of a disciple of Eliseus, Os 9:7 of false prophets and in the sense that their utterances were foolish, Jer 29:26 used by the false prophet Semeias of true prophets.) Finally, it is to be observed that the mention of these companies of prophets in the time of Samuel is not made for its own sake, but only because they happen to enter into the history of Saul. Had they not entered in any way into the life of Saul, nothing probably would have been recorded of them. Inferences, therefore, drawn from the silence of Scripture about similar bodies before the time of Elias are at best ill-founded.

e The company of prophets at Naioth in Ramah was under the presidency of Samuel, 1 Kg 19:20, but their relation to him is not more accurately defined. It is in the time of Elias and Eliseus that we first read of 'the disciples of the prophets', lit. 'sons of the prophets' —an instance of the common Semitic idiom whereby any connexion, physical or moral, is expressed by terms denoting blood relationships. It is surprising how copiously it has been found possible to write on the basis of the scanty information given in the Bible concerning these sons of the prophets. The first mention of them is in 3 Kg 20:35-43 where one, who is also called a prophet, 38, delivers a message of reprehension from God to Achab. They are found only in the Northern Kingdom, at Bethel, 4 Kg 2:3, at Jericho, 2:5, at Galgal, 4:38, by the Jordan where they prepare a more commodious dwelling, 6:1 f. Evidently they were numerous. Fifty are mentioned at Jericho, 2:7, 15 f., one hundred at Galgal, 4:43. Living in common they had also their meals in common, 4:38-44. Some are young, 5:22 ; 9:4 ; some are married, 4:1 (MT, LXX). They are sent on missions by Eliseus, 9:1 ff. However, Eliseus did not live with

the disciples all the time, 4:38 (Galgal), as we find **410e** him living on Mount Carmel, 2:25 ; 4:25, and in his own house in Samaria, 5:9 ; 6:32. After the time **f** of Eliseus and the anointing of Jehu to be king we hear nothing more of organized bodies of disciples of the prophets, though whether this is accidental or because they ceased to exist it is impossible to say. Some have thought the protestation of Amos, 7:14, that he was not 'the son of a prophet', to imply the continued existence of these communities, but clearly a prophet might have one or two disciples without the existence of whole communities, *cf*. Is 8:16. St Jerome looked upon them as the monks of the OT, ' quos monachos in Veteri Testamento legimus ', *Ep. 125 ad Rusticum Monachum*, PL 22, 1076. Also in *Ep. 58 ad Paulinum*, PL 22, 583. In the opinion of the Rabbis the institutions were colleges or schools, whence the now common appellation 'schools of the prophets', for which there is little justification in Scripture and which was unknown to the Fathers, Cornely 278. It is possible, or even probable, that the hundred prophets concealed by Abdias from Jezabel's murderous hatred were members of one of these associations, 3 Kg 18:4, 13. On the other hand, this cannot have been the case with the four hundred prophets who recommended Achab to undertake the proposed expedition to recover Ramoth Galaad and who were not prophets of Baal as they prophesied in the name of Yahweh. As Josaphat refused to recognize them as true prophets of Yahweh, they must have been prophets addicted to the illegitimate calf-worship of Bethel and Dan, 3 Kg 22:6-12. Since persecution strengthens the religious spirit in the strong and fervent as it tends to extinguish it in the weak and lax, it may be that the hostility to the true worship of Yahweh in the Northern Kingdom from the time of Jeroboam I was the driving force which led to the formation of these prophetical associations. On the other hand, as the mention of them is always incidental, generally to the story of Elias and Eliseus—they are never mentioned for their own sake—it would be hazardous to suppose that none such existed simultaneously in the Southern Kingdom. The **outstanding prophets** of this first period were **411a** Samuel, Elias and Eliseus. Others of less importance and fame were Nathan, Gad, Ahias and Micheas. They were consulted by the people about **the affairs of daily life,** as when Saul consulted Samuel about the lost asses, 1 Kg 9:6 ff. ; Jeroboam I consulted Ahias about the sickness of his son, 3 Kg 14:1-13 ; Elias rebuked Ochozias for sending to consult Beelzebub, the god of Ekron (Accaron) whereas he ought to have consulted the God of Israel, 4 Kg 1:2-8 ; Benadad consulted Eliseus about his illness, 4 Kg 8:9 f. And the practice was common : ' In time past in Israel when a man went to consult God, he spoke thus, Come, let us go to the seer ', 1 Kg 9:9. This favour of God to the people was in accordance with the partial purpose for which a succession of prophets had been promised, namely that they should not be tempted to go after the wizards and soothsayers of the Canaanites, Deut 18:10-15. Their predictions also had reference to important **affairs of state.** Samuel foretold the **b** rejection of Saul from the kingly office, 1 Kg 15:26 ; Nathan foretold to David that he would be succeeded on the throne by his own son, 2 Kg 7:12 ; Ahias foretold the rending of the kingdom which was to follow the death of Solomon and Jeroboam's elevation to the throne, 3 Kg 11:29-39. They also took an important part in affairs of state, as was consonant with the fact that the monarchy was theocratic and the interests of Israel were the interests of the God of Israel. This is abundantly illustrated in the history of Samuel both before and after the election of Saul, in the position of Nathan at the court of David and his part in securing the election of Solomon, 3 Kg 1:11-30, in the anointing of Jehu as king at the order of Eliseus, 4 Kg 9:1-10. This activity even extended to the affairs of foreign states. Elias was ordered by God to anoint Hazael as king over Syria (Damascus), 3 Kg

411b 19:16. We do not read of the literal fulfilment of this command, and A Lapide understands the anointing metaphorically. It is reported that Eliseus later announced to Hazael his coming accession to the **c** throne, 4 Kg 8:13 Apart from one important prediction **the Messianic idea** received no further expansion during this period. This was Nathan's promise to David that the kingship should belong to his seed for ever, 2 Kg 7:12-16. No prophecy is more frequently referred to in the OT, Ps 88, Ps 131, 3 Kg 2:4, etc., and it was rightly understood to mean that the Messias was to be of the Davidic line.

d As all the activity of the prophets was aimed at promoting the interests of religion, either directly or indirectly, so in particular they were **defenders of the moral law** and denounced failure in obedience to God and idolatrous or irregular divine worship. Thus an unnamed prophet denounced the worship of Canaanite deities, Jud 6:8-10 ; a man of God rebuked the high-priest Heli for allowing his sons to dishonour the sacrificial worship of the tabernacle, 1 Kg 2:27-36 ; Samuel reproved king Saul for disregarding the divine command and reminded him that God is not pleased with sacrifice accompanied by disobedience, 1 Kg 15:22 f. ; Samuel won the people over from idolatry, at least for a time, 1 Kg 7:3 f., and encouraged them to the practice of true religion while reminding them of the penalties which would follow disloyalty, 1 Kg 12:6-25. Nathan fearlessly denounced to David the iniquity of his adultery and blood-guilt in respect of Urias and proclaimed to him the divine sentence of punishment, 2 Kg 12:1-15. 'A man of God out of Judah' publicly rebuked Jeroboam I for the illegitimate cult he had introduced into the Northern Kingdom, 3 Kg 13:1-5. For the same wickedness Ahias charged the wife of Jeroboam I with a stern message of condemnation and punishment to be delivered to her royal husband, 3 Kg 14:7-16. Equally bold and stern was the denunciation with which Elias met Achab for his guilt in the murder of Naboth and wrongful seizure of his vineyard, 3 Kg 21:17-24. Another royal offender rebuked by Elias was Ochozias of Israel. He had sinned by sending to consult Beelzebub, the God of Ekron (Accaron) 4 Kg 2-17.

e We have, further, records of **literary activity** undertaken by the prophets of this time. Annals, which, like the extant historical writings, will have been religious histories, were written by Samuel, Nathan and Gad, 1 Par 29:29. These contained the story of David's time. That of Solomon's reign was written by Nathan and by Ahias in his 'prophecy' as well as by Addo the seer, 2 Par 9:29. As the work of Addo was written against Jeroboam I, who prevented the people from making pilgrimage to the central sanctuary at Jerusalem and set up forbidden images of Yahweh at Bethel and Dan, and as it is called a 'Vision' like the writings of Isaias and Abdias, it must besides historical records have preserved some at least of his prophetic revelations. The same seer also wrote a record of the reign of Roboam, as did also the prophet Semeias, 2 Par 12:15. Addo, thirdly, wrote a history of Abia in his 'Midrash', 2 Par 13:22. Finally, Jehu, the son of Hanani, seer (2 Par 19:21) and prophet (3 Kg 16:7) chronicled the history of Josaphat, 2 Par 20:34. The titles 'Dibre of Nathan' (2 Par 29:29) and 'Dibre of Jehu' (2 Par 20:34) do not prove the exclusively historical character of these books as is shown by the introductory words of Amos, 1:1, 'the Dibre of Amos', and of Jer 1:1, 'the Dibre of Jeremias,' though it is hardly to be doubted that the proportion of historical to prophetic matter was higher in the books of the older prophets than in those of the later.

412a When the activities of these more ancient prophets are compared to those of the prophets who lived in **the period of extant prophetical writings,** it is found that the latter are essentially the same though with development and change of emphasis. In the first place the old names for 'seer' remain in use. Both occur in Is 30:10 and Amos is called a *ḥōzeh*, Am 7:12. Then

there are still prophets who are not recorded to have **4** put their message into writing. Such was Oded, a contemporary of Isaias, 2 Par 28:9, and Huldah (Holda), a prophetess contemporary with Jeremias, 4 Kg 22:14. Some of the apparent differences between the two periods may be due merely to the accidental circumstance that there was occasion to mention in the records of the older period what there was no occasion to mention in those of the later. As a fact, there is no further mention of companies of prophets nor of numerous disciples of prophets. It is almost certainly accidental that there is no mention of prophets being consulted about **private affairs.** Ezechias may, **b** though it is not recorded, have asked Isaias about the issue of his sickness, 4 Kg 20:1. None of the examples mentioned in the older period was recorded for its own sake, but in each case on account of certain attendant circumstances. People still consulted wizards and soothsayers, Is 8:19, and it is very unlikely that none of the faithful consulted true prophets.

Predictions about **affairs of state** were common. Jonas **c** foretold to Jeroboam II the restoration of the borders of Israel, 4 Kg 14:25. Isaias foretold to Ezechias the delivery of Jerusalem from the threatened attack of Sennacherib's forces, his return to Assyria and subsequent murder, 4 Kg 19:2-7, 32-34. Prophets in the time of Manasses predicted the coming destruction of Jerusalem on account of the wickedness of the king and the people, 4 Kg 21:10-15. And they frequently intervened in affairs of state. Osee condemned alliances with Assyria and with Egypt, 12:1. Similarly Isaias condemned the folly of placing trust in the help of Egypt, 31:1-3. And Jeremias had the unenviable duty of preaching the need of submitting to the hated foreign yoke of Nabuchodonosor, 27:12-17. This intervention **d** extended even to **foreign states.** Jeremias sent messages through their royal ambassadors to the kings of Edom, Moab, Ammon, Tyre and Sidon telling them that God had created the world and its inhabitants, and had given them to Nabuchodonosor, and that therefore they should submit to him under penalty of suffering war, famine and pestilence, 27:3-8. Apart from such direct action, the series of prophecies directed against other peoples is peculiar to this second period. Amos has a series of prophetic threats against Damascus, Gaza, Tyre, Edom, Ammon and Moab, chh 1 and 2. A large part of Isaias 13-23 is occupied by forebodings of evil to Babylon, Philistia, Moab, Damascus, Egypt, Ethiopia, Arabia and Tyre. Jeremias, 46-51, has another similar list of prophecies concerning the nations. See also Ez 25-32. To Jeremias, indeed, at the beginning of his mission God had said, ' Lo, I have set thee this day over the nations and over kingdoms, to root up, and to pull down, and to waste, and to destroy, and to build, and to plant', 1:10 ; *cf.* 25:15. Characteristic among **the themes of prophetic preach-** **e** **ing** in this period is the abundance of **Messianic prophecy,** which had been so scanty earlier. Some outline of this has been given, § 102*h-o*. **Denunciation of iniquity** also plays a far greater part in the mission of these later prophets than it had done with the earlier, as does likewise the annunciation of coming divine chastisement. Indeed, the duty most incumbent on the prophets was to denounce sin and to recall the people from their wicked ways to the true service of God : ' Cry *aloud*, cease not, lift up thy voice like a trumpet, and *declare* to my people their *transgression* and to the house of Jacob their sins ', Is 58:1. To speak humanly, the patience of God was becoming exhausted. ' The Lord hath sent to you all his servants the prophets, *diligently and persistently*, and you have not hearkened, nor inclined your ears to hear ', Jer 25:4. And, therefore, because they persisted obstinately in rebellious and wicked conduct, the hour of final chastisement was approaching. Though God was known to be ' gracious and merciful, patient and of much compassion, and easy to forgive evil ', Jon 4:2, his justice demanded that iniquity should not go unpunished for ever. The **f** reward of sin would be the foreign captivity of the nation

2f and the destruction of the capitals of Samaria and Jerusalem. This is the burden of the message delivered by the prophets from the time of Osee and Amos. The former addressing the Northern Kingdom wrote : ' The Lord shall enter into judgement with the inhabitants of the land ; for there is no truth and there is no mercy, and there is no knowledge of God in the land ; cursing and lying and killing and theft and adultery have over-flowed, and blood hath touched blood ', Os 4:1 f. Therefore shall come another time of bondage like that of Egypt, and Ephraim shall be taken captive to Assyria, Os 9:3. So too Amos castigates the injustice and heartlessness of the men of Samaria who ' oppress the needy and crush the poor ', 2:6–8, 4:1, and their for-bidden image worship, 4:4 f. And because they will not desist from such iniquities, ' now they shall go captive at the head of them that go into captivity ', 6:7, 7:17. ' And I will make Samaria as a heap of stones in the field when a vineyard is planted,' Mic 1:6. So too in the case of Judah : ' Behold every one of you walketh after the perverseness of his evil heart, so as not to hearken to me ; so I will cast you forth out of this land into a land which you know not nor your fathers ', Jer 16:12 f. And more precisely : ' I will give all Judah into the hand of the king of Babylon, and he shall carry them away to Babylon,' Jer 20:4.

g But God had promised from the beginning that he would not utterly reject his people : ' When they *shall be* in the land of their enemies, I *will* not cast them off altogether neither *will* I so *abhor* them that they should be quite consumed and I should make void my covenant with them ', Lev 26:44. The covenant was never to be wholly dissolved and its permanence involved the pre-servation of a **faithful remnant** even in times of the most absolute national infidelity and material disaster. This doctrine of the remnant became a commonplace in the prophetical literature. It was implicit in the Messianic hope and with the promise of return from captivity constituted the main ground for the prophets' words of encouragement and consolation. Thus Isaias, 6:13, speaking of the nation under the figure of a tree felled to the ground, said, ' *the stump thereof* shall be a holy seed '. The nation would not be allowed to perish root and branch ; sinful man could not completely thwart the plans of God. ' I will destroy (the sinful kingdom) from the face of the earth, but yet I will not utterly destroy the house of Jacob ', Am 9:8. And the return from captivity would herald the restoration of the nation. ' I will bring back the captivity of my people Israel and they shall build the *devastated* cities, Am 9:14. ' I will set my eyes upon them to be pacified and I will bring them again to this land ', Jer 24:6. And conjoined with this restoration is the future Messianic hope and all the glory of the Messianic kingdom ; *cf.* § 418a.

h Certain other points of the prophetic teaching have been touched on elsewhere, their **attitude to sacrifices,** § 114*l*, their **universalism,** § 115*g*, their **concern with foreign nations,** § 412*d*. The question of **personal responsibility** cannot be satisfactorily treated in a few lines, yet all reference to it should not be omitted here. The problem is raised by both Jer 31:29 f. and Ez 18:1 ff. Both quote a saying current at the time, ' The fathers have eaten sour grapes and the teeth of the children are set on edge '. The complaint against God was that the generation of the time was being unjustly punished on account of the iniquities of their fathers. The occasion of the complaint was the announcement that God would make them an object lesson to the nations of the earth on account of the wickedness of Manasses, Jer 15:4 ; 4 Kg 24:3. The answer to the complaint is that each man shall die for his own sin. It must be recalled, firstly, that the penalties threatened and imposed for the greater part of the history of the OT were temporal only. Secondly, individual responsibility was recognized in the Covenant where the death of the criminal is imposed for certain crimes, Ex 21:14 ff. Thirdly, the words of the deca-logue that God visits the iniquity of the fathers on the children, Ex 20:5, are not set aside. Jer 32:18, the **412h** very next chapter, repeats them ; Lam 5:7 declares ' Our fathers have sinned and are not, and we have borne their iniquities ' ; our Lord himself says that the principle would be applied to his own generation, Mt 23:35. No one is punished more severely than his own sins deserve. But the iniquities of the fathers may be visited on the children in the sense that prolonged persistence in wickedness may be the cause that the justice of God falls on a nation as it might not have done had it not been for the nation's long past of wickedness. And the solidarity of human society is so close that children inevitably suffer at times, though they are not thereby punished, for the transgressions of their forebears.

It is probable that the **literary activity** of this period **413a** was motivated especially by its Messianic prophecies and by its predictions of the approaching destruction of both the Hebrew kingdoms in punishment for their persistent idolatry and moral iniquity. These messages were not addressed only to contemporaries. It was important that subsequent generations should have a record not only of the new revelations concerning the Messianic kingdom, but also a proof in the writings of the prophets that the destruction of their kingdoms and capitals had been foreseen and foretold and therefore understand that it was brought about by the divine government of the world ; that the Assyrian was indeed ' the rod of (God's) anger ', Is 10:5, and that the Babylonian had been called by him out of the north against all the cities of Judah, Jer 1:14 f.

Besides the extant prophetical writings one at least of **b** the prophets of this period wrote also historical annals as did several of their predecessors. 2 Par 26:22 refers for further information about the reign of Ozias to the history written by the prophet Isaias. The other reference to a writing of this prophet in the same book, 32:32 (erroneously omitted in some copies of DV), is to his account of Ezechias, Is 36–39, 4 Kg 18–20.

A divine command to write is recorded of four prophets, **c** Isaias, Jeremias, Ezechiel and Habacuc. The first was ordered to write concerning two individual pro-phecies, Is 8:1 and 30:8, and only in the latter case is the purpose indicated that it should be for a lasting memorial. The first command received by Jeremias was also concerned only with one prophecy, 30:2–4. On the second occasion, however, the order was to commit to writing the whole series of prophecies which he had received from the first days of his ministry, 36:2. That the universal expression was not intended quite literally is evident from the fact that when king Joakim burnt the volume and Jeremias was ordered to write it all again, ' there were added besides many more words than had been before ', 36:32. Ezechiel's order to write also covered only part of his book, that namely dealing with the rebuild-ing of the temple, 43:11. The command given to Habacuc is recorded in 2:2 of his book. The fact that the prophets whose writings are preserved in the canon, all wrote under divine inspiration, does not necessarily imply that they received an injunction from God to write. A personal decision based on the conviction of the wisdom and utility of committing their prophecies to writing is quite compatible with their inspiration.

The **chronological order of the prophets** is mostly **d** indicated by the information given in the introductions to their books. This is lacking only in the case of Joel, Abdias, Jonas, Nahum and Habacuc. If Jonas is, as seems most probable, the prophet of the same name and parentage mentioned 4 Kg 14:25, he lived under Jeroboam II. From the contents of their writings, Abdias may be dated some time after the destruction of Jerusalem, Nahum some time before the destruction of Nineveh, 612, and Habacuc some time in the 7th cent. The indications given by Joel are patient of different interpretations and he has been dated both very early and very late. See the introduction to the books and also that to Daniel.

413e From Malachias there was a **cessation of prophecy** until the coming of St John the Baptist. Josephus was perhaps unwilling to acknowledge this complete cessation, as he says only that from the time of Artaxerxes I, 465-424, the succession of prophets had not been ' precise ' or ' definite ' (ἀκριβής), presumably meaning indubitable or universally acknowledged, *Contra Apionem* I 8. In the time of the Maccabees the absence of prophets is several times alluded to, 1 Mac 4:46 ; 14:41. And 1 Mac 9:27 implies that this cessation had lasted for a considerable time : ' there was a great tribulation in Israel, such as was not since the day that there was no prophet seen in Israel '. Where God has not revealed his mind, it is hazardous to attempt an explanation, but with due reservations the following considerations may be suggested. The series of Messianic prophecies had presumably reached the term intended by God. There was no further serious danger of idolatry. And the love of the law and of ancestral traditions which was characteristic of the period, and the labours of the Scribes, professional students of the law who first appear at this time, were adequate to keep the people in the main faithful to their religion. Finally, this prolonged cessation of prophecy provoked the keener admiration and a more ready willingness to listen when at long last a new prophet did arise proclaiming the near advent of the Kingdom of God and of the Messias. This cessation after the exile could hardly be due, it seems, to divine punishment, as in general the law was more faithfully observed and religion practised more zealously than previously. The comparative absence of revelation before Samuel's call may have been a punishment of the prevailing lawlessness when every man did what was right in his own eyes, 1 Kg 3:1, Jud 21:24. Among the calamities that were to come on the Northern Kingdom Amos mentions the impossibility of finding the word of the Lord 8:12. And similarly in punishment was foretold the cessation of prophecy at the time of the destruction of Jerusalem, Is 3:1 f., Ez 7:26. And the actual cessation is spoken of Lam 2:9, Dan 3:38 (DV), Ps 73:9. There is, however, here a legitimate hyperbole. Jeremias was in Jerusalem up to its capture, but he was derided, persecuted and disbelieved.

f In later time **the distinguishing garb of a prophet** was a rough mantle woven of hair or a skin worn with the hairy side outwards, such as Zacharias says the false prophets shall no longer wear with intent to deceive, *i.e.* to pretend to be what they were not in fact, 13:4. Such was the sackcloth which Isaias was ordered to remove from off his loins, 20:2, on which passage A Lapide adduces several arguments to prove that it was the prophet's only garment, so that stripped of it he was literally naked. Such was the mantle of Elias, 3 Kg 19:19, 4 Kg 2:13, for this seems to be the reason why he was described as ' a hairy man ', 4 Kg 1:8 (DV, RV), lit. ' a possessor of hair '. It is there added that he had ' a girdle of leather about his loins '. This rough mantle of woven hair or hairy skin would appear not to have been the customary garb of prophets before Elias, as Ochozias was able to recognize Elias by the description, which he would not have been able to do if it had been already usual for prophets so to dress. We read of Joram of Israel wearing a garment of haircloth under his other clothes during the siege of Samaria, 4 Kg 6:30. Such was also the practice of Judith, 8:6. See also Heb 11:37, Mt 3:4 ; 11:8.

g There was **no special rule of life** common to the prophets. Their one rule was to carry out the mission entrusted to them by God. Some we know to have been married, as Isaias, 7:3 ; 8:3, and the prophetess Huldah (Holda), 4 Kg 22:14. So also Osee, 1:2-9 ; 3:1 f. Jeremias, on the other hand, was forbidden to marry, 16:2. The reason given had nothing to do with the merit of celibacy, but was that the sons and daughters born in Jerusalem and Judah should die grievous deaths. The prophets' manner of life must to some extent at least have been influenced by the profession and state of life in which their call found them. The ministry of prophecy was not, of course, hereditary. Only in one case do we read of a prophet being the son of a prophet or seer, namely Jehu the son of Hanani, 3 Kg 16:1 and 2 Par 16:7. (In 3 Kg 16:7 it is probably Jehu who is called a prophet and not his father Hanani—so RV against DV.) Several were priests as Jeremias, 1:1, Ezechiel, 1:3, and Zacharias, 2 Par 24:20 f. Eliseus was a prosperous farmer, 3 Kg 19:19. Amos was a herdman who also looked after sycamore trees, fruit trees allied to the common fig tree, 1:1 ; 7:14.

However the details of their lives may have differed, the prophets had in general an ungrateful and **a dangerous calling.** The least trial that befell them was to meet with disbelief and distrust, Is 7:1-13, to be told to stop prophesying and be gone, Am 7:12 f. Some it was sought to kill, as Elias, 3 Kg 19:2 f., and Eliseus, 4 Kg 6:31 f. Some were imprisoned as Hanani by Asa, 2 Par 16:10, as Micheas the son of Jemla by order of Achab, 3 Kg 22:26 f., and Jeremias, 32:2 ; 37:14 ; 38:6. Others were put to death. In the Northern Kingdom, in the words of Elias' prayer, ' they have slain thy prophets with the sword ', 3 Kg 19:10, 14. The only one mentioned by name as put to death by the sword is Urias, son of Semei, killed by Joakim, Jer 26:23. Zacharias, the son of Joiada, was stoned by order of Joas in the court of the temple, 1 Par 24:20-22, Mt 23:35. The Jews had an ancient tradition that Isaias was sawn asunder by Manasses with a wooden saw. St Jerome on Is 57:1 calls this ' a quite definite tradition ' of the Jews (' quae apud eos certissima traditio est ' ; first attested by Justin Martyr, *Contra Tryphonem* 120). There was also a tradition that Jeremias was stoned to death, St Jerome, *Adv. Jovin.* 2, 37, PL 23, 335. But, of course, the career of the prophets was not one of unbroken opposition. Under good kings, such as David, Ezechias and Josias they were held in honour, 2 Kg 7, Is 37-39, 4 Kg 22:14 ff. And even Jeremias met with protection from princes and people, 26:16.

The Call and Mission of the Prophets—The ministry of the prophets was not hereditary and was independent of any particular state of life, but it was not open to any man of good will to constitute himself a prophet. The revelation of God's will which it involved was **purely supernatural,** and therefore the call to the office could come from God alone. Only in a few cases, however, have we any details about the divine call and mission. Amos in support of his right and duty to prophesy appealed to the divine command : ' The Lord took me when I followed the flock, and the Lord said to me : Go, prophesy to my people Israel ', 7:15. Eliseus was similarly engaged, ploughing with a yoke of oxen, when he received his summons through the intermediary of Elias. The latter had been ordered by God to anoint Eliseus as prophet in his stead. Elias fulfilled the command by casting his mantle upon his successor as a sign that he was called to the same prophetic office, 3 Kg 19:16, 19. Nowhere else except Is 61:1, which is certainly metaphorical, is there mention of anointing as was done in the case of kings and priests, and the manner in which Elias fulfilled his commission points to the conclusion that here also the anointing is to be understood metaphorically. Details of their calls are given by Isaias, ch 6, and by Jeremias, 1:4-10. Ezechiel, without mentioning his mission explicitly, gives details of the time and place of his first vision, 1:1-3, ' and the hand of the Lord was there upon him '.

As the original call was independent of the will of man, so also was **the reception of divine revelations** and messages after the call. A prophet was not always in the prophetic state. Though the mission might be for life, the exercise of the office was intermittent and depended solely on the will of God. The prophet retained, of course, his free will, but it was not within his power to receive a message when he willed.

At times there was a cessation of prophecy (§ 413*e*) when God did not vouchsafe his favours. Often the word of God came unsought, Jer 33:6, Ez 1:3, etc. Sometimes it came at once in answer to prayer, Jer 32:16-25, 26-44; Dan 2:17 f., 19; 9:3-21, 22-27. Sometimes God instructed the prophet to pray and promised a revelation in answer to the petition, Jer 33:2 f. Sometimes a prophet waited for the word of God : ' I will watch, to see what will be said to me ', Hab 2:1. Jeremias on one occasion had to wait ten days for God's reply, 42:4, 7. And, of course, if unworthy men requested a prophet to make enquiry of God for them, he might not deign to reply at all, Ez 14:3. The prophets, therefore, could make petition to God for light and in this sense prepare themselves for a divine revelation, but no natural means could induce a revelation. **Music** had its place in the worship of God as an accompaniment of the liturgical chant, 2 Par 29:25, and could even excite the feelings, as perhaps in the case of the company of prophets, 1 Kg 10:5 (§ 410*c*). But it could also be used to calm a disturbed or irritated frame of mind, as in the case of Saul, 1 Kg 16:16, 23 ; 19:9, and this appears to have been the purpose of Eliseus in asking for the services of a minstrel after his angry interview with the wicked king of Israel, Joram, the son of Achab, 4 Kg 3:13-15.

Divine communications could be made to man either in the sleeping or the waking state. In extolling the pre-eminence of Moses God mentioned **dreams** as one of the ways in which he would reveal himself to lesser prophets, Num 12:6, though the only one related as seen by a true prophet is that in Dan 7:1 ff. In some way which is not explained to us God would make it plain to the recipient that his dream was divinely sent. There is a reference to true prophets receiving such dreams in Jer 23:28. It was easy, however, to make a false claim to have been visited by God in this way, and the false prophets did not hesitate to do so : ' I have heard what the prophets said that prophesy lies in my name, and say : I have dreamt, I have dreamt ', Jer 23:25 ; *cf.* Deut 13:1 ff., Zach 10:2. True dreams were sometimes sent by God to men who were not even Israelites and they required the help of a divinely instructed person to interpret them. We have examples in Pharaoh's two dreams interpreted by Joseph, Gen 41, and in Nabuchodonosor's interpreted by Daniel, Dan 2 and 4.

Intermediary between the sleeping and waking states is the **trance.** In this condition a person is entirely unconscious of what is happening in the workaday world around him and loses for the time being the use of his external senses, but does not lose the use of his reason or clearness of mind. The word ' ecstasy ' has the same meaning except that it is commonly understood to imply that the subject is in a state of supernatural bliss. The Hebrew language possesses no special word to denote this state, but I think there is no doubt that the word *tardēmāh* is used in this sense. This word and its allied forms properly signify a deep sleep, as in Jon 1:5 f. But this sense does not suit its use in Daniel, 8:18 and 10:9, whereas the idea of the prophet's being suddenly bereft of his senses at the words of the Angel fits the context perfectly. For this reason and because deep sleep is not suitable in Gen 15:12, I think that the revelation and vision there recorded were granted to Abraham in a state of trance. His state will have been the same as that of St Peter in ecstasy, Ac 10:10.

According to Plato, speaking of the pagan world, no one ever obtains oracles while **in possession of** his **mental faculties** but only while asleep or under the influence of disease or frenzy, *Timaeus* 71*e*. All the evidence we have of the true prophets of Israel indicates the contrary. There is no reason for thinking that the companies of prophets in the time of Samuel, whatever their state may have been, were proclaiming divine oracles ; § 410*c, d.* And whatever the significance

of Balaam's description of himself as having his **414e** (mental) eye opened as he fell, he was not a prophet of Israel although made use of by God, Num 24:4, 16. Isaias's account of the vision of God upon his throne during which he received his mission is that of a man who may have been rapt out of consciousness of the material world about him but who was in full possession of his mental faculties, Is 6. The same is true of Jeremias's account of his call, Jer 1:4-10. This insensibility to the external world St Augustine calls ' mentis alienatio a sensibus corporis ', *Ad Simplicianum* 2, 1, PL 40, 129.

Certainly not all divine communications were received **f** in a state of rapture or ecstasy. Samuel was asleep when the divine voice awoke him, apparently an externally audible voice, 1 Kg 3:3-8. And a state of rapture is not indicated in Ez 3:22 f., ' The hand of the Lord was upon me and he said to me : Rise, go forth into the plain, and there I will speak to thee ; and I rose up and went forth into the plain '.

The usual mode of communication was by **vision. g** This is one of the modes which God announced that he would make use of with prophets subsequent to Moses, Num 12:6. And what they saw in visions is described by Isaias ch 6, by Jeremias, 1:11-15, and by Ezechiel, 1:4-28, etc. Moreover their entire books are described as visions by Isaias, 1:1, by Nahum, 1:1, and by Abdias, 1:1, although their contents are not confined to visual representations. This fact shows that the word ' vision ' had become practically synonymous with ' revelation '. This is confirmed by the expressions ' the word that Isaias the son of Amos saw ', Is 2:1, ' I will watch to see what will be said to me ', Hab 2:1, ' The vision of Abdias : Thus saith the Lord ', Abd 1:1. This usage is satisfactorily explained if visions were the normal means of divine communication, their predominance causing the term to be extended to other non-visual revelations. A vision might be external like that of the mysterious writing on the wall of Baltassar's dining-hall, Dan 5:5, 24 f., or of the burning bush seen by Moses, Ex 3:2 f. More often the vision was internal, as Ezechiel's vision of the plain scattered over with dead men's bones, ch 37, or Zacharias's vision of Jesus the high-priest standing before the angel of the Lord with ' Satan ' as accuser, ch 3. Other revelations would be by intellectual vision, if the expression may be used after the example of St Augustine, without the image of any corporeal being (' totus animi contuitus aut in corporum imaginibus est per spiritualem, aut in rebus incorporeis, nulla corporis imagine figuratis per intellectualem visionem ', *De Gen. ad lit.* 12, 12, PL 34, 463). For the rest it is not possible to give any detailed explanation of the modality of these visions and revelations, for, as St John Chrysostom has put it, ' he only has any clear knowledge of the matter who has learnt it by experience ', *In Is* 1, 1, PG 56, 14. And only he could know how God communicated the absolute certainty that the message came from him.

In whatever way the word of God came to a prophet, **h** he was under a **moral compulsion to speak** : ' The Lord hath spoken, who shall not prophesy ? ', Am 3:8. Indeed he was under a strict moral obligation to obey the divine behest : ' Whatsoever I shall command thee, thou shalt speak ', Jer 1:7. And the prophet would be held responsible by God for any evil effects of his disobedience, Ez 3:18-20. As the threat given in this passage shows, the prophet retained his freedom, and it was within his power to withhold the word of God committed to him. In fact, so violent was the opposition Jeremias encountered and so bitter the derision which greeted his words that he yielded for a time, at least in thought, to the temptation to disobey : ' I will not make mention of him nor speak any more in his name ', 20:9. But the word of God became as a burning fire in his breast, thus shut up in his bones ; he grew weary with the effort to hold it in and found he could not, *ibid.* An instance of

414h disobedience and its punishment is related 3 Kg 13:20–26.

i In carrying out this duty of announcing the word of God the prophets taught their lessons and drove home their revelations by means of **symbolic actions** in a manner analogous to that by which they themselves had been taught by God by means of symbolic visions (two baskets full of excellent and of rotten figs respectively, Jer 24, four horns, Zach 1:18 f., etc.). The dramatic character of these actions made them most apt to emphasize the meaning of the prophetic utterances and to imprint them on the memory. For instance, Ahias predicting to Jeroboam the division of the kingdom which was to take place after the death of Solomon tore his own new garment into twelve pieces and gave ten to the future king, saying, ' Thus saith the Lord the God of Israel : Behold I will rend the kingdom out of the hand of Solomon and will give thee ten tribes ', 3 Kg 11:30 f. So Jeremias was ordered to break an earthenware pot in the sight of the leading men of the nation and to say, ' Thus saith the Lord of hosts : Even so will I break this city and this people ', Jer 19:10 f. These and similar actions were deliberately performed in view of their symbolical significance. Such significance could also be seen in an accidental occurrence, as when Saul caused a rent in Samuel's mantle. This prompted the seer to say, ' The Lord hath rent the kingdom of Israel from thee this day, and *will give* it to thy neighbour who is better than thee ', 1 Kg 15:27 f. A difficult question arises concerning some of the symbolical actions which God ordered the prophets to perform. On account of their seeming impracticability or impossibility many have considered that such actions were not performed in fact, but were either gone through in a vision or had their effect in the narration much in the same way as a parable. For example St Jerome, *Prooemium in Osee*, was of the opinion that neither Jeremias' journey to the Euphrates to hide a linen girdle in its bank nor Osee's marriages were actually performed. If Isaias was ordered to strip himself literally naked (and not merely to remove his upper garment), Is 20:2 f., the actual performance of the command cannot have been intended as he was to remain in that condition for three years. But a detailed discussion of these and similar cases such as Ez 4:1 ff. must be left to the various commentaries.

j God did not leave to their natural strength and courage the prophets on whom he imposed what was so often a difficult and dangerous task. He gave **special divine assistance :** ' Be not afraid *of them*, for I am with thee to deliver thee ', said God to Jeremias, 1:8. And he gave not only external help, but internal gifts suited to the mission to be discharged : ' I am filled with strength . . . with judgement and power, to declare unto Jacob his wickedness and to Israel his sin ', Mic 3:8.

415a Guarantees of Divine Mission—To the obligation incumbent on the prophets to announce God's word and to the divine authority belonging to their pronouncements corresponded on the part of their hearers an obligation to heed and obey their words. ' He that will not hear his words which he shall speak in my name, I will be the revenger ', said God through Moses, Deut 18:19. An instance of the punishment of one who would ' not hearken to the voice of the Lord ' is given 3 Kg 20:35 f. And Amos foretold to Amasias, the priest of Bethel, what would befall him for his rejection of the divine message, 7:16 f.

b That this message had no natural and human origin in the prophets themselves is attested by the fact that they did not always fully understand their own prophecies, 1 Pet 1:10, and that their predictions were often quite contrary to their natural desires. Jeremias, addressing God, protested, ' I have not desired the day of *disaster* ; thou knowest ', 17:16. His natural wish was that his own true prophecies of calamity and captivity should be false and the words of the false prophet Hananias true that the captives already in Babylon should return and bring back the temple treasures removed by Nabuchodonosor, 28:6. Had **4** prophecy been the product of religious fervour and enthusiasm, there would have been prophets in the time of the Maccabees, when, on the contrary, they were looked for in vain. The kind of prophet produced by the natural stimulus of national danger has been well pointed out by Oehler, 2,266 : ' It is a remarkable phenomenon, that as before the Chaldean destruction of Jerusalem, false prophecy was at its height, and bore a great share of the guilt of that terrible catastrophe, so also, in the dreadful days preceding the Roman conquest of Jerusalem, a number of false prophets again appeared, by whose worthless predictions the people were involved in ruin (Josephus, BJ 6, 5, 2 f.), while the genuine word of prophecy was despised '.

The **power of working miracles** was sometimes conceded by God to his prophets in attestation of the mission **c** entrusted to them. Thus Moses received the power of producing prodigies by means of his rod and in other ways ' that they may believe that the Lord God of their fathers . . . hath appeared to thee ', Ex 4:1–9, 28–31. To convince the people that they had done evilly, as Samuel had told them, God at his prayer sent thunder and rain during wheat harvest, when such phenomena are unknown in Palestine, 1 Kg 12:12–19. When Elias raised to life the son of the widow woman of Sarephta, it was to her a sign of the truth of his mission : ' Now *indeed* I know that thou art a man of God and the word of the Lord in thy mouth is true ', 3 Kg 17:24. Again, when Elias was engaged in his contest with the priests of Baal on Mount Carmel, he prayed God to send fire to consume the holocaust ' that this people may learn that thou *Yahweh art God* '. And when the fire of the Lord fell, the people acknowledged ' They fell on their faces and said : *Yahweh* he is God, *Yahweh* he is God ! ' 3 Kg 18:37–39. As these examples show, a miracle might be worked either directly in proof of the reality of a prophet's mission, or directly in proof of the truth of his teaching or message and so indirectly in proof that he had indeed been sent by God. For other examples see 3 Kg 13:1–5 ; Is 7:11–14 ; 4 Kg 20:8–11 ; and *cf.* Is 38:7 f.

False gods have not **the power of predicting the future. d** ' *Announce* the things that are to come hereafter, and we shall know that ye are gods ', Is 41:23. That is the exclusive prerogative of the one true God : ' New things do I declare ; before they spring forth, I make you hear them ', Is 42:9 ; *cf.* 45:21. It is he alone who can say ' I am the Lord . . . that *bring to pass* the word of my *servants* and perform the counsel of my messengers ', Is 44:24–26. And it is his servants alone who can announce with certainty the things that are to come. For a clear appeal to the supernatural character of prophecy and its distinction from knowledge which could be otherwise acquired see Is 48:1–8. Is 48:3 is an appeal to the fulfilment of ancient prophecies already come to pass : ' The former things of old I declared and they went forth out of my mouth and I made them to be heard : I did them suddenly and they came to pass '.

The thunder and rain in the time of the wheat harvest **e** already quoted as a miracle was also the subject of a prediction quickly fulfilled according to Samuel's words, ' Now then stand and see this great thing which the Lord will do in your sight ', 1 Kg 12:16. Elias predicted to Achab that there would be neither dew nor rain except according to the words of his mouth, a drought which lasted three years and six months, 3 Kg 17:1 ; 18:1, 45, Lk 4:25, Jas 5:17. Micheas the son of Jemla after foretelling disaster to Achab if he undertook the proposed expedition to Ramoth Galaad added, ' If thou return in peace, the Lord hath not spoken by me ', 3 Kg 22:28. The fulfilment of his prediction proved the truth of his mission. For other examples see 4 Kg 6:32 f. ; 8:13–15 ; 4 Kg 19:32–36, Jer 28:16 f.

Many predictions concerned a more or less remote **f**

future, and the unbelieving took occasion from this fact to mock and profess their conviction that these predictions never would be fulfilled. So the iniquitous in Isaias' time spoke of the day of woe he foretold : ' Let him make haste and let his work come quickly that we may see it ; and let the counsel of the Holy One of Israel *draw near and* come that we may know it ', 5:19. So also the contemporaries of Jeremias, ' Where is the word of the Lord ? Let it come ! ' 17:15, with the implication that its fulfilment never would come.

The third guarantee of the reality of the prophets' mission was **the lofty moral character of their teaching** in agreement with our Lord's criterion, ' A good tree cannot bring forth evil fruit, neither can an evil tree bring forth good fruit ', Mt 7:18. The true prophets never flattered the vices or weaknesses of the people, never foretold blessings and prosperity apart from strict reform of their evil ways, never encouraged them in the false belief that God would protect and favour them simply because they were the descendants of Abraham, his Chosen People, and privileged to have his earthly dwelling place in their midst. They thought that they could dwell securely in the shadow of the temple no matter what the wickedness of their lives, because God, they imagined, could never allow his shrine to be desecrated by a pagan foe. Jeremias disabused the people of such vain illusions. ' Trust not in lying words, saying : The temple of the Lord, the temple of the Lord, it is the temple of the Lord ', 7:4. God would not tolerate injustice between man and his neighbour, oppression of the fatherless and the widow, murder, and idolatry. If they persisted in such evil courses, God would destroy the temple as he had already destroyed his shrine at Shiloh, *ibid.* 5-15. So Micheas quotes the bribe-stained judges, the priests who for money explained the law as men desired, and the false prophets whose divinations were guided by the craving of their purses : ' Is not the Lord in the midst of us ? No harm shall come upon us '. And he answers them : ' Therefore because of you, Sion shall be ploughed as a field and Jerusalem shall be as a heap of stones ', 3:11 f.

False Prophets—Such false prophets were, indeed, at times a plague in Israel, and it was probably not always easy for simple and ill-instructed folk to distinguish the pretenders from the true. If they prophesied in the name of heathen gods, only those could be deceived who were themselves tainted by idolatry. That Israelites did prophesy by Baal is attested by Jeremias, 2:8 ; 23:13, and the law ordained that prophets who attempted to lead men astray after strange gods or spoke in the name of strange gods should be put to death, Deut 13:1-5 ; 18:20. The same penalty attached to those who prophesied falsely in the name of Yahweh, Deut 18:20, but in their case detection might not be so easy. Sometimes they could be distinguished by the criterion laid down in Deut 18:22, ' Whatsoever *a prophet* foretelleth in the name of the Lord and it cometh not to pass, *that is a thing which* the Lord hath not spoken, but the prophet hath forged it in the pride of his mind '. An example is furnished by the four hundred prophets of Achab. They all answered in the name of Yahweh that Achab should undertake the expedition to Ramoth Galaad for ' the Lord will deliver it into the hand of the king ', 3 Kg 22:6, 11 f. Micheas the son of Jemla foretold disaster. The death of Achab in battle against the Syrians proved which of the two parties really possessed the word of God. The criterion just quoted was negative. The failure of a prediction proved a prophet to be a pretender, but the converse was not necessarily true. A false claimant to prophecy might by chance make a correct guess as to the outcome of some affair. And it is laid down in Deut 13:1-3 that no heed must be paid to a prophet or dreamer of dreams who should attempt to lead people into idolatry by foretelling ' a sign or wonder and the sign or wonder which he spoke to you come to pass '. The reference here, however, is not to natural happenings but to some manifestation

claimed to be a direct divine intervention. Such **416a** ' portents ' might be due either to natural causes such as sleight of hand or, sometimes, to diabolic agency.

The same passage warns the Israelites to give no heed **b** to ' portents ' in such a case, ' for the Lord your God trieth you that it may appear whether you love him with all your heart and with all your soul '. This does not, of course, imply that God himself worked the sign or wonder in question. It is in accord with the OT manner of speaking by which everything is ascribed to God without mention of secondary causes and without any distinction between his positive will and his permission. The truth which this way of speaking implies is that nothing happens in the world which escapes the overlordship of God. A stronger expression was used by the prophet Micheas the son of Jemla who told Achab that God had put ' a lying spirit ' in the mouth of all that king's prophets, 3 Kg 22:23. When God said, Ez 14:9, ' When a prophet shall be deceived and speak a word, I the Lord have deceived that prophet ', the words could also mean that on account of the prophet's presumption God had caused events to turn out contrary to the prophet's expectation. Some of these false prophets we know by name. There **c** was Hananias the son of Azur who opposed Jeremias, 28:1-17, Achab the son of Colias, Sedecias the son of Maasias, and Semeias, who all three prophesied falsely in God's name to the captives in Babylonia, Jer 29:21, 31. Such men were guilty of lying, consciously proclaiming that to be the word of God which they knew God had not spoken. ' From the prophet even to the priest ', said Jeremias 6:13, ' all are guilty of deceit ', and again 8:10. ' They see vain things and they foretell lies, saying, " The Lord saith " whereas the Lord hath not sent them ', Ez 13:6. The motive impelling these impostors was the simple one of making a livelihood, for the people recognized the material needs of those who helped them in religious matters and did their best to support them. This motive was hinted at plainly by Amasias, the priest of Bethel, when he bade Amos leave the Northern Kingdom : ' Thou seer, go, flee away into the land of Judah, and eat bread there and prophesy there ', 7:12. And so Micheas of the prophets of Jerusalem in his day, ' Her prophets *divine* for money ', 3:11. Indeed he goes further and in the name of the Lord accuses them of extorting money : ' Thus saith the Lord concerning the prophets that make my people err. . . . If a man give not something into their mouth, they *proclaim a holy* war against him ', 3:5. It is not surprising to **d** learn that men of such calibre were apt to be addicts of wine and strong drink, Is 28:7, and let themselves fall into the sin of adultery, Jer 29:23. Such men, as a matter of course, studied to please the people and, unfortunately, succeeded only too well : ' The prophets have prophesied falsehood . . . and the people love such things ', Jer 5:31. For they fell in with the wishes of their hearers who said ' to the seers " See not ", and to them that behold, " Behold not for us what is right ; speak unto us pleasant things ; see *deceptions* for us " ', Is 30:10. Consequently they contradicted the true prophets who foretold calamity in punishment of iniquity : ' They healed the breach of the daughter of my people *in frivolous guise*, saying " Peace, peace ! " *when* there was no peace ', Jer 6:14, also 8:11. And again, ' The prophets say to them : " You shall not see the sword, and there shall be no famine among you, but he will give you true peace in this place " ', Jer 14:13, etc. Such unconditional promises of prosperity were not in the spirit of the true prophets, who demanded obedience to God's law as the condition of divine favour and protection. That these professional prophets made no attempt to carry out the true work of a prophet by striving for the moral reformation of the nation hardly needs to be said. ' The prophets . . . have not laid open thy iniquity ', Lam 2:14. On the contrary ' they strengthened the hands of the wicked that no man should return from his evil doings ', Jer 23:14, an accusation made also by Ezechiel 13:22.

417a Characteristics of the Prophetical Literature—In general the prophetical books set down in summary form the substance of preaching and messages delivered over a course of many years. Parts, of course, like the historical sections in Isaias and Jeremias, were never spoken, and it has been suggested that the prophecies against the nations are literary compositions which were never spoken before an audience. They were not delivered to the nations concerned, but they may well have been proclaimed before suitable audiences in the Holy Land. Even so as they were not intended for delivery to the nations concerned, it is probable that their form is substantially that in which they were first composed. Addresses to the Israelites, on the other hand, which were often put into writing long after their delivery, in many cases probably preserve the substance and not the form in which they were first put before the public. This opinion is confirmed by the literary and often poetic form in which they have been handed down. Poetic form, however, is no certain criterion, as it may have been judged suitable to the dignity of prophecy and more useful as more easily retained in the memory.

b The **lack of chronological order** apparent in the series of prophecies contained within a single book is patient of more than one explanation. An accidental displacement in the troubled times of the exile is quite possible. But it is also possible that the sequence of their prophecies in time did not seem to the writers themselves to be of such importance as necessarily to be followed in composition. That displacement, accidental or deliberate, did occur is plain from the fact that the prophecies against the nations occupy different positions in the Hebrew and Greek texts of Jeremias, in the former occupying chh 46–51 and in the latter chh 25:14–31:44, where the prophecies against the nations are in a different order among themselves. Here as examples of the lack of chronological order may be mentioned that the call and mission of Isaias are narrated only in ch 6 of his book and in Jeremias, chh 35–36, which belong to the reign of Joakim follow chh 32–34, which deal with the reign of Sedecias.

c Among the causes of obscurity in the prophets is the **unannounced change of speaker.** This is not restricted to this class of literature and does not always lead to ambiguity. In 1 Kg 3:4–6 DV makes the sequence plainer by substituting 'he answered' for the original 'and said'. In Ps 133 the first two verses are an address of pilgrims to the ministers of the temple, and the last verse the answer of the ministers. Is 21:2a gives words of the prophet. Then follow the words of God spoken to him in vision, and in 3 Isaias speaks again. Another example : Is 63:1 contains the prophet's question to and the answer of the Messias followed by a renewed question in 2 and the answer 4–6 and then by the prophet's own words, 7 ff.

d It is important to remember **the conditional character of prophecy** even where the form of the announcement is absolute. And this is true whether destruction is foretold or blessing and prosperity. 'If that nation against which I have spoken shall repent of their evil, I also will repent of the evil that I have thought to do to them', and, in the opposite case, 'If a nation shall do evil in my sight that it obey not my voice, I will repent of the good that I have spoken to do to it', Jer 18:8, 10. The preaching of Jonas in Nineveh provides a clear example : 'Yet forty days and Nineveh shall be destroyed', 3:4. But the story relates that on account of the repentance of the Ninevites their city was not destroyed. And Jeremias quotes the prophecy of Micheas, 'Sion shall be ploughed like a field ', 3:4, and explains why it remained unfulfilled. It was because Ezechias and all Judah feared the Lord and besought his face. Therefore ' the Lord repented of the evil that he had spoken against them ', Jer 26:18 f. In the light of history it may be said that the sentence had been suspended and found its fulfilment finally in the destruction of the city by the Babylonians. This example is especially instructive as apart from the

authentic interpretation given by Jeremias we should **4** not have known that the prophecy of Micheas would have been fulfilled earlier had it not been for the prayers of Ezechias and his subjects. It also shows that a prophet may set down a prophecy in his book without indicating whether it was fulfilled or set aside. This characteristic, which is sometimes overlooked, is of manifest importance in any discussion of the fulfilment of prophecy.

Another important fact in this connexion is **the e partial nature of the revelation** made to the prophets. Prophecy and history are quite distinct, and the qualities appropriate to the latter must not be looked for in the former. God asks men for faith and he will not so order his words and his works that they present evidence so demonstrable that the assent of the mind is forced and no loophole is left for cavil. An adequate account of the Messias and of his kingdom was to be left to the history of the NT ; the OT was to offer an adumbration only and that not in one picture of the whole but in the separate delineation of its various features. Moreover, an accurate and instantaneously recognizable picture of the future would have occasioned a grave danger to men's exercise of their free wills when they found themselves actors in the events foretold. This partial nature of revelation made it extremely difficult, if not impossible, for the pre-Christian Israelites to acquire a true composite idea of the personal career and kingdom of the Messias. On the one hand, he is depicted as the warrior-king victorious over his enemies, and, on the other, as one despised, oppressed, and done to death. Later Rabbis have attempted a reconciliation of these diverse elements by postulating a victorious Messias ben David and a suffering Messias ben Joseph. But the NT has shown how both elements could be realized in one and the same person.

Further, **the prophets did not always fully understand f the revelations** which they had themselves received. Even after Daniel had been given an explanation of the vision of the ram and the goat, he remained astonished at the vision and there was no one who could understand it, 8:27. On another occasion when Daniel did not understand a revelation made to him, his enquiry met with the response that the words were shut up and sealed until the time of the end when they would be fulfilled, 12:8 f. Zacharias did not understand the vision of the four chariots and the Angel explained that they were the four winds of heaven, 6:5, but, remarks A Lapide, the prophet was not informed what were the winds or what was their nature, whether literal or parabolical and mystical, and implies that the vision remained obscure even to him, *Prooem.* 2. St Augustine says succinctly that among the Hebrews Messianic prophecies were made ' by some with understanding, by some without ', *De Civ. Dei* 7, 32. And A Lapide was of the opinion that St John himself did not understand the meaning of all the symbols of the Apocalypse.

An important feature to be found nowhere but in the **g** Bible is the ' **compenetration** ' of two persons or two events in the same discourse, namely, **of the type and of the antitype.** The compenetration may be perfect and the words equally applicable to both the type and the antitype. Thus the prohibition ' You shall not break a bone of him ', Ex 12:46, Jn 19:36, is equally applicable and in the same sense both to the paschal lamb and to Christ, the true Lamb of God. Or the compenetration may be imperfect and the words, though applicable to both type and antitype, may be true of the type only in a lower and humbler sense and of the antitype in a full and sublime sense. Thus the words of God spoken through Nathan of Solomon and the theocratic kings, ' I will be to him a father and he shall be to me a son ', 2 Kg 7:14, which were true of them only in the humbler sense of an adoptive sonship, are true of the type, Christ our Lord, in the sublime sense of eternal divine sonship, Heb 1:5. This, of course, is an inference from St Paul's teaching

g implying that the words could not be used of an angel in the sense in which they are true of Christ. In yet another case, the compenetration may be such that the writer intermingles his utterances about the type and the antitype, some being applicable to the one and some to the other. The type and the antitype must have one or more, but not all, features in common; and in these passages it is as if the type and the antitype were depicted with very imperfect perspective on the same canvas, the one visible behind the other but in such a way that it is difficult to discern to which of the two certain features belong. It is in this way that St Augustine explains Ps 71 (72) of Solomon and of Christ, *De Civ. Dei* 17, 8, as does also St Jerome, who illustrates from this Psalm the similar treatment of Antiochus Epiphanes as type and Antichrist as antitype, *Comm. in Dan* 11:21 sqq. (PL 25, 565 f.). The general rule of interpretation in such examples of compenetration is that what cannot be sanely understood of the type in the literal sense is to be understood of the antitype.

a A natural consequence of this compenetration is a **lack of chronological perspective** with the result that the type and the antitype appearing together in the same mental vision seem to have no interval of time between them. This is the explanation, for instance, of the description in Is 40 ff. of the return from the Babylonian captivity and of the glories of the Messianic kingdom in such a way as if both were to be realized simultaneously. The simultaneity is not affirmed nor formally implied, but neither is it indicated that there is to be a long space of time between.

b **Chronological indications** are sometimes given, but in general they appear to be deliberately vague. As our Lord said to the Apostles, ' It is not for you to know the times or moments which the Father hath put in his own power ', Act 1:7. Often the indication is of the vaguest, ' in that day ', Is 17:4, ' at that time ', Is 18:7, ' in those days ', Jer 3:16, ' in the last days ', Is 2:2. Even an expression like ' yet a little while ', Agg 2:7, is far less communicative than it appears at first and may cover a long period of time by ordinary standards. The number seventy does not appear to be given as an exact computation. Tyre is to be forgotten for seventy years, Is 23:15, 17. The king of Babylon and his nation are to be punished and made a desolation after seventy years, Jer 25:12, whereas according to Is 14:1 (MT 13:22) ' Her time is near at hand and her days shall not be prolonged '. Similarly it may be doubted whether the number three is intended as signifying more than a small number. The glory of Moab was to be brought low in three years, Is 16:14. The exact number ' three score and five ' in Is 7:8 is widely recognized as an unjustified gloss ; and it seems not improbable that the number of the fifteen years promised to Ezechias was also not part of the original text, Is 38:5.

c As not all the details of the Messianic kingdom were made known to the prophets, and still less all to any one prophet, many circumstances of the future had to be **described in terms of the existing theocracy**, whence arose a further difficulty of interpretation, especially in pre-Christian times. The centre of the new kingdom is spoken of as Sion, as in the celebrated Messianic prophecy of Is 2:2–4, Mic 4:1–3, ' The law shall come forth from Sion and the word of the Lord from Jerusalem ' ; *cf*. Ps 109(110)2. It is possible that this prophecy is conditional and that, had the Israelites remained faithful and not rejected the long-expected Messias when he did come, Sion would have remained the religious centre under the New as under the Old Covenant. However, the clearly metaphorical character of Is 25:6, where the spiritual blessings of the Messianic kingdom are represented as a rich banquet prepared ' *for all peoples* ' on Mount Sion, may suggest that the location is also not intended in the literal sense. Again, in the Messianic passage Jer 33:14–18 the perpetual priesthood of the Messianic kingdom and its perpetual sacrifice are spoken of in

terms of the typical priesthood of the Old Law and **418c** its animal sacrifices. Similarly in Is 56:6 f. ; 60:7. In this matter we are given a corrective in other passages which show that Levitical institutions are to cease and that, therefore, the mention of them in connexion with Messianic times is to be understood not in the literal but in the typical sense. Thus Jeremias, 3:15–17, foretells that the Ark of the Covenant shall no longer play any part in worship when all nations are gathered together to Jerusalem. Later, 31:31–33, he predicts the passing of the Old Covenant made at Sinai to be replaced by ' a New Covenant ' ; and with the passing of the Old Covenant would naturally pass its distinctive Levitical institutions. And God in Mal 1:10 f. rejects the Levitical priests and their offerings for throughout the world among the Gentile nations a pure oblation is to be offered to his name ; *cf*. § 555*j, k*. These texts, like so many others, obscure before the time of Christ, have been illumined by their fulfilment in Christ.

The prophet Osee, 14:10, alludes to the obscurity of **d** his message, ' Who is wise, and he shall understand these things ? prudent, and he shall know these things ? ' Commenting on these words St Jerome alludes to the difficulty caused by **the use of symbolic names.** Examples are the names of Osee's own children, 1:4, 6, 9, and those of Isaias' sons, Shear-Yashub, ' A Remnant shall return ', 7:3, and Maher-shalal-chash-baz ' Take away the spoils with speed, quickly take the prey ', 8:1. The Messias is spoken of by the typical name of David, Os 3:5 ; Jer 30:9 ; Ez 34:23 f. ; 37:24 f. He is given the symbolic name Emmanuel ' God with us ', Is 7:14, and the glorious names of Is 9:6. But Christ's own name of Jesus is nowhere foretold. This usage rests on the Hebrew conception of names not, as they are with us, as simply distinctive labels, but as connoting a person's function or office. This conception may be illustrated by the change of Sarah's name from Sarai, of Abraham's from Abram, of Israel's from Jacob, of Peter's from Simon.

Another characteristic of prophetic diction is the use **e** of the perfect tense, the so-called **prophetic perfect,** to denote future events—for instance, in the Messianic prediction of Is 9:6 : ' A child *has been* born to us, a son *has been* given to us '. ' This is the custom of all the prophets ', wrote St John Chrysostom, ' to speak of what has not yet occurred as already accomplished ; because they saw with mental vision what was to happen after many years, they narrated everything as they now saw it before their eyes ', *In Gen. 1 Hom.* 10, 4, PG 53, 85. This usage, however, is not confined to the prophets, and is used by others speaking of what they regard as the certain future, *e.g.* in Gen 30:13, ' Women will call me blessed ' (DV, future tense in agreement with the sense). St Augustine gives a more general explanation better in accord with this wider usage. He writes that the event foretold ' is as certain as if it had already happened ', *Enarratio in Ps* 43, n. 9, PL 36, 485.

Unique Character of Israelite Prophecy — Sooth- **f** saying, magic, omen-reading, necromancy, were all rife among the pagan neighbours of Israel, and this prevalence will surprise no one who reflects on the strange hold that superstition has on educated and supposedly enlightened people in our own day. And these practices had a strong hold on the Hebrew people. Even as late as the exile we find Ezechiel, 13:15–23, compelled to denounce the tricks of female sorcerers. But these avocations were no part of Hebrew religion. Indeed they were strictly prohibited, Deut 18:10–14. In general, however, as true religion degenerates, superstition prevails ; and up to the time of the exile the Hebrew people as a nation had never been faithful to their religion for long. The nearest legitimate approach to such practices in Israel is illustrated by Saul's request to Samuel for information about his lost asses, 1 Kg 9:6 ff. The inference seems to be warranted that God condescended to make such matters known through his prophets in order to protect

18a

418f men from the temptation to seek enlightenment through the operations of sorcerers and wizards.

g The Scripture itself speaks of the existence of ' prophets' among the worshippers of pagan gods. Baal had many such in the days of Elias and of Jehu, 3 Kg 18:19, 4 Kg 10:19. But as the sacred books give the same title to the false prophets of Israel, the use of the name in connexion with false religions does not in any way imply recognition of the office. Moreover, the false prophets of Israel claimed to be prophets in the strict sense of communicating divine messages to man, whereas these pagan prophets appear to have had their counterpart in Israel in the companies of prophets of the time of Samuel to whom the title was given in a far wider sense ; § 410c, d. In the case of both, devotion was accompanied by abnormal super-excitation. The prophets of Baal danced or leapt round the altar, thereby, no doubt, working themselves up into a state of frenzy as we read that they cut themselves with knives, 3 Kg 18:28.

Nowhere among the other nations do we find men comparable in character or office to the prophets of Israel who spoke in the name of and with the authority of Yahweh. Certain writers use the term ' prophet' when speaking of the Babylonian *asipu*, but this is apt to be misleading. W. Muss-Arnolt in his *Concise Dictionary of the Assyrian Language* (Berlin 1905) suggests rather 'enchanter' or 'diviner'. *Karl Marti in his book *The Religion of the Old Testament* (English trans., London 1907) 242 writes ' Outside of Israel no men arose who could be called prophets in the sense of the great Israelite prophets '. And the verdict of Eduard König is the same. There is no evidence, direct or indirect, ' of the existence of prophetic personalities comparable to the Hebrew prophets ', EREH 10, 392 f.

ISAIAS

(ISAIAH)

By E. POWER, S.J.

a **Bibliography**—The literature on Isaias is immense. Only a selection from important recent works can be mentioned here. **Commentaries : Chh 1-66**—*F. Delitzsch, Leipzig, 1889[4] ; *A. Dillmann–R. Kittel, Göttingen, 1898[6] ; *K. Marti, Tübingen, 1900 ; *C. von Orelli, München, 1904[3] ; A. Condamin, Paris, 1905 ; S. Minocchi, Bologna, 1907 ; *G. A. Wade, London, 1911 ; N. Schloegl, Wien, 1915 ; J. Knabenbauer–F. Zorell, Paris, 1923[2] ; *B. Duhm, Göttingen, 1923[4] ; F. Feldmann, Münster, 1926 ; *E. König, Gütersloh, 1926 ; *G. A. Smith, London, 1927 ; R. Augé, Montserrat, 1936 ; J. Fischer, Bonn, 1939 ; E. Kissane, Dublin, 1943 ; G. Brillet, Paris, 1945 ; A. Feuillet, DBVS 4 (1947) 647–729 ; L. Dennefeld, Paris, 1947. **Chh 1-39**—*G. B. Gray, Edinburgh, 1912 ; *J. Skinner, Cambridge, 1915 ; *G. Boutflower, London, 1930 ; *O. Procksch, Leipzig, 1930. **Chh 40-66**—*S. Oettli, Stuttgart, 1913 ; *K. Budde, Tübingen, 1922 ; *J. Skinner, Cambridge, 1922 ; N. Peters, Paderborn, 1923 ; *R. Levy, London, 1925 ; *A. Loisy, Paris, 1927 ; *C. C. Torrey, New York, 1928 ; *P. Volz, Leipzig, 1932 ; *H. W. Hertzberg, Hamburg, 1939. **Chh 40-55.** *H. Frey, **b** Stuttgart, 1937 ; *S. Smith, London, 1944. **Special Subjects**—F. Feldmann, *Die Bekehrung der Heiden im Buche Isaias*, Aachen, 1919 ; *K. Budde, ' Zu Jesaja 1–5 ', ZATW 49 (1931) 16–40 ; 50 (1932) 38–72 ; A. Vaccari, ' Visio Isaiae ch 6 ', VD 10 (1930) 100–6 ; 162–8 ; 343–7 ; M.-J. Lagrange, ' La Vierge et l'Emmanuel ', RB 1 (1892) 481–97 ; A. Van Hoonacker, ' La prophétie relative à la naissance d'Immanu-El ', RB 13 (1904) 213–27 ; P. A. Boylan, ' The Sign of Emmanuel ', ITQ 7 (1912) 203–13 ; *H. Guthe, *Zeichen und Weissagung in Jes. 7:14–17*, Giessen, 1914 ; J. Calès, ' Les trois discours prophétiques sur l'Emmanuel ', RSR 12 (1922) 169–77 ; *E. G. Kraeling, ' The Emmanuel Prophecy ', JBL 50 (1931) 277–97 ; A. Vaccari, ' De signo Emmanuelis ', VD 17 (1937) 45–9 ; 75–81 ; A. Feuillet, ' Le signe proposé à Achaz et l'Emmanuel ', RSR 30 (1940) 129–51 ; F. Ceuppens, ' De signo Emmanuelis ', *Angelicum* 23 (1945) 53–9 ; E. Power, ' The Emmanuel Prophecy of Isaias ', IER 70 (1948) 289–304 ; *W. Caspari *Echtheit, Hauptbegriff, und Gedankengang der Weissagung Jes 9:1–6*, Gütersloh, 1908 ; A. Vaccari, ' De nominibus Emmanuelis (Is 7:14 ; 9:3) ', VD 11 (1931) 7–18 ; J. Touzard, ' Isaias 11:2–3a ', RB 8 (1899) 249–66 ; K. Schlütz, *Isaias 11:2*, Münster, 1932 ; *K. Budde, ' Jesaja 13 ', *Festschrift-Baudissin* (Giessen, 1918) 55–90 ; *J. Begrich, ' Jesaja 14:28–32 ', ZDMG 14 (1932) 66–79 ; B. Alfrink, ' Der Versammlungsberg im äussersten Norden (Is. 14) ', Bi 14 (1933) 41–65 ; **c** E. Power, ' The Prophecy of Isaias against Moab ', Bi 13 (1932) 435–51 ; J. Linder, ' Weissagung über Tyrus ', ZKT 85 (1941) 217–27 ; *W. Rudolph, *Jesaja 24–27*, Stuttgart, 1933 ; *J. Lindblom, *Die Jesaja Apokalyse (24–27)*, Leipzig, 1938 ; *M. Brückner, *Die Komposition des Buches Jes. 28–33*, Halle, 1898 ; *W. Caspari, ' Jesaja 34–35 ', ZATW 49 (1931) 67–85 ; J. Linder, ' Zum Canticum Ezechiae ', ZKT 42 (1917) 46 ff. ; F. Zorell, ' Canticum Ezechiae ', VD 2 (1922) 291–4 ; *J. Begrich, *Der Psalm des Hiskia*, Göttingen, 1926 ; F. Feldmann, *Der Knecht Gottes in Isaias 40–55*, Freiburg, 1907, and *Die Weissagung über den Gottesknecht*, Münster, 1913 ; A. Condamin, ' Le

Serviteur de Jahvé ', RB 17 (1908) 162–81 ; J. Fischer, **419c** *Isaias 40–55 und die Perikopen über den Gottesknecht*, Münster, 1916, and *Wer ist der Ebed ?*, ib., 1922 ; *A. Guillaume, ' The Servant Poems in the Deutero-Isaiah ', *Theology* (1926) 2–10 ; 63–72 ; *A. S. Peake, *The Servant of Jahweh*, Manchester, 1931 ; *O. Eissfeldt, *Der Gottesknecht bei Deutero-Jesaja*, Halle, 1933 and ' Neue Forschungen zum Ebed-Jahwe-Problem ', TLZ 68 (1943) 273–81 ; A. Vaccari, ' I carmi del Servo di Jahve ', *Miscellanea Biblica* 2 (Roma, 1934) 216–44 ; F. X. Pierce, ' The Problem of the Servant of Jahweh ', AER (1935) 83–95 ; J. S. van der Ploeg, *Les chants du* **d** *Serviteur de Jahvé*, Paris, 1936 ; *O. Procksch, ' Jesus der Gottesknecht ', *Gedenkschrift-Bulmerincq* (Riga, 1938) 146–65 ; H. Junker, ' Der gegenwärtige Stand des Ebed-Yahwe-Problems ', *Festschrift-Rud* (Trier, 1941) 23–43 ; *C. R. North, *The Suffering Servant in Deutero-Isaiah*, Oxford, 1948 ; *H. Gressmann, ' Die literarische Analyse Deuterojesajas ', ZATW 32 (1914) 254–97 ; J. Touzard, ' L'âme juive au temps des Perses ', RB 35 (1926) 5–43 ; 36 (1927) 5–24 ; 161–79 ; *W. Caspari, *Lieder und Gottessprüche der Heimkehrer*, Giessen, 1934 ; C. E. Simcox, ' The Role of Cyrus in Deutero-Isaiah ', JAOS 57 (1937) 158–71 ; *C. C. Torrey and *J. H. Ropes, ' The Influence of Is II in the Gospels, Acts and Epistles ', JBL 48 (1929) 24–39 ; J. Fischer, ' Der Problem des neuen Exodus in Is 40–55 ', TQ 110 (1929) 111–30 ; *H. Gressmann, *Über die in Jes 56–66 vorausgesetzten zeitgeschichtlichen Verhältnisse*, Göttingen, 1898 ; *K. Cramer, *Der geschichtliche Hintergrund der K. 56–66 im Buche Jesaja*, Dorpat, 1905 ; *A. Zillessen, ' Tritojesaja und Deuterojesaja ', ZATW 26 (1906) 231–76 ; *K. Elliger, *Die Einheit des Tritojesaja*, Stuttgart, 1928 ; *L. Glahn, *Der Prophet der Heimkehr*, Giessen, 1934 ; *G. R. Driver, ' Linguistic and Textual Problems (Isaiah 40–66) ', JTS 36 (1935) 396–406 ; M. Burrows, *The Dead Sea Scrolls of St Mark's Monastery*. Vol. I. *The Isaiah Manuscript and the Habakkuk Commentary*, New Haven, 1950.

Contents—The Book of Isaias contains three separate **e** groups of prophecies addressed to three distinct groups of hearers who belong to different periods. Without prejudging the question of unity of authorship we must thus distinguish Isaias I, chh 1–39, addressed to the prophet's contemporaries, both Jews and Gentiles, *c* 736–700 B.C., Isaias II, chh 40–55, addressed to Jewish exiles in Babylon about a decade before the Restoration, and Isaias III, chh 56–66, addressed to Palestinian Jews recently returned from exile, *c* 538–520 B.C.

Isaias I contains an introductory prophecy, dated **f** *c* 735 B.C., and five collections of prophecies : (1) Prophecies against Judah and Jerusalem prior to the Syro-Ephraimitic war (735 B.C.), chh 2–6, of which the last, recording the prophet's vocation, is earliest in date ; (2) Prophecies, largely Messianic, connected directly or indirectly with the clash between the policies of Isaias and Achaz at a critical period of the Syro-Ephraimitic war, chh 7–12 ; (3) Prophecies against the Gentile Nations : Babylonia, Assyria, Philistia, Moab, Damascus, Kush, Egypt, Edom, Kedar, Tyre, chh 13–23 ; (4) The Apocalypse of Isaias, describing the judgement of the Gentile Nations and the establishment of the Messianic kingdom, chh 24–27 ;

419f (5) Further prophecies against Judah and Jerusalem, dating from the reign of Achaz before 726 B.C. to the Egyptian alliance 702 B.C., chh 28–35. The historical section which concludes Isaias I, chh 36–39, is excerpted from 4 Kg. These collections were not made by the author but by a later redactor. They overlap to some extent. The prophecy against the Northern Kingdom, 9:8–10:4, belongs more probably to the first collection and there is a prophecy against Judah and Jerusalem, 22:1–14, and one against an individual Israelite, Sobna, 22:15–25, in the third. It is doubtful also whether some prophecies in Isaias I, especially the last, 34:1–35:10, and those against Babylon, 13:1–14:23 and 21:1–10, were addressed to the contemporaries of Isaias. On the other hand objections made to Messianic passages should be disregarded. Isaias preaches Messianism in season and out of season. When he predicts the ruin of a nation he usually remembers and frequently mentions the Messianic remnant, the holy seed, which will save Israel from complete destruction.

g Isaias II has for its theme the deliverance of the Jewish exiles from Babylonian oppression which Yahweh will effect in the immediate future through his chosen instrument, Cyrus. The argument frequently takes the form of a judicial contest between Yahweh and the pagan deities. As in the past so also in the present Yahweh alone predicts and performs. The idols know nothing and do nothing. The work is divided into two parts, 40:1–49:13 and 49:14–55:13. In the first the prophet addresses himself to Jacob and Israel, in the second to Sion and Jerusalem. The new exodus from Babylon is celebrated in both parts but the future glories of Sion in the second replace the exploits of Cyrus and the fall of Babylon in the first. The unity of plan is remarkable and makes it easy to recognize that the four poems on the Servant of Yahweh, 42:1–7; 49:1–9a; 50:4–11; 52:13–53:12, are a subsequent addition, composed apparently by the author but inserted by a redactor. They depict the future Messias, not as king and conqueror, but as worker and sufferer. The first two Servant songs interrupt very evidently the context of prophecies in which they were unskilfully inserted. The last two were located more naturally between separate prophecies with which however they have no connexion.

h Isaias III contains prophecies, partly consolatory, partly admonitory, suited to a situation considerably different from that of the exiles. Then the hearers were assured that deliverance from Babylon was at hand and that their sins were expiated and forgiven. Now they complain that final salvation is delayed and are told that their sins are the obstacle to its attainment. The new situation is that of the returned exiles in Palestine in the dark period of the early Restoration. Difficulties about and obstacles to salvation are first discussed, then Sion's future glory is depicted and finally a fervent appeal for divine aid is followed by a description of final judgement and final salvation. It is noteworthy that the Sion poems, chh 60–62, have been apparently subsequently inserted, like the two first Servant poems, in the middle of a prophecy. They contain citations from Isaias II in its final form.

420a **Historical Background**—The history of the periods mirrored in the Book of Isaias will be found in §§ 66a–b, and 121e–i. A brief *résumé* of important events will help the reader to understand the occasion of many prophecies and the historical allusions which they contain. Isaias began his prophetic career in the last year of Azarias, identified, 4 Kg 15:27, with the first year of Phacee, 736 B.C., but possibly a year or two earlier. Judah was then at the height of her prosperity. Azarias had strengthened her military defences, and by his victories over the Edomites and the Philistines secured rich trading outlets on the east and on the west. But foreign connexions and increased wealth had produced grave religious and social disorders, aggravated no doubt during the reign of Achaz, which Isaias denounces in his earliest prophecies.

The clash between the prophet's inspired policy of **4** reliance on God alone and the king's policy of alliance with Assyria during the Syro-Ephraimitic war, 735 B.C., determined the next phase of the activity of Isaias. The danger of extirpation then incurred by the Davidic dynasty was the immediate occasion of the Emmanuel prophecy, the first announcement of the advent of the Messias. The predicted devastation of the Syro-Ephraimitic regions soon followed, 734–733 B.C. Damascus was taken and sacked, 732 B.C. The desolation of Galilee, which like Galaad and Sharon was made an Assyrian province, gave occasion to the second Messianic prophecy. The region of Palestine, first darkened by Assyrian oppression, would be enlightened by the life and teaching of the Messias. Judah and a diminished Ephraim were now vassals of Assyria. Isaias seals his public denunciations of the policy of Achaz, favoured by the people, and confines himself to the instruction of his disciples. One last prophecy during the reign of Achaz, 28:1–29, containing the prediction of the fall of Samaria and the promise of protection to Jerusalem, was mocked by the leaders of the people.

The accession of the pious king, Ezechias, who inaugurated his reign by a great religious revival, 726 B.C., introduced a new era in Judah. Ezechias followed the advice and policy of Isaias, and Judah, though burdened by tribute, was relatively prosperous until the invasion of Sennacherib. In the Northern Kingdom Osee, relying on Egyptian aid, refused tribute to Shalmaneser V, 727–722, son and successor of Tiglathpileser III. Samaria was besieged and finally captured by Sargon II, 721–705, another son of Tiglathpileser III, in January 721. A vassal state which revolted against Assyria usually had its principal inhabitants deported and was made an Assyrian province. To save Judah from such a calamity Isaias strenuously opposed rebellion and foreign alliance. The prophecy of the downfall of Assyria and the salvation of Jerusalem from Assyrian conquest was made. some years after the fall of Samaria, most probably in the first half of the reign of Ezechias, and is closely connected with the third Messianic prophecy. Sennacherib's invasion had been already foretold in 735 B.C. as the punishment of the people's unbelief, 8:5–10. His failure to capture Jerusalem and the destruction of his army are now predicted. The year 713 B.C. is marked by the miraculous recovery of Ezechias from a mortal malady through the prophet's intervention, and a combined movement of revolt against Assyria in several subject states. Embassies from Babylon, then independent of Assyria and ruled by a native monarch, Merodach-Baladan, and from Egypt, where Kushite invaders had recently inaugurated the XXVI dynasty, sought the participation of Ezechias in the projected rebellion. Three prophecies, 18:1–7; 19:1–24; 20:1–6, are connected with the proposed Egyptian alliance to which Isaias was strongly opposed. As Philistia alone paid the penalty of rebellion it is probable that Ezechias was restrained from open revolt by the prophet's remonstrances. Isaias was less successful in his opposition to the Egyptian alliance and the rebellion which preceded the invasion of Sennacherib, 701 B.C. Three prophecies, 29:1–24; 30:1–33; 31:1–9, also denounce this Egyptian alliance. Judah and Egypt will suffer but Yahweh will save Jerusalem from the Assyrians. No personal activity of Isaias is recorded after the retreat of Sennacherib.

In Isaias II, chh 40–55, the scene changes from Palestine to Babylonia, the period from the 8th cent. B.C. to the last decade of the Babylonian captivity. The victorious career of Cyrus the Great, Yahweh's instrument in the liberation of his people, is the historical background of the prophecies. He was originally ruler of the Persian kingdom of Anshan subject to Media and having Susa, later called Persepolis, for its capital. A successful revolt from his liege lord, Cyaxares, whom he captured in battle, made

e him monarch of Persia and Media *c* 550 B.C. Further campaigns in the east and west extended his empire from the Indus to the Halys. Croesus of Lydia was now in danger and formed a defensive alliance with Amasis of Egypt and Nabonidus of Babylonia in 547 B.C. But his kingdom was invaded before he could obtain aid from his allies and his capital Sardis was captured in 546 B.C. We may therefore date the fear of the coast land in particular (Lydia) and of the world in general (Egypt, Babylonia, etc.), recorded in 41:5, in or about 547 B.C. After the fall of Sardis Cyrus secured and extended his conquests in the north and east until 539 B.C. when he invaded Babylonia. Babylon was taken without a battle in July of that year. In the following year an edict of Cyrus, whose religious tolerance was also extended to the Babylonians themselves, allowed the Jewish exiles to return to Palestine, restored to them their sacred vessels and authorized them to rebuild their temple. The former predictions already fulfilled by Yahweh most probably refer at least in part to the early successes of Cyrus. Their fulfilment is a guarantee that the new predictions, the fall of Babylon and the return of the exiles, will also be fulfilled in the near future.

f The historical situation in Isaias III, chh 56–66, is that of the recently returned exiles, 537–520 B.C. Their chief preoccupation is the struggle for existence in a small and devastated region encircled by hostile peoples. They have erected an altar to Yahweh immediately after their return but have not yet succeeded in rebuilding their temple or rewalling their capital. The prophet admonishes, consoles and encourages these mourners in Sion. He does not allude to external events of the period.

a **Authorship and Composition**—The hypercritical theory that the Book of Isaias is made up of fragments composed by authors of different periods from the 8th to the 2nd cent. B.C. and that about one-half at most of chh 1–35 may be attributed to Isaias need not detain us. It arbitrarily minimizes the value of Jewish tradition and ignores the logical sequence of thought which the individual prophecies usually exhibit. It is undoubted however that the book as a whole owes its present form not to Isaias but to a post-exilic redactor, to whom also introductory indications, when not autobiographical or narrated in the first person, usually belong. It is certain moreover that it contains explanatory glosses, easily recognizable for the most part, and some passages of uncertain authorship like 2:2–4. With slight reservations therefore the authenticity of chh 1–35 may be reasonably assumed. The late exilic and early post-exilic periods are too closely connected to raise any time difficulty against the unity of authorship of chh 40–55 and 56–66. Minor differences in language, style, and subject-matter are sufficiently accounted for by the different periods and the different situations with which the prophet had to deal.

b A more vexed question is the unity or diversity of authorship of chh 1–35 and chh 40–66. Jewish tradition strongly supports the unity of authorship by ascribing both collections, united in one book, to the same author, Isaias. The author of chh 40–66 undoubtedly far surpassed all post-exilic prophets. How can it be supposed that he was ignored or forgotten by tradition while they were remembered, that he was not the very famous prophet to whom his works are ascribed ? The Evangelists attribute to Isaias citations from Isaias II (*cf.* Mt 12:17–21) and Isaias III (*cf.* Lk 4:17–19). Ecclus 48:27 f. registers the same tradition. On the other hand the argument from differences in language, style and subject-matter is strong but according to a reply of the Biblical Commission does not establish diversity of authorship ; *cf.* § 49*l*. A more cogent argument is the unique acquaintance and exclusive preoccupation with the exilic and early post-exilic periods attributed to a pre-exilic prophet. Isaias however, unlike other prophets, may have received a special charism by virtue of which he lived in spirit in

these periods. While arguments to the contrary are **421b** indecisive it is imprudent to deny this possibility.

Isaias and his Mission—Isaias (Hebr. *Ye̊ša'yāhū* ' Yah- **c** weh is Salvation ') was born most probably shortly before 760 B.C. Though the Talmudic statement that his father, 'Amōṣ, was a brother of King Amasias is generally discredited he belonged undoubtedly to the noble and cultured class. He received his prophetic vocation most probably in the reign of Achaz. Joatham is mentioned, 1:1, merely as the successor of Azarias, but he reigned during his father's leprosy and probably died before him. The gloomy outlook of the early oracles reflects most naturally the impiety and unbelief of Achaz. The prophet realized that Israel as the people of the All-holy Yahweh should be just and holy, and especially denounced idolatrous practices and social abuses. He was particularly hostile to foreign alliances which led inevitably to religious contamination. His exhortations to repentance and trust in Yahweh were disregarded. And yet if Achaz had followed his inspired policy at a critical period of the Syro-Ephraimitic war the Assyrian would undoubtedly have relieved him of his enemies without the sacrifice of the independence of Judah.

The unbelief of Achaz and the danger incurred by the **d** Davidic dynasty produced the Emmanuel prophecy, announcing and briefly delineating the promised Messias. Isaias had previously predicted the advent of the Messianic kingdom, to be preceded by devastation, deportation and further purification. Only a remnant of the chosen people should inherit this kingdom. Justice and holiness, peace and prosperity are its essential characteristics. It is generally presented as a revival of the idealized kingdom of David. Such a presentation moreover should not be taken too literally. Its realization moreover was conditioned by Israel's acceptance of the Messias. In the fuller revelation of the Servant poems the national element is definitely excluded. The figure of the Messias has some traits borrowed from descriptions of David and Solomon, but his chief characteristics made him in the words of the Psalmist, 8:6, ' little less than God '. He is Emmanuel, ' God-with-us ', born of a Virgin Mother, Wonder-Counsellor (*cf.* 9:5 and 28:29), Mighty God (*cf.* 9:5 and 10:21), Father for ever, Prince of Peace. The spirit of Yahweh abides in him permanently, endowing him with Wisdom and Understanding, Counsel and Might, Knowledge and Fear of Yahweh. His reign will be eternal. It will be distinguished by judgement and justice, the foundation of Yahweh's kingship, Ps 89:15 ; 96:8, by kindness and fidelity, 16:5, characteristic attributes of Yahweh in his dealings with his people. Isaias thus prepares the way for the revelation of Christ's divinity.

The accession of Ezechias in 726 B.C. opened a wide **e** sphere of public activity to Isaias. It cannot be doubted that the zealous prophet inspired and directed the great religious revival with which the pious monarch inaugurated his reign. He may also have saved Judah from participation in the revolt of 720 B.C. and was certainly actively opposed to that of 713 B.C. in which Judah apparently participated, but was saved from chastisement by prompt submission. His opposition to the revolt and alliance with Egypt in 702 B.C. was disregarded by Ezechias who seems to have acted without consulting him. He nevertheless supported the monarch during the critical period of Sennacherib's invasion with the constant assurance that Yahweh would protect his holy city from the Assyrian host. Most, though not all, of the prophecies against the Gentiles belong to the reign of Ezechias. Assyria and Babylonia as oppressors of Israel receive most attention, then Moab and Edom as encroachers on Israelitic territory. Isaias felt deeply the oppression of the weak by the strong. Such oppression was an obstacle to permanent peace and prosperity on earth. Idolatry too should disappear that Yahweh alone might be worshipped by all his creatures. Hence the judgement and chastisement of the Gentiles were necessary for the

421e establishment of the Messianic kingdom. Not all however were to perish in this judgement, for Gentiles would be sharers in the Messianic blessings. Israel was also to be judged and only a small remnant would survive to inherit the Messianic kingdom, 10:22.

f There is no trace of the prophet's personal activity after the invasion of Sennacherib. The Jewish tradition that he died a martyr in the early reign of the impious Manasses is inherently probable, if not fully assured. Nobility of character and religious zeal, eloquence and mastery of language and style all combine to stamp him as the greatest of the Hebrew prophets and writers.

422a The Servant Songs—The four Songs of the Suffering Servant of Yahweh, 42:1–4 ; 49:1–6 ; 50:4–9 ; 52:13–53:12, are the culminating point of OT prophecy. It is now generally admitted that they are a separate composition having a theme of their own, distinct from that of the collection of prophecies of the Restoration, addressed to the exiles of Babylon, in which they were subsequently incorporated. They depict four scenes of a drama in which the history of the Suffering Servant is gradually unfolded. In the first Song he is introduced by Yahweh as his Servant specially dear to him and charged with a mission of spiritual enlightenment to the Gentiles. We see him in the second Song undaunted by the complete failure of his efforts in a spiritual mission to Israel assigned to him by Yahweh. In the third Song a further stage of this mission is presented in which indifference and opposition have become hostility and persecution. In the fourth Song the Sufferings of the Servant are explained as the chastisement of our sins, then the third stage of his vicarious expiation, his Passion and Death, and the posthumous success of his mission to the Gentiles, a numberless spiritual progeny, are depicted.

b The remarkable unity of plan in the drama authorizes several important conclusions. All four Songs have the same author. The first three in particular are unintelligible without the fourth. The additions to the first and second Songs, 42:5–7 and 49:7–9a, were not made by the original author. He would not anticipate in 42:6 the mission to Israel, reserved for the second Song, nor in 49:7 the homage of the Gentiles, reserved for the fourth Song. The use of the perfect tense in the fourth Song does not imply that the Servant belongs to past history. His activity is clearly indicated as future in the first Song. The progressive stages of that activity must therefore be future. The perfects have quite a different explanation as a peculiarity of prophetic visions of future events ; cf. 9:2 ; 14:4 ff., etc. and § 418e.

c The Jews with rare exceptions interpreted the Servant collectively as Israel, relying chiefly on the title, Servant of Yahweh, given to Israel in six Deutero-Isaian passages. The Church from the very beginning, as the Gospels attest, discerned in him a prophetic adumbration of the Redeemer. Only towards the close of the 18th cent., owing to the rise of Rationalism and the denial of supernatural revelation, did the Messianic interpretation begin to be abandoned. It has always been upheld by Catholic scholars and has always found adherents among non-Catholic believers. The critical approach to the problem differs from the Catholic in ignoring the NT and Tradition and seeking the interpretation of the Songs in the psychology of their author and the circumstances of his time. The collective Israel interpretation was at first more popular, usually in a modified form to avoid obvious objections suggested by the contrast in character between the Servant and Israel and the mission of the Servant to Israel. The Servant was assumed to be a part of Israel—the pious element or the prophets or the priests—or an ideal Israel conceived as at once identical with and yet distinct from the real Israel. Duhm's discovery in 1892 that the Servant Songs were not originally a part of Deutero-Isaias deprived the Israel interpretation of its main support and brought individual interpretations into favour. The Songs were now supposed to contain history rather than prophecy and the Servant was identified in turn

with many historical personages. Few of all these **4** interpretations have outlived their authors and none has found general acceptance.

In reality the Anonymous Servant is contrasted with **d** the Israel Servant. He is highly individualized and profoundly real. The new forms of the Israel theory are gratuitous expedients and raise fresh difficulties. Since the sufferings are assumed to be the sufferings of the exile, common to all, how can a part of Israel take on itself the sufferings of the rest or an ideal Israel take the place of the real sufferers ? The drama moreover loses all its movement if the stages of the Servant's expiatory sufferings are only figurative descriptions of the sufferings of the exile. Against the historical interpretations it must be noted that the first Song places the activity of the Servant in the future and that the subsequent Songs depict progressive stages in his career. It is expressly stated in the fourth Song that he transcends all human experience. Individual traits of his description may be found in history but not the whole gigantic figure. The triumph of the Servant's mission to the Gentiles, won by vicarious expiation, promised in the introduction and announced at the conclusion, is the sum total of the drama. Only in the Messianic interpretation is this triumph realized.

Recent Catholic interpreters like Vaccari and Fischer **e** no longer resort to the expedient of textual transposition by which Condamin and Van Hoonacker sought to fit the Songs into the framework of Deutero-Isaias. They recognize the Songs as an extraneous element interrupting the development of the main theme and having a separate theme and unity of their own. They attribute however the Restoration prophecies and the Songs to the same author. An excellent exposition of the arguments on which this conclusion is based will be found in C. R. North, *The Suffering Servant in Deutero-Isaiah*, 161–91. If the linguistic argument for the authorship of the fourth Song is inconclusive, it must be remembered that without this, the last of the series, the other Songs would be unintelligible.

The one point on which there is still disagreement **f** among leading Catholic authorities is the amplitude of the Servant's mission to the Jews. Was it conceived as entirely spiritual and Messianic or as also national and political so that it included the Restoration ? The latter view must be held if with Fischer we attribute the verses immediately following the first and second Songs, 42:5–7 and 49:7–9a, to the original author. It involves no theological difficulty since the Restoration, like other gifts bestowed on the chosen people, was merited by the Messias and may therefore be ascribed to him. We have already noted, however, in § 422b, that from an artistic point of view 42:5–7 and 49:7–9a cannot easily be attributed to the original author since they contain announcements reserved for later Songs. The author moreover assigned repeatedly and with the fullest confidence the mission of the Restoration to Cyrus, the servant and instrument of Yahweh. It is not likely then that he subsequently assigned it to the Servant whose mission is contrasted with that of Cyrus. We prefer therefore to attribute the added verses to a redactor, and with Vaccari to regard the Servant's mission as entirely spiritual and Messianic.

Text and Versions—For the text of Isaias we were **g** almost entirely dependent on the MT, no MS of which is prior to the 10th cent. A.D. In 1947 however a Heb. MS of Isaias was discovered in Palestine and assigned by Albright to the Maccabean period. The fragments of ancient MSS and pre-Herodian pottery revealed by a subsequent investigation of the site established the genuineness of the discovery. The date of the MS is discussed in § 80m. It cannot be doubted that the text is pre-Masoretic. It is particularly valuable as a confirmation of MT with which it generally agrees. It enables us moreover to correct some minor errors, supply some missing words (usually attested also by LXX) but gives little help in establishing the text and determining the sense of the more corrupt and difficult passages. Only variants which affect the sense are here indicated. The MT, though not entirely free from omissions, corruptions and interpolations, is generally good. The Versions are not very helpful. The LXX translator was a poor Hebrew scholar. He renders freely, indulges in paraphrases and in difficult passages omits words and guesses at the sense ; cf. 9:2. It is thus difficult to determine his Hebrew text when a knowledge of it would be most useful. The Syriac version is free and elegant. From the corrections of Vg in the commentary it will be seen that St Jerome was not too successful in rendering the more difficult passages. Our chief help in correcting textual errors is derived from the requirements of the context and the parallelism of verse members. Our knowledge of Hebrew metre is too vague to be helpful. Rigid strophic theories are always hypothetical and often difficult to reconcile with the logical sequence of thought.

There are many difficult problems in Isaias on which esteemed commentators hold different views. In accordance with the scope of this commentary and the restrictions of space we have avoided minute discussions and expounded the views which seemed to us more probable. We are particularly indebted to Fischer's commentary and have often utilized Kissane's translation.

I 1-31 Invitation to Repentance—This vision, though not the earliest of the visions of Isaias, serves as an introduction to his teaching of which it contains the chief elements. Its occasion and date depend on whether the chastisement depicted, 5-9, is an actual fact or a future threat. The first alternative is preferable. The query ' Why will you be smitten more ? ' implies that a severe chastisement has been already inflicted. There is no future verb in the description of foreign invaders devouring (pres. part.) the fruits of the land before the eyes of its inhabitants. The sacrifices and prayers by which they vainly seek relief from chastisement are present not future. Only in 20 and subsequently is future chastisement indicated. The occasion of the prophecy is most probably the invasion of Judah by Israelites, Aramaeans, Philistines and Edomites in 735 B.C., described in 2 Par 28:6-19.

The ingratitude, abandonment of Yahweh and manifold sins of Israel are first described, 2-4. Let them not increase by further iniquity the severe chastisement already inflicted which has reduced them almost to the condition of Sodom and Gomorrha, almost but not entirely, since a remnant survives and restoration may be hoped for, 5-9. Sacrifices, ritual observances and prayers by which they seek to avert disaster are not acceptable to God without a true conversion, 10-15. Let them repent, obey God, be just to their neighbours that their sins may be pardoned, their prosperity restored. Otherwise God will deliver them to the sword of their enemies, 16-20. Jerusalem, once faithful, is now a harlot. Her princes are thieves and oppressors. Chastisement is still needed to separate the dross from the silver, to re-establish justice and fidelity. Sion shall be purified and restored but the wicked will perish miserably in the process of purification, 21-31.

1-4. The date, indicating the entire period of the prophetic activity of Isaias, makes this vision an introduction. 2. LXX has *begotten* instead of ' brought up ' perhaps correctly. Israel's adoption by God and her special privileges add the burden of base ingratitude to her guilt. God's chosen people are inferior in knowledge to the ox and the ass which find their way unaided in the evening from their pastures to their masters' stalls. Only in an accommodated sense can this text be referred to the ox and the ass, popularly associated with the birth of Christ. 4. For ' ungracious ' read ' depraved '. Isaias frequently calls God the Holy One of Israel.

5-9. 5a. ' *Why will you be more smitten, will you increase transgression ?* ' God would prefer to spare them but must punish if they continue to sin. The rod of chastisement produced *bruises and weals and fresh wounds*. The wounds have not been *pressed* to remove foul matter nor *bound up* nor *softened with oil* to relieve pain. 7d. Replace ' enemies ' by *Sodom* and render : ' *And the desolation is like the destruction of Sodom* '. 8. Read *is* for ' shall be ', *booth* for ' covert ' and *besieged* for ' laid waste '. 9. The seed or remnant from which a new nation can arise refers here to the national restoration of Judah.

10-15. 12. For ' appear before me ' read ' *see my face* ', a common expression for visit. The vocalization was most probably altered to exclude the suggestion of a divine image. Read ' *a trampling of my courts* ', a contemptuous characterization of visits to the temple. 13a. Meal-offerings and incense are rejected. 13b. ' *New Moon and Sabbath solemn convocation : I will not abide (the conjunction of) iniquity and sacred assembly* '. Not sacrifices and ritual worship are here reprehended but unrepented sin which makes them unacceptable. 15. Hands were raised, palms upwards, in prayer. The new MS adds : ' *and your fingers of iniquity* ' in parallelism with ' your hands are full of blood ' ; cf. 59:3.

16-20. Cleansing from past sins and amendment of life in dealings with God and with the neighbour are essential elements of true repentance and reconciliation with Yahweh. 18a. ' Come let us reason together '. The pardon is offered on condition of repentance. Scarlet and crimson as colours of guilt are suggested by hands full of blood.

21-31. This vision of the future shows that the condition attached to the offer of pardon was not fulfilled and that further chastisement will be necessary for the purification of Sion. The religious restoration of Sion and the destruction of the wicked are predicted. The relations between God and Sion are frequently assimilated by the prophets to the relations between husband and wife. 21. Harlotry is infidelity. For ' judgement ' read *justice* and for ' justice ' *righteousness*. 23. For ' faithless ' read *rebellious*. 24. For ' I will comfort myself over ' read ' *I will take satisfaction from* '. 25. For ' clean ' read ' *in the furnace* ', a slight but necessary correction of MT. 27. ' *Sion by justice shall be redeemed and her converted ones by righteousness* '. 28. Read ' *shall be destroyed* ', required by parallelism. 29-30. Read the verbs in the 3rd pers. with LXX and Syr. 29. ' *And they shall be ashamed of the terebinths in which they delight and confounded for the gardens in which they take pleasure* ', because the gods whom they worshipped in the trees and gardens were powerless to help them. 30. For ' oak ' read *terebinth*. ' *The strong one* [DV ' your strength '] *and his work* ' are the sinner and his evil designs or the idolater and his idol.

II 1-5 The Universal Messianic Kingdom—The title is an introduction to a collection of prophecies, most probably those of chh 2-6, which all belong to the early period before the Syro-Ephraimitic war. The artificial linking of the following prophecy on the judgement of Yahweh to the description of the Messianic kingdom, 5, seems to indicate the hand of a redactor rather than the more skilled artistry of Isaias. There is no logical connexion between 6 ff. and 2-4. These three verses recur in Mic 4:1-3. It is impossible to determine with certainty who is the original author, Isaias or Micheas or an earlier prophet from whom both have borrowed. The context in Mic is more appropriate and an additional verse, Mic 4:4, completes the picture. On the other hand Mic has parallels to Isaias in ch 5 which may suggest literary dependence. The universality of the Messianic kingdom is taught elsewhere by both prophets and is certainly pre-exilic. In this conflict of arguments the context is the surest guide. The passage is commented on in § 535b.

II 6-IV 6 The Judgement of Yahweh on Judah and Jerusalem—This section contains five prophecies so closely connected that they might be regarded as five parts of a single prophecy. The judgement is first announced as the necessary consequence of sin in general and idolatry in particular, 2:6-21. Its execution is then foretold, on the Israelitic state, ruined by the deportation of its leading citizens and consequent political anarchy, 2:22-3:7, on the men of the upper classes who have oppressed the poor and weak, 3:8-15,

423h on the women of the upper classes guilty of pride and luxury, 3:16-4:1. The happy lot of the remnant, who have survived the judgement, in the Messianic kingdom is finally described, 4:2-4:6. Judah is at the height of her prosperity, 2:7 The prophecies may therefore be dated in the earliest period of Isaias before the Syro-Ephraimitic war.

i II 6-21 Announcement of Judgement—The prophecy is divided into three parts by the refrain. The ruin of Judah is the chastisement of idol worship, 6-11. In the day of judgement appointed by Yahweh the proud and the exalted shall be humbled, 12-19. In that day also idols shall be cast aside by their worshippers, 20. The brevity of the third part and the variations in the refrains are probably due to textual corruption.

j 6-11. 6. ' *Verily thou wilt destroy thy people (the house of Jacob) because they are full of sorcerers and diviners like the Philistines and make alliances with foreigners* '. The perfect ' thou hast destroyed ' is a prophetic perfect, by which a future event is more vividly indicated. ' The house of Jacob ' is probably a later insertion to connect this verse with 5. *Sorcerers* is a correction required by the context. The last member is obscure but probably indicates trading alliances with foreigners as the source of material prosperity and religious corruption. Philistine divination as affecting Israel is exemplified in Ochozias, 4 Kg 1:2. Western commerce had to pass through Philistia to Judah. Ozias' successful war against the Philistines, 2 Par 26:6 f., must have secured him trading concessions. 7-8. Judah's riches and military strength and also her idolatry are the result of foreign alliances. The transposition of *9a* before *8c* is required by the parallelism : ' *And mortal has bowed down and man has abased himself to what his fingers have made* '. **9b.** ' *And forgive them not* ' is most probably a gloss. 10-11. In the refrain for ' pit ' read *dust* and for ' are ' *shall be*.

k 12-19. Not only the pride of man but also the pride of nature (trees and mountains) and of art (towers and ships) will be humbled in the day appointed for judgement by Yahweh. The destruction of God's creatures, abused by sinful man, adds to the terror of the day and manifests the majesty of Yahweh. 12. ' *against all pride and loftiness and all that is elevated and exalted* '. *Exalted* (LXX) is better than ' humbled ' (MT). 13. ' Tall and lofty ' is probably a gloss, interpreting the cedars as the arrogant. Bashan is the region east of the northern Jordan, famous for its forests and its cattle. 16. Tarshish ships correspond to our ocean liners since strong ships were needed for the long voyage to Tartessus in Spain. There is an allusion here to the big ships used by Ozias after re-establishing the Red Sea trade. Read (after ' Tharsis ') ' *and all the beautiful galleys* '. 18. The reference to the destruction of idols, out of place in the middle of the refrain, belonged originally to the third part.

l 20-21. The idolaters take their gold and silver idols with them in their flight from the judgement, but finding them an encumbrance cast them away to the moles and the bats. The text is defective here.

424a 22-III:7 Judgement of the Israelitic State—No trust must be put in man, for Yahweh will deport from Jerusalem the leaders and counsellors on whom the nation's welfare depends, 2:22-3:3. Anarchy will follow, for none will accept the responsibility of rule, 4-7.

b 22-III:3. 22. The instability of man, whose life depends on the breath given him by God, is stated before it is illustrated. Omit the article before ' man ' and render : ' *for why should he be reputed ?* '. III:1. The verb used for deport indicates, 4 Kg 17:23, the deportation foretold by the prophets. The cities, especially the capital, and the upper classes suffered most. After ' Judah ' render : ' *the staff and the stay* ', which mean, not bread and water (a gloss), but men of action and men of counsel. 2. ' *Heroes and warriors . . . soothsayers and elders* '. 3. For ' captain of fifty ' read *army leader* and for ' admirable in countenance ' *magnate*. The

last pair are *skilled magicians and clever sorcerers*. Magicians were influential advisers. **4**

III 4-7. 4. When the leaders are gone, upstarts take **c** command and general anarchy follows. For ' the effeminate ' read *wantonness*. 6-7. The example of the brother, who refuses to accept the responsibility of authority in his father's house through lack of material resources, emphasizes the general destitution.

8-15 Judgement of the Leaders—Sin is the cause of the **d** ruin of the state according to the general law of retribution, 8-11. The sinners, whom Yahweh will punish, are the leaders who oppress the people by extortion and lead them astray by evil example, 12-15.

8-11. 9a. ' *Their partiality has testified against them* '. **e** 9c. ' *Woe to them for they have brought evil on themselves* '. 10-11. The general law of retribution is clear, but one expects a closer parallelism.

12-15. 12. God denounces those who oppress his **f** people and lead them astray. For ' women ' read *usurers*. 13-14a-b. The prophet announces God's arising to judge his people (LXX, peoples MT) and his coming to execute judgement on the elders and princes. Judgement implies righting the wrongs of the oppressed and punishing the oppressors. 14c-d-15. God again denounces the oppression and robbery of his people by their masters.

16-IV 1 Judgement on the Ladies of Jerusalem— **g** Their haughty and wanton deportment shall be punished by disfigurement, 16-17. They shall be stripped of their jewellery and fine raiment, 18-23, be clad in rags and sackcloth and branded as slaves, 24. Sion shall mourn for her sons ; her daughters shall be husbandless, 25-4:1.

16-17. 16d-e : ' *Because they walk with mincing gait and* **h** *make a tinkling with their feet* '. The anklets of 18 are apparently the cause of the tinkling. 17a. ' cover with scabs '. 17b. Some render ' will expose their shame ', others, ' will make bald their foreheads '. Shaving the forelocks was a legal penalty among the Babylonians. There is no evidence for the meaning shame.

18-23. The ornaments were anklets, miniature suns, **i** crescents, ear-rings, armlets, veils, tiaras, little chains (connecting the two anklets and shortening the steps), rich girdles, boxes of perfume, amulets (for protection from the evil eye and other baneful influences), signet-rings and nose-rings. The tiara was probably a band of gold like that of the high-priest. The rendering *veils* is uncertain. 18-21 mention only articles of jewellery. 22-23. The articles of clothing are robes, mantles, shawls, purses, gauze, fine linen, turbans and headveils. Note the similar enumerations in 2:13-16 and 3:2-3. 24c. ' baldness and *instead of rich raiment a girdle of sackcloth, For instead of beauty (shall be) shame* '. The pre-Masoretic MS makes the last member intelligible by supplying *bōšeṭ* ' shame ' omitted by MT and Vss. LXX and Vg also transfer ' beauty ' to 25.

25-IV:1. 25. ' thy men ' : ' *the men of Sion* ' ; ' thy ' : **j** ' her '. The misery of the daughters of Sion suggests that of Sion personified, their mother, and Sion's bereavement deprives her daughters of husbands who will take away their shame. Fecundity was highly esteemed and regarded as a mark of divine favour in OT times. The dearth of husbands recalls the curse of rulers, 3:6-7, and is expressly attributed to foreign invasion.

IV 2-6 The Future Messianic Kingdom—Fertility of **42** the land, holiness of its inhabitants, presence and protection of Yahweh, are its characteristics.

2. The *bud* or growth of the Lord is parallel to the fruit of the earth and therefore designates not the Messias but the rich harvests of Messianic times. This promise of fertility was conditional and was not fulfilled owing to Israel's infidelity. 3. The remnant are the holy who shall survive the final judgement of Yahweh and, purified by suffering, shall inhabit the new Sion. 4a. ' daughter '. Daughter of Sion = Sion (Genit. of definition). The ' blood ' of Jerusalem is the blood-guilt or sin of Jerusalem. Burning implies purification. 5-6. Yahweh's protection is figured by

symbols derived from Exodus. **5.** 'Sion and *over its assemblies* a cloud'.

b **V 1-30 Sin and Chastisement of the Vineyard of Yahweh**—Judah and Jerusalem, compared to a chosen vineyard, have ill repaid the solicitude of Yahweh on their behalf and will consequently be abandoned to their enemies, **1-7.** Six classes of sinners, introduced by 'Woe', are then denounced : landgrabbers, **8-10**, drunken revellers, **11-16**, blasphemers, **18-19**, perverters of right and wrong, **20**, worldly wise, **21**, besotted and corrupt judges, **22-24**. Finally the general chastisement of foreign invasion is announced, **26-30**. **17** and **25** belong to another context. The former is best read after **10**. The latter contains the refrain of 9:7-10:4, and is transferred to that poem.

c **1-7. 1.** '*I will sing about my friend, the song of his love for his vineyard. My friend had a vineyard on a fertile hill*'. The fertile hill, lit. ' horn, son of fatness ', indicates the advantages of fertility of soil and exposure to the sun's heat. **2.** For '' fenced in ' read *dug up*, prepared for planting. The tower was for the watchman. The winepress hollowed out of stone had two parts, one for pressing the grapes, the other at a lower level for receiving the grape juice. ' looked ' : ' *hoped* ' ; ' wild grapes ' : ' *stinking things* '. **4b.** ' *Why when I hoped that it would produce grapes has it produced stinking things ?* ' **5b.** ' wasted ' : ' *grazing land* '. **6.** The briars and thorns are the result of lack of cultivation. **7c-d.** ' *And he hoped for justice and behold bloodshed, and for righteousness and behold oppression* '.

d **8-10.** The Israelite could not be legally deprived of his land which, if expropriated, should be restored in the jubilee year. **8c-d.** ' *field until there is no room left, and you alone are settlers in the land* '. **9a.** ' *In mine ears the Lord of hosts has sworn, Verily many houses shall become ruins, Big and fair they shall be uninhabited* '. **10.** The *semed* (DV ' acre ') was the area ploughed by a yoke of oxen in a day. *Bath* and *ephah* were measures, corresponding respectively to nine gallons and a bushel. The homer contained ten ephahs. So unproductive shall the land be that ten semeds produce only a bath of wine and one homer only an ephah of corn. It must be abandoned to sheep and goats, **17**.

e **11-17.** The sin of the revellers is punished by exile, hunger, thirst and death. Man will be humbled and Yahweh will be exalted on the judgement day. **11b-12.** ' *And tarry in the evening that wine may heat them. Absorbed by the lyre and the lute, the timbrel and the flute, and the wine of their banquets* ', they disregard the work of the Lord, **13**, the threatened punishment. **14a.** ' soul ' : ' maw '. **14c-d.** ' *And down shall go their splendour and their tumult and their din and their revellers therein* '.

f **18-21.** The blasphemers of 18-19 are compared to oxen drawing loads of iniquity and sin. The ropes with which their loads are attached are their mockeries of the prophet's predictions. **20.** The perverse have lost all moral sense. **21.** Those who esteem themselves wise pay no attention to warnings and threats. These three ' woes ' are brief because admonition is useless.

g **22-24.** Corrupt judges, valiant only in their cups, are finally denounced. **24b.** ' *and as chaff perishes in the flame* '. The judges are held particularly responsible for the sins of the people.

h **26-30. The Chastisement of Foreign Invasion**—The invaders described, but not named, are summoned by Yahweh. **26a.** ' nation '. For the Hebrews Mesopotamia was the end of the earth. **27a.** ' *There is none that is weary or stumbles among them* '. **28.** The wheels are the chariots, swift as the whirlwind. Horses, not being shod, needed hard hoofs. **29.** Assyria is the lion, Israel his prey. **30.** Text and position are doubtful. It seems to describe the judgement day : roaring like the roar of the sea, darkness on earth and in the heavens.

i **VI 1-13 Vocation of Isaias**—The position of this vision after chh 1-5 is most probably due to the fact that it served as an introduction to chh 7-12. As the prophecies of chh 2-5 are earlier than those of chh 7-12 they were placed first when the various collections were united. Finally ch 1 became a general introduction.

The rabbinic explanation that the exercise of the **425i** prophetic gift was suspended from the sin of Ozias until his death and that ch 6 describes its resumption is without foundation and generally rejected. If the death of Ozias and the accession of Phacee occurred in the same year, 4 Kg 15:27, the vocation of Isaias must be dated 736. Phacee became king of Israel two years after Menahem paid tribute to Assyria in 738.

The prophet first describes the vision of Yahweh **j** which he saw, **1-4**, then his purification, **5-7**, and finally his mission, **8-11**. The reflexion which concludes the prophecy contains the remnant doctrine, **12-13**.

1-4. That the scene of the vision was the temple at **k** Jerusalem may be deduced from the word *bayit* or house designating the two principal parts of Solomon's temple, the shaking of the door-posts, and the mention of smoke and altar. **1.** The throne implies the kingship of God, explicitly indicated in **5**. ' High and elevated ' may be referred to ' throne ' or to ' Lord ' as in 57:15. The train probably signifies rays of light, Ps 103:1. **2.** ' upon it ' : ' *by him* ' (God). The radical sense of *śārāp* is ' fiery '. The winged *śārāp* of Is 14:29 is a serpent. Serpents are *seraphim* or fiery, Num 21:6, probably owing to the inflammation caused by their bites. Here however the Seraphim are undoubtedly intelligent creatures, **3**, in human form since they have face, feet and hands, **6**, winged attendants of God who sing his praises and accomplish his commands. As they formed God's court they were not merely two individuals but two choirs. They veil their faces and the lower parts of their bodies through reverence. **3.** The trisagion, triple repetition **l** of ' holy ', indicates that God is superlatively holy. Holiness in the OT means separation from what is base or impure. God's holiness is the unique preeminence which separates him from his creatures. Man becomes holy by nearness to God, either ritually as his minister or morally by observing his law. It is only by accommodation that the trisagion is referred to the Trinity. Hosts in the expression ' Yahweh of hosts ' means armies. Yahweh of hosts is the leader of the armies of angels and also of the armies of Israel. In the second part of the song of the Seraphim the omnipresence of Yahweh is indicated. **4.** The song causes the doorposts (or the foundations of the threshold) of the temple to quake. The smoke or cloud was the visible indication of God's presence.

5-7. 5a. ' *Woe is me for I am undone* '. The vision of **m** God foreboded death in the OT. Here moreover God's holiness reminded Isaias of his sins and the sins of his people. He cannot join in the Angels' praises for his lips are unclean. Their cleansing is also necessary in view of his mission.

8-11. The mission must be freely accepted hence the **n** query. Quick decision and firm determination are characteristic of Isaias. His mission is foredoomed to failure, so far at least as its immediate purpose is concerned. His people will not be converted but will be blinded and hardened by his preaching. To understand the language in which this message is conveyed it must be remembered that the sacred writers in tracing the designs of God in the history of mankind attribute to him, often without distinction, both what he directly intends and what he indirectly permits. The All-holy God does not directly intend to blind or harden his people. They blind and harden themselves by refusing to accept the graces which he offers. This refusal renders them less worthy of future graces and less disposed to co-operate with them but never puts them outside the pale of God's Infinite Mercy. Isaias like St Paul cannot believe that the anger of God with his chosen people will endure for ever. He therefore asks ' *For how long, O Lord ?* ' The reply announces foreign invasion and deportation.

12-13. The prophet reflects on the last words of **o** Yahweh. The chastisement of deportation is certain. The remnant to be spared will be further purified and from it will emerge the holy seed of the Messianic

425o kingdom. **12b.** ' *And great shall be the emptiness in the midst of the land* '. **13.** ' *And should there remain in it yet a tenth it will be again for destruction, like a terebinth and like an oak of which, when felled, a stump remains. From its stump will sprout holy seed* '. The distinction of the remnant, the holy seed, from the survivors of the deportation is important.

p **VII 1-XII 6 Trust in God not in Foreign Alliance**— All these prophecies, except one, 9:7–10:4, which may be earlier, are interconnected. The clash between the policy of Isaias, trust in God alone, and that of Achaz, alliance with Assyria, 7:1–13, determines the character not only of the Emmanuel prophecy but also of the others which follow. Yahweh will deliver those who trust in him but alliance with Assyria will be punished by foreign invasion and the devastation of Judah. This double prediction is the theme of the parallel prophecies, chh 7-8. The description of the future deliverer is then further developed, **9:1-6**. This prophecy presupposes the Assyrian invasion and occupation of Galilee in 734. It is appropriately followed by the downfall of the Assyrian oppressor, **10:5-34**. This prediction is later than the fall of Samaria in 721 but prior to the invasion of Judah in 701. It is closely connected with the third description of the Messias and his kingdom of peace which immediately follows, **11:1-16**. The hymn of thanksgiving of the redeemed, **ch 12**, concludes the series.

q **VII 1-25.** The occasion of the Emmanuel prophecy is first narrated, **1-14a**. The prophecy follows in two parts : a message of deliverance from the impending danger, **14b-16**, and of chastisement for the sin of unbelief, **17-25**. This is the traditional interpretation. The modern interpretation, first proposed by E. Reuss in 1874 and accepted by nearly all subsequent commentators, regards the whole prophecy without distinction of parts as a message of chastisement. Articles of Calès (1922), Vaccari (1937) and Feuillet (1940), cited in § 419b, and Dennefeld's commentary (1947) mark a return to the traditional view. Readers will find a fuller discussion of the problem in IER 70 (1948) 289–304.

r **1-14a Occasion of the Prophecy**—When Phacee usurped the throne of Samaria in 736 he altered the previous policy of subjection to Assyria, to an alliance with Damascus against Assyria. Achaz of Judah refused to join the anti-Assyrian league. Phacee therefore and Rason of Damascus plotted to dethrone Achaz and establish an Aramaean partisan, the son of Tabeel, on the throne of Judah. The enthronement of a foreign usurper practically implied, according to the manners of the time, the extirpation of the native dynasty; *cf.* Athalia, 4 Kg 11:1. Now God had promised to David by Nathan's prophecy that his dynasty should last for ever, 2 Kg 7:16, and the promise was fulfilled in the eternal reign of Christ. But it could not be fulfilled if the dynasty of David had been extirpated. Hence the advent of the Messias was a most appropriate sign of the failure of the plot. We can thus understand why the coming of the Messias was first predicted by Isaias at this juncture. The news of the arrival of the Aramaean army at Samaria caused general consternation in Jerusalem. Isaias was therefore sent by God to Achaz to assure him that the plot would fail. But Achaz had already decided to purchase Assyrian support by submission and tribute. The prophet warned him and the House of David that faith was necessary and offered him moreover the choice of a sign, no matter how extraordinary, to confirm the assurance of deliverance. As Achaz refused to accept the offer on the hypocritical pretext of a religious scruple, God declared through his prophet that he himself would give the House of David a sign.

s **1.** The general situation is indicated by a citation from 4 Kg 16:5, 2, the particular moment by the news of the arrival of the Aramaeans at Samaria. ' The House of David ' instead of Achaz emphasizes the danger to the dynasty. **3.** Isaias must take with

him his son, Shear-Yashub (' a remnant will return '), **42** a Messianic sign, 8:18, to the end of the conduit of the Upper Pool, to the highway of the Fuller's Field, south-east of the city (*cf.* 22:11) and there announce deliverance to Achaz. **4.** The hostile kings are called *two tails of smoking firebrands* to show that their end is near. Omit the explanatory gloss which follows. **5.** ' *Whereas Syria has planned evil against thee saying* '. **6.** For ' rouse up ' read, with a slight correction, ' *attack* '. **7.** Note the emphatic repetition. **8-9.** Rason's rule is only over Syria and Damascus, Phacee's over Ephraim and Samaria. Neither will rule over Judah and Jerusalem. The gloss, **8c**, interrupts the context and is erroneous, for Ephraim ceased to be a people 14 years later in 721. **9c.** Note the plural verb to indicate not Achaz alone but the House of David. **10.** ' again ' : ' *further* '. No second meeting **t** of Achaz and Isaias is implied. A prophetic sign is a supernatural manifestation—either a miracle or a revelation or both—by which a prophecy is confirmed. The sign is manifested usually before, sometimes after, the prediction is fulfilled. In the latter case, exemplified in Ex 3:12, its value for the recipient depends on his faith. God knew that Achaz would refuse to choose a sign and gave his own Messianic sign to the House of David indicated by the plural pronoun. Ezechias at least, the heir to the throne, had faith enough to profit by it, since he inaugurated his reign, nine years later, by a great religious revival.

14b-16 The Emmanuel Prophecy—' *Behold the Virgin* **42** *shall conceive and bear a son and she shall call his name Emmanuel. Butter and honey shall he eat that he may know to refuse the evil and to choose the good. Verily before he knows to refuse the evil and to choose the good, the tillage land, whose two kings thou loathest, shall be devastated* '.

The prophecy has two parts : the sign of deliverance, **14b-15**, and the promise of deliverance fulfilled before the manifestation of the sign, **16**. The sign is the Word Incarnate, conceived and born of a Virgin Mother, receiving from her the symbolic name of Emmanuel ' God-with-us ', and endowed from birth with the Messianic attributes of judgement and justice. The deliverance is the devastation of the tillage land of the two plotters against the House of David by the Assyrians two years later in 733.

14b. The Heb. word here translated ' virgin ' is not **b** the technical term, *bᵉtûlāh*, but its practical equivalent, *'almāh*, which means an unmarried maiden of marriageable age, presumed to be a virgin by the strict moral code of the Hebrews. The word never designates a married woman and is sometimes rendered παρθένος ' virgin ' by LXX ; *cf.* § 375d on Prov 30:19 for the one use of the word where text and meaning are obscure. The imposition of the child's name by the mother, contrary to custom (*cf.* 8:3), confirms the conclusion of a virginal conception. Emmanuel necessarily implies by Hebrew usage God's omnipotent aid and consequently deliverance. The word ' behold ', following the mention of a sign, naturally introduces it.

15 contains two members connected by a preposition **c** which followed by an infinitive is usually final, ' that he may know ', and very rarely temporal, ' when he shall know '. The word *ḥem'āh* may mean ' curds ' or ' butter '. In the OT milk and honey usually mean excellent and abundant food. From this some conclude that 15a indicates a period of prosperity, the result of the deliverance announced in 16. Others on the contrary suppose that 15a indicates the absence of tillage and a period of adversity, the result of the chastisement, introduced into 16 by an alteration of the text, which makes Judah the land to be devastated. Both schools of interpreters understand 15b as attainment of the age of reason and connect the verse-members temporally. Emmanuel then would attain the age of reason shortly after the devastation of Samaria and Damascus in 733 or of Judah in 701. Thus the prophecy would determine erroneously the time of Emmanuel's advent and would contradict

c 6:11–13 according to which the Messianic age will be preceded by the devastation of Judah, the deportation of its inhabitants and the further purification of the survivors. In reality the verse has been misinterpreted and simply attributes the Messianic dignity to Emmanuel. Without such an indication, supplied in the two subsequent predictions of the advent of the Messias (9:1–7 ; 11:1–5), this prophecy would be incomplete.

d The attainment of the age of reason confers on a child only moral discernment by which he can choose or refuse both good and evil. Emmanuel receives a higher gift, a practical knowledge by means of which he chooses the good and refuses the evil. This is the gift of the ideal king who loves justice and hates iniquity and is therefore anointed by God with the oil of gladness beyond his fellows, Ps 44:8. It is the practical wisdom of Solomon, the sound judgement which enables a monarch to rule justly. To be instrumental in conferring this gift butter and honey must indicate not corporal but intellectual nourishment. We have an instance of this figurative use in the description of the spouse : ' Honey and milk are under thy tongue ', Cant 4:11. The exact sense is expressed more clearly in an Arabic parallel : ' Thy discourse, if thou graciously favourest me with it, is like the honey of bees and the beestings of camels ', I. Guidi in RB 12 (1903) 243. This parallel and the common origin and ties of language and customs which united Hebrews and Arabs suggest another Arabic parallel, first proposed by H. Lammens (ER 151 [1917, 2] 421) and accepted by J. Calès (RSR 12 [1922] 174), as an explanation of the words of Isaias. The prophet alludes to the *taḥnîk*, lit. conferring of sound judgement. For this purpose the chief of the tribe or some very distinguished person rubbed on the soft palate of the new-born child either chewed dates or, as at Ṭāïf (and in Palestine where dates are not common), a mixture of butter and honey. The custom must have been known to the prophet's hearers like so many other Hebrew customs unknown to us. The infant, who received from God at his birth the gift of sound judgement by means of which he is enabled to rule justly, is evidently the Messias. Judgement and justice (or righteousness) are the foundation of God's kingship, Ps 89:15 ; 96:8, and fundamental attributes of the Messianic king, Ps 71:1 ; Is 9:7 ; 16:5 ; 28:17 ; Jer 23:5.

e **16.** As the sing. often replaces the plur. in Hebrew, especially when a class is designated, the sing. tillage land is intelligible. The emphatic sense of *kî* is supported by the emphatic repetition in 7. The repetition of 15*b* is to inform us that the promise of deliverance will be fulfilled before the sign is manifested. The priority of the deliverance is also expressly indicated in Ex 3:12.

f **Emmanuel is the Promised Messias**—(1) He is the descendant of David in whom the eternity of the Davidic dynasty will be realized. (2) His unique virginal conception and name, Emmanuel, suggest the promised Redeemer. (3) He receives from God the Messianic endowments of judgement and justice. (4) His dominion over Judah ' thy land, O Emmanuel ', 8:8, while Ezechias reigns, can only be by Messianic right. (5) He is identical with the Messias of 9:1–7 ; 11:1–5 and 28:16.

g **The Emmanuel Prophecy a Threat of Punishment ?**— Achaz and his people were undoubtedly delivered once and for all from the two hostile nations whom they feared. This deliverance is predicted by Isaias in the introduction, 7:7, in his address to the House of David, 7:16, and in his address to the people, 8:4. Nevertheless most modern commentators, Catholic as well as non-Catholic, alter the text of 7:16 so as to make Judah the land whose devastation is predicted and interpret Is 7:14*b*–16 as a threat of punishment. The foundation of this interpretation is the curds and honey on which Emmanuel is nourished, supposed to be a consequence of the absence of tillage and thus a sign of the devastation of Judah. It is assumed that

Yahweh substituted for the sign of deliverance rejected **426g** by Achaz a sign of the punishment merited by his infidelity. The popularity of this interpretation necessitates a brief discussion of the difficulties which it involves and the foundation on which it is based.

The most obvious difficulty is the temporal association **h** of the advent of the Messias with the devastation of Judah which occurred many centuries earlier. The prophet would err if he predicted the actual presence of the Messias on earth at the period indicated. It is suggested therefore that that presence predicted is either ideal—Emmanuel is conceived by Isaias as present on earth and eating curds and honey—or hypothetical— if Emmanuel were present on earth he would eat curds and honey. It must be admitted that these interpretations of the prophet's Messianic prediction are forced and unnatural. Can we believe moreover that the sign so definitely promised in confirmation of the prophet's message was never actually given ? Emmanuel, if not really present, did not eat curds and honey.

The restricted horizon of these interpreters presents **i** a further difficulty. They only contemplate the material catastrophe of the devastation of Judah then to be feared. They ignore the far more important spiritual danger of the extirpation of the Davidic dynasty and the consequent extinction of the Messianic hope. It is this danger which explains the character of the sign given by Yahweh, the real advent of the Messias at an undetermined future period, a sign not of punishment but of deliverance by which the promise of salvation from imminent danger is appropriately confirmed. In the modern interpretation on the contrary the announcement of the advent of the Messias at this particular juncture is unexplained. The sole connexion of the Messianic introduction with the rest of the prophecy is the sign of punishment which it is supposed to provide but which was never actually given.

A third difficulty against the modern interpretation is **j** that all the contents of the Emmanuel prophecy, if we abstract for the moment from the disputed question of Emmanuel's nourishment, definitely suggest not punishment but deliverance. The Messias is a deliverer. He comes, as he himself tells us, not to judge the world but to save the world. His God-given name Emmanuel ' God-with-us ' is the regular Hebrew indication of God's omnipotent aid and always implies success or deliverance. The devastation of the kingdoms of Judah's enemies manifestly indicates the deliverance of Judah. We expect moreover in the announcement, made not to Achaz alone but to the House of David, deliverance as well as punishment. In the introduction deliverance is promised, 7:7, and punishment is threatened, 7:9. In the parallel announcement to the people deliverance from present danger is first predicted, 8:1–4, and future punishment is then foretold, 8:5–10. In the prophecy of Nathan, with which the Emmanuel prophecy is very closely connected, an absolute promise of the eternal conservation of the Davidic dynasty is similarly followed by a threat of punishment in cases of infidelity.

The sole foundation of the modern interpretation is **k** Emmanuel's nourishment of curds and honey understood literally as a meagre diet and the sign of adversity and punishment. The literal sense of the expression is, however, rendered very doubtful by the context which indicates prosperity and deliverance and by the regular Hebrew use of milk and honey as a proverbial expression for excellent and abundant food. Support is sought for the literal sense in 21–22 where we read : ' *It will come to pass on that day that every man shall keep one cow and two sheep and owing to the abundance of milk every man shall eat curds—yea curds and honey shall all eat who are left in the land* '. The text is found in a description of the future devastation of Judah, but as interpolations and transpositions are not infrequent in Isaias, its meaning must be determined primarily not from its present context but from its contents. It clearly

426k describes a period in which milk abounds to such an extent that each individual has a constant supply, and milk and honey are the food of all. Such abundance of milk cannot indicate adversity and punishment but is a characteristic of the Messianic period (Is 55:1 ; Joel 3:18). The passage thus appears to be a rabbinic picture of Messianic prosperity, originally a gloss on Is 7:15 explaining how the food of the Messias will also be the food of his subjects. There are two indications that the text is rabbinic rather than Isaian. Such trivial provision for individual needs contrasts with the prophet's more dignified solicitude for the nation as a whole and suggests rabbinism. Milk and honey do not appear as the food of the blessed in the OT but subsequently in 4 Esd 2:19 and later Jewish writers. There is no doubt an element of conjecture in this tentative explanation of a difficult text. The fact remains however that universal ownership of cattle and abundance of milk are not a natural indication of adversity and punishment. The literal sense of curds and honey on which the modern interpretation is founded has little support in these verses.

l Some writers try to solve the difficulties of the Emmanuel prophecy by compenetration. Isaias announces at the same time and in the same words two infants : the Messias to be born in the distant future and an anonymous infant whose proximate advent is predicted. The text however only indicates one child who has Messianic attributes. The anonymous infant is a *deus ex machina*. In genuine cases of compenetration such as an actual king and the Messianic king according to the Antiochian exegetes or the destruction of Sennacherib's army and the fall of Assyria, both persons or events are indicated in the text and are so interconnected in the prophet's mind that he passes naturally from one to the other.

Several positive proofs that Emmanuel is the Messias have been already given. Other identifications of the child whose advent is predicted have been proposed by those who either refuse to admit that the prophecy is Messianic or regard the child as a type of the Messias. It is not difficult to show that these are all exegetically untenable. ' Thy land, O Emmanuel ', 8:8, defines Emmanuel as a single individual. Hence the interpretation of *hā-'almāh* as every maiden and the multiplicity of Emmanuels cannot be admitted. Ezechias cannot be identified with Emmanuel as he was born several years before the prophecy and his mother, a married woman, could not be called *'almāh*. Neither could the wife of Isaias, called prophetess, as the wife of a priest (*khūri*) in modern Syria is called priestess (*khūriyya*), be styled *'almāh*. In any case the sign given to the House of David, a scion of that house, naturally differs from the sign given to the people, a son of the people.

m **17-25 The Chastisement of Unbelief**—The oracle is addressed to the House of David. The chastisement is twofold : Egyptian occupation and Babylonian devastation. There is no reference to the Assyrian invasion of Sennacherib by which the people were chastised, 8:5-10, but not the House of David since Yahweh intervened to save Ezechias and his capital. The chastisement is comparable only to the loss of the ten tribes in the schism, 17. Egyptians represented by flies which abound on the Nile and its branches and Trans-Euphrateans, here Babylonians, compared to the more vexatious bees, will invade Judah. The Pharaoh, Nechao, re-asserted Egypt's ancient claims to Palestine. His slaughter of Josias and subsequent Egyptian intrigues hastened the fall of the House of David.

n **18.** ' hiss for ' : ' *whistle to* '. **19b-c.** ' *in the ravines of the precipices and in the clefts of the rocks and in all the thorn bushes and in all the watering-places* '. **20.** The more terrible invaders were the Babylonians who completely devastated Judah. They were the razor which Yahweh hired. Hair of the feet is a euphemism. ' feet and *even the beard will it* [the razor] *sweep away* '. In 17 and 20 ' the king of Assyria ' is a gloss. Another gloss, 21-22, interrupts the description of the devastation continued in 23 ; *cf.* § 426k. **23-24.** The devastated

vineyards become briars and thorns into which only **4** the hunter in search of game penetrates. **25.** The hill terraces also cultivated, but not productive, when devastated, of briars and thorns like the plainlands, now become pasturage. It must be noted that the Assyrians colonised the provinces which they annexed and did not leave the land untilled. The Babylonians, after conquering Judah, did not colonize it. Isaias depicts therefore, in vivid colours, not an imaginary Assyrian but the real Babylonian conquest of Judah which was the final chastisement of the sins of the House of David.

VIII 1-10 The Prophet's Announcement to the People 4 —This prophecy like the preceding has two parts : a promise of deliverance and a prediction of chastisement. The solemnity of the prophetic announcement is attested by the great tablet, the ordinary script which the people could read, and the legal attestation of two trustworthy witnesses. The chastisement predicted is explicitly the Assyrian invasion of 701 B.C., a heavy calamity for the people of Judah, of whom 200,150 (prob. an Assyrian scribal error for 20,150) were deported.

1-4 The Promise of Deliverance—1. The inscription **b** like those on seals began with a preposition meaning ' belonging to '. The name is rendered ' Haste—booty—speed—spoil ' and denotes the speedy discomfiture of Judah's two enemies explicitly mentioned in 4. **2.** Urias is the high-priest, 4 Kg 16:10, Zacharias may be the father-in-law of Achaz, 2 Par 29:1, or the pre-exilic author of Zach chh 9–11. **3.** The sign, a son with symbolic name, is similar to that of the Emmanuel prophecy. The father gives the name according to custom. **4.** ' his ' (before ' father and mother ') : ' *my* '. Damascus was captured and sacked in 732, Samaria only in 721. The capture of these cities within two years is not here predicted but the devastation of their territories, as in 7:16, regarded as a spoliation of the capitals themselves. *Cf.* 28:1 where Samaria becomes a fading flower by loss of territory. ' strength ' : ' *wealth* '.

5-10 The Chastisement—Because the people of Judah **c** have despised divine aid, compared to the waters of Siloe which flow softly, and have melted with fear of Rason and Phacee, despite God's promise of deliverance, the Assyrians, whose aid they sought, compared to the turbulent waters of the Euphrates, will overrun the entire land, but the flood will only reach the neck, for Jerusalem, the head, will be saved. However numerous and strong the enemies may be their plans will not succeed ' *for God is with us* '. Sennacherib's invasion is here predicted. The waters of Siloe indicate an ancient aqueduct outside the east wall of the city conveying the waters of Gihon to the gardens in the valley.

6. ' taken ' : ' *feared* '. **7.** ' many ' : ' *mighty* ' ; ' he ' : ' *it* ' ; ' his ' : ' *its* '. **8.** ' *And it shall sweep into Judah in a flood and it shall overflow till it reach the neck ; and its spreading margins* '. As Ezechias was then king of Judah it is by Messianic right that the land is Emmanuel's. He is not considered actually present, but the land of Canaan, granted to the chosen people in view of his coming, belongs to him. **9.** ' *Take note* [LXX, preferable to ' be in uproar ', MT] . . . *and be dismayed.* . . . *Gird yourselves and be dismayed* ' (emphatic repetition). **10c.** ' *because Emmanuel* ' or ' *because God is with us* '. In either case the deliverance of Jerusalem from the wrath of Sennacherib is attributed directly or indirectly to Emmanuel.

11-IX 7 The Prophet's Announcement to his Disciples d —This prophecy supposes the recent devastation of Galilee by the Assyrians. The league with Assyria, vindicated by its results, confirms the people in their reliance on human aid. Isaias encourages his faithful disciples to trust in God alone and await patiently the hour of deliverance. He predicts the punishment of unbelief. His prophetic instruction of the people ceases and the formation of his disciples takes its place—a remarkable parallel to the teaching of Christ. By

7d fidelity to Yahweh they will be saved from evil to be finally dissipated where it began, in Galilee, by the advent of the Messias.

e **11a.** ' Verily so hath Yahweh spoken to me when his hand was strong upon me and he warned me not to walk '. **12.** The warning forbids ' calling alliance all that this people calls alliance ' and fearing what they fear. *qeṣer* may mean ' conspiracy ' (against the state by reliance on God alone) or ' alliance ' (with Assyria, the actual state policy). The latter interpretation is preferable as the fear also condemned is the fear of Samaria and Damascus. **13.** ' sanctify ' : ' ally yourselves with ', a correction suggested by the parallelism. **14.** ' sanctification ' : ' sanctuary ', place of refuge. The two houses of Israel are the Northern and Southern Kingdoms. ' ruin ' : ' trap '. There are several references to the stone of stumbling and the rock of offence in the NT (Lk 2:34 ; 20:17 ; Mt 21:42 ; Rom 9:32 ; 1 Pet 2:8). The exact construction of the verbs in **16** is uncertain. Isaias has no more to say to the unbelieving people on the subject of reliance on God rather than on man and therefore binds up his testimony and seals his instructions now reserved for his disciples. **17-18.** He will wait for the Lord, he and his two sons. Shear-yashub is the sign of the Messianic remnant. Mahershallal-hashbaz is the sign of deliverance from invasion. Isaias himself (' Yahweh will save ') bears equivalently the name of Jesus. **19-20.** The disciples are warned to adhere to the testimony and instructions of 16 when people urge them to consult pythons and diviners saying : ' Shall not a people consult their gods, (consult) the dead on behalf of the living ? ' **20b-22** are corrupt and obscure. Vg gives the general sense of a time of calamity and distress, of the night preceding the dawn.

f **IX 1-7 Light after Darkness : The Reign of the Messias**—Galilee was the first part of Palestine to suffer deportation and become an Assyrian province in 734 B.C. Here in the latter days a light shall shine, joy shall abound, oppression shall cease, for the Messias shall come to rule in peace with justice and judgement an eternal kingdom.

g **1-5. 1.** ' Formerly he humiliated the land of Zabulon and the land of Nephtali, latterly he will glorify the way of the sea beyond the Jordan, Galilee of the Gentiles '. Nazareth was in Zabulon. Nephtali lay along the Jordan east of Zabulon. The way of the sea was the trade route from Damascus to the Mediterranean passing through Galilee. Beyond the Jordan means east or west of it according to the context. Here the trade route from Damascus gives the direction and thus indicates the west (Galilee). Some interpreters find in 1b an indication of the three Assyrian provinces recently established : Du'uru (Dor), the way of the sea, Gal'azu (Galaad), beyond the Jordan, and Magidu (Megiddo), Galilee of the Gentiles. But only Galilee's humiliation is mentioned in 1a. It is therefore Galilee's glorification by the life and teaching of the Messias that is predicted in 1b. Dor and Galaad are ignored. **3a** (slightly corrected) : ' Thou hast made exultation great, thou hast made joy abound '. The greatest joys were those of victory and harvest-time. **4.** ' For the yoke of his burden, the rod of his shoulder, and the staff of his work-master thou hast broken as in the day of Madian '. Staff is the staff of office. The terms indicate oppression in general. On the day of Madian cf. Jg chh 8-9. **5a-b.** ' For every boot that tramped in tumult and every mantle rolled in blood shall be for burning, shall be consumed by fire '. War shall be no more.

h **6-7.** ' For a child is born to us, a son is given to us, And sovereignty is on his shoulder, And his name is called : Wonder-counsellor, Mighty God, Father for ever, Prince of Peace. For the extension of sovereignty and for peace without end, On the throne of David and over his kingdom, To establish it and to sustain it in judgement and justice, Henceforth and for ever—The zeal of Yahweh of hosts will accomplish this '.

The Messias and his reign are depicted as present. The indefinite futurity of the event was previously indicated by the distinction of times, 1. Sovereignty resting on the shoulder is most probably the kingly

office imposing duties and thus a burden. The extension **427h** of sovereignty and peace without end express the teaching of Christ in ' Thy kingdom come ' and ' Love one another '. The throne of David recalls Nathan's prophecy and thus identifies the child with Emmanuel. Judgement and justice are characteristic attributes of Emmanuel, 7:15, and of the Messias. The eternal reign of the Messias, implied by the prophecy of Nathan, is here first explicitly indicated.

The Names—Names in the Bible express nature or **i** attributes ; cf. the divine name, Yahweh, Ex 3:14. As the last two names are evidently composite and the second is composite in biblical usage, the first is also composite and there are four names each of two words. These names are an essential part of the revelation. The second word of the first name is a participle and may therefore be a verb or a noun. The sense is practically the same whether we render ' a counsellor of wonderful things ' or ' a wonder of a counsellor '. Mighty God appears always in the OT and even in Is 10:21 as a name of Yahweh expressing his omnipotence. This divine attribute predicated of the Messias implies his divinity. That Isaias understood the implication is uncertain. His hearers probably interpreted the name as superhuman in might. The second part of the third name means either booty or eternity. ' Father of booty ' does not express a permanent quality and scarcely suits the parallel, ' Prince of Peace '. Father of Eternity may mean ' possessed of eternity ', Eternal, or ' Father for ever ', expressing the eternal solicitude of the Messianic king for his people's welfare. The last interpretation is the most satisfactory. Prince of Peace must be understood as implying, in accordance with the full sense of the Hebrew *šālōm*, a reign of peace and prosperity. LXX interpreted these names erroneously : ' And his name shall be called Angel of the Great Council. For I shall bring peace to the princes '. *'Ēl* ' God ' is ' Angel ', *'aḇî* ' father ' is ' I shall bring '. *'ad* ' eternity ' is the preposition ' to ' (cf. the Introit of the Feast of the Circumcision).

IX 8-X 4 + V 25 Sins and Chastisements of Israel **428a** —This prophecy narrates the sins and chastisements of the Northern Kingdom in the past and predicts the final chastisement of complete destruction. It contains five strophes each mentioning a particular sin and ending with a refrain on the necessity of further chastisement. The first part of the last strophe, 5:25, describing the sin, is missing. The date is difficult to determine as the events described are past history. The manner is more reminiscent of the early prophecies, chh 2-5.

8-12 Pride of Israel—The sin (of pride) is described. **b** 9-10, its punishment, 11-12. **8.** Jacob and Israel designate the Northern Kingdom. **9a.** ' And all the people knew, Ephraim and the inhabitants of Samaria, saying '. Read his (Israel's) enemies and omit ' of Rasin '. The verb rendered ' bring in a crowd ' means literally ' weave together ', unite Israel's enemies : Philistines in the south-west and Aramaeans in the east.

13-17 Misgovernment in Israel—**13.** Chastisement has **c** brought no amendment. **14b.** ' Head and tail, palm-branch and rush ' include everybody. **15** is clearly a gloss. **16** indicates the sin : ' They that guide this people are mis-leaders and the guided have been led astray '. **17.** The chastisement must be universal. For ' have joy ' read spare and for ' hypocrite ' godless.

18-21 Civil Strife in Israel—Civil strife is evidenced in **d** Israel by the ten dynasties of the monarchical period as contrasted with the one dynasty of Judah. **18.** Read after ' fire ' ' that consumes ' and after ' thorn ' ' and kindles the thickets of the forest, and they roll up in a pillar of smoke '. **19.** ' troubled ' : ' overturned ' or ' enkindled '. **20.** ' turn ' : ' cut off ' (something to eat). Ephraim and Manasses were rivals.

X 1-4 Unjust Judgements in Israel—Oppression of the **e** lower classes, especially widows and orphans, in the law courts was a common crime. Unjust laws are first reprehended, then unjust judgements. **1b.** ' and to the scribes who write trouble '. **3.** ' glory ' : ' riches '. The

428e sense of **4a** is : (nothing will be left you) '*except to crouch down among the captives or fall among the slain*'.

f **25.** The punishment is introduced by 'therefore' but the sin has disappeared. The place of this fragment in the poem is unknown.

g **X 5-34 Chastisement of the Pride of Assyria**—Assyria, here personified, is God's instrument in the chastisement of Israel. He believes, however, that he is the sole author of his conquests and that he can destroy Jerusalem as he destroyed other cities. His pride will be punished by his speedy downfall and his designs against Jerusalem will be defeated by Yahweh. The unity of the prophecy is indicated by the announcement of the design against Jerusalem in the beginning, **11**, and its frustration in the end, **33-34**. As Judah remained subject to Assyria, **20**, long after the death of Achaz, the limits of date are **717**, destruction of Carchemish, and **701**, Sennacherib's invasion.

h **5-19.** **5.** Assyria is the staff of God's anger, the rod of God's wrath ; '*he is in their hand*'. **6.** '*deceitful*' : '*godless*' ; '*prey*' '*and to leave them to be trodden on*'. The tenses in 6-7 are present. **8.** '*He however thinks not so. And his heart considers not so*'. **9.** Calano is Kullane, east of Syrian Antioch, conquered with Arpad, north of Aleppo, in 740. Hamath on the Orontes was finally subdued in 720. **10.** '*As my hand hath overpowered these kingdoms—and their idols were more powerful than those of Jerusalem*'. The Assyrian assimilates Yahweh to an idol. **12.** The description of Assyrian pride and its punishment is aptly introduced. **13.** Read '*peoples*' ; omit '*of the princes*'. '*as a mighty man I have laid low the inhabitants*'. **14.** '*strength*' : '*riches*'. **15c-d.** '*As if the rod should swing him who lifts it, As if the staff should lift him who is not wood*'. **16a.** The fat ones are the leaders. '*Instead of well-being a kindling shall be kindled like the kindling of a fire*'. **17-19.** A fever shall replace good health. The fire suggests God's wrath consuming the Assyrian warriors as fire consumes the trees of a forest. **18** (after 'flesh') : '*like the wasting away of a sick man*'. Here as in 33-34 there is reference to the destruction of Sennacherib's army.

i **20-27 Messianic Interlude**—The Assyrian remnant, 19, like the Philistine remnant, 14:30, suggests to Isaias the remnant of Israel and the Messianic age. **20.** Then will Israel rely, not as now on Assyria, but on God alone the 'Mighty God' ; *cf*. 9:6. **22.** No matter how numerous the Israelites then may be, only a remnant shall be converted for '*an extermination which overflows with justice* [a purification] *is decreed*'. **23.** '*For an extermination, as decreed, will the Lord Yahweh of Hosts accomplish over the whole earth*'. The second verse extends the judgement to all nations. St Paul cites both verses, Rom 9:27 f., as predicting the small number of converted Israelites. **24-27.** The people are warned not to fear the Assyrians from whose tyranny they will soon be delivered, as they were from Egyptian and Madianite oppression. For the rock of Oreb *cf*. Jg 7:25. **26.** '*lift it up*' : '*take him away*'. Yahweh will remove the Assyrian as he removed the Egyptian oppressor. **27.** 'oil' : '*fat*'. The strength of the neck will burst the yoke laid upon it.

j **28-34 Invasion of Sennacherib**—The abrupt commencement and the eastern deviation from the highway suggest a surprise attack on Jerusalem made by a northern enemy, the Assyrians. Of the places named Magron, Gallim, Laishah, Madmenah and Gabim are unidentified. Ayyath is Hai, et-tell, east of Bethel and 12 m. N. of Jerusalem. **28.** 'into' : 'through'. Machmas where the baggage is left is Muchmas, *c* 8 m. from the capital and separated from Geba by the Wady Suwēnit. **29a.** '*They cross the pass (saying) Geba is our night-quarters*'. *Rama*, er-Ram, 5 m. from Jerusalem on the main road, *is in panic*. *Gabaa*, Saul's capital, Tell el-Ful, east of Rama and 3 m. from the Holy City, *is in flight*. **30.** '*Hearken Laishah, answer Anathoth*'. Anathoth is Anata, 2½ m. from Jerusalem. **31.** The inhabitants of Madmena and Gabim flee to the capital. **32.** The invader halts for the day at Nob on Mt Scopus in full view of Sion which he threatens. **33.** But God

is there to destroy the Assyrians, compared to the trees **4** of a mighty forest as in 18-19. 'earthen vessel' : 'boughs'. The tall trees are felled by the storm wind, and, **34**, the undergrowth is levelled by the axe. When **k** we compare this prediction with its fulfilment we find a remarkable but instructive discrepancy. Sennacherib sought and failed to capture Jerusalem, but he invaded Judah after subjugating Philistia and consequently from the west. From this we learn that the graphic description of the line of march does not indicate the actual route of the future invader but is instead the poetical garb in which the prophecy is wrapped, and by which the invasion is more vividly depicted and the origin of the invader is insinuated ; *cf*. *Institutiones Biblicae* (Romae, 1937⁵) 414 f. It is often difficult to distinguish between ornamental and essential details in a prophecy. There is however no other Assyrian invasion of Jerusalem to which this prophecy can be referred. On the destruction of the army of Sennacherib *cf*. 4 Kg 19:35.

XI 1-16 The Messias, his Reign, his Subjects—This **l** prophecy is closely connected with the preceding oracle. Just as the Assyrian remnant suggested the remnant of Judah, 10:19 f., so the destruction of the forest trees to which the Assyrians are compared recalls the downfall of the House of David and suggests the figure of a shoot or sapling to indicate the Messias. The Messias, **1-5**, his reign, **6-9**, his subjects, **10-16**.

1-5 The Messias—'*But a shoot shall grow from the stock* **m** *of Jesse And a sapling shall sprout from his root, And the spirit of Yahweh shall rest upon him—The spirit of wisdom and understanding, The spirit of counsel and might, The spirit of the knowledge and the fear of Yahweh, And his joy shall be in the fear of Yahweh. Not by the sight of the eyes shall he judge, Nor by the hearing of the ears shall he decide, But he shall judge the lowly with justice And decide with equity for the poor in the land, And he shall smite the oppressor with the rod of his mouth And with the breath of his lips he shall slay the wicked, And justice shall be the girdle of his loins And fidelity the cincture of his reins*'.

1. Both shoot and sapling indicate the Messias, a scion of the dethroned House of David. Jesse, father of David, is the root from which the Davidic dynasty sprang. **2.** The spirit of Yahweh implies that Yahweh is operative as the author of the gifts, whose permanence is expressed by 'rest upon'. The gifts, mentioned in pairs, are intellectual : wisdom and understanding ; practical : counsel and might ; and religious : knowledge and fear of Yahweh. The distinction between wisdom and understanding is not clear-cut, but there is some foundation in Scripture for the explanation of St Thomas that wisdom is knowledge of things in their relation to God, their author and their end, while understanding is knowledge of things in themselves and in their mutual relations. Isaias very probably alludes here to the kingly gift of a 'wise and understanding heart', bestowed by God on Solomon, 3 Kg 3:12. The proper exercise of these speculative gifts is assured by the practical gifts of counsel and might, already indicated in 9:6 by the Messianic titles : Wonder-Counsellor and Mighty God. The religious gifts, knowledge and fear of Yahweh, need no explanation. The last gift is rendered freely 'piety' in LXX and Vg, but literally 'fear of the Lord' in **3a**. This is the origin of the **seven gifts** of the Holy Ghost. The original text has only six gifts, unless we assume, improbably, that the indwelling spirit, **2a**, is intended as a separate gift. Some reject **3a** as a repetition. It has no parallel member. **4-5.** Judgement and justice, the special attributes of the Messianic king, appear in action. **4b.** The Messias like Yahweh operates by his word and by his breath or spirit. 'Earth', '*eres*, is altered to 'oppressor', '*arîṣ*. **5.** The girdle represents activity, hampered by long, loose garments.

6-9. The reign of the Prince of Peace will be a reign **n** of peace. His subjects will be secure from all molestation and particularly from attacks of wild beasts. The peace depicted is to some extent idyllic. Carnivorous animals will not become herbivorous, but the animals created for man's use and benefit and become his n enemies in consequence of sin will return to their allegiance ; *cf.* Rom 8:19 ff. This seems clearly stated in 9 where the wild beasts are declared harmless owing to the universal knowledge of God. **6.** Omit ' and the sheep '. MT has ' fatling ' for ' sheep ' instead of a verb needed and supplied in Vg. **7.** ' calf ' : ' *cow* ' ; supply ' *together* ' after ' feed '.

o **10-16.** The subjects of the Messias will be Gentiles and Jews returned from exile. The authenticity of these verses, especially the prose passages 11–12 and 15–16, has been questioned. No reasonable objection can be made to the conversion of the Gentiles, 11 ; *cf.* 2:2, or to the reoccupation of the promised land, 13–14. Nor is there sufficient reason to exclude a knowledge of the extent of the Diaspora, manifested in the prose passages, from the prophet's vision. **10.** ' beseech ' : ' *seek* ' ; ' sepulchre ' : ' *dwelling-place* '. **11.** ' set ' : ' *lift up* ' ; ' possess ' : ' *acquire* '. Patros is Upper Egypt, Elam Iran, Sennaar (Shinar) Babylonia, Emath Hamath, Islands coastlands and islands of the Mediterranean. **13.** Domestic dissension and foreign molestation shall cease. Judah and Israel are reunited. **14.** The shoulder of the Philistines indicates the foothills west of the mountains of Judah. ' fly ' : ' *swoop down* ' ; ' by the sea ' : ' *to the west* '. **15.** ' lay waste ' : ' *dry up* ' ; ' strength of his spirit ' : ' *heat of his breath* '. ' Strike into ' means ' divide '. Not only will the Red Sea be dried up, but also seven dry channels will be made in the river (Euphrates) for the returning exiles.

p **XII 1-6 Canticle of Thanksgiving and Praise**—The authenticity of this canticle is doubted. The citation from Exodus (2*b* = Ex 15:2) suggests that 4 : *Praise ye the Lord,* etc. is also a citation from the postexilic psalm 104:1. On the other hand the Holy One of Israel in 6 is Isaian. The canticle has two parts, **1-3** and **4-6,** each provided with an introduction. As the song of the redeemed it aptly concludes the Messianic section.
1. ' *I will praise thee Yahweh for though wroth with me thy wrath has turned and thou has comforted me* '. **2.** ' praise ' : ' *protection* '. **3.** ' saviour's fountains ' : ' *fountains of salvation* '. **6.** ' habitation of ' : ' *dweller in* ', used collectively.

a **XIII 1-XXIII 18 Prophecies against the Gentile Nations.**
XIII 1-XIV 27 The Chastisement of Babylon—The authenticity of this prophecy is disputed. The title is most probably due to the redactor. Its correctness, however, is shown by the subsequent mention of Babylon, 19, and the Medes, 17, also by the prediction of the restoration, 14:1-3, which was the sequel of Babylon's fall. Hence the theory that the prophecy originally referred to Assyria but was subsequently adapted to Babylonia deserves no consideration. From the literary point of view the second poem is a masterpiece and eminently worthy of the most grandiloquent of the prophets. It is argued that the Chaldaeans of Babylonia were relatively unimportant during the lifetime of Isaias and for a century afterwards and that the prediction of their destruction would have no interest for his contemporaries. On the other hand he had already foretold the brevity of Assyrian domination, 10:25, the Egyptian occupation of Palestine in 609, 7:18-19, and the Babylonian devastation of Judah, 7:23-25. It would seem therefore that the ruin of Babylon like the ruin of Assyria was within the range of his prophetic vision. It may be noted too that the Persians, unknown to history in the days of Isaias, are not mentioned as the destroyers of Babylon but the Medes, their earlier known associates in world empire. Between the two prophecies against Babylon is a short description of the restoration, 14:1-3. A short prophecy against Assyria follows the prophecies against Babylon, 14:24-27. It is certainly Isaian and probably out of place here.

b **XIII 1-22 Destruction of Babylon**—Muster of the armies of Yahweh, **1-5.** The Day of Yahweh, **6-13.** Panic in Babylon, **14-16.** Massacre of its inhabitants, **17-19.** Babylon a desert for ever, **20-22.**
1-5. 1. The word rendered ' burden ' means most

probably pronouncement or oracle. **2.** ' dark ' : **429b** ' *bare* ' ; ' lift up ' : ' *wave* '. After ' hand ' : ' *and let them enter the gate of the princes* ', the gate of Babylon against which the army of Yahweh is mustered. **3.** ' Sanctified ' means dedicated to a divine mission. ' *I have called my warriors for my wrath, My proudly exulting ones* '. **4.** ' *Hark to the tumult on the mountains.* . . . *Hark to the uproar of kingdoms.* . . . *Yahweh of hosts musters a host for battle* '. **5.** ' to them that come ' : ' *they come* ' ; ' land ' : ' *earth* '. The judgement is first depicted as universal.

6-13. 6. ' howl ' : ' *lament* '. The day of Yahweh is c the day when he shall judge all nations. ' *With the might of the Almighty it comes* '. **8a.** The plur. verb has no subject. Read probably : ' *And all the dwellers on the earth shall be dismayed* '. **8c-d.** ' *They shall gaze at each other in dismay. Their faces shall be inflamed* '. **9.** ' cruel day *in wrath and burning anger* '. **10.** ' brightness ' : ' *constellations* '. **11.** ' *I will visit the world for its evil and the wicked for their iniquity* '. ' infidels ' : ' *the haughty* ' ; ' mighty ' : ' *rulers* '. **12.** ' the finest of gold ' : ' *the gold of Ophir* ', a land in or near South Arabia, famous for its gold. **13.** ' *Therefore shall the heavens tremble and the earth be shaken from its place* '. The firmament was supposed to rest on the extremities of the earth which was itself supported on pillars. Both heaven and earth tremble before the wrath of Yahweh.

14-16. Babylon, a world centre, will have no defence d on the day of judgement. The foreigners will flee from it but the natives will be slain. **14.** Doe and sheep should be plural. **15.** ' come to their aid ' : ' *be captured* '.

17-19. The Medes appear in western Iran in the e 9th cent. B.C. whence they raided Mesopotamia and finally with their allies destroyed the Assyrian empire towards the close of the 7th cent. They were subjugated by the Persians in 549 B.C., but received a privileged position in the empire, being free from tribute. They are depicted as less civilized than the cultured Babylonians. The text of **18a** is corrupt. ' *And youths they slay and maidens they destroy* ' is suggested.

20-22. The prophecy was fulfilled but not immedi- f ately. The city was captured without a battle and continued to be inhabited for a considerable period. **20.** ' founded ' : ' *dwelt in* ' ; ' rest ' : ' *make their flocks lie down* '. **21.** ' serpents ' : ' *owls* ' ; ' hairy ones ' : ' *satyrs* '. These were goat-like demons. A poetical reference to them does not imply their existence. **22.** ' owls ' : ' *hyenas* ' ; ' sirens ' : ' *jackals* ' ; ' temples ' : ' *palaces* '.

XIV 1-3 Messianic Interlude—The total destruction g of Babylon suggests the remnant of Israel by a literary procedure previously noted. The restoration is indicated, **1-2a,** then the Messianic age when Jerusalem is the rendezvous of the Gentiles, **2b-3.** The connexion of this passage with what precedes and what follows is too close and natural to justify its attribution to the redactor. **1.** Omit ' out of ' after ' choose '. Israel becomes again the chosen people. **2.** Read ' *peoples* ', the Medes and Persians.

4-23 Chant over the Dead King of Babylon—The h chant is called a *mashal*, byword or taunt. The king cannot be identified with any Babylonian monarch and may be considered a personification of Babylon as seems indicated 22–23. The Hebrews at this period had no conception of retribution in a future life, but expected that the justice of God would be vindicated on earth. The description of the chastisement of Babylon is not therefore a manifestation of personal or national vindictiveness, but an application of the *lex talionis* and a vindication of divine justice. The chant depicts the universal rejoicing at the death of the oppressor, **4b-8,** his reception in the underworld, **9-11,** the greatness of his fall, **12-17,** the denial of burial to his corpse and of survival to his seed, **18-21,** the absolute and final destruction of Babylon, **22-23.**

4b-8. The tense of the verbs is the prophetic perfect. i **4b.** ' tribute ' : ' *tumult* '. **5.** The plur. nouns indicate several kings or possibly refer to higher officials.

429i 6. ' an incurable wound ': '*strokes without intermission* '. **7b.** '*Men burst forth into song* '. **8a.** '*The cypresses and the cedars rejoice* '.

j 9-11. 9. '*Sheol beneath is astir . . . It arouses the shades for thee, all the chiefs of the earth. It raises up from their thrones all the kings of the nations* '. **10b.** ' wounded ': ' *stricken* '. **11b.** After ' hell ' : ' *the music of thy harps* '.

k 12-17. 12. The king is compared to the morning star, *radiant star, son of the dawn,* to depict the greatness of his fall. The comparison is based on the phenomenon of meteors. **13.** ' covenant ' : ' *assembly* ' ; ' sides ' : ' *recesses* '. The ancient belief in a mount in the extreme north where the gods assembled is referred to in depicting the pride of the king who aspired to be like God. **15.** The depths or recesses of the pit received him instead. **16.** '*They that see thee gaze upon thee and reflect upon thee* '.

l 18-21. 19. '*But thou art stretched out far from thy tomb like abominated carrion, covered up by the fallen, by those pierced by the sword (those who descend to the stones of the pit) like a trampled carcase* '. ' Those who descend to the stones of the pit ' is out of place and should be read before 20. It refers to buried monarchs from whose company this king is excluded. The death in battle without burial of Sargon II of Assyria may have suggested a similar fate for the proud King of Babylon.

m 22-23. Many commentators regard this passage as an addition of the redactor's. It seems preferable to consider it an authentic explanation and emphatic reiteration of the lesson of the chant. **23b.** '*And I will sweep it away with the besom of destruction, saith Yahweh of hosts* '.

430a 24-27 **Chastisement of Assyria**—Prophecies already pronounced against Assyria are briefly reiterated here. **25.** ' In my land ' : in Judah. There is here reference to the destruction of the army of Sennacherib. The outstretched hand recalls the refrain of 9:8-10:4. The purpose of the prophecy seems to be to include Assyria in the judgement executed on all the nations of the earth, clearly indicated in **26**.

b 28-32 **Chastisement of Philistia**—This prophecy is historically important, because it establishes the date of the accession of Ezechias, and still more religiously important, because its literal fulfilment is established beyond all doubt by the Assyrian records. The discovery of the father of Sargon II in 1933 is particularly helpful. The fact that he was not a usurper but the son of Tiglath-pileser III enables us to interpret ' Seed ' in its natural sense as ' son ' or ' descendant '. To understand the oracle we must first correct Vg and read after ' basilisk ' : '*And his fruit shall be a flying serpent* ', **29.** Philistia has suffered from an invader, compared first to a rod and then to a serpent, who has just died. She is not however to rejoice at his death because from the serpent comes a basilisk and from the basilisk a flying serpent to complete the work of destruction. The serpents come from the north, **31**, and are therefore Assyrian kings. As these must be father, son and grandson they are easily determined. Only four kings are in question : Tiglath-pileser III, his two sons, Shalmaneser V and Sargon II, and Sargon's son, Sennacherib. Of these Shalmaneser must be excluded because no son succeeded him. Tiglath-pileser invaded Philistia in 734, Sargon in 720 and 713, and Sennacherib in 701. Tiglath-pileser died in the month of Tebet, Dec.–Jan. 727–726. Ezechias therefore became king in 727 or 726. The years ascribed in 4 Kg to the kings of Judah from Ezechias to Sedecias fill exactly the period from 726 to the fall of Jerusalem in 587. The date of the prophecy may be due to the redactor, but the occasion was evidently the death of the first mentioned Assyrian monarch. Winged serpents are mentioned 27:1 and 30:6, also in the Rās-Shamra tablets. Tree serpents which pass from one date-palm to another are supposed to have originated this popular belief. All the Philistine cities suffered from the invasions though not at the same time.

c 30a-b. The total destruction suggests here as elsewhere the Messianic remnant in Judah. ' the first-born of ' : (with a slight correction) ' *on my mountain* '. **30c-d-31** depict the ruin of Philistia. ' is thrown down ' : ' *tremble* '. Render (after ' north ') ' *and there shall be no straggler in his ranks* '. **32.** The Philistines apparently proposed an alliance with Judah against the common enemy, Assyria. All such proposals were anathema to Isaias whose policy was to trust in Yahweh alone. Ezechias who had just succeeded Achaz followed the prophet's advice and abandoned the foreign alliance policy of his father.

XV 1-XVI 13 Oracle on Moab—Moab is the region **d** between the Dead Sea and the Arabian desert, divided into two parts, northern and southern, by the river Arnon. At the coming of the Israelites northern Moab was part of Sehon's kingdom and was allotted chiefly to Reuben. Southern Moab, subjugated by David, became a vassal state of Israel at the division of the monarchy. Mesha, prince of Dibon, 4 m. N. of the Arnon, organized a revolt against Israel c 853 B.C. and succeeded in wresting all northern Moab from the Israelites. He commemorated his victories by a long inscription (cf. § 80j) in which he boasts of his annexation of Israelitic cities to Dibon, his slaughter of Israelites in Nebo and dedication to his god Chemosh of their sanctuary of Yahweh. Isaias must have been acquainted with the famous inscription to which he apparently makes several references. The Moabites are the only people whom he accuses of boasting, 16:6, exemplified by the inscription of Mesha. He refers to Dibon, Mesha's capital, first as a city, 15:2, then as a capital, 15:9. He represents Yahweh as ironically assigning additions to Dibon and expresses additions by the participle of the verb which Mesha used for ' annex '.

The invasion, 15:1-4, begins with a surprise night **e** attack on the two Moabite cities south of the Arnon, Ar and Qir. Dibon, Nebo, Medaba, Hešbon, Eleale, Yahas, all in northern Moab, are next attacked. The order of mention is without exception from south to north. Yahas alone is unidentified. But it was the headquarters of the Israelites during Mesha's revolt, was captured by him after Medaba, Aṭaroth and Nebo and is associated in geographical lists with cities in the extreme north. The Assyrian invasion is similarly described, 10:28-32. Gray (in the ICC) is undoubtedly right in holding against most commentators an invasion from the south. The Edomites were Moab's southern neighbours and Amos, 2:1-3, had predicted the chastisement of Moab for having burned to ashes the bones of the king of Edom. The flight of the fugitives before the invaders is next described, 5-8. Their temporary refuge in the Jordan valley also indicates an attack from the south. The oracle, 9, ironically assigning additions to Dibon : Edom for the prisoners and Judah for the refugees, is a third proof of an Edomite invasion. Finally envoys are sent from Sela', the Edomite capital, to Sion to dissuade the king of Judah from sheltering the fugitives, 16:1-4a. The rest of the prophecy contains a Messianic interlude, 4b-5, a lament over Moab, 6-12, and a later oracle, 13-14.

XV 1-4 The Invasion—1. ' because ' : ' *yea* ' (em- **f** phatic particle) ; ' silent ' : ' *undone* '. ' Wall ' is a rendering of Qir, el-Kerak. Ar is er-Rabbe. **2a.** ' *The daughter* [inhabitants] *of Dibon hath ascended the high places to weep, On Nebo* [en-Neba] *and on Mēdaba* [Mādaba] *Moab cries aloud* '. Tearing of hair and shaving of beard are signs of mourning also indicated in **3**. ' shall howl ' : ' *cry aloud* '. The laments of Hesbān and El-'Al in the extreme norʻi are heard by their neighbour Yahas. **4b.** '*Therefore are the loins of Moab broken, Her spirit faints within her* '.

5-8 The Fugitives—'*My heart laments for Moab, her* **g** *fugitives flee to Ṣo'ar (the third Eglath). Yea on the ascent to Luhith, they wail as they ascend, Yea on the road to Horonaim they raise cries of distress. Yea the waters of Nimrim have been made desolate ; Dry is the grass, all the herbage, there is no green. Therefore have they made ready their*

g *remnant and their store, They carry them across the Torrent of the Poplars. For the cry hath encircled the boundary of Moab, To Eglaim her plaint, to the Well of the Terebinths her plaint'*. The fugitives flying northwards find a temporary refuge in the Jordan valley where a mountain barrier shields them from their pursuers. The latter however have encircled them and already devastated the Nimrim valley in the north. That is why they take their belongings over the Torrent of the Poplars in the south to reach the ford of the Jordan at el-Goraniyeh for Judah is their last resort. The difficulty of this passage is geographical. The commentators relying on the *Onomasticon* of Eusebius locate Luḥith, Soʻar and Ḥoronaim in the SW. corner of Moab. They are thus obliged to ignore all indications of an invasion from the south and assume instead an Assyrian invasion from the north. In reality however all the streams and towns are in the NW. corner of Moab where traces of the ancient names still survive. Of the eastern affluents of the Jordan Wady Nimrim = Waters of Nimrim and Wady Gharbeh or Poplar Wady (local name of the confluence of W. Hesbān and W. Kefrēn, south-eastern boundary of Israel under Jeroboam II who reconquered Galaad Am 6:14 ; cf. Bi 10 (1929) 216.

h Of the towns Luḥith is located by a Nabataean funeral inscription, ignored by the commentators, CIS Aram —196, discovered in Madaba and commemorating a Nabataean general and the captain of a Nabataean military camp at Luḥith ' in the place where they held office '. Luḥith is therefore near Madaba, probably El-Mheyyet, an ancient fort 5 m. NW. of Madaba guarding the mountain-pass from Moab to the Jordan valley. Horonaim according to Meša's inscription is the last city taken in the revolt after a descent. It is thus very probably Beth-Ḥaran, Tell er-Rame, in the Jordan valley. The local termination *aim* and the West-Semitic alteration of ā to ō explain the later form of the name. Tell-Iqtanu at the eastern end of the valley exhibits an Aramaic equivalent of Soʻar, Qatan ' small ' with a prothetic vowel and the Nabataean noun-ending *u*. Formerly many scholars located Soʻar on biblical evidence in the Jordan valley. The gloss on Soʻar, Eglath-Shalishah ' the third calf ' was apparently suggested by Eglaim, 8, interpreted as ' the two calves '.

i **9 The Oracle**—' *The waters of Dibon are full of blood. Verily I shall assign additions to Dibon : for the fugitives of Moab, Ariel, and for the remnant, Edom.* The *h* added to Edom in MT belongs to the following word and Ariel must be read with LXX instead of MT *'aryēh*. The omission of *l* by haplography left *'aryā* corrected to *'aryēh*. Ariel, lit. ' Hearth of God ', is an Isaian name of Jerusalem, ch 29. The *ar'l* ' altar-hearth ' of the Mesha inscription is probably the same word. The pre-Masoretic MS reads Dibon, MT Dimon, a later form of the same name. St Jerome attests the use of both forms in his time. A recent suggestion that Dimon may be distinguished from Dibon must be disregarded. It was not an obscure city, but Meša's capital, to which he made additions at the expense of Israel. Using the figure of speech called oxymoron Isaias ironically declares that the God of Israel will also make additions to Dibon : Judah, place of exile for the fugitives, and Edom, place of captivity for the remnant. The slain were accounted for, **9a**. What more appropriate additions could be assigned as a punishment to Dibon ? We shall find another example of oxymoron in this prophecy, 16:9.

◄ **XVI 1-4a Negotiations between Edom and Judah—1.** ' *They have sent the lamb of a ruler over the land from Sela' in the desert to the mountain of Sion* '. Sela', lit. ' rock ', is Petra, the Edomite capital. There is question therefore of an embassy and tribute sent by the king of Edom to the king of Judah. Edom was subject to Judah in the early period of Isaias but joined her enemies in the Syro-Ephraimitic war. Tribute was paid in kind. Lamb may be collective. **2.** The envoys were evidently charged with proposals

against Moab, but owing to a textual omission we have **431a** only the conclusion of their message. The dismay of the Moabites (lit. daughters of Moab) at the fords of the Arnon is best explained by a proposed occupation of southern Moab by Edom and northern Moab by Judah. **3-4.** The prophet's opposition to the Edomite proposals is emphatic. **3b-4a.** ' *Conceal the outcasts, Reveal not the fugitives, Let the outcasts of Moab find guest-right within thee* '.

4b-5 Messianic Interlude—Sion's king, consoler of **b** the distressed, suggests to Isaias the future Messias : ' *For the extortioner shall perish, the spoiler shall vanish, The oppressors shall evacuate the land, And with kindness shall a throne be established And with fidelity shall sit thereon in David's tent, A judge who pursues judgement and is swift in justice* '. Note the two pairs of attributes, both divine and Messianic, kindness (*ḥesed*) and fidelity (*'emet*), judgement (*mišpāṭ*) and justice (*sedeq*). The child of 7:15 is portrayed as a reigning monarch.

6-12 Lament for Moab—The sins of Moab are pride **c** and boasting (Meša's inscription). **6.** The last member : ' *Her boasting is unjust* '. **7-10.** Their punishment is the devastation of her famous vineyards. **7b.** ' *For the raisin-cakes of Qir Haresheth [cf. 4 Kg 3:25] shall they wail ; they are all struck down* '. **8.** ' *For the fields of Hešbon languish, the vines of Sibma, Whose choice plants prostrated the lords of the gentiles. To Jazer [Gazzir] they reached, to the desert they wandered, Their branches spread abroad, they passed over the sea* '. Sibma is unidentified but near Hešbon. Qir is the most southerly, Jazer the most northerly of the cities of Moab. The wines exported in all directions were strong enough to prostrate foreign potentates. **9c-10.** ' *For upon thy fruits and thy harvests the huzzah has fallen, And joy and gladness have gone from the garden, And there is no singing, no rejoicing in the vineyards, And there is no treading of grapes in the wine-press, And the huzzah is stilled* '. Note the oxymoron as in 15:9. The *hēdād*, rendered ' huzzah ' by S. R. Driver, is properly the joyous cry of the vintagers, stilled in 10, but the same word indicates also the battle-cry of the invaders, which stills it in 9. Cf. *S. R. Driver, Isaiah : his Life and Times* (London, 1910) 90 n. 3. **11.** ' sound ' : ' mourn ' ; ' brick wall ' : ' Qir Haresheth '. **12.** ' *wearies herself . . . and goes . . . it will not avail her* '.

13-14 Later Oracle on Moab—The new oracle, later **d** than the previous one referred to in **13**, where ' from that time ' should be rendered *formerly*, predicts the (Assyrian) conquest of Moab after three full years. The addition to the prophecy is not dated, nor can we date precisely the Assyrian conquest of Moab, certainly earlier than 713 B.C.

XVII 1-14 Oracle on Damascus (Samaria and Assyria) **e** —Only **1-3** predicts the fall of Damascus. The fall of Samaria is foretold **4-6** and **9-11**. The customary Messianic interlude is **7-8**. Finally the fall of the Assyrian oppressor is prophesied **12-14**. The date is therefore in the period of the Syro-Ephraimitic alliance c 735.

1-3 Damascus—2. As Aroer is a city of Moab, *her* **f** *cities for ever* (LXX) or *the cities of Hadad* (the tutelary god of Damascus) should be read. **3.** ' aid ' : ' the bulwark '. Damascus, defence of Ephraim against Assyria, shall share the fate of Israel.

4-6 Samaria—4. Jacob is a synonym of Israel. ' be **g** made thin ' : ' diminish '. **5-6.** ' *And it shall be as when the reaper gathers the cornstalks and his arm reaps the ears, as when one gathers ears in the Vale of Rephaim [SW. of Jerusalem], and only gleanings are left therein, as when one beats an olive tree and two or three berries (remain) on the top of a bough* '. The meaning is that survivors will be few.

7-8 Messianic Interlude — ' groves and temples ' : **h** ' wooden poles and stone pillars '. The poles were set up to Ashera, the pillars to Baal ; cf. RB 55 (1948) 151 f. **9-11. 9** (corrected after LXX) : ' *In that day thy strong* **i** *cities shall be abandoned as those of the Hevites and the Amorites were abandoned before the children of Israel, and there shall be a wilderness* '. The extirpation of the

431i Canaanites by the Hebrew invaders of Palestine is indicated. **10.** The sin of Israel is abandonment of Yahweh and Gentile contamination, ' *therefore thou plantest pleasant plots and sowest strange shoots* '. **11.** ' *In the day of thy planting thou fencest* (thy plot) *and every morning thou nursest* (thy vines) *but the harvest vanishes in a day of destruction* [MT inheritance] *and pain incurable* '.

j **12-14 Assyria**—The spoiler of Israel and Damascus will be himself despoiled. **12.** ' *Ah, the uproar of many peoples, they roar like the roaring of the sea. And the booming of mighty nations, they boom like the booming of waters* '. The Assyrian empire included many nations. **13.** Omit the first member, a repetition of 12a. ' whirlwind ' : ' *whirling things* '. **14a.** ' *At eventide behold destruction, before morning he is no more* '. The reference is probably to Sennacherib's army.

k **XVIII 1-7 Oracle on Kush**—Kush extends indefinitely southward from the Egyptian boundary at Aswan. Its capital was Napata, its rivers the Blue Nile, the White Nile and the Atbara. As insects swarm about these rivers Isaias calls it the land of the buzzing of wings. The Kushites, long subject to Egypt, established there a Kushite dynasty c 720 B.C. which ruled until the Assyrian conquest. The Kushite king Shabaka, c 716–701, proposed to Ezechias a revolt from Assyria. Isaias, opposed to foreign alliances, calls on the envoys to go forth and announce to their people that the hour of deliverance was not yet, but would be indicated when Yahweh's Assyrian harvest was ripe.

l **1.** ' beyond ' : ' *beside* '. The land lay on both sides ('*ēber* = side) of its rivers. **2.** Sea may indicate either the Nile or the Mediterranean. On the papyrus boats cf. Ex 2:3. (After ' waters ') : ' *Go forth, swift messengers, to a nation of long bodies and gleaming faces, a nation to be feared henceforward, a nation of trampling* [?] *and treading, whose land rivers divide* '. The Kushites were tall, especially as compared to Egyptians, and their dark faces gleamed like polished bronze. Their recent conquest of Egypt is recognized and assures them courteous treatment. ' Go forth ' is more forcible and dignified than ' return '. **3.** They and all are informed that the fall of Assyria will be clearly indicated by signal and trumpet, **4-5**, but not before she is ripe for the harvest of Yahweh. **4b.** He is not only ' *like glowing heat in sunshine and dew cloud in harvest heat* ', which ripen the grapes, but, **5**, is the pruner and tender of his vineyard who ' *before the harvest, when growth is ended and the berry becomes the ripening grape, will cut off the tendrils with pruning-knives and remove and lop off the branches* '. **6.** The Assyrian corpses will be the food of birds of prey in summer and wild beasts in winter. **7.** The Kushites will then send a thank-offering to Yahweh in Jerusalem. Sargon II was aware of simmerings of revolt in Philistia, Judah, Moab and Ammon, incited by Shabaka. He assailed the chief offender, Philistia, in 713 B.C. and captured Ashdod in 711. If Judah actually revolted, contrary to the advice of Isaias, she was saved from chastisement by prompt submission.

432a **XIX 1-24 Oracle on Egypt**—This prophecy first announces the ruin of Egypt, its subjection to a hard ruler and the causes of its downfall, **1-15**, then the gradual conversion of the Egyptians in Messianic times, **16-24**. In the lifetime of Isaias Egypt emerged from a long period of decadence and eager to recover her old influence in Palestine posed as the champion of the smaller states in their resistance to Assyria. Egyptian intrigue at Samaria led to a revolt which ended in the destruction of the Northern Kingdom in 721 B.C. The Kushite envoys of ch 18 sought to foment a similar revolt in Judah. It is natural to connect the present prophecy with this project. Far from releasing Judah from the yoke of Assyria, Egypt would share her fate. The prophecy may be dated 713 B.C.

b **1-4 Conquest of Egypt**—Yahweh is the author of the disaster, provoked by internal discord and lack of counsel, and subjects Egypt to a cruel master, the Assyrian king, Esarhaddon. **1.** ' ascend ' : ' *ride* ' ;

' be moved ' : ' *tremble* '. **2.** Egypt frequently suffered **4** from weakness of central authority and consequent revolts and quarrels of local chiefs. **3.** ' cast down ' : ' confuse ' ; ' wizards ' : ' *spirits of the dead* ', evoked by necromancy. **4.** ' *master* '.

5-10 Bondage of Egypt—The drying up of the Nile, **c** source of all Egypt's prosperity, is not intended literally but symbolically to indicate devastation. Such a phenomenon would affect the fishing, flax and corn industries and produce universal misery. **6-7a.** ' *The streams shall become foul and Egypt's Nile-arms shall diminish and dry up ; The reeds and rushes shall decay, the papyrus beside the Nile shall droop* '. The exact sense of 7a is uncertain. **9b.** ' *The combers and the weavers shall grow pale* '. The combers are women, the weavers men. Egypt was famous for its fine linen. **10.** ' *And her nobles* [lit. foundations] *shall be crushed, and all workers for hire shall be depressed* '.

11-15 Folly of Egypt—The wisdom literature of the **d** Egyptians was known to the Hebrews, and the maxims of Amen-em-ope have left their imprint on the book of Proverbs to which additions were made during the lifetime of Isaias, Prov 25:1 ; cf. § 316e–f. The prophet denies them practical wisdom. **11.** ' wise ' : ' *wisest* ' ; ' will ' : ' *do* '. Tanis in the north and Memphis in the south of the Delta region were ancient capitals of Egypt. **13b.** (After ' Egypt ') ' *the chiefs of her tribes* '. **14.** ' giddiness ' : ' *deceit* '. It is Yahweh who has caused the Egyptians to fail in counsel. **15.** All their efforts shall be vain. On 15b cf. 9:14.

16-24 Conversion of Egypt—*In that day*, repeated five times, means in the Messianic age. Five reappears in the five cities, 18, and must be a round number ; cf. 1 Kg 17:40 ; 21:3. The conversion recalls that of the Gentile nations, Ps 86, who become citizens of Sion by a spiritual rebirth. Egypt becomes a land of Yahweh, another Judah, 24.

16-17. The fear of Yahweh and of Judah where he **f** manifests himself is the beginning of the conversion. Then comes the adoption of the sacred language and revealed religion of Judah in several cities, one of which is particularly holy, like Jerusalem, and called symbolically *the city of justice*. This name, attested by LXX, is critically the most probable. City of the sun (Heliopolis) has little support in the MSS, and city of destruction (MT) is inappropriate. **18.** Egypt has an altar like Judah on which sacrifices are offered to Yahweh and also a memorial stone at its boundary to indicate that it is the land of Yahweh. **22.** It is treated like Judah, smitten for the healing of its sins and, 20, relieved from oppression when it repents. **23.** The reconciliation of Egypt and Assyria depicts the peace of the Messianic age. **23c.** ' *And Egypt shall serve* (*Yahweh*) *with Assyria* '. **24.** The fulfilment of the promise made to Abraham that the Gentiles will be blessed in his seed is indicated when Egypt, *my people*, Assyria, *the work of my hand*, and Israel, *my inheritance*, are equally blessed.

The authenticity of **16-24** is usually denied. But the **g** medium, prose, and the theme, conversion of the Gentiles, are both Isaian. The only indication of date is the reference to Hebrew, the language of Canaan, which must be prior to the adoption of Aramaic as the spoken language and the translation of the Pentateuch into Greek. There can be no allusion therefore to Leontopolis and its temple.

XX 1-6 Oracle on Egypt and Kush—From the **h** Assyrian records we learn that Sargon II invaded Philistia in 713 B.C. to chastise the citizens of Ashdod for having deposed Mitinti whom he had made their king and enthroned a certain Yamani in his stead. Yamani fled to Egypt but was handed over to Sargon by Shabaka. Gath, Ashdudimmu and Ashdod were taken and sacked. Ashdod however only fell in 711 B.C. From Isaias here we learn moreover that the siege of Ashdod was not prosecuted by Sargon himself, whose stay in Philistia was brief, but by his Tartan or second in command. The order to represent symbolically the subjection of Egypt and Kush to Assyria was given to

ISAIAS XXII

Isaias when the Tartan *arrived at* (DV ' entered into ') Ashdod and the three years, estimated in Hebrew fashion, probably coincided with the duration of the siege 713-711. The symbolic action of Isaias impressed more deeply on his people the folly of reliance on Egypt and Kush, doomed themselves to subjection.

2. 'Naked' means without an outer garment. Hair-cloth was usually worn next the skin for mourning. The longer garment cast off must be distinguished from the shorter loincloth retained or subsequently assumed. **3b.** (After ' barefoot ') *'for three years, a sign and a portent concerning Egypt and Kush '.* **4.** ' captivity ' : *' exiles '.* 'The shame of Egypt' is probably a gloss. **6.** ' isle ' : *' coastland ',* as Philistia is indicated.

XXI 1-10 Oracle on Babylon — The mention of Babylon, 9, shows that the fall of that city is here predicted as in chh 13-14. The capture of Babylon, capital of Merodach-Baladan, by Sargon II in 710 B.C., is excluded because the Assyrians were then the enemies, the Elamites the allies of the Babylonians. Here the assailants are Medes and Elamites or Persians, since Cyrus the Great occupied Elam before the fall of Babylon. It is moreover the fall of Babylon in 539 B.C. which, 2, *made all mourning cease.* The compassionate prophet was deeply moved by the terrible calamity ; *cf.* 15:5 ; 16:9-11. The title : Oracle of the desert of the sea (or, of the deserts) is probably derived from the subsequent mention of the desert, from which the invaders came. The calamity is compared to whirl-winds from the desert region south of Judah.

2. God speaks : *' The robber robs and the spoiler spoils ; Invade, Elam, besiege, Media, I have made all mourning to cease '.* **3-4.** (After ' labour ') *' I am prostrated by what I hear, dismayed by what I see. My heart is bemused, shuddering hath seized me. The twilight which was my refreshment he* [God] *hath made a terror to me '.* The evening twilight is meant. **5.** *' They lay the table, spread the carpets, eat and drink. Up ye princes, oil your shields '.* The capture of Babylon during a banquet is recorded Dan 5:30 ; Herodotus 1, 190 ; Xenophon, *Cyropaedia* 7, 5, 15, but not in the Babylonian inscriptions. Banqueters reclined on carpets. Shields were oiled to preserve them from moisture and offer less hold to missiles. **6.** The prophet is ordered to appoint a watchman who, 7, *' when he sees riders in pairs, one on an ass* [the Persians] *and one on a camel '* [the Medes] will pay particular attention. **8.** The watchman expresses his constant vigilance by day and by night. Lion is most probably a corruption of watchman, *'aryēh* for *hārō'eh.* **9.** *' And behold there came riders, pairs of riders ',* the destroyers of Babylon and her idols. The watchman is a dramatic personification of the prophetic vision, an indication perhaps that the prophecy will not immediately be fulfilled. After the prophet dies the watchman remains to see and announce the fulfilment. The prophecy ends with a reference to Babylonian oppression of Israel. **10.** *' My trampled one, my threshing-floor son '.* The threshing of the corn by hooves and sledges is referred to.

11-12 Oracle on Edom—In the title Dumah is prob-ably corrupt. Seir is a mountain range in Edom. The subject of ' calleth ' is indeterminate, a caller. The inquiry is : how far has the night gone ? Is the calamity from which Edom suffers nearly over ? The answer apparently is : the calamity will soon end, but other nights or calamities are still to come. The watcher has no more definite announcement to make and so adds : *' If you want to ask, ask ; come again '.*

13-17 Oracle on Arabia—The oracle is on Kedar, a desert people east of Moab and Edom. Arabia in the title is derived from *"rābāh* ' steppe ' in 13. **13-14.** *' Caravans of the Dedanites who camp in the grove in the steppe, Bring water to meet the thirsty. Dwellers in the land of Teima, Meet the fugitives with bread '.* Dedan (el-'Ela) and Tema were oases in the north Arabian desert. *Grove* (DV ' forest ') may indicate an oasis with its palms. **15.** The fugitives are the more northerly Kedarites who flee *' from the desolate places, from the whetted sword, from the bent bow, from the pressure of battle '.*

17. *' And the bow-men shall be a small remnant. The warriors of Kedar shall be few '.*

XXII 1-14 Oracle on the Valley of Vision—The title, Valley of Vision (*cf.* 21:1 and 13) is taken from 5. The introduction, **1-2a**, gives the occasion of the prophecy, the rejoicing of the citizens on the housetops on the receipt of good tidings, an alliance with Egypt in 713 or less probably the retreat of Sennacherib in 701. Isaias cannot rejoice for he foresees the deportation of the civil and military leaders of Jerusalem and the ruin of the city, **2b-4**. The invasion on the day of Yahweh is depicted, **5-8a**, then the preparations of the citizens on that day to resist the invaders, all useless owing to their abandonment of Yahweh their protector, are described, **8b-11**. Lastly their refusal to obey Yahweh calling them on that day to repentance, their senseless rejoicings and their final impenitence are deplored, **12-14**. ' On that day ', 8b and 12, clearly refers to the day of Yahweh, 5. Thus the whole prophecy (except the short introduction) refers to the future and predicts the conquest of Judah and Jerusalem by the Chaldaeans in 587 B.C. The citizens should not rejoice but mourn since the fall of Jerusalem is only postponed. Penance and trust in Yahweh is their only hope.

1-4. The citizens assemble on the housetops not for mourning but for rejoicing. **2.** ' populous ' : ' boister-ous '. **3.** *' All thy chiefs are fled together, taken captive without bow, All thy strong ones* [LXX] *are taken captive together, they are fled afar off '.* Flee here means depart and being predicated of captives implies deportation ; *cf.* 3:1 ; 6:12. There was no pitched battle with the Babylonians and Jerusalem was taken after a long siege. **5-8a. 5.** *' For a day of tumult and trampling and turmoil has the Lord Yahweh of hosts. In the valley of vision crashing of walls and on the mountain battle-cry '.* Mountain and valley indicate all parts of the city. **6.** *' And Elam takes the quiver, puts* ['āsar for 'ādām] *horses to the chariots, And Qir uncovers the shield '.* Qir is the ancient home of the Aramaeans in south-eastern Mesopotamia. The Elam-ites were allied, the Aramaeans subject to Babylonia, and both were represented in her armies. **7.** The enemies are in the valleys and at the gates of the cities. **8a.** Judah is *unveiled* or without defence.

8b-11. The preparations of the citizens for the day of doom are described : provision of weapons in the armoury, the house of the Forest of Lebanon built by Solomon, **8b**, strengthening of the city walls, **9a and 10**, and assurance of water-supply, **9b and 11a**. These preparations, contrasted with the only efficacious defence of reliance on Yahweh, **11b**, belong to the past, but in the day of doom their uselessness appears. The Old Pool, **11a**, is the Upper Pool, mentioned 7:3 ; 4 Kg 18:17, which received immediately the waters of Gihon. Two canals at different levels conveyed its waters along the east side of the city to the gardens in the east and south. Achaz turned the waters of the upper canal into the city by a tunnel. The Lower Pool resulting is the modern Birket el-Ḥamra. It was between two ramparts, most probably the earlier wall, enclosing the SE. hill, and the later wall of the SW. hill. Ezechias made the Upper Pool and outer canals inaccessible to besiegers and constructed a subterranean canal which conveyed the waters of Gihon into the city. The issue of this canal was more northerly and at a higher level than the reservoir of Achaz. There is apparently no reference here to the canal of Ezechias not yet completed, since the basin at its mouth could not be called the Lower Pool. Thus the two references to the water supply 9b and 11a, originally united, describe two parts of a single operation : the convey-ance of the waters of Siloe, 8:6, by an underground aqueduct into the city and the construction of a basin to receive them in the central valley. It may be assumed that these precautions taken in view of foreign invasion were relatively recent. The presence of King Achaz at the southern end of the Siloe canal, 7:3, may thus be explained by the fact that he was planning or inspecting the operation described above.

12-14. The refusal of the citizens of Jerusalem to obey

433j God's call to penance before the judgement overtakes them will be assuredly punished. The warning is doubtless intended also for the revellers on the house tops.

434a **15-25 Oracle on Sobna, Prefect of the Palace**—Deposition and exile of Sobna, **15-19.** Exaltation of Eliacim, **20-23.** Eliacim's descendants, **24-25.** Sobna and Eliacim are mentioned elsewhere only in the narrative of Sennacherib's invasion. Sobna was then the scribe or secretary, Eliacim the Prefect of the Palace. It is not certain that the Sobna seal discovered at Lakish belonged to this Sobna.

b **15-19. 15-18.** Read 16*b*, where Sobna is described, before 16*a*, where he is addressed : '*Go, get thee unto that minister Sobna, the prefect of the palace, who is hewing himself out a sepulchre on high and carving in the rock an abode for himself. What hast thou here and whom hast thou that thou hewest thyself here a tomb? Behold Yahweh will cast thee violently* [lit. with the cast of a strong man], *wrapping thee well and winding thee well around like a ball, into a wide land. There shalt thou die and thither shall thy splendid vehicles be borne, thou shame of thy master's house*'. **19.** The sentence of deposition follows. Sobna will be cast into exile as a stone is cast from a sling.

c **20-23.** Eliacim receives the office of Sobna. **21.** 'strengthen' : '*gird*'; 'power': '*office*'; omit 'as'. The key is the symbol of office. Being of wood and much bigger than our keys it was borne on the shoulder ; *cf.* note on Jg 3:23. **23.** The peg is either a tent-peg, on which the stability of the tent depends, or a peg or nail in a wall, on which vessels are hung. The epilogue, 24-25, supposes the latter sense, also recommended by the fact that Isaias considers length of office, not importance of services.

d **24-25. 24.** '*And should they hang upon it all the glory of his father's house, the offspring and the offshoot, all the small vessels from the wash-basins even to the pitchers, it shall fail to support on that day*'. This is a prediction that while Eliacim's house, his proximate descendants, will inherit his glory, the smaller vessels or remote descendants will not, for Jerusalem shall fall and its citizens be exiled in the day of Yahweh.

e **XXIII 1-18 Oracle on Tyre**—The oracle contains a poem on the fall of Tyre, **1-14,** and a prose addition on its recovery and conversion, **15-18.** The authenticity of the addition is generally denied. The seventy years' interval between the fall and the recovery is supposed to be derived from the similar period assigned to the Jewish exile by Jeremias. Tyre, though less ancient than Sidon, was the richest and most important of the Phoenician trading cities. It was built partly on the mainland and partly on an island and sustained many sieges before the island city was finally captured by Alexander the Great in 333 B.C. Phoenicia lost its long monopoly of trade in the Mediterranean. The text requires emendation, but not the substitution of Sidon for Tyre with some commentators. The mentions of Sidon are shown by the context and the sequence of thought to be references to the mother city representing Phoenicia in general. The date of the prophecy is uncertain.

f **1-5 General Consternation at the News of Tyre's Fall** —**1.** '*Lament, ye ships of Tarshish, for your haven is destroyed. As they came from the land of Kittim the news was revealed to them*'. Tarshish is Tartessus in Spain, Kittim Citium in Cyprus, both Phoenician colonies. The fall of Tyre deprives the big ships of the haven to which they are returning. *Your haven* is restored from the repetition of this verse in 14. **2-3.** '*Stupefied are the inhabitants of the coastland, the Sidonian merchant who crosses the sea, whose messengers are on mighty waters, whose harvest is the grain of Shihor and whose revenue is the grain of nations*'. '*Have filled thee*' is a corruption of *messengers* and '*the river*' is a gloss on Shihor (waters of Hor), a branch of the Nile. Note the parallelism of Sidonian merchant and inhabitants of the coastland (Phoenicians). **4.** '*Be ashamed, Phoenicia* [lit. Sidon] *for the sea hath said : " Thou hast not travailed nor brought forth nor reared up youths nor brought up maidens "*'. Sidon is the

mother city of Phoenicia, become childless. 'Haven of the sea' inserted after 'sea' in MT is most probably a gloss. **5.** '*The Egyptians shall writhe when they hear of Tyre's fall*'.

6-10 The Fall of Tyre : Yahweh its Author—**6.** 'the seas' : '*to Tarshish*'; 'howl' : '*lament*'; 'island' : '*coastland*'. **7.** '*Is this your joyous city whose origin is of long ago, whose feet have carried her to sojourn afar off?*' Tyre's antiquity and colonies are commemorated. **8-9.** Yahweh has humbled her pride. **10.** '*Pass over to thy land (like the Nile), daughter of Tarshish, thou hast no haven* [MT, girdle] *more*'. 'Like the Nile' is unintelligible. The ship without a haven returns to where it sailed from.

11-14 All Phoenicia is Threatened—Phoenicia was called Canaan by the Phoenicians themselves. **12.** '*Rejoice no more, oppressed virgin, daughter of Sidon*'. Here again Sidon alternates with Canaan. Sidon sailing to Cethim may refer to Lulu, prince of Sidon, fleeing to Cyprus from Sennacherib in 701. **13.** '*Behold the land of the Chaldaeans—that is the people not Assyria—which he founded for the wild beasts. They have erected his siege-towers, razed its palaces. He has made it a ruin*'. The rendering is literal, the sense disputed. There is probably a gloss after Chaldaeans and the ruined city is the Chaldaean capital, destroyed by Sargon II in 710. So shall Phoenicia be destroyed.

15-18. Tyre is here compared to a harlot who recovers her trade after a period of interruption. Trade is not condemned. The sanctification of her gains supposes her conversion to Yahweh. **16.** 'many a song' : '*loudly*'. **17.** (After 'Tyre') '*and she shall return to her hire*'. **18.** 'and be clothed *splendidly*'.

XXIV-XXVII The 'Apocalypse' of Isaias—The unity of these chapters, generally admitted, has been contested by some critics who also regard them as post-exilic. The subject-matter is eschatological : judgement of the nations of the earth and establishment of the Messianic kingdom. The poems contain lyrics, regarded by some as interpolations. Only two lyrics are universally recognized : 25:1-5 and 26:1-6. The latter appears appropriately as the conclusion of the first poem, 24:1-26:6. The former, on the contrary, interrupts the description of the city on the mountain. As it addresses Yahweh in the second person it may originally have introduced the supplication to Yahweh with which the second poem, 26:7-27:13, begins. Condamin proposed this transposition here adopted. The prophecies are distinctly Isaian in character. References to peoples and events are, perhaps designedly, obscure and give no indication of date. The chief reason for denying Isaian authorship is the *a priori* assumption that all references to the judgement and conversion of the Gentile nations in pre-exilic prophets are later additions.

XXIV 1-XXVI 6 Judgement of the Nations and Establishment of the Messianic Kingdom—The prophecy may be divided as follows : Devastation of the earth and punishment of its inhabitants, 24:1-6. Banishment of joy from the earth, 7-13. Salvation of the just and destruction of the wicked, 14-18*a*. Shaking and breaking up of the earth, 18*b*-20. Judgement of the host of heaven and the kings of earth, 21-23. Joy of the nations in the kingdom of Yahweh on Mt Sion, 25:6-8. Yahweh helps his people and humbles Moab, 9-12. Confidence in Yahweh who humbles the proud, 26:1-6.

XXIV 1-6. 1. The earth will be devastated, the works of man destroyed, its surface upset and its inhabitants scattered. Eschatological descriptions are not to be taken too literally. **2.** The opposition of priest and people appears also Os 4:9 and is not post-exilic. **3.** The announcement is prophetic. **4.** '*The earth mourns, decays, the world languishes, decays, both heaven and earth languish*'. **5.** 'changed the ordinance' : '*violated the precept*'. The everlasting covenant is the covenant made with Noe, Gen 9:10 ff., and his descendants which binds all nations. Hence the reference to a new deluge by the opening of the flood-gates of heaven, 18.

c A covenant is a bi-lateral contract imposing obligations not always explicitly indicated. The shedding of blood brought a curse on the earth, Gen 4:11, and was particularly forbidden by this covenant, Gen 9:5. **6.** ' sin ' : ' *pay the penalty* ' ; ' mad ' : ' *consumed* '.

d **7-13.** The general misery is indicated by the lack of wine and of the singing and music of revellers. **7.** ' vintage ' : ' *must* ', new and strong wine. Alter future to present in **9** and **11**. **10.** ' city of vanity ' : ' *city of desolation* '. Cities in general are deserted. The citizens have perished in the day of judgement. Only a remnant is left as on the olive tree after the gathering and on the vine after the vintage. **12b.** ' *and the gates are smitten into ruins* '.

e **14-18a.** The joy of the saved is first depicted, 14–16a, then the fate of the wicked, 16b–18a. **14b-15.** ' *They shall exult in the majesty of Yahweh. Therefore exult in the west, praise Yahweh in the east, praise Yahweh, God of Israel, in the islands of the sea* '. **16b.** ' *And I said : Wasting to me, wasting to me, woe is me. The spoilers spoil, with spoiling the spoilers spoil* '. The repetitions are emphatic. Isaias regards the sins of the world as a personal affliction. ' Secret ' (Vg) supposes an Aramaic text. **17-18a.** Punishment is inevitable.

f **18b-20.** The earth, man's abode, perishes under the weight of his sins. The waters from above pour down on it as at the deluge. The supports on which it is raised above the waters shake. The earth itself shakes and breaks, staggers like a drunken man and finally collapses. Since this catastrophe precedes the establishment of the Messianic kingdom for all the nations on Mt Sion it cannot be understood literally. The judgement is the prophetic message, the description is ideal and poetical. **20.** (After ' man ') ' *it shall rock to and fro like a (frail) hut* '.

g **21-23.** The heavenly bodies, sun, moon and stars, are involved in the chastisement of their worshippers and must disappear for a time, after which they will be again visited and apparently reinstated. With them are associated here as elsewhere the kings of the earth who usurped God's prerogatives and even claimed divine honours. The sun and moon are put to shame by the glory and majesty of the divine king. The personification of the heavenly bodies does not imply that they were regarded as living beings. **22.** ' one bundle ' : ' *prisoners* '. **23.** The ancients are the subordinate authorities.

For 25:1–5 see after 26:1–6.

h **XXV 6-8.** The Messianic kingdom is depicted as a rich banquet for all nations united together on Mt Sion, as a kingdom of peace and happiness free from bloodshed and oppression. **6b-c.** ' *A banquet of rich viands, a banquet of choice wines—Of rich viands full of marrow, of choice wines well refined* '. **7b.** ' *the veil that veils all nations and the screen that screens all peoples* '. All now form one united nation. **8.** The removal of death means most probably the common Messianic blessing of cessation of wars and bloodshed, usually coupled with freedom from oppression.

i **9-12.** The reference to Moab has caused surprise. Some commentators read instead '*ōyēḇ* ' enemy ', others reject the whole passage as a later addition. In reality however the reference is clearly suggested by ' the reproach of his people ', 8. Moab had conquered and appropriated Israelitic territory. Its capital is, for Isaias, Meša's capital, alluded to in **10** by the word *maḏmēnāh* ' dung-heap ', whose radical letters *dmn* suggest Dimon, the alternative form of Dibon, 15:9. The removal of the reproach of his people from all the land requires the chastisement of Moab and the destruction of Dibon. **10b.** ' *And Moab shall be crushed in its place as straw is crushed in the cesspool* ' (lit. waters of dungheap). **11.** Moab's efforts to escape by swimming in the cesspool (DV ' under him ') shall be vain for Yahweh ' *shall lay low his pride despite the cunning of his hands* '. **12.** ' *And the secure fortress [Dibon], its [MT ' thy '] walls he [Yahweh] shall raze, lay low, hurl to the ground, even to the dust* '.

j **XXVI 1-6.** The strength of Sion, the justice and fidelity of its citizens and their trust in Yahweh are celebrated, **1-3.** This trust is secure and eternal, **4-6. 1b.** ' *A strong city have we, for protection hath he set* [or, have been set] *walls and rampart* '. **2.** ' the truth ' : ' *faith* '. **3-4.** ' *Our steadfast purpose thou wilt preserve in peace because we trust in thee. Trust in Yahweh for ever because Yahweh is a rock for ever* '. **5.** ' high city ' : ' *secure city* '.

k **XXV 1-5** and **XXVI 7-XXVII 13 Israel and the Messianic Kingdom**—The preceding prophecy predicted the judgement of the Gentiles and the incorporation of their remnants in the Messianic kingdom, the present is concerned exclusively with Israel and its destiny. The designs of Yahweh are explained and vindicated. The punishment of the proud and mighty is the necessary preparation for the reign of justice on earth, **25:1-5** and **26:7-13.** The people are few and grievously oppressed but let them be patient for a little while and Yahweh will restore their numbers and destroy their oppressors, **26:14-27:1.** Israel is the vineyard of Yahweh. His chastisement of his people is for their good and the expiation of their sins, but their oppressors will be chastised without mercy, **27:2-11.** Israel will recover her ancient territory and worship Yahweh on his holy mountain, **27:12-13.**

l **XXV 1-5.** ' *The designs from afar, faithful and true* ' indicate the general theme, vindication of God's plans. From afar means from of old. **2.** ' to ruin *the citadel of the proud* ', reading *zēḏîm* for *zārîm* ' strangers '. **4c.** ' *For the breath of the mighty is like a winter* [MT ' wall '] *storm* '. **5.** ' *Like heat on a desert land thou shalt subdue the clamour of the proud, like heat in the shade of a cloud the paean of the mighty shall be checked* '.

m **XXVI 7-13.** The just man ardently desires the manifestation of God's justice and its establishment on earth. Injustice must be punished that justice may prevail and that Yahweh alone may rule his people. **7.** ' right ': ' straight ' ; ' is right to walk in ' : ' *straight is the path which thou openest to the just* '. Straight means unimpeded. The general principle of retribution is stated. **9.** ' In the morning ' (Vg) may be correct against ' within me ' (MT) but the tenses are present. **10.** ' *When the wicked is spared he learns not righteousness. In the land he perverts the right and regards not the majesty of Yahweh* '. LXX renders b : ' *Let the wicked be removed from the face of the earth and see not the majesty of Yahweh.* **11.** ' *Yahweh, thy hand is exalted, but they see not. Let them see and be confounded at thy zeal for thy people. Let the fire for thy enemies devour them* '. **12-13.** The final appeal is based on the mutual love of Yahweh and his people.

436a **XXVI 14-XXVII 1.** The prophet laments that the people are few and oppressed, 26:14-18. Yahweh replies that their number will increase and their oppressors will soon be judged, 26:19-27:1. **14.** The dead are clearly those of 19 and therefore Israelites. ' *The dead shall not live, the shades* [inhabitants of Sheol] *shall not rise* '. The sense of ' therefore ' is that they may not rise again. **15.** It follows that the verb ' multiply ' (' *Multiply the people Yahweh, multiply the people, show thyself great, extend the boundaries of the land* ') is a petition, not a statement, and *lû* must be supplied before the verb to give the perfect this sense. **16** (slightly corrected) : ' *Yahweh, with trouble were they visited. Distress and oppression were thy chastisement for them.* **17-18.** The pangs they suffered were those of a fruitless childbirth. **18b.** ' *We do not work salvation on earth and the inhabitants of the earth do not perish* '—a lament for the delay of the judgement on the nations. **19.** ' *Thy dead shall live, my corpse shall arise, They shall awake and exult that dwell in the dust, For thy dew is a dew of light And the land of shades thou overthrowest* '. This, understood literally of a corporal resurrection, would contradict the remnant doctrine according to which the survivors alone inherit the Messianic kingdom. It indicates therefore a national resurrection and the expression, *my corpse*, meaning my dead nation, is intelligible. **20-21.** Patience is enjoined for the judgement which will soon be manifested. **XXVII:1.** Leviathan, the flying serpent, and Leviathan, the tortuous serpent, appear together as mythical monsters in a Rās-Shamra tablet ; cf. Bi 19 (1938) 444 f.

436b They are revealed in 12 as Assyria and Babylonia, and the sea dragon as Egypt.

c XXVII 2-11. Israel will be the fruitful, not the unfruitful, 5:1-7, vineyard of Yahweh, **2-6**. Her chastisement, tempered by mercy, was for the expiation of her sins, **7-9. 2.** '*In that day (shall be) a delightful vineyard, sing to it*'. MT has '*of wine*' instead of *delightful* (LXX). **3.** '*suddenly*' : '*constantly*'. **4.** '*I am not wroth with it. But what am I to do with briars and thorns? I must march against it in combat, I must burn them together*'. **5.** '*Or let it cling to my protection, make peace with me, make peace with me*'. **6a.** '*In days to come Jacob shall take root*'. The world's salvation is from Israel. **7.** '*Has he* [Yahweh] *smitten him* [Israel] *like the smiting of his* [Israel's] *smiter? Or has he* [Israel] *been slaughtered like the slaughter of his* [Israel's] *slaughterers?*' Israel was chastised less severely than her oppressors. **d 8.** The chastisement may be specified as the exile. Text and meaning of *a* are uncertain, but '*the violent wind on a day of scirocco*' in *b*, as a figure of Yahweh's action, supports this view. **9.** This chastisement will expiate the sins of Israel ; the instruments of her iniquity : altar stones, incense altars and Ashera posts will be destroyed. **10-11.** The severer chastisement of the Gentiles, cities and people, is described. 'City' here means every city as in 24:10, 12. Read after 'desolate' '*an abode forsaken and abandoned like a desert*'. **11a.** '*When the branches dry they are broken off : women come and set fire to them*'. The threat of 11*b* cannot refer to Israel.

e 12-13 The Restoration of Israel—The ideal boundaries of Israel, in the north the Euphrates, and in the south the torrent of Egypt, Wady el-'Arish, will be realized in the Messianic period. **12.** 'strike' : '*beat out*' (the ears of corn), a reference to the most ancient method of threshing. All Israel is the harvest. The inclusion of the exiles, lost in Assyria and dispersed in Egypt, in the congregation may be a later addition. The great trumpet calling to judgement, Jl 2:1 ; Soph 1:16 ; Mt 24:31 ; 1 Cor 15:52 ; 1 Thess 4:16, is not mentioned elsewhere by Isaias.

437a XXVIII-XXXV Further Prophecies against Judah and Jerusalem.
XXVIII 1-29 Warning to Jerusalem from Samaria's Fall—Imminent Fall of Samaria, **1-4**. Yahweh Defender of Jerusalem, **5-8**. Mockery of the prophet's message and substitution for promise of salvation of threat of destruction, **9-13**. Futility of human measures of defence without reliance on Yahweh, destroyer of the wicked but saviour of the just, **14-22**. The plan of Yahweh illustrated from husbandry, **23-29**. The prophecy is a unity and is dated by the mockery of the rulers in the reign of Achaz between the Assyrian annexation of Galilee and Galaad, 733, and the accession of Ezechias, 726. Revelry in Samaria would be prior to the siege, 724-721.

b 1-4. Samaria was built on a hill in the middle of a wide valley. *The crown of pride* refers to the strong natural position of the city and *the splendid adornment* to its military defenders, weakened by the loss of Sharon, Galilee and Galaad, and thus likened to a *fading flower*. **1c.** (After 'joy') '*which crowned the hilltop of the rich valley of the wine guzzlers*'. **2a.** '*The strong and mighty one sent by Yahweh*' is the Assyrian who, **2c**, '*casts down to earth with violence*', **3**, tramples on the crown of pride of the drunken Ephraimites, **4**, and seizes the fading flower of its splendid adornment as one seizes and devours an early fig. The early figs appear before the leaves, only on some trees, and are particularly delicious.

c 5-8. 5-6. '*On that day* [when Samaria falls] *Yahweh of hosts will be the crown of splendour and the strength of adornment to the remnant of his people* [the inhabitants of Judah] *and a spirit of justice for him who sits in judgement* [Ezechias] *and strength for those who repel attacks at the gates*'. Yahweh here promises through his prophet to take the place in Judah of the natural and military defences which failed to save Samaria. The definite time indication and the attacks at the gates show clearly that the pas-

sage is not Messianic. *Remnant*, 5, is also definitely indicated by *these also*, 7, as the inhabitants of Judah, not the Messianic remnant. **7a.** '*But these also reel with wine and stagger with strong drink*', like the Ephraimites. **7d.** '*They err in vision, they falter in judgement*'. **8.** Absorbed in the pleasures of the table they see not in Samaria's fall the lesson of reliance on Yahweh.

9-13. 9. Mockers deride the prophet and his message. They deny his claim to revelation and liken him to a stammering child only just weaned. **10.** They mimic his words repeating four times ṣaw, ' command ', and qaw, ' measuring-line ' or ' rule ', and adding twice *a little one is there* to suggest that the monosyllabic sounds are the stammering utterances of a child. ṣaw and qaw probably summarize the prophet's teaching in infantile speech. **11.** Isaias replies : ' *Verily with stammering lips and in foreign tongue will he* [Yahweh] *address this people*'. Foreign invasion is implied. **12.** His message to them was : ' *rest, give rest to the weary and refreshment and they would not hear*'. **13.** He will now speak to them like an infant for their destruction.

14-22. 14. The deriders are *the rulers*, Achaz and his court. **15a.** They say : ' *We have made a covenant with Death, We have made vision with the Underworld*'. The words covenant and vision are suggested by the prophet's appeal to Yahweh's covenant and his own visions. They consulted not Yahweh but the Underworld by necromancy, a common practice against which Isaias specially warned his disciples, 8:19. The *scourge* is Assyrian invasion. Refuge in lies and shelter in falsehood characterized Achaz's policy, 7:12. **16.** The *corner-stone*, the *foundation-stone*, set by God in Sion is undoubtedly Emmanuel. The demand for faith : ' *He that believeth shall not be anxious*' recalls 7:9 just as, **17a**, ' *judgement and justice*' re-echo 7:15. ' *And I have made judgement my measuring-line and justice my plummet*'. **17b-19.** Defence measures of the deriders are futile. **19c.** ' *And it will be sheer terror to understand revelation*'. **20.** Too short a bed and too narrow a coverlet are popular indications of defective measures. **21.** The anger of Yahweh, directed against the Philistines in David's time, 2 Kg 5:20-25 ; 1 Par 14:8-17, will now overwhelm his own people. Mountain of divisions here replacing Baal of divisions, Baal-Perasim, is Râs an-Nādir, NW. of Jerusalem.

23-29. Yahweh is here compared to a husbandman in his dealings with his people. **24.** He ploughs and harrows—temporary operations which prepare the ground for sowing. **25.** He sows *fennel* (DV ' gith ') and cummin and wheat and barley ; but puts *spelt* (DV ' vetches ') on the borders of the wheat and barley as less valuable. Omit ' millet '. **26.** ' *For he instructs him rightly, his God teaches him*'. **27.** He has different ways of threshing : the flail, used with fennel and cummin, **28**, the oxen and the threshing-sledge, used with wheat and barley, but not in such a way as to crush the seed but to separate it from straw and chaff. **29.** His knowledge comes from Yahweh of Hosts ' *wonderful in counsel and great in wisdom*'. As the husbandman has the harvest always in view and acts accordingly, so Yahweh has his Messianic harvest in view, not his people's destruction, in the process of purification by chastisement.

XXIX 1-24 Ariel Besieged, Blinded and Blessed—Isaias first predicts the siege of Jerusalem by Sennacherib and its marvellous deliverance, **1-8**, then depicts the blindness of the people, the insincerity of their worship and the perversity of their designs, **9-16**, and finally describes the new dispensation in the Messianic age, **17-24**. The prophecy must be dated before Sennacherib's invasion, 701, very probably in 702 ; *cf.* 1*b*.
1-8 Siege and Deliverance of Jerusalem—1. ' *Alas, Ariel, Ariel, city where David encamped! Add year to year, let the feasts go round*'. Ariel undoubtedly means Jerusalem. The interpretation, hearth of God, not lion of God, is practically certain. It designates the altar of holocausts in Ez 43:15 f. and here, **2b**, where

the city is compared to an Ariel on which the victims of the siege are immolated. The circle of annual feasts defines the added year as a single year. **2a.** ' Then will I distress Ariel and there shall be sorrow and sorrowing '. **3.** The siege is described : ' Yea I shall encamp against thee in a circle and hem thee in with siege-works and erect walls against thee '. **4.** Ariel will be so humbled that her voice will resemble that of a shade called up by a necromancer from Sheol. The weak voice indicates extreme distress not destruction or death. **5.** It is her enemies who perish. ' them that fan thee ' : ' them that distress thee ' ; ' ashes ' : ' chaff ' ; after ' multitude ' render ' of savage assailants '. They perish in an instant. **6a.** ' By Yahweh of hosts thou shalt be visited with thunder ', etc. Visit may imply chastisement or deliverance. **7.** Here it is deliverance for the terrible besiegers vanish like a dream. The dream clause b should follow c : ' and all her assailants and siege-works [sic] and oppressors '. **8.** The multitude of the Gentiles indicates the various nations in the Assyrian army.

9-16. The prophet now reproaches his hearers for their unbelief and threatens them with the chastisement of increased blindness and insensibility. **9a.** ' Stupefy yourselves that you may be stupefied, Blind yourselves and be blinded '. **10.** ' For Yahweh hath poured out on you insensibility. He hath closed your eyes and veiled your heads '. **11-12.** All vision becomes a sealed book when its meaning is hidden. **13-14.** The punishment of lip-worship without heart-worship will be the withdrawal of wisdom and understanding from the men of counsel on whom public welfare depends. Our Lord applies 13 to the Jews of his time, Mt 15:7-9. Ezechias had revived and imposed the ritual laws, but it was through human respect, as man's command, rather than with sincerity of heart, as God's command, that the people observed them. **15-16.** Finally these unwise counsellors plan in secret and imagine that Yahweh does not know. They forget their dependence on him. The reference is apparently to the intrigues with Egypt and the revolt from Assyria which provoked Sennacherib's invasion. **16.** ' How perverse you are! Is the potter to be estimated as the clay? Does the work say of its maker : He has not made me? Does the pot say of the potter : He does not understand ? '

17-24. The great change in the Messianic age is depicted. **17.** The alteration of forest to fruitful valley (DV ' charmel ') and vice versa is a figure of this change. **18-21.** Lofty are depressed, lowly exalted ; deaf hear, blind see ; wicked are cut off, poor and lowly rejoice. **20a.** ' For the tyrant shall cease to be, the scoffer shall disappear '. **21.** ' They that made a man fail in a suit, that laid a snare for the arbiter at the gate, that turned aside the just unredressed '. **22-24.** Israel will be happy and holy. ' be ashamed ' : ' grow pale '. There shall be no ignorance or sin. ' the law ' : ' knowledge '.

XXX 1-33 Oracle on the Egyptian Alliance—The secret plotting of the diplomats of Jerusalem was denounced in the preceding prophecy, 29:15. Here the plot is revealed as an alliance with Egypt in process of formation. In the following prophecy, 31:1-9, it is an accomplished fact. The three prophecies belong to the same year, 702. The alliance is sinful and futile, **1-7.** Judah's disregard of Yahweh's prophetic warnings will be punished by ultimate ruin, **8-17.** Yahweh will finally establish his people in holiness and prosperity, **18-26,** and chastise the Assyrian oppressor, **27-33.**
1-7. 1. The rebellious children make a plan and form an alliance not sanctioned by Yahweh who has prohibited foreign alliances. **2a.** ' They are on their way down to Egypt without consulting Yahweh '. ' My mouth ' probably means ' my prophet ', Ex 4:16. **2b.** ' to seek refuge in the refuge of Pharaoh and shelter ', and, **3,** all to their own shame and confusion. **4.** ' His [Judah's or Ezechias'] princes have been in Tanis and his messengers are approaching Hanes '. Tanis was the first port of call of the ambassadors, where Taharka was probably in command. They continue southwards to Herakleo-

polis south of Faiyum to meet the Pharaoh, Shabaka. **438b** **5.** ' all shall be '. **6.** The difficulties of the ambassadors' journey through the desert, separating Judah from Egypt, and the costly presents are all in vain. Omit ' the burden of the beasts of Negeb ', an interpolation ; cf. 21:1, 13 ; 22:1. ' in ' : ' through '. **7b.** ' Therefore do I call her the sitting dragon '. Egypt, covered by the Nile, is the inactive sea-dragon, Rahab.

8-17. 8. The prophet is now ordered to write it c (Egypt the sitting dragon ; cf. 8:1 Mahershallal-hashbaz) on a tablet in their presence and record it documentarily as a perpetual attestation. **9-10.** The attestation is needed for the people are rebellious and deceitful preferring false to true revelations. **11.** They bid their prophets : ' Turn aside from the (right) way, decline from the (right) path, remove from our sight the Holy One of Israel '. **12-14.** The punishment of rejecting Yahweh's word and trusting in what is perverse and false will be sudden and complete ruin. The breach swelling out in the wall expresses the suddenness, the broken vessel the completeness. **15.** Conversion to Yahweh and submission to Assyria are essential. **16.** ' And you say : No, but on horses shall we fly—Therefore shall you flee—On swift steeds shall we ride—Therefore shall your pursuers be swift '. Their courage will fail without Yahweh's aid. **17.** ' for fear ' : ' before the attack ' ; insert after ' five ' ' a myriad '. ' mast of a ship ' : ' post '.

18-26. 18. Deliverance is delayed because Yahweh d is a judge who must punish sinners. ' be exalted sparing you ' : ' tarry to show you mercy '. **19a.** ' Because, O people who shall dwell in Sion, you shall weep no more '. Omit ' Jerusalem '. **20.** ' Should the Lord give you bread of affliction and water of distress, no more would your teachers [the prophets] be thrust aside but your eyes would look to your teachers '. The converted remnant will have unlimited trust in their prophets. **21.** The sense is similar. **22.** Idols shall be cast aside even though plated over with silver or covered with gold. **23.** Rich harvests, abundant pasturage, will be assured. The early rain in October–November and the late rain in March–April were uncertain but most necessary for good harvests. **24.** ' mingled provender ', etc. : ' salted fodder '. **25.** Water will be abundant everywhere ' in the day of the great slaughter when the towers fall ', the day of judgement. **26.** Light will abound.

27-33. 27-28. The theophany or manifestation of e Yahweh come to judge the nations is first described. Name is manifestation. The thunder is his voice, the lightning his fiery wrath. The torrent to which his breath is compared reaches to the neck. He comes ' to shake the nations with a sifting of emptiness and put a bridle of error in the jaws of the peoples '. Sifting and bridle are for chastisement, not for purification and guidance. **29.** The Israelites will sing as on the festive night and rejoice as pilgrims ascending to Mt Sion to the sound of the flute. The festive night is most probably that of the Pasch on which sacred songs, later the Hallel, were sung. **30-33** depict the chastisement f of the Assyrian oppressor. **30.** ' terror ' : ' descent ' ; ' the threatening ' : ' a frenzy '. After ' fire ' read ' tempest and rain-storm and hail-stones '. **31.** ' being ' : ' he shall be '. **32.** ' And every stroke [lit. passing] of the rod of punishment [MT ' appointed rod '] with which Yahweh strikes him shall be to the sound of timbrels and harps and in battles of waving will he combat him '. Waving may refer to the sifting of 27 or to the ritual waving of a sacrificial victim. **33.** Assur will finally be consumed by fire. ' For long since is his burning-place made ready, that too is prepared for a king, Deep and wide is its pit, fire and wood abound, the breath of Yahweh like a torrent of brimstone enkindles it '. Topheth, burning place, was the site in the valley of Hinnom (Gehenna), where human sacrifices were offered to Moloch. That place is not directly indicated here but king (melek) alludes to Moloch to whom Achaz sacrificed a son, 4 Kg 16:3. This passage may have contributed to the later use of Gehenna for hell-fire.

XXXI 1-9 Second Oracle on the Egyptian Alliance— g

559

438g This oracle denounces alliance with Egypt and abandonment of Yahweh, **1-3**, who nevertheless will save Jerusalem from the Assyrians, **4-5**. Let Israel be converted for on that day idols shall be put to shame and Assyria shall fall, **6-9**. Reinforcements of horses and chariots were the chief object of the alliance.

h **1.** 'trusted in': 'looked to'. **2a.** 'Yet he too is wise and has brought calamity and not withdrawn his word'. God's wisdom requires that sin be punished. **3.** Egypt and Judah will perish together. 'put down': 'stretch out'. **4-5.** Though Judah is doomed the time is not yet and Yahweh will protect his holy city from the approaching invasion of the Assyrians. Like a lion defending his prey from a multitude of shepherds (the Assyrian hosts), like birds protecting their young, he will save Jerusalem from Sennacherib. 'upon' (after 'whelp') : 'over' ; 'their multitude': 'their shouting'. **6.** The call to repentance is motivated by the promised protection. 'as' : 'to him from whom'. **7.** That day is the day of judgement, similarly described elsewhere as the day when the worthlessness of idols is manifested. It might be referred also to the day of the destruction of Sennacherib's host, a day of judgement for Assyria. **8.** The negative particle after 'flee' is not original. The sense is that whoever escapes the sword will be put to forced labour. The sword is the sword of God, the real author of Assyria's fall. **9.** 'Strength' is lit. 'rock'. The fire and furnace most probably refer to the altar of holocausts, Ariel. There is some obscurity in the prediction, probably due to compenetration. Isaias depicts together two distinct future events, the destruction of Sennacherib's host and the final downfall of Assyria.

i **XXXII 1-8 Justice and Folly**—These verses hardly belong to the preceding or the following prophecy. They seem to embody moral considerations, the contrast between justice and folly. The mention of a king implies a pre-exilic date.

j **1-5 Portrait of Justice**—The whole passage has been interpreted as a conditional sentence : protasis 1-4, apodosis 5. But the construction is grammatically doubtful and more practical consequences than a correct estimation of folly and deceit might perhaps be expected from a reign of justice elaborately depicted. The tenses are present. The princes are the subordinate rulers. **2a.** 'And each (prince) is a refuge from the wind and a shelter from the rainstorm'. A great rock alone affords shade in the desert. **3-4.** The subjects are neither blind nor deaf nor unintelligent. **5.** Folly and deceit are no longer thought noble and honourable.

k **6-8 Portrait of Folly**—**6.** The fool not only speaks folly but 'devises iniquity to practise impiety and speak error about Yahweh'. MT has 'does' for 'devises' against the pre-Masoretic MS and the Vss. He fails to relieve his neighbour's hunger and thirst. **7.** The knaveries (DV 'vessels') of the deceitful are false accusations of the meek and false testimonies against the poor. **8.** 'The noble devises what is noble and by his nobility prospers'.

439a **9-20 Oracle on Sennacherib's Invasion, the Ruin of Judah and the Messianic Kingdom**—The prophecy may be dated in 702 B.C. Lament for the ruin of Judah, **9-14**. Prediction of ultimate salvation, **15-20**.

b **9-14. 9.** 'rich': 'at ease'. **10.** 'Days on a year' apparently means after a year and some days. 'For the harvest time has passed but no harvest is gathered'. **11-14a.** Let the women discard their raiment, put on sack-cloth and beat their breasts over the devastation of the land and the abandonment of pleasant homes and joyous cities. **14b.** 'For fortified hill and watch-tower are become like caves for ever'. Ophel (fortified hill) is generic, not the acropolis of Sion. It indicates the acropolis of Samaria, 4 Kg 5:24, of a Moabite city (Meša inscription). Sennacherib captured many cities of Judah but not Jerusalem. For ever is modified by until in 15.

c **15-20. 15.** It is God who introduces the Messianic age and the new dispensation ; cf. 29:17. **16.** Everywhere shall be judgement and justice, **17-18**, peace and security for ever. 'beauty' : 'abode' ; 'wealthy' : 'untroubled'. **19a.** 'When the forest shall fall headlong'. The reference may be to all the Gentile nations or to Assyria in particular often compared to a forest. **20.** Israel will be blessed with the rich harvests of the Messianic age. On the abundance of water cf. 30:23. The ox and the ass are the harvest workers of 30:24.

XXXIII 1-24 Prayer for and Promise of Messianic Salvation—A prayer for deliverance from oppression, **1-9**. Coming of Yahweh to judge the nations and purify his people, **10-16**. The Messianic kingdom, **17-24**. There is no indication of date unless the covenant is a pact made with an earthly monarch, variously identified with Sennacherib, Artaxerxes Ochus, Antiochus Eupator. It is practically certain however that the covenant of Sinai is meant and that Yahweh who does not save his afflicted people is regarded as not fulfilling his promises. He is similarly regarded as violating his promise to David, Ps 89:40. It is easier to supply Yahweh than an earthly monarch as the omitted subject of the verbs in 8, where moreover he regards not man suggests God as subject. The language and concepts of the prophecy are Isaianic. The devastation of Judah, 8, implies that the prophet contemplates a future period of Israel's history.

1-9. 1. The people are oppressed. 'Woe to thee, destroyer, not yet destroyed, spoiler whom they have not yet despoiled'. **2.** They pray for deliverance, recording Yahweh's ancient benefits to his people. **3-4.** 'At the noise of a tumult the peoples fled, at thy rising up the nations were scattered. And they [Israel] gathered spoil as locusts gather, as locusts leap they leaped upon it'. **5-6** depict Sion in the ideal reign of David, full of judgement and justice. The Messianic kingdom will be a revival of David's. **7-9.** The present distress is contrasted with the ancient security. **7.** The parallelism suggests Salem (Jerusalem) for šalōm (peace). 'Behold the men of Ariel cry without, the messengers of Salem weep bitterly'. **8.** Israel is exiled and oppressed because Yahweh 'has annulled the covenant, has rejected the testimony, regards not man'. **9.** The devastation is not particularized. Only famous places, Lebanon, Sharon, Bashan, Carmel are mentioned. 'shaken' : 'made bare'.

10-16. The prayer receives a dramatic answer. Yahweh comes to judge the world and separate the dross from the precious metal by fire ; cf. 1 Cor 3:13. The judgement of the Gentiles is first announced, **11-13**. **11.** 'You conceive chaff, you shall bring forth stubble'. Read my breath. **12.** 'ashes after a fire' : 'burnt like lime'. **13.** All nations will hear of Yahweh's judgement and recognize his omnipotence. **14-16.** The chosen people also will be judged. **14.** The fire is the fire of judgement, not of hell or purgatory, consuming the wicked but sparing the just. 'of you' : 'of us'. **16.** 'highness' : 'stronghold'.

17-24. The New Sion, its beauteous king and its extensive territory suggest reflections on the past, **17-19**. **17.** 'his eyes' : 'thy eyes'. **18.** 'meditate fear' : 'muse on the terror'. 'Where is the reckoner ? Where is the weigher ? Where is the counter of towers ?' The reference is to the tribute paid by weight to the oppressors, 19, the fierce people of deep unintelligible speech, of stammering senseless tongue. **20.** Sion is like a tent whose ropes and pegs are ever secure. 'solemnity' : 'assembly' ; 'rich' : 'secure' ; 'nails' : 'pegs'. **21a.** 'Nay there Yahweh will be to us a boundary, rivers of wide streams'. Yahweh protects Sion like wide rivers surrounding it through which no warships shall pass. **22.** 'lawgiver' : 'chieftain'. **23.** 'If thy ropes be loosened, they shall not fix a flag-staff nor spread a pennant'. The ropes are tent-ropes, the flag-staff and pennant signals calling for assistance. No attack is to be feared. The blind (conjecturally inserted) and lame considered a sufficient garrison for Jebusite Jerusalem are probably alluded to. **24.** Finally 'no inhabitant shall say : I am sick, and all iniquity is forgiven'. Sickness is regarded as the punishment of sin.

XXXIV 1-XXXV 10 Final Judgement and Final Salvation—The unity of this prophecy is admitted but its

Isaian authorship is usually denied. Ch 34 closely resembles ch 13. Marked hostility to Edom is usually post-exilic. The authorship is a wider problem ; *cf.* § 421*a*. Judgement of the nations, **34:1-4**, of the Edomites, **5-8**, Edom a desert for ever, **9-17**. In Israel salvation, **35:1-4**, healing of evils, **5-7**, return of exiles, **8-10**.

XXXIV 1-4. 1-2. The wrath of Yahweh in the coming judgement is announced to all the nations of the earth. ' killed ' : ' *doomed* ' lit. banned. **3.** The bodies of the slain remain unburied and the mountains stream with their blood. **4.** The heavens are rolled up, like pages of a book-roll, and their hosts, objects of idolatrous worship, *fade away*.

5-8. 5. ' *When* my sword '. Edom is ' *the nation doomed by me for judgement* '. **6.** ' *Yahweh's sword shall be filled with blood, made rich with fat, with the blood of lambs and he-goats, with the fat of the kidneys of rams, for there is a sacrifice to Yahweh in Bosra and a great slaughter in the land of Edom* '. In all sacrifices the blood and fat of the victims were sacred to Yahweh. Their mention here implies the figure of a sacrifice subsequently expressed and located. Bosra, el-Buṣēre, was an important city of Edom. **7.** *The wild oxen* (DV ' unicorns ') and *the bullocks with the bulls* are the nobles. **8.** The day of vengeance and year of retribution indicate the time at which Yahweh will avenge Sion and punish Edom. ' of the judgement ' : ' *of the cause* '.

9-17. Edom shall become a burning-place ; *cf.* 30:33. **9b.** ' *And the land shall become a fire burning night and day* '. This is during the actual devastation. Subsequently Edom shall be barren and uninhabited, the home of wild beasts and fabulous monsters like Babylon, 13:21-22. **11.** The bittern and ericin may be the *pelican* and the *porcupine*. The ibis is the *owl*. ' *And (Yahweh) will stretch over it the measuring-line of desolation and the plummet of devastation* '. **12.** ' *Of kingship they shall speak no more and all her princes shall disappear* '. ' Nobles ' is probably a gloss on princes. **13.** *Palaces* shall grow thorns, fortresses thistles and nettles. ' dragons ' : ' *jackals* '. **14.** ' demons and monsters ' : ' *wild-cats* [?] *and hyenas* ' ; ' lamia ': ' *lilith* ', a female night-phantom of popular belief. **15a.** ' *There shall the arrowsnake make her nest and lay and hatch and brood her eggs*. **16.** ' *Search in the book of Yahweh and read* '. The book probably represents God's decrees.

XXXV 1-4. 1. ' *Let the wilderness and the steppe rejoice, and the desert exult and bloom* '. The verbs are jussives. Join ' like the crocus ' (DV ' lily ') to 2. This early flower marks the end of winter. Israel shall have a luxuriant vegetation like Lebanon, Carmel and Sharon. *They*, **2c**, are the inhabitants of the land, bidden, **3-4**, to take courage for God's vengeance on their enemies and their salvation is at hand. ' *Your God comes as an avenger, God is a recompenser* '.

5-7. Corporal evils : blindness, deafness, dumbness, lameness will be healed in the Messianic age, **5-6**. These verses foretell the healing miracles of Christ, Mt 11:5 ; Mk 7:37 ; Lk 7:22. **6.** ' be free ' : ' *sing* '. **7b** (slightly corrupt) : ' *In the place where jackals lay down will be an enclosure for reeds and sedges* '. The desert will be irrigated.

8-10. The holy way, more exactly sanctuary way, will be *there*, namely in Palestine. It leads to the sanctuary, is free from the intrusion of wild beasts and is found by the least intelligent. Only the pure will travel by it. **8c.** ' *My people shall travel by it and* (*even*) *the simple shall not go astray* '. This *via sacra* in Palestine has no connexion with the way from Babylonia to Palestine. **10** is repeated literally 51:11. Here undoubtedly it completes the picture of the New Sion by describing the return of the exiles.

Appendix to Chh 1-35

XXXVIII 9-20 Canticle of Ezechias—Chh 36-39 have been commented in 4 Kg to which they originally belong. The Canticle of Ezechias however is only found in Isaias. It is called a *miktāḫ* or writing, gener-

ally corrected to *miḵtām*, a psalm title of uncertain **440a** meaning. It commemorates the miraculous healing of Ezechias from a fatal malady in 713 B.C., describing his sentiments before, **10-14**, and after, **15-20**, the prediction of recovery.

10-14. 10. ' *I said : In the noontide* [lit. quiet] *of my* **b** *days I must go, To the gates of Sheol I have been assigned, For the rest of my days* '. Ezechias was then thirty-nine years old. **11.** To see God means to visit his temple. ' rest ' : ' *the world* '. **12a.** ' *My abode is plucked up and taken from me like a shepherd's tent* ', when the shepherd moves elsewhere to find pasturage. **12b-c.** ' *I have rolled up my life like a weaver, He is cutting it off from the thrum, From day to night he delivers me to pain* ' (or, ' he makes an end of me '). Man rolls the web of his life but God cuts off the piece of cloth when life ends. *From day to night* means all day long if pain, in the course of a day if death is meant. **13a.** ' hoped ' : ' *cry out* '. **14a.** ' *I twitter like a swallow, I moan like a dove* '.

15-20. 15. ' *What shall I say ? For he has told me* [the **c** prediction] *and he has accomplished it* [the recovery]. *I shall go through all my years after* [or, notwithstanding] *the bitterness of my soul* '. **16.** ' *Those whom God guards live, And* (*to everyone*) *among them is the life of my spirit, Thou hast healed me and kept me alive* '. The verse is intelligible if ' to everyone ' be omitted. **17.** ' *He has changed* [*mar*] *for me bitterness* [*mār*] *to wellbeing* '. ' that it should not perish ' : ' *from the pit of corruption* '. The dead could not then praise God by public and solemn cult or expect temporal benefits from him. **18-19.** The tenses are present. ' truth ' : ' *fidelity* '. Look for thy truth means expect promised benefits. **20a.** ' *Yahweh will save us* '.

XL-LV Consolation for the Exiles in Babylon. 441a **XL 1-31 The Hour of Deliverance is Near**—This chapter is an introduction to Isaias II, chh 40-55. The scene is changed. Instead of the inhabitants of Judah (8th cent. B.C.) the Jewish exiles in Babylonia (6th cent. B.C.) are addressed. The tacit references to Cyrus imply that he has already begun his victorious career but has not yet defeated Croesus of Lydia, 547, or captured Sardis, 546. Proximate deliverance is foretold, **1-11**, and Yahweh, the deliverer, is celebrated, **12-31**.

1-11. Let the prophet and his adherents console **b** (DV ' be comforted ') the people of Yahweh with the announcement of speedy deliverance. **2.** ' evil ' : ' *servitude* ' (MT lit. military service). *Double* is a poetic hyperbole suggested by compassion and implying severe but not unmerited or vicarious punishment. **3-5.** A herald proclaims the new Exodus, accompanied like the Egyptian Exodus by a manifestation of the glory of Yahweh. A straight and level way must be prepared according to the ancient custom of building a road to welcome a king or conqueror. ' In the desert ' should follow ' prepare ye '. All four Evangelists understand the herald typically as John the Baptist. Literally an angel seems indicated. **3.** ' the paths of ' : ' *a highway for* '. **5.** ' that ' : ' *for* '. **6-8.** A second herald orders the further proclamation that all flesh passes away like grass but the word of Yahweh endures for ever. The spirit or breath of Yahweh is the hot east wind which withers the grass, his word is the promise of deliverance. **9-11.** Finally Sion and Jerusalem personified announce from a mountain top to the cities of Judah the return of Yahweh with the exiles. **9.** Sion and Jerusalem are vocatives. **10.** The exiles are the *recompense* (DV ' work '). The shepherd simile shows God's loving care. He carries the lambs, he *gently leads* the suckling ewes.

12-31. 12. Yahweh is magnificently delineated as **c** supremely competent to fulfil his promise. He is the all-powerful and all-wise creator of all things without assistant or adviser. Weighing with the hand and estimating the earth *at a shalish* (third of an ephah) emphasizes the comparative littleness of creatures. **13.** ' forwarded ' : ' *regulated* '. **15-17.** He is the lord of nations and peoples, mere drops of water, particles

441c of dust, grains of corn before him. The islands are the lands in and around the Mediterranean. All the trees and beasts of Lebanon would not suffice for a burnt-offering worthy of Yahweh. **18-20.** He is exalted immeasurably above all other gods, particularly idols. The description of their fabrication emphasizes their impotence. **19.** The craftsman first casts the idol out of base metal. The goldsmith then overlays it with goldleaf or silver plating. Two misplaced verses, **41:6-7**, are usually inserted here. **41:7.** ' *The craftsman encourages the goldsmith, The tapper with the hammer (encourages) the striker of blows, saying of the welding : It is good. And he fixes it firmly with nails* '. **20** describes the poor man's wooden image, made of sound wood by a skilled carpenter. **21.** Yahweh's exaltation is known to all by revelation from the beginning (from the time of Abraham) and through his creatures *from the foundation of the earth*. **22.** The globe of the earth is the firmament. ' nothing ' : ' *fine cloth* ' or ' *veil* '. **23.** Princes and rulers he sets up and deposes at will. ' searchers of secrets ' : ' *princes* '. **24a.** ' *Scarce were they planted* ', etc. **24b.** The tenses are all past. **25-26.** Yahweh is exalted incomparably over the heavenly bodies, worshipped by man. (After ' see ') : ' *Who hath created these ? He brings forth their host* '. **27-31** set forth the conclusion. Yahweh's chosen people must believe in his providence and trust in his Power and Wisdom. However discouraged they may be, if they hope in Yahweh they shall renew their strength. **27c.** ' *my cause is overlooked by my God* '. **30.** ' shall ' : ' *may* ' ; ' fall by infirmity ' : ' *totter* '.

d XLI 1-29 + XLII 8-12 Yahweh arraigns the Gentiles and their Gods—The first of the Servant poems, 42:1-4, is not a part of this prophecy. The close connexion in thought between 41:27-29 and 42:8-9 shows that the intervening verses interrupt the context. Their contents, commented in § 441i–k, have nothing in common with this prophecy. The argument takes the form of a legal process in which Yahweh arraigns the gentile nations, **41:1-20**, and their gods, **41:21-29 + 42:8-9**. The matter in dispute is : Who has raised up the world conqueror, the still unnamed Cyrus, Yahweh's instrument in the destruction of Babylon and the restoration of Israel, and who has foretold his coming and his exploits ? The answer is : Yahweh alone. The process ends with a paean of victory in which the Gentiles praise and glorify Yahweh, **42:10-12**.

e 1-5. 1. The islands (Mediterranean peoples) and the nations (here apparently eastern peoples) are called to judgement by Yahweh. ' *Hearken to me in silence, ye islands, Wait upon my plea, ye peoples. Let them* [the pleaders] *approach and then speak, Let us come together to judgement* '. **2-5** announce the matter in dispute. The mention of the isles (Mediterranean coast lands) implies that Cyrus' conquest of Lydia has begun. The fear of these lands in particular and the vast military conquests recorded exclude the view of a few commentators that Abraham not Cyrus is referred to. **2.** ' *Who hath raised up from the east one whose steps straightness meets ? Hath delivered up nations before him and subdued kings ? His* [Cyrus'] *sword makes (them) as dust, his bow as driven stubble* '. *ṣedeq* is straightness ; *cf.* Ps 22 (23) 3 where paths of *ṣedeq* = straight paths. The answer to the query is given in **4.** Yahweh is the author of world history from the beginning and likewise to the end. **5.** The nations and especially the ' islands ' (Croesus of Lydia) fear the conqueror. ' They drew near and came ' is a gloss.

f 8-20. 8-10. Israel, Yahweh's servant, his chosen people, the seed of his friend, Abraham, must not fear like the Gentiles. Her salvation is at hand. ' Servant ' is practically equivalent to ' chosen '. **9.** Omit ' in whom '. **10b.** ' *I strengthen thee, yea I help thee, yea I support thee with my righteous* [or, *victorious*] *right hand* '. **11-14.** Through his instrument, Cyrus, Yahweh chastises and extirpates Israel's enemies especially the Babylonians. The tenses of fight, strive, **11**, resist and war, **12**, are past. **14a.** ' *Thou worm Jacob, thou maggot Israel, I am thy helper* '. The epithets worm and maggot

indicate Israel's helplessness without Yahweh's aid. **4 15-16.** Israel will crush her enemies like a threshing sledge and scatter them like a winnowing fan. This is usually interpreted as a conditional prophecy of the future military might of Israel, not fulfilled because she rejected the Messias. It may however indicate the victories of Cyrus, attributed to Israel as the exploits of Yahweh. **17-20.** The new Exodus follows the military exploits. **18.** ' high hills ' : ' *bare heights* ' ; ' plains ' : ' *valleys* ' ; ' impassable ' : ' *arid* ' ; ' streams ' : ' *springs* ' ; **19**, ' thorn ' : ' *acacia* '. The description of the Exodus is based on the Egyptian prototype.

21-29 + XLII 8-9. The gods are now arraigned and **g** their ignorance and impotence are demonstrated. **21-24. 21b.** ' *bring hither your proofs* '. **22.** The gods are challenged to show their previous knowledge of the former things (which Yahweh previously foretold) and of the future things (which Yahweh now foretells). **23.** Such knowledge, even activity for good or evil, would be some defence of their cause. **24.** But they are nothing and do nothing and to choose them as gods is an abomination. **25.** The call and the victories of Cyrus are then foretold. He comes from the north as well as from the east because his empire was north and east of Babylonia. Instead of ' he calls my name ' (MT) we should probably read *I call his name* as in the parallel passage, 45:3. Cyrus was not a monotheist. **26.** Who foretold the victories of Cyrus ? ' thou art just ' : ' *he is right* '. No idol foretold them. **27.** ' *I first announced it to Sion, gave a bearer of good tidings to Jerusalem* '. **28-29.** The false gods cannot advise or answer questions and thus show their falsity. **XLII:8-9.** To me Yahweh belongs the glory of having predicted former things which came to pass and of now predicting new things before they happen. The new things are the mission of Cyrus to destroy Babylon and restore Israel. The former things include very probably earlier and less definite predictions of the conquest of Babylon : Is 13:17 ff. ; 21:2 ff. ; Jer 51:11 ff. or possibly lost oracles.

XLII 10-12. The Gentiles celebrate the victory of **h** Yahweh over the false gods. The prophet anticipates the accomplishment of the new predictions by which Yahweh's sole divinity is manifested to them. **10.** Omit ' that go down to the '. **11b.** ' *Ye tent-dwellers that inhabit Cedar* '. The futures, **11-12**, are imperatives. Cedar and Edom in the east declare God's glory to the islands in the west.

XLII 1-4 The Servant of Yahweh and his Mission— **i** The Servant here introduced is the future Messias, represented not as king and conqueror but as worker and sufferer. Yahweh who upholds him has chosen him, endowed him with his spirit and appointed him instructor of the Gentiles. His mission will be characterized by meekness and sympathy, fidelity and constancy, and will be crowned with success.

1. ' *Behold ! My Servant whom I uphold, My chosen one* **j** *in whom I delight ! I have endowed him with my spirit, He shall announce judgement to the nations* '. ' *Behold* ' may be addressed to the prophet, to Israel or to the Angels. ' Servant ' is an honorary title like ' chosen '. ' Uphold ' implies attachment and support. On the bestowal of the spirit *cf.* 11:2. Judgement is moral and religious discernment, knowledge of right and wrong, a Messianic attribute ; *cf.* 7:15. The voice from heaven heard at Christ's baptism and transfiguration (Mt 3:17 ; 17:5 and parallels) alludes to this verse. **2-4.** ' *He shall not cry nor make any clamour, Nor let his* **k** *voice be heard in the street ; The bruised reed he shall not break And the dim wick he shall not extinguish. Faithfully shall he announce judgement, Not burning dimly nor himself being bruised, Until he have established judgement on earth ; And for his instruction the far coasts wait eagerly* '. The procedure of the Servant in his mission is contrasted with that of a military conqueror like Cyrus. His strength of character is contrasted with the weakness of those whom he instructs and uplifts. The parallelism between judgement and instruction confirms the Messianic sense of the former word. The far coasts (DV islands) are the lands in and around the Mediterranean. Mt 12:17–21 cites this prophecy as fulfilled.

5-7 seem to be a later insertion, not an explanatory afterthought of the original author. **5.** The praise of Yahweh could be intended to emphasize the divine origin of the Servant's mission. Such praises however are often inserted in prophetic discourses without regard to the context. **6.** As Light of the nations means enlightener of the Gentiles, so Covenant of the people means mediator of a covenant between God and Israel. Thus the Servant's mission to Israel, reserved for the second Song, is here unnaturally anticipated. **7.** The darkness could be spiritual, referring to the Gentiles, or material, referring to the Jews in exile. The reference to the exiles, more usually understood, would imply a political mission.

The first section of Isaias 40–55, ended with a canticle of praise, 42:10–12. The second has a similar termination, 44:23. This section describes Yahweh's Zeal, impeded by Israel's Blindness, 42:13-25, Yahweh, Israel's Helper and Redeemer, 43:1-15, Yahweh's gifts to Israel, unmerited and unexhausted, 43:14-44:5, Yahweh the Only God, Vanity of Idols, 44:6-23. **XLII 13-25 Yahweh's Zeal impeded by Israel's Blindness**—Yahweh's designs are benevolent. **13-17 Yahweh's Zeal**—**13.** Yahweh is a mighty warrior, eager for the fray. **14.** Like a woman in travail, forced by her pain to cry out, he can no longer restrain his battle cry. For the MT 'from of old' (DV 'always') read ' at their wickedness'. Render the last member : *I will gasp and pant together*. His breath is the fire of his wrath. **15.** The land of his enemies will be devastated. ' islands ' : ' *arid land* '. **16.** Ways in the desert and light in the darkness insinuate a new Exodus from Babylonia. ' *These are the things which I shall accomplish and which I shall not neglect* '. **17.** Idolaters shall turn back and be ashamed at the impotence of their idols.

18-22 Israel's Blindness—**18.** Those deaf to Yahweh's words and blind to his exploits are the people of Israel. **19.** ' *Who is blind but my servant, and deaf (like my messenger whom I send ? Who is blind) like the covenanted one (and blind like the servant of Yahweh)?* ' This is the only passage of Isaias in which Israel is a messenger to the Gentiles. The triple repetition of blind is not original. The rendering ' covenanted ' is uncertain. The bracketed words are probably interpolated. **20.** ' wilt thou ' : ' *dost* '. **21.** ' *Yahweh wished for his loyalty's sake to make the law great and majestic* ', to make Israel a mighty nation. **22.** Infidelity reduced her to bondage and exile. Yahweh's antecedent designs like prophetic promises and threats may depend for their fulfilment on man's free will. ' the snare of young men ' : ' *ensnared in holes* '.

23-25 The Exile—The prophet earnestly exhorts the people to believe his words, to realize that Yahweh delivered them into bondage for their sins and not to regard the exile as an inexplicable calamity. **25.** (After ' upon him ') ' *the heat of his wrath and of fierce war, which burned him* '.

XLIII 1-13 Yahweh, Israel's Helper and Deliverer—The time of Deliverance has come, **1-2.** The Price of Deliverance shall be paid in full, **3-4.** All the Exiles shall be delivered, **5-7.** Israel shall bear witness before the nations that Yahweh alone is God and Saviour, **8-13.** **1-2.** *But now* indicates a new period when God's wrath gives place to his mercy. Fire and water are figuratively used for dangers of the gravest kind ; *cf.* Ps 65:11. **3-4.** The nations enslaved to form the Persian world-empire are the price of Israel's redemption. Their subjection is necessary for the release of the exiles whom they detain. The release of Babylonian exiles was announced, 40:1-11. Egypt is next in importance. The existence of a Jewish colony at Elephantine on its southern border explains the inclusion of Egypt's southern neighbours Saba and Kush in the Diaspora regions. Egypt was subjugated by Cambyses. The prophet is however not chronicling conquests of Cyrus

but regions of the Diaspora. There is no question of **442c** the Egyptian Exodus here. Egypt was not then sold or subjected as the price of Israel's deliverance. **3.** ' atonement ' : ' ransom '. **4.** ' *Because thou wert precious in my eyes, honoured so that I loved thee* '. ' people ' : ' *peoples* '.

5-7. All exiles shall be able to return. **7.** All called **d** by my name means all the people of Yahweh.

8-13. The nations and their gods are again arraigned **e** before Yahweh's tribunal as in ch 41. Israel, though blind and deaf, is called to witness on behalf of Yahweh. **9a.** ' *Let the nations be assembled and the peoples be gathered together* ', and **9c,** ' *Let them produce witnesses to justify their plea, to announce and say : It is true* '. **10.** For ' my servant ' some read the plural and understand my servants as Israel. Others suppose more probably that a new witness, Cyrus, is adduced. ' I myself am ' : ' *I am He* '. **11a.** ' *I, I am Yahweh* '. Repetitions are a peculiarity of the author's style. **12b.** (After ' heard ') ' *and no strange god among you* '. **13a.** ' *Henceforth also I am likewise God* ' (lit. I am he). ' turn away ' : ' *prevent* '. **XLIII 14-XLIV 5 Yahweh's Gifts to Israel Unmerited f and Unexhausted**—Fall of Babylon the Oppressor, **14-15.** The Old Exodus and the more wonderful New Exodus, **16-21.** Israel's Unworthiness, **22-28.** New Era of Prosperity and Increase in Numbers, **44:1-5.** **XLIII 14-15.** The solemn introduction and conclusion **g** are clear, but the account of the city's fall is obscure. MT reads : ' *For your sake have I sent to Babylon and brought down all the fugitives* [or *bars*] *and the Chaldaeans who rejoice in ships* '. The fugitives could be runaways or Jewish exiles, the bars city defences. The text seems corrupt and incomplete.

16-21. The Egyptian Exodus is first recalled. **17. h** (After ' horse ') ' *the army and the mighty one together* ', and after ' again ' : ' *They are extinguished, gone out like a wick* '. The mighty one is apparently the commander. The former things and the new thing are not here predictions but exploits. The new Exodus will surpass the old. **19.** ' thing ' : ' *things* ' ; ' them ' : ' *it* '. Kissane's alteration of *n^ehārôt* ' rivers ' (MT and Vss) to *n^eṯîḇôṯ* is confirmed by the pre-Masoretic MS. **20.** ' dragons ' : ' *jackals* '.

22-28. 22. Israel has not invoked Yahweh or **i** troubled herself about him or, **23-24a,** offered him un-demanded sacrifices or other costly gifts, but only, **24,** burdened him with her sins and wearied him with her iniquities. The slaughter offerings (DV ' victims ') were the peace-offerings of which the fat only was burned. The oblations were the unbloody food offerings. Incense was both mixed with these and offered separately on the incense-altar. Sweet cane seems to be associated with the incense offering. Sacrifice was undemanded because it could only be offered in Jerusalem. **25.** Yahweh's forgiveness of Israel's sins is entirely gratuitous. **26.** Let Israel plead her cause, prove that she has not deserved her chastisement. **27-28.** She sinned from the beginning and her chastisement was just and inevitable. ' teachers ' : ' *mediators* '. The common view is that the mediators who sinned were Moses and Aaron and that the first father was Jacob. The holy princes are the descendants of David now dethroned and so profaned. Israel was put under the ban and subjected to blasphemous insults.

XLIV 1-5. 1-2. *But now* indicates a change in the **j** attitude of Yahweh. He created Israel, formed her from the womb (made her into a full-grown nation) and helps her. Let her not fear. Jeshurun (DV ' most righteous ') is a pet-name of Israel, used also in Deut, meaning probably ' righteous ' (possibly ' straight ', ' well-formed ') and opposed to Jacob, the supplanter. The Israelites were few. **3-4.** Yahweh here promises to them fertility and fecundity. ' among the herbs ' : ' *like grass* ' ; ' willows ' : ' *poplars* '. **5.** Foreigners will also become Israelites. Some refer this prophecy to apostate or Diaspora Jews, but the assumption of Israel as a new name implies a foreign origin. ' with his hand ' : ' *on his hand* ', a reference to the branding of slaves.

442k **6-23 Yahweh Alone is God, Idols are Vain**—In this prophecy the contrast between the God of Israel and the gods of the Gentiles is developed. Wisdom and Power of Yahweh, **6-8**, Vanity of Idols, **9-17**, Folly of Idolaters, **18-20**, Conclusion and Hymn of praise, **21-23**.

l **6-8.** **6.** Yahweh Alone is God. **7.** '*Whoever is like me let him call out and announce it and set it before me. Who hath announced from of old the things to come and revealed to us what will come to pass?*' The text of *b* is corrected from the context. **8.** Yahweh alone has foretold the future and Israel is his witness. Read after 'besides me': *There is no rock that I know*. Rock frequently indicates God as omnipotent.

m **9-17.** **9.** Idolaters have no profit from their idols. Their witnesses, as contrasted with Yahweh's, are confounded, seeing no exploit, knowing no prediction of their gods. **10.** And yet '*Who forms a god and casts an image except for profit?*' **11b.** '*Let (idolaters) all assemble and take their stand (for judgement), they shall fear and be confounded together.* **12-17.** The inferiority of the idols is not surprising when their origin is considered. **12.** The smith labours with fire and hammer, feels the strain, becomes hungry and weak and if he has no water to drink collapses. The idol cannot help its maker. **13.** The carpenter uses a measuring line to fix the dimensions, a pencil to mark the outline, a knife to carve the wood and thus produces the figure of a man. **14** names the various trees used. **15.** The same species is used indifferently for fuel and for idol. **16-17.** This idea is now expressed more graphically. Half a piece of wood is used for firing, the other half for an idol.

n **18-20.** The folly of idolaters is explained: **18**, He (Yahweh) has veiled their eyes from seeing and their heart from understanding. **19.** They should have concluded that combustible wood cannot be a god. **20a.** '*He shepherds ashes: A deluded heart has led him astray*'. To shepherd ashes or wind, Os 12:2, is to prize what is worthless, the combustible idol, also called lie.

o **21-23.** Israel must take these words of Yahweh to heart, remember his benefits and return to him who has blotted out her sins. **21.** 'forget me not': '*thou shalt not be forgotten by me*'. **23.** All created things are invited to rejoice and praise Yahweh for Israel's redemption. 'hath shown mercy': '*hath done it*'.

443a The third section of the first part of Isaias II, **44:24-49:12**, ends like the others with a short canticle of praise, **49:13**. It contains more definite announcements of the new exploits of Yahweh. Cyrus, Yahweh's instrument for Israel's deliverance, **44:24-45:25**, Powerlessness of Babylonian Idols, Omnipotence of Yahweh, **46:1-13**, Babylon Dethroned and Enslaved, **47:1-15**, Recapitulation of Oracles and Warnings, **48:1-22** + **49:9b-13**. The second Servant poem, **49:1-9a**, is inserted in the last prophecy.

XLIV 24-XLV 25 God's Salvific Design, Cyrus his Instrument—Cyrus is introduced, **44:24-28**, his mission is announced, **45:1-8**, murmuring against a foreign deliverer is condemned, **9-13**, consummation of the design in the conversion of the Gentiles, **14-25**.

b **24-28.** **24-25.** Yahweh's love for Israel, Omnipotence and Omniscience are first emphatically affirmed. **26.** He fulfils the prophecies of his servants (sing. in MT) and messengers, **27**, dries up waters, the Red Sea with possible allusion to the Euphrates. **28.** '*He says to Cyrus:* "*My shepherd who shall fulfil all my desires*"; *to Jerusalem:* "*Be built*"; *to the Temple:* "*Be founded*"'. Cyrus is Yahweh's shepherd faithfully guarding his flock, the exiles.

c **XLV 1-8.** **1-2.** Cyrus is God's anointed as accredited with a divine mission. It is Yahweh who subdues nations before him, ungirds the loins of kings, opens the doors and gates of cities, prepares his way and levels the *mountains* (pre-Masoretic MS and LXX) before him. When long robes are worn activity is difficult without a girdle, which also usually contains weapons. Hence

ungird is weaken, gird strengthen. **3.** While Yahweh desires to make himself known to Cyrus by his gifts and exploits—a clear indication that Cyrus is not a monotheist (*cf.* 41:25)—it is not for his own sake but for Israel's sake that he has chosen him as his instrument. 'call': 'called'. **4.** 'made a likeness of thee': 'given thee titles', shepherd, anointed, etc. **5b.** '*I will gird thee though thou knowest me not*'. **6.** Yahweh makes himself known to the Gentiles by his exploits for his people through Cyrus. A similar design explains the wonders of the Exodus, Ex 7:3-5; 9-16. **7.** There may be a refutation here of the Persian belief in two principles, one of light and good, the other of darkness and evil. **8.** Yahweh produces on earth justice and salvation, personified in Vg. The blessings are Messianic, but are here more immediately associated with the Restoration.

9-13. Murmurs against a foreign instead of a native deliverer are rebellious and unreasonable. Creatures are as clay in the hands of the potter and must submit to their creator's designs. Cyrus will exact no ransom for their deliverance. **9b.** After 'making' (slightly corrected): '*And to its maker, thou hast no skill*' (lit. hands). **11b.** '*Do you ask me to my face about things to come?*' **12-13.** Yahweh can and will accomplish his design fully and gratuitously.

14-25. The ultimate object of the mission of Cyrus, **5**, was to spread the knowledge of Yahweh over the whole earth. Hence the conversion of the Gentiles appropriately concludes his mission. They shall be subject to Israel and Israel's God. The prophecy of subjection to Israel was fulfilled spiritually but not literally because Israel rejected the Messias. Egypt, Ethiopia and Saba are specially mentioned as sold for Israel's ransom, 43:3. **14.** 'Sabaim': '*the Sabaeans*'; 'worship thee': '*pay thee homage*'. Omit 'thee' after 'besides'. That the downfall of his people should lead to the conversion of the Gentiles illustrates, **15**, the mysterious character of the *God who conceals himself*. **16.** Idols bring shame on their worshippers. **17.** Yahweh saves his people. Never more shall they be put to shame. **18.** He has not created the earth *to be a desert* but to be inhabited. **19.** He has not spoken in secret in some dark place like pagan oracle-gods but publicly. He has not asked Israel to seek for nothing him, the remunerator. He has not announced what is unrighteous or untrue. **20.** Let the Gentiles assemble before him. '*Those who carry their wooden idol in procession and invoke a god who cannot save are without intelligence*'. **21.** Let them plead, advance proofs, take counsel together. Yahweh alone foretold the future. He alone is God of truth and salvation. **22.** Let all the ends of the earth then be converted to the one true God. **23.** Nay more, Yahweh hath sworn: '*Before me every knee shall bend and (by me) every tongue shall swear*'. **24.** '*Only in Yahweh, man will say, have I righteousness and strength, Unto him shall come in confusion all those who were incensed with him*'. **25.** '*Through Yahweh shall be just and shall be glorified* [by the converted Gentiles] *all the seed of Israel*.

XLVI 1-13 Powerlessness of Babylonian Idols, Omnipotence of Yahweh—Idols are carried, Yahweh carries his people, **1-4**. Yahweh is Incomparable, Supreme, Idols are creatures, helpless, motionless, useless, **5-7**. What Yahweh has foretold he will assuredly perform through his instrument Cyrus, **8-13**.

1-4. **1-2.** *Bel is bowed down, Nebo is stooped, Animal and beast of burden carry* [lit. have] *their images. Their* [MT your] *burdens are weighty, a load for the jaded, they bow down, they are stooped together, They cannot save their burden, they themselves go into captivity.* Beasts are laden with the humiliated idols and go with them into captivity. Note that *carry* repeated five times, 1-4, is emphatic, suggesting the obvious contrast. Bel, ancient god of Nippur, was identified with Marduk when Babylon became powerful. Nabu, god of Borsippa, was considered the son of Marduk and highly honoured in Babylon. **3-4.** Unlike the gods of Babylon, who must be carried, Yahweh has carried his people from the beginning and will carry them to the end. From infancy (after 'carried' 3) and from the womb mean from birth as a nation.

5-7. 5. '*To whom will you liken me and equal me and esteem me similar that we may be like each other?*' **6.** Not to idols made by men. The subject is they (indeterminate). **7.** The idol is carried, is motionless, cannot hear or help its devotees.

8-13. 8. Rebellious Israelites are warned to *take to heart* the real nature of the idols which they worshipped, and **9,** to remember the ancient predictions and exploits of Yahweh, the only God, **10,** whose counsel is firm, whose word is fulfilled. **11.** Cyrus is compared to a bird of prey swooping on Babylon. '*created*': '*planned*'. **12.** Those *stubborn* Israelites who are far from *salvation* are warned that it is near.

XLVII 1-15 Chant over Babylon Dethroned and Enslaved—The Queen becomes a Slave, **1-4.** Her Mercilessness is requited, **5-7.** Childlessness and Widowhood is her portion, **8-9.** Her Ruin is Sudden and Inevitable, **10-11.** Her Astrologers cannot aid her, **12-15.** *Cf.* Is chh 13-14 and Jer ch 50.

1-4. 1. '*Sit on the ground without a throne, Daughter of the Chaldaean*'. Babylon is called virgin as hitherto intact, daughter as youthful. The Chaldaeans are Aramaean immigrants from the west who became rulers of Babylon in the 7th cent. B.C. **2.** The grinding of corn was the task of the housewife in humble homes, but of slaves among the nobles. (After 'meal') : '*Remove thy veil, strip off thy train*'. The baring of the legs was for the fording of rivers and canals frequent in Babylonia. *3a* is regarded by most commentators as a gloss.

5-7. 5. Babylon after dictating to others must be silent, after ruling others must lie in a dark prison. 'lady' : 'queen'. **6.** The Babylonians like the Assyrians, 10:5 ff., abused their mandate as Yahweh's instrument for the chastisement of his people. **7.** They expected to rule for ever and gave no thought to a day of reckoning.

8-9. Babylon thought herself secure against widowhood and childlessness, now come upon her. 'barrenness' : '*childlessness*', loss of children previously possessed. *9b.* (After 'widowhood') '*In their full measure shall come upon thee, despite the multitude of thy spells, despite the binding-power of thy charms*'. The pagans tried to avert misfortunes by incantations and magical formulae. Such remedies will not save Babylon.

10-11. 10. Babylon thought that her oppression of other peoples would be unpunished. **11.** But evil which she cannot *charm away*, calamity which she cannot *avert by payment*, unsuspected ruin will come suddenly upon her.

12-15. 12. Babylon is now ironically invited to make use of her customary *charms* (DV 'enchanters') and spells. '*Perhaps thou wilt be able to profit from them, Perhaps thou wilt inspire terror by them*'. *13a.* The Heb. word for 'counsels' is generally vocalized to read *counsellors*. These are described as measurers of the heavens (DV 'astrologers') stargazers and New Moon announcers. The astrologers divided up the heavens into zones, according to the signs of the zodiac, and from the movements in these zones of the sun, moon and planets foretold the fate of nations and individuals. They observed the courses of the stars and forecast from them future events. They made monthly calendars of lucky and unlucky days. **14.** But now the astrologers themselves will burn like stubble in the destructive fire of judgement. **15.** '*So have they become to thee with whom thou hast laboured from thy youth. They have erred, each in his own way, there is none to save thee*'. 'Merchants' is probably a gloss.

XLVIII 1-22 + XLIX 9b-13 Recapitulation of Warnings and Prophecies—This prophecy concludes the first part of the second book. It is a final warning against unbelief and a final announcement of proximate deliverance. After a solemn introduction, **1-2,** Yahweh explains his designs in his former revelations, **3-6a,** and in his new predictions, **6b-11.** He then again announces the mission of Cyrus, **12-16,** exacts obedience as a

condition of salvation, **17-19,** and proclaims the new **444a** Exodus, **48:20-22 + 49:9b-13.**

1-2. The people are solemnly addressed : Men of **b** Israel of the tribe of Judah whose God is Yahweh by whom they swear and whom they invoke but without loyalty and righteousness. 'waters' : '*body*', indicating tribal origin. '*Yea they are called by the name of the holy city and put their stay on the God of Israel, Yahweh of hosts*'.

3-6a. Yahweh foretold the former things before **c** their accomplishment because of the obstinacy and perversity of his people who would otherwise be inclined to attribute his exploits to the idols which they worshipped. Pre-exilic idol worship is chiefly referred to but exilic idolatry is included ; *cf.* 46:8. The text of **6a** is doubtful : 'And you, will you not announce?'

6b-11. 6b. '*Now I announce to thee new things, hidden* **d** *things which thou didst not know*'. **7b.** 'before the day when' : '*formerly*'. The new things are the fall of Babylon and the return of the exiles. These were entirely unknown before the oracles of ch 40 ff. that their effect on Israel might be all the greater and the intervention of Yahweh more apparent. **8-9.** It is not through any merit of Israel, completely faithless and called rebel from the womb, that Yahweh has patiently spared her but for his name's sake. **10.** He has refined Israel but not as silver for the dross has not been removed. '*I have tested thee in the furnace of tribulation*'. The exiles have not been fully purified and are thus distinguished from the Messianic remnant. **11.** The ultimate reason of the restoration is God's glory. The reproofs addressed here to Israel re-echo those of 43:22-28.

12-16. Israel is here consoled after being reproached **e** and the destruction of Babylon by Cyrus is again announced. **12.** Yahweh is eternal and, **13,** omnipotent. '*When I called them (into existence) they [the heavens] stood together*'. **14.** The nations are again called to judgement. 'Among them' : among the false gods. **15.** The rise of Cyrus belonged to the former things, his capture of Babylon to the new things. **16.** Omit the gloss 'and now . . . spirits'.

17-19. Before announcing the Babylonian exodus, **f** Yahweh again proclaims his goodwill towards his chosen people, hampered in the past by their disobedience to his commands. If only they had hearkened to his commandments they would be now a great and prosperous nation. **19b.** 'And his name shall not be cut off nor destroyed before me' is not part of the apodosis but an independent statement, probably a gloss.

20-22 + XLIX 9b-13. 20. The deliverance from **g** Babylonian captivity is again foretold in a command to the exiles to flee from Babylon and the Chaldaeans and a jubilant proclamation of their deliverance. **21.** In the new Exodus through the desert they shall not suffer from thirst but like their ancestors shall be miraculously supplied with water. **22** is a gloss derived probably from 57:21. The description of the new Exodus is clearly continued in **49:9b,** after the second Servant song, inserted in a prophecy like the first. It is not the Servant but Yahweh, the Merciful, the Shepherd of Israel, who leads his people and supplies their needs in 49:9b-11 as in 48:21. **12.** The return of the Jews of the Diaspora is suggested by the new Exodus. The land of the Sinites (DV 'the south country') is not China but Syene, Assuan. **13.** The short canticle of praise marks the end of a section.

XLIX 1-6 The Missions of the Servant of Yahweh— **h** The second Servant poem resembles the first in interrupting the context of the prophecy in which it is inserted. The Servant's address to the far coasts which have just been described as waiting eagerly for his instruction marks this poem as the second scene in the drama. The concealment of the sword and arrow indicate that his mission to the Gentiles will not be fulfilled immediately. The failure of his efforts is the first stage of the vicarious satisfaction to be subsequently revealed as the means by which his mission to the

444h Gentiles will be accomplished. His mission to Israel, so far a failure, is now first announced. His all-important mission however is to the Gentiles, not the political mission of the Restoration, assigned to Cyrus, which would be unworthy of him.

i **1-2.** ' *Hearken, ye far coasts, unto me, And give attention, ye distant peoples! Yahweh hath called me from the womb, From my birth he made mention of my name, And he made my mouth like a sharp sword, In the shadow of his hand he hid me ; And he made me a polished arrow, In his quiver he concealed me*'. **1.** The calling and the naming indicate dedication to a particular mission. **2.** The sword and the arrow symbolize the power and penetrating effect of the prophetic word. They are kept hidden or reserved until the time appointed by Yahweh for their use.

j **3-4 & 5c.** '*And he said to me : My servant art thou, Israel by whom I will get myself glory. So was I honoured in the eyes of Yahweh, And my God became my strength. But I said : I have laboured in vain, For nought and to no purpose have I spent my strength. Yet surely my cause is with Yahweh and my recompense with my God*'. **3.** The apparent identification of the Servant with Israel seems to imply that in 5 Israel has a mission to Israel which is impossible. It must be noted however that Israel is here qualified as the means of the glorification of Yahweh. It was in view of the Messias that Israel was chosen and by the Messias that Israel glorified Yahweh. Thus Israel here is not the people but the Messias. In an analogous sense an absolute monarch can say ' L'Etat, c'est moi '. Some less probably consider Israel an interpolation as in LXX 42:1. **5c.** This verse seems to have been misplaced. Its transposition after 3 improves the sequence of thought without altering the sense.

k **5a-b-6.** '*And now saith Yahweh, Who formed me from the womb to be his Servant, To restore Jacob unto him, And that Israel to him should be gathered : Too little is it that thou shouldst be my Servant To raise up the tribes of Jacob, And bring back the survivors of Israel ; So I have made thee a light to the Gentiles, That my salvation may reach to the end of the earth*'. **5a-b.** The common scribal error of *lô'* ' not ' for *lô* ' to him ' has introduced a negation, excluded by the parallelism, into the Vg rendering of the last member. The mission here assigned to the Servant is clearly spiritual, to bring back Israel to Yahweh. In **6** on the other hand a political mission, the restoration of the exiles, seems to be indicated. Many assign both missions to the Servant. It is more natural however to conclude that the political mission, previously assigned with the fullest confidence to Cyrus and here declared unworthy of the Servant, did not form part of his mission to Israel. This mission, whether only spiritual or also political, is subsidiary to the all-important mission to the Gentiles.

l **7-9a.** ' *Thus saith Yahweh, The Redeemer of Israel, his holy one, To him who is deeply despised, Abhorred by all, A slave of rulers : Kings shall see and arise, Princes (shall see and) prostrate themselves, On account of Yahweh, who is faithful, the Holy One of Israel, who has chosen thee. Thus saith Yahweh, In a time of favour have I answered thee, And in a day of salvation have I helped thee, And I form thee and make thee The covenant of the people, To resettle a land, to re-people desolate inheritances, Saying to the prisoners " Come out ", To those who are in darkness " Be enlightened " '*. **7.** The anticipation of the homage of the kings, reserved by the author for the fourth Song, marks this verse as a later addition. ' Despising ' (MT) must be read *despised. Deeply* is literally ' in the soul '. Kings, being seated, stand up, princes, who are standing, prostrate themselves to do homage. **8.** The text assigns to the Servant the mission of the Restoration. But the words ' And I form thee and I make thee the covenant of the people ' are a literal citation of 42:6*b* and seem to be interpolated. If they are omitted the pronouncement is more naturally understood as a prophecy of the Restoration addressed to the exiles and inserted here to facilitate the transition from the Servant Song to the regular theme of the Restoration.

XLIX 14-LV 13. In this second part of Isaias II the oracles are addressed no longer to Jacob—Israel but to Sion—Jerusalem. The theme is the future glorification of Sion. Predictions of the New Exodus interconnect both parts. Two more Servant poems appear, **50:4-9** and **52:13-53:12.**

XLIX 14-L 3 Yahweh is Mindful of Sion and his People—Sion will be rebuilt, **14-17**, and repopulated, **18-21**, and the exiles will return, **22-23**, for Yahweh is Almighty, **24-26**, the Saviour of his people, **50:1-3.**

14-17. Yahweh is ever mindful of Sion as a mother of her child, as a bridegroom who still in the east may have the name of the bride tattooed on his hand. Sion's rebuilders *are coming in haste* and her destroyers and devastators *are leaving* her.

18-21. **18.** The exiles are depicted as already returned. They are the rich raiment, the bridal girdle with which Sion is adorned. **19a.** ' *For thy wrecks and thy ruins and thy wasted land I shall re-establish*'. **20.** Sion, too small for the returned exiles, asks in wonder whence they have come to a mother so long *childless and barren.* **21.** *Exiled and rejected* (DV ' led away and captive '), not in LXX, is probably a gloss. ' I was destitute and alone ' : ' *I was the sole survivor* '. Sion here is the childless mother and rejected bride in Palestine.

22-23. The return of the Jews of the Diaspora is the answer to Sion's query. Their masters will free them and honour them. Kings and queens will *do homage* to them (DV ' worship ') as citizens of the capital of the Messianic kingdom. Sons and daughters are babes in general, borne first in the arms, later on the shoulders.

24-26. **24.** For *ṣaddîq* 'just' (MT) read '*ārîṣ* 'tyrant' (DV ' mighty ') with the pre-Masoretic MS. Deliverance may seem impossible, but what is difficult to man is easy to God. **25.** ' captivity ' : ' *captives* ' ; ' judge ' : ' *contend with* '.

L 1-3. **1.** The complaint of discouraged exiles that Yahweh has abandoned them, 49:14, is unfounded. His repudiation of Sion, his bride, is only temporary. His sale of his people into slavery is also temporary, not the payment of a debt to Babylon but the punishment of their sins. Children were sold into slavery in payment of a father's debt. **2.** Lack of response from Israel to his visitations and the warning of his prophets made the final chastisement of the exile inevitable. But now as formerly he is mighty to deliver. He controls the forces of nature, can dry up seas and rivers and, **3**, turn light into darkness.

4-9 The Suffering Servant : His Obedience, Constancy, and Confidence in Yahweh—The third Song depicts a further stage in the Servant's mission to Israel, marked by persecution and suffering. It is a necessary link between the second and the fourth Songs in which the relation between mission and suffering will be revealed. Now that the dramatic character of the Songs is recognized few commentators follow St John Chrysostom in regarding this one as a record of its author's personal experience. Its resemblance to the other Songs is moreover too obvious to be ignored, and it is attributed to the Servant in an appended comment.

4-6. ' *The Lord Yahweh hath given me A disciple's tongue, That I may know in due season A word for the weary. Morning by morning he awakens my ear That I may hear as a disciple. The Lord Yahweh himself hath opened my ear, I was not rebellious, I turned not back, I gave my back to the smiters, My cheeks to them that plucked my beard, I hid not my face From insult and spitting* '. The text of 4-5 is slightly corrupt but the general sense is clear. For *in due season* (MT) we find ' how to answer ' in LXX. It was in obedience to his Father's will that Christ voluntarily submitted to the scourging, the spittle, and the insults of his Passion.

7-9. '*But the Lord Yahweh helps me, Therefore am I not confounded, Therefore did I make my face like flint, And knew that I should not be put to shame. Near is my Vindicator, Who will take proceedings against me ? Let us stand up together. Who is my adversary ? Let him draw near unto me. Behold ! The Lord Yahweh himself will help me ! Who then can secure a verdict against me ? Behold ! They*

j *shall all wear out as a garment, Moths shall consume them'.* The Servant here proclaims his supreme confidence in Yahweh and in the justice of his cause. He provokes his adversaries to a legal contest before Yahweh who will decide in his favour.

k **10-11** are a comment on the Song of uncertain origin commending obedience to Yahweh and his Servant. **10.** Read *let him hear* for 'that heareth' and *he who walks* for 'that hath walked'. **11.** Those in darkness must seek light from Yahweh, not from the flares of their own kindling. *My hand* is the hand of Yahweh. *This* indicates the punishment of disobedience : *In pain shall you lie down.*

l **LI 1-16 Yahweh encourages the Faithful of Israel**— The prophecy is a dialogue between Yahweh and his faithful followers who need encouragement in their pagan environment. Yahweh's two addresses, **1-8** and **12-14**, are connected by the petition of the faithful that he manifest his might on their behalf as in the days of old, **9-10**. There are several interpolations : **4-5, 11, 15-16**.

m **1-8. 1-2.** Let the faithful exiles, preoccupied by the smallness of their numbers, remember their great ancestors to whom Yahweh miraculously gave a nation for their posterity. Abraham is the rock whence they were hewn, Sara the *quarry* whence they were dug out. **3.** Sion will be rebuilt, her waste places will become fertile, her inhabitants will rejoice. 'a place of pleasure' : 'Eden', Gen 2:8. **4a.** For MT sing. people, nation the versions have plur. in agreement with nations, **4b**, peoples, and islands, **5.** It is clear that an address to the Gentiles has been interpolated. **6.** Though the heavens and the earth with its inhabitants must finally perish Yahweh's salvation and justice will last for ever. 'in like manner' : 'like gnats'. **7-8.** The faithful are further exhorted not to fear their enemies who shall perish, while Yahweh's salvation and justice are eternal. It may be implied here that those finally saved will live for ever.

n **9-10.** Yahweh is asked by the faithful to display his Might as in days of old when he saved his people from the bondage of Egypt. Rahab is Egypt ; *see* note on 27:1. On the interpolated verse **11** see note on 35:10.

o **12-16. 12.** The repetition of *I* in **12** is the answer to the repetition of *Was it not thou ?* in 9-10. 'It is I, even I, who comfort thee' thus begins Yahweh's reply. He admonishes the faithful not to fear man nor forget their Creator nor tremble at the rage of the oppressor whose time is short. **13.** 'As he is prepared to destroy, where is the rage of the oppressor ?' **14-15a.** 'Speedily shall the captive be set free, He shall not go down to the pit of death, Neither shall his bread fail. I am Yahweh thy God'. **15b** = Jer 31:35a. **16** cites from 59:21 ; 49:2 ; Os 2:25 and strangely assigns as mission to the Servant, Israel : 'to stretch forth the heavens and found the earth and say to Sion : Thou art my people'.

p **LI 17-LII 12 The Glad Tidings of Sion's Deliverance** —Sion will no longer drink the cup of God's wrath, **17-25.** Let us rejoice in Yahweh her Saviour **LII : 1-6.** The glad tidings and the New Exodus, **7-12**.

q **17-25.** Jerusalem is exhorted to wake up from sleep after draining to the dregs the chalice of intoxication. She has none to help her among the sons she has borne and reared, all exiled or slain. She has lost her possessions by devastation, her inhabitants by famine and the sword. She has seen her sons lying senseless at the street corners like an antelope caught in a net. But now Yahweh tells her that the cup of his wrath, chalice of intoxication, shall be transferred from her hand to that of her oppressors. Prostration under the feet of the victor was an eastern custom ; *cf.* Jos 10:24.

r **LII 1-6.** Sion is invited to put on festive garments, to rise from the dust of degradation, to loose the fetters of bondage. She was sold into slavery gratis, she will be redeemed gratis. She suffered Egyptian bondage, Assyrian oppression, Babylonian captivity. Yahweh's name is blasphemed as an impotent God. Now therefore will he proclaim his Might by delivering his people.

445s **7-12.** A messenger brings to Sion the tidings of salvation saying 'Thy God is king', foreign domination is ended. Sion's watchmen rejoice to see Yahweh's return to his repudiated spouse. The ruins of the city rejoice in the rebuilding of its walls and houses. Yahweh has manifested to all his Might and Salvation. The scene now changes abruptly from Jerusalem to Babylon. Let the exiles free themselves from contamination and undertake the new Exodus, bearing with them their sacred vessels restored by Cyrus. Yahweh, as in the Egyptian Exodus leads the van and protects the rear of the travellers.

446a **LII 13-LIII 12 Passion, Death, and Triumph of the Servant of Yahweh**—As the Sion theme of 51:17-52:12 is resumed and developed in 54:1-17 the fourth Song like the others has no connexion with the context. It begins like the first with the words 'Behold ! My Servant' and announces his future triumph. It then alludes to the second and third Songs in explaining the cause of his failure and sufferings in his mission to the Jews. Next comes the last scene of the drama, the passion and death of the Servant. Finally the conversion of the Gentiles is announced as the recompense of his vicarious sufferings and sacrificial death. The connexion of all four Songs and the final character of the fourth are clearly manifested.

b **13-15.** 'Behold ! My Servant shall prosper, He shall be lifted up (and elevated) and greatly exalted. As many were appalled at him, For his appearance was debased beneath that of man, And his form beneath that of the sons of men, So many nations shall be amazed at him, Kings shall shut their mouths, Because what had not been told them they see, And what they had not heard they perceive'. The future triumph of the Servant is first announced and then contrasted with his previous degradation. The contrast moreover is between persons as well as periods. Nations and kings clearly indicate the Gentiles. The many who were appalled are the Jews among whom the Servant lived and suffered. **13.** *And elevated*, not in LXX and metrically superfluous, should probably be omitted. **14.** MT 'at thee' after 'appalled' must be read *at him*. **15.** *Shall be amazed* (LXX) is a good parallel to *were appalled*. MT reads : He shall sprinkle (many nations). This spoils the parallelism and 'sprinkle' alone can hardly mean 'purify'.

c **LIII 1-3.** 'Who believed what we heard ? And the arm of Yahweh—over whom was it manifested ? And he grew up before him like a sapling And like a root from an arid soil. No form had he, no majesty that we should regard him, And no appearance that we should delight in him. Despised was he and forsaken of men, A man of sorrows and familiar with sickness, And as one from whom men avert their gaze, He was despised and we esteemed him not'. **1.** Who are the 'we' who esteemed him not, the speakers in 1-9 ? Obviously the Jews who were appalled at his degradation, or at least the better element among them who subsequently recognize their error, not the Gentiles who were amazed at his achievement. This conclusion is confirmed by the equivalence of *our rebellions* in 5 and the *rebellion of his people* in 8. The Servant and the Jews are clearly distinguished. *Cf.* citations in Jn 12:38 and Rom 10:16. This is a regretful confession that the Jewish contemporaries of the Servant neither believed the revelations of Yahweh about his Servant nor perceived the manifestations of his Might. **2.** *Before him* means before Yahweh. The sapling and the root re-echo the sapling from the root of Jesse, 11:1. The suffering Servant is the Messianic monarch. **3.** The man of sorrows is described in general terms. Here as elsewhere the details of the prophetic picture are not all to be understood literally. Sickness is not ill-health, but one of the chastisements of sin. The Servant bore our sickness, the chastisement of our sins.

d **4-6.** 'Yet ours were the sicknesses which he bore, Ours the pains with which he was laden. Though we accounted him stricken, Smitten by God and humiliated, Yet he was pierced through for our rebellions, Crushed for our iniquities ; Chastisement which made us whole was inflicted upon him, And in his stripes was our healing. We all like sheep strayed, We

567

446d *turned each his own way, And Yahweh laid on him the iniquity of us all '*. The doctrine of vicarious expiation, not found elsewhere in the OT but taught by Christ and his Evangelists and especially by St Paul, is the great novelty of this prophecy. **4.** ' Stricken ' is a general term and does not imply leprosy (Vg). **5.** The Servant was crushed by weight of blows. *šālōm* means peace (Vg) but also soundness, well-being, a better parallel to healing.

e **7-9.** ' *He was harshly treated but humbled himself, And opened not his mouth. Like a sheep led to the slaughter, And like a ewe before her shearers, He was dumb and opened not his mouth. After arrest and sentence he was taken off, And on his fate who reflected ? Yea, he was cut off from the land of the living, For the rebellion of his people stricken to death. And they made his grave with the wicked, And with the rich man his sepulchre ; Although he had done no violence, Nor was any deceit in his mouth '*. **7.** In his Passion above all the Servant showed himself ' meek and humble of heart '. **8.** The rendering *arrest* is deduced from the verbal sense of '*ōṣer* which usually means ' oppression '. An alternative rendering is ' by an oppressive [or, unjust] judgement '. A third possible rendering, ' without oppression or judgement ', is excluded by the context, for a criminal's grave implies a judicial sentence and execution. The Heb. *dôr* usually means ' generation ' in the sense of life-time or contemporaries, but cannot indicate the act of generating, the eternal or temporal generation of Christ. Driver's rendering *fate*, adopted here, is deduced from the radical sense of the word, but is not found elsewhere. *To death* for MT ' to them ' is based on LXX and parallelism. *His people* for ' my people ' (MT) exemplifies the frequent interchange of *w* and *y* in Aramaic script. In the pre-Masoretic MS of Isaias these letters are practically identical in form. **9.** *His sepulchre* for the impossible ' in his deaths ' is suggested by the parallelism. Usually *rich man* is similarly changed to evil-doers, but this detail of Christ's Passion may have been revealed. **9b** predicts Christ's sinlessness, 1 Pet 2:22.

f **10-12.** ' *Yet Yahweh was pleased to crush him with sickness ; Truly he gave himself as a guilt-offering. He shall see seed that prolongs days, And the purpose of Yahweh shall prosper in his hand. After his travail of soul he shall see light ; He shall be satisfied with his knowledge. My (righteous) Servant shall make many righteous, And their iniquities he shall bear. Therefore will I assign him the many for his portion, And numberless shall be his spoil, Because he laid bare his soul unto death, And with the rebellious he was numbered ; But he bore the sin of many, And for the rebellious he intercedes '*. **10.** By reading *'emeṭ śām* for *'im tāśîm* we preserve the parallelism of verse members. The correction *'im yāśîm* (' if he give ') suggested by Vg leaves the first member without a parallel. Guilt-offering implies that the Servant's death is sacrificial and expiatory. Seed is understood figuratively as frequently in the OT—a spiritual progeny. **11.** ' *See light* ' means ' live '. Light, not in MT, is from LXX. The pre-Masoretic MS of Isaias has *'ôr* ' light ' after ' see ' where an object is expected. The resurrection was not part of Jewish belief at this period, but the resurrection of the Messias is insinuated in Ps 15:10. *Righteous* before ' Servant ' is probably due to dittography. **12.** Both *rab* and *'āṣûm* can mean ' many ' or ' mighty ', but *rab* means ' many ' four times elsewhere in this Song. *Rabbîm* is apparently a technical term in language relating to substitution when the one is contrasted with the many. *Cf.* Dan 11:33 ; 12:3 ; Mt 26:28 ; Mk 10:45 ; Rom 5:19. For persons as spoil *cf.* Gen 14:21. The reward of a portion among the mighty would be unworthy of the Servant. Christ was numbered with the wicked, Lk 22:37. The change of tense from ' bore ' (perf.) to ' intercedes ' (imperf.) may have no significance but more probably indicates Christ's perpetual intercession, Heb 7:25.

g **The Prophet's Message**—This prophecy is unique among the oracles of the OT. Its Messianism is entirely spiritual without admixture of national elements. It reveals not merely the fact but the manner of the

Redemption. The Redeemer will expiate by his sufferings and death the sins of mankind. The personal character and virtues of the Messias are depicted more fully than elsewhere. His teaching will be rejected by the Jews but accepted by the Gentiles. Though sent to the Gentiles, he lives and labours, suffers and dies, among his own people. Only after his death will his teaching reach those for whom it is primarily intended. The marvellous realization of this complex picture in the Christ of the NT has won for the artist the title of Evangelist.

LIV 1-17 The New Sion—This prophecy develops the theme of 51:17–52:12 in which the salvation of Sion was announced. It predicts not only the Restoration but the future glory of the New Sion in Messianic times. The disgrace of Sion's unfruitfulness is removed, **1-3.** She becomes once more Yahweh's beloved spouse, **4-6.** New and eternal alliance between Yahweh and Sion, **7-10** ; restoration, salvation and security of the New Sion, **11-17.**

1-3. Sion is bidden to rejoice in the numerous progeny that Yahweh will give her now that the period of her abandonment is ended. **1.** ' *bearest* ' : ' *barest* '. **2.** Her tent must be enlarged, its coverings widened, its cords lengthened, its pegs strengthened ; for, **3,** she must extend her boundaries, conquer foreign nations, rebuild ruined cities.

4-6. The shame of Israel's youth, most probably her subjection to various neighbouring nations in the Judges' period, and the disgrace of her widowhood, the Babylonian exile when Yahweh abandoned her, must now be forgotten, for the Omnipotent Yahweh, her Creator and her Redeemer, has taken back his repudiated spouse. **6b.** ' *And the wife of one's youth how could one cast her off* [lit. that she be cast off !] *saith thy God* '.

7-10. The separation and reunion of Yahweh and Sion are depicted as a quarrel and reconciliation of husband and wife. Only for a moment, only in a fit of anger, did Yahweh abandon Sion. His reunion with her will be eternal. As he swore to Noe, so he now swears to Sion never again to be angry with her. Yahweh's solemn covenant with Noe was equivalently an oath. **10a.** ' *Though the mountains shake* ', etc.

11-17. **11b.** The foundations of the New Sion will be of malachite, her walls of sapphire. This is the common interpretation suggested by, **12,** the turrets (?) of rubies, gates of crystal and border of precious stones. MT reads : ' I shall lay thy stones in antimony [for mortar] and found [or, build] thee with sapphires '. *Suns* may be turrets or windows. *Border* is most probably city-wall. The sapphires would then be the material of the buildings within the city. The description is poetical. The magnificence of the New Sion is spiritual rather than material. **13.** Her children will all be Yahweh's disciples, faithful to his teaching and therefore prosperous. **14.** By righteousness will she be protected from oppression and from fear. **15.** ' *If any one assail, it shall be without my will, Whoever assails thee shall fall because of thee* '. **17b.** ' *This is the lot of the servants of Yahweh and their salvation from me saith Yahweh* '. Here first in Isaias ' servants ' (plur.), not ' servant ' (collective sing.), indicates the people of Yahweh.

LV 1-13 Exhortation to accept Salvation—Ch 55 is an epilogue as ch 40 was a prologue to Isaias II. The exiles are finally exhorted by Yahweh to accept the salvation which he offers. Invitation to a new covenant with Yahweh, **1-5.** Conversion alone is necessary for Yahweh is omnipotent, **6-11.** Last announcement of the new Exodus, **12-13.**

1-5. Salvation is here proposed under the figure of food and drink, offered gratis to the hungry and thirsty. **1.** ' *buy* ' : ' *buy corn* '. **2.** Yahweh alone can satisfy his people. **3.** If they accept his offer he will make a new covenant with them and give them *the faithful blessings of David*, that is, gifts promised to and bestowed on David. **4-5.** These gifts are defined as those of Ps 17:44 : ' Thou makest me the head of nations, A people whom I knew not serves me '. The very word, David, means ' leader ', as we learn from the Mari texts. David is here *the witness* (of Yahweh's Omnipotence) *to peoples, the prince and ruler of nations*. These nations were the Philistines, the Edomites, the Moabites, the Ammonites and the Aramaeans whom he subjected. Similarly nations, unknown to Sion, will come to her at her call, thus acknowledging her leadership because of Yahweh, her God. The prophet makes no reference to the prophecy of Nathan or to an individual Messias. There is thus no literary connexion between this reference to David and the fourth Servant poem.

6-11. 6. The exiles are exhorted to seek Yahweh now when he can be found, to call to him now when he is near. **7.** Let sinners abandon their ways and plans and be converted to Yahweh who is rich in mercy and forgiveness. **8.** They are then warned against mistrust in Yahweh, whose ways and plans are very different from and, **9,** far superior to man's ways and plans, and, **10-11,** whose word is all powerful to execute what he announces. The word is compared to the rain and the snow sent down from heaven and accomplishing their mission of making the earth fruitful and providing food for man.

12-13. 12. The Exodus from Babylon will be joyous and peaceful. Let all nature rejoice in it. **13.** Let thorn-bushes become *cypresses* and nettles myrtles. The prophet does not intend these statements literally. Personifications of natural objects are figurative. **13*b*.** '*And it* [the new Exodus] *will be to the glory of Yahweh, an eternal memorial that will never be destroyed* ', because by it Yahweh's Omnipotence will be marvellously manifested to Jews and Gentiles.

LVI 1-LXVI 24 Consolation for the Mourners in Sion —In 55:11-12 Babylonian exiles, in 56:1-8 Palestinian residents are addressed. This change in situation alone explains the different character of the prophecies in Isaias III. The exiles were assured that salvation was at hand, that sins were expiated and forgiven ; the residents complain that salvation is delayed and are told that their sins are the obstacle to its attainment. Salvation, however, in the first case was deliverance from Babylonian captivity and exile, in the second the peace and prosperity of the Messianic age. The exiles on their return found large parts of Judah occupied by foreigners from neighbouring regions especially Edomites. These had introduced strange gods and idolatrous cults. The Jews who had remained in the land would for the most part have abandoned Yahweh or contaminated his worship by heathen practices. Material conditions were equally bad. The land was untilled, the houses in ruins, the neighbours hostile. It is not surprising that the religious spirit of the returned exiles was damped by the difficulties and dangers which surrounded and almost overwhelmed them. The prophecies of Isaias III, partly consolatory, partly admonitory, most probably belong to the dark period of the early Restoration 538-520 B.C. Difficulties about, and obstacles to salvation are first discussed, **56:1-59:20 + 63:1-6.** Sion's future glory is depicted, **60-62.** Yahweh's help is fervently invoked, **63:7-64:11.** Final judgement and Sion's salvation make a fitting conclusion, **65-66.**

LVI 1-8 Consolation for Aliens and Eunuchs—Aliens were non-Israelites residing in Palestine. They could become Israelites by adoption. The Deuteronomic legislation excluded all Canaanites from this privilege, conceded to Egyptians and Edomites after three, to Moabites and Ammonites after ten generations, Deut 23:2-8. Eunuchs were excluded from the community of Yahweh, Deut 23:1. These barriers are now removed, for salvation is universal. *My house*, says Yahweh, *shall be called a house of prayer for all peoples*. Righteousness and obedience to Yahweh's commands are the sole requirements for admission. The final oracle of Yahweh : *Others will I gather with those already gathered*, implies the existence of a nucleus of returned exiles in Judah at this period.

1. Judgement and justice are necessary for salvation. **2.** Sabbath observance became particularly important

in the exilic period when sacrifices and temple ritual **448c** ceased. **3.** The eunuch, compared to a dry tree, will receive, **4,** for his fidelity, **5,** a better reward than offspring. **7.** The holy mount to which the aliens shall be brought is Sion where Yahweh is worshipped. The references to temple and altar are in the future and do not affect the date.

LVI 9-LVII 13 Denunciation of the Leaders and d People of Israel—The Israelites addressed in this prophecy have been variously adjudged to be preexilic, exilic and post-exilic. The exiles are excluded by the character of the land, 57:5-7, whose valleys, projecting rocks and mountains indicate Judah rather than Babylonia, and by the reference to the surrounding nations coming to devour it, 56:9. The iniquities denounced were committed certainly in the pre-exilic and perhaps also in the early post-exilic period. The earlier date is favoured by the contents, the later by the context. A pre-exilic oracle is neither expected nor elsewhere suspected in Isaias III. The prophecy may be divided into : the iniquity of the leaders, **9-12,** the fate of the just, **1-2,** and the sins of the people, **3-13.**

9-12. Through the sins of her leaders Israel is not **e** protected from her enemies figured as wild beasts coming to devour her. The leaders are called watchmen (usually prophets). They are blind and unintelligent, dumb dogs unable to bark, dreamers who lie down and love to sleep. These dogs are greedy, never satisfied, shepherds without intelligence, seeking their own gain, absorbed in feasting and carousing.

LVII 1-2. 1. The death of the righteous and the pious **f** man should be noticed. God saves him by a peaceful death from imminent calamity, the chastisement of sin. ' because ' : ' *and* '. **2** (slightly corrected) : ' *He enters (his tomb) in peace. They rest in their beds who walk straightforwardly* '.

3-13. The people are now addressed. **3.** They are **g** children of a sorceress, brood of an adulteress, because their ancestors practised sorcery and adored false gods. **5.** They themselves worship Baal and Astarte in the woods, Moloch in the valleys. Unchaste practices were associated with the former cult, human sacrifices with the latter. The only site of Moloch worship known to us was in the Hinnom valley. ' who seek your comfort in idols ' : ' *Ye that lust among the terebinths* '. ' high rocks ' : ' *projections of the rocks* '. **6.** ' parts of the torrent ' : ' *smooth ones of the valley* ', probably idols according to the context. The change from ' you ' to ' thou ' is common and has no special significance. **7.** Worship in the high places is denounced. **8*a*.** The memorial set up behind door and door-post was some idolatrous emblem. **8*b*-*c*.** Israel's infidelity to Yahweh is assimilated to adultery. ' discovered ' : ' *uncovered* ' ; ' near me ' : ' *away from me* '. **9.** She worshipped not **h** only Moloch in the Hinnom valley but gods who were far away and gods of the underworld. ' wast debased ': ' *didst go down* '. **10.** Her persistency in her evil ways is described. ' I will rest ' : ' *all in vain* ' ; ' asked ' : ' *grown weak* '. ' Life of thy hand ' seems to mean fresh strength. **11.** Whom did Israel fear so that she forgot Yahweh and *did not fear* him ? The answer is obvious. She feared her oppressors and worshipped their gods. **12.** Yahweh will now expose her heathen righteousness and unprofitable works. **13.** Her idols will not save her or themselves. Only those who trust in Yahweh will possess the land, attain salvation. The last three verses reveal the source of Israel's infidelities and indicate trust in Yahweh as the sole means of salvation. It is not implied that all the Israelites addressed were idolaters.

14-21 Consolation for the Contrite and the Humble— i 14. The call to prepare the way is addressed, 40:3, to the Babylonian and, 62:10, to the Diaspora exiles. That the call here is to the latter seems to follow from 19*b* : ' *Peace, peace to him that is far away* [the exile] *and to him that is near* ' [the resident]. Jerusalem is apparently the central point from which the distances are reckoned and the proclamation is made. **15.** Yahweh's titles : High, Exalted, Enthroned for ever, Holy, differ

448i from those in Isaias II. ' *Though he dwells in the height and is holy* [exalted above man] *he is (nevertheless) with the contrite and humble of spirit to enliven the spirit of the humble and to enliven the heart of the contrite* '. **16.** His wrath is not eternal. ' *For the life-spirit would faint before me and the life-breaths which I have made* '. **17.** Man's sin provoked God's anger at which man rebelled. For ' covetousness ', unexpected here, read ' *for a short time* ', qualifying God's anger. **18.** Yahweh has seen man's 'evil ways and will now heal him, guide him, console him. **19.** ' *To his mourners I shall produce fruit of the lips* ', joy and thanksgiving. Peace and healing to all except, **20 f.**, the wicked who like a troubled sea cannot rest.

449a LVIII 1-LIX 15*a* **Denunciation of the Sins of Israel**— The prophet addresses an established community having its own administration of justice. There is no indication of temple cult nor have walls and ruined dwellings yet been rebuilt, 58:12. Preoccupation about the observation of fast days suggests a situation like that indicated in Zach 7:3, where justice and charity are enjoined as more pleasing to God than fasting. The prophecy thus belongs to the early post-exilic period. Not fasting but justice and charity will bring salvation, **58:1-14.** Injustice and oppression are the obstacles, **59:1-15*a*.**

b **1-3*a*.** The prophet is ordered to announce the sins of the community who ask Yahweh daily why salvation is delayed and like a righteous people call on him for just judgements and help and complain that he disregards their fasting. The four fast days specially instituted to commemorate the fall of Jerusalem are apparently meant ; *cf.* Zach 7:3 ff. ; 8:19.

c **3*b*-7. 3*b*-4.** The prophet replies that their fasting is disregarded because accompanied by trafficking and slave driving (or exaction of debts), by quarrels and strife. ' *You do not fast so far in such a manner that your cry reaches to heaven* '. ' *Is it thus the fast of my choice, A day in which a man afflicts himself ? If a man bows his head like a reed And makes his bed in sackcloth and ashes, Do you call the like a fast And a day of good-pleasure to Yahweh ?* '
6-7. The fast which Yahweh desires is repentance, avoidance of injustice, works of charity. ' bundles that oppress ' : ' *shackles of perversity* ' ; ' burden ' : ' *yoke* ' ; ' despise ' : ' *hide thyself from* '.' ' *Thy own flesh* ' is thy neighbour. Fasting is not condemned but the far greater importance of repentance, justice and charity is emphasized.

d **8-12. 8.** The fast desired by Yahweh will bring salvation, compared to the light which dispels the darkness of misery and the new flesh which grows on an old wound. ' justice ' : ' *salvation* '. **9.** Negative conditions of salvation are first mentioned, then, **10,** positive. ' chain ' : ' *oppression* ' (lit. yoke). To stretch out the finger means to do evil deeds. **11.** Fulfilment of these conditions will assure Yahweh's constant guidance and, **12,** the rebuilding of the ruins of Judah. **11*a*.** ' *Yahweh will guide thee continually, And will satisfy thy desire* [for water] *in the dryland, And will strengthen thy bones* '. The antiquity of the ruins is relative, 587 B.C. **12.** ' rest ' : ' *habitation* '.

e **13-14. 13.** Sabbath observance is also a condition of salvation. The Sabbath is here spoken of as in 56:1-8. ' *If thou turn away thy feet from the Sabbath* [no longer trample on, *i.e.* profane, it] *and cease* [LXX, not in MT] *to do thy business on my holy day* '. **14.** The reward of Sabbath observance will be delight in Yahweh, the Saviour, and full possession of the promised land. ' lift thee up above ' : ' *make thee ride over* ', give thee. The returned exiles only possessed a relatively small part of Palestine.

f LIX **1-3.** It is not because Yahweh lacks might or is deaf to prayer that salvation is delayed. The sins of Israel have put a barrier between the people and their God. It is vain to stretch out blood-stained hands to Yahweh or pray to him with lying lips.

g **4-8.** The prophet now proclaims aloud the sins of Israel. Violence and injustice of various kinds are denounced. The law-courts are corrupt. Nobody *sues in righteousness* or *pleads in truth*. The wicked designs conceived and the evil deeds brought forth suggest the figures of adders' eggs and spiders' webs, which illustrate the unprofitableness of injustice, for the eggs are poisonous and the webs cannot be made into garments. Their hands execute deeds of violence and their feet hasten to shed blood. They plan mischief and destruction. They follow crooked paths, not the ways of peace and rectitude.

9-11. It is because of these sins of the people that judgement is not established and salvation is delayed. Light has not yet come. They resemble the blind feeling their way in the dark. **10*b*.** ' *We stumble at midday as by twilight. In health we resemble the dead* '. **11.** The complaints and longings of the people are likened to the groans of bears and the sighs of doves.

12-15*a*. 12. The prophet speaks as representing the people and makes a public confession of their many sins which bear witness against them. **13.** The sins are declared in less detail than previously : unfaithfulness to Yahweh, deceitfulness to the neighbour, **14,** lack of judgement and justice, of truth and sincerity. **15*a*.** The conclusion seems to mean that practice of virtue and avoidance of evil have alike disappeared.

LIX 15*b*-20 + LXIII 1-6 Yahweh's Judgement on the Gentiles and especially on Edom—The removal of oppression is an essential requisite for the attainment of salvation and is coupled with it in 59:9. Yahweh's judgement on the Gentiles has for its object to secure Israel from oppression. There is no connexion however between the absence of rectitude in Israel, 59:1-15*a*, and the judgement of the Gentiles. Hence 59:15*b* introduces a new theme. The judgement on Edom in particular is part of the judgement on the Gentiles and thus **63:1-6** continues the theme of **59:15*b*-20.** It would seem therefore that the Sion prophecies, chh 60-2, which have a unity of their own, according to most commentators, were inserted in the middle of a prophecy like some of the Servant songs. Yahweh is represented as a warrior before the battle, **59:15*b*-20,** as a vintager after the battle, **63:1-6.** In both passages he fights alone on behalf of righteousness and redeem Israel. Another indication of interconnexion is the almost literal reproduction of 59:16 in 63:5.

LIX 15*b*-20. 15*b*. Yahweh saw that there was no justice for Israel oppressed by the Gentiles. **16*a*.** ' *And he saw that none was there And was astonished that none intervened* ', not to oppose himself (DV), but on behalf of Israel. His support was in his own Might and Justice. Cyrus, whom the exiles knew as Yahweh's instrument, did not aid them after their return. **17.** Yahweh's armour comprises the breastplate of justice, the helmet of salvation, the *tunic* (MT ' garb ') of vengeance and the mantle of zeal. Note the parallelism, vengeance in the cause of justice and zeal for the salvation of Israel, and *cf.* the adaptations in Wis 5:17-20 and Eph 6:14-17. **18.** ' *According to their deserts so will he repay, Wrath to his adversaries, requital to his enemies* '. **19.** West and east mean everywhere. Vengeance is likened to a pent-up stream driven on by Yahweh's breath. **20.** To Sion alone Yahweh comes as deliverer. **21** is usually regarded as a later prosaic addition. It interrupts the sequence of thought and re-echoes passages in Deutero-Isaias ; *cf.* 42:1 ; 51:16.

LXIII 1-6. A victorious warrior advances from Edom whose garments are red with blood and who proclaims himself speaker of righteousness, mighty to save. Edom was the chief usurper of the land of Judah during the exile and was a bitter enemy of the returned exiles. She represents Israel's Gentile oppressors after the fall of Babylon here and ch 34. We first learn whence the warrior comes. **2.** To the query why his garments are red he replies, **3,** that he has, unaided, crushed his enemies like grapes in the wine-press and so stained his garments. **4.** For the time of Yahweh's vengeance on sinners and of Israel's deliverance from oppression has come. **5-6.** Yahweh alone is the conqueror of the Gentiles.

LX 1-LXII 12. The literary unity of these three prophecies on the future glory of Sion is generally admitted. References to the ruins, city walls and temple as still unbuilt assign their date to the exilic or early post-exilic period. Some commentators prefer the former date and regard them as belonging to Isaias II. Others find indications, admittedly inconclusive, of residence in and tillage of the homeland. Literary allusions to Isaias II and more particularly to the Servant poems favour the post-exilic date. They suggest that Isaias II existed in its present form before these prophecies were written. The first, a poetic masterpiece, depicts the glorified Sion as the religious centre of the world. The second is a message of consolation to afflicted Israel. The third expresses the prophet's intense longing for the glorification of Sion. There is no direct connexion between these prophecies and the one which precedes and follows them. The Gentiles are here depicted not as judged or to be judged but as dwelling in darkness and coming to Sion for light. The prophet presents an aspect, not a complete picture, of Messianic times.

LX 1-22 Glorified Sion the Religious Centre of the World—Sion illuminated by the glory of Yahweh, 1-2. The Gentiles thronging to Sion, 3-9. Glorious rebuilding of city and temple, 10-14. Riches and well-being of the new Sion, 15-18. Yahweh Sion's eternal light, 19-20. Righteousness, prosperity and fecundity of Sion's citizens, 21-22.

1-2. 'Arise, be enlightened, for thy light is come, And the glory of Yahweh shines upon thee ; For, behold, darkness covers the earth And gloom the peoples, But upon thee Yahweh shines And over thee his glory appears'. Light indicates knowledge and well-being ; darkness, on the contrary, ignorance and misery. Sion enlightened by Yahweh is the centre and source of religious knowledge and salvation.

3-9. 'And the nations shall walk to thy light And kings to the brightness of thy shining. Lift up thine eyes round about and see, They are all assembled, they come to thee ; Thy sons come from afar And thy daughters are borne on the hip. Then shalt thou see and be radiant, Thy heart shall throb and expand, For the wealth of the sea shall be turned to thee, And the riches of nations shall come to thee. A multitude of camels shall spread over thee, Young camels of Madian and of Ephah. From Sheba they all come, Gold and frankincense they bring And the praises of Yahweh they announce. All the flocks of Kedar are gathered to thee, The rams of Nebayoth are at thy service, They come up with acceptance on my altar, Yea, the house of my glory will I glorify. Who are these that fly like a cloud, Like doves to their cotes ? Yea, to me the isles are gathered And the ships of Tarshish lead the van ; To bring thy children from afar, Their silver and gold with them, For the name of Yahweh, thy God, For the Holy One of Israel, thy glorifier'. The Gentiles recognize the religious leadership of Sion and consequently bring back with honour the Jews of the Diaspora to their homeland and also bring their most precious possessions to acknowledge by gifts their debt to Sion and the glory which she has received from Yahweh. Various Arab peoples dwelling east and south-east of Palestine and particularly the rich merchants of Sheba in south Arabia are first mentioned. Bedouin have only flocks to offer. Then the western lands in and about the Mediterranean, led by Tharshish at the mouth of the Guadalquivir, appear like a cloud in the distance bringing exiles and rich gifts. It is Yahweh who has made Sion the recipient of this homage.

10-14. 'And strangers shall build thy walls And their kings shall minister to thee, For though in my wrath I smote thee Yet in my mercy I had compassion on thee. And thy gates shall be always open, Day and night they shall not be shut, To admit to thee the wealth of nations, Under the leadership of their kings. (For the nation or kingdom that will not serve thee shall perish and the nations shall be utterly devastated.) The glory of Lebanon shall come to thee, The cypress and the elm and the box-tree together, To adorn the place of my sanctuary, And the place of my feet will I glorify. And the sons of thy oppressors shall come to thee bowed down, And they that reviled thee shall prostrate themselves at the soles of thy feet ; And they shall call thee " City of Yahweh ", " Sion of the Holy One of Israel " '. Foreigners willingly offer their services and resources for the rebuilding of the city walls and the temple. There is no mention of the altar erected immediately after the return. **11b.** As these services are voluntary it follows that the kings are conducting the convoys, not being led prisoners, and that the prosaic 12 is a gloss. **13a.** The trees of Lebanon, borrowed from 41:19, are variously identified.

15-18. 'Instead of being an abandoned (bride), A hated **e** (city) with none passing through, I shall make thee glorious for ever, A joy from generation to generation ; Thou shalt suck the milk of nations, Thou shalt suck the breasts of kings, And thou shalt know that I am Yahweh, Thy Saviour And thy Redeemer, the Strong One of Israel. Instead of bronze I shall bring gold, And instead of iron I shall bring silver. And instead of wood bronze and instead of stone iron. And I will make Peace thy prince And Righteousness thy ruler. No more shall violence be heard of in thy land, Devastation and destruction within thy borders, But Salvation shalt thou call thy walls, And Praise thy gates'. The figures of bride, 15, and infant, 16, are lost sight of in the description. Note that **16a** is an echo of 49:23a and **16b** a literal citation of 49:26b. Some consider **17b** (bronze for wood and iron for stone) an interpolation. Prosperity shall abound, Peace and Righteousness shall reign in the new Sion for ever. It is to praise Yahweh that strangers will pass through her ever open gates.

19-20. 'No more shall the sun be to thee light by day, Nor **f** the moon with its gleam give thee light by night, But Yahweh shall be to thee an eternal light And thy God shall be thy adornment. No more shall thy sun set, Nor thy moon disappear, For Yahweh shall be to thee an eternal light And the days of thy mourning are ended'. **19.** The pre-Masoretic MS and LXX have by night, not in MT. As light gives comfort and happiness its appearance marks the end of mourning. The sun and moon become seven times more brilliant in Messianic times, 30:26. Apocalyptic descriptions are not always intended literally. The truth conveyed here is that God is at once the source and the guarantee of the eternal happiness of the blessed ; cf. the heavenly Jerusalem, Apoc 21:23.

21-22 'Thy people shall all be righteous, For ever shall **g** they possess the land, The shoot of my planting, The work of my hands for my glorification. The least shall become a clan And the smallest a mighty nation. I Yahweh will quickly bring it to pass in due time'. The land is Canaan, promised by God to Israel. The returned exiles were preoccupied by the smallness of their numbers. Marvellous fecundity in God's own time is promised them. The prophecy, in its literal application to Israel as a nation, was conditional and depended on their acceptance of the promised Messias.

LXI 1-11 Consolation for Sion's Mourners—The **h** Prophet announces his mission of consolation, 1-3, describes the future glory of Sion, 4-9, and exults in the happiness to come, 10-11.

1-3. The announcement contains echoes of the Servant **i** songs. Some have considered the passage (cited as Messianic in Lk 4:17–19) a Servant song. But it is the prophet who speaks. He is not the Messias but a type of the Messias, announcer of good tidings to the afflicted. **1.** 'Anointed' means 'dedicated'. **2.** The acceptable year of the Lord is an allusion to the Sabbatic year and the Jubilee year in which slaves were liberated. The day of vengeance is the day of judgement on the Gentiles to end oppression. **3.** 'appoint' : ' give joy ' ; ' crown ' : ' adornment ' ; ' spirit of grief ' : ' despondency ' ; ' mighty ones ' : ' terebinths '.

4-9. Ancient ruins shall be rebuilt (cf. 58:12) with the **j** aid of strangers, 60:10, who shall also be shepherds, ploughmen and vinedressers, that the people of Israel may be devoted entirely to the service of Yahweh. They shall be enriched with the wealth of the Gentiles and as their shame was doubled (cf. 40:2b) so shall their reward be doubled. Yahweh will make with them an eternal covenant and all shall recognize them as the people whom he has blessed. **6.** ' pride yourselves ' : ' array yourselves '. **7a.** 'Instead of their shame which was

450j doubled and because insult and spittle was their portion'. Note the allusion to 40:2 (doubled) and to the Servant text 50:6*b*. **8.** 'In a holocaust', lit. in iniquity, may have been originally a participle, *iniquitous*.

k **10-11.** The prophet expresses his jubilation in salvation, conceived as already attained, by a lyrical outburst. In **10** at least he represents the community, clad in the garments of salvation and the mantle of righteousness, compared to the turban of the bridegroom and the wedding dress of the bride. The joy of salvation is the joy of the wedding day. As surely as the earth brings forth its fruits so surely shall Yahweh produce in Israel the fruits of righteousness and renown.

l **LXII 1-12 Longing for the New Sion**—In his ardent desire for Sion's glorification the prophet cannot refrain from repeating his announcement. He describes the glory of the New Sion, **1-5**, appoints watchers to remind Yahweh of his promise, **6-7**, confirmed by oath, **8-9**, predicts the return of the Diaspora, **10-12**.

m **1-5. 1.** The prophet cannot be silent until he sees his predictions fulfilled. Vg personifies justice and salvation. **2.** Sion's glory will be admired by all nations and celebrated by new God-given names. As names express nature and attributes, new names are needed to describe the new Sion. **3.** She shall be a beautiful crown, a royal diadem in God's hand. So Samaria is the proud crown of Ephraim, 28:1, and the city outline is inscribed on Yahweh's hand, 49:16. **4.** No longer shall she be called 'Forsaken' and 'Desolate' but 'My delight in her' and 'Espoused'. These are not the God-given names, but indications of Sion's altered state. **5.** Yahweh will delight in Sion as the bridegroom in his bride ; *cf.* 54:6.

n **6-7.** Watchers are appointed by the prophet over the walls of Sion to remind Yahweh incessantly of his promise to rebuild them. Here as in 21:6 ff. the watchers are a literary device and therefore undetermined. Sion is still unestablished, **7**, and at least incompletely walled.

o **8-9.** Yahweh has sworn that there shall be no oppression in the new Sion and that his people shall enjoy without molestation the harvests which they have planted. The tillage is done by foreigners, 61:5, who serve the Jewish landowners. The mention of the courts of the sanctuary is proleptic.

p **10-12.** The first two verses combine several citations from Isaias II. The way to be prepared might be a sanctuary way in Palestine or a way home from exile. The gates however are more probably those of the centre of interest, Sion, than of unmentioned Babylon. It is therefore the returned exiles who are exhorted to prepare a *via sacra* for the Diaspora Jews. The names in **12** indicate the holiness, happiness and glory of the new Sion.

451a **LXIII 7-LXIV 11 Appeal to Yahweh from his Afflicted People**—This appeal was composed after the ruin of the temple in 587 B.C. and before its reconstruction 520-515. It belongs to the early post-exilic period. The people are distressed and discouraged, conscious of sin and not expectant of proximate deliverance. Yahweh is praised for his mighty deeds in the past, **65:7-14**, and appealed to for aid as the Father of his people, **15-19**, and the God of Miracles, **64:1-5a**. Confession of sins follows, **5b-7**, and renewed appeal to God and Father, **8-11**.

b **LXIII 7-14.** The prophet praises Yahweh in the name of the people. **8.** Yahweh chose them as his people and expected obedience from them. **8b-9a.** '*He became their saviour in all their affliction. Not a messenger nor an angel but he himself delivered them*' ; *cf.* Ex 33 where Yahweh proposes an angel as leader, but eventually leads himself. 'His face' means his presence, himself. On 'carried' *cf.* Deut 32:11. **10-11.** 'the spirit of his Holy One' : '*his holy spirit*'. Frequently in the OT God is conceived as operating by his spirit and as imparting his spirit to man to increase man's strength. The rebellions of Israel in the past and their punishment are commemorated. **11.** '*They* [MT 'he'] *remembered the days of old, Moses his servant* [MT 'people'].

Where is he who brought up from the sea the shepherd of his flock ? Where is he who put within him his holy spirit ?' God's Might (lit. arm) guided Moses and divided the waters of the Red Sea. In **13b-14** the Exodus is further commemorated.

15-19. Yahweh is now called upon to manifest his mercy as in the days of old, to glorify his name by saving his people. **15b.** 'multitude' : '*commotion*'. Commotion of bowels is compassion. **15c.** '*Restrain not thy mercies*'. God is their father. **16.** He alone, not their earthly fathers, Abraham and Israel, can save them. **17.** He is regarded as author of what he could have prevented but did not prevent, error and hardness of heart. He is asked to turn or return, show himself gracious and merciful. **18** (slightly corrected) : '*Why did the wicked possess thy holy mountain and our enemies trample on thy sanctuary ?*' **19.** Yahweh seems to have abandoned them. '*We are become as a people over whom thou didst never rule*'.

LXIV 1-5a. Yahweh is now appealed to as a wonder-worker to descend in a theophany and save Israel from her enemies. **2a.** '*As when fire kindles brushwood, as when fire makes water boil*'. Fire, in particular lightning, accompanies a theophany. **3-4** (omitting the repetition of 1*b*) : '*Shouldst thou do terrible things which we did not expect, which have not been heard of from of old. Nor ear has heard, nor eye has seen a God besides thee who workest for those who hope in thee*'. The work is redemption ; *cf.* 1 Cor 2:9. **5a.** Thou carest for the just who remember thy ways.

5b-7. 5b. '*Behold thou wert angry and we sinned. Thou didst murmur at our iniquity, and we did evil*'. When Yahweh punished them, instead of repenting they continued to sin. Sin takes away a people's strength, makes them like faded leaves before the wind. As past sins are confessed the tenses are past.

8-11. 8. The stressing of the fatherhood of God foreshadows the 'Our Father' of the Gospel. **10.** 'the city of thy sanctuary' : '*thy holy cities*'. **11.** Other cities besides Jerusalem are in ruins and the magnificent temple is reduced to ashes. Divine aid is urgently implored.

LXV 1-LXVI 24. These two chapters are closely related in style and subject-matter and form a fitting conclusion to the whole book. Two classes of Israelites are distinguished, the rebellious who shall perish in the final judgement and the faithful who shall enjoy the Messianic blessings. The purification of Israel and the salvation of a remnant predicted in the prophet's inauguration, ch 6, shall thus be accomplished. The prose passage, **66:18-24**, describes Sion as religious centre of the world and predicts universal worship of Yahweh.

LXV 1-25 Final Purification of Israel : Chastisement and Reward—Yahweh threatens the rebels with chastisement, **1-7**, promises the Messianic kingdom to the faithful, **8-10**, Contrast of the doom of the rebels with the lot of the faithful, **11-16**. Happiness of the elect, **17-25**.

1-7. These threats against the wicked cannot be a reply to the humble petition which precedes and are moreover contrasted with the promises subsequently made to the good, 8-10. They begin therefore a new prophecy.

1a. '*I was accessible to them that asked me not, I was available to them that sought me not*'. The rebellious Jews neither asked nor sought Yahweh always ready to help them. St Paul abandons the literal sense when he applies this text to the Gentiles, Rom 10:20. **3b.** They are accused of sacrificing in gardens, offering incense on bricks, evidently to false gods, **4a**, frequenting graves and holes, practising necromancy, **4b**, eating swine's flesh and other unclean meats, **5a**, saying : '*Stand off, touch me not lest I sanctify thee*' (apparently practising mystic rites which made them taboo to the uninitiated). **5b-6.** These outrages provoke Yahweh's anger and cry out for retribution. 'Bosom' means 'receptacle'. Not only the sins of the rebels but those of their ancestors will be punished.

8-10. The Messianic remnant is here represented as a few good *grapes* (DV ' grain ') in a cluster, not cast aside with the others *because there is a blessing in them.* These are Yahweh's servants. They shall possess his mountains, that is all Palestine. Sharon, **10**, may be a corruption of Yeshīmŏn, a desert west of the Dead Sea.

11-16. 11-12. The rebellious who forsook Yahweh and worshipped Gad and Meni will be slain. Gad is the god of good fortune. Meni is probably identical with the Arabian goddess, Manat, and may be the consort of Gad. ' upon it ', 11 : ' to *Meni* ' ; ' will number ', 12 : ' *destine* '. **13-14.** The lots of the faithful and the rebellious are contrasted. In **15** ' The Lord God shall slay thee ' is probably a gloss. Names are used in imprecations when a person or nation becomes a *mashal*, byword or type of misfortune. Hence Israel's old name must be replaced by a new one. **16.** In blessings and in oaths only the true God will be invoked. MT reads *God of Amen* (fidelity), LXX *God of Truth*.

17-25. 17. The New Heaven and the New Earth indicate a transformation of the universe in which wickedness and oppression will be replaced by righteousness and happiness. Past evils shall be forgotten. **18.** All shall rejoice and, **19**, none shall weep. **20.** There shall be no sickness, no premature death. ' Infant of (a few) days ' means ' shortlived '. Death of a mere centenarian would then be considered premature like the death of an infant or the sudden death of a sinner. **22.** The tree is a figure of longevity. **24.** There will be perfect harmony between Yahweh and his people and, **25**, peace between man and beast. The Messianic kingdom here depicted is material rather than spiritual. The picture is incomplete.

LXVI 1-24 Final Judgement and Final Salvation— Oracle on the rebuilding of the temple, **1-4.** Judgement a surprise to the rebellious, **5-6**, and to the just, **7-9.** The happiness of the just, **10-14.** Fate of the wicked, **15-17.** Sion religious centre of the world, **18-24.**

1-4. The returned exiles were prevented from rebuilding the temple immediately by lack of resources and the hostility of their neighbours. Yahweh consoles the zealous. He does not require a temple for the heavens are his abode, the earth his footstool. What he requires is obedience to his commands. Cult is not rejected but subordinated to obedience. **2.** ' were made ' (MT) : ' *are mine* ' (LXX). The just are contrasted with the wicked, **3**, ' *who sacrifice oxen but also slay their fellow-men, who slaughter sheep but also break the necks of dogs, who combine meal-offerings with swine's blood and incense offerings with idol-worship* '. Dogs and swine were unclean. Sacrifice without conversion, not sacrifice in general, is

vain. Altar of sacrifice without temple indicates an **451n** early post-exilic date.

5-6. The just are warned not to heed the mockery of **o** their wicked brethren who deride them saying : ' Let Yahweh glorify himself that we also may see your joy '. The mockers will be confounded by the sudden manifestation of Yahweh their judge thundering in the city and temple (rebuilt before the final judgement). **6.** ' *Hark to the tumult in the city, hark to the temple, hark to Yahweh dealing retribution to his enemies* '.

7-9. 7. The just in the day of salvation are compared **p** to a mother bearing a child without suffering the pangs of childbirth. **8.** The *land* (DV ' earth ') is the mother, its inhabitants the child. **9.** Yahweh who enables mothers to bear children will not himself be childless.

10-14. 10-11. The prophet is so sure of the future **q** glory of Sion that he invites not only future blessed but present mourners to rejoice with her. ' abundance of her glory ' : ' *breasts of her riches* '. **12.** The immediate source of Sion's well-being is the riches of the Gentiles who will honour her for Yahweh's sake. **13.** Yahweh will be as a mother to his people and ' *they* [lit. you] *shall be comforted in Jerusalem* '. **14** (after ' rejoice ') : ' *and your bones shall sprout like grass* '.

15-17. The last judgement is briefly depicted. Yahweh **r** appears in fire and judges by fire. He is also a warrior whose chariots resemble a whirlwind and who slays many with his sword. **16a.** Read *the whole earth* with LXX after ' judge '. **17.** The rebellious Jews also ' *who sanctified and cleansed themselves for the gardens* [where they worshipped false gods] . . . *ate swine's flesh and abominations* [perhaps creeping things] *and mice* ' shall be consumed.

18-24. This passage is generally regarded as a later **s** addition. It predicts the return to Sion of the Diaspora Jews and the conversion of all nations to Yahweh. *Their works and their plans*, **18a**, *shall be consumed*, **17c.** Omit ' them together with ', **18b.** Yahweh comes to Jerusalem where the Gentiles assemble to see his glory. **19.** He puts a sign on these and sends those who have escaped (the judgement) to the nations : Tharshish (in Spain), Put and Lud (in North Africa), Mesech, Rosh (?), Thubal (in Asia Minor), Yawan (Greece), to make his glory known to them. **20.** They bring back the Jews of the Diaspora with rich presents. **21.** Some of them are made priests and Levites. **22-23.** There will be a new heaven and a new earth for Israel and all flesh will adore Yahweh. **24.** The corpses of the apostates will be seen in Gehenna outside Jerusalem where *their worm dies not and their fire is not extinguished.* This text, in its literal sense, does not teach the eternal punishment of the lost in the next world. Typically, however, it is so interpreted by our Lord, Mk 9:47 f.

JEREMIAS

(JEREMIAH)

By C. LATTEY, S.J.

452a Bibliography—A. Calmet, O.S.B., *Commentarius literalis in omnes libros Veteris et Novi Testamenti*, vol 6, 1735 ; J. Knabenbauer, S.J., *Commentarius in Jeremiam prophetam*, CSS, 1889 ; F. Nötscher, *Das Buch Jeremias*, BB, 1934, and *Jeremias* in the Echter-Bibel, 1947 ; A. Condamin, S.J., *Le Livre de Jérémie*, 1936 ; L. Dennefeld, *Les grands prophètes traduits et commentés* (La Sainte Bible, vol. 7), 1946 ; E. Podechard, *Le Livre de Jérémie : structure et formation*, RB 37 (1928), 181–97 ; *B. Duhm, *Das Buch Jeremia*, 1901 ; *S. R. Driver, *The Book of the Prophet Jeremiah*, 1908² ; *A. B. Ehrlich, *Randglossen zur hebräischen Bibel*, vol. 4, 1912 ; *A. S. Peake, *Jeremiah and Lamentations*, C B¹, 1910–12 ; *A. W. Streane, *Jeremiah and Lamentations*, 1913 ; *L. Elliott Binns, *The Book of Jeremiah*, 1919 ; *J. Skinner, *Prophecy and Revelation : Studies in the Life of Jeremiah*, 1922 (reprint 1940).

b Chronological Scheme—In order that the prophecies of Jeremias may be followed intelligently, it seems necessary to rearrange them for the most part in chronological order. The scheme follows the reigns of the kings. The chronology followed is that of the section on the *Chronology of the OT*.

Part I Josias : 641/640 B.C. : chh 1–20 except 12:7–13:27 ; §§ 456–8.
(Joachaz : 609 : nothing)
Part II Joakim : 609 : chh 26 ; 22–23 ; 25 ; 36 ; 45 ; 35 ; 12:7–13:27 ; §§ 459–60.
(Joachin : 598 : nothing)
Part III Sedecias : 598.
　(*a*) warnings : chh 24 ; 29 ; 27–28 ; 51 ; 59–64 ; § 461.
　(*b*) promises of restoration : chh 30–33 ; § 462.
　(*c*) the siege : chh 21 ; 34; 37–39 ; § 463.
Part IV After the fall of Jerusalem in 587 : chh 40–44 ; § 464.
Part V Prophecies against the nations : chh 46–51 ; §§ 465–7.
Part VI Historical appendix : ch 52 ; §468.

453a The Prophet : his Name and Person—The meaning of the name Jeremias is uncertain. He was the son of Helcias (1:1) but it is very improbable that this was the Helcias who discovered the Book of the Law (4 Kg 22:8), for this would almost certainly have been indicated, and there is no hint of the prophet having close relations with the temple authorities. He was a priest (1:1), a native of the priestly town Anathoth (Jos 21:18), the modern Anata, about 2½ m. NE. of Jerusalem, which was also the home of the high-priest Abiathar, from whom he may have been descended.

b His History—*Prophecy* essentially comprises a revelation and a mission. Jeremias' mission was chiefly to king and people, his revelation was chiefly that of the coming destruction of Jerusalem. He exhorted them not only to repent, but to submit to the overwhelming power of Babylon, with a promise of merciful treatment if they did so, and also in any case of ultimate restoration. The tragedy of his life lay in his not being believed, in the evils coming to pass which he had foretold, in his being treated as a false and disloyal prophet of evil. King Josias he praised (22:15–16) :

against Joakim, who probably meant to kill him (36:26), his language is severe (22:13–19) : the weak Sedecias he tried earnestly to save (38:14–23, etc.).

After the Capture of Jerusalem Nabuchodonosor gave orders that he should be treated well (39:11–12). After the murder of Godolias, the Jew appointed to govern his countrymen under the Babylonians, Jeremias tried to persuade the Jews to remain peacefully in Palestine, but they fled to Egypt, fearing Babylonian reprisals, and forced Jeremias and Baruch to go with them (chh 41–3). The rest of the book is taken up with rebukes and prophecies uttered against the Jews in Egypt and the Gentiles. He was probably stoned to death by the Jews in Egypt. Tertullian (*Adversus Gnosticos Scorpiace*, ch 8 : PL 2, 137) states that he was stoned. St Jerome (*Adversus Jovinianum*, 2, 37 : PL 23, 335) writes that he was stoned by the people when proclaiming the captivity, an evident slip about the time : on Isaias (PL 24, 342) he writes that Jeremias and Baruch died before Nabuchodonosor invaded Egypt, so that the Jewish tradition that the king took him and Baruch to Babylon probably sprang up later. Our Lord may have had Jeremias in mind when he spoke of Jerusalem stoning those sent to her (Mt 23:37 ; Lk 13:34).

The Lachish Ostraca—Nothing has here been said of the ostraca (jar-fragments used, after the manner of the time, for letters) found in 1935 at Tell ed-Duweir, about 25 m. between SW. by W. and WSW. of Jerusalem, probably the ancient city of Lachish. They belong to the last days of Sedecias, and may offer some evidence of a movement in favour of surrendering to Babylon, which was what Jeremias preached ; there is also mention of a prophet, but with no real clue to his identity. It must be enough here to refer to ' The Prophet ' in the Lachish Ostraca, by Prof. D. Winton Thomas (Tyndale Press, 1946), where a bibliography will also be found.

The Prophetic Office of Jeremias : his Sufferings—To appreciate the divine purpose of the message, we must take into account the peculiar character of the messenger, and seldom more than in this case. His was a life of intense suffering, led by one peculiarly sensitive to it. He was naturally emotional and tender-hearted, struck with horror at the fate which it was his duty to proclaim for his beloved city, the chosen city of Yahweh. Often he cries out in pain and bitterness (*e.g.* 8:18 ; 9:1). His life was in danger, even from his fellow-townsmen (11:21). Conscious that his cause was the cause of God, he could pray for vengeance upon his enemies, and, with poetic instinct like the psalmist's, picture what their overthrow would be likely to be in actual fact (*e.g.* 18:21–23) ; but his prayer did not reach out beyond the grave.

His Faithfulness—At all times he remains true to God ; even in his grief he avers that ' thy word was to me a joy and gladness of my heart ' (15:16), and the frequent revelations made to him show that he enjoyed a true intimacy with God. This intimacy, indeed, shows itself at times in a strange manner, perhaps due in part to his disturbed frame of mind : sometimes it is not easy to distinguish his own words from those of God. Thus in 4:19–22 it is Jeremias' heart that is troubled, but God who complains that ' my foolish people have not known me '. Other examples are

9:18 ; 13:20–27 ; 16:19–21. The prophet also at times makes it difficult to distinguish precisely between himself and his people ; *e.g.* in 10:17–25 it is generally agreed that at least 19–20 must be assigned to Jerusalem (or Judah in general).

His Divine Commission—Thus far we have been considering the more subjective aspect of the prophet's ministry ; we may now look at the more objective side, and analyse the characteristics of his prophecies as such. We begin, as the book of Jeremias itself begins, w'th his divine commission, only stopping to notice that he seems by a rare privilege to have been sanctified in the womb, like the Baptist. This would mean that he was freed from original sin and received sanctifying grace even before birth. This appears to be the more likely interpretation of 1:5, though Père Condamin (*ad loc.*) argues that it need only mean 'consecrated for the prophetic office', quoting in support important Catholic authorities. Ecclus 49:9 in LXX and Vg favours this view, but he is mistaken in supposing that the newly discovered Hebrew text of Ecclus necessarily implies it. Such passages as Jer 31:31, and still more Ez 11:19 ; 18:31 suggest sanctifying grace ; but of course there is no strictly systematic theology in the OT.

Neither his mission nor his revelation is limited in any way (1:7) : the former was to include not only Judah and Jerusalem and the kings (17:20) and Israel (31:10) but the Gentiles (1:10), special groups of Jews (42:19), and individuals, *e.g.* Sedecias (37:16).

His Inspiration—The book of Jeremias is more than a record of history and prophecy ; it is also a book of Holy Scripture, written under the divine impulse given to the sacred writer's intellect and will, and with a special providence providing for the writing of it. Such a book need not in whole or part record an antecedent revelation ; in the present case much revelation is embodied, and much mere narrative. There is much sheer prediction, though this again is not essential to inspiration or revelation or even to prophecy as such. Nor of course is it necessary that all prophecy should be recorded ; evidently much OT prophecy, and much prophecy by Jeremias, has not been recorded. Much exhortation is found here, as in the prophetical books in general, with threats and prophecies.

His Secretary—It is unlikely that Jeremias wrote his prophecies with his own hand ; he is bidden write in 36:2, but actually he dictates to Baruch (36:4, 32). There is also record of his writing in 29:1 and 51:60. It may well be that Jeremias used Baruch as his regular secretary, and this may help to account for the mention of Jeremias in the third person ; such an explanation is not really needed, however, for the use of the third person by the prophets is fairly common, perhaps to insist that their words are primarily God's : *cf.* Is 7:3 ; Agg 1:13, etc.

False Prophecies—Some further light is thrown upon the prophetic office of Jeremias and its difficulties from the consideration of the false prophets. He inveighs against them fairly frequently. In 14:14 Yahweh explicitly denies that they have either revelation or mission : *cf.* 23:16, 32. Most important is the Hananias incident, where also revelation and mission are denied (28:15). In his letter to the captives in Babylon Jeremias attacks the false prophets there also (29:9).

Prophetic Symbolism—In Jeremias' ministry, as in OT prophecy in general, a conspicuous part is played by symbolism. It may be enough to point to the two symbols of God's impending action shown him at the outset (1:11–14), and to the Hananias incident (27:2–3 ; 28:10, 13). And the prophet himself may well be reckoned a symbol or type of the suffering Saviour, the Man of Sorrows who likewise wept over Jerusalem (Lk 19:41–44).

The Text : its Arrangement—The time of Jeremias' ministry was a time of great turmoil, and he himself was likewise in a great turmoil ; and this turmoil is reflected in the text as can be seen at once from the chronological arrangement in § 452*b*. The fact that there has been no systematic rearrangement is an argument that we have it in its primitive state. The several portions were probably collected soon after the prophet's death, and it is natural to assign the work of redaction to Baruch.

The Septuagint—This seems to represent an alternative arrangement, for it differs considerably from MT, thus giving us a more valuable check upon the text than it usually provides, and also pushing back the date of the original compilation, the ancestor of both texts. The internal evidence also favours an early date : there is a vivid reality alike in the narratives and the discourses which a later inventor is not at all likely to have achieved.

The Authorship—The tradition of authorship, too, is constant. It is not the manner of OT books, or of NT books either, to quote each other explicitly (though NT often quotes OT) ; but this lends additional force to the explicit appeal in Dan 9:2 and 2 Par 36:21–22 (*cf.* Esd 1:1) to the prophecy of the return from the Babylonian captivity after seventy years. There is also an implied reference to much in Jeremias in Ecclus 49:8–9. NT references are numerous, and are mentioned in their place ; it may be enough here to mention Heb 8:8–12, from 31:31–34.

The Poetry—That much of the text is in poetry is certain ; but the precise character and extent of the poetry is a thorny question, which cannot here be pursued at length, any more than that of textual criticism. In general it seems true to say that the set prophetic utterances are in poetry, while the narratives and God's private communications to Jeremias are in prose.

Note. Jeremias often speaks of the 'Chaldaeans' where he means the Babylonians, and sometimes of 'Chaldaea' where he means Babylonia. The Chaldaeans, originally a distinct race from the Babylonians, were at this time, as the result of long encroachment, the ruling caste among them, and thus the prophet applies their name to the fusion of the two races, and to their common country.

Part I Josias King: 641/640–609 B.C. : chh 1–20, except 12:7–13:27. There does not seem to be any solid reason against assigning these chapters to the reign of Josias, who is mentioned in 1:2 ; 3:6. That much evil already prevailed is clear from this prophecy itself, which is confirmed by 4 Kg 22–23 ; 2 Par 33–34 ; but punishment was postponed out of regard for Josias himself ; *cf.* 4 Kg 22:18–20.

I 1–19 The Call of Jeremias—**1.** For Helcias and Anathoth, see § 453*a*. **6.** His plea that he is a child refers to his lack of skill in speech (*cf.* Moses in Ex 4:10–16), and **8** betrays a certain shrinking fear. He receives encouragement and a symbolic confirmation of his call, based upon a play on the words. **11.** Jeremias sees '*a branch of an almond tree*'. **12.** God answers, ' I will watch over my word ', the word ' watch ' being practically the same in Hebrew as ' almond tree '. **13** seems best rendered, ' I see a caldron *blown upon*', *i.e.* over a fire blown upon, ' from the north '. **14.** God answers, literally, ' from the north shall evil *be blown upon* all the inhabitants of the land ', like a fire being fanned. ' The north ' indicates already the Babylonian invasion. With the call of Jeremias compare that of Isaias (Is 6) and Ezechiel (Ez 2). The call came to Jeremias in 628 B.C., the 13th year of Josias (1:2) ; he thus had forty years of ministry before the city's fall in 587. ' *to whomsoever* ' (with LXX) is a more likely translation. LXX may be right in omitting ' to waste and to destroy ' in 10, and ' the land ' and ' the priests ' in 18 ; but the omission of ' the priests ' may be to avoid disedification, as sometimes elsewhere in the book. **17.** ' *Be not dismayed at them, lest I dismay thee before them* ' ; *cf.* Ez 3:18–20.

There is a reference to 1:7–8 and 1 Par 16:35 in

456b Ac 26:17, and to 1:8 (among other OT passages) in Ac 18:9–10.

c **II 1–VI 30 The Call to Repentance**—The main theme is the faithlessness of Judah, represented as a faithless wife, with invitations to repentance and prophecies of coming doom. Jerusalem, the capital, is prominent, as usual. The years in the desert are represented as the betrothal-time of Yahweh and Israel, when she followed him with love ; though we gather from the Pentateuch and some passages in the prophets (*e.g.* 7:24–25 ; Ez 20:13) that even then her conduct left much to be desired. His benefits at that time should be remembered.

d **2.** '*I have remembered the affection of thy youth*'. **3.** 'Israel *was* holy . . . *whoever devoured him was held guilty* : evils *did* come'. **7.** '*into a fruitful land*', though the word is the same as 'Carmel', to which it was especially applied. **8.** The 'pastors' or shepherds are the rulers. 'by Baal', a word properly meaning 'owner' or 'lord', but a title commonly applied to the local gods of the Canaanites. It probably has a collective sense here, as in Os 2:8 ; for the plur. see Jer 2:23 ; Os 2:13. 'idols', lit. 'things that do not profit' ; in the sing. in 11 ; *cf.* 16:19. **9.** God will '*contend*' (the same verb is repeated) against them as though an accuser in court. **10.** 'Cethim' (Kittim) is probably derived from Kition, the modern Larnaka in Cyprus, whence the name spread. It may here represent the West generally, and Cedar (a nomad tribe to E. of Jordan ; *cf.* 49:28 ; Ps 119:5, etc.) the East. **11.** 'their glory' is God himself ; *cf.* Deut 10:21.

e **14–19. The Punishment of Idolatry**—Israel was not a slave, purchased or homeborn, that he should otherwise have met with such treatment. **15.** The lion was a symbol for Assyria, which had already destroyed the Northern Kingdom (Israel in the narrow sense). **16.** Memphis (Heb. Noph or Moph, Egyptian Mennufer) the ancient capital of northern Egypt, not far from Cairo, and Taphnes (Tahpanhes), the modern Defneh (from Gk. Daphnai) at the NE. of the Delta, stand for Egypt : mentioned again in 44:1 ; 46:14. The translation is uncertain : perhaps, 'shaved the crown of thy head', a shaven head being a disgrace (*cf.* 47:5 ; 48:37). **18.** 'the troubled water' is really a name of the Nile, *Shihor*, as in Is 23:3. In Jos 13:3 ('the troubled water') and 1 Par 13:5 ('Sihor') only the easternmost branch is meant. The etymology is uncertain. 'the river' is the river *par excellence*, the Euphrates. The Hebrews vacillated between Egypt and Assyria 'like a silly dove' (Os 7:11) in the effort to find security, but rather (**19**) should

f have looked to Yahweh. **20.** The 'high hills' and 'green trees' were the centres of idolatrous worship, represented as adultery against Israel's true husband, Yahweh, and all the more fitly because of the impure practices carried on there. **22.** Though she wash herself with '*lye*' (washing-soda), and use much '*soap*', the stain of sin will remain. **23.** 'the valley' is 'the valley of the son of Hinnom' ; see on 7:31. In her adulterous desire for the Baalim she has run after them like '*a swift young she-camel entangling her ways*', running wildly hither and thither, (**24**) like a wild she-ass panting with desire : '*in her heat, who shall turn her back?*' Her lovers (the Baalim) need not trouble themselves ; at her mating time she will herself seek them eagerly. **25.** The prophet cries to her : 'Do not run till thy sandals are worn out, and thy throat parched!' But the answer is a despairing refusal to give up the 'strangers', the foreign gods. **26–27.** The 'stock' is the wooden pole (the 'Asherah') and 'the stone' is the obelisk or pillar, both representing false gods and called 'father', but they would prove of no avail. **28b** is repeated in 11:13a. LXX adds 11:13b here, which Condamin on metrical grounds thinks correct.

g **30. Israel has refused Correction :** 'your sword hath devoured your prophets like a destroying lion'. **31.** '*O generation that ye are, behold Yahweh's word*'. He

has not proved to them a mere desert, or '*a land of thick darkness*'. **32.** For 'stomacher' render perhaps 'sashes' ; Yahweh is the true glory of his bride. **33.** '*How cleverly thou contrivest to win love! Even the bad women thou hast taught thy ways*'. **34.** 'And in thy *hands* is found . . . not in *burglary didst thou* find them', when it would have been lawful to kill them (Ex 22:2), 'but by every *terebinth*'. The reference is to the sacrifice of children at the sacred trees ; *cf.* 19:4–5. **36.** Israel has cheapened herself '*in changing thy way*' ; see on 18. **37.** 'thy hand shall be upon thy head', a gesture of disappointment and disgrace (*cf.* 2 Kg 13:19), because 'Yahweh hath rejected those in whom thou didst trust'.

The Faithless Wife—In the Heb. **III:1** begins simply with the word 'saying' ; it seems most likely that there was a definite reference to Deut 24:1–4, which forbad such a return and is certainly in question. 'many lovers ; *and wouldst thou retun to me?* saith *Yahweh*'. **2.** 'Lift up thine eyes to the *bare heights*' ('bare-heights' is a favourite word of Jeremias), where she prostituted herself to the Baalim, waiting to court them 'as an *Arab*' in the wilderness of northern Arabia (*cf.* 25:24) lies in wait for travellers. **3.** The reference to the rains is in the spirit of much of OT, *e.g.* 5:24. **4.** '*Hast thou not but now cried unto me, "My father, thou art the friend of my youth"?*' She uses the language of wheedling affection, even while going after other gods. God is often spoken of as the husband of Israel, but also (to give a fuller idea of the relationship) as her father, *e.g.* Mal 1:6. **5.** '*Will he retain* (his anger) *for ever*', she asks, '*will he keep* (it) *to the end?*' 'Behold, so thou hast spoken', answers Yahweh, 'but thou hast done evil things, and hast had thy way', lit. 'and hast been able', *i.e.* 'and hast been able' to carry out thy purposes. **6.** Here, as sometimes elsewhere, Israel is distinguished from Judah as the Northern Kingdom (subdued by the Assyrians in 721 B.C.) ; but it could always be used for the whole people. 'high mountain', etc. : see on 2:20. **9.** Judah defiled the land by her reckless readiness for idolatry. 'stones and stocks' : see on 2:26–27. **11.** Judah had less excuse with temple and liturgy, priests and Levites, kings of the line of David, and the warning example of Israel. **14.** The rest of the chapter is an appeal to Judah and Israel together. 'I am your' true Baal : see on 2:8. He will restore them to Sion, but only a 'remnant' (*cf.* 31:7), one from a city, two of a clan (the large units within the twelve tribes).

16. In the Glory of those Days even the Ark will be forgotten, 'neither shall they miss it, neither shall it be made any more'. **18.** 'the land of the north' designates in general the lands to which Assyria took the captives of Israel, and Babylonia those of Judah. **19–20.** How is all this possible with such perversity ? They must call Yahweh 'father' and be faithful to him (*cf.* 1 Pet 1:17). **21.** But now upon the 'bare heights' (*cf.* 2), where they had sinned, 'is heard *the suppliant weeping*' of the Israelites, who are being punished for forgetting their God, but (**22**) accept his invitation to return. **23.** The hills where they sacrificed have proved a delusion, and '*the uproar on the mountains*' of their orgies. **24.** '*The shameful thing*', Baal, has been their curse. **25.** '*Let us lie down in our shame, and let our confusion cover us*', by reason of our sins.

IV 1. Again comes the Invitation to Repentance : 'and if thou wilt put away thy *detestable things* (*i.e.* idols), *and wilt not wander far from me*, (**2**) *and wilt swear in truth* and judgement and righteousness, "As Yahweh liveth", *then* shall the nations *bless themselves by him*', using his name in invoking blessings on themselves, 'and in him shall they glory'.

3. After a preliminary warning not to sow among thorns, (**4**) and to circumcise (not only their bodies, but) their hearts (*cf.* 6:10 ; 9:28, etc.), the prophet turns to his main theme, **the doom of Judah and Jerusalem**, though exhortations to a saving repentance never cease. **5.** The opening of the invasion produces

61 a rush to the fortified cities. **6.** ' Set up a *signpost* ' to guide the fugitives ' *toward Sion : take refuge* ' from the Babylonian invader, **(7)** the lion, ' the *destroyer of nations* ' : **(9)** all shall be panic-stricken. **10.** ' *And they shall say* ', *i.e.* especially the false prophets of 14:15, etc., who complain that the prophecies which they claimed to be uttering from Yahweh have not been fulfilled. MT reads ' And I said ', but Jeremias would never have spoken thus ; the translation follows the Alexandrian MS of LXX ' *thou hast deceived* '. **11.** The invasion is ' a burning wind from the *bare heights* ' (*cf.* 3:2) in the wilderness in the way to the daughter of my people ', a poetical personification for ' my people ' simply, used also with names of cities.

m ' not to fan nor to cleanse ', because such a sirocco would blow away the grain along with the chaff and straw from the threshing-floor, whereas a gentle breeze would leave the grain behind. The ' fan ' was a long wooden fork with five or six prongs, used along with a wooden shovel to throw the mixture of grain, chaff and straw against the wind, thus also ' cleansing ' the grain. **12.** ' *A wind too strong for these things* ', for such winnowing, ' shall come *for me* ' at my command ; ' now will I also myself utter judgements *against* them '. **13.** The horses are swifter than *vultures*. **15.** One messenger brings news of the enemy from Dan in the north ; another ' *announceth calamity* ' from the hills of Ephraim ', only 8–10 miles away. **16.** ' Say ye to the nations, *publish concerning Jerusalem that besiegers* . . . are roaring ' like lions (*cf.* 7). **17.** They are putting up improvised shelters round Jerusalem like those of the guardians of cattle in the open country. **18.** ' *surely* it is bitter, *surely* . . .' **19.** ' My bowels, my bowels ! *Let me writhe ! The walls of my heart ! My heart moaneth within me* ' as it batters against them. **20.** ' *My tents* ' and ' *tent-hangings* ' ; the people's are meant. **26.** ' the *fruitful land* was a wilderness ' ; see on 2:7. **27.** Yahweh himself now speaks, but with the intimation that the destruction is not to be final (*cf.* 5:10, 18 ; 12:15 ; 30:11), which is later (25:11–12 ; 29:10) developed in the promises of return from the Babylonian exile after seventy years. **28.** ' The heavens *shall be dark* '.

n **30** ' thy lovers ' (as in 22:20 ; 30:14) are **Egypt and the other nations** (*cf.* 27:3) inclined to side with the Hebrews against the Babylonians, whom Judah therefore was inclined to court. ' though thou *enlargest thine eyes with antimony* ', blackening the edge of the eyelids above and below in order to increase by contrast the lustre of the eyes and make them look larger. **31.** Here instead will be ' the anguish *as of her that bringeth forth her first child* '. ' daughter of Sion ', see on 4:11. ' gasping for breath ', and crying with outstretched hands, ' Oh, woe is me, for my soul is fainting *because of murderers* '.

o **V 1.** If even one man can be found in Jerusalem that acts justly and makes faithfulness his aim, then will *I forgive her* (*cf.* Gen 18). **4.** The prophet thought that poverty and ignorance might explain the general wickedness, but **(5)** found that even the great men had shaken off the yoke of the Lord. **6.** The animals are the Babylonians. **7.** God himself speaks. **10.** ' *Go up into her vine-rows and destroy* '. Judah is represented as a vineyard ; she is not to be quite exterminated (see on 4:27). **12.** Israel and Judah even deny that God has spoken ; **(13)** according to them the prophets such as Jeremias ' *shall become wind* ', prove mere windbags. ' So be it to them ! ' with a gesture expressing destruction. **14.** ' you ' is Israel and Judah, ' thy ' is Jeremias.

p **16.** The Babylonians are deadly archers ; **(17)** they shall destroy sons and daughters, but there is no suggestion of cannibalism. **21.** *cf.* Is 6:9–10 ; Ez 12:2 ; Mk 8:18, etc. **24.** God ' preserveth *the appointed weeks of the harvest* ', seven in number (Deut 16:9), when there was usually no rain (1 Kg 12:16–19). **31.** ' the priests bear rule *under their control* : the people love to have it so '.

q **VI 1.** ' *Flee for safety, children of Benjamin, from out the midst of Jerusalem* ', which was in Benjamin, the tribe

of Jeremias. ' Sound the trumpet in Thecua ' (Tekoa), **456q** about 12 m. S of Jerusalem, to indicate a place of refuge. ' Bethacarem ' (Beth-haccherem) may be the ' Frank ' mountain 3 m. NE. of Tekoa. The ' standard ' or *signal* would probably be a beacon for the same purpose. **2.** ' The daughter of Sion . . . *will I cut off* '. **3.** ' The shepherds with their flocks ' are the hands of invaders ; ' *they shall feed every one of them, upon what is at hand* ', which shall be so abundant that they will not have to look elsewhere. **4-5.** The enemy are discussing their plans. **7.** ' cold ', *i.e.* fresh. **9.** ' *They shall thoroughly glean* as a vine the remnant of Israel '. The gleaner is bidden turn back his hand *upon the tendrils*, to make sure of leaving nothing behind. In 10 Jeremias speaks, but God in **11c** (' pour it out '). **14.** ' they would heal ' her ruin ' *lightly* ', as if nothing were easier. **15.** ' They shall be confounded . . . *are* not . . . *know* not '.

17. The ' watchmen ' are the Prophets. 21. Yahweh r ' will lay *stumbling-blocks* '. **22-24** are adapted to Babylon itself in 50:41–43. **25.** ' terror on every side ', a kind of refrain in the prophecy : again in 20:3, 10 ; 6:25 ; 46:5 ; 49:29 ; Lam 2:22 ; Ps 30:14. **27.** ' a trier ' (omit ' strong ') or assayer, to test them. **28.** ' *They are all utter rebels*, going about with slanders '. **29-30.** The figure from refining metals is resumed from 27 ; though ' the bellows *blow fiercely*, and the lead ' which has been mixed with the alloy containing the silver ' is consumed ', *i.e.* oxidized, the alloy is so inextricably mixed with the silver that the lead fails to carry it away, and ' the wicked are not separated : rejected silver ', because still impure, ' men shall call them '.

VII 1-X 25 Temple Prophecies—2. God sends Jere- **457a** mias to utter menaces at the temple gate, probably that leading into the inner court (20:2 ; 26:10 ; 36:10). It was built by King Joatham (4 Kg 15:35). **6.** The shedding of innocent blood probably refers to the sacrifice of children in the temple, though ' the valley of the son of Ennom ' (Hinnom) seems to have been the more usual place ; *cf.* 30–31. **7.** ' *I will cause you to dwell* in this place . . . *for ever and ever* '. **9-10.** ' *Will ye steal . . . and then come and stand before me ?* ' *Cf.* Is 56:7 ; Mt 21:13, etc. **12.** For Shiloh, *cf.* Jos 18:1 ; Jg 18:31 ; 21:12. The destruction is also mentioned in Ps 77:60 ; it doubtless took place after the Philistine victory of 1 Kg 4. **16.** The prophet is forbidden to pray for his people, as in 11:14 ; 14:11. God's purpose is fixed. **18.** ' The queen of heaven ' (again, 44:17–19) is Astaroth (probably Ashtart), ' the idol of the Sidonians ' (4 Kg 23:13), worshipped by the Phoenicians and (as Ishtar) by the Assyrians and Babylonians. The Greek name was Astarte. In **22-23** we have the Hebrew idiom of *relative* denial ; God's essential requirement was obedience to his voice, not mere sacrifices in themselves. See the present writer in JTS 42 (1941) 155–165. In **21**, therefore, he is ironical : let them multiply their holocausts, and even eat the flesh (a proceeding forbidden by the Law in the case of these sacrifices) for all he cared ; it was not these outward rites that he really had at heart. **29.** To cut off the hair was a sign of mourning : ' a lament on the *bare heights* ' such as that of Jephte's daughter (Jg 11:37–38). **30.** They have set up their idols even in the temple. **31.** ' The valley of the son of Ennom ', the vale of Hinnom, W. and S. of Jerusalem. ' The *high place* ' (sing.) or idol-sanctuary ' of Topheth ', the site of the burning. **32.** It shall be used for burials ' for lack of room '. **VIII:1-2 Even bones of the dead shall be desecrated,** b being spread out before the heavenly bodies which they had adored. **7.** ' *The stork in the heaven* knoweth her appointed times ' of migration ; and similarly the turtle and swift and (perhaps) swallow ; but ' my people ' do not realize what Yahweh has appointed for this time. *Cf.* Is 1:3. **8.** ' Lo, certainly *unto delusion* hath wrought the *deluded* pen of the scribes '. They put too much confidence in the possession of the

457b Mosaic Law which they copy out, and thus delude others also. **10b-12** practically repeats 6:13–15. **13.** ' I *will utterly consume them* ' : they are like vines bearing no grapes, etc. ' I have appointed those who will carry them off ' into exile : so Condamin, emending a difficult and uncertain text. **14-15** give the dismayed remarks of the people : ' *let us perish* there, for Yahweh our God *hath caused us to perish* '. ' gall ', *i.e.* bile, often used for bitterness of some kind : perhaps ' water of gall ' is the bitter and poisonous juice of the poppy (from which opium is prepared). **16.** The invaders ' *are come* and *have devoured* the land ' : prophetic anticipation often represents the future as present or past. **17.** ' basilisks ', perhaps the ' daboia xanthina ', a beautifully marked yellow viper, the largest and one of the most dangerous in Palestine. **19.** The ' far country ' of the Babylonian exile.

c IX 1-26 The whole chapter seems spoken by Yahweh, except **1**, which rather belongs (as in MT) to ch 8. **2.** ' adulterers ', *i.e.* idolaters. **7.** ' melt ', *i.e.* smelt by severe discipline. **9** repeats 5:9, 29. **10.** ' *take ye up . . . for the pastures of the wilderness* . . . the voice of the cattle* '. **11.** ' a lair of jackals ' ; *cf.* 49:33. **12.** A new sentence begins with, ' *Why hath the land perished* '. **15.** ' wormwood ' or absinth, a generic name for the bitter-tasting ' artemisia ' : often used metaphorically. ' water of gall ', see on 8:14. **17.** ' mourning women ' were ' wise ' or skilful at composing and reciting dirges. **18.** The use of the 1st person offers a striking example of the occasional lack of clear distinction between Yahweh's words and the prophet's own : *cf.* § 454*b*. **24.** *Cf.* 1 Cor 1:31 ; 2 Cor 10:17. **25.** ' I will punish *all them that are circumcised in their uncircumcision* ' of heart. **26.** *Cf.* Rom 2:25–29. These nations practised circumcision, including some Arab tribes who, contrary to Hebrew usage (Lev 19:27) cut the hair off their temples, probably with religious significance (mentioned again 25:23 ; 48:45 ; 49:32). Omit ' in the flesh ' with MT. It is more especially Israel (in view of her spiritual privileges) that is uncircumcised in heart.

d X 1-16 is very probably out of place and perhaps 9:23–26 as well ; the connexion is broken between what precedes and what follows. Jeremias may have written these words to the exiles at a later date. A more surprising sign of the disturbed state of his text (*cf.* § 455*a–b*) is **11**, which is in Aramaic, and originally was probably a marginal note. With **3-5** and **8-9**, *cf.* Is 44:12–17 ; Wis 13:10–14:1. The purpose is mockery of idols, by telling how they are produced. **5.** ' *They are like a pillar in a cucumber-garden, and speak not* ', *i.e.* like a scarecrow : *cf.* Bar 6:69. **9.** ' Tharsis ' is probably Tartessus in Spain ; ' Uphaz ' (or better, with some versions, ' *Ophir* ') is probably SW. Arabia, with perhaps some of the neighbouring African coast. **12-16** are repeated in 51:15–19 : **16.** ' Israel is the *tribe* of his inheritance ' (and in 51:19).

e 17-25 continues from 9:26 (or 9:22). **17.** ' Gather up thy *bundle from the ground* ' in preparation for exile, ' thou that dwellest in *the besieged city* ' of Jerusalem. **18.** perhaps, ' that they may *feel it* '. In **19-25** (see § 454*b*) the prophet seems to be speaking for Jerusalem. **19b.** The sense appears to be, ' But I [=Jerusalem] had said [=thought, as often in Hebrew], ' Well, this is just another misfortune of mine, and I must put up with it '. But it proved far worse than she anticipated. **20.** ' *My tent is despoiled* ', all its supporting cords are broken, there is no one to erect it any more, or to set up the tent-hangings. **22.** ' a lair of jackals ' ; *cf.* 49:33. **25.** *Cf.* Ps 78:6.

f XI 1-XII 6 The Covenant—There is an emphasis on the Mosaic covenant in 11:3, 6, 8, which may well be connected with the reforms following upon the discovery of the ' Book of the Law ' in the temple in the 18th year of Josias (623–2 B.C. : 4 Kg 22:3, 8). **3.** Judah and Jerusalem are to be reminded of the curses contained in Deut 27–28 ; *cf.* 8. **4.** Egypt was the furnace of their suffering ; *cf.* Deut 4:20. **5.** Palestine ' flowed with milk ', chiefly from goats, and wild

' honey ' from the rocks ; the expression is frequent **457b** (*e.g.* Ex 3:8) and implies other advantages. Arabs and Turks have been a blight on the land. **13a** repeats 2:28*b*. Judah has ' set up altars *to the abomination* ', the Baalim. **14.** See on 7:16. **15** probably means : ' *What business hath my beloved* [Judah ; *cf.* 12:7] in my house [the temple], *seeing that she hath wrought wickedness with many* [the Baalim of 13]? *And the hallowed flesh* [the temple sacrifices] *shall pass from thee. When thou dost evil, then thou rejoicest* '. **16.** ' *with sound of great storm he hath kindled fire upon it* ', striking the fair olive-tree with his lightning.

What follows (**11:18-12:6**) has no obvious connex- **g** ion with the preceding : **God reveals to Jeremias the plot of his fellow-townsmen** against him and their punishment. The prophet is perplexed at the prosperity of the wicked ; but God prepares him for still greater trials, such as must befall the elect for their sanctification. **19.** ' *Let us destroy the tree with its sap* '. **20.** ' Yahweh, Lord ' of the angel hosts '. ' reins ' (kidneys) stands for feelings, ' hearts ' rather for understandings. The prophet is fully convinced that his cause is God's, whom he calls upon to vindicate it. **XII:1.** Even after a favourable answer he remains perplexed, like the psalmist in Pss 38, 72. The Book of Wisdom (with 2 Mac 7, etc.) definitely sets forth an other-worldly view, which our Lord stressed still more strongly. **3.** Jeremias prays for strong divine intervention, but worse is to follow : (**5**) ' if in a land of peace *thou hast no assurance*, how wilt thou do in the Jordan fringe ' amid thick bushes and luxuriant vegetation, haunted by lions ? (*cf.* Zach 11:3).
(For 12:7–13:27, see § 460*f–j*.)

XIV 1-XV 21 The Drought—A drought can still be **457** a terrible disaster in the East. We do not know the date of that here in question. **1.** ' word ' in Heb. can mean ' matter, affair ' : ' *concerning the drought* '. **2.** ' Judah mourneth, and her gates [=inhabitants] *languish, they are in mourning garb* upon the ground. . . . **4.** *The tillers of the ground are dismayed*. **6.** . . . the wild asses . . . pant for air like the crocodile ', coming out of the water to breathe, ' their eyes fail ', looking in vain for food. The prophet appeals to Yahweh : **7.** ' *act* for thy name's sake. . . . **9.** Why shouldst thou be as a man *surprised* . . . thy name is called *over us* ', we are thine. But Yahweh answers (**10**) that ' this people . . . have loved to *wander*. . . . **11.** Pray not for this people ' : see on 7:16. **13.** Jeremias lays the blame on the prophets, to whom (**14-15, 18**) Yahweh promises punishment, but without excusing the people. **17.** The term ' virgin daughter ' is often applied in OT to a people, especially to Israel (in Is 23:12 to Sidon), perhaps in the sense of not having been subdued by an enemy.

The prophet, appalled at the message which he is to **b** deliver (*i.e.* 17–18) pleads still more earnestly (19–22) : but his plea is rejected even more decisively (**XV 1-9**). **3.** ' I will visit them with four *families* ' of evils. **4.** ' I will make them a *consternation* to all the kingdoms '. For Manasses' evil reign (698–697 to 643–642 B.C.) see 4 Kg 21 ; 2 Par 33. **6.** ' I am weary of *repenting* ', in the sense of changing my line of conduct, in this case so as to spare ; *cf.* Gen 6:6. **7.** ' *I will winnow them with a winnowing-fork* [see on 4:11–12] in the gates [the cities] of the land ' ; it is implied that the inhabitants have proved worthless chaff : *cf.* Mt 3:12, etc. **8.** ' *I will cause agitation and dismay to fall upon her suddenly* '. **9.** Even the mother of seven is to become childless before reaching the evening of her life. ' The residue ' probably refers to the population in general.

10. Jeremias now bursts out into a lament for himself ; **c** he has incurred general hostility through no fault of his own. ' *I have not lent, neither have men lent to me* '. The Hebrew might exact interest from a Gentile, but not from a fellow-Hebrew (Deut 23:19–20) ; but even if this law were observed (which it was not always ; *cf.* Ps 14:5) friction might arise. **11-14** are difficult ;

8c 13-14 are addressed to the people, and break in harshly here : they are repeated substantially in 17:3-4, where they seem to belong. **12.** ' *Can one break iron, even iron from the north* [indicating the irresistible Babylonians] *and bronze ?* ' But when they come **(11)** ' *verily I will strengthen thee unto good ; verily I will cause thine enemy to make supplication unto thee in the time of evil and in the time of trouble* ', as in 38:14, etc. Jeremias still entreats for himself : **(15)** ' *Avenge thyself for me on my persecutors ; take me not away in thy long-suffering towards them* . . . **(17)** I have not sat in the assembly of merry-makers *and rejoiced* [indicating *because of thy hand* [thy compelling power] I have sat alone, for thou hast filled me with indignation '. Finally he receives a

d more propitious answer : **(19)** ' If thou return to me ', in the sense of being better-minded, ' then shall I bring thee back ', helping thee in this amendment ; ' thou shalt stand before me ' as my minister. ' And if thou bring forth the precious out of the vile [his own or the people's vileness], thou shalt be as my mouth '.

e **XVI 1-XVII 27 Jeremias must prepare for Disaster, trusting in Yahweh : the Sabbath—6.** It was forbidden in Deut 14:1 to mourn for the dead by cutting oneself or making oneself bald ; but the latter practice, at all events, was common (47:5 ; 48:37 ; Am 8:10, etc.). **13.** In exile they ' shall serve strange gods day and night ' in serving the Babylonian worshippers, ' for I will grant you no favour ' in the way of help. **14-15** are repeated in 23:7-8, where they obviously belong. **18.** ' *I will recompense their iniquity and their sin double* ' : omit ' first '. The idols are called ' carcasses ' in scorn. In **19** the prophet speaks of the

f Gentiles, but Yahweh in **21** of Judah, whose sin **(XVII 1-3)** is written deep in their heart, and ' upon the horns of their [idolatrous] altars, *where their children were sacrificed upon the altars of their Asherahs* [false goddesses] *by the green trees* upon the high hills, *the mountains in the fields* '. **2** is difficult ; the translation is based on the present writer's note in ET 60 (1948-9) 52-3. Mention of the sacrifice of children (7:31 ; 19:5 ; 32:35) is to be expected in a passage such as this. **3-4** partly repeat 15:13 f., where the words ' for ever ' are missing, and in view of such promises as 4:27 (see note) should probably be omitted here also. **3.** ' *because of sin* '. **6.** The ' tamaric ' is probably the dwarf juniper tree, whose ' gloomy stunted appearance, with its scale-like leaves pressed close to its gnarled stem, and cropped by the wild goats ' (Tristram, *Natural History of the Bible* [1911] 358) forcibly contrasts with **(8)** ' the tree planted by the waters ' of Ps 1:3. **11.** ' The partridge *heapeth together* ' eggs, laying a large number (Tristram found 26 in a nest, *ibid.*, 225), but they are eagerly sought and easily found, chiefly by men, so that ' *she doth not bring forth* ' young. **16.** ' But I ', the prophet protests, ' have *not hastened after thee with evil purpose* ' against my countrymen (such seems the best text) ; ' neither have I desired the day of man ', the day of man's punishment. **17-18.** But his actual persecutors are the enemies of God ; let him vindicate himself and his prophet !

g The chapter concludes with a commission to Jeremias to urge the **religious observance of the Sabbath**, probably unconnected with the preceding. **20.** ' kings ' in the plural, for the royal family in general, or for future kings : similarly 19:3. The sanctifying of the Sabbath (Ex 20:8-11 ; Deut 5:12-15) was ordered under pain of death (Ex 31:12-17) ; *cf.* Neh 13:15-22.

h **XVIII 1-XIX 15 The Potter's Vessel**—Israel is in God's hand as a potter's vessel **(6)** ; if the vessel be marred, he can make another **(4)**. As Jeremias is to break the vessel, so will God ' break this people and this city ' (19:11). The potter **(3)** ' was doing a work on the stones ', two circular stones on the same vertical axle rotating horizontally, the lower one worked by the foot, the upper and smaller supporting the clay. **4.** ' *And if the vessel which he was making of the clay was spoiled in the hand of the potter, then he would make it again into another vessel* '.

Two great truths are set forth : (1) God is the supreme **458i** author of history : He knows what sort of man or nation he is producing and how they will act **(6)** ; (2) on the other hand a nation is responsible for its own actions, according to which God will treat it **(7-10)**. God is here speaking of his dealings with nations upon the principle of solidarity, which has such deep roots in human nature, and without reference to the next life. The individual is regarded in 17:10, etc. **11.** The divine call to repentance is to all and each, only **(12** : *cf.* 2:25**)** to meet with obstinate perversity. **14-15.** The snow of Lebanon never fails, nor the streams which descend from it ; but Judah is inconstant and fickle, ' sacrificing to *nothingness* ', *i.e.* to idols. **18.** The people resent such language and plot against Jeremias, believing that priest and wise man and prophet will always be there to counsel them. **20.** The prophet had pleaded for them, but now **(21-23)** in utter disgust he makes the divine purpose of punishment, such as it must prove in the concrete, his own.

This divine purpose, and the crimes that have led to **j** it, are now to be proclaimed more emphatically, and **(XIX:1)** a potter's vessel is still the symbol. **2.** ' The Potsherd Gate ' led into ' the valley of the son of Hinnom ' ; see on 7:31. **8.** Every passer-by ' shall be *appalled* ' and (as we might say) ' *whistle* ' ; *cf.* 49:17. On **9** *cf.* Deut 28:53 ; Lev 26:29 ; Lam 4:10. **13.** ' The host of heaven ' are the stars ; see on 8:1-2. **14.** The outer court of the temple, here and in 26:2.

XX 1-18 The Persecution and Complaint of the k Prophet—He is put into the stocks, and upon release foretells evil to Phassur and Judah, and bemoans his own lot. **1.** Phassur, perhaps the father of Gedelias of 38:1, was in charge of the temple ; see on 35:4. **2.** ' The stocks ' were probably a pillory, with four holes for hands and feet, and a collar ; see on 29:26. ' the upper gate of Benjamin ' is probably that of 7:2. **3.** ' Terror on every side ', Magor-missabib, the refrain of the whole book and prophecy ; see on 6:25. **6.** Phassur was one of the false prophets.

In the rest of the chapter **the prophet gives free vent l to his emotions. 7.** ' Thou hast beguiled me, Yahweh '. The verb need not mean more than ' persuaded ' (as in Prov 25:15), but usually implies enticement of some kind into an unpleasant situation. **8.** ' *For as often as I speak, I cry out : I cry " Violence and spoil " !* ' *Cf.* Is 8:3. He is reproached and derided for pointing to the impending evils **9.** ' *But if I say, " I will think no more "* [of the word of the Lord] . . . *then there cometh to be in my heart as it were a burning fire . . . and I am weary* . . . **(10)** *for I hear the whispering of many* . . . " *Denounce* him, we will *denounce* him ", from all my familiar friends, who watch for my stumbling. " Perchance he will be beguiled [*e.g.* into saying something that can be construed as treason] and we shall prevail against him " '. But now **(11)** he rises to the strong conviction that God will succour him. ' My persecutors . . . shall be put to utter shame, *by reason of their failure—an everlasting reproach, which shall not be forgotten* '. **14.** Nevertheless grief overwhelms him **m** once more, so that **he expresses a wish that he had never been born ;** *cf.* Job 3. As Knabenbauer remarks, these imprecations (14-18) are to be understood not literally, but psychologically ; they express an overwhelming anguish at the bitterness of life. **16.** ' the cities which Yahweh overthrew ' are Sodom and Gomorrha (Gen 19:24 f.). Let the man hear the cry of alarm in the morning, and the war-shout of his enemies at noon ! **17.** Would that the prophet's mother had been his grave, and her womb always great !

(For ch 21, see § 463*a*.)

Part II Joakim King : 609-598 B.C. : chh 26 ; 22-23 ; **459a** 25 ; 36 ; 45 ; 35 ; 12:7-13:27. (For ch 25, see § 459*k-m*). Between Josias and Joakim came Joachaz (609 B.C.) who was deported into Egypt after three months (4 Kg 23:30-34) by the Pharaoh Nechao (Necho). Joachaz was Josias' third son ; he is put

459a in the last place in 1 Par 3:15 (under the name Sellum : see § 459*d ad init.*) owing to his insignificance. Necho put Josias' second son Eliacim on the throne, changing his name to Joakim. Ch 26 perhaps belongs to Joakim's first year (26:1). Chh 25 (25:1), 36 (36:1), 45 (45:1) are assigned to his 4th year, and ch 25 to the first year of Nabuchodonosor (25:1), which last is reckoned from the 1st of Nisan (March–April) of 604 ; presumably therefore Joakim succeeded to the throne late in the year, and his 4th year fell mainly in 604.

b   **The significance of this date** lies in the fact that in 605 B.C. Nabuchodonosor, acting for his father Nabopolassar, king of Babylon (who died soon afterwards) defeated Necho at Carchemish (about 260 m. NNE. of Damascus) a great commercial centre and fortress, commanding the principal ford over the Euphrates. He thus became master of western Asia, including Palestine ; the battle was one of the great turning-points in history, leaving Babylon supreme till its conquest by Cyrus, the Persian king, in 539 B.C. Jeremias preached submission, promising that all would go well, but he was not listened to, so that Jerusalem fell in 587 B.C.

c   **XXVI 1-24 Jeremias' Warning and Narrow Escape** —The date is probably 608 B.C. ; but in 28:1 the ' beginning ' of Sedecias' reign is his 4th year, which shows the term to be somewhat elastic. **5.** God sent his prophets, ' rising up early to do so ', *i.e.* insistently and continuously ; similarly in 7:13, etc. **6.** On Silo (Shiloh), see 7:12. **10.** ' the king's house ' was a little below the temple on the eastern hill, and immediately adjoined it ; *cf.* 22:1, etc. **16.** The princes and people save Jeremias ; **(17-19)** certain elders also bring up the case of Micheas (Mic 1:1 ; 3:12). **20-23.** The story of the true prophet Urias illustrates Jeremias' danger ; but **(24)** Ahicam the son of Saphan protected him. Another son of Saphan, Gamarias, was a king's secretary, an important minister of state (36:10–12, 25), and a third son was Elasa (29:3), evidently a friend to the prophet, as was likewise Ahicam's son Godolias (39:14 ; 40:5–6). Ahicam had been trusted by King Josias (4 Kg 22:11–14).

(For chh 27–8, see § 461*e–g*.)

d **XXII 1-XXIII 40 For Kings and Prophets**—(For ch 21, see § 463*a*.) It seems necessary to put 22:1–23:8 here, because the part dealing with the kings, because the memory of Josias' death is recent (22:10, 15–16), and the interest in his own son Sellum is still alive (22:10–12). ' Sellum ' is the name in 22:11 and 1 Par 3, 15, and is that of another king in 4 Kg 15:13 ; he is called Joachaz in 4 Kg 23:30–34 ; 2 Par 36:1–4. Joakim, however, is attacked in the 2nd person, and his end is prophesied (22:13–19), as well as that of his son Jechonias (22:23, 28 ; 37:1, etc. : called ' Joachin ' in 52:31 ; 4 Kg 24:6–15, etc.), who also is addressed in the 2nd person (22:25–26). This passage on the kings leads up to one on the Messianic deliverance (23:3–8), and thus to the false prophets.

e   **6.** ' *Gilead art thou to me, and the top of Lebanon* ', examples of finely wooded regions. **10.** Josias was defeated and slain at Megiddo in 609 B.C. by the invading Pharaoh Necho, who dethroned his son Sellum (=Joachaz) and carried him away to Egypt, whence he was never to return. **13-17.** Joakim is far from imitating the righteousness of his father Josias. **18.** The cries of lamentation are merely the conventional formulae, not intended to have any particular application to Joakim. On his end see also 36:30.

f   There is but little connexion in **20-23** with what immediately precedes or follows. The people are summoned to wail upon the heights (a common place for so doing ; *cf.* 7:29 ; Is 15:2) by which the Babylonians will advance upon Jerusalem, Lebanon in the north, Bashan in the NE., Abarim east of the northern part of the Dead Sea. **20.** ' and cry from *Abarim*, for all thy lovers are destroyed ', for whom see on 4:30. **22.** ' thy pastors ', meaning here and elsewhere the rulers who should feed thee : ' the wind shall

feed ', an ironical expression for scattering them. **23.** Jerusalem has been confident as a bird nesting among the cedars of Lebanon : ' How shalt thou groan ! '

24-30 The Doom of Jechonias—28. The prophet has **g** a word of lament and supplication for him ; but **(29-30)** the stern decree stands. ' barren ' : not in the strict sense, for there is mention of his seed in 28, and of eight sons (or seven, if ' Asir ' means ' Jechonias the captive ') in 1 Par 3:17–18. The word is a rare one, occurring elsewhere only in Gen 15:2 and Lev 20:20–21 : it comes from a root meaning ' to strip oneself ' (BDB), and can well mean ' stripped ' of royal power (as Vg and LXX seem to imply), both himself and his descendants.

XXIII 1-2 The Prophecy passes to an Attack upon h the Kings (pastors) in general. **3-4.** Yahweh will give them better pastors and **(5)** ' raise up to David a righteous shoot ', springing from the ground (rather than a ' branch '). The term is a Messianic title, used again in 33:15 ; Zach 3:8. **7-8** practically repeat 16:4–5, where (as there remarked) they can hardly be in place. This Messianic deliverance shall eclipse the exodus from Egypt, but is conditioned (as always) by 18:7–10.

9-32. The rest of ch 23 contains **an attack upon the i false prophets** with whom in one place (11) the priests are associated. **9.** Jeremias (here as elsewhere) is profoundly moved at the message which he is to deliver. **10.** The ' adulterers ' are so called (as often) primarily because of their idolatry, but secondarily because sexual immorality was often mixed up with the idolatry. The land ' mourneth by reason of *the curse* ', the drought immediately mentioned. The course of prophet and priest ' is become evil, and their power ', their authority, ' *is not right* ' : they abuse it. **13.** The prophets of Samaria ' prophesied *by* Baal ', in his name ; **(14)** but the prophets of Jerusalem are worse, they are as Sodom and Gomorrha. **15.** ' wormwood ' and ' gall ', see on 8:14 ; 9:15. **(19-20** are practically repeated in 30:23 f., where they probably belong ; they interrupt the sense awkwardly here.) **22.** ' But *if they stand in my council* [my intimate circle] *then let them cause my people to hear my words, and let them turn them* [my people] *back from their evil way* '. **23.** God is not *only* near, he is everywhere. **30.** The false prophets (the ' chaff ' of 28) steal God's words from their neighbours (the true prophet, the ' wheat ' of 28) in order to make their own pretended prophecies more plausible. **32.** ' *recklessness* ', rather than ' wonders '.

33-40. In what follows one must understand **the j double sense of the Hebrew word** *maśśā* ', meaning something lifted or taken up, either a ' burden ' in the literal sense, or something taken up on the lips, a prophetic utterance or ' oracle '. **33.** If anyone asks Jeremias what ' massa ' (' oracle ') there is from Yahweh, he is to answer from Yahweh, ' You are my massa (" burden "), and I mean to throw you off '. **34.** In fact, they are not to speak of Yahweh's ' massa ' any more, doubtless because of the rather sinister sense attaching to the prophet's oracles, his ' massas ' ; they may have been protesting that they were indeed ' burdens ' ! **35.** Henceforth they are simply to ask what Yahweh has ' answered ' or ' spoken '. **36.** Again they are forbidden to speak of Yahweh's ' massa ' ; for everyone is making up his own ' massa ' (' oracle '), and thus they pervert Yahweh's own words. **38.** But if they persist in speaking of Yahweh's ' massa ' (' oracle ') in spite of his forbidding it, **(39)** then ' I will take you up ' : this is the verb corresponding to ' massa ', so that the sense is, ' I will make you my " massa " (burden), carry you off, throw you away, and leave you '.

(For ch 24, see § 461*a*.)

XXV 1-38 The Babylonian Supremacy : the Cup of k Yahweh's Fury—As Knabenbauer remarks, there is no need to suppose that Jeremias travelled to all the nations who were to drink the cup, nor even to suppose a vision ; the cup of God's fury is the prophet's

9k denunciation which will be drunk when his prophecies are fulfilled. We may indeed call the Babylonian supremacy itself the cup of God's fury (as appears from 25:9, 11 and especially 51:7), apart of course from Babylon itself, for which see on 12–14. The 23 years of 3 are about 627–605 B.C., both years being included, as usually in ancient calculations. **10** ' the sound of the *pair of millstones* ', circular, 18–24 inches in diameter, the lower one fixed in the ground, the upper one turned by one or two (Mt 24:41) women : their noise was a sound of life in a village.

l **12–14,** and the mention of the king of ' Sesac ' (Babylon) in 26 (omitted by LXX) are thought by some to be later additions, because 15 would follow more naturally after 11, and because of the mention of Jeremias' book of prophecies against the nations in 13, which it may be right to identify with chh 46–51. But in the case of such a disturbed text as this, it is quite possible that the additions were made by the original author ; and it is to be observed that LXX puts chh 46–51 precisely here, roughly as chh 25–31, and that this may be the right place for them, the change being perhaps due to a desire for clearer historical sequence. 25:13 is identical in MT and LXX, except that LXX adds (ungrammatically) a mention of Elam, after which it goes off on to what is 49:35 in MT.

m Jeremias had already prophesied that **the chastisement of the Hebrews was not to be final** in 4:27, etc. (see note) ; now the limit of 70 years is announced **(11–12 ;** *cf.* 29:10), and as for the Babylonians **(14),** ' many nations and great kings *shall use them also as slaves* '. **15.** Disaster and dismay are represented as an intoxicating draught, as often in Jeremias (13:12–14, etc.). **20.** ' all in general ' are the mixed foreign population in Egypt, perhaps especially the foreign mercenaries ; *cf.* 50:37. ' Ausitis ' or Uz, perhaps an Aramaean tribe E. or NE. of Edom. Ascalon, Gaza, Accaron (Ekron), and Azotus (Ashdod) are the Philistine cities in SW. Palestine (*cf.* 47:5). According to Herodotus (ii. 157) the last-named was captured after a 29 years' siege by the Egyptian Pharaoh Psammetichus (666–610 B.C.). Possibly there is some mistake here ; for example, it may have been captured in the 29th year of his reign. **21.** Edom, S. of Palestine : Moab, E. of Dead Sea : Ammon, N. of Moab. These three stretched eastward into the desert. **22.** Tyre and Sidon, the Phoenician cities on the coast to the N. : also the Phoenician colonies on the Mediterranean ' *coastlands* ' are added. **23.** ' Dedan and Thema and Buz ', tribes of N. Arabia ; see on 9:26. **24.** ' Arabia ', the northern part. Omit ' and all the kings of the west ' which in the Hebrew merely repeats the previous words. **25.** ' Zambri ' : omitted by LXX, and not mentioned elsewhere. ' Elam ' : about 200 m. E. of Babylon, N. of Persian Gulf : *cf.* 49:34.

n ' The Medes ' : SW. of the Caspian, NE. of Babylonia and Assyria : about this time their empire reached to the Black Sea and into E. Asia Minor. **26.** ' the kings of the north . . . one with another '. ' Sesac ' or ' Sheshak ', here and in 51:41, is a so-called Atbash cypher for ' Babel ' (Babylon) : the 2nd last letter of the Hebrew alphabet (*š*) is put for the 2nd first (*b*), and the 12th last (*k*) for the 12th first (*l*). It may have been wiser at the time to disguise this direct attack on Babylon ; but this latter is mentioned so freely elsewhere that the use of the anagram seems to have been little more than a literary device. Otherwise we should have to suppose that originally it was used much oftener, but was afterwards discarded. **30.** *Cf.* Am 1:2. Yahweh's ' holy habitation ' is the temple. He shall ' roar against his homestead ' or pasture, meaning Jerusalem and Judah. ' *He shall shout as those treading the grapes* ', but it will be the inhabitants of the earth that he will be treading down. **31.** ' The din ' will be everywhere. **34–36.** The ' shepherds ' are the rulers, as in 2:8, etc. **38.** ' the wrath of the dove ' should probably be ' *the oppressing sword* ', as in 46:16 ; 50:16.

(For ch 26, see § 459*c*.)

XXXVI 1–32 The Reading of the Roll—(For ch 35, **460a** see § 460*d–e*.) This is the most vivid chapter in the whole work. Baruch was Jeremias' faithful disciple and secretary, and belonged to a distinguished family, being the brother of Saraias (*cf.* 32:12 with 51:59), who was ' *captain of the resting-place* ' of the king when travelling (which presumably he would select), or (as we might say) quartermaster, to King Sedecias (51:59). Baruch was taken along with Jeremias to Egypt (43:3–7) : see § 453*c*. The roll which Baruch wrote for Jeremias at this early stage, even the revised roll (36:32), obviously cannot be the whole book as we have it today ; but the fact that the prophet had such a faithful secretary increases our confidence in the genuineness of the whole book. In 45:1–4 there is a special message for Baruch, addressed to him at the time of the writing of the roll. (The Book of Baruch is treated separately.) **3. Forgiveness is still promised to Judah upon repen-** **b** **tance—5.** Jeremias is ' *hindered* ', possibly by some ceremonial uncleanness, from delivering the message himself. **9.** ' The ninth month ', the later Chisleu, roughly our December ; *cf.* 22. **10.** Baruch read the volume ' in the chamber of Gamarias ', for whom see on 26:24. For the ' new gate ' into ' the upper court ', see on 7:2. **12.** For ' the king's house ', see on 26:10. **16.** The princes ' turned in *fear* one towards another '. **18.** Omit ' as if he were reading '. **19.** The princes do not wish the fate of Urias (26:20–23) to befall Jeremias and Baruch (*cf.* 36:26), though **(16, 20)** they feel bound to tell the king. **20.** For ' court ' read ' cabinet ', with a change of a letter ; the king would not be sitting out of doors in December, but in his winter house **(22 ;** *cf.* Am 3:15), doubtless adjoining the rest of the palace. **23.** ' *As often* as Judi had read . . . he cut them with a *scribe's knife* ', used for making and mending reed pens, cutting writing materials, etc. **26.** ' Jeremiel ' is ' the son of *the king* ' (DV ' Amelech '). **30.** On Joakim's end see also 22:18–19 ; in 4 Kg 24:5 he is said to have ' slept with his fathers ', but there is no mention of his burial. **31.** ' *But they hearkened not* ' to God's threats. **32.** ' Many *like* words ' were added in the new roll. Jeremias is ordered to write yet another roll in 30:2.

(For ch 37, see § 463*d*.)

XLV 1–5 The Message for Baruch—(For ch 44, see **c** § 464*f*.) This short chapter practically belongs to the previous section (ch 36), and **(1)** bears the same date (36:1). **3.** Baruch is deeply grieved at what he has had to write ; but Jeremias is to say to him, **(4)** ' *What I have built I am destroying, and what I have planted I am plucking up* '. MT adds what RV renders, ' and this in the whole land ' ; but the translation is uncertain, and LXX is probably right in omitting. **5.** This is no time for ambition, of which Baruch had apparently to some extent been guilty ; but Yahweh will let him escape with his life, whithersoever he goes. The Heb. idiom runs literally, ' I will give thee thy life *as a spoil* ', as something to be snatched up hurriedly and carried away with difficulty. The idiom recurs in 21:9 ; 38:2 ; 39:18.

(For ch 46, see § 465*a–d*.)

XXXV 1–19 The Rechabites—(For ch 34, see § 463*b*.) **d** The Rechabites were a branch of the Cinites (Kenites), who were early associated with the Hebrews, and settled in the S. of Judah (1 Par 2:55 ; Jg 1:16 ; 1 Kg 15:6 ; 27:10). Their ancestor Jonadab, son of Rechab, joined with Jehu (king of Israel 841–814/3) in the extermination of the Baal-worship (4 Kg 10:15–23). The present chapter is our chief source of information about them. Jonadab had bound them to a strictly nomadic life, probably in the main to preserve their religion. They had taken refuge in Jerusalem for fear of the Babylonians and Syrians (35:11 : *cf.* 4 Kg 24:2), which dates the present incident towards the end of Joakim's reign. The ' chambers ' in 2 and 4 are the apartments of priests, etc. ; there is no mention of ' treasures '. **4.** Maasias was one of the **e** three ' keepers of the threshold ' (*cf.* 52:24=4 Kg 25:18), important officials, probably keepers of the temple

460e gates. Sophonias, his son (21:1 ; 29:25 ; 37:3), was even more important, being 'the second priest' (52:24), second only to the high-priest, and apparently in direct command of the temple (29:26), like Phassur in 20:3. **7.** The Rechabites were '*sojourners in the land*', aliens permanently dwelling there, to whom were accorded in the Law practically equal privileges with the Hebrews. **11.** 'Syria' or 'Aram', as always in Hebrew : the capital was Damascus. **19.** To 'stand before Yahweh' would normally mean ministering in the temple. In Hegesippus' account of the martyrdom of St James, the brother of the Lord, quoted by Eusebius in his *Church History* (ii. 23, 7), there is mention of a Rechabite even among the temple priests. There is also mention of a Rechabite at Jerusalem in Neh 3:14.
(For ch 36, see § 460a–b.)

f XII 7–XIII 27 The Waist-Cloth : the Coming Disaster—(For 11:1–12:6, see § 457f–g.) Because of 13: 18 f. it seems more likely that this section belongs to the three months' reign of Joakim's son Jechonias (or Joachin : see § 459d–g). Joakim's mother was Zebida (4 Kg 23:36), of whom we know nothing ; Jechonias' mother was Nohesta (Nehushta, 4 Kg 24:8). Jechonias was only 18 when he succeeded (*ibid.*) ; his youth would enhance the prominence attached to the queen-mother by Eastern custom (*cf.* 3 Kg 2:19), and account for her being mentioned in 13:18 ; 22:26 ; 29:2 ; 4 Kg 24:8, 12, 15. Again, in 12:7–17 the reference is to the bands of Babylonians and Syrians raiding Judah, as in 35:11 ; 4 Kg 24:2 (in which last passage Moabites and Ammonites are also mentioned), so that we should be obliged to place this section, like the preceding one, into Joakim's last years, if in his time at all. In any case this is the most convenient place in which to consider the section.

g 7 Yahweh speaks sorrowfully of having 'forsaken my house . . . and given *the beloved of my soul* into the hand of her enemies' (*cf.* 22:5 ; Mt 23:38), **(8)** because she has turned like a savage beast against him ; 'therefore have I hated her'. **9.** 'Is my heritage', he asks with amazement and pain, 'a speckled bird of prey, *that the birds of prey round about are upon her*' because of her unusual plumage ? Let the wild beasts devour her ! **11.** None consider what the end of such things must be, *i.e.* the desolation of 12–13. **12.** Even 'the bare heights in the wilderness', where Judah courted the Baalim (see on 3:2) will be overrun. **14.** Nevertheless her destruction is not to be final (see on 4:27). And though her enemies are to be plucked out of their own land **(15)** they too will be restored, **(16)** and if they will be converted 'they shall be built up in the midst of my people', being thus in every way united with them, with such presumably as would still be found in Palestine. Even the prophecies against the nations end with promises of mercy (see on 49:39) apart from the special one against Babylon. (The 1st line of Ac 15:16 is from 12:15, but what follows is taken freely from Am 9:11–12.)

h XIII 1 The narrative of the Waist-Cloth presents difficulties—In view of such passages as 25:15–28 (see § 459k) and Ez 4, it can hardly be regarded as certain that Jeremias travelled a few hundred miles to the Euphrates and back in order to hide a waist-cloth in a rock. Some have therefore suggested a vision or dream of some kind. It has also been thought, however, that Wady Fara, about 3 m. NE. of Anathoth, may be meant ; the name represents the 'Parah' (DV 'Aphara') of Jos 18:23. Doubtless for this reason the OT translation published by the Jewish Publication Society of America in 1917 simply retains the Hebrew word 'Perath' in **4–7.** Water penetrated to the buried waist-cloth and spoilt it : **(9)** such also shall Judah and Jerusalem become. **14.** '*I shall dash them one against another, even the fathers and the sons together*'. **15–17.** Let them heed the warning in time.

i XIII 18–19 There follows an apostrophe to King Jechonias and the queen-mother : '*Sit ye down low, for your glorious crowns are fallen from your heads !*' In prophetic vision the prophet sees even the cities of the

south (though the invader was to come from the north) **460i** 'shut up', *i.e.* quite empty, for all the inhabitants have been carried away—a poetical hyperbole.

20–27. The reproaches that follow begin as the words **j** of Jeremias, but (*cf.* § 454b) pass into those of Yahweh. **20.** 'Lift up thine eyes, O Jerusalem [following LXX] and behold those who come from the north'. Her 'flock' are her inhabitants. **21.** 'What wilt thou say, *when he appointeth over thee as heads those whom thou didst teach to be thine intimates ?*' This supposes only a transfer of one word in this difficult line, which also sets the metre right. The nations she is courting (presumably Babylon and other neighbouring nations) will become her harsh masters : *cf.* Ez 23:22–23. Her inhabitants shall be scattered like *chaff* from the threshing floors ; see on 4:11. **27.** '*How long will it yet be, ere thou become clean ?*'
(For ch 14, see § 458a.)

Part III Sedecias King : 598–587 B.C. (a) Warnings to 461 Exiles and Natives : chh 24, 29, 27–28. (For ch 23, see § 459h–j.)
XXIV 1–10 The Exiles with Joachin and those remaining with Sedecias—A strong contrast is drawn between those who had been taken into captivity with Joachin in 598 B.C. (*cf.* 13:18–19 ; 22:24–30 ; 4 Kg 24: 11–17 ; 2 Par 36:8–10) and those who remained behind with Sedecias, entirely to the advantage of the former, who are represented as good figs, while those at Jerusalem are the bad figs. It is natural to suppose that the deportation is a recent event, and that this chapter must be dated near the beginning of Sedecias' reign ; and ch 29 for the same reason, and because of its close connection with this chapter (with 29:17–18, *cf.* 24:8–10). **1.** 'engravers' : more probably 'smiths'. **6.** 'I will set my eyes upon them *for good*', for the purpose of doing them good. **8.** 'So will I *give up* Sedecias'. **9.** '*I will make them a consternation to all the kingdoms*', as in 15:4.
(For ch 25, see § 459k–m.)

XXIX 1–32 The Letter to the Exiles in Babylonia— b (For ch 28, see § 461g.) Jeremias encourages them to settle down contentedly, and (10) promises a return after 70 years ; he deals with some false prophets there. **1.** Why 'the residue', is not clear ; there may have been a massacre. But LXX omit the word. **2.** On 'the queen', see § 460f. 'engravers', see on 24:1. **3.** For 'Elasa', see on 26:24. 'saying' introduces the prophet's letter, which occupies the rest of the chapter, apart from the explanatory note in 29–30.

8–10 The Period of 70 Years for the Babylonian exile **c** had already been mentioned (25:11–12) ; but the false prophets were prophesying an earlier return (*cf.* 27–28, especially 28:4). These 70 years seem best reckoned with Condamin from 605 B.C. to 537 B.C., which would be reckoned as 69 years, and at the round number of 70. By his victory over the Egyptians at Carchemish in 605 B.C. Nabuchodonosor (waging war for his father Nabopolassar, king of Babylon) became master of western Asia. We read in 2 Par 36:5–7 that he took King Joakim from Jerusalem to Babylon as prisoner ; this is not mentioned in 4 Kg 24:1–2, which however makes it clear that the Babylonians were taking prisoners about that time. Berossus, the Babylonian priest of Bel, who wrote about the middle of the 3rd cent. B.C., is quoted by Josephus (*Ant* 10, 11,1 and *Contra Apionem* 1, 19) as stating that Nabuchodonosor had Jewish captives conveyed to Babylon. It seems reasonable, therefore, to date the Babylonian captivity from this episode, and the end of it from the return of the exiles after Cyrus' capture of Babylon in 538 B.C.

12–32 After the 70 Years—12. '*You shall go and pray to d me*'. **15** does not fit in well here, and should probably precede 21, as in the Lucianic recension of LXX, and also in the ordinary LXX text (which however leaves out 16–20 altogether). **17–18.** See § 461a. **21–23.** The two false prophets have been guilty of gross immorality,

61d and are promised dire punishment. **24.** A third false prophet has sent letters from Babylon to Jerusalem, of which the extract quoted must be part of a letter to Sophonias, for whom see on 35:4. He was evidently in sympathy with Jeremias. **26.** He could put anyone 'in the stocks and in the *collar*'; see on 20:2. **28.** 'It is a long time' that the exiles will be in captivity; see on 8–10. **20-30** are parenthetic; **31-32** probably belong to the original letter. Semeias shall have no male issue, in the person of whom he might be said to witness the return from the Babylonian captivity. But perhaps we should end 32 with the LXX: 'there shall not be a man of them (*i.e.* of his descendants) in the midst of you to see the good things which I shall do to you; they shall not see them'.

(For ch 30, see § 462*a–b*.)

e XXVII 1-21 Warning to the five Kings and Sedecias and to Priests and People—(For ch 26, see § 459*a–c*.) It is clear from the mention of Sedecias in 27:3, 12, and from the mention of the captivity of Jechonias in 27:20, that we should read 'Sedecias' in 1 rather than 'Joakim'. The verse may have been taken over by mistake from 26:1. It seems likely also that chh 27–28 are closely connected, and that the time-heading in 28:1 originally belonged to 27:1. The Peshitta actually reads 'Sedecias': LXX omits
f 27:1 altogether, perhaps in perplexity. Since the battle of Carchemish (605 B.C.) the power of Babylon had become overwhelming; but the five kings still hoped to shake off its yoke, and invited Sedecias to join them in the attempt. Jeremias warns all that it will fail. **2.** 'Make the *thongs and bars*' to form a yoke, the 'thongs' being used to bind the 'bars' together: *cf.* Lev 26:13 ('*the bars of your yoke*'), Jer 2:20; 5:5; 30:8. The divine purpose is constantly brought home in Holy Scripture by symbolic action (*e.g.* Gen 9:13; Ac 21:11). In **12** and **16** 'I spoke' refers to Jeremias himself. **19.** 'Thus saith Yahweh of hosts *concerning* the pillars [*cf.* 3 Kg 7:15–22; 2 Par 3:15–17] and the sea [3 Kg 7:23–26; 2 Par 4:2–5] and the bases' (3 Kg 7:27–37; 2 Par 4:14). These were all broken in pieces, and the bronze carried to Babylon (52:17). Other '*articles*' are mentioned in 3 Kg 7; 2 Par 4; for their return, *cf.* Esd 1:7–11.
g XXVIII 1-17 Hananias the False Prophet—See § 461*e*. It has even been suggested that the events in chh 27–28 belong to the same day; in any case this false prophecy was a counterblast to that of Jeremias. **1.** 'Gabaon' (Gibeon), about 5 m. NNW. of Jerusalem. He is called 'prophet', much as we speak of 'fortune-tellers' without belief in their power to tell fortunes. **6.** Jeremias would wish Hananias' prophecy fulfilled; **(8)** still, 'the prophets' of old usually 'prophesied' (omit 'and') threatened calamities, and did not court the people with promises of pleasant things, except as the reward of repentance. **9.** Time will show! **10.** Hananias 'took the *bar* from the neck of Jeremias', meaning the symbolic yoke he wore (see on 27:2), and so in **12** and **13** (where it seems better to read with LXX, 'I shall make'). Jeremias, having now had revealed to him the answer to be given, delivers it to Hananias; of the two essentials of true prophecy, revelation and mission, **(15)** Hananias has received neither, and **(16)** he has 'spoken *treason* against Yahweh' (*cf.* 29:32). **17.** Hananias died within three months; *cf.* 28:1.

(For ch 29, see § 461*b–d*.)

h LI 59-64 The Mission of Saraias—(For 51:1–58, see § 467*e–j*.) Perhaps soon after the events of chh 27–28 (see 461*e–g*) Jeremias writes upon a scroll the evils in store for Babylon, and commissions Saraias to read it there, presumably in private to the Jewish community; he is then to perform the symbolic act of binding a stone to the scroll and sinking both in the Euphrates. **59.** The attempt to draw Sedecias into a league against Babylon (see § 461*e–f*) may have been the cause of Sedecias' journey to Babylon; at that time he may have wished to clear himself from any suspicion of revolt. Saraias was Baruch's brother, and

'captain of the "royal" resting-place' (see § 460*a*). **461h 60.** 'all these words' were obviously written too **i** early to include all the present book of Jeremias; but the expression implies that a copy was preserved, probably containing 50:1–51:58. **61.** '*then see that thou recitest all these words*'. **64.** 'she shall not rise again from the *evil* that I am bringing upon her'. Here the prophecy proper ends. MT adds (*a*) 'and they weary themselves', apparently an interpolation from the end of 51:58; (*b*) 'Thus far the words of Jeremias', probably a compiler's note intended to distinguish the prophecy proper from ch 52.

(For ch 52, see § 468.)

Part III (b) Promises of Restoration—chh 30–33. **462a** (For ch 29, see § 461*b–d*.) These chapters offer a marked contrast to the rest of the book, striking a note of hope seldom present elsewhere (yet see 3:14–19; 16:14–15; 23:3–8).
XXX 1-24 The Restoration of Judah—Judah is mainly in question, though there are some more general references. **2.** Jeremias is commanded to write a second roll, of a very different character from that of ch 36, **(4)** 'words . . . *about* Israel and *about* Judah'. **8.** 'I will break his yoke from off *his* neck', the first 'his' referring to the Babylonians, the second to Jacob, *i.e.* the Israelites, as does 'their' in **9**. The yoke of Babylon was broken by its capture in 539 by the Persian king Cyrus, who allowed the exiles to return. For 'yoke' and 'bands' (*thongs*), see on 27:2. **10-11** are repeated in 46:27–28, but fit better here.

Judah and Israel are not to be consumed utterly: b see on 4:27. **12.** 'Thy hurt is *sore*, thy wound is grievous'. **14.** 'thy lovers': see on 4:30. The last words of 14 occurs again in **15**, and should probably be omitted. 'thy sorrow is *sore*', as in 12. **16.** 'Therefore': because the punishment is from God, he will end it when it has reached the full measure, and punish the wicked whom he has allowed to inflict it. **18.** Yahweh will bring back Jacob's *tents* from captivity: Jerusalem shall be rebuilt upon her own mound, '*and the palace shall be inhabited after its wonted manner*'. **21.** Foreigners shall no longer rule: the native prince 'I shall cause to draw near, and he shall approach unto me': the words imply the priesthood in the Messianic ruler; *cf.* Ps 109:4; Zach 6:13. Who indeed has ever dared to take this office upon himself unauthorized by Yahweh? Lit.: 'for who is this that hath gone surety for his heart [*i.e.* for his courage] to approach unto me?' **23-24** are practically identical with 23:19–20, where they make an awkward interruption; probably they belong only here.
XXXI 1-40 The Restoration of Ephraim—'Ephraim' **c** (6, 9, 18, 20) stands for the Northern Kingdom, of which it was the chief tribe, making up with Manasses 'the house of Joseph'; *cf.* Gen 48; Jos 18:5; Jg 1:22, 35, etc. The Northern Kingdom is also called here 'Samaria' (5) and 'Israel' simply (2, 4, 7, 9, 21) in contrast to Judah (27, 31), so that other words are added for clearness when 'Israel' embraces Judah as well (1, 37), unless mistake be impossible (33). Jerusalem is still to remain the national centre of worship (6).

Shalmaneser V, King of Assyria, conquered the d Northern Kingdom in 721 B.C.; *cf.* 4 Kg 17. **2.** Ephraim *shall find grace* in the desert', used figuratively for the exile: '*I will go that I may cause Israel to rest*'. **3.** 'Yahweh hath appeared from afar', from his dwelling at Jerusalem, 'to me', Ephraim, saying, 'Yea, I have loved thee . . . therefore have I drawn thee' unto me. **5.** 'The planters shall plant, and shall *enjoy the fruit thereof*', lit. 'shall treat as profane' (or common), *i.e.* the fruit. *Cf.* Lev 19:23–25: when a tree was planted, no fruit was to be gathered from it for the first three years, and the fruit of the fourth year was to be consecrated to God, but the owner might eat the fruit of the fifth year, which was then no longer taboo, but profane (common). Thus a period of settled peace and prosperity is indicated.

462d 6. The watchmen on the highlands of Ephraim shall give the signal for the pilgrimages to Jerusalem, thus showing that the schism between North and South is at an end. **7.** ' Cry *aloud at the head* of the [liberated] nations '. **8.** ' The north country ' of the exile of Ephraim was Assyria. Even those who would find it most difficult to travel should return. **9.** They shall return with tears of contrition. ' I shall bring them *unto streams* of water '.

e 15. ' *A voice shall be heard on high* ' : this may well be the right translation, as it has other good support besides Vg ; but the same letters might mean ' in Rama ' (mentioned 40:1), which was about 5 m. north of Jerusalem, not far from Rachel's tomb (*cf.* 1 Kg 10:2 : the reputed site near Bethlehem can hardly be squared with 1 Kg 10) and near enough to justify Mt 2:17–18 in seeing here some indication of a Messianic event, as in Mt 2:15. **16.** Rachel is poetically represented as to be compensated for her sorrow. **18.** ' Hearing I have heard Ephraim *bemoaning* himself ', and saying ' Thou hast chastised me '. **20.** ' *Is not Ephraim my dear son ? Is he not my darling child ?* ' The word ' not ' is twice inserted here, to bring out the sense. ' *For as often as I speak of him, I vividly remember him still* '. **21.** ' *Set thee up guide-posts, make thee waymarks* : set thy heart toward [mark well] the highway, the way by which thou shalt go ' into exile, in order to return by it. **22.** ' *How long wilt thou go hither and thither, O thou backsliding daughter* ', hesitating to make thy peace with God and ensure thy return ?

f And then **a great sign is promised**, so great that it is even called a creation. The verb is in the perfect tense (' hath created '), but it is generally admitted that this is merely another example of the well-known idiom, the ' prophetic perfect ', a vivid manner of representing a prophecy as already fulfilled. The present writer accepts Knabenbauer's explanation in CSS, which he regards as far more plausible than any other, but of course it presupposes that miracle and prophecy are possible. Instead of the initiative being taken by the man, as is usual in human generation, the physical process on the purely human side will be set on foot by the woman, who will ' *press round* ' a man (a meaning given by BDB to the verb in this passage, but with a different implication). The miracle is emphasized by the word used for ' woman ' being an unusual one, which stresses the sexual character. The word for ' man ' (that found in *Gabri-el* ' man of God ') is also an unusual one, implying strength and power ; a cognate word (a fact significant in the present context) is applied as a name to the Messias in Is 9:6 (' God the Mighty '), and directly to God himself in Ps 23:8 (twice) ; Deut 10:17 ; etc. This explanation of the passage is confirmed by the fairly obvious reference which it contains to Is 7:14, which can reasonably be supposed to have been familiar to Jeremias' hearers and readers, as to those of Mic 5:3, immediately after the mention of Bethlehem. Like Isaias, Jeremias passes easily by a process of compenetration from the temporary deliverance to the full Messianic deliverance of which it is a type.

g 23. The blessing shall be addressed to Jerusalem : ' *O abode of righteousness ! O holy mountain !* ' **24.** ' therein ' refers to the whole land of Judah. **25.** ' For I have *sated the* thirst of the weary soul '. **26.** The prophet awakes out of the sleep of ecstasy, which had revealed such pleasant things to him, and opens his eyes : omit ' as it were '. A new prophecy then begins. **27.** Man and beast shall multiply. **29-30.** The solidarity of family and nation and other human units is founded in human nature, and can only be disregarded with peril, nor does God say that he will disregard it ; nor yet was the present generation of the Hebrews free from guilt. But the responsibility of the individual will be the ultimate measure of God's treatment of him ; *cf.* Ez 18.

h 31-34, quoted at length in Heb 8:8–12, as is part of 33–34 in Heb 10:16–17 ; Rom 11:27. From both the passages in Hebrews the conclusion is drawn to **a**

new dispensation, with Christ for high-priest (Heb 8:1 ; **46** 10:21), in place of the old. The passage in Romans throws forward the complete fulfilment of the prophecy to the last stage in the world's history, when Jew and Gentile together will accept Christ (Rom 11:25–32). The prophet is indicating and contrasting the predominant characteristics of the two dispensations ; not that faith and love and forgiveness were entirely absent from the old dispensation, or that proper instruction will be entirely unnecessary in the new. See (*e.g.*) the writer's article on ' The Prophets and Sacrifice : a study in biblical relativity ', in JTS 42 (1941) 155–65. For 36–37, see Rom 11:29, just referred to ; God will not renounce his call of ' all the seed of Israel '. **38.** ' the tower of Hananeel ' (Hananel ; mentioned Neh 3:1 ; 12:38 ; Zach 14:10) was at the NE. corner of the city ; ' the gate of the corner ' (4 Kg 14:13 ; 2 Par 26:9) was at the NW. corner. **39.** Gareb and Goatha (Goah) are not mentioned elsewhere ; the latter presumably marked the SW. corner, and the former some future extension of the city wall to the west. **40.** ' the ashes ' are sacrificial ashes, and the vale of Hinnom is indicated (see on 7:31) : hence it is ' the country of death ', which is probably the right reading, though there is a textual difficulty.

' The horse gate ', however, seems to have been **i** connected with the palace (4 Kg 11:16 ; 2 Par 23:15 ; Neh 3:28), which was south of the temple, so that ' the whole valley ' seems to include the whole broad open depression at the SE. of the ancient city, south of Siloam, and some land round the SE. corner. All this valley ' *shall be holy to Yahweh* ', and shall remain such, with its former infamous rites abolished, sharing in the general consecration of the city to the true God.

XXXII 1-44 The Purchase of the Field—The siege **j** of Jerusalem began in Sedecias' 9th year (39:1 ; 589 B.C.) but was discontinued for a while owing to the approach of an Egyptian army (see on 37:4). Jeremias intended to take advantage of the Babylonians' absence to visit his property in Anathoth, but was arrested on suspicion of deserting to the Babylonians and put into a dungeon (37:10–15), whence upon petition to King Sedecias he was removed to the freer custody of the ' guard-court ' (37:21 ; 38:28). The present incident, which finds him there (32:2, 12), follows upon the events just mentioned, but is best considered here along with the other ' promises of restoration ' in Part III (*b*).

8. Hanameel (Hanamel), the prophet's cousin, offers him the ' redemption ' of a field in Anathoth. If a Hebrew was selling land, it was the duty of his next of kin to ' redeem ', *i.e.* to buy it (see the introduction to the Book of Ruth in WV). This duty Jeremias is ordered by God to discharge, as a pledge that in spite of the capture of Jerusalem (**15**) ' houses and fields and vineyards shall yet again be *bought* in this land '.

1. The date is 587 B.C.—**2.** The Babylonians have **k** resumed the siege of Jerusalem, and Jeremias is still in the guard-court, which formed part of the palace buildings ; *cf.* 38:28. **5.** ' till I visit him ', ambiguous words, possibly Sedecias' softening of the prophet's sterner words (*e.g.* in 21:7). **8.** Hanameel came to the guard-court (see § 462j). **9.** The price of the field was ' *seventeen shekels of silver* ', about £2 2s 6d of our money, but the purchasing power was far greater. (St Matthew, compounding Zach 11:12–13 with Jer 32:6–9 and other verses, sees some foreshadowing in OT of the purchase of the ' Field of Blood ', as in Mt 27:6–10 ; *cf.* Mt 2:15, 23 ; etc.) **10.** ' *And I wrote the deed, and sealed it* '. **11.** ' Then I took the purchase-deed which was sealed, containing the terms and conditions, *and also that which was open* '. ' containing ' is here put for ' and ' in the Hebrew ; such seems the sense. ' terms and conditions ' are probably technical legal terms, the precise sense of which is not clear.

14. The purchase-deed would be enclosed in an **l**

21 envelope of clay, upon the outside of which a duplicate text would be impressed, and the whole put in an earthen jar. Duplicate texts of this kind have been found in Babylonia ; any dispute about the outside text would be settled by breaking the clay envelope before witnesses and referring to the inner text. **12.** Baruch (*cf.* § 460*a*) receives the purchase deed (not a ' book '). **15.** It is in the style of OT prophecy that this prediction should be accompanied by a symbolic act of this kind ; purchase-deeds are to be preserved against the restoration.

m **16-25.** The key to the prophet's prayer is in the last verse ; **Jeremias is perplexed** at what he has been ordered to do, at a time when the Babylonians are about to capture Jerusalem. Yahweh's answer occupies the rest of the chapter. The prayer is full of OT references, too many to give here. In **18**, taken from the decalogue, the text runs on in Ex 20:5 ; Deut 5:9, ' unto the third and fourth generation of them that hate me ', thus applying only to descendants who follow in the wicked ways of their fathers, and it goes on to speak at once of God's mercy. **25.** ' And thou hast said to me ' ; it does not seem to be a question. **26-35.** Yahweh answers that Jerusalem shall certainly receive the punishment she deserves, and recapitulates her sins. The allusion in **32** is of course to false prophets.

36-44. Nevertheless the restoration will come. **40.** ' I will make an everlasting covenant with them, *that I will not turn back from them*, from doing them good '. **43-44.** Only ' fields ' are mentioned, but evidently there is reference to the whole prophecy of 32:15.

n **XXXIII 1-26 The Restoration is to be Full and Messianic**—The story is taken up from the end of ch 32 ; *cf.* 33:1, ' a second time '. Judah and Israel are to be brought back, the Messias is to sit upon the throne of David, and the Levitical priesthood is to continue. Jeremias is still in more or less free custody in the ' guard-court '. **2.** ' Yahweh will do it, will plan it so as to *establish* it '. The figure is really taken from pottery (*cf.* 18:1–6 ; etc.) : lit. ' will form [the vessel] so as to make it firm ', not to be broken. **3.** He will show the prophet ' great things and mysteries '. **4.** He speaks ' *concerning the houses* . . . broken down (to make a defence) a*gainst the siege-mounds* [the ' works ' of 32:24] and *against the sword* '. **5.** The beginning of the verse is difficult ; we should perhaps read, ' Though the Chaldaeans [Babylonians] are coming to fight '.

o **6** refers to the Hebrews : ' I will reveal to them *abundance* of peace and faithfulness ', **God's own faithfulness to his promises. 7.** ' and the captivity of Israel. . . . **(9).** And she [Jerusalem] shall be to me *a name of joy* ', and the Gentiles ' shall fear and tremble ', be filled with great awe. **10.** ' There shall be heard . . . in the cities of Judah, and *in the streets of Jerusalem* . . . **(11)** the voice of joy . . . of them that bring *thank-offerings* '. LXX omit 14–26 ; and **15-16** repeat 23:5–6, where see notes.

p The rest of the chapter offers a difficulty, because it is evident that descendants of David did not ' sit upon the throne of the house of Israel ' (**17**) after the return from the Babylonian exile, and that Levitical priests ceased to offer sacrifices to God (*cf.* **18**) after the destruction of the temple by the Romans. A twofold answer may be given, of which the first part may be called the historical solution, corresponding to the actual facts, and the second, which it is no less necessary to bear in mind, the ideal solution, the scheme envisaged by Almighty God in the case of the Jews accepting their Messias.

q A. The *historical* solution. Christ is the Davidic king, and he shall reign for ever (Lk 1:32–33), though his kingdom is not of this world (Jn 18:36) in the sense that (to put it shortly and roughly) it leaves secular matters to be dealt with by the several temporal rulers. During the time between the exile and Christ's coming, the sceptre (in the sense of a certain autonomy) had not completely passed from Judah (*cf.* Gen 49:10),

though there was an interval during which no descen- **462q** dant of David could be said to be sitting on his throne. On the other hand, during this interval the Levitical **r** priests were sacrificing in the temple, and it is enough to understand the prophecy to refer to the time up to the coming of the Messias. Such a word as ' never ' need not be pressed further than this, for words were not used so absolutely in OT ; in Daniel, for example, the king is often greeted with the wish that he may ' live for ever '. But there were also positive indications that the Levitical priests were not to continue for ever ; it is explained in Hebrews, with reference to Ps 109:4, that Christ himself was a priest ' *after the manner of* Melchisedech ' though of the tribe of Judah (Heb 7) and not therefore a Levitical priest. And there is a manifest rejection of the Levitical priesthood and of the temple in Mal 1:10–11. Even Jeremias speaks of the new age as one in which the ark of the covenant, designed to be the very centre of OT worship, shall be altogether forgotten (3:16), where we should rather have expected him to say that it would be restored. And in his picture of the new covenant in 31:31–34 (quoted in Heb 8:8–12) there is no question of Levitical worship.

B. The *ideal* solution. Thus the prophecy can be **s** explained in the light of history ; and in view of 18:7–10 it could be explained in the light of even graver difficulties. Nevertheless we cannot rightly understand the prophecy unless we allow for the fact that, if we may so put it reverently, the historical solution was God's second-best, and only became history through the Jews' rejection of Christ. If they had accepted him, we may take it that Jerusalem would have become the centre of the Christian Church ; we may imagine Palestine as the independent papal state, and the temple as the mother and mistress of all the churches, with the OT priesthood still retained, though certainly not exclusively. We cannot fill in the details of the picture ; but it drew tears from the Saviour's eyes as he gazed upon the city before entering it in short-lived triumph, even as Jeremias had wept over it, and as those who can scarce forbear to do who are familiar with its history in the Scriptures and after them. ' Hadst *thou* but known ! ' (Lk 19:42.)

It is St Paul's doctrine (Gal 3:26–29, etc.) that **all** **t** **the members of Christ's Mystical Body are one with him,** and thus are the seed of Abraham, and our Lord himself expressed this unity even more strongly at the Last Supper (Jn 17:20–23). Thus the seed of David has increased to countless millions since Christ's death, and the priests and Levites of the new dispensation have also become an immense multitude, though of course by no means so numerous as the faithful.

' The two families ' of **24** are Israel and Judah ; *cf.* 26, and chh 30–31, etc.

(For ch 34, see § 463*b*–*c*.)

Part III (c) The Siege—chh 21, 34, 37–39. That ch 21, **463a** so clearly a siege story (*cf.* 21:4) should have its place so early in the book, is a striking sign of the disturbed state of the work as a whole. (For ch 20, see § 458*k*–*m*.) **XXI 1-14 Sedecias' Enquiry and Jeremias' Answer**— From 21:1 the time appears to be the very beginning of the siege ; afterwards the Babylonians withdraw for a while : *cf.* § 462*j*. **1.** Phassur is not he of 20:1 (the father being different), but of 38:1. For Sophonias, see on 35:4. **4.** ' gather them together ', perhaps the Babylonians : the meaning is doubtful. **9.** The only way is to submit. ' as a spoil ' : see on 45:5. **11.** ' And *concerning the house* '. **12.** ' in the morning ', the usual time for business, while it was still cool. **13.** From the SE. Jerusalem might seem to stand out ' upon a rock above a plain ', but the Hebrew seems to imply a ' tableland ' rather than a rock ; the description applies with difficulty to Jerusalem, but easily to Moab (*cf.* 48:8, 21), so that the verse may be misplaced. **14.** Jerusalem is likened poetically to a forest from its cluster of houses ; *cf.* Is 9:18–19.

(For chh 22–23, see § 459*d*–*j*.)

463b XXXIV 1-22 The Fate of Jerusalem and Sedecias Foretold : the Emancipation of the Slaves—(For ch 33, see § 462n–t.) The city shall be taken and burnt, and Sedecias shall be taken away captive, but shall die in peace and receive the usual funeral rites. He had persuaded the citizens to free their Hebrew slaves, men and women, in accordance with Deut 15:12 (Jer 34:13-15) ; but when the siege was temporarily raised (21 ; cf. § 462j) they brought them back into slavery again (16). God rebukes them and promises punishment. **5.** ' so shall they burn for thee ' the usual spices, etc. ; cf. 2 Par 16:14 ; 21:19. **7.** Only two cities were left, Lachish (Tell ed-Duweir, about 25 m. SW. of Jerusalem) and Azecha (Azekah : Tell ez-Zakariyeh, about 15 m. SW. of Jerusalem). **9.** ' so that they should not serve them, to wit, a man serve his Hebrew brother '. ' to wit ' and the 2nd ' serve ' are inserted for clearness.

c The release probably did not go beyond the requirements of Deut 15:12, which however would doubtless cover the great majority of the slaves. **15.** The act of release was solemnly performed in the temple, **(16)** so that to violate it was to profane Yahweh's name. **17.** They had proclaimed liberty, every man to his brother, etc. ; Yahweh now by way of punishing them for their perjury, proclaims liberty for them from his own service, handing them over ' to the sword and pestilence and famine ' as to their new masters, ' and I will make you a consternation to all the kingdoms of the earth ': see on 15:4. **18-19.** For the sacrificial rite, cf. Gen 15:10, 17. The parties may be calling upon themselves a similar cutting into two is they fail to observe their part of the compact, or the unity of the contracting parties within the same sacred victim may be implied, as in the eating of the same sacrificial meal. **19.** ' eunuchs ' may sometimes mean mere officials, e.g. Putiphar in Gen 39:1.

(For ch 35, see § 460d–e.)

d XXXVII 1-20 Jeremias Arrested : Sedecias' Enquiries—(For ch 36, see § 460a–b.) **1.** It was Sedecia whom (as the text means) Nabuchodonosor had made king. **3.** For Sophonias, see § 460e. Juchal reappears in 38:1. **4.** The Pharaoh Hophra (589-564 B.C. ; cf. 44:30) advanced with an army to relieve Jerusalem. Nabuchodonosor accordingly abandoned the siege for a while, defeated the Egyptians and drove them back to Egypt, after which he resumed the siege and took the city. Cf. Ez 17:11-2 ; Jos., Ant. 10, 7, 3 ; § 462j. **9.** Even if there were left of the Babylonians only ' men wounded ' desperately (lit. ' pierced through '), they would take and burn Jerusalem ; Yahweh's decree of doom stands fast. **11.** Jeremias probably intended to visit his native Anathoth, perhaps to receive an inheritance, **(12)** when he was arrested at the Benjamin gate (mentioned again 38:7), which must have been in the north wall, **(14)** and imprisoned in the house of Jonathan, the king's secretary, ' for they had made that the prison '. **19-20.** Sedecias, however, upon the prophet's request, had him removed to the freer custody of the guard-court, ' and they gave him a daily loaf of bread out of the bakers' street '.

e XXXVIII 1-28 XXXIX 15-18 Imprisonment : Sedecias again consults the Prophet : the Promise to Abdemelech—The removal of Jeremias to the guard-court (37:20) made the publication of his prophecies all the easier. **1.** ' Phassur the son of Melchias ', already mentioned 21:1 ; ' Juchal ' already in 37:3 ; ' Gedelias ', perhaps the son of the Phassur of 20:1. **2.** ' his life shall be to him as a spoil ': see on 45:5. **5.** Sedecias fears to resist the princes : ' The king can do nothing against you '. **6.** So they cast Jeremias into the cistern (so throughout 7:13) of Melchias, which was in the guard-court : an underground pit for storing water, whence Abdemelech obtains permission to release him. **7.** ' the Benjamin gate ', already in 37:12. **10.** ' thirty ' should probably be ' three '. **16.** ' hath made for us this soul ', i.e. these lives of ours. **17.** Even now Sedecias can save himself and his city by surrender. **22.** Many women had been carried away with Joachin in 598 B.C. : the rest shall deride Sedecias :

' Thy friends have prevailed over thee, and set on thee :
Now that thy feet are sunk in the mire, they have turned away from thee '.

26. ' the house of Jonathan ' ; cf. 37:14, 19. **28.** ' Jeremias remained in the guard-court '. ' And it came to pass, when Jerusalem was taken ': these words properly belong to the beginning of the next chapter, where see note.

Abdemelech, the Ethiopian eunuch, had rescued Jeremias from the cistern, where he would probably have died (38:7-13) ; he now receives a message of comfort in return (**XXXIX 15-18**), which however, as indicated in **15**, belongs to the time when the prophet was in the guard-court, and was probably delivered soon after the rescue. **18.** ' thy life shall be as a spoil to thee ' ; see on 45:5.

(39:1-14 follows immediately.)

XXXIX 1-14 The Capture of Jerusalem—The f chapter should begin, as already noted, with the last words of 38:28, and then probably go on to 39:3 ; the intermediate verses interrupt the sense and the sentence (' it came to pass . . . that all the princes '). But 39:4-13 (omitted by LXX) is probably likewise a later insertion, for of course Sedecias would not wait for the chief Babylonian officials to be sitting in state at the gates before attempting to escape. What does happen is that they send for Jeremias, whose story is thus continued.

The two interjected verses, **1-2**, are abridged from g 4 Kg 25:1-4a (=Jer 52:4-7a). The siege began in 589, and ended in 587. **3.** The princes ' sat ' in solemn session to deliver judgements and give directions. Probably there was only one Nergal-sharezer ; the first mention may be a slip for ' Nabusezban ' (Nebushazban) in 13. ' Rabsares ' (Rab-saris) may be a title (' chief of the eunuchs ', or perhaps ' great chief '), and similarly Rebmag (' Rab-mag ', chief of the soothsayers). **4-10** is an abridgement of 4 Kg 25:4-12 (=Jer 52:7-16). **11-13** also offer a difficulty, because Nabuzardan (Nebuzaradan) is not mentioned in **3**, and did not come to Jerusalem till a month after the capture of the city ; cf. 39:2 ; 52:12. There is no difficulty of course in Nabuchodonoscr's order to him in 11-12, but the mention of it is not likely originally to have belonged here. **14.** For Ahicam, see on 26:24. His son Godolias was made ' governor over the cities of Judah ' (40:5), but was murdered by Ishmael and his party (41:2).

The commentary upon the historical matter in this section is reserved for 4 Kg, where it comes in more appropriately.

(39:15-18 precedes 39:1-14.)

Part IV After the Capture of Jerusalem (587 B.C.) : 4 chh 40-4—The folly which had marked the behaviour of the Hebrews towards the irresistible power of Babylon continued to mark it after the capture of their city. The Babylonian treatment of Judah was milder than the Assyrian treatment of the Northern Kingdom in 721 B.C. Those deported seem on the whole to have been treated fairly well, no alien colonists were imported, and the poorer classes (who, left without leaders, were not likely to rebel) were encouraged to settle peacefully on the land under the Hebrew governor Godolias. This Jeremias, who remained in Palestine, likewise encouraged them to do. But Ishmael (41:1), who was of the blood royal and probably hoped with the help of Ammon to mount the now vacant throne, murdered Godolias, and ultimately (41:10, 15) fled back to Ammon. Johanan (41:11) and the other leaders of the Jews fled to Egypt for fear of the vengeance of the Babylonians, in spite of the exhortations of Jeremias to remain in Palestine, and his threats of what would

a otherwise ensue. In Egypt he denounced their idolatry, and warned them that Egypt too would be delivered into the power of Nabuchodonosor. Jer 40:7–43:7 is summed up in 4 Kg 25:23–26.

b XL 1–16 Jeremias remains with Godolias the Governor, who encourages the Hebrews to settle down peaceably. **1.** For Rama, see on 31:15. Nabuzardan (Nebuzaradan) was ' *captain of the bodyguard* ' (again 2, 5 ; 41:10). **4.** He promises Jeremias, ' I will set mine eyes upon thee ', as ordered in 39:12, *i.e.* he will look well after him. **5.** For Godolias, see on 39:14. **6.** Masphath (Mizpah), probably the height Neby Samwil, about 4½ m. NW. of Jerusalem. **7–8.** ' *The captains of the forces which were in the fields, both they and their men* . . . came to Godolias at Masphath ' : and so in 13. **10.** ' I dwell in Masphath (lit.) to stand before the Chaldaeans ', *i.e.* to take orders from the Babylonians, while representing your interests. **14.** The king of Ammon was hostile to Babylon (27:3), and probably hoped that Ishmael might join in resistance.

c XLI 1–18 Ishmael slays Godolias and those with him, and seventy others, but is forced to take refuge with the Ammonites. The Jewish captains prepare to flee to Egypt. **1.** Three months after the capture of the city (*cf.* 39:2), Ishmael (**2**) murders Godolias (**3**) and his Babylonian body-guard with him, ' *even the soldiers* '. **6.** Ishmael feigned sympathy with the eighty men, who were mourning the destruction of the temple. **8.** Subterranean pits were used for storage, (**9**) but the corpses were thrown into a cistern, doubtless built by King Asa to supply Masphath with water when he was fortifying it against King Baasa (3 Kg 15:22). **12.** ' the great waters ' are probably ' the pool of Gabaon ' (2 Kg 2:13), about a mile north of Masphath. **18.** The Jewish captains were afraid of what the Babylonians might do to punish the murder of Godolias.

d XLII 1–22 Jeremias warns the Jewish Captains against fleeing to Egypt, where destruction will overtake them. **1.** For ' Jezonias ' (which is read in MT here from 40:8) read ' Azarias ', as in LXX and 43:2. **2.** ' Let our supplication fall before thee ', which in the Hebrew idiom means ' be laid before thee ', and with success, ' be accepted ', as in 37:19. **10.** ' for I *repent* of the evil ', an anthropomorphic expression of a kind common in Holy Scripture ; in man a change of purpose would be implied, but in God only of conduct. **12.** ' And I will grant you mercy, *that he may have mercy on you, and may cause you to dwell* in your own land ; (**13**) but if you say, " We will not dwell in this land ", *so that you hearken not* to God's voice . . . ' **21–22.** Jeremias sees already that they do not mean to obey his message.

e XLIII 1–13 In spite of Jeremias' Words, the Jews proceed to Egypt, taking Jeremias with them : he foretells the conquest of Egypt by Nabuchodonosor. **7.** Taphnes, see on 2:16. Driver translates (**9**) : ' bury them in mortar in the pavement which is at the entry of Pharaoh's house ', and suggests that the pavement may be the large oblong brick pavement close to the palace-fort built by Psammetichus I (664–610 B.C.), and excavated by Flinders Petrie in 1886. **13.** ' And he shall break the *pillars* ' or obelisks ' of the house ' or temple ' of the sun ', with allusion to that in the Egyptian city On, called Heliopolis (' city of the sun ') by the Greeks, about 6 m. NE. of Cairo. The temple was erected by Thothmes III *c* 1500 B.C., with an avenue of obelisks in front of it, one of which is still *in situ*, and another is ' Cleopatra's Needle ', on the Thames Embankment. An inscription of Nabuchodonosor states that he invaded Egypt in 568 B.C. and defeated King Amasis of Egypt (570–526 B.C.).

f XLIV 1–30 Jeremias rebukes the Jews in Egypt for Idolatry—They will perish there in consequence. The Jews defend their practices. **1.** Magdal (Migdol), on NE. border of Egypt, a little E. of Taphnes, for which (and Memphis) see on 2:16. ' the land of Phatures ' (Pathros) is Upper Egypt (again in 15). **10.** ' *They have not humbled themselves* even to this day '.

464f **14.** (at end) ' none shall return save fugitives ' who also shall be but ' few in number ' (*cf.* 28). **17.** ' every word that is gone forth out of our mouth ' : a solemn expression for a vow ; *cf.* 25. ' the queen of heaven ' : probably Astarte ; see on 7:18. **19.** ' And *when we sacrificed* . . . and *poured out* . . . was it without (the consent of) our husbands that we made cakes to *portray her* [probably with her image stamped upon them, or in her shape] *and poured out* drink-offerings to her ? ' There may well be an allusion to Num 30:7 ff. ; their husbands did not cancel their vows. Obviously 19 is spoken by the women, and the Peshitta and some MSS of LXX mention the fact, but the weight of textual evidence is against the insertion. **23.** ' to idols ' is not in the text, but gives the sense. In 25 LXX reads ' Ye women have spoken ', and this verb and the last two in the verse are in the feminine in MT, so that the whole verse may be addressed to the women. They say, ' *We will surely perform* our vows ' : Yahweh answers ironically, ' *Fulfil then your vows, perform your vows !* ' **26–27** must be understood of the band of idolatrous rebels whom the prophet is addressing (Knabenbauer, Condamin) ; later on there were many Jews in Egypt. **30.** For Pharaoh Ephree (Hophra), see on 37:4. He was deposed by a military revolution and ultimately strangled.

(For ch 45, see § 460c.)

Part V Prophecies against the Nations : chh 46–51— **465a** These belong to the time following the battle of Carchemish (605 B.C.), in which Nabuchodonosor, commanding the Babylonian army as his father's general, decisively defeated the Egyptians under the Pharaoh Nechao (Necho), establishing Babylonian supremacy over the Middle East. Nabuchodonosor shortly afterwards succeeded his father as king of Babylon. These prophecies may originally have followed ch 25, where LXX places them, though not in the same order ; that chapter may in any case serve as a kind of introduction to them, though they so interrupt the story of Jeremias that it has seemed better to keep them here. Such indeed may have been the reason why they came to find their way here, if they were not here originally.

XLVI 1–28 Egypt—1 is the general title of Part V, **b** and 2 of this chapter. **3–4.** A picture of the Egyptians preparing for battle. ' Harness the horses ' to the chariots, an important part of an Egyptian army ; ' the horsemen ' are the cavalry. **5–6.** But almost at once he sees them in flight. ' Terror on every side ' ; see on 20:3. Escape is hopeless. They have been defeated at Carchemish (2) ; see §459b. **7–8.** Egypt was puffed up with pride, but her boasts have come to naught. ' Who is this that riseth up *like the Nile* [in its annual flood] and his waters *toss themselves* like rivers ? Egypt riseth up *like the Nile*, and his waters *toss themselves* like rivers. And he said . . . '. ' The city ' seems to be used (by a Heb. idiom, as in 47:2) for ' cities ' in general, with their inhabitants. **9.** ' *Go up, ye horses* [from Egypt northward] and *rage, ye chariots* ', driving madly ahead. These ' Lydians ' are a people near the west border of Egypt. Mercenaries from these three nations (Ethiopians, Libyans, Lydians) formed the chief part of the Egyptian armies ; *cf.* Ez 30:5, etc. **10.** But the expedition is going to end in Yahweh taking vengeance on them at Carchemish (605 B.C.) ; the death of King Josias (609 B.C.), defeated and killed by the Pharaoh Necho at Megiddo, was still a recent memory. **11.** The balm (balsam) of Galaad (Gilead) is also mentioned in 8:22 (*cf.* 51:8), etc. The Egyptians were famous for their knowledge of medicines. **12.** The Egyptian warriors have stumbled against each other in their flight.

13–26 Jeremias prophesies the Successful Invasion c of Egypt by Nabuchodonosor, which took place in 568 B.C. ; see on 43:13. Sedecias had sought help from Egypt ; *cf.* Ez 17:15. **14.** For ' Magdal ', see on 44:1 ; for Memphis and Taphnes, on 2:16. ' prepare thyself ' to resist the invader. **15.** ' Wherefore

465c hath Apis fled, hath thy strong one made no stand ? ' This on the whole seems the more likely translation. The reference to Apis, the divine bull of Egypt, is apparently preserved in LXX, the translators of which (being in Egypt) would more easily understand it. It implies very little change in MT. Even in the alternative translation (' Wherefore is thy strong one beaten down ? He hath made me stand ') the ' strong one ' is generally recognized to be the Apis bull, the word being often used in OT of bulls, *e.g.* in Ps 21:13 ' many *bulls* have encompassed me : *strong ones of Bashan* have beset me round '. But in 47:3 and 50:11 horses are meant. **16.** The foreign mercenaries (see on 9) will wish to escape home ' from the *oppressing sword* ' : similarly in 50:16.

d **17.** ' Call ye the name of Pharaoh king of Egypt Crash ', the crash of disastrous battle ; ' *he hath let the appointed time* [of grace or of preparation] *pass by* '. **18.** ' so shall he come ', *i.e.* Nabuchodonosor, towering over all. **20.** There shall come upon Egypt ' *a gad-fly* ', Nabuchodonosor with his army. **22.** ' *Her sound shall be like a serpent as it goeth* ', hissing impotently at the wood-cutters who destroy its retreat in the underwood. **23.** The many flourishing cities of Egypt are compared to a forest. **25.** ' Behold, *I will punish Amon* [the god] of *No* [Thebes, the capital of Upper Egypt, now Luxor] and Pharaoh and those who trust in him '. The intervening words are almost certainly an interpolation, as the repetition of ' and Pharaoh ' shows. **26.** The prophecy concludes with a promise of restoration. 27-28 practically repeat 30:10-11, and probably belong there alone ; they do not fit in well here.

e **XLVII 1-7 The Philistines and Phoenicians**—It is implied in **4** that the Phoenicians (Tyre and Sidon) were involved in the general disaster, but the Philistines furnish the main theme. Tyre and Sidon were on the Mediterranean coast to the extreme north of Palestine, and the Philistines to the west of Judah. **1.** ' The word of Yahweh ' is ' concerning the Philistines '. When precisely the Pharaoh, obviously Necho (see § 465a, etc.), ' *smote* Gaza ' on the SW. coast of Palestine is not known. **2.** ' The waters ' are the Babylonians : ' the city ' is used collectively for ' cities ' ; see on 46:8. **3.** ' At the noise of the *stamping of the hoofs of his strong ones* [here horses ; see on 46:15], at the *rattling* of his chariots, at the *rumbling* of his wheels, the fathers look not back ' to carry away their children, their hands hang feebly in their terror. **4.** ' because of *the day that cometh to despoil all the Philistines, to cut off from Tyre and Sidon every helper that surviveth* ', all other helpers having been already cut off from these doomed cities. ' For Yahweh is about to despoil the Philistines, the remnant of the isle of *Caphtor* ', *i.e.* Crete, their home ; they were an Aryan race. **5.** ' Baldness ' and cutting oneself were signs of mourning ; see on 16:6. Gaza, Ascalon, Ekron, Ashdod (Azotus) and Gath were the leading Philistine cities (*cf.* 25:20). ' Ascalon is destroyed : O remnant of Accaron (Ekron), how long wilt thou gash thyself ? ' This seems the most likely translation, but ' Accaron ' implies a change in the Hebrew word, which as it stands can only mean ' their valley ', and is recognized by all to be a scribe's mistake. A lesser change would give, ' O remnant of the Anakim ', older inhabitants of those parts ; *cf.* Jos 11:22 (' Enacims '), etc. **6** appears to be a cry of the Philistines for mercy. **7** is the prophet's answer, that such is the work to which Yahweh has appointed his sword.

466a **XLVIII 1-47 Moab**—The territory of Moab was the high and rich tableland east of the Dead Sea ; but after the Israelite conquest the tribe of Reuben was assigned the territory north of the Arnon, which flows in from the east about the middle of the Dead Sea (*cf.* Jos 13:15-21), territory which had been part of Seon's former kingdom (see on 45). But Reuben did not succeed in holding this territory, so that here and in Is 15-16 cities assigned to it are mentioned as Moabite. Nabo, Cariathaim (which is probably ' the

strong place '), Heshbon (about 14 m. E. of NE. corner of Dead Sea), Horonaim (NE. corner of Dead Sea) and Luith (near E. of Dead Sea, about a third from the S. end) are Moabite cities. **2.** ' *In Heshbon they have devised evil against her* ', *i.e.* Moab. Heshbon is represented as already captured by the enemy, and the sword is to overtake the rest of Moab. **4.** ' *her little ones have caused a cry to be heard* ' ; but perhaps, with LXX and a slight change in MT, ' they make a cry to be heard unto Zoar ', at the extreme SE. of the Dead Sea, and probably now under it, so that the sense would be, ' from one end of Moab (*e.g.* from Heshbon in the north) to the other '. **6.** ' heath ' is probably the juniper ; see on 17:6. But LXX ' wild ass ' (shy and difficult to capture) is a tempting reading.

7. Chemosh (Chamos) was the national god. **8.** ' the valley ' of Jordan towards the Dead Sea, and the main ' *tableland* '. **9.** ' *Give wings to Moab, for she would fain fly away* '. **10.** ' Cursed be he that doth Yahweh's work *negligently* ', *i.e.* the appointed destruction of Moab. **11.** ' Moab hath been *at ease* ', like good wine improved by resting on its own sediment. **12.** ' I will send him men that *tilt up* ' wine-bottles skilfully, so as to let the liquid run off clear, leaving the sediment, ' *and they will tilt him up*, and empty his vessels, and dash his jars in pieces '.

13. Bethel was the rival sanctuary to Jerusalem set c up by Jeroboam in the Northern Kingdom ; *cf.* Am 5:5, etc. **15.** ' they have *gone up into her cities*, and the flower of her young men have gone down to be slaughtered ' like cattle—such is the implication of the word. **17.** ' know his name ' probably implies considerable knowledge of Moab, in accordance with the pregnant sense of ' name ' in Heb. ' strong staff ' and ' beautiful rod ' imply strength, authority, glory. **18-19.** ' daughter of Dibon . . . inhabitress of Aroer ', the inhabitants of these Moabite cities, both a little north of the Arnon. ' bulwarks ', better ' *fortifications* '. **21** ' Judgement is come upon the *tableland* '. **26.** ' Make him drunk ' with terror and despair ; see on 25:15. ' Let Moab fall with a splash into his own vomit '. **27.** ' *For was not Israel a derision unto thee ? Or had he been caught among thieves, that as often as thou spakest of him, thou didst wag thy head* (in scorn) ? ' This ends the verse. **28.** ' Be ye like the dove that maketh her nest in the sides of the hole's mouth '. The text is a little uncertain, but the reference is to the many fissures in the rocky sides of the defiles of Palestine, especially in the gorge of the Arnon, where numberless doves nest.

29-39 contain many reminiscences of Is 15-16, where d also there is question of the doom of Moab, with much that throws light on these verses. References are given to the chief Isaian parallels. **29-30 :** Is 16:6. ' I know his arrogance . . . his boastings are vain, their deeds are vain '. The Heb. is too idiomatic for a close translation. **31 :** Is 16:7. ' I will cry out *for* all Moab, for the men of *Kir-heres* (Is : Kir-hareseth) *will I moan* ', a strong fortress 16 m. S. of the Arnon and 8 m. E. of the Dead Sea. **32 :** Is 16:8-10. The vines of Sabama (Sibmah, probably 2½ m. WNW. of Heshbon) spread out to Jazer (N. of Heshbon?) and SW. over the Dead Sea ; Jazer shall mourn their loss. **33 :** Is 16:10. For ' Carmel ' read ' *the fruitful land* '; see on 2:7. **34 :** Is 15:4-6. A difficult verse, from which some words may have fallen out ; in the light of Is 15:4-6 we may perhaps read, ' Heshbon crieth out, and Eleale [near Heshbon] : even unto Jahaz [about 6 m. S. of Heshbon ?] they have uttered their voice, from Segor [Zoar, see on 48:4] to Horonaim [see § 466a] and the third Eglath [? there may have been three Eglaths near each other] : for the waters of Nemrim also [probably Wady Numeirah near SE. end of Dead Sea] shall become desolate '. **35.** *Cf.* Is 15:2 ; 16:12. **36 :** Is 16:11 ; 15:7a. ' and my heart soundeth like pipes ', such as were used at funerals, ' for the men of Kir-heres [*cf.* 31] : *therefore the abundance that he [Moab] hath gotten is perished* '.

37 : Is 15:2-3. All these are signs of mourning : e

588

'upon all hands are gashes'. See on 16:6. **39.** 'How hath Moab *turned his back with shame!*' **40.** 'One like an eagle [Nabuchodonosor, like (strictly speaking) a griffon-vulture] shall fly, and spread out his wings against Moab'. In 49:22 much of 40*b* and 41*b* are applied to Edom. **41.** The site of Carioth (Kerioth, the native place of Judas Iscariot) is uncertain. With **43–44***a* cf. Is 24:17–18. **45***b***–46** are based on Num 21:28–9 ; 24:17. **45.** 'Beneath the shadow of Heshbon stood *the fugitives without strength*', hoping for protection ; but the city was to prove only the beginning of the conflagration which was to destroy Moab, 'a flame from *the house of Seon*' (or Sihon), another name for Heshbon, from its former king (Num 21:26). This flame 'shall devour *the temples of Moab's head*, and the crown of the head of *the sons of the battle-din*' : 'battle-din' as in 25:31, the reference being to the Moabite warriors : 'temples', perhaps the hair was removed from them with religous significance ; see on 9:26. **46.** Chemosh, see on 48:7. **47.** The prophecy ends with hope of restoration for Moab, as for Egypt (46:26), Ammon (49:6), Elam (49:39), and probably Edom (49:11).

f XLIX 1–6 'On the Children of Ammon'—The tribe of Gad was assigned a territory in Transjordan stretching roughly from the head of the Dead Sea to the north of the Jabbok, the northern part of the former kingdom of Seon (Sihon). In the semi-arid district east of the wide semi-circle of the Jabbok dwelt Ammon, with its capital Rabbath-Ammon (later Philadelphia, now Amman) in a strong position near the source of the river. Under the system of the loose confederacy of tribes, however, Gad was as little able to resist the incursions of Ammon as was Reuben to withstand Moab. King David subjugated Edom, Moab, and Ammon, but Reuben and Gad did not permanently recover.

g 1. Milcom (Melchom) was the national god of the Ammonites, and here represents them. **2.** 'her daughters' are the towns and villages near Rabbath-Ammon. **3.** Hai is apparently an otherwise unknown town near Heshbon, which however was a Moabite city ; some not very successful efforts have been made to emend the text. **4.** 'Why gloriest thou in thy valley?' 'valley' may be repeated by mistake with a verb. Though on a high tableland, Rabbath-Ammon lay between hills. 'delicate' is uncertain. 'Who shall come to me?' This alludes to the strong defensive position of the city ; but (**5**) the enemy shall be all round, 'and we shall be driven away every man *right forth*, and there shall be none to collect them that wander'. **6.** Once more the last word is one of hope ; see on 48:47.

h 7–22 'On Edom'—Edom at this time still inhabited the plateau SE. of the Dead Sea, with the capital perhaps at Teman, near Petra ; but some take Teman for a district. The Nabataean Arabs were soon to drive the Edomites more to the west, so that the later Idumaea cannot be said to correspond at all closely to the earlier Edom. Edom, Ammon, Moab, and Israel, together with the Canaanites, the Syrians (Aramaeans) at Damascus and the Phoenicians in Tyre and Sidon, were all kindred races ; the Arabs, Babylonians and Assyrians, though likewise Semites, were less closely related to the group. The Philistines were not Semites at all. There was always much enmity between the Hebrews and Edomites (*cf.* Ps 136:7) ; but the former were convinced that their cause was the cause of God. With 49:7, 9, 10*a*, 14–16, *cf.* Abd 8 and 1–6.

i 7. The Themanites, and the Edomites in general, appear to have had a certain reputation for wisdom : *cf.* Job 2:11 ; Abd 8. **8.** 'dwell deep down', in inaccessible hiding-places. Esau was the father of the Edomites (Gen 36:8–9) ; Dedan was a district to the SE. of Edom, the inhabitants of which are warned to flee, for fear of sharing Edom's fate. **9.** 'If grape-gatherers come to thee, *they will leave no gleanings ;* if thieves by night, *they will destroy till they have had*

enough'. In Abd the turn of the phrase is different. **466i** **10.** 'I have revealed his secret *places*' : his race is ruined, 'he doth not exist'. These last words have been used to throw suspicion on 11 : but Egypt, Moab and Ammon were not left without hope ; see on 48:47.

12. 'the cup' is that of Yahweh's fury ; *cf.* 25:12, **j** 28:29. 'they to whom it did not properly belong to drink' were the Hebrews. **13.** 'Bosra', an Edomite city about 20 m. SE. of the Dead Sea. 'her cities' are doubtless her smaller neighbours. **14.** The language is figurative. '*and rise up* to battle !' **16** in MT begins, 'O thy trembling', but the word is not found in Abd 3, and the text is uncertain. 'Thou that . . . holdest the height of the hill'. **17.** 'hiss', or, as we might say, 'whistle', to match the parallel word '*be appalled*' (rather than merely 'astonished'). The verse is largely identical with 19:8. **18.** *Cf.* Deut 29:23 ; Gen 10:19, etc. The verse is practically repeated in 50:40.

19. Edom is compared to a flock of sheep, against **k** which he will send a lion (Nabuchodonosor), which will 'come up from the *jungle* of the Jordan [the thick semi-tropical vegetation fringing its banks] *against the established sheepfold : for in a moment I will chase them* [the sheep] *away from it* [the lion]. *And whosoever is chosen* [*i.e.* whosoever I choose] *I will appoint over it*', over the flock. 'For who is like to me' in power ? '*Or who will fix a time for me*', make an appointment to meet me in a trial of strength or in a court of law (*cf.* Job 9:19) ? '*And who is the shepherd that can stand before me*', *i.e.* the ruler that can defend his people from me ? **20.** 'Surely they [their enemies like wild beasts] *shall drag along* [the Edomites like] the little [helpless] ones of the flock ; *surely their sheepfold shall be appalled because of them*'. 19–21 are repeated with variations in 50:44–46. **22.** In 48:40*b*, 41*b* much the same words are applied to Moab.

23–27 'On Damascus'—Damascus, a city of renown **l** and joy (25) in times ancient and modern, situated in a beautiful oasis formed by the streams from the Anti-Lebanon before they lose themselves in the desert to the east, was the capital of Aram (Syria), a powerful kingdom to the NE. of Palestine, until finally subdued by Assyria in 732 B.C. Ben-hadad was the name of several of its kings. Emath (Hamath) was 110 m. N. of Damascus, and Arphad (Arpad) 95 m. N. of Hamath. Evidently all these had refused to submit to Nabuchodonosor, and were to feel his vengeance.

23*b* is difficult and uncertain : Driver renders, 'because of care, like the sea, they cannot rest'. **26** is repeated in 50:30. In **27** 'palaces' of Ben-hadad seems better. The verse may have been partly suggested by Am 1:4, 14.

28–33 'On Kedar (Cedar) and the Kingdoms of Asor m (Hazor), which Nabuchodonosor king of Babylon smote'. For 'Kedar', see on 2:10. 'Asor' may be a collective term denoting village settlements of Arab tribes to the S. and E. of Palestine, as distinguished from the nomadic tribes.

28 contains a summons to the Babylonians to attack, and **29** a promise of booty : the 'curtains' are the tent-hangings. The invaders shall cry out to the natives, '*Terror on every side*' ; see on 20:3. **31** is again a summons to the Babylonians, and **32** a promise of booty. 'their hair cut round' ; see on 9:26. **33.** 'Asor shall be a lair of *jackals*', like Jerusalem (9:11) and the cities of Judah generally (10:22), and Babylon (51:37).

34–39 'Concerning Elam'—For Elam, see on 25:25. **n** The later date assigned to this prophecy marks it out as a subsequent addition, made at a time when the deportations to Babylonia would increase the knowledge of Elam and interest in it.

35. 'The bow of Elam' was 'their chief strength'. **38.** 'I will set up my throne' of judgement, condemning its kings and princes to destruction by the Babylonians. **39.** But here again the prophecy ends with a promise of restoration ; see on 48:47.

467a **L 1–LI 58 'Concerning Babylon'**—The longest and most vehement prophecy is against Babylon. She has been God's instrument for punishing other nations, but she is not to escape punishment herself. The city was captured by the Persian king Cyrus in 539 B.C. It has been too easily assumed by some non-Catholic scholars that Jeremias cannot have written this section, even while they practically admit that it is written in his style. It is a mistake to suppose that a prophet who loved his own chosen country so much could have any really friendly feelings towards its ruthless foe : a still greater mistake, of course, to suppose that real prophecy is impossible, and that therefore these chapters must have been written only a little before the fall of Babylon, when that fall could easily be foreseen. There is some repetition of the main topics, which seems to be due to the author writing under strong feeling.

b **1.** 'In the hand of' is a Heb. idiom for 'by'. **2.** 'a standard', some sort of signal to attract attention. 'Bel', the Babylonian form of 'Baal' (see on 2:8, and *cf.* Dan 14:2), and here probably a title of Marduk (Merodach) supreme god of Babylon. The 'nation' of **3** is spoken of in 51:11, 28 as the Medes, a usage also found sometimes in Greek literature ; the dominant nation was the Persian, but the two were closely united and were together supreme in the Persian empire. Persia proper lay on the eastern side of the Persian Gulf ; Media lay NW. of it, NE. of Babylonia. **4.** Cyrus allowed the exiles to return to Jerusalem. **5.** The words they shall say are, '*Come ye, and let us join ourselves to Yahweh*', etc. **7.** 'because they have sinned against Yahweh', here called 'the abode of righteousness and the hope of their fathers'. **8.** 'be ye as the *he-goats*', leading the way.

c **9.** 'the great nations' are the Persians and Medes and their allies ; 'from thence [by enemies mainly from the north] she shall be captured : their arrows shall be as those of a skilled warrior, *who returneth not empty*' ; *cf.* 2 Kg 1:22. The Persians relied much on the bow. **11–12** are addressed to Babylonians ; 'your mother' is Babylon. '*Because ye rejoice, because ye exult, O ye that pillage mine inheritance : because ye gambol like heifers at grass and neigh like horses* [see on 46:15]', *your mother shall be very ashamed, she that bare you shall be abashed. Behold* [understand here, "men shall say "] *the last of the nations*, a wilderness, a dry land, and a desert'. **14.** The foe is invited to attack. **15.** 'Shout against her round about ! She hath given her hand [in token of submission ; *cf.* Lam 5:6] ; her buttresses are fallen'. **16.** Foreigners settled in Babylon shall flee 'from the *oppressing* sword' ; *cf.* 46:16. **17.** Israel's misfortunes are told in metaphor, but **(19–20)** she is promised restoration and pardon. Bashan, E. and NE. of the Lake of Galilee.

d **21** begins a fresh invitation to attack Babylon. '*Go up against the land of Merathaim, go up against it, and against the inhabitants of Pekod*'. The former is Babylonia, but it is not clear how ; perhaps the name has been adapted somewhat in order to let it mean symbolically 'double (*i.e.* intense) defiance' or 'bitterness'. The latter are mentioned (though DV does not show this) in Ez 23:23 ; they were a people of Babylonia bordering on Elam, and are perhaps mentioned here because the name could suggest 'visitation' or 'punishment'. 'all behind them' should be omitted with LXX and Syr., being probably due to dittography. Yahweh's weapons in **25** are the attacking nations. Words are taken from this verse in Rom 9:22 : see also Is 13:5 ; 54:16. **26.** '*open her granaries : pile her up* [and all inside her] *like heaps* [of corn] *and destroy her utterly*' as an abomination ; *cf.* Deut 13:12–18. **27.** 'her valiant men', lit. 'her young bulls' ; *cf.* Is 34:7. **28.** The liberated Jews shall tell in Sion the vengeance taken by Yahweh on the Babylonians for the destruction of his temple. **29.** '*Call together the archers against Babylon, all that bend the bow : encamp against her round about*'. **30** repeats 49:26. **34.** 'Their redeemer' or vindicator, strictly speaking the

next of kin ; *cf.* the introduction to Ruth in WV. **4** 'to give rest to [not terrify] the earth' : most of the nations had been disturbed by Babylon ; *cf.* Nah 3:19 on Nineveh. **36.** 'her diviners' are doubtless meant : lit. 'her boastings'. **37.** 'the *mixed* people' in the midst of her are the mixed foreign population (*cf.* 25:20) ; but the following words may imply that foreign mercenary troops are especially in question. **39.** For 'dragons' Driver conjectures 'wild cats', from the cognate Arabic word ; and the 'fig fauns' are probably 'wolves'. **40** practically repeats 49:18, and **41–43** are adapted to Babylon from 6:22–24. **42.** 'They lay hold on bow and *javelin*'. **44–46** largely repeat 49:19–21, adapted from Edom to Babylon : in this case the 'lion' is Cyrus.

LI 1 '*I am about to stir up against the inhabitants of* **e** *Leb-kamai the spirit of a destroyer*', *i.e.* of Cyrus : *cf.* 11. 'Leb-kamai' means 'the heart', or in the applied sense, 'the midst', which seems better here, 'of those who rise up against me', and is here an anagram for 'Chaldaea', *i.e.* Babylonia, similar to the anagram 'Sheshak' ; see on 25:26. MT reads 'against Babylon and against the inhabitants', etc. ; but the mention of Babylon should probably be omitted, because it spoils the metre, and because it would be incongruous to insert it before its anagram. Later on it might be thought necessary to interpret the anagram. **2.** 'I will send to Babylon *winnowers*, and they shall *winnow* her, and *empty* her land' by their devastations. For the figure of winnowing, see on 15:7 ; 4:11. **3.** The text is difficult and uncertain ; it may mean that it will be useless for the Babylonians to try to defend themselves. **4.** 'and those pierced through [*i.e.* desperately wounded] in her *streets*'.

5. 'forsaken', lit. 'widowed' : Yahweh is not dead, **f** but has punished their sins, and now will avenge them. **6** is addressed to the Jews in Babylon : 'be not *cut off* in her iniquity'. **7.** The nations 'are mad' from having drunk her wine ; *cf.* 25:15–16, with note. **8.** *Cf.* Is 21:9 ; Apoc 14:8. 'take balm' : see on 46:11. The words are here ironical. In **9** the Jews in Babylon appear to be addressing the other foreigners there : she should have profited by their presence to learn the true religion. 'forsake her' is imperative. 'her judgement' is her punishment. **10.** Yahweh has shown openly the righteousness of our cause. In **11** 'the king of the Medes' is Cyrus ; *cf.* 51:1. 'the vengeance of the temple' ; see on 50:28. **12.** 'against the walls . . . strengthen the watch [invest it closely], set watchers [whose business it will be to see that this is done], prepare the ambushes', perhaps against sorties : *cf.* Jos 8:12 ff. ; Jg 20:29 ff. **13.** 'thy end is come, *the cubit where thou shalt be cut off*', a figure from weaving. **14** should probably read, '*Though I have filled thee* [or perhaps, though thou art filled] *with men* [inhabitants] *as with locusts* [in point of numbers, yet] *they* [the assailants] *shall raise the battle-cry against thee*'. **15–19** repeats 10:12–16, which see.

20–23 should probably be referred to Babylon (rather **g** than Cyrus) ; the tenses can be read as past just as easily as present, and there is no hint of Cyrus in the immediate context ; 24 would then introduce the reversal of Yahweh's action hitherto. Upon this interpretation Babylon is still the cup of God's fury (*cf.* 25:15), or rather (taking the tenses in the past) has been such in the past. **20.** '*Thou wast my mace, my weapon of war, and with thee have I broken in pieces nations, and with thee have I destroyed kingdoms*', and so on, with past tenses. **23.** 'captains and rulers' : better, with Driver, 'governors and viceroys' : the words are of Assyrian origin, and are often used in Assyrian inscriptions of governors of cities or provinces. They are used again in 28 and 57. **24.** '*Nevertheless will I repay*' : Heb. uses 'and' (as here) even where there is a sharp antithesis. **25.** 'mountain' is used metaphorically, as Babylon is in a plain : the reference may be to her towering supremacy in the world, or to her mass of tall buildings. Possibly there is some influence from Ez 35:3 ff. 'which *destroyest*' : the

g verb is repeated. 'a burnt mountain', as desolate as an extinct volcano. **26.** There shall be no further use even for her stones : she shall be ' *desolate* for ever '. **27.** 'Ararat', the Assyrian 'Urartu', roughly the modern Armenia, NW. of Lake Van. 'Menni', the Assyrian 'Mannai', SE. of Lake Van. 'Ascenez' (Ashkenaz : *cf.* Gen 10:3), near the former two : perhaps the Assyrian 'Ashguza'. 'Taphsar', prob-

h ably (with Driver) 'a marshal'. The assailants' horses shall be numerous 'as the *rough* locust'. The Hebrew word for 'locust' probably designates the larva or caterpillar state of the locust, when it is even more destructive than in its winged state. *Cf.* Nah 3:15–17, with WV notes. In this state its wings are enveloped in horn-like sheaths, which project roughly on the back, whence the epithet. **28.** 'the king of Media [Cyrus], *his* governors and all *his* viceroys ', see on 23. **29.** 'shall awake', lit. 'is rising up' for action. **30.** The 'bars' of the city gates. **31.** 'post', from meaning a place where horses were kept in waiting for travellers, came to mean the person so travelling, and then anyone travelling quickly, as in the expression 'post-haste'. Runners from opposite quarters shall meet at the king's palace. **32.** 'And that the *ferries* [across the Euphrates] are taken'. 'the marshes' are perhaps the great reed-beds serving as defences ; or the text here may be faulty. **33.** 'a threshing-floor *at the time when it is trodden*' hard and smooth in readiness for the threshing : soon Babylon will be threshed—a picture of her devastation.

i In **34-35** Jerusalem is bidden speak : **36-50** give Yahweh's answer. **34.** 'devoured' : better, 'troubled'. 'dragon' : the word is used for any great '*monster*' of river or sea, *e.g.* the crocodile (Ps 73:13). **35.** 'and my (wounded) flesh be upon Babylon, *let the inhabitress of Sion say . . . let Jerusalem say*'. **36.** 'her sea . . . her spring', probably alluding to the great lake constructed by Nabucho-donosor for the defence of Babylon. **37** : see on 49:33. **38.** 'They roar . . . they *growl* like lions' whelps'. **39.** While they are gloating over their prey, Yahweh will put them into a sleep whence they shall never awake ; *cf.* 57. **40.** 'like rams with *he-goats*', all the defenders of the flocks. **41.** 'Sesach', see on 25:26. 'surprised . . . astonishment' : rather, '*seized* . . . *appalment*'. **42** signifies the overwhelming numbers

of her assailants ; *cf.* 55. **43.** ' *an appalment, a dry land,* **467i** *a steppe : no man shall dwell in them* . . . pass through *them*'. **44.** 'Bel', see on 50:2 : he will be compelled to disgorge the plunder of conquered nations. **45** is quoted in 2 Cor 6:17, together with Is 52:11. **46.** Understand, 'take heed lest . . . ruler against ruler' : these (with the rumours) will be signs of the break-up of the Babylonian empire. **48.** ' *shall sing for joy over Babylon*'. **49.** ' *Yea, Babylon must fall, O ye slain of Israel : yea* [giving the reason] *the slain of all the earth have fallen because of Babylon*'.

51 gives the answer of the Jews in Babylon ; they **j** are ashamed to return, with strangers in possession of the temple. To this Yahweh answers with his final word of judgement. **53.** 'establish her strength on high' with walls even loftier. **54.** 'and *of* great destruction'. **55.** 'the great voice', the noise of the city's life. the 'wave' of the assailants ; *cf.* 42. 'their voice *maketh an uproar*'. **56.** ' *their bows are broken in pieces*'. **57.** ' *her governors and her viceroys and her warriors*' ; *cf.* 23. 'they shall sleep an everlasting sleep' ; *cf.* 39. **58.** Such is the way in which ' *the peoples labour to no purpose, and the nations weary themselves for* [only to feed] *the fire* ' : omit 'and shall perish' : a quite general statement from Hab 2:13, with which the denunciation of the doom of Babylon concludes.

(For 51:59–64, see § 461*h–i*.)

Part VI The Historical Appendix : ch 52—Most of **468** the matter in this part can be traced to the Books of Kings, and it is generally admitted that it is a later addition, of which Jeremias was not the author. The fall of Jerusalem may be called in a sense the main theme of the book of Jeremias, and perhaps it was thought by some later scribe that it should therefore appear at the end as the grand finale. The contents of the chapter are taken into account in the com-mentary on the Books of Kings, at the relevant passages. **1-27** comes from 4 Kg 24:18–25:21. **28-30** come from some independent source, and are taken into account at the right place in 4 Kg. The extra details about the fittings of the temple in **17-23** are considered under 3 Kg 7. **4-11** and **13-16** have already occurred slightly abridged in 39:1–2, 4–10, but it seems likely (as is noted *ad loc.*) that these verses of ch 39 should be omitted.

LAMENTATIONS

By M. LEAHY

469a Bibliography—*A. W. Streane, *Jeremiah and Lamentations*, CBSC, 1889 ; J. Knabenbauer, S.J., *Commentarius in Danielem Prophetam, Lamentationes et Baruch*, CSS, 1907² ; *A. S. Peake, *Jeremiah and Lamentations*, CBi, 1911 ; G. Ricciotti, *Le Lamentazioni di Geremia*, Torino-Roma, 1924 ; *S. Goldman, *Lamentations* in *The Five Megilloth*, ed. A. Cohen, Hindhead (Surrey), 1946 ; L. Dennefeld, *Les Grands Prophètes* (La Sainte Bible, Tome VII), Paris, 1947, 407-34.

b Title and Place in the Canon—In MT the Book is entitled *'Ēḵāh* (' How ') which is the initial word of the 1st, 2nd and 4th chh. The Rabbis (and St Jerome in the *Prologus Galeatus*) referred to it as *Qînôt* (' Elegies ') and an equivalent title was adopted by LXX (θρῆνοι) and by Vg (*Lamentationes*). In MT the Book is one of the five ' Rolls ' which form part of the third division known as the ' Writings '. (The first and second divisions of the Heb. Bible are known as the ' Law ' and the ' Prophets' respectively.) In LXX, Syr. and Vg, however, the Book comes after Jeremias, among the ' Prophets '.

c Literary Form—Each of the five chh which comprise the book contains twenty-two divisions, which is the number of consonants in the Hebrew alphabet. The first three chh are arranged in strophes of three and the fourth ch in strophes of two verses. In the first, second and fourth chh the opening word of each strophe begins with its respective letter of the alphabet, but in the third ch the same letter begins each verse of a strophe. All the Lamentations with the exception of ch 5 are written in a ' limping ' rhythm, known as *Qînāh* because of its use in this book ; in *Qînāh* rhythm each verse has two parts with, as a rule, three significant words in the first and two in the second.

d Subject-matter—The Book contains laments over the destruction of Jerusalem by the Neo-Babylonians in 586 B.C., and the sufferings endured by the population and the poet himself (*cf.* ch 3) before, during and after the siege. The catastrophe is acknowledged to be the result of repeated transgressions against Yahweh, and thus we find, intermingled with the laments, humble confessions of sin and ardent appeals for mercy and deliverance.

e Authorship—Jewish tradition attributes our book to Jeremias. The LXX has the following preface (not inspired) : ' And it came to pass after Israel was taken captive and Jerusalem laid waste, that Jeremias sat weeping and lamented with this lamentation over Jerusalem, and said ' (*cf.* a repetition of this statement, with a slight addition, in Vg). The Talmud (*Baba Bathra*, 15a) also states that Jeremias was the author. The Greek and Latin Fathers likewise take the Jeremian authorship for granted.

Recently, however, not a few critics, relying chiefly on internal evidence, have sought to show that not all the poems are by the same author, and only some of these critics would admit the Jeremian authorship of any. The following are the principal difficulties against attributing all the lamentations to Jeremias.

f (i) In the first poem the order of the Heb. consonants is the normal one, whereas in the next three chh *Pe* comes before *'Ayin*. This variation would tend to show that the second, third and fourth are not by the author of the first. It may well be, however, that the Hebrew poets enjoyed a certain liberty in the arrangement of the consonants of the alphabet.

(ii) The complaint in 2:9 that the prophets of Jerusalem ' have found no vision from the Lord ' would seem to imply that the author of the second Lamentation is not Jeremias since he, at least, was a prophet. Perhaps, however, the words mean that the prophets have received no vision *of encouragement* from Yahweh.

(iii) Verses 17 and 20 are quoted against the Jeremian authorship of the fourth chapter. In 17 the poet includes himself (note the 1st pers. plur.) with those who expected Egyptian aid whereas Jeremias never did (*cf.* Jer 37:5-10), and in 20 he speaks of King Sedecias with reverence whereas Jeremias spoke of him in disparaging terms, Jer 24:8-10. Those who defend the Jeremian authorship reply that Jeremias in Lam 4 is speaking in the name of the people and interpreting their thoughts.

(iv) The phraseology of Lam varies from that found in Jer. This objection loses some, at least, of its force when it is remembered that the situation as seen by the author of Lam is completely different and so its description necessitates a diction different from that in Jer. The Jews are now suffering severely for their folly. A religious leader—especially one who is himself full of grief—refrains in such circumstances from adding to the sufferings of a people whom he loved by further threats and bitter remarks but, on the contrary, treats them gently, seeks to console, and exhorts them to amend their ways and beg Yahweh's mercy and forgiveness.

On the whole the arguments advanced against Jeremian authorship do not appear conclusive. We do not think, however, that Lam was written as a unity. Commentators point out that the prophecies collected in Jer were originally in circulation as separate compositions. We may reasonably suppose that Lam also was formed by the combination of what were originally five separate elegies composed by Jeremias.

g Doctrine—The author emphasizes the power of Yahweh ; the destruction of Jerusalem is his work for it was he who brought the Neo-Babylonians to be his agents in effecting the destruction, 1:14 ; 2:17 ; 4:11. He lays stress upon the justice of Yahweh, 1:18 ; 3:42, but reminds his readers that, although just, Yahweh is also infinitely merciful, 3:22 f. He frequently states that it is because of their sins and those of their religious leaders that the people are suffering, 1:5, 8, etc. When composing the Office of Tenebræ the Church searched the Bible for words to express our sorrow for Christ in his sufferings ; she could find nothing more apt than these Lamentations.

I 1-22 The First Lamentation—1-11 The Desolation of Jerusalem—1. The city, normally crowded since it was the political and religious centre of the kingdom, now sits solitary, emptied by the exile of many of its inhabitants ; she that was once *great among the nations* is now become as a widow in her unhappiness ; she that was *a princess among the districts* into which the Hebrew Kingdom was divided *is become a bond-servant*, subject to taskwork. **2.** The city weeps bitterly in the night which is normally the time of repose ; she is not consoled by her *lovers* and friends, *i.e.* by her political allies, *cf.* 19. **3.** The inhabitants who remained behind after the destruction of the city chose voluntary exile in Egypt because they found the Babylonian yoke intolerable (*cf.* Jer chh 42 f.) ; Judah *dwells among the heathen*, without, however, finding rest ; all her persecutors *overtook* her *in narrow defiles*. This last clause is to be understood figuratively of the tribulations which hemmed in the people of Judah. **4.** The roads leading up to Sion, once crowded with pilgrims on their way to the solemn festivals, are deserted ; the city-gates, the recognized places of assembly in Eastern towns, are destroyed ; the priests sigh because the temple-ritual has ceased ; virgins are sorrowful because they can no longer take their appointed part in the joyous religious processions (*cf.* Ps 67:26). **5.** Sion's enemies are triumphant and prosper ; her misfortunes are Yahweh's punishment for her sins ; not even her young children escaped captivity. **6.** The daughter (of) Sion (*i.e.* Sion ; we have here the genit. of definition) has lost all her *splendour* ; her princes, weakened by hunger, were an easy prey for the Babylonians. The poet has in mind the flight and capture of King Sedecias and his princes, Jer 39:4 f.

7. Jerusalem *remembers* the days of her affliction and her *wanderings* (DV ' prevarication of ') when her inhabitants fell *into* enemy hands. The reference is to the bitter siege and conquest which left her homeless. The clause ' all her desirable things . . . of old ' should be omitted as a gloss ; there is a line too many and without this clause the strophe gives better sense. The word rendered ' sabbaths ' is not found elsewhere but the context requires some such word as ' extinction '. **8.** Jerusalem has sinned grievously and has become *as one impure, i.e.* ceremonially unclean and therefore to be shunned ; those who once honoured her now despise her ; she herself, painfully conscious of her unsightly condition, *turns aside* to escape notice. **9.** Her filthiness is *in her skirts, i.e.* her sins are exposed for all to see ; in the days of prosperity she reflected not that retribution would inevitably overtake her. The last clause is a cry to Yahweh for compassion, because the enemy *has magnified himself*. **10.** The Babylonians robbed her treasures ; Jerusalem has seen that the heathen are entered into the sanctuary, the heathen concerning whom Yahweh, because of the danger of idolatry, commanded that they should not enter the *community* of his chosen people. **11.** Those who survived the siege are now destitute ; hunger has compelled them to exchange their valuables for food.

12-22 An Appeal for Compassion—In this section, except in 17, Sion is the speaker. **12.** Sion makes a pathetic appeal for pity ; the anguish wherewith Yahweh has smitten her is incomparable. The last part should read : (my *anguish*) *which is severely dealt out to me, wherewith Yahweh has afflicted* (me) in the day of his fierce anger. **13** is a graphic description of the calamities which befell the city. The figures used are those of a fire, a net, sickness ; ' chastised me ', reading *yirdenni*. **14.** ' *Bound* [reading *niṣqad*] is the yoke of my crimes ; *by* his hand [the Lord's] they are *knit* together, *they are come* upon my neck ; *he has made my strength to fail* ; the Lord *has given me over to their* [referring to crimes] *power* [lit. hand ; read *b^eyāḍām*], I am not able to rise '. The crimes of Jerusalem are the poles and cords with which the Lord made a yoke and laid it on her neck ; the sufferings of Jerusalem are but the due punishment of her crimes. The last line but one means that the Lord abandoned her to the fate of sinners (*cf.* Job 8:4). **15.** In two images, that of a solemn feast at which the victims offered are the flower of Sion's army, and that of a winepress in which the blood of the people of Judah is trodden out, the destruction is presented as the work of the Lord as the first cause : ' The Lord *has flouted at* all my valiant men *in* the midst of me ; he has *proclaimed* against me a *festival* ' (DV ' the time '). Read ' *the virgin, the daughter Judah* ' (*cf.* 6). **16a.** Therefore (*cf.* 13-15) does Sion weep. **17.** The poet interrupts the wailing of Sion to affirm that although Sion *spreads* forth her hands in a gesture of entreaty, no one is found to console her ;

Yahweh has decreed concerning Jacob (*i.e.* the nation) *that* **470d** *they that* are round about him should be his (the nation's) enemies. They that are round about him are the neighbouring nations. For ' menstruous woman ' read ' one impure ', *cf.* 8. **18.** Sion acknowledges the justice of Yahweh's judgement. **19** She repeats (*cf.* 2) that her *lovers* deceived her ; her priests and old men perished of hunger. **20.** Sion, betrayed by men, turns to Yahweh. For ' I am full of bitterness ' read ' *I have grievously rebelled* ', and for ' destroyeth ' read ' *renders childless* '. **21.** Her enemies derive special satisfaction from the knowledge that it was Yahweh, in whose special relationship to Israel Sion gloried, who brought this misfortune upon her ; he brought the day that he had proclaimed, the day of Jerusalem's downfall foretold by the prophets (not as in DV ' the day of consolation '). The last clause is an appeal for retribution on her exulting foes : ' *Let them* be like unto me '. **22.** Sion continues her prayer for retribution, pleading that her foes are guilty as well as she.

II 1-22 The Second Lamentation—1-17 The Desola- e tion of Jerusalem and Judah the Result of Yahweh's Anger—1. For the expression ' the daughter of Sion ' *cf.* 1:6. The Lord has brought misery upon the city ; he has cast down from its proud pre-eminence the city of Jerusalem (lit. ' the glory of Israel ') ; he has not remembered his footstool, *i.e.* the temple with the Ark of the Covenant (1 Par 28:2). **2.** He has devastated the *homesteads* of Jacob (here a synonym of Judah) and destroyed the strongholds of Judah ; by delivering them up to the heathen he has deprived the kingdom of its sacred character as his elect (*cf.* Ex 19:6), and the princes of their sacred character as consecrated rulers in the theocratic kingdom. **3.** The horn of an animal is a figure for strength. The Lord has withheld aid from his people against their enemies ; he has brought ruin upon the nation. **4.** He has ranged himself against his people ; his right hand—the hand which shoots the arrows—he has brought into position. MT *niṣṣāb* (' standing ') is to be corrected to *hiṣṣîb* (' he has fixed ') which was read by LXX and Vg. **5.** For ' walls ' read ' *palaces* '. **5b.** (He) has multiplied in Judah *groaning and moaning*. **6a.** And he has *stripped* his *temple-enclosure* as a garden is stripped when its fruit is gathered. **7.** The Lord has caused the destruction of the altar of holocausts, the sanctuary and adjacent buildings ; the joyous singing of the worshippers has given place to the profane shouting of the conquerors. **8.** Yahweh carefully planned and thoroughly executed the work of destruction. A builder uses a line for precision in his work of building ; Yahweh, however, is depicted as using a line for precision in his work of demolition. The rampart and wall are left in such a f dilapidated state that they are said to mourn. **9.** The gates of the city have disappeared without trace ; the whole system of legal administration has ceased with the breaking-up of the state ; Sion's prophets receive from Yahweh no oracle of encouragement. **10.** The old men grieve and mourn in silence ; the virgins are dejected. **11 f.** The poet breaks into tears at the picture of children fainting from hunger and dying in their mothers' arms. The bowels and the liver were, in biblical thought, seats of the emotions. His sorrow was so acute that he could not restrain his emotions (lit. my liver is poured out upon the *ground*).

13. The poet addresses himself to Jerusalem. It would be some comfort for her to know that her disaster is not unparalleled, but the poet can find no example of a like calamity. **14.** The false prophets bear a heavy responsibility for Jerusalem's unhappy state. Had they candidly unveiled her iniquity and foretold its consequences they might have averted the catastrophe which has now befallen her. Instead they deceived her by *oracles of falsehood* (*cf.* Jer 14:13 ; 23:17) and of banishment. The latter are so called because they encouraged a false sense of security which resulted in the people's neglecting to amend their ways and thus having to endure the consequences, *viz.* banishment

470f from the homeland. For ' to excite thee to penance' read ' *to change your lot* ' (lit. ' to bring back your captivity'). **15 f.** recount the malicious glee of Jerusalem's foes. **16.** ' we *have swallowed* her up'. **17.** The poet declares that it is Yahweh who has destroyed Jerusalem ; in the days of old he had decreed chastisement for disobedience (*cf.* Lev 26:14 ff. ; Deut 28:15 ff.).

g 18-22 An Exhortation to supplicate Yahweh—18 f. Sion is requested to cry to the Lord day and night. Emend the first words in 18 to read : ' Cry you (*ṣaʿaqî lāk*) to the Lord, O wall of Sion '. **19** contains a line too many and ' that have fainted ', etc., is to be deleted as a gloss from 11. The apple of the eye is the pupil. The night was divided into three watches of four hours each ; the fourfold division (*cf.* Mt 14:25) is of Roman origin. **20.** Sion, accepting the invitation, supplicates Yahweh to remember that the sufferers are his chosen people, and asks whether he is indifferent to the atrocities which occurred during the siege when mothers ate the children they *were fondling*, and priests and prophets were butchered in the very sanctuary. **22.** Yahweh summoned the terrors of war, plague and famine (lit. *my terrors on every side*) as at other times he summoned the multitude of his worshippers.

471a III 1-66 The Third Lamentation—1-24 A Lament of Personal Woe—1. I am the man that *has seen* (*i.e.* experienced) *affliction*. **6.** The Lord has made him to dwell in dark places like the dead who are cut off from the light of day. **7.** He has hemmed him in by insuperable obstacles. **8.** When he prays the Lord refuses to hear him ; he *shuts* out his request. **9 ff.** describe, again in figurative language, his anguish and perplexity. **12 f.** The Lord is here likened to a hunter, shooting arrows (lit. *daughters of the quiver*) into the poet's body. **15.** Read ' *bitter herbs* ' (DV ' bitterness '). **16.** He has broken his teeth *with gravel*, *i.e.* he has treated him severely, he has *made him to wallow in* ashes. **17 f.** His life is one of unrelieved desolation and he has lost hope. He speaks thus to Yahweh : ' *You have* removed my soul from peace, I have forgotten *happiness* ; And I said (within myself) : my *strength is vanished* as also my hope (which is turned aside) from Yahweh '. **19.** Immediately overcoming his despair, he appeals to Yahweh to be no longer unmindful of his *affliction* and his *wandering about homeless* (DV ' poverty and transgression '). **20.** His soul *remembers them* (*cf.* 19) *without ceasing*, and languishes within him. **21.** ' *This* [what is related in the following two verses] I recall to my mind, therefore *have I* hope '. **22 f.** His hope is inspired by remembrance of Yahweh's unfailing mercies despite the sins of men. (I recall to my mind) that the mercies of Yahweh *have not ceased* (*cf.* Targum and Syr.), *that* (DV ' because') his mercies have not failed. They are ever fresh (23*a*). **24.** Yahweh is his portion, that which alone he desires.

b 25-39 Resignation to the Will of Yahweh—This section teaches that man in the midst of suffering should submit himself to Yahweh and patiently await his help. **27.** It is good for a man *that he bear* the yoke from his youth, that is, that he accustom himself from youth to bear with courage and confidence the trials of life. **28-30.** Let the man, therefore, who is suffering, be resigned and submissive to Yahweh's will. *Let him* sit alone and be silent *when he has laid* it (suffering) *upon him* (28). *Let him* put his mouth in the dust, *perhaps* there is hope (29) ; ' to put the mouth in the dust' is an expression of humble and silent submission—the mouth filled with dust cannot speak. *Let him* give the cheek to him that strikes him, *let him* be filled with abuse (30). **31-33** contain an inducement to resignation to the Lord's will. The suffering will not last for ever, and Yahweh in his mercy will soon grant relief (31 f.) ; he, like a true father, does not cause pain capriciously (lit. not from his heart : DV ' not willingly '). **34-38** contain a further inducement. Injustices are not committed unknown to him ; it is he who permits the wrongs wrought by man—who is he that spoke and *the thing*

was done, when the Lord commanded it not ? (37) ; **47** it is he who sends both prosperity and adversity. *Does not* the Lord *see* (36*b*) the oppression of *mankind* (lit. prisoners of earth, *cf.* Goldman, 89) and the withholding of man's God-given rights and the perversion of justice ? **39.** ' *Wherefore does* a living man *complain*, a man *notwithstanding* his sins ? ' The writer here assumes that a sinful man deserves death, yet the Lord, although he is inflicting suffering, allows him to live.

40-47 The Application to Israel of the above-mentioned c Counsels—40 f. The poet, speaking in the 1st pers. plur., invites his compatriots to examine their consciences and earnestly seek pardon through repentance. **42.** Israel has sinned and God *has not pardoned* because there is no repentance. **43*a*.** God has placed his anger as a screen between himself and his people. **44.** Their sins prevent the return of his favour ; he has *screened himself with* a cloud that their prayer may not penetrate to him. **45 f.** He has humbled the Israelites (MT ' us ' ; DV ' me ' in 45 is incorrect) in the sight of the nations who laughed at their misfortunes. **47.** Fear and *the pit* are their lot, *desolation* (DV ' prophecy ') and destruction. ' Pit ' is a metaphor taken from the hunting of wild animals which were trapped in pits.

48-66 Another Lament of Personal Suffering—48-51. d The poet tells how his eye *runs down* with water because of the ruin of his people (lit. the daughter, my people). He is suffering especially because of the Hebrew women who are completely at the mercy of their captors (51). 51 seems out of place and its original position may have been after 48. The precise meaning of 51*a* is obscure ; it may mean that constant weeping has made him physically ill. **49 f.** His eye *pours down and ceases not, without respite*, till *Yahweh look down and behold from heaven*. **52-54.** The poet, looking back over the past, describes in language which in part at least is figurative (54) the sufferings which he endured at the hands of his enemies. **53*a*.** ' *They resolved to put an end to my life in the dungeon* ' ; *cf.* Jer 38:6-13. **55-58.** While **e** suffering thus he had prayed to Yahweh saying : ' shut not thine ear at my sighing, at my cry ' (56*b*) and Yahweh intervened in judgement, and the verdict in his favour released him from his sufferings. **59.** He now pleads for another intervention of Yahweh in judgement, for if he would only intervene he would grant release from his present sufferings. **60-63.** He goes on to recount the causes of his misery ; his enemies are meanly hostile, they are plotting against him and in all their movements (lit. when they sit down and when they rise up) he is the subject of their taunting songs. **64-66.** He is confident that Yahweh will requite his enemies. 65 : ' *You will give them hardness of heart, thy curse upon them !* '

IV 1-22 The Fourth Lamentation—1-12 A Vivid f Portrayal of the Horrors of the Siege—1. The citizens of Sion once comparable to fine gold and precious and hallowed stones are no esteemed worthless. How is the gold become dim ! how is the *most fine gold* changed ! *how are the hallowed* stones scattered at the top of every street ! **2*a*.** The precious sons of Sion, *comparable to fine gold*. **3.** The *jackals* suckle their whelps, but the inhabitants of Sion do not feed the little children, and are become as cruel as the ostriches who by nesting on sand and not in inaccessible places expose the chicks to danger (*cf.* Job 39:13-16). **4 f.** The little ones and those brought up in refinement suffer from hunger and thirst and are reduced to extreme misery (the verbs are in the present tense). **6.** Sodom was less culpable than Sion seeing that she suffered less ; she was spared a prolonged agony (*cf.* Gen 19:24 f.), and hands *did not fall upon* (lit. whirl round about) her, *i.e.* she was not attacked by the soldiers of an invading army and thus escaped the atrocities frequently perpetrated by them. **7 f.** The poet contrasts the appearance of the nobles (DV ' Nazirites ') before and during the siege. For ' old ivory ' read ' corals '. **9.** Those dispatched by the sword had a better death than they who endured a lingering death by famine. **10.** Starving mothers have *boiled* and eaten their children. **11 f.** The destruction of Jerusalem is the work of the divine anger, although it was widely thought that Yahweh would not permit an enemy to enter the city where his temple stood.

13-16 Insurrection against the Guilty Leaders—14. After the fall of the city, the religious leaders, fearing the wrath of those whom they had deceived, wandered blindly through the streets, not knowing where to seek refuge ; they were polluted with innocent blood *so that people could not touch their garments* (14*b*) lest they contract ceremonial defilement. **15*b*.** They were unwanted even in the lands where they sought refuge : *when they fled away, they wandered here and there : men said* among the Gentiles, ' *they cannot remain* '. **16.** The *anger* of Yahweh scattered them ; people had neither respect for the persons of the priests nor pity for the old men (LXX prophets).

17-20 Futility of the Hope of Help from Egypt— Events showed how vain was their hope : (18*a*) the Babylonians *hunted* our steps so *that we could not walk in our broad places*, *i.e.* those who came into the open spaces had to seek shelter because the besiegers from their siege-towers began shooting arrows and hurling stones at them. **20.** King Sedecias was taken near Jericho (Jer 52:8 f.) : the breath of our *nostrils* (so called because under Sedecias the Jews had hoped to maintain their national life even in a foreign land), *the anointed of Yahweh was taken* in their pits.

21 f. An Imprecation against Edom—The Jews were bitterly hostile towards the Edomites (*cf.* Ps 136:7 ; Abd 10 ff. ; Ez 35:5) ; Edom stood by the Babylonians, and, as a reward, when Judah was conquered, they gave over to her the rural districts. **21** is a sarcastic invitation to Edom to rejoice while it can, for its glee will be short-lived ; it will soon be chastised. The cup is here a metaphor for divine punishment of sin. **22.** The punishment of Sion's sins, *viz.* the agonies endured during the siege and subsequent deportation, is already an accomplished fact, while Edom has yet to undergo the punishment of its iniquity. **22*b*** reads : ' he *will visit* your iniquity, O Edom ; he *will uncover* your sins '.

V 1-22 The Fifth Lamentation—This is not strictly a lament but rather a prayer (Vg entitles it ' Oratio Jeremiae prophetae ') for the Jews—the exiles and **471j** those left behind in Judah—whose unhappy state is recounted (2-18) in order to secure Yahweh's mercy. **2.** Neighbouring peoples have extended their borders into the former territory of Judah (lit. their inheritance). **5*a*.** MT reads : ' upon our neck we are pursued ', but the consonants of the word rendered ' upon ' are identical with those for ' yoke ' and perhaps the text had both words originally. The restored text would read, ' (with) a yoke upon ', etc. **6.** They were engaged to serve the Egyptians and the Assyrians (*i.e.* the Babylonians who acquired the former Assyrian Empire) to procure sustenance, for the exiles had no land to cultivate. **7.** From 16 it is clear that he does not place all the blame on their parents for there he states that the people who were suffering had also sinned. The latter, therefore, merited their own punishment, but on account of the iniquities of their parents they were more severely punished, ' not more severely than they deserved, but more severely than they would have been, had their parents not sinned . . . on account of our solidarity the growing guilt of a sinful race may finally draw down on it a punishment that the hand of God had previously withheld ' (E. Sutcliffe, *The Old Testament and the Future Life*, 1947², 87). **8.** The *slaves* **k** who *rule* were Babylonians who rose to official positions. **9.** The remnant in Judah bring in what little food they can collect in peril of raids by desert nomads who take advantage of the unsettled conditions. **10.** Their skin is *hot* from fever brought on by famine. **11-14** enumerate the atrocities committed by the Babylonians. **13** reads in MT : ' The young men *have carried the mill-stone*, and the children *have stumbled under the load of firewood* '. **16.** They have lost their national prestige. **17 f.** They are full of grief *for this*, namely, for the devastation of the hill of Sion which is such that *jackals wander about* on it.

Sion, Yahweh's earthly throne, is destroyed but **(19)** Yahweh reigns forever, and thus **(20)** there is hope that he will some day restore Judah, his special kingdom. *Wherefore would* you forget us forever, forsake us *for the duration of our days* ? **21.** The poet prays that Yahweh may bring about their moral conversion and their restoration to the homeland. **22.** *Unless* you have utterly rejected us, (and) are exceedingly angry against us. He is convinced that the rejection can be but a temporary one.

BARUCH

By P. P. SAYDON

472a Bibliography—J. Knabenbauer, S.J., *Comm. in Danielem prophetam, Lamentationes et Baruch* (CSS), 1891[1]; 1907[2]; E. Kalt, *Das Buch Baruch* (BB), 1932; L. Dennefeld, *Le Livre de Baruch* in Pirot-Clamer *La Sainte Bible*, 1947, tome vii; *L. St J. Thackeray, *The Septuagint and Jewish Worship*, London, 1923[2], 80–111; *W. O. E. Oesterley, *An Introduction to the Books of the Apocrypha*, London, 1935, 256–71; *O. C. Whitehouse and C. J. Ball in CAP, I, 569–611.

b The Person of the Author—Baruch, Heb. *bārûk* ' blessed ', the son of Nerias, the son of Maasias, Jer 32:12, belonged to a noble family, his brother Saraias being a high official in the court of king Sedecias, Jer 51:59. He is first introduced to us as Jeremias' secretary in 604 B.C., Jer 36:4. Later, he assisted Jeremias in the purchase of a field in Anathoth, Jer 32:12 f. After the fall of Jerusalem and the murder of Godolias he was carried away with Jeremias to Egypt, Jer 43:6. Nothing is known from the book of Jeremias of his later years. It is not unreasonable to suppose that after the prophet's death or shortly before, he went to Babylon with a message of hope to the exiles. From his book we learn that he went to Babylon and in the 5th year of the exile, 581 B.C., came back to Jerusalem bringing his book with him. Baruch was a man of strong character, Jer 43:3, but, apparently, less strong than his master in his resignation to the impending ruin of Jerusalem, Jer 45:3.

c Contents and Structure of the Book—The Book of Baruch, as it is read in Vg, consists of two parts of different origin, chh 1–5 being attributed to Baruch and ch 6 to Jeremias. In LXX the two parts are separated. For the sake of clarity they will be treated here separately.

The **Book of Baruch** proper falls into three parts: (1) a confession of sins and a prayer for deliverance, 1:15–3:8, preceded by a historical introduction, 1:1–1:14; (2) a panegyric on Wisdom, 3:9–4:4; (3) a consolatory message to the exiles, 4:5–5:9.

Although the three parts are linked together by a common historical background, namely, the exile and the desolation of Jerusalem, their literary features are so different that they can hardly be considered as parts of the same theme. Part I is a confessional prayer by the repentant exiles, while Part II is an exhortation to the exiles who are represented as still straying away from the Law, 4:2; in Part III they are assured of the approaching end of their captivity. The three parts seem to be separate compositions originating from the same historical conditions rather than parts of the same theme. This is, to a certain extent, borne out by the fact that the Greek text of Part I closely resembles that of the latter part of Jeremias. If both are the work of the same translator, as Thackeray has maintained (JTS, 1902–3, 261–6), though later he retracted his opinion (*Sept. and Jew. Worship*, 87), then Part I was for some time separated from the rest of the book and united with Jeremias.

The **Epistle of Jeremias**, Bar 6, is a strong denunciation of Babylonian idolatry and a warning to those who were being led into captivity lest they should be impressed by the gorgeous manifestations of idolatrous worship.

d Place in the Canon—In most MSS of LXX Baruch comes immediately after Jeremias and is followed by Lamentations and the Epistle. In the Latin Bible the Epistle forms ch 6 of Baruch and both follow Lamentations.

Original Language—Baruch and the Epistle have been preserved in Greek. St Jerome knew of no Hebrew text (*Praef. comm. in Jer.* PL 24, 680; *Praef. in vers. Jer.* PL 29, 848). But the majority of modern critics maintain that they were both originally written in Hebrew (J. Goettsberger, *Einl.*, 307, 310; Höpfl-Miller-Metzinger, *Intr. Spec.* 454, 457; *O. Eissfeldt, *Einl. in das AT*, 649 ff.; Oesterley, 265 f., 270; A. Robert in DBV (S) 4, 854). The Hebrew origin of 3:9–5:9 and 6 has been disputed by *E. Schürer (*The Jewish People*, 2, 3, 191, 195), J. T. Marshall (HDB, II, 578) on the grounds of the elegance of the Greek language which is not that of a translator. The balance of probability, however, remains in favour of a Hebrew origin. Theodotion's version, made from Hebrew, includes Bar.

Authorship—Catholic writers generally agree in attributing Bar to Jeremias' secretary. Different views are held by J. Goettsberger who attributes 3:9–4:4 to a later author; P. Heinisch who believes that 3:9–4:4 was written after the exile and 4:5–5:9 towards its end (*Theol. und Glaube*, 1928, 696–710) and by A.-M. Dubarle who places the composition of 3:9–4:4 in the middle of the 4th cent. B.C. (*Les Sages d'Israël*, 132).

Non-Catholic critics bring the final redaction of the book down to A.D. 70, though some of the component parts may have an earlier origin. The introduction, 1:2–14, they say, teems with historical inaccuracies. Baruch never was in Babylon. A contemporary writer, as Baruch, would never have associated Nabuchodonosor with Balthassar who was not his son. The altar of sacrifices, which was rebuilt after the return from the exile, Esd 3:2, is supposed to be still standing and sacrifices could be offered upon it. The introduction is therefore considered to be a literary device meant to disguise events much later than the Babylonian captivity. Moreover, it is said that 1:15–2:18 depends on Dan 9:4–19; it is therefore later than 166–165 B.C. Now there is no other event in post-Maccabean history to which the historical introduction can be made to apply except the destruction of Jerusalem by Titus in A.D. 70. 4:5–5:9 depends on the apocryphal Psalms of Solomon (*cf.* 4:37; 5:1, 5, 8 and Ps. Sol. 11:3, 6–8) that were written after the capture of Jerusalem by Pompey in 63 B.C.

These reasons are not convincing. The historical difficulties will be dealt with in the commentary. As regards the literary affinities it is not easy to establish the order of priority. There is evidence in favour of a dependence of Daniel on Baruch. Part II is strongly influenced by Isaias II even in those passages that seem to be related to the Psalms of Solomon.

The origin of the Epistle is generally placed by non-Catholic critics in the Greek period. Babylon of the letter, it is said, is not the magnificent Babylon of Nabuchodonosor, but Babylon in decay as it was in the days of Alexander the Great. Moreover, the prediction of a captivity lasting seven generations or 280 years is inconsistent with Jeremias' prediction of a 70-year captivity. The correction of seven to three does not solve the difficulty. Supposing the text to be correct and reckoning the 280 years from the destruction of Jerusalem in 586 B.C., the captivity predicted by the writer would come to an end in the year 306 B.C., shortly after Alexander's conquest of Babylon. The same view is held by A. Robert in DBV(S) 4, 857.

It is unlikely that the letter was written by Jeremias. The writer displays an intimate knowledge of Babylonian idolatry, such as could not be obtained except through a prolonged sojourn in Babylon. Moreover, the style is by far inferior to that of Jeremias. It lacks the impassioned outbursts, the elegiac tone, the emotional effects, characteristic of Jeremias' style. Compare the Epistle with Jer 10:2–16 which is said to be parallel to it. Had it really been written by the prophet Jeremias, a later editor would have united it to Jeremias' book rather than to that of Baruch.

Taking into consideration the objections against the traditional view of the origin of Baruch and the Epistle I believe that originally they were independent compositions written on four separate scrolls. Bar 1:1–3:8 was written by Baruch and, possibly, interpolated by later editors. Bar 3:9–4:4 and 4:5–5:9 were written during the exile, perhaps by Baruch himself, but as independent compositions. The Epistle too was probably written during the exile by an anonymous writer. The four compositions were united together on account of their common historical background.

Canonicity—Baruch and the Epistle are excluded from the Jewish canon. There is evidence, however, that Bar was accepted by the Jews, though later rejected. Theodotion's version includes it. Moreover, Bar and the Epistle occur in ancient lists, which rigorously exclude the non-canonical books, under the title ' Jeremias with Baruch, Lamentations and the Epistle ' (Swete, *Intr.* 203–10). There is also evidence that Bar was read in Jewish synagogues on certain festivals during the early centuries of the Christian era (Thackeray, 107–11).

Doctrinal Content—The doctrinal element of Bar is common to other biblical books, especially the prophetical writings. The confession, with its threefold element of proclamation of God's justice and power, confession of the people's sins and prayer for forgiveness, is cast in the usual form of confessional prayers, *cf.* Esd 9:5–15 ; Neh 9:6–37 ; Dan 9:4–19. Wisdom, which is identified with the moral law or the Sinaitic covenant, is the source of life and happiness. It is a gift of God, and man cannot acquire it nor find it with all his wealth and labour. Idols are vain things and their worship is degrading.

The **Messianic** doctrine in 2:35 is that of Jer 32:40. 5:1–4 predicts in a fuller sense the spiritual restoration of Jerusalem in Messianic times. The literal Messianic interpretation of 3:38 is based on Vg.

I 1–2 The Title—Probably it refers to 1:3–3:8 only. There is no historical evidence against Baruch's journey to Babylon. The fifth year must be reckoned from 587–586 when Jerusalem was captured and the temple destroyed. Insert ' fifth ' before ' month ' in accordance with 4 Kg 25:8. The book was therefore written in the year 582–581 B.C., the fifth anniversary of the capture of Jerusalem.

3–5 The Reading of the Book—3 f. On that day Baruch read the book before king Jechonias and before all the captives gathered near the river Sedi. Jechonias either enjoyed some liberty and could therefore join the gathering or had the book read to him in prison. The locality of the river Sedi (LXX Sud) is unknown. Probably it was one of the artificial canals of the Euphrates. **5.** Sorrow for their sins, penance and prayer for forgiveness were the effects produced on the hearers.

6–9 A Money Collection—6. In order to obtain God's help more speedily they wished to have prayers offered for them in Jerusalem. So they made a collection of money, **7,** and sent it to the priests and people of Jerusalem. Joakim was not the high-priest, who at that time was in exile, 1 Par 6:15, but the priest at the head of those who remained in Jerusalem. He was,

probably, a relative of Josedek's, the exiled high-priest **473c** whose genealogy, like that of Joakim, is traced back to Sellum (Salom) through Helcias, 1 Par 6:14 f. **8 f.** The subject of ' received ' is Baruch. Baruch, therefore, on the 10th of Sivan (May–June), brought back to Jerusalem some of the temple vessels which Nabuchodonosor had carried off to Babylon, 4 Kg 24:13 ; 25:13–17. Instead of ' bound ', 9, read ' captives ' and transpose after ' the princes '.

10–14 A Message to the Inhabitants of Jerusalem—10. d ' Buy with it holocausts *and offerings for sin* and frankincense and make *an oblation* '. Baruch carried also a message to those left in Jerusalem. Although the temple had been burnt and the altar destroyed, a provisional altar was, most probably, set up on which the priests could perform the liturgical service ; *cf.* Jer 41:5. **11 f.** The exhortation to pray for Nabuchodonosor is an echo of Jeremias' recommendation, Jer 29:7. A difficulty lies in the association of Nabuchodonosor with Balthassar who, as we know with absolute certainty, was the son of Nabonidus. That Nabuchodonosor had a son called Balthassar who died very young is quite possible though there is no documentary evidence. As Balthassar is also represented as Nabuchodonosor's son in Dan 5:2, 11, 13, 18, 22, it is very likely that Balthassar has been introduced here by a later editor from Daniel (W. Stoderl, *Zur Echtheitsfrage von Bar 1–3:8*, Münster, 1922, 21 f.). The expression ' many days ', 12, corresponds to the 70 years of Jer 25:12 ; 29:10. **13.** They acknowledge that their punishment is deserved. Add ' and his indignation ' after ' wrath '. **14.** The book, *i.e.* the confession contained in 1:15–3:8, was to be read in the temple, or on its ruins, on a certain unspecified feast-day, probably the Feast of Booths, sometimes called simply ' the Feast ', 3 Kg 8:2, and on other days of meeting. Thackeray identifies the feast with New Year's Day, and the days of meeting with the Sabbaths intervening between the anniversary of the capture of Jerusalem and the anniversary of its burning, 91–4.

15–II 10 The Confession—It has striking similarities **e** to Daniel's prayer in Dan 9:4–19. **15.** *Cf.* Dan 9:7. God is just and punishment is fully deserved. **16–18.** *Cf.* Dan 9:8, 10. All classes have sinned. The same enumeration occurs in Neh 9:32 ; Jer 32:32. Delete ' nor put our trust . . . obedient to him ', which are not in LXX. **19.** The obstinacy is inveterate ; *cf.* Jer 7:25 ; 11:7. The Syr. reading ' we have rebelled ' is preferable to ' going astray ' ; delete ' we turned away from '. **20–22.** The calamities are the fulfilment of the threats announced by God through Moses, Lev 26:14–39 ; Deut 28:15–68, and later prophets, Jer 11:7 f. ; 16:10–13 ; etc. **II:1 f.** *Cf.* Dan 9:12. The writer develops the thought expressed in 20–22. God has made good the word which he had spoken *against* their rulers and all the people by bringing upon them plagues unparalleled in man's history. **3.** That they would eat the flesh of their own children had been predicted in Lev 26:29 ; Deut 28:53 and Jer 19:9 ; *cf.* also Lam 2:20 ; 4:10 and Jos. BJ 6, 3, 3–4. **4 f.** Another punishment : subjection to foreign powers and oppression. *4a* agrees with Esd 9:7a ; *4b* with Jer 42:9b ; 5 with Deut 28:13. The Israelites were several times under the domination of neighbouring kingdoms, especially Assyria and Babylonia. **6–10.** God is just in inflicting such a severe punishment, because he had forewarned the people. He has therefore kept watch over his plagues and brought them upon his people. The expression ' kept watch ' is a familiar one in Jer ; *cf.* 1:12 ; 31:28 ; 44:27.

II 11–18 The Prayer—After the confession they make **f** an appeal for deliverance from captivity. **11.** *Cf.* Dan 9:15 ; Jer 32:21. God, who, in the past, has delivered them from their enemies, can deliver them now too. **12.** *Cf.* 3 Kg 8:47 ; Dan 9:15. **13.** *Cf.* Jer 42:2. **14 f.** The reason for their deliverance is God's own sake, God's name by which they are called, the intimate relation between God and themselves. They do not ask God to punish their enemies, they simply pray that

473f their Babylonian masters may allow them to return to their homeland. **16 f.** If they are left to perish, there will be none to worship God, because the dead in *Sheol* cannot praise him, Ps 6:6 ; 87:11 ; 113:17. The mention of the ' holy house ', 16, does not necessarily imply that the temple had been rebuilt. The expression ' Look down from thy holy house ' may be paralleled by Is 63:15 where ' dwelling ' (LXX house) means ' heaven '. **18.** A difficult verse. The sense seems to be : Those that are afflicted praise God when they are relieved (Kalt, Dennefeld), or : The repentant people proclaim God's righteousness (Knab., Fillion). The expressions ' a sorrowful heart ', ' to go bowed down ', ' failing eyes ', ' hungry soul ' denote sorrow, humility and repentance ; *cf.* Deut 28:32, 65 ; Prov 27:7 ; Ps 41:10, 12 ; Ecclus 12:11.

g 19-26 God's Past Threats and the People's Obstinacy —They do not deserve God's mercy because they have always spurned his warnings. **19.** *Cf.* Dan 9:18*b*. Their fathers and *their kings* have disobeyed God and have no right to his compassion. **20.** Omit ' But '. They acknowledge that their calamities are the accomplishment of God's threats. **21-23.** In the light of Jer 27:12 ; 7:34 and the underlying Hebrew text read : 21 ' *Bow down your neck and serve* . . . 23 *I will cause in the cities of Judah and in the streets of Jerusalem the voice of mirth . . . bride, and the whole land shall be desolate without inhabitants*'. Jeremias had always advocated a policy of peaceful submission to Babylon, because he knew only too well that resistance meant only destruction and devastation ; *cf.* Jer 27:6-11, 12-15. **24 f.** Read ' *we* ' instead of ' they ', 24, and ' *pestilence* ' for ' banishment ', 25. 24*c* = Jer 8:1 ; 25*a* = Jer 8:2 ; 25*b* = Jer 32:36*b*. They have not heeded Jeremias' advice ; they have revolted against the king of Babylon, and God's threats have come true. In the narrative of the siege of Jerusalem nowhere do we read of the desecration of tombs, but there is evidence of such profanations in the Assyro-Babylonian inscriptions. Jeremias ironically adds that the bones of their kings will be left bleaching in the fields so that they may continue to worship the sun, the moon and the stars as they did in their lifetime. Those who were still living died a terrible death : Lam 2:12, 20 f. ; 4:9. **26.** Another punishment : the destruction of the temple, the pride of their country.

h 27-35 God's Kindness towards his People—God has dealt very leniently with them because he has not exterminated them as they deserved. **28-33.** They recall God's minatory predictions to Moses, Lev 26:14-39 ; Deut 28:62, and his predictions of the people's conversion, Lev 26:40-45 ; Deut 30:1-10. **34 f.** The writer passes on from the national postexilic restoration to the Messianic restoration which is described here with words and ideas borrowed from Jer 31-31:33.

i III 1-8 A Last Appeal to God's Mercy—They have repented ; may God now forgive them and bring them back to their country. **1.** ' A soul in anguish ' and ' a troubled spirit ' are expressions denoting sorrow for sin ; *cf.* Ps 50:19 ; Is 57:15. **2.** The words ' for thou art a merciful God ' are read only in Vg, a few Greek MSS and the Old Latin. **3.** The interrogative form is supported by the parallel passage in Lam 5:19 f. How can God, an eternal and almighty king, let his people be exterminated as if he were unable to save them ? **4.** They are on the brink of the grave on account of their fathers' sins. The correction of ' dead ' to ' men ' is unnecessary, because a desperate condition is sometimes compared to death, *cf.* Is 26:19. **5 f.** If God takes their sins into account, he will punish them accordingly, but this would impair his honour because the heathens will think that he is unable to save them. Therefore they pray God to consider his honour rather than their offences, and they will henceforth proclaim his justice and mercy. **7 f.** It is to this end, that they may praise his name that he has inspired their hearts with sentiments of repentance, reverence and love.

God has promised that he will bring them back to their country when they repent. They have now repented, may he fulfil his promise completely.

9-IV 4 Wisdom leads to Life—Israel was a privileged people because they had a law given by God, such as no other people had. But they have transgressed the law and have consequently sunk into the depths of misery.

9-14 The Transgression of the Law is the Source of their Calamities—9. An invitation to listen to the teaching of Wisdom, *i.e.* to keep the commandments of the Law which is a source of life and happiness, Deut 30:15-20. **10 f.** Remove the point of interrogation to the end of 11. Israel is wasting away in the land of his enemies ; there, in the midst of a heathen people, they have become unclean as by contact with a corpse, Num 19:11 ff. ; they are as good as dead. **12 f.** The answer to the question. Israel has forsaken God, the source of Wisdom. Idolatry was the capital sin of Israel. If Israel had not departed from God, they would have enjoyed peace and prosperity in their land for ever. **14.** Since God's law is the source of peace, Israel must strive after it with all his power. The Law enlightens the mind, strengthens the will in the performance of what is right, and grants length of life, happiness and peace to those who keep it.

15-31 Wisdom is beyond Man's Reach—15. Man must seek Wisdom ; but where does she dwell ? Where are the treasures which she bestows on those who seek her ? *Cf.* Job 28:12. The answer is given further on. **16-21.** Wisdom lies beyond man's reach. Mighty princes, powerful hunters whose hands neither beasts nor birds could escape, wealthy people who trusted in their unlimited riches, silversmiths who produced wonderful works of art were all unable to find the way to wisdom. All these passed away ; and generation after generation strayed away from the right path. **22 f.** The peoples most renowned for their skill, the Canaanites or Phoenicians, Ez 28:4 f., the Themanites, who dwelt in S. Edom, Jer 49:7, the Hagarenes or Ishmaelites, Gen 25:12 f., who sought after earthly wisdom, the merchants of *Madian* and *Thema, who spoke in proverbs* and sought after understanding, have failed to find the way to Wisdom. **24-28.** The immeasurable universe, God's dwelling, does not possess Wisdom, nor were the giants, the renowned men of old, Gen 6:4, the bearers of Wisdom on earth. On the contrary they perished because they lacked Wisdom. God has not placed Wisdom in any part of the immense universe, nor has he chosen any class as messengers of Wisdom. This prepares the way for 32 ff. where the divine origin of Wisdom is declared. **29-31** develop the same thought ; *cf.* Deut 30:12 f.

32-38 Wisdom dwells with God—32-36. God alone, an all-knowing and almighty God, knows Wisdom, Job 28:23. **37.** God possesses Wisdom and has communicated it to the Israelites in the Mosaic Law. Now the sense of the whole section becomes clearer. The Law was given to Israel out of God's love. It could not be acquired by human means. No other people had a Law like it. But Israel transgressed the Law and, as a punishment, they were given up into the hands of their enemies. **38.** In Vg and the Old Latin the subject of ' was seen ' and ' conversed ' is ' he ', *i.e.* God. Hence Greek and Latin Fathers have applied this verse to the Incarnation (Knab. 489). But the context requires ' Wisdom ' as subject of the two verbs. After being communicated to Israel Wisdom remained on earth making her abode amongst men. Some interpreters take the verse for a Christian gloss (Whitehouse, 591 ; Goettsberger, 310). But the personification of Wisdom and the idea of her dwelling among men occur also in Ecclus 24:12-16, and the pretended Christian universalism in contrast with Jewish particularism is neither broader nor different from that of the Wisdom books ; *cf.* Ecclus 24:40-47. The verse, however, refers also, in a fuller sense, to

d the Messias through whom revelation has been brought to perfection.

e **IV 1-4 Exhortation and Conclusion—1.** This Wisdom, which God has bestowed upon Israel, is identified with the book of the commandments, the Law which subsists for ever. Those who hold fast to it will come to life, those who depart from it will meet their own end. **2 f.** A last exhortation. O Israel, hold fast to the Law and walk in its light, lest God should take away from you the advantages of the Law and bestow them upon another people. **4.** But this will never happen, because we shall always do what God has revealed to us.

a **5-V 9 God's Promises of Restoration will be fulfilled** —The writer comforts Jerusalem by the assurance of the approaching end of the exile.

b **5-9a The People punished for their Sins—5.** The writer cheers the depressed exiles who, despite their condition, are still called by the *name* of Israel, a name which recalls a glorious past. **6.** God's punishments are corrective not vindictive. He has given them up into the hands of their enemies, but will not exterminate them. **7.** Idolatry was the inveterate and most heinous sin of Israel. Idols are called demons in Deut 32:17. Omit ' the eternal God'. **8.** Their sin was the more execrable as it was committed against *the eternal* God who had nursed them, and against Jerusalem who had reared them. The figure of God nursing his people is vividly described in Os 11:3 f.; *cf.* also Deut 1:31; 32:10; Is 63:10; for the figure of Jerusalem-mother *cf.* Is 51:18. **9a.** The writer introduces Jerusalem lamenting over her children and comforting them.

c **9b-16 Jerusalem's Lamentations—9b.** Jerusalem addresses the neighbouring cities manifesting the cause of her grief. **10 f.** She brought up her children with joy, but was unable to avert the punishment, and *let them go* into captivity. **12 f.** Her children have been carried away for their sins, and she is like a mother bereft of her husband and children; *cf.* Lam 1:1. **14-16.** Jerusalem again entreats the neighbouring cities to have compassion on her. 15 f. are reminiscences of Deut 28:49 f.; Jer 5:15 ff.

d **17-29 Jerusalem's Message of Comfort to her Children** —**17 f.** Jerusalem can afford no help to her exiled children; God alone can deliver them. **19.** Jerusalem bids farewell to her children on their way to their land of exile. **20.** She has changed the clothes of her happy days for the sackcloth of *mourning*, and she will pray God all her life. **21-24.** She exhorts them to pray to God and feels confident that he will soon deliver them. **25.** The enemies will be conquered and the exiles delivered. It was for a brief moment that God forsook his people, Is 54:7 f. **26.** The children of Jerusalem, brought up with affectionate care are now walking through rough ways and driven like a flock carried away by the enemy. **27.** A repetition of 21. **28 f.** The only condition for their deliverance is that they should seek God with more determination than they had turned away from him.

e **30-V 9 A Message of Comfort to Jerusalem—30.** Jerusalem must not despair. God who has chosen her for himself and given her his name as Yahweh's dwelling-place, will *comfort* her. **31 f.** ' *Woe be to those that have afflicted thee, and rejoiced at thy fall. Woe be to the cities which thy children have served. Woe be to her that hath received thy sons*'. The destruction of the enemies of Israel, especially Babylon, had long before been predicted by the prophets; *cf.* Is 13; 47; Jer 25; 50. **33-35.** The devastation of Babylon is described here with features borrowed from the prophets: thus 33 = Is 51:22 f.; Jer 50:11-13; 34 = Is 47:9; 35a = Jer 51:58; 35b = Is 13:21; Jer 50:39. The word δαιμόνια ' devils ', which occurs also in the parallel passage Is 13:21, probably stands for a word meaning ' wild animals ' as those enumerated in Is 13:21 and Jer 50:39. **36 f.** The exiles will return from all parts rejoicing in their God who has shown his glory by bringing them back to their country. Words and ideas reflect Is 43:5; 49:18; 60:4. The description has its full application in the Messianic restoration. **475e** **V:1-3.** DV and Vg give the sense rather than the exact rendering of LXX: ' Put off . . . and put on *the splendour of the glory of God for ever. Array thyself in the robe of God's righteousness and set a crown on thy head of the glory of the Everlasting. For God will show thy brightness to everyone under heaven*'. Jerusalem will be reinstated in her former glory as a queen adorned with sanctity and ruling with justice over all the world. The outlook is Messianic. *Cf.* Is 52:1; 60; 61:3. **4.** Restored Jerusalem will be called by a new name: ' *The peace of righteousness and the glory of the fear of God* '. She will be the seat of a righteous power, and all her citizens will enjoy peace. **5.** A repetition with slight variations of 36 f. At the end read: ' rejoicing *that God hath remembered them* '. **6.** The exiles will be brought back *as a royal throne*. The Vg and Old Latin reading ' as children of the kingdom ', *i.e.* as royal children, gives a better sense and is supported by Is 49:22 f. **7-9.** All obstacles will be removed, and they will walk *safely*. The tall trees will overshadow them during their march, and God himself will walk at the head of the caravan leading them with joy and protecting them with his mercy and righteousness. The ideas and phraseology recall Is 40:4; 49:9 f.; 52:12; 55:12.

VI The Epistle of Jeremias—The prophet addresses **476a** the Jewish captives warning them against idolatry.

The **Title** does not form part of the Epistle but has been added after Jer 29:1.

b **1-6 Introduction—1.** The captivity was a punishment for their sins, Jer 25:8 f. **2.** This seems to be inconsistent with Jer 25:12; 29:10. But ' seven ' may be a symbolical number having no mathematical value (*cf.* Deut 28:7; Dan 3:19) and ' generation ' may be taken in the sense of an indefinite period of time. *Cf.* the analogous expression ' a thousand generations ', Deut 7:9;, 1 Par 16:15; Ps 104:8. The expression ' seven generations ' is therefore parallel to ' many years ' and ' a long time ', not their equivalent. **3-5.** Omit ' and of stone ', 3. The prophet warns them not to be impressed by the ostentatious processions of the Babylonian gods and by the crowds of worshippers. It is God whom they must worship. **6.** God himself speaks directly. Do not fear these gods, nor seek their protection, because my angel will constantly be with you (*cf.* Ex 32:34), looking after you, or, according to others, he, or I, will not leave your sin unpunished.

c **7-14 Idols are Powerless—7.** Idols have a polished tongue and are all overlaid with gold and silver, but they cannot speak. **8 f.** ' *And they* [the craftsmen] *take gold and make crowns for the heads of their gods* '. The priests did not hesitate to appropriate the gold and silver ornaments of their gods. **10.** They made gifts of them to the hierodules in the temple precincts. They deck *them* [the idols] *as men with garments, these gods of silver, these gods of gold and wood*. **12.** They are richly clothed, but the priests must clean their faces of the dust ' *which is thick upon them* '. **13 f.** They hold sceptres, swords and axes, as is often seen in Assyrian and Babylonian sculptures, but they can make no use of them. Therefore they need not be feared. Transpose these last words to the end of 14.

d **15-22 Idols are Useless and Insensible Images—16-21.** Their eyes are filled with dust; they are locked in temples as a man *condemned to death* for high treason; their interior is *licked up*, worn out; but they do not feel the worms eating up both themselves and their garments. **22.** The refrain; *cf.* 14.

e **23-28 Idols are Helpless and Unconscious of Offences** —**23.** In 7, 50, 56, 70 it is said that idols were only overlaid with gold; but among the many idols there may have been some statuettes made of solid gold. **26.** ' *For if they fall . . . nor if a man set them upright can they move by themselves, nor if they are set crooked, can they set themselves straight* '. They are motionless as the dead, and the offerings made to them are offerings made to the dead. **27.** The priests make any use of the sacrificial offerings, and their wives *salt* a portion of

476e them, but nothing is given to the poor and to the sick. Priests had a share of the sacrificial victims (E. Dhorme, *Les Religions de Babylonie et d'Assyrie*, Paris, 1945, 231 f.). They were also the treasurers of the temple revenue, and sometimes embezzled their gods' property (*Ibid.* 201 f.). **28.** Contrary to the prescriptions of the Jewish Law (Lev 12:4 ; 15:19 f.) women in a state of ceremonial uncleanness could partake of the sacred meals. If idols were true gods, they would never tolerate such profanation.

f 29-39 Further Illustration of the Idols' Impotence—29. How can idols be gods when even women are allowed to minister as priestesses? Jewish legislation debarred women from the altar service. **30 f.** The superiority of the Israelites' God is further emphasized. The Babylonian priests sit, or perhaps *weep*, in the temples with their clothes rent, their heads and beards unshaven and their heads uncovered howling before their gods as at a funeral-feast. All such signs of mourning were strictly forbidden to Israelite priests, Lev 21:5. **32.** This must have been shocking to a pious Jew to whom anything that came near the presence of God became holy. **33-37.** A series of implicit contrasts between the One God of the Israelites and the Babylonian gods. Unlike them God is a just judge rewarding good and punishing evil, Deut 32:35 ; 1 Kg 26:23 ; he sets up kings and deposes them, 1 Kg 2:8 ; he gives riches, 1 Kg 2:7 ; he requires vows to be performed promptly, Deut 23:21 ; he can save from death, 1 Kg 2:6 ; he gives a blind man his sight, Ps 145:8, delivers a man from distress, Is 25:4, helps the widows and the orphans, Deut 10:18 ; Ps 145:9 ; Is 1:17.

g 40-44 The Gods dishonoured by their Worshippers—40 f. The Babylonians dishonour their gods by asking of them what they cannot do. Thus if they hear of a dumb man, they bring him before Bel-Marduk, the great national god of Babylon, entreating him that the man may speak, as if *he can hear them*. And though they are aware, from their own experience, of their gods' impotence, they do *not* forsake them, for they are devoid of sense. **42 f.** They dishonour their gods also by the immoral Ishtar cult. Women with a cord round their waists, sat in the streets, probably near the temples,

burning *chaff*, the smoke of which was believed to possess aphrodisiac properties, and expecting to be accosted by a male worshipper. After having performed her shameful religious duty she reproached her less fortunate neighbour for not having had the same favour. *Cf.* Herodotus 1, 199.

45-51 Idols are the Work of Men's Hands—45. *Cf.* Ps 113:4 ; Jer 10 ; 3 f. ; and esp. Is 44:12-30. Read '*craftsmen*' for 'priests'. **46.** Man is mortal ; how can he produce a god that is immortal and eternal? **47.** Idols therefore are a lie and an object of shame bequeathed by artisans to posterity. **50.** The nothingness of idols will one day be made manifest to all peoples. **51.** '*To whom, therefore, is it not known* . . .?'

52-55 Total Helplessness of Idols—52. Unlike the true God of the Israelites, Deut 17:14 f. ; 28:12,14, the Babylonian gods can neither set up kings nor give rain. **53.** They can neither *plead* a cause nor *redress a wrong* ; they are as helpless as crows flying in mid-air. This is, perhaps, a popular saying meaning : They can plead as much as a crow.

56-64 Idols are utterly Worthless—58. They are absolutely useless. A mighty king, a needful object, a door in a house, a wooden pillar in a royal palace are more useful than false gods. **59-62.** The sun, the moon, the stars, the lightning, the wind, the clouds obey God's commands in all their activities, but idols are utterly powerless.

65-68 The Idols' Powerlessness is further emphasized —Beasts, which are able to move, are better than they. **69-71 Idols are Contemptible Things—**They are like a scarecrow unable to protect a field against robbers ; like a thorny shrub patiently suffering birds to sit upon it ; like a corpse, probably of an infant, cast away in the dark and left to rot. Their purple and *linen* robes are eaten by moths, and they themselves cannot escape the ravages of time, and so they will become an object of shame and reproach to their worshippers.

72 Conclusion—A righteous man having no idols is better than a worshipper of idols. The second term of comparison is implied, and we need not suppose that some words have fallen out. For similar construction, *cf.* Gen 37:27 ; Num 14:3, etc.

EZECHIEL

(EZEKIEL)

By E. POWER, S.J.

Bibliography. I. Commentaries—*R. Smend, Leipzig 1880 ; *A. B. Davidson, Cambridge 1892 ; *C. von Orelli, München 1896 ; *R. Kraetschmar, Göttingen 1900 ; P. Schmalzl, Wien 1901 ; J. Knabenbauer, Paris 1907² ; *H. A. Redpath, London 1907 ; *W. F. Lofthouse, London 1907 ; *J. Breuer, Frankfurt 1921 ; P. Heinisch, Bonn 1923 ; *J. Herrmann, Leipzig 1924 ; L. Tondelli, Reggio-Emilia 1930 ; A. Roelants, Brugge 1930 ; *A. Troelstra, Groeningen 1931 ; *J. Smith, London 1931 ; *A. Noordtzij, Kampen 1933 ; *A. Bertholet, Tübingen 1936 ; *G. A. Cooke (ICC), Edinburgh 1937 ; E. Osterloh, München 1939 ; *J. G. Matthews, Philadelphia 1939 ; M. Schumpp, Freiburg 1942 ; L. Dennefeld, Paris 1947 ; F. Spadafora, Torino 1948.
II. Studies—*A. Klostermann, Ezechiel, Studien und Kritiken 50 (1877) 391–430 ; L. Gautier, La mission du prophète Ezéchiel, Lausanne 1891 ; J. Lajčiak, Ezéchiel, sa personne et son enseignement, Paris 1906 ; *C. Kuhl, Die literarische Einheit des Buches Ezechiel, Tübingen 1917 ; D. Buzy, Les symboles de l'AT, Paris 1923 ; *G. Hoelscher, Hesekiel der Dichter und das Buch, Giessen 1924 ; *C. C. Torrey, Pseudo-Ezechiel and the Original Prophecy, New Haven 1930 ; W. Gronkowski, Le messianisme d'Ezéchiel, Paris 1931 ; *J. B. Harford, Is the Book of Ezechiel Pseudo-Epigraphic ? ET 43 (1931–2) 20–5 ; V. Herntrich, Ezechielprobleme, Giessen 1932 ; *W. E. Barnes, The Scene of Ezekiel's Mission and his Audience, JTS 35 (1934) 163–70 ; A. van den Born, Ezechiel, Roermond-Massiek 1934 ; *J. B. Harford, Studies in the Book of Ezekiel, London 1935 ; H. Pope, Ezekiel and his Visions, Studies 24 (1935) 275–88 ; *G. R. Berry, The Composition of the Book of Ezekiel JBL 58 (1939) 163–75 ; *W. A. Irwin, The Problem of Ezekiel, Chicago 1944 ; *U. Cassuto, L'ordinamento del libro d'Ezechiele, Miscell. Card. Mercati I (1946) 40–58 ; P. Auvray, Le problème historique du livre d'Ezéchiel, RB 55 (1948) 503–19.
III. Texts—L. Duerr, Ezechiels Vision der Erscheinung Gottes, Münster 1917 ; K. Fruhstorfer, Ezechiels Anfangsvision, TPQ 93 (1940) 185–98 ; J. Coppens, Ez 1:18 ; 1:25, Muséon 47 (1934) 259–63 ; *G. R. Driver, Sitting upon Scorpions (2:6), JTS 35 (1934) 54f. ; J. Goettsberger, Ez 7:1–16, BZ 27 (1934) 195–223 ; *J. A. Bewer, Ez 7:5–14, JBL 45 (1926) 223–31 ; *R. Dussaud, L'idole de la jalousie (8:3), Syria 21 (1940) 359 f. ; A. Lemmonyer, Tammouz-Adonis (8:14), RSPT 4 (1930) 271–82 ; *R. Gordis, The Branch to the Nose (8:17), JTS 37 (1936) 234–8 ; P. Joüon, Trois noms de personnages bibliques à la lumière des textes d'Ugarit (14:14), Bi 19 (1938) 283–5 ; B. Mariani, Danel. Il patriarca sapiente, Roma 1945 ; *O. Eissfeldt, Hesekiel, Kap. 16 als Geschichtsquelle, JPOS 16 (1936) 286–92 ; E. Mader, Die Kinderopfer der alten Hebräer und der benachbarten Völker, Freiburg 1909 ; A. Bea, Kinderopfer für Moloch oder für Jahwe ? Bi 18 (1937) 95–107 ; *L. P. Smith, The Eagle(s) of Ezekiel c. 17, JBL 58 (1939) 43–50 ; A. Fernandez, El castigo de los hijos por los peccatos de los padres, EE 2 (1923) 419–26 ; P. Cheminant, Les prophéties d'Ezéchiel contre Tyr, Paris 1912 ; *W. E. Barnes, Ezekiel's Denunciation of Tyre, JTS 35 (1934) 50–4 ; J. Plessis, Les prophéties d'Ezéchiel contre l'Egypte, Paris 1912 ; *W. E. Barnes, Two Trees Become One, JTS 39 (1938) 91–3 ; *G. R. Berry, The Date of Ezekiel 38:1–39:20, JBL 41 (1922)

224–32 ; *J. L. Myres, Gog and the Peoples from the North in Ezekiel PEF (1932) 213–9 ; A. Pohl, Das verschlossene Tor (44:1–3), Bi 13 (1932) 90–2 ; *G. A. Cooke, Some Considerations on the Text and Teaching of Ez 40–48, ZATW 42 (1924) 105–15 ; *T. H. Whitehouse, Ezekiel's Temple and Sacrifices, London 1935 ; *O. Procksch, Fürst und Priester bei Hesekiel, ZATW 17 (1940–1) 99–133 ; *K. Elliger, Die Nordgrenze des Reiches David, PJB 32 (1936) 34–73 ; P. Joüon, Notes Philologiques sur le texte hébreu d'Ezéchiel, Bi 10 (1929) 304–12 ; *G. R. Driver, Linguistic and Textual Problems : Ezekiel, ib. 19 (1938) 60–9 ; 175–87 ; *A. C. Johnson, *H. S. Gehman, *E. H. Kase, The John Scheide Biblical Papyri, Ezekiel, Princeton 1938.

Historical Background—The period with which the **d** book of Ezechiel is chiefly concerned is that which elapsed between the death of Josias, 609, and the destruction of Jerusalem, 587. The fall of the Assyrian empire had been gradual. Long before the capture of Assur, 614, and Nineveh, 612, and the final collapse of Assyrian resistance in Northern Mesopotamia, 607, outlying regions had regained their independence. Shortly before 650 Psammeticus I had driven the Assyrians out of Egypt and laid siege to Ashdod, capital of an Assyrian province in Southern Palestine. His son and successor, Nechao II, led an Egyptian army through Palestine in 609, to aid the Assyrians, his allies, and still more to regain for Egypt her ancient dominion over Syria and Palestine and the control of the great trade routes of the Near East. Josias meanwhile had taken advantage of Assyrian weakness to institute a great religious revival, destroy the idolatrous shrine at Bethel and extend his boundaries northwards. Hoping to maintain his independence he opposed the Egyptians at Megiddo and lost his life in battle, 609. He was succeeded by his second son Joachaz, preferred by the people to his elder brother Eliakim. Nechao after marching to the Euphrates encamped at Riblah on the Orontes, where he received homage and tribute from the Syrian and Palestinian states. Thither he summoned Joachaz, deposed him after a three months' reign and sent him a prisoner to Egypt where he died. Eliakim received from Nechao a new name Joakim (Yôyāqîm) and was made vassal king of Judah, 608–598. After the collapse of Assyrian **e** resistance, 607, the Egyptian army now on the Mesopotamian border had to be dealt with by the Babylonians who also claimed dominion over Syria and Palestine. The crown-prince Nabuchodonosor (Nabu-kudurri-uṣur ' Nabu, protect the boundary ') crossed the Euphrates, defeated Nechao at Carchemish, 606, and pursued the Egyptians through Syria and Palestine to their own borders. Here however he was recalled to Babylon by the death of his father Nabopolassar in May or June 605. On his march through Palestine he had besieged Jerusalem and begun the exile by deporting Daniel and his companions to Babylon in December 606. The fast, instituted to commemorate the anniversary of the calamity, determines the month, in the third year of Joakim (Spring 606–Spring 605) by the Babylonian postdating system, Dan 1:1, but in the fourth (Autumn 606–Autumn 605) by the Hebrew antedating system, Jer 46:2. Joakim paid tribute to the Babylonians for three years but

477e revolted in 602, vainly relying on Egyptian aid. During the rest of his reign he was harried by raids from neighbouring states subject to Babylon. Finally Nabuchodonosor marched a second time against Jerusalem with the intention of deposing and deporting Joakim (2 Par 36:6 mistranslated in Vg). Joakim however had died in Jerusalem before his arrival and been succeeded by his eighteen-year old son Joachin (Yôyākîn) who surrendered to the Babylonians after a mere show of resistance. He was deposed and deported to Babylon after a three months' reign.

f Nabuchodonosor despoiled the palace of its treasures and the temple of its sacred vessels and deported also to Babylon many thousands of the more influential citizens. Ezechiel was one of the deported and dates his prophecies from this event, 597. Joachin was replaced by Matthanias a third son of Josias who received a new name Sedecias and was the last king of Judah, 597–587. He remained subject to Babylon until 589 when Judah, Ammon and Tyre participated in a revolt instigated by the new Pharaoh Hophra (Vg Ephree) more daring than his predecessor Psammetichus II, 594–589. Jerusalem was besieged for the third time by Nabuchodonosor early in 588 and captured in August 587. The citizens were slaughtered and dispersed, the city and temple destroyed by fire. Only peasants and vintagers were left in the land which was not made a Babylonian province but was abandoned to the depredations of hostile neighbours. Sedecias escaped from the city but was captured and taken to Riblah where his sons were slain before his eyes and he himself was blinded and deported.

g The religious condition of Judah during this period was similar to that of nearly a century earlier and was due to the same causes. A great religious revival was followed by a corresponding idolatrous reaction. Pious kings were replaced by impious successors, Ezechias by Manasses and Amon, Josias by Joakim and Sedecias. Foreign alliance or dependence, Assyrian in the earlier, Egyptian and Babylonian in the later period, introduced foreign worship. Old Canaanite religious practices flourished in both periods. The deportation of the best elements of the population in 597 must have aggravated existing evils. There is thus no reason to think that Jeremias and Ezechiel exaggerate in their descriptions of the moral and religious depravity which made chastisement inevitable and sealed the fate of Jerusalem and Judah.

478a **Contents**—The book of Ezechiel is divided into three parts containing respectively threats of chastisement against Jerusalem and Judah, chh 1–24, prophecies against Gentile neighbours, chh 25–32, and promises of a restoration of the exiles, chh 33–48. The threats are varied by denunciations of the crimes committed, practical instructions and rare gleams of hope of a better future. In view of recent theories on the composition of the book a close synopsis of its contents is necessary to give the reader a clear idea of its logical structure.

b In the introduction to the first part, chh 1–3, Ezechiel receives his prophetic mission with appropriate instructions from Yahweh who appears to him in Babylonia enthroned on his heavenly chariot. The first cycle of threats, chh 4–11, begins with a prediction by means of symbolic actions of the siege and fall of Jerusalem and the death and dispersal of its citizens, chh 4–5. The country also from the Egyptian desert to Riblah on the Orontes will be devastated for the sins of its inhabitants, chh 6–7. Transported in a vision from Babylonia to Jerusalem Ezechiel beholds the idolatrous worship which defiles the sanctuary, the execution of the guilty citizens and the destruction of the city by fire. Yahweh abandons his sanctuary and city, but sends through his prophet a message of hope to the exiles to whom he promises a new heart and a new spirit, chh 8–11. The second cycle of threats, chh 12–19, begins with another

symbolical prediction of the fall of Jerusalem and the exile with special reference to the fate of Sedecias. The fulfilment of prophecy is emphatically proclaimed and false prophets are denounced, chh 12–13. The exiles now ask Ezechiel to consult Yahweh on their behalf. He refuses, but exhorts them to a true repentance assuring them that Yahweh spares the innocent when he punishes a nation for their sins, ch 14. There is no hope for Israel, Yahweh's unfruitful vineyard, for the wood of the unproductive vine is useless except as firewood, ch 15. A long historical retrospect of the sins of Israel shows that her punishment is just and inevitable. The lesson is enforced by the examples of Sodom and Samaria, already punished though less guilty, ch 16. Sedecias, a perjurer, doomed to deportation, suggests by contrast a picture of the Messias, ch 17. The exiles, again informed that they will not be punished except for their own sins, are reminded of God's mercy and exhorted to repentance, ch 18. A poetical elegy on three exiled princes, Joachaz, Joachin and Sedecias, aptly concludes the cycle, ch 19. The third cycle opens with another request from the exiles to consult Yahweh on their behalf. Ezechiel again refuses, then denounces their fathers' sins and their own sins, but finally predicts future conversion and restoration, ch 20. The sword of Yahweh, Nabuchodonosor, is next depicted entering the land to exterminate its inhabitants, ch 21. The sins of Judah are again denounced and all classes of her inhabitants are shown to be guilty, ch 22. Another historical retrospect of the sins of the northern and southern kingdoms, Oholah and Oholibah, shows that Judah's chastisement is just and inevitable, ch 23. The last chapter announces the beginning of the siege of Jerusalem and on the same day the death of Ezechiel's wife whom he is forbidden to mourn as a sign to the exiles not to mourn the fall of Jerusalem. The news of that event brought to the exiles by a fugitive will detach Ezechiel's tongue from his palate, give him free use of his prophetic gift.

The second part of the book begins with a prophecy of the destruction of Ammon, Moab, Edom and Philistia, ch 25. Next come three prophecies against Tyre concluding with brief indications of the fall of Sidon and the restoration of Israel, chh 26–28. Finally seven prophecies predict the fall of Egypt and one also her subsequent restoration, though not to her former greatness, chh 29–32.

The promises of restoration commence with the arrival of the fugitive announcing Jerusalem's fall. The teaching on personal responsibility is more fully expounded. Not the remnant left in Palestine and doomed to destruction but the exiles shall possess the land, ch 33. Former shepherds of Israel are denounced. The reign of a new David and the abiding presence of Yahweh are promised, ch 34. The ruin of Edom, implacable enemy of Judah and chief occupier of her territory, is again predicted, ch 35. The restoration of Israel, rebuilding of her cities, multiplication of her seed, gift of a new heart and a new spirit, not through her own merits but for the glorification of Yahweh's name among the Gentiles, are foretold, ch 36. The vision of dry bones restored to life and the symbolical action of joining together two rods figure the revival of the nation by the return of the exiles and the reunion of the sceptres of Judah and Israel, ch 37. The destruction of Gog and his army represents Yahweh's final victory over the pagan world, chh 38–9. Finally the new temple, the new cult and the new holy land are depicted at length, chh 40–48.

Ezechiel and his Mission—Ezechiel (Yᵉḥezqē'l 'God is strong' or 'God strengthens') son of Buzi, was a priest, undoubtedly of the line of Sadoc. He must have been of a certain age and standing to be included among the influential citizens of Jerusalem deported with their king Joachin by Nabuchodonosor in 597. His residence in Babylonia was at Tel-Abib, apparently the chief settlement of the exiles, on the Naru Kabaru or Grand Canal (DV 'river Chobar') south of

Babylon in the vicinity of Nippur. He was married but his wife died on the first day of the siege of Jerusalem, Jan. 588. His custom of dating his prophecies and his adoption of the Babylonian calendar are naturally attributed to the milieu in which he lived and prophesied. He received his prophetical vocation in June 593. His last dated prophecy belongs to the year 571. All our knowledge of him is derived from his own writings, and the dates of his birth and death are unknown. He must have witnessed the religious revival of Josias and the subsequent idolatrous reaction and died in exile.

The mission of Jeremias was to the Israelites in Palestine but that of Ezechiel was to the exiles. He had to maintain Yahweh worship among them and prepare them for the restoration. His task was difficult for they were a rebellious people inclined to idolatry and, in their isolation from temple and cult, accessible to the seductions of Babylonian ritual and pagan environment. Presumption and despair were the chief obstacles to their conversion. They believed that their exile would be speedily terminated and that Yahweh, who had miraculously preserved Jerusalem from the Assyrians, would not allow the Chaldaeans to destroy his city and sanctuary. They believed also that they were being punished unjustly for the sins of their ancestors, and were the innocent victims of national responsibility. Such hearers were little disposed to heed prophetic discourses assuring them of the proximate and certain ruin of the nation and of the need of conversion to obtain a hearing from Yahweh and escape a similar fate. Only when the prophet's authority was established and the exiles' infatuation dissipated by the fall of Jerusalem could his preaching bear fruit. We can understand therefore why he was inhibited in the use of his prophetic gift during a long period and why supernatural manifestations, symbolic actions, parables and popular sayings were particularly necessary to excite interest and secure a minimum of attention from an unprepared and incredulous audience. The many predictions of the fall of Jerusalem and of the destruction and dispersal of the inhabitants of Judah were directed against the presumption of the exiles, the repeated lessons on personal responsibility and divine mercy against their despair. Far from being involved in the ruin of the nation they were to be the nation resuscitated. The many descriptions of the sins of Israel in all its history and in all classes of its population were intended to convince the exiles that her chastisement was just and inevitable. The mass of the Israelites in Palestine were guilty and doomed to destruction. Ezechiel has no mission to preach to them, makes no effort to convert them. His solicitude is for the exiles on whom all his hopes are centred. More fortunate than Jeremias he knows that his labours, at first unfruitful, will be recompensed by a measure of success in the not too distant future.

The view, advanced by Herntrich and Bertholet and defended by Auvray, that Ezechiel's residence in Babylonia before Jerusalem's fall is the invention of a redactor and that his threats of punishment, like those of Isaias and Jeremias, were addressed to the Israelites in Palestine, is based on a misunderstanding of the prophet's mission and character. The three great prophets in their prophecies against the Gentiles distinguish clearly between those against whom oracles are directed and those for whom they are revealed and to whom they are addressed. They did not seek by these oracles to convert the Gentiles but to convince the Israelites that Yahweh would remove the oppressors of his people and thus prepare the way for the Messianic kingdom. Similarly Ezechiel had not like Jeremias a mission to the Israelites in Palestine whose doom he repeatedly announces as proximate and inevitable. His mission was to convert the exiles on whom all hopes of a restoration were based and who had to be disabused of their errors and convinced of God's justice and holiness before they could become the objects of his mercy and the recipients of his favours.

That we learn more of the actual conditions of the **478i** exiles from Jeremias than from Ezechiel is explained by their different characters. Ezechiel, concentrated completely on his main object, gives little information about himself and his surroundings. He is not discursive and self-revelatory like Jeremias. Finally the new view is not commended by the numerous textual alterations required to transport the prophet from Tel-Abib to Jerusalem during the first part of his prophetic career. It should be antecedently well established to justify so many arbitrary emendations.

Ezechiel has been accused of originating the exag- **j** gerated cult of the Law which characterizes later Judaism. The accusation is based on the theory of Wellhausen that the ritual laws of the Mosaic code are a development of the code of Ezechiel. Our increased knowledge of the Ancient East has shown, however, that an extensive ritual developed early in all Eastern religions. Without discussing the date when the legislation of the Pentateuch received its final form we can confidently assume that the ritual laws of Leviticus are earlier than those of Ezechiel. The prophet's code is ideal and selective. He ignores important legal institutions of earlier date and adopts those which suit his purpose. His exclusion of Levi from a tribal portion of the land shows that he regards the whole tribe of Levi as dedicated to the service of the sanctuary. It is most unlikely that later Judaism, while ignoring his descriptions of the temple and the holy land, adopted and developed his legal code. Ezechiel is moreover an eloquent exponent of the need of interior religion. He insists on a sincere conversion to Yahweh, on a new heart and a new spirit.

Many commentators have depicted Ezechiel as a **k** victim of hallucinations, as afflicted with the physical maladies of aphasia and catalepsy. These errors are due, partly to a rationalistic interpretation of supernatural manifestations, partly to a misunderstanding of the texts. His frequent visions and symbolical actions were intended to secure the attention of his incredulous hearers and prepare them for the day when the fulfilment of his oft-repeated prophecies would make them acknowledge his authority and follow his guidance. The visions also taught the necessary lesson that the dominion of Yahweh extended beyond the land of his people to all parts of the world. As Ezechiel's tongue was ' *attached to his palate* ' from the beginning of his prophetic ministry to the fall of Jerusalem, he could not suffer from aphasia while prophetically active but from certain restrictions in the use of his prophetic gift. The binding with cords is another figurative indication of the moral obligation of seclusion imposed on him by Yahweh. It was not catalepsy but Yahweh's command which made him lie on his right and on his left side during long periods. He was also ordered to prepare his own food in the sight of the people during these periods which he could not have done if deprived of all power of movement by catalepsy.

Messianism—As a religious teacher Ezechiel is simple **479a** and earnest and usually enforces his lessons by frequent repetitions. Only his Messianic prophecies require some explanation. They present us with a striking example of the lack of perspective which sometimes characterizes prophetic visions of future events. He sees on the same plane two distinct future events, the proximate national restoration and the remote establishment of the Messianic kingdom and combines these visions in his descriptions of a Messianic restoration. That is why his Messianism is so distinctively national and material and why a literal fulfilment of many of his prophecies cannot be expected since the Messianic kingdom was not national but universal, not materially but spiritually peaceful and prosperous. The Messias is a sprout of the dried up trunk of the Davidic tree which becomes a magnificent cedar, a good shepherd contrasted with the many bad shepherds of Israel, above all a new David. His kingdom is depicted as material and national, the

479a promised land enlarged by the conquests of David. His subjects are the twelve Jewish tribes with an admixture of alien residents. The peace of this kingdom is secured by weakening or destroying hostile neighbours, Philistia, Edom, Moab, Ammon, Tyre and **b** Egypt. The defeat and destruction of Gog and his army after the establishment of the kingdom is an assurance of Yahweh's permanent protection. Material prosperity is indicated by the fertility and fecundity of sterile regions. The new temple is mainly a reproduction of the temple of Solomon. The new laws are Mosaic and national. The conditions of entry into the kingdom are a sincere conversion, a new heart and a new spirit. This picture of a Jewish Messianic kingdom which was never realized may have little appeal for modern readers but was undoubtedly helpful to Ezechiel's contemporaries who needed encouragement to support the trials of exile and prepare themselves for the coming restoration. There is an economy in divine revelation. The expiatory sufferings of the Messias and the exclusion from his kingdom of the Jews who rejected him did not form part of Ezechiel's message.

c **Composition and Authorship**—The logical and for the most part chronological order of the prophecies may well suggest to the general reader that the present form of the book of Ezechiel is that which it received from its original author. A closer study reveals however in this as in other prophetical books the hand of a redactor. The text is sometimes in considerable disorder. Examples will be found in chh 4, 10 and 24. Messianic prophecies in the first part of the book are generally considered later additions (16:57–63 ; 20:33–44 more probably ; 11:14–21 ; 17:22–24 less probably). Other subsequent insertions are 3:16b–21 ; 27:9b–25a ; 28:20–26 ; 39:17–20 ; 46:16–18. For reasons suggested by the context we may well attribute the present position of these passages to a redactor without however denying their authenticity. The present text exhibits moreover a number of minor errors, omissions, amplifications and glosses. There are also many repetitions. Most of these are explained by the fact that Ezechiel often repeats himself to impress his teaching on his hearers but some are more probably later additions.

d Ancient commentators in general and among modern non-Catholics J. Herrmann, 1924, and G. A. Cooke, 1937, in particular defend the substantial authenticity of the prophecies. Only in recent times have other explanations of their origin been proposed, usually too extravagant to need refutation. Hoelscher, 1924, attributes only the poetical parts to Ezechiel and the mass of prose prophecies to a 5th cent. redactor. Torrey, 1930, regards the whole book as a pseudepigraph, composed c 230 B.C., fictionally ascribed to the time of Manasses by its original author and transformed into a post-exilic work by a redactor. Smith, 1931, makes the author a prophet who lived partly in the Northern Kingdom, partly in exile at Nineveh between 722 and 669. Both Torrey and Smith find the idolatrous reaction described by Ezechiel inexplicable after the reform of Josias and therefore transfer the prophecies which denounce it to an earlier historical period. They err in not recognizing that at a later period the same causes produced the same effect. Herntrich, 1932, assigns the promises, especially chh 40–48, to an exilic redactor and nearly all the rest of the book to a prophet who lived at Jerusalem during the years preceding the city's fall. Bertholet, 1936, develops Herntrich's theory. He locates Ezechiel first at Jerusalem during the period of threats, then somewhere in Judah where he prophesied against the Gentiles and finally in Babylonia where he predicted the restoration. He assumes that the prophet only left detached leaves and sketches of prophecies expanded into the present book by his spiritual heirs. It is difficult to believe that the prophet was unable to express himself clearly as Bertholet supposes, and to understand why his editors took such pains to conceal

his long residence in Jerusalem. Ezechiel's repetitions even when accompanied by variations are particularly objected to and attributed to alternative sketches of the same prophecy. Is it not natural for a teacher to repeat himself in order to impress his teaching on his hearers ? Failure to recognize the religious need of a prophet of the exile providentially supplied by Ezechiel is a fundamental error of this and similar theories.

Text and Versions—The Heb. text of Ezechiel is less well preserved than that of any other OT book. Our chief help in re-establishing it is the LXX based on a Heb. text older than MT. Here as elsewhere deeper corruptions are common to MT and LXX. Frequently however the Gk text reveals a gloss or omission in MT and supplies a correction of a corrupt reading. Sometimes the context, sometimes the metre in poetical passages, establishes the superiority of the LXX reading. The qînāh metre more commonly used by Ezechiel is well known, and superfluous additions in MT, omitted by LXX, can be detected. At other times, however, the Gk translator misunderstands the Heb. text or evades a difficulty by an omission or an approximate rendering. No general rule can be given but an intelligible LXX variant is usually preferred to an unintelligible MT reading. Our knowledge of the Gk text of Ezechiel has been increased by the publication of the Chester Beatty (Ez 11–17 with lacunae) and the Scheide (Ez 19–39 with lacunae) papyri dated in the early 3rd cent. before Origen's Hexapla. The fact that the new text has some MT readings not found in our oldest and best Greek MS (B) does not in any way diminish the value of the LXX variants mentioned above. It was previously believed that three Gk translators rendered each a different part of the book. This conclusion, based on the different renderings of the divine names in the MSS, has been upset by the evidence of the Scheide papyrus. We may now ascribe more probably and naturally the whole book to a single translator. The Syriac version occasionally supports corrections derived from LXX. Vg almost invariably follows MT.

I–XXIV Threats : Chastisement of Jerusalem and Judah.
I–III Introduction : First Vision and Vocation.
I 1–28 The Theophany—God appears to Ezechiel in his heavenly chariot. The four living creatures, later called Cherubs, who support his throne are first described, then the chariot wheels, then the throne and finally the figure on the throne. The vision is perceived like a dream not by the outer but by the inner senses. The Cherubim have each four wings, one pair covering their bodies, the other outstretched so that the four pairs of extended wings form the four sides of a square. They have also each four faces like those of a man, an ox, a lion, and an eagle so that they can go face forward in all four directions, N. S. E. W., without turning. Each has moreover two hands under the lower wings and one leg, not jointed and round at the extremity. The legs are attached to wheels which revolve when the chariot is in motion. Each of the four *wheels* consists of two wheels at right angles to each other and can thus revolve in all four directions without turning. Above the Cherubim is a kind of firmament, compared to crystal, and above the firmament the figure of a man enthroned, all fiery and encompassed with a brightness resembling the rainbow.

1–3. Time and place. **1.** The thirtieth year is enigmatical. Suggested reckonings from the birth of Ezechiel and the reform of Josias are unparalleled. Most probably thirtieth is a corruption of the regnal year (12th or 13th) of Nabuchodonosor. **2–3.** The second indication, June 593 B.C., not in the first but in the third person, brings the date into conformity with the other dates of the book, all reckoned from the captivity of Joachin in the first year of Sedecias, 597 B.C., Nisan (March–April) being the first month of the year. The place is the Naru Kabaru, Grand Canal, flowing SE. from the Euphrates in the latitude of Babylon and re-entering it at Nippur. Tel-Abib on this canal was the chief settlement of the Jewish exiles deported with Joachin. **4.** The storm-wind, dark cloud and fire or lightning are the usual accompaniments of a theophany. The vision as the harbinger of evil comes from the north, the region of darkness and calamity. ' a fire infolding it ' : ' *a mass of fire* '. ' amber ' : ' *electrum* ', an amalgam of gold and silver. **5-14.** On the Cherubim *cf.* Ex 25:18 ; 3 Kg 6:23. The Babylonian *kirubu* was an inferior deity who guarded the gates of temples and palaces and might be also an idol-bearer. This monster had the head of a man, the body of a lion or an ox and the wings of an eagle. A few commentators interpret *faces* as aspects and assimilate cherub and *kirubu*. But the wings —the eagle aspect—are distinguished from the faces in the description. Face-forward movement in all four directions without turning requires four faces. The figure of the cherub is based on that of the *kirubu* but is not a reproduction of it. **7.** The jointless legs and rounded soles exclude bending and turning. **8.** Omit ' on the four sides' after wings. **10.** The faces express respectively the intelligence, strength, majesty and swiftness of the Cherubs. ' over ' : ' *to* '. **11.** Omit ' and their faces ', not in LXX and confusing. **12.** The spirit of God directed the movements of the Cherubim. **13a.** ' *And between these living creatures appeared as it were coals of fire which burned like torches* '. Omit **14** (LXX). It was the fire which flashed and moved. **15-21.** The wheels rest on the ground when the chariot comes to earth. ' With four faces ' (unintelligible) : (LXX) ' *by the four* (living creatures) '. **16.** ' the sea ' : ' *topaz* ', lit. eye of Tarshish. The view that the wheels were not double, as already explained, but when seen in perspective seemed to be one within the other is improbable. Work means structure. **17.** Parts are lit. quarters, each facing in a different direction. **18.** Read ' *felloes* ' for ' wheels ' and for ' whole body '. The eyes were most probably ornaments as in a peacock's tail. Some interpret *bosses* instead of *felloes*. Directed by the spirit of God wheels and cherubs moved harmoniously in all four directions without turning. **20-21.** ' spirit of life ' (LXX, Vg) : ' *spirit of the living creatures* ' (MT). **22-28.** The platform resting on the heads of the Cherubim is likened to the firmament, God's footstool ; *cf.* Ex 24:20. Its firmness and colour are indicated by the comparisons. **23.** MT gives the Cherubim three pairs of wings by a dittography, rendered loosely in Vg. ' straight ' : ' *outstretched* ' (LXX). The meaning is that the platform extends as far as the outstretched wings. **24.** Comparisons indicate the noise of the wings when in motion. When let down they remained outstretched. Omit **25.** The voice is premature and the letting down of the wings a repetition. **26.** The spirituality of God is safeguarded by expressions like appearance and likeness. **27.** ' amber ' ' *electrum* '.

The theophany in Babylonia gave an important lesson to the exiles. They shared to some extent the pagan belief that the power and presence of a god were restricted to a particular region. By his majestic appearance in a foreign land Yahweh manifested his Omnipotence and Omnipresence.

II 1-III 15 Call to the Prophetic Ministry—God announces his mission to Ezechiel, constitutes him his interpreter and finally sends him to preach to his fellow-captives at Tel-Abib.

II 1-7 The Task—Ezechiel prostrates himself in fear and reverence before the glory of God. He hears a voice bidding him rise and obeys, strengthened by the spirit. The expression Son of man is equivalent to man. It occurs ninety times in Ezechiel and stresses the littleness of man compared with the greatness of God. **3.** The Israelites are characterized as a rebellious people, not peoples (MT). ' my covenant ' : ' *against me* '. **4.** ' *And the children . . . are of* ', etc.

5. The condition is disjunctive ; ' *Whether they hear* **480h** *or not . . . they shall know* '. **6.** ' Unbelievers and destroyers '. The usual rendering, *briars and thorns* is uncertain. **7b-c.** ' *whether they hear or refuse to hear, for they are a rebellious house* '. House is accidentally omitted in MT.

II 8-III 3 The Message—God presents to Ezechiel **i** a book containing *lamentations, mourning and woe* and orders him to eat it. We thus learn that God is the real author of what Ezechiel preaches and that the divine communications are threats of punishment. The eating of the book is not real but symbolical, since the vision affected only the internal senses. On its roll form *cf.* Jer 36. **8b.** ' *And be not rebellious like that house* '. **9.** The prophet says *a hand* indeterminately to avoid anthropomorphism. **III:1.** ' *Eat what thou findest* '. **3.** The book is sweet as God's gift. *Cf.* ' My yoke is sweet '.

III 4-11 The Sending—Ezechiel is now sent to the **j** exiles, the recipients of his instructions. He is warned that his rebellious and hard-hearted hearers will not heed his words but is strengthened to persevere against all opposition. **5.** The foreigners are ' *deep of lip and heavy of tongue* '. They seem to mumble and stammer. **6.** *Cf.* Christ's words on Capharnaum and Bethsaida (Mt 11:21 ; 12:41). **11c.** ' *Whether they hear or refuse to hear* '.

12-15 The Vision disappears : Ezechiel goes to k Tel-Abib—**12.** (After ' commotion ') : ' *When the glory of Yahweh ascended from its place* '. *berûm* ' in ascending ' replaces *bārûk* ' blessed '. **13b.** ' *and the simultaneous noise of the wheels* '. Omit the rest as an inappropriate repetition. **14.** Ezechiel was not transported to Tel-Abib but a supernatural force uplifted him spiritually and impelled him thither. His bitterness was due to reaction and a realization of the difficulties of his task. **15.** Exhausted by his experiences he remained stupefied for seven days at Tel-Abib until a fresh revelation restored him to his senses.

16-21 The Prophet's Responsibility—Ezechiel is re- **l** markable for his teaching on personal responsibility. The subject is discussed here from the point of view of the prophet, compared to a watchman, and subsequently more fully, 14:12-23 ; 18:1-32 ; 33:1-20. Both prophet and sinner are responsible if no warning is given. Only the sinner is responsible if the warning is unheeded. The punishment contemplated is death. Prolongation of life is the reward of the prophet's fidelity and of the sinner's conversion. The habitual sinner is first considered, then the just man who sins. Conversion is equally necessary and salutary in both cases. **20.** (After ' iniquity ') : ' *And I lay* ', etc. ' *He shall die* ' is the apodosis of the first conditional clause. ' *Because* ' begins the second clause. MT detaches 16a, date of the vision in 22 ff., from 16b, thus suggesting that this passage is a later but not inappropriate addition.

22-27 Silence and Seclusion—These verses may belong **m** to the introduction or to the first cycle of prophecies. Ezechiel is ordered to stay in his house and refrain from preaching. The binding with cords and attachment of the tongue to the palate are figurative indications of the seclusion and silence imposed. As Yahweh is the author of the mutism he must also be the author of the binding ; *cf.* 4:8. **25.** ' *Bonds shall be put on thee and thou shalt be bound with them and thou shalt not go out among them* ' (the exiles). Yahweh as agent is sometimes unmentioned when human agents would be explicitly indicated and he alone can attain his end by imposing on his prophet a moral obligation. There is no reason to suppose that the binders were exiles who thought Ezechiel demented, still less to attribute his silence and seclusion to physical maladies, aphasia and catalepsy. The motive of the precept was the unworthiness and unpreparedness of the exiles. ' *For they are a rebellious house* '.

IV-XII First Cycle of Threats against Jerusalem and 481a Judah.

IV 1-V 17 Symbolical Announcement of the Siege

481a **of Jerusalem and the Exile**—The text must be restored to order. Siege of Jerusalem, **1-3, 7**. Famine during the siege, **10-11, 16-17**, Length of the exile, **4-6, 8**, Unclean foods during the exile, **9-12, 15**, Annihilation of the citizens, **5:1-4**, Explanation of the symbols, **5:5-17**. The determination of the periods represented by days during which Ezechiel lies on his left and on his right side is disputed but only one solution is tenable. As the days represent years they cannot refer to the siege of Jerusalem. Neither can they refer to the iniquity of Judah and Israel during the divided monarchy since Judah's iniquity cannot be reduced to forty years, and Ezechiel represents not the commission but the chastisement of sin. As periods of symbolical expiation they can only refer to the exile. Israel's exile, 721–538, lasted 183 years, Judah's, 587–538, 49 years. The 190 and 40 years preserved by LXX are round numbers in close agreement with these figures. The MT reading 390 probably represents an attempt to equate the combined periods, 430 years, with the length of the Egyptian captivity. The use of Israel as a designation of the Northern Kingdom after the fall of Samaria is exceptional, but not without parallel ; *cf.* Is 11:12. As the prophet was ordered to prepare, cook and eat his food in the sight of the exiles we cannot suppose that he was literally bound or paralysed. He was confined to his house by Yahweh's command, and when he lay down he had to lie on his left side during the first and on his right during the second period.

b **IV 1-3, 7 Siege of Jerusalem**—Ezechiel is ordered to depict on a brick (used in Babylonia for diagrams as well as for writing) Jerusalem in a state of siege. The *siege wall*, which may have been a circle of forts, the mound built up against the city wall, the camps of the besiegers and their battering rams are all depicted. The iron wall encircling and isolating the besieged is represented by the iron griddle, used for baking bread, erected between Ezechiel and the city. The prophet, representing the Babylonians, besieges the city, menaces it with bared arm and prophesies against it. The diagram predicts a future event like the inscription in Is 8:1.

c **10-11, 16-17 Famine during the Siege**—The famine is symbolized by the rationing. Ezechiel is restricted to a daily ration of 20 shekels of bread, about 8 oz, and a sixth of a hin of water, about 2 pints. The drink restriction would be felt most in the hot climate of Babylonia.

d **4-6, 8 Length of the Exile**—As the Oriental faces the east in determining directions the left side indicates the northern, the right the southern kingdom. The expiation is not vicarious but symbolical. **5a.** ' *For I have appointed the years of their iniquity to be unto thee a (corresponding) number of days* '. **8.** ' siege ' : ' distress '.

e **9, 12-15 Unclean Foods during the Exile**—The mixture of wheat and barley, beans and lentils, millet and spelt, was unlawful just as sowing two kinds of corn in one field or using two kinds of cloth for one garment, Lev 19:19 ; Deut 22:9-11. The fuel for baking was also unclean and revolting, Deut 23:13 ff., but a mitigation of this uncleanness was obtained by prayer. The dried dung of animals is still frequently used. Bread is sometimes baked by making a fire over flat stones, spreading the cake on the heated stones and covering it with the embers. The period mentioned is 190 (MT 390) days to which 40 must be added. Food eaten in exile was unclean because sacrifices and offerings of first-fruits by which it was sanctified were impossible.

f **V 1-4 Annihilation of the Citizens**—The last of the symbols refers to siege and exile combined. The shaving of Judah with a razor expressed the completeness of its devastation, Is 7:20. Here the order given to Ezechiel symbolizes the annihilation of the inhabitants of Jerusalem. Some perish within the city by famine and pestilence, others without by the sword ; others are deported but shall not escape the sword. A few are spared from the massacre but even of these

all shall not survive. That this remnant is ignored **4** when the symbol is explained does not justify the conclusion that **3-4** is a later addition. **1a.** ' *Take thee a sharp sword, (as) a barber's razor take it to thee* '. **2.** ' according to ' : ' *after* '. ' knife ' : ' *sword* '. **4.** (After ' with fire ') : ' *And 'thou shalt say to the whole house of Israel* ' (LXX).

5-17 Explanation of the Symbols—The symbols **g** indicate the chastisement of the inhabitants of Jerusalem for their iniquities. Jerusalem was the religious centre of the world. The Jews were God's chosen people united with him by a special covenant. Instead of being an example to the Gentiles they surpassed them in wickedness. Hence their punishment will be without parallel, especially because they defiled Yahweh's sanctuary with idolatrous worship. They shall perish by pestilence, famine, the sword, and attacks of wild beasts. They shall become a byword to the Gentiles, astonished at the severity of their punishment. **6c.** *They* refers to the Jews, not the Gentiles. **7.** ' have surpassed ' : ' *have rebelled more than* '. *The judgements of the nations* indicate the precepts of the natural law. **10.** *Cf.* 4 Kg 6:24-29 and Lam 4:10. **12.** Deportation will not end the punishment. The sword still threatens the exiles. **13b.** When the evils predicted come to pass the sufferers will recognize the prophetic character of Ezechiel's words intended for them as well as for his fellow-exiles. Communications were maintained between the exiles and the Palestinian Jews. *I will be comforted* expresses anthropomorphically Yahweh's satisfaction at the completion of his task. **16-17.** These verses are regarded by some as a later addition. Repetitions, however, are common in Ezechiel. Blood is elsewhere coupled with pest. As distinguished here from blood shed by the sword in battle it may refer to homicides, fatal accidents, judicial executions.

VI 1-14 Announcement of the Punishment of Judah 4—The previous threats of chastisement were directed particularly against Jerusalem and its citizens. Now Judah and its inhabitants are similarly threatened. The hilly character of the land explains why the mountains are addressed. The high places on the hills were conspicuous centres of idolatrous worship. Sword, famine and pestilence are the instruments of chastisement. **3.** ' rocks ' : ' *water-courses* '. The places personified represent their inhabitants. **4a.** ' idols ' : ' *incense altars* ' ; *cf.* Is 17:8. Omit **5a**, a repetition of **4b**. The shrines of the idols are profaned by the bones of their worshippers. **6.** ' *Wherever you dwell, the cities shall be laid waste and the high places shall be desolate that your altars may be laid waste and made desolate and your idols be broken and cease and your incense altars be hewn down and your works abolished* '. **8.** ' *Yet will I leave a remnant in that ye shall have some that shall escape the sword among the nations when ye shall be scattered among the countries* ' (MT). The prophet addresses the Jews in Palestine. He told them in **7** that when the calamity came upon them they should recognize its author. He adds in **9** that a remnant will be converted after the deportation. LXX omits *I will leave a remnant*, already indicated in 5:3. The comparison of idolatry to matrimonial infidelity is common in prophetic literature. ' because I have broken ' : ' *when I break* '. **11.** Clapping of hands and stamping of feet express exultation (*cf.* 25:6), not at the abominations but at their punishment. **13a.** ' your ' : ' *their* '. Ezechiel distinguishes between his fellow-exiles (' you shall know ') and the Palestinians. **14.** Deblatha : *Reblatha*, Riblah on the Orontes at the northern end of David's kingdom identified by Ezechiel with the promised land.

VII 1-27 Second Announcement of the Punishment 4 of Judah and Jerusalem—This prophecy has the same subject-matter as the preceding one. It emphasizes the imminence of the catastrophe, its inevitability, and its enormity. It belongs apparently to the first year of Ezechiel's mission.

1-9. The judgement is imminent. The time, the **4**

day, the evil, the end, is come. **2.** The four quarters of the *earth* indicate the whole world. The prophets frequently depict a particular judgement as part of the general judgement. **3c.** ' *And I will bring upon thee all thy abominations* '. LXX puts **2-3** after **8-9. 5.** ' *Evil upon evil, behold, it comes* ' (slightly corrected). The word rendered ' destruction ' in DV means elsewhere ' crown ' or ' garland '.

10-19. The punishment is inevitable. **10b.** ' *The crown has sprouted, the sceptre has blossomed, pride has budded* '. The reference is probably to the crowning of Sedecias, whose pride brought revolt and ruin. **11,** abbreviated in LXX, is unintelligible. **12.** The buyer rejoiced in satisfying his desire, the seller regretted the surrender of his possessions. They are now equal. **13.** The principle is illustrated by the sale of land which returned automatically to its original owner in the jubilee year. The verse may be a gloss. **14.** ' *They have blown* ', etc. **16.** ' *trembling* ' : ' *mourning* '. **17.** ' *And all knees shall be weak as water* '. **19a.** ' *They shall cast their silver in the street and shall regard their gold as unclean* '.

20-27. The enormity of the calamity appears from the profanation of Yahweh's sanctuary and his complete abandonment of his people. **20-22.** The temple with its *treasures*, desecrated by idolatry, shall be profaned and plundered. ' They ' in **22** is indefinite. ' secret places ' : ' *treasures* '. **23.** ' *Make the chain* ' (MT) for binding captives. ' *and they shall make* ' (LXX). Judgement of blood means blood-guilt. **24.** ' they shall possess their sanctuary ' : ' *their holy places shall be defiled* '. **27.** Omit *The king shall mourn*, not in LXX. Ezekiel never calls Sedecias king. ' judgements ' : ' *deserts* '.

VIII-XI Idolatrous Worship in Jerusalem and its Punishment—In this vision dated a year and two (LXX ' one ') months after the first, August 592 B.C., Ezekiel is transported in spirit to Jerusalem and there beholds : (1) various forms of idolatry practised by the citizens ; (2) the slaughter of all the idolatrous worshippers by destroying angels ; (3) the destruction of the city itself by fire ; (4) Yahweh's abandonment of his city and sanctuary. The vision concludes with a prediction of restoration. The detailed description of the heavenly chariot, mostly borrowed from ch 1, is a redactorial addition. Ezekiel was not bodily but spiritually transported to Jerusalem. He describes supernatural visions, not a series of events.

VIII 1-18 Idolatrous Worship in Jerusalem—Four species of idolatry are mentioned : Idol worship, Animal worship, Tammuz worship and Sun worship, the first of Canaanite, the second of Egyptian and the third of Babylonian origin. Sun worship was common.

1-6. Transported in spirit to the northern gate of the inner court of the temple, Ezekiel looks northwards and sees in the outer court the idol of jealousy set up as a rival of Yahweh and provoking his jealousy by receiving the cult due to him alone. The idol was most probably Ashera, the consort of Baal, set up by Manasses, 4 Kg 21:7, removed by Josias, *ib.* 23:6, and reinstalled by a later king. The reform of Josias like that of Ezechias was followed by an idolatrous reaction. **2.** *Cf.* 1:27. ' of fire ' : ' *of a man* ' (LXX). **3.** ' *he put forth* '. Not the hand but the spirit of God uplifted the prophet. ' near ' : ' *to the entry of* '. The gate was a passage way with buildings on either side. **5.** (After ' gate ') ' *the altar of the idol of jealousy* '. Omit ' in the very entry ' (LXX). **6.** Omit ' thinkest thou '. In **6, 13, 15** ' turn thee ' renders an auxiliary verb expressing repetitions : ' thou shalt see again '.

7-12. In Egypt divinities were commonly represented as animals. Incense was offered by the 70 elders to various Egyptian gods. **8.** Digging through a wall presents no difficulty in a vision. **11.** Omit ' stood ' after Saaphan and ' that ' after them. Jezonias, an important person, is not mentioned elsewhere. **12.** For ' Each in the chamber of his image ' (MT), ' Each offering incense to his image ' is suggested.

The elders say that Yahweh has abandoned them and **483d** they must seek help elsewhere.

13-15. Tammuz was a vegetation god, the Adonis **e** of the Phoenicians, who was supposed to die in the heat of summer and return to life in the spring. The women lament his departure to the underworld. **14.** ' in by ' : ' *to* '. The mourning took place at the northern gate of the outer court. **15a.** ' *Hast thou seen ?* '

16-18. Ezekiel, led back to the inner court, sees **f** in the space between the temple and the altar 25 men with their backs to the temple and their faces to the east adoring the sun. **17.** The sense is : Is it too little for them to perpetrate such abominations in the holy city that they fill the land with violence ? The last member probably refers to idol worship in Yahweh's sanctuary. ' *They present their stench to my nostrils* '. ' Stench ' is literally ' branch '.

IX 1-10 Punishment of the Idolaters in Jerusalem— **g** Ezekiel now beholds six destroying angels slaying, by order of Yahweh, all the idolatrous citizens, but sparing the innocent whose foreheads have been marked with a sign. **1b.** Omit : ' And everyone ', etc. (inappropriate). **2.** The upper gate is the north gate of the inner court. In Palestine the inkhorn of the scribe is still attached to his girdle. The brazen altar erected by Solomon was removed to the north side of the temple by Achaz who put a stone altar in its place, 4 Kg 16:14. **3.** ' Cherub ' : ' *Cherubim* ' (LXX). **4.** *Tau* means mark. It also indicates the last letter of the Hebrew alphabet, shaped like a cross. The text does not refer to the letter or indicate the nature of the mark. Here again Ezekiel teaches personal responsibility. Only the guilty are punished. **6.** ' *The ancients before the house* ' are the sun worshippers. **8a.** ' *And while they were smiting* '. Manifestations of pity and intercession are unusual in Ezekiel. Here they intensify the dramatic effect.

X 1-22 Destruction of the City by Fire—The account **h** is incomplete. It is suggested that the second part was missing or illegible and a redactor filled the lacuna with a second description of the chariot. The only novelties are the names *Cherub* for ' living creature ' and *galgal* for ' wheel ' and the attribution to the Cherubs of the eyes which adorned the wheels. Yahweh's abandonment of his temple is also narrated.

1-7. The angel who had been ordered to mark the **i** foreheads of the innocents is told to take of the fire in the space between the wheels of the chariot and scatter burning coals over the city. **1** is probably interpolated. It repeats 1:26 and interrupts the context. **3.** The right side is the south side. **5.** As the Cherubim have halted, the sound of their wings is surprising. **7.** ' one cherub ' : ' *he* ' (LXX), and after ' Cherubims ' ' *And he took and went forth* ' ; *cf.* 2.

8-17. The Cherubs and the Wheels. **9.** ' to the **j** sight like the chrysolite stone ' : ' *like the brightness of the topaz* '. **11.** ' they first ' : ' *the first* '. **12.** ' necks' : ' *backs* '. ' circles ' : ' *wheels* '. The spirituality of the Cherubim is less apparent than in ch 1. **13.** ' *As for the wheels they were called in my hearing galgal* '. **14.** ' a cherub ' : ' *an ox* '. Ezekiel gets a side view of the chariot which was on the right side of the temple and thus sees first the face of the ox. **15.** ' Living creatures ' is collective.

18-22. Yahweh returns to the chariot which leaves **k** the temple passing through the east gate. **19.** ' it stood ' : ' *they stood* '. **20-21.** The Cherubim are again described. **22.** ' the impulse of every one to go ' : ' *they went every one* '. Omit ' and their looks '.

XI 1-25. This chapter announces the punishment **l** of the wicked counsellors in Jerusalem and the conversion and restoration of the exiles in Babylonia. The two episodes are similarly introduced by proverbial sayings expressing the security of the wicked citizens of Jerusalem and their contempt for the exiles. There is thus a literary connexion between them. The objection that the evil counsellors were already slain in ch 9 ignores the fact that the visions

483 l of the slaughter of the citizens and the burning of the city are prophecies of future events. The visions of the evil counsellors and idolatrous worship do not refer to the future. Moreover the terrible chastisement naturally follows its primary cause, idolatrous worship. The traditional order of the text should be retained.

m 1-13 The Flesh and the Cauldron—Ezechiel sees at the eastern gates of the city 25 of the chief men devising evil counsel. They declare themselves protected from destruction by the city wall as meat in a cauldron is protected from consumption. The prophet announces to them that the corpses of those for whose death they are responsible shall remain within the wall like meat in the cauldron but they themselves shall be deported from the city and slain by the sword. On the capture of Jerusalem in 587 B.C. the principal citizens were deported and some were subsequently executed by Nabuchodonosor at Riblah (*cf.* Jer 52:24-27 ; 4 Kg 25:18-21).

n **1.** Jezonias and Pheltias are mentioned only here, but as princes of the people would be well known to the exiles. **3.** ' *Were not houses lately built ?* ' (LXX, Vg) is preferable to MT : ' The time is not near to build houses '. The reference is to repairs executed under Nabuchodonosor's visit in 597 B.C. **7.** *This* means the city. **10.** The borders of Israel refer to Riblah, the scene of Nabuchodonosor's executions. LXX omits **11-12** possibly as superfluous. **13.** The death of Pheltias at the time of the prophecy was a coincidence.

o 14-21 Who shall possess the Land of Yahweh ?—The inhabitants of Jerusalem say to the exiles : *You are far from Yahweh ; the land is given in possession to us.* The prophet announces that they shall be removed far from Palestine but the despised exiles shall return to it, purify it, and possess it as Yahweh's people. **15.** Omit repetition of ' thy brethren '. 'kinsmen': '*fellow exiles*' (LXX). **16c.** ' *And I have been to them only in a small degree a sanctuary* ', etc. The full observance of Yahweh worship was not possible outside Palestine. **17.** ' you ' : *them* (LXX). **19.** ' one heart ' : ' *a new heart* '. **20b.** ' *They shall be my people and I shall be their God* '.

p 22-25 Conclusion of the Vision—Yahweh abandons Jerusalem—The heavenly chariot appears last on Mt Olivet whence Christ ascended into heaven. Reconducted to Tel-Abib the prophet relates his visions to his fellow exiles.

484a XII-XIX Second Cycle of Threats against Jerusalem and Judah.
XII 1-20 Exile and Devastation—By symbolic actions, Ezechiel predicts (1) the exile in general and the fate of Sedecias in particular, (2) the devastation of the land. He makes public preparations for a departure in the daytime by collecting his belongings and putting them outside his house. He departs by night, passing through a hole which he has made in the wall and simulating blindness. There is some confusion in the text. In the command the evening is the time of departure, in the execution it is the time when the hole was made in the wall. ' Go forth ' (*qal*) and ' carry forth ' (*hiph'il*) are also confused in MT and Vg. Sedecias fled from Jerusalem through a south-eastern gate but was captured and blinded before he was led into exile. The second symbolic action depicts fear and anxiety about food caused by the devastation of the land.

b 1-16 Exile and Fate of Sedecias—**2.** ' provoking ' : ' *rebellious* '. The signs would excite the curiosity of the unbelieving exiles. **3.** Omit ' and remove ' before ' by day '. The preparation was by day, the departure by night. This verse predicts the exile in general. The necessaries would be few : food, water-skin, staff, clothes. **4.** ' furniture ' : ' *belongings* '. Refer ' by day in their sight ' to ' bring forth '. ' that removeth his dwelling ' : ' *to depart* '. **5-6.** These verses refer to Sedecias. **6a.** ' *In their sight thou shalt put (thy baggage) on thy shoulder and go forth in the dark* '. The covering of the face represents the blinding of the king before his deportation. **7.** (After ' dark ') :

' *I put (my baggage) on my shoulder in their sight* '. **10.** The message, lit. ' the prince, this burden (or, oracle) in Jerusalem ', is obscure. **11c.** ' *Into exile, into captivity they shall go* '. **12.** ' *shall carry (his belongings) on his shoulder* '.

17-20. Eating in fear and trembling indicates insecurity of the means of subsistence. **18.** ' trouble ' : ' *trembling* '. ' hurry and sorrow ' : ' *anxiety and fear* '. **19b.** (After ' desolation ') : ' *Because their land and all it contains shall be devastated* '.
XII 21-XIV 11 Prophecy and Prophets—Ezechiel first refutes popular sayings about prophecy. He then inveighs against false prophets and prophetesses. Finally he sets down the conditions required for obtaining answers through a prophet from Yahweh.
21-28 Sayings about Prophecy—The saying ' *The days are prolonged and every vision faileth* ' must cease. Let it be said instead ' *The days are near and every vision is realized* '. **22.** ' in the land ' : ' *about the land* '. The prophecies concern the land of Israel. **23.** ' the word ' (MT) ' the effect ' (DV) : ' *is realized* ' (Syr.). **24.** ' doubtful divination ' : ' *deceitful oracle* '. **25a-b.** ' *I am Yahweh, I shall speak my words, I shall speak and I shall perform and I shall postpone no longer* ' (LXX). The second saying refers particularly to the proximate destruction of Judah and Jerusalem. This prophecy will be fulfilled without delay, not ' *after many days and in times afar off* '.

XIII 1-16 The False Prophets—These are defined as *prophesying from their own hearts*, announcing to the people as the words of Yahweh their own thoughts and wishes, *and seeing not*, having no supernatural vision. They are like foxes in ruins, undermining instead of building, like whitewashers of a wall, hiding instead of repairing weakness. Their punishment will be exclusion from the people and the land of Israel. **2.** (After ' Israel ') : ' *prophesy and say* '. **5.** ' to face the enemy ' : ' *to the breach* '. **6c.** ' *And they expected him to accomplish their word* '. **9.** ' council ' : ' *congregation* '. Written in the book means registered as members. **10.** The wall is the false belief that Yahweh will protect Jerusalem unconditionally. ' dirt without straw ' : ' *whitewash* '. **11.** ' *Say to the whitewashers : there shall be violent rain, hailstones shall fall and the storm-wind shall break forth* '. **13.** The storm is the Babylonian invasion. ' to consume ' : ' *shall fall* '. **14.** Insert ' *you* ' before ' shall be consumed '. **15.** ' I will say ' : ' *it will be said* '. **16.** The prophets are the whitewashers of 15.

17-23. The false prophetesses besides attributing to Yahweh their own inventions and prophesying in his name adopted also Babylonian magical practices. They made bands for the joints of the hand and veils for the head to be used as amulets to avert evil influences. Superstitious belief in the efficacy of these amulets gave the power of life and death to their dispensers. **18.** ' cushions ' : ' *bands* ' ; ' elbows ' : ' *joints* ' (of the hands) ; ' pillows ' : ' *veils* '. To catch souls means to prey upon souls. **18c.** ' *Do you prey upon souls belonging to my people and give life to souls for your own advantage ?* ' The prophetesses promised length of life to the sinners who bought their charms and threatened with death the just who refused them. They also profaned Yahweh by prophesying in his name. **20.** Omit (LXX) as glosses ' flying ' and ' the souls that should fly '. **22.** Justice, not amulets, gives length of life.
XIV 1-11 Worshippers of Idols consult Ezechiel—He is ordered to threaten them with extermination unless they renounce idolatry and not to reply to their queries under penalty of sharing their fate. **3.** ' uncleannesses ' : ' *idols* '. The sense is that their idol worship is external as well as internal. **4.** ' *I, Yahweh, will answer him notwithstanding the number of his idols* '. **5.** The answer has a salutary purpose. **7.** The strangers would be pagan slaves who accompanied their masters into exile. **9.** The prophet who is seduced and answers the demands of idolaters will be exterminated with them. It is Yahweh who seduces

4h him, not positively but negatively, lets him be voluntarily seduced.

i **XIV 12-XVI 63 Total Corruption of Judah and Jerusalem**—Ezechiel first describes the justice of Yahweh in chastising sinful nations, then the sinfulness of Israel, unfruitful vine, ungrateful child, unfaithful spouse. He concludes that her chastisement, severe and inevitable, will be followed by her restoration.

j **12-23 Justice of the Chastisements of Yahweh**—When Yahweh chastises a nation he spares the just but not their sons and daughters. In the chastisement of Jerusalem, however, some will escape into exile to reveal by their manner of life the justice of Yahweh's judgement. Thus the general law of personal responsibility admits exceptions. As some of the guilty are spared here, so the just perish with the wicked, 21:3. **13.** The clauses are all conditional, the apodosis is **14b.** *'They* [alone] *shall be saved'*. **14.** As Israel is an exception to the general rule the instances of just men are sought elsewhere. It is therefore improbable that the prophet Daniel is here indicated. He was moreover a contemporary of Ezechiel while Noe and Job were ancients. Finally the prophet's name is always written Daniel, but here and in 28:3 MT has 'Danel'. This was the name of an ancient Phoenician sage recently revealed by the Rās-Shamra tablets. Most moderns accept the association of the Phoenician Danel with the Edomite Job. It may be assumed that Danel was an ancient historical figure, introduced into Phoenician mythology as Job was introduced into Hebrew Wisdom literature. **22-23.** The conduct and actions of the fugitives must have been evil to convince the earlier exiles of the justice of the chastisement.

k **XV 1-8 Jerusalem, Unfruitful Vine**—The comparison of Israel to a vineyard usually depicts Yahweh's care of his people and their ingratitude and infidelity. Here the point of comparison is the inutility of the unfruitful vine-stock and its consequent destiny, the fire. Both ends, the northern and southern kingdoms, and the centre Jerusalem, captured and sacked in 597 B.C., have been wholly or partially consumed. Yahweh will complete the destruction. **2.** *'What advantage has the vine-tree over any other tree, the vine-branch which is among the trees of the forest?'* **4.** 'reduced to ashes': '*burned*'. **7b.** '*They have gone out*', etc. They have escaped so far but will finally perish.

l **XVI 1-14 Jerusalem, Ungrateful Child**—Jerusalem as capital represents the land of Israel. Ezechiel does not consider the ethnical origin of the Hebrew people. Israel is a foundling. Her father and mother are the previous possessors of the land. The Amorites are the Semitic immigrants who invaded Canaan in the 19th cent. B.C. The Hethites are the northern non-Semitic peoples, Hurrites and perhaps Hittites, who invaded the land in the 18th cent. These possessed Canaan when the patriarchs settled there. **4.** The new-born child is still washed, salted and swaddled by the Palestinian Arabs. Israel as a foundling was neglected. **5.** 'in the abjection of thy soul': '*in disgust for thy life*'. The unwanted child was exposed to death. **6.** *'I saw thee weltering in thy blood and I said to thee in thy blood "Live"'*. Omit last member (LXX). **7.** '*And grow like the plants of the fields*'. 'woman's ornament': '*beauteous maturity*'. **8.** Covering with the extremity of the garment meant betrothal, Ru 3:9. Covenant was espousal. **10.** 'violet-coloured shoes': '*the skin of the sea-cow*'. **12.** 'jewel upon thy forehead'; '*ring on thy nose*'. **13.** Omit last member (LXX). A bride, not a queen, is described. **14b.** *'For it was perfect through my splendour'*. The early monarchy is depicted.

m **15-34 Jerusalem, Unfaithful Spouse**—Judah used Yahweh's splendid gifts ungratefully for adulterous ends. Forms of idolatrous worship, both Canaanite and foreign, are indicated. She even paid her guilty partners instead of being paid by them. **16.** (After 'high places'): '*decked with divers colours and hast played the harlot upon them*'. **17.** 'vessels': '*ornaments*'. **20-21.** Placating false gods with sacrifices of Yahweh's children was the climax of iniquity. Infants were **484m** first slain, then burned as holocausts to Moloch at Jerusalem. **22.** 'after': '*in*'. Correct last member as in 5. **24.** 'common stew': '*altar base*'; 'brothel house': '*high place*'. **26-27** are usually misinterpreted. Ezechiel, describing the sins of Judah, records, after indigenous Canaanite worship, foreign worship introduced by foreign alliances. The first alliance with Egypt was that of Ezechias with the Kushite Pharaoh, punished by the invasion of Sennacherib. Many cities were detached from Judah and incorporated in the Assyrian province of Ashdod. The Egyptians were small in stature but the Kushites who then ruled Egypt were *long-bodied*, Is 18:2, 7. Their stature is here emphasized as giving them a deceptive appearance of strength. *Great in flesh* is 'big-bodied' or 'long-bodied', since *bāśār* 'flesh' is frequently used for 'body', but rarely for *membrum virile*, the inappropriate modern interpretation here. **27.** '*And behold I stretched out my hand against thee, I diminished thy portion and I delivered thee to the desire of thy enemies, the daughters of the Philistines*'. This verse confirms the historical allusion suggested above. **29.** 'Canaan': '*trade*'; cf. 17:4. Babylon was a trade centre. **31.** Cf. corrections in 24. '*Thou hast not been as a harlot seeking* [LXX] *a wage*'. **32-34.** Judah differed from ordinary harlots in seeking and paying her lovers instead of being sought and paid by them.

35-43 The Chastisement of Jerusalem—She shall be **n** handed over defenceless to her paramours who will strip her of everything and, as Yahweh's appropriate agents, will execute on her the sentence pronounced on adulteresses and shedders of blood. **36.** Brass, not used for money (Vg), is unintelligible. 'by': '*and through*'. Bloodshed by human sacrifice is indicated. **37.** 'Hated' may mean 'loved less'. It probably indicates Judah's fickleness in adopting and abandoning false gods. **38b** (corrected). '*And I shall bring upon thee my fury and my jealousy*'. **39.** 'the vessels of thy beauty': '*thy fair jewels*'. **40.** 'multitude'; '*assembly*', a kind of tribunal of the nations. The adulteress is stoned, the shedder of blood has his own blood shed. **41.** 'Women' here means nations and particularly Judah's neighbours who rejoice in her humiliation. **42a.** '*And I shall satisfy my indignation with her*'. Yahweh is depicted as a husband who completely vindicates the wrong done him and is fully satisfied. **43c** is probably interrogative. '*Hast thou not fornicated over all thy abominations?*' Her punishment is merited by continual infidelity.

44-58 Jerusalem compared with Samaria and Sodom o—The justice of the sentence pronounced on Jerusalem is confirmed by a comparison. She has sinned more than Samaria and Sodom. As they were punished her chastisement is inevitable. **44.** Omit 'common'. **45.** The Hittite mother was a heathen. The husbands are national as distinguished from foreign deities. The sisters adopted Canaanite gods and offered them human sacrifices. **46.** 'elder': '*bigger*'; 'younger': '*smaller*'. Not age but extent of territory is indicated. **47.** *Almost*, which begins the second member, must be referred to *all*. Jerusalem has been more wicked than her sisters in *almost all* her ways. **48.** Daughters are minor cities. **49.** 'abundance and idleness': '*careless ease*'; 'put forth': '*strengthen*' (the hand of the needy). **50.** *As thou hast seen* alludes to the still visible ruins of Sodom. **52.** 'Justify' here means render excusable as less guilty. Jerusalem *entreated for* (DV 'surpassed') her sisters by showing the comparative lightness of their guilt. **53.** '*And I will change their lot, the lot of Sodom and her daughters and the lot of Samaria and her daughters and I will change thy lot in the midst of them*'. As the prophecy precedes the fall of Jerusalem, Sodom and Samaria shall be re-established but Jerusalem shall be disestablished. **56-57.** Was not Sodom a byword on thy lips? Now thou art a byword for thy neighbours. 'Syria', Aram (MT); 'Edom' (Syriac). Edom and Philistia were Judah's neighbours. **58.** 'hast borne': '*shall bear*'.

484p **59-63 Re-establishment of Jerusalem**—Yahweh will make a new and eternal alliance with Jerusalem. Her sisters shall become her daughters. She shall never forget her past infidelity. **59.** '*I will deal with thee as thou hast dealt despising the oath*', etc. Chastisement comes first. **61.** Daughters are subject, sisters independent. 'not by thy covenant': not for observance of the covenant. The promise is surprising in this context and most probably a later addition.

485a **XVII 1-24 Fall of Sedecias; Advent of Messias**—Ezechiel announces in a parable the enthronement of Sedecias, his alliance with Egypt and revolt from Babylon, his deposition and deportation. He then contrasts with the perjured and fallen monarch the Messianic king and his universal reign.

b **1-10 The Parable**—Parables like symbols arouse interest. **3.** The eagle is Nabuchodonosor who deposed Joachin and enthroned Sedecias. 'long-bodied': '*with long pinions*'; 'marrow': '*top*'. **4.** Joachin is deported to Babylon. 'top': '*topmost*'; 'Canaan': '*trade*'. **5.** (After 'land'): '*And set it in tillage land beside many waters, (like) A willow he set it*'. Sedecias, comfortably enthroned, is compared to a well-watered willow, but, as a weak ruler, to a lowly vine. **6.** 'grew into': '*produced*'. **7.** The second eagle is the Pharaoh Hophra. **7b.** '*And behold the vine turned its roots towards him and shot forth its branches towards him that he might water it more than (it was watered in) the bed where it was planted*'. **8.** Sedecias' alliance with Egypt was inexcusable. **9.** The consequence of revolt. After 'fruit': '*that all its branches which it shot forth may wither*'. **10.** 'furrows': '*bed*'.

c **11-21 The Interpretation**—The parable narrates the sin and punishment of Sedecias. By violating his oath of allegiance he offended Yahweh whom he had invoked in making it and broke faith with Nabuchodonosor. **12-14.** The future tenses in DV should be past. 'observe it': '*stand*'. **16.** Sedecias died in Babylon. **17.** *Cf.* 9. 'Pharaoh': '*he*' (Nabuchodonosor). **18-19.** The perjury of Sedecias is an offence against Yahweh. **20.** *Judge* is execute the sentence given at Riblah.

d **22-24 The Messianic King**—'*Thus saith the Lord Yahweh: I, myself, will take from the top of the cedar, From its loftiest branches I will crop off a tender twig. I will plant it on a mountain high and elevated. On a lofty mountain of Israel will I plant it. It shall shoot forth branches and bear fruit. It shall become a magnificent cedar. All birds shall dwell beneath it, All winged things in the shade of its branches shall dwell. All the trees of the field shall know that I am Yahweh, That I have brought low a high tree and exalted a low tree, That I have made a green tree wither and a dry tree flourish*'. The Messianic king is a sprout of the Davidic tree, dried up when he appears; *cf.* Is 11:1. He becomes, not a vine like Sedecias, but a magnificent cedar. His kingdom is universal. All nations find shelter therein. All kings recognize its divine origin. *Cf.* the Gospel parable of the Mustard Seed. This promise is appropriate to, and even suggested by, the context.

e **XVIII 1-32 Personal Responsibility**—Ezechiel combats the belief that children are punished for the sins of their parents. Each individual is responsible only for his own sins. Moreover if the just man sin or the sinner be converted, neither the good deeds of the former nor the evil deeds of the latter will be remembered. Finally he invites all to a true repentance assuring them of the Mercy of Yahweh, more ready to pardon than to punish. This teaching on personal responsibility and divine mercy was particularly necessary when over-emphasis on national responsibility and divine justice led to despair. It was more a reminder than an innovation. In the oldest parts of the Bible individuals are rewarded and punished for their own good and evil deeds.

f **1-4.** The Proverb. **2.** '*Why do you repeat this proverb among the children* [LXX, 'land' MT] *of Israel: The fathers have eaten sour grapes and the teeth of the children*

are set on edge?' The proverb attributes injustice to **48** Yahweh and claims innocence for the speakers.

5-9. The just man. The precepts mentioned sum- **g** marize important obligations: purity of worship, sexual purity, social justice and charity. Whoever observes them is just and will be saved from premature death. **6.** The mountains are the high places. **7.** Omit 'to the debtor'. **8.** 'increase': 'interest'. Interest could be exacted from a foreigner but not from an Israelite. **9.** 'truth': '*them*' (LXX).

10-13. The wicked son of a just father. Omit **11a**. **h** The list of sins refers not to omissions but to *these things* (10) which the sinner does. The son dies for his sins and is not saved by his father's justice.

14-20. The just son of a wicked father. This is the **i** case instanced in the proverb. **17.** 'from (injuring) the poor': '*from iniquity*'. **18.** Omit 'to his brother'. **19.** Refutation of the proverb.

21-29. The Convert and the Pervert. God's Mercy **j** to the repentant sinner and the need of perseverance in the practice of justice complete the teaching. God is more pleased to pardon than to punish but repentance is necessary for pardon and no sinner is safe from chastisement. **21.** 'Do penance for' is lit. *turn away from*. **24.** Omit 'shall he live' (LXX). 'prevarication': '*infidelity*'. **26.** Omit 'therein' (LXX). **27.** Omit 'considereth' (LXX). **28.** '*Is not my way*', etc.

30-32. Invitation to Repentance. **30b.** '*Be con-* **k** *verted and turn yourselves from all your transgressions that they may not be to you a stumbling-block of iniquity*'. **32.** For 'him that dieth' many read *the sinner* as in 23.

XIX 1-14 Elegy on the Princes of Judah—This elegy **l** aptly concludes the second cycle of prophecies. It is a poetical composition in *qînāh* or elegiac metre. Each verse has five beats, three in the first and two in the second member. It is also a parable. Two princes are represented as young lions, sons of a lioness, and a third as a vine-branch. Sedecias is the vine branch as in ch 17. The lions, appointed by the lioness, are Joachaz deported to Egypt and Joachin deported to Babylon. Joakim is not mentioned because he died in Jerusalem, 4 Kg 24:5. The view that the second lion represents Sedecias is based on the false supposition that the lioness is Amital, wife of Josias and mother of Joachaz and Sedecias. But the lioness in the midst of lions is not the queen-mother but Judah in the midst of foreign nations. The lioness moreover appoints the second king. Sedecias was appointed by Nabuchodonosor. Finally the second monarch is deposed before the third is mentioned.

1-4 Joachaz—**1.** 'princes' (MT): '*prince*' (LXX). **m** *Thy mother*, 2, 10, shows that the whole poem is addressed to Sedecias. **2-3.** '*What a lioness was thy mother Among the lions! She couched in the midst of the lions, Reared her cubs. She reared one of her cubs Who became a young lion; He learned to rend his prey, He devoured men*'. The detailed description is verified in the lion rather than in the prince. A parable is not an allegory. **4.** '*They summoned nations against him, He was caught in their pit, And they led him in hooks To the land of Egypt*'. Joachaz after a three months' reign was deported by Nechao to Egypt where he died. The lion figure is probably derived from Gen 49:9.

5-9 Joachin—**5.** '*When she saw that she waited And* **n** *hoped in vain, She took another of her cubs And made him a lion*'. Joachin, son of Joakim, like Joachaz was appointed without foreign interference. After a three months' reign he was deported to Babylon where records of his captivity have been discovered in the royal palace; see A. Bea, S.J., in Bi 23 (1942) 78-82. **6-7.** '*He walked among the lions, He became a young lion. He learned to rend his prey, He devoured men, He knew their widows (?), He laid waste their cities, He terrified the land and its fulness, With the noise of his roaring*'. For 'he knew their widows' (MT) 'he preyed in their dens' is suggested. **8-9.** '*The nations round about laid snares for him, They spread out their nets, He was caught in their pit. They encaged him and brought him To the king of*

485n *Babylon, That his voice might be heard no more On the mountains of Israel'*. The nations are the vassals of Babylon.

o **10-14 Sedecias—10-11.** '*Thy mother was like a vine stock in a vineyard, Planted by waters. She was fruitful and rich in branches Owing to the many waters. A strong branch of hers became A ruler's sceptre. His stature dominated Amid the foliage. He was conspicuous by his height And the multitude of his shoots'*. The lion figure is abandoned because Israel is now a vassal state, Sedecias a creature of Nabuchodonosor. **12-13.** '*But she was uprooted in fury, Dashed to earth, And an east wind withered Her branches which were broken off, And her strong branch was dried up And consumed by fire. And now she is planted in the desert In a dry and thirsty land'*. The deposition of Sedecias and the exile are predicted. **14.** '*And a fire came forth from the branch And devoured its shoots'*. Sedecias is made responsible for the fire. Without shoots he can have no successor.

486a **XX-XXIV Third Cycle of Threats against Jerusalem and Judah.**
XX 1-44 Israel's Past and Present Sins and Future Restoration—In August 591 B.C. the elders of Tel-Abib again request Ezechiel to consult Yahweh for them. The prophet again assures them that Yahweh will not hear them or reply to them. He recalls to them instead the sins of Israel and the necessity of conversion.

b **1-4.** The date was about eleven months after the last given, ch 8. **3.** '*answer you*': '*be inquired of by you*'. **4.** '*Wilt thou judge them?*' or '*I will judge them*' (LXX). '*Judge*' means '*accuse*'.

c **5-9. Sins in Egypt. 5.** '*lifted up my hand*' means '*swore*'. '*appeared*': '*made myself known*'. **6.** '*Exuding milk and honey*': producing abundant and excellent food. '*excelleth amongst*': lit. jewel of. **8.** '*provoked*': '*rebelled against*'. **9.** Idol worship merited extirpation. Yahweh spared them that his name as an omnipotent protector might be honoured by the Gentiles.

d **10-17. Sins of the first generation in the desert. 11.** Observance of the law was recompensed by length of life as non-observance was punished by death. **12.** Observance of the Sabbath was particularly important in the exilic period when sacrifices and other ritual observances were impossible. **13.** '*provoked*': '*rebelled against*'. **14.** '*spared them*': '*acted*'. After '*nations*': '*in whose sight I brought them out*'.

e **18-26. Sins of the second generation in the desert.** Though warned they also sinned. Yahweh did not exterminate them for his name's sake. **25.** '*shall*': '*should*'. '*laws that were not good*' are possibly laws not good for them because by their fault they failed to observe them but more probably Canaanite observances which Yahweh gave them, let them take voluntarily. Yahweh's gift of Canaan exposed them to the seductions of Canaanite worship. Cf. 14:9. It would be contrary to the Holiness of Yahweh to impose laws not objectively good. **26.** '*And I polluted them by their own gifts when they caused to pass through the fire all their firstborn to terrify them and that they might know that I am Yahweh*'. God's purpose was to terrify them by the enormity of their crime. St Paul teaches similarly that God allowed sin to abound that man might realize his own weakness and seek divine aid.

f **27-29. Sins in Canaan. 27.** After '*blasphemed me*': '*by their grievous infidelity*'. **28.** Worship in the high places was more usually associated with Canaanite divinities and included licentious practices of Canaanite origin. **29.** The word *bāmāh* '*high place*' is here popularly derived from the verb *ba'* '*go in*', used of conjugal relations and suggesting infidelity to Yahweh. The philological derivation is unknown.

g **30-32. Sins in exile.** The worship of idols made the exiles unworthy of a hearing from Yahweh. **31.** Though human sacrifices were not unknown in Babylonia the reference to Moloch offerings here is surprising and may be an interpolation.

h **33-44. The Restoration.** Yahweh will reassemble his people from the nations among whom they are dispersed and judge them. The wicked shall perish **486h** and the good shall return to Palestine. **35.** '*of people*': '*of the nations*'. The Syro-Arabian desert seems indicated. **37.** '*And I will make you pass under the rod*', the shepherd's rod under which the sheep pass as they enter the fold at night. **39.** After '*Lord God*': '*Do away with* [LXX] *your idols. But after that you shall certainly hear me and you shall no longer profane my holy name by your offerings and your idols*'. **40.** After '*serve me*': '*There I shall accept them favourably and there I shall require your offerings*', etc. The promise here between the sins and their chastisement is unexpected and probably a later addition.

XX 45-XXI 32 (MT XXI:1-37) **The Sword of Yahweh i against Jerusalem and Ammon**—Ezechiel first sees a fire consuming all the trees of Judah, symbol of the sword of Yahweh massacring all the inhabitants. He then describes in verse the sword and its work of destruction. In the third scene Nabuchodonosor (the sword) at the cross-roads consults his oracles to determine whether he shall first assail Jerusalem or Rabbath-Ammon. Jerusalem is designated. Finally Ammon's subsequent chastisement is predicted. This final invasion of Judah began in winter 589 B.C.

45-XXI 7 (MT XXI:1-12) **The Fire and the Sword— j** The fire is a figure, the sword its interpretation. **46.** '*Drop (thy word) on the south*'. **47.** As the forest fire spares no tree, so Nabuchodonosor will spare no person. **XXI:3.** The just perish with the wicked. This prophecy of indiscriminate slaughter by a human agent does not contradict the prophet's teaching of man's individual responsibility before God. Nabuchodonosor neither could nor would discriminate between the just and the unjust. **7.** After '*faint*': '*And all knees shall be weak as water*'.

XXI 8-17 (MT 13-22) **The Song of the Sword**—The **k** text is sometimes uncertain. **9b-10.** '*A sword, a sword is sharpened and polished. It is sharpened to slay; it is polished to flash lightning. Or shall we rejoice? The sceptre of my son despises all wood*'. Wood or tree means sceptre or king. Sedecias despises all kings even Nabuchodonosor. **11-12.** '*I have given it to a butcher* [MT, to be polished] *that he may take it in his hand. It is sharpened, it is polished to be put into the hand of a slayer. Cry and roar, Son of man, for it is (drawn) against my people, against all the princes of Israel; they are vowed to the sword with my people. Strike then thy thigh*'. Striking the thigh expresses grief, Jer 31:19. **13.** '*For what a trial if even the sceptre which despises is no longer! Oracle of the Lord Yahweh*'. The dethronement of Sedecias is predicted. **14-16.** '*But thou, Son of man, prophecy and clap thy hands, Let the sword be doubled, be tripled. It is a sword of slaughter, a sword of great slaughter which surrounds them, that hearts may melt and the overthrown be many. At all their gates I have set the threat* [?] *of the sword. It is made to flash lightning, to slay. Spread terror on the right, place thyself on the left wherever thy edge is destined*'. Clapping hands indicates approval, exultation. **17.** '*I also shall clap my hands, shall assuage my wrath. I, Yahweh, have spoken*'.

18-27 (MT 23-32) **Nabuchodonosor at the Crossroads l** —Ezechiel is ordered to represent graphically the two roads open to the invader. From Riblah on the Orontes they branch off, SW. to Jerusalem, SE. to Rabbath-Ammon. He sees Nabuchodonosor at Riblah directed by his oracles to march on Jerusalem. He marks the Jerusalem road with an arrow in his drawing. **19c.** After '*land*': '*And fashion a signal, at the beginning of the way to the city fashion it*'. The road to Jerusalem alone is marked for the sword of Yahweh. **21.** '*stood*': '*stands*'; '*highway*': '*crossroads*'. The diviners cast lots, conventionally interpreted, consulted the Teraphim, household gods, and inspected the livers of slain animals. **22.** '*In his right hand is the reply, Jerusalem*'. Omit '*to set battering rams*'. '*engines*': '*battering rams*'; '*lift up the voice in howling*': '*raise the war cry*'. **23.** The oracle, disbelieved by the citizens, is confirmed by the remembrance of their iniquity. **24.** '*remembered*': '*called*

486 l to (*God's*) mind' (by further sins). **25.** After 'come' : ' *When iniquity has reached its term* '. **26b.** Lit. ' *this not this* [indicating a change], *exalt the low and abase the high* '. **27.** ' *I will make her a ruin, a ruin, a ruin. Woe to her! She shall remain thus till he come* [the Messias, Gen 49:10], *to whom the right belongs and to whom I shall give it* '. She, according to some Jerusalem, is more probably the Davidic dynasty.

m 28-32 (MT 33-37) **Chastisement of Ammon**—**28c-29.** ' *A sword, a sword is drawn to slay, is polished to flash lightning, amid thy false visions and lying oracles, to put to the neck of profaners, malefactors, whose day has come, whose iniquity has reached its term* '. **30a.** ' *Restore it to its sheath* '. The chastisement is certain but deferred. According to Josephus (*Ant.* 10, 9, 7) the Chaldaeans devastated Ammon five years after Jerusalem's fall.

n XXII 1-31 The Crimes of Jerusalem—Ezechiel first enumerates the various crimes of the citizens. Jerusalem filled with fugitives during the siege is then compared to a melting-pot for base metals. Finally the sins of the various classes, princes, priests, high officials, prophets, common people, are recorded to show that all are guilty.

o 1-16 The City of Blood— Idolatry and bloodshed are the major sins of Jerusalem but many others are here mentioned. **2.** ' dost ' : ' *wilt* '. **3a.** ' *Make known to her . . . and say* '. ' this is ' : ' *Woe to* ' (LXX) ; ' shed-deth ' : ' *hath shed* '. **4.** The sense is : thou hast hastened the day of chastisement and lessened thy years of life. **6.** ' *The princes . . . every one according to his strength, were in thee* ', etc. **8.** ' thou ' : ' *they* ' (LXX). **10.** ' humbled ' : ' *done violence to* '. Omit ' the uncleanness of '. **11.** ' every one . . . father in law . . . brother ' : ' *one . . . another . . . another* '. **12.** ' thou ' : ' *they* ' ; ' increase ' : ' *interest* '. **13a.** ' *I shall put my hands on thy dishonest gain* ' (LXX). **14.** Clapping indicates approval. **16.** ' *And thou shalt be profaned* ' (MT). A slight correction gives : ' *I shall make thee my inheritance* ', an announcement of subsequent pardon.

p 17-22 The Melting-pot—Destruction of base metals is indicated, not testing or refining. **19.** ' I will gather you ' : the country people seeking shelter in the capital. **20.** ' take my rest ' : ' *lay you there* '. **21.** ' burn ' : ' *blow upon* '.

q 23-31 The Universal Corruption—All classes have sinned grievously. There is none to save the nation from destruction. **24.** ' unclean ' : ' *not wetted* ' (LXX), arid and unfruitful. **25a.** ' prophets ' (MT) : ' *princes* ' (LXX). The princes are the lions. The prophets appear later. ' catcheth ' : ' *teareth* ' ; ' souls ' : ' *men* ' : ' hire ' : ' *precious things* '. **27.** ' princes ' : ' *chiefs* '. High officials are meant. Omit ' and to destroy souls ' (LXX). **28.** The prophets have whitewashed concealed weaknesses by false prophecies of security. **29.** The people of the land are ordinary people. For ' by calumny ', ' without judgement ' (a double translation) read ' *wrongfully* '. **30.** There was no saviour like Moses to avert God's wrath.

r XXIII 1-49 Infidelity and Chastisement of Samaria and Jerusalem—Ezechiel develops here the comparison, ch 16, of Samaria and Jerusalem to two sisters espoused by Yahweh and unfaithful to him. The big sister, Samaria, has already suffered for her infidelity from her paramour Assyria. How inevitable then is the destruction of the far more unfaithful Jerusalem by her lover, Chaldaea !

s 1-4 Infidelity in Egypt—The sisters are accused of idol worship in Egypt. **4.** Modern philologists give both names the same meaning ' tent-woman ', Oholah ' tent of her ', Oholibah (with the *yod compaginis*) ' tent in her '. St Jerome rightly renders Oholibah ' my tent is in her ' and understands an allusion to the temple of Yahweh in Jerusalem. In inventing the names Ezechiel must have been influenced by contemporary usage rather than by archaic word formation. The parallel name of Jerusalem, *Hepṣibāh*, is interpreted ' my pleasure is in her ', Is 62:4. Elder and younger

should be big and little. ' I took them *as wives* ' ; **48** lit. they became mine.

5-10 Infidelity and Destruction of Samaria—She **t** became allied with Assyria under Jehu in 841 and more permanently under Menahem in 738. Foreign alliance introduced foreign worship. Revolt from Assyria and alliance with Egypt led to her destruction in 721. **6.** ' *Who were clothed in violet-dyed stuffs, governors and commanders, all beautiful youths* ', etc. **7.** ' uncleanness ' : ' *idols* '. **10.** ' *They uncovered her nakedness . . . she became a byword among women* '.

11-21 Infidelity of Jerusalem—Instead of taking warn- **u** ing from her sister's fate Jerusalem conducted herself still more shamefully in her relations with Assyrians, Babylonians and Egyptians. Achaz introduced the alliance with Assyria, Ezechias made an alliance with Egypt. Alliances with Egypt and Babylonia succeeded each other after the death of Josias. **12.** *Cf.* 6. **14.** ' colours ' : ' *vermilion* '. **15b-c.** ' *And with streaming turbans on their heads and all of them great warriors to look upon, representations of sons of Chaldaea, the land of their birth* '. ' Babel ' before ' Chaldaea ' is probably interpolated. **17.** ' *and her soul was alienated from them* '. **18a.** ' *And her fornications were revealed and her nakedness discovered* '. **19-21.** Jerusalem returns to the sin of her youth by alliance with Egypt.

22-35 Chastisement of Jerusalem—Babylon the para- **v** mour, formerly loved but now loathed, will be Yahweh's instrument in inflicting a most terrible and merciless chastisement. **22.** Omit ' all '. The lovers now loathed are the Babylonians. **23.** For ' nobles, kings, princes ' read *Peqod* (Puqudu) *Shoa'* (Shutu) *Qoa'* (Qutu), peoples east of the Tigris subject to Babylonia. **24.** ' well appointed ' : ' *from the north* ' (LXX). ' breastplate ' : ' *shield* '. Judgements are laws. **26.** Instruments of thy glory are thy jewels. **28.** ' glutted with ' : ' *alienated from* '. **29.** ' full of disgrace ' : ' *bare* ' ; ' disgrace ' : ' *nakedness* '. **32.** The text seems disordered. **33.** ' grief and sadness ' : ' *horror and terror* '. **33a.** ' *And thou shalt drink it and empty it and drain it to the dregs* ' (slightly corrected).

36-49 Recapitulation of the Sin and Punishment of w the Sisters—Some additional sins are mentioned, in particular human sacrifices. **36.** ' dost ' : ' *wilt* '. ' Declare ' is an imperative. **37.** ' offered ' : ' *made pass through the fire* '. **38.** Omit ' on the same day ' (LXX). **39.** ' and ' : ' *they* '. **40.** The strangers to whom a messenger was sent are the Egyptians, Assyrians and Chaldaeans with whom the Israelites sought alliances. **41.** ' thee ' : ' *it* ', the bed. **42.** The text and sense are uncertain. There is question apparently of the reception of the foreigners. **43.** Text is uncertain. Vg renders literally. **45.** ' *But just men will judge them* '. The Chaldaeans are just as instruments of divine justice. **46.** ' multitude ' : ' *assembly* ', a judicial tribunal ; ' tumult ' : ' *ill-treatment* '. **47.** ' *let them kill . . . let them burn* '. **48.** ' Women ' means ' nations '.

XXIV 1-27 Announcement of the Siege and Capture x of Jerusalem—Two symbolic actions indicate the siege. The cauldron previously mentioned is filled with choice meats to be cooked by fire. The choice meats are the principal citizens. Fire is next applied to the empty cauldron to remove the rust with which it is defiled. Complete destruction is indicated. Ezechiel's wife dies suddenly on the day the siege begins. Omission of the usual mourning rites represents the attitude of the exiles on hearing of the city's fall.

1-8 The Full Cauldron—**1.** The date of the beginning **y** of the siege must have been revealed to Ezechiel. It was the 10th of Tebet (Dec.–Jan.) in the 9th year of Sedecias 589–588. Later the Jews celebrated the anniversary by a solemn fast, Zach 8:19. **4.** After ' shoulder ' : ' *fill it with choice bones* '. **5.** Wood, not bones (MT), was piled under the cauldron. **5b.** ' *Boil its pieces of meat and let the bones within it be well cooked* '. **6.** Not the rust but the meat and bones are to be cast out without discrimination since all are for destruction. **7.** There was an ancient belief that blood while exposed

6y called for vengeance on the shedder. **8.** Yahweh is again the author of what he lets happen.

z **9-14 The Empty Cauldron**—The cauldron or the city defies all attempts at purification and must be entirely destroyed. **10.** The text is in disorder. The meat was cooked and the cauldron emptied in 5–6. Here again : ' *Pile up the wood, light the fire, cook well the meat,* (prepare the sauce) *let the bones be burned*'. Similarly the reference to the rust in 6*a* is out of place. It belongs to the burning of the empty cauldron. Heinisch reads 6*a* after 12 and 6*b* after 10*a*. Thus 3–5 and 7-8 refer to the first symbol, 6 and 9-13 to the second. **12.** Omit 'great pains have been taken ', dittography. Attach **13***a*. ' *owing to the defilement of thy lewdness* ' to 12.

aa **15-27 Unlamented Death of Ezechiel's Wife**—By his attitude on the death of his wife, Ezechiel becomes a sign to the exiles. As he is forbidden to lament her death so they are forbidden to lament the destruction of Jerusalem. **17.** MT transposes ' dead ' and ' mourning ' and reads ' men ' for *mourners*. The mourning rites prohibited were baring the head and the feet, veiling the lower part of the face, the mourning meal. **18***a*. ' *And thou shalt speak* ' (LXX), a command executed in 18*c*. **21.** Jerusalem is lit. ' *the glory of your might, the desire of your eyes, the object of your soul's compassion* '. The text is in disorder. **22-23**, in which the prophet speaks, interrupt the speech of Yahweh 21 and 24. **24.** Omit ' of things to come '. **26-27.** The restrictions imposed on Ezechiel's prophetic ministry shall cease when a fugitive from Jerusalem announces the city's fall ; *cf.* 33:21 f.

7a **XXV-XXXII Prophecies against Gentile Nations.**
XXV 1-17 Prophecies against Ammon, Moab, Edom, and Philistia—Like Isaias and Jeremias Ezechiel also predicts God's judgement on the Gentile Nations : Ammonites, Moabites, Edomites, Philistines, Phoenicians, Egyptians. He does not denounce their idol worship but their malevolent attitude towards Yahweh's sanctuary and Yahweh's people, because this hostility is the chief obstacle to a Messianic restoration.

b **1-7 Ammon**—The Ammonites will disappear and Ammon will be a camping-ground for desert dwellers, her eastern neighbours. **2.** ' of them ' : ' *against them* '. **3.** The sin of Ammon is hostility to the temple, the land and the people of Yahweh. **4.** ' inheritance ' : ' *possession* ' ; ' sheepcotes ' : ' *encampments* ', lit. the stone rings surrounding the tents. **5.** ' stable ' : ' *pasturage* ' ; ' children ' : ' *cities* '. **7.** ' people ' : ' *peoples* '.

c **8-11 Moab**—The Moabites will share the fate of the Ammonites. **8.** Omit Seir. **9.** The text is corrupt, but the sense is clear. All Moab will be exposed to invasion. The shoulder is the mountain side protecting on the north Moab and its important cities : Beth-jesimoth (Suwēme at NE. end of Dead Sea), Baal-meon (Ma'īn, S. of Suwēme) and Kiriathaim (Kureiyāt, S. of Baal-meon). **10***b*. ' of the children of Ammon ' : ' *of it* '.

d **12-14 Edom**—The judgement on Edom will be executed by the Jews themselves who subjected the Edomites in the Maccabean period. **13.** ' the south ' : ' *Teman* ', an Edomite city,' perhaps Odroḥ. Dedan is El-'Olah.

e **15-17 Philistia**—God himself will chastise the Philistines. **15.** ' with all their mind ' : ' *with despite of soul* '. After ' destroying ': ' *with eternal* [implacable] *enmity* '. **16.** ' killers ' : ' *Cretans* '. Ezechiel plays on the words *kārat* ' cut off ' and *kerētî* ' Cretan ' equivalent to Philistine.

f **XXVI 1-21 First Prophecy against Tyre : Sin and Punishment of Tyre**—Tyre was the richest and most powerful of the Phoenician cities. It was built on an island nearly half a mile from the shore and was thus impregnable as long as the Tyrians retained command of the sea. It had also dependent cities and considerable territory on the mainland as well as colonies and trading posts in the islands and on the coasts of the

Mediterranean. Its general policy, dictated by com- **487f** mercial interests, was submission and payment of tribute to the imperial invaders of Palestine and friendly relations with its neighbours. Though the Tyrians took part with Sedecias in his revolt against Nabuchodonosor they nevertheless rejoiced at the fall of Jerusalem, a commercial rival whose trade they hoped to inherit. Ezechiel predicts the complete ruin of Tyre and the Babylonian siege of Tyre. The ruin of Tyre is always attributed to Yahweh without mention of human agents. It was finally accomplished by the Saracens in A.D. 1291. Josephus informs us (*C. Ap.* 1, 21) that Nabuchodonosor besieged Tyre for 13 years, *c* 586–574 B.C. We have no direct information on the outcome of this siege. The general verdict of historians that it was unsuccessful, seems to be confirmed by Ezechiel himself in a later prophecy, 29:18. Nabuchodonosor had no fleet and could not assault the island city or intercept its supplies. We must therefore regard the prophet's description of the siege as largely conventional. He magnifies the part played by horses and chariots and makes no reference to the special measures needed for the capture of an island city. A similar use of conventional language in eschatological prophecies is generally recognized.

1-6 Sin and Chastisement—**1.** The date is spring 586. **g** The omitted month must be the 11th or 12th ; *cf.* 33:21. **2.** Tyre rejoices at Jerusalem's fall. ' *Aha, she is shattered, The gate of the peoples. To me hath been turned The fulness of her that was laid waste.* **3.** ' to thee ' : ' *against thee* '. **4.** Omit ' like '. Tyre (Heb. *ṣôr* ; *ṣûr*, means ' rock ') shall become *bare rock*. **6.** The daughters are the cities on the mainland.

7-14 Nabuchodonosor's Siege of Tyre—The long siege **h** is the initial stage of Tyre's chastisement. **7.** ' horsemen and *an assembly of many peoples* '. **8.** The cities on the mainland are first reduced. Wall, mound, testudo or shield formation are ordinary features of a siege. **9.** ' engines of war and ' : ' *the shock of* '. **10.** ' horsemen and *chariot-wheels when he enters thy gates as a conquered city is entered* '. **11***c*. ' *And thy strong pillars he shall lay low* '. **12.** ' they ' : ' *he* '. **13.** ' multitude ' : ' *noise* '. Note the change of subject.

15-18 Effect on Tyre's Neighbours—**15.** They tremble **i** at the news of Tyre's fall. **16.** They exhibit the usual signs of mourning. ' astonishment ' : ' *mourning garb* '. ' ground and *shall tremble every instant and be astonished at thee* '. **17-18.** They chant a lament : ' *How hast thou disappeared from the seas, Famous city ! That ruled over the sea, She and her inhabitants, That spread terror Over all the continent. Now the coasts tremble In the day of thy fall, And the islands in the sea are terrified At thy end* '.

19-21 Oracle on Tyre—**20.** ' *I shall bring thee down to* **j** *those who have gone down to the pit, the men of yore, and set thee in the underworld, the primordial solitudes . . . that thou be no more inhabited, no more subsist in the land of the living* '. **21.** ' to nothing ' : ' *to a terrible end* '.

XXVII 1-36 Second Prophecy against Tyre : Lament **k** **for Tyre**—The city is here likened to a magnificent ship whose construction and destruction are described in elegiac verse. Between the poetic sections is a detailed description in prose of the commerce of Tyre, probably a later addition.

1-9*a* **The Building of the Ship**—**3.** ' mart ' : ' *trafficker* '. **l** The elegy begins **3***c* : ' *Tyre thou hast said : I am a ship, Perfect in beauty.* ' Ship ' (*'oniyāh*) is omitted by haplography after *'ānî*. The comparison suggests insular site and sea trade. **4.** ' *In the heart of the sea thy domain ; thy builders Have made thee perfect in beauty.* **5.** *From the cypresses of Sanir they built All thy planks. The cedars of Lebanon they took To make thee a mast* '. Sanir is Mt Hermon. **6.** ' *From the highest oaks of Bashan They made thy oars. Thy deck they made of ivory inlaid in pine wood From the coasts of Kittim* '. Bashan is northern Transjordan. Kittim, originally the inhabitants of Citium, is by extension Cyprus. The red pine of Cyprus was much used in ship-building. **7.** ' *Of fine linen with embroidered work from Egypt Was thy sail, Violet and purple from the coasts of Elisha Was thy awning* '. ' To be thy

487 l ensign' (after 'sail') is excluded by the metre and by the fact that Egyptian and Phoenician ships had no ensign. Egyptian linen *šēš* was superior to the Syrian byssus. Elisha is most probably Alashiya, usually identified with Cyprus. **8-9a.** ' *The princes* [LXX] *of Sidon and Arwad Were thy rowers, The sages of Simirra were in thee, They were thy pilots, The ancients of Gebal were in thee, They were thy caulkers*'. Simirra is a conjectural emendation of MT Tyre. Phoenician cities : Arwad and Simirra in the north, Gebal (Byblos) in the centre, Sidon in the south, put their skilled men at Tyre's disposal.

m 9b-25a Commerce of Tyre—9b. ' thy factors' : *in thee to exchange thy wares*'. **10.** Nations that gave Tyre military aid are first mentioned, Lud are not Lydians but an African people. Put (DV 'Lybians') is Punt on the southern shores of the Red Sea. **11.** for *gammādîm* (Vg Pygmaei ?) LXX reads *šōmerîm* ' watchmen ' (in thy towers). ' quivers' : ' shields'. **12-24.** The list of peoples is mainly geographical : Tarshish in the far west—Ionia, Tubal, Mosoch in Asia Minor—Thogorma in Armenia—Rhodes, etc. in the Greek Archipelago—Edom, Judah, Israel, Damascus—Uzal, Dedan, Kedar, Saba, Ra'ma, in Arabia—Harran, Kanneh (Calne ?), Eden (Bit-Adini), Assur in Mesopotamia—Media in the far east. **12.** Tarshish supplied silver, iron, tin, lead. **13.** Ionia, Tubal,
n Mosoch gave slaves and bronze vessels. **14.** Thogorma sent draught horses, war horses and mules. **15.** Rhodes (LXX) and the Archipelago provided horns of ivory and ebony, evidently as middlemen. **16.** Edom (LXX) supplied carbuncles, purple, brocade, fine linen, corals and rubies. **17.** Judah and Israel gave wheat, honey, oil, balm and probably tragacanth gum and wax. **18.** Damascus sent wine of Helbon (modern Khelbūn) and wool of Sokhar (unknown). **19.** Omit Dan and Greece and interpret ' Mosel' as = *from Uzal* usually identified with San'a in Yemen. Its products were wrought iron, cassia and calamus. **20.** Dedan (el-'Ola) supplied saddle-cloths. **21.** Arabia and Kedar sent lambs, rams and he-goats. **22.** Saba and Ra'ma gave the choicest spices, gold and precious stones. **23.** Saba is a textual corruption. Render ' Chalmed ' as ' *all the Medes*'. **24.** Costly garments, violet and embroidered robes, carpets of many colours, strong and well-twisted cords were Mesopotamian wares. **25a.** ' *The ships of Tarshish carried thy wares*'.

o 25b-36 Wreck of the Ship—25b. ' *Thou didst fill thyself and wert heavy-laden In the midst of the sea*. **26.** ' south ' : ' *east*'. **27.** Cargo and crew : riches, wares, sailors, pilots, caulkers, traders, warriors, sink with the ship. **28.** ' *At the loud cry of thy pilots The coasts* [?] *tremble*'. **29-32.** Other crews leave their ships, make mourning, and intone a lament for Tyre. **34.** ' *Now thou art wrecked on the sea In the midst of the waters. Thy wares and all thy multitude Have perished with thee*'. **35.** The Mediterranean peoples are stupefied, their kings are terrified. **36.** Rival trading nations rejoice. Metre requires ' *clap their hands*' before ' *and hiss at thee*'.

p XXVIII 1-26 Third Prophecy against Tyre : Sin and Chastisement of the Prince of Tyre—The prince of Tyre is here regarded less as an individual than as an embodiment of the state ; *cf.* Is 14:4-23. The first part of the elegy, **1-10**, is more realistic and better preserved than the second, **11-19**, in which the metre is scarcely recognizable. A short oracle on Sidon, **20-23**, and a prediction of the restoration of Judah, **24-26**, complete the chapter.

q 1-10 Pride and Humiliation of the Prince—2. In his pride he thought himself a god and his island capital the throne of a god. **3.** ' *Wert thou not wiser than Daniel ?* ' ; *cf.* 14:14. ' *None of all the sages equalled thee*'. **4a.** ' *By thy wisdom and thy understanding thou hast gotten thee riches*'. **5.** Wisdom in trading enterprises provided the riches on which his pride is based. **7.** ' strongest ' : ' *most ferocious*'. **8.** ' *They shall bring thee down into the pit, thou shalt die the death of the slain in the midst of the*

sea'. **9.** His death will show that he is a man. **10. 48'** ' Uncircumcised ' : godless. Death without funeral rites was a great calamity.

11-19 Elegy on the Prince—He is fancifully invested **r** with prerogatives denied to mortals. **12.** He is a *perfect seal-ring* on God's hand, exercising divine authority. ' Full of wisdom ' is an unmetrical addition. **13.** ' *In Eden, God's garden, thou wert, All precious stones was thy garment*'. He is Adam before the fall. The list of precious stones, recalling Ex 28:17-20, is scarcely authentic. **14.** ' *In the day of thy creation with the Cherubim I placed thee. Thou wert on the mountain of the gods, thou walkedst in the midst of stones of fire*' (LXX). The prince is in paradise with the Cherubim, its guardians, and on the mountain in the north where the gods assemble ; *cf.* Is 14:13. Ezechiel poetically uses pagan mythology in his imaginative description. The exact symbolism of the stones of fire is unknown. **15.** The prince's state of perfection endured until he sinned. **16.** Then God expelled (lit. profaned) him from the mountain of the gods and the guardian Cherub banished him from the midst of the stones of fire. **17.** Beauty produced pride and pride the loss of wisdom, the folly of sin. **18.** ' sanctuaries ' : ' holiness ' ; ' will bring ' : ' brought ' ; ' will make ' : ' made '.

20-26. The chastisement of Sidon, mother city of the **s** Phoenicians, by pestilence and the sword is briefly predicted. The removal of Israel's enemies is the prelude to the Restoration. **24.** ' stumbling-block of bitterness ' : ' *pricking brier*'. **25.** God will manifest his sanctity to the Gentiles by restoring Israel. This section seems to be an afterthought.

**XXIX 1-16 First Prophecy against Egypt : Ruin and 48'
Restoration**—The prophecy is dated the 12th of Tebet (Dec.–Jan.) 588-587. The pride of the Pharaoh, who is compared to a sea-monster, shall be humbled. Egypt, a weak reed to Israel, shall be devastated and restored, but not to her former greatness.
1-5 The Sea-Monster—*Cf.* Is 27:1. **2b.** ' of ' : **b** ' *against*'. **3c.** ' *The rivers are mine. I made them*' (LXX). The sea-monster, depicted as a crocodile, will be removed from his natural element and cast into the desert, the prey of birds and beasts. **4.** ' bridle ' : ' *hooks*'. **5.** ' gathered together ' : ' *buried*'.

6-12 The Weak Reed—Egypt is denounced as a weak **c** and unstable ally of Israel. **6.** ' Staff ' : support. **7.** ' shoulder ' : ' *hand*' (LXX). **9c.** The Pharaohs claimed divinity. **10.** (After ' sword ') : ' *from Migdol to Syene*', from N. to S. This Migdol was a fort on the NE. boundary. Syene : modern Assuan. **12.** Forty years, not understood strictly, was also the period of Judah's dispersion.

13-16 The Restoration—Egypt shall be restored but **d** not to her former greatness. **14.** ' *I shall change the lot of Egypt and bring them back to the land of Patros*' (Upper Egypt). **16.** The Egyptians will no longer deceive the Israelites by an alliance but will remind them of their iniquity when they turned after them. A weak neighbour is no obstacle to the Messianic restoration.

17-21 Second Prophecy against Egypt : Conquest of e Nabuchodonosor—This is the latest of the dated prophecies, March 571. Nabuchodonosor, Yahweh's servant, is given the land of Egypt as the payment of his unrequited labours in the long and arduous siege of Tyre. The riches of Tyre which he failed to capture will be compensated by the riches of Egypt. **19.** ' multitude ' : ' riches '. **20.** ' Horn ' : strength. The Babylonian conquest of Egypt in 568 B.C. made his fellow-exiles more ready to accept Ezechiel's teaching.

XXX 1-19 Third Prophecy against Egypt : The Day f of Yahweh—This undated prophecy depicts the fate of Egypt on the day when all the nations are judged ; *cf.* Is ch 13. **3.** The time (of the nations) is the day of judgement. **4.** The wounded are those *hors de combat*, whether dead or wounded. ' multitude ' : ' riches '. The foundations are the neighbouring nations who fought in Egypt's armies. **5.** On Put and Lud *cf.* 27:10.

8f Chub is unknown, probably a scribal error. Omit (LXX) ' of the land ' and ' with them '. ' Children of the covenant ' : allies. **6.** ' from Migdol to Syene ' ; cf. 29:10. **7.** ' they ' : ' she ' (LXX). **9.** ' go forth from *me in all haste to trouble the Ethiopians in their security* '. The day of Egypt is the day of her downfall. **11.** ' strongest ' : ' *most ferocious* '. **13.** ' *I will destroy the mighty from Memphis and the princes from the land of Egypt* ' (LXX). **14.** Patros is Upper Egypt ; Tanis (so MT ; DV Taphnis) is in the northern Delta and Thebes in Upper Egypt. **15.** Pelusium was on the north-eastern boundary, Memphis (LXX) south of Cairo. **16.** (After ' Egypt ') : ' *Syene* [LXX] *shall tremble in anguish, Thebes shall be conquered* '. The text which follows is corrupt. **17.** ' they themselves ' : ' *the women* '. Heliopolis (LXX) is south, Bubastes north, of Cairo. **18.** Taphnes was in the northern Delta.

g **20-26 Fourth Prophecy against Egypt : Pharaoh's Arm is Broken**—This prophecy is dated 7th Nisan 587. Egypt will diminish, Babylonia will increase, in might. **21b.** ' *And behold it has not been bound for healing by the application of bandages* '. **22.** (After ' pieces ') : ' *his arms* '. Omit ' which is already broken '. **24.** (After ' Pharaoh ') : ' *so that he shall groan, as mortally wounded groan, before him* ' (Nabuchodonosor).

h **XXXI 1-18 Fifth Prophecy against Egypt : The Cedar is Felled**—The prophecy is dated May 587. Egypt is compared to a magnificent cedar now laid low.

1-9 Beauty of the Cedar—2b-3. ' *To whom wert thou like in thy greatness ? Behold a cedar in Lebanon, Fair in its branches, Lofty in stature, And among the clouds Was its summit* '. Cedar, not Assyria, is the answer to **2b.** Omit ' with thick leaves ' (LXX) ; ' thick boughs ' : ' *clouds* '. **4.** ' *Waters (from above) made him grow, The abyss (beneath) made him increase in height, Making his rivers flow Around the place where he was planted And sending his rivulets To all the trees of the country* '. The ancients thought that springs came from the waters beneath the earth. The trees are symbolical of the neighbouring nations. **5.** Omit ' And his branches were multiplied ' (LXX). ' elevated ' : ' *lengthened* '. **6.** Omit ' when he had spread forth his shadow '. **8.** There is an element of hyperbole in the comparison. Babylonia and Assyria (at an earlier date) were more powerful than Egypt. ' fir-trees ' : ' *cypresses* '. **9.** ' beautiful *by the multitude of his* branches '. ' pleasure ' : ' *Eden* '.

i **10-14 The Felling of the Cedar—10.** ' green and thick ' : ' *into the cloud* '. Pride is punished. **11b** is corrupt. **12.** Insert ' *on the mountains and* ' after ' fall '. ' rocks ' : ' *ravines* '. **13-14.** His fall brings ruin to the nations who depended on him and perish with him. ' among the thick branches and leaves ' : ' *to the clouds* '.

j **15-18 Effects of the Fall**—Nature mourns and men tremble. **15.** Omit ' I covered ' (LXX). The sense is : *I made the abyss mourn over him by keeping back its streams. I darkened Lebanon for him and all the trees of the field languished over him*. **16.** While the nations on earth tremble at his fall those already in Sheol are consoled by his arrival. ' pleasure ' : ' *Eden* '. **17.** ' *They too had to go down with him to Sheol, to those slain by the sword, as well as their descendants who dwelt under his shade in the midst of the nations* '. The Pharaoh's association with those slain by the sword implies privation of burial rites.

k **XXXII 1-16 Sixth Prophecy against Egypt : Lament for Pharaoh**—The date is uncertain, probably spring 586. The Pharaoh, compared to a crocodile, represents all Egypt. The first part of the lament is in verse.

l **1-10 Destruction of the Sea-monster—1.** The date varies in MT and LXX, 11th or 12th month, 586 or 585. **2.** ' *The lion of the nations is come against thee, How hast thou disappeared ! Thou wert like a crocodile in the Nile And didst snort with thy nostrils, Thou troubledst the waters with thy feet And fouledst their streams* '. The

rendering of *2a* is a correction of MT : To the lion of **488l** the nations thou wert likened. But Pharaoh is likened to the crocodile, not to the lion Nabuchodonosor ; cf. 11. **3.** Omit ' multitude of many peoples ', a gloss excluded by the metre. **4.** The crocodile, removed from its natural element, becomes the prey of birds and beasts. **5.** ' hills ' : ' *valleys* '. Ezechiel passes easily from the figure, the crocodile, to the reality, the Egyptians. **6.** The text is confused and unmetrical. ' *I will water the earth with what flows from thee And the watercourses shall be filled with thy blood* '. **7b.** The cosmic disturbances associated with the day of judgement emphasize the greatness of the catastrophe. **8.** ' on thy land ' (MT) : ' *on the earth* ' (LXX). Omit ' when they wounded ', etc., a Vg addition. **9.** ' destruction ' : ' *prisoners* ' (LXX). **10.** ' *When I shall brandish my sword before them and they shall tremble at every moment* '.

11-16 Completeness of Egypt's Destruction—11. The **m** lion of the nations mentioned above is here identified. **12.** (After ' multitude ') : ' *the most ferocious of all nations* ' (in apposition with ' mighty '). **13.** ' that were beside ' ; ' *out of* '. **15.** The sense is : I will make the land, etc. that they may know. **16.** Daughters are here women, the customary mourners.

17-32 Seventh Prophecy against Egypt : Pharaoh in n the Underworld—The last prophecy against Egypt may be dated six weeks after the preceding one. LXX supplies *in the first month*. Pharaoh's descent to the Underworld and his condition there are described. The most noteworthy point is the distinction of two classes in Sheol. The heroes have a privileged position in the upper part of the underworld ; cf. Ps 48:15. The uncircumcised and those slain in battle are at a lower level in the *bôr* or pit. With these are associated the Egyptians and other war-like nations, oppressors of weaker peoples. Israel is not mentioned.

17-21 Pharaoh descends to Sheol—18. ' *I have cast* **o** *her down* '. **19** should follow **21a** (LXX). **20b** is probably corrupt, lit. ' The sword is given. They have drawn her and all her multitudes ' (to Sheol). **21a-19a.** The most powerful of the heroes in Sheol shall say to him : ' *Whom didst thou surpass in beauty ? Go down and make thy bed with the uncircumcised* '. **21b.** ' *With his helpers he has gone down, he has made his bed amid the uncircumcised and those slain by the sword* '. Cf. Is 14:19.

22-32 Pharaoh's Associates in the Pit—22-23. *Assur* **p** *and his multitude* represent king and people. As oppressors they also are in the bottom of the pit. **24-25.** Elam's fate is similar. **26-27.** The Moschians and Tibarenians, always mentioned together, represent the northern nations of whom the Scythians had recently invaded the Near East. **27.** ' *And they lie not with the heroes that fell of old . . . but they have their guilt in their bones for they spread terror by their mighty deeds in their life time* '. **28.** Pharaoh is addressed. **29-30.** Edom, the princes of the north (Syrians ?) and the Sidonians (DV ' hunters ') complete the list. Pharaoh finds some consolation in his associates, oppressors like himself.

XXXIII-XLVIII Promises : Purification and Restora- 489a tion of Israel.

XXXIII 1-33 Conditions of Salvation—Ch 33 is an introduction to the third part of the book. It repeats and develops four instructions already given. The first and second treat of the prophet's functions and personal responsibility. The third and fourth are admonitions addressed respectively to the undeported Israelites in Palestine and to Ezechiel's companions in exile. The occasion of the prophecy was the arrival of a fugitive with the news of the capture of Jerusalem narrated in the third section.

1-9 The Prophet's Functions—The prophet is com- **b** pared to a watchman obliged to be on the lookout and to give warning of the enemy's approach ; cf. 3:16-21 ; 14:9-11. **2.** ' the nearest of them ' : ' *from among them* '. **3-5.** If the prophet gives due warning, the sinner is alone responsible. **6.** If the prophet fails to warn he also is responsible. **7.** ' when thou hearest . . . thou shalt warn them '. **8-9.** The conse-

615

489b quences to the prophet of warning and failing to warn are repeated.

c 10-20 Personal Responsibility—The chastisement of the nation for sins in which the exiles participated causes the latter to despair of pardon. Ezechiel reminds them of the justice and mercy of God who will not visit on them the sins of others and is always ready to pardon repentant sinners ; *cf.* 14:1–8 ; 18:1–32. **12.** Omit ' in his justice ' (LXX). MT has the unintelligible ' in it '. **13-16.** The just must persevere in his justice, the sinner must repent and repair the wrong he has done. **17-20.** God's ways are just and forbid despair. Repentance of evil and perseverance in good will bring salvation.

d 21-29 Admonition to the Undeported Israelites—Ezechiel, informed of the fall of Jerusalem, receives at the same time full liberty of speech in preaching to the people. He rejects the claims of the undeported Israelites to the possession of Palestine. **21.** Correct ' twelfth ' (MT) and ' tenth ' (LXX) to *eleventh* year. The news reached the exiles about six months after the city's fall. **22.** Omit ' and he opened my mouth ', dittography. Ezechiel was in ecstasy from the evening to the following morning when the fugitive visited him as already announced, 24:26. The undeported Israelites argue that Abraham was one, they his descendants are many and being better able to populate and utilize the land have a stronger claim to it. Ezechiel replies that as sinners they are doomed to destruction. Many of them must have suffered in a subsequent deportation, 582 B.C., mentioned in Jer 52:30. **25.** ' uncleannesses ' : ' *your idols* '. **26.** ' *You stood on your swords* ' : you regarded might as right. **27.** The ruinous places are dilapidated towns as opposed to open country, mountain tops, caves.

e 30-33. Ezechiel's fellow-exiles are reproached by Yahweh for their levity in not heeding his words and carrying out his instructions. Omit ' my people ' (LXX). ' *for lies are in their mouth* ', reading *kᵉzābîm* for *ʿᵃgābîm*. **32a.** ' *Behold thou art to them as a troubadour* [*šār* for MT *šîr*] *who has a fine voice and plays well on the harp* '. **33.** Their eyes will be opened in the day of their chastisement.

f XXXIV 1-31 The Bad Shepherds replaced by a New David—In this prophecy Yahweh compares Israel to a flock of sheep, neglected, preyed on and dispersed by bad shepherds. He intends to purify them, to restore them to their old pasturage where they shall find abundant nourishment and where a single shepherd, called David and Servant of Yahweh, shall rule them in peace and holiness ; *cf.* Jer 23:1–8.

g 1-10 The Bad Shepherds—**3.** The shepherds took full remuneration for duties which they did not perform. **4.** They did not assist the weak, sick, wounded and strayed who needed their ministrations, and the strong (LXX) with cruelty they trod under foot. **5.** Omit ' and were scattered '. **8.** The beasts of the field represent the foreign nations. **10.** The shepherds will be called to account and deprived of their office.

h 11-16 Yahweh Shepherd of his Flock—The restoration is predicted. **11.** ' visit ' : ' *look for* '. **12.** As a shepherd reunites his scattered sheep, so shall Yahweh reunite his scattered people. **13.** ' habitations ' : ' *inhabited regions* '. **16.** Yahweh will do all that the bad shepherds failed to do. Omit ' fat ' (LXX).

i 17-22 Judgement and Purification—**17.** The Heb. word for flock includes goats with sheep. Rams and he-goats particularly indicate the ruling classes inclined to egoism. The stronger animals after satisfying themselves trample the pastures and foul the waters. ' *I will judge between sheep and sheep, between rams and he-goats* ' implies the removal of disturbers from the flock. **20.** The fat are the oppressors, the lean the oppressed.

j 23-31 The Messias and his Reign—The Messianic kingdom is often represented as a revival of David's kingdom. The Messias is a new David, servant of Yahweh. His reign will be prosperous and peaceful. The new covenant is a covenant of peace. **23.** Omit

the second ' he shall feed them '. **25.** LXX omits **48** ' secure ' and MT refers ' in security ' to ' dwell '. **26a.** The text seems corrupt. LXX reads : I will set them around my mountains. **29.** LXX reads *šālôm*, MT *šēm* (DV ' renown '). ' a bud of renown ' : ' *a perfect plantation* '. Great fertility is indicated. **30.** Omit ' with them ' (LXX). **31.** ' *You are my sheep, the sheep of my pasturage and I am Yahweh your God* '. ' Men ' is a gloss.

XXXV 1-15 Devastation of Edom—The Messianic **k** restoration is depicted by the prophets as the re-establishment of Israel in all her ancient territory. Edom had occupied a considerable part of Judah after the fall of Jerusalem and aspired to the possession of all Israel. Their chastisement, already predicted, 25:12–14, is again announced as an integral part of the programme of the restoration. **2.** Seir is a mountain range in Edom. **3-4.** Edom will be entirely laid waste. **5.** Edom's sin is perpetual enmity to Judah, manifested particularly in the recent calamity by either slaying fugitives or delivering them to the Chaldaeans, Abd 14. **6.** (After ' God ') : ' *Thou hast made thyself guilty of blood and blood will pursue thee* '. There is a play on the words Edom and *dām* ' blood '. **8.** ' *I shall fill with the slain thy hills and thy valleys ; the slain with the sword shall fall therein* ' (LXX). **10.** The Edomites aspire to the possession of Judah and Israel which belong to Yahweh. **11.** The *lex talionis* will be applied to Edom. Insert *to thee* after ' do ' (LXX). ' *I shall make myself known to thee when I judge thee* '. **12.** ' To consume ' means for our sustenance. **14.** MT is corrupt. Not the whole earth but Edom rejoices. The thought appears clearly in 15.

XXXVI 1-38 Re-establishment of Israel : Pre- 49 **paration of the Land and Purification of the People**—The degradation of Israel was attributed by the Gentiles to the powerlessness of Yahweh, her protector. She must be re-established that Yahweh's name be no longer blasphemed. The devastated land will increase in fertility and the sinful people will be spiritually regenerated. The prophecy was conditional and depended for its literal fulfilment on the co-operation of Israel with the designs of Yahweh. It was spiritually fulfilled in the spiritual Israel, the Church founded by Christ.

1-15 The Mountains of Israel shall be Blessed—**1. b** ' Mountains ' means ' mountainous land '. **2b.** ' *Aha ! Deserts* [LXX] *for ever ! They have become our possession* '. **3.** ' because you have been despised and hated ' (LXX). **4.** ' to the valleys, *to the deserted ruins and the abandoned cities that were spoiled* ', etc. **5.** ' of ' : ' *against* '. (After ' themselves ') : ' *with all the joy of their heart and the contempt of their soul to possess and despoil it* '. **6.** ' ridges ' : ' *ravines* '. **7.** Lift up the hand : swear. **8.** The restoration is depicted as imminent. **9.** ' *I come to you and I turn to you* ', etc. **10.** The fecundity of the remnant is also foretold by Isaias. **12b.** ' *You* [the mountains of Israel] *shall be their inheritance and you shall be no longer deprived of their children* '. **13.** ' suffocated ' : ' *deprived of children* '. **14.** Canaan devoured its children by famine caused by the dryness of its soil.

16-38 Israel shall be re-established and spiritually c regenerated—**16-23.** The motive of the Messianic restoration is first explained. It is not for Israel's sake or through Israel's merits but that Yahweh's holy name be no longer blasphemed by the Gentiles who considered him unable to protect his people. **24.** The exiles will return to Palestine. **25-29a.** The spiritual regeneration of the people is predicted. Washing with water and infusion of God's spirit suggest a baptismal regeneration. **29b-30.** Abundance of the fruits of the earth. **31-32.** The Israelites will be rightly ashamed of their past infidelities. **33-35.** Restoration of inhabitants to the desolate land and empty cities. **36.** The neighbouring nations will recognize the hand of the Lord and no longer blaspheme his holy name. **37-38.** Multiplication of the people. ' *I shall multiply for them men like flocks* '. The comparison suggests the consecrated flocks at the solemn feasts in Jerusalem.

d XXXVII 1-14 The Vision of Dry Bones restored to Life—This vision does not teach the resurrection of the body, though often so interpreted, but the revival of the defunct nation of Israel. The scene of the vision was a plain near Tel-Abib already mentioned, 3:22.

e 1-10 The Vision—**1.** Render '*in spirit*' and omit ' of the Lord '. Read '*men's bones*' (LXX). **3.** '*Shall these bones live?* Omit ' dost thou think '. **5.** Spirit : the breath of life. **7.** ' each one to its joint ' : ' *each to each* '. **9.** ' these slain *that they may live* '.

f 11-14 The Interpretation—The dry bones represent the House of Israel as politically non-existent, not the dead on the last day. The graves were the places where dispersed Israelites lived as strangers in foreign lands. The re-establishment of the exiles in their own land was the revival of the nation.

g 15-28 The Reunion of the Separated Kingdoms—The symbolic action of joining together two rods or sceptres signifies the reunion of the divided kingdoms of Judah and Israel which Yahweh will accomplish. They shall form a single nation, under a single ruler, the new David, in their ancestral territory. Yahweh will make an eternal alliance with them and establish his sanctuary within them. The prophecy is Messianic, spiritually fulfilled in the one true Church.

h 15-20 The Symbolic Action—The names written on the rods are those of the tribal ancestors, Judah and Joseph, whose descendants played the leading part in the kingdoms of Judah and Israel. **19.** ' in his hand ' : MT ' in my hand ', LXX ' in the hand of Judah '. The ruler, David, suggests Judah.

i 21-28 The New Israel—**21-23.** The exiles shall return and form a single kingdom. **24-25.** The new David shall rule over them for ever. **26-27.** Yahweh will make an eternal alliance with them. **28.** From his sanctuary among them he shall become known to the Gentiles.

a XXXVIII-XXXIX Final Victory of Yahweh over the Pagan World—While Israel enjoys peace and prosperity in her native territory and consequently after the restoration, Gog, ruler of the northern nations, leads a mighty army against her. Yahweh protects his people by annihilating the hostile forces when they reach Palestine. The burning of the weapons, the burial of the slain, the feasting of birds and beasts, are described. Ezechiel's chief object is to assure his hearers of Yahweh's permanent protection. He predicts at the same time in language that is largely symbolical a remote future event. The text exhibits repetitions. The feasting on the corpses should precede their burial.

b XXXVIII 1-23 Gog's Invasion of Israel—The army of Gog is first described, then his designs against Israel, and finally his defeat by Yahweh. The nations mentioned are not literally the invaders but represent all the might of paganism.

1-9 Army of Gog—**2.** The name is possibly of Sumerian origin meaning ' darkness '. The northern regions are the regions of darkness. More probably the Gasgas, neighbours of Mosoch and Tubal south of the Black Sea, are indicated. Magog may be mat-Gog, the land of Gog. In Gen 10:12 Magog appears with Mosoch and Tubal among the sons of Japhet. ' of him ' : ' *against him* '. Omit 4*a* = 29:4*a* (LXX). **5.** ' Libyans ' : ' *Nubians* ' (Put). **6.** Gomer are the Cimmerians. Crimea preserves the name. On Thogorma *cf.* 27:14. **7.** The expedition is decreed by Yahweh. **8.** ' be visited ' : ' *receive orders* ' ; ' is returned from the sword ' : ' *was rescued from devastation* '. Israel was waste but is now inhabited.

c 10-17 Designs of Gog—He plans to plunder a peaceful and naturally unprotected people. **12.** ' which hath begun to possess ' : ' *who have cattle and goods* ', are self-supporting, neither traders nor plunderers. The inquiries of the trading nations are explained by the fact that traders attended armies to purchase the plunder. **13.** ' Dedan *and their merchants*, Tarshish *and her traders* '. **14-16.** The repetitions disturb the construction. ' In the latter days ' (*cf.* 8 ' after many

years ') : in the remote future. **17.** Prophecies of the **491c** destruction of Israel's oppressors are meant. Gog only appears here.

18-23 Destruction of Gog and his Army—Yahweh **d** himself annihilates the assailants. The description of the theophany is conventional. Earth trembles, birds and fishes, men and beasts, are terrified, mountains are overturned, rocks are rent, walls collapse. The enemies slay each other, Jg 7:32 ; 2 Par 20:23, perish by pestilence, 4 Kg 19:35, hailstones, Jos 10:11, lightning, Gen 19:24. Brimstone is associated with lightning owing to the sulphurous odour accompanying the electrical discharge (Iliad VIII, 135 ; XIV, 415). **18.** ' wrath ' : ' *nostrils* ', an anthropomorphism omitted by LXX.

XXXIX 1-24 Sequel of the Victory—After a re- **e** capitulation of the preceding prophecy, in which the destruction of the invaders is stressed, the burning of the weapons, burial of the slain and feast of birds and beasts are described.

1-8 Recapitulation—**2.** MT reads ' I will drive thee **f** on ' for ' I will lead thee out '. **3.** The breaking of the bow is a new feature. **4.** ' *I will give* '. **6.** Gog's own land will suffer and the ' islands ' or coastlands of his allies. **7*b*.** Lit. ' nor shall I suffer my holy name to be profaned '.

9-16 Burning of Weapons and Burial of the Slain— **g** The uninterrupted peace following the victory makes weapons useless. Their use for firewood is a reprisal. **9.** ' spears ' : ' *bucklers* ' ; ' pikes ' : ' *spears* '. **11.** ' the passengers ' : ' *Abārim*, a mountain range E. of the Dead Sea. The valley is unknown. **14.** Omit ' to bury ' (MT) but retain ' to seek out ' (LXX). Omit **16*a***, which is a gloss = ' Hamōnah '' multitude '' is also the name of a city ', and *cf.* the last words of 15.

17-24. The Feast of Birds and Beasts—The slain are **h** likened to a sacrificial feast provided by Yahweh. **18.** ' bullocks, *all fatlings of Bashan* '. **21-24.** The causes of the exile and the restoration are set forth.

Fulfilment of the Prophecy against Gog—The pro- **i** phecy will be fulfilled towards the end of a period, regarded by some as pre-Messianic. Gog then represents the Seleucids. The Messianic interpretation seems preferable as Ezechiel contemplates a Messianic restoration ; *cf.* Apoc. 20:7. The judgement of the Gentile neighbours, chh 25-32, was the necessary prelude to the establishment of the peaceful Messianic kingdom. Gog comes from afar to plunder that kingdom already established. He and his army thus represent the forces of evil seeking vainly to destroy the Church founded by Christ.

25-28 Final Prediction of the Restoration—This **j** oracle is a summary conclusion of the restoration prophecies. **25.** ' bring back the captivity ' : ' *change the lot* '. **26.** ' bear ' (MT) : ' *forget* ' (LXX). To bear transgressions would imply chastisement. **27-29.** Yahweh's name will be sanctified by the return of the exiles, their spiritual regeneration and his abiding presence among them.

XL-XLVIII—In this last section of his book Ezechiel **492a** concludes his prophecies on the Restoration with the detailed and magnificent description of the New Temple, the New Cult and the New Holy Land. Catholic tradition has usually regarded this picture as a figurative adumbration in Jewish colouring of the Messianic Kingdom, the Church of Christ. Some modern exegetes propose a more realistic interpretation. It is difficult to suppose that a practical programme for the expected historical restoration is here presented to the exiles. The rebuilders of the temple, guided by prophets, made no attempt to realize the plan of Ezechiel. His legislation which ignored the high-priest and was sometimes at variance with the Mosaic code was never accepted as authoritative. In his description of the New Holy Land there are several features, the temple river in particular, which defy a realistic interpretation. An ideal Messianic Restoration on the lines of Isaias' picture of the New Jerusalem is less open to objection. The prince how-

492a ever scarcely suggests the Messias. His liberty is restricted and possible abuse of his authority is forestalled by legislation. On the other hand Ezechiel, unlike Isaias, never depicts the Messias except as a new David. It seems better therefore, while recognizing the difficulty of the problem, to accept the traditional interpretation. In all his prophecies of the restoration Ezechiel seems to visualize the Messianic period.

b XL-XLII The New Temple—1. The Outer Court and its Gates. 2. The Inner Court and its Gates. 3. The Temple Buildings. 4. The buildings of the Inner Court. 5. The Dimensions of the Sanctuary. The text of these chapters is often corrupt and unintelligible. In the limited space at our disposal we have confined ourselves to a description of the New Temple. A few of the details are necessarily conjectural.

c XL-1-27 The Outer Court and its Gates—Ezechiel is transported in spirit to Jerusalem and ordered to communicate to the house of Israel what is there revealed to him. The date is the 10th Nisan (March–April) 573 B.C. From a high mountain, not determined, he sees the New Temple ; *cf.* Apoc 21:10. An angel in human form, but resplendent, conducts him and takes the various measures with a reed or measuring rod, 6 cubits long, and a cord or tape for longer distances. The wall enclosing *the house* (usually the temple, here the whole sacred area) was a reed = 6 cubits, in thickness and in height. The cubit however was not the ordinary one of 6 handbreadths but contained 7 handbreadths. Render **5** (after ' six cubits ') : ' *of a cubit and a handbreadth each* '. The ordinary cubit was about 17·7 inches, Ezechiel's therefore about 20·65 inches. As the three gates (N. S. E.) were similar, only the eastern and most important is described. It was an unroofed passage-way with walls or buildings on either side. A flight of 7 (LXX) steps led up to the outer threshold 6 cubits long (the thickness of the outer wall) and 10 cubits wide. This gave admission to a corridor 13 cubits wide, flanked on either side by three lodges or guard-houses 6 cubits square and two pillars occupying each a space 5 cubits

d long between the lodges. An inner threshold similar to the outer one led thence into a porch which communicated with the court. The porch was 8 cubits long and 20 wide. Two pillars (DV ' fronts ') facing each other at the entry to the court added 2 cubits to the porch's length and rows of pillars at the N. and S. sides added 5 cubits to its breadth. The whole structure was thus a rectangle 50 cubits long and 25 wide. The guard-houses had barriers or enclosed spaces on the corridor side and doors on the court side. The whole edifice had also diminishing windows (wider outside than inside) looking out on the court. The pillars in the porch were adorned with paintings or sculptures of palm trees. The Outer Court had 30 chambers, fronted with pillars, 42:6, probably adjoining the outer wall and corresponding to the porticos in Herod's temple, and also a paved space all around, extending as far inward as the gates. The distance from these gates to the corresponding gates of the inner court was 100 cubits so that the outer court was 150 cubits wide on all sides.

e XL 28-47 The Inner Court and its Gates—The gates, first described, only differed from the corresponding outer gates in being reached by an ascent of 8 steps instead of 7 and in having their porches not at the inner but at the outer end. Ezechiel, conducted to the E. gate, is next shown the tables on which victims were prepared for sacrifice. Four of these were in the porch, four more outside it in the court, two at each side. They were of cut stone 1½ cubits square and a cubit in height and had knives and other sacrificial implements. They had a border of a handbreadth (LXX ; or hooks ? MT) and were sheltered from sun and rain. Finally Ezechiel enters the inner court and observes two chambers one beside the N. gate facing S., the other beside the S. gate facing N. These are

for the priests, the sons of Sadoc, charged with the **492a** service of the altar. The inner court was 100 cubits long and wide. This measure is obscure and probably incorrect. Other indications show clearly that the inner court, including the temple, was 200 cubits long and wide. The altar of holocausts was due east of the house or temple.

XL 48-XLI 26 The Temple Buildings—Ezechiel's **f** temple like Solomon's had four parts : Vestibule, Hekal (Holy Place), Debir (Holy of Holies), Lateral Building. An ascent of ten steps led to the Vestibule, 12 cubits long and 20 wide. The door, 14 cubits wide, was flanked on either side by a column and a wall 3 cubits long and 5 thick. The door from the Vestibule to the Hekal was 10 cubits wide, the walls on either side were 5 cubits long and 6 thick. The door from the Hekal to the Holy of Holies, entered by the Angel but not by Ezechiel, was 6 cubits wide, the walls on either side 7 cubits long and 2 thick. The Hekal was 40 cubits long, 20 wide, the Holy of Holies 20 cubits long and wide. The lateral building, enclosing the sacred edifice on the N. W. S. sides, rested on a foundation 6 cubits deep and had 3 stories each containing 30 rooms in which the sacred vessels and treasures of the temple were stored. The outer wall was 5 cubits, the inner (that of the temple) 6 cubits thick. Both these walls had their thickness twice diminished by half a cubit to support the floors of the upper stories. Thus the width of the rooms, 4, 5 and 6 cubits, varied with their elevation. Two doors in **g** the outer wall on the N. and S. gave access to the lateral building which was bordered by a paved space of 5 and a free space of 20 cubits. The measures given make the temple 100 cubits long and 50 broad. Only by attaching to its breadth the free spaces of 25 cubits on the N. and S. sides can it be regarded as 100 cubits broad. A building 20 cubits due W. of the sacred edifice is next mentioned. It was 90 cubits long and 70 wide and its walls were 5 cubits thick. It probably served as a store room for wood and a shelter for cattle. All the walls of the vestibule, holy place and holy of holies were panelled and the panelling was adorned with alternating palm trees and cherubs. Two faces of the cherubs, those of the man and the lion, were represented in profile. The holy place and the holy of holies had double folding doors, rectangular in shape. The door of the vestibule was apparently a wooden screen. Before the holy of holies was a wooden altar, 2 cubits square and 3 in height, provided with corners or horns. This was undoubtedly not the Shewbread Table, as is often supposed, but the Altar of Incense. The altar of holocausts is also called table, 44:16. Wellhausen excluded the altar of incense from Solomon's temple, but Ingholt has recently shown that the Canaanite temples had their *ḥammōnîm* or incense altars (*cf.* Is 17:8), also mentioned by Ezechiel, 6:6.

XLII 1-14 The Buildings of the Inner Court—Two **h** large buildings are described parallel to the temple on its N. and S. sides and separated from it by the free space outside the lateral building. The main building in each case 100 cubits long and 20 wide was separated by a corridor 10 cubits wide from a kind of wing, adjoining the court wall, also 20 cubits wide but only 50 in length. The buildings had 3 stories like the lateral building but diminished in width as they ascended. The entry from the outer court was at the east end. The rooms in these buildings served as dining- and vesting-rooms for the priests who were forbidden to eat sacred meats or wear priestly garments outside the inner court.

15-20 The Dimensions of the Sanctuary—The whole **i** space enclosed by the outer wall was a square measuring 500 cubits (LXX) on all sides. MT has 500 reeds = 3,000 cubits. Some commentators suppose a vast unoccupied space surrounding the temple precincts and safeguarding their sanctity. But the free space all round the outer wall is elsewhere estimated at only 50 cubits, 45:2.

XLIII-XLVI The New Cult—Yahweh now enters his temple and prescribes how he is to be worshipped there. 1. The Theophany. 2. The Altar of Holocausts. 3. Prince, Levites and Priests. 4. Offerings. 5. Feasts and Sacrifices. 6. Inalienability of Prince's Domain. 7. Kitchens.

XLIII 1-12 The Theophany—Ezechiel in a vision sees Yahweh solemnly enter his New Temple by the eastern gate. Conducted into the inner court the prophet beholds the glory of the Lord and hears his voice (not an angel's voice DV). Yahweh will dwell for ever among his people. They shall no more profane his holy name by their infidelities, by the corpses of their kings, buried usually in the southern part of the temple hill but sometimes in the palace garden, and by the palaces of their kings separated only by a wall from the sacred edifice. Solomon's temple had no outer court and was separated from his palace only by the single wall of the inner court. Ezechiel is ordered to promulgate the plan and measurements of the New Temple and the laws now revealed to him by which temple service must be regulated. **7.** Supply (after ' son of man ') *thou hast seen* (LXX) and omit ' by the high places ', a dittography.

13-27 The Altar of Holocausts and its Consecration—The Altar is assumed to have been of stone. Underneath was a socle, measuring, outside the altar which fitted into it, a cubit in breadth and height. The altar proper consisted of 3 square blocks placed one on top of the other. The lowest was 16 cubits square and 2 high, the middle 14 cubits square and 4 high, the topmost—the altar surface—12 cubits square and 4 high. *Cf.* § 278c. The altar had horns or projections at all four corners. At the base of all three blocks was a border or rim half a cubit in height. These rims probably formed channels for the reception of the blood. The ascent to the altar was by steps at the E. side. The consecration lasted seven days. On the first day a young bullock was the sin-offering. Its blood was poured on the four horns, on the four corners of the middle and lowest blocks and on the border of the socle round about. The body was burnt outside the sanctuary. After the expiation ceremony a bullock and a ram were offered as holocausts. Similar offerings were made on the following days except that a he-goat was the sin-offering. Not Ezechiel but the priests instructed by him were the consecrators. The salting of the holocausts, not pentateuchal, is noteworthy; *cf.* Mk 9:49.

XLIV 1-31 Prince, Levites and Priests—The prince is the vicegerent of Yahweh who is king of the new theocratic state. Among his privileges is a special place for sacrificial meals, the eastern gate of the outer court. As this gate can never be opened because Yahweh entered by it the king must enter the court by another gate and thus attain the inner entry of the eastern gate. An allusion to a gate of Marduk's great temple in Babylon, only opened twice a year, is generally assumed. Many of the Fathers see in the gate through which God alone passes a figure of our Lady's perpetual virginity. The Israelites are reproached for having permitted foreigners and uncircumcised persons, whom they employed in an inferior capacity as temple servants, to enter and profane Yahweh's sanctuary. The Nethînîm, inferior temple servants of foreign origin, must be replaced by a particular class of Levites, namely, those who formerly exercised sacerdotal functions but are now degraded in consequence of idol worship and infidelity to Yahweh. To these are committed the guardianship of the gates, slaughter of the victims and menial offices in general. They must not discharge the functions or enjoy the emoluments of the priesthood. The priests are no longer all the male descendants of Aaron but a particular class of them, the descendants of Sadoc. Aaron left two sons, Eleazar and Ithamar. Abiathar, high-priest in David's time, was descended from Ithamar. His disloyalty led to the transfer of the dignity to the loyal Sadoc, a descendant of Eleazar,

3 Kg 1:26, 35. The fidelity of Sadoc and his des- **492n** cendants in the service of Yahweh at a time of general apostasy is the motive of their choice as priests in the New Temple. Most of the obligations of the priests will be found in the Pentateuch, sometimes however imposed exclusively on the high-priest whom Ezechiel entirely ignores. Their garments, worn only in the inner court, are of linen. They neither shave their heads nor grow their hair too long. They abstain from wine when serving. Their wives must be Israelites and either virgins or widows of priests. They teach and judge the people. They must avoid association with corpses except in specified cases of very close blood relationship involving subsequent purification. They have no part in the land of Israel but live on the offerings made by the people to Yahweh. Meal-offerings, sin-offerings, guilt-offerings, ban-offerings and first-fruits are specified.

3. ' *Only the prince shall* ', etc. **8.** ' kept the ordi- **o** nances ' : ' *taken charge* '. **10.** ' and have borne ' : ' *shall bear* '. **13.** ' by the holy of holies ' : ' *most holy* '. The most holy things were the meal, sin and guilt offerings, 42:13. **15.** ' *But the Levitical priests* [omitting ' and '], *priests of the tribe of Levi* '. **19.** ' Sanctify ' : practically = pollute. Contact with sacred things was forbidden. **26.** ' cleansed ' : ' *made unclean* '. **29.** Insert *the meal offering* after ' eat '. **30.** The *t*e*rûmāh* or tribute (DV ' meats ') was a special offering levied on all fruits and amounting in rabbinic times to a fiftieth of the harvest. **31.** The food prohibition applied to people as well as priests.

XLV 1-17 Offerings—The land assigned to priests, **493a** Levites, city and prince is first specified, then the prince's obligations and further emoluments. A portion of land 25,000 cubits long and 20,000 broad is first measured. The half of this enclosing the sanctuary and a vacant space of 50 cubits all around it is for the priests, the other half for the Levites. South of this is a space 25,000 cubits long and 5,000 wide for the city. East and west of the entire space already measured, 25,000 cubits square, is the portion of the prince. It extends to the Mediterranean on the W. and the Dead Sea on the E. The ample provision made for the prince is designed to correct the ancient abuse by which monarchs arbitrarily appropriated tribal territory. The prince must not oppress his subjects and must exercise a special control over weights and measures. The shekel was the standard of weight, the bath of liquid, the ephah of dry measure. The prince receives from the people a sixtieth part of their wheat and barley, a hundredth part of their oil and a two-hundredth part of their flocks. In return he must provide all public offerings and sacrifices.

1. ' ten ' : ' *twenty* ' (LXX). **4.** ' suburbs ' : ' *free* **b** *spaces* ' ; after ' houses ' : ' *and for their pasture lands* '. **5.** ' twenty chambers ' : ' *cities to inhabit* ' (LXX). **6-7.** The separation of the sanctuary is the tract of land reserved to temple, priests and Levites. **7.** ' sea ' : ' *west* '. **9.** ' confines ' : ' *exactions* '. **12.** The mine was 50 shekels (LXX) more probably than 60 (MT). **15.** ' of those that Israel feedeth ' : ' *as offering of the families of Israel* ' (LXX). **17.** ' and the sacrifices ' : ' *and the offering* '.

XLV 18-XLVI 15 Feasts and Sacrifices—Two feasts **c** of expiation on the first of the first and seventh months replace the Yôm Kippûr. The blood of the sin-offering, a young bullock, is poured on the corners of the altar blocks, on the doorposts of the hekal and on the gateposts of the inner court. Pasch and Tabernacles are celebrated on the dates assigned by the law but the sacrifices offered are different and are accompanied by offerings of an ephah of meal and a hin of oil. There is no mention of the paschal lamb, barley first-fruits and booths or of the feast of Pentecost. The Sabbath and New Moon feasts are next considered. On these days the eastern gate of the inner court is left open and the prince has the privilege of assisting on the threshold at the sacrifices, invisible to the people, in the outer court. The rule that those who

493c enter the outer court by the northern gate leave it by the southern aims at the maintenance of order and binds prince and people. Six lambs and a ram are sacrificed on these feasts, also a bullock on the New Moon feasts. The usual accompaniment of an ephah of meal and a hin of oil is prescribed except in the lamb offerings when the amount is left to the liberality of the prince. When the prince makes a voluntary offering he may assist at the sacrifice in the porch of the eastern gate. Finally every morning a lamb must be offered as a holocaust together with a sixth of an ephah of meal and a third of a hin of oil. The law prescribed also a similar evening sacrifice and exacted a lesser quota of meal and oil. **19.** ' brim ' : ' blocks '. **20.** ' *on the first day of the seventh month* ' (LXX).

d XLVI 16-18 Inalienability of the Prince's Domain— Only to his sons can the prince give permanently part of his domain. Such a gift made to anybody else is a loan and returns to the prince automatically in the *year of liberty*, the next Sabbatic year when Hebrew slaves were freed from bondage.

e 19-24 The Kitchens—The kitchens for cooking sacrificial meats, sin-offerings and guilt-offerings eaten by the priests in the inner court, naturally attached to the dining-rooms already described, were at the western extremity of these buildings. Only the northern kitchens are mentioned but others on the south side may be assumed. The kitchens for the laity were in four enclosures, 40 cubits long and 30 wide, occupying the four angles of the outer court. Here the flesh of peace-offerings was cooked and eaten.

f XLVII-XLVIII The New Holy Land—The Temple River is first described, then the boundaries of the land, and lastly its distribution.

g XLVII 1-12 The River—It issues from beneath the south side of the threshold of the temple, flows eastward by the Altar of Holocausts and emerges from the sanctuary on the south side of the perpetually closed eastern gate of the outer court. Thence it flows into the Dead Sea, increasing in depth so rapidly that at 4,000 cubits (less than $1\frac{1}{2}$ miles) from the sanctuary it is no longer fordable. The desert which it traverses becomes extremely fertile. The trees on its banks heal with their leaves and bear fresh fruit monthly. The waters of the Dead Sea, healed by its entry, abound with fish. From Engaddi to Enaglaim at the sea's NW. end fishermen ply their trade. Only detached pools of Dead Sea water retain their salt. Ezechiel derives the fertility of desert land, a regular feature of Messianic prosperity, from the abiding presence of Yahweh.

h 13-23 The Boundaries—Ezechiel had previously indicated the northern and southern boundaries when he predicted, 6:14, that the land would be devastated from the desert (between Palestine and Egypt) to Riblah, near Homs, in the latitude of Tripoli and on the southern confines of Hamath. The site of Ezechiel's Riblah where Nabuchodonosor judged his captives on the confines of the land, 11:10, is quite certain. It helps us to identify the sites on the northern boundary and shows that Ezechiel's Messianic kingdom, a revival of that of David, included that monarch's Aramaean conquests. **15-18.** ' *These are the boundaries of the land : On the north side from the great sea* [Mediterranean] *by Hethlon* [Heitala two hours E. of Tripoli], *the entry of Hamath* [Restan midway between Homs and Hamath] *S^edad* [Sadad SE. of Homs], *Berotha* [Bereitan **4** SE. of Ba'albek], *Sibrayim* [Sōmeriye E. of the lake of Homs] *which is between the confines of Damascus and Hamath, Hasar-Enan* [Qaryetain on the road from Damascus to Palmyra] *on the confines of Hauran. And the boundary was from the sea to Hasar-Enan, northern boundary of Damascus and boundary of Hamath. That is the north side. The eastern side was from between Hauran and Damascus and from between Gilead and the land of Israel, the Jordan serving as boundary to the east* [Dead] *sea and Tamar* [Kornub SW. of Dead Sea]. *That is the east side* '. Besides the usual corrections *ṣāpônāh*, a dittography, is omitted in 17. Hauran is the key to **i** the interpretation. It is not Hawwārîn near Qaryetain but clearly a district like Hamath and Damascus, the Assyrian province of Haurina, which had to be included in the Messianic kingdom because it contained Aramaean territory subject to David. Ezechiel gives it a wide extension northwards as far as Hasar-Enan. Berotha and possibly Helam (LXX) are mentioned as Aramaean cities conquered by David, 2 Kg 8:8 ; 10:17. Hamath was the northern, Damascus the eastern boundary of Ezechiel's Hauran. Only at Gilead does the Jordan become the eastern boundary. The southern boundary is the usual one. Meribath-Qadesh ('Ain Qudeis) and the Torrent (of Egypt, Wady el-'Arish) are mentioned. The Mediterranean is the western limit as far as opposite the entry of Hamath. Phoenicia as far north as Tripoli is included.

XLVIII 1-35 The Distribution—Ezechiel begins by **j** giving foreigners settled in the Holy Land a share in its territory. The distinction between Jew and Gentile tends to disappear in the Messianic kingdom. He then assigns a strip of land to each of the twelve tribes, seven to the N. and five to the S. of the previously reserved territory. The order from N. to S. is : Dan, Aser, Nephtali, Manasses, Ephraim, Ruben, Judah, reserved territory, Benjamin, Simeon, Issachar, Zabulon, Gad. Each tribe divides its land by lot among its families and alien residents. Judah and Benjamin have privileged positions next the sanctuary from which the tribes of servile origin on the mother's side, Dan, Aser, Nephtali, Gad are furthest removed. Levi has no portion among the tribes. The Levites therefore in the reserved territory are a tribal unit, not merely degraded priests. Ezechiel's distribution is **k** mathematical. He takes no account of tribes that have disappeared anciently like Ruben and Simeon or recently like those of the Northern Kingdom nor of the variety in the population of the tribes and the fertility of the land. The reconstitution which he contemplates is not practical but ideal or Messianic. A recapitulation of the description of the reserved territory gives new information about the city. It will be peopled by members of all twelve tribes and will measure 5,000 cubits squared if the suburbs extending 250 cubits on all four sides are included. It will have twelve gates named after the twelve sons of Jacob, not the twelve tribes for Joseph and Levi replace Ephraim and Manasses. The reserved territory E. and W. of the city 10,000 cubits long and 5,000 wide on both sides will supply food to the citizens. The circumference of the city wall will be 18,000 cubits and the name of the city will be Yahweh is there.

DANIEL

By P. P. SAYDON

a **Bibliography**—St Jerome, *Commentarii in Danielem Prophetam*, PL 25, 491–584 ; J. Knabenbauer, S.J., *Commentarius in Danielem Prophetam*, CSS, Paris, 1891 ; *F. W. Farrar, *The Book of Daniel*, London, 1895 ; *S. R. Driver, *The Book of Daniel*, CBSC, Cambridge, 1900, rep 1922 ; *K. Marti, *Das Buch Daniel*, Tübingen und Leipzig, 1901 ; P. Riessler, *Das Buch Daniel erklärt*, Wien, 1902 ; *C. Boutflower, *In and Around the Book of Daniel*, London, 1923 ; *J. A. Montgomery, *Daniel*, ICC, 1927 ; J. Goettsberger, *Das Buch Daniel*, BB, 1928 ; *R. H. Charles, *A Critical Commentary on the Book of Daniel*, Oxford, 1929 ; id. CAP, I, pp 625–64 ; H. Junker, *Untersuchungen über literarische und exegetische Probleme des Buches Daniel*, Bonn, 1932 ; *H. H. Rowley, *Darius the Mede and the four World Empires*, Cardiff, 1935 ; *A. Bentzen, *Daniel*, HAT, 1937 ; J. Linder, S.J., *Commentarius in Danielem Prophetam*, 1939, CSS, a revised edition of Knabenbauer's commentary ; G. Rinaldi, *Daniele* (La Sacra Bibbia, S. Garofalo), 1948.

b **The Person of the Prophet**—Our information about Daniel is derived mainly from his book. In the third year of Joakim, king of Juda (605 B.C.), Daniel was led captive to Babylon by Nabuchodonosor. According to Josephus (*Ant* 10, 10, 1), he belonged to the royal family of Sedecias, the last king of Juda. Together with other Jewish youths he was educated at the royal court of Babylon where, however, they all kept to their religious practices. Daniel's extraordinary skill in the interpretation of dreams raised him to a position of the highest authority in the Babylonian empire. His three companions on refusing to worship the golden image were cast into a burning furnace and miraculously rescued. Daniel remained in power during the reign of Darius, who contemplated making him chief minister over the whole realm (6:4). The jealous ministers plotted against his life, but God delivered his faithful servant and brought upon Daniel's accusers the evil they had devised for him. Daniel lived at least till the third year of Cyrus, 10:1 (536–535).

The name Daniel (= 'my judge is God') occurs in the name-lists of the post-exilic period (Esd 8:2 ; Neh 10:7), but there is no evidence that the prophet was one of the exiles who returned back with Esdras. It is generally believed that the Daniel, who is mentioned by Ezechiel as a pattern of righteousness and wisdom (14:14, 20 ; 28:3), is the prophet and the diplomat of the Babylonian court. This identity has recently been disputed mainly on grounds of orthography, the consonantal form of the prophet's name being *dny'l*, while the name of Ezechiel's Daniel is spelt *dn'l*, a form which occurs in the Rās-Shamra tablets ; *cf.* P. Joüon in Bi (1938) 283–5 ; P. Heinisch, *Das Buch Ezechiel*, BB 77 ; Dennefeld, 631.

c **Contents and Analysis**—The general theme of the book is the uniqueness of the God of the Israelites and his superiority over all heathen gods demonstrated by the personal experiences of the prophet himself and by God's prediction of a universal and everlasting reign of peace and justice for those who remain faithful to him. Hence the book falls naturally into two parts, chh 1–6 and chh 7–12. In Part I, which may be called 'the stories section', Daniel relates some of his personal experiences in the court of Babylon in order to show that the God of the Israelites is Almighty and the Only Living God. In Part II, or 'the visions section', he relates his visions and their interpretations.

d In ch 1 the writer introduces Daniel, the divinely gifted interpreter of dreams, and his three companions, the faithful and undaunted worshippers of the true God. In ch 2 Daniel interprets Nabuchodonosor's first dream which symbolized the overthrow of all earthly kingdoms and the setting up of a universal reign. Thereupon Nabuchodonosor acknowledges the superiority of the God of Daniel over all other gods. Ch 3 develops the same theme in a different way. Daniel's companions refuse to worship the idol erected by the king, are cast into a burning furnace, and miraculously rescued from the flames. The king once more acknowledges the power of their God. In ch 4 Daniel interprets another dream to Nabuchodonosor, who is compelled again to acknowledge God's power and righteousness. Ch 5 carries us down to the last days of Babylon. Daniel interprets the symbolical writing on the wall predicting the impending downfall of the Babylonian kingdom. Afterwards (ch 6) Daniel was appointed by Darius the Mede one of the three presidents governing the whole kingdom. On being slandered by envious officials he was cast into a den of lions where he was miraculously preserved from harm. The king acknowledges the power of the God of Daniel, and enjoins all his subjects to honour him.

Part II relates Daniel's four visions. **e**

In the first vision (ch 7) Daniel sees four monstrous beasts emerging from the sea. An angel explains to Daniel their symbolical meaning. They represent four successive kingdoms. From the fourth a king will arise who will seek to exterminate the people of God. But eventually he will be overthrown and the holy people will receive an eternal and universal dominion.

The second vision (ch 8) symbolizes the downfall of the Medo-Persian power, the rise of the empire of Alexander the Great, the sacrilegious arrogance of one of the Greek rulers.

In the third vision (ch 9) Daniel, after confessing the people's sins and praying for the nation's restoration, receives a divine assurance that God's promise will be fulfilled after 70 weeks of years, or 490 years.

The fourth vision (chh 10–12) is a revelation concerning the rulers of the people of Israel down to Antiochus IV, whose conquests and ignominious end are vividly depicted. An age of bliss will then dawn upon the people of God.

Chh 13 and 14 in the LXX and the Vg are an appendix containing the story of Susanna, and the story of Bel and the Dragon.

It appears from this analysis that the two parts differ **f** from one another, not only in their literary form but also in their historical outlook. In Part I the writer is mainly concerned with the Neo-Babylonian empire, and hardly displays any interest in the Persian and the Greek age. Nabuchodonosor is the centre of gravity of chh 1–6. He is the golden head (2:38), the king of kings ruling over the whole earth (2:37 f.), the mighty tree stretching forth its branches to the extremities of the earth (4:17–19). An echo of Nabuchodonosor's greatness and magnificence resounds even in the narrative of the last days of the Babylonian domination (5:18 f.). The general situation of the Jewish exiles is, apparently, uneventful. But in Part II the writer's

494f attention is concentrated on the age of Antiochus IV (175–164 B.C.). The writer is horrified at the sight of the persecuted Israelites, and his sorrow is assuaged not by the remembrance of a glorious past, but by the hope of a brighter future. The Babylonian age has no part in his visions, but he describes the Seleucid domination with a richness of detail unusual in prophecy.

g The Apocalyptic Character of the Book—There are striking differences both in contents and in mode of expression between the book of Daniel and the other prophetic writings. In the latter the reader is moving in a world of realities, among a living community unfaithful to their God, and unresponsive to the prophets' warnings. But in the book of Daniel we are transported into a world of dreams and visions, among monstrous beasts and manlike angels. Future events, which are only vaguely predicted by the other prophets, are depicted in the book of Daniel with a richness of detail which is more appropriate to history than to prophecy.

h Hence it has been the custom to reckon the book of Daniel, especially chh 7–12, with those books which, on account of the revelations which they purport to communicate, have been called *apocalypses*, from the Greek ἀποκάλυψις = 'revelation'. The distinguishing feature of this species of literature, which flourished mostly from the 2nd century B.C. to the 2nd century A.D., producing a plentiful crop of apocryphal writings, is a revelation which, by a literary device, is supposed to have been made by God to some prominent man of antiquity, and kept, for a long time, hidden from the people. The revelation is made to extend over two periods of time, the one prior to the writer's time, the other later; the one relates past history in the form of prediction of future events, the other expresses the writer's hopes in the form of prophecy. On Apocalyptic literature see DBV(S), art. *Apocalyptique*.

i Such a representation of history as real prophecy is, at least apparently, a literary forgery and a gross theological imposture. Modern criticism is, however, less severe. It is generally admitted that pseudonymity does not necessarily imply a falsehood; it may be a literary device, and as such it is quite consistent with biblical inspiration and inerrancy. The book of Wisdom is a well-known example. True it is that the apocalyptic writings are not mere literary pseudographs, in which a writer appears ostensibly under an assumed name. They derive or seem to derive all their authority and influence from the person whose name they assume, and whom they represent as communicating the divine revelation. And in order to strengthen the popular belief in the supposed origin of these writings their authors have also represented God as ordering that these books should be kept hidden until their appointed time.

j It does not seem correct to say that these anonymous writers *intended* to derive all their influence from their assumed names. Nor is it probable that this sort of pseudographic literature was, at the time of its appearance, so shrouded in mystery as is now believed. The fact that many writers during a period of four centuries chose this literary form for the expression of their religious sentiments clearly suggests that writing under an assumed name and representing past history as prophecy was a literary artifice unknown neither to writers nor to readers. The possibility of deception was therefore excluded. The apocalyptic writers derived their influence from their firm belief in God's promises of a better age and from their unshakeable conviction in his universal providence which they expressed in a literary form which was the product of the time. In this way they helped to strengthen the faith of their contemporaries and keep them united together as one soul inseparably attached to God amidst all persecutions. Whether the book may be classed with pseudonymous apocalyptic writings is discussed below, § 495*a–k*.

Position of the Book of Daniel in the Canon—In the **494** LXX and the Vg the book of Daniel ranks fourth among the major prophets, while in MT it is classed among the Hagiographa. St Jerome in the *Prologus galeatus* follows the order of the Jewish Canon (*Praef. in libros Samuel et Malachim*, PL 28, 553 f.). The different position of Daniel in the Greek and the Jewish Canons may be easily explained by assuming that this book received universal recognition when the collection of the prophetic writings had already been closed. The Jews of Alexandria arranged the books of the OT according to criteria of date and literary form, and so Daniel found himself among the prophets.

It is doubtful, however, whether the Jewish order of books is the original one. Josephus seems to include Daniel among the Prophets (*C. Apion.* 1, 8). The oldest Greek lists of books, some of which give the Jewish Canon, enumerate Daniel with the Prophets (*cf.* H. E. Ryle, *The Canon of the Old Testament*, table facing p 292).

The Deuterocanonical Additions—The Greek version **l** of Daniel and the Vg have some sections which are not in the Hebrew-Aramaic text. They are: the prayer of Azarias (3:24–45); the Song of the three children preceded by a prose interlude (3:46–90); the story of Susanna (ch 13); the story of Bel and the Dragon (ch 14). It is generally held by Catholic scholars that these portions were originally written in Hebrew or Aramaic, but did not form part of the original book (C. Julius, *Die griechischen Danielzusätze und ihre kanonische Geltung*, BS, VI, 3/4, 1901). We may add that they originated in the time of Daniel and belonged to the same cycle of Daniel episodes which have come down to us in a Hebrew and Aramaic form. They were translated into Greek, but when the final redaction of the book was made, the original text of these portions was either lost or for some reason inaccessible to the redactor. Of their canonicity, however, there can be no doubt.

The Language Problem—In the Hebrew Bible the **m** book of Daniel is written in two languages. 1:1–2:4*a* and chh 7–12 are in Hebrew; 2:4*b*–6:29 are in Aramaic. The deuterocanonical portions are in Greek. Various solutions have been proposed to explain the trilingual character of the book. The Greek sections are certainly translations from lost Semitic originals. The change from Hebrew to Aramaic and from Aramaic to Hebrew can hardly be attributed to the original writer. Very probably the several episodes and visions circulated on separate leaves in a Hebrew and in an Aramaic form, the one being a translation of the other, and the final compiler put together the stories in that linguistic form that came into his hands.

Text and Versions—The Hebrew-Aramaic text of the **n** book of Daniel has been rather badly preserved, as is shown by the numerous discrepancies from the ancient versions which, in many cases, exhibit a better text. This becomes clearly understandable when we consider that MT represents the last stage of a gradual editorial development which had been going on since the book took a definitive shape about the year 168 B.C. Besides these editorial changes there are others which originated in the time when the book was still in the state of a loose collection of separate narratives. Some of the chronological indications at the beginning of the narratives are, most probably, scribal or editorial insertions. But despite its corrupt state the Hebrew-Aramaic text of Daniel represents on the whole the substance of the original. The earliest version is the LXX, which was made during the latter half of the 2nd century B.C. The translator shows signs of incompetence. Compared with the rival Greek version of Theodotion, it looks more like a paraphrase than a translation (A. Bladau, *Die alexandrinische Übersetzung des Buches Daniel und ihr Verhältniss zum Massoretischen Text*, BS, II, 2/3, p 206). On account of its divergencies from the Hebrew text, the LXX version was never received in the Church (St Jerome, *Comm. in Dan. Proph.* PL 25, 514). The divergencies may,

n however, to some extent, be due to a slightly different Semitic text.

o The LXX version of Daniel was from a very early date superseded by that made by Theodotion, a Jewish proselyte, c A.D. 180. Theodotion's version is probably a revised edition of an older version made from the Hebrew and independent of the LXX (H. B. Swete, *Introduction to the Old Testament in Greek*, p 48). Theodotion places the story of Susanna at the head of the book, and in the *Chester Beatty Papyri*, published by F. Kenyon, the text of Daniel (fasc. vii, pp 17–38), which contains the LXX version and belongs probably to the early 3rd century A.D., places ch 5 after ch 8. But these different arrangements are most likely due to redactors or copyists rather than to a Semitic original.

The Vg is made from the Hebrew-Aramaic text current in Jerome's time, a text which was very closely related to MT. Occasionally Jerome follows Theodotion. The deuterocanonical parts are from Theodotion.

a Date and Authorship—Catholic tradition has always recognized Daniel as the original author of the book. The first heterodox view was that propounded by the Neo-Platonic philosopher Porphyry (died 303), who attributed the book to an anonymous writer living in the times of Antiochus Epiphanes (St Jerome, *Comm. in Dan. Proph.* PL 25, 491). This view, which soon fell into oblivion, was revived with the rise of Rationalism, and is now held, with rare exceptions, by all non-Catholic scholars.

These are their chief arguments :

b 1. The Linguistic Argument. (a) The Hebrew of Daniel is that of a much later age than the 6th century B.C.; it resembles, not the Hebrew of Ezechiel, a contemporary of Daniel, but that of the age subsequent to Nehemias (S. R. Driver, pp lx f.).

(b) The Aramaic represents a later stage of development than that of the Egyptian papyri of the 5th century B.C. and of the book of Esdras (G. R. Driver, JBL, 1926, p 118).

(c) There are at least 15 Persian loan-words and 3 Greek words in Daniel. Now if the Persian words presuppose a period after the Persian empire had been well established, the Greek words demand a date after the conquest of Palestine by Alexander the Great (S. R. Driver, p lxiii).

c 2. The Historical Argument. The writer reveals such an imperfect and inaccurate knowledge of the political history of Babylon during the last years of the Neo-Babylonian empire and the first years of the Persian rule that he cannot have lived in that period. Thus, for example :

(a) A captivity in the 3rd year of Joakim (1:1) is unknown to oriental history.

(b) Baltassar (Belshazzar) is represented as the last king of Babylon and son of Nabuchodonosor (ch 5). In point of fact Baltassar was the son of Nabonidus, the last king of Babylon, and had no relationship with Nabuchodonosor.

(c) Darius the Mede is said to have succeeded Baltasar after the downfall of the Babylonian empire (5:30 f.), and to have ruled over Babylon before Cyrus (6:28 ; 10:1 ; 11:1). In 9:1 he is called the son of Assuerus (Xerxes). It appears that the writer has erroneously introduced a Median kingdom ruling over Babylon between the Neo-Babylonian and the Persian empires. A contemporary writer like Daniel cannot be made responsible for such a gross historical mistake.

d 3. The Theological Argument. (a) OT prophecy is the communication of a divine message directed primarily to the contemporaries of the prophet. Whether it is a message of doom or of hope, it is always intimately related to the cirumstances of the time of the prophet. Now the interest of the book of Daniel is chiefly centred on the age of Antiochus IV, and it brings no message to men of the 6th century. This constitutes a strong presumption that the author of the book of Daniel lived in the period which he describes —that is, in the time of Antiochus.

495d (b) Another distinctive feature of OT prophecy is its relation, close or remote, to the Messianic kingdom and the lack of any determination of time and persons. Hence the principle that prophecy is not predicted history. In the book of Daniel there are a number of prophecies having no apparent relation to Messianic times and many details of time, names, and persons that are unusual in prophecy.

(c) The doctrines concerning the angels, their office, rank and name, the resurrection and the last judgement are presented in the book of Daniel with a distinctness and a development that point to an age later than the exile.

On the ground of these arguments and others of less probative force, such as the position of the book in the Jewish Canon and the complete absence of any allusion to it in the literature earlier than the books of Maccabees, the non-Catholic critical school considers the book of Daniel to be an anonymous apocalypse written at the time of Antiochus Epiphanes, c 168 B.C. Although these arguments, even taken cumulatively, **e** do not compel us to abandon the traditional view, they call at least for a reconsideration of our position. The Danielic authorship, in its strictest sense, can hardly be defended, but, on the other hand, there are no good arguments against the view that there is at least a solid Danielic nucleus. It has been said above that the Aramaic sections are, probably, translations from Hebrew (so Goettsberger, p 9 f.; Linder, p 57). Moreover, recent Catholic commentators are inclined to place the final redaction of Daniel at a much later date than that of the prophet. Now supposing that both the translation and the final redaction were made in Palestine during the Greek period, the linguistic argument will prove only what we actually admit, namely the late date of the final redaction, or, to put it in modern language, the last edition of the book of Daniel. But the origin of the book remains unaffected.

The historical argument, apparently the strongest, is equally inconclusive. That the book contains a number of historical inaccuracies cannot be denied, and it must also be admitted that the efforts made by commentators to defend the accuracy of Daniel are not always successful. Though it is certainly most uncritical and unfair to explain away these historical inaccuracies by laying the blame on copyists, translators and editors, the textual conditions of the MT and ancient versions and the way in which the book, very probably, grew up and was handed down to us must serve as a warning against relying too confidently on certain details which are more liable to scribal manipulation. Thus, for example, there are reasons to believe that the appellation 'Darius the Mede' is a later addition or textual corruption; cf. Lagrange in RB (1904) 501 f.; E. Kissane in *Irish Theol. Quart.* (1919) 57. If this is true, a serious historical difficulty is removed.

The theological argument requires to be treated with reserve. The possibility of prophecy is beyond dispute, so that the question is not whether Daniel *could* foretell future events having no immediate connexion with his contemporaries, but whether he has *actually* done so.

We admit that the prediction of future events having **f** no relation to the Messianic plan of redemption is, at least, not in accordance with OT prophecy in general. Now there is in ' the vision chapters,' especially in ch 11, a mass of historical details couched in prophetic language and yet having no relation to the Messianic kingdom. The assumption that all these historical data are real prophecies would necessarily imply that such irrelevant facts as the marriage of a royal daughter or an unsuccessful political alliance are the objects of a divine revelation, an implication which few, if any, will admit. One feels strongly inclined to consider the prophetic form of certain details as a literary device intended more forcibly to impress upon readers the lesson of history.

In order fully to estimate the real import of the **g**

495g historical or Maccabean standpoint and its bearing upon the date of the book, one must distinguish sharply between the historico-Maccabean and the Messianico-eschatological perspective. The promise of an eternal and universal kingdom to be established upon the ruins of all earthly powers rings throughout the whole book. It is the predominant note, and the point of convergence of all the narratives and visions, whereas the references to the history of either the Babylonian or the Persian or the Greek domination assume a secondary rôle. All these world-empires will be overthrown, the powers of evil will be defeated, and the people of God will enjoy the blessings of a peaceful kingdom established on earth and enduring in heaven for eternity.

h If the prophecies of the book of Daniel are viewed from this twofold standpoint, the theological argument based on the analogy of prophecy loses much of its force. The establishment of the kingdom of God on earth and its consummation in heaven are in themselves independent of the historical circumstances of any particular age, and are the result of God's victory over the powers of darkness symbolized in the person of Antiochus and of all the persecutors of the righteous people. The references to Antiochus IV, and to the Greek period in general, have only a secondary importance, and may be considered as an illustration of the destruction of the enemies of God added by a later writer without any prejudice to the general meaning of the book. In other words, ' the visions section ' may be regarded as the work of Daniel in so far as it foretells the establishment of the Messianic kingdom on earth and its consummation in heaven, while the Maccabean colouring is the work of a 2nd-century editor who adapted Daniel's predictions to the historical conditions of his age.

i It may not be out of place to give here the latest views of Catholic writers on the book of Daniel. J. Nikel believes that the contents of the book go back to the times of the exile, but that the book took its final shape during the Greek age (*Grundriss der Einleitung in das A. T.*, Münster, 1924, p 205). J. Goettsberger holds that the book is made up of two collections, chh 1–6 and chh 7–12, the substance of which goes back to Daniel himself or to his time, but the final redaction of the book was made *c* 300 B.C. Ch 11 has been extensively glossed over (*Das Buch Daniel*, pp 6–8 ; *Einleitung in das A. T.*, p 326). H. Junker thinks that the book is the work of a writer living in the Maccabean age who made use of pre-Maccabean material bearing the name of Daniel. He worked over this older material and illustrated Daniel's visions and symbols by history (*Untersuchungen*, pp 101–7).

j J. Linder explains the Danielic authorship in this manner : 1. The visions were written by Daniel in Hebrew. 2. The narratives were written in Hebrew by Daniel or, at least, in his time, and translated into Aramaic during the Persian age. The translator also rendered ch 7 into Aramaic. 3. A redactor united the two parts together, *c* 300 B.C., and translated 1:1–2:4*a* into Hebrew (p 57). In the latest edition of Höpfl's introduction to the OT it is held that the book in its present form is the work of an unknown writer living *c* 300 B.C., who made use of older material, H. Höpfl–A. Miller–A. Metzinger, *Introductio Specialis in Vetus Testamentum* (Rome, 1946⁵) 482. Dennefeld, 638, without going into details, says in a general way that the book has an apocalyptic character, and received its final form in the Maccabean age, but that its contents go back to the age of the exile.

k Summing up the results of this inquiry into the origin of the book of Daniel, we may say that its formation and transmission had a very eventful history. Daniel himself recorded some of his personal experiences at the court of Babylon. As he did not intend to write a complete autobiography, but to impress upon his fellow exiles belief in the uniqueness of God and his superiority over all heathen deities, the individual episodes, very probably, circulated on separate sheets. They were eagerly read and copied. In course of time these copies were, in varying degrees, retouched and **49** expanded by copyists and editors. The visions were made to apply to the age of Antiochus IV by an inspired writer who lived at that time. These Daniel stories, or many of them, were translated into Aramaic in Palestine, and some of them were probably retranslated into Hebrew. Later they were all translated into Greek. At a certain date the separate narratives were collected into one book according to the form and language which were at hand. It happened that the episode of the idol (ch 3) came into the compiler's hands in its shorter form, and the stories of Susanna and of Bel and the Dragon were either unknown or inaccessible to him. The Greek translators made use of this edition, but either because they wished to have a fuller narrative or for other unknown reasons they adopted the longer redaction for ch 3, and incorporated other stories into their translation.

Doctrinal Value—Though the name Yahweh does not **l** occur in this book, the God of the Israelites is constantly represented as the Only and Living God, an almighty, all-knowing God, the king of kings and the Lord of heaven and earth. He controls all the course of history. He sets up kings and he brings them down. Resistance to his rule ends in destruction ; submission in peace and happiness. God dwells in heaven and rules the world through intermediate spiritual agencies. He permits the righteous to be persecuted only to give them a greater reward if they remain faithful to him.

The **Messianic** doctrine differs sensibly from that of the **m** other prophets inasmuch as it is almost completely absorbed by the eschatological aspect of the kingdom of God. Before the advent of the Messias all hostile powers, and particularly the great persecutor of the people of God, will be utterly overthrown. The Messianic kingdom, unimpressive in its beginnings, will in course of time extend all over the earth. Though established on earth, it will be a spiritual kingdom, based on peace and justice and on the recognition of the Only True God. The rich and varied imagery of temporal blessings, characteristic of other Messianic prophecies, is totally absent. The Messianic king will not conquer the world by the sword, he will be the ' son of man ' and will receive the royal power at the hands of God, who alone has the right to give it ' to whomsoever it shall please him ' (4:14).

The Messianic aspect of the kingdom of God in- **n** sensibly merges into its **eschatological** aspect. The earthly stage of the kingdom of God, in other words the Church of Christ, is only the prelude to its heavenly stage which will last for ever. It is under this eschatological aspect that the kingdom of God, which will be established upon earth, is described as everlasting (2:44 ; 7:18, 27). The inauguration of the heavenly kingdom will be preceded by the destruction of the ' man of sin ' who is generally identified with the Antichrist symbolized by Antiochus. When the Antichrist is overcome, the dead will be called back to life and brought before the final judgement ; the righteous will receive the reward of everlasting life and the wicked will live in everlasting shame.

I, 1 f. Daniel's Deportation—According to Jer 46:2, **4** Nabuchodonosor defeated the Egyptian forces in Syria at Carchemish in the 4th year of Joakim (605 B.C.). Before that year an invasion of Palestine by Nabuchodonosor was therefore impossible. Supposing Jeremias is reckoning the years from the date of accession, while Daniel, following the Babylonian system, is reckoning from the New Year following the accession, the 3rd year of Joakim on the one system would coincide in part with his 4th year on the other. By that victory Syria and Palestine passed under the power of Babylon. While Nabuchodonosor was pursuing the Egyptians down to the borders of Egypt, he received the news of the death of his father, and had to hasten back to Babylon to secure the succession against possible usurpers. On his way back or in his pursuit of the enemy he marched against Jerusalem, very probably

3b to assert his right of dominion over the Judean capital. Joakim came to terms by accepting the status of a vassal king and paying a tribute too heavy for the royal treasury. Some of the temple vessels were carried away to the land of Sennaar, an archaic appellation of Babylonia (Gen 10:10 ; 11:2 ; 14:1, 7, etc.), and placed in the temple of Marduk, the patron-god of Babylon. The words ' and the vessels he brought into the treasure house of his god ' are probably interpolated. The name ' Nabuchodonosor,' Hebrew *Nebukadneṣṣar*, is an alternative form of *Nebukadreṣṣar*, which corresponds to Babylonian *Nabu-kudurri-uṣur*, ' Nebo protect the boundary '.

c 3-7 The Education of Daniel and his Companions—3. In his campaign against Jerusalem Nabuchodonosor took some hostages, *cf.* also 4 Kg 24:1–7 ; 2 Par 36:5–8. It was the custom of oriental kings to have among their pages foreign youths of noble descent. Nabuchodonosor accordingly ordered Asphenez, the chief official of his household, to bring into the court some noble youths of the Jewish captives. **4.** The qualifications required were : absence of any physical imperfection, a comely appearance, and a mental alertness that would enable them to learn quickly and thoroughly all that it was necessary for a page to know. The adjectives ' skilful, acute, instructed ' do not imply three different qualities, but simply serve to emphasize the necessity of their intellectual training. Above all other things the boys had to learn the literature and the tongue of the Chaldeans. The appellation ' Chaldeans ' denotes primarily the people who dwelt SE.

d of Babylon (Gen 11:28, etc.). When Babylon fell into the hands of Nabopolassar, a Chaldean, in 625 B.C., the term Chaldean came to be applied to the subjects of the king of Babylon (4 Kg 25:4–26 ; Is 13:19 ; 23:13, etc.). After the fall of the Babylonian empire it acquired a more restricted sense denoting a special class, the priests of Bel who practised magic arts and were probably of a Chaldean origin. In this sense the word first appears in Herodotus (1, 181, 183), but it never occurs in the OT except in Daniel. It follows that the Chaldean tongue and literature which the Jewish youths had to learn were the incantation texts and the Babylonian language in which they were written. Magic was prohibited by the Mosaic Law (Lev 20:27 ; Deut 18:10–12), but it is nowhere said that Daniel or his companions ever practised this art.

e 5. The course of training was to extend over a period of three years, at the end of which they were to enter the king's service. Their daily food was provided from the king's table. **6.** Among the young nobles were four from Juda. **7.** As a mark of their subjection to another king and to other gods they had their names changed : Daniel ' God is my judge ' was changed into Baltassar, Bab. *balaṭsu-uṣur*, ' (Bel) protect his life ' ; Ananias ' Yahweh is gracious ' into Sidrach, Heb. *Šadrak*, perhaps Bab. *šudur-Aku* ' command of (the god) Aku ' ; Misael ' who is what God is ? ' into Misach, Heb. *Mešak*, perhaps Bab. *mi-ša-Aku* ' who is what Aku is ? ' and Azarias ' Yahweh is a helper ' into Abdenago, Heb. *'abed nego*, Bab. *'abed Nebo*, ' servant of (the god) Nebo '. For the practice of changing the name of high public officials in a foreign country or under a foreign power *cf.* Gen 41:45 ; 4 Kg 23:35 ; 24:17.

f 8-16 The Loyalty of the Youths to their Religion— 8. Certain foods were prohibited to the Jews (Lev 11). Moreover the meat, whether prohibited or not, and the wine might have been offered to the gods before being served. Partaking of such food was a violation of the Levitical law and a recognition of the heathen deities. In order to avoid the possibility of contamination Daniel asked to be allowed to abstain from the meals provided from the royal table. For other instances of abstention from heathen food *cf.* Tob 1:12 ;

g Jud 12:2. **9 f.** The request, bold though it seemed, aroused in the official a feeling of sympathy. He would willingly have acceded to his request, but as responsible for their health he might incur the king's displeasure if they should not look as well as the other boys of their age. **11-13.** Daniel repeated **496g** his request through a subordinate official who had the immediate care of the boys, and proposed a ten-day experiment. The word ' Malasar ', Heb. *hammelsar* is either a proper name, Bab. *amelu-uṣur* ' (Bel) protect (thy) servant ' or a title denoting a particular office, perhaps ' keeper, warden '. **14-16.** As the result was satisfactory, Malasar kept them on a vegetarian diet. God's intervention is naturally implied.

17-20 Daniel and his Companions introduced to the h King—17. God rewarded the youths' steadfast attachment to their religion by an extraordinary wisdom. This wisdom was not the superstitious art of divination (5), but the knowledge of those moral and practical principles that were necessary for the high positions which they were later to occupy. Daniel in particular was endowed with the power of interpreting dreams and visions. This remark is a prelude to the following narratives and serves also to stress the fact that Daniel's exceptional skill was not the result of his training in the literature of the Chaldeans but the gift of God. The science of dreams was highly appreciated in a country where so much importance was attached to them. **18.** At the end of the three years they were introduced to the king who (**19**) after conversing with them found them superior to all the others, and chose them as his personal attendants. **20.** Whatever the king asked them, they invariably proved far superior to all the magicians and enchanters in his realm. The superiority of the God of the Israelites is implicitly asserted.

21 does not necessarily imply that Daniel died in the **i** 1st year of Cyrus, as this is contradicted by 10:1. These chronological indications are very probably editorial additions ; see note to 10:1.

II Nabuchodonosor's Dream—The object of the dream **497a** is to show how all earthly kingdoms will pass away and upon their ruins God will set up a universal and everlasting kingdom. Though the king did not understand the meaning of his dream, he acknowledged the superiority of Daniel's God. The story is parallel to that of Pharaoh and Joseph, Gen 41.

1-12 The Magicians unable to interpret the King's b Dream—1. The date is inconsistent with 1:5, 18. In the second year of Nabuchodonosor Daniel and his companions had not yet completed their course of education, and could not therefore be involved in the condemnation of the wise men (13). The difficulty is not solved by the assumption of a double way of reckoning which would make Nabuchodonosor's second year coincide with the third year of Daniel's education (Goettsberger, p 19 ; Driver, p 17). Other interpreters introduce textual changes and read *sixth* instead of *second* (Montgomery, p 141), or *twelfth* (Linder, p 133 ; *Marti, p 7 ; *Farrar, pp 143 ff.). The date is probably an interpolation. Nabuchodonosor had a dream which agitated his mind and interrupted his sleep. Dreams were regarded by many peoples of antiquity as divine communications, and their meaning was therefore a matter of the greatest importance. The Babylonians, the Assyrians, and the Egyptians had professional dream-interpreters. **2 f.** The king summoned the **c** whole class of *magicians, enchanters, sorcerers* and Chaldeans and requested them to tell him his dream and its interpretation. It has been supposed that the king had really forgotten his dream, and that only a vague and confused impression was left in his mind (Knab.). Probably the king simply pretended to have forgotten his dream only to test the magicians' skill. Naturally the magicians were unable to meet the king's first demand. The word ' Syriac ' in 4 is a gloss based on the false assumption that Syriac, *i.e.* Aramaic, was the language of the Chaldeans. The change from Hebrew into Aramaic in 4*b* cannot therefore be due to a writer living in the 6th century B.C. **5 f.** The king insisted that they should recount the dream themselves. ' *The word from me is sure* ', i.e. I proclaim an irrevocable sentence : ' If you will not tell me the dream and its interpretation, you shall be *cut into pieces* and

497c your houses shall be *made a dunghill*'. Although the severity of the punishment was in accordance with the times, we must not imagine the king as an insensate despot making impossible demands. He believed that an exceptionally important divine communication had been made to him, and wanted to make sure that there was no falsehood in the magicians' interpretation. The threats were, however, balanced by the promise of great rewards if they succeeded in telling the dream **d** and its interpretation. **7-9.** The reason for the king's unusual demand is now made clear. He felt that the dream portended some very important event, and in order to have a guarantee of the truth of the interpretation he insisted that the magicians, endowed, as they were believed to be, with an extraordinary wisdom, should tell him his dream. He repeated his threats. *The sentence is irrevocably given.* In vain do you seek to gain time to have an opportunity to concoct a false interpretation. **10 f.** In order to defend themselves the magicians put forward two arguments : (i) no monarch had ever made such a demand to his magicians ; (ii) no human being, but the gods alone who do not dwell upon earth, can satisfy the king's demand. Implicitly they acknowledged a superhuman wisdom in Daniel, who later told the dream and its interpretation.
e **12 f. The King's Order**—The king burst out into anger and ordered that all the wise men should be slain. A decree was issued to that effect.
f **14-23 Daniel promises to interpret the Dream—14 f.** On that occasion Daniel displayed remarkable prudence and discretion. He immediately sought Arioch, the chief of the royal bodyguard, and inquired the reason of this decree. It may appear strange that Daniel, though found to be ten times wiser than all the magicians of Babylon (1:20) was not summoned with the other wise men. But it must be remarked that Daniel is consistently separated from the king's magicians, and is introduced only when they fail (*cf.* 4:3-5 ; 5:7-13). His wisdom is a gift from God, not a superstitious art. His separateness reflects God's separateness from, and superiority to, the gods of the Chaldeans. **16** raises a serious difficulty. Daniel could not enter the king's presence without being introduced, as is expressly stated in 25. The difficulty is removed by deleting with Theodotion the words ' went in and ' and reading : ' Daniel desired of the king', etc. **17 f.** Daniel communicated the matter to his companions, and urged them to pray that the merciful God might reveal to them this secret and deliver them from impending death. The LXX add ' fasting and penitence ' to prayer. **19-23.** God answered their prayer, and Daniel praised God, confessing his wisdom, his might, his providence, his sovereign power over all kings, his unlimited knowledge and his favour towards them.
g **24-28a Daniel introduced before the King — 24.** Having the king's secret in his hands, Daniel requested to be brought in before him. **25.** Arioch immediately introduced Daniel, who, **26**, declared to the king, **27, 28a**, that though the wise men could not answer the king's demand, there was a God in heaven who could reveal all secrets and who had in reality revealed future events to the king. The expression ' in the latter times ' denotes the Messianic age (*cf.* Is 2:2 ; Mich 4:1). Therefore the revelation refers ultimately to the establishment of the Messianic kingdom on earth.
h **28b-35 The King's Dream—29.** Daniel refers to the natural causes which gave shape to the king's dream. After the fall of the Assyrian empire and the collapse of the Egyptian forces in Syria Nabuchodonosor, who was then ruling over a vast and powerful kingdom, was one night pondering over future conquests or the possibility of hostile attacks. As all his speculations proved fruitless, God revealed to him in a dream what was to happen till a far distant future. **30.** Daniel will tell this portentous dream not because of any superior natural wisdom, but only in order that the king may know the meaning of his dream. **31-35.** The

dream was this : The king saw a colossal and extra- **i** ordinarily bright statue standing before him ; its appearance was terrible. The head was of fine gold ; the breast and the arms of silver ; the abdomen and the hips of bronze ; the legs of iron and the feet partly of iron and partly of clay. While he was wondering at that statue, a stone was cut out from a mountain without any human agency and smote the statue on its feet, breaking it to pieces. Nothing was left of the statue ; the fragments were carried away by the wind, and the stone became a great mountain filling the earth.
36-45 The Interpretation of the Dream—36. The **j** plural ' we ' refers probably to Daniel and his companions, but *cf.* for the use of the plural 2 Cor 1:4-14. **37 f.** The golden head symbolized Nabuchodonosor's kingdom, a powerful and a glorious kingdom. The title ' king of kings ' was common in the Persian age ; *cf.* Esd 7:12. Nabuchodonosor is represented with a certain rhetorical exaggeration as a universal king who, however, has received his kingdom from God. Nabuchodonosor is in reality the greatest king of the Neo-Babylonian dynasty with which he is here identified. **39 f.** The other metals symbolize three other successive kingdoms. The second is described simply as inferior to Nabuchodonosor (omit ' of silver ', 39) ; the third as ruling over all the earth, and the fourth will be strong and destructive as iron. **41 f.** The composite structure **j** of the feet and toes—iron and clay—indicates that the fourth kingdom will be divided into two parts of unequal power of resistance. **43.** An attempt will be made by intermarriages, to give a greater stability to the two rival kingdoms, but alliance will prove as unsuccessful as the intermingling of iron and clay. **44 f.** When all those kingdoms are overthrown, God will set up another kingdom different from all the others. It will be indestructible and eternal, it will ever be in the hands of one people, and will supersede all earthly kingdoms. It appears from 44 that the fifth kingdom will be set up while the other four are still standing. But both the simultaneous destruction of the four kingdoms and the appearance of a fifth kingdom ' in the days of those kingdoms ' are details required by the nature of the image not by its meaning. Daniel solemnly affirms the truth of this interpretation.
46-49 Acknowledgement of God's Superiority and k Elevation of Daniel and his Companions—46. The king deeply impressed by this interpretation and recognizing a superhuman knowledge in Daniel, bowed down to him and ordered that divine honours be given to him. It is idle to inquire how such a strict monotheist as Daniel could accept divine honours, or whether he accepted them at all. The writer's concern is to emphasize Nabuchodonosor's acknowledgement of the supremacy of Daniel's God, an acknowledgement manifested outwardly by the homage paid to Daniel, God's representative. St Jerome (*ad loc.*) pointedly remarks that the king worshipped not so much Daniel as God in Daniel, and refers to Acts 14:10-17 and to a similar fact related by Josephus in *Ant* 11, 8, 5. **47.** The titles ' a god of gods ' and ' a **l** lord of kings ' must be taken here in a polytheistic sense. **48.** Nabuchodonosor kept his promise (6), and bestowed rich gifts on Daniel. He also promoted him to the post of governor of the most important *province* of Babylon, and made him chief of the whole guild of magicians. This last office simply stresses Daniel's superior skill in the interpretation of dreams without implying necessarily that he practised magical arts. **49.** Daniel did not forget his companions. At his request they were appointed to high offices in the province of Babylon, while he remained at court as the king's chancellor. For the expression ' in the gate of the king ' *cf.* Est 2:19, 21 ; 3:2.
Appendix I. Historical Meaning of the Dream—It is **m** universally admitted that the four kingdoms symbolized by the four metals are four historical kingdoms, but there is no agreement about the identification of the kingdoms. The theory prevalent in Catholic exegesis

and which is already found in St Jerome (PL 25, 504, 530) identifies them as : 1. Neo-Babylonian ; 2. Medo-Persian ; 3. Greek ; 4. Roman. Non-Catholic commentators, with a few exceptions, identify them as : 1. Neo-Babylonian ; 2. Median ; 3. Persian ; 4. Greek. Amongst recent Catholic interpreters there is a growing tendency to identify them as : 1. Neo-Babylonian ; 2. Medo-Persian ; 3. Alexander ; 4. Alexander's successors ; Lagrange, RB (1904) 503 f. ; D. Buzy, *Les symboles de l'Ancien Testament*, 1923, pp 266–80 = RB (1918) 403–26 ; M. Becher, VD (1924), 206–10 ; L. Dennefeld, *Le Messianisme*, 1929, p 173 ; J. Chaine, *Introduction à la lecture des prophètes*, 1932, p 260.

As none of these theories is free from difficulties we must try to establish certain facts. It is generally agreed that the four kingdoms of ch 2 are identical with those of ch 7. It is also universally admitted that the first kingdom is the Neo-Babylonian or the reign of Nabuchodonosor, the greatest representative of the Neo-Babylonian dynasty. The fourth kingdom of ch 7 cannot be the Roman empire, because the beast symbolizing it is slain before the establishment of the Messianic kingdom. Even in ch 2 the Messianic kingdom is represented as following the destruction of the statue. The fourth kingdom of ch 7 is certainly the Greek empire, the identification resting mainly on the identity of the fourth beast with the he-goat of ch 8, which symbolizes the Greek empire (8:21). Both beasts are characterized by a small horn growing greater and stronger and making war against the holy people.

While upholding the Greek theory with many Catholic interpreters, we disagree with them in their separation of Alexander's reign from that of his successors. The Jews made no such distinction. For them there was only one Greek empire represented mainly by Antiochus IV. As the horns are a natural feature of the beast, the domination of Alexander's successors must be considered as a part of one empire and not as a separate empire symbolized by a different beast. Moreover, since in ch 8 the Medo-Persian empire is represented as one empire symbolized by one beast, so must it be represented by one beast or by one metal in the other visions. Any attempt, therefore, to split up the Medo-Persian empire into two separate and successive kingdoms is against the writer's view of history. For an exhaustive discussion of the various theories, see H. H. Rowley, pp 61–173, where the view current in Protestant exegesis is strongly defended.

On account of the difficulties which confront all these theories one feels inclined to ask whether the number four is a historical number or rather, to a certain extent, schematic (Junker, p 9). In fact, Daniel seems to be predicting not a definite number of historical kingdoms, but *all* the historical kingdoms, whatever their number, from Nabuchodonosor to the establishment of the kingdom of God. These kingdoms are distributed into four periods, and in 7:2 are related to the four winds which have certainly a meaning of universality (*cf.* Zach 6:1, 5 ; Apoc 7:1). The schematic plan is also evinced by the fact that the writer displays no interest in the second and third kingdoms. He gives no clue for their identification. Their only function in the writer's plan is to succeed one kingdom and be succeeded by another. Therefore it is at least probable that, while the first and fourth kingdoms represent two definite and historical kingdoms, the second and third are intended to fill up the period intervening between the fall of Babylon and the Greek domination. A similar interpretation has been proposed by St Augustine for the ten horns in 7:7, which, according to him represented all the kings of the Roman empire (*De Civ. Dei* 20, 22 ; PL 41, 695 f.).

Appendix II The Messianic Kingdom—Catholic exegesis has from very early times identified the fifth kingdom symbolized by the stone with the Messianic kingdom. There seems to be an allusion to the Messianic interpretation in Hermas, *Similitudes*, 9, 2.12. The Church has made extensive use of Daniel in the office of Christ the King. The Messianic kingdom is described as a **498e** spiritual or divine, universal and eternal kingdom. The destruction of the hostile powers is not necessarily simultaneous, but a time will come when all opposition will be overcome and the Church of Christ will spread over all the earth. The kingdom of Christ must be considered in both its earthly and its heavenly stage. The *sensus plenior* of the prophecy includes all the stages of development of the Church until its consummation in heaven.

Although the coming of the Messianic kingdom is **f** closely associated with the collapse of the fourth kingdom, which we have identified with the Greek empire, we must not take this chronological succession in a strict sense. Future events are generally revealed without any distinct indication of their dates, and consequently the Messianic future is, not infrequently, represented as following immediately upon historical events which in reality are separated from it by a long interval. Therefore we must not infer that Daniel expected the foundation of the Messianic kingdom immediately after the fall of the fourth kingdom. The expression ' in the days of those kingdoms ' has no strict chronological bearing on the establishment of the Messianic kingdom, see note to 2:44.

III—The object of this chapter is twofold : (i) to **499a** illustrate the uniqueness and supremacy of the God of the Israelites ; (ii) to lay down a rule of religious conduct, namely, the faithful must choose martyrdom before apostasy. For later references to the story see 1 Mac 2:59 ; Hb 11:34.

1-7 The Erection and Dedication of the Golden Idol—1. **b** In the LXX and Theodotion the story is dated ' in the eighteenth year of Nabuchodonosor '. This date corresponds to the 19th year of Nabuchodonosor according to the Jewish system of computation, the year of the fall of Jerusalem (2 Kg 25:8 ; Jer 52:12). If the date is genuine, the statue was probably erected to celebrate the king's victories and to honour the patron-god of Babylon. The statue was very likely a colossal stele partly sculptured at the top and overlaid with gold. The dimensions, *c* 90 feet in height and *c* 9 feet in breadth, are to be referred to both the part presenting human lineaments and to the pedestal. The image was erected outside the city of Babylon, in the plain of Dura. **2 f.** For the ceremony of the solemn dedication of the statue the king summoned all the high officials of his kingdom among whom were naturally Daniel's companions. A great crowd was also present. **4-7.** A proclamation was then made that as soon as the signal should be given all were to fall down and worship the statue. Disobedience would be punished by burning. The furnace was probably a lime-kiln with an opening at the top for the escape of smoke (22), and another at the bottom for supplying the furnace with fuel. There is an allusion to a similar form of punishment in Jer 29:22.

8-12 The Accusation against the three Jews—Daniel's **c** companions refused to obey the king's order. On seeing this some of the Chaldeans or magicians (see 1:4) stimulated by jealousy, maliciously slandered (lit. ' ate the pieces of ') the Jews who stood so high in the king's favour. The reason why Daniel has no part in this story may be either that the Chaldeans were afraid of him on account of his very high position, or that he was not present at the ceremony.

13-18 The Jews' Courage and Faith—13 f. The king, **d** wishing to prove the truth of this charge, ordered the Jews to be brought before him, and inquired whether they really refused to worship his god. **15.** It was not a mere inquiry ; it was a command ; and the Jews were once more ordered to bow down and worship the statue under penalty of being burnt alive. If the statue was erected after the capture of Jerusalem (see 1) it was certainly intended to express the superiority of Bel over Yahweh, a superiority which is clearly implied in Nabuchodonosor's defiant words : ' Who is the God that will deliver you from my hands ? ' The inconsistency of these words with Nabuchodonosor's

499d recognition of the God of Daniel as the God of gods and the Lord of kings (2:47) is perfectly compatible with the polytheistic belief of Nabuchodonosor.

e **16.** To the king's command they replied unhesitatingly : We have no *need* to answer thee concerning this matter. They believed in God and trusted in him, and refused to discuss the question whether he could deliver them. The king had challenged God's power, but their faith remained unshaken. **17.** They expressed their loyal attachment to their God in the most explicit terms : ' *Whether* our God, whom we worship, is able to save... **18.** *or not*, be it known to thee, O king, . . .' These words do not imply a doubt about God's power, but are to be understood from the king's point of view. Whether God is able, as we believe, or not, as you think.

f **19-23 The three Jews in the Burning Furnace—19.** On hearing this the king's countenance was disfigured with rage. He ordered that the furnace, one of the many brick-kilns round the town, should be heated seven times more than was necessary for ordinary purposes. **20 f.** The strongest men of the army were then commanded to bind the three Jews clad as they were in their mantles, their tunics, and their headgears, and throw them into the fiery furnace. **22 f.** While they were being thrown in, the executioners perished in the flames that were fiercely bursting forth through the top opening of the kiln.

g **24-90 The Miraculous Deliverance of the three Jews—** This section is not found in MT ; *cf.* § 494*l*. It consists of three parts : the prayer of Azarias (25-45), a historical interlude (46-50), a song of praise and thanksgiving (51-90).

h **24-45 The Prayer of Azarias—**This is a confession of the Israelites' sins and God's justice and a prayer for deliverance. For similar confessions *cf.* 9:4-19 ; Neh 9:6-37 ; Bar 1:15-3:8. It is out of its historical context. Azarias could not possibly stand up in the midst of the flames unless the flames had been rendered harmless, but it was in v 50 that the angel in response to Azarias' prayer ' made the midst of the furnace like the blowing of a wind ', and then the three Jews broke out in a hymn of praise. There are some textual variations between LXX and Theodotion. The prayer was probably made while the men were being bound and the furnace was being heated (Linder, p 193 f.). **24** reads better after 50. **25.** The words ' in the midst of the fire ' have been added to make the prayer fit in with its present context. **26-28.** God deserves all praise because he is just in all his dealings with his people, just in his commandments, in his punishments, in his warnings, in his threats and promises ; *cf.* Deut 32:4. **29 f.** Azarias confesses the people's sins : apostasy from God and transgression of his law, **31,** and the justice of God's punishments. **32 f.** The people, for their sins, were given up into the hands of their godless enemies, and particularly into the hands of Nabuchodonosor, the most wicked of all ; confusion and shame *have befallen* the servants and worshippers of God, who cannot even express their grief. **34-36.** Azarias implores God's mercy and forgiveness. Total extermination of the people would mean a breach of God's covenant with the Patriarchs and consequently bring disrespect upon his name. **37-40.** He describes in moving terms the miserable condition of the people. They were reduced to a contemptible number ; they had none to govern them, no prophets, no temple, no liturgical service whereby they could propitiate God. The only thing they could offer was a contrite and humble heart, which they hoped would have the same propitiatory effect as the Levitical sacrifices. The words ' there is no prophet ' seem to point to the Maccabean age when there were no prophets (1 Mac 4:46). But though both Jeremias and Ezechiel were still living when Jerusalem was captured, the episode may have been written when the two prophets were dead, and there was none who could speak in the name

j of God. **41.** Repentance is accompanied by the purpose of a new life. **42-45.** At last they appeal to God's goodness and mercy, praying him to deliver them from their enemies, to bring shame and disgrace upon their oppressors in order that all may know that he is the only God on all the earth. Although the prayer hardly fits in with its historical context, it cannot be said to be inconsistent with it. It is a national, penitential prayer, which may well be applied to the three Jews. Azarias is speaking on behalf of his people. He identifies himself with his people, and prays God to deliver them from their enemies.

46-50 Historical Interlude—46-48 are, very probably, a duplicate account of 22 f. derived from another source. There is therefore no contradiction between the two passages. Theodotion, from whom this section is derived, omits v 22 in which the death of the executioners is recorded. The apparent contradiction in Vg is due to the fact that St Jerome has combined in his translation two texts, the Aramaic text and Theodotion's Greek version. **49 f.** are the sequel to 45. In response to Azarias' prayer the angel of the Lord came down into the furnace with the three Jews—the prayer having been made while they were being bound (see § 499*h*)—produced a cool breeze in the midst of the burning furnace, and they were unscathed by the flames. The miraculous deliverance is represented as being due to the angel's driving the flames out of the furnace. This, however, is rather a popular representation of God's protective power and omnipotence.

51-90 The Song of the Three Children—This is a litany psalm, as Ps 135, made up of two parts, distinguished from one another both by their contents and the form of the responsory. The first part, 52-56 with 57, is read in the Sunday office at Lauds II ; the other part, or 57-88*b*, with two additional verses and without the responsories, is read in the Sunday office at Lauds I. The responsories are probably liturgical additions (*Liber Psalm. cum cant. Brev. Rom.*, Romae, 1945, 338). We need not suppose that the song was composed by the young men themselves. They may have simply recited a hymn of praise which they had learned before ; there is, therefore, no contradiction between 53 and 38.

51-56. They praise the God of their fathers, the God of the covenant, who has manifested his sanctity and magnificence by his presence in the temple of Jerusalem and on the throne of Israel, an all-seeing and all-knowing God whose heavenly throne rests on the cherubim (Ez 1:10 ; 11:22), and whose glory fills the heavens.

57-90. This is an invitation to all creatures to praise God. **57.** The works of the Lord are the works of creation, *i.e.* all created things which are enumerated in the following verses from the angels and heavens to the earth and men, and ultimately to the three Jews. **58.** The angels, the noblest of all creatures, lead the chorus of praise. Vg follows LXX, but in Theodotion 58 and 59 change places. **59-73.** The heavens, abode of rain (Gen 1:7) and all the celestial bodies, the sun and the moon, the stars, showers and dew, the *winds*, fire and heat, cold and *frost* (LXX), dew and hoar-frost, frost and cold, ice and snow, night and day, light and darkness, lightnings and clouds are next called upon to praise the Lord. The two pairs, ' cold and frost ' and ' dew and hoar-frost ' in 67 and 68 are omitted by the Vatican MS of Theodotion, and very probably are to be deleted as repetitions.

74-81. The earth with its mountains and hills, its vegetation, its fountains, its seas and rivers, and all that moves in the waters, its birds, its beasts and cattle join in this hymn of praise. **82-87.** Man comes last and in this order : all men in general, the people of Israel, the priests, the ministers of the Lord, the righteous people, the pious and oppressed worshippers of God. **88-90.** Conclusion. It is strange that the three Jews should be addressed in the second person and referred to in the first person in the same verse. Reading the first person throughout the sense would be : Let us all, now and forever, praise God who has delivered us from the abode of the dead and from impending death, from the midst of the flames, from the midst of the fire (note the parallelism). **89** is a well-known liturgical versicle; *cf.* 1 Par 16:34, 41 ; 2 Par 7:3, 6 ; etc. **90.** A last invitation to praise God is made to all the worshippers of the true God, whether Israelites or Gentiles.

91-97 (Aram. 24-30) The King's Recognition of the True God—91 (24). The king was sitting opposite to the side-opening of the furnace watching the execution of the sentence. On seeing four men walking in the furnace he was astonished and rising up from his seat asked his ministers whether it was not the fact that three men had been thrown into the furnace. Theodotion and LXX add that the king heard the men singing. **92 (25).** The causes of the king's astonishment were : there were four men instead of three ; their bonds had been burnt away and they were walking freely in the midst of the fire ; they were uninjured by the flames ; the fourth man looked like *a son of the gods, i.e.* an angel (so expressly LXX). All this becomes perfectly understandable if 49 f. are considered as a part of the original narrative. **93 (26).** What the ministers' reply was we are not told. Naturally they did not know more than the king himself. Hence the king was bound to attribute the deliverance of the three men to a divine intervention, and called them out of the furnace, addressing them as the ' servants of the Most High God'. Nabuchodonosor recognized the God of the Israelites as the supreme god, but not necessarily as the Only God. **94 (27).** Then all the high officials gathered around the three Jews, and were astonished that they had not even the smell of burning on them. The truth of the miracle was thus evidenced by the king and his ministers. **95 (28).** The king extolled the God of the Israelites, who had protected his faithful servants, and praised the courage of the three young men who had *frustrated* his order and faced death itself that they might not depart from their God. **96 (29).** Nabuchodonosor once more recognized the power of the Israelites' God and his supremacy, and issued a decree threatening with the most severe punishment those who should speak against this God. The king's confession is that of a polytheist who believes in one god without excluding others. **97 (30).** The three Jews were reinstated in their former posts.

98 (31)-IV 15. Nabuchodonosor's Second Dream— This episode is another illustration of the supremacy of the God of Israel recognized by a heathen king. **98-100 (31-33).** The royal proclamation, though placed at the beginning of the narrative, is in reality the result of the king's psychical experiences related later. After addressing all his subjects who, according to diplomatic style, are represented as dwelling in all the earth (*cf.* 6:25), the king manifests his intention to make known the wonderful deeds of God, the Most High (*cf.* 3:93). The body of the edict is made up of two couplets after the manner of the Hebrew Psalms (*cf.* Ps 144 [145] 13), and betrays a Jewish origin. **IV 1-4.** After having extended his conquests as far as Egypt and embellished Babylon with magnificent streets and buildings, Nabuchodonosor was enjoying a quiet life, and was ' flourishing in his palace' as a mighty tree stretching forth its boughs far and wide. The date ' in the eighteenth year', given by LXX is an insertion from 3:1. One night the king was, perhaps, complacently imagining himself or his capital Babylon to be like a mighty cedar tree affording shade and shelter to men and beasts. For the comparison of a powerful empire with the cedar tree *cf.* Ez 31:3-9. Then he saw a dream which was, naturally, provoked by his heated imagination, but the meaning of which he could not understand. The magicians were unable to interpret the dream. The fact that Daniel, who had been made chief of the magicians (2:48), was not consulted first, as was to be expected, is meant to emphasize Daniel's independence of, and superiority to, all the idolatrous and superstitious wise men of Babylon (see notes to 2:14-28*a*, 48).

5 f. As the magicians were unable to interpret the **500c** dream, Daniel was *at last* called before the king. Daniel's Babylonian name Baltassar, Heb. *Bēlt*ᵉ*šaṣṣar,* is linked up with the name of the Babylonian god Bel, which, very probably, was originally a component element of Daniel's full name *Bel-balaṭsu-uṣur* ' (Bel) protect his life'. Daniel is described as being possessed of ' the spirit of the holy gods', considered as a source of inward illumination (*cf.* Gen 41:38). **6*b*** must be read, with Theodotion : ' hear the visions and tell the interpretation of them'. **7-15.** The king relates his dream. He saw a mighty tree which grew higher and stronger, till it reached to heaven and extended over all the earth. It afforded nourishment and shelter to all the beasts and fowl of the earth. While the king was wondering at that tree, a holy ' watcher' came down from heaven. The term ' watcher' or better ' wakeful one' denotes an angel, the angels being ever vigilant and ready to perform God's commands (St Jerome *ad loc.*). This appellation first occurs in Daniel, but became common in later literature. In the apocryphal book of Enoch angels are called ' holy watchers' (15:9), ' watchers of heaven' (12:4 ; 13:10). The angel with a loud voice ordered the tree to be **d** cut down. But a stump was to be left encircled with a metal clamp. The last figure most likely marks a transition from allegory to reality. As the cutting down of the tree symbolizes the calamity which was to befall the king, the metal band must certainly refer to the physical restraint imposed upon him or to the iron bonds with which he had to be bound during his madness. The king, not the symbolic tree, *will feed on* the grass of the field, be wet with the dew, and dwell among the wild beasts (omit ' in the grass of the earth', 12). His heart, which according to Hebrew **e** psychology is the organ of intellect, will be made like that of a beast. This state will last seven years, a time expression denoting a period of an unspecified duration. The king's doom is irrevocably fixed by God at the request of the holy watchers, who form a sort of divine council (*cf.* 3 Kg 22:19 ff. ; Job 1-2). The scope of the angels' demand was the manifestation of the sovereignty of God, who alone had the power to set up kings on the throne and to raise up over the earthly kingdoms even the humblest of men. Having related this dream, the king pathetically requested Daniel to give its interpretation.

16-24 The Interpretation of the Dream—16. On hear- **f** ing the ominous dream, Daniel, to whom God had revealed its meaning, was *for a while appalled* or perplexed at having to announce to the king his impending calamity. The king perceived his embarrassment and encouraged him to speak out. Daniel began by expressing the desire that the disasters portended by the dream might be averted from him and fall upon his enemies. **17-19.** Then he proceeded to interpret the dream. The tree symbolized the king as the personification of a vast and powerful empire. **20-22.** As the tree was cut down, so will the king fall from his pride and glory ; he will be driven away from his city into the wilderness where he will live in company with the beasts and in a beastlike manner until he recognizes that God, the Most High, the true and only God, is the supreme ruler and that it is from him, not from other deities, that kings receive their power. **23.** The stump left in the earth symbolizes the king's restoration to power which will follow his recognition of the divine origin of all human power. ' Heaven' is a metonym for God common in later Judaism ; *cf.* 1 Mac 3:18, 19, 50, 60, etc. **24.** Then Daniel advised the king to atone for his iniquities by good works and alms-giving ; by this means God would perhaps prolong the king's prosperity. The theological doctrine of the meritoriousness of good works is clearly implied ; *cf.* Tob 4:11 ; 12:9.

25-34 The Fulfilment of the Dream—25-27. The king **g** did not give heed to Daniel's warning, and the doom, which had been foretold, fell on him. After a twelve-month respite for repentance Nabuchodonosor was one

500g day walking upon the roof of his palace in Babylon and admiring the great city and the magnificent buildings which he had erected. He was a great builder, and his utterance in 27 is reminiscent of the high-flown expressions by which he records his architectural achievements. His inscriptions contain the following phrases : ' My dear Babylon, the city which I love ' ; ' the palace, the wonder of the people, the seat of royalty ; the abode of happiness '. **28 f.** The king had no sooner uttered the boastful words than a mysterious voice announced to him the immediate fulfilment of **h** the dream. **30.** At that very moment he was seized by a sudden attack of mania and had to be driven out to dwell with the beasts in the open fields. Nabuchodonosor's malady is scientifically known as ' lycanthropy ' or ' insania zoanthropica', a form of insanity in which the patient imagines himself to be a beast and behaves like a beast. The king's external appearance became, to a certain extent, similar to that of a beast. His unkempt hair grew thick and rough like an eagle's feathers, and his uncut and hooked nails like claws. **31 f.** At the end of an unspecified period of time (see 22) Nabuchodonosor recovered his human consciousness. He lifted up his eyes to heaven and his reason was restored to him. He then praised the living God, acknowledging his everlasting domination and kingdom, the worthlessness of all men, God's irresistible power in heaven and on earth and the helplessness of all men before him. The ideas expressed here by the king occur in other books ; *cf.* 31*b* and Ps 144 (145) 13 ; 32*a* and Is 40:17 ; 32*b* and Is 24:21 ; 32*c* and Is 43:13 ; 45 :9 ; Job 9:12 ; Eccles 8:4. **33.** The king was welcomed back to his kingdom by his ministers, reinstated in his former majesty and *splendour*, and restored to even greater glory. **34.** In the final doxology the king recognizes the justness of God, who punishes those who, like himself, walk haughtily before him. As has been remarked at the beginning of this chapter, the royal proclamation in 3:98–100 is the chronological sequel to ch 4. This, however, is not a sufficient reason for transposing 3:98–100 after 4:34. The writer has preferred a logical to a chronological nexus.

i **Appendix—Nabuchodonosor's Madness.** Against the historicity of this chapter it is objected by non-Catholic interpreters that (i) there is no historical evidence of Nabuchodonosor's insanity in contemporary documents ; (ii) the narrative serves a didactic purpose.

j To these objections it is replied : (i) there is no reason for supposing that Nabuchodonosor could not suffer from the particular form of insanity which is described in ch 4, and which is indisputably attested by medical observation ; (ii) we possess no complete biography of Nabuchodonosor ; contemporary documents hardly record anything else except his architectural achievements, and we must not expect the royal scribes to record the weaknesses of their royal masters ; (iii) a story about Nabuchodonosor, bearing a certain resemblance to the biblical account and accredited by some interpreters, is told by Megasthenes (*c* 300 B.C.), and preserved by Eusebius (*Praep. ev.* IX 41 ; PG 21, 761) ; (iv) the didactic character of a narrative is by no means inconsistent with its historicity. The view held by some recent commentators (Riessler, p 44 ; Goettsberger, p 41) that Nabuchodonosor in ch 4 stands for Nabonidus who, for some years, lived in retirement in the Arabian city of Tema is not probable.

501a **V Baltassar and the Fall of Babylon**—This chapter is remarkable for its historical difficulties. On reading it without any reference to other historical information one will hardly escape the impression that Baltassar (Belshazzar) was the sole supreme ruler of Babylon ; that he was the son of Nabuchodonosor ; that he held a festival on the eve of the fall of Babylon, and was slain on that night, and that he was succeeded by Darius the Mede.

b All this is inconsistent with the available historical information. In the inscriptions Baltassar is invariably called ' the son of the king ', but never ' the

king '. It appears that he was never elevated to the **5** throne either as co-regent with his father or as subordinate king. The statement which is met with in the inscriptions that Nabonidus entrusted the kingship to Baltassar does not imply more than a delegation of a limited power to be exercised during the king's absence from the capital (S. Smith, *Babylonian Historical Texts*, 1924, pp 84, 88). Moreover Baltassar, so far as contemporary evidence goes, was neither the son nor the grandson of Nabuchodonosor, nor was he in any way related to him. Lastly, it is unlikely that a king would hold such a festival when the invading army of the Persians was approaching Babylon and many cities had already fallen to the enemy. From **c** the Nabonidus-Cyrus Chronicle we learn that the troops of Cyrus entered Babylon without fighting. After some weeks Cyrus himself entered the city proclaiming peace to all (H. Gressmann, *Altorient. Texte zum A.T.*, 1926², p 368). There is nothing in the cuneiform records suggesting that Babylon offered any resistance to the Persians, and that Baltassar was killed in battle. The succession of Darius the Mede is definitely contradicted by all we know of the history of that period. See on the whole question H. H. Rowley, *The Historicity of the fifth chapter of Daniel*, JTS (1931) 12–31.

Those who uphold the historicity of the narrative **d** argue at length that since Baltassar was invested with royal authority, he could well be called king, though in point of fact he is never so called in the inscriptions. Moreover, though there is no evidence of a blood relationship between Nabuchodonosor and Baltassar, it is reasonable to suppose that Nabonidus, Baltassar's father, and a usurper of the throne of Babylon, had married a daughter of Nabuchodonosor or his widow in order to strengthen his position. S. Smith propounds the theory that queen Nitocris, mentioned by Herodotus, 1, 185, was the mother of Nabonidus, and became the wife of Nabuchodonosor after being deported from Harran to Babylon, *Babylonian Historical Texts*, 43–45. Nabonidus was consequently the son of Nabuchodonosor's wife, and in a legal sense the son of Nabuchodonosor. Consequently Baltassar was the grandson of the latter. As regards the capture of Babylon, the cuneiform documents have not preserved a full account of the event. But it seems to be established that the Persians entered the city during a night revel and that a prominent personage, perhaps Baltassar himself, died on that occasion (C. Boutflower, *The Historical Value of Daniel v and vi*, JTS [1915] 43–60, and *In and Around the Book of Daniel*, pp 114–41 ; B. Alfrink, *Der letze König von Babylon*, Bi [1928] 187–205 ; *R. P. Dougherty, *Nabonidus and Belshazzar*, New-Haven, 1929 ; Linder, pp 244–52).

Let us try to find a middle course. Baltassar certainly **e** was not king, and it may be granted that he was not even co-regent with his father. But he was invested with a certain measure of royal authority, and consequently he could be called king at least in a sense corresponding to that limited degree of authority. To the popular mind Baltassar was the king of Babylon, especially in the absence of his father. Though, speaking with historical accuracy, the title was inappropriate, it can hardly be said to be untrue. This popular use of the royal title may have been determined by the didactic character of the narrative. Daniel's object was to draw a contrast between the proud but religious and repentant Nabuchodonosor and the sacrilegious, godless, and unrepentant Baltassar, and between the different fate which befell the two rulers. Nabonidus, the actual king, did not make a good contrast with Nabuchodonosor, and so his rôle had to be played by his son, who is therefore represented as king. This contrast explains also the reason why Baltassar is described as the son of Nabuchodonosor. We need not suppose that Nabonidus married Nabuchodonosor's widow or daughter. Baltassar's **f** popular appellation of king made him a successor of Nabuchodonosor, who consequently was a predecessor of Baltassar. This relation of ' predecessor-successor ' which ordinarily but not necessarily implies that of ' ancestor-descendant ' or ' father-son ', seems to be the only one involved in Daniel's narrative. The question of the possibility of the festival may be dismissed in a few words. We do not know whether it was simply a state banquet or a religious feast which had to be kept in spite of adverse conditions. The circumstances of Baltassar's death are not known from cuneiform documents. The fact that the troops of Cyrus entered Babylon without fighting does not exclude the possibility that Baltassar was killed either by the Persians or by the Babylonians for some unknown reason. The question of Darius the Mede will be dealt with in the next chapter.

1-4 Baltassar's Feast—1. No indication is given of the occasion or the date of the feast. The date may be determined from 30 f. The fall of Babylon is now placed with certainty on the 16th of the month Tishri (= 12th October) of the year 539 B.C. The name of the king is *Bēlšaṣṣar*, Bab. *Bel-šar-uṣur* ' Bel protect the king ', (Belshazzar) and must therefore be distinguished from the Babylonian name of Daniel. In Vg and DV Baltassar represents two different Babylonian names. See note on 1:7. The extraordinary number of guests was in accordance with the custom of oriental monarchs. The king was seated at a higher table facing the guests. **2-4.** When he *tasted* the wine, not necessarily when he was drunk, he sacrilegiously ordered the sacred vessels of the temple of Jerusalem (1:2) to be brought into the banquet-hall. According to Babylonian custom women were admitted to these banquets, though under Persian and Greek rule they were not allowed to sit at table with men. The concubines were wives of an inferior rank. Insult was added to profanation when the sacred vessels were used for libations to the Babylonian gods amidst the songs and chants of the revellers.

5 f. The Writing on the Wall—5. When the revelry was at its height the king saw the appearance of a man s hand moving slowly upon the wall opposite to him and tracing some letters on the white plaster, which was lit up by candles. **6.** At that sight he was alarmed, grew pale, and began to tremble so violently that his knees struck one against the other. We are not told whether the guests saw this vision, as the writer was not concerned with them.

7-9 The Magicians unable to read the Writing—The order of these verses seems to be disarranged, because the magicians are twice introduced to the king. W. Baumgartner in Kittel's *Biblia Hebraica*, 3rd ed., transposes 8*a* between 7*a* and 7*b*. The existing order, however, may be retained if we assume that the royal decree contained in 7*b* was brought to the magicians' knowledge by the king's ministers. Rewards were promised to the successful interpreter. Purple and the golden necklace were worn by persons of high rank ; *cf.* Est 8:15 and the apocryphal 3 Esd 3:6. The meaning of the title ' third ' is not clear. Some explain it as the third after Nabonidus and Belshazzar ; others the third after the king and the queen-mother. But the Aramaic word *talti* (16, 29 *talta*), which is apparently related to *tᵉlataya*, Heb. *šalîš* ' third ', is probably a loanword from Hittite *šalliš*, a word denoting a high official in close attendance on the king ; *cf.* A. Cowley in JTS (1920) 326 f., Montgomery 256. The magicians were unable to explain the words, though presumably they could read them. The king's agitation increased and produced bewilderment and confusion among the guests.

10-16 Daniel before the King—10-12. The queen-mother, who was not with the king's wives mentioned in 2, entered the banquet-hall and advised the king to summon Daniel, a man whom she knew to be endowed with a divine spirit (see 4:5), and who, for his singular wisdom, was made chief of all the magicians by Nabuchodonosor (2:48), and from whom no secret was hidden. **13-16.** Daniel was therefore brought before the king, to whom he appears to have been personally unknown. The king repeated his promises and declared the magicians' failure to read the writing.

17-28 Daniel Interprets the Writing—17. Daniel **501k** promised to read the writing, but refused to accept any gift from the impious king. **18-21.** He recalled Nabuchodonosor's fate and his submission to God, the supreme ruler of all the earth (*cf.* 4:25-34). **22-24.** He then reproached the king for his irreligious spirit. The doom was inexorable ; no respite for repentance was offered. **25-28.** The inscription on the wall was : *mᵉnē', mᵉnē', tᵉqēl uparsîn*. The repetition of the first word and the plural ending of the last are not attested by Theod., Vg and Josephus (*Ant* 10, 11, 3), and are not held to be original by Charles and Montgomery, who believe that the words were originally vocalized as nominal forms *mᵉne', tᵉqel, pᵉrēs*, and were interpreted by the Greek translators as passive participles. Hence the sense is : Number(ed) : God has numbered the days of thy domination and brought them to a close. Weight (or weighed) : weighed art thou in the balance of divine judgement and found wanting. Division (or divided) : thy kingdom is divided or taken away from thee, and given to the Medes and Persians. This is the oldest interpretation which is already in Jerome. A recent interpretation, which is more common, **l** though hardly more probable, reads the first word as a passive participle meaning ' numbered ', and the other three as names of weights, *mᵉne'* being the equivalent of Heb. *māneh*, the mina ; *tᵉqel* being the Aramaic form of Heb. *šeqel*, the shekel ; and *parsîn* being the plural or dual of *pᵉrās*, a late Jewish name for the half-mina. Hence the sense : Numbered : a mina, a shekel and (two) half-minas. The proportion of the weights is 60, 1, 30 + 30. The mina represents the flourishing reign of Nabuchodonosor ; the shekel is Baltassar ; the two half-minas are the Medes and Persians considered as one kingdom. So Riessler, Goettsberger, Linder, Marti, Driver, Boutflower, Bentzen. If the inscription contains a threat, as it certainly does, the first interpretation agrees better with the context.

29. The king keeps his promise and bestows rewards upon Daniel. There is no contradiction between 17 and 29. Daniel would not let himself be influenced by the promise of rewards in the interpretation of the mysterious writing.

30. The divine sentence was swiftly carried into effect. On that same night Baltassar, the last king of the Neo-Babylonian dynasty, was murdered, and the power passed into the hands of Darius the Mede.

Appendix—Darius the Mede. Darius the Mede is **m** represented in 5:31 as the immediate successor of the last king of the Neo-Babylonian empire. Comparing this statement with 6:28, where Darius is mentioned before Cyrus, and with 11:1 where the 1st year of Darius is supposed to have preceded the 3rd year of Cyrus (10:1) it is inferred that the writer has interposed a Median empire between the Neo-Babylonian and the Persian, and a Median king ruling between Baltassar and Cyrus. This is a glaring misconception of history. There is indisputable historical evidence that Cyrus was the first king of Babylon after the collapse of the Neo-Babylonian dynasty. The Persian troops entered Bablyon on the 16th of Tishri (= 12th October) ; Cyrus entered Babylon on the 3rd of Marchesvan (= 28th October), and in the contract tablets, the earliest of which is dated 24th Marchesvan (= 19th November) Cyrus is already called ' king of Babylon '. There is therefore no room for an interregnum following the fall of Babylon.

Some interpreters believe that the name Darius the **n** Mede is a textual corruption or later addition, and that Darius Hystaspes is the real name of the king (M.-J. Lagrange, RB [1904] 501 f. ; E. J. Kissane, *The Irish Theological Quarterly* [1919] 43-57 ; J. Goettsberger, p 49). But the majority of Catholic interpreters retain the name, which recurs in 9:1 and 11:1, and endeavour to discover the person represented by that name. They argue that the man called Darius was not an independent sovereign, as the Aramaic text says simply that he *received* the kingdom, *i.e.* the

501n power, but not that he *succeeded* (Vg) to the throne of Baltassar. His position was therefore that of a governor or an associate king or a subordinate king. Consequently he is identified with Gobryas, the general who led the Persian army into Babylon (DBV art. *Darius le Mède*) ; with Cambyses, the son of Cyrus, whose name is sometimes associated with that of his father on the contract tablets and is called ' king of Babylon ', while Cyrus is ' king of lands ' (Boutflower, pp 142–67) ; with Astyages, the last king of Media, captured by Cyrus who, however, spared his life and appointed him governor or viceroy of Babylon (B. Alfrink, *Darius Medus*, Bi [1928] 316–40 ; Linder, pp 279–81) ; with Cyaxares, the son of Astyages, according to Xenophon, *Cyr.* I, 5, 2, etc. (Knabenbauer, pp 171–3). On all these identifications see H. H. Rowley, pp 7–53.

o Non-Catholic interpreters mostly try to find an explanation in the confused historical conceptions of the writer, who, living a long time after the events related by him, was unable to distinguish true historical facts from confused and distorted traditions (Marti, 42 ; Driver, 70 ; Charles, 139–46 ; Rowley, 54–60 ; Bentzen, 28 f.).

p While recognizing the insufficiency of any of the identification theories and refusing on the other hand to ascribe an historical error to the inspired writer, I feel inclined to admit the existence of a confused historical tradition attributable, however, to later editors, who have put together the separate episodes fitting them into a historical framework corresponding to the conceptions of their own time. That the book of Daniel has seriously suffered at the hands of copyists and editors is admited by all, and though it is not always possible to distinguish additional - elements, certain verses are so loosely connected with the context that they clearly betray their origin. Thus the name Darius the Mede in 12:1 is regarded as a gloss by some interpreters. The chronological indication in 10:1 betrays a late origin, and many other chronological indications are to be treated with reserve. That Darius the Mede is a creation of ignorant scribes has recently also been admitted by H. Höpfl–A. Miller–A. Metzinger, *Introductio Specialis in V. Testamentum* (1946⁵), 484 f.

502a **VI Daniel in the Lions' Den**—The story is parallel to that narrated in ch 3. Both stories stress the supremacy of Daniel's God and the duty of observing the religion of the Only God even in the midst of persecutions. But while ch 3 dwells on the negative duties of religion, ch 6 deals rather with its positive duties.

b **1-9 (Aram 2-10) The Ministers' Plot against Daniel—1.** Darius, obviously Darius the Mede previously mentioned, appointed 120 satraps or governors over his empire. Herodotus (III, 89) says that Darius Hystaspes (521–485 B.C.) divided the empire into 20 satrapies, but in Esther 1:1 Xerxes is said to have ruled over 127 provinces. **2.** They were in charge of the king's revenue, and over them there were three chiefs, one of whom was Daniel. **3-5.** Through the assistance of God Daniel distinguished himself by his ability and integrity and the king contemplated entrusting him with the administration of the whole empire. The two other ministers, who could not tolerate a foreigner being raised above them, plotted against his life. Since his conduct as a statesman was above suspicion, they devised a plan to bring his religious conduct into

c conflict with the law of the king. **6-9.** They certainly knew that Daniel used to pray to his God at fixed hours. They therefore *came in concert* (6 ; so probably with Montgomery against Vg-DV ' craftily suggested ' and the usual rendering ' rushed ') to the king and requested him, apparently on behalf of all the governors, to issue an irrevocable decree to the effect that anyone who, for thirty days, should make petition to either god or man save to the king alone should be cast into the lions' pit. The unsuspecting king signed the decree. The object of the conspirators was to make Daniel appear before the king guilty of a capital offence.

They were not in any way concerned with the religious **5** practices of the other subjects of the king, so we must not take into serious consideration certain questions, why, for example, Daniel was not consulted on this matter, or why the decree was to remain in force for thirty days only, a period which was insufficient for its promulgation throughout the whole empire. There are not sufficiently clear indications that the Persian kings considered themselves as gods ; *cf.*, however, Linder, p 286 and note 1. The irrevocability of the decree of a Persian king is attested by Est 1:19 ; 8:8. Lions were kept by the Assyrians and Persians for hunting.

10-13 (11-14) Daniel Faithful to his God — 10. The **d** jealous ministers having secured the king's assent hastened to inform Daniel. Daniel, however, was not daunted, but kept faithfully to his religious practices. The place for prayer was the upper room of the house (*cf.* Acts 1:13 ; 9:37, 39, etc.), having latticed windows. His face was turned towards Jerusalem, the dwelling-place of the God of the Israelites (3 Kg 8:48). In later times the three hours for prayer were : (i) early in the morning, at the time of the morning sacrifice ; (ii) in the afternoon, about three o'clock, at the time of the evening sacrifice ; (iii) in the evening at sunset (E. Schürer, *A History of the Jewish people in the time of Jesus Christ*, 2, 1 p 290, n 248). **11.** At one of the fixed hours of prayer the two ministers *went in concert* (the same verb as in 6) to a place where they could see Daniel through the latticed window, and found him praying to his God. A practical illustration of the principle later proclaimed by St Peter : ' It is not just, in the sight of God, to hear man rather than God ' (Ac 4:19). **12 f.** They denounced him to the king immediately.

14-18 (15-19) Daniel Condemned to the Lions' Pit—14. **e** The king felt sorely grieved that his able and loyal minister had fallen a victim to the plotters' jealousy through his own rashness, and strove all day to deliver him. But his pleading was of no avail. **15.** The conspirators insisted on the irrevocability of the decree and demanded the death sentence against Daniel. **16.** At last the king had reluctantly to yield. The death sentence was pronounced, and Daniel was cast into the lions' pit. The king hoped that God would deliver his servant. **17.** The mouth of the pit was closed with a stone, which was then sealed with the signet-ring of the king and his ministers that nothing might be done *concerning* Daniel, *i.e.* that neither the king nor the ministers might tamper with the seals, lift up the stone, and rescue Daniel or kill him if un-injured by the lions. **18.** The king went back to his palace, but his grief was so great that he refused all food and spent a sleepless night. The meaning of the Aramaic word for ' meat ', Vg *cibi*, is uncertain. Other meanings equally doubtful are : ' musical instruments ', ' dancing girls ', ' concubines '. The general sense is that ' the king did not indulge in his usual diversions ' (Driver, 77).

19-23 (20-24) Daniel Delivered—19 f. Early in the morn- **f** ing the king hastened to the pit and called Daniel with a sorrowful voice to find out whether God, the living God, could rescue his faithful servant. **21 f.** Daniel was safe, and acknowledged the power and justice of God, who, through the agency of his angel, had rendered the lions harmless and thus rewarded the right-eousness and faithfulness of the king's minister. For later references to Daniel's deliverance *cf.* 1 Mac 2:60 ; Heb 11:33. **23.** The king's decree, which the ministers claimed could neither be repealed nor altered, was declared null and void by God himself. Daniel was brought out of the pit and, to the king's joy and astonishment, was found unhurt. The lions' den was a pit dug in the open air, having a lateral entrance closed with a stone and a partition wall with a door in it. A perpendicular shaft surrounded by a wall gave air and light to the lions' compartment. It was through this shaft that the king spoke to Daniel, but it was through the lateral entrance that Daniel was cast into, and brought out of, the pit.

g 24 Daniel's Accusers Condemned—The punishment meted out to the false accusers was according to the principle of retaliation. But the slaughter of their families, though in conformity with primitive conceptions of justice (*cf.* 2 Kg 21:5–9) and Persian practices (Herod. III, 119) is against the principle of personal responsibility inculcated in Dt 24:16 ; Jer 31:29 f. ; Ez 18. We are not to suppose that all the 120 governors with their families were thrown into the pit. The LXX are probably right in making the two colleagues of Daniel the only victims.

h 25-27 (26-28) The King's Acknowledgement of the God of Israel—The phraseology of the edict is very similar to that of Nabuchodonosor s edict in 3:98–100 and 4:31–34. Daniel's God was to be regarded as a living and ever-enduring God, whose sovereignty was not transferable, and who manifested his power by wonderful signs, especially by delivering Daniel from the lions. **28 (29) Conclusion**—Daniel *prospered* in the reign of Darius and Cyrus. This closing remark at the end of the stories section is most likely due to the editor who collected the Daniel episodes narrated in the first part of the book ; *cf.* 1:21.

a VII-XII The Visions—This section is marked out from the preceding (chh 1–6) by a change in the literary form and the historical and prophetical outlook of the writer. The prophetic message is given in the form of visions, and develops at length a theme already foreshadowed in Nabuchodonosor's first dream, namely the destruction of all hostile powers and the establishment of a universal and abiding kingdom. The writer is not merely a theologian teaching the basic doctrine of the uniqueness and supremacy of the God of Israel, he is also and above all a prophet predicting the triumph of God over all the anti-theocratic powers, the establishment of a spiritual kingdom upon earth, and its glorious consummation in heaven. On account of their higher theological importance, the interpretation of the visions is represented as given by God through the ministry of an angel. Chronologically the visions run parallel with the episodes narrated in chh 5 and 6, but the chronological indications, which have no bearing on the meaning of the visions, may be later additions.

b VII The Vision of the Four World Empires—This vision is parallel to Nabuchodonosor's first dream. There are, however, appreciable differences between them. The writer's standpoint in ch 2 is the Babylonian age, in ch 7 it is the Maccabean age, or at least an age of religious persecution. In ch 2 Nabuchodonosor's glorious kingdom will be followed by successive periods of decadence leading to the setting up of a more glorious kingdom. In ch 7 this glorious kingdom will be preceded by an age of persecution and the extermination of a godless persecutor at the end of a succession of kingdoms. On the supposed mythological associations underlying the several features of the vision see H. Junker, pp 29–65.

c 1-8 The Vision—**1.** On Baltassar, king of Babylon, see § 501*g*. 1*b* read : *And he wrote the dream.* **2.** In his night vision Daniel saw the four winds of heaven (*cf.* Zach 2:6 ; 6:5) stirring up the great sea, which is not the Mediterranean as in Jos 9:1, nor any other particular sea, but the world with its turbulent nations (*cf.* Is 17:12 ; Apoc 17:15). The winds represent the harmful forces, the disturbing influences, the enemies of peace and order coming from all directions. **3.** Four monstrous and ravenous beasts, all different in appearance, came up from the sea. The connexion between these beasts and the evil powers which they represent is quite natural, and we need not go back to ancient mythology to explain it (*cf.* Is 27:1 ; 30:6 ; Ez 29:3). **4.** The first beast was a lion with eagle's wings. The lion and the eagle symbolize the mightiest powers on earth. Representations of winged lions are common in Assyrian and Babylonian art. But its wings were plucked off, and it was made to stand erect upon two feet like a man, and a man's heart

or intelligence was given to it. This last detail, which **503c** is a clear allusion to 4:13, has led interpreters to believe that the plucking off of the wings and the lifting up of the beast into an erect position denote the humanization of the beastlike king symbolized by the lion (Goettsberger, p 54 ; Dennefeld, 675 ; Driver, 81 ; Marti, 49 ; Bentzen, 32). This interpretation is **d** incompatible with the historical fact that Nabuchodonosor had a man's heart during all his period of conquest, and it was only when his career of conquest was over that a beast's heart was given to him (Charles, 176 f.). Supposing the reference to 4:13 to be an interpolation made on the ground of the identity of the first beast with Nabuchodonosor (Junker, p 39), the other details may be easily explained as signifying the degradation or humiliation of the king or kingdom symbolized by the first beast. **5.** The second beast was like a bear raised up on one side and having three *ribs* between its teeth, and it was incited to devour more prey. The bear is described as lying down with one of its sides raised higher than the other. Some interpreters represent the beast as raising itself on one of its sides before springing on its prey (Driver, p 82 ; Montgomery, p 288), or erect on its hind legs in an aggressive posture (Junker, p 41).

The three ribs are the remains or a large mouthful of **e** the prey. Interpreters have endeavoured to find out the symbolical meaning of the several features of the bear. Thus the two sides, one higher than the other, are believed to represent the unequal strength of the Medes and the Persians, the two constituent parts of the Medo-Persian empire (Linder, p 300 f.). The three ribs are referred to the kingdoms of Lydia and Babylonia conquered by Cyrus, and Egypt conquered by Cambyses (Linder, p 301). The command to devour is an allusion to the destructiveness of the Medes (Is 13:17 f. ; Linder, 301). It is better, however, not to press the meaning of these details, which after all are only natural features of the beast. **6.** The third beast was like a leopard having four wings on its *sides* and four heads. The leopard is remarkable for its swiftness (Hab 1:8), but this symbolical leopard with its four wings is represented as very much swifter than the swiftest animal. The four heads have been **f** taken to typify the four Persian kings referred to in 11:2 (Goettsberger, 54 ; Dennefeld, 676 ; Charles, 178 ; Bentzen, 33), or the four divisions of Alexander's empire (Linder, 301). It is perhaps preferable to take the four heads as indicating the four winds or directions and signifying an immense domain extending in all directions (Driver, p 83 ; Montgomery, p 290). With the words ' power was given to it ' the figure passes into reality. **7 f.** The fourth beast was unlike the others in its fierceness and unlike any known creature in its appearance. While the seer was contemplating the ten horns of the beast, another and a smaller horn grew up *in* the midst of them, rooting up three of the other horns. It had eyes like the eyes of a man and a mouth speaking haughtily.

9-14 The Divine Judgement—The second act of this **g** drama opens up in heaven. Those dreadful beasts no longer play havoc in the world. They are judged and killed, in other words the heathen powers are overthrown and the world domination is given to the ' son of man '. **9.** The seer imagines a large hall with thrones set for the judges or counsellors. Then the chief judge, or God himself, represented as an aged man, took his seat. Though the expression ' ancient of days ' does not necessarily imply the idea of eternity, in the present text it presupposes it and must be explained as the analogous expressions in Job 36:26 ; Ps 55:19 ; 102:25 f. ; Is 41:4. He was clad in snow-white raiment, and his hair was white like clean wool. His throne and its wheels were blazing flames and dazzling light (*cf.* Ez 1). **10.** A stream of fire was coming forth from before him to devour and consume those against whom the death sentence should be pronounced. Myriads of angels stood in attendance ever ready to execute God's orders. The court sat,

503g and the indictment was read to the accused, *i.e.* all the misdeeds of the four symbolical beasts were recalled **h** as if they were read in a book. **11 f.** The construction is awkward but the sense is clear. While the seer's attention was concentrated on that majestic sight of the divine court, the beast was condemned to be burnt on account of the arrogant and blasphemous words which the little horn was uttering. Although the destruction of the beast naturally implies that of its horns, the implication does not go beyond the figure. The seer is concerned only in the little horn which he identifies with the fourth beast, but is uninterested in the fate of the other horns. The other beasts survived for an unspecified time after their power had been taken from them. The expression ' a time and a time ' denotes a fixed but unspecified period of time.
i 13 f. When all the beasts had been destroyed, one like a man or a human being was seen coming with the clouds, and therefore from heaven not from the tumultuous sea, and was presented before the aged judge. The expression ' Son of Man ', which is rare in Aramaic but common in Hebrew, especially in Ezechiel, means simply an individual, a member of mankind ; *cf.* Num 23:19 ; Ps 80:17 ; Is 51:12, etc. This mysterious man was invested with royal power, not as the successor to the throne of any of the heathen rulers, but as a universal sovereign whose power would be everlasting, untransferable, and imperishable. See § 504*d–g*.
j 15–17 The Interpretation of the Vision—15. Daniel was anxious to know the meaning of this vision. **16.** He approached one of the angels and asked him about all these things. Angels sometimes appear as interpreters of visions, *cf.* Zach 1–6 ; Ez 40–48. **17.** The four beasts represent four *kings* either individually or as the personification of their empires. **18.** The destruction of these kings or kingdoms is not explicitly recorded, but is implied in the statement that the kingdom will be received by the saints of the Most High in everlasting possession. The ' saints ' are the servants and the worshippers of God, united to him by the bonds of submission and obedience, and participating in some way in his sanctity. Though the Israelites are primarily intended, the expression has a universal meaning including all those who will **k** submit to God's sovereign rule. These loyal subjects of the kingdom of God are said to receive the sovereignty inasmuch as they will be freed from all foreign dominations and will enjoy all the blessings of a peaceful kingdom under a righteous king. There is, therefore, no contradiction between 18 and 14, where the royal power is given to the Son of Man. **19 f.** Daniel was not satisfied with this summary explanation, and requested further information about the fourth beast and its horns, and especially the small horn. **21 f.** These verses are an amplification of 8 and 11. In his description of the little horn, the seer passes insensibly from the figure to reality. The king symbolized by the little horn was making war against the faithful servants of God in order to bring them over to his gods. He prevailed, at least for some time, and many Israelites abandoned the religion of their fathers. But that was only for a short time. God came to the rescue of his people ; judgement was given in their favour, and they acquired once more their religious liberty.
l 23. The fourth beast represents a kingdom which will be different from the others, both in its character and its destructive operations. **24.** Ten kings will arise out of this kingdom or king ; then another will arise *different* from all the others, and will bring down three of the ten kings. **25.** He will speak haughtily against God, the Most High, and will wear out his faithful servants by oppression and persecution. He will attempt to interfere with the liturgical service of the Israelites by suppressing the religious festivals that were prescribed on fixed days. The period of the persecution will last for ' a time and times and half a time '. From very early times this vague and obscure

time indication, which occurs again in 12:7 and in **5** Apoc 12:14, has been interpreted as denoting one **r** year, two years and one half-year. Therefore the saints will be delivered into the hands of the persecutor for three years and a half. This approximately agrees with 8:14, where it is said that the profanation of the temple and the abolition of worship will last for 2,300 evenings and mornings, or 1,150 days which make up approximately three and a half years. Moreover this indefinite time expression is equated with ' forty-two months ' in Apoc 13:5. Some interpreters, however, prefer an indefinite and symbolical sense ; *cf.* the analogous expression ' three and a half days ' in Apoc 11:9, 11. **26 f.** At the close of the three and a half years of persecution judgement will be given against the persecutor, his domination will be taken from him and he will disappear for ever. Then the saints will take over the domination (see 18), which will be universal and everlasting, and which they will hold under the sovereignty of the Son of man.
28 Conclusion—The concluding remark, ' Hitherto is **n** the end ' corresponds to the introductory words in 1*b*, ' This is the beginning '. Daniel was distressingly agitated by this vision and its interpretation, and kept the matter in his mind.
Appendix I—The Four Empires. For the various identi- **5** fications see § 498*a*. The Roman theory identifies the ten horns with ten kings or kingdoms arising out of the Roman empire, and the little horn with the Antichrist (Linder, p 302 ff.). The Greek theory, which is adopted here in the form proposed in § 498*c*, identifies the fourth beast with Alexander's empire. The great Macedonian general overran all Western Asia, smashing all opposition like a fierce beast trampling under its feet all the animals of the fields. The ten horns are his successors of the Seleucid dynasty. The little horn is Antiochus IV, the eleventh successor of Alexander on the throne of Syria. The number ' ten ' has not necessarily an exact mathematical value. The three horns are three prominent personages whom Antiochus displaced in order to secure the throne. The historical background of this identification is provided by the books of Maccabees. Antiochus IV made war against the people of God, and, in a sacrilegious endeavour to stamp out the religion of the God of Israel, abolished the liturgical worship and desecrated the altar of sacrifices. The period of religious persecution lasted approximately three years and a half, the altar being desecrated on the 15th of the month Casleu (= December) 168 B.C. (1 Mac 1:57), and rededicated on the 25th Casleu (1 Mac 4:52), and the edict forbidding all religious observances being issued a short time before (1 Mac 1:43–56). Antiochus died a few months after the rededication of the altar.
Antiochus, however, and his impious achievements **b** do not correspond exactly to the description of the little horn. The death of Antiochus did not bring about either the end of the Syrian domination or the rise of a universal and abiding kingdom. Considering the close resemblance between the ' Man of Lawlessness ' or the Antichrist, as described by St Paul in 2 Thess 2:3–12, and the little horn, we hold that the little horn in its literal, historical, and obvious sense represents Antiochus IV, but in a fuller and adequate sense it is the Antichrist of whom Antiochus was but a faint image ; see J. B. Orchard, *St Paul and the Book of Daniel*, in Bi (1939) 172–9. It follows that the complete victory of the righteous people and the establishment of an ever-enduring kingdom will not be perfectly realized before the end of the world. The fact must be stressed that Daniel's outlook extends much further than the Messianic age.
As regards the other kingdoms no definite identifica- **c** tions are proposed. The writer is wholly uninterested in them. He is also indifferent about the fate of the remaining seven horns of the fourth beast. It appears, therefore, that the quaternary number of the beasts arising out of the four principal winds or parts of the world is meant to express the universality of earthly

powers, and particularly the anti-theocratic powers, ruling over the Jews, and culminating in the person of Antiochus, which will be definitely destroyed before the establishment of the kingdom of God.

Appendix II—The Son of Man. The expression is used (i) in poetry as a synonym of ' man ' and in parallelism with it, Num 23:19 ; Is 51:2, etc. ; (ii) in Ezechiel with a diminutive sense implying inferiority, unworthiness in relation to God ; (iii) in the plural to denote ' mankind ', Gen 10:5 ; 1 Kg 26:19, etc. (ii) and (iii) are obviously inadmissible in Dan 7:13, where the expression seems to be intended to mark the contrast between the representative of the fifth kingdom and those of the other four. The latter were symbolized by monstrous beings emerging from the sea, the former is represented by a manlike being coming from the clouds.

Before proceeding to identify the Son of Man we must determine whether the expression is used in a collective or in an individual sense. Two considerations seem to require a collective sense. 1. As the beasts symbolized kingdoms not kings, so must the Son of Man represent a kingdom not a king (P. Riessler, 70 ; Buzy, *Les symboles . . .* 291 ff.; Goettsberger, 56). 2. In 18, 27, the kingdom is given to the people of the Most High, therefore the Son of Man who in 14 receives the kingdom is in reality the whole community of the people of God. Other interpreters prefer to combine the two senses, considering the Son of Man as representing both king and subjects as forming one indivisible whole or one empire, Lagrange, RB (1904) 506. In 7:13 the Son of Man is an individual receiving the power to rule over the holy people, while in 18 and 27 the holy people, on account of their intimate association with their king are represented as reigning with him, *cf.* Apoc 20:4, 6. There is therefore no contradiction between the individual sense of the vision and the collective sense of its interpretation.

Catholic exegesis has always recognized the Messias as the king designated by the title ' Son of Man '. The strongest argument for the Messianic interpretation is unquestionably the evidence of Christ himself who appropriated not only the appellation, but also the royal prerogatives attributed to the Son of Man by Daniel. Thus Christ will be a king and will sit at the right hand of God, Mt 16:28 ; 19:28 ; Lk 22:69 ; he will come in the clouds, Mt 24:30 ; 26:64 ; Mk 13:26, 14:62 ; Lk 21:27 ; he will judge all men, Mt 25:31–46. There can be no doubt that Christ derived this title from Dan 7:13, and interpreted it in a Messianic sense by appropriating the prerogatives and functions of the heavenly being that appeared to Daniel in human form ; *cf.* F. Rosanliec, *Sensus genuinus et plenus locutionis ' Filius Hominis ' a Christo Domino adhibitae* (Rome, 1920) 86–109.

The Messianic interpretation of Dan 7:13 was also maintained by Jewish tradition from very early times. In the apocryphal book of Enoch there are in the ' Parables ' section (37–71) written in the 1st century B.C. numerous references to the Son of Man derived from Daniel and applicable to the Messias alone. In rabbinic literature the Messias is sometimes called ' Anani ' from Heb. *'ānān* ' cloud ', with reference to Dan 7:13. The Messianic doctrine of 7:13 f. is the establishment by God of a kingdom which will be entrusted to the Messias. It will be a universal and everlasting kingdom, and therefore spiritual, established on earth and enduring in heaven for eternity. It will be established on earth some time after the death of Antiochus IV, and perpetuated in heaven after the destruction of the Antichrist.

VIII The Vision of Two World Empires—The prophetic outlook, which in the preceding vision extended over the four world empires, is now narrowed down to two. The imagery and, in a certain measure, the doctrinal standpoint of the two visions are also different. In ch 7 the seer is predicting the end of persecution and the establishment of a new kingdom ; in ch 8 he is vividly depicting the persecution of the holy people

and the desecration of the sanctuary by Antiochus, **505a** but has hardly a word of hope for his oppressed people. Therefore ch 8 cannot be regarded as a doublet of ch 7 (Montgomery, 324), nor an explanation of the second and third kingdom of the first vision (Linder, p 329), but an independent vision consistent with the first in its general significance, but having its proper scope and outlook.

1 f. Introduction—The vision is dated in the 3rd year **b** of Baltassar, probably an editorial insertion. Daniel was transported in spirit (*cf.* Ez 8:3 ; 9:24) to the citadel of Shushan (Susa) in the province of Elam, and there he saw a vision while he was *near the stream* Ulai. Susa was the capital of Elam (Neh 1:1 ; Est 1:1), rebuilt by Darius Hystaspes (521–485 B.C.), and the winter residence of the Persian kings. The stream Ulai is the Eulaeus of the classical writers which flowed close to Susa (Pliny, *Hist. Nat.* 6, 27). The place therefore provided a suitable setting for the vision.

3-12 The Vision—3. Daniel standing near the stream **c** Ulai saw on the opposite side a ram with two horns, one higher than the other. As the ram symbolized the Medo-Persian empire (20), its unequal horns represented the two powers separately. The higher horn, representing Persia, came up after the other one, the Persian empire being stronger than the Median and coming up later. **4.** The ram butting to the west, the north, and the south, and advancing irresistibly in all directions represented the victorious march of Cyrus, who extended his conquests as far as the Black Sea and Egypt. His irresistible power made him undertake any military expedition, and success made him exceedingly great and powerful. Some interpreters see a correspondence between the three directions of the ram's advance and the three ribs in the bear's mouth (7:5), and between its unequal horns and the bear's unequal sides (Linder, p 329 f.). The correspondence seems rather far-fetched. **5-7.** While **d** Daniel was looking attentively at the ram, a he-goat, having a conspicuous horn between its eyes, came swiftly from the west and dashed against the ram, beating it down to the ground. The he-goat is the Greek empire (21) and the horn is Alexander the Great. The expression ' he touched not the ground ', which is reminiscent of Cyrus' swift advance (Is 41:2 f.), vividly describes the rapidity of the march of Alexander, who in a few years subjugated all Western Asia as far as the borders of India. **8.** When the he-goat had grown so powerful, its dreadful horn was broken, not in a fight but through an ordinary, unspecified cause, and in its place four *other* horns came up. When Alexander had reached the peak of his glory he fell ill and died in Babylon in the year 323 B.C. at the age of thirty-two years. On his death his empire was divided between four of his generals—Cassander, Lysimachus, Seleucus and Ptolemy. This settlement was arrived at in 301 B.C. after many wars among the rival generals. The first two had no part in the history of the Jews. **9-12.** The history of the Seleucid dynasty is passed over, **e** and mention is made of one king only, Antiochus IV (175–164 B.C.), the little horn which made war against Egypt (the South), Parthia (the East), and against the ' Beauteous Land '. The last expression for Palestine occurs again in 11:16, 41 and in Jer 3:19 ; Ez 20:6 ; Zach 7:14. On the wars of Antiochus with the Jews read the books of Maccabees. The little horn growing greater and greater until it reached the stars of heaven represents the arrogance of Antiochus and his insolent attack on the religion of the Jews, many of whom fell victims of his arrogance like stars hurled down from heaven. Antiochus' first attack was directed against those Jews who professed the religion of Yahweh. His second attack is now directed against God himself, the prince of the *host* or stars, whose daily sacrifice he abolished, and whose sanctuary he profaned, treating it irreverently as a worthless thing. On the daily sacrifice see Ex 29:38 ff. ; Num 28:3 ff. ; on the abolition of divine worship see 1 Mac 1:47 ; on the

505 f profanation of the temple by Antiochus see 1 Mac 1:21-24, 49, 57; 4:36-59. **12a** is obscure and corrupt. The sense of Vg is that the suspension of sacrifices was a punishment of the people's sins, a sense which is not in conformity with the context. A probable interpretation is: An armed garrison was wickedly placed by Antiochus in the neighbourhood of the temple for the purpose of suppressing more effectively the divine worship (Driver, 117; Goettsberger, 62). By emending the first word of 12 *ṣābā'* ' army ' into *ṣᵉbî* ' beauty ', and shifting it back to 11, an equally good sense is obtained: Antiochus treated irreverently not only the temple but also all Palestine, ' the land of beauty ' (*cf.* 9) and the dwelling-place of Yahweh by erecting ' altars throughout all the cities of Juda ' (1 Mac 1:57). Then 12 is made to read thus: ' and the iniquity (instead of " in iniquity ") was set upon the place of the daily sacrifice ', the allusion being to the abominable idol erected on the altar of sacrifice, 1 Mac 1:57 (Linder, 337). Antiochus will also try to stamp out the true religion by destroying the books of the Law which embodied the true religious and moral principles (1 Mac 1:60). Success will crown this iconoclastic campaign.

506a 13 f. Duration of the Desecration of the Sanctuary— In the meanwhile Daniel overheard one angel asking another: How long will this profanation last? And the answer was: ' Unto evening and morning 2,300 ' (MT omits ' days '). This peculiar time expression is interpreted in two ways. It denotes either 2,300 days or 2,300 evenings and mornings, *i.e.* 1,150 days. The first sense is adopted by LXX, Theod., Vg, and by many ancient and modern interpreters. This period, which according to the context must coincide with the entire period of persecution, is reckoned from Antiochus' campaign in Egypt in March 169 B.C. and his subsequent attack on Jerusalem (1 Mac 1:18 ff.) to the peace terms offered by Lysias to the Jews (1 Mac 6:58-61) in July–August 163 B.C., an interval of six years four months, or *c* 2,300 days (Linder, 342 ff.). This interpretation fails to take into due consideration one important fact. The vision is entirely centred on Antiochus, the greatest persecutor

b of the Jews. Therefore the 2,300 evening-mornings cannot be made to extend beyond Antiochus' death in 164 B.C., nor, on the other hand, can they be made to commence before the persecution broke out in 169 B.C. It seems more probable that the expression ' evening-morning ' denotes two separate time units, and that the number 2,300 is the sum of 1,150 evenings and 1,150 mornings. The chief reason for this interpretation lies in the fact that the daily sacrifice, the suspension of which is emphatically predicted, was offered twice a day, in the morning and in the evening. Therefore the number 2,300 represents the total of daily sacrifices which will not be offered. As 1,150 days correspond to *c* three and a half years, this period is generally identified with the time and times and half a time of 7:25. The sanctuary was rededicated on nearly the same day in which it had been desecrated three years before (1 Mac 1:57; 4:52).

c 15-27 The Interpretation of the Dream—15. The subject of the conversation between the angels was the duration of the persecution, but Daniel wished to understand more fully the meaning of the whole vision. An angel in a human form suddenly appeared standing at some distance from him. In Heb. there is a play on the word *geber* ' man ' and Gabriel ' man of God '. **16.** A voice like that of a man came from between the banks of the stream Ulai requesting Gabriel to explain the meaning of the vision to Daniel. This is the first time that an angel is called by a proper name in Scripture. He is mentioned also in 9:21 and in Lk 1:19, 26. **17.** Daniel is addressed as ' son of man ', a title denoting, as in Ezechiel, the weakness or inferiority of human nature in relation to God or the

d angels. The vision deserved careful attention because it dealt with events which would take place ' in the time of the end '. This expression, which occurs again

in 11:35, 40; 12:4, 9, means simply ' the appointed time ' which, according to the context, is the time of wrath (19), or the time of Antiochus' persecution. The expression, which seems to connect the end of the persecution with the end of the world, has been purposely chosen to denote two distinct but interrelated periods of time. As the death of Antiochus marked the end of a period of persecution and the dawning of the Messianic era, so will the elimination of Antichrist at the end of the world be followed by a reign of everlasting happiness in heaven. Both the end of the persecution and the end of the world are intended. **18.** As the angel spoke, Daniel swooned or fell stunned to the ground, but was soon raised to his feet. **19.** The vision deals with the time of persecution which is defined as a time of *wrath*. According to OT conceptions all the calamities which befell Israel during their long history were the manifestation of God's wrath for their sins; *cf.* Is 5:26; 10:25; 26:20; and for the times of Antiochus *cf.* 1 Mac 1:67; 2:49; 3:8, etc. **20-25.** Then follows the historical interpretation of the vision. The great horn of the he-goat is Alexander the Great. After Alexander's death his empire was divided between four of his generals, none of whom, however, had the power of Alexander. As Daniel is concerned only with the Seleucid dynasty, the words ' after their reign ' (23) refer only to this dynasty.

At a certain time, when the sins of the Jewish people, especially the sins of apostasy (*cf.* 1 Mac 1:11-16) have reached full measure (*cf.* 2 Mac 6:14), the wrath of God will come upon them in the form of a persecution by Antiochus, a bold-faced king, skilled in the art of dissimulation and duplicity (*cf.* 1 Mac 1:31). The words ' but not by his own force ' (24) are probably interpolated from 22. If genuine, they imply that Antiochus will become powerful either by intrigues or by divine permission. His devastation of the land of Israel and the suppression of religious institutions will be greater than can be imagined. He will rid himself of his political opponents (' the mighty '), and will exterminate the pious Israelites. Through his cunning he will successfully practise deceit, and in his mind he will devise great, presumptuous schemes; he will kill many *unawares* and, after making a stand against God, the Prince of princes, he will fall not in war nor by a natural death but by divine intervention; *cf.* 1 Mac 6:8-16; 2 Mac 9:5-28. By a slight textual emendation partially based on LXX this sense is obtained: **24.** '. . . he shall destroy the mighty ones. **25.** *And against the holy people shall his policy be directed, and he shall cause craft to prosper in his hand*' (Charles). **26.** The angel confirms the truth of the vision which is called the vision of the evenings and mornings (*cf.* 14), because it was intended to reassure the persecuted Jews that the end of the persecution would soon come. For similar asseverations of the truth of a vision *cf.* 10:1; 11:2; Apoc 19:9; 21:5; 22:6. Daniel is then commanded to write down this revelation and to close up and seal the scroll until the time of its fulfilment shall come.

27 Conclusion— The disclosure of the gloomy future of his people caused a painful shock to Daniel, who felt even more distressed because there were many details which he could not understand.

IX The prophecy of the Seventy Weeks— The vision of ch 8, compared with that of ch 7, was far from reassuring. It foretold persecutions, profanation, destruction, and though all this would have an end, it was not said plainly how and when the end would come. Daniel wished for further enlightenment, and in his anguish he turned to God, confessing the sins of his people which had been the cause of all their sufferings, implored him to forgive them, and to deliver them from their oppressors. We may distinguish two parts: the prophecy, 24-27, and its general background, 1-23. The general background is the age of the exile; the prophecy refers to the Messianic age, though its particular setting is the Maccabean age.

7b 1-3 Introduction—The prophecy is dated in the first year of Darius the Mede, therefore a short time after the fall of Babylon (5:31). In **1** Darius is called the son of Assuerus. In reality Assuerus, the Greek Xerxes, was the son of Darius I and the grandfather of Darius II. These chronological introductions are best accounted for as the work of ignorant scribes. In that year, when the prediction of the fall of Babylon made by Jeremias (25:12) had already been fulfilled (5:31), and the fulfilment of the promise of the restoration of Jerusalem after its 70 years punishment (Jer 29:10) was eagerly expected, Daniel, assuming the rôle of his repentant people, turned his face in the direction of Jerusalem and prayed God to forgive their sins. It appears that at that time there was already a collection of canonical books, of which the prophecies of Jeremias formed part. If the 70 years are reckoned from the year of the prophecy of Jeremias, or the 4th year of Joakim (605 b.c., Jer 25:1), they close in the year 535 b.c. But the number 70 has not necessarily an exact arithmetical value (A. Condamin, *Le Livre de Jérémie*, p 197).

c 4-19 Daniel's Prayer—The prayer is modelled after a type which seems to have been common in times of national calamity and which is characterized by these features : confession of sin, acknowledgement of God's justice, appeal to his mercy, and a prayer for deliverance. Examples of such public prayers are Esd 9:6–15 ; Bar 1:15–3:8 ; Dan 3:25–45. **4b** agrees almost verbally with Neh 1:5 and Deut 7:9. **5 f.** Daniel confesses the nation's sins, which are forcibly expressed by five synonymous verbs. The gravity of the sins is heightened by two circumstances : they refused to listen to the prophets' warnings, and all classes of the people have sinned. For the phraseology *cf.* 3 Kg 8:47 ; Deut 17:20 ; Jer 44:4, 21 ; Neh 9:34. **7 f.** God is righteous, and the faithless people must bear the shame and disappointment of being driven out of the land of their fathers. **9-11.** Daniel does not try to conceal or to extenuate the people's guilt. All have sinned, and the curses impending over transgressors of the Law (Lev 26 ; Deut 28 : 15 ff.) have now fallen upon them. In their hopeless plight Daniel makes an appeal to God's compassion and forgivingness. **12-14.** are an expansion of 10 f. **15-19.** The confession now passes into a prayer for deliverance. The seer emphatically reaffirms the people's guilt, and, implicitly, their repentance and prays that God may look favourably upon Jerusalem and the mountain of the temple which had become an object of derision to all heathen peoples around them. Then he makes a stirring appeal to God's honour. God's temple in Jerusalem lay in ruins as if he were unable to protect it.

e 20-23 The Apparition of the Angel—The angel Gabriel, whom Daniel had seen on a previous occasion (8:16), was sent from heaven and ' flying swiftly ' (so Vg and the ancient versions) came to Daniel at the time of the evening sacrifice to make him understand clearly the things he desired to know. In **22** read *came to* (LXX) for ' instructed me '. By way of introduction the angel said that as soon as Daniel commenced his prayer a divine revelation was made in response to Daniel's desire, and he came to communicate it to him because he was a man *greatly beloved*.

f 24-27 The Prophecy of the Seventy Weeks—After the fall of Babylon Daniel expected the immediate release of the exiles and the restoration of the monarchy of Israel. His expectations, though derived from Jeremias' predictions, were not yet fully realized, and he therefore turned to God for illumination. God predicted another restoration, a spiritual one, which would come after a longer period than predicted by Jeremias, and would be preceded by an age of persecution. There is therefore a relation of contrast between the object of Daniel's prayer and that of the angel's revelation, and we see no reason for regarding 4-19 and 20 as an interpolation and linking 21-27 with 3, making the prophecy an appendix of ch 8 (Marti, 64 ; Charles, 226 f. ; Goettsberger, 69 ; Bentzen, 41 f.). The

interpretation of this most difficult prophecy will be **507g** based on these two main premisses : the historical standpoint is the Maccabean age ; the prophetic perspective is Messianic and eschatological. For a discussion of MT and the ancient versions see Linder, pp 364–73. **24.** It is universally admitted that the 70 weeks are 70 seven years' periods (*cf.* Lev 25:8), or 490 years. Most interpreters hold that the 70 weeks are a definite period, as is shown by their irregular division into three parts 7 + 62 + 1 (25, 27), of which the last part is further subdivided into two halves (27). The mathematical value of the number 70 provides the basis for the chronological determination of the coming of the Messias and his death. But very probably the number 490 is simply an intensification of the 70 years of Jeremias (Junker, p 85), which in its turn is the product of two symbolical numbers 7 and 10 ; *cf.* the analogous numerical intensifications in Gen 4:15 ; Mt 18:22. This period of time has been *decreed* upon the people and the city, *i.e.* it has been decided that 490 years shall pass before the restoration takes place. This restoration will be characterized by **h** (i) the finishing of transgression, *i.e.* the sin of apostasy and the religious persecution ; these will be definitely checked ; (ii) the ending of sin ; sin will be shut up, sealed up and thus prevented from doing any harm ; (iii) *atonement* for iniquity ; atonement is here used in the sense of appeasing God offended by sin. God will be appeased by the death of Antiochus for the sins of apostasy, and by the death of his only Begotten Son for the sins of all mankind ; hence Vg–DV ' iniquity may be abolished ' is a good paraphrase. To this threefold negative element corresponds a threefold positive element consisting in (i) the bringing in of everlasting righteousness, *i.e.* the recognition of God's supreme rights and the performance of the duties deriving therefrom ; (ii) the fulfilment of vision and prophet, or, according to others, the sealing up, the end of prophecy ; (iii) the anointing of a thing most holy, *i.e.* the rededication of the temple and the altar of sacrifice or the consecration of a mystical temple of the Messianic age, or the anointing of Christ the Messias, that is the inauguration of his ministry.

The end of the persecution, however, marked only the **i** beginning of a national spiritual restoration which attained its full development only in Messianic times. The Maccabean interpretation of 24 is therefore only partially true, while the Messianic interpretation, which was always common in the Church, is the only perfectly true one. It follows that the Messianic restoration need not necessarily be placed in the last week. **25.** The 70 weeks are divided into three periods of unequal duration, 7 and 62 to which another week is added in 27, each being characterized by some particular event. The first seven weeks are to be reckoned from ' the going forth of the word '. The ' word ' is the divine oracle or divine communication made through Jeremias concerning the 70 years' captivity and the return of the exiles to their land (Jer 25:11 f. ; 29:10 ; *cf.* also Jer 30:18 ; 31:38). As these prophecies were uttered between the years 605–588 b.c. it is from these broad limits that the 7 weeks are to be reckoned. We purposely allow this latitude **j** to the *terminus a quo* because we do not attach a strict mathematical value to the number of weeks. So with differences of detail Goettsberger, p 69 f. ; Höpfl–Miller–Metzinger, p 490 ; J. Chaine, *Intr. à la lecture des prophètes*, 262 f. Other interpreters, however, who refer the whole prophecy directly and exclusively to the Messias, take the ' word ' in the sense of ' edict ', and identify it with the edict issued by Artaxerxes I in the year 458 b.c. for the rebuilding of Jerusalem (Esd 7:1–7, 11–26) ; Knabenbauer, Linder. This brings the last of the 70 weeks to the years a.d. 26–33, an exact Messianic date. But if ' word ' is a royal edict, it should be identified with Cyrus' edict in 538 b.c. (Esd 1:1), which, being the first, was far more important than subsequent edicts by **other**

507j Persian kings. Though the building of Jerusalem is not expressly mentioned in Cyrus' edict, it is naturally implied (*cf.* Esd 5:1 ; Agg 1:4). Moreover the words *leḥāšîb weliḇnôt* do not mean ' to rebuild ' but ' to bring back (from captivity) and to build ' ; *cf.* Jer 29:10.

k Now the permission to return to their land, to build the house of God and, naturally, their own homes was first granted by Cyrus. The first interpretation is therefore considered preferable, especially on the ground of the fact that the 70 weeks are an extension of the 70 years of Jeremias, and must therefore have the same starting-point. From the date of Jeremias' prediction concerning the return from the exile and the building of Jerusalem to the coming of an anointed prince 7 weeks or 49 years will elapse. The Messianic interpretation identifies the anointed prince with Christ the Messias. But as 49 years, from whatever date they are reckoned, are too short an interval for the coming of Christ, the 7 weeks are, on the strength of the punctuation of Theod. and Vg, added to the 62 weeks, and thus the interval between Artaxerxes' edict and the coming of the anointed prince is made to extend **l** over 69 weeks or 483 years. There is, however, no reason for departing from MT, which divides the verse at ' seven weeks '. It is the interpretation that must be based on the text, not the text to be made to conform to a particular interpretation. We prefer the Massoretic punctuation which gives a good sense and, accordingly, identify the anointed prince with Cyrus. The main argument for this interpretation is that we have in this prophecy a gradual unfolding of God's plan of restoration which was to commence with the release of the Jewish exiles by Cyrus, and to reach its culmination in the Messias, the point of convergence of Daniel's predictions. Cyrus is actually called the anointed of the Lord in Is 45:1. From Jeremias' predictions, 605–588 B.C., to the end of the exile in 538 B.C. approximately 49 years have passed. After the first 7 week-years a period of 62 week-years will commence during which Jerusalem will be rebuilt, square and moat, *i.e.* provided with broad spaces and ditches round about. But times will be hard ; *cf* **m** Esd 4 ; Neh 4, 6. If the 62 week-years are reckoned from the year 538 B.C. they end in the year 104 B.C., a date which has no particular significance. To avoid the inconvenience some interpreters make the 62 weeks run parallel with the 7 weeks, thus pushing back the *terminus ad quem* to the year 171 B.C., the year in which an anointed one (26), the high-priest Onias III, was murdered (*M. Thilo, *Chronologie des Danielbuches*, Bonn, 1926, 14). But the text obviously demands that the 62 weeks be reckoned consecutively to, not concurrently with, the 7 weeks. The Messianic interpretation adopts the Vg punctuation , and combines together the two periods of 7 and 62 weeks, making their sum of 483 years to start from 458 B.C. Such a way of reckoning renders the distinction of the two periods meaningless.

n As a period of 490 years divided into three consecutive periods of 49, 434 and 7 years respectively, characterized by certain definite events, cannot be made to fit into the historical framework of the last five centuries B.C., it is perhaps preferable to explain the 62 weeks as a vague, indefinite quantity having no precise arithmetical value. It is a fact that all these numerical operations of Daniel ultimately rest on the 70 years of Jeremias. The first operation is the multiplication of 70, which is the product of 7 by 10, by the symbolical number 7. The product 490 is therefore symbolical, though, of course, not without a broad historical value. The writer then goes on to work on this symbolical number dividing it into three unequal quantities. The first, 7 weeks or 49 years, is primarily symbolical, secondarily and approximately historical. The last week or 7 years, divided into two equal parts, is also symbolical, though at the same time very nearly historical. The remaining 62 weeks are the remainder of the subtraction of 8 (7 + 1) from 70, and their rôle is to fill up the interval between the events of the first 7 weeks and those of the last week. What the seer had **5** in mind was the prediction of certain historical events and their chronological sequence, but not their exact dates. The 62 weeks therefore correspond to the period intervening between the return of the exiles in 538 B.C. and the cutting off of an anointed one, whether this is the high-priest Onias III, murdered in 171 B.C. (2 Mac 4:34), or Christ killed in A.D. 30 or 33. **26.** A slight emendation of the last two words of 25 based on LXX and their transposition to the beginning of 26, would give this sense : ' *At the end of the times* ', *i.e.* after the 62 weeks, etc. (Charles, Goettsberger). After the lapse of 7 and 62 weeks an anointed one will be cut off, ' and the people that shall deny him shall not be his '. The words between inverted commas are a paraphrase of a two-word elliptical and obscure Hebrew phrase which literally means : ' and shall have naught '.

If the anointed one is the Messias the sense is : The **p** cutting off of the Messias will bring about not his end but that of his enemies (Knabenbauer, p 256), or : The Messias will be cut off not for his own guilt (Linder, p 406). If the anointed one is Onias III the sense is : He will have no legitimate successor, or no one to defend him, or though he has committed no fault, etc. The identification of the anointed one may help us to reach the meaning of this enigmatic expression, but absolute certainty will perhaps never be attained. Interpreters identify him either with the Messias or with the high-priest Onias III, according to their particular system of interpretation. Though neither the city nor the temple were destroyed after the death of Onias, both suffered considerably ; *cf.* 1 Mac 1:31, 32, 38 ; 3:45. 26*b* is also referred to the destruction of the city and the temple by Titus in A.D. 70. And his (or its) end will be *in an overwhelming flood*. If these words are referred to Antiochus, the sense is that he will be swept away by a divine judgement as by an overwhelming flood ; *cf.* 1 Mac 6:8–16. If they are referred to the temple and city, they denote their complete destruction. The war and its concomitant devastations, that are determined by God, will continue till the end, *i.e.* the time appointed by God. **27** is **q** a detailed description of some of the events referred to in 26 as taking place after the 62 weeks. During the last week the leader or prince referred to in 26 will make a strong covenant with many, the allusion being to the co-operation which he found in many of them ; *cf.* 1 Mac 1:11–15, or to the establishment of the religion of the New Covenant by Christ. For three and a half years he, Antiochus, will cause all sacrifices to cease (1 Mac 1:54 ff. ; 4:52), or after three and a half years—the duration of Christ's public ministry according to a probable theory—Christ will abolish all sacrifices of the Mosaic Law by his sacrifice of the cross. Not only will the sacrificial worship be suspended or replaced, but ' an abomination of desolation ' will also be set up on the *pinnacle* of the temple. The expression has a general meaning and denotes any **r** abominable idolatrous object or sacrilegious action causing horror to the faithful. It occurs four times in Daniel (8:13 ' the sin of the desolation '; 9:27 ; 11:31 ; 12:11), always in connexion with the suspension or abolition of worship. The author of 1 Mac referred it to the heathen altar set up by Antiochus on the altar of sacrifice (1:57), while in the Gospels (Mt 24:15 ; Mk 13:14 ; Lk 21:20) it has a broader meaning and denotes, most probably, the profanation of the temple by the Zealots a short time before the siege and fall of Jerusalem in A.D. 70 (*cf.* Jos BJ 4, 3). This temple profanation will last for a fixed time, *i.e.* until the time determined by God, after the lapse of which the divine wrath will be poured out completely destroying the horrible abomination. The beginning of a new age is tacitly implied.

Appendix—The Messianic Interpretation of the Prophecy 50 of the 70 Weeks. (For the various interpretations see F. Fraidl, *Die Exegese der Siebzig Wochen Daniels in der alten und mittleren Zeit*, Graz, 1883.) The various interpretations may be grouped under two headings, the

a Maccabean interpretation and the Messianic interpretation. The first restricts the prophetic perspective to the age of Antiochus IV, the persecutor of Judaism. The other refers it exclusively to the Messianic age.

b Both interpretations have a side open to attack. The Messianic interpretation, which has always enjoyed the greatest favour in Catholic exegesis, seems to overlook the undeniable allusions of the prophecy to the Maccabean age and its relation to the general plan of the visions, while, on the other hand, the Maccabean interpretation ignores the fundamental fact that Daniel's interest, though centred on the age of Antiochus, extends far beyond the limits of that age, and that the restoration described by him, especially in 24, by far exceeds the rededication of the temple in 165 B.C. The combination of the two systems will give a more satisfactory interpretation. To the prophet who was yearning for the temporal restoration of his people the angel promised a spiritual restoration described

c with Messianic characteristics. But as the temporal restoration, following the release from the exile, was preceded by years of suffering, so was the Messianic restoration to be preceded by a period of persecution and oppression. The thought of the oppression called forth some particular facts of the persecution period. When this period is over, the Messianic era will dawn upon the faithful Jews. This general sense of the prophecy falls into line, not only with the historical situation of the prophet as described in 9:2 ff., but also with the general plan of the visions which consists in the prediction of a period of persecution, the destruction of the persecutor, and the beginning of a new era.

d In the light of these general considerations we give the following exposition of the prophecy. The Messianic restoration will be accomplished after a longer period than that predicted by Jeremias for the end of the exile. The first step will be the release of the Jewish exiles and the commencement of a new national and religious life. Then, after some time, persecution will break out. The highest representative of the Jewish religion—the high-priest Onias III—will be assassinated, an attempt will be made to extirpate Judaism, many Jews will forsake the religion of their fathers, the temple service will be suspended, and this will last for some time. At last the persecutor will be taken away and the restoration described in 24 will be gradually effected. The date of the coming of the

e Messias is not indicated. The Messias will inaugurate his kingdom upon earth some time after the end of the persecution. But there are in this prophecy, as in the other visions, three different perspectives combined into one : the Maccabean, the Messianic, and the eschatological perspective. The persecutions of the Maccabean age will lead to the Messianic restoration; the Messianic kingdom or the Church of Christ will be attacked during all her long existence, but all her enemies will in the long run be utterly overthrown and the kingdom of Christ will enter upon its final and glorious stage in heaven. The same line of interpretation, with some differences of detail, is taken up by M.-J. Lagrange, RB (1904) 514 ; (1930) 179–98 ; J. Goettsberger, 74 ff. ; L. Bigot, DTC, IV, 75–102 ; F. Ceuppens, *De prophetiis Messianicis in Antiquo Testamento*, 505–21 ; Höpfl, *Intr. Sp.*, ed. 5a, 490 f. ; J. Chaine, 262 f., Dennefeld, 686 ff.

a **X–XII The Revelation of the History from the Beginning of the Persian Rule to the End of the Times—** This revelation is a brief survey of the history of the Persian and the Seleucid reigns and of the diplomatic relations between the Seleucids and the Ptolemies. It is carried down to the time of Antiochus, whose end is also mentioned. The prediction of the triumph of the righteous at the end of the world closes the revelation. Unlike the other symbolical visions, this is a direct communication by the angel Gabriel to Daniel.

b **X 1–XI 1 Introduction. The Apparition of the Angel** —**1.** That this chronological indication, at least in its present form, is a late editorial note is made clear by the designation of Cyrus as ' king of Persia ' which came **509b** into use during the Greek period. The usual title of the Persian kings during the Persian domination was ' king of Babel ' (S. R. Driver, *Introduction to the Literature of the Old Testament*, 9th ed., p 546). The revelation dealt with the hardships which were to befall the people in times of war. Daniel paid careful attention to the revelation as its importance naturally required. **2 f.** Daniel received the revelation after a three-week mourning. The motive of Daniel's mourning was his anxiety about the fate which was ' to befall his people in the latter days ' (14). He abstained from delicious food, from flesh and wine and ointments, these being marks of joy and happiness ; Pss 103 (104) 15 ; 31(32) 6 ; etc. **4.** After the three-week **c** fasting Daniel was, on the 24th Nisan, on the banks of the *Euphrates* ' the great river '. **5 f.** There he saw what he thought was a man. The description is reminiscent of Ez 1:13. The superhuman being was an angel, and most probably the same one who had appeared to him before (8:16 ; 9:21). **7–9.** The cause of the terror was not the vision, which Daniel's companions did not see, but perhaps a flash of lightning and a thundering noise which preceded the vision ; cf. Acts 9:7 ; 22:9. Daniel lost consciousness and fell upon the ground. **10.** Daniel returns to his senses and is raised up by the angel to a semi-prostrate position. **11.** Then the angel addressed Daniel, the *greatly beloved* man and bade him stand upright and pay attention to his message. **12.** Daniel was anxious **d** about the future destiny of his people ; he prayed God and fasted, and his prayer was heard by God. A clear example of the efficaciousness of prayer accompanied by fasting ; cf. Tob 12:8. **13.** The angel explains the reason of his delay. All nations had their own tutelary angels. The tutelary angel of the Jews received a divine message to Daniel, but the angel of the Persians stood in his way and tried to intercept the message. The conflict went on for 21 days, and the angel of the Persians seemingly prevailed. But at the critical moment Michael, an angel of a higher rank, or an archangel (Jude 9), came to his help, and the angel of the Jews prevailed there beside the *prince* (LXX, Theod., Syr.), i.e. the patron-angel of the Persians. This sense is obtained by reading *hôṭartî* (LXX, Theod.) instead of *nôṭartî* (MT), and giving it the intransitive meaning ' to excel ' hence ' to prevail '. This war between the angels (see also 20), who, for the very reason of their being tutelary angels, are considered as God's ministers, is a dramatic representation of the nations' opposition against the people of God and of God's absolute control of all the nations.

14. After being delivered from his rival, the patron- **e** angel of the Jews came straight to Daniel with his message. The expression ' in the latter days ' denotes both the near and the remote future inclusive of the Messianic age, because the events of these future days need still to be manifested by another vision. **15.** As the angel spoke, Daniel cast his eyes to the ground and was speechless. **16 f.** A touch by the angel restored to him his power of speech, **18 f.**, and after another touch he completely regained his vigour. **20–XI 1.** These verses are probably disarranged. Montgomery (p 416) followed by Linder (p 438) rearranges them provisionally thus : 20a, 21a, 20b, 21b, 11:1. Another possibility is that in 20–11:1, as in the whole chapter, we have a redactional combination of two slightly different forms of the same narrative (Junker, p 99). The angel calls Daniel's attention by a rhetorical **f** interrogation (**20a**) ; he then declares that he will announce to him what is written in the book of truth (**21a**), the destinies of mankind being, as it were, written by God in a book and therefore inalterable. The object of the angel's announcement is : continuation of the war with the angel of the Persians, and, when this war is over, the beginning of another war with the angel of Greece, which will end with the victory of the revealing angel aided by Michael, the

509f great patron angel of the Jews (**20b, 21b**). **11:1** is interpreted in different ways. The simplest interpretation is that Gabriel has helped Michael from the first year of Darius the Mede. This is hardly consistent with the context, which represents Michael as the helper. Others prefer to remove *1a* as a gloss and to read : ' standing as a helper and as a defence for me ' as a continuation of *21b* (Montgomery, 416 ; Junker, 99 ; Bentzen, 44).

510a **XI 2 The Persian Age**—The history of the Persian domination is reduced to three, obviously the first three, of Cyrus' successors : Cambyses (529–521), Darius I (521–485), and Xerxes (485–465). Of the wealth of Xerxes and his military expedition against Greece in the year 480 B.C. there is evidence in the classical writers (*cf.* Herod 7, 20–99). It cannot be inferred that the prophet knew only of four Persian kings, of whom Xerxes was the last. As he was not particularly interested in the history of all the Persian kings, he chose to mention four on account of the relation of the fourth king with Greece, whose interference in Palestine he intended to narrate at greater length.

b **3 f. Alexander the Great** (336–323 B.C.)—**3.** A powerful king ruling over an immense empire and crushing all resistance is a very appropriate description of Alexander the Great. **4.** The suddenness of the fall of Alexander's short-lived empire is vividly depicted. After his untimely death his kingdom was broken (*cf.* 8:8 ' the great horn was broken ') and divided between his generals, none of whom had any blood relationship with Alexander or enjoyed his power. Like these generals, none of their successors were of Alexander's kith and kin. His illegitimate son Heracles and his posthumous son Alexander were both murdered in 309 and 311 respectively.

c **5–20 The Conflicts of the Seleucids and Ptolemies**—Coele-Syria was for many years the bone of contention and the scene of many wars between the kings of Syria and the kings of Egypt. **5.** The king of the south is Ptolemy I, son of Lagus, who, after Alexander's death, secured Egypt for himself and ruled first as satrap (323–305) and then as king (305–285). Seleucus I Nicator, another of Alexander's generals, was one of Ptolemy's princes or captains. At the convention of Triparadisus in 321 he received the satrapy of Babylon ; in 316 he fled to Egypt, where he became Ptolemy's general ; in 312 he recovered his satrapy and extended his dominion over all Asia Minor. He made Antioch the capital of his kingdom. Seleucus' empire was thus **d** *more extensive* than that of Ptolemy. **6.** After some years hostilities broke out between Ptolemy II Philadelphus (285–247) and Antiochus II Theos, grandson of Seleucus I (261–246), over the possession of Palestine. In order to bring about a peaceful settlement Ptolemy II gave his daughter Berenice in marriage to Antiochus II, who had divorced his wife Laodice. After her father's death Berenice was divorced by Antiochus, and later murdered with her child by Antiochus' first wife **e** (Jerome *ad loc.*). **7–9.** Ptolemy III Euergetes (247–222) and Seleucus II Callinicus (246–226). *After some time* (these words are to be transposed from the end of 6 to the beginning of 7) Ptolemy III, brother of Berenice and therefore ' a scion of her roots ', arose in the place of Ptolemy II, and with a view to avenging his sister's murder marched into Syria, reached its outer defences, entered into Seleucia and Antioch, the stronghold of the king of Syria, and returned to Egypt with a rich booty. He had to desist from attacking the king of Syria on account, very probably, of an insurrection in Egypt. After two years Seleucus II made a reprisal attack against Egypt, but was defeated and had to retreat to his land.

f **10–19. Antiochus III the Great** (223–187). **10 f.** Seleucus III Ceraunos (226–223), the son and successor of Seleucus II, was killed during a campaign in Asia Minor, and was succeeded by his brother Antiochus III, who resumed the war with Egypt. His conquests of the Egyptian possessions in Syria (219) were like an overflowing flood. Antiochus then (217) moved in **5** the direction of Egypt, and met the forces of Ptolemy IV at Raphia, on the borders of Egypt and Palestine, where he was defeated with heavy losses (Polyb., 5, 86). **12.** Though the army of Antiochus was almost annihilated, the king of Egypt did not follow up his victory. **13 f.** Antiochus III raised another army, stronger than the former, and after some years (204) marched against Ptolemy V (204–180), who was still an infant, with a great army and much *war equipment*. The many who will rise up against the king of Egypt are Antiochus III, Philip V of Macedon his ally, and many insurgents in Egypt, who were dissatisfied with the rule of Agathocles, the prime minister of the infant king Ptolemy (St Jer.). These were joined by a band of Jewish apostates who had forsaken the law of God and adopted Hellenistic laws and customs (1 Mac 1:11–15). By their anti-religious attitude they pre- **g** pared the way for the Hellenization policy adopted later by Antiochus IV, and so they unintentionally contributed to bring about the fulfilment of the prophecies on the persecution by Antiochus IV. But their plans will fail. **15.** After the parenthesis of 14 the prophet reverts to Antiochus' campaign. The historical interpretation of this verse is given by St Jerome (*ad loc.*) : Antiochus met the Egyptian forces near the sources of the Jordan (198), and defeated Scopas, Ptolemy's general, who took refuge in Sidon. Antiochus then besieged Sidon, and, as the Egyptian army was unable to raise the siege, Scopas surrendered to Antiochus. **16.** After his successes in Syria Antiochus took possession of Palestine ' the glorious land ', carrying destruction in his hand, the allusion being probably to the threat of an invasion of Egypt.

17. Antiochus never invaded Egypt. Though he **h** purposed to acquire all the dominion of Ptolemy, he preferred to come to equitable terms with him owing to the interference of Rome. So he made an alliance with him, giving him his daughter Cleopatra in marriage, which was celebrated at Raphia in 192. The unusual expression ' a daughter of woman ' probably denotes Cleopatra's excellent character and administrative qualities. By this political marriage Antiochus intended to simulate friendship with Ptolemy hoping to get a peaceful footing in Egypt without irritating the Romans. But *his plans* were foiled, for Ptolemy's generals, distrustful of Antiochus' show of friendliness, were constantly on their guard, and Cleopatra was on the side of her husband rather than on that of her father (Jerome). Antiochus never got possession of Egypt. **18 f.** Antiochus made many **i** successful expeditions in the coast lands of Asia Minor. In 191 he was defeated by the Romans at Thermopylae, and again in 190 at Magnesia by the general Lucius Cornelius Scipio, the prince *who* not only *checked Antiochus' arrogance*, but made him submit to humiliating terms of peace. Antiochus met an ignominious end in 187 at Elymais in Persia, where he was killed after plundering the temple of Bel. **20.** Seleucus IV Philopator (187–175). Antiochus III was succeeded by his son Seleucus IV, *who sent an exactor to the glorious kingdom*. The allusion is to the mission of Heliodorus, the prime minister of Seleucus, to the land of Judah, in order to plunder the temple of Jerusalem (2 Mac 3:1–40). Seleucus met an inglorious end after twelve years of an uneventful reign.

21–45 Antiochus IV Epiphanes, the great Persecutor of **51** **the Jews** (175–164)—The writer's interest in the age and person of Antiochus IV is evinced by the abundance of details with which his story is retold. Antiochus was the brother of Seleucus IV, and for fourteen years a hostage at Rome. At Seleucus' request the Romans released Antiochus and took Demetrius, a son of Seleucus, in his place. While Antiochus was on his way to Syria, Seleucus was killed and Antiochus hastened to seize the throne which legitimately belonged to Demetrius, Seleucus' son. On Antiochus' relations with the Jews see 1 Mac 1:11–6:16 ; 2 Mac 4:7–10:9. For an appreciation of his character see

a F. M. Abel, *Antiochus Epiphane* in *Vivre et Penser* (= RB) 1re série (1941), 231–54.

b **21 Antiochus' Accession**—To the Jews Antiochus was not a *theos ephiphanes* ' a manifest god ' as he boastfully called himself, but a despicable man. He had no right to the throne ; he arrived at Antioch unexpected and usurped the throne by intrigue.

c **22-24 His Rise to Power**—**22.** The army which will be *completely* destroyed is probably that of Heliodorus, who, after having murdered Seleucus IV, attempted to oppose Antiochus and to seize the throne. The prince of the covenant is the high-priest Onias III, murdered in 171 (2 Mac 4:34). **23** probably describes Antiochus' duplicity. He would enter upon alliances, and then would play his allies false, and was able to rise to power by means of a small army and a few partisans. **24.** He was a senseless spendthrift. In order to replenish his empty coffers he would, *in time of peace*, enter and loot the most opulent of the cities ; he devised plans against fortified places, but this was to last only until the time fixed by God. Antiochus' prodigality is well attested by ancient historians (*cf.* Livy, 41, 20 ; Polyb., 26, 10 ; 1 Mac 3:30).

d **25-28 Antiochus' first Egyptian Campaign, 170-169 B.C.** —*Cf.* 1 Mac 1:17–20. The war was provoked by Ptolemy VI Philometor acting on the insensate advice of his ministers. Antiochus defeated the young king between Pelusium on the borders of Egypt and Mt Casius, captured the fortress of Pelusium, and went on to occupy the whole of Egypt. Ptolemy, while attempting to escape, fell into the hands of Antiochus. Into this disastrous war Ptolemy was led by two of his most trusted counsellors, probably his guardians Eulaeus and Lenaeus. In order to achieve the complete subjugation of Egypt, Antiochus cunningly simulated friendship with Ptolemy, whom he lavishly entertained at table and maliciously pretended that he only intended to restore him to his throne. But Alexandria held out and Ptolemy Physcon (Euergetes II), brother of Ptolemy, was proclaimed king. When Antiochus departed from Egypt, the two brothers Philometor and Euergetes were reconciled, and Antiochus' plan of a complete and permanent occupation of Egypt was foiled. On his way back to Syria Antiochus made a detour to Jerusalem and plundered the sanctuary (1 Mac 1:21–24).

e **29-30a Antiochus' second Egyptian Campaign, 168 B.C.** —When the two brothers Ptolemy VI and Euergetes II had been reconciled, Antiochus marched once more towards Egypt, but the issue was quite different from that of the previous campaign. The Roman Senate, to whom the two brothers had appealed, sent the legate Popilius who, on his arrival at Alexandria, ordered Antiochus to withdraw from Egypt immediately. The words ' the galleys and the Romans ' are a correct interpretation, not a translation, of Hebrew which means ' the ships of Kittim '. Kittim denotes primarily the island of Cyprus (Gen 10:4), and in a wider sense the islands and coasts of the Mediterranean Sea (Jer 2:10 ; Ez 27:6), and later the western maritime peoples (1 Mac 1:1 ; 8:5) ; *cf.* also Num 24:24.

f **30b-39 Antiochus' Persecution of the Jewish Religion and his Impiety**—**30.** After being unceremoniously turned out of Egypt, Antiochus set himself to Hellenize the Jewish nation. A pro-Hellenic party had already arisen among the Jews (1 Mac 1:12–26). Antiochus *gave regard to* them. **31, 32a.** Antiochus' forces supported by Jewish apostates set to their task, profaning the sanctuary, which was fortified as a stronghold, abolishing the daily sacrifice and setting up an abominable idol on the altar of sacrifices ; *cf.* 1 Mac 1:46–57. The impious men of Juda who had violated the covenant were then made apostates by means of deceitful promises. **32b.** The faithful Jews were strong enough to challenge their persecutors ; *cf.* the stories of Eleazarus (2 Mac 6:18–31), and that of the mother

g and her seven children (2 Mac 7). **33-35.** Those that remain loyal to God, *i.e.* the party of the Assideans (1 Mac 2:42) or the godly, will teach others the right

course. Many of them will perish, but the party will **511g** be saved from complete extermination through the assistance of the small band of the Maccabees. Many joined the ranks of the Maccabees *insincerely*, fearing the drastic punishment of Juda (1 Mac 3:8 ; 6:21–27 ; 7:5-7) and became traitors to their people when opportunity arose. Many will fall, but death will come upon them not as a punishment but as a means of cleansing and purifying them, as gold is purified by fire, until the time appointed by God. For a fuller historical interpretation read the Books of Maccabees.

36-39. These verses describe Antiochus' self-deifica- **h** tion and self-identification with Zeus Olympios or Jupiter Capitolinus, and his self-exaltation over the gods of his fathers and the God of the Jews. His insolence towards God and his worshippers will last as long as God is wrathful with his people. The description of Antiochus' anti-Jewish campaign corresponds perfectly to that of the little horn in ch 7 and the he-goat in ch 8 ; thus : he will do what he likes, 8:25 ; he will exalt himself, 8:10, 11, 25 ; he will speak haughtily, 7:8, 25 ; he will have a short-lived success, 7:25 ; 8:12, 24 f. during the time of God's wrath with his people, 8:12. This is further evidence for the identification of the little horn and the he-goat with Antiochus. Antiochus assumed the title of *theos epiphanes* ' the Manifest God ' in 169 after his victorious campaign in Egypt. From 169 to 166 he is represented on coins with the emblems of the deity, and the inscription is *Antiochos Theos Epiphanes*. But from 166 onwards his figure is that of Zeus Olympios and the inscription is ' King Antiochus, God Manifest, Victory-bearer ' (F. M. Abel, *loc. cit.*, 245 f.). Antiochus made Jupiter Capitolinus or Zeus Olympios **i** the chief and only God of all his empire. Consequently the local Syrian deities, especially Apollo, the tutelary god of Syria, and Tammuz (Adonis), the *beloved* of women, a Phoenician deity so-called because its annual festival was celebrated especially by women, fell gradually into discredit. Instead of the god of his forbears he will worship the god of the *fortresses*, very probably Jupiter Capitolinus, who had appealed to his imagination so strongly during his prolonged sojourn at Rome, and to whom later he built a temple near Antioch and gave rich gifts (Livy, 41, 20 ; 42, 6). **39a** in MT is obscure and probably corrupt. As it stands it means : ' He will make a bulwark of *fortifications* with the help of a foreign god '. A slight textual emendation will give this sense : ' *He will place as defenders of the strongholds* (of Judah) *a people of a foreign god* ', the reference being to the foreign soldiers who garrisoned the fortresses of Jerusalem and Judah ; *cf.* 1 Mac 1:33 ; 3:36, 45. The king's favourites were greatly honoured by him, and to them he distributed the land in return for services and, possibly, for a bribe ; *cf.* 2 Mac 4:8–10:24.

40-45 The End of Antiochus—Apparently these verses **j** relate another expedition against Egypt after 168. So Goettsberger, p 87, following Porphyry (Jerome, PL 25, 598). Many Catholic interpreters regard them as a recapitulation of the chief events of Antiochus' reign from 171 to his death (Linder, p 474). This opinion may, perhaps, be improved upon if we assume that 40–45 are a duplicate and shorter relation of Antiochus' campaigns added to the longer one, 21–39, by an editor. **40.** ' *The time of the end* ' is not the close of Antiochus' reign, but the time appointed by God for the execution of his designs ; *cf.* 8:17. The allusion is to the first Syro-Egyptian war ; *cf.* 25–28. **41.** On Antiochus' invasion of the ' glorious land ' see 28. For strategical reasons three peoples were not attacked. The Edomites and the Ammonites were the enemies of Judah (1 Mac 5:1–8). **42 f.** He reduced many lands **k** under his power ; he appropriated the treasures of Egypt, and the Lybians and Ethiopians were among his *tent-followers*. The historical allusions are obscure. **44.** The tidings coming from the north and the east are the rumours of the insurrections of the Armenians and the Parthians (1 Mac 3:37). He crossed the

511k Euphrates to the east, arrived at Elymais in Persia, and there he attempted to plunder the treasures of the temple of the goddess, but was driven off by the people of the place. Then the news reached him of the defeat of his forces in Palestine by Judas Maccabeus (1 Mac 6:1–7 ; 2 Mac 9:1–3). *Enraged* at these reverses Antiochus ordered his troops to march into Palestine, threatening the people of Judah with utter destruction (2 Mac 9:4). He was taken ill and died at Tabae in Persia (Polyb., 31, 11). **45a.** 'And he will plant the tents of *his palace* between the Sea and the Holy Beauteous Mountain', *i.e.* Mount Sion ; this statement refers to Antiochus' plan of campaign against Judah. Actually Antiochus never came to Jerusalem after his last expedition in the east. **45b.** Antiochus' plans of attack upon Jerusalem will not be carried out, because he will come to *his end* in Persia. Antiochus death is narrated in 1 Mac 6:8–16 ; 2 Mac 9:5–28.

512a XII 1–3 The Final Triumph of the Righteous—The end of the persecution will be followed by a period of bliss. The faithful Israelites, the martyrs of the religion of the One God, will be raised up to everlasting happiness, and the wicked to everlasting shame. The chronological succession of the end of the persecution and the resurrection must be understood according to the principles of the prophetical perspective ; see § 498*e*, *f*. **1.** In the time appointed by God for the duration of the persecution, the archangel Michael, the patron-angel of the Jews (10:13, 31), will take up the cause of the faithful Jews. It will be a time of unprecedented distress. Another and a more violent persecution seems to be predicted. But the angel is here looking to the far distant future, and predicting the affliction which will befall the righteous at the end of the world, *cf.* Mt 24:21 ; Mk 13:19. Thus the age of Antiochus **b** merges insensibly into that of Antichrist. From that persecution only those will be saved whose names are written in the book of life, *i.e.* the true worshippers of God, who are enrolled for eternal life. For the figure of the book of life or the book of God *cf.* Ex 32:32 ; Ps 68(69) 29 ; Is 4:3. **2.** The doctrine of the resurrection and the last judgement is clearly stated, though still in an undeveloped form. The passage is a direct reference to all the Israelites who are represented in this chapter as falling into two classes, the pious and the unfaithful (12:10). There is no reason, therefore, for taking the word ' many ' in a partitive sense, as if the resurrection were restricted to the persecutors and the persecuted ; *cf.* E. F. Sutcliffe, *The OT and the Future Life*, 139 f. The dead will be raised up from their sleep in the grave for everlasting life or for shame and everlasting *abhorrence* according to their deeds. Although the universal resurrection is not explicitly asserted, it is at least implied in the eschatological outlook of the prophet, and in the application by Christ of 2*b* to the last judgement, which will certainly be universal (Jn 5:29). **3.** Those who are ' learned ' and those who teach others the way of righteousness form, according to the law of parallelism, one class comprising all those who have a practical knowledge of God and obey his law (*cf.* 11:32, 35).

c 4 The Closing up of the Vision—On the sealing of the book *cf.* 8:26. When the appointed time comes, many will *go through* the book, and, on seeing that their sufferings had been predicted long before and their victory assured, their knowledge of God's universal providence will be increased.

d 5–13 Conclusion—5. After the last vision had been closed up, two other angels appeared standing on each bank of the Euphrates. Their rôle was probably to act as witnesses of the oath guaranteeing the truth of the revelation (7). **6.** Daniel asked the angel clad in white (10:5 f.) when these extraordinary things would be accomplished. **7.** Before answering the angel lifted up both hands to heaven appealing to the Living God to confirm the truth of what he was about to say. The answer was the same as in 7:25. A further time determination is added which, however, is very vague. The *shattering* of the *forces* of the holy people refers, if

the text is sound, either to the persecution of Antiochus **5** or to the persecutions of the last days. Persecution will cease when the holy people appears to be annihilated. By emending the text this sense may be obtained : When the power of the oppressor comes to an end, *i.e.* when Antiochus is dead, persecution will cease, Antiochus being the last persecutor. **8.** Daniel **e** asks for further particulars about the *last* events preceding the end which will come as foretold in 7. **9.** The angel refuses. The revelation is now closed and sealed up, and nothing can be added to it. When the appointed time comes, the readers will understand what Daniel did not. **10.** But all will not understand. The ' wise ' (11:32, 35 ; 12:3), who will *purify* themselves, make themselves white and refine themselves through sufferings and persecution, will understand that the time of their deliverance is approaching ; but the wicked will not understand. **11 f.** These verses seem to break **f** the sequence of ideas and are considered by most non-Catholic critics as early interpolations meant to correct the statement of 8:14. But if 12:11 is a correction of 8:14, and 12:12 of 12:11, we should expect further corrective statements seeing that the deliverance was not accomplished at the end of 1,335 days. The two verses contain different computations of the same period predicted in 8:14, and must be regarded as integral parts. The two time indications of 1,290 and 1,335 days point immediately to the Maccabean restoration, mediately to the Messianic restoration, ultimately to the final triumph of the righteous at the end of the world. **13.** The prophet will not live till the time of the promised restoration. He will rest in the grave, but will rise up to enjoy the blessings of an everlasting age.

XIII, XIV The Deuterocanonical Appendices—The **5** stories of Susanna and of Bel and the Dragon were collected by the Greek translators from a cycle of Daniel traditions and incorporated into the book of Daniel as an appendix, but they did not form part of the original book. The stories, as they are read in the LXX and in Theod.–Vg, differ from each other in their position in the book and in certain details, the differences being mostly attributable to the liberty with which the text was handled by translators and copyists. Jerome is very careful to note that ch 12 is the end of the Hebrew book of Daniel, and that the following stories are translated from the Greek version of Theodotion.

XIII The Story of Susanna—In the LXX and the Vg **b** it follows ch 12, but in Theod. it stands at the beginning of the book. This position is against the context, and has no claim to originality.

1–4 Susanna's Virtue and Social Condition—1. The **c** story is located in Babylon during the exile. **2 f.** Susanna is introduced as the daughter of Helcias and the wife of Joakim, a beautiful and a God-fearing woman, trained up in the law of Moses. **4.** Her husband was one of the most distinguished Jews, and it was in his house that the exiles met for the purpose of administering justice and teaching the law. It is not incredible that Jews possessed houses in their land of exile ; *cf.* Jer 29:5.

5–14 The Two Lustful Elders—5. The Jews in their **d** exile seem to have been allowed to retain their own laws and institutions. The time indication ' that year ' either refers to a date which has not been preserved, or has a general meaning ' in a certain year '. Jewish tradition has identified them in with the two false prophets mentioned in Jer 29:21–23. The quotation is either an unwritten prophetic saying or an allusion to some passage such as Jer 23:14 ff. **6–14.** The description of the two elders' lustful desires is most realistic. They saw the woman many times and felt a passion for her. They wilfully indulged in their sensual desires, forgetful of the law of God and unmindful of the punishment for such sexual offences. Fully conscious of the impropriety of their desires, they tried to conceal them from one another. Their uncontrolled passion betrayed them, and one day they had to disclose their common

d feelings. This strengthened their passion, and together they planned how to satisfy their desires.

e 15-27a Attempted Seduction—This part of the narrative is condensed by the LXX into three verses corresponding to Vg 19b, 22b, 23. What a contrast between the lewd old judges enjoying the highest authority and the lofty moral principles of the helpless woman. The two men accosted her and were repulsed; they threatened her, but she trusted in God and stood firm in her resolution. The unfaithful wife was punished by death, Lev 20:10; Deut 22:22.

f 27b-43 Susanna falsely Accused and Condemned to Death—On the following day the two judges, while hearing the causes in Joakim's house, summoned Susanna before them. She well knew the reason of the summons and came accompanied by her sorrowful household. The unveiling of the suspected adulteress was prescribed in Num 5:18, though in later times the Mishna, tr. *Sota* 1, 5, forbade the uncovering of a handsome woman. The judges played the part of witnesses by laying their hands upon the head of the accused, *cf.* Lev 24:14. Then followed the act of indictment as concocted by the perjured judges (36-40). As according to a principle of Jewish juridical procedure, a witness could not be the judge, the sentence of death was passed by the credulous multitude. Susanna protested her innocence and appealed to God's supreme tribunal.

g 44-60 Susanna Acquitted—Appeal from the people's verdict was admitted, and a youth called Daniel appeared as counsel for the defence. Before a capital sentence was carried out fresh evidence had to be asked for (Mishna, tr. *Sanhedrin* 6, 1.2), Daniel came forward protesting that he was not responsible for the death sentence, and remonstrated against the rashness with which sentence had been passed on an honourable woman, declaring the judges' evidence to be utterly false. The astonished people hurried back to the place of judgement, and the elders, obviously not the two false witnesses but their colleagues on the bench, made Daniel sit down among them, recognizing in him a superior knowledge which none but God could give. Daniel cross-examined the witnesses separately.

h The way in which Daniel addressed the elders, recalling their past misdeeds and his denunciation of the first evidence before proving its inconsistency with the other, show clearly that divine inspiration was the source of his knowledge. In Greek there is a play upon the words: 'mastic tree (σχῖνος)' and 'shall cut in two (σχίσει)'; 'holm tree (πρῖνος)' and 'cut in two (πρίσει)'. For examples of paronomasia in Hebrew *cf.* Jg 7:25; 10:4, etc. The paronomasia of the Greek text lends no support to the theory of a Greek original. When the people saw that the two witnesses were convicted of perjury they burst out in voices of praise to God who had saved an innocent woman from death.

i 61-64 The two Judges Condemned to Death—The death penalty was inflicted on the perjured judges according to the prescriptions of Deut 19:18-21.

j XIII 65-XIV 22 The Stories of Bel and the Dragon—These two short stories, connected to each other in time and place but wholly unrelated to the story of Susanna, form a single narrative closing the book of Daniel. In Theod. they follow immediately after ch 12, and are preceded by the title 'Vision 12'. In LXX they follow 'Susanna' and bear the title, 'From the prophecy of Habakuk, the son of Jesus, of the tribe of Levi'. The lesson which the two stories are intended to convey is the supremacy of the One, Living God and the nothingness of all heathen gods; *cf.* ch 6.

k XIII 65-XIV 1 Introduction—The last verse of ch 13 is not the conclusion of the Susanna story but the introduction to the following narrative. Astyages was the last king of Media; he was defeated and made prisoner by Cyrus, who annexed his kingdom to his own before the death of Astyages. As this verse is almost identical with 6:28, and the narrative of ch 14 is closely related in meaning to that of ch 6, it has been

conjectured that ch 14 originally followed after ch 6 **513k** (Goettsberger, p 8). When ch 14 was later separated from chh 1-6, a new introduction became necessary, and so 6:28 was repeated in 14:1 with the name Darius changed into Astyages. Daniel is always represented as enjoying the favour of his heathen sovereigns, *cf.* 2:48; 5:29.

2-12 The Idol Bel and his Priests—**2.** Bel, a shorter **l** form for Bel-Marduk 'the Lord Marduk', was the chief of the Babylonian pantheon. To him the Babylonians offered 12 'artabas' (= *c* 164 bushels or 6 hecto-litres) of fine flour, 40 sheep and 6 vessels (RV 'firkin' = *c* 9 gallons, which is almost the exact equivalent of the Greek μετρητής) of wine (LXX 'oil') every day. The daily offering of such ample provisions to the gods was a part of the Babylonian ritual; see *G. C. Gadd, Babylonian Myth and Ritual* in *Myth and Ritual* (Oxford, 1933) 42. **3.** Cyrus for political reasons worshipped, besides his own god, the gods of his conquered peoples; Daniel, however, worshipped no other god but his own, **4,** who was the only God, creator of heaven and earth, all other deities being the work of man's hands. **5.** Bel was believed to be a living god, and the proof was the enormous quantities of food daily consumed by him. **6.** Daniel ridiculed the argument. Clay and brass do not eat. **7-12.** The king began to suspect some fraud, but the priests assured him of their god's voracity and proposed to put the matter to a test. As they penetrated into the temple by a secret entrance, they never suspected that their fraud could be detected.

13-21 The Fraud Detected and the Priests put to Death m —The result of the test was, needless to say, contrary to the priests' expectations. Truth came to light and the priests had to acknowledge their crime. According to the condition laid down by themselves (11) they were put to death together with their wives and children. The acknowledgement by the king of the superiority of the God of Daniel is implied in the king's action. But the destruction of the temple (21b) is, very probably, a Jewish insertion. It is not mentioned in the LXX, and Herodotus (1, 183) relates that the temple was pillaged by Xerxes.

22-42 The Story of the Dragon—The word 'Dragon' **n** denotes here, like the Greek δράκων, a large serpent. There is ample evidence of serpent-worship in Babylon, though so far there is no evidence that live snakes were worshipped as gods; *cf.* S. Landersdorfer, *Der Drache von Babylon* in BZ (1913). But it is not improbable that they were.

22-26 Daniel Kills the Dragon—If a metal idol was not **o** a god, a live serpent certainly was, and Daniel was therefore requested to worship the serpent. Daniel refused and asked to be permitted to kill the serpent without any weapon, and to show that the serpent was no more a god than Bel. The king believing in the immortality of the serpent-god granted the permission, and after a short time the serpent was dead.

27-31 Daniel in the Lions' Den—On seeing that their **p** gods were being destroyed the Babylonians became furious, and demanded the death of Daniel. The king tried to save him, but had to yield. On the lions' den see note to 6:23. **30b** in LXX follows after v 1.

32-38 The Intervention of Habacuc—While in the **q** den Daniel was miraculously fed through the agency of Habacuc. The words 'a prophet in Judaea' are a gloss intended to identify Daniel's Habacuc with the homonymous prophet. The identity cannot be admitted for chronological reasons. The Habacuc episode, though loosely connected with the context, prepares the way for the miraculous liberation of Daniel.

39-42 Daniel's Liberation—On the seventh day, when **r** the people's indignation had begun to cool down, the king went to the den to mourn for Daniel. To his amazement he saw him unhurt sitting amidst the lions. Recognizing the superiority of Daniel's God the king ordered that Daniel should be immediately taken out of the den, and that the same punishment be meted out to those who had plotted against Daniel's life.

OSEE

By P. P. SAYDON

514a Bibliography—St Jerome, *Commentarii in Osee Pro-phetam*, PL 25, 815–946 ; *W. R. Harper, *Amos and Hosea*, ICC, 1905 ; E. Tobac, *Les Prophètes d'Israël*, 1919, Vol. I, 195–242 ; D. Buzy, *Les Symboles de l'Ancien Testament*, Paris, 1923, 33–93 ; *S. L. Brown, *The Book of Hosea*, WC, 1932 ; articles on Osee by L. Fillion in VDB, L. Clamer in DTC, *A. B. Davidson in HDB. For a fuller bibliography see 409b and Knabenbauer–Hagen, *Commentarius in Prophetas Minores*, CSS, Vol I, 7–14, 24–8.

b Name and Life of the Prophet—The prophet's name Osee (Heb. *hôšēaᶜ* ' salvation, deliverance ', Gr. ' Ωσῆε) is identical with that of the last king of Israel (4 Kg 17:1) and with the original name of Josue, Moses' successor (Num 13:17). Of his place of origin, social position, and other circumstances of his life nothing is known beyond what can be gleaned from his book. He is described as the son of Beeri, 1:1. His interest in the Northern Kingdom, his intimate knowledge of its political and religious conditions and the absence of any mention of Jerusalem bear evidence of his Israelitish origin. As most of the metaphors and images in Osee's book are taken from agricultural life (*cf.* 4:16 ; 6:3 ; 8:7 ; 9:2, 10, 16 ; 10:1, 11–13 ; 13:3 ; 14:6–8), it has been inferred that the prophet was a farmer. The inference, however, does not seem to be sufficiently warranted, as the prophet's peculiar imagery may be due to his profound love of nature. He married Gomer, the daughter of Debelaim, from whom he had three children.

c The story of **the prophet's marriage** has, since the days of St Jerome, been a subject of controversy. It has been repeatedly asked whether the prophet in the first three chapters is relating history, vision, or allegory. Long lists of names may be drawn up in support of the several interpretations which may be grouped in two classes : the literal and the non-literal. In favour of the non-literal interpretation it is urged : (*a*) that it is inconceivable that a prophet of Yahweh should dishonour himself by such a shameful marriage or that God himself should command a union so repugnant to the moral sense ; (*b*) that the domestic events narrated in 1:3–9 took too much time to serve as the basis of a moral lesson to the people ; (*c*) that the prophets were sometimes commanded by God to perform actions which it was impossible to perform except in a vision, *cf.* Ez 4:9–17 ; (*d*) that the close connexion between the act itself and its symbolical meaning, 1:2, clearly suggests that the prophet's main concern is the religious state of his people, not the story of his domestic life.

d To these arguments the supporters of the literal interpretation reply : (*a*) what is in itself repugnant to the moral sense remains so even if it is the object of a vision or an allegory ; (*b*) the moral lesson is based not so much on the symbolical names of Osee's children as on his marriage ; (*c*) from the fact that certain actions commanded by God could not be performed except in a vision it cannot be inferred that all actions commanded by God to his prophets were performed in a vision, *cf.* 3 Kg 22:11, etc. ; (*d*) this is true, but does not show that the prophet's marriage was not real.

e All are agreed that the prophet's marriage has a symbolical meaning. A distinguishing feature of a symbolical action is its unusual and extravagant char-acter. Thus Ahias rends his new garment in 12 pieces, **5** 3 Kg 11:30 ; *cf.* also Is 20:2 ; Jer 19:10. The symbolical action is really a dramatic representation of an abnormal moral or religious situation intended to make the people realize the situation more vividly. Such actions, which no man under normal conditions will do, may be performed either actually or in a vision. They are considered to be performed in a vision when the moral lesson is intended for the prophet alone. But when the lesson is intended for the people, the symbolical action must be considered as really performed (Buzy, 21).

f The application of these considerations to Osee's marriage shows that it was real. No one will deny that marriage with a woman of evil character is out of the common run. All will likewise agree that the moral lesson inherent in Osee's marriage was intended for the people not for the prophet who needed no proof of the people's wickedness. The people must have been shocked on seeing the prophet bringing home a dishonoured wife and, it is reasonable to suppose, manifested their disapproval, thus providing him with an opportunity to insist on the hideousness of their faithlessness to Yahweh despite Yahweh's immense love for them.

The literal interpretation may, however, be given another form. Gomer was, at the time of her marriage, of an irreproachable character. She is called ' a wife of fornications ' on account of her later misbehaviour. After having borne three children she loved another man and was sent away by her husband. But Osee still loved his erring wife and after some time bought her back. This interpretation does not weaken the demonstrative force of the symbolical action, because the queerness or unusualness inherent in the symbolic action may well consist in Gomer's misbehaviour and in her being divorced and taken again by her husband. For a fuller discussion of the different views see Buzy, 33–93 ; P. Cruveilhier, RB (1916) 342–62 ; A. Reigner, RB (1923) 390–7.

g Osee was called to the prophetic ministry during the reign of Jeroboam II (783–743 B.C., Kugler, *Von Moses bis Paulus*, 164). As the prediction of the fall of Jehu's dynasty made at the beginning of Osee's ministry, 1:4, was fulfilled in 743 B.C. with the murder of Zacharias, Jeroboam's son and successor, the prophet must have begun his ministry at least some years before 743. All are agreed on this. But opinions differ on the question of the duration of his ministry. According to 1:1 it extended till the reign of Ezechias (721–693 B.C., Kugler, *op. cit.*, 163). Many interpreters, however, on internal grounds, reduce Osee's ministry within narrower limits. The fall of Samaria in 722–721 is represented as a future event, 8:5 f. ; 9:5–8 ; 14:1. The people of Israel turning for help to Assyria, 5:13, 6:11, 8:9, still enjoy a certain measure of political independence which they lost in the reign of Phacee, 736–732 B.C. There is no allusion to the war of Phacee of Samaria and Rasin of Damascus against Achaz of Judah in 734 B.C. These facts suggest that Osee's ministry did not extend beyond the reign of Manahem, 742–737 B.C., and consequently the words ' Achaz and Ezechias ' in the superscription are to be regarded as interpolated (Hoonacker, 1 f., 12). Osee's ministry is, therefore, made to cover a period of approximately ten

644

g years, 747–737 or 745–735. But as the texts upon which this opinion rests may be interpreted differently (*cf.* L. Gry, *Osée VII, 3 sqq et les dernières années de Samarie*, RB (1913) 191–206 ; Robinson, 45, 51) the opinion which extends Osee's ministry till the fall of Samaria still retains its degree of probability.

h **The Historical and Religious Background**—Osee lived and prophesied in a time of internal political decadence and general moral corruption. The long and prosperous reign of Jeroboam II was the last flash of glory enjoyed by a crumbling kingdom. Zacharias, Jeroboam's son and successor, was murdered by Sellum after a six-months' reign, 4 Kg 15:10. Sellum himself was killed by Manahem who succeeded, with the aid of Assyria, in maintaining himself in power for six years, 742–737 B.C. (4 Kg 15:17). His son Phaceia was murdered by Phacee after two years, 4 Kg 15:23–25. Phacee entered on a military alliance with Rasin of Damascus against Assyria, 4 Kg 16:5 ; Is 7. But Tiglath-pileser defeated the allied armies, captured Damascus, overran the northern territory of Israel and deported the inhabitants to Assyria, 4 Kg 15:29. The Northern Kingdom, reduced more or less to the territory of the tribe of Ephraim, became a vassal-state of Assyria. The loss of political independence provoked a strong feeling of hostility against Assyria which made the people turn for help to Egypt. The intrigues and manœuvres of the pro-Egyptian party were largely responsible for the downfall of Ephraim. Phacee, the leader of this party, was assassinated by Osee, a loyal pro-Assyrian who became king of Israel and paid unfailingly his annual tribute to the Assyrian monarch so long as Tiglath-pileser lived. But on the accession of Shalmaneser V (727 B.C.) Osee fell into the trap of the anti-Assyrian party and refused to pay tribute. This was tantamount to an act of revolt. Osee was deposed, and after a three-year siege Samaria fell to the Assyrians in 721 B.C.

i The religious situation may be described as a confused medley of a perverted Yahweh-worship and an idolatrous Baal-worship due to a misconception of the true character of Yahweh. The calf-worship was the official cult. Though not originally an idolatrous worship, the calf being intended only as a representation of Yahweh, it was certainly against the prescriptions of Ex 20:4 and led most naturally to idolatry. When, later, king Achab, who had married a Phoenician wife, introduced Baal-worship into his kingdom, 3 Kg 16:30, not only was a new form of religion, characterized by its licentious cult, set up in the kingdom of Israel, but the Yahweh cult itself became evermore contaminated by idolatrous influences. As in the days of Elias, 3 Kg 18:21, the people worshipped Yahweh as well as the Canaanitish deities. They still kept the Sabbath and held their annual festivals, 2:11, offered sacrifices to Yahweh, 5:6, 8:13, and swore by Yahweh, 4:15. They worshipped Yahweh at Bethel, 4:15, and burnt incense and gave themselves up to debauchery on hilltops, 4:13 f. ; they made idols of silver and gold, 8:4 ; 13:2. Yahweh, their God, was conceived as one among other gods. He demanded sacrifices which they offered punctiliously, but he had no regard, they thought, to their moral conduct and internal dispositions. Hence religion came to be considered as the performance of acts of worship rather than a- system of religious truths and moral precepts. Osee's preaching was directed mainly against the calf-worship, but in point of fact it was Baal-worship which constituted the heinous infidelity of Israel.

j **Contents and Analysis**—The theme of Osee's book is the expression of a strong reaction of love against ingratitude. Yahweh loved his people in spite of their unworthiness ; he loved them still despite their backslidings ; he threatened to cast them off ; but, though they were not responsive to his persistent appeals, his wrath was that of a loving father ever ready to receive his repentant children into his arms. It is difficult to give a logical division of the whole book. Chh 1–3 are easily distinguishable from the rest. The prophet's

affection for his unfaithful wife represents in a dramatic **514j** manner Yahweh's love for his ungrateful and unfaithful people. The remaining chapters contain, in an abridged form, some of the prophet's discourses loosely connected with one another, but all subordinated to the central theme—God's love and the people's ingratitude. Chh 4–8 form one group of discourses in which the prevailing thought is Israel's guilt with occasional references to punishment. The prophet denounces the depravity of the people which he traces back to their ignorance of God and to the bad example of the priests, ch 4. He then arraigns in a special manner the kings and the priests, the leaders of the nation, who are held responsible for the general degradation of public life, 5:1–14. If Israel will repent sincerely, God will forgive them, but at present their sins appear to be beyond remedy, 5:15–6:11a.

Revolutions, anarchy, and decay of national strength **k** are the disastrous consequences of their having forsaken God, the only source of their strength, and turned for assistance to foreign powers, 6:11b–7:7 and 7:8–16. The prophet denounces once more Israel's most grievous sins : idolatry, an unlawful dynasty and foreign policy, and announces imminent punishment, ch 8. In chh 9–14:1 the leading idea is this imminent punishment with frequent references to Israel's sins. While the people are rejoicing in their harvest feasts, the prophet announces the exile into Assyria or Egypt, 9:1–9. He recalls Israel's inveterate wickedness and depicts with gloomy colours the dire punishment which will soon be meted out to them, 9:10–17. Altars and sacrifices will not avert the coming doom ; on the contrary they only serve to increase Israel's guilt, 10:1–8. Punishment can be averted only by a change of life, 10:9–11:1. In a moving discourse, one of the finest passages of the whole book, the prophet recalls God's incessant care for Israel since their early days and depicts the reaction of God's love to Israel's ingratitude, 11:1b–11. The two last discourses, 11:12–12:14 and 13:1–14:1, develop some of the leading ideas of the whole book, Israel's infidelity, the unchangeableness of divine purpose, punishment. 14:2–10 form the conclusion of the book. After having atoned for all her sins Israel will repent, return to God, and enjoy God's favour once more.

Doctrinal Contents—These may be grouped under **l** two headings : God and Religion. Though Yahweh is generally represented as the God of Israel, 3:5, 4:6, 12, etc., and the only source of their welfare and salvation, 2:8, 21 f., 13:4, he is also the only God, 13:4, while the Canaanitish Baals and all other deities are nothing but the work of man, 8:4–6 ; 13:2. Osee's **monotheistic doctrine** was not a creation of his own or of the prophetic school of the 8th century B.C., but the basis of the religion of Israel from its very beginning. Idolatry was the result of the people's ignorance of Yahweh, 4:6, *i.e.* the people fell into idolatry on account of their misconceptions of the true nature of Yahweh whom they considered as one of the local Canaanitish deities. The prophets did not introduce a new doctrine but simply endeavoured to recall the people to the monotheism of their forefathers ; *cf.* M. J. Lagrange, *La nouvelle histoire d'Israël et le prophète Osée*, RB (1892) 208 ff.

The **relation between Yahweh and his people** is repre- **m** sented under the figure of a covenant, 6:7, or of a marriage, 2:2 ff. The figure of a marriage which occurs first in Osee, and was probably suggested to him by his domestic experience, became common in later writings, *cf.* Is 54:6 ; Ez 16 ; and the Canticle of Canticles. In NT times the bridegroom is Christ and the bride the Church, *cf.* Jn 3:29 ; 2 Cor 11:2 ; Eph 5:23–32 ; Apoc 21:9. This symbolical marriage was contracted out of God's immense love for the people of Israel. As God's plans are unchangeable, so is the marriage bond indissoluble. He will never put away his bride though she may prove unfaithful. In point of fact the Israelites were never completely rejected by God : they were punished with the exile for their

514m infidelity, but afterwards they were taken up again by God and restored to their former rights and privileges. God's punishments are corrective, not vindictive. He punishes the sinner in order to make him acknowledge his sin and repent of it. He is represented as a loving father who cannot divest himself of his affection for his children even if they prove untrue to him. God is ever ready to receive the repentant sinner. Osee's conception of Yahweh as the God of love approaches very closely to the sublime doctrine of St John on Christ's love ; *cf*. I Jn 4:7–21.

n The **religion** of Osee considered in its practical aspect includes two elements, the sacrificial worship and the moral law. Osee apparently condemns sacrifice, 6:6 ; *cf*. Is 1:11–14. In reality, however, he only condemns those popular forms of worship that are either idolatrous or infected with idolatrous influences. This is made clear by his strong denunciation of the immoral cult-practices, 4:13 f., and the unlawful forms of worship, 7:14, 8:4–6, 11, 10:1 ff., 13:2, characteristic of the Canaanitish religion. Sacrifice and all other external acts of worship are acceptable to God only when they are accompanied by a true knowledge of the Only God and his law and a sincere love for God and men. In other words it is the internal disposition of the worshipper that renders the external act acceptable to God.

o The **moral law** of Osee covers the greater part of the decalogue. The fifth, sixth, seventh and eighth commandments are clearly implied in 4:2. Image-worship is forbidden, 8:4 ff. ; 10:2, 5, 8 ; 13:2. The law of the Sabbath rest or festival is referred to in 2:11.

p Osee's **Messianic** doctrine is closely connected with his conception of the indissolubility of the marriage bond between Yahweh and his people. The people will be punished by exile but will not be utterly destroyed. After having atoned for their infidelity they will be reinstated in their position of people of God. This restoration, however, as described by the prophet, lies beyond the historical horizon of the post-exilic age. As the prophets do not generally distinguish between the near and the distant future, the historical post-exilic perspective and the Messianic perspective represent one restoration commencing with the return from the exile and culminating in the deliverance by the Messias and the establishment of a universal kingdom upon earth. The main features of the Messianic restoration are : (i) an everlasting covenant established on justice and righteousness ; *cf*. also Jer 31:31–34. (ii) the people will be innumerable as the sands of the sea, 1:10. (iii) the calling of the Gentiles is typically predicted, *cf*. 1:10 ; 2:24 and Rom 9:25 f. ; I Peter 2:10. (iv) the Messianic people will be under one king of the Davidic dynasty, 3:5. On 6:3 and 11:1 see the commentary.

q Osee's **Character**—Osee was a man of a strongly emotional character and a deeply religious temperament. He is rightly called the prophet of love as St John is the Apostle of love. He was a loving husband and a loving father. His sensitive nature finds expression not only in his efforts to woo back his erring wife, but also in passionate outbursts of paternal love (11:8) and in the pathetic images by which he describes Yahweh's care for Israel (11:2–4). But his affections were centred mainly on Yahweh. His strong love for Yahweh provoked in him violent outbreaks of anger against his ungrateful people. Justice demanded that the people should be punished. But love reacted to the claims of justice and triumphed. Transferring his human feelings to God the prophet pictures Yahweh threatening his people with severe punishment, but saving them from utter destruction. As the prophet could never be brought to keep his wife away, so Yahweh would not reject his people for ever.

r **Text and Style**—The Hebrew text of the book of Osee has been badly preserved and this to a certain extent accounts for its obscurity. Some passages may be confidently emended with the help of the LXX, but others are corrupt beyond emendation, and critical conjecture is the only means to make the text yield a **5** reasonable sense. The Vg, though representing a form of text older than that of our MT, is of no help for the restoration of the original text. To the corrupt and unintelligible passages St Jerome added a number of mistranslations, thus 4:6 *conticuit* for *periit* ; 7:10 *humiliabitur* for *respondebit* ; 10:14 Salman is erroneously identified with Salmana of Jg 8 ; 11:8 *protegam* for *tradam* (deliver up) ; 12:7 *Chanaan* for *mercator* ; and others which will be noticed in the commentary. Osee's style is described by St Jerome as ' commaticus ', *i.e.* made up of short and abrupt sentences ' quasi per sententias loquens ' (Praef. in XII Proph., PL 28, 1015). This is due not so much to a defective literary skill as to the prophet's strongly emotional nature, to conflicting and sometimes uncontrolled feelings and to his profound religious temperament. Though Osee's prophetic utterances are cast in a rhythmical form, they cannot be reduced to uniform metrical standard, and all attempts to rearrange the text metrically involve so many textual alterations as to render the rearrangement unacceptable.

A. I–III Osee's Marriage and its Symbolical Meaning **5** —The prophet relates a personal experience of domestic life in order to outline more effectively the message which he is about to bring to his people, a message of love for an unfaithful people.

I Superscription—See § 514*g*.

2, 3a Osee's Marriage—At the beginning of his **b** ministry Osee was commanded by God to marry ' a wife of fornications '. For the meaning of this appellation see § 514*f*. The children share their mother's disgrace, although the appellation ' sons of fornication ' does not necessarily mean that they were born in adultery. There is nothing in the text suggesting that they were illegitimate. It is probable that the symbolical meaning of Osee's marriage reacted upon the literal sense of the origin of his children so that a new symbolical meaning completely absorbed this literal sense. The prophet's children, representing as they did a people untrue to its God, are called adulterine in the same sense as their mother, the nation of Israel, is called adulterous because of her unfaithfulness to Yahweh. God explains the reason of this perplexing command. The people of Israel had turned away from Yahweh and gone after foreign gods as a wife who goes astray. In order that the people may realize the hideousness of their behaviour, the prophet is to marry a woman of disreputable character and thus excite a feeling of horror in their insensible hearts. Obeying God's command Osee married Gomer, the daughter of Debelaim. The names of daughter and father have no symbolical meanings.

3b-9 His Children—3b-5 The first son was called **c** Jezrahel. This symbolical name refers to the events narrated in 4 Kg 9:21–26, 30–37 ; 10:7–11. The sanguinary deeds there recorded were to be avenged by the downfall of Jehu's dynasty and the extinction of the kingdom of Israel. Two points deserve consideration. First, the birth of Osee's firstborn fell in the last years of Jeroboam or in the six months of the reign of his son Zacharias, the last of Jehu's royal descendants. Consequently Osee began to prophesy during the last years of Jeroboam II. Secondly the prophet considered the overthrow of Jehu's dynasty as the beginning of a period of political decadence to culminate in the extinction of the Northern Kingdom. It cannot, therefore, be inferred that he expected the end of the kingdom of Israel to come with the downfall of Jehu's dynasty, especially as he lived under other kings after the fall of Jehu's house. The place of the collapse of the Israelite forces will have been the Vale of Jezreel which stretches from the town of Jezreel, the modern Zerin, in a SE. direction down to the Jordan. Jezreel, not Samaria, is mentioned here on account of the massacre perpetrated by Jehu and of its assonance with Israel.

6. The prophet's second child was a daughter, whom he **d**

called by God's command 'Without mercy', thus symbolizing the inexorable doom impending over Israel. Times without number had God shown mercy to his people ; but there is a limit to God's mercy and that limit has been reached. **7.** God will, however, have mercy on the house of Judah. This parenthetical remark interrupts the narrative of the prophet's domestic story and is considered by many critics as an interpolation (Harper, Robinson) or as a transposition from ch 2 (Hoonacker). It extends the prophetic outlook beyond the political conditions of the kingdom of Judah. The house of Judah, *i.e.* the Davidic dynasty, will never be permanently cut off. As a political power it will be overthrown, but a time will come when, through the assistance of God and without military help, it will be restored to its former, and even to a brighter, splendour. The perspective is obviously Messianic. **8 f.** The third child, a son, was called 'Not-my-people', a name symbolizing the total rejection of Israel. As the Israelites have refused to recognize Yahweh as their only God, Yahweh will no longer regard them as his people.

10–II 1 Promise of a Brighter Future—10. All of a sudden the prophet's outlook becomes brighter, and the rejection is represented as a temporary punishment which will be followed by a magnificent restoration. The people of Israel will increase to extraordinary numbers and will be taken up again by God as his sons, the sons of a living God who can protect them from all evil. **11.** The kingdoms of Judah and Israel will be reunited under one leader and will come up to Jerusalem from their land of captivity, because the day of Jezreel, a day of humiliation for the old Israel, will be a day of triumph for the new Israel. Although the prophet has clearly in view the return from the captivity, his vision extends to the Messianic age, when the children of Israel, the 'Israel of God' (Gal 6:16) or the Christians, will be the object of the divine favour and will become numerous as the sand of the sea (Rom 9:25 f. ; 1 Pet. 2:10), forming one kingdom under one king, the Messias.

II 2–13 Gomer's Conjugal Unfaithfulness—After having borne three children to her husband, Gomer broke the conjugal bond. The children remained with their father who did all he possibly could to bring his wife back to him. This is the literal and historical sense. Symbolically, Gomer is the nation, the children are the individual Israelites, the husband is Yahweh. **2.** The prophet urges his children to expostulate with their mother that she may put away her effrontery and her lewdness. **3.** He threatens her with exspoliation and death. The day of her nativity is the time of the Exodus, the beginning of Israel's national life. Adultery was punishable by death (Lev 20:10) which is expressed here by the image of a dry and barren land. In 4 ff. there is an imperceptible transition from the historical to the symbolical sense. On the one hand Osee threatens his faithless wife, on the other Yahweh threatens the people for their idolatry.

4 f. Yahweh will no longer show any mercy to his people. Both individually and collectively (children and mother) they have forsaken their God. The literal sense here is entirely absorbed by the symbolical sense. It is not the prophet who threatens to suppress all natural affection towards his innocent children ; it is Yahweh who is about to withdraw his favour from an unfaithful people. If we admit this sense in **4** we need not infer (Hoonacker, 16) that Osee's children were born in sin. **5b–10.** From the faithless nation the prophet insensibly goes back to his faithless wife. She regards her lovers as the source of all her material well-being. Her husband, who still loves her, tries to call her back, and his efforts are represented metaphorically as a blocking up of all the roads leading away from home. Unable to find the path to her lovers she returns to her husband whom she is bound to acknowledge as the bestower of all blessings. As all his gifts have been put to wrong uses, in future he will withdraw his gifts from her. Moreover he will reveal

her abject condition to her lovers who will be powerless to help her. **11–13.** Now the figure of the erring wife fades away and that of the nation again becomes prominent. The joyful celebrations of Israel will cease ; the vineyards and fig trees, believed to be the reward of her gods, will be devastated. God will punish the people for having worshipped the Baals in whose temples they arrayed themselves in jewels and sacred garments. Although the literal and the symbolical meanings run into each other, the symbolical sense is the more relevant. The people have gone after the Canaanitish gods and God called them back by some unspecified calamity. They will recognize the helplessness of their gods and will return to their God. *Cf.* the parable of the prodigal son, Lk 15:11–32.

14–25 The Last Act of the Drama of Divine Love— The prophet's wife goes off the stage and the only actors are Yahweh and the nation of Israel. When the people of Israel have paid the penalty of their faithlessness, God moved by their miserable condition will come once more to their rescue. He is represented as a husband wooing his erring wife. **14.** In order to win her over he will lead her to the wilderness and there he will speak to her words of love. The wilderness is a figure for the land of exile. The figure is reminiscent of the first betrothal of Yahweh to Israel in the wilderness of Sinai. **15.** In the land of exile Israel will repent and will be reconciled to her spouse who will give her back her *vineyards*, *i.e.* her former possessions, and the Vale of Achor will be for her a ray of hope. The reference is to Jos 7:25 ff. The first entrance of Israel into Palestine through the valley of Achor was accompanied by disaster, but the second entrance will be entirely successful. The restoration will be complete. In that quiet place Israel, overwhelmed by the irresistible power of God's love, will joyfully and submissively respond to her husband's appeals, as she did in her younger years. **16 f.** In that day—an expression used to introduce the Messianic age—Israel will no longer call Yahweh 'Baali', *i.e.* my Baal, but '*iši* 'my Husband'. Baal (lit. 'master') has sometimes the meaning of 'husband', *cf.* Gen 20:3, Lev 21:4, etc., and is therefore a synonym of '*iš* 'man, husband'. But Baal is also used to denote the Canaanitish deities and its use is condemned on account of its heathen associations. *Cf.* the NT conception of the Church as the Bride of Christ, Eph 5:32. In Osee's time Yahweh was worshipped under the name and by the cult of Baal (see § 514*i*), but the future relation of Israel to Yahweh will be that of a faithful spouse, and all memory of the Baal-worship will be wiped out.

18. The relations between Yahweh and the new Israel are described as a covenant ; *cf.* also Is 55:3 ; Jer 31:31–34 ; 32:40 ; Ez 16:60 ; 34:25 ; 37:26. One feature of this covenant is peace and security ; *cf.* Is 11:9 ; Ez 34:25 ; Mic 5:9 ff. **19 f.** The covenant is also represented as a permanent betrothal established on justice and righteousness and on God's love and mercy. To this betrothal both parties will remain faithful, and the people will acknowledge their God as the Yahweh of the Old Covenant, a God true to his promises. A fuller and deeper knowledge of God is another characteristic of the Messianic age ; *cf.* Is 11:9 ; Jer 31:33. Therefore a new era commencing with the post-exilic restoration and reaching its fullness in the Messianic age will dawn on the reborn Israel. **21 f.** It will be an age of abundance. Jezrahel, *i.e.* Israel, will ask for temporal blessings, these will ask the land to yield an abundant crop, the land will ask the heavens to send the rain in its proper season, the heavens will ask God to be allowed to pour rain on the earth, and God will respond in faithful love. **23 f.** are a striking contrast with ch 1. Jezreel, the scene of the overthrow of the Northern Kingdom, became a name significant of God's planting (lit. 'God sows') his people again on their land. They will become once more the people of God and the object of his favours.

516e III 1-5 Gomer's Reconciliation to her Husband—
Gomer had deserted her husband (2:2) and was living with another man. Her rightful husband bought her back, but for some time she had to live in seclusion. This seems to be the historical meaning of ch 3 (Harper, Robinson, Hoonacker, Tobac). According to another interpretation, which may be traced back to St Jerome (PL 25, 842), the woman of ch 3 is not Gomer, hence Osee is said to have married twice (Crampon, 736 f; Knab. 60; Buzy 72–88). The first interpretation is more probable as it fits in better with the historical and symbolical meanings of chh 1–3.

f 1. The sensitive soul of Osee could not divest itself of its warm affection for his faithless wife. He loved her still, as the Lord loved Israel though she abandoned him and worshipped the Canaanite gods. The phrase ' lovers of raisin-cakes' characterizes the Baal-worshippers. **2.** Unable to resist the impulse of his heart he bought her back for 15 shekels (c £2) and one homer and a half (12 bushels) of barley. Supposing the ordinary price of barley was a little less than one-half shekel per seah (4 Kg 7:18), or one-third of a shekel per seah, the price of one homer and a half (45 seahs) would be 15 shekels which added to the 15 shekels in money give an amount of 30 shekels, which was the price of a bondmaid (Ex 21:32). It may therefore be inferred that Gomer had become a slave concubine of her master and was afterwards redeemed by her husband by the payment of a fixed sum.

g 3. Gomer had now to give up her past licentious life and lead, for a certain time, a quiet life (DV wait) preparing herself to be reinstated in her conjugal rights. MT reads : ' . . . many days thou shalt sit still for me . . . and I also (will sit still) for thee'. Vg and DV reproduce the sense rightly though not literally. Both wife and husband, though reconciled, will live in a state of isolation for some time before re-establishing their old relations. This temporary separation is, of course, a punishment inflicted by the husband upon his faithless wife. Very probably the historical sense is, to a large extent, absorbed by the symbolical sense, i.e. the verse expresses not so much Osee's behaviour to his reconciled wife as Yahweh's attitude towards repentant Israel. **4 f.** The symbolical sense is formally declared. The people of Israel will not be restored to their former rights as soon as they turn back to Yahweh. For some time they will be denied Yahweh's familiarity. They will have to live, as it were, in seclusion, deprived of their political leaders and of the objects of their worship. In v 4 read 'pillars' for DV 'altars'. When the period of seclusion is terminated, the children of Israel united under one king (cf. 1:11) of the Davidic dynasty attach themselves again to their God trembling with joy before the Lord and his bounty. The prediction of Israel's post-exilic restoration foreshadows the Messianic age with all its spiritual blessings. This is borne out by the fact that the king of the restoration is called simply David, an appellation of the Messias (cf. Jer 23:5 ; Ez 34:23 f. ; 37:24 f.) and by the indefinite time-indication ' in the last days ' which usually denotes the Messianic times (cf. Is 2:2 ; Jer 23:20 ; Mic 4:1, etc.).

517a B. IV-XIV 1 Comminatory Discourses—In plain but vehement language the prophet denounces the sins of the people and threatens them with punishment.

b IV 1-14 The Sins of the People and their Cause—The prophet addresses the people and their religious leaders announcing Yahweh's judgement or contention with them. **1 f.** This judgement is called for by their sins : (i) lack of truth, i.e. honesty in dealing with one another ; (ii) lack of mercy or love for one's fellow-men ; (iii) lack of knowledge of God, not mere theoretical knowledge, but practical knowledge consisting in obedience to God's law and the performance of duties towards other men ; (iv) cursing or swearing ; (v) lying (iv and v may be combined as the sin of false swearing) ; (vi) killing ; (vii) theft ; (viii) adultery ; (ix) house-breaking (DV ' have overflowed ') ; (x) frequent murder.

3. The people will be punished by drought and famine. In 3d read ' all the fish will perish.' The land and the animals are frequently associated with men in punishment ; cf. Is 16:8 ; 24:3–6 ; Am 8:8, etc. **4.** Vg may be interpreted in two ways : The moral depravation is so deeply rooted that the people is like one who stands out against the priest, the representative of God ; reproof is of no avail, correction hopeless ; or let no one contend with God over the severity of the punishment ; they fully deserve it because their sin is comparable in its gravity to that of resisting the authority of the priest. But the context represents the priest as the source of all the moral corruption not as the lawful representative of God. Hence it is perhaps preferable to emend 4b slightly and translate Heb. thus : ' Let no one find fault (or : surely, none finds fault) with the people ; let no one reprove them : it is with thee, O priest, that I have a quarrel ; or My people are like their priestlings '. The priest is to blame more than the people because he has neglected his duties. **5** is obscure. Heb. reads : Thou (O priest) shalt stumble by day, and the prophet too shall stumble with thee by night, and I will destroy thy mother. Priestlings and false prophets will be punished alike. The ' mother ' is either the nation (Knab.) or the whole priestly clan (Harper). **6.** The people have perished morally on account of the sins committed owing to their ignorance of God's law. It was the priests' duty to learn and to teach the law of God, the torah (3 Kg 12:31 ; 13:33 ; Agg 2:12 ; Mal 2:7), the basis of which was the belief in, and the worship of, Yahweh, the God of the Alliance and the Only God. The priests have wickedly neglected this instruction, and since they have shown such unconcern for God's honour, they will be rejected from the priesthood. The subject in ' thou hast forgotten' refers to the priest against whom the rebuke is directed, not to ' mother ' of 5 (Vg). The children are the individual priests. The northern priesthood was certainly illegitimate (3Kg 12:31) and its rejection by God implies a more severe punishment. **7.** Their sins increased in proportion to their number, but God will cover with shame the glory with which they have bedecked themselves. This is the general sense of Vg though somewhat vague. Many scholars adopt the Syriac reading ' they exchanged ' for ' I will change ' and interpret : They have exchanged their glory, i.e. Yahweh and his worship, for an ignominious idol-cult. This reading recommends itself both for its excellent sense and for its parallelism to the first half of the verse. Others, on the strength of Jewish tradition, moreover substitute ' my glory ' for ' their glory'. The sense remains substantially the same. **8.** The priests encouraged idolatry. As a portion of the sin-offering went to them (Lev 6:25 f.) they would have been deprived of a substantial source of income if the people offered their sacrifices in the temple of Jerusalem. Idolatry was therefore a lucrative business for the priests who fed greedily on the sins of the people. For ' souls ' read ' greed '. **9.** The priests will therefore be punished with the people. **10.** The priests' desires will be unsatisfied ; disappointment will be their reward. This is the general sense though the meaning of Heb. yiprōṣû ' they break through, they spread out, they increase ' (DV ' they have not ceased ') is not clear.

11-14. Debauchery and drunkenness played havoc among the religious institutions of the Israelites. The people, led astray by a spirit of apostasy from God, turn to wooden images for advice and consult their divination rods. They worship their gods on hilltops with all the immoral ritual of the Canaanites. But the young, inexperienced women will be punished with less severity, all responsibility resting with their elders, whose example they follow, and with the priests, who encourage the licentious cult of the Canaanites. A people having no knowledge of God's law will perish (14c).
15-19 A Warning to Judah—15. The prophet warns those of Judah not to follow the example of Israel.

f They are to have no connexion with Galgal and Bethaven, important places of idolatrous worship, cf. 9:15; 10:5; 12:11. Bethaven ('house of iniquity') is an ironic designation of Bethel ('the house of God') which was raised to a centre of calf-worship by Jeroboam (3Kg 12:29; cf. the Hebrew of Am 5:5 'Bethel shall become [Beth]aven'). Swearing by Yahweh was not sinful (Jer 4:2); the prohibition is obviously restricted to swearing by Yahweh considered as a calf-god. **16.** The obstinate Israelites have become like an unmanageable heifer; is it now possible that Yahweh will lead them like a lamb to spacious pasture-lands? For the interrogative sense see GK § 150a. **17.** The prophet goes on addressing Judah. Ephraim, a designation of the Northern Kingdom very common in Osee, is associated with idols; let him meet his fate alone. **18** is corrupt. By introducing a slight textual change in 18a and adopting the LXX reading in 18c we translate: *Those of Ephraim are a band of drunkards*; they give themselves up to harlotry; *they prefer their shame to her pride, i.e.* Yahweh-worship. **19.** Calamity will fall upon them like a storm-wind which will carry them away from their country and there they will have to acknowledge the uselessness of their idolatrous worship.

g **V 1-14 The Doom of Israel is Inevitable**—The moral corruption and the faithlessness of the people encouraged by the priests and the rulers have reached such a stage that a sincere return to Yahweh appears to be impossible and therefore no human power can avert the impending punishment.

1. The prophet arraigns the priests, the people, and the royal family. A sentence has been passed upon them because they have become like a snare on *Mt Maspha* and a net spread upon Mt Thabor and a *deep pit dug in Shittim* (**2**). God will *punish* them all. The metaphors 'snare, net, pit' denote the artful and insidious devices by which both priests and rulers entrapped the unwary Israelites in the meshes of idolatry. **3 f.** But though they have been thus ensnared, their internal dispositions are not hidden from God. They are hardened sinners; the spirit of apostasy has so overwhelmed them that they are unable to appreciate the holiness and justice of Yahweh and to return sincerely to him. **5.** Their arrogance is evident on their faces; their confidence in their gods and their stubborn resistance to the warnings of the prophets will in the long run bring about their destruc- **h** tion and that of Judah. **6 f.** They may try to avert the disaster by sacrifices, but these will do them no good as they are not accompanied by internal dispositions of repentance and obedience (1 Kg 15:22). Yahweh has left them because they have treacherously broken the pact with him, as a woman breaking the marriage bond. The children begotten during this period of conjugal or religious infidelity are naturally *illegitimate* and in a short time they and their possessions will be utterly destroyed. **8.** The suddenness of the destruction is vividly represented by a series of imperatives 'Blow the cornet', etc. As all the places mentioned here are situated near the border line of the kingdoms of Judah and Israel, the enemy is represented as having already occupied almost all the Northern Kingdom and is approaching its southernmost border, unless we are to believe that the attack on Israel will come from the south, *i.e.* from Judah (Knab. 92). The last sentence of 8 means that the enemy is already at the frontiers of Benjamin, which probably stands for Judah. **9.** Devastation will be the fate of Ephraim, as it is surely predicted.

i **10-14** present another aspect of the dismal picture of the degeneration of Israel and Judah. The princes of Judah have become like those who displace landmarks. The moving of the boundary stones of landed property was expressly forbidden (Deut 19:14; Prov 22:28). Here, however, it denotes any encroachment upon the rights of God or man. **11.** Even those of Ephraim, since they chose to go after the abominable gods of other nations, are guilty of deeds of violence and iniquitous judgements. **12.** Internal disintegration **517i** will be their first punishment. In Osee's time national deterioration had already set in. **13.** When Judah and Ephraim realized the seriousness of their internal political situation, Ephraim looked to Assyria for help, and Judah, which very probably must be supplied as the subject of the verb 'sent', turned for assistance to an anonymous king whom Vg and DV have dubbed 'the avenging king'. It is impossible to identify this avenger. The Heb. *Yareb*, seemingly a proper name, is either a nickname meaning 'contender, bellicose' or a corruption of *rab* 'great'. 'The Great King' was a title of the kings of Assyria (cf. Is 36:4). **14.** But all human efforts are unavailing. Ephraim and Judah are like a prey in a lion's claws; who dares to rescue it?

15-VI 11a Israel's Present Wickedness and Future 518a Repentance—The contrast between Israel returning to God (**6:1**) and Israel hardened in sin (**6:7 ff.**) has led some interpreters (Harper, Brown) to believe that Israel's conversion was not sincere. But there is nothing in the text suggesting such insincerity. The sense is: Israel will repent. Will God forgive them? Their past conversions were shortlived and their present conditions are such as to provoke God's anger rather than his mercy. God will forgive when Israel has adequately atoned for its sins.

V 15-VI 3 Israel's Repentance—Yahweh is repre- **b** sented as returning to his heavenly abode and abandoning the people to their fate until they *atone* for their offences. The prophet has the captivity in view. **VI 1-3.** There deprived of all human help they will acknowledge their fault and turn earnestly to God, recognizing him as the author of their calamity and the source of their life and welfare. They feel confident that God will deliver them in a very short time. For the use of the numerals in the expression 'after two days: on the third day' see Lk 13:32. The passage has been interpreted by many of the Fathers as a prediction of Christ's resurrection (Knab., 102 f.). This interpretation cannot be accepted except as an accommodation of the literal sense which foretells the national and religious revival of Israel after the exile (Tobac, 228-30). In the liturgy of Holy Week the passage 6, 1-3 is read at the beginning of the Mass of the Presanctified by an accommodation to the imminent resurrection of Christ. The conversion of Israel is also represented as an earnest effort to obtain a better knowledge of God. They feel confident also that God's aid will be as certain as the morning light, and his aid will be as beneficial as the autumn rain and the spring rain which are so necessary to agriculture, and were amongst the blessings promised by God to the faithful Israelites, Jer 5:24; Jo 2:23.

4-6 God's Refusal of Pardon—But God still hesitates **c** before granting his pardon. In order to understand this attitude of God, one must place the two events—repentance and refusal of pardon—in their proper chronological sequence. **1-3** represent the future sincere dispositions of the people, while **4-10** represent their present insincere dispositions. Therefore 1-3 and 4-10 represent two separate periods in the religious history of Israel, the one referring to the contemporary age of idolatry, the other to the exilic age and to the Messianic age of restoration.

4. The people are unworthy of forgiveness because **d** their *piety*, *i.e.* their love for God and for their fellows, is transitory as a morning cloud and as the morning dew which disappear quickly. This refers to the present and past not to the conditions predicted in 1-3. **5.** On account of their inconstancy God punished them by means of the prophets who, like stone-cutters, dealt heavy blows on the people by delivering God's sentence against them. The commination of the death penalty was made in order that the justice of God's judgement (read 'my' for 'thy') might become manifest when punishment came.

6. Their lack of a genuine piety is emphasized by **e** God's rejection of their acts of worship. Sacrifices are not acceptable unless they are accompanied by a true

518e knowledge of God and a sincere love for him; *cf.* Is 1:11–15; 66:3; Mic 6:6 ff.; Mt 9:13; 12:7.

f 7-11a Israel's Obstinacy—7. The people are hardened in sin. Like Adam in Eden they broke the covenant in the land where they had received so many benefits. The adverb ' there ' seems to require a place-name in the first half-verse, hence some interpreters read instead of Adam a place-name such as Adom (Jos 3:16), Edom, Adamah, etc. The LXX take '*āḏām* for a common noun and translate ' as men (usually do) '. Hoonacker goes further giving the expression ' as men ' the meaning of ' shamefully ' (*bassement*), a meaning which recurs in Job 31:33 (*cf.* P. Dhorme, *Le Livre de Job, ad loc.*). **8.** Galaad, probably Ramoth-Galaad E. of the Jordan, is a city of *mischief*-workers, *marked* with bloody *footprints*. **9** is corrupt. The sense seems to be : The priests are a band of robbers lying in wait for the pious Israelites passing through Sichem on their way to Jerusalem to worship Yahweh on the prescribed festivals (*cf.* St Jerome *ad loc.*). **10.** The general situation is one of the utmost moral corruption. Instead of ' the house of Israel ' modern commentators read ' Bethel ' (*cf.* 10:15 ; Am 5:6). The leading sanctuary of Bethel was a centre of apostasy and immoral cult. **11.** The sense and connexion with the context are obscure. If 11*b* is shifted to the beginning of ch 7 the sense of 11*a* will be : O Judah, set a harvest (*i.e.* a punishment, *cf.* Jer 51:33) for thee, or : prepare thyself for punishment. But Heb. is : Judah too, a harvest is reserved for thee, or, more plainly : A harvest is reserved for Judah too. This sense links v 11 with v 4 providing an answer to the question there put. What will God do to Ephraim and Judah ? Ephraim's sins demand a punishment ; Judah too will be punished for having committed the same sins.

g 11b–VII 2 Hopelessness of Repentance—11b. God's efforts to bring the people back to him, **7:1,** and to heal the disease of Israel served only to lay bare the wickedness of the people who persisted obstinately in their evil course practising falsehood, house-breaking, and highway robbery. **2.** They did not even consider that God took their sins into account, and yet all their misdeeds stood around them and were committed in his presence.

h VII 3-7 Conspiracies—3 f. The prophet passes from the consideration of social disorders to political disorders. The people, or their political leaders, deal treacherously with their king. While they rejoice the king by an outward show of devotion, they are inwardly *raging* like a burning oven and plotting against his life. When their plans are mature, the conspirators wait for an opportunity to carry them out, just as a baker ceases to kindle and *to stir the fire* from the kneading of the dough until its leavening. **5.** On a certain day, perhaps the king's birthday, the princes, *i.e.* the ringleaders, while banqueting with the king, went mad with wine and joined hands with *assassins*. **6 f.** Their hearts were really *burning* (LXX), as an oven, with intrigue. At one time their violent passion seemed to have *abated*, but all of a sudden it burst out like a blazing furnace devouring their rulers. **3-7** are an allusion to the eventful times which followed the death of Jeroboam II. Four kings had fallen victims of conspiracies, and yet none of them had turned to Yahweh for assistance. For the history of the last kings of the Northern Kingdom *cf.* 4 Kg 15:8–31 ; 17:1–6.

i 8-16 The Foreign Policy of Israel and its Result—8. Israel in her utter helplessness wanders farther from Yahweh seeking for aid from foreign nations. But instead of being relieved, she becomes plunged deeper into difficulties. Ephraim has become entirely imbued with a pagan spirit and now she is like a cake which is not turned while it is being baked and is therefore half-scorched and half-raw, consequently unfit for any use. **9.** The moral strength and the temporal prosperity of Israel have been absorbed by those very nations with which it came into contact, and now it is powerless like an old man whose hair begins to turn grey. Yet they do not understand that their own perversity has reduced them to this wretched state.

10. Their arrogance is manifest on their faces, and **51** they refuse to return to Yahweh. **11.** Their foreign policy is one of indecision. Like a dove heedless of danger they turn now to Egypt and now to Assyria. **12.** But no human help will avail them. As they wander away, God spreads his net over them and brings them down like birds and punishes them as the prophets have previously announced, or, according to others, as their wickedness deserves.

13. Destruction now awaits the ungrateful people. **j** Though God has delivered them many times, they speak evil of him by misrepresenting him and making him like to the Baals. **14.** They never sincerely cried to Yahweh, but howled on their couches while eating the sacrificial meals, and *made incisions on their bodies* (*cf.* 3 Kg 18:28) while crying deliriously for material blessings. **15.** Yahweh gave them strength to win their victories (omit DV ' chastised ') and yet they shamefully associated him with the conquered Baals. **16.** The inanity of their confidence in other gods and foreign nations is further emphasized. They turn *to them, i.e. gods, who can afford no help,* and are like a bow which shoots the arrow in a swerving direction thus missing its mark. Theirs will be a disastrous end. Their political leaders, and chiefly the pro-Egyptian party, will perish by the sword of Assyria, and Egypt will delight in their downfall.

VIII 1-14 Israel's Sins and the Coming Doom—This **5¼** chapter is a general indictment of Israel. The main charges are : violation of the covenant, unlawful dynasty, calf-worship, foreign policy, idolatrous worship. **1.** The prophet is commanded to sound the alarm because the enemy, obviously the Assyrians, swift as an eagle, is about to fall upon the land of Israel, Yahweh's abode. First charge, **2 f.** As they have spurned Yahweh's law and service, Yahweh will not listen when they cry to him, but will leave them to the mercy of their enemies. Second charge, **4a.** Their kings were not of the Davidic and only rightful dynasty. This is said of all their kings, not of the last kings only who were usurpers. Third charge, **4b-6.** The calf-worship was introduced by Jeroboam I (3 Kg 12) and remained the official cult till the downfall of the kingdom. God wrathfully rejects the calf of Samaria which is a god of their own manufacture, and therefore no god at all. It will be *shattered to pieces* (**6**). Fourth charge, **7-10.** Israel's foreign relations lead **b** them to their own destruction. Their policy is as senseless as the sowing of wind, but the result will be as disastrous as the reaping of a whirlwind (*cf.* Gal 6:8). The perspective is that of the Assyrian captivity. They are like a crop having no ears and therefore yielding no meal. Their material prosperity is being swallowed up by their foreign allies (*cf.* 7:9) and they have become useless as a worthless thing that is thrown away. V 9 emphasizes the folly of Israel's foreign policy by contrasting them with a wild ass. The wild ass is fond of his unrestrained, natural freedom, shunning the habitations of men and the company of other animals (*cf.* Job 39:5–8), but the Israelites, though separated by God from all other nations, were losing their national independence by seeking the help of Assyria to whom they also gave *love-gifts*. But though they go bargaining for unprofitable alliances, they will not escape punishment. God will gather them as wood for the fire (*cf.* Ez 22:20 f. ; etc.), and they will cease for a while from *anointing* (LXX) kings and princes. **11-14.** **c** Fifth charge : Idolatrous worship. The temple at Jerusalem was the only lawful place of sacrifice (Deut 12:5–7). Jeroboam I chose the cities of Bethel and Dan (3 Kg 12:28 f.), but altars were set up in many other places. The Levitical prescriptions for the sacrificial worship were accounted as those of a stranger and therefore not binding. **12** is a clear allusion to the existence, in Osee's time, of a written code of laws which is commonly identified with the Levitical legislation contained in the Pentateuch. These sacrifices were not acceptable to God who threatened his idolatrous worshippers with captivity in Egypt. As there is no evidence in the historical books of a captivity in Egypt following the downfall of the Northern Kingdom, interpreters believe that the punishment, *i.e.* the Assyrian captivity, is announced in figurative terms recalling the early servitude of the children of Israel in Egypt (Knab., Hoonacker), or that many Israelites will flee to Egypt, when the Assyrians fall upon their land, and will live there in exile (Robinson, 35). It may be that the prediction of a double captivity in Egypt and in Assyria (*cf.* 9:3, 6 ; 11:5) corresponds to the two opposite parties, the Egyptian and the Assyrian. Whichever party prevails, the people will be punished with captivity. Israel has forgotten God and built *palaces*. Judah too, over-confident in human strength, has increased the defences of his country. But God will destroy both palaces and defences (*cf.* Am 2:4 f.).

IX:1-9 Prediction of the Exile—The prophet predicts the exile in clear and unequivocal language. **1.** While the people celebrate their harvest festivals and express their gratitude to the gods from whom, they believe, all their material blessings come, the prophet severely condemns these heathenish rejoicings and announces their coming end. **2.** The land will no longer yield its produce. **3 f.** The people will have to quit their homeland, and will be taken captive to Egypt (8:13) and Assyria, an unholy land. There, far from Yahweh's land, they will be unable to offer him sacrifices. Their bread will be like bread eaten in a house of mourning and therefore unclean (Num 19:14). It will be a bread which, not being presented in the house of the Lord as firstfruits, will be deprived of its spiritual character and will serve only to satisfy their *hunger*. **5.** Their festivals will no longer be celebrated. **6.** They will flee to Egypt (8:13 ; 9:3) and die in Memphis, while their dwellings and all their treasures in the land of Israel will be left to nettles and thorns.

7. When the days of punishment come, the people will learn by experience whether the prophet was mad or not. It was the enormity of their sins and their *hardened stubbornness* (7) that made his warnings excited like the utterances of a madman. Some interpreters believe that the prophet is alluding to the false prophets, who have always promised peace and prosperity, but will be convicted of folly and insanity when punishment comes (Knabenbauer). **8.** Though he was the watchman of Ephraim, living in close intimacy with God, he encountered everywhere stiff opposition. **9.** Their sins have matched the heinous crime of Gabaa (Jg 19), but will not be left unpunished (*cf.* 8:13).

10-17 Israel's Early Corruption—Israel has been ungrateful to God ever since the early days ; conversion has become hopeless.

10. God found Israel in the wilderness with that joyful satisfaction with which one finds a bunch of grapes or a first ripe fig when they are not expected. Though he loved them dearly, they were faithless. The episode of Beelphegor (Num 25:1-3) was the beginning of a long series of backslidings. Man is like the things he loves, and so Israel became detestable like its gods. **11.** The unrepentant Ephraim will now lose his glory with the swiftness of a fleeing bird. The glory of Ephraim is that signified by his name which is similar in sound to *pārāh* ' to increase ' hence ' fruitfulness ' (*cf.* Gen 48:19). In other words no more will there be birth, pregnancy or conception in Ephraim. **12.** And the children whom they may now be bringing up will be taken away. **13.** Ephraim was indeed destined to become a country great and prosperous as the city of Tyre, but in point of fact he will bring out his children to slaughter. Tyre is hardly an appropriate term of comparison, hence the text is variously emended and translated. Hoonacker translates : ' As a hind has its little ones destined for prey, so must Ephraim lead out his children to slaughter '. The sense is in perfect harmony with the context. **14 f.** Unable to repress his indignation at the people's depravity and his horror at the coming destruction the prophet utters a dire imprecation for the total extinction of the people (*cf.* 11). They practised Baal-worship in Galgal and

in other places (4:15 ; 12:11) ; there God felt an irrepressible aversion to them. **519f**

16 f. sum up God's dreadful message. Ephraim is like **g** a tree which will bear no fruit because it is smitten by wind, heat, and worms, and its roots are dried up. They will be cast away by God and dispersed among the nations.

X 1-8 Israel's Prosperity, Idolatry, and Ruin—The **h** theme of this discourse is that treated before : God's tender love for his people, the people's unresponsive attitude, and the impending disaster.

1. Israel has been prosperous like a luxuriant and **i** fruitful vine ; but the more prosperous she became, the more altars she built. **2.** Men's hearts are divided between Yahweh and Baal, or, according to others, are ' false, deceitful ' ; they must be punished. **3** is a confession which the people will make (' now they shall say ') when punishment overtakes them. Then they will acknowledge that it was the helplessness of their kings and their lack of fear of Yahweh that have brought about the national crisis. **4.** The court diplomacy consists in words without truth, false oaths, and alliances with foreign nations ; but punishment will spring forth like poisonous weeds in the furrows of a field.

5 f. Their powerless gods will be carried to a foreign **j** land. The inhabitants of Samaria will be seized by terror on account of the *calf* of Bethaven (*cf.* 4:15), they will mourn over it, and its priestlings will *howl* because both their god and its precious ornaments will be carried to Assyria and given as a present to the Great King (*cf.* 5:13).

7 f. Samaria is inexorably doomed ; the king, like a **k** chip on the waters continually tossed by the waves, is unable to stand the onslaught of the conflicting political parties. Ruin cannot be averted. All the high-places will be destroyed and overgrown with thorns. And the people terrified at the approach of the Assyrian army will prefer to be buried under the crumbling mountains than to fall into the hands of their enemies.

9-XI 1a Repentance and Forgiveness still Possible— **l** Though Israel has sinned from her early days, there is still time for her to return to Yahweh and secure his favour once more. If she persists in her evil ways, ruin will soon overtake her.

9 f. are very obscure. Gabaa is again mentioned (9:9) **m** on account of the outrage narrated in Jg 19. This is the general sense : There, in Gabaa, the Gabaaites took up a defiant attitude believing that war would not overtake them. But God *will come* (DV ' according to my desire ') to punish the children of iniquity (the words ' the children of iniquity ' being transposed from 9 to 10), *i.e.* the Gabaaites, and on that day he will rally against them the peoples, *i.e.* the tribes of Israel except that of Benjamin, to exact vengeance for the double crime of adultery and murder. In other words, Israel has from the very beginning taken the wrong way believing she would escape God's punishment. But the day will come when God will rally the Assyrian armies against them to take vengeance on their wickedness.

11. Contrasting the past with the future of Israel, the **n** prophet compares Ephraim to a heifer to which was assigned the easy work of threshing. But the heifer became unmanageable and God had to lay a yoke on her fair neck making her draw the plough and the harrow. In other words the unyielding Israel will exchange the favours she has enjoyed for the hardships of captivity. Read ' Israel ' for ' Judah '.

12. The impending ruin can be averted only by a **o** change of life. Israel must sow in righteousness by living up to the standards of justice, reap *according* to piety by love of man and God, and break up the fallow ground by stirring up their insensible hearts, cleansing them of evil habits and preparing them to receive the seed of a new moral life. To such a change of life Israel is encouraged by the promise of the benevolence of God who will come to teach righteousness if they but seek him. There is always time to

519o repent, and God is ever ready to forgive the repentant sinner. As the teaching of righteousness is often represented by the prophets as one of the functions of the Messias (Is 2:3 ; 28:9 ; 30:20, etc.) we may see in **12b** an allusion to Messianic times.

p **13-15.** So long as they directed their activities to evil-doing, disappointment was their reward. They have trusted in their *chariots*, **13b** (LXX), and in the multitude of their warriors, but these will not save them. **14a** must be connected with **13b**. **14b** introduces a new period which is continued in **15**. As Salman destroyed Beth Arbel in war when the mother, *i.e.* the land, was laid waste with the children, *i.e.* the cities, so will it be done to you, O house of Israel. Salman, erroneously identified by Vg with Salman of Jg 8:5, is probably Salamanu, king of Moab, mentioned in the annals of Tiglath-pileser III (745-727). He must have destroyed the town of Arbela E. of the Jordan, near Pella, and massacred its inhabitants. And the king of Israel will pass away as suddenly as comes daybreak after the night, **XI :1a.**

520a **XI 1b-11 God's Tender Love for Israel**—This is a very touching picture of God's loving care for his people. Israel, Yahweh's son, was brought up most tenderly. But he wandered away and Yahweh threatened him with destruction. But how can Yahweh destroy his beloved son ? He will punish him, but then he will take him up again. The post-exilic and the Messianic restorations are blended together.

b **1b** Yahweh loved Israel from his early year, and called him out of Egypt. This is applied in Mt 2:15 to the return of Christ from Egypt. It is remarked, however, that the verb *qārā'* 'to call' must have the same meaning as in 2 where it means 'to appeal to'. Moreover, the preposition *min* may have a local meaning 'from' and a temporal meaning 'since'. For these reasons Hoonacker translates : 'I made appeals to my son since Egypt'. Other appeals were subsequently made, but Israel turned away offering sacrifices to the Baals. This makes excellent sense, but the force of Matthew's application is considerably weakened.

c **1b, 2** may be interpreted thus : God called Israel out of Egypt to follow him. Afterwards, when Israel began to turn away from Yahweh, others, *i e.* the prophets, called them after Yahweh. The two actions of calling out and calling on are two aspects of, or two consecutive stages in, the process of the religious upbringing of Israel. Though the departure from Egypt is nowhere in the OT represented as a type of Christ's return from Egypt, Osee provided the ground for the typical meaning of that event by expressing God's attitude towards the young Israelite nation in a form that is applicable to the return of Christ, the true son of God, from Egypt. Consequently Matthew's words : 'That it might be fulfilled' must be taken in the sense of the fulfilment of a typical prophecy rather than an accommodation of a biblical passage to an historical event. **3.** After having called Israel to be his son Yahweh guided the first experiences of national life, like a father leading his child by the hand, though they failed to recognize Yahweh's protection and care.

d **4.** *I used to draw them with cords of man and with bands of love, and I was to them as one who lifts up the yoke from upon their jaws and I bent to him and gave him to eat.* The figure is that of a team of bullocks drawn by cords, that are suitable for a man rather than for an animal, and relieved of the yoke in order that they may eat. But the expression 'he lifts the yoke from upon their jaws' is a difficulty. By reading '*ûl* 'a little child, a suckling' for '*ōl* 'yoke' a better sense and a more gracious picture is obtained. Yahweh used to draw his little child close to him by humane and gentle cords (the image being that of a mother carrying her child against her hip bound with cords to prevent it from falling), and he was to him as one who lifts a babe to his cheek, bends to it, and gives *it* to eat. **5.** Unmindful of all this affection Ephraim fell away from Yahweh and is now threatened with exile. Instead of 'not' read 'to him' and transpose to the

end of v 4. **6.** The sword *will whirl* in their cities destroying the *bars* of their gates (perhaps better 'their children') and devouring (their inhabitants) on account of their *counsels*, *i.e.* their religious conduct and foreign policy. **7.** Those who survive will long for deliverance, but they will have to bear the yoke of captivity. This is the sense of MT, Vg and DV, but modern scholars regard the verse as corrupt. Hoonacker emends and translates thus : 'My people will be hanged near their habitations, and in the sight of those who go up to their cities : none shall remove them'. This sense completes the picture of wholesale destruction described in 6. **8.** Yahweh is horrified at the thought of having to reduce his people to such pitiful conditions, and a struggle breaks out between his justice and his mercy. He is reluctant to *deliver up* the child whom he has fondled in his arms and destroy him as Adama and Seboim, two cities mentioned in connexion with Sodom and Gomorrha (Gen 14:2, 8 ; Deut 29:23). **9.** God's love prevails. He will not exterminate his people because he is a merciful God not a revengeful man ; he is holy and therefore he will keep the promises made to the Patriarchs ; he will not *exterminate*. **10 f.** These protestations of mercy, though expressly addressed to Israel or Ephraim, are really made to Judah as well. The people as a whole was never destroyed. They were led into captivity ; the northern tribes were absorbed by other nations, but the people of Judah were brought back to their homeland to start on a new life preparatory to the Messianic restoration. When the people have atoned for their sins in the exile, they will turn to Yahweh who, like a roaring lion, will summon his scattered people and they will come back hurriedly from the western coastlands (DV 'the children of the sea '), and from every land where they may be detained.

12-XII 2 Israel's Faithlessness and Punishment— **f** Here too we have the same elements as in other speeches : idolatry, obstinacy, foreign alliances and impending punishment. A new feature is a digression on the patriarchal history.

12a. Yahweh is represented as surrounded by false- **g** hood and treachery. **12b** is obscure. The sense of DV is : Judah remained faithful to God with the saintly men, *i.e.* the patriarchs, prophets, etc., and thus turned out a witness against Israel. This sense however is doubtful, as Osee's estimate of Judah is mostly unfavourable, *cf.* 5:10, 12:14 ; 6:4, 11 ; 8:14. By reading *qᵉdēšîm* instead of *qᵉdōšîm* we obtain this sense : Judah is still inconstant with God, but faithful with the temple-prostitutes. Interpreters emend and translate the text in different ways.

XII : 1. The unprofitable policy of Ephraim who, by **h** means of endless falsehood and fraud, tries to gain the favour of Assyria and Egypt, to whom he makes presents of oil, is compared to the vain efforts of a senseless shepherd tending the wind and pursuing the burning sirocco.

2. Yahweh has a quarrel with Judah (read prob. 'Israel') ; he will punish Jacob, *i.e.* his descendants the Israelites according to their deeds.

XII 3-14 Jacob and his Descendants—In this passage **i** we have a contrast between the patriarch Jacob and his posterity. Jacob was always faithful to God who protected him and delivered him from his enemies. His descendants in Egypt were also delivered because they were faithful to Moses, God's prophet. But the Israelites of Osee's time were unfaithful to their God, and were delivered up by God into the hands of their enemies because of their unfaithfulness.

3, 4a. Jacob's divine election and the assurance of **j** divine help are illustrated by two well-known episodes (Gen 25:22-25 ; 32:24-28). **4b.** In Bethel Jacob received the promise of a numerous posterity (Gen 35: 1-15). **5.** A doxology recalling God's own attestation in Ex 3:15. Mark the contrast. Bethel once consecrated by a divine apparition has now become a centre of idolatrous worship. **6** probably refers to a promise to Jacob on his way to Haran (Gen 28:10-22).

g *By the help of thy God thou wilt return* (to thy land); be kind therefore and just with men and faithful to God. **7 f.** But Jacob's descendants, like *a merchant* using unfair means, took to all sorts of fraudulent dealings; they have made a *fortune*; but all their gains are insufficient for the expiation of their iniquity. **k 9.** The God of Ephraim, however, is Yahweh, the God of the covenant, ever the same, true to his promises and just in punishing sin. **9b** is taken for a promise by Knab. following St Jerome. The people will peacefully dwell in tents as in the days of the Feast of Booths. The context however demands a threat. The people will have to wander away from their country and live in tents. **10.** As they have persistently refused to listen to God's warnings, God *will destroy them* by means of his prophets, *i.e.* God will threaten them with destruction through the ministry of his prophets, *cf.* 6:5. **11** is obscure. The sense seems to be: Will their false gods deliver them? No, because Galaad is a *nest of iniquity* (6:8) and in Galgal the people practise a vain cult, offering sacrifices to powerless bull-gods. Their altars will be turned to heaps of rubble. **l 12 f.** The prophet turns to Jacob. Though Jacob had to flee to Aram and work hard tending flocks in order to win a wife, God always delivered him from all dangers. After many years Jacob's sons became a numerous people in Egypt and God brought them out under the leadership of Moses, and through the ministry of Moses they were kept safe. **14.** Now this people, Ephraim, has bitterly provoked God's anger by their unyielding attitude and will therefore have to pay the penalty for their offences.

m XIII 1–XIV 1 Utter Destruction the Fate of Israel— This speech develops the usual theme: faithlessness, punishment, and the helplessness of their king.

n 1 marks a contrast between Ephraim's glorious past and his miserable present. In the period of the Judges the numerical strength of the tribe of Ephraim gave it a certain pre-eminence over the other tribes. But they became guilty of Baal-worship and incurred the death penalty. **2.** They have kept sinning up to the prophet's time making silver images. **2b** is obscure in DV and probably corrupt in MT. By supplying the word Elohim 'gods', which can easily have fallen out, MT may be rendered: these [the idols] they call gods; (to them) they sacrifice; men kiss the calves (*i.e.* worship the calf-gods). **3.** Extermination will be their reward. For 'chimney' read '*window*'. **o 4.** Despite their faithlessness God asserts his right over them. He is their God and their only saviour since their coming out of Egypt. **5.** In the desert he took them up and kept them in close relationship with them. For 'I knew them' LXX reads 'I shepherded them', which agrees better with 6. It denotes God's unceasing care for his people in the wilderness. **6.** But when they arrived in Palestine and enjoyed to the full the blessings of a prosperous life, their heart was lifted up and they failed to recognize the source of their prosperity (*cf.* Deut 8:11–15; 31:20; 32:15). **7 f.** The ungrateful people will be consumed as a prey devoured by a wild beast. **9.** DV makes good sense; but MT agrees better with the context: *I destroy thee, O Israel; yea, who will save thee?* **10.** The king is powerless. There is a reference here to 1 Kg 8:4 ff. and implicitly to the separation of the ten tribes from the house of David. **11.** God gave the northern tribes a king to their own perdition, and now is about to take him away in order to deprive them of the help in which they trusted. **p 12.** Ephraim's sin is kept for the day of reckoning, like a treasure tied up and hidden for safe custody until the time to use it arrives. **13.** When that time arrives, the nation will be seized by internal convulsions comparable to the pangs of a woman in travail. But instead of bringing joy to the mother the child, an unwise son, will be an occasion of further sufferings because he will not have the strength to stand in the mouth of the womb (Vg etymologically and literally 'in the breach of the children') at the

proper moment, *i.e.* the child will not have the strength **520p** to come to light. Ephraim is compared both to the mother and to her child. The internal troubles of the nation will be a cause of further affliction. **14.** But Osee cannot bring himself to believe that God will exterminate his people. Looking further into the **q** future he sounds a reassuring note of hope. God will not leave his people in the hands of death for ever; one day he will bring them back to life. He will prevail over death which will be powerless to detain its captives. **14b.** *Where are thy plagues, O death? Where is thy destruction, O Sheol?* The promise of a new life is irrevocable. Read 'repentance' for 'comfort' and *cf.* Ps 109:4. This promise had its first fulfilment in the return from the exile, but reached its complete fulfilment in Messianic times; *cf.* 1 Cor 15:54–57. Many modern commentators interpret the verse in the sense of a threat. 'Shall I redeem them from the hand of Sheol? Shall I deliver them from Death?' A negative answer is implied. Death and Sheol are then commanded to let loose their plagues on earth because repentance is hopeless. **15** takes us back to a time preceding the final catastrophe. Though Ephraim may be *flourishing (as a plant) among reed-plants*, a scorching east wind from the wilderness will sap the source of its vigour and fruitfulness. Vg read *yaprîd* 'he separates', but *yaprîaḥ* 'he flourishes' was probably the original text; '*aḥîm* 'brothers, prob. stands for '*āḥû* 'reed-plants.' Even if Ephraim were as strong and flourishing as a reed-plant in the waters, he would not escape destruction. The wind represents Assyria which will carry off all the treasures of Ephraim. **XIV:1.** Osee winds up his discourse by setting forth God's judgement once more. Samaria will have to atone for her unfaithfulness by a dreadful punishment. MT need not be interpreted in an optative sense.

C. XIV 2–10 Israel's Conversion—This last discourse **521a** forms the conclusion of the book according to the general plan of the prophetic books in which punishment is followed by pardon and destruction by restoration. **2–9 The Triumph of Yahweh's Love—**The repentant **b** people will at last confess their sins and sincerely return to Yahweh. Yahweh's love will triumph over their wickedness, God will receive them with paternal affection and will bestow his blessings upon them. **2.** As Israel's apostasy brought about her downfall, her return to God will raise her up again. **3.** The people will return with words of repentance on their lips: Forgive all iniquity, accept what is good, and we will pay the *fruit* of our lips (Heb. and Vg 'calves'), *i.e.* words of praise and thanksgiving. **4.** They will no longer look for help to Assyria, nor will they rely on Egypt and its cavalry. They will no longer call the idols made by themselves 'our God', because in God and in God alone will they, as orphans, find support. **5.** Their conversion being complete and **c** sincere, God will take them again into his favour. He will heal their *apostasy*, *i.e.* he will stir up again in their hearts their former affection for him and he will love them of his own free will because he is no longer wrathful with them. **6 f.** Forgiveness reinstates them in their friendly relations with God, and they will enjoy again the blessings of God's benevolence. **8.** *Once more* they will dwell under his shadow, *i.e.* the children of Israel will dwell peacefully in their country under the protection of the new Israel compared to a tree (*cf.* v 7); they will flourish *as* the corn and will blossom as a vine and their *fame* will spread far and wide as the fame of the wine of Lebanon. **9.** Ephraim will cast idols away and Yahweh will respond to their cries, and will *look after them*. Yahweh *will be* as an evergreen cypress, their protector and the only source of their prosperity.

10 Conclusion—The practical lesson which anyone of **d** wisdom and discernment must draw from God's dealings with his people is that God's ways are right and lead man safely to life. The righteous walk in them and attain life; but the wicked meet their own death.

JOEL

By P. J. MORRIS

522a Bibliography—J. Knabenbauer, § 409*b* ; A. Van Hoonacker, § 409*b* ; *S. R. Driver, D.D., *Joel and Amos*, CBSC,1915 ; *S. L. Brown, *A New Commentary*, London, 1928 ; V. Ermoni, art. Joel, DBV ; M. Faulhaber, art. Joel, CE.

b The Prophet and his Date—Joel (Yahweh is God) son of Pethuel, from his frequent and exclusive references to Judah and Jerusalem, Sion and the Temple and the priestly ministrations, seems to have prophesied in Judah, probably in Jerusalem itself. No explicit indication is given of the period in which he lived. Older commentators mostly assign him to the 9th or 8th century B.C., probably under Joas (836–797). Modern critics prefer a date following the reforms of Nehemias and Esdras. His position in the Hebrew canon between Osee and Amos favours an early date. On the other hand, the absence of any reference to a king, the complete silence about the Northern Kingdom, the fact that the Babylonians and Assyrians do not appear as the actual enemies of the people, the assumption that the people knows no God but Yahweh and no worship but the Temple worship, harmonize better with a post-exilic date. Jl 3:2 seems to allude to the Exile as to a past event. The numerous allusions or reminiscences of other biblical and especially prophetical books, create a presumption that Joel is the borrower. It cannot be said, however, that any of these arguments is decisive.

c Contents—The prophecy falls into two parts : 1–2:17 ; 2:19–3:21, with 2:18 serving as connecting link. The first part consists of two discourses : 1:1–20, in which Joel describes a terrible locust plague and exhorts priests and people to penance ; and 2:1–17, in which he repeats these thoughts more emphatically : these plagues are but the harbingers of greater scourges in the Day of Yahweh. The people does penance, turns to Yahweh, and he is appeased (18). In the second part, he promises prosperity, deliverance from the plague, the teacher of justice (2:19–27), an outpouring of the Spirit, and salvation (2:28–32, MT 3:1–5). He will judge the nations who have afflicted the Chosen People, in the valley of Josaphat (3:1–21, MT ch 4).

d Interpretation—Commentators, generally, are agreed that Jl 2:28–3 refer to Messianic times and the end of the world. There is less agreement as to the interpretation of chh 1–2, and their relation to the rest of the book. The Fathers and ancient commentators saw in the locust swarms of chh 1–2, a mere figure of future enemy invasions. Some moderns (*e.g.* Van Hoonacker) regard the whole prophecy as apocalyptic, and the locusts of chh 1–2 as a purely ideal vision of the signs preceding the Day of Yahweh. It seems, however, much more probable that ch 1 describes an actual locust visitation. In general, prophecy springs from contemporary conditions. Joel's question in 1:2 f., and his reiterated calls to penance and prayer are more intelligible in the hypothesis of an actual calamity. The depredations described are characteristic of destructive insects and of drought, not of war havoc. The realistic accuracy of his descriptions of the locusts and their ravages is undisputed. The horrors of a locust plague of exceptional severity might well evoke a vision of the calamities preceding or accompanying the Day of Yahweh. The latter concept in the prophetic writings is 'capable of embracing within itself by force of compenetration any particular crisis and Messianic times and the end of the world' (Fr Lattey on Mal 4:23, WV). In Jl 2:28–3, the Day of Yahweh embraces the Messianic era and the consummation, without any distinction of chronological perspective (*cf.* Ac 2:17–21). The cosmic disturbances associated implicitly with the Day of Yahweh in 1:15, and explicitly in 2:11 are associated in Is 13:9–10 with the fall of Babylon, and in Jer 4:23–24 with the misfortunes threatening Judah and Jerusalem. Particular crises are described in much the same terms as the final Judgement, either because they are types of the latter or because both events are combined in the same prophetic view. It would be a mistake to take too literally the images of cosmic ruin. They are part of the vocabulary of apocalyptic symbolism, which is hyperbolical in character.

It seems that the calamities of ch 1 represented for Joel a first rehearsal or anticipation of the Day. This thought dominates his discourse of ch 2, where he gives a fuller description of the signs of its approach and a more urgent call to repentance (2:1–17). The signs are depicted in imagery borrowed from the recent locust visitation, but the viewpoint shifts to the future and the vision takes on a more ideal character. Moreover new elements enter into the vision. In the supplications placed on the lips of the priests (17), and in Yahweh's answer (19), there is mention of Judah's 'reproach among the nations'. Modern critics refer this to the locust plague and translate 17 : ' give not thy inheritance to reproach that the nations should make proverbs of them'. The reproach of Judah is, however, foreign domination, not a passing locust scourge to which the enemy nations themselves might at any time be subject. The Vg version : ' that the heathen should rule over them' is fully justified (see commentary). In 20, Yahweh's promise to expel ' the Northerner' appears to refer to a hostile human power (see commentary). It is true that the locust imagery is retained here, and this has led some commentators (*e.g.* Knabenbauer) to see in the locusts of ch 2 merely a figure of enemy nations. It may be, however, that we have here merely another aspect of compenetration. The locusts and their ravages symbolize indistinctly the disasters whether natural or political which presage the Day of Yahweh. The comparison of the locust swarms with an invading army would readily lead the prophet's thought to the vision of the heathen invaders of Judah as harbingers of the Day, and in v 20, the two ideas are blended. The reference to the enemy nations is also demanded by the unity of the book. It is for relief from the disasters of the locust plague and from foreign domination that the people does penance and turns to Yahweh (18), and in consequence the Day of Yahweh becomes a day of blessing and triumph for Judah, and of definitive judgement for the nations. The future blessings are conceived as the reversal of past calamities. The marvellous fertility of the Messianic age will compensate for the locust ravages (2:19–27) as a symbol and accompaniment of the spiritual blessings to be ushered in by the outpouring of the Spirit (2:28–32) ; and the reproach of Judah is removed by the definitive judgement and destruction of the nations in the valley of Josaphat (ch 3).

Doctrinal Value—Joel has the distinction of supplying the first biblical text of the first apostolic sermon (Ac 2:16–21). The passages from 1:13 f. and 2:17 ff. are still used in the Lenten liturgy. Notable Messianic passages are 2:23 ' the teacher unto justice', and 2:28 ff, on the outpouring of the Spirit. The popular belief that the universal judgement will take place in the valley of Josaphat owes its origin to Jl 3:2, 12.

The Teacher unto Justice, 2:23. In the midst of the material blessings promised to Judah, there is included (v 23), the promise of ' the teacher unto justice' (*hammôreh liṣᵉdāqāh*). Many moderns read : ' the former rain in just measure ', on the grounds that the context treats of the gifts of the earth, and that *môreh* means the autumnal rain. *Môreh*, however, means ' one teaching ' in Is 9:14 ; 30:20, and this is its more usual meaning. *ṣedeq* or *ṣᵉdāqād* regularly signifies a moral or juridical quality. The autumnal rain is the object of a distinct promise in 23*c*, and would be redundant here. The promise of the teacher unto justice fittingly opens the discourse to the children of Sion. It presents a strong parallel with Is 30:20. Most Catholics interpret the promise directly of the Messias, Knabenbauer of the prophets generally, including Christ.

The Outpouring of the Spirit, 2:28–32. St Peter in his Pentecostal sermon (Ac 2:17–21) quotes Jl 2:28–32 as fulfilled in the miraculous gift of tongues. He quotes it according to LXX, substituting ' in the last days ' for ' after this ' of MT. Probably the latter phrase merely marks the transition from the consideration of material to that of spiritual blessings and does not indicate chronological sequence. The abundant outpouring of the Spirit is a feature of Messianic times (*cf.* Is 32:15 ; 44:3 ; 59:21 ; Ez 36:27 ; 39:29 ; Zach 12:10). In the past the Spirit had been manifested chiefly in the form of prophecy bestowed on a restricted group, and dreams and visions were among the principal means of divine communication. In the Messianic age the Spirit will be poured out abundantly on all. The gift of prophecy includes not only the prediction of the future, but also speaking under divine influence for instruction, exhortation and consolation. St Peter's interpretation is not exhaustive. He sees in the gift of tongues an initial and visible fulfilment of the prophecy and the manifest inauguration of the Messianic era. In Acts and Epistles the Holy Spirit is exhibited not only as the principle of prophecy and the charismatic gifts, but also and especially of the life of grace. All these varied manifestations of the Spirit are adumbrated in the words of Joel, and all classes and conditions will share in them : ' the servants also and the handmaids '. In the context the words ' all flesh ' may refer immediately to the Israelites, the people of Yahweh, but of themselves they have a universal significance. St Peter does not as yet indicate this explicitly. It is clear from Ac 2:36 that he understands the formula ' call upon the name of the Lord ', of faith in Christ as the condition of salvation ; but it is left to St Paul to reveal the universal significance of this text in Rom 10:13, where he shows that there is no distinction between Jew and Gentile, and that faith in Christ constitutes the one way of salvation for all men.

The Valley of Josaphat, 3:2, 12. The belief that the universal judgement of mankind will take place in the valley of Josaphat rests on Jl 3:2, 12, the only passages where it is mentioned in the Bible. Some commentators think that the reference is to the place where king Josaphat defeated the peoples of Moab, Ammon, and Edom (2 Par 20:20 ff.). A very ancient tradition identifies the valley of Josaphat with part of the Cedron valley east of Jerusalem. The belief that this will be the scene of the Last Judgement, survives in popular Jewish and Moslem as well as Christian eschatology. Joel, however, says nothing of a universal judgement, but speaks only of a judgement on the heathen enemies of Israel. According to its etymology (*Yᵉhôšāpāṭ*) means ' Yahweh judgeth ', and most com-

mentators nowadays hold that it is merely a symbolic **522i** name for the place where Yahweh will execute judgement on the enemies of his people.

I:2–II:17 A Locust Plague heralds the Day of Yahweh ; 523a a Call to Penance.
2–4 An Unprecedented Visitation—Addressing the people, Joel invites the oldest to testify if they have ever experienced or heard tell of a calamity like this. Its memory deserves to be handed down to succeeding generations. In four successive swarms, locusts have destroyed the crops. **4.** Four words in the Hebrew designate locusts, but their precise meaning is unknown. According to their etymology, the names may indicate various aspects of the locust's destructiveness, *viz.*: the shearer, swarmer, lapper, finisher.
5–12 All Classes mourn—The drunkards are roused **b** from stupor to mourn the loss of the sweet wine. In strength and multitude the locusts resemble an invading nation, *cf.* Prov 30:25 f. For destructiveness, their teeth are like a lion's (*cf.* Apoc 9:8) and their jaw teeth *as of a lioness*. They have ravaged the vine, made the fig tree *a broken thing*, and stripped bare the bark. The community (conceived as ' daughter of Judah ') is to lament with the inconsolable grief of a virgin bereft of her betrothed. The priests mourn, because the daily sacrifices—the meal-offering and drink-offering —have ceased (*cf.* Lev 2:4 ; Ex 2 29:40–41 ; Num 28:3–8). The ground ' mourns ' because its chief products, corn, *new wine, fresh oil* (*cf.* Deut 7:13) are destroyed. The husbandmen and vine-dressers are bidden mourn, because harvest, vintage and fruit-crop have perished. Drought completes the desolation. **6b,** ' a lion's whelp ': RV ' a great lion '; Heb. *lābî*, alongside *'aryēh* as in Gen 49:9 ; Num 24:9, probably signifies *lioness* here. **10.** ' confounded ': RV ' dried up '. Heb. *hôbîš*, occurs here and in 12 of the vine ; in 17 of the corn ; in 11 of the labourers. It is the Hiph'il of *yābaš* (' to be ashamed ') rather than a derivative of *yābēš* (' to be dry '). *Is confounded*, *i.e.* wears the look of one ashamed. The verbs in **11a** are best read as imperatives. **12c** lit. ' Joy is confounded (away) from ', etc.
13–20 A Call to Penance—The prophet summons the **c** priests to a solemn lamentation (*cf.* Jer 4:8). They are to *lie all night* in sackcloth in token of penance (*cf.* 9), to proclaim a solemn fast, convoke a national religious assembly, and cry to Yahweh : Alas for the day ! for the Day of Yahweh is near and it shall come as devastation (*šōd*) from the Almighty (*šaddai*). The locust visitation portends its approach, but by penance, fasting and prayer the punishment may be averted. The sacrificial food, the joyous offerings are cut off from the Temple. Drought completes the ruin. Barns and storehouses are dilapidated for lack of use. The domestic animals groan for want of pastures ; the cattle are bewildered ; the sheep suffer. The prophet cries for help to Yahweh, because the pastures of the wilderness are burnt up. The wild beasts look up longingly to Yahweh, for the water-courses are dried up and the pastures withered. **14.** ' Sanctify ': *qiddēš* is used for ' convoke, decree ', either because of the holiness of the object in view or of the religious rites which inaugurated it. 15–20 probably contain the tenour of the supplications the community are to address to Yahweh. **16a.** ' before *our* eyes . . . *our* God.' In 19, it is the community regarded as a single collectivity which speaks, or the prophet in the name of the nation. **17a** is uncertain. LXX: the heifers leap at their stalls ; RV : the seeds rot under their clods ; Van Hoonacker : the presses are become filthy under their refuse. **18.** *How the beasts groan* ! LXX, omitting one letter : What shall we put in them ? *viz.* the barns, etc., of 17. **20.** ' As a garden bed . . . rain ' is wanting in MT and LXX. The verb *'ārag* which is rendered by DV following Vg ' look up to ', means ' to ascend ', and then ' to desire ' as in Ps 41 (42) 2. St Jerome has expressed this desire by the added comparison : ' as a garden bed ', etc., influenced

523c perhaps by the cognate noun *arûgāh* (' a garden bed ', *cf.* Ex 17:10) and by Aquila. St Jerome remarks ' Aquila signifies this by one word, saying ἐπρασιώθη (become green like flower-beds) '.

d **II:1-11 The Day of Yahweh is near**—Sound the alarm-horn on Sion's hill for the Day of Yahweh is near, a day of darkness and gloom, of clouds and *thick darkness*. The locust legions, strong and numerous, appear with the swiftness of dawn spreading on the mountains. It is an unparalleled invasion. They advance like a prairie fire ; before them the country is like *the garden of Eden* ; behind them, desolation. Nothing escapes them. They look like horses and their course is that of horsemen (or, *steeds*). The sound of their advance is as that of chariots on the mountains, as the crackling of flame in the stubble, like an army in battle array. Panic grips the populations. Irresistibly and in ordered ranks they advance, assault the city, scale the walls, enter the windows of houses. Cosmic disturbances accompany them. They are the army of Yahweh, harbingers of his dread day, and his voice resounds in their onset.

Here as in ch 1, the imagery is based on the habits of locusts. The image of darkness, traditionally associated with the Day of Yahweh, may be suggested (**2**) by a cloud of locusts obscuring the sun and darkening the sky ; the fire and flame (**3**), by the appearance of a country ravaged by locusts ; the locust's head resembles that of a horse (**4** ; *cf.* Apoc 9:7). The comparison with chariots is suggested by the noise of a locust-flight heard from afar ; the crackling sound by the noise of their eating (**5**). Their irresistible, ordered advance has often been described. **6b** ' like a kettle ': *all faces gather in beauty*, i.e. lose colour and freshness (*cf.* Nah 2:10). **7c**, *they march everyone in his ways : and they entangle not their paths.* **8b.** For ' in his path ' Van Hoonacker suggests ' *in his breastplate* '. **8c.** *they burst through the weapons, and break not (their ranks).* **9.** In the East, windows consist merely of an opening with lattice work.

e **12-17 The Judgement may still be averted**—Even now the judgement may be averted. In the name of Yahweh, Joel summons priests and people to penance and prayer to ward off the menace. They must return to Yahweh by a sincere conversion of heart ; their repentance must show itself not only outwardly, but above all inwardly. Yahweh's character is such that he is ready to pardon those who turn to him (*cf.* Ex 34:6 ; Jon 4:2). Perhaps he will turn back from the path of judgement and leave behind him the means of offering and libation. Sound the trumpet as signal for a public fast and assembly. None must be absent from oldest to youngest ; even the newly married must leave their *nuptial tent*. In the court of the Priests, let the priests supplicate Yahweh with tears to spare his people and inheritance, and deliver them from the yoke of foreign domination. **12.** *And even now*, etc. The heart was for the Hebrews the centre of intellectual life. Conversion to God, therefore, implied the submission of man to God with all his powers and faculties. **13.** ' Rend your hearts and not (only) your garments.' Joel does not condemn external signs, but insists on the necessity of interior dispositions, *cf.* Os 6:6 for a similar turn of phrase. ' Ready to repent of the evil ', *viz.*, which he inflicts or threatens. **16.** ' Sanctify the Church ', *i.e.* call a sacred assembly. **17.** ' Between the porch and the altar ', *i.e.* the porch of the sanctuary (3 Kg 6:3), and the altar of holocausts in front of it (3 Kg 8:64) ; in the inner court, therefore, or court of the priests. The priests would address their prayers towards the sanctuary. For ' rule over them ', many moderns read ' make proverbs of them ', *i.e.* an object of mockery. The verb *māšal* could mean this, but with *beṭ* of the object it regularly means ' rule over ', etc. (*cf.* Knabenbauer, p 223). The reproach of Judah is foreign domination (*cf.* Jer 24:9).

f **18-III:21 Yahweh's Answer to his People's Prayer**—The assembly is held and Joel states its happy

results. Appeased by the repentance of the nation, Yahweh promises the blessing of bounteous harvests. Judah will no longer be an object of reproach among the nations. He will remove ' *the Northerner* ' into the wilderness south of Judah, with his forepart towards the Dead Sea and his rear towards the Mediterranean. The locust imagery remains in the picture of putrefying carcasses. The motive for his chastisement is pride (lit. ' great things ').

18-20 The Judgement is averted—**18.** It is assumed, not expressly stated that the assembly is held. **20.** ' The Northerner ' (*haṣṣepônî*) : some suppose this to refer to the locusts as coming on this occasion from the north, instead of as usual from the south or south-east ; but this would not justify the unqualified application to them of the description ' the Northerner '. Moreover our passage has analogies with Jer 1:13-15 ; 4:6 ; 6:1 ; Ez 26:7 ; 38:6 ; 39:2, which announce the enemy, the evil from the north. The Jews saw in Jl 2:17 an allusion to Gog and Magog. Joel, therefore, seems to have in view enemy peoples, a human power. This harmonizes with vv 17, 19*b* and 20*c*, which can only be understood of actions inspired by pride.

21-27 Promise of Material Blessings—Developing the promise of v 19, Joel addresses : (1) the land : its trials are ended, and there is room henceforth only for joy ; (2) the animals : the burnt up pastures are springing forth again ; (3) the children of Sion, who are promised ' the teacher unto justice ' (see § 522*g*), and the autumnal and spring rains (conditions of a fruitful harvest). The threshing floors will overflow with wheat, the presses with *new wine* and *fresh oil*. Yahweh will restore the years devoured by the locusts. Plenty will replace want, and thus they will know that Yahweh is in the midst of his people, protecting them against hostile attack, and will realize the unique character of the God of Israel. The repeated assurance ' my people shall not be confounded for ever ' (**26c** ; **27c**) implies a return to the promise of the deliverance of the people from foreign domination.

28-29 The Outpouring of the Spirit—With the material blessings, symbol of the felicity of the Messianic age, there will be an abundant effusion of spiritual gifts (see § 522*h*).

30-32 The Day of Yahweh—Terrifying prodigies, on earth the ravages of war, eclipses and blood-red moons in the heavens, portend the Day. The true worshippers of Yahweh alone will escape the judgement of condemnation and share in the Messianic blessings ; for in mount Sion and in Jerusalem there will be survivors, as Yahweh has said (*cf.* Abd 17), as also among the Jews of the Dispersion who are called by Yahweh.

III:1-16a The Judgement of the Nations—In the time when Yahweh will restore Israel, he will contend in judgement with the nations gathered in the valley of Josaphat (see § 522*i*), for their crimes against his people. He will requite the Phœnicians and Philistines for enriching their palaces with the plundered treasures of Judah, and for selling the Jews as slaves to the Greeks. Yahweh will redeem the children of Judah, who will in their turn sell their enemies in slavery to the Sabaeans. The nations are challenged to muster for battle in the valley of Josaphat. The surrounding nations are summoned ; but Joel prays Yahweh to send his celestial warriors down for the battle. Yahweh answers the call. He will judge the nations hostile to his people. By their wickedness they are ripe for the harvest of judgement. Multitudes throng in the *valley of decision*, because the Day of Yahweh is near. Cosmic upheavals accompany it ; in thunder and earthquake Yahweh will speak from Sion and Jerusalem.

1-2. The reference here seems to be to the Babylonian Captivity. Israel here as in 2:27, 3:16, is the name of the people of God as such. **3.** ' Cast lots ' : *cf.* Abd 11 ; Nah 3:10. ' Put in the stews ', i.e. sold as salary to a harlot. ' Sold for wine ', i.e. cheaply, for a passing sensual gratification. **4.** ' But what have you to do with me ? ' Lit. ' And also what are you to me ? ' **4b** indicates that the sense is : What can you do against me ? ' The districts of the Philistines ', *i.e.* the division of the territory according to their five chief towns. **5.** ' My silver ', etc., either the Temple treasures or treasures which are Yahweh's because Judah is his inheritance. ' Your temples ' (or ' palaces '). **6.** ' to . . . the Greeks '. Syrian slaves, among whom Jews would be reckoned, were much sought after in Greece, *cf.* 1 Mach 3:41 ; 2 Mach 8:11. **7.** ' for which ' you have sold them. **8.** The Sabaeans : a people of SW. Arabia with whom the Jews had trade relations (*cf.* 3 Kg 10:2, 10 ; Jer 6:20). **10.** A reversal of Mich 4:3 ; Is 2:4. **11.** From round about, *i.e.* Philistines, Phœnicians, Edomites. ' There will the Lord cause ', etc. ; read ' *Make thy warriors go down, O Lord* '. ' The strong ones ', *i.e.* the warriors of Yahweh : the angels. **13.** Yahweh speaks to his strong ones (*cf.* Mt 13:24 ; Apoc 14:15).

16*b***-21 The Glorification of the People of God**—It is implied that the nations are destroyed, but Yahweh will be a refuge and a stronghold to the children of Israel. Thereby Israel will experience that Yahweh is its God, dwelling in its midst on Sion. Jerusalem will be unprofaned by the presence of the heathen or foreign conqueror. The land will be blessed with marvellous fertility. The arid water-courses of Judah will flow ; a fountain issuing from the Temple will water the Valley of the Acacias. The enemy countries, of which Egypt and Edom are types, will become barren wastes, because they have shed the blood of inoffensive refugees in their land ; and Judah will be inhabited for ever. Yahweh will avenge their blood and will not grant impunity : and he will dwell in Sion.

18. ' The mountains shall drop down sweetness ', etc., *cf.* Amos 9:13. The fountain issuing from the Temple is a symbol of divine blessing, *cf.* Ez 47:1 ; Zach 13:1 ; Apoc 22:1. ' The torrent of thorns ' : Heb. *naḥal haššiṭṭîm*, Wady of the Acacias. *Naḥal* means a rocky water-course dry except in the rainy season. Some identify the place with Abel Shittim, the camping site of Israel opposite Jericho (Num 33:49) ; others with the Cedron valley. Acacias grow in dry soil, and the meaning seems to be that even the deserts will become fertile, a further symbol of felicity. **21.** MT : ' I will cleanse their blood (which) I have not cleansed ', *i.e.* Yahweh will no longer permit the oppression of his people which he so often suffered in the past. Van Hoonacker reading *wᵉniqqamtî* for *wᵉniqqêtî* in 21*a* : ' I will avenge their blood and I will not grant impunity '. This is much the same as LXX. By his punishment of the Egyptians and Edomites God shows that he avenges the crimes, which he appeared for long to have passed over. The book ends with the promise already repeated more than once, that Yahweh will dwell in Sion.

AMOS

By M. LEAHY

524a Bibliography—J. Knabenbauer, S.J., *Commentarius in Prophetas Minores I* (CSS), Parisiis 1886 ; *W. R. Harper *Amos and Hosea* (ICC) 1905 ; A. Van Hoonacker, *Les Douze Petits Prophètes*, Paris 1908 ; J. Touzard, *Le Livre d'Amos*, Paris 1909 ; *E. A. Edghill, *The Book of Amos* (Westminster Commentaries), London 1914 ; *W. Nowack, *Die Kleinen Propheten* (HAT), Göttingen 1922³ ; *T. H. Robinson, *The Book of Amos, Hebrew text*, London 1923 ; *E. Sellin, *Das Zwölfprophetenbuch, Hosea-Micha* (KAT), Leipzig 1929 ; *R. S. Cripps, *The Book of Amos*, London 1929 ; *S. R. Driver, *Joel and Amos* (CBSC), Cambridge 1942².

b Historical Background—Jeroboam II (the first king of that name is always called the son of Nabat) reigned over Israel when Amos delivered his prophecies in the Northern Kingdom, 1:1 ; 7:10. He was the fourth ruler of the dynasty founded by Jehu. Israel under Jehu and his successor Joachaz suffered much at the hands of the Syrians. During Jehu's reign Hazael of Damascus overran and took possession of the transjordanic part of Israel, *viz.* Bashan and Galaad, 4 Kg 10:32 f. ; during the reign of Joachaz Hazael reduced Israel still more by decimating its armies and by wresting from it various cities, 4 Kg 13:7, 25. Hazael's son and successor Benhadad III continued the aggressive policy of his father, and during the first years of the reign of Joas who succeeded Joachaz Israel had still to suffer. A change came, however, when the Assyrians under their energetic king Adadnirari III (805–782) resumed their policy of expansion towards the west. The Assyrian expeditions with the resulting devastations weakened Syria. Assyria then withdrew and with the exception of some minor incursions into Syria was fully occupied with wars against the kingdom of Urartu on its northern borders.

Taking advantage of Syria's weakness and Assyria's inactivity as far as Israel was concerned, Joas was able to recover the cities which Joachaz had lost, 4 Kg 13 :25, and his successor Jeroboam II succeeded in restoring the border of Israel from the approach to Hamath, a Syrian town on the Orontes to the Sea of the Arabah, the Dead Sea, 4 Kg 14:25. The limits of the old Davidic kingdom, except for Judah and Edom, were thus regained, and Israel, besides receiving tribute from subject states, was free to devote its energies to reconstruction, to international commerce and to private enterprise.

c Date of the Prophetic Activity—The superscription (*cf.* 1:1) informs us that Amos delivered his oracles sometime in the period when Jeroboam of Israel was contemporaneous with Ozias of Judah. Jeroboam II was co-regent of Joas of Israel from 793 to 782, and he reigned alone thereafter until 753, while Ozias of Judah was co-regent of Amasias of Judah from 791 to 767, was sole ruler thereafter until 750, and had Joatham as his own co-regent until 740 (so Thiele in the *Journal of Near Eastern Studies*, July 1944). The earliest date, therefore, of Amos' prophetic activity would be 791, and the latest 753. The further statement that Amos came on the scene ' two years before the earthquake ' (1:1b) would have dated his preaching for his early readers but is of little help to us in defining the date more precisely since earthquakes were not infrequent on the coast of the Mediterranean. The internal evidence of the book, however, points to the latter part of Jeroboam's reign as the period to which the discourses of Amos are to be assigned. It was a period of great wealth and luxury, and hence Jeroboam's battles must have been already fought and won.

The Life of Amos—(*a*) **Private Life.** Amos was a common man, not necessarily poor, but presumably not in high social position. We are told in 1:1 that in private life he was a *nôqēd*. This same word is applied to Mesha, king of Moab in 4 Kg 3:4. Its meaning is seen from the cognate word in Arabic which applies it to one who raises a peculiar breed of stunted sheep valued for their excellent wool. In 7:14 Amos declares that he was a *bôqēr* (cattle-tender), but this may be as scribe's error for *nôqēd*. We learn from 1:1 that Amos pastured his sheep in the neighbourhood of Tekoa, the modern *Tequʿa* lying on an elevated Judean hill six miles south of Bethlehem. From 7:14 it appears further that the future prophet was employed in dressing sycomore trees (not our trees of the same name). The fruit of those trees resembles a fig in shape and size and grows in clusters. The dressing probably consisted in nipping (LXX κνίζων ; Vg *vellicans*) the fruit, and so releasing an injurious insect which prevents it from ripening. The trees grew in the lower part of the semi-wilderness which slopes down from Tekoa to the Maritime Plain on the west and to the Dead Sea on the east. In this region of moor and semi-desert Amos lived, and his writing is rich with imagery from the life of the sparsely-inhabited Judean uplands : the wagon swaying under its load of sheaves, 2:13 ; the roaring of the lion, 3:4 ; the snaring of birds, 3:5 ; the shepherd rescuing remnants of a sheep from a lion ; 3:12 ; a serpent lurking in a cranny of the house, 5:19 ; an ever-flowing stream, 5:24 ; rocks on the hill-side, 6:13 ; a basket of ripe summer-fruit, 8:1.

(*b*) **Public Life.**—Amos himself tells us that he was actually engaged at his ordinary occupations when Yahweh said to him : ' Go, prophesy to my people, Israel ', 7:15. In obedience to the divine call Amos, though a Judean, went to the Northern Kingdom, there to prophesy against the social and religious vices of the nation. The main scene of his public preaching was the royal sanctuary at Bethel. Here he met with opposition from the local priest Amasias. The latter denounced him to Jeroboam, who seemingly took no notice of the partly-distorted report which he received from his priest. Whereupon Amasias, addressing Amos contemptuously as a visionary, exhorted him to leave at once for his native Judah and there earn his living. Amos replied that he was no professional prophet, nor did he pretend to any trained skill in prophesying, nor derive his commission from any society of men. There and then the prophet daringly predicted enemy invasion, barbarous treatment of Amasias's own wife by the invading soldiery, the massacre of his children, the confiscation of his land, and his death outside the borders of Palestine. Finally Amos predicted the captivity of Israel. When his mission was concluded, the prophet returned home and there placed on permanent record the substance of the speeches which Israel refused to heed.

The Social and Religious Conditions censured by Amos—(*a*) **Social Conditions.** The nation comprised but two classes of people, *viz.* the very rich and the very poor. The former lived in houses of hewn stone panelled with ivory ; they partook of sumptuous banquets and looked with disdain on their unfortunate brothers and sisters at the other end of the social scale. The poor were in dire distress and, as the inequality in the distribution of wealth increased, their lot became more wretched still. They were, moreover, oppressed and exploited by the rich. Over a period of years the agricultural population had suffered losses not only from the Syrian hosts which overran the land, but also from the drought, the blasting and the blight which affected the crops, *cf.* 4:7–9. Some people were therefore compelled by financial distress to borrow money for which they had to pay a high rate of interest and in addition to mortgage their holdings of land. Failure to meet the money-lender's demands resulted in foreclosure. Although the laws of Israel (Lev 25:25 ff.) decreed that the former owner could at any time redeem the land for money and that at the year of jubilee it was to be returned free, nevertheless the administration of those laws was, in the days of Amos, in the hands of a corrupt executive which was not above accepting bribes from the wealthy. When the borrower of money had no land he was compelled to mortgage his person, and failure to repay resulted in slavery. The wealth derived from slave-labour, from the excessive interest charged on loans, from exorbitant rents, and from commercial deceit went to provide further luxuries for the rich and their already well-pampered women-folk.

(*b*) **Religious Conditions.**—The Israelites worshipped at the shrines of Bethel, Galgal, Dan and Beer-sheba. We gather from Amos that this worship, though nominally that of Yahweh, was in reality that of a god invented by the imaginations of the worshippers. Yahweh as Amos knew him was a different being from the Yahweh whom he saw the people worship, for their conceptions of him were decidedly false. The popular idea of Yahweh was so radically erroneous that it could no longer be said that he was worshipped by Israel ; *cf.* *L. B. Paton, JBL 13 (1894) pp 80–90. Since Amos regarded the god who was worshipped by the great majority of the people as other than Yahweh, there was no reason to single out for particular condemnation the symbolism of the bull-calf, for if the god who was worshipped was not Yahweh, it was a very minor question, indeed, whether or not this god should be worshipped under the form of a calf. We should note the following passages : 3:14 speaks, not of the purification of a perverted worship of Yahweh, but rather of the entire abolition of the cult at Bethel (*cf.* 7:9 ; 9:1–4) ; in 4:4 f. Yahweh is not pleased with the sacrifices offered because he does not regard them as offered to himself (*cf.* 5:21 ff.) ; in 5:4 f. Yahweh is clearly distinguished from the god whom the Israelites worship, for here Yahweh declares that it is he whom they must seek if they are to survive as a nation, and not the god whom they adore at the sanctuaries (*cf.* 8:14).

The Doctrine of Amos—(*a*) **Yahweh is the Creator and Governor of the Physical Universe.** He formed the mountains and created the winds, he can in a moment darken the sky with his clouds, 4:13. He made the constellations Pleiades and Orion ; he causes day to alternate with night, 5:8. He controls nature to the advantage (*cf.* 9:13) or disadvantage of man (*cf.* 4:6–11). His power over nature is manifested in the phenomenon of the waves which at his command inundate the land, 5:8 ; *cf.* 9:6.

(*b*) **Yahweh is God of all Nations.** He is a universal God for he determines the destinies of the nations of the earth. He brought the Philistines from *Caphtor* (i.e. either Crete or Carpathos near Rhodes) and the Syrians from *Qir*, 9:7 ; he caused the Amorites to flee before the Israelites, 2:9 ; he will send the Syrians back whence he brought them, 1:5 ; he will raise up a nation (*viz.* Assyria) to invade Israel, 6:15. Yahweh will likewise judge all nations : he will

chastise not only Israel and Judah but likewise all the **525d** peoples in the vicinity for their acts of inhumanity which are breaches of the laws of universal morality, 1:3–2:3. Those heathen nations Yahweh will punish not as God of Israel and not because they have offended against his chosen people (*cf.* 1:6 ff. ; 2:1 ff.) but he will arraign them as their God.

(*c*) **Yahweh, the God of the Universe, is in a Special e Way the God of Israel.** Israel alone he knew, for he freely chose this people from among the nations of the earth and with them entered into a covenant, 3:2 ; his will he had clearly made known to them through the covenant laws and also through the voice of the inspired prophets, 2:11 ; 3:7. Israel, however, is not to imagine that the special choice of Yahweh carries with it immunity from judgement. Against those who for example thought, as the Moabites did of Chemosh, that his existence was bound up with theirs and that, therefore, their preservation was vital to him, Amos insisted that Israel is Yahweh's people not through any natural necessity but solely through his free choice. In fact Yahweh's judgement on his chosen people will be a rigorous one, because his relations with them involved special obligations which they failed to honour.

(*d*) The moral attribute of Yahweh on which Amos **f** lays most emphasis is his **righteousness.** While the prophet Osee regarded Israel's sin as especially an outrage on divine love, Amos thought of it as especially a provocation of divine justice. Yahweh being himself pre-eminently just will not tolerate injustice in the world over which he rules. But Yahweh is also a merciful and loving God, for the exhortation ' seek ye me and ye shall live ' (5:4*b*) is the invitation of one who waits with loving heart to receive back his erring children.

Amos' Familiarity with Israel's Past—The words ' his **g** brother ' in 1:11 show that he was acquainted with the story of Jacob and Esau, Gen 25. From 2:8 we may infer that he knew of the law against retaining pledged garments over night, Ex 22:26. He knew of the Exodus and the Conquest, 2:9 f. ; 3:1 f. ; 5:25 ; 9:7. He was acquainted with the history of David, 6:5.

Biblical Citations from Amos—The book is referred to **h** in Tob 2:6 and a citation made from 8:10 ; in Ac 7:42 f. where Am 5:25 f. is quoted from the ' book (DV ' books ') of the prophets ', *i.e.* the twelve Minor Prophets regarded by the Hebrews as one book ; in Ac 15:16 f., a quotation from Am 9:11.

Division of the Book—The book may conveniently be **i** divided into four sections as follows : (1) A prologue (chh 1–2) which comprises a series of prophecies against Israel's neighbouring states and against Israel itself. (2) Chh 3–6, further oracles against Israel. (3) Five visions interspersed with some addresses, chh 7–9. (4) An epilogue describing the restoration of David's kingdom, 9:11–14.

I 1 Superscription—see § 524*c*. **526a**

2 The General Tenor of all Amos' Utterances— **b** Yahweh *roars*, *i.e.* proclaims his anger against sinners. His voice is as loud and as awe-inspiring as the roar of a lion in the act of springing upon its prey, and as the peals of the rolling thunder (*cf.* Ps 17:14). The voice comes from Sion, Yahweh's earthly abode. The terror which it inspires is described figuratively as drying up vegetation.

3–II 5 The Crimes of the Nations and the Inevitable c Punishment—In each of the oracles against Israel's neighbouring states the prophet follows a fixed pattern, *viz.* ' Thus saith Yahweh : For three crimes of . . . yea, for four, I will not *revoke* it (*i.e.* the sentence of doom) ; because . . . (one specific sin and the punishment are here mentioned) '. In the expression ' For three crimes of . . . *yea*, for four . . . ' the two numbers together suggest a large but indefinite number. One specific transgression is mentioned as a typical example. All the nations will be punished by fire which symbolizes the devastations of war, and

526c Damascus and Ammon by exile also. Damascus is charged with ravaging Galaad ; Philistia with seizing whole groups of people in time of peace and selling them to Edom ; Tyre with slave-trading with Edom, a sin aggravated by the crime of perfidy ; Edom with undying hatred of Israel ; Ammon with massacring the pregnant women of Galaad ; Moab with desecrating the corpse of an Edomite king, and Judah with rejecting the Law, neglecting Yahweh's commandments, and worshipping idols. The whole context makes it clear that Amos regards the acts of the heathen nations as transgressions against the moral law.

d 3-5 Judgement on Damascus—Damascus was one of the many states of Syria. Threshing instruments of iron (DV ' iron wains ') were frequently composed of heavy planks joined side by side by means of wooden cross-pieces, and studded underneath with basalt or iron teeth. They were pulled by oxen over the heaped-up corn on the threshing-floor ; the corn was thereby shelled and the straw cut into pieces. The charge against Damascus is probably not to be taken literally, but rather as figuring the cruel treatment meted out to the inhabitants of Galaad. **4 f.** In punishment Yahweh will send the flame of war (for fire as a symbol of war, *cf.* Jg 9:20) into the royal palaces once occupied by *Hazael* and *Benhadad III*, the two recent kings who caused such suffering to Israel. He will cause an invading enemy to break the bar which fastened the city gates, in other words, to prize open the fortifications. Moreover, Yahweh will extirpate from the plain of *Aven* (DV ' the idol ' ; LXX ' On ') whoever dwells there, and from the house of *Eden* (DV ' pleasure ') the supreme official, and the people will be taken into exile to *Qir* (DV ' Cyrene '). The three places mentioned here cannot now be identified with any certainty ; the first may be the plain between Lebanon and Antilebanon, while the site of Eden may have been where now is Jubb 'Adîn, 25 m. NE. of Damascus. The district called Qir may be the land of the Karites between the Tigris and the Euphrates.

e 6-8 Judgement on Philistia—Four of the five federated city-states are mentioned, Gath being omitted. The sin with which Philistia and pre-eminently Gaza is taxed is that of carrying off *whole groups of captives to deliver them over to* Edom, presumably to be resold to Arabia. In those days Edom must have been engaged in the slave-trade. The text does not say that the sufferers were Israelites. Yahweh, through his prophet, declares that those city-states will be devastated and *what remains* of the Philistines after such devastation will perish subsequently.

f 9-10 Judgement on Tyre—Tyre's sin, likewise that of slave-trading, is aggravated by the crime of perfidy. Since there is nothing in the context to suggest that the captives delivered up to Edom were Israelites, it seems that the ' covenant of brethren ' which the Tyrians disregarded was one formed with other Phoenician cities. Moreover, it may not have been a specific treaty but rather one of mutual obligations enjoined by kinship.

g 11-12 Judgement on Edom—Edom, with hereditary and unchecked hatred, persecuted Israel, its blood-relation (*cf.* Gen 25). Theman here refers not to a district of Edom but as sometimes in the Bible (*cf. e.g.* Jer 49:20) to the whole kingdom. Bosra was an important Edomite city, probably represented by the present-day town of *El-Buṣaireh*, 20 miles SE. of the Dead Sea. It has been urged that according to the historical books of the OT Edom, until the period of the Exile, suffered more from Israel than the latter from Edom. However, it must be remembered that not all the occurrences of the unsettled period of the Israelite monarchy are referred to in the Bible.

h 13-15 Judgement on Ammon—Ammon's crime is that with the sole intention of acquiring more land its inhabitants massacred pregnant women of Galaad. *G. R. Driver in JTS 39 (1938) 261 objects to the rendering ' they have ripped up women with child ', one of his reasons being that the verb *bāqaʻ* (rip up)

in its *qal* form as here is elsewhere applied to breaking into a country. He suggests that the noun *hārôṭ* (pregnant women) is the name of a district belonging to Galaad. For this crime *their king* (DV ' Melchom ' ; so also Syr.) and his princes are doomed to an ignominious captivity. Against those critics who retain the reading ' Melchom ', the name of the national god of the Ammonites, may be urged that the words adjoined, *viz.* ' his princes', point to the king, that the condemnation is not because of the nation's idolatry, and finally that the references in other judgements are to the civil rulers, *cf.* 1:5, 8 ; 2:3. Rabba stood on the site of the modern Amman, capital city of Transjordan.

II 1-3 Judgement on Moab—The Moabites desecrated a royal corpse, that of a king of Edom, by cremation. Nothing further is known of this act. In ancient times such an indignity was looked upon as a heinous crime which called for vengeance. Yahweh will punish this inhumanity, although Edom was actually the enemy of Israel, Yahweh's chosen people ; see *g* above. The exact location of Carioth, referred to again in Jer 48:24, 41 and also mentioned on the Moabite Stone, is unknown. The Carioth to which the family of Judas belonged would be in Judah. The trumpet, the horn of a cow or a ram, was sounded on various occasions, but principally when danger threatened.

4-5 Judgement on Judah—The people of Judah are charged with revolting from Yahweh, and allowing themselves to be led astray by their idols (lit. ' their lies ') which their forefathers worshipped. The idols were images of Yahweh or, perhaps, the reference is to other gods.

6-16 The Crimes of Israel and the Sentence—The prophet, whose mission was to Israel, prefaces his oracles against the Northern Kingdom by a rapid survey of its neighbouring states, and thus skilfully leads up to a climax. The Israelites would have been only too pleased to hear the sins of their neighbours denounced and to agree that the threatened punishment was well deserved. Having thus gained the attention and good-will of his audience, Amos unexpectedly points to their own transgressions of the same moral laws against which their neighbours have offended. Israel's crimes are aggravated by ingratitude for Yahweh's special favours. Punishment is inevitable. **6b.** The money-lenders sold into slavery the honest man who was forced by circumstances to borrow, and at the appointed time was unable to meet their demands, and they sold the needy man for a trifling debt (lit. ' a pair of *sandals* '). The clause ' they sold the poor man for a pair of shoes ' does not mean that the price obtained for the poor man was something trifling, because assuredly those rapacious money-lenders would get as much, not as little, as they could. A less probable interpretation of the clause is based on the custom of casting a shoe on a piece of land as a sign of taking possession (*cf.* Ru 4:7 ; Ps 59:10 ; 107:10). This interpretation makes Amos refer to the cheating of the poor out of their land (*cf.* Is 5:8), and is supported by the LXX reading of 1 Kg 12:3 : ' from whose hand have I taken a bribe, and a shoe ? ' which are the words of a protestation made by Samuel. **7a.** The rich ground down the poor ; the lowly found their modest purposes thwarted. **7b.** The young woman was probably the servant-maid of the house (the word ' same ' is not in MT). Amos gives but another example of the oppression of the poor by the rich. The master and his son have carnal relations with the maid. This abuse is a profanation of Yahweh's holy name for it is an act inconsistent with his infinite holiness. Some commentators hold that the young woman is one of the prostitutes who were a feature of the Canaanite ritual at the shrines. Those who had intercourse with one of those prostitutes were thought to place themselves under the patronage of the particular deity which she represented. The inevitable consequence of this crime was that Yahweh's name, in virtue of his connexion with Israel, was brought into discredit. Deut 23:17 prohibits the practice. **8.** The civil code of Israel (*cf.* Ex 22:26 f. ; Deut 24:12 f.) decreed that if a poor man was obliged to pawn his outer cloak the creditor must restore it to him before sundown, for use at night when it was often his only covering. Those whom Amos condemns reclined during the sacrificial banquets on clothes held in pawn in contravention of the law. They believed, perhaps, that if the garment could be used in a religious service the needs of worship would supersede those of civil law. At the sacrificial banquets the wine they drank was purchased with the money of those whom they had *mulcted*. In this verse as in the preceding the emphasis is on the oppression of the poor. Amos uses the words ' the house of their *god* ', for he wishes to insinuate that there was nothing in common between Yahweh and the god whom those people worshipped as Yahweh.

9-12. The people's guilt is enhanced by the benefits conferred upon them by Yahweh. The name ' Amorite ' is here used as a general designation of the pre-Israelite population of Canaan on both sides of the Jordan (*cf.* Jos 24:18). **10.** It was Yahweh who cared for them during the forty years in the wilderness and eventually led them into the promised land. **11 f.** He raised up men who taught them by their doctrine (prophets) and example (*Nazirites*). The Nazirites were men consecrated to God, and one of their vows was to abstain from wine. The Israelites, however, debauched the Nazirites and commanded the prophets to be silent.

13-16 Judgement is pronounced on Israel—13. *Behold I will make it* (*i.e.* the ground) *sway under you as a wagon sways that is full of sheaves.* Many interpretations of this difficult verse have been put forward ; the one here adopted involves the slight change of one consonant, *viz. 'ayin* to *pe*, in both verbs (*cf.* Robinson, p 18). The swaying ground denotes Yahweh's coming in judgement. **14 ff.** Against the divine visitation the Israelites cannot stand : *refuge will fail the swift* ; *the valiant will not be able to assert their strength* ; *the warrior* (DV ' the strong ') will not save himself ; *the bowman will be routed* ; *neither the infantry nor the cavalry will secure their safety* ; *even the most courageous will cast away his armour and rush from the battlefield in attempted flight.* The sentence will surely be accomplished ; it is ' the oracle of Yahweh ' (DV ' saith the Lord ').

III 1-8 The Certainty of Chastisement on Israel—1. This oracle, though primarily intended for the Northern Kingdom, seems also to include Judah. **2.** In the preceding discourse (2:6-16) the prophet foretold the destruction of Israel. Those who heard him refused to believe him. Yahweh had chosen the Israelites from among all nations to be his own, and therefore they could count on him to preserve them. They had fallen into the habit of thinking after the manner of the heathen (*cf.* 4 Kg 18:33 ff. ; also the Moabite Stone) that each nation had its own god who would not readily punish his own people, unless perhaps he was angry with them for some reason not related to their moral conduct. Yahweh is surely not angry with Israel, for the people are duly performing the ritual and supplying an abundance of sacrifices. Amos retorts that because Israel is Yahweh's special people, the morally guilty nation is all the more deserving of punishment.

3. *Will two walk together unless they know one another* (so LXX) ? There can no longer be fellowship between Yahweh and his people because the latter have broken off friendly relations ; their election was for service, and they have failed to give it. The words of MT and Vg which mean that two do not meet unless they have made an appointment may be relevant if spoken to the inhabitants of the sparsely-populated district of Tekoa, and not, as here, to the throngs who frequent Bethel. **4 f.** The judgement threatened by

Yahweh is an awful reality and will most certainly **527a** come to pass. Amos represents it as already in execution. A lion only roars when it is springing upon its prey ; Yahweh has roared, so his prey is at hand. **5.** *Will a bird fall to the earth* (omit with LXX ' into the snare ') *when there is no trap for it ? Will a bird-snare spring up from the ground and have taken nothing ?* Yahweh has set the trap, and Amos envisages Israel as actually caught. **6 f.** The sound of a horn is the signal of approaching attack, and the people of the city are terrified because they know that attack is certain. The calamity (DV ' evil ') which Yahweh has threatened to send upon his people is equally certain, for the voice of the prophet, who is but proclaiming what Yahweh has revealed, has sounded the alarm. **8.** Amos summarizes his discourse. The lion *has roared* ; Yahweh, represented by a lion, has made known his vengeance and Israel's ruin is real. Yahweh, the author of this imminent calamity, has told his prophet, and the prophet cannot refrain from proclaiming it.

9-15 The Doom of Samaria—9 f. The crimes of the **b** Israelite aristocracy are such that those who inhabit the palaces of the great nations of the earth, *viz.* Assyria (so LXX ; DV ' Azotus ') and Egypt— heathens all and given to luxurious living—are invited to assemble on the mountains of Samaria (*i.e.* the whole Northern Kingdom). They are to look over the land and *mark* the great tumults (DV ' many follies ') and especially the social crimes committed there. Wrong-doing has become second nature to the many who store up in their mansions the wealth they have amassed by violence and rapine. **11.** Because of those crimes, for the existence of which there is ample evidence, *an enemy will encircle* ($y^e s \bar{o} b \bar{e} b$) *the land and will strip from thee thy strength, and thy mansions will be plundered.* **12.** *Thus saith Yahweh :* As the shepherd saves from the mouth of the lion two legs or a bit of an ear, so shall the children of Israel who inhabit Samaria be saved with (only so much as) the corner of a divan or the cross-piece from the leg of a couch. This, that of *N. Herz in JTS 15 (1914) 262, seems the most probable rendering of a difficult verse. The word *biḏmeśeq* (DV ' of Damascus ') is divided into two by Herz and pointed differently, *viz. baḏ miśśôq*. Amos institutes a comparison between the bits of the sheep rescued by the shepherd from the lion and the scraps of their expensive furniture saved by the voluptuous Israelites from the catastrophe which will overtake them. A shepherd was held responsible by the owner for the safety of every sheep. It was, however, recognized that he could not altogether prevent damage by lions, so if he could produce any fragment of the carcase with the marks of the lion's teeth, he was absolved from restitution (*cf.* Ex 22:13). **15.** This verse seems out of place after 14 and originally probably followed 12. Their beautiful mansions will be destroyed. The winter house and the summer house were probably parts of the same building, the latter being an additional apartment built on the flat roof of the winter house (*cf.* Jg 3:20 ; Jer 36:22). Houses of ivory were those panelled or adorned with ivory (*cf.* 3 Kg 22:39 ; Ps 44:9). A slight change in the Hebrew word for ' many ' gives us ' ebony ', and this may have been the original reading. Those stately mansions, with their divans and couches, were for him, who owned but a mountain-hut with a sleeping-mat, symbols of excessive luxury. **13 f.** The well-to-do nobles of Assyria and Egypt who in 9 above were bidden to come and note the wickedness of Samaria are here invited to hear and affirm the divine sentence given in 14. Yahweh, the God of hosts, declares that in the day in which he will punish Israel for its transgressions he will also destroy the altars of Bethel, the chief shrine of the Northern Kingdom. The Northern Kingdom is here called ' the house of Jacob '. In Amos it is also referred to as ' house of Israel ', ' house of Joseph ', ' house of Isaac ' (in 7:9, 16 where DV reads ' idol '), Samaria. The title ' Yahweh, God of hosts ' or more frequently simply ' Yahweh of hosts '

527b is pre-eminently a prophetic title of Yahweh. The word 'host' is, in the Bible, applied to (i) an army of men, (ii) a company of angels and (iii) the army of the heavenly bodies. Although differences of opinion exist as to the original meaning of the title 'Yahweh of hosts', there seems to be no doubt that for Amos it designates Yahweh as the Ruler of the hosts of heaven and earth (cf. LXX παντοκράτωρ). The 'horns' of the altar were horn-shaped projections from the four corners. At the oblation of the victim the priest touched the horns with his finger which was dipped in the victim's blood.

c IV 1-3 Amos Censures the Women of Samaria—He likens these well-pampered and wanton upper-class women to the kine of *Bashan* (DV 'fat'), Bashan being a district beyond the Jordan noted in OT times for its well-nourished flocks and herds, Deut 32:14 ; Ps 21:13 ; Ez 39:18. Those lazy women fatten upon the poor ; they imperiously urge on their husbands (DV 'masters') to provide the means of indulgence by fair methods or by foul, not caring what their luxuries cost their less fortunate sisters. Yahweh, however, will cause them to suffer for such conduct. *They will be led away with hooks, and the last among them with fish-hooks* (2b)— the image is now that of fish being hauled out of their native element. Their departure from the city will be through breaches made by an attacking enemy in the walls, each woman going straight before her for she is being dragged out by the enemy, and they will be *chased towards Mt. Hermon*. The Heb. of *3b* gives no clear meaning ; it reads ' ye will cast towards Harmon '. *Harmon* (DV Armon) is unknown. The emendation followed is that of Van Hoonacker, p 234.

d 4-13 The People's Zeal in Worship—The stark contrast between the sedulous performance of religious services and simultaneous moral wrong-doing manifests their belief that provided they did not fail in his ritual, Yahweh would overlook their evil lives. **4 f.** The invitation is ironical. The transgression lies in the very fact of going to Bethel and to Galgal, not in the making of incorrect offerings at those shrines. The offerings mentioned, *viz.* morning sacrifices, tithes every three *years* (DV 'days' : the plural 'days' is used sometimes in the OT in the sense of 'years' : Lev 25:29 ; Jg 17:10 ; 2 Par 21:19), thank-offerings *without* (see note below) leaven and free-will offerings were all according to the law. **5a.** The law (cf. Lev 2:11) decreed that leaven might not be consumed upon the altar as part of a sacrifice. Here, however, the context seems to show that the Heb. preposition, *min*, is not partitive, meaning ' from ', *i.e.* ' made up of ', but rather privative, meaning ' without ' (cf. Robinson, p 24). **5b.** *Proclaim free-will offerings* (cf. Lev 7:16 ; Deut 12:17), *make them known*. This also was the correct procedure laid down in the law (cf. Deut 12:18) that members of the offerer's household and others were to partake of the sacrificial banquet, and, of course, they had to be notified. The statement ' for so you love ' (DV ' for so you would do ') refers not to the clause immediately preceding, but rather to the ironical invitation as a whole ; the people are ever ready to go to those shrines.

e 6 ff. Yahweh on his side showed his displeasure by sending various chastisements, famine (6), drought (7 f.), blight (9), epidemic disease (10) and earthquake (11). The divine visitations had not, however, the desired effect, for the people continued to worship a god who in reality was not Yahweh. The refrain ' you have not returned to me ' is repeated after the description of each visitation ; the repetition seeks to impress the fact upon the listeners. **6c.** ' And I also have given you *cleanness* of teeth in all your cities ' : the teeth were clean because of lack of food. **7 f.** On one occasion Yahweh withheld the rain which usually falls in Palestine in the form of heavy showers in the months of March and April. The corn thereby suffered a serious setback and could not fully recover. On another occasion Yahweh caused the winter or ' former ' rains to fall in one place and not in an adjoining district. This he did in order that the people might observe that the lack of rain in some parts was not a mere accident. Only in those comparatively few cities where the rains fell did the water-cisterns contain water, and the inhabitants having but little to spare from their own wants could not satisfy those from the neighbouring towns who, weakened by thirst, *staggered* (DV ' went ') in to find water. **9.** The grain and fruit crops were destroyed by the sirocco and by a blight. In addition locusts ravaged all herbage. **10.** The fourth divine visitation comprised a pestilence after the manner of the pestilences which are endemic in the marshy lands on the Egyptian frontier. In addition there was warfare in which Israel's choice young men were slain together with their captured (or, according to G. R. Driver in JTS 39 (1938) 262, collected) horses. The air was filled with the stench of unburied corpses. Yet, notwithstanding, the people failed to learn that, in Yahweh's eyes, zeal in worship does not compensate for wickedness of life. **11.** From the terrible visitation of an earthquake Israel emerged like something charred.

12 f. Since the above calamities failed to teach Israel that the real Yahweh is a righteous God, a worse disaster will come. The nature of this disaster is not stated but is deliberately left indefinite by the word *thus* (DV, ' these things '). As man fears the unknown more than the known, ignorance of the nature of threatened disaster inspires greater fear. Let Israel expect forthwith to meet an offended God, coming to execute vengeance ; he is omnipotent and omniscient. **12b.** *because I will do this to thee, prepare to meet thy God, O Israel.* **13.** This is the first of three doxologies given by Amos, the others being 5:8 f. and 9:5 f. Yahweh made the mountains and the wind ; *he declareth unto man what is his musing*, for he can penetrate the secrets of the human heart ; *he maketh the dawn darkness*, by causing clouds to appear ; he rides on the high places of the earth, *i.e.* on the thunder-clouds as they sweep over the hill-tops (cf. Mic 1:3) ; Yahweh, the God of hosts is his name.

V:1-6, 8, 9 A Dirge, Israel's Coming Destruction—The prophet utters a dirge (**1b-2** ; MT, 2) over fallen Israel, as if it were already ruined. He then declares briefly how (3) and why (**4 f.**) Israel will come to that abject state. Finally, Amos exhorts his hearers to do, even at this eleventh hour, what heretofore they have neglected to do, *viz.* to seek Yahweh, who is the Creator and Governor of the physical universe and the Ruler of the world of men (**6, 8 f.**) Verse **7** is out of place and should immediately precede 10.

1a. *Hear this word which I take up for a dirge over you.* In Hebrew poetry a dirge has a special rhythm, for the lines of the verse have each five beats or accents with the caesura as a rule after the third ; this is known as qinah rhythm.

1b-2. *She is fallen to rise no more, the virgin of Israel ;*
She is forsaken upon her own land, none to upraise her.

The nation as a whole is personified under the figure of a virgin. **3.** Ninety per cent of Israel's fighting forces will be destroyed. **4 f.** Israel merits the fate which has just been pronounced against it, because the people did not observe the moral law of Yahweh, who, being himself righteous, demands above all else right-living from men. **6.** Amos turns in exhortation to the people to seek Yahweh that they may live, that the nation may not be overthrown by war (here symbolized by fire). The prophet hoped that even at this late hour the nation might find the real Yahweh. **8.** *Pleiades* (DV ' Arcturus ') and Orion are two constellations mentioned again in Job 9:9 ; 38:31 f. The participles with which, in MT, this verse and the following verse open are in apposition with Yahweh mentioned in 6. **9.** Lit. ' Who causes devastation to smile upon the strong, and devastation comes upon the stronghold '. G. R. Driver in JTS 39 (1938) 262 suggests that the verb ' causes to smile ', which is unsuited to devastation, should be emended to ' wreaks ' (hamm*e*gabbēl). For ' comes ' read with all the versions ' causes to come '. If men defy the will of Yahweh, then though they be strong and live in strong fortresses, he will destroy them.

7, 10-17 Amos censures the Corrupt Judges—The sense seems to demand that the word ' woe ' be supplied (*cf.* 5:18 ; 6:1) at the beginning of **7,** *Woe to them that turn judgement to wormwood, and cast justice to the ground.* Amos is referring to the corrupt administration of law. Wormwood, a species of the genus Artemisia, is a bitter plant (*cf.* Deut 29:18 ; Jer 9:15 ; 23:15). **10.** They who sit in judgement at the gates of the city hate him who pleads the cause of the innocent. **11.** Judges were bribed by the landlords to give decisions against the tenant farmers ; the latter were thus required to hand over *exactions of grain* (DV ' choice prey '), *i.e.* an extortionate share of the produce of their land. Yahweh, however, will not suffer such crimes to pass with impunity ; the corrupt judges will not live to enjoy the houses and vineyards on which they have expended their unjust wealth. **12.** Israel merits the judgement threatened in 11. **13.** Things have come to such a pass that, lest he provoke greater evils, the prudent man *is keeping silence.* **14 f.** contain a call to repentance. A necessary condition of Yahweh's active love is the moral uprightness both of their private and of their public lives when they are acting as judges of the people. If this condition is fulfilled, perhaps Yahweh will have mercy on the remnant of Joseph. The Northern Kingdom had already been reduced to a remnant because the life of the nation had gradually been sapped by exploitation and oppression on the one hand, and luxury and dissipation on the other. Some, *e.g.* de Vaux, RB 30 (1933) 528, say that the ' remnant ' in 15 is what will be left after judgement. **16 f.** The opening word ' therefore ' would suggest that the prophet, before delivering the sentence contained in these verses, paused for some sign from his audience that they were prepared to implement the condition necessary for national life. As no indication that they would do so was forthcoming, Amos predicted a calamity which would cause wailing and lamentation in town and country-side.

18-27 Yahweh is roused to Anger by the Worship at the Shrines—The sinful nation will be severely chastised, and that by Yahweh himself, whose ethical character the people have entirely neglected. **18.** The expression ' day of Yahweh ' is of frequent occurrence in the prophets, where it means the day on which Yahweh will notably intervene in historical events ; *cf.* A. Jones, ' The Eschatology of the Synoptic Gospels ' in *Scripture*, vol. 4, pp 222 ff. There may be many such interventions and, therefore, many ' days of Yahweh '. Amos' contemporaries looked forward to a day when Yahweh would intervene and confer upon his special people some crowning victory. Amos, however, makes known that on the day about to come Yahweh will procure the victory of righteousness over sin by chastising the morally guilty nation. **19 f.** The day of Yahweh will bring in ineluctable disasters ; a man will escape one peril only to fall into another ; calamity will seek out its victims even in their homes. **21 ff.** Yahweh will not spare them for their zealous discharge of ritual observances. Their sacrifices, festivals, sacred chant and music are condemned. We should note that the condemnation here is not absolute in the sense that such acts do not belong to the religion of Yahweh. We have here rather a relative condemnation, a condemnation, namely, of the cult practices at the northern shrines ; *cf.* C. Lattey, JTS 42 (1941) 155 ff. The Israelites who worshipped at those shrines thought of Yahweh in much the same way as the Canaanites thought of Baal or the Moabites of Chemosh. Yahweh was simply a tutelary god who loved Israel only, and would always protect it against other nations, all of whom he hated ; he was a god whose demands were satisfied by a show of ritual. Yahweh rejected the religious practices of those Israelites because their idea of him was so erroneous that he did not consider the worship as given to him-

self. **24.** *But let judgement roll down as the waters, and* **527i** *justice as a never-failing torrent.* The real Yahweh desires the constant and universal practice of social righteousness. Amos does not deny that the real Yahweh likewise demands sacrifices ; we have here another example of the usage by which biblical writers emphasize too exclusively ; *cf.* Ac 5:4*b*. **25 f.** The answer to be expected to the question in 25 is ' no ' which is, however, a relative ' no '. The prophet speaking for Yahweh does not deny that the Hebrews offered sacrifices during the forty years in the desert, but he denies that those sacrifices were genuinely offered to Yahweh. The worship during that period was only nominally that of Yahweh for actually it was the worship of false gods. We should note that the prophet is speaking in general terms of the nation as a whole ; there were, no doubt, many individuals who were genuine worshippers of Yahweh. **26.** This verse is obscure. In MT (taking the consonants only) there is mention of the Assyrian deities *Sakkuth* and *Kaiwan*. *Sakkuth*, besides being the god of war, was the god of the sun and of light ; *Kaiwan* was the planet Saturn. It is extremely unlikely that Assyrian deities were worshipped in the desert. We might gather, however, from Deut 4:19 and 17:3 that the Israelites in the desert were given to sun and star worship, and a scribe copying this passage in Amos after the fall of the Northern Kingdom to the Assyrians might have introduced into the text these Assyrian names. **27.** Israel is doomed to a captivity in the unknown regions beyond Damascus.

VI 1-15 The Condemnation of the Conceited and **j** **Wealthy Aristocracy**—**1.** *Woe to them that are at ease in Sion and in security on the mount of Samaria, the men of repute of the first of the nations, unto whom the house of Israel comes* (*viz.* for judgement). The ' men of repute ' are the nobles or the ruling classes. Israel is referred to as the first of the nations in ironic allusion, perhaps, to Israel's own opinion of itself. **2.** Why would the nation's leaders be conceited ? Let them look at *Calneh* (*Kullanhu* in NE. Syria), *Hamath* (on the Orontes) and Gath (in Philistia) and observe their equally prosperous condition. And yet those latter states are smaller in extent than Israel. *Are there better* (*i.e.* more flourishing) *than these kingdoms ? Is their territory greater than your territory ?* **3.** *You that thrust off the evil day, and cause the seat of violence to come near.* They refuse to believe that the nation will perish, while at the same time they hasten by their actions the day when *violence* will rule the land. **4-6.** They lounge in extreme luxury ; *they devise for themselves instruments of music as David did* (5*b*). And while they are so conducting themselves their eyes are blinded to the affliction of Joseph, *i.e.* to the physical misfortunes and sufferings of their brethren (*cf.* 4:6 ff.). Or, perhaps, the reference in 6*b* may be to the moral corruption of Israel.

7-15. Yahweh will chastise the proud nobles ; their **k** land will experience war and siege with the attendant evils of pestilence and devastation. **7*b*.** *And the revelry of them that stretched themselves will cease.* **9 ff.** A household of even ten men will be wiped out by a plague. Before the last of the ten succumbs a kinsman of one already dead, *his burner*, will arrive at the house to burn his relative's pestilence-infested body and will be told by the survivor that he is the only one still alive. He will further be requested to keep silent for the name of Yahweh must not be mentioned. **11*b*** is the language of despair, as if the case was hopeless and it was useless to pray. **13.** The end of the nation is only what is to be expected. A condition of affairs exists which is as unnatural as the galloping of horses upon rocks or the ploughing of a sea with oxen. *Do* horses *gallop upon rocks ? Does one plough the sea with oxen ?* The adopted reading of this second clause involves a division into two and a different vocalization of the one Hebrew word, *viz.* *babbᵉqārîm* to be read *bᵉbāqār yām.* **14.** They rejoice in their material prosperity (lit. ' a thing of nought ') and they boast of their national power. The ' horn ' is a figure used to denote power, *cf.* Deut 33:17 ;

527k Ps 74:5. **15.** The torrent of the desert was some river which flowed into the Dead Sea from the south.

528a **VII:1-3 The Vision of the Locusts**—In chh 7 ff. Amos recounts what he had seen and heard in five symbolical visions. With regard to the first two visions, they ' are parallel with the list of inflictions in 4:6–11, others might have been added, but those two were typical of all the efforts which had been made to turn Israel from her evil way. . . . These (*i.e.* the first and second) visions are not premonitions of coming disaster, but rather interpretations of actual afflictions' (Harper, p 164). **1.** *Thus the Lord Yahweh showed me : and, behold, he was forming locusts in the beginning of the shooting up of the late corn-crop : and, behold, it was the late corn-crop after the corn-crops of the king.* The meanings here adopted for *leqeš* (DV ' latter rain ') ; current rendering ' late grass ') and for *gizzê hammelek* (DV and current rendering ' the king's mowing ') are those of E. Power in Bi 8 (1927) 87–92. The corn-crops of the king were those sown in the winter months prior to the 20th of January on which the king made a levy. The late corn-crop was that sown between the 20th of January and the end of February. The prophet wishes to declare that the locusts were being formed ' at such a time as to destroy the entire corn-crop. . . He represents them therefore as coming when the late crop is beginning to spring up . . . that is to say at the exact time when they shall naturally destroy the late-crop itself as well as the more developed earlier crop. If the invasion were earlier the late crop still underground would be safe : if it were later the early crop might have been already reaped ' (E. Power, p 89). **2 f.** *And they were making an end* (so *C. Torrey, JBL, 13 (1894) 63, who divides and vocalizes differently the first nine consonants of MT) *of devouring the green herbage* of the land (2*a*) but Amos interceded with Yahweh. He urged the insufficiency of the nation's resources and Yahweh put a stop to the destructive work.

b **4-6 The Vision of a Devouring Fire**—Yahweh called out that punishment by fire should overtake Israel for its crimes. The fire devoured the great deep, *i.e.* the mass of water which according to popular conception lay below the flat earth. It *would have eaten up the land of Israel* (DV ' a part '), but the prophet prayed and Yahweh again averted disaster. **4b.** The Heb. word rendered ' a part ' in DV means literally ' the portion ', *viz.* that given by Yahweh to his chosen people (*cf.* Mic 2:4) ; so Targum.

c **7-9 The Third Vision (Iron)**—The same Heb. word, *viz.* '*anāk*, occurs four times in the description of this vision, and in DV it is rendered once by ' plastered ' and three times by ' mason's trowel '. The meaning of the word is much disputed, and various meanings have been proposed, for which see J. M. Rinaldi in VD 17 (1937) 82 ff. The rendering ' iron ' (*cf.* LXX ἀδάμας) given by A. Condamin in RB 9 (1900) 586 ff. seems the most probable. Amos beheld Yahweh stationed upon a wall of iron, with iron in his hand. The wall of iron symbolizes the invincible might of the enemy (*viz.* Assyria), Yahweh's instrument in the coming destruction of Israel. The iron which he holds and which he will place in the midst of his people (*cf.* 8) is the destroying sword. **8b.** Yahweh *will not pardon them* (DV ' plaster them over ') *any more.* **9.** The hill-top sanctuaries of *Isaac* (DV ' the idol ') will be destroyed, and the royal house will perish.

d **10-17 A Biographical Narrative**—This section which describes the clash between Amos and Amasias, the priest of Bethel, gives us information concerning the life of Amos before his call to prophesy, his prophetic activity and the reception accorded to him. This information is noted in the general Introduction, § 524*d, e.* We might remark here that Amos did not say as Amasias reports him as saying (*cf.* 11*a*) that Jeroboam would die by the sword. What Amos had said referred to the house of Jeroboam (*cf.* 9*b*). This whole section is closely connected with the preceding vision, for in explaining the third vision Amos pre-

dicted ruin for the dynasty to which Jeroboam belonged.

VIII 1-3 The Vision of the Basket of Summer (*i.e.* Ripe) **Fruit**—Amos sees a *basket of summer fruit.* The summer fruit is a symbol of Israel ripe in its sins and ready to be devoured. There is a play upon the Heb. words *qayiṣ* (summer fruit) and *qēṣ* (end) of similar sound. Amos sees *qayiṣ*, but this brings to mind *qēṣ*, the end which is to come upon Israel. **3.** *The singing women* (*šārôt*) *of the palace will howl* in that day, saith the Lord Yahweh ; *many will be the corpses ; in all places they will be cast forth ! Hush !*

4-14 Dishonest Merchants exposed and Retribution threatened—This section is in the form of an address giving reasons why the end referred to in the explanation of the previous vision is coming. Avaricious, dishonest, and mean traders are impoverishing the poor. Yahweh's anger is aroused and he swears that Israel will suffer a terrible retribution. **5.** The merchants are irritated when they have to suspend business on the festivals of the *New Moon* (DV ' the month ') and of the Sabbath, for on those days they may not open (*i.e.* display for sale) the *wheat.* They are thus deprived of an opportunity of engaging in their nefarious practices on those days. On business-days they diminish the *ephah* (which was equivalent to about eight gallons of dry measure), *i.e.* the measure by which they sold, and they enlarge the *shekel* (which was about 160 grains), *i.e.* the weight used for weighing in the silver received from the buyer ; they use false balances. **6.** They buy from the money-lenders (*cf.* 2:6) the poor whom they themselves have so impoverished that they cannot repay what they owe. Finally these dishonest men sell the refuse of the wheat that is not fit for bread. **7.** Yahweh has sworn *by* the pride of Jacob that the wickedness of Israel will not go unpunished. The expression ' the pride of Jacob ' is ironical, insinuating that the pride of Jacob (*i.e.* Israel) is so unalterable as to be the suitable reinforcement of an oath.

8 ff. The terrestrial and celestial wonders are not foretold literally but are received prophetic imagery to depict Yahweh's coming in judgement. An earthquake will shake the land, the movements of which are compared to the undulations on the surface of the Nile (so Van Hoonacker). The generally accepted opinion maintains that the term of comparison is the annual rising and fall of the Nile, but one could hardly compare the short rapid shakings of the earth when it quakes with the gradual change of the waters of the Nile at the annual inundation. The land *will rise, all of it, as the Nile and it will be tossed and will fall* (reading the verb *šāqaʿ* as in 9:5) as the *Nile of Egypt* (8*b*). **9.** The theophany in the day of Yahweh will be accompanied not alone by an earthquake but also by a complete eclipse of the sun at noon-day. **11 ff.** A most terrible chastisement is here threatened : the people will rush about from one part of the country to the other, from the Dead Sea to the Mediterranean, from the north even to the west, seeking through a prophet an oracle from Yahweh. They will seek in this national crisis to know Yahweh's will, but they will seek in vain. **14.** Such will be the punishment inflicted on those who now swear by a god who is Yahweh only in name. They have failed to recognize his true nature ; they have localized him in different sanctuaries and correspondingly broke him up as it were into different deities, *viz.* the *god* of Samaria, the god of Dan, the god of Beer-sheba. MT has the words ' the guilt (DV ' sin ') of Samaria ', but the word ' guilt ' is due probably to the intentional substitution by a scribe, just as *bôšet* (' shame ') was deliberately inserted in place of ' Baal ' in 2 Kg 2:8 ; 11:21 ; Os 9:10 ; Jer 3:24 ; 11:13. Translate **14b** by *As surely as thy God, O Dan, lives* ; *As surely as thy* (*divine*) *patron, O Beer-sheba, lives.* To get the reading ' your patron ', *derek* (' way ') is to be emended to read *dôdᵉka.*

IX 1-6 The Vision of the Smitten Sanctuary—The

people are assembled for worship in a sanctuary. The prophet sees Yahweh standing beside the altar and commanding that the building be thrown down on those assembled. The few who manage to escape death here will not ultimately elude the divine anger. Though they were to dig through to *Sheol*, or climb to the heavens ; though they were to hide on Mount Carmel, or go down to the bottom of the sea ; though they were to flee to a foreign land, they would not escape the avenging justice of Yahweh who is all-powerful. **1a.** *Strike the capitals* (which held up the roof) *that the thresholds may tremble, and cut them off on to* (DV ' for there is covetousness in ') *the head of them all*. **3.** The serpent is the sea-monster Leviathan which, according to the ancients, dwelt in the depths of the sea (*cf.* Is 27:1). **5 f.** This is the third of the doxologies which celebrate the power and majesty of Yahweh, the author of the forthcoming searching and rigorous judgement. **5.** Yahweh touches the earth in the phenomenon of lightning, *cf.* Ps 143:5 f. Yahweh is the author of the phenomenon of earthquake when the land *rises up, all of it, as the Nile and falls as the Nile of Egypt, cf.* 8:8*b*. **6a.** *It is he that builds his upper chambers in the heavens, and that has established upon the earth his vault* (DV ' bundle '). The vault is the sky conceived by the ancients as an arch resting at its extremities on the earth. **6b.** Yahweh has power over the waves. **7-10 Israel not immune from Destruction**—Amos points out that Israel by nature, or in its natural state, is in Yahweh's eyes on the same level as far-distant Ethiopia. Yahweh gave their first beginnings to all nations (Israel, Philistia, Syria) and, independently of his free choice which has ordained otherwise, Israel is no more to him than any other nation. The *Philistines* who came from *Caphtor* and the Syrians from *Qir* were hated by the Israelites. **8a.** The ' sinful kingdom ' is Israel. There is, however, no implied contrast with Judah. **8b.** The Israelite people will not be wholly destroyed. Although in 9:1–4 judgement falls on all without distinction, it is clear from the body of the prophecy that the sins of the upper classes determined the fate of the nation. The doctrine of a remnant which will be spared and eventually return from Exile to Palestine to form there the nucleus of the new Israel is implicit in this clause. **9 f.** Though there were, no doubt, many faithful followers of Yahweh, chiefly among the poor whose cause Amos champions, the nation as a whole was corrupt and both the faithful and the wicked would suffer the disaster of exile. The purpose of the exile was two-fold : to punish the nation for its crimes, and to sift out and destroy the wicked elements. Yahweh will

sift the house of Israel among all the nations, *as though* **528i** *it were shaken in a sieve*. The nations were the various subject peoples of the vast Assyrian Empire among whom the exiles were planted. We should note that MT makes no mention of corn, and it is probable that the comparison is to the sifting of sand by a sand-screen. The latter allows the fine sand to pass through and retains all the stones. The nations are Yahweh's sieve. Among them Israel is shaken ; the good element represented by the pure sand passes through, falls to the ground, and is preserved, while the un-worthy element represented by the stones fails to pass through and is cast away. Of the loyal adherents of Yahweh who went into exile some fell away under adversity while the others became yet more purified and more attached to their religion. These latter (their descendants) will be reinstated in the home-land. The sinners of 10 are the stones which are cast away. The threat that the sinners will die by the sword is to be understood figuratively ; they will no longer be reckoned among the people of Israel.

11-14 A Promise of Restoration—This promise is **529a** concerned with the faithful minority which together with those of the kingdom of Judah who survive the Babylonian Exile will be re-established in their ancient home. **11.** Amos sees, rising up beyond the ruin of Judah (*cf.* 2:5), the re-building of the dynasty (lit. ' hut ') of David which would cease to function on the capture of Jerusalem (586). In a coming era Yahweh will restore to its former splendour the dynasty of David ; he will heal the schism which took place in the days of Roboam (*cf.* 3 Kg 12). **12.** This verse is concerned with the pre-eminence of the restored king-dom in the future. Its glory will consist in the pos-session of what remains of Edom and also the nations, all of which belong to Yahweh. The reference is to the future conversion of the gentiles (*cf.* Is 2:2, etc.). **13.** The superiority of this future kingdom is described **b** under the figure of an extraordinary fertile soil. The harvest will be so bounteous that the reaping will not have been completed when the ploughing for the next season's crops is due to begin, and the vintage so abundant that the cereal-sowing will arrive before the vintage has been finished. The vineyards will pour down streams of *sweet wine*. **14.** Yahweh *will restore the fortunes* (DV ' bring back the captivity ') of Israel (*i.e.* the united kingdoms). The people will work to beautify their country, confident that they will no more be removed from their native land. The golden age which Amos has in mind is the Messianic era (*cf.* Ac 15:16 f.), the age of great spiritual blessings, figured by images of the most abundant plenty.

ABDIAS

(OBADIAH)

By S. BULLOUGH, O.P.

530a Bibliography—St Jerome, *Commentarii in Abdiam Prophetam*, PL 25, 1097–1118 ; *E. B. Pusey, *Minor Prophets*, 1860 ; Knabenbauer, S.J., *cf.* § 409*b* ; Condamin, S.J., *L'Unité d'Abdias*, RB 9 (1900) 261 ff. ; Van Hoonacker, *cf.* § 409*b* ; *J. Bewer in ICC, 1912 ; *H. C. O. Lanchester in CBSC, 1918 ; *H. Wheeler Robinson in *Peake's Commentary*, 1920.

b This is the shortest book in the OT, consisting of a single chapter, but St Jerome wrote (on v 1) that ' quanto brevius est, tanto difficilius '. The considerable **difficulty of the Book** arises from its brevity, from the references to historical events not easily identifiable, from the absence of any date or autobiographical material, from the problems raised by parallels elsewhere, and lastly from several grave textual obscurities.

c About **the Prophet himself** St Jerome reports a Jewish tradition that he is the same as the steward of King Achab, who bore the same name, who sheltered the hundred prophets, 3 Kg 18:3–16, and whose tomb was shown at Samaria together with those of Eliseus and John the Baptist. The prophet's name in MT is '*Obadyāh* (that of the man in 3 Kg is, with a negligible variant '*Obadyāhû*), and it appears in AV as Obadiah. The name means ' Servant of Yahweh '. There are in all 12 characters in the OT (chiefly in the lists in Par) bearing this name or its variant. The tradition about the pronounciation seems to be quite unstable, various forms of Abdias or Obadiah being current : LXX, according to the codices and in the different texts, provides many variants of both patterns, and for the 12 persons Vg has 4 times Abdias, thrice Obdia, twice Obedia, once Obadia, once Obdias and once the acc. Obdiam. It is impossible seriously to identify the prophet with any of the other 11, and it must be admitted that beyond the prophecy itself nothing is known of the author.

d The **Theme of the Book** is the pride of Edom (the neighbouring kingdom to the south, and akin to Judah being descended from Esau), 2–4, and their destruction, 5–9, on account of their unbrotherly attitude to Judah at the time of the latter's calamity, 10–14, which will bring on them God's wrath, 15–16, and retribution from Judah, who will triumph over all nations, 17–21. This last section envisages the restoration of all Israel and concludes with a Messianic sentence on Yahweh's universal kingship.

e **The Jeremias Parallels**—Jer 49:7–22 is also a prophecy against Edom, wherein are some sections which are almost verbal parallels with Abd, not, however, in the same order. The parallels are these (3*b* and part of 5 have no parallel) :

Abd	1*b*	2	3*a*	4	5*a*	5*b*	6
Jer 49:14		15	16*a*	16*b*	9*b*	9*a*	10

Some literary dependence must be supposed, either of one on the other, or of both on an older source. The supposition will depend on the date assigned to Abd. There are some isolated phrases with parallels in **Joel** : in Abd 11 & Jo 3:3, Abd 15*a* and Jo 1:15, Abd 15*b* and Jo 3(4):4 and Abd 17 and Jo 2:32 (3:5).

f The **Problem of the Date.**—The only fair treatment is to place before the reader the principal evidence in Abd on which he may base a conjecture. A date must be sought when the following circumstances may be verified : (1) Edom feels secure, but ruin is coming upon her at the hands of her former allies, 1–9, (2) Jerusalem has been invaded by foreigners, and men flee from the city, 11–14, (3) Edom meanwhile stood aloof and even joined the invaders, 10–14, (4) Both Israel and Judah are in captivity, 20. The inheritance of Palestine and the punishment of Edom by the returned exiles is seen in the future, 15–16, 17–21.

There are three main groups of opinions : (1) *A pre-exilic date*, emphasizing the hostility of Edom (*e.g.* Knabenbauer). Edom began (and continued) a state of revolt against King Joram of Judah *c* 847 B.C. ; 4 Kg 8:20–22 ; 2 Par 21:8–10. About the same time the Philistines and Arabs invaded Judah and Jerusalem itself, 2 Par 21:17, and since Edom was still in revolt it may be supposed that they joined the invaders. Amos' prophecies against Edom (esp. 1:11 on their hostility), dating from about 760 B.C., look back to these events, and similarly Joel's remarks about deportations by Tyrians, Sidonians and Philistines, Jo 3(4):2–7, refer to this period, so that Joel, Amos and Abdias form a more or less contemporary group in the 8th cent. B.C. The position assigned by tradition to Abdias among the XII is also adduced in support of this date. On this theory Jeremias was of course long posterior to Abdias. Calamity upon Edom is to be taken as a threat, not as a past event.

(2) *An exilic date* (held by St Jerome and many since), emphasizing the invasion of Jerusalem, which is identified most easily with the catastrophe of 586. Edom's hostility is not indicated in the historical account of 586, but it is clearly suggested in contemporary exilic documents such as Lam 4:21–22 ; Ez 35 (the whole ch has the same theme as Abd, esp. v 5) ; and Ps 136(137) 7 (' filiorum Edom in die Jerusalem, qui dicunt : Exinanite, exinanite '), a Ps which at any rate in its present form is plainly exilic. The calamity that overtook Edom is supposed to be at the hands of the Babylonians (whom they had supported in 586) after the fall of Jerusalem when they penetrated into Egypt, overrunning Moab and Ammon *en route*, Jos, *Ant.* 10, 9, 7, and therefore probably Edom also. On this theory the Jeremias parallels are contemporary, and both may depend on older sources reflecting the earlier troubles with Edom in the time of, *e.g.*, Amos. The identification of place-names of the Babylonian exile in Abd 20 is connected with an exilic date for Abdias (6th cent.).

(3) *A post-exilic date*, emphasizing the chastisement of Edom (*e.g.* Wellhausen and many moderns, incl. Van Hoonacker). Here the captivity of Jerusalem is regarded as past, and the chastisement of Edom by her former allies is beginning. A connexion is made with Mal 1:2–4, written *c* 480 B.C., where Edom is described as already devastated, and although Petra, one of the principal cities of Edom, was not occupied by the Arabs until 312, as Diodorus Siculus relates, 19, 94, it is easy to suppose Arab invasions of their territory long before this, especially as already *c* 444 we find an Arab element of some importance in Palestine offering resistance to the work of Nehemias at Jerusalem, Neh 2:19 ff. The Edomites may well at first

have made common cause against Judah with the Arabs in Palestine, only as the Arabs grew stronger to be abandoned by them and eventually defeated. On these suppositions Abd is dated a little before Malachias, *c* 500 B.C., and the texts in Jeremias are of course older, though it is unlikely that they are source of those of Abd.

A few authors (*e.g.* Hitzig) place the book as late as the ruin of Petra in 312 and claim that the deportation of Jews refers to that by the Egyptians about this date, recorded by Josephus in *Ant.* 12, 1, 1.

The Unity of the Book, small as it is, has been questioned, chiefly on the grounds of chronological incoherence, it becoming thus possible to assign each section to the most convincing date. P. Condamin, RB 9 (1900) 261 ff., demonstrated the unity of the book on a metrical basis, and although one might admit the incorporation of older material, esp. in the opening verses, it seems unnecessary to postulate a multiplicity of authors.

The **style** is regular classical Hebrew without obvious signs of either archaic or late post-exilic diction, if one excepts the word *qeṭel* in 9, which occurs only here. Its root is unknown in the earlier books and is found only in Job 13:15 ; 24:14 and Ps 138 (139) 19. The metre is in some places regular but in others inconsistent, while certain sections appear to be in prose. The text of some verses is uncertain.

1 Introduction—The ‘ vision ’, *i.e.* prophecy ; *cf.* § 414*g*.

‘ *A report we have heard from Yahweh, and an ambassador among the nations has been sent* ’ ; the LXX and the Jer parallel have ‘ I have heard ’. After ‘ Thus saith . . .’ we expect a divine utterance, which this section appears not to be. Van Hoonacker (henceforth written Van H.) takes the section, together with the substance of the report, ‘ Arise . . .’, as an ‘ aside ’, introducing Yahweh’s words in 2. Others take the three sentences ‘ Thus saith. . . . We have heard. . . . An ambassador . . .’ as a triple introduction to the divine utterance ‘ Arise . . .’ (thus Schegg, and Mgr. Knox’s translation suggests this). Knabenbauer, following LXX ‘ I have heard . . .’, takes the speech as beginning at that point, and as the utterance at once of God and the prophet.

2-4 Edom’s Pride—2. Jer 49:15 for ‘ exceeding ’ has ‘ among men ’. 3. MT reads ‘ The pride of thy heart hath *deceived* thee ’. ‘ Rock ’ (singular), *Sela*‘ has no article in Abd (though it has in Jer 49:16*a*), and is perhaps a proper name (*cf.* RVm) as in Jg 1:36 ; 4 Kg 14:7 and Is 16:1, where Vg translates ‘ Petra ’ (with capital), though DV has ‘ rock ’ except in Is : ‘ from Petra of the desert ’. The identification with the present Petra in Transjordan, an Edomite stronghold (*cf. i supra*), is doubtful since there were several such rock-hewn cities in that area, as St Jerome (on 4) already observed. ‘ Who *is saying*, Who shall . . .’ is not in Jer.

5-9 Edom’s Fate—Difficult verses. In **5** the Jer parallel (49:9) has the thieves and grape-gatherers in inverse order, and their activities are not a question but a statement : the grape-gatherers will not leave a remnant, the thieves damage till they have had enough. This yields a more reasonable sense. Furthermore the awkward ‘ How wouldst thou have held thy peace ? ’ (HT ‘ How art thou destroyed ! ’) does not appear at all, and the Vg mistranslation here perhaps makes it suspect—Van H. transfers the sentence to the beginning of 6. Jer seems here to have preserved a better reading, and in view of this and the next v here, the meaning seems to be not that something will be left, but that Edom will lose all at the hands of invaders under the figures of thieves and grape-gatherers. I would therefore reconstruct as follows : *If thieves come to thee, if raiders of the night, shall they not steal their fill ? If grape-gatherers come to thee, shall they leave a remnant ?* **6** : the last Jer parallel (49:10), and no longer verbal in Hebrew. Knox,

translating Vg, sees a contrast to the preceding : **530o** 5 ‘ at least they had been content to carry off what needed them . . .’, 6 ‘ But now, see how Esau is ransacked . . .’, which offers an explanation of Vg. **7.** In HT this verse begins with ‘ Even to the border ’, **p** which enables some (incl. Van H.) to attach the words to the end of 6. St Jerome noted but rejected this possibility. Yet it simplifies translation : ‘ *sought out his hidden things even to the border* ’. If, however, the phrase really belong to 7, the question arises, whose border is indicated ? The abandonment of Edom by her allies is described. If it is the allies’ border, then the sense is that Edom’s delegates (or refugees) are turned out of those lands ; if it is Edom’s own border, the probable meaning is that the Edomites are turned out of their own land, at least as far as their own border, or else that Edomite conquerors are driven back within their own borders (*cf.* Knox) ; but in any case the rendering is forced and requires much supposition. ‘ They that eat with thee ’ is an artificial translation in Vg : MT has simply *laḥmᵉḵā*, ‘ thy bread ’, which might conceivably be attached to ‘ men of ’ : ‘ men of thy peace, thy bread ’, but this is unsatisfactory and various emendations have been proposed. Van H. attempts to derive a word from a cognate root (found in Syriac and Arabic) and translates ‘ tes associés ’. Since, however, LXX ignores the word, I prefer to omit it as a dittography of the preceding word. ‘ There is no understanding in him ’ is by some considered to form part of the rhetorical question in 8. **9.** ‘ And **q** thy valiant men, *O South*, shall be afraid, *so that* man may be cut off from the mount of Esau ’ : the ‘ South ’, *Têmân*, represents Edomite territory (*cf.* Am 1:12, where linked with Bosra), and their dismay will itself be the cause of their own failure.

10-14 The Reason of the Calamity is Edom’s un- **r** brotherly conduct towards Judah. **10.** ‘ For (= because of) the slaughter ’ in MT is part of 9, but LXX and Vg rightly include it in 10. Abdias has a slight peculiarity of style according to which such brusque juxtapositions of nouns and verbs are not unusual : *e.g.* 5 ‘ If thieves . . . if raiders ’, 7 has no conjunctions, and 12 ‘ in the day of thy brother, in the day of his estrangement ’, so that here ‘ for the slaughter, for the *violence* ’ (HT has no ‘ and ’) is not surprising. **11.** ‘ When thou stoodest *aloof* ’ (*cf.* Knox). **12.** DV’s ‘ his leaving his country ’ = Vg ‘ peregrinatio ’ : MT *nôker*, ‘ estrangement ’ only here, but *cf.* the cognate *nēker* only in Job 31:3 where it is parallel to ’*êd*, ‘ misfortune ’, which occurs in 13 here. The word therefore does not necessarily refer to an exile (*cf.* Knox). ‘ *Enlarge not thy mouth* ’, perhaps in laughter, though ‘ mouth ’ may merely mean ‘ words ’ (as in Deut 17:6), and so the phrase may mean ‘ talking big ’, ‘ be not arrogant, or taunting ’. **13.** ‘ Thou shalt not be sent out against his army ’, probably ‘ *Lay not a hand upon his glacis* ’ : In MT the active verb ‘ stretch out ’ has a fem. ending, for which read *yāḏ*, ‘ a hand ’. The word *ḥêl*, ‘ glacis ’, occurs together with ‘ wall ’ in Lam 2:8 (Vg ‘ antemurale ’, DV ‘ bulwark ’), and Nah 3:8, where, as here, Vg has read it as *hayil*, ‘ strength ’.

15-16 The Day of the Lord, a frequent notion in the **s** prophets, sometimes considerably developed from the day of triumph of Judah to the eschatological notion of the everlasting Day of the Lord at the end cᶜ time, *cf.* esp. §§ 554*a–b* and 551*i*. The meaning here seems to be chiefly the first, though ‘ all nations ’ in 15 and the last words of 21 suggest a more universal application. The wider horizon from this verse to the end has suggested to some that this section is a later composition. Yet the theme of the condemnation of Edom continues : as Edom has done, so shall it be done to her, she shall share the fate of the nations. **16.** ‘ As you have **t** drunk ’, probably the cup of bitterness (a common figure, *cf.* Jer 25:16 ; Mt 20:22). ‘ You ’ most probably refers to Judah, and then the nations in their turn shall drink the same cup, and become nonentities, when Judah triumphs (Van H., Knox, others). Some,

530t however (*e.g.* Knabenbauer) understand the phrase of Edom having joined the drunken orgies of the invaders of Jerusalem, and of the nations then holding similar orgies in Edom (though Knabenbauer himself in the second member sees the cup of bitterness). ' Sup up ', *lā'û*, a verb occurring only here and of uncertain meaning. The various readings of LXX suggest a faulty text. Some would read *bāl⁰'û*, ' swallow down ', which is easy.

u 17-21 The Triumph of Judah—17. ' Salvation ' : *p⁰lêṭāh*, might mean this, but usually indicates a ' *remnant* that is saved '. **18.** Jacob stands for Judah, and Joseph for the Northern Kingdom, as does Ephraim in 19. It is important to note that 17–19 envisage a restored Israel without ' partition ', who will inherit once more the whole of Palestine including its outlying districts. Israel's vengeance upon Edom is pictured also in Ez 25:14. **19.** A geographical description of the triumph of the united Israel : southwards they shall possess Edom (Esau), westwards Philistia (on the coast), northwards ' *Ephraim shall possess the country of Samaria* ' (this reading involves the rejection of the accusative ' the country of ' before ' Ephraim ', which certainly looks like a confusion), and eastwards Benjamin (the area north of Jerusalem) shall possess

v Galaad (which is across the Jordan). **20.** The extension north and south is further described together with the return of the exiles. A very difficult verse. Many emendations have been proposed. An obvious one is to read *yîr⁰šû* ' shall inherit ' for *'ᵃšer*, providing at least a verb for the first section. The most convincing for *haḥēl hazzeh* is Bewer's reading *baḤᵃlaḥ*,

' in Halah ', which is the place in Assyria whither Israel had been deported, 4 Kg 17:6 ; 18:11 ; 1 Par 5:26, DV ' Hala '. This provides the balance of another place-name, and supports an exilic date for the book. With these emendations the text can be translated, but a slight shuffling provides the following lines with a perfect parallelism :

> ' *And the captivity of the children of Israel which is in Hala shall inherit Canaan as far as Sarepta* [far north of Palestine] ;
> And the captivity of Jerusalem which is in Sepharad shall inherit the cities of the south '.

There remains the problem of *S⁰pārad* : the name comes only here in the OT, and in later Hebrew it indicates ' Spain ' (so that Spanish Jews are still called Sephardim, as opposed to the Ashkenazim or Jews of Central and Eastern Europe). St Jerome said that the Jew who taught him told him it meant the Bosphorus, whither (he said) Hadrian had deported the Jews. St Jerome himself, however, adds that the obvious meaning is somewhere in Babylonia. Modern commentators have suggested Šaparda in Mesopotamia (mentioned in Sargon's inscriptions). Upholders of a date in the Persian period prefer to identify with Sparda (= ? Sardis) in Asia Minor (mentioned in the Behistun inscriptions). **21.** ' Saviours ', the title applied to the heroes of old, Jg 3:9, 15, who delivered the people, though LXX reads the passive, ' those who are saved '. The book ends on a Messianic note, ' And the kingdom shall be for the Lord '.

JONAS

(JONAH)

By E. F. SUTCLIFFE, S.J.

Bibliography—T. E. Bird. *The Book of Jona* (WV, 1938); A. Condamin, S.J., ' Jonas ' in DAFC ; A. Feuillet, ' Les Sources du Livre de Jonas ' and ' Le Sens du Livre de Jonas' RB 54 (1947) 161–86 ; 340–61 ; P. J. B. Schaumberger, C. SS. R., ' Das Bussedikt des Königs von Ninive bei Jonas ' 3:7–8 ' in *Miscellanea Biblica II* (Roma, 1934) 123–34 ; on a modern, legendary 'Jonas' see E. König ET 17 (Aug. 1906) 521, Lukyn Williams ET 18 (Feb. 1907) 239, E. F. Sutcliffe Mn 153 (1929) 165 f. ; see also the bibliography § 409*b*.

The Prophet Jonas—It is recorded that Jeroboam II (782–753) ' restored the borders of Israel . . . according to the word of the Lord the God of Israel, which he spoke by his servant Jonas, the son of Amathi, the prophet, who was of Geth, which is in Opher ', 4 Kg 14:25. As this prophet and his father have the same names as the prophet of our book and his father, it can hardly be doubted that they are the same persons. Our prophet was, therefore, probably a contemporary of Jeroboam and a member of the Northern Kingdom. Nothing further is known of him beyond what is recorded in our book.

The Author—If there is no conclusive argument that Jonas was himself the author of the book, neither is there that he was not. Only he could have been the source of the story narrated and it is perhaps more probable that the frank delineation of the prophet's shortcomings is from his own pen than from that of another. The statement that ' Nineveh was a great city ', 3:3, does not prove that the narrative was written after 612 B.C. when the city was destroyed, any more than St John's remark that ' Bethania was near Jerusalem about fifteen furlongs off ', 11:18, proves that Bethania was no longer near Jerusalem nor of the same distance away at the time he wrote his Gospel. The sacred writers often speak in this way of the precise point in hand while prescinding from other aspects of the question. The knowledge of Hebrew usage at different times and places is too scanty for any decisive argument to be derived from the occurrence in the book of certain Aramaisms. The allusions to late psalms in Jonas' prayer are of doubtful evidential value, since it is probably a later addition ; and the argument from borrowings or allusions is apt to be a two-edged weapon.

Doctrine—The central doctrine of the book is the universality of Gods' love and providence extending beyond the bounds of the Chosen People to pagan nations. It contains also the important type of Christ's Resurrection, Mt 12:40. Yahweh is the God of heaven, who made earth and sea. All is subject to his rule. He sends the storm, calms the sea, provides shade and destroys it. Nineveh, a pagan city, is entirely in his power. His wisdom has means to secure the compliance of unwilling man. Evil displeases him and calls for just punishment, but he is merciful and moved to pardon by the penance even of pagans, and he hears their prayers for temporal benefits. His loving providence embraces all his creatures including infants and dumb animals. His desire is to spare them all.

The Historical Character of the Book—The Book of Jonas occurs among the prophetical writings but has the form of historical narrative. The explanation is that a prophet is one who has a mission from God and delivers the message that God puts into his mouth.

Jonas was sent by God to Nineveh and preached as **531e** God bade him, 1:2 ; 3:2. He uttered one prediction, 3:4, but such foretelling of the future is no necessary part of a prophet's function ; see § 409*e*.

Is the narrative intended to set forth actual happenings or is it a pious fiction designed to teach a lesson ? The guidance given by the Church shows the possibility of such literature as symbolic history being inspired and canonical ; see §§ 52*j*, 53*l*. The question is an open one. Until recent times, however, the historical character of this narrative was never seriously doubted in the Church. Now several Catholic authors, such as Van Hoonacker and Condamin, have denied or questioned it. They explain the book as a parable or in some similar way.

The following reasons may be urged in favour of the **f** historicity of the narrative. The story is narrated in the same simple direct way as are, for instance, the historical narratives of Elias and Eliseus. Not only does our Lord say, ' As Jonas was in the belly *of the sea-monster* three days and three nights, so shall the son of man be in the heart of the earth three days and three nights ' ; not only does he speak of the men of Nineveh doing penance at the preaching of Jonas in exactly the same way as he speaks of the queen of the South coming to hear the wisdom of Solomon ; he goes beyond what is found in the Book of Jonas and adds that ' the men of Nineveh shall rise in judgement with this generation and shall condemn it ', Mt 12:40–42. If the men of Nineveh did not do penance but are only imagined to have done so, what force would there be in Christ's words ?

Moreover, the prophet Jonas is shown to have acted in ways far from virtuous. He is disobedient to Yahweh's command, 1:3 ; he is angry at God's pardon of the Ninevites, 4:1 ; he shows impatience at his own physical discomfort, 4:8 ; he even addresses God disrespectfully, 4:9. If Jonas was guilty of these defects, it is intelligible that they should have been put on record, as have so many defects of the Apostles in the NT. But if Jonas did not act thus at all, the narrative would be inexplicable. It is hardly credible that an inspired writer should, without any basis in fact, have cast such aspersions on the character of one known from the Books of Kings to have been a prophet of God.

Some of the great Fathers speak strongly on the matter. St Augustine in answering a query sent by a friend mentions that the story of Jonas was derided by the pagans. He proceeds : ' The answer to this is that either belief must be withheld from all divine miracles, or there is no reason why this should not be believed. We should not believe that Christ himself rose on the third day, if the faith of Christians feared the jeers of pagans. But as our friend has not asked the question whether it should be believed that Lazarus was raised on the fourth day or whether Christ himself rose on the third day, I find it very astonishing that he sets down the incident about Jonas as incredible, unless perchance he thinks it easier for a dead man to be raised from the tomb than for a living man to be preserved in the great belly of a beast ', PL 33, 382. Similarly St Jerome : ' I am not unaware that some will consider it incredible that a man threatened with ship-wreck could have been preserved three days and

531f three nights in the belly of a sea-monster. These, of course, will be either believers or unbelievers. If they are believers, they will be obliged to believe much greater things : how three youths cast into a furnace of blazing fire were so completely unharmed that not even their clothes smelt of fire . . . and much of the same kind ', PL 25, 1132. Again St Cyril of Jerusalem, speaking of Jonas saved in the fish and of Christ's resurrection, says : ' If the former is credible, so is the latter ; if the latter is incredible, so is the former ', PG 33, 848.

St Gregory of Nazianzen treats the story as historical, PG 35, 505–8, 953 ; 36, 596. The fact that he draws an allegorical meaning from the name of Joppe, PG 35, 508, is comparable to St Gregory the Great's mystical interpretation of St Peter and St John running to the sepulchre as denoting the Church and the Synagogue respectively. In both cases the historical character of the facts is presumed. Theophylact gives an allegorical interpretation of the story proposed, he says, by ' some ' and based by them, he is careful to add, on the historical character of the narrative, PG 126, 960 f. The first part agrees verbally with the allegorical exposition of St Gregory of Nazianzen, PG 35, 508.

g In favour of the fictitious character of the book it is urged that though miracles as such constitute an argument neither for nor against its factual character, still some of the miracles narrated appear bizarre and unworthy of the wisdom of God. It may be answered that if an inspired author had so regarded them, he would not have invented them. Moreover, is it surprising that God should have worked a remarkable miracle as the type of our Lord's resurrection, itself the central miracle of the Christian faith ?

That the book has an important lesson to teach is not, of course, a proof of its being parabolic. That the fatherly care of God embraces not only the Hebrews but even the pagan nations hostile to Israel is a lesson more cogently taught if God actually sent a prophet to preach penance to the Ninevites than if such a mission is merely a pious imagination. But it is urged that this lesson points to a time of narrow nationalistic outlook on the ground that a prophet's message is directed against prevailing tendencies, and that the book is thus indicated as post-exilic and non-factual. Against this may be quoted striking pre-exilic expressions of universalism such as Is 2:2–4.

Another argument urges the absence of many details said to be required in a narrative meant to be historical, such as where on the coast Jonas was restored to land, and the name of the king of Nineveh. This seems to rest on a misunderstanding of the nature of Hebrew historical narrative. History in the Bible is never related for its own sake, but for its religious significance. Consequently, as can be observed also in the Gospels, it did not occur to the sacred writers to set down many facts that we moderns should like to know.

Finally the inherent improbability of certain features of the story is said to favour its purely didactic character. But truth is stranger than fiction, and a writer composing his own story would presumably take pains to conform with verisimilitude. Certain other points are touched on in the notes and in § 531c.

532a **I 1-3 The Flight of Jonas**—To avoid the unwelcome task of preaching repentance to the Assyrians, who were the enemies of his people and whose capital was Nineveh, Jonas decides to escape as far from Palestine as possible. He, therefore, takes ship for Tarshish, probably Tartessus in Spain, at the other end of the then known world. As he proclaims himself to be a worshipper of Yahweh, ' the God of heaven, who made both the sea and the dry land ', 1:9, he cannot have imagined that he could escape from God. Still, in fleeing from the Holy Land he was escaping from the face of the Lord, as God had there manifested himself in an especial manner and he appears to have hoped that after this sign of determined reluctance God would leave him alone. ' To stand before the face of God '

is to be in his special service ', 3 Kg 17:1 ; 18:15, and this special service Jonas wished to avoid.

4-10 Jonas in the Storm—' Jonas *had gone* down into the *hold* of the ship ' and fallen into a deep sleep before the storm arose. Like our Lord, also overtaken in sleep by a dangerous storm, Jonas was not awakened by its violence. He was overcome by the fatigue and emotion of his flight ; *cf.* Lk 22:45. The lot fell on Jonas, as St Jerome says, not through any power inherent in the method of casting lots, but ' by the will of him who guided the chances of the lot ' ; *cf.* Act 1:26. To discover the nature of his crime the sailors interrogated him. They knew whither Jonas was going, but asked ' *Whence comest* thou ? '.

11-16 Calm over the Sea—Whatever Jonas' defects, he displays true magnanimity in his readiness to die that the crew may be saved. The peril of the storm brings home to him the gravity of his disobedience. Seeing that the others are in danger on his account, whereas he alone deserves punishment, he suggests to the sailors to remove him from the ship by casting him overboard. From the moral point of view this is similar to the action of a person who jumps into the sea from a burning ship. The sailors repay generosity with generosity, pagans though they were, and at the risk of their lives attempt to row back to land. As the men were polytheists, their prayers and sacrifices to Yahweh do not prove that they embraced the religion of Israel, only that they acknowledge his to have been the divine power that saved them.

II 1-2 The Great Fish—It is not said either here or in the Gospels what kind of great fish it was that swallowed Jonas. Both the shark and the sperm whale are found in the Mediterranean and are capable of swallowing a body bigger than a man's. The period of three days and three nights signifies in Hebrew usage a part of three days including the whole of the second day; *cf.* Est 4:16 ; 5:1 ; Mt 12:40. As Jonas prayed in the belly of the fish, 2:2, it does not seem possible to hold that he died and was restored to life.

3-10 Jonas's Prayer—The prayer recorded does not purport to give exactly the prayer the prophet prayed. Reminiscences of the psalms readily occur in the prayers of those who constantly recite them. Jonas cried out of the belly of Sheol (or the underworld), but this does not imply his actual death ; *cf.* Ps 85:13, ' Thy mercy is great towards me ; and thou hast delivered my soul out of the lower hell '—the prayer of one delivered from what was only imminent danger of death. To be cast away out of the sight of God's eyes is to be far removed from his temple, where he had deigned to manifest his presence. The mountains are spoken of as sending their roots down into the depths of the sea. Those that observe empty vanities are the worshippers of idols, and such forsake God the source of all mercy.

III 1-4 Jonas preaches in Nineveh—This time Jonas has learnt his lesson and at once obeys the divine command. According to Diodorus Siculus II 3 the circumference of Nineveh measured 480 stadia and Herodotus V 53 assigns 150 stadia to a day's march. These figures have suggested the idea that ' a great city of three days' journey ' meant one so great that three days would be required to pass round its circumference. But this does not fit the following words that Jonas began ' to enter the city one day's journey '. This shows that the three days are used hyperbolically of the time required to pass through the city. No one will have supposed that the city actually extended in a straight line for some 60 miles. See also on 4:11. The message preached by Jonas quickly became known throughout the city and the inhabitants believed and began to do penance. Although the sentence of destruction was preached in an absolute form of words, the Ninevites understood that God would revoke his sentence and spare them if they did penance, 3:9. Jonas also knew that the sentence was conditional, 4:2. ' Forty days ' is the reading of HT and Vg, ' three days ' that of LXX.

5-10 The Effect of the Preaching—The fast was observed presumably from sunrise to sunset in accordance with oriental custom, and was to last till God's pardon was assured by the continued safety of the city.

Surprisingly enough, the story has been classed as didactic fiction on the ground that there is no record in the Assyrian monuments of any change from polytheism. But our text does not hint at any such conversion, and the repentance from wrong-doing was not likely to be recorded. The conversion may well have been aided by calamities that befell the Assyrians about the middle of the 8th cent. The records of several years speak of civil disturbances and pestilence. It is surprising that the animals should have been included in the fast and covered with sackcloth. Some think that the mention of them in connexion with the sackcloth is an accidental repetition from the previous verse ; but this explanation is not necessary. We ourselves garb our horses in black at funerals. As regards the fast, it would appear that the Ninevites wanted universal penance and universal manifestations of it without considering philosophically what the effect of the animal fast could be. And Schaumberger has shown that it accords perfectly with known Assyrian custom.

IV 1-4 Jonas grudges Nineveh Its Pardon—Jonas would not have attempted to avoid his mission, had he believed that God would actually destroy the city. He was guilty of an unforgiving spirit, a certain national vindictiveness. As he knew God's mercy, patience and readiness to forgive (*cf.* Ps 85:5 ; Jl 2:13), he had foreseen the pardon ; but when it actually came, he was so moved by chagrin that he grew tired of life. **532h** God's expostulation meets with no response in the heart of the angry prophet. Subsequent events force him to see reason.

5-11 Jonas' Lesson concerning his Fault and the i Loving-kindness of God—In 5 omit ' then ', an addition in DV and against the sense. Jonas had gone out of the city after his preaching and before it was plain that God had granted a pardon. Hence some think that this verse was originally after 3:9. But although misplaced in the chronological order of events, the verse is in its original position. Hebrew writers—and this important point is often overlooked—attend at times more to the grouping of their matter than to chronological sequence. 5 is entirely in place as introduction to the account of the marvellous growth and destruction of the broad-leaved plant that gave him such welcome protection from the fierce heat of the sun, for which purpose the shack he had put up for himself was inadequate. This plant is called ' ivy ' in Vg for the simple reason that St Jerome could not find a more suitable equivalent in Latin. Probably it was the castor-oil plant or a gourd. Worms quickly destroyed it—not ' a worm ', as Hebrew often uses a singular noun in a collective sense. **11.** By this incident God brings home to the prophet what were the divine sentiments towards the inhabitants of Nineveh, pagan city though it was, and how loth he was to destroy the men—and the beasts—he had made. The number of inhabitants cannot be computed from the figure given for infants and small children. The expression denotes graphically and hyperbolically the great size of the city. On the number 120 = 60 × 2 see on Gen 6:3.

MICHEAS

By K. SMYTH, S.J.

533a Bibliography—See § 409*b*.

b The Prophet—Micheas is the sixth of the Minor Prophets in MT and Vg, but follows Osee and Amos in LXX : that is chronologically better, for he was a younger contemporary of Osee, though his long ministry covered nearly the same years as that of Isaias (*c* 740–695). His name 'Who is like Yahweh' is not uncommon. It had been borne by a ninth-century prophet (3 Kg 22), from whom he is distinguished by the epithet 'the Morasthite', after his birth-place *Môrešet-Gat*, a village about 30 miles SW. of Jerusalem.

c His Message—Two prophecies of Micheas' deeply impressed his countrymen : the threat to Jerusalem, and the promise of a Saviour from Bethlehem. Both are at the heart of his message ; which is, that Israel's hope would indeed be fulfilled, but only after deep humiliation and loss. Like Amos and Osee, he had to warn Israel that 'the Day of the Lord', for which the people longed, would be 'Darkness and not Light'. It would not be a triumphant vindication of Israel, in view of the promises, by a divine judgement upon the nations, but a grim purging of Israel, in view of her sins, by a catastrophe which would indeed involve the world. Israel was not to advance in unbroken prosperity to the place of rest, but was to meet with a disaster in which both the bearers and the object of the promises were to be transformed ; and the Day of the Lord was to come finally, not by human merit, but only from the mercy of God.

d With his contemporary Isaias, Micheas now proclaims that Israel is to be reduced to a 'remnant' before she can be worthy of the 'faithful mercy' promised of old to Abraham (Mic 7:20). To the scattering of the Northern Kingdom must be added the ruin of Jerusalem itself (3:12) ; and the ultimate gathering together of the sundered and exiled Kingdoms will be the work of a mighty Ruler from a tiny village. Thus in the womb of 'a Mother' (5:3) the promised Salvation takes the form of a Saviour, whose history is mysteriously eternal.

e The doom of Samaria and Jerusalem is placed in a cosmic setting (1:2), because it is prelude and route to the establishment of the new Sion to which all nations stream (4:1 ff.). For this Israel is to be prepared by a change of heart, when not merely her sin is purged (7:19), but even her reliance on human aids (5, 9 ff.) and her attachment to local and transitory religious forms give way to adoration in spirit and truth (6:6). Parallel always is the execution of judgement on the nations *superbe delirantes*, blinded by their brief triumphs (4:12), yet coming to feel the weight of God's hand (4:13 ; 5, 5 ff. ; 7:13). Thus they too learn 'to be ashamed of their strength', and come in humble reverence to adore (7:16 f.).

f Micheas therefore announces a Universal Judgement, which strikes the Northern Kingdom first, then overwhelms Judah, and envelopes the nations. Sent as he was, however, to Jerusalem, he is chiefly occupied with exhorting his own people of the south. The fate of the nations is in the background, but part of the one process of redemption. They are broken, judged and taught by one who rules in the might of 'the Lord of all the earth'. Micheas' vision, for all its limitations, is still of God's great plan : ' to enclose all in disobedience, that he may have mercy on all ' (Rom 11:32).

This is the inner unity of Micheas' message. His statement indeed is often fragmentary and obscure ; this arises from the very pregnancy of his oracles, which are but the representative summaries of a long ministry. But a deeper source of obscurity lies in the fact that one great principle was not yet made clear : that suffering is not merely the punishment of sin, but the very means of redemption. Only when the woes of the world are revealed as shared and sanctified by the Just Servant of God are they seen in their true and necessary relation to redemption. But enough was revealed to Micheas to give a consistent picture of the ways of God to men.

The Unity of the Book— The misgivings of some critics, therefore, with regard to the unity of the book, need not be taken seriously. They were based on the principle that no pre-exilic prophet could combine hope of salvation with threat of doom. But here they offended gravely against all religious sense. For no prophet could seriously seek to convert his people by holding out only unconditional threats of irreparable disaster. But the critics missed also the whole trend of prophecy as the historical facts show it. How vivid and widespread were the hopes raised by the traditional promises to Abraham, in whose seed all the nations of the earth should be blessed, is amply shown by Amos' challenge to the common view of the ' Day of the Lord ', and by Osee's and Isaias' efforts to correct the principles of that hope. Micheas had a like task. There is no question of their denying the hope of Israel. They are its spokesmen, but have to re-affirm the necessity of Israel's keeping the Covenant in purity of heart. If they foresaw her failure, it was only to proclaim that God indeed would make good his promises ; now by saving but a remnant in the shadow of the Cross.

I-III Sin and Punishment of Israel — The first section of the prophecy attributes the ruin of Samaria to the sins of the Northern Kingdom, and threatens Jerusalem with a like fate. The Temple itself will not save Judah ; for the presence of the Holy One of Israel is regarded perversely as a shield for sin, and not recognized as a call to repentance.

1:2-5 The Wrath to come—Not only the earth and the nations, but God himself witnesses against the sins of Israel. **3-4.** And when his holiness flames forth to destroy sin, it is more terrible than thunderstorm and earthquake. **5.** Such a judgement will come upon Israel, whose two capitals have been no better than idol-shrines corrupting the land.

6-9 The Doom of Samaria—**6.** Of the city crowning the hill there will be left only a few stones : *and* there vineyards may be planted, so bare will the site remain. **7-9.** Her *riches* will go with her idols : for they came from worldly trading and must go back to the profane traffic of the nations. The city had already been sacked by 720. But Micheas sees that the ruin is final and that the shadow darkens over Jerusalem also.

10-16 The Invasion in Vision—The enemy threatens the city from the south-west, and the names of the towns in his path become omens of disaster. Micheas

672

34d begins with a reminiscence of David's lament over Saul and Jonathan (2 Kg 1:20)—as if we should say : ' If you have tears prepare to shed them now,' though here it is said that tears are vain. **10.** In *Beth-le-'Aprāh* ' House of Dust' there will be cause for grief. **11.** *Šāphir* ' Beautiful Place ' must fly in disorder ; *Ṣa'anān* (as if ' Landscape ') has no escape ; *Beth-hā-'Ēṣel's* (as if ' Bystand ') *mourning will deprive you of the stay* which she seemed to promise. **12.** ' *Though she has yearned for good things, she that dwells in Mārôt'* (' Bitterness '), yet is evil coming upon her '. **13.** Lachis must *yoke the steed to the chariot* (*rakš*) and fly. The great station on the route to Egypt is called the beginning of sin ; the reason is not clear. **14.** Therefore must Israel give up *Mōreset-Gat* ; lit. give farewell-presents for it, that is, the portion given away with a bride. *Mōreset* may suggest ' bride ' as well as ' inheritance '. And *Akzib* (the town's name means a river which fails in summer) is truly a deceitful hope. **15.** God will bring *one who dispossesses* to take over Maresa, whose name again suggests ' inheritance ' : and once more shall Israel be homeless and hunted like David in the caves of Odollam. **16.** Hence Micheas bids Israel mourn. Isaias (chh 10 and 15) uses the same literary form to describe invasions ; Micheas here adds the note of inevitability to disaster by linking it to the very names of the threatened towns.

e II:1-5 The Doom and its Cause — **1.** Men have set their hearts on sin ; the evil which they *plan*, they execute vigorously *because their hand has strength* to do so, and they know no other law. **2.** They evict the poor from their holdings, demolishing their cottages to make way for great estates, *cf.* Is 5:8. **3.** But God too has his plans ; and upon the nation which tolerates such things, he will lay a still heavier yoke. **4.** The day will come when Israel itself is despoiled and her grief echoed mockingly : ' We are laid waste and spoiled ; the portion of my people is changed : *how it departs from me! To the infidel he divides our land'*. **5.** And none of the Chosen People shall be left, to cast measuring-line on a plot of the Promised Land.

f 6-7 The Covenant and the Doom—**6.** Like other prophets, *e.g.* Amos (*cf.* Am 5) and Isaias (*cf.* Is 28), Micheas was contradicted. False prophets now speak, insisting that Yahweh has committed himself to the protection of Israel. ' *Prophesy not, they prophesy : one may not prophesy such things. Confusion shall not come upon us.'* **7.** Therefore the house of Jacob flatters itself that the Lord is not impatient ; such is not his way. And Micheas must reaffirm the true terms of the Covenant : ' Nay rather, it is with him who walketh uprightly that God makes good his word '.

g 8-10 The Doom and its Justice — **8.** They have forfeited their claims upon God by their violence and injustice : have taken away the cloak from off the coat *from them that passed harmless, from men averse to war.* **9.** They have driven out unprotected women, and taken from the children the rich blessings which God had designed for his people. **10.** Therefore the Promised Land can be no lasting city or place of rest, *cf.* Deut 12:9 ; it has been defiled by sin, and it shall be *devastated*, grievously *devastated.*

h   11. Knowing himself disdained, Micheas denounces the spirit of the times : ' *If a man going after windy falsehood should lying say : I will prophesy to thee of wine and strong drink'*, that is, encourage the people in their coarse and sensual habits, ' *he indeed could be prophet for this people'.*

i 12-13 Refugees and their Miraculous Salvation—This is a fragment out of its context ; it would suit better 4:6 ff. For its promise of restoration could well follow upon a threat of punishment, but hardly upon a denunciation of sin. The imagery is taken from the raising of a siege. **12.** All who have fled before the invader God has gathered in a place of safety, like sheep in the fold : ' *it shall hum with men'.* **13.** And then from behind their defences, they shall march out in triumph, their king, protected by the Lord, leading

them, as Moses under Yahweh's guidance led the **534i** Exodus. The prophecy refers at least typically to the Messias. Such a scene was enacted at the time of Sennacherib's invasion 701.

III:1-4 Micheas before the Princes — **1-3.** The **j** judges whose duty it was to uphold justice have only plundered the people. Their savagery is compared to the butchering of cattle for food. **4.** But the time of distress will come, when they will cry in vain to the Lord, as the poor have cried in vain to them.

5-8 True Prophet against False — The false prophets **k** make all depend on their receiving gifts. Flattering the great and conniving at injustice, they insist that all is well ; though in reality the encouragement which they give is as dangerous as a serpent's bite (**5a**). ' Bite with the teeth and preach peace ' may however be taken with **5b** and then would mean : As long as they may eat their fill, they answer ' All is well '. But if anyone refuses them gifts, they denounce and menace him. **6-7.** They were never inspired instruments of revelation. But they had a certain semi-official standing, beside the priests, as exponents of the revelations contained in the Sacred Books. They constantly travestied the Covenant by reducing it to a charm against danger, and surrounded their oracles with the apparatus of wizardry. They could point to prosperity as a proof of their words of comfort. But ' the Day of the Lord, darkness and not light ' would disgrace and destroy them. They will be able to give no explanation of their former assurances ; and like the prophets of Baal on Carmel, at the time of testing, they will call in vain on their God. **8.** In face of these sycophants, who dared not oppose the holiness of God's law to the sins of the great, the true prophet stands forth conscious of his divine call, with authority to challenge the world ; he has strength from the Spirit of the Lord, he has a keen sense of justice, he has courage to denounce a nation's sins.

9-12 The Fall of Jerusalem—Accused of one great **l** conspiracy of venality, fraud and oppression, now prince and judge, as well as prophet and priest, are confronted with the most terrible threat of all, the destruction of the Holy City and the Temple. It amazed and shocked them like a blasphemy. **10.** But the real offence against the inviolable holiness of God was to strengthen and embellish his city through forced labour and unjust exactions. **11.** It was a delusion to rely on God the essentially holy, in order to sin with impunity. **12.** Therefore, for the sins of the nation's representatives, only possible because the people as a whole were ready accomplices, the nation's centre and sanctuary shall be reduced to a wilderness.

For a similar threat to the Temple, a hundred years later, priests and false prophets demanded the death of Jeremias. He was only saved by the intervention of some of the Elders, recalling the prophecy of Micheas and asking : ' Did then Ezechias, the King of Judah, and the whole people, kill him for it ? Was not Ezechias rather moved to fear the Lord and to placate him, so that God was pleased to repent of the evil with which he had threatened them ? ' (*cf.* Jer 26). Thus the people were moved to repentance, and Micheas had the reward of the true prophet : the conversion effected by his preaching averted for a time the punishment which he had foretold.

IV-V Messianic Hopes—Micheas never revoked his **535a** sentence of doom. It was but suspended, and as the Assyrian armies swept through the land on various campaigns between 720 and 700, the execution of the sentence must often have seemed imminent. But Micheas was granted a vision full of splendid hope, which shone steadily beyond and above the dark ways ahead. He saw that God would establish before the eyes of all men, a universal Kingdom of justice and peace. And he saw something of the coming of the Kingdom. There would be disaster first, and the people of God sadly diminished. But there would

535a come at last a 'King from the hand of God', sent to save and make prosper the Kingdom of God.

b **IV:1-5 The Messianic Jerusalem Centre of the World's Worship**—**The last days** are the final stage of revelation. They run from the time of the last great intervention of God in human history, when all types and shadows have been fulfilled, when no more revelation will be added, when the New and Eternal Testament is in force : from the foundation of the Church to the end of the world. **1.** Under the image of a Jerusalem towering above the surrounding hills, Micheas sees the divinely appointed source of light and holiness revealed to all men. It is 'prepared', that is, 'established', high above the hills, supreme and conspicuous as it is enduring. **2.** It is only from the New Sion that God will teach men his truth and the way of life : here appears the Church Visible with all the notes of Universality, Uniqueness and Divine Authority. **3-4.** There too God arbitrates and gives judgement for the destinies of nations ; by the heavenly light of which Sion is the centre, all can direct their actions. The crude appeal to force is outlawed. No happy age of universal disarmament and mutual trust has ever in literal fact graced the pages of history. But the prophecy does not speak of material good things. The promise of the New Testament is Eternal Life, and the spiritual blessings which lead to it. And in fact the Church is in glad and quiet possession of infallible truth which no error can endanger, and of sanctifying graces which neither unworthy ministers can impede nor human frailty exhaust. Thus in the indefectible holiness of the Church of Christ, each Christian finds that heavenly peace which the world can neither give nor take away. And this is promised by the 'Lord of Hosts', as if solemnly invoking all his power and majesty. **5.** The call to the Kingdom is universal ; though as yet the peoples are still serving their idols, they are bound to follow the example of Israel and worship the one true God.

c **6-7 Exile and Salvation**—The vision changes from the lofty and distant prospect of Messianic peace, to the dark and painful ways through which it must come. The most flourishing, extensive and populous part of the Holy Land, the Northern Kingdom, had already been ravaged, and great numbers of the people transported. Judah too was suffering from the Assyrian campaigns. Under Sennacherib only Jerusalem itself escaped. To prophets like Isaias and Micheas, for whom North and South made but one indivisible 'People of God', the First Exile had already begun. It is then of a crushed and diminished Israel that God promises now to make a 'Remnant', the vigorous nucleus of a new Kingdom, which will never fail, for it is protected by God's own royal power.

d **8-10 A Call to Confidence in God**—**8.** '*And thou, Tower of the Flock, Hill of the Daughter of Sion, unto thee shall it come, yea, the former realm shall return.*' After all losses, the rule of Israel will expand again to the full extent of God's promises, symbolized of old in the dominions of Solomon. **9.** She must not despair ; there is yet on the throne a ruler from the house of David, to whom God had sworn 'I will establish the throne of his kingdom for ever' (2 Kg 7:13)—and so in the King they have a sign of God's protection. **10.** But there is indeed cause for grief. Incredible disaster must come first. For now (the future vividly present to the prophet) the city must surrender to its foes and the inhabitants march out defenceless, to be exiled and scattered among the towns of the Assyrian Empire, notably Babylon. Not in Jerusalem will they find salvation (*cf.* 2:10) ; they will not in the end be preserved from exile, but exiled and then delivered. It is a greater sign of God's power to raise from the dead than to preserve from death.

e **11-V 1 Quare Fremuerunt Gentes!**—From regarding a particular event, the Exile, the vision changes to embrace the whole course of history : seeing the kingdoms of this world massed against the Kingdom of God.

Once more the future is vividly present. The enemies **53** of God's people assert the sovereignty of their gods. **11.** 'Let her be *profaned*, that we may gloat over Sion's ruin.' Her inviolable holiness is to be proved a sham ; in her moment of weakness, they can ask (*cf.* 7:11) 'Where then is her God?' **12.** But their brief triumphs are only apparent. In reality they are gathered together only to work out God's purposes ; they shall not crush the Kingdom of God, but they themselves shall be crushed '*like sheaves on the threshing-floor*'. **13.** God can raise up what seems to have gone down in ruin. And to fallen Sion the call will come, to rise up and *trample upon* those sheaves. For her God is 'Lord of the whole earth' and all nations must learn, if needs be by being broken, that all their work and wealth is to be dedicated to the service of God. **V:1.** But before turning to the Messias, under whom the Kingdom shall prevail, Micheas mourns once more the disasters of Israel ; she is called *Robber-daughter*, because herself so long engaged in robbery (*cf.* chh 2 and 3).

V 2-6 The Ruler from Bethlehem — Just as the **f** threat of doom pronounced over Jerusalem (3:12) gave way to the serene contemplation of the new Jerusalem to which all nations stream ; so now to the humiliation of Sion's king (4:14) succeeds the triumph of the Messias. God will intervene to restore the promised realm to Sion. But now his power is to be enshrined in the person of a Ruler who arises, not from royal Jerusalem, but from lowly Bethlehem. It was indeed 'a little one among the *seats of the clans* of Judah' ('thousands' is used here locally, like the English 'hundreds' or 'tithings'). It had figured as David's birthplace, but was too inconsiderable to play any further part in the history of the royalty. First Hebron and then Jerusalem had been chosen as seat of David's government. But Bethlehem was to be glorified by the birth of the Messias. Hence, Mt 2, the Jews answer the Magi according to the implications of the prophecy : 'And thou, Bethlehem . . . not the least among the princes of Judah', that is, not least in dignity, though small in size. So the Epiphany hymn :

> O sola magnarum urbium
> Maior Bethlehem, cui contigit
> Ducem salutis coelitus
> Incorporatum gignere.

2a. The solemnity of the moment calls for the place's full title : Bethlehem, of (the district of) Ephrata, of Judah ; to add 'Ephrata' and 'Judah' was immemorial when speaking of Bethlehem. All texts and versions read Bethlehem, though LXX adds 'house of' before Ephrata—an insertion found elsewhere in the Greek. Thus this striking prophecy is as well-established as it is definite. Bethlehem means 'House of Bread' and Ephrata, 'Fruitful'.

2b. There the Ruler, raised up by God's power, **g** marching out in God's cause ('unto me') will appear. Jewish and Christian tradition always understood this, rightly, of the birth of the Messias in Bethlehem. Thence indeed the Ruler goes forth in the flesh ; but his personal history does not begin there. For he has been going forth from of old ; he has an origin hidden in the depths of eternity. 'His going forth' is plural in the Hebrew, and suggests 'activities, appearances'. The word is used of the sun's setting out on its course (Ps 18:7) ; of companies marching out, and, in the common phrase, 'goings out and comings in', to denote activities in general. 'From the beginning' etc. are the widest possible terms for eternity, used of the strictly divine (Prov 8:23), though of patriarchal times (Is 51:9). To the coming Ruler, then, are ascribed activities of old, such as were the interventions of the Angel of Yahweh in the destinies of Abraham, Jacob, Moses, etc. ; *cf.* Is 63:9 'The Angel of his face saved them . . . all the days of old'. This teaches the heavenly pre-existence of the Ruler, previous to his birth in Bethlehem. Thus it foreshadows 1 Cor 10:12

535g 'From the spiritual Rock which followed them they drank: but the Rock was Christ'. '*Goings forth*', however, may also be taken as equivalent to an abstract noun 'origin': hence Vg and Syr. *egressus*. It would then mean 'His origin, that is, birth, is most ancient'. This is of course implied above; to have been active, he must have existed from of old. The full literal sense, as expounded by Catholic tradition, is the eternal origin of the Son from the Father. Many moderns follow the later Rabbis in reducing the meaning of 2c to 'His ancestry shall be the ancient (Davidic) one'. But this would not distinguish the coming Ruler from Ezechias or his son; and the antiquity of David's family was no greater than that of other Israelite clans, all deriving from the Patriarchs. To understand it of his having 'ancient titles to royalty' is to re-write the text. It is to be noted against the modern interpretation that 'origin' here cannot mean source, *e.g.* dynasty, in the sense of something preceding and distinct from that which comes forth. It means only the person himself, but viewed at his origin, birth or going forth. The person of the Ruler, then, must be mysteriously eternal.

h 3. Because it is God's plan to raise up a Saviour, not from royal Sion, but from Bethlehem, he will leave Israel at the mercy of her enemies, *till a Mother bears child*. Then begin God's blessings, with the return of the Child's exiled brothers. Abrupt and succinct, this prophecy evidently supposes a great current of Messianic prophecy then familiar to all. It harmonizes perfectly with Isaias 7:14. There is the same sign of deliverance: the appearance of a Mother, the coming of the Child, then the return of the exiles; *cf.* Is 7:3 'A Remnant will Return'. Through the centuries which prophetic vision has to pierce, only figures gigantic in their import can be distinguished. But, however indistinctly perceived, a Woman looms large throughout the great prophecies of Redemption. In the Proto-Evangel Gen 3, in Isaias and in Micheas salvation comes through one who always associates with himself a Mother. Thus the Catholic Church follows out fundamental lines of revelation in the honour paid to the Virgin Mary, Mother of God, and in acknowledging her significance in the economy of Redemption.

i j 4. The Ruler takes his stand to guard his kingdom, as the Shepherd takes a commanding position to guard his flock. He is not merely invested with authority from God, like Saul or David, but he embodies marvels of divine majesty and might (*cf.* Is 11:2). And so his people *dwell secure*, for now (again the future made vividly present) his power and prestige shall embrace the whole earth. For Isaias, the ruler is the Prince of Peace (*cf.* Is 9 and 11). Micheas now sums up the Messianic blessings in words alluded to in Eph 2:14; '*And he shall be peace*' (5a), that is, source of peace. Should then the Assyrian, named here because forerunner and representative of the enemies of God's people, attempt to invade the land, there will be an abundance of great leaders to ward them off. 5b. The numbers rising in gradation signify 'enough and more than enough'. 6. They will even lay waste the hostile countries; thus the Messias, using human means, just as his own human nature is instrument of God, is to bring victory. Ps 44 too associates human princes with the work of the Messianic King: 'Constitues eos principes super omnem terram'.

k 7-9 Israel Supreme — Like rain which men can neither bring down nor hinder, like the lion whom none dare challenge, the new Kingdom is absolutely independent of man and his works. Its mission is divine. Therefore the Church can neither depend on human aid, nor be subject to the temporal power, nor need she fear it. Note that it is not said here that Israel will be a blessing to the nations nor again, that Israel will be a menace to them, as if the beneficial effect of rain (7) were contrasted with the ravages of the lion (8). The point of the comparison is that they cannot be con-

trolled by man: and so the Church must be sovereign **535k** and supreme. The section ends with a conventional cry of triumph (9).

10-14 The Land in Messianic Times — After the **l** Prince and his victories (2-6), and the People's role in the world (7-9), Micheas describes the Land (10-13), ending with a glance beyond its borders (14).

Israel had long relied on armament and fortified city 'in forgetfulness of his Creator' (*cf.* Os 8:14). Now all that shall be swept away. **10-11.** It is not a period of devastation that is here foretold, but the disappearance of martial installation. The gates of the city lie open day and night (*cf.* Is 60) because God alone is the one and sufficient defence. The Kingdom is not of this world, and needs no worldly weapons. **12-13.** Not only shall the worship of the true God prevail, but he shall be rightly worshipped. No superstitious elements shall debase the true religion. This prophecy echoes the long campaign of Isaias and Micheas against pagan infiltrations into the cult of Yahweh. The statues (12) were the large stone pillars of the Canaanite cult, the *maṣṣēbōt*; the groves (13) were the *'ašērîm*, wooden emblems of a female divinity set up beside the altar of Baal. These had been copied in Israel's own sanctuaries; and the reforms of Ezechias bear witness to Micheas' successful polemic against the forms of worship used on the 'High Places'. **14.** Finally Micheas returns to the universal call of the nations (*cf.* 4:1 ff.; 5:4) with the warning that the call can be disregarded by them only to their own ruin. Christ and his Church are necessary to the world, even for the kind of peace which the world seeks.

VI-VII The Trial, Sentence and Pardon of Israel — **536a** A judicial process was announced against Israel in 1:2, which was continued in fact to the end of ch 5. Now the process is resumed, almost in formal terms, with dramatic changes of speaker. A serener tone, both in grief and joy, may be noted; there is more sadness than anger in the prophet's denunciations, more tenderness than jubilation in his promises.

VI 1-2 The Prophet speaks — He is to make his **b** accusation *over against* the mountains, so that all nature, witness of the enduring goodness of God, may witness to Israel's ingratitude.

3-5 Yahweh speaks — This moving complaint is beauti- **c** fully adapted in the Improperia of Good Friday, to express the feelings of the suffering Redeemer. It is one of the express biblical foundations of devotion to the Most Sacred Heart of Jesus, whose unrequited love calls for reparation (*cf.* 6) — God has never burdened the people with costly sacrifices; on the contrary, he has delivered them from slavery; the curse which Balac intended, he turned to blessing on the lips of Balaam (Num 22); brought them miraculously across the Jordan, from Setim to Galgala and so into the Promised Land. These things are to be remembered; constant meditation on the mysteries of Redemption provides the great motives for a loving service of God.

6-7 The People ask Counsel — Can they placate **d** Yahweh with gifts? They are ready even to give up their firstborn to the good pleasure of God; this either a reminiscence of Abraham's generosity, or perhaps, since every firstborn was 'holy unto the Lord', implying that they will renounce their privilege of buying him back from the service of the Temple. Under the next king, Manasses, human sacrifice was offered to idols. Micheas therefore must have used this figure of speech at a time when there was no danger of its being mis-used to condone something utterly abominated by the prophets. It is therefore an indication that it was written before the time of Manasses.

8-9 The Prophet answers — Justice, charity and care- **e** ful obedience to God come first. Integral and acceptable worship is a union of outward offering with interior dedication of the will. The material gift is precious in the sight of God (*cf.* Ps 49) only by reason of the religious attitude which it embodies. Addressing

536e men whom he is accusing of ingratitude and injustice, Micheas urges a truth often expressed in Sacred Scripture : 'The victims offered by sinners are hateful to the Lord' (*cf.* Prov 15:8). He does not belittle their gifts, but demands that their lives be all that their gifts imply. So too our Lord, when he says : 'He that believes in me, believes not in me, but in him who sent me' (Jn 12:44), does not exclude belief in himself, but points to all it implies.

f 10-16 Yahweh speaks—The people are totally corrupted by injustice and fraud (**10-12**), therefore he condemns them to deprivation and famine (**13-16**). For Jerusalem has committed all the crimes by which the kings of the North brought ruin on Samaria. Therefore she shall be the object of *the world's* scorn.

g VII 1-6 The Prophet—Like one in the stripped and deserted vineyards at the end of autumn, he finds no fruit of good works, to which he might appeal to avert the anger of God. **2.** This recalls our Lord's comment on the world before its Judge : 'When the Son of Man comes, think you that He will find faith upon earth ? ' **3.** '*The evil of their hands they do well ; the prince is exigent, the judge demands bribes, the magnate tells what he wants, and they intrigue together.*' **4-6** describe the breakdown of civil and family loyalties ; *cf.* Mt 10:36. Therefore the city is ripe for the destruction, which the Day *promised by the watchmen* (**4b**), the prophets, will bring.

h 7-10 The People repents—Made the mouthpiece of the prophet's hope, they proclaim their confidence in **530** God, known of old as Saviour, who will hear the cry of the contrite heart (**7**) and raise up in mercy what he has cast down in anger (**8**). Humbly confessing that in punishing them, God has only vindicated his justice, they may hope that now he will vindicate his promises. Only the capital had escaped Sennacherib's ravages, and an enormous tribute had to be paid.

11-13 The Prophet's Comfort—**11.** 'The day will **i** come when thy *defences* are built up ; in that day *shall thy boundary reach far and wide.*' **12.** Israel will hold universal sway (*cf.* 4:1 ff.). For '*from Assyria and from Egypt, from Egypt and even from the River* (Euphrates) ; from sea to sea and from mountain to mountain', that is, from the ends of the earth (*cf.* 5:4) all nations shall come to pay homage. **13.** Whereas the pagan world ' which disobeys' (5:14) must pay the penalty and be laid waste.

14-17 The Prophet's Prayer—**14.** The isolated people **j** is now confined to poor land on Carmel, west of Jordan ; may it regain the rich pastures on the east, which the Promised Land of old included ! **15-17.** May God show again his power in miracles, not merely to help Israel, but to reveal his Godhead to the nations, and so make his worship universal !

18-20 Magnificat !—Micheas' name means ' Who is **k** like God ? ' And he sums up his message in rapt and joyous adoration of his incomparable Majesty. God is most wonderful in his mercy and his love, in his infinite and enduring fidelity.

NAHUM

By S. BULLOUGH, O.P.

7a Bibliography—St Jerome, *Commentarii in Naum Prophetam*, PL 25, 1231–72 ; J. Knabenbauer, S.J., *cf.* § 409*b* ; Van Hoonacker, *cf.* § 409*b* ; *S. R. Driver in CBi, 1906 ; Dom Hugh Bévenot, O.S.B., in WV, 1937.

b The Prophet—All we know is that he was an ' Elcesite ', MT *'Elqōšî*, AV ' Elkoshite '. The place is unknown in OT, but there are three main theories of the identification of Nahum's home.
(1) *Alqush*, about 24 m. N. of Nineveh, where Nahum's tomb is still shown, and is a place of pilgrimage for Christians, Mohammedans and Jews. There is, however, no evidence of this tradition before the 16th cent., and although a birthplace near Nineveh might seem to be supported by Nahum's apparently accurate topography of that city, 2:6(7), and his graphic account of its calamity, it is more probable that this identification was made later on account of his prophecy.
(2) *Elcesi*, a village in Galilee, was proposed by St Jerome (prologue). He writes of ' usque hodie in Galilaea viculus, parvus quidem et vix ruinis veterum aedificiorum indicans vestigia ; sed tamen notus Judaeis, et mihi quoque a circumducente monstratus '. Perhaps = modern el-Kause near Ramah in Galilee (WV, xxiv). Although Carmel and Lebanon are named in 1:4, a Galilean village is unlikely at the time of Nahum, whose interest furthermore centres on Judah, 1:15 (2:1) and 2:2 (3).
(3) *Elqosh* ' beyond Bêth-gabrē of the tribe of Simeon ' is the solution given in *The Lives of the Prophets* attributed (doubtfully) to St Epiphanius, a native of Judaea (403) (PG 43, 409 reconstructed text). Bêth-gabrē probably = the modern Beit-Jibrin (Eleutheropolis), 20 m. SW. of Jerusalem ; about 6 m. E. of this village there is a well called Bir-el-Qaus (Driver). This is the most likely identification. The prophet's name *Naḥûm* means 'comfort', an expanded form being 'Nehemias '.

c The Date of the Prophecy—The mention of the fall of Thebes (No-Amon ; in Egypt) as a past example, in 3:8–10, gives us 663 B.C. as a *terminus a quo*, while the fall of Nineveh in 612, described as impending, gives us a *terminus ad quem*. But the period may be further narrowed by the consideration that Nahum alone among the prophets has no word of vituperation for the Jews, which may indicate the period after 622 when Josias' reforms were in full vigour : his only word to Judah, 1:15 (2:1), is an exhortation to the observance of festivals ; *cf.* 4 Kg 23:21. Nahum's prophecy may have been occasioned by the beginning of Assyria's collapse with the fall of Asshur, 50 m. S. of Nineveh, to the Medes under Kyaxares in 614. A date in this period would make Nah a little later than Soph, contemporary with Jer and a little earlier than Hab.

d The Problem of the Acrostic Poem—Several of the Pss (§ 335*e*), Lam and Prov 31:10–31 are constructed as an alphabetical acrostic, each verse or section beginning with a new letter. It has been observed that Nah 1 contains traces of a similar construction, and since Bickell in 1880 various attempts have been made to reconstruct the text on the basis of the whole alphabet. As it stands, the Heb. text from 1:2 to 1:9 provides an acrostic (with certain lacunae) of the first half of the alphabet. After 1:9 the provision of an

acrostic requires considerable alteration of the text **537d** and shuffling of lines. On these suppositions the opening poem reaches to 2:2 (3), excluding 2:1 (2). (Note that in LXX, Vg and English Bibles 1:15 = HT 2:1, with consequent different verse-numbers in ch 2 ; Heb. vv are placed in brackets in this commentary.) An example of a complete acrostic reconstruction is to be found in Van H. Authors are, however, divided, and the difficulty is that the acrostic in 1:2–9 is so convincing that it is hard to ignore it, while the evidence after this is so vague that it is hard to admit it. It is generally supposed that the section 1:2–2:2(3) represents either a complete acrostic poem, or else part of one followed by another non-acrostic fragment, the whole being prefixed to the prophecy on Nineveh by way of introduction. Authors are also divided about whether the introductory poem or poems are by Nahum himself, or by another, but there is no direct evidence against his authorship, and it seems most likely that he himself made use of relevant sections of other poems of his own to serve as an introduction to his main prophecy. Indeed Nahum's vivid style seems to run through the whole book.

Theme and Analysis of the Book—On the above basis **e** 1:2–15 with 2:2 (1:2–14 with 2:1, 3) are the introductory poem or poems, the theme of which is the power of God and consolation of Judah. The main prophecy begins at 2:1 (2), excludes the misplaced 2:2 (3), and continues to the end of the book. The theme is the fate of Nineveh, the oppressor.

The Style is highly coloured and poetical, representing **f** some of the most vigorous poetry in Hebrew literature, making use not so much of rare words as of unexpected forms, especially of verbs. The metre is often excited and irregular, and the ring of the words, to which we call attention occasionally in the commentary, is by no means entirely obscured in translation.

I 1 The Title—' The burden ' : *cf.* § 550*c*. ' Elcesite ' : **538a** see § 537*b*.
2–15, II 2 (2–14, II 1, 3) **The Introductory Poem(s) : b a Description of God's Power.**
2–6 The Lord is mighty—**2.** This verse begins with *aleph* ('*Ēl*), starting the acrostic. ' Jealous ', a word which with its by-form is used only of God : Knox, well, (explaining) ' a jealous lover '. The Basic OT (1949) has ' who takes care of his honour '. **5.** ' The earth hath quaked ', MT *tiśśā*' ' is lifted up ', so RV ' upheaved '. **6.** ' Are melted ', reading *niṣṣᵉtû*, ' are smashed '.
7. The Lord is good to those that trust him, ' *a refuge* ' **c** in the day of trouble.
8–11 The Lord is Severe—**8.** ' The place thereof '. **d** LXX provides a solution : ' *his rebels* and enemies darkness shall pursue ', so that we can read *bᵉqāmāw*, translating ' make an end of *those who rise against him*, and . . .' ; *cf.* Ps 17 (18) 49. **9.** ' Ye '—God's enemies in general : the poem has no particular application. ' Not a double affliction ' : one is enough to annihilate them. **10.** From the Vg reading ' like (*kᵉ*) thorns ', and *kôh*, ' so ', we can reconstruct, ' *For as tangled thorns* [which burn easily], *so at their drink* [*kôh bᵉsob'ām*] *the drunk have been consumed* '. **11.** ' Contriving treachery in his mind ' : HT ' Counsellor of Belial (= worthlessness) ' ; *cf.* 1:15.

538e **12-15, II 2** (12-14, II 1, 3) **The Second Introductory Poem (or second part of the one): the Consolation of Judah**—The analysis of these verses is difficult and the text uncertain: 13, 14, 15 (2:1), 2:1(2), 2(3) seem to be addressed alternately to Judah and to the oppressor. 2:1(2) (to the oppressor) begins the main prophecy, and it is usually supposed that 2:2(3) (to Judah) should follow upon 1:13, or 1:15 (2:1). The following is an analysis fairly generally held (Van H., WV and *cf.* Driver): 1:12-13 and 2:2(3), the consolation of Judah through her deliverance from the oppressor. 1:14, an oracle against the oppressor. 1:15 (2:1), the promise to Judah of peace. It may be that 14 and 15 are fragments of another poem altogether, used by Nahum to conclude his introduc-

f tion on a hopeful note. **12.** Difficult: DV = MT almost literally. LXX is very different and the whole passage is doubtful. In any case for ' he shall pass ' read ' *they shall pass away* ', adding the pl. termination. **13.** ' His rod with which he struck *thee* '. **II 2** (3). ' Rendered ' for Vg ' reddidit ', *restored* '. ' Pride ',

g or glory, or majesty (WV). **I 14.** WV alters to the 3rd person, ' concerning *him* ' (the oppressor), which eases the transition from the previous v, if this v is indeed part of the same poem. ' The house of thy *gods* '. **15** (2:1). An Isaian figure (52:7), with the exhortation to Judah that suggests the period of reform. ' Belial ', usu. an abstract noun ' worthlessness ' as in 11, and very rarely, as here, applied to a particular person (*cf.* 2 Kg 23:6 and perhaps Job 34:18); Basic OT, well, ' the good-for-nothing man '. The reference is of course to the detested officials of the Assyrian army of occupation, who now will no more be seen in the land.

h II-III The Main Prophecy.

II 1-6 (2-7) **The Attack on Nineveh—1** (2). ' He that shall destroy ', lit. ' The Scatterer ' in MT and Vg. To revocalize as *mappēṣ*, ' shatterer ' (*cf.* Jer 51:20, and the verb 9 t. in 51:21-23) is perhaps more expressive (so WV, *cf.* RV, Basic OT ' crusher '). ' *The Scatterer is come up before thee! Fortify the fortress! Watch the way! Gird* [lit. strengthen] *thy loins! Confirm thy strength!* ' A series of ironic commands to the now hapless oppressor. **3** (4). ' The shield . . . is *reddened* '—either by the sun (WV, *cf.* 1 Mac 6:39), or being of copper, or painted. ' Scarlet ', the colour of the military cloak (*cf.* Mt 27:28 and Xenophon, *Cyrop.* 6, 4, 1) and of more recent soldiers' uniforms. ' The reins ': the simplest emendation is to *lappīdôt*, ' torches ': ' *his chariots are like* [reading *k^e*] *the fire of torches* ', though admittedly the word occurs in the next v. ' The drivers ', reading *pārāšim* for MT *b^e rôšîm*, ' fir trees ' = (?) ' spears ' (RV); ' are stupefied ', lit. ' reel ' as of a drunken man, and so ' *act wildly* '. **4** (5). A typical Nahum verse with its colourful verb-forms. **5** (6). ' Muster up ' (*cf.* WV) for Vg ' recordabitur ' which = MT. The problem is to whom the verse refers: either to the desperate defenders, whose confusion makes them ' stumble ', who man the walls and prepare a ' covering ' (a word found only here, presumably part of the fortifications); or else to the Babylonian attackers, who ' disappear among the embankments ' (WV for ' stumble ', *i.e.* stumble deliberately), attack the walls and prepare the ' mantelet ' (RV) or shelter for those who work the battering-ram. **6** (7). ' The gates of the rivers ' = MT lit., indicate either (1) ' river sluices ' (WV), letting in the water—and *cf.* references to the flooding of Nineveh at its fall in Ctesias and Diodorus Siculus (see Van H.), or (2) ' moat-sluices ', emptying them —and remains of dams and sluices are still visible, or (3) gates where the river Khusur or the canal passed through the city—vulnerable points (see Driver), or (4) ' bridge-gates '. Probably the reference to flooding is the most likely, esp. in connexion with the figure in 8(9). The temple, or the palace, is melted (lit.).

i 7-10 (8-11) **The Sack of the City—9** (10). ' *Plunder silver! Plunder gold! And there is no end to the store* '

(WV)—the cries of the invaders are imagined—' *it is* **5** *more precious than all articles of delight!* ' MT *kābôd*, ' precious ', is not represented in Vg and may be a corrupt copy of the preceding or following word. This v finds a striking parallel in line 45 of the Babylonian tablet (now in BM), commemorating the fall of Nineveh (publ. 1923 by C. J. Gadd).

10 (11). Again typical of Nahum's vigorous Hebrew. **j** (N.B. in BOW 1914 Douay text ' lions ' is misprinted for ' loins '.) ' The faces of all of them *become drawn* ' (lit. withdraw beauty). The word for ' beauty ', *pā'rûr*, occurs only here and in the same phrase in Jo 2:6, and not with *parûr* ' a pot ' !

11-13 (12-14), **III 1 The Lions' Den is destroyed— k** **11** (12). ' Feeding place ', MT *mir'eh*, ' grazing '. But lions do not graze, and *me'ārāh*, ' cave ' (of wild beasts in Is 32:14) is usually proposed. ' To enter in ', *lābî'*, is more likely another word for *lion* (as ' lioness ' in 13), spelt identically. There are 4 different words for ' lion ' in these vv. **13** (14). ' Behold I come against thee ', a phrase common in Jer and Ez for God's reproof. ' Thy chariots ': we expect the lion figure to continue and could read with Davidson and Driver *sib^e kēk* or *subb^e kēk*, ' thy thicket ', used in Jer 4:7 of the abode of a lion. ' Thy messengers ', once more the occupying power. **III 1.** The wicked city is still seen as a lions' den, full of ' rapine '—the same word as ' prey ' and cognate with ' rapine ' in 12(13) above.

III 2-7 The Disgrace of the Harlot—The fate of the **l** city is now described under a new figure. **2-3** are particularly colourful examples of Nahum's excited style. **3.** ' *Horseman mounting, flame of sword, flash of spear, heap of slain, mass of corpses: no end to the bodies, men stumble among them* '. **4.** ' *Mistress of* witchcraft '. **6.** ' An example ', ' a *gazing-stock* ', ' a public show ' (Knox).

8-10 The Warning of the Fate of No-Amon—8. m This was the city in Egypt, near the modern Karnak, known to the Greeks as Thebes. Amon was the god in whose honour its great temple was built. No = Egyptian *net*, ' city ', so sometimes merely called ' No ' as in Jer 46:25; Ez 30:14 ff. In Ez 30:15 occurs the famous pun on the god's name, *h^a môn Nô* ', ' the *multitude* of No ', which gave rise in rabbinic tradition to the identification here of Amon and ' multitude ', whence Vg ' populorum ' and AV ' populous No '. St Jerome, writing ' Alexandria ', is conscious of the anachronism and explains that he is merely giving the modern name—though the identification happens to be wrong. ' Rivers ', the proper word for the Nile (on which Thebes is situated), and referring to the many branches and canals. ' Sea ', the vastness of the Nile. ' Riches ', reading *ḥayil* ' strength ' for *ḥêl* ' glacis, rampart '. ' Waters are its walls ', reading *mayim*, which is better than MT *miyyām*, ' from the sea is its wall '. **9.** Cush (Ethiopia, S. of Egypt), Egypt itself . . . Put (Africa) and the Libyans. Put is always translated ' Libya ' in the versions, except here, where the Libyans (*Lûbîm*) are also named. **10.** We cannot but remark once more on Nahum's sturdy-sounding verb-forms here. No-Amon (Thebes) was captured by the Assyrian Ashurbanipal in 663, and this completed for the time the subjugation of Egypt begun about 10 years previously by his father Esarhaddon. The disaster, though some 40 years before Nahum's prophecy, was evidently still fresh in men's memories.

11-19 Final Apostrophe to Assyria—11. ' Be de- **n** spised ', a word usually meaning ' hidden ' and of doubtful meaning here. **13.** ' The gates ', *i.e.* the mountain passes forming entrances to the land, *cf. e.g.* the ' Cilician Gate '. **14.** Ironic commands to fortify the city; *cf.* 2:1(2). Clay was kneaded with the feet. HT has ' *Walk in the mud, and trample in the clay, seize the brick-mould* ' (probable meaning of this last), mentioning two kinds of material: excavations, *e.g.* those near Nineveh itself in 1935, show the use of sun-dried mud-bricks, as well as of fired clay-bricks (v. Bévenot in WV).

15-16. But the fortifications will be of no avail, for 'There fire shall devour thee, sword *shall cut thee off, young locust devour thee*'—this last reading involves the omission of *kaph* before the locust, and a masc. verb. The young locust (*yeleq* 'bruchus'), before it can fly, is the most destructive : ravaging the land it becomes a mature insect (*'arbeh*), strips off its wing-sheaths and flies away (*v.* Driver). So far the locust is the scourge of Nineveh. Now, with sarcastic imperatives, it is symbol of what Nineveh might be : now if thou wouldst, '*be numerous as the young locust* (and destroy), *be numerous as the mature locust* (and fly to safety), *multiply thy merchants as the stars of the sky—the young locust bares* (its wings) *and flies away !* ' All thy mercantile glory is of a sudden disappeared, as a swarm of locusts that has taken to flight. For ' thou hast multiplied ' in 16 it is preferable to read an imperative. **17.** ' Thy guards . . . thy *scribes* ', two Assyrian titles of un-

certain meaning, probably connected with Assyrian roots of these meanings. The second is found only here and in a by-form in Jer 51:27 (Vg Taphsar), but has nothing to do with *ṭap*, ' children ', as Vg here. All will be lost like a swarm of locusts : merchants, soldiery, scholars. ' Locusts of locusts ', spelt differently in Heb., the second form being found besides only in Am 7:1, and being probably no more than a correction of the first, not found elsewhere. ' Their place was not known ' is certainly the correct reading ; MT has ' his place was not known ; where are they ? ' the latter phrase being a corruption of the plur. suffix to ' their place '. **18.** ' Thy princes *have slept* ', with LXX. ' Thy people are *scattered*', so Jerome in his commentary, though Vg has ' latitavit '. **19.** Lit. '*There is no dimming of* thy destruction ' (Vg ' non est obscura contritio tua '), an unusual phrase, the noun occurring here only, though from a root of established meaning.

HABACUC

(HABAKKUK)

By S. BULLOUGH, O.P.

539a **Bibliography**—St Jerome, *Commentarii in Abacuc Prophetam*, PL 25, 1273–1338 ; J. Knabenbauer, S.J., *cf.* § 409*b* ; Van Hoonacker, *cf.* § 409*b* ; *S. R. Driver in CBi, 1906 ; Dom Hugh Bévenot, O.S.B., in WV, 1937.

b About **the Prophet himself** we know nothing. He may, or may not, be identified with the prophet Habacuc in Judah who in Dan 14:32–38 was miraculously transported to the lions' den in Babylon. Chronologically it is possible, though the king in Dan is unnamed and so the story undated. Pseudo-Epiphanius' *Lives of the Prophets* puts Habacuc's birthplace at Bethzocher, which may be the same as Bethzacharam in 1 Mac 6:32 f., the modern Beit-Sakariyeh not far from Bethlehem and the traditional ' Hill of Habacuc ' (*cf.* on 2:1). The prophet's name is in Hebrew *Ḥᵃbaqqûq*, of peculiar form and uncertain meaning.

c The **Divisions** of the book are clearly marked. The first part, 1:2–2:4, is cast in dramatic form, being a dialogue between the prophet and God. There follow the ' Woes of the Wicked ', 2:5–20, and lastly the Canticle, ch 3.

d The **Theme and Manner** of Habacuc are quite his own. He is deeply preoccupied with the age-old problem of injustice on earth and God's apparent inactivity. A definite rhythm of thought runs through the whole book. At first there is the dialogue in which the problem is stated, and on the answer coming from God that he will indeed intervene, the problem is pushed a stage further with the consideration of the wickedness of him whom God sends to punish the evil. Habacuc has a manner of soliloquizing—in 1:14–17 he broods over the iniquities of the coming invader, and in 2:1 he speaks to himself. The argument culminates in God's reassurance that, come what may, it is the faithfulness of the just man that will count in the end, 2:4 ; this is the passage that is quoted three times by St Paul. In the next section, the ' Woes ', the prophet once more turns to reflect upon men's wickedness, and he formally stigmatizes certain sins. Finally, in the Canticle we find Habacuc's thought still running to the same rhythm, though here presented in lyric form : the prophet again asks God to come, 3:2, and then describes the might of his power, 3:3–11 ; he considers his terrible judgement, 3:12–15, and confesses his own terror, 3:16–17, but in the end, as before, he feels reassured that trust in God, come what may, will bring consolation.

e The **Date of the Prophecy**—Habacuc's argument is so perennial that it fits every age, not least our own. The reference, however, to the Chaldaeans (Babylonians) places it at a time of their ascendancy, but evidently before their invasion of Palestine. It was the victory of the Babylonians at Carchemish, under Nabuchodonosor (Nebuchadnezzar) in 605 that made them masters of Western Asia. It was not long, before Nabuchodonosor invaded Palestine and King Joakim ' became his servant three years ', 4 Kg 24:1, which cannot have been later than 602–599 (the latter's death). We can therefore suppose Habacuc to have prophesied between the years 605 and 602. This is further borne out by the fact that since Josias' death in 609 his religious reforms had been set aside and his successors Joachaz and Joakim both ' did evil

before the Lord ', 4 Kg 23:32, 37, and Habacuc's **5.** words in 1:2–4 and 2:5–19 certainly reflect the unhealthy moral condition of those reigns.

Suggestions, however, have not been wanting, which place the prophecy later, during the exile (the prophet's name is claimed as a Babylonian type), or even as late as the time of Alexander, though the moral reflexions are by most regarded as early. The Canticle is frequently held to be late, especially by those writers who regard the psalms to be mostly of late post-exilic composition.

I 1 The Title —' Burden ', *cf.* § 550*c*. ' The prophet ': **5** only Hab, Agg and Zach receive this formal title in the heading.

I 2–II 4 The Dialogue. **b**

2–4 The Prophet speaks, uttering his complaint that there is strife and injustice in the world, while God remains silent. **2.** ' *I shout to thee " Violence! " and thou savest not* '. **3.** Vg and, still more, LXX have a better disposition of the phrases than MT, and we follow them in reading the infinitive ' to see ' rather than ' thou shalt see ' of MT. ' *Why dost thou shew me iniquity and trouble, to see ruin and violence ? Before me there is strife, and contention is raised* '. The last word here, from *nāśā'*, must be read in the Niph'al—the Qal is never intransitive. **4.** ' Therefore *teaching grows numb,* and judgement *goes out no more* '. ' Prevaileth against ' is a doubtful word : in Pi'el = ' lie in wait for '.

5–11 God's Answer—He will intervene, eventually. **c** His intervention came with the Babylonian invasions. **5** is quoted in Acts 13:41 with reference, of course, to Christ. **6.** Chaldaeans, *Kaśdîm*, or Babylonians. **7.** ' Burden '—something raised up, probably ' dignity ' (RV). **8.** ' Their horses are *swifter* than leopards ; and *keener* than evening wolves *are* their horsemen '. The word *pāšû* (DV ' shall be spread abroad '), of doubtful meaning, should be omitted as a doublet of *pārāšâw*, ' his horsemen '. The repetition of this word is probably also a doublet, so that we proceed at once ' *They come* from afar . . .' (*cf.* the neat rendering of Basic OT). **9.** ' terror goes before their face '—a **d** most likely suggestion of Van H.'s. **10.** In 7–11 the use of sing. and plur. for the Chaldaeans is irregular. So here : ' *He shall mock at kings* '. **11.** ' *Then he sweeps by as a wind and passes through* ' (with RV). Bévenot in WV has a brilliant suggestion : ' *and he sets up his altar to his god* ' (*cf.* Jer 11:13), which pictures the pagan invader entering the holy city. The reconstruction explains every letter in MT.

12–13 The Prophet speaks again, explaining further **e** his concern : indeed the Lord will intervene, but what of the injustice of the appointed scourge itself ? **12a.** ' We shall not die ' = MT and all older Vss, but this is one of the 18 *Tiqqûnê Sôpᵉrîm* or Corrections of the Scribes, included in the Massoretic notes, where the text was deliberately altered to avoid an apparent irreverence (*cf.*, *e.g.* Pope, *Aids*, 1, 165). The supposed original here was ' *Thou shalt not die* ', altered to avoid the suggestion of such a possibility. This is probably the true reading, and is followed by WV, Basic and many moderns. **12b.** Vg lit. (= MT) ' *and a strong one* [lit. rock] *to give correction thou hast founded him* '. God as a refuge or protection is often addressed as

e 'Rock', *e.g.* Ps 17(18) 3, 47; 18(19) 15 (Vg 'adjutor', NP 'Petra'), but here it apparently indicates the scourge appointed by God. Some, however, as RV, WV and Basic, translate 'O Rock' as addressed to God, but the Heb. as it stands hardly warrants this. **13**. The clumsy last word in MT is omitted by LXX, probably rightly, reading 'when the wicked devoureth *the just*' (WV).

f **14-17 The Prophet's Reflexions** on the ruthlessness of the coming scourge. **14**. '*He will* make men like fishes': 'he' is the wicked of 13, and is surely to be read here (with WV and Basic), since the fishing figure continues in 15-17 in the 3rd person. The words for the fishing tackle are all rare, but their meaning is obvious from the context. **16**. He deifies his weapons (*cf.* 11 if the text is there right); Driver notices that according to Herodotus 4, 62 (rather than 59-60) the Scythians were wont to offer sacrifice to a scimitar as a symbol of Ares. 'Portion . . . fat and *food rich*'. **17**. MT '*Shall he* therefore . . . ?'

g **II 1 The Prophet's Soliloquy**—'Watch' from root 'to guard', and 'tower' either = fortified place (Vg, RVm), or = watch-tower (DV, RV), from another root 'to guard'. Bévenot says that the traditional 'Hill of Habacuc', about 3 m. S. of Jerusalem, not far from Bethlehem, is a magnificent vantage-point, WV, xxv and 33. '*what answer he (yāšîb* for '*āšîb) will return to my argument*' is given by the Syriac, and is followed by Van H., WV, and Basic, and is preferable to MT, LXX and Vg.

h **2-4 God's Answer**—**2**. The prophet is to write the message plainly, 'that he may run that readeth' (AV, RV), that it may be read quickly and easily. Hence the well-known saying. **3**. MT 'For *a* vision is yet *for the appointed time*'. It is not certain what 'vision' is referred to. It may be (1) the oracle of 4 (the most likely), or (2) the theophany of ch 3, or (3) the fulfilment of the threats in 1:5-11, or (4) the Messianic triumph at the end of time. 'Apparebit in finem, et non mentietur : si moram fecerit, expecta eum, quia veniens veniet' is used of the coming of Christ in the Advent liturgy (3rd Sunday, Resp. i at Matins), and similarly 'Qui venturus est veniet, et non tardabit' in Resp. iii and vi. The latter passage is quoted in Heb 10:37, also according to LXX, introducing the important quotation of 4. St Jerome here deliberately wrote 'visus' rather than the feminine 'visio', because of the application to Christ.

i **4**. 'He that is unbelieving': probably we should read (with Van H. and WV) '*he fainteth*', lit. 'is covered', which corresponds to LXX. 'The just man shall live by his *faithfulness*'. The Heb. word conveys this rather than 'faith', though, as Bévenot observes, 'faith' = belief in the divine mysteries, is a NT conception legitimately developed from the OT idea of faithfulness to the divine precepts. Basic has 'good faith'. St Paul quotes this passage in Rom 1:17, Gal 3:11, Heb 10:38. In Rom and Gal 'his' is not included, but LXX here has 'my faith' and Heb. transfers the possessive to 'my just one'.

j **The Woes of the Wicked 5-19.**
5-6a i Woe to the Proud and Deceitful—**5**. Difficult. Probably : 'Woe to [*hôy*] the treacherous, the proud man, and arrogant' (*yōneh* with LXX). The first Woe results therefore from this reconstruction. **6a**. 'Dark speech', Vg 'loquelam aenigmatum', two nouns, 'taunt' and 'riddles', in HT. '*One shall say*' I would attach to the preceding.

k **6b-8 ii Woe to the Usurer**—**6b**. 'Thick clay': MT '*abṭîṭ*, 'usury' (only here, but *cf.* '*abôṭ* in Deut 24:10-13). **7**. 'Bite', so HT lit. ; but from this root is the word *nešeķ*, 'usury' (piece bitten off), so here 'thy debtors'. The Chaldaeans seem in particular to be the cruel usurers here, who will, however, come to a bad end.

l **9-11 iii Woe to the Embezzler**—**9**. 'Him that *getteth ill-gotten wealth*'. **10**. 'Confusion' = 'shame'. 'Thy soul hath sinned' is a quite unhebraic notion, but translate, as in Prov 20:2, '*Thou forfeitest thy life*' (so Van H., Driver, WV). **11**. 'The stones will cry out',

Lk 19:40, on the lips of Christ, takes up the figure **540 l** from here. 'The timber', a rare word found only here (LXX 'beetle' !), MT continues '*from the wood(work)*', but Jerome follows Symmachus and Theodotion (*v.* his comm.).

12-14 iv Woe to the Extortioner, *cf.* Mic 3:10 of **m** Jerusalem. **13**. 'These things', *i.e.* town and city. '*For the people labour for the fire, and the nations toil for nothing*', *cf.* Jer 51:58 of the useless labour of Babylon, which will so shortly be destroyed. **14**. The parallel in Is 11:9b guides us to a better rendering '*filled with* [acc.] *the knowledge of* the glory'.

15-17 v Woe to the Debauched—**15**. 'Woe to him **n** that giveth his *neighbour* to drink *from the cup of his wine, and getteth drunk, in order to* behold *their nakedness.*' I would read *ḥamrô* 'his wine'; *cf.* Deut 32:14; Is 27:2, and Aramaic. **16**. In the context of drinking, the familiar figure comes easily of the 'cup of the Lord' (*cf.* 'calix in manu Domini,' Ps 74(75) 9). 'Shameful vomiting' : 'disgrace'. **17**. '*For violence done to* [as in 8] Lebanon'. 'Terrify *thee*', *cf.* LXX. 17b is a repetition of 8b.

19, 18, 20 vi Woe to the Idolater—**18** evidently fits **o** after 19, which begins this Woe. 'A molten and false image' : '*An idol and a teacher of falsehood*'.

III The Canticle of Habacuc is a lyric psalm of great **p** poetical power, somewhat loosely attached to the rest of the book, though the dominant ideas reoccur. The text in MT is frequently uncertain, but Vg generally preserves a surer reading ; it will not be possible, however, here to explain fully all the details of reconstruction of MT that are involved. In general pattern and in several characteristics the canticle resembles the Psalms, especially in the presence of presumed musical directions at the beginning and end, and the indication *selāh* in 3, 9 and 13. Hence some suppose that it is a liturgical fragment appended to this book. The Canticle appears in the Breviary at Lauds (II) on Friday. The Canticle may be summarized thus : The poet contemplates God's power and asks for his mercy, **2**, he pictures his coming in majesty, **3-4**, and the terrible effects upon nature, **5-11**, the punishment of the wicked, **12-14**, and his final triumph, **15**. Finally the prophet expresses his fear, **16-17**, but immediately also his trust in God's mercy, **18-19**.

1 The Title—'For ignorances', *Šigyônôt*, *cf.* in the **q** title of Ps 7 *Šiggāyôn* (Vg 'Psalmus'). Probably a musical term, of uncertain meaning. Some connect with the root *šāgāh* or *šāgag*, 'wander', hence Vg 'error', or 'in a wandering (free) rhythm' (Driver) ; or with an Assyrian root 'mournful' (WV). Many leave untranslated.

2 Introduction—WV and NP (1945) after LXX read **r** 'I have heard thy report, I have seen thy work', with better parallelism. For 'in the midst of the years bring it to life' LXX has the peculiar reading 'in medio duorum animalium', a text preserved in the Dominican Breviary (5th Resp. at Christmas Matins), though not in the Roman, which does, however, retain 'ut animalia viderent Christum natum'. This text is probably the origin of the traditional ox and ass at Bethlehem. 'In the midst of the years' means either (1) in the course of history, or (2) in a few years' time, or (3) now—between past and future. 'Thy work', to be revived, is God's work of mercy.

3-4 The Theophany—**3**. 'South . . . Pharan', towards **s** Sinai, the site of the original theophany. **4**. 'Horns', a symbol of power, and *cf.* Moses' countenance 'horned' after the vision, Ex 34:29 f., 35. 'Hid', a doubtful word.

5-11 The Effects on Nature—**5**. 'The devil', *rešep*, **t** 'a flame': Jerome tells us that the Jews claimed this as the name of a prince of devils (like Beelzebub), and the one who tempted Eve. **6**. 'Melted', a doubtful word, *yattēr*, which we should perhaps read from roots *nātaṣ* or *nātaš*, 'break down' or 'root up', both used of nations. 'The *eternal* hills were bowed down ; *his journeys are eternal*'. **7**. 'Tents of Ethiopia *under*

540t affliction ' ; ' under ' with an abstract noun is otherwise unknown. Among emendations proposed that of Nowack and WV (*cf.* Van H.), of *yîrᵉʾûʿ* (the tents) shall fear ' for *rāʾîṯî*, ' I saw ', should be noticed.

u 8b. ' *That thou ridest* upon thy horses, thy chariots *of salvation* ', a kind of apposition, GK 131r. **9a.** MT ' *Nakedly thy bow is aroused* '. **9b.** Difficult. I would suggest ' (the bow) *full of [siḇʿaṯ] arrows* ', though admittedly this usage of ' rods ' has no warrant, and connect *ʾōmer* with the next sentence. **9c.** I would read *ʾāmartā* (from 9b) *lannᵉhārôṯ baqqᵉʿû ʾereṣ*, ' thou saidst to the rivers, " Cleave the earth " '. **10.** Sudden floods in the dry wadys after a severe storm are a source of terror to the desert tribes (*cf.* note in Driver, 99). ' The deep ' (2nd time), MT ' *on high* ': and note that it is a distinct word in Vg. **11.** In the brilliance of God's storm the sun and the moon have no further function : ' *for light*, thy *arrows go ; for brightness, the flash of thy spear* ' (*cf.* Van H.). For God's arrows *cf.* Pss 7:14 ; 37(38) 3.

v 12-14 The Effects on the Wicked—13a. ' With *thine anointed* ': LXX omits ' with ', perhaps rightly. It may refer (*cf.* the parallel) to the people or to the king or to his Messianic successor. **13b.** The house of the wicked is imagined as a man, whose head is struck off, laying bare the neck ; though NP and many for ' neck ', *ṣawwāʾr*, read *ṣûr* ' rock ' (of the foundations). **14.** Perhaps we should read *párāšāw*,

' his horsemen ' for ' his warriors '. RV, WV and **5** many understand the staves (or sceptres) as belonging to the victim, though NP, Basic and others emend to ' thy staves '. *Maṭṭeh*, ' staff ', is not, however, used of a spear-like weapon, any more than of an arrow (*cf.* 9b), but only for support in walking, and (occasionally, figuratively) for beating. LXX has ' in ecstasy '—?

15. God's Triumph—' *Thou treadest* the sea *with thy* **w** horses, in the *surge* of many waters '. ' Surge ' from root *ḥāmar* as in Ps 45(46) 4.

16-17 The Prophet's Fear—16b. ' Rottenness *enters* **x** my bones, and beneath me falter *my steps* ', reading *ᵃšûrai* with Wellhausen and others. **16c.** ' *I will* rest '. LXX is more probable ' the people *around me* '—perhaps *negdî*. **17.** The picture of the desolation that will follow God's scourge.

18-19 The Prophet's Consolation—18. He who trusts **y** will rejoice, ' in the God *of my salvation* '; Jerome, interpreting directly of Christ, leaves the word untranslated, to show the connexion between the Holy Name and its meaning. **19.** ' *And upon my heights he will have me tread* '. The ' conqueror ' and ' singing psalms ' are but musical directions often found in the Psalter : ' for the choirmaster, on *nᵉgînôṯ* ' (perhaps a musical instrument), as in the title of *e.g.* Ps 4 (DV ' unto the end, in verses '). The last verse in Vg is lovely poetry.

SOPHONIAS

(ZEPHANIAH)

By S. BULLOUGH, O.P.

a **Bibliography**—St Jerome, *Commentarii in Sophoniam Prophetam*, PL 25, 1337–88 ; J. Knabenbauer, S.J., *cf.* § 409*b* ; Van Hoonacker, *cf.* § 409*b* ; *S. R. Driver in CBi, 1906.

b **The Name and Person of the Prophet**—Sophonias, MT S*e*panyāh, transliterated in AV as Zephaniah. Vg follows LXX. The name means ' The Lord has treasured '. The prophet was of royal descent, 1:1. He does not appear elsewhere in OT, nor is his great-grandfather Amarias, son of King Ezechias, mentioned in the historical books.

c **The Date** is given in the title as ' in the days of Josias, king of Judah ', 640–609 B.C., 4 Kg 22:1. It was in his 18th year (622) that he had the great religious reform, abolishing idolatry, repairing the temple and restoring its worship, finding ' the Book of the Law ' in the temple, and restoring the observance of its precepts and of the prescribed festivals, 4 Kg 22:3–23:25. Sophonias' references to idolatry, 1:4 ff., and his appeals to the people to return to the worship of the true God (*e.g.* 2:3) are indications of a date probably just preceding the reform of 622 : indeed Sophonias' preaching may have contributed to it. He was thus a contemporary of Jeremias, who began his work in the 13th year of the reign, 627, Jer 1:2, and also of Nahum. Nahum was wholly occupied with the impending fate of Nineveh, but Sophonias merely mentions it as a dreadful warning to Judah, 2:13–15. In fact disaster came to Nineveh within 10 years, in 612.

d **The Theme of the Book** is a call to the people to repentance, and an assurance of God's love for them, esp. 3:15–17, but the approach is through the direst threat of calamity : the technique is that of the ' hell-fire sermon '. God's judgement is presented in 1:7–18 in terms of the ' Day of the Lord ' (' Dies irae dies illa '), a figure frequently used by the prophets, esp. previously by Jo Am and Is (whence Soph may have got the idea), and later by Jer (only his later work, 46:10 and Lam), Abd Ez Zach and Mal (*cf.* § 542*e*). There is danger in the air : Assyria, the mighty power, has already devastated Palestine just 100 years before, and her own catastrophe will come with that of all the nations. Judah, if she remain faithless, will share in their fate (as in fact she did some 36 years later, in 586), but the Lord will remember the faithful remnant, and will restore them to glory, and indeed all the nations will come to adore him in the end. It is here, just for an instant, that Soph opens out a wider eschatological view, 3:9–10.

e ' The great and abiding **religious value** of the book consists in the profoundly earnest moral tone which pervades it, and in the prophet's deep sense of the sin of his people and of the stern need which impels Yahweh, who would only too gladly rejoice over his people, if it would permit him to do so, 3:17, to visit it with a discipline which will purge away its unworthy members ' (Driver, 106 f.).

f The simplest **division of the Book** is according to its chapters : I The Threats of God's judgement, II The Call to Repentance, with examples of the calamities around them, III The Denunciation of Jerusalem, again with examples, 6–7, a promise of the recognition of the true God among the nations, 8–10, and of the salvation of the faithful remnant, 11–13, concluding **541f** with the song of consolation, 14–20.

The Unity of the Book—The older critical school (from **g** Kuenen, 1889, to Marti, 1904) rejected various portions of the book, sometimes a verse here and there, sometimes a longer section, as post-exilic additions or interpolations. Driver (1906) considered many of these opinions ' arbitrary ' (p 109) ; he himself limited the interpolated glosses to 2:7*b*, 11 and 3:9–10, 18–20, sections which, he felt, either fail to continue the argument of the context or represent a post-exilic viewpoint. Van Hoonacker considers 2:7*b*, 10 and perhaps 11, and a phrase in 3:10 to be later glosses. These writers represent a moderate critical view. Generally speaking, however, the book presents a literary unity. The style is regular of the period, but the text is in several places very insecure, notably 2:2, 6, 14 ; 3:1, 5, 10, 18, 19.

I 1 The Title—Sophonias has the longest genealogy **542a** of any of the prophets, probably in order to include his royal forbear, Ezechias. The fact that there are four generations in his line after Ezechias while in the royal line there are but three (Manasses, Amon and Josias) is explained when we remember that Manasses reigned 55 years, 4 Kg 21:1.

2-6 The Threat against Judah and Jerusalem—3. **b** ' Shall meet with ruin ' : MT and Vg have a noun, but a verb is better, probably we should read a *hiph'il* ' I will overthrow '. **4.** Although the foregoing threat might apply to every land, here Judah and Jerusalem are specifically mentioned. ' Wardens of the temples ' : Vg ' aeditui ', which Jerome explains, adding ' vel fanatici ' (wardens of a ' fanum ') ; HT has the word reserved for pagan priests. The contemporary account of Josias' reform, 4 Kg 23:5, includes their elimination (Vg there ' aruspices ', DV ' soothsayers ', together with all worshippers of Baal, or of sun, moon or stars (*cf.* 5). ' With the priests ' or read *mē'im*, ' from among the priests ', *i.e.* at the same time shall be eliminated the degenerate priests of Yahweh who were turning to idolatry. **5.** Acc. to MT ' swear *to* the Lord . . . swear *by* Melchom ', which is awkward. Omit ' swear ' the first time : ' *who adore the Lord and* (at the same time) *swear by Melchom* '. This points to idolatrous worship being practised together with that of Yahweh. Melchom (MT, AV Milcom) was the god of the Ammonites, 3 Kg 11:5, 7, 33 ; 4 Kg 23:13, one of several Semitic deities (as Moloch) whose name derives from *melek*, ' king '.

7-9 The Day of the Lord : calamity will come on **c** that day, the victim of the sacrifice being Judah and the guests her foes. **8.** ' Visit upon ' = ' punish ' (common). ' The king's sons ' : LXX, ' *the king's house* '. This is the more likely reading since at the time of his reform King Josias was but 26 years old —he was 8 when he ascended the throne, 4 Kg 22:1 —and would hardly have had sons capable of serious iniquity. One notices that the young king himself does not come under the condemnation. ' Strange apparel ', *i.e.* alien idolatrous customs. **9.** ' that *leapeth* over the threshold ' refers either (1) to a pagan superstition (*cf.* that in 1 Kg 5:5) (Driver), or (2) to rapacious courtiers hastening to cross the threshold of the king's palace (Van Hoonacker), or (3) connect-

683

542c ing with what follows in Vg, to arrogant entrance to the temple (St Jerome). HT for ' of the Lord their God ' is simply ' *of their lord* ', which may refer to the king, and supports (2) above.

d 10-13 The Dismay of Jerusalem—10. The Fishgate, mentioned in Neh 3:3 ; 12:39 ; 2 Par 33:14, was in the N. wall not far from the NW. corner. Jerusalem is approached from the N. by an invader. ' The Second ', thus lit. MT = ' *the second quarter of the city* ' (also named in 4 Kg 22:14 ; Neh 11:9) was probably a new section added to the city (*cf.* Knox ' the New Town '), perhaps that enclosed by the new outer wall of Manasse, 2 Par 33:14, which included the Fishgate. **11.** ' The Morter ', only found here, Prov 27:22 (a mortar for grinding), and Jg 15:19 (a cavity in a jaw-bone). Presumably it refers to a valley either shaped like a mortar, or where the inhabitants will be pounded, or both. ' Wrapped up in silver ' = ' rolling in money '. Vg read *nᵉlôṭê* for *nᵉṭîlê* ' laden ' in MT. **12.** The figure of the Lord cleansing the city, using lamps to illuminate the murky corners.

e 14-18 The Day of the Lord is Near—14. ' The voice ' in Heb. often = ' the sound ', and sometimes (as perhaps here and in 10) an exclamation ' Hark ! ' **15.** ' *Dies irae dies illa* ' comes from this verse, developing the meaning to the eschatological sense of the Day of Lord at the end of the world. **16.** The trumpet (' *tuba mirum spargens sonum* ') has become through the Gospel, Mt 24:31, and St Paul, 1 Thess 4:15 ; 1 Cor 15:52, a familiar feature of the picture of the Parousia (*cf.* also Handel's *Messiah*, n. 48). **18.** God's ' jealousy ' : the traditional translation covering the senses both of zeal for his people and of exclusive claim to worship (*cf. e.g.* Ex 20:5) : Knox, well in this context, ' his slighted love ', also in 3:8.

f II 1-3 The Call—1. Judah is to come together in unity (*cf.* 3:9), and as a nation is to turn to God. ' Not worthy to be loved ' : ' *undesirable* ' from an obscure Heb. root (so Jerome), or more probably ' *unabashed* ' as in Targumic Hebrew, Pss 34(35) 4 ; 68(69) 7 in Targum ; Driver. **2.** Difficult : MT ' Before (*i.e.* scarcely) the decree is born, the day passes like chaff ', but the figure of windblown chaff is hardly applicable to the Day. LXX ' Before you become like a flower which passes ' suggests that for the unlikely ' the decree is born ' LXX read *lō' ṭihyû* ' you shall not become '. Now the conjunction *bᵉṭerem* (' before ') may be used with a negative, as it is twice later in this verse, so that this reading brings the phrase into line with the syntax of the whole verse. The word ' day ' is not in LXX. We can reconstruct, therefore (with Nowack), ' *Before you become like blown* (or passing) *chaff* '.

g 4-7 The Fate of the Philistine Cities—4. 4 are named, but not the 5th, Geth (Gath), which had apparently ceased to exist after the 8th cent., *cf.* § 550*e*. ' At noonday ' : in broad daylight, with no difficulty whatever. This seems more likely than a reference to siesta-time or the discomfort of midday heat, which are the usual interpretations. **5.** ' O nation of *Kerethites* ' (or Cretans ; *cf.* LXX), probably Cretan emigrants in Philistia ; *cf.* Am 9:7, Deut 2:23. St Jerome rejected the reading ' Cretans ', saying that ' Chorethim ' means ' perditorum ', following Aquila, Theodotion and Symmachus. **6.** LXX ignores the ' sea-coast ' and for *kᵉrôṭ* (a word otherwise unknown) read *Kereṭ*, ' Crete ', as the subject of the fem. verb. Again we can take Kereth to indicate Cretans in Philistia and translate ' *And Kereth shall be pastures of shepherds* '. **7.** Philistia shall belong to ' *the remnant of the house of Judah* '—the first indication in Soph of the triumph of Judah over the neighbouring lands, a theme that returns in 9. The sentence about the ' captivity ' seems to many writers to be a post-exilic gloss, though it may be part of the prophet's view of the coming disaster.

h 8-11 The Example of Moab—Moab will be punished for their hostility to Judah (*cf.* Abdias on Edom) and will eventually be dispossessed by the remnant of Judah. **9.** ' Dryness ' (or perhaps ' a field '), ' thorns ' **5** and ' heaps ' are all rare words of uncertain meaning. **11.** Yahweh's triumph over the false gods—he will ' consume ' them (probable meaning of a rare verb).

12 The Example of Egypt—MT ' Cush ', LXX Vg **i** ' Ethiopians '. These sections make the circuit of the compass : Philistia to the W., Moab to the E. (beyond the Dead Sea), Egypt to the S., and finally Assyria to the N.

13-15 The Example of Assyria—13. ' The north ', a **j** common designation in Is, Jer and Ez. The invaders came round the northern edge of the desert. Even Assyria will succumb. For ' the beautiful city ' HT has Nineveh, the Assyrian capital. **14.** The animals are a famous crux (*cf.* Knox in CR 30 [1948] 220), but the main point is that they are descriptive of desolation. They have been variously identified. The voice (*qôl*), esp. of the porcupine, is unlikely, and Marti suggested reading *kôs*, ' owl '. The best reading is, I think, ' *pelican, porcupine, owl, crow* ', all of which might be found in ruins (St Jerome assures us that there is a desert species of ' onocrotalus ' or pelican). ' I will consume her strength ' represents a reading '*erzeh 'uzzāhh* for MT '*arzāh 'ērāh* ' one has stripped off the *cedar-work* ', *i.e.* panelling, doors and window-frames. **15.** ' Wag his hand ', a gesture of contempt or pity : ' Shake his head ' would be to us more expressive, as is also Knox's ' Shake his fist ', though this is rather a gesture of rage.

III 1-7 The Denunciation of Jerusalem—1. ' *Ho !* **k** *Defiant and polluted ! The merciless city !* ' DV ' redeemed ' : there are two roots *gā'al*, ' to redeem ' and ' to defile ', and the second (though only found in exilic or post-exilic books, Lam Dan Esd Neh Mal and Is [59:3 and 63:3]) is the more likely here. ' The dove ' : but it is much more probably the fem. participle of *yānāh*, ' to oppress ', whence the above translation (*cf.* RV). **3-4.** Judgement on her princes, judges, prophets and priests. The judges are ' evening wolves : they left nothing for the morning '—' so voracious are they ' (Driver). The verb for ' left ' occurs only here and is of doubtful meaning, but this is the usual translation. The prophets are ' *wanton, men of deceits* '. **5.** ' *Morning by morning he gives his judgement* '. The rest in DV represents MT, but the text is uncertain ; LXX adds a phrase that raises critical problems for both LXX and MT. The phrase ' bring to light ' is foreign to Heb., and I suspect that ' to light ' and ' shall not be hid ' (or perhaps the Heb. means ' has not failed '), as well as the LXX addition, are corrupt doublets of ' he knows no iniquity ', so that perhaps the original HT ran ' . . . gives his judgement and knows no iniquity '. **6-7.** The example of the nations : their fate is to be a warning to Judah. ' Their ways ' : ' their *streets* '.

8-13 The Promise—8. ' *Therefore wait for me, saith the* **l** *Lord, for the day when I rise as a witness* ' ; *cf.* LXX. God as a witness for or against men is a familiar notion, esp. with the judgement that follows, whereas the ' everlasting resurrection ' would be obscure. Others (as RV) read *lᵉʻad*, ' for the prey '. ' *My judgement is to assemble nations and gather kingdoms* ', without articles in HT. **9.** ' *For then I will restore to the peoples* [pl.] *clean lips* ', *i.e.* all the nations will serve Yahweh. ' With one shoulder ' = HT literally ; Knox ' straining at a single yoke '. The shoulder in OT is usually in a context of bearing a burden. **10.** DV represents MT (though lit. ' daughter of my **m** dispersed ones '), but the context is hardly of dispersed Jews and rather indicates pagan nations. Further, LXX ' among my dispersed ones ' leads us to suspect the text. It was Ewald who first observed that a frequent parallel to Cush (Vg here Ethiopia) is the land of Put = Libya, or perhaps the Egyptian Punt, Somaliland, Nah 3:9 ; Jer 46:9 ; Ez 30:5 ; 38:5 ; *cf.* Gen 10:6 ; DV ' Libyans ' or ' Libya ' in these texts (but ' Africa ' in Nah), and he proposed reading *Pûṭ* here in place of *pûṣai*, ' my dispersed ones ', which

m provides a tolerable text. But I consider that the word *'aṭārai*, 'my suppliants', is as it stands not only of uncertain meaning (it occurs only here and LXX translated 'I will receive') but fails to fit the context, and is probably a doublet of *'ēber*, 'beyond', with the letter *mem* 'from' belonging to *Pūṭ*, so that the original text may have been 'From beyond the rivers of Cush, from Put they will being my offering'. Van Hoonacker, accepting MT, rejects the reference to the dispersal as a gloss. **11-13.** 'In that day', when God shall greet the faithful Israel, she shall stand before him purified, with occasion no more for shame, as so often in the past, for her crimes she shall commit no more. Précis of St Jerome's comment: Thou shalt no longer be ashamed of thy former sins, when the Gentiles believe and the scribes and Pharisees and the proud are no longer in thy midst, but rather the poor, such as fishermen, who will be the remnant.

n 14-20 The Song of Consolation—**15.** 'The Lord hath *withdrawn the judgements against thee*' (*cf.* GK 135*m*). **17.** 'The Lord thy God *is in the midst of thee, mighty to save*'. The phrase 'He will be silent in his love' is a line of poetry.

o 18. 'The triflers that were departed from the law', *nûgê mimmô'ēḏ*. *Nûgê* is, however, a *niph'al* participle (only here and Lam 1:4) of *yāgāh*, 'to be sorrowful', *cf.* the attempted translation of RV. But the reasonable reading is preserved in LXX, which attached the phrase to the preceding and read *kîmê mô'ēḏ*, 'as in the days of a feast', *cf.* Os 12:9(10). The rest of 18 is also difficult: HT, LXX and Vg are all different: HT 'I have gathered from thee: they have been a burden upon her, a reproach'. The best plan is to accept the idea of LXX 'I have gathered thy smitten ones', and for MT *mimmēk*, 'from thee' to read *makkayik*, 'those that smite thee': '*And I will remove* [gather] *those that smite thee*: *they have been a burden upon thee* [2nd person], *a reproach*'. It is not clear what HT St Jerome had to work upon. **19.** Also difficult. Vg seems to have the true reading **p** by supposing the word *kālāh*, 'destruction' (as in 1:18): '*I am making destruction of all . . .*' Israel is seen under the figure of a flock of sheep, some of which are lame, others lost. 'The land of their shame' supposes the absence of the article before 'the land'. **20.** The reference to 'captivity' again (*cf.* on 2:7) suggests to some that 18–20 are post-exilic, though it may be just a part of the prophet's view of Judah's calamity and her subsequent peaceful restoration according to God's loving promises.

AGGEUS

(HAGGAI)

By S. BULLOUGH, O.P.

543a Bibliography—St Jerome, *Commentarii in Aggeum Prophetam*, PL 25, 1387 ff. ; Van Hoonacker, *cf.* §409*b* ; *S. R. Driver in *The Century Bible*, 1906 ; *W. Emery Barnes in CBSC, 1917 ; *R. H. Kennett in *Peake's Commentary*, 1920.

b The Background to the Prophecy—There is hardly a Book in the OT that is easier to place in its historical setting than Agg, for each of its four prophecies is carefully dated. The prophet's name is in Hebrew *Haggay*, probably connected with the word *ḥag*, a feast day (whence Jerome interprets ' festivus '), AV Haggai, LXX 'Αγγαῖος, from which Vg Aggaeus and DV Aggeus. Nothing is known of him apart from his book and the references to his preaching and that of his contemporary Zacharias, and to the good effect thereof and the fulfilment of their prediction of prosperity, in Esd 5:1 and 6:14. But Aggeus stands out clearly as a forceful character, who addressed the leaders and the people of Judah in a time of religious

c crisis. It will be easiest to understand the work of Aggeus and Zacharias if we set it upon the large background of their time, the first century of Persian rule in Palestine. The following table shows the history of the rebuilding of the Temple, the principal preoccupation of Aggeus. (Note that Hebrew months do not coincide with ours, since the first day is about the middle of our month, so that two month-names stand for one Hebrew month, *cf.* § 83*i–j*.)

586 Destruction of the temple and deportation to Babylon.

538 **Cyrus** conquers Babylon (reigns till 529).

537 (1st of Cyrus) Decree authorizing return under Zorobabel and Jesus (Esd 1:2 ; 2:2).
7th month (Sept.-Oct.) Altar built (Esd 3:2).

536 2nd month (Apr.-May) Work of rebuilding begins (3:8). Foundations are laid (3:10). Older men remember the former temple (3:12 *cf.* Agg 2:4). The Samaritans hinder the work, and the building stops ' all the days of Cyrus . . . even until the reign of Darius ', *i.e.* from 536 till 520 (Esd 4:5, 24).

529 **Cambyses.**

521 **Darius I Hystaspis** (till 485).

520–19 (2nd of Darius) Aggeus and Zacharias prophesy (Esd 5:1).

1/6/2, *i.e.* 1 Aug.-Sept. 520, *Aggeus I* (Agg 1:1).
24/6/2, *i.e.* 24 Aug.-Sept. 520. His message takes effect and work starts again (Agg 2:1 ; Esd 5:2).
21/7/2, *i.e.* 21 Sept.-Oct. 520. *Aggeus II* (Agg 2:2).
8th month, *i.e.* Oct.-Nov. 520. *Commission of Zacharias* (Zach 1:1).
24/9/2, *i.e.* 24 Nov.-Dec. 520. *Aggeus III, IV* (Agg 2:11, 21). Work resumed on the foundations (Agg 2:19 ; Esd 5:16).
24/11/2, *i.e.* 24 Jan.-Feb. 519. *The Visions of Zacharias* (Zach 1:7). Note Zach 4:9, ' The hands of Zorobabel *have* laid the foundations of this house, and his hands shall finish it '.

518–7 (4th of Darius).
4/9/4, *i.e.* 4 Nov.-Dec. 518. *The Enquiry made to Zacharias* (Zach 7:1).

516–5 (6th of Darius).
3/12/6, *i.e.* 3 Feb.-Mar. 515. Completion of the temple (Esd 6:15).

499 Revolt of the Ionians. 5

490 (32nd of Darius) Marathon : Greeks repulse the Persians.

485 **Xerxes I :** 480, Thermopylae, Persian victory ; 480, Salamis ; 479, Plataea, Greek victories. *These are of interest here in view of the mention of the Greeks in Zach 9:13.*

464 **Artaxerxes I.**

458 (7th of Art.) Esdras arrives in Jerusalem (Esd 7:8).

445 (20th of Art.) (Mar.-Apr.) Nehemias arrives (Neh 2:1, 11). (Aug.-Sept.) The wall of Jerusalem is finished (Neh 6:15). Neh 3 describes the wall, *cf.* Zach 14:10.

The immediate occasion of the prophecy of Aggeus is **d** probably the beginning of the disintegration of the Persian Empire that showed itself in the reign of Darius (in his first nine years as recorded in the Behistun Inscription), and culminated in the war with Greece. (For a full treatment of this, see Barnes xxxiv-ix.) This will have been the sign for a bid for local independence in the provinces, the rights of minorities and a strengthening of local government.

Theme—It was now seventeen years since the first exiles **e** had returned, and although the altar had been erected, the work on the temple site had been abandoned through difficulties with the local population. Zorobabel, who had been appointed governor by the Persians, and Jesus, the high-priest, had shared the general discouragement of the people. It was left to Aggeus to see the grave peril to the whole treasure of the Hebrew revelation. The temple with its liturgy had always been the centre of the Jewish worship of the True God. If this life of the people without a temple were allowed to go on, their fidelity to God would be threatened. Aggeus rose up, a man of courage and hope, before a discouraged, defeated, deported and barely reinstated people, who were struggling to bring back their civic life to normal. Now he addresses the governor and the high-priest, now the whole people. He takes them to task, encourages them, rallies their hopes, promises them the rewards of God's blessing and brings them to a realization of God's designs for them.

The central figure in the message is **Zorobabel**, son **f** of Salathiel (Esd 3:2, 8 ; 5:2 ; Mt 1:12 ; Lk 3:27), son of Jechonias (thus called in Jer 22, 1 Par 3:16–17 and Mt), otherwise Joachin (4 Kg 24:15), the king of Judah who was deported into Babylon. Zorobabel was therefore of the royal line of Judah, as the Gospel genealogies show, though Mt traces Zorobabel and Salathiel through the kings to Solomon, son of David, and Lk traces them to Nathan, son of David by Bethsabee (2 Kg 5:14 ; 1 Par 3:5). This double descent from David may be the reason of the coupling in Zach 12:12 f. of the ' house of David ', *i.e.* the royal house through Solomon, and the ' house of Nathan '. Zorobabel had been appointed governor (*peḥāh*) of the Persian province of Judah at his return with the first exiles. He first appears in the 7th month after the return under Cyrus in 537 (Esd 3:2), having been listed (Esd 2:2) first among those who returned. It was he who superintended the first effort at rebuilding the temple in 536 (Esd 3:2, 8 ; Zach 4:9), and so is probably to be identified with Sassabasar (*Šešbaṣṣar*), the leader (*nāśî'*) of Judah appointed by Cyrus to

f bring the people back (Esd 1:8, 11), especially in view of Esd 5:14, 16 ' Sassabasar . . . appointed governor (*peḥāh*) . . . laid the foundations of the temple '. It was also Zorobabel who completed the work in 518 (Esd 6:15 ; Zach 4:9). It would seem that already **g** **Salathiel,** his father, was born in exile, for no sons of Jechonias (Joachin) are mentioned at the exile, although he had wives before leaving (4 Kg 24:15) even at the age of eighteen (4 Kg 24:8) (' 8 ' in 2 Par 36:9 must be a mistake). Jeremias, however, called him ' barren ' (22:30), but adds that ' not a man of his seed shall sit upon the throne of David '. Lk (3:37) makes Salathiel to be of Neri, otherwise unknown, and **h** so of Nathan and David. With Zorobabel is closely linked the **high-priest Jesus,** son of Josedec. Josedec was the high-priest who was taken to Babylon by Nabuchodonosor along with Jechonias (1 Par 6:15), who in turn was the son of Saraias (6:14), killed by Nabuchodonosor (4 Kg 25:18–21). So the high-priest Jesus was in direct descent from the priestly tribe of Levi (1 Par 6:1–15). His name is always written ' Jesus ' in Vg and DV of Agg and Zach (and Ecclus 49:14), following the LXX form Ἰησοῦς (adopted in NT) of the Hebrew name *Yᵉhôšuaʿ* or Joshua (AV, RV), in the other Hebrew parts of the OT always written Josue by Vg and DV, even when this priest is referred to in Esd (2:36 ; 3:2, 8, 9 ; 4:3 ; 5:2) and Neh (12:1), in which passages, however, the Hebrew is *Yēšûaʿ* (RV Jeshua), which is the Aramaic form that our Lord would have used. It is in Zach (esp. in 6:13, and see § 547c and § 548f) that we see the ideal ' Church and State ' relation built upon Zorobabel the prince and Jesus the high-priest, with the ' counsel of peace between them both '.

i This brings us to the **Messianic ideas** in this book. Zorobabel is a Messianic figure throughout Agg and Zach, as guardian of the Chosen People, as rebuilder of God's house, and in particular in the closing verses of Agg as the one who has restored the dignity of the house of David after the disgrace of 586. (The share of the high-priest Jesus in the Messianic role is more developed in Zach : § 547c and § 548f.) Zorobabel is to be a ' signet ' on God's hand (Agg 2:24 ; Ecclus 49:13), and to be the leader in God's triumph over the Gentiles in the Messianic age. In this connexion comes the famous passage : ' And the desired of all nations shall come ' (Agg 2:8, see § 544g), traditionally interpreted of the future Redeemer of the world, who was to be born of the stock of David through the line of Zorobabel. God is addressing the governor and the priest, and is telling them how he will move heaven and earth and all nations, and through the Redeemer **j** will fill the new temple with glory (2:7–9). Here we should note the **typical sense** in the traditional interpretation of the new temple, to be rebuilt by Zorobabel and Jesus, not merely as the centre of Jewish worship, but as a type of the universal Church of Christ, whither all nations will come to adore : ' Great shall be the glory of this last house more than of the first, saith the Lord of hosts : and in this place I will give peace ' (Agg 2:10). For the development of this idea in Zach, see esp. Zach 2:11 ; 8:22–23 ; 14:16–21 ; and § 545d, e.

k **Brief Analysis**—First prophecy : the temple must be rebuilt (1:1–11). Appendix : the effect : work begins (1:12–2:1). Second prophecy : the people are encouraged in their work (2:2–10). Third prophecy : the people must examine their consciences (2:11–20). Fourth prophecy : the promise to Zorobabel (2:21–24). **l** The **Text** of Agg presents few difficulties, and there is no dispute over the date, authorship or unity of the book.

a **I 1–11 FIRST PROPHECY : the Temple must be Rebuilt** (1/6/520)—Addressed first to Zorobabel and Jesus, and after v 4 to all the people. **1–4 The Temple is still in Ruins**—The date shows the passage of seventeen years since the first abortive attempts to rebuild after the return of the exiles under Zorobabel. In the face of Samaritan opposition the

work had been abandoned, and Aggeus is calling the **544a** people to task. **1.** Darius I Hystaspis, king of the Persians 521–485, relative, but not direct descendant of Cyrus who captured Babylon in 538 and released the Jews. He was the Darius who sent the expedition against Greece, which was defeated at Marathon in 490. For Zorobabel, see § 543f. ' Governor ', *peḥāti*, is apparently a loan-word from the Assyrian *paḥāti*, a governor, and is used only twenty-eight times in OT (4 Kg, Esd, Neh, Est, Is, Jer, Mal and here, always of Assyrian, Babylonian or Persian governors or satraps ; 3 Kg 10:15 ; 2 Par 9:14 of Solomon's governors ; 3 Kg 20:24 of Syrian captains). For Jesus, see § 543h. **2.** ' The Lord of hosts ', a favourite phrase of Agg, occurring no less than fourteen times.

5-7 The People are to consider their Ways : they **b** have had many troubles, but now if they will obey things will change.

8-11 God is commanding them to set to work on the **c** rebuilding, and God will reward them. Perhaps the fact that it is only timber that is to be fetched indicates that the stonework was there, but in ruins. **10.** MT lit. ' heavens withheld from dew (*mittal*) ', read *tallām* ' withheld *their* dew '.

12-II 1 APPENDIX : The Effect of the Prophecy : d Work begins (24/6/520, i.e. 23 days after the words of Aggeus)—**12.** ' to them ' is not in MT. **13.** ' And Aggeus, the *mal'ak̲-Yahwēh* with the *mal'ᵃk̲ût̲-Yahweh* to the people, spoke, saying : " I am with you, saith Yahweh " '. The word *mal'ak̲*, lit. ' messenger ', is used in a technical theological sense of an angel (cf. Gk). Frequently in the OT we find the *mol'ak̲-Yahweh* speaking in the person of Yahweh himself (e.g. Gen 16 Num 22). And it appears to be so here. (The word *mal'āk̲ût̲*, ' message ', occurs only here, and LXX and Vg read *mimmal'ᵃk̲ê*, ' from among the angels of '.) But the *mal'ak̲-Yahweh* is always a supernatural being or a manifestation of Yahweh himself (cf. Zach 1), and this cannot be applied to the prophet here. Some simply omit the words, as copied from the following words. If the text is right, it is the only time that a prophet receives this title. Jerome records the opinion that Aggeus actually was an angel, but prefers to consider it a special title here. I would suggest the omission of the first letter of *l'êmôr* ' saying ' (the previous word begins with this letter), and read *'āmar*, translating : ' *And Aggeus said :* " *The Angel of the Lord, with the message of the Lord to the people, said :* ' *I am with you, saith the Lord* ' " '. **II 1.** The printed Hebrew Bibles, followed by AV and RV make this v 15 of ch 1, so that it reads : ' . . . did work on the 24th day of the month in the sixth ' (' month ' at the end is not in HT). LXX and Vg attach, awkwardly, to ch 2 ; their verse-numbers of ch 2 are therefore one higher. Yet the Hebrew Bibles have a paragraph mark after v 14, which some attribute to a feeling of conflict with 2:19, but the point is rather that the work *began* on 24/6/2, and that the *foundations were laid* three months later on 24/9/2 (2:19). The work in 2:1 is the preliminary work of clearing the site (Driver).

II 2-10 SECOND PROPHECY : The People are En- e couraged (21/7/520)—**2-6 Encouragement, and Comparison to the Temple's former Glory—2.** In the date DV omits the day, though it is in HT and Vg. **4.** Cf. Esd 3:12–13 : it is suggested that Aggeus had seen the original temple sixty-six years before, and was therefore now an old man (Pusey). **6.** ' The word ' *'et̲-haddāb̲ār* with accusative prefix, made by Vg to be the object of ' perform ' in v 5, necessitating the parenthesis. RV adds ' *according to* the word '. ' Covenanted ' is simply the word ' cut ', the usual verb in Hebrew with *b rît̲* ' covenant '. It is easier to omit the accusative prefix *'et̲* as a dittography of the two preceding letters, and to read *habb̲ᵉrît̲* ' the *covenant* which I made ', taking ' perform ' absolutely : i.e. ' work '. LXX omit the whole phrase ' the word . . . Egypt '.

7-10 The Messianic Age will come, and the New f Temple will be more Glorious—' Yet one little while,

544f and I will move'; MT lit. 'Yet once, a little is it, and I will shake'. LXX omit 'a little is it', and read '*Yet once I will shake*', and the passage is so quoted by St Paul in Heb 12:26 f. This is probably the best reading. St Paul quotes the passage as Messianic, emphasizing the 'only once more' of the Second Coming of Christ : 'There was no escape for those others, who tried to excuse themselves when God uttered his warnings on earth, still less for us, if we turn away when he speaks from heaven. His voice, even then, made the earth rock ; now, he has announced to us that it shall happen again, only

g once' (Heb 12:25–26 KNT). **8.** 'The **desired of all nations** shall come': in HT the verb is plural, from which it would appear that the noun is a collective : 'the desirable things' (RV), referring to the gifts brought to the temple. Strictly the word means the desire, and is only used of the thing desired here and perhaps 1 Kg 9:20. The traditional rendering of Vg, followed by AV, referring directly to the personal Messias, the longed-for Redeemer of all nations, and used at Lauds on IV Sunday of Advent (2nd ant.), needs the alteration of the plural verb *bā'û* to the singular *bā'*. Jerome claims to have read HT as he translates it, for he remarks on the reading of LXX, which corresponds to our present HT. **9.** This verse admittedly bears out the interpretation of v 8 of the temple treasures.

h **11-20 THIRD PROPHECY : The People must examine their Consciences** (24/9/520)—The date is that of the laying of the foundations (v 19), three months after the work had been begun on the site, although some preliminary work on the foundations had already been done in 536 (Esd 3:10).
11-14 Two Examples from Ceremonial Uncleanness —12. 'Ask the priests for *guidance*' : the word *tôrāh* means something taught, hence frequently of the Law of Moses or the Pentateuch, but here in a general sense. 13-14. *Casus 1* : 'If a man carry home some blest meat (his share after a sacrifice) in his garment (*i.e.* in the pocket formed above his belt by the double breast of his tunic), and with this garment touch other food at home, does this other food count as blest food ? ' Obviously not. But *Casus 2* : 'If a man be ceremonially unclean because he touched a corpse (lit. unclean of a soul—a legal phrase, Lev 22:4 ; Num 5:2 ; 9:10), and then touch these things, do they become ceremonially unclean? ' Yes, for what is

holy hallows only what it itself touches (Lev 6:27), while what is unclean infects not only the person in contact with it, but whatever he touches as well (Num 19:22) : 'uncleanness had thus a greater infectious power than holiness. So it is thus with the people' (Driver).
15 The Moral from these Examples—Because the people are unclean, all that they touch is unclean, including their work and their acts of religion in the past.
16-18 Yet they have not learnt their Lesson—Let them consider their tribulations during these years of remissness about building the temple (*cf.* 1:5–7). **17** is a description of their want. The verse starts with an impossible word in MT : *mihyôṭām*, 'from their being', with no connexion with the rest of the sentence. RV and RVm attempt to translate it ; others emend to 'who were you' or 'how fared you', based on LXX, but little sense results. I would omit the word as a miscopy of *min-hayyôm* ('from this day') in the line above. The verse then reads : '*One went to a heap of twenty, and there would be ten ; one went to the vat to draw fifty* (insert *from*) *the press, and there would be twenty*'. The measures are inserted in the Versions as an explanation. **18.** 'There was none among you that returned to me' : MT 'There is not (accusative prefix) you to me', an awkward phrase. The parallel (including the blight and mildew) in Am 4:9, and also LXX here, have '*and you did not return to me*', reading *weʾlō šaḇtem ʾēlay*.
19-20 God's Blessing follows on their good Resolution to rebuild the temple—19. 'From the day that . . .' identifying the day of the foundation with the day of the prophecy. **20.** '*Is there still seed in the granary ? Is any more* (reading '*ôḏ* with LXX) *the vine or fig or pomegranate or olive tree not bearing?* (reading *nōśēʾîm* with LXX)'—a rhetorical question to express their fruitfulness.
21-24 FOURTH PROPHECY : The promise to Zorobabel (24/9/520), see § 543*f*, *i*—**24.** 'A signet', Driver : 'a mark of honour and distinction, given by a monarch to an important minister, as a mark of confidence and authority' (*cf.* Gen 41:42 ; Est 3:10). In Jer 22:24, when God rejects Jechonias (Joachin), he says that if he 'were a ring on my hand, I would pluck him thence'. Here God's Messianic promises to the house of David after the degradation of Jechonias are transferred to his grandson Zorobabel, who thus becomes a type of Christ.

ZACHARIAS

(ZECHARIAH)

By S. BULLOUGH, O.P.

Bibliography—St Jerome, *Commentarii in Zachariam Prophetam*, PL 25, 1415 ff. ; Van Hoonacker, *cf.* § 409*b* (so often quoted that I have abbreviated Van H.); *S. R. Driver in *The Century Bible*, 1906 ; *W. Emery Barnes in CBSC, 1917 ; *R. H. Kennett in *Peake's Commentary*, 1920 ; Touzard in RB (1913) 285–94, (1917) 123–33.

The Person of the Prophet—Zacharias, Heb. *Z^eḵa-ryāh* ('Yahweh remembers'), AV & RV Zechariah, probably a younger contemporary of Aggeus (§ 545*j*), is mentioned precisely elsewhere only in Esd 5:1 and 6:14, as preaching with Aggeus. He was commissioned by God to preach, in the month between Aggeus' 2nd and 3rd prophecies (in the 8th month 520). He is given in Zach 1:1, 7 as the son of Barachias (*Bere-kyāh*), son of Addo ('*Iddô*). Whether the Addo ('*Iddô*) in Neh 12:4, one of the priests who returned with Zorobabel in 537, is the grandfather of the prophet cannot be proved. If he is, then his youth is shown by the presence of his grandfather among the returning exiles, when Zacharias himself would not be above his twenties, and his thirties at the time of his first prophecies. Esdras, however, calls him simply ' the son of Addo' (instead of grandson as in Zach). But in Neh 12:16 in the list of the priests who returned with Zorobabel, under the group of (DV) Adaia (Heb. '*Iddô* as in v 4) the first name is Zacharia, in Heb. identical with the name of the prophet. Whence it has been supposed that 'son of Addo' shows membership of a group of priests, rather than son- or grandsonship. In which case the prophet is himself already one of the priests who returned, and the argument about his age is not so obvious. Anyway he seems to belong to a priestly family, and his interest in ceremonial matters has been observed, *e.g.* the lamp in ch 4, the garments and headgear of the high-priest in chh 3 and 6, and the fasts in chh 7–8. We should note a coincidence in Is 8:2, where one of Isaias' witnesses (*c* 740 B.C.) is (DV) ' Zacharias the son of Barachias ', but in Heb. the names are slightly different (*Z^eḵaryāhû* and *Y^eḇerekyāhû*), perhaps names that ran in a family ? And see on Mt 23:35.

Historical Background—The prophecies of the first part of the book are dated as are the prophecies of Aggeus, and occur in the same or in the succeeding two years (2nd and 4th of Darius, 520–518 B.C.), and Zacharias joined Aggeus in calling for a rebuilding of the temple, *e.g.* in the 1st Vision (1:16), 5th Vision (4:9), and Conclusion to the Visions (6:12–13), and for a mending of the people's ways, *e.g.* 1:3–6, 6th Vision (5:3–4), and 7th Vision (5:6–8) ; so that with respect at least to the first eight chapters the historical background is exactly the same, and the reader is asked to turn to the outline of the period in § 543*c*. The relation of the latter part of the book (chh 9–14) to the period will be discussed in § 545*j*.

Division and Theme of the Book—The book falls obviously into two parts, chh 1–8 and chh 9–14, and the style and treatment are notably different in the two parts, but there are certain themes that run through the whole. Both parts are essentially **Messianic** in character : in the first part (as in Aggeus) Zoro-babel is presented as a Messianic figure, by his restora-tion of temple-worship and of prosperity to the land

a type of the Redeemer who will restore all things **545d** (*cf.* § 543*f, i*) ; in the second part there is no more mention of Zorobabel or of the need of restoring the temple (this work was apparently by then completed —in 515, *cf.* § 545*j*), and the Messianism is one that looks directly into the future at the Redeemer to come and to the triumph of the **New Jerusalem,** a notion in which the twin ideas of the Church of Christ on earth and the everlasting Jerusalem of Heaven are fused in a picture of an earthly restoration (see esp. 2:11 ; 8:22–23 ; 14:16–21 with notes). In the first part Zorobabel receives the Messianic title of *ṣemaḥ* ' branch, shoot, bud (DV **Orient**) ' (3:8 ; 6:12, see § 547*f*) ; while in the second part the Messias is announced as ' the **King** ' (9:9) (a title never applied to Zorobabel), and this Messianic King will be ' just and victorious ', and ' his power shall be from sea to sea ', but in contrast he will be ' poor and riding upon an ass ' (*ibid.* § 550*g*), and in the last chapter Yahweh himself shall stand upon the earth, shall go forth to fight and ' shall be king over all the earth ' (14:3, 4, 9). The Messianic promises in Aggeus to Zorobabel have but a suggestion of the universal rule of the Messias (Agg 2:7–8, 22–24), and this is little more apparent in the first part of Zach (*e.g.* 8:22–23), but the **universality of the Messianic Kingship** is striking in 9:9 f. and in ch 14. A Messianic role is further acted by the prophet in the second part, in the type of the **shepherd** rejected by the rulers (11:4–14), a passage whose Messianic nature is attested by the NT (Mt 26:15 ; 27:9). Again in the first part the prophet looks back on the years of oppression and misery, and sees in the joint rule of Zorobabel the prince and of Jesus the priest a new era of prosperity (esp. ch 8), marking the end of the dark period since 586, and typifying the Messianic age to come. In the second part he looks forward through the trials and tribulations of future history to the happiness of the Messianic age, identified mysteriously at the end with the ' **Day of the Lord** ' (14:1, 4, 6, 7, 8, 9, 13, 20, 21), when (according to our reading of 14:6, see § 554*c*) ' there shall be a great light ', day that shall be neither day nor night, but everlasting light. In this apocalyptic ch 14 we see Zacharias' **eschatology,** identifying with typical prophetic ' compenetration ' the restoration of Jerusalem with the first and the second coming of Christ. *Cf.* here Malachias' teaching on the ' Day of the Lord ' Mal 4:1–3, § 555*i*.

Thus the Messianic theme, though differently treated **e** in the two parts of the book, runs through the whole. Another theme that appears all through the book is that of **God's Providence,** *e.g.* in Yahweh's zeal for Jerusalem (1:14 ; 8:2), his dwelling in their midst (2:10 12 ; 8:3), his vigilance symbolized in the seven eyes engraved on the stone (4:10), his care for his people (8:7–8), his control of the nations (9:4 ff. ; 12:2–6 ; 14:12–15) and his bringing victory to Judah (*ibid.*) and his purifying of Jerusalem (13:2, 9). Linked with the Messianic idea of the restored Jerusalem is the theme, common to both parts of the book, of the **return of the exiles** (*e.g.* 2:6 and 9:12) and the **promise that the nations also will come** (*e.g.* 2:11 ; 8:22–23 and 10:10 ; 14:16–19). **God's forgiveness** is also taught in both parts, *e.g.* 8:11–15 and 10:6 when Yahweh will no longer punish the people. Yet this

545e depends upon their conduct (1:3 'Turn to me, and I will turn to you') : the need is for a **spiritual religion,** *i.e.* not merely external ritual, but a change of heart. This teaching is most important in Zach : truth, mercy, fair judgement are urged, and 'let not a man devise evil in his heart' (1:4 ; 5:3–4 ; 7:5–10 ; 8:16–19), *i.e.* the intention is important : a central point of Christ's teaching in the Sermon on the Mount, *e.g.* Mt 5:22, 28. These passages should be compared with James' definition of religion clean and undefiled before God, in his Epistle (Jas 1:27). In this teaching Zacharias anticipates that of the NT.

f To sum up therefore the foregoing : the principal **religious teaching** of Zacharias consists in the Messianic theme, in 1–8 under the type of the restoration of Jerusalem and temple-worship under Zorobabel, in 9–14 under the figure of the new and everlasting Jerusalem and of the universal kingdom of Yahweh, and under the type of the shepherd rejected (and contrasted with the type of the Antichrist in 11:15 ff.) ; in the showing of God's providence and forgiveness ; and in insistence upon religion not merely concerned with external rites, but with a right attitude of heart and a cultivation of truth and mercy.

g **Literary Forms**—The notable difference between the two parts of the book is largely due to difference in literary form. Chh 1–6 are a series of *visions* or dreams (1:8 ' by night '), each with a distinct message. Van Hoonacker (pp 579 ff.) considers these to be a special literary form, in which the prophet puts his preaching into the form of visions, frequently transported in imagination to events of the past, and that this particular form of preaching is proper to Zacharias. He adopts this view, rather than the commoner one that the chapters simply represent an account of actual visions received, because several of the visions seem to refer to past events, the revelation of which by means of a vision seems rather pointless, whereas it is easily explicable if they are a literary device intended to bring home graphically to hearers the situation in the past. On the other hand it can be claimed that it is not the fact of the past event, but the message involved, that is the object of the revelations if they are real visions. Be that as it may, the vision-form of chh 1–6 naturally involves a different style. A notable feature of these visions is the introduction of an *interpreting angel*, as in Dan 7:16 ; 8:16 ; 9:21 ff. and in Apoc 17:1 ff. ; 21:9. The phrase ' that spoke in me ' is peculiar to Zach (1:9, 13, 14 ; 2:3—not in DV ; 4:1, 5 ; 5:5, 10 ; 6:4) and its precise significance is uncertain. It is only paralleled in Num 12:2, 8 of God speaking to Moses. 6:9–15 is a *symbolic action* connected with the theme of the visions. Chh 7–8 again have the special literary form of an *enquiry* made to the clergy (*cf.* Agg 2:12–14), followed by the prophet's answer on the need of a spiritual religion. This also may be either the record of an actual enquiry or a literary device. The literary forms in chh 9–14 are the more familiar styles of OT prophecy, including the *enactment of the roles* of the good and foolish shepherds (11:4–17) which may be compared with the symbolic action of 6:9–15 and with Osee's marriages (Os 1:2 ff. ; 3:1 ff.), with Micheas' going naked (Mic 1:8), Isaias' going barefoot (Is 20:2), his writing the name of his son (Is 8:1), and Ezechiel's many symbolic actions, *e.g.* eating the book (Ez 3:1), drawing a plan (4:1), moving his furniture (12:3), etc. We find also in the second part of Zach *prophecies* (' burdens ') against Judah and the nations, and passages of *apocalyptic description* (esp. ch 14), which are familiar features of prophecy.

h **Analysis**—In view of the complicated nature of this book, a fairly full analysis is desirable here. (**N.B.**—I have added an asterisk to references where an alteration in the order of the text is called for. Many such shufflings have been proposed. Those made in the 4th Vision [the lampstand] and in the parable of the foolish shepherd receive general acceptance. Explanations will be found in the commentary.)

FIRST PART A : The Visions 1–6

(After each vision is printed in italics the gist of the angel's interpretation)

Introduction : 'Turn from your evil ways' 1:1–6 (dated 8/520)

1st Vision : The Angel & the 4 Horses 1:7–17 (dated 24/11/519)
  (*Jerusalem shall be rebuilt*)

2nd Vision : The 4 Horns and the 4 Smiths 1:18–21 (HT 2:1–4)
  (*The oppressors shall be destroyed*)

3rd Vision : The Man with the measuring-line 2:1–13 (HT 2:5–17)
  (*The exiles shall return to Jerusalem, and the nations shall come*)

4th Vision : The Lampstand 4:1–3, 11–14 *
  (*The Temple shall be restored by Zorobabel & Jesus*)

5th Vision : The high-priest 3:1–8
  (*Jesus is called to his new work in the temple*)
  The Stone 3:9*a* ; 4:4–10 ; 3:9*b*–10 *
  (*The temple shall be rebuilt by Zorobabel*)

6th Vision : The Flying Scroll 5:1–4
  (*The land shall be purged of injustice*) ·

7th Vision : The woman in the barrel 5:5–11
  (*Iniquity shall be removed far away*)

8th Vision : The 4 Chariots 6:1–8
  (*The oppressors shall be chastised*)

Conclusion : Symbolic action : Jesus and Zorobabel, and ' the counsel of peace between them both '.

FIRST PART B : An Enquiry and its Answer 7–8

(i) An Officer's enquiry about fasting 7:1–3 (dated 4/9/518)

(ii) The Prophet's answer : Truth and Mercy are more important than fasts 7:4–8:23
  (In the past the people rejected God's commands of Truth and Mercy, and therefore they were punished : but now he gives the Messianic promises as an incentive to these virtues. In the Messianic age fasts will be turned into holidays)

SECOND PART A : The First ' Burden ' 9–11 with 13:7–9

(i) The Triumph of Judah 9–10
  (*a*) Prophecies against various cities of Palestine 9:1–8.
  (These cities will either be humiliated or destroyed, while Judah will prosper)
  (*b*) The Messianic hope for Jerusalem 9:9–10
  (Jerusalem shall rejoice, for her Messianic King, poor and humble, will come)
  (*c*) The Triumph of Judah 9:11–10:12
  (The exiles will all return, and Judah in spite of her past infidelity shall have victory and prosperity)
  Interlude : the Destruction of the Forests 11:1–3

(ii) The Shepherds (two parables enacted) 11:4–17 ; 13:7–9
  (*a*) The rejection of the good Shepherd 11:4–14
  (The Shepherd is appointed, but the flock is doomed by its owners. The Shepherd breaks his two symbolic rods, and is rejected by the owners)
  (*b*) The fate of the foolish Shepherd 11:15–17 ; 13:7–9 *
  (The foolish Shepherd has no care for the flock, and is stricken down. The flock is scattered, but a remnant shall remain faithful)

SECOND PART B : The Second ' Burden ' 12–14 less 13:7–9

(i) The fall of Jerusalem shall be a calamity to the nations 12
  (Jerusalem in her fall shall wreck other nations, but shall eventually triumph, though she shall mourn over the rejected Messias)

(ii) The cleansing of Jerusalem 13:1–6
  (Idolatry and magic will be cast out, and the
  ex-prophet shall turn husbandman)
(iii) The Day of the Lord 14
  (Jerusalem shall be captured and the people
  shall flee, but the Lord shall come. Judah and
  Jerusalem shall be restored in the Messianic age,
  and though her enemies will be discomfited, yet
  a remnant of the nations shall adore the Lord)

Historical Allusions in IX-XIV —The allusions to current events at the time of the dated prophecies of the first chapters are for the most part quite obvious (including events back to 586, and mention of Babylon in 2:7 and 6:10) ; but the allusions in the latter part are particularly important for the dating of chh 9–14. *Assyria* (a defunct power since 612) is mentioned in conjunction with Egypt in 10:10 f. The *Jebusites* (a tribe in Jerusalem, which ceased to exist in the time of King David *c* 1000) are mentioned in 9:7. The *Philistines* (a people resident along the sea-coast, for long rivals to the Hebrews in Palestine, and who apparently received a new prosperity in Persian times —*v*. EBCB art. Philistines) are named among the Palestinian cities in 9:6. *Ephraim* (9:10, 13 ; 10:7) and the *house of Joseph* (10:6) apparently stand for the Northern Kingdom or the ten tribes, who were taken into captivity in 722. The earthquake in the time of *Ozias, king of Judah* (14:5) took place *c* 750. The *sons of Yāwān* (Ionia or Greece) are mentioned in 9:13. This is an important allusion, for although the name occurs as far back as Gen 10:2, it seems in earlier passages to connote a remote race, and not a great power as it does here. Although Greece begins to appear in world history about the time of Marathon (490) (see table in § 543*c*), the reference here raises a special problem (see § 550*j*). References to *David* or his house as symbols of power (12:7, 8, 10, 12 ; 13:1) suggest a time when there was a Davidic ruler (such as the kings or Zorobabel). Finally we should remind the reader of the following dates to which there are possible allusions : 586 Captivity. 537 Return under Zorobabel. 515 Completion of the temple. 458 Return under Esdras. 444 Walls of Jerusalem finished. 333 Alexander's victory over the Persians at Issus (Greek domination). 197–142 Seleucid power in Palestine. 175–161 Maccabean revolt.

The Dating of IX-XIV—In view of the varied historical allusions in these chapters, it is not surprising that there are varied opinions on their date. What may be called the *traditional view* is that they are by Zacharias himself, composed after chh 7–8 (518), and probably after the completion of the temple in 515 (since mention of this matter is absent from the second part of the book). The fact that there are certain themes that run through the whole book (§ 545*d, e*) supports this view. If it is true that Agg 2:4 suggests that Aggeus in 520 was an old man who remembered the temple of sixty-six years before, and that he died before its completion, since he does not mention this fulfilment of his desires, it may well be that Zacharias was a much younger man when they both began to prophesy in the year 520 (Esd 5:1), and indeed he always has second place. Further, if Addo of Neh 12:4 was his grandfather, Zacharias would be at most in his thirties in 520 (but *cf*. § 545*b*). It is then quite possible that he would still be preaching even forty years later at a time when the political scene was changing considerably.

I would maintain therefore that the vision or dream writing of the first part, with all its hopes in a new era, is the work of a young man (of about thirty) in 520–518, while the more forbidding and remotely hopeful prophecies of the second part are the work of the older man (of about seventy), when the future of the Persian Empire had become less secure, after the revolt of Egypt in 486, the death of Darius in 485, and the failure of the expedition against Greece (Salamis 480, Plataea and the final Ionian revolt in

the year 479). It is likely that Zorobabel was dead **545k** —he is not heard of later than 520 (Agg 2:1 ; Esd 5:2), though Zacharias in his earlier prophecy promised that he would complete the temple (Zach 4:9), which happened in 515 (Esd 6:15, though Esd does not mention him here by name). If Zorobabel was dead before 490 (he had become governor in 537), it would explain the absence of the Zorobabel theme in the second part of the book. It would appear from the references to the house of David in ch 12 that his successors in government were also of the royal line. By the time of Esdras, however (458), this was not so any more, but nothing is known of the government of Jerusalem between Zorobabel and Esdras. The difference in style and treatment between the two parts of the book is also explained by the difference in the author's age and the changing political circumstances. The famous reference to Greece in 9:13 may conceivably be interpreted in the light of current affairs. The allusions to Assyria (10:10 f.) must be taken either as archaisms, or else as general terms for the imperial rulers of Mesopotamia, be they Babylonians or Persians. Similarly allusions to Ephraim or Joseph have to be understood as symbolic complements to Judah, completing the whole of the ideal Israel ; and the Jebusite in 9:7 has to be taken as a symbol for a race absorbed into Israel.

Van Hoonacker, holding that the visions in 1–6 are **l** a special literary form, maintains that allusions to nations or events of the past are either deliberate archaisms or part of the *mise en scène* deliberately staged for graphic effect. He finds this method in both parts of the book (*e.g.* his exegesis of the destruction of the forests and identification of the shepherds in ch 11 with a *mise en scène* of 586, *cf.* § 545*g*). On this principle Van H. explains the 1st–5th visions as staged in exilic times, through the destruction of Babylon (2nd vision) to the gradually more settled life at Jerusalem after 537, and again the 6th–8th visions as beginning before 586 (Babylon therefore taken literally in the 7th vision), and ending with the chastisement of Babylon in 538 in the 8th vision. Similarly the enemies of Judah in 12:2 ff. refer to difficulties in building during the years 536–520, already past at the time of writing, and the apocalyptic scenes of ch 14 are a merging of the 586 situation and present difficulties into a picture of the future. With this theory Van H. is easily able to defend the Zacharian authorship of the second part of the book, and seems to consider it to have been written only shortly after the first part, *Yāwān* in 9:13 being taken as a later interpolation (see § 550*j*) ; Van H. pp 579–81, 650–62. A *semi-traditional view* is that of Barnes (pp xiv–xxii), who **m** holds that though the second part is by a different hand ('Zechariah the disciple'), it was written shortly after the first, and certainly before the time of Nehemias (444). Indeed in the views expressed above under *k, l, m*, the time of writing is *after* the dated writings of the first part (520–518), probably *after* the completion of the temple (515), and certainly *before* the time of Esdras (458) or Nehemias (444), when the rule of the Davidic line had already ceased.

Since the *denial of the unity of the book* in the 17th cent. **n** there have been many opinions, frequently dividing the book into many fragments. Almost all commentators agree in accepting the dates given in the book for chh 1–8. With regard to chh 9–14, there are three chief schools of those who hold that they are not by the author of the first part. (1) The older **o** critics, *e.g.* Hitzig (1863) and Ewald (1868) held that these chapters are chiefly *pre-exilic*, later absorbed into the book of Zach. Their claims are based principally on pre-exilic historical allusions, including the deportation of the ten tribes by the Assyrians in 722. (2) Driver **p** (1906, pp 228–35), following Stade (1882) and Nowack (1904), places these chapters *in the time of Alexander*, after his victory over the Persians in 333. This is suggested in the first place by 9:13 (Greece), but also by the absence of any reference to Zorobabel or the

545p temple, by the different Messianic treatment and by the state of war, siege and plunder reflected in this part of the book. Ephraim stands for the Diaspora, and Assyria for oppressing powers in general, probably Persia. (The traditional view, of course, also takes

q these names as symbolical.) (3) The third school is represented by Kennett (1920, in Peake, p 579), following Wellhausen (1898, and his art. Zechariah in EBCB, 1907) and Marti (1904), who all date these chapters *in Maccabean times*, about the year 170, claiming that this period is faithfully reflected in ' Deutero-Zechariah', and that Greece in 9:13 refers to the Seleucids, as also does Assyria. Kennett writes that there is no record in post-exilic times of such storm and stress as Zach depicts, until the second cent. Arguments from the classical Hebrew style of Zach are countered by the example of the classicism of Ecclus, *c* 180 B.C. The solution of the difficult problem of the identity of the shepherds in ch 11 depends upon the school to which the exegete belongs (see § 551*b*, *e*, *h*).

r Although one can admit the possibility of the various identifications suggested above, it seems to me probable that the names of the oppressing nations quite *symbolically* for the forces of evil in the world, while Judah (including Ephraim and Joseph in chh 9-10, representing the fullness of the New Israel of the Redemption) stands for the power of Christ in the world, against which the gates of hell will not in the end prevail. In this case many names could, and were intended to, carry several simultaneous identifications in history, past, present or future.

s **Text**—The Hebrew of Zach is in good classical style, with no obvious signs of either archaic or late usage. There is a difference of vocabulary and phraseology between 1-8 and 9-14, but no more than might be expected from the different treatment and different subject-matter, or from the youth and age of the same author ; and there are indeed notable analogies. (For the elaborate linguistic arguments both ways, see Van H., pp 657-60.) The text is frequently unsound—often they are small points that do not affect the sense (and most of these we shall omit to mention in the commentary) ; in many places the LXX or Vg have the better reading, but quite often the corruption is already reflected in those versions. In some passages the Hebrew is simply not patient of the traditional translation, or even of the effort of the RV, and certain critical emendations are almost universally recognized, while for other passages various proposals old and new will have to be put forward. In chh 3-4, and in the placing of 13:7-9, a transposition of verses seems to be demanded by the sense.

t **Interpretation**—It is well to bear in mind that Zacharias is one of the most difficult and enigmatic books of the OT. St Jerome himself several times laments (though not without humour) the difficulty of interpretation. For instance in the Prologue to ch 6 (the last vision) he says : 'Ab obscuris ad obscuriora transimus', and on 10:1 : ' Omnis hic locus obscurus et dubius est, et debet nobis lector ignoscere, si in his quae ambigua sunt, et nos pendulo incedimus gradu'. When he faces ch 11 he writes : ' Transimus ad Libanum, et ad duas virgas, tresque pastores . . . et ad triginta argenteos . . ., et ad stulti vasa pastoris, et caetera . . ., quae tantis sunt contexta mysteriis, ut misericordia Dei et tuis indigeamus orationibus'. Sometimes even the literal sense or allusion is obscure, but sometimes the spiritual sense is plain, as in certain Messianic passages or in the references to the new and eternal Jerusalem ; sometimes indeed it is guaranteed by NT or liturgical usage, but at other times we also must leave God's word a mystery and commend ourselves to his mercy.

FIRST PART A : The Visions I-VI

546a **I 1-6 Introduction**—**1.** The date : the 8th month (Oct.-Nov.) 520, the month between the second and third prophecies of Aggeus. Darius I Hystaspis, King

of the Persians, 521-485 (*v.* § 544*a*). Zacharias, his **5** person and parentage, § 545*b*. **3.** ' Turn ye to me, and I will turn to you ' is commented on by St Thomas in I-II 109, 6 ad 1, where he says that although it is true that ' man turns to God by his free will, yet not unless God turns to him ' (*i.e.* by the gift of habitual grace, ' the principle of meritorious action', *ibid.* corpus). He quotes Lam 5:21, ' Convert us, O Lord, to thee, and we shall be converted'. **4.** ' Turn ye from your evil ways and from your wicked thoughts', a summary of the teaching of the 'former prophets', rejected by the people in the past.

7-17 1st Vision : The Angel and the Horses—The **b** object of this vision is to show Yahweh's vigilance through his emissaries (**11**), and to convey his message of zeal for Jerusalem (**14**, **17** ; *cf.* 8:2) and his promise that the temple and city would be rebuilt (**16**). As so often (and quite patently in ch 14, where the events described are after the final coming of God), Jerusalem is to be understood in the spiritual sense of the Church first on earth and then in heaven. The literal sense here of course refers to the need of rebuilding the temple in Jerusalem, which was not in fact completed until 4 years later (see § 543*c*).

7. The date 24/11/2 (519). Note the Babylonian name of the month (Jan.-Feb.), only here and 7:1 in Agg or Zach ; it had probably become current among the returned exiles. **8.** Myrtle, a shrub standing 3-4 feet high. ' Bottom ' is an old English word (still found in place names) for ' valley or hollow'. Note the definite article, probably indicating a particular hollow near Jerusalem. The word is generally used of the depths of the sea or a river (*cf.* 10:11). The three horses behind were *bay* (red), *sorrel* (RV, *i.e.* mixed white and bay) and *white*. **9.** ' Spoke in me ' is literal, and the expression is peculiar to Zach, see § 545*g*. **10.** ' The man ', *i.e.* the rider on the front horse. **11.** ' The Angel of the Lord ' is now identified with the front rider, and is distinct from the Angel that spoke ' within ' the prophet. The other three riders are God's emissaries who have been to inspect the earth, and have found that ' all the earth is inhabited ', in contrast to the desolation of Jerusalem. **12.** ' 70 years ' —67, to be exact, since 586.

18-21 (HT 2:1-4) 2nd Vision : The 4 Horns and the c 4 Smiths—(In Hebrew Bibles ch 2 begins here.) The horns are the powers that have scattered Judah into exile (*cf.* horns on the beasts=nations in Apoc 13:1, 11), and the *craftsmen* are come to repair the damage. **18.** (1) Horns (of an animal) are a metaphor for power, so that ' to lift up the horn ' is a usual metaphor for ' to act haughtily', as in v 21 (4). **19.** (2) ' Spoke *to* me ' here in DV, although HT and Vg have ' in me ' as usually in Zach. **21.** (4) ' Scattered Judah *so that no man* lifted up. . . .'

II 1-13 (HT 2:5-17) 3rd Vision : The Man with the d Measuring Line—*Cf.* Ezechiel's ' man with a measuring reed in his hand' who takes the prophet in spirit about Jerusalem (Ez 40 ff.). The restored Jerusalem, after the return of the exiles, will be too great to be (figuratively) contained within walls (**4**) : Yahweh himself will be the wall (protection) (**5**), so the services of the young stonemason will not be required. The exiles are to come from Babylon (**6-7**), for there were many who had not yet returned : Esdras' party did not return until 38 years later (in 458, Esd 7-8, *v.* § 543*c*). **4.** (8) The young man is the stonemason of v 1. **6.** (10) ' The north ', frequently used by the prophets (esp. Jer) as a vague description of the lands of the exile. Actually of course invaders from across the Euphrates (Assyrians, Babylonians, Persians) would follow the fertile crescent, cross the Euphrates in its upper reaches and enter Palestine from the north, rather than come direct from the east across the desert. The Vg reading ' I have scattered you into the four winds ' supposes *bᵉʾarbaʿ* for MT *kᵉʾarbaʿ* ' according to the four winds '. But the LXX reading *mēʾarbaʿ*, and *ʾāsaptî* for *pārastî* (' I have scattered ') is preferable, with the translation : ' *From* the four winds I have *gathered* you '. **8.** (12) ' After glory ' is very difficult. RV ' After glory hath he sent me ', AV as DV. Driver makes the whole phrase a parenthesis, and takes ' to the nations ' with ' saith the Lord '. Among various emendations the most satisfactory is that of Van H. *kōḇēḏ* (' suffering ', *cf.* Is 21:15) for *kāḇôḏ* (glory). The words of the prophet (speaking of Yahweh in the third person) are identified with God's authority (' Thus saith . . .') (as in 3:2 and 8:20–22). Translate : ' After the *suffering,* he (Yahweh) hath sent me (Zach) to the nations who rob you, for whoever touches you, touches the apple of *his* (Yahweh's) eye '. The word for the apple of the eye is not the usual one, and occurs only here. The third person suffix is in MT (and in Jerome's commentary). **10** (14) refers presumably to the restored temple. **11.** (15) The nations shall come : a Messianic idea, *cf.* § 545*e.* Here the restoration of Jerusalem as the centre of universal worship (*cf.* esp. 14:16–19) can only be fully understood in the spiritual sense of the universal Church of Christ. **13.** (17) *Cf.* the ' silence in heaven ' of Apoc 8:1.

This verse leads on most easily to the vision beginning ' And the angel . . . waked me ' (4:1), after the silence. Some shuffling is anyway necessary in chh 3–4 ; 4:11–14 are clearly the explanation of the Lampstand in 4:1–3, so that the dialogue beginning in 4:4 must refer to something else : I would therefore attach 4:4–10 to the ' Stone ' passage in 3:9 (*v.* further explanation in § 547*g*). I have chosen to place the Lampstand vision first, in view of the wakening after the silence.

IV 1-3 ; 11-14 (chh III and IV 4-10 follow) 4th Vision : The Lampstand—2-3. The **vision** of a ' *lampstand all of gold, and a reservoir upon the top of it, and its seven lamps above it, and seven pipes to the lamps which are upon the top thereof* '. **2.** ' *Lampstand* ' with seven lamps : the same word is as used of the ' seven-branched candlestick ' of the temple (Ex 25:3 ff. ; 37:17 ff.), wherefore it is taken here as a figure of the temple and its worship (*cf.* the point of the next vision : its restoration), ' and in a more sublime sense ' (Challoner) of the Church of Christ. ' Reservoir ' *gullāh* (a bowl). The *mappiq* in the *he* is probably an error, supposing a word *gōl* with suffix : ' *its* bowl '. (After the words ' above it ' MT has again ' seven ', rightly omitted by LXX and Vg.) **3.** ' And two olive trees *beside* it.'

11-14. (for vv 4–10 see § 547*g–i*). The **interpretation** follows with its usual dialogue (*cf.* 1:9 ; 1:21 ; 2:2 ; 4:4 ; 5:2 ; 5:6, 10 ; 6:4). **12.** ' Olive branches ', properly ' ears ' as of corn. ' Beaks ', a word occurring only here, related to the word for ' pipe ' or ' spout ' in 2 Kg 5:8 and Ps 41(42):8. ' In which are the funnels of gold ', MT lit. ' which empty from upon them the gold '. RV adds the word ' oil ', supposing a poetic diction quite inadmissible after the mechanical description of the apparatus. Vg read a noun for the verb ' empty ', but the sense arrived at is unlikely. Either a phrase has dropped out, or better, we must for ' from upon them ' read the word *mûṣāqôṯ* ' pipes ' (as in v 2), translating : ' *which empty from the pipes of gold* '. **14.** ' Sons of oil ', *i.e.* full of oil (*cf.* Is 5:1 ' son of fatness ', DV ' fruitful place '). This word for oil is used of oil freshly pressed from the olive, not that prepared for anointing, so probably here (Kennett) the idea is not that of anointing, but of fruitfulness.

The Lampstand, a figure of the temple, is supplied with oil by the two fruitful olive trees, obviously Zorobabel and Jesus, the restorers of the temple and its worship : *cf.* the next vision (5th) and the concluding prophecy (6:9–15 § 548*d*), where is emphasized the Messianic significance of Zorobabel (*cf.* Agg 2:24 and see § 543*i*) and Jesus, combining between them the kingly and priestly power, fulfilled together in Christ. The ' two olive trees and the two lamps that stand before the Lord of the earth ' of Apoc 11:4 are there connected with the temple, and are presumably

taken from this passage. Jerome mentions a traditional **547c** interpretation of the two trees as the OT and NT.

III 1-8 5th Vision (first part) : The high-priest— d In the *first part* of this vision the prophet sees the high-priest rebuked by God for his slackness, symbolized by his slovenly liturgical attire (a matter of interest to Zacharias the priest). His iniquity (4), presumably his remissness over rebuilding the temple, is removed and he is reclothed with new vestments, symbolizing his preparedness for the restoration of temple worship. In the *second part* he sees the cornerstone for building, which is to be put in position by Zorobabel, lying before the high-priest (9*a*). The interpretation of the whole vision is in 4:4–10 and 3:9*b*–10.

1. Jesus, the high-priest, see § 543*h*. ' Satan ', in **e** Heb. ' *the* Satan ', *i.e. the* Adversary *par excellence.* Used without article for any adversary, *e.g.* in Num 22:22, 32 (Balaam) of the angel standing in the way. **2.** Satan is rebuked : Jerusalem is to belong to Yahweh and not to him. The high-priest is a ' firebrand plucked out of the fire ', *i.e.* having narrowly escaped destruction at Satan's hands (same metaphor in Am 4:11). **4.** The high-priest's ' iniquity ' is his remissness. In 4:9 the work is obviously begun, but not yet finished—this is 24/11/519, and Aggeus' preaching had its effect in starting the work on 24/6/520 (Agg 2:1), five months before to the day. But work was apparently slow, for they needed encouragement again on 21/7/520 (Agg 2:2), after less than a month. Jesus is to be prepared for his new work in the restored temple. **5.** ' He said : Put . . .', MT ' I said : They will put . . .'; Vg better. **7.** The angel is speaking : ' Some that are now present here ', *i.e.* other angels, members of the celestial court to which Jesus is now admitted. Here is a compenetration of the ideas of the earthly and the heavenly Jerusalem. ' I will give thee *maḥlᵉḵîm* ' ' walks ' (of place or distance : a rare word, only in Ez 42:4, 4 ; Neh 2:6 ; Jon 3:3 and here). Probably best translated as in AV and RVm : ' *places to walk among these that stand by* '. **8.** *Men of portent* ', the assistant priests with a glorious future before them.

' The **Orient** '—one of the Messianic titles, here applied **f** to Zorobabel (*cf.* Agg 2:24, *v.* § 543*i*) as restorer of the temple, and so, by compenetration applied to Christ, saviour not only of Israel but of the world (*cf.* § 550*g*). Zachary in the Benedictus (Lk 1:78) refers to Christ as the ' Orient ' (AV RV ' Dayspring ') (*cf.* the ' O Antiphon ' for Dec. 21), Gk ἀνατολή, sunrise, east ; this is the word here in LXX for Heb. *ṣemaḥ*, meaning a ' *shoot of a plant* ' and used Messianically in Jer 23:5 ' I will raise up to David a just *ṣemaḥ* ' (LXX ἀνατολή, Vg germen, DV branch) and Jer 33:15 (LXX A ἀνατολή, B βλαστός, *al.* κέρας, Vg germen, DV bud). (AV & RV have ' branch ' in all passages, but RVm adds in Zach ' or shoot, or sprout ', and in Jer 23 ' or shoot, or bud '.) It is doubtful whether ἀνατολή can mean the rising of a plant, and the origin of the LXX and Vg rendering remains obscure, though the title has been accepted by NT usage and liturgical tradition. The title occurs again in 6:12, where the reference to Zorobabel is quite obvious.

III 9a IV 4-10 III 9b-10 5th Vision (second part) : g The Stone—9a. The mention of Zorobabel (' Orient ') in 3:8 brings a new stage in the vision : the building-stone for the temple, laid in the vision before the high-priest, and engraved with 7 eyes, a sign of Yahweh's vigilance as explained in 4:10, in the interpretation of the vision. (These two references to the 7 eyes are the key to the present rearrangement.) Barnes mentions a stone engraved with 7 eyes found at Gezer, the device was therefore known to Palestinian masons ; *cf.* PEF (1908) 201. (Mention should be made of Wellhausen's view that the reference is to a precious stone with 7 facets, a diadem for Zorobabel's crown.) **IV 4-5.** The familiar dialogue, obviously not part of the Lampstand vision, for that has its dialogue in 4:11–13. In the order as the text stands, this vision (of the high-priest and the Stone) alone

547g has no dialogue : I therefore maintain that ' these things ' (4:4) refer to the happenings to Jesus and to the presence of the stone before him. The whole vision is concerned with the restoration of the temple, which is the theme of the interpretation 4:4–10. **6.** ' Not by *force* nor by might ', *i.e.* not by human effort alone will the rebuilding of the temple be done,

h but by the spirit of Yahweh. **7.** Zorobabel as civil governor is to lay the final stone himself. A very difficult verse. MT lit. ' Who art thou, mountain the great, before Z., for flatness ? And he shall bring out the top stone—noises—grace, grace to it '. RV's attempt : ' . . . before Z. *thou shalt become a plain*. And he shall bring forth the head stone *with shoutings of* " Grace, grace to it ! " ', which, although adopted by Van H., undoubtedly forces the Hebrew. LXX ' . . . before Z. *for setting upright* ? And *I* will bring out the stone *of inheritance, equality of* grace, grace to it '. Syr. ' . . . before Z., *but like a plain*, and he brought out the head stone *of equality* and *of mercy* '. These divergent readings at least suggest weaknesses in the text, rendered also suspect in its first words by the absence of the article to ' mountain ', while the adjective has it. Some would read here *weṣamtî 'eṭ hāhār* ' and I shall set the mountain ', but I feel that the mountain is quite out of place here, and for *mî 'attāh har* (' who art thou, o mountain ') I would read *kî nāṭattî hā'eben* ' For I have set the stone '. The LXX ' for setting upright ' points to a verb such as *leyaššar* (Piel) for *lemîšôr* (' for flatness '), and the LXX, Syr. and Vg ' equality ' suggests a word from root (I) *šāwāh*, for which I would propose *weṣiwwāhh* ' and he will place it ' from root (II) *šāwāh*. Further, the repeated *hēn* (' grace ') offers for one of them the reading *wehinnēh* ' and behold '. I would therefore translate the reconstructed verse : ' *For I have set the great stone before Zorobabel to erect straight, and he will bring out the top stone and will place it, and behold it has beauty* '. This reconstruction preserves the theme of the building-stone throughout. If, however, we retain the reading ' mountain ', it must be understood of *obstacles* to

i Zorobabel's work, which will be *smoothed out*. **9.** The promise to Zorobabel that he indeed will finish the work of rebuilding the temple, to be fulfilled 4 years and 1 month afterwards (3/12/515 Esd 6:15, *cf.* § 543*c,f*). **10.** ' Little days ', *i.e.* days of insignificant things, small beginnings. Those who once despaired will now rejoice. ' Tin plummet ', lit. ' the stone, the tin ' (in apposition). This is not the usual word for a plummet as in Am 7:7, and it stands awkwardly. Van H. reads *habbāḏûl* (' reserved ') for *habbeḏil* (' tin '), but I would suggest *haggeḏôlāh*, translating ' . . . see the *great* stone (referred to above, and immediately afterwards) in the hand of Zorobabel '. This reading brings us easily to the stone with 7 eyes, which in turn leads us back to III 9*b* where Yahweh himself will engrave the 7 eyes, symbolizing his vigilance, and ' take away the iniquity of that land ', *i.e.* Judah, ' in one day ', *i.e.* quickly and completely. Jerome takes the stone itself, pierced, as a type of Christ, who will ' take away iniquity in one day '. **10** completes the whole with a picture of peace and prosperity in the Messianic age, with husbandmen calling to one another from under their fruitful trees.

548a **V 1–4 6th Vision : The Flying Scroll**—Yahweh's judgement on the thief and perjurer : part of the work of cleansing the land. *Cf.* the moral exhortations to truth, justice and mercy in 1:4 ; 7:5–10 ; 8:16–19, and see § 545*e*. **1.** ' Volume ', *i.e.* a scroll that can be rolled up. **2.** Obviously here unrolled, showing its full dimensions : 30 × 15 ft. **3.** ' Shall be judged as there is written ', MT lit. ' has been cleared out (more frequently used of acquittal) from now according to it (*mizzeh kāmôhā*) '. For this last Wellhausen proposed *zeh kammāh* (' how long ? '), translating : ' How long has the thief gone unpunished ? ' **4.** ' I *have brought* it forth, and it shall come . . . '

b **5–11 7th Vision : The Woman in the Barrel**— Under another figure the iniquity of the land is

removed. The evil woman in the barrel of iniquity is removed to Babylon, ' the proper home of all that is evil ' (Driver). **6.** ' Vessel ', *i.e.* a grain measure or barrel, an ephah (RV) (*'êpāh*) = about 7 gallons (*cf.* § 82*j*). ' Their eye ', lit. from Heb. *'ênām*. RV ' their resemblance ' (Driver adduces Num 11:7 and Lev 13:5 for the meaning ' appearance ', *i.e.* what appears to the eye), but much better read with LXX *'awônām*, and translate : ' This is their *iniquity* in all the *land* '. **7.** ' Talent ' Heb. *kikkār* = something circular (*cf.* RVm), perhaps simply the lid of the barrel, but the word came to be used regularly of the leaden weight, a talent (108–130 lbs), and all the Vss convey this. Barnes comments : ' Those who sinned by fraud are appropriately punished by measure and weight '. **8.** ' Weight ', lit. ' stone '. **9.** It is probable that the two women have no special significance, but are merely a vivid part of the picture of the transportation of the barrel to Babylon. If, however, we adopt a *mise en scène* of 586 for this vision (v. § 545*l*), then they obviously represent the Babylonians. ' Kite ', Vg milvus, which Jerome avers is the meaning of *hasîḏāh*, though LXX has ' hoopoe ' and RV and BDB ' stork '. In other passages it is translated heron (LXX, Vg) or pelican (LXX), onocrotalus (a kind of pelican, Vg—DV bittern) or kite (Vg). **11.** ' Sennaar ', where Amraphel had been king (Gen 14:1), *i.e.* the territory of Babylon (so LXX here). It is either a symbol of all that is evil, or to be taken literally if the vision refers to 586.

VI 1–8 8th Vision : The 4 Chariots—God's chariots go forth to punish the oppressing nations. **1.** The chariots come out from between *the* two mountains of brass. In v 5 we understand that they came from the presence of Yahweh. Barnes therefore suggests that the prophet is using a current Babylonian idea (reflected in the Koran ch 18) that a brazen or copper rampart divided earth and heaven. Others suggest that the article indicates a well-known image, or an unrecorded part of the 1st Vision (Driver), or that they stand for the ' brazen ' strength of God's abode (Kennett, *cf.* Jerome), or the fabulous metallic wealth of remote regions (Van H.). **2–3.** The 4 horses are *bay, black, white* and *dappled* (' spotted ' of sheep in Gen 31:10, 12 ; Vg here has ' varii ' as for the sorrel horse in 1:8. DV here ' grisled ' and ' speckled ' in 1:8 for the sorrel horse). The dappled horses are also described as ' strong ' (*'amuṣṣîm*, only here and v 7, and probably a corrupt repetition of *'aḏummîm* ' bay ', and so probably to be left out, as in Syr.). **5.** ' Go forth *from standing* before the Lord '. **6.** ' That in which were ', MT lit. ' which in it '. These words have little connexion with the sentence and make little sense : probably they are corrupt copies of the preceding word and the following article : the participle (' went forth ') after the horses is anyway plural. Read ' The black horses *were going forth* '. **6–7.** The mission of the horses : (1) the *black* ones are going forth to the north, (2) the *white* ones *to the west* (I would read *'aharônāh, cf.* Num 2:31, for the almost meaningless *'aharêhem* ' after them '), (3) the *dappled* ones to the south, and (4) the *bay* (reading *'aḏummîm, cf.* v 2, for *'amuṣṣîm* ' strong '—the bay would otherwise be unmentioned) sought to walk about the earth. **6 & 8.** ' The north ' = Babylonia (*cf.* 2:6 § 546*d*), visited by the black horses, is singled out. The collapse of Babylonia at the hand of Cyrus in 538 springs to the mind, when Yahweh's wrath against Babylonia is ' quietened '. Other kingdoms have been assigned to the other horses, notably (if we retain ' after them ') the white horses who went after the black (Cyrus) being identified with Alexander, those who went to the south with Egypt, and the bay (or strong) horses who went through all the earth, with the Romans (v. Challoner, following Jerome).

9–15 Concluding Prophecy : a Symbolic Action— Jesus the high-priest is to be crowned with crowns made from gold and silver belonging to returned exiles, as a sign of his priestly dignity and authority ; and

d (12) with him is to be united in the rule of the restored Jerusalem the man whose name is ' the Orient ', who shall build the temple, *i.e.* Zorobabel. This again looks ahead to the Messianic hope of the New Jerusalem and its divine leader, Christ **(13)**, uniting in himself the priestly and the kingly dignity (Jerome). Lastly, the nations shall contribute to the building of the new temple (*cf.* Agg 2:7 ' the Desired of all nations ', *v.* § 544*g*), which can hardly be understood but in the spiritual sense of the New Temple, the Church of Christ.

e 10. ' Of the captivity ', *i.e.* of the body of the returned exiles : Holdai (who reappears in v 14 as Helem—both names otherwise unknown), Tobias, Idaias, and Josias the son of Sophonias (who reappears as Hem—Heb. *ḥēn*, which is probably a corrupt repetition of the following word *ben* ' son of ', so in v 14 read simply ' *and to the son of* Sophonias '). **12.** ' The Orient ', *ṣemaḥ*, Messianic title as in 3:8 (*q.v.* & § 547*f*). The reference to Zorobabel as builder of the temple (*cf.* 4:9) is obvious here. ' Under him ', a usual Heb. idiom for ' where he stands '. ' Spring up ', a verb from the root of *ṣemaḥ*, ' a shoot ', translated ' Orient '. **f 13.** ' And he shall be a priest upon his throne '. For ' on his throne ' read with LXX ' at his right hand ', translating : ' *And there shall be a priest* (Jesus) *at his* (Zorobabel's) *right hand, and the counsel of peace shall be between them both* '. This last sentence, speaking of two people, bears out the LXX reading. The passage is important as representing the ideal government, with the ' counsel of peace ' between priest and prince, Church and State, but the emendation from the LXX is necessary for its proper understanding.

FIRST PART B : An Enquiry and its Answer VII-VIII

a VII 1-3 The Occasion : an Officer's Enquiry about Fasting—1. The last date in Zach, 4/9 (Nov.-Dec.)/4 (518), exactly midway (2 years and 3 months) between the resumption of work on the temple at the insistence of Aggeus (24/6/520) and its completion (3/12/515), and just over 1¾ years after the visions (see § 543*c*). **b 2.** MT lit. ' And there sent *Bēt-'ēl* (or, the house of God) *Ṣar-'eṣer* and *Regem Meleḵ* and his men to entreat . . .' LXX & Syr ' And there sent to Bethel . . .' For *Regem* the LXX has various corruptions in various MSS, and Syr has *Raḇmāḡ*. The place Bethel (as RV) is unthinkable. Van H. reads Beth-Israel, but Wellhausen's suggestion is that it is the first component (the name of a deity) of the following Babylonian name *Ṣar-uṣur* is very convincing. In Jer 39:3, 13 we have the name *Nērgal-šar'eṣer* who has the title of Rab-mag among Babylonian officers, who are called *Rabbê* and *Ṣārê hammeleḵ* ' officers of the king '. *Nergal* is of course the name of a Babylonian deity. In this case we might suppose the first component was *Baitil*, the name of another deity. And for *Regem* we can read *Raḇ*, a usual word for a Babylonian officer. So the passage reads : ' *And Baitil-šar-uṣur, an officer of the king, and his men, sent to entreat* . . .' The sing. verb here and in v 3, and the sing. suffix ' his men ', are thus also explained. The man must have been a Jew who had obtained a commission in the army during the exile, and returning to Jerusalem to the half-built temple, had a question about liturgical observance. **c 3.** ' Weep ', *i.e.* ceremonial mourning observed on the 10th day of the 5th month (July-Aug.), the day of the destruction of the temple in 586 (Jer 52:12 ; 4 Kg 25:8) ; ' *sanctifying myself* ', *i.e.* fasting (omit ' or ' according to MT). **His question is whether now that the temple is being rebuilt he must still observe the day of mourning over its destruction ?** Kennett remarks that it is odd that an enquiry is made in November about a fast-day in July, and suggests that the text should include the other fasts mentioned in 7:5 and 8:19, *viz.* 9/4 (Jerusalem taken Jer 52:6), 3/7 (Godolias

murdered Jer 41:2—Barnes states that the 3rd day **549c** was only fixed in rabbinic times) and 10/10 (siege began 4 Kg 25:1).

VII 4-VIII 23 The Prophet's Answer : Truth and d Mercy are more Important than Fasts—four sections, each introduced by ' And the word of the Lord came to Zacharias '.

VII 4-7 In the Past, were Fasts kept for God ?—5. e ' These 70 years ', *i.e.* 68 since 586. **7.** Did not the ' former prophets ' (*cf.* 1:4) preach the same thing before the exile, ' when Jerusalem was as yet inhabited and *quiet* . . . and there were inhabitants towards the *Negeb* (proper name of S. Judah) and the *Shephelah* (a definite area, the lowlands [RV] W. of the Judaean mountains) ' ?

8-14 God commanded Truth and Mercy by the hand **f** of the ' former prophets ', and forbade evil devices in the heart **(9-10)** (this doctrine of Zach on intention is important, *cf.* NT teaching, see § 545*e*), but the people refused to obey ; so God punished them with exile. In **11** ' they *gave a stubborn* shoulder ', same phrase in Neh 9:29. ' Stubborn ' as in Os 4:16 of a heifer unwilling to work (DV ' wanton ') ; *cf.* the phrase ' to give the cold shoulder '.

VIII 1-17 And now God is giving Messianic Promises g as an Incentive—He will no longer punish them (*cf.* § 545*e*). On the contrary he makes to them seven promises, each beginning ' Thus saith the Lord of hosts '. **2. 1st promise :** Yahweh is zealous for Jerusalem. **3. 2nd promise :** he is returning thither, with his presence in the temple. ' City of Truth ', *i.e.* Faithfulness, from the same root as Isaias' well-known phrase ' the faithful city ' (Is 1:21, 26). **4. 3rd promise :** he will give prosperity in the Messianic age, longevity and offspring. ' Staff in his hand for very age ' (RV) : longevity as a sign of prosperity. **5.** ' One of the very few indications in the OT of a love for children as such ' (Kennett). **6. 4th promise :** Yahweh assures them of his power to do this. ' Hard ' in the sense of ' difficult '. **7. 5th promise :** he will bring back the exiles to Jerusalem, ' and they shall be my people and I will be their God '=almost verbally Jer 7:23. 2 Cor 6:16 quotes either Zach or Jer. (Similar passages are Ex 6:7 ; Lev 26:12 ; Ez 37:23, 27 ; *cf.* Deut 27:9 ; Ps 32(33):12 ; 143(144):15.) **9. 6th promise :** he will bring prosperity instead of the curse of former days before the rebuilding of the temple had begun. **10-11.** In those days unemployment and class-warfare were rife : now it will be so no longer. **12.** ' But there shall be the seed of peace : the vine shall . . .' A difficult passage. MT lit. ' For the seed of peace, the vine shall . . .' The text as it stands can be translated by the insertion of a verb as in DV & RV, or else with the ' seed ' and the ' vine ' in apposition (as in the lit. trans. above). The LXX however for ' the seed of ' (*zera‛*) has ' I will show ', whence the word has variously been emended into a verb or participle : reading *zārûa‛* ' peace is sown ' (Barnes) ; *'ezrᵉ‛āh* ' I will sow peace ' (Wellhausen) ; *zar‛āhh šālôm* ' her seed is peace '; but I would prefer *'ezrᵉ‛ēhā bᵉšālôm* ' I will sow her (the remnant) in peace ' (*cf.* Zach 10:9 of ' sowing ' the exiles among the nations) ; or perhaps reading *yizraḥ* ' peace will dawn '. **14. 7th promise :** he will no longer afflict the people, but they must obey his commands to **truth and mercy**, and **avoid evil in the heart and perjury**. (*Cf.* 7:9-10 and also 1:4 ; 5:3-4, the Vision of the Scroll.)

18-23 The Answer to the Officer's Enquiry—19. h The fasts (see note on 7:3 § 548*c*) shall be turned into holidays—' only love ye truth and mercy ', which is much more important. **20** ' *Yet nations shall come* ' (reading '*ôḏ* with LXX as in MT, but omitting '*ªšer*. Vg read '*aḏ* '*ªšer*). **21-23.** ' And the inhabitants *of one* (fem. *sc.* city) *shall go to another* (fem.) ', and not only the land, but the Gentile nations shall come to worship Yahweh. This again is only fully understandable of the Church of Christ which embraces all nations.

SECOND PART A : The First ' Burden '
IX-XI with XIII 7-9

550a For the discussion of the authenticity and the date of this part of the book, see § 545*j–q*. For its distinct Messianism § 545*d*, for its literary forms § 545*g*. The **general theme** of chh 9–14 is that God will bring happiness and prosperity to Judah, especially with the advent of the Messianic King, but discomfiture or absorption to her enemies (9–10) ; yet Judah will reject her shepherd and have a bad ruler (11) ; but finally, though Jerusalem will be destroyed, she will yet be cleansed and restored, and the remnant of the nations will join her in adoring Yahweh (12–14).

b The precise **interpretation** of these various elements is difficult, for there is much prophetical ' foreshortening ' in the time-perspective, from the past events of 586, through the present of the restoration of the Jewish nation and worship, to the future settling of the country, the further future of Christ the Redeemer and the New Jerusalem, his Church, and the remote future of his second coming in the calamitous end of the world. These various perspectives must be kept in mind when reading these chapters. Although the identification of particular persons and events is difficult, the symbolic meaning of the whole, the final triumph of God's cause and of right in the world, and the defeat of evil, is plain enough (*cf.* § 545*r*). The first ' Burden ' falls into two parts with an interlude. Ch 9 is textually the most difficult in the book.

c **IX-X The Triumph of Judah.**
IX 1-8 Prophecies against Various Cities of Palestine, as a prelude to that on Jerusalem (*cf.* Am 1:3–2:3 as a prelude). **1-4** mention cities of Syria, **5-7** Philistine cities of SW. Judaea. **1.** ' Burden ', *prophecy* or (RVm) *oracle*, a common title in prophecy (Is, Jer, Ez, Nah, Zach, Mal), Heb. *maśśā'*, from the verb *nāśā'* ' to lift up ' (the voice), distinct from *maśśā'* a burden (that is lifted up). Perhaps here

d it stands alone as a title (see translation below). Among the **Syrian cities**, ' Hadrach ' is found only here, and is usually identified with Hatarika, an area of Syria mentioned in Assyrian inscriptions, or with Hazrach of an Aramaic inscription. For ' the eye of a man ' *'ēn 'āḏām*, we should doubtless read (with Klostermann) *'ārê 'ārām* ' the cities of Aram (Syria) '—a generally accepted emendation. For ' Israel ' *yiśrā'ēl* (which seems irrelevant) the reading *śem'ōl* ' left ', *i.e.* ' north ', has been suggested. So the reconstructed verse reads :

> ' An Oracle.
> *The word of Yahweh is upon Hadrach,*
> *And Damascus is his resting-place ;*
> *For to Yahweh belong the cities of Syria*
> *And all the tribes of the North* (or *Israel*).

2. Either (1) translate MT ' Emath (Hamath) also shall border on her ', or else (2) follow LXX and Vg, reading *big*ᵉ*bûlāhh* ' within her border ', the sense being (in either case) that even this city in the very north of Palestine will border on Yahweh's land. But (3) Kennett's reading ' Emath *and* G*ᵉ*bal ' (*cf.* Ez 27:9), a Syrian city on the coast=Byblus (one of the four provinces of Phoenicia) is attractive. The Syrian cities mentioned are therefore Hadrach, Damascus, Hamath, (Gebal), Tyre and Sidon. **3-4.** The vast riches of Tyre and Sidon shall also belong to Yahweh. These were the centres of Phoenician trade, which prospered greatly under Persian rule (EBCB art. Phoenicia). Tyre was captured by Alexander in 332, and some understand the impending disaster of this event (§ 545*p*) ; but the general idea that the great kingdoms of the earth will have no future in the Messianic age can be taken as a purely symbolic meaning.

e **5-6.** The **Philistine cities** near the coast will also fall under Yahweh's judgement. Four cities are mentioned : Ascalon, Gaza, Accaron (Ekron), Azotus (Ashdod) ; the fifth, Geth (Gath), had apparently ceased to exist after the Assyrian invasions of the 8th cent. and is

not mentioned after Am 6:2 and Mic 1:10. But the cities mentioned here continued in prosperity, first as vassals of the Babylonians and then of the Persians. A vassal-king at Gaza (**5**) is still named in Babylonian times, and Herodotus (*c* 450) describes the city as very prosperous (EBCB art. Philistines, Gaza). **6.** ' The divider shall sit ' (Vg ' separator '), Heb. *mamzēr*, only here and Deut 23:2 among those forbidden entry to the church or assembly. It is usually understood to mean a ' bastard ' (DV there has ' mamzer ' with explanation), so here ' *a bastard race* ' (RVm) or *half-breed shall dwell in Azotus* ' (*cf.* LXX). One of the calamities that will befall Philistia : and indeed from the beginning they seem to have mixed with the local population, a mixture probably increased by the invasions from the east (EBCB, *ibid.*). **7.** ' Abomination ' : Ez 33:25 speaks of the heathen inhabitants of Palestine during the exile committing various abominations, including eating the blood of their victims. ' Governor ' *'allûp* : probably should be pointed *'elep*, translating : ' He (Azotus) shall be as a *tribe* in Judah ' (Driver), which is completed by the parallel sentence : ' And Accaron as a Jebusite ', *i.e.* treated as a fellow citizen, as were the Jebusites in Jerusalem before the time of King David (Jos 15:63). The difficulty is to see clearly the fate of the Philistines : Syria is to be struck by Yahweh and her wealth appropriated, while Philistia shall fear, lose her king, her race and religion, and apparently be incorporated into Judah.

8. MT ' And I will encamp for my house *miṣṣābāh* **f** from one passing and returning '. BDB suggests a noun (*cf.* *maṣṣāb*) meaning garrison, translating : ' I will encamp as a watch for my house ' (*cf.* RVm), but for ' encamp ' *ḥānîtî*, read *hinnaḥtî* (Hiph. of *nûaḥ*) ' set ' (*cf.* LXX ' leave posted '), translating : ' *I will establish a garrison for my house, from those who pass and return* ' (*i.e.* the occupants of the land) : for Jerusalem is now mistress of Palestine, and uses the inhabitants for her own purposes. The Vg DV AV and RV are attempts to translate *miṣṣābāh* as if it were *miṣṣābā'* (' from an army ') ' For now *I am watching* ' : the perfect in Heb. here expressing conditions acquired before, but of which the effects still remain in the present (GK 106*g*).

9-10 The Messianic Hope for Jerusalem — Here the **g** thought suddenly broadens out from the narrow sphere of Palestinian affairs to the Messianic idea of world peace, and the **King** ' who will come to thee, poor, and riding upon an ass '. ' From the Jewish hopes opens the universal destiny for all men ; . . . the prophets . . . no longer speak only to their own race, but speak a sign of contradiction to the whole world (sono contradittori che parlano al mondo) ', Paolo Orano, *Ebrei in Italia* (Rome, 1937) 33–4. The Saviour-King who will be poor is indeed a contradiction to the previous verses, as was his entry into Jerusalem to the Jewish hopes of the time, founded on too literal an interpretation of the prophets' foretelling of the final victory of Judah. Indeed, the mystery of the combination of mightiness and lowliness was not to be fulfilled until Christ himself. Mt 21:5 quotes this passage, combined with Is 62:11, ' Tell the daughter of Sion, behold thy Saviour cometh '. Note that Mt 21:2 has *two* animals as in Zach, and that the ass and colt already appear in the Messianic passage about Judah in Gen 49:11. The verse ' Exsulta satis . . . ' is used in the Liturgy as Communion-verse at Christmas (2nd Mass), and Offertory on the 3rd Sunday of Advent. **9.** ' Saviour ' Niph. Ptcp. lit. ' having been saved ', *i.e.* ' victorious ' (Driver), otherwise follow LXX and Vg, reading *môśîa'* Hiph. Ptcp. ' saviour ' (of God in Is 43:11 ; 45:15, 21 ; 63:8). **10.** The Age of Peace. ' The *River* ', *i.e.* the Euphrates, the edge of the civilized world.

IX 11-X 12 The Triumph of Judah—The exiles shall **h** all return, and Judah, in spite of her past infidelities, shall have victory and prosperity. This brings us back to Palestinian affairs, and the general idea of God's victory.

11-12 The Return of the Exiles—'Blood of thy testament', *i.e.* the daily sacrifices, by whose intercession the remaining captives are returning. MT '*I have sent forth*'. The sharp contrast between the desolation of a waterless pit, and the hope that the captives should have in God, who will restore them to a double prosperity.

13-16 The Victory of Judah—It is not patent who the vanquished are. They may be identified with various oppressors (§ 545*i-q*), or may be a pure symbol of the forces of evil, while Judah and Ephraim stand for the power of good. Such a symbolical interpretation makes Zacharias's message a message for every age (*cf.* § 545*r*). **13.** The famous reference to the Greeks : ' *For I have bent my bow, O Judah, I have filled it* (i.e. fitted the arrow), *O Ephraim : and I will rouse thy sons, O Sion, against the sons of Greece*'. 'Sons of' *cf.* LXX. 'Greece.' Heb. *Yāwān, i.e.* Ionians. The name occurs in Is Dan Ez and Jo among the prophets, but its presence here, evidently indicating a power hostile to Judah, is difficult to explain in a passage written even as early as 480 or 479 when the Greek victories over the Persians, although in fact showing the first assertion of Greek power, can nevertheless hardly be considered to constitute a threat to the nations of the East. The phrase certainly suggests a background of the time of Alexander the Great (*c* 333) or of the Seleucids in Maccabean times (*c* 170), and this is one of the elements in the arguments for a late date for these chapters (*cf.* § 455*p, q*). If, however, we date this part of the book in the old age of Zacharias, *c* 480 (*cf.* § 545*k*), although the reference to Greek power is just conceivable, it is much more likely that the phrase is a marginal gloss inserted at a later age to give point to the prophecy. This view is strongly supported by considerations of metre and parallelism in that verse, which without the gloss would run as follows :

*I have bent my bow, O Judah—I have filled it, O Ephraim :
I will rouse thy sons, O Sion—I will make thee as a sword
of a hero*

Cf. Van H. *in loc.*, who, however, follows Vg (and DV) in taking Judah and Ephraim as accusatives, standing for the bow and arrow respectively. **15.** ' With stones of the sling ' : ' with ' is not in HT, but is rightly suggested in LXX. ' They shall be inebriated', *hāmû* ' they have made a noise ' (*cf.* RV), but tense and sense are unsuitable. LXX (B) has ' them ' (*hēmmāh*), and LXX (A) has ' their blood ' (*dammām*), according to which we can translate : ' *And they shall drink them* (or *their blood*) *like wine* '. ' Bowls ' lit. ' tossing-vessels ' AV ' basons ' (Ex 27:3 ; 38:3 where DV ' fleshhooks '), temple utensils in which the blood of the sacrificial victims was collected and tossed against the sides of the altar, thus drenching also the ' horns ' (EBCB art. Sacrifice 26, *cf.* Lev 1:5). The use of these sacrificial words supports the reading ' their blood ' above. The whole verse is a wild metaphor, ' but it reflects, no doubt, the *animus* with which a people that had suffered much regarded its oppressors ' (Driver). **16.** ' Yahweh . . . will *deliver them, his people, like a flock* '. ' For holy stones ('*aḇnê-nêzer* : stones of consecration) are lifted up'. Van H. : ' les mots ne disent rien du tout ', but many explanations have been attempted : royal or priestly crowns (*cf.* RV), magic charms, etc. Van H. reads '*āḇaḏ nōṣêr*, ' the guardian has perished ', but I think that less violent and more suitable is *bᵉnê-nêker* ' foreigners ' (as in Is 56-62, Ez, Neh). I would also derive *miṯnōsᵉsôṯ* (lifted up) from the root *nûs* to flee (*cf.* Ps 59[60] 6), though it is usually connected with *nês* ' an ensign ' and so considered to mean ' lifted up '. Read of course the masculine *miṯnōsᵉsîm* and another *mem* for the preposition ' from '. I would therefore translate : ' *For foreigners are fled from upon his land* ' —the final relief at the departure of the invaders.

IX 17-X 2a The Prosperity of the Land after its Deliverance—**17.** ' *For how great is his* (Yahweh's) *goodness, and how great is his beauty ! Corn shall make the young men flourish, and new wine the maids* ' (RV). ' Spring forth ' from the root ' to fructify, hence, to flourish '. ' Elect ' *baḥûrîm*, a usual word for ' young men ' (*i.e.* choice, in their prime). **X 1.** ' Rain in the latter season ' *malqôš*=rain in Mar.–Apr., as opposed to *yôreh* or *môreh*=rain in November. ' Snows ' *ḥᵃzîzîm* only here and Job 28:26 ; 38:25 variously translated by LXX and Vg as ' phantasies ', earthquakes, uproar, snows, storms, thunder. Probably=*lightning* (RV). **2a.** ' Diviners have seen a lie *and told idle dreams* '.

X 2b-7 God was Angry at the People's Past Infidelity, but now will give them the Victory—**3.** ' Shepherds ' : chief leaders ; ' buck-goats ' : subordinate leaders. **4.** ' *Corner stone . . . tent peg* ' as essentials (*cf.* figure of the priest in Is 22:23–25). ' Exacter '=ruler even in a good sense. **6.** ' And will *answer* them '.

8-12 God will assemble the Exiles and make them Prosper—**10.** The exiles are to be gathered both from ' Assyria ' (an archaism for Babylonia, see § 545*i, k, o*, unless it refers to those deported in 722) and from Egypt. In fact, during the exile, after Godolias the governor appointed by the Babylonians had been assassinated as a ' collaborator ' by Jewish partisans, many of these, in spite of Jeremias' warnings, fled into Egypt for fear of reprisals by the Babylonians (4 Kg 25:26, and in full detail Jer 41:17 to 44:30, with a prophecy of the calamities to come upon Egypt and the return of a remnant 44:28). ' Galaad and Libanus ' : an archaism for Palestine. ' Place shall not be found ' because of their multitude (*cf.* 2:4). **11.** MT lit. '. . . pass over the sea, straitness ' (apposition). Many would read for *ṣārāh* ('straitness') *Miṣrayim* (' Egypt '), and translate : ' over the sea of Egypt '. ' The River ' *yᵉ'ôr* (without article), almost a proper name for the Nile. (*Cf.* 9:10 for Euphrates.) **12.** ' Shall walk ' *yiṯhallāḵû* : probably we should read with LXX *yiṯhallālû* ' shall glory '.

XI 1-3 Interlude : The Destruction of the Forests—A difficult fragment to place. The destruction of Palestine does not seem to attach to the preceding or to the following themes. It is probable that the cedar is merely a symbol of height, and the oak of might (*cf.* Am 2:9), the shepherds of leadership and the lions of strength, to be applied to the oppressors, the place-names being irrelevant and merely adding colour to the metaphor. **2.** ' The fenced forest ', lit. ' cut off ', *i.e.* ' *inaccessible* ' (Driver), on the steep hillsides of Libanus. **3.** ' The pride of the Jordan ' : its thick undergrowth once the lair of lions. The same phrase occurs in Jer 12:5 ; 44:19 ; 50:44 (DV AV, ' swelling '), in the last two places, also connected with lions.

XI 4-17 with XIII 7-9 The Shepherds (two parables enacted by the prophet)—Driver : ' This prophecy is the most enigmatic in the OT '.

XI 4-7a The Task of the Good Shepherd—God addresses Zacharias who is to play the part of the shepherd appointed by God. **4.** Jerome's paraphrase : ' Feed the flock of the slaughter, *i.e.* now let it prosper and grow, for soon it will be killed by enemies, the Romans who have taken possession of it and own it by right of victory. They will kill the sheep, and sell what they have spared not through pity, but through desire of the price of them '. He adds that these things came about in the time of Hadrian (*i.e.* after the rejection of Christ). That the shepherd is a type of Christ is shown by the NT use of vv 11 and 12 (*q.v.*). The immediate identification of the shepherd and the owners (v 5) or buyers (vv 7, 11 emended) depends entirely upon the theory held about the *mise en scène* (586, post-exilic, 330 or Maccabean) or purely symbolic interpretation (§ 545*f, l-r*). The owners may be (1) foreign oppressors (Babylonians, Persians, Alexander or Seleucids), ór (2) the very heads of Israel who betray the people, or (3) in general, God's enemies past, present or future. Similarly the shepherd may be (1) Yahweh himself, who permits the castigation by the oppressor, or (2) a good leader (*e.g.* Onias for the Maccabean scene), or (3) simply the symbol of

550m

n

o

551a

b

551b God's goodness in the world. In every interpretation the Good Shepherd is rejected, and thus is a type of Christ.

c **5.** The verbs in MT are confused between sing. and plur. (DV all plur.), probably due to the fact that sing. and plur. forms for 'shepherd' and 'owner' with suffixes are often identical (GK 93*ss*). 'Blessed be the Lord' is either cynical, or (Kennett) a euphemism for 'cursed', *i.e.* we don't care. **7a.** 'For this, O ye poor of the flock' *lākēn ᶜᵃnîyyê hass'ôn* ; LXX 'into Canaan', which suggests *likᵉnaᶜᵃnîyyê hass'ôn* '*for the buyers of the flock*' ('Canaanites' frequently for merchants, *e.g.* 14:21). This emendation is generally accepted.

d **7b-11 The Symbolic Action of the Shepherd—7b.** The two shepherd's staves are named 'Beauty' and '*hōḇᵉlîm*', lit. 'Ropes'. *ḥeḇel* frequently means 'a plot of land', measured by rope—so LXX here. BDB '*union*', Van H. '*liaison*', *i.e.* a tying together (RV 'bands', RVm 'binders'). Kennett compares the naming of the staves with the modern cartoon where **e** objects are symbolically inscribed. **8.** The identification of the three shepherds cut off in one month is very difficult, and again depends on the *mise en scène*. Three worthless leaders with very short reigns, or a short-lived ruling clique, are sought. For pre-722, Zacharias, Sellum and Manahem (4 Kg 15) are proposed ; for pre-586 Joakim, Joachin and Sedecias ; or Joachaz (Sellum), Joakim and Joachin (Jechonias) (4 Kg 23-24 ; Jer 22) (Van H.) ; for Persian times three unknown high-priests (Driver) ; for Maccabean times, Jason, Menelaus and Lysimachus (2 Mac 4) ; or the sons of Tobias ; or the satellites of Simon the Benjamite who fought against Onias (2 Mac 3) (Kennett). Others suggest three foreign powers, such as the Assyrians, Babylonians and Persians, or the Persians, Greeks and Romans ; or else three oppressing kings, such as the three Seleucid emperors of Maccabean times who all met their death within a month of (*i.e.* 30) years : Antiochus Epiphanes, Antiochus Eupator and Demetrius I (Wright). Lastly it may be that no identification is intended—'part of the furniture of the allegory' (Kirkpatrick)—or that the meaning is wholly allegorical, of *e.g.* the triple power of king, priest and prophet, brought to an end by Christ, the Good Shepherd. (For all this, see Driver, p 254.) 'My soul was *shortened, i.e. impatient* in their regard, and their soul *felt loathing* in my regard'. **10.** The symbolic action of the breaking of the staff 'Beauty', thus making void 'my covenant which I had made with all *the peoples*' (RV). The action signifies 'that the covenant which he (Yahweh) had (metaphorically) made with the nations that they should not molest Israel was now annulled' (Driver). The breaking of the first staff is therefore the sign for calamities to come upon Israel *from without*, just as the breaking of the second staff (v 14) heralds disruption and tribulations *from within*. **11.** 'The poor of the flock' read 'the *buyers*' as in v 7. 'That keep for me' *hassōmᵉrîm 'ōṯî* 'that *were watching* me' (BDB), but Van H. reads cleverly *haśśōḵᵉrîm 'ōṯî* '(the buyers) that *were hiring* me' (*cf.* next verse).

f **12-13 The Rejection of the Good Shepherd**—These verses, quoted in Mt 26:15 and 27:9 show the typical interpretation of Christ to be authentic. **12.** 'They weighed for my wages' LXX *ἔστησαν* 'appointed', and thus quoted by Mt. 30 *šᵉqālîm* = about £4-£6. **13.** 'Statuary' *yōṣēr i.e.* modeller, usually of clay, *i.e.* '*potter*' (RV). LXX has 'foundry', Syr. 'treasury' whence some propose the reading '*ōṣār*. '*Cast it to the potter—the magnificent price at which I was priced by them !*' (*cf.* WV on Mt 27:9). The reference to the potter is enigmatic, but the buying of the 'potter's field' (Haceldama) (Mt 27:7) is regarded as its fulfilment.

g **14 His Second Symbolic Action**—He breaks the staff 'Union', thus symbolically breaking the union of the flock.

h **15-17 with XIII 7-9 The Prophet acts the Part of the**

Foolish Shepherd—In so far as the Good Shepherd is a type of Christ, Jerome's opinion that this shepherd stands for Antichrist seems correct. Not only will he mislead the flock, but in the end he will be smitten and only a remnant of the flock will be saved (see esp. the continuation of this prophecy in 13:7-9). If an immediate historical identification is sought, it will follow those of the shepherds of vv 4 & 8 (*q.v.*). For 586 Sedecias is proposed, who was the last king of Judah and fled from the besieged city (4 Kg 25 ; Jer 21) (Van H.) ; or for post-exilic times an unknown high-priest ; or for Maccabean times Jason or Menelaus. **15.** 'Instruments' *kᵉlî* often used for 'things', *i.e.* 'accoutrements'. **16.** 'Scattered', correctly reading *hanniddaḥaṭ* (*cf.* Ez 34:4) for the impossible *hannaᶜar*. 'Which standeth', *i.e.* in good health. 'Break their hoofs'-either to prevent them walking, or for fattening (Van H.), or else by driving them cruelly over rough places. **17.** 'O shepherd *of worthlessness*' : Vg's 'idol' follows a particular use of *'ᵉlîl* for a 'worthless god'. This verse, on the fate of the Foolish Shepherd, with its reference to the sword, so obviously attaches to 13:7, where the subject of the shepherd's fate by the sword is resumed, that one does not hesitate to consider 13:7-9 displaced. **XIII 7.** 'The man that cleaveth to me', lit. 'a man, my companion', *i.e.* the leader of my people. 'Strike the shepherd . . .' is quoted by Christ (at Gethsemani) in Mt 26:31 ; Mk 14:27. It is an 'accommodation', *i.e.* merely an apt quotation, for of course the foolish shepherd is *not* a type of the Redeemer. NT has 'I will strike', a reading of 3 codices of the LXX in Zach, and probably right ; *cf.* 'I will turn' which follows. 'Against the little ones', *i.e.* the flock, who shall be destroyed except for a remnant who will remain faithful. This picture of the work of Antichrist coincides esp. with that of Mt 24 ; Mk 13 ; 1 Jn 2 ; Apoc 11:7 ff.

SECOND PART B : The Second 'Burden' XII-XIV less XIII 7-9

XII (i) Jerusalem shall fall, yet she shall triumph— Again the prophetical perspective is difficult to see (*cf.* § 550*b*) : the earthly Jerusalem shall indeed suffer, and the nations with her, but she shall rise as the New Jerusalem of Christ 'coming down out of heaven from God' (Apoc 21:2, 10), symbolized in the warlike triumph of this chapter. Or again, if the earthly Jerusalem represents the Church of Christ, then the reference is to the Church's suffering and martyrdom amid the torments of the world, to be replaced by Christ's final victory.

1-3 The Fall of Jerusalem will be a Calamity to the Nations—1. 'Burden' : title, see on 9:1. **2.** 'Lintel of surfeiting', *saṗ raᶜal*. There are two words *saṗ* : (1) cup, (2) threshold. The root *rāᶜal* means 'to tremble, totter, reel'. LXX has here 'tottering porches' ; Barnes '*quaking threshold*' ; RV '*cup of reeling*' (Driver & Van H. understand of intoxicating drink, Barnes of the cup of God's wrath that causes men to stagger, if the sense 'cup' is right), *cf.* Is 51:17, 22 *kôs tarᶜēlāh* 'cup of reeling' (RV) (DV 'cup of deep sleep'). Be it in the sense of an intoxicating cup or a dangerous place to stand on, her fall will wreck the nations. 'And Judah also . . .', MT 'And also against Judah'. Vg rightly omits 'against', giving a sense consonant with v 7 and 14:14, where even Judah joins in the fight against Jerusalem. **3.** Jerome says that still in his time many Palestinian villages kept a heavy stone for weight-lifting contests.

4-9 Jerusalem shall triumph—Note the reiterated **c** phrase 'In that day' in each of these promises of victory (vv 4, 6, 8, 9), and *cf.* the formula in the promises of ch 8. **5.** 'Let the inhabitants . . . be strengthened for me', lit. 'be a strength for me', but the usage is doubtful. Probably for '*amṣāh lî* we should read '*emṣᵉ'āh lᵉ* (with Stade, BDB *cf.* LXX) '*may I be found sufficient for* the inhabitants'. **6.** 'Firebrand amongst *cut corn*'. **8.** ' That hath offended ', Vg ' offenderit ', *i.e.* ' *stumbled* '. ' As David ', *i.e.* as strong and valiant. These references to David (vv 7, 8, 10, 12 ; 13:1) suggest that the ruling house was still that of David (and of Zorobabel) : § 545*i, k*.

10-14 But they shall mourn over the Rejected Messias —In all the triumph of the New Jerusalem there will remain the note of mourning as a reminder, like the wounds in the Body of the Risen Christ, or the permanent Crucifix in our churches. **10.** ' They shall look on me whom they have pierced ' : quoted (with ' on *him* ' '*ēlāw* probably rightly for '*ēlay* ' on me ') in Jn 19:37 after the death of Christ, with reminiscences of Zach in Apoc 1:7. Note that Jn quotes from HT, not from LXX which here has ' insulted ' for ' pierced '. If we follow Jn's reading ' on him ', we can understand the passage of a person of whom God is speaking. 12:10-11 with 13:6-7 is the Lesson of the Votive Mass of the Passion or of the Five Wounds. ' Plangent eum quasi unigenitum ' is used at Lauds on Holy Saturday (2nd ant.) and on the Compassion of Our Lady (5th ant.). **11.** Adadremmon is a place otherwise unknown, in the valley of Mageddon (Megiddo). 2 Par 35:22-25 mentions the death of King Josias near Mageddon and the lamentations that had become an institution in Israel. **12-13.** The *royal* house of David, and of Nathan son of David, and the *priestly* houses of Levi and of Semei, grandson of Levi. One recalls the position of Zorobabel and Jesus in Aggeus and the first part of Zach, and notes the mention of Nathan as interesting, since in the Gospel genealogies of Zorobabel, Mt traces the line to David through Solomon, but Lk through Nathan (*cf.* § 543*f, h*). The separation of the men and women was part of the penitential solemnity (*cf.* Ex 19:15 before the giving of the Law).

XIII 1-6 (ii) The Cleansing of Jerusalem.

XIII 1-3 Idolatry and Magic shall be cast out—1. ' There shall be a *spring* '. ' For the washing . . . ', lit. ' For sin and for uncleanness ' (RV). The latter word is *niddāh, cf.* in Num 19:9, 13, 20, 21 *bis* ' the water of *niddāh* ' in ceremonial purification (RV ' separation ', DV variously ' aspersion, expiation, purification '). The sense is that the city shall be purified of both moral and ceremonial transgression. **2.** ' False ' is inserted, after LXX & Vg ' pseudoprophetas '. **3.** ' Prophesy ', *i.e.* in the manner of the false prophets. In the Law (Deut 13:6-9, 18:20) a false prophet is punished with death, and his own family are to be the first to denounce him.

4-6 The ex-Prophet shall turn Husbandman—4. The prophet shall be ' confounded ', *i.e.* ' *ashamed of his own vision* ', and **5.** he will abandon his profession and take to husbandry, ' for Adam is my example ' *kî* '*ādām hiqnanî*, lit. ' for a man (or Adam) acquired (?) me ' (Hiph. of *qānāh* ' possess ' only here). LXX has ' begot me ', which shows that the text is doubtful, though it may be that LXX is merely associating this passage with ' I have possessed a man ' in Gen 4:1 (birth of Cain). Most would read with Wellhausen *kî* '*ǎdāmāh qinyānî* ' *for the earth has been my possession* '. **6.** ' These wounds in the midst of thy hands ', lit. ' between thy hands ', *i.e.* arms, *i.e.* on thy breast ? The text is used, in an accommodated sense (*i.e.* the ex-prophet is *in no way* a type of Christ : *cf.* §§ 102*p*, 551*j*) of Christ in the Liturgy (Lesson of the Votive Mass of the Passion or of the Five Wounds). Perhaps it is, in the literal sense, connected with the selfinflicted wounds of ecstatic prophets, *cf.* the enaction of a parable by a prophet in 3 Kg 20:25-43, or the prophets of Baal at their sacrifice in 3 Kg 18:28 (Van H. & Barnes after Marti).

7-9 Conclusion of the Fate of the Foolish Shepherd —Generally regarded as attaching to 11:17, because of the continuation of the ideas and vocabulary from there. These verses are commented with ch 11 (§ 551*h, j*).

XIV (iii) The Day of the Lord—In this last prophecy are gathered together the Messianic notions of the

victory of Judah (**11-12**), and the earthly Jerusalem **554a** itself rebuilt (**10**), with the restored worship of Yahweh at Jerusalem, in which the nations will take part (**16-21**), by ' compenetration ' eschatologically identified with the New Jerusalem that will rise after the calamities of the Last Day (**1-5**), when the Day of the Lord will dawn, the day of everlasting light (**6-9**, see exegesis of 6). If we understand Jerusalem in the Messianic spiritual sense of the Church of Christ, then calamities to the Church at the end of time are foreshadowed, when even her own people (Judah **14**) will fight against her, but in the end, when the Day comes, she will be transformed into the New Jerusalem of Heaven (*cf.* §§ 550*b*, 552*a* and 545*d*). If we seek to identify the events historically, the matter will depend once more on the period of the *mise en scène* (see § 545*l–r*).

1-5a The Capture of Jerusalem and the Flight of the b People—1. ' *A Day is coming for the Lord* '. The idea of the Day of Yahweh includes the eschatological calamities gradually turning into the everlasting Day (*cf.* Mal ch 4, § 555*i*). **3-4.** These apocalyptic vv are used on Advent Ember-Wednesday at Matins (3rd Resp.). **4.** ' A very great *valley* '. **5a.** MT lit. ' And you shall flee to the valley of *my* mountains, for the valley of the mountains shall reach unto '*āṣal* '. Vg read '*eṣlô* ' unto next-to-it ', which explains DV and is probably the best reading. RV follows LXX and translates as an unknown proper name. For ' my mountains ' *hārai* Wellhausen suggested *ḥinnôm* : ' Flee to the Valley of Hinnom (Gehenna) ', which lay to the SW. of the city. The earthquake referred to is mentioned in Am 1:1 and occurred *c* 750 B.C.

5b-9 The Coming of the Lord—Phrases from these **c** verses appear in the Advent Liturgy : in the Communion verse for Ember Friday (see note on v 6), and on Sundays I (Lauds 3rd ant.) and II (Matins 2nd Resp.). **5b.** ' And all the *holy ones* with him ' (MT ' with thee ') is usually taken to mean the angels. **6.** A difficult verse. MT lit. ' There shall not be light *yeqārôt* (' precious ' fem. pl.) *weqippā'ôn* (' and congelation ', or Ktib *yiqpā'ûn* ' shall congeal '). LXX & Vg read for *yeqārôt* a word related to *qôr* ' cold ', probably a better reading. Most other attempts (such as AV RV RVm) connect ' precious ' with ' glorious ' or ' bright ' and refer to the stars. The next verse, however, far from suggesting darkness or night, speaks of perpetual light. In fact the liturgical text (Adv. Emb. Fri. Comm.) differs greatly from Vg and reads ' Et erit in die illa lux magna '. On the basis of all this I am inclined to reject the negative and consider the two difficult words as a doubled corruption of a word such as *gāḏôl* ' great ' (*cf.* Is 9:2), translating : ' And it shall come to pass in that day, that there shall be *a great light* ; (**7**) and there shall be one day . . . not day nor night ', *i.e.* the eternal light of the Messianic age, when the Kingdom of Christ is fully arrived. If we retain the negative, the passage must be explained (with Jerome) by Is 60:19 ' Not the sun, but the Lord, will be your light '. **8.** ' East sea ', *i.e.* the sea ' in front ', the Dead Sea. ' *Western* sea ', *i.e.* the sea ' behind ' (DV ' last sea '), the Mediterranean. Hebrew compass-points assume that one faces east.

10-11 The Restoration of Judah and Jerusalem—10. d ' And he shall encompass all the land, even to the '*Arābāh* (almost a proper name for the barren part of the lower Jordan valley), *from Gabaa* (Jos 21:17—6 m. NE. of Jerusalem) *to Remmon* (Neh 11:29—35 m. SW.). This describes the Kingdom of Judah. Now the city : ' *From the gate of Benjamin* (N.—Jer 37:12 road to Babylon), past the former gate, *to the corner gate* (NW.—Jer 31:38 ; 4 Kg 14:13 ; 2 Par 26:9) ; *from the Tower of Hananeel* (NE.—Jer 31:38 (mis-spelt in DV) ; Neh 3:1 ; 12:38), *to the king's winepresses* (SE.—probably in the " king's garden " by Siloe Neh 3:15) '. *Cf.* the description of the wall in Neh 3.

12-15 The Discomfiture of the Nations that fought e against Jerusalem—13. ' Take the hand ', *i.e.* to kill

ZACHARIAS XIV

554e him. **14.** Even Judah is in the fight against Jerusalem at the end : see above § 554*a*, and *cf.* 12:2 (Vg & DV) and 12:7, although here (as in 12:2) the meaning may be ' *at* Jerusalem ' (RVm), perhaps fighting *for* her.

f 16-21 The Remnant of the Nations shall adore the Lord—The most striking exposition of the universal Messianism of the second part of Zach (see § 545*d*), only fully intelligible of the Church of Christ embracing all nations (*cf.* § 545*e*, and esp. 2:11 ; 8:22-23). **16.** ' The Feast of Tabernacles ', *i.e. Sukkôṭ* or Booths, in early October, commemorating the homeless wandering in the wilderness (Lev 23:39-43). **17.** ' No rain ', a major calamity to an agricultural population. **18.** ' If the family of Egypt go not up, nor come (omit with LXX in MT " neither shall it be "), *upon them shall be* the destruction wherewith . . .' **19.** ' This shall be the *sin-offering* ' (*cf.* the use of *niddāh* in 13:1). **20.** MT lit. ' In that day upon *meṣillôṭ* the horses holy to the Lord ' : *meṣillôṭ* ' things that tinkle ' (BDB), so

RV ' bells ', part of the bridle (which is the translation of LXX & Vg). For *'al* ' upon ', probably read *kōl* ' all ' : ' *all* the bells of the horses shall be holy ', but RV takes ' holy to the Lord ' as an inscription on the bells ; *cf.* on the high-priest's mitre (Ex 28:36-38). Some would avoid both the bells and the horses (*sûs*), which indeed seem rather unlikely in the context of temple utensils, and read *'al maṣliṭ* (a word invented from root *ṣālāh* ' roast ' : I would prefer *ṣēlāḥôṭ* ' dishes ' as in 2 Par 35:13) *weṣîr*, translating : ' *On the dishes and pots " Holy to the Lord " '*. In other words, so widespread will be the worship of Yahweh that the commonest things will be used in his service, and the liturgical ceremonies of Jerusalem will require a multitude of utensils. **21.** ' Merchant ' Heb. Canaanite, *cf.* emendation in 11:7, 11 (§ 551*c*). The meaning is either that foreigners (Canaanites) shall be excluded, or else traffickers in the sense of those whom our Lord himself drove out from the House of God. Jerome decided in favour of the latter.

MALACHIAS

(MALACHI)

By E. F. SUTCLIFFE, S.J.

Bibliography—St Jerome, *Commentarii in Malachiam Prophetam*, PL 25, 1541 ff.; L. Reinke, *Der Prophet Malachi* (1856); J. Knabenbauer, S.J., *cf.* § 409*b*; Van Hoonacker, *cf.* § 409*b*; C. Lattey, S.J., *The Book of Malachy*, WV, 1934; E. F. Sutcliffe, S.J., *Malachy's Prophecy of the Eucharistic Sacrifice*, IER 5 Ser 19 (1922) 502–13; *J. M. Powis Smith, *The Book of Malachi*, ICC, 1912.

The Name and Person of the Prophet—It cannot be said for certain that there was a prophet with the personal name of Malachias. St Jerome in the Prologue to his commentary on the book mentions, and himself adopts, the opinion of the Jews that the author was Esdras, PL 25, 1541 f. The Aramaic paraphrase of Pseudo-Jonathan inserts the name of Esdras in the first verse, and the LXX in place of Malachias has 'of his messenger'. It thus appears that early Jewish tradition retained no memory of a prophet named Malachias, a strange fact if a prophet of that name exercised his ministry after the exile and was the last of the long line of prophets before the coming of John the Baptist. On the other hand analogy suggests that the title of the book must contain a personal name, and, as such, 'Malachy' of MT is quite suitable. Etymologically it could mean 'my messenger', but a child would not be given a name with such a meaning. The LXX and the Vg have the form Malachias, which supposes the Hebrew to be an abbreviation for 'Messenger of Yahweh', just as Phalti, 2 Kg 25:44, is an abbreviation of Phaltiel, 2 Kg 3:15. There is no probability in the suggestion that the name has its origin in 3:1; and that there was no firm tradition among the Jews concerning Esdras' authorship is shown by the attribution of the book to Mardochai in the Babylonian Talmud, *Megillah* 15*a*.

Date of the Book—All are agreed that Malachias flourished after the Exile, and was the last of the prophets whose writings are preserved in the OT. The name of *pehah* given to the governor of Judea, 1:8, agrees with the usage of the Persian period, but the word occurs earlier, Jer 51:28. The similarity, and in part, the identity of the abuses which Malachias on the one hand and Esdras and Nehemias on the other strove to correct point to the prophet having laboured about the same period as they. But there is considerable divergence of opinion among writers who attempt to fix the time of his activity more exactly.

According to the traditional and more common opinion Esdras returned to Jerusalem in the 7th year of Artaxerxes I, 459–458 B.C., and continued his labours until the arrival of Nehemias in the 20th year of the same Persian king in 446–445 B.C., Neh 3:1; 8:2. In the 32nd year of Artaxerxes I, Nehemias returned to court, Neh 13:6, and later again came back to Jerusalem, Neh 13:7. If we start from the return of the exiles under Cyrus, 537–536 B.C., it is possible to exclude certain periods for the activity of Malachias. In his time the Temple had been rebuilt, 1:10, but this rebuilding was not completed until the 6th year of Darius I, 516–515 B.C., Esd 6:15. Moreover the neglect of divine worship and the contempt of the altar rebuked by Malachias, 1:7, would not have been possible for a number of years after the dedication of the Temple, which had been celebrated with enthusiasm, Esd 6:16.

The period immediately following the reform of Esdras **555c** may also be excluded, as he caused the people to put away their foreign wives, Esd 10, and the reform must have had some lasting effect. However, Nehemias, during his first stay at Jerusalem, found the same abuse in existence, Neh 6:18, and after his second return took strong action in the matter, Neh 13:23–30. Malachias' denunciation of such marriages, 2:11, could therefore fall only either before Esdras' reform or sometime thereafter. Moreover the expenses of the Temple were met out of the royal exchequer in the time of Darius I, Esd 6:1, 9, 13, as they were in the reign of Artaxerxes I after the return of Esdras from Babylon, Esd 7:15–17, 20–23. If the order of Darius was faithfully carried out till the close of his reign in 486 B.C., Malachias' prophecy, if written before the reform of Esdras, would date from some time after this year, as the offering of cheap defective victims, Mal 1:8, indicates that the expenses of the Temple worship fell on the Jews themselves. But it is by no means certain that the royal provision was adhered to for so long. The decree of Artaxerxes had ceased to be of effect by the time of Nehemias' first sojourn at Jerusalem, as he found it necessary to institute an annual tribute of a third of a shekel for the maintenance of the Temple services, Neh 10:32 f. The period of Nehemias' governorship from the 20th to the 32nd year of Artaxerxes may also be excluded as, on the one hand, Nehemias expressly says that for all that time he had refused to be a charge to the people by eating 'the yearly allowance that was due to the governors', Neh 5:14 f., and on the other hand, it is clear that Malachias wrote while the payment of such dues was in force, Mal 1:8. The evidence is not adequate to enable us to fix the date of Malachias with certainty, but the more probable period is that preceding the reforming activity of Esdras.

I omit a discussion of the question on the basis of the reconstruction of the history proposed by Van Hoonacker according to which the reforming activity of Esdras followed that of Nehemias, as there appears to be no adequate ground for departing from the chronological order indicated in the Bible. (See § 289*i*–*q*.)

Theme and Analysis of the Book—The theme of the **d** book is briefly that God loves Israel, though Israel questions the existence of this love. The sins of the priests and the people are such that they prevent God showing his favour. If they will repent, they shall again feel the effects of the divine benevolence. The Jews even dare to question God's justice. This leads to the prediction of God's coming as a fire both consuming the wicked and refining the good. The book may be analysed more in detail as follows.

The Jews are dissatisfied with God. They question the existence of his love for them, which, however, is manifest by the favour shown to them in comparison with the hard lot of the descendants of Esau, the brother of their own progenitor Jacob, 1:2–5. But God is prevented from showering his favours on the Jews, for they do not render the honour and reverence that are his due. The priests despise his name by offering polluted sacrifices. It were better for the Temple to be closed and an end put to these useless offerings, for in the whole Gentile world a pure offering is made to his name which is honoured throughout

555d the world, 1:6-14. If the priests do not amend their ways, they will bring a curse upon themselves and the deepest shame, 2:1-4. Of old the priestly caste was true to God's covenant with them and merited the prosperity attached to its faithful observance. The present generation of priests, on the contrary, has itself offended and has occasioned the sin of others, 2:5-9. Among the iniquities of the people are marriages with pagans, 2:10-12, and the divorce of their legitimate wives, 2:13-16.

The accusation has even been made that God favours the wicked, and the existence of a just providence ruling the world has been questioned : ' Where is the God of justice ? ' 2:17. The answer is quickly given. After his messenger God will come himself to his temple. Who then will be able to stand before him ? He will come as a refining fire. When he has purified the priesthood, they will again offer a worthy sacrifice. He will come for judgement against sorcerers, adulterers, perjurers, and oppressors of the weak, 3:1-5. God has not changed and hates evil always, whereas the Jews are contumacious in their iniquity. None the less, if they will repent, God will again turn to them. They must pay their dues of tithes and offerings, 3:6-10. Due observance will bring its reward from God in renewed prosperity, 3:11 f. Again are mentioned the accusations against God's just government of the world, 3:15. True worshippers are written in a book of remembrance before Yahweh ; they shall be his special possession on the great day that is to come. God will spare them. Then will men again recognize the different lot of those who do, and of those who do not, worship God, 3:16-18. The day that is to come will consume the evil-doers like stubble, but the sun of justice will shine on the good, who will triumph over the wicked, 4:1-3.

An exhortation to remember the law of Moses is followed by the prophecy that Elias will be sent before the great and terrible day of the Lord to work harmony of spirit between the fathers and the sons lest God at his coming strike the land with an anathema.

e Doctrinal Content—There is no systematic exposition of doctrine, and the points touched on were indicated by the needs of the time. The Jews were in a relatively miserable condition. They were under foreign rule ; had no prosperity ; crops for some time had been poor owing to lack of rain and the devastations of locusts, 3:10 f. As a consequence they tended to lose faith in God. It had always been the faith of Israel that God is the just ruler of the world who rewards good and punishes evil. In their sad estate many put the blame on God instead of on their own sinful conduct.

f It is this frame of mind that explains the prophet's insistence in his **teaching about God** on the old truth that ' Yahweh is ⬤ magnified beyond the borders of Israel ', 1:5, and in part its repetition 1:11, 14. The same applies to the emphasis with which it is taught that God does reward virtue, 2:5 ; 3:10-12 ; 4:2 f., and punish wickedness, 2:3 ; 4:1. It must be remembered that the doctrine of retribution after death had not yet been revealed, and the mystery of God's government was correspondingly more obscure. God is just ; yet, though he never punishes more than sin deserves, he sometimes treats sinners with love that they do not deserve. Thus God visited Edom with severe chastisement for theirs were ' borders of wickedness ', 1:3 f., yet Israel was not visited with signs of equally severe divine displeasure, though Malachias has many denunciations of Jewish iniquity, and though Edom and Israel were both descended from Jacob, 1:2. God has a special love and care of those who serve him and treats them as a father with mercy, 3:17.

g Turning to the **teaching about man**, we may note first that all men have equal rights before God, though in the context this is said of the Jews only, 2:10. Men are under an obligation to honour and reverence God, 1:6, by the due observance of the prescribed ritual, 1:7 f., and by the payment of tithes and offerings imposed by law, 3:8, 10. At the same time to be pleasing to God man must avoid evil, sorcery, adultery, perjury, oppression of the weak, 3:5. Divorce is hateful to God, 2:14-16, where see note. The hardness of heart of the Israelites had led Moses to tolerate divorce in certain conditions and under certain safeguards, probably to avoid the worse evil of murder, Deut 24:1-4, but even there strong language is used of the divorced wife who has remarried. In Malachias' time these divorces seem often to have been occasioned by another great evil, namely, marriage with pagan wives, to whom it was desired to give the place of honour in the home, 2:11 with note. Such divorces were not sanctioned by the law of Deuteronomy.

Priests have a mission from God, for they are his messengers or angels, 2:7. They should carry out their ritual and sacrificial duties with exactness and reverence, 1:7, etc., should teach the law of God with fidelity, 2:6, 8, and be the means of helping men to live good lives, 2:6.

The day of the Lord is the subject of important prophecies, 3:1-5, 4:1-3. It is essential here to remember that the full truth was not always revealed to the prophets even on subjects concerning which they had profound truths to teach. So it was in this instance. Malachias foretells that the Lord is to come, but he does not distinguish between his first and his second coming, between his coming to save the world and his coming in the clouds of heaven for judgement. This is connected with the fact already mentioned that the truth about rewards and punishments had not yet been revealed nor consequently that judgement is to follow the end of each one's life on this earth. Consequently Malachias foretells the destruction of the wicked and the blessedness of the just on the great and terrible day of the Lord, but he does not make it plain to his readers that this day is to be far removed in time from the day on which the Lord will come to his temple. Similarly he does not make it plain that the prophet whom God is to send before the great and terrible day of the Lord, 4:5, is not he who is to be sent to prepare the way of the first coming, 3:1. Now after the revelation of the New Testament we know that this first messenger was John the Baptist, who came in the spirit of Elias. This is an example of ' compenetration ', by which two events separated in time are fused into one picture just as in old paintings objects separated in space are represented without regard to perspective.

Even more striking and arresting than these prophecies of the coming of the Lord is that in which is foretold the offering of a pure sacrifice throughout the gentile world, **the sacrifice of the New Covenant.** The Jewish priests of the day were offering polluted and defective sacrifices ; the animals they offered to God were such as they would not have dared to offer to the Persian governor for the maintenance of his household, 1:7 f. It were better if the gates of the Temple were closed and the fire not kindled upon the altar to no purpose. God rejects the Jewish sacrifices : ' I have no pleasure in you, saith the Lord of hosts, and I will not receive a gift of your hand ', 1:10. The honour and reverence that God had a right to expect above all from his chosen people is withheld by them, but from the rising of the sun to the going down thereof his name is great among the Gentiles, and in every place a pure oblation is offered to his name, 1:11 with note. The Jewish sacrifices are rejected, and in their place God accepts a pure oblation made throughout the Gentile world and therefore by the Gentiles themselves. In the light of history there is only one sacrifice that corresponds to this prediction, and that is the sacrifice instituted by the Angel, or Messenger, of the New Covenant, 3:1 and Jer 31:31. This is a pure oblation, for the victim is none other than the Son of God made man, who is mystically immolated upon the Christian altar by the sword of the word, and it is offered throughout the Gentile world by priests of the non-Israelite order of Melchisedech.

This interpretation, which is that of the Council of

Trent, Sess. 22 cap. 1, and of the earliest Christian tradition as evidenced by St Justin, *Dial. cum Tryphone* 117, is only confirmed by the various attempts to give the passage some other application. It has been held that Malachias is referring to the worship paid by the nations each to its own supreme divinity, as by the Romans to Jupiter, the Greeks to Zeus, and the Persians to Ahura Mazda, and that inasmuch as they worshipped a supreme god they were in reality adoring Yahweh, the one true God. Apart from other passages of the Bible this idea runs counter to Malachias' own teaching. His condemnation of marriage with ' the daughter of a strange god ', 2:11, that is with a pagan woman, is clearly also a rejection of all pagan cult. Another view maintains that the reference is to sacrifices offered by Jews scattered throughout the pagan world. This again is quite untenable. We know of only two such Jewish temples—at Elephantine and at Heliopolis. Had there been many, we should certainly have record of others. And had the Jews considered such temples legitimate in spite of Deut 12:1-14, the destruction of the Temple at Jerusalem would not have put an end to all Jewish sacrifices, but from the year A.D. 70 the Jews have abstained from all sacrifice. Moreover the cult of Elephantine would certainly not have been called pure by Malachias as the degenerate Jews there worshipped Ashim-Bethel and Anath-Bethel as well as Yaho (Yahweh) ; *cf.* A. Vincent, *La Religion des Judéo-Araméens d'Eléphantine* (1937) 562, 622 ff., 654 ff. Yet a third attempt has been made to interpret the prophecy of the sacrifices of praise, that is the prayers and hymns, offered to God by the pious Jews of the Diaspora. For one thing it is gratuitous to suppose that the Jews who had remained abroad were more pleasing to God than those who had remained in or returned to the Promised Land, and secondly, it is illegitimate to understand terms normally used of material sacrifices in a metaphorical manner where there is no indication in the text, as there is not in our passage, that the terms are being used in any other than their ordinary sense. It is thus clear that Malachias' words do not refer to any sacrifices of his own time, whether sacrifices of the Gentiles, or sacrifices, material or metaphorical, of the Jews. He speaks of the future Messianic age.

l Text and Style—The text of Malachias is on the whole well preserved though textual corruptions are not lacking as well as divergences between the Hebrew text and the early versions. These, of which the more important are noted in the commentary, as well as the poetic diction employed, render it impossible at times to be certain of the prophet's exact meaning. His style is that of poetic prose, not that of poetry. The attempt to fit his words into the mould of metre can be successful only by the aid of a violent and arbitrary handling of the text, though it is not denied that certain parts have the parallelism and metre proper to poetry. Specially characteristic of Malachias is his use of dialogue.

a I The Title—'The *oracle* of the word of the Lord ' occurs besides only Zach 9:1 ; 12:1. The name of Israel, which had been used of the Northern Kingdom, is now used of the Jewish community as a whole. God deals with men through men, as here through one of his prophets.

b 2-5 God's Special Love of Israel—Throughout the longer part of their history the Hebrews expected the good to be rewarded by temporal prosperity. Consequently their present plight led them to question God's love for their nation. But God's love was shown by the far greater severity with which he had justly punished the iniquity of Edom and the comparative leniency shown to Israel, though the two were brother nations descended from Jacob and Esau, the two sons of Isaac. **3.** Probably it was by recent incursions of the Nabateans that Esau's mountain home had been made a wilderness and ' his inheritance *a desert pasture* '. **4.** Neither is God prepared to show to Edom in the future the clemency extended to Israel. **5.** If the Jews

had foolishly thought that the arm of God was short- **556b** ened, they would see that ' the Lord *is* magnified *beyond* the border of Israel '.

6-9 Israel's Sinful Sacrifices—6-7. ' *A son honours* **c** *his* father and *a servant reverences* his master '. Yet Israel treats God with neither honour nor respect ' saith the Lord of hosts to you, O priests, who despise my name. *Yet you say :* Wherein have we despised thy name ? You offer polluted *food* upon my altar, *yet you say.* . . .' Israel was in fact no more worthy of the favour of God than sinful Edom. Contempt of God's name is contempt of God himself for whose person the ' name ' often stands practically as a synonym. **8.** ' If you offer the blind for sacrifice, *there is no harm !* ' The statement is either ironical or repeats the thought of the negligent priests. By law nothing blemished was to be offered in sacrifice, Deut 15:21. They would not dare to offer a defective animal in fulfilment of civil obligations. ' Offer it to the Governor ! Will he be pleased with it or show thee favour ? ' **9** is not an exhortation to repentance, but is ironical. While you continue to act thus, if you try to propitiate God ' *will he show favour to you ?* ' Clearly not !

10 f. Jewish Sacrifices replaced by a Universal and **d** **Pure Oblation**—' O that one among you would shut the gates and that you would not kindle the fire upon my altar to no purpose '. God rejects the Jewish sacrifices. **11.** The word ' for ' shows that the universal and pure oblation is to replace the existing Jewish sacrifices, a fact which of itself shows that Malachias is not thinking of any other existing sacrifices but of the future Messianic Age ; see § 555*j*. ' From the rising of the sun even to the going down *thereof* ' is a geographical expression signifying universality. The MT reads : ' and in every place *muqtar muggaš* to my name and a pure oblation '. In essentials this agrees with the Vg in spite of the different position of the conjunction and the possibility of varying opinions about the grammatical form and meaning of *muqtar*. The LXX translates, probably correctly : ' In every place incense is offered to my name and a pure oblation '. It is certainly worthy of remark that whenever the Sacrifice of the New Testament is offered with full ritual, the use of incense is an integral part of the sacred function.

12-14 Further on Sinful Sacrifices—12. It was the **e** priests who defiled the altar or table of the Lord by their unworthy sacrifices, but, as men are apt to do, they seek the cause of the evil results of their own actions elsewhere. The DV of 12*b* is a free rendering of a doubtful Hebrew text, but gives substantially the sense intended. **13.** ' *And you say :* " *Look ! What a trouble ! and you have been sniffing at it and bringing what was robbed both lame and sickly* " '. The verbs denote repeated action in the past and continued into the present. The robbery might be that of legal injustice committed to the knowledge of the priests by the persons presenting the victims. The suggestion that the Hebrew word for ' robbed ' has here the sense of ' mutilated ' offers a sense that suits the passage but lacks adequate linguistic confirmation. **14.** Worse still than the irreverence of offering defective victims is the conjunction therewith of perjury : ' Cursed is the deceitful man who has in his flock a male *which he vows*, and offers to the Lord in sacrifice *a defective female* '. Victims for peace-offerings were allowed to be of the female sex, Lev 3:1, but males were considered to be the more honourable sacrifices, Lev 1:3 (where only males are allowed for a holocaust). And if a male were vowed, it was obviously sinful to offer a female. The antithesis seems to demand that vocalization of the HT which signifies a defective female. The alternative vocalization, which signifies a blemished male, renders the previous emphatic mention of the sex quite pointless.

II 1-3 Commination against the Priests—1. The **557a** commandment to the priests is probably that implicit in the passage, namely, to amend their ways and give

557a honour to God by the due performance of their duties. **2.** If they will not listen, God says ' I will send *a curse* upon you', which St Jerome understands to refer to poverty in contrast to the ' blessings ' they had hitherto enjoyed. The alternative explanation that God will curse what the priests bless is very improbable, as God would not curse the pious folk who sought the priests' blessing in virtue of their office. **3.** What follows clearly threatens the priests with the most ignominious treatment as merited by their very irreverent conduct towards God, but the detail has been understood in different ways, with different vocalizations of the noun and different consonantal readings of the verb. St Jerome took it that the shoulder of the victim which belonged to the priests by right, Deut 18:3, was to be cast at them ignominiously together with the dung of the sacrificial victims. Other suggestions are that God threatens to hew off the arm raised in blessing, or to cut off seed and posterity or to restrain the seed in the soil from giving its crop. No interpretation is convincing.

b **4-9 The Ideal of the Priesthood now Debased—4.** God gives this commandment either that his covenant may abide with Levi (as in the DV and RV ; for this use of the verb *cf.* Lev 22:26 ; 1 Kg 6:1, etc.) or because his covenant was with Levi. In any case the latter sense implies the former as its consequence. On the covenant with Levi, *i.e.* the priestly caste, *cf.* Num 25:12 f. **5.** ' My covenant was with him of life and peace, and I gave *them to him, of reverence and he revered me'.* Both parties to the covenant, both God and Levi, were faithful to their undertaking. **6.** On the duty of the priests to teach, *cf.* Lev 10:11, Deut 31:10-13. **7.** The priest is ' the angel of the Lord of hosts ', a phrase that occurs nowhere else. It is possible that in denouncing the wickedness of the priests Malachias was denouncing his own order, and that here he explains the function of the priest in a phrase borrowed from his own name. The priests were, **9,** unjust ' *respecters of persons* in the law ', *i.e.* in its administration. On the judicial function of the priestly office *cf.* Deut 17:8-11, 2 Par 19:8.

c **10-12 Marriages with Pagans—10.** God was the common father of all Israelites ; ' Israel is my son, my firstborn ', Ex 4:22. He was ' the Creator of Israel ', Is 43:15. This was a grave reason why each should not ' *deal treacherously* with his brother ', as all Israelites were brothers. The internal dissensions connected with the mixed marriages here condemned are illustrated by Neh 6:17-19. The covenant of the fathers refers to that entered into between Yahweh and the nation, Ex 19:5 f. ; 24:8. This bound them into one social unit with mutual obligations. **11.** The daughters of strange gods are pagan women, and marriages with them ' profaned the *sanctuary* of the Lord ', *i.e.* the people of Israel, Ps 113 (114) 2, which was to be ' a holy nation ', Ex 19:6. Marriage with the pagan inhabitants of the Promised Land was forbidden on account of the danger of perversion to idolatry, Ex 34:11-16 ; Deut 7:1-4. Such marriages were a grave menace after the exile, Esd 9:1 ff. ; Neh 6:18 ; 10:30 ; 13:23 ff. **12.** The phrase translated ' both the master and the scholar ' signifies totality by the combination of opposites. In the HT it is literally ' awaker and answerer ', which has an interesting parallel in Arabic, ' In the city there is neither caller nor answerer ', *viz.* no one at all. Three times in his commentary St Jerome calls this last verse a curse, and he must have written in agreement with HT ' Disperdat ', *i.e.* ' May the Lord cut off the man that hath done this '.

d **13-16 The Evil of Divorce—13.** St Jerome with the ancient Rabbis rightly explained the covering of the altar ' with tears, with weeping, and *with groaning* ' as caused by the harsh treatment of husbands divorcing their legitimate Jewish wives. The expression is, of course, metaphorical, as women did not have access to the altar. And this injustice is a further reason why God tells the Jews that he no more regards sacrifice

nor accepts ' *it with favour* at your hands '. The marriage covenant or contract was sacred and God was a witness how it was kept, as he tells the sinful husband, ' between thee and the wife of thy youth, *against whom thou hast acted faithlessly'.* **15.** This verse is obscure and has been variously interpreted. The meaning intended by St Jerome and the DV is this : Did not one and the same God who made man (Adam) make also woman (Eve), and did he not breathe into the first woman of the same breath that he breathed into Adam, Gen 2:7 ? And what was God's purpose in uniting the sexes except that they should raise up children to God ? As so much of Malachias is in dialogue form, and in particular in the form of objections raised by the Jews, and as moreover a Jew could not fail in this connexion to recall the dismissal of Agar by Abraham, it is probable that the prophet's meaning is : Did not one do this, who yet was not lacking in the spirit of God ? (It is perhaps not accidental that Abraham is twice spoken of as ' one ', Is 51:2 ; Ez 33:24.) Then the answer is given : ' But what was that one's purpose but the seed of God ? ' Abraham acted with divine permission in the interest of Isaac, the child of promise, Gen 21: 10-12. This agrees better with the following exhortation : ' Look then to your spirit and *deal not faithlessly* with the wife of thy youth '. **16.** The interpretation of this verse also is difficult. The DV follows that of St Jerome according to which an objection is raised from Deut 24:1 with the answer implying that if God there tolerated divorce it was because of the hardness of men's hearts. Translate : ' *When a man dismisses (his wife) out of hatred . . . he covers his garment with injustice'.* Therefore ' *take care of your spirit and act not faithlessly'.*

II 17-III 7 The Coming of the God of Justice and of 5 His Messenger—17. Filled with the idea that virtue is rewarded with temporal welfare during life and falsely priding themselves on their innocence, the Jews called in question the very justice of God when they compared their low estate with the prosperity of unbelieving nations such as their rulers the Persians. At least, they ask, if God *is* just, where is he ? We see no sign of his presence. **III:1.** God answers that he will come, but they are not fit to receive his coming. ' Behold I send my *messenger* and he shall prepare the way before *me'*, *cf.* Is 40:3. This was John the Baptist, as our Lord explained, Mt 11:10. ' And *suddenly* the Lord whom you seek (*cf.* 2:17) shall come to his temple, and the *messenger of the covenant*, whom you desire, *behold! he cometh!* ' The suddenness of the Lord's coming shows that the majority will not allow the forerunner really to prepare the way in their hearts. The Lord and the messenger of the covenant are one. Christ himself instituted the New Testament, Mt 26:28. So there is here a striking witness to the divinity of our Lord. **2.** But the people are unworthy : ' Who shall be able to *endure* the day of his coming ? And who shall stand *when he appears ?* ' **3.** Malachias speaks of the priesthood of the new covenant in terms of the old ; *cf.* Is 2:2-4, and Gal 3:29 where all Christians are ' the seed of Abraham '. God says that he will come in judgement, **5,** where there appears to be compenetration of the first and second comings of Christ ; *cf.* however what the Baptist said of Christ, Mt 3:10. **6-7.** The God of justice does not change : ' For I *the Lord have not changed*, but you, sons of Jacob, *have not made an end* [reading the *pi'el*] ; from the days of your fathers you have departed from my ordinances '. How could God treat them with special favour ? Yet he is always willing to receive back the repentant sinner. The Jews however will not even recognize the existence of their sin : ' *In what matter* shall we return ? '

III 8-12 Tithes and Retribution—8 The DV ' afflict ' b is due to St Jerome's having introduced here a far-fetched Messianic allusion, his words ' affiget ' and ' configitis ' being intended as an allusion to the Crucifixion ; *cf.* his commentary. ' Shall a man *rob*

b God?' for withholding the Temple dues was equivalent to depriving God of his rights. They were robbing God 'in tithes and in *oblations*'. **9.** '*With a curse you are cursed, for it is I whom you rob*'. The curse was precisely that of want, as the sequel shows. The punishment fell on that in which they sinned. Their undue attachment to property led to God's withholding temporal prosperity. **10.** If they are faithful to their duty, God will give in abundance the fertilizing rain essential for the crops of Palestine. 'The flood-gates of heaven', here probably a poetic phrase, signified originally, Gen 7:11, the apertures in the firmament the opening of which allowed the upper waters to descend on the earth in the form of rain—the simple scientific hypothesis of a primitive age. **11-12.** Not only will the soil be fruitful, but its produce will be protected from 'the devourer', the locusts or other destructive agencies. Obviously these blessings will not be bestowed if the duty of tithes and oblations is fulfilled, but other obligations already stressed are neglected. The passage is a good example of the usage by which biblical writers at times stress the point in hand as if it were the only one and prescind from all other aspects of a question—a characteristic important to bear in mind to avoid serious misinterpretations. Nehemias also complained of the non-payment of tithes and of its disastrous effect on the Temple worship, Neh 13:10-12. Storehouses for the tithes and oblations were prepared in the reign of Ezechias, 2 Par 31:8-12.

c **13-15 Complaints against the Providence of God**— **13.** The prophet returns at greater length to the blasphemous sayings mentioned in 2:17. In spite of their sins many claimed to be obeying God's law and complained that they did not receive the anticipated temporal reward. **14.** They claimed also to have been walking sorrowful before the Lord, perhaps, that is, to have been observing fasts, *cf.* Ps 34 (35)13; Mt 6:16. As St Jerome pointed out long ago, these are not the words of those ' that feared the Lord ' of 3:16, for ' if they feared the Lord, they would not say those things '.

d **16-18 The Virtuous are God's Special Possession**— **16.** It is surprising that the contrary conversation of the virtuous is not reported in detail, but its substance can be readily understood from the context. It is also to be remarked that the word ' then ' is vague and unsatisfactory, and probably covers an ancient and deep-seated corruption of the text. The LXX emendation, if such it was, is not happy for by substituting ' these things ' it puts the previous blasphemies into mouths that could never have uttered them. St Jerome suggests that this LXX reading must be understood ironically of those who falsely boasted their **558d** worship of God, but against this is the fact that the same phrase is used of the really virtuous later in the same verse. It seems clear that what the Lord heard the pious say was judged by him worthy of remembrance for the purpose of reward. **17.** In Ex 19:5 God had promised that the whole people would be his peculiar possession if they would obey his voice. But the condition had not been fulfilled and here the same promise is restricted to the good. That even the good require the clemency of God shows that none are entirely without sin. **18.** On the day that God manifests this special favour for the just, he says to all, ' You shall *again* see the difference between the just and the wicked'.

IV 1-3 The Day of the Lord—In the HT the remaining **e** verses of Malachias are numbered consecutively with the verses of ch 3. **1.** The punishment that is to come on the wicked is spoken of in strong metaphorical language which, if taken literally, would suggest their annihilation. ' It shall not leave them root nor branch '—another phrase implying universality by the mention of opposites. **2.** The sun of justice is the sun that brings the reward of justice ; *cf.* Ps 23 (24)5, where the Vg has translated the same word by ' mercy '. There is ' *healing* in his wings ', which are the sun's spreading rays ; *cf.* the winged sun-disk of Egypt. The just shall gambol for joy ' like calves of the *stall* ', *i.e.* well-fed and freed from their confinement.

4 Exhortation to obey the Law—That this monition **f** comes rather unexpectedly does not prove it to be a later gloss. If an editor could judge the place not unsuitable for its insertion, so could the original author.

5 f. The Coming of Elias—Elias had been carried **g** up in a fiery chariot by a whirlwind to heaven, 4 Kg 2:11. He is to come again to restore religious harmony and unity among all. As already explained, the doctrine of future retribution had not been revealed in the time of Malachias, who consequently merges in one picture both the first and the second comings of Christ, first to save and secondly to judge the world. It is in accordance with this that the disciples with the Scribes took this passage to refer to the coming of the Messias. When the Transfiguration had brought vividly to their minds that the Messias was already with them, they asked : ' Why then do the Scribes say that Elias must come first ? ' Our Lord answered : ' Elias indeed shall come and restore all things ; but I say to you that Elias is already come '. Then they understood that Christ spoke to them of the Baptist, Mt 17:10-13. In this way our Lord manifested the truth that there are two precursors as there are two comings.

1 and 2 MACCABEES

By T. CORBISHLEY, S.J.

559a Bibliography—J. Knabenbauer, S.J., *Commentarius in duos libros Machabaeorum*, Paris, 1907 (CSS) ; H. Bévenot, O.S.B., *Die Beiden Makkabäerbücher*, Bonn, 1931 (BB) ; L. C. Fillion, *Les Livres des Machabées*, Paris, 1900 ; F.-M. Abel, O.P., *Géographie de la Palestine*, Paris, 1933–8 ; *id.*, *Topographie des Campagnes Machabéennes*, RB 32–5 (1923–6) ; F. X. Kugler, S.J., *Von Moses bis Paulus*, Münster in Westf., 1922, pp 301–413 ; Donatien de Bruyne, O.S.B., *Le texte grec . . .*, RB 31 (1922) 31–54 ; 39 (1930) 503–19 ; *Fairweather and Black, *The First Book of Maccabees*, Cambridge, 1897 ; *W. O. E. Oesterley (1 Mac) and J. Moffat (2 Mac) in CAP ; *J. W. Hunkin (1 and 2 *Maccabees*), in *A New Commentary on Holy Scripture*, ed. Gore, Goudge and Guillaume, 1928 ; CAH, vol. VIII, ch. XVI ; *Schürer, *The Jewish People in the Time of Christ*, Div. I, vol. I, 1890 ; M.-J. Lagrange, O.P., *Le Judaïsme avant Jésus-Christ*, Paris, 1931 ; D. Schötz, O.F.M., *Erstes und Zweites Buch der Makkabäer*, Echter Bibel, Würzburg, 1948.

b General Introduction—In many ways the Books of Maccabees are amongst the most easily intelligible of the OT. The story they have to tell—the account of the successful resistance of the Jewish people to a foreign tyranny—is one which is characteristic of human history in all ages, with this important difference that in Mac great stress is laid upon the religious nature of the uprising and upon the assistance received by the Jews from God. There are few difficulties of interpretation, and very few passages of great theological importance. Such difficulties as occur are mostly of minor historical detail, though there are a number of perplexities raised by the fact that the two books often treat of the same incidents from slightly different points of view. But, since the Church has appointed readings from these books to provide the Scripture readings for the First Nocturn during the whole month of October, the commentary will have no small practical value.

The **title Machabaeus**, strictly appropriated to Judas, the third son of Mathathias, is thought to be derived from the Heb. *maqqābāh*, meaning a ' hammer '. It was afterwards used of the whole family of Mathathias, and eventually came to be applied by the Fathers to the seven sons and the mother whose story is told in 2 Mac 7.

c Historical Background—The general situation has been described elsewhere (§ 68*b–h*), but a somewhat more detailed account of contemporary history is necessary **5** for an adequate understanding of the Books. After the death of Alexander the Great in 323 B.C., his vast empire split up. The wars of his successors, lasting for some forty years, eventually resulted in that pattern of Eastern Mediterranean states which was to endure until Rome absorbed them all. Apart from Macedonia, mistress of most of the Greek mainland, the two great powers in the Middle East were Syria, with its capital at Antioch, ruled by the Seleucid dynasty (so called from its founder Seleucus), and Egypt, with its capital at Alexandria, ruled by the Ptolemies. Between these two lay Palestine, at first belonging to Egypt, but shortly after 200 B.C. falling to Syria, as the result of the vigorous policy of Antiochus III, who, no less than his successor Seleucus IV, respected the Jewish religion. But Antiochus IV (Epiphanes = the Illustrious) began a policy designed to secure political unity by the imposition on his heterogeneous kingdom of religious and social uniformity. This involved requiring of the Jews certain practices which were an abomination to the devout. Unfortunately, within the Jewish people there were always to be found many who were prepared to sacrifice the Law of God for their own ambitious ends, and a ' Hellenizing party ', prepared to admit the requirements of Antiochus, sprang up and split the unity of the nation.

The theme of the Books of Maccabees is the history **d** of how a single family, rallying the forces of resistance, managed to prevail over the ' collaborationists ', backed by the might of Syria. This success was due to several factors : first and foremost was the genuine religious fervour of the faithful party ; second, the leadership and military skill of Judas and his brothers ; and third, the chronic civil strife within the kingdom of Syria itself. It is necessary to give some account of this if we are to follow the story of the Books at all clearly.

The table below will make it clear that when Antiochus IV ascended the throne he was usurping the power that should have descended to his nephew. This nephew subsequently challenged the claim of the son of Antiochus IV and became Demetrius I. This was the beginning of a series of dynastic quarrels which considerably helped the Jewish revolt and eventually led to the downfall of the power of Syria. A further factor that must be noted is the enmity between Syria and Egypt. The latter country was never reconciled to the loss of Palestine and open war broke out on more than one occasion.

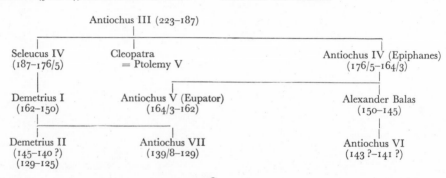

	Antiochus III (223–187)		
Seleucus IV (187–176/5)	Cleopatra = Ptolemy V		Antiochus IV (Epiphanes) (176/5–164/3)
Demetrius I (162–150)	Antiochus V (Eupator) (164/3–162)		Alexander Balas (150–145)
Demetrius II (145–140 ?) (129–125)	Antiochus VII (139/8–129)		Antiochus VI (143 ?–141 ?)

9f Meanwhile, in the background, the threat of Rome was a constant reality. Although not yet prepared to assume direct responsibility for any Asiatic territories, the Roman Senate was concerned to secure her interests in the Levant by playing off one power against another. Thus, when Syria seemed likely to prevail against Egypt, it was Rome's envoy, Popillius Laenas, who stayed her advance. The defeat of Antiochus the Great at Magnesia in 190 B.C. had been so absolute that it secured the prestige of Rome in the East for nearly a century. Incidentally, too, it saddled the Syrian kingdom with a debt which seriously hampered the warlike preparations of the Seleucids. We may well believe that Rome would welcome any *rapprochement* with the Jews, so long as it did not involve active intervention in the revolt.

g A few words may be added concerning the politico-religious situation in Judaea itself. After the annexation of the country by Antiochus the Great, there remained a fairly strong pro-Egyptian party, represented amongst others by the high-priest and the 'traditionalists' generally. Against these stood the 'progressive' Hellenizing party, with the wealthy Tobiad family at its head. It seems to have been the policy of Antiochus III and Seleucus IV to try to conciliate the former by showing deference to the religious susceptibilities of the Jews and by financial support of the temple. This policy was reversed by Antiochus IV, possibly owing very largely to the intrigues and suggestions of the Tobiad family and their supporters.

10a **Chronology**—The problem of Maccabaean chronology has been discussed by different scholars, with different results. The Seleucid era is taken as the basis of dating in both books, but there is some uncertainty about the precise determination of this era. The most probable conclusion seems to be that the author of 1 Mac reckons his years from Nisan to Nisan, and that the first year of the Seleucid era (*sc.* the era dating from the reign of Seleucus I) runs from Nisan 312–Nisan 311 B.C., whilst for the author of 2 Mac the reckoning is from Tishri to Tishri (Nisan = March/April; Tishri = Sept./Oct.). Thus any event falling between Nisan 1 and Tishri 1 in any given Julian year would be attributed to different years by the different books. This will account for a number of apparent discrepancies as that in 2 Mac 13:1 and 14:4 events appear to be dated a year earlier than in the corresponding passages of 1 Mac. (Knabenbauer has a good short discussion, with references to the standard authorities; Bévenot is slightly fuller but comes to the same conclusion.)

(For **560b** see p 708)

c **The Figures found in Maccabees**—Non-Catholic critics often treat the figures given by the authors of Mac as entirely unreliable. But allowing for the possibility of occasional textual corruption and even conceding, with Bévenot, that the recurrence of multiples of 10,000 in the figures given for the Syrian armies suggests that, sometimes at any rate, there has been a misunderstanding of the Heb. *rᵉḇāḇāh* (= like the Gk μύριος, sometimes 10,000, sometimes merely a very large number), it is desirable to point out that it is unsafe to reject the existing numbers merely on *a priori* grounds. Despite the cynic, God is not always ' on the side of the big battalions', as has been proved time and again in history, from the days of Marathon down to the 20th cent. On the contrary, given a resolute command and a people convinced of the righteousness of their cause, there have been any number of well-attested examples of a relatively small force securing a resounding victory over what might have seemed impossible odds. Remembering then that the Jews were fighting on a terrain well-known to them, often in hill-country suited to a guerilla type of warfare and favouring the defence, that they were inspired by an intense patriotism coupled with an even more intense religious fervour, we should expect to find them succeeding against larger Syrian armies, presumably composed as a rule of mercenary troops, and those not necessarily **560c** the best at the king's disposal (since he had so many other commitments).

Occasional apparent discrepancies between 1 Mac and 2 Mac have been treated in the commentary. For a fuller discussion of the problem *cf.* Bévenot, 34 ff., Cornely-Merk, *Introd. Compendium*, Parisiis, 1927⁹.

Doctrinal Content—The Books of Maccabees, being **d** primarily the story of men of action, refer only incidentally to points of doctrine. But there are passages which give glimpses into the beliefs of the devout Jews of the time. The chief contribution is made by 2 Mac 7, the well-known account of the 'seven Maccabees'. From this it is certain that the Jews possessed a clear conviction not merely of **survival after death**, but of eternal life (7:36), in contradistinction to the punishment (by implication eternal) which awaits the wicked. Thus, in 36, Antiochus is warned that he will receive ' just punishment', whilst in 14 he is told that he will ' have no resurrection unto life'. Moreover, the 'resurrection of eternal life' (9) will include the **restoration of bodily existence.** Thus the third son says : ' I hope to receive them [tongue and hands] again from him' (11), whilst the mother assures her children that God will restore to them ' both breath and life' (23).

The passage in 2 Mac 12:43-46, which describes **e** how Judas sent money to Jerusalem ' for sacrifices to be offered for the sins of the dead', is so well known as to call for little comment, for nothing short of complete scepticism can explain away the clear doctrine there expressed that, of those who have ' fallen asleep with godliness', some will need prayer ' that they may be loosed from sins'—the most definite expression of a belief in **Purgatory.** It is obvious then from ch 7 and 12:43 ff. that there existed in the mind of Judaism in the 2nd cent. B.C. a profound conviction of **immortality,** of **eternal punishment for sin,** of the **resurrection of the body** and of an **intermediate state of purification** after death. Even Razias who misguidedly committed suicide rather than fall into the hands of his enemies hoped for such immortality, 14:46.

Two other passages call for comment. The first is **f** 7:28, a clear statement of the doctrine of **creation** *ex nihilo.* Whether we read with Rahlfs οὐκ ἐξ ὄντων ἐποίησε or prefer the reading ἐξ οὐκ ὄντων which is to be found in a number of Gk MSS, supported by Vg, the meaning is substantially the same. And it is mere pedantry to see in the passage a Philonian restatement of the Platonic μὴ ὄν and not a natural conviction based on Gen 1:1.

The remaining passage is 1 Mac 2:51 ff., with its **g** anticipations of St Paul, especially Heb 11:1 ff., whilst both 1 Mac 2:52 and Rom 4:3 repeat Gen 15:6. The passage in Mac seems to be of importance for the whole subject of **faith and works,** and has perhaps not received sufficient attention from the theologians.

THE FIRST BOOK OF MACCABEES

Composition—The original language was almost cer- **561a** tainly Hebrew, as is inferred from the number of Hebraisms in the existing Greek version. A few of these are indicated in the commentary. The author, clearly a devout and believing Jew, with a first-hand knowledge of Palestine, seeks to tell in a straightforward manner the story of his people's deliverance from the danger of perversion. Whilst entirely alive to the providential nature of that deliverance, he nowhere emphasizes or exaggerates the preternatural element in the story, but is content to show the operation of natural causes—the tenacity and skill of Judas and his brethren, the dissipation of the Syrian forces, the moral support of Rome—whilst at the same time stressing the importance of the religious spirit with which the Jewish leaders imbued their followers.

The **date of composition** cannot be determined with **b**

SYNCHRONISTIC TABLE

560b B.C:	Seleucid Era		1 Mac	2 Mac 560b
323		Death of Alexander the Great	1:8	
175	137	Antiochus Epiphanes succeeds	1:11	(4:7)
174	138	(Hellenization begins)	(1:12 ff.)	(4:8 ff.)
172	140	'First' expedition against Egypt by Antiochus Epiphanes :		4:21 f.
		Epiphanes in Jerusalem		4:21
171	141	Menelaus becomes high-priest		4:24
169	143	Epiphanes' 'second' expedition against Egypt	1:21	5:1
168	144	Temple plundered	1:23	5:15 ff.
167	145	Apollonius in Jerusalem	1:30	5:24
		'Abomination of Desolation'	1:57	6:2
166	146	Revolt of Mathathias	2:27	
		Death of Mathathias	2:70	
		JUDAS MACHABAEUS leader	3:1	8:1
165	147	Victories over Apollonius	3:11	
		(at Bethoron) over Seron	3:23	
		(at Emmaus) over Nicanor and Gorgias	4:3 ff.	8:9 ff.
		(Antiochus Epiphanes in Persia)	3:37	
164	148	Lysias defeated	4:28-34	? 11:1-12
		TEMPLE PURIFIED	4:52	10:1-8
163	149	Successes in Idumaea, Galaad, etc.	5:1 ff.	8:30 ff.
				12:18-25
				10:24-38
				12:26-31
		Death of Antiochus Epiphanes :	6:16	9:28
		Antiochus V (Eupator) succeeds	6:17	(11:22, 3)
162	150	Judas attacks the citadel	6:20	
161	151	Eupator in Judaea : takes Bethsura	6:31 ff.	13:1
	(149)	Demetrius I lands in Syria	7:1	14:1
	(150)	First attempt to impose Alcimus (Bacchides)	7:1-25	14:4
		Second attempt (Nicanor)	7:27 ff.	14:14 ff.
		Defeat of Nicanor (13 Adar)	7:43 ff.	15:28
160	152	Third attempt to restore Alcimus (Bacchides)	9:1	
		Death of Judas	9:18	
		JONATHAN leader	9:31	
		Expedition across Jordan	9:39 ff.	
159	153	Alcimus orders destruction of the Soreg :	9:54	
		his death	9:56	
158	154	'Two years peace'	9:57	
157	155	Bacchides fails at Bethbessen :	9:68	
		peace	9:70	
152	160	Alexander Balas lands at Ptolemais	10:1	
		Jonathan high-priest	10:21	
151	161	War between Demetrius I and Alexander	10:48 ff.	
		Death of Demetrius	10:50	
150	162	League between Ptolemy and Alexander	10:57	
147	165	Demetrius II lands in Syria	10:67	
		Apollonius in Judaea : defeated by Jonathan	10:69 ff.	
146	166	Breach between Ptolemy and Alexander	11:1 ff.	
		Death of Alexander Balas	11:18	
145	167	Demetrius II succeeds	11:19	
144	168	Jonathan at Ptolemais	11:24	
143	169	Tryphon rebels against Demetrius	11:39	
		Jonathan supports Demetrius	11:44	
		Tryphon puts Antiochus VI on the throne	11:54	
		Antiochus confirms the privileges of Jonathan :	11:57	
		Demetrius's generals are defeated by Jonathan	11:73 ; 12:30	
		Alliance with Rome renewed	12:1 ff.	
142	170	Capture of Jonathan		
		SIMON leader of Jews	13:8	
		Tryphon driven off :	13:24	
		'Liberation of Israel'	13:41	
141	171	Citadel taken	13:51	
140	172	(Demetrius in Persia : capture)	14:1, 3	
		(18 Elul) Simon honoured by public inscription	14:27	
139	173	Letters to Simon from Antiochus	15:1 ff.	
138	174	Antiochus VII lands in Syria	15:10	
		Death of Tryphon		
137	175	Cendebaeus defeated by Simon's sons	15:10	
135	177	Death of Simon :	15:14-16	
		JOHN HYRCANUS succeeds	15:23	

b any preciseness, but there is no need to suppose that it was much later than the reign of John Hyrcanus, who died in 103 B.C. The Book must certainly have been completed before Rome became hostile to the Jews, in view of the attitude of the writer to the Romans, which would have been unthinkable after Pompey's entry into the temple in 63 B.C.

c Contents—After a brief introduction (1:1-10) giving the broad historical setting of the events to be narrated, the author first describes the causes leading up to the revolt headed by Mathathias, with a brief account of his achievements and death (1:11-2:70). He then (3:1-9:22) narrates in some detail the activities of Judas, first of all under Antiochus Epiphanes (3:1-6:17) and then under Antiochus Eupator and Demetrius I, concluding with an account of the death of Judas. The next section is devoted to the deeds of Jonathan (9:23-12:54), and the last section is concerned with the work of Simon, closing with his death and the succession of John (13:1-16:24).

2a I 1-10 Prologue : Alexander's Empire divided at his Death—The account of the rise of the Syrian kingdom naturally begins with the pivotal fact of Alexander's conquests. These started in 332 when he began his march from Greece (' the land of Kittim ', used in the OT of the Greek-speaking lands ; cf. 8:5, Gen 10:4, Jer 2:10), and included the whole of SW. Asia as far as the Punjab, as well as Egypt. They are impressively indicated in 2-4. The phrase in 1 ' who first reigned in Greece ' cloaks an obscurity in the Gk, but the meaning is probably that he was the first ruler of the ' kingdom of the Greeks ' (11 and cf. ' Greece ' in 6:2), i.e. of that Hellenistic kingdom which was constituted by his conquests, and of which Syria seems to have been regarded as the legatee. The evidence that Alexander formally divided his empire before his death is not convincing, and 6 must be understood to refer to the arrangements which he made in his lifetime for the administration of the different satrapies ; the actual division into the constituent kingdoms of Macedonia, Syria and Egypt was the result of the wars of the Diadochi, Alexander's generals and their successors, which began soon after his death and produced misery and devastation for forty years (10).

b 11-16 Antiochus Epiphanes : Attempted Hellenization of Palestine—Antiochus the Illustrious (Epiphanes) seized the throne of Syria in 175 B.C., and a party in Judaea lent themselves to his design to Hellenize the Jews. The internal situation amongst the latter is more fully developed in 2 Mac ; cf. § 559c-g. The desire of the Hellenizing party to co-operate with Antiochus doubtless represents an attempt to curry favour, but must also be understood as the latest manifestation of the chronic tendency amongst the Jews to assimilate themselves as much as possible to the religious and social conditions of their neighbours. The institution of the (characteristically Greek) gymnasium led to a desire to conceal the traces of circumcision, a desire with obvious religious implications (15 f.). The practices hinted at in the words ' sold themselves to do evil ' (sc. were prostituted) remind us of one of the great moral dangers of the new tendencies. The Greeks were notoriously given to unnatural vice.

c 17-42 Antiochus invades Egypt : he pillages the Temple and Jerusalem is sacked—This attempt of Antiochus to aggrandize himself at the expense of the young king of Egypt was checked by Rome, 168 B.C. 2 Mac 5:5 makes it clear that it was the behaviour of some of the Jews during his absence which provoked the king's anger. 23. For the ' golden altar ' and other objects cf. 3 Kg 7:48, 50. They had been removed by Nabuchodonosor (2 Par 36:7) and restored by Cyrus (Esd 1:7 ; 5:14).

26-29, 38-42 afford a very good example of the way in which the author of 1 Mac rises from the plain prose of his narrative passages to a style which is reminiscent of the more poetical portions of the OT. **562c** It is interesting to compare Ps 78, which may have been composed at this time.

The ' chief collector of his tributes ' (30) is apparently the Apollonius of 2 Mac 5:24, where he is styled Μυσάρχης ; cf. ad loc. It seems probable that we should read captain of the Mysians here too, the presumed original Heb. śar hammussîm having been misread as śar hammissîm.

In 35 is described the fortification known as the castle or citadel (ἄκρα). It is referred to frequently in accounts of the later campaigns. Its precise situation is uncertain, but the more common opinion is that it was situated close to the temple (cf. 4:41), near its southern or possibly south-western end. (The ' city of David ' is often identified with the region of Mount Sion, but 7:32 f. suggests that the author distinguished them.) **38.** ' An evil devil ' : a source of annoyance, a constant threat.

43-67 Hellenization enforced by Antiochus—The **d** policy indicated here (and more fully described in 2 Mac 6 and 7) was meant to produce a uniform religious and social system as an important factor in the unification of the very heterogeneous Syrian kingdom ; cf. Roman Emperor-worship propaganda. In making their heroic stand the Jewish victims of the persecution anticipate the later Christian martyrs and all Confessors who maintain the rights of God as against those of Caesar. **45.** Many ' consented to his service ', sc. to the form of worship prescribed by the king, possibly though not necessarily including worship of himself as a manifestation of Zeus. According to Josephus (Ant. 12, 5, 5) the Samaritans actually addressed Antiochus as θεός ἐπιφανής ' God made manifest '. **47-51** describe the attack made upon all forms of Jewish worship of the true God, and the legal observances which were its safeguard. Circumcision, the sign of the individual's belonging to Yahweh, was naturally a practice ruthlessly forbidden by the Syrian authorities. **51.** The Vg reading justificationes Dei is represented in the Gk by δικαιώματα = prescriptions, ordinances (of the Law). This is one of a number of passages in which the name of God is found in Vg though not in LXX. The author of 1 Mac seems to have been most scrupulous in his avoidance of the sacred Name.

57. Note the way in which the date of this infamous **e** act is perpetuated. The equivalent date is between 10 and 17 Dec., 167 B.C. The ' abominable idol of desolation ' was, according to Josephus, an idol-altar actually built upon the altar of sacrifice in the temple. 2 Mac 6:2 would suggest that the altar was consecrated to Zeus Olympios. The Gk says simply βδέλυγμα ἐρημώσεως = abomination of desolation, and it is not clear why Vg renders abominandum idolum desolationis. For the expression abomination of desolation cf. Dan 9:27 ; 11:31 ; 12:11 ; Mt 24:15, etc. **62** bears out Josephus—' the altar which was upon the altar of sacrifice ' (LXX τὸν βωμόν, ὃς ἦν ἐπὶ τοῦ θυσιαστηρίου). In addition to the altar in the temple, the Syrians set up statues (Hermae ?) and shrines in the streets of Jerusalem and other cities of Judaea (57-58 ; cf. Josephus, Ant. 12, 5, 4). The reading in **64** is a little doubtful, but it seems probable that we should emend ' houses ' to servants (οἰκείους not οἴκους), so that not only were the mothers put to death but also those in any way connected with the rite of circumcision. According to Josephus they were crucified.

II 1-14 Mathathias and his Sons—So far we have been **f** told of the cruelties of the Syrians, and the emphasis has been laid on the defection of the Hellenizers rather than on the resistance of the faithful. **1.** Now we come to the account of active opposition, initiated by one family from Modin, some 15 m. NW. of Jerusalem. Doubtless there were many such centres of resistance, but it is the incident described in 23-25 which marks the beginning of organized rebellion, resulting in the liberation of Judaea. Joarib, from whom Mathathias was descended, is mentioned in 1 Par 24:7 as receiving

562f by lot the first of the 24 courses of the priesthood. Simeon is called by Josephus (*Ant.* 12, 6, 1) the son of Asmonaeus, but it is thought that Asmonaeus (*ḥasmōnay*) is a collateral form of Simeon; hence the family is frequently called Hasmonean. **2-5.** Gaddis = Lucky; Thasi = Zealous; Machabaeus (*cf.* § 559*b*) = Hammer; Abaron (? Avaron) = Beast-sticker (*cf.* 6:43 ff.); Apphus = Cunning. In **7-13** we have another example of the poetical side of 1 Mac.

g **15-26 Modin: the Incident of the Apostate Jew**—As a member of the priestly family, Mathathias was naturally invited to set an example to the rest by offering sacrifice at the bidding of the king. His refusal is in marked contrast to the conduct of Menelaus, the high-priest, (2 Mac 5:15). **24.** 'His wrath was kindled *in accordance with the requirements of the law.*' **Phinees,** *cf.* Num 25:7, 11.

h **27-48 Beginnings of Revolt**—'The mountains' (28) and 'the desert' (29) are probably to be located E. and S. of Hebron, in a general direction SW. from Jerusalem. The incident recorded in **32-38,** the slaughter of the Jews who refused to resist on the Sabbath, stamps the movement as essentially religious, and reminds us that we are here dealing with a holy war and with no mere nationalistic uprising. **38.** 'So they gave them battle on the Sabbath' = the Syrians *attacked* the unresisting Jews. **40.** After that gesture it was no contradiction that the Jews should come to see that the service of God demanded that they should be prepared to fight even on the Sabbath.

42. The 'congregation of the Hasidaeans' (*Ḥᵃsîdîm* = the Pious) who now join Mathathias are the forerunners of the later Pharisees. (A Lapide suggests that they were a sort of Military Order, like the medieval Knights Templar, but there is no need to suppose that they were more than a sect of specially devout Jews who, in this moment of national peril, rallied to the cause of God; *cf.* Lagrange, 56, 272). The 'sinners' and 'wicked men' of **44** are the Hellenizing Jews, whilst the 'sons of pride' (*i.e. the proud*—by a common Hebraism) of **48** are the Syrians and others who arrogantly oppose God's law. Another Hebraism 'yielded not the horn to the sinner', which may mean either that *they did not give way to the wicked* or that *they did not allow the wicked to triumph*, is one of the numerous indications of an underlying Hebrew original.

i **49-70 Death of Mathathias**—The moving exhortation of the dying Mathathias is worthy to rank with many noble passages in the Bible. The OT examples referred to in **52-60** are recorded in Gen 22:2; 41:40; Num 25:13; Jos 1:2; Num 14:16; 2 Kg 2:11; Dan 3:50; 6:22. **52** is of particular interest with reference to Gen 15:6 and Rom 4:3.

563a **III 1-26 Judas Machabaeus succeeds his Father: his Early Successes**—The eulogy of Judas in **1-9** has been reconstructed in Hebrew by C. F. Burney to produce an acrostic poem with the initial letters JHUDH HMKBY (JTS [1919–20] 319ff.). The reconstruction involves some manipulation of the existing text.

10. It was Apollonius who was responsible for the sack of Jerusalem (1:29; 2 Mac 5:24). According to Josephus (*Ant.* 12, 7, 1) he was governor of Samaria. But this may be a mere inference from the present passage. **13.** Seron (= Hiram) is described by Josephus as governor of Coele-Syria. The mention of Bethhoron (**16**) suggests that he came by the regular route from the coastal plain to Jerusalem. The town itself, consisting of an upper and a lower half, lies some 10 or 12 m. NW. of Jerusalem. It was on the line of Josue's famous pursuit of the Amorites (Jos 10:10), and by it the Philistines marched against Saul (1 Kg 9:17). The weakness of the army of Judas and the fact that Jerusalem itself was strongly garrisoned by the Syrians (1:35) suggest that the march was no more than a surprise raid, which succeeded because of its very boldness. The time for regular campaigns of reconquest had not yet come.

In **18** 'the God of heaven' (Vg 'Dei caeli') and in **5**
22 'the Lord' ('Dominus') are not found in the Gk, which has simply *heaven* and *himself*, in accordance with the practice mentioned in § 562*d* of avoiding the use of the Name.

27-41 Counter-measures of the Syrians—Lysias, com- **c** missioned by Antiochus to take the necessary steps, sends into Judaea an army under Ptolemy, Gorgias and Nicanor. Hitherto, against the scattered resistance of isolated bodies of Jews, Antiochus had been able to enforce his will without any great military power. The realization that a more organized form of resistance, under a leader of obvious capacity, had to be broken, leads to more elaborate measures. The parallel passage (2 Mac 8:8 ff.) informs us that Ptolemy was governor of Coele-Syria, having presumably replaced Seron after his failure. If the number 40,000 is authentic, this large force must have been divided between Nicanor and Gorgias (*cf.* 2 Mac 8:9), the latter of whom was in command of the Syrian fortresses in Idumaea (2 Mac 10:14; 12:32) at least in the following reign, and he may well have received this command from Lysias at this time.

The Persian expedition referred to in **31, 37** ('the **d** higher countries' = *the inland regions*) was intended not merely to recoup the king, whose exchequer had been drained by the large indemnity imposed on Syria by the Romans after Magnesia (190 B.C.), but also to repress the rising power of Mithridates I, who had succeeded to the Parthian throne in 171 B.C. and was becoming too powerful for a mere vassal of the Seleucid kingdom. 'It is probable that to Antiochus the Jewish trouble seemed a small enough affair compared with the Parthian menace in the East. Some modern scholars speak sarcastically of the Jewish books which represent the events in Judaea as the things of central importance in the world and pretend that Antiochus' chief preoccupation was the ill-success of the local government forces in dealing with the Jewish bands. No doubt from the point of view of Antiochus the Jewish books greatly exaggerate the importance of events in Judaea, just as from the point of view of the Persian king, we may believe, the Greek books greatly exaggerated the importance of the battle of Marathon. In regard to the influence destined to be exerted on the subsequent history of mankind, the Greek books and the Jewish books were right. Of all that was happening in the kingdom of Antiochus, the events in Judaea were by far the most important in their consequences for the mind of man in the ages to come' (CAH 8:513 f.).

In **41** 'servants' represents παῖδας of the Gk, but the Syriac reading suggests that the original text had πέδας 'fetters' which suits the context better. For 'Syria' read *Edom*, the error being due to the confusion of *resh* and *daleth* in the Hebrew original. The Edomites were traditional enemies of Israel; and for Edomite activity in the slave-trade see § 526*e*. 'Strangers' are the Philistines, thus regularly referred to in LXX; *cf.* 4:22, 30; 5:66.

42-60 The Mustering of the Jews—In face of the **e** threat from the NW. (Emmaus, 40, the site of the Syrian camp, is some 15 m. WNW. of Jerusalem, according to the identification with the modern 'Amwas; others would place it at El-Qubeibe, some 8 m. NW. of the capital, which would agree with the 60 furlongs of Lk 24:13) Judas drew out his forces as far as Mizpah (Maspha), a sacred site associated with Samuel (1 Kg 7:5 f.) and probably to be identified with Nebi Samwil, some 6 m. NW. of Jerusalem. There they besought the help of God. There is some difficulty in **48.** The accepted Gk reading is καὶ ἐξεπέτασαν τὸ βιβλίον τοῦ νόμου περὶ ὧν ἐξηρεύνων τὰ ἔθνη τὰ ὁμοιώματα τῶν εἰδώλων αὐτῶν, which is adequately rendered by Vg: 'et expanderunt libros legis de quibus scrutabantur gentes similitudinem simulacrorum suorum', *sc.* 'they laid open the books of the law *concerning those things about which the Gentiles were accustomed to consult*

43e *their idol-images'*. The meaning of this is not certain, but Wellhausen, followed by Bévenot, suggests that the Jews opened their sacred books in order to find some reassuring message, even as the Gentiles were accustomed to consult oracles. (2 Mac 8:23 would bear out this interpretation.) This gives a reasonable sense and it is hardly necessary to emend. DV mistranslates.

In 49 ' stirred up ' = *summoned*. The exemptions in **56** are in accordance with the prescriptions of Deut 20:5 ff. **59** reminds us that it is at once a right and a duty to resist to the death where the enemy is bent on religious and political oppression. **60.** Gk simply says : ' *as it shall be the will in heaven* '.

44a IV 1-25 Defeat of Gorgias (and Nicanor) at Emmaus —The parallel passage (2 Mac 8:24 ff.) makes it clear that Gorgias was here acting in concert with Nicanor, and that Judas scored a double victory, apparently over the force led by Nicanor, at Emmaus, and then over the force led by Gorgias, which had attacked the Jewish camp, S. of Emmaus ; *cf.* 57. If Gorgias had already been appointed to the command in Idumaea, the attack would be from the S. concerted with Nicanor's advance from the N. But it is possible that Nicanor and Gorgias advanced together from the coast as far as Emmaus, and that Gorgias there attempted a turning movement. In any case Judas scored a brilliant victory in compelling the Syrian army, greatly superior in numbers, to withdraw from Judaea. **7-16** describe the victory over Nicanor's force, which is pursued as far as Gezer (Gezeron : Tell Jezer), a distance of 5 m. The plain of Idumaea is used apparently of the region W. of Judaea ; Idumaea normally refers to the district to the S. of Judaea, but *cf.* 1 Mac 5:59 where Gorgias, ' commander of the strongholds in Idumaea ', is found in command in the neighbourhood of Jamnia. For the attack on Nicanor Judas apparently divided his force, taking with him 3,000 lightly armed men (**6**) out of the 6,000 he had in all (2 Mac 8:15 LXX, where Vg and DV have 7,000). The remainder were doubtless left to protect his rear against the attack by Gorgias, which did not develop, when Gorgias realized that Nicanor was in flight. (' His men ' in 20 is not in the Gk, which says simply : ' *when he saw that they* [*sc.* Nicanor's men] *were in flight* '.) Gorgias fled and Judas plundered his camp at leisure. In **24** the Gk says : ' *they blessed heaven* '.

b 26-35 Defeat of Lysias at Bethsura—Lysias with a still larger army now advances from the region SW. of Jerusalem. In **29** the MSS favour the reading Idumaea as against the Judaea of Vg and DV : Bethhoron is presumably a corruption of Bethsura, *i.e.* Beit Sur, N. of Hebron and some 22 m. SSW. of Jerusalem (*cf.* 2 Mac 11:1-15), though the fortress for the possession of which this battle was presumably fought seems to have been situated a little farther to the west.

c 36-59 Entry into Jerusalem : Purification of the Temple : Encaenia—Stationing a force to prevent interference on the part of the garrison in the citadel (**41** ; *cf.* 1:35), Judas carefully purifies the temple. He destroys the idol-altar (' the stones that had been defiled '), dismantles the altar of sacrifice, and stores away the constituent stones until the time when some prophet should arise who could be consulted as to their further disposal. A new altar is built and everything renewed for the temple-worship. The Feast of Dedication is celebrated on 25 Casleu, three years to the day since the setting up of the abomination of desolation (1:62). This encaenia—the renewal of the altar—became an annual feast ; *cf.* Jn 10:22. Josephus (*Ant.* 12, 7, 7) calls it the Feast of Lights. For the parallel passage *cf.* 2 Mac 10:1-8.

d 60-V 8 Fortification of Sion and Bethsura : Campaigns against Idumaeans, etc.—The temple mount is fortified against the citadel-garrison ; Bethsura (*cf.* 4:29) is occupied and strengthened, presumably as a preliminary to the campaign described at the beginning of ch 6. There seems to be a slight textual error in **564d 61.** A phrase has been repeated in the Gk text which **e** has given rise in Vg to the reading *munivit eum ad custodiendam Bethsuram*. What was meant is simply : *munivit Bethsuram*—' *he fortified Bethsura* '.

Having secured the Holy City, Judas now proceeds to extend the area of his conquests. He is encouraged to do this by the persecution of the Jews settled amongst the heathen peoples of Idumaea and elsewhere : the *sons of Esau*, *sc.* the Edomites living in Acrabatane, a ridge SW. of the Dead Sea ; the *sons of Bean* (*cf.* Num 32:3 ; Vg Beon, LXX Baian), living in Baal Meon, E. of the Dead Sea ; the *sons of Ammon*, NE. of the Dead Sea, led by Timotheus. This campaign against the Ammonites is more fully described in 2 Mac 10:16-38. (Bévenot does not accept the identification of Gazer [Jazer] here with Gazara in 2 Mac 10:32, but it seems simpler to do so. In Num 32:3 it occurs in close connexion with Hesebon and Beon [Baian], and is probably situated some 23 m. ENE. of Jericho.)

V 9-54 Campaigns in Galilee and Galaad—Dividing **565a** his forces into three parts, Judas plans campaigns to deliver the faithful Jews in Galilee and in Galaad, the district E. of Jordan. Simon is given the task of rescuing those in Galilee, and this he successfully achieves (**21-23**) ; Joseph is left with a garrison to protect the base in Judaea, but with strict orders not to undertake any offensive action—his disobedience in this respect being punished (**56-62**) ; Judas himself marches into the regions E. and NE. of Jordan and wages a highly successful campaign.

The details of the campaign are difficult to follow. **b** In **9** we are apparently informed that all the Jews who had escaped massacre had taken refuge in Dathema. In **26, 27** we learn that many of them were shut up in Barasa . . . ' and in the rest of the cities of Galaad '. Wellhausen suggests cutting the knot by emendation, reading *were gathered together from* in place of ' were shut up in ' (**26, 27**), whilst in 27 he would read *this city* or *stronghold* (*viz.* Dathema) for ' these cities '. The latter suggestion is probably necessary ; but there does not seem to be any need for the other changes suggested. The situation seems to be as follows. Many Jews had been massacred ; but the earliest reports (**13**) were exaggerated. It appeared later that, in addition to those besieged in Dathema, there were others imprisoned in different cities in Galaad, doubtless awaiting execution (**26**). Judas set out first of all to relieve Dathema ; but on receiving news from the *Nabataeans* (**25**) : the famous nomad tribe, later to become predominant in Transjordania : *cf.* 2 Cor 11:32), he turned aside to attack Bosor first. Since Judas took Bosor (**28**) it is clear that it must have been in possession of the people of Galaad, and therefore there must be some corruption in **27** which suggests that they were attacking their own cities. Therefore it seems necessary to accept some emendation of that verse on the lines of Wellhausen's suggestion, or at least to understand ' cities ' in **27b** (Gk has τὰ ὀχυρώματα) of Dathema alone. ' Them ' refers not to cities but to the Jews—πάντας τούτους not πάντα ταῦτα.

As to the location of the places mentioned, the follow- **c** ing seem to be the most acceptable suggestions. Dathema = ? Characa, *sc.* El-Kerak, some 45 m. E. of the Sea of Galilee ; *cf.* 2 Mac 12:17. Bosora (Barasa = Bosor in 28), presumably the most southerly of the places referred to, since Judas, coming up from the S. attacked it first, may be identified with Bostra (Busra eski-Sham), some 50 m. ESE. of the Sea of Galilee and about 12 m. from Dathema (= El-Kerak), the ' fortress ' of **29**, a night's march away. Carnaim is probably Sheikh Sa'ad, some 23 m. E. of the Sea of Galilee, whilst Raphon (**37**) seems to be El-Rafe, some 17 m. NE. of Carnaim. Ephron (**46**) which Judas attacked on his return march, seems to be situated a few miles E. of the upper Jordan, since Bethshan (**52**), the modern Beisan, is the same as the

565c ancient Scythopolis, and is apparently not far from Ephron. The other places mentioned have not yet been satisfactorily identified.

13. The land of Tubin (*cf.* Tubianites 2 Mac 12:17) was apparently the region immediately to the E. of the Sea of Galilee.

Of Simon's brilliant campaign in Galilee, we are given tantalizingly little information. Even the locality of Arbatis (**23**) is uncertain ; but presumably it lay somewhere in N. Samaria. Possibly it is Narbata, 10 m. NE. of Caesarea.

d 55-68 Joseph suffers Defeat : Judas restores the Situation—On his return to Jerusalem Judas found it necessary to undertake a campaign in the coastal plain to restore the situation which had been weakened by the defeat suffered by Joseph in consequence of his rash and disobedient sortie against Jamnia. According to 2 Mac 12:8, Judas had undertaken an expedition against Jamnia not long before his march into Galaad, and possibly Joseph and his associate thought that it would be an easy matter to imitate that sortie. But not only were they not of the Hasmonaean house, they were acting contrary to orders, and their attempt met with disaster. Judas marched S., took Hebron (Chebron), some 20 m. S. of Jerusalem, and then turned W. towards *Maresa* (*cf.* 2 Mac 12:35), which should be read for ' Samaria ' in **66**. Having displayed his power as far as the coast at Azotus, he returned to Jerusalem. 'The aliens' (**66**) and 'strangers' (**68**) are the Philistines.

e VI 1-17 Death of Antiochus Epiphanes—In 2 Mac this event is recorded before the purification of the temple, but there is no doubt that it actually occurred after it. (For the reconciliation *cf.* 2 Mac 9:1 ff.) Correct Vg and DV (**1**) in accordance with a few Gk MSS (so Bévenot) : ' *he heard that there was in Elymais* [= Elam] *in Persia, a city greatly renowned for its wealth of silver and gold* '. It seems probable that this attempt on the temple of the goddess took place early in the king's absence, since one of his motives for going to ' Persia ' was to raise money (3:31), so the reports of the disaster to Lysias (**6** ; *cf.* 4:26 ff.) and of the purification of the temple (**7** ; *cf.* 4 :36 ff.) and of the capture of Bethsura (*ibid.* ; *cf.* 4:61) are rightly described as having reached him later. It is probable, then, that some considerable interval elapsed between the attack on the Persian temple and the king's death, though it is interesting to note that, in his account of the death of Antiochus, Polybius (31:11) speaks of him as having been ' driven mad, as some say, by certain manifestations of divine anger. . . .'

The circumstances of the usurpation of the Seleucid throne by Antiochus Epiphanes made it necessary for him to take steps to secure the succession to his son, since the lawful heir, Demetrius, was now of an age to claim his rights, as he subsequently did (ch 7). Antiochus had left his son, of the same name, in the care of Lysias (3:33). Now, for some reason, he entrusts his affairs to Philip (**14**). This was to give rise to a struggle between Lysias and Philip, from which the Jews were to benefit (**63**).

566a 18-47 Eupator in person invades Judaea—Judas, having fortified the temple mount (4:60), now proceeds to reduce the citadel, held by a Syrian garrison and a number of apostate Jews. On an appeal from the garrison, the king,. who has just succeeded to the throne, raises an exceptionally large army and marches to its relief. Once again the line of march is from the S., and the key-fortress of Bethsura (*cf.* 4:61) is invested. Its actual surrender is not mentioned until **49**, but the fact that the battle between Judas and the king's forces was fought at Bethzacharias (**32 ff.**), which is N. of Bethsura, shows that the position must have been at least neutralized. Notice the fascination exercised upon the mind of the writer by the elephants, stimulated to battle by the sight of ' blood ', even if it is only the juice of grapes and mulberries. The presence of 32 men (**37**) on each beast is a manifest impossibility and the reading is best explained as

a corruption of ' 2 or 3 ' men. Fairweather suggests **56b** that in the original HT ' two chosen men ' was read, and the same consonants would give the existing reading : a similar confusion is indicated in 1 Par 11:11 ; 2 Kg 23:8. **40.** ' was distinguished by ' = ' *marched separately along* '. **43.** Eleazar, son of Saura, is, according to the Gk reading, ὁ Αὐαραν, the Eleazar Abaron (2:5) or Avaran, meaning probably ' beast-sticker ', a name presumably given to him posthumously because of this exploit. He was therefore the brother of Judas.

48-63 Siege of Jerusalem : Peace—After the reduc- **b** tion of Bethsura and the victory of Bethzacharias, the king made his way without difficulty to the Holy City. Fortunately for the Jews the siege he began had to be broken off because of the approach of Philip (*cf.* 14), who resolved to enforce his claim to the title of regent conferred upon him by the late king, against Lysias, the acting regent. The possibility of an attempt by Demetrius to claim the throne (7:1) was an added reason for coming to some arrangement with the Jews. After concluding an armistice the king treacherously orders the destruction of the fortifications of the temple mount. **51.** ' pieces ' = *pieces of artillery* (σκορπίδια).

VII 1-25 Demetrius : Intrigues of Alcimus, etc.— **c** Demetrius' landing at Tripolis (so 2 Mac 14:1) ' with a few men ' (Polybius says there were 16 in all) is made the occasion of a difficulty, since 2 Mac 14:1 speaks of ' a great power and a navy '. But this is an artificial objection. Presumably Demetrius would have an army waiting for him. Marching upon Antioch (2 : ' the house of the kingdom of his fathers ' ; *cf.* Dan 4:30, where a similar expression in Gk is used of the capital Babylon), he is welcomed by the army who put to death Antiochus Eupator and Lysias. Approached by a deputation from the Hellenizing party of the Jews, headed by the high-priest Alcimus, he appoints Bacchides, governor of Coele-Syria (the *land beyond the river Euphrates, sc.* from the point of view of Persia), to undertake the task of suppressing Judas. By treachery, Alcimus and Bacchides at first prevail, especially persuading the Hasidaeans not to resist (**13** : ' the *Hasidaeans were pre-eminent amongst the* [*faithful*] *Israelites* ', *cf.* 2:42 ; the implication is that their example would be followed by others). But the ensuing massacre causes a revulsion of feeling, and though Bacchides leaves Alcimus the support of an army (**20**), presumably to suppress Judas and his party, the latter manages to restore the situation.

19. Crampon suggests that ' from ' is a mistake for **d** *to* Jerusalem. According to him the Hebrew *min*, used here (as in Gen 11:12 ; 13:11 ; Is 22:3, etc.) of motion towards has been mistranslated as meaning away from. The correction will enable us to understand Bethzecha as a suburb of Jerusalem (*cf.* Josephus, *Ant.* 12, 10, 2—Berzetho, perhaps the same as the later Bezetha : Josephus, *BJ* 5, 4, 2). **24.** ' coasts ' : ' *regions* ' (Vg ' fines '). ' They ceased to go forth any more into the country ', *sc.* to vex the faithful ; or possibly, by means of some exemplary punishment, he prevailed on those who were seeking to desert from his army to stay and fight.

26-50 Defeat and Death of Nicanor : ' Nicanor's Day ' **e** —In response to a further appeal from Alcimus, Demetrius sends a fresh force under Nicanor. According to 2 Mac 14:19 ff., Nicanor is at first friendly and only resorts to violence under pressure from the king. (This Nicanor is apparently to be distinguished from the Nicanor of 3:38, etc., since the latter was fighting in Judaea at a time when, according to Josephus, the other was with Demetrius in Rome.) It is not known where Capharsalama (**31**) was, but some identify it with the Khirbet Deir Sellam, some 5 m. N. of Jerusalem. We do not know in what direction Judas had withdrawn on the dismantling of the temple fortifications by Eupator (6:62). After this first defeat, and in spite of the assurances of the priests of their loyalty to the king, shown by their offering sacrifices for him

(33 : *cf.* Esd 6:10), Nicanor seeks to suppress the Jews by force. In a final battle at Bethhoron (*cf.* 3:16) or Adasa (Adarsa) [**40 :** according to Josephus, *Ant.* 12, 10, 5, this is some 4 m. from Bethhoron], Nicanor is killed, ' first in the battle '. This need not mean that Nicanor was the first casualty in the whole engagement, especially as Josephus says that he fell ' at length ', but merely that, in the closing stages of the fight, as soon as Nicanor fell, the rest fled. It is possible that the Gk text means *Nicanor the general was slain*. The pursuit to Gazara (**45** ; *cf.* 4:15) covered a distance of some 20 m. Then they sounded *the solemn trumpets* (*cf.* 4:40 ; Num 31:6). **46.** ' they pushed them with the horns ' (Vg ' *ventilabant cornibus* ') is a misunderstanding of ὑπερεκέρων, sc. ' they outflanked *them* '.

This great victory over Nicanor was celebrated with a special thanksgiving service, which became an annual festival, held on the anniversary (13 Adar) even in the time of Josephus (*Ant.* 12, 10, 5). It lapsed later possibly because of the immediate proximity of Purim (14 Adar).

VIII 1-32 Alliance with Rome—It was entirely in accordance with Rome's foreign policy in the eastern Mediterranean at this time that she should have encouraged the Jews in their revolt against the Syrian power. Whilst reluctant to assume any responsibilities which would require warlike action on her part, she was glad to foster any tendencies which would weaken the stronger powers. The treaty negotiated between Judas and the Senate is precisely what we might have expected. ' Doubts have been thrown on its existence on the ground that to recognize the Jewish state as an independent power would have been a *casus belli* between Rome and Demetrius, and that, as a matter of fact, the Romans let the Hasmonaeans down before Demetrius without giving them any help. These objections have no force in view of the fact that Rome behaved in just the same way with regard to the rebel Timarchus. . . . The Senate had indeed no intention of intervening by armed force in Syria ; it desired only to embarrass Demetrius by giving countenance to his enemies ' (CAH 8:519).

The general impression of Rome's power, prestige and moral qualities recorded in **1-16** is not vouched for by the sacred writer as necessarily accurate in all its details, but simply as what Judas heard (**1**), as he doubtless did. Any inaccuracy in detail therefore in no way relates to the inerrancy of Scripture. **2.** ' Galatia ' may, as Mommsen held, refer to the subjugation of Cisalpine Gaul by Rome in 190 B.C., but there seems no reason to refuse the more natural identification with Galatia in Asia Minor, which would be of greater interest to the Jews. We know of a campaign in that district conducted by Manlius Volso in 189 B.C. ' Large sums, sometimes amounting to 200 talents, were extorted from numerous cities ' (CAH 8:228 f.). **3.** Spain was annexed in 201 B.C., but only partially pacified at the time. **4.** ' had conquered places that were very far off from them '. So Vg ; LXX says : ' the *place* [Spain] *was very far off from them* '. ' The kings from the ends of the earth ' are presumably the Carthaginian *leaders*, Hannibal and Hasdrubal, coming from Spain. **5.** ' The king of the Chittim (Ceteans = Greeks in general ; here Macedonians : *cf.* 1:19) refers first to Philip V defeated at Cynoscephalae in 197 B.C. and then to Perseus defeated at Pydna in 167 B.C. **7.** Antiochus the Great was defeated at Magnesia in 190 B.C., but was not actually taken alive. ' that which was agreed upon ' (Vg ' constitutum ' is in Gk διαστολὴν) apparently = *a division of the land*. **8.** ' Indians and Medes ' must be corrupt. Risberg suggests Pisidians and Milyans ; Crampon, with greater probability, Ionians and Mysians. **9-10** refer to the Aetolian War of 191-188, the general being M. Fulvius Nobilior. The details of **15-16** are not entirely accurate. The Senate did not meet daily, and there were of course *two* consuls. But in the absence of his colleague, either of them

might be described, as in effect he would appear to **567b** the eyes of a visiting foreigner, as supreme head of the state.

17. Eupolemus may be the Palestinian Jew who wrote on OT subjects at this time (*cf.* Schürer, 3:474 -477 ; 2 Mac 4:11). Jacob (LXX Akkos or Akkhos) : a name in a priestly family. If Eleazar is the hero of 6:43 ff., this Jason will be a nephew of Judas. Meyer suggests the martyr of 2 Mac 6.

For the treaty, *cf.* Bévenot *ad loc.*, who gives an interest- **c** ing comparison with a treaty concluded between Rome and Astypalaea in 105 B.C. (Text in Hicks : *Man. Gk. Hist. Inscrr.*, 347-9). The text of **26** and **28** presents some difficulty. A clearer parallel seems to be required than is given by the existing text. Thus Romans in **26** seems to require *Jews* in **28**, whilst ' they shall observe their orders without deceit ' (**28**) is the counterpart of the obscure phrase in **26** : ' they shall obey their orders without taking anything from them '. But there is no clear explanation of the origin of the corruption. Knabenbauer is perhaps right in seeing in these passages indications that there was no strict equality envisaged. In both cases, it was Rome who would decide the nature of the obligations incumbent both upon herself and on her partner ; nor were the Jews to hope for any return for their assistance.

IX 1-22 Death of Judas—It seems not unlikely that **d** the speed with which Demetrius acted after the disaster to the army of Nicanor caught Judas unawares. Nicanor had fallen on 13 Adar and in the first month of the following year, *sc.* Nisan, a fresh Syrian army was already in Jerusalem (**3**). Even allowing for an intercalary month, this gives only a few weeks for the news of the defeat to reach Antioch, for the raising of a new army and for the march S. through Galilee. **2.** ' Galgal ' is most probably a corruption of *Galilee* (*cf.* Josephus, *Ant.* 12, 11, 1 ; in Jos 12:33, the reverse corruption has occurred, Galgal in the Heb. having become Galilee in LXX). Arbela (Arabella) is the modern Khirbet Irbid or Arbed, not far from the W. shore of the Sea of Galilee and near the Horns of Hattin, site of the great Christian defeat by Saladin in A.D. 1187. Masaloth (Heb. *mᵉsillôt*) is the steep descent from the caves in this region ; *cf.* Josephus, *BJ* 1, 16. **4.** Berea, perhaps El-Bireh, 10 m. N of Jerusalem, is not far from (**5**) Laisa (El-'Ashshy). **15.** ' The mount Azotus ' of DV is an attempt to smooth out the difficulty of Gk and Vg ' the mountain of Azotus ', that city lying in the maritime plain. The error probably arose in the Heb. original, 'ašdōd (Azotus) being confused with 'ᵃšēdôt ' he pursued them even to the *mountain-slopes* '.

It seems clear that Judah had some premonition that this was to be his last battle. There is a lack of his customary confidence in the words he addresses to his few followers, and though there is no lack of courage in his day-long resistance, it is surprising to find him deceived by the old trap of the retreating right wing and the encircling left. For the sepulchre at Modin, *cf.* 13:25 ff.

23-31 Election of Jonathan—The death of Judas was **568a** a great blow to the cause. ' The wicked ' and ' the workers of iniquity ' (the Hellenizing Jews) took heart, and the prevailing scarcity (**24**) was apparently used by Bacchides as an opportunity to bribe those in need to come over to his side ; *cf.* Josephus, *Ant.* 13, 1, 1. There seems to be a striking personification in **24** : ' *the very land itself went over to the side of Bacchides* ' (*cf.* Os 9:2 *vinum mentietur eis* ; Hab 3:17 *mentietur opus olivae*, etc.). **25** suggests the appointment of quislings as local officials. The reference to the absence of a prophet (**27**) recalls 8:46 and the anticipations, not necessarily of the Messias, but at least of some spiritual leader. The sad plight of the Jews was made more obvious by the lack of any leader. Hence the election of Jonathan (**30**), who took upon him the *leadership*. It seems strange that there was no automatic succession.

1 MACCABEES IX

568b 32-57 Jonathan Leader : Bacchides and Alcimus again in Judaea : Death of Alcimus : Bacchides withdraws
—Jonathan seems to have succeeded to the leadership of Judaea in circumstances not unlike those which prevailed when Judas was chosen. It is true that the temple was freed from its pollution, but the Jewish army was forced to take to the desert (**33** : Tekoa is some 5 m. S. of Bethlehem, Asphar 3 m. further S.), whilst Jonathan sent his brother John with a caravan, including, as Bévenot suggests, their wives and children, as well as their treasures, to seek safety with the Nabataeans, who had shown themselves friendly on a previous occasion ; *cf.* 5:26. However, one tribe or party amongst them, *the sons of Jambri* (the name Ya'amru is conjectured on a Nabataean inscription), sallied out of their stronghold at Madaba, some 12 m. E. of the N. end of the Dead Sea, and captured the whole party. Jonathan undertook a punitive expedition against them (**38 ff.**), and on his return was intercepted by Bacchides who had crossed the Jordan (**43 : 34** has apparently crept into the text by an erroneous copying of **43 :** it has no connexion with what has preceded). Bacchides contrived to force the Jews into a position between his army and the marshy lands on the E. bank of the Jordan near its mouth. In the ensuing engagement Jonathan personally attacked Bacchides. After the Syrian force had been driven back some distance, the Jews succeeded in crossing the Jordan back to their own country. But Bacchides proceeded to hold the whole region down by a series of forts (**50, 52**), stretching from Dok, the fortress of Jericho, and including Emmaus (*cf.* 3:40), Bethhoron (3:16), Bethel (which is Beitin, some 10 m. N. of Jerusalem, watching the old road from Jericho), Timnath (Tell Tibneh, some 12 m. NW. of Bethel) and Phara (the Pharathon of Jg 12:15 ; being the modern Far'ata, W. of Sichem) ; Thopo (LXX Tephon) is unidentified. For Bethsura and Gazara *cf.* 4:29 ; 4:15 ; ' the castle ' is the citadel of Jerusalem (1:35, etc.).

c The action of Alcimus referred to in **54** is thought to be the destruction of the Soreg, the low wall separating the Court of the Gentiles from the inner Court to which the Jews alone were allowed access. Such an action would symbolize his desire to Hellenize the temple, and, though not as drastic as the setting up of the altar to Zeus by Antiochus Epiphanes, would be most repugnant to devout Jews. His paralysis and death put an end to the project. The departure of Bacchides is not explained, but presumably he felt that the military occupation of the land had been adequately secured, whilst the death of the high-priest may have relieved him of any necessity to persevere with a religious policy for which he had no inclination. At any rate Judaea was untroubled for two years (**57**).

d 58-73 Return of Bacchides : Treaty—However, the intrigues of the Hellenizers against Jonathan went on and eventually they prevailed upon Bacchides to return with an army. Again Jonathan was forced to take refuge in the desert, after eluding an attempt to capture him. In **61** for ' he apprehended ' Gk reads συνέλαβον ' *they apprehended* ', which may refer either to the party of Bacchides—as Josephus interprets it—or, more probably, to the faithful Jews, the ' authors of the mischief ' being the Hellenizers. Bethbessen (**62**) is Khirbet Beit Bassa, some 3 m. ESE. of Bethlehem. Bacchides besieged the Jews here, being apparently supplied by the local Bedouin. Jonathan divided his forces, leaving Simon to hold the fortress whilst he himself attacked the allies of Bacchides, under their leader Odares (LXX Odomera), and thus cut off the supplies on which the Syrians depended. The success of this attack, coupled with a victorious sortie by Simon, forced Bacchides to raise the siege. **69** rather implies that Bacchides had entered upon the expedition with some reluctance (*cf.* 57, 59), and Jonathan found little difficulty in arranging a favourable peace. With his final withdrawal, Jonathan was able to establish a semi-independent principality with its

military centre at Michmash (Mukhmas, about 7½ m. SE. of Bethel), and to set about reducing the power of the Hellenizers. But the citadel of Jerusalem was still held for Demetrius, and 10:6, 7 implies that Jonathan was not authorized to raise troops and was required to give hostages for good conduct.

X 1-47 Demetrius and Alexander Balas bid for the Support of Jonathan—Demetrius, already surrounded by hostile powers in Pergamum, Cappadocia and Egypt, now finds himself threatened with civil rebellion, when a young man, claiming to be the son of Antiochus Epiphanes and backed by the king of Pergamum, makes a bid for the Seleucid throne. Deciding to conciliate Jonathan, he formally recognizes what was a *fait accompli*, the independence of Jonathan, by withdrawing the garrisons from Judaea, with the exception of Bethsur and the citadel, and the Jewish leader soon establishes himself in the Holy City, rebuilding the fortifications of the temple mount. Alexander, on his side, goes even further, appointing Jonathan to the high-priesthood, which has apparently been vacant since the death of Alcimus, and giving him the title of king's friend, presumably with something of the status of a client-king of the Roman Empire. Demetrius goes further still by remitting the tribute due to him. The crowns (**29**) were sent as tokens of submission, the charge being generally commuted to a money-payment. The three cities (*regions*) of Samaria-and-Galilee (**30**) are named in 11:34—Ephraim, Lydda and Ramathaim. We get a clue in **36** to this astonishing liberality on the part of Demetrius—shortage of man-power. Ptolemais (**39**) was hardly in the king's gift, being then occupied by the supporters of Balas (**1**), and it seems likely that the king was thus hoping to embroil the Jews with his rival. The sums mentioned in **40** and **42** (£3,200 and £1,067 respectively) together with the different amounts of tribute referred to in **29** and **30** give some indication of the material value to the king of the Judaean dependency.

48-66 Jonathan's Relations with Alexander and b Ptolemy—Jonathan's decision to support Alexander may have been dictated not merely by doubts as to the sincerity of Demetrius (**46**), but also by the realization that, with the support of Egypt, the former was more likely to prevail, as indeed happened. But in spite of his victory over Demetrius (**48-50**), ' it was a sign of the subordination to Egypt which marked the new state of things in Syria that Alexander seems to have resided more in Ptolemais than in Antioch ' (CAH 8:324). The scene described in **59-62** indicates that Alexander still felt the need to cultivate the friendship of Jonathan, possibly foreseeing the coming breach with Ptolemy. In addition to other marks of honour, Jonathan receives the titles of First Friend, General and Ethnarch (**65**), *sc.* he receives formal confirmation of his position as leader of the military forces in Judaea and as civil governor in that area.

67-89 Jonathan defeats Apollonius, General of Deme- c trius II—With the attempt of Demetrius II to regain his father's throne, the position of Jonathan is once more threatened. Apollonius, governor of Coele-Syria tries to suppress the Jewish high-priest, but not only does the latter with the help of his brother Simon force Apollonius out of Joppe, but he also succeeds in reducing several Philistine towns. ' As one that was making a journey ' (**78**) is obscure and no satisfactory explanation can be suggested. It may mean that Apollonius travelled to Azotus with a small escort, like a simple traveller, though when he got there he did not stay but joined his large force of cavalry in the plain outside the city. The purpose of this is not clear. Josephus helps us to understand what happened next (*Ant.* 13, 4, 4). Apollonius posted 1,000 of his cavalry in a wady (' privately ' **79**). Jonathan drew up his army in a hollow square, with orders to remain on the defensive (**80, 81**), until the enemy cavalry were exhausted and much of the ammunition used up. Then he attacked the infantry, unprotected by the cavalry, and routed them. As a result of this

714

c success Jonathan was honoured with the title of Kinsman, receiving the appropriate insignia. Accaron (Ekron), 12 m. NE. of Azotus was given to him as a private estate (89).

d **XI 1-19 Alexander and Ptolemy at War : Death of Both**—It is not certain what precise policy Ptolemy had formulated when he invaded Syria. According to Diodorus and Josephus he originally intended to help his son-in-law Alexander against Demetrius. Probably he was merely hoping to turn the situation to his own advantage, and to that end was prepared, if it should prove more profitable, to sacrifice his son-in-law. Jonathan prudently supported the invader, escorting him as far as the river Eleutherus, the boundary between Phoenicia and Syria proper (7). Having got possession of Antioch and formed a league with Demetrius, Ptolemy joined battle with Alexander, who was defeated and fled into Arabia (? in the neighbourhood of Palmyra ; there is a Palmyrene inscription bearing the name Zabdiel ; 17), where he met his end. However, Ptolemy himself died a few days later, of wounds received in the engagement, and the way was clear for Demetrius to assume the crown. The Egyptian garrisons in the coast-towns (3, 18 : 'they that were in the camp' ἐν τοῖς ὀχυρώμασι) are the *inhabitants* of these cities.

e **20-37 Jonathan is reconciled to Demetrius II**—Apparently Demetrius did not feel himself strong enough to break with Jonathan, who played his cards skilfully and persuaded the king to renew the concessions made by his father, numbering him amongst *his chief friends* (27), and remitting the tribute from Judaea and the three Samaritan districts (10:30 ; 11:34) on payment of 300 talents (approx. £97,500). The king ratified his decision in letters addressed to Jonathan himself and to Lasthenes (the Cretan who had been responsible for the operations leading to his restoration), who is styled, after the oriental fashion *kinsman* (31) and *father* (32). The districts mentioned in 34 are Apherema (Ephraim : 2 Kg 13:23 ; 2 Par 13:19 ; Jn 11:54), some 6 or 7 m. N. of Bethel, Lydda (Ludd) NE. of Jamnia and Accaron, and Ramatha (probably the Arimathaea of Mk 15:43, etc. = Beit-Rima, between Lydda and Shechem, or possibly Rentis, a little further W.). 'Instead of' is not clear, but the meaning probably is that the Jews were to receive the produce from these places instead of having to pay tribute themselves.

f **38-53 Jonathan supports Demetrius against Tryphon**—The Cretan mercenaries who had put Demetrius on the throne became a source of odium to the Syrians, especially to the army (38), who felt themselves disgraced by their presence ; Diodotus 'the Rake' (Tryphon), who had been a governor at Antioch under Alexander, took this opportunity to set up a rival to Demetrius. He concerted a plot with an Arabian Emalchuel (conceivably an associate of the Zabdiel with whom Alexander had taken refuge, possibly having his son with him), to proclaim Alexander's son king as Antiochus VI. Jonathan at first continued his support of Demetrius, but later changed his allegiance, perhaps because the latter, who had undertaken to withdraw his garrisons from the strongholds of Judaea (41, 42 : *cf.* 10:12) and from the citadel of Jerusalem, failed to implement his promise. Moreover Antiochus showed a readiness to confirm and to extend the privileges enjoyed by the surviving Hasmonaeans (55 ff.).

g **54-74 Jonathan supports Antiochus VI against Demetrius : Victory in Galilee against the latter's Generals**—Antiochus conferred a marked honour upon the Jews by appointing Simon governor of the whole coastal region from below Tyre to the frontiers of Egypt. In connexion with this appointment Jonathan marched through Coele-Syria ('the land beyond the river'; *cf.* 7:8) to Philistia. Ascalon opened its gates to him, and when Gaza resisted he compelled it to surrender hostages ; after this he marched, presumably on reconnaissance, as far N. as Damascus. Meanwhile

Simon regained control of Bethsura (*cf.* 4:29, etc.). **569g** These operations were directed against Demetrius and his partisans, ostensibly on behalf of Antiochus, though of course the Jews would benefit directly from this extension of the power of their arms.

Meanwhile the generals of Demetrius invaded Galilee **h** and Jonathan marched against them, to the region of Cades, some 15 m. N. of Genesar (67—the first mention in Scripture of the Lake of Gennesareth). Hazor (Asor) is some 3 m. SW. of Cades. At first, taken in the rear as well as meeting opposition from in front, the Jews began to run away ; Jonathan and two of his fellow-officers stood their ground and by their example restored the situation, and apparent defeat was turned into victory. Absalom (70) is perhaps the man referred to in 2 Mac 11:17. Calphi = Alphaeus (Mt 10:3).

XII 1-23 Embassy to Rome and Sparta—Jonathan **570a** decided to make the most of the favourable turn of events ('the time served him', or as we should say, fortune was on his side : 1) by strengthening the bonds with Rome and also by forming other alliances. The ambassadors chosen were to go to Rome first and to Sparta on their return journey, which was performed under a safe-conduct given by the Romans (4). The letters were sent in the name of Jonathan the highpriest and 'the ancients of the people'—the *gerousia* mentioned by Josephus (*Ant.* 12, 3, 3 : ? *cf.* 2 Par 19:8), later the Sanhedrin, a name which is first found in Josephus (*Ant.* 14, 9, 4) under Hyrcanus II—the priests and the people as a whole. The Onias of 7 is Onias I, a contemporary of Arius I of Sparta (309–265). Josephus (*Ant.* 12, 4, 10) misplaces this document hopelessly. In 9 the Jews make it plain that the kinship alleged by the Spartans to exist between the two nations does not alter the fact that they themselves possess the revelation of God, which is their chief hope and comfort, though they are not unwilling to accept the friendship of Sparta. The statement that the Jews had prayed for the Spartans is an interesting and valuable sidelight on the spirit of genuine Jewish piety, which was by no means so exclusive as is sometimes suggested by its more Pharisaical aspects ; *cf.* Bar 1:11. 15 is a more explicit expression of the confidence the Jews had in the aid of God, as being of incomparably greater value than any human alliance. At the same time, they do not reject any natural assistance that is compatible with their supreme allegiance. The statement in the letter of Arius to Onias (21) that the Spartans were descended from Abraham need not be taken too seriously. It is little more than a conventional opening, like the term *kinsman* (11:31) ; the passage often referred to in Josephus (*Ant.* 14, 10, 22), in which the Pergamenes speak of friendship existing between their ancestors and the Jews in the days of Abraham is another such empty compliment.

24-38 New Campaign against the Generals of Demetrius **b** —The fact that Jonathan was able to intercept the invading army in the land of Hamath (26), *sc.* on the middle Orontes, is a striking indication of the reality of Jewish might at this time. True, the Syrian army made its escape by means of a stratagem (by leaving fires burning in their camp to create the impression that they were still there even after they had retreated), but the general effect was a real victory for the Jews. The success of Jonathan against the Zabadaeans, somewhere to the NW. of Damascus, is also a measure of his power.

39-54 Simon's Successes in the South and in Judaea : **c** **Jonathan is betrayed to Tryphon**—Simon (11:59) had been made governor of the coastal regions S. from Tyre, and in this capacity he prevents an incipient defection of Joppe to the party of Demetrius. He then proceeds to blockade the citadel in Jerusalem and to strengthen the fortifications of the city. The brook (37) is Cedron. Caphetetha (37) is obscure, and no certain interpretation can be given. One suggestion is that it means *hunger-wall* and may have

570c formed a part of the blockading works. Adiada is 3 m. E. of Lydda, dominating the Shephelah or low hills between the coastal plain and the central range of Judaea. Vespasian had a fortified camp here during the siege of Jerusalem (Josephus, *BJ* 4, 11, 1).

Tryphon, who had put Antiochus VI on the throne, now plans to make himself king. As a first step he decides to remove the support which Jonathan was likely to give to the young king, and to that end he invades Palestine. He gets as far as Bethshan (= Scythopolis ; 5:52) before he is checked. Realizing that Jonathan is too strong to be overcome by force, he tricks him into dismissing his army and then entraps him at Ptolemais. In spite of the first report (**50**) Jonathan is not killed immediately (*cf.* 13:23).

571a **XIII 1-11 Simon succeeds Jonathan**—After being chosen to succeed his brother as leader (? and high-priest, *cf.* 13:36 ; 14:35), Simon first completes the fortification of Jerusalem and then garrisons Joppe with fresh troops, possibly because the former garrison was likely to support Tryphon. **11.** Absalom : *cf.* 11:70.

b **12-30 Tryphon invades Judaea, puts Jonathan to death and usurps the Kingdom of Syria**—Simon, hearing that Tryphon was preparing an expedition against him, occupied the position fortified by his brother on a previous occasion (Addus, 13 = Adiada 12:38), and after Tryphon's treacherous offer to release Jonathan in exchange for a ransom and on surrender of hostages, convicted him of deceit. When the invasion took place by the road from the coast (Ador = Dura, 5 m. WSW. of Hebron), Simon, moving on interior lines, managed to keep between Tryphon and the capital (**20**), to prevent the relief of the citadel-garrison. Eventually Tryphon was compelled to withdraw beyond the Jordan. (**22** in Vg is corrupt : ' non venit in Galaadi-tim ' apparently by haplography for something like *non* venit [*propter nivem sed solvit et* venit] in *Galaadi-tim* : *sc.* he failed to reach Jerusalem because of the snow but departed and reached Galaad.) There he killed Jonathan, and having buried him at Bascama (= ? Tell-Bazuk, NE. of the Sea of Galilee) returned to Antioch. Vg and DV say that he also slew the sons of Jonathan ; this is not in LXX, but is probable.

Jonathan's remains were rescued by Simon and buried at Modin, his native place (2:1), in a sepulchre which, according to Josephus (*Ant.* 13, 6, 6), still stood in his day. Traces of it are to be found in modern times (DBV IV 1186 f.). The monument carried trophies to symbolize Jonathan's might by land and sea.

c **31-53 Simon seeks the Favour of Demetrius II : his Successes**—The usurpation of the Syrian crown by Tryphon led Simon to restore his support to Demetrius. The latter granted complete autonomy to the Jews—' the yoke of the Gentiles was taken from Israel ' (**41**)—and the event was noted by being taken as the starting point for a new chronological era, as is testified by some extant copper coins of Simon. All that remained was to expel the garrison from the citadel and from *Gazara* (4:15). ' Gaza ' of **43** must be a mistake, as that town was not occupied until 96 B.C.—nearly 50 years after this date ; Josephus (*Ant.* 13, 6, 7 ; *BJ* 1, 2, 2) reads *Gazara* = Tell Jezer, some 6 m. S. of Lydda and virtually the key of Judaea. Macalister (*The Excavation of Gezer*, I, 209) discovered there the remains of a Maccabean palace, bearing a Greek imprecation, calling down fire ' upon the palace of Simon '. The seal was set on the work of the Has-monaeans by the final reduction of the citadel at Jerusalem (**50**), for so long a thorn in the side of the faithful Jews (1:35, etc.). The feast which was in-stituted on this occasion is no longer kept. Simon then proceeded to fortify the mount *opposite* the citadel (**53**). (According to Josephus the people actually levelled the mount of the citadel ; but this was pro-bably done later.) John, famous in history as John Hyrcanus, succeeded his father as governor of the coastal district and commander-in-chief of the Jewish **57** army.

XIV 1-15 Judaea under Simon—The defeat of **d** Demetrius by the Parthian king, Mithridates I (Arsaces (**2**) being a name assumed by all the Parthian kings, after the founder of the dynasty) still further strengthens the position of Simon. The occupation of Joppe (**5**) gives a valuable outlet to the sea, a fact presumably underlying the nautical features of the family sepulchre at Modin (13:29). The possession of Gazara, Bethsur and the *citadel* (**7**) gives him the keys of Judaea. The different strongholds are pro-visioned and fortified (*he provided them with all the gear necessary for their fortification* **10**), and although the language of **4** is to be explained as rhetorical exaggera-tion, since the peace was broken towards the end of his reign (15:39), this time is undoubtedly one of great peace and prosperity. Above all, of course, it is a time when the Law is carefully observed and offenders *destroyed* (**14**).

16-24a Renewal of Alliances with Rome and Sparta e —It seems desirable, as Bévenot suggests, to read **24a** before **16**. As we shall see, **24b** is certainly corrupt, and there is no evidence to suggest that Simon sent two embassies at this time, whereas 16 follows naturally on 24*a*. The order of events then is : Embassy to Rome ; renewal of Roman alliance (**24a**, **16-19a**) ; on their return the ambassadors visit Sparta (**21**), and the Spartans send a letter renewing the pact made with Jonathan (12:23). Apparently the same ambassadors were employed as on the previous occa-sion (**22** ; 12:16).

24b-49 Inscription in Honour of Simon—' The people **f** of Rome ' (Vg ' Populus Romanus ') is a copyist's error. The Gk says simply *the people*, and the context demands that the *Jewish* people be understood. **48** bears this out.

There are a number of perplexities in the passage, due to some extent to the fact that the inscription may have been a Hebrew translation of a Greek original, and the Hebrew finds some difficulty in expressing the long sustained syntax of the proclama-tion ; there are also several slips on the part of copy-ists, either of the Gk or of Vg. The general sense is however clear enough. The document gives a brief summary of the services rendered by the Hasmonaean family in general (**29-31**) and of Simon in particular (**32-35**) ; it then describes the honours already con-ferred upon him (**35**), his further services (**36-37**), and the confirmation of his office by Demetrius II (**38**). ' And he heard ' (**40**) is based on the authority of the better Gk MSS, which read ἤκουσε, but there can be little doubt that the other reading ἠκούσθη (= *it has been heard by the Jews*) is correct since (*a*) Demetrius was a prisoner in Parthia at this time (**3**), and even if he had heard of the embassy to Rome, he could have done nothing about it ; (*b*) he had already con-firmed the appointment of Simon as high-priest (13:36). (Bévenot suggests that *Spartans* should be read in **40** in place of ' Romans ', since the latter had not called the Jews ' brethren '. Perhaps *Romans and Spartans* should be read.) It will be necessary to modify the syntax of **41**, omitting ' that ' and read-ing : ' So the Jews and their priests have consented that he should be their prince and high-priest from generation to generation ', *sc.* the high-priesthood and kingship of Simon are made hereditary ; *cf.* **25** ' What thanks shall we give to Simon and his sons ? '

27. ' At Asamarel ' (Vg *in Asamarel*, LXX ἐν ἀσαραμελ) **g** seems to imply an original Heb. form *śar ʿam ʾēl* = ' Leader of the people of God ', as a title conferred on Simon. Read therefore, ' Simon the high-priest *and leader of the people of God* '. This will, it is true, introduce into 1 Mac the only explicit mention of the Name of God, but in such a case as this it is pro-bably no more difficult than, say, in the parallel Israel. **28.** It has been proposed to omit the first ' and ' reading ' in a great assembly of the priests of the people ', thus giving a better balance to the sentence. **34.** Gazara is actually some 17 m. from Azotus, but their territories may have been adjacent.

In **48**, by a happy mistranslation, DV restores the original sense, obscured by Vg 'in loco celebri': the Gk ἐν τόπῳ ἐπισήμῳ must mean 'in a conspicuous place'. A copy was to be placed in the Temple Treasury—the very word of the Gk is preserved in Jn 8:20 'in gazophylacio'—which presumably included archives as well as actual treasures. It was put in safe keeping, as the possession of Simon and his descendants.

XV 1-14 Antiochus VII seeks the Support of Simon against Tryphon—Antiochus, brother of the captive Demetrius, was a man of energy for all his extreme youth (he was only 20 at the beginning of his reign), and soon took in hand the defence of his kingdom against the usurping Tryphon. His letter to Simon before his landing is an explicit and formal recognition of all existing privileges (including one not previously mentioned, that of coining money; though we know that Simon had been striking coins at least a year before this). Landing in Syria he drove Tryphon before him as far as Dora (Tanturah, 9 m. N. of Caesaraea), where he blockaded him (**10-14**).

15-24 Various Letters from Rome in Support of the Jews —The authenticity of the first letter (**16-21**) is upheld by a curious mistake of Josephus, who puts a similar document, bearing the names of Lucius Valerius as consul, and of Numenius and Alexander as ambassadors, into the reign of Hyrcanus II (*Ant.* 14, 8, 5). The Lucius of **16** is presumably L. Calpurnius Piso, consul in 139 B.C. Ptolemy is Euergetes II, king of Egypt 145–116. For the allusions in **17**, **18**, *cf.* 14:24. Demetrius was, of course, by now a prisoner, but the news of his capture could not have reached Rome before the embassy left. Attalus II, king of Pergamum, 160/159–139/138 B.C.; Ariarathes V of Cappadocia, 163–*c* 130 B.C.; Arsaces (*cf.* 14:2) = Mithridates I king of Parthia, 171–138; Lampsacus, a Mysian town on the Hellespont; but more probably we should read with LXX *Sampsame*, a town on the Black Sea coast, E. of Sinope: Delos, Samos and Cos are islands in the Aegean, Rhodes the chief island of the Dodecanese group; Sicyon, neighbour of Corinth, had naturally become much more important since the destruction of the latter place in 146 B.C.; Myndos, Cnidus and Halicarnassus are all situated in (the lastnamed being the capital of) Caria, in the SW. corner of Asia Minor; Phaselis is a seaport in Lycia, E. of Caria; E. of Lycia is Pamphylia, with Side an important harbour; Aradus is an island, containing a town of the same name, off the Phoenician coast; Gortyna is in the island of Crete; Cyrene is the capital of Libya in N. Africa. As will be seen the names are arranged in no recognizable order, and it would be interesting to know what were the relationships existing between Rome and these scattered communities, most of them outside the limits of the Roman Empire, though well within her sphere of influence.

25-XVI 10 Antiochus VII breaks with Simon: his General, Cendebeus, is defeated by the Sons of the High-Priest—Once Antiochus had pinned Tryphon down (15:14), he apparently felt strong enough to demand reparations for the extra-Judaean annexations (**28**: *cf.* 12:33; 13:43) and even for the citadel of Jerusalem, which he claimed as part of his kingdom. Simon's answer is entirely justified, though we have no means of judging how far 100 talents (£32,500) would provide an adequate compensation for the loss of Gazara and Joppe. The seaport at any rate represented a serious loss to the Syrian king, but the Jews were entitled to recoup themselves for the extensive damage that had been inflicted on their country under the Syrian domination. The issue could be decided only by force, and whilst Antiochus pursued Tryphon (who first escaped to Orthosias, N. of Tripolis, but was captured and compelled to commit suicide; *cf.* Strabo 14:668), he left the management of the

Jewish affair to Cendebeus, whom he made supreme **572c** commander (ἐπιστράτηγος) of the coastal plain, presumably the position which Simon, with a slightly different title (στρατηγός) had formerly held (11:59). Having occupied Jamnia, he proceeded to construct a strong base at Gedor (= Kedron, 7½ m. NE. of Azotus) to command the route into Judaea. John, who had been appointed commander-in-chief of the Jewish forces, with his headquarters at Gazara (*cf.* 13:14), then came to consult his father, Simon, who left the conduct of military affairs in the hands of his two sons, Judas and John. For the first time we hear of cavalry employed by the Jews (**4, 7**). The victory, which occurred in the plain between Modin and Kedron (Gedor of 15:39), was followed by pursuit as far as Azotus. The towers into which some of the Syrian army fled are similar to those mentioned in 4 Kg 17:9; 18:8. Vg and DV say that John burnt the towers; LXX says the city (αὐτήν).

XVI 11-24 Death of Simon: John succeeds—Ptolemy, **d** the son of Abobus, was possibly an Idumaean (Bévenot), but the treachery of this attack on Simon is a melancholy conclusion to the noble story of the efforts of the Maccabees on behalf of their country. Fortunately the attempt of Ptolemy to betray his people into the hands of Antiochus as the price of his own elevation to the high-priesthood was foiled by the energy of John, who established himself in Jerusalem in succession to his father. It is true that Antiochus was able to impose tribute on the Jews for a time, in return for their continued occupation of the disputed strongholds of Joppe, Gazara and the rest (*cf.* 15:30), but the strength of Syria was waning and John's reign marks the beginning of a period of independence which was not finally ended until the coming of Rome; *cf.* §§ 69 ff.

15. Doch (Dok) is a fortress on a height a little to the NW. of Jericho. **19.** Ptolemy apparently sought to bribe some of the officers in John's army to desert. **24.** Nothing is known of 'the book of the days of his priesthood', which was presumably some sort of official journal.

THE SECOND BOOK OF MACCABEES

Introduction—The author of the Second Book expli- **573a** citly states that he is merely summarizing the five books of Jason of Cyrene, and there is no reason to doubt that these would be composed in Greek, so that the original language of the epitome would almost certainly be Greek. This is borne out by certain expressions almost of the nature of puns: *e.g.* ἄγειν ἀγῶνα, 4:18; εὐημερίαν δυσημερίαν, 5:6; κρεμάσαντες ἐκρήμνισαν, 6:10, etc. **The author's aim** is quite clearly to glorify Judas Machabaeus as the instrument of Divine Providence, the other members of his family receiving scarcely a mention. The story closes at the period of Judas's triumph.

The tone of the book is different from that of the First. **b** Where the author of the First Book is content to tell a straightforward story—though this does not imply that there are not passages of real elevation in his work—the author of the Second is far more sententious and much more prone to stress the supernatural or preternatural elements in the events narrated. His style is more florid and even turgid; where the former writer is careful to use reverential paraphrase for the Name of God, the latter uses the term freely; where the former acknowledges frankly the need for Sabbath warfare, the latter adopts a more conservative attitude. In sum, the difference might be expressed by saying that the author of the Second Book is bent on 'edification', whereas the author of the First prefers to let the facts speak for themselves, though he is nonetheless deeply conscious of the divinity shaping the ends of man.

573c Contents—Prefixed to the actual narrative portion are two or three letters (**1:1-2:19**), and a brief foreword by the epitomist (**2:20-33**). In **3:1-7:42** he outlines the events leading up to the outbreak of the revolt. The rest of the book is taken up with the account of the exploits of Judas Machabaeus, the first part (**8:1-10:8**) dealing with events in the reign of Antiochus Epiphanes, the second (**10:9-15:37**) with those under Eupator and Demetrius I. (Though *cf.* on **9:1**, where it is shown that the events of part at least of ch 10 relate to the previous reign.) The last three verses of the Book form the epitomist's own epilogue (**15:38-40**).

d Date of Composition—The evidence for the date of composition is inconclusive, but, in spite of Willrich's theory which would make Jason a contemporary of Philo, it is most natural to suppose that the Book (or at least Jason's history) was composed whilst the effects of the Maccabean liberation were still felt and before the conquest by Rome. It is possible that the author of the 'five books' is the Jason of 1 Mac 8:17 (? nephew of Judas), who was sent on the embassy to Rome. Some even suggest that the work was composed by Jason on that occasion to support the case of the Jews at Rome (*cf.* Cornely, *Introductio* II i n. 155). This, of course, is a speculation without proof or possibility of refutation, but it is at least as well based as any other. If we press the words in 15:38—'from that time the city being possessed by the Hebrews'—it will be necessary to conclude that the history was written before the death of Judas and the ensuing 'great tribulation in Israel' (1 Mac 9:27).

To the epitome of Jason's work are prefixed certain letters (1:1–2:19) of a later date (see the commentary). The date of the latest of them (possibly 125 B.C. : *cf.* on 1:10) naturally makes the date of composition of the Book as we have it at least as late as that. But it is not necessary to suppose that the Second Book is any later than, if indeed it is as late as, the First.

574a I 1-II 19 Introductory Letters—It is not clear whether there are two or three letters prefixed to this Second Book, but the best division seems to be that of Meyer and others : (i) **1-7a** : a greeting from the Jews of Jerusalem to those at Alexandria. This letter concludes : (Given) 'when Demetrius reigned, in the year 169'.

(ii) **7b-10a** : 'We Jews wrote to you. . . .' This is a letter urging the Alexandrian Jews to observe the Feast of Dedication, 25 Casleu (*cf.* 1 Mac 4:59), to celebrate the purification of the temple by Judas. The letter concludes (10a) : ' In the year 188.' (So almost all the MSS : many modern scholars would emend to 148, as in two inferior MSS ; this would mean that the letter was written about the time of the actual purification of the temple (*cf.* 1 Mac 4:52), which would give more point to the letter. We do not know why such a letter should have been written forty years later.)

(iii) **10b-2:19** : an account of the death of Antiochus and a record of the Nehemias fire-miracle.

The second letter marks the defection of Jason (*cf.* 4:7 ff.) as the occasion of the beginning of the trouble. **8a** is a summary statement of the sufferings of the Jews : ' they burnt the gate ' (1 Mac 4:38 ; 2 Mac 8:33) and ' shed innocent blood ' (1 Mac 1:39) and in general of the persecution. There is no mention of the battles fought by Judas. The whole emphasis is on the answer to prayer. **8b** obviously refers to the purification of the temple (*cf.* 1 Mac 4:50-1).

The third letter is undated and the only chronological indication (apart from the events narrated in 12-17) is the address to Aristobulus (**10**), who is known (from Clem. Alex., *Strom.* I 22, PG 8,893 ; Euseb. *Praep. Evang.* 9, 6 ; etc.) to have been a Peripatetic philosopher and to have dedicated an allegorical interpretation of the Pentateuch to Ptolemy Philometor (180–146 B.C.), which would seem to imply a date for the letter earlier than the year 146 B.C.

Who is ' the king ' (**11**), ' Antiochus ' (**14**) ? The obvious answer is Epiphanes, since he was certainly the chief oppressor of the Jews. The only difficulty is that the account of his death (**15-16**) does not seem to agree with that given in 9:1-16. For this reason some would find here an account of the death of Antiochus the Great ; but all the evidence goes to show that he treated the Jews well. Moreover, a reading of this passage and of 9:2 strongly suggests that the same incident is being referred to in both places. Bévenot suggests that, for motives of prudence, the writer of the letter thought it unwise to refer to recent incidents, and elected to repeat the well-known facts about the death of Antiochus the Great, leaving it to the recipients of the letter to read between the lines, seeing in the death of the former king a premonitory example of the way in which God punishes all impiety. This seems more satisfactory than to say, with Knabenbauer, that in the letter we have an account, based on an early and exaggerated report, of what had happened to Epiphanes in Elam—a view which is difficult to reconcile with the writer's inerrancy ; or to cut the knot by arguing, as does Emmanuel Sa, that this letter is not necessarily inspired, any more than are the letters quoted elsewhere from the Romans, Spartans, etc.

There are a number of textual difficulties in the letter. **c** **10.** Bévenot follows Torrey in suggesting that the original reading was ' *the Senate of the Jews* ' (not ' the Senate and Judas '), as in some Syriac MSS (**11, 12**). The Gk means : ' *Having been rescued by God from great dangers, we give him great thanks as though we were set against the king ; for he himself has expelled those who were set against (us) in the holy city* '. (Vg and DV are, as will be seen, strangely at fault in **12,** in which the Gk has no mention of Persia.) The word παρατασσόμενοι ' set against ' is suspicious in 11, being obscure in the context and coming so close to παραταξαμένους of 12. The simplest change would be to read παρατασσομένῳ in 11 (' as though he [God] were set against the king ') ; but some deeper corruption seems probable.

The second part of the letter (1:18-2:19) deals with **d** two main themes—the ' fire-miracle ' of Nehemias and the concern of Jeremias for the safety of the Ark of the Covenant. The relevance of these incidents (not elsewhere recorded in OT) is obvious ; they must have been the theme of much speculation at the time of the dedication of the temple, so similar in many ways to the dedication which had taken place on the return from the Babylonian Captivity. For the general circumstances of this return *cf.* Esd and Neh. This particular incident is presumably derived from the (lost) memoirs and commentaries of Nehemias (**2:13**). **20.** ' As they told us ' would more naturally be ' *as they told Nehemias* ' ; the corruption of διεσαφησανveεμια into διεσάφησαν ἡμῖν. There can be little doubt that the ' thick water ' (**21**) is to be explained in conjunction with the name ' Nephthar ' (**36**) as being some kind of inflammable substance akin to naphtha, which is found in Persia. The continuity between the temple fire and the new fire kindled at the time of the return is to be understood as meaning that the materials which had produced the former fire had been preserved and served for this first kindling of the sacrificial flame. The actual kindling, it is implied, was miraculous (*cf.* 3 Kg 18:38). The author apparently connects the name ' Nephthar ' with the root *ptr*, meaning ' to separate '.

23. Jonathan is apparently the Johanan of Neh 12:22. The Jonathan mentioned in Neh 12:11 belongs to a later generation.

There is nothing in the extant writings attributed to **e** Jeremias to bear out the statements in **2:1-12** except for the Epistle of Jeremias in Bar 6. The connexion of **1-7** with what precedes and what follows is presumably that the story of Jeremias' hiding the Ark, etc. leads up to the passage in 7, which is appropriate to the circumstances of the letter, as are the references

to Moses and Solomon (cf. Lev 40:32 ; 3 Kg 8:11 ; **575d**
Lev 9:24 ; 2 Par 7:1 ; Lev 10:16 f.).

f II 20-33 Author's Prologue—With **20** we come to
the actual words of the epitomist. The central theme
of the letters quoted has been the purification and
dedication of the temple, and the author now proceeds to show how this is the climax of the life-work
of Judas, related at great length in the five books of
Jason of Cyrene, and here summarized for the benefit
of those who might not have either the time or the
inclination for a reading of such a lengthy history.
For Jason, cf. § 573d. Here it will suffice to add a word
on Inspiration. Since Jason's original work is not
to be regarded as having been inspired, the epitome
of it which constitutes the greater part of 2 Mac must
be understood to be inspired in the sense that the
necessary guidance is afforded to the editor to ensure
that only such things appear as are in accordance
with the mind and intention of the Holy Spirit, the
Supreme Author of the Holy Scriptures.

III 1-40 Peace under Onias III and Seleucus IV broken :
Frustration of the Attempt to rob the Temple—The
politico-religious situation here implied was roughly as
follows. After the annexation of Judaea by Antiochus III (c 200 B.C.), both he and his immediate
successor Seleucus IV sought to conciliate the tradi-
tionalist pro-Egyptian party, headed by the family
of Onias, the high-priest, whilst the Tobiad party,
representing the ' progressive ' Hellenistic idea, was
making its way to power by a close *rapprochement* with
the Syrian authorities. This involved, as we shall
see, the betrayal of the religious faith and traditions
of the Jews. Thus Simon (**4**), whether he was or was
not of the Tobiad family, was certainly of that party,
and set out to ingratiate himself with the governor
of Coele-Syria, Apollonius *of Tarsus* (**5** : Apollonius
is apparently the same as the Apollonius son of Menestheus [4:21] and a change from *of Tarsus* to *of Thraseas*
may easily have occurred), by informing him of the
wealth of the temple. (The Syrian kings were acutely
embarrassed financially as a result of the indemnity
imposed on them by the Romans in 188 B.C. ; cf.
1 Mac 3:29 ; 8:7 ; 2 Mac 8:10.) The king, informed
by Apollonius, entrusts the affair to Heliodorus, who
is mentioned in inscriptions as the king's vizier. The
amount of money in the temple was equivalent to
something like £855,000 of our money (£130,000 +
725,000), part of it forming a sort of benevolent fund,
whilst the rest had been deposited there, presumably
for safety, by a member of the Tobiad family. This
suggests that Simon was prepared to betray his associates as well as the deserving poor. Hyrcanus is
mentioned in Jos., *Ant.* 12, 4, 2-11. ' Son of ' may
mean no more than *descended from*.

The vivid description of Heliodorus's sacrilegious
attempt and its frustration is a characteristic passage
(**14-29**). The ' cloistered virgins ' (**19**) came to the
gate-towers, etc. Onias (Vg and DV) is a curious slip ;
the Gk has τοὺς πυλῶνας. In any case, Onias was
presumably with the priests before the altar (**15**) and
inaccessible to women. Heliodorus (**23**) ' *began to
execute* ' (imperfect). There is nothing in the Greek
corresponding to sacrifice ' of health ' (Vg ' hostiam
salutarem ') ; it says simply θυσίαν (**32**).

IV 1-22 Onias denounces Simon : Jason usurps the
High-Priesthood: Introduction of Hellenizing Practices
—**4**. ' Apollonius was outrageous ' (Vg ' insanire ') is
a rendering of most of the Gk MSS μαίνεσθαι, now
universally given up in favour of μενεσθέως (son
of Menestheus ; cf. **21**) ; ' which increased ' (Vg ' ad
augendam ') is a mistranslation. Read : ' *considering
that Apollonius son of Menestheus was seconding the wicked
designs of Simon*'.

The death of Seleucus was, as we know, brought about
by this Heliodorus, who sought to make himself king
(Appian, *Syr.* 45). But (**7**) Antiochus IV, with the
help of neighbouring kings, succeeded in expelling him
and ascended the throne. Jason (a Greek name

adopted by him, presumably as resembling his original **575d**
name Joshua) shows his Hellenizing tendencies. The
attempt to obtain the high-priesthood held by his
own brother and his attempt to bribe the king by
means of the temple funds show the depths to which
the official leaders of the Jews had sunk, and set in
an even stronger light the fidelity and self-sacrifice
of the Maccabees. **8**. 360 talents = £117,000 ; 80
talents = £26,000—this sum apparently to be paid
annually : 150 talents = £49,000. **9**. The distinction
between ' a place for exercise ' and ' a place for youth '
appears to be that the former was for adults, the
latter for youths of 14–18. ' Antiochians ', either
because enjoying certain special privileges associated
with their Syrian citizenship or as a mere empty title.
11 supports the statement of 3:2 about the exemptions
allowed to the Jews by previous Seleucid kings ; cf.
Jos. *Ant.* 12, 3, 3 f. We know nothing of John, but
the reference to Eupolemus is interesting as being
connected with an incident, the embassy to Rome
(1 Mac 8:17 ff.), which is later than the victory over
Nicanor with which 2 Mac concludes. If Jason of
Cyrene were the Jason of that embassy he would have
personal acquaintance with this Eupolemus.

12. ' Brothel houses ' repeats the insinuation of 1 Mac **e**
1:16, but there is no very good reason for accepting
this translation here. The Gk is ὑπὸ πέτασον (' in a
πέτασος ') and the πέτασος, the characteristic Greek
hat, is probably to be understood as a symbol of Greek
ways in general. Bévenot suspects that ὑπὸ πέτασον
has come in by dittography from the preceding ὑποτάσ-
σων. ' The castle ' is not the Syrian-occupied ἄκρα of
1 Mac 1:35, etc., but probably the site of the later
Antonia. **14**. The Gk has : ' *hastened to be partakers
of the unlawful exercises in the arena, after the proclamation
of the discus-contest*'. **15** means that they ceased to
care for their traditional glories and thought only
of winning a name for excellence in Greek pursuits.
16. ' *they got into a dangerous situation, finding enemies and
oppressors in those whose mode of life they envied and whom
they sought to imitate in all things*'.. **19**. Vg and DV
mistranslate : Gk = ' *The accursed Jason sent representatives* [spectatores, which has become *peccatores* in Vg],
Antiochians [cf. **9**] *as though from Jerusalem* [i.e. representing Jerusalem], *taking 300 didrachmas for the sacrifice
to Hercules* ' (= the Tyrian Melkart). **20**. Since 300
didrachmas = £16, ' making of galleys ' must be
understood rather as contributing to the equipping
of them. **21**. ' to treat with the nobles ', etc. : rather,
' *for the enthronization of Ptolemy Philometer* '—πρωτοκλίσια
—which occurred in 172 B.C. What Antiochus understood (from Apollonius) was that Ptolemy was ' hostile
to his [Antiochus's] interests (ἀλλότριον τῶν αὐτοῦ γεγονέναι
πραγμάτων).

23-50 Jason is replaced as High-Priest by Menelaus— **f**
Menelaus : Josephus says he was also called Onias and
was a brother of Jason : this is clearly a confusion.
Jason had replaced his brother Onias (cf. 4:7, 10).
Menelaus is thought to be a member of the Tobiad
family, which is borne out by the fact that when he
flees, he goes to the ' country of the Ammonites ' (**26**),
where the Tobiads are known to have had a stronghold. **27**. Sostratus was the Syrian governor of
Jerusalem. **29**. The Gk means : ' *Menelaus left his
brother Lysimachus as his deputy and Sostratus left Crates
(governor of the Cyprians) as his*'. ' Governor of the
Cyprians ' may mean that he was in command of a
body of Cyprian mercenaries. **30**. Tarsus and Mallos
are both in Cilicia. Onias had gone to Antioch some
time before (**4**). **33**. Daphne is a suburb of Antioch,
with a sacred precinct, some 5 m. SW. of the capital.

The pillaging of the temple by Menelaus (**32**) and
Lysimachus (**39**) enrages the people and goads them
to an outburst against their leaders. Some threw ashes
(**41**) ' *upon the supporters of Lysimachus* '. According to
LXX, Ptolemy (**45**) is the son of Dorymenes ; cf.
1 Mac 3:38.

V 1-27 Beginnings of Persecution—The preceding **576a**
chapter gives a very good idea of the disorders caused

576a by the unscrupulous conduct of the Hellenizers at Jerusalem, and it is hardly surprising that Antiochus should have decided to intervene in person, on his return from his Egyptian expedition. The invasion referred to in **1** is the second only in the sense that the contemplated expedition, mentioned in 4:21 f., counts as the first ; *cf.* 1 Mac 1:20 ; Dan 11:28. For the portents of **2, 3** *cf.*

> Fierce fiery warriors fight upon the clouds
> In ranks and squadrons and right form of war. . . .
> The noise of battle hurtled in the air,
> Horses did neigh and dying men did groan.
> (Shakespeare : *Julius Caesar*, II 2)

5. Jason had fled into the country of the Ammonites (4:26) when Menelaus had been awarded the high-priesthood by Antiochus. Now, hearing that the latter was dead, he attempts to regain his position, but unsuccessfully. **8.** Aretas, king of the Arabians ; *cf.* 1 Mac 5:25. **9.** 'Kindred sake'—an allusion to the letter of 1 Mac 12:21, in which the Spartans claimed kinship with the Jews.

b Antiochus not unnaturally interprets the revolt of Jason against Menelaus as an attack upon his own authority, and after his reverse in Egypt he is in no mind to brook insubordination in Palestine. This first persecution therefore had as much a political as a religious motive, though the two were closely connected. He also desired to get into his possession the treasures he had heard of (3:7), some of which he had been promised, but had not received (4:8 ff., 27). For the attempt of Heliodorus, *cf.* 3:14 ff. **21.** 1,800 talents = £585,000. **22.** Philip, who now replaces Sostratus (or Crates, 4:29) as governor of Jerusalem, is mentioned as persecuting the Jews savagely (6:11). **23.** The Samaritans, too, are oppressed. Gazarim = Garizim ; *cf.* Jn 4:20. **24.** Finally, Antiochus sends Apollonius (two years later ; *cf.* 1 Mac 1:30) to stamp out all opposition to the new religious policy. 'That hateful prince' is a mistranslation of Μυσάρχην, *i.e. commander of the Mysians*' ; *cf.* on 1 Mac 1:30. We know from Polybius that there was a corps of Mysians in the Seleucid army (Polybius 31:3, where he describes a procession at Antioch, which took place a few years after these events, in which 5,000 Mysians took part). **27.** Judas Machabaeus now appears, with a small group of nine companions (presumably including his father and brothers ; *cf.* 1 Mac 2:1). 'The pollution' referred to is of course the contamination of heathen practices ; *cf.* 14:3.

c **VI 1-31 Measures by Antiochus to introduce Hellenism : Martyrdom of Eleazar**—The general features of the situation have been discussed in 1 Mac 1:43 ff. ; *cf.* in particular 1 Mac 1:57 for the 'abomination of desolation', the altar to Jupiter Olympius (**2**). **4.** LXX : '*The temple was full of debauchery and revelling by the Gentiles, who dallied there with harlots and would lie with women in the sacred precincts, bringing in objects that were unbecoming*'. **5.** Diodorus (34:1) describes how a sow was slain on the altar and the Jews forced to partake of it. **6.** LXX : '*neither could any man*', etc. **7.** The king's birthday was celebrated *every month* (LXX). The feast of Bacchus was the Dionysia, probably kept in the autumn. **8.** '*by the suggestion of Ptolemy*' (4:45), who appears to have been in charge of religious propaganda. **10** apparently refers to the incident described at greater length in 1 Mac 1:63 ff. **11.** 'They made a conscience' : '*they scrupled to defend themselves* by reason of the religious observance of the day'.

d The martyrdom of Eleazar, familiar to all Catholics and particularly to those who recite the Divine Office, being the subject of the first lessons read on the Monday in the fifth week of October, calls for little general comment. **19.** The 'torture' is more strictly 'the instrument of torture' (τύμπανον), either a rack, perhaps cruciform (Wilcken), or a bastinado ; *cf.* 30. The verb formed from the Gk word (ἐτυμπανίσθησαν) is used in Heb 11:35, which seems to be a reminiscence

of this passage. **20.** 'Considering' (Vg 'intuens') seems to be intended to represent προπτύσας '*spitting out*' (the swine's flesh). The division of 19-20 is misleading. '*He went voluntarily to the torture, spitting out the flesh : showing* [some word seems to have dropped out] *in what way* [or, *in the way in which*] *those ought to go who are resolved to refuse whatever it is not lawful to eat, in spite of one's love of life*'. **21.** 'The bystanders' are, according to the Greek, '*those commissioned to*' require this eating of unlawful meats. **23.** Vg and DV do not adequately render a difficult original, which may be corrupt, but as it stands seems to mean : '*forming a noble conclusion, worthy of his age and his advanced years, and of the added distinction of his grey hairs*'. **28.** According to LXX he was not 'carried' but '*went unfalteringly to the rack*'.

VII 1-42 The Seven Brothers—In the Breviary this passage is closely linked with the story of Eleazar, and the same spirit breathes through both. Comment is again almost superfluous. The faith and constancy of the brothers and of their mother speak for themselves, as also does their certainty of immortality. The only points requiring some elucidation seem to be the following. **1.** The presence of the king has been regarded by some as casting doubt upon the historicity of the whole incident. But, whilst it is true that the king had left Jerusalem after the plundering of the temple more than two years before (5:21), we do not know that he may not have revisited it on some later occasion. Alternatively the incident may have taken place at Antioch, as the Roman Martyrology for 1st August assumes.

The barbarous nature of the punishment need hardly surprise us : for roasting, *cf.* Jer 29:22 ; for scalping, *cf.* Herodotus 4:64 ; for cutting off of hands, feet, etc., *cf.* Xen. *Anab.* 1:9:13. Antiochus III had thus treated his own cousin (Polybius 8:23).

11 is, of course, most important as evidence for Jewish faith in **the resurrection of the body ;** whilst **14** does not imply that there would be no resurrection for the wicked, but only that there would be no resurrection to the life of happiness but to eternal death. **28.** 'made them out of nothing' is represented in most of the Gk MSS by οὐκ ἐξ ὄντων ἐποίησεν sc. '*did not make them out of existing matter*', but some MSS, as well as the Syriac, have the form implied in Vg ; in any case it seems reasonable to suppose that the same idea underlies either form of expression. **36.** '*have drunk of eternal life, under God's covenant*' (reading πεπώκασιν for πεπτώκασιν), which gives good sense and makes the Gk smoother.

VIII 1-7 Early Successes of Judas—What has preceded is largely introductory to the main purpose of the book, which is to recite the achievements of Judas Machabaeus. The latter at first necessarily confines himself to local action against isolated positions. This would involve some splitting of his forces, and may explain why, although 6,000 is given as the number of men raised (**1**), in 1 Mac 4:6 Judas has only 3,000 men in a later engagement against Gorgias ; *cf. ad loc.* **6.** 'commodious' : the most important strategically.

8-23 Measures and Counter-measures of Apollonius and Judas—**8.** Philip : the governor of Jerusalem (5:22 ; 6:11), apparently appointed to bring about the religious changes desired by Antiochus. For Ptolemy, *cf.* 1 Mac 3:38 ; 2 Mac 4:45 ; 6:8. **9.** Nicanor and Gorgias, 1 Mac 3:38, etc. For the whole passage, *cf.* 1 Mac 3:27-60. **10.** The tribute : *cf.* 1 Mac 8:7 ; 2 Mac 3:7. According to Polybius 21:17, the period of payment was 12 years (from 188 B.C., the date of the treaty of Apamea), but we know from Livy (42:6) that in 173 B.C. Apollonius was at Rome apologizing for the delay in paying, and although the report of his speech on that occasion seems to imply that he was bringing the final instalment ('*omne advexisse*'), it may be that the Romans had granted a moratorium and that he was bringing the payments up to date. **11.** One motive for this expedition against the Jews is then to raise money by taking and selling slaves. For the slave-dealers accompanying the expedition, *cf.* 1 Mac 3:41. **13.** Not all the Jews who left the forces of Judas were cowards or deserters ; *cf.* 1 Mac 3:56. **16.** 7,000 : 6,000 in Gk ; *cf.* 1. **19.** Sennacherib : *cf.* 4 Kg 19:35. **20.** Of the battle against the Galatians we have no other mention, but presumably it occurred during a campaign fought by Antiochus III in Media against a rebel satrap, Molon, in 220 B.C. Molon is known to have had a force of Galatians in his army (Polybius 5:40–43). The Jews would presumably constitute a part of the mercenary army under Antiochus ; there is much evidence to show that the Jews often served as mercenaries under the Hellenistic kings.

There is some corruption at the beginning of **23.** LXX says : *Eleazar also*, which looks like a clumsy attempt to introduce a fourth captain (**22**) to make up the total of 6,000 men ; but it may be authentic. The verse goes on : ' *having read the holy book and given the watchword " The Help of God", himself commanding the first company* [*sc.* he is the ' fourth ' captain], *he attacked Nicanor*'. **22.** 'Joseph' should almost certainly be *John*. Judas had no brother Joseph ; *cf.* 1 Mac 2:2. **24-29 Victory over Nicanor (and Gorgias)**—This victory is described at greater length in 1 Mac 4:1–25. The two accounts are derived from different sources, since 1 Mac says practically nothing about Nicanor, whilst Gorgias and Lysias, not mentioned in 2 Mac, there play a more prominent role ; *cf.* 1 Mac 3:38, etc. **30-36 Defeat of Timotheus and Bacchides**—**30-33** appear to be wrongly inserted here. **34-36** clearly refer to the events immediately following on the defeat of Nicanor. Moreover, the reference to Jerusalem, etc. in **31-33** should be connected with ch 10. In 1 Mac 5:6–8 there is a reference to a campaign against the Ammonites, under Timotheus, apparently shortly after the temple purification, and this may be part of the same campaign.

IX 1-29 Death of Antiochus Epiphanes—The insertion here of the account of the death of Epiphanes should not be taken to imply that the author regarded it as preceding the temple purification ; *cf.* 10:9. It certainly did not do so, as is clear from 1 Mac 6:1–17. Possibly Jason, or his epitomist, did not wish to break the story of the successes of Judas, and therefore anticipated the interpolation of the fortunes of Antiochus. Moreover, there is evidence to suggest that Jason was not very careful about chronological sequence ; and in any case he may have inserted here a complete account of the adventures of Antiochus in the East, which had begun some time before and would naturally close with the account of his death, which the epitomist has extracted.

2. Since the city where the temple was is said to have been in Elam (Elymais 1 Mac 6:1 ; *cf.* Polybius 31:11), the name Persepolis must be understood to mean not the well-known capital of Persia, but simply a Persian city, *i.e.* a city of the Persian Empire (= Persia). **3.** According to Polybius, Antiochus died at Tabae (? = Gabae, near Aspadana, which ought perhaps to be read here for ' Ecbatana '). If, as suggested § 577*f*, the campaign against Timotheus took place after the temple purification, then Antiochus must have heard the news of this too, but the author suppresses this fact since he has not yet dealt with the incident.

In spite of the somewhat rhetorical nature of the description of the king's sufferings and remorse (**8-17** : as we have said, such treatment is characteristic of 2 Mac), it is an excess of sophistication to doubt its veracity. Nor need there be any difficulty in accepting the authenticity of the letter addressed to the Jews (**19-27**). The general nature of the terms in which it is couched suggest that it was intended as an appeal to the different countries composing the king's realm, and we may well believe that where ' Jews ' stands in this version (**19**), other copies would insert Syrians, Phoenicians, and the like. ' Subjects ' (Vg ' civibus ') should be replaced by some such term as fellow-

citizens. Antiochus at times condescended to a style **577h** of conduct which seemed to express a desire to show his ' democratic ' spirit ; *cf.* Polybius 31:4. **29** has caused some perplexity. According to 1 Mac 6:14, 55–56, 63, Philip was made regent and succeeded in occupying Antioch, but was driven out again by Lysias. According to Josephus (*Ant.* 12, 9, 7) he was captured and killed by Antiochus V (Eupator). Possibly he went to Egypt before his attempt to seize power, with the object of concerting measures with Ptolemy.

X 1-8 (9) Purification of the Temple : Encaenia— **i** For the events of this passage *cf.* 1 Mac 4:36–59, where they are treated at greater length. The ' two years ' of **3** is not to be taken literally, since the actual interval was three years precisely ; *cf.* our own expression ' a couple of years '. **9** bears out what was said in § 577*f-g* about the death of Antiochus following the temple purification.

10-23 Victories over the Idumaeans, etc. — 11. **578a** The ' appointment ' of Lysias was merely the formal ratification of an existing situation, though it is significant as reversing the decision of Antiochus Epiphanes (1 Mac 6:14) to replace Lysias by Philip. It was of course Lysias who took the initiative in all this (1 Mac 6:17). **12.** Ptolemy is governor of Coele-Syria (*cf.* 8:8), but is probably not Ptolemy son of Dorymenes (1 Mac 3:38, etc.). **14.** Gorgias is now governor of Idumaea ; *cf.* § 563*b*. The ' strangers ' are the Philistines. **15.** For ' Jews ' read, with LXX, ' *Idumaeans, occupying the most advantageous strongholds, harried the Jews, and, receiving the Hellenizing refugees from Jerusalem, tried to keep up their activities*'. **16-19.** For Judas's exploits *cf.* 1 Mac 5:3–5.

The incident of **19-22** is in keeping with the general **b** purpose of 2 Mac, the contrast between the virtue and wisdom of Judas and the weakness and corruption of those about him. Doubtless there were such traitors ; but it would be wrong to suppose that Simon was one of them. Certainly he was not put to death with the traitors (**22**), and the part he plays in 1 Mac is sufficient testimony to his uprightness and general worth. **19.** ' Joseph and Zacchaeus ' may be a corruption of Joseph son of Zacharias ; *cf.* 1 Mac 5:56, where he is concerned in a dangerous act of insubordination. **20.** The 70,000 *drachmas* possibly represent the ransom of 700 men at the normal rate of a mina a head. The total is something less than £4,000.

24-38 Defeat and Death of Timotheus, Leader of the **c** **Ammonites**—It was suggested in § 577*e* that the account of the campaign there mentioned against Timotheus had been displaced, and should occur after the purification of the temple (*sc.* after the early verses of this chapter), possibly forming part of this campaign. (It ought to be stated that not all interpreters accept the identification of the Timotheus of 8:30 with the Timotheus of this chapter.) At any rate, the capture of Gazer (1 Mac 5:8 = Gezer) seems to be the incident described in **32-37**. ' In a certain place ' (**37** : Vg ' in quodam loco ' ; LXX ἔν τινι λάκκῳ) : ' *in a pit*'.

XI 1-38 Defeat of Lysias : Treaty—It seems probable **d** that this campaign of Lysias is the one described in 1 Mac 4:26–35, *sc.* before the death of Antiochus Epiphanes and the purification of the temple. (Its dislocation is another example of the confusion of the source employed by the epitomist [*cf.* 8:30 ; 9:1–29], although of course there is no error expressed or indeed implied. The writer is giving the story of what happened, but is not particularly concerned with problems of chronology.) It seems clear that Lysias is here acting, not in conjunction with the king, who is not mentioned, but on his own responsibility. (In ch 13 the young king is mentioned, although there Lysias must still have been largely responsible for the operations.) Moreover, Bethsura (**5**) is almost certainly the place mentioned in 1 Mac 4:29. Further, the first of the letters (**16-21**) reads as though it were sent off in the absence of the king ; *cf.* 18 ' whatsoever

578d things could be reported to the king' implies some difficulty of communication, whilst there is some MS authority for reading 'I have granted as much', etc. The date of this letter (21) is towards the end of a month Dioscorus, which is thought to be a novel form of (or a mistake for) Dystros (= Adar). The second letter (22-26) must have been written shortly after the receipt of the news of the death of Antiochus Epiphanes, since it reads like a proclamation at the beginning of a new reign. Eupator and still more Lysias would be aware of the danger threatening from Egypt and from Philip (9:1-29) and would be anxious to conciliate the Jews. This second letter is addressed to Lysias, but obviously with the intention that it should be communicated to the Jews, as a sort of covering letter for the following one. The letter (27-33) to the Jews from the king, dated 15 Xanthikos (= Nisan) is intended to provide a safe-conduct for those Jews desiring to travel between Jerusalem and Antioch, presumably on their return from the Passover celebrations. Menelaus will be the high-priest of 4:23 ; 5:5, etc.

e The last letter (33-38) from the Roman ambassadors bears the same date, possibly by a mere coincidence, though it may be an error in copying. Quintus Memmius is otherwise unknown. Titus Manilius is probably T. Manlius Torquatus, known to have been an ambassador in Egypt about 164 B.C. ; he may have received some commission in connexion with Syrian affairs.

579a XII 1-31 Fresh Outbreaks : Punishment of Jamnia and Joppe : Defeat of Timotheus—This is a very confused chapter and bears all the signs of being a mere collection of disconnected material concerning campaigns with no sort of interrelation. The events of 10-31 are certainly those recorded in 1 Mac 5:24-53, whilst the events of 3-9, which have no connexion with the generals mentioned in 2 and, as we shall see, do not lead naturally to 10, are entirely without a firm chronological reference. Further, the mention of Timotheus, mysterious as are his appearances and disappearances (2, 10, 18, 24), strongly suggests that this passage should be read before 10:24-37, a passage which ends with an account of his death. Some would cut the knot by supposing that this is a different Timotheus, which is possible, but (a) the fact that he is operating in the same vicinity and (b) the statement in 10:24 that he had already been overcome by the Jews are reasonable grounds for maintaining the identification. (However cf. Bévenot, Introduction, § 9.)

b Of the generals mentioned in 2, nothing more is heard of any except Timotheus. Nicanor is probably different from the Nicanor of ch 14. The hostility of the coast towns to the Jews was of course nothing new, but there is no evidence as to what occasioned this fresh outburst. But in that world of intrigue (Egypt-Syria, Philip-Lysias, Antiochus-Demetrius) there would be many occasions for minor party incidents.

c The outline of events dealt with in 10-31 is more clearly indicated in 1 Mac 5:24-53 and it will suffice here to resolve one or two minor problems. **9.** ' 240 furlongs ' seems corrupt for *340*. **10.** The nine furlongs cannot, of course, be reckoned from Jamnia or even from Jerusalem (8, 9), as the fighting next described occurred in Transjordania. Something has clearly been omitted, either by the epitomist or by a copyist ; cf. 17. **13.** Casphin is probably the Casphor of 1 Mac 5:26, which may be the modern Khisfin, some 10 m. E. of the Sea of Galilee. **17.** The 750 furlongs can hardly be reckoned from Khisfin, and it seems likely that 17 should come between 9 and 10, so that the 750 furlongs will be reckoned from the neighbourhood of Jerusalem, which would bring them within striking distance of the Tubianites ; cf. Tubin 1 Mac 5:13. Characa is probably El-Keraᴋ = Dathema of 1 Mac 5:9, etc. **20.** For 120,000 the Old Latin reads 12,000, almost certainly correct. **21.** Carnion = Carnaim (1 Mac 5:9). **27.** Ephron, cf. 1 Mac 5:46. **29.** Scythopolis is called

Bethshan in 1 Mac 5:46. **31.** The Feast of Weeks = Pentecost (32).

32-46 Defeat of Gorgias—This is apparently paralleled by 1 Mac 5:65 ff., although Gorgias is not there mentioned (but cf. 1 Mac 5:59). We know that he was in command in Idumaea (' the land towards the South ', 1 Mac 5:65), whilst Maresa (35) is some 12 m. ENE. of Hebron (Chebron, 1 Mac 5:65). Again in 1 Mac 5:66 it is thought that for Samaria, Maresa should be read. Esdrin (36) is probably another form of the name Azarias (cf. 1 Mac 5:60), whilst the incident of the idol-amulets (40 ' donaries ': Vg ' donaria ': LXX ἱερώματα) seems to be connected with the reproof of 1 Mac 5:62.

43-46 is of course one of the best-known passages in Mac. Its dogmatic importance is considerable, testifying as it does to a clear-cut and confident belief in personal immortality and in the value of **intercessory prayer for the dead.** The force of the words is strengthened rather than weakened by the objection that ' such an idea is unparalleled in Jewish literature '. Here is no vague echo of a conventional platitude but a definite statement of the writer's personal conviction, the witness of one consciously taking sides in a debate about the fact of survival. As is well known the Sadducees rejected the doctrine of the resurrection of the body (Mt 22:23), and it may well be that it was during this period of struggle between the orthodox party, represented especially by the Hasidaeans (1 Mac 2:42), later to become the Pharisees, and the Hellenizing party within the priesthood, constituted by the sceptical Sadducees, that the doctrine of personal immortality began to assume a sharper definition. To that definition such a passage as the present may well have contributed. The gesture of Judas would of course become widely known, and would serve to deepen and strengthen the faith that it yet presupposed.

The number 12,000 drachmas, which would represent between £600 and £700 is suspect. Most of the Gk MSS. read 2,000. Even this figure it is interesting to contrast with the 300 drachmas which was all that could be raised for the Tyrian festival (2 Mac 4:19).

For Pharisees and Sadducees cf. Lagrange, 56, 304 ff., 353 ff.

In **45 f.** Vg is a little tendentious. The Gk means : ' So, looking at the splendid reward [Χαριστήριον = reward as an act of gratitude] laid up for them that had fallen asleep in godliness [those who, although sinful, had given their lives for the defence of the truth]—a holy and godly thought—he made an offering of propitiation to the end that they might be loosed from their sin '.

XIII 1-26 Eupator in Person fails : Peace—According to the parallel passage (1 Mac 6:18 ff.), the occasion of this expedition was an appeal from the garrison in the citadel at Jerusalem, which Judas was attempting to reduce. The presence of Menelaus with the army (comparable to that of Alcimus with Bacchides, 1 Mac 7:9, 12) suggests that he knew that he could not hope to hold the position of high-priest by any personal merit and that the Hellenizing party in Jerusalem was not strong enough to support him : he could come only as the nominee of a foreign power. The deceitfulness (εἰρωνείας, 3) consisted in the fact that he pretended to be inspired with patriotic motives but was a mere self-seeker. He was put to death at Beroea (Aleppo)—the name has dropped out of the Vg text —but probably, as the account in Josephus implies, at the end of the campaign, when (23) Antiochus was seeking to conciliate the Jews ; Ant. 12, 9, 7 ; cf. 1 Mac 6:59. The account of the death of Menelaus is not clear, but suggests that he was killed by being buried alive in (? smouldering) ashes.

b It has to be admitted that in **22, 23** Jason, or his epitomist, glosses over what would have been a serious reverse for the Jews but for the rebellion of Philip. But it is true that this fact, coupled with the prolonged resistance of Bethsura and the military skill of Judas, prevented the king from reaping the fruits of his victory and turned what might have been a disaster to the Jewish cause into a reason for thanksgiving. The king did withdraw, having been weakened (**23, 24;** 1 Mac 6:60).

Was Judas appointed governor of the coastal districts, as Simon was afterwards (1 Mac 11:59)? There is no mention of it in 1 Mac, and the Gk text says that Antiochus appointed Hegemonides governor. Some emend Hegemonides to ἡγεμόνα, which was presumably read (? by error) in the version underlying the Vg rendering. On the whole, it seems safer to conclude against the view that he was actually appointed. **25.** 'He' is apparently Antiochus. 'The men of Ptolemais were much displeased with the treaty, *for they were angry about certain points which they desired to have abrogated*'. The reading of the latter part is not certain but the above seems to be the sense.

XIV 1-14 Intrigues of Alcimus—For Demetrius *cf.* 1 Mac 7:1 and § 559*e*; for Alcimus (**3**) *cf.* 1 Mac 7:5. 'In the time of mingling' is incorrect; the Gk is ἐν τοῖς τῆς ἀμειξίας χρόνοις, *sc.* in the early days of the persecution when the Jews who desired to remain faithful shunned all dealings with the heathen; *cf.* 38; 1 Mac 1:53; 2:33; 2 Mac 5:27. **4.** 'boughs *which were customarily used in* the temple'.

There were apparently three attempts to restore Alcimus, two by Bacchides (1 Mac 7:8 ff.; 9:32 ff.) and this attempt by Nicanor (after the failure of the first attempt by Bacchides (1 Mac 7:25 ff.), but before his second attempt, which was successful).

15-36 Relations between Judas and Nicanor—The account here given of the attitude of Nicanor to Judas is much fuller than that in 1 Mac 7:26 ff. The preliminary skirmishing round Dessau (an unknown locality: does the reading Lessau, found in some MSS, suggest the truth, *sc.* Laisa, near Bethhoron: *cf.* 1 Mac 9:5?) is not mentioned in 1 Mac, which also suggests that Nicanor was hostile to Judas from the beginning and that his friendship (**24**; *cf.* 1 Mac 7:27) was hypocritical. But 1 Mac has compressed, omitting the earlier phases. Thus 1 Mac 7:26*b* ff. will correspond with **30** here. **26.** A word in the Gk has been overlooked in Vg: 'seeing the love they had to one another *and taking the agreements they had made*'.

'assented to the foreign interest' means *was hostile to* **580e** *his interests* (the phrase used of Ptolemy in 4:21). 'Successor': more probably *deputy*; *cf.* 4:29.

37-46 Death of Razias—This passage has perplexed **f** the moralists, and has been cited by heretics either as a defence of suicide (so the Donatists : *cf.* Augustine, *Contra Gaudentium* 1:26–31) or as proving that 2 Mac is not inspired. But whilst we must condemn the act of Razias as objectively wrong, we may with the author praise the determination to die rather than to risk apostasy. That he was in good faith is clear from **46**. The words in **44**, 'upon the midst of the neck' should be 'on the midst of *his flank*' (or possibly '*into a hollow place*', *sc.* the empty space formed by the parting of the crowd).

38. Vg has misled the translators of DV. The Gk **g** means : '*Formerly, at the time when the Jews were not consorting with the heathen* (*cf.* **3**), *he had made the choice of Judaism*' (κρίσιν εἰσενηνεγμένος τοῦ Ἰουδαϊσμοῦ; RV: 'had been accused of cleaving to the Jews' religion'; Bévenot : 'he had aimed at maintaining the purity of the Jewish religion').

XVI 1-37 Defeat and Death of Nicanor—Judas, who **h** had withdrawn from Jerusalem in a NW. direction *towards* Samaria (κατὰ Σαμάρειαν, **1**), had taken up a position at Adarsa (1 Mac 7:40), due N. of Jerusalem, having eluded Nicanor's army at Bethhoron. The parallel passage (7:26 ff.) deals more at length with the military operations, 2 Mac as usual being interested in the more 'edifying' details—Judas's dream and prayer (11–16; 21–24). In **28** (apparently) : *they recognized Nicanor lying in his full armour*. **37.** '*The 13th day of the 12th month* (*called in Syrian Adar*), *the day before Mardochaeus's day*'; *cf.* 1 Mac 7:49. **38.** The Jews did not retain possession of Jerusalem for long (1 Mac 9:23 ff.), but there was no return to the former desecration of the temple precincts and in comparison with that the mere military occupation of the capital was a relatively tolerable matter. (If we press the meaning we must suppose that the Book was completed before the death of Judas.)

38-40 form a delightful and entirely characteristic **i** Epilogue : *cf.* the epitomist's Prologue (2:20–33).

THE TEXTUAL CRITICISM OF
THE NEW TESTAMENT

By J. M. T. BARTON

581a Bibliography—M.-J. Lagrange, O.P., *Introduction à l'étude du Nouveau Testament. Deuxième partie : Critique textuelle, II. La critique rationnelle*, EB, 1935 ; H. J. Vogels, *Handbuch der neutestamentlichen Textkritik* (1923) ; L. Vaganay, *An Introduction to the Textual Criticism of the New Testament* (E.T., 1937) ; *F. Kenyon, *The Text of the Greek Bible* (1937) ; *K. Lake and S. New, *The Text of the New Testament* (6th ed., 1928).

b Meaning of the Term—Textual criticism, also called lower criticism, is that which deals with the establishment of the best available text of a work that has (at least in many instances) been handed down in manuscript form and copied by many hands. (Higher criticism studies the literary contents of the text established by lower criticism.) It has, as its secondary purpose, to account for the variant readings that are to be detected on comparing one copy with another, and, so far as may be, to trace these readings to their respective archetypes.

Necessity—In a work such as the collection of New Testament books, textual criticism is made necessary by the disappearance, probably for all time, of the original autographs of the Apostles and other NT writers. These autographs, and their first copies, have perished, in ways that would include (*a*) destruction by Christians in time of persecution to prevent the manuscripts from falling into the hands of heathens, (*b*) destruction by the persecutors themselves, and, doubtless in great measure, (*c*) ordinary wear-and-tear, by the daily use made of the precious writings in the Christian communities to which they were addressed. The copies that have come down to us are always, in some degree, imperfect copies, since ' owing to the frailties of the human hand and eye and brain, it is impossible to copy large quantities of matter without making mistakes ', Kenyon, 9. Among various causes that have led to erroneous copying one may mention confusion between letters (*e.g.* the Greek capitals Θ and O), dittography (*i.e.* accidental repetition of one or more letters), transposition of letters, and homoeoteleuton (*i.e.* the omission of a line owing to the use of several words or clauses successively with repetitions or similar endings). There are also many cases where deliberate alterations have been made by the copyist in the interests, real or supposed, of accuracy, elegance, sound doctrine, and so forth ; *cf.* Lagrange, 32–40 ; also RB 41 (1933) 481–98.

c External Form of the Greek Codices—Throughout the first two Christian centuries the NT writings were, doubtless, circulated on rolls or sheets of papyrus. Sheets, rather than rolls, seem to be the normal form even as early as the second century. The pith of the plant's stem was cut into long strips. These, laid first vertically and then horizontally, were gummed together into a single sheet, which, after drying and rubbing down with ivory or a shell, was ready for use. The horizontal strips were mostly used for writing, as the lines were better marked and the sheet could more easily be rolled inward on that side (known as the *recto*, the back being named the *verso*). The ordinary size of a sheet was 9–11 inches by 5–5½. Thus a short letter (*e.g.* 2 Jn) could be written on a single sheet, or, where more space was needed, two or more sheets could be fastened together to make a roll. The following lengths in feet have been calculated for NT documents : Rom 11½ ; Mk 19 ; Jn 23½ ; Mt 30 ; Lk and Ac 31–2. By way of comparison, a book of Thucydides would occupy a roll of 30–5 ; a book of Plato's *Republic* little more than half of this.

The custom of using a scribe to take down letters at dictation was widespread. For some evidence of St Paul's habits, *cf.* 2 Thess 3:17 ; 1 Cor 16:21 ; Col 4:18. Gal 6:11 may indicate that he wrote this epistle with his own hand.

From the second cent. onwards the codex form (*i.e.* sheets of papyrus arranged in quires and pages) came gradually to replace the roll ; by the end of the period of the persecutions vellum or parchment began to be used for the better type of book ; in the eighth cent. *charta bombacina* or paper was brought in from the East. The ink (*atramentum*, Gr. *melan, melanion, graphikon melan*) was applied with a reed (*kalamos*), later by a quill.

The principal division of the codices, according to the manner of their writing, is into uncials (lit. ' inch-long ' letters) or majuscules, in which the script employed is made up of separated capitals, very elegantly inscribed, and into minuscules, also called cursives, which are written in a running hand, with ligaturing of the letters. It would be a mistake to regard MSS in uncials as invariably older than those in cursive script. In fact, cursive writing existed already at an early date, but was mostly employed for private letters rather than for literary composition. In the ninth cent., Theodore the Studite (759–826 ; *cf.* DTC 15 [1946], 287–98) or some other worker in the Studium monastery at Constantinople, invented an especially beautiful cursive hand that became dominant in the Byzantine empire. Unfortunately it was all so much alike that it is often difficult to tell one MS from another on the ground of writing only. It is not to be inferred that an uncial is necessarily more important than a cursive, since it has been frequently established that many uncials are witnesses to a late text, whereas many cursives have derived from a very early one. Among NT cursives of special importance may be mentioned 33 (9th–10th cent., considered by Eichhorn and Hort as the best in this script), and those of the family 1 (associated with the name of Kirsopp Lake) and family 13 or Ferrar group. ' In short,' writes Professor Lake, ' it is neither the date nor the script of a MS which determines its value for the critic, but the textual history of its ancestors ' (*op. cit.*, 12).

It may be added that the minuscules vastly outnumber the uncials. Gregory's list, published in 1908, claims that there are some 4,000 NT codices comprising 161 uncials, more than 2,000 minuscules, 1,556 lectionaries (*i.e.* service books containing a large amount of Scripture, though not continuously or always in the order found in NT documents), and 14 papyri. These figures have been greatly increased during the intervening forty years, as a result of more recent discoveries and assignments, so that, for example, the latest list includes 2,429 minuscules and 1,678 lectionaries. *Cf.* Kenyon, *Our Bible and the Ancient Manuscripts*, 1939 ed., 106 ; F. M. Braun, O.P., *La Sainte Bible*, 10 (1946), 485–7.

The Division of the NT Text—Ancient divisions into *stichoi* or ' sense lines ' and *per cola et commata* (that is, e respectively, by clauses in a sentence and minor divisions) may here be ignored. Only two methods of division are genuinely important for our purpose, *i.e.* those into chapters and verses. The chapter division is attributable to Stephen Langton, archbishop of Canterbury (*d.* 1228). It was first made in the Latin Vulgate, but later passed into use in the Hebrew and Greek texts. The Complutensian or Alcala polyglot (published 1522) has chapter divisions. The verse divisions were first attempted by Santes Pagnini, O.P. (*d.* 1541), in a new rendering of the Bible published at Lyons in 1527. Later the Parisian printer, Robert Estienne, whose name so frequently occurs in its Latinized form of Robertus Stephanus, published in 1551 a Greek NT printed at Geneva, in which the division into verses was the work of Stephanus himself. In 1555 he published a complete Latin Bible, in which he used Pagnini's verse division for OT proto-canonical books, while employing a modified form of this for the NT and the OT deuterocanonica. It is generally admitted that these chapter and verse divisions are critically valueless, frequently spoil the sense, and would, in many cases, be better away. They are, however, invaluable for reference purposes.

The MS Codices of the NT—In the absence of the original MSS and the first copies of the NT writings we are thrown back upon MS codices of a later date that give a more or less faithful copy of the text. Some of these are of early date (the most ancient more or less complete ones, being of the 4th cent.), whereas, as is well known, the MS codices of the Latin and Greek classics are of much later date. Few NT codices include the whole of NT ; most of them contain only a part, *e.g.* the Gospels, or the Acts and Catholic epistles or the Pauline writings or the Apocalypse. Many are no more than lectionaries that contain such parts of the Gospels and apostolic writings as were customarily read in the liturgy.

Codices are divided according to their contents into pure and mixed. Pure codices give only the original Greek, whereas mixed codices, in addition to the original text, give commentaries or *scholia* or versions (these last including bilingual codices such as Greek and Latin or Greek and Syriac). There are also codices known as *palimpsests* (from the Greek *palin* = 'again' and *psaô* = 'to scrape'), or rescripts, *i.e.* documents in which original MS has been rubbed out and new writing superimposed. Perhaps the best known example of a palimpsest is the famous Codex C (*Codex Ephraemi rescriptus*), a fifth cent. MS of the whole Bible which in the twelfth cent. was used again as writing material for some works of St Ephraem the Syrian Doctor (*d.* A.D. 373). Fortunately it has been found possible to recover the older (that is, usually, the more valuable) text by means of chemicals or ultra-violet ray photography.

Some of the codices have names pointing to their past or present place of storage (*e.g.* Vaticanus, Alexandrinus, Sinaiticus, Claromontanus) or their former owners, *e.g.* Coislinianus (from Coislin, a former bishop of Metz), and Laudianus (after Archbishop Laud of Canterbury).

The manner of referring to the various codices has varied, and there are, at the present time, several methods of reference. Since the time of Dr John Mill (*d.* 1707) and, in particular, since Wettstein's great edition of 1752 ff., it has been customary to use letters of the Latin alphabet to designate uncials and Arabic numerals for cursives. The system was improved by Tischendorf and Scrivener, who added the Greek letters from Gamma to Omega and the Hebrew letters from Aleph to Daleth. So A = Codex Alexandrinus, B = Codex Vaticanus, C = Codex Ephraemi rescriptus, D = Codex Bezae or Cantabrigiensis (presented to the Cambridge University library in 1581 by Theodore Beza, the Reformation scholar), and Aleph = Codex Sinaiticus.

Gregory, whose enumeration of MSS has already been cited, in his book *Die griechischen Handschriften des N.T.*

(Leipzig, 1908), retains the old capitals (Aleph, A–Z, **582a** Gamma–Omega) for the 45 oldest uncials, or uses numbers 01–045 ; for the remaining uncials he used the numbers 046–0161. Minuscules are designated by the numbers 1–2292, with the addition of the letters e (= *evangelium*), a (= *apostolicum*) or p (= *paulinum*) to indicate the part of NT contained in a particular codex. Lectionaries are shown by Arabic numerals preceded by 1. Papyri are noted by the letter P followed by Arabic numerals from 1–14.

More recently still, Freiherr Hermann von Soden (1852–1914) distinguished three classes of codices by the Greek letters δ (= *diathêkê*) for the whole NT, ε (*euangelion*) and α (*apostolos*). He also designed an ingenious but highly complicated system for showing at a glance the absolute or relative dating of a codex. Thus numbers 1–49 stand for codices dating from the fourth to the ninth cent. ; 50–99 are tenth-cent. codices. In later codices the first number shows the century. So δ1 = Codex Vaticanus of the fourth cent. ; δ2 = Codex Sinaiticus, also of the fourth ; δ3 = Codex Ephraemi of the 5th cent. ; δ121 = an 11th-cent. codex.

For ordinary use the oldest method is perhaps the **b** most important, but either of the two later systems has something to recommend it. On the whole the balance of approval among textual critics inclines towards Gregory's relatively simple and easily memorized system.

For a list of the chief MS codices reference may be made to the work of Sir Frederic Kenyon on *The Text of the Greek Bible*, which has in ch 3 a sufficiently full account of the ' Manuscripts of the New Testament '. For a short list of Gospel MSS, *cf.* F. M. Braun, *op. cit.*, 486, in which the MSS are divided into four groups, after the manner of Lagrange's *Projet de critique textuelle rationnelle du N.T.*, RB 41 (1933) 481–98. These are (1) The B group (a moderate and generally faithful revision of the now unavailable originals)=*les bons* (*i.e.* codices B, Aleph, C, T, Z, L and Daleth (for Mk). (2) The A group (a thoroughgoing revision in the interests of stylistic excellence ; the prototypes of the famous *textus receptus* of the Renaissance humanists) = *les antiochiens* (*i.e.* A, E[e], Omega, Daleth [non-Marcan] H[e], V, G[e]). (3) The D group (a thorough revision with an eye to harmonization and simplified readings) = *divers* (*i.e.* D[e] and W [Mk 1–5:30]). (4) The C group (occupying a position intermediate between B and D) = *césaréen* (*i.e.* W. N. Theta, Pi, K[e]). These groups will be more fully explained in the following section on the families of Gk codices.

It may be added that the highly important Codex **c** Aleph or Sinaiticus, acquired by the British Museum from the Soviet authorities in 1934, is well described in the pamphlet *The Mount Sinai Manuscript of the Bible*. The most sensational discovery of recent times is that of the Chester Beatty papyri, first publicly announced in *The Times* (19 Nov. 1931), and fully discussed in Kenyon's *Recent Developments in the Textual Criticism of the Greek Bible* (1933). This discovery is valuable in three ways. It carries the date of the Greek Bible back for some decades and provides a substantial portion of 3rd-cent. NT MSS ; it shows a text free from all suspicion of Byzantine revision and not manifesting the prominent Western variants ; and it confirms the early use of the codex form of book by the Christian community.

The Families of Greek Codices—It is common know- **d** ledge that there is a considerable variety of readings between the numerous NT codices, but it was not until the time of Albert Bengel (1687–1752) that the problem was simplified by dividing the different codices into *families*. The term is clearly explained by Kenyon, *Text of Greek Bible*, 11 : ' If in a given manuscript of any work some words are wrongly transcribed, or a passage omitted, every manuscript copied from it, or from copies of it, will have the same mistake or the same omission ; and if among the extant manuscripts we find that several have the same important mistake or

582d omission, it is legitimate to argue that they are all descended from the manuscript in which that mistake or omission was first made '. That is, we may assign the various MSS to different families or groups with characteristic types of readings, much as Shakespearean scholars distinguish the text of *Hamlet* in the pirated First Quarto of 1603 from that of the Second Quarto of 1604, and both of these from the readings of the

e First Folio of 1623. Bengel divided the codices known to him into Asiatic and African, a grouping that roughly corresponds to Westcott and Hort's later divisions into Syrian and Alexandrian. J. J. Griesbach (1745–1812) developed the 'family' hypothesis on lines still recognized as essentially sound. He classified three groups of MSS, *i.e.* (1) the Alexandrian or Origenian, so called because the type occurs principally in Origen's quotations, in codices A, B, C and L, and in the Egyptian (Bohairic and Sahidic) versions; (2) the Western, so styled because its characteristic readings are found in the Latin Fathers and in Codex D; (3) the Constantinopolitan, the text of the great majority of Greek MSS. He judged the last to be less valuable than the other two, but his principle was that, in default of any exclusion on grounds of internal criticism, a majority verdict of two to one among the groups was to be accepted. K. Lachmann (1793–1851) made further progress by excluding a great mass of the extant MSS as containing a text that was palpably late. So, for practical purposes he divided the MSS between two great families, the Eastern (A, B, C, etc., and Origen) and the Western (D, D^2, D^3, the Old Latin, Vulgate, etc.). The editions of Tregelles and Tischendorf (1815–74) depend for their principles mainly upon Lachmann.

f The Cambridge scholars, Brook Foss **Westcott** (1825–1901) and Fenton John Anthony **Hort** (1829–91), were responsible for the most important edition of modern times. The edition was first projected in 1853, but was not made public until 1881. It was accompanied by a long introduction by Hort on the critical principles guiding the selection of MSS. Neither scholar was, however, a specialist in palaeography or comparative philology. They did, in the event, succeed in arranging and explaining the quantity of codices amassed by Tischendorf.

By applying a variety of tests (such as the evidence of conflation in the Patristic use of the NT, and of internal criticism) they were able to distinguish four types of text. These were, first, the *Syrian* (not to be confused with Syriac), which is that of the vast majority of MSS, and which, in their view, was an eclectic text, following now one earlier text, now another, and frequently combining two texts into one by *conflation* (*i.e.* the fusing together of readings). An example of this is Lk 24:53, where one set of early authorities (Aleph, B, C, L, with the Coptic versions and the Sinaitic and Palestinian Syriac) have ' blessing God ', Codex D and the Old Latin versions have ' praising God ', and the majority of MSS (*i.e.* the *Syrian* group, including Codex A, twelve other uncials, all the cursives, Vg and other versions) have ' praising and blessing God '. Westcott and Hort further distinguish three pre-Syrian texts, *i.e.* the *Alexandrian*, the *Western* and the *Neutral*. Of these the first is the least important, since the changes made in it are very slight and it almost certainly depends upon the Neutral tradition. The other two, however, are very early, and go back as far as we have knowledge of distinctive texts. On Westcott and Hort's showing there was a time, earlier than the fourth and probably earlier than the middle third cent., when the NT text was transmitted in two great traditions—the Western and the Neutral. Then a group of copyists or editors, probably in Syria and possibly at Antioch, produced an eclectic text that sometimes follows the Western, sometimes the Neutral, and sometimes, as in the examples they give, combines the two by conflation.

g Of the two earliest and most important types of text, they regard the Western as a very early and very

corrupt source, a product of free interpolation and paraphrase at a time when the need for scrupulous preservation of the original text was still imperfectly appreciated. For them the **Neutral text** (as found in the great uncials Aleph and B and some other MSS) is the most reliable text. One exception, however, they make, for they lay stress upon the Western text's *omissions* or ' non-interpolations ', on the ground that a text that is so prone to interpolate and expand would never omit except for some critically excellent reason. In the interval since 1881 their methods and results have been so often attacked that it is important to realize that, in certain vital respects, their work remains unshaken, though all but seventy years have passed since the definitive issue of their introduction and text.

In the first place, it is not open to doubt that the vast majority of extant MSS represent a later text. Kenyon (*Text of the Greek Bible*, 203) prefers to style it the Byzantine recension, since this title ' makes no assertion as to its origin, but merely records the unquestioned fact that it is the text which dominated the whole Church of the Byzantine Empire '. Secondly, it is all but equally certain that the Neutral tradition represents an exceedingly pure and early stage of the text, and that it has in its favour the oldest vellum MSS of any size, *i.e.* Codices Aleph and B. Later criticism, however, tends to regard their contention regarding the quasi-innate superiority of the Neutral family not as altogether unfounded but as insufficiently proved.

The Neutral text is, indeed, one that comes as regards its main representative, from only one corner of the Christian world, and is thoroughly attested by only one version, *i.e.* the Memphitic or Northern Egyptian version, for the earlier Egyptian version (*i.e.* the Sahidic) does not give it such definite support. The three chief Fathers who bear witness to it (Clement, Origen and St Cyril of Alexandria) are all Alexandrians, and of these Clement has been shown, since Westcott and Hort's time, to have an unexpectedly large Western element in his text. So far as can be ascertained all the MSS giving this type of text were written or copied at Alexandria. In spite of Hort's surmise that ' B and Aleph were both written in the West, probably at Rome ' (*op. cit.* 267), it can hardly be doubted that B was written at Alexandria, and that, though Aleph was probably written at Caesarea, it is based upon an Alexandrian text, brought to Caesarea by Origen when he left Alexandria in A.D. 231.

There is, in fact, ample evidence for the view that the Neutral family may represent the revised, as contrasted with the unrevised text. True, as Kenyon writes : ' If it is the result of editorial handling, the editor was one who was seeking an original text. It is not harmonistic, it does not cultivate smoothness of phrase, it does not seek additions. It may be described as an austere text'. (*Recent Developments in the Textual Criticism of the Greek Bible*, 85.) In any case, it is a local, not a universal text, and is to be controlled with the help of other texts. Of these the most notable is the large Western group, principally found in the Greek uncials D (Gospels and *Acts*), E^2 (*Acts*) and D^2 (Pauline epistles) with a number of Old Latin MSS, and, as regards a large number of their readings, the Old Syriac versions (Sinaitic and Curetonian). Of these the Old Latin and Old Syriac are by no means in complete agreement ; many of the readings of the oldest Syriac version are aligned with B rather than with the Latin group. Yet the evidence of the versions supporting it does at least go to show that the Western text, in one form of another, has a greater claim to be heard than Hort ever suspected, and this not only in its omissions but in its additions. At times, in fact, it seems to give a purer and less revised reading than the so-called Neutral family.

In recent years, as a result of work by Kirsopp Lake, Blake, Streeter and others, a new group has been identified—the **Caesarean family**, made up of the so-called Koridethi MS (Theta), the Washington c codex (W), two groups of minuscules known as families 1 and 13, certain other minuscules (*e.g.* 28, 566 and 700), and the Chester Beatty papyrus 45. Textually this group hold a position intermediate between the Neutral and Western families, though in its major variants it usually sides with B. It derives its importance from its association with Origen, Eusebius and the school of Caesarea. But the examination of this text and the determination of its type are still incomplete.

It does not follow from these data that the NT text is an uncertain one. It is far better attested than any other work of ancient literature and the difficulties arise rather from an excess than from a defect of evidence. Most of the variants are quite trivial in character, so that, in Hort's phrase, the amount of substantial variation ' can hardly form more than a thousandth part of the entire text '. (The New Testament in the Original Greek, *Introduction*, 2.)

d On the whole, the conclusion must be, in the present state of our knowledge, that, whereas the Byzantine and Western texts show abundant traces of free editorial revision, this is less evident in the Neutral and Caesarean families. Their revision was the work of scholarly editors, who desired an authentic text rather than an easy one. These texts have neither the substantial additions of the Western, nor the harmonizing and stylistic alterations of the Byzantine. We can regard them as the best available for the recovery of the authentic (or earliest obtainable) text of the NT, while relying, as opportunity offers, on such sporadic readings of other MSS as can be shown to be of early date.

In this work of reconstructing the text, we rely not only on texts and versions, but on patristic quotations. So Irenaeus quotes the NT about 1,800 times, Clement of Alexandria 2,400 times, Origen some 18,000 times. The shorter quotations are sometimes an unreliable guide to the text, since the Fathers frequently quote from memory. But the longer quotations, when there is agreement among witnesses of an early date, are a most valuable guide to the primitive text as it first came forth from its inspired authors.

e **Printed Editions of the Greek NT**—The *editio princeps* of the Greek NT is vol. V of the Complutensian (Alcala) Polyglot, finished 1514, published in 1522, and later re-edited in the Antwerp Polyglot of 1571 and by Gratz at Tübingen in 1821.

Almost simultaneously (1516) Erasmus produced a Greek text with a Latin version and notes. His claim to have used the oldest and best codices is unsubstantiated, and the last six verses of the Apoc (wanting in his MS) were supplied by translating the Vulgate into Greek ! The famous ' Three Witnesses ' text (1 Jn 5:7–8) was inserted in the third (1522) edition on the authority of a solitary Greek MS, the Codex Montfortianus or Britannicus (61 ; 15th or 16th cent.). A little later, the Aldine edition (Feb. 1518/1519) was published by Aldus Manutius at Venice, and the Paris edition (1534) by Simon Colinaeus.

Robertus Stephanus printed four editions. The third (1550) is the *editio regia*, dedicated to King Henry II, and in the fourth (1551) the division into verses first occurs. For the text he used mostly Erasmus revised according to the Complutensian Polyglot. Theodore Beza (*d.* 1605) produced many editions of NT (*e.g.* 1565, 1582, 1588, 1598) based mostly on Stephanus, though with some use of MSS and Fathers.

f In 1623 Bonaventure and Abraham Elzevir printed at Leyden a mixed text based on Stephanus and Beza. **583f** In the preface to the second (1633) edition occur the words : ' Textum ergo habes nunc ab omnibus receptum : in quo nihil immutatum aut corruptum damus '. This *textus receptus* was, until comparatively recent times, much esteemed and frequently reprinted.

The first really critical edition seems to have been that of John Mill (1645–1707), who in the year of his death issued the third (*regia*) edition of Stephanus with an apparatus including some 30,000 variants, drawn from 78 MSS. The great Richard Bentley (1662–1742) never carried out his project for a critical edition. The work was later undertaken with varying degrees of success by Wettstein (who first established the system of reference to MSS by letters and numbers), Bengel and Lachmann. The last set aside the evidence of the printed texts, in particular that of the *textus receptus*, and sought to recover the text in existence in the 4th cent. His first edition came out in 1831 ; his second, with notes on the readings added by the great philologist Philip Buttmann, of *Lexilogus* fame, appeared in 1842 (vol. I) and 1850 (vol. II).

Of later editors one must specially mention Tischendorf, **g** whose eighth edition (1864–72) has yet to be superseded by the new Oxford text, of which the first volume (Mark) and the second (Matthew) appeared respectively in 1935 and 1939. It has met with severe criticism, and it seems unlikely that such a task can be continued by a single editor. *Cf.* T. W. Manson JTS 43 (1942) 83–92.

Westcott and Hort's text is excellent, but there is no full *apparatus criticus*. The notes on selected readings are a poor substitute for a complete justification of the text adopted by these scholars.

Of recent non-Catholic texts one need only mention the late Eberhard Nestle's ' resultant ' text, based on majority verdicts of the three editions of Tischendorf, Westcott and Hort, and Bernhard Weiss. It was first issued in 1906, and the sixteenth (1936) edition contains a reasonably full *apparatus*.

Up to the year 1834 Catholics had taken little part in these labours. In that year appeared the Greek NT of Scholz (*d.* 1852), a Catholic critic who examined and partially collated nearly 1,000 MSS. Authorities differ regarding his care and competence as a collator ; Gregory says that his collations are very good. (*Canon and Text of the New Testament*, 1907, 452.)

Among recent editors mention should be made, **h** though only as an awful warning, of Fr Brandscheid's *Novum Testamentum graece* (*editio altera, emendatior*, Freiburg i/B, 1901), in which the Greek is corrected according to the Latin, surely a critical monstrosity ! The two latest and best editions by Catholics are those of the celebrated Bonn professor, Dr H. J. Vogels, published at Düsseldorf (1920 ff.), and that of P. Augustin Merk, S. J., *Novum Testamentum Graece et Latine*, published at Rome in 1933 (sixth edition, 1948). Neither of these editions is wholly satisfactory, and it is to be hoped that some other Catholic scholar of repute may, sooner or later, attempt the production of a text with an apparatus fuller than that of Vogels and less complicated than that of P. Merk. In the article mentioned above Professor Manson has argued forcibly for the use, as a medium of collation, of the *textus receptus*, which fulfils the twofold criterion of being old enough to be in no danger of becoming out of date, and of making fairly certain that such variants as appear in the apparatus will be really significant.

THE JEWISH WORLD
IN NEW TESTAMENT TIMES

By J. L. McKENZIE, S.J.

584a Bibliography—J. Bonsirven, S.J., *Judaïsme Palestinien au temps de J.-C.*, 1934² ; *Bousset-Gressmann, *Religion des Judentums im NT Zeitalter*, 1926³ ; *R. H. Charles, *Religious Development between the Old and the New Testaments*, nd ; *A. C. Deane, *The World Christ knew*, 1946 ; M.-J. Lagrange, *Judaïsme avant J.-C.*, 1931³ ; *W. O. E. Oesterley, *The Jews and Judaism during the Greek Period*, 1941 ; *E. Schürer, *Jewish People in the Time of Christ* (Eng. tr.), nd.

b Introduction—At the beginning of the Christian era Jerusalem and Judaea were the centre of the Jewish world. Outside of Palestine, Jewish settlements were found in most of the large cities of the eastern Roman Empire, and in Babylonia. The largest and most influential communities were in Babylonia and Egypt. While the Jews living abroad were somewhat assimilated to the Gentile population of the cities in which they dwelt, the powerful influence of Palestinian Jewry imposed on Jews everywhere a unity of religious belief and practice which gave Judaism a distinctive character, and prevented its absorption by Greco-Roman culture.

c Sources—The principal contemporary sources for the history of Judaism are :
A. Flavius Josephus (*b.* A.D. 38), the Jewish historian ; fought in the rebellion of A.D. 66–70 ; was taken and pardoned by the Romans, and became a client of the Flavian house. In the *Jewish Antiquities* and the *Jewish War* Josephus has preserved much information about pre-Christian Judaism not found elsewhere ; but he is uncritical in his use of sources.
B. Rabbinical Writings : (*a*) The *Mishnah*, a collection of the oral traditions of the Rabbis by which the Law was interpreted, amplified, and applied to particular situations. These traditions are *Halakhic* (legal) or *Haggadic* (doctrinal). Since the collection was not made until the close of the second cent. A.D., it must be employed with caution to determine Jewish ideas of the NT period. (*b*) *Midrashim*, or interpretations of the Scriptures.
C. Apocalyptic Literature. A great number of works appeared during the period 200 B.C.–A.D. 100 which, under the pseudonym of ancient figures (such as Henoch or Esdras), pretended to be predictions of the downfall of the great heathen powers and the establishment of the Jewish kingdom of God. It is uncertain how far these works represent the prevailing sentiments of Judaism of the time.
D. The New Testament, especially the Gospels.
E. Profane historians. Tacitus (*Historiae* V) gives a brief sketch of Judaism. Other Roman historians (Suetonius), and satirists (Horace, Juvenal) allude to Jewish beliefs and practices. These works, which exhibit a profound anti-Jewish prejudice, are biased and inaccurate ; but they indicate a common attitude towards Judaism among the Gentiles.

d Palestinian Judaism—Up to the fall of the monarchy in 586 B.C., the Hebrew religion and the Hebrew nation had been identified. The restoration of the Jewish commonwealth under the Persians in 538 B.C. did not restore the original conditions. In NT times many more Jews lived dispersed in Gentile lands than in Palestine itself. The language of Palestinian Jews was no longer Hebrew, but Aramaic (another Semitic

language closely akin to Hebrew) which was spoken throughout most of the Near East. Palestine was now, instead of an independent state, a province of a world empire, with a much smaller area than that ruled by the Hebrew monarchies. The territory in which Jews formed a majority of the population was limited to Judaea, Galilee and Peraea. This territory was an island in a sea of Gentile populations which surrounded it on north, east and south. Most of the Palestinian Jewish population belonged to the humbler peasant and tradesmen's classes. The loss of political independence meant that Judaism became a religion ; the kingdom of God, the theocracy, existed only as an ideal to be realized in some distant future. But the consciousness of the identity of religion and nation survived in Judaism to express itself in two different directions : the political nationalism of the Hasmonaean period (165–163 B.C.) and of the Zealots who rebelled against Rome in A.D. 66, and the religious nationalism of the Pharisees.

It was in these four centuries, and in Palestine, that Judaism developed those distinctive traits which made it unique in the ancient world. Several factors contributed to this : the successful effort of the Jews in Babylon to resist assimilation ; the feud with the Samaritans, in which the Jewish community closed itself against any foreign admixture ; the promulgation of the Law by Esdras, by which Jewish life was based upon the strict observance of the Law ; and the Maccabean wars, in which the threat of Hellenization was successfully resisted by violence, and a short-lived Jewish state was established.

The effort of the Jews to retain their distinct identity and to preserve themselves against foreign influence resulted in a characteristic exclusivism. Palestinian Judaism refused any contact with Gentiles beyond that of bare necessity—a theory which was never abandoned, although it was impossible to reduce it to practice. The Jew was required by law to do business with his own, to marry his own, to enjoy social relations with his own. Any contact with a Gentile caused ritual impurity. Gentiles defiled land, houses and food. The obligations of justice and charity were not as strict towards Gentiles as they were between Jews. Just those features of Jewish law and ritual which emphasized the separation of the Jew from the Gentile were most insisted upon. The Gentiles usually, and not always without reason, thought the Jews were haughty.

Social and Economic Conditions in Palestine—The social and economic conditions of Palestine in NT times were generally similar to those which were found throughout the eastern Roman Empire, especially to those of the neighbouring regions of Syria and Egypt. It is the opinion of some writers that Palestine was one of the most prosperous countries of the empire ; but it is difficult to be certain about this. Palestine was an agricultural country. Its principal crops were wheat and barley, of which there was normally an annual surplus for export. Besides the grains, Palestine produced fruit in abundance : olives, figs, grapes, dates. In NT times the forests of Palestine had not yet been destroyed ; and, while it is a question how rich this resource of Palestine was, we can be certain that timber was abundant in comparison with modern times. The pasturing of sheep and goats, mentioned so frequently in the OT, was still carried on, but it no longer had the economic importance which it possessed under the Hebrew monarchy. Palestinian Jews in NT times were not engaged in trade and commerce on a large scale. Outside of Jerusalem, there was no Jewish city of any importance ; and Jerusalem itself was not a great market. Trade and commerce were centred in the cities of the coast and in the Decapolis, which were the ports of entry for foreign goods and the agents of export for Palestinian products. These cities were entirely or predominantly Greek. The cities on the shore of the Lake of Galilee were also important trading centres for the region ; but here again there was a large Greek population. In Jerusalem itself there were a few wealthy Jewish merchants and bankers ; but they were a small minority. Their economic importance, of course, was out of all proportion to their numbers.

Palestine at the time of Jesus had probably reached the peak of its population in ancient times. Exact figures are not available ; two million (including Trans-jordan) would be a conservative estimate. The country had enjoyed peace since the Roman conquest by Pompey in 63 B.C., and had not yet suffered the horrors of the revolt of A.D. 66–70, which left the country ravaged and depopulated. In spite of the emigration of Jews to foreign countries, conditions were favourable to a rapid growth of population.

The population of Palestine was not racially homogeneous ; indeed, it had never been. Of the three divisions of the country, Judaea, Samaria and Galilee, Judaea was the most Jewish both in population and in ideas and practice. Samaria was regarded by the Jews themselves as an alien enclave—a judgement which was hardly accurate ; the mixed origins of the Samaritans were more Hebrew than anything else, and the religion of the Samaritans was a schismatic Judaism. Galilee was so mixed as to be cosmopolitan. Its cities were mostly Greek, its rural areas mostly Jewish ; but there was a free interchange between city and country. This was reflected in the language of the three regions ; it is probable that Judaea spoke mostly Aramaic, while Greek was probably as important in Galilee as Aramaic. Some scholars think Jesus and his Apostles, like most of the Galileans, were bilingual. Among themselves, however, Jews employed Aramaic.

The prosperity of the three regions was proportionate to their Gentile population. Galilee, blessed with a more fertile soil and with better communications to the outside world, was the richest part of the country. The great trade route which connected Egypt with Damascus, Syria and Mesopotamia passed up the coast without touching Judaea and Samaria directly ; it then turned north-east and went through the heart of Galilee. The route from Damascus to Arabia was easily reached from Galilee, while the route from Arabia to Gaza ignored Judaea altogether. Hence Judaea retained its Jewish insularity, and looked with some suspicion on the Galileans as half heathen.

There was a certain tension between Jerusalem and the Judaean countryside, and still more between Judaea and Galilee. Jerusalem was the residence of the priestly aristocracy and the wealthy merchants and landlords, whose wealth was built upon the labourers and the peasants. It was also the centre of Jewish learning, where the most distinguished rabbis were found. Their legal decisions were binding on the poor workers, for whom the Pharisaic interpretation of the Law was often impossible. Jerusalem had the typical urban contempt of the countryman. In one feature Galilee excelled Jerusalem, and that was Jewish nationalism. It was in Galilee that the revolt broke out in A.D. 66. The ruling classes of Jerusalem, whose position depended on political and economic stability, were of necessity linked with the government, whether it was the government of Herod or of a Roman procurator. The Gospels contrast the enthusiasm of the Galileans for the Messianic kingdom with the coldness of the men of Jerusalem. **584i**

It is difficult to speak of social classes among Palestinian **j** Jews ; for even in NT times the Jews had begun to manifest that social solidarity which has been so characteristic of them throughout their subsequent history. Theoretically, the Jews were a democratic society ; at the time of Jesus the Hasmonaean aristocracy was practically extinct, and the Herodian aristocracy was never accepted by the Jews. The Jewish aristocracy was composed of a few priestly families, who were also the wealthy families. This does not mean that all the priestly families were wealthy ; they were not. Pride in Jewish blood was so great that any Jew who could vindicate his ancestry regarded himself as socially the equal of any other. Practically, of course, things did not work out this way. The Jewish aristocracy was an aristocracy of wealth rather than of blood. At the same time there was the aristocracy of the masters of the Law, which was not coterminous with the aristocracy of wealth. Jewish social classes were fluid and hard to define ; but there were divisions and a certain social unrest beneath the superficial unity of Palestinian Judaism.

It was quite otherwise with the economic classes, which **k** had reached a fixed stratification in NT times. There were no middle classes between the wealthy and the poor ; and both wealth and poverty were extreme. Wealth came from commerce and ownership of land ; since these remained in the same families, fortunes grew through successive generations. Dives of the parable, Lk 11:19 ff., was an extreme example, but the wealthy could recognize themselves in his portrait. Whether they were, as a class, as insensitive to the needs of the poor as Dives of the parable is open to question. Almsgiving was much recommended by the rabbis ; but we can be certain that whatever almsgiving was practised did nothing to remove the horrible social blight of poverty.

The employments of the poor were agriculture, the crafts, and unskilled labour. The Lake of Galilee gave employment to a large number of fishermen, whose product was consumed throughout Palestine ; this class is of interest to the reader of the Gospels because the first disciples of Jesus were chosen from it. Jesus himself was a craftsman, and not on the lowest rung of the economic ladder ; the craftsmen were better off than others. In a village like Nazareth Jesus may have been the only man to practise his trade ; in Jerusalem he would have had his shop in one of the bazaars in which it was customary for merchants of the same wares and workers of the same craft to congregate. Some writers speak of whole villages devoted to a single craft.

Beneath the craftsmen we find the peasant. The **l** peasant tilled the soil of a wealthy landowner who probably resided in Jerusalem. The peasant himself resided in a village with other peasants, each of whom had his strip of land in the neighbourhood. The yield, of course, was not to be compared with that of modern agriculture. The peasant had to meet the rent, the taxes and the tithes. We do not know what the rent may have been ; the taxes paid to Rome were 25 per cent of the yield. The tithes for the Temple came to 22 per cent of the remainder. The peasant was expected to pay a second tithe for the poor ; it is thought that this was rarely paid. Nor is it likely that the full Temple tithe was always paid. If the rents corresponded to these obligations—as they probably did—it is not hard to calculate how much was left for the peasant.

Rents, taxes and tithes were paid in kind. Taxes were not collected by the Roman officials themselves. The estimated revenue was based on a census ; we read of such a census in the year of the birth of Jesus. The taxes were then farmed out to speculators, the 'publicans' of the Gospel, and the contract was awarded to the highest bidder. The tax-farmer was then free to collect as much revenue as he could ;

584l his profit, of course, was what he collected above the price he paid for the contract. He could appeal to the Roman military to enforce his requisitions.

m Beneath the peasant was the unskilled labourer, the ' hireling ' of the Gospel. Slavery in Palestine was comparatively rare ; Jewish sentiment was opposed to the enslavement of one Jew by another, and the country was not wealthy enough to import large numbers of slaves from abroad. But the very existence of slavery depressed the unskilled labourers. They hired themselves out for whatever work was available, usually by the day. There was always a large number of unemployed ; and competition depressed the income of the labourer still more. But it is not likely that the difference between this proletariat and the skilled worker was really great. The poverty of the mass of the population of Palestine probably did not differ much from that of the average population of the Empire, but it was appalling. On the other hand, we must not judge the attitude of these people towards their poverty by our modern ideas. They were born to it, and economic stratification prevented any higher ambitions. A drought, a war, an insect plague inevitably meant slavery or starvation ; but the poor were accustomed to face such dangers as a normal part of life.

Furthermore, the dignity of manual labour was much praised by the rabbis. The fact that a man earned his living by manual labour was not a social stigma. Not only Jesus and St Paul, but many of the great rabbis practised a trade ; and they were accepted in the homes of the great because of their knowledge of the Law. The poor, if we may judge from some Gospel passages, had very free access to the homes of the rich.

n Below the unskilled labourers were the social outcasts. Like the Samaritans, a Jew of mixed origin, or a Jew who took on Greek ways, was an object of disdain. A tax-farmer like Matthew or Zacheus was a moral leper. The sick, the crippled, the aged and the orphans who had no families to support them were at the mercy of an unfeeling world. Beggars were common. There were always men who were discontented with Roman rule, or who had fallen under the suspicion of the authorities, who fled to the desert and a life of banditry, preying impartially on Jew and Gentile alike. There was often a strong bond of sympathy between such bandits and the poor and the extreme nationalists.

Debt was an additional curse on the poor. Since their margin was so small, any emergency threw them into the hands of the moneylenders ; and we have no reason to believe that the Scribes could not circumvent the law prohibiting interest between Jews. The interest rates were probably exorbitant, although we cannot give exact figures ; we know that the honourable Brutus charged 50 per cent in Rome. While this did not always result in personal enslavement, it did mean economic enthralment for the peasant, who lived at subsistence level, or less, when he fell into debt. There is no historical evidence that the law of jubilee, with its universal remission of debt, was ever observed.

One effect of the general poverty was (surprisingly) that early marriages were the rule. A boy or girl of twelve years was regarded as grown enough to leave the home ; the family wished to be rid of them as soon as possible. If the boy could not find a trade from his father or his relatives, he was cast into the great reservoir of the unemployed. Early marriage and childbirth were followed in the natural course by premature senescence, which meant that more helpless persons were thrown upon society.

o The food of the poor was very simple. Only the few wealthy could afford the luxury articles of diet imported from abroad. The staples of the poor were wheat or barley bread and dried fish. Meat was a rare treat. Vegetables—leeks, lentils, beans—and dried fruit were Palestinian products. Wine was produced in Palestine and was in common use, although the best wine was exported. The poor man

would scarcely have more than one set of garments : the tunic, which was his ordinary dress, and a cloak for inclement weather and for sleeping. The houses of the poor were of stone, one or two storeys, usually shared by several families ; the very poor might share a room among several families. The houses, even in the villages, were built very close together ; only narrow alleys were left for passage and for the disposal of refuse. The site of the village was determined by the availability of water ; it would be an unusually favoured site if there were more than one well. The water supply was supplemented by cisterns.

It is important to understand this background of the Gospels and the early expansion of Christianity. Christianity was the only movement of any kind in ancient times which arose in the masses. Jesus himself, like his first followers, belonged to the poor, and he spoke to them in the first place. They listened to him, because he was one of themselves. When Christianity spread into the great cities of the Roman Empire its appeal was to the poor ; and it reached the upper classes from below.

The Temple and the Priesthood—The Temple of Jerusalem, as the one place where sacrifice could be legitimately offered, was the official centre of Jewish worship. It was the desire of every pious Jew, whether in Palestine or abroad, to visit the Temple at one of the great annual feasts ; and we are told that many travelled long distances to gratify this desire. The second Temple, dedicated in 516 B.C., stood until the erection of the Temple of Herod at the beginning of the Christian era. This great structure, planned on a truly magnificent scale, was completed shortly before it was razed to the ground by the Romans in A.D. 70 (but *cf.* comm. on Jn 2:20 *infra*).

The priesthood enjoyed a position of great importance, certainly greater than it had under the monarchy. The priesthood was a distinct hereditary order. Priests might marry women of non-priestly families ; but they must be undefiled virgins or widows of pure Israelite extraction. The high-priest might marry only an undefiled Israelite virgin. Contact with death was prohibited, since this caused ritual uncleanness. The priests had to be free of any physical defect which marred their appearance or disqualified them to perform priestly functions. They were inducted into the sacerdotal office by a rite of consecration called ' filling of the hands ', in which they received in their hands portions of the sacred flesh of the sacrificial victim. Since the number of priests was far in excess of that necessary for the Temple service, they were divided into twenty-four courses, each of which served in turn. Within the courses there were further divisions into specialized offices, which involved a difference in rank. The Levites, like the priests, were a hereditary order. They were entrusted with subordinate duties (singers, janitors, servants of the priests).

The priests and the Temple services were maintained by revenues from the people. To the priests belonged first-fruits and the first-born of animals, and the money paid for the redemption of first-born sons ; portions of sacrificial victims ; tithes on all produce or profits ; voluntary and votive offerings ; and a half-shekel annual tax on every male Israelite over twenty years of age. The Jerusalem Temple, like many pagan temples, was used as a place of safe deposit for money and valuables. The Temple had its own police force, the jurisdiction of which was not limited to the Temple.

The power of the high-priest was much increased during the post-exilic period. Under the imperial governments of Persia, Syria and Rome the high-priest was the supreme native magistrate under the provincial authorities. The Maccabees were a priestly family ; and in Simon (140 B.C.) the offices of high-priest and head of the independent Jewish state were united. This double dignity was retained by the succeeding members of the Hasmonaean dynasty (except Alexandra) until its fall before Pompey (63 B.C.).

c This overweening power of the high-priest met with an actively hostile reaction from the Pharisees, and it created a deep cleft between the sacerdotal aristocracy and the mass of the people. This cleft was widened by the Hellenistic inclinations of priestly families, both before and after the Maccabean wars. After the Roman conquest the high-priests were appointed by the Roman authorities. By political manoeuvering the members of a few priestly families kept the appointment for themselves. The influence of high-priests after their term of office (such as Annas) was very great.

d The worship of the Temple was conducted in a sumptuous manner, and the contributions of the people to its support were heavy. The chief daily services of the Temple were the burnt-offering on behalf of the people each morning and evening, and the offering of incense daily at the same time. The Levites accompanied these offerings with vocal and instrumental music. There was always a large attendance of the public at these daily services. On the Sabbath and the major festivals more numerous victims were offered. It is characteristic of post-exilic Judaism that the expiatory and propitiatory purpose of sacrifice was emphasized rather than the joyous and grateful sentiment of many pre-exilic offerings. The attitude of the pious Jew towards the ritual of the Temple is expressed in Ecclus 50:1 ff.

e The Scriptures—It is impossible to determine exactly when the first collection of sacred books was made. The Jews, under the leadership of Esdras, bound themselves to the observance of the Torah, or Law of Moses, Neh 8–10. The date of this event is uncertain (*cf.* §§ 289*i–q*, 297*a–d*). It is clear from the prologue of Ecclus that a collection which included ' the Law, the Prophets and the Writings ' was in existence in 130 B.C. We do not know by what authority it was determined which books should be included in the collection. The sacred books should have been in the custody of the priesthood, and it is to them that the first collection should in all probability be attributed. But we find that the Scribes subsequently asserted their authority to exclude books from the collection. The vagueness of this determination is seen in the existence of two canons . the Palestinian canon, represented by the OT in Hebrew, and the Alexandrine canon represented by the OT in Greek, which contained books not admitted into the Palestinian collection.

f The influence of the sacred books on Judaism cannot be overestimated. The Law was the entire basis of Jewish life and piety. Both the Law and the Prophets formed the material of the synagogue lessons. The use of the Psalms in the Temple liturgy and in the worship of the synagogue coloured the language and the attitude of Jewish prayer. The ordinary Jew was familiar with the text of the sacred books. Mohammed called Judaism ' the religion of the book '. To the Jew his books comprised all wisdom and learning, and a complete code of right conduct.

g The Law—The five books of Moses, called the *Tôrah*, were the most highly venerated of the sacred books. *Tôrah* actually means ' instruction ' or ' doctrine ' rather than ' law ' ; and a large portion of the books of Moses is narrative. From the narrative portions as well as from the legal portions were deduced conclusions about God, his Providence, and human conduct. ' Law ', however, expresses accurately the attitude of Judaism towards these books. The basis of legal observance was faith in the covenant of God with Israel and in divine retribution. The minute regulations of the Law extended to almost every detail of life ; and what the Law did not explicitly touch was covered by applications, sometimes quite far-fetched, of general precepts. As a matter of fact, the laws of the Mosaic code were never intended to be such a universal and detailed guide of conduct. The extension of legal obligation into every detail of private and public life could not but result in an externalizing of religion to some degree. By some Jews mere external

observances were esteemed as grave as duties of piety, **585g** justice and charity. From the fact that the greater number of precepts is prohibitive it follows that there was a certain negative character about Jewish observance.

Special emphasis was placed on those observances **h** which were distinctive of Judaism : circumcision, the Sabbath, and legal cleanliness. Circumcision was not, in its origins, a peculiarly Jewish practice ; but in pre-Christian centuries it had become such a mark of Judaism that Jews who wished to adopt the Greek way of life and Greek manners resorted to a painful surgical operation in order to rid themselves of the sign of their religion. The Sabbath observance was understood to mean a complete rest from all activity. Even food should be prepared on the preceding day. The distance which one might walk was restricted to 2,000 cubits (about 3,000 feet) ; by leaving a bundle of food, however, one was considered to establish a temporary domicile which enlarged the scope of travel. A whole block of houses, or a quarter of a city, might be considered as a single residence. There were 39 kinds of work classified as violations of the Sabbath rest. The weight which one could lift without violating the Sabbath was determined. It is not surprising that the Roman authorities found it simpler to exempt the Jews from military service than to adjust military discipline to the Jewish Sabbath.

The obligation of legal cleanliness was, if observed **586a** strictly, an almost impossible burden. The obligation of cleanliness was originally intended for the priests actually officiating in the sanctuary. Its extension to all Jews of any state or occupation meant either constant ablutions or constant uncleanness, which rendered one unfit for religious exercises. There were various degrees of uncleanness according to the nature of the object touched, and six kinds of water were distinguished for purification from these various degrees. Contact with Gentiles, or with the dead, or with certain diseases, or with a person who had contracted uncleanness, or any sexual process were all defilements. Food had to be protected against uncleanness, in addition to the dietary regulations, which meant in practice that it could not be handled by Gentiles. Generally, the laws of cleanliness were simply not observed, especially where Jews and Gentiles dwelt together.

From the Law was deduced the obligation of wearing **b** *ṣîṣît*, fringes at the corners of the outer garment ; *tᵉpillîn* (*phylacteries* in the NT), boxes containing small scrolls on which were written Ex 13:1–10, 11–16 ; Deut 6:4–9, 11:13–21, attached to the head and the arm by straps ; and of placing at the door-post *mᵉzûzôt*, small boxes containing scrolls on which were written Deut 6:4–9, 11:13–21. The devout Jew was obliged to recite the *Shema*, Deut 6:4–9, 11:13–21 ; Num 15:37–41, the Jewish profession of faith, each morning and evening. Fasting was characteristic of Jewish legal piety as a token of repentance and as an expression of petition in difficult times. Some annual fasts were of general obligation, but most fasting was done out of private devotion. The Law imposed the celebration of the three annual ' pilgrim-feasts ' (at which pilgrimages were made to the Temple): Passover, in remembrance of the Exodus of the Hebrews from Egypt ; Pentecost, in remembrance of the giving of the Law ; and Tabernacles, in remembrance of the sojourn of the Hebrews in the desert. The original agricultural character of these feasts disappeared completely. Besides these there were the New Year, and what became the greatest Jewish feast, the Day of Atonement (*Yôm Kippûr*), when expiation was made for the sins of the whole people.

The Law, however, was more than a series of minute **c** regulations of external conduct. It was possible for Hillel to sum it up in the rule, ' Do not to another what you would not have him do to you ', and for the Saviour to point out as its greatest and first commandment, ' Thou shalt love the Lord thy God with thy

586c whole heart', and as the second, 'Thou shalt love thy neighbour as thyself'. But the vast number of precepts—they were reckoned at 613—certainly helped to create a characteristic feature of Judaism, a deep sense of sin and guilt. This sense of sin undoubtedly can be traced back to the Exile itself, and to the teaching of Jeremias and Ezechiel, who insisted on the truth that the national disaster was due to the sins of the people. The prayers of Judaism are filled with confessions of sin and cries of repentance. Contrary to pre-exilic practice, sacrifice was viewed chiefly as an atonement for sin. The Law furnished a definite measuring-rod of righteousness. Hence, if the prescriptions of the Law were observed, it was possible for the Jew to develop a feeling of self-righteousness ; and we find this sentiment marching side by side with the sense of sin.

d The Scribes—The study and interpretation of the Law was in the hands of those who are called in the Gospels Scribes and doctors of the law. Originally the interpretation of the Torah was the function of the priests ; but the Scribes as such were not priests, although priests were included in their number. Once the Law was accepted as the basis of Jewish life, it was necessary to determine its meaning, and to apply it, as far as possible, to any situation that might arise. Hence came the Scribes. The name is first given to Esdras, ' a ready scribe in the law of Moses '. The Scribes had no official position ; and their opinions had no authority except that of personal influence and public opinion. But this authority was enough. They were legislators, teachers and judges. They sat ' in the chair of Moses ', and were addressed by the title of *Rabbi* (master). The study of the Law was, in the eyes of the devout Jew, the highest occupation of man (*cf.* Ecclus 39:1–11). It was not remunerative ; many of the Scribes, who did not enjoy an independent income, were quite poor and supported themselves by a trade. Their function was ' to build a fence around the Law ' : to protect the perfect observance of the Law by additional regulations. These regulations were formed by deducing them from the text **e** of the written Law. There were two kinds of interpretation : the *Halakhah*, an interpretation, application, or extension of the precepts of the Law into a rule of conduct ; and the *Haggadah*, an amplification of the narrative and doctrinal portions of the Law by the addition of legend, speculation or sheer imagination. The Haggadah was especially concerned with the future and the heavenly world, about which it pretended to give much information. The Halakhah was always based, at least in appearance, on an inference or a deduction from the written Law, however far-fetched these conclusions might be. Thus conclusions were formulated from single words or letters, or even from punctuation or the order of the words. By adding the numerical values of the single letters, and by redividing the sum, new words or sentences could be formed (*gematria*), from which a precept could be deduced. The same end could be reached by inverting the letters according to the alphabetical order in reverse, and forming new words. The regulations thus formulated grew into a second legal system, the oral law, which was proposed as of equal authority with the Law of Moses ; indeed, the beginning of oral tradition was attributed to Moses himself.

f The oral law was the object of tradition. A distinguished scribe would gather around himself a group of disciples who preserved his teaching, and in their own generation amplified it. Until after the beginning of the Christian era there was no written basis for the teaching of the Scribes. Memory was all-important. The schools of the Scribes were by no means uniform in their interpretation of the Law. Difference of opinion was a constant cause of quarrels ; a quarrel between the schools of Hillel and Shammai is said to have issued in fatal violence on one occasion. These two schools were, according to the Jewish sources, the

principal schools of the last century B.C. The school of Hillel was mild in its interpretations ; that of Shammai was inexorably rigorous. These two tendencies were active, whether these two men were their creators or not.

Much of the casuistry of the Scribes is judged unfavourably by moderns. There are many allusions in the Gospels to the over-emphasis they placed on external observances (tithing mint, anise and cummin, and neglecting mercy, justice and faith), the devices by which they evaded obligations of the Law (*e.g.* the evasion of the obligation of supporting one's parents by consecrating one's goods to the sanctuary), and the hypocrisy which masked their refusal to live by their own precepts (binding intolerable burdens on men, while refusing to lift a finger). They treated those who were ignorant of the Law, or who did not observe it, with a lofty contempt. But among their number were found some who were ' not far from the Kingdom of God '. It is thought that the first Jewish Christians must have included a not inconsiderable number of men who, like St Paul, had devoted their lives to the earnest study of the Word of God, and who attempted to live by this Word as they understood it.

The Sanhedrin—The Aramaic word *sanhedrin* is identical with the Gk *synedrion*, assembly or council. When this institution arose cannot be definitely determined. From earliest times local government had been conducted by a council of the elders, men whose age, rank and wealth gave weight to their decisions. It was probably not before the Greek period (after 330 B.C.) that the Jerusalem council, called the Sanhedrin, came to wield legislative and judicial authority for all Judaea, and to claim the same authority not only for Palestinian Judaism, but also, so far as the dispersed Jews consented, for Judaism of the Diaspora as well. The presidency of the Sanhedrin was vested in the high-priest, who was the supreme native magistrate under the imperial governments. The original composition of the Sanhedrin was exclusively aristocratic : members of the high-priestly families, and the ' elders ' of the lay aristocracy. It was probably during the Hasmonaean period that scribes also were admitted. These classes are the ' chief priests, elders and scribes ' of the Gospels. In NT times the party of the Pharisees was in the ascendancy in the Sanhedrin. The number of its members was seventy-one. Members were admitted either by co-option or by appointment of the imperial government ; the method is not certainly known. The competence of the Sanhedrin was originally very broad, including all religious questions, and all civil and criminal cases which the imperial government did not reserve to its own officers. Before the Roman period (63 B.C.) these reservations were very few ; and the Romans limited the civil authority of the Sanhedrin to Judaea proper. But even the Hasmonaean rulers quarrelled with the Sanhedrin, and these quarrels, on occasion, broke out into armed strife ; and Herod and the Roman government restricted the jurisdiction of the Sanhedrin very considerably. Capital crimes (except trespassing in the Temple area) were removed from its competence. It was the supreme authority in determining the interpretation of the Law, both oral and written ; these decisions were valid for the Diaspora. It had its own police force.

The procedure of the Sanhedrin favoured the accused. In capital cases, the arguments of the defence were heard first, and favourable testimony was irreversible. Unfavourable testimony could be reversed. A delay of one day should intervene between the trial and a sentence of condemnation. A majority of one sufficed for acquittal ; a majority of two was required for condemnation.

The Hasidim—In the Maccabean period there appears a party among the Jews known as the Assideans (Heb. *ḥāsîd*, ' pious '). They were a group devoted to the perfect observance of the Law ; and, while they took active part in the Maccabean revolt, they refused to fight on the Sabbath, even in self-defence. Under the Hasmonaean rulers they appear again as hostile to the pretensions of the priestly rulers. They represent the sentiments of the lower classes as opposed to the aristocracy. It was from this group that there evolved the far more famous Jewish sect, the Pharisees.

The Pharisees — The name (Aramaic *perûšîm*, ' separated ') was probably given to the sect by their enemies as a term of opprobrium. It became, however, the accepted designation of the group. They were called ' separate ' because of their exact observance of all the prescriptions of the Law, which set them apart not only from the Gentiles, but also from less observant Jews.

Distinctive Pharisaic tenets are reported by the ancient sources as follows. *Firstly*, the acceptance of the oral law, ' the traditions of the ancients ', as of equal validity with the written law. This meant in practice that most of the Scribes were Pharisees. Pharisaic interpretation was generally more rigorous and imposed all the precepts of the Law as equally grave. *Secondly*, belief in human freedom under the control of divine Providence. This problem was attacked by the Pharisees, if we may trust Josephus, by affirming both terms of the antinomy : human freedom, and effective control by divine Providence. *Thirdly*, belief in the resurrection of the body. *Fourthly*, belief in the existence of the angels. It is doubtful whether these last two points should be called peculiarly Pharisaic doctrine.

Pharisaism was a religious, not a political, movement. But the struggles of the Pharisees with the Hasmonaean dynasty made them prefer a friendly and liberal foreign government to an enlargement of sacerdotal power ; and they lived peaceably under Herod and the Romans as long as the imperial government did not interfere with perfect observance. The kingdom of God, they believed, would be established by divine intervention, not by human efforts. Government by foreign powers was divine punishment for the sins of the nation, and as such should be accepted submissively ; but, on the other hand, it was a profanation of the Holy Land and of the Chosen People, and an obstacle to the establishment of the kingdom of God. As such, it should be overturned by rebellion. Since there was no such thing as a Pharisaic political policy, Pharisees were active in all the wars and rebellions of the Jews from the Maccabees to the insurrection of Bar Kochba in A.D. 135.

It was Pharisaism which imposed its permanent stamp upon Judaism. The great catastrophe of A.D. 70, in which the city and the Temple were destroyed by the Romans, wiped out all other parties in Palestinian Judaism. But even before that date the Pharisees dominated Judaism. Their perfect observance of the Law won them the admiration, if not the affection, of the mass of the people ; and their opposition to the sacerdotal aristocracy, which was often dishonest and rapacious, put them on the side of the common people. Their emphasis on the study and the observance of the Law, and on exercises of piety which were independent of the Temple, made it possible for Judaism to survive as a religion after the disappearance of the priesthood and the Temple liturgy. They were not democratic, and did not intend to be ; but their aristocracy was spiritual, as they understood it. Unfortunately their spiritual aristocracy too often degenerated into mere pride. The haughtiness of the Jew towards the Gentile was found sevenfold in the Pharisee. Their withdrawal from profane contact meant, in practice, withdrawal from the human râce. The Gospels show them in an unfavourable light. The Pharisees, nevertheless, represent what had once been the highest and purest form of Judaism.

The Sadducees—The origin and meaning of the name are uncertain. The Sadducees were the party of the priestly aristocracy, which claimed descent from Zadok. The party seems to have arisen from community of interests. The wealth of the priestly families made common cause for them with other wealthy and conservative circles. They were concerned with preserving the high state of the priesthood. The Pharisees were not anti-sacerdotal nor anti-ritual ; their strict interpretation of the Law allotted ample revenues to the priests. But they opposed the political activity of the priesthood, and set up a standard of legal observance which the priests were unwilling to follow. Hence the Sadducees rejected the oral tradition, and admitted only the written law as valid ; they had, however, their own traditions, and included Scribes in their party. The difference was not in the theory of interpretation, but in the binding force of tradition. In penal laws and in some Levitical laws the Sadducees were more rigorous than the Pharisees. Their religious beliefs were more conservative, clinging to older forms of Jewish doctrine. This was not based on any theological principle ; it was a consequence of their worldliness, and of their lack of any real interest in religious questions. Of all parties and classes of Judaism, the Sadducees were the most favourable to Hellenistic culture. According to Mt 22:23, Ac 23:8, and Josephus, the Sadducees denied divine Providence, the resurrection of the body and the existence of angels.

Like the Pharisees, the Sadducees had no political policy ; priests appear both in rebellion against the imperial government and working in collusion with it. But they were politically active ; their politics, however, had no principle except the advancement of their party and the preservation of sacerdotal wealth and power.

The Sadducees had little influence on the common people, nor, apparently, did they seek it ; they were more concerned with dealing dexterously with the imperial government. They had no lasting influence on Judaism ; with the destruction of the Temple in 70 A.D. the priestly party disappeared altogether from history.

The Essenes—The existence of this sect is affirmed by Josephus. According to his testimony they were a group of men who withdrew from ordinary life to dwell in communal groups in the wilderness. They practised celibacy. Their life was abstemious, spent in labour and the study of the sacred books. They practised numerous ablutions. They took no part in the sacrificial worship of the Temple, although they contributed to its maintenance. Candidates were submitted to three years' probation. They practised perfect community-ownership of goods. They took no oaths, abstained from the common practice of anointing, and wore white garments. At daybreak they invoked the sun, which they must have addressed as a visible symbol of the Deity ; but we cannot ascertain the meaning of this remarkable ceremony. We know nothing of any special doctrines ; Josephus says that they took a vow of secrecy. They would appear to be an extreme wing of the Pharisaic movement. They are not mentioned in the NT ; and they had no influence on Christianity.

The People of the Land—This designation was originally applied to the inhabitants of the rural districts of Palestine, often of mixed Jewish and Gentile extraction, who were affected only slightly, or not at all, by the religious reforms of Esdras, and still less by the Pharisaic movement and the oral law of the Scribes. In NT times the designation was extended, in a contemptuous sense, to all of any class or position who were ignorant of the Law or careless of its perfect observance. To the Pharisees, ' this muititude that knows not the Law is accursed '. The people of the land were the ' publicans and sinners ' with whom the Saviour mingled freely, unlike the Pharisees ; they were the ' little ones ' to whom the Father revealed what he had hidden from the wise. The mass of the people, sustaining itself in poverty by hard labour, was unable to listen to the instruction of the Scribes,

588d or to execute the precepts of the Law. The people of the land were habitually unclean. It was in them, nevertheless, that the essence of Judaism was found : life according to the moral principles of the Law, the simple piety of daily prayer, Sabbath observance, synagogue worship, and occasional visits to the Temple, and the hope in the kingdom of God to come. It was to such that Jesus addressed himself, and by whom he was at first so cordially received. Unlike the Pharisees, he associated freely with them and taught them ; it was a feature of his ministry worth notice that ' the poor had the Gospel preached to them '. For he was himself a member of their class, and from them came his apostles.

e **Judaism of the Diaspora**—The name Diaspora (Gk ' dispersion ') was given to those Jewish communities which were settled outside Palestine. The dispersion of the Hebrews abroad began with the deportations of the conquered by the Assyrian and Babylonian rulers in the eighth, seventh and sixth cent. B.C. Many of the early exiles lost their identity as Hebrews, and were absorbed by the population of the area where they dwelt. The Babylonian exiles, however, in large measure retained their distinctive character, adhered to Jewish religious beliefs and practices, married their own and dwelt in Jewish communities. During the Greek period there was a great migration of Jews to foreign countries for trade. By the last century B.C. large Jewish communities had been established in Syria, Egypt, Asia Minor, Mesopotamia, Babylonia, Persia, Greece and Italy. The number of Jews of the Diaspora is estimated in millions. Their language was Greek ; it is thought that most of them were ignorant of Hebrew or Aramaic. The largest communities were found in the great cities, such as Antioch, Alexandria and Rome. The most important Jewish centre outside of Palestine was in Alexandria ; it was notable not only for its numbers and wealth, but also for its intellectual activity.

f Most of the Jews of the Diaspora were engaged in trade. They dwelt in separate quarters of the large cities, and were granted privileges of self-government under their own ethnarch by imperial and municipal authorities. This was an extension of the policy of the Hellenistic states and the Roman Empire of granting freedom to private religious associations. The Jews were really separate independent municipalities, and had the power of arrest for offences against the Law. While they did not always possess citizenship, their importance in commerce brought them so many privileges that they were often in a better position than the citizens themselves. Under Julius Caesar (*d.* 44 B.C.) the Romans initiated the policy of conferring Roman citizenship throughout the empire ; and many Jews, like St Paul, possessed this right in addition to their Jewish privileges. This world-wide network of Jewish communities, most of which were wealthy and influential, looked to Palestine for religious leadership, and to Jerusalem as its spiritual capital. Without the contributions of the Diaspora to the support of the Temple the priesthood could scarcely have maintained itself.

g The privileges of the Jews and their commercial success were not without accompanying troubles. They aroused the envy of the native population, which was further inflamed by Jewish exclusivism. In more than one instance this ill-feeling erupted into rioting, as at Antioch, Alexandria and Caesarea, and in charges laid against the Jews before municipal and imperial authorities. At Alexandria there was an almost perpetual feud between Jews and Gentiles ; the great Jewish philosopher Philo once led a delegation to appeal to the Emperor Caligula (A.D. 37–41). The Jews were expelled from Rome more than once, and elsewhere had their privileges revoked. Up to A.D. 70, however, these troubles were only temporary ; and the Jews always regained what they had lost.

589a **The Synagogue**—This characteristically Jewish institution (Gk *synagoge*, meeting-place) was the centre of religious life in the Jewish communities of the Diaspora. Synagogues existed in Palestine also ; every village of any size had its synagogue, and larger cities and towns had more than one. When and where the synagogue arose is not known ; it may have been in the time of Esdras (the 5th or 4th cent. B.C.), and it probably had its roots in the meetings for prayer and discourse conducted by the Jews in Babylonia during the Exile. The purpose of the synagogue was reading and instruction in the Law ; it presupposed that those present were unable to attend the worship in the Temple. Elementary schools for children seem to have been a normal complement of the synagogue ; the Law was the only subject of study. The meetings were held on the Sabbath and on feast days ; in later Judaism week-day meetings were added. The synagogue was governed by the elders of the synagogue ; in strictly or predominantly Jewish communities these may have been identical with the civil authorities. The management of the synagogue and the maintenance of order in the services was in charge of the ruler of the synagogue (Gk *archisynagogos*). None of the officials were priests ; the synagogue was a lay organization. There were no officers appointed to conduct the synagogue services ; members of the congregation were called upon to read the Law, to explain it, to lead the prayers. Originally the services were **b** conducted in private dwellings ; in NT times communities of any size possessed a synagogue building. Many of these were large and built in a grand style. The principal articles of furniture were : the ark or chest in which the scrolls of the Law were kept, the tribune on which speakers and readers stood, lamps, horns and trumpets for ceremonial purposes. Men and women sat in separate groups. The service began with the *Shema*, the Jewish profession of faith. There followed a prayer, the reading of the Torah in Hebrew, a translation or paraphrase of the passage in the vernacular, and an explanatory discourse. If a priest were present he concluded the service by giving the sacerdotal blessing. The Law was so divided that the whole was read in the course of three years.

It is impossible to overestimate the part of the synagogue in maintaining Jewish unity of faith and nation. The synagogue was a regular place of meeting for Jews everywhere. Visitors from elsewhere were invited to read or to deliver the discourse, especially if they came from Palestine. Hardly any other single factor is equally responsible for the resistance of Judaism to the assimilative force of Greco-Roman culture.

The Septuagint—The name (Lat. ' seventy ') is given **c** to the translation of the OT into Greek made probably during the 3rd and 2nd cent. B.C., and is based on an unfounded legend that the translation was the work of seventy-two men. This was the most important contribution of the Diaspora to Judaism, from which it passed to Christianity. Most of the Jews of the Diaspora had no facility in reading Hebrew. There was, besides, a desire among many Jews to present their own sacred books to the cultivated world of the time. This monumental work made it possible for Jews abroad and for Gentiles to consult the Scriptures. The LXX enjoyed great authority among the Jews of the Diaspora, equal to that of the original text ; and its translators were believed to have done their work under divine inspiration. The LXX is quoted frequently in the NT, and the indirect influence of its language has, in the words of Swete, ' left its mark on every part of the NT '. The Christian Church adopted the LXX as its own Bible with so much enthusiasm that its use was abandoned by the Jews after the 1st cent. A.D.

Jews and Gentiles—The exclusivism of the Jews and **d** their resistance to Gentile culture was not and could not have been entirely successful. That Judaism was affected by ideas from foreign sources is certain ; the extent of this influence cannot be determined exactly.

Hellenistic culture is the name given to the diffusion

of the Greek language, learning, arts and customs throughout the East and the Mediterranean littoral following the conquests of Alexander (d. 323 B.C.). The culture of Greece, thus presented to a world-wide audience and adopted by it, shook off its peculiarly Greek traits and became universal. The kingdoms of Syria and Egypt, one or the other of which ruled Palestine from the death of Alexander to the Maccabean wars, were both Hellenistic.

The impact of Hellenistic culture on the Jews had different effects in Palestine and in the Diaspora. Palestinian Judaism, which had erected itself into a tightly homogeneous community, was better able to resist it than the Jewish communities which supported themselves by commerce in the large Hellenistic cities. Again, we must distinguish between the externals of Hellenistic culture and the religious and philosophical ideas of Hellenism. Judaism both at home and abroad was at first swamped under the externals of Hellenistic culture. The common articles of trade and of daily use, food, clothing, furniture were Greek in name and in style. A great number of Greek personal names appear among the Jews in the Hellenistic period (Andrew, Philip, Alexander), many of them altered from a Hebrew name of similar sound (Joshua and Jason). Even such definitely Jewish buildings as synagogues were erected in the Hellenistic architectural style. Because of the severe restrictions of the Law on the use of images, the Jews seem to have been touched very lightly by the plastic arts of Greece ; but there was much study of Greek literature and philosophy, even in Palestine. Civil government in Jewish communities adopted many features of Hellenistic cities. Even in Palestine many Jews enthusiastically adopted Greek costume and such Greek practices as athletic contests, baths and theatres. The members of the sacerdotal aristocracy were the leaders in this movement of Hellenization ; it was they, also, who abetted Antiochus Epiphanes in his efforts to impose Hellenistic worship, which led to the Maccabee rebellion. As a result of the wars of the Maccabees, Palestinian Judaism cast off many of the externals of Hellenism ; the Pharisees professed to reject it entirely, the Sadducees were still sympathetic, and the people of the land were more or less Hellenized according to their environment. But Palestinian Judaism admitted no real infiltration of Hellenistic thought, and very little even of Hellenistic literary forms. The Scribes and Pharisees refused to learn anything from the Greeks.

The same cannot be said of Judaism of the Diaspora. The principal literary works of the Diaspora which have survived are the Book of Wisdom (written 150–50 B.C.) and the writings of Philo of Alexandria (b. about 30 B.C.). For the question of Greek influence on Wisdom cf. §§ 388–9. That Philo was a student of Greek philosophy, and that he looked on it with favour, is evident from his works. His aim was to show that the Law, the sum of all wisdom for the Hebrew, was a philosophy like Platonism or Stoicism. In details his thought shows the effects of Greek philosophy. If Philo is a true example of Alexandrine Judaism, then the assimilation of Greek thought had gone far. But Philo remains a Jew ; and the amazing conglomeration of peculiarly Hebrew and Greek ideas in his works issues in strange confusions—which may aptly illustrate the confusion of many a Jew in the presence of the wisdom of the Greeks.

Other foreign influences on Judaism are less certain. From Babylonia the Jews acquired a number of ancient superstitious practices, some of which have survived into modern times ; but it cannot be said that Babylonia contributed anything to Jewish religious beliefs. The influence of Persia has been seriously discussed. These resemblances have been noted between Judaism and the religion of Zarathushtra : belief in a world destiny, a final conflagration, an evil spirit, a final judgement of good and wicked, the ultimate triumph of good over evil, and the resurrection. A closer study of these resemblances shows that many of them are specious ; that no connexion can be found through which Persia could have influenced Judaism ; and that the roots of these doctrines are found in the Scriptures and the traditions of Judaism. The whole question is fully treated by Lagrange, *Judaïsme*, 388–409. **589h**

Proselytism—Judaism of the NT period was moved by two opposing tendencies : the nationalist, particularist, exclusivist tendency by which Judaism formed a tight front against the Hellenistic world, and the intrinsic universalism of the doctrines of Judaism. The Jews had only to read their sacred books to realize that their God was the one true God of all mankind, and that all men should know him, all races and tongues should serve him ; from Zion proceeded revelation for the whole world. At the beginning of the Christian era particularism, represented by the Pharisees, had triumphed ; there was no sect or movement within Judaism which stood for universalism. But the inherent tendency towards universalism could not be suppressed ; and it found an outlet in proselytism, the admission of Gentiles to the practice of the Jewish religion. **590a**

There were several obstacles to proselytism. Besides the particularist spirit of official Judaism, there was the obstacle of anti-Jewish prejudice. Jewish exclusivism was the one force which opposed the Hellenistic amalgamation of many nations, cultures, languages and religions into one universal, supranational culture ; Gentiles recognized this, and resented it. Even before the Christian era, and more frequently afterwards, Greek and Latin literature show not only numerous anti-Jewish allusions, but formally anti-Jewish compositions, which the Jews felt themselves obliged to answer. There is a striking similarity between the anti-Jewish prejudice of the ancient world and modern anti-Semitism, which is not an effect, nor even a by-product of Christianity. But there were also favourable factors. Gentile prejudice moved many of the Jews of the Diaspora to present Judaism in the manner best calculated to attract Gentiles, by suppressing any emphasis on Jewish external practices, such as circumcision and the Sabbath, and expounding the real essence of Jewish doctrine : the pure concept of the one supreme God, and lofty standards of Jewish morality. Such a presentation was sympathetically received by many Gentiles. Among educated Hellenistic circles the old Greek polytheism had been done to death by the criticisms of the philosophers ; Platonism and Aristotelianism conceived of God in an abstract and impersonal fashion, but freed of the debasing traits of the ancient gods of the Greeks ; and Greek philosophers, from Socrates to the Stoics, had worked out a system of morality which was not unworthy of comparison with Jewish morality. But philosophy alone left a religious hunger ; and the Hellenistic world was very receptive to oriental religious cults, even to such fantastic rites as those of Mithra or of the Great Mother. Furthermore, the breakdown of nationalism in the Hellenistic world separated religion from the nation. All religions appealed to a wider audience, and there was a tendency to identify all gods. Judaism, then, came before the Gentiles with the aura of mysticism which the Greeks attributed to the Orientals. **c**

There were two classes of proselytes : 'fearers of God', and true proselytes. The fearers of God accepted the Jewish doctrine of God and the Scriptures, attended the synagogue, and observed the Sabbath and the dietary laws ; but they were not required to submit to circumcision nor to undertake the complete observance of the Law. These were probably far more numerous than the true proselytes. The true proselytes, by adopting Judaism in its entirety, actually became Jews ; they included one oriental royal family. **d**

Proselytism was not limited to the Diaspora ; in spite of Pharisaism there were proselytes in Palestinian Judaism as well. Here Pharisaism was somewhat inconsistent with itself ; the Gospels credit it with proselytizing zeal, in spite of its narrow religious nationalism. No more striking example of proselytism

590d can be found than that of John Hyrcanus (135–104 B.C.), who forced the Edomites to submit to the full yoke of Judaism.

Proselytism did not solve the tension between universalism and particularism. Judaism did not assimilate the Gentiles. The true proselyte, by becoming a Jew, not only adopted Jewish beliefs and practices, but had to abandon his Hellenism and enter the Jewish community. Judaism was still a nation as well as a religion, and one could accept it on no other terms. Once the missionary activity of Christianity reached the Greco-Roman world, and especially after the Jewish rebellion of A.D. 66–70, we hear little of proselytism among the Jews.

e Apocalyptic Literature—During the last two centuries B.C. there arose among the Jews a form of literature called apocalyptic (Gk *apokalypsis*, ' revelation '). While most of this literature is of Palestinian origin, it cannot be identified with any of the sects or schools of Palestinian Judaism. But it represents a school of thought, of undetermined diffusion and influence, whose religious outlook extended far beyond the Law. Apocalyptic literature is a development of a type of literature which first appears in the canonical books of the prophets, Is 24–27, Jl, Zach 9–14, Dan, and is found also in the NT Apocalypse of St John. In form, apocalyptic literature is always proposed as a secret revelation made in the distant past and just now discovered. Hence it is studiously mysterious, cloaking contemporary events under obscure names and figures. These can usually be identified. The occasion of these writings was the national troubles of the Jews during these centuries, and they are written to bolster the hope of the nation that the hand of God would rescue it from its tribulations. The apocalyptic writings promise a great divine intervention in world history, by which heathen nations will be destroyed, sinners will be punished, and the faithful rewarded with life **f** everlasting in the Jewish kingdom of God. This is a development of the Messianic hope in the prophetical books of the OT (*cf.* § 102*h–o*), and, when this literature follows the lines of legitimate development, it exhibits religious traits of remarkable power and beauty ; but in its ferocity towards the Gentiles and its hope of a kingdom of God filled with material pleasures, sometimes of a gross type, it cannot be regarded as a legitimate development. In addition, the apocalyptic writings are a mine of speculation, in the form of prediction or occult revelation, on the mysteries of nature, the early history of the human race and the Jewish people, and the problem of sin and divine justice. The outlook of the apocalyptic writers is entirely national ; divine justice finds its fulfilment in the supremacy of the Jewish nation as the kingdom of God. The best known of these works are the Books of Henoch, the Assumption of Moses, the Apocalypses of Baruch and Esdras, and the Testament of the Twelve Patriarchs.

591a Beliefs of Judaism—It is impossible within the limits of this sketch to present a complete summary of the doctrines of Judaism, as they are complicated by wide variations between different periods and different centres. The doctrines discussed below are characteristic of the NT period. They are treated under four heads : God, angels and demons, Messianism, and eschatology.

A. God—The Jewish conception of God is based, first and foremost, on the OT ; and the OT is filled with an overpowering sense of the divine presence and the divine activity in the world. God is the supreme lord of nature and of history. He is personal, with a personal interest in his creatures which the OT often describes in language which is altogether human. He is the supreme reality, as real to the ancient Hebrew as himself. But in the NT period the simple faith of the ancient Hebrew had been somewhat modified ; and the influences which operated upon Jewish belief in God are not always easy to trace.

b The existence of God was not, for the Hebrews, a speculative question. In all Hebrew literature there is no effort to demonstrate the existence of God. Herein Judaism was a true child of the ancient faith of the Hebrews, with its sense of the divine reality ; and it was unacquainted with the curiosity of Greek philosophy, which, once it had destroyed the gods of the ancient polytheism, was under the necessity of constructing a supreme being from its own intellectual processes. When the fool said, ' There is no God ', Ps 13:1, he denied not the existence of God, but his effective government of the world. The author of the Wisdom of Solomon, who was certainly acquainted with Greek philosophy, calls ' ignorance of God ' folly, Wis 13:1 ; but he means ignorance of the true nature of God, not of his existence.

The Divine Names—The proper personal name of the **c** God of the Hebrews was *Yahweh* ; *cf.* § 165*a*, *b*. In NT times this name was never uttered except by the priests in a few liturgical functions. It is uncertain when its use was abandoned ; it seems to have occurred between the 5th and 3rd cent. B.C. Nor is it easy to assign a reason for this avoidance of the traditional name. The opinion that it was due to an exaggerated fear or reverence is not accepted by many modern scholars. Some believe it was to protect the name from profanation by use in magical formulae ; others, that it was abandoned from a monotheistic scruple. The deities of heathendom were distinguished from one another by their personal names (Zeus, Apollo, Aphrodite, etc.) ; in order that the God of the Hebrews might not be esteemed one of many, his distinctive personal name was suppressed for the more universal ' God ' or ' Lord '. Yet even these designations were used with restrictions. ' God ' (*elōhîm*) is not used outside the Bible. ' Lord ' (*ădōnāi*, Gk *kyrios*) is used only in the Bible and in prayer. In extra-biblical Jewish literature and, we may suppose, in Jewish conversation, God was usually designated by circumlocution : the Name, the Place, the *Shekinah* (dwelling), the Power, the Heavens, the Most High, the Holy One (this last usually followed by the doxology ' Blessed be He '). Such modes of speaking certainly suggest a great advance in reverence, not to say timorousness, over the bold addresses of many of the Psalms (which, however, were used liturgically during this period), and an increasing reserve in converse with God. They suggest also a more remote sense of the divine personality and presence.

Monotheism—The belief in one only God as the basis **d** of religion distinguished Judaism both from Gentile religions and from Greek philosophy. There was no ancient religion which did not admit and worship a plurality of gods. Many schools of Greek philosophy professed belief in the existence of one supreme being. This conviction, however, was the fruit of philosophical speculation ; Judaism based its belief on the revelation of the one God whom it worshipped. This fundamental doctrine is expressed in the *Shema* (Deut 6:4), which the devout Jew recited twice daily : ' Hear, O Israel, the Lord our God is one Lord '.

As the Jews came more closely into contact with the **e** great Gentile cultures of the ancient world, their rigorous monotheism responded to these cultures, which, from every point of view except that of religion and morality, were superior to their own, by a vigorous polemic against polytheism. The Jews thus protected themselves against the powerful attraction which these cultures exercised, and asserted their own superiority. Examples of such polemic already appear in the OT, and are found with more frequency in the extra-biblical Jewish literature of the last centuries B.C. Nor does it seem unfounded to see in monotheism the basis of the harsh judgement which Judaism passed against heathendom, and of the Jewish tendency to condemn Gentile culture root and branch as essentially sinful. Certainly the religious beliefs and the moral principles of Judaism were far superior to the religion and morality of the other ancient nations ; but the Jews were austerely intolerant of Gentile culture as a whole, and blind to any elements of good which it

91e might contain, because it was based on the folly of polytheism.

f **The Divine Attributes**—Extra-biblical Jewish literature lays particular emphasis on three divine attributes : majesty, spirituality and holiness. The OT speaks with sublime eloquence of the majesty of God ; extra-biblical Jewish literature echoes the OT, but with a difference. In the OT Yahweh, while majestic, is not remote ; transcending the world, he is not an abstraction. The God of Judaism is more remote from human affairs, less personal and more abstract. This does not mean that Judaism made no effort to penetrate the majesty of God ; a favourite subject of Haggadic speculation was the heavens and the divine glory, which are more than once described in some detail. There were seven levels of the heavens ; the seventh was the abode of God himself. These speculations were regarded as the most difficult and advanced, to which the student must not be admitted until he has been well prepared.

g It is difficult to analyse the Jewish conception of the spirituality of God. The OT, like the Hebrews who were its authors, is material-minded ; it exhibits no concept of purely intellectual activity such as was developed by Greek philosophers. Yet the OT and Judaism were always aware that God is a spirit, no matter how often they may speak of God's eye, or ear, or hand, or mouth. But we find that Judaism hesitates to employ such metaphors of God. Many of the vivid anthropomorphisms of the OT are suppressed by abstraction and circumlocution in LXX. What was lacking in Judaism was a positive concept of spiritual reality. The Hebrew concept of life was animal ; they had no philosophy by which they might formulate an idea of rational or intellectual life. Hence the denial of material composition in God left only an abstraction ; and this was another step towards making the divine reality more remote and less personal.

h The holiness of God is a peculiarly Hebrew idea, for which English has no adequate word. Holiness is not so much a divine attribute as divinity itself ; it is everything which distinguishes God as such from his creatures. In modern language, it is the divine transcendence. It is more than moral goodness, although this element is not excluded ; it is the physical and moral superiority of God over his creatures. In Judaism the moral aspect of holiness received greater emphasis. One of the titles of God used most frequently in the rabbinical literature is ' the Holy One '.

a The doctrine of **Providence** in Judaism was, in many ways, well developed. No truth is proposed in the OT with more emphasis, both by discourse and by narrative, than the truth of the intervention of God in human affairs. The dominant thought of Jewish belief in Providence was that whatever happens is the work of God. This doctrine, however, was applied principally to events on a national or world-wide scale : the history of the Jews, in particular, and of the great world-empires of ancient times. The idea of the action of God on the individual soul was much less well developed. In this, as in other doctrinal questions, the Jewish mind was more interested in the external. The question of the relation of the doctrine of Providence to human liberty and responsibility was not solved in Judaism, or, rather, not raised. Josephus says that the Pharisees occupied a middle position between the Essenes, who denied human liberty, and the Sadducees, who denied Providence ; but most scholars think that Josephus has over-simplified the teachings of these parties. In Judaism, as we know it from the extant literature, human liberty and responsibility are asserted together with the truth that all that happens is the work of God ; the apparent antinomy is ignored. A consequence of Jewish faith in divine intervention was a ready belief in stories of the marvellous and miraculous. Exaggerated credulity appears on almost every page of rabbinical and apocalyptic literature, which abound in anecdotes of the marvellous which are not only grotesque, but, **592a** often enough, indecorous, yet all calmly attributed to God.

The doctrine of Providence implies divine omniscience **b** and foreknowledge of human events, and this Judaism affirms ; and from the doctrine of the divine foreknowledge flows the doctrine of predestination. Here Judaism advanced far beyond the doctrinal basis of the OT, especially the apocalyptic literature, which reveals future events as antecedently decreed and determined. The election of Israel as the Chosen People implied the reprobation of the Gentiles, who are, consequently, regarded as hopelessly beyond the pale of salvation.

A counterweight to the depersonalization of God is found in the emphasis laid by Judaism on the divine goodness and mercy. Jewish prayer is full of expressions of thanksgiving for the divine benefits. And while Judaism is highly conscious of sin, it also has deep faith in divine mercy to the repentant sinner. But the divine mercy was not thought to reach all sinners. Judaism divided all mankind into two classes : the good, whose occasional falls were quickly repented and easily forgiven, and the wicked, who were impenitent and obdurate. For these God neither had nor could have any mercy. Among the obdurate sinners were included all Gentiles and the Hellenizing Jews ; for the Pharisees, all who did not observe the Law were accursed. These harsh views of the official circles of Judaism had little or no effect on the piety of the ordinary Jew.

Another effect of the abstract and transcendental con- **c** cept of God was the personification of certain divine attributes. This has a basis in the OT : the spirit of God brooded over the surface of the waters (Gen 1:2), the Lord sends forth his word to do his work, Is 55:11, the wisdom of God is his helper in the work of creation, Prov 8:22 ff. ; and many other texts could be cited. In the OT these personifications are not really distinct from God himself ; they are poetic and imaginative locutions about the divine attributes as manifested in creation. In Judaism such personifications are used very frequently, especially the spirit, the word (*Memra*), the wisdom, the *Shekinah* (dwelling, *i.e.* presence). The spirit is the creative force ; by the *Shekinah* God is present everywhere. With one exception there is, in the thought of Judaism, no real difference between these personifications and God himself. They are used as substitutes for the divine name, and they permitted the Jews to speak of the external works of God without attributing these to him directly. The exception is Philo of Alexandria, who seems to have treated the personified attributes as beings intermediate between God and the angels, with a distinct reality of their own.

B. Angels and Demons—Angels are mentioned fre- **d** quently in all the books of the OT, both early and late. They appear as bearers of the divine revelation, as executioners of the divine judgements, and as the heavenly retinue of God. Judaism expanded the doctrine of the angels far beyond the basis of the OT. The angels were conceived as spiritual beings, at least in the sense that they were not composed of gross terrestrial matter ; but here again the Jews lacked a positive concept of spirituality, and did not elaborate the idea beyond that of the mere negation of body. The speculations of the Haggadah abound in descriptions of the material form of angels, which was certainly thought to be invisible to the mortal eye ; they are described as gigantic winged human forms. In the rabbinical writings the angels are given a fiery nature, based on a misunderstanding of Ps 103:4. The theory of angelic choirs already appears in the Books of Henoch ; seven choirs are mentioned in 1 Henoch, nine in 2 Henoch. The names of seven archangels are given : Uriel, Raphael, Raguel, Michael, Sarakiel, Gabriel and Jeremiel. Michael is the guardian spirit of Israel (*cf.* Dan 10:21).

The interest of Judaism in the angels corresponds to **e**

592e its feeling that God was remote. In the OT, where the sense of God's present reality is so pervasive, the angels play a relatively small part. In Judaism there was a need to multiply intermediaries. Many operations which the OT ascribes to God directly are attributed to angels in Judaism. This appears in LXX, where the angel of the Lord sometimes replaces the divine name of the original Hebrew, and in some uncertain passages of the MT, where the divine name and the angel of the Lord have become inextricably confused. In the speculations of the Haggadah the functions of the angels have been notably expanded beyond the doctrine of the OT. Judaism also describes them as the divine retinue ; but the imaginative expansion of detailed description lacks nothing for fullness. The angels preside over the elements of the material universe, and over the celestial bodies—a quaint view which survived into the Middle Ages, when, fused with the Aristotelian theory of separate intelligences, it resulted in the theory that the movements of the celestial spheres were governed by angels. They presided over nations, each of which has its guardian spirit—a deduction from Dan 10:20 f. They intervene actively in history and are the agents of the miraculous. But their most important function was that of intermediaries of the divine revelation. In the older prophetic books the prophet speaks the word of the Lord which he himself has heard. In the books of Zacharias and Daniel, however, an ' interpreting angel ' appears, who communicates the word of the Lord, or explains the meaning of the visions of the seer. In the apocalyptic literature the interpreting angel is the usual medium by which the seer is informed of heavenly things.

593a It may almost be said that the OT contains no demonology, so rare and so obscure are the allusions to a world of evil spirits. The demonology of Judaism was more indebted to foreign sources than to the OT. Here again the Haggadic speculations supplied what was missing in authentic sources. Like the angels, the demons were known by name ; the chief of the evil spirits was Satan (mentioned in Job 1 and 2, and Zach 3, but not certainly as an evil spirit) ; the Heb. word means ' adversary ', ' accuser '. Satan appears to be identical with the Mastema mentioned occasionally in extra-biblical Jewish literature. Another evil spirit frequently mentioned is Beliar or Belial. The Heb. word *beliya'al* probably means ' useless ' ; in the OT a ' son of belial ' is a good-for-nothing, *i.e.* wicked person. The origin of the evil spirits was a subject of great interest in the Haggadah. Obviously they could not have been created evil, so their wickedness was attributed to some sin. The most commonly accepted belief was that they were the ' sons of God ' of Gen 6:1–4, who sinned with the ' daughters of men '.

Ordinary Jewish belief was disfigured by a great deal of superstition, which was probably of Babylonian origin. Babylonian demonology was very highly developed. Almost every conceivable evil, mishap, or inconvenience was attributed to demonic malevolence ; and the innumerable demons which threatened human welfare could be warded off only by incantations and magical rites. Such incantations and magic were practised among the Jews ; the wearing of amulets against demons was very common.

b **C. Messianism**—The Messianic conception of the Jews may be defined with Bonsirven as ' the conviction that the chosen people of God cannot disappear, that it will attain its peak and reach the fullness of the ideal predestined for it by God only in a future more or less remote, at " the end of days " ' (*Judaïsme* I, 341). The stream of the Messianic hope runs all through the OT. Its fullest development in extra-biblical literature is found in the apocalyptic books. There are many allusions in the NT to the Messianic expectation ; and it is clear from these allusions that the form which it took in NT times was material, temporal and national, rather than spiritual, eternal and universal. This conception we may trace in the literature, especially in the apocalyptic writings.

The Messianic future was called the ' days of the **5** Messias ', or ' the end of days ', although two different conceptions lay beneath these two designations. The days of the Messias looked principally to the national restoration of the Jews ; the end of days looked rather to the universal consummation of the world. In both of these the accomplishment of the Messianic future was the effect of a direct divine intervention, a cosmic manifestation of God in his majesty and power ; this divine intervention, rather than the work of the Messias himself, was the cause of salvation. The Messianic era was to be initiated by the precursor of the Messias, who was Elias, the angel of the covenant (based on Mal 3:1, 4:5 ; *cf.* §§ 555–8 ; 670–1). The coming of the Messias was preceded (or accompanied) by the Messianic tribulations. This was based on the apocalyptic predictions in the prophetic books of the OT (such as Is 24–27) ; this period was of indefinite duration, and was filled with temporal and spiritual calamities, convulsions of nature, the triumph of the wicked, etc. The coming of the Messias coincided (in a general way) with the end of the world ; and the belief that this was near seems to have been widely accepted in NT times. Jewish speculation was much interested in trying to determine when the consummation would come, and several calculations are found. The most popular seems to have been that which reckoned the duration of the world at seven periods of one thousand years each (after the seven days of creation) ; the last period, the millennium, was initiated by the coming of the Messias, and the establishment of a kingdom of material and sensible joy on earth. After this period, the just were to be translated to ' the world to come '. This belief in a thousand years of earthly joy was accepted by some of the Fathers of the Church and by many Christians during the earlier centuries of our era.

The Messianic kingdom is, in every conception, **d** identified with the kingdom of Israel restored to Palestine from the dispersion ; but extra-biblical Jewish literature exhibits great confusion in its descriptions of the Messianic kingdom. With Bonsirven, these conceptions may be classified, although it is impossible to eliminate some overlapping (*Judaïsme* I, 418 ff.). **Conceptions of the Messianic Kingdom—A.** Messianism of two periods : ' the days of the Messias ', in which the kingdom of Israel is restored and the Gentile nations destroyed, occur on earth. ' The world to come ' is realized in a supraterrestrial universe, where the just are rewarded with all joys.
B. Transcendental Messianism : in this conception there is no Messianic kingdom upon earth. The scene of salvation is heaven or paradise.
C. Eschatological Messianism : this is a contamina **e** tion of A by B. In this form, which exhibits several variations, the resurrection and the judgement are transferred from ' the world to come ' to the Messianic times upon earth ; or, the days of the Messias are prolonged into infinity, with no sharp division between the days of the Messias and the world to come ; or, the present world is transfigured into the transcendental world to come, with no change of scene from earth to heaven.

Eschatological Messianism was the most common belief among the Jews in NT times. The other conceptions are found in two of the most important apocalyptic works, besides other writings : Messianism of the two periods is found in the Apocalypse of Esdras, and the Books of Henoch (which are not a literary unity) contain both transcendental and eschatological Messianism. In the apocalyptic writings the fate of the heathen nations is treated with some uncertainty. At one time they are destroyed in the war which the Messias (without any human aid or earthly power, but by the miraculous intervention of God) wages against them ; at another, they are preserved through the Messianic times, during which they war against the Messias and the kingdom of God upon earth, to meet final judgement and destruction in the world-catastrophe of ' the end of days '. As a matter of fact the apocalyptic writers were much less interested in the fate of the nations than in the restoration of the kingdom of Israel.

The centre of the national hope was the Messianic kingdom, the ' kingdom of God '. In the OT Yahweh himself is king of Israel (*cf*. Pss 92 ; 94–99). The kingdom of God is identical with the Jewish kingdom, whether it be located on earth or in heaven. In Messianism of two periods and eschatological Messianism the kingdom of God on earth is established in Palestine. The centre of the Messianic kingdom is Jerusalem, expanded in size and rebuilt with becoming magnificence. The whole face of the country is to be transformed in the Messianic times. A semi-arid country, it will abound with streams of water and will be prodigiously fertile. Material felicity and the satisfaction of all sensible desires will prevail, and, with all the Gentile nations destroyed, universal peace will reign. But the kingdom is not exclusively of this material and national character. The establishment of the kingdom presupposes a moral renovation of the people ; the wicked have no place in the kingdom. The worship of God will be carried out in the Temple with all solemnity, and the wealth of nations will be laid under contribution to serve his cult.

The Messias—The Heb. word *māšîḥᵃ* (Gk *christos*) means ' anointed one '. This title is not applied to the expected deliverer in the OT (some exegetes think the word is applied to him in Dan 9:25). In the OT it is used of kings and priests, the sacredness of whose office was indicated by a rite of consecration in which anointing was used. In the books of Henoch and Esdras the Messias is pre-existent in heaven before his appearance on earth ; he is superhuman, occupying a position between God and man, but not identified with either ; and he is endowed with transcendental properties. In the books of Henoch (where he is also called the Elect One) he appears suddenly and supernaturally in the glory of his triumph ; but this view was not generally accepted in Judaism. The more traditional conception represented the Messias as coming to war against the enemies of Israel, and to establish the kingdom of God on earth. In the Psalms of Solomon, which belong to the 1st cent. B.C., he is represented as a human king, a great warrior, who reigns over the restored kingdom of Israel in Palestine. There is an element of vagueness in the conception of the Messias as king, in spite of the fact that the coming of the Messias king is characteristic of the Messianic hope in the OT, and is mentioned very often in the prayers of Judaism. He will reside in Jerusalem, govern his people, and give judgement in legal cases. But his work as an agent either of spiritual or of material blessings remains undefined. Bonsirven points out that he is not represented in extra-biblical Jewish literature as a miracle-worker. In rabbinical literature, unlike apocalyptic, the transcendental and superhuman qualities of the Messias are suppressed, and his pure humanity is emphasized.

The idea of a suffering Messias escaped Judaism entirely. It is not found in apocalyptic literature, and only a few allusions appear in the rabbinical writings. It is quite probable that the idea was suppressed as much as possible after the preaching of Christianity. The few allusions which exist are based on Is 53. But the reconciliation of the suffering servant of the Lord there described with the Messianic king was too difficult ; and so we find the sufferings attributed to another Messias, the son of Joseph. The Messianic king is the Messias, the son of David, although he is once said to be the son of Levi, hence a priestly king. This idea probably arose as a consequence of the union of royal and sacerdotal dignity in the Hasmonaean dynasty.

This brief summary can do no more than indicate the wavering and uncertainty of Jewish ideas about the Messias, who was sometimes human, sometimes superhuman, sometimes earthly and national, some-

times transcendental and universal. This vagueness in the mind of Judaism itself shows why the Messianism of the Gospels was proposed with such caution and reserve. **594b**

D. Eschatology—Belief in retribution of divine justice for good and evil is basic in Jewish doctrine ; and nothing did more to sustain the religion of Judaism through the centuries during which the national life was extinct and the Jews submitted to Gentile empires both at home and abroad. The concept of God exhibited in the OT and in Jewish belief was that of one who is not indifferent to right and wrong, but imposes his moral law on all men, who rewards its observance and punishes sin. But divine justice certainly is not manifest in this life ; hence there must be a continuation of life beyond the grave, in which the good receive their reward and the wicked pay the penalty of their misdeeds. One of the most remarkable features of the OT is the almost complete absence of this doctrine in the pre-exilic books. Yet the few sketchy allusions to a future life which we find there do not permit us to conclude that the religion of the OT lacked any idea of eschatological retribution. When the doctrine reached a fuller development, it was based on that firm faith in divine justice which pervades the entire OT. It can be said with certainty that Judaism is not indebted to any foreign religion for its doctrine of retribution and the future life. Of all the ancient peoples, the conception of the after life was most completely developed by the Egyptians ; but there is no trace in the OT, or in the literature of Judaism, of any Egyptian influence in this field of belief, although the Hebrews throughout their history were in contact with Egypt ; *cf*. Sutcliffe, *The OT and the Future Life*, London, 1947².

It is difficult to disengage Jewish eschatological beliefs **d** from the Messianic hope, since the establishment of the Messianic kingdom was the ultimate act of divine retributive justice ; hence the present division is somewhat artificial. It may be justified, however, as a consideration of the individual destiny of the good and the wicked, while the Messianic faith is more concerned with the national destiny.

As indicated above, the ' days of the Messias ' follow the establishment of the Messianic kingdom on earth ; they are, therefore, a transition between ' this world ' and ' the world to come '. It is in the world to come that the just receive their full reward ; the Rabbis say of certain sinners that they have no part in the world to come. But just as there is confusion concerning the earthly and the heavenly kingdom of God, so likewise there is uncertainty whether the recompense of the righteous begins with death or the resurrection. Where the earthly Messianic kingdom is emphasized it is obvious that the resurrection must precede any reward of the just.

The Judgement—The retribution is preceded by a **e** judgement of good and evil. The judgement on all mankind precedes the establishment of the Messianic kingdom. More generally God, and not the Messias, is the judge. This conception of a general judgement is based on the ' Day of the Lord ' in the prophetic books of the OT (*e.g.* Am 5:18 ff.). It is the principal act in all the Messianic-apocalyptic schemes, by which God defeats his enemies and vindicates his people ; but there is no agreement on its precise place in the end-process. While it is a universal judgement, the apocalyptic literature treats it as a judgement of the wicked alone. The record of the righteous deeds of the good is kept in the book of life. The judgement, as already indicated, deals with nations as well as individuals ; hence there is a confusion of national and ethical elements in the idea of the judgement. Judaism never arrived at the idea that men were weighed in the judgement purely on their ethical merits.

Life after Death—The ancient Hebrew conception of **595a** the nature of life after death was extremely vague at best. Hence, when the question was asked concerning the state of the just between death and the resurrection,

595a which was to come at 'the end of days', it is not surprising that there was no certain answer. More generally, the just were thought to remain in a state of suspended animation. An exception to this is the Book of Wisdom (*cf.* Wis 3:1 ff.). Outside of this book the ancient concept of Sheol survived in Judaism, at least as far as the intermediate state was concerned. Sheol was the receptacle of all the dead ; it was a place of neither joy nor pain, but simply the negation of human life as it is known by experience. For the just, it is true, Judaism conceived it as a state of quiet repose ; but the wicked were not really punished in Sheol, since their pains were reserved for the period following the general judgement. In the Books of Henoch we find four compartments in Sheol : for the just who died as martyrs, for the other just, for the sinners who were not punished on earth for their sins, and for the sinners who were punished on earth for their sins ; these last do not rise. The Fourth Book of Esdras describes seven joys of the just and seven tortures of the wicked until judgement. The doctrine of the rabbinical writings was the most refined. Here the judgement takes place at death, and the just are rewarded immediately in heaven, or in Eden, the location of which is undefined.

b **The Resurrection of the Righteous**—It is impossible to state when belief in the resurrection of the dead arose in Judaism. Not all the apocalyptic writings contain this belief ; and even in the NT period it was not universally accepted. Judaism never arrived at a consistent position on the universality of the resurrection. The righteous arise to share in the joys of the intermediate terrestrial kingdom ; the place of their ultimate reward is uncertain. It is located in heaven, or in a supraterrestrial Paradise or Eden, or on the renovated earth, or in a terrestrial Eden. The eschatological Paradise is depicted after the manner of the primitive Paradise of Gen 2, with the tree of life and the waters of life. The reward of the just consists in eternal life, understood in the minimal sense : continuation of life in the body. This eternal life is free from pain ; it is a life of quiet repose in the satisfaction of all sensible desires. According to some Rabbis, the bodies of the just will be endowed with colossal size in the resurrection. The risen just will be free from sin and perfect in all virtue. According to the Rabbis, their chief joy will be the study of the Law. A hint of higher things is seen in the belief that the ultimate happiness of the just lies in communion with God. Some Rabbis distinguished seven degrees of the just (accommodated to the seven heavens) ; only the seventh and highest degree 'see God'. This conception is not that of the beatific vision in Christian theology.

c **Punishment of Sinners**—There is equal or greater divergence about the punishment of the wicked. Judaism wavers between annihilation or eternal punishment after the judgement, or limits eternal punishment to notorious sinners, such as apostate Jews or Gentile persecutors ; or the wicked are believed to remain in Sheol. For those whose wickedness is less than supreme, there may be temporary punishment, followed by release or annihilation. The place of the punishment of the wicked is *Gehenna* (or *Tophet*). The former name (Heb. *Gê-hin-nōm*) belonged originally to the ravine SW. of Jerusalem, which was regarded as accursed and defiled by the human sacrifice which had been offered there under the Hebrew monarchy. It was used, consequently, as a place to cast unclean refuse. There is much Haggadic speculation on the location and the dimensions of Gehenna. The chief torment of the wicked was fire ; and Haggadic speculation never wearied of conceiving new tortures for the damned.

These details should not obscure the fact that there was in the ancient world no other belief which had the moral force of Jewish belief in divine retribution.

d **Jewish Morality**—Jewish morality was erected on the firm basis of faith in the moral character and the retributive justice of God. There was no other religion of the ancient world which proposed a true religious basis for ethics. The religious motive of ethics in Judaism was based not only on reverential fear, but on the love of God, ' the first and greatest commandment of the Law'. The Law itself was the complete rule of conduct. The Law was imposed upon Israel as a part of the covenant ; in return for the election of Israel as the people of God, the people undertook the obligations laid upon them in the Law. The emphasis which Judaism placed upon the Law as a rule of conduct induced a change in the conception of sin. In the prophetic literature sin is a personal offence against God, rebellion, adultery against the divine love ; in Judaism sin is a legal transgression. These two conceptions are not mutually exclusive ; it is a question of emphasis. The obstacle to right conduct was called in the rabbinical literature *yēṣer hā rā'*, the ' evil inclination'. By the Law this inclination was brought under control, which was at best imperfect.

Here, as elsewhere, only some of the more characteristic features of Jewish morality can be noticed.

Social Relations—The Law commands the Jew to love his neighbour as himself. But the question of the scribe, Lk 10:29, ' Who is my neighbour?' was never answered by Judaism. Generally, the neighbour meant a fellow-Jew ; Gentiles were not included in the obligations of justice and charity. Harsh as this statement may seem, it summarizes Jewish theory on social relations, as far as the theory was formulated ; but the practice of Jews, especially in Gentile communities, did not correspond with the theory. To admit that Gentiles deserved the same consideration as Jews would have seemed to be a denial of the very covenant of election. Hence the rule of conduct was to abstain from social relations with Gentiles ; friendships should be formed only within the Jewish community. The obligations of justice and charity were relaxed towards Gentiles, to a degree which was never determined exactly. One could take advantage of the error of a Gentile in a business transaction, or, according to some authorities, deceive him. Lost articles, or even stolen goods, need not be returned to their Gentile owners. Usury might be exacted from Gentiles. There was no obligation to protect them from death or injury, and no prohibition against taking vengeance upon them. No gift was to be made to them ; and, in theory, salutations were not to be extended to them. The danger of ' profaning the name ' (*i.e.* of bringing trouble against the Jewish community) was admitted as a reason for giving Gentiles equal treatment with Jews. These and similar determinations were largely—but not entirely—theoretical ; in many instances Jews and Gentiles lived together in harmony.

An effect of the legal distinction between Jews and Gentiles was a solidarity within the Jewish community which, apart from its exclusiveness, is one of the most pleasing features of Jewish morality. The Jew in need could count on the help of his Jewish neighbour, even at the cost of great inconvenience. Almsgiving was a sacred duty, much inculcated in the oral Law, and it was regarded as a highly meritorious means of expiating sin. The Jew was supposed to share in the joys and sorrows of his neighbours : to attend their family festivals, to grieve with them in a disaster or a bereavement, to visit the sick, to assist the imprisoned.

The treatment of slaves, both according to the Law and in practice, was far more humane than in any Gentile code. Ancient slavery was pure chattel slavery, and the owner was responsible to no one for the life of his slave. While the Law made a distinction between Jewish and Gentile slaves, the Jewish owner did not enjoy, even over his Gentile slaves, the right of life and death. The owner was forbidden to inflict any permanent injury, and such an injury would give the slave the right of freedom ; but no punishment was enjoined if a slave died, through oversight, from severe treatment.

Family Morality—To the Jew marriage was the fulfilment of the precept, ' Increase and multiply ', Gen 1:28. Children, as many as possible, were God's blessing upon a marriage ; and it was a duty to procreate a large family. Consanguinity, impotence and difference of religion were impediments which prohibited marriage. Polygamy was permitted under the Law ; but it seems that it was practised rarely in NT times, for economic reasons, if for no other ; only the wealthy could afford a harem. And there are indications that monogamy was regarded as a higher ideal.

The position of the Jewish wife was, in general, higher than that of the wife in Greco-Roman culture. The misogyny of the Talmud is so profound as to be amusing ; but it is an indirect testimony to the freedom of women. In theory the wife was, under Jewish law, the property of her husband ; but the prevailing practice of monogamy was a protection of her position, although she was in every respect absolutely dependent upon her husband. In theory, also, Jewish law was ruled by the double standard ; unlawful intercourse was not regarded as adultery unless the woman was married. Divorce was permissible under the Law ; but the scribes were divided on the meaning of the ' shameful thing ' which is assigned in Deut 24:1 as a reason for divorce. The school of Shammai permitted divorce for adultery only ; the school of Hillel is credited with the opinion that divorce was permissible if a wife cooked badly, or if the husband found another woman who pleased him more. Divorce was a privilege of the husband alone.

Children were bound very strictly to revere and obey their parents, and to support them in their old age. The power of the father was not unlimited, as in Roman law, which conferred on the father the dominion over life and death ; but, according to the Law, rebellion or grave irreverence was a capital crime, to be decided by a court of law. Exposure of infants, especially female, which was so common in Hellenistic communities, did not occur among the Jews. The father controlled the marriage of his children through the law of the purchase of the bride.

Both in law and in practice Jewish family morality was immeasurably superior to the family morality of Hellenism. It kept the Jewish family together as a stable and tightly knit unit, in which the members supported one another, and the substantial obligations of parents and children were observed. The family was also a religious unit, in which common prayers were recited and the festivals celebrated. The family solidarity of the Jews must be reckoned among the reasons for the sturdy resistance of Judaism to assimilation.

Individual Morality—Among the distinctive features of Jewish individual morality we may notice Jewish esteem of chastity, and Jewish esteem of wealth. It is fairly safe to say that chastity was nowhere esteemed in the Hellenistic world except among the Jews. With them an unmarried girl was supposed to be a virgin, and her seducer could be legally compelled to marry her or to pay the purchase price. A betrothed virgin or a wife was punished by death, according to the

Law, for unchastity ; and, while it is not certain that **596d** this penalty was usually inflicted, Judaism did esteem chastity as the crowning virtue of woman. The death penalty was laid upon the male accomplice also, if the woman were a betrothed virgin or a wife. A woman was either an unmarried virgin, and protected by the property rights of her father, or a wife, and subject to the property rights of her husband. Prostitution was strictly forbidden. The unnatural vice which so disfigured Hellenistic culture was forbidden by Jewish law. On the other side we have the esteem of wealth, which **e** was regarded as a sign of God's blessing ; poverty was a curse, and a probable sign of sin. In this connexion it is fair to notice that the average Palestinian Jew was extremely poor. In most employments he competed with slave labour ; he had, as Canon Deane puts it, no margin, and was separated by not much more than one day's wages from destitution ; a minor disaster could reduce him and his family to slavery. In such circumstances, it is easy to understand that Judaism was somewhat loose in its standards of honesty, especially where Gentiles were concerned, and why it tolerated almost any way to turn a penny which was less than actual theft. One will scarcely find in extra-biblical Jewish literature a forthright condemnation of avarice. The wealthy aristocracy lived in opulence, and were envied and hated at the same time. The poor man could console himself with dreams of the Messianic kingdom, in which every man would be rich.

In summary, Judaism did impose upon its followers a standard of morality which was far above anything in the world of its times. The average Jew was by all known standards a good man and a religious man.

Jewish Piety—The sources for the religion of Judaism **f** do not offer us much information about the personal religion of the average Jew, ' the people of the land '. Yet the Law, the cult, and the doctrines of the rabbinical and apocalyptic writings do not tell the whole story. Jewish piety appears at its best in the prayers which have been preserved. From these it is evident that the Jew lived in close personal communion with God. God is addressed not only as creator and king, but also as father. He is solicitous for his creatures. Jewish prayer never omits the elements of adoration, praise, and thanksgiving for past mercies, and offers its petitions with full confidence that they will be heard. Judaism, as is evident from its Messianic aspect, is a religion of hope and confidence. Prayer occupied a very large part in the life of the Jew ; the *Shema* and the *Shemōneh 'Esrê* (the ' eighteen benedictions ') were to be recited daily ; prayer was offered at meals and at the beginning of important activities. The Jew was not ashamed to pray in public, although the Pharisees carried external devotion to the point of mere display. The consciousness of sin and professions of repentance are never lacking ; and there is firm confidence in the goodness and mercy of God. There is a strong sentiment of resignation to the will of God ; the evils which come upon the people are the just punishment for their sins, and repentance will hasten the coming of the Messianic kingdom. Judaism is a religion of external observance ; but it also fostered a genuine interior piety unique in its time.

THE PAGAN WORLD
IN NEW TESTAMENT TIMES

By W. REES

597a Bibliography—General : *R. Livingstone, *The Legacy of Greece* (1922) and *The Pageant of Greece* (1923) ; *T. R. Glover, *The Ancient World* (1935) ; *L. Whibley, *A Companion to Greek Studies* (4th ed. 1931) ; *J. E. Sandys, *A Companion to Latin Studies* (3rd ed. 1921) ; *M. Rostovtzeff, *Social and Economic History of the Roman Empire* (1926). **Government :** *CAH* vol. x (1934) ; *F. B. Marsh, *The Founding of the Roman Empire* (1932) ; *H. Stuart Jones, *The Roman Empire* (1908) ; *Sir H. Maine, *Ancient Law* (about 1868 ; Everyman's Lib. 1917) ; *H. Grose Hodge, *Roman Panorama* (1944) ; **Religion :** *T. R. Glover, *The Conflict of Religions in the Roman Empire* (1909) ; *Farnell, *An Outline History of Greek Religion* (1921) ; *W. K. C. Guthrie, *Orpheus and Greek Religion* (1935) ; *F. G. Church, *The Trial and Death of Socrates* (1880) ; *Warde Fowler, *The Religious Experience of the Roman People* (1911). **Morality :** *E. R. Bevan, *Stoics and Sceptics* (1913) ; Epictetus's *Discourses* (various translations, *e.g.* Carter in Everyman's Lib.) ; *S. Dill, *Roman Society from Nero to Marcus Aurelius* (1905). **Habits and Customs :** *Friedländer, *Roman Life and Manners* (Eng. tr. in 4 vols, 1908–13).

INTRODUCTION

b The Hellenization of the East—We must first recall some facts of history. Civilization appeared in the East some time before 3000 B.C., but it was not till after 1000 B.C. that the first whole nation of Europeans, the Greeks, became civilized. They had learnt much from the East, but they soon surpassed their teachers and made some important innovations (widespread education, democratic government, etc.) which the East had never known. Soon after 500 B.C. the Persians marshalled all the strength of the East to conquer Europe. The small Greek states, inspired by Athens, utterly defeated them. From that time onwards the eastern nations in deed though not always in words recognized the Greeks as the foremost nation in the world. Europe had overtaken and outstripped the East. In the next century the Greeks under Alexander the Great conquered the Persians and founded an empire stretching from Egypt to India. It soon broke up into several portions, but Greek kings maintained themselves in Egypt, Syria and Asia Minor, and proceeded to plant their European culture among the ancient nations of these lands. A Greek ruling class established itself all round the eastern Mediterranean. New Greek cities arose, and the Greek language, Greek manners and ideas, went on spreading for centuries till all the educated class was Greek in culture, though no longer, for the most part, of Greek blood.

c Roman Intervention—But the Greek states proved unequal to the task they had undertaken, the Europeanization of the Near East. They decayed and their work was in danger of perishing, when a stronger power came to the rescue. This was Rome. The Romans were the second nation in Europe to become civilized. It was to Greece, to Athens especially, that they owed their civilization. They adopted the Greek culture in all its fullness in the 2nd cent. B.C., and in the next century they undertook the direct government of the eastern Mediterranean lands. As soldiers, statesmen and lawyers they had valuable gifts denied to the Greeks, and under their patient supervision Greek civilization was at last solidly established in these lands. The process was more than half completed in the times of the NT. A similar process is at present taking place in these countries, but today the work is only beginning : in our Lord's time it was far advanced. These countries,. including Palestine, were far more European then than they are now. Only the Jewish religion had not been submerged by the flood from the west.

The Strata of Society—There are therefore three things to be distinguished in these countries : first, the national characteristics of the native races (Phrygians, Syrians, Egyptians, etc.) ; secondly, the Greek culture and language which were being overlaid on these ; thirdly, the Roman government which was using its influence to promote the Greek penetration. Society was therefore complicated and changing : the old and Asiatic was everywhere losing ground before the new and European. In country districts the lower classes—small farmers, labourers and slaves—lived much as their ancestors had lived a thousand years before, spoke the Egyptian or Lydian or other language, kept up many old customs and worships, and no doubt resented both Greek fashions and Roman rule. Their gentry and middle class had adopted Greek ways and the Greek language, and regarded themselves as Greeks. They were estranged from their own uneducated countrymen, whom they looked down upon as practically a different and inferior nation, and though they did not welcome Roman rule they felt nearer to the Romans than to the mass of their own backward countrymen. In all towns of any size Greek was the official language and all the townspeople had at least a smattering of it. At the top of the social scale stood the Romans—that is, the Italian or half-Italian officials, officers, merchants and visitors. Their status as members of the ruling race caused them to be treated with a special respect, and they themselves, though men of very varying merits and culture, were apt to assume an air of superiority over even the choicest spirits among the subject races.

The eastern Mediterranean world was therefore a complex world : a foundation of many races, some decadent and some backward, a civilization derived from Greece, and a Roman political framework into which all was being fitted.

GOVERNMENT

Roman National Tradition and its Expansion—The national character of the Romans was narrower and duller than that of the Greeks, but surpassed it in some valuable qualities, the so-called civic virtues, the qualities that make a good citizen—industry, shrewdness and dexterity, thrift, everyday honesty, fidelity to promises, attachment to home and country and courage to defend them, obedience to law and authority, dislike of change and novelties, respect for the rights and possessions of others, and firmness in vindicating one's own. Such a character is not showy, but it wears well and can endure storms. The faults to which it is liable are narrowness, rigorism, arrogance, callousness,

e avarice, coarseness and intemperance—faults which are all too common in Roman history. Yet this was the character which had made the Roman state the strongest that the world had yet seen.

f This national character or tradition did not spring from the blood but was hammered out slowly under the pressure of circumstances, or rather, of Providence. It was already formed by 300 B.C. within the small Roman state. It became in a century or two the character of an Italian nation, a compound of many races among which the Romans were only one. By the Christian era the descendants of the original Romans were degenerate, but the tradition was still vigorous and still expanding. Its chief representatives were now the people of the Italian country towns. In the 1st cent. A.D. it took hold of the leading men in the adjacent lands, especially France and Spain. Few of them had a drop of Roman or Italian blood, but henceforth when we speak of Romans we mean chiefly these men. They had a right to the name for they carried on the great tradition of civic virtues and public service.

g **Autocracy and Emperor-worship**—The Roman Empire, the mighty state established by the Romans, now encircled the Mediterranean and had lately been advanced northwards to the Rhine and Danube. Shortly before the birth of Christ, its government had become an autocracy. It was the form of government which both Greeks and Romans of an earlier age, when they lived in small democratic or aristocratic states, had hated with a fanatical hatred. But autocracy was considered the only practicable government for a large state—it was reserved for the English to solve that problem by means of representative assemblies. So first the Greeks, and now the Romans also, had to submit to despotism. Hatred of it continued long among the educated of both peoples, kept alive by their earlier literature, especially the oratory, which was the chief study of young men of the wealthier classes. To soothe them, the despots kept much of the language and forms of republican days: the Roman monarch was not called King but only First Citizen and Commander-in-chief. The mass of the population, however, both in Italy and elsewhere, felt little discontent. They were not sufficiently educated to make painful comparisons between the present and the past, and they enjoyed more material comfort than they had in republican times.

h The power of the Roman emperors (as we now call them) depended on their control of the armed forces, not on hereditary title or on election. The army alone could oppose or dethrone the emperor, and with its support he could defy the opinions and wishes of civilians. Over them his power remained absolute, and neither custom nor law ever placed any effective limit on it. The reigns of the bad emperors present a hideous picture of tyranny and servility. The ancient senate or council of nobles still remained. It was not hereditary, but consisted of those who had held the chief offices of state. To be a senator was the highest ambition of a public man, but the senate seldom dared to disagree with the emperor.

In the eastern provinces of the empire it had long been the custom to treat kings as gods, to offer sacrifices and incense to their statues, and to build temples to them. These eastern countries now paid the same honours to the emperors. The earlier emperors repudiated any claim to divinity and forbade such worship in the west (Suetonius, *Aug.* 52, Tac. *Ann.* 4, 37), but they tolerated it in the east, and in time it inevitably spread and came to be regarded as a political necessity. To refuse to worship the emperor was considered disrespectful, disloyal, and therefore treasonable. It became a capital crime.

i **The Central Government and the Provinces**—Italy and to a lesser degree Egypt (on which Italy depended for corn) came directly under the emperor's control, and so did a great deal of the finances and military supervision throughout the empire. These many calls

upon him led to the growth of an enormous bureaucracy. It consisted of men who owed everything to the emperor, his own slaves and freedmen (*i.e.* liberated slaves) or men of humble origin whom he had advanced and enriched. Under some weak or suspicious emperors freedmen became millionaires and in effect prime ministers of the empire. The empire, apart from Italy, was divided into thirty or forty provinces. Each province had its governor who was appointed by the emperor or through his influence, and usually held his post for a period of one to three years. The bigger provinces were governed by senators, the smaller ones, like Judaea, by men of the next highest class, the 'Roman knights'. In this way men who had lived in the servile atmosphere of Roman society and scarcely knew what freedom meant, found themselves for a short time raised to the position of despots. Not a few, as we should expect, succumbed to the temptations of power, and ruled as tyrants. While they were in office, there was no remedy except rebellion. After their departure their subjects could accuse them to the emperor. Under a just or a jealous emperor we may believe that provincial government was tolerable, but even under Augustus there were some scandalous cases (Velleius II, 117, Seneca, *De Ira* II, 5).

j **The Mission of Rome and the Growth of Roman Law** —The establishment of Roman autocracy came after a miserable sixty years of misgovernment and civil war. Autocracy brought the blessings of peace, order, and security, blessings which hardly anybody then living had experienced before. We cannot wonder that many Romans were more inclined to welcome these blessings than to repine at the loss of the old constitutional government. They found consolation in the thought that Fate had given supreme power to Rome not for the sake of the Romans only, but also of the many nations that Rome now governed. This glorious destiny seemed both to justify and compensate for the sacrifice of liberty. Rome had been divinely chosen to give peace, unity, and order to the world. The truth of this belief is beyond any doubt and appears much more clearly to us than to the Romans of Christ's time : Rome was God's instrument first for the civilization of Europe, then for its Christianization, as the breaking down of frontiers all round the Mediterranean made the spread of the Gospel immensely easier. ' Thou hast given a single home and country to the separated nations of the earth. What was once a world, thou hast made into a city '. So a later poet described it. We must not on that account shut our eyes to Rome's faults : Assyria and Babylonia were also God's instruments, as we are expressly told by the very prophets who denounce their sins and foretell their punishment.

k The deep desire of the world for peace and the lofty conviction of the mission of Rome were most finely expressed by the Roman poet Virgil who died about fifteen years before our Lord's birth. Other nations, he says, could outshine the Romans as artists and men of science, but Rome is divinely called and specially endowed to rule the world and to maintain peace and just government in it. It was a noble hope, a glorious ideal, only imperfectly realized, but the very proclamation of the ideal by Virgil and others no doubt inspired many a Roman and many a Roman-minded Spaniard or Greek to labour for its fulfilment.

l The Roman mind was conservative yet progressive, that type of mind which almost refuses to admit that anything ought ever to be changed, yet does in fact carry out revolutions which are the most radical and permanent, because they are the most gradual, careful, and detailed. Thus the Roman lawyers professed to remain faithful to their ancient code drawn up in the 5th cent. B.C., and declared their dislike of all abstract moral or political principles such as those of the Greek philosophers. But by a gradual process they embodied in their own law a more complete application of these very principles (especially those of the Stoic philosophy—see § 601*c*) than any Greek state had ever

597i

597 l done. It was the Roman who could grasp at once the broad principle and the mass of prosaic and tedious detail, and who combined an endless patience and willingness to compromise with a tenacity of purpose which persisted from century to century. However, it was not until A.D. 212 that Roman Law became the law applicable to all the free population of the empire, who then all became Roman citizens.

598a Distinction between Roman Citizens and Provincials— —We know that the Roman citizens numbered about five millions in the time of Christ (*Res Gestae D. Aug.*, 8) while the whole population of the empire may have been anything from fifty to a hundred millions or even more, about equally divided between slaves and free men. Throughout the provinces there was a sharp distinction drawn between citizens and non-citizens or 'provincials' as they are usually called. Roman citizens were privileged both by custom and by law. Firstly, whether they were Italians or not, they shared in the respect, influence and social importance which naturally go to members of a ruling class. Secondly, they alone were within the sphere of Roman civil law, while the provincials were allowed on the whole to keep the laws or customs which they had before the Roman conquest. But in their relations with the provincials the Roman governors still retained not a little of their original character of military commanders of conquered territory. They had a summary jurisdiction of such a wide kind over both their property and their lives as almost to justify us in saying that the provincials lived under perpetual martial law. Any action which was construed as being directed against the government could be punished with extreme penalties (crucifixion, enslavement, exile, confiscation, flogging, etc.) at the governor's discretion and without

b appeal. It was this power, the so-called *coercitio*, that was used in the case of many Christian martyrs. Every government must be armed with some such power in time of grave emergency, but its mere retention (even if infrequently used) through long periods of peace and security seems utterly contrary to the best traditions of European states, ancient or modern; and we have no proof that its use by Roman governors was very infrequent. From this dangerous power the Roman citizen was largely protected: he must be dealt with according to much more detailed and well-defined laws, and on a capital charge he could appeal to the emperor's court. The Roman franchise was rarely bestowed on whole districts, but it was often given to individuals for some public service or eminent merit, to the original citizens of the Coloniae (see § 598h) and to every soldier enrolled in the legions (*i.e.* heavy infantry).

c Roman Taxes—Various taxes were paid to the Roman government. *Tributum* was the general name for direct taxes, which were paid in one form or another by all provincials over the age of fourteen, but not by Roman citizens. In some cases it took the form of income-tax (about 10%), in others it was a property-tax (about 10% of the annual value), and in Egypt it was a poll-tax of apparently moderate amount. The chief indirect taxes, paid both by citizens and provincials, were: (1) Customs duties, usually from 2% to 5% of the value of goods, levied not only on the empire frontiers but also on the boundaries of the eight or nine large customs-areas into which the empire was divided. (2) An excise of 1% on goods sold by auction and of 4% on the sale of slaves. (3) A legacy duty of 5%, not paid by near relatives or on small legacies. (4) A tax of 5% on the value of a slave emancipated by his owner. For the purpose of assessing the *tributum* a census of all the provinces was taken every fourteen years.

d These taxes are light in comparison with those we pay. If they ever did become burdensome under the empire, as they had sometimes been under the republic, it was due to abuse of the method of collecting, or to some local causes. For the *tributum* each district was assessed at a certain sum, and the local authorities

were left to collect this in their own way and by means **5** of their own servants. The indirect taxes in each area were leased out to a firm or firms of (generally Italian) financiers, who undertook to pay a certain sum into the treasury and collected the taxes through their employees or slaves. These tax-farmers were the *publicani* in the proper sense, but the word came to be loosely applied to the actual collectors employed by them or by others. These indirect methods of collection no doubt saved trouble to the government, but they placed temptations in the way of both municipalities and tax-farmers. The central government probably kept a sharp eye on the intermediaries, for we hear little about rapacious taxation. We hear more complaints about the governor's right of requisition, *i.e.* compulsory purchase or hire of anything (including labour) needed for the administrative staff or the forces.

The Roman Army—The empire had a standing army **e** of at least 250,000 men. About three-quarters of these were stationed on the most vital frontiers, the Rhine, the Danube, and Syria. The forces were everywhere divided about equally into legions and auxiliaries. A legion consisted of about 5,000 men, who were all Roman citizens. They were infantry carrying considerable armour (helmet, breastplate, greaves, and shield) and furnished with a short sword and two six-foot spears (*pila*), used mainly for throwing. They served for twenty years and were provided with a livelihood afterwards. The auxiliaries consisted of cavalry, archers, slingers, etc., divided into units of 500 or 1,000 men. They were not Roman citizens as a rule. Lastly, there were the emperor's guards, 10,000 or more in number, housed in barracks in the suburbs of Rome.

The Roman army had once been a citizen-army **f** raised by general conscription. It was now a professional army, and the majority of its men were no longer of Italian blood. The power of conscription was always retained, but in ordinary times it was never enforced in Italy, and probably very seldom in the provinces, for enough volunteers seem to have been forthcoming to fill the ranks. No doubt most of the officers were still of Italian origin, and Roman discipline and training were maintained in all their sternness and efficiency. But the ordinary soldier's chief loyalty was not to Rome but to the person of the emperor, or to his own legion or commander. A short period of military service was still essential for every man who wished to hold high office at Rome, but the vast majority of men had no experience of it. Peace and security had made it possible for a great state to free the bulk of its population from military service— probably for the first time in the history of the world.

The Romans had now no maritime enemies but some naval squadrons were kept up, mainly as a protection against pirates. They were based on about six ports, including Alexandria, and Seleucia, the port of Antioch.

Municipal Government and Coloniae—Municipal **g** government was a shadow of the bygone city-state. But owing to Roman influence the democratic elements in the city constitution had vanished, even in Greek lands. The civic officials were chosen not by popular vote but by the city council, of which they then became members for life. The officials were not only unpaid but were required and often compelled, by express promises in advance, to contribute substantially to various public expenses, the construction or repair of public buildings, the cost of festivals and amusements, etc. Half the money which nowadays would be raised by rates came out of the pockets of the city officials. Only the wealthy therefore could hold such offices, and each municipality was in fact a plutocracy. The poorer citizens took the comforts provided for them and were apparently contented, or at least resigned.

Scattered throughout the provinces were towns called **h** *coloniae*—towns founded fairly recently by the Roman government, many as homes for soldiers discharged after the wars of the century before Christ. In theory they were small fragments of Italy : the original settlers were all Roman citizens, only Roman law was valid, the official language was Latin, and the town was to some extent outside the sphere of the provincial governor. Later on we find the descendants of the first citizens forming a privileged class amidst a mixed population of non-citizens, and clinging proudly to Latin tradition or sentiment. St Paul visited several of these towns : Pisidian Antioch, Philippi and Corinth were among them.

Survey of the Eastern Countries about A.D. 50— There were sixteen provinces, six or seven dependent kingdoms, and many smaller principalities. These last two groups were in much the same position as the native states in India before 1947. The province of Egypt was thoroughly Greek in its towns, and the fine city of Alexandria was a leading centre of Greek culture and learning, and the second largest city in the empire. The province of Syria was especially important because of its army of about 50,000 men guarding the frontier on the Euphrates. It was rich and populous, and full of Greek cities. Antioch, its capital, was the most beautiful of the great cities of the empire, and the third in size—a city adorned with miles of marble colonnades and with garden suburbs, and set amidst magnificent scenery. Eastern Cilicia (St Paul's home) was now joined to the province of Syria. Beyond the Euphrates lay the large empire of the Parthians, stretching to India. It was a feudalized state, whose king seldom had sufficient power over his great vassals to become a serious danger to the Romans. Asia Minor contained five provinces and three good-sized kingdoms. The coastal districts were nearly all Greek, the inland parts were more backward. The west formed the large and prosperous province of Asia, full of Greek cities. The province of Galatia in the centre of the peninsula was rapidly becoming Greek, but Cappadocia to the east was still a wild and lawless country with hardly any towns. Cyprus formed a separate province, thoroughly Greek.

In Europe the southern half of modern Greece made up the province of Achaia, thinly populated owing to centuries of emigration, but still the most cultured land in the world. Athens drew crowds of students, Romans and Greeks, and was full of masterpieces of art, but the new and rather upstart city of Corinth, a busy, commercial, and half-Italian place, was the capital of the province. The province of Macedonia stretched across the peninsula to the Adriatic and its eastern half was far more civilized than the other. North of the Aegean Sea the province of Thrace was still semi-barbarous except for the coast-line.

Merits and Demerits of the Roman Empire—The Romans gave several centuries of unprecedented peace to all the countries round the Mediterranean ; they found south-western Europe a semi-barbarous land and raised it to civilization ; they were the first imperial race who made any attempt to consider the welfare of their subjects, and they ultimately raised these subjects to the same level as the rulers ; they worked out an unsurpassed code of civilized law ; and they unconsciously smoothed the way for the spread of Christianity. On the opposite side of the account we have to admit that there were five centuries of autocratic government, alien to the earlier traditions of civilized Europeans ; that methods of government were brutal and inhuman as compared with the previous usages of both Romans and Greeks ; that the evils of a plutocratic society were present—extreme contrasts of riches and poverty, and the steady vulgarization of the higher classes.

RELIGION

Ancient paganism was not one in teaching and organization as Catholicism is, nor was it made up of exclusive and independent sects as was earlier Protestantism. It was a great jumble of many worships and doctrines, base and noble, crude and refined, competing yet seldom persecuting, continually borrowing from one another yet distinguishable. Modern Hinduism is just such another jumble. We must first look at the chief ingredients which went into the mixture. There were six of these : the four chief national religions of the Mediterranean world (those of Egypt, Syria, Greece and Rome) together with certain influences which came into Greek religion from outside, and lastly Greek philosophy.

Egyptian Religion—The religion of Egypt was the most ancient of the pagan religions. At its highest level it had taught the immortality of the soul and a judgement after death, and it had exalted one supreme god (the sun-god Ra) so greatly as to approach to monotheism. But these wholesome elements were embedded in a mass of gross or trivial superstition—animal-worship, endless magical formulae, etc. Under Greek influence some attempt was made to detach them, and two divinities, Isis and Serapis, became well known as far west as Italy. Their worship encouraged the expectation of a future life and included some ascetical and perhaps moral preparation for that life.

Syrian Religion—The religion of the Syrians and Phoenicians, the paganism against which the Jewish prophets had fought, was the lowest of the great national religions. But it still survived in Syrian villages, and colonists had carried it to Cyprus, Tunisia and Sicily. It was a religion which exploited human fear, lust, and ferocity, and it is hard to discover any good side to it. In the past at least it had encouraged human sacrifices, and perhaps infants were still sometimes burnt in honour of Moloch. It still continued to promote and consecrate the foulest immorality, and its temples still had their sacred prostitutes.

The primitive religions of Asia Minor are little known to us. They seem to have resembled that of Syria in many respects. The chief divinity was a goddess worshipped under many names. In Egypt, Syria and Asia Minor the most famous temples had in the course of ages acquired immense riches—vast estates and thousands of slaves. Guarded by popular veneration, these great possessions had survived and even increased amidst all the political changes. By the time of Christ the head-priests who governed them had come to rank as great noblemen in Egypt and as semi-independent princes in Syria and Asia Minor.

Greek Religion—The Aryan tribes who conquered Greece and Italy in the Bronze Age introduced their ancestral religion into both countries and gave it the most honourable position there. It was a religion of many gods or spirits, who seem to have been associated with some natural object or with some portion of man's life (birth, marriage, harvest, war, etc.). Above them all was the supreme god, the sky-god Deus or Dius. This ' Aryan religion ' had a very different history in the two countries. In Italy it was added to rather than changed, but in Greece changes came rapidly. Various gods and religious practices which the Greek invaders found in the country were accepted into the religion of the conquerors, and the result was complete polytheism : the sky-god, Zeus, still retained a nominal presidency, but seven or eight other divinities held a position almost of equality, and we may believe that for each district its own chief local god quite overshadowed Zeus. There was a general belief in a life after death, but it was imagined as a vague shadow of this life. There was a rough moral code, for the gods rewarded courage, honesty and hard work. But while the intellect and the moral sense had as yet made no progress among these early Greeks, their imagination was awake and soon reached an astonishing degree of poetical refinement. Countless stories were made up, in which the gods appear as essentially human figures, more powerful, dignified or graceful than the common run of men, but neither better nor wiser. Imagination often proved stronger than

598 l

m

n

o

p

598p reverence. This stage of Greek religion would very likely have been outgrown and forgotten in time if a supreme poet, Homer, had not embodied a multitude of these stories in his two great epic poems, some time between 950 and 750 B.C., and by so doing made them immortal. He had no idea of being a religious teacher, but in fact he became the most compelling religious teacher that the Greeks ever had. The fascination of his poetry bound them fast to his earth-born gods for a thousand years and frustrated all the efforts of religious reformers. The whole notion of the Divine was lowered, and the vital distinction between the Divine and the human, so easy even to the ignorant among us, remained blurred to the majority of Greeks.

q Homer often tells of gods disguised as men, and often of semi-divine beings ('heroes'), the offspring of a divine and a human parent. Many families claimed to have a god among their ancestors. There were many cases too in Greek history of distinguished men who after their death were worshipped as gods or demi-gods. Alexander the Great was persuaded by his courtiers that none but a god could have begotten him, and he claimed and received divine worship during his lifetime. It soon became the custom in Asia and Egypt to treat kings and even governors as gods. In consequence of all this, all kinds of ideas about a fusion or union of the divine and human, about incarnate gods and deified men, were trite and commonplace to the Greek mind. It was only to the Jew, with his much loftier and truer notion of the Divine, that such an idea was a startling novelty.

Later movements shook, though they could not overturn, the Homeric theology. There are two of these which need special description, the Mysteries and Greek philosophy.

599a **The Mysteries**—This is the general name given to various religious rites which seem first to have become important in the 7th cent. B.C. Their special marks were these : (1) They were not public rites open to all the members of a community, but secret rites to which worshippers were only admitted after certain preparations, and on certain conditions, among which was an oath of secrecy. (2) They appealed much more to the emotions than did the ordinary observances, and in many cases there was a definite process for developing excitement or even hysteria. (3) They awakened a new interest in the future of the soul and several of them offered a clearer hope and a more definite teach-

b ing on this subject. Some of these rites may have had their root in the earliest Greek religion itself, some probably sprang from pre-Greek cults ignored by the 'Homeric religion' while others no doubt came from neighbouring countries (Thrace, Egypt, Asia Minor) or even from farther afield (Persia or India). Many of them were certainly connected with some divinity who was believed to be author of fruitfulness, Demeter the goddess of harvest, Dionysus the vine-god, etc., and the yearly cycle of the seasons was transformed into the story of a god or goddess who died and rose again to life. Such stories of death and resurrection are found in nearly all the religions of the Near East. Represented in solemn ceremonies or in some form of religious drama, they could easily be the occasion of strong emotion, and could suggest a hope that the worshipper too might somehow share in the god's victory over death.

c We can guess some of the reasons which led to this development. No doubt it was an attempt to meet some desires left unsatisfied by Homer. Apparently a need was felt for some sort of revelation about the unsolved problems of life, especially the problem of the soul's destiny, and for some sort of religious discipline, and again for some larger scope for religious feeling—in short a vague longing for a religion which could engage the whole personality, including intellect, will, and emotions, those sides of human nature to which little had been offered by the Homeric religion. That religion had indeed made a strong appeal to the senses

d and imagination, but no more. It is to the honour of the Mysteries that they provided some satisfaction for this wider longing, though a very imperfect one, as it seems to us. We can see how vague or false were the 'inner truths' which they taught, and how unhealthy and dangerous was the excitement which some of them stimulated. At their best they created a confident and cheerful faith in immortality, with the sobering idea that future happiness depended on present action, partly at least on moral action. Their first introduction met with some opposition, but eventually some such rites were established in most of the Greek states. For a time even the average man seems to have been stirred by them, but before long they became a part of religious routine, except for some of the more thoughtful spirits who continued to find an inspiration and comfort in them throughout the centuries down to the final extinction of paganism.

Greek Philosophy—In the 6th cent. B.C. a new kind of 'wisdom' was heard of among the Greeks, a genuine invention of their own, and a startling one. Certain Greeks of Asia Minor put forward theories which attempted to explain the origin of the world in terms of mere matter without reference to any divine power whatsoever. They were materialists and practically atheists. This was the unpromising beginning of Greek philosophy and this materialism continued for centuries as *one* of the strands in it. But other theories, idealistic and even mystical, soon appeared. Here we can only mention Pythagoras (about 530 B.C.). He was influenced by the Mysteries, but introduced some doctrines apparently new to Greece, especially the notion that the soul was destined to inhabit a succession of bodies, some human and some animal. This was bound up with the view (derived perhaps from India) that matter was essentially evil and that the union of soul and body was a calamity or punishment. Pythagoras organized his disciples into semi-monastic societies, which lasted for a century or two.

A new chapter begins about 430 B.C. with the appearance of Socrates the Athenian. He wrote nothing and some branches of his teaching are uncertain, but he was the greatest personality in the whole story of ancient philosophy. An unwearied searcher for truth and a devastating critic, deeply religious, immensely interested in the practical implications of philosophy, possessing at once the zeal of a lonely prophet and the exquisite sympathy, urbanity and humour of a perfect man of the world, he made an indelible impression on the ancient world both by his life and by his death—he was executed on the charge of impiety. He and his great pupil Plato were much impressed by the Mysteries and by the teaching of Pythagoras, and helped by these they reached a belief in one God and in a perfect spiritual world, and worked out a higher moral code than the Greek world had yet known. They did not reject the old Greek religion, but had hopes of purifying and reforming it. They failed : their arguments and their eloquence could not induce the masses to give up the Homeric theology. Few other thinkers even attempted such a reform. When we come to the next great philosopher, Aristotle, who lived during the middle of the 4th cent. B.C., we can see that philosophy and religion are parting company : he attempted, independently of religion, to erect a theology and morality on sound rational foundations, and produced the firmest system of pure philosophy which the ancient world knew, the system which the great Catholic thinkers of the Middle Ages were able to adapt to Christian truth. Two other philosophies arose which had the widest influence of all in Roman times—Stoicism and Epicureanism (see § 601*b, c*).

Thenceforth philosophy and religion went their separate ways without an open quarrel. Men who desired an intellectual basis for their beliefs and a more enlightened morality lost interest in religion. They paid outward respect to it, they regarded it as good and necessary for the ignorant and unintellectual, but they themselves drew all their inspiration from some philosophy. In the 2nd cent. B.C. it seemed that before long even the ignorant would cease to care for religion and that it would disappear altogether. Two or three generations however before the birth of Christ the tide began to turn. Educated society, especially in Italy, was frightened at the prospect of a godless populace and a general dissolution of all religious scruples. A revival of paganism, based more on policy than on conviction, had definitely begun when our Lord was born, and continued steadily for two or three centuries, gathering more and more sincerity as it went on. The Roman government did all in its power to promote it. But the cleavage between religion and morality still remained serious at the time of the Apostles.

Roman Religion—The ' Aryan religion ' which the Italic race had brought into Italy (see § 598o) had received considerable additions at an early date from Etruscan sources and the mixture which resulted formed the early Roman religion—a polytheism like the Homeric religion, but the Italians had not the vivid imagination which created the Greek mythology. If there ever were any Italian stories about Jupiter, Juno or Vesta, they disappeared without leaving a trace. There was an elaborate ceremonial, and a special veneration for many very primitive divinities such as Saturnus the patron spirit of sowing, Ceres who presided over harvest, Vesta the protectress of the hearth, and for a multitude of others, and the ancient sky-god of the Aryans still remained at the head of the pantheon under the name of Jupiter. With a few additions from Greece and elsewhere, this religion remained the official religion of the Roman state, respected even by non-Romans for its close connexions with Roman public life, and with the mighty power of Rome.

There was the same rough moral code that we find in early Greek religion. Long before Christ the Romans had identified each of the greater Greek gods with some Roman god and in this way had grafted on their own religion the whole Homeric mythology with all its imaginative appeal and also all its disadvantages. Its connexion with the state kept the Roman religion alive in Italy and gave it an honourable position in the Latin provinces of the west, but Greek, Egyptian and Asiatic cults were now competing with it in Italy and ultimately all gained a firm foothold there. For emperor-worship see § 597h.

The Resulting Confusion. Moral Standards—Such were the chief materials which were joined together to form the patchwork of ' pagan religion '. Every conceivable mixture of them was to be found in the same family or even in the same mind. One member of a family might frequent the ancient temples of Jupiter or Poseidon, another might put all his hopes in one of the Mysteries, a third might care only for Isis, and a fourth might be a Stoic and look with tolerant superiority on all the rest. Or again the same person might successively, or even simultaneously, try to drink from all these fountains. There was no definite moral standard associated with religion in general or with any one religion. The most diverse moral levels could claim to be equally pious and devout. We find pagans who attain to a serene and refined piety which might almost remind us of a Victorian parsonage, and we find others who can still call themselves devout though sunk in superstition or lust. There is a similar contrast in Hinduism between the austere mystical Brahmin and his grosser co-religionists.

There were other grave weaknesses : there was no controlling authority either in teaching or government, no organization, hardly what can be called a clergy, and no theology.

Authority, Theology—In Egypt and in Rome some sort of central authority had once existed, but had long ceased to operate. The religious authority of the emperor as head of the Roman state-religion was exercised occasionally, but only to protect Italy from un-Roman devotions. As a rule every temple was independent and secure from all interference except when the civil power intervened to repress disorder.

No pagan denied the right of the state to interfere in **600c** religion, and the worship of the emperor also implied an acknowledgement of such a right. Yet if we call the emperor the head of the pagan religion, he was a head that rarely governed.

In Egypt, Syria and Asia Minor we find a large body **d** of professional clergy—priests whose priestly office was the main business of their lives. Even in Egypt they seem to have counted for little as a spiritual force, and elsewhere for even less. Among the Greeks and the Romans the majority of the priests were not professional : they had secular work to do, more urgent and exacting than their sacred duties. Their priesthood was a side-occupation, which might add dignity to a public career or provide a graceful occupation for old age. In such circumstances little special training or knowledge would be necessary or possible. With such a clergy and with the severance between religion and philosophy, it is natural that no body of pagan theology ever grew up. The appeal of religion was to the senses, imagination and emotions : it provided hardly anything to satisfy the intellect or win the heart of a thinking man, hardly any rational foundation for faith and devotion, or incentive to holiness. There was an intellectual and spiritual mediocrity about the pagan religion. In its whole history it did not produce one great spiritual book comparable to the best which Mohammedanism or Hinduism have to show. Those which come nearest (the works of Plato, Epictetus, Marcus Aurelius, Plotinus) are essentially philosophical works pathetically trying to catch the spirit of religion. We cannot therefore class ancient paganism among the great non-Christian religions of the world.

Let us glance at some of the externals of paganism :
Temples—By far the commonest type throughout the **e** empire was that which evolved by the Greeks of the 5th cent. B.C.—the oblong building of white marble or light-coloured stone, with low-pitched roof supported on every side by pillars. Its wide prevalence even in alien lands far away from Greece is a remarkable proof of the power of Greek artistic tradition, for it embodied the most characteristic qualities of this tradition—an infinitely delicate sense of proportion and harmony, and an extraordinary self-restraint. Other peoples have perhaps had as deep a feeling for beauty, and have expressed it as finely in their architecture, but in *this* style the Greeks have had no equals. A Gothic cathedral would no doubt have shocked them as something florid and riotous. In the same way if we, nursed in our very different traditions, were to come upon a well-preserved temple in the midst of a Greek city (not a picturesque and famous ruin in the wilderness) our first feeling might well be that the building was tame and plain. Time and effort would be needed to appreciate its beauty.

The temple was regarded as a house for the god, not **f** for his worshippers, and therefore the interior (usually one chamber, the *cella*) was not on the same scale as that of our churches. One of the very largest interiors, that of the temple of Artemis at Ephesus, was 145 feet by 65. In the *cella* stood the chief statue of the god. It was frequently of a large or even colossal size— that of Athena in the Parthenon at Athens is said to have been forty feet high including its pedestal. In some of the bigger temples the *cella* seems to have been wholly or partly open to the sky—in other cases the light must have come mainly from the open door. The *cella* was often adorned with other sculpture, with votive offerings or with paintings. The altar stood in the open air before the entrance. It was on the open space before the temple, not inside it, that crowds gathered at festivals.

Statues of the Gods—Greek tradition aimed at depict- **g** ing the gods as beautiful or noble *human* figures, and the great sculptors had carved some of their masterpieces to be erected in temples. But some lewd or bestial forms remained even among the Greeks, and many nightmare shapes continued to inhabit the temples of Egypt and Asia. What degree of idolatry

600g was there—how far did the pagan believe that the statue was the god? We may be sure that hardly any educated man held such a belief. The making of divine images was carried on quite openly, and every god had many images. An educated man could not believe that Apollo, for example, was identical with some one statue, or that he somehow inhabited or animated a thousand statues. But no doubt some such beliefs did survive among the uneducated masses, especially in the more backward countries. Against these latter pagans the denunciations of the OT writers were still valid.

h **Sacrifices**—Sacrifice was a constant part of pagan worship. Animals of various kinds, cakes, meal, fruit, wine, milk, honey and flowers were among the things offered to the gods. Some gods did not receive animal sacrifices. Many of the things offered were either destroyed in the ceremony (the wine poured out, etc.) or became the property of the temple authorities and were consumed or sold by them. But an animal, after a portion had been burnt on the altar, was usually eaten by the worshipper and his friends at the temple or near it, and so a sacrifice would normally lead to a dinner. In the same way great public sacrifices often involved public dinners. These public sacrifices were often accompanied by elaborate ritual, with rich vestments, incense, chants and musical instruments. Greek sacred choral music had once reached a high artistic level, but it is doubtful whether these masterpieces were often heard now. Greek tradition scarcely regarded any religious festival as complete without a series of athletic contests, but this association of religion and athletics never became popular in the west. The Greeks also were very fond of religious processions which often walked surprising distances.

i **Prophecy and Oracles**—Some temples had a reputation for curing diseases, and drew many pilgrims on that account. But many more pilgrims travelled to the numerous shrines which claimed prophetic inspiration, *i.e.* an oracle of some sort. Oracles were found in abundance both in east and west. Delphi was the most celebrated in Greek lands; one of the most frequented in the west was the great temple of Fortuna at Praeneste close to Rome. Many methods were used: trance-talk, dreams, lots, interpretation of sounds animate or inanimate, etc. Some oracles seem to have regularly used fraud or equivocation, but as a rule there was nothing worse than ignorance and superstition.

j Prophecies and omens meet us everywhere in ancient paganism. Whenever an animal was sacrificed, its internal organs were examined for omens, and even the sober Roman religion used an elaborate system of divination from the flight of birds. The higher religions have generally tried to repress man's foolish belief that he can peer into the future. The blind guides of ancient paganism shared this belief, no doubt. They certainly encouraged and exploited it. (See Dill: *Roman Society from Nero to Marcus Aurelius*, 451–73.)

MORALITY

601a **Moral Ideals in the Time of Christ**—I have said that the highest moral ideals were founded on philosophy, not religion. The two noblest efforts of philosophy had been those of Plato and Aristotle (§ 599*f*, *g*), but at the time of Christ both these philosophies were in eclipse. Another system, that of the Stoics, had come to dominate the world. Next to Stoicism the widest appeal was probably made by the philosophy of Epicurus, who taught just before 300 B.C. He had given a new shape to the materialism and atheism which we noticed in early Greek thinking (§ 599*e*).

b **Epicurus** taught that atoms, falling aimlessly through space, had combined by pure accident to form this present world, which was bound in the course of ages to break up again by the separation of the atoms.

Man therefore must not labour to please any god or to prepare for any future for himself or for his race. He had only his own single earthly life to think of. The highest proper motive for his action was pleasure. In the catalogue of pleasures Epicurus gave the foremost place to those of the intellect and imagination, but such a philosophy would, even at its best, encourage a refined individualism, and at its worst might serve as excuse for almost any degree of sensuality. Its most eloquent exponent was a Roman, the poet Lucretius, who, fifty years before the birth of Christ, attacked all religion as the greatest curse of human society, and pleaded against it with a fervour worthy of an evangelist. In the century before Christ many eminent Romans had been Epicureans, but there were not so many in the following century.

Stoicism: Its Teaching and Influence—The Stoic philosophy had been built up by three men of whom none was a thinker of the first rank. The world, according to the Stoics, was a single living being, whose soul was God—indeed the world could rightly be called God. Every part of it, man included, was a part of him, and was in itself as incomplete and worthless as a finger severed from the body. Each man therefore existed purely for the sake of the world and had no claim to any individual happiness here or hereafter: the hope of immortality was foolish. Moreover, as man had no true individuality, there was no such thing as free will. All his actions were determined by the motion of the Whole to which he belonged. But once a man recognized his insignificance and heartily acquiesced in it, he came into his true greatness, for though a fragment, he was a fragment of God. Nothing could thwart him as long as he subordinated himself utterly to the Whole. By acknowledging himself to be nothing he became omnipotent. He had within himself all that he needed for a perfect life. He was not only invincible against temptation and suffering, he was insensible and inaccessible to them. Pleasure and pain, health and sickness, riches and poverty, were all alike to him. They were 'indifferent' to him. This doctrine of the self-sufficiency of the soul and the indifference of its environment was the core of Stoic morality. Thus the false idea that God is one with the world led to the two opposite results of unnatural self-effacement and unnatural self-exaltation. Moreover the Stoic outlook was limited to this present life almost as much as that of the Epicureans: perfect happiness must be found here and now if it is to be found at all.

This erroneous and sombre philosophy had gained immense influence among educated and half-educated pagans when our Lord was born, and it continued to dominate men's minds for another two centuries. It pervaded the atmosphere of the time and reached countless persons who were not formal adherents of any philosophy. A class of philosophical missionaries had come into existence, men who preached moral philosophy in popular language, not to students but to all who cared to listen. Their teaching, though somewhat mixed, was more Stoic than anything else, and through them the Stoic catchwords and the outlines of Stoic morality reached many of the uneducated. Thousands became half-Stoic without realizing it. Stoicism appealed to the Romans more strongly than any other form of Greek philosophy. Its stern maxims found an echo in their national character. In short no other moral code exercised such a wide influence in antiquity, and this influence was nearly at its height in the time of Christ.

With all its faults Stoicism must have done immense good. It overrode racial differences and taught a brotherhood of men. It encouraged justice, public spirit, courage and self-control. It supported society when ancient sanctions of morality were weakening. It must have saved many a prosperous man from sensuality or arrogance, and many an unfortunate one from servility or despair. But the ordinary man must always have been repelled by its uncompromising doctrine of self-sufficiency and by its cheerless outlook on the future : it made such enormous demands on men and offered so little in return. It was more suited to strong self-centred characters than to the diffident and sociable, who are more numerous. For these or other reasons Stoicism failed to win the masses, and ultimately declined and disappeared.

I have described the outstanding moral ideal. Turning now from theory to practice, I will content myself with sketching a few aspects of pagan society which bring out the moral differences between it and ours.

Comparison of Ancient and Modern Moral Conditions—In some details the Roman world compared favourably with ours. National rivalries and hatreds within the empire, though not dead, were hardly ever carried to the point of bloodshed. Religious persecution had hitherto been a rare thing. Drunkenness never seems to have become the curse which it has been in northern countries. Gambling was moderate compared to its present-day scale. Duelling, which has been till lately a serious evil, was almost unheard of among the civilized nations of antiquity.

On the other side there were evils which are unknown or less known among us :

Despotism—To what I have said already (§ 597*g*) I need only add that the sight of irresponsible power wielded on a vast scale, when there was not in the world a single state governed constitutionally or democratically, must have been a corrupting influence, aggravated by the lapse of generations. The political ideals of Greek statesmen and thinkers (one of the most valuable things that Greece had given to the world) seemed lost for ever, and the loss was a great *moral* loss.

Slavery—Slaves formed a large proportion, a third or even more, of the population of the more civilized provinces. There were slaves in every household except the poorest, and there were often hundreds working for a rich man. Great gangs of slaves tilled the large farms of Italy and Africa, and laboured in mills and factories, where they were often trained to a machine-like efficiency which would be impossible with free workmen. These industrial slaves seem in many cases to have been treated little better than animals, and naturally became brutalized and savage beings. Household slaves received a more humane treatment ; some were highly educated or trained in medicine or the arts. But even in this milder form slavery offered terrible temptations to cruelty and lust. Both law and custom had sought to limit the owner's power, but in practice such restrictions seem for some reason to have been of little use. At any rate we still find cases where slaves are brutally maltreated or killed with impunity. Slaves who had done good service were often liberated, and such freedmen were now accepted nearly everywhere as equals by freeborn citizens. Some public offices however were closed to them. The supply of slaves had always to be maintained by importation. Barbarian chiefs outside the empire sold their captives or subjects to dealers who resold them at the great slave-markets. Rebels within the empire were sometimes reduced to slavery as a punishment.

Infanticide—Pagans were still permitted by their laws to allow a newly born child to die if its father did not wish to bring it up. Several indisputable cases occur in or near the time of Christ, but it is impossible to say how common the horrible practice was. If we may judge by the indifferent tone in which it is referred to, it would seem to have been not rare.

The Amphitheatre—The inhuman sports of the amphitheatre were one of the worst blots on the Roman world. It was the Etruscans who first amused themselves by making slaves or prisoners of war fight one another to the death. The practice was copied by the Romans and became one of their national sports. The Greeks in general looked upon it with aversion, and many cultured Romans came to loathe it, but they reluctantly gave the populace what it enjoyed. The amphitheatre was invented for the murderous pastime and numerous ruins justly perpetuate the memory of Roman brutality. The sport spread to all parts of the empire except Greece. Its victims were of several classes : slaves bought for the purpose, criminals who were not Roman citizens, subdued rebels, prisoners taken in wars with the frontier tribes, etc., and sometimes volunteers from among the free citizens. Some of the slaves (called ' gladiators ') were carefully trained for the exhibition, but many of the performers received no special training. After every victory, whether over foreign tribes or rebels, it became the custom to set large numbers of prisoners to kill one another in the amphitheatres. There were also fights between men and animals and the slaughter of unarmed men by animals. High Roman officials were compelled by custom to provide such entertainments and to preside at them in person. In Italy and the western provinces not only men but women also, even the Vestal Virgins themselves, could and did witness these massacres. Great multitudes were enabled frequently, without personal risk, to gloat over the agonies of others : it was a perfect training in cruelty and cowardice, and a plentiful crop of both appeared in due time.

Relations of the Sexes—In the Asiatic provinces long ages of polygamy had inevitably robbed women of the honour and respect which are their natural right. European influence had now restored monogamy, but had not yet restored women to their rightful position. They were a depressed class even among the upper, or Greek, portion of society. They were unequal partners in their own homes, and counted for very little outside them. A wife had her own rooms in the house and did not meet her husband's guests or eat with them. Roman tradition however, which prevailed in the western provinces, gave much greater freedom and importance to women. Unmarried daughters could not indeed choose their husbands, but after marriage women lived on something like an equal footing with men. The influence of women in Roman history is considerable.

Roman law allowed either husband or wife to dissolve the marriage at will, by merely making a short statement before witnesses. In the eastern provinces the husband alone could use this easy method, while the wife could only obtain divorce by legal process. The richer classes both in East and West made extensive use of these powers, and marriages were freely made and unmade. Children usually remained in their father's care and endured, as best they could, a succession of stepmothers. There were laws imposing severe penalties on adultery in which a married woman was involved, but they seem to have been seldom enforced. With this exception, unchastity in a man, married or single, was regarded as a small fault or none. We should have expected the Stoics to teach a higher standard of male morality, but they did not : a great Stoic moralist like Epictetus contents himself with advising moderation in immorality. Greek opinion on the subject of certain incestuous unions and on homosexual vice had sunk into a state of disgraceful laxity, little better than that of the Asiatics. The Romans still looked on such things with a severer eye, but they never used their power to attempt any reform in the eastern provinces, and moreover their own standard was now declining. Finally there was the consecrated unchastity surrounding many temples in Syria and Asia Minor : the Romans did not interfere, but they successfully resisted any westward spread of these abominations.

HABITS AND CUSTOMS

Education—Schools throughout ancient times seem to have been practically always private schools, not those of the medieval and modern type controlled by

601k

602a

b

c

602c some sort of corporation. Although we hear, especially in the eastern provinces, of municipal grants of money towards schools, the master seems to have depended largely on the fees of his pupils. The average slave seems to have received very little education, and for free men education was entirely voluntary. The proportion of illiterate persons seems to have been much bigger than in western Europe today. We know little about the education of women, but many Roman women of the richer class were certainly well-educated.

d Education was in three stages as with us. After elementary education up to twelve, a boy spent about four years at a secondary school, where the chief study was the works of the poets, Greek poets in the East, and both Greek and Latin poets in the West, where the Greek language was a regular part of a liberal education. Other subjects (history, geography, mythology, astronomy, etc.) were included incidentally in the reading of the poets. Greek boys seldom learnt Latin, but received considerable training in athletics and music, subjects which the Roman schools neglected. The next stage, for those who wanted it, was a period devoted to the study of rhetoric—a survival from democratic days. The students wrote speeches for imaginary occasions and delivered them with the prescribed intonation and gestures. Bad models were often followed and sophistry or a florid style was the frequent result. The training explains why it was as natural for the average Greek or Roman to declaim or to quibble as it is for the average modern to sentimentalize or over-analyse. In Greek lands philosophy might be substituted for rhetoric. Endowed professorships of both subjects existed in various places, and some Greek cities, especially Athens, Alexandria, Tarsus and Marseilles, had a reputation for learning and drew crowds of students, though there was not the organization of a modern university.

e Occupations—Both Greeks and Romans held manual work in greater contempt than we do (Aristotle, *Politics* 3, 5. Cicero, *De Officiis* 1, 42). The Romans indeed regarded all work done for a salary or a fee as somewhat dishonourable. They had less scruple about profits gained by trade, and it was the Roman middle class who carried industry and finance to a pitch of efficiency never reached before. They used many of the devices of modern finance—bills of exchange, banking, insurance, and joint-stock companies. Mines, factories and large-scale farming were conducted with skill and rigid economy. Slave-labour was employed, ruthlessly trained and disciplined. Its efficiency and cheapness enabled many articles to be produced almost as economically as in the modern world with all its machinery, and gave big industry much the same advantage over the small man. There is no doubt that the free workmen, especially the semi-skilled or unskilled, were in a bad position. Such men were seldom employed in large enterprises or as household servants. They worked singly or in small groups. They had therefore little chance of forming the associations by which modern workers have improved their condition, and moreover the government forbade all such association except for worship or mutual insurance. In special distress the workman had nowhere to turn except to private charity. Public hospitals and poor relief did not exist. Free corn and occasional free meals could be obtained in some large cities, but that was all.

f Cities—The first century of the empire was one of the great building ages of the world. Many new cities were founded and old ones were adorned with modern buildings. The majority of the great new buildings were intended for utility, comfort or luxury. There were theatres, amphitheatres, baths, town-halls, lawcourts, market-buildings, and in some cultured cities public libraries. Every town of any size had its public baths (with halls and shady walks often attached) for frequent bathing was now the fashion everywhere. Immense sums were spent on water-supply and drainage. But we do not find great schools or colleges or hospitals. Except in frontier areas, city-walls and fortresses were non-existent or neglected. Antioch was a mighty stronghold, but Corinth was an open city. A modern visitor to the cities of this time would at once be struck by the number of colonnades or pillared walks. They formed some part or adjunct of most large buildings, and they lined the principal squares and streets, roofing in what we should call the pavement. Old cities like Rome and Jerusalem had many crooked narrow streets, but the newer ones (Antioch, Ephesus, Troas, Thessalonica, Philippi, Caesarea, etc.) were better planned, with straight and broader streets. Big cities had many pleasure-grounds, public and private, in their outskirts, with groves, grottoes, ornamental waters, and of course colonnades. Antioch is said to have been the only city with street-lighting and perhaps only Rome had a well-organized fire-service. Rome had over a million inhabitants, Antioch and Alexandria at least half a million each, Jerusalem perhaps a hundred and fifty thousand.

Houses—The sharp contrast between riches and poverty is very evident here. In the towns the poor lived in buildings of wood or sun-baked brick, and the villages in many parts of the empire were clusters of miserable huts, round or square. The houses of the wealthy were as big and as luxurious as those of eighteenth century Europe, but in an inferior style. Beauty and even grandeur were sacrificed to piecemeal display and tasteless comfort. There was a want of order and dignity. Every moderate-sized town-house was built round a small courtyard : the big houses enclosed several, and larger, courtyards. The best rooms were on the first floor, which was often the highest. The façade towards the street was plain. Country houses had even less unity, and were rambling collections of fine and luxurious parts. The Romans loved the country much more than the Greeks, and a wealthy Roman often had five or six houses in the country or by the sea. In big cities, especially Rome, the poorer middle class lived in huge tenement-houses of six or seven storeys. Everywhere the furniture would appear scanty to us, except in well-to-do dining-rooms where a number of huge couches, holding three reclining persons each, would fill most of the room.

Daily Routine, Meals, etc.—Very early rising was the rule, in order to have the coolest hours for work. This was compensated for by a sleep after lunch. There were usually three meals. Breakfast was a very light meal, there was a substantial lunch about noon, but the largest meal was eaten some time between four and seven o'clock, generally after a bath. It was eaten in a leisurely manner and then people seem usually to have retired for the night. Greek tradition favoured simplicity and moderation in food and drink, but the Romans were less abstemious and coarser in their taste. Both Greeks and Romans regularly mixed their wine with two or three times its volume of water, usually hot water. Beer was drunk in several countries, but distilled liquors were unknown. The custom of reclining at the evening meal was now universal among men, both rich and poor. The diner lay on his left side, his feet pointing away from the table, and handled his food with his right hand, using his fingers or a spoon. Couches were used in the richer houses, cushions or rugs in the poor ones. Women and children, if they were present, sat on the edge of couches or on some kind of low seat.

Dress—Dress throughout the empire, both male and female, consisted essentially of two garments : (1) A shirt-like garment, reaching to the knees for men, to the ankles for women (*chiton, tunica*), made usually of white or light-coloured cloth. Women wore a belt with it, men often did. (2) A large piece of woollen cloth, irregular oblong in shape and longer than a blanket (*himation, pallium*). This was wrapped round the body over the *chiton*, rather like a shawl but in one prescribed way. Women drew it over both shoulders, men over the left shoulder only, as a rule. It was usually coloured, more brightly for women than for men, but Roman citizens on ceremonial occasions wore a voluminous white *himation* called a *toga*. Men engaged in active work wore the *chiton* only, so as to have the arms free. Women out-of-doors drew the *himation* over the head to form a sort of hood. Men went bare-headed or wore a cap or a flat broad-brimmed hat. Greek custom favoured sandals but shoes or boots were common in the west. Clean-shaving had been the fashion for centuries, and was still rigidly maintained by the Romans, but beards were no longer rare in the east. Short hair was the universal rule for men.

Recreation—The Greeks had early acquired a passion for athletic sports (running, boxing, wrestling, etc.) and these had become an essential part of all liberal education in the eastern provinces. Athletic contests were included in all festive celebrations. Every city had its public gymnasium for training in these sports (not in our 'gymnastics'). It was nearly always the individual, of course, who competed : ball-games and other team-sports never became highly developed. Greek sports were copied in the west, but only one of them, chariot-racing, became popular there. Music, especially choral singing, had been intensely cultivated by the Greeks and was still kept up, though with less enthusiasm. The Romans cared much less for it. The plays of the great dramatists were still performed in Greek theatres but the Roman populace would no longer listen to such things. Little was seen on the Roman stage except dumb-show acting, ballet-dancing and buffoonery. In Greek cities large crowds would attend displays of skill by fashionable professors of rhetoric. Dancing was left to children and professional dancing-women : it was not a pastime for respectable adults. I have said enough elsewhere (§ 601*k*) about the amphitheatre.

Travelling—Roman roads, the first metalled roads **c** ever made, but rough and narrow compared with ours, were spreading all over the empire. Harbours were being built or improved. Highwaymen and pirates were fast disappearing. Travel was becoming easier and safer, but even the Romans could not make land-travel nearly as fast as it was in our stage-coach days. Sea-travel was quicker and therefore cheaper. There were plenty of ships which carried both passengers and cargo. They were sailing-ships—only warships were propelled by oars. But navigation was still so backward that it was necessary to suspend all sailing between November and March. During that time Rome was almost cut off from the provinces. Yet travelling was easier than ever before. The removal of national frontiers helped towards the same result. More people travelled for pleasure, and among the richer Romans we now hear of a class whom we may call tourists ; they travelled chiefly in Italy, Greece and western Asia Minor. In these areas comfortable hotels came into existence. Elsewhere only rough accommodation was to be found, and travellers endeavoured to stay in private houses whenever possible. The Romans had not the Greek passion for exploring. They never troubled to trace the European coast-line beyond Denmark, and though their armies often marched through the Alpine passes, no Roman attempted or desired, as far as we know, to scale the peaks.

THE GOSPELS AND NON-CATHOLIC
HIGHER CRITICISM

By E. GUTWENGER, S.J.

604a Bible criticism is of various kinds ; one kind is concerned with textual criticism ; another with the exegetical explanation of the Bible text ; and the third, higher criticism, with the origins of the biblical books. Higher criticism of the gospels, then, investigates the authorship of the gospels, the date of their composition, and the sources which account for the content and form of the gospels. It is on its sources that the historical reliability of a book is largely dependent.

It should be noticed that in the treatment of the gospels exegesis and higher criticism may easily overlap. In the rationalist *Lives of Jesus*, for instance, the authors undertake to explain the various events and discourses recorded in the gospels ; such an undertaking might be classed as exegesis. However, they do not stop short there. Being rationalists, they ascribe the supernatural elements in the gospel stories to a human proclivity to invent myths and legends, and so must needs pass judgement about the historicity of certain passages or whole books. Such work is higher criticism. Considering the fame enjoyed by some of the *Lives of Jesus*, I have thought it better not to disregard them altogether in this article, especially as the development of higher criticism was deeply influenced by them.

b Of course, the problems of higher criticism are treated also by Catholic scholars. This paper, however, is concerned with the criticism that comes from the pens of non-Catholic authors. To avoid confusion it should be noted at once that our attention will be focussed on tendencies which are hostile to the views of tradition. There are, and have been, non-Catholic scholars whose opinions coincide more or less with ours—great names such as Bishop Lightfoot, Theodor Zahn, etc. To write an essay on non-Catholic higher criticism and in it to discuss only radical views is, therefore, a little unfair. As this paper is partly a criticism of the critics and the space allotted to it very limited, I must content myself with offering my apologies to the non-Catholic authors who defend the historical basis of Christianity, but to all appearances are here not distinguished from those who are more inclined to attack than defend. When in the following pages we speak of ' higher criticism ' without further modification we mean to designate the radical views and opinions. It is, of course, impossible in a few pages to give a detailed description of all attacks delivered against the gospels in the course of two centuries. This will be only a very rough sketch. The number of authors encountered in the course of our exposition will be small. To mention all is impossible, for their name is legion.

c Higher criticism owes its beginnings and rise to two different problems, one of which was of a philosophical, the other of a literary nature. The first problem is that of **the possibility of miracles.** With the advent of rationalism a marked change had taken place in the attitude towards the supernatural. Mysteries were said to be against the autonomy of the human intellect and were relegated to an obscurantist limbo. Miracles in particular met with scorn. It was the English rationalists, the deists of the 18th cent. (John Toland, Thomas Woolston, etc.), who gave them special attention. Their opinion was that the physical laws of the universe had been once and for all imposed by God upon nature. Now he must respect them, so much so that any interference on his part is impossible. Some of them

asserted that a body of truth exists which shows the same inviolable necessity as pertains to mathematical propositions. Physical laws form a part of that body of truth. Hence it is impossible for God to deviate from them. Since miracles are events not in conformity with the physical laws of nature, it came to be regarded as a safe principle that miracles do not happen. But what about the miracles in the gospels ? The deists set to work to make them look like natural events. The raising of the dead was said to have been a cure from lethargic slumber which had the appearance of death. The resurrection of Our Lord was done away with as a piece of fiction and his appearances were relegated to the realm of deceptive visions seen by highly imaginative dreamers. English deism exercised a considerable influence upon such French writers as Voltaire and the Encyclopaedists, who in their turn waxed sarcastic and violent as well. The result was that confidence in the gospels was undermined. Henceforth they were treated with great liberty, but little reverence. Although the rationalist foundation for the impossibility of miracles fell later into disrepute, each subsequent generation of higher critics repeated oracularly that miracles do not happen.

Side by side with the philosophical approach there was a new literary interest in the gospels. Three facts were calculated to stir the minds of scholars. Mention should first be made of the **discrepancy of the evangelists** in narrating certain facts. That here lay one of the reasons for discounting the gospels is borne out by Conyers Middleton's *Reflections on the Variations which are found among the Four Evangelists in their different Accounts of the same Facts*, 1752. Middleton shows himself no longer content with the exegetical rule advocated by St Augustine and St Jerome. The rule amounted to this. Whenever the evangelists are inconsistent in the report of a certain event, we should rather think of different events similar to each other, which occurred at different times and under different circumstances. Middleton is inclined to explain the discrepancies of certain narratives as caused by inaccuracy or faulty memory (*cf.* R. H. Lightfoot, *History and Interpretation in the Gospels*, 1935, p 4). In his pamphlet, *The Age of Reason*, 1796, Thomas Paine, the popularizer of Middleton's ideas, went to the extreme by affirming that the gospels could not have been written by eyewitnesses, and that they were wrongly attributed to Matthew, Mark, Luke and John.

Another point to which due attention was given has come to be known as the **synoptic problem.** When reading the first three gospels everyone will quickly perceive that to a large extent the same events and the same sayings of Our Lord are put down in each of them, that the synoptic writers follow largely the same order and, describing the same event, often use the same vocabulary. The obvious, though not necessarily right, explanation of this phenomenon seemed to be to admit the mutual dependence of the synoptic writers on one another. As a matter of course the question arose : Who is dependent on whom ? As early as 1782, in his *Marcus non epitomator Matthei* J. Koppe defended the priority of Mark, a theory which later was to be accepted unanimously as a dogma of higher criticism. Still, before that came to pass, other combinations were to be tried. J. J. Griesbach, who by the way was the first to use the term 'synoptic gospels', maintained in his *Synopsis*, 1797, that Luke was dependent on Matthew, and Mark on both Matthew and Luke. The important point to be noticed is the easy way in which the savants of the age separated themselves from the historical evidence provided by the documents of early Christian literature. On the whole it must be said that both in its origins and in its later development higher criticism has signally failed in respect for external historical evidence about the composition of the gospels. Right from the beginning it put its trust in its power of literary analysis rather than in the broader approach which includes analysis and historical tradition alike.

The similarities between the first three gospels had led to the synoptic problem ; so likewise the dissimilarity between the synoptic writers and St John led to the **Johannine problem.** It very early became an acute question who should be trusted more as a source of historical information, the synoptists or St John. In recording the sermons of Our Lord St John shows a propensity to abstractness which is foreign to the synoptists. Sometimes he indulges in theological speculation and uses the term 'logos' of which much was made by the Stoa, Philo, the Gnostics and Neo-Platonists. Moreover, certain points of doctrine, as the divinity of Christ, the supernatural life, etc., are more stressed by him than by the other evangelists. Can we assume that the fourth gospel was written by an eye-witness ? One of the first to raise his voice against the fourth gospel's being a work of the Apostle John was the Anglican divine E. Evanson in his *Dissonance of the four commonly received Gospels*, 1792. He was not long alone. Soon German critics began fiercely to deny the Johannine origin of the fourth gospel. An important event in radical criticism was C. G. Bretschneider's *Probabilia de Evangelii et Epistolarum Joannis Apostoli Indole et Origine*, 1820. However, for a time the further progress of radical views was arrested by F. Schleiermacher who for philosophical reasons defended the authenticity of the fourth gospel. His contention was that Christianity would remain inexplicable if the portrait of Christ as painted by the synoptists were the only one to be admitted. He compared the first three gospels with Xenophon's account of Socrates, the fourth gospel with Plato's account, and drew the obvious conclusions. Some decades later the attack was reopened by Strauss and has never ceased since.

After showing the sources and initial attempt of what came to be known as higher criticism, we must give a brief sketch of its further development. The strongest impulse proceeded from the doctrine of rationalist philosophy, as will become increasingly obvious. A year of great importance was 1778. In this year G. E. Lessing finished the edition of the *Wolfenbuettel fragments*. As librarian in Wolfenbuettel he had discovered the MSS of Hermann Samuel **Reimarus**, late professor of oriental languages in Hamburg (d. 1768). Out of the bulky heap of notes left by Reimarus he chose and published four sections dealing with biblical matters, the last of which was entitled *Vom Zwecke Jesu und seiner Juenger*. It is not easy to exaggerate the sensation caused by it, for Reimarus had applied the rationalist principles without regard to the susceptibilities of the public.

Jesus, so he tells us, must be stripped of all supernatural qualities. His mission needs to be interpreted by the Messianic ideas current among the Jewish populace at his time. Those ideas were political. Therefore Jesus must be regarded neither as the Son of God nor as a prophet, but as a Jewish Messiah bent upon establishing an earthly kingdom to deliver his people from the Roman yoke. Miracles he never worked. The miraculous events of the gospels were nothing but ordinary cures later magnified and heralded as supernatural occurrences, or were pure inventions. They served to let him appear as great as the prophets of old, to whom the power of performing miracles had

been ascribed by the Old Testament writers. That **605b** Jesus himself believed his political mission to have been a failure is shown by his words : ' My God, my God, why hast thou forsaken me ? ' It was his disciples who changed his idea of an earthly and political Messiahship into that of a spiritual one. To do it successfully they resorted to deception on a grand scale. They stole his body from the tomb and proclaimed that he had risen from the dead. And in order to remove all ignominy from his death, they made it a religious event by declaring that it had been the death of a suffering and spiritual redeemer. Of course, they are also the inventors of the miracles in the gospels. Therefore, not Jesus, but his disciples founded the Christian religion. As might be expected, the final judgement which Reimarus passes on the gospel is not friendly. According to him the entire gospel is nothing but a clever piece of fraud.

The objections against Reimarus's interpretation of **c** the gospel story are fairly obvious. Reimarus makes it the basis of his work that miracles are impossible. Yet, this is in flagrant opposition to any sound philosophy, which, in admitting the omnipotence of God, must likewise admit the possibility of miracles. Further, that Jesus necessarily adopted the current ideas of a political Messiah, is a postulate without any foundation. Reimarus approaches the question of the historical value of the gospels with definite prejudices, namely, that Jesus was not divine and that he cannot have had other ideas about the Messiahship than Reimarus permits. Such a method does not lead to explaining, but to explaining away. No wonder that Reimarus even fails to explain how the grandiose deception on the part of the disciples was possible.

Reimarus's attempts at depicting the historical Jesus set the general pattern in accordance with which many of the subsequent *Lives of Jesus* were written. We need not discuss here those authors who went so far as to assert that Jesus never existed. The evidence of the gospels, of St Paul, the Apostolic Fathers, the Talmud, Josephus Flavius, of Tacitus, Suetonius and Pliny are sufficient to dispel any doubt as regards the existence of Our Lord. No serious scholar and, for that matter, no sound-minded man will pay attention to books in which scepticism gets the better of an author's wits.

Of little more interest nowadays are the critics of the **d** early 19th cent. who were influenced by Kant's doctrine then gaining ground on all sides. In 1793 Kant had published his *Religion within the bounds of mere reason*, in which he set down the rule that we should not ask what the evangelists had actually written, but what they should have written in conformity with the demands of a purely natural religion. Such an approach, he said, even if it should do violence to the text, would be better than a literal interpretation (Ed. Cassirer, vol. 6, p 255). Kant, true to himself, repeats the axiom of Protagoras that man is the measure of all things, and lends his hand to mould God to the image and likeness of man. The result was a number of rationalist and naturalist *Lives of Jesus*, in which Christ was depicted as a simple, good-living citizen. This was in perfect accordance with Kant's ideas. For he had taught that secularist morality was identical with religion.

A new event profoundly affecting the study of the **e** gospels was *Das Leben Jesu kritisch bearbeitet* by David Friedrich **Strauss**, published in two volumes in 1835–1836. His method can briefly be summarized by stating that he reduces to myth whatever bears the hallmark of the extraordinary in the gospels. He is not the originator of the mythological method. There were others before him who employed it. But he certainly is its greatest exponent.

Strauss distinguishes two classes of the evangelical myth, the pure myth and the historical myth. The existence of the pure myth he assigns to two causes. One of them is the prophetic portrait of the Messiah in the books of the Old Testament. This portrait was minutely elaborated during the centuries between the Babylonian exile and the time of Jesus.

605e The decisive step that accounts for the existence of the gospels took place when the portrait of the Messiah was projected upon Jesus and he was increasingly identified with it. Then the second cause came into play, consisting in the impression made by the character, deeds and fate of Jesus, and modifying the Old Testament portrait of the Messiah in the minds of the people. In opposition to the pure myth, the historical myth is based on a historical fact embellished to mythical proportions by the use of elements taken from the messianic portrait of the Old Testament.

f In order to allow for the development of the gospel myth Strauss holds that the present gospels originated at a rather late date, *i.e.* in the middle of the 2nd cent. In this he follows his teacher, F. C. Baur, of whom we are going to speak presently. It must be kept in mind that the growth of myth and legend that surrounds many a historic person, requires a considerable amount of time. Supposing that the synoptic gospels were written within the three decades after the death of Christ, the mythical theory would have to be ruled out of court. This was perfectly understood by Strauss. Therefore he presumes a late date for the gospels.

Strauss maintains that in the name of history the myth of Jesus must be exposed, but he expressly affirms that he does not intend to do away with Christianity altogether. In the *Concluding Dissertation* of his *Life of Jesus* he endeavours to rebuild by philosophical speculation what, so it seems to him, he has destroyed by historical criticism. To achieve his purpose he uses Hegel's thought laid down in the latter's *Phenomenology of the Mind* and *Philosophy of Religion*. The religious idea taken in the Hegelian sense is independent of historical phenomena. The infinite spirit of God and the finite spirit of man are identical. The infinite spirit is true, but not real, whereas the finite spirit is real, but not true. The true and real existence of the spirit is obtained in the identity of the infinite and finite spirit, that is in God-man. God-man means the whole human race. But there remains an opposition between the finite and infinite that leads to conflict, suffering and death of the God-man. That the final unity may be achieved, a way must lead back from death. It does so, in resurrection and ascension. These difficult ideas need to be shown to the simple-minded in a historical figure to whom is attributed by way of myth what in the realm of philosophy is expressed in abstract ideas.

g It is clear that owing to an unsound philosophical tradition Strauss is under a bias as regards supernatural events. In accepting so late a date as 150 for the origin of the gospels he stands in downright opposition to facts, as will become clear in the course of this article. Between the death of Christ and the composition of the gospels there was actually no time for the development of myth. Moreover, on his own suppositions Strauss fails to give a satisfactory explanation why it was Jesus who was identified with the Messianic portrait of the Old Testament in the belief of the people. There have been other men who pretended to be Messiahs. At the time of the second Jewish war (132–5) there was Bar Kochba. He was proclaimed as Messias by R. Akiba, one of the most famous rabbis of all times, and enjoyed the full support of the Pharisees. But posterity did not crown him with the wreath of Messianic myths. Surely there must have been something supernatural in the character and life of Jesus to prompt people to identify him with the Messiah who had been foretold by the prophets of old.

606a We must call attention now to the teacher of D. F. Strauss, Ferdinand Christian **Baur**, the founder of the younger Protestant school of Tuebingen. Of the many books he wrote his *Kritische Untersuchungen ueber die kanonischen Evangelien*, 1847, must be mentioned here. Whereas Strauss had borrowed mainly from Hegel's philosophy of religion, Baur makes ample use of both Hegel's philosophy of religion and philosophy of history. According to the German idealist, historical developments proceed in the rhythm of thesis, antithesis and synthesis, that is to say, a historical fact, in which a certain tendency finds its embodiment (thesis) and calls its opposite (antithesis) into existence. The ensuing conflict between both leads finally to a higher unity (synthesis), wherein both are brought into harmony with each other. Baur applies this doctrine in his explanation of the development of Christianity. He tells us that there was a profound antagonism between the followers of St Peter, who were Judaizing particularists, and the followers of St Paul, who were anti-Judaizing universalists. At the time when the conflict reached its climax the Petrine faction produced the Apocalypse, the epistle of St James and the Aramaic gospel according to the Hebrews. Paul, the leader of the opposite faction, wrote four epistles (Gal, 1 & 2 Cor, Rom) which are his only authentic ones. The gospels in their present form no longer show the same marked opposition as the documents just mentioned. We have, therefore, to assume that they are of a later date. Baur assigns their origin to the years 130–70, when the opposite tendencies of the Petrine and Pauline faction fell into abeyance and a kind of compromise was being reached. According to Baur the chronological order of the gospels is Matthew, Luke, Mark, John. The reasons for the rearrangement of the traditional order are as follows. Matthew still shows a trace of the Judaizing tendency, while Luke bears the stamp of Paulinism. Mark is neutral and, therefore, must have been written after Matthew and Luke. The latest gospel is that called after St John, which is both neutral and more advanced in doctrine than Mark. The implication of so late a dating is, of course, that gospels were written by unknown writers and not by those whose names they bear.

Baur was enormously successful. Although widely abandoned with the advent of the historico-critical school, his ideas were kept alive right into the 20th cent. by some Dutch critics.

Baur's historical method is too much influenced by Hegelian thought. To look everywhere for the verification of the dialectic process from thesis to antithesis and synthesis leads finally to the construction of situations which need not have existed at all. In fact, there is no documentary evidence for the violent opposition between a Petrine and Pauline faction as alleged by Baur. The gospels not only betray no trace of it, but as Harnack rightly pointed out show all the signs of primitive Christian tradition, a fact which had been overlooked by Baur. He makes also too little of the evidence provided by the early Christian writers. The evidence is quite clear and outspoken. Not only did the Apostolic Fathers allude to our canonical gospels, but Papias, *c* 120, reports the words of the Elder who almost certainly is identical with John the Apostle. We are told that Matthew wrote in Hebrew (= Aramaic) and that Mark, the interpreter of Peter, wrote down what Peter had preached in Rome about Jesus. For accurate information about Papias I must refer the reader to Dom Chapman's *John the Presbyter and the Fourth Gospel*, 1911. But our chief witness is St Irenaeus. For he knew the tradition of Asia Minor, where he came from, of Rome and Gaul. Besides, he was conversant with the writings of Papias, and as a youth had heard St Polycarp the disciple of the Apostle John. He again *c* 185 testifies to the authenticity of the gospels and to the order in which they were written. It is the traditional order. In all this he is supported by the tradition of Italy, Africa and Alexandria as represented by St Justin († *c* 165), the old Latin prologues, the Muratorian fragment (*c* 180), Tertullian (†220), Clement of Alexandria († *c* 215) and Origen (†253).

About the dates of the gospels Baur is absolutely mistaken. From the ending of the Acts of the Apostles we can deduce that they were written before St Paul was released from his long captivity in 63. In the introductory verses to Ac St Luke refers to his gospel as already written. Hence the year 60 is the approximate date of it. The second gospel was composed when Peter preached at Rome, *i.e.* between 55 and 58. Before that time Matthew, the first evangelist, wrote. For John's gospel the year 90 indicates roughly the date of its origin (*cf.* §§ 678a, 725d, 744f, 777–9).

Baur's disciples saw the one-sidedness of their master's approach to the gospel problem, and slowly began to take stock of the evidence provided by the early Christian writers.

Here is the place to insert a short account of the *Vie de Jésus*, 1863, by **Ernest Renan,** not indeed because Renan's scholarly merits are by any means outstanding, but rather because his *Life of Jesus* enjoyed an unrivalled popularity and is much read even today. Renan's was an artistic temperament. Viewed from a literary angle there are passages of great beauty in his book, though sometimes marred by a saccharine sweetness not infrequently met with in devout pictures imported from France.

Renan made use of a more advanced criticism. The gospels, he thinks, are on the whole authentic, at least the discourses in Mt came from St Matthew's pen and the anecdotes in Mk were written by St Mark himself. He does not doubt the authenticity of the third gospel. St John is blamed for having substituted obscure metaphysics for the simple words of Jesus.

In its general trend the *Life of Jesus* betrays the influence of Strauss as Renan himself candidly admits. But instead of Strauss' Messianic myth he introduces the pious legend to account for the supernatural in the gospel stories. ' That the gospels are in part legendary, is evident, since they are full of miracles and the supernatural.' The rationalist principle that miracles do not happen is of unquenchable vitality. Under Renan's hands Jesus is again pedantically deprived of all that belongs to the sphere of the supernatural and extraordinary, and is turned into ' l'homme idéal '.

Of the greatest import for higher criticism was the advent of the so-called **historico-critical school** that originated in the circles of liberal Protestantism. It might be useful to sketch the philosophical background of that brand of Protestantism in order to enable the reader better to appreciate an attitude of mind which at times seems rather reckless. In the beginning of the 19th cent. Friedrich Schleiermacher had made the attempt to save religion in the philosophical revolution then taking place. He thought it imperative to arrive at a compromise with Kantian philosophy. Kant had banished religion from the sphere of theoretical knowledge. Schleiermacher accepted the verdict, identified religion with ' mysticism ' and made it a function of sentiment. In England this doctrine was developed by S. T. Coleridge, F. D. Maurice and Matthew Arnold. In Germany Albrecht Ritschl became the champion of religious sentiment. As he is the founder of liberal Protestantism he naturally influenced the theology of the historico-critical school. A central position in Ritschl's system is held by the ' judgements of value'. He maintains that religious judgements are independent judgements of value based exclusively on the feelings of approbation or disapprobation. These feelings are elicited by religious conceptions which are approved of or disapproved of according to whether the conceptions stand in relationship to the highest good, the kingdom of God, or not. Religious conceptions which arouse the feeling of approbation are of religious value and worthy of becoming objects of faith. The question whether they have objective reality is neither of import nor capable of solution. Considering the doctrinal basis of liberal Protestantism one understands the famous distinction between the Christ of history and the Christ of faith, a distinction which is voiced, wherever higher criticism has established itself. The implication in the distinction is this. If from the standpoint of historical research Christ must be reduced to insignificant proportions, his importance remains nevertheless untouched from the standpoint of religious value. No wonder that liberal Protestants treated the gospels and the Christ of history

at times very recklessly. After all, in their opinion no **606f** harm could be done to religion, since it was not based on history.

Within the circles of liberal Protestantism the so- **g** called historico-critical school came into prominence in the field of higher criticism. While hitherto the *Lives of Jesus* had kept pride of place in the literary activity of the critics, a noticeable change occurred now, as the interest was shifted to more literary problems. The greatest representative of the historico-critical school was **Adolph von Harnack** (†1930) whose reputation became international. The intensive study of the literary aspects began roughly about 1870. English scholars took a very active part and the names of many of them became known abroad. Nevertheless, with a few exceptions, it would be wrong to assign them to any definite school, such as the historico-critical school, since they either kept aloof from subscribing to any of the philosophical systems which formed the backbone of the current schools, or remained more independent and conservative in their criticism. It is worth mentioning that Harnack subjected the dates of the gospels to fresh investigation. He assigned Luke to the year 60 and Mark to the preceding decade. Matthew he inclined to place later than 70. His authority was such that his results were accepted by many. Nevertheless others objected on the ground that the prophecies of the destruction of Jerusalem in Mark and Luke made it imperative to assign those gospels to a time after the actual destruction. According to rationalist premises prophecies, too, do not happen. Harnack's opinion coincided with the rationalist slogan, but he thought it possible that at the time of the composition of Mark and Luke the destruction of Jerusalem no longer lay beyond the limits of a clever guess.

In what follows I propose to sketch the treatment by **607a** higher critics of certain literary questions in such a way that the reader may be introduced to the opinions which are now current.

In connexion with **the synoptic problem** heated discussions had raged as to whose gospel was chronologically the first. As we saw in the beginning of this article, the priority of Mark had its defenders as far back as the 18th cent. It was, however, Christian Hermann Weisse in 1838, who tried to find a more solid basis for that hypothesis. His arguments were perfected by Heinrich J. Holtzmann in the latter's *Die synoptischen Evangelien*, 1863. Harnack and his school followed him. The acceptance of the priority of Mark by men like F. C. Burkitt, Sir John Hawkins, Dr W. Sanday and Canon B. H. Streeter made the hypothesis popular in England. Today the priority of Mark is considered as an established fact by the higher critics. I shall here set out the main arguments for the priority of Mark and shall suggest their weakness in each case.

First argument (considered by Holtzmann as the chief **b** argument) : Nearly the whole matter reported in Mark can be read in Matthew, and half of the matter is included in Luke. That goes to show that both Matthew and Luke borrowed from Mark, which fact necessitates the priority of Mark.

But Mark could equally well have borrowed from Matthew, since nearly the whole of Mark's matter is contained in Matthew. The more detailed description of certain events in Mark is accounted for by the information which Mark received from St Peter.

Second argument : The order of events in Mark is to a great extent the same as in Matthew and Luke. When Matthew differs from Mark, Mark is upheld by Luke, and vice versa, when Luke differs from Mark, Mark is upheld by Matthew. This again shows that Mark was used as a model by Matthew and Luke alike.

But Mark can have followed Matthew and can have made some changes in the order of events for reasons of his own. Luke on the other hand, instead of following Matthew, could have followed Mark where the latter differs from Matthew. Sometimes Luke follows neither Matthew nor Mark.

607c *Third argument* : Supposing the priority of Mark, one can nearly always explain why a certain event is not recorded either in Matthew or Luke. But if the priority of Mark is denied and Mark is supposed to have utilized Matthew, no satisfactory reason can be given for the omission of certain events in Mark.

No one will assume that St Mark, the interpreter of St Peter, wrote down in his gospel all the events of which he had knowledge. Therefore, even on the supposition of the priority of Mark there must be a reason why he omitted to record certain events. That reason remains a satisfactory reason for the omissions, even when the priority of Mark is denied.

Fourth argument : The style of Mark is rather uncouth, while that of Matthew and Luke is rather polished. There is a strong indication that Matthew and Luke have improved upon the style of Mark. Some Aramaic words are contained in Mark, whereas Matthew and Luke omit them nearly always. Further, Matthew and Luke show more urbanity of expression than Mark, when referring to Christ or the Apostles.

d These and similar details of style in Mark are satisfactorily explained by Mark's having been the interpreter of Peter. Mark could have used the gospel according to St Matthew and at the same time recorded certain events as he had heard them from St Peter. It is arbitrary to suppose that anyone who copies from another writer must necessarily improve upon the latter's style. The opposite may happen. But there is no evidence to show that our Greek translation of Matthew was already in existence. Perhaps Mark used the Aramaic original. Nothing, therefore, can be deduced from his uncouth Greek.

There are some other minor arguments for the priority of Mark. But it is fair to say that they run on the same lines as those just mentioned. With particular reference to the last argument based on Mark's style, Canon Streeter states that he is unable to comprehend how anyone can retain the slightest doubt of the original and primitive character of Mark. However, if Canon Streeter and, for that matter, the other higher critics had examined the synoptic gospels with a broader attitude of mind, they would have soon discovered the boomerang-quality of their proofs. There are clearly two different possibilities of explaining the facts which the higher critics try to turn to their advantage. The question which of the gospels is the oldest, is a historical question. The choice between the two possibilities should be guided by historical evidence which is amply provided in early Christian literature. But historical evidence is in favour of the priority of Matthew.

e The presumption of the higher critics is that one synoptist must have copied from the other ; that in the first century people must have had their eyes glued on books, and that similarities can be exhaustively accounted for and must be accounted for by reference to extant written texts. However, it stands to reason that all three synoptic writers may have drawn from oral tradition transmitted in more or less rigid forms, or from lost documents which contained the primitive catechesis of the Church. There are not only similarities, but many dissimilarities in the parts that are common to all three synoptic gospels. And these dissimilarities cannot satisfactorily be explained if the solution be based exclusively on the mutual dependence of the evangelists. The higher critics are inclined to treat the synoptic gospels as a chemical compound which they divide up into the Markan matter, the collection of the sayings of the Lord (Logia, Q) to account for discourses found in Matthew and Luke, but not in Mark ; and finally a special source for Matthew and another for Luke to explain those parts which are found only either in Matthew or Luke. Others are even content to derive Matthew's and Luke's material solely from Mark and Q, the latter being a hypothetical source. Such procedure may be in accordance with the requirements of Occam's razor. But when writing the gospels, did the evangelists themselves conform to Occam's razor as understood by the higher

critics ? To find the right answer in matters such as this a shred of external evidence is more valuable than all speculations built upon internal evidence alone, *cf.* §§ 610–5.

A few words must be added here about **the Logia**, a hypothetic document often designated simply as Q. The Logia are supposed to be a collection of the sayings of Jesus, and St Matthew is said to have been its compiler. In the first gospel, so many critics maintain, a substantial part of the Logia of Matthew is embedded. That is why the first gospel is called the gospel according to St Matthew, although, as it stands, it was not written by St Matthew, but by a person or persons unknown. The originator of the Logia-theory was Schleiermacher. He based his proof on the Papias fragment about Matthew : ' Matthew composed the Logia in the Hebrew dialect, and each translated them as he was able '. Schleiermacher maintained that Papias referred to a collection of sayings of Jesus. His theory gained many followers and up to recent times it was based on lexicographical grounds, that is to say, that ' sayings ' was considered the right translation of the Greek term ' Logia '. But wrongly so. Fr John Donovan gives the result of his research into the meaning of Logia as follows : ' Hence the inevitable conclusion that Papias was making use of an expression in already fairly common use, and that he used it with that definite meaning, *i.e.* Christian revelation as couched in the Gospels ' (*The Logia in Ancient and Recent Literature*, 1924, p 37). The Protestant scholar Gerhard Kittel in his *Theologisches Woerterbuch zum Neuen Testament*, 1938, refers on page 145 to the Logia-theories and states that the appeal to the fragment of Papias must be disallowed. Of course, even if the appeal to the fragment of Papias were given up, the old theory would enjoy a new lease of life through the acceptance of the modern solutions of the synoptic problem in which it is stated that Matthew and Luke are based upon Mark and Q. If apart from the priority of Mark, anyone likes to assume that there existed a collection of the sayings of Jesus before the gospels were written, he is entitled to do so. But if he maintains that St Matthew compiled only those sayings and not the gospel, he is contradicted by historical evidence.

However, in order to defend their theory, many **g** critics maintain that the present gospel according to St Matthew shows all the characteristics of Hellenistic origin, and therefore can never have existed as an Aramaic original. Such a contention does not square with the facts. Jewish traits are abundant in Matthew's gospel. In its plan, phraseology, use of the Old Testament and general background it clearly indicates that it was written for Jewish readers (*cf.* Rev. C. Lattey's *Introduction* to *The Gospel according to St Matthew*, WV, 1928). Hence, there is nothing to upset the traditional view that Matthew was originally written in Aramaic. On the contrary, it is supported by internal evidence.

In popular writings one can come across the statement that the Aramaic Matthew was identical with the apocryphal ' gospel according to the Hebrews '. The few fragments which have been preserved from this apocryphal book reveal a notable divergence from our Matthew. But it seems that there was sufficient resemblance between the two to make St Jerome think, at least for a time, that it was the original Matthew. Nowadays the ' gospel according to the Hebrews ' is generally regarded as a secondary document which was used by a Jewish Christian sect who were known as Nazaraeans (*cf.* M. R. James, *Apocryphal New Testament*, 1926, p 1). Hence there is no support for the view that our Greek Matthew is the original work of an unknown writer, who made very free use of the Aramaic gospel according to the Hebrews.

As regards the **Johannine question**, contemporary **h** criticism is concerned not so much with the date of the origin of the fourth gospel as with the question of authorship and historicity. After all, the dating will follow automatically if the Johannine authorship is h established. In the estimation of higher criticism the Johannine question is still regarded as unsettled. The German radical critics delivered violent and repeated attacks against the Johannine authorship and the historicity of the fourth gospel, with Harnack in the van. That the attacks broke down, or in other words, that the negation of Johannine authorship and of the historicity of the fourth gospel was not commonly accepted by non-Catholic higher critics is due to a group of very able defenders in England : Bishop Lightfoot, Principal J. Drummond, Dr V. H. Stanton and Dr W. Sanday. It is still instructive to read the publications of both parties, and to observe on the one side neglect of all evidence which conflicts with the preconceived scheme, and overstatement of whatever is favourable to it, while on the other the discussion is carried on with a careful weighing of all the available evidence.

i The radicals made much of the fact that Christian literature in the first half of the second century, and particularly St Justin, show only scanty allusions to the fourth gospel. Had the Apostle John been its author, they argued, it would have been alluded to with the same frequency as the other gospels. As it is, during the period referred to, it cannot have been regarded as of apostolic origin. Drummond provided a telling answer :

' But why then, it may be asked, has Justin not quoted the fourth gospel at least as often as the other three ? I cannot tell, any more than I can tell why he has never named the supposed authors of his Memoirs (= gospels), or has mentioned only one of the parables, or made no reference to the Apostle Paul, or nowhere quoted the Apocalypse, though he believed it to be an apostolic and prophetic work. His silence may be due to a pure accident, or the book may have seemed less adapted to his apologetic purposes ; but considering how many things there are about which he is silent, we cannot admit that the argumentum a silentio possesses in this case any validity ' (*Inquiry into the Character and Authorship of the Fourth Gospel*, 1903, p 157).

j From the period preceding St Justin there is St Ignatius of Antioch († c 110), whose thought and style are steeped in the gospel of St John. It is worth while mentioning that in 1935 a papyrus-fragment was published, which contains Jn 18:31-33, 37-38. It shows that St John's gospel was circulating in Middle Egypt in the first half of the second cent. (C. H. Roberts, *An unpublished Fragment of the Fourth Gospel*). The mere fact that the papyrus was found in that part of the world suggests that it must have been held in repute very early. Incidentally it also does away with theories which propose a late date for the fourth gospel. In this connexion mention should be made of Tatian and Irenaeus. Tatian, a disciple of St Justin, wrote about 170 a gospel harmony, the Diatesseron, in which he made ample use of the fourth gospel and thus testifies to its apostolic origin. St Irenaeus who had so great a knowledge of early Christian tradition clearly establishes the Johannine authorship of the fourth gospel. Unfortunately, he is often treated as if he had been born in the year in which he wrote, or as if the book by Papias and a brief intercourse in his early years with Polycarp had been his only sources. ' It is like Nero wishing that Rome had one neck, in order that it might be cut at a single stroke', writes Dr Sanday.

k Against the authorship of St John the critics have cited the de Boor fragment (7th or 8th cent.), probably an extract from the chronicle of Philip of Side, who flourished in the 5th cent. The fragment runs as follows : ' Papias says in the second book that John the theologian and his brother James were killed by the Jews '. Georgius Hamartolus (9th cent.) repeats the story of the violent death of John, but lets it take place under the reign of Nerva, after John had written his gospel. The de Boor fragment does not say that James and John died at the same time. Papias may have been commenting on the words of Jesus to the sons of Zebedee that they would drink of the cup from **607k** which he himself was to drink. James died as a martyr. And St John had somehow to be turned into a martyr too. Perhaps Papias had only meant to say that his death was hastened by the persecution of the Jews. Whatever the explanation of the de Boor fragment may be, it is certain that St John did not die along with his brother James (in the year 42). The premature death of St John was unknown to Irenaeus, Victorinus and Eusebius who were familiar with the work of Papias, and is clearly contradicted by Ac 12:2, Gal 2:9 and Polycrates. The latter, bishop of Ephesus, wrote c 180 to Pope Victor and claimed John as one of the great lights of Asia who had died there, ' John who lay upon the breast of the Lord and became priest wearing the golden frontlet, and was witness and teacher '. The radical critics appeal also to a Syriac martyrology of the 5th cent., which has recorded under 27th December: ' The Apostles John and James at Jerusalem '. The Syriac martyrology, however, has been shown to be an abridgement of, and a careless translation from a Greek martyrology of the 4th cent. which says nothing to the same effect (V. H. Stanton, *The Gospels as Historical Documents*, vol. 3, pp 113-7, also John Donovan, S.J., *The Authorship of St John's Gospel*, 1936).

l Of course, the radical critics also find arguments in considerations of internal evidence. However, from the use of the Logos-idea nothing can be deduced that tells against Johannine authorship. Logos-speculation had its roots not only in Greek philosophy ; rabbinic learning too, based on the books of wisdom, had developed its hypostasis of a Memra. It was an easy step for Philo to bring about a synthesis of Jewish and Greek thought on that matter. The Gnostics took up the Logos-idea and talked about the first emanation from the divine substance. In a word, the atmosphere was charged with Logos-speculation. No wonder that in the prologue to his gospel St John corrected these ideas, and set down a Christian Logos-doctrine.

Much has been said and written about the style of the fourth gospel, which seems fundamentally different from the simple accounts of the other evangelists. But we must not forget that the fourth gospel is the work of old age. For many years the author had been meditating on the words of Jesus, particularly on those dealing with his divinity and the supernatural life. From the discourses of Our Lord he chose those which served his purpose, to prove the divinity of his Master. And he related them in a manner which is intent more on the doctrinal structure of the discourses than on the actual words in which they were spoken.

m However, the radical critics have made up their minds that the fourth gospel is not the account of an eye-witness. Harnack, J. Moffat, B. W. Bacon, etc., bestow the honour of authorship on John the Elder, whom they declare to be different from John the Apostle. Others follow Alfred Loisy. Being a thoroughgoing allegorist Loisy denies that the fourth gospel gives any history at all. Not even the beloved disciple is a historical person, though the gospel proclaims him as its author. ' He is the young Church, to whom was entrusted the heritage of Judaism and Jewish Christianity '. According to Loisy the real author is unknown, but must be some one of the converts from Jewish Hellenism in Ephesus or Antioch. His theory is fantastic. But the most fantastic theory of all perhaps is given by Dr Robert Eisler in his *The Enigma of the Fourth Gospel*, 1938. He maintains that the author of the fourth gospel is identical with the Johanan, who in 37 was chosen to act as high-priest by the Roman governor Vitellius. During the revolution of 66 Johanan commanded one of the five Jewish armies occupying Gophnitis and Acrabatene. After the destruction of Jerusalem, however, he settled down in Ephesus, adopted some kind of Christianity and produced the fourth gospel, with Marcion (the Luther of the 2nd cent.) as his secretary. Dr Eisler's notes of triumph bring to mind nothing so much as the blaring fanfares of a travelling circus—so far removed

607m are they from the true notes of sound higher criticism.

It might be worth while mentioning that at the present time there seems to be a growing tendency to establish an Alexandrian provenance for the fourth gospel.

608a A short account must now be given of the **Proto-Luke hypothesis,** all the more as it has its origin in England. Canon B. H. Streeter was the first to state it in an article in the Hibbert Journal for October 1921. It was more fully expounded in his *The Four Gospels : A Study of Origins*, 1924, and in Dr Vincent Taylor's book, *Behind the Third Gospel*, 1926.

Canon Streeter points out that in Luke we find a number of sections which are independent of Mark and must, therefore, be derived from other sources ; the sections are Lk 3:1–4:30 ; 6:20–8:3 ; 9:51–18:14 ; 19:1–27 ; and the accounts of the Last Supper, of the Passion, the Resurrection and the appearances. Now Streeter's contention is that all these sections taken together form a complete gospel, the Proto-Luke. He is inclined to regard St Luke as its author. ' The non-Markan sections represent a single document, and to Luke this was the framework into which he inserted, at convenient places, extracts from Mark '. Chapters 1 and 2 were taken from a special source. So far his hypothesis is a brilliant piece of work, although remaining in the realm of mere probabilities. In elaborating Streeter's theory Dr Taylor assigns Proto-Luke to the years 60–5. Mark he dates about the year 68. In this manner the final composition of St Luke's gospel would have to be placed in the eighth decade of the first cent. In fact, Canon Streeter assigns it to the year 80. Those dates are too late, as may be gathered from what we had to say about the dating of the gospels on a previous page.

b I must now take the reader back to the beginning of this century to recall certain important events which have not yet been mentioned. When the priority of Mark was accepted by the leading lights of higher criticism and by the rank and file as well, a new vista seemed to be opened to the writers of the *Lives of Jesus*. If Mark was the source of the other synoptic gospels, then, it was said, he must be nearest to historical truth, and consequently every future *Life of Jesus* must needs be based upon him. The older authors at once became antiquated from the critical point of view, because they had drawn from other gospels as well. But as events were to show, not even Mark escaped unscathed. In his *Das Messias-Geheimnis in den Evangelien*, 1901, W. Wrede criticized the rationalist method. For it had induced people to consider as historical in the narrative only what they could understand, and to explain away all that bore the stamp of the supernatural. But, so Wrede's contention ran, Mark himself did not make any such distinction. Hence, every passage would be controversial from the point of view of historical truth. Wrede does not deny that Mark had historical matter at his disposal. But at the time when Mark wrote, the portrait of Jesus had already been idealized and altered by the early Christian community. Mark then arranged and interpreted his material in accordance with his own theological ideas and the beliefs of the Christian community. Henceforth, in criticism, it would be necessary to distinguish carefully between the historical material that had been transformed by, and according to, the beliefs of the community, and the redaction of the evangelist which had been guided by theological ideas. The reader will notice how Strauss's evangelical myth begins to reappear in disguise.

c **J. Wellhausen** went a step further. His theory is as follows. Mark's gospel consists of little narratives which had been written independently of each other. The older a narrative is the less its historical content has suffered from transformation by the community and the nearer it is to historical truth. Mark collected the narratives and cemented them together by passages which are of his own invention. But this is not all.

His book was repeatedly revised ; so that in our present gospel we no longer possess the Ur-Mark, the primitive Mark. It is, therefore, imperative to distinguish the following parts in the gospel : old layers and new layers of tradition, and the several layers of cement put in by subsequent editorial redactions. So far so good. But who was to disentangle truth from fiction, history from theology ? The road which was meant to lead to historical certainty ended in bewilderment and scepticism. Of course, it is quite arbitrary to assert that in his gospel Mark only wrote about the ideas of the early Christian community, but not about the historical Christ ; more arbitrary to presume that the early Christians had lost interest in the historical portrait of their Master. In fact, as has been seen, Mark wrote the recollections of St Peter, who had been an eye-witness, precisely to satisfy the historical interest of the Christians. Anyhow, Wrede and Wellhausen led up to a development which reached its height in the eschatological school (as represented by Albert Schweitzer) and in the school of form-criticism.

Along with the critical studies just sketched went research into the meaning of the kingdom of God. Ritschl's system had become very popular, and the idea of the kingdom of God held an important part in it. No wonder that during the last two decades of the 19th cent. a number of monographs had been published about the exegetical meaning of the kingdom of God. A number of scholars based their investigation on the supposition that in his Messianic ideas Christ cannot have been different from the rest of the Jewish people. Here a principle of Reimarus was taken up again. Further, they presumed that the Messianic ideas current at the time of Jesus must be looked for in the Jewish apocryphal writings. Accordingly, it was maintained that Jesus thought of the kingdom of God as a new era to be brought about by a cataclysm in which the present world would be destroyed. He never considered himself as the Messiah of an earthly, but of an eschatological kingdom.

In his book *The Quest of the Historical Jesus*, 1926[2] (first German ed. in 1906), **Albert Schweitzer** synthesized the eschatological interpretation and the advanced criticism of Wrede and Wellhausen. The message he has to give is a message of scepticism. There is no hope, he proclaims, that we shall ever discover the historical Christ in the contradictory passages of Mark. The only thing we know is that Jesus preached the eschatological kingdom of God which he at first thought would be realized during his life-time. Then the conviction dawned upon him that he must suffer for others, so that the kingdom might come. The ethics preached by Jesus were a provisional code for the short interval that separated the world from its destruction. Thus by a peculiar use of external evidence Schweitzer turns the kingdom of God into an eschatological dream. And by a peculiar neglect of external evidence he denies the historical truth in Mark. The way in which Schweitzer tries to accord Jesus a place in the religious life of man, belongs to the mysteries of a philosophy whose avowed purpose it is to do away with mysteries. Schweitzer concludes his book by saying : ' He (Jesus) commands. And to those who obey Him, whether they be wise or simple, He will reveal Himself in the toils, the conflicts, the sufferings which they shall pass through in His fellowship, and, as an ineffable mystery, they shall learn in their own experience Who He is '.

A straight line leads from Wellhausen's analytical experiments to **form-criticism** (Formgeschichte), the chief representatives of which are Martin Dibelius and Robert Bultmann. In England form-criticism has found a friend in Prof. Robert Henry Lightfoot (*History and Interpretation in the Gospels*, Bampton Lectures, 1934). The form-critics accept the thesis that not only Mark, but all the synoptic gospels, consist of independent units artificially linked together. The units themselves are considered to have been handed down by way of oral tradition until they were committed to paper. Just as the faith of the early Christians ' developed ', so the units underwent a transformation which kept pace with the growth of the ideas of the community. In fact, the student of these units does not directly deal with the historical Jesus, but with opinions which prevailed among the early Christians. The first task to be performed is to take the units out of the gospel-frame and to class them in different categories as their literary form may require. The following categories are of importance : the paradigm (Dibelius) or apophthegm (Bultmann), *Novelle* (Dibelius) or miracle-story (Bultmann), parenesis and legend. The paradigm or apophthegm is a narrative leading up to a word of Jesus in such a manner that Christ's saying is clearly the chief feature, Mk 2:1–12 ; 3:1–6. The *Novelle* or miracle-story relates an act of power ; the incident itself remains the main subject of the narrative, Mk 1:40–45 ; 4:35–41. The parenesis is concerned with isolated words of Jesus spoken for the instruction of the people, as the Sermon on the Mount and the parables. Legends, of course, are of no historical significance whatsoever. They are met with in the stories of the infancy of Jesus, of the resurrection, etc. Now the supposition is that by studying the form of a narrative it is possible to discover its primitive content and to strip it of subsequent growths. For it is held as a principle that primitive literary expression is made in one of the categories just described. The form-critic, of course, must endeavour to establish the typical form of each category. By comparison he will recognize what elements in a narrative conform with its type and will consider them as parts of the original story, while he will remove such elements as are alien to the pure type. When this has been done, the form-critic looks for the ' Sitz im Leben ' of the different categories. ' Sitz im Leben ' is perhaps best translated as a permanent situation of the Christian community conditioned by special aims which are embodied in missionary and catechetical activity, worship of the religious hero, or in apologetic defence.

Dibelius allows that the sayings of Jesus were handed down by oral tradition, whereas Bultmann seems to maintain that in the beginning of the Christian community a collection of edifying sayings was made for teaching purposes, which only later were put into the mouth of Jesus. According to Dibelius the historicity of the paradigm depends on the knowledge and the intention of the preacher. But although the paradigm clearly belongs to the time of primitive preaching it does not therefore necessarily represent objective truth. After all, the preacher had to persuade his audience, a fact that forced him to adapt his stories to his aim and to exclude neutral objectivity. Bultmann derives his apophthegms mainly from the discussions of the Palestine Christian community. After analyzing the apophthegms he is convinced that many of them were originally isolated sayings subsequently put into a fictitious setting. Only when the words cannot be understood without the scene we have to consider them as one complete conception. Writing about the *Novellen* Dibelius assigns their ' Sitz im Leben ' to a tendency to show the superiority of Jesus in relation to pagan gods. For they too were believed to have performed miraculous healings. About the historicity of the *Novellen* he says only that they are further removed from historical truth than the paradigms. With this Bultmann agrees. He also thinks that the miracle-stories are of Hellenistic origin and must have later penetrated into Christian tradition.

In the description of the literary form of the gospel units the form-critics have shown much shrewdness. But in their conclusions they are as arbitrary as possible. The whole theory of Dibelius and Bultmann is built on the supposition that the early Christians had no biographical interest in the life of Jesus and that a strange transformation of the portrait of Jesus occurred at a time when plenty of eye-witnesses were still alive. *Sic volo, sic jubeo.* External evidence is absolutely neglected by the form-critics. Instead we meet with a welter of unfounded hypotheses put down as facts with a breath-taking naivety (*cf.* Laurence J. McGinley, S.J., *Form-Criticism of the Synoptic Healing Narratives,* 1944).

Here our hurried journey along the highways and byways of higher criticism is over. Literary criticism of the gospels is a useful study if carried out in the right spirit and guided by sound principles. For it allows us to see or, at least, to guess how the evangelists set to work when they produced the books which have been the inspiration and consolation of untold numbers of Christians. Such a study quite naturally carries its heavy weight of responsibility and should not be considered as the obvious ground on which to erect sensational, but unfounded theories. The radical brand of higher criticism has failed to be guided by sound principles of investigation. It draws its life from the obsolete speculations of a rationalist era, and clings desperately to its dogma of the impossibility of miracles. Proceeding from such a philosophical bias its historical method is of necessity vitiated. External evidence is often neglected altogether if it is seen to lead to conclusions that are contrary to the tenets of rationalism. Or, if some obscure and questionable evidence can be turned to the support of radical views, it is chosen in preference to the clear utterances of trustworthy and venerable writers. Higher criticism has suffered under its own arbitrary method. No lasting achievement can be gained in the historical field, if research is not guided by safe principles. That is why we perceive a continuous flow of divergent views in higher criticism. Higher criticism set out to destroy confidence in the gospels, but on a balanced view of the evidence, it has only succeeded in destroying confidence in itself.

THE SYNOPTIC PROBLEM

By B. C. BUTLER, O.S.B.

610a Bibliography—*Sir J. Hawkins, *Horae Synopticae* (1909²); *F. C. Burkitt, *The Gospel History and its Transmission* (1906); *W. Sanday (ed.), *Oxford Studies in the Synoptic Problem* (1911); *H. G. Jameson, *The Origin of the Synoptic Gospels* (1922); *B. H. Streeter, *The Four Gospels, a Study of Origins* (1924); H. J. Chapman, *Matthew, Mark and Luke* (1937); B. C. Butler, *The Originality of St Matthew*, Cambridge (1951); *A. Huck, *Synopse der drei Ersten Evangelien*, Tübingen (1922⁶). See also Lagrange's Introductions to his commentaries on St Matthew's and St Luke's Gospels; C. Lattey, *The Synoptic Problem* (Appendix 2, The Synoptic Gospels, WV, 1938).

b The Synoptic Problem is posed for us by the similarities between the first three Gospels, leading us to ask whether any, and if so what, connexions, literary or oral, direct or indirect, between these Gospels or any two of them must be supposed to have given rise to some of these similarities. The facts may be stated in summary fashion as follows :

A Through a total of about 200 verses, mainly comprising discourse and scattered about in various parts of the Gospels, there runs a strong similarity or even virtual identity, between Mt and Lk, in content, presentation and language, but there are no parallels for most of these verses in Mk. They constitute what we shall here describe as the ' Q ' material or the ' Q ' passages.

c **B** (1) Mk contains 673 verses. The substance of over 600 of these is found also in Mt, and of about 350 of them in Lk.

(2) Where a section of Mk has parallels in both Mt and Lk, the majority of Mk's actual Greek words is usually found in both Mt and Lk, or at least in one of them. And where a section of Mk is parallelled in only one of the other two, there still remains a marked parallelism of wording and phraseology between Mk and the parallel Gospel. This parallelism of wording and content is combined with a similarity of approach to the incidents recorded that comes out most clearly if contrasted with Jn's highly individual approach.

(3) The order of Mk's sections or incidents is generally found also in Mt or Lk or in both.

(4) Where all three Gospels are parallel, there is frequent agreement of all three in wording, etc. There is also frequent agreement of Mt and Mk with disagreement of Lk, and of Mk and Lk with disagreement of Mt. But the agreements of Mt and Lk with disagreement of Mk are strikingly rare.

(For the above summary I am largely indebted to B. H. Streeter, *The Four Gospels, a Study of Origins*.)

d The full force of these data is only appreciated when the original Greek text of the three Gospels is carefully studied, set out if possible in parallel columns with Mk as the middle column. The extent of similarity is too great to be explained by identity of purpose and coincidence. Some hypothesis of connexion is necessary. And such connexion may be direct or indirect. Thus, if documents X and Y are connected, the reason may be either that the author of one used the other, or that X or Y was used in oral teaching by some unknown person, whose oral teaching then became the source of Y or X. And obviously the missing link might be not oral teaching but a document

Z, copied from X or Y and itself copied by Y or X. Or again, such oral teaching or document Z might be the common source of X and Y.

It should be taken as a principle of scientific documentary criticism that non-extant conjectural sources are not to be supposed, if a hypothesis of direct connexions will satisfy the internal evidence without violence. Thus at one stage of synoptic study it was suggested that the cases, relatively few, where Mt and Lk, though parallel to Mk, yet show agreements against Mk, might be partially explained on the hypothesis of a lost second edition of Mk. But the difference between the two editions would have been slight and this is now a generally discarded hypothesis, though the agreements mentioned still require explanation or removal. On the other hand, the conjecture that the Q passages are to be explained by appeal to a conjectural lost document has found wide favour and is dealt with in the next section.

e A purely oral theory can hardly do justice to the character and extent of the parallels and similarities ; and it must suppose a Greek oral tradition more rigidly fixed than we have any right to assume. Moreover it is equivalent, critically speaking, to the hypothesis that all three Gospels are derived, in their Marcan sections, from an Ur-Evangelium, a conjectural lost original Gospel. Now it can be shown that such an Ur-Evangelium must turn out to be indistinguishable from either Mt or Mk or Lk :

f For a careful consideration of the evidence referred to in B(4) above shows that Mt and Lk, though connected in the passages where both are parallel to Mk, are not directly connected with each other but indirectly by means of a document or oral teaching practically identical with Mk. Otherwise we cannot explain why the agreements of Mt and Lk against Mk are not nearly as frequent as those of each with Mk against the other—in fact the former set of agreements is relatively so small that reputable scholars have tried to remove or explain them all away. Indirect connexion by means of a document or oral teaching practically indistinguishable from Mk means either that both Mt and Lk used such a source or that such a document used either Mt or Lk (or something indistinguishable) and was itself used by the remaining Gospel of the three. Thus we should be driven to hold that the oral tradition used by all three Evangelists was practically indistinguishable from one of them ; *i.e.* that one of the Evangelists succeeded in preserving the tradition exactly and each of the others only with considerable modification. Such a conjectural source is thus critically worthless and an unjustifiable hypothesis. Most students who will take the trouble to study the evidence in detail will further agree that it does not adequately deal with the facts available.

g **Alternative Solutions**—We have seen that the similarities between the first three Gospels may be due either to a common oral catechesis or to written documents or to dependence of two of them on the third or to a mixture of all these factors. The main solutions are :

(1) **The Traditional Solution,** according to which Mark depends on Matthew in the main, and the

chronological order of writing was Matthew, Mark, Luke ; *cf.* Aug. *De Cons. Evang.*, 1, 2, 4 (PL 34, 1044). This is the solution vindicated in the course of the present article against its chief rival.

(2) **The Two-Document Hypothesis,** which is maintained in substance by almost all non-Catholic scholars at the present day (though with some doubts as to the unitary nature of 'Q'), and its elaboration in the Four-Document Hypothesis of Streeter (*op. cit.*) and V. Taylor ; *cf.* also §§ 604*e*, 607*a–g*.

(3) Other recent solutions (based on varying degrees of literary dependence and oral tradition), which deserve mention as having found favour with many Catholic scholars anxious to reconcile the priority of Mt (§ 679*a–f*) with the Two-Document Hypothesis, are :

(*a*) Mk and Lk depend on Aramaic Mt, Mk also on St Peter's catechetical teaching, Lk also on Mt (Vannutelli) ; (*b*) dependence of Mt, Mk and Lk on a more or less fixed oral catechesis (Lattey and others) ; (*c*) dependence of Aramaic Mt and of Mk on oral catechesis ; of Mt on Mk ; and of Lk on Mk and parts of Mt (Vosté and others ; a partial dependence of Mk on Aramaic Mt is admitted as possible by Simon-Dorado and others, and a full dependence is thought possible by Merk and others). A history of the Synoptic Problem and a survey of proposed solutions will be found in Cornely-Merk, *Compendium Introductionis* ; it should, however, be noticed that modern English non-Catholic scholarship looks back to Lachmann (1835) as the decisive figure in the history of the problem, which is not discussed by the Fathers, except for a statement of St Augustine (*supra cit.*) that Mk appears to be an abbreviation of Mt.

It may be well to point out that, except the Two-Document Hypothesis with its descendants and the Traditional Solution as restated in this article (for which see also Jameson and Chapman, *op. cit.*), few of the proposed solutions take due note of the crucial fact of the relative non-agreement of Mt and Lk 'against Mk' in the main body of the material common to all three evangelists. It is this fact that makes it extremely difficult to deny dependence as between Mt and Mk. The errors of the Two-Document Hypothesis are due to the fact that, while misinterpreting this crucial datum, it does not push far enough the detailed comparison of Mt and Lk in the 'Q' passages and of Mt and Mk, and in consequence reaches conclusions that are inconsistent with the external evidence.

An initial difficulty in accepting the Traditional Solution arises from the hypothesis of the existence of Q. If Q does not exist or can be shown to be identical with Mt, then the way is clear to proving Mk's dependence on Mt. The topics will therefore be treated in this order.

I. The So-called Q Passages

Most modern scholars outside the Church adopt the Two-Document Hypothesis as the fundamental solution of the Synoptic Problem. This hypothesis explains the facts summarized in § 610*c* by supposing that Mk is the earliest of the extant Gospels and that it was copied independently by the authors of Mt and Lk. This supposition may be expressed diagrammatically thus :

(*a*)   Mk
        /   \
      Mt   Lk

As was pointed out above, the relative absence of agreements of Mt and Lk against Mk throughout the sections where all three Gospels run parallel drives us to accept either the connection expressed in the above diagram or one of the two following :

(*b*) Mt   (*c*) Lk
        | |
       Mk   Mk
        | |
       Lk   Mt

In other words, Mk must be the connecting link between Mt and Lk in what we may call their Marcan sections. But the alternatives (*a*), (*b*) and (*c*) are all equally probable on the evidence as so far stated.

The Two-Document Hypothesis then proceeds to **b** explain the Q material by supposing that Mt and Lk depend separately on a document, conjectured but not known to have existed and commonly called 'Q', which contained mainly sayings and discourses of our Lord. This must have been a Greek document, as the wording of the Q passages in Mt and Lk is often identical or so closely similar as to rule out the supposition of independent translation from a non-Greek original. Thus for the Q passages we should have the following diagram of relationship :

and for the whole Two-Document Hypothesis :

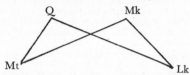

We have however already observed that a non- **c** extant document ought not to be conjectured if the data can be satisfactorily explained without recourse to it. We therefore ask whether Mt and Lk may not be directly connected in the Q passages, and the following arguments tend to show that in fact Lk is directly dependent on Mt.

(1) If Q existed its subject-matter to some extent overlapped that of Mk. For there are five passages where all three Gospels are connected but where agreements between Mt and Lk against Mk are too numerous to be regarded as coincidences, so that connection through Mk will not satisfy the data : (*a*) Mk 4:30–32 *cf.* Mt 13:31–33 and Lk 13:18–21 ; (*b*) Mk 9:42 *cf.* Mt 18:6, 7 and Lk 17:1*b*, 2 ; (*c*) Mk 3:23–30 *cf.* Mt 12:25–32 and Lk 11:17–23, 12:10 ; (*d*) Mk 6:8–11 *cf.* Mt 10:9–14 and Lk 10:4–11 ; (*e*) Mk 12:28–34 *cf.* Mt 22:34–40 and Lk 10:25–28.

The phenomena to be explained in these passages are : agreements between all three Gospels ; agreements between Mt and Lk against Mk and between Mt and Mk against Lk ; relative absence of agreements between Mk and Lk against Mt ; and the fact that the passages in Lk are not in their Marcan context, whereas it is observed that where Mk and Lk are directly connected they nearly always follow the same order of incidents.

Now just as we saw that in the passages referred to **d** (§ 610*c*) the relative absence of agreements between Mt and Lk against Mk compels us to suppose that in *those* passage Mt and Lk are connected not directly but by means of Mk or a source indistinguishable from Mk, so in dealing with *these* passages we shall naturally conclude that the relative absence of agreements between Mk and Lk against Mt, coupled with the difference of context in Lk as compared with Mk, is due to the fact that Mk and Lk are not here directly connected, but indirectly by means of a document indistinguishable from Mt. In other words, that in these passages either Lk is Mt's source or *vice versa*.

(B. H. Streeter, a Two-Documentarian, is driven to **e** conclude that in such passages Mk and Q 'overlapped', *i.e.* told the same story each in his own words— Streeter does not believe that either copied the other

611e —and that Lk used Q for these passages while Mt 'conflated' Q and Mk. But on passage (a) he comments: The differences between the Mk and Q versions of the parable 'are entirely unimportant . . . no one antecedently would have expected that Matthew would take the trouble to combine the two versions'. And as regards passage (d) he points out 'the almost meticulous care with which Matthew conflates Mark and Q—the only real additions he has to make are the words "gold" and "Gomorrha"'. In other words, the Q hypothesis here lands us into complications that are unnecessary and absurd.)

f (2) The sermon in Lk 6:20–49 is clearly the same sermon as the Sermon on the Mount (Mt 5–7). Each begins with Beatitudes and ends with the simile of the two houses; and there is hardly anything (the Woes and about three longish verses) in Lk's sermon that is not parallelled in Mt's. Mt's sermon is far longer than Lk's, and one effect of the absence from Lk's sermon of much that is found in Mt's is that Lk's is almost completely lacking in special Jewish setting and relevance and appears as a discourse of charity towards one's fellowmen. We have already seen in § 611d that Mt and Lk are probably directly connected, and if we ask which is more likely to have copied this Sermon from the other, the answer is already clear. Either our Lord preached a sermon of universal, non-particular relevance which Mt has expanded in length but narrowed in scope, set back into a Jewish thought-world and made relevant to Palestinian controversies, thus transforming it into a quasi-original Christian manifesto against the Jews of our Lord's own time and place (and this despite the fact that the Gospel is written in good Greek); or Lk has transformed a sermon of the latter type into a shorter one on a more generalized theme. Closer inspection confirms the supposition that Lk is the borrower:

g Lk's language shows traces of Mt's (6:23 'reward'; 6:24 ἀπέχετε; 6:27 'to you I say who hear', cf. Mt 5:43, 44). Some passages found in Mt's sermon appear in other contexts in Lk 11:33; 16:18; 12:33 f.; 12:22–31, and these passages in Lk seem secondary when compared with the corresponding passages in Mt's sermon. Finally, at the end of his sermon Lk says 'When he had finished all these words', which corresponds with Mt 7:28. Bht this formula is one which Mt uses on four other occasions in his Gospel.

(3) A similar Mt formula (occurring 6 times in Mt) is found in Lk's parallel (13:28 f.) to Mt 8:11 f. Again Lk 9:57–10:24 appears to show Lucan editing of material borrowed from Mt 8:19–22; 11:21–23, 25–27; 13:16 f.

612a (4) Lk's divergences from Mt in his Q passages are nearly always towards typical Lucan style or otherwise apparently less primitive than their equivalents in Mt. The criterion of poetical form led *C. F. Burney (The Poetry of Our Lord, O.U.P., p 7) to conclude that in most Q cases ('though not in all') Mt preserves the more original form of our Lord's sayings.

On the whole, we may conclude that the hypothesis of Lk's direct dependence on Mt in the Q passages is one which not only explains but is required by the evidence, and the conjectural Q document is therefore an unnecessary and undesirable hypothesis. It is doubtful whether it would have had such a vogue in modern criticism if it had not been accepted as a corollary of the dependence of Mt and Lk on Mk. For if Mk is held to be original, Mt has many additions in Marcan passages which can be conveniently derived from Q; but if Mt does not depend on Mk there is no need to seek for a source for these 'additions' other than that from which the author (or translator) of Mt obtained the contexts in question.

II. Mk's Dependence on Mt

b Scholars who admit literary connexion between the first three Gospels are almost all agreed that Lk depends on Mk, not vice versa. Students who wish to test this dependence may note Lk 4:38 f., cf. Mk 1:29–31 (our Lord in Simon's house; Mk has already described Simon's call, but in Lk this call is not mentioned till the next chapter); Lk 4:23, where the people of Nazareth know of our Lord's ministry at Capharnaum, first described by Lk at 4:31 ff.; Lk 20:38–40, apparently telescoping Mk 12:28–34 (Lk 10:28 also seems to borrow from Mk 12:34). A more general argument is that where Lk is not running parallel to Mk, he lacks clear historical outline and the apostles lose their individuality and become lay-figures. We note that the Preface of Lk refers to other written accounts of Christian origins, and it is natural to suppose that Mk is one of these, and that the author of Lk had seen it.

c Accepting Lk's dependence on Mt in the Q passages and on Mk where Mk and Lk are parallel, we now seek to discover whether, where Mt and Mk are parallel, Mt depends on Mk or vice versa. In this inquiry we have no third document to help us.

It is to be noted that whereas Mt has (after the first two chapters and apart from the last few verses of his Gospel) few incidents that are not found also in Mk, he has a great deal of teaching and discourse that is absent from, or very inadequately represented in, Mk. Mk has very little teaching and very few incidents that are not parallelled in Mt. An examination of the parallel passages and contexts in cases where Mt has a large section of discourse and Mk little or none gives decisive reasons for inferring that Mk depends on Mt.

d (1) Mk 12:38–40 cf. Mt 23:1–36. That this is a genuine pair of parallels is shown by the identity of context and by the identical phrases 'greetings in the market-places', 'first-seats in the synagogues' and 'first-couches in banquets'. (Mt 23:14 [cf. Mk 12:40] is omitted by Huck. But it has strong support from Lk 20:47, Lk being dependent on Mt 23 in the context.) But Mt could not have invented 'they make broad their phylacteries and enlarge their fringes' out of Mk's 'who wish to walk about in robes'. The phylacteries and fringes are genuine Jewish 'local colour' and the rhythmical parallelism in Mt is Semitic. Mk, writing probably for non-Palestinian and largely non-Jewish Christians, substitutes the bizarre phrase 'walk about in robes'. Further, through his omission of Mt's 'love' he has awkwardly left 'wish' to govern first a prolate infinitive and then a series of nouns in the accusative case. Finally, as Mk is excerpting from a long discourse he introduces his brief extract by 'And in his teaching he said'; cf. a similar phenomenon at Mk 4:2, again due to the fact that the author is excerpting from Mt.

e (2) Mk 13:33–37 cf. Mt 24:37–25:46. Identity of context again shows that parallelism is genuine. But nearly everything in these five verses of Mk is explicable by reference to the two parallel chapters of Mt, though the parallels are dispersed through 61 verses of Mt as follows: Mt 25:13, 14, 15; 24:45; 25:15 f.; 24:45 (the faithful servant set over the household, i.e. St Peter or his successors par excellence, i.e. perhaps the door-keeper, or key-bearer of Mk 13:34b); 24:42, 43, 50; 25:5, 32. It is preposterous to suggest that Mt succeeded in expanding Mk's five verses into his own 61; it is a counsel of despair to question the fact of connexion between the Gospels at this point; but it is easy to see how Mk might telescope and abridge Mt's long **f** discourse into his own five verses. This telescoping process has led to one incongruous result: in Mt we have the simile of a thief who comes at an unpredictable hour of the night, and the apostles are told that even so the Son of Man will come at an unexpected moment, and that therefore they must be ready for him whenever he comes—otherwise he may find the rulers of his church abusing their authority. Mt also gives us the simile of an absent master who returns (not at an unexpected hour of the night; there is no reason why a traveller must get home after nightfall, but) after much time. His arrival causes no surprise to his servants, with whom he goes through their accounts.

Now Mk, by rather rough-and-ready telescoping, has conflated these two disparate similes. He presents us with an absent master (whose absence was foreseen as a long one, hence he assigned special work to each of his servants) and an instruction to the doorkeeper to 'keep vigil', because he does not know 'at what hour of the night' his master will return; 'lest coming suddenly he finds you sleeping'. Is the doorkeeper to watch *every* night? But supposing the master chose to return by daylight? The conflation of thief and absent master is patent and not really to be doubted.

(3) Mal 3:1 is quoted in Mk 1:2b in such a context as to suggest that it is from Is. It is also quoted (in the same non-LXX Greek version) in Mt 11:10, where it is integral to its context, a highly-wrought piece of our Lord's teaching. It is so obvious that Mk has taken it from Mt and misplaced it that Two-Documentarians are driven to suggest either that both evangelists got it from a conjectural written source (but this is the old evil practice of hypothesizing sources to escape the difficulties in which their theory has landed them) or that the half-verse is not authentic in Mk; but there is no MS authority for the excision and this is tantamount to a confession that the verse must be in its original setting in Mt and not in Mk, i.e. that in Mk it depends on Mt.

(4) Mk 4:21-25 is a collection of short sayings with parallels for the several items at different points in Mt (Mt 5:15; 10:26; 7:2, cf. 6:33; 25:29). Bishop Rawlinson thinks that the Mt contexts seem generally more appropriate than the Marcan. And note that whereas Mk 4:24a is parallel with Mt 7:2, Mk 4:24b (not very well placed in Mk) is found in Mt three or four verses earlier than 7:2 (6:33) in a context to which it convincingly belongs. This cannot be a coincidence and the conclusion in favour of Mt's priority is inevitable unless (with some MSS) we excise the phrase from Mk—but neither Rawlinson nor Huck nor Souter resorts to this surgical operation; the omission is probably due to homœoteleuton.

(5) Mk 8:27-33, cf. Mt 16:13-23; St Peter's confession of faith. Mk omits our Lord's praise of St Peter and the 'Thou art Peter', etc. In so doing he destroys the antitheses of Mt ('Thou art the Christ . . . Thou art Peter'; 'Blessed art thou . . . Satan'; 'flesh and blood have not revealed it unto thee but my Father in heaven. . . . Thou savourest not the things of God but the things of man'; 'Thou art Peter and upon this rock I will build my Church . . . Thou art a stumbling-block to me'), although in each case he retains one member of the antithesis, usually the second. It is absurd to suggest that Mt took Mk's passage and from it elaborated his own highly symmetrical structure, Semitic in every detail, by adding the missing members of the antitheses, each usually *before* the Marcan word or phrase with which it is thrown in contrast.

(6) Mk 13:9-13 cf. Mt 10:17-22; 24:9-14. The Marcan passage is in the same context as Mt 24:9-14; but its real parallel is Mt 10:17-22. Burney (pp 118-120) states that this section of Mk is distinguished from the rest of the chapter in which it occurs by its rhythm, and that though Mk 13 as a whole is eschatological this section is not, but coheres as to its content with the setting given to it in Mt 10. Burney is a Two-Documentarian and is reduced to suggesting, here and elsewhere, the dependence of Mk on Q. But obviously the evidence suggests that Mk has taken a passage of Mt and put it into a context for which neither its rhythm nor its subject-matter really fits it.

(7) In view of the foregoing evidence, it is not surprising that Mk 4:1-34, a collection of three parables of which two are found in Mt 13:1-50 together with five other parables not given by Mk, shows at its beginning and at its end indications that it is an incomplete reproduction of a collection of parables: 'He taught them many things in parables, and *in his teaching* he said unto them . . . And *with many such parables* he spoke the word to them'.

Mt 13 contains seven parables, of which six fall into **613e** three groups of two, the Parable of the Sower having no partner. Mk 4 has the Parable of the Sower and that of the Mustard Seed (coupled in Mt with the Parable of the Leaven); Mk 4 also contains the Parable of the Seed growing secretly, which is absent from Mt. It seems probable that this is the missing partner of the Sower Parable, and we should thus have a collection of eight parables in four pairs. Mt gives all but one of the collection; perhaps this one was missed by the original recorder of this Sermon of our Lord, but was remembered in substance by an oral informant of Mk.

A small point in this section confirms the view that **f** Mk here excerpts from Mt. Mk 4:13 and 21 appear to refer to the disciples as 'them'; but in 34a the same pronoun, though naturally it would be taken as referring to the same persons, must mean the crowds. This awkwardness is due to Mk's copying and omissions from Mt, where the ambiguity does not exist, since Mt mentions the crowds before referring to them as 'them' in 13:34, cf. Mk 4:34a.

(8) Mk 11:20-25 cf. Mt 21:20-22. After the Withering of the Fig Tree both Gospels put into our Lord's **g** mouth a short exhortation to faith. To it Mk appends v 25: 'And when you stand praying, forgive if you have anything against anyone, so that your Father, who is in the heavens, also may forgive you your trespasses'. To this the parallel in Mt is Mt 6:14 f., a comment on the Our Father (ibid. vv 9-13): 'For if you forgive men their trespasses, your heavenly Father will forgive you also; but if you do not forgive men, neither will your Father forgive your trespasses'. The verse has no relevance to its context in Mk, but is of course in perfect place in Mt. This is the only occasion on which Mk uses 'Your (or my) Father who is in the heavens' for God; Mt has it 13 times, and in seven other places has 'Your (or my) heavenly Father'; and it has been pointed out that this is a typically Jewish expression. The final proof of Mk's dependence **h** on Mt here is in the following parallelisms of language:

(a) 'When you stand praying . . . if you have anything against anyone' cf. Mt 6:5, 'When you pray . . . they love to pray standing in the synagogues' and especially Mt 5:23 'If you bring your gift to the altar and there remember that your brother has something against you . . .' It may be observed that Mk's limitation of the injunction to forgiveness to occasions when one 'stands praying' is, to say the least, odd; Mt, loc. cit., envisages the situation of a man about to engage in a solemn religious act who happens to remember that he is at variance with another.

(b) Mk's 'Your father which is in the heavens' is not **614a** strictly parallel to Mt 6:14, from which the rest of the phrase comes, but to the opening words of the Lord's prayer ('Our Father who art in the heavens') a few verses earlier in Mt. All these phenomena are explained easily by the theory of Mk's dependence; on the opposite theory they cannot be adequately explained. (Bishop Rawlinson appears to think that Mk is here dependent on the Lord's Prayer as currently known among Christians; but this does not explain Mk's links with Mt 6:14, 5; 5:23. And we do not know that the Lord's Prayer was current at this time except in Mt.)

(9) Mt is full of Aramaisms, both where he is parallel **b** with Mk and where Mk has no parallel, and many of these Aramaisms are missing from the corresponding passages of Mk. E.g. 'heavens' is Hebrew-Aramaic, not Greek, and Mt has it 55 times—32 times in the formula 'Reign of the heavens', a formula completely eschewed by Mk; yet 11 of these cases in Mt are in passages where Mk is running parallel. Again Mt continually uses τότε ('then') 89 times, of which 51 are in passages to which Mk has a parallel, but of these 45 are eschewed by Mk. Now τότε is a regular LXX translation of the Aramaic 'eḏayin or bē'ḏayin. It is hardly conceivable that Mt added 45 times this Greek translation of an Aramaism to a Greek text

614b copied from Mk. The most reasonable explanation of these Aramaisms in Mt is that they are due to the Aramaic (written or oral) source that he is translating.

c The converging force of the above evidence is strong enough to compel us to admit the dependence of Mk on Mt. It remains to suggest an explanation of the conversational tone of Mk as compared with Mt's careful literary finish. It would seem as though there lies behind Mk an oral teacher, who based his lectures on the text of Mt, omitting material that lay outside the scope of an immediate eye-witness of our Lord's public ministry and private intercourse with his apostles, omitting also most of the discourses, as being matter that an individual could not trust to his memory to corroborate in detail, and adding a little from his own memory to what he found in Mt. It is remarkable that this oral teacher has omitted everything in Mt that could redound to the credit of St Peter, but has been careful to include whatever reflected discredit

d upon him. The scheme of dependence, taking into account both the A and the B evidence, is therefore as follows :

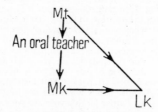

I should not, however, wish to exclude the possibility that the author of Mk revised his record of the oral teacher's discourses by direct reference to Mt.

Mt, the earliest of the Gospels, is naturally also the one most deeply rooted in the Palestinian situation contemporary with our Lord and with the earliest days of the Church in Judaea ; its Greek is also such that it can very probably be supposed to be translated from an Aramaic original. Both Mk and Lk tend to bleach out the Palestinian-Jewish colouring that would be unfamiliar and irrelevant to their Greek-speaking, largely Gentile, readers. Mk gives only the public ministry of our Lord, and mainly incidents not discourses, because such was the material that the oral teacher could confirm by his own memory. Lk makes Mk the backbone of his Gospel, perhaps out of respect for the oral teacher on whom he knew it to depend. He is able however to add a narrative of the birth of St John Baptist and our Lord, and of the childhood of our Lord, derived, it would seem, ultimately from our Lady ; and other material derived partly from the circle of Herod's court and partly from Palestinian sources that he may have tapped during St Paul's two-years detention in Caesarea. He also secured a copy of Mt and was thus enabled to add considerably to the teaching of our Lord that he had already derived from Mk and other sources. But he will not spoil his narrative of our Lord's birth by conflating with it the account in Mt, which appears to be derived ultimately from St Joseph. Lk is the most Hellenistic and at the same time the least ' three-dimensional ' of the Synoptic Gospels.

Conclusion—The above investigation has been presented without recourse to external arguments (*cf.* §§ 677–8, 724, 744–5). It remains to point out that our solution gives us the traditional order of the Gospels. It throws open the possibility that Mt is, as tradition suggests, a translation of a Semitic original. It renders easier the traditional attribution of Mt's Semitic original to St Matthew the Apostle. It strengthens the traditional assertion that Mk contains a record of St Peter's teaching at Rome. It enables justice to be done to the evidence adduced for the dependence of Gal on Mt 16 (H. J. Chapman, R Bn, 1912) and of 1 and 2 Thess on Mt (J. B. Orchard, Bi, Jan. 1938). It thus helps very considerably over the question of the dates of composition of the first three Gospels. Mt will be earlier than Gal and 1 and 2 Thess, and its Aramaic original, if it had one, will be still earlier. A great many loose theories concerning a long period of oral transmission of the story of Christian origins will be undermined, and we can now watch the Christian Gospel story in its actual evolution from the Palestinian to the Hellenistic Church, an evolution seen to be not one of corruption by accretion, but of universalization by omission.

THE PERSON AND TEACHING OF
OUR LORD JESUS CHRIST

By Dom A. GRAHAM

a **Bibliography**—The secondary authorities to which this study is indebted are acknowledged in the text. Among the best Catholic works available in English are the following translations from the French : Lagrange, *The Gospel of Jesus Christ*, 2 vol. ; Grandmaison, *Jesus Christ*, 3 vol. ; Lebreton, *The Life and Teaching of Jesus Christ*, 2 vol. For a comprehensive bibliography, see DTC, 8, Pt 2, 1408–11. A list of non-Catholic works will be found in Peake, *Commentary on the Bible*, 670–1.

b The subject will be dealt with under the following headings :

    I   Method and Point of View
    II   Outline of the Life of our Lord
    III   Jesus : the Messias and Son of God
    IV   The Teaching
    V   Some Special Points :
        (*a*) The Kingdom of God
        (*b*) The Parables
        (*c*) The Miracles
        (*d*) Our Lord's Knowledge
    VI   The Mystery of Jesus

I Method and Point of View—In what spirit are we to approach a study of the significance of our Lord Jesus Christ ? Have we to make choice between, on the one hand, adopting an attitude of scientific detachment, self-consciously aware of, and not unwilling to parade, the latest results of contemporary scholarship, or, on the other, giving proof of our loyalty by confining ourselves to the merely devotional and edificatory aspects of the gospels ? There is perhaps no need to pose so sharp a dilemma. It may be difficult, but surely not impossible, to combine a critical temper of mind with whole-hearted allegiance. Modern criticism often presents a picture of Jesus scarcely to be reconciled with Catholic orthodoxy ; but this has little to do with the critical approach as such (by which we understand the attempt to attain objective truth in the light of evidence), to which the Church shows no hostility. Rather it is because the critics have all too often been imbued with, or have unconsciously accepted, a rationalistic philosophy which can find no place for divinely revealed mysteries and the supernatural order. The Hegelian idealism and Positivist scepticism (an aberration against which the scholar and savant, absorbed in the minutiae of research, has continually to be on his guard) which, until lately, have pervaded Protestant systematic theology, impose far more crippling limitations upon the mind intent on discovering the essential Christian message than the dogmas of the Church are supposed to do.

c A typical example of this limited approach is provided by a recently published ' exposition of the Gospels in the light of modern research ' (*Major, Manson, Wright, *The Mission and Message of Jesus*—Macmillan, London, 1940). The authors tell us, with a suggestion of great impartiality, that they ' are not concerned to make the Gospels affirm the declarations of the traditional creeds nor to teach the traditional scheme of salvation ' ; and they appeal to the dictum of Archbishop Frederick Temple : ' If the conclusions be prescribed, the research is precluded '. This is

well enough so far as it goes, but it is based on an **616c** assumption which appears to have escaped the notice of those who appeal so confidently to it. What seems to be taken for granted is that the inner essence of Christianity will yield itself to ' research ', or at least *modern* research. In other words, those who study Christian origins in this spirit are guilty of a far more flagrant *petitio principii* than can be charged against the ' older orthodoxy '. The Catholic Church has never held that her teaching about Christ, as formulated in the Nicene Creed and the definition of the Council of Chalcedon, can be logically deduced from the written gospels in the same way as, for example, the character of Socrates may be inferred from the writings of Plato and Xenophon. The Church's faith **d** in Christ, though truly if inadequately expressed in the *verbum Dei scriptum vel traditum* (Dz 1792), has for its object the inner recesses of his personality, far beyond the reach of human evidence and escaping rational analysis. Thus there is a sense in which it is true to say that the Gospels are the result, and not the cause, of Christian faith. This is a position by no means unassailable on philosophical grounds, as Catholic theologians are well aware, but it is not touched by those who imagine that they can reconstruct the ' historical Jesus ' solely on the basis of modern scholarship. The researches of the past century, fruitful as they have been in many respects, have conspicuously failed, and must of their nature fail, to reach finality as to the significance of Jesus. The reaction towards the traditional theology of the Incarnation, embodied in such thinkers as Barth and Brunner, though raising a whole set of difficulties of a different order, is a striking evidence of the insufficiency of the Liberal Protestant attempts at discovering the heart of the Christian message.

The scholastic theologians evolved an axiom which, **e** though of universal application, is especially relevant in our present context : *cognitum est in cognoscente secundum modum cognoscentis* ; ' the object known is in the mind that knows it according to the measure of that mind '. So much depends upon the point of view, upon the temper in which we approach the object of our study. Learning, be it acknowledged at the outset, is an essential pre-condition ; but it is not the only one. *Sanday, in his *Outlines of the Life of Christ* (p 240), well expresses this point : ' It should be needless to say that the Life of Christ can be written only by a believer. Renan had all the literary gifts— a *curiosa felicitas* of style, an aesthetic appreciation of his subject, and a saving common-sense which tempered his criticism ; but even as literature his work is spoilt by self-consciousness and condescension, and his science was not of the best '. The same writer tells us that he knows of no *Life* which possesses ' such a balance and combination of qualities as to rise quite to the level of a classic '. And he adds significantly : ' What is wanted is a Newman, with science and adequate knowledge '.

Though the Church is committed to a certain view **f** about the person and life-work of our Lord, she is in no way opposed to the scientific investigation of Christian origins. On the contrary, as the utterances of recent Popes go to show (*e.g.* Pius XII, *Divino afflante Spiritu*), she warmly encourages these researches,

616f provided they be conducted with due regard to the exigencies of their object. Indeed her consistent rejection of any ' double standard ' of truth—whether it be the 13th cent. contention that what is true for theology need not necessarily be true for philosophy, or the modernist opposition between the ' Christ of faith ' and the ' Jesus of history '—implies a submission to historical evidence far more radical than can be claimed by those critics who, bringing to their study preconceived theories and *a priori* categories, arrange their findings accordingly.

g As the present writer has written elsewhere, ' The historic revelation of Christianity can be considered from two points of view. We may look at it from without, as a series of facts and truths of peculiar interest, but nevertheless as no more than particular events in the general story of our race. Or, having received the gift of faith, we can study them from within and see that they are realities of eternal significance ' (*Love of God*, 78). The Catholic scholar is free, should he so choose, to adopt the first line of approach—the science of Apologetics is in fact chiefly concerned with it—whereby he prescinds from, without abandoning, the act of faith. Furthermore the Church's insistence on the unity of all truth, the principle that a fact of revelation cannot conflict with a fact of human history, precludes the manipulation of evidence to secure the desired conclusion. A strictly revealed dogma, so St Thomas teaches (ST II, 2, Q. i, Art. 5), can no more be demonstrated by purely rational argument than can a truth accessible to reason be said to form an object of faith.

h Thus though historical research and individual reflection may tell us much about Christ our Lord, may—and, as we hold, should—dispose the mind to the acceptance of the Church's faith concerning him, they cannot pronounce decisively either for or against the truth of the inner content of that faith. This is a revealed mystery of which the inherent possibility, let alone the fact, cannot be rationally established. Having spoken of the motives of credibility which lead up to belief in Christ, St Thomas adds these significant words : ' But when a man, led on by these motives, makes the act of faith, then can it still be said that not in virtue of any of them does he believe : neither on account of the evidence of reason, nor through the witness of the Law, nor as moved by what has come to him through preaching, but solely on account of the truth itself—*propter ipsam veritatem tantum* ' (*Comm. in Joan.*, cap. IV, lect. v, 2). Not only St Peter (*cf.* Mt 16:17), but each member of the faithful, confesses Christ to be the Son of the living God because the Father has revealed it to him.

i The Catholic belief concerning the person of our Lord received final formulation in A.D. 451 at the Council of Chalcedon (Dz 148). Here the doctrine of the two natures in one divine Person was defined, that Jesus Christ is ' consubstantial with the Father in respect of his deity, consubstantial with us in respect of his humanity . . . as the Lord himself taught and the symbol (Nicene) of the Fathers handed down to us '. Anyone who shares the convictions of the present writer must hold that a study of the NT evidence will always lead ' to a better appreciation of the Chalcedonian definition ' (*Lowther Clarke, Divine Humanity*, p v). But whether or not this be accepted, it has yet to be shown that such a standpoint involves any distortion of the scriptural accounts. The Fathers of the Council maintained in the 5th cent., as the Church maintains today, that they drew up an article of faith which did justice to the oral and written tradition about our Lord. They were concerned with nothing but this. Those who think them mistaken may profitably inquire whether they themselves are not pre-judging the issue, though from different premisses, by the same process with which they charge the orthodox theologians. To be prepossessed with the desire to accommodate Jesus to the grasp of the modern mind, or to rule out in advance the possibility of such a

divine intervention into human affairs as the Catholic doctrine of the Incarnation implies, or to hold antecedently that miracles do not happen, or to think that antiquity means obscurantism and modernity enlightenment—all or any of these positions must, on the grounds of objectivity alone, have a gravely incapacitating effect upon a mind striving to understand the gospels.

Writing some forty years ago of the Christological work performed by the early Church Councils, Sanday remarks : ' The decisions in question were thus the outcome of a long evolution, every step in which was keenly debated by minds of great acumen and power, really far better equipped for such discussions than the average Anglo-American mind of today ' (*op. cit.*, 226). This judgement, which might also have included the average German mind, has lost nothing of its truth. But it must not be thought that on this account the Catholic student is left free to ignore the positive results of recent scholarship. On the contrary, he owes it to himself to assimilate them ; for unless the Church's dogmatic teaching on the Incarnate Word is, as it were, filled in and illustrated by the NT narrative, considered in its literal and concrete meaning, he will be in danger of forming an abstract and quite unreal notion of the personality of our Lord. Thus, though the official Catholic doctrine has never failed to give full recognition to the complete humanity of Jesus, the same cannot be said of the conceptualizations and elaborations of that doctrine by individual theologians —and these have not been without influence on the minds of believers. The following criticism of Peter Lombard's Christology is interesting, not only for its own sake, but because it may suggest reflections of more general application : ' His view illustrates the general tendency of later Greek theology, which he generally follows, to assign an excessive predominance to the Deity in Christ ; a tendency resulting from an *a priori* method of reasoning in regard to the Incarnation, drawing conclusions not from the picture in the Gospels, but from the probable conditions under which an incarnation of Deity may be supposed to have occurred ' (*Ottley, The Doctrine of the Incarnation*, 521).

The dogmatic formulas, precious though they are as affording an anchorage to the mind, do not exempt us from the task of re-thinking the gospels for ourselves under the guidance of the Church. We have, in our own intelligence and imagination, to avoid each of the opposing departures from the central truth into one or other of which men are bound to fall when they lose their balance on the knife-edge of orthodoxy. On the one hand, Docetism (of which Monophysitism is a form), which regards the Incarnation as a theophany, Christ's human nature a mere appearance, or at best a veil to the Divinity—for which in consequence Jesus is not truly man. On the other, Adoptianism (which lies at the root of Nestorianism), the prototype of humanitarian Christianity, which holds that the humanity was in some way divinized, taken up into union with the Deity—whence it follows that Jesus is not truly God. We shall be preserved from both these errors in turning to the evangelical witness and finding there disclosed to us the Jesus of history, who is also the Christ of faith.

II Outline of the Life of our Lord—According to St Matthew (2:1) and St Luke (2:4) our Lord was born in Behtlehem, a town in Judaea some six miles south of Jerusalem. The date can only be calculated approximately. When in the 6th cent. Dionysius Exiguus equated the Roman year 754 with 1 A.D. he could not have been correct. Mt (2:1) tells us that the birth of Jesus took place ' in the days of King Herod ', and we know from Josephus (*Ant.*, 17, 8, 1) that Herod died in the spring of the year corresponding to 4 B.C. Time must be allowed for the infant days in Bethlehem prior to the massacre of the Innocents, followed by the flight to, and sojourn in, Egypt which

c ended with Herod's death. Estimates of the interval which had elapsed between the Nativity and this latter event have varied from as much as three years to as little as a few weeks. (Fuller treatment of the point may be looked for in the art. *Chronology of NT Times*, §§ 674–6.) It is certain, however, that our Lord could not have been born later than the early months of the year 4 B.C.

d We learn from Lk, who wrote his account, ' having diligently attained to all things from the beginning ' (1:3) of the coming of the shepherds to the new-born Babe and of the hymn of praise—' Glory to God in the highest '—sung by ' a multitude of the heavenly army ' (2:13). On the eighth day (*cf.* Lev 12:2–4) the Child was circumcised and given the name of Jesus. After the prescribed forty days Jesus is brought by Mary his mother to the Temple at Jerusalem for her purification ' according to the law of Moses ' (Lk 2:22 ; *cf.* Lev 12). At the same time she presents her Child to God (*cf.* Ex 13:2) and, not being able to afford the offering of a yearling lamb for a holocaust, she was allowed to substitute in its place two young pigeons (Lk 2:24 ; *cf.* Lev 12:8). The Purification, though combined with the Presentation by Lk, as it is in the Liturgical Feast (Feb. 2nd), had originally no connection with it.

The devout Simeon, a strict observer of the law and a man of deep personal piety, was watching in the Temple at this time, together with Anna ' a prophetess '. They were true representatives of that class who awaited in hope and holy fear the coming of ' the consolation of Israel ' (Lk 2:25). Simeon, under divine inspiration, recognizes the Babe as the long expected Messias ; he saw in him not only the promised Saviour of his people, but one who would also bring the light of revelation to the Gentiles. In veiled language he foretells the future of the Child : his Messianic mission will be no popular triumph ; not all will accept him, though all will be affected by him. Men's response to his message will be the test of the sincerity of their own inmost thoughts. He will meet with opposition and contempt, and a sword of anguish will pierce his mother's heart.

e St Matthew now takes up the story with material peculiar to himself. He tells us of the visit of the ' wise men from the east ' (2:1), of their interview with Herod which was the prelude to the massacre of the Innocents, of their journey to Bethlehem guided by the star, and of the act of homage paid there to the new-born Child (2:11). The NT tells us no more about them, except that, avoiding Jerusalem and Herod, ' they went back another way into their country ' (v 12). On their departure, Joseph, warned by an angel in sleep, takes the Child and his mother by night into Egypt, where they remain until Herod's death. It is after this event that the Holy Family make their way to Nazareth in Galilee, whence Mary and Joseph had journeyed to Bethlehem, and it is with this northern town that the name of Jesus is ever afterwards to be associated.

f St Luke alone lifts the veil, if but for a brief moment, from the years which shroud the ' hidden life '. He notices, like a good physician, that ' the child grew and waxed strong ' (2:40), that he was ' full of wisdom ', and that his mental and physical development won him favour with both God and man (v 52). In a word he passed through the normal stages of boyhood and youth in a way to delight all who came in contact with him. From Joseph he would learn the carpenter's trade, from Mary many of the domestic arts ; but most of all would his heart be in his studies at the synagogue school at Nazareth. Since their return from the Babylonian exile and the growth of the synagogue system, every Jewish community of any size was provided with a school attached to its synagogue in which all male children were taught the Law. In consequence the level of popular education in the Judaism of our Lord's time was, within its limits, intellectually, morally and spiritually higher than that of any other contemporary civilization. Quite apart **617f** from the sources of knowledge later to be discussed, Jesus gained familiar acquaintance with the OT scriptures by the wholly human process of studying and learning them by heart. Judged by the standards of his own country and time, our Lord was well educated ; he would express himself normally in Aramaic, the language in common use, but he no doubt also spoke, when occasion demanded, in Greek and Hebrew. The taunt that he had ' never learned ' (Jn 7:15) was the unworthy gibe of defeated disputants wishing to discredit an opponent. It had little substance in fact.

One incident in our Lord's boyhood has been recorded **g** by St Luke. A Jewish boy became responsible for the discharge of his religious duties, which as a circumcised Jew he was bound to perform, at the age of twelve years. It was then that he acquired the status of a ' Son of the Law '. So we find Jesus at the feast of Passover, at Jerusalem with Mary and Joseph. An oriental child at the age of twelve is well able to take care of himself ; doubtless this knowledge, and perhaps some confusion in the arrangements of the home-going caravan, caused his parents to lose contact with him for a time. The rediscovery in the Temple presents a scene as significant as it is charming. Save as an infant in arms, this was possibly the first time our Lord had ever been within its walls, and he is reluctant to depart. He recognizes it as his Father's house (Lk 2:49) ; the consciousness of his unique sonship with God, as expressed in the first of his recorded words, is already upon him. We may note that his role ' in the midst of the doctors ' (v 46) was not (the surely unattractive one) of the youthful teacher correcting and supplementing the ignorance of his elders. Rather does Jesus show himself, as befitted his age, as the seeker after knowledge. Absorbed as he was in thoughts of religion, he would—with boyish modesty, as we may well imagine—raise points with these experts in Jerusalem which possibly his teachers in the synagogue at home in Nazareth had been unable to settle. They in their turn would inquire his reasons for asking, good humouredly testing what he knew and weighing how much he deserved an answer. It is at his responses to these questions that we find him as the youthful doctor ; they ' were astonished at his wisdom and his answers ' (v 47). The curtain now descends and is not raised again for some eighteen years or more.

The Public Ministry—Possibly the autumn of A.D. 27 **618a** is the date indicated by Lk 3:1, when John, the son of Zachary and kinsman of Jesus, was found baptizing and preaching repentance on the banks of the Jordan not far from Jericho. Israel, which had lived these hundreds of years by the written law, without a prophet to kindle their hearts to fervour (Ps 73:9), once again heard the voice of prophecy. John had assumed the famous garment of camel's hair (Mk 1:6 ; Mt 3:4), the official garb of the prophet (Zach 13:4), which perhaps no one living had seen before. His mission, as can be gathered from Josephus as well as from the gospels, created an immense popular stir : so far as outward and immediate effects were concerned, it may well have been more impressive than that of Jesus himself. The burden of his message, preached with great personal asceticism and forebodings of an imminent revelation from God, was ' Repent . . . the kingdom of heaven is at hand ' (Mt 3:2 KNT). He demanded uncompromisingly what the prophets before him had demanded, a change of heart, a more serious attention to what his hearers knew to be their religious duty ; but his teaching did not seem to imply any radical criticism of the existing order, nor did it contain anything fundamentally new. John felt himself to be the precursor of the Messias ; but our Lord was in no real sense the continuer of his work. Jesus understood and appreciated John, while at the same time insisting on the superiority of his own mission in its inspiration and vital significance.

618b Yet 'Jesus came from Nazareth of Galilee and was baptized by John' (Mk 1:9). Sinless himself (Heb 4:15), he nevertheless wishes to be identified with a sinful people. John demurs, conscious at least of a holiness which made such a baptism incongruous ; but Jesus insists, for he must, in Matthew's characteristic phrase, 'fulfil all due observance' (3:15 KNT). The voice of the Father and the coming of the Holy Spirit, which accompanied the baptism, were a manifestation that this was Israel's Messias, and also perhaps, though not exclusively, a consoling and strengthening experience for Jesus himself (Mk 1:11 ; Mt 3:17 ; Lk 3:22). John the Baptist realized in some measure what was taking place (Jn 1:32 f.), though not, it would seem, in a way to exclude a later mood of impatience at the Messias' seeming tardiness in establishing his kingdom (Mt 11:3). There is no evidence that this theophany, striking as it was, made any impression on, or was intended to impress, the onlookers at the baptism. Before setting out on his Messianic mission, the consciousness of which had ever been before him, our Lord 'led by the Spirit' (Lk 4:1), undergoes temptation in the wilderness.

c These temptations afford a moving testimony to Jesus's kinship with ourselves (Heb 4:15). What was their nature and purpose ? Strictly speaking they are a prelude to, rather than a part of, the Public Ministry. They took place when Jesus was alone, and presumably we should have heard nothing of them had he not thought fit to recount the experience to his disciples. There is indeed a dramatic appropriateness in these particular temptations coming at this point. Our Lord had just heard the voice of the Father and received an outpouring of strength from the Holy Spirit, both alike encouraging to his human nature—apt, by the very fact that it was human, to shrink from an office so fraught with suffering and danger—to go forward on his predestined task of bringing salvation to Israel. Was it not to be expected that the forces of evil (cf. Eph 6:12) should conspire together to oppose the projected work, if not by direct attack, then at least by infecting its motives and perverting its object ? If the good deed was not to be frustrated, might not wickedness secure a more subtle triumph by ensuring that it should be done for the wrong reason ? Satan was bent upon undoing what Jesus, the Lord's anointed, had been called to carry through. Our Lord, in the literal meaning of the phrase, was being tempted to abandon his vocation.

d We may conjecture that Jesus, during the days of retreat in the desert, was anticipating in his mind all that was involved in the work to which he was about to set his hand. He would have the light of a knowledge derived from the union of his human nature with the Godhead ; even as man his mind would enjoy, in virtue of its unique holiness, a divine illumination possessed by no other ; but surely this does not exclude a mental review of what lay before him, natural to any man in such a situation, even though he had ever in mind the plan eternally foreordained by the Father. In the midst of these reflexions Satan comes to interpose his counsels.

The first temptation consists in an invitation to our Lord to use the power given him by his Father to satisfy his own personal needs. He has been fasting and is hungry—why not change these stones into bread (Mt 4:3) ? Some have seen in this suggestion an even wider significance. Jesus is being tempted to use the Messianic office as a means of securing economic relief for the numerous poverty-stricken people of Palestine, and so to gain popularity and acceptance with them. However that may be, his reply, an appeal to Deut 8:3, gives no encouragement to any conception of the Messias which would apply the materialistic test of temporal prosperity. The second temptation is a crude appeal to his miracle-working powers ; let him make some spectacular display, like jumping from the pinnacle of the Temple in Jerusalem, and so win followers by an appeal to the vulgar desire for excitement. Jesus, as we know, will work many miracles, but not one of them in this spirit ; he makes no concessions to those who seek the wonderful for its own sake (cf. Mt 16:4) and the kind of self-display which directly tempts God is to him an abomination. Again he appeals to Scripture (Deut 6:16). The last temptation perhaps suggests recourse to political means, a response to the expectations of the fanatical Zealots who looked to the Messias to overthrow the Roman and Herodian power. The tempter is dismissed with the invocation of the first and greatest of the commandments : 'The Lord thy God shalt thou adore, and him only shalt thou serve' (Mt 4:10 ; cf. Deut 6:13).

e The impossibility of assigning any precise chronological sequence to the Public Ministry is now generally admitted. The length of time spent by Jesus in Judaea before he began to preach in Galilee is uncertain. St John gives us some details of what happened : a striking testimony from the Baptist (1:29 ff.) ; the preliminary call of the first disciples (v 38 ff.) ; the driving of the traders out of the Temple precincts (2:14 ff.) ; the discussion with Nicodemus (3:1 ff.)—unless this took place, as seems likely, at the last Passover festival (§§ 771a, 736c, 765d). There is also the first miracle, the 'sign' in Cana of Galilee (2:1 ff.), the changing of water into wine, before we reach the obviously parallel passages in the synoptists. But if St John's account is really patient of chronological treatment, room must be found for the visit to Jerusalem just alluded to (2:13 ff.), the final witness of the Baptist (3:23 ff.) 'in Ennon near Salim', and the conversation with the Samaritan woman (4:6 ff.) before the opening of the Galilean ministry, which is the preoccupation of the first three evangelists (Mk 1:14 ; Mt 4:12 ; Lk 4:14 ; cf. Jn 4:45).

f Jesus began to teach in the synagogues (Lk 4:15), and not until later in the open air. St Luke gives us a vivid account of his early preaching at Nazareth. The Master takes as his text the famous passage from Isaias (61:1–2), which speaks of the gracious mission of the Servant of Yahweh, and asserts that it is now being fulfilled ; that is to say, in veiled language, he makes the Messianic claim. We find him next at Capharnaum. Here he made a deep impression by reason of the novel method of his teaching. His manner was original ; instead of citing authorities and learned commentators, as did the scribes, he delivered his message directly and, as it were, on his own responsibility. 'You have heard that it was said to them of old. . . . But I say to you . . .' (Mt 5:21). At Capharnaum he exorcizes a demoniac, who testifies to his Messiahship, and his reputation spreads throughout Galilee. Here also he heals Simon's mother-in-law and many others brought to him after the Sabbath sunset. There followed the remarkable healing of the leper at the latter's own request. This created such a stir among the people that the popular demand would have forced Jesus's work of preaching to become purely a ministry of healing. For this reason he kept away from the towns and 'retired into the desert and prayed' (Lk 5:16). It may have been that our Lord visited the Galilean synagogues before returning to his temporary base at Capharnaum. His increasing fame has drawn upon him the attention of official Jewish ecclesiasticism as represented by the Pharisaic party. The cure of the paralytic (Mk 2:1–12 ; Mt 9:2–8 ; Lk 5:17–26), whereat Jesus declares the sick man's sins forgiven and for the first time in the gospels ascribes to himself the title 'Son of Man', creates an unfavourable impression on the minds of Pharisees who witness it. The call of Levi with the feast that follows, at which our Lord is found consorting with tax-gatherers and non-observers, causes a second clash. With the dispute about fasting and two conflicts over Sabbath observance, in which Jesus clearly places conformity to the Law on a lower plane than the common kindness of relieving human necessities, the attitude of the

Pharisees hardens into uncompromising hostility. They took counsel with the Herodians to be rid of him—for Sabbath-breaking is a capital offence. It is this combination of ecclesiastical and political power, originating in the Sabbath dispute, which will finally bring about the wrecking of the Galilean ministry (Mk 7:24 ; Mt 15:21).

Meanwhile, with the common people, our Lord's popularity grew. The crowds are so great that, to gain some relief, possibly also as a precaution against sudden arrest by his enemies, he resorts to the device of preaching on the lakeside from a boat. It was Simon Peter's (Lk 5:3). We now reach one of the key-points of the ministry, the choosing of the apostles following upon a night spent in prayer (Lk 6:12). Knowing that his work could only reach its final issue after his death, Jesus selects by a deliberate act of his will (Mk 3:13) twelve to be especially trained by himself (v 14). As he was acting on a mandate from the Father, so they in their turn would continue his mission (cf. Jn 17:18). Simon Peter's name comes first on the list of all three synoptists (Mk 3:16 ff. ; Mt 10:2 ff. ; Lk 6:14 ff. ; cf. Ac 1:13). Having gathered the twelve about him, to them in particular but also to all who would afterwards call themselves his followers, our Lord delivered the teaching contained in the Sermon on the Mount—the 'Charter', as it has been called, 'of the Kingdom of God' (Mt 5-7 ; Lk 6:17-49).

If we follow St Luke's order, we shall place the cure of the centurion's servant at Capharnaum and the raising of the widow's son at Naim as the next important events in the Galilean ministry. The latter miracle was performed out of sheer compassion ; no request came from the mother and no act of faith was demanded. The onlookers were deeply moved ; Jesus's reputation was spreading throughout Palestine. Reports of him had reached as far as Machaerus, on the mountains overlooking the Dead Sea, where John the Baptist was imprisoned. Possibly to banish a temptation to doubt, possibly in order to reassure his own disciples, John sends to Jesus to inquire whether after all he is the promised Messias (Lk 7:20). Our Lord replies, not by a direct affirmative, but by appealing to his works, leaving John to draw the inference, as he easily could (Is 29:18 ff. ; 35:5-6), that in Jesus part at least of the Messianic office was being fulfilled. It may have been shortly after this, while still in Galilee, that the feet of Jesus are anointed by the sinful woman and we get the 'golden saying' : 'Many sins are forgiven her, because she hath loved much' (Lk 7:47).

Our Lord now begins to preach the Kingdom of God, no longer in the direct manner of the Sermon on the Mount, but in figures of speech, extended similes, known as parables. We touch here on a much-discussed question—See § 625g infra—as the reasons for adopting this method are obscure. It will be sufficient to suggest in this place that, wishing in the short time at his disposal to concentrate on the formation of an élite, Jesus directed his attention to gathering about him the more stable and thoughtful among his hearers. This view, at any rate, finds support in the Parable of the Sower (Mt 13:3 ff. ; Lk 8:5 ff.). At the end of the day's teaching in parables he does not alight from his boat-pulpit but, in order doubtless to escape being thronged by the crowd, crosses over to the eastern shore of the Lake. On this journey he stills the suddenly-rising tempest, filling his disciples with awe by his power over the elements. Arrived at the farther side, in 'the country of the Gerasenes', our Lord exorcizes an unhappy demoniac. The cured man wishes to become a disciple ; but Jesus bids him rather to go and relate his good fortune to his friends. Sent thus on a sort of apostolic mission to the Gentiles —for he comes from Decapolis—the happy man begins to publish abroad the 'great things Jesus had done for him' (Mk 5:20). Returning once more to the western shore of the Lake, the Lord raises to life the daughter

of Jairus and, while on his way, cures the woman with **619c** haemorrhage as a reward for her great faith. This time he enjoins that no one shall be told of it.

Nazareth is next visited and, if we may follow La- **d** grange in reading two visits into Luke 4 (the first vv 16-22a ; the second vv 22b-30, parallelled by Mk 6:1-6, Mt 13:54-58 ; cf. Jn 4:44 ; 6:42), it is on this occasion that Jesus is scornfully rejected by the townsfolk ; the Prophet is without honour in his own country. There now follows, after the failure at Nazareth, a third significant stage in our Lord's ministry (in line with the call of the disciples and the change from popular to parabolic teaching) : he calls the Twelve about him, arms them with effective power (δύναμις) and official authority (ἐξουσία), delivers a charge, and sends them to preach the Kingdom of God through the tetrarchy of Herod Antipas. The Baptist had by this time been beheaded, and Herod, fearful and superstitious, hearing of the activities of Jesus, wonders whether it can be that John has risen from the dead. The possibility of hostile action from Herod causes Jesus to withdraw with his disciples away from the populous towns ; but the crowds follow him to the remoter countryside. On one such occasion, when he has attracted no less than five thousand people, moved at the thought of their hunger, he feeds them all from five barley loaves and two fishes—a miracle recorded by all four evangelists (Mk 6:30-34 ; Mt 14:13-21 ; Lk 9:10-17 ; Jn 6:1-15). So great was the enthusiasm that the zealots among the crowd, reckoning they had found the leader for their political revolution, would have acclaimed him King. But he withdrew from them and hid himself (Jn 6:15). The same night he again demonstrates his mastery over nature by walking upon the waters to rejoin his disciples. The next day, with much appropriateness, having first healed many sick on the lakeside (Mk 6:53, 54 ; Mt 14:34-35), he preaches the discourse on the Bread of Life (Jn 6:22 ff.), in which he indicates his intention of giving his flesh and blood to be men's food and drink. Notwithstanding the previous demonstration of supernatural power, many find it a hard saying and follow him no longer (Jn 6:67).

If St John's gospel really aims at chronological sequence **e** (following the ancient gospel harmonies, we invert the order of chapters 5 and 6), it would seem reasonable to place a visit to Jerusalem, with the Sabbath-day cure of the paralytic at the pool of Bethesda, before the three attacks made by Jesus upon Pharisaic legalism and rabbinical casuistry (Mk 7:1-23 ; Mt 15:1-20). Immediately afterwards he withdrew, a refugee, 'into the coasts of Tyre and Sidon' (Mk 7:24), where he cures the daughter of the Syrophoenician woman. Turning south-east, but avoiding the territory of Herod Antipas, he enters the Decapolis ; near the borders of the Lake he has brought to him a deaf-mute, whom he cures to the delight and wonder of the crowd. Not far from Bethsaida he feeds four thousand people from seven loaves and a few fishes—a miracle which Mk is careful to distinguish from the previous feeding of the five thousand (8:19)—and then crosses the Lake to the western shore. Here he is confronted by the hostile Pharisees ; disregarding his wonderful works of healing, they demand 'a sign from heaven' as proof of his Messiahship. Jesus, who would never attempt to compel belief merely by a display of the marvellous, refuses to be put to the test in this way. 'A sign shall not be given to this generation' (Mk 8:12). Crossing the Lake, he warns his disciples against the leaven of the Pharisees and Herodians. As if to reprove their slowness to comprehend his meaning, on arrival at Bethsaida he restores sight to a blind man : a cure which he seeks to effect in private and one— like the healing of the deaf-mute : also peculiar to Mk 7:32 ff.—not presupposing the patient's faith.

We now reach what is in many respects the central **f** point of the Public Ministry : the acknowledgement of Jesus as the Messias by Simon Peter at Caesarea Philippi, together with the Master's felicitation and

619f promise of the headship of the Church (Mt 16:13–20; *cf*. Mk 8:27–30; Lk 9:18–21). Jesus himself, having first prayed on the journey, chooses the moment for eliciting the supreme act of faith from his disciple; but he will not allow the 'Messianic secret' (as Mk seems to see it) to be spread abroad. 'And he strictly charged them that they should not tell any man of him' (Mk 8:30). He begins to enlighten them as to the true significance of his Messianic office, 'the Son of man must suffer many things' (Mk 8:31). The impressionable yet devoted Peter is horrified at such a prospect and would banish it from his Master's mind; only to receive from him words of rebuke no less telling than had been those of approbation shortly before. The office of Messias, contrary to popular expectations, involves no temporal triumph, but rejection by the nation and a shameful death. Those who would follow him must likewise take up their cross. There will be a glorious resurrection one day, but only for him 'that shall lose his life for my sake' (Mt 16:25). A week later, perhaps to banish the depression and bewilderment of the disciples, taking apart Peter, James and John, Jesus is transfigured in glory before them. Moses, representing the Law, and Elias, who stands for the Prophets, are present. 'In this scene all that was most divine in Israel's past does homage to the new prophet and upholds what he has foretold about the scandal of his death' (LGJC, Eng. Tr., vol. I, 269). On their way down from the mountain he enjoins his three favourite disciples to silence concerning what they have witnessed. In answer to their puzzled questioning about the teaching of Scripture, he tells them that Elias has already come in the person of the Baptist.

620a Our Lord next cures the epileptic boy. His teaching to the disciples now has for its constantly recurring theme the coming Passion, and he tells them that he who would be great among them must be the servant of all. They must learn also not to reject the co-operation of others who do a good work in the name of Jesus. He urges them to deeds of neighbourly charity and to the practice of self-discipline, so that the danger of scandal-giving be avoided. The method of fraternal correction is made clear, with the invoking of the authority of the Church (Mt 18:15–18) and the need for a forgiving spirit emphasized and illustrated by a parable (Mt 18:23 ff.). Arrived at Capharnaum, the Lord pays the Temple dues (Mt 17:23 ff.) at the same time imparting a lesson to Simon Peter. The Galilean ministry has come to an end, a tragic failure. Jesus laments the fate of the cities of the lakeside, Capharnaum, Corozain, Bethsaida, where he has preached in vain, and 'steadfastly set his face to go to Jerusalem' (Lk 9:51). We find him there for the feast of Tabernacles (Jn 7:10 ff.). His teaching in the Temple precincts is the occasion of a plot to arrest him. Presently he cures the man blind from birth by sending him to wash in the pool of Siloe, a miracle in keeping with his character as 'the light of the world' (Jn 9:5). Now also he reveals himself as the good shepherd who lays down his life for the sheep (Jn 10:14–15).

b Much of the material to be found in Lk 9:51–18:14 can perhaps be placed after St John's account of the visit to Jerusalem for the feast of Tabernacles. Here we find our Lord dealing with aspirants to discipleship, the mission of the 'seventy-two, the most striking declaration, Johannine in its sublimity, of the intimate relationship between himself and the Father (Mt 11:25 ff.; Lk 10:21 ff.)—which such critics as Harnack and Wellhausen, flying in the face of the manuscript evidence, arbitrarily reject as a very early interpolation! In close succession are recorded the greatest of the parables, that of the good Samaritan (Lk 10:30 ff.), the charming encounter with the sisters Martha and Mary—which the Church Fathers have allegorized as the type of the 'two lives', that of action and that of contemplation—and Jesus teaching the disciples how to pray. Two further cures are followed by the odious charge of the Pharisees, so effectively refuted, that Jesus performs his good works with the aid of black magic. This gross slander, to be urged from the Jewish side for centuries (*Klausner, *Jesus of Nazareth*, pp 18–54) testifies to the ever increasing hostility of the Pharisees. In their culpable blindness they are sinning against the light.

Abandoning the attempt to win over the Pharisaic party, our Lord gives instruction to his disciples on their preaching of the Gospel; he emphasizes the supreme value of the human soul and the need for being ever on the watch. His gaze is fixed more and more upon the future, on the Passion, the baptism wherewith he is to be baptized, and the urgency of the Gospel dominates his thought. The curing of the deformed woman on the Sabbath (Lk 13:10–17) serves only to deepen the gulf between Jesus and official Judaism. We find him again at Jerusalem for the winter feast of the Dedication (Jn 10:22 ff.); this was the last great feast prior to the fateful Passover the following spring. He speaks of himself openly as the Son of God, uniquely one with the Father, to meet only with hostility and rejection (Jn 10:30 ff.). Thereafter he withdraws into Peraea, east of the Jordan. In his teaching he now speaks of the condemnation which awaits those who have refused to accept him and of their place being taken by many from 'the east and the west and the north and the south' (Lk 13:29). Undeterred by a warning from Herod, Jesus proceeds on his healing mission until the appointed hour at Jerusalem. He still dines with certain of the Pharisees, still insists without compromise on the claims of the Kingdom, while bidding men think what they do before counting themselves his disciples. Yet his message is softened by a wonderful revelation of divine mercy, illustrated by the parables of the Lost Sheep and the Prodigal Son (Lk 15).

It may be that our Lord's teaching concerning riches and the right treatment of the poor, as well as the reminder that even the most faithful of his disciples must acknowledge that they have nothing in which to glory, was delivered shortly before the final approach to Jerusalem (Lk 17:11). On his way he heals the ten lepers, he teaches the people that the Kingdom of God has already come, warns them of the advent of the Son of Man in judgement, urges them to persevere in prayer. The story of the Pharisee and the Publican, the teaching on marriage and divorce, Jesus's touching welcome to the little children, his admonition against the love of riches, the illustration of the entire gratuitousness of the divine gift by the parable of the labourers in the vineyard, are what precede the raising of Lazarus at Bethany (Jn 11). This miracle is the occasion for Caiphas, with the leaders of the Sanhedrin, to resolve to do away with him. Political expediency demands his removal; Jesus is now an outlaw of his own nation, virtually under sentence of death.

For the third time our Lord forewarns his disciples of what lies in store for him, while encouraging them with the prediction of his resurrection (Mk 10:32 ff.; Mt 20:17 ff.; Lk 18:31 ff.); but they, fearful and perplexed, fail to grasp his meaning. He lingers awhile on the northern outskirts of Jerusalem, preaching and teaching, before going up to Jerusalem to celebrate the momentous Pasch. He has still to rebuke James and John for their worldly ambition and remind his followers that precedence in the Kingdom goes, not with earthly prestige, but in the measure of willingness to serve. Let them weigh the implications of the fact that 'the Son of Man . . . is not come to be ministered unto, but to minister and to give his life a redemption for many' (Mk 10:45). Near Jericho he cures the blind Bartimeus in dramatic circumstances. In the town itself we have the vivid, attractive, half humorous scene of the Lord's visit to the house of the tax-gatherer, Zachaeus. Here, in an atmosphere heavy with expectation of the imminent coming of the Kingdom—did not Jesus's advance upon Jerusalem suggest some political *coup d'état*?—he tells his audience of tax-gatherers the parable of the pounds and talents ; his outward triumph is not yet, but let his enemies beware of what is involved in their rejection of him. There remains only the anointing at Bethany, where the Master's defence of Mary's seeming extravagance brings to a head the resolve of Judas to betray him, before the Messianic entry into Jerusalem on Palm Sunday. As he draws near he weeps over the city, now about to precipitate its doom.

It is at this point, appropriately enough, that our Lord's words assume an unsurpassed grandeur and poignancy (*cf.* Jn 12:20-36) ; even the Gentiles within the Temple precincts are seeking him out. The events of Holy Week include the cursing of the barren fig tree (an acted parable symbolizing the Lord's anger with Israel, whose religion flourishes outwardly but bears no genuine fruit) and the claim before the agents of the Sanhedrin to derive his authority from the same source as John the Baptist. His teaching has for its chief theme the Jews' rejection of their Messias ; it embraces the parables of the two sons (Mt 21:28 ff.), the wicked husbandman (partly an allegory and most striking evidence of Jesus' claim to a unique divine sonship), the eschatological parable of the wise and foolish virgins (Mt 25:1-13), as well as the two discourses on the destruction of the Temple and the coming of the Son of Man in judgement. He defends the resurrection of the dead against the Sadducees, and counters, with vigour and great dialectical skill, the polemic of the Sanhedrin representatives and the Pharisees, to the confusion of his enemies and enthusiastic admiration of his friends. He is not to be caught in the dilemma between the apparently rival claims of God and Caesar ; rather he challenges his questioners in their turn to give him an explanation of David's Messianic Psalm (Ps 109 ; Mk 12:35 ff.). Nor does his argumentative mastery fail to make its impression : with at least one member of his learned audience he is able to lift the controversy to the highest level of religion (Mk 12:28 ff.). Undaunted to the last, he denounces in their own citadel of Jerusalem the hypocrisy of the scribes and Pharisees, commenting pointedly on the value of the widow's mite cast into the Temple treasury (Mk 12:41 ff.).

The climax is at hand. On the Wednesday of Holy Week Judas Iscariot agrees with the high-priest's faction to betray his Master for money. The evening of Maundy Thursday the Lord celebrates the Paschal Supper and institutes the Eucharist (Mk 14:22-24 ; Mt 26:26-28 ; Lk 22:19-20) ; on the same occasion he washes the disciples' feet, urges upon them the need for humility, and delivers the ever memorable discourses recorded in Jn 13:31-14:31 (see also Jn 15-17). No paraphrase or summary can convey the sublime level at which the greatest of all tragedies is now moving. From the moment of the assembly in the Upper Room, through Gethsemane, until the last word on the Cross is spoken, our eyes are fixed, in awe and wonder, on the 'Hero of Calvary'. Every sentence in the gospel-narrative should be pondered, as throwing light upon the most significant twenty hours in world history. They close, according to St John, with the pregnant words of Jesus : ' It is consummated ' ; to which is added ' And bowing down his head, he gave up the ghost ' (19:30).

On the events of Easter day we have not the space to linger. As Lagrange observes (*op. cit.*, vol. 2, 283) : ' The four evangelists relate, each in his own way, how the tomb of Jesus was found empty, to the great astonishment of Christ's friends. . . . The difficulty of harmonizing the four accounts has been greatly exaggerated. Nothing is more simple provided we do not stick at unimportant details, provided also we pay attention to the way in which each gospel is composed.' The risen Lord appears to Mary Magdalen, to the two disciples on the road to Emmaus, to Peter and then to the rest of the apostles (1 Cor 15:5). He appeared to them in Jerusalem eight days later, when the ' doubting ' Thomas was present ; in Galilee

also, on the shores of the Lake, where Peter, atoning **620h** for his thrice-spoken denial, makes his threefold profession of love ; and on the mountain-side (Mt 28:16 ff.) to give them the great commission to teach all nations, promising his abiding presence. There were other appearances, as we learn from St Luke (Ac 1:3), before the final moment near Jerusalem when, having foretold the Pentecostal outpouring of the Spirit, giving the apostles his blessing, ' he departed from them and was carried up to heaven ' (Lk 24:51).

III Jesus : the Messias and Son of God—' What **621a** think you of Christ ? Whose son is he ? ' (Mt 22:42). This most momentous of questions was posed by Jesus himself to the Pharisees. They evaded an answer to it and their example, at least in its refusal to consider the evidence without prejudice, has subsequently been followed by many students of his life. It has been said that ' Neither the question " What is the historical value of the Gospels ? " nor its corollary " What was the historical character of Jesus ? " ' (as we understand the problems) were raised in the Middle Ages or in the time of the Reformation ' (Klausner, *op. cit.*, 75). Both questions were discussed by the English Deists, notably Thomas Woolston (1669-1731), and solved according to the principles of that philosophy. The gospel miracles were explained away and Jesus looked upon as a great prophet, whose task it was to illuminate more profoundly the ' natural religion ' existing in all men and among all nations. This line of thought was followed up by Voltaire and a group of eighteenth-century French rationalists ; they not only rejected the miracles but looked with disfavour upon the high ethical code of the NT : these ' barefaced inventions ' of ' artful priests ' (hence ' priestcraft ' and the corresponding French term ' prêtres rusés ') were devised with a view to the domination and exploitation of the masses. Jean Jacques Rousseau, while allowing Jesus to be a ' divine man ' and strongly opposing the contemporary theory that he owes his existence to the fertile imagination of the evangelists, is content to rank him as a ' sage hébreu ', along with Socrates, a ' sage grec '.

In contrast with these views, Reimarus (1694-1768), **b** in a work published posthumously by Lessing (1778), tried to explain Jesus, not as a Son of God or as a prophet or lawgiver, but simply as a Jewish Messias. Strauss (1808-74) finds the most satisfactory explanation for the gospel miracles, not in the fact that they actually occurred, but in the ' legend-creating faith ' of the first Christians. He was supported in this theory by Ferdinand Christian Baur, the founder of the Tübingen School. Bruno Bauer (1809-82) gained a reputation as an authority by first propounding the provisional hypothesis that Jesus *might* have existed, thence working gradually to the conclusion that he was no more than the product of Mk's able imagination ! In 1863 appeared Renan's *La Vie de Jésus*, which ran to twenty-three editions in the author's lifetime. Klausner justly describes it as ' rather a historical novel than a work of scholarship ' ; its Hero is depicted as a philosopher-poet, a liberal with all the characteristics of a French rationalist of the eighteen-sixties. This set the fashion for a number of ' Lives ' written from a liberal angle, presenting a *modernist* Jesus adapted to the prejudices and sensibilities of the modern man.

As a contrast to this ' modernism ' comes the work of **c** Johannes Weiss, and still more pronouncedly in the same direction, of Albert Schweitzer. They stress the importance of eschatology in Jesus's Messianic consciousness. For Schweitzer this is the root-principle of explanation : our Lord's teaching is fundamentally an ' interim-ethic ', a moral code applicable only to the short intervening period between this ' present world ' and the world to come—the ' Days of the Messiah ', when family, state and property cease to have any value. Jesus himself was bound up almost entirely with the beliefs of his own people, time and

621c country. In 1905 Julius Wellhausen propounded the view that ' Jesus was not a Christian : he was a Jew. He did not proclaim a new faith, but taught men to do the will of God. According to Jesus, as to the Jews generally, this will of God is to be found in the Law and the other canonical scriptures '. A few years earlier Harnack, in his *What is Christianity?* (E.T.), had argued a contrary thesis, that Jesus rose so far above contemporary Judaism as to be all but untouched by it. Again we are confronted with a modernist and a philosopher who emphasized, on little more than a humanitarian level, the paramount importance of the Fatherhood of God. This is the Jesus, as Klausner remarks, of the liberal and anti-Jewish Germany of the early twentieth century. *Cf.* §§ 604-9.

d But these aberrations need not detain us. Whatever the partial truth embodied in them, they do violence to the sources and leave much of our data unexplained. In general they are based upon an antecedent denial of the supernatural and an idealistic philosophy which, notwithstanding the learning and personal integrity of those who hold them, preclude an objective consideration of the evidence. ' To this flow and return of opinion Catholic historians of Christian origins no longer pay much heed. For the last fifty years Catholic science, thanks to its own labours and those of non-Catholic scholars, has made very great progress. Matured, on the other hand, through the Modernist crisis, it has become aware of the critical soundness of its positions ' (Lemonnyer, *The Theology of the NT*, Eng. Tr., 17).

e Whom then do the NT records reveal Jesus to be? That he both thought of and finally proclaimed himself to be the long-awaited Messias no serious student can doubt. Of the denial of this (based on such texts as Mk 8:30 ; Mt 16:20), that our Lord never regarded himself as the Messias and only after his death was acclaimed as such by his disciples, Klausner truly observes : ' . . . had this been true, it would never have occurred to his disciples (simple-minded Jews) that one who had suffered crucifixion (" a curse of God is he that is hanged ") could be the Messiah ; and the Messianic idea meant nothing whatever to the Gentile converts. *Ex nihilo nihil fit* : when we see that Jesus's Messianic claims became a fundamental principle of Christianity soon after his crucifixion, this is a standing proof that even in his lifetime Jesus regarded himself as the Messiah ' (*op. cit.*, 255-6).

f According to the Johannine account Jesus is recognized as the **Messias**, ' him of whom Moses . . . and the prophets did write ' (Jn 1:45 ff.), from the early days of his ministry. He does not, however, appear to have wished to divulge his Messianic character to the people at large ; he never unequivocally ascribes to himself, in the hearing of the Jewish crowds, one of the common names of the Messias. He knew that such a disclosure would give rise to the popular demand that he should fulfil the role generally assigned to his office ; as in fact happened when a group of enthusiastic zealots, seeking the realization of their political and materialistic aims, would have acclaimed him King of Israel (Jn 6:15). After one of his exorcisms we find it recorded : ' And rebuking them he suffered them not to speak ; for they knew that he was Christ ' (Lk 4:41). His self-effacement was such that he would conceal his own identity rather than allow a premature revelation of it to prejudice his mission of convincing men of the paramount claims of his heavenly Father and the dire need of their own souls.

g But the simple folk could not refrain from ascribing to him the most popular of all the Messianic titles : ' Is not this **the son of David** ? ' (Mt 12:23). So in effect the act of recognition had come from the woman of Samaria (Jn 4:29), from the Canaanite woman (Mt 15:22), above all in Peter's great confession (Mt 16:16). Jesus responds by a miracle to the prayer of the blind men at Jericho, with its salutation to the ' Son of David ' (Mt 20:30). The acclamations which burst forth at the triumphal entry into Jerusalem were expressly Messianic. To the protesting Pharisees Jesus replies : ' I say to you that if these shall hold their peace, the stones will cry out ' (Lk 19:40). That he knows himself to be the Messianic Son of David emerges from the difficulty he propounds to the Pharisees over the meaning of Ps 109, as does also a disclosure on the mystery of his personality as yet hardly suspected even by his own disciples (Mt 22:42 ff. and parallels). Finally, at his trial, our Lord answered an explicit question from the high-priest with a no less explicit answer : ' Art thou the Christ, the Son of the Blessed God? And Jesus said to him : I am ' (Mk 14:61). This was the ' blasphemy ' for which ' they all condemned him to be guilty of death ' (v 64).

It must be acknowledged, however, that the title by which our Lord most frequently described himself was **The Son of Man.** This designation appears sixty-nine times in the synoptic gospels alone and is employed probably on forty distinct occasions (*Driver, HDB 4, 579). A whole literature has arisen on the meaning of the title ; here the briefest note must suffice (*cf.* Lemonnyer, *op. cit.*, 65 ff. ; Allo, *Le Scandale de Jésus*, 52-6). In Hebrew *son of man* means *man* (*cf.* Ps 8:5) ; but in Aramaic, the language spoken by our Lord, the phrase is often no more than the idiomatic equivalent for *I, myself* (*cf.* Mt 5:11 and Lk 6:22 ; Mt 8:20 and Lk 9:58 ; Mt 11:19 and Lk 7:34, etc. ; in Jn 6:26 ff. Jesus uses both ' I ' and ' Son of Man ' in turn). Notwithstanding this, as Lagrange observes, the familiar expression assumes on the lips of Jesus a suggestion of mysteriousness. ' Whom do men say the Son of man is ? ' (Mt 16:13). In the comparison between the Son of Man and John the Baptist— Mt 11:18-19 ; Lk 7:33-34—we get an impression of a reserved meaning which cannot be exactly expressed. The formula even hints at something of superhuman grandeur when we hear of ' blasphemy ' against the Son of Man (Mt 12:31 and parallels). In such passages as Lk 5:24 ; 6:5 ; 11:30 ; 19:10 and Mt 13:37 the meaning seems to pass from an emphatic ' I ' to that of a personal appellation ; while designating Jesus, it simultaneously manifests the powers with which he considers himself invested and the mission which he claims as his. In other words ' the Son of Man ' has become a Messianic title. The equivalence of ' Son of Man ' and ' Messias ' is taken for granted in Mk 14:61 ff. (*cf.* Mt 26:63 ff. ; Lk 22:66 ff.). The phrase is used with a clear reference to Dan 7 when the Son of Man appears in the character of judge (Mt 13:36 ff. ; Lk 17:24 ; Mk 13:26) ; but if we consider the great Messianic declaration cited above (Mk 14:61), in relation to its parallels (Mt 26:64), and especially Lk 22:69, we discover a Messianic title connected with Dan 7 which is not necessarily eschatological : what is referred to is a permanent state of Christ without reference to the Parousia. Finally, in contrast with the glorious vision of Daniel, Jesus relates himself as ' Son of Man ' to the Suffering Servant in the prophecies of Isaias (Is 42 : 1-14 ; 49:1-6 ; 50:4-9 ; 52:13-53:12). This connexion is clear on the three distinct occasions on which our Lord announces his future Passion : after the confession of Peter (Mk 8:31 ff. ; Mt 16:21 ff. ; Lk 9:22 ff.), following upon the Transfiguration (Mt 17:22 ; *cf.* Mk 9:31 ; Lk 9:44), and lastly near Jericho when he is going up to Jerusalem (Lk 18:31 ff. ; Mt 20:18 ff. ; Mk 10:33 ff.). The following texts should also be consulted : Lk 17:24 ; Mk 9:11 ; Mt 12:39 ff. ; 16:4 ff. ; Lk 11:29 ff. The linking of the destiny of the Messias with the Suffering Servant of Isaias, as foretold by the prophets (*cf.* Lk 24:46), is by implication to show that the Messianic ' Son of Man ' has another office besides that presaged by the exalted figure of Dan 7.

A further and scarcely less significant title ascribed to Jesus in the gospels is that of **Lord.** This is found frequently in Mt and Lk, but also in Mk (7:28 ; 11:3 ; and implicitly in 12:35 ff.). Nor does the evidence support the theory of W. Bousset that this appellation, directly signifying divinity, was only conferred upon Jesus after the Resurrection—and then by the earliest Hellenistic communities, who had been familiarized with it through the worship of the emperors and the phraseology of the mysteries. Often it may well be no more than a courtesy title : as perhaps in its use by the Canaanite woman, Mk 7:28. But of its meaning on the lips of Jesus himself in such a passage as Mk 11:3 there can be no doubt. ' Say ye that the Lord hath need of him '—*viz.* the colt. The context is Messianic and the title must be so too—the Lord (Maran, Kyrios) is, in the usual Court language of Syro-Greek royalties, the reigning monarch. Here it signifies the Messianic King, as his disciples must have been very clearly aware.

We have yet to consider the meaning of the term **Son of God,** which is applied to Jesus with comparative frequency in the synoptics. It should be noted that neither in the OT nor in the later Jewish literature does the formula appear as a distinctively Messianic title. Even the sonship referred to in Ps 2:7 is not unique ; for Israel and Cyrus are addressed elsewhere in much the same language. What is its NT significance ? The Petrine confession—' Thou art Christ, the Son of the Living God ' (Mt 16:16)—surely implies an acknowledgement of divinity as well as of Messiahship. Jesus is the son of God in a natural, and not (like every good Jew) merely in a moral, sense. The same interpretation is supported by the theophanies at the Lord's Baptism (Mk 1:11 ; Mt 3:17 ; Lk 3:22) and Transfiguration (Mk 9:7 ; Mt 17:5 ; Lk 9:35), by Mk 13:32, ' But of that day or hour no man knoweth, neither the angels in heaven, nor the Son, but the Father ', and by the affirmative reply to the High-priest's question (Mk 14:61 ; Mt 26:63 ; Lk 22:70). In Mt 11:25-27, which might be mistaken for a passage in St John (*cf.* Jn 10:15—and, though the context is different, Lk 10:21), the Father and the Son are placed upon the same plane and are, as it were, strictly proportioned to one another. With reference to the not immediately significant Mt 18:20— ' For where there are two or three gathered together in my name, there am I in the midst of them '— Lagrange recalls an utterance of the Rabbi Chananiah: ' Where two are seated together, intent upon the Torah, glory (Yahweh) is in the midst of them '. There is thus suggested a parallel between the presence of Jesus and the presence of Yahweh. Before leaving the synoptics we may note the centurion's confession of faith after the death of Jesus : ' Indeed this man was the Son of God ' (Mk 15:39). See the interesting comment on this text in *Hoskyns, *The Riddle of the NT*, 91).

Supplementing the already abundant evidence of the synoptics, St John leads us with ever deeper insight into the mystery of the personality of Jesus. Leaving aside for the moment the theological introduction (Jn 1:1-14), we find in the Johannine narrative two attributes of Christ standing out in marked relief : *Light* and *Life*, especially the latter. Mt (4:16, citing Is 9:1) tells us that ' the people that sat in darkness hath seen great light ' ; for Lk (2:32) Jesus himself is ' the light which shall give revelation to the Gentiles ' (KNT). But the exposition of this sublime theme was left to St John. ' I am the light of the world. He that followeth me walketh not in darkness, but shall have the light of life ' (Jn 8:12). ' As long as I am in the world, I am the light of the world ' (9:5). Jesus is the light because he is the Truth, illuminating the minds of those who accept him (*cf.* 14:6 ; 18:37). ' I am come, a light into the world, that whosoever believeth in me may not remain in darkness ' (12:46).

' Life eternal ', which, in the synoptics, is synonymous with the Kingdom of Heaven, *i.e.* of God (Mk 9:44 ; Mt 19:16 ; Lk 10:25, etc.) becomes in the fourth gospel one of the chief attributes of Christ. ' And as Moses lifted up the [brazen] serpent in the desert, so must the Son of Man be lifted up [on the Cross] : that whosoever believeth in him may not perish, but

may have life everlasting. For God so loved the world, 622d as to give his only begotten Son : that whosoever believeth in him may not perish, but may have life everlasting ' (Jn 3:14-16). Nor are we justified in restricting the concept of Christ as the ' Life ' within the limits of Messianism ; the texts taken cumulatively demand the recognition of Jesus as endowed with the very life of the Godhead. The life which the Father has in himself the Son likewise has in himself (Jn 5:21). The eucharistic discourse, Jn 6:35 ff., carries us far beyond purely Messianic conceptions. Jesus here speaks of himself according to his human nature, richly endowed with the Father's gifts, but at the same time in the character of ' Son '. ' As the living Father hath sent me and I live by the Father : so he that eateth me, the same also shall live by me ' (v 58). In this context the *I* and the *me* can refer only to the person of the Son, conscious of an equality in nature with the Father. This unique relation of sonship, clearly indicated in isolated texts in the synoptics (*cf.* Mt 11:25 ff. ; Lk 10:21), is one of the chief themes of the fourth gospel. St John testifies to it, both as recorder of Jesus's own words and as their interpreter.

In the colloquy with Nicodemus, Jn 3:11 ff., we find, e in veiled and designedly thought-provoking language, the full doctrine of the Incarnation—affirmed not, as we might have expected, of the Son of God, but of the Son of Man. It is he personally who ' descended from heaven ' ; and we are told of the continuing presence in heaven—' in the bosom of the Father ' (Jn 1:18)—of the Son of God who, as Son of Man, is living on earth. He dramatically illustrates his claim to equality with the Father in his Sabbath-day cure of the infirm man at the pool of Bethesda ; nor did his enemies fail to draw the correct inference. ' My Father worketh until now ; and I work. Hereupon therefore the Jews sought the more to kill him, because he did not only break the Sabbath but also said God was his Father, making himself equal to God ' (Jn 5:17-18). In the verses which follow our Lord implicitly accepts the charge ; while derogating nothing from the profound submission which he in his human nature owes to God, he at the same time acknowledges the unique relation to the Father in which the Son is placed by the Incarnation. Considerations of space preclude further citation ; the following texts should be consulted as illustrating the same doctrine : Jn 6:44 ff. ; 8:42 ; 10:24-38 ; 14:8 ff. ; 16:15 ; 17:21—for all of which, see Comm. *in loco.*

With the NT doctrine of the Trinity we are not here f directly concerned, but it is impossible to discuss the Person of Christ without allusion to the **Holy Spirit.** We recall that in the early Church the Holy Spirit, plainly disclosed as a divine Person (*cf.* 1 Cor 6:19 ; Rom 8:9), takes literally the place of Jesus (*cf.* Ac 4:31 ; 5:32 ; 8:29 ; 9:31 ; 10:19 ; 16:6, etc.). That our Lord intended the Spirit to have this role, to act as his interpreter and the fulfiller of his mission, is clear from the striking passages in St John (Jn 15:26 ; 16:7 ff. ; *cf.* Lk 24:49) referring to the Paraclete. As the Father has ' sent ' the Son for the world's salvation (Jn 3:17 ; 4:34 ; 5:23, etc.), so likewise, and for the same purpose, the Father and the Son ' send ' or ' give ' the Holy Spirit to Jesus's disciples (Jn 14:16, 26 ; 15:26 ; 16:7).

The NT synthesis of the revealed teaching on the g Personality of Jesus is to be found in the Prologue to St John's gospel (1:1 ff. ; see Comm. *in loco*). The Johannine doctrine of the *Word*—which is ' the Word of God ' (Apoc 19:13)—has a close connexion in the writer's mind with one of the central themes of the gospel : the identification of Christ with ' life eternal '. This is evident from what is said in 1 Jn 1:1 ff. : ' That which was from the beginning, which we have heard, which we have seen with our eyes, which we have looked upon and our hands have handled, of the word of life '. The Prologue starts from the pre-existence of the Word with God, passing thence to speak of the part played by the Word in the creation of the world,

622g to rest finally on the thought that the Word has become incarnate in Jesus Christ. The familiar *light* and *life* motif is enunciated : ' the life was the light of men ' (v 4). Christ is introduced, closely linked with the historical witness of the Baptist (vv 6–8), implicitly as the Word (v 14), explicitly as the Light ' which enlighteneth every man that cometh into this world ' (v 9). The ' grace and truth ' (v 14) which come from the Word's being made flesh (' That is to say, the Word of God ceased to be expressed in a literature or in a prophecy, and became embodied in human flesh, and there the OT was fulfilled ', Hoskyns, *op. cit.*, 218) signify humanity's participation in Light and Life. The ' finality ' of Christ, the fact that he is the unique revealer of the secrets of the Godhead, is the real conclusion of the Prologue ; it is the central truth of the Gospel : ' No man hath seen God at any time : the only begotten Son who is in the bosom of the Father, he hath declared him ' (v 18). This was the tremendous import of the ' Messianic secret ' which Jesus, with the incomparable pedagogical skill of the Master, gradually made known to his disciples, until it bore fruit in the post-resurrection faith of the reluctant Thomas : ' My Lord and my God ' (Jn 20:28). From that day to this these words have summarized the authentic confession of Catholic Christianity in the Person of Jesus Christ.

623a **IV The Teaching**—The teaching of Jesus is embodied in his own Person ; there exists an organic continuity between himself and the doctrine he propounded. Christ is the ' vine ', his disciples are the ' branches ', drawing all their vitality from union with him (Jn 15:1 ff.). The whole of the ' fourth ' gospel is an illustration of this thesis. He who is the Truth and the Life is also ' the Way ' (Jn 14:6). (We know that, from the first, practical discipleship meant precisely following ' the way ' : *cf.* Ac 16:17 ; 18:26 ; 19:23 ; Heb 10:20, etc.) To attempt to formulate a Christian philosophy or ethical system which should be valid independently of faith in Christ himself is an idle and presumptuous task. This is why the Church has ever been at pains to base her morality upon dogma, the practical Christian life upon a personal belief in, and surrender to, our Lord himself. The content of his teaching, despite implications of inexhaustible richness and subtlety, is in its broad outlines supremely simple. It is hardly patient of schematization, though its main drift is inescapably clear. With a one-pointedness which has embarrassed those who have looked in the NT for what it refuses to give—a metaphysic, a philosophy of culture, a programme of social reform —Jesus's utterances bear without exception upon his mission as Israel's Messias and the Saviour of the world. In other words his message was wholly and exclusively religious, even while he gave to religion a boundless range and depth and raised it to a position of supremacy over every department of men's lives.

b ' Salvation is of the Jews ' (Jn 4:22). It is against the background of the OT that our Lord's life-work must be seen. What is there foretold of the Kingdom, or *Rule*, of God—See § 625a–f *infra*—and of the office of the Messias, was consciously realized by Jesus, though in a manner so elevated and transformed as to escape the grasp of those who refused to accept him as their teacher. Thus the fault of those who rejected him lay, not in their failure to anticipate that this was the kind of Messias pointed to by the prophetic writings, but in their unwillingness to receive him as the interpreter of the prophets. ' This is my beloved Son in whom I am well pleased. Hear ye him ' (Mt 17:5). But this they would not do. Our Lord's awareness of his being the unique Master is evident from Mt 23:8–10 ; ' for one is your master, Christ '. His teaching, owing to the imperfect comprehension of the disciples, would need to be amplified and elucidated by the Holy Spirit whom he would send (Jn 16:12–13) ; in default of Christ's grace they could not hope to apprehend it (2 Cor 3:14) ; it would

remain no more than words unless God himself opened the ears of their understanding (Ac 16:14). While the initiative lay ever with the Lord to draw whom he would to the Father (Jn 6:44 ; *cf.* Mk 3:14), the chosen ones yet remained free to accept or reject the call (Jn 6:68–69).

The indispensable prerequisite of discipleship was **c** living **faith**—an acknowledgement that the supreme revelation of God was to be found in Jesus, together with trusting self-abandonment to him. Not without this condition of soul could a fruitful response be made to the Sermon on the Mount (Mt 5–7 ; Lk 6:20–7:1 ; 11:33–36 ; 14:34–35), the ground-plan of the Christian life. The Beatitudes (Mt 5:3–11), offering a pledge of future and even present happiness, could be realized only as the goal of detachment from the world and adherence to God's law. They portray Christian morality at once in its most uncompromising and most attractive form : not as an arbitrary code of prescriptions and prohibitions, but as an invitation to goodness founded upon the vision of man's final destiny. The great paradox of the Gospel emerges : if we would save our lives, we must first of all lose them (Mt 10:37–39)—that is, abandon them to the cause, in the loving service of God and man. If the grain of wheat is to fructify it must fall to the earth and die (Jn 12:24–25).

The moral integrity implied in the Sermon on the **d** Mount and the faith which it presupposes form the basis of our Lord's later teaching on the meaning of the Kingdom of God. This comprises substantially, whether as illustrated by the parables or as more directly affirmed in the Last Supper discourses, obedience to the first two commandments of the Law. ' Hear O Israel : the Lord thy God is one God. And thou shalt love the Lord thy God with thy whole heart and with thy whole soul and with thy whole mind and with thy whole strength. . . . Thou shalt love thy neighbour as thyself ' (Mk 12:29–31). Thus we find Jesus in continuity with the loftiest teaching of the OT (*cf.* Deut 6:4–5 ; Lev 19:18) ; he is the fulfiller, not the destroyer of the Law. **Love** is truly the sum and substance of the Gospel, but it is a love no more to be identified with the *philanthropia* of the ancients than with modern secular humanitarianism. Unlike these fundamentally irreligious counterfeits, Christian love is impregnated with religion, its vivifying principle lies in whole-hearted devotion to the all-holy will of God. Our good works must be performed, not for their own sake, still less for the pleasure which comes from beneficent action, but so as to be pleasing in the sight of our heavenly Father, who ' seeth in secret ' (Mt 6:1, 3, 18). This was indeed the whole motive-force of the life of Jesus himself : ' I am not alone, because the Father is with me ' (Jn 16:32) ; ' I do always the things that please him ' (8:29) ; ' My meat is to do the will of him that sent me ' (4:34).

The God of Jesus Christ is the God of Abraham, **e** Isaac and Jacob. As a successor to, though himself infinitely greater than, the prophets (Mt 12:41 f.), he accepts the divinely given Mosaic Law, while spiritualizing it and shaping it to his own ends in virtue of the still higher authority with which he knows himself to be vested. The OT legislated for the exterior actions of men ; Jesus is concerned with the inner motives and desires (Mt 5:27 ff.). It is not only adultery but lust, not only murder but hatred, it is the well-springs of evil and not merely their outward consequences which are proscribed. These new ordinances reach a deeper level than the old ; they are more exacting and yet easier to bear, because they are imposed not as an outward constraint but as evoking an intimate conversion of the heart ; the response they demand is that of children and sons rather than of servants (Jn 15:15), the rule of fear has given place to the reign of love (1 Jn 4:18). In the soul wholly dedicated to God virtue comes to birth all but spontaneously ; the divine life flourishes as it were by second nature. ' Come to me, all you that labour and are burdened : and I will refresh you. Take up my yoke upon you and learn of me, because I am meek and humble of heart : and you shall find rest for your souls. For my yoke is sweet and my burden light ' (Mt 11:28–30).

Nothing illustrates this most encouraging truth more clearly than our Lord's attitude towards **sin.** See, for example, the touching incident related in Lk 7:36–50, with its ' golden saying ' : ' Many sins are forgiven her, because she hath loved much ' (v 47). He was the Lamb of God who had come to take away the intolerable weight of human sinfulness (Jn 1:29, 36) ; he came as one offering service to others, not demanding it for himself, ' to give his life a redemption for many ' (Mk 10:45). Here, in what is often regarded as the most primitive of the gospel records, we find the doctrine of the Redemption elaborated by St Paul (1 Thess 5:9–10 ; 1 Cor 6:20 ; Rom 5:6–21 ; 8:29–32, etc.). But if Jesus is our redeemer, he is also our judge (Mt 16:27 ; 24:30–31), rewarding the good and punishing the guilty (Mt 25:34 ff.) ; the role which the Jews knew to be the prerogative of God the parables show him claiming for himself (Mt 13:37–42). It is thus noteworthy how the moral teaching of the NT implies its Christology ; we can only appreciate at their due weight our Lord's commandments and promises by reference to the divine authority vested in his person.

The cosmic import of the revelation brought by Jesus is disclosed in the Johannine formula of ' life eternal '. Whatever the possibility of the soul's immortality apart from its union with God, Christ came to give point and meaning to the religious destiny of man. The aspirations for a supra-temporal existence, the longing for a security and purposefulness which the world of its nature cannot give, were fulfilled in him. ' Have confidence. I have overcome the world ' (Jn 16:33). ' This is eternal life : That they may know thee, the only true God, and Jesus Christ, whom thou hast sent ' (17:3). So he had promised from the time he began to preach : ' Blessed are the clean of heart : for they shall see God ' (Mt 5:8). He had come that we might ' have life and have it more abundantly ' (Jn 10:10). But at how great a price ! The good shepherd was to give his life for the sheep (v 11). The Son of Man must be raised on the Cross before he can draw all men to himself (Jn 12:32). It was thus that the world and all it stood for should be brought to judgement, the dominion of sin and death conquered (v 31). To these assurances of Jesus was added the Father's confirmation in the triumph of the Resurrection ; the sacrifice of the Cross had been accepted ; sin being blotted out by Christ's blood, man was redeemed ; in the same act death was vanquished and the prince of this world ' cast out '.

The redeeming mission of Jesus, however, was not yet accomplished. In the glory of the resurrected and ascended Christ we recognize the first fruits of that life eternal which he had promised to his disciples ; but it is needful that the faithful should follow in his footsteps here on earth, likewise carrying their cross, if they would have place with him in the Kingdom. Nor has he left them to make this arduous journey alone. On the night before he died, foreshadowing the sacrificial act of the morrow, he ' took bread and blessed and broke and gave to his disciples and said : Take ye and eat. This is my body. And taking the chalice, he gave thanks and gave to them, saying : Drink ye all of this. For this is my blood of the new testament, which shall be shed for many unto remission of sins ' (Mt 26:26–28). To which he added the charge : ' Do this for a commemoration of me ' (Lk 22:19). Faithfully the apostles obeyed : twenty-five years later we find St Paul recalling to the Corinthians what he had ' received of the Lord ' (1 Cor 11:23), *viz.*, the institution of the **Eucharist.** And he makes clear, in virtue of the grave responsibility of those who receive it, the transcendent holiness of the sacrament : ' whosoever shall eat this bread,

or drink the chalice of the Lord unworthily, shall be guilty of the body and blood of the Lord. . . . For he that eateth and drinketh unworthily eateth and drinketh judgement to himself, not discerning the body of the Lord ' (vv 27, 29).

It is in the sacramental setting of the Last Supper, as enshrining the gift of his body and blood, that the Lord imparts to the disciples his most intimate and fundamental teaching. ' A new commandment I give unto you : That you love one another, as I have loved you, that you also love one another ' (Jn 13:34). This is the essence, the ' religious philosophy ' of the Gospel. The injunction to mutual love is no novelty ; but that we shall love ' *as I have loved you* '. That is unique. True, Jesus had said it before in other contexts, but never so expressly or so movingly. We have to imitate the love of a Saviour who ' came not to call the just but sinners ' (Mk 2:17), a love destitute of all self-righteousness, full of exquisite compassion for the weak and feeble. For us it must be a *fraternal* charity, based upon equality and fellowship, without tincture of patronage or paternalism. ' All things therefore whatsoever you would that men should do to you, do you also to them. For this is the law and the prophets ' (Mt 7:12). Mercifulness is supreme among God's attributes ; in bidding us to aim at the perfection of his heavenly Father (Mt 5:48), our Lord is in fact inviting us to imitate his mercy : ' Be ye therefore merciful, as your Father is merciful ' (Lk 6:36). This is what is implied in the love of Jesus, which we must make our own. St John, with the Last Supper discourse lingering ever in his memory, recalls the life-giving truth : ' And we have known and have believed the charity which God hath to us. God is charity and he that abideth in charity abideth in God, and God in him ' (1 Jn 4:16).

It was likewise at the Last Supper that Jesus spoke, as never before, of his intimate relationship with the Father and of the Father's love for the disciples. ' And the glory which thou hast given me I have given to them : that they may be one, as we also are one. I in them, and thou in me : that they may be made perfect in one : and the world may know that thou hast sent me and hast loved them, as thou hast also loved me ' (Jn 17:22–23). This is the plane upon which the fatherhood of God and the brotherhood of man, in which some would epitomize the Christian message, must be conceived. Here also we find the authentic source for the loving communion between God and the individual soul which has inspired the Catholic mystics and saints throughout the centuries. ' If any one love me, he will keep my word. And my Father will love him : and we will come to him and will make our abode with him ' (Jn 14:23). ' I will love him and manifest myself to him ' (v 21). ' But the Paraclete, the Holy Ghost, whom the Father will send in my name, he will teach you all things and bring all things to your minds, whatsoever I shall have said to you ' (v 26). Thus is signalized the presence of the Blessed Trinity within the human spirit, to give countenance to that quasi-experimental knowledge of God which is the reward of the life of charity. We note how the evangelical mysticism is to be distinguished from its numerous counterfeits, ranging from philosophical neo-Platonism, through aestheticism and the various forms of ' nature mysticism ', down to the eccentricities of the theosophists. Jesus lays down the condition for the aspirant to such a grace ; he must ' keep my word '. ' He that hath my commandments and keepeth them, he it is that loveth me ' (Jn 14:21). For all his tenderness he is terribly in earnest, uncompromising in the demand for sincerity and truth as manifested in practical conduct. He can admit to discipleship the sinful and morally weak, but not the poseur or religious dilettante. ' Not every one that saith to me, Lord, Lord, shall enter into the kingdom of heaven : but he that doth the will of my Father who is in heaven, he shall enter into the kingdom of heaven ' (Mt 7:21).

624d   The religion of Jesus is above all a worship of God
' in spirit and in truth ' (Jn 4:24), but he knew too
well the needs of sense-bound human nature to leave
his disciples without the aid of an external cultus.
The clear evidence in the gospels for the institution
of Baptism (Mk 16:16 ; Mt 28:19 ; Jn 3:5) and the
Eucharist—which the texts show to have been a
sacrifice as well as a sacrament (Mk 14:22–24 ;
Mt 26:26–28 ; Lk 22:19–20 ; 1 Cor 11:23–25)—
indicate that he willed these ordinances to be the
indispensable channels of the Christian life. Moreover
he did not wish his disciples to live in isolation from
one another ; he formed them into a living and
hierarchic society, his Church. At Caesarea Philippi
he had promised to make Simon Peter its rock-
foundation (Mt 16:18–19), and a little later he gave
to all the apostles the power of ' binding and loosing '
(Mt 18:18). The content of this power is explained
in the post-resurrection commission to remit and
retain sins (Jn 20:23), while Peter's primacy is finally
confirmed in his appointment as shepherd of the flock
(Jn 21:15–17).

e   The apostles were not enthusiastic volunteers, self-
chosen for their task of continuing Christ's mission ;
they had been the object of a particular election on the
part of Jesus (Mk 3:13–14), as he reminded them at the
Last Supper (Jn 15:16). This initial choice had been
the starting point of a special formation, the nature
and course of which we can follow from the NT
records. Closely grouped around the Master, they
were the auditors of his discourses and witnesses to the
miracles, repositories of the mystery of the Kingdom
(Mk 4:11). To the crowds he spoke in parables, to
the apostles he revealed all (Mk 4:34), or as much at
least as they were capable of grasping ; for there were
many things beyond their comprehension, which the
coming of the Holy Spirit would reveal to them
(Jn 16:12–13). He prepared them for their subsequent
labours by a preliminary mission in Galilee
(Mt 10:1–42). Peter was their selected leader ; all
the lists of the apostles show his name first (Mk 3:16 ff. ;
Mt 10:2 ff. ; Lk 6:14 ff. ; Ac 1:13) ; upon him, as
we have seen, the Church was to be built, unshakable
and invincible by the powers of evil (Mt 16:18). To
Peter Jesus gave the keys of the Kingdom and the
office of binding and loosing (v 19) ; it was he who
was charged in a special manner to support the other
members of the apostolic college (Lk 22:31–32), to
feed the lambs and the sheep of Christ's flock (Jn
21:15–17).

f   Our Lord himself had sown the seed ; the reaping
of the harvest lay with the apostles. Witnesses to the
life, death and above all, the resurrection of the Son
of God, they were to gather in the fruits of his work,
as well as dispense to others what they had received
from him. Armed with his authority—' He that
heareth you heareth me : and he that despiseth you
despiseth me ' (Lk 10:16)—and with the assurance of
his abiding presence, they were commissioned to preach
the ' good news ' to Israel and to all the world (Mk
16:15, 20 ; Mt 28:19–20).

625a V Some Special Points (*a*)—The brief outline of the
teaching of Jesus given above can be summarized,
from another point of view, as his preaching of the
Kingdom of God (or ' of Heaven '—a reverential
periphrasis ; the terms are synonymous). That the
Messianic age would see the realization of the Kingdom
was clearly the expectation of Israel (*cf.* Lagrange, *Le
Messianisme chez les Juifs*, Paris, 1909). We may accept,
with certain provisos, the judgement of Loisy that
' Jesus brings the message of God ; he does not preach
himself. He brings the good tidings which the Father
sends to men, *viz.* that the time is fulfilled and the
Kingdom at hand ', *Loisy, Les évangiles synoptiques*
(Paris, 1907) 434. In this respect at least the synoptics,
especially Mk, show him in continuity with and as the
fulfilment of the preaching of John the Baptist. ' Do
penance (*i.e. repent*), for the Kingdom of heaven is

at hand ' (Mt 3:2 ; *cf.* Mk 1:15). Throughout his **e**
ministry it is the Kingdom which dominates his
thought. To the disciples, as to the multitudes, he
speaks of little else. ' Jesus went about all Galilee,
teaching in their synagogues and preaching the
gospel of the Kingdom ' (Mt 4:23). ' To other cities
also must I preach the Kingdom of God : for therefore
am I sent ' (Lk 4:43). It is the same message which is
committed to the apostles (Mt 10:7) and disciples
(Lk 10:9–11). ' This gospel of the Kingdom shall be
preached in the whole world ' (Mt 24:14). Finally we
find him appearing to his disciples after the Resurrection ' and speaking of the Kingdom of God ' (Ac 1:3).

What is our Lord's conception of the Kingdom ? **b**
Space will allow only the briefest answer to this very
large question. First it must be said that his teaching
can be appreciated only against the background of the
OT development of the doctrine of the Kingdom ;
cf. *Orr, *Kingdom of God*, HDB 2, 844–4. He takes
from this all its most elevated and spiritual elements,
more particularly as these were set in relief by the
great Hebrew prophets, and gives them a new setting
in relation to his own person. It was his harking back
to the prophetic teaching, so much neglected in the
political and materialistic conceptions of contemporary
Pharisaism, which was responsible for much of the
hostility and misunderstanding experienced by Jesus
at the hands of the religious leaders of his day. Though
it must also be remembered—and this intensified the
conflict with those who would not admit him as
Master—that he was conscious that his own teaching
on the Kingdom contained radically new elements,
of transcendence and universality, incompatible with
the maintenance of the old order ; it was useless to
patch a worn-out garment with new cloth, idle to pour
newly fermenting wine into old wine-skins (Mt 9:16–17).

The scriptural imagery in which the Kingdom is **c**
portrayed is frequently suggestive of the pomp and
circumstance of earthly kingship. Indeed it could
hardly be otherwise, the more so when we consider the
exalted place held by King David in Jewish history
and legend. Nor is this notion repudiated by Jesus ;
but the fundamental conception of it is the rule or
dominion of God, the absolute primacy and control of
the divine will which that implies, God and man being
respectively what they are. The Greek word βασιλεία
may mean both ' kingship ' and ' realm ', and the
synoptics appear to use it now in one sense now in
the other ; but it is important to notice that these
closely related ideas merge in the more fundamental
one just mentioned, *viz.* God's unlimited mastery and
lordship as manifested in nature and providence.

The teaching of Jesus presents the Kingdom of God **d**
under a number of aspects, it contains subtleties and
shades of thought which cannot be reduced to a single
formula. He spoke of the ' mystery ' of the Kingdom
(Mk 4:11 ; Mt 13:11 ; Lk 8:10). It is a *heavenly*
Kingdom that is suggested in the Beatitudes (Mt
5:3–10). ' Rejoice for your reward is very great in
heaven ' (v 12 ; *cf.* Lk 6:20 ff.). The *realm* of God,
something into which one enters and not simply his
' kingship ', is indicated, *e.g.* in Mt 5:20, ' For I tell
you that unless your justice abound more than that
of the scribes and Pharisees, you shall not enter into
the Kingdom of Heaven '. Entry into it is the equivalent of being ' saved ' (Mk 10:23 ff. ; Lk 18:24 ff.).
Moreover the state of soul needful for making entrance
is the product, not of nature, but of grace ; a spiritual
re-birth is demanded (Jn 3:5 ff.). Again the Kingdom
has a supra-mundane and eschatological aspect ; the
just are received into it ' at the end of the world '
(Mt 13:40 ff.). The way into this Kingdom, in which
an eternal banquet is enjoyed (Mt 8:11 ; Lk 13:29),
is through the Resurrection (Mt 22:30 ; Mk 12:25 ;
Lk 20:36), and at the time of the Parousia (Mt 25:1–46) ;
after a solemn judgement (v 31 ff.), Jesus will drink
anew the fruit of the vine with his own (Mk 14:25 ;
Mt 26:29). The risen just will there lead the lives
of angels (Mt 22:30) ; they will shine as the sun

(Mt 13:43) and enjoy perfect felicity (Mt 5:3 ff. ; Lk 6:20 ff.). Thus the *Regnum Dei*, considered as a divine realm, culminates in the transcendent and eschatological reign of God over his elect in heaven, which is the Kingdom as described in the apocalypses and in rabbinical literature.

Nevertheless the Kingdom of God is already, at least in part, realized upon earth. ' The Kingdom of God is come upon you ' (Lk 11:20). That the true believers are already ' in the Kingdom ' is clear from Lk 7:28. No doubt it does not yet exist in its full splendour ; men cannot point to it, ' Behold here, or behold there' (Lk 17:20–21) ; but the same verses show that it is already within Israel. Yet the ' Thy Kingdom come ' of the Lord's Prayer (Mt 6:10 ; Lk 11:2) tells us that its fruition is still to be looked for in the future. What seems to be suggested, and the lessons of the parables bear this out, is that the coming of the Kingdom means the progressive development of the Kingdom already in being. Nor does this view need to be abandoned in the light of the apparent difficulties arising from such a text as Mk 8:38–39 (*cf.* Lemonnyer, *op. cit.*, 42 ; *Dodd, *The Parables of the Kingdom*, 53). We cannot enter into details here concerning the Parousia and the general eschatological teaching of Jesus ; but there are good grounds for supposing that he implied that there would be several parousias or ' comings ' of the Kingdom, and of the Son of Man, ' in power '—the Resurrection was certainly one of these—before the final coming for the Last Judgement. The close inter-connexion between the eschatological discourses and the predictions of the fall of Jerusalem warrant the interpretation that the coming of the Kingdom ' in power' points to a particular development of the already existing Kingdom of God on earth, a development bound up with the disappearance of the Jewish nation.

The kingship of God is concerned chiefly with his rulership over the hearts of men, but, as we have already seen, in Mt 16:18–19 God's Kingdom, or Realm, appears under the form of a ' Church ', that is, a visible and organized society. Compared to a building, the Kingdom-Church has Peter and the apostles as its foundation (*cf.* Eph 2:20–21) ; it is opposed to, and impregnable by, the forces of evil (Mt 16:18). And this close relationship between the Kingdom and Christ's Church emphasizes the still more intimate connexion between it and his own person. Jesus clearly knows himself to be not only the founder of the Kingdom, but the possessor of it ; it is *his* Kingdom as well as the Father's, and he is the Lord and Ruler over it (Mt 13:41 ; 16:28 ; 20:21 ; 25:34, etc.). It is thus closely linked with the OT theocracy, with God's kingship over a chosen people and its exercise through visible representatives. Typically, though imperfectly, shadowed forth in the descendants of David, it is now wholly realized in the Messianic King, by reason of his being completely at one with God (Mt 11:27 ; Jn 4:34 ; 5:30 ; 6:38, etc.). The new theocracy has Christ for its living embodiment ; he is the prototype of the new relationship of sonship with God into which men are invited to enter through him. So that, in the profoundest sense, the Kingdom of God may be said to have existed on earth from the first moment of the Incarnation. The full realization of the Kingdom is in the measure of men's union with Jesus, in faith and love, in obedience and submission to his rule, which is the same thing as doing the Father's will, in the ever deepening reality of their vital contact with him, as of branches with their parent vine (Mt 7:21–23 ; 8:10 ; 11:28–30 ; 16:24–25; Jn 15:1–8, etc.). Whence there follows the ' transvaluation of all values ' involved in the very nature of the Kingdom. Christ's sovereignty was exercised, not by violence and earthly power, but by lowliness, by service and deeds of mercy, above all, by the invincible witness to truth in the face of a hostile world and at the price of bitter suffering (Mt 11:4–6, 29 ; 18:3–4 ; 20:25–28 ; Jn 18:36–37). So likewise is his Kingdom to be ruled ; not by compulsion and tyranny, but by the patient and steadfast testifying to the Gospel, and the all-conquering influence of love over hearts freely submitted to its sway (Mt 22:37–40 ; Jn 14:15 ; 15:15).

625f

(*b*) A very large portion of our Lord's teaching on **g** the Kingdom of God was embodied in **parables.** Indeed he is acknowledged on all hands to be the supreme master of the art of inculcating doctrine by happy illustrations from the events of everyday life. The term *parable* means ' a placing of one thing beside another ' with a view to comparison. In employing this method Jesus not only conformed to the usage of the Jewish rabbis, but showed his appreciation of the truth that concrete examples are more effective instruments of instruction than abstract principles. *Longum est iter per praecepta, breve et efficax per exempla* (Sen. *Ep.* 6). A large proportion of the parables have the Kingdom of God as their theme, though the allusion is clearer in some than in others. The more explicit ones open with the formula, ' The Kingdom of heaven (or ' of God ') is like to . . .' Such are the parables of the good seed and cockle (Mt 13:24 ff.) ; of the grain of mustard seed (vv 31 ff.) ; of the leaven (vv 33 ff.), and a number of others (vv 44 ff. ; Mk 4:26). But the use of parables, which are of a simplicity often more apparent than real, gives rise to two important questions, the answer to which throws much light upon the mission and message of Jesus. How are the parables to be interpreted ? And what was their purpose ?

It is now generally admitted that the allegorical **h** interpretation to which the parables were submitted by the Church Fathers was not seldom arbitrary and unconvincing. It consisted in taking every term in the story as a cryptogram for an idea, and so decoding the whole term by term. (For a typical example from St Augustine, see his *Quaestiones Evangeliorum*, 2, 19 ; paraphrased by Dodd, *op. cit.*, 12.) This method gave scope to much ingenuity, and was even justifiable as a vehicle for the exposition of doctrine valid enough on other grounds, but it gives little help when we are concerned to elucidate the literal meaning of the text. It must, however, be borne in mind that the borderline between a strict parable, a story told to illustrate a single main lesson, and an allegory, containing many significant points, is not always clear-cut. This is evident from those cases in which we have our Lord's own interpretations—see the Sower (Mt 13:4 ff.) and the Tares (Mt 13:25)—where many of their several features are explained. Nevertheless it is probable that the typical parable, whether it be a simple metaphor, or a more elaborate similitude, or a full-length story, presents one single point of comparison ; its details are not intended to have independent significance. Thus, in the parable of the importunate friend (Lk 11:5–8), we are not meant to ask who is represented by the friend arriving from a journey, or by the children in bed ; these and other details serve merely to build up the picture of a sudden critical need calling for an urgency otherwise untimely and out of place. Even in the Sower the incidental features would seem in the first place to be no more than the setting for a single main picture—that of the vast amount of wasted labour which the farmer must face, and so throwing into relief the satisfaction brought by the harvest, in spite of all.

The remarkable realism and vividness of the parables, **i** their faithfulness to nature, the fact that they are not far-fetched and artificial analogies, are due to the affinity which does in truth exist between the natural order and the spiritual order. The Kingdom of God is, in many respects, intrinsically *like* the processes of nature and the daily life of men. We may note also, as illustrative of our Lord's pedagogical method, that the parable has the character of an argument, in that it entices the hearer to a judgement upon the situation depicted, and then challenges him, directly or by implication, to apply the judgement to the matter in

625i hand. A famous example of this is Nathan's story of David (2 Kg 12:1 ff.) about the poor man's ewe lamb which was stolen by the rich man—with its dramatic conclusion ' Thou art the man '. So was it with the parables of Jesus ; always there is an underlying question, explicit or implicit. ' What do you think ? If a man has a hundred sheep. . . .' ' What do you think ? A man had two children. . . .' We are invited to a judgement on the imagined situation and so to grasp, by a process of active assimilation, the lesson intended ; see Dodd, *op. cit.*, 22–4. Whence we are led to the further question : what was our Lord's motive in teaching by parables ?

626a The foregoing remarks have already suggested a partial answer. Jesus, a master of pedagogy, wished to persuade his hearers by evoking an assent based on their own reflexions. But we must note that, while he preached to the multitude in parables, he reserved their explanation to his disciples (Mk 4:33–34 ; Mt 13:34 ff.). Why did he indulge in this apparent mystification ? Not because there was anything esoteric in his doctrine ; our Lord had no ' secret ' teaching exclusively for the initiated (Jn 18:19–21). His message was for all ' according as they were able to hear ' (Mk 4:33). Without doubt, ' He that hath ears to hear, let him hear ' (v 9) ; but the implication of this saying is that many would comprehend imperfectly or perhaps not at all (*cf.* Jn 1:5). Nor need this unresponsiveness always have been due to malice or bad faith. As Grandmaison remarks (*Jesus Christ*, E. Tr., 2, 41), ' With many of those who heard Jesus, it was less a case of grave sin against the light than an attitude suggested to·them and almost forced upon them by the prestige of the scribes and doctors who were enemies of the Gospel. It was a temporary attitude, a heaviness which the leaven of the Gospel could eventually lighten. For such men (and they were legion) this teaching, whose enigmatic nature did not demand—as a clearly expressed instruction would have demanded—the immediate decisions of which they were as yet incapable, this teaching, given in parable and metaphor, though apparently a punishment, was in reality a great act of mercy. They were sent back to wait for a more favourable season, and were not excluded from the Kingdom of God. Meanwhile the idea of the Kingdom was kept before them, and its character explained to them " according as they were capable of understanding." '

b Thus there is disclosed to us a divine forbearance in the ministry of him who would not break the bruised reed or extinguish the smouldering flax (Mt 12:20 ; Is 42:3). But a dark saying still remains to be explained : ' To you it is given to know the mystery of the Kingdom of God : but to them that are without, all things are done in parables : That seeing they may see and not perceive ; and hearing they may hear and not understand : lest at any time they should be converted and their sins should be forgiven them ' (Mk 4:11–12 ; *cf.* Mt 13:10–17 ; Lk 8:9–10. On this and the whole question of the parables, see Buzy, *Introduction aux Paraboles Evangéliques*, especially 233–86). Here it should be observed that the Semitic idiom, of which the gospel Greek is the expression, finds no place for the distinction, familiar to the Church Fathers and theologians, between what God positively wills and what he permits. To the Jewish mind everything happened because God had so decided, so decreed. But the economy of mercy, which is the Gospel's chief characteristic, as well as the light subsequently thrown on the matter by the theologians (*Vid.* S. Aug., *Tract. 53 in Joan.*, PL 1774 *seq.* ; S. Thom., *Expos. in Joan.*, 12, lect. 7, Parma edit., 10, 519), rules out the possibility of a divine predestining to sin and damnation.

c We must nevertheless not overlook the fact that there is such a thing as the ' hardening of the heart ', a sinning against the light which brings with it the penalty of God's withdrawal of grace. Among ' those without ' who listened to the parables there were certainly proud and self-interested men deter-

mined to resist Jesus at all costs. They could be won over by nothing ; therefore their doom was pronounced. Whatever the possibility of a last-minute repentance for individuals, the final consequences of such a general attitude are inescapable ; and our Lord was concerned to impress upon his hearers the fearful urgency of his message, not to make allowances for those who rejected it. Set for the rise and fall of many in Israel, he embodied in his own person the most tremendous ' crisis ' with which mankind could be presented. Following the method of the Jewish rabbis, he put it before his hearers in those strong contrasting phrases which alone could give expression to it. Moreover the synoptic writers, confronted with the patent results of widespread rejection, had good reason for throwing into the sharpest relief the words of Jesus. St John also, in his sorrowful epilogue to the Public Ministry, records the fulfilment of Isaias' predictions concerning the blinding of the eyes and the hardening of the hearts (Jn 12:37–41). It was the darker obverse side of the Gospel picture, the dread alternative to the experience of believers : ' Blessed are your eyes because they see, and your ears because they hear ' (Mt 13:16).

(*c*) A word remains to be said with regard to the **miracles,** or ' signs ', which our records show Jesus as having worked habitually throughout his ministry. A discussion on the miraculous as such is outside the scope of this study (see Grandmaison, *op. cit.*, 3, 97–154 ; Michel, DTC, 10, pt 2, 1798–1859 ; de Tonquédec, DAFC, 3, 517–78 ; *Bernard, HDB, 3, 379–96) ; here we must confine ourselves to a brief note on the fact, the significance, and the purpose of the gospel miracles. (For an acute critique of recent attempts to explain away the miraculous element in the NT, see Allo, *Le Scandale de Jésus*, 57–100.) In the first place it must be observed that our Lord's miracles form an integral part of the evangelists' story ; they have nothing of the character of decorative embellishments ; were they eliminated the whole narrative would have to be recast on different lines—a consequence which has been clearly seen, and boldly acted upon, by many modern critics. This notwithstanding, the judgement still remains true that ' we cannot construct a consistent picture of the life of Jesus Christ from the gospels, if we do not take account of his miraculous powers, however those " miraculous " powers are to be explained. . . . We cannot contrive any theory by which we may entirely eliminate the miraculous, and yet save the historicity, in any intelligible sense, of those wonderful narratives ' (HDB, 3, 389).

The miracles have often been classified as ' miracles of healing ' and ' cosmic miracles '—a division which, though roughly applicable, is not wholly satisfactory. Whether all our Lord's cures are to be ranked technically as ' miracles ' depends upon our definition of that term and, in particular, upon the account we give of demoniacal possession, with which so many of his healings were concerned (see Grandmaison, *op. cit.*, 3, 128–40). Among this class we find the cures of the demoniacs (Mk 1:23 ff. ; Mt 8:28 ff. ; 15:21 ff. ; 17:14 ff.), of the impotent man at the Pool of Bethesda (Jn 5:2 ff.), of the man with the withered hand (Mt 12:10 ff.), of the woman with the spirit of infirmity (Lk 13:11 ff.), of the dumb man with a devil (Mt 9:32 ff.), of the man ' possessed with a devil, blind and dumb ' (Mt 12:12 ff.). Perhaps even more striking than these, in that they allow less of a ' natural ' explanation, are the cases of the centurion's servant (Mt 8:5 ff.), of the palsied man (Mt 9:2 ff.) ; of the deaf and dumb man (Mk 7:32 ff.), of the blind (Mk 8:22 ff. ; Mt 9:26 ff. ; 20:30 ff.), and the very remarkable instance, which occasioned such a stir at the time, in Jn 9:1 ff. Here we may note also the cures of the dropsical man (Lk 14:2 ff.), of the fever patient healed with a touch (Mt 8:14 ff.), of the woman with a haemorrhage (Mt 9:20 ff.), of the lepers (Mt 8:2 ff. ; Lk 17:11 ff.), and of the servant Malchus (Lk 22:50 ff.). Most arresting of all are the three instances of the restoration of life : to Jairus's daughter (Mt 9:23), to the widow of Naim's son (Lk 7:11 ff.), and to Lazarus (Jn 11:43).

The ' cosmic ' miracles, *i.e.* those worked upon nature as distinct from man, include the first ' sign ' of all, the transformation of water into wine at the marriage feast (Jn 2:1 ff.), the stilling of the storm (Mt 8:26) and the walking on the sea (Mt 14:25), the feeding of the five thousand (Mt 14:19) and of the four thousand (Mk 8:1 ff.), and the blasting of the fig tree (Mt 21:19). In addition there are the remarkable ' coincidences ' of the great draught of fishes (Lk 5:1 ff. and Jn 21:6 ff.) and the finding of the stater in the fish's mouth (Mt 17:24 ff.). Finally, in a class apart and transcending all others, is the Resurrection of Jesus himself. This was the credential to which the Church continually appealed (Rom 1:4 ; 4:24 ; 1 Pet 1:21). Over and above the explicit testimony of the evangelists, the Resurrection is presupposed in all the apostolic epistles ; it is likewise the burden of the apostolic sermons recorded in Acts (2:32 ; 3:15 ; 10:40 ; 13:34 ; 17:3, 31 ; 26:23). It would be hard to surpass the circumstantiality of St Paul's account of it in 1 Cor 15:3–8 (*cf.* Rom 8:34 ; 14:9 ; 2 Cor 5:15 ; 1 Thess 4:13). So confident is he, that he appeals to the fact of the Lord's resurrection as a *reductio ad absurdum* of those who would deny that we too shall rise again (1 Cor 15:13 ff.). It is from the actual historic event that he draws forth its spiritual and symbolic meaning : ' that, as Christ is risen from the dead by the glory of the Father, so we also may walk in newness of life ' (Rom 6:4 ; *cf.* Phil 3:10 ; Col 3:1).

It should be unnecessary to point out that our Lord was not a wonder-worker, a thaumaturge, in any ordinary sense. This role, precisely the one which the devil had tempted him to assume (Mt 4:3–7), was explicitly rejected by him (Mk 8:11 ff. ; Mt 16:4). If there was to come a time when, in a last vain attempt to win over the incredulous, he would point to his wonderful deeds as proof that he came from God— ' though you will not believe me, believe the works ' (Jn 10:38 ; *cf.* Allo, *op. cit.*, 95–6)—he did not parade them in this light, as being, so to say, ocular demonstrations of divinity. Proofs and evidences to the well-disposed they certainly were, and have always been so regarded by the Church ; but their probative force is not compelling. Human pride is impervious to the appeal of miracles ; in such an atmosphere they can often afford a motive for disbelief. That the miraculous element in the gospels is nowadays sometimes looked upon as an obstacle rather than an aid to faith is no peculiarly modern phenomenon ; it was the experience of Jesus himself. His enemies, who could not gainsay the facts, were anxious to ascribe them to the agency of Satan (Mt 12:24). The Galilean prophet might well have cured a man blind from birth ; but what of that ? The point to consider was that he had offended by doing so on the Sabbath (Jn 9:1 ff.) ! Of what use are miracles to this temper of mind ?

The truth is that the miracles are as much, nay more, manifestations of God's love than demonstrations of his power. Power in subordination to love, love declaring itself in power—is the key to the understanding of the miracles. The preternatural works of Jesus were almost without exception beneficent deeds—to alleviate human misery or to further the interests of the Kingdom. They were not arbitrary interferences with the course of nature, a show of divine might without reference to the needs of the situation or the saving character of Christ's mission. On the contrary they were outpourings of God's favour, wholly of a piece with the mercy and loving kindness which received their supreme embodiment in the person of Jesus. For this reason he himself seems almost to make light of his miraculous healings, or to desire at least to keep them secret (Mk 7:36 ; 8:26) ; there was a moment when the people would have acclaimed him as the mighty wonder-working Messias of their earthly expectations (Jn 6:14 f.), and he openly rebuked

them for seeing in his miracles no more than the **627b** alleviation of material necessities (v 26). Our Lord's wonderful works were thus symbols of God's goodness, and only goodwill could rightly respond to them. Considered as mere evidences, they were not sufficient to produce belief ; there was needed also the inward enlightenment of the mind and heart for which they were the occasion. For all the persuasive power of the miracles of Jesus, they would not of themselves have sufficed to make the refusal to accept him inexcusable, had they not been accompanied for the unbelievers by an interior grace of illumination (S. Thom., *Expos. in Joan.*, 15, 5, 4, Parma edit., 10, 573).

From the viewpoint of Christian apologetics it should c be remembered that the supreme motive of credibility is not the miracles, but the personality of him who worked them. This was the influence which could subjugate all hearts, a light irresistibly alluring to those who did not voluntarily close their eyes. The charm and majesty of the mere presence of Jesus, his unblemished purity, the serenity which distinguished him from the OT prophets, the manifest goodness at once so accessible and so resourceful, the incomparable teaching, proclaimed with such divine assurance, in a manner so different from that of the Jewish rabbis— these are what constituted the most impressive ' miracle ' of all. Even had there been no miracles men should still have believed in Jesus Christ ; for he bore within his own person, and could bring to bear upon the soul, the appeal and illumination of the ' first Truth ', loved instinctively by every creature. To resist this inward impulsion is suicide for the intelligence, a sin only to be explained by perversity of heart. ' If any man do the will of him [that sent me], he shall know of the doctrine, whether it be of God, or whether I speak of myself ' (Jn 7:17 ; *cf.* Allo, *op. cit.*, 93 ff.). *Cf.* also §§ 87–91.

(*d*) In this brief note we shall treat exclusively of the d **knowledge present to the human mind of Jesus.** It should be observed that the Church's magisterium and the dogmatic theologians have laid down certain principles for the guidance of scriptural exegetes (Dz 2032–5 ; 2183–5). A comprehensive statement of these principles may take the form of the commonly accepted theological thesis that ' the soul of Christ possessed every species of knowledge and human science which accorded with his dignity and are not contrary to the end for which he became incarnate ' (Dickamp, *Theologicae Dogmaticae Manuale*, 2, 312). It is now generally admitted that, in addition to the normal human knowledge acquired from sense experience, our Lord possessed two other forms of knowledge : that gained from God's direct infusion into his mind of ideas or ' species ', so giving him an insight comparable to that of the angels, and—most enlightening of all—the knowledge resulting from the direct contemplation of God in the Beatific Vision. For he was a *comprehensor* as well as a *viator* ; he dwelt in the heights of heaven even while making his journey on earth.

Our Lord's human knowledge, though not amounting e to the omniscience which is the prerogative of the Godhead, cannot be said to have involved ignorance or error ; it did not embrace the infinite realm of possibilities known only to the divine mind, but it substantially included all actual events, past, present and to come. Such would seem to be involved in the plenitude of knowledge proper to the Incarnate Word. ' No man hath seen God at any time ; the only begotten Son who is in the bosom of the Father, he hath declared him ' (Jn 1:18). ' Amen, amen, I say to thee, that we speak what we know and we testify what we have seen ' (3:11). The divine authority embodied in Jesus, constituting God's final self-disclosure to the world, demands that we recognize in him unequivocal Truth. He was, as St John tells us, ' full of grace and truth ' (1:14) ; from this there follows the possession of that supreme degree of knowledge which is the

627e basis of our confidence in, and acceptance of, what he taught. This is the source of the otherwise inexplicable self-assurance of Jesus ; for all his humble subjection to the Father, he comes before us throughout his ministry as complete master of the situation ; there is no hesitation, no uncertainty of touch. He was conscious from the beginning of his Messianic dignity, clearly aware of all that pertained to him as God the Son made man.

f It is clear, however, that our Lord did not always choose to reveal the full content of his knowledge. That he practised a certain deliberate ' economy ' in his teaching is evident from Jn 16:12 ; perhaps the most famous example of this is Mk 13:32 : ' But of that day or hour no man knoweth, neither the angels in heaven, nor the Son, but the Father ' (on the various interpretations of this text, see Diekamp, *op. cit.*, 322–3 ; Hugon, *Tractatus Dogmatici*, 2, 475–7). Briefly it may be said that the Son had not received from his Father the commission to communicate the precise date of the Parousia and from that point of view, the only one which concerned his ministry, was within his rights in professing ignorance of it (*cf.* Lagrange, *Saint Marc*, 326–7). Here it may be recalled that the ecclesiastical magisterium has explicitly condemned the proposition that ' the natural sense of the evangelical texts cannot be reconciled with what our theologians teach concerning the infallible knowledge and science of Christ ' (Dz 2032) ; but it should be noted that the Church, by this very declaration, is as much concerned to preserve ' the natural sense of the evangelical texts ' as to safeguard the deliverances of theology. Nothing must be allowed to whittle away the clear evidence of Jesus's acquired and experimental knowledge. May it not be that the *a priori* processes habitual with theologians can make them insufficiently appreciative of what was implied in our Lord's perceptual experience in the workaday world of space and time ? Even the youthful St Thomas was disposed to underestimate the reality of Christ's acquired knowledge (*In Sent.* 3, d. 14, q.l, a. 3, sol. 5), though he afterwards revised his opinion (*Summa* 3, q. 9, a. 4).

628a However this may be, as a safeguard against the unconscious Docetism into which too concentrated attention on the higher forms of knowledge might lead us, the great text from the Epistle to the Hebrews remains a reminder that our Lord shared the fullness of our humanity : ' he learned obedience by the things which he suffered ' (5:8). From boyhood, like the rest of us, he ' advanced in wisdom ' (Lk 2:52). As a man, though revealing the keenest natural intelligence and superlative powers of sense observation, as illustrated by the similitudes and parables, he could yet experience wonder (Mk 6:6 ; Lk 7:9). In all this there was no play-acting ; the mind of Jesus was really enlightened by his contacts with nature, with man and human affairs, by a mode of knowledge which had not hitherto been his. That these concepts acquired by his intellect were themselves bathed in a light issuing from the divine sources of knowledge already mentioned we cannot for one moment doubt ; but this theological schematization, though valid within its limits, must not be interpreted to mean the monstrosity of a series of wholly distinct departments of knowledge within our Lord's mind. Having all the perfections due to the Incarnate Word, his human consciousness was wholly at one with itself ; there were no lines of cleavage, no elements at variance one with another. But into the inner harmonies of the mind of Jesus we cannot presume to enter. We are brought face to face with the legitimate *refugium in mysterium*, the ' refuge in mystery ' which ultimately confronts every believer when contemplating the only begotten Son of God.

b **VI The Mystery of Jesus**—It has been well said that the gospels portray in Jesus Christ ' a Person who, despite his obvious humanity, impresses us throughout as being at home in two worlds ', *Illingworth, Divine Immanence* (1904) 50, and *cf.* Grandmaison, *op. cit.*, 2, 329. He was a man of his age, a pure Jew, with all the ardour and intensity of his race. He was not a ' superman ', nor yet, as some have thought, an apparition from some higher realm clothed in human flesh. Everything points to his being a sharer in our common clay. He was tired and hungry, could rejoice familiarly with his friends and weep with them in sorrow ; when he chose, he could speak out vehemently against his enemies, yet be prostrated in anguished apprehension at the prospect of his torments. The evidence shows him to have had a mother and near relatives ; he plied a trade ; there is nothing remote or inaccessible about him. On no reading of his character could he be described as a shadowy and colourless figure ; so remarkable was the impression of vitality upon his contemporaries, that they were moved alternatively to worshipping admiration or passionate hatred. In a word, if the colloquialism may be allowed, he was one of ourselves : ' consubstantial (of the same substance) with us according to humanity ' (Dz 148).

But together with all this he was immeasurably more. Notwithstanding his approachableness, the disciples, save when they forgot themselves, looked upon him with something akin to awe. There was about his person the fascination of the numinous, the All-Holy was present within him—' Depart from me, for I am a sinful man, O Lord ' (Lk 5:8). He knew and declared himself to be more than a prophet, which was the highest ideal of manhood in his day ; for the prophetic formula ' Thus saith the Lord ' he substitutes the ultimately authoritative ' *I* say unto you '. Nor does he show the least trace of having scaled to these heights as it were from below ; in this sense he is no ' hero ' who has raised himself, or been raised in the common estimation, above his fellows by his outstanding exploits. The divine quality within him is not the result of an achievement : it is something already given, a fact. The marvellous deeds, the mastery of their performance, the incomparable sayings, embodied though they be in the texture of human life, issue from a source that is more than human ; the deep underlying serenity, undisturbed by the surface turmoil and conflict, points rather to the Godhead's ' striking downwards ' than to a human individual's aspiring to the heights. Jesus acts and speaks as one for whom heaven is his native element, the Deity a personal possession : ' consubstantial with the Father according to divinity '.

Yet there is no suggestion that divinity and humanity are anything but harmoniously united. Deeds and words, and the whole conduct of the Public Ministry, hold together with utter consistency ; never was a life led with more complete unity of purpose. Jesus could experience both depression and elation, but of a ' split personality ' there is not a trace. He is equally poised, at one with himself, when being acclaimed by the crowd and when standing before Pilate ; the personal ' I ' comes as naturally to his lips in the familiar instructions to the disciples as when united in prayer to his heavenly Father ; there is one sole *ego*, in whatever heights or depths it may be said to dwell. How is this duality in oneness to be put into words ? ' One *person*, two *natures* '—such is the traditional Catholic formula, attempting to express the inexpressible. It is inevitably inadequate to what it represents ; nor can any analysis of its terms yield the fullness of the knowledge of Jesus available only in the inspired scriptural texts. The statement is in no sense offered as the conclusion of a demonstration of the truth of the Incarnation ; for, as has already been said, this is a mystery of faith not susceptible of rational proof. But it was believed by those responsible for its formulation, as it is held by the vast majority of Christians today, to be a proposition in comprehensible language which does least injustice to the evidence of Scripture. Nor have recent attempts to suggest alternatives or substitutes given the least grounds for supposing that the modern mind has fundamentally a better understanding of Christ our Lord than the Fathers at Chalcedon. The Catholic formula can be assailed, but, from the nature of the case, it cannot be refuted. The mystery of Jesus remains—a subject more proper for adoring contemplation than theological disputation. It is the supreme glory of the Church to have made full allowance for this mystery : **628d** at one and the same time, guarding the inner secret of the Lord's personality from the desecrating hands of the rationalists and unbelievers, and presenting to the world in intelligible terms the Truth by which alone it may hope to live : ' This is eternal life : that they may know thee, the only true God, and Jesus Christ, whom thou hast sent ' (Jn 17:3).

CHRISTIANITY IN APOSTOLIC TIMES:

DOCTRINE AND PRACTICE

By M. BÉVENOT, S.J., (§§ 630-5 ; 638-9 ; 655-60)

AND

Dom RALPH RUSSELL, (§§ 636-7 ; 640-54)

629a Bibliography—St John Chrys., *Hom. on Ac. and on St Paul's Epistles*, PG 60-3 ; DBV(S), *Agape* (Thomas), *Apostolat* (Médebielle), *Baptême* (d'Alès and Coppens), *Charismes* (Lemonnyer), *Citations de l'AT dans le NT* (Venard), *Confirmation* (Coppens), *Eglise* (Médebielle), *Eucharistie* (Coppens), *Evêques* (Marchal), *Expiation* (Médebielle), *Extrême-Onction* (d'Alès), *Foi* (Antoine), *Gnose* (Cerfaux), *Grâce* (Bonnetain), *Hellénisme* (Bardy), *Israël* (de Vaux), *Jésus-Christ* (Lebreton), *Jud. pal. au temps de J.-C.* (Bonsirven), *Justice et Justification* (Descamps and Cerfaux) ; DTC, *Confession* (Mangenot), *Espérance* (Harent), *Esprit-Saint* (Palmieri), *Eucharistie* (Ruch), *Justification* (Lemonnyer and Rivière), *Mariage* (Godefroy), *Messe* (Ruch), *Ordre* (Michel), *Paul* (Colon), *Péché originel* (Gaudel), *Pénitence* (Amann), *Prédestination* (Lemonnyer), *Primauté du Pape* (Glez), *Rédemption* (Rivière) ; DAFC, *Eglise* (de la Brière), *Mystères païens et S. Paul* (Jacquier), *Eucharistie* (Lebreton) ; DAC, *Agape* (Leclercq), *Fractio Panis* (Cabrol) ; Dict. de Spiritualité, *Charité* (Prat).

b L. de Grandmaison, S.J., *Jésus Christ* (tr. 1934, 3 vols) ; M.-J. Lagrange, O.P., Commentaries on Mt, Mk, Lk, Jn, Gal, Rom ; E. Jacquier, *Les Actes des Apôtres* ; E.-B. Allo, O.P., Commentaries on 1 Cor, 2 Cor, Apoc ; F. Prat, S.J., *The Theology of St Paul* (Eng. Trans.) I (1933²), II (1927). J. Lebreton, S.J., *History of the Dogma of the Trinity* (tr. 1938 of 8th ed., Vol. I, *Les Origines du Dogme de la Trinité*), *La Vie chrétienne au premier siècle de l'Eglise* ¹⁴ (1928), *The Living God* (tr. 1923 of *Dieu vivant*) ; J. Lebreton and J. Zeiler, *The History of the Primitive Church* (tr. 1942-4, 2 vols) ; BJP, BEJC, BER, BEP ; L. Cerfaux, *La Théologie de l'Eglise suivant S. Paul*² (1948) ; F. Amiot, *L'Enseignement de S. Paul*⁴ (1946) ; G. Thils, *L'Enseignement de S. Pierre*³ (1943) ; J. Chaine, *Les Epîtres catholiques*² (1939) ; C. Spicq, O.P., *Les Epîtres pastorales* (1947) ; ' Verbum Salutis ' series, especially F. Amiot, *Epître aux Gal.*, *Epître aux Thessaloniciens* (1946) ; J. Huby, S.J., *Les Epîtres de la Captivité* (1935) ; U. Holzmeister, *Comm. in Epistolas SS. Petri et Judae*, I (1937) ; WV Appendices.

c K. Adam, *The Spirit of Catholicism* (tr. 1934²) ; E. Mersch, S.J., *The Whole Christ* (tr. 1938 of *Corps mystique du Christ*), *La Théologie du Corps mystique*² (1946) ; F.-M. Braun, *Jésus* (1947), *Aspects nouveaux du Problème de l'Eglise* (1942)—tr. and revised under title of *Neues Licht auf die Kirche* (1946) ; M.-J. Congar, O.P., *Esquisses du Mystère de l'Eglise* (1941) ; Y. de Montcheuil, S.J., *Aspects de l'Eglise* (1949), *Mélanges théologiques* (1946) ; J. Coppens, *Les Harmonies des deux Testaments* (1949) ; H. de Lubac, S.J., *Histoire et Esprit* (1950), and notes in *Origène, Hom. sur la Genèse* (1943), *Origène, Hom. sur l'Exode* (1947) ; J. Daniélou, *Sacramentum Futuri* (1950) ; L. Bouyer, *The Paschal Mystery* (tr. 1950, of *Le Mystère pascal*) ; Bandas, *The Master-Idea of St Paul's Epistles* (1925) ; E. Tobac, *Le Problème de la Justification dans S. Paul* (1908) ; J. Guillet, *Thèmes Bibliques* (1950).

d J. Crehan, S.J., *Early Christian Baptism and the Creed* (1950) ; J. Coppens, *Imposition des Mains* (1925) ; *Catholic Faith in the Holy Eucharist* (Cam. Sum. School, 1928, ed. Lattey, S.J.) ; P. Batiffol, *L'Eucharistie* (1920) ; W. Goossens, *Les Origines de l'Eucharistie sacrement et sacrifice* (1931) ; M. de la Taille, S.J., *The Mystery of Faith* (tr. of *Mysterium Fidei*) I (1947), II (1950) ; E. Masure, *The Christian Sacrifice* (tr. 1944 of *Le Sacrifice du Chef*) ; J. Bonsirven, S.J., *Le Divorce dans le NT*

(1948) ; H. Rahner, S.J., *Griechische Mythen in Christlichen Deutung* (1944) ; O. Casel, *Le Mystère du Culte dans le Christianisme* (tr. 1946).

*O. Cullmann, *Les premières Confessions de Foi chrétienne* (1943), *Le Mystère du Culte dans le Christianisme* (tr. 1946 of *Das Christliche Kultusmysterium*), *Le Christ et le Temps* (1947), *Königsherrschaft Christi u. Kirche im NT* (1941), *Urchristentum und Gottesdienst* (1944) ; *C. H. Dodd, *The Apostolic Preaching* ; *E. Hoskyns and N. Davey, *The Riddle of the NT* (1931) ; *R. Newton Flew, *Jesus and His Church* (1943²) ; *J. Moffatt, *Jesus Christ The Same* (1942) ; *F. J. Foakes Jackson and *Kirsopp Lake, *The Beginnings of Christianity*, I, *The Acts of the Apostles* (5 vols, 1920-33) ; *K. E. Kirk (ed.), *The Apostolic Ministry* (1946) ; *L. Thornton, *The Common Life in the Body of Christ* (1941) ; *W. Davies, *Paul and Rabbinic Judaism* (1948) ; *W. Flemington, *The NT Doctrine of Baptism* (1948) ; *H. Lietzmann, *Messe und Herrenmahl*² (1949) ; *J. Jeremias, *Die Abendmahlsworte Jesu*² (1949) ; *G. Dix, *The Shape of the Liturgy* (1943) ; *Bible Key Words*, tr. from KTW : *K. L. Schmidt, *The Church* ; *G. Quell and *E. Stauffer, *Love* (1950) ; ICC.

Introduction—The purpose of this article is to try to present the NT data as a whole, in so far as it reveals the life and thought of the early Christians, in the first decades subsequent to our Lord's earthly ministry. Such an approach is in harmony with the most recent trends in biblical scholarship generally, *viz.* that, instead of looking for the differences between the various books, and even within the same book, one starts with the presumption that this body of writings has, for all its variety, a common source in certain historical facts, and testifies to the emergence of a way of life, of a new outlook on creation and beyond—in fact, to the ' originality ' of Christianity. This ' modern ' realization of the fundamental unity of our sources (*cf.* JTS 45 [1944] 85-7) is one of the periodical ' re-discoveries ' of what Catholics have always taken for granted thanks to their sense of continuity with the past.

This sense of **continuity with the past** is in fact the key to the way in which Catholics normally come to understand the nature of the Church which Christ founded. They do so primarily from their contact with the living Church of today to which they belong, and they learn not only from what they are told, but from what they see and find out from experience of her ; *cf.* Dz 1793-4. But they can also read and study and analyze the sacred text *as if* they had not the developed teaching of the Church to fall back upon ; in difficulties, they can consult the works of her scholars, which reveal the progress constantly being made in the understanding of the ancient world, as new fields are opened up by archaeology, the study of comparative religions and philosophies, of linguistics, papyrology, and the rest. This progress means a better understanding of the details, but the main lines of the picture remain, and as these often stand out all the clearer under the light of the new evidence, the Church's serene confidence in the truth of the message which she proclaims today is repeatedly vindicated.

Not that the whole of modern Catholic doctrine and practice is to be found within the pages of the NT. Even if all that was said or done in those times had been written down in them, we should not expect to find direct testimony to everything that we now believe and do. If 'Scripture and Tradition' are the sources of our Faith and Catholic life, that life has not been static, but has developed, as all life develops, from the day of Pentecost until now. Nevertheless, if what we now express and do is *more*, what we have is not *other* than what the first Christians enjoyed.

A final word of introduction is perhaps necessary. As Catholics, who recognize the doctrine of inspiration and therefore are assured of **the historical accuracy of the NT**, we naturally take our four gospels as narrating the earliest events in our period, then the first part of the Acts of the Apostles, then most of the epistles strung along the latter part of the Ac, and lastly the rest of the NT writings. To assess correctly the theories of non-Catholic critics, and indeed to enter into the minds of the NT writers ourselves, we have to remember that the gospels were not written at the precise time when the events were taking place, and that St Luke compiled the first part of the Acts anything up to thirty years after Pentecost. St John wrote his Gospel towards the end of the 1st cent. Those who, for a century and more, have called in question the truth of these accounts, have been using a sound enough principle, *viz.* that a writer is bound to be affected by his present *milieu* even when he is trying to record accurately what happened in the past. But not only have many of these critics grossly exaggerated the effect on the NT writers of the development of the Church about them when they were recounting its origins, but, to make such exaggeration plausible, they have always pushed the dates of those writings as late as they possibly could. One of the great merits of the historian *A. Harnack was his refutation of the current dating of the Gospels, which the Tübingen School placed in the 2nd cent., and his assigning to them dates well in the first—though, even so, much later than can reasonably be admitted (*cf. The Synoptic Problem*, §§ 610–15, and *The Chronology of NT times*, §§ 674–6). The more modern school of *Form-Criticism*, while calling attention to some useful features in the construction of the Gospels, makes of these a sort of folk-lore created by the Christian communities around the quite ordinary events of the life of a merely human Christ. It treats the gospels as if they were merely the projection of the religious experience of the communities, and makes little or no account of the decisive part played by those who were the *witnesses* of the events themselves. This complete inversion of the process which produced the Gospels, after attracting much attention for some years, met with attacks from so many quarters that its influence is on the wane. Indeed the progress of NT scholarship today is such that our assumption that the Synoptics and the Acts are in substance historically accurate can hold its own whenever the evidence is not parcelled out according to pre-conceived theories but accepted as it stands, its various parts converging in one complex whole.

The **main divisions** of this article will be as follows :

I THE FIRST THIRTY YEARS (§§ 631–4)
    Origins and expansion
    Obstacles
    Impact on individual converts

II THE COMMUNITY OF THE FAITHFUL (§§ 635–9)
    Corporate character of their religion
    Their ' Communion ' in its many senses
    The ' Charismata ' and the common faith

III THE HOLY TRINITY (§ 640)
    JESUS THE LORD (§ 641)

IV THE REDEMPTION (§§ 642–9)
    In the Old Testament
    The Gospels
    St Paul
    St John

V THE SACRAMENTS (§§ 650–4)   **630e**

VI THE MINISTRY (§§ 655–9)
    The Mystical Body and Authority
    The Apostles—Peter
    Their Successors

VII SOME PRACTICAL ASPECTS (§ 660)
    The Family
    Slavery
    Property and Poverty
    Attitude to the State

I THE FIRST THIRTY YEARS

(This section has been put into the mouth of an in- **631a** telligent, not unsympathetic observer, who, about A.D. 60, has been asked for an account of this new ' Christian ' religion.) ' It all began with **the young Rabbi from Nazareth**, if he could be called a Rabbi at all, for he had been through none of the ordinary training. For all that, he made quite a stir during his short campaign of preaching—two or three years at most, until the opposition of the Jewish religious authorities could stand his unauthorized activities no longer, and they had him executed by the Roman Procurator on a trumped-up charge of fomenting disaffection towards the emperor. This, of course, only shows how powerful had been the effect of his preaching and how widespread his influence had become. The fact was that he knew the mind of the people, and striking a note of authority and independence, searched their hearts implacably, not sparing their prejudices and foibles any more than he did the formalism and hypocrisy of their official leaders. He laid down maxims which he taught them to remember, and illustrated his ideas with telling little stories which generally had much more in them than appeared on the surface, so that they were treasured and repeated by those whose confidence he had won. Free as he was from any violence of gesture, or incitement to mass demonstrations, his open-air preaching in the Galilean countryside, on the mountain slopes or by the lake, recalled the memory of the Hebrew prophets of old. This was enhanced by the perfectly well authenticated stories of the cures which he worked instantaneously on the fever-stricken, the cripples, and the blind, not to mention a few cases of his raising the dead to life. His enemies, of course, put this down to magic or devilry, but this latter accusation, prompted by his strange power with the possessed, was neatly rebutted by his question : ' Can Satan cast out Satan ? If a kingdom be divided against itself, that kingdom cannot stand ', Mk 3:23–24.

' Whether or not he foresaw that with the manifest **b** antagonism of the Jewish priests and Pharisees he was riding for a fall, it is clear that he made provision that his ideas should be perpetuated and his memory endure. Soon after he had acquired a fairly regular following, **he picked out twelve** from among them, who by sharing his life and receiving a more thorough instruction and training might carry on his work after him. They were mostly fishermen of no education, only one or two being of a slightly better class. As one might have expected, he had no small trouble in getting them to grasp his own lofty principles ; to the very end he had constantly to correct their misconceptions as to the true character of his message, and to help them to an ever truer estimate of the significance of his own life and personality. With one of them he failed completely : the priests bribed him and he enabled them to arrest his Master at dead of night out of sight of the crowds who revered him ; but this act of black treachery was almost his last, for remorse and suicide removed him from the scene. The rest of the Twelve, the Apostles as he had called them, thus showing his intention to use them in future missionary work, were utterly devoted to him, and if they were lacking in understanding and unstable in an emergency, he knew he could rely on their love to bring them back sorrowfully but loyally

631b to him. This was particularly true of the one whom he had specially chosen as his deputy and called 'the rock', meaning him to be the foundation of the new brotherhood of his followers, and who in fact took such a leading part in the resurgence of the movement a couple of months after the Rabbi's execution. It is also said that the Rabbi promised that they would each be endowed with that same superhuman power by which he himself had cast out devils and worked his cures.

c 'Certainly the results corresponded with what he seems to have planned for. Unexpectedly, dramatically even, the whole of Jerusalem was one day stirred by the emergence into its streets of some 120 men and women, under the leadership of the original Apostles (their number having been made up to twelve again by a special election), who fearlessly maintained that, so far from having been finally silenced, Jesus of Nazareth had been raised up again from the dead by God, had been seen by them more than once, and was now at the right hand of God, inspiring them to speak what they knew without fear, as all could see for themselves. And they quoted the prophets to show that the whole series of events of the past months had been preordained by God, and that, responsible as the city had been for the murder of him whom they must now recognize to be the long-expected Christ, they should repent and by baptism attach themselves to their company so as to live henceforth as he had instructed them. Of course, many who heard them upheld their first conviction that these men were all drunk, but the fact remains that some 3,000 rallied to them that very day, and a couple of thousand were added to them when their leader, Cephas ("the rock"), cured a cripple in his master's name near the Beautiful Gate of the Temple. It all testifies to the influence which Jesus had really had despite his apparent failure. Besides, there was the fact of the disappearance of his body from its guarded tomb—which the chief priests were unable to explain away—and the number of independent witnesses of his resurrection provided evidence which could not be gainsaid. What is more, Jerusalem was crowded at the time for the feast of Pentecost, so that the pilgrims on returning home prepared the way in far distant parts for the coming of the authorized missionaries later on.

d 'But, in the city, organization began at once. Filled with a strange zeal, most of the new sect began leading a kind of communal life, selling their property and putting the money into the common pool, so that the poor among them were at first well cared for. The deficiencies of the experiment only appeared with time. [See § 660q]. Officials, later called deacons, ministered at the common meals, leaving the Twelve free to devote themselves to their more spiritual ministrations. Preaching went on in spite of the arrest and punishment of the leaders on two occasions; and the particularly outspoken harangue of Stephen, one of the deacons, at his arrest, led not only to his being lynched then and there, but to a general persecution which spread for a while from the city to other centres. The Apostles stayed in Jerusalem, but many others fled and carried with them their new message, so that new centres sprang up throughout all Judaea and Galilee and Samaria, Ac 9:31; there was perhaps one already at Damascus, Ac 9:2, 19. In Palestine the names of Lydda, Joppe and Caesarea occur to one, Ac 9:32, 36; 10:1 ff., and quite early one began to hear of "the churches of Judaea" in general, Gal 1:22. The "Gospel" was also preached in Phœnicia, Cyprus and Antioch, Ac 11:19; 15:3; and this opened a new chapter in the history of the expansion.

e 'For with few exceptions all that one hears of it is connected with the activities of Saul, previously their persecutor, who as Paul has come to be known as the Apostle par excellence. He broke new ground first in his own country of Cilicia, Ac 9:30, Gal 1:21–23, Ac 11:25, whence he was fetched by Barnabas to help in the development of a Church of a new kind, that of Antioch, where for the first time a new kind, that of Antioch, where for the first time

there was a large access of Gentiles, Ac 11:20–26. The three missionary journeys which he undertook from this base cover a period of some ten years, during which time he devoted most attention to southern Galatia, Corinth and Ephesus, the two latter, as cosmopolitan ports, being particularly important for more distant contacts. But he had also preached in Cyprus, later to be developed by Barnabas and Mark, Ac 15:39; founded flourishing churches at Philippi and Thessalonica in Macedonia, and developed, either personally or through his helpers, the growth of Christianity in the province of Asia, the hinterland of Ephesus. He could in fact summarize his labours by saying: "My own work has been to complete the preaching of Christ's gospel, in a wide sweep from Jerusalem as far as Illyricum", Rom 15:19 KNT. Meantime, other missionaries had founded the flourishing Church of Rome to which he addressed these words, and no doubt other churches too of which one hears, though details of their origins are wanting. Certainly, it is an interesting movement, and I should be surprised if it had not a great future before it.'

Of these 'other churches', something can be added to round off the account of our benevolent observer. Thus the northern parts of Asia Minor are covered by the address of 1 Pet: Pontus, Galatia, Cappadocia, Asia and Bithynia. But Paul's own work was not completed yet. Besides the incidental preaching he was able to do as a prisoner in Caesarea, Malta and Rome itself, he planned to go to Spain, Rom 15:23, 28, and may well have realized his project, as later evidence suggests (1 Clem. 5 and *Frag. Murat.* 38–9). He certainly preached in Crete and provided for further developments there, Tit 1:5. No doubt eastern Syria had been evangelized already and perhaps Alexandria and Cyrene. At least centres had been established along most of the Mediterranean littoral before Paul's death, an achievement which speaks highly not only for the devotion of the first missionaries, but for the authenticity and vitality of the religion which they taught.

Conversion to Christianity—If we know something of the geographical spread of Christianity, we have little to enable us to estimate the number of its adherents, after the first days. That it was notable in the various cities can be estimated by the opposition aroused. At Philippi: 'These men are convulsing our city', Ac 16:20; at Thessalonica: they 'have turned the world upside down', 17:6 WV; at Ephesus: 'This Paul, by persuasion, hath drawn away a great multitude, not only of Ephesus, but almost of all Asia', so that there was a great riot, instigated by the silversmiths, whose craft of making models of Diana's temple was 'in danger to be set at nought', Ac 19:24–27; and in Rome the leading Jews, though obviously unacquainted with the doctrines of 'this sect', could at least report that it was 'everywhere decried', Ac 28:22 KNT. Far more important are the questions: why did people become Christians at all, and what did their conversion mean to them?

Though it is true that every conversion is ultimately something quite personal, and the interplay of grace and circumstances will vary in almost every case, some general indications can be given of the motives of the early converts, whether Jews or Gentiles; of the circumstances which favoured their believing, and of those which formed obstacles to be overcome. Of course, those who lived in Palestine and especially in Jerusalem, and who had thus come under the direct influence of our Lord himself, had special motives not offered to the rest of the world. They had been brought up against the facts in a way that made it impossible to evade them. If the earnestness of the new disciples is patent, one senses the bad faith of those most opposed to them, Ac 4:3, 14–22; 5:17–18, 24, 26, 33, 40; 6:11–14; 7:54, 57–58; 8:1, 3 (*cf.* 9:5)—also Lk 2:34 (*cf.* P. Gaechter, *The Hatred of the House of Annas*, in Theological Studies VIII [1947] 3–34). One cannot therefore reduce the motives of the converts, here or elsewhere, merely to there being 'something in the Christian message which *appealed* to them ' : essentially it proclaimed facts which might or might not appeal, but in face of which each must decide what his own attitude should be. Indeed, their objective reality was of a kind that demanded not merely the cold recognition of their truth, but a complete re-orientation of life in response to them, and called therefore for immediate action.

Consequently, any argumentation which the Apostles might use, any miraculous sign which attended their preaching, was no more than paving the way to that essential personal response, not so much to the Apostles' appeal, as to the personal appeal of Christ, manifested in his life, death and resurrection, whereby God was reconciling mankind to himself, 2 Cor 5:19, etc. These were the objective facts to which the Apostles testified : it rested with their hearers to humble themselves beneath the mighty hand of God, that he might exalt them in his own good time ; casting all their care upon him, for he had care of them ; *cf.* 1 Pet 5:6-7. It meant a recognition and a personal acceptance of Christ and of all his intentions and purposes, a love for him which took the exigencies of his love for granted, and therefore the repudiation of their sinful past as a necessary preliminary. It was all this which the Apostles, following our Lord's teaching, meant when they spoke of Faith—of believing—the faith that finds its expression in love, Gal 5:6 KNT ; *cf.* BEJC, ch 10. It was of such Faith that our Lord had said : ' This is eternal life : that they may know thee, the only true God, and Jesus Christ, whom thou hast sent ', Jn 17:3 ; and St Paul : ' It is only through the Holy Spirit that anyone can say, Jesus is the Lord ', 1 Cor 12:3 KNT.

The Mission in Palestine—It was some such unanalysed process by which the 3,000 Jews were converted on the day of Pentecost. As was suggested above, § 631c, the crowds addressed that day received the full impact of the divine manifestation. The minds of most had already been prepared by our Lord's preaching, and by their own friendly, hostile, or vacillating attitude towards him. And now, they saw these men who had been so cowed since the crucifixion, boldly asserting his innocence and their loyalty to him, challenging thereby the authority of the Jewish leaders who had condemned him. These ' simple men, without learning ', Ac 4:13 KNT, were handling the Scriptures with confidence, and showing them that this Jesus, whom *they* had crucified, had been raised by God from the dead according to what had been prophesied of the Messias. And that this was no mere fanaticism on their part, but a divinely inspired fervour, was clear from the fact that they spoke in the various languages of their hearers—a sign from God that all should hear them. These Jews then, recalling Jesus's patent goodness, his preaching, his kindly miracles on behalf of the sick and the afflicted, contrasting his modest uprightness with the shameless insincerity of the charges made against him, and above all conscious of their own share, great or small, in the responsibility for his cruel death—no wonder that their consciences were stung, and that they turned to Peter and his fellow-Apostles and asked them what they should do. ' Repent, Peter said to them, and be baptized, everyone of you, in the name of Jesus Christ, to have your sins forgiven ; then you will receive the gift of the Holy Spirit ', Ac 2:37-38 KNT.

It is clear that, so far as rested with the Apostles and their future helpers, it was the presentation of Christ's life, death and resurrection as the long-awaited **fulfilment of the ancient prophecies,** which was to be their most cogent argument with the Jews. But as the Jewish expectation had been for a ' redemption ' and a ' kingdom ' of a very different sort, the Holy Spirit came to the assistance of the Apostles with **miracles** of many kinds to bear witness to the divine favour which their ministry enjoyed ; *cf.* Heb 2:3-4. There was the healing of the cripple at the Beautiful Gate, Ac 3 ; *cf.* 4:30 ; and there were the many miracles wrought by the hands of the Apostles, so that men hurried out their sick into the streets that Peter's mere shadow

might fall across them and cure them, and sick and **632e** possessed were even carried in from the neighbouring town to be healed, Ac 5:12-16. All these happenings would be referred to, later, in confirmation of their own witness to Christ's life and resurrection, and would in their turn serve as ' motive ' for men's turning wholeheartedly to Christ. Nor did such miracles stop there. A few of those recorded in the Acts may be recalled here : the deliverance of the Apostles from prison, 5:19-25, as also that of Peter alone later, 12:6-11 ; the great wonders and signs of Stephen, 6:8, and his ecstatic vision of ' the heavens opened and the Son of man standing on the right hand of God ', which so exasperated his judges and earned for him the first martyr's crown, 7:55 ff. ; Philip's cures in Samaria of the possessed, the paralytic and the lame, and the manifestations there of the Holy Spirit at the prayer of Peter and John—important as an offset to the ' spiritualism ' of Simon the magician, 8:6-13, 14 ff. (*cf.* 10:44-48 ; 19:6) ; at Lydda, St Peter's cure of Aeneas the paralytic, and at Joppe, his raising of the pious Tabitha to life, 9:32-41—primarily simple acts of kindness, it would seem, yet potent on the minds of the inhabitants, 9:42.

One must not belittle the importance of these ' signs **f** and wonders ', but equally one must not exaggerate the part which they played in the work of conversion, any more than we should exaggerate that of our Lord's own miracles, *cf.* Jn 4:48 ; 20:29 ; also Mk 13:22 ; Apoc 13:13-14 and BEJC, 457-62. Many as they appear when thus collected together, they were in fact only occasional—spread over a considerable time and space—in comparison with the constant preaching of the Apostles, so that many of their converts will never have actually seen a miracle—and it is always easier to evade a report than to repudiate a personal experience. Consequently, it was chiefly the preaching itself of the word, and the unconscious example of the Apostles and their disciples in their life together (*cf.* §§ 636-7) which, with the grace of the Holy Spirit, turned the hearts of their hearers to Christ, and made Christians of Jews and Gentiles alike (Mt 7:15-20 ; 12:33-37 ; and Ac 20:18-21, 31-35 ; and *passim* in St Paul).

The Mission in Gentile Lands—Our Lord's last words **633a** had set the programme : ' You shall be witnesses unto me in Jerusalem, and in all Judaea and Samaria, and even to the uttermost parts of the earth ', Ac 1:8. They had not looked beyond the immediate task before them, nor indeed had he told them either *when* they should begin to ' make disciples of all the nations ', Mt 28:19 WV, nor on *what conditions* the Gentiles should be admitted into the Church. They could wait on events, relying on the guidance of the Holy Spirit. It was only after some ten years that the visions and other signs, attending the conversion of Cornelius, intimated to Peter, and through him to the mother Church of Jerusalem, that **Gentiles might be received without circumcision** and the other peculiarly Jewish practices, Ac 10-11:18 ; and it was another ten years—after the first successes at Antioch and after Paul's first mission to Cyprus and the cities of Galatia—that this was publicly recognized as a general principle, Ac 15.

The importance of this recognition for the Gentile **b** mission cannot be exaggerated. Hitherto it had been taken for granted that the Jewish religious customs should be preserved except where they had been explicitly modified by our Lord, and that a Gentile would have to adopt them if he came to believe in Christ. And as hitherto many devout ' God-fearing men ' (*cf.* 13:16 etc.) had come to believe in the God of the Jews and in his promises, but had been deterred from full participation by the requirement of circumcision and of their many taboos, so now they will at first have listened wistfully to the announcement of the Messias' actual coming and still have felt unequal to the sacrifice. To such as these the door was now opened, and they had a dauntless champion in Paul, who would brook no attempt on what he called the liberty which

633b they enjoyed in Jesus Christ, Gal 2:4 KNT. He indignantly rejected the accusation that he was making things too easy for them, and merely courting the goodwill of men, 1:10 ; there was a principle at stake, the nature of which had, at least now, been made patent to all. It affected the presentation of Christianity to the Jews themselves. For St Paul was the first who, to the argument that the prophecies had been fulfilled in Jesus, added the further fact that ' in him everyone that believeth is justified *from all those things from which ye could not be justified by the Law of Moses* ', Ac 13:38 WV. Implicit as it had been before, the radical inefficacy of the Law now took a central position in the apostolic witness to Christ, as they proclaimed to the Jews the absolute necessity of his grace.

c If this had a place in the message to the Gentiles too, it was only a subordinate one of explanation, when they were being introduced to the Scriptures and to the historic background of Jesus, and when the relationship of Christianity to Judaism was explained to them. What was inevitably central was the Person of **Jesus Christ,** depicted above all as **crucified,** and thereafter raised from the dead and one day to return to judge the deeds of men, Gal 3:1 ; 6:14 ; 1 Cor 1:23 ; 2:2 ; Ac 17:31 ; Rom 2:12–16 ; 14:9–12 ; *cf.* 2 Cor 5:10 ; 2 Tim 4:1, etc. At Athens, St Paul approached his subject by an appeal to the spirituality and transcendence of God, Ac 17:22–27 ; *cf.* 14:15–17, and to memories of poetical intuitions of God : ' In him we live and move and have our being '—' for we are also his offspring ', Ac 17:28 ; but his poor success there led him to concentrate on the great central message of salvation through the historic deeds of Christ ; discarding the wisdom of the world for the foolishness and the weakness of God, 1 Cor 1:17–25 ; 2:1–5.

d As in the Palestinian days, so now, far afield, the preaching was supported by occasional **miracles,** Ac 13:8–12 ; 14:8–18 ; 14:19–20 ; 16:16–34 ; 19:11–20 ; 28:3–6, *cf.* Mk 16:18 ; Ac 28:8–10. But it is clear enough that neither Paul nor the others relied on such interventions. (At Corinth, where he spent 18 successful months, no miraculous cures are recorded.) He relied on **his own example of charity and hard manual work** to supplement the spoken word : he would at times appeal to these later (*e.g.* 1 Thess 1:5–6 ; 2:1–12 ; 1 Cor 4:1–4, 9 ; 11:1), and if he wanted to invoke God's intervention, he always had the story to tell of his own conversion : Ac 9 ; 22 ; 26, and often referred to it in his epistles, from Gal 1:13–16 to 1 Tim 1:12–17. So much, then, we may glean of the character of the first impact of Christianity on the Jewish and Gentile minds of the time. Its force can be estimated only against the background provided by three of the preceding articles : The History of Israel, 130 B.C.–A.D. 70, §§ 69 ff. ; The Jewish World in NT Times, §§ 584 ff. ; The Pagan World in NT Times, §§ 597 ff.

e **The obstacles** which it had to overcome were many and various. **The Jews** not only had to spiritualize their ideas of the Messianic Kingdom, but to acknowledge a *suffering* Messias, 1 Cor 1:23 ; *cf.* § 642*g–j.* (One way in which this ' stumbling-block ' may have been removed has recently been suggested in terms, however, perhaps too exclusive. ' Only upon the interpretation of that judicial murder on Calvary as the *deliberate offering of the Messianic Sacrifice by the Messianic High-priest* was any proclamation of Jesus as Messiah by or to Jews *possible* at all ', *Gregory Dix in The Apostolic Ministry,* ed. K. E. Kirk [1946] 247–8.) Besides this scandal of the cross, their fierce national and cultural isolationism soon felt a like scandal at the admission of Gentiles on an equality with themselves—and, in the Gentile cities, at the speedy predominance of the Gentile element, with its consequent depreciation of ' the custom of our fathers ', *cf.* Ac 21:21 ; 28:17.

f But, quite obviously, the **obstacles to conversion** were even more numerous **among the Gentiles.** Idolatry, in all its forms, public and private, filled the air they breathed ; *cf.* Rom 1:23. State occasions, holidays,

military life, celebrations of all kinds were unthinkable without their appropriate acts of worship and sacrifice, *cf.* 1 Cor 8 ; 10:14–11:1 and § 600*h.* To the great gods of the Greco-Roman pantheon were now being added, even in the West, the divinities of the imperial house, so that observance of the State religion became more than ever identified with civic loyalty. This may have had a genuine hold on the masses, but even those who had little respect for the gods were not necessarily any nearer to Christianity. On the contrary. The general religious scepticism of the educated classes, the widespread pessimism and escapism of the times, the licentiousness, whether cloaked in religious respectability or naked and unashamed, the cruelty and rapacity—characteristics only rarely mitigated by some nobler or gentler qualities to be found in the best Roman and Hellenist types—all these (*cf.* Rom 1:26–32) militated against serious attention being paid to the outpourings of a Levantine babbler, who made tents for a living. Moreover, no sooner had he secured a group of adherents, than he was liable to assault from interested parties, who might raise the cry that these Jews were ' recommending customs which it is impossible for us, as Roman citizens, to admit or to observe ', Ac 16:21 KNT, or even that ' all these folk defy the edicts of Caesar ; they say that there is another king, one Jesus ', Ac 17:7.

This accusation of **political ambitions,** echoing the accusation made during the Passion, was natural and spontaneous in a pre-Christian atmosphere, when it was taken for granted that the omni-competent State controlled, and in great part initiated, all religious manifestations. Christ's disjunction of the things that were God's from those that were Caesar's—an unparalleled innovation at the time (*cf.* J. Lecler, *L'Eglise et la Souveraineté de l'Etat* [1946], esp. 18–22)— was blackest heresy and rebellion ; it was a captious distinction, subversive of the State. How great was this obstacle, not merely as an inflammatory slogan, but as setting the whole machinery of State power in motion against the Christians, the next 250 years were to show. Already in NT times, when emphasis on the responsibility of Rome for the judicial murder of Christ could scarcely be avoided (*cf.* *S. Liberty, ' The Importance of Pontius Pilate in Creed and Gospel ', JTS 45 [1944] 38–45), the Apostles were at pains to clarify the Christian attitude and to show not only that the Christians were loyal subjects of Caesar, but that the Roman officials, once they had understood their case, had treated them so far with toleration, and indeed with friendliness, Rom 13:1–8 ; 1 Tim 2:1–4 ; Tit 3:1 ; 1 Pet 2:13–17 (*cf.* Prat, II, 321–6 [1927 ed.]. Thus Ac, probably intended, in part at least, as an historical apologia for Paul as he awaited his trial in Rome, conveys a very favourable impression of the Roman officials with whom he had come in contact). The optimism which this implied persisted *e.g.* in Clement's prayer for the ruling powers—in spite of Nero and Domitian—and even later (*cf.* 1 Clem 61). On the other hand, the fearsome descriptions of the almost contemporary Apoc, were perhaps needed to remind the faithful that State persecution had been foretold by our Lord, Mt 10:18–20 ; Lk 12:11–12 ; 21:12–15 ; *cf.* Jn 15:18–20 ; 16:20–22, 33 ; and § 660*s–u.*

Telling against the acceptance of Christianity in a more personal way, were those half-religious, half-family or social **customs** which were interwoven with everyday life, and to which the more conservative spirits were piously attached. To become a Christian was to ostracize oneself in one's own home or set. As to the **Mystery Religions** (§§ 599*a–d,* 645*d*) and the multitude of small semi-religious **guilds** (in some of which national and even class distinctions were done away with), they expressed and responded to the gathering need of something more personal in religion than the official cults had ever provided. The Mysteries, in general, encouraged the sense of need for purification, promised a personal immortality and made use of secret symbolic rites and ' dramatic ' representations, which may well have made a deep impression at the time of initiation (*cf.* L. de Grandmaison, S.J., *Jésus-Christ* [Eng. trans. 1934] III, 349–72 ; 319–46, etc.). The small religious guilds will have encouraged a fraternal atmosphere among their members and revealed to them the unexpected pleasure of comradeship across the barriers maintained in ordinary life. Both types can be seen as providential preparations for Christianity, with its doctrines of sin, redemption and immortality, its sacraments and the ' comprehensiveness ' of its membership—its cohesion through charity. On the other hand, the secrecy and the emotionalism on which they were based, and the fact that, up to a point, they *did* satisfy a need hitherto unprovided for, will have so attached their members to them, that their minds were closed to further religious search : their ' religious experience ' would be proof even against a religion which actually met their deepest, if unappreciated, needs to the full. Those who did come from the Mystery Religions to Christianity may appear to us to have found in them a preparation for their new faith ; while still under their spell, they did not feel it so. But the crucial obstacle was that, while all these ' mysteries ' and guilds were compatible with the official and in fact with any other kind of religion (§ 600a), Christianity was all-inclusive, allowing no religious side-lines for the adventurous individualist. It demanded a renunciation never insisted on before.

Such, in brief, were some of the chief influences which we can discern at work during the first thirty years, facilitating or impeding the acceptance of Christianity. The success actually achieved by the Apostles' preaching depended less on the exterior conditions of the time than on **the plain truth of the ' good news '**, the Gospel, which they preached, *i.e.* the life and death of Christ with all its cosmic implications. It was not the beauty and sublimity of a moral ideal which converted men ; it was the revelation of God's love, made concrete for us on the cross and authenticated by the resurrection, which was recognized to be *true*, and which therefore challenged them to respond becomingly. It was no philosophical system that had been devised by men (*cf.* 1 Cor 1:18 ff. ; Justin, *Apol. I*, 14, 5) ; it was no myth which by its symbolism put beautiful thoughts into the minds of the initiates ; it was historical facts, playing out a divine drama in the very midst of mankind and directed towards their hearts, which ultimately motivated the conversion of such numbers of Jews and Gentiles of every type, and were at the root of the subsequent growth and persistence of the Christian Church.

The Individual—Before asking *what* were the doctrines which so inspired the early Christians, *cf.* §§ 640–54, it is necessary to consider *in what setting* they were learnt. Otherwise it might be thought that the essence of Christianity consisted in believing certain ' doctrines ', and that the Church came into being by the subsequent coming together of those who were so like-minded, *cf.* § 655a. Such an individualist conception of Christianity would overlook the concrete reality of the setting in which the early Christians found themselves from the first. In fact, to try to distinguish between what Christianity meant to the new converts as individuals, and what it meant to them as members of a body, is not so easy as one might expect. The response to the first preaching, the compunction, the request for Baptism and the open witnessing to Christ made when receiving it, these were all certainly the individual's own acts, but they were stimulated by the preacher or by the example of men already Christian. In the very act of reception, he was received into the body of the faithful, and even his most personal actions, his private prayer, his self-denial or all those things ' done in secret ' according to our Lord's commands, Mt 6:3–4, 6, 18 ; *cf.* 1 Cor 14:28 ; 1 Pet 3:4, became indissolubly connected with the whole life of the Christian community. Ever since Pentecost, it was not a question of individuals, who had come to believe in Christ, banding themselves together so as to form a ' Church ' ;

it was a question of the Church, which had then come **634a** into being, gathering into her already existing life new members who were thus admitted to share in it, (*cf.* *O. Cullmann, ' Le Baptême—agrégation au Corps du Christ ', in *Dieu vivant*, 11, 45–66 ; *cf.* § 650m).

But if the distinction between the ' individual ' and the ' community ' is in part an artificial one, so that neither can be adequately treated without the other, it remains true that the acceptance of the ' good news ', the self-commitment, and the obligations undertaken were intensely personal—as was indeed, thereafter, the sharing in the life of the community itself. A short outline of the personal response of the individual to the appeal of Christ's personality and work at the very beginnings, will prepare for the consideration of the individual within the community, §§ 635–9 ; *cf.* §§ 655–60.

The first Christians, being Jews by race and up- **b** bringing, were naturally in the first place seized by the realization that Jesus of Nazareth was **their Messias,** *the* Christ, after all. The tension of expectation, which for so many centuries had supported and yet tried them by its very length, was suddenly resolved, and a flood of joy filled their hearts. What they knew of his life, his goodness and his miracles, had prepared the way for the recognition of the truth ; now, the manifestations of Pentecost and the witness borne by his closest disciples to his resurrection and ascension, removed all hesitations—reversed, all the more completely, their possibly adverse estimate of him which his humiliations and crucifixion had provoked. As he had conquered death, so now was he sitting at the right hand of God, and would return on the clouds of heaven for the judgement of the whole world. Such was the first κήρυγμα, the first apostolic preaching (*cf.* *C. H. Dodd, *The Apostolic Preaching*, 1936) in its briefest outlines, but in what a new light did Jesus's life appear now, and what a transformation did their understanding of the Sacred Books undergo ! The chaotic, contradictory-seeming prophecies and types of the Messias found their unified realization in him : what had been taken literally was now seen to be fulfilled in a higher, spiritual way ; what had been overlooked—the suffering servant, for instance —was now seen to be central, Is 42:1–4 and Mt 12:16 ff. ; Is 61:1 and Ac 4:27 : and many things which had seemed to be but accidental details in their history, became types of realities ' fulfilled ' in him. This mutual illumination of the life of Jesus and their memories of the past, not only acted as a guarantee to them of the reality of his Messiahship, but intensified their certitude of God's loving care of his Chosen Race throughout its history, of which now they were participating in the undreamt-of culmination. Truly could they now appreciate all that he had told them of ' their Father who was in heaven ', *e.g.* Mt 6 ; 7:7–11. The first Gentiles to become Christian had, themselves, **c** much of the Jewish background ; even the sheer pagans who, very soon, began to come, were introduced to that background, so that without the travail which the Jew must go through, the Gentile too could come to appreciate the economy of the divine condescension and his own inclusion in the new non-racial ' Chosen People '. With their distinct antecedents, both faced the same Jesus who ' went about doing good ', Ac 10:38, the same divine intrusion in history.

Repentance for the past, absolute faith and confidence **d** for the future formed the natural response evoked by this divine initiative. Let the Apostles and his other close friends tell them more of him, tell them what to do. And so they learned and practised. Baptism first, then the ' breaking of the bread ' which he had told them to do ' in commemoration of him '. Hereby they became ' partakers of the body of the Lord ', yielding themselves to his now hidden influence to make them ' put on his mind ', ' put *him* on ', so that they too might live as the sons of God, which they had become by Baptism. They must leave their old life, with its sins and concupiscences and darkness, and come into the light shining upon them from the face of Christ, led

634d by the Spirit in fulfilling all things whatsoever he had commanded. Their new life opened up vistas of unbounded possibilities : they could, and must, **grow in the knowledge of Christ**, cf. Eph 4:12–16 ; Phil 1:9–11. If to all had been preached ' a Christ crucified ', the implications, the hidden depths of this were not to be appreciated in a day. If all had undergone a radical, divinely wrought transformation, if to all could be rightly attributed the title of ' saints ', that gave to each new capabilities and responsibilities. Each, in his own measure, must ' live up to ' what had been done for him, and ' realize ' his own capacities to the full.

e Each had received an earnest of what he might expect, each was encouraged by the fact that Christ ' was offered because it was his own will ', that ' he was wounded for our iniquities . . . by his bruises we are healed ', and that he had ' given his life a redemption for many ', Is 53:7, 5 ; Mt 20:28. It was the **love** of him and the **hope** that he inspired, which roused them to follow his example along the narrow way, as also his assurances that there would be much treasure laid up for them in heaven, Mt 10:38 ; 16:24 ; 7:13–14 ; 4:12 ; 6:20 ; 19:21 ; cf. Lk 10:20. Not at once would they analyse out all the elements of their new life in Christ : all they felt was that it sprang from what they *knew* of him, what he had shown himself to be despite all appearances to the contrary, and for that reason they could compendiously sum up their response to him in the one word, **Faith** in him. Faith could not but ' work by charity ', Gal 5:6, and if the works of the Law were impotent to achieve justification, Rom 3:19 etc., Faith understood in that pregnant sense, could do so, and thereafter pursue *its own* law, Rom 3:27 ; 8:2, 7 etc. (cf. Prat, I, 172–4; 180–1; II, 311–21), accomplishing its own works, since faith if it have not works is dead in itself (cf. Jas 2:14–26 ; §§ 643*i–k*, 647*h–n*, 648*l–n*).

II THE COMMUNITY OF THE FAITHFUL

635a This personal, individual life, though based on the fuller understanding of the first Commandment of the Law which our Lord had revealed both in his own actions and in his teaching, is no more than an abstraction when considered apart from the realities of concrete life, and cannot itself be fully realized apart from the second ' which is like unto the first ' : ' Thou shalt love thy neighbour as thyself ', Mt 22:36–39. Indeed, not merely historically, but in the very nature of things, to follow Christ meant joining others who were *already* following him, and it therefore involved entering into a whole system of relationships already established among them. The new disciple, who joined the Christians of his town or city, found himself received into a company of men and women united not only by their common faith and worship, but also by a certain general goodwill, an interest in one another's good, Phil 2:4, a mutual helpfulness in which he was now privileged to share. As he found himself receiving much from them, so was he encouraged in his turn to give, 1 Pet 4:8–11 : to enter into this new life where the principle, if not always the practice, was to look not to their own ends, but to those of Jesus Christ, cf. Phil 2:21. But despite his new realization of the Father's love revealed in Christ, despite his new love for Christ and his efforts to put on that mind which was his, and despite the promptings and help of the Holy Spirit which he could not deny, he found the ' old man ' strong within him still, and mutual criticism, backbiting, if not open disputes, 1 Cor 1:11 etc. ; 2 Cor 12:20 ; 1 Pet 2:1 (cf. Jas 4)—to mention only less grievous failings—still came easily or were easily joined in. Only by seeing the day-to-day life of his immediate Christian surroundings in a wider setting, would he be enabled to hold his own against that life of the flesh, that spirit of the world on which he had thought to turn his back for good. This was provided by the bold teaching which completed what he knew of his union

with God through Christ in the Holy Spirit, and which laid down for all the principle of unity in charity, the positive practice of ' peace ' among themselves. Out of the fact that he now was living by the life of Christ rather than by his own unaided powers, came the natural corollary that his fellow-Christians were living by that same life too, that he and they were *all* ' in Christ '.

The reality of this, itself as mysterious and elusive to **b** the mind of the natural man (ψυχικός) as was the reality of his personal union with Christ, was inculcated by a variety of metaphors. None of these, by itself alone, quite covered the whole truth, and they only combined up to a point, but between them they provided a vast field for meditation and gratitude and joy, and at the same time an incentive to action which in its turn deepened the realization of the mystery. Unity based on charity was meant to exist, and indeed already existed, radically, not only among the Christians he knew but among all Christians wherever they might be. For all were ' in Christ ' : they formed the living body of Christ ; each being united to him by his Spirit, they were all united to one another as **members of his body,** he being at once their Head and continuing to live his life in and through them too. If each personally was to grow into the likeness of him who was the image of the invisible God, Col 1:15, so was each to grow within his body, subservient to and also subserving the good of the whole. That process was going on all the time, and must go on ; purification, mortification of the flesh (if the spirit were not to be done to death by its warring members), and in all activities an ever greater docility to the indwelling of the Spirit, according to the capabilities of each and to the needs of the other members ; a process never done with, for its term must be the re-presentation of Christ in the perfection of order prevailing among his members—a maturity measured by the flawless perfection of Christ himself, cf. Eph 4:13. (The crystallization of the mystery in the form : ' the body *of Christ* ' was due to St Paul. For a close discussion of its genesis and purport cf. L. Malevez, S.J., ' L'Eglise, corps du Christ ' in *Science Religieuse* [war-time RSR 1944] 27–94.)

The same reality was represented in two other **c** metaphors both closely allied to the first, and each mixing unawares with it : that of **a building**—and in particular a sanctuary like that of the Holy of Holies— and that of the bride of Christ. The conjunction of the ideas of the Body of Christ and of a sacred building goes back, it seems, to Christ himself. It would have been difficult to guess what really underlay the garbled saying of Jesus which the false witnesses attributed to him, Mt 26:61 ; Mk 14:58 ; but St John gives us both his words and their significance : ' Destroy this *sanctuary* and in three days I will raise it up ', Jn 2:19— ' He spoke of the *sanctuary* of his body ', 2:21 (cf. A. M. Dubarle, O.P., ' Le Signe du Temple ' [Jn 2, 19], RB 48 [1939] 21–44).

The memory of these words, 2:22, enabled the first Christians to add fresh developments to their understanding of the sacred ties that bound them to one another—along with and beyond those provided by the idea of their being the members of the body of Christ. The Spirit coming with love-streams into their hearts, Rom 5:5 ; Gal 4:6, already suggested that they were, each of them, a sanctuary of the Holy Spirit, 1 Cor 3:16–17 ; 2 Cor 6:16–18 (cf. 1 Cor 6:19, of their own bodies) ; now they could see themselves as living stones being shaped to fit into one another to build up and adorn a new *sanctuary* (ναός, not ἱερόν)—and all the numerous associations of the word would give to Jew and Gentile alike a fresh appreciation of the sacred character of their mutual relations already implied, under another aspect, by the idea of their being the Body of Christ (cf. Eph 2:14–22 : Jew and Gentile reconciled in the flesh of Christ—making one body— built together upon and in Christ to form a holy sanctuary, the dwelling of God ; and especially 1 Pet 2:5, in its context). Thus in their common development the Christians could see Christ at work rebuilding the sanctuary of his Body (in Jn 2:19 and Rom 4:25 the same word [ἐγείρω] is used of raising up the sanctuary and of Christ's rising [from the dead] for our justification—δικαίωσιν *not* δικαιοσύνην) ; and as they knew his life to be in them, they must co-operate with him in the building. The idea became so familiar for expressing all the influence for good which they might have on one another, that the word ' building ' by itself could stand for all—a use which survives with a now weakened sense in the word ' edifying '. Some of the ways in which the idea was woven into the texture of their minds will appear below ; (*cf.* Prat, I, 302–7, § 660).

The danger of a sort of ' Pan-Christism ' following from their being the ' members of Christ ' was probably remote enough : it was in fact eliminated by the insistence that Christ was the *Head* of the Body, and that among the stones which made up the sanctuary, he was the one *which crowned the summit.* (*Cf.* KTW I, 792–3, ἀκρογωνιαῖος, and especially PEQ July–Oct 1946, 103–15, Edwin E. Lebas, ' Was the Corner-Stone of Scripture a Pyramidion ? ' for the rich implications of the true meaning). This combination of identity and difference is perhaps most strongly brought out in the ' **Bride of Christ** ' metaphor (*cf.* Is 62:5 ; Os 2:19–20, and Malevez, 81 [§ 635*b*]). In the OT, the marriage-idea was not uncommon to express the relation between God and his chosen people, but it was practically confined to the correlative ideas of God being a jealous God and of Israel being either faithful or adulterous. That the Christians constituted the Body of which Christ was the Head, suggested a richer development of thought which left the old in the background (however *cf.* 2 Cor 11:2–3) ; the wife was subject to her husband as to her ' head ', 1 Cor 11:3 ; Eph 5:23, and yet he looked upon her as ' bone of his bones and flesh of his flesh ', Gen 2:23, the two being ' in one flesh ', *ib.* 24 ; so too while the Christians as a whole were subject to Christ as to their Head, they were made to realize that as ' members of his body, of his flesh and of his bones ', they were the object of his special love and self-sacrifice in the task of their purification by him, *cf.* Eph 5:22–32.

These highly spiritual conceptions—to which should be added the relation of the vine to the branches (if recorded only by St John, Jn 15:1 ff., not for that reason remembered by him alone)—were not relegated to the sphere of speculation, but were made to enter into their practical daily lives. No doubt their application to Jewish life alone or to pagan life alone would in either case have meant a revolution of outlook and practice : but besides they challenged the historic antagonism which divided the Jewish world from the Gentiles. Racial exclusiveness, the consciousness of a cultural tradition of divine origin, higher moral standards—all tended to make the Jew look upon the non-Jews as ' sinners ' *par excellence, cf.* Gal 2:15 ; while the Greco-Roman world of the time looked on the Jews as at best a nuisance for their narrowness, and at worst the scum of the earth. Both had now to learn to live together ' in Christ ', for Christ had **broken down the barrier** that separated them, replaced their age-long antagonism by his peace, uniting them to God by his Blood on the Cross, and so of the two creating a new man by their reconciliation in his one Body, Eph 2:13–16. They must face the world together as one man : the world before knew ' the Jew ' ; let it now know ' the Christian '.

The importance of this Christian unity manifests itself in the very language of the NT. A study of the uses of the word ' Communion ' will show how active was the idea from the very first and how deeply rooted it became wherever the Church established itself.

Communion manifold—Those entering the Pentecostal community found themselves sharing a **life in common :** ' They were persevering in the doctrine of the Apostles and in the *communion : the breaking of the bread and the prayers.* . . . All they that believed were together

and had all things common ', Ac 2:42, 44. On the day **636a** which recalled the giving of the Old Law the Holy Spirit had taught them the meaning of Christ's new commandment ' that you love one another as I have loved you ', Jn 15:12. As St Paul would say : ' The love of God has been poured out in our hearts by the Holy Spirit which we have received ', Rom 5:5, KNT (ἐκχέω as in Ac 2:17 ; 33*a* ; Tit 3:6 ; *cf.* Jl 2:28). In descriptions of the first congregation their world ' unanimous ' constantly recurs, Ac 1:14 ; 2:46 ; 4:24 ; 5:12 : 15:25 ; *cf.* MMV, ὁμοθυμαδόν. From interior union of heart and soul, 4:32, flowed exterior union : they lived ' all together ' (ἐπὶ τὸ αὐτὸ, 2:44, 47) exemplifying and fulfilling that perfection in unity for which their Lord had died and prayed, Jn 11:52 ; 17:23 ; 1 Jn 5:8 ; *cf.* DBV(S), *Eglise*, 600–1. He had asked for it ' that the world may believe that thou hast sent me ', Jn 17:21, 23, and the sight of this united congregation, living in the manner of his disciples a common life of faith, prayer, sacrifice, praise, love and practical charity under the direction of the Apostles, reinforced the witness of the latters' preaching and miracles so as to win ' *goodwill with all the people* ', the Lord adding converts daily ' *to the same unity* ', Ac 2:47 ; *cf.* 5:13*b* ; Pet 2:12 ; 3:16.

The words ' communion ' (κοινωνία), ' companion ' **b** (κοινωνός), the verb ' to have communion in ' or ' partake of one undivided thing ' (κοινωνέω) and its practical synonym ' share with those who also have their shares ' (μετέχω with its derivatives ; *cf.* Lk 5:7, 10 ; 2 Cor 6:14 ; Heb 2:14 ; MMV, 350, 351, 405, 406 : KTW, III, 789–810 and esp. the profound study by *L. S. Thornton, The Common Life in the Body of Christ*) are rendered in our versions by fellowship, communion, communication, participation, partners, sharers, partakers, etc. This variation fits the shades of meaning in the contexts, but the original repetition of the words showed how that meaning expanded with the Christian life. We can trace the expansion from the moment when Peter, with James and John, his ' *sharers in common* ' in the fishing business leave all things to follow the call of Jesus, Lk 5:7, 10, to when Peter's Second Epistle tells Christians that in accordance with the promises of him who has called us we have become ' *sharers in common* ' in the divine nature, 2 Pet 1:3, 4 ; *cf.* Chaine, *Les Epîtres catholiques*, 40–3. For everything belonged to those who were Christ's : Paul, Peter, the world, life, death, things present and things to come, 1 Cor 3:22, 23.

The ' **Communion** ' of the Christians was therefore **c** far deeper than the ' communism ' of goods in some philosophic brotherhood. ' It was the sharing of a common life whose source was in God ', Thornton, 6. It was a communion, sharing with Christ and one another in everything divine and human. Communion of life with Christ is ' the master idea, one might almost say the unique idea ' of the first Epistle to the Corinthians, who had been ' called through God into the *communion* of his Son ', 1 Cor 1:9 (*cf.* Allo, *Sec. ép. aux Cor.*, 343). Therein was ' communion in the Gospel ', Phil 1:5 (*cf.* 1 Cor 9:23) ; ' communion of spirit,' Phil 2:1 ; (*cf.* Heb 6:4) ; ' communion of faith ', Phm **6** (*cf.* Tit 1:4 ; Rom 1:12) ; ' communion of the sufferings of Christ ', Phil 3:10 ; 1 Pet 4:13 (*cf.* 2 Cor 1:7). In common they shared Christ himself, Heb 3:14, and his promise, Eph 3:6, grace, Phil 1: 7 (*cf.* 1 Cor 10:30), their heavenly vocation, Heb 3:1, salvation, Jude 3, their training in tribulation, Heb 12:8 ; Apoc 1:9, each other's sufferings, trials and consolations, 2 Cor 1:7 ; Phil 4:14 : Heb 10:33, their own apostle, Phm 17, his apostolic work, 2 Cor 8:23, and their future glory, 1 Pet 5:1. There was a corresponding communion in sin which throws light on this by contrast, Mt 23:30 ; Eph 5:5–11 ; 1 Tim 5:22 ; 2 Jn 11 ; Apoc 18:4. In this Christians could not share : ' For what *share* hath justice with *licence*, and what *communion* hath light with darkness ', 2 Cor 6:14 : ' if we say that we have *communion* with him and walk in darkness, we lie . . . but if we walk in the light as he is in the light, we have *communion* with one another ', 1 Jn 1:6, 7.

By communion with those sent by Christ they **d**

636d entered **communion with the Divine Persons** themselves: 'What we have seen and heard', affirms St John, his gaze rising to Christ as principle of life in his eternal pre-existence and his Incarnation, 'we declare unto you, that you also may have *communion* with us, and our *communion* may be with the Father and his Son Jesus Christ', 1 Jn 1:3. Thus Christ's prayer is fulfilled : 'that they may be one in us', Jn 17:21 ; *cf.* 1 Jn 5:20. And since Christ is in us through his Spirit whom he imparts to us, Rom 8:9, 10, those who share in Christ, Heb 3:14, share in the Holy Spirit, 6:4. Thus St Paul desires for the Corinthians that 'the grace of the Lord Jesus Christ and the charity of God and the *communion of the Holy Spirit* be with you all', 2 Cor 13:13.

e Returning now to the primitive community, we find that the spiritual communion was the source of the temporal one : 'The multitude of believers had but one heart and soul. Neither did anyone say that aught of the things which he possessed was his own, but all things were common unto them. . . . Neither was there anyone needy among them', Ac 4:32, 34*a*. The Communion found expression in a **community of goods** which supplied the wants of all. This **Christian 'Communism'** sprang from love, not compulsion. That it was voluntary is shown by the examples given : the generosity of Barnabas and the humbug of Ananias and Sapphira, 4:36–5 :10. St Peter's words to Ananias make this plain : 'Unsold, the property was thine ; after the sale, the money was at thy disposal', 5:4, KNT. On the other hand, such generosity is the mark of genuine Communion.

f Next it had to be shown that the **Communion** was **universal.** Although the way was opened by St Peter's admission of Cornelius and the Gentiles with him to baptism without imposing the Mosaic Law, the Judaizers seem to have interpreted the case as exceptional. But when Paul and Barnabas came to consult the Apostles about their work among the Gentiles, James and Cephas and John 'gave to me and Barnabas the right hands of *communion* : that we should go unto the Gentiles and they unto the circumcision', Gal 2:9. This historic moment in the history of the Church's expansion proclaimed **Communion of Government** (as we speak of bishops being in or out of Communion with the Apostolic See), for the apostolic authority was shared in common while the spheres of apostolate were distinguished. These seem to have been merely geographical—the other Apostles, for the time at least, were to go on working in Palestine while St Paul went to the nations. But the gesture of communion was crucial, for it showed 'the riches of the glory of the mystery' which Paul preached to the Gentiles, a mystery 'now revealed by the Spirit to (God's) holy apostles . . . that through the gospel preaching the Gentiles are to win the same inheritance, to be made part of the same body, to share the same divine promise, in Christ Jesus', Eph 3:5, 6, KNT. Like a wild olive, grafted into the Jewish stock, they had communion in the root and riches of the olive, Rom 11:17. The Communion was visible and it was Catholic.

637a And from this Catholic Communion there flowed immediately a universal, practical charity, a 'sharing in common' like that in the primitive community. The other Apostles only asked St Paul 'to remember the poor', that is the Jerusalem Christians then in poverty, 'which', he adds, 'was the very thing I had set myself to do', Gal 2:10, KNT. In consequence he embarked upon one of the major enterprises of his career, 'the crown of his work in the East'. Why should this great missionary, with all the world to win for Christ, spend so much time and risk his life over a collection ? Because it manifested and fostered the 'Communion' of the universal Church, since it embodied the evangelical charity and sacred service (λειτουργία) which the Gentiles owed the mother church and won the latter to thankfulness 'glorifying God for the obedience of your confession unto the gospel of Christ and for the simplicity of your *communion* unto them and unto all ; 2 Cor 9:12, 13 ; *cf.* Allo, *in loc.,*

and in RB 45 (1936) 529–37, *La portée de la collecte pour* **e** *Jérusalem dans les plans de S. Paul.* No wonder that St Paul comes back to this Collection in four epistles and preached such a beautiful 'charity sermon' about it, 2 Cor 8:4–9:13 ; *cf.* Gal 2:10 ; 1 Cor 16:1–4 ; Rom 15:25–28 ; Ac 24:17. It was purely voluntary and with perfect spiritual realism he calls it 'a Communion' : '*Macedonia and Achaia have spontaneously determined to make a communion towards the poor of the saints in Jerusalem . . . and indeed it is they who are their debtors. For if the Gentiles have had communion in their spiritual goods, they owe it to them to serve* (λειτουργῆσαι) *them with their temporal goods*', Rom 15:26–28 ; *cf.* 1 Cor 9:11 ; 2 Cor 8:4. Upon the Communion is founded the delicacy of Christian charity : the poor saints have put the rich in their debt for the faith itself, and it is the latter's privilege to serve them, as the Philippians were privileged to help St Paul himself, Phil 4:14, 15, συγκοινωνήσαντες. Christians were taught to practise this 'communion' with their teachers and with one another, Gal 6:6 ; Rom 12:13 ; 1 Tim 6:18 ; Heb 13:16.

'They were persevering . . . in the *Communion* : *the* **b** *breaking of the bread*', Ac 2:42. **The fountain-head of the 'Communion',** the bond of Christian charity, is **common sharing in the Eucharistic sacrifice and banquet,** *cf.* §§ 652*g*–653*d*. Perfecting the incorporation with Christ and with one another begun by baptism, it is the sign and source of the Communion of the congregation. Because Christ was truly present beneath the sign (*cf.* 1 Cor 11:24, 25, 27) they came into Communion with him (*cf.* Jn 6:56) the one Food making them one : 'The chalice of benediction which we bless, is it not the *communion* of the blood of Christ ? And the bread which we break, is it not the *communion* of the body of Christ ? *Because there is one bread, we in our multitude are one body, for we all have a share from the one bread*', 1 Cor 10:16, 17 ; *cf.* Ign. Ant., *Philad.,* 4 ; *Smyrn.,* 7, 1 ; *Did.,* 9, 4. St Paul contrasts this with the Jews' 'communion' in their altar by eating the sacrifice and the pagans' 'communion' with devils by eating sacrifices offered to idols, 1 Cor 10:18–21 ; *cf.* Heb 7:13. 'The unity of the Mystical Body is the fruit of the true Body which we have received', Aquin., ST, 3, 82, 9, ad 2.

This is why St Luke, disciple of St Paul and a very **c** accurate writer, juxtaposes 'the communion' and 'the breaking of the bread', Ac 2:42. The expressions explain and enfold each other : the 'communion' has its active centre in 'Holy Communion', and 'Holy Communion' expands into the 'communion'. At Jerusalem, the Upper Room being no longer large enough, the Apostles went from house to house (*cf.* 5:42) and with the celebration of the Eucharist went the sharing of ordinary food in a Love Feast, *cf.* § 652*f*. 'Breaking bread from house to house, they *took their share of food* with joy and gladness', 2:46. First celebrated at a Supper, the Eucharist imparted its 'communion' to the food shared in common.

To sum up : In the vision of the Christian 'Com- **d** munion' and its expansion into every relation of human life is contained the Gospel message of love. Perfect fruit of the sacrifice of Calvary, love poured out by the Holy Spirit, this Communion in and with Christ and each other brought forth the Catholic charity of the Church. It embraced alike the life of the Spirit which has Communion with the Persons of the Holy Trinity and the practical charity extended to the needy, *cf.* 1 Jn 3:17 ; Jas 2:15, 16. Nurtured by the Gospel, fed by the Eucharist, the union of love in each congregation and in the whole Church reinforced the sign of the unity of faith.

But how to reduce these spiritual ideas to common practice was not at all obvious. If they must present a common front to the world, at least general lines of conduct were necessary. How should former pagans behave towards their unconverted friends ? How were the Jewish Christians to treat the other members of their race ? And how were both to regard the social customs and practices which they each found the others wishing to preserve within their new unity in Christ ? That their new-found unity presented **innumerable problems** which no neophyte could be expected to solve for himself, may be illustrated by the questions about meats offered to idols, *e.g.* 1 Cor 8-10, and by the question of the preservation of the Jewish ritual taboos among the Christians in general, Ac 10-11 ; 15, and especially Gal 2.

But the neophyte was not left to himself : if a new orientation had been given to his life with the coming of faith, that did not exhaust the help and guidance that he might expect from the members of the body into which he had been admitted. Not indeed from the first members he might chance upon, but from such as were looked up to by them as having the right to decide such questions, those in fact to whom they already turned for the fuller knowledge of Christ's Gospel. If it was only natural that the neophyte should look to others for **guidance,** it was no surprise to see even Christians of long-standing recognizing certain among them as exercising authority over the rest. The very idea of their all helping to constitute the Body of Christ implied the very opposite of egalitarianism : if all the parts of the human body are interdependent, some nevertheless control others, some help to bind the rest into one whole as do the ' joints and *ligaments* ', Col 2:19, to ensure, through vital continuity with the head, the harmonious growth of the whole man, *cf.* Eph 4:12-16. Each could share in the life of the whole, and as the neophyte could see that very varied functions were exercised by the different members of the community, so he was encouraged by the teachers among them to find his own appropriate place in relation to the rest. What was *his* charisma, the special gift which the Holy Spirit had made him, to be used for the general good ? For the union which he had entered was no static one : growth and development were of its very essence ; he must himself contribute to them along with the rest.

The Charismata—The guidance of **the Holy Spirit** had been continual from the first, now in explosive manifestations, now in quiet interior seductive ways, the manner of his help being adapted to times, places, persons and circumstances. There was the grand transformation scene of Pentecost, the wind, the tongues of fire outwardly heralding the new boldness of the Twelve, who preached fearlessly to the Jews of the whole world the meaning of the judicial murder which their leaders had committed, in that very place, only a few weeks before. The conversion of three thousand on the spot completed the outward evidence of the Spirit's action. There were the miracles in the name of Christ (Ac *passim*) which not infrequently accompanied and confirmed the early apostolate ; there were also visions, such as those of Stephen, Ac 7:55, of Peter, Ac 10:9-16, and of Paul, Ac 9 (*cf.* Ac 22 ; 26), and the latter was guided more than once in his apostolate by the Holy Spirit, Ac 13:2-4 ; 16:6, 7, 9-10 ; 20:22-23 (*cf.* 21:4 ; 10-14) ; *cf.* also 18:9-10 ; 19:21 ; 23:11 ; 27:23-24. Other outward manifestations occurred at times on the bestowal *par excellence* of the Holy Spirit, ' Confirmation ', Ac 8:14 ff. ; 19:6 (*cf.* 10:44 ff.), not to mention the exorcism of evil spirits, Ac 8:7, 13 ; 16:16 ff. ; 19:13 ff. ; *cf.* 5:1-11 ; 13:8-11. These wonders were not predictable, and might at first suggest a completely haphazard choice by the Holy Spirit of the human instruments of his activity. Yet we can notice at once that the vast majority of cases ' happened ' through the Apostles—above all, through Peter or through Paul ; other intermediaries were exceptional, and even so were in some way associated with the former.

But what characterized all these extraordinary interventions of the Spirit was that though they might at the moment call attention to the person of those who were so moved by him, yet their total effect was the advantage of the body of the faithful in numbers or in fervour. It was by an easy transition of thought that

the same term was applied to any activity or endowment **639b** which benefited the community as a whole. Indeed it was by this characteristic that the activity of the Spirit was to be distinguished from manifestations of false or dubious origin. Hence we can define these gifts (or **charismata**) as being functions exercised either continuously or momentarily, which, whether extraordinary or not, of their nature tended to the building up of the body of the faithful, either locally or universally. It is a mistake to confine the word, as so many modern exegetes do, to extraordinary manifestations and, above all, to deny it to functions exercised in virtue of a special appointment to office by election or nomination. It had a much wider scope, as an analysis of St Paul's teaching on the subject shows.

Thus (*a*) *charismata* were not only extraordinary gifts : **c** for instance, in the list of Rom 12:6 ff., are mentioned ' he that exhorteth ' (ὁ παρακαλῶν), ' he that dispenseth ' (ὁ μεταδιδούς), ' he that sheweth mercy ' (ὁ ἐλεῶν), and the list includes ' him that *presideth* ' (ὁ προϊστάμενος), 8. Encouragement, almsgiving, works of mercy can be inspired by the Spirit of Christ without supposing any preternatural manifestations ; *cf.* 1 Pet 4:11. So too the ' presidency ' of a Christian community. ' Even those charismata which were essentially extraordinary —like prophecy—were not equally so in all their manifestations. When the prophet was exercising οἰκοδομή (edification) and παράκλησις (exhortation) and παραμυθία (comfort), 1 Cor 14:3—which constituted undoubtedly his most regular function—this use of his charisma came to no more than fulfilling his office of preacher ' (A. Lemonnyer, O.P., art. ' Charismes ' in DBV(S) 1, 1241). In fact, unless this be admitted, we should indeed have the preaching of the κήρυγμα [the glad tidings of God's intervention, by the coming, death and resurrection of Christ,] and of the διδάχη [the instruction of the faithful in the new way of life consequent on it], but we should have no record of the ordinary sermon of exhortation and encouragement such as even the best instructed of the faithful require and appreciate. The prophet would rarely be foretelling the future, less rarely he would be really inspired with some immediately relevant message from God, but mostly he would devote himself to the general edification of the Christian assembly by homily or by hortatory explanation of the Scriptures.

This distinction is important in more ways than one. **d** Just as the special guidance which St Paul at times was given by the Holy Spirit in his travels, in no way dispensed him from ordinarily ' planning for himself ', so the charisma of **prophecy** was recommended as one worthy of ambition—and therefore as one which could be prepared for and practised without any ecstatic or astounding impulse of the Spirit. The fact that prophets themselves were subject to control by others (*cf.* 1 Cor 14:29 and Allo, *ibid.*), points to the possibility of an all too human initiative in certain cases, as also do our Lord's warnings against false prophets, Mt 7:15 ; 24:11, 24 ; Mk 13:22, which St Paul in various ways reiterates, Ac 20:29-30 etc. ; *cf.* 1 Tim 4:1-2 ; 6:3-5, 20. If then a true charisma of the Spirit might be exercised while the full consciousness of one's initiative remained, and if its supernatural source did not necessarily reveal itself in its external effects, it was also possible for delusion and even malice to produce a counterfeit ' prophesying ', not always easy to detect.

Such a possibility was still more obvious in the case **e** of the charisma of ' **tongues** ' as it is usually named. It gave more trouble to St Paul than any other, 1 Cor 12-14. Its name and certain of its characteristics led to its being identified with the faculty of speaking in many languages granted to the Apostles on the day of Pentecost, Ac 2. But a closer study of St Paul's words and of the quasi-technical use of the word γλῶσσαι at the time, shows that a foreign tongue need have nothing to do with this charisma ; *cf.* Allo, *Première Epître aux Corinthiens*, Excursus XV, 374-84, and Comm. An address in a foreign tongue at a gathering of Christians would not have led the chance visitor, unlearned or in-

639e fidel, to treat them as madmen, 1 Cor 14:23. Rather was it an apparently ecstatic condition in which articulate or inarticulate utterances were voiced, of which the general character could be grasped (prayer, thanks-giving, etc.) but not the precise meaning. The γλῶσσαι, strictly speaking, were not entirely foreign expressions nor a mere magical jargon—which no one could have understood—but rather unfamiliar words of little or no currency, rare or archaic expressions in some dialect, neologisms and startling compounds, even exaggerated circumlocutions (Allo, *loc. cit.* 379, 381). A love of display, memories of similar ecstatic transports in the pagan mystery religions, sheer hysteria might all contribute to produce a parody of the real mystical gift ; that is why St Paul is so anxious that such mani-festations should be properly controlled and so insistent on the indispensable gift of Charity and the far more beneficial gift of prophecy, 1 Cor 14:13, 26–33 ; 13 ; 14:1–5.

f The fact that the charisma of 'tongues' was an extraordinary manifestation of the Spirit's action, as was also that of 'prophecy', at least on occasion, so fascinated certain minds in fairly modern times, that they identified all action of the Spirit as being necessarily manifested by extraordinary outbursts, and maintained that the life of the primitive Church was wholly guided by such spiritual interventions, so that law and reason played no part in its organization. How arbitrary is this conception of 'pneumatic anarchy', as they called it, is clear from the consideration of the lists of the charismata which St Paul enumerates, or even of the few mentioned above ; and whatever success the theory enjoyed, was due to its falling in with the desire to do away with all idea of juridical authority in 'genuine' Christianity. If it has been treated here at some length, it is because reminiscences of the theory still befog the minds of many, though such treatment is out of all proportion to the place which these extraordinary transports held in the life of the early Church. In our records, the references to them are few, and, if kept in perspective, have a real importance ; but though, like miracles, they then had a larger place in the Church's life than they have today, they were subject to control, tested and submitted to definite regulations as to their exercise even by the most charismatic of men, the Apostle St Paul.

g (*b*) The foregoing discussion has incidentally suggested that quite ordinary pursuits—works of charity, spiritual and temporal—were regarded as depending on the 'gifts' of the Spirit, and there is no reason for thinking that they were regarded any differently when undertaken in a regular way as the result of some quite human **appointment to office,** whether by election or nomination. Sometimes, no doubt, as in the case of Barnabas and Saul, a special prompting of the Holy Spirit intervened, Ac 13:2 ; but there is no ground for thinking that this was more than exceptional, still less that it was the rule. It is only a pre-conceived system which requires that juridical appointments should be regarded as a *pis-aller* resorted to when charismatic endowments had begun to wane, or which sees an opposition between such appointments and the free agency of the Spirit—between office and 'charisma', as if the Holy Spirit might not freely make such appointments the occasion for the bestowing of his gifts. If not Matthias, then the Seven may be quoted as examples, and he would be rash indeed who refused a charisma to the πρεσβύτεροι 'appointed' by Paul and Barnabas 'in every church', Ac 14:22, especially as a 'charisma' attaches to him 'that *presideth*', *cf.* § 639c. Timothy's consecration to office was a very formal investiture, even if prophecy (but of what kind ?) paved the way to it : Paul certainly regarded the charisma which Timothy had received, as having been conferred by himself when he headed the presbyters in imposing hands upon him, 2 Tim 1:6 ; 1 Tim 4:14 ; *cf.* C. Spicq, *op. cit.*, 322–3.

h Such considerations, which will be resumed when the Ministry is treated of below (§§ 656h, 657h), must

not be understood to belittle the direct, at times startling interventions of the Spirit. Insistence on the matter-of-factness of some of the gifts is intended only to correct the tendency to level up all the gifts to the plane of the extraordinary, not to level them all down to the commonplace. It is the *diversity* of the gifts which must be kept in mind : there were the highest as there were the lowest. And among the highest (ranking, indeed, even above the 'presidency') stand 'the *utterance* of wisdom (σοφία) through the Spirit', and 'the *utterance* of knowledge (γνῶσις) according to the Spirit', 1 Cor 12:8—that wisdom which was no milk for babes, but solid food for 'grown-ups' in the spirit, learnt from the Holy Spirit, spoken in words of his teaching—incomprehensible, 'foolishness' to the natural man (ψυχικός), 1 Cor 2:6–3:4 and Allo *in loc.* This 'wisdom' did not consist of the knowledge of certain facts withheld from the generality of the faithful, for all received from the Spirit the same faith in God's dealings with men in the person of Christ, along with their Baptism into his Body—it was no esoteric knowledge ; but it consisted in the deeper penetration into God's designs and into the harmony of their various parts, through the possession of the intuition (νοῦς) of Christ (*cf.* Allo *1 Cor* Excursus V : and Comm. on 1 Cor 2:6–3:4 ; § 634d). It was the fuller, yet never exhausted, understanding of the faith such as all should strive for : it might, besides, be crowned by the charisma of the 'utterance' of this wisdom (λόγος σοφίας, λόγος γνώσεως, 1 Cor 12:8), whereby the 'adult' souls might converse of the divine plan with the mentality of Christ himself, 2:16, being con-formed to him and growing ever more conformed to him thereby.

III THE HOLY TRINITY

The difference between the first Christians and their contemporaries is immense. They are not confined within the shadows of the Law, or the speculations of Greek philosophy, or religious systems which are only symbols of the cosmic cycle. God has entered human history in Person, explaining, altering and summing it up, not only enlightening but transforming the faith and life of man. 'In these last days he hath spoken to us by his Son', Heb 1:2 ; *cf.* Rom 16:25 ; Eph 3:5 ; Col 1:26 f.

God is no longer, as for the Pharisees, 'une monade inféconde, isolée dans sa majesté', Lagrange, *Le Judaïsme*, 590. Nor is he only the One Creator, whose spirituality, eternal power and divinity are manifested to human reason by his creation, Rom 1:19 f. ; *cf.* Wis 13:1–9 ; Ac 14:15 ff. ; 17:22 ff. By the revelation of the 'Son of the living God' men have passed beyond the stage when they knew him only in unity of essence. He is **the Living God,** living above anything that 'flesh and blood' can conceive, Mt 16:15 ff. ; Jn 17:6 ; Gal 1:15 f. ; 1 Thess 1:9 f. ; 1 Jn 1:2. The NT is the revelation of One God in Three Persons and of our union with him. The Mystery of the Holy Trinity is the 'substantia Novi Testamenti', Tertullian, *Adv. Prax.*, 31.

Henceforth Christians are and know themselves to be the **children of the living God,** Rom 9:26 ; Os 1:10, dwelling in his house which is the Church, 1 Tim 3:15, his city, the heavenly Jerusalem, Heb 12:22 ; Apoc 21:2, each his temple, 2 Cor 6:16. The New Law rests on the state of sonship to which they have been raised. Born of the Spirit by baptism, Jn 3:5 f., 'even now the sons of God', 1 Jn 3:1 ff., they are free with the freedom which Christ has won for them, Gal 4:21–5:1 ; Jn 8:36, 'sons in the Son', living in him their new, Trinitarian life, *e.g.* Jn 15:1 ff. ; Rom 6:4 ; 8:29 ; 1 Jn 5:20.

The Son has revealed his Father to these sons in the context of their own life, Mt 11:25 ff. ; Lk 10:21 f. ; 1 Cor 1:24–31. They are to pray 'Our Father' to him who knows their needs, for the tender heart of a father is only a type of his, Mt 7:11. To be truly his sons, they must do good and be perfect like him, forgiving as he forgives, 5:44-48. But the Beloved, Only Son revealed his Father not only in their life but in the Divine Life, as ' My Father '. He glorified him by manifesting his proper name of ' Father ' to these new brethren ' that the love wherewith thou hast loved me may be in them and I in them ', Jn 17:1-6, 26 ; *cf.* especially Cyr. Alex., *In Joann.*, PG, 74, 497-501. To him the Son refers all things, *e.g.* Jn 6:65 ; 8:28 ; Apoc 2:28. Now they know him as he is, he from whom every family group in heaven and on earth is named, **the Father who begets a Son**, Eph 3:14 f., 1 Jn 1:3. The Spirit of the Son continues to reveal this Father to them, teaching them to cry, Abba, Father, Gal 4:4 ff. ; Rom 8:14 ff. He is the first principle and last end of the redemptive work, *e.g.* 2 Cor 5:8 ff. To him all praise must ascend, Eph 1:3-14.

As the son reveals the Father, so **the Father reveals the Son**, *e.g.* Mt 3:17 ; 16:17 ; 17:5 ; 2 Pet 1:17. The Mystery of the Father is inseparable from that of the Son, Mt 11:25 ff., Lk 10:21 f. ; Jn 5:23 ; 1 Cor 1:30 ; 1 Jn 2:23. ' I am in the Father and the Father in me ', Jn 14:11 ; 17:21. In the Son we see the Father and through him we go to the Father, Jn 1:18 ; 14:4-14 ; Rom 5:1 f. Both are revealed together because the Son, in whom is the fullness of the Godhead, received from the Father all that the Father has, Jn 5:26 ; 16:15 ; Col 2:9.

But the **Mystery of the Father and the Son is revealed by the Holy Spirit.** He comes forth from God and sounds the depths of God, 1 Cor 2:10 ff. He glorifies and bears testimony to the Son, Jn 15:26 ; 16:14 ; 1 Cor 12:3. By receiving this ' other Paraclete ', the ' Spirit of truth ' whom the Son sends from the Father and the Father sends in the name of the Son, the disciples know that ' I am in my Father and you in me and I in you ', Jn 14:16-20, 26 ; 15:26 ; 1 Jn 4:2-6, 13 ff. For this knowledge is essentially loving knowledge. The mutual knowledge of the Father and the Son is not separable from the love whereby the Father loves the Son and is loved by him. Therefore men can share it only in the unity of the love of the Holy Spirit, who pours the love of God into their hearts, Rom 5:5. As later theology recognized, he is the bond of love in the Trinity, the Person who is the mutual love of Father and Son. He is not an intermediary between us and the Son, who is the only Mediator. But as the Spirit of Love he assimilates us to the union of the Son and the Father. In other words he perfects our adoptive sonship by the spirit of filial love, and thereby shows us that we are in the Son and the Father, Gal 4:6. As Paraclete, Advocate, he assures our spirit that we are sons of God and intercedes for us with groans beyond all utterance, Rom 8:15 f., 26 f. Hence his presence in us is the ' first-fruits ' of the new creature divinized in the Son, 23 ; 2 Cor 1:22 ; Eph 1:14, and by contrast he proves the sin of the world and the defeat of the devil, Jn 16:8-11. This communication of the Spirit, the Love of the Divine Persons, is the supreme gift of the glorified Christ to his own, and enables them to understand divine love and their Master's parting injunction to mutual love : ' These things I have spoken to you that my joy may be in you, and your joy may be filled. This is my commandment that you love one another as I have loved you . . . Just Father . . . I have made known thy name to them and will make it known ; that the love wherewith thou hast loved me may be in them, and I in them, 15:11 f. ; 16:20 ff. ; 17:25 f. ; Rom 8:9 ; Bouyer, 134-40, here followed closely.

The NT keeps constantly in view **the order of the Divine Persons,** but approaches the Mystery from various points in their to-and-fro relationship, descending from the Father or ascending to him : ' I came forth from the Father and am come into the world ; again I leave the world and I go to the Father ', Jn 16:28. ' God hath sent the Spirit of his Son into *our* hearts crying, Abba, Father ', Gal 4:6. Again, it is through the Son

that we have access in one Spirit to the Father, **640g** Eph 2:18, and St Paul will turn from him through whom all graces come, to their source in the Father's love and thence to their communication in the Spirit : ' The grace of our Lord Jesus Christ, and the charity of God, and the *communion* of the Holy Spirit be with you all ', 2 Cor 13:13.

Already **we share in the divine nature,** 2 Pet 1:4. **h** As the Father has life in himself, he has given the Son to have life in himself and to bestow life upon whom he wills, Jn 5:21, 26 ; *cf.* 1:4. We have this life in the Son, 1 Jn 5:11 f., in whose life we shall be saved, Rom 5:10. He bestows and nourishes it by the gift of himself in the Eucharist, Jn 6:40, 57 f. It constantly grows, 2 Cor 2:16. Though now hidden with him in God, it shines out through suffering, and will be manifested in glory when he who is our life appears, 4:10 f. ; Col 3:3 f. The Father has given us the Spirit who is inseparable from Christ to dwell within us as first share of our inheritance as sons and earnest money of the eternal life which finally will absorb even our bodies, 2 Cor 1:22 ; 5:4 f. ; Eph 1:13 f. ; Rom 8:5-17. He constantly intercedes for the fullness of our sonship, 8:23, 26 f.

This revelation is made, **this life communicated in i the Body of Christ.** There the gifts which come from all the Divine Persons are distributed by the Holy Spirit, the offices by the Son who is the body's Head, and all activity derives from the Father as ultimate source : ' There are varieties of gifts, but the same Spirit. And there are varieties of ministrations, and the same Lord. And there are varieties of workings, but the same God, who worketh all in all ', 1 Cor 12:4, WV. It is upon the unity of the Holy Trinity that the rich, organic unity of the Body is founded. Animated by one Spirit it tends to the one end of eternal possession of God, takes its existence from the one Lord in whom all are incorporated, and forms one family, all sons of the one God who is the Father of all, Eph 4:3-6 ; *cf.* Huby, *in loc.* Thus its members attain to divine intimacy, 2:18 f., and the visible unity of the Body, based on a sharing in the unity of the Persons abiding within it, is an open manifestation of the Son's mission from the Father, Jn 10:30 ; 17:11, 21-26.

Further, **the Holy Trinity is the source of the sacra- j mental life** of the members of the Body. The final, universal command of the omnipotent Son of God had been to baptize ' in the name ' of the Three Divine Persons, Mt 28:19 ; *cf.* § 650e. Thus baptismal salvation is wrought by the Divine Persons, the Father sanctifying through the Son in the Spirit, 1 Cor 6:11 ; Tit 3:4 ff. Again, the Father makes the disciples firm and anoints them in Christ, sealing them by the earnest of the Spirit whom he pours into their hearts, 2 Cor 1:21 f. The sacramental reference here recognized by modern exegetes is suggested in another way. As Christ ' through eternal Spirit ' offered himself to God and so won eternal redemption, Heb 9:12 ff., as he consecrated himself (ἁγιάζω) a victim that his Apostles might be ' consecrated in truth ', Jn 17:19, so Paul, his sacred minister (λειτουργός), with the priestly office of the Gospel (ἱερουργοῦντα), prepares the Gentiles to be consecrated by the Holy Spirit and offered to the Father, Rom 15:16 ; Phil 2:17 ; *cf.* Eph 5:25 f.

All this, taken with what will be said on the part of **k** the Father, the Son and the Spirit in the work of redemption, on union with the Son, and on the gift and fullness of the Sprit, shows **a constant teaching,** which fully confirms the authenticity of Mt 28:19. That text, in which the revelation given at Jesus's own baptism shone out in full splendour (Lebreton, *The Living God*, 104) finds its echo in many others, often containing a baptismal reference, where the Three Persons are mentioned together and distinguished from all created being, § 650g ; Prat, II, 132 ff. and Note S. Given the rigorous monotheism of the Christians, the only formula for this relative opposition and mutual compenetration is Trinity in unity, 138, and there is ample material to justify and make necessary the technical terms of

640k later theology : nature, person, consubstantiality, procession, relation, circuminsession.

l Thus is revealed not an abstract God but God One in Three Persons. The Son, in speaking of God as ' my Father ', also reveals himself as Son. The Father, bearing testimony to his Beloved Son, reveals himself as Father. In the ' life of the Spirit ' is revealed the Holy Spirit who testifies to the presence of Father and Son. So **the Christian life,** coming from the whole Trinity and within the unity of the Trinity, **involves relations to each of the Divine Persons.** The members of Christ's Body are taught to realize these relations individually and collectively. They know that all in them is the work of the Father (Phil 2:13 ; 1 Thess 2:13) who predestines them to be conformed to the image of his Son, Rom 8:29, and that the graces of the life of the spirit come to them from the Spirit who is given by the Father to the Son and by him rendered back to the Father ; *cf.* 1 Cor 12:1–11 ; 2 Cor 3:4 ff. ; Gal 3:5 ; Eph 4:3 ff. ; 1 Jn 4:13.

m This life of the Divine Persons within them is to be the reason for their Christian living. Because God works in them, they must work at their salvation with fear and dread, Phil 2:12. Because they are sons in the Son, they must walk with the freedom and love of sons, Gal 4:4–7. And the indwelling of the Spirit is their motive for hope, Rom 5:5, purity, 1 Cor 3:16 f. ; 6:19, avoiding pagan ways, 2 Cor 6:14, and for steadfastness in doctrine, 2 Tim 1:14. Thus will they be built up in Christ into one holy sanctuary and spiritual dwelling place of God, Eph 2:21 f. ; 1 Pet 2:5.

n So too **St John sees the Holy Trinity in the Church** present and consummated, the heavenly Jerusalem. The Father penetrates all the city with his glory, the Lamb lights it with his doctrine, and the Holy Spirit, represented by his operation as the water of life flowing from the throne of God and of the Lamb, gives to the Tree of Life its fecundity, Apoc 21:22–22:5 (*cf.* Allo, *in loc.* ; Jn 7:38 f.), while from within the Church, the Spirit cries ' Come ' to Jesus, Apoc 22:17, 20.

o This deep Trinitarian life is proclaimed in the salutations of epistles, grace, peace and mercy coming simultaneously from the Father and the Son, Rom 1:7 ; 1 Cor 1:3 ; Gal 1:3 ; 1 Tim 1:2, in the Spirit, 1 Pet 1:2. It is at the heart of contemplative prayer, Rom 8:26 f. It breaks out in the prayers to Christ and canticles in his honour (*e.g.* Ac 1:24 ; 7:59 f. ; Eph 5:14 ; 1 Tim 3:16 ; Apoc 5:9 f.) and in **Doxologies.** These abbreviated hymns, reserved for the Jews to God, are usually referred to the Father, *e.g.* Rom 11:36 ; Gal 1:5 ; Phil 4:20 ; 1 Tim 1:17 ; 1 Pet 5:11 ; Apoc 7:12. But when the thought is fixed on Christ, they apply directly to him, Rom 9:5 ; 2 Tim 4:18 ; 2 Pet 3:18 ; Apoc 1:6 ; 5:9–13 ; *cf.* 7:10, God and the Lamb. When both are mentioned together, Christ as the Head of the Church is the Mediator through whom honour, glory, and thanks are given to the Father, Eph 3:21 ; Jude 25. St Paul seems to provide a norm for such prayers : ' Whatsoever ye do in word or in work, do all in the name of the Lord Jesus, giving thanks to God the Father through him, Col 3:17, WV ; *cf.* *Chase, The Lord's Prayer in the Early Church, Texts and Studies,* 1, 3, 168–76 ; Prat, II, 119–24 ; Lebr., HDT, 265 f.

641a Jesus Christ the Lord—Jesus Christ is the centre of all that is old and new in the NT revelation. On his divinity in the Gospels *cf.* §§ 616–28. On the earliest Christian teaching about him *cf.* § 817c–e. It contains two elements : the apologetic presentation shown in the preaching of Peter, Stephen and Paul, and the belief of the Christian community, which comes out in prayer, worship, ways of speaking and living, and in the common faith assumed by the epistles. All preachers of new doctrine naturally lead their hearers on from what they already acknowledge. Christ himself did so, Lebr., HDT, 259 ff. The new faith consummated the old : ' Jesus does not separate the Christians from God, he unites them . . . never has prayer been more confiding and filial, or union with God closer ', 266.

The Resurrection was the decisive proof of the Messianic dignity of Jesus and the supreme manifestation of his divine Sonship, 261 f. He was ' marked out Son of God by resurrection from death ', Rom 1:4, WV ; *cf.* *Sanday-Headlam, Rom., in loc.* Hence the NT often repeats that God raised him from the dead, and St Paul takes the Resurrection as the final proclamation of the Sonship already declared at the Baptism and Transfiguration, Ac 13:33. But it was not the Resurrection which made him Christ and Son ; he had been so in his life-time, *e.g.* Mt 16:16 ; 21:37 ; 26:63 ; Mk 13:32.

The Conversion of St Paul is of cardinal importance for the development of NT doctrine. The revelation he then received was recognized by the other Apostles as coinciding with that given to St Peter, Gal 2:7 ff. ; Mt 16:16 f. His faith was the same as theirs, 1 Cor 15:11 ; Gal 2:6, and as that of churches he had not visited, Rom 1:12. The Judaizers, who would have pounced upon his slightest deflexion from monotheism, could accuse him only about Jewish observances. He who had met the chief Apostles and lived with Barnabas, Mark and Luke, must have been fully informed on the life and words of Jesus. In fact, they were constantly in his mind, BEP, 19–27. Modern scholars have shown that he knew Mt and later Lk, *cf.* Chapman, RB, 36 (1912) reproduced in DR, 36 (1937) 432 ff. on Gal 1:15 ff. ; 2:7 ff. and Mt 16:16 f. ; Orchard, Bi, 19 (1938) 19 ff., with Buzy, RSR, 28 (1938) 473 ff. on 1 and 2 Thess and Mt 24, 25 ; B. C. Butler, *St Paul's Knowledge and Use of St Matthew,* DR, 66 (1948) 367 ff. ; Spicq, *op. cit.,* cxliii–cliii.

But while the first disciples had passed from the earthly life of Jesus to his exaltation, Paul had been ' seized ' by the ' Lord of glory ' whom he had seen, Phil 3:12 ; 1 Cor 2:8 ; 9:1. From this revelation his doctrine expanded homogeneously. It had pleased God ' who called me by his grace to reveal his Son in me that I might preach him among the Gentiles ', Gal 1:15 f. To them he preached first Christ risen from the dead, living and heavenly, possessing and communicating the Spirit, Ac 17:31 ; 1 Cor 2:2 ; 15:1–4, and after that Christ true man who fulfilled the Messianic prophecies, *cf.* 2 Tim 2:8 ; Spicq, clix. Although he is ready to start with Messianism when preaching to the Jews, Ac 9:22 ; 26:22, it moves into the background in the epistles, and from the moment of his vision Jesus is for him the Transcendent, the Infinite, Prat, *op. cit.,* II, 112 f.

' **The entire work of Paul** is fundamentally only a **Christology,** since it all centres in the Person or the mission of Christ ', 424. His theology does not derive from syncretism, nor from a distinction between Jewish ' flesh ' and Hellenic ' spirit ', nor from ' Lutheran ' principles on Justification. Such intellectual systems are far too narrow for this great mystic, 477 ff., ' Theologies of St Paul ' ; BEP, 35 ff. His Gospel is summed up in ' the mystery of God, Christ, in whom are hid all the treasures of wisdom ', Col 2:2 f. ; BEP, 49 ff.

' **Lord** ' is the title for Christ which Paul uses most (at least 260 times, isolated or as ' the Lord Jesus ' or ' Jesus Christ our Lord ', BEP, 51 ff.). Its Palestinian origin is shown by its use in the Gospel data (where it passes from an honorary to an exclusive sense, *e.g.* Mt 22:43), in the primitive community, *e.g.* Ac 1:21 ; 2:36, and in the Aramaic prayer formula ' Maranatha ', 1 Cor 16:22 ; *cf.* Apoc 22:20. Hence *W. Bousset (Kyrios Christos)* was wrong in claiming that its origin was Hellenistic and accounted for belief in Christ's divinity, Lebr., HDT, 268–80 ; KTW, *Kyrios,* III, 1045–82. ' Who art thou, Lord ', had been Paul's first cry on seeing the risen Jesus, followed by total submission : ' Lord, what wilt thou have me to do ', Ac 9:5 ; 22:10. The title ' Lord ', familiar from LXX, may be applied to the Father, usually under OT influence, *e.g.* Rom 9:28, but St Paul clearly marks it as Christ's : ' There are varieties of gifts, but the same Spirit. And there are varieties of ministrations, and the same Lord. And there are varieties of workings, but the same God, who worketh all things in all ', 1 Cor 12:4 ff., WV ; *cf.* Eph 4:4 ff. This divine name is given by a strict monotheist fully conscious of pagan usage : ' We know . . . that there is no God save one. For even though there are gods so-called . . . as indeed there are ' gods ' many and ' lords ' many—yet for us there is only one God, the Father, from whom come all things and for whom we live ; and one Lord Jesus Christ, through whom come all things, and through whom we live ', 1 Cor 8:4 ff., WV. Jesus is Lord to whom all belongs and to whom Christians give themselves completely, doing all in his name, Rom 14:7 ff. ; 1 Cor 7:22 ; Col 3:17. To confess him as Lord is an act of faith proceeding from the Holy Spirit, 1 Cor 12:3 ; *cf.* Mt 16:17 ; Gal 1:16, and necessary for salvation, Rom 10:9 f. ; *cf.* Phil 2:11.

The name ' God ', in continuity with OT monotheism, is normally reserved to the Father, the ultimate Principle of the Godhead. Jesus is called **' Son of God '** nineteen times. He is the Son of the Father's love, Col 1:13 ; Eph 1:6, the ' Beloved Son ' of the Gospels. He is the pre-existing, divine Son, *e.g.* ' God (sent) his own Son in the likeness of sinful flesh. . . . Seeing that he hath not spared his own Son . . . how can he fail to grant us all things with him ', Rom 8:3, 32, WV ; 1:3 f. ; 2 Cor 1:19 f. ; Gal 2:20.

But sometimes **he is called God directly,** as in the culmination of Israel's privileges : ' From whom is Christ according to the flesh, who is over all things, God blessed for ever ', Rom 9:5 ; *cf.* Com. *in loc.* ; Durand, RB, 12 (1903) 550–70 ; KTW, III, 106 (Stauffert). That ' the manifestation of our great God and Saviour Jesus Christ ', Tit 2:13, refers wholly to him is accepted by nearly all modern exegetes, Spicq, *in loc.* ; KTW, IV, 544–46 (Grundman). On Ac 20:28 *cf.* Com., *in loc.* ; but R. Schnackenburg, in *Episcopus* (Munich Univ. *Studien*, 1949) recognizes ' God ' as the Father, and translates ' the blood of his own ', *cf.* MMV, ἴδιος. OT texts concerning God are applied to Christ, *e.g.* Rom 10:9–13 ; 1 Cor 10:9. The Spirit of God, who spoke in the prophets, is the Spirit of Christ, Rom 8:9 ; 1 Pet 1:11, and God's coming, tribunal, Gospel, Church and Kingdom are Christ's, 1 Thess 3:13 ; 2 Thess 1:9 f. ; Rom 14:10 ; 2 Cor 5:10 ; Rom 1:1, 9 ; 1 Cor 1:2 ; Rom 16:16 ; Eph 5:5 ; Prat, II, 130. The supreme efficacy assigned to his Passion is another sure proof of belief in his divinity ; *cf.* § 647c ; Lebr., HDT, 310.

Christ's divinity is shown again in the great Christological texts. Phil 2:5–11, ' the most complete expression of St Paul's thought ' (Prat, II, 129) sets forth his divine, pre-existing life, his life of trial and his glorified life, *cf.* 2 Cor 8:9. God's own Son was born of a woman, Gal 4:4, and coming into the world to save sinners, appeared in the flesh, 1 Tim 1:15 ; 3:16. In terms closely resembling the Prologue of St John's Gospel, Col declares that all things were created through him and for him, and he is the sovereign head of the Church, his Body, possessing the plenitude of graces to bring universal peace and reconciliation ; ' in him dwelleth all the fullness of the Godhead corporally ', Col 1:16–20 ; 2:9, WV.

Paul had been sent to teach the Gentiles **the Mystery of Christ's divine life in the Church.** It was an expansion of that first revelation : ' I am Jesus whom thou persecutest ', Ac 9:4 f. ; 1 Cor 15:9 ; Eph 3:3–7 ; Col 4:3. **' In Christ Jesus '** occurs 164 times in his epistles. Occasionally it means little more than ' Christian ', *e.g.* Gal 1:22 ; 2 Cor 12:2, or by Heb. idiom ' in ' expresses Christ's agency in redemption, *e.g.* 5:18 f. ' through Christ . . . in Christ '. But usually it involves the doctrine of the Body of Christ and our real, mystical inclusion by baptism in the Saviour who died and has risen for us, *e.g.* Rom 6:3 ; 2 Cor 5:17 ; Gal 3:26 ff. ; sometimes his presence in us is indicated, *e.g.* Rom 8:9 ff. ; 2 Cor 13:3 ff., Prat, II, 297 ff., 391–5 ; . Malevez, RSR 30 (1944) 35 ff. Further, Christ is the principle of life and growth in the organism of the Church, Eph 4:7–16 ; *cf.* Col 3:4.

The mystery of the Infinite Person of the Saviour **641j** including all men within himself is apparent in the doctrines of the Second Adam, Rom 5:12–19 ; 1 Cor 15:45–9, and of the summing-up of all creatures in Christ, Eph 1:3–14 ; Col 2:9 f. ; 2 Tim 1:9 f. ; *cf.* BEP, 89 f., 101–3 and § 646*b–g*.

' The unsearchable riches of Christ ', Eph 3:8, were **k** shown forth to the various churches by their Apostle. To the conceited, sophisticated Corinthians he preached Christ crucified, the Power and Wisdom of God, 1 Cor 1:23 f., 30 f. To the Colossians, troubled by angel-worship, he laid open his universal primacy and Mediatorship. When the Galatians were falling back under the Law, he urged the liberating power of his redemptive grace. An exhortation to humility and service passes into the famous text : ' Let this mind be in you which was also in Christ Jesus. . . .', Phil 2:5 ff. The great dogmatic epistles show Christ the centre and sum of human history. Against the terrible fact of universal sin, Rom sets God's free, loving justification through the redemption in Christ Jesus, the Second Adam restoring the life of grace to those who died in the first, Rom 3:22–5 ; 5:12–21. Eph praises the Father's eternal design to sum up all things in Christ, making him head of the Church which is his body and his fullness ; in this one Body Jews and Gentiles, alike sons of God, have access in one Spirit to the Father, Eph 1:10, 22 f. ; 2:16 ff. In face of a temptation to return to the temple liturgy and undue worship of angels, Heb celebrates the perfection of Christ's Sonship, sacrifice and priesthood : ' He, being the flashing forth of his glory and the very expression of his being, sustaineth all things by God's word of power ' ; ' Jesus Christ is the same, yesterday and today, yea, and for ever ', Heb 1:3 ; 13:8, WV ; *cf.* § 647*e*.

By the time of the Pastorals, these great doctrines did **l** not need developing again. Christology was expressed under themes already familiar in the Church : confessions of faith, baptismal professions or liturgical hymns, Spicq, clix. But now the title **Saviour** comes into its own. The OT had reserved it to God (*cf.* Lk 1:47), and the NT given it to Christ as Messias, Lk 2:11 ; Ac 5:31 ; 13:23, and as saving his Body, the Church, Eph 5:23, and our bodies, Phil 3:20. The Pastorals often apply it to God, Saviour of all by his redemptive design, and to Christ, the Mediator of the mystery of salvation, *e.g.* 1 Tim 1:1 ; 2:3 ff. ; 2 Tim 1:10 ; Tit 3:4, 6 ; *cf.* 2 Pet 1:11 ; 1 Jn 4:14. When St Paul speaks of ' the epiphany of the glory of our great God and Saviour Jesus Christ ', Tit 2:13, he seems deliberately to choose in connexion with his ' epiphany ' or ' manifestation ' ' the greatest title the NT has bestowed upon Jesus ', Spicq, clxii. For Christianity was now entering into conscious conflict with world paganism. All peoples were required to unite in celebrating the emperor's birthday or accession (' epiphany ') as of the ' god manifest ', the ' great god ' bringing favour (χάρις), salvation (σωτηρία), peace and fair hopes to his subjects ; the imperial cult had its priests and hymnology ; there were also the ' saviour-gods ' of the ' mystery religions ', *cf.* Lagr., *S. Luc*, 74 f. ; Allo, *L'Apocalypse*³ 225 ff. ; § 645*d*. To such pretensions the Christians opposed their own ' imperial proclamations ' of Christ and God, 1 Tim 1:17 ; 6:14 ff., and their own hymnology, *cf.* 3:16 ; Pliny, *Ep.*, X, 96 ' carmen Christo quasi Deo '. For the Lamb will conquer the kings ' because he is Lord of lords and King of kings ', Apoc 17:14 ; 19:16, and all creation sings : ' To him that sitteth upon the throne and to the Lamb, benediction and honour and glory and power for ever and ever ', 5:13 ; *cf.* 4:9 ; 7:12 ; Spicq, clxii–iv, 264 ff.

IV THE REDEMPTION

The riches of the Redemption were not brought to **642a** Christians confined within legal explanations or in a few formulae. Formulae were indeed given : ' Faithful

642a is the saying, and worthy of all acceptance, that Christ Jesus came into the world to save sinners ', 1 Tim 1:15, WV. But they were seen against the background of OT prophecy, 1 Cor 15:3, and the doctrine of the sinfulness of the whole human race, and their redemption in the Second Adam, through whom they have access in one Spirit to the Father. Moreover the doctrine was embodied in an institution, the central act of Christian worship, the Sacrifice of the New Covenant, wherein Christians renewed, as Christ had commanded, the ' memorial ' of his sacrifice on the Cross, and ' showing forth ' his death, waited for his coming, *cf.* 1 Cor 11:23–26. As the OT and the Gospels look forward to Christ's redeeming sacrifice, so St Paul and St John look outwards from it to the vast horizons of salvation, God's New Covenant, the Kingdom which the glorified Christ offers to the Father, the whole world consummated through him.

b **The OT was God's fatherly and merciful preparation** of his design to save the world through his Son. Though it had in it nothing of final achievement, it was the introduction to a ' better hope by which we draw nigh to God ', Heb 7:19. Christ himself, ' beginning at Moses and all the prophets ' had shown that the Messias ought to ' have suffered these things and so enter into his glory ', Lk 24:25–35. The strands of this design are gathered together in the NT.

c The moral law and the reality of sin and of the judgements of God had been inculcated by the **giving of the Commandments**, *cf.* Rom 3:19 f. ; Gal 3:19. The Law was holy, and the Commandment holy, just and good, Rom 7:12. Though the Israelites constantly transgressed, they were as constantly called back to repentance through the mercy, compassion and fidelity of Yahweh and his tender love for Israel, his unfaithful spouse, *e.g.* Ex 34:6 f. ; Deut 7–11 ; Mic 7:18 ff. ; Os 2:19 f. ; 11:1, 4. If they return to him, he takes away their sins, Ac 10:43 ; Jer 31:33 ; Dan 9:24. He will give them a new heart and spirit, Ez 11:19 ; 36:26, since before his omnipotence they are like clay in the potter's hand, Is 29:16 ; Jer 18:6 ; Rom 9:21. His prevenient action goes before their co-operation : ' Make me to return and I will return, for thou art Yahweh, my God ', Jer 31:18 ; *cf.* Lam 5:21 ; Ez 18:31 ; DBV(S), *Grâce*, 734–7. ; 839–41.

d **Sacrifice,** which is natural to man, was freed for the Hebrews, at least in principle, from magical associations. For God himself had instituted the rites and was moved by the humble prayer and obedience which they embodied. But their repetition and multiplicity (bloody and unbloody sacrifices, holocausts, peace-offerings, offerings for sin etc., *cf.* Heb 8:3 ; 9:9 ; 10:5–10, and §§ 104–15) suggested deficiency, Heb 10:1–4.

e **Expiatory sacrifices,** to avert punishment due to sin, almost all involved the offering of **blood**, Heb 9:22. Blood, the vehicle of life, God's most precious gift, was so sacred that men were strictly ordered to abstain from it, and it was reserved for the altars, Gen 9:4 ; Lev 17:10–14 ; Deut 12:23 ; Ac 15:29. When life had been forfeited by sin, the victim's blood, offered in substitution, obtained pardon and alliance with God, Lev 17:11 (lxx) ; *cf.* 1 Jn 1:7 ; Apoc 1:5 ; 7:14. On the great **Day of Atonement** (Kippurim), the purification of the sanctuary and the people depended on the presentation of blood before God, and the high-priest entered the Holy of Holies to perform this, his highest office, Lev 16:15 ff. ; Heb 9:7–14. The immolation of a victim for sin contained an element of penal substitution, but the central act was the pouring forth of the blood, symbol not of death but of the offering of life. Symbols of love, alliance and union were therefore dominant, *cf.* DBV(S), *Expiation*, 74–6 ; *Westcott, *The Ep. of St John*, 34 f. ; *The Ep. to the Heb.*, 295 ff. As bond of brotherhood between men, blood was also the symbol of the Covenant between God and his people and of his protection, Ex 12:13 ; 24:3 ff. ; Heb 9:19. This holy union was imaged in the **Peace-Offerings,** followed by a meal conceived to be shared between God

and the worshipper, a sacrament of fellowship. But since the efficacy of these sacrifices depended on the sincerity of the offerers, the prophets tried to arouse corresponding dispositions of heart and insisted that sacrifices were useless without them ; *cf.* Lattey, *The Prophets and Sacrifice*, JTS 42 (1941) ; §§ 155–65. Thus ' the sentiment of reconciliation and of love impregnates the whole symbolism of sacrifice and makes us already understand why, in preparing by ancient figures the salvation of the human race, God willed that there should be " no redemption without the shedding of blood " ', DBV(S), 81 ; Heb 9:22.

Abraham's Heroic Faith, and his obedience, particularly in sacrificing Isaac, had founded the destinies of Israel and thereby the salvation of the world, Gen 15:6 ff. ; 22:16 ff. ; Ac 3:25 ; Rom 4:1–22 ; Heb 11:8–12, 17 ff. The merits and prayers of the Patriarchs and other great heroes were also a source of expiation, *e.g.* Gen 18:22–32 ; Ex 32:13 f. ; Num 11:2 ; Jer 15:1 ; Ez 14:14. The doctrines of solidarity and substitution here implicit were developed by Jewish theology in its teaching on **' the merits of the Fathers '.** The prayers of God's great servants continued to intercede for his people, 2 Mac 15:12–14, without removing individual responsibility and need for conversion, *e.g.* 1 Kg 26:23 ; Jer 32:19 ; Ez 18:1–32. The belief in expiation by suffering, especially by the blood of martyrs, is attested for Palestinian and Hellenistic Jewry by 2 Mac 7:37 f., and by rabbinical writings about the beginning of the Christian era, *art. cit.*, 105–8 ; Lagr. *Le Messianisme chez les Juifs*, 236 ff. In the apocryphal 4 Mac Eleazar says ' may my blood be an instrument of their purification and take my life as ransom for theirs' (καθάρσιον . . . ἀντίψυχον). God accepts the lives of the mother and her sons as ' ransom of the sin of the people. . . . Through their blood and their expiatory death (ἱλαστηρίου θανατου) Divine Providence has saved Israel ', 17:20 f. ; *cf. art. cit.*, 108 ; BJP, II, 98.

The Gospel of the Suffering Servant linked the doctrines of sacrifice and merit at their deepest level. A mysterious and incredible theme, Is 53:1 ; Jn 12:38 ; Rom 10:16, the sweet and humble offerer takes on himself the faults of all the straying sheep without contracting their stain, and God delivers up his Servant in compassionate love, only to exalt him as the head of a glorious humanity. His life will be a ' sin-offering ' ('āšām) and thus ' the ritual act of the shedding of blood is joined with the noblest interior virtues to become the most perfect symbol of religion . . . the ideal expiatory sacrifice ', DBV(S), *art. cit.*, 99–100 ; Is 53:4–12. The Servant is distinguished from the ' many ' whose sins are pardoned on account of his self-sacrifice ; *cf.* § 446*f* ; *art. cit.*, 91–7 ; R. Murphy, *Second Isaias : the servant of the Lord*, CBQ 9 (1947) 262 ff. The Isaian prophecy, echoed in Zach 12:10–13:1, is continually in the thoughts of the Great Servant himself as the Passion approaches, and in the apostolic preaching, *e.g.* Mk 9:12 ; Ac 3:13 ; 8:32 ; 1 Cor 15:3 ; Heb 9:28 ; 1 Pet 2:22–5 ; 1 Jn 3:5. The Servant's history, and especially the Crucifixion, are imaged with amazing precision in the Psalms, *e.g.* Ps 22 (Vg 21) ; DBV(S), *art. cit.*, 100–5. The Just One offers himself to God as a victim whose heroic obedience is more meritorious than OT sacrifices, Ps 40(39) 7–10, where LXX suggests the thought of Heb 10:5–10 that God had prepared his body to be a victim replacing those of the Old Law, *cf.* Lagr., *Notes sur le messianisme dans les Psaumes*, RB² (1905) 54. The Messias, though not of Aaron's family, is priest in the manner of Melchisedech, Ps 110(109) 4 ; Heb 5:10 ; 7.

Why then was a Suffering Messias a Scandal to the Jews?—Rom 9:30 ff. ; 1 Cor 1:23. For all their advantages over the Gentiles, Rom 9:4 f., only a ' remnant ' recognized him. This too had been prophesied, *e.g.* Rom 9:27 ; 11:5 ; Is 10:22. Prophecy, always fragmentary, does not force its recognition upon the will, and contemporary Judaism had fashioned a Messias after its own image. The sense of God's free, profound action upon the soul (still preserved nobly by Philo in Alexandrian Judaism ; *cf.* DBV(S), *Grâce*, 926 ff.), was replaced by an exaggerated idea of the dignity of man : his actions demanded in strict justice a divine salary from a far-off, divine Master, and with only the Law's external help, he could keep that Law and triumph over evil. The wide charity of the Law itself was degraded into legal formalism. The privileges of Israel, which had been guarded by segregation from other nations, were made exclusive. The universalist understanding of the prophetic visions was abandoned. All that surpassed the natural order and the racial horizon was shut out by a personal and national pride which became the bitter enemy of the Gospel of grace, BJP, II, 318–25 ; DBV(S), *Grâce*, 930–7.

Thus a total incomprehension of the redemptive death of the Suffering Servant is shown by Contemporary Rabbinical Writings. He would be a warrior or a wonder-worker. His humiliations were ascribed to the Jewish people or their adversaries. How could he be a victim of love who would make void the ancient ceremonies and open God's kingdom to all nations ? St Paul himself, while a disciple of the Rabbis, did not understand the universalist chapters of the prophets ; *cf.* Eph 3:5. Though the ' just remnant ' of prophecy would appeal to the prophets (*cf.* Ac 3:13 with Is 42:1 ; ch 53 ; and Ac 8:32 with Is 53:7 f.), the sectarianism of the Pharisees would never ' sacrifice the Law to a text of Isaias ', Lagr., *Le Messianisme chez les Juifs*, 251.

This spirit implacably opposed and crucified Jesus, recognizing that his mission, life and teaching condemned it. Jesus, usually so mild, revealing the merciful and bountiful God, Friend and Lover of men, denounced its justice as insufficient for the kingdom of heaven, Mt 5:20, and its professors as hypocrites, blind guides, whited sepulchres, vipers ; summing them up in the parable of the Pharisee and the Publican and warning his disciples against them. It cast forth and killed the Son and heir of the Vineyard of Israel, seeking to take his inheritance, and thus rejected the corner-stone of God's building, Mt 21:33–45 ; *cf.* Is 5:1–7 ; Ac 4:11 ; Rom 9:32 f. It is the key to that opposition of darkness to the Light which goes through the Gospel of St John. It continued to persecute the early Church, tried to restrict her universalism and subject her to the Law, and pursued its great enemy, the Apostle of the Gentiles. It explains the vehement warnings of Gal against falling under the yoke of the Law, the treatise on the universality of sin and on God's gracious justification in Rom, and the teaching of Heb on the transcendence of Christ's mediatory Priesthood and expiatory sacrifice. This spirit re-appears in early heresies, and in the Pelagian attempt to ' make void the Cross of Christ '.

a The Gospel of Grace—St Paul's developed theology on the initiative of the Father and the universality of sin and salvation for Jew and Gentile was rooted in the Gospel revelation. We now deal with the Gospels, *cf.* §§ 645*b*–649 for Paul. Isaias had been a universalist long before Paul, and Simeon in heralding the salvation brought by Christ ' set himself exactly in the horizon of Isaias ' (Lagrange), Lk 2:30–32 ; Is 40:5 ; 42:6 ; 49:6 ; 52:10 ; Ac 13:47. The Precursor also took his manifesto and his images from Isaias when he sought in preaching judgement and repentance from sin to ' prepare the way of the Lord ' by opening mens' hearts to grace, Mt 3:1–12 ; Mk 1:2–4 ; *cf.* Is 40:3–5 ; 59:5, etc. Jesus carrying forward the message, required **repentance** and **belief** : ' The appointed time has come and the Kingdom of God is near at hand ; repent and believe the gospel ', Mk 1:15, KNT.

b ' Grace ' (χάρις)—The word is not in Mt and Mk, nor Jn, apart from the Prologue, and seems not to have been used by our Lord, DBV(S), *Grâce*, 715–1 ; *cf.* 727–48 for Hebrew terms. The Good Shepherd taught in words his flock understood. Grace is God's free gift. The verb ' *give* ' (δίδωμι) with its derivatives (KTW,

δίδωμι, etc., II, 169) in the technical sense of God giving **643b** man all he has and specially what he cannot gain of himself, is characteristic of the entire NT. ' It is given ' or ' will be given ' or ' given ' constantly recurs. ' It is given ' to the Apostles to know the mysteries of the Kingdom, Mt 13:11 ; *cf.* 1 Jn 5:20. The Kingdom itself is given, Mt 21:43. God's love is not a sentiment but a ' giving ', *e.g.* 7:11 ; Rom 8:32 ; 1 Jn 3:16. The Father gives : ' God so loved the world as to give his only begotten Son ', Jn 3:16 ; ' a man cannot receive anything unless it be given him from heaven ', Jn 3:27 ; ' no man can come to me unless it be given him by my Father ', 6:65 ; ' behold what manner of love the Father hath *given* to us, that we should be called and should be the sons of God ', 1 Jn 3:1. Christ's love is the gift of his life, Mt 20:28, of himself, Gal 1:4, of his body in the Eucharist, Mt 26:26 ; Lk 22:19. The Holy Spirit is ' given ' and ' received ', *e.g.* Lk 11:13 ; Jn 3:34 ; 7:37 ff. ; Ac 1:8 ; 2:38 ; 1 Cor 2:14.

Although the gift is gratuitous, it does not exclude **c** recompense, ' **merit** ', itself the fruit of grace, or ' demerit '. This is marked by the compounds ἀποδίδωμι and ἀνταποδίδωμι with their nouns, Mt 6:4, 6, 18 ; 16:27 ; Rom 2:6 ; 12:19 ; 2 Tim 4:8, 14 ; Apoc 22:12. It is shown in the parables, *cf.* Mt 20:13 ff. ; Lk 17:7 ff. with Mt 25:14 ff. ; Lk 19:12 ff. To him who has, more will be given, Mt 25:29. Though God, always master of his gifts, rewards a hundredfold, making the servants enter their Lord's own joy, 5:12 ; 19:29 ; 25:21 ; Lk 6:38, there is correspondence between merit and reward, *ib.*, the merciful obtain mercy, those who pardon are pardoned, those who acknowledge Christ will be acknowledged, if they lose their lives for him, they will save them, the humble will be exalted, and the watchful servants will be served by the Master himself. In short, God crowns men's merits, but in doing so, crowns his own gift, Rom 11:35 ; Col 3:24 ; 1 Thess 3:9, DBV(S), *Grâce*, 717–22, 969–71.

Man takes or receives God's gift (λαμβάνω and δέχομαι **d** are practically synonymous, KTW, II, 49) and may thus welcome or reject ' the word ', Mt 13:20 ; Mk 4:16, 20, a person representing Christ, Mt 10:40 f. ; 18:5 ; and the Kingdom, Mk 10:15. ' Giving ' and ' receiving ' are used for the whole order of grace : ' What hast thou that thou hast not received ? And if thou hast received, why dost thou glory as if thou hadst not received it ', 1 Cor 4:7 ; Eph 4:7 ; Jas 1:17.

Salvation from sin (*cf.* § 645*i*) is an aspect of the Gospel **e** of Grace which draws out the true meaning of the Messianic concept and distinguishes it from material notions. Jesus came to save men from sin, *e.g.* Mt 1:21 ; 1 Tim 1:15. Those who accept him, enter the way of salvation, *e.g.* Mk 16:16 ; Lk 13:23 ; Ac 2:21, 47, which leads, for those who persevere, to final salvation, *e.g.* Mt 10:22 ; 24:13 ; Lk 8:12. It is all in the story of the Samaritan woman : the sinner, the prayer, the Giver, the ' gift of God ', the ' fountain of water springing up into life everlasting ' which Jesus will give if she asks, Jn 4:10 ff., *cf.* § 645*g*.

The Devil and the World—Sin is of the devil ; *cf.* **f** 1 Jn 3:8. Opening the vision upon the fecundity of the creative act, Scripture shows myriads of incorporeal spirits, *e.g.* Mt 13:41 ; 25:41 ; Lk 2:13 ; Heb 1:6. The wicked angels, hurled from heaven, hold sway on earth through man's infidelity, *e.g.* Apoc 12:7 ff., 12 ff. Though ' the world ' can mean God's creation, or humanity, Jn 3:16 ; 2 Cor 5:19, it usually stands for the ' whole world ' dragged thus under the power of the devil, 1 Jn 5:19, WV ; *cf.* 2:15 ; Rom 3:19 ; Jas 4:4 (whom St Paul even calls ' the god of this world ', 2 Cor 4:4) and under his demons, ' *world-masters* of this darkness ', Eph 6:12. This ' mystery of wickedness ' is working among the ' children of unbelief ', 2 Thess 2:7 ; Eph 2:2. The adoration of devils under cover of ' the elements of the world ' was the reason for the Christian horror of idolatry's empty gods, 1 Cor 10:19 ff. ; Gal 4:3, 8 f. ; Col 2:8, 20 ; *cf.* Huby, *in loc.* From this fundamental point of view Christ came ' to destroy the works of the devil ', 1 Jn

643f 3:8. Hence his meeting with Satan in the desert Temptations, Mt 4:1–11, the tremendous encounter of the exorcisms, when the 'strong man' is driven from his usurped dwelling, 12:29, the passing on to the disciples of the power whose exercise draws forth Jesus's words 'I saw Satan like lightning falling from heaven', Lk 10:18, and the final death struggle with 'the prince of this world', Jn 12:31; 14:30; 16:11. On the Cross he triumphed, like a Roman conqueror, over the world and the powers of darkness, 33; Col 2:14 f. It is against them, not merely against 'flesh and blood', that we who are bidden to share his victory, have our warfare, Eph 6:12; 1 Pet 5:8; 1 Jn 2:13. But one who is 'born of God' and keeps himself from sin, cannot be touched by Satan, whom God will crush under our feet, Rom 16:20; cf. Gen 3:15; 1 Jn 3:9; 5:4 f., 18; Apoc 2–3; 15:2; 21:7; Bouyer, 98–104, here followed.

g **The Kingdom of God**—Cf. §§ 625a–f, 678f, g, the concept chosen by Jesus because familiar to his hearers, ' is above all, a gift ', SB, I, 180f. It is 'given' by the Father, Mt 21:43; Lk 12:32, and comes silently from God in his chosen time, Mt 6:10; 10:7; 12:28; Ac 1:7. A man must ' receive ' it as a little child, Mt 18:3; and thereby enters the phase of the Kingdom leading to the glorious consummation prepared by the Father for his children, 25:34. Indeed it is the property of the ' poor in spirit ', the ' little children ', 5:3; 19:14. Within it, the bankrupt sinner is forgiven his debt, 18:27, and the Father distributes rewards and places as he pleases, 20:1–16, 23. It is a marriage feast, invitations to which are issued first to special guests, then to all, 22:1 ff. It can be taken away and given to others, 21:43. One may be shut out from it, 25:10, or cast out, 13:41 f.; 22:13, for even some of those in the Kingdom will not be ' worthy of the age to come ', Lk 20:35; 2 Thess 1:5. Christ's parables are symbolic revelations of the Kingdom, a revelation which is itself a gift, Mt 13:11, 34 f.; cf. M. Hermaniuk, La Parabole évangélique, 274–301. Although the Kingdom-concept and the teaching by parables were unfamiliar to Gentiles and are hardly mentioned outside the Gospels (but cf. 1 Cor 15:24 f.; Col 1:13) they lie behind the rest of the NT.

h **Repentance** (μετάνοια), 'a change of sentiments' from sin to God, is the negative aspect of ' **being converted** ' (ἐπιστρέφω) the turning of the heart from evil to good, a new orientation from self to God, cf. Is 6:9 f.; Mal 4:6; Mt 13:14 f.; Lk 1:16 f.; 22:32; Ac 9:35; 28:26 f. The relations of God and his people in the OT had shown this regular rhythm: infidelity, punishment, conversion, pardon, the help of Yahweh. What Jesus wished to transform was the heart, or will, the free centre of man's dispositions, Mt 5:8; 12:34; Mk 7:21; 11:23; Lk 8:15; Ac 2:37 f.; Rom 2:5. Like the Baptist, he began his preaching by this call to repentance, Mt 3:2; 4:17. He sent his Apostles to preach it, Mk 6:12, and it was always a first part of their message, Ac 2:38; 5:31; Rom 2:4; Heb 6:1. St Luke gives beautiful examples: the sinful woman, the publican, the prodigal son, Zachaeus, the good thief.

i **Faith**—The positive disposition required by Jesus is called belief in himself, Mt 18:6, in God, Mk 11:22, in the Gospel, 1:15, or simply ' believing ', Mt 21:22; Mk 5:36; Lk 8:12 f. In OT faith, though a fundamental virtue, was rarely mentioned, e.g. Gen 15:6; Ex 14:31; 2 Par 20:20; Is 7:9; cf. Heb 11. But with Christ's coming religion is self-giving to a Person and his message. ' Faith ' describes the normal Christian attitude (250 times in NT). **To believe** (300 times) is to accept the Gospel, and Christians are ' believers '. Since the believer logically conforms himself to the way of salvation, Christ often says ' thy faith hath saved thee ', e.g. Mt 9:22, and faith is equated with charity, Lk 7:47, 50 (but cf. 1 Cor 13:2, 8); § 648l; DBV(S), Grâce, 968; ZLG, πίστις.

This faith is not blind confidence, for its motive is the divine authority of a witness accredited by God. Jesus never told men to shut their eyes and believe, but to open their eyes and hearts to the motives for believing: his miracles or ' works ', Mt 11:2–6; Jn 5:36; 10:25, 37; 14:11, the witness of prophecy, e.g. 5:39, his own character, 8:46 f., his doctrine, whose divine origin is apparent to men of goodwill, 7:17; cf. 46; Mt 7:28 f. The Resurrection was final confirmation, Rom 1:4. The dialogue with Nicodemus illustrates the process: he admits that the signs done by Jesus prove him a teacher from God, and when he demurs at a hard doctrine, he is taken back to this motive: Christ's witness is God's, Jn 3:2, 11.

When faith is strong, it brings the trust united with **j** certainty which procures miracles and ' moves mountains ', Mt 17:19 f.; 21:21 f.; 1 Cor 13:2. The miracles, as the nature of many of them shows, are not the result of ' faith-healing '. It is for a man's spiritual good that Christ frequently demands the act of faith, and he rewards it by forgiveness or miracles, Mt 9:2 ff., 20 ff., 27 ff., and punishes its absence by withholding them, 12:38 f.; 13:58; Mk 6:5 f.

The faith given to the word of Jesus must be given **k** to that of his appointed witnesses, Mt 10:40; Mk 16:14; Lk 10:16; Ac 1:8; 2:32, as a condition of salvation for all to whom the Gospel is preached, Mk 16:16 f.; Ac 2:38–41; 2 Thess 1:10. It was always needed to obtain and live in accordance with the Messianic blessings, 2 Cor 13:5; Gal 2:20; cf. further § 648e–n; DBV(S), Foi, 291–4.

Justice—Righteousness, conformation to God's will, is **l** an interior aspect of the Kingdom: ' Seek first his Kingdom and justice ', Mt 6:33; cf. 3:15; 5:20; BEJC, 140; KTW, II, 200 (Schrenk). It forms a principal theme of the Sermon on the Mount which describes the dispositions comprising it: ' poverty of spirit ', gentleness and humility, 5:3, 5, hunger and thirst after ' justice ', love of mercy and peace, patience, generosity and forgiveness, 5:6 f., 9, 33–47, purity and goodness of heart, 5:8; Lk 8:15. The ' just ' are those in whom God takes pleasure, the opposite of sinners, e.g. 18:9; 20:20. These fundamental dispositions of simplicity, humility, purity and confident love are the reason why ' unless you be converted and become as little children you shall not enter into the kingdom of heaven, Mt 18:3, for to such it belongs, 19:14. They are to grow to the perfection of the Heavenly Father, 5:48, Jesus himself being the model, 11:29; cf. 1 Cor 11:1. Opposed to them are hardness and insensibility, fickleness, love of riches, care for this world and especially pride and self-sufficiency, e.g. Mt 13:19 ff. The teaching of St Teresa of Lisieux is thus the heart of the Gospel.

Jesus came to proclaim the ' Jubilee Year ', the **e** Messianic ' Day of Salvation ' to an evil generation, slaves of sin who thought themselves free men, 16:4; Lk 4:18–21; Is 61:2; cf. Jn 8:34 ff; Rom 6:16–20. The ' Sinners' Friend ', sent to call them to the repentance which all needed, Mt 9:13; 11:19; Lk 13:2–5, he asserted his authority to forgive sins by working the cure on the paralytic, Mt 9:2 ff, and entrusted the same mission of forgiveness to his Apostles, 16:19; 18:18; Jn 20:21 ff. For the sinner, all was made easy: ' My yoke is sweet and my burden light ', Mt 11:28 ff. But Jesus gave his death as the price.

The Redemptive Death of Jesus is no Pauline inter- **f** polation, but in the very fabric of the Gospels, cf. DBV(S), Expiation, 114–33; BEJC, 219 ff.; J. Lilly, The Idea of Redemption in the Gospels, CBQ 9 (1947) 255 ff.; *A. Rawlinson, St Mark, 108–111. It was not the course of events which showed Jesus that he would die. Early in his public life (and the context is purely Jewish), he had foretold that his disciples would mourn when the bridegroom was taken from them, Mt 9:15. Asked for a sign, he declared ' destroy this temple and in three days I will raise it up ', Jn 2:19; Mt 26:61, so linking the Resurrection with the day when his body would become the central sanctuary of the New Law, cf. A. M. Dubarle, Le Signe du Temple, RB 48 (1939) 21–44. While he was preparing men's minds to accept a truly religious kingdom, and to acknowledge himself, he did no more than hint at his death, as by the ' sign of Jonas ', Mt 12:39 f. ; 16:4, the ' baptism ' he had to undergo, Lk 12:50, the ' cup ' to drink, Mt 20:22, the ' lifting up ' of the Son of man, Jn 3:14, and the answer to an attempt to frighten him, Lk 13:31 ff.

But once he had obtained Peter's vital confession, ' from then ' (and the typically Semitic passage is in all the Synoptics), ' Jesus began to show to his disciples that he must (δεῖ) go to Jerusalem and suffer many things . . . and be put to death and the third day rise again '. Mk adds ' and he spoke the word openly '. The shock to the Apostles appears from Peter's reaction. But Jesus called together his disciples with the crowd and insisted that he who would come after him must also be ready to take up his cross, Mt 16:16–27 ; Mk 8:29–38 ; Lk 9:20–26. The redemptive programme is suddenly unfolded. We are on the watershed whence the horizon opens upon the Cross and the Resurrection.

On the journey to Jerusalem Jesus repeated his prophecy with increasing detail, e.g. Mt 17:22 f. ; 20:17 ff. These scenes with their vivid touches about the terror of the Apostles and their fear to ask him questions, Mk 9:32 ; 10:32, part of the web and woof of the Gospel story, are supplemented by the record that the great figures of the OT spoke of these things with Jesus at the Transfiguration, Lk 9:31 (cf. Mk 9:9 ; Mt 17:9–13), by the little double prophecy that Mary of Bethania had anointed him for burial and would be remembered for it in all the world, 26:6–13, and by the allegory of the vineyard whose rebel husbandmen kill the Lord's son, Mt 21:33 ff. ; cf. Is 3:14 ; 5:1 ff. Jesus's anticipation is not the natural depression of one whose mission is failing, for he joins the Resurrection to his death. Nor is it due to his reading of prophecy, for he always speaks from direct knowledge. But the Scriptures, especially the ' Gospel of Isaias ' on the suffering, death and glory of the Servant, are continually in his mind, and he uses them to show that the Son of Man ' must ' suffer, cf. Is 53 with Mt 26:24, 54 ; Mk 9:12 14:49 ; Lk 18:31 ; 22:37. The lesson would bear fruit, 24:27, 45.

In this context Jesus sums up his own plan and purpose to his Apostles, angry over the ambition of the sons of Zebedee : ' The Son of man hath come not to be served but to serve, and to give his life a ransom for many ', Mt 20:28 ; Mk 10:45, WV ; cf. DBV(S), Expiation, 123–33 ; Lagr., S. Marc, in loc. ; KTW, IV, 343–51 (Buechsel) ; HRCS. λύτρον, which in LXX translates kôṭer, or words associated with pāḍāh and gā'al, means a price paid, a compensation offered, the deliverance of men by ransom or substitution, cf. HRCS ; Eus. Praep. Ev., PG, 21, 85, mentions Phoenician kings sacrificing their dearest son as a λύτρον, and it was used for the price paid to a temple for manumission. Vg's ' redemptio ' is an exact translation. Jesus did not say how, or from what, men were to be ' redeemed ', but no man of that evil generation could give compensation for his own soul, Mk 8:37 f. ; 9:19. So the ' service ' of the Suffering Servant is the reconciliation of ' the many ' to God by the offering of his life ; cf. Is 53:11 f. Here is the doctrine of the Redemption in germ, as contemporaries could begin to understand it. It will be developed organically by St Paul, but there is no trace of an interpolation of his characteristic doctrines on sin, death, etc. Nor is there contradiction with men's need for repentance. They have but to believe and love, but the Good Shepherd gives his life for his sheep (Jn 10:11 ; cf. 15:13) and so abundantly does he redeem them, that his devotion calls forth similar love and service ; cf. Mk 8:31 with 34 ; Phil 2:5–8 ; DBV(S), art. cit., 131 f.

f The Sacrifice of the New Covenant—The fact and doctrine of the Redemption were enshrined by Jesus in the Eucharistic rite which he instituted at the Last Supper. By celebrating it and entering into the sentiments of Jesus, the faithful commemorate his Passion as he intended they should, and are filled with the same mind as that with which he went to Calvary, 1 Cor 11:26. What he did and said showed his death

to be an expiatory sacrifice ; cf. DBV(S), art. cit., **644f** 133–45 ; Eucharistie, 1146–215 (Coppens) ; DTC, Eucharistie, 989–1121 (Ruch) ; Commentaries on Mt 26:26–29 ; Mk 14:22–25 ; Lk 22:15–20 ; 1 Cor 11:23–25 ; texts compared by BEJC, 230–37.

Between two prophecies of his death and in circum- **g** stances dominated by the thought of Calvary (Mt 26:21, 29 ; Mk 14:18, 25 ; cf. Lk 22:15–18) Jesus taking the cup had said, ' This is my blood of the Covenant which is shed for many ', Mk ; Mt adds ' for the remission of sins '. ' Blood shed ' is used for violent death, e.g. Gen 4:8 ff. ; 1 Kg 25:31 ; Is 59:7, and the sacrificial meaning is clear from the words added. The parallelism, and the words ' for you ' added in Lk and 1 Cor, show that his body also is offered ; cf. Jn 6:51. The ritual separation of body and blood shows the immolation of the victim, followed, as in all such sacrifices, by the pouring forth of the blood. ' Many ' does not exclude ' all ', cf. § 739h.

The Covenant—(διαθήκη, cf. KTW, II, 105–37 **h** (Beham) ; DBV(S), Expiation, loc. cit.) which holds a central place in biblical theology, is the gracious pact of alliance and union made between God and his People. (διαθήκη thus means for Jews ' Covenant '— Sinaitic, Messianic, or simply God's, cf. L. da Fonseca, S.J., Bi, 8 (1927) 290–319 ; 9 (1928) 26–40 ; 143–60, for this meaning in 396 cases in LXX and almost always in NT). The prophets had foretold a ' new ' and ' everlasting ' Covenant, and contemporary Jews were expecting it ; cf. Is 55:3 ; 59:21 ; 61:8 ; Jer 31:31 ff. ; Ezech 16:60 ; Os 2:18 ff. ; M. Schechter, Documents of Jewish Sectaries ; Lagr. RB, 9 (1912) La secte juive de la Nouvelle Alliance, 213–40 ; 321–60. The ' blood of the Covenant ' must be that of this Covenant (1 Cor and Lk add ' new '), the eternal union and friendship between God and men, wherein he is their Father and they his children, the ' marriage ' of Os 2:18–20 ; Mt 22:2 ff. ; 25:1 ff. ; Eph 5:25–32 ; Apoc 19:7–9. Blood, symbol of union because bond of brotherhood, had been used to ratify the Old Covenant, Ex 24:6 ff. Jesus now gives his own blood as sacrifice of the New Covenant, not merely as sign but as real, mediatorial cause, Heb 8:6–13 ; 9:15–23. ' What assurance of divine friendship ! ' DBV(S), 141 f. To Greek audiences διαθήκη would also suggest its other meaning ' testament ', Heb 9:15 ff., and the Fathers say that Jesus left himself to his own. The Paschal character of the Supper shows further that the saving blood of Jesus is that of the true Paschal Lamb, Mt 26:17 ff. ; Mk 14:12 ff. ; Lk 22:7 ff. ; cf. Jn 1:29 ; 13:1 ff. ; Is 53:7.

Communion with God was given by the sacred meal **i** after sacrifice ; cf. 1 Cor 10:18–21 ; Philo, De Spec. Leg., I, 221. ' Drink ye all of it. For this is my blood ', Mt 26:27 f. Christ commands what Moses had forbidden ! The Law of Fear gives place to the Covenant of Love ! The sanctity of the blood, which had made the faithful abstain from it, is the motive which invites them. Man's bold and impotent desire for union with God, symbolized in sacrifice, is fulfilled. While the sacramental form takes all repugnance from the senses and deepens the mystery for the spirit, the faithful who eat Christ's Body and drink his Blood become in truth brothers of God, DBV(S), 142–3.

Critics, who deny the divinity of Jesus, cannot accept **j** such conclusions and try to cut the account of the institution of the Eucharist from the Gospel data as ' Pauline '. Yet it was kept in memory by a repetitive rite, the specific and essential act of Christian worship, Ac 2:42, 46 etc., and it was transmitted by the earliest tradition, 1 Cor 11:23 ff. Upon it converge all the lines of the symbolism of OT sacrifice, of the national sense of sin, of prophetic hope, of the redemptive power of the merits of the Just and of Jesus's own teaching upon the purpose of his Messianic work. It is expressed in simple language free from ' Paulinisms '. It shows Jesus loving his own even to the perfect act which consummated his devotion, Jn 13:1. Far from contradict-

644j ing his early preaching on the Fatherly love of God, it is its supreme revelation. ' God so loved the world as to give his only begotten Son ', Jn 3:16 ; ' *God makes known his love towards us because when as yet we were sinners, Christ died for us* ', Rom 5:8. With Jesus, all is redemptive : his words revealing the Father, his miracles leading men to the faith, his Person drawing them to repentance, above all his blood which he sheds for many. ' Here, like avenues ending in a cross, join the perspectives opened by the teaching of Jesus on the end of the Law, on the new justice and the religion of the new man, on the reconciliation of the world to the Father in heaven, and on the part of the Son of man in this religion and this reconciliation. The blood of a sacrifice sealed this new covenant, and the Victim of this sacrifice was the Son of man ', Batiffol, *L'Enseignement de Jésus*[4], 248 f. ; *art. cit.*, 145. *Cf.* further on the Last Supper, §§ 652*g*–*i*, 653, 657*f*–*h*.

645a **The first message** of the Apostles to their fellow-Jews was of the realization of the Messianic hope, whose meaning was deepened by the new understanding given by the Spirit. Jesus is the only Saviour, and his gifts the promised remission of sins, and the Spirit, Ac 2:38 ; 4:12 ; 10:43. Calvary, which might have seemed the negation of his Messiahship, was part of his work in the ' determined design of God ' and the Resurrection its divine consummation ; both were fulfilments of prophecy, 2:23 f. ; 3:18 ; 4:25–28 ; 8:28–35 ; 13:27 ; Is 53. Accordingly the primitive catechesis taught that Christ died for our sins and rose according to the Scriptures, 1 Cor 15:3 f.

b **The Redemption in St Paul**—St Paul handed on the faith which he had received, *ib.*, 11. This faith looked outwards from the redeeming sacrifice and the cosmic glory of the Resurrection to the salvation of all mankind. It saw in them the love of the Father of the human family who sent his own Son to save the world, the loving obedience of the Beloved Son even to the death of the Cross and his consequent glorification as risen Head of a new humanity, and the universal extension of sin and death (from which the Law could not deliver) overcome at last by the grace of the universal Mediator, in whom the Father sees the whole race of his redeemed sons, Jews and Gentiles, made one through the action of the Spirit. Incorporation in the Body of Christ came by the grace of baptism, that sharing in the dying and rising of Christ which expands into the individual and corporate life of Christians. This life, guided by the Spirit of Christ, led to the final triumph over concupiscence and death by glorious, bodily resurrection with him on the Day of his final Coming. This is true **Paulinism**. *Cf.* Rom 8:14–23 ; 1 Cor 3:23 ; 15:28 ; Col 3:11.

c **The Mystery**—'We speak of the wisdom of God embodied in a mystery, that hidden wisdom which God devised before the ages unto our glory ; a wisdom which none of the rulers of this world hath come to know. . . . To us God hath revealed it through the Spirit ', 1 Cor 2:7 f., 10, WV. It was granted Paul to preach to the Gentiles the universality of this Mystery, the wonderful variety of God's wisdom manifested in the unsearchable riches of Christ and their incorporation in him, Eph 3:2–11 ; Col 1:25 ff. ; 2 Tim 1:9–11 ; Tit 1:2 f. ; *cf.* Rom 16:25. Contained in his original vocation, Ac 9:6, 15, formulated already in 1 Cor, this teaching attains its full development in the Epistles of the Captivity ; *cf.* DTC, *Paul*, 2356.

d **This ' Mystery ' is utterly different from the Mystery Religions**—*Cf.* §§ 599*a*–*d*, 633*h*, 652*e*. The former Pharisee fully shared the Jewish horror of pagan rites and apotheoses, and his enemies were able to accuse him only of setting aside the Law, never of compromising with pagan belief, *e.g.* Ac 12:20 ff. ; 14:8–18 ; 26:5 ff. ; Rom 2:22 ; 1 Cor 5:11 ; 6:9 ; 10:7, 14–21. Pagans who became Christians had to abandon idolatry and henceforth share repugnance for it, 1 Cor 8:4 ff. ; 2 Cor 6:14 ff. ; Eph 5:7 f. ; 1 Thess 1:9 ; Lagr., *Les origines du dogme paulinien de la divinité du*

Christ, RB, 45 (1936) 5–33. Besides, the ' mysteries ' were rites open only to initiates which it was profane to reveal. But ' the Mystery ' in NT means principally God's hitherto secret purpose in his dealings with men which he now wills to be revealed by his Apostles to all who have ears to hear it ; *cf.* *J. A. Robinson, *St Paul's Epistle to the Ephesians*, 240 ; MMV μυστήριον. The ' mysteries ' of God were understood by spiritual Christians not because they were a privileged class but because they had reached spiritual maturity at which all should aim, 1 Cor 2:6 ; 3:1 ff. ; Heb 5:11 ff. The rites of the ' mysteries ', expressing vague, human desires for God and immortality, may have remotely prepared their transcendent fulfilment. But contemporary ' mystery cults ' were magical, often immoral and usually required no change of life, whereas Paul subordinated salvation to faith in the historic Christ and crucifixion of the flesh with its vices, Gal 5:19–24. Neo-Platonist syncretists who at a later date tried to attribute approximately Christian ideas to these rites, met with indignant repudiation from writers like St Justin and Tertullian. These deities of vegetation or totemistic myth had no historic life, death or resurrection, nor was there any idea of justification through the merits of a suffering God. There is no evidence that Mithraism, which developed after Christianity, had any influence upon it. St Paul's use of the word ' mystery ' is not surprising, as it had passed into common speech, *cf,* Lagr., RB 16 (1919) 157–217 (Eleusis), 419–80 (Attis), 29 (1920) 420–46, review of *Loisy's *Les mystères païens et le mystère chrétien* ; Grandmaison, *Jésus Christ*, III, 319–46, ' Gods who died and came to life ', 349–77, ' The Pagan Mysteries ' ; Allo, *L'évangile en face du syncrétisme païen : Les dieux sauveurs*, RSPT 15 (1926) 5–34 ; DA, *Mystères païens et S. Paul* ; DBV(S), *Baptême*, 883–6, 903–20 ; *Eucharistie*, 1156–63, 1193–209 ; *Expiation*, 3–48 ; *Gnose*, 690–701 ; *Grâce*, 707–14 (full bibliography) ; KTW, II, 334 f. (Oepke), IV, 810–19 (Bornkamm).

e We must not confine the doctrine of the Redemption within the limits of theories which theologians may elaborate with much freedom. They are presented and discussed by J. Rivière, *Rédemption*, DTC, 1912–2004, with an abundant bibliography ; *cf.* ET 47, 246 ff. (different views), 48, 267 ff. (bibliography). The ground is thus cleared and objections based on mistaken notions are removed. The idea that the Redemption puts constraint upon the good and loving Father from whom its whole design proceeds is as crude and false as that of a vindictive God calming his wrath by punishing his innocent Son. The Father reconciles humanity to himself through his Beloved Son, their new head, 2 Cor 5:18, and the Son crowns a life of devotion and solidarity with fallen man by a sacrifice of perfect obedience which gives back to his Father the honour and worship (violated by sin) which just order requires in man, constitutes him the Mediator of his brethren, and wins for himself the glory which the Father had destined for him, and for men the pardon they need. This act of reconciliation is not extrinsic to men. So effective is it that it calls forth their love and gives them grace to co-operate freely in the redemptive work itself, Phil 2:5 ; Rom 8:17 ; DTC, 1962 ff. Metaphors, such as the buying back of mankind at the price of Christ's blood, are only metaphors, whose legal implications are not to be pressed. Equally mistaken is any attempt to confine Christ's sacrifice within the categories of OT sacrifices, for while it fulfils them all, it utterly transcends them. However, Rivière's own theory of satisfaction needs incorporating, in our view, into the Mystery of the Total Christ, *cf.* Mersch. *Théol. du Corps Mys.*, chh 10, 11.

f The word '**Redemption** ' (ἀπολύτρωσις) is mainly positive in meaning. Five times out of seven in St Paul it stands for the wide process by which God gives us in Christ graces destined to expand in the glory of heaven, Rom 3:24 ; 8:23 ; 1 Cor 1:30 ; Eph 1:14 ; 4:30 ; *cf.* Lk 21:28. This shows that even when it is called ' the remission of sins ', Eph 1:7 ; Col 1:14, it has

f not that predominantly negative sense which etymology from slave-manumission suggests. In fact St Paul's use of the word goes back to the OT, where *gā'al* is liberation from Egyptian captivity and especially the free Messianic liberation to be accomplished by God, the Redeemer of Israel, BEP, 144 f.

g This deliverance from spiritual danger into true happiness, implying a spiritual transformation, is also called **Salvation**, *cf.* § 643*e*. Perfectly realized only in heaven, it strictly stands for 'eternal life', being opposed to 'death', 'perdition', or 'wrath', *cf.* 1 Cor 3:15; 2 Cor 7:10; Phil 1:28; 1 Thess 5:8 f.; 2 Thess 2:10. But in a wider sense it means the entry into Christian 'justice' of those who are 'saved in hope' and continue to work out their salvation in fear, *e.g.* Rom 8:24; 1 Cor 15:2; Phil 2:12; 1 Tim 4:16; *op. cit.*, 145 f. Salvation is due to God, 1 Cor 1:21; 1 Tim 2:4, to Christ, Ac 4:12; Rom 5:9; Heb 7:25, and comes through grace, Eph 2:5, faith, *e.g.* Ac 16:31; Rom 10:9, baptism, *e.g.* 1 Pet 3:21; Tit 3:5, 'the word', Jas 1:21; 1 Pet 2:2, an Apostle, Rom 11:14; 1 Cor 9:22, a husband or wife, 1 Cor 7:16, one of the faithful, Jas 5:20; Jude 23, attention to Christian doctrine, 1 Tim 4:16; *cf.* ZLG, σαῴζω.

h St Paul's term 'Grace' now comes into its own (at least 100 times, apart from Heb, and 100 in rest of NT) *cf.* § 643*b-d*. God is always first in giving, Rom 11:34. The Incarnation with the Redemption is the 'gift' of God *par excellence*, founding the gratuity of the whole order of grace, which is the absolutely free gift of God's merciful love, 3:24; 5:8; 8:32; Eph 2:4-8; 2 Tim 1:9 f.; 1 Jn 4:9 f. Thus grace is the divine goodness shown in the promise made to Abraham, Gal 3:18, and realized in the Incarnation, 2 Cor 8:9 and specially in Christ's death, Gal 2:21. It is communicated to men, Rom 5:15 ff., by faith and baptism, and by those divine gifts which enable Christians to live their lives and fulfil their functions as members of the Christian community. The Christian state may simply be called 'grace', Gal 5:4; *cf.* Rom 6:14 f. 'Grace thus appears as the common factor found in the diverse acts of the process whereby God raises humanity to himself. . . . This idea . . . . strips of their prestige the so-called juridical theories of the Redemption', BEP, 147.

Hence Grace and Redemption may be taken as objective or subjective. St Paul sees these points of view together: men are 'justified freely by his grace, through the redemption that is in Christ Jesus, whom God hath proposed to be a propitiation, through faith in his blood', Rom 3:24 f.

i We are redeemed from **Sin**—*Cf.* § 643 *f.* As Apostle of salvation St Paul is intensely aware of the universal extension of sin in human history and society and his biblical education is illumined by his experience of the triumph of Christian grace in the tortured conscience of a great Pharisee vainly striving to keep the Law; *cf.* Rom 7:5–25. In Rom 1–3 he vividly depicts the sinful state of both Jews and Gentiles—for he knew what sin was like in the great cities of the empire. He uses to express it the LXX vocabulary: lawlessness (ἀνομία, the preponderating notion), impiety, impurity, error, disobedience, fall, transgression, and most frequently 'sin' (ἁμαρτία): in plur. personal sins, in sing.: Sin personified and the power of sin, *op. cit.*, 107 ff. Concupiscence, or evil desire, is so much a factor in sin that it can be called 'sin', *e.g.* Rom 6:12; 7:7 f.; *cf.* Dz 792; KTW, III, 171.

j Whence comes sin's universality and man's inclination to evil? OT attested the facts, Ps 51(50) 7; Job 14:4, 17 ff., and contemporaries believed in an 'evil heart' or 'tendency' in man which had to be fought; but of **original sin** there are but vague traces in Jewish literature, which explicitly affirms only that the first sin had physical consequences, BJP, II, 12–23. It was consciousness of solidarity with Christ which illumined the moral solidarity of all men with Adam—a doctrine perhaps too hard to bear (*cf.* Jn 16:12) till the Redemption was accomplished and understandable only in

terms of the Redemption. 'As in Adam all die, so in **645j** Christ all shall be made to live', 1 Cor 15:22, WV, expressed solidarity in death with Adam, but this is not only a solidarity in punishment. Sin entered the world through one man's fault and passed into all through solidarity with him, Rom 5:12–21. Starting from the accepted premises that without sin there is no retribution and that death is retribution for sin, St Paul argues to the universality of sin from the universality of death even in the time between Adam and Moses when no personal sins were committed which fell under the direct condemnation of a Law, 12–14. Therefore 'all had sinned' and 'through the disobedience of the one man the many were constituted sinners', 12, 19, WV; *cf.* Dz 789. This difficult doctrine is set in the context of the abundance of Christ's grace whereby 'we exult in God through our Lord Jesus Christ'. St Paul does not refer to it directly again (not in Rom 8:20–23, nor Eph 2:3) but describes the Redemption as remission of personal sins, Eph 1:7; 2:1–6; Col 1:14. As practical pastor of souls, he directs his attention to the virulence of the 'law of sin and death' in us, and our deliverance by 'the law of the spirit of life', Rom ch 7; 8:2; BEP, 109–15; Prat, I, 213-21; II, 57 ff., 221 ff.

The Flesh—in OT *bāśār* means the living matter of the **k** bodies of animals and men, and suggests their weakness compared with God, Gen 6:3; Is 31:3; *cf.* Jl 2:28. St Paul uses 'flesh' for the elements of the body, Rom 2:28; 1 Cor 15:39, the body itself, 1 Cor 5:5; 2 Cor 4:11; Eph 2:14, the human person, *e.g.* Eph 5:29, life, *e.g.* 2 Cor 10:3, the race, *e.g.* Rom 9:3, human nature taken together, *e.g.* 3:20, and in its creaturely limitations as 'flesh and blood', 1 Cor 15:50; Gal 1:16; Eph 6:12; as distinguished from God but holy (Christ's human nature, Rom 1:3; 9:5); he also uses 'flesh' in some opposition to God as the merely natural, 4:1; 2 Cor 11:18, as natural generation opposed to that by God's promise, *e.g.* Rom 9:8; finally as 'the carnal', opposed to God or divine life in man, *e.g.* 7:5; 8:1–13; Gal 5:16–24, subject to sin and inclined to it, Rom 7:18, 25, and its instrument, *e.g.* 8:3, 12 f.; Gal 5:13; Eph 2:3. There is no physical division between body and spirit. St Paul's sources are not in Greek thought, but in Gen, where all things are good. There is a proud carnal mind, Col 2:18, a fleshly wisdom, 2 Cor 1:12; *cf.* 1 Cor 1:17; 3:3, sins of the flesh include sins against charity, Gal 5:16–22, and 'spirit' may be defiled as well as 'flesh', 2 Cor 7:1. Therefore 'the flesh' is the entire man disordered by sin, contrasted with 'the spirit' as the same man remade by grace; these correspond to 'the new man' and 'the old man', BEP, 106 f.; Prat, *op. cit.*, II, 71–4; 402–4. *W. Davies, Paul and Rabbinic Judaism, 19 ff.

The Law in St Paul means habitually the Mosaic **l** Law, with its 'commandments' and 'decrees', Rom 7:8–13; Eph 2:15; sometimes 'Scripture', *cf.* Rom 3:19; 1 Cor 14:21; other meanings, Prat, I, 224 ff. A Jew would not distinguish the natural and the Mosaic Law. The Law is God-given, and to have received it was a glory for the Jews to whom it brought moral enlightenment, Rom 9:4; 2:17–20. It is true, holy, just, and even 'spiritual', inspired by God, 2:20; 7:12, 14, 16; 1 Tim 1:8. It is 'for life', Rom 7:10; he who does the commandments will live, Gal 3:12; Lev 18:5; Lk 10:28. It leads men to faith in Christ and bears witness to justification, Gal 3:24; Rom 3:21. The justice that comes through faith, far from making void the Law, establishes its basis, 31, for 'God sent his Son in the likeness of sinful flesh . . . that the *justice* of the law might be fulfilled in us who walk . . . according to the spirit', 8:3 f. So the commandments remain, fulfilled by charity, 13:8, 10; Gal 5:14; Mt 5:17–20. Finally, there are just Israelites (and just pagans) whose observance of the law is not without faith and grace, Rom 2:13 ff.; 26 ff.; 10:5; *cf.* Heb 11 on OT 'faith'.

Why, then, does St Paul attack the regime of the **m**

645m Law, as of a law of sin and death, powerless before the flesh to do more than add to concupiscence the attraction of the forbidden fruit, Rom 8:2 f. ; 3:20, a letter which kills, opposed to the life-giving spirit, 2:27, 29 ; 7:6 ; 2 Cor 3:6 f. ? He is opposing dialectically the ' economy of the Law ' to the ' economy of grace '. The Judaizers, by forcing all to submit to the whole Mosaic Law, would have frightened away the Gentiles from Christ, and corrupted the supernatural character of Christianity by changing submission to the Person of Christ into submission to the jurist, divine grace into a commercial system of retribution, and God's justice into their own ; *cf.* Rom 10:3 ; Jn 10:34 f. ; BEP, 135–42. The ' Jew ' is thus the man who thinks he can fulfil the commandments by mere force of will, Rom 2:17 ff., and so transforms the Law into a system which brings only cursing and death, Gal 3:10, 13 ; Deut 27:26. In this sense no man is justified before God by the works of the Law but only by faith in Jesus Christ, Gal 2:16 ; 3:11 ; Rom 1:17 ; 3:20 ; *cf.* Ps 143 (Vg 142):2 ; Hab 2:4.

n If by giving knowledge of sin the Law is not to be simply a spur to sin, and so call forth divine wrath, Gal 3:19 ; Rom 5:20 ; 1 Cor 15:56 (*cf.* KTW, I, 765 f.), it must be brought into relation with Christ, and the total divine economy of **the Promise**, BEP, 136. The Promise, made to Abraham and realized in Christ, is not annulled by the Law which was promulgated in the interval, Gal 3:14 ff. The Law is inferior to the Promise and the Gospel, being given by the mediation of angels and Moses, not by the unitive act of the Son of God, 19 f., 22. For him it prepares, 24 ; he is its fulfilment, Rom 10:4 ; after him its regime gives place to that of faith and sonship, Gal 4:1–7, and its servitude to the liberty which Christ has won for us and gives us by the Spirit, 5:1, 13 ; 2 Cor 3:17. Those who are led by the Spirit are not under the Law made for transgressors, Gal 5:18 ; 1 Tim 1:9, but they are not without a divine law, for they are under Christ's, 1 Cor 9:20 f. Thus the commandments abide, fulfilled in Christ by the spirit of love, Rom 13:8, 1 Cor 9:8 ff. ; Gal 5:14 ; the ceremonial law gradually fell into abeyance, BEP, 141 f.

To sin and its consequences God's answer is ' the gift given in the grace of the one man, Jesus Christ ', Rom 5:15, WV.

646a The Redemption is a Mystery of Divine Love, totally expressed in the Father's supreme gift : his Beloved Son. The initial Mystery, the incomprehensible excess of goodness and generosity, is that God loved sinners and gave up his own Son for them, Rom 5:8 ; 8:32, 39 ; Eph 2:4 ff. ; 1 Jn 4:8 ff. From this everything flows like a second creation, as gratuitous as the former but more splendid, 2 Cor 4:6 ; *cf.* Gen 1:3 ; Rom 8:19–23 ; 12:2 ; Gal 6:15 ; Eph 2:10.

The Father's Love initiates the whole redemptive work, and in him it ends : ' All things are of God who hath reconciled us to himself by Christ. . . . God was in Christ, reconciling the world to himself ', 2 Cor 5:18 f. ; Rom 11:36. From him ' ye have your being in Christ Jesus ', 1 Cor 1:30, WV. ' When the fulness of the time was come, God sent his Son . . . that we might receive the adoption of sons. *And the proof that you are sons is that* God hath sent the Spirit of his Son into *our* hearts, crying : Abba, Father ', Gal 4:4 ff. ; Rom 8:14 ff. St Paul cannot thank him enough for his immense kindness, and from and to his praise moves the most splendid of the texts on the divine purpose, celebrating the glory and magnificence of the overflowing grace he has given us in his Son, Eph 1:3–14 ; *cf.* Col 1:12 ff. ; Tit 3:4 ; Prat, *op. cit.*, II, 85–89 ; Mersch, *Théol. du Corps Mys.*, I, 325–9, here followed.

b The Love of the Son—' If God is the unique first principle of the Redemption as he is of grace, Christ is the unique first principle in Redemption as he is in grace . . . the action of his humanity is the first, unique, universal principle ', *op. cit.*, 333. For Redemption is ' in Christ Jesus ', Rom 3:24 ; 1 Cor 1:30 ; Col 1:14, a mystery of unity in him who includes

all within himself *cf.* § 641*j*. The ' summing-up ' of all **6** things in the Beloved is expounded in Eph 1:3–14 with constant repetition of the words ' in Christ ', BEP, 97–103. ' In him it hath pleased the Father that all the fulness should dwell, and through him to reconcile all things to himself, alike the things on earth and the things in heaven, making peace through the blood of his cross ', Col 1:19 f., WV ; *cf.* 2:9 ; Jn 1:16 f. But if Redemption is thus expressed in terms of the Mystical Christ, its source is the Personal Christ, who ' hath loved us and delivered himself for us ', Eph 5:2 ; *cf.* Gal 2:20, loved the Church, his Body, with a burning love like that of bridegroom for bride, and died for her, Eph 5:23–32. From God's side all is union and love.

Jesus is the only Mediator—The word passed beyond **c** its juridic sense of an arbiter or negotiator between two parties with whom he had something in common (as Moses negotiated the acceptance of the Law between God and the people, Ex 19:3 ff. ; Gal 3:19 f.) to indicate a much more intimate relation. Jesus is the Mediator of the New Covenant as the victim which the parties set between them as divine representative and guarantee, 1 Cor 11:25 ; Heb 8:6 ; 9:15 ; 12:24. Still more deeply, the sacrificial mediation of the God-man, in whom the fullness of the Godhead is incarnated and the fullness of mankind recapitulated, is founded on a communion of total solidarity. This mediation fulfils God's universal will to save, for ' there is only one God and only one mediator between God and men, Jesus Christ, who is a man, like them, and gave himself as a ransom for them all ', 1 Tim 2:5 f., KNT. From him flow all supernatural graces, Rom 1:5 ; 5:21, peace, 5:1 ; justice, Phil 1:11 ; strengthening, 2 Cor 1:5 ; confidence, 3:4 ; the gift of the Spirit, Tit 3:6 ; victory, Rom 8:37 ; 1 Cor 15:57 ; eternal life, Rom 5:17, for by him are all things and we by him, 1 Cor 8:6 ; Prat, II, 166–70 ; BEP, 89–92.

Christ, in whom is realized God's eternal decree to **d** save mankind is the Mediator of **Predestination**, Eph 1:3–14 ; 3:11. This high mystery involving the absolute freedom of God's love and grace given in fullness to the Son and then, without regard to previous ' works ', to the brethren who are to be conformed to him, is set forth as a *message of encouragement*. But it needs to be understood !

We must distinguish Scriptural data from later **e** theological developments. Since it was not till late in the OT that the future life was revealed, the idea of Predestination is only adumbrated there by ' the Book of Life ', Ex 32:32 ; Ps 69(68) 29 ; Dan 12:1, an image recurring in Phil 4:3 and Apoc 3:5 ; 17:8 ; 20:12, 15 ; 21:27. The Gospels imply it, Mt 20:23 ; 24:24 ; 25:34 ; Lk 10:20 ; Jn 10:29. It is contained in the great subjects of hope : the Messianic blessings and the Kingdom of God. In this context it finds its theologian in St Paul, whose rabbinic training emphasized God's eternal dispositions, BJP, I, 188–91 ; BEP, 93–103, here followed ; *cf.* DTC, *Prédestination*, 2809–15.

Rom chh 9–11 envisage the Messianic election of **f** Israel in function of the unbelief of the Jews and the call of the Gentiles. This is also a call to Christian grace, and therefore to salvation and glory, but cannot simply transpose what St Paul says into terms of individual salvation. Besides, his warnings show that God's call does not guarantee perseverance, Phil 2:12, he knows that some pagans practise ' justice ', Rom 2:27, and that God wishes all men to be saved, 1 Tim 2:4, and he always assumes personal responsibility. For predestination to be a motive of hope, it is enough that God wishes his loving call to lead to eternal happiness.

Predestination is totalitarian, bringing with it all sub- **g** sequent graces, **though man remains free.** ' We know that for them that love God he worketh all things together unto good, for them that are the called according to his purpose. For those whom he hath foreknown, them he hath predestinated to bear a nature in the image of his Son's, that he should be first-born among many brethren. And those whom he hath predestinated,

646g them he hath also called : and those whom he hath called, them he hath also justified : and those whom he hath justified, them he hath also glorified ', Rom 8:28 ff., WV. God's love is expressed in his ' vocation ' or ' election ', Eph 2:4 ; 1 Thess 1:4, which results from his purposive design (πρόθεσις ; Rom 9:11 ff. ; Eph 1:11 ; 3:11 ; 2 Tim 1:9), man giving a return of love, 1 Cor 2:9 ; 1 Jn 4:19. To show that all graces come from God's free choice, St Paul in human fashion distinguishes five decisions or acts of God : prevenient, elective ' knowledge ', involving friendship ; cf. 1 Cor 8:3 ; 13:12 ; Gal 4:8 f ; BEP, 96, n. 2 ; DTC, art. cit., 2813 ; predestination (προορίζω, determine beforehand, cf. Ac 4:28 ; 1 Cor 2:7 ; Eph 1:5, 11 ; KTW, II, 702) ; efficacious calling to Christian grace ; (e.g. 1 Cor 1:9 ; 1 Thess 5:24 ; cf. Rom 9:12 ; KTW, III, 488–97 for OT terms) ; justification (the first realizing of this calling) ; and ' glory ', whether possessed already or in hope, 5:2 ; 8:18.

h There is no basis in St Paul for the Calvinist doctrine of positive reprobation. What he says about collectivities or OT typical figures in the Messianic scheme cannot be simply applied to the eternal lot of individuals. As to the latter, ultimately nothing escapes God's will, but their ' rejection ' or ' hardening ' is due to personal or national sin and abuse of grace, cf. 1 Cor 1:23 f. A just judgement upon wilful obstinacy and hatred of the truth allows those who have refused the light to be further deceived in the course they choose, 2 Thess 2:9–12 ; cf. Rom 1:24–28 (pagans), 11:7–10 (Jews). In this sense those who reject the apostolic preaching are called ' those who perish ', 1 Cor 1:18 ; 2 Cor 2:15 ; 4:3. But far from decreeing their sin in order that they might be damned, Rom 11:11, God shows much patience towards them, 9:22. The mystery of his predestined choice of souls on whom he will have mercy remains, 9:19 ff. But while he has prepared glory for the elect, 23 ; Mt 25:34, the eternal perdition of the damned is caused by their own sinful choice, BEP, 122 ff.

647a **The New Adam** is the Apostle's ' most complete, fruitful and original picture of the redeeming mission of Christ ', Prat, II, 171. As we have borne the image of the man from slime, so we shall bear the image of the heavenly man who has become ' quickening spirit ', 1 Cor 15:21 f., 44–49. As the first brought the universal reign of sin and death, so through the second, ' the gift in grace of the one man, Jesus Christ ', grace superabounds and reigns unto life everlasting, Rom 5:12–21. Thus the Father has ' delivered us from the power of darkness and hath transferred us to the kingdom of his beloved Son ; in whom we have redemption, the forgiveness of our sins ', Col 1:13 f., WV.

b **Why did Christ die ?**—To overcome the world's proud wisdom by the folly of the Cross, 1 Cor 1:18–31, to show the abundance of God's love and kindness for us, Rom 5:8 ; 8:31–39 ; Eph 2:4–7, to give us a model, Phil 2:5–11 ; Eph 5:1 f. The principal reason was to save sinners, e.g. 1 Tim 1:15 ; 1 Cor 15:3 ; Gal 1:4 ; cf. Mt 20:28 ; Lk 15:1 ff. ; 19:10 ; Jn 3:17 ; 1 Jn 4:10. To every aspect of sin, there will be a corresponding aspect in redemption, reconciliation being the most fundamental : ' God was reconciling the world to himself in Christ ', 2 Cor 5:18 f. ; Col 1:19–22. Reconciled now by his cross in one body to God, all men have access through him in one Spirit to the Father, Eph 2:15–18, cf. Prat, II, 190.

c **By what did Christ redeem us ?**—His Passion redeems, e.g. Rom 3:24 f. ; 1 Cor 6:20 ; Gal 3:13 ; 1 Tim 2:6, satisfies for sin, Rom 4:25 ; 1 Cor 15:17 ; Eph 5:2, and abolishes death, Rom 6:9 ff. ; 1 Cor 15:54–57 ; 2 Tim 1:10 ; cf. Lebr., HDT, 310. He himself refers to his death in terms of the sacrifice of the Covenant, e.g. Mt 26:28 ; 1 Cor 11:23 ff., and St Paul in terms of the sacrifices of Expiation and the Paschal Lamb, Rom 3:25 ; 1 Cor 5:7 ; cf. Heb 9:13 f. Through his blood we have remission of sins, reconciliation, peace and the graces of salvation and justification, e.g. Rom 5:9 f. ; Eph 1:7. Christ crucified, ' the lamb slain in the

midst ', ' a propitiation . . . in his blood ' is the centre **647c** of the Redemptive tableau and the focus of Christian love, e.g. Apoc 5:6 ; Rom 3:25. But NT shows that the fullness of his Redemptive activity is constituted by his life of humiliation, poverty and obedience, culminating in his death on the Cross to fulfil his Father's command and triumphing in his exaltation, Phil 2:5–11 ; cf. Jn 5:30c ; 10:18c ; Rom 5:19 ; 2 Cor 8:9. His sacrificial will began with the Incarnation, sanctified us through the offering of his body once, and eternally presents his offering for us at the Father's right hand, Heb 10:5–14 ; cf. 7:28. This idea of sacrifice in its widest extension is suggested by other texts in which Jesus ' gives himself up ' for us, Gal 1:4 ; 2:20 ; Eph 5:2, 25 ; 1 Tim 2:6 ; Tit 2:13 f. Moreover his death is inseparable from his Resurrection: **d** ' Christ was delivered up for our sins and rose again for our justification ', Rom 4:25 ; 2 Cor 5:15. He had himself foretold that he ' must ' die and rise again, and that he would be ' consummated ' the third day, Mt 16:21 ; Lk 13:32. The Apostles' insistence on the Resurrection is repeated in St Paul's constant declaration that the religion of the risen Christ fulfils the hope of Jews and Gentiles in a future life, Ac 23:6 ; 24:21 ; 26:23 ; 28:20 ; 1 Cor 15:12–22. Christ is ' life-giving Spirit ', ' the Son of God in power ', with whom even now we have been raised and made to sit in heavenly places, 15:45 ; Rom 1:4 ; Eph 2:5–10. Thus the efficacy of his death is joined with the power of his Resurrection in baptism and the Christian life, Rom 6:4 ; Phil 3:10 f. ; Col 2:12 ; 1 Pet 1:21 ; Apoc 1:18. St Paul even gives greater present importance to his Resurrection : ' If when we were enemies we were reconciled to God through the death of his Son, all the more, once reconciled, shall we be saved by his life ', Rom 5:10, WV ; cf. 8:34.

Heb celebrates the Redemption by demonstrating **e** the transcendence of Christianity over the Old Law in the **Priesthood and Sacrifice of Christ.** As the OT showed, a priest must come from among men and be called by God, ' appointed as a representative of men in the things that refer to God, that he may offer gifts and sacrifices for sins ; as one who can be mild with the ignorant and erring, since he himself is encompassed with weakness ', Heb 5:1–4, WV. Jesus is the perfect priest. Sharing our flesh and blood, perfected by the sufferings and death in which he experienced obedience, he has become the cause of eternal salvation to all his brethren, 2:10 ff., 17 f. ; 4–14 f. ; 5:7 ff. The priestly role of the Messias, typified in Melchisedech, appears in the royal dignity of the priesthood of the Son of God who made propitiation for the people's sins and sits at God's right hand, pleading for us before the Father, 1:3 ; ch 7 ; 9:24 ff. ; cf. Ps 2:7 ; 110 (Vg 109):1, 4 ; Gen 14:17 ff. A priest must offer sacrifice, Heb 8:3. The sacrifice of Jesus, 8:1–10:18, fulfils and takes the place of all bloody and unbloody sacrifices of the OT, 9:9 ; 10:5, 8 ; cf. § 64d, e. In the great sacrifice of *Kippurim* the high-priest after expiating sin by the blood of victims might once a year penetrate into the Holy of Holies. Jesus, offering himself once, gained by his own blood eternal redemption and entered heaven which he opens to all. This sacrifice, being perfect, is unique, redeeming once for all the sins committed both before and after it, 9:6–15 ; cf. Rom 3:25 ; 6:10, for the divine Person communicates eternal effects to his sacrificial will, Heb 9:12 ff. ; 13:8 ; DBV(S), *Expiation*, 190–202.

The New Life in Christ Jesus—There is now Redemp- **648a** tion for all men ' in Christ Jesus '. Their incorporation in him is one process described under various heads : the Gift of the Spirit—Faith—Justification—Baptism.

The Gift of the Spirit—Christ completes his redemptive **b** work by sending the Spirit from the Father, Jn 15:26 ; 16:7 ; Ac 1:8 ; cf. § 651b. ' Christ hath ransomed us from the curse of the Law . . . that in virtue of faith we may receive the promised Spirit ', Gal 3:13 f., WV. Thus when no controversy imposes another termino-

648b logy, entry into Christian life is described as the coming of the Spirit : ' Let me be content with asking you one question, Was it from observance of the law that the Spirit came to you, or from obeying the call of faith ? ', 3:2, 5, KNT.

c **Spirit**—(379 times in NT, 145 in St Paul) can mean : the superior, thinking principle in man, often opposed to ' flesh ', so ' mind ' and also ' a manner of thinking ', *e.g.* Mt 26:41 ; 1 Cor 2:11 f. ; incorporeal natures—God, the soul, angels, devils, *e.g.* Mt 10:1 ; Jn 4:24 ; Ac 23:8 ; Heb 1:14 ; the OT *rûah*, divine Principle or Force, and this is possessed by Christ, Rom 1:4 ; 1 Cor 15:45 ; 2 Cor 3:17 f. ; *cf.* BEP, 59, 61. Finally it means a distinct, divine Person, highest revelation of this Divine Principle, and man under his influence with ' spiritual ' graces and functions, and all that we call ' the supernatural life ', *e.g.* Rom 7:14 ; 1 Cor 9:11 ; 15:44 ; Gal 5:22 ; Eph 1:3 ; 1 Thess 5:19 ; Jud 19. These last senses of man's ' spirit ' and ' the Spirit ' acting within him are often hard to distinguish, just because the latter is constantly in view. Generally he is called ' the Spirit of God ', ' the Spirit of Christ ' and ' the Holy Spirit ' (but this can mean, his communication, *e.g.* Ac 6:5 ; 2 Cor 6:6). His Person is clearly indicated when distinguished from the Divine Essence or the other Persons, *e.g.* 1 Cor 2:10 ; 12:4 ; 2 Cor 13:13 ; *cf.* Prat, *op. cit.*, II, 405 ff., 435 ff. ; BEP, 74 ff. ; § 640*f*. In him Christian life flows from the Holy Trinity itself.

d **He is the Spirit of the Son,** and makes Christians sons too, filling them with the spirit of sonship, and pouring the love of God into our hearts, Gal 4:6 ; Rom 8:15 f. ; 5:5. He inspires the word of the preacher and its reception and marks it by his wonders, 1 Thess 1:5 f. ; Rom 15:19. His coming is a call to holiness and a seal, a pledge of final Redemption, 1 Thess 4:7 f. ; 2 Thess 2:13 ; Rom 8:23 ; Gal 5:5 ; Eph 1:3. All are baptized in one Spirit to make one body, 1 Cor 12:13 ; 6:11. Dwelling in them as in his temple, he transforms them, giving them a new life, 1 Cor 3:16 ; 6:11, 19 ; 2 Cor 3:6 ; Tit 3:5 f. He knows and reveals the deep things of God, 1 Cor 2:10 ff. ; Jn 16:3 ; 1 Jn 2:27, and aids their weakness by praying with them, Rom 8:26 ; *cf.* Mt 10:20. Where he is, there is liberty, 2 Cor 3:17. Henceforth they are to believe, hope, love, live and walk in the Spirit, Gal 5:5 f, 16–25 ; Rom 5:2–5 ; 8:4. For the giving of the fullness of the Spirit *cf.* § 651.

e **Faith**—St Paul develops the Gospel concept, *cf.* § 543*i–k*. Faith ' in Christum ', self-giving to Christ, *e.g.* Gal 2:16*b*, brings faith ' in Christo ', an interpenetration of the believer and Christ, *e.g.* 3:26 ; *cf.* 1 Tim 1:14 ' faith and love in Christ Jesus '. ' The faith of Christ Jesus ' seems to be faith which has Christ as object and lays the foundation of a life in common, Gal 2:16*a*, 20 ; 3:22 ; Rom 3:22, 26 ; Eph 3:12 ; Phil 3:9. Faith must profess doctrines about Christ, *e.g.* he is ' Lord ' and God has raised him from the dead, Rom 10:9. Thus it ascends through him to the Father, 4:24 ; Col 2:12 ; BEP, 177 ff. ; *cf.* Prat, II, Note V for other meanings of ' faith ', such as ' the Faith ', the object of belief, Gal 1:23.

f The preambles of faith are proved to the Jews from miracles, prophecies and memories of Christ's life, Ac 2:15–36 ; 17:2 ff., and to pagans by a rational approach to God's unity and Providence, 17:23 ff. ; *cf.* 14:15 ff. ; signs of power accompanied Paul's apostolate, 2 Cor 12:12 ; *cf.* Rom 15:19. Christians must show their faith's divine origin by the holiness, purity, gentleness and charity of their lives, and be able to give an account of it, 1 Pet 2:12–3:16. God's witness to Christianity makes belief a moral obligation, but men can refuse to ' obey the Gospel ', Rom 10:16 ; 1 Cor 15:15 ; 2 Cor 4:4 ; 1 Jn 5:10.

g **Faith is the Gift of God**—the initial grace of salvation which comes from his free call, Gal 1:15 f. ; Eph 2:8 ; Phil 1:29 ; Tit 1:1, though men must accept it to be worthy of eternal life, Ac 13:46, 48. Normally one must hear to believe, but God sends the preacher and it is Christ's ' word ' which he speaks, Rom 10:14–18.

This ' word ' is faithfully transmitted by the Apostles **648** and must be accepted as God's : ' When you had received from us the word of the hearing of God, you received it not as the word of men, but (as it is indeed) the word of God ', 1 Thess 2:13 ; *cf.* Rom 1:4 f. ; Heb 4:2. It ' worketh in you that believed ', ' living and energizing and keener than any two-edged sword ', ' a judge of the thoughts of the heart ', 1 Thess 2:13 ; Heb 4:12, WV ; *cf.* Jn 12:48 ; Apoc 19:15. Acceptance is itself a grace, for the fundamental confession ' Jesus is Lord ' can be made only ' in the Holy Spirit ', 1 Cor 12:3 ; *cf.* Gal 3:2.

h **God's gift requires men's co-operation,** as in the typical case of Abraham, Gal 3:6 ; Rom 4:3, 10, and they should be obedient to it, Rom 1:5. Their faith is a homage, Phil 2:17 ; it comes from the ' heart ', Rom 10:9 f. ; it grows and becomes strong, 2 Cor 10:15 ; Col 2:7 ; 2 Thess 1:3 ; or loses vitality, 2 Cor 13:5. It should be sound and wholesome, firm against evil influences, 1 Cor 16:13 ; Tit 1:13 ; 2:2, and used as a defensive armour, Eph 6:16 ; 1 Thess 5:8. It brings knowledge of divine truth which is veiled from unbelievers, 2 Cor 4:2–4 ; Phil 3:8–10. It launches a man into a new life, lived with ardent confidence in God, 2 Cor 1:9 ; 2 Tim 1:12 ; Heb 10:23 f., and issues in ' the work of faith ', 1 Thess 1:3. Because he has faith Paul does not fear to speak his mind, 2 Cor 4:13, and Christians must profess theirs openly, Rom 10:9 ; Phil 2:11.

i ' Faith is a *basis* of things hoped for, a *demonstration* of things not seen ', Heb 11:1 ; *cf.* ZLG ; DBV(S), *Foi*, 298. It is thus **indispensable for salvation,** first of the three great virtues by which we share in the life of God, for without ' faith it is impossible to please him ', 11:6, WV ; *cf.* Rom 1:16 ; 10:9 ; 1 Cor 13:13. It gives to hope the certainty which rests on divine testimony, Heb 11:4 ff., yet it is not vision, for it concerns things still invisible ; *cf.* 1 Cor 13:12 ; 2 Cor 4:18 ; 5:7. Such was the faith of Abraham and of all the just of the OT, Rom 4:19 ff. ; Heb 11:2–40.

j Christians believe in ' the truth ', *e.g.* 2 Thess 2:12 ; Eph 6:14, 16 ; 1 Tim 2:7. St Paul is always anxious that they should grow in knowledge, wisdom and spiritual understanding as the perfect development of their Christian life, 1 Cor 2:5 ff. ; Eph 1:17 ff. ; 3:17 ff. Col 2:2 f. **The intellectual element in faith** is also shown by the historical facts to be believed, 1 Cor 15:3 ff. ; 1 Thess 4:14, and by injunctions to keep the apostolic ' traditions ' and the ' deposit ', 2 Thess 2:15 ; 3:6 ; 2 Tim 1:14 ; 2:2. The idea of **orthodoxy in faith** emerges from Paul's constant warnings against ' another Gospel ', Gal 1:6–9, and specious doctrines leading them astray from the true faith they had learnt, Rom 16:17 ff. ; Eph 4:14 f. ; Phil 1:27 f. ; Col 2:6 ff. ; Heb 13:9. The object to be believed consists in revelation as a whole, and particular doctrines, such as Christ's resurrection and ours, Rom 6:8 ; 10:9 ; 1 Cor 15:12 ff. ; 1 Thess 4:14.

k What has been said shows the inadequacy of the Lutheran definition of faith : ' a technical term to express reliance on Christ for salvation ', HDB, I, 830. For views of modern Protestants *cf.* Prat, II, 233 f. Some make faith an attitude of sentiment, but others see in it a conviction of spirit, an adherence to the truths of the Gospel, and so they converge with Catholic doctrine, which never regards faith as purely intellectual, *cf.* Lagrange, *Ep. aux Rom.*, 137.

l **Faith and Justification**—Why does St Paul often attribute justification to faith ? Faith was constantly demanded by Christ, founds a life in common with him, *cf.* §§ 648*e*, 643*i*, and had been the first, well-remembered and critical disposition in conversion. Besides, Paul argues against the Judaizers from the great OT type, Abraham, whose ' faith was reputed to him unto justice ', Gen 15:6, and applies Hab 2:4, *e.g.* Gal 3:6 ff. ; Rom 1:17 ; 4:3 ff. Justifying faith is ' living ' faith, working through charity, which is often mentioned with it, Gal 5:6 ; 1 Cor 13:13 ; 1 Thess 5:8 ; 2 Tim 1:13 ; contrast faith without charity, 1 Cor 13:2, 8.

So Paul's emphasis on faith does not exclude other elements in justification and salvation. NT ascribes these to faith, *e.g.* Jn 3:16 ; Ac 16:31, but also to repentance with faith, Mk 1:15, faith with baptism, 16:16, repentance with baptism, Ac 2:38, baptism, Jn 3:5 ; 1 Cor 6:11 ; Eph 5:26 ; Tit 3:5, grace, Jn 6:44 ; Rom 11:6 ; Eph 2:5 ; Tit 3:7, keeping the commandments, Mt 19:17 ; Rom 2:13, and final perseverance, Mt 10:22 ; Apoc 2:10 ; DTC, *Foi*, 72-5.

Faith and Justice—Justice is spoken of as 'of ', 'from ', 'through ', 'by ' and 'upon ' faith, *e.g.* Rom 4:11 f. ; Gal 2:16 ; Rom 1:17 ; 3:28 ; Phil 3:9. From God's side faith 'is reputed to ' justice because they are two stages in one gracious operation. From man's side, faith, the co-operative use of intellect and will to adhere to God in Christ, is the last disposition for justification, which is itself the freely accepted work of grace. Hence faith is 'the foundation and root of all justification ', Dz 801.

Faith and Works—' Man is justified by faith without the works of the Law ', Rom 3:28 ; Gal 2:16, expresses St Paul's usual contrast between grace and merely human effort. This faith is accompanied by charity and good works 'in Christ Jesus ', Gal 5:6 ; Eph 2:10. But some abused St Paul's language to calumniate him, Rom 3:8. St James knew others who made faith a 'dead ' thing, mere intellectual adhesion without good works. He insists that Abraham was justified by works coming from faith when he showed himself ready to sacrifice Isaac, Jas 2:14-26 ; *cf.* Heb ch 11. St Paul safeguards the principle that faith comes from grace, St James the need to put it into practice. There is conflict only with the Lutheran doctrine of ' justification by faith alone ', BEP, 201-5.

Justification, though not the preponderating element in St Paul's doctrine, is an essential one, as is shown by the controversial concentration of Gal and Rom, and other allusions, *e.g.* Ac 13:38 f. ; Gal 2:15 ff. He used familiar OT words and phrases, 'just ', 'justice ' and 'justification ' to insist against the Pharisees that salvation is always initiated by God, that the first step in the Christian life comes entirely from grace, and that man cannot 'glory ' as if it were due to him for mere human works done under the Law, Rom 3:21-27 ; 4:2 ; 8:30 ; Eph 2:8 f. ; *cf.* Bonsirven, *op. cit.*, 199 ff. ; KTW, II, 176-229 ; IV, 649 ff. It was because the Jews did not know God's justice and sought to establish their own, that they did not submit to God's, Rom 10:3. Yet Abraham, the great OT type, had 'believed God and it was reckoned to him justness. Now to him that worketh, his reward is not reckoned as an act of grace, but as a debt ; but to him that worketh not, but believeth in him that justifieth the impious, his faith is reckoned justness ', 4:3 ff., WV ; Gal 3:6, 18.

Scripture, as Catholic theology has always recognized, does not oppose 'justice ' to 'mercy ' and 'grace ', DBV(S), *Grâce*, 1271. Justice is often associated with mercy in God and man, and in the second part of Is is parallel with salvation, *e.g.* Ps 85 (84) 10 f. ; 116 (114) 5 ; 145 (144) 7 ; Os 2:19 ; Mic 6:8 ; Is 45:8, 21-26, *art. cit.*, *supra*, 733 f. Hence 'the justice of God ' which is the theme in Rom, is not ordinarily that whereby he judges (as Rom 3:5 ; Ac 17:31), still less vindictive justice, but justice which brings salvation, Rom 1:16 f. It is God's activity in justifying men whom he pardons on account of Christ's death, and is opposed to 'wrath ', *art. cit.*, 1011. But it takes from man all boasting save 'in the Lord ', *e.g.* Rom 2:23 ; .3:21-27 ; 1 Cor 1:29 ff.

God does not simply declare men just, covering non-imputed sins by the justice of Christ, as earlier Reformers asserted, DTC, *Justification*, 2131-54 ; 2192-207. In OT the sense which LXX renders ' justify ' (δικαιόω) is almost always 'recognize as just ', (man also 'justifies ' God), and the passive has the intransitive meaning 'to be ', or 'become just ' ; where God 'declares a man just ', he is so. St Paul transforms these OT concepts by deepening them. **God makes men just.** The justice of God, received in Jesus and flowing from the gift of faith, becomes our justice and redemption and source of eternal life, Rom 3:24 f. ; 5:17 f. ; 1 Cor 1:30 ; 2 Cor 5:21 ; Tit 3:7. Although 'to justify ' has a declaratory, eschatological sense in Rom 2:13, it usually stands for God's initial act in conferring 'the gift of justice on one who has believed, asked for and received baptism ', Lagrange, *Ep. aux Rom.*, 122-41. Our 'justice ' is therefore a spiritual condition due to a profound divine action, Gal 3:5 ff. ; Rom 4:3 ff. It is Christian communion and participation in Christ taken in its beginning—though also in its being and end : 'That I may gain Christ and be found in him, not having for my justness that which is from the Law, but that which is through faith in Christ, that justness which cometh from God, based upon faith —that so I may know him, what the power of his resurrection, what fellowship in his sufferings, and become one with him in his death, in the hope that I may attain to the resurrection from the dead ', Phil 3:9 ff., WV ; BEP, 210. Such is St Paul's legitimate development of Hab 2:4, Gal 3:11 f. ; Rom 1:17 ; Heb 10:38 ; *cf.* § 640j.

God justifies the impious, Rom 4:5, not merely by simple pardon, but by a gracious transformation so radical that they are as really just as they were formerly sinners, as free of sin as a dead man of earthly punishment for crime, 'there is now no condemnation for those in Christ Jesus ', 3:24 ff. ; 5:18 f. ; 6:7 ; 8:1 ; 1 Cor 6:11 ; 1 Pet 4:1 f. This is a bestowal of divine life which removes evil by surmounting it. In place of sin with its wages of death, grace reigns through a living justice with hope of life everlasting, Rom 5:21 ; 6:23 ; Tit 3:7. Free now from sin, the just man must give himself to the service of this saving justice whose fruit is holiness and whose term is heavenly glory, Rom 1:16 f. ; 5:9 ; 6:19, 22 ; 8:30. The Kingdom of God is 'justice and peace and joy in the Holy Ghost ', 14:17.

Justification by Faith and Baptism—Faith and baptism are closely connected, and there is no 'unresolved conflict' in St Paul between them. Faith leads to, and cannot be separated from baptism, its efficacious symbol, which identifies the believer with Christ ; baptism is the sacrament of faith, for to be baptized one must believe, Mk 16:16 ; Eph 1:13 f. ; Col 2:12. Tradition and the Liturgy show this in practice. When opposing Jewish concepts, Paul attaches justification to faith ; when speaking of Christians, he shows it received in and through baptism and the gift of the Spirit, 1 Cor 6:11. This leaves room for the Catholic doctrine that justifying faith includes baptism of desire, Lagr., *Ep. aux Rom.*, 149-52.

St John, prior to St Paul as witness to Christ, certainly knew his writings, and seems to have illustrated them in his use of the Gospel data. But he **has his own approach to the Redemption.** For St Paul we must 'die to be born ', for St John we must ' be born to live ' DBV(S), *Jean, Evangile*, 817 ; *Epîtres*, 804, citing *Ed. Reuss, La théol. joh.*, 143. The seed of God, which is eternal life, is received by the children of God in their new birth from the Spirit, 1:12 ; 3:3, 5 f. ; 1 Jn 3:9. By believing Jesus to be the Son of God, they will have life, Jn 20:31 ; *cf.* Jn 2:20.

For St John, as for St Paul, **all flows from the Father's love and all returns to the Father.** 'God is love ', and has been the first to love us, proving the greatness of his love by sending his only begotten Son as propitiation for our sins and those of the whole world, Jn 3:16 ; 1 Jn 4:8 ff., 14, 16, 19 ; Rom 3:25 ; 5:8 ; 8:32. The Father loves the Son and has given all into his hand, Jn 3:35 ; 5:20 ; 15:9, and the Son loves the Father, does his will always, and glorifies him through the Cross which is his own triumph, 3:14 ; 12:32 ; 13:31 f. ; 14:31. In the Resurrection the Father glorifies the Son, and the Son, 'the Resurrection and the life ', glorifies the Father by imparting his own glory to those whom the Father has given him, 7:39 ; 11:25 ; 14:13 ; 15:8 ; 17:1-5 ; *cf.* Phil 2:6-10 ; 2 Cor

649b 3:18. His Father's love will be in them, as he is, and they will see his glory, Jn 1:14 ; 17:22, 24. ' In this we have known *love* : *in that* he hath laid down his life for us ; and we ought to lay down our lives for the brethren ', 1 Jn 3:16. St John holds up love's divine model to urge brotherly love, where St Paul (but *cf.* Phil 2:5 ff.) tends to stress pardon to inculcate trust, Rom 5:5–11 ; 2 Cor 5:18 ff. ' The diversity of approach only brings out the fundamental identity of teaching : the powerlessness of man, the prevenient action of God, the initiative of the Father, the love of the Son, the mission of salvation embracing the entire life of Jesus and consummated by his death ', and his Resurrection, DBV(S), *Expiation*, 229 f.

c St John is as conscious as St Paul of **Sin** (*cf.* § 645*i, j*) which he expresses in the vivid contrasts of present judgement : Light and darkness, Life and death, Truth and the lie, from on high and from below, heavenly and earthly, God and the devil. Men of evil works love the darkness and will not come to the light, Jn 3:19 f. ; 12:46 ff., nor take the life given by Jesus, 3:36 ; 5:24, 40 ; 6:53, nor believe him when he speaks the Truth, nor for its freedom shake off sin's slavery, 8:32–37, 40–46 ; *cf.* Rom 6:16 ; 2 Thess 2:10 ff. ' He that doth sin is of the devil . . . to this end was the Son of God manifested, that he might undo the works of the devil ', 1 Jn 3:8. This is no dualism, for if men are ready to do God's will, they see that Jesus's doctrine is from God, Jn 7:17, the Saviour of the world draws them to himself, 4:42 ; 12:32 ; 1 Jn 4:14, and they pass from the flesh to the spirit, from death to life, Jn 3:3–8 ; 5:24.

d Though the Baptist had pointed to the ' Lamb of God who takes away the sin of the world ', it was only on the Cross that he was shown as the true Paschal Lamb, 1:29, 36 ; 19:34–37 ; Ex 12:46 ; *cf.* Is 53:7. Jesus at first speaks of his **redemptive death and resurrection** in veiled terms, Jn 2:19 ff. ; 3:14 f. ; 7:33 ; 8:28. It is chiefly in the parable of the Good Shepherd that he shows his intention of laying down his life for his sheep under a free, tender love for them which goes with his love for his Father's will, 10:14–18. When in his last days Gentiles sought to speak to him, he foresaw his coming exaltation when he would draw all men to himself and the grain of wheat in dying would bring forth much fruit. Then, after a momentary anticipation of the terrors of Gethsemani, he bade his Father glorify his name, 12:24–32 ; *cf.* 15:8. The expiatory effects of his death were foretold in the last oracle of a high-priest, 11:50 ff.

e **The life of the Church is the fulfilment of the Redemption**—It is in a baptismal context that Jesus declares he must be ' lifted up ' that those who believe in him may have eternal life, 3:14 f. The work of the Incarnation, the Son given, the Word made flesh, which is consummated in his expiatory death, is continued in his Eucharistic mystery, 6:51 ; 1:14 ; 3:16. The Last Supper is its liturgical setting, and there the divine Priest-Victim's self-consecration consecrates the ministers of his redemptive work, 17:17 ff. ; *cf.* Ex 29:1 ; Lev 8:14–33 ; Mt 23:17 ; Heb 2:11 ; 10:10. Its effect will be the sending of the Paraclete, Jn 16:7, and the indwelling of all the Divine Persons, 14:16–26. Finally, the Cross is both sacrifice and source of sacrament, for the blood and water which flow from the Saviour's pierced side betoken baptism and the Eucharist, 19:34–37 ; Zach 12:10–13:6 ; 1 Jn 1:7 ff. ; 5:6. Those who are nourished by his sacrificed body and blood and abide in him, will have eternal life, Jn 6:51–58. Thus ' the apostle of love, the doctor of religion " in spirit and in truth " keeps fundamentally the same language as St Paul ', DBV(S), *art. cit.*, 202–24.

f **Redemption as Union**—Sin causes disunity, Satan's scattering of God's flock, Jn 10:12 ; 16:32 ; *cf. e.g.* Gen 11:1 ff. ; Jer 10:21 ; Zach 13:7 ; Mt 12:24–30 ; 26:31 ; Lk 15:3 f. Jesus died to gather God's scattered children into one and give them peace in himself, Jn 11:52 ; 10:16 ; 16:33 ; *cf.* Eph 2:15 f. Sharing the glory of the Crucified, they enter the very unity of the Son with the Father, their own unity being a visible proof of his mission : ' The glory which thou hast given me, I have given them, that they may be one, as we are one—I in them and thou in me—that they may be perfected in unity, in order that the world may know that thou hast sent me ', Jn 17:20–23, WV. **The object of the Redemption** is the At-one-ment with the Divine Persons of that Communion which is the Church, *cf.* §§ 636, 637.

Christ who shed his blood in redemptive love is risen and reigns for ever, and Christians reign with him, sharing his resurrection and eternal Priesthood, while they await his coming, Apoc 1:5–7 ; 20:6 ; *cf.* Eph 2:4 ff. ; 1 Pet 1:3–9. They have ' washed their garments in his blood ', triumphing through his sacrifice by a work which is also their own, Apoc 7:14 ; 12:11. John had never forgotten his first sight of the Lamb of God, Jn 1:29, and in ' the most brilliant prophetic vision in the Bible ' he sees amid the Throne and the whole company of heaven a Lamb ' as it were slain ', yet standing in symbol of life, with the seven horns and eyes of universal power and knowledge, while the twenty-four ancients who represent mankind and myriads of angels and every creature praise and adore him : ' For thou wast sacrificed, and didst redeem to God through thy blood men from every tribe and tongue and people and nation, and hast made them a kingdom and priests to our God, and they shall reign upon the earth '! Apoc 5:6–14, WV ; *cf.* DBV(S), *art. cit.*, 234–42.

V THE SACRAMENTS

Baptism—Critics have tried to break the links between the acts and interventions of Jesus and the NT doctrine of baptism ; *cf.* Dz 2039. But St Paul assumes that the rite and its efficacious symbolism were familiar to the Christian communities. Union with the historic Person of Jesus, requiring moral co-operation on the highest plane, is altogether different from the vague, magical Pantheism of the ' mystery rites ', and Jewish and Christian horror of paganism would have repelled any infiltration ; *cf.* DBV(S), *Baptême* (Coppens), 903–20 ; § 645*d*.

Others would derive it from ritual, Jewish washings. The practices of the Essenes have been cited, but this small Pharisaic sect had no provable influence on Christianity, DBV(S), *Esséniens* (Marchal), 1109–32. The bath of the proselytes came into use in the 1st cent., and was a rite of transition from the legal impurity of idolatry to a new, juridical state ; the Talmud compares it with the emancipation of slaves. Although the proselyte is called a ' new-born babe ', *e.g. Yeb.* 22*a*, this is far from the spiritual re-birth of Jn 3:1–10 ; Tit 3:5 ; 1 Pet 1:23 ; 2:2, which Jewish critics themselves call ' magical ', Prat, *op. cit.*, II, 466 ff. ; DBV(S), *Baptême*, 892–95 ; JE, *Baptism*, 499 f. ; *A. Edersheim, *The Life and Times of Jesus*, II, App. 12.

Such rites were given a deeper meaning in **the baptism of John,** which was a true preparation for the Kingdom, a symbolic act in the manner of the Hebrew prophets, realistically understood by those who received it as embodying their repentance and its acceptance ; *cf.* *Flemington, 22. Jesus himself submitted to it at the inauguration of his public life, the primitive preaching recalled it, *e.g.* Ac 10:37 (*cf.* Heb 6:2), and the stress which the Evangelists laid upon this baptism of Jesus with the accompanying manifestation of the Three Divine Persons and of the Divine Sonship of Jesus, shows how significant it was for Christian baptism. The Baptist himself said he was preparing for one greater than he, who would ' baptize in the Holy Ghost and fire ', Mt 3:11 ; Mk 1:7 f. ; Lk 3:16 ; Jn 1:31, 33 ; *cf.* Ac 19:4. ' Fire ' was the image of divine, purifying work in souls, Deut 4:24 ; Is 1:25 ; Mal 3:2 f. That water was also part of Christian baptism is attested by the word βαπτίζειν and by *e.g.* Jn 3:5 ; Ac 8:36 ; 10:47 ;

d Eph 5:26. The rite made ready by the Baptist was employed by the disciples of Jesus, Jn 3:22–26, though whether as a continuance of John's baptism (*cf.* Ac 19:3 ; Chrys., PG, 59, 167), or as that of the Spirit (Aug. PL, 33, 178) is controverted. Our Lord himself commented upon the Baptist's enigmatic prophecy : ' Amen, amen I say to thee : unless a man *be born of water and Spirit*, he cannot enter into the kingdom of God ', Jn 3:5. The Spirit, principle of God's creation of life, Gen 1:2 ; 2:7 ; Ezech 37:5 ff., now gives that higher life of divine sonship which is contrasted with the life transmitted through the flesh, Jn 3:6 ; *cf.* 1:13 ; 6:63. The rite through which this was effected is assumed to be familiar to the hearers of the Gospel.

e The life of the Spirit was given in its fullness after the glorification of the Redeemer, Jn 7:39, and it was then he gave his **command to baptize universally :** ' All authority in heaven and on earth has been given to me ; you, therefore, must go out, making disciples of all nations, and baptizing them in the name of the Father and of the Son, and of the Holy Ghost ', Mt 28:18 f., KNT ; *cf.* Mk 16:15 f. This universalism is in line with the prophetic tradition, Is 49:6 ; Hab 2:14 ; Lk 2:32 ; 3:6, the restriction of the Apostles to Israel, Mt 10:5 ff., being lifted now that Jesus's power shines forth in splendour. The Trinitarian doctrine forms a natural conclusion to the Synoptic data, and the frequency of explicit or implied Trinitarian formulae in St Paul—often in connexion with Baptism —shows they were familiar to the earliest Christians. The text in our form is in all MSS and ancient versions, and is quoted by Cyprian, Origen, Tertullian, Hippolytus, Irenaeus and Theodotus. Hence *F. Conybeare's attempt (ZNTW, 1901, 275–88 ; HJ, 1902, 102–8) to prove from shorter, free citations in Eusebius and others that the Trinitarian and baptismal references were post-Nicene interpolations should never have found support ; it was disposed of by *F. H. Chase, *The Lord's Command to Baptize*, JTS 6 (1905) 481–521 ; 8 (1907) 161–84 ; *cf.* Lebr., HDT, I, Note 4, 436–9 ; DBV(S), *Baptême*, 859–64, 920–1, and Com. on Mt 28:18.

f But if Christ prescribed the Trinitarian formula, why do Ac speak of ' **baptism in the name of Jesus** ' ? This is held to disprove the authenticity of Mt 28:18 f. even by *Flemington, 108 f., who shows that baptism must have come from a command of Christ. Others assert that the use of ' the name ' was a magical exorcism. But in Heb. ' the name ' is the person, and *cf.* §§ 645*d*, 650*h*. By rabbinical usage, ' in the name ' had a causal or a final meaning, SB, 590, 1045 f. on Mt 10:41 ; 28:19, and some have held that the Trinitarian liturgical form was not ordered by Jesus, but only baptism ' into union with ', or ' by a consecration to ' the Divine Persons, Lebr., HDT, 257 f., 439 ; *J. Armytage Robinson, JTS 8 (1906) 195.

g But that the Trinitarian form was actually employed is at least strongly suggested by the constant NT allusions to the Trinity in relation to the baptismal rite or its effects, *e.g.* Ac 2:22–39 ; 10:34–38 ; Rom 15:16 ; 1 Cor 6:11 ; 12:4 ff., 13 ; Eph 4:4 ff. ; 2 Thess 2:13 ff. ; Heb 10:29 ; 1 Pet 1:2 ; 2:5 ; 4:14, and perhaps Paul's question to the men at Ephesus, Ac 19:2 f. The long-standing difficulty is removed if it is recognized that ' baptism in the name of Jesus ' refers, not to the action and words of the baptizer, but to the confession of faith made by the adult receiving baptism. J. Crehan, S.J., *op. cit*, has shown that the Baptist had required faith in him who was to come, 19:4, Paul was baptized ' calling upon his name ', 22:16, and Christians were those who ' call upon the name of the Lord ', *e.g.* 9:14, 21 ; Rom 10:12 ; 1 Cor 1:2. The invocation seems postulated by St Peter, Ac 2:21, 38 ; 10:43 ; 1 Pet 3:21, as by the reading, certainly older than Irenaeus, ' I believe that Jesus is the Son of God ' in Ac 8:37, and by St Paul, *e.g.* Rom 10:9 ; *cf.* Phil 2:10 f. J. Coppens, DBV(S), *Baptême*, 872 ff., gives another explanation : baptism ' in the name ' was baptism ' on the authority

of Jesus ' as foundation or efficacious source (*ἐπί* or *ἐν*), **650g** or ' into the Mystical Christ ' (*εἰς*). The use of the Trinitarian formula, as enjoined by our Lord, remains untouched.

The administration of **baptism** was **the normal h conclusion of apostolic preaching**, Ac 2:37 f. ; 8:12 ff., 32 ff.; 9:18 ; 10:44 ff. ; 16:14 f. ; 19:1 ff. The NT presupposes it alike in Pauline and non-Pauline churches, *e.g.* Rom ch 6 ; 1 Cor 1:13 ff. ; 12:13 ; Gal 3:27 ; Eph 4:5 ; Heb 6:2 ff. ; 1 Pet 3:20 f. This could be due only to the initiative of Christ, *art. cit.*, 863 f. Baptism was a bath of purification and sanctification which **incorporated men into the Messianic Kingdom**, 1 Cor 6:9, 11, an effect expressed subjectively by confession of Jesus as Lord and by the moral conversion foretold by the prophets. It accorded a share in the remission of sins, the gift of the Spirit and the Table of the Lord, Ac 2:38, 41 ; 5:31 f. ; 10:43, and rescue from the power of the devil—though Ac mentions this only once, 26:18, showing how far baptism was from being a ' magical ' exorcism. The simple exposition of baptism as a purification from sin and a new birth was easily understood by the first converts and is recalled by St Paul, 1 Cor 6:11 ; Eph 5:26 ; Tit 3:5 ; Heb 6:2 ; 10:20.

But the aspect expressed by baptism ' into Christ ', **i** *e.g.* Rom 6:3 ; Gal 3:27 ; *cf.* 1 Cor 12:13 ' into one body ', and by the reception of the Spirit, showed that the baptized entered into communion with their risen Lord. Moreover Jesus himself had suggested a connexion between baptism and his Passion by describing it as a baptism preparatory to glory, and to the ' fire ' he would cast upon the earth, Mk 10:38 ; Lk 12:50. When he entered into his glory as ' life-giving Spirit ', 1 Cor 15:45, he baptized ' in the Holy Spirit and fire ' (*cf.* Mt 3:11 ; Lk 3:16) those to be born of ' water and the Spirit ', Jn 3:5. St Paul can assume as part of the common faith that **the power of Christ's redeeming death and resurrection pass to the baptized in the act of baptism**, Rom 6:3 ff. ; 1 Cor 1:13 ; Col 2:11 f. ; *cf.* Heb 10:22. They have been crucified with Christ, Gal 2:19, baptized into his death so that they have died mystically with him, so that with their ' body of sin ' destroyed, they live no longer ' in the flesh ' but ' in the spirit ', Rom 6:3, 11 ; 7:5 f. ; 8:9 ; Col 2:20 ; 3:3. They have been buried with him beneath the baptismal waters to rise gloriously with him to a new life, to ' put on Christ ', Rom 6:4 f. ; Gal 3:27 ; Col 2:12 f. ; *cf.* Is 61:10.

The development of the graces of baptism as a **j** sharing in Christ's death and resurrection provides Christians with their life-programme, *e.g.* Rom 6:4, 6–18 ; Col 2:20 ; 3:1, 3. Their baptism is the source of a new morality. St Paul, writing to those already baptized, drops the mention of repentance. He appeals to the new life they have begun in decisive contrast to the old, 1 Cor 6:9–11. At baptism they crucified their flesh with its passions and lusts, Gal 5:24, and henceforth, led by the Spirit of God who dwells in them, they must wage deadly war on their concupiscence, Rom 8:8 ff., 13 f. They are ' dead ' to sin and their real life is hidden with Christ in God, 6:2, 8, 11 ; Col 3:3. As sons of God, they must suffer with the Son that his life may appear in them, and they be glorified with him, Rom 8:15–17 ; 2 Cor 4:11 ; Gal 3:26 f. ; 2 Tim 2:11. Their baptismal life means freedom, not freedom to sin but freedom from sin, Rom 6:12 ff. ; 8:2. The old Law of fear and the discipline of servants went in baptism, and their new life as sons is directed by the Spirit of adoption of sons, Gal 2:19 ff. ; 4:6 f. To live by the Spirit, they must walk by the Spirit (for only thus will they possess the Kingdom of God) and his fruits are charity, joy, peace . . ., Gal 5:21–25 ; Rom 8:6–10. Thus, reflecting the glory of the Lord, they will be progressively transformed by his Spirit from glory to glory, Rom 5:2 ; 2 Cor 3:18. In a word, Christians must ' become what they are ' ; baptism is a ' sacrament of realized eschatology ', which leads to the final consummation.

650k Therefore **Baptism accomplishes a real, sacramental Change**—(indicated by the aorist, *e.g.* 1 Cor 6:11 ; 12:13, and by comparison with circumcision, Col 2:11 f.). Primarily it is not the act of the faithful but the sanctifying act of Christ received by them once for all. It effects what it symbolizes. It washes away sin, Ac 22:16 ; 1 Cor 6:11, but it does more. Death to sin coincides with spiritual resurrection, both flowing from the receiving of the Spirit, *art. cit.*, 899. Thus begins a life ' in Christ ', ' in the Spirit ', which is, by participation, really divine. The baptized son of God is caught up by the merciful love of the Father, through the death and resurrection of the Son and in the outpouring of the Holy Spirit to share the life of the Most Holy Trinity. Towards the close of his life, St Paul summed up baptismal theology in a passage which is an inspired comment on Our Lord's command to baptize in the name of the Divine Persons : ' When God our Saviour manifested his kindness and his love for man, he saved us . . . out of his mercy, with the bath of regeneration and with renewal by the Holy Spirit, whom he poured out on us richly through Jesus Christ our Saviour, in order that justified by his grace we might become in hope heirs of everlasting life ', Tit 3:4-7, WV.

l The initiatory efficacy of baptism is further shown by the term ' Seal (*Sphragis*) of the Spirit ', though it would seem to apply rather to the post-baptismal gift of the Spirit, who is the earnest and pledge of eternal life, 2 Cor 1:21 f. ; Eph 1:13 ; 4:30 ; *cf.* Rom 4:11 ; 2 Tim 2:19 ; Coppens, *Imposition des mains*, 267-75. These passages are the Scriptural basis from which the Fathers developed the doctrine of the seal, the ineffaceable mark on the soul which we call ' character '.

m If Gal and Rom emphasize the mystical union with Christ effected by baptism for the individual, 1 Cor, Eph and Col show **baptism creating the new society**, the Kingdom of God in preparation, the ' **glorious Church ' which is the Body of Christ**. For we are not baptized as isolated individuals. By one baptism we are all baptized into one Body and one Spirit, in which we all go to the Father, all fellow-citizens of the heavenly city, members of the family of God, brethren whose eldest brother is Christ, 1 Cor 12:13 ; Eph 2:16-19 ; 4:4 f. ; 5:26 ; *cf.* Rom 8:29 ; Gal 3:26 ff. The Christians were taught to realize vividly the unity which they had entered in baptism. St Paul uses it to heal splits in the congregation, 1 Cor chh 1-3 ; *cf.* 1:10-17 ; 3:4 ff, 22 f., and develops from it the whole doctrine of the Mystical Body, 12:13 ff. ; Eph 4:3-7.

n Christians henceforth are to live in the hope of eternal life given them by baptism. This hope is the theme of 1 Pet, a ' baptismal homily ' written to encourage them in trial, *cf.* 1 Pet 1:3-9, 21 ff. ; 2:9 f. ; 4:13 f. ; 5:10 ; Thils, 124 f. We live in the time granted for repentance to a world already judged by God, 2 Pet 3:9 ; Jn 16:8-13 ; 1 Cor 11:32. Baptism is the ' antitype ' of the Flood, 1 Pet 3:20 f., a judgement through water, introduced by the preaching of penance (*cf.* 2 Pet 2:5, Noe ' herald ' of justice '), effecting that destruction of unbelief and sin which will be consummated by the catastrophic final judgement of fire, Mt 24:37 ff. ; Lk 17:26 f. ; 2 Pet 3:5 ff, and saving through water those who have a mystical participation with the Just One, 1 Pet 2:18, 20 ; Justin, *Dial.*, 138, 2. The Spirit who moved over the waters of creation, Gen 1:2, and was typified by the dove with its olive branch over the waters of the Flood, has appeared again over the waters of the baptism of the Anointed, and renders fruitful for eternal life those waters from which are born a new race with whom God makes Covenant, Mt 3:16 ; Mk 1:10 ; Lk 3:22 ; Jn 1:32. Thus this fragment of the primitive catechesis draws its baptismal theology from the whole story of God's dealings with men. It was richly developed by the Fathers and the Liturgy and illustrated by the figures of Noe, type of Christ, and the ark, type of the saving Church, in the catacombs, *cf.* Daniélou, *Déluge, Baptême, Jugement*, in *Dieu vivant*, VIII, 97-112.

o There is no direct NT evidence for the **baptism of infants**. But the Jews were accustomed to ' baptize ' **6** converts' children with their parents on the ground that action on behalf of another is permissible if obviously for his good. Anyhow, Christians, regarding baptism as the entry to the New Covenant (*cf.* Col 2:11 ; 1 Pet 3:21 ; Justin, *Dial*, 43) would have given baptism in place of circumcision. Further, paedo-baptism follows upon the theological concept of baptism as aggregation to the Christian community, and membership of the Body of Christ is suggested when St Paul tells children how to behave ' in the Lord ', Eph 6:1 ; Col 3:20. We may therefore infer, even apart from early tradition, that the ' households ' baptized included children ; *cf.* Ac 16:33 ; 18:8 ; 1 Cor 1:16 ; and two good complementary studies, *Flemington, 130-47 ; *O. Cullmann, *Le baptême des enfants et la doctrine biblique du baptême*, in *Dieu vivant*, XI, 45-66.

The Fullness of the Spirit—Foreshadowing but not yet **6** revealing his distinct Personality, the OT had spoken of the Spirit of Holiness, the Spirit of God whom he had put among his people to guide them and teach them to do his will, *e.g.* Is 63:11, 14 ; Ps 142:10. The outpouring of the Spirit upon all flesh would be the characteristic of Messianic times, Jl 2:28-32 ; Ac 2:17-21. Since NT ascribes to him the Incarnation itself, Lk 1:35 ; prophetic inspiration, *e.g.* 41, 67, 2:27, baptism, *e.g.* Mt 3:16 ; 1 Cor 6:11, the remission of sins, Jn 20:23, and the gift of grace, Ac 11:16 ff. ; 15:8 f., his action is not restricted to a special occasion. But the fullness of the Spirit was given after the glorification of the Son, Jn 7:39 ; 16:7.

The Baptist's words ' he will baptize you in the Holy **l** Spirit and fire ', which had rung in the ears of the first disciples, were echoed by Jesus himself before he ascended, Mt 3:11 ; Mk 1:8 ; Lk 3:16 ; Jn 1:33 ; Ac 1:5 ; 11:16. In his lifetime he had told his own that the Spirit of their Father would speak through them, and that they would receive the ' living water ' of the Spirit, Jn 7:37 ff. ; *cf.* 4:13 ff. On the night before he died he had declared that he would send them from the Father the Spirit of Truth who proceeds from the Father, whose coming would be so vital for them that it was better that he himself should die. For though they would see him no more, this **other Paraclete** would bear witness to him, glorify him by receiving of his, and by showing it to them, lead them into all truth, 15:26 f. ; 16:7, 13 ff.

The preparation of the Father and the Mysteries of **c** the Son were accomplished at **Pentecost,** when God who had ' sent his Son ' in the Incarnation, sent the ' Spirit of his Son ' to complete the work in his sons by adoption, *cf.* Gal 4:4 ff. ; DBV(S), *Grâce*, 980 f. The Holy Spirit, ' the promise of my Father ', clothed them with power from on high, Is 44:3 ; Ez 39:29 ; Lk 24:49 ; Ac 1:4 f., 8, to make them ' spiritual ' witnesses of Jesus with light to understand and fortitude to preach, Jn 14:26 ; 16:12 f. ; Ac 2:33 ; 4:29 ff. ; 1 Cor 2:11 ff. The whole Church was at prayer round Peter, the Apostles and the Mother of Jesus, Ac 1:13-16 ; 2:1, when the mighty wind of the Spirit, Gn 1:2 ; 3 Kg 19:12 ; Jn 3:8, filled the whole house, and on each of them rested the tongues of fire. Fire symbolizes divine presence, light, warmth, purification, rapid spread, Ex 3:2 ff. ; Is 4:4 ; 6:6 ; Ez 1:4 ; Mt 3:11 ; Lk 12:49 ; Heb 12:29. The tongue is the organ of witness, Rom 14:11 ; Phil 2:11. All the 120 present, ten times the Apostles' number, were ' filled with the Spirit ' and spoke in different tongues, Ac 2:4, 17 f. ; Chrys., PG 60, 43 ; Aug., PL 38, 1230. Thus, as in Confirmation, Sacrament of ' Catholic Action ', the bestowal of the Spirit made all co-operators in the work of the Apostles, the divinely chosen teachers and rulers of the community, Ac 1:2 ; 2:42 ; 6:3. All were needed for the conversions about to begin.

In the Mystical Body thus manifested the Holy Spirit **d** is the Soul, *Mystici Corporis*, 25, 32, 55, 77 ; *Divinum Illud*, ASS, 29, 649 f., and from him stream those graces which he distributes there as he wills, 1 Cor 12:4-31 ;

Rom 12:3–9 ; Eph 4:1–16. The **graces of Confirmation** were shown in the fortitude and deep understanding of the Scriptures of St Peter's first sermon, and in the corporate life of charity which reinforced the witness of the Apostles' preaching and miracles, Ac 2:14–36, 43–47 ; 4:32 f. To be ' filled with the Spirit ' did not primarily signify exterior ecstasy. It goes with faith, wisdom, grace and fortitude, its special mark being joy, *e.g.* 6:3–10 ; 11:24 ; 13:52 ; 1 Thess 1:6. The ' fruit of the Spirit ' is ' love, joy, peace, patience, *kindness*, goodness, faith, *gentleness, temperateness* ', Gal 5:22. The Church is built up by this inner encouragement, this παράκλησις of the Spirit, rather than by human activity, Ac 9:31 , 1 Cor 14:3, 5.

The Holy Spirit was given to others by **the imposition of the Apostles' hands** with prayer, the case of the Samaritans showing the distinction from baptism given by a deacon, Ac 2:38 ; 8:15 ff. So Paul imposed hands on the men at Ephesus after their baptism, 19:1–6. This rite normally followed baptism, for it is mentioned as part of Christian initiation in Heb 6:1 f., and Ac imply that the situation of the Samaritans was unusual. Two distinct rites are indicated by the aorists in 1 Cor 12:13 : ' In one Spirit all we . . . were baptized into one Body ; and were all given to drink of one Spirit ', WV. Birth into the spiritual life of the Body by baptism is completed by the ' mission ' or ' seal ' of the Spirit, who is ' poured out abundantly upon us ' after the ' bath of regeneration ', 2 Cor 1:22 ; Eph 1:13 ; 4:30 ; Tit 3:5 f. Similarly the Synoptics, who certainly regard Christ's baptism in the Jordan as prefiguring the rites of initiation, distinguish his baptism from the descent of the Spirit, Mt 3:16 ; Mk 1:10 ; and two sacramental graces may be inferred from St John's Gospel, since we must be re-born of the Spirit before sharing his special mission and indwelling, Coppens, *Imposition des Mains*, 210 ff. While, therefore, baptism makes a man a Christian, *cf.* Ac 8:36 ff. ; *Ep. Barn.*, 11, 11 ; Hermas, 9, 16, 4 ; Justin, *Apol.*, 1:61, the whole NT supports the authenticity of Ac 8:5–25 ; 19:1–6 ; *cf. op. cit.*, 258 ff. ; DBV(S), *Confirmation*, 122–9, 135 ff., 141–7. But the Holy Spirit is master of his gifts, and his effusion upon the first Gentiles preceded their baptism, Ac 10:44 ff. ; 11:15 ff.

The Holy Eucharist, Christ's supreme gift of himself, fulfilment of all man's instincts of worship and sacrifice expressed in Jewish and pagan rite, is the representation by his Church under efficacious signs of his own sacrifice on the Cross and the source of the life of his Mystical Body. Bond of union between the members of the Body and their risen Head, it is the bond of union between the members themselves, and the joyful pledge of their resurrection, *cf.* Cyr. Alex., *Adv. Nest.*, 4, ch. 5, PG 76, 189–97. ' Sanguis Christi, novum testamentum ', Florus, *Expositio Missae*, ch. 61. The Eucharist ' sums up in its richness everything which St Paul in Eph unites in the one word " Mystery ", that is to say the whole content of the designs of God upon the world, revealed and realized in Christ ', H. de Lubac, S.J., *Corpus Mysticum*, 224.

' That God who gave life to the world by his Son should not have wholly withdrawn him from the world, that the flesh which saved it should still sustain it—does not that seem worthy of his goodness ? Does it not seem consistent with the very right plan of the Incarnation ? It is, moreover, the only right meaning of Scripture ', Lagrange, *The Gospel of Jesus Christ*, I, 235. Far from contradicting the historical records, it appears in all of them as **an essential part of the life of Jesus and the perfect revelation of his love ;** *cf.* § 644*j*. While it recalls previous Jewish practices and beliefs, it is closely joined to salient features of Jesus's own teaching : the Messianic banquet, the new Covenant, his supreme gift of the new manna, the heavenly bread, true bread of life, DBV(S), *Eucharistie*, 1211. This does not explain away the Eucharist, which comes from an historical initiative of Christ. But it helps to show why the minds

of the Apostles, prepared already, Jn 6, and probably **652b** further instructed by the discourse at the Supper of which we have only essential fragments, were open to understand their Master's supreme act. Besides, the Gospels themselves attribute the full intelligence of the Mysteries of Jesus and specially of the Eucharist to belief in his words under the inspirations of the Holy Spirit, Jn 6:44–7, 63 ff. ; 14:26 ; 16:12 ff. ; *cf.* 16:9 ; 1 Cor 2:14 f. ; *art. cit.*, 1168, 1212.

Heretical Opinions—Luther kept the Real Presence, **c** but with ' consubstantiation '. Zwingli is father of the purely ' symbolic ' interpretation, Calvin of the ' dynamic '. Liberal Protestants and Rationalists tend to admit that the Pauline churches had the realist, Catholic interpretation, but ascribe it to influences from primitive religion or the ' Mysteries '. In their view, Jesus was free from sacramental concepts. As the Gospel account of the Institution abounds in them (since Jesus foresees his death as having a sacrificial, expiatory value), they argue against its historicity : (*a*) Jesus was too humble to institute a memorial of his passion ; (*b*) the order to repeat the rite is not given by Mt and Mk, but only by Paul and Lk ; (*c*) Paul knew he was innovating, for he traced this order to a direct revelation from Christ, 1 Cor 11:23 ; (*d*) various hypotheses are then proposed to account for the origin of the Eucharist. Without going so far, Peake's Commentary says ' it is doubtful if we ought to say that (Jesus) ordained the sacrament ', 669. *Cf.* Dz 2045.

But **the evidence of the sources** is that Jesus instituted **d** the Eucharist and ordered its repetition. There are no good reasons for setting aside this evidence. (*a*) If Jesus was God—this is the real issue—he foresaw his expiatory death and showed a truly divine humility by setting himself beneath sacramental signs that men might commemorate his passion by offering him again and entering communion with him. (*b*) Mt and Mk customarily reproduce a shorter, liturgical text. The Apostles would not have repeated the Lord's Supper without his command, but there was no need to mention it in the rite. Paul's less polished text may show an earlier tradition. (*c*) He says, not that he received a direct command from Christ, but that ' I received *by tradition from the Lord* ' (παρέλαβον ἀπὸ τοῦ Κυρίου) ' *what I also handed on as a tradition to you* ' (παρέδωκα), 1 Cor 11:23 ; *cf.* 15:3 ; Gal 1:9 ; Col 2:6 ; 4:17 ; Phil 4:9 ; 1 Thess 2:13 ; 4:1 f. ; 2 Thess 3:6 ; full discussion in Allo, *Prem. Ep. aux Cor.*, exc. 12. He thus attests both the Jerusalem tradition and its origin ' from the Lord '. (*d*) Since the sources stand, the hypotheses fall ; *cf.* for these DBV(S), *art. cit.*, 1147–67, 1192–210.

The most frequent hypothesis is of a dependence of **e** the Eucharist on the ' Mystery Religions '. But *cf.* § 645*d* for these, and 1 Cor 10:20 for Christian horror of pagan rites, which makes any derivation from them impossible. Moreover an abyss divides the real, highly spiritual union with the historic Christ effected by eating his Body and drinking his Blood from the vague union with a mythical deity conceived as present at a banquet or as extending protection to the initiated.

The ' Agape '—Everyone agrees (except Baumgartner, **f** but *cf.* Allo, exc. 10), that the Lord's Supper at Corinth was either the Eucharist or joined with its celebration. Some rationalist critics held that it was simply a fraternal banquet manifesting the union of the members of the Church and analogous to those of the pagan brotherhoods ; others, that the idea of a relation to the death of Christ was introduced into it by Paul, and from this came the attribution of a sacramental effect to the receiving of the bread and wine (von Dobschütz, Loisy). Early Christian writers distinguish clearly the consecrated elements from what was eaten and drunk besides, the Greeks holding that this meal came before, the Latins after the Eucharist. St Thomas thought the meal an abuse which Paul forbade. Among modern Catholics there are two main views : (1) There is no evidence that the Eucharist in Pauline churches was connected with an Agape (Batiffol, L. Thomas, Coppens, H. Connolly). The

652f Corinthians had perhaps expected to be praised for introducing a meal which recalled the Last Supper, but Paul poured scorn on what may have been a pagan infiltration : ' Do I praise you ? ' 1 Cor 11:22, and forbade the custom as soon as he heard of it : ' If anyone is hungry, let him eat at home ', 11:34. For these authors the evidence for an NT Agape is confined to Jud 12 and 2 Pet 2:13, where the text is doubtful and need not refer to an actual feast. Moreover there is no trace of an Agape in the formal celebration of the Eucharist on ' the first day of the week ' at Troas. A long sermon is followed (after its interruption) by the ' breaking of the bread ' and only incidentally by the ' tasting ' of some food, Ac 20:7-11. (2) Others (Funk, Allo, Leclercq) hold that the ' Lord's Supper ' was a fraternal feast which normally culminated in the Eucharist. Jewish meals were ceremonial. Christians did not repeat the Paschal Supper, because Jesus had substituted a new, incomparably higher sacrifice. But they naturally kept the supper framework. The ' breaking of bread ' in Ac 2:46 is in the context of a meal. However, among Gentile converts abuses arose. They were suppressed by Paul at Corinth, but led eventually to the separation of Eucharist and Agape, e.g. Pliny, *Ep.* X, 96. (Had Paul already ordered this separation at Troas ?) The injunction to hungry Corinthians to eat at home first so that they may not mind waiting for others, 1 Cor 11:33 f., suggests a meal rather than the Eucharist alone.

g ' **The Breaking of bread** ' with blessing and giving of thanks was the customary sign of union in formal Jewish meals. Noted in Christ's feeding of the multitude by all Evangelists with obvious symbolic reference to the Eucharist, Mt 14:19 ; 15:36 ; Mk 6:41 ; 8:6 ; Lk 9:16 ; *cf.* Jn 6:11, it comes in the scene at Emmaus, Lk 24:30, 35, and in Ac 27:35 (where the point is that Paul eats openly before pagans). It is mentioned in all accounts of the Institution, Mt 26:26 ; Mk 14:22 ; Lk 22:19 ; 1 Cor 11:24, and became the most ancient technical term for the Eucharist, *cf.* DAC, *Fractio Panis* (Cabrol), 2104, n. 6 ; *Did.*, 14, 1.

We are told that the Pentecostal community ' were persevering in the doctrine of the Apostles, *the communion, the breaking of the bread* and the prayers ', Ac 2:42. Were this an ordinary meal, not a religious act, it would not be joined with the other elements of Christian teaching, life and worship in which they ' persevered '. In the Gk, ' the breaking of the bread ' is in apposition (without ' and ') to ' the communion ', *cf.* § 637*b, c*. St Luke is using the same term as his master St Paul : ' The bread which we break, is it not the *communion of the body of Christ* ', 1 Cor 10:16 ; *cf.* Jacquier, *Actes,* 87. Ac 2:46 continues : ' *persevering* with one accord in the temple and breaking bread from house to house, they *took their share* of meat with gladness and simplicity of heart '. ' The breaking of the bread ' related at Troas was the purpose of the gathering, 20:7, 11.

h Some critics (*Lietzmann, *Messe und Herrenmahl*) allege that the primitive Church had two Eucharists : the ' breaking of bread ' alone in Acts, which continues the meals taken by Christ with his disciples, and the ' Lord's Supper ' introduced by Paul, who connected it with the Last Supper and Christ's death. But the evidence from post-apostolic writings for a double rite shows no more than that from the 2nd to the 4th cent. some heretical sects and some particular churches, under ascetic and doctrinal influences of non-Christian origin, innovated by celebrating under one kind, DBV(S), *art. cit.*, 1171. In reality ' to break bread ' was a Jewish expression for a meal which St Paul himself uses to include the Cup, 1 Cor 10:16, and Paul's own ' breaking bread ' in Ac 20:11 explains 2:42. While ably refuting the two-rites theory, *O. Cullmann (*La Signification de la sainte Cène*, in *Revue d'histoire et de philosophie religieuses* [1936] 1-22), put forward the view that St Paul had attached the Eucharist to the Last Supper and the death of Christ in accord with his theology of the Redemption, whereas the ' breaking of

bread ' in Acts was a joyful derivation from meals with the risen Christ.

Cullmann was right in stressing the importance of these meals in primitive Christianity. He opened the way to the valuable synthesis : *Signification eschatologique du Repas eucharistique*, by Y. de Montcheuil, S.J., RSR 33 (1946) 10-43, reprinted in *Mélanges théologiques*. The occasions for collective apparitions after the Resurrection are often meals which the risen Jesus takes with his Apostles, whose authoritative witness they guarantee, Mk 16:14 ; Lk 24:30, 41 ff ; Jn 21:12 f. ; prob. Ac 1:4 ; 10:41. These meals form a link between the Last Supper and the celebration of the Eucharist in Acts. The joy of those who shared them sprang from union with their Lord present in their midst, from union with one another, and from certainty of the Resurrection, first fruits of the glorious coming of that Kingdom in which they already participated. How could the Apostles forget either the Last Supper or those meals with their risen Lord when they celebrated the Eucharist ? A meal is a religious act, and Christ's meals in the Gospel have a religious, and in the broad sense a sacramental character, for by them he is in communion with men. Sharing his meals, the sinners he came to pardon have a foretaste of the Messianic banquet, Mt 9:10-15 ; Mk 2:16 f., Lk 15:1-32. Food and drink are God's gifts. Our daily bread, enjoyment of a divine gift, becomes the promise of a total gift. The meals at the multiplication of bread and at Cana look forward to the Eucharist, Bouyer, *Quatrième Ev.*, 87 ff. By saying that he would not eat the Pasch again until it was fulfilled in the Kingdom of God, nor drink of the fruit of the vine until the Kingdom of God came, Lk 22:16 ff., a kingdom which he disposed to them that they might eat and drink at his table in it, 30, he set the final consummation in eternity, but he envisaged also his kingdom on earth, wherein the divine banquet of the Eucharist replaces and fulfils Jewish figures, *cf.* Lagrange, *in loc.* Already ' we have tasted the heavenly gift and the powers, of the world to come ', *cf.* Heb 6:4 f. ; 2:5. The risen Christ, present to the eyes of faith, is our host as well as our food. Thus this chain of meals leads to the eternal banquet, and the first Christians seem to have regarded the Eucharist as its anticipation, *cf. art. cit.*, followed closely.

But St Paul did not create a new Eucharist. Christ's resurrection is inseparable from his death, *cf.* Lk 24:26, and both are to be seen ' less as past events than as present mysteries ', *art. cit.*, 25 ; *cf.* Rom 6:9-12 ; Gal 2:19 f. ; 5:24 f. It is by sharing his Cross that we share his glory, *cf.* Rom 8:17. What St Paul does is to bring out from tradition Christ's own words of institution and the double repetition of the command ' Do this ', to remind the fickle Corinthians that the Eucharist is a representation of the Last Supper. Therefore ' as often as ye eat this bread and drink of the cup, ye proclaim the death of the Lord, until he come ', 1 Cor 11:23-27, WV. The final perspective lighting up the Mystery is still the glorious Coming, 26 ; *cf.* Jn 6:54. The pledge of this Coming is the sacrificial act of the New Covenant, the ' remembrance ', or effective memorial of the Last Supper, 1 Cor 11:24 f., which carries the community into Christ's kingdom, bringing sentiments of holy fear, repentance, joy and fervent charity. This doctrine Paul had preached from the first, 33, and yet nobody could say that the Eucharist at Corinth was ' sad ' ! It remains the doctrine of the Church : ' Unde et memores, Domine, nos . . . sed et plebs tua sancta . . . tam beatae passionis, nec non et ab inferis resurrectionis, sed et in caelos gloriosae ascensionis . . . '.

The Real Presence is affirmed by the words ' This is **b** my body ', ' this is my blood ', *cf.* §§ 720*a, b*, 739*g, h* ; *Aquin ST*, 3, 75 ; *In 1 Cor, in loc.* and Allo, *op. cit.*, exc. 12. The version ' this *means* my body ' is false to the original, and contradicts all early Christian tradition. The view that the bread only symbolizes the Mystical Body also distorts the words and fails to account for

b 'this is my blood'. For St Paul's whole treatment, particularly vv 26 'you proclaim the death of the Lord', 27 'guilty of (or 'accused for') the body and the blood of the Lord', and 29 'not discerning the body of the Lord' (μὴ διακρίνων τὸ σῶμα, 'without distinguishing the body from other food', WV) shows that 'the faithful entered into direct relation with the personal body and blood of the Saviour', Allo, exc. 11, 296. 'The body of Christ' and 'the blood of Christ' (unless the context determines that the former means the Church) always imply his death ; cf. Rom 3:25 ; 5:9 ; 7:4 ; Col 1:20 ff. ; Heb 10:5, 10. It is from Communion in the true Body, 'the *unique* Bread', 1 Cor 10:17, that the Mystical Body results, cf. § 637b. In the analogous passage 'they drank of the spiritual rock that followed them ; and the rock was Christ', 10:4, the point is that it was the Person of Christ who accompanied them and was symbolized by the rock, cf. Allo, *in loc.*

c The Eucharist is a true sacrifice, a representation of the Saviour's Sacrifice : 'Do this *for my remembrance.* . . . You *proclaim* the death of the Lord until he come', 1 Cor 11:24–26 ; Dz 938. The ritual elements of the sacrifice are identical with the Body and Blood of Christ, cf. § 644*f–j*. In 10:18–21 St Paul compares the drinking of the chalice of the Lord and the sharing of his 'table' with the Jewish and pagan sacrifices, the point being that to share ceremonially in the thing sacrificed, is to share the sacrificial act and all that it implies, ICC. Like the pagans and the Jews, 18, the Christians too have an altar, and they cannot share in this 'table' and in that of devils, 21 (where 'table' certainly means 'altar' in opposition to that of the devils, and to the Jewish θυσιαστήριον) ; this is sometimes the meaning in OT, and cf. Philo, *De Spec. Leg.*, I, 221. Every time they share the Lord's Supper, they effectively 'proclaim his death until he come', just because his Presence is real, though mysterious and needing 'discernment'. Finally, the statement that this is 'proclaiming the death of the Lord', together with the repetition of Christ's command and words, is good evidence that the words uttered by him at the Last Supper were repeated at the Lord's Supper to represent his death, Allo, 294.

d St Paul unites in one movement of thought the presence of Christ in the Eucharist and the effect upon the communicants. Because they communicate in Christ really present, under effective symbols, their communion is the source of their unity, 10:16 f. ; cf. Jn 15:1–11 ; *Did.* 9, 4 ; *Aquin.*, ST 3, 73, 3 ; § 637b, c. This leaves no room for the members of the one body to be selfish individualists, any more than to share in a false cult, 1 Cor 10:20 f., 24, 28 f. The Eucharist, being a spiritual food and drink, like its figures, the manna and the water from the Rock, confers communication of the Spirit and increase of charity, 10:3 f., 17 ; cf. 15:50 ; 2 Cor 13:13. But it does not work as magic, and requires moral co-operation, 1 Cor 10:5 ; 11:17. Let a man examine his conscience before he receives it, 28 ; cf. 2 Cor 13:5 ; DBV(S), *art. cit.*, 1186–7.

e Thus the rich Eucharistic doctrine of the NT must not be split into isolated elements by heresy or one-sided piety. Christ is a Person, not a kind of impersonal force. He is the friend around whom his own gather in joy, the host at the Supper at which he gives himself. The commemoration of his death must not be separated from his real Presence, nor that presence from the Sacrifice wherein it becomes real, nor must individualism diminish the sense of a communal banquet. When his coming occupied the horizon, men tended to forget that they must go to him by his death. Now that his coming seems delayed, they forget that they already share in his resurrection. But all these values are in St Paul's doctrine of that breaking of bread which is the communion of the Body of the Risen Lord, who the night before he suffered offered himself under symbolic rite, and commanded his Apostles who supped with him to do what he had done ; cf. de Montcheuil, *art. cit.*, 37 ; § 657*f–h*.

The unique sufficiency of the sacrifice of the Cross **653f** compared with those of the Old Law, and of the one, eternal priesthood of Christ compared with the Levitical, is brought out by Heb, cf. 10:10, 'we have been sanctified through the offering of the body of Jesus once for all', WV ; 7:27 ; 9:26, 28 ; 10:1 ff. This is the point of departure of the Catholic doctrine on the identity of the sacrifice of the Cross and that of the Eucharist, which is a real re-presentation of that Sacrifice, with the same Victim and the same high-priest, who offers himself by the ministry of his priests under those same symbols under which he offered himself at the Last Supper ; cf. Dz 938, 940. The Protestant objection that Heb shows that the Eucharist is not a sacrifice, misapprehends this combined doctrine of Heb, 1 Cor and the words of Institution. Deeper examination shows the Eucharistic implications of the epistle. The sacrifice of the Cross is described in the sacrificial terms used by Christ as the Last Supper : offering his body, Heb 10:10, and his blood, 9:12, 14, the Mediator of the NT offers the blood of the New Covenant for the remission of sins, 9:15, 18 ff. ; 10:29 ; 12:24 ; 13:20. The comparison of Christ's priesthood with that of Melchisedech suggests the sacrifice under symbols of bread and wine. Moreover, his priesthood is not extinguished by his death, 7:15, 24–27. The sacrifices described as proper to Christians, 13:15 f., exclude only those of the Law, and can well be understood in function of the Eucharist. In communion with Christ, 3:14, in and through the blood of the great Priest-Victim, 10:20 ; 6:19 f., we have the way opened to the heavenly sanctuary, and are thus already citizens of the heavenly Jerusalem, and companions of the angels and saints, 12:22 ff. ; cf. 1 Cor 1:9 ; 10:16 ff., 21. In the new dispensation the humblest Christians are far more privileged than the Jewish priests, for 'we have an altar from which they are not entitled to eat who serve the Tabernacle', Heb 13:10, WV. This altar would seem to be the Cross, but we 'eat' from it by the nourishment of the Eucharist.

St John's account of Christ's discourse on the Eucharist **g** in ch 6 is not his only reference to it. For his facts are also symbols with many values, and though he does not repeat the Synoptic narrative of the Institution, his Gospel is shot through with allusions to the rite which was centre and source of the Christ-life of the churches for whom he wrote. The Incarnation is prolonged by the Eucharist : In the Word 'was life . . . he was in the world . . . the Word was made flesh' . . . 'The bread which I will give is my flesh for the life of the world . . . he that eateth my flesh and drinketh my blood hath eternal life', Jn 1:4–14 ; 6:51, 54. As Yahweh is married to his people, so Jesus, the bridegroom, 3:29, chooses water and wine at a marriage feast to be the first sign whereby to manifest his glory, 2:11 ; cf. 1:14, and on the Cross blood and water issue from his side as his last sign prefiguring baptism and the Eucharist, 19:34. It is a sign to which John renders solemn testimony, 35 ; cf. 1 Jn 5:6–9. Using the traditional symbol for the People of God, Jesus after the Last Supper declares that he is the true vine in which his disciples must abide, Jn 15:1–11 ; cf. 6:56, a Eucharistic reference recognized by early Christianity, *Did.*, 9, 2. By his sacrifical death he consecrates both himself and those Apostles whom he has commanded to renew his sacrifice, 17:19 ; cf. § 649e.

The Eucharistic Discourse itself had been preceded **h** by demonstrations of Christ's power over bread and over his own body. It builds up from the multiplication of bread and the figure of the manna to Christ as the bread from heaven and finally as divine food, really present under sacramental signs. Upon this Real Presence he insists by declarations about 'eating my flesh' and 'drinking my blood', 6:53–58. The only metaphorical meaning in Scripture and Semitic languages for 'eating the flesh' of someone, 'to destroy by calumny', is here impossible. Nor will Jesus explain that what he has said is metaphorical, as, *e.g.* in Mk 8:14–21. Instead he repeats it six times,

653h Jn 6:53–58. He lets the worldly-minded crowd and many disciples leave him rather than withdraw this, his best gift, only appealing to the latter to exercise that faith which is given by the Spirit of God, 60–66. The 'spiritual mentality' of St John does not contradict but confirms the Real Presence by the words : ' It is the spirit which giveth life ; the flesh profiteth nothing ', 63, WV. ' The flesh ', *i.e.* mere human, weak, ' carnal ' understanding and action, *e.g.* Mt 16:17 ; 26:41 ; Mk 14:38 ; Jn 1:13 ; Gal 1:16 ; 1 Cor 15:50 ; *cf.* § 645*k*, is not the same as ' my flesh ', and it is precisely ' the spirit ', *i.e.* man under the impulse of the Spirit of God (*cf.* § 648*b, c*) who believes the reality of Jesus and his words : ' every spirit which confesseth that Jesus Christ is come in the flesh is of God ', 1 Jn 4:2 f. For the Spirit bears witness, and he ' is one ' with ' the water ' and ' the blood ', 5:6, 8. Lastly, the sacrificial character of the Eucharist is affirmed as decisively as anywhere in St Paul : ' The bread which I will give is my flesh for the life of the world ', Jn 6:52 (Vg).

i St John's doctrine is thus identical with St Paul's, but individually expressed. What distinguishes it is the stress upon the present effect of the Eucharist, the eternal life already given to him who eats Christ's flesh, the abiding in him, the actual relation of the communicant to him : ' You can have no life in yourselves unless you eat the flesh of the Son of man, and drink his blood. The man who eats my flesh and drinks my blood enjoys eternal life, and I will raise him up at the last day. . . . He who eats my flesh, and drinks my blood, lives continually in me, and I in him. As I live because of the Father, the living Father who has sent me, so he who eats me will live, in his turn, because of me ', 6:54–58, KNT. The life which will flow from this communion in the resurrection is in more distant perspective, 52, 55, 59, and it remains for the Supper Discourse to show—how magnificently !—that if we live in Jesus, we live in one another, 13:34 f. ; 14:20 ; 15:9–12 ; 17:21 ff.

j **Conclusions**—Christ, therefore, is truly present beneath the symbols, and there is a true sacrifice which originates from the Lord himself. Catholic exegetes have thus answered both Protestants and Rationalists. Their further task is to display among the riches of NT doctrine and symbolism all the values intended by the Spirit of God. Prefigured by the manna, the vine of Israel and the ancient sacrifices, and foretold by the last prophet as the Clean Oblation to be offered in every place, Mal 1:11, the Eucharist was instituted in the context of the Paschal meal and anticipated the Messianic banquet. Moreover, the Last Supper draws ' into unity the three apparently unrelated notions of the new Kingdom (established by a new Covenant), the suffering Messias, the Bread of Life. For this reason it is the almost indispensable key to the Messianic plan. It so declares the essence of the mission of Jesus and so communicates its effects that it becomes the central liturgical act of the Kingdom which Christ founded : Do this in commemoration of Me ! ', R. Dyson, S.J., and A. Jones, *The Kingdom of Promise* (1946) 165. That act re-presents ' for the remission of sins ' the death of the Saviour, the universal source of salvation. Men share in the new, risen, eternal life of their Head by renewing his sacrifice, and by participating in his Body and Blood. The sacrifice of Christ's Church is the source of her life and unity. Body and Bride of Christ, she comes forth from his side on the Cross and is nourished by his very flesh, Eph 5:29 f. ; Gen 2:21–24. As in the primal Paradise God gave the first pair to eat of the tree of life, so now Christ will give to him who conquers ' to eat of the tree of life which is in the Paradise of my God ', Apoc 2:7, that tree of life which gives its fruits and leaves for the healing of the nations, all spiritual promises for time and for eternity, 22:2 ; *cf.* Allo, *in loc.* ; Jn 6:52.

k **The Day of the Lord**—day of the Resurrection and Pentecost, first day of the week, is already in Ac 20:7 the day of public service ' when we were gathered together to break bread ', WV, *cf.* 1 Cor 16:2 ; *Ep.*

Barn., 15 ; Ign., *Magnes.* 9, 1 ; Justin, *Apol.* I, 67 ; Pliny, *Ep.* X, 96, ' stato die '. This is the ' day of the Lord ', the Lord glorious and risen, when St John saw the heavenly liturgy, Apoc 1:10 ; chh 4 and 5 ; *Did.*, 14, 1. As baptism succeeded circumcision, and the era of grace and liberty that of the Law, so the Lord's Day succeeded the Jewish Sabbath, the shadow being fulfilled in the reality of Christ, Col 2:16 f. ; *cf.* Gal 4:10 ; Tertull., *Adv. Jud.*, 6. Historically, the Christian liturgy completes the Sabbath's, and the vigil began on the evening of the Sabbath and ended at dawn after the celebration of the Eucharist ; *cf.* Ac 20:7–11. Thus the Passion, Resurrection and Ascension of Christ were celebrated by the whole community in unison, leading to the glorious Day of the Lord, itself a joyful anticipation of the final day of his return. For the Jews the eighth day of the cosmic week, for the pagans the ' day of the sun ' (*cf.* Justin, *Apol.* I, 67), the Christian Mystery of the Lord's Day in its indestructible originality fulfilled, and its liturgy could borrow from, the Jewish world of history and the pagan world of nature. Here are the materials for the restoration of the sense of the Mystery of Sunday, *cf.* DAC, Dimanche (Dumaine) ; H. Rahner, S.J., *Griechische Mythen in Christlichen Deutung*, reviewed by J. Daniélou, RSR 34 (1947) 380 ; La Vie Spirituelle, n. 317, *Le huitième Jour* (1947).

Penance—*Cf.* DTC, *Pénitence* (Amann) ; *Confession* (Mangenot). The Gospels are full of invitations to repentance as a prelude to entering the kingdom. Jesus delights to be among the sinners he has come to save, and explicitly claims the power to forgive sins in the case of the paralytic of Capharnaum ; *cf.* Mt 9:2–8 ; Mk 2:3–12 ; Lk 5:18–26. To Peter and the Apostles he promises the power of ' binding and loosing ' in contexts which involve the intervention of the rulers of the Church, Mt 16:18 ff. ; 18:15–18. After the resurrection he bids them preach repentance in terms so absolute as to include cases of relapse (*cf.* 28:18 ff. ; Lk 24:47 ff.) and expressly confers on them his own life-giving mission of peace with authority to remit or retain sins, Jn 20 :21 ff. This recalls the promise of the power to bind or loose, and the alternative indicates a judgement, upon due knowledge of the offence and the dispositions of the sinner ; *cf.* Dz 894, 899, 913. Confession of sins, so constantly practised by sinners in the OT, had been required in some form by the Baptist, Mt 3:6 ; Mk 1:5.

The power of forgiveness was first exercised through baptism, Ac 2:37 ff. But the cases of Ananias and Sapphira, 5:1 ff., and of Simon, 8:18 ff., and the attempts of Saul, probably sometimes effective, to make the faithful ' blaspheme ', 26:11, show that something further was needed. Temporary or definitive excommunication was practised by the Jews and had been required by Jesus himself to preserve the purity of faith or morals ; *cf.* Mt 5:29 ; 18:17. Experience proved the need for it ; *cf.* Ac 5:11 ; 3 Jn 9 ff. St Paul uses his power of binding to excommunicate the sinner, both to cleanse the community, 1 Cor 5:13, and in hope of his ultimate good, 1 Tim 1:20 ; *cf.* 2 Tim 2:17. He mentions sins which carry this penalty, 1 Cor 5:11 ff., citing Deut 13:5, LXX. Exclusion from or reconciliation to the Body of Christ was the essential fact involved, those outside being in Satan's kingdom. To the sinner of 2 Cor 2:5–11, he grants remission of punishment, to be made through the community ; *cf.* Allo, *in loc.* How this was done, we do not know. Nor can it be proved that the confession of sins mentioned, Ac 19:18, and recommended, Jas 5:16 ; 1 Jn 1:8 ff., was sacramental. Some attribute to penance the laying on of hands in 1 Tim 5:22.

While the Apostolic Church was conscious of her power to remit sins, and there was repentance even for great sins, Apoc chh 2, 3 ; 1 Jn 1:7, 2:2, she expected that the baptized would be ' dead to sin ' and not fall grievously again, Rom 6:2–23 ; Col 3:1–11. In Heb 6:4–8 ; 10:25 ff. ; 12:16 f., apostasy is spoken of as if irremissible. Rigorist heretics used such texts. But Jewish forms of speech must be remembered, and the natural insistence, with a community tempted to apostatize, upon the moral impossibility of forgiveness in a state when faith in the only sacrifice efficacious for sin was lacking. Moreover some texts seem concerned with that wilful blindness which in practice makes subsequent appeals useless. Such apostasy may be the ' sin unto death ' of 1 Jn 5:16 f., prayer for the remission of which is not forbidden but not enjoined. ' Blasphemy against the Holy Spirit ' is the attribution of divine works to the devil, a hardened rejection of God's light which precludes the conditions for forgiveness, though a miracle of accepted grace might remove the sin ; *cf.* on Mt 12:31 f. ; Mk 3:28 ff.

Marriage—God, the author of marriage, joins man and wife to be ' two in one flesh ' in a permanent union, image of that ' marriage of God and his people ' which is recalled by the parables of the marriage feast of the Son, Gen 1:27 f. ; 2:18–24 ; Mt 22:2 ff. ; 25:1 ff. In this normal Christian vocation (a ' charisma ', 1 Cor 7:2, 7, 24), the love of husband and wife, a total mutual self-giving unto death, symbolizes and is modelled on the love of Christ and his Bride and Body, the Church, Eph 5:22–33 ; Apoc 19:7 ; *cf.* § 635*d*. The sacramental grace of marriage between Christians, here suggested (Dz 969 ; Prat, II, 271–4), enables them to give Christ's own love to each other, for they marry ' in the Lord ' ; *cf.* 1 Cor 7:39. Thus their home will be a fruitful cell of the Mystical Body.

Though Moses had allowed divorce ' by reason of your hardness of heart ', Jesus had re-enacted the **natural indissolubility of marriage,** Mt 5:31 f. ; 19:7 ff.; Mk 10:3 ff. ; Lk 16:18. Mk, Lk and Paul admit no exception and for explanation of Mt, *cf.* Com. *in loc.* and J. Bonsirven, S.J., *Le Divorce dans le NT* (1948). In a society where the Law had kept the standard of morals high, Jesus needed only to correct its imperfections. But with converts from paganism, St Paul had often to insist on the duties of marriage. The little dogmatic treatise in 1 Cor 7 is based upon and amplifies the teaching of his Master.

He defends marriage against scrupulous Corinthians and heretics, 1 Cor 7:28, 36 ff. ; 1 Tim 4:3 f. It is to be held in honour and kept in holiness, free from any impurity, 1 Thess 4:4–8 ; Heb 13:4. The conjugal duty is a debt owed by either party to the other ; lest they be tempted, they should not abstain save by mutual consent and for a time, to give themselves to prayer, 1 Cor 7:3 ff. The law of the Gospel on the identity of their essential rights and duties, frees the wife from her old, humiliating dependence. She is the equal of the man in all that concerns the unity, fidelity and indissolubility of marriage, 10 f. By their mutual, irrevocable gift, they belong to each other, not to themselves, and Paul gives commands and counsels equally to both, 2 ff. But he firmly maintains the hierarchy in the home. The husband is the head, as Christ is head of the Church, but he is not the irresponsible master. He must love and cherish his wife with tender respect, as she must reverence and be subject to him, 1 Cor 11:3, 7 ; Col 3:18 f. ; 1 Tim 2:11 f. The wife wins her salvation by her Christian motherhood, 15. St Peter adds that husbands must be wise and honour their wives as co-heirs of the grace of life, 1 Pet 3:7 ; *cf.* further § 660*c–e*.

St Paul gives no command to marry, but ' an exhortation dictated by prudence ', 1 Cor 7:2–6, 26 f. ; *cf.* Allo, *in loc.* Those who cannot be continent should marry, 9. Once married, the Lord commands them not to separate, and if they do, to remain unmarried or be reconciled, 10 f. The bond holds while the other party lives ; in case of death, there is freedom to marry again, only ' in the Lord ', *i.e.* normally to a Christian, 39 ; Rom 7:2 f. For moral reasons, he wishes young widows to marry and have families, 1 Tim 5:14.

Virginity—Yet to remain unmarried for the Gospel's sake is a better state since it makes possible an undistracted devotion to the interests of Christ, 1 Cor 7:1, 8, 25 f., 32–35, 38, 40. This is Christ's own **654h** invitation, but it requires a special grace, Mt 19:12 ; 1 Cor 7:7 ; *cf.* Apoc 14:4 ; Dz 980 ; § 660*g*.

The ' Pauline privilege '—Conscious that he speaks by **i** the Spirit, St Paul gives an apostolic ruling. A baptized Christian, married before baptism to an unbeliever who now consents to their living peaceably together, may not break off the marriage, for the family relations are sanctified by the believing partner. But if the unbeliever (with whom lies the initiative) breaks it off, the marriage may be dissolved for the peace of the Christian party, who should not be enslaved by the possibly chimerical hope of converting the other, 1 Cor 7:12–16, 40 ; 14:37 ; § 660*f*.

For **Order**, *cf.* §§ 657*f–h*, 659 ; for **Extreme Unction,** *cf.* Com. on Jas.

VI THE MINISTRY

Introduction—Reference has already been made to **655a** those whom the neophyte would find in every Christian community, and who, by whatever name they might be called, were obviously the guides, the leaders, the teachers of the rest, § 638. It was once fashionable to maintain either that whatever influence these men had was due to the unpredictable influences of the Spirit, or that, if they held some sort of regular office in the community, this was held from the community itself. In both these views, a fundamental pre-supposition was that a Christian community formed itself by *individual* Christians coming together so that they might help themselves and one another to live their faith better. By thus assembling, they created a Christian ' assembly ', an ἐκκλησία, a Church ; and just as the local Christian Church came into being by the union of individual Christians, so too the universal Church was conceived of as arising from the union of the many local churches through mutual recognition, *cf.* § 634*a*. Today, **the individualism** which permeates this reconstruction is being more and more abandoned : it was, of course, particularly useful to those who, for whatever cause, denied that the creation of a Church ever held a place in Christ's intentions. As Loisy said : ' Christ proclaimed the coming of the Kingdom of God ; and it was the Church which appeared in its place ', *L'Evangile et l'Eglise* (1902) 111. It is now recognized that it is impossible to eliminate such an intention from Christ's mind without doing violence to the historical evidence of the NT records, and the possibility is at once re-opened that the leaders, the ' officials ' who are there mentioned incidentally in the local churches, exercised their influence and authority not merely through the invisible working of the Spirit or because of a delegation of power by the local community, but chiefly as the result of a commission ultimately traceable to our Lord himself (*cf.* F. M. Braun, O.P., *Aspects nouveaux du Problème de l'Eglise* [1942] ; German ed. with supplementary matter : *Neues Licht auf die Kirche* [1946]).

But before this question could be investigated on its **b** own merits, another ghost had to be laid, which had been haunting ecclesiology for nearly two centuries. In these last years, the **eschatological problem** has been working itself out to a more reasonable issue. That Christ founded no Church seemed obvious to those who made of him an apocalyptic prophet, predicting the end of the world and the final judgement within the lifetime of his hearers. The Kingdom of God would only be inaugurated after the judgement, but ' the Kingdom of God was at hand ', hence the consummation was not far off. No need then for a Church during the few years that remained : Christ merely taught an ' Interim-Ethics ', and if the Parousia, the Second Coming, did not occur as expected, and the Christians built a Church instead, this Church could scarcely be said to have been instituted by Christ. The fundamental question is dealt with in §§ 670–1 ; suffice it to say here first that no one who ascribes such a

813

655b delusion to Christ can explain the *unwavering* belief of the early Christians in his word even after they had come to realize that he had misled them ; and secondly, that the new line of interpretation which is now showing itself is a substantial return to Catholic tradition (*cf.* *O. Cullmann, *Christus und die Zeit* [1946] ; trans. *Christ et le Temps* [1947]). Between the Resurrection and the Second Coming is placed, as part of Christ's own outlook and that of his disciples, *an intermediate period*, which, however, already belongs to the final economy. The duration of this intermediate period was left quite undetermined in Christ's prophecies, so that he was neither himself deceived nor did he mislead his hearers. It is in this period that the Church was to function, and Christ indeed could and did speak of ' his Church '. (*Cf.* Braun, *op. cit.*, Excursus III, *L'eschatologie néo-testamentaire dans la pensée protestante contemporaine*. Also the criticism which the new ideas call for : *ibid.* chap IV, §§ 1 and 2).

656a The Mystical Body and Authority—The fact that all Christians could be called ' saints ', obviously neither implied that they were finished products of perfection, nor that their ' sanctity ' bestowed on them complete independence from any human interference. Not even their title to be called ' a royal priesthood ', Exod 19:6 ; 1 Pet 2:5, 9 ; Apoc 1:6 ; 5:10, did this : such a title only brought out what was implicit in that of ' the saints ', for sanctity is not inert but essentially self-communicative : indeed a ' sanctity ' which rests in itself and does not in some way try to communicate, priestwise and royally, the divine largesse to others, is not sanctity at all. All this finds its place in the reality, already considered, of the Body of Christ, which his Church is. For the members not only all co-operate (as might nations who had no thought of surrendering each its own sovereignty) : their co-operation will often realize itself within a relationship of authority and subordination. However, just as the Church, which is rightly called a society, **is** a society *sui generis*, so too the authority and corresponding subordination which it entails, are themselves *sui generis*, and may not be equated with those which prevail, for instance, in the State, in all various forms ; *cf.* M.-J. Congar, O.P., *Esquisses du Mystère de l'Eglise* (1941) 47–52 ; H. Chirat, *L'assemblée chrét. à l'âge apost.* (1949) 50 ff.

b This was made clear by **our Lord** himself on more than one occasion. There were indeed to be among his followers some who should be ' greater ' than others, or ' first ' or ' leaders ', Mt 20:26–27 ; Mc 10:43–44 ; Lk 22:26, but they should not on this account ' lord it over ' the rest, as did those among the Gentiles who wielded power. On the contrary their position demanded of them the greater service towards others ; was not his own example eloquent enough ? He, the Son of Man, had not come among them to be waited on by them : he had come to do *them* service, to give his life in ransom for them ; he, their Master and Lord, had laid aside his tunic to wash their feet, like any slave ; while they sat at table, he was serving. He was not the less their Master and Lord for performing this lowly task ; if they were to follow his example, as he had told them, that need not exclude every kind of distinction between his followers, not even that wherein some should have authority over others ; but it did involve excluding that pride and self-aggrandisement which is so wont to be coveted by those who enjoy authority, Mt 20:25 ff. ; Mc 10:42 ff. ; Lk 22:24 ff. ; Jn 13:12 ff. (*cf.* § 597*g*–*i*). So too, from their very context, must be explained such passages as Mt 23:8 ff. : it is not the bearing of this or that title which our Lord forbids his Apostles (' Rabbi ', ' Father ', ' Teacher '), it is the arrogance with which the Scribes and Pharisees preened themselves, that he here pillories. Fathers and Teachers they must be : but the greater they are as such, the more thoroughly must they become the servants of all (*ibid.*).

c Much of the fragrance of Christ which enriches the epistles of **St Paul** comes from this blending of authority and humility. In his ' interpretations ' of the Scrip-

tures he could rival the best of the *Rabbis* (*cf.* J. Bonsirven, S.J., *Exégèse rabbinique et exégèse paulinienne* [1939] *passim*) ; he was a *father* to more churches than that of Corinth, *cf.* 1 Cor 3:1–2 ; 4:15 ; and what did he do but *teach* on all his missionary journeys, in all his letters, in the special instructions which he gave to his missionary deputies, *cf.* 1 Cor 4:17 ; 2 Tim 3:14 etc. ? He could threaten to come with a rod if his ' children ' began putting on airs, 1 Cor 4:18–21 ; none more sure than he that he taught the pure Gospel, Gal 1:6–10, that it was for him not only to ' make every mind surrender to Christ's service ', but also to be ' prepared to punish rebellion from any quarter ', 2 Cor 10:5–6, KNT.

But he manifested in his own person how fully such ' authoritarianism ' could be impregnated with what is one-sidedly called ' the spirit of Christ '. When the Corinthians were threatening to split up into rival factions claiming to have Apollo, or Paul, or some other as their ' authority ', St Paul's distress showed itself in the way that he rebuked them. They were lowering themselves by thus placing their ' glory ' in mere men : like everything else in the world, life and death included, the Apostles and their helpers had been placed at *their* service, all for *them* ; and *their* pre-occupation should be to live for Christ, and so for God, by the way they used all that God had placed at their disposal— including those mysteries of his, of which the Apostles were merely the stewards, accountable to him for their ministrations, *cf.* 1 Cor 1:11–13 ; 3:21–4:5. The Apostles were merely ministers, assistants, in God's work among them ; to him alone must be ascribed the increase : it was not for Paul or for Apollo to take credit for the richness of the harvest, or for the beauty of the building ; these belonged to God, 1 Cor 3:3–9 ; *cf.* 2 Cor 4:5, 7, 15 ; 5:17–20.

Thus, just as our Lord himself constantly sought to turn attention away from himself and ascribed all that he said and did to his Father (Lebr. ODT I [1927⁷] 309), so too St Paul manifests an exquisite humility, above all when he is vindicating his authority against the calumnies of those who attacked his apostolate. *All* those called to such a work had become ' the refuse of this world, the offscouring of all ', 1 Cor 4:13, yet he least of all would think of complaining, having previously ' persecuted the Church of God ' and thus being the least of all the apostles, as he was indeed the last, ' one born out of due time ', 1 Cor 15:8–9. He had worked all the harder for that, or rather the grace of God working with him, *ibid.* 10 ; but he showed his sense of peculiar obligation to preach which the ' violence ' of his conversion had imposed on him : if preach he must, he would do it ' free of charge, not making full use of the rights which gospel preaching gives me ', 1 Cor 9:14–18, KNT (*cf.* Allo *in loc.* ; also Paul's great ' boasting ' apologia, 2 Cor 10–13 etc.). In every way he tried to adapt himself to the various conditions and needs of those he would win to Christ, 1 Cor 9:19 ff. : ' I have made myself everybody's slave, to win more souls ', *ibid.* KNT ; so much so that it was easy for his critics to accuse him of opportunism, of ' courting the favour of men ', Gal 1:10, KNT. His fierce repudiation of such a charge (*e.g.* Gal) brings out all the more how, for all his humility in dealing with his converts, he was loyal to the commission he had received to teach and to direct them.

This blending of authority and self-abasement, coming as it did from our Lord himself, was not confined to St Paul. **St Peter** in his first epistle, teaches and exhorts objectively and peremptorily : yet his deep humility can be sensed in the way he praises his hearers who are so full of love for Christ, though they have never even seen him, let alone known and lived with him as he has done, *cf.* 1 Pet 1:8 ; or again when he lays down rules for the ' *presbyters* ', reckoning himself merely as one of them, and revealing his own outlook when he tells them not to lord it over their charges, but to set an example to their flock ; *cf.* 1 Pet 5:3. Such phrases have given occasion to some to belittle

CHRISTIANITY IN APOSTOLIC TIMES

f Peter's authority; like Paul, he will have been familiar enough with having his words and actions misrepresented; *cf.* 1 Pet 2:15; 3:14; 4:14, especially when most nearly imitating his Master; *cf.* 3:16–18.

g The Catholic Church is often accused for her insistence on the authority of her accredited officials. Perhaps two considerations will put this matter in a clearer light. One can scarcely 'lord it over' others unless one is in a position to do so, *cf. sup.* § 656*b*. That our Lord warned his disciples against it implies that they might be in such a position, *i.e.* so far from excluding it, his words imply that authority is to be exercised within the body of his followers. But those in such a position may abuse it in one way or another; that is why he puts before them the idea—his own—of humble service, which they should themselves adopt; whether they do so or not, the authority is theirs (*cf.* his reply to Peter, contrasting the conduct of the faithful and wise steward with that of one who is disloyal and violent: Lk 12:39–46).

Secondly, the repudiation of human authority among Christians can be maintained in the face of the evidence of the NT only by an exaggerated personification of the Gospel revelation. Because Christ is the Word of God in person, not only is a personal authority ascribed to Scripture (the 'word of God' in another sense), but the *preaching* of the Gospel too (the 'word of God 'once more) is given a personality—often indistinguishable from that of Christ himself. Thus where Catholics see the human instrument exercising authority because commissioned by God to do so, others see only 'the Word' with all its binding force and exigencies as well as its appeal and challenge. This 'power of the Word' is not denied by the Catholic Church: the fact that in her teaching the three great realities—Christ, the Scriptures, the preaching of the Gospel—have always been seen the same name, shows her awareness of the inner relationships between them; but the experience of nineteen centuries prevents her from forgetting the warnings of Paul, of John, of Peter, of Jude, and those indeed of Christ himself, to beware of false prophets, of men who come speaking in his name, liable to deceive, if possible, even the elect, *cf.* § 639*d*. That is why Christ made the preaching of the Word [the Gospel] contingent on an office. There were Gnostics and others even in apostolic times who also professed to proclaim 'the Word': but how were ordinary folk to know the difference? Since it was the Word [*i.e.* Christ] who gave the Apostles their authority, their 'office' was indeed contingent on 'the Word'; but that office in turn had as its essential function to guarantee, for the generality of the faithful, the proclamation of the Word [*i.e.* the Gospel] in all its purity. Again, if it was through the power of the Word [*i.e.* of Christ] that the Apostles had their authority, their approval of those who were, in their turn, raised to an office in the Church was itself but a prolongation of the activity of the Word. And, in fine, if the power of the Word [the Gospel] was manifested in its preserving itself among the children of men, it did so precisely through constantly renewed officials, upon whom was laid the charge of preaching the Word and guarding it against all corruption (*cf.* §§ 639*f, g*; 657*h*). One might then say that, from God's point of view, indeed, the office was contingent on the Word; but from the point of view of the ordinary faithful (for whom the Word was given), the Word was contingent upon the office.

In the brief survey of the origins of the ministry, which is all that is possible here, what has just been said of the place of the ministry in the organic harmony of the mystical Body, and of the nature of the authority exercised by its members, must be understood where reference to these topics is not explicitly made. (See also §§ 635, 638*b*, 639*f–h*.) The full presentation of the evidence does not confine itself to the analysis of a small handful of texts, but embraces in a wide sweep the whole economy of the Redemption as manifested in the two Testaments and in the early Church. In this way, justice can be done, at one and the same time,

to the demand for *a spiritual appreciation* of Christ's **656i** Church and to the implication of *a firm human structure* which, historically, underlies the words of the Apostles, and, in the first place, those of Christ himself. It is to this 'exterior' element of the Body of Christ that we can now turn our attention.

What Christ had done: (i) the Apostles—If the first **657a** things which the early Christians were taught were the facts about our Lord: his Messiahship (at least), his saving death and resurrection, his promised return to judge the world; if the faith in him as 'Lord', and repentance and Baptism were the essentials for admission to the new company, it is clear that their instruction did not stop there. We hear from the first that they were 'persevering in the doctrine of the Apostles', Ac 2:42, and what was said above of their growing in the knowledge of Christ (§ 634*d*), suffices to explain why St Luke (or his very early source) used these terms to express what they learnt. We have the qualifications of an Apostle, as then envisaged, in St Peter's address at the election of Matthias: one 'who has companied with us, all the time that the Lord Jesus came in and went out amongst us, beginning from the baptism of John, until the day wherein he was taken up from us ... a witness with us of his resurrection', Ac 1:21–22.

The 'doctrine of the Apostles', then, was what the **b** Apostles had learnt through being with our Lord during his public ministry: they were the men who had lived in closest intimacy with him, had heard his teaching and been witnesses of his life and of his wonders of power and lowliness, *cf.* Heb 2:3. If they tried chiefly to reproduce his words, they could not do so apart from the incidents which so often occasioned them, and inevitably they would be led on to recall other memories in response to their hearers' questions: 'Why did he do that?' 'What did he do then?' And even if they had wanted to, they could not have escaped explaining the privileged position which they had held at his side, if they were to satisfy the curiosity of the new believers—and not merely their curiosity, but the natural human need to fit into the newly-forming pattern of their minds, the position of these 'witnesses' from whose lips they knew they were receiving the truth. After all, the Twelve *had* been chosen by our Lord in order that they 'should be with him, and that he might send them to preach', Mk 3:14.

The very way in which St Peter expressed the need of **c** replacing Judas, likewise implies that the Twelve were, in our Lord's mind, to have an official status among the disciples. Others had 'companied with' them throughout his public life, and a still greater number had been 'witnesses of his resurrection', yet only one was to 'become with us a witness of the resurrection': the emphasis, therefore, must be put on 'with us', and the meaning be 'join us as one of the *official* witnesses of the resurrection'. The number Twelve had to be made up again; our Lord had used this number to represent the totality of Israel with its twelve tribes, Mt 19:28; Lk 22:30; *cf.* Apoc 21:12, 14; Peter and his fellows could not foresee that a thirteenth was destined to be added to them by the unquestionable choice of our Lord himself; the place intended for Judas was vacant owing to his irretrievable loss (James of Zebedee's place, on the contrary, was not made vacant by his death, Ac 12:2, since death for Christ spelt salvation: he had merely occupied his throne of judgement before the others, and there was therefore never any question of replacing him); at the moment, the intentions of Christ could only be realized by an appeal to him to show which of the two selected as fulfilling the conditions, was the object of his choice, Ac 1:24; *cf.* Lebr. ODT I [1927⁷], 347 *n.* 1. (On the Twelve *cf.* esp. P. Gaechter, S.J., 'Die Wahl des Matthias', ZKT [1949] 318–46, and, with some slight reservations, *K. H. Rengstorf in KTW *s.v.* δώδεκα; also *s.v.* ἀπόστολος; on the Twelve with Paul [and

815

657c perhaps Barnabas] as being the only Apostles strictly so-called, *cf.* WV III, Appendix II, ' The Ministry in the Apostolic Church ' : ' Apostles ', 226–9 and 242 *n.* A slightly different view : A. Médebielle, ' Apostolat ' in DBV[S] I, 579–81).

d The presentation of the Apostles by the Synoptists harmonizes perfectly with what Ac etc. imply, without being conditioned by it. They are usually called by them ' the Twelve ', or merely ' the disciples ', and not ' the Apostles ', because while with our Lord they were as yet hearers and, save for one short experimental mission, never acted *as* ' apostles ' before Pentecost, Mt 10:5 ff. ; Mk 6:7–13, 30–31 ; Lk 9:1–6, 10 ; Lk 10:1–17 mission of the seventy-two (?). Yet when Christ first ' chose out twelve—whom he would—from among his disciples ', it is explicitly stated by Lk that it was he who named them ἀπόστολοι, 6:13. The Hebrew word which this represents, *šālîaḥ*, meant ' one entrusted to fulfil a task, acting in the name of the sender ' (hence, he is ' not above him who sent him ', Jn 13:16 ; at the same time, ' he that receiveth you receiveth me ', Mt 10:40, and ' he that heareth you heareth me, and he that despiseth you, despiseth me ', Lk 10:16 ; *cf.* Mt 10:14–15). The task entrusted to them, most solemnly, Mt 28:18, was summarized as that of ' making disciples of all the nations, baptizing them . . . : teaching them to observe all that I have commanded you ', Mt 28:19–20, WV ; and again as that of ' preaching to all the nations repentance and forgiveness of sins in the name of the Christ, beginning from Jerusalem ', *cf.* Lk 24:47.

e But this, of course, was only a summary. Mt concludes a selection of parables and of their explanation to ' the disciples ' with our Lord's words : ' " Have ye understood these things ? " they say to him : " Yes ". He said unto them : " Therefore every scribe instructed in the kingdom of heaven is like to a man who is a householder, who bringeth forth out of his treasure new things and old " ', Mt 13:51–52. (*N.B.* The Apostles are the ' scribes ' of Christ's new order : *e.g.* Mt 23:34 compared with Lk 11:49.) What may be called their pastoral duties are summed up in Mt 18, where **their authority within the Church** is canonized : ' " Whatsoever you shall bind upon earth shall be bound also in heaven " ', 18:18, not merely the power of excommunication—implied directly by the immediate context —nor, at the other extreme, merely a ratification of all that *Christians in general* may do which ' conforms to the principles of charity, union and concord ' (G. Lambert, S.J., ' Lier-délier ' in *Vivre et Penser* [war-time RB], III [1943–4] 101, where the specific significance of the contrasted terms is unjustifiably set aside), but a real power, replacing that claimed by the Scribes, of making authoritative decisions binding in conscience, which is promised by our Lord to those in general who will act on behalf of ' the Church ', and immediately, here, to the Twelve whom he is instructing for their future work (Mt 18:1 ; *cf.* the parallel ch in Mk, especially 9:34. So Catholic exegetes generally ; also *J. Jeremias in KTW, *s.v.* κλείς, 751–2, who calls attention to the fact that in Tit 3:10, the final decision rests not, apparently, with the community as such, but with Titus, acting with full power on behalf of the Apostle). This power was not confined to teaching and administration, but included a priestly power to forgive sins through the Spirit, when the sinner gave sufficient evidence of repentance ; a power expressly conferred after the resurrection, Jn 20:21–23, and perhaps already hinted at in Mt 9:8 : the crowds, after the healing and *forgiveness* of the paralytic, ' glorified God that gave such power to men '. (K. Adam, ' Zum ausserkanonischen und kanonischen Sprachgebrauch von Binden und Lösen ' in TQ 96 [1914] 49–64 ; 161–97). Protestants generally deny this forgiving power, but this denial is reduced to a question of words when it takes this form : ' Through the Spirit, whom Christ bestows upon his authorised messenger, it is *Christ* who acts *immmediately* as the forgiver ' (Jeremias KTW, *ibid.* 753). By the power of Orders the priest

acts, in fact, as the minister of Christ, and not in his **e** own name, nor merely as a Church official enforcing external discipline.

But the greatest priestly power, which our Lord con- **f** ferred on those whom he had attached closest to him, was that of enacting a liturgical worship far surpassing, and intended to displace, the most solemn sacrifices of the temple. Its institution was of so all-embracing a character that some have seen in it the moment of the creation of the Church itself (*cf.* *F. Kattenbusch, ' Der Quellort der Kirchenidee ' in *Festgabe für A. von Harnack* [1921] 143–72). At least it manifests, in its pregnant details, our Lord's **intention to initiate a society** comparable in its inner and external unity to the children of Israel whom on Sinai God had chosen to be *his* ' people '. Later, there had been promised them a new covenant, to replace the old one which they had broken, whereby in a far more intimate sense ' he would be their God and they his people ', Jer 31:31–33 ; Heb 8:7–13, WV ; *cf.* Dt 26:17–18 etc. Our Lord came, and he had proclaimed the terms of the new relationship with their Father in heaven ; he had appealed to the chosen race as a whole—to Jerusalem especially—and they had refused, *cf.* Mt 23:37 ; Lk 13:34 : the old garment had become torn, the old bottles cracked, and new ones had to take their place, *cf.* Mt 9:16–17 par. He had chosen the Twelve and he now inaugurated, for them and for all those who through their word should believe in him (*cf.* Jn 17:20), a rite which, beyond its own inherent sacredness, would be a perpetual memorial of the new covenant which God was sealing with them through his mediatorship.

Next day he was to ' give his life a redemption for **g** many ', Mt 20:28 ; ' by his own blood ' he was to ' obtain eternal redemption ' and to ' cleanse our conscience from dead works, to serve the living God ', *cf.* Heb 9:12, 14. Moses, with the blood of the sacrifices in bowls beside him, had, of old, ' taken the book of the covenant and read it in the hearing of the people : and they said : " All things that the Lord hath spoken we will do. We will be obedient " '. The blood, as being the force of life, was to symbolize the vital bond between God and his people. Moses had already poured half of the blood on the altar (representing Yahweh) ; and now ' he took the blood and sprinkled it upon the people, and he said : " This is the blood of the covenant which the Lord hath made with you concerning all these words " ', Ex 24:5–8 ; *cf.* Heb 9:18–20.

So too Christ, pre-enacting his sacrifice of the morrow, **h** after distributing the bread, which he had blessed with the words : ' This is my body given for you ', passed round the cup as he uttered the history-charged words : ' This cup is the new covenant in my blood, which is being shed on your behalf ', Lk 22:20, WV ; 1 Cor 11:25, WV ; *cf.* Mt 26:28 ; Mk 14:24 and § 644*f–j*. Here was no gift merely to be partaken of by individuals, it was also **the pledge of the eternal covenant** to which generation after generation would adhere, a covenant sealed not with ' the blood of goats and of oxen ' as of old, but with his own blood, when he ' offered himself unspotted unto God ', Heb 9:13, 14. He thus showed that he was forming a new ' people of God ' (*cf.* Deut 29:12–13), a new ' nation ' which was to possess ' the kingdom of God ', of which the Jewish nation, through its representatives, had proved itself unworthy, *cf.* Mt 21:43 ; ZLG, *s.v.* διαθήκη ; L. G. da Fonseca, ' Διαθήκη—foedus an testamentum ? ' in Bi 8 (1927) 299–301, 421–3, 435–40. [The *parallelism* is what is most significant in this connexion. The word ' covenant ', suggesting as it does a certain equality between the parties to it, is clearly inadequate when God is one of those parties ; yet it is irreplaceable. Anxiety to safeguard God's sovereign initiative has led Protestants to neglect certain aspects in both ' covenants ', and to reduce the meaning merely to ' a proclamation of the sovereign will of God in history whereby he establishes the relationship between himself and mankind in accordance with his intent to save'; (*e.g.* *G. Quell and *J. Behm in KTW, *s.v.* διαθήκη). Full justice is done to this consideration by Jos Schmid in LTK, *s.v.* 'Testament in der Bibel'. For the richness of content of the new 'covenant' even already as prophesied in the OT, *cf.* P. van Imschoot, ' L'esprit de Jahvé et l'alliance nouvelle dans l'ancien testament' in ETL XIII (1936) 201–20 ; *cf.* also § 644*h*.]

If Calvary was the efficient cause of ' the new people ', individuals being transformed and drawn together by its reconciling power, the symbolic rite which so vividly manifested this fact—for the reality of Christ's presence under the separate elements is an essential part of the *symbolism*—was of itself most apt to become the supreme act of worship of his new people. That it should be so, was determined by himself, Lk 22:19 ; 1 Cor 11:25, and in view of the position and the powers which he had already given or was to give to his future Apostles, it was to them that he entrusted the celebration of this rite and the care for its perpetuation. As in so much else, he left the details to them, or rather to the Holy Spirit who was to guide them hereafter in his place, Lk 24:49 ; Jn 14:16–17, 26 ; 16:12–15 WV : and if from the bare words : ' This do ye in remembrance of me ', one might (as some have done) consider this command as addressed to all the faithful indiscriminately, the fact remains that the early Church never so considered it, but regarded it as a commission entrusted first to the Apostles, and by them in turn, to such as they appointed to share in this and other functions which they had been privileged to receive. Once the privileged position of the Apostles is recognized as having constituted a many-sided ' office ' in the life and organization of the early Christians, their own celebration of the Eucharist and their responsibility for the choice of the men who, along with other functions, should celebrate and administer it as the Church expanded, seem so inevitable that only the strongest contrary evidence—which is lacking—could lead one to doubt it (*cf.* §§ 639*f*, *g* ; 656*h*).

(ii) **Peter**—The responsibilities, which our Lord entrusted to the Twelve alone, sufficiently indicate that he meant them to exercise a sacred authority within the whole body of his disciples. We must now ask ourselves whether, within the group of the Twelve itself, he did not give to one of them responsibilities beyond those which he laid on the rest. No one can seriously call in question that the NT as a whole gives to Peter a unique position among the Apostles—whatever be the nature of that position ; one has only to re-read the Gospels and the Acts, with an eye open to whatever concerns Peter, to appreciate the cumulative force of this evidence (conveniently collected by V. Johnson in *One Lord, one Faith* [1929], chh 10–11). Taken as a whole, it forms the background of the more important incidents (which alone can be treated here), showing not only the special attention which our Lord devoted to him, but the sense of the writers (reflecting that of the early Church) that what concerned Peter in some way concerned all.

This attitude of the Evangelists, revealed in the numerous incidents and sayings which they record about Peter, finds its natural explanation in the fact that on three occasions our Lord expressly singled him out for a special commission, Mt 16:13–23 ; Lk 22:31–34 ; Jn 21:15–23. In each case he takes the initiative, in each case Peter is separated off from the rest, and in each case the distinction between the office and the man is brought into relief by a rebuke from our Lord's lips immediately after. It is clear that the Evangelists understood the incidents in this way, and the attempts to discredit their presentation of them are gradually being dropped simply in the name of biblical scholarship.

At Caesarea Philippi, Mt 16:13–20, Peter alone answers Christ's question aright, not as a spokesman cognisant of the mind of all the Apostles, but under a divine illumination not apparently accorded to the rest. To his personal confession Christ responds with a promise to him personally, couched in figurative **657k** language, its three metaphors combining to express a single unmistakable reality. Peter was to do for Christ's ' Church ' what **the rock** does for the house that is built on it : if floods and winds beat upon it, the house yet stands owing to the stability it derives from the rock, *cf.* Mt 7:24–27. Until the consummation of the world, even the elect would be imperilled by seducers, traitors, false prophets, Mt 24:5, 10, 11, 22, 24 ; the wicked one would be snatching away the word of the kingdom sown in men's hearts, Mt 13:19 ; the good seed would be oversown with cockle by the devil, or choked by the thorns of the deceitfulness of riches, Mt 13:25, 39 ; 13:7, 22—yet none of these attacks of the power of Satan would succeed in destroying the Church because of the strength which it derived from Peter. Yet how could one man prevail against such odds, how could he support the burden of the Church ? The next two metaphors give us some clue. As far as it was possible for any man, Peter was to replace Christ in the exercise of authority over all his followers ' until he come ', 1 Cor 11:26, *cf.* Lk 12:41–48. The keys entrusted to a man have always been a symbol of delegated authority. And, finally, the same is expressed by the power given him of ' binding and loosing ', which only secondarily refers to that of forgiving sins (as does that of ' the keys ' too), but primarily means the right of making authoritative decisions, binding in conscience (*cf.* ' shall be bound also in heaven ', *i.e.* in God's sight), whether they be doctrinal (*e.g.* ' this is forbidden '—' that is allowed '), or disciplinary, *viz.* applied to individual cases, *cf.* Mt 18:17 ; SB I 739. Christ's intention is clear : Peter was to have authority over all the members of his Church. His promise is likewise clear : that through that authority the Church would be preserved from ruin. How this was to be, who should explain ? As with all Christ's work, we know enough, we cannot understand all : the mystery remains. (Leading Protestant scholars now recognize the historicity of this passage and its personal reference to Peter : *cf.* K. L. Schmidt, KTW, *s.v.* καλέω, III, 523 ; and Braun, Excursus II, *Tu es Petrus*.)

During the Last Supper, Lk 22:31–34, our Lord's **l** words to Peter imply a commission of similar import under quite different figurative expressions. Satan is to attack them all ; Peter is singled out as the special object of Christ's prayer so that the rest may count on him for the strength they need : **his faith shall never fail**. This will be due to the office which he holds, for his personal conduct is not guaranteed : within a few hours he will three times deny his Master. But on *his* faith will theirs be grounded : the parallelism with ' Thou art Christ ', Mt 16:16, *par.*, at least suggests that it is not merely trust in Christ that is in question, but objective truth which the Father revealed.

Lastly, at the lakeside after the resurrection, Jn **m** 21:15–17, Christ makes Peter the **shepherd** of his flock. Some have tried to turn the significance of this event, by making it merely a reinstatement in his apostolic office : Peter had forfeited it by his triple denial, he now makes amends by a triple profession of love, and is restored to his place among the other shepherds. Such an exegesis overlooks certain essential details of the situation. Never before had any of the Apostles been treated as ' shepherds ' ; Christ reserved that office to himself : he alone was ' the good shepherd ', Jn 10:11 ff. (*cf.* Mt 26:31 and Mk 14:27) : he was defending *himself* in the parable of the lost sheep (Lk 15:1–7, *cf.* Mk 6:34). The Apostles were still only the ' little flock ', Lk 12:32—' sheep ' sent in the midst of wolves, Mt 10:16. Our Lord even seems to have deliberately avoided calling them shepherds, Mt 9:37–38 ; *cf.* 36. But on this occasion, when he was about to leave them for good (*cf.* Jn 20:17) to single out one from his little flock and to tell him to ' shepherd ' his lambs and sheep, could only convey the meaning that he was appointing one of them to take his place among them. It was thus that his intention to gather his ' other sheep that were not of this fold ' was to be

657m realized, since he, personally, had not been ' sent but to the sheep that are lost of the house of Israel ', Mt 15:24 : the place of Peter in the admission of the Gentiles, Ac 10:1–11 ; 15:7–12, shows him as fulfilling his Lord's purpose that there should be ' one *flock* and one shepherd ', Jn 10:11, 14, 16. Later, others too, no doubt, came to be called ' shepherds ' of his Church, but that was a natural evolution of the term which did not detract from what the seven at the lakeside had understood its first application to mean.

n The importance of the incident is further brought out not only by the acknowledged solemnity of our Lord's thrice repeated address : ' Simon, son of John ' —which would have been out of place if he were merely exacting reparation for his fall—but by the fact that the command to ' feed my sheep ' was repeated *three* times, and that in the presence of *witnesses*. The solemn repetition of a formula engaging oneself, or entrusting some charge to another, or indeed expressing any binding decision, was, *if spoken three times before witnesses*, the seal of validity, giving the act a legal irrevocability. Before memory and the spoken word were replaced by documents and signatures, that was the recognized way of making good a juridical disposition. It can be traced in Gen 23:3–20 ; it still characterizes marriage, divorce, etc., in parts of Palestine and in various Muslim lands (*cf.* P. Gaechter : ' Das dreifache " Weide meine Lämmer " ' in ZKT 69 [1947] 328–44). The impressiveness of the scene lay in Peter's being made conscious of his personal unworthiness of such a charge, and in Christ's bringing home to him that the trust he was placing in him called for uttermost loyalty and devotion to himself. But, at the same time, the manner in which Christ laid this charge upon him was calculated to indicate its being the deliberate establishment of a juridical office—of a real delegated power. This however in no way made Christ's own power and activity superfluous, as is sometimes thought to be the Catholic view. If Peter was chosen to be the rock on which the Church is built, it is continually from Christ, not from himself, that he has that strength ; if he holds the keys, they are Christ's keys, and it is only in his name that he can use them ; if he is to confirm his brethren, it is due to Christ's praying for him that his faith shall not fail ; and if he is to feed the flock, it is Christ's sheep that he is to feed and on his behalf. In a word, Peter's position does not mean that he (or anyone else) can dispense with Christ ; but it does mean that he is the Vicar of Christ, able to act visibly for him, so long as Christ is only invisibly among his own.

o Some description has already been given of **Peter's later activities** and of the spirit in which he carried them out (§§ 631*b*, *c*, 636*f*). Furthermore, a wonderful coherence is given to the first half of Ac, and to the varying relations between the local churches of Jerusalem and Antioch, if that unique position of Peter in those times is once recognized. The people of Palestine and Syria were men with a keen sense of legitimate authority and rights, and a close scrutiny of what happened in those years reveals where that authority was felt to be ; *cf.* P. Gaechter, ' Jerusalem und Antiochia ' in ZKT 70 (1948) 1–48. Much might be said too of the often neglected testimony to Peter's position by his fellow Apostle Paul in 1 Cor and Gal : even the circumstances and the form of the rebuke which he publicly administered to Peter at Antioch enhance, if anything, our estimate of the prestige in which Peter was generally held ; *cf.* X. Roiron, ' Saint Paul témoin de la primauté de saint Pierre ' in RSR 4, 1913, 489–531 ; A. Médebielle in DBV(S) II 620–2.

p To suggest that the leadership of the Church passed from Peter to Paul, is to miss the force of all this evidence. No doubt Paul fills the centre of the picture in the latter part of Ac, whereas Peter had done so before ; but St Luke became Paul's companion for several years, and wrote of what he could vouch for. He could not have known all that Peter was doing at the time ; what he

does give suggests anything but a loss of authority on the part of Peter. Of course Peter did not ' behave as a tyrant among slaves, but as a leader among brethren ' ; and if the Catholic doctrine is true that *all* the Apostles were infallible, there was little call for Peter to assert himself in a way that *to us* would be unmistakable. At least, at the Council of Jerusalem, when Paul's course of action was being investigated, it was Peter who gave the decisive word, after which ' all the multitude held their peace ', Ac 15:12. That James thereafter pronounced in favour of the principle thus decided on, and found a formula (later abandoned) to give practical effect to it, is altogether insufficient evidence for regarding him as superior to either of the great Apostles. And later, Paul did nothing to correct his own disciples at Corinth for the obvious esteem in which Peter was held among them : ' Cephas ' was not to be monopolized by one party—he belonged to all : he was ' theirs ' as much as Paul himself and Apollo were theirs, 1 Cor 1:12 ; 3:22.

But perhaps the most striking indication of Peter's **q** position in the early Church, is the importance which was attached to his having been made by Christ the rock on which he was building his Church. Nothing shows this more clearly than the fact that they felt it necessary, quite early on, to *translate into Greek* the name which Christ had given to Simon. It is clear, from St Paul's normal usage, that among those who understood Hebrew or Aramaic, the Grecized form Κηφᾶς was fully adequate ; and it had become so current as a mere name that its *significance* (' rock ') could fall into the background. We use the names Mr Smith or Mr Miller without advertence to their significance. In normal every-day use, the *meaning* of a person's name does not matter, and thus it was that the name Κηφᾶς came to be used among all Christians, even by those who knew only Greek. Hence, except for some quite exceptional circumstance, there was no need to create **a new (Greek) name** for him : Κηφᾶς distinguished him adequately from everyone else. There can be only one explanation for the introduction of the name Πέτρος : the need to convey the significance of the incident at Caesarea Philippi, when Christ told him that he was to be the rock on which he would built his Church. Κηφᾶς would do for any other passage ; it would do here for those who understood Hebrew or Aramaic, but it would not do for anyone else : Πέτρος was substituted in order to make intelligible the promise that he was to be the Church's πέτρα. Hence, the fact that a new Greek name was created for him shows both the historicity of that event and the importance attached to it from the first ; and every time the name ' Peter ' occurs, it is a testimony to it ; *cf.* H. Rheinfelder, ' Philologische Erwägungen zu Matth 16:18 ' in BZ 24 (1938) 139–63 ; A. C. Cotter, ' Tu es Petrus ', CBQ IV (1942) 304–10.

Successors of Peter and of the Apostles—It is quite true **r** that we are unable to quote any words of Christ which explicitly direct Peter to see to it that Popes should succeed him, or which lay down that monarchical bishops should replace the others. This is however no cause of embarrassment. In fact, the record of any such words would be extremely difficult to harmonize with the rest of the NT. If anything is clear about our Lord's teaching on his Second Coming, it is that, for whatever reason, he wanted to leave his followers in *complete* uncertainty as to its date. Nothing which he said need have conveyed to his hearers, then, the idea that many centuries were to pass before that event. It might be near, it might be distant : the essential thing for them was to be always ready. He created that state of alertness which he meant to be permanent in his Church. But it is obvious that any kind of direction or pre-occupation shown by him with regard to the men who should succeed them, would have lifted the veil at least to this extent that they could have said to themselves : ' Anyhow, *we* shan't be alive when he comes '. But there is never a trace of any such assurance—quite the contrary. Even such expressions as

'Behold I am with you all days, even to the consummation of the world', would tell them nothing : they would not have been any the less perfectly fulfilled had the end come after no more than ten or twenty years ; cf. §§ 670-1.

Even those Protestants who today are more ready than Luther to admit that the 'Tu es Petrus' granted special privileges to Peter, and who recognize that he and the other Apostles were chosen by Christ to form 'at least that much stable organization which no human society can in fact dispense with', (e.g. *G. Gloege, *Reich Gottes und Kirche im Neuen Testament* [1929] 375), nevertheless will not hear of their having transmitted their powers to others by what is known as Apostolic Succession. In their view, such powers as the Apostles had were strictly personal, bestowed on them because necessary for the inauguration of the Church ; but after their death, those who served the Church were not to have 'authority' strictly so called, nor any clearly defined functions, but their activities would be such as their own devotion might suggest—more or less subject to their being so commissioned by the body of the faithful. Christ will have foreseen the possibility of a multiplication and grading of offices thus arising, and their appearance cannot be taken as being a betrayal of his intentions, nor as constituting a break-away from his dispositions ; cf. Gloege, op. cit., 362 ff. This at least allows for 'non-biblical' offices (cf. inf. d), but as regards its main contention, closer consideration shows its inherent weakness, quite apart from the contrary evidence. To Catholics, at least, it seems obvious that, if the Church is to preserve its identity and unity during its rapid expansion and throughout the adaptations which varying conditions called for, it must have had within itself something guaranteeing the course of its structural development. 'Such an inherent prerequisite, already operative in the time of the Apostles, can only have been the authority and power with which the Apostles were the first to be invested'. Furthermore, 'if what the Apostles had received from Christ was not transmitted to others ; if on the contrary offices of a new type took their place, how can one possibly still speak of the *one Church* having maintained its identity through the changes of time ? There is no getting away from the contradiction involved', F. M. Braun, *Neues Licht auf der Kirche* (1946) 162, n. 4.

But even *K. L. Schmidt, who decisively rejects the idea of an early evolution from a charismatic to a juridical conception of Church and ministry—such as R. Sohm and A. Harnack have so influentially sponsored—(*Revue d'histoire et de philosophie religieuses*, 17 [1937] 335 f. ; Braun 98-9) refuses to admit Apostolic Succession, because it would lead to the usurpation, by men, of the authority which belongs to God alone, 316 f. But this is entirely beside the point. The possibility of an abuse of power does not touch the question whether God, as the founder of a visible, lasting Church, did not entrust certain men with powers which were by that very fact in some sense divine. Still less does it touch the question whether they were to transmit those powers or not. If they were to act in his name at all, they must appeal to a *jus divinum* for doing so. That was what the Twelve did ; Paul did the same : and no one calls it usurpation. And if Jesus intended such power to continue, as being necessary for the later life of the Church, that was what their successors did too ; cf. F. M. Braun, op. cit. 166, n. 1.

But is Apostolical Succession 'unbiblical', as Schmidt and others contend ? In a sense, yes, and the reason is not far to seek. The idea was not primitive, and we have seen why not (sup. a). But, further, nearly the whole of the NT was written by Apostles, and both letters and narratives deal with the Church in what was still its missionary stage. That means that the direction of the local churches did not depend on the officers (of whatever kind) who might be there, but depended essentially on missionaries *from outside*, i.e. ultimately, on the Apostles themselves. What local

organization there was could only be of a provisional **658d** character, and until this was replaced by some stable organization of at least relative independence, there could be no real question of *successors* to the Apostles. Διάκονος, πρεσβύτερος, ἐπίσκοπος were all terms which of themselves might have a very general or a very particular meaning ; and they were all used of men obviously subordinate to the Apostles at the time. It is therefore highly unhistorical to deny the existence of a stable office on the basis of the silence of the biblical documents (which concern a period when such an office was most unlikely to have existed), and then to refuse to consider the subsequent evidence for it because it is 'unbiblical' (cf. Braun, op. cit. 163, especially, n. 2, with its quotation from *O. Linton). John, in his old age, might have been more explicit : that he was not, was due, no doubt, to his seeing no importance in writing down what everybody knew and could see with their own eyes. (Yet Diotrephes seems to have been one whose right over his own Church was recognized by John—however tyrannously he was exercising it, 3 Jn 9-10.) The evidence of Clement of Rome and of Ignatius taken together and that of the rest of the second century clearly record that the Apostles transmitted the powers which they had received from Christ to those men who, one in each city, came alone to bear the name ἐπίσκοπος, and who were assisted in the execution of the various functions of their office by πρεσβύτεροι and διάκονοι subordinate to them. But this takes us outside the NT evidence.

The Local Ministry—The provisional character, how- **659a** ever, of most of the ministry mentioned—casually, for the most part—in the apostolic writings, does not imply that they were unimportant for the particular stage of the Church's development in which we find them. Indeed there is no sufficient reason to doubt that some of the functions entrusted to them were considered permanent, even though their exercise remained in subordination to apostolic control, §639f, g. We have already seen something of the activities of the **Deacons**, § 631d, but we know very little of their specific functions (the seven, Ac 6:1-6 ?—if so, then the preaching of Stephen, 6:8-7:60, and the missionary activities of Philip, 8:5-13, 26-40, seem far to exceed the 'serving of tables' to which they had been so solemnly appointed). The only explicit references to an *office* of διάκονοι are Phil 1:1 (coupled with ἐπίσκοποι) and 1 Tim 3:8-13 (chiefly concerned with the minimum qualifications for the post—which, however, implies incidentally that it was by Timothy or some other with like authority that they were appointed). We notice too that the accomplished deacon will be a man of acquired stability and of fearless eloquence, 13, which reminds us of Stephen again).

We know a little more about the πρεσβύτεροι (**Presby- b ters**). That they held a fully recognized position in the various communities, when Luke was writing, is clear from his not having felt it necessary to explain who they were when he first mentioned them, Ac 11:30. Paul appointed presbyters in the churches which he founded, Ac 14:22 (Luke took this as understood after the first mention, cf. 20:17). At least in Jerusalem, they had a big share in the affairs of the Church, though subordinately to the Apostles (cf. the Council, Ac 15:2, 4, 6, 22-23 ; 16:4 ; also 21:18). Spiritual functions are ascribed to them by St James, 5:14. However, there can be no doubt that it is to the presbyters that other titles likewise refer, and these tell us a little more of their functions. The Thessalonians (1 Thess 5:12-13) are told to appreciate those 'who labour among you' (τοὺς κοπιῶντας ἐν ὑμῖν, cf. 3:5 ; Col 1:29) 'and are over you in the Lord' (καὶ προϊσταμένους ὑμῶν, cf. Rom 12:8) ; both these characteristics are ascribed to the *presbyters* in 1 Tim 5:17) 'and admonish you' (καὶ νουθετοῦντας ὑμᾶς, as Paul himself was wont to do, e.g. Ac 20:31, 1 Cor 4:14). They should be the object of a particular love because of their responsible function. They, in their turn, must 'admonish

659b the disorderly, encourage the faint-hearted, support the weak, show patience towards all ', 1 Thess 5:14, WV.

c The idea of ' being over ' the others recurs in various forms : οἱ ἡγούμενοι, Heb 13:7, 17 ('obey your superiors and be subject to them ', WV), 24 ; it is implied of ' the house of Stephanas ' at Corinth, 1 Cor 16:15–18 ; it became canonized in the word ἐπίσκοπος ' overseer ', from which is derived our own word *bishop* as well as the French *évêque*. It is now almost universally admitted that ἐπίσκοπος and πρεσβύτερος at that time were designations of the same persons ; the evidence is Ac 20:17, 28 ; Tit 1:5, 7, and Tit 1:6–9 compared with 1 Tim 3:2–7. As bishops appointed over the flock by the Holy Spirit, they are to ' shepherd the Church of God ' ; they are to be prepared for the attacks of wolves from without (*cf.* Mt 10:16 ; Jn 10:12), and guard against perverse teaching from within, Ac 20:28–30 (*cf.* Mt 7:15 : our Lord's warning against false prophets as being wolves in sheep's clothing). This care for the Church of God over which they are to rule—as does a father over his home—is again enjoined on them by St Paul in 1 Tim 3:4–5 ; as is also sound teaching and the defence of their flock against perverse doctrines, Tit 1:9–16 (*cf.* ' some as shepherds-and-teachers ', Eph 4:11, WV. For a more detailed treatment, *cf.* C. Spicq, *Les épîtres pastorales* [1947], *Introd.* ch 4 and 84–91 ; also §§ 918–25).

d The word ' presbyter ' and not ' priest ' has been used here to represent πρεσβύτερος, because the fact that they were ' priests ' is not implied by the Greek word and can only be deduced indirectly, chiefly from evidence later than the NT. We can exclude the idea that any and every Christian could celebrate the Eucharist, and on the other hand it is clear that others besides the Apostles did so. Thus, besides the obvious importance of ' the Lord's Supper ' and the *a priori* probability that it was celebrated in all the churches, we know that it was celebrated at Corinth at a time when Paul was not there, nor apparently any of his close companions, 1 Cor 11:20 ff. It is but a step to say that those who presided at the rite were of the number of those to whom had been entrusted the care of the local church itself. Hence the justification of the translation ' priests ' in DV and WV.

e But were they not perhaps bishops, too, in our modern sense, at least as far as Orders were concerned ? If opinions are still divided on the point, generally it is denied, and for several reasons. If 1 Tim 4:14 suggests that Timothy had been given the ' charisma ' of his office ' by prophecy with imposition of hands of the *presbyters* ', this is not decisive, because, as we saw above, § 639*f*, in 2 Tim 1:6 Paul speaks of the same grace as being in him ' by the imposition of *my* hands '. Moreover, the commission to Titus to appoint ' presbyters ' in Crete, Tit 1:5, suggests that these had not themselves the power to create other ' presbyters '. Confirmation of this view may perhaps be found in the fact that St Paul's praise of such as ' desire the office of a bishop ', 1 Tim 3:1, is more easily understood if it is the lower order of the priesthood that is in question : certainly the tradition of the Church has always looked askance at those who seek after prelacy ; *cf.* U. Holzmeister, Bi 12 (1931) 41–69. The same would apply to ' the house of Stephanas and of Fortunatus and of Achaicus ', who were the ' first-fruits ' of the Church of Corinth, and who seem to have volunteered their services, 1 Cor 16:15. And we may well have a reference to them in that other letter to the Corinthians written by the Church of Rome forty years later, in which the Apostles are described as instituting in the districts and cities which they had evangelized, ' bishops and deacons ' selected from ' the *first-fruits* ' of their labours. For it is clear that these ' bishops ' had not the power to transmit their office to others, since it came only as an afterthought to the Apostles that these, in time, might have to be replaced—and they made provision accordingly, entrusting this power to certain ' outstanding men ', 1 Clem 42:4 ; 44:2–3. This may well refer to such men as St Paul's close companions whom

he frequently sent to act in his name in the churches which he had founded, *e.g.* Timothy, Titus, Epaphroditus, Phil 2:25 ; Epaphras, Col 1:7. Of these we have seen that the first two had the power to create presbyters, though neither as yet was attached to any single church, as were the monarchical bishops later.

All this is in keeping with the missionary conditions which prevailed in NT times. Without later evidence, we could not tell in what form the special powers accorded to the Apostles and especially to Peter were to be preserved. Jerusalem may have been taken as the model : it is there that with James, the presbyters and the Seven, we see the first outlines of that structure : ' Bishop—Priests—Deacons ' which became the universal rule for local churches from the second century on. (*Cf.* the WV appendix already referred to.)

VII SOME ASPECTS OF EARLY CHRISTIAN LIFE

Reference has already been made (§ 655*b*) to the theory that Christ taught that the end of the world was near and that the counsels which he gave to his disciples should not be treated as principles intended for a Church which was to endure for centuries, but as ' Interim-Ethics ', *i.e.* directions of conduct to be observed during the ' interim ', the few years at most, which separated them from the great cataclysm and his Second Coming. This ' consistent ' Eschatology, as the theory is called, supposes that the early Christians lived on the tip-toe of expectation, so that their outlook was coloured by a sense of the futility of all earthly happenings, and normal life was for them a thing of the past. No doubt, their new faith profoundly altered both their outlook and their conduct, but the evidence which we have of their social outlook, of their attitude to the family, to property, to slavery, to the State, goes to show that their understanding of our Lord's teaching was not connected with any fevered expectation of the world's dissolution. The questions which they ask St Paul generally spring from the ordinary problems of life ; his answers blend the highest spiritual conceptions with a fund of sound commonsense : he does not invoke ' eschatology ' at every turn.

Actually the evidence for the social life of the first Christians is sparse and scattered. But this fact is of itself significant. The NT writers say little of the externals of their social life for the simple reason that there was little to say : Jews continued to observe their customs, and Gentiles too, save where these involved manifest sin or offended against Christ's ' new ' precept to love one another. Whatever certain modern writers have maintained, Christ was no advocate of social revolution in the accepted sense. The fire which he came to cast on the earth was a new spirit which might bring about great changes in time, but which could from the first burn brightly in Caesar's household and among the slaves of testy masters as well as among the saints in Jerusalem. Hence for any complete survey of their practice in ordinary life, our records would need to be supplemented by what we know of the Jewish and Gentile social customs of the period (*cf.* §§ 584–603): here we shall only make some gleanings from what happens to be recorded in the NT. What is valuable to us is the new spirit that is there revealed, a spirit which transformed men's lives without any previous change in the conditions in which they were placed.

(i) **The Family**—Apart from the possibility of divorce and re-marriage, there was nothing to change in the essential structure of the Jewish home. Taught by nature itself and by their Scriptures, the Jews already had a religious conception of the relations existing between the various members of the household. The position of **the father** as the loving master of the family is sufficiently indicated by our Lord's using it to illustrate God's dominion and providence over all men :

'If you, evil as you are, know well enough how to give your children what is good for them, is not your Father in heaven much more ready to give wholesome gifts to those who ask him?' Mt 7:11, KNT; 'thus, therefore you shall pray : " Our Father . . ."', Mt 6:9. And the dignity and responsibility of human fatherhood was all the more emphasized when after years of familiarity with our Lord's poignant teaching on the nature of God's Fatherhood, the faithful were told by St Paul that it was after him that all other fatherhood was so named, Eph 3:15. Affection and charity in the father required no abdication of authority : his was the responsibility of the good ordering of the home, 1 Tim 3:4 ; indeed failure in this was a disqualification from any office in the Church : 'for if a man know not how to rule his own house, how shall he take care of the church of God?' 1 Tim 3:5 ; cf. 3:12.

The wife, then, is subject to her husband, Eph 5:22 ; 1 Tim 2:12 ; 1 Pet 3:1, yet shares with him the ordering of the home, 1 Tim 5:14 ; Tit 2:5. He may be a pagan, but in any case she can lead him to esteem the Christian life by her loving reverence for him and the quiet modesty with which she fulfils her duties. These inner virtues rather than artificial adornment will win her husband over to Christ, 1 Tim 2:9-10 ; 1 Pet 3:1, thus will even the pagan husband be sanctified by the Christian wife, 1 Cor 7:14. So far are the early Christians from regarding conjugal relations as sinful (cf. 1 Tim 4:3-5) or as forbidden in view of the 'shortness of the time', 1 Cor 7:29, that child-bearing is regarded as one of the means whereby a mother works out her salvation, 1 Tim 2:15—to mention but one instance of the NT teaching on marriage ; cf. § 654d-g.

Together the parents have the responsibility of bringing up **their children** and providing for their future, 2 Cor 12:14. If love for them is characteristic of the mother, Tit 2:4, the father's authority must be tempered by a loving prudence : 'Fathers, do not irritate your children, that they may not lose heart', Col 3:21, WV ; 'You who are fathers, do not rouse your children to resentment ; the training, the discipline in which you bring them up must come from the Lord', Eph 6:4, KNT. On this model, St Paul would have his disciples see in himself a father, who loves them even when he corrects, 1 Cor 4:14-15, 21. This training and correction of the young, with all that it involves of repression and pain, is taken as a matter of course : it serves in fact as an illustration of the trials of life being but part of God's education of us in sanctity, Heb 12:4-13. On their part children must learn that to honour and obey their parents is the road to happiness, Eph 6:1-3, besides being the way to please our Lord, Col 3:20. Jewish parents in particular will have felt it their duty to warn them of our Lord's displeasure at casuistic evasions of the fourth Commandment, Mt 15:3-6.

The continuity of tradition in a Jewish family turned Christian, may be illustrated by the place which the OT retained in the upbringing of children. Though Timothy's father was a pagan, Ac 16:1, he had, as a child, learnt from his Jewish mother Eunice to esteem the Sacred Scriptures, and she no doubt had so been taught by her own mother Lois, 2 Tim 1:5 ; 3:15-17. The value which St Paul attached to that early training, and the indispensable light which the OT throws on our Lord's life and work (as he himself had so often shown ; cf. esp. Lk 24:25-27) suggest that the 'argue, obsecra, increpa', 2 Tim 4:2, which St Paul addressed to his beloved disciple included exhortations to parents to use the OT in fostering their children's 'faith in Christ Jesus'. The place of the OT in the life of the post-apostolic Church makes it probable that such training was also adopted in Gentile-Christian homes from the first.

That the acceptance of the Gospel might lead to **the break-up of homes** was fully understood from Christ's own warnings ; cf. Mt 10:34-37 ; Lk 12:52-53 ; 14:26. Even a beloved wife or husband might have to be given up, and we have indirect evidence of this occurring from St Paul's permission to the new **660f** Christian to remarry when his or her former partner refused to acquiesce in the change, 1 Cor 7:12-16 ; cf. § 654i on the 'Pauline privilege'. We have to wait for later times for evidence of Christians being delivered to death by their own family. But as far as possible the old relationships were to be preserved. 'According to what the Lord has assigned to each, in whatever state God's call found him, therein let each one pursue his course', 1 Cor 7:17, Allo. Nevertheless, this introduced, paradoxically enough, one great change in the Christian social outlook owing to the new attitude towards continence.

Its origin was undoubtedly the attractiveness of **g** Christ's own purity and that of his Mother, and also his recommendations of an ideal offered to volunteers who would and could take it, Mt 19:12. But St Paul's exaltation of **virginity** for both sexes, 1 Cor 7 ; cf. 6:12-20 (without prejudice to marriage also being a God-given charisma, 1 Cor 7:7), and his own practice (ibid.) not only imply a general repudiation of sins of the flesh in a world which even divinized them, but, together with many other indications, show that from the first there existed those who, as if by instinct, were so taken up with the things of the Lord, how they might please him, cf. 1 Cor 7:32, that marriage or remarriage had by comparison lost its appeal. (That their number was considerable is clearly implied in Apoc 14:1-5.) One can easily understand how in pagan cities especially (cf. § 602a, b), this new idea of itself sufficed to mark off the Christians as odd people even in the circle of their personal friends ; it also created a new problem among the Christians themselves. The men would naturally offer to help the Church leaders, and some would in time enter their ranks themselves as deacons or presbyters ; but many of the young women or even the elderly ladies may at first have been at a loss what to do. Few would be able to accompany the missionaries and see to their wants in their travels ; cf. 1 Cor 9:5, also Rom 16:1-2(?). At home they might divide their time between the functions of a Martha and a Mary, Lk 10:38-42, but many would be restless and wish to assert themselves at the conferences and meetings of the Ecclesia, even more perhaps than did their married sisters ; cf. 1 Cor 11:3-15 ; 14:34-35 ; 1 Tim 2:12.

We know a little more about the Christian **widows h** than about the virgins of the time. Their needs early led to the appointment of the Seven, Ac 6:1-6, in Jerusalem ; and at Joppe they were the special object of Tabitha's industrious charity, 9:39. St Paul's recommendation to them not to remarry was not intended to be binding, 1 Cor 7:8-9, 39-40 ; in fact later he preferred young lonely widows to do so, especially if they had no one at all to support them, and that because they tended to become gossiping busy-bodies, relying on the support of the faithful instead of doing some helpful work, and sometimes giving no small disedification to non-Christians. But those who had genuinely set their hope in God and dedicated themselves to prayer, were to be the objects of respect and solicitude, so that the Church must relieve such as were in need. From among the older of them (over sixty, St Paul says) would be enrolled those who were officially designated 'the Widows', ladies who, by the way they had brought up their children, and their open hospitality and personal devotion to those in distress had won the respect of all, 1 Tim 5:3-16 ; cf. Spicq in loc. To them especially was entrusted the care of the other widows and of the poorer homes in general, and also the instruction of the young married women in their domestic duties ; cf. Tit 2:3-5.

(ii) Slavery—Slaves, for all who could afford them, **i** were an integral part of home life (cf. § 601i), and nowhere does the slow, leavening power of Christianity manifest itself better than in the history of slavery. St Paul could say 'there is neither bond nor free . . .

660i for you are all one in Christ ', Gal 3:28, without proclaiming Emancipation. But he laid down such principles as would at once mitigate the lot of the slaves of Christian masters, gradually lead the State to recognize a slave's inherent rights, and finally abolish the institution wherever Christian civilization has had its way and has not yet been repudiated.

At first then, the general rule stood : ' Let every man abide in the same calling in which he was called. Wast thou called, being a bondman ? care not for it ', 1 Cor 7:20-21 ; and, according to the more common interpretation (Allo *in loc.*), he even recommended the slave not to avail himself of a chance of manumission. But deep were the changes which Christ's adoption of the form of a slave made in the outlook of masters and slaves alike. Where both were Christian, the reciprocal duties could be performed as between conscious members of Christ. The slaves were to obey fully, as thereby fulfilling God's will for them ; not, therefore, only in their master's presence as if there were only him to please, nor in a slovenly way or to the master's loss, but with a will, and with a single eye serving the one Master, Christ, from whom they would not fail of their reward, Eph 6:5-8 ; Col 3:22-25. The same spirit must guide their masters : the slaves had rights, whatever the world might think ; accordingly they must be treated with justice—nay more, with equity ; to tyrannize with fierce threats was to forget that master and slave alike had the same Master above, who was no respecter of persons, Eph 6:9 ; Col 3:25 ; 4:1. Unheard of as it was in the pagan world, this new bond between them was but the minimum for Christians ; the generosity possible in a Christian towards a stealing, runaway slave is outlined in the delicate and warm-hearted appeal which St Paul addressed to Philemon.

j But masters were not always Christian, nor were even these always kind. Harsh and unjust punishment was to be accepted without outburst of curse or threat ; let the slaves glory to be following in Christ's footsteps who, guiltless as he was, meekly submitted to cruel injustice in atonement for the sins of all and as an example to themselves, 1 Pet 2:18-25. In so doing, and indeed in all their conduct as loyal, trusty servants, they would actually be *apostles of Christ* by manifesting the attractiveness of the Saviour's teaching, Tit 2:9-10. Service of God, imitation of Christ, the conversion of their masters—the implanting of such ideals in the hearts of slaves, was a greater triumph for Christianity than any immediate campaign for the abolition of slavery could have been. Indeed the sudden destruction of an institution of so many centuries' standing would have scarcely been less unjust and immoral than its maintenance without any qualification, *cf.* Prat, I, 275-9.

k (iii) **Property and Poverty**—Here, if anywhere, the influence on the early Christians of Christ's own teaching and example is manifest. What they knew of him must, then, first be summarized if we are to appreciate their outlook on worldly possessions, on the rich and on the poor. Our Lord's teaching on the subject focussed his two main preoccupations—men's attitude to his Father, and their attitude to their neighbour : the two great commandments of the law. Rich and poor alike needed that **detachment from worldly goods** which is the obverse of the filial trust in God's providence which he hymned with such loving art, Mt 6:24-34 ; Lk 12:22-33. Thus would they earn the blessing of the ' poor in spirit ', Mt 5:3. He never condemned wealth as such, and could count some who were rich among his friends—Joseph of Arimathea, Nicodemus, the family at Bethany, Zachæus. For all that, he kept warning his disciples of the dangers inherent in riches, and his condemnation of the vices of the rich was second only to his denunciation of hypocrisy. ' The care of this world and the deceitfulness of riches and the pleasures of this life ' were the thorns which choked the word and made it fruitless, Mt 13:22 ; Mk 4:19 ; Lk 8:14 ; the woe against the rich, Lk 6:24, and the parable of Dives and Lazarus, Lk 16:19-31, were both directed against those who looked for their ' consolation ' in riches alone—God did not enter the picture : they had given all their love to Mammon and become slaves ; *cf.* Mt 6:24 ; Lk 16:13. The irony of the parable of the rich fool adds the reminder that no man can count on the morrow to enjoy his riches, be they never so great, Lk 12:13-21. And so ' how hard is it for them that trust in riches to enter into the kingdom of God ! ' And lest any ever forget it, ' it is easier for a camel to pass through the eye of a needle . . . ', Mk 10:23-25. So did he emphasize the dangers of wealth, if divorced from a dominating docility to God's grace, 10:26-27 ; *cf.* BEJC, 165-71—' disponibilité '.

Such docility was contained in his exhortations to his disciples ' not to be solicitous ' ; it would secure their being ready for any sacrifice which conscience might demand, Mk 8:36 ; Mt 18:8-9. But there was a further step possible, suggested to the generous, whereby, apart from any such demand, they permanently renounced the security of any regular income which might be theirs, in order to devote themselves undividedly to the cause of God. In favour of this **voluntary poverty** there was his own example, Mt 8:20 ; Lk 9:58, and he expected it of those who, during his public ministry, attached themselves most closely to himself. So with the fishermen, Mt 4:20, 22, so with Matthew, Lk 5:28. This is especially clear from his invitation to the rich young man that, ' if he would be perfect,' he should ' sell what he had and give to the poor and come follow me ', Mt 19:16-23 ; Mk 10:17-25 ; Lk 18:18-25. It meant living on casual alms, as he and the Apostles did, *cf.* Mt 10:8-10 ; Mk 6:8-9 ; Lk 9:3 ; 10:4, 7-8 ; Jn 12:6, and, since they must be prepared for rebuffs, it called for a more acute sense of their dependence on God for all they needed, Mt 6:11. They could thus sympathize, as he did (*cf.* 2 Cor 8:9) with those who were poor by force of circumstances, but who might yet be taught to find a special blessing in their condition by the heightened trust in God which it called for (so the first beatitude according to Lk 6:20). They would learn by experience what it meant to ' seek first the kingdom of God and his justice ', Mt 6:33 ; they would also learn to love their neighbours as themselves, Lk 10:27.

This second commandment was likewise ' fulfilled ', Mt 5:17, by our Lord, and he had every right to call it his very own ' new commandment ', Jn 13:34 ; 15:12. For he extended the scope of the word ' neighbour ' to include even one's enemies, Lk 10:29-37, and that of the word ' love ' by emphasizing the range to which disinterestedness could go. It is within this setting that falls the **use of worldly goods in succouring the poor**. The ideal was to give without hope of any return, Lk 6:30-35 ; 14:12-14, and whereas the Jews already showed sensitiveness for the feelings of the poor and recommended that charity should be dispensed secretly lest they be put to shame, our Lord went further by recommending not only the sacrifice of the admiration which almsgiving would evoke, but even that of the self-satisfaction which the act of kindness might engender, lest it detract from the single-minded love which had prompted it : ' When thou dost alms, let not thy left hand know what thy right hand doth ', Mt 6:3. Generosity in giving he inculcated in every way : never more persuasively than when he promised to take any kindness done to others as done to himself, Mt 25:35-41 ; *cf.* 10:40-42. If that was the spirit in which they were to give away what was their own, it was clear enough that there must be no thought of remuneration when they were dispensing what was not their own but God's : ' Preach . . . " The Kingdom of heaven is at hand ". Heal the sick, raise the dead, cleanse the lepers, cast out devils : give as you have received the gift, without payment ', Mt 10:7-8 KNT. They were not forbidden to receive alms or hospitality : these were only to be expected, for ' the labourer has a right to his maintenance ', 10:10c ; *cf.*

Lk 10:6–7. And, in fact, having set out with no provision for themselves save trust in providence, they wanted for nothing, and so learnt their lesson ; *cf.* Lk 22:35–36*a*.

Poverty and the Apostles—This outline of the Gospel teaching tells us already much of the Christian attitude to property in apostolic times. As the Apostles had learnt from our Lord, so they taught ; and the chance references that we have in their writings suffice to show that it was an ideal which—with exceptions—the Christians tried to fulfil. The need of detachment and the dangers of riches are especially emphasized by St James, who underlines the transitoriness of wealth, Jas 1:10, the folly of counting on the morrow, 4:13–15, and the self-importance which it breeds, 2:1–7 ; 4:16. His seemingly unqualified condemnation of riches as such, paralleling that of our Lord, is in fact directed against those who were defrauding labourers of their pay, and against the self-indulgence which riches facilitate, 5:4–6. So too St Paul, while warning against the love of riches as being the root of all evils, 1 Tim 6:9–10, takes for granted in the same epistle, that some of the faithful are wealthy men, and gives them sound advice accordingly, 6:17–19 ; *cf.* P. H. Furfey, ' *Plousios* ' and *Cognates in the NT*, CBQ 5 (1943) 243–63.

In their preaching and the use of their powers of sanctifying and of healing, the Twelve continued to ' give as they had received the gift, without payment ' (*cf.* Ac 8:18–24) and they depended on alms for their support, as the Lord had ordained, 1 Cor 9:4, 14 ; 1 Tim 5:18. The prominence given to Barnabas's action, Ac 4:36–37, suggests that he had heard the story of the rich young man—and not in vain, but had ' sold what he had and given to the poor ', the better to follow Christ. Later, we find him in St Paul's company, both of them working with their hands and even waiving their right to be supported by the faithful, that their preaching might be both freer and more persuasive (1 Cor 9:6, ' Or is it I alone and Barnabas who have not the right *to forbear from work* ? ' WV). The great-hearted Apostle himself lets us know what distress his missionary labours involved (*cf.* 2 Cor 4:8–18 ; 11:23–28) and how complete was his poverty, 6:10. Yet, in addition, he supported himself by his tent-making ; for ' what I claim is yourselves, not anything you can give ', and ' for my own part, I will gladly spend and be spent on your souls' behalf, though you should love me too little for loving you too well ', 2 Cor 12:14, 15, KNT.

An incidental effect of this untiring labour alongside his preaching was his being in a position to correct certain abuses as they occurred. Thus he could rebuke effectively those at Thessalonica who, on the pretext that the final consummation was at hand, refused to do any more work and relied on the support of the community, 1 Thess 4:11 ; 2 Thess 3:6–12—' if any man will not work, neither let him eat '. Again, to the presbyters at Miletus, he referred to his manual labour as having provided both for himself and for his companions, Ac 20:34, and he encouraged them : ' so labouring, you ought to support the weak ' by recalling our Lord's words, ' It is a more blessed thing to give rather than to receive ', 35. This possibility of helping others was the motive which he proposed even to the naturally light-fingered, when urging them to honest work, Eph 4:28. In this way he fought the pauperism and idleness which the general charity of the faithful might easily have induced in certain quarters.

This **charity**, after all, was what was most striking in the life of the early Church, and most clearly reflected the ' new Commandment '. It is significant that the first practical thing which the converts of Pentecost did was to have ' all things in common. Their possessions and goods they sold and divided them to all, according as everyone had need ', Ac 2:44–45 ; *cf.* 4:32, 34–35. By thus freely selling what they had, and putting it all into the Apostles' hands—or whatever part they chose—for distribution, Ac 4:36–37 ; 5:4, they were giving reality to the central doctrines of

Christ and manifesting that they were indeed his **660q** followers. From the first there was a ' daily ministration ', 6:1, and the number of the disciples increasing, special officials were appointed, as we have seen, §§ 631*d*, 659*a*, 660*h*, to deal with it. The spiritual conception, which the Apostles had of this seemingly merely administrative work, is shown by the fact that they wanted for it only men ' full of the Holy Ghost and wisdom ', 6:3.

It is usual to stress the fact that this voluntary kind of ' communism ' (Ac 4:32, ' Neither did anyone say that aught of the things which he possessed was his own : but all things were common unto them ') did not outlive the enthusiasm of the first days, and to suggest that the recurrent poverty of ' the saints ' in Jerusalem was due to the initial recklessness. What seems far more important is that the spirit and the practical charity of this first experiment not only persisted in Jerusalem, but became characteristic of all the churches from then on. If Luke recorded the appointment of the Seven for the daily ministration of the poor, Ac 6:1–6, and the responsibility of the *presbyters* for the relief of the famine-stricken brethren of Judaea, Ac 11:28–30, this was not merely bygone history which had no counterpart in the life of the churches as he knew them. Paul nobly fulfilled his promise to James, Cephas and John to ' be mindful of the poor in Jerusalem ', Gal 2:10 ; Rom 15:25–28, 31 ; Ac 24:17. We know how practical were the measures he took to collect contributions from Galatia, 1 Cor 16:1, Macedonia, 2 Cor 8:1–4, and Greece, 1 Cor 16:1–4, and how exquisite was the art of his persuasion which, while playing on their sense of rivalry, or their self-respect, or even their own interest, could appeal to the highest spiritual motives for generosity : ' our Lord Jesus Christ, being rich, became poor for your sakes ', 2 Cor 8:9, ' God loveth a cheerful giver ', 9:7 etc. (on 2 Cor 8–9 *cf.* Prat, I, 149–52, and E. B. Allo, *La portée de la collecte pour Jérusalem dans les plans de S Paul*, RB 45 [1936] 529–37. We notice, in passing, how he insists on the *voluntary* character of the offerings, *cf.* § 637*a*).

But all this implies the existence in each of the **r** churches of a practical care for their own needy members, not only exercised by individuals, but regularly administered by the recognized officials. One need not appeal, as an illustration of this, to the Agape—understood as a common meal, connected with the Eucharist, when an opportunity was given to the well-to-do to succour the poor (it has been seriously questioned whether the practice existed at all in NT times ; *cf.* L. Thomas, *Agape* in DBV(S) I, 134–53 ; *cf.* 652*f*). Rather is it to be recognized in countless scattered indications : the Apostles' exhortations to charity, the care of the members of Christ's Body for one another, the fact that the ' good works ' characteristic of the faithful were predominantly those exercised in charity to the neighbour (*e.g.* Rom 12:8*b*, *d*, 9*a*, 13, 17, 20 ; Jas 2:4–17 ; 1 Jn 3:17) ; so for instance Tabitha, Ac 9:36, and especially in the Pastorals (Spicq Excurs. XIII, esp. 294), where Timothy is to exhort the wealthy ' to be rich in good works, to be open-handed and generous ', 1 Tim 6:18 WV. These exhortations are no doubt primarily directed to the personal exercise of charity, but the existence of the deacons as officials in the Church (*cf.* § 659*a*) and the matter-of-fact reference to those, especially widows, who were a charge upon each Church, 1 Tim 5:16, are proof of ordered organization —too well known everywhere to need any further recording. But even if there were no such indications, the existence of such a ' social service ' in all the early churches would have to be pre-supposed as alone explaining the universal practice of the Church as testified in post-apostolic times (*cf.* L. Prunel, *Les Pauvres et l'Eglise*, DAFC III, 1673–7). Such a practice cannot have grown up everywhere independently, but must be the continuation, with developments no doubt, of what was done from the first under the Apostles in response to the Master's teaching and example.

660s (iv) **Attitude to the State**—The early Christians were not ' politically-minded ', nor was it proposed to them as an obligation to be so. For all that, Christ had introduced a revolution in political thought by distinguishing between the religious and the secular spheres (*cf.* § 633*g*). Hitherto, among Jews and Gentiles alike (if in different ways), the two had been inseparable, in principle at least ; the exemptions which in practice the Jews enjoyed at the time, were real derogations from that principle. ' Render to Caesar the things that are Caesar's, and to God the things that are God's '. If, in the context, Mt 22:16–22, Christ was primarily rejecting the opinion that loyalty to the true God demanded, or at least permitted, the refusal to pay tribute to the Roman State, he at the same time made clear that there was a religious sphere over which the State had no rights. ' We ought to obey God rather than men ', Ac 5:29, was the first echo of this, repeated against the State's claims to omni-competence by the martyrs of every century.

t　　But the novelty of this and the emphasis on ' liberty from the Law ', especially by St Paul, called for instruction on ' the things that *are* Caesar's ', lest liberty degenerate into anarchy. As Christ had said to Pilate ' Thou shouldst not have any power against me, unless it were given thee from above ', Jn 19:11, so St Paul writes, ' Every soul should subject itself to the ruling powers, for there is no power except from God. Those that exist have been established by God ', Rom 13:1 (Boylan). And when his life was at stake he (like his Master) recognized the Roman authorities by his appeal to Caesar, Ac 25:10–11 (*cf.* § 598*b*). Thus he insisted that it was not because of the sword which they held that the authorities should be paid taxes etc. (*cf.* § 598*c–d*), but as a matter of conscience, since they were acting as God's ministers, Rom 13:2–7 ; *cf.* Prat, II, 320–6. A further reason for civil obedience was given by St Peter : the edification of the pagans through the exemplary conduct of the Christians, 1 Pet 2:12–17. This also seems to be the main reason for St Paul's rebuking the Corinthians for haling their fellow-Christians before the pagan courts (1 Cor 6:1–6 ;

cf. Prat, I, 103–5 ; Allo *in loc.*) and not, as Cullmann suggests, any disparagement of those courts themselves —which even he recognizes as having been ' quite legitimate ' (*Christ et le Temps*, 142, 145).

It was indeed part of the duties of Church leaders to admonish the faithful ' to be subject to princes and powers, to obey at a word, to be ready to every good work ', Tit 3:1. If prayers for all men were to be offered by the faithful, ' kings and all that are in high station ' were to be specially mentioned, since on them depended whether the Christians could live their lives in peace and quiet, 1 Tim 2:2. For the fact remained that, though they had their power from God, they could abuse it, and our Lord had foretold that ' synagogues, and magistrates and powers ', Lk 12:11, and ' governors and kings ', Mk 13:9 ; *cf.* Mt 10:18, would beat them and put them to death. But this was to be their opportunity : they were not to fear ' them that kill the body and are not able to kill the soul ', Mt 10:28, they were not beforehand to ' take thought how or what to speak ' for the Spirit of their Father would be speaking in them—thus would they be enabled to witness to the truth before kings and the whole pagan world, Mt 10:18–20. They had the example before them of ' Christ Jesus, who gave testimony under Pontius Pilate, a good confession ', 1 Tim 6:13, and who through his death had given them a hope which overcame the fear of death itself, Heb 2:14–15.

Maybe, the Christians saw angelic powers—for good or ill—behind the authorities of the State ; but these powers were all now subject to Christ's kingship, Phil 2:9–11, so that any victory of theirs was only apparent and temporary (*cf.* 1 Cor 15:24–28 ; Cullmann, *op. cit.* and *Königsherrschaft Christi*, 1946[2] ; for the satanic powers in the world *cf.* L. Bouyer, Le Problème du Mal, in *Dieu vivant* 6, 17–42).

This is graphically pictured in the Apocalypse : the beast may ' make war with the saints ' and overcome them, 13:7, but the great army stretching unbroken from earth to heaven marches onward, hailing the Lamb, as it were slain, seated upon the throne.

EPISTLES OF THE NEW TESTAMENT

By Dom BERNARD ORCHARD

Bibliography—(1) **General**—J. E. Steinmueller, *A Companion to Scripture Studies*, 3 vols, New York, 1943[1]; *cf.* vol 3, pp 241 f. and 353 for exhaustive bibliography; Höpfl-Gut, *Introductio Specialis in N.T.*, Rome, 1938[4]; Cornely-Merk, *Compendium Introductionis in S. Scripturae Libros*, 2 vols, Paris, 1934[5]; also E. Beurlier, art. *Courrier*, DBV II 1089 f., and art. *Lettre missive*, DBV III 189–96; H. Höpfl, art. *Authenticité*, DBV (S).
(2) **Epistles of St Paul**—F. Prat, S.J., *The Theology of St Paul* (Engl. trans.), 2 vols, London, 1927; *idem*, DAFC, *Paul (Saint) et le Paulinisme*; J.-B. Colon, DTC, *St Paul*; J.-M. Vosté, O.P., *Studia Paulina*, Desclée, Rome, 1928; *W. J. Conybeare and J. S. Howson, *The Life and Epistles of St Paul*, 2 vols, London, 1898[2]; *Sir W. Ramsay, *St Paul the Traveller*, London, 1935[18]; *K. Lake, *The Earlier Epistles of St. Paul*, London, 1930[2].
(3) **The Catholic Epistles**—J. Chaine, *Les Epîtres Catholiques*, Paris, 1939[2] (Etudes Bibliques), but lacking 1 Pet and Jas; *cf.* also Charue, *Les Epîtres Catholiques*, in *La Sainte Bible* (L. Pirot), vol 12, Paris, 1938; and for devotional reading only, R. Eaton, *The Catholic Epistles of SS Peter, James, Jude and John*, London, 1937.

There are twenty-one canonical epistles in the NT, of which fourteen form the **Pauline Corpus**, *viz.* Rom, 1 and 2 Cor, Gal, Eph, Phil, Col, 1 and 2 Thess, 1 and 2 Tim, Tit, Phm, Heb. The first nine are often referred to collectively as **The Epistles to the Churches**; Eph, Phil, Col, Phm as **The Epistles of the Captivity**; 1 and 2 Tim, Tit as **The Pastoral Epistles**. The remainder (Jas, 1 and 2 Pet, 1, 2 and 3 Jn, Jude) are usually known as **The Catholic Epistles**.

THE EPISTLES OF ST PAUL

Their Number—It is a curious fact that the Acts of the Apostles, our chief source for the life of St Paul, does not once refer to any of his Epistles. Out of all the letters and treatises that he must have composed during the course of his thirty years' ministry there have come down to us only fourteen which the Church accepts as genuine and canonical. That he wrote a great many more seems an obvious inference from his intense activity and solicitude, and we have certain knowledge of at least one other letter, now lost, addressed to the Corinthians prior to our 1 Cor (*cf.* 1 Cor 5:9); whilst he probably wrote yet another letter to them between our two canonical epistles (*cf.* 2 Cor 2:3–9; 7:8–13). It also seems likely that he wrote several epistles to the Philippians (*cf.* Phil 3:1), as St Polycarp assumed (Ep. ad Phil 3:2), and that he wrote an epistle to the Laodiceans (Col 4:16), unless this be, as some think, identical with the Epistle to the Ephesians. Some apocryphal correspondence was also foisted on to St Paul in the early centuries, *e.g.* letters to the Churches of Alexandria and Laodicea (which the Muratorian Canon says were written to aid the heresy of Marcion), an epistle of Paul and Barnabas to Cyprus, a series of letters between Paul and the Corinthians, and another between him and Seneca, *cf.* § 94*b*, *h*. But the Pauline Corpus as we now have it has been a clearly defined body of writings from at least as early as the middle of the 2nd cent. For St Polycarp quotes from

nearly all the letters of Paul in his short letter to the **661c** Philippians (at the same time supposing *their* acquaintance with them); St Justin Martyr utilizes all, or nearly all, of them, and they were freely drawn on fifty years earlier by Clement in his Epistle to the Corinthians and by Ignatius of Antioch. Furthermore, they are all expressly mentioned in the Muratorian Canon (except Heb), and all except 2 Thess, the Pastorals and Phm are found in the recently discovered Chester Beatty papyri (3rd cent.), in which Heb occurs between Rom and 1 Cor.

Genuineness—A distinction is occasionally made **d** between the genuineness and the authenticity of the Epistles, in which case, their authenticity implies that their contents correspond to facts and are not fictitious, whilst genuineness means that their reputed author is the real author. Their authenticity is guaranteed by the fact that every Council of the Church which has dealt with the Canon of Scripture has included all fourteen epistles, *cf.* Council of Rome (A.D. 381), IIIrd Council of Carthage (A.D. 397); *cf.* also Letter of Pope Innocent I to Exsuperius (A.D. 405), Dz 84, 92, 96; *cf.* §§ 15*i*, 94*l*. The same Councils also accept the Pauline authorship, *i.e.* the genuineness of all fourteen epistles, though the IIIrd Council of Carthage makes a rather peculiar reference to Hebrews: 'Pauli apostoli epistulae tredecim eiusdem ad Hebraeos una'. For further treatment of the authorship of Heb see § 928*a*–*f*.
Outside the Church, however, the position in recent years has been quite otherwise. There was a period in the last century when the Tübingen school of critics (who, led by F. C. Baur, denied the genuineness of all except Rom, 1' and 2 Cor, and Gal) exerted very considerable influence in England and America. The excesses of certain Dutch critics, who went so far as to deny the genuineness even of these, led to a healthy reaction among non-Catholic critics of all nations towards the recognition of the Pauline authorship of the majority. Chief among those who stemmed the initial force of rationalist criticism was the anglican Bishop Lightfoot, whose work deserves honourable mention here. Today there is almost universal recognition among non-Catholic scholars of the genuineness of all the Pauline Corpus save the Pastoral Epistles and Heb (*q.v.* for a fuller discussion).

Order in the Canon—The order of St Paul's Epistles **e** as found in modern Catholic bibles is not chronological but follows the order adopted by the Council of Trent (PL 34, 31), in which the epistles are ranked in descending order based on the dignity of the Church addressed and the length of the contents. The same order is to be observed in the Epistles for the Sundays after Pentecost in the Roman Missal, at least as far as the Epistles to the Churches are concerned. It is not known who first adopted this order.

Chronological Order—This is still much in dispute. **f** Whereas the majority of Catholic writers would still put Gal after 1 and 2 Thess, an increasing number would reverse the order and make Gal the earliest (*c* A.D. 49), placing it between the First Missionary Journey and the Council of Jerusalem, *cf.* JRB 28 (1944) 154–74. There is general agreement that 1 and 2 Cor preceded Rom. Regarding the Epistles of the Captivity, the majority view is that Col, Phm

661f and Eph were all composed about the same time during St Paul's first imprisonment at Rome and entrusted to the same messenger, Tychicus, for delivery (Eph 6:21 f. ; Col 4:7 f. ; Phm 12), and that Phil was written about the end of it. Then came Heb, and then the Pastorals, probably in the order 1 Tim, Tit, 2 Tim.

g The form of the epistles is the same as that of the secular letters of the period, which normally contain an introductory paragraph giving the name of the writer, the name of his correspondent, and a greeting (χαίρειν, ' health '). Heb alone lacks this introduction ; a middle portion containing the main message, and a concluding paragraph bidding farewell (ἔρρωσθε) and giving messages from friends. But St Paul never concludes with the date as so many of the papyri letters do. Two brief examples of this common form are in Ac 15:23–29 ; 23:26–30. Paul, however, changes the pagan greeting ' health ' into χάρις καὶ εἰρήνη, ' grace and peace ' (1 and 2 Tim add ἔλεος, ' mercy '), and in the conclusion he alters the pagan ' farewell ' into some variant of the valediction, ' The grace of our Lord Jesus Christ be with you '. In the majority of his letters the main part is divided into two sections, the former dealing with points of dogma or with his relations to the Church in question, and the latter dealing with special difficulties proposed for his solution.

h Method of Composition—As a general rule St Paul followed the ordinary custom of the wealthy and educated classes in dictating his letters. In Rom 16:22, for example, his amanuensis adds a greeting of his own and reveals his name as being Tertius. A study of 1 Cor 16:21, 2 Thess 3:17, Col 4:18, shows that he was wont to add a sentence or two in his own handwriting at the end of a dictated epistle, both as a mark of special affection and as a sign of genuineness. Sometimes, however, he would write the whole epistle himself, as in the case of Phm (*cf.* 19). It has been calculated that it would have taken him a good two hours to dictate 1 Thess and more than eleven hours to dictate Rom (*pro rata* for the other epistles) ; and since it would have been impossible for him to have dictated for such lengths of time without suffering many interruptions, attempts have been made to discover by careful analysis where these pauses or interruptions occurred (*cf.* E. Stange, *Diktierpausen in den Paulusbriefen*, ZNTW 18 (1917) 109–17). For as Professor J. H. Moulton has well said, ' Paul's habit of dictation, combined with the casual character of his letters, made his writing practically identical with his speaking ' (*Peake's Commentary*, 592). The process was carried too far by the German ' sound-analysis ' school, which attempted to distinguish between the parts dictated by Paul himself and the conjectural interjections and additions of such bystanders as Silas and Timothy. Their researches have nevertheless served to emphasize the value of reading the Epistles aloud as an aid to understanding them. The time taken to compose them must have varied enormously ; for whilst Rom would seem to have occupied the leisure moments of the Apostle for a considerable period, Galatians bears all the marks of haste as if it had been dashed off at a single sitting.

i What other aids to composition did St Paul have ? It is more than likely that he followed the contemporary practice of keeping a copy of each epistle in a special letter-book and that he referred to it from time to time when composing later epistles. This would help to account for certain similarities of ideas and speech in, say, Gal and Rom, *cf.* Deissmann, *Licht vom Osten*, 4, 200. Express quotations from the OT (LXX) (as opposed to tacit quotations and allusions) are confined almost entirely to Rom, 1 and 2 Cor, Gal, and the freedom with which he quotes, adapts and combines texts from the LXX suggests that he usually quoted from memory. Quotations from the Heb are very rare, *cf.* Prat, *op cit.* I, Note B. On the other hand Vaccari (*Institutiones Biblicae*, p 163) says

that Heb follows the LXX, but the other thirteen epistles ' ad textum hebraicum respiciunt et sensum liberius reddunt '.

Did St Paul carry about with him rolls or codices of the LXX ? The existence of first cent. codices has not yet been proved, but he may well have had a travelling chest containing the rolls of the LXX. In any case he would have had access to copies in the synagogues of such large cities as Ephesus and Corinth. It is the opinion of the present writer that St Paul also possessed a copy of St Matthew's Gospel in Greek, which he utilized in composing 1 and 2 Thess, *cf.* Bi 19 (1938) 19–42 ; B. C. Butler, *St. Paul's Knowledge and Use of St Matthew*, DR (1948) 367 ff.

Writing Materials and Methods—It seems probable that the secretaries, to whom Paul and the other Apostles normally dictated their letters, wrote with a reed in the Greco-Roman manner. The reed was cut exactly like the goose-quill of later times, and was dipped in ink prepared from charcoal or soot mixed with gum and dissolved in water when required for use. The material for writing was normally papyrus, though leather was used for writings requiring to be preserved, papyrus being perishable by nature. *Papyrus* was made from the fibrous pith of a water plant found in the Nile (though now no longer found in Egypt). Horizontal and vertical layers of thin strips of pith were fastened together by Nile water, glue and pressure, and were then polished. The recto side had the top fibres lying horizontally, and the verso had the top fibres lying vertically. The recto was the side primarily intended for writing, though not infrequently a papyrus roll was inscribed within and without (*cf.* Ezech 2:9). The sheets of papyrus were fastened together side by side to make a roll, the average length of which was about 35 feet with a depth of 9 or 10 inches, *cf.* § 21*g, i.*

At the beginning of a roll there was usually a blank column to permit handling, the writing then proceeding in columns of 2 to 3 inches width in the case of literary works. Letters, if short, would be written on a single sheet very much like a modern letter to look at, except for the absence of addresses. There was no separation of words one from another, little punctuation ; there were few paragraphs, no capital letters or accents and very few breathings. Shorthand was certainly known and practised, but there is no proof that it was used in the NT documents (*cf.* art. *Tachygraphy*, Oxford Classical Dictionary, 1948). It should also be noted that whereas the roll seems to have been universal for secular books up to the 4th cent., the codex (or modern book) form seems to have predominated for the NT writings from the 2nd cent., probably on account of its easy mode of reference to all passages required in liturgical worship.

Vellum, a very enduring material for writing and made from the skins of calves, lambs and kids, was not used in NT times, and only came into use in the 4th cent.

The Jews had no organized post in the modern sense, and among the Romans the post was reserved exclusively for the Emperor and his officials. Private letter writers, therefore, like St Paul, had to rely for delivery on special messengers or on friendly travellers.

Style and Language—German critics such as Deissmann have devoted much time to discussing the question whether St Paul's Epistles are really private letters, *i.e.* not intended for the general public, but sent in response to some particular message or to meet some particular situation, and specially directed to the needs of a particular person or group ; or whether they are better regarded as literary products making use of the epistolary form as a convenient vehicle for conveying instruction to a nascent and struggling Christian community ; though Deissmann, *op. cit.*, p 232, concludes that they are ' real non-literary letters ', they are, in fact, unique in so far as they combine both characteristics, though in varying degrees in particular cases. For on the one hand

2c they are most intimate, revealing his ardent affection for and devotion to his converts, and at the same time most practical in the answers they give to requests for help, advice and encouragement in the troubles and difficulties of the hour ; on the other hand, it is quite clear that he intended them to be read to the whole Church, 1 Thess 5:27, and even to be communicated to other Churches, Col 4:16 ; and hence he deliberately worked much doctrinal instruction and close theological argument into them, *cf.* A. Steinmann, *Der hl Paulus und seine Breife*, in *Die Briefe an die Thessalonicher*, Bonn, 1935. (Nevertheless it is very important to note that he does not give but *presupposes* a knowledge of fundamental doctrines, *e.g.* in Phil the divinity of Christ comes in incidentally as something known to the readers and serving merely to emphasize a lesson of humility ; *cf.* also his references to the oral teaching he had already given to his readers, 1 Cor 11:2 ; 2 Thess 2:15 ; 3:6 ; 1 Cor 11:23 ; 15:3, etc.)

d St Paul wrote all his epistles in good idiomatic contemporary Greek (the so-called *Koine* or common dialect), of which he had a thorough command, *cf.* § 21*a*. His famous reference to himself in 2 Cor 11:6 as being ' rude in speech ' (ἰδιώτην τῷ λόγῳ) merely meant that he made no attempt to impart to his writing or speech that Attic elegance and polish which his Corinthian critics seemed to revere. Actually, his language and style strike a successful mean between literary Greek and the common speech of contemporary life, and it was he who first adapted the Greek tongue to the sublime doctrine of the Christian religion, B. E. Allo, RSPT 23 (1934) 29–39. Precisely because his writing is practically identical with his speaking we often find in his letters that looseness of construction which is common in the ordinary converse of even the best educated. Hence there is no reason for surprise or disparagement if we find what the strict grammarians would label as blemishes of style, *e.g.* semitisms (the use of the abstract for the concrete, substantives for adjectives), transpositions of words (*e.g.* Gal 3:19), anacolutha (*e.g.* 1 Thess 1:8), strings of words to illustrate his meaning (*e.g.* Rom 1:29 f.), rhetorical questions, unheralded asides, parentheses and digressions (*e.g.* Rom 5:12–13 ; Gal 2:3–6). Hence we may very well agree with 2 Pet 3:16 that in St Paul there ' are certain things hard to be understood ' even by his contemporaries who were in a far better position than we are to fathom his meaning. Nevertheless his obscurity should not be exaggerated, and though doubts will continue to remain over the meaning of texts here and there, the grand lines of Pauline theology are clear beyond all dispute, *cf.* Prat, *op. cit. passim.*

Sources of his Teaching—It is sufficient here to state that there is no contradiction between his teaching and that of the Evangelists and St Peter. St Paul, the chosen instrument of divine Providence in the initial spread of the Gospel, framed the vast synthesis of Christian theology through the power of his great intellect, illumined by grace and trained in the schools of rabbinic theology. The elements of his synthesis **662e** were derived from (*a*) the direct revelation of Christ, *cf.* Gal 1:15 f. ; 1 Thess 4:15 ; this element, however, should not be overstressed, for the great bulk of facts relating to the life and teaching of Christ he had derived naturally from (*b*) the teaching and converse of the Apostles and disciples, *cf.* 1 Cor 11:23 ; 15:3 f., (*c*) his study of, and meditation on, the OT in the light of the known facts about Jesus and the special personal revelation he had received, (*d*) the main stream of Jewish theology, in which he had been carefully educated by Gamaliel. The view, very popular some years ago, that his thought was much influenced and formed by hellenistic syncretism has now been largely abandoned, *cf.* E. Jacquier, DAFC IV 964–1013 ; Prat, art. *Paul et Paulinisme*, DAFC. Whilst he must have had some acquaintance with the pagan mystery religions and certainly used (in special connotations of his own) some of the words which they employed as technical terms, *e.g.* (γνῶσις, μυστήριον, φωτίζειν), yet his hatred of all pagan contamination was so thoroughly Jewish that he would have rejected with horror the idea of borrowing pagan doctrines or rites. Moreover he takes it for granted that Christian communities which he had not founded share his faith and characteristic doctrines, such as the mystical effects of baptism, Rom 1:12 ; 6:3 ; he expressly says that he preaches the same truths as the other apostles, 1 Cor 15:11 ; and that they had found nothing to reprehend in his doctrine, Gal 2:6.

THE CATHOLIC EPISTLES

f The term ' Catholic ' might mean either ' canonical ' or ' addressed universally ' to the Catholic body and not to a particular Church or person (in this case, excepting 2 and 3 Jn), but most likely it means an epistle ' accepted by the Catholic Church '. The term was also sometimes used of the genuine epistles of St Paul, but proved to be most convenient as a designation of the non-Pauline letters received by the Catholic Church. The term, which first appears in a mutilated portion of the Muratorian Canon in reference to Jude and 1 Jn, is first found in reference to all seven in Eusebius, HE, II, 23, 24 f.

Order in the Canon—In the most ancient codices and catalogues these seven epistles are always found together, and very often they are found bound up in a separate codex following Acts. But in the West they were as a rule placed after the Pauline Corpus. As regards the order of these epistles among themselves, the DV (following Vg) takes the order adopted by the Greeks in the 4th cent., which was perhaps based on Gal 2:9, though that adopted by the Council of Trent, which ranks them in order of apostolic dignity, *viz.* Pet, Jn, Jas and Jude, was at one time more usual in the West.

The Chronological Order may have been Jas, 1 Pet, Jude, 2 Pet, 1, 2, 3 Jn.

The authenticity of these Epistles is very little disputed at the present time except for 2 Pet (*q.v.*).

THE LIFE OF SAINT PAUL

By D. J. O'HERLIHY

663a Bibliography—St John Chrysostom, *De Laudibus S. Pauli*, Montfaucon 2, 562–618 ; Boudou, *Les Actes des Apôtres*, Paris, 1923 ; Camerlynck-Vander Heeren, *Commentarius in Actus Apostolorum*, Bruges, 1923 ; Jacquier, *Les Actes des Apôtres*, Paris, 1926 ; Lusseau-Collomb, *Manuel d'Etudes Bibliques*, Tome V, Paris, 1938–41 ; Amiot, *L'Enseignement de Saint Paul*, Paris, 1938 ; Bläser, *Das Gesetz bei Paulus*, Munster, 1941 ; *Conybeare-Howson, *The Life and Epistles of Saint Paul*, 1862 ; *Deissmann, *Paulus, eine kultur-und religions-geschichtliche Skizze*, Tübingen, 1925 ; *Foakes-Jackson, *The Life of St Paul*, 1927 ; Fouard, *Saint Paul and his Missions*, 1907 ; Fouard, *Last Years of Saint Paul*, 1911 ; Holzner, *Paul of Tarsus* (Eng. tr. of *Paulus, sein Leben und seine Briefe*), St Louis, 1946 ; Lattey, *Paul*, 1938 ; Maritain, *Saint Paul*, 1942 ; *Morton, *In the Steps of Saint Paul*, 1936 ; Murillo, *Paulus et Pauli Scripta*, Rome, 1926 ; Pieper, *Paulus, seine missionarische Personlichkeit u. Wirksamkeit*, Münster, 1929 ; Prat, *La Théologie de Saint Paul*, Paris, 1923 ; *Ramsay, *The Cities of St Paul, their Influence on his Life and Thought*, 1907 ; *Ramsay, *St Paul the Traveller and the Roman Citizen*, 1908 ; Ricciotti, *Paolo Apostolo*, Rome, 1948 ; *Schonfield, *The Jew of Tarsus*, 1946 ; Tricot, *St Paul, The Apostle of the Gentiles*, 1930 ; Vosté, *Studia Paulina*, Rome, 1928 ; WV, *The Acts of the Apostles : St Paul's Epistles to the Churches*, 1939 ; *Hastings, *Dictionary of the Bible* ; Vigouroux, *Dictionnaire de la Bible* ; Bover, *De mystica unione ' in Christo Iesu' secundum B. Paulum*, Bi I (1920) 309–26 ; Vitti, *L'Eloquenza di S. Paulo colta al vivo da S. Luca negli Atti*, 22, 159–97 ; Allo, *La Portée de la Collecte pour Jérusalem dans les plans de Saint Paul*, RB 45, 529–37 ; Benoît, *La Loi et la Croix d'après Saint Paul*, RB 47, 481–509.

b Birth and Education—St Paul was born in the city of Tarsus at the dawn of the Christian era. Tarsus was the capital of Cilicia, Greek in language and Roman through the favour of Caesar. Distinguished for commercial advantages no less than for literary attainments, the town on whose coins civic pride had stamped the boast ' First and Fairest and Best ' was ' no mean city '. Like most trading centres in the Greco-Roman world, it had its Jewish colony, and the future Apostle was born in the ghetto. It appears that the boy was given two names at birth, Saul, after the greatest man of his tribe, and Paul, in token of the Roman citizenship which he inherited. For a provincial such citizenship implied a very special privilege, conferred for service and goodwill to the Roman cause or purchased for a substantial figure. As became one born into a strict Jewish family, Saul's early formation was on traditional lines, and it is not likely that he attended the lyceums that were preparatory to enrolment in the Tarsus university. But he could not altogether escape the influence of a pagan and prosperous city. Temples and theatres abounded outside the quarter inhabited by his race ; popular quotations occur in his writings ; and the imagery of trade, athletics and war may partly be based on the memories of childhood. Together with two names, he had two languages from his youth—Aramaic being the home-language of the stricter Jew in Asiatic lands and Greek the language of the synagogue in the Mediter-ranean world. He would shortly become acquainted with Hebrew.

For the purpose of graduating as a master of the Law in the ghetto of his native city he was sent to Jerusalem to complete his studies. Possibly some members of the family resided in the Holy City where at a later stage his sister's son saved his life. The Schools of Hillel and Shammai—two rabbis of the Herodian period—were then in the ascendant and Saul joined the former under the direction of Gamaliel I. He was fortunate in having as teacher one whom the Mishnah eulogizes and of whose repute St Luke preserves an echo, Ac 5:34. While more attention was paid in the schools to the utterances of men than to the word of God, yet Saul acquired, at the feet of Gamaliel, an incomparable knowledge of Hebrew lore and made his own the peculiarly Jewish methods of argumentation which he was later to employ with advantage in presenting the Christian message to his compatriots. And apart from progress in knowledge, he was to preserve from the home of Pharisaism a burning zeal for the integrity of doctrine and tradition and for a rigorous observance of the Mosaic legislation, ' according to the justice that is in the law, conversing without blame ', Phil 3:6 b. It appears that he left Jerusalem some time before the Baptist inaugurated the movement which Jesus took over and dominated. The years of Pilate's procuratorship are obscure in the life-story of Saul. From scattered notices in his writings it is legitimate to conclude that he devoted his adolescence to acquiring a fuller knowledge of the Law and to advancing more and more along the path marked out for him by his teacher in Jerusalem. His zeal will have found an outlet in the school attached to the local synagogue and he may have been consulted as a legal expert by the Tarsus sanhedrin of which he was not a member on account of his age.

Conformably to the Talmud recommendation, ' He that hath a trade in his hand, to what is he like ? he is like a vineyard that is fenced ', he had been initiated into the occupation of his father, the local craft of making tents and cloaks out of Cilician cloth and he remained a manual labourer to the end. He supported himself in this way, even when he was actively engaged in preaching the Gospel (1 Cor 9:12 b), and may have wished to emphasize in his person the dignity of manual labour against the tendency of Roman society to relegate handwork to slaves. He never married (1 Cor 7:7). We have no knowledge of his personal appearance apart from the description in the apocryphal Acts of Paul and Thecla : ' a man of little stature, thin-haired upon the head, crooked in the legs, of good state of body, with eyebrows joining and nose somewhat hooked, full of grace, for sometimes he appeared like a man, and sometimes he had the face of an angel '. Many writers think that they find, in St Paul's writings and in St Luke's account of him, evidence that he suffered from shortness of sight or from some affliction of the eyes. The ' stake in the flesh ' of 2 Cor 12:7 connotes a form of physical illness, about which it is difficult to be precise. The Latin Fathers suggested headaches while modern writers are divided between epilepsy and malaria. But whatever the malady was, it is interesting to reflect that the volume of his achievement was accomplished, not in the strength of a healthy body, but in the face of a disability that caused him much distress.

Conversion—While Saul tarried in Tarsus, epoch-making events took place in Palestine. The long-awaited Messias came, preached for the appointed time and was rejected by his own. His disciples, dispirited by the death of their master, were comforted by his reappearance and transformed by the effusion of the Holy Spirit. In the knowledge that the Jews had made a tragic mistake in rejecting the Messias, they set themselves to the task of repairing the error and of converting Israel to its Lord and Saviour. But the leaders of the Jews were in no mood to accept the advice of Galilean fishermen and, moreover, were disturbed at the increasing success of the new Gospel. The preaching of a young deacon set a seal on their opposition to its progress. It is interesting to notice that among the Jews represented as disputing with Stephen were some from the synagogue of the Cilicians, and Saul may have been among them and may have lent himself to the campaign which culminated in the trial before the council. The speech of Stephen on this occasion is drawn from the very writings which he was charged with discrediting and is unique among the discourses in the early chapters of Acts. It throws conciliation to the winds and impeaches Israel without reserve : ' You stiffnecked and uncircumcised in heart and ears, you always resist the Holy Ghost. As your fathers did, so do you also ' (7:51). His death —whether as a result of a sentence passed by the sanhedrin without competence or as an act of mob violence which the leaders did nothing to prevent— was the signal for a violent persecution which resulted in the scattering of the infant Church and continued to rage until Pilate's successor was securely invested in office. Saul kept the garments of those who stoned Stephen and he ' was consenting to his death ' (7:59). The pogrom saw him emerge in the role of chief inquisitor, raiding the synagogues and invading the sanctuaries of domestic life in a grim determination to extirpate the new religion. Nor was he satisfied with a local extirpation : he would reach as far as Damascus whither, it was thought, some Christians had fled to escape the fury which reigned in Jerusalem. Armed with letters of credence from the high-priest and an escort, he hastened northwards and was struck down by a miracle in the midst of his frenzy and converted to the faith he persecuted. That St Luke regarded this event as of capital importance in the life-story of St Paul is evidenced by the circumstance that he tells it three times, once in his own words (9:1-19) and twice in those of St Paul (22:3-21 and 26:9-19). Too often have these parallel passages been examined in a captious spirit. In fact, the differences to be noted in them are merely circumstantial and far from raising any doubts about St Luke they are rather an index to his veracity for a suspicious writer would have taken care to remove them.

The supernatural character of the conversion is placed beyond all reasonable doubt by the various historical details and statements of Acts as well as by the testimony of St Paul and the tradition of the Church. Rationalist critics, avowed opponents of the supernatural, are compelled to find an explanation for the episode in harmony with their preconceived opinions and many adopt the view made popular by Renan, to wit, that Paul merely recognized that Jesus was the Son of God. Others contend, with more reverence but not more reasonableness, that Saul imagined, under the stress of emotion, that he saw him who, the Christians believed, had risen from the dead. Neither St Paul, however, nor his biographer retain any vestige of this alleged emotional urgency. Saul was ' ignorant in unbelief ' (1 Tim 1:13) and was firmly convinced that he had to do many things against Jesus (Ac 26:9). Ananias openly claims that Jesus had appeared to Saul on the way (Ac 9:17) and Barnabas tells the Apostles how

Saul saw the Lord and how the Lord spoke to him **664d** (Ac 9:27). Saul himself is certain of having seen Christ, arguing thence to his status as an Apostle (1 Cor 9:1) and to equal rank with Peter, James and the Twelve (1 Cor 15:8). If Christ did not really **e** appear to Saul on the way to Damascus, then Saul who says that he saw Jesus either wished to deceive his hearers or was himself deceived. No one suggests that he was a deliberate liar, and the case for self-deception is excluded by the factual statements of Acts as well as by the strength and consistency of his post-conversion career. It would be strange indeed if illusion could have created or conserved the life of the Apostle of the Gentiles. Much has been written about the psychological preparation of the Apostle, as if he had long been impressed by the beauty of Christianity and recently touched by the heroism of Stephen. But whatever the influence of Stephen's prayers—' Si Stephanus non orasset Ecclesia Paulum non habuisset ' —it is difficult to attach any great importance to this ' psychological preparation ' in view of the concordant testimony of Acts and Epistles which represents the conversion as something sudden, startling and unforeseen.

In the city of Damascus whither he was led by his **f** companions Saul received a commission : he was set apart to carry the name of Jesus ' before the Gentiles and kings and the children of Israel '. At this early stage he perceived that the name of Jesus was the only saving name. The jealous champion of the Law saw in a flash its utter helplessness as an instrument of salvation and became convinced that men could not be saved except through faith in Jesus Christ who had been crucified in the name of the law. It is interesting, too, to notice that the words which he heard on the road to Damascus—' I am Jesus whom thou persecutest ' (Ac 26:15)—enshrine the doctrine which he made peculiarly his own, that the faithful make up one body of which Jesus is the head, continuing through time the work of redemption.

When he had recovered from the ordeal in the house **g** of Judas and had been baptized by Ananias, he withdrew for a time to Arabia (Gal 1:17). Returning to Damascus he preached the divine sonship and Messianic character of Jesus in the synagogues. But the Jews were unwilling to be taught by a renegade and in an effort to kill him sought help from the soldiery of the Ethnarch of Aretas. It was then that the disciples took him and let him down in a basket from a window in the wall. He went to Jerusalem to see St Peter and had difficulty in overcoming the suspicion in which he was held by some Christians. But Joseph Barnabas, ' a good man ', vouched for him to the Apostles, and a fifteen-day association with their leader clearly demonstrated that Saul also was among the prophets. A vision accorded to him in the temple enlightened him further in respect of his future career and he left for Tarsus. The length of time that was allowed to pass between his conversion and his official summoning to the work of heralding forth the Gospel gave him an extended insight into the way of providence on the one hand, and on the other hand into the workings of grace in the human heart, thus constituting a suitable preparation for the office of preaching to a world which ignored Providence and had become insensible to divine inspirations.

The beginnings of the apostolate to the heathen world **h** are curiously interesting. St Peter, appropriately, had taken the first steps in this direction, receiving Cornelius the Centurion into the Church, but that he had done what Jewish Christians found hard to bear is proved by the circumstance that he had to justify his action on his return to Jerusalem. At Antioch-on-the-Orontes, one of the chief cities of the Greco-Roman world, refugee Christians, unauthorized, proceeded to address themselves to the heathen, and with a fair measure of success. Barnabas was sent from the Mother-Church to foster the beginnings of the predominantly Gentile community, and on being satisfied that there was a

664h wide field of apostolate, he secured the services of Saul whom he had befriended a few years before and of whose destiny he was not unaware. Under their combined fostering the word of the Lord increased and the disciples became numerous enough to attract the attention of the public. It was here that they were first called 'Christians'. Perhaps it was at this time that Saul, during an errand of mercy in Jerusalem, became the recipient of the visions and revelations to which he refers in 2 Cor 12:1-4. But Antioch was to be his base and thence, set apart by order of the Holy Ghost, he sailed on the first missionary journey.

665a **First Missionary Journey**—The itinerary was through Cyprus (the home-island of Barnabas), Perge in Pamphylia, and the Galatian towns of Antioch, Iconium, Lystra and Derbe. It ought to be noted that in the course of the expedition the leadership of the party, hitherto directed by Barnabas, passed to Paul, the name which his biographer uses from this point onwards. St Jerome reckoned that the change of name commemorated the victory over Sergius Paulus in much the same way as Scipio was called Africanus from the conquest of Africa. The failure of the Jews to accept the Gospel was borne in on Paul at this early stage of his missionary endeavour : 'To you it behoved us first to speak the word of God : but because you reject it and judge yourselves unworthy of eternal life, behold we turn to the Gentiles' (Ac 13:46). Despite opposition, the work of the missionaries was not without fruit for God stood by them and rendered witness by miracles to the words that proclaimed his grace. They revisited the communities which they had established and consolidated the work by appointing priests in every Church.

b **Circumcision and Mosaic Observances**—The applause which greeted the return of the delegates to Antioch was short-lived, for 'some, coming down from Judea, taught the brethren : That, except you be circumcised after the manner of Moses, you cannot be saved' (Ac 15:1). It is difficult to state in precise terms the facets of the problem which now embarrassed St Paul and continued for a decade (but see Comm. on Gal., §893c-f) to disturb his churches. He had founded communities in southern Asia Minor on the basis of the absolute equality of Jew and Gentile, for to become a full member of the Christian Church faith and baptism alone were necessary. Others—the name 'Judaizers' has been coined to indicate them—held that such membership was not complete and that circumcision was necessary as well as baptism for the full possession of the privileges of the Christian state. The point of view might easily be current in Palestine: the Palestinian Gospel—that according to St Matthew —represents Jesus as perfecting, not abrogating, the Law (5:17). Jesus himself was circumcised : and the Church of Jerusalem, under the guidance of the pious James, had not ceased, in spite of persecution, to hope to win the Jews to Christianity on the sole basis of accepting Jesus as the Messias. 'It was one thing to let a small group of Gentiles be received into the Church without circumcision in consequence of a manifest divine intervention, but quite another to have multitudes entering the Church upon the simple condition of faith all over the world' (WV 2, 218).

c For Paul the question was one of policy as well as of principle. To accept the Judaistic claim was to make nugatory his whole mission to the Gentile world, and to renounce the hope of gaining that world for Christ. But above all, the thesis of the Judaizers struck at the nerve-centre of the Gospel, denying by implication the intrinsic merit of the Cross. To set up national or racial prerogatives within the Christian Church was an outrage to his conviction that Christ died for all without distinction and, in the light of his intimate experience, both before and after his conversion, he was satisfied that a religion, whose motive-power was Law, would never bring men to God.

d To remove the occasion for disquiet, it was deemed expedient to go to Jerusalem and consult the Mother-Church. Paul and Barnabas represented the Antioch community that stood for freedom from the Law (cf. Comm. on Gal for discussion of mutual relation of the visits mentioned in Ac 11 and 15, and Gal 2, §895c). In the Holy City the Apostles recognized Paul's title to apostolic rank and approved the method employed by him in preaching to the Gentiles.

At an official assembly St Peter took the initiative and spoke in favour of gentile freedom, 'why tempt you God to put a yoke upon the necks of the disciples which neither our fathers nor we have been able to bear' (Ac 15:10). He was supported by St James, the alleged patron of the Judaizing party, who sought confirmation of the ruling in the OT. Yet James thought it wise to add certain prohibitions with a view to respecting the feelings of Jews in mixed communities. On these lines, as the rescript sent to the churches shows, agreement was reached and the commendation of Paul and Barnabas together with the repudiation of their opponents made it clear that the victory was theirs. The choice of Judas and Silas to be bearers of the apostolic decree may have confirmed all this, for in Silas Paul found such a kindred spirit that he chose him, in place of Barnabas, as his chief companion on the second missionary journey.

Second Missionary Journey—They traversed Syria and Cilicia and the Galatian towns evangelized on the first journey. Forbidden to preach in Proconsular Asia, they struck north to the frontier of Bithynia. This district they were not allowed even to enter, so they turned west again, skirting Mysia and reaching the coast at Troas where a heavenly vision called them to Macedonia. At this point in the narrative of Acts occurs the first 'we-section', indicating that St Luke was already in the party ; Timothy had been taken on at Lystra. They reached Europe at Neapolis, the terminus of the well-known Egnatian highway, and hurried to Philippi which was the foremost town in that part of Macedonia. The ministry there had three phases : 1, the preaching at the river bank with the conversion of Lydia ; 2, the expulsion from a slave girl of a divining spirit followed by the flogging and imprisonment of the preachers ; 3, the conversion of their jailer. The Philippi ministry is significant in that it was here, in a Roman colony, that Paul first insisted so strongly on his Roman citizenship. The converts mentioned specifically by Luke differ in social rank and religious education and serve to illustrate the Pauline maxim that in Christ there is neither Jew nor Greek, bond nor free, male nor female. And the sequence of their conversion is symbolical of the progress of the Gospel outside Palestine—through the ghettos of the dispersion on to the Greek world and to Rome, the centre of civilization. Paul and Silas moved west along the main road to Thessalonica, the Macedonian capital, and here they preached for a short time and with some success among the heathens. But the hostility of the Jews forced them to flee to Berea and we find Paul for a brief moment at Athens —sorrowful and alone—before making Corinth, on the maritime route between Rome and the East, the real centre of missionary endeavour at this time. The exordium of his discourse to the Athenian philosophers survives to show that he could use the language of the higher culture when occasion required, but anxiety to be of service to all was checked, in his relations with paganism, by an innate repugnance for anything to do with the worship of idols. He spent eighteen months at Corinth, plying with Aquila and Prisca the trade of tent-maker, by which means he avoided becoming a burden to the converts and running the risk of being equated in their minds with the travelling sophist or sordid politician. On meeting with opposition from the synagogue, he changed, under divine inspiration, a Jewish mission for a predominantly Gentile and fruitful one : 'And the Lord said to Paul in the night, by a vision : Do not fear, but speak. And hold not thy peace, because I am with thee and no man shall set upon thee, to hurt thee. For I have much people

g in this city' (Ac 18:9–10). It was from the capital of Achaia that he wrote the two Epistles to the Thessalonians.

a **Third Missionary Journey**—After his return to his base on the Orontes, the third journey was undertaken almost immediately. He passed through ' the country of Galatia and Phrygia' and sought out Ephesus where he held disputations in the synagogue for three months and later in the house of a certain Tyrannus for upwards of two years. The circle of believers slowly widened and the Gospel, thanks to the new converts, was carried into the valley of the Lycus with the formation of Christian groups in the cities of Colossae, Laodicea and Hierapolis. To this period are assigned the major Epistles—Galatians to the beginning, unless it be assigned to a date before the Council of Jerusalem (*cf.* § 893*c–f*), Romans to the close, and the Corinthian Letters in between. All are occasional writings with the exception of Romans which is a treatise setting forth with clearness and distinction the fruit of his meditation on the central problem of the time—the relations between the Church **b** and the Synagogue. At the end of the Ephesian ministry, Paul ' purposed in the spirit, when he had passed through Macedonia and Achaia, to go to Jerusalem, saying : After I have been there, I must see Rome also ' (Ac 19:21). The work of evangelizing the East had been completed. From Jerusalem to Illyricum (Rom 15:19) he had fully carried out the preaching of the Gospel in the eastern world, and now he was determined, when he had handed over in Jerusalem the money contributed by the Gentile Churches to the poor of the Mother-Church, to seek a field of preaching in the extreme west where Christ had not been known. Paul obviously attached much importance to this subsidy for the benefit of the poor of Jerusalem, no doubt as a concrete proof of the loyalty of Gentile Christians to their fellow believers **c** in Judaea. He little guessed that his visit to Rome would be delayed for some years, and that ultimately he would arrive thither, as a prisoner, on appeal to Caesar. Yet the future was casting its shadows before. At Ephesus a notable disturbance almost cost him his life (Ac 19:23–31) ; at Corinth a change of plan was rendered necessary by the knowledge that the Jews were plotting against him (Ac 20:3) ; and in the course of the return journey from the Aegean the Holy Spirit, in city after city, testified that bondage and affliction awaited him (Ac 20:23).

d **Arrest and Imprisonment**—He arrived in Jerusalem in time for the feast of Pentecost and as he was completing with others a ritual purification, undertaken on the advice of James, Asiatic Jews stirred up the multitude and ' laid hands upon him, crying out : Men of Israel, help : This is the man that teacheth all men everywhere against the people and the law and this place ; and moreover hath brought in Gentiles into the temple and hath violated this holy place ' (Ac 21:27–28). And they would have beaten him to death but for the timely intervention of the Roman Tribune. From the steps of the fortress of Antonia Paul addressed the mob in the vernacular, recalling his education at the feet of Gamaliel, his zeal for the Law of Moses, how he had persecuted the Christians, and how he had been converted. His subsequent reference to the divine commission to preach the Gospel among the Gentiles, though he himself pleaded to be allowed to preach in Jerusalem, roused the Jews to fury, whereupon the Tribune gave orders to bring him into the fort and to examine him under the scourge.

e This was a contravention of the ' Lex Porcia ', and the Tribune, on being made aware of the circumstance, found himself in an embarrassing situation, not unlike that of another Roman in the presence of a greater than Paul. To escape from it he presented the prisoner to the sanhedrin, without result, and Paul, for his part, was comforted by a voice from heaven : ' Be constant ; for as thou has testified of me in Jerusalem, so must thou bear witness also at Rome ' (Ac 23:11). At this point a plot to kill the Apostle was discovered, whereat **666e** the Tribune had Paul spirited away by night to Caesarea, the residence of the Roman Governor.

Palestine had been re-attached to the Province of Syria **f** at the death of Herod Agrippa I in 44, and it was unfortunate that at this time the Governor should have been a wicked man and a time-server. Tacitus notes with cruel precision the character of Felix before whom Paul now stood : ' Antonius Felix, per omnem saevitiam et libidinem, ius regium servili ingenio exercuit ' (Hist 5, 9). After some days the high-priest arrived in Caesarea with a pleader, Tertullus, who led the prosecution and urged that Paul was a disturber of the peace which Felix had been at pains to establish in Palestine. Paul denied having caused any disturbance in Jerusalem and while admitting that he served God ' according to the way which they call a heresy ' (Ac 24:14) affirmed his belief in the Law and the Prophets, and the general resurrection, and stressed his endeavour at all times to have a conscience void of offence in regard of God and man. The Governor, though he had no doubt about the prisoner's innocence, adjourned the case giving orders that Paul be kept in bonds but treated with indulgence. He would later come to appreciate the wisdom and independence of the prisoner but in the hope that a ransom would be paid for the freedom of one so influential he kept the Apostle in chains. On his removal from office two years later things began to happen under the determined and energetic rule of his successor. Flavius Josephus con- **g** trasts Festus favourably with his predecessor (BJ 2, 14) and his prompt handling of the present case compares to advantage with his predecessor's dilatory tactics. The NT portrait of his character reveals that curious combination of contempt and fear which Roman officials usually exhibited in their relations with the Jews. To the Jews of Jerusalem Festus replied that the prisoner was in custody at Caesarea and that there he would remain. Yet, when the accusations broke down in Caesarea, he showed himself willing and even anxious to oblige them. But Paul, sensing a danger to his life, of which Festus must have been unaware, appealed to Caesar, thus overriding the jurisdiction of the Governor's court. Soon after this **h** the prisoner had an opportunity of which he gladly availed himself to state his case and his mission before a distinguished audience, King Herod Agrippa II and Berenice. The apologia is a model of moderation and prudence, remarkable for the respect shown to his hearers and to the Law which he venerated but whose domination was now at an end : ' But being aided by the help of God, I stand unto this day, witnessing both to small and great, saying no other thing than those which the prophets and Moses did say should come to pass : that Christ should suffer and that he should be the first that should rise from the dead and should show light to the people and to the Gentiles. And as he spoke these things and made his answer, Festus said with a loud voice : Paul, thou art beside thyself : much learning doth make thee mad. And Paul said : I am not mad, most excellent Festus, but I speak words of truth and soberness. For the king knoweth of these things, to whom also I speak with confidence. For I am persuaded that none of these things are hidden from him. For neither was any of these things done in a corner. Believest thou the prophets, O king Agrippa ? I know that thou believest. And Agrippa said to Paul : In a little thou persuadest me to become a Christian. And Paul said : I would to God that both in a little and in much, not only thou, but also all that hear me this day, should become such as I also am, except these bands ' (Ac 26:22–29).

He was taken away by sea, bound for Italy, and Luke **i** who accompanied him has left a detailed report of the long and dramatic journey. For some obscure reason—none better has been put forward than the traditional one, that, having brought the matter up to the moment of writing, there was nothing more to say—Luke's narrative breaks off with the master in

666i Rome, where ' he remained two whole years in his own hired lodging '. His imprisonment was no bar to the progress of the Gospel. The ' word ' spread among the jailers and even into the imperial residence, and the prisoner became well-known throughout the
j whole Pretorian camp. It was a period, too, of literary activity, four Epistles named from the imprisonment having survived. To the Philippians, a dear and docile congregation, he writes out of the fullness of his heart of the peace and spiritual joy which he wishes his children to share. In Ephesians he celebrates the Trinity of Eternal Love coming forth for man's salvation, and hymns the primacy of Christ and the grace-plenitude that flows from him to the Church. Colossians is a less objective exposition of Christ's pre-eminence, for in the Lycus valley philosophy had made an effort to draw the Christian Faith within its own sphere and to absorb it as it had done with so many pagan mythologies—hence the frequent warning against the danger of being cheated by plausible speech or deprived of their rights by philosophy and vain deceit. Alone among his extant writings the letter to Philemon is addressed to a private individual on a personal matter. It bespeaks from him a kindly welcome for an unprofitable slave. While an extraordinary freshness and charm make it, in the literary order, a pure gem, it has an enduring value in that it gives an insight into Paul's approach to social and political evil. To this period, also, belonged the preparation of the hieratic dissertation called Hebrews which was later dispatched from Italy.

667a **Release and later Journeyings**—He was released at the end of two years and Spain may have had the benefit of his preaching, if only for a brief space. A visit to the extreme west is recorded in the first-century Epistle of Clement (5:5-7) and St John Chrysostom echoes the tradition in *Epist. ad Hebr. Praef.* From scattered references in the Pastoral Epistles it is possible to fix some of the stopping places in Paul's last missionary tour eastward. At Crete he left Titus behind to set in order what was still defective ; Ephesus was to have the benefit of Timothy's kindly rule. From Macedonia he wrote to these delegates counselling them to be good ministers of Christ Jesus, able to exhort with sound doctrine and to rebuke the gainsayers. He wintered in Nicopolis, sending thence Titus to Dalmatia after his successful work in Crete. On the return, he touched at Troas, remaining some time with Carpus ; at Miletus where Trophimus had to be put ashore on account of illness ; and at Corinth
b where Erastus remained. During the journey to Rome or on arrival there he was rearrested, and the honourable custody of a few years before gave way to imprisonment in one of the city's dungeons where it was none too easy to locate him. The temper of the times had changed so much in Rome that Christians were in mind and spirit like people besieged ; in the press of contemporary events faith alone sustained them. Paul's last surviving letter—to the well-beloved Timothy whom he besought to come to him with all speed—gives us to understand that he is awaiting the end, without that expectation of release which we find in the Epistles of the captivity, but with the quiet assurance that ' there is laid up for me a crown of justice which the Lord the just judge will render to me in that day ' (2 Tim 4:8).
c **Martyrdom**—Tradition has it that he was beheaded at Aquae Salviae, a few miles outside the walls of Rome, and that friends had him buried in a cemetery half-way back to the city. Over the *cella memoriae* erected by an early Pope a Roman Emperor built a vast basilica in the fourth century and we still possess Constantine's laconic epitaph : PAULO APOSTOLO MART. . . .
d **Paul's Relations with the Twelve**—At the same time and in the same city, though by a different method, St Peter suffered martyrdom, and throughout the centuries Rome combines the cult of the two and jealously guards their tombs. It is sometimes alleged

that this posthumous association is not justified by their relations during life and that the Antioch ' incident ' (Gal 2:11-14) is only one of many which might have been recorded. But the ' incident ' creates no difficulty if properly understood. More serious is the charge that Paul, being cast in a different mould, never became quite one with the other Apostles and that, being a Hellenist, he was obviously tempted to introduce pagan conceptions into a Christianity that was still unformed and defenceless. Such a theory is a distortion of the facts. Paul was a Jew by race, ' circumcised the eighth day, of the stock of Israel, of the tribe of Benjamin, an Hebrew of the Hebrews ' (Phil 3:5) and despite the straying of Israel and the misfeasance of her leaders he cherished to the end a strong and tender love for his kinsmen according to the flesh (Rom 9:1-5). And if it is wrong to cut him off from his race and his upbringing, it is pernicious to suggest that he was independent of Christianity in its earliest form. Paul did not differ from the other Apostles in his appreciation and preaching of the Gospel : ' For whether I or they, so we preach : and so you have believed ' (1 Cor 15:11) ; ' And I went up according to revelation and communicated to them the Gospel which I preach among the Gentiles : but apart to them who seemed to be something : lest perhaps I should run or had run in vain ' (Gal 2:2). It would make this section too long to outline the arguments for the view that 1 Thess echoes the rhythms of the primitive catechesis which was a source of the Gospels. The connexion of baptism with the death and resurrection of Christ is taken by many to indicate a ' Hellenizing ' tendency, but the proof that the viewpoint is not exclusively Paul's is that he takes for granted that the symbolism is familiar to the Romans and Colossians, who were not his converts. The evidence of the Epistle to the Romans is decisive, for that Epistle implies the possession by the Romans of the full tradition of Christian teaching, even in regard to abstruse points. This highly didactic document closes with a warning against false teachers who arouse dissensions and set up obstacles ' contrary to the doctrine which you have learned ' (16:17). If, on occasion, as in Gal 2:6-7, Paul uses language which appears to be uncomplimentary to his predecessors in the apostolic office, it behoves us to inquire if this was not occasioned by the employment of their names by Judaizers in the interests of party propaganda and as a drag on the wheels of progress.
Missionary Methods—Paul had an advantage over his fellow Apostles in that he had an early and reliable biographer. Not that Acts is a biography in the strict sense ; it is rather an apologia defending St Paul from the criticisms of his detractors. Its summary character is made clear by a perusal of the Epistles to Corinth, where the author recalls the true circumstances of the apostolic life and wherein ' the word overflows from the fulness of love and contemplation ' : ' For I think that God hath set forth us Apostles, the last, as it were men appointed to death. We are made a spectacle to the world and to angels and to men. We are fools for Christ's sake, but you are wise in Christ : we are weak but you are strong : you are honourable but we without honour. Even unto this hour we both hunger and thirst and are naked and are buffeted and have no fixed abode. And we labour, working with our own hands. We are reviled and we bless. We are persecuted and we suffer it. We are blasphemed and we entreat. We are made as the refuse of this world, the offscouring of all, even until now ' (1 Cor 4:9-13). ' Of the Jews five times did I receive forty stripes save one. Thrice was I beaten with rods : once was I stoned : thrice I suffered shipwreck : a night and a day I was in the depth of the sea ' (2 Cor 11:24-25). Of these humiliating experiences, Luke recalls only a few (Ac 14:18 ; 16:22-23) and of other obstructive influences, he barely preserves an echo. Yet, thanks to him, we are made familiar with the method of evangelization conceived

7g by the master, and catch a glimpse of the genius displayed in its execution. It was Paul's policy to concentrate, after the manner of a general, on strategic points, organize them thoroughly, and make them a base for further operations. He was in the habit of revisiting the scenes of his former labours and when prevented from doing so, kept in touch by letter or by chosen delegates.

h The dispersion of Israel has been looked on in the light of a providential preparation for the Gospel. The synagogues of the Hellenistic world gave him a platform whence he could reach not alone his kinsmen according to the flesh, but also that fringe of the Gentile world which had been attracted to the religion of Yahweh. It is possible to trace in Acts the story of the failure of the Jews to believe, in view of which failure they ought not to have complained when the missionaries turned to the Gentiles : ' To you it behoved us first to speak the word of God : but because you reject it and judge yourselves unworthy of eternal life, behold we turn to the Gentiles ' (Ac 13:46 ; *cf.* 17:5–9 ; 18:6 ; 19:9 ; 28:24–29). While he announced the revelation of the Son of God to all, his message took on different aspects with different audiences. To the Jews, he spoke of the history of salvation, how Israel had been chosen to be the carrier of the Messianic Hope, and how that Hope had been fulfilled in Jesus of Nazareth (Ac 13:16–41). To the Gentiles, he dwelt on the eclipse of religious truth, pointing out the folly of idolatry and its attendant vice, and the necessity of turning in worship to the One True God who in those days had called men to their primal obligations through an accredited representative, his Son Jesus Christ (Ac 14:14–16 ;

i 17:22–31). The teaching is found in more developed form in the Epistles that carry his name and that are sometimes called ' the foundation-documents of Christianity '. While these Epistles were written for a definite purpose and to meet particular needs, it is obvious that they presuppose general instruction. They follow on what he and others had already orally taught, assuming a knowledge of much of which they themselves say little, and in that assumption creating difficulty for commentators. It is essential, therefore, to place them against a background of Church life and in a setting of Christian tradition which was in existence before they were written. A direct appeal to that tradition is made twice in 1 Cor, the first, 11:23, being of peculiar interest, because it shows that the Mass was being said and Holy Communion received for some twenty-five years before the abuses in Corinth provoked this written account of the institution of the Eucharist. We should resist the tendency to regard these letters as systematic formulations of Christian belief, for most of them were occasional, in the sense that they were prompted by, and written with reference to, a particular situation. It is a tribute to the genius of their author that writings so produced should constitute a heritage of perennial

j value. Concerning his status as a writer it ought to be observed that ancient classic literature offers no precise parallel to the Pauline letters, either in structure or in tone. There is a freedom and variety in them that have no ancient analogy except in the letters which the discovery of Egyptian papyri has recently disclosed. Though the style has not been universally admired, owing to its anacolutha and parenthetic interruptions, it carries an impression of power and sincerity that a more polished diction would not secure. An attentive reading of the Pauline ' corpus ' compels the conclusion that the author, while remaining a stranger to the figures and forms of the rhetoricians, was fully alive to the possibilities of the plastic speech of Hellenism. His was a talent remarkable for lyrical utterance combined with an ability, sometimes displayed, to match the graceful order of ideas with a formal beauty of expression.

8a **Fellow-workers**—Paul was careful in the choice of collaborators. It seems, indeed, that loyalty to him

and use of his methods were demanded of all those **668a** in close association. Many-sided men, like Barnabas, did not feel at home with one whom nature had fashioned for the first place. Talented speakers, like Apollo, must have thought it strange to see eloquence set aside in order that the Christian Thing might stand forth for what it was, a ' showing of the Spirit and power ' (1 Cor 2:4). Among those of whose services he constantly availed himself were : the timid and affectionate Timothy, his ' truly-beloved son ' : Titus, a stronger character, highly valued because ready for every kind of work : Silas, of whom we know little beyond the circumstance that he shared with his leader the double privilege of Jewish blood and Roman citizenship : and Luke, the ' beloved physician ', who shielded the master from criticism. These men, whatever their natural talents, became under inspiring leadership lieutenants of very high quality. Trained under his eye and profiting by his example they were able to extend his work and, if need be, to take his place. It is interesting to notice in connexion with these fellow-workers that some of them, if not all, were the converts of other men, and this confirms Paul's strong unity with those who went before.

Character and Genius—However much we admire the **b** impetus given to early Christianity by the missionary labours of St Paul, it would be unjust to allow the greatness of the work to obscure for us the character of the worker. St John Chrysostom, having commented on the Pauline writings with a mastery and an eloquence that have never been surpassed and seldom equalled, composed seven panegyrics on the Apostle. The keynote of Chrysostom's admiration is struck in the opening panegyric where he declares that no tongue is adequate to sound the praises of St Paul. In an enthusiastic passage at the end of the commentary on Romans, he prostrates himself in spirit before the tomb of the Apostle at Rome and eulogizes the remains which guard that city ' more powerfully than tower or rampart ' (in *Epist. ad Rom.*, hom 32 (PG 60, 679)).

No writer in English has written more beautifully **c** about St Paul than J. H. Newman. Under the caption ' St Paul's characteristic gift ', he says : ' To him specially was it given to preach to the world, who knew the world : he subdued the heart, who understood the heart. It was his sympathy that was his means of influence : it was his affectionateness which was his title and instrument of empire '. In virtue of this gift of sympathy the Apostle was able to spread about his person an aura of fragrance and to exercise on his fellows a kind of magnetic attraction : ' For whereas I was free as to all, I made myself the servant of all, that I might gain the more. And I became to the Jews, a Jew, that I might gain the Jews : To them that are under the law, as if I were under the law (whereas myself was not under the law), that I might gain them that were under the law. To them that were without the law, as if I were without the law (whereas I was not without the law of God, but was in the law of Christ), that I might gain them that were without the law. To the weak I became weak, that I might gain the weak. I became all things to all men, that I might save all ' (1 Cor 9:19–22). Human nature, even in its unregenerate state, was an open book to him. Though he had never been a heathen and was no longer a Jew, yet he was a heathen in imagination and a Jew in the history of the past. Scattered throughout his writings there are specimens of the tender affection which his great heart had for all his kind, and what a mixture of admiring love and plaintive denunciation did the thought of his own race inflict upon him ! (Rom 9:1–5).

The consciousness of exalted office—dealing in priestly **d** fashion with the Gospel of God—was to him a personal humiliation, for he realized that he himself was weak and one of the sinful race for whom Christ died : ' But we have this treasure in earthen vessels, that the

668d excellency may be of the power of God and not of us ' (2 Cor 4:7). As a consequence he used his awful apostolic power only at the call of duty, rejoicing to exhibit himself on that footing of human weakness which he shared with his hearers and converts. That is why he found himself in a position to conceive such great love of the brethren. After the pattern of Almighty God and in imitation of Jesus Christ he cherished to a high degree the virtue of compassion, and a character which was impetuous and unyielding by nature became gentle and affectionate under the **e** influence of grace. The affection in which he held his own converts was as tender as it was strong. With the unselfish love of a mother he brought forth the image of Christ in the souls of the Galatians (Gal 4:19) ; with the devoted sympathy of a nurse he cherished the Thessalonians and recaptured the language of infancy in order the better to be understood (1 Thess 2:7) ; with the strong solicitude of a father he exhorted and adjured all to walk worthily of the God who called them to his kingdom (Eph 4:1). How he rejoiced at the orderly array of the Colossians and grieved at the thought of their being cheated and led astray ! (Col 2:4–5). 'His mind ', says Newman, 'was like some instrument of music, harp or viol, the strings of which vibrate, though untouched, by the notes which other instruments give forth '. How he deplored divisions and abhorred enmities in the Christian body ! (1 Cor 1:10–12). These he conceived as an offence against nature, and above all as injurious to the Saviour who died to **f** restore the unity of mankind. Fraternal charity was always in his thoughts, and no man hymned it as well or practised it so assiduously : 'If I speak with the tongues of men and of angels, and have not charity, I am become as sounding brass or a tinkling cymbal. And if I should have prophecy and should know all mysteries and all knowledge, and if I should have all faith, so that I could remove mountains, and have not charity, I am nothing. . . . Charity is patient, is kind ', etc. (1 Cor 13). Christian altruism owes its noblest expression to him : 'Let each esteem others better than himself ; each one not considering the things that are his own, but those that are other men's ' (Phil 2:3–4) ; and Christian humanism its motto : 'For the rest, brethren, whatsoever things are true, whatsoever modest, whatsoever just, whatsoever holy, whatsoever lovely, whatsoever of good fame, if there be any virtue, if any praise of discipline : think on these things ' (Phil 4:8).

669a Such high and noble sentiments flowed spontaneously from St Paul's appreciation of the Christian Mystery. His mind worked by intuition, and he saw more clearly than others the universal efficacy of the redemption. If salvation is for all men, and if in Christ there is neither Jew nor Gentile, it is because the power that works salvation is not the Law of Moses but faith in him who 'was delivered up for our sins and rose again for our justification ' (Rom 4:25). The Law of Moses was holy and just and good, but it was powerless to save. And how unequal to the struggle with sin were those who had nothing but that law to help them Paul explained by a vivid description of the conflict between the higher and the lower self occasioned by the commands of God's positive legislation (Rom **b** 7:14–25). In further setting aside the claims of Jewish propaganda he stressed the primacy of the life of grace over external observances, and showed himself more deeply acquainted with the spirit of the Gospel than many of his contemporaries. Christians, therefore, though freed from the Mosaic Law, were not free from all law, for they were subject to the law of the Spirit and had to keep their minds fixed on the things of the Spirit. The freedom of the sons of God is another intuition which appears constantly in his writings. The death of Christ set men free from the tyranny of sin and the grave, and the Christian lives a new life in union with the Risen Christ. In virtue of that union the Christian gives glad and willing service,

inspired and borne along by the Holy Spirit. The **6** 'slaves of Christ ' are the only men who are truly free, for 'where the Spirit of the Lord is, there is liberty ' (2 Cor 3:17).

'Slave of Christ Jesus ' was the title which he himself **c** loved beyond all others. From the time that his eyes were opened after the blinding experience on the road to Damascus, he saw only Jesus. Henceforth faith in a crucified Lord was the power that charged his energies, the star that shaped his course, the wings that gave him flight. In a striking passage in Colossians, he recalls the primacy of Christ with the object of confirming the teaching given to that Church by Epaphras : 'In whom we have redemption through his blood, the remission of sins ; who is the image of the invisible God, the firstborn of every creature : for in him were all things created in heaven and on earth, visible and invisible, whether thrones, or dominations, or principalities, or powers : all things were created by him and in him. And he is before all, and by him all things consist. And he is the head of the body, the church, who is the beginning, the firstborn from the dead ; that in all things he may hold the primacy. Because in him it hath well pleased the Father that all fullness should dwell ; and through him to reconcile all things to himself, making peace through the blood of his cross, both as to the things that are on earth, and the things that are in heaven ' (Col 1:14–20). What an impression the passage gives **d** of the deep religious life that is centred in Jesus ! Existing before the world of men and of angels, present to his followers from the beginning of this life and their goal in the next, Jesus was the object of Paul's heartfelt praise and undying love :

'Who shall separate me from the love of Christ ? Shall tribulation or distress or famine or nakedness or danger or persecution or the sword ? ' (Rom 8:35).

'For to me, to live is Christ : and to die is gain ' (Phil 1:21).

'With Christ I am nailed to the cross. And I live, now not I ; but Christ liveth in me ' (Gal 2:19–20).

'But God forbid that I should glory, save in the cross of our Lord Jesus Christ, by whom the world is crucified to me and I to the world. . . . From henceforth let no man be troublesome to me ; for I bear the marks of the Lord Jesus in my body ' (Gal 6:14–17).

'If any man love not our Lord Jesus Christ, let him be anathema ' (1 Cor 16:22).

To think so magnificently of Jesus, to be wise with that **e** wisdom which is none other than Jesus and him crucified, to be urged on by an enthusiasm and a personal love for Jesus that still burns and inflames across the centuries : all this was granted to Paul, so much so that the phrase 'in Christ Jesus ' occurs as a refrain in his writings and recapitulates all his thoughts. Old age did not wither nor custom stale the beautiful relationship. From the darkness of a Roman prison he spoke of the light that the Saviour brought, shedding rays of life and immortality through the gospel which he had been appointed to herald (2 Tim 1:10). And though he felt that the end was at hand, he was not put to the blush, because Jesus, to whom he had given his confidence, was no stranger to him, and had the means to keep his pledge safe (2 Tim 1:12). The imagination is busy with the picture of the old man Paul in prison. Did the memories of thirty years of toil in the service of the Lord crowd in upon him ? some painful, appeals unheeded, invitations spurned and grace rejected : others consoling, so many of the same mind, cherishing the same bond of charity, and the peace of God watching over their hearts and minds in Christ Jesus. One thing is certain : he had fought the good fight, had finished the race, and had redeemed his pledge. He could look forward to the future with calm and serenity: 'The Lord hath delivered me from every evil work : and will preserve me unto his heavenly kingdom, to whom be glory for ever and ever, Amen ' (2 Tim 4, 18).

THE NEW TESTAMENT TEACHING ON
THE SECOND COMING

By E. J. HODOUS, S.J.

Bibliography—M.-J. Lagrange, O.P., *Le Judaïsme avant Jésus-Christ*, Paris 1931[3] ; J. Bonsirven, S.J., *Le Judaïsme Palestinien au Temps de Jésus-Christ*, Paris 1934[2], Vol. 1 ; J. Bonsirven, S.J., *Les Enseignements de Jésus-Christ*, Paris 1946[3], ch 8, 315–55 ; F. Prat, S.J., *The Theology of St Paul*, tr. John L. Stoddard, 2 vol., London 1933 ; C. Lattey, S.J., *St Paul and his Teaching*, London 1930, ch 5, *The Second Coming*, 113–54 ; Billot, *La Parousie*, Paris 1920 ; A. Feuillet, *Le Discours de Jésus sur la ruine du Temple*, RB Vol. 55 (1948) 481–502 ; 56 (1949) 61–92 ; *The Westminster Version of the Sacred Scriptures*, New Testament (London, various dates). General commentaries : *Cursus Sacrae Scripturae* (Paris, various dates) ; *Verbum Salutis* Series, Paris 1927 ; **The Expositor's Greek Testament*, ed. W. Robertson Nicoll, Grand Rapids, Mich., nd ; *Albert Schweitzer, *The Quest of the Historical Jesus*, London, 1926[2] ; *C. H. Dodd, *The Parables of the Kingdom*, London, 1935 ; *The Apostolic Preaching*, London, 1944[2].

That Jesus Christ, the Son of God Incarnate, will come gloriously at the end of the world ' to judge the living and the dead ' is as established a dogma of Catholic Theology as is the dogma that he has already come and has redeemed mankind. To the Catholic exegete the definiteness of these two dogmas is of great help. It limits for him the field of established truth in which to concentrate the energies of his study, and spares him from investigating theories which are clearly condemned as false. His is not the task to deny with Wrede that Jesus was the Messias ; nor to suppose with Wellhausen that Jesus could not determine whether he was or was not the Messias ; nor to ponder with some moderns on just what occasion the Messianic consciousness of Jesus first asserted itself and what psychological phenomena initiated that consciousness. He concerns himself little with the theories of the so-called Eschatological School which in substance maintains that Jesus, who neither was the Messias nor claimed to be such, would become the Christ only in the future when he would found his Kingdom in glory. There are, of course, varying opinions within this school sustained each in their own fashion by Baldensperger, J. Weiss, Loisy, Bousset, Wernle and others. The Catholic scholar, though recognizing what worth they have, will not wholly ally himself with the teachings of Karl Barth who, influenced by Kierkegaard's subjective cognizance of objective reality in preference to an appreciation of historical incidents, would so exaggeratedly impregnate time with Christ that he would ignore if not dissolve the resurrection of the dead, the Second Coming and the historic Judgement of the world into a kind of evolutionary process which is going on today whereby the human race is being resurrected in Christ who is always resurrected and being approved by God's judgement in the fact that Christ has yielded himself to the judgement of God and has taken away all malediction in a constantly flowing stream of reality amongst men. Barth does not seem to sustain that the Second Coming is to be an historical incident (*Karl Barth, *Dogmatics in Outline*, SCM Press, London 1949). *Dr Oscar Cullmann's *Christ and Time* (Westminster Press, Philadelphia 1940), on the other hand, while fundamentally agreeing with Barth's position as to the time-compenetrating meaningfulness

of religious dogma, and the stress on Christocentricity, seems to allow the Second Coming to remain as an historical event to come. It is obvious that the Catholic scholar will agree neither with orthodox Judaism—that the personal Messias is still on his way to establish the Kingdom of Israel—nor with liberal Jews who suppose that the Parousia is the general dispensation of God's Providential Presence in the affairs of mankind. There is indeed much confusion and disagreement in modern non-Catholic thought concerning the Second Coming of Christ. The Catholic is spared much of this confusion.

However the very definiteness of the dogma of the Second Coming may tempt the Catholic exegete to pronounce too readily in favour of the Parousia while he is interpreting texts which are, by the intention of both God and the hagiographer, left objectively obscure. Consequently he may be confused, if not shocked at what seem contradictions to him expecting a clearly enunciated programme of future events where he finds but vague and incompletely revealed truths. Paramount amongst these confusing texts is Christ's Eschatological Discourse over the destruction of Jerusalem Mt 24 ; Mk 13 ; Lk 21.

The Coming in the OT—It is not our purpose here to discuss just which OT prophecies refer strictly to a personal Messias ; but there are indications in the ancient Scriptures which do at least typically imply that he is to come into the world, Arising from Bethlehem Ephrata the Messias will be the ruler of Israel, Mic 5:2, Wonderful, a Counsellor, God the Mighty, the Father of the world to come, the Prince of Peace, Is 9:6. He will come in the clouds of heaven, Dan 7:13, in majesty and glory, Agg 2:8, 10, and yet riding on the foal of an ass, Zach 9:9. He will strike the earth, Is 11:4, and move its foundations, Agg 2:7, for he will manifest wrath and come in judgement, Is 2:4. The day of his arrival will be one of darkness and fire, a terrible day, Jl 2:30, 31 ; Mal 4:1. And again it will be a day of peace, Is 2:4 ; 9:7 ; 11:6–9 ; Os 2:18 ; Agg 2:10, and of sweetness, Jl 3:18, at which men should rejoice, Soph 3:14, 16. It will be a day of light, Is 9:1, 2, 6 ; 11:10, 12, of law, Is 2:3 ; 59:21, of justice, Is 11:4, 5 ; Os 2:19, of wisdom, Is 11:2. Yes, he will be in our midst, Soph 3:17 ; Zach 2:11, to save us ; Jl 2:32 ; Abd 17, 21 ; wash us of sin, Zach 13:1, 2, and care for us as a shepherd, Zach 13:7, and gather a remnant together, Soph 3:13 ; Zach 13:9, and this forever, without end, Is 59:21 ; and yet, shoot of Jesse that he is, Is 11:10, born of a maid, Is 7:14, he will be pierced, Zach 12:10, and Elias will precede him, Mal 4:5, 6.

No prophecy *explicitly* states that he will come to the world twice ; and whatever else the people of the Old Dispensation may have derived from these prophecies, they never concluded that he would establish a purely spiritual kingdom amidst suffering and trial, that he would then depart into heaven to sustain his triumph in the hearts of men through long and laborious centuries, and that finally he would come anew to establish his universal victory at the Parousia.

The Coming and Christ's Contemporaries—Like their forefathers Christ's contemporaries both expected a Messias and were confused about how he would come, how establish his kingdom. Herod the Great, Mt 2:4,

670e John the Baptist, Jn 1:20; Lk 3:15, Andrew, Jn 1:41, the Samaritan woman, Jn 4:25, the very enemies of Jesus, Jn 10:24—all give testimony to that expectation. The perplexities which they harboured with that expectation are also recounted in the NT texts. Some, obviously with Mic 5:2 in mind, thought he was to come from Bethlehem, Jn 7:42, while others contended that ' when the Christ cometh no man knoweth whence he is ', Jn 7:27—an idea implying perhaps that he would appear suddenly in the clouds of heaven or from the sun, as the apocrypha, 4 Esd and the Apoc of Baruch, suggest. There certainly seemed to be a rather common conviction that at his coming, God's Kingdom would be restored to the Jews with material prosperity as well as with spiritual peace, Mt 3:2; Lk 19:11; Mt 20:21, and that the Messias would rule that Kingdom, Mt 2:2; Lk 19:38; Jn 1:49; 6:15.

f **The Coming and Christ's Disciples**—That the disciples of Christ too kept awaiting some such prosperous Messianic Kingdom on earth is manifest throughout the gospel narrative; and only gradually did Christ reveal his plans to them, leaving the while many perplexities to obscure their minds till the day of Pentecost. In what we might call the first phase of his public life he seems to support and foster their expectations. He was manifesting his glory and the disciples believed in him, Jn 2:11, 23, believed that he was the ' king of Israel ', Jn 1:49. He asserts his authority at the first cleansing of the temple : ' Destroy this temple (shrine) and in three days I will raise it up ', Jn 2:19—a challenge, taken at the time, as the boast of a powerful monarch, Jn. 2:22. Miracles, exorcisms, cures of various kinds follow so that ' all men seek thee ', Mk 1:37. He proclaims an exquisite doctrine and outlines a plan of triumph in which the poor, the meek, the afflicted will be liberated from their miseries, in which law will be happily and perfectly fulfilled and the members of the kingdom will be as secure as a house built on rock, Mt 5-7. Those who will not belong to this kingdom will, on the last day of the current age, be cast out into eternal punishment and the loyal adherents of the triumphing King will shine as the sun, Mt 13:41-43. Storms he conquers, the dead he raises to life, Mk 4:39; 5:41, 42, food he increases, Jn 6:11-15, and promises even better bread which will give his followers an endless life in his Kingdom, Jn 6:54-59. At least twice did he send out his disciples to proclaim his Kingdom and shower men with its blessings : ' And going, preach, saying : The kingdom of heaven is at hand. Heal the sick, raise the dead, cleanse the lepers, cast out devils ; freely have you received, freely give ', Mt 10:7, 8; Lk 10:9, 11. If we continue the reading of Mt here, Mt 10:17-23, it is on this occasion that Jesus made the following statement : ' You shall not finish all the cities of Israel till the son of Man come '. All commentators, Catholic and non-Catholic, agree that the coming to which reference is made is puzzling. They fluctuate. Some think that the text means that the Apostles will not cover all of Israel on this mission before Jesus comes to recall them from their work. ' No thorough work can be done till—a universal gospel for humanity has begun to be preached ' is Lutteroth's interpretation cited in the *Exp. Gk Test., while Durand suggests that the destruction of Jerusalem as the first phase of the supreme triumph may be here hinted.

g For about three-fourth's of his public career Christ stressed the blessings of the triumphal Kingdom which he was establishing, and the disciples cherished the thought that their expectations of a victorious Messias were being fulfilled. But ' from that time Jesus began to show to his disciples, that he must go to Jerusalem, and suffer many things from the ancients and scribes and chief priests, and be put to death, and the third day rise again ', Mt 16:21; Mk 8:31. This we may call the second phase of the public life, the phase in which Christ proclaims that his triumphant Kingdom will not be established before his death. Peter and the other disciples are thoroughly shocked at this disappointment

to their hopes, Mt 16:22, 23; Mk 8:32, 33. To confirm their confidence in a triumphing King, Christ is transfigured before them. How gladly would they encamp with this victorious Messias, flanked by Moses to perfect the Judaic religion, and by Elias who was to usher in the new age ' before the coming of the great and dreadful day of the Lord ', Mal 4:5. But what followed upon the vision presented them with the problem of when that victorious reign would begin ; they had to readjust their expectations since these would be fulfilled after the Messias' death—but *when* after his death ?

At the Resurrection ?—Immediately after the vision **h** on the mount Jesus said to his disciples, ' Tell the vision to no man, till the Son of man be risen from the dead '. Would the triumph perhaps begin at the Resurrection ? The disciples ' were questioning together what that should mean : When he shall be risen from the dead '. Now the Pharisees and scribes believed that the dead would rise to the Messianic age, that God's enemies would then be destroyed, and that Elias would usher in the new era. Were the Pharisees right and was this transient appearance of Elias what Malachy had foretold ? Christ answers that the Pharisees are partly right, ' Elias when he shall come shall restore all things '. Yet neither were the Pharisees entirely correct nor were the disciples in imagining that this was the prophesied return of Elias. ' But I say to you that Elias is already come, and they knew him not, but have done unto him whatsoever they had a mind. So also the Son of man shall suffer from them. Then the disciples understood that he had spoken to them of John the Baptist '. (For these various texts, see Mt 17:1-13 ; Mk 9:1-12.) John the Baptist, then, whose work the Pharisees did not recognize, was Elias ushering in the Kingdom ; John died ; Christ too will die ; but he will rise again. His Resurrection, then, will likely inaugurate the new age when all men will rise to share the glory of the King. Indeed the Kingdom of God is close at hand !

Succeeding passages in the gospels corroborate the **i** theory that the disciples misapprehended not only the nature of the Kingdom's triumph but also the occasion on which that triumph would be ultimately disclosed ; the same passages indicate that Christ was gradually revealing more clearly the spiritual nature of the Kingdom without reassuring them what would be the progression and sequence of events by which its spiritual triumph would advance to its complete manifestation. The Apostles were eager to know when the material victory would appear ; Christ insists that the spiritual victory is being won in every event of time. All that he said was true ; yet when applied to the fulfilment of their human aspirations, all that he said was poorly understood.

They were ambitious to be great in the kingdom they anticipated. ' And when they were in the house, Jesus asked them : What did you treat of in the way ? But they held their peace, for in the way they had disputed among themselves which of them should be the greatest ', Mk 9:32, 33. How well too Christ's words in Lk 12:37, speaking of the master's return from a wedding feast, fitted their misconceptions : ' Blessed are those servants, whom the Lord when he cometh, shall find watching. Amen I say to you, that he will gird himself, and make them sit down to meat, and passing will minister unto them '. When Christ tells the Pharisees that ' the kingdom of God cometh not with observation ', that it is ' within you ', that he must first die and then be revealed with the majesty and extensiveness of the lightning flash, Lk 17:20-37 ; when he says to the Apostles, ' Amen I say to you that you who have followed me, in the regeneration, when the Son of man shall sit on the seat of his majesty, you also shall sit on twelve seats judging the twelve tribes of Israel ', Mt 19:28 ; when he told them of a certain nobleman who ' went into a far country, to receive for himself a kingdom, and to return ' (Lk 19:12-27)—they could always stimulate their hopes that when he and the rest

670i of men should arise from the dead the new age of the world would begin ; they could fire their ambitions that they would be head officials in that glorious reign. Not only does the mother of the sons of Zebedee, but James and John themselves, give expression to their expectations : ' Grant to us, that we may sit, one on thy right hand, and the other on thy left hand, in thy glory ', Mk 10:37, ' in thy kingdom ', Mt 20:21.

j Christ's triumphal entry into Jerusalem was that of a conquering king ; and his very words convey the idea that after his death will follow the glory. The final conquest of his enemies will be the last day of the prevailing disorder. ' The hour is come that the Son of man should be glorified. . . . Now is the judgement of the world : now shall the prince of this world be cast out. And I, if I be lifted up from the earth (in the crucifixion) will draw all things to myself. He that despiseth me, and receiveth not my words, hath one that judgeth him ; the word that I have spoken, the same shall judge him in the last day ', Jn 12:23–50. Nor did Christ's Eschatological Discourse dispel the misapprehensions about his Resurrection and the End of the world being coincident. It only added the further misapprehension that the temple's destruction would be the first of the victories signifying that the revivified Messias was beginning his reign in a rejuvenated world.

k Common Catholic Opinion on the Eschatological Discourse—All exegetes find Mt 24, 25 ; Mk 13 ; Lk 21 somewhat distressing to analyze because the gospel accounts seem to fluctuate back and forth between the exposition of Jerusalem's destruction and the Second Coming at the end of time. We shall here summarize the perplexing texts in their sequence and the usual interpretation of those texts.

It is supposed that at least in Mt 24:3 the Apostles asked about two distinct events : ' Tell us when shall these things be (the destruction of the temple) ? And what shall be the sign of thy coming (parousia) and the consummation of the world ? ' Christ answers :

(1) Watch before each event, Mt 24:4 ; Mk 13:5 ; Lk 21:8.

(2) False christs, wars, opposition between nations and kingdoms, earthquakes, famines, terrors and great signs from heaven will be the beginnings of sorrows, Mt 24:5–8 ; Mk 13:6–8 ; Lk 21:8–11. Comment : These occurrences are harbingers certainly of the Parousia, but probably, in a minor degree, of the temple's ruin.

(3) Before ' all these things ' you will be persecuted ; but whoever perseveres to the end will be saved, Lk 21:12, 13 ; Mt 24:9–13. Comment : Before the harbingers mentioned above you will be persecuted, and he who perseveres to the end of his life, or to the end of the persecutions will be saved.

l (4) The gospel must be preached to all nations, and then will come the end, Mt 24:14. Comment : This is a transitional sentence introducing the change of theme from the end of the world to Jerusalem's destruction. When the gospel has begun to be preached to all nations Jerusalem will be destroyed ; and when it has been preached to all, the end of the world will come.

(5) The abomination of desolation will indicate the end of Jerusalem's religious domination, Mt 24:15–21 ; Mk 13:14–19 ; Lk 21:20–24.

(6) For the sake of the elect those dreadful days will be shortened, Mt 24:22 ; Mk 13:20. Comment : The dreadful days pertain first to the siege of Jerusalem ; but since this is a sentence which makes a transition back to the world's destruction, the dreadful days contemplate too the end of the world.

(7) Then beware of false christs. For as lightning comes out of the east and appears even to the west, so shall the coming (parousia) of the Son of man be. Wherever the body shall be, there shall the eagles also be gathered together, Mt 24:23–28 ; Mk 13:21–23. Comment : ' Then ' may mean at the end of the world ; or if translated with the meaning of ' after that ' it signifies after Jerusalem's destruction without specifying how long after. The ' parousia ' is Christ's Second Coming which will be as obvious as the presence of a carcase where birds of prey are wheeling aloft. The carcase in this case may imply the dead and corrupting world. **670 l**

(8) And immediately after the tribulation of those **m** days, Mt 24:29, in those days, Mk 13:19, there shall be signs, Lk 21:25—the sun, moon, stars will be affected and the powers of heaven shaken. Comment : The ' immediately ' probably refers back to Mt 24:22, 23 and the passage is speaking of the end of the world.

(9) And then the sign of the Son of man will appear in heaven. Your redemption is at hand, Mt 24:30, 31 ; Mk 13:26, 27 ; Lk 21:27, 28. Comment : This is the Second Coming.

(10) Even so when you see all these things, know that it is at the door. This generation will not pass away till all these things have been accomplished, Mt 24:33, 34 ; Mk 13:29, 30 ; Lk 21:31, 32. Comment : Authors here are thoroughly divided. All these things may, they maintain, refer to either destruction or to both. If it refers only to the temple's destruction ' generation ' is to be taken literally ; if it refers to the end of the world, ' generation ' is figurative for either the Jewish race or Christ's enemies or his followers.

(11) But of that day and hour no one knows . . . but the Father only. As in the days before the flood . . . even so will the coming (parousia) of the Son of man be, Mt 24:36–39 ; Mk 13:32. Comment : The Second Coming is meant.

(12) Mt 24:40, 41 has here the passage of the two men and two women : one will be taken and the other left. (Lk has it, perhaps in a better context—Lk 17:34, 35). Comment : At the end of the world one will be taken to be rewarded ; the other left for punishment.

(13) That day will come as a snare upon all who dwell on the face of the earth. Watch for you do not know at what hour your Lord will come, Mt 24:42–51 ; Mk 13:33–37 ; Lk 21:34–36. Comment : This is the Second Coming.

(14) Here Mt 24:45–51 ; 25:1–30 has three parables : The Householder, the Virgins, the Talents. Comment : The first probably is explaining the coming at the particular judgement, the second applies probably to the Second Coming, the third may refer to either the particular or the general judgement. (Lk has the parable of the Talents in 19:12–27.)

(15) Mt 25:31–46 is definitely a description of the Last Judgement.

Modern non-Catholic Opinion—Modern non-Catholic **n** opinion has veered away from such strict analysis and adaptation to two distinct incidents. This fact is exemplified by the comments of the Expositor's Greek Testament which we shall use in our summary of non-Catholic thought.

The disciples ' accept the fate predicted for Jerusalem, and now desire to know the when and how ? ' Consequently their question ' took for granted that all three things (the temple's destruction, the parousia and the completion of the prevailing age) went together ' (pp 288, 289). Christ answers, therefore, in accord with the meaning of the question :

(1) Be watchful ;

(2) False christs etc. will antecede the temple's destruction ;

(3) And before it is destroyed you will be persecuted ;

(4) The gospel must be preached to all nations before the temple's downfall ;

670n (5) The abomination of desolation will be the sign that it will fall ;

(6) But those dreadful days will be shortened for the sake of the elect ;

(7) Then, at Jerusalem's destruction, beware of false christs, for his judgement on that occasion will, like the lightning flash, be clearly manifest, definitive and true ; and when the eagles of the Roman armies gather together over Judaism, it will be a carcase beyond redemption ;

(8) And immediately after Jerusalem's destruction the very powers of heaven will be shaken. Physical imagery here represents social and religious upheavals. Thrones, temples, all God's establishments of the past, will fall in one vast national ruin ;

(9) Then the sign of the Son of man will appear. On what the sign is commentators do not agree ; but the statement as such is not indicative of a physical event so much as a comforting assurance that when Jerusalem falls Christ's victoriousness will manifest itself.

(10) When you see all these things know that Jerusalem's downfall is at hand.

(11) Of when this will happen there is no communicable knowledge, but be comforted, for the victory over Jerusalem will come to the unexpectant Jews as the judgement of the flood came upon the carefree contemporaries of Noe.

(12) In this catastrophe one will succumb and another be spared.

(13) But watch for you know not when the Son of man will come to destroy Jerusalem in judgement.

(14) Lessons of the parables : The Householder—whenever Christ comes in judgement he is as unexpected as the master of a house returning from an expedition ; the Virgins—also refers to any judgement of Christ ; the ' long delay ' in the parable of the Talents teaches that the judging presence of Christ may not manifest itself in punishment for a great period of one's life.

(15) Mt 25:31-46 is a story picturing the fact that Christ is a victorious judge. It is not the prediction of an historical event.

o The modern non-Catholic tendency is to avoid taking this discourse as prophetic of an historic Second Coming.

[In recent years Professor *Dodd has replaced *A. Schweitzer as the leader of the ' eschatological school of Protestant writers ', and his theory of Realized and Futurist Eschatology demands a note.

Professor Dodd argues that the apostolic *Kerygma* asserted a Realized Eschatology, *i.e.* the message of the first days of the Church was that the Last Things (the *Eschata*) are already upon us, that we are living already in the Last Times ; and he goes on to argue that the Futurist Eschatology, the doctrine of the Second Coming of Christ at the end of history, was only put forward, if not invented, later on when the first hopes of the imminence of the final transformation and resurrection had been disappointed.

Now in the former assertion there is indeed a great truth. We *are* really living in the *Eschata*, in the Last Age (*cf.* 1 Jn 2:18), the Kingdom *has* come down upon earth, and the whole life of the Church *is* eschatological. The Mass itself is in a real sense a pledge of the Second Coming. We are already ' come to the heavenly Jerusalem, . . . and to God the judge of all and to the spirits of the Just made perfect ' (Heb 12:22-23). Nevertheless, it is quite false to assert that the Apostolic *Kerygma* did not include the doctrine of the temporal Second Coming of Christ as the central fact which will sum up and conclude this Last Age. For these facts are clearly embedded in Mt 24, 25 ; Ac 17:31 ; 1 Cor 15 ; 1 Thess 4:15-5:11 ; 2 Thess 1:3-2:14, as well as in the constant teaching of the Church. Professor Dodd's view has to ignore the plain fact that sane men like St Paul not only knew that Christ had come but also expected him again historically at some unknown but possibly imminent date in the future.

But a Realized Eschatology that leaves room for the Second Coming is a valuable factor in Christian thought and life, which is in frequent danger of being neglected. There is no doubt that the apostolic *Kerygma* did stress the importance of the Second Coming for the Christian Life. Though it is true that for the first generation of Christians the perspective was confused by the foretold destruction of Jerusalem (itself a Coming of Christ in power), yet for St Paul and for his generation the only thing that mattered for every Christian was readiness to meet Christ at the Last Judgement, *cf.* Introd. to 1 Thess, § 914*g-l*. And it is the same for us today.

There is thus no need to explain away or diminish the force of texts which stress the imminence or importance of the Second Coming and Final Judgement, for this is the one moment of history towards which the life of every Christian must be oriented. The Apostles and the Church neither were themselves deceived nor have they deceived others ; but being in ignorance of the time of the Second Coming of Christ in Judgement they constantly directed the faithful (as the Church still does) to the precept of Christ : Wherefore be you also ready, because at what hour you know not the Son of Man will come (Mt 24:44)—Gen. Ed.]

A Proposed Solution—No Catholic can ignore the **67** Second Coming of Christ (*cf.* Tridentine Profession of Faith, DB 994 ; response of Bib. Comm., June 18, 1915, DB 2179 sqq.) ; no Catholic can doubt that some of the details mentioned by Christ in this discourse will be fulfilled at this Second Coming. But no exegete should make little of the fact that here as indeed in all his teaching, Christ's chief concern is not to stress the moment of temporal occurrences, but rather to emphasize the spiritual meaning of all events in history and to encourage men to live out that meaning when the various events take place. He does not state when Jerusalem will be destroyed nor when the present age of the world will end ; he does reveal that the destruction of Jerusalem and all other historic events signify that he is conquering the world by the fact that he is present in it—Christ is triumphing while all history rolls on to the glorious manifestation of that triumph in the Messianic Age. Since his victoriousness preeminently began with his death and resurrection and since he did not explain to his followers that he would first ascend into heaven and then return to proclaim his triumph, they sustained the hope that onward from the time he and mankind arose again, he would, while present with them, expand his Kingdom, conquer his enemies and majestically proclaim himself Lord of all on earth forever.

b Because the expression ' all these things ' occurs several times in this context, it is well to consider what the expression meant to the Apostles. ' All these things ' should mean, everything as it is. To the Jew it meant not only the entire pile of masonry, all the paraphernalia of the temple—the altars, the shewbreads, the incense, the various courts, the vestments of the priests, the veil before the Holy of Holies, the sacrifices ; but it also meant the whole Providential economy of Jahweh over his people and man's proper response to that economy—a religious response expressed openly by this material establishment which God himself had ordained. ' All these things ' meant religion, life lived in the service of God in the arrangement of things during the current age. It was so easy for the Apostles to hope that the Messianic Kingdom with its new life would arise when all these things fell. Upon the collapse of Judaism must come the triumph of the Messianic King.

When, therefore, Christ told them that the temple would be completely destroyed, they asked two questions about what they thought would be one event : When will Judaism collapse and what special indication

b will there be to show us that the close of the age is the beginning of your triumph ? ' Tell us when shall these things be ? And what shall be the sign of thy coming (παρουσία — presence) and of the consummation (συντέλεια) of the world (τοῦ αἰῶνος—of the age) ? ', Mt 24:3. ' And what shall be the sign when all these things shall begin to be fulfilled ? ', Mk 13:4 ; Lk 21:7. Christ's discourse follows :

c (1) Let us under all circumstances watch.
(2) Here are the circumstances which will arise throughout history, one phase of that history being the temple's destruction : wars, opposition between nations and kingdoms, earthquakes, famines, terrors and great signs from heaven. (For these events at the siege of Jerusalem, see Josephus, *Ant.* 20, 8 ; *Wars*, 6, 5.)
(3) Before ' all these things '—all the existing economy is ended—before not only Jerusalem's destruction but also before the whole mode of life which prevails today is destroyed, you will be persecuted. He who perseveres to the end of the persecutions and trials or dies in them will be saved, will have the security of my Kingdom.
(4) After the gospel is preached to all nations the end of the world's domination will come, and I shall reign triumphant. In the process of triumphing and spreading the gospel you will be hated by all but God will always provide for you.
(5) The abomination of desolation will be the sign of triumph over Jerusalem.
(6) That my faithful followers may continue the triumph, the destruction wrought upon Jerusalem will not become universal ; the days will be shortened and human affairs will become normal again.
(7) Then, when Jerusalem has been destroyed and a state of normalcy and quiet triumphing has ensued in men's affairs do not be led astray by any false christs no matter what wonders they perform, because my triumphing presence will always be as widely and obviously manifest as the lightning flash is across the sky. Wherever the world's enmity against me has died there will lofty souls be gathered together to celebrate the victory.
d (8) And as soon as those days in which I was winning the victory amidst oppression are over the cataclysm of the world will follow.
(9) At the time of this cataclysm which spells the end of the prevailing age, the sign of the Son of man will appear. He will assert himself as glorious judge. Then the fact that you have been redeemed from the slavery of this world into the household and kingdom of God will be magnificently manifest.
(10) And in a manner similar to the sprouting of the fig tree all these things which I have been telling you portend my success—it is near, even at the door. By success, here—the ' it '—Christ does not mean necessarily the final manifestation of the victory but rather the progressive winning of it. Therefore when you see Jerusalem destroyed, when you endure persecutions, when the gospel is being spread and earthquakes and famines prevail—recognize that I am advancing the victory. And when the final cataclysm ends this age, appreciate that I have won. All history has this one meaning : Christ triumphs. This generation, mankind, will not pass by without experiencing that I am victorious in all the upheavals of time. Heaven and earth are passing arrangements ; what I am teaching you will not pass away.
(11) But out of the day and hour when all these various victorious incidents will occur, no one has communicable knowledge ; that is not to be revealed beforehand. And as ordinary as were the days when Noe was working with God, preparing to save his family, so will my Presence keep pro-

ducing its effects amidst the ordinary affairs of **671d** human life ; and as in the days preceding the flood, so men will continue the ordinary course of their worldly lives without acknowledging that my Presence is within the world quietly effecting its victory toward the final manifestation.
(12) While it is so progressing here are some examples **e** of how quietly it works : of two men in a field one welcomes my Presence to himself, and one keeps himself free of it (παραλαμβάνεται and ἀφίεται are probably middle, not passive voice). Similarly the case of two women.
(13) Lk 21:34—Take care not to have your hearts overcharged with drunkenness and the cares of this life lest that day—the period in which I am quietly effecting my victory—catch you off-guard ; that you may be able to keep your stance facing the Son of man. Keep awake, therefore, because you do not know under what circumstances your Lord keeps coming along the pathway to his victory. Like a householder on guard against a thief, however he may come, be you watchful that if I come suddenly to inquire whether you are striving victoriously with me, you may be ready to assure me that you are doing your part. Mk 13:33–37—The reference here is likely to Christ's coming at death to the individual.
(14) The parables of the Householder, of the Virgins and of the Talents are best explained if they are taken not to refer primarily to the Second Coming because in each parable there are significant details which cannot be verified at the end of the world. The ' coming ' spoken of in the parable of the Talents likely refers to some crises in history, like the Reformation, when Christ multiplied the supernatural gifts in his saints to increase their beneficent influence whilst others who had not used the grace he had given them lost it.
(15) And whenever the Son of man finally reaches the majestic celebration of his triumph amidst the angels, when he is finally enthroned as victorious King of all mankind in history, then he will judge all men of all nations ; and those who have co-operated in his campaign will inherit citizenship in the glorious Kingdom. Whatever was done in favour of or against others was done to him because throughout history he was always present amidst the affairs of men, Mt 25:31–46. Those who were dissident will not share the endless life of happiness in his Kingdom.

In this long discourse Christ only partially answered **f** the problems which were bothering the disciples. He did say that Jerusalem's destruction would be but the beginning of a period of suffering and struggle during which every disintegration of hostile power would be the sign of his continuing conquest, enduring till the glory of his Kingdom would be completely manifested. He did not tell them at what time relative to his resurrection the triumph would come. They still hoped that it would be when he and mankind arose from the dead.
Christ's Subsequent Revelations—Nor did any subse- **g** quent statement of his make that point clear. Everything he said and did left open the possibility of their prejudiced hopes. We may paraphrase thus :
' I shall not eat the pasch again until it be celebrated in its completed form in the Kingdom of God, nor drink of the fruit of the vine until I drink it fresh when the Kingdom flourishes ', Lk 22:15–18 ; Mt 26:29 ; Mk 14:25.
' I am now giving you my blood which is being shed. It is the blood of the new kind of Dispensation. I am disposing my Kingdom to you that you may enjoy its blessings and govern the whole of Israel. Now (when my death is impending) I am beginning to be glorified, and God will glorify me at once ', Lk 22:20, 29 ; Mt 26:27 ; Mk 14:24 ; Jn 13:31, 32.

671g ' From heaven (after my death) I shall send you the Advocate of truth to help you carry on. I keep coming to you, too ; not the world but you will keep seeing that I am living and you will keep living. You will know in the day while the triumphing is in process that the Father, I and you are in one another. Indeed if anyone love me in this wise I shall keep manifesting myself to him ; he will know of my triumphing presence. Hence I am leaving peace, a harmony of order, with you. I am on my way to my Father and yet I keep coming to you as victor ; you really should be glad that I am going to my Father. I told you this that when we are so advancing victoriously you may believe that everything was planned by me just as it occurs ', Jn 14:1–31.

h ' As the branches grow by the strength of the vine, so you will fructify by my power because I am the vine. Your abiding in me and bringing forth fruit is the glorification of the Father and your joy ', Jn 15:1–11.

' It is expedient for me to depart in death so that the Spirit of Truth come to help you to glorify me ', Jn 16:7–15. Now the disciples ask what Christ means when he says, ' A little while and you will not see me ; and again a little while and you will see me '. They can understand by the first ' little while ' that he is soon to die ; but the second ' little while ' after which they will see him puzzles them. Hitherto the Apostles seem to have taken the three days between Christ's Death and Resurrection in a figurative sense to represent a period of time, an age of the world, an economy of things, as ' day ' is frequently taken in the NT (*e.g.* Mt 26:29 ; Lk 1:80 ; 6:23 ; Jn 8:56 ; 2 Cor 6:2 ; Eph 4:30 ; 1 Thess 5:5,8 ; Heb 3:8 ; 4:7–9 etc.). Was Christ here indicating that the time between his death and resurrection was to be literally three days ? They ask him what he means by that ' little while '— and he answers merely that when he returns they will rejoice. He did not tell them that his resurrection would take place after three days, to be taken literally, that it would not be contemporaneous with the time when all men would rise from the dead. Indeed the fact that the disciples did not believe that he arose literally on the third until they had actually seen him, seems to indicate that they continued to consider the three days figuratively since he did not now tell them what he meant by the ' little while '. The disciples admit on this occasion of the Last Supper that Jesus is clear on one point—namely, that he comes from God, and is returning to him—and to this Christ adds, ' Have confidence, I have overcome the world ', Jn 16:16–33.

i Nor does the last prayer of Jesus explicitly inform them of his ascension and Second Coming : Begin glorifying thy Son, O Father, and keep glorifying him by his success in winning over humanity while he reigns in heaven. These men have understood that I came forth from thee and they have believed that I am thy Messias even though I came otherwise than as they had expected. I do not ask that thou lift them out of the world into some sort of glorious kingdom, but that thou sanctify them in truth in the midst of the world as it is. Let them thus carry on the victory, until it is won. I pray that all believers may share my glory—the unity of love binding thee, Father, and me into one ; may they share that love with us, Jn 17:1–26.

Nothing which occurs or which he says before his death tends to dissuade the disciples that their preconceptions of the Kingdom are wrong. Christ says, in Mt 26:32, that after he is risen again he will go before them into Galilee—but he does not assure them that his resurrection would antedate the new age when all men would be risen from the dead. In Mt 26:64 and Lk 22:69 Jesus asserts before the high-priest and the council that he will come in glory hereafter—but hereafter might be at his resurrection. Before Pilate he explains that his Kingdom is not of this world— which could mean that it is unlike any kingdom which now flourishes ; a Kingdom, that is, characterized by truth, Jn 18:36, 37. Indeed that perplexing text inserted in the narrative at the time of Jesus' death,

Mt 27:52, 53 : ' And the graves were opened : and **6** many bodies of the saints that had slept arose : and coming out of the tombs after his resurrection, they came into the holy city, and appeared to many ' may be indicative of the satisfaction which the disciples derived when they saw that their expectations were not entirely unfulfilled. What their hopes had been and how completely those hopes had been frustrated by the fact that the Body of Christ seemed to have been lost, is expressed by the disciples on the way to Emmaus before they acknowledged that Jesus had risen : ' But we hoped that it was he that should have redeemed Israel : and now besides all this today is the third day since these things were done '—and even his Body is gone, Lk 24:21–24. The only comfort they got from Christ's response was that Christ ought to have suffered these things and so begun his glorious reign, Lk 24:26.

After Christ's Resurrection—Once the resurrection **j** became a proved reality to the disciples and as the resurrection of mankind had not yet taken place, they had to make a new adjustment in their expectations : he would now establish the flourishing Kingdom amidst unresurrected mankind. What he told Magdalene : ' I am not yet ascended to my Father. But go to my brethren, and say to them : I ascend to my Father and to your Father, to my God and your God ', Jn 20:17— that statement seemed to imply that he would establish his triumphant reign on earth now after his resurrection and only then return to his Father.

Again, that important meeting in Galilee of which he had spoken before his death, Mt 26:32 ; Mk 14:28, which the angel had announced to the holy women at the tomb, Mt 28:7, with the request that Peter be present at the meeting, Mk 16:7, the assembly which Jesus himself had planned when he appeared to the women—was not that to be the formal inauguration of his Kingly reign on earth ? In a sense it was such an inauguration—but not quite in the sense which the Apostles had anticipated. He said that Peter would be led captive and die. (As to his words about John's fate, see commentary on Jn 21:22.)

Yet their experiences in Galilee did somewhat con- **k** firm the disciples in their hopes of Israel's proximate restoration. Though some at first hesitated to pay him the homage of the Messias King setting out on his triumphant march, nevertheless he assured them that such he was : ' All power is given to me in heaven and in earth. Going, therefore, teach ye all nations . . . teaching them to observe all things whatsoever I have commanded you ; and behold I am with you all days even to the consummation of the world '—the Gk of which (ἕως τῆς συντελείας τοῦ αἰῶνος) rather conveys this idea : until the present age (either which I am inaugurating, or in which we are now living) has realized its destiny of perfection, Mt 28:18–20. Mk 16:15–18 explains the security and characteristics of the age now beginning : devils will be cast out, new tongues spoken, serpents and poison will cause no hurt, and the sick will get well. Shortly before this incident Jesus at Emmaus explained that all that had happened to him up to the present happened according to the plan of his campaign : ' Thus it is written, and thus it behoved Christ to suffer and to rise again from the dead the third day '. The future plan was that the disciples should preach and extend the power of his reign the world over, once they were endued with power from on high, Lk 24:46–49. Eager to have their hopes soon fulfilled, the disciples at the Ascension asked him : ' Lord, wilt thou at this time restore again the kingdom of Israel ? ' And Jesus responded that that secret they were not to know, Ac 1:6–7.

What continued faith these men had sustained in the **l** Messias amidst many disappointments ! They had first expected the kingdom of Israel to be restored to its glory by him when Jesus began his teaching career. He revealed that he must die, but will rise again on the third day. They trusted this new revelation but misunderstood its true significance. The first age of the Messias having closed with his death, a second period would ensue, a time for them of struggle and suffering while he was reigning from heaven. The downfall of Jerusalem would be the beginning of the second period during which the battle for certain victory would be won. And then (they thought) the third stage, Christ's third day, when he and all mankind would rise from the dead and he would proclaim his triumph in the glorious kingdom on earth. But he rose literally on the third day and not all mankind rose with him. With unfailing trust they made their readjustments. Now the risen Christ would establish himself gloriously on his throne amidst unresuscitated mankind. But he departs from them into heaven and they are stunned. Then the last revelation about his victory is made : ' This Jesus who is taken up from you into heaven shall so come as you have seen him going into heaven ', Ac 1:1-11. Now the plan is clear, the meaning of redemption unfolded. There will be a **Second Coming** which will usher in not a material Israel but **the restored spiritual Kingdom of God.** This is the eternal glorious Kingdom of Heaven which the Messias has been promising and which he opened up to his followers by his teaching, his life, his death, his resurrection, his ascension. This now is the completely revealed truth which they must teach. Mankind must prepare for the Second Coming at the end of time, when Jesus will come to judge the living and the dead.

The Apostles explain—This truth concerning the Second Coming of Christ, clarified and developed through the years by contemplation and progressive divine revelation, the Apostles shared with their followers, making it for posterity a prime topic of the Church's deposit of faith. Peter and Paul and James and Jude and John in their writings often refer to it—sometimes explain its details, 1 Cor 1:8 ; 2 Cor 1:14 ; Phil 1:6 ; 2:16 ; Col 3:4 ; 1 Thess 1:10 ; 2:19 ; 2 Tim 1:12, 18 ; Tit 2:13 ; Heb 10:25 ; Jude 1:14, 15 ; 1 Pet 1:5, 7 ; 4:13 ; 5:4, 6 ; 1 Jn 2:28 ; 3:2 ; Apoc 16:14. We do well to study what they say. **When?**—At the close of the last age of the world, the Messias, they taught, will come again. The period of Christianity when, as Joel says, ' Your sons and your daughters shall prophesy, and your young men shall see visions, and your old men shall dream dreams ' (Jl 2:28 quoted in Ac 2:17) ; the age when grace shall abound and completed revelation prevail, when men while waiting for the redemption of the body shall enjoy ' the first-fruits of the Spirit ', Rom 8:23, when, sanctified by truth, men shall be some beginning, Jas 1:18, of the creature God ordained them to be ; the time which John figuratively calls a thousand years when the devil shall ' no more seduce the nations ', Apoc 20:3 (in that not heathenism but Christ's principles will flourish amongst the peoples) ; the years between Christ's ministry on earth and the end of the world—this era was considered by the Apostles, in the divine dispensation of the economy of salvation, to be the last age of the world, Gal 4:4 ; Eph 1:10 ; Col 1:26 ; Heb 1:2 ; 1 Pet 1:20 ; 1 Jn 2:18. At its close, after the vicissitudes of time shall have been accomplished ' in the dispensation of the fulness of times ' God will re-establish in Christ all things that are in heaven and on earth, Eph 1:10.

On this occasion the dead will rise and the general judgement take place, Ac 4:2 ; 10:42 ; 17:31, 32 ; 23:6 ; 24:15, 21 ; Rom 2:16 ; 14:10 ; 1 Cor 3:13 ; 4:5 ; Phil 3:11 ; 2 Thess 1:7-10 ; 2 Tim 4:1 ; Heb 6:2 ; 10:27 ; Jas 5:3 ; 1 Pet 4:5 ; 2 Pet 2:9 ; 1 Jn 4:17 ; Jude 1:6, 14.

Not soon—But the Apostles admittedly did not know when this will ensue because the date was never revealed to them, Ac 1:7. St Paul said that that day would come as a thief in the night, unexpectedly, 1 Thess 5:2 ; that apparently it is not close at hand : ' Be not easily moved from your sense . . . as if the day of the Lord were at hand ', 2 Thess 2:2.

And yet there are texts which seem to teach an early advent : ' The time is short ', 1 Cor 7:29 ; ' for yet a little while and a very little while and he that is to

come, will come, and will not delay ', Heb 10:37 ; **671n** ' behold the judge standeth before the door ', Jas 5:9 ; ' I come quickly ', Apoc 3:11 ; 22:7, 12, 20. But when read in their contexts these statements explain themselves.

In 1 Cor 7 Paul is not discussing the Parousia at all. He is answering the Corinthians' question whether celibacy is required for the service of God. Though personally Paul prefers celibacy because of its many advantages, v 8, yet he recognizes that ' the Lord hath distributed to every one ' his individual way of life— ' as God hath called every one, so let him walk ', v 17. Indeed every social or physical condition in life can be a means of serving God—being circumcised or uncircumcised, bond or free, married or single. ' Brethren, let every man, wherein he was called, therein abide with God ', vv 18–25. Now follows a sentence, v 29, to introduce the assurance that sorrow, joy, commercial entanglements, marriage or celibacy, whatever one's lot may be (μεμέρισται in v 33)—all eventualities of life, if properly accepted and employed, can and should help a man (v 35) ' to attend upon the Lord without impediment '. This sentence reads in English ' the time is short ' ; the Gk, however, has ὁ καιρὸς συνεσταλμένος ἐστίν and may be correctly translated as ' the opportunity (of serving God) has been arranged '. Whatever the state and circumstances of one's life, they offer an opportunity arranged by God to help one attend upon the Lord ; they are not an impediment. Clearly in this context St Paul is not teaching the proximity of the Parousia.

The context of Heb 10:37 offers an equally simple **o** solution to the difficulty it seems to engender. The sacrifices which could not delete sin are past ; the one sacrifice of Christ which wiped away sin and makes grace possible to those who believe in him has been offered. ' Let us draw near (to Christ) with a true heart in fulness of faith ', v 22, and ' Do not lose your confidence which hath a great reward ', v 35. To confirm such persevering confidence in his readers, the author of Hebrews stresses the fact that the trials of life and its persecutions are after all brief in comparison with the eternal and assured reward with Christ (cf. 1 Cor 2:9) : For yet a little while, indeed a very little while and he that is to come will come—it really will not be long. It is disputed whether the author is speaking of the shortness of time of an individual's life or of the brevity of history in comparison with the eternity of reward. The point is unimportant ; but telling is the fact that he is not teaching that the Second Coming of Christ is historically close at hand.

Jas 5:9 also gathers its significance from its context. The Apostle is exhorting the poor who are being oppressed by the worthless rich to be patient because ' the coming of the Lord is at hand ', v 8—ἡ παρουσία τοῦ Κυρίου ἤγγικεν—the Lord has come close, abides with you ; and as Judge, he likewise is present with the oppressors, estimating their wickedness : ' Behold the judge standeth before the door '. It is because the ever-watchful eye of Christ is with men that in the gold they unjustly garnered the rich have stored up wrath against the last days, Jas 5:3.

Of the Apocalypse texts, ' I come quickly ', Apoc 3:11 ; 22:7, 12, 20, little need be said. Apocalyptic prophecy is characterized by a lack of chronological perspective ; it stresses rather the supernatural, eternal significance of events, frequently under glaring figurativeness. The ἔρχομαι ταχύ, therefore, is probably emphasizing the prompt eagerness of Christ to bring to accomplishment the eternal meaning of the human history which the treatise has been discussing in variegated forms, but always without consideration of time sequence or time proportions.

ANTECEDENTS OF THE PAROUSIA—No matter **p** how inadequate the explanation of the preceding few texts may seem, a glimpse at the many and great antecedents of the Parousia which the Apostles taught in addition to Christ's predictions, Mt 24:5-12, 29-31,

671p must settle the matter that they cannot have anticipated the end within a brief space of time.

Man of Sin—St Paul, 2 Thess 2:3, 4, tells us that before the last day a revolt must come first ' and the man of sin be revealed, the son of perdition, who opposeth and is lifted up above all that is called God, or that is worshipped, so that he sitteth in the temple of God, showing himself as if he were God '. What this apostasy is and who is the man of sin has been the subject of much dispute (Prat, II, 372). Many commentators favour some outstanding revolt, led by some individual man. That may be correct ; it is unwise, however, to close one's mind to other possible interpretations. Probably St Paul, employing compenetration in his prophecy, is synthesizing into one picture the heresies and all anti-God movements of the ages which Christ had foretold, Mt 24:10–12, 24, even as John seems to have done in Apoc 13. Perhaps St Paul too is epitomizing mankind, drenched with sinful pride and rebellion against God, into one typical heresiarch or atheist. St John certainly seems to have epitomized when he asserted that every spirit which denies Jesus is the spirit of *the* Antichrist ' of whom you have heard that he (or it) cometh and is now already in the world ' (Gk of 1 Jn 4:3). Again he writes (2 Jn 7) : ' Many seducers are gone out into the world, who confess not that Jesus Christ is come in the flesh : this is a seducer and an antichrist ' (but the Gk has ' *the* seducer and the 'Antichrist '). Nor in the Apocalypse does John necessarily individuate the beast, which may be Antichrist, by ascribing to it the number six hundred and sixty-six, the number of a man, Apoc 13:18. Varied and perplexing as the explanations of this number are, it is probable that the digits ' six ' represent the completeness of man's perfection in the natural vegetative, animal, and intellectual order, whereas the digits seven would indicate man's entire perfection including elevation through faith and effective grace into the supernatural state. The rebel, then, would be represented as man highly developed in nature, but so proud of his acquired perfection as to spurn God and substitute himself for God.

q Cosmic Manifestations—Of the cosmic cataclysms which are to precede Christ's Second Coming this may be said : The Apostles were merely reiterating what Joel had prophesied, Ac 2:20, or what Christ had foretold, Mt 24:29 ; Mk 13:24 ; Lk 21:25, when they spoke of the sun's becoming black and the moon's changing into blood and the stars' falling from heaven, Apoc 6:12, 13. Although the sun's darkening may figuratively imply the rejection of God's revelation throughout history, and the moon's becoming blood typify the persecutions of the Church, which, like the moon to the sun, reflects God's revealed light, yet it may be that these physical catastrophes are literally to ensue at the close of time's drama. [Nevertheless it is now generally agreed that these expressions are conventional apocalyptic language descriptive of the cataclysm of Judgement and Renewal at the End, and that we are not to expect their literal fulfilment as historical events !—Gen. Ed.]

The Final Resurrection : How?—Somehow or other the corporeal condition of man will then be spiritualized. St Paul, 1 Cor 15:35–57, describes this transformation in the faithful as follows : As a seed sown in the ground gives up its seminal vitality and is changed and developed into a product with a new kind of life, so too the weak, natural body is laid to rest to corrupt dishonourably as an earthy, mortal substance but will rise celestial, supernaturalized, incorruptible, glorious as a heavenly orb, powerful and immortal.

r Will all die and rise ?—It seems quite clear that not all men will die before the general judgement. The Greek of 1 Cor 15:51–53 makes precisely this point : ' We shall not all asleep (die) but we shall all be changed. . . . For this corruptible body must needs put on incorruption and this mortal body immortality '. 1 Thess 4:15, 16 conveys the same idea, *cf*. WV, III, 221–3 ; Prat, I, 140. Although Heb 9:27 and

Rom 5:12 assert that all men must die, they are merely stating the general principle that everyone is mortal without proclaiming actual death in the case of each individual even under unique circumstances. [The Apostles' Creed confirms the Church's belief that there will be some persons living at the Second Coming in the words : From thence he shall come to judge the living and the dead.—Gen. Ed.]

Will the Wicked rise ?—To this the Apostolic answer is affirmative. Firstly, several texts, Ac 10:42 ; 2 Tim 4:1 ; 1 Pet 4:5, speak of the judgement of ' the living and the dead ' ; and while it is true that these texts may mean the physically living and dead, they do not exclude the notion of the morally good and wicked. The just are said to be alive in Jn 5:24 ; 6:47 ; Rom 6:11, 13 ; 8:6 ; 11:15 ; 2 Cor 2:16 ; 4:10, 11 ; 1 Jn 3:14 ; 5:12, 13, 16 ; and the sinful are said to be dead in Rom 8:6 ; Eph 2:1, 5 ; Col 2:13 ; 1 Tim 5:6 ; 1 Jn 3:14, 15 ; 5:12 ; Apoc 3:1 ; 20:5, 12. Secondly, Jn 5:28, 29 says explicitly : ' And they that have done good things shall come forth unto the resurrection of life ; but they that have done evil, unto the resurrection of judgement '.

The Parousia described—It remains only to find a more detailed description of Christ's Second Coming, if we can gather one from the NT. When ' the kingdom of this world is become our Lord's and his Christ's, and he shall (begin to) reign for ever and ever ', Apoc 11:15, when earth and heaven shall have fled away, Apoc 20:11, when ' time shall be no longer ', Apoc 10:6, and ' the mystery of God shall be finished ', Apoc 10:7—the mystery of the Providential economy of salvation which was Christianity's dispensation of grace and life to men—Christ will come with the souls of ' all his saints ', 1 Thess 3:13, ready to unite themselves to bodies re-formed and ' made like to the body of his glory ', Phil 3:21. He will appear as the ' King of kings and Lord of lords, who only hath immortality, and inhabiteth light inaccessible ', 1 Tim 6:15, 16, ' sitting on the right hand of the power of God and coming in the clouds of heaven ', Mt 26:64. ' And then shall appear the sign of the Son of man in heaven . . . and they [all men] shall see the Son of man coming in the clouds of heaven with much power and majesty. And he shall send his angels with a trumpet and a great voice : and they shall gather together his elect from the four winds, from the farthest parts of the heavens to the utmost bounds of them ', Mt 24:30, 31. He will appear announced ' with the voice of an archangel and with the trumpet of God ', 1 Thess 4:15, and ' in a moment, in the twinkling of an eye, at the last trumpet . . . we shall be changed ', 1 Cor 15:52.

The Trumpet of the Archangel—This picture can be amplified. In the OT trumpets announced the ark of the covenant 2 Kg 6:15 ; 2 Par 5:13, announced the king 4 Kg 11:14 ; 3 Kg 1:34, 39 etc., and the coming of the Lord, Ex 19:16, 19 ; 20:18. They were sounded at festivals, Ps 80:4, proclaimed victory, 2 Par 20:28, expressed joy, 2 Par 23:13, declared grief and destruction, Os 5:8 ; 8:1 ; Jl 2:1 ; Am 3:6 ; Soph 1:16, initiated Day of Atonement, Lev 25:9 ; Is 58:1 ; Jer 4:5 ; Jl 2:15, assembled the people, Num 10:1, 2. It is befitting, then, that a trumpet-call should announce the final coming of the King, should summon mankind—initiating an eternal festival of victory for the just, declaring grief and destruction and endless expiation for the wicked. Fitting too it is that the voice of an archangel should make that proclamation with the trumpet of God. Whoever this high herald may be, he will perform a function similar to that of the precursor of the glorified Messias of whom Mal 4:5 says : ' Behold I will send you Elias the prophet, before the coming of the great and dreadful day of the Lord '—Elias whose second coming John the Baptist prefigured when the Kingdom of God was proclaimed for the first time, Lk 1:17 ; Mt 11:14.

The Sign of the Son of Man—Ancient writers favour the idea that this sign is a luminous cross. We u venture to suggest that the return of Elias, forerunner as he is to be, may be the sign indicating that the Son of man is about to appear.

The Kingdom delivered up—And then after the passing of this world, the only real significance of which is to be a reflection of the Word—' and all things were made through him, and without him was made not a single thing that was made ', Jn 1:3—when the whole world shall have been judged whether it made all things reflect the Word through the mediating grace of Christ who personally linked humanity to divinity in the Incarnation and, as a Mediator, bound the material, passing creation to the unchangeably eternal God—then the marriage of the Lamb will ensue, Apoc 19:7–9, directly to God. St Paul well describes the consummation of Christ's mediatorship by this direct union with God in 1 Cor 15:24, 28 : ' Afterwards the end, when he shall have delivered up the kingdom to God and the Father, when he shall have brought to nought all principality, and power, and virtue. . . . And when all things shall be subdued unto him, then the Son also himself shall be subject unto him that put all things under him, that God may be all in all '

v **The Millennium**—The question may arise : Is this beatific state the thousand years of which Apoc 20 speaks ? Such a deduction is impossible because the period of the Apocalypse is not eternal. Satan is represented as bound for that span of time ; the faithful are to live and reign with Christ as his and God's priests while the rest of the dead live not till the thousand years are finished. This is the first resurrection. But when the thousand years are finished Satan will be loosed and do battle all over the earth. Finally he and his aides will be vanquished and cast into the pool of fire and brimstone.

It is the misunderstanding of this passage of Apoc together with notions gathered from some apocrypha which caused a rather widespread and crude doctrine to originate and even flourish in many Christian communities in the early days of the Church. Urged by the hopes which the Apostles themselves had originally cherished of the restoration on earth of a glorious Messianic Kingdom of Israel, and not having, as had the Apostles at the Ascension and Pentecost, those hopes transformed into an appreciation that Christ's conquest and reign was to be entirely of a spiritual character, men like Cerinthus and his followers of the 1st cent. A.D. envisioned a reign of a thousand years of sense pleasure and earthly happiness. Papias is said to have been a millenarist in this sense and St Irenaeus himself was also infected by similar tenets. Tertullian and the Montanists were exponents of this belief and there are indications of its existence amongst others in both East and West until the age of Jerome and Augustine when millenarianism became patently untenable within the Church.

In these early years its advocates coloured the belief with varying details of their own fancying : some would have it come after six thousand years, equivalent to the six days of creation ; others would have it begin in a less

distant future. Again there were those who would not **671v** insist on a thousand years' duration, while the less imaginative took the number literally. The faithful would participate in its joys and only after it had run its course would the second resurrection of all mankind and the universal judgement take place.

In more recent times some Protestant sects had revived **w** millenarianism in variously modified forms. Amongst these may be mentioned the Anabaptists, Zionists, Mormons and Adventists. At present when religious vagaries abound and apocalyptic ideas flourish some fanatics like Jehovah's Witnesses are tainted with all sorts of chiliastic confusions including a belief in the literal battle of Gog and Magog. The Church completely spurns crass, sensuous millenarianism in all its forms as vacuous speculations nor may a Catholic align himself with any such erroneous movements.

But what is to be said of a kind of ' spiritual millenarianism ? ' The Rev. Raphael Eyzaguirre (Apocalipseos Interpretatio Litteralis, Rome 1911) has recently attempted to revive a modified and spiritual as opposed to an historical and material millenarianism [but his views have failed to find support.—Gen. Ed.].

But Father R. J. Loenertz, O.P. (The Apocalypse of **x** St John, tr. H. J. Carpenter, O.P., New York 1948) has what seems to be a better and more common interpretation of this chapter of Apoc. According to him (pp 134–6) the age of Christianity from its earliest years till the end of the world is the thousand years, when Satan is chained and restrained, working as he does through his dupes but checked by the grace of Christ which is sanctifying mankind (cf. 2 Thess 2:6, 7). This bringing of mankind back to the life of grace is the first resurrection ; the second will be the resurrection of the body at the end of time. ' Towards the end of the Messianic era ', he says, ' in the very last days, the predominance of Evil over Good in the world will be appalling ' (p 135). Then will follow the manifest triumph of Christ at the last judgement and in eternal beatitude.

Conclusion—Throughout the Christian era Christ **y** keeps coming to men in many ways—at the individual's death in the particular judgement, with special graces in the crises of life and of history, in moments when sacraments are received, in the quiet of profound and loving prayer. All this Jesus foretold when he spoke of his coming and lasting presence amongst men. He provided that his followers be consoled with the truth that his constant victoriousness will culminate in a Second Coming. But just as he had only gradually unfolded the divine plans to his Apostles, so he has left many details of the Second Coming still to be revealed to mankind on the last day. ' It is not for you to know the times or the moments, which the Father hath put in his own power ', Ac 1:7. Why does the Messias still keep the glories of his Second Coming partly veiled ? That our faith may grow more firmly rooted in the truths which are revealed ; and, above all, that throughout our lives we may be spiritually on the watch, dominated not by the fear of death so much as by the hope of Life, the hope of the Parousia.

THE 'BRETHREN OF THE LORD'

By S. SHEARER, C.P.

672a Bibliography—Articles in DAFC; DBV; CE; CSAB 3; WV 4; F. Prat, S.J., RSR 17 (1927) 127–38; J. Chapman, O.S.B., JTS 7 (1906) 412–33; A. G. Murray, O.S.B., CR 23 (1943) 351–6; E. F. Sutcliffe, S.J., CR 23 (1943) 494–8; M.-J. Lagrange, OP, *Commentary on St Mark*, 4th ed. 79–93; P. F. Ceuppens, OP, *Mariologia Biblica*, 192–201; *J. B. Lightfoot, *Commentary on Galatians*, Dissertation II; *J. B. Mayor, *Commentary on St James*, Introduction.

b Introduction—Much controversy has arisen over the references to the 'brethren' of our Lord in several passages of the NT (*e.g.* Mt 12:46; Mk 6:3; Jn 7:3; Ac 1:14; 1 Cor 9:5). It is the purpose of this article to show, in the light of Scripture and tradition, that these 'brethren' of our Lord were not his full brothers, sons of Mary and Joseph, nor even his half-brothers, sons of Joseph by a former marriage, but at the most his cousins.

The word **brother** is used in a very wide sense in Sacred Scripture. When applied to relations, it is not restricted to meaning brother german or half-brother, but is also used of a nephew or cousin. Thus Lot is described as the 'brother' of his uncle Abraham (Gen 14:14) and Jacob as the 'brother' of his uncle Laban (Gen 29:15). The sons of Cis are described as the 'brethren' of their cousins, the daughters of Eleazar (1 Par 23:21–2). When 4 Kg 10:13 speaks of forty-two 'brethren' of king Ochozias, it would seem to embrace more remote degrees of kindred. The reason for this ambiguous usage lies in the fact that neither Hebrew nor Aramaic had a special word to signify 'cousin'; they either used the word 'āḥ (brother) or a circumlocution such as 'son of (paternal) uncle' or 'son of the brother of the mother'. Hence to avoid excessive clumsiness the word 'brethren' was indispensable for denoting a group of cousins of different origin.

c The NT writers, schooled in the primitive Aramaic catechesis, would find it natural, like the authors of LXX, to render the word 'āḥ in all its various meanings by the one Greek word ἀδελφός. It is obvious, therefore, that where this word occurs its meaning must be determined by the context or by other sources in Scripture or tradition. Now there is nothing in the contexts in which the phrase 'brethren of the Lord' is used to make us suppose that it means brothers in the strict sense. On the contrary, such a supposition gives rise to a host of difficulties in other parts of the NT narrative and is quite irreconcilable with the firm tradition of the first four centuries as to the perpetual virginity of our Lady.

d The 'Brethren' are not the Children of Mary—When the angel came to Mary to seek her consent to becoming the mother of Jesus, her first question was: 'How shall this be done, because I know not man?' (Lk 1:34). This has been taken from earliest times as an indication that she had made a vow or at least a firm resolve to preserve lifelong virginity, even in marriage. Even Loisy (*Les Evangiles Synoptiques*, I, 1907, 290) admits the reasonableness of this, the common interpretation, which alone brings out the full meaning of Mary's words.

A careful perusal of the Gospels makes it clear that Mary kept her resolve, having no further children after the virginal birth of Jesus.

In the account of the finding of our Lord in the temple, for example, it appears that at the age of twelve he is her only child (Lk 2:41 ff.). To the inhabitants of Nazareth he is known, seemingly in an exclusive way, as 'the son of Mary' (Mk 6:3). And it is significant that this title is reserved to him alone in the Gospels; though others are referred to as his brethren, they are never referred to as sons of Mary.

Again, the whole attitude of his 'brethren' to our Lord suggests that they are his elders. They give him advice as to how to make his public life a success (Jn 7:3, 4); they seek, for his own benefit, to restrain his activities (Mk 3:21). Such behaviour among Jews is understandable only on the supposition that the 'brethren' of Jesus are senior to him in age. But this necessarily implies that they are not the children of Mary, for Lk 2:7 describes Jesus as her firstborn.

Another strong indication that Jesus is Mary's only son is the fact that when dying on the Cross he entrusted her to the care of St John (Jn 19:26, 27). It is hard to see why he should have made this provision for his Mother if his 'brethren', of whom at least four—James, Joseph, Simon and Jude—were alive at the time, were also her natural sons. As Lightfoot puts it, 'Is it conceivable that our Lord would thus have snapped asunder the most sacred ties of natural affection?'

Two objections drawn from the Gospel accounts of the birth of our Lord have been urged against interpreting the phrase 'brethren of the Lord' in any other than the strict sense. The first is based on a literal translation of Mt 1:25: 'And he (Joseph) knew her not till she brought forth her first born son'. It is argued that the natural inference is that Mary and Joseph afterwards lived together as husband and wife, so that it is their children, the natural fruit of their union, who are known as the 'brethren' of Jesus. Such an interpretation, though in itself possible, is by no means necessary. Many instances could be quoted from Scripture of the use of the word 'until' without any implication as to the future. Thus in 2 Kg 6:23 it is said that 'Michol, the daughter of Saul, had no child until the day of her death'; the implication is not that she had children then or afterwards. Or again, when 1 Mac 5:54 speaks of the Maccabees offering thanksgiving sacrifices 'because not one of them was slain till they had returned in peace' it does not imply that any of them were slain afterwards. Other examples can be found in Gen 8:7, Deut 34:6, Jdt 12:9, etc. All that can be gathered from Mt 1:25, therefore, is that Joseph played no part in the conception of Jesus. KNT is supported by many modern translators (*e.g.* Joüon, Buzy) in rendering the passage simply: 'and he had not known her when she bore a son'.

The second objection concerns the use of the word 'firstborn' in Lk 2:7. Jesus could not be called Mary's firstborn, it is argued, unless other children—his 'brethren'—followed him. But this is to insist on giving the word a meaning which it need not possess, for, in the well-known words of St Jerome, '*primogenitus est non tantum post quem et alii sed ante quem nullus*' (*Contra Helvid. 10*). In Lk as in LXX πρωτότοκος is equivalent to the Hebrew *bᵉḵōr*, which does not imply any relation to younger brothers but is used in an absolute sense for 'that which openeth the womb' (Ex 13:2, Num 3:12, etc). Thus the first male child of a marriage was called the 'firstborn' immediately after its birth, and it retained that name even if it remained the only child. This usage of the word is illustrated in a Greek inscription found in 1922 on a stele at Tell el Yehoudieh in Egypt, and probably dating from shortly before the birth of Christ, which tells of the death of a woman, Arsinoe by name, in bringing her 'firstborn' into the world (cf. Bi 11 [1930] 373–90).

The Scriptural witness to the fact that Jesus is Mary's only son remains, therefore, unshaken. But there is in addition the strikingly unanimous witness of Christian **tradition.** From the very beginning of the Christian era Mary's virginity was recognized in the name universally given to her—the 'Virgin Mary'; so that St Epiphanius could write in the 4th cent. : ' Has there ever been anyone who pronounced the name of holy Mary who would not immediately add, " the Virgin " ? . . . The name of virgin has always been given to her, nor will it ever be changed ; for she remained ever undefiled ' (*Adv. Haer.* 78, 6, PG 42, 705). Any suggestion to the contrary was stigmatized by the early Fathers as ' madness ', ' sacrilege ', ' heresy '.

The tradition of the first four centuries is well brought out in the controversy between St Jerome and Helvidius who, writing about 380, had attacked the perpetual virginity of Mary by asserting that the ' brethren of the Lord ' were sons of Mary and Joseph, born after the virginal conception of Jesus. St Jerome at first refused to reply to a doctrine that was ' novel, wicked and a daring affront to the faith of the whole world ' ; but when he was finally prevailed upon by friends to write his masterly treatise *De Perpetua Virginitate B. Mariae* (PL 23, 193–216) against Helvidius, he was able to show the falsity of the latter's teaching not only by convincing exegetical arguments (some of which have been outlined above) but by an appeal to the testimony of ' Ignatius, Polycarp, Irenaeus, Justin Martyr and all the other learned men going back to Apostolic times ' who had written on the subject. Helvidius claimed the support of two writers—Tertullian and Victorinus of Pettau ; but St Jerome showed that even these were of no avail, for Tertullian was a heretic and Victorinus had been wrongly interpreted. Helvidius was effectively silenced and never ventured a reply. Indeed, little more was heard of his theory, until it was revived in modern times.

The ' Brethren ' are not the Children of St Joseph— In the same way, little more was heard until recent times of the theory of Origen, Clement of Alexandria, St Epiphanius and some other early writers who, in defending the doctrine of the perpetual virginity of our Lady, had maintained that the ' brethren of the Lord ' were our Lord's half-brothers, sons of St Joseph by a former marriage. St Jerome condemned the holders of such a view as ' following the ravings of the apocryphal writings '. One can hardly imagine him speaking thus if the theory were widely held or supported by a well-defined tradition.

Mary, the mother of James and Joseph, was alive at the time of the Passion (cf. Mt 27:56, Lk 24:10). But if James and Joseph are the sons of St Joseph (of which, as St Jerome pointed out, there is no indication in Scripture), we should have to conclude that this Mary was his divorced wife. This, in view of the character of St Joseph as portrayed in the Gospels (' a right-minded man ', Mt 1:19, etc.) is quite unthinkable. It is not surprising, then, that the *sensus Ecclesiae* is certainly that St Joseph preserved perpetual virginity and had no wife except Mary.

It remains to show that **The ' Brethren ' of our Lord were his Cousins.** This has been the view most commonly held since St Jerome's time ; but it must not be thought to have originated with him. The Christians of his day, and he himself, had no doubt that what he taught was the true tradition, which had been inarticulate until the attack on it by Helvidius.

Only four of the ' brethren ' are explicitly named in the Gospels—James, Joseph, Simon and Jude (Mt

13:55 ; Mk 6:3 ; cf. Gal 1:19). Of these, we may **673b** concentrate for the moment on James. In the account given by the Synoptics of the women who were present at the Crucifixion, we learn that his mother was named Mary (Mt 27:56 ; Mk 15:40) ; and it would appear from the obviously parallel account in Jn 19:25 that she is to be identified with Mary (the wife) of Cleophas.

A difficulty urged against this is that elsewhere **c** (Mt 10:3, etc.) James is described as ' (the son) of Alphaeus ' ; how, then, could Mary his mother be wife both of Alphaeus and of Cleophas ? One solution is that she was twice married. The more usual solution, however, is that Alphaeus and Cleophas (or, as the Greek has it, Clopas) are the same person ; the Aramaic name Halphai could have different renderings (just as the French name Louis is rendered in Latin by Ludovicus or Aloysius) ; or Alphaeus could have taken a Greek name closely corresponding to his Jewish name (just as Saul took the name Paul).

It may be regarded as probable, therefore, that **d** James is the son of Mary and Cleophas. Now Mary may well be the sister of our Lady (see Table 1, note), which would make her son the cousin german of our Lord. But in any case, if the witness of Hegesippus, the 2nd cent. historian, is correct, we can trace a relationship between our Lord and James through Cleophas. Eusebius, writing in the 4th cent., quotes a statement of Hegesippus in which Clopas is described as the paternal uncle of our Lord ; this would mean that Cleophas is the brother of St Joseph, and, indeed, Eusebius elsewhere quotes Hegesippus as asserting this (*Hist. Eccl.* 4:22, 4 ; 3:11, 1). James would thus be the nephew of Joseph and cousin of Jesus, Joseph's putative son.

The Relationship of James to Joseph, Simon and Jude— **e** James and Joseph are clearly uterine brothers (Mk

Table 1 **f**

Suggested relationship between our Lord and James through Mary of Cleophas :

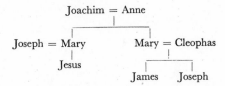

Note—This table is based on the supposition, made by many commentators, that Jn 19:25 identifies our Lady's sister with Mary of Cleophas. Other commentators object that it would be strange, if not impossible, for two children of the same parents to possess the same name, Mary.

Table 2

Suggested relationship between our Lord and James through Cleophas :

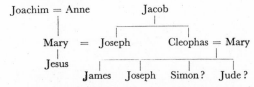

Note—It will be seen that it is not impossible for both Tables 1 and 2 to be correct ; two sisters, Mary the Mother of Jesus and Mary the Mother of James, could have married two brothers, Joseph and Cleophas. There is, of course, the tradition that Mary and Joseph were related before their marriage.

673e 15:40, 47 ; 16:1). The position of Simon and Jude is not so clear. However, they are always named together, next to James in the list of the Apostles and next to James and Joseph in the list of the ' brethren of the Lord ' ; Simon is called by Hegesippus the son of Cleophas (Eusebius, *Hist. Eccl.* 3:11, 1) ; and Jude gives himself the title ' brother of James ' in the first verse of his own epistle (*cf.* also Lk 6:16). It is, then, at least probable that they are full brothers of James and Joseph, having the same parents, Mary and Cleophas, and therefore bearing the same relationship of cousin to our Lord.

If the four outstanding ' brethren ' can thus be shown with great probability to be really cousins of our Lord, it would seem a legitimate inference that the whole *turba* (to use St Jerome's term) of those who are called ' brethren of the Lord ' deserve that name only in a broad sense—they are related to our Lord at the most as cousins.

Such an explanation is the only one which safeguards both the dogma of the perpetual virginity of our Lady and the tradition of the Church as to the perpetual virginity of St Joseph. It is in accord with the Scriptural use of the word ' brethren ', is based on strong Scriptural arguments, and has the great majority of ecclesiastical writers to support it.

(For **673f** see Tables on p 845)

THE CHRONOLOGY OF
NEW TESTAMENT TIMES

By T. CORBISHLEY, S.J.

See table on next page.

Note—Final certainty in this matter is still unattainable. The table on p 848 gives the conclusions which seem most naturally compatible with all the evidence. Certain alternative views preferred by the editors have been added as an Alternative Chronology.

It should be explained that the traditional B.C.–A.D. dating is late and incorrect. It was calculated by the monk Dionysius Exiguus (*c* 520), apparently on a hasty deduction from Lk 3:1 and 3:23. The consequence is that, since he decided that the year of Rome 753 was the year of Our Lord's birth, whereas that event took place some years earlier, we are compelled to make the paradoxical statement that Our Lord was born several years 'B.C.'.

Bibliography—In addition to the works referred to in the course of this article, the following should be mentioned. Holzmeister: *Chronologia Vitae Christi* (Rome, 1933) is a complete handbook to the whole problem of Gospel Chronology. All the ancient sources and all modern works bearing on the subject, with very few exceptions, are listed or referred to there. Most of the discussions on individual points are to be found in the ordinary periodical literature and in the standard commentaries and dictionaries, especially, HDB : Chronology ; DBV(S) 'Chronologie'. The article on *Chronology, Biblical* in the Catholic Encyclopaedia is still valuable in the NT sections. A recent work, *The Chronology of the Public Ministry of Jesus*, by George Ogg, Camb. Univ. Press, 1940, has its value.

A. Pivotal Dates from Secular History

1. The Death of Herod the Great—This took place (Josephus, *Ant.* 17:191 ; *BJ* 1:665) after he had reigned thirty-four years from the death of Antigonus (A.U.C. 717), and thirty-seven from the time when his claim to the throne had been acknowledged by the Triumvirs at Rome (A.U.C. 714) ; therefore his death cannot have been later than A.U.C. 751, and the date 750 seems more probable, in view of the ancient method of addition and subtraction ; this would also square more easily with other chronological indications in Josephus.

2. The Governorship of Pilate—This lasted ten years, and came to an end some months before the death of Tiberius (March 16, A.D. 37), *cf.* Josephus, *Ant.* 18:89. It is not clear whether the beginning of Pilate's period of office falls in A.D. 26 or 27.

3. The 'Fifteenth Year of Tiberius'—Augustus died in August, 14 A.D.. It is true that Tiberius had been associated with him in some vague manner, described by Tacitus as ' collega imperii ' (*Ann.* 1:3), but the scene described in *Ann.* 1:11 suggests that his succession to the imperial power was by no means automatic, and it is generally agreed that, as Fotheringham puts it : ' All our evidence points to one conclusion, that the regnal years of Tiberius throughout the whole Empire were reckoned from his succession to full imperial authority [Sept. 17, A.D. 14], not from his co-regency with Augustus ' (JTS 35 [1934] 150). The most probable view seems to be that the 15th year of Tiberius runs from the autumn of 28 to the autumn of A.D. 29. This would be the normal Roman way of reckoning. Tacitus, *Ann.* 4:1 (' C. Asinio, C. Antistio consulibus nonus Tiberio annus erat ') makes it possible to hold that the 15th year of Tiberius = A.D. 29. On the other hand, in the neighbourhood of Syria, it is possible that the first year of Tiberius = the fraction between his accession in September and October 1, A.D. 14, since the Syrian rulers dated their regnal years generally in this way. Fr Sutcliffe (*A Two-Year Public Ministry*, p 143 f.) accepts this view, and concludes that the 15th year of Tiberius ran from Oct. 1, 27 to Sept. 30, A.D. 28. It may also have run from Nisan 28 to Nisan 29.

4. The Death of Herod Agrippa I—The usual date **d** given for this event is A.D. 44. If that is correct, it must have occurred very early in the year. Josephus (*Ant.* 19:350) says that Herod died in the (54th year of his life and the) 7th of his reign. In *Ant.* 19:351 we are told that the king had reigned for four years under Gaius Caesar. This cannot be four full years, since Gaius himself reigned from March 37 to Jan. 41. Again in *Ant.* 19:343 Josephus tells us that when he died Herod had completed three years as king of all Judaea, and in *Ant.* 19:351 we learn that the king reigned three years under Claudius. Presuming that the same system of reckoning was employed throughout the reign, it seems to follow from all the foregoing evidence that Herod Agrippa's first year ran from his accession in late March or early April, A.D. 37, presumably after Nisan 1, to Nisan 1, A.D. 38. In this way, his fourth year will have run from Nisan 40 to Nisan 41, so that when Gaius died in Jan. 41, Herod Agrippa had completed most of his fourth year. (If we reckoned that his first year ran from his accession to Oct. 1, 37, then, when Gaius died, Herod Agrippa would be well on into his fifth year.) Whether he began a new reckoning on his taking over Judaea in Jan. 41, we cannot tell. If he did, then he would have completed three years at the beginning of Nisan 43, since his first year would run from Jan. to Nisan 1, 41. The ' seven years ' of his whole reign would in that case be about six on our reckoning. But if the calculation was carried right through from the beginning, then his seventh year would be concluded by the beginning of Nisan 44. In any case, then, his death occurred early in 44, if not soon after Nisan 1, A.D. 43. (*Prima facie*, Ac 12:3 ff. suggests that the death of Herod Agrippa occurred soon after the Passover ; but the διέτριβεν of 12:19 may imply an indefinite length of time.) (Traditionally, of course, the imprisonment of Peter is ascribed to A.D. 42.)

5. The Famine under Claudius—Cassius Dio (60:10, **e** 11) tells us that there was a serious famine in Rome in A.D. 42. Josephus refers to a famine in Judaea at some period in the procuratorship of Fadus and/or that of Alexander. Niese reads ἐπὶ τούτου which would make the famine fall under Alexander, who succeeded Fadus apparently in A.D. 46. But the MSS read ἐπὶ τούτοις, which was apparently read by Eusebius and Cassiodorus. Niese, presumably on grammatical grounds, prefers the reading of the 10th cent. Epitome. If we restore ἐπὶ τούτοις we may suppose the famine to have begun in Judaea under Fadus, who became procurator on the death of Herod Agrippa I, in A.D. 43 or 44.

6. The Proconsulship of Gallio—An inscription exists **f** which makes it certain that there was a Gallio govern-

	Events of Secular History		Events of Sacred History		Alternative Chronology
A.U.C.		B.C.			
714	Herod the Great recognised at Rome by the Triumvirs	40			
717	(Oct.) Herod takes Jerusalem	37			
742	P. Sulpicius Quirinius consul	12			
744	P. Sulpicius Quirinius, governor of Syria	10			
746	Sentius Saturninus, governor of Syria	8	Nativity of Jesus Christ		
748	P. Quinctilius Varus, governor of Syria	6	Flight into Egypt		
750	Death of Herod the Great : Archelaus succeeds him in Judaea : Herod Antipas becomes tetrarch of Galilee	4	Return from Egypt		
		A.D.			
759	Archelaus deposed : Judaea becomes a Roman province under procurators. Quirinius, as governor of Syria a second time, holds census of Judaea	6	Christ, at the age of 12, goes up to Jerusalem with his parents		
767	(Sept.) Tiberius succeeds Augustus	14			
780	Pontius Pilate, procurator of Judaea	27		27	(autumn) St John Baptist begins his ministry
781		28	(or early 29) St John Baptist begins his mission	28	(Jan.) Christ is baptized First Passover of Public Life Cleansing of the Temple
782	Coss. C. Fufius Geminus, L. Rubellius Geminus	29	Christ is baptized	29	Second Passover of Public Life (cf. Jn 6)
783		30	First Passover of Public Life	30	(7 April) The Crucifixion
784		31	Second Passover of Public Life	31–32	Martyrdom of Stephen Conversion of Paul
785		32	Third Passover of Public Life	32 ?	Paul in Arabia
786		33	(3 April) Crucifixion	33–34?	Paul returns to Damascus
787	Herod the tetrarch at war with Aretas IV of Nabataea	34	Martyrdom of Stephen : Conversion of Paul	34	Escapes from Damascus
788		35	Paul in Arabia	35	? Conversion of Cornelius
789		36	Paul returns to Damascus		
790	End of Pilate's term of office : Tiberius dies : Herod Agrippa I becomes king of Trachonitis, etc.	37	Escapes from Damascus First visit to Jerusalem	37 ?	Paul brought from Tarsus to Antioch
791		38			
792	Deposition of Herod the tetrarch	39			
793		40	? Conversion of Cornelius		
794	Claudius emperor : Herod Agrippa I, king of Judaea	41			
795	Famine at Rome	42	Paul brought from Tarsus to Antioch	42	Peter in prison (Ac 12)
796	Death of Herod Agrippa I	43	Peter in prison		
797	Fadus, procurator of Judaea	44	Paul's 'Famine Relief visit' to Jerusalem (?)		
798	Famine in Judaea	45			
799	Alexander, procurator of Judaea	46		46–47	'Famine Relief visit' to Jerusalem (Ac 11:30)
800		47			
801	Cumanus, procurator of Judaea	48			
802		49	'Council of Jerusalem' : Paul's third visit		
803		50	(spring) Paul arrives in Corinth		
804	Gallio, proconsul of Achaia	51	(autumn) Paul before Gallio		
805	Felix, procurator of Judaea	52			
806		53			
807	Nero succeeds Claudius	54			
808		55			
809		56			
810		57	Paul's first captivity—Jerusalem and Caesarea		
811		58			
812	Festus, procurator of Judaea	59	Voyage to Rome begun : winter in Malta		
813		60	Paul arrives in Rome		
814		61			
815	Albinus, procurator of Judaea	62	Paul released		
816		63			
817	Gessius Florus, procurator of Judaea : Great Fire at Rome	64	Christians persecuted at Rome		
818		65			
819	Jewish War begins	66			
820		67	Martyrdom of SS Peter and Paul (?)		
821	Death of Nero	68			
822		69			
823	Jerusalem captured by Titus	70			

ing Achaia in A.D. 52. (It is impossible to discuss it briefly, but a full account is to be found in *The Beginnings of Christianity* by F. Jackson and K. Lake, Vol V, note xxxiv.) The more probable conclusion is that Gallio entered on his term of office in the summer of A.D. 51, the normal term being one year.

B. The Chronological Indications given in the NT Documents

1. The Birth of Christ—We know that this occurred before the death of Herod the Great, *i.e.* before 750 A.U.C. A more precise dating depends upon the view we take of Lk 2:2. Lagrange (*ad loc.*) holds that Lk is here distinguishing the census connected with the Nativity from the one which we know to have taken place in 759 A.U.C. (= A.D. 6), when, on the deposition of Archelaus, Judaea was turned into a Roman province. (This latter census is the one referred to in Ac 5:37 ; *cf.* Josephus, *Ant.* 18:1 ff.) Lagrange's argument is that we must take πρώτη in Lk 2:2 as having a comparative force. This is possible Greek, and if we accept that rendering then the passage ceases to have value for any chronological argument. I have argued elsewhere (*Klio* 27 (1934) pp 122–48) for the view that P. Sulpicius Quirinius (= 'Cyrinus' of Vg) was governor of Syria from 743–46 A.U.C. There remains the odd fact that Tertullian (*Adv. Marcionem* 4:19) connects the Nativity census with the name of Sentius Saturninus, governor of Syria from 746 (?)–48. The most natural interpretation of all the evidence seems to be that Our Lord was born in the year shared by Quirinius and Saturninus, his successor, *viz.* 746 A.U.C. (= 8 B.C.).

2. The Duration of the Public Ministry—The interminable discussions on this topic suggest that finality cannot be attained by the internal evidence of the Gospels themselves. In default of such conclusive evidence it seems more satisfactory to try to establish the *termini a quo* and *ad quem*. The *terminus a quo* is, of course, the fifteenth year of Tiberius, discussed above. *The terminus ad quem* is the Crucifixion. Now, according to Fotheringham's well-known article (JTS 12 [1910–11] 120), the only possible years for the Crucifixion during the whole period of Pilate's government are A.D. 30 and 33. The argument is based on astronomical considerations, showing that it is only in these two years that Nisan 14 can have fallen on Friday. As between the years 30 and 33, the following seem to be the deciding factors.

(*a*) The earliest date at which John the Baptist can have begun his preaching, even if we take the minimum interpretation of the 15th year of Tiberius, is the spring of A.D. 28. It will therefore be impossible to fit the Baptism of Christ and the Forty Days' Fast in before the Passover of that year. Therefore the earliest date for the First Passover of the Public Ministry will be that of A.D. 29. If we accept 30 as the date of the Crucifixion, this can only be done by returning to the generally discredited view of a one-year Ministry.

(*b*) 'Geminis consulibus'. There is an old tradition dating back to the middle of the 2nd cent. A.D. that the Crucifixion took place 'Geminis consulibus' sc. in the consulship of C. Fufius Geminus and L. Rubellius Geminus. At first sight this would suggest that the astronomical evidence is worthless and that we must accept A.D. 29 as the date of the Crucifixion. But the tradition may have another significance. The ancients did not possess our scientific interest in problems of chronology, and were usually content with a vague indication of time ; 'suffered under Pontius Pilate' is all that the early Christian officially professed. Now we have seen above that the year 'Geminis consulibus' corresponds roughly to the 'fifteenth year of Tiberius' (if indeed it is not actually identical with it), and it is reasonable to hold that 'Geminis consulibus', as an alternative for 'the fifteenth year of Tiberius', was early regarded as the date of the 'accepted year of the

Lord'. Whether or not that year was to be regarded **676c** as a strict calendar year or not would seem to them unimportant. Without pressing the matter, then, it seems fair to conclude that 'Geminis consulibus' strengthens the case for the identification of the 'fifteenth year of Tiberius' with at least the major part of A.D. 29.

(*c*) There is an interesting passage in Josephus (*Ant.* **d** 18:113 f.) which may bear on this question. At a date which cannot be earlier than 34 and may be as late as 36, Herod the Tetrarch is at war with Aretas IV, the father of Herod's first wife. One reason which precipitated hostilities was the repudiation of that wife in favour of Herodias. In the passage in question, a disaster which befell the arms of Herod is attributed to divine justice avenging the execution of the Baptist. It would seem desirable, in view of this passage, to accept the latest possible date for the death of John, to bring it as close as may be to the events of 34.

On the whole, then, the more probable date for the Crucifixion would seem to be A.D. 33 ; according to Fotheringham, the precise date would be April 3. But A.D. 30 is a possible date.

One or two further points remain for elucidation. **e** What of Lk 3:23—'*Jesus had now reached the age of about thirty*' (KNT) ? On any system which takes account of all the evidence, it must be admitted that Lk cannot mean that Christ was precisely thirty at the time of his baptism. Nor does he say so. The expression is vague, and may mean no more than that he was, as we say, 'in the thirties'. Actually, if we accept the end of A.U.C. 746 for the date of the Nativity, and April 786 A.U.C. for that of the Crucifixion, our Lord will have been in his fortieth year at the time of his death, a fact which may shed a little light on the mysterious passage in Irenaeus (*Adv. Haer.* II:32:5) : 'From his fortieth or fiftieth year a man verges upon maturity (declinat iam in aetatem seniorem) ; and Our Lord possessed this when he taught, as John declared, according to the witness of his Gospel and of all the elders who conversed in Asia with John, the Lord's disciples'.

There remains the difficulty of Jn 2:20—the 'forty-six years' of the Temple's building. Owing to the difficulty of determining with certainty the *terminus a quo* for the calculation of this period, the passage is not yet valuable for determining the precise date of this, the first Passover of the Public Ministry. (Rev. E. F. Sutcliffe, S.J. : *A Two-Year Public Ministry* [1938] pp 149–53 : argues for A.D. 28. Fr E. Power, S.J. [*Biblica* (1928) 257 ff.] has argued for A.D. 30. On somewhat different grounds, I came to the same conclusion [JTS 36 (1935) 22 ff.]. But until the chronological scheme of Josephus' account of the reign of Herod the Great has been finally established, any conclusion based on his writings must remain provisional.)

3. The Date of St Paul's Conversion—Attempts have **f** been made to establish this from the reference to the 'ethnarch' of Aretas at Damascus. Some would argue that that official can only have been in existence after A.D. 37, when Caligula put Damascus under the jurisdiction of the Nabataean king. But the status of Damascus and the extent of the power of the Nabataean king during all this period are far from clear. The passage in Gal 1–2 is still a cause of perplexity. The famous second visit, 'after fourteen years' (from conversion or from the former visit ?) must presumably be either the 'Famine Relief visit' of Ac 11 or the 'Council of Jerusalem' visit of Ac 15. Dom Bernard Orchard (JRB 28 [1944] 174) has collected the authorities for the view that the Relief visit occurred in A.D. 46/47, but in Ac that visit seems to be so intimately associated with the death of Agrippa that I find it hard to separate the two events by as much as three years. Moreover, since we know that the famine was felt at Rome as early as A.D. 42, it is not unnatural to think that, even apart from the prophecy of Agabus, the inhabitants of Palestine would have received some warning of an impending shortage, and that the

676f Christians would be making preparations before the actual incidence of the famine, so that St Paul might easily have gone to Jerusalem some little time before the actual famine there, even if this did not occur before 45.

g With some reluctance, I feel that we are on safer ground in identifying the second visit referred to in Gal 2:1 with that of Ac 15, leaving the question open whether the ' fourteen years ' refer to the interval after conversion or since the first visit. I would myself put the conversion in 34 : the events of Ac 1–8 cannot have occupied more than a year. If 3,000 were converted at Pentecost, it would surely not be long before the numbers rose to 5,000, Ac 4:4 ; and the material needs of the community must have been felt fairly soon (Ac 6 : appointment of deacons) ; nor need we suppose that a long interval elapsed between Stephen's appointment and his execution. Paul's escape from Damascus (after three years—Gal 1:18) will thus have occurred in 36 or 37. It may be possible to associate the precautions of the ethnarch of Aretas with the war then raging between this king and Herod. We know that at this time the Nabataeans controlled the easterly trade-routes to Damascus from the south (*cf.* A.H.M. Jones : *The Cities of the Eastern Roman Provinces*, p 292) and the growth of their power at this time was sufficient to warrant a full-scale campaign by the governor of Syria. This was scheduled for A.D. 37, but was not undertaken because of the death of Tiberius (Jos. *Ant.* 18:124). But the whole incident is too mysterious to serve as a solid basis for argument, *cf.* Ac 9 ; Gal 1:15–2:10 ; Ac 11:25–30 ; 2 Cor 11:32 ; Ac 15.

4. The Council of Jerusalem—The Gallio inscription referred to above makes it probable that Paul came to Corinth in the spring of 50, which provides a clue to the date of the Council of Jerusalem a few months earlier.

The rest of the dating of the story of Ac depends largely on the dates of the different procurators of Judaea mentioned by Josephus. He is vague on the subject, but the years given in the table may be taken as probable.

THE GOSPEL OF JESUS CHRIST ACCORDING TO
ST MATTHEW

By A. JONES

Bibliography—J. Knabenbauer, S.J., *Evangelium secundum Matthaeum*, CSS, Paris 1892–3 ; M.-J. Lagrange, O.P., *Evangile selon Saint Matthieu*, Paris 1927[4] ; P. Joüon, S.J., *L'Evangile de Notre-Seigneur Jésus-Christ*, Paris 1930 ; F. Prat, S.J., *Jésus-Christ*, Paris 1933 ; J. Bonsirven, S.J., *Le Judaïsme Palestinien*, Paris 1935[2] ; Abbot J. Chapman, O.S.B., *Matthew, Mark and Luke*, London 1937 ; John Donovan, S.J., *The Logia in Ancient and Recent Literature*, Cambridge 1924 ; J. Dean, *The Synoptic Gospels*, WV, 1938 ; J. M. Bover, S.J., *El Evangelio de San Mateo*, Barcelona 1946 ; D. Buzy, S.C.J., *La Sainte Bible*, Vol 9, Paris 1946 ; E. Osty, *Les Evangiles Synoptiques*, Paris 1947 ; P. Benoit, O.P., *L'Evangile selon Saint Matthieu*, Paris 1950 ; A. Feuillet, P.S.S., articles on Eschatology in : RSR 35 (1947) 303–27 ; 36 (1948) 544–65 ; NRT 71 (1949) 701–22 ; 806–28 ; RB 56 (1949) 61–92 ; 340–64 ; 57 (1950) 43–62 ; 180–211 ; *W. C. Allen, *St Matthew*, ICC, 1912 ; *A. Plummer, *An Exegetical Commentary on the Gospel according to St Matthew*, London 1915 ; *A. H. McNeile, *The Gospel according to St Matthew*, London 1915 ; *A. Edersheim, *The Life and Times of Jesus the Messiah*, London 1927 ; *G. D. Kilpatrick, *The Origins of the Gospel according to St Matthew*, Oxford 1946 ; *M. Black, *An Aramaic Approach to the Gospels and Acts*, Oxford 1946 ; *F. W. Green, *The Gospel according to Saint Matthew*, Oxford 1947 ; B. C. Butler, *The Originality of St Matthew*, Cambridge 1951.

**I Authority and Authorship of the First Gospel ;
1 Early Witness to its Authority**—Already at the end of the 1st cent. and during the first years of the 2nd, the gospel we know as Matthew's had won special prominence. The allusions of Clement of Rome (*1 Ep. ad Cor.*, A.D. 95) of the Epistle of Barnabas (A.D. 100–30), of Ignatius of Antioch (*d.* A.D. 115), of the *Didache* (*c* A.D. 100), clearly reflect the text of the First Gospel. Nor are these reflexions confined to the discourses (λόγια) of our Lord (*e.g.* Ignatius, *Ep. ad Smyrn.* 1:1 ; *cf.* Mt 3:15). The authority of Mt's text is even underlined by the phrase 'as it is written' (ὡς γέγραπται) which is technical for the canonical writings of the OT (*Ep. Barn.* 4:14, alluding to Mt 22:14). Though the name of the Apostle is not yet used in connexion with these texts this early preference for the First Gospel, in Rome and in Antioch, does not favour a recent or obscure origin.
2 Early Witness to Matthean Authorship—From the mid-2nd cent. at least, and probably from its beginning, the title 'according to Matthew' (κατὰ Ματθαῖον) was current ; there is no trace of any other name in connexion with the First Gospel. Explicit evidence comes from Irenaeus writing before the end of the 2nd cent. : he declares that Matthew not only preached to the Hebrew (*i.e.* Aramaic) speaking public but also produced for them a written gospel in their own tongue (*Adv. Haer.* 3:1 ; quoted by Eusebius, HE 5, 8, 2). Origen (writing *c* A.D. 233), severe critic though he was, accepts the truth of the already rooted tradition (ὡς ἐν παραδόσει μαθών) that the apostle-publican Matthew wrote the First Gospel in Hebrew characters for converted Jews (*cf.* Eus., HE 6, 25). This witness becomes a commonplace in the 4th cent. (Eus., HE 3, 24, etc. ; Cyril of Jerusalem, *Catech.* 14, 15 ; Epiphanius, *Haer.* 30, 3, 6 ; 51, 5, etc. ; *cf.* texts and references in Lagrange, Mt xi–xv).

3 Testimony of Papias—Ματθαῖος μὲν οὖν ʽΕβραΐδι **677d** διαλέκτῳ τὰ λόγια συνετάξατο (?συνεγράψατο). ʽΗρμήνευσε δ'αὐτὰ ὡς ἦν δυνατὸς ἕκαστος (quoted by Eus., HE iii. 39) : 'Matthew wrote an ordered account of the oracles (λόγια) in the Hebrew tongue and each interpreted those oracles according to his ability'. This is the earliest known explicit witness to the Matthean authorship of the First Gospel. It comes from Papias, Bishop of Hierapolis, who wrote a five-volume work : *Explanation of the Lord's Discourses* (or : *of the Oracles about the Lord*). The date of Papias' birth was probably A.D. 60 (Chapman) or 70 (Lagrange) and his book is commonly dated *c* 125. He was in touch with the immediate disciples of the Apostles (Irenaeus). The precise sense of his term λόγια ' oracles ' has been much disputed (*e.g.* WV I xviii–xxii) but it is becoming increasingly recognized that Papias was not attributing to Matthew merely a collection of our Lord's words (the hypothetical document originally dubbed ' Q ' in critical circles). It may be that Papias chooses the term λόγια because the discourses are to form the theme of his book (though see WV *l. c.*), but it by no means follows that Papias denies to Matthew anything more than discourses. There is a growing reluctance to credit the existence of a document containing our Lord's words without any factual background and, moreover, its existence was not even suspected by those who originally used Papias' evidence. ' From his context it is quite clear that Eusebius took it [the term λόγια] to mean the Gospel according to St Matthew. The same is true of Irenaeus. This interpretation seems the most satisfactory one, especially as we know that the Gospel was used by Ignatius some twenty years before Papias wrote. Nor can the ascription κατὰ Ματθαῖον be later than Papias' time. Hence the presumption is that Papias by τὰ λόγια means our Gospel ', Kilpatrick, 3. *Cf.* also § 607*f.*

For those, therefore, who deny that the Apostle **e** Matthew wrote a gospel at all it remains only to refuse the witness of Papias. This is done on the alleged authority of internal evidence. Before we examine this internal evidence and the legitimate conclusions to be drawn from it we should do well to make some preliminary and cautionary observations. In the first place, Papias' is not the only evidence that remains to be explained away. Even granted that Irenaeus was its unwitting victim we are still faced with the conviction of the critical Origen who claims not Papias only, but a whole tradition in its support ; Eusebius, too, mistrustful of Papias on other points, accepts his evidence on this without question. Secondly, in questions of this kind both internal and external evidence must be respected and not manipulated. Thirdly, the historical evidence is stubborn on two points which are not necessarily connected—Matthean authorship and Aramaic original ; the ' critical ' hypothesis must reject both, however, if its arguments are to hold ; in fact it argues from the Greek to the non-apostolic authorship of the same. Here there is danger of confusing the issue because the traditional view is not tied down to the detailed identity but only to the substantial identity of the Greek translation with its apostolic, Aramaic, original. Fourthly, the firm tradition insists that our Greek Matthew is a translation. If it is right in so doing we are already in presence of a complex problem to which we might reasonably

851

677e expect a complex answer. It will not therefore be wise to dismiss such an answer lightly as a ' cumbersome hypothesis '. We shall outline the possible solution below.

f **II Original Language of the Gospel**—Papias, Irenaeus, Origen, Eusebius, Jerome, all bear formal witness that the First Gospel was written by Matthew ' in the Hebrew tongue ' or ' in his mother-tongue '. It is fairly clear that by ' Hebrew ' is here meant not the classical Hebrew of antiquity, but the cognate Aramaic, the contemporary Palestinian vernacular. For this use of the term, see the early ecclesiastical writers and, in the NT, Ac 21:40 ; 22:2 ; 26:14 ; Jn 19:13, 17, 20. Hebrew, indeed, would have been inaccessible at this time to all but scholars. Intrinsic evidence also excludes a Hebrew original since, in that hypothesis, quotations from the OT would have been taken verbatim from the Hebrew text (see below). A development of the argument for an original Aramaic Matthew may be found in Chapman, 182-214.

Despite this evidence the existence of a Semitic original is commonly denied on the ground that our Greek Matthew is manifestly not a translation. The arguments are not convincing. The Greek is clear but inelegant and repetitive : it may well be that of translation ; occasional ingenuities of phrase (*e.g.* 21:41) are not beyond the powers of a translator ; the handling of OT quotations points rather towards an Aramaic original than away from it. This last point calls for some elaboration : it is argued that the First Gospel makes use of the Greek Bible, the Septuagint, thus betraying its Greek origin. It may be answered, first, that this phenomenon too may be ascribed to the fact that the translator leans towards his familiar Greek OT. It may be argued further with Lagrange (Mt, cxvii-cxxiv ; and *cf.* Chapman, 261-93) that the First Gospel's use of the OT is in fact an indication of Semitic origin. The form of ten of Mt's quotations betrays the influence of the Hebrew text and in six of these cases, 1:23 ; 2:6, 18 ; 12:18-21 ; 13:35 ; 21:5, no adequate reason can be assigned for such recourse to the Hebrew other than the fact that it, and not LXX, was already used in the work which lay before the translator's eyes. The most natural explanation of such citations, notes Lagrange, is that ' Matthew (*i.e.* the Apostle) writing in Aramaic had before him the Hebrew text with which he was familiar and which he uses with a certain freedom '. At times the translator reproduces this characteristic of his original, at others (especially when the quotation is paralleled in the other Synoptics) he prefers the LXX form.

678a **III Date of Original and of Translation**—That Matthew was the first of the four to write his gospel is the firm persuasion of antiquity. This puts the Aramaic Matthew before A.D. 62 (the date of Luke). External evidence does not allow of any further precision : the testimony of Eusebius (HE iii. 24. 6) is too vague and that of Irenaeus (*Adv. Haer.* iii. 1. 1) too uncertain of interpretation (*cf.* WV I xvii-xviii) to admit of a conclusion. The Greek Matthew was probably written several years before A.D. 70, see below. If therefore we allow twenty years or so for the development of our Gk Mt from its Aramaic original, A.D. 40-50 would be an appropriate date for the latter.

The Gk Matthew was certainly well established in the first years of the 2nd cent. : the seven letters of Ignatius (A.D. 115 or earlier) use the Gk text as we know it. On this score alone it is difficult to believe that the translation was made later than A.D. 90. The arguments of Kilpatrick, especially pp 101-23, for A.D. 90-100 are not compelling : the situation which our gospel was designed to meet was already developing before the Synod of Jamnia in A.D. 90. In view of the fact that our Gk Matthew contemplates the Jewish catastrophe as something still to come a date some time before A.D. 70 is probable. The translator who, as will be seen, uses a certain freedom (*cf.* 21:39 note), would doubtless have allowed his language to be influenced by that event had it already taken place. Indeed,

recent comparative studies of Matthew and Paul have suggested a date earlier than the latter's first epistles (*i.e.* before A.D. 51) for a Gk translation of Aramaic Matthew ; see Chapman, DR (1937) 432 ff. ; Orchard, Bi (1938) 19 ff. ; Butler, DR (1948) 367 ff. ; *cf.* Dodd, ET (1947) 293 ff. Whether this translation or one of these translations (*cf.* the evidence of Papias) is identical with our Gk Matthew or whether it is only the precursor and source of the same will have to be decided on other grounds. If we accept the argument for our Gk Matthew's dependence upon Mark (*cf.* § 679a) we shall have to put Gk Matthew after A.D. 60 (probable date of Mark) and thus reject the identification.

IV Pertinent Replies of the Biblical Commission— (19th June, 1911) ; § 50a-g.

1. The Apostle Matthew is truly author of the Gospel that bears his name.
2. Tradition amply shows that Matthew wrote before the other evangelists and in the language of the Palestinian Jews.
3. The date of the original Matthew is not later than the fall of Jerusalem (A.D. 70) and tradition is best satisfied if we place it before Paul's coming to Rome (*c* A.D. 60).
4. Matthew did not compose merely a collection of our Lord's discourses, but a gospel in the strict sense.
5. Our Gk Matthew is substantially identical with the original. This is the legitimate conclusion from the fact that the Greek text was treated as canonical by the Fathers and ecclesiastical writers and by the early Church herself.

V Structure of the Gospel—It has been truly said that ' if any passage or section is to be found in our Gospel as well as in another, our Gospel is the one in which it may most easily be found '. This is the result of Matthew's highly systematic arrangement. Prescinding from the prologue (the Infancy narrative of chh 1-2) and from the epilogue (the Passion and Resurrection account of chh 26-28) the Gospel appears to fall naturally into five great parts. The evangelist marks these divisions with the repetition of a stereotyped formula (or its near equivalent) used nowhere else in the Gospel : ' And it came to pass when Jesus had ended these words . . . ', 7:28 ; 11:1 ; 13:53 ; 19:1 ; 26:1. Each part has its predominantly narrative section followed by a long discourse for which the narrative forms an apt preparation thus :

1.	i. Narrative	chh 3-4	(The indispensable preliminary *mise en scène*).
	ii. Discourse	chh 5-7	(Inaugural Discourse : the ' Sermon ').
2.	i. Narrative	chh 8-9	(Opening of our Lord's ministry ; miracles).
	ii. Discourse	ch 10	(Instruction for Apostles' ministry).
3.	i. Narrative	chh 11-12	(Opposition to the ' Kingdom ').
	ii. Discourse	ch 13	(Kingdom's mysterious nature explains opposition).
4.	i. Narrative	chh 14-17	(Formation of disciples and of Peter).
	ii. Discourse	ch 18	(Duties of the disciples).
5.	i. Narrative	chh 19-23	(Mounting opposition of Judaism).
	ii. Discourse	chh 24-25	(Messianic Judgement on Judaism, etc.).

VI Characteristic Theme—One might hesitate between two possible titles for our Gospel : the ' Gospel of Fulfilment ' or the ' Gospel of the Kingdom ' but, in effect, these are but two aspects of the one theme. The coming of the Kingdom is a fulfilment of the old promises and the Kingdom itself is not an entirely new thing, but a perfecting of the old. There is true continuity here as Mt insists in one sentence which he alone quotes : ' The kingdom of God shall be taken from you, and shall be given to a nation yielding the fruits thereof', 21:43.

The Gospel of Fulfilment—Mt sees both Kingdom and King not as unforeseen and unprepared phenomena, but as the supernatural climax of a divine plan announced and developing in the history of Israel. On twelve occasions the evangelist formally asserts that the old Scriptures were 'fulfilled' in Jesus and his work (1:22; 2:15, 17, 23; 4:14; 8:17; 12:17; 13:35; 21:4; 26:54; 27:9; *cf.* 3:15 note). From the first verses of the Gospel this is evident. The descent of Jesus from Abraham, not traced back to Adam as in Lk, implicitly links our Lord with the promise of Genesis (Gen 13:15; 17:8; *cf.* Gal 3:16) and the Infancy narrative is punctuated with OT references eagerly sought out to reduce the surprise of the early opposition to the Messias, 2:15, 17, 23. Alone among the evangelists Mt, 4:15, sees the opening of our Lord's public preaching as the shining of the great Messianic light already spoken of by Isaias (9:1), and the first works of healing as the prophesied function of the Isaian 'Servant of God', Mt 8:16–17. This second passage with its hint of suffering prepares the reader for the remaining OT citations chosen for circumstances more sombre: our Lord's withdrawal from the opposition of his people's leaders, the blindness of the people themselves, the flight of his own disciples, the mortal treachery of one of them—even these are not the frustration of the divine plan, but its fulfilment, 12:17; 13:35; 26:54, 56; 27:9.

As for the new order itself, it too is a fulfilment of the old and not its destruction, 5:17; ritual laws may pass, but the ancient moral code is protected, 15:3–6, and reinforced with a strong inner spirit, 5:20–48; though the new era is on a higher plane the old had looked towards it, 11:11–13. The message of the new Kingdom is addressed first to the subjects of the old, 10:5 f.; if it passes from Israel it is through Israel's fault, 21:28–44, and even our Lord's farewell words to his people hold a hint of hope for the nation elect of old (23:39 note). The very refusal of its Messias by Israel is no break with the past, but rather the climax of its melancholy history: Israel's response to God's invitations was never generous, 23:35, and Matthew's readers, largely converts from Judaism, need not be surprised nor scandalized that their own nation as a body has rejected the new offer, 23:34.

The Gospel of the Kingdom—51 times (as against 14 in Mk, 39 in Lk) Mt speaks of 'the Kingdom', but whereas Mk and Lk consistently use the expression 'Kingdom of God', Mt uses it, at most, 5 times only and prefers (32 or 33 times) 'Kingdom of the Heavens'. This last is almost certainly the formula used by our Lord himself (Lagrange, Mt, ci, cv–cvi), the plural form of 'heavens' reproducing Aramaic (and Hebrew) usage and the term itself being the contemporary respectful equivalent for 'God', 1 Mac 3:60; 4:24. Since the two expressions are in practice synonymous it follows that the phrase 'Kingdom of the Heavens' does not necessarily imply a kingdom in another world than this. Nevertheless the expression lends itself of its very nature to a certain ambiguity and the context will have to decide the exact formality of its use in any given passage. Sometimes it is the Messianic kingdom of God on earth, sometimes the apotheosis of that kingdom in heaven, sometimes the recognition of God's royal rights by the individual soul. The perspectives will often merge since the kingdom on earth is designed as the antechamber to the kingdom in heaven, *e.g.* 8:11–12. In some cases the distinction will be clear as when the kingdom of the Son (the kingdom on earth) is distinguished from the kingdom of the Father which is in heaven (*cf.* 1 Cor 15:28); this is most deliberately done in Mt 13:41–43. Thus to the kingdom of the Son refer 13:41; 16:28; 20:21, and *cf.* 19:28; to the kingdom of the Father: 13:43; 25:34; 26:29. On occasions the characteristics of the kingdom are such as to exclude a formal reference to heaven; thus, in the case of the parables of ch 13, the coexistence in

the kingdom of good and bad, the hidden nature of the **678f** kingdom, its slow and secret growth. Similarly the disciples' ambition in 18:1–4 clearly has an earthly kingdom for its object; the same may be said of the request of the sons of Zebedee, 20:21. Likewise when the kingdom is said to have come, 12:28, or when it is given a human authority, 16:17–19, the aspect of a kingdom on earth is foremost. It is upon this aspect **g** that Mt's emphasis lies because, for him, the kingdom is successor to God's ancient kingdom which was Israel, a kingdom of God upon this earth. The kingdom is on the threshold when the Baptist speaks, 3:2, and his words are echoed by our Lord, 4:17, with whose ministry the day of Sion's kingdom had dawned (11:5; *cf.* Is 35:5; 61:1). It has manifestly come with the great work of exorcism, 12:28, and is a matter of present experience, 13:16–19. But its 'coming', though hidden and constant like the great works of nature, may break through into observable history in spectacular fashion from time to time; in this sense it may have many 'comings'. Such a thrust is said to be near at hand, 16:28; 24:34; when the old temple falls the new kingdom will be known for its excelling successor (ch 24 notes). Matthew's gospel is therefore in some sort a theology of history, a sustained reflection upon the origin and nature and fortune and final destiny of the permanent and permeating force which God, through Christ, has infused into the affairs of the world. The Epistle to the Romans sees this revolutionary thing as the saving justice of God manifested in his Son, the gospel sees it as God's kingdom established by the Son; its theology is less elaborate than St Paul's, but it is no less profound and its arrangement admirable. The skilful synthesis and distribution of our Lord's discourses provides the reader with a growing understanding of the Kingdom which is Mt's central theme. His first discourse describes the true subjects of the Kingdom and their spirit; his second instructs its missionaries; the third illustrates its hidden but irresistible power; the fourth the mutual obligations of its citizens; the fifth its establishment in power upon the ruins of Judaism—nor does this last discourse end until the king ushers his faithful subjects into the lasting kingdom of his Father. It is small wonder that the marked preference for the gospel of Matthew in the early Church has remained to this day, because it is the gospel of God's kingdom on earth, the 'ecclesiastical gospel', the gospel of 'the Church'.

VII The Composition of Greek Matthew—The Two- **679a** Source Theory (Two-Document Hypothesis) with varying modifications is accepted in non-Catholic critical circles as a demonstrated thesis. Rejecting the historical evidence of an original Aramaic gospel it affirms two principal sources of Gk Matthew: (1) Mark's gospel, incorporated almost *in toto*; (2) A written document containing principally the sayings of our Lord (document 'Q') which is the supposed source of non-Marcan matter common to Mt and Lk. Harnack maintained that Q consisted almost exclusively of our Lord's discourses, but it is more commonly held today that Q contained narrative matter also, that it was an embryonic gospel. In addition to these two sources at least one other is usually postulated for those parts of Gk Matthew not found in either Mk or Lk—a source of Semitic origin. The Two-Source theory has been rejected by the Biblical Commission, § 51*a–b*, which notes that it lacks historical foundation. The Commission, however, permits free discussion of all hypotheses which respect the points mentioned in its decree of 1911, § 50*a–g*.

Catholic scholars, fully aware of the problem and **b** equally respectful of the data of historical tradition are not agreed upon the solution of the problem. The Oral Tradition Theory considers the Synoptic phenomenon adequately explained by the uniformity of the original spoken gospel. This was 'a traditional outline of the life of Christ and of his chief sayings, current at Jerusalem both in Aramaic and Greek'. It is claimed that the hypothesis is confirmed by the language of the

679b gospels themselves which displays a colourless uniformity in sections common to the three Synoptics as opposed to the marked individuality of other passages. The tenacious oriental memory is credited with the preservation of the order of events and content of discourses found to be the same in the three Synoptics. Stress is laid upon the differences which, it is said, the theory of written sources finds it difficult to explain. ' Memory explains both the likenesses and the differences in the Synoptic gospels, but the hypothesis of documents does not sufficiently explain the differences such as we have them in the concrete ' ; *cf.* WV I 371–82. The Aramaic gospel of Matthew and, through it, the Greek preserve for us the Aramaic form of the original spoken gospel.

c The majority of Catholics think this explanation insufficient to account for a similarity which is striking and sustained. In addition to the part played by oral tradition they invoke some form of Mutual Dependence of one written gospel on another. Within this school of thought are two widely differing opinions. The first is a return to Augustine's view that Mk is, in effect, an abridgement of Gk Mt. ' The Gk Mt served as Mk's chief source in the sense that Peter, when preaching in Rome, had the Gk Mt before him, and adapted it in his own way to his hearers' needs ', Chapman, xxi. Mark was Peter's stenographer, *ibid.* 89–92. In this theory Gk Mt is considered as an independent translation of the Aramaic original and a discussion of its ' composition ' lies outside the range of the Synoptic Problem.

d The second of the two ' Mutual Dependence ' theories is adopted here. It enjoys the advantage of combining the historical data with what appear to be the more assured findings of recent inquiry into the internal evidence. The following summary of the theory, which is offered as a probable solution, is based upon the outline-presentation of Père Benoit O.P., 12–30. The source which the critics call ' Q ' is no other than the original Aramaic gospel, discourses and events, of the Apostle Matthew. This gospel presented the Jerusalem catechesis which was the framework of Peter's preaching, the preaching which Mark committed to writing. Composed in Aramaic, as its Semitic flavour often suggests, it was very soon translated into Greek (*cf.* § 678*a* : the alleged dependence of Paul on Gk Mt). There were, doubtless, many such translations (Papias). These translations were used by our three evangelists each of whom adjusted his source to his purpose. Thus Mark, for example, omitted many sayings of our Lord, notably the opening discourse, and arranged the narrative-matter in his own way. In this Luke followed him fairly closely but filled in many of his omissions of discourse. The Gk Mt completely reorganized the narrative-sequence and, to some extent, the discourses—though apparently his arrangement of five great discourses is due to his source, the Aramaic Mt.

e The vindication of this hypothesis cannot here be pursued in detail and a few general remarks must suffice. The theory rightly insists that the *Two-Source* position has a fatal weakness : its rejection of the distinction between our Gk Mt and an Aramaic original vouched for by firm historical evidence. It agrees, however, that oral tradition alone is not capable of explaining the similarity between Mark and Gk Mt (the latter has all of but little more than Mark's narrative ; its order from Mt 14 is identical ; 45 verses of Mk, one-fifteenth of his gospel, are remarkably similar in form to their counterpart in Mt ; 23 rare words are found only in the parallel places of Mk and Gk Mt). It agrees also, and in this it is opposed to the former of the Mutual Dependence opinions, that the form of *narrative* in Gk Mt is dependent upon Mk and not *vice-versa* (its less vivid and more correct style, its signs of transposition, its doublets, etc.). Attention is called, on the other hand, to contrary phenomena— the Gk Mt is more Semitic in character than Mk who also shows signs of having abridged the Mt-narrative

in places. This cannot be due to a dependence of Mk on Gk Mt, as has been shown ; it must therefore be due to Mark's dependence upon the common source (the Aramaic catechesis). The same apparently contradictory phenomena occur in the *discourses* and lead to the same conclusion : dependence of Greek Mt on Mk and dependence of both on a common source. It is regarded as fairly probable that Mk knew and used the catechesis not only through the medium of Peter's preaching but also in its written form in the original gospel of Mt. As for the translator of Mt, he too ' knew this primitive tradition in the Aramaic gospel of Mt which was probably already translated. He undertook to present this gospel more fully than Mk, his predecessor, of whose work however he made considerable use. Employing this Gk text of Mk he adjusted it when his prudence suggested, omitting those descriptive details which did not further his essential purpose which was doctrinal and at times preserving the flavour of his Aramaic original. He made use also of Mark's sequence which was, to a great extent no doubt, the sequence of Aramaic Matthew ; this he sometimes followed, sometimes manipulated. From the original gospel of Mt he took over the discourses in their entirety, even adding to them with the help of other traditions ', Benoit, *op. cit.*, 20–1.

As for the relationship of Gk Mt with Lk, it seems impossible to suppose any direct dependence of either upon the other in view of their notable differences (*e.g.* the Infancy narratives, the genealogies, the wording of the Our Father, etc.). Their similarities are, therefore, best explained by a common written source of their non-Marcan material containing (as we have noted) not only discourses but also events. This source is the early translation, or better ' translations ', of the original Matthew. In addition to this source a second is postulated which Luke took bodily into his ' great intercalation ', Lk 9:51–18:14, but which the Gk Mt quarries for the structure of his great discourses.

If this conception of the facts is approximately correct it follows that our Gk Mt is not a mere translation of the Apostle's original Aramaic gospel ; nevertheless it maintains the same fundamental structure and the same substantial teaching. Indeed any hypothesis which rejected the substantial identity of our Gk Mt with the apostolic work would collapse before the historical evidence. It is undeniable that the earliest ecclesiastical writers unanimously accepted our Gk gospel as the reliable presentation of the Apostle's Aramaic work. It may be added that they received the Greek text as sacred and canonical.

Inspiration of Mt.—It seems probable that the immediate, though not necessarily exclusive, object of the Church's pronouncements relative to ' sacredness and canonicity ' is the Greek version, since this is the form of the Gospel in ecclesiastical use from the first century onwards, the well-known ' evangelium Matthaei '. If this view is exact then we possess a work inspired in its entirety and not simply a translation substantially identical with an inspired original.

For further discussion see *The Synoptic Problem*, §§ 610–15 ; also §§ 604*d*–*f*, 607*a*–*g*.

A. I:1–II:23 Prologue : Infancy of the Messias. I 1-17 Genealogy of Jesus the Messias—1. A brusque opening in headline-form introduces the Gospel. It refers perhaps to the whole gospel (WV ' book of the coming '), more probably to the genealogy only (KNT ' record of the ancestry ') or to the genealogy together with the conception-narrative ; *cf.* 1:18. The use of ' Christ ' (not ' the Christ ') as a proper name became common after our Lord's death (it is frequent in St Paul). The term is the Greek equivalent (χριστός) of the Aramaic *mᵉšîḥā'* (Gk transliteration Μεσσίας) meaning ' anointed ', technical at this time for the prophesied King. The most popular title of this King, representing his basic characteristic, was ' Son of David ', 2 Kg 7:12–17 ; Is 11:1 ff., etc. Its vindication for Jesus is the goal of Mt's genealogy. ' Son of Abraham ', whether immediately qualifying 'Jesus Christ' or 'David', implicitly presents Jesus as fulfilling in his person the Abrahamitic promise, Gen 12:3 ; Gal 3:16.

2-6a First Series : Abraham to David : Patriarchal List—*Cf.* 1 Par 1:27–2:15 where, as here, the list is incomplete since only three names occur between Phares and Naasson to cover the period (at least 215 years) of the Egyptian sojourn.

6b-11 Second Series : Solomon to Jechonias : Royal List—*Cf.* 1 Par 3:5–16 where, unlike here, the list is complete, placing Ochozias, Joas, Amasias, between Joram and Ozias (or Azarias) and naming Joaqim as also Sedecias. The historical situation summarized in 11 f. is this : *about the time of the deportation to Babylon,* 598, Josias, 638–608, was succeeded by his son Joachaz, 608, whose successors were Joaqim, brother of Joachaz, 608–598, Jechonias (or 'Joachin') son of Joaqim, 597, finally Sedecias brother of Joachaz, 598–587). Jechonias, aged 18, was taken captive to Babylon in 598 and was released 37 years later. Zorobabel, 12 f., headed the returning exiles in 537.

12-16 Third Series (Jechonias to Jesus) : Dethroned Davidic Family—For Salathiel and Zorobabel *cf.* 1 Par 3:17–19 ; Esd 3:2. From Abiud onwards Mt's source must have been family archives, carefully preserved in Jewish circles and easily challenged by hostile readers. **17.** Three series of fourteen generations are punctuated by two national crises : the inception of a divinely guaranteed Davidic dynasty in the 10th cent. and the Babylonian exile in the 6th.

Notes on the Genealogy—(*a*) *Purpose.* The genealogy does not prove Messiaship, but vindicates for Jesus its prerequisite condition, *viz.* Israelitic stock traceable to the patriarch of the whole race and, in particular, royal Davidic descent. But the singular manner of our Lord's conception, 18–25, introduced a special difficulty : though Mary was evidently of Davidic family herself (*cf.* Rom 1:3 ; Prat, I, 77), ancient (and particularly Jewish) genealogical usage ignored descent from the female line. Mt, therefore, gives the ancestry of Joseph, reputed and legally registered father through whom alone the Davidic descent of Jesus could be juridically established. (*b*) *The term 'begot'.* Used of mediate natural generation in *e.g.* 8 ('Joram begot Ozias') and possibly of legal ('levirate' ; 22:25 note) generation in 12 ('Salathiel begot Zorobabel' *cp.* Esd 3:2 with 1 Par 3:19). (*c*) *The women in the genealogy.* Contrary to usage and therefore with a purpose four women are named : Thamar, Rahab, Ruth, Bethsabee ; *cf.* Gen 38 ; Jos 2 ; Ru 1–4 ; 2 Kg 11. Their common quality is apparently that of alien blood : Rahab Canaanite, Ruth Moabite, Thamar probably Canaanite, Bethsabee probably 'Hittite' like her first husband. Their mention prepares us for an association of the Gentiles with God's designs—an association subsequently emphasized by the incident of the Magi (ch. 2). (*d*) *Fourteen generations.* The number is taken from the OT record of the first series and deliberately, 17, applied to the second and third as a symmetrical aid to memory. It may have been a further recommendation (or happy accident ?) that 14 is the first multiple of the sacred number 7 (favoured by Mt) and the numerical equivalent of the Hebrew consonants of David's name (DWD, 4 + 6 + 4). (*e*) *Defect of the third series.* The third series is apparently one name short unless we count Jechonias twice—as king, 11, and as dethroned civilian, 12, Augustine, PL 34, 1076 and WV note to Mt 1:17. Alternatively (Buzy) Jechonias need not be counted as beginning the third series if Mary be reckoned one of the fourteen ; this is not improbable in view of the singular quality of her motherhood. A third solution (*Allen ; Lagrange) reads Joaqim for Joakin (Jechonias) in 11 (translator's carelessness ?). Besides solving the numerical question, this gives point to the mention of 'brethren', 11, since two of Joaqim's brothers reigned. (*f*) *The conclusion of the genealogy.* The evangelist studiously avoids the phrase 'Joseph begot Jesus' : Joseph figures only as the legal husband of Mary. The text is critically certain. The Syriac

variants (all careful to insert the word 'virgin' with **680g** 'Mary') are the result of subsequent effort to combine the legal paternity of Joseph and the virginal motherhood so clearly asserted in 18–25. The Sinaitic Syriac reads 'Joseph to whom was betrothed Mary the virgin begot Jesus'. That it intends no more than a legal begetting is clear from its care to render the Greek of 1:18 (' before they came together ') by ' at a time when they had not come together ', thus safeguarding the perpetual virginity of Mary even more scrupulously than the Gk ; *cf.* RB 19 (1920) 349–52. (For the conciliation of Mt's genealogy with Lk's, Schmid [Das Evangelium nach Matthäus, Regensburg 1948] rejects the 'levirate' solution and invokes the defects in the family tables implicitly cited by Mt and Lk.)

18-25 The Virginal Conception of the Messias—This **h** passage more clearly explains the situation suggested in 16. Joseph appears as witness of two things : first, of his own assumption of legal paternity (this fact alone justifies the presence of Joseph's genealogy in Mt) ; second, of his virginal relationship with Mary and of his heaven-sent conviction of the virginal conception. **18.** Betrothal (*qiddûšîn*) in Jewish law conferred the status of husband and wife (hence the terms of 19 f.). A child conceived during this period was regarded as legitimate unless disowned, but the marriage was regarded as incomplete until the husband formally ' took possession ' (the *niššû'în*) of his bride by taking her to his home. This he was free to do at any time, 2 Kg 3:14 ; *cf.* Edersheim, I, 353–5. After Mary's return from her cousin's house, Lk 1:39–56, but before Joseph had taken her to his home her condition became clear (' she was found ' or, in the weakened sense of the Heb. verb, ' she became ', Joüon). Mt adds with reverent haste what was revealed later, 20, that the child was God-begotten. **19.** That denunciation was **i** a legal duty in the circumstances cannot be proved ; nor does the text suggest that Joseph sacrificed legal scruples (' and '—not ' but '—' not willing to make her case public '). It suggests rather (Lagrange) that precisely because Joseph was ' just ' (*i.e.* aware of duties to God and neighbour and, in this case, to Mary) he did not place the matter before the village-court. Such a course, though not necessarily involving condemnation (a woman might be pronounced blameless in such cases, Deut 23:25 f.) meant publicity for Mary, unwelcome and evidently incompatible with Joseph's ' justness '. Why incompatible ? Presumably because ignorance of the facts coupled with knowledge of Mary's character made of mere publicity an injustice. St Joseph's attitude is to be observed : there is no word of complaint or even of inquiry. The evangelist leaves us with the impression of a patient instrument of God. Another course remained open : to give Mary her freedom by a bill of divorce before two witnesses (19:7 note) without the publicity of the court. To this course Joseph was inclining. His delicacy is admirable —communicated to him, no doubt, from his knowledge of Mary. He cannot believe her blameworthy ; he knows nothing of the Annunciation (Mary had been silent and absent for three months, Lk 1:39 ff.) ; he can think only of some unknown cause, perhaps supernatural, certainly consistent with Mary's character. **20.** There remained a third possibility : to celebrate **j** the *niššû'în* and thus acknowledge the child as his own. From this, evidently, Joseph shrank ; perhaps because it would put him publicly in a false position. The angel reassured him. He could now without scruple adopt this third course because the child, though not his, was his more than any man's. It was the child of his betrothed. His patience and obedience make Joseph a model of Christian men ; his unique relationship to the child makes him our powerful intercessor. **21.** Joseph is to assume the duties of parent (*cf.* Lk 1:31, 63) and impose the name 'Jesus' (in Heb.: *Yᵉhôšûa'* or *Yēšûa'*). The name means ' Yahweh is Salvation '. The salvation is to be not from Herod nor from Rome but ' from sin '. We are warned from the outset that the child's kingdom is not of this world, Jn 18:36,

680j contrary to the popular Messianic idea which our Lord was to find so difficult to eradicate. This same work is assigned to God himself in Ps 129:8 (Lagrange)—one of many hints (*e.g.* 23 with note) preparing us for a **681a** greater revelation of the child's true dignity. **22-23.** All this *has taken place*, says Mt (for whom the Incarnation is an abiding thing) in such a way as to fulfil the prophecy of Isaias, Is 7:14. Over seven centuries before, the prophet had announced a Davidic king to be born of a young woman (a ' virgin ' LXX) by divine intervention, Is 7:14. His contemporary, Micheas (Mic 5:3-5, *cf.* § 535*h*) had alluded to the same event. Mt recalls this quality of the Messias which had been allowed to fall into the background in Jewish Messianic tradition (Lagrange, *Le Messianisme*, 223). The incompatibility of virgin-birth with physical descent from the Davidic male line is resolved in Mt by legal descent through Joseph's adoption. The child's name is to be Jesus, but he is to be ' called ' (*i.e.*, in Semitic idiom, the true description of his mission, or even of his personality, is to be) '*Immānū 'El*, or ' With Us (is) God '. Of all the numerous OT theophoric names (*e.g.* Josue ' Yahweh is Salvation ' ; Johanan ' Yahweh has been Gracious ') this name, found applied only to the Isaian child, Is 7:14 ; 8:8, is the one most strangely suitable to describe the real personality of Jesus. In order to bring it down to the level of other theophoric names it has to be reduced by paraphrase (though this is not impossible) to, *e.g.*, ' God is by our side to help '. Mt (for his Aramaic-speaking readers) or his translator **b** (for Greeks) interprets the Hebrew term. **24-25.** Though the *niśśū'in* took place very soon, perhaps on the following day, this marriage was not consummated. Mt makes this statement of the period which directly concerns him, his purpose being to safeguard the virginal nature of the conception and birth of Jesus. Of the period following the birth he says nothing. His sentence would be best paraphrased : She brought forth a son without having relations with Joseph. The Semitic turn of phrase (DV ' till ') while denying the action for the period preceding the verb ' brought forth ' implies nothing for the period which follows it ; *cf.* Gen 8:7 ; 1 Tim 4:13, etc. ' These words cannot be taken to imply that it (the virginity of Mary) was not afterwards preserved ', *Green, 106. For the word ' firstborn ', unauthentic here, *cf.* Lk 2:7 note.

c **II 1-12 The Magi—1.** Mt's first indications of time and place are given incidentally as if already known to readers, but recalled with a view to the subsequent story. The child was born during the reign of Herod the Great, 37-4 B.C., at Bethlehem of *Judaea* (scene of David's birth and anointing, 1 Kg 16:13 ; 17:23), 6 m. S. of the capital. The **Magi** (DV ' wise men ') were originally a Median priestly tribe of clairvoyants who retained their functions under their Persian conquerors. The term later became general, Dan 1:10 ; Ac 8:9 ; 13:8, for astrologers, sorcerers, etc. of all nationalities. We may translate ' sages ', since Mt clearly does not intend a derogatory sense. Their homeland (' the East ') is most probably the district just beyond Jordan and the Dead Sea, *i.e.* Nabataean Arabia which at that time reached as far north as Damascus. (For this use of ' the East ' *cf.* the early Palestinian writers : Justin, Origen, Epiphanius.) Here Jews and Arabs speaking similar dialects formed a mixed population. The nature of their gifts confirms their Arabian origin : Arabia was renowned for its gold, 1 Kg 9:28, incense, Jer 6:20, and myrrh, Pliny, *Hist. Nat.*, 12, 30-5. The time of the Magi's visit is to be put after the Purification, Lk 2:33-38, which took place forty days after our Lord's birth, since Joseph plainly would not have taken his charges to the capital after the warning of 13 (see note). It was probably not more than a year after the nativity **d** (16 note). **2.** The appearance of a new and brilliant star *in the eastern sky* (ἀνατολή in the sing. as in 9, not plur. as 1) sends the Magi in a westerly direction to the Jewish capital. Evidently they were aware of the high pitch of Messianic expectation among their Jewish neighbours (witness the many pseudo-Messiahs after

Herod's death). Possibly also (though Mt is silent) the Magi received a special revelation. The ' star ' (ἀστήρ) cannot mean a group or conjunction of planets (ἄστρον) ; this excludes Kepler's conjunction in 7 B.C. of Saturn, Jupiter, Mars. Halley's comet, 12 B.C., is apparently excluded by its date. The comet-hypothesis in general (Origen, *Contra Celsum*, 1, 58, *cf.* Patrizi, *De Evangeliis*, 3, 309-54) is difficult to reconcile with the description of the star's behaviour in 9 unless (with Lagrange) we grant that Mt intends no more than a popularized account of an extraordinary but natural phenomenon. For the majority of Catholic exegetes the star is a special creation as, indeed, the text most naturally suggests. **3.** The common, general stir (DV ' trouble ') no doubt takes the form of anxiety in Herod, of excitement in the populace. **4.** The Sanhedrin, the supreme Jewish advisory body of 71 members, was composed of three groups in approximately equal force : the chief priests, *i.e.* the high-priest in office, the deposed high-priests and the heads of the twenty-four priestly classes ; the ' scribes ' (' doctors of the Law '), Pharisee in persuasion, specialists in the Mosaic Code and instructors of the people ; the ' ancients ' or prominent laymen. Since these last are not mentioned here, it is probably not a formal meeting of the Sanhedrin, rarely consulted by Herod and unnecessary to his present purpose. Herod's question does not imply his faith in the prophets, but his appreciation of the dangers of the popular belief. Any pretender, especially with an appearance of prophetic backing, was seen as a peril by Herod, who did not over-estimate his own popularity. **5.** The answer to the question may not have come as promptly as appears from the brief account of Mt. The birthplace of the Messias was the subject of diverse opinions (*cf.* Jn 7:27, 42) among the people and presumably among their teachers. In Jewish written tradition there is no evidence of the Bethlehem birthplace before the 3rd cent. A.D. (Lagrange, *Le Messianisme*, 222). The prophecy (Mic 5:1, 3 ; *cf.* § 535*f-g*) was doubtless quoted verbatim by the scribes. Mt is content with substantial fidelity ; moreover he adapts the text to the circumstances. For him Bethlehem is no longer ' insignificant among the clans of Judah ' because the Messias has been born there ; when Micheas wrote, the greatness was still to come. **7-8.** Herod betrays a superstitious anxiety though he is careful to make his further inquiries in private—there is excitement enough already, 3. He attaches importance to the time of the star's appearance, evidently presuming that it coincides (if it has any significance at all) with the time of the birth. His plans are already made, but his assumed appearance of leisure, 8, ultimately defeats its own end. **9-10.** The star reappears (*cf.* ' and behold ')—it had evidently not led the Magi to Jerusalem. It stands now in the southern sky in the direction of Bethlehem. Mt's text, literally interpreted, gives the impression of a light visibly advancing southwards (unless we translate, with Patrizi, ' *had* gone before them '). This impression is heightened by the apparent implication that it was the star which showed the actual dwelling (though read ' over the place ' KNT, rather than ' over the spot ' WV). If this is correct, the ' star ' is a luminous body in the lower atmosphere. **11.** The Magi enter the *dwelling* (οἰκία). This is either a new abode or possibly still the cave-stable (*cf.* the 2nd cent. tradition recorded by Justin, *Contra Tryphonem*, 78, 5), not an unusual home for Orientals. Joseph though he may have been present is not mentioned ; with this delicate touch, Mt recalls the virginal conception and Mary's incomparable closeness to the child. Note the similar indications of 2:13 f. The verb ' adored ' (προσκυνέω), frequent in Mt, does not necessarily imply divine honours ; yet the emphasis of the expression ' falling down they adored ' is suggestive, and the offering of incense, usually reserved to the divinity even among the pagans, strengthens the suggestion, Prat, I, 105 f. The gifts are probably products of the Magi's native land (*cf.* Gen 43:11)—indispensable for visits to a king. The 'frankincense' (*i.e.* 'precious' incense) is, like the myrrh, a resin. Myrrh, a perfume, Cant 3:6, was used in powdered form as a deodorant at burials, Jn 19:39, and, mixed with wine, as a narcotic, Mk 15:23—hence its suggestion of mortality adopted in later symbolism : 'gold for the king; incense for the God; myrrh for the mortal'. **12.** *Being warned* in sleep the Magi went home not by the way they had come (probably from the direction of Moab *via* Jericho) but either by making for the south of the Dead Sea by way of Hebron or by effecting a crossing from its western shore at En-gedi.

II 13-15 Flight into Egypt—13. The circumstances (delay would have been fatal) and the terms (' behold ' following the aorist participle and preceding the historic present : ' appeareth '—*cf.* the same construction in 2:91) suggest that the flight took place very soon after the Magi's departure, probably the same night. Five or six days' travelling would take the holy family to the frontier of Egypt, now an Imperial Prefecture with a Jewish population of about one million concentrated especially in Alexandria and Heliopolis. As a refuge from oppression at home Egypt was convenient and traditional, 3 Kg 11:40 ; 4 Kg 25:26. **14.** Mt's narrative, not being an edifying fable, preserves a sober silence (unlike the apocryphal gospels) on the details of the journey. There is no ancient, constant tradition relating to their new home. **15.** Mt implicitly anticipates the return the better to space his OT quotations, 15, 18, 23. It might be noted here that, as in 18, rather than ' the incident being made to fit the quotation ' (*A. J. Grieve, Peake's Commentary on the Bible*) it would be less false to say that the quotation, Os 11:1, is made to fit the incident. The original text (not LXX which reads ' his [Jacob's] children '—unsuitable to Mt's purpose) refers in the strictly literal sense to the end of the Egyptian exile for Israel (God's ' son ', *cf.* Ex 4:22 f.). The text is not a formal prophecy since the tense of the verb, faithfully preserved by Mt, is past. Mt, therefore, introduces the original situation merely as a providential rehearsal of the present event, thus calling our attention to a fuller sense of ' son ' than Osee could have imagined.

II 16-18 Massacre of the Innocents—16. The sacrifice of a few children to the safety of his throne meant nothing to Herod (for a summary of his appalling record, see Schürer, 2, 1, 401-16) ; his own sons had suffered in the same cause. Bethlehem and *district* (the term excludes neighbouring villages, *cf.* RB 8 [1899] 422 ; 9 [1900] 435) had a population of about 1,000 (now over 7,000) which, allowing for the high infant-mortality rate, would bring the number of children of two years and under to about 20. The age of the victims indicates that the star had appeared not more than two years before—probably about one year, Herod callously leaving a safety-margin on either side. **17-18.** The text, Jer 31:15, quoted here *ad sensum*, poetically presents Rachel (mother of Benjamin and of Joseph, the father of Ephraim) lamenting the fate of her children on their way into exile. She mourns from her tomb near Rama in Benjamin, 1 Kg 10:2 f. Rama lies 5 m. N. of Jerusalem and was the mustering place for the exiles on their way to Babylon, Jer 40:1. For Mt the circumstances are similar—the maternal lament of Rachel is echoed now in Bethlehem. Nevertheless, he does not allege a literal fulfilment of prophecy, otherwise he would have omitted ' in Rama '. The quotation receives added point from another tradition (represented by what is probably an ancient but incorrect gloss in Gen 35:19) which places Rachel's tomb near Bethlehem ; *cf.* Abel, *Géographie de la Palestine* (Paris 1938) 425 f.

II 19-23 From Egypt to Nazareth—19. Herod died shortly before the Pasch (April 12 in that year) of 4 B.C. For his last days *cf.* Schürer I, 1, 462-7. Archelaus (the elder of his sons by Malthace) was assigned Judaea and Samaria and named king in Herod's will, being saluted as such on his father's death, Jos., *Ant.* 17, 8, 2. He had to wait perhaps six months for the confirmation of Augustus (U. Holzmeister, *Chronologia Vitae Christi*,

Rome 1933, 49) who granted him the title of ethnarch **682c** only. The length of the Egyptian sojourn during the period between the Magi's visit and the accession of Archelaus was probably at least six months because at the time of the Magi's visit there is as yet no sign (*cf.* 2:8) of Herod's fatal illness contracted probably in Sept. of 5 B.C. (Holzmeister, *op. cit.,* 25). That the sojourn was not prolonged after Herod's death seems clear from 19 (*cf.* 2:13) and perhaps accounts for the use of ' reigned ' (22 : βασιλεύει) which possibly suggests that Archelaus's title of ' king ' had not yet been formally reduced to that of ' ethnarch '. **20.** The word ' they ' (though possibly a plural of generalization, Joüon) is perhaps best explained as a deliberate reference to the similar situation of Moses in Ex 4:19 f. **21-22.** Joseph evidently intended to return to Bethlehem, if not to settle there at least to order his affairs. He was doubtless on the coast-road (Egypt-Gaza-Azotus) when he heard of the accession of Archelaus who had a bad reputation, not undeserved (Schürer, I, 2, 40). Judaea was still no place for a Messianic claimant and Joseph proceeded to his old home in Galilee. This was Nazareth, Lk 2:4, lying in the hills on the northern fringe of the plain of Esdraelon, *c.* 20 m. W. of Tiberias. The insignificant village, mentioned neither in Josephus nor Talmud, is the *Naṣraṭ* (not *Nazraṭ*) of the Syriac versions. (For a similar Gk transcription of the sibilant *cf.* the Zogora of LXX with the Heb. *Ṣō'ar* in Gen 13:10). The place was known to Julius Africanus (*c* A.D. 160-*c* A.D. 240). Nazareth was to be the scene of our Lord's childhood and youth. **23.** The term ' Nazarene ' (Ναζωραῖος) **d** might be more exactly transcribed ' Nazoree '. Its termination thus suggests a member of a sect (*cf.* Pharisee, Sadducee) rather than an indication of origin ; *cf.* Magdalene, *i.e.* of Magdala. It is probable that the term ' Nazoree ' was first applied to the disciples after our Lord's death, Ac 24:5, with a measure of contempt for the provincial origin (*cf.* Jn 1:46) of the founder of the ' sect '. When the word became common its hostile sense would diminish (*cf.* ' Quaker ') and it might well have become synonymous with the strictly geographical term ' Nazarene ' originally used of Jesus himself (Prat, I, 119)—hence its use throughout Mt, Ac, Jn (Mk uses ' Nazarene '). Nevertheless, it was always possible to recall the original, contemptuous flavour of the expression, and it is probable that this is Mt's intention here (Lagrange). If this is so, he wishes to say that the obscurity of his Master's home, though now a subject of derision, should not be unexpected to those who knew the prophets. These, rightly read, had spoken of a Messias humanly inglorious, Is 53, Ps 21. It is perhaps less probable that the term ' Nazoree ' contains a verbal reference to the ' sapling ' (*nēṣer* ; DV ' flower ') from the Davidic root, Is 11:1. This would make the ' prophecy ' little more than a punning coincidence and would scarcely justify Mt's plural ' prophets '.

B. III 1-IV 11 The Messianic Prelude. **e**
III 1-12 Herald of the Messias (Mk 1:2-8 ; Lk 3:1-18) **—1-6.** ' In those days ' (Mt's vague formula is given precision in Lk 3:1) an ascetic who achieved fame and respect among his compatriots (Jos., *Ant.* 18, 5, 2 ; 21, 2, 6) inaugurated his penitential message in the mountainous, arid district east of the Jerusalem-Hebron road. He demanded a change of heart (μετανοεῖτε) as the necessary disposition for receiving an imminent divine gift—' the kingdom of the heavens ' (' of God ' throughout Mk & Lk, but Mt's form is probably the Baptist's and our Lord's ; *cf.* Lagrange 47). This realm and rule of God is the goal of Messianic prophecy (*cf.* § 678d). John preached penance preparatory to the kingdom because he was the divinely appointed herald to the king. He personified the disembodied voice, Is 40:3, that heralded the return from pagan Babylon and the establishment of the new religious era of Judaism, itself a foretaste of, and preparation for, the new era declared by John. **4.** The

682e garb suggests the prophet. John's outer garment is woven of camel-hair ; *cf.* Zach 13:4. He wears a loin-cloth (possibly ' girdle ', RSR 23 [1933] 589–98) of skin ; *cf.* Elias, 4 Kg 1:8. His food is of the simplest : the easily caught locust (a winged insect some two inches long, eaten still by Bedouin) and the insipid tree-gum (perhaps of the tamarisk, common on the

f Jordan banks). He baptizes in the Jordan near Jericho, of easy access from the capital. It was his impressive proclamation of the kingdom that drew the crowds, Jos., *Ant.* 18, 5, 2. His baptism was not the Jewish ceremonial bath removing Gentile defilement, a rite too narrow for John's horizon (*cf.* 9) ; nor had it the *ipso facto* efficacy of Christ's sacramental baptism. It held a place between the two, characteristic of its period which was one of transition from ' ceremonial washings ' to the ' better times ' of inner, sacramental, re-birth ; *cf.* Heb 9:10. By accepting it the Jews acknowledged, in formal ritual fashion, their conviction that the kingdom was at hand and their willingness to admit and (implicitly) to remedy past guilt. Thus they became subjects of the era of preparation announced by John and this act of willing submission would earn

g God's grace. **7-10.** Mt, having given, 2, the two themes of John's preaching, now proceeds to expand them in the Baptist's own words. The first theme, penance, is urged against the Pharisees and Sadducees. Neither of these two parties could afford to ignore the popular religious movement. The **Pharisees** (*i.e.* Separatists—from the common herd by reason of their legalistic punctilio) stood for the Law and for the traditions that had accrued to it. They held no official religious or political position in the Jewish State ; as professional and orthodox ' holy men ' their influence with the people was enormous. The **Sadducees** (*i.e.* ' sons of Sadoq ', representative of the priestly line ; *cf.* 3 Kg 2:35 ; 1 Par 6:8-15 ; Esd. 3:2, Ez 40:46) were the rationalists of the day, Mt 22:23, and, as such, unpopular. Nevertheless, almost all members of the priestly families, including the high-priest himself, were Sadducees. Both parties were concerned in the Jewish governing body, the Sanhedrin (more powerful now than under Herod). The high-priests were members of that assembly and the Pharisees exercised a strong influence in it through the scribes (see on 2:4). The Pharisees though loathing the occupying Power prudently repressed their nationalism ; the more cynical Sadducees were indifferent to any regime provided it left them in office. The Pharisees were, perhaps, more concerned with the religious aspect of the Baptist's movement but, like the Sadducees, they would fear its taking a political turn disastrous alike to the State and to their own interests.

h They come, therefore, as spies not as devotees and John knows it. He ironically asks : Who can have taught the Teachers ? They have clearly come with subtle and venomous intent (' vipers ', *cf.* Ps 13:3). They cannot escape the *coming wrath* of the Messianic judgement without a profound change of heart with its appropriate change of life (' fruit corresponding to repentance ', Joüon). Provoked, evidently, by their pompous attitude the Baptist interjects : ' *Bear not the appearance of those inwardly saying " We are the sons of Abraham ! " '* They are priding themselves on a divine gift in receiving which they were as passive as the stones on the river bank. He then, 10, resumes the invitation of 8. The axe of the Messianic judgement already threatens the fruitless trees but there is still a short time for repentance. The ' fire ' that awaits the felled trees is not explicitly the fire of hell but a metaphor indicating in general the punishment reserved for those who do not

i take the present opportunity. **11-12.** John now turns to address the crowd (*cf.* Lk 3:15 f.) who conjecture his Messiahship to assure them that he and his baptism will not bear comparison with the real Messias and the baptism to come. John is less than a slave, unworthy to bear his shoes. His baptism is only an expression of, and stimulus to, repentance ; the baptism of the coming Messias will be a steeping in the Holy Spirit, a pro-

foundly purifying fire (*cf.* the Messianic purification of Mal 3:2 f.), not merely touching the surface like water. ' And fire ',(being without the preposition, is explanatory of ' Holy Spirit '). John thus foretells the outpouring of the Holy Spirit, Ac 2:3, of which the sacrament of Baptism is one means. This purifying action on the individual soul produces a distinction between those who accept and those who refuse it. Hence the Messianic action is like a winnowing-fan (or fork) : the grain is thrown into the air and the wind carries off the light chaff. The perspective is final : those not purified by the fire of the Spirit will be consumed by the fire of the wrath of God, Is 66:24.

III 13-17 Baptism of the Messias Son of God (Mk 1:9–11 ; Lk 3:21 f.)—Our Lord comes from Nazareth, 2:23, to associate himself by baptism with all who thus expressed their readiness for the Messianic era. As his kinsman, Lk 1:36, John very probably knew him personally. He is evidently aware of the sanctity of Jesus and (as Mt suggests, *cp.* 11, 14) of his Messiahship. Of this last, however, John was not formally assured until after the Baptism, Jn 1:33. The strange inversion of roles shocks John (Mt only), but our Lord assures him that *for this occasion* (ἄρτι) it must be accepted since it is the divine will (' Justice ': δικαιοσύνη, *i.e.* observance of the due order established by God). ' Why had the institutor of the new Baptism to receive the old. . . . ? This is precisely the question that Mt answers and the one that lies at the root of his gospel. It is not by a coincidence that this same evangelist has here, 15, used " fulfil " as in 2:15, 17, 23 ; 5:17. Jesus did not come as a revolutionary innovator, he came to perfect the old order. Just as he submitted himself to the Law, so he accepted the conditions preparatory to the Messianic age—the principal condition appearing as a baptism of repentance. It was God's design for a period of transition ', Lagrange. **16-17.** Where others had delayed in order to confess their sins, 6, the innocent Christ does not, but, being baptized, ' forthwith ' leaves the water. The heavens (the clouds ?) were torn apart, Mk 1:10, like a veil before him to give passage to the descending and approaching Spirit. The shape of a dove is fitting for the brooding and creative Spirit (Gen 1:2 note). Its appearance at this decisive moment in conjunction with the voice of the Father and the person of the Son would symbolize, for a Christian writer familiar with Baptism and its formula, the second creation—the re-birth through water and the Holy Ghost. Whether the dove was seen and the voice heard by the bystanders is not clear, but the Baptist's function as herald of the Messias and his own words, Jn 1:32–34, suggest at least that it was John alone who saw the full significance of both. The words of the Voice, *cf.* Is 42:1 but note the significant substitution of ' Son ' for ' Servant ', do not imply that the divine sonship of our Lord dates from the Baptism. Had this been Mt's intention he would aptly have completed his echo of Ps 2:7 (' Thou art my son ') with its following words : ' This day I have begotten thee '. It is the voice of the Father testifying to John (and the bystanders ?) and at the same time encouraging his incarnate Son with a new expression of his love. The descent of the Spirit is the Son's investiture for his heroic office ; *cf.* Is 42:1 ; 61:1 ; Lk 4:18.

IV 1-11 The Messias challenged : the Temptations (Mk 1:12–13 ; Lk 4:1–13)—**1-2.** The Spirit who had appeared at the Baptism now leads Jesus to his encounter with the personal power of evil, naturally hostile to the Messianic plan. The single combat is to be engaged on the devil's own ground—the desert ; *cf.* 12:43. According to a tradition dating back to the 5th cent. this is the lonely, barren, mountainous district between Jerusalem and Jericho. **3-4.** *First Temptation.* Our Lord's unbroken fast of forty days (model of our Lenten fast, and *cf.* Moses in Ex 34:28 ; Elias in 3 Kg 19:8) provides the occasion for the first temptation. The devil has evidently heard the Voice, 3:17, because he echoes its phrase : Son of God. His words ' If thou be the Son of God ', though perhaps only half-understood, are only an affectation of doubt. They seek to goad our Lord to a self-assertive and unnecessary (11) display of power. The word ' tempt ' (lit. ' to put to the test ') is therefore here to be understood in its usual sense of stimulating to evil rather than in the possible sense of seeking information, 22:35 note. Our Lord, who later was to create bread for the multitudes, refuses to work such a miracle in his own interest and declines to demonstrate his powers to the devil. He is content with a quotation from Holy Writ, Deut 8:3, to show his perfect detachment from everything but God's will. The text in its original setting declares that the manna had shown that God could dispense with the ordinary means of sustenance when necessary ; its basic lesson is calm trust in God. Our Lord refuses to anticipate God's providence and later, 11, his trust is amply vindicated. In the circumstances, his retort, unlike the dictum of Jn 4:34, refers rather to physical life than to the life of the spirit. **5-7.** *Second Temptation.* The devil now takes our Lord to Jerusalem, *c* 20 m. from the traditional site of the first and third temptations. He causes him to stand (ἐστήσε, *cf.* 18:2) on a projection of the temple roof (πτερύγιον)—probably on the SE. corner of the outer temple about 300 feet above the valley of the Kedron. Jesus has already used a Scriptural text to express his confidence in God ; the devil adroitly joins issue on this very point. But the situation (' cast thyself down ') would turn the confidence of the psalm quoted, 90:11, into presumption. Our Lord counters with a quotation (Deut 6:16 referring to the incident of Ex 17:7) which supposes that the Son will not thus seek to wrench a miracle from the Father. Miracles must not be the condition of our trust in God : such an attitude is ' tempting ' God, *i.e.* ' putting him to the test '. **8-11.** *Third Temptation.* Satan stakes all. The traditional scene is Djebel Qarantal, a few miles NW. of Jericho. This mountain, walling-in the plain of Jericho, looks eastwards across Jordan to the hills of Moab. The devil now appeals to earthly ambition and his boast of political power (*cf.* 2 Cor 4:4) does not today appear empty. **10.** But this is the only power he can offer and our Lord refuses it. His kingdom is not of this world. He names the devil for what he is—Satan. (In Heb. satan—rendered διάβολος in Gk—means an enemy, 1 Kg 29:4, or legal accuser, Ps 108:6, and in post-exilic literature the archenemy of man, 1 Par 21:1,and his accuser before God, Job 1:6–2:7.) Jesus quotes the great principle of Hebrew monotheism, Deut 6:13, anticipating his own declaration that it is impossible to serve two masters, Mt 6:24. Satan leaves him ' for a time ', Lk, to return in other guise, Mt 16:22 f., Lk 22:3, 53. The ' ministry ' of the angels appears in Mk 1:13 (' were ministering ' WV) to extend over the forty days' fast. It is evidently not a ministering of food. In Mt also it is possible that the service (διακονεῖν) is to be taken in the more general sense, 25:44, of a support which rendered food unnecessary.

Notes on the Temptations. (a) Messianic Significance. —There are three occasions of temptation, but the underlying suggestion is one : to take the crown without the cross. But since this is directly opposed to the divine plan (*cf.* Is 53:2–12 ; Zach 12:10 ff.) the crown can only be an earthly one. The devil, fully aware of the Messianic atmosphere, seeks to make the approaching attack on his kingdom harmless. Experience had taught him all he had to lose when men took the hard way and the prophets had pointed this way to the establishment of the Messianic kingdom. It was for him to urge the easy and deceptive way. There is a crescendo in his temptations. He suggests first the reasonable satisfaction of bodily needs (certainly not gluttony after forty days' fast) by means of a miracle before one witness only. The second is an invitation to a more spectacular display of power. The choice of the distant temple for the scene of the second temptation evidently has point : it suggests the achievement of popular Messianic acclaim by means of a public prodigy worked in the sacred precincts. In each case our Lord

is called upon for an unwarranted provocation of God's **683f** power. The instinct of the tempter is sound : he probes for the defects which normally accompany human qualities, assuming that where he finds great trust in God he will find presumption. Having failed, in the first two temptations, to reveal presumption he begins to suspect the strength of the quality of which it is usually the defect. The third temptation, therefore, attacks the quality of trust. It invites to total apostasy from God and reliance upon Satan himself. **(b) Mode g of the Temptations.** It seems clear that the evangelists intend to describe temptations with the three distinct, objective actions mentioned. They do not convey the impression of a general ' psychological struggle from which Christ emerged with a clearer and higher idea of his Messianic mission '. But how did Satan communicate his suggestions ? The texts hint (but do not formally state) that Satan was visible—probably in human form (*cf.* παραλαμβάνω, *i.e.* to take as companion, 4:5, 8). The vision of ' all the kingdoms of the earth ' appears to be presented as a miracle worked upon the imagination, Lk 4:5. On the other hand, the journey to the temple seems more than visionary (though see Lebreton in DBV(S) 4 991). There is, however, no suggestion of levitation in Satan's action. The verb παραλαμβάνω, like its Aramaic equivalent *d^ebar*, in no way implies taking hold of another physically, by the hand for instance (Joüon). **(c) Nature and further h Purpose of the Temptations.** By reason of the hypostatic union our Lord was incapable of sin nor, being without original sin, could he be tempted from within by concupiscence (*i.e.* by the inordinate desire consequent upon original sin). He could be tempted, therefore, not by the lower nature itself, but only by the exterior suggestion of the Enemy ; *cf.* ST 3, 41, 1, ad 3. The devil's proposition could be presented to our Lord's senses or imagination and so to his judgement. But, in virtue of the hypostatic union, the judgement being affected by no intrinsic unbalance would unerringly perceive, and the will inflexibly reject, the inordinate suggestion. In allowing even this satanic approach our Lord warns us that the holiest may be tempted but leaves us a model of firmness in dealing with Satan. Lastly, he draws as near to our condition as his sinlessness would permit so that, through human experience, he could ' sympathize ' with us, Heb 4:15 ; *cf.* ST 3, 41, 1 corp.

C. IV 12–XIII 58 The Messianic Light shines on Galilee. 684a IV 12–25 Introductory.
IV 12–17 Capharnaum and Opening of the Ministry (Mk 1:14–15 ; Lk 4:14–15—Mt briefly introduces us to the Public Ministry with a glance at its first scene, 4:12–17, its first collaborators, 4:18–22, its first acts and their initial effect, 4:23–25. The Temptations had followed immediately upon the Baptism, but some months now elapse (for the events of this interval, *cf.* Jn 1:19–3:36) at the end of which Jesus withdrew from Judaea to Galilee. The immediate occasion of this withdrawal was the arrest of the Baptist (*cf.* 14:3–12) ; the silenced herald is succeeded by his Master and the work of the kingdom goes on. **13.** By way of Samaria, Jn 4:3 ff., and Cana, Jn 4:46 ff., our Lord went back home to secluded Nazareth ; *cf.* Lk 4:16 ff. He soon left there to make his headquarters in Capharnaum (Tell Hum on the north-west shore of the ' sea ' of Galilee) a busy little market-town on the Damascus–Egypt highway and situated in the old tribal district of Nephthali which bordered on that of Zabulon ; both districts lie north and west of the Lake. **14–16.** Mt **b** solemnly announces the advent of the Messianic age. He calls attention to the Messianic (Emmanuel) section of Isaias from which he has already quoted, 1:22 f. The text, Is 8:23–9:1, contrasts the Assyrian devastation of northern Palestine, in 734 B.C., with the future Messianic deliverance. ' The way of the Sea ' (ὁδὸν Θαλάσσης: better ' on the sea-road ' KNT) probably describes, in the original text, the district of Zabulon and Nephthali through which the road (the ' Via

684b Maris' of the Crusaders) passes from Damascus to the Mediterranean Sea at Acre. For Mt, however, thinking of Capharnaum-on-Sea ($\pi\alpha\rho\alpha\theta\alpha\lambda\alpha\sigma\sigma\iota\alpha$, 13), the 'sea-road' is apparently that which runs along the west coast of the 'sea' of Galilee. The district called 'Beyond-Jordan' is doubtless the province of Gilead on the east side of Jordan facing Zabulon and Nephthali; this too was overrun by the Assyrians. 'Galilee of the Gentiles' (the Isaian $g^e lil$, i.e. 'district' of the Gentiles had become a proper name) probably refers to a non-Jewish district of western Galilee. These precisions are of Isaias rather than of Mt who quotes the prophecy as a whole, content to see it broadly verified in the fact that our Lord's ministry opens formally in Galilee. **17.** The Messianic age (our Lord uses the same words as the Baptist in 3:2) has passed from prophecy to fulfilment. It is 'at hand'—a phrase probably equivalent in itself (as certainly in the context, cf. Mk 1:15 'the time is accomplished') to 'is here'.

c 18-22 Call of the First Four Disciples (Mk 1:16-20; Lk 5:1-11)—Mt here (though cf. 8:14-17) passes over the first miracles, Mk 1:23-34, being content with a general reference, 23 f. But he evidently regards the call of the Four (introduced parenthetically) as a necessary part of his summary introduction to the Galilean ministry. The ready obedience of the Four is more easily explained if we bear in mind their previous familiarity with Jesus, Jn 1:35 ff. For the detail, cf. Mk 1:16-20 notes.

d 23-25 Epitome of our Lord's Missionary Activity (Mk 1:39; 3:8-10; Lk 4:44; 6:17-19)—The verses are a summing-up, and in part an anticipation, of our Lord's missionary activity before the evangelist proceeds to present the great charter of the new kingdom, 5:1-7:29, and the power of its founder, 8:1-9:34. **23**, repeated almost exactly in 9:35, appears to prelude the personal work of Jesus as 9:35 introduces the mission of the apostles (Lagrange). His activity, doctrinal and miraculous, spreads from Capharnaum throughout Galilee and his reputation as a wonder-worker beyond the borders of Israel ('Syria'—probably the non-Jewish district to the south of Hermon). The preaching is the good news ('gospel', $\epsilon\vec{v}\alpha\gamma\gamma\epsilon\lambda\iota ov$) of the kingdom. The miracles were of all kinds: 'too numerous and too varied to be explained by faith-healing. It is incredible that all the sick laid in the streets were neurotic patients', *Plummer. Attempts to ascribe the miracle-narratives to the pious inventive genius of the later Christian community are not only gratuitous, but overlook the fact that the miracle-narratives formed part of the very earliest Christian teaching, e.g. Ac 10:38. **25.** By way of immediate introduction to the Sermon Mt suggests the audience. Crowds follow our Lord; they come not only from Galilee, but from the Ten Towns ('Decapolis'). This last was a confederation of Greek-speaking cities, all east of Jordan facing Galilee except Scythopolis; cf. Schürer, 2, 1, 94-6. They come also from Judaea, even from its capital, and from the district (Peraea) which faces it across Jordan.

685a V 1-VII 29 Sermon on the Mount.
Structure and Content—The discourse, four times as long in Mt as in Lk, appears to have been expanded by the evangelist according to a fairly recognizable plan. Internal criticism and comparison with Lk's gospel indicate Mt's deliberate insertion of some passages of our Lord's discourses spoken on other occasions. This is in accord with the evangelist's habit of synthesis (cf. Introduction, § 678c). But Mt has not been haphazard: though the connexion in some places is loose, the discourse as it stands is a connected whole and Mt proposes it as such. According to Lagrange the imported passages are as follows: 5:13-16 (Lk 14:34 f.; 11:3); 5:18 (Lk 16:17); 5:25-26 (Lk 12:57-59); 6:7-15 (Lk 11:2-4); 6:19-34 (Lk 12:33 f.; 11:34-36; 16:13; 12:22-32); 7:7-11 (Lk 11:9-13); 7:22-23 (Lk 13:26 f.). The Sermon, pronounced in substance in the first few months of the Galilean ministry, sounds the keynote of the new Age which our Lord has come

to introduce. The new spirit (and with this our Lord is chiefly concerned) is to be gentle, 5:3-12, generous, 5:21-24, 38-47, thorough, 5:27-30, simple, 5:33-37, and above all sincere, 6:1-6, 16-18. It must not be arrogantly censorious, 7:1-5, but rather mistrustful of self, 7:13-14, yet sober, prudent, discriminating, 7:15-20, and, finally, energetic, 7:21-27. In short, the spirit of one always consciously imitating his perfect and watchful Father, 5:48. Since this fatherhood of God pervades the discourse, 6:4, 9, 15, 18, 26, 32; 7:11, implicit appeal is made throughout to filial love. Love is to be the mainspring of the new era—and love can ask more than fear can command. God, through his prophets demanded less of a people that had to be mastered by awe; when the time was ripe he, through his Son, asked more of those who were made free by love; cf. Augustine, PL 34, 1231. The new spirit is thus at variance with the Pharisaic ideal by reason of the emphasis laid upon the spirit at the expense of the letter of the Mosaic Code and of the casuistry that had gathered about it. The Law does not pass, on the contrary its moral commands remain, but the fullness of time demands a new perspective. The Law, of its nature, could not go deep enough into the heart of man; its Pharisaic interpretations had spread too widely over his external actions. Hitherto there has been a wrong emphasis and an imperfect law. On our Lord's attitude to the Law cf. the interesting study of *P. Lestringant, Essai sur l'Unité de la Révélation Biblique (Paris 1942) 44-62. **Analysis. (1) The New Spirit: Basic Qualities and Rewards**, 5:3-12—The selfless outlook, having little to attract externally, must first be presented with prospect of heavenly reward (Beatitudes). 13-16 are a parenthetical warning to the preachers of the new spirit. **(2) The New Spirit and the Old Law: perfecting, not opposing**, 5:17-48. (i) The principle laid down, 5:17-20. (ii) The principle explained by examples, 5:21-48. (a) Murder and 'internal' murder (anger), 5:21-26. (b) Adultery and 'internal' adultery (impure thoughts etc.), 5:27 f. (c) Divorce once restricted now abrogated, 5:31-32. (d) Oaths once regulated now declared unnecessary, 5:33-37. (e) Strict justice gives way to mercy, 5:38-42. (f) Limited charity to break its old bounds, 5:43-47. **(3) The New Spirit and Hypocrisy**, 6:1-6, 16-18. (i) Example taken from almsgiving, 6:2-4. (ii) From prayer, 6:5-6; followed, 6:7-15, by a development on the subject of prayer. (iii) From fasting, 6:16-18. **(4) Interlude on the Demands of the New Spirit**, 6:19-34. These verses occupy a central place in Mt's arrangement. They describe the outlook that the new spirit demands—the single heart and the will confidently surrendered to the Father. **(5) The New Spirit in Action**, 7:1-27. (i) Its social manifestation (charity, prudence), 7:1-6, 12. (ii) Its difficulties and unpopularity, 7:13-14. (iii) Its opponents, 7:15-20. (iv) Its true possessors, 7:21-23. (v) Reward of action; penalty of lethargy, 7:24-27. Note: 7:7-11, absent from Lk's sermon, on the efficacy of prayer, have no clear connexion with the context.

V 1-12 Introduction and Beatitudes—1-2. 'The mountain' which served as our Lord's pulpit was evidently a hill near Capharnaum (cf. 4:13; 8:1, 5) dominating the plain of Genesar. It is perhaps near et-Tabgha, about half an hour's walk from Capharnaum (DBS 1, 947-50). Among the audience were many besides his more regular followers, 7:28. **3-12.** The sermon opens with a series of magisterial pronouncements which, in rhythmic prose, describe and approve the new spirit that our Lord is to preach. The form chosen ('Blessed', Latin: 'Beati'; hence 'Beatitudes') is biblical; Ps 1:1; 111:1; Prov 3:13 etc. The qualities mentioned are so clearly the product of one, consistent, spiritual outlook ('many facets of one diamond') that the shades of difference are at times very faint. The number of Beatitudes is reckoned variously as 7 (by elimination of 4), 8 (retaining 4), 9 (reckoning all the 'Beati' formulae, even that of

11), 10 (as a new 'Decalogue'). The last is the least probable and the choice probably lies between 7 (Lagrange) and 8 (Pirot, Buzy). **3.** The 'poor in spirit' of Mt (*i.e.* lowly in their own estimation) renders the sense of Lk's 'poor' (probably the original form of the dictum) since 'poor' in biblical language indicates all in adversity (rich and poor) who humbly turn to God; *cf.* *Plummer 64. It is for such that the kingdom, even now awaiting them in heaven, is designed; *cf.* Is 61:1. **4.** The term 'meek' (πραεῖς) in its OT background seems to imply much the same as 'poor' (πτωχοί) but lays more emphasis on manly resignation to adversity and less on the adversity itself. The reward in its original setting (Ps 36:11, almost verbatim) is of prosperity in the land of promise. In this context, however, 'the land' is a reward as spiritual as the kingdom of heaven, 3, or the vision of God, 8, and indeed the qualities our Lord demands (meekness etc.) are unlikely to win political success. **5.** The third blessing (reckoned in the second place by many ancient manuscripts and modern authorities, *cf.* WV) is for those who have cause to lament (without complaint, as is clear). It is a challenge and an answer to the problem of suffering. The promised 'comfort', as the atmosphere of the promises shows, will far exceed the sorrow, Jn 16:20. **6.** The eager desire for 'justice' will be more than satisfied. This 'justice' may be the state of the soul described in the Sermon ('justness' WV) or possibly the manifestation of divine justice when God is to reward the poor, the meek, the afflicted; *cf.* DBS 1, 935. **7.** The 'merciful' (*i.e.* forgiving, sympathetic, etc. to others) will obtain God's pardon which, to meet man's needs, must be and is infinitely greater than man's; *cf.* 18:23–25. **8.** From the heart come (in Heb. metaphor; *cf.* RB 31 [1922] 493–508) thought, plans, memory, affections; its 'cleanness' (*cf.* Ps 23:4) means, therefore, a freedom from blemished purpose. This purpose is, as the reward shows, the search for God. Nothing short of the direct vision of God will be its recompense, envisaged already in the OT, Ps 16(17) 15 (HT), more clearly in the New, 1 Cor 13:12; 1 Jn 3:12. **9.** The 'peacemakers' are those who by patience and, if necessary, by judicious intervention spread their own inward peace about them. These shall be called (*i.e.* 'shall *be*', in Heb. idiom) children of God—made in the likeness of the God of peace, 1 Thess 5:23, whose Son by nature is 'the Lord of peace', 2 Thess 3:16. **10.** Persecution endured for the sake of the religion of which our Lord is the founder and object (*cf.* Lk 6:22, 'for the Son of Man's sake') is pronounced a blessing (*cf.* Ac 5:41) because it establishes a claim to the kingdom of heaven. This last phrase (10*b*) echoes that of 3*b*; if this is the Semitic literary device known as 'inclusion' (the ending of a discourse as it began, *cf.* 15:2–20; 16:6–11; 18:10–14; 19:4–8; 19:13–15), it is probable that the Beatitudes finish here. **11-12.** An expansion of the last beatitude with the warmth and appeal of personal address and the added consolation of suffering with God's chosen prophets. **13-16.** dealing with the responsibilities arising from the world-importance of Christian discipleship (*cf.* Mk 4:21; 9:50; Lk 14:34–35; 8:16; 11:33) have no close connexion with the context. The world (the 'earth') is henceforth dependent for its moral well-being on the preservative influence of the Christian disciple. If this 'salt' become insipid (as the impure salt of common Palestinian usage could), there is nothing in the world to restore its savour. It is so much rubbish to be cast out into the street (the oriental refuse-bin). Even the world as it passes spurns the disciple who has lost his fervour. The comparison changes to light, like salt a necessity of life. The disciples have the social obligation (not incompatible with personal humility, *cf.* 6:1, 5, 16) of lighting the way to the Father by their example for a world in darkness. If they shirk this responsibility they thwart their public purpose; they will be as useless as a lamp hidden behind the flour-bin ('bushel'; μόδιος actually means one peck in dry

measure; here used for the jar that contains it). The comparison of the hill-town is surprising here and may be a separate saying of our Lord inserted in this place for convenience. The image recalls Mt 16:18. **685g**

V 17-48 New Spirit and Old Law. **h**

V 17-20 The Principle—17. The solemnity of our Lord's opening pronouncements and his clear intention of inaugurating a new religious movement make it necessary for him to explain his position with regard to the Mosaic Law. He has not come to abrogate (καταλύειν) but to bring it to perfection (πληροῦν), *i.e.* to reveal the full intention of the divine legislator (*cf.* 22:40 note). The sense of this 'fulfilling' will become apparent from the few samples he chooses, 21–48; the object of it is the total expression of God's will in the old order ('the Law and the Prophets'). Here, as the context shows, the emphasis is rather on the moral life in the new kingdom than on the fulfilment of prophecy in the person of its founder. **18.** Far from dying (our Lord proceeds, in this parenthetical verse) the old moral order is to rise to a new life, infused with a new spirit. Not its tiniest letter (the letter *yod* = *i*, in the square alphabet of our Lord's time) nor ' flourish' (KNT) of a letter (narrowly distinguishing letters like *kaph* and *beth*) is to pass away. It is as durable as the heavens and the earth themselves (*cf.* Lk 16:17, εὐκοπώτερον). **19,** pursuing the statement of 17 (*cf.* **i** 'therefore') insists that this re-born Law will be enforced with no less rigour. The Christian disciple is perforce always a teacher by his example, 13–16: neglect even of the minutiae will be noticed and will do damage. The new order is to be distinguished by the perfection of its inward spirit, 21–48, but it will not dispense with external works. By its exacting standards the careless disciple will be accounted less than his more scrupulous brother. The 'kingdom' in this and the following verse would appear to be the new kingdom of Christ on earth in which the Law and the Prophets find their goal and their deepest sense. **20.** Membership of this kingdom imperatively demands a sanctity more generous than that of the leading exponents of the Mosaic Law because its ideals are higher and its spirit more profound.

V 21-26 First Example of the New Spirit: Thou shalt **j** not kill—21. For the prohibition *cf.* Ex 20:13; Deut 5:17 and, for its sanction, Ex 21:12; Lev 24:17. The old Law, being a law, could control effectively only external acts. The new spirit reaches down to the innermost part of man and its sanctions are of the spiritual order. This double truth is expressed in Semitic fashion by our Lord in three parallel and synonymous sentences without crescendo, but with cumulative effect. For internal anger or a sharp, angry word man is to be accountable before the tribunal of God (ἔνοχος τῇ κρίσει . . . τῷ συνεδρίῳ) and thus liable to divine punishment (ἔνοχος εἰς τὴν γέενναν). The tribunals mentioned (DV 'the judgement' and 'the council', *i.e.* Sanhedrin—perhaps respectively local and central courts) are terms symbolic of God's judgement as the last sanction (hell-fire) shows and as the context demands. The Aramaic word 'Raca' (*rêqa'* or 'empty-head') means much the same as the 'fool' (μωρός) of the later part of the verse. The Aramaic **k** *Gêhinnâm* (DV 'hell'; γέεννα), *i.e.* 'Valley of Hinnom', a ravine touching Jerusalem on the south, was the ever smouldering rubbish-dump (*cf.* 2 Kg 23:10) of the city. In some non-Christian Jewish writings it becomes the place of punishment for the wicked. Used symbolically it is opposed to eternal life by our Lord himself, 18:19. The shock of the phrase in our context is lessened if we remember that our Lord is simply saying in striking language that the smallest faults of enmity are matter for accusation before a divine tribunal in whose competence lies even the extreme spiritual penalty. Naturally the tribunal will judge of greater or less. Nevertheless our Lord seems to imply that even internal anger can be murderous and so of mortal guilt (*cf.* ST II, 2, 158, 3 ad 2). The virtue of charity, therefore, comes before all ceremonial pieties, even that of sacrifice ('gift').

685k 25-26. It is a matter of spiritual prudence, too, as our Lord parabolically explains (*cf.* Lk 12:58–59). We owe a debt of charity ; the prudent debtor will attempt an amicable arrangement before the matter comes to court and so to imprisonment. The solemnity of our Lord's warning suggests the spiritual application of the parable.

686a V 27-30 Second Example : Thou shalt not commit Adultery (Mt 18:8 f. ; Mk 9:43, 47)—The prohibition (Ex 20:14 ; Deut 5:15 ; *cf.* Lev 20:10 ; Deut 22:22) in the polygamous society of Moses' day attached to the wife but not to the husband (over whom none of the wives had exclusive rights)—unless, of course, he sinned with the wife of another. Hence the punishment of Lev 20:10 ; Deut 22:22 is appointed only for a wife and her accomplice. Our Lord, who is directly addressing men, again condemns the internal act even if unaccompanied by external effect (DV ' to lust ', πρὸς τὸ ἐπιθυμῆσαι, *i.e.* ' to the point of lusting '). He is the first to point this out (the Rabbis quoted in this connexion, SB 1, 299, are post-Christian). The energetic language in which our Lord warns against the occasion of sin must not be taken literally, such language has its freedoms : the left eye, for instance, is no less a danger than the right. ' Right eye ' and ' right hand ' clearly mean all we hold most dear. If these are a trap (σκάνδαλον) in the moral path they must be put aside.

b V 31-32 Third Example : ' Let him give her a bill of Divorce ' (Lk 16:18 ; Mk 10:11 f., Mt 19:9)—Deut 24:1-4 mitigated the evils of divorce by demanding of the husband a formal renunciation of rights in the interest of the dismissed wife. Our Lord, attacking the matter radically, roundly denounces divorce itself as incompatible with the new spirit. The whole tone of the Sermon and the magisterial ' But I say to you ' lead us to expect a fundamental reform. Clearly our Lord is not simply taking sides in a rabbinic dispute. Rather is he robbing those disputes of meaning. (See § 708*b-d*, 19:3-12).

c V 33-37 Fourth Example : ' Thou shalt not forswear thyself ' (Mt only)—The Old Law, Ex 20:7 ; Deut 23:21 ; Num 30:3, forbade perjury and infidelity to solemn vows made to the Lord. This was good so far as it went, but such external vehemence should be unnecessary in the new regime of inward sincerity of mind and honesty of purpose. Henceforth, therefore, it will involve a disrespectful use of God's name amounting to a usurpation of what belongs to God. The disrespect is no less if the Name be casuistically avoided, as when the Pharisees swore by heaven and by the temple. They even sustained the validity of oaths made to the detriment of justice as when, *e.g.* a husband vowed to deprive his wife of conjugal rights. (This last practice was so common that it may account for the juxtaposition of Divorce and Oaths in the Sermon, Lagrange.) Man, therefore, has no right to pledge what is God's. He must not swear even by his own body, for over this, too, God has dominion, not man : the youth cannot make his dark hair grey, nor the old man his white hairs black. Our Lord asks for a simplicity of speech that reflects the equable spirit : ' *Let your word " Yes " be " Yes " ; your " No "*, *" No "* ' (*cf.* Jas 5:12). Extravagant vehemence proceeds from a disordered state of human relations (' is of evil ') and has no place in the new order. In this, it should be noted, our Lord is giving a general rule of Christian life ; moreover, his clear-cut phrases must be interpreted with the finesse that all aphorisms demand. Thus, for example, it was no less clear to him than it is to us that some answers cannot be ' Yes ' or ' No ' without misleading. Thus, also, he is not attacking juridical procedure in which oaths are calmly and respectfully taken. Yet even here the necessity for such oaths issues from a defect which, though characteristic of human societies, should be absent from the kingdom whose charter our Lord defines.

d V 38-42 Fifth Example : ' An eye for an eye ' (Lk 6:29 f.)—The Mosaic code (Lev 24:19 f.) sanctioned the existing practice of vendetta, but restrained it by the principle known in Roman Law as *talio* (*cf.* Lat. ' talis ', Eng. ' retaliation ') : the compensation was not to exceed the damage. This principle of personal vindication, effective in primitive conditions and the unpoliced State, had probably taken the shape of pecuniary compensation in gospel times. Our Lord, again speaking for the individual Christian soul and not for governments, subordinates strict justice to generous charity. Four little examples illustrate his point. Here again allowance must be made for the vigour of his language : he himself did not literally ' turn the other cheek ', Jn 18:23, but his prayer, ' Father forgive them ', Lk 23:34, shows what he means. The second picture, **40,** is of the law-court where a man is sued for his *undergarment*—' Let him take thy cloak, too ! ' The third, **41,** is of a man (or his beast) temporarily requisitioned for State service by way of errand or transport (ἀγγαρεύσει DV ' force ', is technical in this sense). Let such a one overcome his natural resentment by doing more than he is forced to do. As for the borrower (the fourth picture, **42,**) our Lord recommends neither the worldly prudence of a Polonius nor (for the whole context would protest) the investments of a Shylock.

V 43-47 Sixth Example : ' Thou shalt love thy neighbour and hate thy enemy ' (Lk 6:27 f.)—Only the first half of this sentence is found in the OT, Lev 19:18. Bearing in mind the sharp Semitic antithesis, the occasional Heb. use of the word ' hate ', Gen 29:31 ; Mal 1:2 f., and the hint of ' permission ' often contained in the future tense, we may thus render the second half of the sentence : ' but need not love thy enemy ' (Joüon). The old Law, addressed primarily to a nation, secondarily to individuals, was perforce at war with pagan foreigners inasmuch as they were a menace to the purity of race and religion, Deut 23:6. Moreover, by the *lex talionis*, § 686*d*, it committed to individuals the punishment of enemies (' hate ' in the juridical order). For the OT and the Rabbis, the ' neighbour ' is the Israelite. For our Lord (*cf.* Lk 10:36) the word admits of no exception. ' Jesus was the first to teach mankind to regard everyone as a neighbour and to love him ' (SB I, 354). Our Lord recommends not tolerance but positive beneficence : ' *Love your enemies and pray for them that persecute you !* ' This shorter version of 44 is to be read with the best manuscripts ; *cf.* WV. **45.** In this we shall be in the likeness of God—demonstrably his children—*because he* (not ' who ' DV), with his sun and rain, feeds the lands of friend and enemy alike. If we refuse this, in what are we superior to the despised publicans (9:9 note) or the pagans ? If we salute only those of our *clique, what generosity is this ?* (τί περισσὸν ποιεῖτε). (For the Aramaic flavour of 43-48, *cf.* *Black, 137–9.) **48.** By way of conclusion to his programme of the new perfection our Lord refuses to set bounds to the ideal. The children are asked to aim at the completeness of their spiritual capacity. When, in their measure, they achieve this they will be like their Father who possesses (though he eternally and of necessity) the fullness of his being.

VI 1-6 (7-15) 16-18 The New Spirit and Hypocrisy—The essential inwardness of the new era does not exclude the practice of external works with their danger of ostentation. Our Lord, therefore, warns his followers : *Do not perform your acts of piety* with a view to admiration. This intention robs the act of its spiritual value. For illustration our Lord takes three practices : alms, prayer, fasting, characteristic of Jewish piety, Tob 12:8. Each illustration is constructed on the same clearly marked plan : the practice, its abuse, condemnation of the abuse, advice ; 2-4 ; 5-6 ; 16-18. 7-15, a self-contained instruction on prayer, break the sequence of these illustrations and have apparently been drawn into this place by the mention of prayer in 5-6 (Buzy, *Klostermann, Lagrange). This hypothesis is confirmed by the fact that they are grouped about the ' Our Father ' which is elsewhere in Lk, 11:1-4.

2-4. Almsgiving. The hypocrite (ὑποκριτής, actor)

has many subtle ways of publishing his philanthropy ('sounding a trumpet' is metaphorical). Such conduct assumes the character of a mere transaction : he has bought public admiration ; the business is finished ; he has signed the receipt (the common technical sense of ἀπέχω ; DV 'has received') ; he can expect no more. The striking and original picture of secrecy (the right hand hiding its beneficence from the left) even suggests the unhealthiness of reflecting upon one's own good deeds. But nothing goes unseen of the Father (DV 'seeth in secret', *i.e.* seeth what is secretly done) and the reward will come. **5-6. Prayer.** Jesus does not condemn the practice of praying in public assemblies, Lk 18:10—the words of 6 are as hyperbolic as those of 3. Nor does he condemn the practice (in use among Moslems) of praying in the streets. He condemns the practice of deliberately striking a pious attitude for public notice.

7-15. Digression on Prayer (Lk 11:1-4)—First a warning, 7-8, then the ideal prayer, 9-13. **7-8.** There must be no gabbling over empty formulae. This is superstition like that of the pagans who feared to omit from their prayer the name of one god or the mention of one request. The Christian is not forbidden to lay his needs before God (though he already knows them) but he should do so in simple, general terms, and in a trustful spirit. Needless to say, repetition of such simple prayer as the Rosary is by no means discouraged provided it does not become mechanical. We use repetition not to secure God's attention, but to sustain our own. **9-13. The Ideal Prayer.** Mt's text of the 'Our Father' is longer than Lk's. There are three prayers for the glory of God ('hallowed be thy name, thy kingdom come, thy will be done') with an expansion ('as in heaven so on earth') and three personal requests : for food, forgiveness, freedom from temptation, with an expansion of this last (' but deliver us from evil'). Lk has neither of the expansions and omits 'Thy will be done'. The Jewish colouring of Mt's text (obscured in Lk's, *cf.* *Allen, 58) and its Semitic balance powerfully suggest that Mt represents the original form of the prayer, abbreviated and simplified by Lk. Lk, however, has probably given the prayer its exact chronological setting. Most of the phrases of the prayer are to be found in Jewish sources (*cf.* SB 1, 406-25) but its simple brevity and the deliberate exclusion of the spirit of Jewish nationalism (markedly present, *e.g.* in the great Jewish prayer, the *Tephillah* or *Shemoneh Esre*) prove that though the body may be Jewish, the soul is Christian (Buzy). The tenderness and trust of the whole prayer are revealed in the bold word 'Father'. The phrase '*our* Father' draws our Lord's followers together as children of one family. It is fitting that the first ejaculations should be addressed to the Father's honour which, however, is always inseparable from man's benefit. The Christian prays that the holiness of the divine 'name' (*i.e.* in Semitic expression, the person as known and revealed) may be recognized. Since this 'holiness' is not only God's sacred remoteness, Lev 10:3 etc., but his absolute moral perfection, Ez 36:21 ff., the recognition means man's practical acceptance of his Father's commands. **10.** The second petition implies the same recognition but, this time, rather of God's kingship establishing itself increasingly in the hearts of men. The third (' thy will be done') declares clearly what is latent in the first two : effective acknowledgement of God as Father and King is accomplished by filial and loyal subjection. May this be as perfect as that of the angels ! (Ps 102:19 ff. ; Lagrange). **11.** The second half of the prayer also has three members which, unlike those of the first half, are direct petitions for our needs. Of these, the first (' Give us this day our supersubstantial bread' : τὸν ἄρτον ἡμῶν τὸν ἐπιούσιον δός ἡμῖν σήμερον) is a request for the simple necessaries of life, embraced in the term 'bread'. The word 'supersubstantial' (Vg translation of ἐπιούσιον which, however, it renders 'daily' in Lk 11:3) suggests 'excellent', 'special' (περιούσιον) as it did for Jerome (PL 26, 43 ; *cf.* Prat II,

35 note) and favours a Eucharistic reference. Nevertheless, the word ἐπιούσιος (so far found only once elsewhere and with meaning uncertain, *cf.* JTS 35, 377) will not bear this translation. Etymologically it means either ' necessary for subsistence' (ἐπί + οὐσία) or ' for the day that lies before us' (ἐπί + ἰοῦσα, *i.e.* ' belonging to the coming' day, *cf.* Prov 27:1, LXX). This second meaning, though in itself more probable, makes the phrase ' this day' redundant. It may therefore be preferable to accept a third explanation (*Black, 149-53) and read ' Give us our bread *day by day*' as a more exact rendering of an Aramaic idiom (wrongly translated in the Gk) which runs literally ' of today and the following day'. **12.** The next petition is for i forgiveness of sins, called ' debts' in Mt and in common Jewish parlance (Lk has simplified to ' sins'). We ask forgiveness on conditions that must make us reflect on our own conduct towards those who have injured us (*cf.* 14 and 18:32-35). **13** is probably one petition put negatively and positively (the latter being omitted by Lk). It asks that our Father should not ' lead' us into temptation. Since God tempts no man, Jas 1:13, the phrase ' lead us not' may be understood ' permit us not to go' (in the Semitic manner, *cf.* Joüon & WV note). Nor does the word ' temptation' necessarily imply a direct invitation to sin ; it may indicate circumstances which, for us, prove to be an occasion of sin. The prayer ends with a final cry for deliverance from all moral evil (probably—in view of Mt's usual sense of τὸ πονηρόν—not ' from the evil one'). The word ' Amen' is a later, liturgical addition. So also are doxologies like : ' For thine is the kingdom . . .', probably added (*Plummer) to avoid ending the prayer with the word ' evil'. **14-15** explain and underline in antithetic parallelism (*cf.* § 313e) the condition of divine forgiveness implied in the petition of 12.

16-18. Fasting. The last of three illustrations j contrasting true with merely professional piety. The time will come when our Lord's disciples will, like the Pharisees, form a compact body of religious men. Like the Pharisees they will fast, 9:15. Our Lord warns them against the faults into which many of the Pharisees fell. Far from wearing gloomy looks and pulling long faces (ἀφανίζω ' to disfigure', or possibly ' to hide' with a veil as in certain Jewish fasts) the disciple should take the greatest care to disguise his piety. The image used by our Lord even suggests the appearance of one on his way to a banquet !

19-34 Deep Root of the New Spirit : Absolute Trust 687a (Lk 12:33-34 ; 11:34-36 ; 16:9-13 ; 12:22-31)—It is not improbable that Mt has gathered to this place various sayings of our Lord. Nevertheless they constitute here a compact discourse pervaded by the one ideal : abandonment to the Father and the futility of all else.

19-21. Experience shows the uselessness of trust in worldly goods. Hoarded stuffs are the prey of moth and ' rust' (βρῶσις, lit. an ' eating' ; more probably a variety of moth, or possibly ' decay') ; hoarded valuables are the prey of thieves. Not so (continues our Lord with elaborate Semitic antithesis) the treasure earned on earth, banked in heaven—real but intangible. Why not amass material goods ? Because, says our Lord, 21, such conduct shows that the heart is not set on God alone. His reasoning assumes that his hearers recognize this last duty at least. **22-24.** This sense of due proportion comes from a sound mind (' heart' ; *cf.* 5:8 note) which guides the soul as the *sound* (ἁπλοῦς) eye, like a *lamp*, shows the body its way. But if the eye itself be diseased (or ' evil', since the moral atmosphere hangs over the terms of the parable), ' then what darkness ! '. It is already implied, 21, that exclusive choice must be made between God and gold. Each is in practice a jealous master. The slave of two masters is in an impossible position. Their interests are sure to clash : he will have to declare openly for one or the other (' hate', ' love') or, at least *consult the interests of* one (DV ' sustain' ἀντέχομαι, *cf.* 1 Thess 5:14) and slight the other. **25-34.** Because this divided service is im- b

687b possible, we must renounce not only the anxious pursuit of wealth as an insurance against future need but also anxiety about our present wants, for even this divides the heart. The central idea of the passage is therefore freedom from anxiety ($\mu\epsilon\rho\iota\mu\nu\alpha$, preoccupation) and the word keeps recurring, 25, 27, 28, 31, 34. ('Mammon', more accurately 'mamon', is a Greek transliteration of the Aramaic *māmônā*, frequent in the Palestinian Talmud and *cf.* Ecclus 31:8 where *māmôn*, late Hebrew, means 'wealth'. The Semitic form—instead of the usual Gk word $\pi\lambda o\hat{v}\tau os$—is left here possibly because 'Mamon' is personified, Joüon) . **25.** The two primary needs are food and clothing. Food keeps the soul (life, $\psi v\chi\acute{\eta}$) in the body, clothing protects the body itself. Our Lord's argument is briefly expressed. It implies that, since soul and body are '*greater gifts*' (KNT) than their necessities, God who gave the gifts can and will surely sustain them by providing for their needs. Naturally, this does not exclude placing our needs trustfully before God ; *cf.* 6:11 ; 7:11. Jesus goes on to demonstrate his point from God's conduct towards even his lesser creatures—the birds (proving the 'food' point ; 27 belongs to this little section) and the flowers ('clothing';

c 28-30). **26.** Even animals make prudent provision and our Lord does not condemn them. He is attacking only worry—an exclusively human failing and inexcusable because man alone is conscious of a Father in heaven and of his own rank in the Creator's order. **27.** If this argument does not convince, appeal may be made to the obvious uselessness of *being anxious* ($\mu\epsilon\rho\iota\mu\nu\hat{\omega}\nu$ as in 25 ; DV 'taking thought'). This will not *add to life a single span*. $\hat{\eta}\lambda\iota\kappa\acute{\iota}\alpha$, DV 'stature', may equally mean 'age'; $\pi\hat{\eta}\chi vs$, DV 'cubit', *i.e.* the Hebrew measure *c* 1½ ft, may be used metaphorically for a span of life-time ; *cf.* Ps 38:6. 'Age' is certainly more probable in the parallel place in Lk 12:25 by reason of the preceding parable, Lk 12:16–20 ; it is perhaps more probable here also (*cf.* 25) especially as length of life, not of figure, is the common anxiety.

d **28-30.** The 'lily of the field' (called 'grass' or 'herb' in 30) is a simple flower (not, therefore, the gladiolus etc.). It is possibly the wild narcissus or the mayweed with its daisy-like flower (*anthemis*) ; *cf.* RB 54 (1947) 362–4. These are more beautiful in their God-given simplicity than Israel's richest potentate in his man-made splendour ; 3 Kg 10. If the Creator so cares for his creature, how much more the Father for his children ! Man's years outlast the season of the flowers and, at the end, he is to be gathered into the granary of eternity, 13:30, whereas the dead herb is destined only to serve man's humbler needs. The inference is obvious : only those (so many !) with less than a modicum of trust could fail to see it. **31-33.** Bringing to a close his attack on these daily anxieties our Lord tells his Jewish audience that such preoccupation reduces them to the level of heathens and, moreover, insults the providence and love of the Father. The kingdom and its *justness* must be the first object of daily care. The kingdom in this connexion is the way of life God requires of his subjects—a way that our Lord has been explaining ; *cf.* 5:20. Provided (and this is understood) man calmly pursues his labour, God will provide. **34.** Do not add today's anxiety to the morrow's sum of worry ; *the morrow will have anxieties of its own* (WV). God's providence allows a certain daily measure of difficulty ; the prudent proportion should not be upset. Since 34 speaks of difficulties in general—*kakía*, DV 'evil'— and not merely of anxieties ; since also it speaks not of the present but of the morrow, it has a viewpoint rather different from 25–33. This, *plus* its omission by Lk possibly indicates that the words were originally spoken in another context.

e **VII 1-27 The New Spirit in Action**—Before the concluding exhortation to action, 13–27, our Lord gives two pieces of advice for those to whom he has explained the new spirit. The first, 1–6, concerns the relationship of the Christian with his fellows ; the second, 7–11, of the Christian with God by prayer. There is no clear connexion of the sections within the chapter nor of this chapter with the preceding.

1-6 Judge not ! (Lk 6:37-42)—Condemnation of our neighbour (like forgiveness ; 6:12) brings a like answer from God. In this sense (but *cf.* Lk 6:38 note) the rabbinic saying 'measure for measure' is true, SB 1, 444 f. But even on the human plane such procedure is unjust and absurd. By a remark involuntarily echoed in our own conscience our Lord shows it. Psychologically we are quick to see (and to magnify) our own faults in others ('lynx to our neighbours, mole to ourselves ', La Fontaine, *Fables*, 1, 7 ; *cf.* Lagrange). We see the *splinter* ($\kappa\acute{\alpha}\rho\phi os$, a dry particle of sawn wood) in his eye and miss the *plank* in our own—this is the true proportion and it escapes us. Yet we kindly (and hypocritically) offer to remove what we are too blind to see. **6.** Yet a discreet assessment of our fellow's dispositions is sometimes necessary as when, for instance, there is danger of sacrilegious profanation. Indiscretion in such matters may turn indifference to malevolence, thus uselessly harming our neighbour, injuring ourselves, wasting what is precious and sacred. Our Lord speaks, as it seems, of prudence in expounding the mysteries of the kingdom ; he himself later, 13:10-15, shows the example. The principle was applied in the early Church (*cf. Didache*, 9, 5) to the question of non-admission of the unbaptized to the Holy Eucharist. Our Lord compares the indiscretion to that of offering sacred (sacrificial meat ?) or precious things to mere brutes which turn on the giver with disappointed ferocity. The comparison is a general one. We should not seek therefore to identify the 'swine', *e.g.* with pagans, nor the 'dogs' with lapsed Christians, nor to regard the terms as a pointed insult. The animals together represent the religiously unappreciative ; their distinction is merely graphic and stylistic in the manner of Semitic parallelism. This parallelism will be all the more marked if we accept the not improbable suggestion (adopted by *Black, 146–8) that the Aramaic has been mistranslated or subjected to interpretation and originally read : 'Give not a precious ring (Aram. *qᵉdāšā*') to dogs '. Our present text ($\tau\grave{o}$ $\ddot{\alpha}\gamma\iota o\nu$, DV 'that which is holy ') supposes an original Aramaic *qudšā*'.

7-11 Prayer Sure of a Hearing (Lk 11:9-13)—In Lk this passage is not included in the Sermon, and it is unexpected in this place in Mt, though it would aptly follow 6:33. **7-8.** It is a constant divine law that prayer is never unanswered. Provided we pray as our Lord taught his disciples, 6:9–13, a door will be opened to us (by God, as in the similar use of the impersonal in 2, 19). **9-11.** To doubt this would be to insult our Father. Even human fathers, with all their imperfections, are capable of perfect paternal love. How much more the heavenly Father who is perfection itself ! He will not disappoint the hungry children with a stone that looks like bread nor with a serpent (equally useless for food) which has perchance been netted with the fish ; *cf.* RB 55 (1948) 195–8. The 'serpent' may be identified with the *tropidonotus tesselatus*, sometimes hooked, and presumably netted, in the Lake of Galilee. Hence (in the absence of any similarity, comparable to the bread-stone similarity, between the 'serpent' and any known Galilean fish) the fish-serpent juxtaposition). **12. The Golden Rule** (*cf.* Lk 6:31)—The whole message of the ancient Scriptures which our Lord had come to fulfil (5:17 note) is summed up : In all things that concern our fellows (practical charity, forgiveness, kindly judgements, etc.) our best available standard of conduct is the treatment we should like to receive (though perhaps do not) from him. This eliminates the interest we have in ourselves or rather shares it with our neighbour, thus restoring the balance. Mt evidently takes this love of neighbour to include the love of God which is its true motive, 22:34-40. For a negative form of the Golden Rule *cf.* Tob 4:16. The original setting of the maxim is perhaps, as in Lk 6:31, after the 'retaliation' section, 5:38–42, though it would as suitably follow the 'Judge not' passage, 7:1–5. The falling cadence at the end of the verse and the echo of

887h 5:17 give the impression that the Sermon proper is now at an end. This prepares us for the concluding exhortation to serious action.

888a **13-27 Call to Action**—The Christian must not follow the majority, 13-14, nor run after every specious teacher, 15-20, nor be content with mere professions of loyalty or even with the grace of miracle-working, 21-23. He must do the will of the Father as declared by the Son, otherwise his efforts are wasted, 24-27. **13-14.** (Lk 13:23 f.). Our Lord does not minimize the difficulty of the Christian way of life, but laments the fewness of those who in fact follow it. He uses images familiar to Jewish teachers (SB 1, 461 ff.). The ' city-gate ' (πύλη), or possibly ' defile ' (Joüon), through which we enter upon the way is as narrow as the path is narrow (' strait ') to which it leads. That there are few who walk this way is a fact of experience. It does not follow that only these reach the goal—who can calculate the mercy of God ? Our Lord does not intend to define the number of the ' elect '—a question which he refuses to answer in Lk 13:23 f. It is the practical solution that counts : Strive to enter by the narrow door, Lk 13:24. The answer to the theoretical question is not useful to man ; God reserves the know-
b ledge to himself, ST 1, 23, 7 *corp.* We know that ' God wishes all men to be saved ', 1 Tim 2:4, and this is solid foundation for our hope. **15-20.** Beware of false guides ! *cf.* Lk 6:43-44. Again there is no close connexion with what precedes, but the passage has been drawn into this place by the idea of finding the right way, 14. Our Lord here deals not with the personal morals of those who falsely claim to bear a message from God (false ' prophets '), but with the damaging effects of their teaching. Doubtless he has the Pharisees in mind, but he is providing for the more distant future, too. These false teachers will bear the appearance of belonging to the flock of Christ, hence the danger. Heresies live on their modicum of truth. But underneath that skin, error devours the duped victim. Yet how recognize the false teacher ? A little patience and the effect of their work (' fruit ', by an abrupt change of metaphor) will betray them. That grapes and figs do not appear on thorns and thistles is a commonplace of experience. And *so indeed* it is with *any* tree (DV ' even so, every '). It does not, 17, nay cannot, 18, produce fruit alien to its nature. The *rotten* tree (σαπρός, decayed, or corrupt in the moral sense *cf.* Eph 4:22) will bring forth ' evil ' (πονηρός, wicked) fruit. The adjectives, which are susceptible of a moral interpretation, have been chosen with a view to the application of the comparison. **19.** Parenthetically Mt prophesies the punishment of these false teachers (or possibly the certain elimination of their teaching) in the
c words of the Baptist, 3:10 ; *cf.* Lk 3:9. **20.** The passage closes as it began (*cf.* 16a), summing-up what has been said (' inclusion '). **21-23.** Lip-service etc. insufficient ; Lk 6:46 ; 13:26 f. Our Lord is passing to his concluding appeal for serious action. He has just spoken, 15-20, of false teachers ; he speaks now of the danger of *self*-deception—the danger of presuming upon the privilege of belonging officially to the fellowship of Jesus. **21.** (Lk 6:46). The gates of heaven do not open to the urgent cry : Lord, Lord ! (*cf.* 25:11 note) but to those who do the will (good pleasure) of God. Jesus, with quiet assurance, uses the phrase ' *my* Father ', as again in 26:39, 42. He teaches the disciples to say ' *our* Father ', 6:9, but studiously avoids the phrase himself—his sonship is not of the common sort. **22-23.** (Lk 13:25, 27). Not even preaching on the authority of Jesus (DV ' prophesied in thy name ') nor exorcism nor miracles worked through that same authority will, in themselves, qualify preacher or wonder-worker for entrance when he comes to stand at heaven's gate. Unless such a one has also ' done the will of the Father ', our Lord will *openly declare* that even while working these prodigies the man was never truly of his company. Jesus himself significantly assumes the power of expulsion from the kingdom of those who, ignoring the will of the Father, have worked nothing

but iniquity (ἀνομία, *cf.* Ps 6:9). **24-27.** Concluding **688d** Appeal (Lk 6:47-49). Two parables in elaborate antithesis. The man who hears and acts upon our Lord's teaching has a firm dwelling. The torrential winter rains, the streams in flood, high winds (like those that brought houses down in Jericho in 1912, Lagrange) will not disturb it. Not so the man who builds on thin, crumbling earth (ἄμμος). **28-29.** Mt rounds off the Sermon with the formula he reserves for the end of his five great groups of discourse, 11:1 ; 13:53 ; 19:1 ; 26:1. All were amazed at the matter of the discourse and the manner of the Teacher. They were used to the Scribes and Pharisees who repeatedly appealed to the authority of Scripture and of the teachers of repute who had preceded them. But our Lord had interpreted, even modified, the Scriptures, 5:21-47, and this without appeal to any authority (DV ' power ') but his own.

VIII 1-IX 34 The Messias at Work in Galilee—The **689a** light that dawned on Galilee, 4:15 f., with the teaching of Jesus, chh 5-7, now shines also through his works, chh 8-9. Mt selects as samples ten miracles. He recounts them in one group though (after the first three) with significant interruptions. Between the leper, 8:2-4, the son of the centurion, 5-13, Peter's mother-in-law, 14 f., there is no pause in the narrative. Mt then makes general mention of many miracles, 16 f., and tells of the sobering demands made by Jesus of two enthusiastic would-be followers, 19-22. Our Lord and his disciples then cross to the east side of the Lake, 23, and three more miracles are narrated : the calming of the storm, 24-27, the Gadarene exorcisms, 28-34, and (back in Capharnaum) the paralytic, 9:1-2. This last is followed by the disputes on forgiveness of sins, 3-8, and, after Matthew's call, 9, on our Lord's association with sinners, 10-13, and, finally, on the fasting question, 14-17. The last four miracles : Jairus' daughter, 18-19, 23-25, the issue of blood, 20-22, the blind men of Capharnaum, 27-30, the dumb demoniac, 32-33, are interrupted only by comments on the effect of our Lord's miracles, 26, 31, 33-34. Mt, indeed, makes a point of noting the human reactions to this prodigious display of power. The confidence of those in trouble, 8:2, 8, 16 ; 9:2, 18, 21, 28, the astonishment of the multitudes, 8:27 ; 9:8, 26, 31, 33, and, on the other hand, the cavils of some, 9:3, 11, 24, culminating in blind hostility, 9:34. In this section, therefore, we have not merely a list of miracles arranged systematically to prove our Lord's powers. The miracles are narrated not, as it were, statically, but with a view to the dynamic development of our Lord's ministry in itself and in its impact upon the public. As for the exact placing of the events in time, Mt's general procedure and the fact that he is here selecting only samples of our Lord's miracles forbid us to expect rigid chronological sequence. This last, however, is not entirely ignored. Matthew's vocation, for example, is doubtless placed in its actual setting. The order of events is vastly different from Mk's (*cf.* *Allen, xiv-xvii). For Mt's independence of Mk, *cf.* §§ 610-15. For more ample historical detail on the miracles of chh 8-9, *cf.* commentaries on Mk and Lk.

VIII 1-4 The Leper (Mk 1:40-45 ; Lk 5:12-16)—By **b** placing the miracle in this setting (after the Sermon) Mt illustrates the power of Jesus, and at the same time his respect for the Law ; *cf.* 5:17. **1.** This verse may perhaps be reckoned as part of the conclusion of the preceding account of the Sermon. In any case, it implies no close chronological connexion with the miracle, which took place probably before the Sermon. **2.** The term ' leprosy ' was used of skin diseases of many degrees some of which were curable, though the cure had to be certified by the priests, Lev 13:2 ff. For description and distinction of various forms of ' leprosy ' *cf.* Lev 13-14. Leprosy in the ordinary sense of the word, however, was the incurable disease eating away the extremities and covering the body with running sores until eventually the flesh rotted away. This second sense seems to be demanded here by Luke's

689b 'full of leprosy', Lk 5:13. The leper had no right to approach : the precautions of the Law required that he live apart and never appear in public without warn-**c** ing. **3.** Our Lord's pity overlooks the legal fault. Moved by the man's faith he touches the repulsive body. Aware of his own authority and of his power to heal, he fears neither legal contamination, Lev 15:7, nor physical. The cure is immediate. **4.** Careful as ever, 9:30 ; 16:20 ; 17:9, to preclude popular excitement our Lord binds the man to silence ; vainly however, Mk 1:45. The injunction does not necessarily exclude the presence of the 'multitudes' (8:1, though see note) who may have been at some distance ; or possibly our Lord forbids only a formal declaration made before the priests had pronounced. Indeed, though the man was cured he was not legally pure before such pronouncement. The Law must be respected : first, medical examination by the priests in Jerusalem, then the complicated ritual of purification. The 'gift' (sacrifice) was, for the poor, of one lamb or two turtle-doves ; *cf.* Lev 14:1–32. The purpose of this last command is to afford to the official representatives of Judaism the opportunity of recognizing both the power of Jesus and his scrupulous respect for the Law.

d VIII 5-13 The Centurion's Servant (Lk 7:1–10)—Mt tells in summary fashion the more detailed story of Lk. The incident took place after the Sermon ; *cf.* Lk 7:1–2. **5.** The centurion (commander of one hundred men, approximately ' sergeant-major ') though not a Jew, 10–12, was well-disposed to Judaism and had contributed to the building of a synagogue in Capharnaum, Lk 7:5. He was an officer, perhaps, of a Roman garrison at Capharnaum or possibly of the army of Herod Antipas, tetrarch of Galilee and Peraea. **6-8.** A valued servant had been struck with paralysis (a general term covering, *e.g.* arthritis, meningitis). Having heard of the miracles of Jesus (*cf.* 4:23) the centurion enlists Jewish friends to ask him to visit the sick man (Lk ; Mt's account is shorter). Repenting his own action with its appearance of a brusque summons he hastens to forestall the visit and (through his friends ; Lk) professes his unworthiness. The humble words of the pagan soldier have passed to the lips of the Christian priest. **9.** The soldier knows what discipline is : he takes orders and gives them, and obedience is unquestioned (a man ' under authority ', one used to the atmosphere of military discipline). It is possible, however, that the original Aramaic read less awkwardly ' a man *that hath authority*, and soldiers are under my **e** charge ', *Black, 116 f. **10.** As man, our Lord was capable of wonder : ' although nothing was hidden from Christ yet a thing could come freshly to his experiential human knowledge, and so produce wonder ' (ST 3, 15, 8 *ad* 1). Israelites had shown their faith in him, 4:24, but the centurion's quiet conviction of his power to heal at a distance was a new experience. **11-13.** *Cf.* Lk 13:28 f. The faith of this Gentile recalls to Mt the words of our Lord (used probably on the occasion assigned to them by Lk) lamenting the fate of ' the sons of the kingdom ', of those who would naturally be expected to inherit the blessings of the Messianic age. The images of the banquet (for ' sit down with ' translate ' feast with ' WV) and of the darkness are familiar in Jewish description of the world to come. Nevertheless, Mt's formula ' kingdom of the heavens ' (*i.e.* ' of God ') does not exclude the kingdom on earth ; nor does it appear to do so in this place—especially as there is an allusion to those ' from east and west ' who, Mal 1:11, are to become subjects of a kingdom of God on earth. Many of the Gentiles will inherit the promises made to the patriarchs and finally share their reward. Ironically the very children of the patriarchs will, as a body, be excluded. In the darkness that lies outside the kingdom shall be despair and fear : *the* weeping and *the chattering* (*i.e.* from fear, rather than ' gnashing ' from disappointed rage ; *cf.* Lagrange, *Comm. Lc.*, 390) spoken of in the Jewish eschatological literature. Though, in that literature, the phrases are used in

connexion with a future, entirely transcendent order, **689**e we are not thereby forced to restrict our Lord's thought to the same limits. For him the ' kingdom ' inherited by the Gentiles is the kingdom of which he is the centre here and hereafter.

14-15 Peter's Mother-in-law (Mk 1:29–31 ; Lk 4:38 f.) **f** —In the interests of his logical plan Mt, unlike Mk and Lk, ignores details of time and circumstance. Actually the miracle preceded those of the leper and the centurion's servant. Simon (Mk ; Lk) called ' Peter ' (Mt ; *cf.* 4:18) though a native of Bethsaida, Jn 1:44, lived with his brother Andrew (Mk) in Capharnaum. The brothers invited our Lord (with James and John ; *cf.* Mk) to take refreshment in their home. The woman, cured in the height of fever (Lk), prepares a meal for *him* (αὐτῷ). This detail is mentioned in Mt's summary account not as a picturesque circumstance, but to prove that the cure was instantaneous and complete.

16-17 Various Cures and Fulfilment of Prophecy (*cf.* **g** Mk 1:32–34 ; Lk 4:40–41)—After sunset, as soon as the Sabbath with its enforced rest was over (Mk ; Lk) the people flocked thither with their sick. The miracle at Peter's house was soon known in the village. Our Lord's exorcisms, unlike the elaborate Jewish ceremonies, were worked by a simple command. Of the ' Servant of God ' who was to suffer the prophet had said : He has taken our sufferings upon himself and has burdened himself with our sorrows, Is 53:4. Mt (who quotes here from the Heb. text and not from LXX) applies the words, as the context clearly shows, to the removal of human sufferings. It is not clear that Mt means that our Lord undertook to endure these sufferings since the text as used here might be satisfied by our Lord's taking it upon himself to annihilate the suffering. Yet the Isaian prophecy means that the Servant himself assumed the suffering due to others (thus expiating human sin) and this sense would not escape the Christian reader fully aware of the Passion and its spiritual significance. Under the obvious sense of the quotation in this passage there lies, therefore, a profound dogmatic sense ; *cf.* Lagrange.

18-22 Demands of Discipleship (Mk 4:35 ; Lk 8:22 ; **h** 9:57–60)—The date of the departure across the Lake and of the two miracles, 8:23–27, 28–34, is uncertain but it is placed much later in the Ministry by Mk and Lk. The incident of the two would-be disciples, 19–22, is perhaps correctly placed in Lk 9:57–60. **18.** The ' multitudes ' surrounding Jesus are not necessarily the people of 16. Indeed, there is a ring of finality in 17 and, in any case, Mt does not mention the time of departure for the eastern side of the Lake. **19-20.** On the way to the boat (Peter's ?) a scribe (*cf.* 2:4 note) enthusiastically offers himself as a permanent disciple. Our Lord while not rejecting the offer warns him of the consequences of discipleship. It means sharing the homeless existence that Jesus is now embarking upon. Even the marauding fox and the wandering bird have their headquarters. Not so ' **the Son of Man** '. This **69** is Mt's first use of this strange title ; he uses it 33 times in all. The expression (*cf.* Ps 8:5 where ' *a son of man* ' means ' a mere human being ') is used by our Lord on about 40 occasions to emphasize his humanity and at the same time to surround it with a mysterious dignity. Its Messianic implication will appear only when it is placed in the setting of Daniel's prophecy ; *cf.* 26:64 note. Probably our Lord took the expression from Daniel (where ' one like a son of man ' is the symbol of the coming kingdom), giving it definition (' *the* Son of Man '). It is possible, too, that our Lord chose this title because he ' perceived the last consequences of the Messianic synthesis of lowly Servant, Is 53, and glorious Son of Man, Dan 7:13 f., thus accepting what Judaism in its retrospect upon its own prophetic history had refused to see or failed to grasp ' *W. Manson, *Jesus the Messiah*, London 1943, 117. On the ' Son of Man ' title ; *cf.* §§ 621*h*, 728*b*, 740*h*, 746*d*, 829*f* ; also Lagrange, *Ev. Mc.*, 1929, cxlix–cli ; Joüon, 601–4 ; *Plummer, xxv–xxviii ; *T. W. Manson, *The Teaching of Jesus*, 211–36 ; 258 ff. ; A. Charue, *L'Incrédulité*

des Juifs dans le Nouveau Testament, Gembloux, 1929, **Da**
40-6 ; *C. H. Dodd, The Parables of the Kingdom,
London 1935, 81-110. **21-22.** Of the scribe's reaction
to our Lord's words we know nothing. Now another
person, one of the disciples (Joüon) and therefore expected
to accompany Jesus on his journey, asks leave to stay
and bury his father. The respite he asks is evidently
short since, in Palestine, burial follows very soon after
death. But when God calls neither comfort must be
considered, 19-20, nor even the most sacred human
ties : Leave the burial of the dead to those who are
not alive to the greater interests of God : (WV note).

b 23-27 Stilling the Tempest (Mk 4:36-41 ; Lk 8:22-25)
—Storms come suddenly on the Lake of Galilee. Itself
more than 600 ft below sea-level, it is surrounded by
high hills. The differences of temperature produce
sudden, high winds from the north-west. The waves rose
high over the ship (KNT) but Jesus, taking the opportunity
of a brief rest, was undisturbed. When the frightened
disciples awakened him, he first (Mt) calmly rebuked
the lack of faith shown in the cry ' We are perishing ! '
They should have known they were safe with him,
awake or asleep. Erect on the pitching boat he rebuked
winds and sea as if they were unruly servants. Mt says
that ' the men ' marvelled—a strange expression to use
of the disciples (though cf. Joüon citing Heb. use for
' the men ' = ' they '). It is possible, therefore, that
Mt is rounding-off his account of the miracle, as in
9:8, 26, by noting its effect upon the general public
who would be informed by the disciples. Mt is more
systematic and less picturesque throughout than Mk.
For details, therefore, cf. Mk 4:36-41.

c 28-34 The Gadarene Demoniacs (Mk 5:1-20 ; Lk
8:26-39)—They disembark in the district of Gadara
(Mt ' of the Gadarenes ' ; Mk ' Gerasenes ' ; Lk
' Gergesenes '), a town of the Decapolis on a height
c 6 m. SE. of the Lake (now Um Qeis). It was a well-
known town, even called ' the metropolis of Peraea '
by Josephus (Bell. Iud. 4, 7, 3 and cf. Schürer, 2, 1,
100-4) and perhaps for this reason Mt (or his translator) uses the name to indicate vaguely the place of
disembarkation on the ' lakeside '. This place was
probably at a spot called Moqâ Edlô where, after thirty
yards of shore, the bank rises sharply to hills in which
are natural caves possibly once used as tombs, 28. A
mile or two to the north lies the deserted hamlet of
Chorsia (el-Korsi cf. Abel, Géographie de la Palestine,
Paris 1938, 2, 300), doubtless the ' city ' of 33 f. It
lies on the east side of the Lake facing Magdala ; its
name probably accounts for Mk's ' country of the
Gerasenes '. **28.** Mk (followed by Lk) mentions only
one demoniac, presumably the more violent of the two
and around whom the account, as Mk received it, had
centred. Mt has evidently an independent source of
information. **29.** The devils resent the pressure of
the power that confronts them (Mk ; Lk). They cry,
through the possessed : Why dost thou meddle with us ?
(KNT). They complain that our Lord has invaded
their territory before ' the time ' of their final expulsion
to hell. Meanwhile they claimed the right to exercise
their malignity on earth without interruption (cf. the
Jewish apocalyptic writings, e.g. Book of Jubilees, 10:8 ;
d Henoch 10, 12-14). **30-31.** In this predominantly
pagan district the Talmudic prohibition against the
rearing of pigs would be, as elsewhere, ignored. In any
case, it is not said that their owners (much less their
consumers) were Jews. For lack of a nobler object of
their essential malignity the spirits ask to be sent into
(or ' among ', Joüon) the herd (2,000, Mk) of swine.
32. Our Lord worked no second miracle to restrain
the devils from the pigs. He was concerned with the
salvation of human beings. Moreover, his rights over
property were sovereign and the demoniac action,
which he at least tolerated, was calculated to emphasize
both the blind malignance of evil and his own mastery
of it. These lessons, had they been learned, were more
precious to the inhabitants than all their pigs. **33-34.**
But the lessons were not learned, though the scared
herdsmen took the story straight to the village. Fear

(Lk) lost the villagers their great chance, and they asked **690d**
our Lord to go. Here again Mt's account is summary.
He has not the vivid description of the demoniac's
violence, Mk 5:3b-5, nor the subsequent history of the
exorcized, Mk 5:15-20. He is concerned with the fact
of the miracle and with its effect upon the public.

IX 2-8 The Paralytic (Mk 2:1-12 ; Lk 5:17-26)—The **e**
series of miracles is continued and Mt still notes the
wonder of the people, 8, 26, 31, 33. Yet a discordant
note is now struck—the opposition of the Jewish
religious leaders, 3, 11, 34. Mt, like Mk, connects the
three incidents that follow (the paralytic, the call of
Matthew, the fasting-question) but, unlike Mk,
narrates them before the Jairus's daughter miracle.
Mt's scheme is not chronological ; moreover he is as
usual less detailed than Mk. For his dogmatic purpose
he tells only the essentials.

1. Our Lord re-enters the boat and again (Joüon) sails
across the Lake back to ' his own town ' Capharnaum,
which he had chosen as his centre (cf. 4:13) on the
western shore. **2.** The house was packed (Mk) and
the bearers of the paralytic were forced to carry him
up the outside staircase on to the flat roof. Part of this
they removed, lowering the man through the gap (cf.
Mk 2:4). Our Lord was touched by the faith of the
paralytic and his friends. This faith, manifested by
their extraordinary conduct, is more obvious in Mk
than in Mt who omits the ' roof ' incident. It seems
from our Lord's first words that the paralytic's hopeful
courage is failing him at the thought of his unworthiness. The belief probably prevailed then (as later,
cf. SB 1, 495, and Jn 9:2) that sin was the cause of
disease and that pardon must therefore precede cure.
3-4. The declaration that the man's sins are even now **f**
being forgiven (ἀφίενται) or are forgiven from this
moment (ἀφέωνται) is actually a remission (cf. 3, Mk 2:7).
The thoughts of the Scribes (and of the Pharisees ;
Lk) are not merely troubled by our Lord's words, but
actively and spontaneously hostile (' evil ' 4). His words,
they consider, do an injury to God (βλασφημεῖ) since
only the Offended can forgive the offence (Mk). That
our Lord reads their thoughts is only the beginning of
their discomfiture. Note that whereas ' Pharisee ' is
the term for a school of thought, ' Scribe ' is that of the
profession of students and teachers of the Mosaic Law.
Not all the Scribes were Pharisees (some were Sadducees) nor all the Pharisees Scribes. From the time of
the Babylonian exile (6th cent. B.C.) the study of the
Law intensified and the profession of Scribe grew
steadily in importance. With the Law as his text-book
he expounded what we should call dogmatic and moral
theology (haggadah and halakah). The Scribe was not
fully-fledged until, after study from childhood, he
attained his fortieth year. He received the title of
' Rabbi ' and his authority was said to be greater than
that of the Law itself (cf. U. Holzmeister, S.J., Historia
Aetatis Novi Testamenti, Rome 1932, 187-92. The
qualified Scribe had his disciples who acted as preachers,
instructors, etc. in the smaller towns, SB I, 496-8).
5-7. The Scribes were thinking that it was easy to use **g**
a formula whose effectiveness no one could either verify
or contest. It was impossible to prove that the sins
were in fact forgiven ; our Lord, therefore, proves that,
where results can be checked, his formulae are not
empty. Hence he deserves credence as God's envoy
even when he speaks of the invisible world. He concedes that to pronounce one formula (forgiveness) is as
easy as pronouncing the other (physical cure) but defies
their incredulity in the first case by confronting it with
startling results in the second. ' He claims the power
to forgive sins without saying whether it is in his own
name or in God's. Yet he does not say that he has
received the power, but simply that he has competent
authority. The most natural conclusion is, therefore,
that he claims a divine prerogative ', Lagrange, Marc,
37. The term ' son of man ' (8:18 note) clearly does
not mean in this place : Man (i.e. mankind in general,
cf. Aramaic : bar 'nāšā') since our Lord is vindicating
a special prerogative for himself, just as his miracle of

690g healing is a special prerogative. Nor is it, of itself, a Messianic title. Used in this context it means that our Lord, though *a man among men*, claims to exercise on earth the very authority that God wields from heaven. It is already a hint of the doctrine of the Incarnation. **8.** The people are impressed by the miracle (' seeing it '), not by the invisible remission of sin. Filled with reverential awe they praise God for this miraculous power given to a ' son of man ' like themselves. Unlike the Scribes, 3, they forget the more significant part of the episode—the claim to remit sin.

691a **9-13 Call of Matthew** (Mk 2:13–17 ; Lk 5:27–32)— **9.** Capharnaum lay at the place on the busy Damascus road where the province of Antipas touched on his brother Philip's—hence the custom-house near the lakeside (Mk). Here were collected the tolls and dues. The publicans (τελῶναι), in the Gospel sense, were agents of the head-publicans (ἀρχιτελῶναι ; *cf.* Lk 19:3) who in turn were the representatives of those who bought from the State (in this case, from Antipas) the right to collect taxes. The demands of their masters and their own greed caused the agents to exploit the opportunities offered by ill-defined taxation and the ignorance of their victims. This conduct together with their professional association with Gentiles explains the common Gospel-phrase ' publicans and sinners '. Matthew (Heb. Mattai, prob. abbreviated from Mattatiah or ' gift of God ') appears in the lists of Apostles (Mt adds ' the publican ' ; *cf.* 10:3 note). There is no doubt that he is to be identified with the ' Levi ' of the parallel places in Mk, Lk. Two names for one person (even two Semitic names, like ' Matthew' and ' Levi ') were not uncommon (*e.g.* 1 Mac 2:2–5 and *cf. Corp. Inscr. Sem., Aram.* 158 ; 486 quoted by Lagrange, *Marc*, 42). The evangelist is not ashamed to make open reference to his old profession, but Mk (followed by Lk) uses the less-known name possibly **b** out of consideration (Jerome). **10.** To celebrate the great occasion Matthew invites his new master to a banquet (Lk) together with many old business-fellows and ' sinners ', careless livers, at least in the eyes of the legalist Pharisees. **11.** The Pharisees were certainly not sitting at table. It is possible that, in the fashion of the country, they stood at the door and watched ; or perhaps they had the facts only on hearsay and their objections were put some time after. They did not venture (*cf.* 9:3–8 !) to attack our Lord directly, but addressed their rabbinical scruples to the disciples. **12-13.** Our Lord's answer was in proverb-form. Others may fear the contagion of legal or spiritual ' disease '—not so the One who had come (*i.e.* into the world—a hint of pre-existence, *cf.* Lebreton, *History of the Dogma of the Trinity*, Eng. trans. 1, 210 f.) to cure it. ' Read and comprehend the prophet,' he says : ' It is devotion I desire and not sacrifice '. The quotation (Os 6:6 ; from the Heb. as in 12:7 where it recurs more aptly) is used to emphasize God's over-whelming preference for true inward devotion over the external observances even of the Law. The argument is the more cogent in that the prohibition of eating with Gentiles is found not in the Law, but in Pharisaic practice. The appreciation of this text should make them understand how much closer to God's mind is our Lord's conduct than their ungenerous cavils.

c **14-17 The Fasting-Question** (Mk 2:18–22 ; Lk 5:33–39)—**14.** It is not clear that the incident followed immediately upon the preceding (*cf.* Mt's usual vague ' then ' and Mk 2:18 note) though it is aptly mentioned in this place. The prime movers are, doubtless, the Pharisees (*cf.* Mk), but ' the disciples of John ' also take part. That our Lord's disciples do not fast is an opportunity of attack for the Pharisees ; for the disciples of the Baptist it is perhaps only a difficulty. (On the prominent place given to fasting in Jewish piety *cf.* Bonsirven, 2, 281–6 ; Edersheim, 1, 662–3.) The question has a Semitic form (*e.g.* Is 5:4) better rendered ' *How is it that thy disciples do not fast when we and the Pharisees fast so often ?* ' (KNT). **15.** Our Lord answers that fasting, which bears the aspect of sorrow, ill

becomes the joy the disciples feel in the presence of **6** their master. Time enough for fasting (the first hint of the Passion) when the Master has been taken away from them (ἀπαρθῇ. *cf.* Is 53:8 αἴρεται). The image Jesus uses is that of a wedding-feast ; *cf.* 22:2 note. The idea of the bridegroom would recall the Baptist's words, Jn 3:29, to the Baptist's disciples. The ' children of the *bridal-chamber* ' (in this case, our Lord's disciples) are the *bᵉnê haḥuppāh* or friends of the groom charged with the supervision of the celebrations. **16-17.** Our Lord's **d** defence of his disciples is driven home by two comparisons. Both point to the one conclusion, namely, the imprudence and impossibility of uniting incompatibles: the new and the old. The patch (τὸ πλήρωμα : DV ' fulness ') of undressed (' new ') cloth tears away from the cloak. Wine that is not completely fermented bursts the *wineskins* (of sheep- or goat-hide) rubbed thin by long use. In either case the imprudence is disastrous to both new and old. This dictum of our Lord's is loaded with consequences, gradually appreciated by the Apostles when the time came for the definitive break with Judaism. For the present, however, the principle has immediate application only to the Pharisees' fasting-observance.

18-26 The Woman with the Issue of Blood. Jairus's e daughter (Mk 5:21–43 ; Lk 8:40–56)—Mt uses a transitional formula (18 ; *cf.* 12:46) not to be taken as deliberately indicative of chronological sequence. The incidents in this section are (Mk, Lk) to be placed immediately after 9:1*b*. **18-19.** A prominent official of the Capharnaum synagogue (Mt ἄρχων ; Mk and Lk : εἷς τῶν ἀρχισυναγώγων) named Jairus (Mk, Lk) *prostrated himself* before Jesus asking a cure for his daughter, who was on the point of death (Mk, Lk) or (Mt—a celebrated difficulty) ' even now dead '. Our Lord and his disciples set out for Jairus's house. On the way (Mk and Lk only) news was brought that the girl had died, but Jesus reassured the father. Mt, according to his custom, telescopes the whole incident. This explains his divergence from Mk–Lk in reporting the words of Jairus. He is content to sum up the successive thought, fear, faith of the father in one sentence which he puts on Jairus's lips. Augustine, *De Consensu Evangelistarum*, 2, 28, 66, PL 34, 1110 f. : ' It is in the interests of brevity that Mt makes Jairus ask the Lord to do what in fact he did. . . . The two (Mk and Lk) give what Jairus actually said, Matthew what he wished and thought. . . . From examples of this kind we deduce a most useful and absolutely indispensable principle (of interpretation), *viz.* . . . that (a writer) does not lie if he makes a person say what that person wishes rather than what he actually said '. **20-22. f** Meanwhile, before news is brought of the child's death, a woman with a chronic haemorrhage, Lk 8:43, comes stealthily and timidly, but with great faith to touch our Lord's cloak. To escape embarrassing notice, partly too because the malady conveyed a legal im-purity, Lev 15:25–27, she touches the very edge of his outer garment—one of the multi-coloured tassels (*ṣîṣiṯ*) worn by pious Jews at the four corners of the cloak (Num 15:37–41 ; on our Lord's dress *cf.* Eder-sheim, 1, 620–6). She is immediately cured (Mk ; Lk) ; not mere physical contact but her faith had already merited the miracle (Mt). But she has not escaped notice. Our Lord knows what has happened, Mk 5:30 ; Lk 8:45, though Mt does not suggest that this knowledge is supernatural. **23.** With Peter, James and John (Mk ; Lk) our Lord enters the house of the dead girl and encounters the confused noise of the wailing sympathizers and the dismal music of pro-fessional *flute-players* (indispensable at Jewish funerals ; *cf.* SB 1, 521). **24.** He dismisses all this apparatus (' Get ye hence ' ; WV) as useless. There is no cause for mourning ; the girl is only asleep. Our Lord was to use a similar phrase of Lazarus, Jn 11:11. In each case he avoids the term ' dead ' because neither the girl nor Lazarus was irreparably dead (the usual implication of the word). That she is not still alive, however, is perfectly clear, Mk 5:35 ; hence the mocking incredulity. **25.** When at last the mourners are persuaded to leave, our Lord, in the presence of the father and mother and of his favoured three (Mk), took the dead child by the hand (Mt ; Mk ; Lk). **26.** Our Lord had taken precautions against undue publicity (24 f. and Mk 5:43) possibly because such a miracle might have provoked a Messianic crisis (*cf.* Lagrange, *Le Messianisme*, 176 ff.) yet, as Mt is accustomed to note, the *report* spread through the district.

27-31 The Two Blind Men of Capharnaum—(Mt only). The episode has, of its nature, certain similarities with that of the blind men of Jericho, 20:29-34, with which it is too confidently identified. The one common element that might be thought significant is the 'Son of David' cry which (if it be not imported from 20:31 —Lagrange) is natural enough at a time when miracles were inducing a Messianic atmosphere. **27.** As Jesus leaves the house of Jairus, two blind men (two for mutual support—a not uncommon sight in Palestine) hail him as Son of David, *i.e.* as Messias ; *cf.* 1:1 note. **28.** It is perhaps for this very reason that our Lord does not acknowledge their cry (*cf.* note to 26) but waits until he reaches 'the house' (probably Matthew's ; *cf.* 9:10) before he speaks to them. The 'pity' they have asked of the Son of David is clearly the gift of sight and our Lord asks only if they believe in his power to heal. They answer 'yes', adding a term of profound respect ('Lord' ; Gk : κύριε ; Aramaic : *mâri*). **29.** The cure proves they have not lied. It will be noticed, however, that the faith though perfect did not work the miracle, but was our Lord's required condition. **30.** Jesus most strictly enjoins secrecy—the more strictly, no doubt, because they had already openly proclaimed his Messianic character. But Mt notes (again !) that they could not resist the temptation.

32-34 The Dumb Demoniac (*cf.* Lk 11:14-15)—When the two cured of blindness had left the house there was brought in a man whom diabolic possession had made dumb. The exorcism was effortless (contrast the Jewish exorcisms ; Edersheim, 2, 770-86). The remark of all : ' Never was the like seen in Israel ', is the result of this last of a series of miracles. It makes a fitting and characteristic epilogue to chh 8-9, yet Mt is forced also to note the wicked obstinacy of the spiritual leaders of the people. Their remark, too, is doubtless typical of their attitude to all the preceding miracles, and our Lord later exposes its intellectual dishonesty (12:22-37, see notes).

35-38 The Need for Missioners (Mk 6:6*b* ; Lk 10:2 ; *cf.* Jn 4:35-38)—From our Lord's work amongst the people Mt is now passing to his preparation of the Apostles. The Twelve had already been chosen before the Sermon (*cf.* Lk 6:12 ff.) and had witnessed our Lord's work among the people—too much for a single human being. **35-36.** Experience in Galilee (and beyond ?) showed the desperate case of the people. Our Lord was deeply moved (ἐσπλαγχνίσθη) for they were *harried and abject* (KNT) like shepherdless sheep ; *cf.* 18:12-14. Their spiritual pastors had failed them. **37-38.** The metaphor changes (*cf.* Lk 10:2 which perhaps retains the words in their true chronological place) but, shepherds or harvesters, men are needed for the work. Otherwise the sheep will perish and the harvest rot where it stands. As with his other gifts, so with this : God will provide if we ask. By the Incarnation the divine Son accepted certain human limitations. The world has a duty to pray for men to help our Saviour. It is his own command.

X 1-42 Missionary Instruction—Our Lord calls together the chosen Twelve (1-4) to regulate their conduct on their first, and local, missionary journey, 5-16 ; 40-42 ; further instructions, 17-19, relate to a more distant future and a wider mission where they will meet not contempt only but inexorable and universal persecution, 17-23. Conscious of the Son's example and of the Father's loving vigilance the disciple must not capitulate, 24-33 ; his old life may be torn up by the roots, but he shall find a new, 34-39. Mt's well-knit discourse is probably a synthesis of our

Lord's missionary instructions given on different **692c** occasions.

X 1-4 The Twelve (Mk 3:13-19 ; Lk 6:12-16 ; *cf.* **d** Ac 1:13)—Mt does not narrate the call of the Twelve (*cf.* Mk 6:7 ; Lk 9:1) but presupposes it and mentions their names in passing. The section is but a summary introduction to the discourse. Here alone Mt calls them ' Apostles ' (*i.e.* ' envoys '), elsewhere ' The Twelve '. The number is chosen evidently because it suits our Lord's plan of campaign but it has the further advantage of symbolizing the twelve patriarchs of the new Israel. All four lists of the Apostles (Mt ; Mk ; Lk ; Ac) agree in placing Simon, Philip, James (' the Less ') at the head of each group of four. The members of each group are the same in each list, but within the group the names are interchanged in the various lists. Mt gives the names in pairs (*cf.* Lk), suggesting that this was the order of their sending. Mt (only) describes Simon Peter as ' the first '—a phrase unnecessary at the head of a list unless it indicates pre-eminence of dignity, *Plummer, 147. The name *Peter* (*cf.* 16:18 note) was probably conferred (Knabenbauer, Lagrange) and explained (Lagrange) on this occasion ; *cf.* Mk 3:16. *Andrew* (like Philip) bears a completely Greek name, evidently not an uncommon custom in ' Galilee of the Gentiles ' where Greek was freely spoken. Had other considerations not intervened, Andrew should have appeared at the head of the list because he was the first to come to Jesus, Jn 1:40. *James* and *John* both bear Hebrew names. James (Jacob) ' the Greater ' was martyred under Agrippa I in A.D. 44, Ac 12:1 f. ; John (' the beloved disciple ') lived to write the Fourth Gospel towards the end of the century. *Philip*, like **e** Peter and Andrew, was a native of Bethsaida, Jn 1:44. *Bartholomew* (Bar-Tolmai, *i.e.* son of T.) is commonly identified with the Nathanael of Jn 1:45 on the grounds that Nathanael is associated there (as Bartholomew here) with Philip and because Nathanael is grouped with the Apostles in Jn 21:2. *Thomas* (Aramaic : *t^e'ômā* ; Greek : δίδυμος, Jn 11:16, ' the twin ') precedes *Matthew* (unlike Mk ; Lk) possibly for politeness' sake ; modesty may account, too, for Mt's insertion of ' the publican ' (and see note to 9:9). *James of Alpheus* (possibly James, son of Cleophas, *cf.* Jn 19:25) is called ' the Less ' or ' the Small ', Mk 15:40, to distinguish him from James, son of Zebedee. He is probably to be identified with the Apostle, ' brother of the Lord ', first bishop of Jerusalem (*cf.* Gal 1:19 ; Ac 15:13). *Thaddeus* is apparently an Aramaic name (' stout ' ?) and another name for Jude (brother) of James, Lk 6:16. The surname Thaddeus (Mt ; Mk) or the addition ' of James ' (Lk) distinguishes him from Judas the traitor. *Simon the Cananean*, better ' the Zealous ' (Aramaic : *qana'na*) or possibly ' the Zealot ' (WV), *i.e.* former member of the active Jewish nationalist party. *Judas Iscariot*, *i.e.* ' man of *Qeriyôth* ', a soubriquet derived from his father, Jn 6:71. *Qeriyôth* is an unidentified village of Judah, Jos 15:25. Judas himself probably lived in Galilee like the other Apostles.

5-16 Instructions for the Local Mission (Mk 6:8-11 ; **f** Lk 9:2-5 ; *cf.* Lk 10:4-12 ; Mt 11:24)—**5-6.** In the divine plan Israel was to be first beneficiary of the Messianic offer, Rom 1:16 ; the Apostles, therefore, are not yet to walk the roads leading to non-Jewish districts (' the way of the Gentiles ')—neither northwards to pagan Syria nor south to Samaria, mixed in population and diluted in Yahwism since the Assyrian colonization of the 8th cent. ; *cf.* Jn 4:7. The mission is confined to Galilean territory. Mk and Lk, writing for Gentile readers, delicately omit the prohibition. **7-8.** The theme of the preaching is summed up in a sentence. It is the Baptist's theme (3:2 note) and our Lord's, 4:17. Miracles will guarantee the genuineness of their message. Their missionary purpose must not be obscured or defeated by the passing of money ; the power of miracle and doctrine had cost the Apostles nothing. **9-10.** Our Lord's advice for the journey is **g** not ' practical ' in the usual sense, but consists in a complete reliance on Providence. No need for gold,

692g silver, *copper* in their *girdle-pouches* (DV 'money in your purses') ; nor *food-satchel* nor warm clothing (*cf.* Mk 6:9) but barefoot and unarmed ('nor a staff'). Mk, 6:8–9, allows shoes and a staff. It would be difficult to prove that Mk and Mt are speaking of different varieties of shoe and staff (*cf.* however, Knabenbauer *in loc* ; Power, Bi 4 [1923] 241–66 ; WV note). It is more probable (Maldonatus, Lagrange, Prat, Buzy, Bover) that the general sense, and not the actual words, is preserved by each evangelist and worded according to his scope (*cf.* Augustine's words quoted on 9:18–19). Thus Mt's atmosphere is of complete detachment, Mk is more practical ; the substance of each is the same, *viz.* no undue anxiety but reliance upon Providence. The supernatural powers of the Apostles cannot be sold or bought, 8, but for the labour involved in their exercise, and in the preaching of the gospel they deserve their *upkeep* (*cf.* Lk 10:7 ; 1 Tim 5:17–18 ; Gal 6:6 ; 1 Cor 9:13–14). Providence will see that this is provided. **h 11-15.** Arrived at his destination the Apostle having found a respectable (DV 'worthy') house should lodge there until he leaves the town lest he appear restless or fickle or over-particular in material things. 'Peace!' (*šalôm*) is the common oriental greeting, but on apostolic lips it takes a religious significance ; it is efficacious if its recipients be worthy. In biblical writings, ' peace ' is the sum of all blessings. This apostolic blessing (like God's own word, *cf.* Is 55:11) cannot be robbed of its intrinsic power by the unworthiness of the person addressed : it returns to the giver that he may confer the rejected benefit on some worthy house. The despised blessing even becomes a curse : the last Judgement will show that such rejection of the good news of the Kingdom is a crime greater even than the typical wickedness of ' the cities of the plain ', Gen 19. Meanwhile, the Apostle will show symbolically that the unworthy house, though evidently Jewish, is no better than pagan territory. The gesture of ' shaking the dust from the feet ' is exclusively Jewish, practised on return to the Holy Land after journeys on the ' impure ' soil of paganism. It is ironical that the gesture should be turned against Jews (*cf.* also Paul in Ac 13:51) ; the Holy Land itself is not proof against uncleanness. It becomes clear that the old order of a confident national religion is passing ; *cf.* 3:9. **16.** The sombre possibility of rejection leads, through this transitional verse, to the prospect of active persecution. Good is not violent ; evil is (the opposition is brought out symbolically by ' sheep ' and ' wolves ') ; the only defence of the Good, therefore, is the prudence of the serpent quick to perceive attack and to elude it, together with the moral armour of innocence (of which the dove is symbol) which robs the attacking Evil of its pretexts.

693a 17-23 Persecution Prospect (Mt 24:9, 13 ; Mk 13:9–13 ; Lk 21:12–17, 19 and *cf.* Lk 12:11 f.)—The horizon widens and darkens and the tone of the passage suggests that Mk and Lk (as even Mt in summary fashion, 24:9, 13) have rightly placed its delivery at the end of our Lord's life. **17-20.** The terms (kings, governors, testimony to the Gentiles) though possibly explainable of Jewish territory (*cf.* 10:5) hint at a wider field. Parenthetically, 19–20, the Apostles are assured that they may still rely on Providence in their official defence of the gospel-message. No anxious thought (μὴ μεριμνήσητε, *cf.* 6:27) will be necessary ; the Spirit of their Father will suggest their line of defence. The readiness of the Apostles to face trial with courage will be a guarantee of their doctrine. We should notice how, in the remainder of this chapter, our Lord presents himself as the focus of devotion ; *cf.* ' for my sake ' etc., 18, 22, 32 f., 37 f., 39. The emphasis would be unique and intolerable in the mouth of a merely human prophet. **21-23.** Domestic dissension (not the formal overthrow of the old authorities spoken of in 10:35 where Mic 7:6 is quoted) will result because it is a new and practical religion with a defined rallying-point (' for my name's sake ') that is to be preached, not merely a philosophical system. Perfect endurance (*cf.* on 24:13) will

alone secure salvation : hence the preacher must **6** persevere though hounded from town to town. He need not fear that he will exhaust the cities, his places of refuge, before the ' Son of Man ' intervenes on his behalf ; *cf.* on 16:28. **24-33 Moral and Physical Violence ; Intrepidity** (*cf.* **b** Lk 6:40 ; 12:2–9 ; *cf.* Mk 8:38 ; Lk 9:26)—Fear of calumny must not prevent the preaching of the mystery of the Kingdom, 24–27 ; fear of death must not deter the confessors of Christ, 28–33. The tenor of the words suggests that they concern the period after our Lord's death. **24-25.** A tiny parable, lightly ironical, warns the disciples that at least they may expect no better treatment than their Teacher. They should be satisfied with the same. Indeed, lacking their Master's personal dignity, the slaves may expect worse—he had already been accused of alliance with ' the prince of devils ', 9:34. Vg, DV read ' Beelzebub ', identifying the ' Beelzebul ' of the Gk text with the name of the god of Accaron, 4 Kg 1:2 f. ; 6:16. Beelzebub is probably the Heb. form of the Assyrian *bêl dabâbi* (an opponent in a process of law). The name was chosen by the Philistines perhaps because this god was adored, in placatory fashion, as man's adversary (Heb. šatan) in the final judgement. The correct reading of all the Gk NT texts is ' Bee(l)zebul ' which appears to be related to the *B'lzbl* (actually *Ẓbl-B'l*) of the Ras-Shãmra-Ugarit texts, *i.e.* the prince-god (prince, Ugaritic *zbl*, *cf.* Gen 30:20 ; god, *b'l*). Since the pagan gods are reckoned as demons, 1 Cor 10:20, the term Beelzebul becomes equivalent to ' the prince of devils ' (*cf.* 9:34 ; 12:24 ; Mk 3:22 ; Lk 11:15). *Cf.* Zorell, *Lexicon Hebraicum*, 1947, *Ba'al* ; *Ẓ^ebûl*. The name is therefore apt for the arch-enemy of the true God. **26-27.** Repeated calumny may lead to self-doubt **c** which, however, is excluded in this case by the knowledge that the perfect Master was thus attacked (' therefore fear them not '). Another reason for confidence in these circumstances is that the truth will prevail either when the gospel-message triumphs on earth or at least in the final account, 32 f. With this for comfort let the knowledge of the Kingdom, confided in the intimacy of the apostolic circle (*cf.* 13:11) be boldly and publicly declared ! **28-31.** God alone, not the devil (*cf.* Jas 4:7) is to be feared, for only with his permission can both soul and body be consigned to perdition (not to ' destruction ', *i.e.* to annihilation, since the idea of the annihilation of the soul would be strange to Jewish theology ; *cf.* Bonsirven, 1, 527–9). The apparent harshness of 28*b* is due to the vigour of Semitic expression which does not distinguish the permissive from the positive will of God ; *cf.* 13:15 note. A second consideration to cast out fear is that the disciple is not lonely and abandoned among his enemies—he who creates and cares for the sparrows is his Father and cares for every fibre of his being. If the persecutor triumphs over the body (his only sphere, *cf.* 28) it is only because the Father permits it ; such treatment is only a mysterious form of the Father's care. **32-33.** By way of conclusion to the gist of the discourse (enduring loyalty to the Son and to his teaching, 17–31) our Lord sounds a personal note. On the basis of fidelity to his own person (a point of considerable theological importance) he is to be counsel for the defence or prosecution before the Father-Judge who, with the Son, will be watching from heaven. **34-39 The New Loyalty and the New Affection** (*cf.* **d** Lk 12:51–53 ; 14:25–27 ; 17:33)—Our Lord introduces an important modification into the current hope of Messianic days : the peace he brings is between God and man, not between man and man, as the world might give, Jn 14:27, and as the Jews expected ; *cf.* Bonsirven 1, 442–4. The dividing sword is his doctrine (*cf.* Heb 4:12) ; its supernatural edge cuts, if necessary, through the natural domestic loyalties (*cf.* Mic 7:6 where the words are a lament for the chaotic state of Samaria). For himself personally, not for his Father only, our Lord boldly claims man's whole heart, 37— it is the claim of God. Even the grim prospect of a crucifixion (all too familiar in Galilee since the ruthless suppression of the recent outbreaks, cf. Jos., Ant. 17, 10, 10) must be faced. But again (cf. 23, 32) the section closes with a word of comfort (in paradoxical form due to the epigrammatic omission of distinctions) : he that *hath found* (*i.e.* secured, procured) his (natural) life shall lose his (supernatural) life ; he that *hath lost* his (natural) life for my sake—not through any other considerations as a Stoic might sacrifice it—shall find a supernatural one.

40-42 Sharing the Work and Reward of the Ministry (Lk 10:16 ; cf. Mt 18:5 ; Mk 9:37 ; Lk 9:48 ; Mk 9:41)—These concluding vv follow naturally upon 14 : the ' reception ' (cf. 14) is not so much a material welcome (cf. 42) as a docility to the apostolic message (cf. Lk 10:16 : ' he that *heareth* you ') which is that of Christ and his Father. It is a meritorious reception of one who speaks on behalf of God (' prophet ') if it is accorded not from merely natural politeness but from a supernatural motive recognizing God's truth and God's sanctity in the person of his ministers (' in the name of ', *i.e.* precisely as, because he is ; cf. Joüon *ad loc*). Even material help, 42, given with the same motive to an insignificant and weary Apostle will associate the giver with the work, and therefore with the reward, of the Apostle.

a **XI 1-30 The New Order : Its Reception**—The Baptist's message, 1-6, evokes his praise as the usher of the Kingdom, 7-15, though neither he nor his Master could please the demonstrably ill-disposed, 16-19. This last thought makes Mt place here, 20-24, the denunciation of the sophisticated who scorned the preaching of the Kingdom. The same thought leads by contrast to the praise of the Wisdom which chose to reveal the mystery of the Kingdom to the simple by means of the omniscient Son, 25-27. To all such the Son addresses his appeal, 28-30.

b **XI 1-6 The Baptist's Message** (Lk 7:18-23—**1-2.** The usual formula (cf. 7:28 ; 13:53 ; 19:1 ; 26:1) closes the discourse of ch 10 and the Baptist's question serves to introduce the theme of ch 11. John's arrest (cf. 14:3 ff.) had been the signal for our Lord's preaching of the Kingdom, 4:12 ; it was the end of the old order. Word had come to John of our Lord's Galilean activity and it is important to notice (in view of the interpretation of what follows) that it is this activity which provokes the Baptist's question. This question is put through the medium of two, Lk 7:19, disciples. **3.** They ask : ' Art thou the Coming One ? ' (*i.e.* the one destined to come ; cf. the underlying Aramaic participle, Joüon). It is not clear from either NT or Rabbis that the phrase in this form was ' a common Messianic title ' (cf. the names of the Messias in Bonsirven 1, 360-9) but the Baptist had already referred, 3:11, to Christ as ' the one coming after me ' and had indicated him as the Messias. He certainly does not begin to doubt this now—he is no ' reed shaken by the wind ' ; nor, evidently, is he suspecting for the first time that Jesus may be the Messias. It remains *either* that the Baptist is hinting at the need for more incisive Messianic action (as, for instance, the outspoken denunciations of Mt 23) in accordance with John's own zealous Messianism (cf. 3:10-12) *or* that, himself content with our Lord's gentle method, he sends his disciples for their own instruction. This last view is forced to suppose that when Jesus asks the disciples to ' tell John ', 4, he

c enters into John's little plan. **5.** The disciples are privileged to witness miracles, Lk 7:21, which our Lord himself significantly sums up in Isaian Messianic terms ; cf. Is 26:19 ; 29:18 f. ; 35:5 f. That the poor (*i.e.* the simple and docile, cf. 5:3 note) have the good news (εὐαγγέλιον ; gospel) announced to them is another sign that the ' acceptable year ' of the Lord has indeed come, Is 61:1 f. ; cf. Lk 4:18 f. The Messias is in their midst ; there is no room for John's disciples to doubt it nor for the Baptist to urge a more explicit Messianic declaration. **6.** Our Lord's person and procedure, therefore, are justified in advance by prophecy ; to those of goodwill (which sharpens understanding) they are no snare (' scandal ') in the way of faith.

7-15 Our Lord's Panegyric of the Baptist (Lk 7:24-28) **694d** —The Baptist is praised not so much for his personal sanctity as for the part he has so faithfully played in the divine scheme. He is the strong bridge between the old and the new order. It is through no fault of his incorruptible temper and unassailable integrity if that bridge has not been used.

7-8. Galilee itself had been stirred by the Baptist's preaching (he had baptized as far north as Salim ; cf. Jn 3:23) and Galileans like Andrew and Simon had been among his disciples, Jn 1:40. All knew well enough that John was an envoy of God otherwise they would not have sought the desert scenes of his activity ; clearly they did not go to admire the scenery of the Jordan banks (*i.e.* the ' waving reeds '—a feature of the scenery happily chosen to suggest, by contrast, the Baptist himself imprisoned now for inflexible principle). They sought a man, then ? Yes, but they could not have sought him for any human dignity in him—otherwise, why the ' desert ' and not the palace ? **9-11a.** They knew him, therefore, for one with a super- e natural message, but they did not suspect as our Lord now assures them that of all the prophets John is the greatest, or indeed something greater than a prophet— a herald who proclaims the present king. John is the messenger (' angel ' DV) of the Messianic age : the messenger announced by the last of the prophets (Mal 3:1 ; ' a commonplace of Messianic prophecy ' ; and cf. Edersheim 2, 736 f.). The Lord's words in Malachy's text (cf. § 558a) run : Behold I send my messenger and he shall prepare the way before me. By changing the pronoun Jesus significantly identifies his own coming with that of ' the Lord ' in Malachy. In the order of prophetic preparation for the Messianic Kingdom none had such pre-eminence. That John worthily fulfilled the function is supposed throughout, but our Lord is not speaking of his sanctity ; it would be idle, therefore, to introduce the question of, *e.g.* our Lady's excelling sanctity in connexion with the text of 11a. **11b-15.** f Yet (still in the order of dignity and not of sanctity) the members of the Kingdom (already in existence on earth as 11b certainly implies) are more highly privileged (' as sonship excels servitude, cf. Gal 4:4-7 ', WV note). **12.** *Now* (δὲ) from the time of John's arrest (his ' days ' are the days of his unhindered preaching) when our Lord began to proclaim the Kingdom up to the present moment of Christ's speaking these members have been and are occupying the Kingdom. And this by dint of earnest effort (' violence ') for indeed it is a kingdom which yields only to attack by storm. It is possible to understand the ' violence ' and the ' bearing away ' in a hostile sense, *e.g.* WV, not KNT. The verse then becomes a denunciation of the Pharisaic opposition which seizes upon the Kingdom and bars its entrance to the simple folk who would come to it. Yet such an image is strained and the thought foreign to the context which is concerned with the praise of John's work. The interpretation would compel 12 to be read as a parenthesis since the idea of opposition does not enter until 16. **13.** This is happening before their eyes because (γὰρ) the time for prophecy has ended (the ' days ' of the Baptist, now over, were its last stage) and the prophesied Kingdom is now a reality. **14.** This being so, the audience is asked to give a docile assent to the surprising proposition that the ' Elias ', herald of the Kingdom in Mal 4:5 f., is none other than the Baptist ; see on 17:11 ff. **15.** This passing of one epoch into another is mysterious : the crisis must be attentively studied to be appreciated.

16-19 God's Wisdom misconstrued and vindicated g (Lk 7:31-35)—The discourse on the Baptist and the Kingdom suggests a reference to the Baptist's reception and to that of the Kingdom, *i.e.* of our Lord, its representative. The reception of each by the élite of the nation was unfavourable (cf. Lk 7:29 f. ; Mt 9:10 f.) and the attitude of our Lord's contemporaries (' this generation ') reminds him of petulant children who refuse to join in any game of ' pretend ' no matter how wide the choice offered—grave or gay. The com-

694g parison is adroitly chosen since the game of ' funerals ' recalls the stern Baptist while the merrier game suggests the less unbending conduct of Jesus ; *cf.* 9:10–15. Divine wisdom, effecting the design of salvation through both John and Jesus, is *vindicated* by its result (' works ' WV ; not ' children ' DV—probably a harmonization with Lk 7:35). Its effect is to demonstrate the insincerity of the opposition. The same message was delivered by John and Jesus, each using a different approach ; the rejection of their contrasting methods showed that it was the message itself that was rejected. Childish obstinacy had clearly been at work but the loving wisdom of God had done all that was possible : it stood vindicated by the manifest ill-will of its opponents.

695a **20-24 Condemnation of the Sophisticated** (Lk 10:13–15)—The chronological place of this discourse is doubtless towards the end of the Galilean ministry, but logically it follows admirably the attack made upon those who had rejected Wisdom's offer and introduces a description of those who accept that offer. **20.** Matthew's vague ' then ' introduces the condemnation. The towns are not attacked for their immorality (in the narrow sense of the word) as their unfavourable comparison with Sodom, Tyre, Sidon, shows. Their crime is spiritual obstinacy. God's offer, so clearly supported by signs, had brought no change of heart (' penance ', *cf.* 3:2 note). **21.** Corozain (Chorazin) and Bethsaida, towns of the lakeside, had seen much of our Lord. The ruins of the former (Khirbet Kerâzeh) stand on the slopes *c* 2 m. N. of lakeside Capharnaum ; Bethsaida (et-Tell) was near the lakeside on the east bank of the Jordan as it enters the Lake. On the question of two ' Bethsaidas ' *cf.* Mk 6:45 and Abel, *Géographie*, 2, 279–80. Our Lord's miracles were signs of the imminence of the Kingdom, 11:4–6, and the necessary preparation for the Kingdom was penance, 4:17. The Kingdom (and, therefore, the miracles) were first offered to Israel, but Israel refused the penance. Tyre and Sidon themselves, coastal cities of pagan Phoenicia and typical of those beyond the pale, would not have so refused. **22.** In the final assessment of guilt, therefore, rejection of a divine invitation will turn the scale. It is clear how far our Lord is from the national Messianism of his contemporaries and how exactly the Apostle of the Gentiles interpreted him. **23.** Capharnaum, privileged to be the adopted home of the Messias, 4:13, earns a separate condemnation and the most opprobrious comparison (Sodom !). Its pride (*cf. e.g.* Abd 1:4) is as high as its fall will be abysmal (*cf.* Is 14:13, 15). Yet this is not so much a prophecy of destruction, material and spiritual, as a declaration of exact and public assessment of worth when the time comes— the term ' hell ' is here, like ' heaven ', metaphorical.

b **25-30 Revelation to the Simple** (Lk 10:21–22)—The Son thanks his Father that the revelation is given to ' little ones ', 25–26. The essence of this revelation is the knowledge of the Father through the Son, 27. The Son, therefore, appeals for simple trust in himself, 28–30. The framework of the section recalls the more elaborate appeal for the wisdom of the Law in Ecclus 51:1–17 (prayer of thanksgiving), *cf.* Mt 11:25–26 ; 51:18–30 ; the wisdom of the Law ; *cf.* the knowledge of the Father in Mt 11:27 ; 51:31–38 ; the appeal, *cf.* 11:28–30. Nevertheless, the wisdom our Lord asks for does not come from study, however sacred, but from personal abandonment to him—to the Son who reveals more than the Law could ever give. The passage fits excellently into the context of the whole chapter though Lk probably gives it its historical place after the return of the Seventy-two (perhaps nine months after the Baptist's embassy). Certainly Mt's vague ' at that time ' contrasts with Lk's precise ' at that moment '.

c **25-26.** Our Lord praises (DV ' confesses to ') his Father as the overruling Providence of the great plan now shown to be in action. The praise is not for the ' hiding ' but for the ' revealing ' (in the Semitic manner ; *e.g.* Is 12:1). The simple folk, and especially the disciples, have humbly received both the Baptist and

Jesus despite the objections lodged by the sophisticated **695** and astute, 11:18 f. Their simplicity has earned an intuition from God that pierces the difficulties ; *cf.* 1 Cor 1:19–31. **27.** This verse has the tone of our Lord's words as reported by the fourth evangelist and has therefore been called ' the Johannine aerolite ' ; its undoubted authenticity is valuable confirmation of John's fidelity in reporting the substance of Christ's discourses. That the sentence is found also in Lk shows that it has strong roots in the Christian tradition, and its content is in complete accord with Mt's Christology. ' If we add the fact that a similar use of the Son—the Father occurs in Mk 13:32, this usage as a traditional saying of Christ is as strongly supported as any saying in the Gospels ' (Allen, p 123). The dogmatic force of the passage can hardly be overstated, especially if we remember that our Lord is implicitly identifying himself with the Wisdom of God (*cf.* his use of Ecclus 51). The Son possesses the fullness of the Father's knowledge (πάντα παρεδόθη). The bold statement that only the Father is adequate to know the Son puts both on the same transcendent plane. Moreover, the Son alone knows the Father and uses his absolute discretion in making the Father known according to the capacity of his hearers. **28-30. The Great Appeal** (Mt only). **d** The Son asks for devotion to his own person and acceptance of his yoke as of his comfort. This is not the language of a prophet, but of the Son who holds unique relationship with the Father, 27. The ' yoke ' (current metaphor for the Law ; *cf.* Jer 5:5 ; Ecclus 51:34 ; Ac 15:10) is that of the New Legislator. It is easeful (χρηστός) because he perfects the Law, 5:17, making outward observance subservient to inward spirit and thus developing a law of love, available and attractive to all of goodwill, 5:3 ff. Being *his* yoke it brings, too, the gift of his help. He asks for obedient disciples (μάθετε ἀπ'ἐμοῦ, DV ' learn of me ') because (not ' that ') he is the perfect master—not overbearing nor of an exclusive caste (unlike the Pharisees) but *gentle* and of a lowly condition willingly embraced (' humble of heart ').

XII 1-45 Divine Wisdom against Human Sophistica- **69 tion**—Four incidents, 1–8 ; 9–14 ; 22–37 ; 38–45, furnish our Lord with an opportunity to show his divine wisdom in action against the ' wisdom ' of this world ; *cf.* 11:25–27. They show how simple and kind is the one, how tortuous and ruthless the other.

1-8 First Sabbath Question : the Ears of Corn (Mk 2:23–28 ; Lk 6:1–5)—**1-2.** To judge by the order of Mk and Lk (Mt uses his vague ' at that time ', *cf.* 11:25 ; 14:1) it is shortly after the call of Matthew. Jesus and his disciples take a short Sabbath walk (about half a mile) through the fields. Reaping and threshing were two of the thirty-nine works forbidden on the Sabbath. Later rabbinic casuistry regarded plucking the ears as reaping, and rubbing between the hands (Lk) as threshing (Edersheim 2, 56, 783). The watchful Pharisees were already of this persuasion. **3-4.** Refusing to enter into casuistical discussion Jesus solves the question on the principle that necessity excuses from such ' positive ' law. He makes this principle irrefutable for his audience by citing the example of the great David, 1 Kg 21:1–6. From the anger of Saul David had fled to Nob of Benjamin where the Tabernacle then was. Achimelech the high-priest allowed him to eat of the twelve loaves called often ' of the face ' (because placed in God's presence in the sanctuary) or ' of proposition ' (προθέσεως, *i.e.* ' placed before ' ; *cf.* Lev 24:5–9). This offering was renewed weekly, the withdrawn loaves being eaten (by reason of their sacred character) by the priests. Yet David's necessity prevailed over this positive law and the exception had the high-priest's sanction. **5-6.** Our **b** Lord adds (Mt only) that the temple-sacrifice offered on the Sabbath, Lev 23:25 ; 24:8–9 ; Num 28:9, is a literal infringement of the sabbath-rest. A remark inviting the obvious retort : the temple service stands alone and clearly transcends all other duties. But the retort is boldly anticipated : There is *something greater* (μεῖζον) than the temple here. The presence of Jesus turns the field into a sanctuary. The saying opens up limitless horizons (Lebreton). In conjunction with other sayings (notably Jn 2:19 ; *cf.* Dubarle, RB 48 [1939] 21–44) it offers the person of Jesus as the great substitute for the old sanctuary—a substitution already hinted in Messianic prophecy (*e.g.* Is 28:7–22 ; Mic 3:12–5:1 ; Ez 11:16 ; Dan 9:23–27 ; *cf.* Feuillet, RB 56 [1949] 70–5 and notes to Mt 24:30). **7.** (Mt only). The quotation is telling (Os 6:6 ; *cf.* on 9:12–13, where it has been used already). These Pharisees have not penetrated the spirit even of the old Law. Otherwise they would not have allowed their legal scruples to oust prudent and charitable judgement of the guiltless disciples. **8.** Why guiltless ? Because their master, the Son of Man (§ 690*a*), is Master (κύριος) of the divinely instituted Sabbath and can dispense at will. ' Taken in the light of the preceding verses this claim to be " Lord of the Sabbath ", like so much else in the gospel, cannot adequately be explained by anything short of Christ's divinity' (WV).

c 9–14 Second Sabbath Question : Withered Hand (Mk 3:1–6 ; Lk 6:6–11)—On another Sabbath (Lk) in the *synagogue* (prob. of Capharnaum, *cf.* Mk 1:21 ; 3:1) a man with a withered hand was present, probably asking a cure. The scribes and Pharisees (Lk) are there to trap our Lord in act (Mk, Lk) and speech (Mt). In their eyes only danger of death could excuse the administration of extraordinary remedies on the Sabbath (Edersheim 2, 59–60). **11–13.** (Mt only). Our Lord's reply (clear in sense but Semitic in form and awkwardly translated) is not explicitly abstract and final (unlike 8) but primarily practical and deterrent. It halts the Pharisees by making them see their scruples in due perspective. In the case of a beast, their own property, no Sabbath-scruples ; in the case of a man, a mere individual to them, a singular delicacy of conscience ! Underlying the argument however (and explicitly in Mk 3:4) there is also the principle that a good act is permissible at any time. Our Lord, far from condemning the procedure in favour of a sheep implicitly approves it as a dictate of common prudence. It is a frontal attack upon Sabbath-casuistry, for which in general *cf.* Edersheim 2, 777–87. On our Lord's sorrow and anger on this occasion *cf.* Mk 3:5. **14.** For the Pharisees this act of defiance following on the others (*cf.* 9:4 ff. ; 9:11 ff. ; 12:2 ff.) was the last straw. Already decided on our Lord's death they are now concerned only with procedure. This they discuss with the supporters of Antipas ('Herodians' Mk 3:6, see note).

d 15–21 The Gentle Messias (*cf.* Mk 3:7–12 ; Lk 6:17–19)—Jesus knew (either naturally or supernaturally) the murderous mind of his enemies ; he therefore withdraws to the country districts. When the appointed time came he would deliberately walk into the enemy camp (Mt 20:17–19 ; Lk 13:22, 33 ; Jn 11:16) ; meanwhile there was work to do ; *cf.* 10:23. He did not intend that he should be ' made known ' as the Messias and popularly so acclaimed. He was no demagogue but the gentle ' Servant of God ' described by Isaias, Is 42:1–4 ; 41:9. In the form of this quotation Mt is influenced partly by the Heb. text, partly by LXX, partly by his own purpose in using it. Thus ' My beloved ' (' my chosen one ', HT, LXX) recalls the ' beloved son ' of the Baptism ; *cf.* 3:16–17 where the ' spirit ' also appears. ' He shall not contend ' (' provoke dispute ') is a reasonable adjustment (' shout aloud ', HT, LXX) to fit the withdrawal of our Lord, 15, from unseemly and useless dispute with the Pharisees. The ' Gentiles ' of 21 (lit. ' nations ', ἔθνη as in LXX) replace the ' islands ' (*i.e.* ' distant lands ') of HT ; it is an equivalent but more suitable expression for a Gospel which is to close with the words ' teach all nations '. The general sense of the passage here, as in Isaias, is that the ' Servant of God ' will *expound* (God's) *integral truth* to the nations outside Israel (' shew judgement ', 18 ; ' judgement ', κρίσις rendering the Heb. *mišpāṭ,* a word which here embraces the whole revelation

of God to his people, *cf.* Kissane, *The Book of Isaiah,* **696d** 2, 35 f.). **19.** The triumph of this ' Servant's ' mission will come not by noisy propaganda, 19, nor by harsh measures, 20. On the contrary, he will be tender with the (spiritually) weak and prudent with the souls in which the divine light is flickering out—the ' injured reed ' and the ' *smouldering wick* ' (DV ' smoking flax '). This is to be his firm policy right to the end when he shall *establish God's truth victorious* (by his Resurrection ?). Thenceforward the whole world will find its hopes in his ' name '—in his Person as revealed by his works and by those who tell of them.

22–24 Exorcism and Pharisaic Calumny (Lk 11:14–15 ; **e** *cf.* Mk 3:22)—**22.** The miracle is similar to that of 9:32–34 with the added detail (absent from Lk 11:14) that the possessed man was not only dumb but blind. It is possible that Mt returns to the same miracle here (in the context of the condemnation of the Pharisees) to tell of the controversy merely hinted at in 9:34. Alternatively (Prat, 1, 313) 9:32–34 may be an anticipation. It is possible that we have two distinct miracles but this hypothesis would seem to imply that our Lord did not reply to the grave calumny of 9:34. This would be surprising. **23.** Among the crowd there are tentative murmurs : *Is this man perhaps* (μήτι—only half-incredulous) the Son of David ? (the Messias ; *cf.* 1:1 note). **24.** With the Pharisees are scribes from Jerusalem (Mk)—evidently the plot, 14, goes forward and the Jerusalem Sanhedrin is in action. ' This man ', they say, scornfully echoing the crowd's phrase, ' is himself possessed by the prince of devils [Mk] who, through him, casts out the minor demons '. The accusation is desperate and (as our Lord will show) absurd. For ' Beelzebub ' *cf.* 10:25 note.

25–30 Our Lord's Retort : Significance of his Exorcism f (Mk 3:23–27 ; Lk 11:17–23)—Jesus, supernaturally aware of the Pharisees ' mind, first demonstrates the absurdity, 25–26, and dishonesty, 27, of the charge. He then passes to the positive conclusion to be drawn from his exorcisms, 28–29, and throws down a challenge, 30. **25.** The general principle is axiomatic : a divided kingdom (as Israel knew to its cost) is devoured piecemeal by its foes ; indeed civil dissension in even smaller communities (civic or domestic) is calamitous. **26.** The particular and topical application is obvious. The great ' Adversary ' (*šāṭān* ; *cf.* 4:10 note) of all goodness is himself no exception. Our Lord appeals implicitly not to a single instance of exorcism (which Satan might instigate for his own subtle ends) but to repeated examples ; *cf. e.g.* 8:16. If this were a set policy it would be the policy of a fool which Satan is not. Satan, therefore, does not cast out himself (*i.e.* his satellites)— the paradoxical expression underlines the contradiction in the Pharisaic argument. **27.** The argument, moreover, issues from prejudice. The Pharisees were the spiritual leaders of the nation at large. Among their disciples, therefore (' children '—a Semitism) were some who at least claimed to enjoy a certain success in exorcism (Jos., *Ant.* 8, 2, 5 ; Ac 19:13–14 ; Mk 9:38). Why did not the Pharisees denounce *them* ? Such exorcists are therefore living witnesses and (were the question put to them) perforce judges of their own spiritual teachers. **28.** Satan excluded, there remains **g** the one alternative—the spiritual power of God. That our Lord freely wields this power, without effort or restriction, is clear proof that he is the founder of a new era—the ' kingdom of God ' (usually ' of the heavens ' in Mt but here used to balance the phrase ' spirit of God '). **29.** How can it be otherwise since our Lord is already pillaging Satan's kingdom ? Satan, therefore, must be helpless. He is helpless not because weak or careless but because Jesus, stronger than he, has overcome him just as a robber may overpower a strong and vigilant householder. This victory has already taken place (with the Incarnation ?) ; it remains only to gather the spoils. **30.** It is a climax of history, a time for decisions. There are only two possible choices—God or Satan. Our Lord speaks with a calm assurance of dignity which recalls his manner of speech

696g in Jn. He will not accept tolerant neutrality nor benevolent suspension of judgement. The words are addressed probably to the waverers, hardly to the Pharisees who are clearly his enemies. The 'gathering' and 'scattering' metaphor is obscure. It is probably neither agricultural nor pastoral but general : all work is dissipation of energy when not united with the cause of Jesus.

697a 31-32 Blasphemy of the Spirit (Mk 3:28-30 ; Lk 12:10)—The meaning of ' blasphemy of the Spirit ' is to be determined by the context. In the first place, it is blasphemy *against* (objective genitive) the holy Spirit ; *cf*. 32. But, secondly, what precisely is the sin in question ? The context (to which 31-32 are closely tied ; *cf*. ' therefore ' in 31 and even more explicitly Mk 3:30) is decisive. The sin referred to is one of which an example has just been furnished by the Pharisees. They have perversely attributed to Satan what is clearly the work of God. This is only one example of conscious, hardened rejection of God's proffered light—the root-vice of the Pharisees (*cf*. Jn 9:41 ; 3:19 f.) as of others. This is the direct affront of the Spirit of wisdom ; *cf. e.g.* 1 Cor 2:10-13. It is the sin ' that remaineth ', Jn 9:41. Why does it ' remain ' ? Why is it unforgivable ? Of its very nature. Man cannot be saved without the gifts of God, one of which is forgiveness. If these gifts are perseveringly refused nothing can be done. ' It is called " unforgivable " because of its very nature it precludes those things (*i.e.* the dispositions) which induce forgiveness. However, we cannot thus exclude the power and mercy of God which can find a way of forgiveness . . . by which, as it were miraculously, he heals such sinners ', ST II, 2, 14, a. 3. Even in this hypothesis of a ' quasi-miraculous ' grace the sinner is presumed to accept it. At that moment and to that extent he ceases to affront the Spirit ; he ceases to be a blasphemer of the Spirit because he has (though tardily) accepted God's light. Our Lord's statement is therefore literally true : it shall never be forgiven because it refuses to be forgiven. The ' *word against the Son of Man* ' is, though grave, forgivable. To assail the human conduct of our Lord (*e.g.* 9:11 or even 16:22) is an insult to his compassionate humanity but it proceeds from a misreading of God's ways. It may presuppose a religious, if indocile, spirit. It finds some excuse in the fact that the Word has taken flesh and is, to that degree, veiled. But an attack upon the Son of Man who manifestly wielding the power of the Spirit is conscious malice—an attack upon the Spirit himself.

b 33-35 Attack upon Pharisaic Hypocrisy (*cf*. Lk 6:45)—33. A maxim already used by our Lord, 7:17-20, is now given a different turn. It is a direct assault on the Pharisees for their blasphemous words, 24, an appeal, in the spirit of 30, for a downright attitude and for clear issues. Nature knows no deception : from good fruit one may argue a healthy tree. Not so the Pharisees. From their customary pious discourses one would not guess at their inward corruption. They are as dangerous, therefore, as a *brood* of vipers. Let them reform inwardly or at least show their corruption outwardly in speech. The form of 33 is awkward. *Black, 148 f., suggests the Aramaic original : A good tree makes, *i.e.* produces, good fruit etc.—the participle for ' makes ' having been read as an imperative. **34.** They are an unnatural and repellent phenomenon because words are customarily the ' *heart's overflow* ' (KNT) and if the store of the heart is good, the mouth dispenses what is good (35).

c 36-37 The Idle Word (Mt only)—In the present context our Lord's words sound a grave warning for the Pharisees. If every *casual* (ἀργός, *i.e.* do-nothing, lazy) word will be accountable for (the text does not necessarily imply ' condemned '), how searching will be the examination of considered pronouncements like the deliberate blasphemy of the Pharisees ! **37** has the ring of a proverb, particularly as '.thou ' replaces the ' you ' of the previous verse. The ' words ' are a sure criterion of acquittal (' justification ') or condemnation

since, if we except the Pharisaic monstrosity of 34, they **696** are the index of the heart, 34, 35.

38-42 Attack upon Pharisaic Unbelief (Lk 11:29-32) **d** —**38.** After the rebuff of the Pharisees, 24-34, others continue the conversation (' answered and said ', *cf*. the Aramaic idiom '*aneh wᵉamar, i.e.* ' spoke up and said ', in which there is no suggestion of answering a question but merely of reacting to certain circumstances or words ; *e.g.* Dan 2:26). They ask for a convincing proof of our Lord's Messianic mission—a ' sign ' of their own choosing more startling than the miracles so far witnessed ; see 16:1, § 703*f*. **39.** Ignoring the veneer of politeness our Lord directly attacks the questioners as representatives of an evil and ' adulterous ' race, faithless to God, Israel's spouse ; *cf*. Os 2 ; Ez 16, etc. A sign will indeed be given but, as a race, they shall reject it ; *cf*. 41. **40.** The sign is the Resurrection though the word is not spoken, and the allusion remains cryptic until the event unveils it. If we remember that analogies are not designed to be urged too far, the likeness is striking between the OT presentation of Jonas's story and our Lord's' burial (though again the term is not used) and Resurrection. As the fish (κῆτος, sea-beast KNT) swallows Jonas so the earth shall swallow-up the Son of Man. The disappearance is ' for three days and three nights ' in each case. In Jon 1:17 this phrase may or may not indicate 72 hours ; Heb. usage makes the expression ambiguous (*cf. e.g.* Est 4:16 with Est 5:1 and the Jewish method of reckoning part of a day, month or year for the whole ; SB I, 649). In our Lord's case it certainly does not indicate 72 hours as the evangelist, though faithfully recording the expression, well knew, 16:21 ; 17:23 ; 20:19. In any case, the general analogy is enough and this point should be remembered also when it is objected that Jonas was body and soul in the fish and our Lord's body only in the tomb or when it is urged that ' the heart of the earth ' is as deep in the earth (and therefore Limbo ?) as the ' belly ' is in the fish. **41.** The **e** example of the Ninevites will rise accusing at the final reckoning. (It is possible, however, that the words ' in judgement ' have been added by the Greek translator ; the original Aramaic would then read simply ' shall rise with this generation ', *i.e.* in the Aramaic idiom ' dispute with, reproach ', Black, 97.) It will put the incredulous Pharisees to shame—their missionary was not a mere prophet but the Son of Man himself. **42.** *Cf*. 1 Kg 10:1 ff. This fresh contrast is of another order : it suggests not the impenitence of the Pharisees but their refusal to recognize the true wisdom offered them. The queen of Sheba (in SW. Arabia, called the Yemen, *i.e.* ' the south ') travelled far to hear one whose wisdom, though proverbial in Israel, did not compare with this.

43-45 Hypocritical and Cynical Pharisees warned of f their Danger (Lk 11:24-26)—By means of a comparison suggested by the present exorcism incident, 22-24, Jesus warns his opponents against a false sense of security. There is peril in over-confidence—in the calm assurance of the Pharisees conscious of Israel's privileged status, unconscious of spiritual need. They cannot afford to refuse the help of Jesus who alone opposes Satan with the Spirit of God, 28-29. **43.** The unclean spirit (' unclean ' as opposed to the ' holy ' Spirit) appears as a tenant not necessarily evicted but perhaps simply seeking a change of residence. **44.** He finds the waterless countryside unsuitable and decides to return to his old home. To his delight it is still *untenanted* (σχολάζοντα), cleaned and *decorated* (κεκοσμένον). **45.** Anxious to share his good fortune (there is no suggestion of gathering forces for a battle) he invites a whole band (' seven '—the number of completion) of like-minded spirits. Packed with this unclean horde the house is made dirtier than ever. Applied to this ' wicked generation ' the comparison invites it to consider the possibility that the God-favoured house of Israel may, through sheer indifference, be open—with vacant possession—to Satan. Such indifference will make the state of Israel more desperate (though not yet hopeless) than its condition was before God's call of Abraham. The unprivileged pagans will be in better case.

46-50 True Kindred of Christ (Mk 3:31-35 ; Lk 8:19-21—**46.** The episode has no obvious logical connexion with the rest of the section nor is it clear that it took place at this time : Mt's apparently precise indication (' as he was yet speaking ') is, in reality, his own vague connecting formula, 9:18 ; 17:5 ; 26:47. Mt, who is primarily interested in our Lord's pronouncement, 48-49, does not say why his ' brethren ' sought him (see Mk 3:21 where the ' friends ' are probably relations, *i.e.* ' brethren ' ; *cf.* Mk 3:31-32). Of this passage Lagrange pointedly remarks : ' The presence of our Lord's mother on this occasion no more proves that she shares the sentiments of the others than does her presence at the foot of the Cross '. She is there simply because she wants to be near him. **47-48.** The house (*cf.* 13:1) is full, Mk 3:20. Mary and the ' brethren ' are outside. Our Lord is informed. (47 is unnecessary and absent from MSS B & S and from the early Syr. versions. It is excluded, probably rightly, by Hort and von Soden. Our Lord takes up the words of his informant to drive home a lesson. **49-50.** With a gesture and a word he sets the example of complete detachment (enjoined on his followers in 10:37) in the interests of the Father. He acknowledges no kinship but with those who are obedient and therefore genuine children of the one Father. His mother was dear to him for the same reason, Lk 1:38. For such he uses the nearest and dearest terms—brother, sister, mother—but ' father ' is reserved for his Father in heaven. The terms ' brother ' and ' sister ' in 12:50 do not necessarily define the word ' brethren ' of 12:46 f. which (*cf.* Mk 3:32 ; 6:3) is actually to be understood of ' relations ' in general. To indicate relationship of affection our Lord was restricted to the terms ' brother ', ' sister ' because the terms of more distant relationship (' cousin ', ' aunt ', etc.) would be absurd used in a figurative sense.

XIII 1-53 The Parables of the Kingdom—The foregoing chapter presented our Lord and the Pharisees ; in ch 13 our Lord turns to ordinary folk. In contrast with the direct teaching of the Sermon, chh 5-7, his teaching is now in ' parables '. They are of various kinds, but the subject throughout this ' day of parables ' is one—the kingdom of God, the great subject of our Lord's preaching, 4:17 ; 10:7 ; *cf.* Lk 4:42-43 ; 10:9 ; Ac 1:3. The term ' parable ' (παραβολή) means ' comparison '. The Gospel parables may be defined as : fictitious though likely stories designed to clarify a moral lesson or doctrinal truth by means of comparison ; *cf.* Prat, I, 320-1 ; 549-54. The parable is a comparison to be taken as a whole ; its details are inserted merely to make the story live. In this it is distinguished from the allegory which is a chain of metaphors of which each link has its own significance. It follows that the lesson of the parable inclines to simplicity and clarity ; the lessons of the allegory are multiple and tend to obscurity. Yet some allegories may be clear and some parables obscure by reason of the circumstances of their utterance or of the difficulty of the subject treated. The gospel parables, especially those concerning the Kingdom, often contain allegorical elements. This phenomenon has been used to prove that such parables have been decorated with allegory by the evangelists. Jesus, it has been claimed, would not have used allegory since it would obscure his message. In this theory the evangelists, anxious to explain to pagan and Jew the blindness of the Messias's own people, have deliberately obscured the parables with allegorical elements. The theory is exaggerated. Allegory and parable are similar literary forms and the intrusion of allegory into parable is a natural process (*C. H. Dodd, *The Parables of the Kingdom*, London 1936). Moreover, the mixture of the two is equally characteristic of the rabbinic ' parables ' in the first centuries of the Christian era ; *cf.* D. Buzy, *Introduction aux Paraboles Évangéliques*, Paris 1912, 148-54.

1-2 The Setting (Mk 4:1 ; Lk 8:4)—Mt's phrase ' the **698b** same day ' may be as vague as his other phrase ' at that time ', or (if intended to be exact) may apply only to some of the parables in the chapter. Leaving the house (*cf.* 12:46 ; on this ' house ', Matthew's own with some probability, *cf.* Lagrange, *Mt*, lxxvi f.) our Lord goes down to the lakeside. So that all may see and hear he addresses the throngs from one of the boats moored there.

3-9 The Sower (Mk 4:3-9 ; Lk 8:5-8)—**3-4.** In Palestine the farmer sows after the first autumn rains (usually November). His hedgeless fields are bordered, and often traversed, by stony paths. Willy-nilly some seed, scattered from his basket, must fall on the track (' on ' rather than ' by '—παρά is probably a mistranslation of the ambiguous Aramaic *'al* ; *cf.* Lk 8:5 where the seed is ' trodden under foot ', Black 120). The greedy Palestinian sparrow is not slow to seize it. **5-6.** Even in Galilee the stony soil lies thin on outcrops of rock. The very lightness of such soil favours too rapid growth (perhaps within a few hours) and the sun, still strong in November, will shrivel the delicate shoot unsustained by moisture from a deep root. **7-8.** The Palestinian farmer prefers to cut his weeds. The result is disastrous : they stifle everything in the vicinity. As for the more fortunate seed, it is a mistake to look for botanical precision in a parable. Our Lord's figures are selected at random to illustrate the abounding virtue of the seed. In special cases one seed may produce (even in Palestine) two or three hundred grains of cereal (Bi 8 [1927] 84-5), but the ordinary Palestinian farmer (from whom our picture is taken) is content with an average yield of 12 to 1. **9.** Far from wishing to puzzle his audience our Lord seriously asks them to reflect upon his words. His formula (again in 11:15 ; 13:43, *cf.* Deut 29:4 where the absence of the listening ' ear ' suggests guilt) implies that in these matters goodwill facilitates understanding ; *cf.* Jn 3:21.

10-17 Purpose of the Parables (Mk 4:10-12 ; Lk **c** 8:9-10—**10.** The disciples (not only the Twelve ; *cf.* Mk 4:10, WV) seem puzzled at this indirect method of teaching. Their question, however, was not put until they were alone with Jesus, Mk 4:10. **11.** The notion of the ' kingdom of heaven ' embodies the hidden design (μυστήριον) of God. The mass of the Jewish people were ill-prepared for a direct and sudden revelation of its profound nature. The indirect teaching by parable must for the time suffice ; direct light would only blind. But the inner circle of disciples, willing to be taught and destined to teach, can and must be told. It should however be noticed that this inner circle was not a closed circle. It was open for all who heard the parables to show their goodwill by making further inquiries. **12.** Our Lord observes that a worldly practice, common but not admirable, here finds its spiritual application. The rich are flattered with gifts, the poor suffer violence and loss. Those who accept and are rich in the gifts of God (which include docility, pliant will, generous heart) amass further treasures ; *cf.* Jn 1:16. The spiritual pauper has only himself to blame (*cf.* ' Ask and it shall be given ', 7:7) —and this explains how an axiom of unjust worldly practice can have its counterpart in the spiritual order. He is said, by a paradoxical hyperbole, to lose what he has—which is nothing. The application of this dictum to the present situation seems to presuppose some fault (as it does in 25:29 where it is used again) on the part of the people at large. **13.** This fault is a lack of spiritual **d** perception. Confronted with this, our Lord did not withdraw as he did from the actively malignant Pharisees, 12:15. He mercifully remained to do what he could in the circumstances. Like stupid children the people could learn only from little stories—analogies which, though helpful, could not plumb the depths of the mysterious ' Kingdom '. **14-15.** *Cf.* Is 6:9-10. Isaias had been thwarted by the same dispositions. His experience rehearsed that of the Messias-Prophet as the OT history in general was a rehearsal of the Messianic

698d era. Mt reproduces the LXX version (translate : *Assuredly* you shall hear . . . *assuredly* you shall see but . . .). This softens the harsh (but heartbroken) irony of the Semitic imperatives : Hear and understand not ! See and comprehend not ! Harden the heart. . .' (*cf.* Is 6:9 with notes). The words expand, by more literal quotation, those of 13 and like them they explain why our Lord is forced to use parables. Whether the purpose of the parables is of chastisement or of benefit is much discussed. In effect we cannot exclude either **e** element. The difficulties of the texts, however, (especially Mk) must be resolved in the light of three certain facts. First : our Lord's own love for this people ; his mission is mercy not judgement ; he has come to save that which was lost, 18:11. Second : the parable is designed not to obscure but to clarify ; absolutely speaking, it is not the most direct and efficient form of teaching, but relatively to the capacity of the audience's mind and heart it may be the only possible one ; the only alternative would be silence. Third : graces refused become matter for condemnation. The question is treated at some length in, *e.g.* Buzy, *Introduction aux Paraboles*, 231–413 ; A. Charue, *L'Incrédulité des Juifs dans le Nouveau Testament*, Gembloux 1929, 141–4 ; Durand, ER 107 (1906) 256–71 ; Lagrange RB 7 (1910) 5–35 and *L'Evangile de Jésus-Christ*, Paris 1932, 168–71 ; Lebreton, *Life and Teaching of Jesus Christ* (Eng. tr.), London 1935, 239–53 ; F. Prat, *Jésus-Christ*, 1, 340–1 ; Skrinjar, Bi 11 (1930) 291–321 ; 426–49 ; 12 (1931) 27–40. **16-17.** Our Lord does not praise the docility of the disciples, but invites them to be grateful for God's free gift. Born in less happy times men as just as they and even the prophets could only peer into the great dim future, 1 Pet 1:10 ff. In that future, now present, the disciples are privileged to live and not only to live but to be the pupils of the Master in the new era ; *cf.* ' therefore ' in 18.

699a **18-23 The Sower Parable explained** (Mk 4:13–20 ; Lk 8:11–15)—' *You* therefore ', says our Lord, ' hear ye the parable '. Actually it is the *meaning* of the parable that they are about to hear, but in Aramaic there is no exact expression for ' significance, explanation ' ; *cf.* similar defective phrases in Mk 4:10 ; 9:10 ; Lk 8:11 ; Joüon 86 f. The seed is the doctrine (λόγος) of the Kingdom, sown by our Lord and later by the Apostles. For three classes of men it remained fruitless. **19.** In some it is a total lack of spiritual appreciation. The ' word ' lies unregarded. Satan alone benefits. ' This is he that *was sown* by the wayside '. ' The various kinds of soil represent the various kinds of hearers. But since the fate of the seed really represents the spiritual fate of the hearers, the seed and the hearers are in part identified ', WV. **20-21.** In others there is a thin layer of spiritual perception, but the superficial are given to sudden and ephemeral enthusiasms. The quick growth is not of deep root and soon disappears ; the personal sacrifice entailed and even active opposition ' presently ' (*i.e.* ' immediately ', εὐθύς) prove a snare in the moral path of such men. **22.** The third category is of those in whom the root strikes deepest. Yet here too the seed will not come to maturity if side by side with it grow preoccupation with the affairs of the world and particularly with the seductive *glamour* (WV) of riches. **23.** Not all the successful seed bears the same fruit, but in all cases it is abundant ; *cf.* 8 note.

b 24-30 The ' Cockle ' (Mt only)—The parable has a setting similar to the previous one and completes it. **24.** From the outset our Lord makes it clear that he is speaking of the Kingdom ; contrast 3. But, in the rabbinic manner, the term of the comparison is said to be ' a man who sowed ' when, in reality it is the whole situation which is thus compared ; *cf.* also 13:31, 33, 45, 47 ; 20:1 ; 22:2 ; 25:1. **25-26.** The ' cockle ' is the *lolium temulentum* (so named from its effect of dizziness on men and cattle)—more accurately not ' tares ' (KNT) but ' darnel ' (WV). It is sown secretly and in spite. The weed is indistinguishable from the wheat until its more slender ear appears. **27-29.** This plant (rare in England) is common in Palestine, but the servants are astonished at the amount. The farmer himself immediately senses the hand of an enemy, but it is too late, or too early, to act : the roots of weed and wheat are intertwined. **30.** He must wait until the ears are ripe and then the wheat, which grows higher than the weed, may be cut near its head while the sickle leaves the weed untouched. It is unusual to sheave weeds, but then it is unusual to sow them : it is an unusual operation to meet an unusual case. Nevertheless there may be allegory here though the sheaving is not mentioned again in the explanation ; 40 mentions only the gathering and burning. For the explanation of the parable see notes to 37–42.

31-32 The Mustard-Seed (Mk 4:30–32 ; Lk 13:18–19)—Once again it is not precisely to the seed that the Kingdom is compared but to the whole situation ; see on 24. It would seem wiser, therefore, not to attempt to emphasize the pungency or other property of the seed except its apparent insignificance which is an integral part of the parable. This would be allegory without warrant. In the world of nature, as in the word of history, insignificant beginnings may be misleading. It is so with the world-event known as the Kingdom of Heaven. The human activity of our Lord was limited, its immediate results unspectacular. The mustard-plant is the *brassica nigra* of the botanists. The seed, proverbially tiny (*cf.* 17:20 and SB 1, 669) is not in fact the smallest known, but our Lord is not giving a lesson in botany. It is the smallest of the familiar seeds, DBV 5, 1601. Its bush is common on the banks of the Jordan and of the Galilean Lake, often reaching a height of 12 ft and therefore called a ' tree ' by the Arabs ; *cf.* Biever, *Conférences de Saint Etienne* (1911) 281. That the ' birds of *heaven* come and dwell in its branches ' recalls the prophecy of Ez 17:22–24 where the ' tree ' (a cedar) is the future Messianic kingdom and ' every bird and winged thing ' the people of all the nations. This reminiscence seems to warrant for the ' birds ' the allegorical sense of all peoples.

33 The Leaven (Lk 13:20–21)—The preceding parable stressed the contrast between small beginnings and enormous end ; the present one covers the intermediate process. The Kingdom's development is not a matter of almost inevitable, natural growth from its Old Testament beginnings. It is the issue of forces intrinsic to the element (the yeast) now for the first time implanted in the world. These forces work powerfully, secretly, in every corner. The yeast is small compared with the dough, perhaps one ounce to sixteen or seventeen pounds of flour nowadays in Palestine : *cf.* Buzy, 178. The ' measure ' chosen by our Lord for his parabolic purpose is the σάτον (Aram. *sā'tā* ; Heb. *se'āh*), which is one-third of an *ephah*. The ' three measures ' are therefore equivalent to one *ephah*. the unit of capacity slightly more than our ' bushel ', RB 28 (1931) 212. This large amount is chosen to illustrate not the size of the kingdom (*cf.* previous parable) but the power of the ' yeast '.

34-35 Parabolic Teaching foreshadowed (*cf.* Mk 4:33–34)—Mt again seizes the opportunity of pointing out the reflexion of the New Order in the Old. The psalmist in 77(78) 2, about to expound the mystery of God's way with his people, dubs his exposition a ' parable ' (*māšāl* ; LXX παραβολή ; in this case a didactic poem). Struck by the word itself, so apt to the teaching he describes. Mt points to the divinely constituted precedent. He insinuates the uniformity existing between the teaching method in the word of God of old and that of the Son of God now. But he insinuates, too, as elsewhere when he quotes the OT, that the psalmist's words would be more profoundly true on our Lord's lips. This last point appears to be emphasized by the form in which Mt puts the second half of the quotation. Unlike the first half it is not identical with LXX but seems to be a more impressive translation of the Heb. ' Enigmatic things of old ' (HT, LXX—referring in the psalm to the early days of Israel's history) becomes : ' Things concealed from

876

e the time of the foundation' of the world; *cf.* 25:34. The psalmist (' Asaph ' is named in Ps 77:1 and called ' prophet ' in 2 Par 29:30) had a much more restricted purpose. Our Lord's doctrine is not contained within the temporal or spatial bounds of Israel.

36-43 Cockle Parable explained (Mt only)—Not all the elements of the parable are allegorical. The sleepers of 25, for example, are not careless pastors; nor does the ' binding ' of 30 indicate that not one of the wicked shall escape. Such applications may be tentatively made, and were often made by the Fathers, but they were not made by our Lord. He explains the allegory of the main elements only. The conditions described in the parable are said to be those of the early Church, *e.g.* by *G. D. Kilpatrick, *The Origins of the Gospel according to St Matthew*, (Oxford 1946) 97; 107. The implication is that the parable, in its present form, is not traceable to Christ. This position, however, makes no allowance for our Lord's divine foreknowledge and refuses him even human foresight. It also ignores the fact (*cf.* 1 Cor 5:2) that in the early Church the ' cockle ' was not always allowed to go unmolested until the ' harvest '. This attitude of the early Christians makes it evident that they did not consider our Lord as laying down exhaustive legislation for a fully constituted society. It makes it still more evident that the parable-allegory is not the invention of the early Church. Moreover, the objection forgets that the problem of God's tolerance (*cf.* note to 13:39) was not to rise only in the distant future—one of the Twelve was already a traitor, as Jesus knew; *cf.* Lagrange, *Mt.* **36.** Dismissing the multitudes our Lord returns to the house; 13:1 note. The disciples, emboldened by his words, 11, ask a more detailed explanation of the parable of which, doubtless, they already have the general meaning. **37-38.** The field is the world—or that part of it in which the Son of Man has sown. The seed is not now the Word, as in 19, but every ' citizen ', every loyal subject, of the Kingdom (in Semitic phrase : ' child of the kingdom '). The ' cockle ' is the offspring of evil (or ' of the Evil One ' ?) *i.e.* evil deeds and evil men alike; 41 note. **39.** The Evil One himself is the spiteful enemy of the Son of Man, attacking him indirectly and by stealth. The explanation takes a leap to the end of the world; the intermediate period of growth is not mentioned, presumably because here it is not significant. It appears, therefore, that the object of the parable is not to define the duties of the leaders in the early Church but simply to explain God's tolerance of evil. The angels who execute God's judgements (Bonsirven 1, 235) gather the crop, wheat and weed. **40.** The emphasis on the fate of the ' cockle ' (40-42; the ' wheat ' goes unmentioned) is in accord with the purpose of the parable : the exercise of retribution is only delayed. **41.** The Son of Man must present a perfect Kingdom to his Father, hence it is he who executes judgement (*cf.* Jn 5:27) through his ministers. (This quiet assumption of authority should not go unnoticed.) These will cleanse the Kingdom of scandals (of acts constituting a moral snare for the faithful) and of those responsible for them (*cf.* the same distinction in 18:7; *cf.* also in HT, Soph 1:3 of which our Lord's phrase is probably a reminiscence : ' I will destroy . . . scandals together with the wicked '). **42.** The cockle will be cast into the ' furnace of fire ', a contemporary synonym for the place of the damned, Bonsirven 1, 537. The ' weeping and gnashing of teeth ' sorts ill with the suggestion of burning, but the phrase is stereotyped in Mt (8:12; 22:13; 25:30; in which places it is more naturally associated with the ' exterior darkness '). **43.** Finally a word of comfort for the disciples. Their future glory is expressed in terms familiar to Jewish thought (Dan 12:3; Wis 3:7 and the uninspired 4 Esd 7:97; and *cf.* Bonsirven 1, 520 f.). The Kingdom thus purified now passes from the hand of the Son and becomes the kingdom of the Father; *cf.* 1 Cor 15:24. For the concluding formula *cf.* 13:19 note.

44 The Treasure (Mt only)—Mt records this and the **700a** following parable without either preamble or explanation. Doubtless the two were proposed to all, like the previous parables. Explanation was scarcely necessary; they are already sufficiently clear. A man finds buried treasure, struck perhaps by his random spade, in another's field—not an unlikely experience in a country familiar with invasion and flight; *cf.* Jos., BJ 1, 7, 5, 2. He buries it again for security and *in his joy* (WV) goes off and sells his possessions (the significant trait of this parable as of the next). He buys the field, clearly without acquainting the owner (landlord or employer, presumably) of his discovery. The morality of his action need not be discussed : it lies outside the purpose of the parable which is to teach that the Kingdom is worth the sacrifice of all worldly possessions (*cf.* 10:37-39).

45-46 The Pearl (Mt only)—A pendant of the former **b** parable with the same moral. The parable naturally finishes with the acquisition (again, at all costs) of the single and valuable pearl. The merchant may have turned connoisseur but, in any case, he is parabolically pictured as retaining the pearl; suggestion of re-sale would have injured the parable.

47-50 The Drag-Net (Mt only)—From pictures of **c** farm and kitchen and market-place our Lord turns to that of lake-fishing, equally familiar to the Galileans. The net (often about one-quarter of a mile in length and about 6 to 10 feet in depth) is sustained by cork floats and weighted with lead. The men on shore pay out the net as the boatmen, holding the other end, describe a wide arc in the lake until they disembark further along the bank. The net, now semicircular, is evenly drawn towards the shore by both parties. Of the thirty or so species of fish in the Lake of Galilee none is *worthless* (σαπρός) though the cat-fish (*clarias macracanthus*) being scale-less was not eaten by practising Jews, Lev 11:9; Deut 14:9. It is unnecessary, however, to seek ichthyological exactitudes : the moral of the parable demands a mixture of bad and good (as in the ' Cockle ' parable) and the picture becomes subservient. **49-50.** The application of the parable is similar to that of the ' Cockle ' (without the epilogue concerning the ' just ') of which it is a twin. Both parables make it clear that the Kingdom exists amid earthly conditions before it reaches its final stage of perfection.

51-52 The Scribe in the Kingdom (Mt only)—The **d** disciples assert that they have grasped the implications of the foregoing parables of the Kingdom. Our Lord in reply defines the advantage of such understanding. It is only when he possesses this comprehension of the Kingdom (διὰ τοῦτο) that the ' scribe ', thus instructed, becomes comparable to the careful householder. Old garments have not been destroyed but put away in his *store-cupboard* ready for emergencies. The new must not be used to patch the old, 9:16, but the old has its subservient uses. The ' scribe ' (or law-learned) of the new order (*cf.* 23:34), unlike his counterpart of the old, has the essentials of the Old Law at his finger-tips precisely because he possesses the knowledge of the Kingdom which is the perfection of the Law, 5:17. He is in a position to expound the working-out of God's design not only in its preliminary expression (the Mosaic dispensation) but in its present activity (the Kingdom in being) and even in its consummation, 39-43; 49-50.

53-58 Hostile Reception at Nazareth (Mk 6:1-6a; **e** Lk 4:22b-30)—**53-54.** From the account of the parables Mt (having already, in chh 8-9, narrated the miracles of Mk 4:35-41; 5:1-20, 21-43) takes us straight to Nazareth, our Lord's home-town; *cf.* 21:11, Mk 1:9. It is Jesus' second visit; *cf.* 4:13 and Lk 4:16-30. His teaching in their *synagogue* astounds them, 7:29 note. They know he has not been trained in the rabbinic schools at Jerusalem. Moreover, they have heard of miracles worked, though not at Nazareth (another source of complaint; *cf.* Lk 4:23-29). **55-56.** With the public our Lord passed for the son of Joseph the

700e carpenter (τέκτων—joiner and housebuilder ; *cf.* Höpfl, Bi 4 [1923] 41–5). His ' brethren ' are known to the people of Nazareth : James, Joseph (or Jose ; Mk 6:3), Simon, Jude. James is called ' brother of the Lord ' in Gal 1:19 ; nevertheless he is certainly not a son of our Lady but of another Mary (' of Cleophas ', *cf.* Mt 27:56 ; Mk 15:40 ; Jn 19:25) who is also the mother of Joseph (Jose) ; *cf.* §§ 672–3. If the first two named are only cousins (the Greek term ' brethren ' represents the more general Aramaic '*aḥ*) it is scarcely likely that Simon and Jude, named last, are closer relations (Lagrange, *L'Evangile*, 193–4. On the question of the ' brethren ' of the Lord ; *cf.* §§ 672–3). **57-58.** Contemptuous familiarity was a psychological obstacle. Our Lord sadly notes this irrational but common attitude. He works only a few unspectacular cures (Mk), evidently upon some of the few who accepted him. He could give nothing (*cf.* note to Mk 6:5) to those who refused his gifts.

701a **D. Round and About Galilee : Formation of the Apostles—XIV 1-XX 16.**
XIV 1-12 Antipas, Jesus, the Baptist (Mk 6:14–29 ; Lk 9:7–9 ; 3:19–20)—**1-2.** Antipas (called ' Herod ' on his coins), son of Herod the Great by Malthace the Samaritan, was tetrarch (' ruler in that quarter ' KNT) of Galilee and Peraea (4 B.C. to A.D. 39). He was living probably in his new town of Tiberias on the SW. bank of the Lake when reports of our Lord's activity became too persistent to ignore. Only guilty superstition could have prompted his absurd conjecture, if, indeed, it is to be taken seriously ; *cf.* Lk 9:9. His courtiers had other ideas, Mk 6:15. **3-4.** The imprisonment of John had taken place before our Lord began his Galilean ministry, 4:12. Its cause was John's denunciation of Antipas's adulterous marriage, Lev 18:16 ; 20:21. Herodias was the wife of his half-brother Philip—not Philip, tetrarch of Trachonitis and Iturea, Lk 3:1, but a private individual. To make the case worse, Antipas, though the Baptist does not mention it, was the uncle of Herodias. **5.** Mt, unlike Mk, content with general statements of events, does not mention the murderous intent of Herodias, though *cf.* 8. Nor does he represent as adequately as Mk 6:20 the vacillating character of Antipas, fascinated by John, half-persuaded by Herodias, held back by fear of John's many supporters. This perplexity seems to have lasted for nearly a year.
b **6.** The scene was the banquet-hall of the fortress-palace of Machaerus (*Mkāwer ; cf.* Jos., *Ant.* 18, 5, 2). The castle, rebuilt by Herod the Great, lay between Callirhoe and the Arnon. It stood in the mountains of Moab on the southern border of Antipas's Peraean dominion, *cf.* Abel 2, 371 f. The occasion was the birthday of Antipas ; *cf.* Schürer, 1, 2, 26 f. In place of the usual courtesans danced Salome, daughter of Herodias by her first husband ; *cf.* Jos., *Ant.* 18, 5, 4. This condescension of a young princess of the blood (perhaps about fifteen years old at the time, certainly not more than twenty) was doubtless instigated by the far-sighted Herodias. **7-8.** Antipas fell into the trap. The girl's mother then instructed her (προβιβάζω : not ' instruct *before* ', DV ; and *cf.* Mk 6:24) to ask for the head of the Baptist who lay in the dungeons. The girl herself pertly added ' here, in a dish ' ; *cf.* Mk 1:24–25. **9.** The unexpected and cold-blooded request sobered Antipas. He was being rushed into an act which did not suit his policy, 5, nor entirely answer his feelings, Mk 6:20. He was a king (tetrarch in fact, ' king ' in popular speech ; *cf.* Holzmeister, *Historia Aetatis Novi Testamenti*, Rome 1932, 54) and a royal, if drunken, oath could not be recalled—if uttered in public ! **10-11.** The courageous Baptist died a martyr's death for the sanctity of marriage. His head went fitly back to the woman who had schemed so carefully for it. **12.** Antipas possibly silenced his strange conscience by allowing the disciples of John to bury the body. For the subsequent history of Antipas, Herodias, Salome, *cf.* Jos., *Ant.* 18, 5, 1–4.
c **13-21 First Multiplication of Loaves** (Mk 6:31–44 ;

Lk 9:10*b*–17 ; Jn 6:1–15)—**13. If** Mt's formula is not a transitional *cliché* it implies that our Lord's suggestion of repose for his disciples (Mk) was reinforced by the fate of the Baptist, 12, and the sinister reflexion of Antipas, 2. The people were evidently excited ; Antipas might act ; our Lord used his human prudence and retired to a place ' apart ', *i.e.* not so much secluded as removed from the crowds. He and his disciples were on the west side of the Lake (*cf.* 22, 34), presumably near Capharnaum, Mk 6:32. They quietly withdrew from Antipas's territory and sailed to that of Philip the tetrarch, to the neighbourhood of Bethsaida Julias in Gaulanitis ; *cf.* Lk 9:10. The crowds, not to be thwarted, followed on foot ; doubtless they had observed whither the boat was heading. The distance (*c* 6 m.) was almost twice that by sea, but the disciples, in need of rest, were in no hurry and the crowd arrived first, Mk 6:33. Its numbers had increased as it went. **14.** Our Lord's heart could never resist suffering. In the broad, uncultivated plain that lies to the SE. of Bethsaida between hills and sea he healed the sick. He taught the simple folk, too, Mk 6:34. **15.** The work went on until late afternoon (' evening ' : ὀψίας, *cf.* 23). Our Lord took no heed but the hungry disciples called his attention to the fact that the time (for refreshment ?) had slipped by. They were perhaps not thinking solely of the multitudes ! **16-17.** The Master's command must have left them dumbfounded. It was Peter's brother, Jn 6:8, who told of the boy with the five cheap (barley) loaves and the two dried fish. This remark of Andrew's was not meant to be helpful—Philip had already calculated that two hundred days' labour would not buy the necessary provender. **18-19.** The plain of Bethsaida is green in spring at the time of the Pasch, Jn 6:4, and all sat down on the grass in companies, Mk 6:40, at our Lord's bidding. He evidently wished to give the impression of a formal meal and, in the same spirit, he invoked a blessing like the father of a family. The breaking of the bread also, being mentioned by all four evangelists, is evidently significant : our Lord repeated this action just one year later, at the Last Supper, 26:26. It would appear that the ceremony was deliberately symbolic of the Holy Eucharist but the symbolism is our Lord's : the very sober account of the evangelists suggests historical intention on their part and not mere symbolism. Moreover, the presence of the fish and the absence of wine does not suggest that we have here a *mere* symbol of the Eucharist. (On the opinions of non-Catholic critics *cf.* Lagrange, *Mt*, 170 f.) Whether the bread increased in our Lord's hands or in the Apostles' does not appear. **20-21.** The prodigality of God's gifts does not excuse human waste and the remnants are gathered up. They fill twelve baskets (the property, perhaps, of the twelve Apostles) whereas the original amount had been carried in one—the boy's. The ' baskets ' here are ' hampers ' in 15:37 (second multiplication) and the distinction is preserved when our Lord recalls the two miracles, 16:9–10. It would seem that the distinction is not merely literary : ' The κόφινος of 14:20 appears to have been a strong wicker " basket " ' (as used for farmwork) ' the σφυρίς of 15:37 a larger " hamper " used chiefly for food (*cf.* Ac 9:25) ' (WV note to Mt 16:9–10).
22-33 Our Lord (Mk 6:45–52 ; Jn 6:16–21) **and Peter** (Mt only) **walk on the Waters—22-23.** The miracle of the loaves had dangerously excited the people, Jn 6:14 f. It was important that the Apostles should not share their political frenzies ; our Lord therefore dispatched them boatwards (εἰς πλοῖον) while he sent the people home. He did not rejoin the Apostles who evidently waited at the lakeside until night fell (Jn 6:17. In Mt and Mk ὀψία as in 15, but here, apparently, bearing the meaning ' night ', *cf.* Lagrange, *Mk*, 173). Instead, he slipped away from the crowd to pray in the hills surrounding the plain. **24-25.** The Apostles left without him, but made poor progress against the high (Jn) and contrary wind. Driven, no doubt, off their course they were in mid-

e lake (over 3 m. out ; Jn) making little headway. There was only one way to rejoin the dispirited Apostles and our Lord took it. The time was between 3 and 6 in the morning—the 'fourth watch' of the night according to the Roman reckoning used by the Jews at this time, SB 1, 688 f. **26-27.** The cry of the Apostles : ' It is a ghost' proceeded from the apparent impossibility of any other explanation. The familiar
f voice calmed and convinced. **28-31.** Peter now appears for the first time with his high qualities and their endearing human defects. He is devoted to his Master and sublimely confident in him but, conscious suddenly of self, he cries out in fright. The hand of Jesus is ready and his reproach gentle : ' Of little faith ! ' If this could be said of Peter for his momentary fear, what of us ? asks St Jerome, PL 26, 104. **32-33.** To Peter on the water and now to the Apostles in the boat it is clear that they are safe with their Master : the wind drops as he joins them. The Apostles (' those in the boat ', *cf.* 22) are carried away. They confess the divinity of their Master (*cf.* § 50*g*), who with divine power has walked the waters ; *cf.* Job 9:8. Their confession is, however, a sudden outburst due to the pressure of miracle upon miracle. Peter's calm and considered profession in 16:16 is clearly regarded by Mt as of much higher quality, 16:17 ; and *cf. Scripture*, 1 (1946) 32 f.
g 34-36 Miracles at Gennesaret (Mk 6:53–56)—Stretching for *c* 4 m. along the west side of the Lake between ' Ain Tabgha and Magdala and less than 2 m. S. of Capharnaum is a rich plain about 2 m. broad at its widest part. It is not improbable that the name of this plain was Gennesar and that the name *Gennesaret* (not ' Genesar ' DV), with the feminine suffix, is that of a village in the vicinity of Capharnaum (Lagrange, *Mk*, 177). The inhabitants immediately *recognized* our Lord who was well known in neighbouring Capharnaum. As usual, they ran (Mk) to fetch their sick. Many were healed by the touch of the tassel (κράσπεδον ; *cf.* 9:20 note) of his cloak.
a XV 1-20 Legal Cleanness and Purity of Heart (Mk 7:1–23).
XV 1-10 Attack and Counter-attack (Mk 7:1–13)—**1-2.** The quiet atmosphere of the last two chapters is now broken upon by the renewed attack of the Pharisees who meanwhile have not been idle. This time reinforcements for the local Pharisees have come from Jerusalem itself in the person of Scribes. (The distinction is Mk's ; Mt is not concerned with this detail.) These complain that the disciples do not observe the prescribed ceremonial handwashings before, during and after the meal (' when they eat bread '—a Semitism). These prescriptions were carefully laid down not in the Law but in the **oral** tradition of the ' ancients ' (*i.e.* of the early Rabbis). Towards the end of the 2nd cent. A.D. they were codified in written form in the Mishnah (tract : *Yadayim* or ' Hands '). Such traditions were held in even higher esteem than the Law itself, SB 1, 692 ; for the minutiae of the handwashing ordinances, *cf.* SB 1, 689–705, Edersheim 2, 9–12. **3.** Our Lord declines an aimless discussion of sophistries and sharply attacks the spirit that prompted the objection. As once before (12:7 note) he might have denounced explicitly the legal zeal that had suffocated charity. Instead, he fights them on their own ground and shows how this blind devotion to ' the tradition of the ancients' had driven them to ' transgress ' (he uses their own word, 2) the law of God himself. He supports the
b accusation with one example. **4.** The law of God on duties to parents was unequivocal (the citations are from Ex 20:12, or Deut 5:16, and Ex 21:17). **5.** This, most certainly, God said ; ' *whereas* you *say that if anyone should utter this sentence to father or mother : " Any property of mine from which you might draw benefit is* Qorban ", *then he will not (need to) honour his father* '. Mt obscures the already involved sentence by translating the technical term ' Qorban ' (' offering, gift ' consecrated, *i.e.* to God) ; Mk keeps the Aramaic term and explains it. The use of this word ' Qorban ', though not implying that the property in question would be actually given

to the temple, had the effect of a sacred oath isolating **702b** that property from any claims. That these claims included those even of filial duty was the opinion of at least some of the Rabbis in our Lord's time (*cf.* Babylonian Talmud, *Nedarim*, 3, 2 ; *cf.* also Edersheim 2, 21 ; Bonsirven 2, 163, note 7). Later reforms may have been due to criticism such as our Lord's in the present passage. To sustain the validity of such a vow, therefore, was in effect (though the Pharisees would not deduce this conclusion in so many words) to relax the divine command always to honour father and mother, 4*a* ; indeed such an oath is equivalent to a curse, 4*b*. It declares null (ἀκυροῦν : DV ' made void ') the divine law. **7-9.** Again sacred history repeats itself (13:14 f. **c** note). Isaias, 29:13, had also been confronted with hypocrites and his denunciation applied equally to this Messianic age. The quotation, practically identical with Mk 7:6 f., is from LXX, slightly adjusted though not abbreviated. It is given a slightly different turn. The prophet (*cf.* HT) had complained of the Law observed from human motives ; the evangelists complain of the Law unobserved through human ' traditions '. On the lips the word ' Qorban ' has a pious sound but, as our Lord's example shows, it may hide the heart's contempt for the express will of God.
XV 10-20 The True Perspective (Mk 7:14–23)—We **d** observe three grades of teaching adapted to three classes of listeners. The malevolent have their charge rebutted, and no more, 3–9 ; the ordinary folk, now gathered together by our Lord, receive positive, though prudently veiled, instruction with an invitation to reflect upon it, 10–11. To the disciples, interested enough to ask, Jesus explains himself more fully, 15–20. **10-11.** It seems odd that our Lord should summon the crowd to hear this one sentence. It is possible, therefore, that Mt and Mk have selected it from a longer discourse. The dictum of 11 would remain obscure for the multitude who, it seems, were unaware of the circumstances, 1–2, that prompted it. Moreover, for those imbued with the food-distinctions of the Law (Lev 11 etc.) the implications of 11*b* would be unthinkable. The startling implications are there nevertheless, as Mk 7:19 observes. But the immediate application of our Lord's saying is determined by the context. The unwashed hand, thought the Pharisees, communicates its uncleanness to the food and so to the eater. There is no suggestion, 2, that the food itself was illegal and consequently our Lord's retort to the crowds does not explicitly touch the Mosaic distinction of foods but only the superstitious precautions of the ' tradition of the ancients '. He affirms that to eat with clean or unclean hands can have no moral significance because the very food handled has none. He will explain later, 18–19, what he means by ' what cometh out of the mouth '. **12-14.** (Mt only but *cf.* Lk 6:39). The **e** disciples are perturbed ; the recognized religious leaders, evidently present in the crowd, have taken serious offence at ' this word ' of 11. Perhaps they saw more clearly than the simple folk that our Lord's words touched not only the ' tradition ' but—in their logical conclusion—the Law itself. What they could not see was the possibility that certain elements of the Law might be transient and ill-suited to the fullness of time. Such incomprehension was excusable and the Apostles long shared it ; *cf.* Ac 10:9–15. Not blindness only but refusal to see was the sin of the Pharisees, Jn 9:41. They would not lower themselves by humbly asking explanations. But their whole regime, being not of God, would pass and our Lord warns the disciples against setting any store by hostility even on the part of those who were the accepted guides. Only the blind would mistake those for guides who are blind themselves. Jesus, therefore, opens his disciples' eyes to the blindness of the Pharisees and urges them to have nothing to do with them (ἄφετε αὐτούς, *i.e.* ' leave them to their own devices '). **15-16.** It is Peter who speaks up (' answering ', in the Aramaic sense) and asks an explanation of the ' parable ' (here, as sometimes in OT, enigmatic saying) of 11. He speaks for the

879

702e disciples. Our Lord reproaches them : *At this* **f** *stage* (ἀκμήν) *are even you uncomprehending?* **17.** With unusual energy and realism (Lagrange) our Lord declares that food, of itself, is an object indifferent to the spiritual soul ; it is matter only for the digestive process. **18.** Of no spiritual import, therefore, what goes into the mouth but what proceeds from it. For the mouth is the overflow of the inmost heart, 12:34, and the heart, in Semitic idiom, is the factory of evil or good intent. **19.** Having reached this point in the reasoning there is no further need for the opposition (into the mouth ; out of the mouth) of 17–18. The sins mentioned in 19 are therefore not confined to sins of the tongue. They are embraced by the term ' *wicked purposes* ' (WV ; DV ' evil thoughts ') and include four sins of act and two (false witness ; blasphemies) of the tongue. **20.** Our Lord (in Mt, not Mk) rounds off the whole controversy with a concluding reference to its starting-point, 2—the Semitic literary phenomenon known as ' inclusion ' (*cf*. Lagrange, *Mt*, lxxxi).

703a **XV 21-28 The Canaanite Woman** (Mk 7:24–30)—**21.** This incident, one of the most touching in the gospel and treated with a delicate realism unusual in Mt, takes place in the pagan *district* of Tyre and Sidon ; *cf*. 11:21 note. This Phoenician territory borders Galilee on the north. It is possible that our Lord leaves Israelitic ground to give his disciples the respite which they had been recently denied, 14:13 note. **22.** Mt uses the term ' Canaanite ' (Mk ' Syrophoenician ') to under-line the significance of a miracle worked for one who belonged to the hereditary enemies of Israel. The term is not inaccurate : this district, colonized by Canaan-ites, Gen 10:15, was still basically Canaanite. The woman salutes our Lord with the Messianic title ' Son of David ' ; see on 1:1 ; 9:27. The phrase must have spread with his reputation beyond the confines of Israel, 4:24 note. **23.** (Mt only). The realistic reference to the disciples' intervention is strangely absent from Mk. Mt's Greek translator is evidently independent of Mk here. Since it is not his habit to enter into detail of this kind, it is clear that the detail is not invented ' to heighten the effect ' (*Allen, 169) but rather that the translator has under his eye ' a second and longer account (than Mk's) '. Yet even here the lifelike quality of the incident is due as much to what is implied as to what is expressed. Our Lord's silence (we gather) naturally drives the poor mother to the disciples. These are more concerned to rid themselves of the annoyance but, as our Lord's reply in 24 hints, they suggest that the only way to do so is to dismiss her with the request **b** granted. **24.** Our Lord's personal concern (like that of the Apostles on their first mission ; 10:6 note) is with Israel. His remark recalls that made to his mother at Cana, Jn 2:4, where, evidently, the tone was sufficiently kindly to encourage. **25.** In any case, the woman's quick eyes have seen him at last open his mouth. She seizes the slight advantage and falls at his feet with a cry for pity. **26.** The words of Jesus are not as harsh as they read and they seem deliberately to invite a riposte. That they are a little parable turned into allegory only by the situation lessens the shock of the words. (On parable and allegory *cf*. notes to ch 13.) Moreover, the term ' dogs ' (κυνάρια not κύνες) would be better rendered ' little dogs ', ' pet dogs ' ; it serves to bring out the importance of priority for the children yet eliminates the absolute idea of contempt. **27.** Never-theless the remark would have checked one with a vestige of pride (contrast Naaman, 4 Kg 5:11–12) as our Lord well knows. But the woman's simple humility rises to the occasion and there is wit in her reply : ' *How true* ' (or : ' Please ! ' *cf*. Phil 4:3 ; Phm 20 ; Benoit) ' *Lord ! for the little dogs also get their meal—from the crumbs that fall* '. The woman quaintly turns the parable to her own advantage : it is true, she implies, as far as it goes, but it has not been taken far enough. As a mother she knows that she would not thus rob her children of bread, but she also knows their table-manners and how the floor is kept clean. **28.** The Sacred Heart is won by a faith that stood so sharp a

test. When the woman got home she found her child **70** well again (Mk).

XV 29-31 Cures at the Lakeside (*cf*. Mk 7:31–37)— **c** Jesus with his disciples leaves the district of Tyre and Sidon for the Lake of Galilee ; for this journey *cf*. Mk 7:31. The scene of the miracles appears to be the NE. side of the Lake where the hills fall to the plain. The sick were *laid down* at his feet (not ' cast down ' ; the Semitic verbs for ' to throw '—*e.g*. Aramaic *rᵉmāh* —are often used in the sense of ' to put, place ' ; Joüon, 101). In 31, ' the maimed healed ' should be read (Merk etc.) though omitted by Vg, DV, WV. From the fact that the crowds praise ' the God of Israel ' it would be bold to argue that they were pagans ; *cf*. Lk 1:68 ; Ac 13:7.

XV 32-39 Second Multiplication of Loaves (Mk 8:1–10) **d** —The evangelists plainly record the multiplications as two separate miracles. Each narrates them in close succession (Mt chh 14–15 ; Mk chh 6 and 8) and subse-quently refers to them as two separate events, Mt 16:9–10 ; Mk 8:19–20. If the unexpectant attitude of the disciples on this second occasion seem surprising, we should remember the months that had elapsed since the former miracle, the occasions on which the disciples must have since gone hungry without a miracle being worked, their very proper diffidence in asking for a miracle, 23. **32.** The disciples therefore leave it to our Lord to comment on the hunger of the crowds. He does so. Their provisions are exhausted after three days with him, far from their homes (Mk). Jesus proposes a dilemma : they have no food here yet he will not send them elsewhere. He is clearly inviting the dis-ciples to ask for a solution like the previous one, 14:19. So far, the text does not exclude (rather it suggests) a previous multiplication of loaves. **33-34.** The disciples' remark is cautious, perhaps even a sly suggestion : Whence should we [emphatic] have . . . ? They express their own helplessness, not necessarily his. Moreover, their answer to our Lord's question : How many loaves ? is not the helpless one of 14:17 (' only five ') but simply ' Seven ', as if in this case the infor- **e** mation was not regarded as useless. **35-37.** The multi-tude (4,000 here, 5,000 in ch 14) sat on the ground— there was no ' green grass ' as on the previous occasion, Mk 6:39 ; it was summer. The number of *hampers* (WV ; see on 14:20) corresponds, not to the number of the Apostles (unlike 14:20) but to the original number of loaves, thus more directly signalizing the abundance of the miracle. **39.** It appears that our Lord sets sail for the western bank of the Lake since it is on this bank that he would be most likely to meet the Pharisees, 16:1, and since it is to the eastern side that he later sails, 16:5, to go to Caesarea Philippi, 16:13, *via* Bethsaida Julias, Mk 8:22. But the point of arrival, Magadan, (' Dalmanutha ' in Mk) is unknown. It is probable however (Abel 2, 373) that the form, certainly authentic, represents ' Magdala ' (*cf*. 27:55 note) just as the ' Migdal ' of Jos 15:37 is transcribed ' Magada ' in the Vatican Codex. (Mk's ' coasts—*i.e*. district—of Dal-manutha ' may represent an Aramaic original : *liglîlā'* *dilmᵉʿōnāṭēh* or ' to the place of his abode ' ; *cf*. RB 53 (1946) 373–84 and Mk 8:10.)

XVI 1-12 Leaven of the Pharisees and Sadducees **f** (Mk 8:11–21 ; Lk 12:54–56 ; *cf*. Mt 12:38–39 ; Lk 12:1*b*)—The incident of 1–4 serves as introduction to the lesson of 5–12. **1.** Pharisees and Sadducees forget their differences and make common cause against the new teacher. The situation is similar to that of 12:38 ff. (see note) but the Sadducees here take the place of the Scribes, our Lord's answer is notably different and the reference to Jonas is curt (on the ' doublet ' question *cf*. Lagrange, *Mt*, liv). They issue a cynical challenge (' tempting ', *i.e*. putting to the test). They demand a Messianic sign descending from (Mt : ἐκ) the physical heavens. This ' sign ' is possibly a repetition of the ' manna ' miracle of Mosaic times (*cf*. Jn 6:30 ff.) which times were in Jewish tradition (Edersheim, 1, 176), a re-hearsal of the Messianic age ; in particular, the Messias was to bring down manna from heaven for his people ;

cf. Lagrange, *Jn*, 175. Their ill-will had contrived to explain away our Lord's miracles (*e.g.* 9:34 ; *cf.* Jn 9:18–29) and he refuses to work wonders at their dictation ; *cf.* his similar attitude in Lk 23:8–9. **2-3.** He ironically concedes their ability to recognize natural portents in the heavens but adroitly invites them to discern supernatural portents on earth among the blind, the lame, the deaf (*cf.* 11:4 f.), announcing the new Messianic day. **4** has possibly (Buzy, Lagrange) with the exception of the ominous, valedictory phrase, been imported hither by translator or copyist from 12:39. **5.** Jesus and his disciples sail for the eastern shore of the Lake. Distracted by dispute or by unexpected departure the disciples had not made their usual provision : only one old loaf lay in the boat, Mk 8:14. **6-7.** Jesus bids his disciples beware of the corrupting element ('leaven', *cf.* 1 Cor 5:6) which is the outlook ('doctrine') of his recent questioners. The word 'leaven' reminds the disciples who exclaim : 'We have forgotten the bread !' (omit 'because' : the ὅτι of 7 is probably recitative). **8-12.** After witnessing the two miracles of the loaves (14:17–21 ; 15:34–38 with notes) the disciples needed no great faith to exclude worry about material things ; still less should they have implicitly attributed this worry to their Master. Our Lord has only to repeat his original remark (doubtless with an emphasis on its second half) to make its metaphorical meaning clear. Doctrinally the Pharisees and Sadducees had little in common, the ' doctrine ' therefore is their common cynicism, so recently displayed, with regard to the ' signs of the times '. Our Lord's warning is not unnecessary : unlike the Pharisees and Sadducees the disciples did not ignore his Galilean miracles but they were inclined to forget them and to miss their full significance, 8–10.

13-20 Peter's Profession and Primacy (Mk 8:27–30 ; Lk 9:18–21)—**13.** After reaching the east bank of the Lake and after the cure of the blind man at Bethsaida Julias, Mk 8:22–26, our Lord takes his disciples to the *district* of Caesarea Philippi on the extreme northern frontier of Palestine, 2 or 3 m. E. of Dan. Here in fertile country rises one of the largest sources of the Jordan. It is a natural site for the sanctuary of Pan (hence Panias ; Arab. Baniyas) built there by the predominantly Greek population in the 3rd cent. B.C. In our Lord's time the town itself was new-built by Philip the tetrarch in 3–2 B.C. and named Caesarea in honour of Caesar Augustus. It boasted a temple to Augustus built by Herod the Great *c* 20 B.C. Here where ' men worshipped side by side the forces of nature and the incarnation of political power ' the divinity of Christ was first clearly professed ; *cf.* SHG 473–8. Our Lord asks for the rumours of his identity, not to inform himself but to lead up to his next question. In Mt (' Son of Man ' ; Mk and Lk : ' I ') we are already prepared for ' Son of God ' which is to follow, 16. **14.** In Galilee at Antipas' court there was a superstitious rumour of the Baptist's resurrection. Other circles felt the Messianic atmosphere and thought of Elias the precursor (but *cf.* 17:10 note) or of Jeremias, Israel's champion at a time of national crisis (*cf.* 2 Mac 15:13–16) ; the Messianic age was associated, too, with the return of other prophets ; *cf.* 4 Esd 2:18. It is strange that none mentions rumours of the Messias himself which must have been recently circulating ; *cf.* **b** Jn 6:15). **15-16.** Our Lord expects more from his companions and pupils, but it is only Peter who makes the decisive and immediate reply acknowledging his Messiahship. In Mt (only) he goes on to profess the divinity of his master ; *cf.* § 50g. Peter's formula ' the son of the living God ' is found, with slight variation, on the lips of Caiaphas, Mk 14:61, and for its acceptance Jesus is declared guilty of blasphemy. He accepts it here and in terms which make it clear that Peter's conception of his dignity is not merely a deduction of Messiahship from adequate human premisses ; *cf.* 11:4–6. **17-19.** Human considerations (' flesh and blood ') such as reasoning from miracle and prophecy could have led Peter to a confession of Messiahship—no

great marvel there. That the Father, not the Son, had **704b** revealed shows how profound was the significance of Peter's words even if Peter himself had not yet fully sounded their depth. By this revelation the Father had singled out Peter as the natural foundation for his Son's society and our Lord, as ever, follows his Father's lead. Faith in the divinity of Christ must henceforth be a criterion of the true society of Christ. The Son of God now echoes and outdoes the generosity of the son of Jonah. At last he explains the name (apparently of his own invention) promised to Simon at the first encounter, Jn 1:42, and confirmed on the occasion of Simon's call, Mt 4:18 ; *cf.* 10:2. The name **c** in Aramaic is *Kēphā*, *i.e.* ' Rock ' or ' Stone '. The Greek translator judged πέτρος ' stone ' more suitable, being masculine in form, for Simon's name and kept πέτρα ' rock ' for the foundation-material demanded by the metaphor. The original language, however, leaves no room for distinction : Thou art *Kepha* and upon this *kēphā*. . . . The ' church ' (ἐκκλησία, the customary LXX rendering of the Hebrew *qāhāl*, *i.e.* religious assembly, congregation) is the new society of Christ's faithful answering to, and supplanting, the OT *qāhāl*. Simon is to be the ultimate authority on earth of this society which is itself the hierarchical body described in 18:15–18. By reason of this rock-foundation the malignant powers will not prove stronger than (κατισχύσουσιν) the citadel-society. The phrase ' gates of Hell ' needs some explanation. The term ' gates ' in Hebrew is often used of the fortified city itself (Gen 22:17 ; 24:60 ; Is 14:31, etc.) ' Hell ' (Hades), dwelling-place of demons (four times in this sense in the Apocalypse, *cf.* Allo, *L'Apocalypse*, Paris 1933, 101, and *cf.* Lk 16:23) is not merely ' death ' (an idea which would confuse the warlike image) but the activity of forces hostile to the cause of Good. The promise is therefore not one of immortality for Peter (Harnack)—a meaning that would require also (against the natural construction of the sentence) that the pronoun ' it ', 18, be referred to ' rock ' and not to ' church '. In 19 the metaphor changes : the besieged citadel founded on a rock now becomes the Kingdom with its Chancellor to whom Christ will in due time commit his own keys, Jn 21:15–17. The gift of the keys implies responsible stewardship as the keys of Eliacim, Is 22:22, implied stewardship of the Davidic household. This idea serves as a bridge from the rock-metaphor to the more direct definition of Peter's powers (Lagrange). These powers **d** are of effective ' binding ' and ' loosing ' in the spiritual order on earth. The ' binding and loosing ' (rabbinical terms for excluding from (' binding ') or granting readmission to the community or for declaring forbidden or permitted according to the Law) must be understood as containing all that is implicit in the gift of the keys, *i.e.* all powers necessary to the well-being of the kingdom including any positive legislative power which may prove necessary in the future. (On the authenticity etc. of the Petrine text *cf.* Bi 1 (1920) 240–64 and DBV(S) II, 546–64.) **20.** The title ' Son of God ' refers to our Lord's personal dignity, the term ' Christ ' to his function. The latter might politically excite the crowds ; it alone, therefore, is the direct object of his prohibition.

21-23 First Passion Prophecy. Peter rebuffed (Mk **e** 8:31–33 ; Lk 9:22)—**21.** Caesarea Philippi marks a turning-point of the Apostles' faith. Our Lord now ventures to break the strange news of his approaching Passion. The titles ' Messias ', ' Son of God ', were to the Apostles far removed from the idea of Israel's official rejection (through the Sanhedrin) and from the prospect of death. All three Passion predictions, 16:21 f. ; 17:21 f. ; 20:18 f., are accompanied by a prophecy of resurrection which, however, seems to be overwhelmed in the Apostles' mind by the shocking prediction preceding it. Moreover, the nature of this resurrection is relatively vague and its prospect remote ; *cf.* their mentality perhaps with Martha's, Jn 11:23–24, 39. **22-23.** Peter ' taking him ' (προσλαβόμενος—drawing him to one side or, possibly, ' trying to be helpful ')

704e remonstrates : ' Mercy on you ! ' (ἵλεώς σοι, i.e. ... εἴη ὁ θεός : ' may God be merciful to you '). But Peter is a snare (' scandal ') in the path traced by the Father and willingly taken by the Son ; our Lord orders him out of the way. Peter cannot yet appreciate (οὐ φρονεῖς) God's ways. He is unwittingly playing the part of their great adversary (śāṭān). Through him Satan, who had left our Lord only ' for a time ', Lk 4:13, renews the original temptation, 4:1-11. The faithful report of this rebuke is a tribute to the candour of the evangelist who has just reported the promise of the primacy.

f **24-28 Death the Way to Life** (Mk 8:34-38 ; Lk 9:23-26)—Like master, like man : the disciple must himself be prepared to shoulder a cross in imitation of Christ. The saying is even more natural in this passage than it is in 10:38 (see note) because it here follows a prediction of the Passion. **25.** The exhortation is reinforced by a prospect of the great issues involved (cf. 10:39)—no less than the loss or gain of eternal life. **26.** How great is this gain appears from a literary balance of the world's riches against the supernatural life of the soul ; it appears too from the obvious inability of those riches to purchase that life. That ' soul ' here is regarded as the principle of supernatural, not merely natural, life is clear from the context and, on the dogmatic side, from the unanimity of Catholic interpretation ; cf. § 52h and A. Bea, Bi 14 (1933) 435-47. **27.** Man cannot buy eternal life : it will be awarded according to his works, i.e. according to his loyalty to Christ's cause, 25. The fitting judge of this loyalty is Christ himself. Of him, with his cross, one might be tempted to be ashamed (Mk, Lk) but the true dignity and reward of his following will appear from

g his glory and his sentence in the final judgement. **28.** This sentence, though juxtaposed to 27 was perhaps originally a separate dictum, as Mk 8:39 seems to hint. In the present context it appears to imply that the dignity of Christ's discipleship will be manifested even before the final judgement, nay, in the lifetime of some of the bystanders. The Kingdom of the Son (not ' of the Father ', cf. 13:43 note) will establish itself shortly ' in power ' (Mk ; cf. 1 Cor 4:20). This power, following the ' weakness ' of the Cross, 1 Cor 1:23-25, manifests itself progressively from the Resurrection onwards, Rom 1:4 ff. To those who could see it the glory of this spiritual Kingdom on earth was already plain in St Paul's time, e.g. 1 Thess 2:12, Eph 2:6 f. The destruction of Jerusalem in A.D. 70 served only to show that the Kingdom stood alone. The presence on earth of such a kingdom, acknowledging Christ as its king, will be evidence that the Son of Man has entered into (ἐν for εἰς as often in biblical Greek) his kingdom, i.e. has been solemnly invested as King in heaven. It will be the realization of Daniel's vision in which the ' coming ' of one like a ' son of man ' was a coming not to earth but to the Ancient of Days on his heavenly throne to receive power and a kingdom. See notes to Dan 7:13 ff. ; Mt 8:19-20 ; 26:64.

705a **XVII 1-9 The Transfiguration** (Mk 9:1-8 ; Lk 9:28-36 ; cf. 2 Pet 1:16 ff.)—**1.** The Father had already revealed the divinity of his Son to Peter, 16:17, he now, about one week later, reveals it more publicly. As his companions our Lord takes (παραλαμβάνει ; cf. 4:5, 8) the three favoured witnesses of one of his greatest miracles, Mk 5:37, and of his deepest distress, Mk 14:33. The ' high mountain apart ' is not Hermon but, according to a 4th cent. tradition, probably Tabor, a few miles SE. of Nazareth and two or three days' direct journey from Caesarea Philippi ; it rises, symmetrical and isolated, about 1,000 ft above the plain. **2.** Before the eyes of the disciples the aspect of Jesus was profoundly changed (μετεμορφώθη), the result of an inner brilliance affecting even his garments (read, with the best MSS : ' white as light '). **3.** Moses the legislator and Elias the prophet-champion of Yahwism (cf. Ecclus 48:1-10) show by their presence that the old order is not destroyed but fulfilled in the person and work of Jesus —fulfilled even in the ' scandal ' of the Cross, the subject of their converse with him, Lk 9:31. Wearied

with the climb in the August heat the three Apostles **7(** are asleep ; they waken to see the vision (Lk). **4. b** Peter's suggestion is a wild one (Mk, Lk), based apparently on the assumption that Moses and Elias have come to stay and to herald Jesus in his glory. ' It is fortunate we are here ', he says (tr. Osty, Les Evangiles Synoptiques, Paris 1947). He means that, being there, he and his companions will be able to improvise lodgings (huts of branches). He forgets that such guests need no shelter. **5.** As in the OT (cf. Ex 24:15 ; 33:9-11 etc.) the cloud is the visible manifestation of the divine presence. It envelops them all. The Voice repeats the words spoken at the Baptism, 3:17, and approves Peter's profession, 16:17, but the added command (' hear ye him ') warns the Apostles against questioning the words of the Son ; cf. 16:22. **6-9.** The glory passes and Jesus is once more the familiar friend. He enjoins silence : the vision is not to be spoken of until after the Resurrection, presumably to avoid premature and mistaken Messianic enthusiasm. Few, knowing of the Transfiguration, would learn to appreciate the necessity of the Cross.

10-13 The Precursor (Mk 9:10-12)—The appearance **c** and disappearance of Elias have been troubling the Apostles. He had appeared after our Lord and disappeared without furthering our Lord's mission in any way. This was not the Elias, herald of the Messias, depicted by the Scribes (cf. Edersheim 2, 706-9 : SB 4, 764-98) from their reading of the prophet Malachy (Mal 4:5-6 ; DV). Our Lord grants the expression of the scribal teaching : Elias is to come and restore (i.e. bring back to perfection) . ., but he corrects its perspective. This herald-Elias has already come in the person of the Baptist. The ' great day of the Lord ' before which Elias was to come, Mal 4:5, is therefore the day of Messianic visitation. Jesus declares the profound sense of the prophecy (missed by the Scribes) : not the person but the spirit of Elias returns—in the person of the Baptist ; cf. Lk 1:17. (With many Catholic commentators, e.g. Lagrange, Pirot, Allo, Van Hoonacker, we find here no justification for asserting the physical return of Elias before the final judgement.) Our Lord then turns this discussion to advantage : if the great Elias is the martyred Baptist, it is not surprising that the glorious Messias should prove to be the crucified Son of Man. The fate of the Baptist was a hint of God's Messianic plan. John was a precursor in more ways than one.

14-20 The Possessed Epileptic (Mk 9:13-28 ; Lk **d** 9:37-44a)—**14.** It seems that the night was spent on the hill, Lk 9:37. On the following day Jesus and the Three descend to find a crowd gathered round three groups : the nine Apostles, certain Scribes (Mk ; their presence suggests Galilee rather than the Hermon district), and a father with his son. The boy has all the symptoms of epilepsy, Mk 9:17-25, called ' lunacy ' by the ancients by reason of its periodicity. **15-16.** In the absence of Jesus the father has approached the disciples, without success ; he now eagerly approaches the Master. Our Lord's tone is one of lament rather than of rebuke. His words ' are not merely those of a man among men ; it is a divine being speaking—one whose own home is heaven ', Lagrange, Lk, 277. The lament embraces the whole faithless and misguided (DV ' perverse ') human race among whom our Lord came to work. It is immediately evoked, however, by the impotence of his own Apostles (their own fault, cf. 18-19) and perhaps by the malevolence of the carping Scribes, Mk 9:13. **17.** The child was not only epileptic but possessed, since our Lord not only cures but exorcizes, Mk 9:34 ; Lk 9:43. The father, however, does not distinguish the two states nor does our Lord instruct him. Jesus did not come to teach the natural sciences. **18-19.** The Apostles puzzled at their inability to exorcize (their first failure ?) ask the reason. Our Lord underlines his earlier hint (' unbelieving ' generation ; 16)—lack of confidence in God. The tiniest grain of such ' faith ' (cf. 13:32) can work the impossible. He uses the current rabbinic hyperbole of ' moving

d mountains' (SB 1, 759), suitable to their situation at the foot of Tabor. **20.** This verse is probably to be omitted with the 4th cent. uncials B and S as a harmonization with Mk 9:28, where see note.

e 21-22 Second Prediction of the Passion (Mk 9:29-31 ; Lk 9:44*b*-45)—' *While they were still together in Galilee* ' (KNT) or ' while they were gathering together (at some rendezvous) in Galilee ' (συστρεφομένων αὐτῶν) and about to leave for Jerusalem, our Lord again warns the disciples of his death. ' Betrayed [better ' delivered '] into the hands of men ' takes the place of the ' suffering from the ancients, scribes, high-priests ' of the first prediction (16:21, see note). The phrase suggests a terrible fate, 2 Kg 24:14, and there is pathetic irony in the juxtaposition of ' Son of Man ' and ' the hands of men '.

f 23-26 The Temple Tax (Mt only)—**23.** From Tabor it is a full day's walk direct to Capharnaum. On their arrival, Peter is approached by the tax-collectors for the tribute which, in the absence of Jesus and the Apostles, has evidently become overdue. The ' didrachma ', or two-drachma silver-piece (WV ' florin ') is the annual subscription towards the upkeep of the temple. (1 Greek drachma = ¼ stater = ¼ Jewish shekel = 1 Roman denarius. The denarius was the recognized daily wage of a labourer ; *cf*. Mt 20:2). This tribute affected all male Jews at home and abroad, aged twenty and over. The subscription was traditional (*cf*. Ex 30:11-16 ; Neh 10:32-34), the amount fluctuating. The diffident approach of the collectors (who were usually local men) may be due to respect for the dignity of their great townsman ; they were aware that priests at least were not forced to pay the temple-tax. **24-25.** Peter, knowing his master's custom, unhesitatingly answers ' Yes ' and goes into the house (his own ? *cf*. 9:10, 28 ; 13:1, 36) where Jesus is staying. Our Lord forestalls (DV ' prevented '—a Latinism) Peter's words. He already knows Peter's difficulty—either supernaturally or because he has overheard the conversation. He frames a small parable in the form of a question the answer to which is obvious. ' Tribute ' (τέλος—customs dues) and ' custom ' (κῆνσος —direct, capitation, tax) would certainly not be exacted of members of an oriental royal family—the royal children are *exempt*. Now the temple-dues are a tribute ' which each offers to God ', Jos., *Ant*. 18, 9, 1. It is therefore clear (especially to Peter who has recently confessed the divine sonship) that Jesus is exempt. **26. g** Nevertheless, refusal to pay would savour of impiety for those ignorant of our Lord's dignity and rights. Doubtless the necessary money could have been obtained by ordinary means but the miraculous means chosen has the advantage of avoiding the ' scandal ' while yielding nothing to the principle (' the children are exempt ') because the money does not come from the apostolic purse after all. The miracle is certainly one of supernatural knowledge, probably more, though the *hemichromis sacra* of Lake Galilee has been found with *e.g.* pebbles in its mouth (*cf*. Buzy 233 ; Prat 1, 455). Simon here (as the disciples elsewhere ; 12:1-8) is associated with the immunity of One who is greater than the temple. (The incident of the ' stater ' miracle is discountenanced in many circles as a pious story later [*c* A.D. 97 ?] elaborated partly to clear up early difficulties on the relationship of early Church and State—*cf*. Kilpatrick, *Origins*., 41 f.—partly to enhance the dignity of Peter and of the Roman church. This accusation is subject to the general remarks regarding ' Form Criticism ' [*cf*. § 33*k-o*] but in particular it should be observed that late invention is improbable for this passage. After the destruction of the temple in A.D. 70 the tax remained but was diverted to the temple of Jupiter at Rome ; Jos., BJ 7, 6, 6. Against this background the argument of Jesus [resting on the fact that the collection was for his Father's temple] would be meaningless.)

a XVIII 1-35 Instructions on the Kingdom : Its Spirit and Organization—Our Lord addresses himself principally to those who were to carry on his work.

His discourse is far from being a systematic and ex- **706a** haustive charter for the Church's leaders, but it inculcates certain fundamental dispositions : childlike spirit, 1-4 ; care for the simplest of the faithful, 5-9 ; for the wayward zeal, 10-14, but salutary firmness and exercise of full authority, 15-20 ; and all this without personal rancour, 21-35.

1-4 Importance of Simplicity (Mk 9:32-36 ; Lk **b** 9:46-48)—Despite (or even because of ?) the promise to Peter of primacy in the Kingdom, 16:19, the Apostles debate, not without personal interest, the question of precedence. The dispute takes place on the way to Capharnaum (Mk) and the Apostles are ashamed to tell our Lord (Mk, Lk) who, however, knows their thoughts. Mt characteristically ignores these details and summarily presents the incident in the form of Jesus' own question and answer. **1.** The question concerns present dignity, not degrees of reward in heaven (*cf*. Mk 9:33 : ' which of them *was* greatest ' WV). The ' kingdom of heaven ' is, therefore, the kingdom in its earthly stage. This is shown also by the theme of the whole chapter which deals with mutual relations of the disciples on earth. **2.** The child is a flesh-and-blood parable. Ambition is not a common trait of childhood. See Chrysostom's further developments in the moving homily 62 *in Mt*, Roman Breviary, July 20. **3.** Our Lord's words are particularly stern in Mt ' *Unless you become like little children again* ' (KNT ; στραφῆτε not ' be converted ' but ' turn back '), far from achieving eminence in the Kingdom you cannot even qualify for entrance. Ambition in this matter defeats itself ; *cf*. 20:20 ff. with note. **4.** The greatest stature in the Kingdom (*i.e.* true dignity before God) is paradoxically that of the man who ' *makes himself small* ' (Joüon ; ταπεινόω, *cf*. Lk 3:5). High function in the Kingdom absolves no one from personal humility.

5-7 Obligations towards the ' Little Ones ' (Mk **c** 9:37, 42 ; Lk 9:48 ; 17:1-2)—**5.** The ' child ' suggests all, young or old, who have simple faith in our Lord. He therefore passes to the duties of the Twelve towards the least sophisticated of the faithful. Care devoted to such, if it be given because they belong to Christ (ἐπὶ τῷ ὀνόματι) as his chosen ones, becomes an act of devotion to our Lord himself. **6.** The care for the ' little ones ' demanded in 5 is explained by its opposite vice—the providing of a snare (' scandal ') in the moral order by one's own conduct—bad example or direct seduction. This is a danger for those destined to occupy high place in the community. Better that those who so seduce should be securely out of the way of doing harm— weighed down in the depth of the sea. The ' millstone ' (lit. ' ass-mill ') in question is the lower of two stones which is ' like a hollow inverted cone with a wide hole at the narrower end allowing the flour to fall through when the grain has been crushed against its sides by the upper millstone ' (Lagrange, *L'Evangile*, 269). The mill is set in motion by an ass harnessed to a beam. This hollow cone could be put on a man collar-fashion. **7.** Human nature being what it is, ' scandal ', given and received, is inevitable, but woe to the giver because he takes the evil initiative !

8-9 Ruthless Elimination of Moral Obstacles (Mk **d** 9:42-48)—The transition to this new idea is made, in Semitic fashion, by means rather of a word (' scandal ') than by a direct logical connexion with 5-7. A similar thought has been expressed in 5:29-30, but here the context (dealing with mutual relations in a society) suggests that the ' hand, foot, eye ' further represent those dear to us who may prove occasions of sin. Our Lord's words are severe because so much is at stake : Life or Everlasting Fire. The ' life ' is the unending life of the world to come (*cf*. Wis 5:15 f. ; 2 Mac 7:9, 36 ; Bonsirven 1, 517-26) where sacrifice of mortal life and limb will be repaired. Everlasting fire or the hell (gehenna) of fire (5:22 note) is proposed as the one alternative without prospect of end, and this was the prevailing Jewish belief, but *cf*. Bonsirven 1, 538-41 for its more exact description.

706e 10-14 The Sheep Astray (*cf.* Lk 15:3-7)—After the short digression on ' taking scandal ', 8-9, our Lord returns to the care for the ' little ones ', 5-7, with a parable to which Luke (Lk 15:3-7, note) gives a different emphasis. **10.** These ' little ones ' (5, note) are not contemptible ; they have their representatives at the court of God to plead vindication of their wrongs or neglect. That these angel-representatives are also companions of the just on earth (*cf.* Ps 90:11) is a doctrine found in rabbinic writings (Bonsirven 1, 233 ; Edersheim 2, 752) : the just man on his journey is accompanied by two good angels, the wicked by two evil spirits. Later Rabbis speak of angels assigned to the permanent care of each individual (SB 3, 437 f.). Here our Lord clearly speaks of angelic advocates in Heaven and, if we take into account the background of Jewish angelology, implies that they accompany their charges on earth. This doctrine of ' guardian angels ', based on our text (and *cf.* Ac 12:15), is not defined by the Church, but is consecrated in her practice and is held to be *proxima fidei*. On the manuscript evidence editors rightly omit **11** as an importation from Lk 19:10. **12-14.** The parable speaks for itself. The lesson is implicit : if the Father thinks so much of these ' little ones ', how far should the disciple be from despising them ! The shepherd is, of course, not a perfect image of God ; his impetuosity in leaving the ninety-nine, his disproportionate joy in finding the one, are very human qualities. Yet, by their very excess they serve admirably to illustrate the Father's concern for his ' little ones '. The disciples' duty is clear : not only the negative obligation of averting scandal, but the positive one of leading the ' little ones ' back to the fold when they stray.

f 15-18 Exercise of Correction (Mt only)—This duty of seeking the straying Christian (' brother ') is to be exercised with discretion. **15.** The sinner (prob. omit ' against thee ', WV, and *cf.* Lagrange *ad loc*) must be won back to God (' gained ') as sweetly as may be. If there be no need for public reprimand, charity forbids it : one must *show him his fault* (WV) privately. **16.** In juridical matters the old Law required at least two witnesses : ' it is by the deposition of two or three witnesses that the case is to be established ', Deut 19:15. The principle is transferred to this affair which is not yet juridical. The persons called are therefore not witnesses of the fault but are called in as independent opinions helping not to convict but to convince the sinner of his fault. **17.** Only in the last resort must the matter be brought to official notice—this for the sake of the individual and of the community. Our Lord prudently and naturally provides for the future (as in 16:17-19, notes) when he will be no longer at hand to settle difficulties. His ' Church ' appears as a compact, defined body with powers to exclude the recalcitrant from its society. After such a sentence the sinner stands outside the Society as the pagans and the Jewish tax-gatherers (' publicans ' ; *cf.* 9:10 f., note) are beyond the pale of the Synagogue. For Jewish ideas on fraternal correction, *cf.* Bonsirven 2, 231. **18.** 15-17 were addressed, in the singular, to any Christian ; now our Lord addresses the Apostles (' you ' ; *cf.* 18:1), not the members of the Church at large. He associates their powers with Peter's without prejudice to Peter's exclusive custodianship of the keys or to his function as the one foundation, 16:17-19. The apostolic body, with Peter, is given wide powers which include that of formal excommunication or reconciliation.

g 19-20 Mystical Presence of Jesus (Mt only)—Though the connexion with the preceding may be loose (*cf.* ' again I say to you ') it seems probable that the words, in Mt's context, still have reference to the Apostles. They appear to guarantee efficacious help for any agreed course of action ($\pi\rho\hat{a}\gamma\mu a$) concerning which the Apostles ask divine assistance. Most commentators, however, refer our Lord's promise to the prayer of the faithful in general and refuse any close connexion with 18. **20.** In any case, the reason why the Father's help is certain is based on a general principle : the

beloved Son himself whom the Father always hears, Jn 11:42, is mystically present in the tiniest gathering convoked to do him honour (' in my name ' ; $\epsilon\dot{\iota}s$ $\tau\dot{o}$ $\dot{\epsilon}\mu\dot{o}\nu$ $\dot{o}\nuο\mu a$, not $\dot{\epsilon}\nu$ $\tau\hat{\omega}$ $\dot{\epsilon}\mu\hat{\omega}$ $\dot{o}\nu\dot{o}\mu a\tau\iota$, suggests the idea of appurtenance, consecration, devotion to). We may compare the words with the rabbinic saying (*c* A.D. 135): ' When two are together and discussing the Law, the Glory [*i.e.* God himself] is in the midst of them '. Our Lord takes the place of the Law as the purpose of the gathering and assumes the role of the Glory itself.

21-35 On Forgiveness (*cf.* Lk 17:3b-4)—**21-22.** The instruction on reconciliation of erring brethren, 15-18, has said nothing of repeated faults. It is Peter (naturally enough, in view of his position, 16:17 ff.) who seeks precision on this matter, though he introduces a personal note (' against me ') hitherto absent ; *cf.* 15, note. Seven is a round (Semitic) number and therefore, Peter thinks, generous. It is not generous enough for the spirit of the Kingdom. Our Lord multiplies and multiplies the sacred number to leave the impression of limitless pardon. Repeat them as he will, our neighbour's offences against us can never compare with ours against God—and still God forgives. Nevertheless, our forgiveness of neighbour is the condition of God's pardon of us. This is the lesson of the parable which follows.

23-35 The Heartless Debtor (Mt only)—The parable is a drama in three scenes : Mercy, 22-27, Cruelty, 28-30, Justice, 31-34, with an epilogue, 35. **23.** Because this notion of pardon is so indispensable it is possible to represent the Kingdom in terms of Mercy and Justice. The time has come for the king's officials (provincial governors or financial administrators) to settle their account with the Treasury. **24.** At the very outset one is brought to the king's presence who owes nearly three million pounds (10,000 talents ; one talent is a weight of silver equivalent to 6,000 Greek drachmas—more than a labourer could earn in fifteen years ; *cf.* 17:23, note). The sum is fantastic even for a highly-placed official ; its choice has in view the application of the parable to our debt towards God. **25-27.** The king, using his royal prerogative, orders the man and his family to be sold into slavery and a small percentage of the debt to be paid for the sale of his person and possessions. The king, though he knows the absurdity of the man's wild promises, relents ; he remits the whole debt—a kingly gesture. **28-30.** The contrast that follows is emphatic and detailed. The forgiven debtor meets his equal, not his subject ; he is owed a paltry sum—one six hundred thousandth of his own forgiven debt ; he assails his fellow-debtor with violence, not giving time to speak ; he spurns him when his attitude and words (ironically the image and echo of his own) must have recalled the recent interview with the merciful king. Finally he throws his debtor into prison to force him to raise the money by some means (selling-up, borrowing, etc.). **31-34.** The shocking contrast between the king's conduct and his servant's is made explicit in this third tableau. The matter is reported to the king who exacts the rigorous justice which the merciless servant has just demanded. The unhappy man is handed over to the torturers who will force him perhaps to disclose some hidden reserves. He is handed over ' until he should *pay* '. There is no likelihood that he will be able. **35.** The epilogue is on a threatening note, but it plainly identifies the Father with the king whose first characteristic is limitless mercy, 23-27. The enormity of our debt to the Father is immeasurable : it is represented arithmetically only because a parable in human terms demands it and because the figure serves to dwarf our neighbour's ' debt ' to us. But the Father lays down two firm conditions, and only two : that we ask for forgiveness ; that we exercise it ourselves. The first condition is implicit in the parable, the second explicit. The parable is the graphic development of the pregnant and sobering prayer ' Forgive us *as* we forgive ', 6:12. And the forgiveness must be ' from our hearts ', profound and absolute. ' I forgive but I cannot forget ' is not a Christian saying.

▲ XIX 1-12 The Divorce Question.

1-2 From Galilee to Judaea (Mk 10:1 ; Lk 9:51 ; cf. 17:11 ; Jn 10:40–42)—The common plan of the synoptic gospels gives preference to the Galilean ministry, omitting the various visits of our Lord to Jerusalem, Jn 2:13 ; 5:1 ; 7:2 ; 10:22. After the visit of Jn 10:22 (for the feast of Dedication in December) John says, 10:40, like Mt and Mk, that Jesus went ' beyond Jordan '. It is probable that the journey described by Mt and Mk took place in September and that it included Jn's two visits to Jerusalem—for Tabernacles (Sept.–Oct. ; Jn 7:2) and for Dedication, Jn 10:22. In 19:1 Mt rounds off his fourth group of discourses with his familiar formula, 7:28, note. Our Lord seems (Mk) to go first into Judaea and from there to the plain just across Jordan, Jn 10:40, which, though strictly part of mountainous Peraea and under Antipas's jurisdiction, was commonly regarded as the ' district ' of Judaea.

3-12 Divorce (Mk 10:2–12 ; cf. Mt 5:31–32)—**3.** The Pharisees ' put him to the test ' (KNT). Their question must be seen against its background. In our Lord's time were two schools of thought divided on the question of sufficient motive for divorce in the full sense. The followers of the Rabbi Shammai allowed it on grounds of adultery only. Those of Hillel (Shammai's pre-Christian contemporary) for less grave, even trivial, reasons ; see Edersheim 2, 331–5. The controversy turned on the interpretation of Deut 24:1. There the Mosaic Law prescribed that a husband give his wife a ' bill of divorce ' (*sēper keṛîṭuṭ*, lit. ' document of cutting-off ') if he discover in her ' some uncleanness ' (*'erwaṭ dābār* ' indecency of (in) something '— apparently some sexual irregularity). This last phrase was the subject of bitter argument. It appears that in the 1st cent. A.D. the school of Shammai was gaining ground at least among the ordinary folk in Palestine, and that divorce was more common in the upper classes. The Pharisees' question is therefore equivalent to : ' Is Hillel right ? Can divorce *for any cause whatever* be tolerated ? ', or : ' Is a man permitted to send away his wife *however the case stands* ? '. **4-6.** To their chagrin our Lord pronounces for neither school but, as in 15:3 f., goes straight to the act and words of God, Gen 1:27 ; 2:24. Having created a woman for Adam, God (through the inspired author) had insisted that the union was even closer than that of blood. It produced, as it were, one single and indivisible person (' one flesh '). Our Lord emphasizes his conclusion claiming that no man, not Shammai nor Hillel, dare interfere with the express will of God. **7.** The answer was disconcerting. It struck at the practice of divorce itself. Whether the questioners be of the Hillel or of the Shammai school they are forced now to defend common ground. They in their turn appeal to Scripture, Deut 24:1. Their implication is that our Lord's conclusion from Gen is in plain opposition to the enactment of Moses himself. **8.** Jesus removes the contradiction by correcting their terms. Divorce was not a Mosaic ' command ' but a toleration of existing custom. This custom itself was due to Israel's ' hardness of heart ', *i.e.* (cf. Deut 10:16 ; Jer 4:4 ; Ecclus 16:10) to a moral immaturity insensitive to God's will—a will made plain, as our Lord says, in Gen 1:27. The Mosaic ' bill of divorce ' made the best of an existing situation by demanding a formality which restrained hasty action and which safeguarded the divorced wife from recall at her divorcing husband's whim. **9.** Our Lord restores the stability of the primal institution on his own authority, ' I say to you ' ; cf. 5:21–44. His attitude is so uncompromising, indeed, that the disciples are shocked, 10, as they would never have been had he merely declared for the severe view of Shammai. Moreover, his words as reported by Mk, 10:11 f., and by Lk, 16:18, and used by Paul, 1 Cor 7:10 f., contain no hint of an exception made for adultery. It is in the light of these certain facts that the obscure ' exceptive ' clause

of Mt, here and 5:32, must be explained. In view of the marked Jewish tone of Mt's words it seems probable that he is nearer to the *ipsissima verba* of our Lord. In any case, an evangelist would not have been so bold as to intrude an exception of his own making nor so stupid as to contradict his own context. It is still less likely that Jesus is reversing his uncompromising attitude with a casual parenthesis thrown out *en passant*. It follows that the so-called ' exceptive ' clause (μὴ ἐπὶ πορνείᾳ) cannot permit re-marriage on the ground even of adultery. Its positive explanation is, however, a matter of dispute. The ' classical ' Catholic explanation takes πορνεία (DV ' fornication ') as being here ' adultery ', as it is a question of married persons. The disputed clause is not strictly an ' exception ' but *reserves* the case of adultery (that it is a ' reservation ' appears more clearly from the παρεκτός—' setting aside ' —of 5:32 than it does from the awkward μή of 19:9). It does not positively provide for the case of adultery. This provision, however, must have been made at some time, explicitly or implicitly, by our Lord. It consists in separation *a mensa et toro* and is found explicitly in Paul, 1 Cor 7:10. The reservation was made to avoid the impression that our Lord was imposing the hardship of living with a faithless partner. An alternative Catholic explanation (recently revived, amended and given rabbinic background by J. Bonsirven, S.J., *Le Divorce dans le Nouveau Testament*, Tournai 1948) objects that the usual OT and NT word for ' adultery ' is μοιχεία. It maintains that πορνεία here means concubinage (cf. 1 Cor 5:1)—incestuous marriage within the degree forbidden by the Mosaic Law, Lev 18:1–17. In such a case a man in dismissing (divorcing) the woman is not only guiltless but is actually doing his duty. Our Lord inserts the clause in order to hint that the Mosaic injunctions remain (cf. CR 20 [1941], 283–94).

10-12 The more Perfect Chastity (Mt only)—**10.** In **f** private (cf. Mk 3:10) the disciples express their concern. Such severity is unheard of. If such be the position (DV ' case ') of the married state, marriage is too dangerous because irrevocable. **11.** Our Lord does not withdraw his severe pronouncement but (doubtless to the disciples' surprise) passes from their own phrase (' not expedient to marry ') to an even higher teaching. All this *doctrine* (' word ') of the due perspective on marriage and its expediency or non-expediency can be fully appreciated (WV ' taken in ' ; χωρεῖν) not by the carnal man but by those alone whose understanding is of God (' given ') ; cf. 13:11. **12.** For (says our Lord, explaining that such an understanding and perspective is so given) not accident of birth alone nor malice of men (the case of the first two classes of eunuch) but the high motive of the Kingdom (cf. 1 Cor 7:32) has succeeded in inducing virginity—and, in this last case, of free choice. To these last the divine sense of due proportion has been ' given ' and put into practical effect, not by self-mutilation but by self-denial. Our Lord thinks, perhaps, of the Baptist and of others who like Jeremias, Jer 16:2, have thus sacrificed themselves in the interests of the Kingdom. He is proposing an ideal foreign to Judaism which held marriage as a sacred duty for all men, Bonsirven 2, 207 f. Let him who is capable of appreciating the true order of values apply his faculty to this case ! WV ' He that can take this in, let him take it in ' ; χωρεῖν as in 11. It is fairly evident that Jesus is not appealing only for speculative appreciation : a gentle invitation underlies his words.

13-15 Blessing the Children (Mk 10:13–16 ; Lk **709a** 18:15–17)—**13.** Our Lord has just shown himself the champion of family-life ; it is perhaps not without significance that the mothers bring their babies and little children (παιδία) for a blessing. The disciples were used to the throngs of sick but now ' even the little ones ' (Lk 18:15 ; WV) are brought. They rebuke the children, or rather (Mk) their parents, for this waste of their master's time and strength. **14.** It is one of the rare occasions when our Lord shows himself really dis-

709a pleased with his disciples ('he was indignant' Mk) : 'Leave the little children alone!' (ἄφετε). This adult contempt is misplaced ; their elders should not interfere but rather watch how he loves their simplicity and learn themselves to imitate it, 18:1–4, notes. He takes the children into his arms (Mk) and touches their head with a murmured blessing.

b 16-22 Counsel of Poverty (Mk 10:17–22 ; Lk 18:18–23) —**16.** A young man of wealth and (Lk) position who, no doubt, had been watching and listening hurried after our Lord (Mk). Jesus had spoken, 14, of a necessary disposition for the Kingdom—a disposition less tangible than the observance of the Decalogue ; this has perhaps brought uneasiness to the youth's mind. ' Master ', he asks (not ' good ' master, DV), ' what good work am I to do . . .? '. He evidently wishes to feel an assurance of salvation. **17.** Our Lord's rejoinder is verbally uncertain ; probably the original form is found in Mk 10:18, Lk 18:19. In Mt it is obscure though even here there remains the *prima facie* difficulty (' One is good ') against our Lord's consciousness of his divinity—a difficulty, it should be noted, that was not grave enough to trouble the early Church which did not shirk the text ; *cf.* Lagrange, *Mt*, 373 ff. Mt's formula seems to imply that the youth leans too heavily upon one who, as he thinks, is a Rabbi and no more. Our Lord declines this compliment to his human nature ; *cf. e.g.* 20:23 ; 23:9. He seeks to put the inquiring soul into immediate contact with God who is personified Good. God himself, the one absolute Good, is the model of sanctity ; *cf.* 5:48. Nevertheless, our Lord goes on, in magisterial tone, to exercise the sovereign authority of his human office by confidently pointing the way to eternal life.

c 18-19. He doubtless surprises the youth when he lays down as necessary conditions the elementary prohibitions of the Decalogue, Ex 20:13–16 ; *cf.* Deut 5:17–20. But he passes then to positive commands that admit of degrees of perfection in their observance. First, the young man's duty to his parents (Ex 20:12a ; *cf.* Deut 5:16a) ; secondly, the great precept of charity towards one's fellows, Lev 18:19, not found in the Decalogue. **20-21.** In view of the last, and difficult, command the youth's confident reply appears hasty but evidently has little trace of self-sufficiency since (Mk) our Lord's affection is aroused. The young man has a generous heart and our Lord invites it to a perfection exceeding what is, absolutely speaking, necessary to eternal life. If the youth is content to have his treasure (and so, all his heart ; *cf.* 6:21) only in heaven, then he is fit for our Lord's inner circle, 27. **22.** The young man, who might have become an Apostle, was taken aback (' his face fell ' Mk) and went away dismayed.

d 23-26 Danger of Riches (Mk 10:23–27 ; Lk 18:24–27) —**23.** The departure of the youth is the occasion of a sad warning to the disciples. It is *with difficulty* that the rich shall enter the kingdom of heaven. The saying surprises after our Lord's distinction of moral precept, 17 ff., and counsel of poverty, 21. He speaks, however, not of impossibility, 26, but of difficulty. Nor does he condemn the rich young man but illustrates from his case how riches may grip and even suffocate the heart. **24.** Indeed, for merely human reason it is inconceivable that those whose heart is possessed by riches should enter the Kingdom. Our Lord expresses this with a slight adaptation of the Jewish proverb (Edersheim 2, 342) that ' a man even in his dreams does not see an elephant pass through a needle's eye '. **25-26.** He has deliberately provoked the astonishment of the disciples in order to impress on them the spiritual menace of riches. If possessions are such an obstacle —and there are few who have no possessions—who can be saved ? Our Lord (in words reminiscent of Gen 18:14 ; Job 42:2 ; Zach 8:6) explains that divine grace accomplishes the humanly impossible. Grace may leave the riches but loosen their grip on the heart.

e 27-30 Reward of Renunciation (Mk 10:28–31 ; Lk 18:28–30)—**27.** During this discussion Peter's mind has turned to the situation of himself and of his companions. They have accepted the invitation, 4:22, refused by the rich young man. What reward ? A natural and honest question, if somewhat brusque. **28.** The solemn promise surpasses expectation. Its meaning turns on the sense of the word ' regeneration ', ' rebirth ' (παλιγγενεσία) used in NT only here and in Tit 3:5 (of the ' new birth ' by Baptism in the Christian era). A similar idea, though not the term, is found in the OT (' the new heavens and new earth ' of Is 65:17 ; 66:22) referring, in apocalyptic style, to the Messianic age. The reference is pointed by Paul, 2 Cor 5:17, for whom the Christian era here on earth is already a ' new creation '. It appears probable, therefore, that our Lord refers to the Kingdom established on earth rather than to the world to come and the last judgement. This opinion (adopted by WV) is supported by the similar text of Lk 22:28–30 which also refers to the kingdom of the Son on earth—not ' of the Father ' in heaven ; *cf.* 13:43, note. The Son of Man seated on his *glorious throne* recalls Dan 7:9 and (as in 26:64 ; see note) refers to our Lord's presiding from heaven (*cf.* Ps 109(110) 1 quoted in 22:43 f.) over his Kingdom on earth. Associated with him in this royal function of judgement (*i.e.* of government, *cf.* Ps 71(72) 2 etc.—the Last Judgement is reserved exclusively to the Son in Jn 5:27) are the Twelve. This office they are to exercise on earth (and, doubtless, when they pass from earth and the Church remains) ; they will be thus associated with their master in heaven. Since the horizon has not yet widened for the Apostles, 10:5 ; 15:24, our Lord speaks in terms of Israel. It will be clear to them later, 28:19, that the sphere of their authority is to be the whole world—the Israel ' of God ', Gal 6:16. Our Lord addresses the Twelve as a body. He has already hinted at the defection of Judas, Jn 6:71, but this is not the place to mention it ; moreover, their number was later supplied by the election of Matthias, Ac 1:26. **29.** In the new era the Apostles occupy a privileged position but those who have imitated their detachment, leaving family or estates for Christ, will have their abounding reward too. The reward, though on earth (Mk) is clearly of the spiritual order since it is compatible with persecution, Mk 10:30. And finally (closing the whole section as it opened ; *cf.* 16) in the world to come ' life everlasting '. **30** introduces the following parable which serves also to conclude, 20:16, note.

XX 1-16 Parable of the Vineyard Labourers (Mt only) —**1.** Not the householder but the whole situation in which he figures is comparable to the Kingdom, 13:24, note. He goes to the bazaar at daybreak (ἅμα πρωΐ) to find men standing waiting for hired work. Since we are in parable and not in allegory (see note to ch 13) it is unnecessary to seek an individual significance for the ' vineyard ', though in the allegory of Is 5:1–7 it represents Israel. **2.** After the usual bargaining, no doubt, the day's wage is formally agreed upon (a circumstance to be remembered in view of what transpires)—a denarius, 17:24, note. **3-5.** At nine, noon and three p.m. (the hours are reckoned from 6 a.m.) the man returns to the bazaar. His first visit was presumably at 6 a.m. The times, however, are merely schematic and should not be scrutinized for hidden meanings. No sum is now mentioned other than a ' fair wage '. In human affairs one would expect three-quarters, one half, one quarter of a denarius respectively. **6-7.** One hour before sunset (the time-scheme is violently broken into to emphasize the lesson) the man hires the last of the unemployed— more, it would appear, from pity than from need. **8.** The foreman is evidently given two unusual instructions. The first, though this is mentioned later to suspend the interest, is to give the same wage to all— and herein lies the point of the parable. The second is to begin with the ' last ', with the late-comers. The purpose of this odd procedure is to hold back the first-comers as witnesses, hostile and critical, who will make objection and thus pave the way to the master's reply. This reply, 13–15, holds the lesson of the parable. **9-12.** The disgruntled bystanders complain only of the most extreme case of 'injustice', though they might have complained of the other later groups. These 'last' have worked for one hour, and that in the cool of the evening! **13-15.** The master addresses the chief grumbler. His gentle tone ('friend') recalls that of the Prodigal's father addressing the elder son, Lk 15-31, nor is there irritation in 'go thy way' (against KNT: 'away with thee!'; ὕπαγε; cf. e.g. 8:4). He calmly reminds him of the agreement, duly observed by both parties. 'It is my wish', he says, 'to give the last what I have given to the first'. When justice has been done, should anyone complain if kindness plays its part? The eye (of the mind) should not see evil where there is only good. If it does, it must be a diseased eye. **16.** Jesus has explained by parable his initial epigram: 'Many there shall be: first, last, and last, first', 19:30, and concludes: 'It is in this way (DV 'so') that the last shall be first and the first last'. It may be that we have in this parable only 'a striking picture of the divine generosity which gives without regard to the measures of strict justice', Dodd, 122. In this case the parable insinuates a mistrust of works for their own sake (perhaps as a corrective to the reward promised in 19:27-29) to the advantage of the divine liberality. The concluding sentence, stripped of its violent contrast imposed by paradoxical form, implies simply that 'first' and 'last' (long or short service) merge into one another before God—not that he is indifferent to the distinction but that his mercy refuses to be restrained. (The ominous: Many are called but few are chosen, is perhaps not authentic here—Mark omits—but drawn from 22:14, where see note.) The 'murmurers' of 11 do not necessarily figure the Pharisees; they may appear only with a parabolic purpose (8 note) similar to that of the Elder Brother in Lk 15:25 ff. This general lesson may not exhaust the parable. In Lk 13:30 the dictum of Mt 20:16a is connected with the personnel of the Kingdom to which there may also be reference here. If so, the late-comers are the Gentiles (cf. Lk 13:29) who will flock to the Kingdom ahead of the mass of Israel; cf. Rom 11:25 f. And this because, although the whole Jewish race has been 'called' to the Kingdom, only a few—the 'remnant' spoken of by the prophets, e.g. Is 1:9—have deserved to be 'chosen' to belong to it; cf. Feuillet, RSR 34 (1947) 303-27.

E. Jerusalem XX 17-XXV 46.
XX 17-19 Third Prediction of the Passion (Mk 10:32-34; Lk 18:31-34)—**17.** Passing from the plain across Jordan (19:1-2, note) our Lord hurries ahead of his apprehensive disciples and of others who follow (Mk) towards Jerusalem which lies on the western mountains before him. He turns to them as they follow and, for the third time (cf. 16:21; 17:22-23), speaks to the disciples alone (κατ᾽ ἰδίαν) of his coming Passion and Resurrection. **18-19.** The prophecy is more detailed than before. The death-sentence is to be engineered by the Sanhedrin and executed by the Romans. Mocking, scourging and (Mt only) crucifixion appear now for the first time. For the Apostles our Lord evidently wishes to soften the harsh notion of such an inglorious Messias by showing that he goes to his death consciously and freely. There is no remonstrance this time; cf. 16:23. It is clearly useless.

20-28 Ambition of the Sons of Zebedee (Mk 10:35-48; Lk 22:25-26)—**20.** Zebedee's wife, probably the Salome of Mk 15:40 (cf. Mt 27:56), falling on her knees before Jesus (KNT; DV 'adoring') has evidently some great favour to ask. Her presence suggests that of the other holy women whom we find later at the Cross and at the tomb. **21.** Mother-like she is interested in her sons' career, but it appears that she profoundly misreads its true character. Our Lord's 'kingdom' though doubtless spiritual is for her, as for the expectant Jews in general, a place also for honours as the world knows them—a Religion-State. For James and John (cf. 4:21) she asks the first and second rank in the King's hierarchy. **22.** The mother has asked

but the sons are answered: presumably they had **710b** confided their hopes to her, possibly even prompted her to ask. Though there is ambition here to be corrected, our Lord does not display the indignation he reserves for the Pharisees, 23:6. It must, therefore, have something of simplicity in it. Moreover, it is accompanied by docility since the brothers profess themselves ready to drink our Lord's own bitter cup; cf. 26:42. The 'cup' is a Hebrew metaphor for destiny—happy, as in Ps 15(16) 5, or unhappy, as in Ps 74(75) 9. **23.** Like all our Lord's worthy followers, 10:38 f., the brothers are to share his cross—an imitation of Christ which does not always suppose a martyr's death. James was in fact beheaded in A.D. 44; John suffered torture and exile; cf. PL 2:49; 26:143. Nevertheless our Lord, speaking as the envoy of his Father, reserves to the Father's eternal decree the honours of the Kingdom. He himself has already designated the primate of the Kingdom on earth, 16:18 f., but here he answers the question as it has been put, Mk 10:37, and speaks of the Kingdom in its final, glorious stage. **24-27.** Nor will Jesus tolerate the **c** spirit of ambition in his kingdom on earth. This spirit shows itself in the indignation of the ten even more than in the request of the two. It is a commonplace of political kingdoms that rulers are heavy-handed and their ministers officious ('their great ones domineer' WV). There will be rank in our Lord's kingdom, 16:18 f.; 19:28, but it must not be used for selfish ends. Let all know who would seek that rank that it is the rank of *servant*, 26, even of *slave*, 27. **28.** In this too (cf. 22) our Lord is the model—Lord by nature, servant by deliberate choice, Jn 13:13 ff. He has already hinted, 18, 19, 22, the lengths to which he is prepared to go in this service; now he states it clearly, and his phrase contains, in germ, the whole dogma of redemption later developed by Paul. The Servant is to give his life in ransom (DV 'redemption')—one life for the many. The Greek word used (λύτρον) is found twenty times in LXX where its meaning is variously the sum offered either in compensation for injury, or for the purchase of an object, or as the price of a slave's manumission. It is the term used (in Num 3:12; LXX) even of human beings—the Levites, substituted for the firstborn in the temple-service. The evidence of contemporary profane Greek literature shows that the most natural sense of the word in our Lord's time was certainly that of a slave's ransom; see texts quoted in DBV(S) 3, 126. The idea of a human life offered as ransom (λύτρον) is found in the 1st cent. A.D. (Philo of Byblos). Moreover, our Lord's phrase must be read in the light of contemporary Jewish thought not unfamiliar with the idea of an expiatory death, 2 Mac 7:37 f. The same idea of expiation is found in Is 53:10 where, as here, the expiation is the function of a Servant—the 'Servant of Yahweh'.

29-34 The Blind Men of Jericho (Mk 10:46-52; **d** Lk 18:35-43)—**29.** Our Lord, making his way from Peraea, 19:1, towards Jerusalem, 20:17, passes through Jericho, the beautiful garden-town adorned architecturally by Herod the Great and by Archelaus. It lies little more than 5 m. to the W. of Jordan and 15 to the E. of Jerusalem but in the plain 3,300 ft below the capital. The approach of the Paschal season brought crowds to the neighbourhood. **30-31.** On the way out of the town two blind men sit begging. Hearing that the passer-by is Jesus, the wonder-worker from Nazareth, they cry loudly for pity and refuse to be quieted. They address him as 'Son of David', an indubitably Messianic title, and Jesus this time does not enjoin silence (contrast 9:30; see note). Open proclamation of Messiahship is no longer untimely: our Lord is himself about to enter Jerusalem as Messias, 21:1-9; he is himself to raise the question of the Messias in public, 22:42 ff., to speak openly as Israel's saviour, 23:37-39, and solemnly to declare himself, 26:64. **32-34.** The faith of the blind men is encouraged by our Lord's call and by his gentle question, and they dare to give definite shape to their vague hopes. As

710d at Capharnaum, 9:29, the fingers of the Light (*cf.* Jn
e 9:5–6) touch the blind eyes. *Note on the Synoptic
accounts* : There seems no reasonable doubt that
Mt, Mk, Lk all speak of the same incident though only
one blind man is mentioned in Mk, Lk. It is probable
that Mk, consciously or unconsciously, omits the
second because he is interested in the first whom he
evidently knows ('Bar-Timaios' Mk 10:46). Lk,
though here somewhat independent of Mk, follows
him in this detail. The exact place of the miracle is
uncertain : going out of Jericho (Mt, Mk), approaching Jericho (Lk). It may be (Prat 2, 182, with hesitation) that one was healed on the way in, the other on
the way out. Or (Pirot, *La Sainte Bible*, Paris 1946,
IX, 532) Lk may refer to the Herodian Jericho, Mt, Mk,
to the old, deserted site a mile or two NNW. and
through which our Lord would pass to the inhabited
Jericho. It is perhaps more likely that the inspired
authors are content with a vague indication ('near
Jericho')—an attitude which they so often adopt
towards the chronological order of events ; *cf.* Lagrange,
L'Evangile, 418, footnote 2.

f **XXI 1–11 Triumphal Entry into Jerusalem ; Sunday**
(Mk 11:1–11 ; Lk 19:29–40 ; Jn 12:12–19)—**1.** From
Jericho Jesus had gone to Bethany, on the eastern slope
of Olivet nearly 2 m. from Jerusalem. There, on the
Saturday, he had been anointed by Mary ; *cf.* Jn
12:1–8 ; Mt 26:6–13, § 719*b*. It is now Sunday, Jn
12:1, 12. Bethphage lay higher up the eastern flank
of Olivet nearer Jerusalem and between Bethany and
the summit, a summit which from its 2,500 ft looks
downwards and westwards, across the Kedron valley,
upon the temple 200 ft below. The old steep road
from Jericho to Jerusalem passed to the right of Bethany
and through Bethphage. **2.** Bethphage is the village
that the disciples have almost reached (1 : εἰς, *i.e.*
towards) ; it lies ' *straight ahead* ' (DV ' over against
you '). Just inside the village, our Lord assures them,
they will find an ass and her foal tethered. **3.** If any
watchful bystander object, they are to say that ' the
Master ' (ὁ κύριος) needs them ' *but will straightway send
them back* ' (WV ; where see note) when he has finished
g with them. **4–5.** Mt (and Jn 12:15) is struck by the
literal fulfilment of the prophecy of Zacharias, 9:9. In
view of the sombre prospect of the Passion, Mt introduces the citation not with the ' shout for joy ' of
Zacharias, 9:9*a*, but with the sober words in which Isaias
announces the Saviour in 62:11. The promise to ' the
daughter of Sion ' (Jerusalem) is fulfilled. The substance of the prophecy is the humble advent of the
triumphant King, but our Lord chooses to fulfil it to
the letter and so to declare his Messianic character.
The Hebrew prophecy (here translated from the Heb.,
not incorporated from LXX) displays the parallelism
(synonymous here) inherent to Heb. poetic form. We
should therefore read : ' upon an ass, yea [not ' and ']
upon a colt '. That this is the meaning of Mt is
evident : a translator of the Hebrew would not so misread the poetic device nor would an intelligent writer
intend the absurdity of a rider using two mounts
apparently at the same time. The ' ass ' of 5 is therefore equivalent to the ' colt ', as the prophetic context
demands, and not to the she-ass of 2. This last is the
beast of burden (WV ; DV ' of her that is used to the
yoke ') of 5. **6–7.** The colt was not yet broken in,
Mk 11:2, note ; its dam is brought only to steady it.
Nevertheless it seems from the text as it stands that the
two disciples, 1, made their cloaks into saddles for both
beasts (7 : ' upon *them* '). This is odd but possibly it
was done to leave our Lord the choice of mount. On
the other hand, many competent commentators (*e.g.*
*J. Weiss, *Klostermann, Lagrange, Joüon) prefer to
read the singular ' upon *it* ' (the colt) with some not
h unimportant MSS and versions. **8.** The news of our
Lord's approach has spread to the capital where he
was expected, Jn 11:55 f., for the Paschal feast. The
excited crowd collecting at Bethphage is thus reinforced
by another from Jerusalem, Jn 12:12, which escorts
Jesus down the western slope of Olivet, across the

Kedron and up the opposite slope to the temple. Some **710c**
paved his path with their cloaks in sign of reverence,
4 Kg 9:13, others with branches broken from the olives
in the fields. Those who came from Jerusalem waved
palm-branches, Jn 12:13, which, as they set out, they
had torn from the trees in the warm Kedron valley.
9. At the feast of Tabernacles it was customary for
the people to carry branches in procession and to wave
them as they sang ' Hosanna Yahweh ! ' (*cf.* Edersheim
2, 159) and the branch itself was called ' the hosanna ',
SB 1, 845–50. The crowd now, waving branches,
associates the action with the word ' Hosanna ! ' an
abbreviated form (*hôšaʻ-na*) of the biblical *hôšîʻah-nnā*',
Ps 117(118) 25, lit. : ' Oh save ! ' or ' Oh be propitious
to . . . ! ' Their cry is : ' God save the Messias ! '
and (26 of the same psalm with a slight change) :
' Blessed be he that cometh in the name of the Lord ! '
—*i.e.* with the Lord's glory in view. In the final cry
' Hosanna in the highest ' the ' hosanna ' is a mere shout
of joy, the phrase being equivalent to ' Glory (to God)
on high ! ' ; *cf.* Lk 19:38. **10–11.** (Mt only). The
capital is in a turmoil : the triumphal approach has
been seen and heard. There are visitors from abroad
who know nothing of the new prophet. Probably they
have heard his Messianic rank acclaimed and they ask
only his identity.

12–13 Cleansing the Temple ; Monday (Mk 11:15–17 ; **71c**
Lk 19:45–46 ; *cf.* Jn 2:13–17)—If the episode is the
same as that described by Jn, it is probably Jn who gives
it its actual chronological setting, *viz.* at the beginning
of our Lord's public life. Mt who (like Mk, Lk)
mentions only this one journey to Jerusalem would be
bound to insert the incident here if he was to narrate
it at all. And indeed the priests, though custodians of
the temple, do not here (15 ; though see 21:23) refer
to the incident which perhaps suggests that it did not
take place at this time. For this opinion *cf.* among
Catholic authors : Calmès, Buzy, Lagrange ; *cf.* also
Braun, RB 38 (1929) 178–200, followed by Dubarle,
RB 48 (1939) 21–44. On the other hand, in view of the
notable differences between Jn's account and that of
the Synoptics, it is possible that our Lord took this
action twice—the need for it would certainly recur
(thus, amongst Catholic commentators, Durand, Prat,
Pirot). **12.** At festal times temporary booths were
erected in the great outer court of the temple where
tradesmen turned pilgrim piety to profit. The
materials for sacrifice, animal and bloodless, were sold
in noisy market with the usual oriental haggling. Some
sold oxen and sheep, Jn 2:14, others doves, the sacrifice
of the poor ; *cf.* Lev 12:8. Since Tyrian coinage only
was accepted for temple-offerings, Roman and Greek
coins were exchanged at a fee by the money-changers
who set up their tables in the court. Jesus drove out
the animals and their anxious owners. He was content
to up-turn the tables of the money-changers and the
chairs of the dove-sellers. It is to these, it seems, he
speaks. **13.** All three Synoptics remember the striking
words : the joyful prophecy of Isaias, 56:7, joined to the
subsequent lament of Jeremias, 7:11. The Jews themselves had profaned the temple by making of it an
unseemly and dishonest market.

14–17 The Official Protest (Mt only)—The chief priests **b**
and the scribes though of different schools of thought
(Sadducee and Pharisee repectively ; *cf.* 2:7–10 note)
are at one. They are irritated by the miracles but
particularly by the shouts of the children. Echoing
the cry of their elders, 9, doubtless without understanding, they hail Jesus as the Messias and he suffers
it. In answer to the objectors he clearly approves it.
He sends the scribes back to their Bible, Ps 8:3, leaving
them to complete the quotation (' that
thou mayest destroy adversaries '). The Heb. text of
the psalm declares that the tiniest children acknowledge
the Creator's glory ; those who do not are the Creator's
adversaries. The implication is sharply pointed by the
present circumstances and recalls our Lord's appeal
for simplicity, 18:3, 14. LXX (quoted by Mt) renders
substantially the same sense as HT, but more clearly

underlines our Lord's approval of the children's cry : ' Out of the mouths of babes . . . *thou hast brought forth perfect praise* ' (WV). **17.** On this note Jesus leaves them. He spends the night at Bethany (1, note) where his friends Martha and Mary and Lazarus lived.

18-22 The Fig-tree and Its Lesson ; Monday-Tuesday (Mk 11:12-14, 20-24)—It is characteristic of Mt that he presents the miracle and the lesson to be derived from it without breaking up the episode as Mk does in 11:15-18. In view of this telescoping process there is no need to stress the ' immediately ' of 19, though the word may in fact be intended literally. **18-19.** On the Monday morning our Lord left Bethany for the city. The fig-tree stood, perhaps, on the slopes of Olivet ; it was in leaf, as it would be at the Paschal season (beginning of April). Our Lord had evidently not broken his fast as he approached the tree. He knew, as well as the evangelists knew, that ' it was not the season for figs ' (Mk 11:13)—the figs are not ripe till June (for details *cf.* Lagrange, *Mk*, 293 ; HDB 2, 6). He laid a curse on the tree. There is no impatience in the words since he expected no fruit and it would be a curious sentimentality that could read cruelty there—especially as the insentient tree becomes a signpost for man. The tree withers. The unusual severity of our Lord's tone, the strange rebuke addressed to a mere tree—a tree, moreover, obedient to the Creator's law—betray the fact that his action is entirely symbolic. It resembles the extraordinary symbolic actions of the prophets, *e.g.* Is 20:1-6, Jer 13:1-11. But our Lord did not explain it. The action, so far as we know, stood isolated. It was only on the following day (Tuesday ; Mk 11:19 f.) that our Lord chose to draw from the incident a further, personal lesson for the disciples, 21 f. The meaning of the symbol, therefore, can be decided only from its foregoing and subsequent historical context. Israel has welcomed its Messias, on the previous day, with wild enthusiasm. In a day or two it will reject him. Judaism is condemned by Jesus for its deceptive, fruitless show (*cf.* 21:43)—a show that should normally have proclaimed its spiritual summer, Cant 2:12 f. When, in the course of the week, the Apostles heard our Lord's rejection of Israel and his condemnation of the vine-dressers who refused his fruit to the Master, they would come to understand, Prat 2, 206. **20-22.** Meanwhile the present lesson for the disciples, struck by the display of power rather than by the symbolism, is strong faith to carry them through this difficult week and beyond. Nor is this lesson entirely independent of the symbolism since our Lord has implicitly demonstrated his power over his enemies (*cf.* 26:53) by causing this figure of hostile Israel to wither. Underlying the exhortation to faith is this invitation to believe in the power of their master when, in the Passion, he is to appear most powerless. Nevertheless, the explicit invitation is to faith in their own power through prayer, or rather an invitation to pray with lively faith. This will move all obstacles—and what obstacles lie ahead for the disciples ! With his eyes on Olivet (' this mountain ') Jesus uses the common rabbinic hyperbole for accomplishing the impossible : ' rooting-up mountains ' ; *cf.* Edersheim 2, 376, note.

23-27 Our Lord's Authority officially challenged ; Tuesday (Mk 11:27-33 : Lk 20:1-8)—**23.** The priests particularly are concerned at our Lords unauthorized temple-teaching, possibly also (if his cleansing of the temple was recent) at his assumption of authority over the sacred precincts by expelling the buyers and sellers. With representatives of the other sections of the Sanhedrin (including scribes ; *cf.* Mk) they ask if he acts on his own initiative or at least (and they deem this impossible) to name his accreditor. **24-25.** After the manner of rabbinic discussion Jesus answers question with question, not disrespectful to the established authority but pointed enough for those who wield that authority dishonestly. The question concerns the mission of the Baptist. He sums up this mission in the word ' baptism '—significantly, because this baptism was a rite preparatory for Jesus' own

work, 3:11 f. Whence did the ' authority ' of the **711e** Baptist derive ? They had once asked that question themselves, Jn 1:25, but since that day to the day of John's martyrdom it had become increasingly plain to those of good faith that John was a man of God and his work ' of heaven ', heavenly. **26.** The objectors, over-anxious to save their face, miss the implication of the question—namely, that if John's mission was supernaturally accredited so also was that of the one he announced (Jn 1:29-37 ; 3:25-30 ; 5:33 ff.). They assume instead that Jesus will attack them for never having countenanced John, 3:7-10, § 682g-h. On the other hand, the public esteem in which the Baptist was held (*e.g.* Ac 19:3 ; Jos., *Ant.* 18, 5, 2) kept them from denying to John the status of prophet. **27.** The weak reply, surely damaging in the ears of those present, reveals that they are guided only by motives of policy. To such dishonest witnesses our Lord need make no answer ; let honest bystanders judge between them ! Nevertheless, he pursues the theme of the Baptist in the parable that follows.

28-32 Parable of the Two Sons (Mt only)—**28-30.** The **f** significant point of the parable is the contrast between a farmer's two sons : one, beginning with flat refusal, ends with obedience ; the other, in appearance at least readily submissive, is in effect recalcitrant. **31.** There can be no doubt which did the will of the father ($\tau o \hat{v} \pi a \tau \rho \acute{o} s$: the application of the parable begins to peep through at this place). Swiftly upon the inevitable answer comes the devastating application. The publicans (9:9, note) who had listened to the Baptist, Lk 3:12, and the women of evil life who had come to the Saviour, Lk 7:36 ff. ; Jn 4:4 ff. ; 8:2 ff., *are going* into the Kingdom even now. There is as yet no sign (and this is a warning) that our Lord's interlocutors are on their way. **32.** It was John's preaching that tested the ' I will not ' of the sinners and the ' I go ' of professional just men. John had come ' in the way of justice ' ($\dot{\epsilon} \nu \ \dot{o} \delta \hat{\omega} \ \delta \iota \kappa a \iota o \sigma \acute{v} \nu \eta s$), *i.e.* respecting the traditional Law. He spoke, too, the old prophetic language of penance. Despite this, the learned in the Law did not listen. The repentance of public sinners should have shamed them ' *but even when you saw that, you would not relent and believe him* ' (KNT).

33-46 Parable of the Wicked Husbandmen (Mk **g** 12:1-12 ; Lk 20:9-19)—From the lighter warning of 31 to a prophecy of ruin, 43, which concludes a parable that contains many allegorical details. **33.** To those familiar with Is 5:7 the image inevitably suggests Israel, vineyard of God. The stone well, the hollowed rock whence the juice of the pressed grapes passed through stone channels to a deeper rock-basin, the stone watch-tower, all are present in Is 5:1-2. These details appear in the parable, not with any allegorical significance but with the purpose of establishing the identity of the vineyard by literary reminiscence of Isaias. The listeners are now in a position to see the meaning of what follows. In his absence the owner, clearly God, commits the vineyard to farmers accountable to himself. These farmers are the centre of the story. **34-36.** It would appear from 43 that the vineyard, through the negligence of the husbandmen, had yielded nothing. In any case, to thwart the Master they maltreat or murder his servants who ask for the produce—the fate of the prophets, 23:30-31, § 714h. But the Master has superhuman patience. He sends even more servants but to no better effect. **37.** The climax of gentleness is to send his son to persuade them. They will surely respect him. The event is to turn this hope to irony. **38.** The sight of the son only stimulates their hate. If he is removed, their possession will be for ever undisturbed. His existence threatened their possession just as our Lord's threatened the position of the Jewish leaders, Jn 11:47-53. **39.** In Mk (probably nearer the original words here) the son is first murdered and then cast out. In Mt and Lk the subsequent detail, Heb 13:12 ff., has perhaps influenced the order of words. In either case, the Son is cast out of the vineyard that was his own ; *cf.* Jn 1:11. **40-41.** It is already obvious **h**

711h what the Master will do when the time of reckoning comes, but in Mt our Lord invites his hearers to pronounce, implicitly, their own sentence. God will choose other, more honest, workmen who will promptly render the produce. As for the wicked husbandmen, they shall meet an end proportioned to their wickedness. **42.** Our Lord's quotation is taken, like the 'Hosanna' cry of 9, from Ps 117(118) 22 f. In the psalm the saying, probably a proverb, seems originally to refer to Israel rejected like a useless stone by the nations as they founded their pagan polities. But in God's surprising plan and in God's building, Israel is the conspicuous angle-stone crowning and uniting the two high walls. The unexpected issue of 41 is, therefore, not without precedent in God's providence. That is why, 43, our Lord has no hesitation in pronouncing his startling prophecy. The kingdom is to pass from the Jewish leaders and apparently from the Jewish people as a race. It will go to others who, as God's new planting, will produce the fruit for which their leaders will faithfully render timely account ; **i** *cf.* 41. **44.** The allegory of the stone, interrupted by the parenthetical 43, is resumed or rather given a new direction. Note, however, that 44 may be a gloss from Lk 20:18. The setting of the allegory has invited the hearers to see the cast-out Son, 39, in the rejected stone, Ac 4:11. But the 'stone' is no longer considered as part of a building, it is considered in two prophetic connexions differing from this and differing from each other. In the first, Is 8:14, the 'stone' is 'one against which one might strike one's foot . . . a symbol of trouble' (*cf.* Kissane, *The Book of Isaiah*, 103) ; this 'stone' is God himself who becomes a severe judge for those disloyal to him. In the second, Dan 2:34-45, the 'stone' is God's future, lasting kingdom, symbolized and summed-up in 'one like a Son of Man'—a boulder rolling down to the destruction of earthly kingdoms. Our Lord, therefore, warns the opponents of God and his Kingdom with three intimidating texts, 42, 44, which he applies to himself and to his work. **45-46.** The words were too pointed to be mistaken. His enemies knew that it was at them that the last parable was directed. The preceding one had been explicitly applied to them by our Lord himself, 31 f.

712a XXII 1-14 Parable of the Wedding-Feast (*cf.* Lk 14:15-24)—This parable-allegory, unlike 21:33-44, is not directed against the Jewish leaders as such, though there is an ominous echo of 21:38-41 in 22:6-7. It is addressed to all and relates to the personnel of the Kingdom. The distinguished ones favoured with the invitation refuse, those of no distinction take their place. But even among these (Mt only) some are unworthy and so excluded. **1-2.** 'Once more Jesus began to speak to them in parables ', in parabolic form. The situation about to be described (*cf.* 13:24, note) presents one aspect of the Kingdom. Jewish literature (*cf.* Edersheim 2, 425 f.) likened the Messianic era to a feast (*cf.* Is 25:6) and the Messias himself to a bridegroom wedded to Israel ; *cf.* the Targum on Ps 44(45) 2 (3) ; Edersheim 2, 718. It is clear at the outset, therefore, that the 'king' is God and the 'son' the Messias. **3-5.** It was usual in the East to remind invited guests when the time drew near. The servants, presumably the Prophets, warn the chosen people that the *marriage-feast* (γάμοι) is imminent. With great forbearance the king overlooks the refusal and sends a second group of servants to say that the feast stands waiting. This circumstance indicates that the second group of servants is representative of God's envoys in the new order ; *cf.* the invitation of 3:2 ; 10:7. The *oxen and fatted animals* suggest a feast of royal proportions, but the invited are more interested in their worldly cares. **b 6.** Others (and the strange violence of the action suggests allegory) not content with insulting the servants (and through them their king) actually murder them. This treatment the Baptist had experienced and the Apostles been taught to expect, 10:28. **7.** The king's patience is at last exhausted and his revenge terrible : death for the murderers and ruin for their

city. The 'city' is plainly not the king's capital which **7** is elsewhere—perhaps (if the allegory has influenced the picture) in heaven itself. But it is as unnecessary to localize the 'city' as it is to localize the 'vineyard' of 21:33. The subsequent destruction of Jerusalem in A.D. 70 by the armies of Vespasian (God's instrument) would give the words a significance perhaps missed by their first hearers. **8-10.** The scene shifts to the palace. The king orders his servants (those of 3 or others) to bring in those who have not shown themselves unworthy of the royal honour. They are gathered indiscriminately from ' *the street-crossings* ', not chosen as Israel was chosen—we think automatically of the Gentiles ; *cf.* Lk 13:29. Sinners and just alike, all are called, though not all found worthy. The *bridal-hall* is full. **11-13.** In Mt, 10, not in Lk, our Lord describes **c** the execution of the king's command, 9, with a view to developing a warning for the newcomers ; *cf.* Rom 11:19-21. One is found unsuitable when the king surveys the guests. The lack of attire befitting the occasion is not surprising since the guests had been hurriedly and indiscriminately assembled. The king's sentence, therefore, is justified only if we assume that somehow or other the lack was culpable. Allegory is not concerned to explain such details. We are expected to see immediately that the 'wedding-garment' is an allegorical element representing fitness for the Kingdom ; lack of such fitness is obviously culpable and requires no explanation. The man has no excuse to offer. The king passes sentence and the banquet begins or rather is resumed under new conditions, *i.e.* it now becomes a banquet in which all are perfect. We are reminded of the parables of the Drag-net and of the Wheat and Cockle (*cf.* 13:39-40, 48-49) where the discrimination of bad and good is postponed until the Final Judgement. The banquet which is the Messianic era on earth passes into eternity with its worthy members. **14.** It is difficult to see how the 'many called, few **d** chosen' (*cf.* 21:17, note) sums up either part of the parable. In the first part, 2-7, many are called but all refuse ; in the second, 8-13, though the one man no doubt represents a class of persons, we are left with the clear impression that relatively ' many ' are chosen. Unless we treat the remark as a disjointed appendix (with Buzy, *Mt*, 295 f.) it would appear that it applies to the two parts taken together, Prat 2, 228. In the perspective of the parable and in the range of the experience of our Lord's audience the invitation to the Kingdom has gone out to many—to the whole nation of Israel—and the nation as a whole has refused. Add to this the thought that even in the ' nation ' next invited, 21:43, there are some unworthy, 22:11 ff., and the ' many called, few chosen ' appears in its due proportions. It is to be remembered also that the term ' few ' is relative ; they are ' many ' in 8:11. Moreover, the dictum refers not directly to the number of the saved (a question our Lord refuses to answer ; Lk 13:23) but primarily to the members, and worthy members, of the Messianic kingdom on earth. The rest is the secret of the Father. *Note* : we have explained the parable as a unity. There are, however, reasons for holding that Mt has fused one parable (1-10 with the exception of 6-7) with two fragments related in theme. The parable is found in Lk 14:16-24, the fragments concern the ' murderers ' (Mt only) 6-7) and the ' wedding-garment ' incident (Mt only) 11-14). *Cf.* Buzy, RB 41 (1932) 38-43.

15-22 The Tribute Question (Mk 12:13-17 ; Lk **e** 20:20-26)—**15-16.** The Pharisees seek to trap Jesus with a question. To hide the trap they do not approach him themselves but send their students (not yet Rabbis). With these are the Herodians, a political and not a religious sect, supporters of the Herodian princes ; in this respect they did not share the Pharisees' outlook which was anti-Herodian. Both parties were at one, however, in their interim policy of subservience to Rome. It was to their common interest to scotch a movement which threatened or seemed to threaten the *status quo*. They open the debate with a compliment calculated to disarm. They insist, tendentiously, upon the Master's well-known independence of thought (*e.g.* 7:29) and outspoken expression even against the person of the ruling power, Lk 13:31 f. It seems from this emphasis that they hope for an anti-Roman decision which later they were forced to fabricate, Lk 23:2. The word 'tribute' (κῆνσος) here apparently embraces all taxes (capitation, land-tax, etc.) payable to the civil power. The question is dishonest: Pharisees and Herodians had long since adjusted their conscience to the payment. But it presents Jesus with a dilemma. Should he advise non-payment, as they hope and expect, he becomes indictable to Rome. The pseudo-Messias, Judas the Galilean, had perished for this very cause, twenty years before in A.D. 7. Should he advise payment he loses his Messianic credit with the people for whom Messianism spelt independence of foreign yoke. **18.** Our Lord, knowing the insincerity of the question, could refuse to answer but does not. **19.** As usual (*e.g.* 21:31-40) he asks the objectors to contribute to their own downfall and they show him a silver denarius (*cf.* 17:23-26, note), the Roman coin with which the taxes were so often paid. **20.** The coin was probably of Tiberius (A.D. 14-37) with, on the obverse, the laureate head of this emperor and the inscription: 'Ti(berius) Caesar Divi Aug(usti) F(ilius) Augustus' (HDB 3, 427 f.). **21.** Plainly the coin came from Caesar, it is right that it should be *returned* (ἀπόδοτε) to him. These civil transactions are on one plane, God's rights on another. There is no inevitable clash, provided (as was the case in the relationship of Rome and Jewry) that the civil demands did not encroach upon the duties of man to God. **22.** The answer is a simple one. But it amazes the adversaries because they have no suspicion of the simple principle from which it emerges. Messianism is for them inevitably a political movement and their dilemma, 17, consequently exhaustive and fatal. It is the spiritual nature of our Lord's Messianism that provides the third alternative which is, not compromise, but due delimitation of spheres; *cf.* Jn 18:36 f.

23-33 Bodily Resurrection attacked (Mk 12:18-27, 34*b*; Lk 20:27-40)—The Sadducees, 3:7-10, note, now appear on the scene not, as the Pharisees had attempted, to involve Jesus with the political authorities, but with a question of Jewish doctrine and practice. They seek either to score a point off the Pharisees by winning his support or else, if our Lord defends the Pharisees' doctrine, to make game of him. The Sadducees, despite the fact that from their ranks the priests were chosen, believed the one God to be uninterested in his creation. They therefore denied divine providence, the immortality of the soul and the resurrection of the body. The Pharisees' doctrine of bodily resurrection was firmly held but, to judge by certain texts, crass (Bonsirven 1, 482-5). In the question put to our Lord, therefore, another dilemma is implied: either a very material conception of resurrection or no resurrection at all. As before, our Lord has a third alternative to propose, 30, which proceeds from the high spirituality of his mind. **23-27.** The Sadducees quote Deut 25:5 enunciating the 'levirate' law. They propose a case in which each of seven brothers, all being childless, had successively equal rights over the one wife. What when these rights become simultaneous after death? It reduces the idea of bodily resurrection to absurdity! **28-30.** The objection shows ignorance of God's power to raise man and woman bodily to the chaste condition of the angels who, being immortal, need not to reproduce their kind. **31-32.** It shows ignorance, too, of the very Scriptures they have ventured to quote. Our Lord chooses a text from Ex 3:6 (not, *e.g.*, from the clear text of Dan 12:1-2) perhaps because, as is highly probable, the Sadducees accepted only the Pentateuch as having full canonical authority. In its original setting, the revelation in the 'burning bush', the text strictly implies that the God who was now speaking with Moses was the same God as his ancestors adored. Here our Lord draws out its

fuller sense after a fashion no Rabbi could resent. The **713b** living God could not be named after a dead thing; yet God himself uses the title 'God of Abraham'. Abraham, therefore, still lives. Nor is it only of the *soul's* continuing life that our Lord speaks. In the first place, this is not the difficulty, 25, 28; in the second place, Jewish theology did not distinguish immortality and bodily resurrection, 2 Mac 12:43 f. Thus the Pharisees, believing in immortality, accepted resurrection; the Sadducees denied the first and therefore the second. There was no third school. It is against this theological background that our Lord's argument must be read. If Abraham lives at all (and the Exodus text proves that he does) he lives with a view to bodily resurrection. And indeed even outside this background but within the total OT context the words of Exodus are significant. Setting aside explicit texts (*e.g.* Pss 15(16) 10-11; 48 (49) 16; 72(73) 24) the whole OT protests that God could never desert his servants—he is their God as he is the God of Abraham. Neither Abraham, therefore, nor any other faithful servant can perish utterly. **33.** Again the admiration (*cf.* 22) and again, it seems, because the objectors have not grasped the simple principle, *viz.* the spiritual nature even of bodily resurrection. Evidently the Sadducees had never thus heard their difficulty answered by the Pharisees.

34-40 The Great Commandment (Mk 12:28-34*a*; *cf.* **c** Lk 10:25-28)—**34.** The new approach to Jesus has in Mt the air of a conspiracy unless we read (Lagrange) against the weight of MS evidence: the Pharisees ' gathered about him ' (ἐπ' αὐτόν) instead of ' gathered together ' (ἐπὶ τὸ αὐτό). In this latter reading the Pharisees are presented as pursuing the attack (though, *cf. infra*, they have chosen an unsuitable representative). The former reading shows them somewhat conciliated by the repulse of the Sadducees. **35-36.** One versed in the Law puts a question probably debated in the schools (SB 1, 900-5). The 613 commandments of the Law were subdivided into ' light ' and ' grave ', infringements of the latter being expiated only by death. These again were subdivided into small and great. Our Lord's questioner is concerned only with the greatest of all. In Mk 12:28 he seems sincere; in Mt the word ' tempting ' suggests the opposite. The solution lies perhaps in the wide sense of this word (πειράζων; perhaps ' probing ', ' sounding ', *cf.* Prat 2, 222); or possibly the lawyer's initial hostility softened as the conversation advanced. **37-38.** The words of the commandment, Deut 6:5, were familiar: they opened the twice-daily prayer—the *Shema'*; *cf.* Mk 12:29. They urged the submission of the heart (in Hebrew idiom, the centre of intelligence) and the soul (principle of sensitive faculties—emotion etc.) to God. And this ' with thy whole strength ' (Mt's ' mind ' is probably due to the Greek translator). **39.** It is more surprising that our Lord joins to this the love of neighbour, Lev 19:18. The fact that he speaks of the ' second ' commandment without being asked shows his unwillingness to separate the two. Love of neighbour and love of God are child and parent. The two commandments are ' like ' because true love of neighbour is but an overflow of true love of God. As our Lord is the first to present these two precepts as one so he is the first to give the widest meaning to the word ' neighbour '; *cf.* his explanation of the term on a similar, but apparently not the same, occasion in Lk 10:25-37. **40.** From this double support hang (κρέμαται) ' Law and Prophets '. The last phrase significantly repeats 5:17 so that ' we now understand what this divine system was that Jesus had come not to destroy but to bring to perfection. It was essentially the law of charity ' (Lagrange, *Mt*, 432). **41-46 The Messias Son and Lord of David** (Mk **d** 12:35-37*a*; Lk 20:41-44)—**41-42.** The recent question, 17, has betrayed a political conception of the Messias, 22, note; our Lord now invites reflexion. That the Messias was to be of the Davidic dynasty was the constant teaching of the prophets, Is 11:1; Jer 23:5; Ez 34:23 etc., and there is no hesitation in the Pharisees' reply. **43-46.** Yet in the Davidic psalm 109

713d (110) were written the inspired words : ' Yahweh said to my lord : Sit at my right hand '. The Pharisees evidently admitted that the Davidic ' my lord ' referred to the Messias. The Rabbis of the next two centuries, probably influenced by our Lord's argument repeated and developed by the early Christians, did not. The psalm-verse, especially with its suggestion of the Messianic throne of Dan 7:29, emphasized the transcendental nature of the Messias. ' Son of David ' is therefore not an adequate description of him. Our Lord leaves them with this thought. If honestly pursued it could take the Pharisees and others (*cf.* Mk 12:35) from ideas of a political Messias to the notion of one whose work was to be as spiritual as his origin.

714a XXIII 1-36 Discourse on the Scribes and Pharisees (Mk 12:38-40 ; Lk 20:45-47 ; *cf.* Lk 11:37-54)—The whole chapter is a warning to those who are or may be deceived by the worst elements in Pharisaism. It is with this in view that our Lord mercilessly exposes them. Note, however, that the recurrent ' Woe ! ' is not a curse but a portentous expression of grief ; *cf.* 24:19.

b 1-7 The Pharisees and their Victims—1-4. When the scribes and Pharisees faithfully expound the Law it is on the teaching-chair of Moses that they sit (ἐκάθισαν, aorist equivalent to the Semitic stative ' imperfect ' ; Black, 93). Accordingly they must be obeyed. But this obedience should not lead to imitation because they are hypocrites at heart. The letter of the Law they observe, not without ingenuity, but not its spirit ; *cf.* Jn 7:19-23. On the contrary, the casuistic interpretations of the Law that over-burdened the conscience of others, Ac 15:40, served to extricate the Pharisees themselves from many an obligation ; *cf.* Edersheim 2, 777. They take pains to make neat and heavy parcels and to lift them on to the shoulders of others. With their own shoulders, nay with their own fingers they will not carry them an inch ; *cf.* Lagrange, *L'Evangile*, 337. **5-7.** (Mk 12:38-39 ; Lk 20:48.) Their show is hollow though it is the basis of their prestige. They seek to impress others with their zeal for the Law by making their phylacteries more noticeable. The ' phylacteries ' (φυλακτήρια, *i.e.* safeguards, amulets ; Aram. *t͏ᵉphillîn*, literally ' prayers ') were tiny, oblong, leather-covered cases containing four strips of parchment on which were written the texts, Ex 13:1-10, 11-16 ; Deut 6:4-9 ; 11:13-21, the monotheistic profession of faith. Here the word is evidently used to include the ribbons or thongs by which the cases were fastened, one to the forearm, another to the forehead, at the time of morning-prayer. The practice derived from an unduly literal interpretation of Ex 13:9, 16. Our Lord condemns neither phylacteries nor tassels, 9:20-22, § 691*f*, but only the ostentatious piety that makes them conspicuous. The low respectful bow in sight of all, the title Rabbi (' master ', ' teacher ') delighted the scribes and Pharisees.

c 8-12 Danger of Imitation (Mt only)—Our Lord turns to his disciples. As he had not condemned phylacteries so in 7 does he not forbid the title ' Rabbi ' but the vain complacency taken in it. It is in this sense that the injunction of 8 is to be understood. Our Lord is not out to reform current nomenclature ; he is concerned with the spirit, not with the letter. But the use, 9, or acceptance, 8, 10, of any adulation that threatens to intrude between man and God is sternly forbidden. All human titles are only shadows of God's authority from which they derive, Eph 3:15. Unless this is clearly understood, ' call no one on earth " *Abi* " ', ' father ', a term sometimes used of the great Rabbis ; *cf.* Edersheim 2, 408-10. Note that our Lord is not a grammarian regulating the use of terms : he is a doctor of the spirit. He forbids any acknowledgement of fatherhood that obscures the fatherhood of God, nothing more. If we make no allowance for the concreteness and brevity of his phrases we reduce either them to absurdity (*e.g.* 6:3) or him to inconsistency (*e.g.* Jn 18:23, *cf.* § 686*d*). He would not forbid a human son to use the word ' father ' nor would he forbid the term if addressed to one who is God's

representative ; in this second case, indeed, it serves **7** to remind its user of the fatherhood of God. Nor must the Christian disciple pose as an independent spiritual guide (10, καθηγητής). He himself is subject to one Teacher (διδάσκαλος, 8) and one Guide, 10 —our Lord himself (the term ' Christ ', if a scribal insertion, nevertheless renders the sense rightly). They have one Father who is in heaven. The principle of graded authority remains (11 ; *cf.* 20:26, note) but the spirit in which that authority is wielded must be one of humility. For 12, *cf.* 18:4, note.

13-31 The Seven Woes—13. *First Woe : opposition* **d** *and obstacle to the Kingdom.* A general denunciation. Our Lord's anger is explained by the harm he sees done to simple folk. The formalism of scribes and Pharisees has blocked the entrance even to our Lord's own kingdom. It has darkened the public mind and made it incapable of appreciating the need for inward religion or even of recognizing its presence. **14.** An insertion from Mk 12:40. **15.** *Second Woe : proselytism to bad purpose* (Lk 11:52). Not content with obstructing entrance to the Kingdom, the Pharisees seek, with immense zeal, to draw ignorant pagans down to their own level and to make them too consciously sin against the proffered light of Christ. On the intense and successful Jewish proselytism of this period, *cf.* Schürer 2, 2, 303-27. Often twice as fanatical as the born-Jew the newcomer is twice as surely established in the infernal dominion (' son of ' in this Semitic sense = ' belonging to '). **16-22.** *Third Woe : casuis-* **e** *try ; a sample.* **16-19.** The Scribes and Pharisees, blind themselves, have absurdly assumed the role of guide. To illustrate the blindness our Lord chooses an example (or contrives a characteristic, if non-existent, case) of their attitude to vows. On the annulment of these they were an ingenious court of appeal. The terms of the vow were closely scrutinized without regard to the original intention of the one who had made it. Their verdict would be either : ' It is nothing ' (it is no vow) or ' He is under obligation '. Two individual illustrations of this attitude are given, 16, 18. Vows naming the gold (apparently the votive-offerings) in the temple and vows naming the sacrifice (' gift ') on the altar. These are declared ' valid ' ; vows on the temple or altar itself are declared void. But our Lord turns the casuistry against them, 17, 19. If they are determined to make these distinctions (though distinctions in this matter are out of place, *cf.* 20-22), surely the house of God and his chosen altar are more sacred than man's possessions. These last are sacred only when, and because, they become offerings. Even casuistry should have reached a conclusion contradictory to that of the scribes. **20-22.** But, in truth, there is no room for it. A sacred vow, whatever its terms, is made in the presence of God. And (22—a final thrust), contrary to the explicit decision of the Jewish doctors, the invocation of ' heaven ' in place of the divine name makes not the slightest difference. It is the intention and not the word that tells. **23-24.** *Fourth Woe : false perspectives* **f** (Lk 11:42). **23.** The minutiae of the tithe-laws (based on Lev 27:30) on all comestible plants were truly astonishing, Edersheim 2, 412. Even the small seasoning herbs, ' mint, dill, cummin ', were not forgotten. The practice is not condemned, nor is it enjoined, despite the misleading Semitic downrightness of the phrase ' these things [' justice ' etc.] you should have practised without neglecting the other [tithe] '. But it surely should not be found incompatible with the weightier matters of the Law—justice to one's neighbour (κρίσις, *i.e.* *mišpāṭ* ; *cf.* Deut 10:18), sympathy for him (ἔλεος), good faith in dealings with him [πίστις ; *cf.* Ps 32(33) : 4 ; Gal 5:22(23)]. **24.** This fantastic situation is illustrated in massive hyperbole. Such conduct is compared to that of one who would carefully filter from his cup a tiny gnat (lest he incur some legal impurity) leaving there a camel. Attention is sometimes called to the play on words (*gml'*, *qlm'*, *qml'* ; respectively ' camel ', ' gnat ', ' filter ' ; *cf.* Lagrange, *Mt*, 447) which probably indicates that the saying

g was proverbial. **25-26.** *Fifth Woe : formalism* (Lk 11:39-41). Meticulous ceremonial care to avoid legal impurity (*cf.* Mk 7:4 ; Schürer 2, 2, 106-11) was not matched by moral scruples. The surface of the crockery was, no doubt, clean, but it held the product of plunder and the means of intemperance : ' *within they* [the vessels] *are filled from* [ἐξ] *robbery and excess* '. First things first : see that what is within (τὸ ἐντός) is morally pure ; it will then confer all necessary purity upon the surface of the container. **27-28.** *Sixth Woe : hypocrisy* (*cf.* Lk 11:44). The ' inner ' and ' outer ' contrast of 25-26 leads on to a formal accusation of hypocrisy. The comparison, deliberately nauseating, is borrowed from the tombs whitened with chalk four weeks before the Pasch to warn pilgrims of the danger of contact and legal impurity ; *cf.* Num 19:16. The eye sees them gleaming in the sun but they cover corruption. By the same paradox the Law-abiding Pharisee is full of law- **h** lessness (ἀνομία) ; *cf.* 1-7, note. **29-33.** *Seventh Woe : murder of God's envoy* (Lk 11:47-48). As in 23 it is not the act of honouring their great ancestors, 29, that is condemned but present murderous intention which lays bare the hypocrisy of their protestations. They admit, 30, that it was their fathers who murdered the prophets but seek to disclaim responsibility. Never- theless, they and our Lord know their murderous intent in his regard ; *cf.* 21:38, 45. The situation of their ' fathers ' has reappeared and their conduct shows, 31, that they are worthy sons and that their protest, 30, is empty. Bitterly ironical, our Lord urges them to their deadly work : their fathers have killed the servants, 21:35, 36, it is theirs to complete the work and kill the Son. In these words, recalling those of the Baptist (33 ; *cf.* 3:7) but unexpected and terrible on the lips of our Lord, the crafty Pharisees are warned **i** of the judgement that condemns to hell. **34-36.** *The crime and its punishment* (Lk 11:49-51). To this end (*i.e.* of 32 ; 33 is parenthetical) our Lord in his turn (ἰδοὺ ἐγώ, emphatic) is sending (*cf.* 10:16) his own ' prophets ' to declare the divine message and ' wise men ' and ' scribes ' (*cf.* 13:52) to apply it. The old order will repeat itself, and with it the opportunity for sacrilegious murder. **35.** Thus the chosen race will fitly bear the responsibility for all the innocent blood shed *on the ground* in the whole course of sacred history. The names of Abel and Zacharias are chosen because Abel's murder is the first mentioned in the Scriptures, Gen 4:8, and that of the priest Zacharias, 2 Par 24:20-22, the last in the Hebrew order of books. In each case there is question, as here, of a just reckoning to be made, Gen 4:10 f. ; 2 Par 24:22. The reference to Zacharias is certainly to the priest of 2 Par 24:20—' son of Joiada ' and slain in the temple precincts (*cf.* Lk 11:51)—and not to the prophet, who is called ' son of Barachias ' in Zach 1:1. There are some faint indications that the reading ' son of Barachias ' in Mt is not original : the phrase is absent altogether from the Sinaitic MS and from four cursives ; it becomes ' son of Joiada ' in the ' Gospel of the Nazarenes ' known to Jerome and thought by him to be the original Matthew. Its absence from the parallel place in Lk suggests to many critics that it may be an ancient and mistaken gloss (*e.g.* *Allen, *Plummer, *Loisy). This theory is accepted by many Catholic exegetes. The question remains unsolved. **36.** For all these crimes the nation shall shortly answer. The fall of Jerusalem came forty years later.

j **37-39 Lament for Jerusalem** (Lk 13:34-35)—**37.** The sorrow underlying the anger of the denunciations rises to the surface. The city of God, 5:35, assassin of his envoys (*cf.* 30, 34 ; 2 Par 24:20 f. ; Jer 26:20 ff. ; 4 Kg 21:16, etc.) and finally rejecting the reconciliation through the Son ! By repeated appeal to Jerusalem (unmentioned in the Synoptics but told in Jn) our Lord has used the most anxious care to protect his own. **38.** The city with its temple (' your house ') will be left forsaken as the prophet had threatened, Jer 22:5—a repetition of the sorrows of the Babylonian exile. **39.** But Jesus does not yet speak openly of material ruin.

He speaks rather of the spiritual loss his absence will **714j** bring. They have heard his last appeal. His mission to them is over. Yet, it seems, he ends on a note of invitation. If Jerusalem should come to hail him as her King, as many on Sunday had saluted him (*cf.* 21:9, note), she will find him. But not till then. The words are perhaps merely a farewell exhortation though many (as Prat, Lagrange) see in them a promise of the future conversion of Israel to Christ—a conversion which is in fact prophesied by Paul, Rom 11:25. For barren resentment of Jewry we should substitute prayer.

XXIV 1-52 Discourse on ' the End ' (Mk 13:1-37 ; **715a** Lk 21:5-36).

XXIV 1-3 The Question and its Background (Mk 13:1-4 ; Lk 21:5-7)—**1.** Our Lord leaves the temple by the eastern gate, and, crossing the Kedron, climbs the slope of Olivet. Turning to look backward down upon the temple buildings the disciples, admiring provincials, exclaim at their massive beauty. **2.** Our Lord's reply is disconcerting. This Herodian temple, begun more than forty years before (20/19 B.C.) and not completely finished until thirty years later (A.D. 64) was even now threatened with total ruin—it was burned and overthrown in A.D. 70. **3.** The remark is unexpected and the disciples walk on, perhaps in silence, perhaps in agitated discussion until, reaching the summit, all stop to rest. Our Lord's four privileged disciples (Mk) put the double question : ' When ? ' ; ' What warnings ? '. It is difficult to determine whether these questions refer to one event, the time and herald-signs of the destruction of Jerusalem, or to two, the time of the destruction of Jerusalem and the signs of the end of the world. Luke's words and to a slightly less extent Mk's seem to suggest one ; Mt's suggest two. It is usual to reconcile the two forms of the question, Mt as against Mk, Lk, by pointing out that for a Jew the destruction of the temple would spell the end of the world itself. In this hypothesis the dis- ciples thought that the two events were to be simul- taneous, and our Lord in his reply treats of them together because the first is a figure of the second (' end of a world ', ' end of the world ') ; nevertheless, it is claimed, he removes the disciples' chronological con- fusion. It is said that two separate events are certainly discussed in the discourse because one is described as local, imminent, foreseeable through historical happen- ings while the other is universal, of unknown date, without warning signs.

Another and important theory has been recently **b** presented by A. Feuillet [RSR 34 (1947) 303-27 ; 35 (1948) 544-65 ; NRT 71 (1949) 701-22, 806-28 ; RB 55 (1948) 481-502 ; 56 (1949) 61-92, 340-64 ; 57 (1950) 43-62, 180-211]. It is a revival of Augus- tine's tentative opinion (PL 33, 904-25), later adopted by Calmet and Le Camus, but revised and supported with powerful new arguments. The theory defends the unity of the discourse and holds that the reference throughout is to the destruction of Jerusalem with its double aspect : the end of the old order (' times of the Jews ') and the opening of the new (' times of the Gentiles '). The hypothesis does not deny the possi- bility of a further sense (fuller ? typical ?) in the discourse. Indeed it follows from the nature of the case that the divine judgement which closes the first act of world-history (the Age of Israel) is the destined model or type of the Last Judgement which is to mark the end of the next (the Age of the Gentiles). This fusion of perspective is in the style of the prophets. For them the ' Day of Yahweh ' (*i.e.* of Yahweh's judgement) has a shifting perspective, the reason being that this ' day ' is considered more from the theological, transcendental, plane than from the historical and contingent point of view (*cf.* Scripture, 4 [1950] 222-30, 264-73). But the hypothesis denies that the two themes (end of Jerusalem, end of the world) are juxtaposed so that one part of the discourse refers to the end of Jerusalem, the other to the end of the world ; it does not deny that the themes are superimposed

715b (Benoit). St Paul, therefore, could resume certain phrases of the discourse and refer them to the end of the world. Strictly literal interpretation, the theory claims, is satisfied by the historical reference (destruction of Jerusalem) and, in fact, sometimes demands such a reference (*e.g.* 24 ; 16-20). The following commentary will briefly state both views. Regarding the form of the disciples' question Feuillet, emphasizing the text of Mk, Lk, insists that it is explicitly concerned with the destruction of Jerusalem and that Mt's form is capable of the same interpretation. The phrase 'thy coming' (παρουσία, a term not used in the gospels except Mt 24) has in the Greek papyri the meaning of a royal visit. Paul certainly uses the word for Christ's final coming at the end of the world (1 Cor 15:23 etc.) but it may be that in this case as in others he has taken over Mt's terminology and adapted it to the final coming, RB 56 (1949) 75-6, note. On the resemblance between Mt and Paul ; *cf.* *Dodd, ET 58 (1947) 293 ff. and critique in DR 66 (1948) 367-83 ; on the likeness of terminology between Mt 24 in particular and 1, 2 Thess *cf.* Orchard, Bi 19 (1938) 19-42 ; the last author concludes that Paul in his apocalyptic 'has used the same words, ideas and phraseology (as Mt), reshuffled them, and set them down in their new combination'. The 'consummation of the world' (συντελεία τοῦ αἰῶνος) sounds more decisive for the end of the world reference than does the term ' parousia '. Nevertheless the word αἰών signifies not the physical world or universe, but ' era, epoch ' of human history ; for Paul's use *cf.* Allo, *Vivre et Penser*, 1ʳᵉ Sér., 1941, 179. The ' era ' here might therefore be that of the old dispensation. In 28:20, where the perspective changes, it is the new, Messianic era.

c 4-14 The Beginning of Sorrows (*cf.* Mk 13:5-13 ; Lk 21:18-19)—Our Lord does not yet reply directly to the disciples' question : he is concerned primarily with spiritual issues and with the conduct of the disciples. **4-5.** He supposes his own death after which many would come usurping the title that belonged to him—as in fact they did, with grievous results for themselves and their followers. For these political, pseudo-Messiahs who appeared in considerable numbers before the destruction of Jerusalem *cf.* Jos., BJ 2, 13, 4 ; 6, 5, 4 ; Lagrange, *Le Messianisme*, 21-7. **6-7.** Still anxious to warn his own rather than to foretell the future, our Lord speaks of the inward peace the disciples must preserve in a troubled world. The prophetic style he uses does not call for minute verification though this is not lacking for the years before A.D. 70. It was a period savage in its wars, ferocious in its very peace (Tacitus, *Hist.* 3, 2, 1) with war's usual concomitants : plagues (Tacitus, *Annales* 16, 13) and famine (Ac 11:28 ; Jos., *Ant.* 20, 2, 5) ; even earthquakes (in towns of Asia Minor, A.D. 61-2 ; Pompeii in A.D. 63 etc.). All this does not closely concern the Apostles, as the Jerusalem catastrophe will ; *cf.* 15 ff. The ' end ' of Jerusalem with its final break with the old order is still to come. **8.** These calamities are ' the beginnings of *the pangs of childbirth* ' (ἀρχὴ ὠδίνων). The world is in travail for a new age (*cf.* Mic 4:9-10 ; Apoc 12:2) though the pangs have not reached their climax ; *cf.* 15, note. The sentence, though ominous, is designed to console the disciples ; *cf.* Jn 16:20-22. **9.** Pursuing the theme of his disciples' conduct (*cf.* 10:17-23, notes) Jesus fortifies them against the future by showing that their fate is neither outside his knowledge nor divorced **d** from his interests (' for my name's sake '). **10-12.** Under the pressure of persecution many shall *fall away* and even hand one another over to the persecutors. In this divided field religious impostors (*cf.* 5) reap a rich harvest. (Such a situation in fact developed some years before the Destruction of Jerusalem ; Rom 16:17-18 ; Gal 1:6-9 ; 2 Cor 11:13 etc.) Faced with this disedifying spectacle the love of God will freeze in the hearts of many. **13.** But he will save his soul (*cf.* Lk 21:19) who has *endured perfectly* (or ' to the end ', *i.e.*—in this context—to the end of life, not of Jerusalem.

Nevertheless, the phrase εἰς τέλος—not εἰς τὸ τέλος **7**—probably signifies ' completely, perfectly ' like the ἕως τέλους of 2 Cor 1:13 and, possibly, the εἰς τέλος of Jn 13:1). **14.** But before the ' consummation ' (τέλος : ' the end ') which, in view of the following verses, probably now means the end of Jerusalem, the good news of the Kingdom must be announced to the whole world (ἐν ὅλῃ τῇ οἰκουμένῃ). This last phrase, suggesting to modern ears the inhabited world as we now know it, is already used, equivalently, in Rom 1:8 ' in the whole world ' and the testimony ' to all nations ' finds its echo in Rom 1:5. Paul registers this universal preaching as a *fait accompli* as early as A.D. 60, Col 1:23, ten years before the fall of Jerusalem. The verse does not hint, therefore, that the perspective has passed beyond the fall of Jerusalem. Through all the hostile circumstances described, 5-12, the gospel will go steadily forward. 14, too, thus holds a note of consolation for the disciples.

15-28 The Great Tribulation (Mk 13:14-23 ; Lk **7** 21:20-24)—At last our Lord proceeds to answer the disciples' question but he is still concerned primarily with practical advice and comfort. **15.** The prophet Daniel (Dan 9:27 ; *cf.* 11:31 ; 12:11) had spoken of the ' devastating hateful thing ' which ' will be upon the temple ' (LXX). The words were verified in 168 B.C. (*cf.* 1 Mac 1:57 ; 2 Mac 6:1-5) by the conduct of the hellenizing tyrant Antiochus Epiphanes who set up in the temple an idol and altar to Olympian Zeus. Our Lord speaks of a repetition of such sacrilege and he invites the reader of Daniel to penetrate the deeper prophetic sense of the allusion. (Possibly it is the evangelist himself who invites to this or to an attentive consideration of our Lord's words.) If Jesus is referring explicitly to the desecration of the temple (' in a holy place '), the warning would be recognized by the Christians when, in A.D. 68, the Jewish Zealots tyrannized in the temple which they had turned into a fortress. If he is referring to the desecration of the sacred soil of Palestine, it would be the Roman armies bearing down on Jerusalem in A.D. 69 that would be the signal for flight ; *cf.* Lk 21:20. **16.** The Christians are to flee from Judaea to the mountains (across Jordan, seemingly). In effect they did leave Jerusalem for Pella before the siege, Eus., HE 3, 5, 3. **17-20.** Haste will be imperative. Should anyone be taking his ease, eastern-fashion, on the flat-roof let him run down the outer staircase but not go into the house to encumber his flight with baggage. Should he be at work in the field let him not wait even to pick up his cloak. And alas for those forbidden by necessity or by love to leave their burden behind ! The disciples must pray that God's judgement be tempered with mercy. In winter, rushing torrents would stay their flight ; sabbath-scruples (*cf.* Ex 16:29), still felt by the Christians in the early days of the Church, would restrict it to less than one useless mile. Many exegetes will see in **21** the beginning **b** of a discourse on the end of the world, 21-32. If this is so, its opening conjunction γάρ (' For ') is a merely formal connective after the manner of apocalypse (*cf.* *e.g.* Dan 11:45 with Dan 12:1). Others prefer to see a close connexion (WV makes one sentence of 20-21) and refer 21 to the destruction of Jerusalem. In support of this reference is the parallel Lk 21:23*b*. The ' great tribulation ', it is urged, like the ' great distress ' of Lk 21:23*b*, may still be the concomitant of the destruction. The extravagance of the terms (not, however, entirely absent from 6-7 which certainly refer to the period before the destruction) is not incompatible with this restricted reference. The prophets present local historical events connected with the fortunes of God's people in grandiose language ; *cf.*, *e.g.* the ' apocalypse ' of Is 24-27 dealing with the overthrow of the arch-enemy, Assyria. ' The mere mention of a world-judgement is no proof that the section deals with the end of time. Every intervention of God is a world-judgement ' ; Kissane, *The Book of Isaiah* (Dublin 1941) 1, 267. See terms very like those of Mt and referring to the destruction of Jerusalem by Nabuchodonosor,

e Bar 2:2 ; *cf.* Is 13:6–10 ; Jer 4:23–26 ; 30:7. **22.** This verse may suggest the period immediately preceding the end of the world ; the time, with its physical trials and moral seductions, 24, is mercifully to be shortened ; otherwise the salvation of the chosen Christian faithful would be threatened. The mention of these ' elect ' is said to prove that the destruction of Jerusalem is not here referred to since the ' elect ' can be neither the Jewish factions besieged in Jerusalem nor the Christians, because these last left Jerusalem before the siege, 16, note. Nevertheless the argument is not peremptory : Chrysostom (*Hom. 76 in Mt*) identifies the ' elect ' with Christians who remained in Jerusalem and explains that it was owing to their presence that God shortened the siege and so preserved a remnant of the Jews. Alternatively it is possible to identify this ' remnant ' itself with the ' elect ' of 22 and 24. The ' remnant of Israel ' is the recurrent theme of the prophets (RB 42 [1933] 562–39) ; it indicates the survivors of the particular national calamity the prophet has in mind, some of whom, not all, will prove worthy of God's promise. In this view the calamity is the destruction of Jerusalem and the ' elect ' are the surviving Jews for whom the offer of the Messianic kingdom still lies open. St Paul (Rom 11:7 ; *cf.* Rom 11:15) names the ' remnant ' ' the elect ', but refers the term to those Jews who have already (*c* A.D. 56) embraced Christianity. This is because, in his perspective, the crisis has already occurred—the advent, death, resurrection of the Messias ; this crisis is entirely a spiritual one, and its ' survivors ', therefore, are necessarily those who have actually entered the Messianic kingdom. Our Lord's perspective is different : the crisis is national and yet to come. This difference of perspective means, as in the case of the prophets (*Scripture* 4 [1950] 223–4), that the personnel of the ' remnant ' is different also. The prophetic flavour of the passage is perceptible : divine decree has ' cut short ' (*cf.* Dan 9:24) the time of tribulation (the siege of Jerusalem lasted five months)—otherwise no single inhabitant ('no flesh' ; *cf.* Jer 12:12) would have survived. **23–25.** The words are addressed indeed to **d** the apostles but only in so far as these represent the faithful who live to see the end (of the world ? of Jerusalem ?). The pseudo-liberators, 5, appear again. Their deceits are described in the terms of Deut 13:1 where the false prophet *announces* (Heb. *nāṭan* ; LXX δῷ ; Mt δώσουσιν ; DV ' shew ') various portents. The fulfilment of such predictions, however, is to be taken only as a trial of faith permitted by God, Deut 13:2–3. Their purpose (DV ' inasmuch as to ', but ὥστε here is probably purposive as in 10:1 ; 27:1 ; *cf.* Mk ' in order to deceive ') will be to win supporters even among the ' elect '. The reappearance of the ' deliverers ' in this part of the discourse argues for a reference to a second epoch—the end of the world. But, on the other hand, it may be that our Lord's intention is simply to indicate that they multiply, as might be expected, as the threat to Jerusalem grows more alarming. **26.** The impostor must be left severely alone under whatever guise he present himself : whether coming like a second Moses from the desert, as happened under the procurators Felix, A.D. 52–60, and Florus, A.D. 60–2 (*cf.* Jos. *B.J.* 2, 13, 4 ; *Ant.* 20, 5, 10) or hidden in the *store-rooms* (the inmost rooms) surrounding his preparations with the mystery sometimes expected of the Messias (Lagrange, *Le Messianisme*, 221–4). **27.** The ' lightning ' image suggests a suddenness which might forbid reference to the destruction of Jerusalem which, 15, gives warning of its approach. Yet the argument is not conclusive since the suddenness is not such as to exclude a period of activity for pseudo-messiahs, 24, and the ' lightning ' image is used by the prophets, Is 30:27 ff. ; Zach 9:14, of divine judgements in the course and not at the end of history. The ' coming ' (παρουσία, 3, note) of the Son of Man is therefore not necessarily a coming for the final and universal judgement ; it may be his

coming for the judgement upon Israel. **28.** A sentence **716d** in proverb-form reminiscent of Job 39:30. It possibly means that the final coming of the Son of Man will leave none untouched (Buzy) but similar language is used by the prophets to describe divine judgement on Jerusalem (Jer 7:33 f. etc.) in which case the ' carcase ' is Jerusalem where the birds of prey will have work to do.

29–31 After the Tribulation (Mk 13:24–27 ; Lk **e** 21:25–27)—Almost all commentators refer 29–31 to the end of the world theme. The new theory, however, maintaining the single reference of the whole discourse, insists that Jesus still speaks of the fall of Jerusalem or rather of its counterpart which is the establishment of the Messianic kingdom in power. **29.** The consequence of the great disaster is expressed in the prophetic style we have already noted, 21. The serried ranks (*ṣᵉbā'ôṭ i.e.* ' marshalled hosts ' ; DV ' powers ') of God's heavenly army are in turmoil. As in Is 13:6–10, foretelling the ruin of Babylon, the very heavens are presented as involved in the catastrophe. All agree that these stereotyped terms of prophecy and apocalypse are not to be taken literally whether the reference be to the end of the world or to the end of Jerusalem. It follows that 29 does not settle the problem. It should be noticed, however, that Peter, Ac 2:19 f., uses the very similar language of Joel 2:30 f. not of the end of the world but of the new era formally and spectacularly inaugurated on Pentecost Day. For Peter, Joel's ' great and manifest day of the Lord ' has come with the Messianic age. It is instructive (*cf.* 31, note) that Joel heralds this ' day ' with a trumpet, Jl 2:1. **30.** **f** Commonly taken as decisive for the end of the world reference. The Son of Man appears as sovereign judge ; the sign is of his triumphant and avenging Cross ; the lamentation is not of repentance, which would come too late, but of despair. The opposed view makes ' the coming of the Son of Man in the clouds ' (*cf.* Dan 7:13) refer (as in 26:64 ; see note) to the glorious establishment of his kingdom on earth. The ' mourning of the tribes ' is taken from Zach 12:10–14 where the ' mourning ' is not of despair but of repentance for the death of one untimely slain, apparently of David's house. The repentance is followed, Zach 13:1 ff., by an era of grace. These references to Daniel and Zacharias, it is claimed, both suggest the Messianic era rather than the end of the world (*cf.* the grouping of the same texts in Apoc 1:7, probably in the same sense ; Allo, *L'Apocalypse*, 61). The ' sign of the Son of Man in heaven ' is taken to mean the rallying-signal which is the Messias himself (σημεῖον as in Is 11:12). It is a sign perhaps experienced rather than ' seen ' ; *cf.* 26:64, § 720g. It is a ' heavenly ' sign (once asked for and now to be given, *cf.* 12:38 ff., § 697d), like the ' coming in the clouds ', because the Son of Man's heavenly glory is perceived in the triumphal establishment of his kingdom on earth. The mourning, as in Zach 12:10, is consequent upon the realization of the glory of the Son whose death is thus shown to have been a hideous crime. In this theory, therefore, the sign is ' Christ the King seen in symbolic vision bearing the marks of his shameful death now as glorious wounds—a vision which forces itself upon the attention of men '. **31.** The gathering **g** of the elect is variously interpreted according to the sense given to the word ' elect ' (22, 24, notes). It is usually understood as the fulfilment of the Christian hope for the end of time, 1 Thess 4:17 ; 2 Thess 2:1, while the ' trumpet ', 1 Thess 4:15 f., is to awaken the faithful who are supposed dead (Buzy). The second hypothesis, which has referred 30 to the conversion of the nations (' all tribes of the earth ') who perceive that Christ has risen and reigns, asserts that 31 calls attention to those other members of the Messianic kingdom—the ' remnant of Israel ' (22, note). The ' trumpet ', it is held, is only the signal that the Messianic era has opened ; it is the rallying-call for God's people precisely as in Is 27:13. We are reminded that in the Jewish daily prayer (*šᵉmōnê 'Esrê*, 10)

176g the 'trumpet' of 31 and the 'sign' of 30 are joined in a petition for the coming of the Messianic age : ' Sound the great *trumpet* for our deliverance and raise a *standard* for the rallying of our exiles ! '. The ' trumpet ' in Mt, as so often in the Apocalypse (Allo, *L'Apocalypse*, lxi, 122 f.), unlike the ' last ' trumpet of 1 Cor 15:52, announces perhaps the intervention of God in the course of history and not at its end. In this view the symbolical trumpet is to rally Christ's own elect—the remnant of Israel dispersed over the known world.

717a 32-35 Parable of the Fig-tree (Mk 13:28-31 ; Lk 21:28-33)—On the assumption that the preceding verses refer to the end of the world the context of this section causes difficulty, particularly in view of 34. Some (Lagrange, Buzy) suggest that our passage refers back to the destruction of Jerusalem section ; others (Prat) find this procedure arbitrary and, yielding to the force of the context, apply 32-35 to the end of the world (34, note). The view which holds for the destruction of Jerusalem theme throughout the discourse claims to offer the more natural explanation of the text, with Lagrange, and also to save the context, with Prat. **32-33.** Just as the happy season of summer has its herald-signs, Cant 2:12 f., so the establishment of the Messianic era, counterpart of the destruction of Jerusalem, has its portents, *viz.* ' all these things ', 33 ; *cf.* ' these things ' in 3. The events of 5-28 will, as they mature, proclaim the imminence of the Kingdom whose powerful establishment is described, according to the Feuillet view, in 29-31. **34.** And indeed none of ' these things ' is far distant. All shall take place within the lifetime of many now living (' this generation ' ; *cf.* 11:16 ; 12:39 ; 17:7 etc.). Here, as in 23:36 f., our Lord appears to intend a chronological indication ; the alternative explanation (Knabenbauer, Prat) of ' this generation ' as ' the Jewish race ' is less probable. **35.** That ' heaven and earth shall pass ' may mean that the old order is to give way to a new world (19:28, note)—the Messianic era, 29. Possibly, however, 35 which is apparently parenthetical and occurs elsewhere (5:18, note) has no reference to the symbolism of 29 and indicates that our Lord's words (his doctrine in general) are more stable than the physical universe.

b 36-41 The Deluge Comparison (Lk 17:26-27, 30, 34-35 ; *cf.* Mk 13:32)—**36.** A return to (Lagrange) or continuation of (Prat) the end of the world theme ; or (Feuillet) a continuation of the destruction of Jerusalem theme. Our Lord refuses an exact date though in 34 he seems to define a date within 30-40 years. From this apparent incompatibility the inference is usually drawn that 34 and 36 refer to two different events, respectively the destruction of Jerusalem and the end of the world. It is admitted however (Ricciotti, *Vita di Gesù Cristo*, Milan, 1946, 641) that 36 is unexpected in its present place. For this reason, and for others, Feuillet emphasizes the indefiniteness of the time-indication in 34 as opposed to the refused precision (' day and hour ') in 36. He concludes that 34 and 36 may refer to the one event—the establishment of the Messianic kingdom, the great ' day ' of Yahweh according to the prophets. He underlines the close similarity between 36 and Ac 1:7 f. where our Lord, asked the time of this establishment, refuses to give it and says only (Ac 1:8 ; *cf.* Mt 24:14) that the Gospel must first be spread abroad (RB 56 [1949] 87 f.). In either case, the exact day and hour is the Father's secret. No man, no angel, *not even the Son* (this last phrase, certainly authentic in Mk 13:32, is probably authentic in Mt) knows that. The crescendo is instructive, but there remains the dogmatic difficulty of our Lord's proclaiming his ' ignorance '. It should however be remarked in passing that the inclusion of the phrase is a strong witness to the complete honesty of the evangelists. The difficulty (similar to that of 19:17 ; 20:23 ; *cf.* §§ 709*b*, 710*b*) is to some degree solved if we remember that it is the constant practice of the incarnate Son to claim no knowledge beyond that which the Father has instructed him to use. This is true even of

the gospel of John who indubitably teaches the divinity of Christ ; *cf.* Jn 7:16 ; 14:10. On the dogmatic side it may be said (A. Durand, S.J., NRT 71 [1949], 497-503) that in the incarnate Word were two planes of knowledge—divine and total on one plane, human and limited on the other ; direct communication between the two being established only by his supernatural ' infused knowledge '. This last was infused in proportion to the dignity of the man-God and to the needs of his redemptive work (*e.g.* knowledge of his own divinity and Messianic character ; gift of prophecy). It is doubtful if the knowledge of the time of the world's ending or of the *exact* ' day and hour ' of Jerusalem's destruction was thus needed ; *cf.* Dz 2183-5. **37-39.** No one knows the hour *because* (γάρ) in the divine decree the exact time of the coming (παρουσία) is uncertain and sudden. This ' coming ' is to overtake people at their usual occupations, careless of impending disaster. **40-41.** The sudden event ' will make a sharp distinction between the fate of individuals who up to that moment were in close association ' (Dodd, *The Parables of the Kingdom*, London 1936, 87). The sense of ' taken ' and ' left ' will depend upon the identification of the disaster. For those who accept the end of the world context the terms mean ' taken to God ', ' left unaccepted '. In the destruction of Jerusalem hypothesis, ' taken ' means ' swept away by the catastrophe ' and ' left ' means spared (as Noe was ' left ', Gen 7:23) to form part of the chosen ' remnant ' (RSR 35 [1948] 555-8).

42-44 The Surprised Householder (Lk 12:39-40 ; *cf.* Lk 21:34-35)—This, like the deluge-comparison, 39, presents a man overtaken by disaster. It warns the disciples to *be wakeful* (γρηγορεῖτε). Though you do not know the hour (*cf.* 36), proceeds our Lord, *this ye know* (at least), *i.e.* you can appreciate this, namely, that if a householder knew exactly when (ποία φυλακῇ) the thief would come he would be prepared. The saying is strange because the disciples themselves do not know ' the hour ', 36. We are evidently to understand the suppressed implication that the householder, if forewarned of the event but ignorant of the exact hour, would watch all night. As before, 4 ff., our Lord is concerned with the conduct of his disciples. The coming disasters will overwhelm their hope and faith and lead them to rash action (*cf.* 25-26) unless they stand in calm fortitude awaiting the hour of deliverance ; *cf.* Lk 21:28.

XXIV 45-51 The Parable of the Stewards (Lk 12:41-48) —It is probable that the parable was not spoken on this occasion and that Lk gives its correct setting. It is drawn hither in Mt by an analogy of subject—the ' watchfulness ' enjoined upon the disciples, 42, in preparation for a divine ' coming '. But the ' coming ' in this case is to the individual not to a community, as in Lk. The parable is a diptych. **45-47.** The first picture presents the faithful superintendent of the household, always giving ' *them their food in due time* '. He is found so doing when his master comes. From supervision of the servants he is promoted to superintendence of all his master's affairs. This steward would appear to represent the disciple placed by Christ, the Master (ὁ κύριος), in a post of responsibility. The coming of the Master (it is not described as a ' return ' ; Dodd, 159) lacks the solemnity of the ' coming ' of 24:27, 30. It does not, therefore, suggest more than the ' coming ' to each individual—the time of reckoning which is death. The word ' blessed ', 46, and the extravagance of the reward for simple duty, 47, suggest allegory : the disciple, faithful to his earthly responsibilities in the Kingdom, will be associated in heaven with the glorified Son of Man presiding thence over his earthly kingdom ; *cf.* 19:28, note. **48-51.** In the companion-picture the steward sees in his master's absence an opportunity for oppression and debauch. The master's ' delay ' of 48 is probably but ' a necessary part of the dramatic machinery to produce the situation desired ' (Dodd). In the hypothesis that the ' coming ' of the Master is the End of the World, the

f ' delay ' is taken as an indication that the End may be ' long a-coming '. The ' separate him ' of 51 is difficult (διχοτομήσει ; WV ' cut him asunder ') though the sawing asunder of a slave's body was a punishment not unknown in the Greek and Roman periods ; cf. Black, 190. Possibly it is allegorically figures severe punishment ; possibly it is to be rendered ' cut him off ' (KNT), i.e. from the association with the reigning Christ in heaven, 47. His *lot* is henceforth with the ' hypocrites '. This last term invites us (cf. 23:13, 15 etc.) to think of the scribes and Pharisees who had cut themselves off from the Kingdom, 23:13. The ' weeping and gnashing of teeth ' (cf. 8:11-13, note) has already been associated with individual reprobation, 22:13, and recurs, significantly, in 25:30.

a **XXV 1-13 The Ten Virgins** (Mt only ; but cf. Lk 12:35-39)—The ' coming ' of the Master described in 24:45-51 is now presented as the coming of the Bridegroom. Here again the ' coming ' lacks the pomp of 24:29-31 and we think instinctively of the ' coming ' that tests the individual—death. **1-4.** The kingdom of heaven considered in the stage just described (i.e. of the Master's coming to examine the conduct of his servants ; 24:46, 50 ; this seems indicated by the τότε ὁμοιωθήσεται ; DV ' Then shall . . . be like ') resembles the situation about to be outlined ; cf. 13:24, § 699b. The general background is that of a marriage but wants detail and has elements of improbability (Buzy, 326 f.) that perhaps suggest allegory. It is not entirely clear that the ' virgins ' are bridesmaids since no bride is mentioned throughout (omit ' and the bride ' from 1 ; WV) and, unless we intrude our knowledge of Palestinian marriage-custom, there is no hint that the virgins go to the bride's house first ; it is to the groom's they go. The parable is concerned only with the relationship of virgins and groom. The tiny clay *lamps* hold little oil. The prudent young ladies, foreseeing possible delay, carry small refuelling vessels also. Such lamps are eminently unsuitable for the open-air procession. They are introduced into the parable deliberately, possibly because the more practical torch would not bring in the necessary idea of replenishing-vessels, possibly as symbols of vigilance, Lk 12:35. The *bridegroom* (called ' Lord '—κύριε—in 11 ; cf. 7:22 ; 24:50) is Christ himself (cf. 9:15 ; 22:2 ; Eph 5:25 ff. ; Apoc 19:7-9 ; 21:2. For rabbinic ideas of the Messias wedded to his people cf. Edersheim 1, 722 f. ; Brierre-Narbonne, *Les Prophéties Messianiques de l'A. T. dans la* **b** *Littérature Juive*, Paris 1933, 22 f.). **5-8.** Wearied with waiting all *grew drowsy* and fell asleep. This detail serves to underline the delay of the groom. It is not reproved : both wise and foolish have allowed themselves to be overtaken by sleep. The guilt does not lie in this but in the carelessness that had made no provision for all eventualities. The wise, though asleep, are prepared. Nor need the delay of the groom hold an allegorical significance (cf. 24:48, note) ; it perhaps merely emphasizes the prudence that had provided for it. **9.** The rather selfish complacency of the prudent may not be admirable but (as elsewhere ; cf. Lk 16:8) it is only their one quality (of preparedness) that is set as a model. It emerges that this quality is a personal one and cannot be supplied by others (note the emphatic pronouns of 3, 7, 9 : ' their *own* lamps ', ' for yourselves ', ἑαυτῶν, ἑαυταῖς). **10-13.** It is too late now : the groom's arrival (like the Master's in 24:50) has caught them unprepared. The wise go in with the groom to the *marriage-feast* ; cf. 22:2, note. The door fast-shut, the invocation ' Lord ', the strange and solemn repudiation by the bridegroom, are all unlifelike and betray the application of the parable. This is explicitly made in 13 : prudent provision for the Lord's coming, whenever it be.

c **14-30 The Talents** (cf. Lk 19:11-27)—Our Lord had said, 24:45, that the true servant must be faithful and prudent. The parable of the Virgins illustrates the prudence that makes the Christian live with a view to the coming of the Bridegroom. The parable of the Talents illustrates the faithfulness required of each Christian in the administration of goods committed **718c** to him by the Master. **14-15.** The ' watchfulness ' mentioned in 13 is necessary because (For it is as when ' : ὥσπερ γὰρ) the situation under discussion is comparable to the one about to be described. In proportion to the financial ability of each of his servants (with the intention, therefore, of their making profit for him) the Master commits to them various sums. A huge sum to the first, a small fortune to the second, a not inconsiderable amount to the third. For the ' talent ' cf. 18:24, § 707b. **16-17.** The first and the second lose no time (the ' immediately ' of 15 is to be taken with 16 : *Straightway he that had received . . . ;* WV) in doubling each his master's money by hard work. Presumably this result was achieved only ' after a long time ', 19, when the master returned ; cf. 25:5 ; 24:48, note. **18.** The third hid his talent, doubtless in the form of current coins, in a hole in the ground for safety. **19.** The long absence of the master throws into relief the sustained diligence of the first and second servants and the persistent laziness of the third. **20-23. d** The faithful conduct of some few business-matters (the amounts, though huge, are as nothing to the master and in comparison with the reward) is rewarded by a post of greater importance. The application of the parable shines through the sentence : Enter thou into the joy [i.e. the joyful banquet ; Joüon, 157 ; cf. 25:10, note] of thy Lord ! The faithful servant shares with Jesus (cf. 25:34) the joy of the Father's kingdom and apparently (cf. 25:21, 23) is associated with the King's administration of the earthly kingdom so long as it lasts ; cf. 19:28, note. **24-25.** The lazy servant throws the responsibility upon the master. Experience tells him, he suggests, that the master is an exacting man. It seems that he stops short of an accusation of dishonesty. He develops the term ' exacting ' in two farming-images : ' reaping where thou hast not sown ', ' *garnering where thou hast not winnowed* ' (WV). They are operations in which the master has had no personal share, from which nevertheless he expects profit. It is the classical objection to the ' capitalist '. The servant alleges that his timidity proceeded from a knowledge of this. He considers that the return of the talent absolves him from blame. **26-27.** The master immediately unmasks the true motive of the servant's conduct : sloth. Even granted this caricature of himself, he argues, the servant should have had the wit and will if not to trade, as the others have done, at least to bank the money. On Jewish bankers cf. Edersheim 2, 463 f. The master would thus have received the *interest.* **28-29.** To the first servant, who has shown **e** himself able to bear great responsibility, the master transfers the idle ' talent '. Yet the servant has already ' entered into the joy of his Lord '. One, therefore, again receives the impression (cf. 21, 23) that ' the faithful servant of Christ is awarded a stewardship of a higher order in heaven (cf. Lk 16:9-12) and associated more closely than ever with the furthering of the Kingdom's interests ' (Feuillet). In human affairs responsibility is increasingly added to the able and willing. This is true, *mutatis mutandis*, of the Kingdom, 29. **30.** The punishment is directly contrasted with the reward. The lazy servant is thrust out from the joy and light of the king's banquet-hall ; cf. 8:12, § 689e. The parable primarily teaches that God's gifts, of nature and especially of grace, are held in stewardship and must not be allowed to lie idle. They are to be used to further his kingdom ; cf. 5:13-16. It emerges, secondarily, that the standard of God's judgement is relative to the opportunities offered : ' the greater the gifts, the greater the account demanded ' (Gregory the Great, PL 76, 1106).

XXV 31-46 The Last Judgement (Mt only)—The pre- **f** ceding parables have dealt with God's particular assessment of the conduct of individuals—an assessment which is repeated throughout the course of the earthly Kingdom's history as each individual comes to his account. Our Lord now passes to a description of the universal and final Assize. ' Between 24:1-44 and 25:31-46

718f there is this in common, *viz.* that in each case a collective judgement closes an era in the history of salvation, and there is a solemn intervention of the Son of Man. . . . But the analogy stops there. . . . The first tableau, 24:1–44, presents a purely collective judgement, taking place in time, without any reference to sanctions in the eternal world ; this is followed by a new stage in the history of man's religious evolution—a new cosmos. The second tableau describes a judgement not only collective but individual also ; when it is finished, human history is at an end ; man goes to eternal life or to eternal loss', Feuillet. Contemporary Jewish thought, too, appears to distinguish a judgement inaugurating the Messianic era (' days of the Messias ' ; *cf.* 19:28, § 709*e*) and another judgement, strictly eschatological, which introduces the eternal world, Bonsirven, I, 486–93. Even the second of these has, for the Rabbis, a tinge of nationalism : Israel would receive preferential treatment from God the Judge, Bonsirven I, 500–3. Our Lord, speaking here of this second and final judgement, shows no trace of nationalism. The judgement by which the kingdom of the Son is purified before becoming the kingdom of the Father is decided exclusively on religious grounds. **31.** Of this final judgement the Messias had not been imagined as the independent Judge. Our Lord, however, unhesitatingly assumes this office. He goes further (*cf.* 40, 45) and decides the issue on man's attitude to himself. This situation ' constitutes a declaration (of divinity) almost as solemn as the one he was to make when he presented himself to the Sanhedrin as Son of God ',

g Lagrange. **32–33.** Man is fitly judged by the Son of Man and the judgement is universal. The ' sheep ', for their mild expression and docility, are a suitable image of the faithful followers of Christ the shepherd, Jn 10:3, 4, 27. They are distinguished from the ' goats ' (*cf.* Ez 34:17), mistrustful of eye and intractable of conduct, aptly chosen as their wicked counterpart. The right hand then, as now, was considered as the place of favour. **34.** The ' king ', the enthroned Son of Man of 31, invites the good to the kingdom of his royal Father. They are blessed of (*i.e.* ' by ' or ' belonging to ' ; *cf.* Jn 11:29) that Father who, in his eternal decree had foreknown his own and prepared for their happiness ; *cf.* 5:4, note. **35–36.** Why this reward ? Because the King himself had been by them fed, harboured, clothed ; visited in sickness and in captivity. The Son of Man thus identifies himself with the cause of all men whom, as the Servant of God, Is 53, he purchased with his death. **37–40.** Christian disciples at least could not doubt that they had done these things for the love of Christ, Mk 9:40, nevertheless they could not have realized, without our Lord's assurance, that these were favours personal to him. This was all the more remarkable in that the visible objects of those favours were often their own enemies and perhaps his ; *cf.* our Lord's own instructions in 5:46. But the astonishment of the just at the judgement is merely a literary presentation of the lesson. In effect, after this revelation of our Lord's, they will henceforth see Christ

h in all the needy, friend or foe. **41–46.** The sentence of the wicked, expressed more briefly than the invitation of the just, is a terrible one. Instead of ' Come ! ', ' Depart ! ' ; in place of the Kingdom, ' everlasting fire '. God had prepared for man the Kingdom, not the fire, Wis 2:23 f. ; this last was prepared only for the rebellious Satan (*cf.* 2 Pet 2:4 ; Jude 6) and his satellites whom, in rabbinic tradition, the archangel Sammael (Satan) had dragged with him to their doom, SB I, 983 f. The Jewish texts do not agree on the eternity of punishment (Bonsirven I, 538–41) but our Lord's terms clearly suggest a definitive separation of good from bad when the last and solemn judgement is declared.

719a F. The Passion XXVI 1–XXVII 66.
XXVI 1–5 The Conspiracy (Mk 14:1–2 ; Lk 22:1–2)—
1–2. The long discourse of chh 24–25 is over (note Mt's familiar formula ; *cf.* 7:28 ; 11:1 ; 13:53 ; 19:1). It

is Wednesday, two days before the Friday of our Lord's death. **3–4.** Even as our Lord is speaking (if Mt's usually vague ' then ' is here intended as a chronological note ; otherwise *cf.* Jn 11:47–53) the Sanhedrin holds an informal meeting in the *palace* (not ' courtyard' ; *cf.* Joüon, 159 f.) of its president Caiaphas (Iosepos Kaiaphas), high-priest from A.D. 18–36). **5.** Haste is imperative yet the impending feast of the Pasch, anniversary of the birth of the nation, is an obstacle being a time of Messianic excitement. Moreover, the Galilean pilgrims and others have triumphantly escorted Jesus into the city on the previous Sunday. Had Judas not intervened it seems that the arrest would have been deferred.

6–13 Anointing at Bethany (Mk 14:3–9 ; Jn 12:1–8)— Though the incident took place on the Saturday before Palm Sunday, Jn 12:1, Mt and Mk place it in this Passion-context as a prophetic rehearsal of the burial-rites. **6.** The host bears the common name of Simon, one of ten such in NT. He has suffered from some form of leprosy (*cf.* 8:2, § 689*b*), hence his soubriquet. He was possibly the father of Martha, Mary and Lazarus (*cf.* Jn 12:2–3) but more probably all three were guests at Simon's house. **7.** From a flask of onyx (' alabaster-box ') Mary pours the ointment that would have cost a contemporary labourer his whole year's salary or a Roman legionary sixteen months' pay (300 denarii ; Mk 14:5). **8–9.** It would have bought bread for thousands, Jn 6:7. The extravagance shocks the utilitarian but it is a salutary warning that the protest is most loudly voiced by Judas, Jn 12:4, who had no love of the poor, Jn 12:6. **10–11.** Jesus is far from opposing efforts to conquer pauperism ; he simply remarks a fact : the disciples will have ample opportunity after he has gone to care for the poor. **12–13.** Consciously or unconsciously, Mary has lovingly enacted a prophecy of our Lord's death. The generous tone of his prediction, remarkably fulfilled, is in sharp contrast to the mean protest of 9.

14–16 Judas at Work (Mt only)—Mt resumes the thread of the historical narrative after the break in 6–13. Presumably it is still Wednesday. The traitor, reproachfully called ' one of the twelve ', was the only non-Galilean Apostle, 10:1–4, § 692*e*. He had evidently reached the conclusion that nothing material was to be gained from associating with a Messias who preached sacrifice and who had so little appreciation of the value of money, 9. The sum agreed upon for the treachery is the equivalent of 120 denarii ; *cf.* 7, note. The ' pieces of silver ' are staters ; *cf.* 17:24, note. The sum was a natural one for the priests to choose because the Law laid it down as the price for a human person (a slave ; Ex 21:32).

17–19 Preparation for the Supper ; Thursday (Mk 14:12–16 ; Lk 22:7–13)—All the evangelists are agreed that our Lord died on the day preceding the Sabbath, *i.e.* on Friday, Mk 15:42 ; Lk 23:54 ; Jn 19:31. The day of the Supper is therefore certainly Thursday. **17.** The ' feast of the Azymes ' (*i.e.* of ' unleavened bread '), so called from the week's abstention from leavened bread, was celebrated from the evening of 14th Nisan to the evening of 21st Nisan. On the evening of the 14th the paschal lamb was slain and the paschal supper celebrated with unleavened bread. The term ' feast of the Azymes ' (alternatively ' feast of the Pasch ') was applied in particular to the first day of the week's feast, from sunset 14th to sunset 15th. The ' first day of the Azymes ' (Mt) ' on which it was necessary that the pasch should be killed ', Lk 22:7, is evidently used here (as *e.g.* in Josephus) in the wider sense of the phrase to include the whole day on the evening of which the paschal supper was eaten. It seems evident (Mk 14:14 ; Lk 22:11 ; see however WV I, 362–5) that our Lord actually celebrated the Jewish paschal supper ; *cf.* J. Jeremias, *Die Abendmahlsworte Jesu*, Göttingen, 1949². Nevertheless, John 18:28 makes it clear that our Lord's enemies celebrated the paschal supper on the evening of the following day, Friday, and the Synoptics themselves describe

9d the Friday morning as such a busy time for priest and Pharisee (Sanhedrin meeting, delation to Pilate, etc.) that it is difficult to imagine Friday being the 15th Nisan, one of the greatest feasts of the calendar with abstention from business and work. It seems probable that our Lord and the Galilean pilgrims celebrated the paschal supper on the day before the Jerusalemites, *i.e.* on the evening of Nisan 13th. If it were celebrated at all it would be with unleavened bread (essential to the paschal rite) and therefore the evangelists may speak of Nisan 13th as ' the first day of the Azymes '.

e *Cf.* §§ 739*e*, 768*a–c*. **18.** Our Lord is outside the city (perhaps he has spent the night in prayer on Olivet, *cf.* Lk 21:37 ; Jn 18:2) but it was obligatory to eat the paschal lamb in Jerusalem, Bonsirven 2, 123. The disciples (Peter and John ; Lk 22:8) are therefore sent into the city to one whose name the evangelists suppress, perhaps for prudence' sake. It appears from Mt (' the Master saith ') that the man was a friend of our Lord and willing to put a private room at his disposal despite the crowded conditions of the town at festal times. The hour of our Lord's destiny has struck (his ' time '—as in Jn 7:6-8).

f 20-25 Prophecy of Treason (Mk 14:17-21 ; Lk 22:14, 21-23)—**20.** When the sun had set (*cf.* Ex 12:8), the thirteen *lay* at table. The guests would lie on mats or mattresses, resting on the left arm, the right being used for eating. If the order was that of the Roman *triclinium*, three sides of the square (or oval) were used by the guests, the fourth being left open for convenience of service. (For positions at table *cf.* Jn 13:23 ff., § 802*g*). Judas, keeping up appearances, was still with the Apostles, but in the course of the meal our Lord attempts to touch his conscience. **21-23.** Our Lord's answer to the question of the troubled Apostles insists on the intimacy, not the identity, of the traitor. The traitor is at table now ; he *has dipped* (or ' is dipping ' as in Mk 14:20 ; *cf.* Joüon 162) his herbs (first course of the paschal meal) in the dish of sauce that passes round the table. **24.** That the Son of Man goes freely to his death (*cf.* Jn 8:14, 21 f. etc.) is no excuse. **25.** Judas probably puts his question in a low voice or possibly in concert with the others, 22. The answer is not a direct affirmative (Aramaic has *hên* or *hēn* for ' yes ') but it agrees with the statement made and at the same time calls attention to the fact that the first speaker had provoked agreement ; it therefore implicitly invites the first speaker to salutary reflection ; *cf.* 26:64 ; 27:11. Judas must have left the table almost immediately—his knowledge of discovery would make his position intolerable ; it is therefore improbable that he was present for the institution of the holy Eucharist. Lk 22:21 gives the impression that Judas was still at table for the Institution but his phrase is placed before the Institution by Mt 26:23 and Mk 14:18.

a 26-29 The Holy Eucharist (Mk 14:22-25 ; Lk 22:15-20 ; *cf.* 1 Cor 11:23-25)—The Holy Eucharist appears to have been instituted within the framework of the paschal supper, but its importance eclipses the traditional Jewish elements which go unemphasized, therefore, in the gospel accounts. The institution took place probably when the principal course (the lamb) was over, 1 Cor 11:25. **26.** The bread is unleavened—the only type available after the noon preceding the paschal supper. Our Lord blesses it (or ' gives thanks ' over it : εὐλογήσας, εὐχαριστήσας in Lk 22:19 and 1 Cor 11:24) and breaks. As he gives it to the disciples (Lk 22:19 ἔδωκεν λέγων) he says ' This [that I hand to you] is my body '. In view of the clear belief and practice of the early Church it is becoming increasingly old-fashioned to question the plain meaning of the words ; the present custom is rather to deny that Jesus spoke them and to credit them to Paul the ' sacramentalist ' ; *cf.* Coppens DBV(S) 2, 1150 f., 1155 f. **27.** The chalice was in all probability the third cup of the paschal supper. It followed the eating of the lamb and, being itself followed by a long blessing, was called ' the chalice of benediction ' ; *cf.* 1 Cor 11:16.

28. A new covenant had been promised through **720b** Jeremias, Jer 31:31 ; the old Sinaitic covenant had been sealed with the sacrificial blood of animals (Ex 24:8 ' Behold the blood of the covenant ! '). Both reference and inference are unmistakable—the new covenant is now being liturgically concluded with the sacrificial blood of Christ. The sacred blood is considered either in the state of being shed or as now dedicated to its shedding (ἐκχυννόμενον, present participle, possibly with future meaning ; Joüon 163). The Apostles (' Drink ye all *from* it ') are to make the sacrifice their own and thus achieve its purpose which (most fully expressed by Mt) is the expiation of the sins of many (ὑπὲρ πολλῶν) by the death of One (*cf.* 20:28). **29** is placed by Lk 22:18 before the Institution, probably rightly because the reflexion is more naturally made before the thought of the Apostles has been raised to the higher plane of the chalice of Christ's blood. The reason for its present place in Mt and Mk is that each, concerned only with those elements of the Last Supper which were to endure, does not speak of the first half of the paschal celebration. Consequently the cup, though the third, is mentioned only once and the dictum of 29 used by Jesus of an earlier cup, is perforce joined with the Eucharistic cup. ' This fruit of the vine ' (the phrase is taken from the Jewish ritual benediction) seems, therefore, to refer to the unconsecrated cup : our Lord declares his imminent death and the happy reunion in the eternal Kingdom (' of my Father ') where all is new, Apoc 21:1, 5. *Note :* St Luke appears to have in mind the ' Kingdom ' on earth, the Church, and the Eucharistic banquet which is the ' Pasch ' of the Messianic era ; *cf.* RB 48 (1939) 357-93.

30-35 Prediction of Desertion and Denial (Mk **c** 14:26-31 ; *cf.* Lk 22:31-34 ; Jn 13:36-38)—**30.** The Jewish paschal supper ends with the singing of the ' Hallel ' (' praise ') psalms, 113:8-18 ; 114-117 (Vg), and, the religious rite over, conversation turns to other topics. At the Last Supper it is our Lord who discourses, Jn 14:1-17:24, but the discourse is not reported in the Synoptics. The time is probably about 10 p.m. and the little company passes through the town in an easterly direction, crosses the Kedron valley and turns left along the western slope of Olivet. A walk of nearly a mile brings them to Gethsemani. **31.** Either on the way or while still in the supper-room (*cf.* Lk Jn ; Mt's ' then ' is often merely stylistic and not chronological) the disciples are told of their impending desertion : ' You will all *lose courage over me* ' (KNT). Our Lord quotes Zach 13:7 to illustrate the general principle that the flock owes its strength and unity to the shepherd (especially this flock to this shepherd). The illustration is borrowed from the history of king Sedecias, a timid ' shepherd ' who, attacked by the Babylonians, abandoned the capital and its inhabitants to their fate, 4 Kg 25:4. **32-35.** In the general consternation the Resurrection prophecy again goes unheeded as also, it would appear, 28:10, the Galilean assignation. Peter's indignation outdoes his respect and draws upon him a detailed prophecy of his own moral fall. The ' cock-crow ' in Mt is probably the second—the dawn-crow at about 5 a.m. Mk mentions two, 14:30 ; the earliest cock-crow at paschal time is reported as 2:30 a.m., Lagrange, *L'Evangile*, 542. Between 35 and 36 there is a pregnant silence. Our Lord leaves the event to make reply, 25:56.

36-46 Gethsemani (Mk 14:32-42 ; Lk 22:40-46)— **d** **36-38.** They come to a *plot of land* (χωρίον) at the foot of the western slope of Olivet, facing the temple ; a garden, Jn 18:1, called ' the oil-press ', *gaṭ šᵉmānî* (m), doubtless because of some rustic installation among the olive-trees. Eight of the Apostles remain near the gate but Peter, James and John, witnesses of Jesus' glory (17:1-2 ; *cf.* 2 Pet 1:17-18) are invited to see him in his suffering. The prospect of his passion brings distress and dismay (WV) and mortal sadness. He asks his friends to remain wakeful with him. **39-44.** In an attitude of complete prostration but with his human

720d will deliberately turned to the Father he asks that the cup of sorrow (cf. 20:22) may pass him by if this may be done without upsetting the divine redemptive plan. There are two wills in Christ : the divine will and the human will. We may distinguish a double act in the human will : the act of the will which may be called 'instinctive' (*voluntas ut natura*) and the deliberate, considered act (*voluntas ut ratio*). Our Lord's instinctive will, true to its nature, shrank from suffering and death considered in themselves ; his deliberate will embraced them for the sake of what they were to bring : the redemption of man in the way God willed it. 'Placebat enim Christo secundum voluntatem divinam . . . ut voluntas naturalis in ipso et voluntas sensualitatis secundum ordinem suae naturae moverentur' (ST 3, 8, 6). With the restlessness of sorrow he seeks the solace of his disciples but he asks them to pray not for him but for themselves. Peter's loyalty, so eagerly expressed, 35, is not enough : without prayer, fear for bodily security will overwhelm the will. In his second prayer our Lord uses the words he taught his disciples to say, 6:10. **45-46.** His first words, 45a, are perhaps a question : 'Are ye going to sleep on (τὸ λοιπόν) and take your rest?' (*Plummer, *Mt*, 371) and he awakes them with 'Behold . . .', stirring them to activity with ' Rise . . .'. Others prefer the tone of melancholy resignation to the disciples' weakness : ' Very well, then, sleep ; (it is too late to worry what you do), the hour has struck . . . ; let us go to meet the traitor '.

e **47-56 The Arrest** (Mk 14:43-50 ; Lk 22:47-53 ; Jn 18:2-12)—**47-49.** Judas was familiar with this garden and with our Lord's habits, Jn 18:2. He knew, too, that Jesus would not have gone to Bethany because paschal night was to be spent in Jerusalem or in the immediate neighbourhood. He now leads what is (to judge by their impromptu weapons) a casual gang hired for the purpose, but there is evidently an escort of Roman soldiery, Jn 18:3. The kiss (natural enough from disciple to master) is ostentatious (κατεφίλησεν) to avoid mistakes. **50.** The clipped, and therefore obscure, Greek phrase (ἐφ' ὅ πάρει ; lit. ' for what thou art come ') is interpreted as a question by DV (and KNT) ; more probably it is an exclamation either fully expressed (' for what a purpose art thou come ! ', WV) or, perhaps better, cut short by emotion, e.g. ' (A kiss), friend, for such a purpose ! ', Lagrange. Lk 22:48 appears to render this last sense. **51-54.** Peter's half-parried blow at Malchus, Jn 18:10, is rebuked by our Lord. Firstly, it is useless—violence must always take the consequence of violence and, in this case, the power is apparently on the wrong side. Secondly, it is unnecessary and undesired—the Son does not choose to exercise his power : twelve times six thousand armed angels, not eleven impotent Apostles, waited his word. But how, were he to give that word (' how, were it so . . . ? ' KNT), would this consort with the prophecies (e.g. Is 53) of a meekly suffering Messias ? **55-56.** Our Lord objects to the absurd drama of his arrest and to the show of violence. It implies that he is a dangerous bandit. Yet it must have been clear from his general habit of public teaching (' daily ' in the temple ; cf. especially Jn 7:14 ; 8:2, 20, 59 ; 10:23) that he was no secret conspirator and that he could have been seized at any time. He thus lays bare the leaders' fear of overt unpopular action, 26:5. The evangelist notes on his own account, 56, what our Lord had already said, 54—the whole incident is a prelude to the fulfilment of prophecy. He does not deem it necessary, however, to point out that the flight of the Apostles verifies our Lord's recent forecast, 31.

f **57-68 Before the Council** (Mk 14:53-65 ; cf. Lk 22:54-55, 63-71 and Jn 18:12-14, 19-24)—**57-58.** The prisoner is taken back along the Kedron to the Gate of the Fountain at the SE. angle of the city-walls and so up the graded road to the palace of Caiaphas in the SW. quarter of the city. For Caiaphas cf. 26:3-4, §719a. To judge by the Talmud (cf. Edersheim 2, 533f.) night-trials were illegal, but details like this are dwarfed by the monstrous injustice of the whole process. Peter has followed at a safe distance ; having reached the *palace* (αὐλή ; DV ' court ') he ventures into the court, Mk 14:54, to await the upshot (τέλος). **59-62.** All three classes of the council are represented (chief priests, elders, scribes ; cf. 57). This council (or ' Sanhedrin ' —the Greek συνέδριον in Aramaic form) totalling 71 members was the supreme judiciary body of the Jewish nation and met under the presidency of the reigning high-priest. For capital trials a quorum of 23 sufficed, according to the Mishna, Sanhedrin 4:1 ; it is not, therefore, necessary to understand ' whole council ' strictly. The object of the meeting is to formulate a capital charge to present to the procurator, who alone had power to order execution of sentence ; cf. Jn 18:31 ; Schürer 1, 2, 57 f. ; Jos., *Ant.* 20, 9, 1. For appearance' sake the formalities had to be observed (Num 35:30 etc.) and eventually the necessary two witnesses are found though even these are not in complete agreement, Mk 14:59. They pervert our Lord's words, slightly in words, profoundly in sense ; cf. Jn 2:19. The high-priest is not satisfied ; he seeks a capital charge and hopes to condemn our Lord from his own mouth : ' *Answerest thou naught ? What is it that these men allege against thee ?* ' (WV). **63.** Jesus, ignoring the trumped-up charge of the witnesses, will not refuse an answer to an independent and formal demand from the highest authority (' by the living ', and therefore avenging, ' God ') : ' Tell us if thou be the Christ, the Son of God ! '. The Rabbis never give the title ' Son of God ' to the Messias (Bonsirven 1, 366 f.) and the Jewish writings about our Lord's time are shy of it, Lagrange, *Le Messianisme*, 104 f. The titles ' Son of God ', ' Christ ', are therefore probably not equivalent for Caiaphas. But the term ' Son of God ' had been used of our Lord in his own circle, Mt 16:16 ; Jn 11:27, and the fact was known outside that circle, 27:39-40. It is probable that Caiaphas, aware of all this, adds the title to the term ' Christ ' and so feels his way to a charge of blasphemy, a capital crime, Deut 13:2-6. **64.** Mt's ' thou hast said it ' is equivalent to Mk's ' I am ' with a faintly ironical touch as if Caiaphas by using the terms already assumed their truth. Taking this fictional assent as starting-point our Lord proceeds to build upon it. ' *Moreover* ', he says solemnly, ' from now onwards (ἀπ' ἄρτι, cf. 23:39) you shall be witnesses of ' the situation described by Daniel. ' See.', in regard to apocalyptic vision is not so much physical vision as intellectual appreciation. The sentence is better punctuated : ' You shall see " the Son of Man ", Dan 7:13, " sitting on the right hand of the Power " [i.e. of the Almighty ; cf. Ps 109(110) 1] and " coming upon the clouds of heaven " ', Dan 7:13. This punctuation by indicating a mere juxtaposition of tableaux removes the confusion of imagery. In effect, the ' sitting at the right hand ' and the ' coming upon the clouds ' indicate the same thing. The twin-thrones for God and the Messias suggested by the psalm (and cf. Dan 7:9) indicate a participation in the divine administration of the world. The same idea is found in the Daniel text where one ' like a son of man ' ' comes ' (i.e. to the Ancient of Days for investiture, not to the earth for Judgement) riding on the clouds to receive his Kingdom. In Daniel there is no suggestion of a ' coming ' in a distant perspective of ' Last Judgement ' : it is a question of the new Messianic era. Jesus, too, speaks of the new era which begins now (ἀπ' ἄρτι) on earth ; its glory is paradoxically inaugurated by the whole process of the Passion itself ; cf. Jn 12:31-33. **65-66.** The second of Caiaphas's two questions (Christ ? Son of God ?) may have been asked after the reply of 64 as in Lk 22:66, 70. In any case, it is clear that the high-priest takes our Lord's transcendental Messianism for capital blasphemy. Jesus, therefore, is not claiming a mild, political Messianity though Caiaphas will find the ' Messias ' admission useful before the pagan tribunal. He tears his garments, from the neck downwards for a palm's length, in the ritual manner prescribed for the hearing of blasphemous speech. For the religious court the case is clear, Lev 24:16 ; it remains to secure sentence from the procurator, 27:1. **67-68.** Mt leaves us to understand that our Lord was blindfolded ; *cf.* Mk 14:65 ; Lk 22:64. Those who strike him (not necessarily the Sanhedrists, even in Mt) defy him to use his prophetic or clairvoyant gifts ; *cf.* Ac 23:2 for similar action of another high-priest.

69-75 Peter's Denials (Mk 14:66-72 ; Lk 22:56-62 ; Jn 18:17, 25-27)—Peter is in the open-air courtyard round which the palace was built (αὐλή as in 58 but here further defined by ἔξω). Meanwhile, Jesus is on trial in an upstairs room, Mk 14:66, of the building itself. In the light of the fire, Lk 22:56, Peter is recognized by a maid ; his public denial is not less real for being indirect. He moves from the light towards (εἰς) the gate and another maid (the portress ?) challenges him. The denial is formal this time. Then (' about an hour later ' ; Lk 22:59) Peter is once more at bay among many accusers. His Galilean dialect (confusion of the gutturals : ḥeth ʿayin, ʾaleph ; difficulty with the vowels : a, i, o) proclaims him a northerner. The third denial is emphasized by oath and straightway signalized by the crowing of the cock for the second time ; *cf.* Mk 14:68-72. It is a bitter reminder of our Lord's words, 26:34.

The evangelists do not, as a rule, purpose to give the exact words of speeches—of accusations and denials in this case—nor the exact order of events. From 26:34 we should expect three denials, but the combined gospel accounts suggest more by naming five different accusers at least. The solution probably lies (*cf.* Prat 2, 355 f.) in assigning the multiplicity of accusers to three groups only, thus :

First Denial : in the courtyard (Mt, Mk, Lk) by the fire (Mk, Lk). Accused by a maid (Mt, Mk, Lk), the portress (Jn). The cock crows for the first time (Mk).
Second Denial : in the forecourt (Mk) near the door (Mt) a little later (Lk). Accused by the same maid (Mk ' *the* maid ') whose accusation is supported by others (Jn) including another maid (Mt), a man (Lk).
Third Denial : apparently by the fire again, a little later (Mt, Mk), after about an hour's time (Lk). Accused by the bystanders (Mt, Mk) including another man (Lk) and a relation of Malchus (Jn). The cock crows for the second time (Mk) immediately (Mt, Mk, Lk, Jn).

XXVII 1-2 Jesus and Pilate (Mk 15:1-15 ; Lk 23:1-25 ; *cf.* Jn 18:28-19:16).

XXVII 1-2 Jesus delivered to Pilate (Mk 15:1 ; Lk 23:1 ; Jn 18:28)—The second meeting of the Jewish council (Luke, simplifying, records only one) was at dawn, Lk 22:66 ; it was evidently short because it was still early morning when Jesus reached Pilate's residence, Jn 18:28. The meeting was held probably in the Sanhedrin's assembly-hall (the *gazith*), on the southern side of the ' court of the Israelites '. Its purpose was to pass sentence of formal condemnation in legal day-session (57-58, note) and to formulate a charge which would impress the governor. They decided upon a political one (27:11 ; *cf.* Lk 23:2). In the Roman province of Judaea only the procurator (Pontius Pilatus, A.D. 26-36) could order execution of the death-sentence (SB 1, 1026 ; *cf.* Holzmeister, *Historia*, 82-4). Normally resident at Caesarea Palestinae, the procurator established his military headquarters (' praetorium ') in Jerusalem for the dangerous periods of the great feasts. In the year of Christ's death at least this praetorium was probably established in the Antonia, the fortress abutting on the NW. corner of the temple-enclosure.

3-5 Fate of Judas (*cf.* Ac 1:18-20)—The whole incident, 3-10, presented parenthetically, serves to underline the Sanhedrin's contempt for justice and the hypocrisy of its members. **3-5.** Mt's ' then ', as so often, is vague—the time may be after the condemnation by Pilate. Possibly Judas had thought that the evidence would prove insufficient for condemnation or possibly his crime came home to him only when he saw its fruit and handled the bribe. Filled with remorse (not true ' repentance ' because empty of hope) he sought to dissociate himself from the affair by proclaiming his Master's innocence. The unscrupulous cynicism of the judges showed the attempt hopeless and drove him to a desperate decision. The money was now worse than useless ; he flung it down in (εἰς) the temple (ναός, a word which, to judge from its use in Jn 2:20, may include the temple buildings such as the *gazith*). The place of his suicide is unknown. **721b**

XXVII 6-10 Scruples of the Unscrupulous (Mt only)— **c** **6-8.** The Law, Deut 23:18, forbade the price of chastity to be put to sacred use ; the Sanhedrists now extend the principle to blood-money—it must not be put into the temple-treasury (*qorbānā*, Aram. ' offering '). With it they buy ' Pottersfield ' (hitherto a well-known name, evidently, and doubtless so called because it contained potter's clay) ; thenceforth it was called in Aramaic *ḥᵃqēl dᵉmā* ' field of blood ' because bought with blood-money, but *cf.* Ac 1:18 f. This cemetery for strangers (probably Jews who died on pilgrimage in Jerusalem—pagans were the Romans' affair) lay on the southern slope of the Hinnom valley. **9-10.** Mt, as usual, hastens **d** to associate the OT with the event ; *cf.* Zach 11:12-13 ; Jer 18:2-4 ; 19:1-2 ; 32:7-9. The prophet Zacharias, a true shepherd of Israel, is assessed by the false shepherds, the political authorities, at the mean price of thirty pieces. It is an insult to God whom Zacharias represents. ' Throw it to the potter ! [*i.e.* to the cheap shop] a fine price at which to be assessed by them ! '. The words are God's. The striking similarity of situation and the concurrence of the ' thirty pieces ' with ' the potter ' call Mt's attention to a text which he freely adapts, apparently from the Hebrew text : ' *And they* [the priests—the prophet himself, ' I ', in HT of Zach] *took the thirty pieces of silver, the assessment at which he was assessed* [lit. ' of one assessed ']—*they were of Israel who assessed him—and gave them to the potter's field* ' (Zach ' and I threw them into the potter's workshop ' ; trans. Van Hoonacker). Mt adds, in Zacharias's name, ' as the Lord directed *me* ', betraying the original ' I ' of the preceding verbs in HT. In so doing he underlines the fact that the hand of God was in the first situation and therefore prepares us for a higher, Messianic, significance. The Rabbis, too, applied the passage messianically but the thirty pieces of silver become the thirty precepts given by Moses to Israel, Edersheim 2, 736. *The attribution of the text to Jeremias,* strongly supported by the MSS (though *Ta* ; *33* ; Φ ; *157* ; *a* ; *b* ; syrsin ; peš. omit ' Jeremias ') is strange. It is possible, however, that the text is a fusion of Zach and Jer. Jer 32 recounts the purchase of a field, symbolic of confidence in Judah's rehabilitation ; Jer 19:11 has a curious *rapprochement* of the potter's vessel and Hinnom ; Jer 18 tells of a visit to a potter of which (according to Van Hoonacker, *Les Douze Petits Prophètes*, Paris 1908, 677) the text in Zach is an ' adaptation '. In this case, Mt assigns the text to Jer (as Mk 1:2-3 assigns a composite Is–Mal text to Is only) as being the more ' important ' prophet or as heading the fifteen prophets in the Jewish canon of the time (SB 1, 1029 f. ; for this opinion *cf.* Knabenbauer, Buzy, Bover, WV, KNT, etc.). If the reminiscence of Jer seem **e** too slight to make this view acceptable, it still does not follow that formal error is to be attributed to the evangelist himself. Indeed, according to Lagrange, *Mt*, 515, it is ' psychologically improbable ' that the evangelist, who appears to have adjusted a Hebrew text which he had in front of him, could have made such a mistake. From purely rational considerations, therefore, it is not improbable that the name of the prophet was inserted by an early copyist misled by the faint echoes of Jer. It has been recently suggested (G. Courtade, S.J., DBV(S) 4, 542) that, in any hypothesis, the principle of inerrancy remains untouched since the mind of the evangelist (?) is not formally to teach the derivation of the prophecy from Jeremias, he merely uses the name ' Jeremias ' *en passant* ' without guaranteeing its exactitude '. Augustine's explanation, PL 34, 1175, is not dissimilar : he

721e concedes that the use of the name may have been an initial inadvertence of the evangelist which, however, subserved the purpose of the Holy Spirit who wished to inculcate the unity of the prophets. In this case, the categoric statement of the inspired writer which is guaranteed by inspiration is : ' It was said by one of the prophets ' ; to this he adds, equivalently : ' by Jeremias, I think '.

f **11-26 Jesus before Pilate** (Mk 15:2-15 ; Lk 23:2-5, 18:25 ; Jn 18:28-40 ; 19:1-15)—The scene is Pilate's praetorium, the residence of the commander-in-chief with adjoining barracks. In this year it was apparently established not in the palace of Archelaus, the dispossessed Herodian, but in the Antonia ; *cf*. 2, § 721*a*. Jn 19:13 names the place of judgement ' Lithostrotos ' ' paved place ' and ' Gabbatha ' ' eminence '. The terms admirably fit the recently excavated court attached to the Antonia : it is a paved space more than 50 yards square and occupies the highest point of the city's eastern side ; *cf*. Jn 19:13, note. **11-14.** The interview takes place on some terrace of the Antonia looking on the street since the Jewish leaders are present but do not enter the building, Jn 18:28. The accusation is a political one (the ' tribute ' question ; *cf*. Lk 23:2) prejudicing the title ' king of the Jews ' to which, however, our Lord does not refuse claim (' Thou sayest it ', *cf*. 26:64, note). John's fuller account, 18:33-38, explains how Pilate, despite the claim to kingship, remains unconvinced of our Lord's guilt —a kingdom of ' truth ' (whatever that be ! *cf*. Jn 18:38) is not a political entity within Pilate's competence. Our Lord answered none of the accusa-

g tions ; calumny's best answer is silence. **15-18.** Pilate is impressed and seeks to apply the Roman *abolitio* (suspension of criminal proceedings) in our Lord's favour. Such a concession was made on certain festal occasions (κατὰ δὲ ἑορτὴν) in the provinces (*cf*. the papyrus of A.D. 80 for a similar occurrence in Egypt, *Papiri Fiorentini* 1, Milan 1906, 113). Pilate offers the one alternative (there were others possible, *cf*. Mk 15:7) of the murderer Barabbas (' Jesus Barabbas ' is a probable reading ; *cf*. Vaganay, *Textual Criticism of the New Testament*, London 1937, 193-6). The contrast, he thinks, will decide the case in favour of Jesus Christ. He appeals to the people because he has been informed, reliably enough, that the cause of our Lord's arrest was precisely the leaders' envy of his popularity with them. **19.** (Mt only). For the evangelist the incident of Pilate's wife (Claudia Procula by name according to the apocryphal gospels) underlines the malice of Israel —a pagan woman pleads the cause of Jesus against his own people. For Pilate it confirms his own uneasy wonder by thickening the atmosphere of mystery. For the Jewish leaders it provides an opportunity of

h organizing their supporters. **20-23.** The modern technique of mob-management shows how a multitude, even well-disposed, can yield to a vociferous and violent minority—moreover, Barabbas was suffering for a nationalist cause, Mk 15:7, and would have noisy supporters among the crowd. **24-25.** By an action familiar to Jews, Deut 21:6, and Gentiles, Herod 1:33, Pilate disclaims responsibility, saying : ' *I am innocent of this blood* ' (WV). It is an act rather of private superstition than of public administration. This latter Pilate is as impotent to decline as the Jews are powerless to assume. It is before God and not before Tiberius that the Jews take responsibility upon themselves and their descendants. **26.** Mt omits Pilate's further attempt to release our Lord after the scourging, Jn 19:4-15. The scourge was normally the prelude of the cross. Its leathern thongs usually carried pieces of bone and metal. The naked victim's hands were tied to a low column ; this bent position made the executioner's work easier and more efficient. In Roman practice the number of blows was limited only by the endurance or taste of the executioner. It was not uncommon for victims to die under the lash.

722a **27-30 The Mockery** (Mk 15:16-20 ; *cf*. Jn 19:2-3)— **27-28.** Our Lord is brought from the paved outer court

into the praetorium properly so called, *i.e*. to an inner court of the Antonia, Mk 15:16, which appears to be that in which the barracks were placed. Only the off-duty men of the *cohort* would be present (the ' cohort ', σπεῖρα—there were five in Judaea, one permanently resident in the Antonia—was larger in the minor provinces of the empire than the ' cohort ' which formed part of a ' legion ' ; it mustered sometimes nearly one thousand men). Our Lord has evidently been allowed to dress after the scourging, but now his outer garments at least are replaced by a crimson military cloak symbolizing ironically the imperial purple, Mk 15:17. **29-30.** The emphasis is on the ridicule rather than on the pain of the crowning. The ' thorn ' is, with some probability, the *poterium spinosum* which abounds about Jerusalem and was used then, as now, for firewood ; its spikes are slender. The form of the ' crown ' may have been that of a head-dress, as in the 2nd cent. representation in the Catacomb of Praetextatus, though the phrase πλέξαντες στέφανον suggests a fillet ; but *cf*. RB 42 (1933) 230-4 ; DAC 5, 4141 ; 1150. The earliest (5th cent.) representations of the Crucified show him without the crown ; it was perhaps laid aside with the reed (his ' sceptre ').

31-32 The Way to Calvary (Mk 15:21 ; Lk 23:26-32 ; Jn 19:17*a*)—**31.** Jesus carried his own cross, Jn 19:17, from the praetorium, **31**, until the procession left the town, **32**. The shape of this cross is not certainly known. The X, Y and T forms were in use, but in our Lord's case the T-shape with upward prolongation of the vertical (*crux immissa*) is witnessed by the best authority (Irenaeus, *Adv. Haer.* 2, 24, 4) and leaves room for an inscription ' over his head ', **37**. The transverse beam was called the *patibulum* and, in Rome at least, it was customary for the criminal to carry only this beam. This may be true of our Lord ; the σταυρός of Jn 19:17 may mean *patibulum* only. In the middle of the upright was usually a small block to serve as a seat and so take some weight from the hands which were sometimes bound to the *patibulum*, but usually nailed, as in our Lord's case ; *cf*. Jn 20:25, 27 ; Lk 24:39. In Christian art the seat has become a foot-support, doubtless for aesthetic reasons. There is no reason to think that our Lord's feet were nailed together : all representations of the Crucified up to the 12th cent. show them nailed separately. (But *cf*. Barnes, The Holy Shroud of Turin, London 1934.) **32.** Simon, born in Cyrene (N. Africa ; a town with a large Jewish colony) is conscripted (ἀγγαρεύω, *i.e*. to press into governmental service) into carrying the cross in place of our Lord (*cf*. Lk 23:26, note) who seems to have collapsed.

33-34 Crucifixion and Derision (Mk 15:22-32 ; Lk 23:33-43 ; Jn 19:17*b*-27)—**33.** Golgotha (simplified form of Aramaic *gulgoltā* ' skull ' ; Latin ' calvaria ') was the name for the mound, rising about 15 ft. from the surrounding soil, just outside the city-walls (*cf*. Vincent & Abel, *Jérusalem Nouvelle*, 89-300) and about half a mile from the Antonia. **34.** It was the custom for pious women (SB 1, 1037 f.) to administer narcotics to condemned criminals. The ' gall ' (χολή) of Mt is used, as in LXX, in a general sense : bitter drug (more precisely ' myrrh ', *cf*. Mk 15:23). Our Lord refuses the alleviation. **35.** The soldiers take their customary perquisite of the criminal's possessions, but Mt (strangely) does not call attention to this fulfilment of Ps 21(22), 19, though the text has been imported into Mt by some few MSS from Jn 19:24 and is found in Vg and DV. **37.** The exact form of the inscription is not known (four different forms are found in the four gospels) but would certainly include the name of the crucified and the charge (' cause ') : Jesus, the ' king of the Jews ' ; this proves too laconic for the chief priests' liking. **38.** The episode of the *brigands* (λῃσταί), like the gesture and words of the passers-by and the mockery of the priests are all verbally reminiscent of OT passages (Is 53:12, *cf*. Lk 22:37 ; Ps 21[22], 8 ; Wisd 2:13, 18 ; Ps 21[22], 9) but in no case does Mt remark the fact. **39-40.** Criminals were usually crucified by the roadside for a warning. The passers-by *railed at*

22c *him, tossing their heads* (WV), *i.e.* in derision ('Vah', οὐά, is a cry of ironic admiration 'Ha!'; it is absent from the Greek text of Mt but present in Mk 15:29). **41-44.** Representatives of the Sanhedrin are there to see their work carried to its conclusion. Unlike the vulgar public they do not hurl their taunts directly at the Crucified. They (or Mt, interpreting their thoughts) use the words by which the sufferer is mocked in Ps 21 (22), 9.

d XXVII 45-50 Death (Mk 15:33-37; Lk 23:44-46; Jn 19:28-30)—**45.** From noon until three in the afternoon darkness covers Jerusalem and its horizon (not 'the whole inhabited earth'—ἐπὶ πᾶσαν τὴν οἰκουμένην, but 'the whole land'—ἐπὶ πᾶσαν τὴν γῆν, *cf.* Ex 10:22; Prat 2, 409). It is clear that the evangelist thinks of a miraculous event; possibly the frequent April 'black sirocco' occurred in this year with miraculous intensity (Pirot, *La Sainte Bible*, ix, Paris 1946, 596). The miracle should have reminded the scribes of the darkness associated with the great day of God's judgement in the prophetic writings (Jl 2:10; Am 8:9; Is 13:10; Jer 15:9). **46.** *'Elî 'Elî lᵉmāh šᵉbaqtānî* are the opening words in Aramaic (*'Elî* is the Hebrew form also) of Ps 21(22). Doubtless our Lord continues the psalm in silence. The fact that the words are a quotation removes the dogmatic difficulty. The psalm is not a cry of despair but, on the contrary, a hymn of supreme confidence in God despite profound suffering. As in our Lord's case the divine 'forsaking' in the psalm is no more than a poetical expression of acute physical and mental pain to which God has 'abandoned' the psalmist without, however, having 'turned his face away', Ps 21(22), 2, 25. In our Lord's mouth, indeed, the words are not even a complaint because his intention is simply to show that the fruitful martyrdom of the innocent psalmist was a shadow of his own; *cf.* NRT 70 (1948) 137-49. It is worth noting, however, that the mental shock that the words, coming from the God-man, must produce, powerfully argues the fidelity of the evangelists who ran this risk in the interests of **e** honest report. It will be observed that in our explanation of this quotation on our Lord's lips the question does not formally arise of his enjoyment of the beatific vision even during the passion (the common opinion of theologians). That the uninterrupted beatific vision in the highest faculty of the soul is compatible with bodily, mental and even spiritual suffering (*e.g.* the uselessness of his passion for some souls) becomes clear to our intellect, not to our imagination, if we remember that the formal object of the vision and the formal object of the suffering are different. Compare the simultaneous joy and sorrow of a parent whose son leaves home to become a priest. (And *cf.* § 720d.) **47-49.** Misunderstanding (deliberately?) the *'Elî*, articulated with the difficulty of a dying man, the Jews, 47, 49, think or affect to think that this 'Messias' may have his precursor-Elias at hand; 17:10 ff., notes. A soldier, moistening a sponge with the sour wine (*posca*) of his flask, places the sponge on the end of a long reed (or javelin? *cf.* Jn 19:29, note). He was moistening our Lord's lips with it (ἐπότιζεν); others, apparently Jews, adopting the Elias-jest, bid him to desist—not wishing to spoil the atmosphere of empty expectation. In Mk 15:36 the soldier, too, weakly makes his compassionate action part of the joke. **50.** At about three in the afternoon when, a few hundred yards away, the paschal lambs of the old rite were being slain in the temple, the Lamb of God died; *cf.* 1 Cor 5:7. His last cry was loud and clear. Lk 23:46 tells us what it was: 'Father, into thy hands I commend my spirit'.

51-54 Prodigies after the Death of Jesus (Mk 15:38-41; Lk 23:45b, 47-49)—**51.** The veil of the temple (ναός) may be the curtain of the inmost sanctuary, the Holy of Holies, of the appearance of which nothing certain is known; or possibly the enormous and elaborate curtain to the outer sanctuary, the Holy Place; *cf.* Jos., BJ, 5, 5, 4. If the first, the priests, many of whom were converted, Ac 6:7, could verify and report the prodigy. The symbolism seems to favour this inner **722f** veil, Heb 10:20 f.; *cf.* 9:7, 25. If God used secondary causes (Mt does not say) we may possibly think of the gale, miraculous now in intensity, that dissipates the black sirocco of spring, 27:45, note. **52-53.** The earth, too, was torn (Mt, alone, mentions the earthquake) and opened some of the rock-tombs: vertical earthquake-fissures are still to be seen in the rock of Calvary (Vincent & Abel, *Jérusalem*, 2, 186). It seems probable that the bodily resurrection and apparition of many dead just ones did not occur until after our Lord's resurrection (*cf.* 1 Cor 15:20-23) and that it is mentioned here because the earthquake prepared their exit from the tombs. **54.** The manner of our Lord's death, the darkness, the earthquake, all impress the pagan guards. They confess the justice of the title 'Son of God' with which they had heard Christ's foes ironically taunt him, 27:40, 43, however little they may realize all this title holds.

55-56 The Holy Women (Mk 15:40-41; Lk 23:49)— **g** The Galilean women stood watching from some distance: Mary of Magdala (el-Mejdel on the lakeside *c* 3 m. N. of Tiberias) whom our Lord had exorcized, Lk 8:2; Mary, mother of James (the 'Less') and of Joseph, 13:53-54, note; the mother of the sons of Zebedee (20:20, note) probably the 'Salome' of Mk 15:40.

57-61 Burial (Mk 15:42-47; Lk 23:50-56; Jn **h** 19:38-42)—**57-58.** The sacred body had to be removed and buried before the first stars announced the beginning of the Sabbath, Jn 19:31. It would be about four o'clock in the afternoon when Joseph, sympathetic throughout to our Lord, Lk 23:51, approached Pilate to whom, as an influential member of the Sanhedrin, Mk 15:43, he would have access. He was of Arimathea (Ramathaim; *cf.* 1 Kg 1:1, 19 etc.) *c* 12 m. N. of Lydda. **59-61.** He had purchased a worthy linen shroud, Mk 15:46, and Nicodemus, Jn 3:1-15, had bought a quantity of spices, Jn 19:39, to place on the shroud and round the body. In the presence of the women, and doubtless with their help, they laid Jesus in Joseph's own unused tomb about fifty yards from the cross. The more well-to-do Jews cut the family tomb in the rock, usually on the side of a slope; a low entrance closed by a thick disc of stone led to the vestibule which in turn led to the tomb proper by a small communicating cavity. Joseph's tomb had one shelf on the right of the entrance, Mk 16:5, for the reception of the body. For a description of the contemporary tombs of Abu Gosh *cf.* RB 34 (1925) 275-9. The two Marys (56; *cf.* Mk 15:47) remained. Others of the holy women prepared spices for a further and less hurried anointing, Lk 24:1.

62-66 The Tomb-Guard (Mt only)—A night passes **i** —the night of Friday, the 'parasceve' or 'preparation-day' of the Sabbath. On the Saturday there is no formal meeting of the Sanhedrin (Mt does not mention 'ancients') but it occurs to a few of the priests and Pharisees that the dead 'impostor' promised his resurrection after three days; *cf.* 12:40. The disciples must be prevented from removing the body during these crucial three days. The first 'imposture'—our Lord's claim to Messiahship and more—had been effectively answered by crucifixion; the second (resurrection, possibly to be alleged by the disciples) would be more difficult to counter should the body be stolen. Pilate, who sounds tired of the whole affair, allows the Jews to use their supporting posse of Roman troops (*cf.* Jn 18:12) for the guardianship of the tomb. The stone is then joined to the surrounding rock, presumably by means of a tape and the official seal.

G. XXVIII 1-20 The Resurrection and after—The **723a** women see the angel and the empty tomb, 1-8; the Magdalen sees the risen Christ, 9-10; the tomb-guards are bribed into silence, 11-15; the Eleven meet our Lord in Galilee, 16-17, and from him they receive the universal mission, 18-20.

1-8 The Empty Tomb; the Angel (Mk 16:1-9; Lk 24:1-9; *cf.* Jn 20:1)—**1.** The sabbath-rest was

723a observed, Lk 23:56. When the Sabbath was over (ὀψὲ δὲ σαββάτων : *after the sabbath* ; WV) as the sky was lightening towards sunrise on ' the first day of the week ' (Sunday ; *cf.* SB 1, 1052) the women (Mk 16:1 ; Lk 24:10) including Mary the Magdalen and Mary the mother of James, 27:56, came to watch at the tomb (Mt) with a view, no doubt, to completing the hasty anointing of Friday, Mk 16:1, Lk 24:1. **2-4.** Before their arrival as it seems (2-4 are probably parenthetical) a considerable earth-tremor declared the advent of the angel in human form. His purpose was to declare the physical Resurrection of Christ and to confirm his message by the spectacle of the empty tomb. He therefore rolled away the stone not to enable the already risen Christ to emerge (*cf.* Jn 20:19, 26) but to allow the women to enter. Mt gives the impression that the angel was still seated on the stone when they arrived but that he preceded them into the tomb (ἐκάθητο, δεῦτε ἴδετε). Terror made the guards powerless to interfere ; it is probable that they made off citywards before the coming of the women since the angel and the women ignore them completely and there is no trace of their presence in Mk 16:1-8 or Lk 24:1-8 ; and see

b on Mt 28:11. **5-8.** But for the women (true seekers of *the crucified one*) there was no cause for such terror (' Fear not *you* '—emphatic). The Lord's promise was fulfilled ; *cf.* 16:21 ; 17:22 ; 20:19. Escorted by the angel they saw the empty tomb for themselves. The physical body had risen. Now they were to tell the disciples that the risen Christ would be found in Galilee. (7 is better punctuated thus : ' . . . say to his disciples : " He is risen and behold he will go before you into Galilee [will be there when you, his disciples, arrive] ; there you shall see him ". Lo, I have told you ', *i.e.* There, that is all ; Joüon). It is possible that the verb ' go before ' (προάγειν) is to be translated ' lead, conduct ' (Braun, *Jésus*, Paris 1947, 190-4) in which case Mt clearly supposes that our Lord appeared to the disciples in Judaea. But in any case it is Mt's plan to describe only the Galilean episode. By a kind of factual ' inclusion ' (§ 702), he presents Galilee as the starting-place of the universal mission as it had been the starting-place, 4:12-16, of the first, restricted preaching of the Kingdom. Hence he is careful, unlike Lk and Jn, to report the angel's message concerning the Galilean rendezvous and to reinforce it, 10, with our Lord's instruction to the same effect.

c 9-10 Magdalen and the Risen Christ (*cf.* Mk 16:9-11 ; Jn 20:11-18)—Some Catholic authors identify this apparition, the first mentioned by Mt, with the apparition to Magdalen alone, Jn 20:11-18. In this hypothesis Mt attributes to the women-group (as opposed to the ' brethren ' in 10 ; *i.e.* the disciples ; *cf.* 12:49) what happened to their single representative. Such a ' plural of category ' is perhaps not unfamiliar to Mt ; *cf.* 2:20 ; 24:8 ; 27:44 ; Levesque, RB 25 (1916) 13-16. The identification would also explain Lk 24:22-24 where it seems that the women had reported no more than the angel and the empty tomb. Other Catholic authors (*e.g.* Bover, SJ, *El Evangelio de San Mateo*, Barcelona 1946, 518-20) oppose the identification and explain (*cf.* Buzy, *Mt*, 384) that 9 refers to a second visit of the women (without Magdalen). Whatever the solution, it must take account of the extreme telescoping of Mt's last chapter.

d 11-15 The Guard bribed (Mt only)—As the women were still on their way, certain of the guard were in touch with the priests. It is probable that the guard had already left for the city before the women arrived at the tomb ; 28:2-4, note. The Gk tenses used do not contradict this suggestion (' whilst they [the women] were on their way [from the tomb] the guards *having reached* the city told . . .'). The situation of the guards is awkward : the true, supernatural, explanation of their discomfiture would be laughed at in a court-

martial. The priests, therefore, have no difficulty in **723** bribing them to suppress an explanation that would have been useless in any case. The main point of the priests' instruction was the alleged theft by the disciples. This the soldiers agreed to and this story became the current explanation in Jewish circles ; *cf.* 15 and Justin, *Contra Tryphonem*, 108. The ' sleep ' excuse is thrown out carelessly as a suggestion. It could be used only before the general public ; clearly if it came to an official inquiry (14 : ' if the case should be brought before the Governor ') sleeping on duty would be no adequate excuse. The priests undertake, in this case, to *bribe* in high places (for πείθω ' persuade ' in this sense, *cf.* 2 Mac 4:45 ; 10:20).

XXVIII 16-17 Galilee : Apparition to the Eleven e (Mk 16:15-18)—The Eleven remained in Jerusalem until the end of paschal week, Jn 20:26, when, naturally, they went back to their homes with the assurance, 7, 16, that they were not leaving the risen Christ in Jerusalem. Mt is aware of the fact (though, like the other evangelists, he does not report Christ's own words) that our Lord had indicated a particular ' mountain ' in Galilee. The ' mountain ' is doubtless the high ground above the Lake (as in 5:1 ; 14:23 ; 15:29)—perhaps, fittingly, the hill of the Discourse which inaugurated the Kingdom, 5:1. ' Some doubted ', says Mt. It is probable that he is simply recording a fact (mentioned by the other evangelists, Mk 16:11, 13, 14 ; Lk 24:11, 21 ff. ; Jn 20:25) without reference to this particular occasion. The reason may lie in the summary nature of Mt's final chapter (Buzy) or possibly the phrase is to be translated : ' they, *the very ones who had doubted*, adored ' ; *cf.* Abel, *Grammaire du Grec Biblique* (Paris 1927) 119.

18-20 The Universal Mission (Mk 16:15-18)—**18. f** The obedience unto death of the man-Christ has resulted in the Resurrection which constitutes his formal investiture as king of the kingdom of heaven and earth, *cf.* Phil 2:8 f. Sovereign powers were his before (11:27 ; *cf.* Jn 3:35), a necessary consequence of the Incarnation, but now the Son of Man has formally taken possession of his throne, Dan 7:14. The Resurrection inaugurates the new and worldwide epoch of the Kingdom. The Kingdom has come ' in power '. **19.** Consequently (οὖν) the old restriction of apostolic preaching, 10:5 f., is abrogated. Enrolment of disciples (μαθητεύσατε ; DV ' teach ye '), baptism, religious and moral instruction are for Gentiles also. The exact conditions of Gentile-reception will cause difficulty later (*cf.* Ac 15) but the principle is already clear. The rite of enrolment is baptism according to Mt (all MSS and versions) and Mk 16:16, and indeed the rigorous and universal practice of the early Church is explainable only by the historical fact of Christ's command. ' In the name of ' is not ' on the authority of ' (ἐν τῷ ὀνόματι ; *cf.* Ac 2:38 ; 10:48) but ' by way of consecration to ' (εἰς τὸ ὄνομα). By baptism ' the neophyte becomes the property, and therefore the *protégé*, of the person named '. It therefore seems probable (Prat 2, 567) that the Trinitarian formula was necessary for the efficacy of the rite, and it is attested early in the 2nd cent. (*Didache*, 7:1 ; Justin, *Apol.* 1:61). It is possible, however, that our Lord is not prescribing the exact formula to be used but describing the effects of the rite—consecration to the blessed Trinity ; *cf.* Lebreton, *History of the Dogma of the Trinity*, 1, 439. **20.** Faith and ritual are not sufficient. There are obligations of the moral order. ' In a few words our Lord initiates a regime hitherto unknown to the ancient peoples : a doctrine not only religious but, at the same time, moral ', Lagrange, *Mt*, 545. His precepts and his spirit are known to the Apostles who will, nevertheless, need the light and force of his presence in the hard days ahead. These will be with them until the era of the Messias on earth draws to its close. The promise has held good for two thousand years.

THE GOSPEL OF JESUS CHRIST ACCORDING TO
ST MARK

By J. A. O'FLYNN

Bibliography—*Catena in Marci Evangelium*, ed. Cramer (Oxonii 1840) ; Maldonatus, *Comm. in Quattuor Evangelistas*, Tom. 1 (Brixiae 1597) ; J. Knabenbauer, *Evang. sec. Marcum* (Paris 1894) ; M.-J. Lagrange, *Evangile selon saint Marc* (Paris 1947⁴) ; J. Huby, *Evangile selon saint Marc* (Paris 1929) ; Simon-Dorado, *Praelectiones Biblicae, Nov. Test.*, Vol. 1 (Turin 1947⁷) ; J. Kleist, *The Gospel of St Mark* (Milwaukee 1936) ; *C. H. Turner, *Marcan Usage*, JTS 25–9 (1924–8) ; *H. B. Swete, *The Gospel according to St Mark* (London 1913³) ; *W. C. Allen, *The Gospel according to St Mark* (London 1915) ; J. Schmid, *Das Evangelium nach Markus* (Regensburg, 1950²) ; Bonsirven, *Les Enseignements de Jésus-Christ* (Paris 1946).

Modern Importance of Gospel of St Mark—Until the 19th cent. the Gospel of Mark was rarely made the subject of extended commentaries such as were written on the other Gospels. The explanation for this neglect of the Second Gospel and apparent lack of interest in its narrative lies in the fact that Mark contains very little material which is not found also in the Gospels of Matthew and Luke, who give much additional information about the discourses and deeds of Christ. Only two miracles, 7:31–37 ; 8:22–26, one parable, 4:26–29, and the incidents recorded in 3:20 f. and 14:51 f. are peculiar to Mark ; in all, only some sixty verses of the Gospel are without parallels in the other Synoptics. In modern times, however, the Gospel of Mark has come to hold a foremost place in Gospel studies. Some have been particularly attracted to it by the vividness and realism with which scenes are depicted. But it is the critical study of the literary relations between the Synoptic Gospels which has been mainly responsible for focusing attention on Mark in the last century. Non-catholic critics are practically unanimous in holding that Mk was written before the other Synoptics, and that it was used as a source by the authors of the First and Third Gospels. It was formerly the general verdict of critics that Mark's narrative shows fewer traces of subsequent interpretation intermingled with the primitive record of Christ's Life and Teaching than do the other Gospels, and consequently, that Mk should be regarded as our most reliable source of information for the simple historical facts concerning the Person and Mission of Christ. That critical estimate of the historical worth of the Second Gospel has been called into question by more recent critics, especially by writers of the ' Form-criticism ' school. According to these, even Mk does not bring us into such immediate contact with the facts of Christ's life as was commonly supposed by earlier critics. The author of the Gospel is regarded as primarily a compiler or editor who has brought together scattered fragments of oral tradition and, with the aid of various editorial connecting phrases, fitted them into an artificial, chronological and geographical framework in which details of time and place are quite unhistorical. Supporters of this theory maintain that the fragments of oral tradition now loosely linked together in the Gospel were, for the most part, the creation of the Christian community. They are a reflexion of the faith and of the religious needs of the first Christians rather than an objective record of authentic sayings of Christ and the historical facts

of his Life, *cf.* 'The Gospels and non-Catholic Higher **724b** Criticism ', §§ 607*a–e*, 608*b–c*, 609*a–d*, 610–615.

External Evidence of Authorship—Against such denials **c** of Marcan authorship and refusal to recognize the organic unity and historical value of the Second Gospel, and also against critics who contend that the Gospel embodies one or more earlier written documents (Proto-Mark etc.) or that it is the result of successive rehandlings of a basic document, we have clear evidence, both external and internal, that the Gospel is the work of a single author, Mark, that it faithfully reproduces the oral catechesis of St Peter and should, therefore, be accepted as a reliable source within the limits of the author's purpose. The tradition of the early Church is unanimous in declaring that Mark, the disciple and interpreter of St Peter, was the author of the Second Gospel. Evidence of this tradition is to be found not merely in the explicit assertions of the fathers and ecclesiastical writers, but also in the quotations and allusions occurring in their writings, in the use of the Gospel by heretics, and in the title ' according to Mark ' attached to the Gospel in the manuscripts and early versions. The internal evidence of the Gospel itself provides remarkable confirmation of the external testimony ; *cf.* ' Replies of the Biblical Commission ', § 50*h*.

The oldest surviving testimony to Marcan authorship **d** is that of Papias, who wrote a work entitled *Expositions of the Oracles of the Lord*, about A.D. 125. His words, which have been preserved by Eusebius (*H. E.* 3, 39, 15), are as follows : ' And this the Elder used to say : Mark, having been the interpreter of Peter, wrote accurately, though not in order, all that he remembered of the things said or done by the Lord. For he had neither heard the Lord nor been his follower, but afterwards, as I said, he was the follower of Peter, who gave his instructions as circumstances demanded, but not as one giving an orderly account of the words of the Lord. So that Mark was not at fault in writing certain things as he remembered them. For he was concerned with only one thing, not to omit anything of the things he had heard, and not to record any untruth in regard to them '. Papias here quotes, at least in the first sentence of the passage, the statement of an Elder (presbyter) called John. Whether the Elder was John the Apostle or, as many authors hold, a disciple who had known the Apostles, his statement takes us back to the 1st cent. and to the contemporaries of Mark. The main points of the passage are that Mark, who was a disciple and interpreter of Peter, put the oral catechesis of Peter into writing, and that the lack of ' order ' in the work was due to its dependence on Peter's preaching. Apparently some had found fault with Mark's work because it lacked ' order ' ; probably it was being compared unfavourably with the Gospel of Matthew in which the material is arranged in a systematic, logical order (*cf.* Prat, *Jésus-Christ*, 1, 17). In reply to this criticism, Papias points to the fact that Mark's purpose in writing was simply to reproduce faithfully the teaching of Peter. Papias is undoubtedly speaking of the canonical Gospel of Mark. The ancient writers who were acquainted with the work of Papias never mention any other Gospel of Mark, and the internal evidence of the Second Gospel is in complete harmony with what Papias says of the absence of ' order ' in Mark's work and its close dependence on St Peter.

724e In later writers we find similar unhesitating affirmations of the close relationship between Mark and Peter and the dependence of the Second Gospel on Peter's preaching. St Justin, who wrote in Rome about A.D. 150, makes clear his conviction that Mark's Gospel depends on Peter, though he does not name the author. Dealing with the change of Simon's name to 'Peter' and the title 'Boanerges' given to James and John, he gives the *Memoirs of Peter* as the source in which these points are found (*Dial. c. Tryph.* 106). Actually the only passage in which the matters in question are mentioned together is Mk 3:16 f. (*cf.* Vaganay, *L'Evangile de Pierre*, 151 f.). No other Evangelist tells us that the sons of Zebedee were called 'Boanerges'. From Irenaeus (†A.D. 202) we have the statement that after the death of Peter and Paul 'Mark, Peter's disciple and interpreter, himself also left us in writing the preaching of Peter' (*Adv. Haer.* 3,1,1). Clement of Alexandria says : 'When Peter had publicly preached the word in Rome and promulgated the Gospel under the inspiration of the Spirit, many of those who were there besought Mark, as one who had long been a companion of Peter and remembered his words, to write down what he had said. Mark did this and gave the Gospel to those who had asked for it. When Peter learned of it he did nothing either to hinder or to encourage it' (in Eus. *H. E.* 6, 14, 6). Tertullian (†220), Origen (†254), Jerome (†420) and other early writers all stress the relationship of Mark's Gospel to the oral catechesis of St Peter.

f Internal Evidence—When we turn to the Gospel itself we find a number of features which confirm the external testimony. The general scheme of the Gospel, beginning with the mission of John the Baptist and continuing till the Ascension, corresponds with Peter's address at the reception of the Gentile Cornelius into the Church, Ac 10:34–43, and with the conditions which Peter laid down when a successor to Judas was about to be appointed, Ac 1:22. Miracles, as a divine seal on Christ's mission, are given particular prominence in Mark ; *cf.* Ac 2:22 ; 10:38. It is noteworthy that Peter stands out from the group of disciples who were in close touch with Christ. He is mentioned by name on four occasions (1:36, 11:21 ; 13:3 ; 16:7), when the other Synoptics do not mention him ; after a brief account of the mission of John the Baptist and the Temptation of Christ, Mark tells of the call of Peter and Andrew, 1:16 ; Peter is first in the list of the Apostles, 3:16, and first of the three who were present at the raising of the daughter of Jairus, 5:37, at the Transfiguration, 9:2, and at the Agony, 14:33 ; he answers on behalf of all at Caesarea Philippi, 8:29 ; he calls Christ's attention to the withered fig-tree, 11:21 ; after the Resurrection he is mentioned specially by the Angel in the instructions given to the women, 16:7. There is nothing, however, to suggest that the author wished to present Peter in a particularly favourable light. On the contrary, we are told of the stern rebuke which he received when he protested against the prediction that Christ should suffer, 8:33 ; his denials of Christ are recorded faithfully, 14:66–72, but there is no mention of his walking on the waters, Mt 14:29, of the praise he received from Christ when he was promised the Primacy, Mt 16:18 ff., or of the incident of the coin with which to pay the temple-tax for Jesus and Peter, Mt 17:24 ff. These latter incidents did particular honour to Peter, and their omission from Mark's Gospel is to be explained by the fact that Peter, in his humility, did not dwell on **g** them in his preaching. Although tradition states clearly that Mark was not an immediate disciple of Christ, many incidents in the Gospel are described so vividly and with such realistic detail as to suggest the narrative of an eyewitness. Mark's Gospel is considerably shorter than Mt or Lk, but in narratives which are common to all three Synoptics Mark usually gives more details than do the others ; *cf.* 2:1–12 ; 5:1–20, 21–43 ; 9:13–28, and parall. in Mt and Lk. A notable characteristic of Mark's style is the use of an indefinite plural in describing the movements of Christ and the disciples, this being followed immediately **72** by a verb in the singular referring to Christ alone ; *cf.* 1:21 ; 5:1, 38 ; 8:22. This peculiarity of style is readily intelligible if we suppose that Mark is reporting the words of an eyewitness who said, *e.g.* 'we came to Capharnaum . . . and *he* (Christ) entered the synagogue and taught', 1:21 ; *cf.* C. H. Turner, JTS 26 (1925), 225 ff. ; Chapman, *Matthew, Mark and Luke*, 61 f. Mark's narrative is direct, simple and graphic, but these qualities cannot be attributed to the literary skill of the author. His style lacks variety and the range of his vocabulary is limited ; frequent redundancies of expression, lack of grammatical sequence and omission of connecting particles suggest everyday speech rather than literary art. The unimportant details which make the narrative so realistic were not inserted for literary effect, but simply because they were part of what Mark had heard from Peter, the eye-witness who remembered vividly the scenes at which he had been present. Apart from some minor variations, the distinctive stylistic and linguistic features are to be found uniformly throughout the whole Gospel, except in 16:9–20. This must be regarded as a definite pointer to the unity of authorship of the Gospel. By way of summary of the internal evidence it can be said that many features of the Gospel positively confirm the external testimony to its authorship, and that there is nothing incompatible with the traditional view. Most non-Catholic critics support the Marcan authorship.

Life of St Mark—Tradition stresses particularly the **7** close relations between Mark and St Peter, but in the passages of the NT which refer to Mark, and which actually furnish most of our information about his life, his relations with Paul and Barnabas are much more prominent. Only two passages, 1 Pet 5:13 ; Ac 12:12, mention or imply close association between Peter and a disciple called Mark. This is significant as an indication that the tradition of Marcan authorship of the Second Gospel and its dependence on Peter is not merely a conclusion derived from the evidence of the NT. Several passages of Ac and the Pauline Epistles refer to a disciple who is sometimes called 'John', Ac 13:5, 13, sometimes 'John who is surnamed Mark', 12:12, 25 ; 15:37 f., sometimes 'Mark', Ac 15:39 ; Col 4:10 ; Phm 24 ; 2 Tim 4:11. In Ac it is clearly the same person who is sometimes given his Hebrew name John, and on other occasions, the Roman surname Mark. It was not unusual at the time to have two names ; *cf.* Mk 2:13 ; 3:16. In Col 4:10 we are told that Mark was a cousin of Barnabas ; this information fits exactly with Ac 15:37–39 which shows that there was a bond between Mark and Barnabas. Mark was the son of a woman called Mary to whose house Peter came when he was released from prison by an angel, Ac 12:12. The house was a meeting-place of the Christians. Peter was evidently known to the household, and could count on their attachment to himself. Mark must, therefore, have been known to Peter. It is probable that, with other members of his family, he had been baptized by the Apostle ; this may be the reason why Peter calls him 'my son', 1 Pet 5:13. About the time, apparently, of Peter's escape from prison (A.D. 41) Paul and Barnabas came to Jerusalem with the assistance contributed by the Christians of Antioch, Ac 11:29 f., and on their return they took Mark with them. When they set out on the first **b** missionary journey (*c* A.D. 45) Mark accompanied them as an assistant and remained with them until they reached Perge in Pamphylia. There, for reasons which are unknown, Mark separated from Paul and Barnabas and returned to Jerusalem, Ac 13:5, 13. Paul was so seriously displeased by his conduct that when it was proposed by Barnabas that Mark should rejoin them on the second missionary journey (*c* A.D. 50), Paul refused to take him. The result of this dissension was that Barnabas took Mark and revisited Cyprus, while Paul was accompanied by Silas in revisiting the other districts which they had evangelized, Ac 15:36–41. For some ten years after this the NT is silent about

b Mark. It was probably in this period that Mark became the follower and interpreter of Peter. The stern attitude which Paul had adopted towards Mark did not cause permanent estrangement. We find Mark was in Rome when Paul was first imprisoned there (A.D. 61–3). Together with two other disciples of Jewish origin he was praised by Paul as a fellow-worker for the kingdom of God who had been a comfort to him. Paul also refers to a proposed visit of Mark to the church of Colossae, Col 4:10 f., Phm 24. It was probably about this time that Peter wrote from Rome his first Epistle, in which he refers to Mark as ' my son ', 1 Pet 5:13. The fact that Peter sends greetings from Mark to the Christians of Pontus, Galatia, Cappadocia, Asia and Bithynia suggests that Mark was known in these districts, presumably because he had taken part in evangelizing them. During Paul's second Roman captivity (A.D. 66–7) he wrote to Timothy, who apparently was at Ephesus, instructing him to come and to bring Mark ' for he is useful to me for the ministry ', 2 Tim 4:11. We have no certain information of other events of the life of Mark. The tradition that he was one of the seventy-two disciples contradicts the testimony of Papias. Eusebius and Jerome record a tradition that he was the founder of the church of Alexandria. Many exegetes are of opinion that Mark was the young man in Mk 14:51 f.

c **Destination of the Gospel**—The statements of Clement of Alexandria and other early writers that Mark put Peter's oral catechesis into writing for the Christians of Rome is borne out by the evidence of the Gospel itself. It is clear that Mark did not write for Christians of Jewish origin ; his Gospel is silent about the Mosaic Law and its relation to the NT economy ; unlike Mt, it rarely points to the fulfilment of the OT prophecies, 1:2 1. ; 15:28 ; very little of Christ's denunciation of the scribes is recorded, 12:38–40 ; Jewish customs are explained for the benefit of readers, 7:3 f. ; Aramaic words and expressions are translated, 3:17 ; 5:41 ; 7:11, 34 ; 9:43 ; 14:36 ; 15:22, 34 ; we are told that the Jordan is a river, 1:5, that Mt Olivet stands over against the temple, 13:3, that the Parasceve is the day before the Sabbath, 15:42. This omission of matters of special interest to Jews, and the addition of information superfluous even for those Jews who lived outside Palestine, show that the Gospel, like the instructions of Peter which it reproduced, was intended primarily for Christians of Gentile origin. It has also been noted that Latinisms occur in the Greek of Mark (cf. 2:23 ; 10:33 ; 11:32 ; 14:65 ; 15:15, 19), and that a number of borrowed Latin words are used, e.g. *legion*, 5:9, *speculator*, 6:27, *denarius*, 6:37, *sextarius*, 7:4, *census*, 12:14, *praetorium*, 15:16, *centurion*, 15:39, 44. Specially notable is 12:42 where we are given the Roman equivalent of Greek coinage. It is natural to think that Rufus, the son of Simon of Cyrene, 15:21, who obviously was known to the readers of the Gospel, is the Rufus to whom Paul sends greetings at Rome, Rom 16:13. All these features of the Gospel are readily intelligible in the traditional view that Mark wrote Peter's instructions for the Christians of Rome.

d **Place and Time of Composition**—The testimony of Clement of Alexandria, Jerome and other early sources that Mark wrote his Gospel in Rome finds support in the internal evidence ; cf. § 725c. Chrysostom, PG 57, 17, states as hearsay the opinion that the Gospel was written in Egypt, but this is improbable. As to the time of composition of Mark, opinion is divided. The Biblical Commission, § 50m, has rejected the view that the Gospel was written after the destruction of Jerusalem in A.D. 70. In actual fact, there is nothing in the Gospel to indicate that Jerusalem had been destroyed, or even that the revolt of A.D. 66, which led to the final catastrophe, had begun when the Gospel was written. On the contrary, the manner of reference to the ' loaves of proposition ', 2:26, and, in particular, certain expressions in the eschatological discourse, ch 13, clearly imply that the city and temple were still standing when Mark wrote. Some Catholic writers hold that

the Gospel was written as early as A.D. 42–5. But the **725d** majority nowadays favours the view that it was written in the period A.D. 53–63. This view accords with the known facts of Mark's life and with the evidence of tradition concerning the order of composition of the Synoptic Gospels. It does not seem likely that Mark could have been the companion and interpreter of Peter in Rome before c A.D. 53, cf. §725b. Consequently, the composition of the Gospel cannot be placed before that time, and the latest date is fixed by its relation to the Gospel of Luke. Modern critics agree with ancient tradition in maintaining that Mark's Gospel was written before the Third Gospel. Now Luke wrote his Gospel before Ac, which was composed towards the end of Paul's first Roman captivity, c A.D. 63 ; see § 50n. The statement of Irenaeus that ' after their [Peter and Paul's] death, Mark . . . left us in writing the preaching of Peter ' constitutes a difficulty against this view, as it is generally accepted that Peter's martyrdom did not take place before A.D. 64. Various solutions of this difficulty have been propounded. Probably Irenaeus was less concerned with the exact time of composition of Mark's Gospel than with its authority as the continuation of the preaching of Peter.

Canonicity and Authenticity of Mk 16:9-20—The **726a** Biblical Commission, § 50i, has declared that the reasons adduced by critics to show that the last twelve verses of Mk were not written by Mark do not justify the assertion that they are not to be accepted as canonical and inspired, nor do they *demonstrate* that Mark was not the author. For Catholics the canonicity of Mk 16:9–20 is not open to doubt, as the passage fulfils the conditions laid down by the Council of Trent in the decree on the Canon of Scripture, EB 409. It was at all times accepted by the Church as inspired and forms part of the Latin Vulgate. The question of literary authenticity, *i.e.* whether Mark was the author, is a distinct problem from that of canonicity and inspiration. In the MSS and patristic writings we find evidence of four different forms of ending to the Gospel. (1) The Gospel ends at 16:8 in the Gk codices *Vaticanus* and *Sinaiticus*, in one Syriac MS (*syr-sin*) and in some MSS of the Coptic and Armenian versions. Both Eusebius and Jerome state that 16:9–20 was missing from many Gk MSS. (2) A Short Conclusion. One MS (*k*) of the Old Latin version introduces after 16:8 the words ' They recounted briefly to the companions of Peter the things which had been commanded them. After this Jesus appeared and through them sent from East to West the holy and incorruptible preaching of eternal salvation '. This short ending is found together with the canonical conclusion in a few Gk MSS and in some MSS of the Coptic and Syriac versions. (3) The Freer-Logion. In the Gk codex W(ashington) a fairly long passage, beginning with the words, ' But they declared themselves, saying, " This age of iniquity and incredulity is under the domination of Satan " ', is inserted after 16:14. Jerome knew of Gk codices which included this passage. (4) The Canonical Conclusion. This is **b** found in all Gk MSS except *Vaticanus* and *Sinaiticus* ; it is included in all Vg MSS and in all MSS of the Old Latin version except *k* ; it is also found in the Syriac, Coptic and other early versions, with the exception of the MSS already mentioned. Justin, Irenaeus, Tatian, Epiphanius and Chrysostom were acquainted with it. Ambrose, Augustine and later Latin writers also have this passage. This external evidence is, on the whole, strongly in favour of the authenticity of the canonical conclusion. Furthermore, it is highly improbable that the Gospel originally ended at 16:8 with the abrupt final phrase ' for they were afraid '. At the same time, the variation in the manuscript and patristic testimony, taken in conjunction with the internal evidence of 16:9–20, suggests that the present final section is not the *exact* original ending. There is a break in the continuity of the narrative between 16:1–8 and the final section, which is not written in the usual style of Mark ; cf. on 16:9–20. It has been suggested that Mark left the Gospel unfinished at first, or that the

726b original conclusion was lost (*cf.* C. H. Roberts, JTS 40 (1939) 253–7), and that Mark himself later supplied the present canonical conclusion. But the lack of continuity and change of style militate against the view that Mark wrote the section as it stands. Some authors favour the opinion that when the original ending was lost the present conclusion was added by another inspired writer. In an Armenian MS of the 10th cent. the note ' of the presbyter Ariston ' is written in before 9–20. Possibly the opinion which is least open to objection is that when the original ending was lost, the canonical conclusion was supplied from memory, and by reference to the other Gospels, by a contemporary who had known the original. This would account for the change of style and lack of continuity.

c **Purpose and Teaching**—Mark's primary purpose in writing his account of ' the sayings and deeds of the Lord ' was to provide the Christians of Rome with a faithful record of the teaching of St Peter. The Gospel is not directly apologetical in its aim or its method of treatment of the life of Christ. It was written for people who already believed that Jesus was Son of God and Saviour of mankind. Its purpose is not so much to prove that Jesus was the Messias and Son of God as to narrate the facts of Christ's ministry on earth as Mark had learned them from the preaching of Peter. As a consequence of Mark's dependence on instructions given by Peter to an audience which consisted mainly of Gentiles, we find that the Gospel stresses particularly the events of Christ's life which were calculated to impress a pagan audience. Unlike Mt, which constantly appeals to the fulfilment of the prophecies of the OT in order to prove to Jews that Jesus was the promised Messias, the Second Gospel gives prominence to those things which show forth the divinity of Christ. It is noteworthy that there is a striking similarity in theme between Mark's Gospel and the discourse delivered by Peter in the house of the Gentile Cornelius —' Jesus Christ, who is Lord of all . . . God anointed him with the Holy Spirit and with power, and he went about doing good and healing all that were oppressed by the devil, for God was with him. . . . And he commanded us to preach to the people and to testify that it is he who has been appointed by God to be judge of the living and of the dead ', Ac 10:34–43.

d The dominant theme of the Gospel is indicated in the opening words : ' The beginning of the Gospel of *Jesus Christ, the Son of God* '. This is the Evangelist's affirmation of his own belief in the divinity of Christ. In the Gospel, by a simple narrative of Christ's ministry, Mark puts before the reader facts which leave no room for doubt that the Christian faith in Jesus Christ, true God and Sovereign Lord, is well founded. The divine sonship of Christ is proclaimed by the Father at the Baptism, 1:11, and at the Transfiguration, 9:7 ; the demons who call Christ ' the Holy One of God ', 1:24, ' the Son of God ', 3:11, ' the Son of the Most High God ', 5:7, fear him and obey his command ; Christ is the Lord of the Sabbath, 2:28 ; he cured the paralytic in order to prove that he possessed the divine prerogative of forgiving sin, 2:10 ; in the Parable of the Wicked Husbandmen, 12:1–12, and in his reply to the high-priest, 14:62, Christ claimed to be God. The divine power of Christ is manifested in his miracles. Mark's Gospel has been called ' the Gospel of Miracles ' because of the high proportion of the narrative devoted to the miracles of Christ. Despite its brevity, the Second Gospel gives most of the miracles recorded in the other Synoptics, and adds two others, 7:31–37 ; 8:22–26. In the performance of miracles, whether healing the sick and afflicted, 1:31 ; 2:11 f. ; 5:28 f. ; 6:56 ; 7:32 ; 8:22 ; 10:52, or controlling the forces of nature, 4:39, 6:48, or in his complete mastery of the evil spirits ,1:24–27, 34 ; 3:11 f., 22–27 ; 5:1–15 ; 9:16–27, Christ acts as the Supreme ' Lord of all ', Ac 10:36. The reader of the Gospel must echo the words of the centurion, ' Indeed this man was the Son of God ', 15:39.

The portrait of Christ which emerges from the Gospel of Mark is not, however, exclusively that of the Son of God. There is no question of making the divinity stand out at the cost of obscuring his humanity. In fact, no other Evangelist gives more tangible proofs of the reality of the human nature which Christ had assumed at the Incarnation. Christ is ' the Son of Man ', 2:10 ; he eats, 2:16, and sleeps, 4:38, like ordinary mortals ; he feels compassion for the leper, 1:41, and for the crowds who have nothing to eat, 8:2 ; he is moved to anger and grief by the blindness of the Pharisees, 3:5 ; he wonders at the lack of faith of the people of Nazareth, 6:6 ; he is indignant with the disciples and shows his affection for the children, 10:14–16 ; in Gethsemani Christ is sorrowful and dismayed, and in his prayer that he might be spared the ordeal of the Passion he submits his own will completely to the will of the Father, 14:33–36. Mark is not the Evangelist of Christ's divinity merely. His is the Gospel of the Incarnate Son of God who ' came not to be ministered unto, but to minister and to give his life a redemption for many ', 10:45.

I 1–13 Preparation for the Public Ministry. **1–8 John the Baptist ;** *cf.* Mt 3:1–12 ; Lk 3:1–18 ; Jn 1:19–28—**1–4.** The exact construction of this passage is uncertain. Some take 1 as the title of the Gospel, while others connect it more closely with 2–3. It appears to be more satisfactory to treat 2–3 as a parenthesis and to link 1 with 4 ; *cf.* Turner JTS 26 (1925) 146. Mark means to declare that the mission of John the Baptist was the prelude to the Gospel and also the fulfilment of prophecy : ' Mark has made the preaching of John the commencement of the Gospel ' (Basil, *Adv. Eun.* II 15). **1a.** ' The Gospel of Jesus Christ ' here means not the written record of his life and teaching, but the good news (εὐαγγέλιον) of the coming of Jesus Christ, the glad tidings of salvation brought by Jesus, the promised Messias. **1b.** ' Son of God '. These words are missing in a few ancient witnesses to the text and are omitted in some critical editions, but the evidence does not justify the omission. In the Synoptic Gospels the title ' Son of God ' applied to Christ does not necessarily imply belief in his divinity ; *cf.* Lk 4:41. In the present context, however, it is rightly understood as an affirmation by Mark of the divinity of Christ, in which he clearly believed ; *cf.* § 726c. Mark is speaking here in his own name, not merely reporting the words of others. **2–3.** The prophetic passage in 2 is taken from Mal 3:1. Of the numerous solutions put forward to explain how the words of Malachias are included under the name of Isaias the most probable seems to be that this is an interpolation which has found its way into the present context from Mt 11:10 (Lk 7:27), where Christ applies these words to the Baptist. A scribe who was familiar with them in Mt or Lk may have included them here because of their application to the Baptist ; *cf.* Lagrange, *Saint Marc*, 3 f. **3.** In this passage from Is 40:3 the prophet announces the return of the exiles from Babylon and depicts Yahweh as about to lead them through the desert back to Palestine. The voice of a herald proclaims the coming of Yahweh so that a road may be prepared. This imagery is derived from the custom of sending a herald to proclaim the forthcoming visit of a king so that his subjects might put badly-kept roads into a proper state of repair. The words of Isaias are here applied to the Baptist. He is the herald who announces the coming of the Messias and urges the Jewish people to make due preparation to receive him. **4.** The baptism of John was a rite which symbolized the interior renovation which he preached as the fitting preparation for the Messias. By *penance* we are to understand not mere penitential exercises or regret for past sins but the true repentance (μετάνοια) which consists in a change which brings the mind and heart of man into conformity with the law of God. **5.** The preaching of the Baptist naturally aroused the hopes of the Jews and clearly evoked an enthusiastic response from many. The effect of John's words was heightened by his dress which recalled the prophet Elias, 4 Kg 1:8, and by the asceticism of his life. Locusts are still eaten by the Bedouin of the desert. Wild honey may have been either the honey collected by wild bees or the sap of certain shrubs. **7-8.** Some who heard the Baptist speak wondered whether he was not the Messias ; *cf*. Lk 3:15 ; Jn 1:19. In reply to such surmises John insisted that he was an inferior, unworthy to perform even the most menial tasks for the Messias. The baptism of the Messias would impart the Holy Spirit and is thus incomparably superior to the baptism of John, which was a merely preparatory rite, an external washing symbolic of interior conversion. Some writers understand the reference to the ' baptism with the Holy Ghost ' as a metaphor signifying the copious outpouring of the gifts of the Holy Spirit not merely in the Sacrament of Baptism but in the entire economy of salvation to be established by Christ ; *cf*. Ac 1:5. The prophets had spoken of the copious effusion of the Holy Spirit as a characteristic of the Messianic age, Is 44:3 ; Jl 2:28 ; Zach 12:10. **9-11 The Baptism of Jesus ;** *cf*. Mt 3:13-17 ; Lk 3:21 f. ; Jn 1:30-34—In coming to John to be baptized, Jesus, who had no need for repentance, gave an example of humility and showed his approval of the mission of the Baptist ; *cf*. 11:29-33. Moreover, it was the divine purpose that John, on the occasion of the baptism, should receive unquestionable evidence that Jesus was Messias so that he might make him known to the Jewish nation, Jn 1:30-34. The baptism marks the inauguration, with clear divine approval, of the public ministry of Jesus who is Messias and Son of God. **10.** The descent of the Spirit on Christ recalls instances from the OT, Jg 3:10 ; 6:34 ; Is 11:2 ; 42:1, where persons called to the performance of arduous tasks are given the special assistance of the Spirit. In the case of Christ the descent of the Spirit is a sign of the divine origin of his mission and a pledge of divine assistance. It is not to be understood as signifying an addition to the fullness of grace already possessed by Christ. Neither the descent of the Holy Ghost nor the voice of the Father brought about a change in the Person or dignity of Christ. These external manifestations were the public authentication of his divine mission and Messianic dignity. **11.** ' Beloved ' : ἀγαπητός. In classical Gk and in LXX, where it frequently translates the Heb. *yāḥîd*, this word has also the meaning ' only ', ' only-begotten '. Jesus is always well-pleasing to the Father because he is the eternal, only-begotten Son of God ; *cf*. Jn 1:18. Some early heretics interpreted the events at the baptism in the sense that the ' god-Messias ' then descended on the man Jesus of Nazareth, remaining with him till the Passion. Modern rationalists say that it was at the baptism that Jesus became conscious of his Messianic dignity and mission. He descended into the Jordan a mere man, but came up from the waters convinced that he was Messias. Such interpretations are a denial of the divinity of Christ and have no foundation in the narrative of Mark. Jesus did not become Messias or Son of God at the baptism, but it was then that God solemnly introduced the beloved Son in his Messianic role. **12 f. The Temptation of Jesus ;** *cf*. Mt 4:1-11 ; Lk 4:1-13—Mark gives only a summary account of this incident. Satan wished to discover whether Jesus was the Messias and, if possible, to lead him from the path of suffering which God had ordained as the course to be followed by the Redeemer. Our Lord allowed Satan to tempt him, ' for since he himself has suffered and been tempted he is able to assist those who are tempted ', Heb 2:18 ; ' For we have not a high-priest who cannot have compassion on our infirmities, but one tried in all things as we are, except sin ', Heb 4:15. Mark alone mentions the wild beasts whose presence suggests the desolate character of the region to which our Lord had retired.

I 14-III 19 Beginning of the Public Ministry.

14-15 The Return to Galilee ; *cf*. Mt 4:12 ; Lk 4:14*a* ; 727e Jn 4:1-3—John had been thrown into prison by Herod Antipas, the ruler of Galilee and Peraea, whom he had denounced because of his adulterous union with Herodias, Mk 6:17-29. This reference to the imprisonment of the Baptist indicates the time of Christ's return to Galilee, while Jn 4:1-3 shows that the growing enmity of the Jews had made it advisable for Jesus to withdraw from Judaea. In Galilee Jesus proclaimed the good news that the Messianic kingdom foretold by the prophets was at hand. The time appointed for the establishment of the kingdom was come and all are exhorted to prepare themselves for entry into it by repentance and acceptance of the glad tidings proclaimed by Christ. This call to repentance, first issued by the Baptist and repeated by Christ, was in itself a corrective to the popular misconceptions of the nature of Messianic salvation which proved such an obstacle to the success of Christ's ministry among the Jews. **16-20 The Call of the First Disciples ;** *cf*. Mt 4:18-22 ; Lk 5:1-11—It is uncertain whether the narrative of Lk refers to the same incident as that recorded by Mk and Mt. We know from Jn 1:35-42 that Peter, Andrew and John were already followers of Christ. Here, however, they receive a special call to become immediate disciples. The redeeming mission of Christ was not to end with his own death and departure from this earth. Hence he selected as intimate companions and witnesses of his life and teaching a number of disciples who, after his departure, would be the duly accredited teachers of the Gospel, bringing the knowledge of salvation to all men. **21-34 Preaching and Miracles in Capharnaum ;** *cf*. f Mt 4:13-17 ; 8:14-17 ; Lk 4:31-41—**21-22.** The synagogue meeting on the Sabbath, with its ritual of prayer and readings from the OT followed by an instruction, was a characteristic institution of post-exilic Judaism. The ruler of the synagogue had authority to invite a member of the congregation to address those present. In this way Christ was given many opportunities of making his message known to the Jews. Mark repeatedly draws attention to the astonishment of those who heard Christ speak, 1:27 ; 6:2 ; 11:18. Listeners were impressed by the fact that he spoke ' as one having power ', as a teacher qualified to speak and decide questions in his own authority, whereas the Scribes were accustomed to repeat the traditional views and constantly cited the opinions of the great rabbinical teachers of the past. **23.** The miraculous cure of the demoniac was a confirmation of the supernatural ' power ' which he possessed. **24a.** *What is to us and to thee ?* This idiomatic Hebrew phrase normally expresses dissent or protest of some kind ; *cf*. Jg 11:12 ; 2 Kg 16:10 ; 19:22 ; Mt 8:29 ; Mk 5:7 ; Lk 4:34 ; Jn 2:4. The demons had now come to realize that Christ was the ' stronger one '. Lk 11:22, who would overcome Satan, and they protest against his coming to destroy their power over men. **24b.** ' The Holy One of God '. Though there is no evidence that this was an accepted title of the Messias, it is possible that this was the sense intended by the demon ; *cf*. Lk 4:34, 41 ; Jn 6:69. Christ, of course, was ' the holy one of God ' in an altogether unique sense. **27.** ' *What is this ?* (*This is*) g *a new teaching with authority, and he commands even the unclean spirits and they obey him* '. The authority of Christ was evident not merely in the manner of his teaching but in the fact that the demons obeyed his command. **32.** ' After sunset ', when the Sabbath had ended, the sick and those possessed by demons were brought to Christ. According to the teaching of the Scribes, even the carrying of the sick was a violation of the law of sabbath rest. **34.** The demons knew now that Jesus was the Messias, Lk 4:41, but they were forbidden to proclaim this fact The chief reason for this ' injunction of silence ', Mk 3:12 ; 5:43 ; 7:36 ; Mt 8:4, is to be found in the prevalent misconceptions of the nature of the Messianic kingdom and of the role of the Messias. The Messianic

727g hope had at this time taken a strongly nationalistic and materialistic colouring. The Messias of popular expectation was a great national leader who would break the yoke of foreign domination. In these circumstances an open declaration of Christ's claims to crowds who were raised to a high pitch of enthusiasm by his teaching and miracles, would almost inevitably have led to a clash with the Roman authorities ; *cf.* Jn 6:15. It was necessary for Jesus to proceed with caution, winning the attention of the people by his marvellous doctrine and striking miracles, gradually instilling into their minds by means of parables and other instructions the true spiritual concept of the Messianic kingdom and bringing them to understand that the Messias foretold by the prophets was a suffering Messias. The reluctance of the Jews to abandon their erroneous notions of the kingdom is strikingly exemplified in the case of the disciples, Ac 1:6.

h 35-39 Preaching and Miracles throughout Galilee ; *cf.* Mt 4:23 ; Lk 4:42-44—**35.** It is possible that in departing from Capharnaum Jesus wished to allow the enthusiasm of the crowds, who were still ill-instructed about the nature of the kingdom, to moderate. He also wished, as the Evangelist tells us, to preach the message of salvation in other parts of Galilee. **36.** Mark is the only Evangelist to mention that Peter was among those who went to find Jesus—a characteristic Petrine touch in the second Gospel.

40-45 Healing of a Leper ; *cf.* Mt 8:1-4 ; Lk 5:12-16 —The Mosaic Law, Lev chh 13-14, gave extensive regulations concerning leprosy, including under this name a number of curable skin-diseases as well as the malady nowadays known by that name. The leper was compelled to lead an isolated life, wearing a special garb and giving notice of his approach by crying out ' Unclean ', in order to prevent contagion. Anyone who claimed a cure from leprosy was obliged to go before the priest who would verify the cure and, presumably, give some certificate of legal cleanliness. **43.** Our Lord cured the man but *he spoke sternly to him*, because he had violated the prudent regulations of the Mosaic Law in thus coming into contact with others who might receive the contagion. **44.** The man is commanded by Jesus to carry out the regulations laid down by the Law. ' For a testimony to them '. Some interpret this phrase in the sense that the priests, seeing that the man had been cured, would have clear testimony that Christ had worked a miracle. It is more probable, however, that the phrase refers to an official attestation of freedom from leprosy which the man would receive from the priest in order to reassure those who had previously known him as a leper.

728a II 1-12 Healing of a Paralytic ; *cf.* Mt 9:2-8 ; Lk 5:17-26—The dispute with the Scribes which took place on the occasion of this miracle was the first of a series of such conflicts, 2:1-3:6, and gives the earliest indication in Mk of the growing opposition to our Lord. Christ's miracles and teaching had aroused the enthusiasm of the people ; he had begun to form his own group of disciples and conducted his mission in complete independence of the traditional religious guides of the Jews. He thus incurred the suspicion of the Scribes, the recognized interpreters of the Law, who now watched him continually, and ultimately, together with the Pharisees and Herodians, determined to put him to death.

1-5. As soon as the crowds learned of Christ's return to Capharnaum they thronged to the house in which he was staying. The bed on which the paralytic was carried was a mat or pallet used as a stretcher. An outer stairs gave access to the flat roof of the house, and it was not difficult to make an opening, as it was a simple structure of tiles, flat stones and rubble resting on cross-beams. Christ rewarded this remarkable display of faith by remission of the sins of the paralytic. **9-10.** The cure of the paralytic and the forgiving of sin both equally demanded divine power. But it was easier to *claim* the power implied in the words, ' Thy sins are forgiven thee ' than to *claim* the power

to cure the paralytic. **The latter claim could easily** be put to the test. Consequently, the miraculous cure should be taken as proof that Christ, the Son of Man, had the power on earth to forgive sin. It is noteworthy that while all four Gospels give numerous examples of the use of the title **Son of Man** by Jesus to designate himself, they do not give any instance of its application to him by others. In the rest of the NT the title is found only three times, Ac 7:56 ; Apoc 1:13 ; 14:14. These passages appear to allude directly to the figure mentioned in the vision of Daniel, ' I beheld therefore in the vision of the night, and lo, *one like a son of man* came with the clouds of heaven ', Dan 7:13 ; *cf.* Lattey, *The Book of Daniel*, 83. In Hebrew and Aramaic usage ' son of man ' means ' a man ', ' a member of the human race ' ; *cf.* Ps 8:5. The common view of exegetes until the last century was that Jesus called himself ' the Son of Man ' in order to emphasize the human nature and lowly way of life which he had assumed at the Incarnation. Nowadays it is widely held by Catholics that the use of this title was part of the scheme of progressive revelation and instruction followed by Christ in his teaching. Because of the prevalent misconceptions about the Messias and his kingdom it would have been imprudent to claim publicly the title of Messias ; *cf.* 1:34. By designating himself as ' the Son of Man ' Jesus gradually prepared the way for the revelation of his identity as the suffering Messias and also the Son of God. The unusual form of the title (lit. ' the Son of the Man ') as employed by Christ, and its frequent repetition were calculated to focus attention on his person, ' *the man that I am* '. His humanity is thus affirmed not merely when there is reference to sufferings and humiliations, 9:12 ; 10:33, but also when he claims power to forgive sin on earth or authority over the divine institution of the Sabbath, 2:28. It seems probable that a limited section of Jews, who recognized the Messianic sense of Dan 7:13 f., referred to the Messias as ' Son of Man ', but the expression was not in common use among the people at the time of Christ as a title of the Messias. It could be used, therefore, without the risk of provoking a popular upheaval. Moreover, when closely linked with the vision of Daniel, it pointed to the heavenly origin of Jesus, who was not a merely human Messias but the Son of God ; *cf.* 13:26 ; 14:62.

13-17 The Call of Levi ; *cf.* Mt 9:9-13 ; Lk 5:27-32 —It is clear from Mt 9:9 ; 10:3 that Levi the publican and the Apostle Matthew are one and the same. The NT gives several examples of this double nomenclature, *e.g.* Simon–Peter, Saul–Paul, John–Mark, Joseph–Barnabas. It may be that Mk and Lk used the name Levi here because they did not wish to draw attention to the fact that one of the chosen twelve had previously belonged to a class hated by the Jews. The ' publicans ' of the Gospels were local agents of the person who had bought from the State the right to collect the taxes in a particular area. Jews who took the position were commonly regarded as renegades from Judaism. The phrase ' publicans and sinners ' in practice meant ' publicans and other sinners '. **15-16.** The banquet given by Matthew provided the Scribes and Pharisees with another opportunity to attempt to discredit our Lord. They were greatly concerned with questions of ritual purity and sought scrupulously to avoid contact with all possible sources of legal defilement. The question put to the disciples was intended to create a prejudice in their minds against Jesus by suggesting that he was blameworthy in associating with persons whom the Pharisees regarded as sources of defilement because of their contacts with pagans and disregard of the Law and pharisaic traditions. **17a.** Christ's ministry is compared to that of a physician ; the physician must come into contact with the sick who need his ministrations, and similarly, Christ, the physician of souls, must associate with sinners. **17b.** The salvation of sinners is the object of Christ's mission. The self-righteous Pharisees, by their pride and obstinate opposition to the claims and teaching of

Jesus, are excluding themselves from the blessings of Messianic salvation.

18-22 A Question concerning Fasting; *cf*. Mt 9:14–17; Lk 5:33–39—Fasting was well known to the Jews as a sign of repentance and mourning. The Mosaic Law had prescribed only the Day of Atonement as a general day of fasting, but custom had introduced other days and the Pharisees boasted that they fasted frequently. **18.** The question put to our Lord was intended to place him in an unfavourable light by contrasting the conduct of his followers with the ascetic practices of the Pharisees and of John's disciples. **19-20.** Christ uses a simple illustration to show that fasting by his disciples is inopportune while he is with them. At a wedding celebration no one expects the companions of the bridegroom to fast, because it is a time of joy. Similarly, while Christ is with the disciples, fasting is out of place. But when he is taken away, *i.e.* after his Passion and Death, then the disciples will fast in token of sorrow. It is in this spirit, in association with the sufferings and death of Christ, that the Church orders times of fasting. **21-22.** In these two illustrations Christ taught that the spirit which would animate his followers is incompatible with the spirit which inspired pharisaic observance. 'Raw cloth' is the new material which has not yet been fulled in order to prevent shrinking. Such material is quite unsuitable for patching old garments, because when it shrinks it will make an even larger rent in the old garment. 'Bottles': Gk '*wineskins*'. Skins of animals were commonly used in antiquity as containers for liquids. New unfermented wine must not be put into old wineskins, which are worn and inelastic, as the fermentation may cause them to burst. The disciples were being prepared for a new life animated by a spirit totally different from that of the Pharisees. In the economy to be established by Christ fasting would be practised as a sincere expression of repentance, not as a display of righteousness.

23-28 The First Dispute about the Sabbath; *cf*. Mt 12:1–8; Lk 6:1–5—The observance of the obligation of abstaining from work on the Sabbath, which is the subject of this dispute, figured frequently in conflicts between Christ and his opponents; *cf*. Mk 3:1–6; Lk 13:10–17; Jn 5:9–18. The Mosaic Law, Ex 20:10, had forbidden work on the Sabbath in order to give men relief from their daily labours and to enable them to share in the public worship of God. But the Scribes, by excessive rigour in the interpretation of this law, had made the observance of the Sabbath an intolerable burden. Christ showed, Mt 12:5, 11, that the Scribes were inconsistent in their interpretation and that they had lost sight of the fundamental purpose of the law. **23-24.** The action of the disciples in plucking the ears of corn and rubbing out the grain is taken as a violation of the prohibition of work on the Sabbath. **25-26.** Christ disregards casuistic discussion of the law of sabbath rest and considers the essential nature and purpose of the law. In effect, his answer means that the law of abstention from work is not an absolutely rigid and immutable regulation based on the nature of things. It is rather a positive ordinance intended to benefit mankind. The letter of the law must not be insisted on against the demands of charity and the needs of men. 'Loaves of proposition'. Twelve loaves were placed on the table of the sanctuary each Sabbath and when changed at the end of the week were to be eaten by the priests, Lev 24:5–9. The incident from the biblical narrative, 1 Kg 21:1–6, illustrates forcibly the point that the letter of the law should not be allowed to stand in the way of the urgent needs of men. 'Under Abiathar the high-priest'. According to the text of 1 Kg 21:1–6 it was the priest Achimelech, not his son Abiathar, who gave the loaves to David. Some suggest that the phrase is not authentic. Others take it to mean 'in the time of Abiathar' or 'in the biblical passage about Abiathar'; *cf*. Mk 12:26; Rom 11:2. Abiathar was closely connected with David as the high-priest of the time (*cf*. Knabenbauer, *Evangelium sec. Marcum*, 87–9). He figures prominently in the

biblical narrative and was presumably present on this occasion. We are not here dealing with a word for word citation from the OT, but rather with a general allusion to an incident which illustrates the point of doctrine which Jesus wished to inculcate. **27.** The fundamental principle is that the law of sabbath rest was intended to benefit mankind. Its observance is subordinate to the needs of men, who were not created merely in order to observe the Sabbath. **28.** Further, the Son of Man, *i.e.* Jesus the Messias and Son of God, has authority to interpret or even to abrogate the Sabbath. In declaring himself ' Lord of the Sabbath ' Christ claims authority over a divine institution, thus making an implicit claim to divinity. **728f**

III:1-6 Cure of a Man with a Withered Hand; *cf*. Mt **g** 12:9–14; Lk 6:6–11—**1-3.** Here again the question at issue is the observance of the law of sabbath rest. The hostility of the Pharisees has increased; they now spy on Christ to see whether he will perform a cure on the Sabbath so that they may accuse him of violation of the Law. **4.** This question means, Is it permissible to perform a good deed on the Sabbath in contravention of the letter of the law, or must one allow evil to happen, by refraining from action in order to keep the letter of the law? May one take action to save life on the Sabbath, or should assistance be withheld despite danger to life? It was admitted in practice by the Pharisees that one should assist a person whose life was in danger. The principle thus established had obviously a far wider application in all cases where the needs of mankind seemed to conflict with the positive law. **5.** Mark alone notes the anger and grief of Christ on this occasion, 'blindness of their hearts': Gk '*the callousness of their hearts*'. The silence of the Pharisees is proof of their obduracy. **6.** The first mention of a plot against our Lord. The Herodians (*cf*. Mt 22:16), were either a party who supported the dynasty of Herod, or persons of influence at the court of Herod Antipas, the ruler of Galilee. Christ was within Herod's territory at this time and the sanction of the tetrarch would have been necessary for the success of any scheme to bring about his death.

7-12 Enthusiastic Crowds come to Jesus; *cf*. Mt 4:24 f.; **h** Lk 6:17–19—This section gives a vivid picture of the excitement caused by Christ's teaching and miracles. The crowds came from districts far removed from Galilee, and even from outside Palestine, in order to avail his miraculous healing powers. They so pressed upon him that it was necessary for him to address them from a boat moored near the shore. In Mt 4:24 f. and Lk 6:17–19 this account of the coming of the crowds to Jesus (7–8) leads on to the Sermon on the Mount. For a discussion of the absence of the Sermon on the Mount from Mk, especially in relation to the Synoptic Problem, see Vaganay, RB 58 (1951) 5–46. **11-12.** The casting out of demons was not merely a work of mercy, but a proof that Jesus was mightier than Satan. Later Jesus pointed out that the breaking of Satan's power was a sign that the kingdom of God had come; *cf*. Lk 11:20. The title ' Son of God ' suggests more forcibly than ' Holy One of God ', 1:24, the unique relation between Christ and the Father. There is no certainty as to the precise sense intended by the demons, but probably they had some notion of Christ's divinity by this time. Christ did not refuse the title but for motives of prudence (*cf*. 1:34) forbade the demons to proclaim it.

13-19 The Call of the Twelve Apostles; *cf*. Mt 10:1–4; **i** Lk 6:12–16; Ac 1:13—The twelve disciples now specially chosen by Christ were to be the duly accredited witnesses who would proclaim the message of salvation after the death of Christ. Hence the solemnity attached to their calling. Luke tells us that Christ spent the whole night in prayer beforehand. Mark emphasizes that the choice came from Jesus; *cf*. Jn 6:70; 15:16. **14-15.** The number *twelve* had symbolic significance in relation to the twelve tribes of Israel. The Apostles would be the rulers of the new spiritual

728i Israel, the Church which Christ was about to establish. Their companionship with Christ during his public life, their intimate knowledge of his teaching and acquaintance with his supernatural powers, fitted them in a special way to be the authentic witnesses of the good news of the Redemption. The power of working miracles would be a confirmation of their teaching ; they shared in the ministry of Christ even during his life on earth ; *cf.* Mk 6:7 ff. **16.** It is significant that Simon (Peter) is placed first in all the lists of the Apostles, though there is some variation in the order of the others, with the exception of Judas who is always placed last. **17.** ' Boanerges ' is probably a defective transcription into Greek letters of the Aramaic *B^enê-r^eḡēš* ' Sons of thunder ' = The Thunderers. This title may be explained by the incident recorded in Lk 9:54, which suggests the fiery disposition of the brothers. Some writers take the expression as a reference to their eloquence, and especially to the theology of John, the author of the Fourth Gospel. **18.** ' Simon the Cananean '. Lk calls him ' the Zealot ', translating the Aramaic *Q^enānā* of which the Gk Καναναῖος is a transcription. It is unlikely that Simon belonged to the fanatical political group known as Zealots. The word refers rather to a personal trait of character or to zeal for the Law ; *cf.* Ac 21:20 ; Gal 1:14.

THE MINISTRY IN GALILEE AND ADJOINING DISTRICTS

729a **20-30 Different Attitudes towards Christ—20-21** are found only in Mk. The crowds are still enthusiastic and so eager to be with Christ that it is impossible for him and the disciples to take their meals. This eagerness of the crowds is a contrast to the anxiety shown by the persons mentioned in 21, and still more to the blasphemous accusations of the Scribes and Pharisees. **21.** ' Piety adds to the difficulty of this passage ; for the mind shrinks not merely from believing but from the very thought that Christ's relatives said or considered that Christ was mad ', Maldonatus. The usual interpretation is that relatives (or followers) of Christ, disturbed by reports, came out to take charge of him. The following points are to be noted. (1) The phrase οἱ παρ'αὐτοῦ does not necessarily mean relatives (friends). It has a wider usage which would include disciples, followers, members of a household. It is not certain that the persons designated by this phrase are the same as ' his mother and brethren ', 31. Even if they are, there is no reason for thinking that our Lady shared in the sentiments of the others, though she would naturally wish to be present when the welfare of her divine Son was in question. (2) ' For they said ', rather, ' *For people were saying* '. If this be correct, then 21*b* refers to reports which reached Christ's friends, not to an expression of opinion by them. (3) ' He is become mad ' is too strong as a translation of ἐξέστη. This verb is used by Mark to describe the astonishment and awe caused by the teaching and miracles of Christ, Mk 2:12 ; 5:42 ; 6:51. In the present context a more satisfactory rendering would be ' *he is beside himself* '. Those who came to seize Christ may have thought that his conduct, *e.g.* neglect of his health, 20*b*, was imprudent. ' For not even his brethren believed in him ', **b** Jn 7:5. An alternative explanation, which would obviate the difficulties of the usual interpretation, was put forward by Hartmann, BZ 11 (1913) 249–79. The gist of his interpretation is conveyed by the following translation : ' *When they who were with him (in the house) heard (the crowd), they went out to control it [the crowd]. For they said, it [the crowd] is out of hand* '. A strong argument against this interpretation is drawn from Marcan usage. In no other instance in Mk do we find the *singular* of the pronoun αὐτός used when referring to the crowd (ὄχλος). It is always the *plural* (αὐτούς, αὐτοῖς) which is found ; see MacRory, IER 65 (1945) 1–5 ; Fahy, *ibid.* 6–15. We must take it, therefore, that the pronoun in the phrase κρατῆσαι

αὐτὸν ' to lay hold on him ' refers to Christ. If Mark intended to refer to the crowd he would have used the plural αὐτούς ; *cf.* CBQ 4 (1942) 357–9.

22-30 The Scribes calumniate Our Lord ; *cf.* Mt 12:22–33 ; Lk 11:14–22—**22.** The Scribes from Jerusalem had probably been sent by the Sanhedrin to spy on our Lord. The blasphemous charge that Christ was in league with Satan in expelling the demons shows the blindness and obduracy of his opponents. It also indicates the indisputable character of the evidence that Christ had really performed these miracles. ' Beelzebub ' is the name given to the god of Accaron in 4 Kg 1:2 f. It appears in the Ras-Shamra tablets also as the name of a pagan divinity ; *cf.* R. Dussaud, *Les Découvertes de Ras Shamra et l'Ancien Testament* (Paris 1937), 69. It is uncertain how this name came to be applied to the prince of demons. In the Greek MSS of the Gospels the name usually appears in the form ' Beelzebul ', which is variously explained as ' lord of the dwelling ', ' lord of dung ', ' lord of flies '. Some think that Beelzebul is a corruption of the Aramaic form Beelzebub, which means ' enemy ', ' accuser '. It would correspond, therefore, to the Hebrew ' Satan ' = Adversary, and διάβολος = Accuser. **23-26.** The illustrations introduced here by Christ show the absurdity of the blasphemous charge which had been levelled against him. Every kingdom or household which is torn by internal strife will come to ruin. If Christ is in league with the prince of demons in order to cast out devils, then the kingdom of Satan is divided against itself and its collapse cannot be far off. It was clearly absurd to suppose that Satan would be willing to destroy his own kingdom in this way. **27.** This parable points to the only correct conclusion from Christ's power over the demons. The ' strong man ' is Satan, the ' prince of this world ', Jn 12:31. But Christ ' a stronger one ', Lk 11:22, has come and overcome Satan. The expulsion of demons from men is the proof of Christ's victory and the sign of the destruction of Satan's kingdom.

28-30 Blasphemy of the Holy Spirit ; *cf.* Mt 12:31 f. ; Lk 12:10—In this context ' blasphemy ' is to be understood in accordance with the primary sense of βλασφημεῖν ' to slander, calumniate '. It is clear from 30 that ' blasphemy against the Holy Ghost ' is the sin committed by those who attributed to the power of Satan the expulsion of demons by Christ. These miraculous works of mercy were so clearly due to the beneficent operation of divine power that to attribute them to Satan was a calumny of diabolical malice. Unlike other blasphemies or sins which might be partially excused by ignorance, passion or inadvertence, this was a sin of wilful malice and blindness to the light. As long as such a mentality persists, pardon is impossible, not because of any limitation on the power or mercy of God, but because those who are guilty of this sin refuse to respond to the promptings of grace.

31-35 The Mother and Brethren of Jesus ; *cf.* Mt 12:46–50 ; Lk 8:19–21—**31.** According to the usual interpretation, Christ's mother and brethren are the persons referred to in 21 as ' friends ', and their arrival is the sequel to the facts there described. **33-35.** These words of Christ are not a repudiation of the ties of blood nor a refusal to acknowledge the duties which arise from such relationship. Christ condemned the casuistry which made it possible for undutiful children to evade the obligations imposed by the Fourth Commandment, Mk 7:9–13, and when dying on the Cross showed his solicitude for his mother, Jn 19:26 f. Here, however, he wished to inculcate the doctrine that the claims of natural kinship are subordinate to the primary duty of performing God's will. ' His brethren '. Other references to the brethren of Christ are to be found in Mk 6:3 ; Mt 12:46–50 ; 13:55 f. ; Lk 8:19–21 ; Jn 2:12 ; 7:3, 5, 10 ; Ac 1:14 ; 1 Cor 9:5 ; Gal 1:19. The evidence of the NT and of Tradition leads to the conclusion that the ' brethren ' were cousins of Christ. The precise degree of relationship and also the question whether they were related to

Christ through our Lady or through St Joseph remains uncertain ; *cf.* Lagrange, *Saint Marc*, 79–93 ; Holzmeister, *De S. Joseph Quaestiones Biblicae* (Romae 1945) 40–67 ; *cf.* also §§ 672–3.

IV:1–34 Teaching in Parables ; *cf.* Mt 13:1–52 ; Lk 8:4–18—**1–2.** The enthusiasm of the crowds for Christ is undiminished as they gather again to hear his teaching. The sloping shores of an inlet of the lake would have provided a natural amphitheatre for the crowds whom he addressed from a boat moored near the shore. This was not the first occasion on which Jesus made use of parables (*cf.* Mk 2:19–22 ; 3:23–27), but both Mk and Mt seem to indicate this day by the lake-shore as the ' day of parables ' in a special way. Mark records only two of the ' parables of the kingdom ' which are found in Mt 13, but he has one parable, 4:26–29, which is not found in the other Evangelists. **3–9.** The Parable of the Sower depicts a situation familiar to Christ's audience. The cultivated land was not fenced off by walls or hedges, the only boundary marks being stones fixed at intervals. The ' wayside ' was frequently nothing more than a rough path. Seed which fell on it had not even a light covering of earth to protect it from the birds which, according to modern observers, sometimes snatch the seed as it is falling to the ground from the sower's hand. Much of the soil of Palestine is stony, with frequent outcroppings of rock or only a light covering of soil over the underlying rock. The seed which fell there sprang up quickly but, because of the lack of moisture, the corn withered in the burning heat of the sun. The thorn-growths were not uprooted in the preparation of the soil. Usually they were burned together with the straw which remained after the preceding harvest, but roots left in the earth and seed which had fallen to the ground produced a new growth which smothered the grain-crop. **9.** This phrase is used by Christ (*cf.* Mt 11:15) to impress upon the listeners the importance of what he has said and to urge them to ponder upon its meaning.

10–12 The Reason Jesus spoke in Parables ; *cf.* Mt 13:10–15 ; Lk 8:9 f.—**10.** This question about *the parables* was put to Jesus by ' *those about him with the twelve* ' at a later stage, when the crowds were not present. **11a.** ' The mystery of the kingdom of God ' is the secret design of God for establishing the Messianic kingdom. It is called a ' mystery ' because it proceeds from the inscrutable wisdom of God whose hidden purpose is not ascertainable by human reason apart from divine revelation. Knowledge of this design of God, of the nature of the kingdom, the manner of its foundation, the conditions of entry into it, is given to the disciples on whom would fall the duty of proclaiming the kingdom after Christ's death. By their docility and faith in Christ they had shown that they were fitted to receive a more profound and clearer understanding of God's design. **11b.** ' Those outside ' are not neglected ; they are taught in parables. The expression ' those outside ' includes Christ's avowed enemies, the Scribes, Pharisees and Herodians, and also the crowds who, though attracted by Christ and impressed by his teaching and miracles, had not become faithful followers. It was not Christ's intention, in teaching through parables, to prevent them from understanding his doctrine. The Evangelist tells us that Christ spoke to them in parables *according to their capacity to understand*, 33. Parables, by their very nature, are calculated to arouse the interest and to enlighten, but a certain effort is called for if one is to grasp the truth enshrined in the imagery of the parable. In adopting parables as a method of instruction Christ took account of the dispositions of ' those outside ' and of their mistaken notions of the kingdom. Prevalent misconceptions of the role of the Messias and of the character of his kingdom made it necessary to propound the true doctrine to the people in a manner which would neither destroy such goodwill as could be found among them nor provoke a conflict with the Roman authorities ; *cf.* 1:34. Christ's appeal for earnest consideration of his teaching, 9, was not to be dismissed lightly in view of the manifest signs of God's approval which his **729g** mission had received. Men of goodwill would reflect on the parables and be enlightened. Those who, like the disciples, sought further explanation would receive it from Christ. But for the ill-disposed, who neglected the grace thus offered to them, the parables would be the occasion of a further hardening of their hearts. **12.** In its original context in Is 6:9 f. this **h** passage predicts the failure of the prophet's mission, a mission of mercy which, because of the blindness and obduracy of the Jews to whom he was sent, resulted in further hardening of their hearts. At first sight the passage seems to mean that the *purpose* of the prophet's mission was to blind and harden. But the text must be understood in accordance with Hebrew idiom and the Hebrew conception of divine causality in which little account was taken of secondary causes. The final result of God's merciful action in sending Isaias is stated as if it were the purpose of his mission. Actually of course, that foreseen result was brought about by the evil dispositions of those to whom he was sent ; *cf.* Kissane, *The Book of Isaiah* (Dublin 1941), Vol. 1, 75 f. The situation contemplated in the text of Isaias has a parallel in the mission of Christ. He too came on a mission of mercy and taught ' those outside ' in parables, because that was the method most suited to their dispositions and capacity for understanding his doctrine ; *cf.* Vosté, *Parabolae selectæ D. N. Jesu Christi* (Romae 1933).

13–20 Explanation of the Parable of the Sower ; *cf.* **730a** Mt 13:18–23 ; Lk 8:11–15—The key to the meaning is given in **14.** The seed represents the message of the kingdom which Christ is preaching. As the fate of a seed depends upon the type of soil on which it falls, so the success of Christ's teaching and the growth of the kingdom depend upon the dispositions and loyal co-operation of those who hear him. If his message is to bear fruit it must find a fruitful soil in the minds and hearts of the listeners. This lesson had a special significance for the Jews of the time of Christ. Many of them imagined that membership of the Chosen People, irrespective of moral qualifications, would secure entry into the Messianic kingdom, but the parable emphasizes the necessity of good dispositions.

21–25 The Mystery of the Kingdom will be revealed ; **b** *cf.* Mt 5:15 ; 7:2 ; 10:26 f. ; 13:12 ; 25:29 ; Lk 8:16–18—The instructions contained in the parables of the Lamp, 21, and of the Measure, 24, appear to be directed specially to the Apostles and disciples. **21–23.** The knowledge of the kingdom which has been given to the disciples, 11, is not for them alone. They are ' the light of the world ', Mt 5:14–16, and as the function of a lamp is to give light, so it will be the function of the disciples to proclaim to all mankind the knowledge of Christ and his teaching which has been entrusted to them. For the moment ' those outside ' are incapable of appreciating the doctrine of the kingdom, but the time will come when that knowledge will be proclaimed from the housetops, Mt 10:26 f. **24–25.** The semi-proverbial statements of 24b and 25a contain a warning which recalls the teaching of the Parable of the Talents, Mt 25:14–30. Knowledge of the kingdom is a favour from God which, like all God's graces, demands the co-operation of man if it is to be understood and to prove fruitful. The measure of understanding and fruitfulness is in proportion to the attention and goodwill with which the message is received. Those who make use of the knowledge they have received will be granted an increase. This teaching obviously has a special interest for the disciples who would have the duty of preaching to others.

26–29 The Seed growing by Itself—In this parable, **c** which is found only in Mk, the central point of comparison with the kingdom of God is the manner in which the seed, once it has been sown, grows to maturity without further intervention from the sower. While he goes about his daily round, the seed, through its own hidden energies, develops in the soil until it is fit for harvesting. The chief lesson of this parable appears

730c to be as follows : just as the seed develops gradually until it has formed the full-grown ear ripe for harvesting, so the kingdom of God established on earth by Christ, will develop gradually, but none the less surely, until it reaches the final consummation. This doctrine of the gradual but persistent growth of the kingdom was a timely corrective to the false ideas of those who looked for an immediate and highly dramatic inauguration of the Messianic kingdom. The parable inculcates patience and confidence in the mysterious plans of God who will secure the growth of the kingdom without the aid of violent revolutionary upheavals or the theatrical manifestations which were part of popular expectation.

d **30-32 The Mustard Seed ;** *cf.* Mt 13:31 f. ; Lk 13:18 f.—The mustard seed, though not absolutely the smallest of all seeds, was proverbial for its smallness, Mt 17:20. From this tiny seed, however, grows a plant which attains the dimensions of a tree. Flocks of birds gather on its branches to eat the ripe grains of mustard seed. This growth from small beginnings provides the term of comparison in the present parable. The kingdom has an apparently insignificant beginning ; the preaching of the Gospel is an apparently inadequate method of inaugurating the Messianic age. But Christ foretells a remarkable development to which history bears testimony in the spread of the Gospel and the growth of the Church. He also discredits mistaken ideas of a sudden manifestation of the kingdom in all its fullness, and directs attention to the latent powers which achieve this extraordinary expansion.

e **33-34 Concluding Remarks on the Parables ;** *cf.* Mt 13:34 f.—**33b**. ' *According to their capacity to understand* '. These words make it clear that the evangelist did not consider that the purpose of the parables was to blind and harden ; *cf.* 4:10-12. The reason for failure to understand the doctrine of the kingdom propounded in them must be sought in lack of goodwill and failure to give due attention to Christ's teaching. His mission had evident marks of divine approval and, consequently, his teaching merited the most earnest consideration. **34.** The disciples showed their goodwill by seeking explanations, 10, and they received from Christ the fuller knowledge which would not have been refused to 'those outside' if they had seriously sought it.

f **35-40 The Storm on the Lake ;** *cf.* Mt 8:18, 23–27 ; Lk 8:22–25—Mark's narrative mentions several details not found in the other Synoptics, *e.g.* ' they took him as he was, in the boat ', ' other boats accompanied him ', 36, ' he was in the stern sleeping on a cushion ', 38. These unimportant details which make the narrative more graphic without affecting the substance of the story, clearly imply that the evangelist's information came from an eyewitness. This internal evidence is in complete harmony with the tradition that Mk is a record of the preaching of Peter. The realism and graphic quality of the narrative, as well as certain other features of the second Gospel, are traceable to the eye-witness Peter. **37-38.** In the sudden violent storms which sweep down on the Lake of Galilee waves rise to a height of more than six feet and small craft caught in these squalls are in grave danger. **39.** ' *Be silent ! be muzzled !* ' Christ addresses the winds and waves as if they were living things. **40.** The disciples were not completely lacking in faith—their appeal to Christ shows that they relied on him to help, 38—but their faith was still imperfect. **40b.** The disciples were awed by this manifestation of the power that Christ possessed over the forces of nature, a power which in the OT is attributed to Yahweh. The Fathers see in the boat tossed upon the waters a symbol of the Church subjected to persecutions and trials.

g **V 1-20 Expulsion of the Demons in Gerasa ;** *cf.* Mt 8:28-34 ; Lk 8:26-39—Once again it is noteworthy that Mark's account of this and the subsequent incidents, 21-43, is characterized by touches of realism and graphic detail which immediately suggest that the evangelist's information came from an eye-witness. **1.** ' *And they came to the opposite shore of the lake, in the territory of the Gerasenes* '. Instead of *Gerasenes*, which is the best supported reading in Mk. some witnesses to the text read *Gadarenes* (*cf.* Mt 8:28) or *Gergesenes* (*cf.* Lk 8:26). The latter reading is most probably an emendation due to Origen (*cf.* PG 14 270). While it is clear that the cure of the demoniac was performed on the eastern shore of the lake, the place has not been identified with certainty. It is unlikely that the name ' Gerasenes ' should be connected with the well-known city of the Decapolis called Gerasa (modern Jerash) which lies some 30 m. to the SE. in Transjordan. It has been suggested, however, that the territory of Gerasa reached the lake shore and that the lake side inhabitants were therefore called Gerasenes. But the town to which the Gerasenes belonged was evidently close to the lake ; *cf.* 5:14 ; Lk 8:27. At the place called *Moqâ Edlô* on the eastern shore a steep descent comes to within a short distance of the water's edge, 13. In the vicinity there are numerous caves which may have been used as tombs, 3. About a mile north of *Moqâ Edlô* there is a place called *Kursi*. It is probable that this name should be traced back to the Aramaic form of Gerasa and that the present Kursi indicates the site of the town of the Gerasenes ; *cf.* Lagrange, *Saint Marc*, 132–6. **2-8.** We have here a particularly striking manifestation of Christ's power over the demons. The possessed man, who was previously uncontrollable and had doubtless rushed out to molest Christ and those with him, Mt 8:28, was now subdued and *prostrated himself*, 6, before our Lord, who commanded the unclean spirit to depart from him. The demon, dismayed at the destruction of his malignant tyranny over men, 3:23–27, adjured Jesus not to torment him ' before the time ', Mt 8:29—' not to command them to go into the abyss ', Lk 8:31. This appeal appears to reflect the belief that demons were allowed to roam the world to harass and tempt men till the day of judgement. Some commentators are of opinion that the ' torment ' is the deprivation of the malicious pleasure which the demons derived from harassing those who were possessed. ' *Son of God Most High* ' was not a current Messianic title. The demon evidently recognized the exceptional dignity and superior power of Christ. It would seem, however, that he did not yet know the full significance of the title ' Son of God ' as applied to Christ. If he had understood he would not have adjured Christ by God, as by One who was Christ's superior. ' Most High ' was the name given to the God of the Jews by Gentiles who did not know his real name ; it was also used by the Jews to emphasize the transcendence of their God. **9-10.** The Roman legion numbered up to 6,000 men. Here the word signifies a very large number and suggests the power of Satan. But despite their numbers, the demons are compelled to beg Christ not to drive them from the district. **11-13.** The inhabitants of the territory east of the Lake of Galilee were mostly pagans (*cf.* Jos., *B.J.* 2, 18, 5), and, consequently, unaffected by Jewish traditions or by the declarations of the Mosaic Law, Lev 11:7 ; Deut 14:8, that swine were unclean animals. The loss which Christ permitted the demons to inflict on the owners of the swine should be judged in the same way as other material losses and afflictions which God permits for a higher purpose. The inhabitants of the district were rid of the malignant power of Satan, and were granted an exceptional opportunity of coming to recognize Christ as the divine envoy who would liberate souls as well as bodies from the dominion of Satan. **14-17.** Consideration of the loss which they had suffered outweighed even the evidence of the miracle, and the inhabitants asked Christ to leave their territory. **18-20.** The man who had been freed from the demon was probably a pagan. His presence among Christ's immediate followers would have given the Scribes and Pharisees an opportunity to arouse opposition to the public ministry among the Jews. Moreover, Christ had a special mission for this man to his own people. By making known to them how great things Jesus had done for him, he would arouse their interest in the

i Person and mission of Christ, thus preparing them for the message of salvation. The proclamation of Christ's wonderworking power among the pagan inhabitants of the Decapolis did not involve the risks of political upheavals which were to be feared among the Jews ; *cf.* 1:25, 34 ; 3:12.

j **21-43 The Daughter of Jairus and the Woman with the Issue of Blood** ; *cf.* Mt 9:18-26 ; Lk 8:40-56—Both incidents illustrate the importance of unwavering faith in Christ. **21.** '*And when Jesus had again crossed in the boat to the other side*', to the western shore, the crowds gathered to him with an eagerness which is in striking contrast to the attitude of the Gerasenes. **22.** Jairus was either the chief official who presided at synagogue services or one of the elders who were responsible for the administration of the synagogue. **25-29.** The disorder of normal menstruation from which this woman was suffering made her legally unclean, Lev 15:25. It would have been embarrassing for her to tell her affliction to Christ in the presence of the crowd. The people might have driven away and ill-treated one who exposed them to the danger of contracting legal defilement. Consequently, she had recourse to this means whereby she hoped to secure the benefit of Christ's miraculous power without being observed. The Gospels mention other cases where cures were sought by touching Christ. 3:10, or his garments, 6:56 ; Mt 14:36.

k **30-34.** Jesus knew '*that power had gone forth from him*' ; he was aware that the miracle had been performed. The question 'Who hath touched my garments ?' was intended to make it clear to the woman that she had not obtained the cure as a magical result of contact with Christ's garment without his knowledge or consent. The miracle was granted in answer to the faith of which she had given such striking proof. Christ, of course, knew by supernatural knowledge who had touched him. His action in looking round 'to see her who had done this', and the question in **30***b* are to be understood in the light of his experimental knowledge. He had assumed a real human nature at the Incarnation and, by the use of his senses and intelligence, acquired knowledge experimentally in the same way as other men. **35-36.** The messengers did not think that Jesus could restore the girl to life. Jesus, however, reassured Jairus ; all will be well if his faith remains unshaken. **37.** These were the three Apostles who were privileged to be witnesses of the glory of Christ at the Transfiguration, and were also his companions at the Agony. **38.** The 'tumult' was caused by the lamentation of relatives and neighbours together with the cries of the professional mourners. **39-40.** The girl was really dead, as the mockery of the listeners shows, but her death is likened to sleep because she was about to be restored to life. **41.** Mark alone gives the actual Aramaic words *ṭᵉlîṭā*, 'maiden', *qûmî* 'arise' spoken by our Lord. **43.** Christ again imposed silence on the witnesses of the miracle. The time was not yet ripe for the fulfilment of his command : 'For there is nothing hidden that shall not be made known, and nothing has been kept secret but in order that it should be brought to light', 4:22.

1a **VI 1-6 Jesus at Nazareth** ; *cf.* Mt 13:53-58 ; Lk 4:16-30—Commentators are not in agreement on the question whether Lk, which records a visit to Nazareth early in the Galilean ministry, deals with the same incident as Mk and Mt. It is difficult to understand how, in the course of a single visit, the people of Nazareth changed so suddenly from admiration of Christ's wisdom to scepticism and murderous hostility. A possible solution of the problem is that the accounts of two separate visits have been joined together. On the occasion of his first visit, Mt 4:13, Jesus was well received, Lk 4:16-22. But on this later occasion the atmosphere was less friendly. His townsmen were disappointed and jealous that Jesus had left Nazareth and favoured Capharnaum and other cities with his miracles. They refused to recognize the superiority or extraordinary mission of one who had grown up amongst them and, finally, tried to kill him, Lk 4:23-30.

1. 'His own country' (Gk '*His fatherland*'), *i.e.* **731b** Nazareth ; *cf.* 1:9, 24. In paying this visit to Nazareth Christ's purpose was to preach the kingdom of God. He was accompanied by the disciples who would have learned a useful lesson for their own ministry from the rejection of Christ by his townsmen. **2.** The people of Nazareth were all the more astonished at Christ's wisdom because they knew that he had not attended a rabbinical school. **3.** These questions reflect the change from admiration of Christ to scepticism and ill-will. He had returned to Nazareth with the reputation of a prophet and wonder-worker, but his townsmen *took offence.* Their attitude was that they knew his relatives and his own humble way of life too well to accept him as a divinely appointed teacher. 'The carpenter'. This is the only passage in the Gospels which reveals this fact of the hidden life of Christ. 'The son of Mary'. The form of the expression in Gk, ὁ υἱὸς τῆς Μαρίας, indicates that Jesus was the only son of Mary. 'Brother . . . . sisters', *cf.* 3:31-35, § 729*e*. **4.** Jesus answered the scepticism of the people of Nazareth with a proverb which is a particular application of the familiar truth that jealousy and familiarity create a prejudice against one who is well known. His words disclose the real reason for the offence they have taken at him and also affirm his own claim to be a prophet **5.** Christ's power to work miracles was not limited or lost, but faith, which his townsmen lacked, was normally demanded for the exercise of this power. **6.** Christ's wonder was real ; the attitude of his townsmen was something new in his human experience.

7-13 Mission of the Twelve ; *cf.* Mt 10:1, 9, 11, 14 ; **c** Lk 9:1-6—**7.** Christ had chosen the Twelve to be with him and that he might send them to preach, 3:14. They had been in his company for a considerable time, and as a further step in their preparation for the task which lay before them, 16:15-20, they are now directly associated with his personal ministry. In order to lend authority to their message of repentance, 12, Christ gave them power over the unclean spirits. **8-9.** The meaning of these instructions is that they are to undertake their task in a spirit of complete detachment from material or personal considerations, with entire trust in divine providence. The verbal discrepancy between Mk, which allows a staff and sandals, and Mt and Lk, which forbid shoes and even a staff, does not affect the sense. 'Each one wished to convey that Christ had commanded the Apostles to take nothing more than was needed for immediate use', Maldonatus, *Comment. on Mt 10:10.* **10-11.** When they have found hospitality in a respectable house the Apostles are to remain there. Changing from one house to another would lay them open to the charge of inconstancy and be likely to cause jealousies and contentions. By 'shaking the dust from their feet' they would signify the breaking off of relations and refusal to accept any further responsibility for people who had shown themselves unworthy ; *cf.* Ac 13:51. **12-13.** The **d** proclamation of the message of repentance and the driving out of demons emphasize the spiritual character of the kingdom for which the preaching of the disciples is a preparation. 'Anointed with oil'. According to the Council of Trent (Sess. 14, *c.* 1, Dz 908), the Sacrament of Extreme Unction is 'insinuated' in this passage ; *cf.* Jas 5:13 ff. Oil was commonly used at the time in the dressing of wounds, etc. Here, however, it is clear that there is question of an anointing which has results far beyond those customarily associated with ordinary medical treatment. It is probable that the Apostles were acting in accordance with a definite instruction of Christ. The anointing which they practised foreshadowed Extreme Unction in somewhat the same way as baptism by the Apostles during Christ's life, Jn 4:2, foreshadowed the Sacrament of Baptism.

14-16 Herod's Opinion about Jesus ; *cf.* Mt 14:1 f. ; **e** Lk 9:7-9—**14a.** 'and he said'. According to another Gk reading, '*and people were saying*'. Herod Antipas,

731e tetrarch of Galilee and Peraea, had undoubtedly heard of Christ before this, but the mission of the Twelve had created a stir throughout the whole country and speculation about Jesus was rife. While some were of opinion that he was the Baptist risen from the dead, others, recalling the teaching of the Scribes, Mk 9:10 f., though+ it was Elias who had come to prepare for the Messias. Others regarded Christ as a prophet like one of the prophets of old. Herod's guilty conscience drove him to accept the opinion that the Baptist had risen from the dead.

f 17-29 The Death of the Baptist ; *cf.* Mt 14:3-12 ; Lk 3:19 f.—Mark had previously referred to the arrest of the Baptist, 1:14. This account of the circumstances of his arrest and death is introduced here in order to explain Herod's statement. Herod had married a daughter of Aretas, king of the Nabataeans, but while on a journey to Rome became infatuated with Herodias the wife of Philip, a half-brother of his, who lived as a private citizen. When Herod's wife became aware of his intention to divorce her she fled to her father, while Herodias abandoned her husband and went to live with Herod. The Law, Lev 18:16 ; 20:21, expressly reprobated such a union, and John did not hesitate to denounce it. He thereby incurred the enmity of Herodias who ' *nursed a grudge* ' against him, 19, and wanted to have him put to death. But she was forced to bide her time because ' *Herod stood in awe of John . . . and protected him, and was greatly perplexed when he heard him, and still listened to him gladly* ', 20. The celebration of Herod's birthday with a banquet for ' *the high officials, tribunes and chief men of Galilee* ', 21, gave Herodias her opportunity. Her daughter Salome, the child of her marriage to Philip, became the instrument of her evil designs. It was beneath the dignity of one of her rank to appear in the role of dancer at these festivities, but the performance was a pleasant novelty for guests accustomed to professional entertainers. Herod, evidently feeling obliged to show his appreciation in princely fashion, made an extravagant promise and rashly confirmed it with an oath. Herodias took full advantage of the situation, knowing that it would be difficult for Herod to reject even the outrageous request which Salome was instructed to make. Herod was grieved by it because of his esteem for John, but through shame before the guests and a superstitious fear of violating his oath ' *he was unwilling to refuse her* ', 26. Thus the malice of Herodias finally triumphed over the weakness of Herod. According to Josephus (*Ant.* 18, 5, 2), the defeat which Herod subsequently sustained at the hands of Aretas was thought by many Jews to be a punishment for his treatment of the Baptist. **29.** The place where the disciples buried the body of John is not known. In the 4th cent. the tomb of the Precursor was venerated near Samaria ; *cf.* Theodoret, HE 3, 7.

g 30-44 Return of the Twelve and Feeding of the Five Thousand ; *cf.* Mt 14:13-21 ; Lk 9:10-17 ; Jn 6:1-15 —30-33. Mk here resumes the account of the Apostles' mission from which it digressed at 14. As a result of the activity of the Twelve, fresh throngs were coming to Christ so that the disciples ' *had not time even to eat* ', 31. It was solicitude for the Apostles, not any fear of Herod's intentions, which prompted Christ to take them away by boat to an uninhabited place near Bethsaida, Lk 9:10, where they could rest from their labours. But the crowds saw from the shore the direction they had taken and, surmising their destination, followed on foot. Mk alone has the detail that the crowds had arrived before Christ and the disciples, 33b. **34-44.** The Feeding of the Five Thousand is the only miracle recorded by all four evangelists. **34.** Though the presence of the crowd ended the prospect of a period of rest, Jesus did not resent this nor seek to go elsewhere. He had pity on them ' because they were like sheep without a shepherd ' (*cf.* Ez 34:5). Christ was the Messianic shepherd foretold by Ez 34:23, and in fulfilment of that role he began to give them instruction. They had been neglected by those whose duty it was

to give them guidance. **37b.** ' *Are we to go and buy* 7 *two hundred denarii worth of bread, and give them to eat ?* ' **39.** ' companies ' : συμπόσια, ' groups (of guests) ' ; ' green grass ' is to be found in Palestine only in the spring. This indication of the time of year at which the miracle was performed agrees with John's statement that the Pasch was near, Jn 6:4. **40.** ' ranks ' : πρασιαί, *garden-plots* or *flower-beds*. The crowds when arranged in groups on the ground, which at this season would have had a rich carpet of flowers, looked like garden-plots in orderly arrangement. **41.** ' blessed '. The usual formula of blessing was ' Blessed be Thou, Yahweh our God, King of the universe, who hast caused the earth to bring forth bread '. The multiplication of the loaves was a foreshadowing of the Eucharist and, together with the walking on the waters, 47-52, was a manifestation of power which made an admirable prelude to the Eucharistic discourse, Jn 6:26-72.

45-52 Jesus walks on the Waters ; *cf.* Mt 14:22-33 ; h Jn 6:16-21—**45a.** Jesus *compelled* the disciples to leave lest they should be carried away by the misguided enthusiasm of the crowds who wanted to make him king, Jn 6:14 f. The miracle just performed by Christ was of the spectacular kind which, according to popular expectation, would mark the coming of the Messias. **45b.** ' *to go ahead of him to the other side towards Bethsaida* '. Bethsaida-Julias, near which the miracle had taken place, was on the north-eastern shore of the Lake. This text seems to mean that there was another Bethsaida on the western shore. But there is no historical or archaeological evidence to support this. If the point of departure of the disciples was on the south side of the small inlet near the place where the miracle took place, then the text can be explained without reference to the western shore or to a second Bethsaida. Lagrange (*Saint Marc*, 172) suggests that πρὸς Βηθσαΐδάν means ' *opposite Bethsaida* '. Some MSS omit ' to the other side '. **50.** ' All saw him '. There was no possibility of an illusion, yet the disciples could not understand how Jesus was walking on the waters. **52.** They had failed to appreciate the full significance of the miracle of the loaves in so far as it shed light on the person of Jesus. ' For their heart was blinded ' (*cf.* 3:5) ; their understanding was dull. They lacked insight and penetration. Clearly the disciples were not witnesses whose imaginations were easily excited, and the value of their testimony is thereby enhanced.

53-56 Jesus returns to Gennesareth ; *cf.* Mt 14:34-36 —**53.** ' *Having crossed over, they reached land at Gennesareth and moored the boat* '. The plain at the north-west of the Lake was called Gennesar. It was renowned for its fertility. **55-56.** Once more we see the unbounded enthusiasm of the crowds as they bring their sick to be healed by Christ.

VII 1-23 Controversy on Rabbinical Traditions ; *cf.* 73 Mt 15:1-20—The Pharisees, 3:6, and Scribes, 3:22, had previously been discomfited by Christ, but they evidently thought that the failure of the disciples to perform the ritual washing of hands before eating provided a suitable opportunity for renewing their attack. **2.** ' common ' = defiled, ritually unclean. ' they found fault '. This phrase is not found in the majority of the MSS. **3-4,** which are peculiar to Mk, give an explanation for the benefit of non-Jewish readers who would not understand why it should be considered blameworthy to eat with unwashed hands. The Pharisees were concerned not merely with the observance of the written regulations of the Mosaic Law concerning legal defilement, but also with the traditions of the ancients, interpretations of the written law and further regulations handed down by the Rabbis of the past. It was one of these rabbinical traditions, which the Pharisees regarded as no less binding than the Law itself, that the disciples had violated. **3.** ' Often ' πυκνά. A more probable reading is πυγμῇ = ' with the fist '. Some take this expression to mean ' vigorously, thoroughly ' : others interpret it as ' the finger-tips ' or ' up to the elbow ', signifying a ritual

32a washing. **4.** '*And they do not eat what comes from the market without sprinkling it*'. The phrase ' and of beds ' is probably not authentic. All these rules concerning the legal cleanliness of persons, foods and vessels were part of the fence around the Law which had been erected in the post-exilic period. They were intended to secure unquestionable legal cleanliness. **5.** The Pharisees and Scribes, while not directly charging Jesus with violations of the traditions of the ancients, imply **b** that he is responsible for his disciples' conduct. **6-8.** Jesus challenges the principle of these traditions and denounces the insincerity and hypocrisy which characterize the conduct of the Pharisees. The words in which Isaias, 29:13, denounced the insincerity of his contemporaries in their worship of God are applicable to Christ's opponents. In their eagerness to maintain traditions which had their origin in the opinions of earlier teachers, they neglect the essential obligations of God's law. **9-13.** Here Christ gives an actual example of the way in which adherence to rabbinical tradition nullified God's law. The Fourth Commandment strictly commanded children to honour their parents, an obligation which undoubtedly included the duty of rendering them assistance when they were in need. But rabbinical casuistry made it possible for undutiful children to evade their duty to parents under the pretence of respect for tradition. **11-13.** ' *But you say, if a man say to his father or mother, " Whatever help you might have had from me is Corban "* (*that is a gift to God*)*, you no longer allow him to do anything for his father or mother, nullifying the word of God by your tradition* '. The Hebrew word ' Corban ' meant a ' gift ' or ' offering ', especially a gift dedicated to God. To declare that something was ' Corban ' meant that it was dedicated to God and, therefore, withdrawn from profane uses. From this lawful practice of dedicating things to God a grave abuse had arisen. People pronounced the word Corban to signify that they would not do something which was perfectly lawful or even obligatory. The Talmud gives examples of such ' Corban ' oaths or vows, *e.g.* ' Corban, if thou wilt have any advantage from me ', *i.e.* I swear that thou wilt not have any assistance from me. According to rabbinical tradition, such an oath or vow was binding, even though the course of action to which person bound himself was contrary to the Law of God. Thus an undutiful child who said to a parent, ' Corban, if thou wilt have any assistance from me ' (*cf.* 7:11) was regarded as bound not to assist them. In this way the Pharisees nullified the precept of the Decalogue by their tradition. It was absurd that they should criticize the disciples for infraction of a merely human tradition concerning legal defilement.

c 14-23 True Principles concerning Defilement—14-16. Christ summoned the crowd and invited them to pay serious attention to his words. In 15 he states the fundamental principle that real defilement, moral defilement, is not caused by externals such as food, but by what comes from within, 20-23. The first part of this statement, 15*a*, was easy to understand in the light of the case which had been challenged by the Pharisees. But the second part, 15*b*, was not so easy to grasp—the disciples do not appear to have understood it—because ' the things that come from within a man ' might have referred to sources of defilement such as leprosy. **17-23.** Here Jesus sets forth clearly, in answer to the disciples, the meaning of the statement in 15. **18-19.** Food, like other externals, cannot of itself defile a man morally. It does not enter into or contaminate the seat of man's moral life. *Making* (*declaring*) *all foods clean.* This is a parenthesis inserted by Mark to explain the significance of Christ's words. His teaching means that the distinction between clean and unclean foods is abrogated. This was a radical change for persons accustomed to the Mosaic Law and Pharisaic tradition. It was only gradually that the full implications of Christ's teaching were grasped ; *cf.* Ac 10:9-16, 28 ; 11:1-10. **20-23.** The heart, as the seat of moral life, is the source whence proceed the evil thoughts and affections which cause moral defilement. ' From here the new law

according to the spirit takes its beginning ' (*Catena in* **732c** *Marc.*).

24-30 The Syrophoenician Woman ; *cf.* Mt 15:21-28 **d** —This was one of the few occasions on which Christ went outside Palestine. The district of Tyre and Sidon, part of ancient Phoenicia, now belonged to the Roman province of Syria. The population was pagan, and though the report of Christ's miracles had reached there, 3:8, it does not appear that it was his intention to preach the Gospel in the district. He may have wished to proceed quietly with the instruction of the disciples. **24.** ' Coasts ' : ὅρια = ' districts ', ' *territories* '. **27-28.** The ' children ' represent the Jews to whom Christ's personal mission extended ; *cf.* Mt 15:24. The ' dogs ' represent the Gentiles. The comparison is based on a familiar domestic scene, but the woman was probably well aware of the contempt which Jews had for the Gentiles and their gods. It is not certain that at the time of Christ the Gentiles were called dogs by the Jews. With profound humility and understanding she turned the image to her advantage—her request was only for a crumb of consolation, something which would not be missed from the rich feast offered to the Jews. **29-30.** Christ granted her request as a reward of her strong faith and deep humility.

31-37 The Cure of a Deaf-Mute—This incident is **e** recorded only by Mark whose account is again characterized by vivid touches suggesting the story of an eyewitness. **31.** Jesus had been in the Decapolis previously, 5:20, and his fame had been spread there by the man whom he had freed from diabolical possession. **32.** ' Dumb ' : μογιλάλος = ' speaking with difficulty ', ' with an impediment of speech '. **33.** ' *Taking him aside from the crowd* '. In the exercise of his miraculous powers Jesus avoided ostentation. His humility in this respect was a contrast to the pretensions of false messiahs who sought to win the favour of the people by extravagant promises of miraculous deeds. The prevalent misconceptions of the nature of Messianic salvation explain the measure of silence and secrecy with which Christ sought to veil his miracles and his own identity at the beginning of his ministry. In the present instance there was an additional reason. The gestures employed by Christ in curing this man were very appropriate to the cure which he was about to perform. But pagans might have mistaken their significance and have interpreted them as part of a magical rite. Some consider that the purpose of these gestures was to arouse in the man the faith required from those who sought the benefit of Christ's power. Jesus could have cured this man by a word, even at a distance, *cf.* Mt 8:8-13, but the actions performed in this case place in clear light the efficacious participation of his humanity in his miracles. This would not be so clear if he had cured the man by a mere word. **34.** ' Ephpheta ' : ἐφφαθά is a transcription of the Aramaic form *'eppᵉtaḥ* = *'etpᵉtaḥ* = ' Be thou opened '. Here again Mk gives the Aramaic word spoken by our Lord. **36.** The command of silence emphasizes the humility of Christ. He knew, of course, that the command would not be obeyed, but the disciples would have learned from Christ's example the lesson that they were not to seek personal renown from the exercise of the powers that they would enjoy. **37.** The crowds in their enthusiasm apply to Christ the words of Isaias, 35:5 f., concerning the Messianic age.

VIII 1-9 Feeding of Four Thousand ; *cf.* Mt 15:32-39 **f** —This second multiplication of the loaves and fishes appears to have taken place while Jesus was still in the Decapolis. Many critical writers assert that there was only a single multiplication and that this second account is simply a recension of the earlier one, 6:34-44. It is quite clear, however, that the evangelist intended to tell of two distinct incidents ; *cf.* 8:19 f. The general resemblance between the two accounts is not surprising, and there are important points of difference. This miracle was performed in the wilderness, while the first took place near Bethsaida-Julias with towns and villages nearby. Here it is Christ himself who takes the initiative, whereas previously it was

732f the disciples who suggested that the crowds should be sent away. There is also a difference in the numbers of those who were fed, the number of the loaves and fishes and the number of baskets of fragments which were left over. It is urged that the attitude of the disciples as expressed by their question ' Whence can anyone fill them with bread here in the wilderness ? ' is difficult to explain if they knew of an earlier multiplication. It must be remembered, however, that a considerable time had elapsed since the first multiplication and that it had not been the practice of Christ to work miracles to meet the everyday needs of the people. Clearly it was only by a miracle that the crowds could be fed. The question of the disciples, in effect, leaves the matter in the hands of Christ.

g **10-12 The Pharisees ask for a Sign from Heaven;** cf. Mt 15:39–16:4 ; Lk 11:16, 29–32 ; Mt 12:38–42 ; Lk 12:54–56—**10.** Dalmanutha is not otherwise known. In Mt 15:39 the best Gk MSS read ' Magadan '. No satisfactory identification of either place has been put forward. The presence of the Pharisees suggests that the incident in 11 took place on the western shore ; cf. 13. It is possible that there is some corruption in the form of the name ; cf. RB 53 (1946) 372–84. **11.** In asking for a sign from heaven the Pharisees had in mind some striking manifestation like the manna, Ex 16:12 ff., or the fire which fell from heaven, 3 Kg 18:22 ff. Such a sign, because of its unquestionable divine origin, would provide a dramatic confirmation of Christ's claims. It was commonly believed that the coming of the Messias would be accompanied by some outstanding sign of this kind. ' tempting him ' : ' putting him to the test '. The demand of the Pharisees was not prompted by a sincere desire for enlightenment. They had become the enemies of Christ because he acted independently of them and opposed their assertions. They had even attributed his miracles to the power of Satan. But they saw clearly that Christ was claiming to be an envoy from God, and now seek to put his claim to the test. **12.** Christ sighed because he knew of the evil intention of the Pharisees. If they had been men of goodwill they would not have needed any other or more dramatic signs than the miracles which Christ had already performed. He refused to grant a sign such as they sought. If he had granted it, some of them would still have remained unconvinced. Moreover, a sign of this kind would have encouraged false Messianic hopes, whereas Christ wished them to prepare their hearts for the kingdom.

h **13-21 The Leaven of the Pharisees and of Herod;** cf. Mt 16:5–12 ; Lk 12:1—**14.** It was a normal precaution to take provisions when crossing over to the eastern shore of the Lake of Galilee. **15.** The Jews regarded the fermentation caused by leaven as a kind of corruption. For this reason leaven was removed from their homes during paschal time. The Law forbade the inclusion of leaven in some of the offerings made in the temple, Lev 2:11. Christ here uses the word ' leaven ' in the metaphorical sense of a principle of moral corruption ; cf. 1 Cor 5:6 ff. ; Gal 5:9. The leaven of the Pharisees was hypocrisy, Lk 12:1. They were extremely concerned with the externals of religion but neglected the essential interior spirit. The leaven of Herod was the spirit of worldliness, preoccupation with pleasure and political ambitions. **16-21.** The disciples failed to understand Christ's warning, and thought that he was referring to their failure to bring provisions. Christ took them to task for their slowness in comprehending the significance of the wonderful events which they had witnessed. His words were a reminder that they should have learned by now to trust him, even for their material needs. Mark's insistence on the disciples' lack of understanding (cf. 6:52) is a noteworthy confirmation of the reliability of the Gospel. The evangelist makes no attempt to present a flattering picture of Peter and the other Apostles by omitting mention of their faults and weaknesses.

i **22-26 Cure of a Blind Man at Bethsaida**—This incident

is recorded only by Mk. As he had done previously in **7** the case of the deaf-mute, 7:31–37, Jesus takes the blind man aside, performs a certain ritual and forbids divulgation, 26. The reasons for secrecy are presumably the same as in the former instance. Christ performed both miracles out of compassion, and did not wish to give any occasion for misunderstanding about the nature of his mission. **24.** ' And as he began to see he said, " I see men ; for I see them as trees, (but) walking " '. Evidently the man had not been blind from birth. Various explanations have been put forward for the fact that Christ performed this cure slowly and by degrees. Some hold that the degree of healing corresponded to the man's faith in Christ. It is probable that Christ meant to teach a lesson to the disciples. They were to learn that spiritual enlightenment is usually a gradual process. It had been so in the case of the disciples themselves, and it would be thus also with those to whom they would preach the Gospel. The disciples could hardly have failed to see the Messianic significance of healing the eyes of the blind ; cf. Is 35:5.

27-33 Peter's Confession : Prediction of the Passion ? **and Resurrection ;** cf. Mt 16:13–23 ; Lk 9:18–22— Caesarea Philippi was a new city built by Philip the tetrarch on the site of the ancient Paneas, near the sources of the Jordan. In this pagan district Christ was away from the malicious intrigues and demands of the Pharisees, and could discuss freely with the disciples the fundamental question of his own identity and mission. **27-28.** The opinions about Christ correspond to the rumours which circulated at the court of Herod, 6:14–16. Those among the crowds who had formerly thought of Jesus as the Messias, Jn 6:14 f., may have abandoned the idea because he refused to manifest himself as the conquering Messias of popular expectation. **29.** Peter makes a clear confession that Jesus is the Messias. Neither Mk nor Lk give the additional phrase, ' Son of the living God ', nor do they report the promise of the Primacy to Peter. The silence of Mk on the latter point is due to dependence on Peter whose humility prompted him to omit from his preaching matters which brought honour to himself (Eusebius PG 22, 217). **31.** This prediction of the Passion and Resurrection was intended as a corrective to false ideas of a triumphant Messias. Now that the disciples firmly believed that Jesus was the Messias, it was necessary that they should understand that he was a suffering Messias (cf. Is 53) who would be rejected by the leaders of the Jews. **32-33.** Peter understood the meaning of this word which Christ ' spoke openly ', but he was obviously taken aback by the prediction of the fate of Jesus at the hands of the Jews, and ' began to remonstrate with him '. He was rebuked by Christ because his protest showed that his thoughts were out of harmony with the divine plan. It was God's will that the Messias should suffer. ' Satan ' : ' adversary '.

34-39 How to be a Follower of Christ ; cf. Mt 16: **?** 24–28 ; Lk 9:23–27 ; Jn 12:25—The teaching of this section is closely connected with what has gone before. As the Son of Man must suffer, so also must those who take him as their leader. **34.** ' Deny himself ' : treat himself as a stranger, renouncing his own interests. ' Take up his cross ' : the disciple must be ready to face even death by crucifixion. **35-36** explain why the disciple must be prepared to sacrifice even life itself. ' Life ' and ' soul ' translate the same word ψυχή, which can mean life, soul, oneself. In the context there is an underlying antithesis between physical life and the life of the soul. The person who sacrifices his life for the sake of Christ will secure the eternal life of the soul. To have saved one's life, or even to have gained everything that this world can offer, is of no avail if eternal life has been lost. **37.** Nothing that a man may gain in this world will enable him to buy the life of the soul ; once that has been lost in death, man has no means or power to redeem it. The Pontifical Biblical Commission replied in the negative to the question whether it was lawful to assert that the words of Christ found in Mt 16:26 and Lk 9:25 (cf. Mk 8:36 f.) in the literal sense do not refer to the eternal salvation of the soul, but merely the temporal life of man ; see § 52h. **38.** Whoever refuses to follow Christ because of the sacrifices which this involves, shows thereby that he is ashamed of Christ and his doctrine. At the day of Judgement Christ will disown those who have been ashamed to follow him. **39** (Gk 9:1). From here to the end of ch 9 the verse numbers in the Vulgate differ by one from the numbers in the Gk text. The opening words ' And he said to them ' are a transition formula and indicate that 39 is an independent statement not closely connected with 38. **39b.** *until they see the kingdom of God come* (ἐληλυθυῖαν : *established*) *with power* ; cf. Mt 16:28 ' until they see the Son of Man coming in his kingdom ' ; Lk 9:27 ' until they see the kingdom of God '. The coming of the kingdom in power is not to be understood as the Parousia, when Christ will come as the Supreme Judge ' in the glory of the Father with the holy angels ', 38 ; cf. Mt 25:31 ff. None of the features usually associated with the coming of Christ in final judgement on the world is mentioned here. Neither can the coming of the kingdom be explained satisfactorily as a reference to the Transfiguration, Resurrection or Pentecost. These events belonged to the immediate future, but the words ' there are some standing here who shall not taste death ' etc., point to a more remote period. Christ was speaking of a striking manifestation of power related to the establishment of his kingdom on earth. If he had one particular manifestation in mind, it is probable that the destruction of Jerusalem was the event in question. It marked the end of the ancient economy. Together with the expansion of the Church through preaching of the Gospel to the Gentiles, ' God adding his testimony by signs and wonders and manifold deeds of power, and impartings of the Holy Spirit, according to his will ', Heb 2:4, it constituted a striking proof that God had established his kingdom ' in power ' on earth ; cf. Feuillet, NRT 71 (1949) 709–15.

IX 1-7 The Transfiguration ; cf. Mt 17:1–8 ; Lk 9:28–36—**1-2.** This is the only place, outside the Passion narrative, where Mark gives a precise indication of the date. The six days are counted from Peter's confession at Caesarea Philippi which is now confirmed by the events at the Transfiguration. The same three Apostles were present at the raising of the daughter of Jairus and were also with Christ at the Agony. A tradition coming from the 4th cent. identifies the high mountain as Tabor in Galilee. ' Transfigured ' : μετεμορφώθη, ' transformed '. The glory of the divinity which was normally veiled is allowed to shine forth. The Apostles are made ' eye-witnesses of his majesty ', 2 Pet 1:16, ' we saw his glory ', Jn 1:14 ; cf. Phil 2:6 f. Even Christ's garments shared in the radiance proceeding from the glory of his divine Person. **3.** Moses and Elias represent the Law and the Prophets. By their presence they testify to the continuity and harmony between the Old Dispensation and the New Covenant inaugurated by Christ who had come ' not to destroy the Law or the Prophets . . . but to fulfil ', Mt 5:17. **4-5.** ' *It is well that we are here* ' : the exact purport of the phrase is uncertain. Peter may have thought that this vision was the beginning of the glorious reign of the Messias. In his confusion and eagerness he offered to provide three huts for Christ, Moses and Elias. **6.** The voice of the Father, coming from the cloud which is the external manifestation of God's presence (cf. Ex 16:10 ; 19:9, 16), repeats the declaration made at the Baptism, Mk 1:11. This is the culminating point of Mark's Gospel. ' Hear him ' : henceforth they owe obedience to Christ, not to the Law and the Prophets which have rendered testimony to him through Moses and Elias. The Transfiguration of Christ, together with the appearance of Moses and Elias and the declaration by the Father, was a confirmation of all that Christ had taught them concerning his own Person and his relation to the Old Law. It

was undoubtedly intended to strengthen the faith of **733d** the Apostles and to prepare them for the trials of the Passion. According to Leo the Great (PL 54, 310) the chief purpose of the Transfiguration was to remove the scandal of the Cross from the hearts of the disciples. ' He reveals his glory so that they may no longer be distressed by their own death or the death of the Master '. (*Catena in Marc.*)

8-12 The Return of Elias ; cf. Mt 17:9–13—**8-9.** The **e** command of silence was particularly necessary here because this manifestation of Christ's glory would have made it all the more difficult to understand the prediction of his sufferings. After the Resurrection all these things would be seen in proper perspective. **10.** According to a belief based on Mal 4:5 f. Elias was to come before the Messias to prepare for him ; cf. Justin, *Dial. c. Tryph.* 49. But they have now seen Elias come after Christ, not before him, and he has disappeared without carrying out the expected preparation for the Messias. **11-12.** ' [*If*] *Elias comes first and restores all things, and [then] how is it written of the Son of Man that he must suffer many things and be despised ? But I say to you that Elias has come, and they did to him what they would, as it is written of him* '. The majority of ancient commentators concluded from this passage that the prophet Elias in person will return before the second coming of Christ ; cf. Skrinjar, VD 14 (1934) 361–7. It is difficult however, to maintain this interpretation in view of Christ's statements that Elias has come, 13, and that John the Baptist is ' Elias who is to come ', Mt 11:13 f. Moreover, we are told that the disciples understood that the Elias of whom Christ spoke was the Baptist, Mt 17:13. It seems more satisfactory to take the opening phrase ' Elias comes first ' etc. as a concessive clause. Christ grants that the Scriptures speak of the coming of Elias, but they also foretell the sufferings of the Messias (cf. Is 53 ; Ps 22). If it were true that Elias in person was to come and restore everything in preparation for the coming of the Messias, how then explain that the Messias should suffer ? The fact is that the precursor of the Messias foretold by Scripture has already come in the person of John the Baptist, who is figuratively called Elias ; ' and he will go before him in the spirit and power of Elias ', Lk 1:17. The restoration which he carried out in preparation for the Messias did not save him from sufferings similar to those which befell Elias, his prophetic prototype ; cf. 3 Kg chh 17–19. Similarly, all that has been foretold about the Messias must be fulfilled. His mission must be understood in the light of the prophecies concerning his sufferings.

13-28 Cure of a Possessed Boy ; cf. Mt 17:14–21 ; Lk **f** 9:37–43—Here again it is noteworthy that the narrative of Mk is much more detailed than the accounts of the other Synoptics. **13.** The dispute with the Scribes was about the failure of the disciples to cure the boy. **17.** ' dasheth him ' : ' *casts him down* '. The symptoms of the boy's illness correspond to those of epilepsy. In Mt 17:15 his condition is described by the word σεληνιάζεται which was in common use to designate epilepsy. But it is clear from Christ's words, 24 f., that the boy was also possessed by the demon. **18.** The complaint uttered by Christ applied to all present. All of them, in different degrees, were lacking in faith. **19.** ' troubled him ' : ' *threw him into convulsions* '. **20-23.** This further description of the boy's state is found only in Mk. **22.** ' If thou canst believe ' : lit. ' This if thou canst ', *i.e.* ' *as for being able* '. The phrase refers back to ' If thou canst ', 21. **23.** The father realizes the imperfect nature of his faith but appeals to Jesus to help him nonetheless. **25.** ' Greatly tearing him ' : ' *throwing him into violent convulsions* '. **27-28.** The power of casting out demons which the disciples had received did not operate after the fashion of magic. Christ expelled demons by a simple command because of his divine power. The disciples had failed to cast out this demon because they relied excessively on themselves, forgetting that they were only instruments of divine power. They should have recourse to God in prayer, with faith,

733f Mt 17:18–20, and humility. **28.** ' This kind ' : it is uncertain whether this means demons in general or a particular class of demons whom it is especially difficult to expel. ' and fasting ' : these words are missing from a few important MSS.

734a **29–31 The Second Prediction of the Passion** ; *cf*. Mt 17:22 f. ; Lk 9:44 f.—The Galilean ministry is now at an end and the last journey to Jerusalem about to begin. **30.** Jesus avoided the crowds ' *for he was instructing his disciples* '. The renewed prediction of the Passion was necessary because this was an aspect of the role of the Messias which the disciples found it difficult to understand. Like the doctrine of the necessity for personal sacrifices by the followers of Christ, it did not accord with popular expectations.

b **32–36 Jesus Checks the Ambition of the Disciples** ; *cf*. Mt 18:1–5 ; Lk 18:46–48—This and the succeeding sections to 9:49 give instructions on a variety of topics without any strict logical sequence. It is not necessary to hold that all were spoken in the same circumstances. **32–33.** The discussion among the disciples may have arisen from the promise of the Primacy made to Peter a short time previously, Mt 16:18 f. **34.** Christ sets before them the ideal of humble and devoted service of which he himself had given the example ; *cf*. Lk 22:24–27 ; Jn 13:13–15. In his kingdom selfish ambition for preferment is out of place. Greatness in the kingdom will be estimated not by the distinction of high position, but by the degree of devoted service. **35–36.** The child represents the humble and unimportant among those whom the disciples will be called to serve. Whoever receives such little ones with kindness for Christ's sake, receives Christ and the Father who sent him. If humble service brings so great a reward, ambition for the highest places in the kingdom is misplaced. Mk alone mentions that Christ embraced the child.

c **37–39 Use of the Name of Jesus** ; *cf*. Lk 9:49 f.—**37.** The phrase ' in my name ', 36, probably recalled to John's mind the incident of the man who was casting out devils in the name of Jesus and had been ordered by the disciples to desist because he did not belong to their group. Jesus disapproves of their action and recommends a more tolerant attitude. One who performs miracles in Christ's name thereby recognizes Christ's authority, and is unlikely to speak ill of him. The dispositions and faith of such a person may be imperfect, but his miracles are a commendation of Christ and his teaching. Unlike the Scribes and Pharisees who were irreconcilable in their opposition, he is making common cause with the disciples. **40–41.** Here Christ returns to the theme of 36. The smallest service rendered to the disciples because they are Christ's followers, will not go unrewarded. But whoever scandalizes those who believe in Christ, especially children, will incur a dreadful punishment.

d **42–49 Avoidance of Scandal**; *cf*. Mt 18:6–9 ; 5:29 f. ; Lk 17:1 f.—The followers of Christ are to avoid causing scandal to others, and they must also be prepared to sacrifice anything which is a cause of scandal to themselves. The hand, foot and eye represent particularly dear possessions. But nothing, however precious or useful, is to be spared if it is a cause of scandal. ' Life ', 42, 44, is identified with ' the kingdom of God ' in 46. This is the true, eternal life which the just will attain as a reward for faithful service. The place of punishment is the hell of unquenchable fire, γέεννα, Gehenna. The Gk word is formed from the Aramaic *Ge-hinnam* = the valley of Hinnom. This was the name of the valley to the south of Jerusalem where at one time children were offered in sacrifice to Moloch, Jer 7:31. Later it was made the dumping ground for the refuse of the city. The fire which burned there constantly and the worms which fed on the refuse became symbols of the torments inflicted on the wicked, and in the apocalyptic literature the name Gehinnom was applied to the place where the wicked were punished ; *cf*. 4 Esdras 2:29 ; Enoch 27:2. In Is 66:24, which is quoted in 47, the prophet alludes to Gehinnom as a

symbol of the place of condemnation where rebels against God are punished ; *cf*. Kissane, *Book of Isaiah*, 2, 327 f. **48a.** ' For everyone shall be salted with fire '. Some take this phrase closely with 47 and interpret it in the sense that the fire of hell preserves as well as punishes. It has power to preserve, like salt, so that those who go to hell will not be destroyed by the fire, but will be punished for ever. Others take this verse as the conclusion to 42–47. The words ' salted with fire ' refer to the purifying effect of the voluntary renunciations and sacrifices made by the disciples who will be like acceptable sacrificial offerings which have been sprinkled with salt, Lev 2:13. **48b.** Critical editions of the text omit ' and every victim shall be salted with salt ' as a gloss. **49a.** Similar expressions are to be found in Mt 5:13 ; Lk 14:34. Salt is used to season and preserve foods, but if it should lose its saltness it is no longer of any use. **49b.** This final admonition links up with the dispute among the Apostles. The imagery is based on the idea of salt as seasoning and as a symbol of friendship. A ' covenant of salt ' meant a perpetual covenant, Num 18:19 ; 2 Par 13:5. If the disciples have within them the salt of the true Christian spirit, they will be at peace with one another. They will not dispute about the highest places. This was all the more necessary in those who are the ' salt of the earth ', Mt 5:13, as their example would influence so many others.

X 1–XIII 37 Journey towards Jerusalem and Last Ministry in Jerusalem.

X 1 Ministry in Judaea and Peraea ; *cf*. Mt chh 19–20 ; Lk 9:51–18:34—' *And departing thence he came into the region of Judaea and beyond the Jordan* '. This mention of a journey into Judaea and Peraea is probably to be understood as a general reference to a period of missionary activity which took place in the interval between the end of the Galilean ministry and Christ's arrival in Jerusalem for the Pasch at which he was put to death. The visits to Jerusalem for the feasts of Tabernacles, Jn 7:14, and Dedication, Jn 10:22, may belong to this period. For some time Christ had concentrated on the instruction of the disciples, but now he resumes the teaching of the multitudes as formerly.

2–12 The Question of Divorce ; *cf*. Mt 19:3–12 ; 5:31 f. ; Lk 16:18—Mk's account differs from Mt in two main points ; he omits the words ' for every cause ', Mt 19:3b, from the Pharisees' question, 2, and also the clause ' except it be for fornication ', Mt 19:9, from Christ's reply, 11. The reason for the omission is presumably that these phrases referred to matters which were primarily of interest to Jews and would scarcely be intelligible to Gentile readers. **2.** The Mosaic Law, Deut 24:1–4, permitted a man to divorce his wife ' if she did not find favour in his eyes because he found in her a shameful thing '. If a man decided to repudiate his wife, the Law commanded him to give her a ' bill of divorce '. The marriage was then regarded as dissolved, and both parties were free to contract new marriages. But though all Jews agreed that divorce was allowed, they differed in their interpretation of the ' shameful thing ' (Heb. *ervat dābār*) which justified a man in repudiating his wife. According to Shammai, adultery was the only legal cause. Hillel and his school allowed divorce for far less serious reasons. The Pharisees, probably having some knowledge of Christ's views, hoped to force him into open contradiction of the Mosaic Law. **3–5.** Jesus knew their evil intention and asked what Moses had commanded. Actually Moses had merely permitted divorce, but had commanded that the woman who was repudiated should be given a bill of divorce which would regularize her position. This legislation did not grant the Hebrews the right to repudiate as a privilege. It simply tolerated an abuse which was due to their evil dispositions. Divorce did not correspond to the primitive institution of marriage. **6–9.** God's will in regard to marriage and divorce is shown in the primitive institution of marriage as recorded in Gen 1:27 ;

2:24. Man and woman united in marriage are linked by bonds as real and permanent as those which unite members of the same family. Divorce, therefore, is contrary to God's law. **10-12.** Here, in answer to the disciples, who were naturally surprised by teaching contrary to that which all Jews accepted, Jesus reaffirms that neither partner is set free through divorce to marry again. Husband and wife are on an equal footing in this respect. According to Jewish law it was only the husband who had the right to initiate divorce proceedings. In Roman law, at the time of Christ, the wife had the same right as the husband ; *cf.* J. Bonsirven, *Le Divorce dans le Nouveau Testament* (Tournai 1948) ; U. Holzmeister, Bi 26 (1945) 133–46.
13-16 Jesus blesses the Children ; *cf.* Mt 19:13–15 ; Lk 18:15–17—Mk alone mentions that Jesus was *indignant* with the disciples. They probably thought that by keeping away the children and their mothers they would save him from an intrusion which would interfere with the more important work of teaching. **14-15.** The simple confidence and docility natural to the child must be possessed, as the result of deliberate choice, by all those who seek to enjoy the blessings of the kingdom of God. **16.** As in 9:35, Mark is the only evangelist who mentions that Jesus embraced the children.
17-22 The Rich Young Man ; *cf.* Mt 19:16–22 ; Lk 18:18–23—**17-18.** It would seem that this man was impressed by the preceding incident and now wants to know what conditions he must fulfil in order to have a share in the kingdom. The expression 'receive life everlasting' (*cf.* 9:42, 44, 46 ; 10:30) corresponds to 'enter the kingdom', 15, and probably refers to membership of the kingdom on earth as well as to enjoyment of the eternal reward of the just. '*Why callest thou me good ? No one is good but God alone*'. These words are not a disavowal of a claim to divinity. According to many commentators, Christ intended by them to give a hint of his divine nature. It was not the custom of the time to add the epithet 'good' to the title 'Master' (Rabbi, Teacher). God alone is the absolute good. If Jesus deserves the title 'Good Master', it is because he is more than a merely human teacher. Others hold that Jesus did not intend by these words to suggest anything about his own divinity. He answered in accordance with the state of mind of this enquirer who had come to him as to an outstanding human teacher. The flattering title by which he was addressed gave Jesus an opportunity of turning the man's thoughts to God, the supreme good and source of all goodness, to whom all honour is due ; *cf. Catena in Marc.* **21.** '*Jesus fixed his gaze upon him and loved him*'. This detail is found only in Mk and again points to an eye-witness as the source of the evangelist's information. The man was good and sincere, but it was still possible for him to aim higher by carrying out a counsel of perfection. Renunciation of worldly goods would be compensated by treasure in heaven. **22.** 'He shows him that the reward is great, and great indeed is the recompense for following him' (*Catena in Marc.*). '*His face fell at the saying and he departed in grief*'. His attachment to his possessions was such that he was not prepared to make the sacrifice proposed by Christ.
23-27 The Danger of Riches ; *cf.* Mt 19:23–26 ; Lk 18:24–27—These verses forcibly point the moral of the preceding incident. **23-24.** '*With what difficulty shall they who have riches*' etc. The repetition of this pronouncement, which amazed the disciples, leaves no room for doubt about the meaning and the importance of Christ's statement. Riches are not evil in themselves, but man has only a stewardship of this world's goods. Undue attachment to wealth is a form of idolatry and inconsistent with true service of God. 'You cannot serve God and mammon', Mt 6:24. **25.** The paradoxical expression 'a camel passing through the eye of a needle' may have been a proverbial phrase signifying an impossibility. The Talmud has a similar expression—'an elephant passing through the eye of a needle'. **26-27.** The disciples understood that Christ

was speaking literally of an impossibility. But what **735e** is humanly impossible does not exceed the power of God. With the aid of grace, and by attaching himself to God as the supreme good, the rich man can be saved.
28-31 The Reward of those who leave all to follow f Christ ; *cf.* Mt 19:27–30 ; Lk 18:28–30—**28.** Peter's question follows naturally from the incident of the rich man and the subsequent statements of Christ. It seems to invite approval of the action of the disciples in abandoning everything to follow Christ. **29-30.** A twofold reward is promised to those who have abandoned earthly interests and family ties 'for the sake of Christ and the Gospel' : first, 'a hundred-fold now in this time . . . with persecutions' ; second, 'in the world to come life everlasting'. The clause 'with persecutions' shows that the hundred-fold recompense in this life is not to be understood in terms of earthly happiness. According to St Jerome (PL 26, 139), the meaning of the hundred-fold reward is that whoever abandons fleshly things for Christ's sake will receive a spiritual recompense whose value by comparison with earthly things is as a hundred to a small number. A more satisfactory explanation would appear to be that Christ had in mind the spiritual kinship and the bond of charity which unites all those who make the sacrifices demanded from every true disciple ; *cf.* 8:34–38. The true follower of Christ acquires a new kindred far more numerous than those whom he may have abandoned for the sake of Christ and the Gospel. In this new relationship, dominated by charity, all are 'brothers', Mt 23:8, and 'children of God', Jn 1:12 ; Ac 2:44 ; 4:32. The recompense granted in this life does not, however, exclude suffering and persecution at the hands of men. Christ foretold that his followers would suffer for his name's sake, that they would be hated because they belong to him ; *cf.* Mt 5:11 ; 10:24 ; Lk 6:22 ; Jn 13:16 ; 15:19. **31.** Some take this as a warning to the Apostles, who are now in the first places because they have left all things to follow Christ, lest through presumption they should fall to the lowest places hereafter. More probably, however, the 'first' are those who, judged by the world's standards, hold the highest places in this life, the rich, Pharisees, members of the Sanhedrin. Hereafter, these will be in the lowest places, while the Apostles, who are of no account in the world's estimation, will take the highest places.
32-34 Third Prediction of the Passion ; *cf.* Mt g 20:17–19 ; Lk 18:31–34—**32b.** '*And Jesus was walking before them, and they were dismayed, and those who followed were afraid*'. Here we have a vivid picture of Christ going forward resolutely to face the sufferings which awaited him in Jerusalem. Mark is the only evangelist who mentions the dismay of the disciples and the fear of those who were accompanying Christ. **33-34.** This prediction of the Passion is more detailed than the earlier ones, 8:31 ; 9:30. The statement that the Son of Man would be handed over to the Gentiles and put to death implies that he would die by crucifixion. But the assurance of final triumph is contained in the words '*after three days he shall rise again*'. These predictions of the Passion, though disconcerting for the disciples, put the doctrine of the suffering Messias clearly before them. Later, the fulfilment of these prophecies in Christ's Passion and Resurrection confirmed their faith.
35-40 The Request of James and John ; *cf.* Mt h 20:20–23—**35-37.** The request of the disciples was made through their mother, according to Mt. Their petition was for the highest places in the kingdom next to Christ. Despite his teaching about the Passion and the sacrifices which would be demanded from his followers, 8:34–38, they did not appreciate fully the place of sufferings in the Messianic kingdom. **38.** The metaphorical expression '*drink the cup*' could signify either joy or affliction. In this context it obviously refers to the endurance of suffering. 'Baptism' : lit. 'immersion'. This metaphor conveys the idea of

735h being overwhelmed by sorrows. **39-40.** James and John will be associated with the sufferings of Christ, but it is not part of his mission as Messias to assign places in the kingdom. These are assigned in accordance with the eternal decree of the Father. As Messias, the capacity in which he had been approached by the two brothers, Jesus carries out the decrees of the Father—he does not alter them. **40***b***.** ' To you ' : these words are not authentic, and should be omitted.

i 41-45 The Obligation of Service by those in Authority ; *cf.* Mt 20:24-28 ; Lk 22:24-27—**41.** The other Apostles were annoyed by the pretensions of James and John. Jesus took the opportunity of teaching the Twelve the lesson of humble service of those whom they would rule. **42-44.** ' *You know that those who are regarded as rulers of the Gentiles lord it over them, and their great ones domineer over them* '. The Apostles will have authority in the Church, but in the exercise of that authority they are not to imitate rulers and high officials who rule tyrannically and arbitrarily in their own interest. Rather they should make the service of those entrusted to them the ideal of their office. In that way they will imitate ' the Son of Man who came not to be ministered unto, but to minister '. **45***b***.** ' to give his life a *ransom* for many '. In these words Christ states the purpose and redemptive value of his death. The use of λύτρον in profane Gk and in LXX confirms the translation ' ransom ', *e.g.* the price paid for the redemption of a slave. The death of Christ, therefore, is like the price paid to redeem from slavery. The slavery in question is slavery to sin. Christ's sufferings and death are an expiation of the sins of men. ' for many ' : ἀντὶ πολλῶν ' *instead of many* '. The preposition ἀντί conveys the idea of substitution ; Jesus pays the price of redemption for ' many ' who are unable to pay it themselves. ' Many ' is here used as a contrast to the *One*, the Son of Man, who suffers for the multitude. No one is excluded from the benefit of his redemptive sacrifice ; *cf.* 14:24. There is a clear connexion between these words of Christ and the teaching of Isaias concerning the sufferings of the Servant of Yahweh, Is 52:13–53:12.

j 46-52 Cure of the Blind Man Bartimeus ; *cf.* Mt 20:29-34 ; Lk 18:35-43—Mk again excels in its vivid presentation of the incident. **46.** ' And as he went out of Jericho '. Mk and Mt agree in saying that this miracle was performed as Jesus was leaving Jericho, while Lk states that it took place when he was drawing near Jericho. The explanation of the discrepancy is that Mk and Mt are referring to the ancient city conquered by Josue, through which Jesus had just passed, while Lk is speaking of the new Jericho built by Herod, in which Christ was about to be received by Zacchaeus. The miracle was performed on the way between these two places ; *cf.* Ketter, Bi 15 (1934) 411–18. Bartimeus means ' son of Timeus '. Mk records the name probably because the man was known in the Christian community. **47.** ' Son of David ' was the most widely used title of the Messias ; *cf.* 12:35-37 ; Jn 7:42. It was a title which recalled the promises made to David, 2 Kg 7:8-16. **51.** ' Rabboni ' = *My Rabbi* (Master) ; *cf.* Jn 20:16. **52.** ' *Thy faith has saved thee* ' : this statement refers primarily to the restoration of the man's sight, but he was probably also granted the light of salvation, for ' he accompanied him [Jesus] *on the way* '.

736a XI 1-11 The Triumphal Entry into Jerusalem ; *cf.* Mt 21:1-11 ; Lk 19:29-44 ; Jn 12:12-19—Here Jesus presents himself to the people as Messias, fulfilling one of the clearest Messianic prophecies, Zach 9:9, in the manner of his triumphal entry. On this occasion Jesus makes no attempt to withdraw from the crowds, and openly approves of their acclamations, Lk 19:39 f. He was truly the Messias, though not the Messias of popular expectation. He had not come to establish an earthly kingdom. This modest and peaceful triumph would not have caused any alarm to the Roman authorities. **1.** ' And when they were drawing near to Jerusalem, *to* (at) *Bethphage and Bethany on the Mount*

of Olives '. Bethphage was between Jerusalem and Bethany, near the summit of Mt Olivet, and is probably the village mentioned in 2. **2-6.** It is noteworthy that Jesus himself took the initiative in making these preparations which were intended to fulfil the prophecy of Zacharias ; *cf.* Mt 21:2 f. **3***b***.** ' *The Lord hath need of it, and will at once send it back hither* '. **7-10.** It was an extraordinary mark of honour to spread their garments on the road before Jesus ; *cf.* 4 Kg 9:13. ' Hosanna ' : Heb *hôša'-nā'* = ' Save, we pray ' ; *cf.* Ps 117:25 ;85:2. The expression had become a cry of acclamation. Here it is a triumphant salutation of Jesus as Messias. He is coming in the name of the Lord (*cf.* Ps 117:26) to restore the kingdom of David, *i.e.* to establish the Messianic kingdom. For the Jews, the coming of the kingdom of David represented the fulfilment of the Messianic promises. **11.** As was fitting on this occasion, Jesus visited the temple where he would have noted the abuses which profaned the sanctuary, but owing to the lateness of the hour and possibly in order to allow the excitement of the crowds to die down, he took no action till next day. Meantime he retired to Bethany with the Twelve.

12-14 The Barren Fig-Tree ; *cf.* Mt 21:18 f.—This incident is to be understood as a symbolic act or parable in action. Such a method of teaching or giving a warning was familiar to the Jews from the OT ; *cf.* Is 20:1-6 ; Jer 13:1-11 ; 27:1-11. Some have held that Christ was not really hungry on this occasion, that he merely simulated hunger in order to lead up to the miracle he was about to perform ; *cf.* Maldonatus, *Commentary on Mt 21:18*. But there is no sufficient reason for departing from the obvious meaning of the evangelist's words. Christ's hunger was real, and made a very natural starting point for the symbolic action. He did not, however, expect to find fruit on the tree ' for it was not the time for figs ', 13. This strange act on his part, as well as the malediction and subsequent withering of the fig-tree, forms part of the symbolic action. They were intended to impress upon the mind of the Apostles something the sense of which they did not immediately perceive. The chief lesson of the incident is that those who fail to yield the fruit of good works which Christ seeks will be punished ; *cf.* Lk 13:6-9. This lesson applied in the first instance to the Jews who failed to answer his call, but it has an application for all time, especially to Christians. It is probable that the withering of the fig-tree was also intended to be a timely reminder of the power of Jesus. He could have used his power to destroy his enemies, but refrained from doing so and went forward voluntarily to his death : ' the fig-tree was withered for the sake of the disciples in order that they might be encouraged. . . . It was necessary that he should give proof of his power to punish, so that the disciples might learn that although he had power to wither the Jews, he submitted voluntarily ' (*Catena in Marc.*).

15-19 Christ drives the Sellers from the Temple ; *cf.* Mt 21:12-17 ; Lk 19:45-48 ; Jn 2:13-17—It is uncertain whether John and the Synoptic writers are dealing with one and the same incident or two distinct occurrences, one at the beginning of the public ministry (Jn), the other at the final Pasch (Synoptics). Among those who hold that there was only a single expulsion of the sellers, there is a difference of opinion as to the time at which it took place. The majority favour the view that it was at the beginning of the public ministry. They argue that John gives the exact historical setting, while the Synoptic writers, who were less concerned with matters of chronology, relate the incident in connexion with their one description of a visit of Jesus to Jerusalem during the public ministry. **15.** Mk, more precise in details of information than Mt or Lk, connects the driving out of the sellers from the temple with the day after the triumphal entry, 12. The fact that Mk gives the precise day is an indication that an expulsion of the sellers from the temple did take place at the final Pasch. Animals and other things required for the sacrifices were being

86c bought and sold. The money-changers took foreign money in exchange for the coinage in which the tax for the temple was paid ; *cf.* Mt 17:23-26. These commercial activities, conducted with all the clamour of an oriental market-place, were a profanation of the sanctuary. **16.** This detail is found only in Mk ; evidently people carrying loads were taking a short cut through the temple area. **17.** The Scriptural passages are quoted from Is 56:7 and Jer 7:11, ' *Is my house a robber's cave ?* ' Trafficking within the temple precincts, with its exploitation of the pilgrims, had, in effect, turned the place of prayer and worship into a haunt of robbers. **18.** Christ's action was considered an infringement of the authority of the priests, who were responsible for the administration of the temple. The Scribes should have approved the example of zeal for God's house which Jesus had given, but because of their conflicts with him they joined with the priests in seeking a way to bring about his death. **19.** Christ withdrew from the city each evening probably in order to prevent any attempt by the Sanhedrin to seize him before the time when he would voluntarily yield himself to the power of his enemies.

d 20-26 The Withered Fig-Tree : Faith and Prayer ; *cf.* Mt 21:19*b*-22—**20-21.** Mk again gives more precise information than Mt, mentioning that it was next morning that the disciples noticed that the fig-tree was withered, and that it was Peter who drew Christ's attention to it. **22-23.** Jesus did not explain the symbolism of the incident of the fig-tree, but in the words ' *Have faith in God* ' he drew attention to that faith which is an essential prerequisite for the performance of deeds of power such as the withering of the fig-tree at his command. By confident faith in God, through whose power miracles are wrought, even that which seems impossible will be accomplished, provided it is reasonable and useful for the kingdom of God ; *cf.* Mt 17:20. **24.** In prayer also it is necessary that we should have confident faith that our requests will be granted. ' Believe that *you have received* ' (ἐλάβετε) expresses the confident assurance that the petition will be granted. **25.** ' Stand to pray ' : standing was the ordinary posture in prayer. To pray on bended knees or prostrate on the ground was a sign of insistent supplication. The disciples are reminded of their duty to forgive others before seeking from God forgiveness of their offences against him, Mt 6:14 f. Thus prayer will be inspired by charity as well as by faith. **26** is not found in the best Gk MSS.

e 27-33 Jesus is questioned about His Authority ; *cf.* Mt 21:23-27 ; Lk 20:1-8—**27-28.** The group who approached Jesus were probably an official delegation from the Sanhedrin, the Jewish supreme council, which was constituted from representatives of the priestly families, the Scribes and the lay aristocracy of the Jews (the ancients). Their question about Christ's authority may have arisen from his action in driving the buyers and sellers from the temple. Responsibility for the administration of the temple rested with the priests, and Christ had acted without their authority. **29-30.** Instead of giving a direct reply, Jesus put to the delegation a question which would have set them on the right track if they were conscientiously seeking information. They should have had no difficulty in recognizing the heavenly origin and authority of the mission of John the Baptist. A similar conclusion was indicated in the case of Christ, especially as the Baptist had borne witness to him, Jn 1:29-37 ; 3:25-30. **31-33.** They were not prepared to consider the question in accordance with the evidence. They had shown no enthusiasm for the mission of John. To admit its heavenly origin now would have been to condemn themselves, and yet they dared not deny it because of the popular belief that John was a prophet from God.

f XII 1-12 The Parable of the Wicked Husbandmen ; *cf.* Mt 21:33-46 ; Lk 20:9-19—In this parable Jesus made it clear to the deputation from the Sanhedrin that he was aware of the plot to put him to death, and warned them that this crime, which was the climax

of Israel's ingratitude and disobedience to God who **736f** had given so many favours to the chosen people, would bring dire punishment. Their privileges would pass to the Gentiles. ' Therefore I say to you that the kingdom of God shall be taken from you and shall be given to a nation yielding the fruits thereof ', Mt 21:43.

1. The careful preparation of the vineyard (*cf.* Is 5:1 f.), which was equipped with everything necessary for protection and for the extraction of the wine before being handed over to the husbandmen, symbolizes the lavish favours which God had extended to the chosen people. **2-5.** The servants represent the prophets and others who spoke in God's name to the chosen people, urging them to remain faithful to the covenant and to obey God's law, but constantly received ill-treatment at their hands. **6-8.** ' The beloved son ' (*cf.* 1:11 ; 9:6) is Christ. The contrast with servants throws into relief the fact that Christ claims divine sonship in an altogether unique sense. He is the Son and Heir, Heb 1:1-4, and, like God the Father, enjoys full rights over the vineyard because of his divine nature. **9.** By the death of Christ the old order is abrogated. In the new dispensation which replaces it the privileges of the Jews are extended to the Gentiles. ' The vineyard is let to us on condition that we yield fruit to God in due season ', Jerome, PL 26, 158. **10-11.** In the original context of Ps 117:22 f. the stone rejected by the builders represents Israel which, though despised by the pagan empires, was destined to play a decisive part in God's providential design ; *cf.* Calès, *Le Livre des Psaumes*, 2 (Paris 1936⁶) 402. In like manner, Christ, though rejected by the leaders of the Jews, holds a position of supreme importance in the Messianic kingdom. His triumph over his enemies would be complete. ' Head of the corner ' : the corner stone which joins two walls, an essential element in the building. **12.** The significance of Christ's words was quite clear to the representatives of the Sanhedrin and they would have attempted to seize him were it not that they feared the people.

13-17 The Tribute to Caesar ; *cf.* Mt 22:15-22 ; Lk **g** 20:20-26—The tribute in question was the poll-tax, payable to the imperial treasury, which had been imposed by the Romans after the deposition of Archelaus in A.D. 6. The tax was resented by many Jews on patriotic grounds. It created a real problem of conscience for those who thought that the payment of tribute to a pagan overlord was inconsistent with the theocratic conception of God as the only true ruler of Israel. The Zealots, led by Judas of Galilee, refused to pay the tax on this ground ; *cf.* Jos., *Ant.* 18, 1, 1 ; *B.J.* 2, 8, 1. **14b.** ' *Is it lawful to pay tribute to Caesar or not ? Should we give* (it) *or should we not give* (it) *?* ' In practice, the Pharisees as well as the Herodians (*cf.* 3:6) submitted to Roman overlordship and paid the tax. The sole purpose of their hypocritical question was to trap Christ. They knew his Messianic claims, and interpreting these in accordance with the popular conception of the Messias as a national hero who would overthrow foreign domination, they felt that Jesus would declare that the tax should not be paid. They could then ' deliver him up to the authority and power of the governor ', Lk 20:20, as an agitator against Roman rule. **15-17.** The use by the Jews of Roman coinage stamped with the image of the Emperor and bearing his name and titles was a sign of acceptance of Roman dominion. In the words ' Render therefore to Caesar the things that are Caesar's and to God the things that are God's ' Christ teaches that the practical recognition of Roman authority implied in the payment of the tribute to Caesar was not incompatible with duty to God. This reply of Christ embodies a principle which has a wider application to the relations between the demands of civil authority and the fulfilment of obligations to God. The obligation of submission to the civil power is limited by the primary duty of conforming our conduct to the law of God ; *cf.* Rom 13:1-7 ; 1 Pet 2:13-17.

18-27 The Resurrection of the Dead ; *cf.* Mt 22:23-33 ; **h** Lk 20:27-40—**18.** This is the first mention of the

736h Sadducees in Mk. They were the section of the Jewish nation who had been influenced most deeply by Hellenism. Members of the sect belonged mainly to the priestly families and upper classes ; *cf.* Ac 5:17. Under the Romans they gave ready submission to the established order. One of their number was regularly selected as high-priest at this time. In religious matters, ' the Sadducees say that there is no resurrection, nor angel, nor spirit : but the Pharisees confess both ', Ac 23:6–10 ; *cf.* Jos. *Ant.* 18, 1, 4. They also differed from the Pharisees in their refusal to attach importance to the traditions of the ancients ; *cf.* Mk 7:1–4. According to some of the Fathers (Jerome PL 26, 165), they accepted only the first five books of the OT ; *cf.* Schürer, *Geschichte*, 11⁴, 480 f. In numbers and influence with the people they were altogether inferior to the Pharisees. **19-23.** The imaginary case submitted to Christ was intended as a *reductio ad absurdum* of the doctrine of the resurrection. The case was based on the Mosaic Law concerning levirate marriage, Deut 25:5 f. If a man died without issue, his brother was commanded to marry the widow. The first son of this marriage was regarded as the offspring of the dead man, thus perpetuating his name. Fictitious cases like that submitted to Christ were probably put forward by the Sadducees in their controversies with the Pharisees in order to ridicule the idea of the resurrection.

i 24-25. The denial of the resurrection by the Sadducees shows that they do not understand either the teaching of Scripture or the power of God. They misconceive the manner of existence of those who rise from the dead. Their question is futile because it supposes that life in the resurrection is merely a prolongation of the conditions of the present life. But the power of God will so transform the risen body that ' they cannot die any more, for they will be like angels, and are sons of God, being children of the resurrection ', Lk 20:36. Marriage is an earthly institution for the conservation of the human race. In the resurrection, however, men will be immortal and like angels in their freedom from preoccupation with marriage and other temporal matters. **26-27.** ' in the bush ' ; ἐπὶ τοῦ βάτου = ' *in (the passage about) the (burning) bush* ', Ex 3:2 ff. This method of quoting Scripture was used in the absence of chapter and verse divisions ; *cf.* Rom 11:2 ; Mk 2:26. The selection of a text from the Pentateuch rather than, *e.g.* Dan 12:2 or Is 26:19, may have been due to the refusal of the Sadducees to recognize the authority of the rest of the Jewish Scriptures. In its original context, the passage quoted, Ex 3:6, means that God, who reveals himself to Moses, is the God whom the Patriarchs worshipped. The argument here proceeds on the basis that God's declaration contains the assurance that he has not ceased to be the God of the Patriarchs ; he has not forgotten his promises nor their loyal adherence to the covenant concluded between them and God (*cf.* Heb 11:16) ; he will not abandon to death those who served him, for ' he is the God of the living, not of the dead '. In the actual state of Jewish belief, death was a penalty and the life of Sheol was considered an imperfect form of existence. It was inconceivable that God should fail to re-unite the souls and bodies of those whom he loved. The resurrection is part of the recompense due to Abraham and the other Patriarchs for their faithful service. God is faithful and just, and he will make them live again ; *cf.* Lagrange, *Saint Marc*, 319 f.

j 28-34 The Greatest Commandment ; *cf.* Mt 22:34–40 ; Lk 10:25–28—**28.** Mk does not suggest that this question was prompted by hostility to Jesus. The Rabbis enumerated 613 precepts of the Law, 248 commands and 365 prohibitions. These were further classified into ' light ' and ' grave ' ; *cf.* Mt 23:4, 23. The question of the relative importance of these precepts, which included religious laws and ritual ordinances as well as expressions of the natural law, was a subject of discussion among them. **29-30.** The commandment to love God with all their powers, Deut 6:4 f., was quite familiar to the Jews as it was part of the mono-

theistic profession of faith which every faithful Israelite **736j** recited twice daily. This profession of faith was known as the *Shema* from the first word of the passage (Heb. *š^emaʿ = Hear !*). The importance of the command to love God may have been obscured by the fact that in the *Shema* it was immediately followed by passages from Scripture which dealt with temporal prosperity and with the wearing of tassels upon garments (Deut 11:13–21 ; Num 15:37–41). **31.** ' *The second is this :* **k** thou shalt love thy neighbour as thyself. There is no other commandment greater than these '. The command to love the neighbour, quoted from Lev 19:18, is introduced here because, in the teaching of Christ, it is inseparable from the command to love God. ' If any man says " I love God " and hates his brother, he is a liar. . . . This commandment we have from him, that he who loves God should love his brother also ', 1 Jn 4:20 f. ; *cf.* Jn 13:34 f. ; Rom 13:8–10 ; Gal 5:14. In Lev 19:18 the ' neighbour ' is a Jew, a compatriot. Christ, however, made it clear in the Parable of the Good Samaritan, Lk 10:29–37, that ' neighbour ' included all men without exception ; *cf.* Mt 5:43–47. The twofold precept of charity is the greatest commandment. It sums up all man's duties to God and to other men. **32-34.** These verses are found only in Mk. The prophets (*cf.* Is 1:11–20 ; Jer 6:20 ; Os 6:6) had taught that the interior spirit of religion and fulfilment of the moral law were superior to the external ritual of sacrifice. That teaching, however, had not received due emphasis in the rabbinical schools. The Scribe showed understanding in deducing from Christ's words the superiority of the law of charity over ceremonial worship. His good dispositions won the approval of Jesus, but we do not know whether he entered the kingdom by becoming a disciple of Christ.

35-37 The Origin of the Messias ; *cf.* Mt 22:41–46 ; **l** Lk 20:41–44—**35b.** ' How do the Scribes say that the *Messias is son of David ?* ' It was not simply in order to confound his opponents that Jesus raised this difficulty about the origin of the Messias. He was then engaged in teaching in the temple, and ' the great multitude listened to him gladly ', 37. Rather he wished to direct attention to an important aspect of Scriptural teaching concerning the Messias which the Scribes had overlooked. The prophecies had foretold that the Messias would be a descendant of David ; ' son of David ' was the most popular title of the Messias ; *cf.* 10:48 ; Jn 7:42 ; Rom 1:3. It was a title, however, which suggested a merely human Messias who would restore the temporal kingdom of Israel. Jesus did not question the belief that the Messias would be a descendant of David, but he quoted a passage of Scripture, Ps 109:1, which indicated that the Messias would be something more. ' *The Lord* [Yahweh] *said to my Lord* [Adoni] ', *i.e.* the Messias. If David, to whom the Psalm was attributed, calls the Messias his Lord, then the Messias is assuredly more than a ' son of David '. The fact that the Messias is to sit at the right hand of God points to the same conclusion. The answer to the difficulty, 37, is contained in the doctrine of the Incarnation. The Messias is both God ' the Lord of David ', and man ' the son of David ' ; *cf.* 14:62.

38-40 Denunciation of the Scribes ; *cf.* Mt 23:1–39 ; **m** Lk 20:46 f.—The preceding section (736*l*) gives an instance of how the Scribes had failed in their role of teachers of the people. Here they are condemned for their bad example, which was all the more reprehensible in those who set themselves up as zealous defenders of God's law. The vanity of the Scribes showed itself in their seeking after marks of honour to which they claimed a right as models of legal righteousness. **40.** ' Who devour the houses of widows *and make* pretence of long prayers '. In their avarice the Scribes did not refrain from victimizing the most defenceless section of the community. They gained possession of the property of widows, either by using their expert knowledge of the law in order to defraud them, or by a pretence of piety which was calculated to impress. Their hypocrisy in making long prayers

737b only adds to their guilt. The vanity, avarice and hypocrisy of the Scribes are directly opposed to the humility, detachment from wealth and sincerity of spirit inculcated by Christ.

41-44 The Widow's Mite ; cf. Lk 21:1-4—The building known as the Treasury was situated within the temple area. In it were kept the treasures of the temple together with vessels and vestments used in the services. Apparently it was also used as a place of safe keeping for the property of private individuals ; cf. 2 Mac 3:10. According to the Talmud, there were thirteen trumpet-shaped receptacles for offerings for the temple. Christ, showing his knowledge of hidden things, drew the attention of the disciples to the offering made by the widow in order to inculcate once again the importance of the intention of the heart in the service of God. The moral worth of the mite offered by the widow is measured by the sacrifice which she made.

XIII 1-37 Prophecy of the Destruction of the Temple and of the Coming of the Son of Man ; cf. Mt chh 24-25 ; Lk 21:5-36 ; 17:20-37—This prophecy, the longest discourse of Christ recorded in Mk, is usually referred to as the Eschatological Discourse or Synoptic Apocalypse. It was spoken in reply to the question of the disciples about the time of the destruction of the temple, 4, and in it Christ tells of signs preceding that event and also speaks of the coming of the Son of Man. The chief problem in interpreting the discourse is to determine whether certain passages should be understood of the destruction of the temple and events connected with it, or of the coming of the Son of Man as Judge at the end of the world.

A majority of writers at the present day hold that Christ dealt both with the destruction of the temple and the coming of the Son of Man in final judgement in this prophecy. Some writers contend that the manner in which the predictions concerning these two events are combined in a single prophecy, with abrupt transitions from one theme to the other, shows that Christ believed that the destruction of the temple and the coming of the Son of Man at the end of the world would be contemporaneous.

737b Most modern Catholic exegetes hold that the evidence of the discourse itself indicates that Christ made an important distinction between the two events. The destruction of the temple would be preceded by signs which would serve as a warning to the disciples to escape from impending disaster, 14-17. This local calamity, from which they could escape by flight elsewhere, would come to pass ' before this generation passes away ', 30. Christ, however, gave no information about the time of the coming of the Son of Man, 32. That event would be sudden and unexpected. It would concern ' the elect . . . from the uttermost part of the earth to the uttermost part of heaven ', 27. There would be no warning signs. Constant readiness is demanded—' Take heed, watch. For you know not when the time is ', 33. While Christ did not reveal the time of the Second Coming, his words convey sufficient information to put the disciples on their guard against identifying it with the time of the destruction of Jerusalem. In their minds, the overthrow of the temple and the end of the world were closely linked (cf. 13:4 ; Mt 24:3). Christ, by insisting that the time of the Parousia is uncertain, while at the same time declaring that the destruction of the temple would take place before ' this generation passes away ' and also by prescribing different attitudes for his followers in relation to these events, intended to dispel the confusion in the Apostles' minds ; cf. Lagrange, *Saint Marc,* 332-354 ; id. *The Gospel of Jesus Christ,* 2, 170 ff. ; Grandmaison, *Jésus-Christ,* 3, 61-96, 251-9 ; Bonsirven, *Les Enseignements de Jésus-Christ,* 330-55.

737c Some prefer to interpret the intermingling of themes and sudden transitions from one to the other as an instance of the lack of perspective which is a well-known feature of the prophecies of the OT. Because of the absence of perspective, the prophecies do not bring into clear relief the time-interval between future

737c events in the way that history sets out events of the past in their chronological sequence. On this theory, Christ would have accommodated himself here to the limitations of ordinary prophetical utterance without in any way implying that the destruction of the temple and his own Second Coming would take place in the same period. But if it be admitted that the prophecy has a twofold theme, the considerations put forward in the preceding paragraph would seem to exclude this explanation.

A number of ancient writers and some moderns do not admit that Christ spoke of two distinct themes in this prophecy. Some hold that throughout the discourse Christ has primarily in mind the coming of the Son of Man at the last Judgement. It is difficult to see how this interpretation can be reconciled with the question of the disciples, 4, and the words of Christ, 14-19. Even if it be granted that the destruction of the temple is a symbol which prefigures the end of the world, it seems to be quite clear that this local calamity in Jerusalem and Judaea is treated as an independent event with its own importance and significance, and not merely as a symbol of a greater upheaval at the end of the world.

737d Another explanation, which hitherto had few supporters, has recently been restated and strengthened with fresh arguments by A. Feuillet ; cf. RB 55 (1948) 481-502 ; 56 (1949) 61-92, 340-64 ; 57 (1950) 62-91, 180-211. He holds that the prophecy deals throughout with the single theme of the destruction of the temple. The coming of the Son of Man ' in the clouds with great power and glory ', 26, is not to be taken as Christ's coming at the Parousia, but as the inauguration of his reign, the coming of the kingdom in power ; cf. Mk 8:39 ; 14:62 ; Dan 7:13. This coming is the counterpart of the judgement of condemnation inflicted on the Jewish nation in the destruction of the temple and the calamitous events connected with it. With the disappearance of the temple, the ancient economy, already abrogated by Christ's death, comes to an end, and the new era of universal salvation, ' the times of the nations ', Lk 21:24, is inaugurated. Further references to this interpretation will be found in the Commentary.

737e **1-4 Occasion of the Prophecy ;** cf. Mt 24:1-3 ; Lk 21:5-7—Herod the Great had undertaken the restoration of the temple in an attempt to win the favour of the Jews. The splendour of the buildings and the dimensions of the huge blocks of stone used in the work of reconstruction are described at length by Jos., *Ant.* 15, 11, 3 ; *B.J.* 5, 5, 1-2. Christ's prophecy was fulfilled to the letter when Titus, after the capture of Jerusalem in A.D. 70, ordered that the city and temple should be razed to the ground ; cf. Jos., *B.J.* 7, 1, 1. **4.** The first question of the Apostles refers to the destruction of the temple. In the second question the words ' all these things ' have been taken commonly as an indication that the Apostles visualized the destruction of the temple as part of a greater upheaval, the end of the world ; cf. Mt 24:3. Feuillet maintains that the form of the Apostles' second question, even as found in Mt, does not necessarily imply that they intended to ask about the time of the end of world as a distinct subject. The expressions used might be understood of the Messianic age ; cf. RB 55 (1948) 486 ; 56 (1949) 344-7.

737f **5-13 Advice for Times of Distress ;** cf. Mt 24:4-14 ; Lk 21:8-19—Christ did not reply immediately to the questions put to him. He took occasion first to warn the Apostles against the dangers of deception by false Messiahs and to remind them of the difficulties which they would encounter in preaching the Gospel. Such advice was necessary lest they should be led astray by the expectation that the end of the world, with the coming of the Son of Man in glory, was at hand. In the period between the death of Christ and the fall of Jerusalem many impostors arose and took advantage of the intense Messianic expectations of the time to promise a decisive intervention of God (cf. Lagrange, *Le Messianisme,* 21 ff.). The same period was marked

737f by wars in the Roman Empire, disturbances in Palestine, earthquakes and famines (*cf.* Ac 11:28 ; Jos., *Ant.* 20, 5, 2–3). Tacitus (*Hist.* I, 2–3) describes it as an age ' rich in calamities, made terrible by battles, torn by civil strife, cruel even in its peace. Four emperors perished by the sword. Three civil wars, many foreign wars . . .' ; (*cf.* Jos. *BJ Proem.* 2). Christ's words apply in the first instance to the trials of this troubled period before the fall of Jerusalem. **8b.** *These things are the beginning of birth-pangs.* The trials of which Christ has spoken are only the beginning : the great tribulation, 19, is still to come. The figure of the pains of childbirth contains an element of consolation. Just as the pangs of childbirth are followed by joy that ' a man is born into the world ', Jn 16:21 f., so the trials which reached their climax in the fall of Jerusalem will lead to joy. They are the pangs accompanying the birth of a new world, the kingdom of

g God on earth ; *cf.* Lagrange, *Saint Marc* 337. **9–13.** Christ's followers will be subjected to persecutions and will incur the hatred of Jews and Gentiles (*cf.* Mt 10:16–23), but they will have the special assistance of the Holy Spirit when they are summoned before tribunals to answer for their faith in Christ and their preaching of the Gospel of salvation. If they remain faithful to the end, they will save their souls. **10.** The immediate context suggests that ' first ', πρῶτον , is not to be interpreted as ' before the end of the world '. Christ is still speaking of the period of the ' beginning of birth-pangs '. The preaching of the Gospel to all the nations can be explained as the evangelization which had already taken place in the Apostolic age before the fall of Jerusalem ; *cf.* Rom 1:5, 8 ; 10:18 ; Lagrange, *Saint Matthieu* 461. Feuillet (RB 55 [1948] 492–3) points out that the bringing of the Gospel to the nations should be envisaged particularly as the evangelization of Jews dispersed throughout the Roman empire. As God's chosen people, they would have the opportunity, before the catastrophe of A.D. 70, of knowing the Gospel.

h **14–18 The Sign of the Destruction of the Temple ;** *cf.* Mt 24:15–20 ; Lk 21:20–24—**14.** This gives the answer to the disciples' question, 4. ' The abomination of desolation, standing where it ought not '. It is not certain how this sign of the imminent destruction of the temple was fulfilled. The expression ' abomination of desolation ' comes from Dan 9:27 (*cf.* Dan 11:31 ; 12:11) where the prophet is speaking of something which would cause defilement of the temple : *cf.* Lattey, *The Book of Daniel*, 91, 101–2. In 1 Mac 1:57 the expression is applied to the profanation of the temple by Antiochus Epiphanes who erected a statue of Zeus Olympius within the sanctuary in 168 B.C. Presumably Christ had in mind a sacrilegious profanation of a similar character. It is noteworthy that the Gk text of Mk reads ἑστηκότα (masc.) in apposition to βδέλυγμα (neutr.). This sense-construction may be intended to suggest that the abomination is not an inanimate thing but an intelligent being. A number of authors hold that the invasion of Judaea and the subsequent siege of Jerusalem constituted the abomination of desolation ; *cf.* Lk 21:20. Others find the sign in the crimes committed by the Zealots who seized the temple in A.D. 68 and converted it into a fortress. They murdered two high-priests as well as countless others and caused the cessation of the daily sacrifices ; *cf.* Jos., *B.J.* 4, 5, 1–3 ; 6:3 ; 5, 10, 5. **14b.** ' He that readeth, let him understand '. This may be a statement of Christ directing attention to the profound significance of the prophecy of Daniel, 9:27. More probably it is a parenthesis by Mk inviting the reader of the Gospel to pay attention to the practical lesson of Christ's warning. **15a.** According to Eusebius (HE 3, 5, 3), the Christians, warned by a revelation, fled from Jerusalem before the siege and took refuge at Pella, across the Jordan. **15b–18.** These words of Christ emphasize the urgency of the warning to fly from the catastrophe about to overwhelm the city.

738a 19–23 Great Tribulations : False Christs and False

Prophets ; *cf.* Mt 24:21–28—Exegetes are far from **7** unanimous in their interpretation of this passage. Many hold that at 19 there is a transition from events at the fall of Jerusalem to the trials before the end of the world. They argue that it is no longer a question of saving one's life by flight from a local calamity, but of a great tribulation, 19, from which no one could be saved if the Lord did not shorten the time, 20. In this tribulation it is apparently the eternal salvation of the elect, 20, 22, which is the important issue. The fresh warnings against impostors are taken to imply that the situation is different from that contemplated in 5 ff. On the other hand it is pointed out that Josephus (*BJ Proem.* 4) describes the fall of Jerusalem in terms very similar to those used here. Furthermore, 19 f. are logically connected with the preceding verses (*cf.* ' γὰρ ' ' for ')—they give the reason for the hasty flight urged in 15 ff. The most natural break in the discourse appears to be in 23—' Take you heed, therefore : behold I have told you all things beforehand '. The warnings against impostors, 21 f., may be simply a resumption and development of the earlier admonitions. Feuillet (RB 55 [1948] 485) notes the correspondence between ὅταν, 14, and τότε in 15 and 21, and also between ἐν ἐκείναις ταῖς ἡμέραις, 17, and αἱ ἡμέραι ἐκεῖναι, 19. This evidence indicates that 14–23 form a unity and that 19–23 deal with happenings at the time of the destruction of Jerusalem. **20.** ' no flesh (no one) should be saved '. In the context of the destruction of Jerusalem this must be taken in a relative sense, ' no inhabitant of Jerusalem or Judaea '. ' The elect ' : Feuillet (RB 55 [1948] 498–502) holds that ' the elect ' are the remnant of the chosen people whom God will preserve from death in the great catastrophe, so that at least a ' remnant ' (Is 1:9 ; *cf.* Kissane, *The Book of Isaiah*, I, p 10) of the Jewish race would enter the Church ; *cf.* Rom 9:27–29 ; 11:1–7. For their sake the time will be shortened.

24–27 The Coming of the Son of Man ; *cf.* Mt **b** 24:29–31 ; Lk 21:25–28—The language and imagery used in this passage are frequently found in the prophetic and apocalyptic descriptions of God's intervention in judgement upon cities or nations ; *cf.* Is 13:10 ; 24:18 ff. ; 34:4 ; Ez 32:7 ; Am 8:9 ; Jl 2:10, 30 f. ; Agg 2:22. The language is metaphorical, and the striking imagery of disturbances in the heavenly bodies was intended to suggest the power and majesty of God. Christ makes use of this accepted terminology in order to describe the coming of the Son of Man. His words need not be taken literally as an enumeration of signs in the heavens which will precede the end of the world. They are rather the recognized mode of signifying that God is about to intervene. **26–27.** It is commonly held that the divine intervention in this case is the coming of the Son of Man at the end of the world. Christ, the Son of Man, will then come in glory as the Supreme Judge and gather his elect to himself from the whole earth ; *cf.* 1 Thess 4:15 f. ; 1 Cor 15:51–53. Against **c** this interpretation Feuillet (RB 56 [1949] 61–82) argues that nothing in the text indicates such a complete change of perspective between 19–23 and 24–27. There is no hint of a prolonged interval between the great tribulation and the coming of the Son of Man. On the contrary, the repetition in 24 of the phrase ἐν ἐκείναις ταῖς ἡμέραις (*cf.* 17, 19), and the presence of the time-particle τότε (*cf.* 15, 20) corresponding to it in 26 and 27, suggest that the coming of the Son of Man will be contemporaneous with the great tribulation. Feuillet finds the key to the meaning in Dan 7:13–14, to which Christ obviously alludes here. In the prophecy of Daniel the coming of ' one like a son of man with the clouds of heaven ' is a symbol of the establishment of God's kingdom on earth. The destruction of the temple by the Romans is God's judgement on the chosen people and brings the old order to an end, but it also marks the inauguration of the new era of salvation, the establishment of the Messianic kingdom on earth and its extension to all nations. This is the joyful and consoling aspect of the birth-pangs represented by the destruction of Jerusalem. The gathering of the elect is explained by Feuillet as the entry into the Church of the 'remnant' of the chosen people who believe in Christ. Together with the great mass of Gentile converts this minority will form the new spiritual Israel, the Church (ἐκκλησία = assembly, gathering) founded by Christ. Other passages of Scripture also employ the figure of 'gathering' to describe Christ's redeeming mission ; *cf.* Jn 11:51 f.

28-31 The Parable of the Fig-Tree : the Time of the Destruction of Jerusalem ; *cf.* Mt 24:32-35 ; Lk 21:29-33—**28-29.** When the leaves appear on the fig-tree men know that summer is near. Similarly, when the disciples see these things coming to pass they will know that it (' the kingdom of God ', Lk 21:31) is at hand. The phrase ' these things ' corresponds to the question of the disciples ' when shall these things be ', 4, and probably refers to the abomination of desolation and the destruction of Jerusalem rather than to the happenings foretold in 5-8. When the disciples see these things coming to pass they will realize that they herald the establishment of the kingdom. Feuillet (*art. cit.*, 83) emphasizes that the purpose of the parable is to bring home to the disciples that the destruction of the city and temple is not an unqualified disaster, inasmuch as to the eyes of faith it spells the coming of the Messianic age. **30.** ' This generation ' has been interpreted in a variety of senses : the Jewish nation, the human race, the community of the faithful (the Church), the generation of Jews contemporary with Christ. If Christ is speaking here of the end of the world (ταῦτα πάντα γένηται), the meaning would appear to be that the human race, or the Jewish nation, or the Church would still exist at the Second Coming. It is difficult to see the precise force of such a statement or how it fits the immediate context. Probably ' all these things ' alludes to the destruction of Jerusalem. Christ meant that it would come to pass before the contemporary generation of Jews had passed away ; *cf.* 8:12, 38. ' Generation ' frequently has a pejorative sense (*cf.* ZLG. *s.v.* γενεά), and it may be that it has that nuance in the present context. The destruction of Jerusalem is regarded as the punishment of the evil generation that rejected Christ ; *cf.* Mt 23:35 f. Not more than forty years elapsed from the time Christ spoke until the fall of Jerusalem in 70 A.D. **31.** An emphatic declaration of the permanency and truth of all Christ's teachings.

32-37 The Time of Judgement: the Need for Constant Vigilance ; *cf.* Mt 24:36-51 ; Lk 21:34-36—**32.** Christ has announced the sign which will precede the fall of Jerusalem and foretold that that catastrophe would take place during the lifetime of his contemporaries. Now he declares that no one except the Father ' knows about that day or that hour '. The Arian heretics appealed to this text as proof that Christ did not know the time of the day of Judgement and, therefore, could not be God ; *cf.* Maldonatus, *Comment. on Mt 24:36*. Many modern writers (*cf.* Feuillet, *art. cit.*, 87) explain the passage in the sense that Christ revealed the general period (this generation) in which the temple would be destroyed but gives no information as to the precise time (the day or the hour). But the opposition here is not simply between a general indication of the period, 30, and a precise date, 32. There appears to be a contrast between two distinct situations. In one case, there will be warning signs and the general period is revealed : in the other, there are no signs and no information is given about the time. Hence the admonition, ' Take heed, watch. For you know not when the time is ', 33. It is unlikely, therefore, that Christ had the same event in view both in 30 and 32. The day and hour of which he spoke was most probably the Day of Judgement ; *cf.* Lk 10:12 ; **f** 2 Thess 1:10 ; 2 Tim 1:12, 18 ; 4:8. The statement that the Son, *i.e.* Christ, does not know the time of the Second Coming is to be interpreted in the sense that it was no part of his Messianic mission to reveal this information to men. Christ, as a divine Person, knows

all the secrets of the Godhead, but it was not the will **738f** of the Father that he should make known to men the time of the Last Judgement. **33-37.** Because the time of Christ's coming in judgement is not revealed, constant readiness is necessary. This admonition, which is enforced by a parable, was not intended for the Apostles alone—' what I say to you, I say to all : watch ', 37.

XIV 1-XV 47 The Passion, Death and Burial of Christ. 739a XIV 1-2 The Plot of the Sanhedrin ; *cf.* Mt 26:1-5 ; Lk 22:1 f.—The Pasch, *i.e.* the ceremony at which the paschal lamb was eaten, was celebrated on the evening of the 14th Nisan. ' The Azymes ', or the feast of unleavened bread, began on the 15th Nisan and lasted seven days. In practice, the whole period from the beginning of the paschal ceremony to the end of the Azymes was referred to either as the Pasch or the Azymes. According to an ancient tradition (*cf. Catena in Marc.*), this meeting of the Sanhedrin was held on the Wednesday before Christ's death.

3-9 The Anointing at Bethany ; *cf.* Mt 26:6-13 ; Jn **b** 12:1-8—From Jn we know that this incident took place on the day before the triumphal entry into Jerusalem, six days before the Pasch. Mk and Mt place the account of the anointing between the plot of the Sanhedrin and the betrayal by Judas because of its relation to the burial of Christ, 8, whom the Sanhedrin had now decided to put to death. The incident also throws light on the conduct and motives of Judas. **4.** ' *Some were indignant* '. From Jn 12:4 f. we know that Judas protested against the waste of precious ointment which might have been sold for the benefit of the poor. **6-9.** Christ defended Mary from the charge of prodigality brought 2gainst her under the pretence of solicitude for the poor. Her action was a gesture of homage to him. In view of the nearness of his death, no one should find fault with the lavishness of the expenditure. Opportunities to assist the poor would never be lacking, but Christ would not be visibly present among them much longer. In fact, though Mary may not have realized it, this anointing was an anticipation of the anointing of Christ's body which, in accordance with Jewish custom, should have been performed before burial. It would seem that, because of the haste with which the burial of Christ was carried out (Lk 23:54 ; Jn 19:42), certain of the customary preparations for burial were not completed ; *cf.* 15:46-16:1 ; Lk 23:56-24:1. **9.** The woman who anointed Jesus was Mary, sister of Martha and Lazarus, Jn 11:2 ; 12:2 f. It is doubtful whether she should be identified either with Mary Magdalen or with the un-named sinner who anointed Christ on another occasion, Lk 7:37 ff ; *cf.* O'Rahilly, *The Family at Bethany*, 181-92.

10-11 The Betrayal by Judas ; *cf.* Mt 26:14-16 ; Lk **c** 22:3-6—By offering to betray Jesus to the Sanhedrin, Judas solved for them the problem of ' *how to seize him by stealth* ', 1. There has been much speculation concerning the motives which prompted the betrayal. In Jn 12:6 love of money is indicated, and disillusionment of false Messianic hopes and disappointed ambition probably also played a part. Both Lk 22:3, and Jn 6:71 f. ; 13:2, 27, refer to the influence of Satan upon the conduct of Judas.

12-16 Preparation for the Pasch ; *cf.* Mt 26:17-19 ; **d** Lk 22:7-13—**12.** For the paschal meal, in addition to the lamb which was to be slaughtered in the temple, it was necessary to provide unleavened bread, bitter herbs, wine, and a sauce called *ḥarôseṭ*, made from fruits, nuts, spices and vinegar. Four cups of wine at least were prescribed. The third cup, taken after the eating of the lamb, was called the ' cup of blessing '. During the meal the Hallel Psalms (113-118) were recited, and the head of the family explained the significance of the ceremony, which commemorated the Exodus. **13-15.** From Lk 22:8 we know that the disciples sent to prepare for the Pasch were Peter and John. Jesus had probably made an arrangement with the householder to whom they were directed. The directions

739d for finding the place were a test of the disciples' faith in Christ, and gave proof of his divine knowledge. He may have avoided mentioning the householder's name or the exact place in order to keep it from Judas, lest he should reveal it to the Sanhedrin beforehand.

e A number of texts in the Synoptics and Jn put it beyond doubt that Christ died on a Friday ; *cf.* Mt 27:62 ; Mk 15:42 ; Lk 23:54 ; Jn 19:31. The Last Supper took place on the previous evening. That Christ intended to celebrate the Jewish paschal feast is clear from the accounts of the preparations ; *cf.* 14:12–16 ; Mt 26:17–19 ; Lk 22:7–13. The words ' With desire have I desired to eat this Pasch with you before I suffer ', Lk 22:15, confirm that Christ and the Apostles actually partook of the customary paschal meal. In the evangelists' account of the Last Supper the traditional ritual of the Jewish Pasch is overshadowed by the institution of the Eucharist which is the Pasch of the New Covenant. The Mosaic Law, Ex 12:6, prescribed that the paschal lamb was to be slain about sunset on the 14th Nisan and eaten that night. Taking this regulation in conjunction with the Synoptic account one would conclude that Christ died in the afternoon of the 15th Nisan. But from Jn 18:28 it is clear that the Jews had not eaten the Pasch on the day that Christ was put to death. That day was the day of preparation, *i.e.* the eve of the Pasch, Jn 19:31, 42. Moreover, the first day of the paschal feast, the 15th Nisan, was a day of sabbath rest on which it was not lawful to hold a trial. The Synoptics, Mt 27:32 ; Mk 15:21, 46 ; Lk 22:26 ; 23:56, mention various other activities which also appear to be inconsistent with the supposition that the day of Christ's death was the first of the paschal feast. Various solutions have been put forward to explain the difference in practice between Christ and the Jews on this occasion. Some, indeed, have denied that Christ celebrated a real paschal meal, while others have held that Christ and the Jews celebrated the Pasch on the same day. But the evidence already adduced indicates that neither view is tenable. Whether Christ anticipated the legal date of the Pasch by one day, or the Jews postponed it to the evening of the 15th Nisan remains uncertain. It is possible that there was a divergence in regard to the fixing of the date of the Pasch, which depended upon observation of the new moon fourteen days earlier ; *cf.* Lagrange, *Saint Marc*, 354–63 ; Prat, *Jésus Christ*, 2, 507–20 ; *cf.* § 768*a–c*.

f **17-21 Announcement of the Betrayal ;** *cf.* Mt 26:20–25 ; Lk 22:21–23 ; Jn 13:21–30—**17-18.** The announcement of the betrayal was made during the paschal celebration which began after sunset. Among the Jews at this period the ancient practice of standing while partaking of the paschal meal, Ex 12:11, had given way to the Greek and Roman custom of reclining on couches at table. **19-20.** The expression ' *one who dips with me in the dish* ' has the same meaning as ' *one who eats with me* ', 18*b*, = one who partakes of a meal with me. These words did not reveal to the other Apostles that Judas was the traitor, as they could apply to anyone present at the meal. In accordance with oriental practice, each one helped himself from a common dish. **21.** Christ, in fulfilment of the divine command, was going voluntarily to his death which had been foretold by the prophets. God foresaw from all eternity the part which Judas would play, but the crime of betraying Jesus, which Judas committed by his own free act, was none the less heinous.

g **22-25 The Institution of the Eucharist ;** *cf.* Mt 26:26–29 ; Lk 22:19 f.—Mk's account here is almost verbally identical with that of Mt, while Lk closely resembles 1 Cor 11:23–25 and includes the command of Christ, ' Do this in commemoration of Me '. **22.** In the sentence, ' This is my Body ' the subject ' this ' (τοῦτο), *i.e.* the bread which Christ held in his hands, is identified with the predicate ' my Body ' (τὸ σῶμά μου). In Aramaic, the language in which Christ spoke, the copula ' is ' (ἐστιν) is not expressed, but the sense is the same. The evangelists and St Paul express faith-

fully in Greek the meaning of Christ's words. That these words are to be taken literally, signifying that the bread has been changed by divine power into Christ's body, follows no less from the impossibility of giving any reasonable figurative interpretation to them than from the emphasis with which it is stated that this is Christ's own body, not a mere figure of it, but the body that suffered for men : ' This is my body, [the body] which will be given for you ', Lk 22:19. **24.** The same point is made even clearer in the consecration of the chalice : ' This is my blood, [the blood] of the covenant, [the blood] which will be shed for many '. The cup contains the blood of Christ, the same blood which is to be shed in the sacrifice which inaugurates the new covenant between God and men. The participle ἐκχυννόμενον is used proleptically with reference to the shedding of Christ's blood on Calvary. ' of the new testament '. ' New ' may be here an interpolation from Mt. The Mosaic covenant was inaugurated by the shedding of blood, Ex 24:4 ff. ; Christ inaugurated the New Covenant, which replaces the OT economy, by the sacrificial shedding of his own Blood on Calvary —' by a single offering he consummated for ever those that are being sanctified ', Heb 10:14. ' for many '. The word ' many ' does not imply that some are excluded from the benefit of Christ's sacrifice ; it simply marks a contrast between the multitude who are to be redeemed and the One who died for all ; *cf.* 10:45. **25.** In these words, which Luke places before the account of the institution of the Eucharist, Jesus reminds the Apostles that this is a farewell banquet, for his death is imminent. But he will triumph over death, and they will be with him again in the happiness of the eternal kingdom. Christ uses a metaphor familiar to the Rabbis, comparing the kingdom of God to a banquet. The wine at that banquet will be ' new ' ; it will belong to a new order of things. Some see in this passage an allusion to the Eucharist which would unite them with Christ even here on earth.

26-31 Prediction of the Scandal of the Apostles and Peter's Denials ; *cf.* Mt 26:30–35 ; Lk 22:33 f. ; Jn 13:36–38—**26.** The hymn sung on this occasion was the second part of the Hallel, Pss 115–118, which brought the paschal supper to a close. **27-28.** The defection of the Apostles predicted by Christ was not an abandonment of faith in him ; it was rather a temporary faltering in their loyalty, caused by discouragement at seeing him fall into the hands of his enemies. Together with the warning that they would be scandalized, Christ gave the Apostles the reassuring reminder of the triumph of his Resurrection. The scriptural quotation in 27*b* is from Zach 13:7—' Sword . . . strike the shepherd, and the sheep of the flock will be dispersed '. **29-31.** Peter's protestations of unshakeable loyalty were sincere, but relying excessively on his own strength and placing his own loyalty above that of the other Apostles, he failed to heed the warning words of Christ. The others also protested their loyalty. Mk alone mentions the second cock-crow ; *cf.* 14:72.

32-42 The Agony in the Garden ; *cf.* Mt 26:36–46 ; Lk 22:39–46—**32.** Gethsemani is situated at the foot of the western slope of Mt Olivet. The name means ' oil-press ', an installation for extracting the oil from the olive. **33-36.** The three Apostles who were with Christ at the Agony had earlier been witnesses of the Transfiguration and of the raising of the daughter of Jairus. **33*b*.** ' *He began to be dismayed and distressed* '. ἀδημονεῖν (' to be distressed ') suggests repugnance, disgust. The Passion and Crucifixion which were now imminent, were the immediate cause of the Agony of Christ. His hour had come ; the Passion with all the accompanying humiliations presented itself so vividly to his mind that he was filled with anguish and dismay. He was also conscious of the unbelief of the Jews, the betrayal by Judas, the scandal of the Apostles, the ingratitude of men, the burden of sin which he had to expiate by his sacrifice. At the Incarnation he had assumed a real human nature : it is in accordance with that nature to shrink from suffering and death. Christ's

a prayer that he might be spared 'this chalice', the ordeal of the Passion, is at once a manifestation of the shrinking of his human nature from the sufferings which lay before him, and a measure of the anguish caused by the thought of them. The prayer, however, is conditional—'he prayed that if it were possible, the hour might pass from him'. His human will was in complete accord with the will of the Father—'not what I will, but what thou wilt'. Despite the repugnance of his human nature to suffering, Christ, by a meritorious act of obedience, voluntarily submitted to the Passion which had been decreed by God for the salvation of men. 'Though Son, he learned obedience from the things he suffered, and having been made perfect, he became the author of eternal salvation to all those who obey him', Heb 5:8 f. This narrative puts beyond question the fact that Christ had a true human nature, and a human will distinct from and yet completely obedient to the will of the Father ; Vosté, *De Passione et Morte Jesu Christi* **b** (Romae 1937) 7–56. **37–42.** Christ returned to seek comfort in the company of the Apostles whom he had asked to keep watch with him. This seeking for comfort in the presence of friends, and the restlessness shown in the repeated coming and going of Christ are characteristic of one who is deeply distressed. The Apostles, despite their protestations, had failed to keep awake. Mark, 37, notes that Christ's gentle reproof was addressed especially to Simon Peter. This first failure to live up to their protestations of loyalty, 29–31, taught the Apostles the lesson that good intentions are not enough. Human nature is weak and liable to fail in time of trial. Constant vigilance and prayer for God's help were necessary if they were to remain steadfast in their loyalty to Christ in the far greater trials which lay before them.

c 43–50 The Arrest of Jesus ; *cf.* Mt 26:47–56 ; Lk 22:47–53 ; Jn 18:2–11—From Jn we know that a detachment of Roman soldiers under the command of a tribune was present at Christ's arrest. If resistance were encountered, they would have given all necessary support to the representatives of the Sanhedrin who came armed with swords and clubs to seize Jesus. Judas led them to Gethsemani because he knew that Jesus frequently resorted there with the disciples, Jn 18:2. In the darkness even those who had seen Christ previously might have failed to identify him among the Apostles. The sign which Judas arranged was the customary form of respectful greeting. **47.** Jn 18:10 tells us that it was Peter who drew the sword in defence of Christ. **48–49.** Jesus did not resist arrest or attempt to escape, but made a dignified protest against the methods employed against him by the Sanhedrin. If they had a charge against him because of his teaching or claims, they could have summoned him openly before their tribunal. There was no need to come with an armed band as if Christ were a malefactor from whom violent resistance was to be expected. Force, indeed, would have been useless if Christ chose to resist, *cf.* Mt 26:51–54 ; Jn 18:4–6. All that was taking place, however, was in accordance with the prophecies of Scripture ; *cf.* Is 53:7, 12.

d **51–52.** Only Mk records this incident of the unnamed young man. He may have been roused from sleep by the crowd and followed them with a linen cloth (σινδών) wrapped about him. The fact that he followed our Lord in these circumstances suggests that he was a disciple or, at least, sympathetic to Christ. It is unlikely that mere curiosity explains his actions. Many writers hold that this is a personal reminiscence of the author of the Gospel, and identify the young man with Mark himself. The insertion of this personal anecdote, which is not closely linked with either the preceding or the subsequent narrative, would be equivalent to the setting of Mark's signature to the Gospel. The view is not certain, but it gives a reasonable explanation of an otherwise baffling narrative. It appears to be clear that we cannot identify the young man who figures in this incident with any of the Apostles—they had all fled, 50.

53–65 Jesus before the Sanhedrin : the Religious 740e Process ; *cf.* Mt 26:57–68 ; Lk 22:54, 63–71 ; Jn 18:13, 19–24—Jn informs us that when Jesus was arrested he was brought first to Annas, who had held the office of high-priest from A.D. 6 till 15 when he was deposed by the Roman Governor, Valerius Gratus. The high-priest at the time of the Passion was Caiphas. He was son-in-law of Annas and held office from A.D. 18 till 36. The interrogation of Christ by the high-priest, Jn 18:19–23, was probably an informal examination intended to obtain some evidence which could be used against Jesus when he was brought to trial before the Sanhedrin or the Roman Governor. The Sanhedrin had extensive judicial power. It was competent to pass sentence of death on certain charges, but had not the right to execute the sentence ; *cf.* Jn 18:31 ; Holzmeister, *Hist. Aet. N. Test.* (Rome 1932) 82–5 ; *id.,* Bi 19 (1938) 43–59, 151–74. The Romans reserved that power to their own representative in the subject territories. Consequently, when the Sanhedrin had pronounced sentence of death on Christ on the charge of blasphemy they were obliged to seek ratification and execution of the sentence from Pilate, the Roman Governor, who had the right to review the case in order to satisfy himself that the verdict should be executed.

According to Mk 15:1 and Mt 27:1 there were two **f** meetings of the Sanhedrin, one during the night at which Christ was condemned, the other next morning before he was brought to Pilate. Lk makes no mention of the night session : his account of Christ's condemnation is connected with the meeting of the Sanhedrin held in the morning, Lk 22:66–71. The precise relation of Lk's account to the narrative of Mk and Mt is uncertain. Some authors deny that a formal trial of Christ by the Sanhedrin took place during the night. According to the Talmud it was unlawful to hold a trial by night. On this view the condemnation of Christ took place at the formal trial held in the morning, as described in Lk. The other two Synoptic writers have anticipated in their narrative, giving the story of the condemnation along with their account of certain preparatory investigations conducted by the high-priest and the maltreatment of Christ during the night. Others hold that the second session of the Sanhedrin was necessary in order to remedy the illegality of the trial by night, or because it was not permitted to pronounce a condemnatory sentence at the session in which an accused was found guilty. It is possible that the Sanhedrin, having condemned Christ at the night session on the charge of blasphemy, met again next morning in order to formulate charges which would ensure that Pilate would ratify their verdict and execute the death sentence. Like Gallio at Corinth, Ac 18:12–16, Pilate might have refused to take any action on a charge of a purely religious nature. It was decided, therefore, at the morning session to bring Jesus before Pilate as a political offender because of his Messianic claims ; *cf.* Mk 15:2 ; Lk 23:2. **53–54.** The usual meeting-place of **g** the Sanhedrin was a hall situated at the western side of the temple area. On this occasion, however, possibly because the gates of the temple were shut at night or because of the desire for expedition and secrecy, the representatives of the three groups which formed the Sanhedrin met in the house of Caiphas. Peter, having overcome the panic which caused him to abandon Christ, now followed at a distance and was brought into the courtyard of the high-priest by another disciple, Jn 18:15. **55–61a.** In the Law, Num 35:30 ; Deut 17:6 ; 19:15, it was laid down that a man could not be condemned to death except on the concordant evidence of two or three witnesses. The testimony of the first witnesses against Christ was conflicting. The two witnesses who testified that Christ had said he would destroy the temple misrepresented what he had actually said, Jn 2:19. His words were ' Destroy this temple ' not ' I will destroy this temple ' etc. Moreover, as explained in Jn 2:21, he was speaking of the temple of his own body. Here too the witnesses failed

740g to agree in their testimony. It was not necessarily blasphemous to predict the destruction of the temple or even to say, ' I will destroy the temple '. But the charge brought against Christ would have created prejudice against him among the people. The Sanhedrin would no doubt have regarded it as sufficient ground for condemning Christ to death. Jeremias had been threatened with death for predicting the destruction of the temple, Jer 26:6 ff. One of the charges brought against St Stephen was that he had said ' Jesus of Nazareth will destroy this place ', Ac 6:14. When the witnesses failed to agree, Caiphas tried to elicit some statement or explanation from Christ in the hope that he would compromise himself in the hearing of the Sanhedrin. But Jesus remained silent : there was no case for him to answer. **61b-65.** Caiphas, having seen **h** the debacle of the false witnesses, feared that the plot of the Sanhedrin might fail completely. He sought, therefore, to obtain from Christ an avowal of his claims which would immediately be condemned as blasphemous by the Sanhedrin. They could then pass sentence of death without reference to any other witnesses. ' Art thou the Messias, the Son of the Blessed One ? ', 61b. Jesus was not bound to answer this question, even in deference to the authority of the high-priest. But silence at this time might have been misinterpreted as a disavowal of his claims. Therefore he replied, ' I am. And you shall see the Son of Man sitting at the right hand ' of the Power and coming with the clouds of heaven '. The expressions ' the Blessed One ' and ' the Power (of God) ' were used by the Jews as substitutes for the name of God. Christ's answer, with its allusions to Ps 109:1 and Dan 7:13, is a clear affirmation both of his Messianic dignity and his divinity. He is not a merely human Messias, but One who will take his place at the right hand of God, sharing his power. He is Son of God in an altogether unique sense. The Sanhedrin understood that Christ was claiming divinity, making himself equal to God ; cf. Jn 5:18. The high-priest rent his garments, this being the customary gesture to express horror at hearing a blasphemy. Merely to claim to be the Messias was not in itself blasphemy nor punishable by death. It was because Christ claimed to be Son of God in the strict sense, making himself God, Jn 10:33, that the Sanhedrin found him guilty of blasphemy and condemned him to death. **65.** From Mk it appears that some members of the Sanhedrin began the maltreatment of Christ, spitting upon him and mocking his prophetic power and knowledge of hidden things by striking him when blindfolded and asking him to name the one who had struck him.

i 66-72 Peter's Denials and Repentance ; cf. Mt 26:69-75 ; Lk 22:54-62 ; Jn 18:15-18, 25-27—The fact that all four evangelists record this incident, in no way seeking to mitigate Peter's fault, is a remarkable tribute to their reliability. Peter was Head of the Church when the Synoptic Gospels were written, and had won the crown of martyrdom for his faith in Christ when John wrote his Gospel, yet there is no attempt to gloss over his lapse. It is also noteworthy, as an indication of Peter's humility, that the denials are narrated so fully by Mark, whose Gospel is a record of Peter's preaching. All four evangelists agree in recording that Peter denied Christ on three distinct occasions. There are differences in the details of their accounts, but these do not affect the substance of the narrative, nor can they be urged as instances of contradictions between the Gospels. We are not obliged to suppose that Peter uttered only a single denial each time he was challenged. It is altogether more reasonable to hold that, in his panic and confusion, he blurted out denials in different forms especially when challenged by several persons at once. There was room for more than one accurate, though incomplete, account of the denials. None of the evangelists purports to give an exhaustive account. Each one recorded the incidents in his own way, giving the sense of the challenges to Peter and of his denials rather than the actual words.

66-69. The first denial took place when Peter, who had **74** joined the servants gathered round the fire in the courtyard, was challenged by the portress who had admitted him to the high-priest's house at the request of another disciple. Mark alone mentions the crowing of the cock after the first denial. Peter moved from the fire towards the entrance porch where, after an interval, he once more encountered the portress, who was joined by others in charging Peter with being a disciple. **70-72.** Some time later Peter was again with the group around the fire. The peculiarities of his speech betrayed the fact that he was a Galilean, and he was identified as a disciple by a relative of Malchus, whose ear he had cut off in Gethsemani. This time Peter sought to strengthen his denials with oaths and curses, calling down God's punishment on himself if his statement was not true. The crowing of the cock reminded Peter of the warning words of Christ, who at that moment was being led away from the hall where he had appeared before the Sanhedrin—' and the Lord turning looked at Peter ', Lk 22:61. The Apostle realized the gravity of his fault and showed his repentance by his tears. **72b.** ' He began to weep ' (ἐπιβαλὼν ἔκλαιεν). The exact sense of ἐπιβαλών is uncertain, but it probably refers to a sudden overwhelming outburst. ' He burst into sobs and wept ', cf. MMV s.v.

XV 1-15a Jesus before Pilate : the Civil Process ; **74** cf. Mt 27:11-26 ; Lk 23:1-25 ; Jn 18:28-19:16—**1-5.** Mk is extremely concise at this point and needs to be clarified by reference to the other evangelists. **1.** Probably the chief purpose of the morning session of the Sanhedrin was to decide what charges should be brought against Christ at the tribunal of the Roman Governor ; cf. § 740f. Knowing that they could not count upon unquestioning acceptance by Pilate of their own verdict on a purely religious charge, the Sanhedrin kept the charge of blasphemy in the background and brought Christ before Pilate as a political offender— ' we have found this man perverting our nation and forbidding to pay tribute to Caesar and asserting that he is the Messias, a king ', Lk 23:2. As the representative of Rome, Pilate was obliged to take notice of these accusations. **2.** The Messianic claim of Jesus had been represented to Pilate as a claim to political kingship of the Jews, and, consequently, sedition against the Emperor. **2b** ' Thou sayest it ' (σὺ λέγεις). According to some authors this is a non-committal answer = ' It is you who say it '. More probably it is to be understood as an affirmative = ' It is as you say '. A fuller account of the questioning of Christ by Pilate, given in Jn 18:33-38, shows that Christ explained that his kingship was not an earthly one in opposition to the authority of Rome. Pilate was satisfied that the charge of sedition was unfounded. **3-5.** Having reached the decision that Jesus was **b** not guilty of sedition, Pilate should have brought the trial to an end and set him free. But when he announced that he could find no crime in him, Lk 23:4 ; Jn 18:38, the chief priests persisted, ' he is stirring up the people, teaching throughout all Judaea, beginning from Galilee even to this place ', Lk 23:5. Pilate, knowing that the anxiety of the Sanhedrin for the interests of Rome was a pretence, questioned Jesus again, probably hoping to discover the real motive of the animosity of the Jews. But Christ remained silent : he had already made his position clear to Pilate. **6-11.** The sending of Christ to Herod Antipas, Lk **c** 23:6-12, was the first of Pilate's attempts to find a way out of his difficulty. He knew that Jesus was innocent and was anxious to set him free, yet he was afraid to offend the Jews, lest they should denounce him to the Emperor for negligence in dealing with a political agitator. It was by playing on this fear that the Jews finally succeeded in securing the condemnation of Christ, Jn 19:12 f. Having failed to transfer responsibility for the case to Antipas, Pilate now had recourse to another expedient. The custom of releasing at the paschal feast a prisoner selected by the people appeared to provide a way of escape from his embarrassing position. If the people selected Christ, the Sanhedrin would have no pretext for denouncing Pilate. It was natural to expect that the crowds who had acclaimed Christ a few days previously would now exercise their privilege in his favour. But the chief priests stirred up the people to ask for Barabbas then in prison ' *with the rioters who had committed murder in the riot* '. We cannot tell by what means the crowd were incited to ask for Barabbas in preference to Christ. It is difficult to understand how that choice could have been made by people who had acclaimed Christ at the triumphal entry into Jerusalem. Probably it was the rabble of the city along with the servants of the Sanhedrin who asked for Barabbas. Some are of opinion that Barabbas was not simply a brigand or common criminal, but a prominent figure in a revolutionary group striving to overthrow Roman power in Palestine. By presenting him in the guise of a national hero the chief priests would have been able to influence the people to ask for his release. The Gospels are the only source which inform us that the Roman authority in Palestine recognized the custom of liberating a prisoner at the Pasch. Similar customs are known to have existed elsewhere in the Greek and Roman world. A remarkable parallel to the Gospel story is found in an Egyptian papyrus from c A.D. 85 which quotes the statement of the Governor of Egypt to a man on trial before him—' You deserved flagellation . . . but I pardon you as a favour to the people ' (Deissmann, *Licht vom Osten*, 229–30). **12-15a.** The unexpected turn of events disconcerted Pilate. Forgetting that he alone was the competent judge in the case, he asked what they wished to have done to Jesus. When they called for his crucifixion, Pilate again declared that Jesus had committed no crime which merited the death penalty. But the clamour continued and Pilate finally gave way to the demand under the threat of delation to the Emperor, Jn 19:12 f.

15b-20a The Scourging and Crowning with Thorns; *cf*. Mt 27:26–31 ; Lk 23:16, 22 ; Jn 19:1–3—Scourging was a normal preliminary to the execution of the death sentence. It was also inflicted sometimes in order to extort a confession, or as a distinct form of punishment for offences which did not merit the death penalty. One form of scourge had leather thongs weighted with fragments of bone ; another consisted of light chains with balls of lead at the end. Roman law did not impose any limit to the number of blows which might be inflicted. In Palestine, where there were no lictors, the scourging was done by soldiers. From Lk and Jn we know that Pilate had not yet sentenced Christ to death when he ordered the scourging. He intended to set Christ free after the scourging, believing that this compromise would appease Christ's enemies. **16.** ' *And the soldiers led him into the courtyard, that is, the praetorium, and called together the whole cohort* '. The name ' praetorium ' was originally given to the tent of the commander-in-chief (praetor). In later use it applies to any place where the Emperor or his military representatives exercised the functions of their office. It is disputed whether the praetorium where Christ was mocked and condemned to death was in the palace of Herod or in the fortress Antonia adjoining the temple. The palace of Herod was the usual residence of the Procurators when they visited Jerusalem. It is probable, however, that at the Pasch and other great feasts Pilate moved into the fortress Antonia where he could more easily keep the crowds under observation and take prompt action to quell disturbances. Recent archaeological findings appear to favour this view ; *cf*. Vincent, RB 42 (1933) 85–113.

17-20a. The pitiable condition to which Christ was reduced by the scourging aroused no sympathy in the soldiers. In a mock coronation and parody of homage they ridiculed his claim to be king. The purple garment, probably a soldier's scarlet cloak, represented the royal purple ; the crown of thorns and the reed placed in Christ's hand, Mt 27:29, represented the crown and sceptre. It was probably on their own initiative that the soldiers indulged in this brutal mockery of Christ. **741f** After the scourging and mockery Pilate brought forth Jesus wearing the crown of thorns and the purple garment, Jn 19:4 f. He thought that the sight of his wretched state would satisfy the Jews' desire for punishment. But they still cried out for his crucifixion. Pilate, intimidated, passed the death sentence.

20b-41 The Crucifixion and Death of Jesus ; *cf*. Mt **742a** 27:31–56 ; Lk 23:26–49 ; Jn 19:16–37—The evangelists do not give a detailed account of the crucifixion, because their readers were familiar with this form of punishment. It was well known in the Roman empire, particularly as the penalty for slaves condemned for serious crimes, though freedmen or provincials found guilty of sedition and, sometimes, even Roman citizens were put to death in this way. The more common type of cross consisted of two lengths of timber, an upright and a crossbeam. These were not fixed together in the familiar form of cross until crucifixion took place. In Rome, the condemned person, stripped of his garments, carried the crossbeam to the place of execution, being subjected to indignities and ill-treatment on the way. A placard announcing his crime was carried before him or hung from his neck. At the place of execution, it seems that the hands of the condemned person were fastened to the crossbeam, usually with nails, and then he was lifted on to the upright beam which was already in position. A projecting block on the upright served as a ' saddle ' to support the body ; the crossbeam was secured to the upright at the top or in a socket lower down, and the feet were nailed or tied with cords. Death was sometimes hastened by breaking the legs or by other means ; *cf*. Holzmeister VD 14 (1934) 149–55, 216–20, 241–9, 257–63. Christ was crucified by four Roman soldiers, Jn 19:23, under the command of a centurion, Mk 15:39. We know from Jn 20:20, 25, 27 and Lk 24:39 f. that his hands and feet were fastened with nails. On some points it is uncertain how far the manner of Christ's crucifixion may have differed from the usual Roman practice. It is widely held that Christ carried the whole Cross, not merely the crossbeam. Mk 15:20 ' they put his clothes on him, and led him out to crucify him ' indicates that Christ was still clothed in his own garments on the way to Calvary. Most of the ancient writers believed that Christ was completely naked on the Cross. But it is not improbable that, in Palestine, the Romans respected Jewish feeling and custom in this matter and allowed some kind of covering.

20b-32 The Crucifixion—Christ was led forth from the **b** praetorium carrying his cross, but when the soldiers saw that he was too weak to carry it to the place of execution they exercised their right to requisition services and compelled Simon of Cyrene to carry it for him. The mention of Simon's sons shows that they were known to the Christians of Rome for whom Mark wrote his Gospel. Rufus was probably the man to whom St Paul sent greetings in Rom 16:13 ; *cf*. 725c. ' Golgotha ' is the Gk transcription of the Aramaic word ' *gûlgûltā* ' = ' skull ' ; Latin, ' Calvaria '. The name probably alludes to the shape of the slight eminence on which the crucifixion took place. **23.** It was a Jewish custom to give wine mixed with myrrh to condemned persons in order to deaden their senses (Strack-Billerbeck 1, 1037). Christ refused to alleviate his sufferings in this way. **24.** In accordance with accepted practice, the garments of the crucified became the spoil of the soldiers who executed the sentence. **25.** ' *Now it was the third hour when they crucified him* '. This appears to contradict Jn 19:14, which informs us that it was about the sixth hour when Pilate condemned Christ. Some hold that the discrepancy is due to a copyist's error. Probably, however, Mk is following a division of the day into four periods of three hours each, *cf*. 15:1 (morning) ; 15:25 (the third hour) ; 15:33 (the sixth hour) ; 15:34 (the ninth hour). ' The third hour ' covers the whole period from about nine until midday. Christ was condemned before midday, and the soldiers took him straightway to

742c the place of crucifixion. **26.** The inscription placed on the Cross was the official placard proclaiming the charge on which Jesus had been condemned. **27.** The crucifixion of the robbers on either side of Christ seems to have been intended to throw contempt on his claims by associating him with common criminals. This added humiliation was a literal fulfilment of the prophecy of Is 53:12 ' he was counted with the evil-doers '. **28** is missing in some MSS and it is doubtful whether it is authentic. **29-30.** Calvary was outside the walls but close to the city, Jn 19:20. The passers-by who railed at Jesus had probably been turned against him by garbled reports, put out by the Sanhedrin, of what he had said about the temple and what had transpired at the trial. **31-32.** The chief priests and Scribes ridiculed Christ's kingship and taunted him with the miracles he had performed. By paying this involuntary tribute to his supernatural power they condemned themselves. ' He rose from the dead and you did not believe : even if he were to descend from the cross, you would not believe ', Jerome, PL 26, 211. **32b.** Lk 23:39-43 informs us that one of the robbers rebuked his fellow for reviling Christ. It is possible that both robbers at first joined in insulting him, but that one of them later repented of his conduct. More probably the plural ' robbers ' in Mk and Mt 27:44 is indefinite. The evangelists simply mention another quarter from which insults were offered to Jesus without intending to specify the exact number of those who took part.

d 33-41 The Death of Jesus—33. The evangelist evidently regarded the darkness, which began at midday and lasted until Christ's death three hours later, as a portent caused by special divine intervention. It was a sign of the judgement of God on those responsible for the crucifixion of Christ. The Jews should have recalled passages in the writings of the prophets, *e.g.* Am 8:9, where the imagery of the darkening of the sun is used to describe the intervention of God in judgement upon men. It is not possible to determine the exact nature or the immediate cause of the phenomenon. The darkness was not the result of an ordinary eclipse of the sun. This was impossible at the Pasch, as the moon was then at the full. Some hold that God miraculously withheld the sun's rays ; others think that God prevented the rays of the sun from reaching the earth by interposing dense layers of cloud. Lagrange (*Saint Marc*, 432) suggests a miraculous intensification of the gloom brought about in Jerusalem at the beginning of April by the clouds of sand and dust blown by the sirocco. **33b.** ' Over the whole *land* '. It is not necessary to hold that the darkness extended to the whole earth. Many writers think that the reference is only to Judaea. Probably the evangelist meant simply that the whole horizon was darkened—he was not thinking

e of the exact geographical extension. **34** gives the Aramaic translation of the opening verse of Ps 21 (22). This Psalm is the prayer of the just man who, though surrounded by enemies and in deep distress, looks confidently to God for deliverance. The words ' My God, my God, why hast thou forsaken me ? ' are a cry of distress wrung from the just man by the taunts and sufferings which God allows his enemies to inflict on him. There is no note of despair in that cry : confidence in God remains unshaken ; *cf*. Ps 21:10, 25. Christian tradition recognizes the Messianic sense of the Psalm, which finds complete fulfilment only in Christ : ' it contains the whole Passion of Christ ' (Tertullian, *Adv. Marcion*. 3, 19). Christ, the Just One *par excellence*, made the cry of the Psalmist his own on the Cross with far more perfect sentiments of submission and confidence in God. The desolation felt in the human soul of Christ is given expression in the Psalmist's words. But there is no question of despair or of abandonment of the humanity by the divinity. Christ was abandoned by God only in the sense that God did not spare him the sufferings of the Passion and Crucifixion, but allowed his enemies to work their will on

f him. **35-36.** The bystanders who said ' he calleth Elias ' had confused the word ' Eloi ' = ' my God '

with the name ' Elias '. This may have been a genuine mistake, though the Scribes who were present could scarcely have failed to recognize the words of the Psalm. It was a common belief, Mk 9:8-12, that the prophet Elias would return to anoint the Messias and make him known to the world. The idea that Jesus, as he hung on the Cross, was calling to Elias for assistance, gave a fresh opportunity for sarcastic gibes. One of the soldiers, hearing Jesus say ' I thirst ', Jn 19:28, soaked a sponge in the mixture of water and vinegar called *posca* which was the soldiers' ordinary drink, and raised it to Jesus' lips. The soldier was moved by compassion, but apparently because of hostility among the bystanders to this kind deed, he sought to excuse his action by joining in the mockery—this relief to the crucified would give Elias time to come to his assistance ! **37.** The words which Jesus uttered in a loud voice were probably ' Father, into thy hands I commend my spirit ', Lk 23:46. Many patristic writers and modern exegetes regard this loud cry uttered at the point of death as indicative both of the divinity of Christ and of the fact that he died of his own free will. It is not clear, however, that in the circumstances the loud cry just before death necessarily implies more than human power in Christ. The words spoken show that he retained full consciousness and complete self-control to the end. Christ's death was voluntary : he had the power to lay down his life and the power to take it up again, Jn 10:17 f., but he freely accepted and fully carried out the divine plan for our redemption, knowing that this involved his own death on the Cross. His last words are a renewed expression of his voluntary acceptance of the sacrifice of his life for the redemption of men. **38.** It is uncertain whether the veil which was rent in two was the outer veil which hung at the entrance to the sanctuary, or the inner veil which separated the Holy Place from the Holy of Holies. The exact significance of this event is also doubtful. According to some, the rending of the inner veil was a manifestation of God's power which signified that by the death of Christ the way into the heavenly sanctuary was thrown open and the Mosaic economy with its ritual was abrogated ; *cf*. Heb 6:20 ; 9:9 f. ; 10:19 f. Others, holding that it was the outer veil which was rent, interpret the event as a sign that by Christ's death the mysteries which concerned the Church were revealed, the inner veil remaining as a symbol of the truths to be revealed in the heavenly kingdom. **39.** The centurion was impressed by the bearing of Christ during the Passion, by the rapidity of his death and by the loud cry which he had uttered before dying, and also by the darkness and the earthquake, Mt 27:54. He had heard of Jesus' claim to be the Son of God, and in the manner and circumstances of his death saw proof that the claim was well-founded. It is doubtful whether the centurion understood the full significance of the title, ' Son of God ' ; *cf*. Lk 23:47, ' Indeed this was a just man '. His confession at least attests the honest conviction that Jesus was innocent and that he was no ordinary human being. **40-41.** We know from Jn 19:25 that our Lady was near the Cross. Of the other women who saw the Crucifixion Mark names only the three who came to the tomb to anoint Christ's body on the morning of the Resurrection.

42-47 The Burial of Jesus ; *cf*. Mt 27:57-61 ; Lk 23:50-56 ; Jn 19:38-42—It was the Roman custom to leave the bodies of those who were crucified to decay on the cross or to be devoured by wild animals and vultures, unless friends obtained permission to remove a body for burial. Jewish law, however, prescribed that the body of one hanged should be buried the same day, Deut 21:23, and this regulation was applied also to those who were crucified ; *cf*. Jos., *B.J.* 6, 5, 2. **42.** The crucifixion of Christ took place on Friday (*cf*. § 738*e*). ' Parasceve ' : παρασκευή = ' preparation ', *i.e.* the day of preparation for the Sabbath. The obligation of sabbath-rest began at sunset, and as the Sabbath on this occasion coincided with the first day of the Pasch, it was all the more imperative, in the eyes of the Sanhedrin, that the bodies of the crucified should be buried before sunset, as the Law prescribed. Consequently, they asked Pilate to hasten death by breaking the legs of the victims so that the bodies could be taken away, Jn 19:31-37. If our Lord's friends had not intervened his body would probably have been cast into a common grave with the bodies of the two robbers. Joseph of Arimathea, though a member of the Sanhedrin, had not consented to their decision and deeds ; he was a good and just man, and, secretly, a disciple of Jesus, Lk 23:50 f. ; Jn 19:38. Availing himself of his standing as a member of the supreme council of the Jews to have access to the Roman Governor, he secured permission to take away the body for burial. **44.** Pilate was surprised that Jesus had died so quickly. Persons condemned to death by crucifixion usually lingered on the cross for a much longer period, sometimes even for days. Jesus, however, had endured exceptional sufferings and torments from the time of the Agony in Gethsemani. **46.** In removing the body of Christ from the Cross and preparing it for burial, Joseph had the assistance of Nicodemus, Jn 19:39. Christ's burial-place was a tomb newly hewn out of the rock in which no body had previously been laid. It belonged to Joseph and was close to Calvary, Jn 19:42. The Gospels, Mk 15:46 ; Lk 24:12 ; Jn 20:5, 12, bear out the presumption that it resembled other Jewish tombs of the period, some of which can still be seen near Jerusalem. An outer chamber or vestibule hollowed out in the rock is connected by a low doorway with the inner or burial-chamber which contains recesses for the bodies. At the entrance to the tomb a large circular stone standing on its edge could be rolled into position to close the tomb or rolled aside into a groove cut in the rock. The customary Jewish ritual of preparation of a body for burial included washing and anointing and wrapping of the body in grave-clothes. The Gospels give the impression that the preparations for the burial of Christ were carried out hurriedly. The sabbath rest began at sunset, and there was no time to spare. The very brevity of Mk's narrative suggests haste.

XVI 1-18 The Resurrection and Apparitions of Christ ; cf. Mt 28 ; Lk 24 ; Jn 20-21—**1-8.** The Women at the Tomb. When the Sabbath ended at sunset on Saturday the women bought unguents with which to anoint Christ's body. Mary Magdalen and Mary the mother of James and Joseph had watched the placing of Christ's body in the tomb. They must, therefore, have known that a mixture of myrrh and aloes brought by Nicodemus had been used in the burial, Jn 19:39 f. But apparently they felt that, because of the haste on that occasion, the burial rites had been performed only in a summary, even provisional fashion. They proposed to complete the rites by anointing the body. **2b.** 'the sun being now risen' ; cf. Jn 20:1 'when it was yet dark'. This discrepancy is eliminated in some MSS of Mk which read ' as the sun was rising '. According to some authors, who hold that the women purchased the unguents on their way to the tomb on Sunday morning, Jn refers to the time when they set out, Mk to the time when they reached the tomb. Probably both evangelists should be understood as referring to the brief period after sunrise before darkness disappears completely. **3-8.** The stone at the entry to the tomb had been rolled back by an angel, Mt 28:2. It was quite natural that the women should wonder how they would have it removed, as it was very large. A man would probably have needed some kind of lever to roll it back. Mary Magdalen may have reached the tomb ahead of the others. Apparently she did not delay when she saw that the stone was rolled back, but immediately went to Peter and John, Jn 20:2 ff. The other women, possibly believing that the stone had been rolled back by some of the disciples, entered the tomb. A young man, i.e. an angel, seated on the ledge at the right side of the tomb told them that the crucified Jesus of Nazareth whom they sought had arisen from the dead, and instructed them to inform ' the disciples

and especially Peter that he goeth before you into Galilee '. **743b** The special mention of Peter, recorded only by Mk, was a sign that he had been forgiven and retained his position as head of the Apostles. The women were so filled with fear that they delayed in delivering the angel's message ; cf. Mt 28:8 ; Lk 24:9.

9-18 Apparitions of Christ—At this point there is a **c** break in the continuity of Mk. The abrupt final phrase in 8 ' for they were afraid ' leaves the story of the women unfinished. In 9 Mary Magdalen is introduced and identified, Lk 8:2, as if this were the first time she has figured in the narrative. The statement that Christ had arisen, 9, is not linked with the angel's words. The whole final section of the Gospel, 9-20, appears to follow a different plan from that of 1-8. Instead of the typically Marcan narrative, with picturesque detail and other graphic touches, we have a rapid, detached summary of events between the Resurrection and the Ascension. A number of the words and expressions which occur in the passage are not found elsewhere in Mk. In view of this internal evidence, it has been questioned whether this is the original ending of the Gospel and whether it comes from the pen of St Mark ; cf. § 726a, b.

9-11. The appearance of Christ to Mary Magdalen **d** is described more fully in Jn 20:11-18. ' appeared first to Mary Magdalen '. This statement does not exclude the possibility of an earlier apparition to our Lady. The evangelists were concerned with those apparitions which had a certain public, official character. The appearances to the Apostles were the foundation of the Church's teaching, and those to Mary Magdalen and to the other women were a reward for their fidelity and a preparation for the manifestation of Christ to the Apostles and disciples ; cf. Lagrange, *Saint Marc*, 449. **12-13.** The apparition to the two disciples is described at length in Lk 24:13-35. ' he was manifested in another *form* '. It seems that Christ's outward appearance had undergone some change which made it difficult to recognize him ; cf. Jn 20:14 ; 21:4. **14.** The narrative has emphasized the unwillingness of the Apostles to believe the reports of the Resurrection. Their unbelief is overcome only by the appearance of Christ in their midst ; cf. Lk 24:25-43 ; Jn 20:19-28. Christ reproached them for their unbelief and hardness of heart. The rebuke is more severe than any other administered to them by Christ ; cf. Mk 4:40 ; 8:17. In view of his repeated prophecies of the Passion and Resurrection, they should have been more ready to accept the word of those who had seen the risen Christ. **15.** The command given to the Eleven **e** is similar to that which was addressed to them by Christ at the mountain in Galilee where he had directed them to meet him, Mt 28:16-20. The narrative here, 15, does not mark clearly the change to a scene different from that described in 14. This does not imply, however, that the author meant to convey that these instructions were given to the Apostles on the occasion when Christ first appeared to them. The account is simply a summary which does not purport to give precise indications of time or place. The Apostles are commanded to preach the Gospel of salvation to all men throughout the world. The Gospel and the salvation which it brings are for all without exception. **16.** Those who hear the message of the Gospel must accept it with faith and be incorporated with Christ by baptism, if they are to share in the supernatural salvation which he has merited by his death. Refusal to believe the Gospel means rejection of the proffered salvation and involves eternal condemnation. **17-18.** **f** When sending the Apostles on a temporary mission in Palestine, 3:14 f. ; 6:7, 13, Christ gave them power to cast out demons in order to strengthen the appeal of their preaching. Now he promises to believers miraculous signs to guarantee the truth and divine origin of the doctrine which they had accepted ; cf. Heb 2:4. The promise is made to the community of the faithful rather than to each individual believer. In the early days of the Church, possibly because of a greater need

743f for extraordinary signs in order to move a sceptical and hostile world to which the Gospel and Church were still new, some of these manifestations of miraculous power were more frequent than in later times. But Christ's promise is not limited to a particular period. In every age miracles have given proof that Christ abides with the Church. ' cast out devils ' ; *cf.* Ac 8:6 f. ; 16:16 ff. Irenaeus (*cf.* Eus., HE 5, 7, 4–6) and other early writers speak of numerous instances of casting out demons. ' speak with new tongues ' ; *cf.* Ac 2:3 ff. ; 10:46 ; 19:6 ; 1 Cor 14. ' take up serpents ' ; *cf.* Ac 28:3 ff. ; Lk 10:19. ' shall lay their hands upon the sick ' ; *cf.* Ac 28:8.

g 19 The Ascension ; *cf.* Lk 24:50–53 ; Ac 1:9–11— ' after he had spoken to them ' : this does not mean that the Ascension took place immediately after Christ had given the Apostles the command to preach the Gospel throughout the world. In this brief summary the author does little more than allude to the different events without marking the changes of time and place. ' *has taken his seat at* the right hand of God ' ; *cf.* 14:62. In this metaphorical expression the author proclaims his faith in the divinity of Christ ' who was manifested in the flesh, justified in the Spirit, revealed to angels, proclaimed among the nations, believed in the world, taken up in glory ', 1 Tim 3:16. The glorified Christ sits at the right hand of God, equal to the Father in dignity and power.

20 Conclusion—The Apostles had evidently preached the Gospel in many districts outside Palestine when these words were written. Christ was no longer visibly present on earth, but he assisted the Apostles and set the divine seal on their preaching by the miracles which followed it, Heb 2:3 f., thus fulfilling the promise, ' Behold I am with you all days, even to the consummation of the world ', Mt 28:20.

THE GOSPEL OF JESUS CHRIST ACCORDING TO

ST LUKE

By R. GINNS, O.P.

a **Bibliography**—*Commentaries*: Origen, PG XIII, 1801 ff.; St Cyril of Alexandria, PG LXXII, 475 ff.; St Ambrose, PL XV, 1527 ff.; Ven. St Bede, PL XCII, 307 ff.; Lagrange O.P., *S. Luc* (1921), *Gospel of Jesus Christ* (G.J.C.), (1938); Knabenbauer S.J. (1896); Schanz (1883); *Plummer, ICC (1910); *Edersheim, *Jesus the Messiah* (1886). *Introduction*: CE, *St Luke*; *Ramsay, *Luke the Physician*; *Hobart, *The Medical Language of St Luke* (1882); Burrows, *The Gospel of the Infancy*, Heythrop, 1940.

b **Author**—'Thirdly, Luke the Physician, by nation a Syrian of Antioch, whose praise is in the gospel, and who himself was a disciple of the Apostle Paul, wrote (*volumen condidit*) in the districts of Achaia and Boeotia, seeking material from the ancients (*quaedam altius repetens*) and, as he admits in his preface, writing rather from hearsay than from eye-witness'. Thus St Jerome in his commentary on Matthew sums up the unvarying tradition traceable as far back as the Muratorian Fragment and the *Adv. Haer.* of St Irenaeus which date from the 2nd cent. Firm tradition, backed by internal evidence, shows that Luke was also the author of Acts. His name—Lucas, Λουκᾶς—is in all probability an abbreviation of Lucanus or of Λούκιος, the latter being the Greek form of the Latin Lucius, which is the sort of praenomen that would be assumed by a Greek on the acquisition of Roman citizenship. He may have been a freedman if not a full Roman citizen. Some wish to identify him with Lucius of Cyrene, Ac 13:1, in view especially of Cyrene's repute as a centre of **c** medical study. 'Luke the most dear physician', Col 4:14, was St Paul's companion during the Roman imprisonment (61-3), and there is much to be said for Harnack's suggested translation, 'the beloved Luke, my doctor'. There is good reason for thinking that the Apostle stood in need of medical attention, and it may have been in such capacity that Luke accompanied him. The attribution of Syrian nationality to Luke should not be exaggerated; it probably indicates no more than the enjoyment of citizen rights at Antioch, the Syrian capital. To all intents and purposes Antioch was a Greek city, owing its foundation to the Alexandrine conquest of the East. Josephus speaks of 'the Macedonians and Greeks who were the inhabitants' of the city (*Ant.* 12, 3, 1), and it became the main channel for Greek culture flowing eastwards. Thus its situation and character were ideal for the spread of the Gospel westwards, for the introduction to a Greek world of a faith which had such origins as the faith of Christ. It was there that the disciples lost their national character and appellation, and under the new Greek title of Χριστιανοί were recognized as a group distinct from the Jews; Ac 11:26. This is in complete accord with the character and spirit of the third Gospel, and it seems likely that its author was one of numerous Greeks who first accepted faith in Christ at Antioch; **d** Ac 11:20. We incline to the opinion that Luke was of European origin, perhaps descended from Greek or Macedonian colonists settled in Antioch. He was very familiar with Antiochian events; Ac 11:19-27; 13:1; 14:18-21, 25; 15:22-35; 18:22. Confirmation is added by the manner in which Paul groups him with his Greek disciples (Col 4:14, Phm 24), and by the irreproachable Greek style of Lk and Ac which

marks off their author clearly from the other NT **744d** writers, all of Hebrew origin (except perhaps the writer of Heb). Luke's association with Paul and the Apostles is affirmed by Scripture and tradition. Jerome's words 'whose praise is in the gospel' are taken from 2 Cor 8:18, and the nameless preacher (there is no question of a written gospel) is traditionally identified with Luke, who remained Paul's constant companion from about 50 to the Apostle's death in 67. Their first recorded meeting was at Troas when Paul **e** was about to begin his first mission to Europe, Ac 16:10. Luke goes to Philippi, remains there to carry on the work at Paul's departure, and is there collected by him on the last return to Jerusalem, *c* 58; Ac 16:10-40; 20:5 ff. Remaining in Palestine during Paul's imprisonment at Caesarea, 58-60 (some hold that the Gospel was written at this time) he accompanies him to Rome for the appeal to the imperial law-courts, staying there for the two years while the case awaits trial. On the successful outcome of the appeal it may be surmised that Luke joined him during his few remaining years of apostolic work, for we find him still with Paul during the latter's second imprisonment at Rome, 2 Tim 4:11, which ended with the Apostle's martyrdom. A tradition traceable to *c* 200 states that Luke wrote his Gospel in Achaia, where he had preached, and that he died in Bithynia (probably a mistake for Boeotia). Later traditions make him a painter and one of the Seventy-two, the latter most unlikely.

Date—This may be fixed with reasonable certitude **f** from the evidence provided by Luke himself. He wrote Ac after the Gospel, therefore if we can fix the date of Ac this gives the latest limit for Lk. Now the evidence of Ac forces us to the conclusion that it was written in or shortly before 63. For the chronology of St Paul we base our conclusions on the work of Brassac (*Une Inscription de Delphes et la Chronologie de St Paul*, RB [1913] 36-53, 207-17) who fixes the first Roman imprisonment 61-3. Now it is against all likelihood, and at variance with the known character and style of Lk, that he would have left his reader in doubt about the outcome of Paul's appeal to Caesar, had he known it when he finished Ac. The arbitrary suggestion that he left the question pending because he had in mind to write a 'third treatise' has no foundation. On the contrary, the decision of the Biblical Commission (*cf.* § 51*i*) directing Catholic scholars to the evidence in favour of dating Ac towards the end of the first Roman imprisonment has all the reason on its side. Added confirmation is provided by the fact that Ac throughout shows the Roman authorities in an accommodating attitude towards the Church; there is no suggestion of the violent persecution which began under Nero after the fire of Rome, July 64, a persecution which put the faith under the imperial ban and brought St Peter to martyrdom. There are **g** two objections to consider, the first hardly meriting serious attention, *viz.* that Lk shows dependence on Josephus and therefore must have been written not earlier than the end of the 1st cent., but the asserted dependence is unproven. The second, more grave, is Irenaeus' assertion (*Adv. Haer.* 3, 1, 1) that Mk did not write his Gospel until after the deaths of Peter and Paul. But as Lk is the third and shows a clear dependence

744g on Mk, it follows that Lk would have to be dated in or after 67, the date of Paul's martyrdom. Efforts have been made to interpret the words of Irenaeus in a manner more favourable to an earlier date (*cf.* Chapman, JTS [1905] 563 ff.) ; but with Lagrange we prefer to doubt the unsupported assertion of Irenaeus. Rationalist critics on *a priori* grounds demand a late date because of Lk's more detailed description of the destruction of Jerusalem in A.D. 70. Our conclusion is that Lk was composed before the end of 63 ; Harnack said *c* 60.

h Contents and Plan—Lk completes the trio of the Synoptic Gospels and as such follows the general scheme of Mt and Mk : the preaching of John the Baptist, the Baptism and Temptation of Jesus, the ministry in Galilee and the Transfiguration, the journey up to Jerusalem, the ministry in and around the Holy City followed by the Passion, concluding with the Resurrection and Ascension. Such appear to have been the lines of the primitive catechesis of the Gospel indicated by Peter at the first meeting of the Apostles after the Ascension, Ac 1:21–22. Thus most of Mk is contained in Lk ; in addition Lk contains much of that which distinguishes Mt from Mk. But further, Lk contains a good deal wholly proper to itself that we owe to Luke's diligent researches into the origins of the Gospel story ; it is twice as long as Mk and considerably longer than Mt. Of its twenty miracles six are proper, as are eighteen of its parables. The long Infancy Narrative, which forms one-eighth of Lk, is completely proper save for a word or two in Mt. Finally the long Journey Narrative, 9:51–18:30, erroneously called the Peraean Ministry, is to a large extent Lk's own. Like Mt and unlike Mk, he gives a number of the discourses of Jesus ; but while Mt prefers to gather the discourses and sayings into a unity, Lk follows a different kind of order, distributing them throughout his narrative and placing them in their suitable settings. ' In Mk (and in Mt if he knew the whole of it) Lk would find proof of a considerable gap. Mk is not unaware of the fact that Jesus had preached in Judaea, but he chooses to restrict himself to Galilee. . . . Lk discovered what had happened during a mission of Jesus in Judaea covering several months, and he has given an account of it, but place, occasions, characters, no longer stand out as they would in an account by St Peter . . . Hence in this whole section, peculiar to Lk and of priceless worth, we do not get the details that characterize the story

i of the lake-side ' (Lagr., GJC I 5). The purpose of the Gospel is defined in its opening words which recall Jn 20:30–31 ; Lk has gone to great pains in searching out the exact origins of the Gospel history and in setting everything down ' in order ', so that his reader may know the security of the truths in which he has already been ' catechized ', *i.e.* instructed by word of mouth ; the word plainly suggests the primitive catechesis of the Gospel and, according to Harnack, should here be taken in its strict sense : ' The third Gospel is, in the full force of the term, an *evangelium εὐαγγέλιον*, *i.e.* the announcement of good tidings. These good tidings tell of the Messiah's coming and of his work, which is to offer salvation to mankind. In Ac Luke has told how these good tidings spread from Jerusalem and, after various wanderings, reach Rome itself. In the Gospel he has shown how the good tidings came down from heaven to Jerusalem first of all, then to Nazareth and eventually to Bethlehem. The word then spreads over all Israel and finally comes back to Jerusalem, where the work of salvation is brought to its fitting completion ' (Lagr. *Lk* xxxiv). Lk falls easily into six clearly defined parts which we follow Lagrange in entitling thus :

(1) The Infancy Narrative, the dawn of salvation, 1:5–2:52.
(2) The investiture of Jesus with his Messianic office, 3:1–4:13.
(3) The manifestation of the Saviour in Galilee, 4:14–9:50.

(4) Insistent preaching on salvation, 9:51–18:30. **7**
(5) Arrival at Jerusalem and the Passion, 18:31–23:56.
(6) The Resurrection and Ascension, 24:1–53.

Sources—Luke indicates them himself : first many **7** written accounts of the Gospel history, and secondly those persons ' who from the beginning were eyewitnesses and ministers of the word ', 1:1–2. Ancient commentators were inclined to interpret ' word ' as the proper name of the Son of God after the fashion of Jn's prologue, but Lk and Ac commonly use it to mean the teaching of doctrine. We need not conclude (though some have done so) that Lk disapproves of the written documents to which he refers, hence we need not exclude Mt and Mk from among them. It is antecedently probable that there were a great many written accounts of the life and teachings of Jesus, in whole or in part, during the early years of the Church ; it would be surprising if there were not. Knowing Luke as we do from his writings, it is also antecedently probable that such a careful writer and exact historian would neglect no opportunity of familiarising himself with what had been written on a subject he had so much at heart. He tells us, 1:3, that he had been a diligent inquirer ' from the beginning ' ἄνωθεν—not to be confused with the ' from the beginning ' ἀπ' ἀρχῆς of 1:2. Origen says that ἄνωθεν should be translated ' now for a long time ', *i.e.* the matter had been a preoccupation of Lk since the time of his conversion years before. His opportunities of consulting those who had **b** come into contact with Jesus may be gathered from a consideration of Luke's own history. He spent long periods in Palestine, Antioch and Rome. It will be observed that whenever St Paul mentions him, Mark is always in the company ; Col 4:10, 14, Phm 24, 2 Tim 4:11. Luke mentions others who could have furnished him with information : Joanna, wife of Chusa, Herod's steward, Susanna, and ' many other (women) who ministered unto (Jesus) of their substance ', 8:3. With regard to the Infancy Narrative it is difficult to avoid the conclusion that the repeated remark of 2:19 and 2:51 is intended to indicate that the Mother of Jesus herself is the direct or indirect source of his information. Some modern scholars maintain that the Semitic character of the Infancy Narrative shows that Luke used an Aramaic written source ; it is possible but there are other explanations of Lk's Semitisms. As Plummer so well says, Lk is the most versatile of all the NT writers. He can be Hebraistic in describing Hebrew society and Greek when describing Greek society. His relationship to Mt and Mk in the parts **c** common to him and them is disputed among scholars of the greatest authority. In our opinion the following brief conclusions seem best to account for the facts. First that Lk shows dependence on Mk for much material and order of events, though without any slavish copying. Where the Synoptists march together Lk prefers the order of Mk, omitting however and transposing where his purpose requires. His aim is chiefly to present Jesus the Jewish Messias to his Gentile readers as the divine Saviour of all mankind, and to present him in a manner calculated to inspire confidence in those hitherto considered by the Jews as outside the pale, sinners and objects of divine wrath by their very birth ; *cf.* Eph 2:3 ; Gal 2:15. This stands out in the sections peculiar to Lk ; in parts common to Lk and Mk his omissions create the same impression. He passes over details which tend to leave an impression of severity towards non-Jews, *e.g.* the incident of the Gentile woman of Syro-Phoenicia, Mk 7:25 ff. For a similar reason he omits things too characteristically Jewish to be of interest to Gentile readers. Again it is characteristic of him to pass over **d** details unbecoming to the dignity of Christ, *e.g.* the attribution of madness by his relatives, manifestations of human emotion (though not always) ; he omits remarks derogatory of the dignity of the Apostles ; he dislikes repetitions and abundance of detail, and finally

5d he leaves out larger passages which would no doubt hinder him from including those proper parts which he intends to add to the narrative of Mt and Mk. His relation to Greek Mt is harder to define, but again, considering the antecedent probabilities, it is hard to believe that a man of Luke's disposition and opportunities could have remained ignorant of such an important document as Aramaic Mt, the only account at that time known to have been written by an Apostle.

e Official Catholic teaching (*cf.* § 50*e*) is that our Gk-Mt is substantially identical with Ar-Mt, but who translated the latter and when is a matter of conjecture. It may not have existed in Greek at the time of Luke's writing, but there could have been no great difficulty in the way of his learning the contents. As he would have known that its chief advantage over Mk was the fact that it contained a long collection of the discourses of Jesus, there is nothing improbable in the supposition that he may well have obtained or found a Greek translation of these discourses. In the large sections of Mt and Lk devoted to the sayings of Jesus (reckoned as one sixth of each Gospel, though the sayings are scattered through Lk) the similarities are so obvious that there seems to be either interdependence or else a common source for both. In reply to those who maintain that Gk-Mt seems rather dependent on Lk than *vice-versa*, it may be said that this can be explained by the possibility that the Greek translator made use of Lk in those parts common to Lk and Ar-Mt. For fuller discussion of the relations between Mt, Mk and Lk see article on *The Synoptic Problem*, §§ 610–5.

f Character of the Gospel—Bearing in mind who the author is—not merely a healer of men's bodily ills but a 'beloved physician'; a convert from Gentile paganism to faith in a Christ who is a divine healer of men's spiritual maladies; a devoted follower of St Paul, the preacher of universal salvation in Christ Jesus—this Gospel manifests precisely the character to be expected of it. Plummer points out that its first words recall those with which Hippocrates begins his treatise *On Ancient Medicine*, and we may note that the benign spirit of Lk calls to mind the old Hippocratic oath taken by medical students. They swore that they would honour and obey their teacher, care for his children in need, help their patients to the best of their ability, never supply them with poison or perform unlawful operations, never abuse their position but always enter a house as a friend and helper. Biblical critics, orthodox and unorthodox, join in praising Lk as the most touching and beautiful book ever written, outstanding for its note of joy at the loving-kindness of God and for its deep sympathy with the sorrows of suffering humanity. But Luke is no mere sentimentalist. He insists with repeated emphasis also on the necessity of absolute self-surrender for all who would profit by the goodness of God and the tenderness of the Saviour. It is a Gospel of renunciation of a most stark character, and the chief example of that is the **g** Saviour himself. Attention may be drawn to the following salient points : (1) Luke's qualities as a genuine historian and literary artist of great merit; (2) his insistence on the joyful character of the good tidings of the Gospel, the solution of both the moral and social evils of the world; (3) his emphasis on the necessity of prayer, exemplified by additional instances in the life of Christ; (4) the important place he assigns to those women who were associated with Christ, to his Mother first of all. Tradition has made Luke the patron of Christian art, and even if he never wielded the painter's brush, without question he has used his pen with an art that has furnished the chief inspiration of Christian painters all down the ages, providing them with the subjects of which they are fondest : the childhood of Jesus at Bethlehem, Nazareth and Jerusalem, the widow's son, the prodigal, the disciples at Emmaus. In like manner the liturgy of the Church draws largely from Lk : the *Gloria in excelsis*, *Benedictus*, *Magnificat*, *Nunc Dimittis*, while the Joyful Mysteries of the Rosary give us the Infancy Narrative in the form of prayer. **745g** Few writers have stood such severe tests of historical accuracy as Luke, yet he comes out triumphant under every test. Adverse critics have repeatedly attacked **h** him as unreliable and even dishonest, but in every case it is the critics who are eventually put to shame. Even Harnack has to blush for 'the truly pitiful history' of their criticisms and the party prejudice which blinds them to the facts that tell against them. Today every biblical scholar worthy of repute accepts with little reserve the verdict of Ramsay that Luke is a great and accurate historian. Every advance in scholarly research has so far completely justified the claim with which Luke begins his Gospel, that like a good historian he has verified his facts before setting them in order. That order is not a chronological stringing together of unrelated facts, a procedure which would have offended both the canons adopted by the classical historical models which he consciously imitates, and also the spirit of rational philosophy characteristic of the Greek world in which he had received his education. Not that Luke lightly neglects chronological sequence ; but what he chiefly seeks is the logical concatenation of events out of which grows the object he always keep in view, ' that thou mayest know the *security* of those things in which thou hast been catechized ', 1:4. This intro- **i** duces us to the second point above noted, the joyful character of Lk. It is not mere human history but the divine history of man's salvation, summed up here in the word *evangelium* εὐαγγέλιον, a word he never uses, but its verbal form εὐαγγελίζειν is found in such significant places as 1:19 ; 2:10 ; 3:18 ; 4:18, 43 ; 7:22. εὐαγγελίζεσθαι is the LXX rendering of the Hebrew *biśśar* ' to gladden with good tidings ', a favourite word of St Paul, Luke's master. No one can read Lk without realizing that this is the key-note of his Gospel, the gladness that God's loving-kindness stirs up not only on earth but in heaven also. At the birth of Christ the whole celestial court turns out to celebrate the event ; when a sinner turns back to God with repentance there is public holiday in heaven ; *cf.* 15:7, 10. The special note of joy in Lk is due to the fact that the good tidings of salvation are offered to all who are well-disposed, without distinction of race, sex or social standing, to Gentile as to Jew, to slave as to free. It is what we should expect from a disciple of St Paul, for in certain respects Luke stands in relation to Paul as Mark, *interpres Petri*, stands to the chief of the Apostles. It might be said that Lk is the gospel of Paul with all the asperities taken out of it. In Lk as in St **j** Paul the disposition required in those who wish to profit by the Gospel, which is ' the power of God unto salvation ', Rom 1:16, is that complete self-surrender to Christ which Paul calls faith. Lk continues the development of this theme in his own beautiful fashion ; *cf.* the repetition of ' thy faith hath saved thee ', 7:50 ; 8:48 ; 17:19 ; 18:42. In heaping up demonstrations of how deep is the love of God's merciful heart he seeks to give sinners that confidence in approaching God, as the publicans and sinners gladly draw near Jesus, which is essential for their happiness. His Gospel is a long drawn out example of that phrase which appears in the splendid passage from Tit 3:3–7 used in the liturgy of Christmas Day, ' when the goodness and kindness φιλανθρωπία of God our Saviour appeared '. But the goodwill of God demands a corresponding goodwill on man's part, and Luke therefore insists even more strongly than his fellow evangelists on the necessity of renunciation of all things to follow Christ's example. There is no enervating softness here ; *cf.* 9:51–62. In Luke's teaching ' there is no room for the flabby-minded in the Kingdom of God ' ; let each one reckon up the cost beforehand. No other Gospel, for example, insists with such emphasis on the duty of the rich towards the poor ; the rich are urged to use their wealth to make friends and patrons among the poor, God's special friends. Friends are what God desires, and friends naturally turn to one another with confidence in their needs. Thus Lk returns continually to the **k**

745k subject of prayer, the soul's communion with God. The model of prayer, as of all else, is our Lord ; Lk adds to the examples provided by the other Gospels, showing how Christ turned to his Father with prayer at all the great crises of his life : at the Baptism, before the call of the Apostles and the founding of the Church, before Peter's confession, at the Transfiguration and the Crucifixion. Joined to those two proper parables the Importunate Friend and the Pharisee and Publican, we have a regular treatise on prayer, showing that it must be a confident and persevering cry for God's mercy from the depths of our need, not a declaration of our own self-sufficiency. In speaking of prayer we may note that, though no Jew, Luke shows great appreciation of the purpose and meaning of the temple liturgy with which he shows a remarkable familiarity. Indeed his Gospel begins in the temple and ends there with the characteristic words, ' they went back into Jerusalem with great joy, and were always in the temple (praising and) blessing God '. In a word Luke betrays a literary art and a sensitive delicacy of feeling which is perhaps demonstrated by nothing so much as
l the place he assigns to women in the Gospel : Elizabeth and Anna the prophetess, the woman who was a sinner, the women from Galilee who followed Jesus and ministered to his needs, the women of Jerusalem who wept over him at the Passion, and most of all the Mother of Jesus. With sublime art he conveys the truth of the virgin motherhood of Mary, telling us more by his silence and delicate reserve than by his words. In accordance with his insistence on the universality of salvation, Luke gives his Gentile readers to understand that from now on women are to receive a new dignity such as the ancient world refused to accord them ; a world in which Jewish Rabbis could still seriously discuss the problem of whether women had souls ; a world in which the pagan attitude to womanhood bore fatal fruit in that list of anti-social evils drawn up by St Paul, Rom 1:26–32, a passage which ends on a terrifying note : ' hateful to God, without affection, without fidelity, without mercy '. Of all this the Gospel of Luke the disciple of Paul, is the complete antithesis.

746a Doctrinal Witness—We must recall Luke's standpoint : he intends to write a well-ordered history of the origins of the Christian faith for one who is probably already a Christian disciple, a convert from paganism like himself. His aim therefore is not to teach the truths of the faith, but to confirm the credibility of the truths his reader has already learned. ' The sacred text ', writes Cardinal Newman in the *Apologia*, ' was never intended to teach doctrine but only to prove it, and if we would learn doctrine we must have recourse to the formularies of the Church, *e.g.* to the Catechisms and the Creeds '. Lk ought, therefore, to contain clear indications of the faith of the first generation of Christians. Now the central point of the Christian faith is the belief that in the person of Jesus God has become man to save the world by the cross from the consequences of sin, and further to establish on earth the means by which those who accept him as their Saviour may enter with him into God's kingdom of eternal life. Luke therefore makes an appeal to the prophecies of the OT and to the miracles and supernatural events of the Gospel history as a guarantee of the truth that the coming of Christ was a divine intervention in the world for the good of mankind ; ' God hath visited his people ' is the characteristic note, 1:68, 78 ; 7:16. Plummer, strangely enough, thinks that Luke is not interested in the fulfilment of prophecy, writing as he does for Gentiles ; nothing could be further from the truth.
b Continually Luke insists, in the words of Jesus, that Christ is fulfilling a preordained role clearly foretold by the Scriptures ; that is the note on which the Gospel ends with greatest emphasis ; 24:20–21, 25–27, 44–46. In that last chapter Luke shows how our Lord had disappointed his disciples in their hopes, hopes which they believed were founded on the prophecies. But he has disappointed them not because he has not fulfilled

the prophecies but because he has fulfilled them so **7** perfectly. In other words the Messias they were looking for was not the Messias foretold by the Scriptures ; hence ' he opened their understanding that they might understand the Scriptures ', 24:45–48. If that is how Luke ends, it is also how he begins. The first two chapters draw largely on the OT in all its parts ; but the book of Malachias, the last of the prophets, is most used. Indeed Lk might almost be called the continuator of Malachias : ' the Old Dispensation runs gently into the New as a river runs into the sea, so gently that one fails to notice where the one ends and the other begins ' ; *cf.* Mal 4:5–6 and Lk 1:16–17. In a striking way he shows the continuity of God's saving work, as though ' to link the present with the past and future, as with a golden chain of promises that bound the Holy City to the Jerusalem that was above, which in type had already descended and in reality would soon descend from heaven ' (Edersheim). (1) **Jesus the Son of c God**—It may be said that while agreeing with Mt and Mk in recording the proofs of Christ's divinity, Lk provides us with further indications of early Christian usage in expressing belief of this truth. He has the habit of giving Jesus the title of ' the Lord ', reserved to God alone in the LXX. It is common enough in St Paul and is found in Jn several times ; but its special significance in Lk is seen with reference to the declaration of the angel in 1:34–35, a declaration understood so clearly by rationalist critics that they wish to eliminate it as a gloss or later addition to the original Gospel. There is no doubt that Lk means Son of God in the proper sense of the word, *i.e.* having one nature with the Father. Indeed he has omitted many details of Mt and Mk which might tend to arouse difficulties about this central truth in the mind of a Gentile reader, *e.g.* signs of human emotion in Christ, the declaration of his inability to work miracles at Nazareth because of the unbelief of his fellow-townsmen, the ignorance of the Son about the last day, his cry of dereliction on the cross. The critics accuse Lk here of a dishonest attempt to create a false impression, but the accusation takes little account of the fact that the same Lk has allowed his divine hero to be tempted by Satan, to weep over Jerusalem, to sweat blood in human agony, to die on a cross. (2) Moreover in Lk, **d** as in Mt and Mk, Jesus is the **Son of Man**. The reader is referred to the commentaries on Mt and Mk for the discussion of the origin and Messianic meaning of this mysterious title, still a subject of much divergence of opinion (§§ 690a, 740h). Of the eighty times it appears in the gospels Lk comes second to Mt (31 in Mt, 24 in Lk, 14 in Mk, 11 in Jn). In Lk as in the others, the expression is used only by Jesus of himself, never of anyone else. The NT writers do not use the title when referring to our Lord, nor does it seem to have been in use among the first Christians (one exception in Ac 7:55). A comparison of parallel texts in the Synoptists shows that in the mouth of Jesus it is taken as a synonym of ' I ', though it is on comparatively rare occasions that he employs it. In Lk, as in Mt and Mk, it is found on the occasions where our Lord wishes to lay emphasis on what he is about to say of himself, *e.g.* that he has authority to pardon sin, 5:24, his authority is higher than that of the Mosaic Law, 6:5, but that he is preordained by his Father to suffer the humiliation of the Passion, 9:22, as a condition of entering into the glory of his Resurrection, 24:7. A good study of its usage will be found in *The Study of the Gospels* by *J. A. Robinson, pp 49 ff. It is evident then that our Lord uses the title with a Messianic significance, though it cannot be said to have been a traditional Messianic title. ' When he calls himself Son of Man Jesus simply means " the man that I am " so as to draw attention to his person without assuming the title Messias openly, and so to say officially. It is evident that the most glorious of the Messianic prerogatives are consistent with this title ; but, in addition, its unassuming character, which so well lays emphasis on his human nature . . .

agrees admirably with his predictions of the sorrowful Passion . . . And when he wishes to allude to his triumph, very naturally he may remind his hearers of the words of Dan 7:13 and Ps 109, two texts which indicate a person who is associated with the glory of God ' (Lagrange). The title therefore contains the whole secret of the Incarnation. It is as though Jesus says that he, man as they see him to be, exercises powers which are the prerogative of God himself ; but at the same time he is in subjection to God who wills him to suffer and die for the redemption of the world, and so to be glorified. (3) **The Kingdom of God and the Church**—As Luke is also author of Ac where the formation of the infant Church is so evident, we should expect him to keep that in view in the Gospel. With special emphasis he develops the notion of the Kingdom of God as the reign of God's will over the lives and actions of men here, with a view to their entrance into the perfect Kingdom of God in the hereafter, where complete happiness is found in the restoration of that ideal condition in which God's benevolent designs are fulfilled without any contrariety of man's will. Hence the establishment of God's Kingdom means the destruction of Satan's kingdom. That is also the work of the Church, which by its organization and supernatural help brings all things into subjection to God through Christ, a theme Luke had so often heard developed by St Paul. He emphasizes the truth that the Kingdom of God is a newly established order in the world, begun in the person of Jesus and completed by his Passion and Resurrection. Among men the Kingdom embraces all those who voluntarily surrender themselves to the will of God as revealed through the life and teachings of Christ. These men, as Luke shows here and in Ac, are not a haphazard group who do not recognize one another, but a visible, organized society with duly appointed leaders whose office it is to rule in the newly established Kingdom as the ministers of Christ. He insists more than Mt and Mk on the deliberate will of Jesus in the choice of the Apostles, an act preceded by a night of prayer, 6:12-13. He adds to Mt and Mk by foreshadowing the development of the hierarchy in recording the appointment of seventy-two additional ministers of Christ, 10:1-24. Regarding the question of Peter's primacy, if he omits the witness of Mt 16:17-19, he provides equally strong evidence of his own, 5:10 ; 22:31-32. The latter text is as strong as that of Mt in affirming the infallibility of Peter, and is all the more significant in that it immediately precedes the prediction of Peter's fall, thus furnishing the reader with no excuse for misunderstanding the precise nature and purpose of infallibility. It carries us back to the opening words of Lk, who writes in order to provide Theophilus with *security* of faith, which is the purpose of infallibility. (4) **The Catholicity of the Church**—No reputable scholar now seriously calls into question the fact, well-established by sound tradition and internal evidence, that the author of Lk and Ac was Luke the companion of St Paul. It would be strange if there were no reflexion in the Gospel of Luke's relation to his master. Those who still maintain that the essence of Paul's doctrine is that the righteousness which comes to man from the sacrifice of Christ is not a real gift, but the mere legal imputation of righteousness which leaves the sinner still buried in his sins, will of course find it hard to see a reflexion of such a doctrine in Lk. On the contrary Lk leaves us in no doubt about the real mind of St Paul : that Jesus, Son of David according to the Flesh and Son of God according to the Spirit, Rom 1:3-4, died for the salvation of every man, Jew and Gentile, Greek and barbarian, slave and free, Gal 3:26-29 ; that his Passion is the source of pardon for sin and the cause of reconciliation with God for everyone who believes in Christ with a faith that implies total surrender of self to his influence and guidance. This is the faith that saves ; Lk 5:20, 7:50, 8:48, etc. Everyone agrees that Lk, much more than Mt and Mk, echoes the teaching of St Paul concerning the universal character of the redemptive work of **746f** Christ. Such additions as 3:6 and the omission of incidents like those found in Mt 15:21-28, Mk 7:24-30 which might create a contrary impression on his Gentile readers, serve to emphasize the point. Indeed one might almost say that the impression given by Lk is that if there is any privilege at all it is in favour of the Gentile, the sinner, and the outcast. It must have been after reading Lk that Celsus wrote so bitterly attacking the faith of Christians, whom according to Origen's *Contra Celsum* he makes to say : ' Let no educated person come, none wise, none sensible. . . . Whoever is a sinner, or ignorant, or a fool or under malign influence, him the Kingdom of God will accept. . . . Why was Christ not sent to the innocent as well as to sinners ? What harm is there in not having sinned ? ' Some critics have refused to believe that Luke was the author of the Gospel because it makes no reference to the Judaizing controversy so prominent in Ac, a quarrel that touched so closely this question of the universality of the Church. But Lk is a careful historian who in the Gospel writes ' in order ' of the origins of the Gospel history ; the fact that he omits to speak of a thing that is of much later date merely supports his claim to be an objective historian. Moreover the Judaizing controversy, though of importance for a convert Jew and for convert Gentiles under Jewish influence, was of no importance for Theophilus and his fellow Greeks, the more so in view of the fact that the quarrel had .been authoritatively settled at St Paul's instance a dozen years before Lk wrote his Gospel.

I 1-4 The Prologue—The opening words furnish a **747a** good indication of the author's character, style and aim : he is a careful writer, he possesses an excellent Greek style, his aim is to furnish his reader with reliable information that will guarantee the credibility of things already learned by word of mouth. This probably refers to instructions in the Christian faith—doubtless the primitive gospel catechesis (*cf.* κατηχήθης in 4) which Theophilus had already received. It may well be that Luke is writing not for a single person, but adopts the current fashion of dedicating literary works to some distinguished personage. There are unverifiable traditions about Theophilus ; all that can be gathered here is that he seems to be already a Christian, and that his title (κράτιστος ' most excellent ') indicates an imperial official of the Roman administration ; *cf.* Ac 23:26, 24:3, 26:25. Lk's second ' treatise ' is also addressed to him, Ac 1:1. His name means ' the beloved of God ' and some have held that Theophilus is a fictitious personage symbolizing the Gentile Christian. In his prologue Luke shows him the reason why he can rely upon the truth of what he is about to read : the writer has ' from the beginning ' (ἄνωθεν, 3) of his Christian life investigated carefully the whole history of the Gospel handed down by those who assisted at its fulfilment ' from the beginning ' (ἀπ' ἀρχῆς, 2). Ancient commentators saw in ' the word ' of 2 a reference to the Word, *i.e.* the Son of God ; but it seems more probable that Lk means the life, miracles and doctrine of Christ (*cf.* Ac 2:21-22). That is Lk's usual meaning of ' word '.

I 5-II 52 The Infancy Narrative—The importance **b** attached to this part by the author may be gathered from the fact that it comprises more than a tenth part of the whole Gospel. It is entirely peculiar to Lk save for a few words in Mt's Infancy Narrative. Some critics maintain that it did not form part of the original Lk because it differs in language and style from the rest ; others hold that Luke has incorporated with little change an Aramaic source discovered in his investigations. But evidences of Lucan authorship are as frequent here as in the rest of Lk and in Ac. The alleged Aramaisms are rather Hebraisms, accounted for by the deliberate imitation of the style of the LXX which Lk everywhere betrays (*cf.* Plummer's remark above, 745*b*). It is one of the marks of his great literary and artistic ability. A special reason for the Hebraic style here is the fact that in these introductory

747b chapters Lk links up the New Dispensation with the Old, the New Law with the Mosaic Law, intending thus to show the continuity of God's saving work. He draws largely on the thoughts and words of the OT and carries the mind back to the beginning of Genesis. There may have been written sources such as that suggested above, but the only positive indication of any source at all is the repeated remark about Mary's

c remembrance of events, 2:19, 51. Why has Lk made this great addition to what appears from Mt and Mk to have been the accepted form of the primitive catechesis of the Gospel? First, for the reason indicated; secondly, because it was inevitable that questions should have been asked among Christian disciples about the early history of the Saviour; thirdly, because Lk insists throughout on the character of the Gospel as the good tidings of salvation, and the Infancy Narrative emphasizes that point, *cf.* 1:19; 2:10–14. Hostile critics see here an obvious attempt to find a marvellous origin for the hero of the Gospel, after the manner of the pagan mythologies. Lk answers them himself by the simplicity and sobriety with which he surrounds the cradle of the child Jesus, who shows no signs of precocity or abnormality in himself and, apart from the modest incident of 2:41–52, remains in obscurity till about his thirtieth year; nothing mythological there. The chief lesson is the reality of the Incarnation, *i.e.* that a person, divine by origin and nature, becomes a child like other children. The marvels and supernatural interventions here narrated are not for his sake but for the sake of others. He works no miracles, for miracles are meant to confirm the truth of teaching, and it is not yet time for him to teach.

d I 5-25 Annunciation of John the Baptist's Birth—The Gospel good tidings are revealed within the framework of the Mosaic dispensation. As of old an angel appears. The message is to a Levitical priest, at Jerusalem, in the temple, during the offering of the daily sacrifice of the lamb. Lk begins as he ends in the temple, and here he shows great familiarity with the temple ceremonial. The names of Zachary (Yahweh hath remembered) Elizabeth (God hath sworn), John (Yahweh is gracious), all bear out the idea of continuity, linking present events with the past. The thoughts suggested by these names are repeated again and again in the Magnificat, Benedictus and Nunc Dimittis, canticles made up of a mosaic of phrases from the Law, the Prophets and the Psalms, *cf.* 24:27, 44. The words of the angel to Zachary, 1:16–17, pick up the thread dropped in the final words of Malachias, 4:5–6, the last of the Prophets of the Old Law. That prophet was not concerned with the Jewish Messianic hope of a coming King, the Son of David; he foresaw the coming of God in person, 3:1 ff., the passing of the temple worship and priesthood, the spread of a purer worship among the Gentiles, 1:10–11; inveighing against a corrupt priesthood and people, he foretold the coming of a better state of affairs, 1:6 ff.; 2:8–11; 3:3–4, and concluded with an exhortation to remember the Law of Moses, 4:4.

e 5-7. Lk re-echoes all this, beginning by presenting us with an ideal Jewish couple, a Jewish priest and his wife, the antithesis of the priests and people censured by Malachias; of blameless life, exact in the observance of the Mosaic Law, but deprived of the blessing of offspring. **8-10.** The great number of priests (Josephus boasts that there were 20,000) necessitated their division into groups for the purpose of temple ministry (*cf.* 1 Par 24:1–19), each group serving for a week at a time; even so the number was still so large that the chief offices were assigned by the drawing of lots. On the day of the Gospel's beginning Zachary had drawn the lot of offering incense in the sanctuary before the sacrifice of the lamb, an office held so honourable that no priest exercised it twice. Zachary had waited till old age for the privilege. **11-17.** Having strewn incense on the fire in the Holy Place it was his duty to bow towards the Holy of Holies and retire; he is arrested by the vision of an angel who announces that his prayer is granted. What prayer? During the offering of incense both priest and people (10*b*) prayed in a set form for the coming of the Messias and the redemption of Israel. But Lk certainly seems also to indicate a prayer expressive of the desire of offspring, despite the advanced age of Zachary and his later doubts, 18. In fact the birth of John was an answer to both prayers (*cf.* 14), which sets the note of joy running all through the Gospel. John, though a priest by birthright, is not to claim his privilege: he will follow the example of the Sons of Rechab who of old recalled Israel to the example of the patriarchs by refusing to forsake the nomadic life of the desert; Jer 35:1 ff. He shall be filled with the Holy Ghost, a specially Lucan phrase (53 times in Lk and Ac). Ecclesiastical tradition interprets this of John's cleansing from original sin. The influence of the Spirit of God continually recurs in the Infancy Narrative, 1:35, 41, 67; 2:25, 26, 27. In the work for which God has designed him John is to be another Elias, like Elias another 'converter' or 'restorer' of the people; *cf.* 1:17; 3 Kg 18:37; Mal 4:5–6. He will be like Elias in fiery zeal, in rebuking princes, in calling Israel to repentance (μετανοία, change of mind), in living in the desert on what God sends him. Jewish tradition held that Elias would come to anoint the Messias; *cf.* Mt 17:10 ff.; Mk 9:10 ff. But the main idea of the angel's words is that of Mal 3:1; John is the forerunner of God himself. **18-22.** For doubting the word of an angel, and such an angel, 19, Zachary is stricken dumb, deaf too in view of 1:62. The punishment is also to serve as a sign of the reality of the vision and guarantee of its fulfilment. 'To bring these good tidings', lit. to announce the *evangelium* or gospel, ἐυαγγελίζεσθαι, a favourite word of Lk and Paul, not in Mk and Mt (except Mt 11:5). **23-25.** There is no suggestion that the child is conceived in any but the normal way, though the special intervention of God is indicated in 1:36–37. Why does Elizabeth hide? Not for shame, because her shame is taken away, 25. Partly, perhaps, because her condition at her advanced age would have aroused comment. There are divine secrets here, and Mary is to be the first sharer of them (39 ff.).

26-38 Annunciation of Christ's Birth—By this second announcement that just recorded is now given its proper place and explanation. John's mission is to prepare Israel for the coming of God. As the same angel is sent to Mary we are led to anticipate that the message concerns the same object, *viz.* that the one now announced is he for whose coming John is to prepare. After due preparation of Mary's mind the angel affirms this in clear terms, 35.

The objections raised by rationalist critics against this verse lend emphasis to its significance. Some hold that Lk has borrowed the idea from pagan sources: others that the words are a tendentious interpolation by a later hand, though there is no MS authority for the suggestion. By the latter it is argued that the idea and terminology are completely un-Hebraic, since Spirit in Hebrew is feminine and therefore could not have been used to express the active principle in conception; that the words contradict the reading of 3:22 in Codex Bezae, 'thou art my son, this day have I begotten thee'; and finally, even if 35 is authentic, it means no more than that a child, conceived in the normal way, is to receive the sanctification of the Spirit like John, 15.

To the first of these criticisms it may be answered that the instances adduced from pagan literature are not in fact parallel. There is many a story of unions between gods and human beings, but there is none relating a virgin birth. The contrast moreover between the sublime description of St Luke and the gross legends of paganism should not be overlooked; *cf.* Douglas Edwards, *The Virgin Birth in History and Faith*, London 1943. The second criticism is answered above; to the third it may be said that Luke is writing in Greek, not Hebrew, and there is no proof that he used a Semitic written source ; to the fourth, that the critics have yet to prove that Codex Bezae merits the importance they attribute to it ; to the last, that a mere reading of Lk is sufficient contradiction.

26-28 The time is fixed with reference to John's conception. Note the contrasts, a literary device of which Lk is a past master. The annunciation of the Forerunner is made in circumstances of great splendour and dignity : to a priest, at Jerusalem, in the temple, at the hour of solemn sacrifice : that of the Master in circumstances of poverty and obscurity : to a poor girl, 2:7, 24, in a wretched village of no account, Jn 1:46, with no external accompaniments of splendour and dignity. 'Simplicity is the condition that befits the advent of the Incarnate Word to mankind, whom he comes to serve' (Lagr. GJC 1, 16), *cf.* 1 Cor 1:17-31. Current Jewish ideas of Messianism are contradicted from the outset : a Messias springing from among the Galileans, regarded with contempt among the Judaean Rabbis even for their very *patois* ; his birth announced in a village never mentioned in the OT, or the Talmudic writings, or even in Josephus. Lk does not indicate why Mary and Joseph had settled there : in fact he gives us no history of them at all, for he does not allow mere human interest to overshadow the great central fact to which he directs our attention. The Gospel is not a biography of Jesus but a history of the establishment of the Kingdom of God upon earth. He sees the importance of noting that Joseph is of Davidic origin, as he is to become the legal father of Jesus. But Joseph has not yet assumed the legal paternity of Jesus, and Mary is therefore of Davidic origin too, in view of 1:32 and 69, confirmed by Rom 1:3 ; 2 Tim 2:8, and the ancient tradition which makes Joseph and Mary related. **28.** The contrast is now reversed : the angel's attitude to Mary differs greatly from that to Zachary. 'Full of grace,' κεχαριτωμένη, a word (replacing Mary's name in the salutation) meaning one endowed with favour or grace, χάρις, in permanent fashion. It is God's favour which is indicated here. St Paul had already developed the idea of the divine graciousness of God which endows men with a supernatural quality making them pleasing in his sight as his children. The doctrine of the Church is that Mary, after her Son, is the most completely endowed with divine grace, through her divine maternity becoming the channel of all the graces received by others. 'Blessed art thou among women ' is probably a gloss here from 42. **29.** Mary is troubled, not, like Zachary, by the vision but by the unaccustomed salutation : *cum esset humilis non tam alta de se sapiebat* (Aquin). **31.** Lk with artistic reserve abstains from saying that Mary, like Zachary and the other actors in the Infancy Narrative, is a pious Israelite looking for the redemption of Israel, or that she is filled with the Holy Ghost. That is all taken for granted. We may be sure that the words of 31 must have recalled to her Is 7:14 and thus prepared her for what follows. The description of the child goes by ascending degrees, and could leave no doubt in the mind of a Jew that the Messias was in question ; Son of David was his most common title. **33.** 'Kingdom,' βασιλεία, 'kingship ' or 'reign ' in an active sense. **34.** Here again Mary differs from Zachary. Her question indicates not doubt but belief, and the reason she gives for her question would be meaningless unless it supposes, as Catholic tradition holds, that she had a previous compact with Joseph about the observance of virginity. If it be objected that such a thing would be at complete variance with accepted Jewish thought, we answer first that the Incarnation and all its circumstances were also at variance with prevailing Jewish Messianism and thought. The whole Gospel shows this. Secondly, it is false to assert that the observance of virginity was utterly foreign to Jewish ideas of the time. Such sentiments as here manifested by Mary (and it is to be concluded that Joseph was of the same mind)

were shared by other Jews, such as the well-known **748d** sect of the Essenes as Josephus makes plain, *Ant* 18, 1. Some object that, in such a case, why had she allowed herself to be betrothed to Joseph ? We may reply that she may have been left with little choice in the matter owing to the tyranny of established custom, even though she had made her vow before the betrothal. Moreover, knowing Joseph as she did, she may have acted with all the more confidence of finding in him a guardian of her virginity. In the divine design, as Mt indicates more expressly, the betrothal and subsequent marriage of Mary and Joseph were to serve as a protection for mother and Child. Her question, therefore, demands how God's design in her regard stands with respect to her proposal of virginity. The purpose of her vow was the pleasure of God and she will not observe it against his will. The reply of the angel is that God's design will not affect her vow, since the Child is to have no father but God. **35.** In the OT the Spirit of God appears on **e** the scene when things are to be brought to life or a special power from God is to be given for the fulfilment of divine purposes ; *cf.* Gen 1:2 ; Num 24:2 ; Jg 3:10 ; 6:34 ; 1 Kg 10:6, 10 ; Ps 103:30 ; Is 11:2, etc. An overshadowing cloud is the traditional symbol of the divine presence and mysterious action ; Ex 19:9, 16 ; 13:21, etc. ; 3 Kg 8:10-12 ; Is 6:4 ; Lk 9:34 ; Ac 1:9. Three possible readings of 35*b* ; omit ' of thee ': (1) ' the holy one to be engendered shall be called the Son of God ' ; (2) ' the one to be engendered shall be holy, he shall be called the Son of God ' ; (3) ' the one to be engendered shall be called holy, he shall be the Son of God '. The force of ' therefore ' falls only on the first phrase ; Jesus is the Son of God not because of his temporal but because of his eternal generation. **38.** Lk shows Mary as the first example of that total surrender to the will of God which is the essential characteristic of the Kingdom of God.

39-45 The Visitation—Unlike Zachary Mary has **f** asked for no sign, though she receives a sign. When Lk emphasized the haste with which she goes to Elizabeth, those critics are very obtuse who make Lk say that she ' proceeds to verify the sign '. St Ambrose understands him better : *non quasi incredula de oraculo, nec quasi incerta de nuntio, nec quasi dubitans de exemplo, sed quasi laeta pro voto, religiosa pro officio, festina pro gaudio.* Mary's charity provides an occasion for the meeting of the chief actors in the drama and for the supernatural intervention by which Elizabeth and her son are moved to acknowledge and pay homage to Mary's Child. Ain Karim, 5 m. west of Jerusalem, has the best claim to be the site of Zachary's home. **41-45.** Just as Mary is miraculously informed about Elizabeth, so Lk seems to indicate that the latter learns Mary's secret by the revelation of the Holy Ghost. ' Blessed (εὐλογημένη) art thou among women ', a Hebraism for ' more blessed art thou than all women '. In saluting Mary as ' the mother of my lord ' Elizabeth is at least recognizing the child's Messianic dignity. **45.** ' *Happy* (μακαρία) *is she that hath believed that these things shall be accomplished* ', etc. Elizabeth seems here to be comparing the faith of Mary with the hesitation of Zachary, rather than assuring her that the angel's words shall be fulfilled.

46-56 The Magnificat—Many recent attempts have **g** been made to prove that this canticle really belongs to Elizabeth, because three Latin MSS attribute it to her and because of its similarity to the canticle of Anna, 1 Kg 2:1-10 ; Elizabeth is held to be much more in the situation of Anna than our Lady. The weight of evidence (all the Greek MSS) in favour of the attribution to Mary is overwhelming, and to put the Magnificat on Elizabeth's lips would be, as Lagrange says, to falsify the whole context of Lk. The canticle is Mary's quiet answer to Elizabeth's congratulations ; it is as though she says : ' There is no reason to congratulate me. It is all the work of the Lord. My good fortune consists in the fact that he has deigned to notice one so small as I am '. 48 is an echo of 38.

748g If the Magnificat owes its inspiration to the canticle of Anna, its ideas and their expression are drawn from the OT generally, especially the Psalms : *cf.* Ps 23:8 ; 30:8 ; 33:4, 11 ; 68:31 ; 70:18 ; 88:11, etc. The speaker is saturated with the thoughts of the ancient Scriptures. The keynote is that God is gracious especially to the poor and lowly, and Mary, who has called herself ' the slave of the Lord ', insists on keeping that place ; ' because he hath regarded the *lowliness* (not, humility) of his *slave*, therefore all generations will call me happy '. She confesses that since God is her Saviour, 47, she needs salvation ; that is the doctrine of the Church : as a child of Adam she needed her Son's redemption which gained her the preventive grace saving her from incurring the stain of all sin, original and actual. **50.** The fear of God in OT phraseology means what we should call the service of God. **51-53.** A faithful echo of the canticle of Anna ; if that canticle is Messianic in outlook, much more so is the Magnificat which carries us back to the promise made to Abraham, Gen 12:3 ; 17:7 ; 18:18, a promise foreshadowing the universalism of the Gospel. Note that Mary refrains from any prophecy about the role of her Son the Messias. In 55*b* ' to Abraham and his seed for ever ' are not governed by ' spoke ' ; the words follow on from ' mindful of his mercy ' with 55*a* as a parenthesis.

h 57-67 Birth of John the Baptist—In a few words Lk conveys realistically the religious joy with which the Jews celebrated a boy's circumcision, the ceremony admitting him to spiritual communion with Israel and a share in the promises to the patriarchs ; it was a deed of contract between him and God ; *cf.* Gen 17. 'No domestic solemnity', says Edersheim, 'was so important or so joyous as that in which the child had laid upon it the yoke of the Law, with all of duty and privilege which this implied'.

i 68-79 The Benedictus—Like the Magnificat, a chain of the principal thoughts running through the OT, a canticle completely in harmony with the character of Zachary as painted by Lk, as the Magnificat harmonizes with the character of Mary. It marks the recovery of his speech last used to pronounce the ritual prayers offered by priest and people at the sacrifice of incense nine months before. These prayers included the Eighteen Benedictions which sum up the hopes of Israel, and Edersheim points out (*op. cit*, I 158 f.) how the Benedictus echoes the main thoughts of the Jewish prayer. It is worth noticing how it further turns round the ideas signified by the names of Zachary, Elizabeth and John. The canticle falls into two distinct parts divided in sense : 68–75 repeat the general theme of the Magnificat without referring to what belongs to Mary ; 76–79 are addressed to John and his vocation. **68-69.** The visiting of his people by God is Lk's theme ; *cf.* 7:16. It is a common OT phrase ; God visits to help, save, judge, pardon, show mercy. The same is true of ' horn of salvation ', a symbol (borrowed from the bull) of strength and power. Here Zachary joins Elizabeth, 42–45, in paying homage to the child of Mary, the Son of David, whose name Jesus (Jehoshua, Yahweh is salvation) is thus clearly indicated. The testament of 72 is the covenant between God and Abraham, between God and Israel on Sinai (*cf.* Lev 26:42), as the oath of 73 is that made to Abraham at the time of the famous promise, Gen 22:16–18. Our English translation seems to leave 71–75 hanging, but they are consecutively dependent on the verbs of the preceding **j** vv, being explicative of their content. **76-78** echo Mal 3:1 ; 2:6–7 and 4:2, and foreshadow the preaching of John, Lk 3:3 ff. **78.** ' The Orient ', ἀνατολή, is used for the rising of the sun or a star (*cf.* Is 9:2 ; 60:1–2 ; Zach 3:8 ; 6:12) and recalls Mal 4:2, ' unto you that fear my name the sun of justice shall arise *with healing* in his wings ', a text that would appeal to a physician. **79** naturally flows from this and is suggested by Is 9:2. Only with light can the wayfarer guide his steps straight ; *cf.* 3:4. The chief feature of the Benedictus is that the Messias, born in the house of David, appears in the character of a Divine Being, and thus serves to confirm 1:35. **80.** Lk, after his fashion, sums up a long history in a few well-chosen words ; *cf.* 2:52 ; 3:19–20. The ' spirit ' is the Divine Spirit which filled John from the womb and now leads him into the desert (*cf.* 3:2 ; 4:1) to be prepared for his mission. John lays no claim to his priestly rights ; the passing of the temple and the Law is foreshadowed.

II 1-20 Birth of Jesus—After the rough chronological indication of 1:5 (reign of Herod the Great, 37–4 B.C.), Lk here furnishes a more precise date for the birth of Christ, the occasion of a general census of the Roman empire commanded by Caesar Augustus. He adds a qualifying phrase in 2:2 which has given rise to much difficulty. Cyrinus (a Greek form of Quirinius) was Publius Sulpicius Quirinius, a Roman official of obscure provincial origin who by his military prowess rose to the consulship. He was certainly governor or legate of the imperial province of Syria in A.D. 6 when a census was made in Judaea preparatory to the incorporation of that kingdom in the province of Syria, an event remembered on account of the Jewish revolt it occasioned. This census is recorded in Ac 5.37 and is therefore not to be confused with that mentioned here. It has been objected that secular history knows nothing of a general census ordered by Augustus or of a census in Judaea about the time assigned to the birth of Christ, 6–4 B.C. ; indeed that such a census was impossible because Herod was then the acknowledged king of Judaea. Finally it is denied that Cyrinus was governor of Syria at the time. For a full treatment of the difficulty, *cf.* *Ramsay, *Was Christ born at Bethlehem ?* ; Lagr. *Luc* 65 ff. ; CE *St Luke* ; Ricciotti, *Life of Christ* 167 ff. ; *Scripture*, vol i 77 ff., vol iii 76 ff. We may sum up here by saying that historical research tends to confirm the accuracy of Lk. It is certain that Augustus instituted a financial reform especially with regard to taxation abuses in the provinces, and set up a professional civil service for that purpose. He set himself to acquire exact knowledge of the financial resources of the empire of which at his death in 14 A.D. he left a written account (Tac. *Ann.* I, 11 ; Suet. *Aug.* 28). The only way of obtaining such information was by a census of inhabitants and their wealth, and it was natural that he should begin with the provinces immediately under the imperial control. There was such a census in Gaul in 12 B.C., in Egypt 10–9 B.C. It may be concluded that the case was similar in Syria, the command of which was reckoned highest in rank of all the imperial provinces. It has long been admitted by responsible scholars that Cyrinus twice held authority in Syria, the first time in conjunction with Sentius Saturninus, 9–6 B.C., and there is documentary evidence in favour of this (*cf.* Lagr. *S. Luc* 65–6). Lk does not say that Cyrinus himself conducted the census ; if it was begun under Cyrinus it would take long to complete in view of the manner in which it was made. There still remains the objection that Judaea was an independent state until A.D. 6 and not a part of the empire. But the real fact is that Herod was merely a client-king, completely dependent on the goodwill of Augustus, who at first saw in Herod a convenient ruler of a state that formed one of the frontiers of the empire. As Ramsay says, to all intents and purposes Herod's kingdom was part of the Roman world, and consequently there is nothing improbable in the idea that it was included in the command for a general census. Moreover it does not follow from Lk that the census in Judaea was conducted by Roman officials. A census made by native officials at the command of the emperor need not have caused any great stir, particularly when we remember that in the neighbouring country of Egypt there appears to have been a system of 14-yearly enrolments for taxation purposes (*cf.* S.H.R. Wallace, *Taxation in Egypt from Augustus to Diocletian*). In conclusion it may be said that a writer of proved carefulness like Luke would not have been guilty of such an error as could easily have been detected by those for whom he wrote. Early critics of the Gospel like Celsus never question his statement, while early Christian writers like St Justin (a Palestinian) appeal to the Roman records in proof of it. **1.** ' The whole world ', lit. all the habitable (world), a commonly accepted phrase for the empire ; *cf.* Ac 11:28, etc. **2.** ' This enrolling was first made *while Cyrinus was* governor of Syria '. To avoid the difficulty it has often been suggested that the Greek could be translated ' this enrolment was made before Cyrinus was governor ' ; *cf.* Jn 1:30. But others maintain that such a translation is untenable, and in view of the above there seems no necessity for it. **3.** The method of enrolment indicated here was not the Roman method, but it was the custom in Egypt and was allowed by the Romans. **5.** Critics object that here again Lk is at fault, since there was no need for the wife to accompany her husband. But it is obvious from Mt 1:18 ff. that her presence with Joseph would seem advisable, not to speak of the fact that they would see in the circumstances a fulfilment of prophecy. **6.** No indication is given of the time spent at Bethlehem, but it would be an anachronism to suppose that the census was conducted with modern efficiency. The impression is that the caravanserai of Bethlehem was full because of the census. **7.** The bare record of the fact of the birth of Jesus ; Lk ' with indescribable appropriateness and delicacy draws a veil over the most sacred mystery ' (Edersheim). In this he is worlds away from the apocrypha which have none of his reserve ; they introduce a midwife to bear witness to the virginity of Mary and the miraculous birth. Lk's only indication of anything exceptional is that Mary herself ' brought forth her firstborn son and wrapped him in swaddling clothes ', the normal clothing for a new-born infant with which she had come prepared. The constant tradition of the Church has always been that neither the conception nor the birth of Jesus was in any way detrimental to the perpetual virginity of Mary. Lk does not indicate anything different in his use of ' firstborn ', which represents the Hebrew *bᵉḳōr*, a word suggesting not so much later children as the Mosaic legal obligations connected with a firstborn son. He already has in mind what has to be said about the Presentation, 22 ff. Moreover he carefully avoids all reference to the ' brothers ' and ' sisters ' of Jesus found in Mt and Mk. There is no trace in the Church of growth in the dogma of the perpetual virginity of Mary. For a treatment of the question see under Mt 1:25, 13:55-56, Mk 6:3 ; Lagr. *Mc* 3:32. **8.** Bethlehem is a centre for shepherds ; Lk may have in mind 1:51-53, for shepherds were ' under the ban of Rabbinism on account of their necessary isolation from religious ordinances and their manner of life which rendered strict legal observance unlikely ' (Edersheim) ; *cf.* Jn 7:48-49. In the OT frequent divine manifestations are made to shepherds, like Abraham and Moses ; these shepherds prove docile to the voice from heaven like those of old, very different from the Rabbis. **10.** ' Behold I bring you tidings of great joy ' ; compare Greek with 1:19. ' *The Glory of the Lord* ', 9, which shone around them recalls 1:78-79 and Is 9:1-2. **11.** ' A saviour who is *Messias* lord ' ; as there in no article in Greek before Lord, we may perhaps understand ' Messias Yahweh '. Were Lord used as a common name we should expect it before Messias. Adverse critics are reduced to the suggestion that Lk has here mis-translated a hypothetical Aramaic document which had ' the Messias of Yahweh '. But why has he not mistranslated in 2:26 ? **13.** The angels' song recalls Job 38:7 and Is 6:3, both significant texts. In Job the angels sing at Creation ; the birth of Christ is the beginning of a new world, as we shall be reminded again in 3:21 ff. ; *cf.* Jn 3:3, 5. **14.** Three possible renderings : (1) as in DV ; (2) ' Glory to God in the highest and on earth : peace to men of good will ' ; (3) ' Glory to God in the highest ; peace on earth ; good will to

men '. (3) is possible only if εὐδοκία ' good will ' is in **749f** the nominative in the Gk text, as was the common reading among the Greek Fathers. But the strength of MS evidence (א B A D W) is on the side of the reading εὐδοκίας, *bonae voluntatis* is as in Vg. Hence the choice is between (1) and (2). It is objected that the order of the Gk excludes (2), but that is questionable. If we divide the words after ' earth ', the angelic song forms a distich, each line of which begins with the significant word ' glory ' to God, ' peace ' to men. There is much to be said for the traditional English rendering which divides the words after ' highest '. In this case the angelic song forms a distich in which each term has its parallel, heaven opposed to earth, glory opposed to peace, God opposed to men. Who are the ' men of good will ' ? Apparently those well disposed towards God. But two objections are raised against this interpretation : first, although Lk makes it clear that good dispositions are required for entering the Kingdom of God, yet the spirit of the Gospel, here especially, is that the good tidings are for all ; secondly, it is maintained that εὐδοκία is always used of God's will in Scriptures (but *cf.* Rom 10:1 ; Phil 1:15). It is probable then that the meaning is ' peace to men who are thus made the objects of divine favour '. **17.** The shepherds ' *made known* the word ' ; DV follows Vg which mistranslates ἐγνώρισαν as ' they understood '. **19.** Here and 51 are the only indications of Lk's sources of the Infancy Narrative.

21-24 Circumcision and Presentation of Jesus and g Purification of Mary—The Saviour just given to Israel now comes forward as the appointed heir of the promise made to Abraham, confirmed in the institution of the rite of circumcision. Here, as in the case of his birth, the narrative is marked with great simplicity. The precise prescriptions of the Law are followed ; Gen 17:12 ; Lev 12:3. As the firstborn, Jesus is God's property, consecrated to God as a sacrifice. Parents could redeem, *i.e.* buy back, such a child from God at the price of five shekels of silver ; Num 18:15 ; Ex 13:2, 12 ; Lev 12:4 ff. ; Lk makes no reference to this part of the ceremony but indicates that instead of the lamb prescribed to be offered as a sacrifice by the mother, Mary offers what was known as ' the poor woman's offering '. Mary seeks no exemption from the Law although, as Catholic tradition teaches, there was no cause for Levitical purification in her case (*cf.* ST, III, 37:3, 4). The subjection of Christ to the Law recalls Mt 3:15 ; Gal 4:4-5 ; Rom 8:3 ; Heb 2:14-17. **22.** ' Her purification ' ; here DV follows Vg, but the Greek has ' their purification ', which is difficult. As neither Jesus nor Joseph needed purification, the explanation must be that Lk is thinking rather of the Levitical ceremony of presentation and redemption than of Mary's purification, which is mentioned only because of the Presentation. There was no need for a woman to make a special journey to the temple for purification.

25-35 Holy Simeon. The Nunc Dimittis. Forebodings h of Opposition—A man after the type of Zachary and Elizabeth, aged, pious, looking for the fulfilment of God's promises in the true spirit of the OT. All such, Lk points out, are under the special influence of the Spirit of God, and through that influence it is Simeon's office to welcome the Lord to his temple, Mal 3:1, and to acknowledge Jesus as the promised Messias. **25.** ' The consolation of Israel ', abstract for the concrete ; *Naḥam* or ' Consolation ' of Israel was a traditional idea associated with the Messias, *Māšîaḥ ha-Mᵉnaḥēm,* God's ' Anointed Comforter '. **26.** ' The Christ of the Lord ', *i.e.* the Messias (the anointed one) of Yahweh, a common expression of the OT for the kings chosen by God to reign over Israel. This title is paralleled in the Nunc Dimittis by ' thy salvation ', *i.e.* the child Jesus, the Saviour. Here, as already in 1:41 ff., 67 ff., Lk seems to indicate that the Holy Spirit gives light regarding the divine mystery ; Simeon recognizes the Christ of the Lord despite the circumstances which run

749h counter to current Jewish Messianism. Lk shows no hesitation, after what he has said, in using the words 'parents', 'father and mother'. It follows from the narrative that Joseph has assumed legal parenthood of **i** Jesus, a thing that Mt declares more explicitly. **29-32.** The Nunc Dimittis, a third canticle preserved for us by Lk alone, and like the former ones used daily in the liturgy. This closes the Church's day, as it closed Simeon's day. Simeon sees further than Zachary; salvation is prepared not only for Israel but for all nations, according to the promise to Abraham, and the light is already shining in their face. The Nunc Dimittis starts where the Benedictus leaves off with the idea of light shining in the darkness. This canticle too breathes the spirit and echoes the words of the OT; *cf.* Gen 15:15; 46:30; Tob 3:6; Is 9:2; 42:6; 49:6. **33.** The wonder of Mary at least can hardly be surprise, if Lk is to be interpreted as an intelligent author, after 1:26 ff. Some suggest it is surprise that Simeon seems so well informed; but it is more likely that it is simply the Lucan style of recording astonishment at the manifestation of the supernatural; *cf.* 1:63; 2:18, 33; 4:22; 8:25, etc., and in Ac frequently. Or is it anticipatory of 34-35, which is the first hint of opposition? So far all has been on a note of joy and welcome; now there is a promise of tragedy, strife and the sword. Simeon thus gives a more complete picture of OT predictions. Note 'is set' (κεῖται) is preordained; perhaps he has in mind such texts as Is 8:14; 28:16; Ps 117:22; *cf.* Mt 21:44. Some have put 35*a* in parenthesis for fear of attributing anything derogatory to Mary; Origen and some of the ancient commentators, thinking of Mk 3:21, interpreted the words as foretelling that she would be tempted to doubt her Son. But it seems more probable that 35*b* applies to all the preceding; as Jesus will later say, contact with him reveals all hearts, *i.e.* the dispositions of soul in each one. There can be no neutrality; everyone must come to a decision. The same idea is in the Magnificat. But it is only natural that the heart of Mary will be pierced with sorrow by the opposition shown to her Son. Tongues of enemies are like a sharp sword, Ps 56:5; 63:4.

j 36-38 Anna the Prophetess—Another of the little group of people on the threshold of the tomb who 'looked for the redemption of Israel'.

39-40 Return to Nazareth—It is difficult to find a satisfactory reconciliation of Lk with Mt 2:1-20. If Lk is not ignorant of these events (and he can hardly be if there is any force in the conclusions drawn from 2:19, 51) then we can only suppose that he has deliberately omitted here, as elsewhere, in view of his plan and aim. The adoration of the Magi might seem fitted to strengthen his thesis of the universalism of the Gospel; but Lk has a different type of people in view, the poor, the wretched, the sinner. In any case 39-40 in no way denies Mt 2:1-20, for it is in characteristic Lucan style, summing up the infancy of Jesus before he proceeds to the next event; *cf.* 1:80; 3:18-20. Note that only to Jesus and Mary has he attributed the grace of God. Catholic theology teaches that the soul assumed by the Word of God was informed by sanctifying grace in all its fullness; that Christ, as the 'author and finisher of faith', Heb 12:2, had all the requisite *gratiae gratis datae*; and that as Head of the Church he is the source of all the graces given to men (ST III, 7-8). The Child was also full of wisdom, of which an example will now be given by Lk.

750a 41-52 Jesus in the House of his Heavenly Father—The only incident we are allowed to learn of the hidden life, therefore of great significance in the mind of Lk. Neither women nor children were bound by the precept commanding a triple annual appearance at the temple; *cf.* Ex 23:14-17, Deut 16:16. Boys fell under the obligation when they became 'sons of the Law' at thirteen, but it was customary to anticipate this age by a year or two. It seems that Lk's intention is to show this incident as the first appearance of Jesus in the temple since the Presentation. The whole incident is full of mystery. Jesus 'remained' in Jerusalem of his own accord; no Jewish boy of twelve would easily be lost, but as the pilgrimages were made in village parties, it is not surprising that Jesus was not missed at first especially as the men and women folk perhaps travelled apart; he might have been with either party, *cf.* 44. It is another indication of Lk's about the reality of the Incarnation; Jesus behaved as an ordinary boy. **46-47.** It was the custom for the Rabbis, especially at great feasts, to give sermons and lessons on the Law and tradition in the surroundings of the temple, as the Moslems do today in mosques. It was among the listeners who readily joined in discussion with the Rabbis that the Child was found, his answers showing such wisdom that all the hearers are ' *out of themselves* ' with amazement. **48.** Mary and Joseph are also amazed—not the same word as above but an even stronger one in Greek, expressing the idea of shock; but Lk gives the reason in 48*b* : Jesus has never behaved so to Mary before. It is to be remembered that with her, as with others, Jesus had conducted himself as a normal child; his divinity was to her, as to us, an object of faith and not vision. **49.** ' *What reason had you to search for me? Could you not tell that I must needs be in the place which belongs to my Father?* ' (KNT). An answer surely given with an affectionate smile. The emphasis is on 'search'; where would you expect a child to be but in his father's house? Lk has here 'in the things of my Father' ἐν τοῖς τοῦ πατρός μου, which could in other circumstances mean 'my father's affairs', but here certainly means 'my Father's house' (so the ancient commentators). 'Father' (God) here is a reply to 'father' (*i.e.* Joseph) in 48, and the evident sense is that Jesus at the age of twelve is conscious of his Divine Sonship, a thing that will be confirmed from heaven in 3:22. Another point of importance is the fact that Jesus takes it for granted that Mary and Joseph will know what he means; it is in the light of this plain fact that we must interpret 50; if Mary does not understand, then the events of 1:26-38 lose most of their point. 51*b* also throws light on the point. 'They learnt only gradually what his Messiahship involved (*cf.* 2:34-35) and this is one stage in the process. From the point of view of her subsequent knowledge, Mary recognized that she and Joseph had not understood' (Plummer ICC on 2:51). **52.** Lk ends the Infancy Narrative with a last emphasis on the reality of Christ's human nature: 'Jesus *made progress* in wisdom and *stature* and *favour* with God and men'. God's favour is shown by grace, and though Christ had the plenitude of grace from the beginning of the Incarnation, yet as he advanced in life he showed greater effects of the grace that was in him. His human mind advanced in wisdom, because as man he acquired knowledge by experience, as it is proper to man to do.

III 1-IV 13 The Investiture of Jesus as Messias—It was fitting that there should be a public manifestation of Jesus as the promised Messias, Son of David, King of Israel. But in the secret designs of God the Messias was to be also God's only begotten Son, and this too had to be officially declared. In accordance with the ideas of the time it was fitting that Christ should be preceded by a herald, especially as it was expected that Elias should perform in some sort that office by anointing the Messias. We are already prepared by Lk to see John in that character. Here Lk begins what is held to be the primitive form of the Gospel catechesis, and up to 9:50 he follows Mk faithfully while making such omissions and additions as suit his purpose.

III 1-20 Preaching of John the Baptist—(Mk 1:1-8; 6:17-29; Mt 3:1-12; 14:3-12). Lucan additions are the detailed chronological indications, 1-2, examples of John's advice to the people and their questioning about his character, 10-15; he anticipates after his fashion by completing the story of John without mentioning his death, 18-20. He omits things unsuitable for Gentile readers: details of John's food and clothing, and the confession of sins by those baptized.

The latter omission is dictated by the fact that all this is merely preparatory for Christ's baptism, and there can be no question of confessed sin there.

The '15th year of Tiberius' may be taken as A.D. 27–8. Augustus died 19 Aug. A.D. 14 and was succeeded by Tiberius. The remaining months of that year would count as the first year of Tiberius ; and if, as seems likely, Lk reckons according to the Seleucid calendar which was current in Syria, the new year would begin on 1 Oct. Thus October of 27 to October of 28 is the 15th year of Tiberius. John began his ministry after 1 Oct. of 27 and the baptism of Jesus took place before the Pasch of 28. Allowing for three Paschs in the ministry of Jesus, this would date the Crucifixion at the Pasch of the year 30. If the birth of our Lord was in 6 B.C., and many think it could not have been later, he would have been 33 at the time of his baptism. Lk says 'about thirty'. He has been accused of error in the historical details he here gives : first by including Ituraea in the dominions of Philip, son of Herod the Great ; secondly, by making Lysanias the tetrarch of Abilene ; thirdly, by joining Annas with Caiaphas in the office of the high-priesthood. But it is now proved (cf. Lagr. Lk 101–2) that, although Ituraea proper was outside the dominions of Philip, the country of the Ituraeans included the district of Panias which was formerly part of Herod's kingdom and passed to Philip, who there built Caesarea Philippi. With regard to Lysanias, the critics formerly held that the only person of this name connected with the district of which Lk speaks had been dead for sixty years. But later research has found a Lysanias of Abilene which corresponds exactly with Lk's Lysanias ; cf. CE St Luke, and Scripture, vol. iii. 35. There is also good reason for Lk's inclusion of Annas along with Caiaphas (read 'high-priest' with Gk, not plural as in Vg and DV). Annas was deposed by the Roman authority in 15, Caiaphas, his son-in-law, appointed in 18 ; but such was the repute of Annas, added to the fact that by Mosaic Law the high-priesthood was for life, that many Jews still acknowledged him as the real religious chief ; cf. Ac 4:6 ; Jn 18:13. **4-6.** By extending the quotation from Is 40 further than Mk and Mt, Lk includes words useful for his universalizing theme. **10-14.** These specimens of John's advice considerably modify the uncompromising character of him we gather from Mt and Mk. Lk points out, 18, that John's preaching was the authentic Gospel good tidings, *evangelizabat, εὐηγγελίζετο.* The counsels of John are thoroughly in accord with the spirit of Jesus, 6:30 ff, and explain the character of that penance which is demanded in Mk as a preparation for the kingdom, μετανοία, a thorough change of disposition, signified by a baptism of total immersion which symbolized not only a washing but a rebirth, *i.e.* a new life. John's kindness to the despised publicans and soldiers (probably the soldiers used by the tax-gatherers to enforce their demands, and therefore Jews) anticipates the attitude of Jesus.

21-22 Baptism of Jesus—(Mk 1:9-11 ; Mt 3:13-17). As in Mk with the following differences : Jesus prays and Lk seems to connect the marvellous events with this prayer ; the Spirit descends ' in bodily form ' which might seem to make Lk agree with Mt in showing the events as a public demonstration from heaven of the character of Jesus, while Mk is interested in the scene only as it concerns Jesus, though he does not exclude others explicitly. Ac 10:38 may be a reference to this incident. Some non-Catholic critics show great attachment to the reading of Codex Bezae and a few later MSS in 22, ' thou art my beloved son, this day have I begotten thee ' ; it favours their contention that originally it was believed that only at the Baptism did Jesus become Son of God, *i.e.* Messias, or that only now does he become conscious of his vocation and mission. Consequently he is not the Son of God in the proper sense. But the reading has no support in the older Greek MSS and is found only in Lk, where it is a clear gloss from Ps 2:7. The reader is referred here and later to the commentaries on Mt and Mk for the parts **750f** common to them and Lk. The appearance of the Spirit above the waters recalls Gen 1:1 ff. This is the παλιγγενεσία, Mt 19:28 ; Tit 3:5, the beginning of a new world, which is the Kingdom of God.

23-38 The Genealogy—(cf. Mt 1:1-17). Having given **g** a clear indication of Jesus' divine origin Lk proceeds to describe his human descent. Difficulties of reconciliation arise from the comparison of Lk's genealogy with that of Mt. There are two chief differences first to be noted : Mt is content with showing his Jewish readers that Jesus is a true Son of Abraham ; Lk traces his origin back to Adam, intent on presenting Jesus as the universal Saviour. Secondly Mt traces his descent through Solomon, Lk through David's son Nathan. The two lists of names then meet again at Salathiel the father of Zorobabel, parting once more until they reach Joseph, the foster father of Jesus. Mt's list contains 42 names divided into three groups of 14, Mt 1:17 ; Lk's contains 77 in the Gk text, 76 in the Vg. The difference of number need cause no great difficulty, as it is not necessary to suppose that either evangelist has wished to include all the ancestors of Jesus. A comparison of the two genealogies of Esdras, 1 Esd 7:1 ff. and 1 Par 6:1 ff., shows that several names are omitted in the former. The dissimilarities of Mt and Lk led many scholars to suggest that the former traces the descent of Jesus through Joseph, the latter through Mary who was also of the house of David. But this is rejected by the majority of scholars on the ground that it does not accord with the words of Lk 3:23, and that it is contrary to the ancient and traditional interpretation. Lk, then, having declared that Joseph was only the reputed father of Jesus, proceeds to trace the descent of Joseph, as does Mt, though each gives a different name for the father of Joseph. It is necessary to observe that no reasonable **h** understanding of the genealogies is possible without taking into consideration two facts : first, that ancient Semitic ideas of kinship differed greatly from our own ; secondly, that both Mt and Lk are concerned to show that Jesus was a son of David in the eyes of the Jewish law. But according to Jewish ideas there was no objection to the inclusion of adoptive or legal parents in a genealogical tree. Thus Julius Africanus, a Christian who lived in Palestine during the 3rd cent., has left it on record that he gathered the following facts from the memories of the kindred of our Lord. Mathan, Mt 1:15, married Estha and begot a son Jacob. Estha, left a widow, was married by Melchi, Lk 3:24, who thus became the father of Heli. Heli died childless, and in accordance with the law of the levirate (cf. Deut 25:5-6 and Mt 22:23-27) his widow was taken to wife by his half-brother Jacob. Their son was Joseph who, according to Jewish law, was reckoned as the legal son of Heli (cf. Eus., HE 1, 7). This explanation is unacceptable to those who wish to explain divergences between the two genealogies by the proposal to regard that of Mt as following the *legal* line of royal succession and inheritance of the Davidic promises, and that of Lk as following natural descent. For a fuller discussion of the problem and suggested solutions, cf. CE *Genealogy in the Bible* and *Genealogy of Christ*, also Lusseau et Collomb, *Manuel d'Etudes bibliques*, IV Cap 10, Paris 1938. We may conclude by drawing attention to the fact that the Jewish adversaries of our Lord never denied his Davidic descent. **23.** ' beginning about the age of thirty ', *i.e.* beginning his mission of teaching ; thus falling in with traditional Jewish ideas according to which it was unfitting that a man should come forward as a religious master before the age of thirty.

IV 1-13 The Temptation—(Mt 4:1-11 ; Mk 1:12-13). **i** Before dealing with this incident it will be well to recall the development of Lk. In 1:17 the mission of John is announced in the terms of Mal 3:1, ' he shall go before him (*i.e.* Yahweh) in the spirit and power of Elias '. In 2:49 the child Jesus is shown to be conscious of his divine Sonship. In 3:16 we find the

750i application of 1:17, identifying Jesus in some way with Yahweh. All this is crowned by 3:21–22 where the divine Sonship of Jesus is declared from heaven and he is shown as one possessed by the Spirit of God who henceforth conducts him in the work of his Messianic mission, 4:1, 14, 18 ; 5:17. The work of the Messias is to establish the Kingdom or Reign of God, and in consequence to destroy the reign of the devil, *cf.* 1 Jn 3:8. Hence the dramatic effect of this meeting between the two opposite champions at the beginning of the ministry, when Jesus goes out to meet his adversary in the desert, the place popularly considered as the special preserve of the evil spirits. The incident was held to be of importance in the early catechesis of the Gospel (the disciples could have learned it only from Jesus) and Lk not only incorporates it, but neglects Mk's brief summary in favour of the detailed source followed by Mt. But he differs from Mt both in order and by notable additions. He emphasizes that Jesus comes from baptism 'full of the Holy Ghost' but, omitting Mk's strong expression ' the Spirit drove him out ', he says ' Jesus was led by the Spirit *in the* desert for the space of forty days, *what time he was* tempted ', etc. Like Mt he seems to show that Satan had heard the words from heaven at the Baptism, though Satan does not understand ' Son of God ' in its proper sense ; this he could do only by faith or
j revelation. St Augustine tells us that the devils knew only so much about our Lord as he willed them to know by means of his operations ; hence their conclusions were at best conjectural. But Satan, convinced that Jesus was the Messias, attacks him on the point which is the Messias's chief concern, the establishment of the Reign of God of which he is to be the living embodiment. Hence the temptations take the form of persuasion to use his miraculous powers unduly *i.e.* not subject to God's will ; to seek the aid of human power and glory like a false Jewish Messias. Lk characteristically omits Mk's reference to the beasts, 1:13, according to his manner of omitting things derogatory of the dignity of Christ ; but he omits the angels also. He concludes by the warning that Satan has not given up the contest : ' having *completed every kind* of temptation the devil departed from him *till a favourable opportunity* ', or perhaps ' till the time appointed ', *i.e.* by God, who determines the course of events in the career of Jesus, a notion of frequent occurrence in Lk. There will be further attacks ; *cf.* 22:3, 28, 40–44, 53.

751a **IV 14–IX 50 Manifestation of the Saviour in Galilee** —In most of this section Lk runs parallel with the Galilean ministry in Mk, making such additions and omissions as his plan and aim require. His most notable additions are such as emphasize the character of Jesus as the Saviour of all men, especially of those most in need. In Mt and Mk the person of Jesus is hidden behind the proclamation of the Kingdom of God. Lk represents (though written shortly after Mk) a later stage in the growth of the Christian mind, when attention became much more fixed upon the person of our Lord (note the early Christological controversies). Thus this part opens with the sermon at Nazareth, found later in Mt and Mk, where Jesus draws the minds of the hearers to himself and his relation to God. In doing this Lk postpones the preaching at Capharnaum and the call of the disciples, Mk 1:14 ff., and so creates difficulties of reconciliation.
b **14–30 Preaching at Nazareth**—*Cf.* Mt 13:53–58 ; Mk 6:1–6 which are not strict parallels ; Lk passes over the visit to Nazareth mentioned there by Mt and Mk. But there are indications, 23, that he has here anticipated the chronological order, and it is hardly likely that there were two different visits to Nazareth followed by two rejections. Augustine is for the identity of 4:16–30 with Mk 6:1–6. Why has Lk anticipated ? Perhaps (1) to make Jesus speak for himself and declare what his mission is ; (2) to give an example of the treatment Christ will receive ; *cf.* Jn 1:11 ; (3) to

demonstrate the Pauline thesis (Lk being a disciple of Paul) that salvation shall pass from the Jews to the Gentiles. The two examples given, 26–27, are of Gentile origin, and the effect of these examples was similar to that so often produced by Paul's declaration of his thesis in Ac. The incident may be meant here as an early fulfilment of the threat in 13, though perhaps the connexion between 14 and 18 is the best explanation of the insertion of this incident. 15 sums up Mk 1:14 ff. until Lk is ready to rejoin Mk at 31. 16–17 show familiarity with the customs of the synagogue, where men of reputation for learning and piety were invited to read and expound the Scriptures on the Sabbath. The repute of Jesus is already established, 14–15. Despite the apparent meaning of 17*b* it is possible that Lk means the passage read was the Haphtarah or part of the Prophets assigned to that day, though it is questionable whether set pieces were at that date appointed for each day. The quotation in 18–19 seems drawn from various places in Isaias ; *cf.* 61:1–2 ; 58:6 ; 42:7. Is Lk quoting freely from memory or does the quotation contain parts of our Lord's exposition of the passage read ? Omit from DV ' to heal the contrite of heart ' and ' the day of reward ', which are not in the Greek. Is 61:2 speaks of ' day of vengeance ' ; characteristic of Lk to omit this. **21.** The text from Isaias is a proclamation (in 61:1 it is the servant of Yahweh who speaks, in the other places it is Yahweh himself) and the words of Jesus mean that the proclamation predicted by Is 61:1 ff. is now being made, and the maker of it is himself. He thus establishes the character of his Messiahship, one in genuine accord with the OT ; he is no Messias after the vulgar notions of popular rabbinic tradition. In fact he has a very different sort of work to do. Later on, 7:19 ff., he will have occasion to remind John the Baptist of this same truth, when he will quote the same thoughts from Isaias. Note that the Hebrew word for ' anointed ' is *Mešiḥa* ; for ' anointed by the Spirit ', *cf.* Ac 10:38, a possible reference to the Baptism. As the ceremony of anointing in the OT signified divine choice and endowment with power or authority from above, the word Messias came to bear this meaning rather than the fact of being anointed. There is a further veiled reference to the fact that the time of Messianic divine favour is inaugurated in the person of Jesus by ' the acceptable year of the Lord ', 19. **23.** Here, as in Mk 6, the Nazarenes cannot reconcile this aspect of Jesus with the obscurity of his origin. He makes them say ironically : ' You had better begin to uplift yourself before you begin to uplift others ', then answers one proverb with another, proceeding with examples from the OT which point the moral that the fact of being a Jew does not necessarily bring God's favour. As St Paul has said already, neither circumcision nor uncircumcision count any longer, but the faith exemplified in these two examples ; *cf.* 3:8 ; Ac 7:51–54 ; 22:21–22.
31–44 Ministry in Capharnaum—(Mk 1:21–39). The parallels in Mt are scattered ; 4:13–14, 23 ; 7:28–29 ; 8:14–16. It will be noted that Lk and Mt never agree together against Mk where all three narrate the same incidents. The following peculiarities may be observed : in 38 Lk brings in Simon without introduction (an anomaly for so careful a writer) having omitted the call of the disciples already given by Mk. But Theophilus has already received the primitive catechesis, so Lk allows himself some latitude. In 40 there is the interesting addition that Jesus cures by the imposition of hands, a detail of importance in view of the ceremony in use by the Church from earliest times ; *cf.* Ac 6:6, 9:12, 17, 13:3, and Lk 13:13. There is a characteristic variation in 43 : ' *I must bring the good tidings* (*evangelizare*, εὐαγγελίσασθαι not κηρύσσω of Mk 1:38). **44.** The weight of MSS evidence is in favour of ' Judaea ' ; ' Galilee ' is doubtless due to a copyist's correction ; *cf.* Mk 1:39 ; Mt 4:23. Judaea creates no real difficulty since Lk uses it in 1:5 to signify the province containing ancient Juda with Samaria and

Galilee. Moreover he may have additional information about the extent of the ministry such as is seen in Jn.

V 1-11 Miraculous Draught of Fish : Call of the Disciples—There is no trace of this miracle in Mk and Mt, but the call of the disciples is paralleled in Mk 1:16-20 ; Mt 4:18-20, so far neglected by Lk. The conclusion is the same in all three Synoptists, and it is unlikely that the disciples were called twice. It has been suggested that Lk has taken great liberties with chronology by anticipating the miracle of Jn 21:1-14 in order to provide a suitable setting for the call of the disciples ; but the two incidents are altogether different. Others suggest, on account of the similarity between 5:3 and Mk 4:1 ; Mt 13:1-2 (followed in both by the Parable of the Sower), that Lk has anticipated the time of the miracle in order to throw light on 10*b*. It may be noted that this is not the only instance of Mk's omission of incidents that do honour to Peter. The miracle is of a nature likely to impress fishermen ; note the progress from ' Master ' in 5 to ' Lord ' in 8. Christ's miracles were done that men might recognize in him *virtus divinitatis*, and it is a quality of divine power that all creatures should be subject to it (ST III, 44, 4). Peter has fished all night, the proper time for fishing, without success ; Jesus fishes in daylight, the wrong time, with marvellous success. To a Semitic mind, power of command over the sea and its inhabitants would suggest divine power ; *cf*. Gen 1:1 ff. and Ps 92. This may give the key to Peter's exclamation, 8*b*. The thought of the Spirit of God dominating the primeval waters, the Creation, the subjection of creatures to man (*cf*. Ps 8), man's loss of this power through sin (*cf*. Rom 8:18-23), Peter's failure and our Lord's success : all this leads up to the conclusion that Jesus stands in very special relationship to God. It is worth noting that the first disciple called by our Lord begins with an avowal of sinfulness ; though Jesus has cured the sick and reigned over the lower nature, his true mission is to cast out sin and make God reign in the souls of men. Despite Peter's declaration he is called to be associated with the work of Christ. But the force of the incident is this : that Peter and his fellow-disciples are to remember that the plan and method of that work are of God's design. As in the capturing of fish, so in the capturing of men for God's Kingdom, God's way will be found at variance with human standards : a lesson Peter and the rest were very slow to learn. As for Jesus, so for his associates, absolute surrender to the will of God is required. **11**. The lesson goes home. The call is not restricted to Simon ; but Simon is clearly made the leader, for to him alone is addressed : ' Fear not ! from henceforth thou shalt catch men '.

12-16 Healing of the Leper—(Mt 8:1-4 ; Mk 1:40-45). Here Lk takes up again the thread of Mk which he had dropped in order to insert 5:1-11. Mt inserts the Sermon on the Mount before this incident. Lk's omissions of the signs of emotion and severity in Jesus noted by Mk are characteristic. But he makes the retirement to the desert, apparently caused by the unwelcome attention of the crowd in Mk 1:45, a voluntary withdrawal, indeed a matter of habit (according to the grammatical construction of the Greek).

V 17-VI 11 A Series of Disputes with Adversaries—Having thus shown how Jesus gathers around him a little group of sympathetic followers whom he chooses as fellow-workers, Lk proceeds to bring out the contrast that there was another group hostile from the very first. Here begins the description of our Lord's relations with the Scribes and Pharisees, the representatives of official Judaism. It is crystallized in a series of disputes which result in two effects : the adversaries begin as various factions but unite against Jesus, and end by a determination to destroy him (6:11, more strongly stated in parallels Mk 3:6 ; Mt 12:14). Here again Lk follows the order of Mk 2:1-3:6, while the parallels in Mt are scattered. The reader is

referred therefore to the commentaries on Mt and Mk **751h** except for the peculiarities of Lk to be noted.

17-26 Healing of the Paralytic—(Mk 2:1-12 ; Mt 9:1-8). The chief differences between Lk and Mk are that while Mk does not mention the presence of the Scribes and Pharisees until late, Lk prepares the scene in his usual orderly manner. Note his introduction : having gathered his audience he writes ' the power of the Lord [Yahweh] was *that he* [Jesus] *should* heal ', as though again to indicate that God is directing affairs. The difference of DV and Vg here is due to the reading αὐτούς ' them ' instead of the more probable αὐτόν ' him '. Lk's literary emendations have sacrificed the vivid character of Mk's narrative. He omits the graphic description of digging a hole through the earthen roof of the house, and makes our Lord address the paralytic as ' Man ' instead of the affectionate ' Son '. The presence of Scribes and Pharisees from Judaea and Jerusalem is perhaps the reason of ' Judaea ' in 4:44 ; but in 5:17 Judaea must be accepted in its restrictive sense. **23**. As in Mk the comparison is not between miracle and miracle but between the *saying* and the *external manifestation* of the saying's result. As forgiveness of sins shows no external manifestation, it does not lay the speaker open to ridicule if he falsely claims to forgive sins. But healing of disease must be externally shown. Our Lord vehemently rejects the accusation of blasphemy, and will not allow that his words of forgiveness have been merely declaratory. For ' Son of Man ', see § 746*d*.

27-32 Call of Levi the Publican—(Mt 9:9-13 ; **i** Mk 2:13-17). Like Mk, but unlike Mt, Lk refrains from identifying Levi with Matthew ; he adds the phrase ' leaving all things ', 28, which is reminiscent of 5:11. **30**. Read ' the Pharisees and *their* Scribes ' following the preferable reading of Mk 2:16 ' the Scribes of the Pharisees ' ; the Sadducean party also had its own Scribes who were laxer than the former in interpreting the Law. **32**. Lk adds that to which Jesus calls sinners, penance μετανοία, change of mind or conversion. The word has already been mentioned in John's preaching, 3:3 ; *cf*. 1:16-17. It will be noted that the account of these disputes serves to bring out the nature of our Lord's mission. Having just laid claim to the power of absolving men from their sins, a claim to divine power in the eyes of the Pharisees, 21, he now throws down a challenge to his adversaries by choosing for his intimate disciple a man like Levi, one of that class hated all over the ancient world for its anti-social activities. Lucian groups them with adulterers, procurers and people who overturn the world. Levi was rather a *portitor* or collector of the customs tax called *portorium* (probably for Herod Antipas) than a *publicanus*, *i.e.* one of the rich financiers who farmed the government taxes. Apparently Levi has done well ; he is rich enough to hold a great feast (δοχή reception) to celebrate his calling, at which Jesus and his disciples mix with Levi's colleagues and other guests, classed as ' publicans and sinners ' by Mk. This (in Lk) appears to give rise to a double complaint : first about incurring ceremonial defilement by mixing with people who are careless of the legal requirements of Judaic Law, secondly about the failure to observe the fast.

33-39 Dispute about Fasting—(Mt 9:14-17 ; Mk **752a** 2:18-22). Each of the Synoptists approaches this incident from a different angle. In Lk the disciples of John do not appear on the scene except in the words of the opponents of Jesus ; in Mt it is the disciples of John who make the objection. Lk adds the interesting detail about the special prayers of John's disciples ; he remembers this in 11:1, at the beginning of the instruction on prayer. He understands the objection in the same way as Mk and Mt : if Jesus is setting himself up as a religious leader in Israel, teaching and gathering followers, why does he not follow the example of accepted leaders like the Pharisees or John the Baptist, instead of mixing with such doubtful characters

752a as the publicans ? The fast in question is evidently not the Day of Atonement, which was the one annual day of obligatory fasting for all, Lev 16:29. We know that the Pharisees had special fast days (*cf.* 18:12) and it is not surprising that the followers of such an ascetic as John fasted. There were four or five fasts kept by the devout, such as the anniversary of the destruction of Jerusalem, and the day in question seems from 34 (*cf.* Mt 9:15) to have been an occasion of mourning. As in Mk and Mt, Jesus answers with one of those striking illustrative parables which mark all his encounters with Pharisees, *cf.* 31*b*. There is strong allegorization in the parable of 34, where Jesus makes the striking claim that his presence with his disciples creates a new situation which calls for joy rather than mourning (fasting) ; *cf.* 10:23. Not that he condemns fasting as such ; far from it, for the days shall come when fasting will be suitable for his disciples—a veiled prediction of his Passion. But the present situation is like a wedding feast, he the bridegroom, the disciples like 'the children of the *bride-chamber*', *i.e.* the guests or rather the friends of the bridegroom whose business it is not to be sad but to celebrate the marriage of their **b** friend. **36-39.** With Mk and Mt, Lk adds further parabolic utterances (Lk alone here uses the name 'parable ') by which Jesus explains his attitude to the traditional observances of Judaism. Note 36 : ' no one *having torn a patch from* a new garment putteth it upon an old garment ', rather different from Mk 2:21 and Mt 9:16 ; but it brings this parable into line with the second : both new garment and old ruined, like new wine and old skins both lost. **38b.** 'and both are preserved ', a gloss from Mt 9:17. The meaning of these parables is much disputed, but it seems to be this : Jesus is indeed setting up as a religious teacher, but not like his adversaries. Everybody had noticed this already ; *cf.* 4:32, 'they were *amazed* at his *teaching*, for his *word* was with *authority* ', and ' not as the Scribes ', adds Mk 1:22. Jesus now says that his teaching is such that it must be put into new men, *i.e.* into minds not fixed in the grooves of traditional prejudices. His call of Levi, a publican, has just demonstrated this. He does not condemn the old Mosaic observances (as Mt makes clear in 5:17-20 and Lk will indicate later, 16:16-18) ; they are good in themselves but they have served the purpose for which God gave them. Indeed, if allegory is pressed here, they must be judged to be getting rather old and worn-out. Note the concluding words of Lk in 39 (proper to him ; *cf.* Jn 2:10), where our Lord seems to express a feeling of sympathy for the Jews who find a difficulty in contemplating the abrogation of what they had been taught to look on as sharing the very eternity of God himself. Jesus has yet to make them realize that the Mosaic Dispensation loses nothing of its honour in finding its perfection and completion in him. But it would be false to conclude from these parables that he has any intention of preserving it : to add the Gospel on to the frame-work of the old observances would only spoil both.

c VI 1-11 The Lord of the Sabbath—(Mt 12:1-8 ; Mk 2:23-28). This is the last of the disputes recorded by Lk and Mk at this time, postponed by Mt to a more advanced stage in the conflict between Jesus and his adversaries, and it concerns a question to which the latter attached such importance that the result of the dispute drives them to madness and brings things to a head, 11. It is a commonplace that the Rabbis had rendered the law of the Sabbath so intolerable a burden by their complicated and puerile legislation (Edersheim, Append. xvii) that they defeated their own professed purpose to make the Sabbath not only a day of rest but of delight, when Jews should wear their best clothes and eat their best food. Exaggeration ran rife, some Rabbis holding that even the tortures of Gehenna were suspended on the Sabbath, while if one kept two Sabbaths perfectly salvation was assured. And the Mishnah (*c* A.D. 200) taught that desecration of the Sabbath was a crime deserving death. As much of this would appear trivial to Gentile minds there was no need for Lk to add with Mk ' the Sabbath was made for man and not man for the Sabbath '. For the rest he follows Mk closely, avoiding the difficulty of reconciliation with 1 Kg 21 by omitting mention of Abiathar. There is no entirely satisfactory explanation of ' secondfirst Sabbath ', and the best MSS omit ' second-first ' ; it is probably a combination of different glosses. One suggested view is that it means the first Sabbath of the first month (Nisan) the new sacred year, the first ' first Sabbath ' being the first of the month Tišri, in which the civil year began. The objection made to our Lord is that the action of his disciples is equivalent to reaping ; sillier things are found in the rabbinic books. He refuses to descend to discussion on the casuistical point and lays down in reply the broad ethical principle that *nulla lex positiva, e'iam divina, obligat cum magno incommodo*. Since Law is a dictate of the reason for the common good of man, when the observance of positive law is found to be for the harm of the community it is right to dispense with it. The example seems, to Jewish minds at least, rather an extreme one, but our Lord chose it doubtless to draw attention to himself and his mission. Note his startling conclusion : ' I, as Son of Man, have authority over the Mosaic Law which you all hold to have been given by God '. It is this that probably leads to the determination to destroy him, 11. The miracle in the synagogue, 6-10, provides another application of the principle Jesus has just laid down ; there was no pressing need for a cure on that Sabbath day, but he wishes to show his adversaries that their very principles are wrong. It is certainly wrong to do evil on the Sabbath, not because it is the Sabbath but because evil is against the moral law. But not all good things may be done on the Sabbath ; some are forbidden by God's positive law given to Moses. Therefore one must consider what was the legislator's purpose, *i.e.* the good of man, and where that is seriously frustrated by the observance of positive law, then the legislator does not intend the law to stand. This is an example of our Lord's ' teaching with authority ', 4:32, which caused so much admiration. The Rabbis had drowned even the Ten Commandments in a sea of positive prescriptions, never seeking principles but only some text or rabbinical authority on which to base their teaching. Note the Lucan details : it was the man's right hand, 6, Jesus again manifests supernatural power in reading thoughts, 8, Lk omits that Jesus looked around ' with anger ', Mk 3:5.

12-19 Call of the Apostles—(Mt 10:1-4 ; Mk 3:13-19). Having broken with the representatives of official Judaism, Jesus now groups around himself new followers—a Church. Lk is peculiar in giving the impression of something of grave import ; it calls for a night spent alone in the mountain ' in the prayer of God '. This is characteristic : *cf.* 3:21 ; 9:18 before confession of Peter, 9:29, etc. Lk records in Ac how this practice was kept up by the Church ; 13:3. He emphasizes (here and in Ac 1:2) the deliberate choice of the Twelve from a greater number ; there were 120 disciples gathered for Peter's address in Ac 1:15 ff. He insists on the name bestowed, Apostles (not referred to till later in Mk 6:30) and throughout Lk and Ac he shows a preference for this title, contrary to the practice of the other evangelists. Insistence on the note of choice recalls God's choice of the twelve patriarchs (*cf.* Ac 13:17) and emphasizes the idea that something new is beginning, the new Israel of God (*cf.* Gal 3:7-9 ; 6:16). His order of Apostles differs from Mk and Mt, as these differ from each other ; but all observe the same three groups of four, and the same names head each group, Peter's name always heading the first group. Thaddaeus of Mk, Lebbaeus of Mt, is ' Jude of James ' in Lk, identified with the Jude of Jn 14:22, the author of the Epistle. Doubtless like others of his time he enjoyed several names, and it is natural that the early Christians should have avoided the name he shared with the traitor. Finally, Lk follows

Mk in omitting to identify Matthew with Levi the publican.

17-49 Discourse on the Qualifications of a True Disciple—Usually called the Sermon on the Plain because of 17a. Lk here forsakes Mk who has no collection of sayings of Jesus. Is this the same discourse as the Sermon on the Mount in Mt 5-7 ? But the first question is whether these two sermons are here as our Lord gave them. A common opinion today is that both are a collection of his principal sayings which must have been often repeated. Both in Mt and Lk they appear in an artificial setting ; cf. Mt 4:23 ff. with Lk 6:17 ff. In both there is a similar *mise en scène*, in both the same beginning and the same conclusion. Mt makes collections of sayings, parables and miracles. Lk, who prefers a different sort of order, has distributed much of Mt's sermon through his Gospel, putting sayings in their due setting, whether chronological or logical we do not know. St Augustine seems to conclude that Mt and Lk have both taken the inaugural sermon of Jesus to his chosen disciples, each editing it after his own fashion and purpose, § 745a. In Lk the sermon is addressed to disciples and would-be disciples ; it forms a programme of the dispositions required of them. **20-26.** Like Mt he begins with the opposition existing between the spirit of Jesus and the spirit of the world, exemplified by the Beatitudes to which here Lk adds the Woes (reserved by Mt to much later ; cf. 23:13 ; Lk is a lover of contrasts) Those animated by the spirit of this world seek riches, comfort, pleasure and honour ; the disciple is to look for happiness (the Beatitudes begin with μακάριοι, 'happy are ye ') in the midst of poverty, privation, tears and persecution. Lk agrees with Mt in proceeding to show Jesus predicting the inevitable clash between these contrary spirits. **27-36.** Here, as in Mt 5:44-48, the disciple is warned that persecution is to be met with charity alone, a superhuman charity which involves detachment from worldly considerations, which demands that absolute surrender of self insisted on so often in Lk. **37-45.** As in Mt 7:1 ff., warning against the temptation to judge oneself better than others, even while meeting hatred with goodness, mercy and generosity of an extraordinary kind. The disciple must strive to make others better by his example, even correcting them when necessary ; but let him begin the work of improvement and correction with himself. Only the good can do good. **46-49.** Conclusion as in Mt 7:21-27 ; let all set to work, not satisfied with listening to their Master but eager to carry out his teaching loyally. Such is Lagrange's summary of the discourse. It will be noted that Lk omits Mt's references to the Old Law ; he has not the latter's precise purpose of showing our Lord as the long-foretold Messias, and showing him in this sermon like a new Moses giving a New Law from the mountain.

20. Lk puts simply 'poor' for Mt's 'poor in spirit' ; it is clear from the whole sermon that he is not preaching social revolution or beatifying material conditions as themselves the sources of happiness. As in Mt emphasis is here laid on the interior dispositions of soul. Unorthodox critics argue from 20-38 that this teaching anticipates ' a speedy end of the age and the early advent of the Kingdom of God ' ; a literal application of this teaching ' would be to invite anarchy '. But there is no indication that Jesus is laying down precepts to be followed by all, nor even counsels of perfection which absolve his followers from their social duties. But ' if these words were a little oftener practised in imitation of the Saints, society would rather gain than lose by such heroic examples of charity ' (Lagrange). We have just seen the enormous influence exercised by Gandhi, a non-Christian, who practised some of these teachings heroically. **22.** ' when they shall *excommunicate* you (cf. Jn 9:22 ; 12:42 ; 16:2) and *insult* you, and *proscribe* your name as evil ' etc., recalling the proscriptions so common at the beginning of the Roman empire. **32-34.** Lk substitutes ' sinners ' for ' publicans ' and ' Gentiles ' in Mt 5:46-7. **35.** Difficulty

about true reading here ; it is maintained that the **752i** Greek will not bear the translation of DV and Vg ; ' thereby ' is a gloss. Some translate ' nothing despairing ' or ' despairing of none ' or ' making none despair '. But although ἀπελπίζειν is not found elsewhere with the Vg meaning, there is no doubt that such meaning best fits the context. **36.** Substitution of ' merciful ' for Mt's ' perfect ' : characteristically Lucan.

VII 1-10 The Centurion's Servant—(Mt 8:5-15, not **753a** in Mk ; affinities with Jn 4:46 ff., but probably different incident). The incident well suits Lk's aim of showing how the Gospel benefits are extended to the Gentiles. This Gentile centurion is presented in a particularly favourable light even at the expense of Israel : his humanity towards a slave, his religious spirit and kindness to Judaism, the reverence and humility he shows towards Jesus, and finally his ' great faith '. The Church uses his humble confession daily in the administration of Holy Communion. What is the faith on which he is congratulated by our Lord, a faith such as Jesus had not yet found among his fellow-Jews (even the Apostles are not excepted) ? Note that from now on Lk begins to record examples of faith ; cf. 7:50 ; 8:25, lack of faith ; 8:48, 50. The centurion argues from his own situation to that of our Lord, with all that it implies. He is one fixed τασσόμενος in a system of authority having superiors above and inferiors below. Whoever Jesus may be, the centurion recognizes him as one set in a system of authority of which the head and source is God, and Jesus has power to exercise this authority to do such a thing as here suggested. In other words the centurion admits our Lord's special relationship to God and the divine character of his mission, a thing that the Jews refuse to do. At the same time he admits his unworthiness as a Gentile to profit by close contact with this Jewish thaumaturge ; his Jewish friends doubtless left him in no doubt about the essential holiness of Israel and the essential sinfulness of Gentiles ; cf. Gal 2:15 ; Eph 2:1-3 ; Lk 6:32-33 with Mt 5:47. The incident is surely the same both in Mt and Lk despite the differences, e.g. that in Mt the servant is called a ' boy ', that he is a paralytic, that the centurion comes himself to ask for the cure ; such differences, which St Augustine reconciles, do not militate against the identity. Mt has drawn the conclusion in 8:11-12 which we might have expected Lk to draw ; but his parallel to Mt 8:11-12 comes much later, 13:28-30.

11-17 Widow of Naim—Only in Lk. The Gentile **b** centurion had recognized in Jesus a person endowed with the mysterious power belonging to God alone, therefore one coming from God. The incident at Naim ends with the same conclusion on the part of Jews : ' God hath visited his people' ; cf. 1:68, 78 ; Ac 15:14. In these last two incidents Lk may be said to sum up what any honest witness might have gathered from the life and actions of Jesus. Naim lies about 8 m. SE. of Nazareth and not far from Sunam where Elias raised the dead boy to life, 4 Kg 4, a fact which is enough to make the rationalist critics throw doubt upon Lk's incident. But neither Eliseus nor any other prophet had raised a dead person to life by a word ; note the prophets' extraordinary labours in 3 Kg 17 and 4 Kg 4. Plummer remarks that most of the recorded cases of the raising of the dead in Scripture were for the sake of women ; cf. Heb 11:35. **13.** Note ' the Lord ' a sudden appearance of the phrase after the constant use of ' Jesus ' ; doubtless Lk's witness to early Christian usage. Here Lk forsakes his usual reserve in speaking of our Lord and says he was ' moved with *compassion* ' (not, mercy) ἐσπλαγχνίσθη, a word used only of Jesus in the Gospels and only here applied by Lk to him (but see 10:33 and 15:20). **17.** Judaea again, perhaps used in its restricted sense in view of the sequel ; John's disciples come from the south where their master is in prison at Machaerus, Herod's castle lying east of the Dead Sea.

18-35 Jesus and John the Baptist—(Mt 11:2-19, cf. **c** Lk 16:16). One of the first cares of our Lord's disciples

949

753c was to determine and record the relationship of their Master to John the Baptist, and therefore what attitude they should adopt to John's followers. That a lack of understanding between the two groups sometimes survived is proved by Ac 18:24-26 ; 19:1 ff., where as late as A.D. 54-5 persons claiming to be disciples of John appear to be ignorant of the necessity of Christian discipleship. Mk, writing for Roman Christians, has no need to clear up this point and omits this incident narrated by Lk and Mt. In a certain way John the Baptist had overshadowed Jesus by appearing in the traditional garb of a prophet, frightening people with thundering denunciations like a prophet, attracting them by his courage and burning enthusiasm ; while Jesus appeared in a very modest manner, quietly preaching in the synagogues ; *cf*. 11:28-30 ; 12:15-21. It was necessary then to record the fact that John, great as he was, had his *raison d'être* in his relationship to Jesus ; in the designs of God, as in fact, he pointed to

d Jesus ; *cf*. Jn 1:6-9, 15, 26, 29, etc. But this incident fulfils another purpose in Lk, at one with his theme of Jesus as the manifestation of the goodness and mercy of God. To understand the sense of the question put to Jesus by John's disciples it is necessary to refer to John's preaching, in which he had announced 'a Coming One', ὁ ἐρχόμενος, who was to baptize with the Holy Ghost and fire, who was to separate the wicked from the good. To escape the formidable judgement that was foreshadowed men had to change their lives by penance (μετανοία 'conversion'), for the Coming One was pictured with an axe in his hand to cut down unfruitful trees. As indicated above, the mission of Jesus seems to bear no relation to such a grim foreboding. Indeed there is more than a suggestion here that, if Jesus is the Coming One, why does he not save his witness from prison and death? *Cf*. Jn 11:37. Traditional exegesis is not inclined to admit that John himself is in doubt ; his question is for the sake of his followers in view of his coming death, so that he may pass them on to Jesus. It must be confessed that at first sight the Gospel seems to give the opposite

e impression. But there is a third explanation based on the difference between the method of John and that of Jesus, of which we have just spoken. In other words John, as Mt 11:2 says, having heard while in prison of the miracles of Jesus which serve to confirm what has been revealed to himself of the person and mission of Jesus, feels a certain surprise and perhaps impatience. Why does Jesus hesitate to declare himself and to use his mighty power to cleanse the threshing floor in the vigorous way that John has foretold ? At any rate the reply of Jesus, addressed be it noted to John, seems to suppose that such was the sense of John's question. God's work must be done only in God's way. What that way is has already been indicated in 4:16 ff. **20.** The question is not whether Jesus is the Messias ; John had never used the word of him. But although 'the Coming One' was not a current name for the Messias it certainly suggests a Messianic significance. Hence, although 22 is generally made a fulfilment of Isaian Messianic prophecies in 35:5, 61:1, it may be noted that there is not much identity between these texts and 22. Moreover these texts were not traditional Messianic texts for the Jews ; hence 22 must be read in the light of 21, a Lucan addition. Jesus bids his questioners not to form their conclusions from what they see in his appearance, 23, but from his works which, as they might know from the Scripture, manifest the benign hand of God working in the world. This is Lk's thesis, and Jn's too : 'If you will not believe me, believe the works'. The answer seems also to indicate that Jesus has not come as the executor of divine vengeance, which the preaching of John might seem to indicate. The same is gathered from the sermon at Nazareth, 4:18-21, which refers to the same texts in Isaias. In a word, John had announced Jesus as the one through whom the Spirit of God should be poured out upon the world ; our Lord replies that his works prove that this is now taking place in his person ; *cf*. Jn 7:39. Lk

reproduces with great similarity the panegyric of John as in Mt. This is the Church's answer to the disciples of John : John was great because he was the forerunner of a greater : the greatest of the prophets because nearest to Christ, who was the *raison d'être* of all the prophets ; *cf*. 16:16. (See commentary on Mt for exegesis of these verses.) **29-30.** Proper to Lk ; not a Lucan parenthesis, but a continuation of our Lord's words ; *cf*. Mt 21:32. Therefore, 'and all the people hearing (John), *even* the publicans . . .'. The meaning is that the despised common people (*cf*. Jn 7:49) and even publicans fell in with God's benevolent designs for man's salvation (for John's baptism was part of the divine Messianic plan), while the religious leaders '*nullified God's purpose in their regard*' by rejecting John's baptism ; *cf*. 20:1-8. **31-35.** Parable and application as in Mt. (Omit 'and the Lord said' ; not in Gk.) It is a parable, not an allegory, otherwise it would have to be turned round. It is the Pharisees who are like disagreeable children, finding fault whatever is proposed, whether it is John coming in ascetic manner to help them, or Jesus who comes to their aid leading a normal life. But happily there are others, more in harmony with God and divine wisdom, who therefore recognize the hand of God wherever it appears, whether in John fasting, or in Jesus eating and drinking with sinners. Thus 'wisdom is *vindicated*' by all such, for they are her true children.

36-50 The Sinful Woman anoints Jesus—The similarities between this story and those recorded in Mt 26:6-13 ; Mk 14:3-9 ; Jn 12:1-8, have led to the opinion that the four evangelists narrate the same incident. Latin tradition since the time of St Gregory the Great has been in favour of identity ; the general tradition among the Greeks (except for Origen) is that Lk's incident is altogether different and most modern Catholic commentators adopt this view. It must be admitted that the divergences seem irreconcilable. If Lk omits Mk 14:3-9 in his parallel place, that is only in accordance with his common practice of avoiding repetition of similar incidents. The impression is given that this is a woman of abandoned life and well-known as such, though the word 'sinner' would not necessarily mean that for a Jew. Note the relation of this story to 7:29. If Lk omits to name her, that is only in harmony again with his delicate reserve. There is nothing in Lk which justifies identifying her with Mary of Magdala, 8:2, or Mary of Bethany, 10:38 ff. Greek tradition generally distinguishes them all. **38.** She comes in to seek Jesus and render him this act of reverence and affection. Why ? Presumably, especially in view of 29-35, because she is one of those who have 'justified God' in recognizing Jesus as God's minister for her salvation. She manifests the penance (μετανοία 'conversion') to which he calls sinners ; *cf*. 5:32. The pouring of sweet ointment on the head of an esteemed person was no extraordinary thing ; it is noteworthy that she presumes only to put it on his feet ; *cf*. Mt 26:7, Mk 14:3. **40-43.** The application of the parable is certainly that love is consequent on forgiveness, though the opposite seems to be stated in 47*a* ; hence the traditional interpretation that charity removes sin, despite the apparently opposite meaning of 50 which Protestant commentators have used to support the doctrine of justification by faith alone. But 47*b* shows that 47*a* cannot mean what it at first sight appears to mean, for in that case 47*b* would be without purpose. Hence 47*a* must mean, 'wherefore I say to thee, (it is manifest) *her* many sins *have been* forgiven because she (shows clear signs that she) hath loved much'. Note what is claimed here in a veiled manner : she was a sinner, Jesus declares her sins have been forgiven, the love she feels in return is shown to Jesus. At the least, then, she treats him as representing God. Note the significance of anointing in the OT, *i.e.* God's elect, God's representative, priest, king, prophet, Messias especially. A further conclusion Simon is left to draw for himself : he has treated the woman with contempt as one

1 separated from God, *cf.* 18:9, but if Jesus may conclude from the woman's behaviour that God has forgiven her, Simon too may conclude from his own behaviour towards Jesus that God has not forgiven him. Lk again draws attention to the supernatural power of Jesus in reading thoughts, 40. Simon objects that Jesus must be ignorant of the woman's character ; Jesus replies that he knows very much about her, even that her sins have been taken away. **50.** Faith here and elsewhere in Lk is not the mere intellectual assent to truths about God under the influence of the will, but an attitude of the whole man, mind and will and affections, towards God, a compound of faith, hope and charity ; a belief in God not merely as existing, but as rewarding and full of solicitude for the good of man ; *cf.* Heb 11:6. It also includes a certain attitude towards Christ as God's representative at least ; in a word, it sums up the thesis of Lk, God visiting his people in the person and work of Jesus to save them. That is the note on which the incident terminates.

a VIII 1-3 Women Disciples of Jesus—A brief description, peculiar to Lk, of a preliminary journey of ministry with the Twelve and a group of women. Taken with v 4 (*cf.* Mt 13:2 ; Mk 4:1) it furnishes the *mise en scène* for the parables which follow here as in Mk and Mt. Joanna appears in Lk alone, here and again at the sepulchre, 24:10. All the women have been healed by Jesus of diseases either of body or soul. It does not follow that Mary of Magdala, on the west coast of the Lake of Galilee, has been healed of moral disease ; but as seven signifies completion in Semitic thought, it follows that she has been either a great sufferer or a great sinner. Lk gives no ground for her identification with the sinful woman of 7:36-50.

b 4-18 Teaching in Parables—(Mt 13:1-23, 5:15, 10:26, 25:29 ; Mk 4:1-25). Lk here takes up again the thread of Mk and runs parallel for a considerable space, while Mt's parallels are scattered. We have already seen examples of our Lord's fashion of using argumentative parables to silence the Pharisees ; here begin his illustrative parables, *i.e.* throwing light on the nature and characteristics of the Kingdom of God which he has preached from the start ; *cf.* 4:43. Light is needed because the subject is one of mystery, 10, and his parables are the means by which he brings the hidden things to light, 16-18. It is surely in accordance with the clear drift of these words that we must interpret the difficulty of 10, where Lk is much briefer than Mt 13:10-15, Mk 4:10-12, probably in view of his Gentile reader. He could not omit the warning altogether, seeing that it left such a strong impression on the mind of the early Church. All the Evangelists record it, St Paul insists on it, Ac 28:25 ff., Rom 11:8. The most reasonable explanation of this enigmatical saying of our Lord is that given by Chrysostom (PG 57, 467) and Aquinas (ST III, 42, 3), *i.e.* the parable is of its very nature apt to enlighten the mind, and its enigmatic form is intended to excite the interest of the hearer. But for the same reason it serves as a sifting process, its enigmatic form ensuring that only those who are well disposed to the speaker and keen on finding out the truth will take the trouble to apply their minds seriously in order to see the meaning of the comparison. Therefore Jesus uses such phrases as ' he that hath ears to hear let him hear ' and ' take heed therefore how you hear ', as though to say : ' Think well on this : it needs your close attention '. It is only in the above sense that obscurity may be said to be the object of the parables. (For further commentary see Mt and Mk *in loc.*)

c 19-21 The Mother and Brethren of Jesus—(Mt 12:46-50 ; Mk 3:31-35). Lk postpones further parables and inserts this incident which comes earlier in Mk ; but it is very well placed here just at the moment when our Lord has made his disciples the confidants, as it were, of his family secrets (*cf.* Jn 15:15). He omits reference to ' brother and sister ', perhaps to avoid arousing unprofitable questions in the mind of his reader ; **754c** the word ' brethren ' could have a wider meaning in Greek than children of the same mother and father. The dogmatic tradition of the Church maintains the virginity of both Mary and Joseph. For *The Brethren of the Lord* see Lagr., *S. Marc* (1911) 72 ff. and GJC I, 203-5, and §§ 672-3.

22-56 Various Miracles—(Mt 8:23-34 ; 9:18-26 ; Mk 4:35-5:43). These four miracles demonstrate in an ascending scale the supernatural power of Jesus and the growing recognition of him by his disciples as one who is a depository of divine authority to be exercised at will. There is a further clarification of the meaning of faith, 25, *i.e.* such an attitude to Jesus as to one through whom God is intervening in the world for man's good that his mere presence even when asleep gives sufficient ground for confidence ; *cf.* also 48 and 50. The following peculiarities of Lk may be noted : the Greek has ' Master ! Master ! ' in 24, giving a realistic air to the disciples' cry. **43.** Luke the physician characteristically omits Mk's remark about the woman being rather the worse for the attention of the doctors. **48.** ' *Thy faith hath saved thee* ' as in 7:50, and again in 18:42.

IX 1-50 Stages in the Formation of the Apostles— d Passing over Mk's account of the visit of Jesus to Nazareth, having dealt with that in 4:16 ff., Lk continues to follow the general lines of Mk's narrative while omitting numerous incidents. The omissions are dictated partly by the fact that he has in mind to include a large section, 9:51-18:30, not found in Mk and Mt, although parts of it are scattered through Mt. He therefore omits incidents which are more or less duplications of things already described, *e.g.* the walking on the sea, the second feeding of the multitude ; he passes over the dispute with the Pharisees about purification and the incident of the Canaanite woman's daughter, the former as of no interest to the Gentile reader, the latter because of the apparently hard words spoken by Jesus regarding non-Jews. The mission of the Apostles is followed by the report of what Herod thinks about Jesus, which prepares for the question of what the Apostles themselves think. This leads to Peter's confession, whereupon the Twelve are taken aside for further instruction of a more advanced character. They have reached the stage where they are strong enough to hear the prediction of the Passion, which is to be drilled into them henceforth. The Galilean ministry in Lk, which had opened with the declaration from heaven at the Baptism, closes with the same declaration at the Transfiguration.

1-6 Mission of the Apostles—(Mt 10:1, 9-11, 14 ; **e** Mk 6:7-13). Here Lk follows Mk pretty closely, but substitutes that the Apostles went out ' announcing the good tidings ' for Mk's ' they preached that men should do penance '.

7-9 Herod's Perplexity—(Mt 14:1-2 ; Mk 6:14-16). The indication given in 6 is sufficient to explain the stir that would naturally be caused through Galilee and disturb Herod, whose perplexity would be better accounted for if Lk had not omitted Mk's story of John's execution. **9b**, proper to Lk, prepares us for another special incident added by him in the Passion narrative concerning Herod's interview with Jesus, 23:7-12.

10-17 Feeding of the Multitude—(Mt 14:13-21; Mk 6:30-44). There is little change from Mk here (except of a literary character) beyond the introduction of the miracle in 10b-11, where the mention of Bethsaida indicates a special source ; Lk is often careless of topography, and even here he does not tell us how the scene changes from Bethsaida to the desert place of 12.

18-27 Confession of Peter—(Mt 16:13-28 ; Mk 8:27- **f** 39). Lk neglects the mention of Caesarea Philippi ; the incident might have taken place near Bethsaida according to the information he gives us. But he adds to Mk and Mt by saying that Jesus was occupied with

754f prayer. Thenceforward he follows Mk save for a change in the words of the confession and his characteristic omission of the reprimand of Peter, Mt 16:22–23; Mk 8:32–33. Arising from prayer Jesus questions the disciples about the opinion of the crowd (in Mk and Mt 'men') concerning him. The answers recall exactly the opinions already given in 8, where it will be noted that nobody had suggested that he was the Messias; therefore the confession of Peter, in the name of the rest, stands out all the more significantly. Lk's record of the confession is more complete than Mk's, less than Mt's; but it is consistent with what has gone before; *cf.* 2:11, 26, also Ac 10:38. It adds nothing in reality to Mk's simple formula; and in view of what Lk has told us regarding the origin and person of our Lord, nothing can be concluded, from his omission of Mt's words 'the Son of the living God', adverse to his teaching on the divinity of Christ. In any case, we have said that it seems certain Lk bases himself on Mk's narrative rather than upon Mt's in

g his account of the Galilean ministry. **21–23.** Here Lk, like Mk and Mt, shows our Lord imposing silence on the disciples about what is called the Messianic Secret. The reason for this is plain: as Jesus has already said 7:22–23, he wishes people to judge of him and his mission from the character of his works and not to be led astray by their preconceptions. Moreover he has to guard himself against the misplaced enthusiasm of the crowd (*cf.* Jn 6:14–15), based as it is upon false conceptions of the true role of God's Messias, conceptions which seem to persist in his own disciples right up to the end; *cf.* 24:19 ff.; Ac 1:6; Mk 10:35 ff. (not in Lk). His own disciples are the first to be taught that the Messias is to complete his destined work in a shocking manner, described by the repeated predictions of the Passion, the first of which appears in 22. Those who have been associated with him in this work must be conformed to the example of their Master in this respect. The prediction of 22 is sufficient to indicate what sort of death he must die, for if the Elders, the High-priests and the Scribes (representing the three sections of the Sanhedrin) are to reject Jesus, that means execution by the only power that has authority to put to death, *i.e.* the Roman governor. All doubt is removed by the words of 23, where Lk adds that the disciple must bear his cross 'daily'. This verse must be read with the fact in mind (it was surely in the minds of the disciples) that only twenty years before 2,000 Jews had been crucified under the legate Varus for rebellion (Jos., *Ant.* 17, 10, 10). The penalty of crucifixion had become very common in the provinces of the empire after the death of Julius Caesar, and was common in Judaea under every procurator. **27.** Lk concludes with the mysterious promise (in Mk and Mt with remarkable differences) which is interpreted by some of the Fathers as referring to the Transfiguration; others see in it a reference to the fall of Jerusalem, the signal for the complete release of the Church from the shackles of Judaism and the consequent extension of the Kingdom of God in the Gentile world.

755a 28–36 The Transfiguration—(Mt 17:1–8; Mk 9:2–8). As Lagrange says, it is impossible to read the Gospel without seeing the relation of this scene to the parallel scene in Gethsemani: 'they stand in opposition to one another like strophe and antistrophe, but the Transfiguration serves as a sure pledge of Christ's future glory, while Gethsemani shows him to us in the lowest depths of human abasement'. The incident must be joined with the prediction of the Passion; these predictions always end (except in Lk 9:44*b*) with a promise of resurrection, and it is the glory of the risen Christ that is foreshadowed in the Transfiguration. The chief additions in Lk are characteristic: our Lord is again at prayer while the events begin to happen (*cf.* 3:21); his Passion is the subject of his conversation with Moses and Elias, who like Jesus (32) appear in glory; the disciples are heavy with sleep as at Gethsemani; it is only when Moses and Elias are on the

point of departure that Peter breaks in with his suggestion. **28.** Lk is less definite than Mk and Mt about the time, but such is his manner. **30–33.** Here, contrary to his usual custom when parallel with Mk, he is much more detailed; Lk evidently attaches much importance to the incident. 'They spoke of his decease', ἔξοδος, Vg *excessus*. The Gk word is used for death in 2 Pet 1:15; Wis 3:2, 7:6. There is little doubt about its meaning here, and the importance of the incident in Lk's eyes may be gathered from its relation to 24:25–27, 44–47. Moses and Elias, who as Tertullian says certainly stand for the Law and the Prophets, appear 'in glory', ἐν δόξῃ (*cf.* 2:9), *i.e.* dwelling with God. They confirm the prediction of the Passion just made by Jesus, thus declaring that such is the design of God. *In transfiguratione illud principaliter agebatur ut de cordibus discipulorum scandalum crucis tolleretur* (St Leo the Great). **33.** Lk's remark that Peter speaks only when he sees Moses and Elias departing justifies the translation, 'Master, it is a good thing that we are here', which is grammatically correct: a good thing, because he and his companions can build some sort of shelter against the sun (σκηνή 'tent' or 'booth') for Jesus and his visitors from heaven. He wishes to detain them. What do they want shelters for? Surely because Peter is under the impression that, supported by such undeniable witnesses as Moses and Elias, Jesus is about to inaugurate his Messianic manifestation to the world (*cf.* 20). The lesson of 22–27 has not yet gone home, as subsequent events will prove. Lk adds, with Mk, that Peter does not know what he is talking about. **34.** The cloud comes as if in answer to Peter's words, here as elsewhere signifying the divine presence; he had suggested making shelters and the divine cloud covers them. God now enters on the scene and speaks as he spoke with Moses on Sinai about the Law, of which Christ is the end; Gal 3:24; *cf.* Ex 19:9 ff. **35.** MS authority is divided between 'beloved' (only) ἀγαπητός and 'elect' ἐκλελεγμένος. The former looks like a borrowing from Mk and Mt or from 3:22. 'Elect' is a traditional Jewish Messianic title; *cf.* 23:35 and Is 42:1. The relation between the Transfiguration and the Confession of Peter is emphasized here by the similar command of silence (implied in Lk, explicitly stated in Mk and Mt) with which they both conclude.

37–50 Further Instruction of the Apostles—(Mt 17:14–23; 18:1–5; Mk 9:14–41). The recent events inspire the questions of the disciples now recorded by Mk and Mt but omitted by Lk, who proceeds immediately with the story of the epileptic boy which Mk describes in very great detail to the disadvantage of the Apostles. Lk characteristically passes over what seems to discredit the Apostles and makes the addition that the boy is an *only* son; a similar addition in the case of Jairus's daughter. But he does not fail to include the somewhat surprising outburst of our Lord in 41, 'O faithless and *twisted* generation, how long . . .'. To whom is the reproach addressed? To all. To the disciples who have been attempting the cure during the absence of Jesus with Peter, James and John, but have failed through lack of faith and due means (Mk 9:28–29 omitted by Lk); to the father whose faith is so imperfect (Mk 9:22–23 omitted by Lk); and to the Scribes who have been attacking the disciples as Mk alone shows, 9:14. Lk's abbreviations necessarily obscure the meaning at times. 43*b* is very Lucan; *cf.* 7:15. Similarly 44, 'all were astonished at the *greatness* of God'.

44b–45 Second Prediction of the Passion—(Mt 17:21–22; Mk 9:30–31). Lk makes our Lord take occasion from the recent astonishment and admiration to renew his warning about the future, introducing it with the emphatic 'Lay up in your ears [not hearts] these words'; here, but not in Mk and Mt, the warning is the more serious from the omission of all reference to the Resurrection. Lk is very emphatic about the way the disciples are at a loss.

46-48 Dispute about Precedence—(Mt 18:1–5; Mk 9:33–7). Though Lk, like Mk, omits to record the bestowal of the primacy on Peter at his confession, it is tempting to think that this dispute had its occasion there. 'In a few words Jesus teaches them what are the conditions necessary for spiritual power. He who has the right to command must exercise that right only in the general interest; he is the servant of all' (Lagrange). Lk adds that the really great man is he who makes himself less than others.

49-50 The Unknown Exorcist—(Mk 9:37–41). The instructions conclude as in Mk (not in Mt) with a word about the attitude to be adopted towards those who believe in Jesus but are outside the circle of his chosen disciples. The man in question seems to have been successful in his use of Jesus' name; hence he must have been a true follower. Lk abbreviates again. So ends the Galilean ministry in Lk.

IX 51-XVIII 30 Insistent Preaching of Salvation on the Way to Jerusalem—Here begins a very distinctive part of Lk, mostly proper to the third Gospel and comprising about one-third of the total. Unjustifiably it has been called the Peraean Ministry, for only some of its incidents take place east of the Jordan; others have called it the Samaritan Ministry because of the special reference it makes to the people of that district. Perhaps its best name is the **Journey Narrative**, though it appears to deal with more than one journey; but we have seen that Lk has special sources, and certainly Jn knows of several journeys to Jerusalem. But it can be said that Lk is here concerned principally with the progress of Jesus to Jerusalem for the purpose of fulfilling the divine decree of the Passion which he has begun to announce; cf. 9:51; 13:22; 17:11; 18:31. It is the final events at Jerusalem that Lk has in view all the time, and this it is which gives unity to the section. It is largely composed of discourses, containing thirteen parables proper to Lk. Scattered here and there are some of the *logia* or sayings contained in the Sermon of Mt chh 5–7. Characteristic of this part, and somewhat of a change from the preceding, is the severity of our Lord's language on occasion; cf. 9:57–62; 11:42–52; 12:20, 56; 13:5, 26–35; 14:26–35. It may be an indication of his source that Lk here shows very little care for topography; the Apostles are named but once, even Peter, James and John rarely appearing. Finally this section contains some of the finest examples of Lk's writing, e.g. 15:1–32.

IX 51-X 24 Proclamation of the Kingdom of God—The opening verse sets the tone for the whole section. 'Assumption'; the same word (in its verbal form) is used in Ac 1:2 and Mk 16:19 for the Ascension and in the LXX for the taking up to heaven of Henoch and Elias. **52** recalls Mal 3:1 with its reference to Elias and John the Baptist (cf. Mal 4:5 and Lk 1:17; 7:27); in Samaria Jesus and his disciples are in a locality which speaks of Elias. Hence the suggestion of James and John, **54**, is a remembrance of 4 Kg 1:10 ff. Note the introduction of 'the disciples James and John' as though they had not yet appeared in Lk. There is very strong MS authority against the inclusion of 55*b*–56*a*. Cf. Mt 8:19–22. What is said of Jesus in 51 is demanded of all would-be disciples. He '*fixed* his face to go *towards* Jerusalem' in spite of those who tried to persuade him to the contrary; cf. Mk 8:31 ff.; 10:32–4; Jn 11:7–8. So too those who wish to follow him must tread down all obstacles. There is no room for the flabby-minded in the Kingdom of God. 'Let the dead bury their dead'; a hard saying, suggesting to the mind of some commentators that those not preoccupied with the Kingdom of God are spiritually dead; cf. Jn 5:21–29; 11:25. But it may be no more than an enigmatic way of saying that Jesus demands disciples who are ready to renounce home and family ties for the Gospel. This was addressed to a man already called. Such is the meaning of 62: it is impossible to plough a straight furrow unless the eyes are fixed steadfastly on the mark set up by the plough-

man. 'Fit' i.e. 'well-placed' and suitable for the **756b** work that has to be done.

X 1-24 Mission of the Seventy(-Two)—(Cf. Mt 9:37– **c** 38; 10:7–16, 40; 11:21–23 for parallel ideas.) This is proper to Lk although many of the instructions are contained in Mt's mission of the Twelve, a point that need surely cause no surprise. Jesus has therefore gathered round him a large number of disciples 'fit for the Kingdom of God'. In Ac 1:15 Lk shows us 120 disciples gathered at Jerusalem immediately after the Ascension. The disciples are sent out two and two like the Apostles in Mk 6:7, but with this difference that the Seventy-two are sent to prepare for the coming of Jesus himself. MSS differ about the reading seventy-two or seventy. **4b.** The absorbing thought of the preacher must be his mission; he must have the appearance of a man on a most urgent journey, looking neither to right nor left; cf. 4 Kg 4:29. Their message is urgent indeed: 'the Kingdom of God *hath come near*', the proclamation with which Jesus begins his preaching in Mk 1:15; this is its first appearance in Lk. **12.** 'In that day'; 'in the day of judgement' in Mt's parallel 10:15; understood of the great Messianic Day when God shall appear to vindicate his rights; cf. Dan 7:13 ff. **13-15.** The mention of the Cities of the Lake, after 9:51–52, seems out of place; the context is more natural in Mt 11:21–23.

17-24 Return of the Seventy-two—There is a general **d** feeling of joy in which Jesus notably shares, the reason being the subjection of the devils to his disciples, a sign that the Reign of God has begun; Satan's power over men is broken by their power over him. **18** indicates that Jesus was acting through his disciples when they used his name. There is a common opinion that here he was warning them against the danger of pride, but that seems to be contradicted by 19, words echoing Ps 90:13 and paralleled in Mk 16:17–18. DV's translation of 18 is confusing; what Jesus says is: 'I was watching Satan falling like lightning-from-heaven', referring to the swiftness of the collapse of Satan's dominion over men brought about by the preaching of the disciples. **20.** The disciples are not forbidden to rejoice over the subjection of the devils; here as in 21*b* we have the Semitic idiom of comparison: 'rejoice more that your names are written in heaven than that . . .'; 'I thank thee Father that thou hast revealed these things to little ones more than . . .'. 'Names written in heaven'; cf. Ex 32:32; Ps 68:29; Is 4:3, etc. Greek cities kept an exact written roll of those with right to citizenship. **21-23.** Remark- **e** able verbal parallels with Mt 11:25–27 and 13:16–17. There is a characteristic addition in 21 where the joy of Jesus, like the whole action of his Messianic career, is attributed to the Holy Ghost; cf. 4:1, 14, 18. For the rest see the commentary on Mt where the context is different and very suitable, i.e. after our Lord's explanation of the purpose of the parables which hide the secret of the Kingdom from the unworthy; but to the disciples it is given to know the mystery of the Kingdom, and the very heart of that mystery is the truth of the Incarnation to which reference is here made. This clear affirmation of the divinity of Christ (and in Mt) is a source of great embarrassment for rationalist critics; some have maintained, without the least support from the MSS, that a later hand has added these words from the teaching of Jn. But, as more orthodox critics have said, the teaching of Lk and Mt here provides one of the closest links between the Synoptic and the Johannine teaching on the person of Jesus. Its affinities to the Fourth Gospel are obvious, yet it comes to us embedded in the earliest Palestinian document Q, probably the earliest of the evangelical sources. We may agree with this while awaiting better proofs of the existence of Q. Note especially that here Jesus is no longer 'the Son of Man', but 'the Son' absolutely.

25-37 Neighbourly Charity—This teaching concludes **f** with the parable of the Good Samaritan, proper to Lk, but the incident which calls forth the parable finds a

756f somewhat similar parallel in Mk 12:28–31 ; Mt 22:34–40. Some hold that Mk's and Mt's incident is altogether different on account of the very obvious discrepancies. In Mk and Mt the Scribe poses a question, as though commencing a mere academic discussion, about the most important precept of the Mosaic Law ; we are to remember that, as traditionally interpreted, the Law comprised some 300 positive precepts and some 300 negative ones. Lk's Scribe begins with a more pleasing request : what was he to do to gain everlasting life ? ' Tempting ' need not be taken in a bad sense ; ἐκπειράζειν will easily stand the meaning of ' finding out by examination '. The mention of everlasting life, new in Lk, comes well after 20 and the recent echoes of Jn who harps on that note. **26.** Jesus deals with the man in a friendly way, referring him to the Law of which as a Scribe he is an accredited master. What does the Law say, for the way to life depends on the Giver of that Law ? **27.** The Scribe replies as any Jew might have replied by quoting Deut 6:5, for these words are the beginning of the *Shema*, the ritual prayer required to be said by every Jew twice a day. But how many Jews would have added the words which echo Lev 19:18 about brotherly love ? The Law, it is true, insisted on this point, but it drew little attention from the doctors of the Law. Such a combination of texts is nowhere found in the rabbinical writings ; the prevailing Jewish attitude towards the non-Jew was one of bitter contempt ; *cf.* Mt 5:43. **29.** Therefore it looks as if the question of the Scribe here was dictated by his discontent with the common view on this point. Lk seems to present us with another of those pious Jews who have more thoroughly penetrated the true spirit of the Old Law, hence a kindred soul with Jesus.

g 30-37 The Good Samaritan—Though proper to Lk it echoes thoroughly the teaching of his fellow Synoptists ; *cf.* Mt 5:43 ff. ; 9:13 ; 12:7. The significance of the parable is tremendous when we recall the attitude of the Jews to the Samaritans ; *cf.* Ecclus 50:25 ff. ; Jn 4:9 ; 8:48. Here the Jews, even priests and Levites, are not only compared unfavourably with a Samaritan, but a Scribe is bidden to sit at his feet and learn the true meaning of the Law. Remember that the Samaritans too followed the Pentateuch and looked on Moses as their teacher. The contrasts are strong : on the one hand the wounded Jew ; the priest and the Levite who, as they lived on the offerings of the faithful, were the more obliged to the offices of neighbourliness. On the other hand a hated Samaritan, passing through an unfriendly country and therefore excusable if he hurried to get out of it ; but not content merely to render first-aid and leave the victim, he carries him to the inn and undertakes all the charges, paying what was the equivalent of two days' wages, Mt 20:2, and promising to return in case there was more to pay. **36-37.** If Jesus concludes by turning the Scribe's question around the other way it is for two reasons : first because the sense of the question was, how far does the obligation of neighbourly love extend ? The answer (provided by the Samaritan) is : to everyone in need, Jew or non-Jew, friend or enemy. Secondly, by thus raising the Scribe's question to the sphere of general principles regarding charity and mercy, there is no room left for rabbinical casuistry about Jews and non-Jews, Samaritans and Gentiles. Every man is my neighbour, more particularly the man in need. The parable has always been a common field for allegory : Christ as the Good Samaritan, the wounded man as the human race robbed and despoiled by the devil, oil and wine the Sacraments, the inn the Church, etc.

757a 38-40 Martha and Mary—Proper to Lk. There is great divergence of opinion about the significance of the incident ; some think that here Lk intends to show that works of charity are not sufficient : faith is also required ; others that the recent parable illustrates the second part of the Scribe's answer in 27, while this incident shows how God is to be loved and sought first of all by contemplation, and thus the contemplative life has a pre-eminence over the active, etc. **38.** Lk as usual neglects topographical details, but Jn 11:1 ff. and 12:1 ff. show that the place is Bethany near Jerusalem. Doubtless the parable of the Good Samaritan was spoken on the way up from Jericho to Jerusalem which passes through Bethany. Martha is shown as the mistress of the house ; Mary appears for the first time ; *cf.* § 753g. The law of hospitality, much insisted on in the East, would require both sisters to be occupied with the care of providing a meal for the unexpected guests, and it may be taken for granted that Jesus was accompanied by his disciples. **40.** Martha is distracted or preoccupied with attention to the preparation of the meal : Lk in no way suggests that she is indifferent to the teachings of Jesus. ' Much serving ' does not mean that the guests were already at table ; our Lord is teaching. Mary too is distracted, torn away from the thought of the meal by absorption in the words of Jesus. The scene and the words of Martha indicate a situation of friendly familiarity, and it would be as false to interpret her complaint in too serious a manner as it would be to read a grave rebuke into the reply of our Lord. It would be very unlike him to rebuke a woman who, if she is busy, is busy for the sake of him and his friends. Moreover he was a guest ; she was the hostess. **41.** Note here again ' the Lord ' and in 39. ' Martha, Martha, thou art *full of care and trouble* about many things ; but *there is need of few things or of one (only)* '. Such seems to be the preferable, as it is the more authoritative, reading of the Greek. The repetition of Martha's name gives the reply an affectionate tone ; the ' many things ' is an obvious reference to the ' much serving ' above, while the ' few things or one (only) ' is an equally obvious contrast. In fact the plain literal meaning in the circumstances must be that Jesus bids Martha not to go to such trouble for the sake of her unexpected guests ; it is embarrassing for them to be the cause of it. One dish alone would satisfy their needs. He concludes with the almost humorous remark of 42b : ' for Mary hath chosen *a good* part *and she shall not be deprived of it* ' merely in order that she may join in all these preparations which are really unnecessary. It follows that Mary has really chosen well in preferring to listen to his words. The shorter reading of 42a, adopted by Vg and DV, favours the more common interpretation, *viz.* that Jesus is here teaching the severe lesson that solicitude about the needs of this life stands in the way of ' the one thing necessary '. Objections to that interpretation are that it would be out of place in the circumstances ; secondly, what is ' the one thing necessary ' here ? Listening to Jesus like Mary ? But our Lord often warns that merely *hearing* his words is of no profit, and here it is Martha who is *doing* the work of ministering to the Lord. We may note in conclusion that until 1950 this passage was the Gospel of the Assumption of our Lady who, in the fulfilment of her maternal office towards her Son, played the part of Martha as well as that of Mary. But like Mary, she ' kept all these things in her heart ', 2:19, 51.

XI 1-13 Teaching on Prayer—The material collected here, except for the parable of the Importunate Friend, is found in Mt 6:9–13 and 7:7–11. We have already noted Lk's insistence on prayer, particularly in the life of our Lord (*cf.* 1:10, 46 ff., 68 ff. ; 2:14, 20, 29 ff., 37 ; 3:21 ; 6:12 ; 9:18, 29 ; 10:21 ; 22:32, 42–44 ; 23:34 ; 24:53), most of these cases being proper. Here in a short treatise he sets before us the example of Jesus, the model of prayer taught by him, the conditions required for efficacious prayer, *i.e.* perseverance and faith in the goodness of God. **2-4.** In the *Our Father*, as in the Beatitudes, Lk shortens the form given by Mt. Some hold that Lk's form is the more primitive, that of Mt being amplified for liturgical purposes (*cf.* the addition in the Syriac version, ' for thine is the kingdom ' etc., which is a liturgical addition). But the fact that Mt's form is the one adopted in the liturgy probably shows that it is the more primitive ; Lk has the habit of abridging. See Mt 6:9–13 for commentary. **5-8.** By teaching his disciples to begin their prayers with the word ' Father ', Jesus wishes to inspire them with confidence ; there are two things looked for in the person from whom we seek favours : the ability to do what we require and the goodwill to do it for us. But if God is our Father, then he has our good at heart, and if he is a heavenly Father then there is no need to doubt his ability. To drive home this lesson Lk records a delightful parable for the full understanding of which it is necessary to put oneself in the circumstances of the time : a house of one room, beds spread on the floor, scant means of artificial lighting, all of which go to render more obvious the untimeliness of the request. Allegorization induces conclusions very unworthy of application to God ; it is a clear parable with an evident meaning : unwearying and confident prayer. **9-13.** But for an added example in 12 and the remarkable variation in 13*b* Lk gives this teaching as in Mt 7:7-11. The change from Mt in 13*b* is very characteristic in view of Lk's insistence on the part played by the Holy Ghost : ' how much more will your Father from heaven give the good Spirit (Mt " good things ") to them that ask him ' ? The influence of the Spirit, as in Gen 1:2 ; 2:7, is always represented as productive of good. The chief good the disciple is to ask in prayer is that he may be like his Father in heaven, and this will be accomplished by the reception of God's Spirit, as Lk has so often heard from St Paul, Rom 8:9 ff., etc. **14-54 Beginning of Denunciations of Scribes and Pharisees**—Here begins a series of incidents common to Lk and Mt but found very scattered in Mt. Mk has but one parallel, the accusation of using diabolical agency of diabolical agency in Jesus, Mk 3:22-27, an incident put by Mt and Mk in the Galilean ministry. The first series of disputes with the Scribes and Pharisees, 5:17-6:11, ended with the threat against our Lord's life ; here is the first fulfilment of that threat, an effort to discredit the undeniable miracles he has worked by making out that he is a tool of Satan. That is the key to the very strong condemnations he utters in reply, for such an accusation is a blasphemy against the good Spirit just spoken of, 13. **14-28 Satan does not fight Satan**—(Mt 12:22-30, 43-45 ; Mk 3:22-27). Lk omits to say who the adversaries are, but we learn from Mt and Mk that they are Scribes and Pharisees. In Lk the Pharisees do not appear till the denunciations begin in 37-39. As in Mt the accusation of using diabolical agency arises out of the cure of the dumb man (also blind in Mt) ; both Synoptists attribute the defect of the man to diabolical influence. The ancient Semites, like the modern Arabs, attributed disease to demonic influence, especially such diseases as induce an apparent change of personality, like madness. Rationalist critics maintain that our Lord was subject to the same superstition, and it is common for orthodox scholars to reply that he merely accommodated his language to the current notions of his time. But that cannot be true of all the cases in the Gospels, for our Lord accepts diabolical possession as an objective reality as the Church does still. The fact is that there is nothing theologically wrong in attributing all human ills to diabolical agency from the Fall downwards. By consenting to sin man has subjected himself to the dominion of Satan; Jn 8:34, Rom 6:12-14 ; the purpose of the Incarnation is to deliver man from the consequences of the Fall and to destroy the reign of Satan through the re-establishment of the Reign of God. All this is reflected here. The only differences between Lk and Mt are Lk's additional demand for a sign from heaven (found later in Mt 12:38) and the unexpected change of Mt's ' Spirit of God ' to ' finger of God ' in 20 ; Lk's expression echoes the cry of Pharaoh's magicians in Ex 8:19. The demand for a sign is logical after the accusation ; Jesus is required to show a sign that he acts through the Spirit of God and not through the evil spirit. The conclusion in 23 is a very stern hint for the adversaries ; if they have so sided against Jesus when he casts out a devil, is not that in itself a

sign that they have taken sides with Satan whose reign, **757f** as is shown in the allegorical application of the preceding parables, our Lord has come to overthrow ? **24-26.** This corresponds very closely with Mt 12:43-45, **g** a passage which is variously interpreted. In Lk it seems to express by means of a parable the lesson that the Jews, in refusing to accept the Kingdom of God inaugurated in the person of Jesus and his victory over Satan, have placed themselves in a worse position than that in which they were before ; *cf.* Jn 9:41. It reinforces the warning of 23. **27-28.** Lk alone. In the context of Mt and Mk the Mother and brethren of Jesus are here brought in (earlier in Lk 8:19-21). This suggests that our Lady's appearance may have inspired the good woman's words of admiration at the victory of our Lord over his enemies : ' Happy mother ', she cries, ' that bore such a son '. The reply of 28 is the same in effect as that in 8:21 ; Jesus does not deny the woman's affirmation, but he declares that exact fidelity to the will of God (of which he knew better than anyone Mary was so outstanding an example) is cause for greater happiness. **29-32 Jonas as a Sign of the Son of Man**—Close **758a** correspondence here with Mt 12:38-42, save that Lk has put earlier, 11:16, the demand for a sign. He omits all reference to the whale and application to the Resurrection. The sign of Jonas is his preaching to the Ninevites, Jon 3:1 ff., whom he converts to such thorough-going penance. The Jews come out badly by comparison with the pagan Ninevites, and even with the Queen of Sheba. Note the growing severity of the reproaches and the significance of the claims : Jesus is superior to the Prophets, greater than Solomon. **33-36 Jesus is a Light for those who receive him**— (Mt 5:15 ; 6:22-23). Lk has already used 33 before in the context on the use of parables, 8:16-17, but the verses are well-placed here where our Lord tells the Jews why they fail to see what is staring them in the face ; their dispositions are evil. There is plenty of light, and he is that light. The moral application is well drawn out in Jn 3:19-21. **36b.** ' the whole (man) shall be *lit-up as when the lamp enlighteneth thee with its shining brightness* '. **37-54 Denunciation of Pharisees and Scribes**— **b** (Mt 23:4, 6, 13, 23, 25-26, 29-31, 34-36). The section concludes, as does the former series of disputes, with violent rage on the part of the adversaries of Jesus and renewed efforts to close his mouth. On this occasion battle is joined more earnestly ; he sees that it is time to show them up for what they are, hypocrites, and therefore a danger to their fellow Jews. From the start we are surprised to see him breaking out into an attack on the Pharisee who has invited him to dinner. Note here again ' the Lord said ', 39. **41.** An obscure verse but evidently with the meaning that external observance is useless without interior observance ; Is 58 ; Mt 5:20 ff. Hence ' *give in alms that which is within* ' (*i.e.* inside the cup and platter) ; this would make them cleaner than all their repeated purifications ; Ps 40:1-2. **47-48.** Lk makes this more difficult to understand than the parallel in Mt. But perhaps he turns it into a piece of irony. While the Jews show honour to the Prophets by building their tombs, they are seeking an opportunity of killing Jesus, who is the Prophet of the Prophets ; *cf.* 11:32. **53.** ' And as *he went out thence*, the Pharisees . . .' **XII 1-59 Dispositions required in those who seek** **c** **Salvation**—Jesus declares that everything turns on this question of the soul's salvation, for which a man must be prepared to face any loss, to renounce every other good whatsoever. Therefore, too, all must be* on the watch constantly for the coming of the Lord, for the chance once lost is lost completely. **1-12 Instruction concerning the Future Preaching of the Disciples**—(Mt 10:26-33 ; 12:32 ; 10:19-20). In the introductory verse we are shown a great crowd (μυριάδες, lit. ' tens of thousands ') so pressing round Jesus that they tread on one another ; Jesus renews his warning to the disciples of the leaven

758c (*i.e.* teaching) of the hypocritical Pharisees, and proceeds with instructions which find a very exact parallel in Mt. The particular points worth noting here are as follows : in 4 Jesus addresses his followers as ' my friends ', new in Lk (*cf.* Jn 15:15) ; in 8–9 ' the angels of God ' take the place of ' my Father in heaven ' in Mt 10:32–33 ; in 12 ' the Holy Spirit ' corresponds to ' the Spirit of your Father ' in Mt. Mt's context for the sin against the Holy Ghost is more suitable than Lk's ; in Mt it comes immediately after the accusation of using diabolical agency. Here Lk seems to have the disciples rather than adversaries in view, as though to say that a disciple who, after having believed in Jesus and received the Holy Ghost, should then deny him would be guilty of an unforgivable sin ; *cf.* Heb 6:4–6. It is not a question of a sin of its nature unforgivable, for Lk knows that Peter himself will deny his Master. But the prospect here is of one who appears before God still denying Christ. Further 11–12 indicate that, since the Holy Spirit will speak through the disciples when they are brought before hostile judges, to deny Jesus then would be to sin against the Holy Ghost, *cf.* Mk 13:11.

d 13-34 The Detachment required in a Disciple—The section begins with an incident found only in Lk, followed by another of his special parables. The incident of 13–14 recalls the story of Moses in Ex 2:11–15. The teaching of the Parable of the Rich Fool is in tune with the note that runs all through these later discourses, the supreme importance of the soul and its salvation. If Lk omits the solemn warning of Mk 8:37, Mt 16:26*b*, it is here in a more graphic form. **21.** ' Rich towards God ' ; either the using of one's wealth for God's service ; or laying up treasure in heaven in the form of spiritual goods ; or, more probably, using wealth for almsgiving to those whom Lk makes the special friends of God ; *cf.* 12:33 ; 16:19 ff. As St Ambrose finely says, ' the hands of the poor, the houses of widows, are storehouses that endure for ever '. **22-34.** Parallels in Mt 6:25–33 ; 19:21, with but little change. The ravens and the lilies are contrasted with the Rich Fool. In 25 ἡλικία seems best rendered by ' span ' (of life) or ' age '. Thus the Rich Fool is again recalled ; he could not extend his life in order to enjoy his hoarded goods. **29b.** An addition to Mt, or rather another expression for solicitude ; to be ' lifted up on high ' is to be suspended, therefore ' be not in suspense ' about your needs. **31.** Omit ' and his justice ' which is a gloss from Mt 6:33. **32.** A Lucan addition, thoroughly in keeping with this section, 9:51–18:30, which is remarkable for its alternation of severity and tenderness in the language of our Lord to his disciples ; *cf.* 12:4, 7. For those who are faithful to the spirit of the Beatitudes which are here recalled the Kingdom of God is assured, *cf.* 6:20. **33-34.** Lk here repeats the thought of Mt 6:19–20 and concludes with the same warning : set all your thoughts and desires on the all-important object. In Semitic imagery the ' heart ' is the seat of consideration, not of affection.

e 35-59 The Necessity of Watching—According to his usual fashion our Lord concludes his instruction with a call to action ; *cf.* 6:46–49. The insistent note is one of ' watching ' but the Greek γρηγορεῖν does not mean watching like a spectator ; it is rather to be awake and active, ' looking alive ' as we say. Thus the loins are to be girt, *i.e.* the skirts of the garments lifted up in preparation for labour and marching, as when the Israelites ate the first Pasch in Egypt, Ex 12:11 ; as the master in 37*b* girds himself to wait on his faithful servants. The parable (35–38) is peculiar to Lk in this form, but it contains the same lesson as the somewhat similar parable in Mt 25:1–13 which is proper to Mt. There is a strong note of allegory in 37*b*, for it is not the human fashion for a master to wait on his servants ; but this is the Master of 22:27 and Jn 13:5. The conclusion then is that the disciple must be ready for his Master's coming and not weary if he is long a-coming, a conclusion with which Mk

ends the instructions of Jesus on the eve of the Passion, 13:33–37. But Lk omits the saying of Mk 13:32 and Mt 24:36 concerning the uncertain time of the coming of the Son of Man, the secret of which is reserved to the Father alone and not shared even by the Son according to Mk. **41-46 :** parallel with Mt 24:45–50 save for the introduction and the conclusion. This is the sole appearance of Peter in the Journey Narrative. The answer given by our Lord to his question seems to be a fuller explanation of the words of Mk 13:37, the conclusion of a similar instruction. Some see an allegory in the parable of 42–44 : Peter is the steward set over all the other servants of the Lord. **47-48.** Proper to Lk. Peter has asked whether his Master's warning is meant for others besides the disciples. Here Jesus appears to say that everyone will be dealt with according to his correspondence with the light he has received ; if the disciples have been shown special favour (*cf.* 10:23–24) then so much the more will be expected of them. The same lesson is applicable to the Jews in general who have been privileged to see and hear Christ. **49-50.** Proper to Lk but recalling Mk 10:38–39 ; the patristic explanation is that the reference is to the fire of charity, since our Lord has come to baptise in the Holy Ghost and with fire ; *cf.* 3:16 ; Rom 5:5. Lk may be recalling again the prophecy of Malachias to which he refers so often earlier ; in Mal 3:2–3 the prophet foresees the coming of the angel of Yahweh ' like a refining fire ' separating the good from the bad. This would carry on the idea of discrimination referred to in 42–48, where emphasis is laid on the standard of discrimination, *i.e* fulfilment or non-fulfilment of the will of God. The thought of his Father's will perhaps here suggests to Jesus what the fulfilment of that will entails for himself, and hence explains 50. Comparison with Mk 10:38–39 seems to show that the baptism here spoken of refers to the Passion. In what sense is our Lord ' straitened ', *i.e.* hemmed-in, constrained, afflicted, until that baptism be accomplished ? Perhaps it is an echo of Jn 12:32–34. Or is the source of his affliction the fact that while some accept his teaching, so many refuse ? This is suggested by the theme of **51-53**, which recalls the words of Simeon, 2:34–35 ; Jesus is a sign of contradiction. ' To give peace on earth ' must not be interpreted as an infinitive of purpose, but of consequence ; Lk has not forgotten the message of 1:79 ; 2:14 ; 7:50. Mt includes this warning of our Lord in the instructions given at the mission of the Apostles ; 10:34–36. **54-59.** Parallels in Mt 5:25–6 ; 16:2–23. The discourse thus concludes with a warning to the crowd about the urgency of the teaching just given ; it is high time to be reconciled with God ; the judgement of God looms and the result of that judgement is inescapable. Let them read the signs of the times, *i.e.* the appearance of John the Baptist and the coming of Jesus.

XIII 1-9 A Call to Repentance—Proper to Lk, carrying on the theme of the discourse just concluded. The fate of Israel is at stake, and the Jews will no longer find any advantage over other men. Indeed they will have the mortification of seeing themselves excluded from the Kingdom of God, while those whom they have despised as outcasts from God will be received, 25–30. Therefore while there is time let them bring forth fruits of repentance, a lesson emphasized by the Parable of the Fig-tree. The allegorical application is clear ; Israel is receiving the most careful attention from the Divine Gardener, as the presence of Jesus proves, but failure to respond will entail speedy and final punishment. The note of impending disaster is increasing. **1.** On Pilate's slaughter of the Galileans, *cf.* § 72*c*.

10-17 Further Dispute about the Sabbath—Proper to Lk. The miracle which arouses the dispute exemplifies the above remark concerning God's continued efforts to save Israel ; but the response it calls forth from one who represents the leaders of Israel confirms the doleful prognostications of Jesus. In using the words ' whom

Satan hath bound these eighteen years' he does not indicate diabolical possession, though they seem to indicate supernatural knowledge on his part, for the miracle was not asked for. See note above (§ 757f) on disease and diabolical influence.

18-30 Three Parables of the Kingdom—The first two are among Mt's collected parables of the Kingdom, 13:13-33 ; Mk 4:30-32, omitted in the Lucan parallel and reserved for this place where they are connected with the present context ; cf. 12:32 and 51 ff. The comparisons which insist on the smallness of the beginnings serve to recall again the blindness and obstinacy of the majority of the Jews, and so provide an introduction to the third parable which foreshadows the reprobation of the Jews and the welcome accorded to the Gentiles ; parallels in Mt 7:13-14 ; 25:11-12 ; 7:22-23 ; 8:11-12 ; 19:30. It will be noted that here, as often in the Journey Narrative, the teaching is occasioned by an interruption from the audience ; 10:25 ; 11:1, 27, 45 ; 12:13, 41 ; 13:1.

24-25. Omit 'but' at the beginning of 25 (not in Gk) and join the two verses together as one parable, according to some commentators, though they appear separately in Mt 7:13-14 and 25:10-12. The entrance to the Kingdom is narrow in the sense described by our Lord, i.e. severe renunciation is the condition of entrance. **26** gives a strong allegorical turn to the parable, thus identifying Jesus with the master of the house who admits to or excludes from the Kingdom. **28.** 'There', i.e. in that place which means exclusion from the Kingdom ; outside the door, where they are shut out from the society of the patriarchs and consequently no longer true children of Abraham ; cf. 16:22 ; 3:8 ; Gal 3:7 ff. ' Weeping and gnashing of teeth ', here alone in Lk but oftener in Mt, expressing sorrow and terror ; βρυγμός means the chattering of teeth with fear rather than gnashing them with rage. **30.** As in Mt 19:30 and 20:16.

31-35 Lament over Jerusalem—Cf. Mt 23:37-39, where there is almost verbal correspondence with 34-35. Mt has the better context, where Jesus is at or near Jerusalem, while in Lk he is in Peraea, the territory of Herod Antipas ; Peraea however extended to the west of Jordan and its frontier approached Jerusalem. He is in the neighbourhood of Machaerus where Herod had executed John ; hence perhaps the warning in 31. It does not seem clear whether these Pharisees are well-disposed, or merely plotting to get Jesus into Judaea and within their power. His answer fits either case ; he will not go up to Jerusalem until the time appointed for him to die there, and until that time nothing shall stop him from carrying out the mission bestowed on him by his Father. **32.** The day here spoken of is not to be taken as the natural space of time. ' I am consummated ', τελειοῦμαι, ' I reach the end '. **35.** Omit ' desolate ', which has been added from Mt 23:38. ' Your house ' seems to mean the temple ; a foreboding of the cessation of the Mosaic worship. **35b** seems to foretell the greeting on Palm Sunday (cf. 19:38) but its parallel in Mt 23:39 follows Palm Sunday. Hence the conclusion of the commentators that our Lord is here speaking of a future event that will take place after his Passion ; according to some, his second coming ; according to others, the time foretold by St Paul, Rom 11:25, when the Jews shall be converted and recognize Jesus as the Messias.

XIV 1-6 Healing of the Dropsical Man on the Sabbath —The miracle and the following counsel given to the Jews, 7-14, find no parallel in Mt and Mk. Lk seems to make them the setting for the Parable of the Great Supper which carries on the theme of the previous two chapters : the refusal of the Jews to accept Jesus and the consequent prediction of the incorporation of the Gentiles in the Kingdom of God. After the miracle Lk places the comparison of 5 which he had omitted in 6:6-11, his parallel with Mt 12:9-13 ; Mk 3:1-6, where it appears. The Greek reads ' son or ox ' in place of Vg and DV ' ass or ox ' ; but the meaning remains the same : a work of charity and mercy such

as Jesus had performed was a fulfilment rather than a **759d** breach of the Sabbath.

7-14 Advice on Humility and Charity—It may seem **e** strange to find our Lord as a guest in the house of an important Pharisee after the recent denunciations ; but it may be explained by the fact that he is still in Peraea where perhaps the local Pharisees have had little previous contact with him. Lk gives a picture of the Pharisees which is quite in accord with the character of them painted by non-biblical Jewish writings. We are not to suppose that our Lord is advising them to practise false modesty in order to get the better of their fellows. It is suggested that he is again attacking their hypocrisy because they seek an opportunity for self-aggrandisement even in the exercise of the sacred obligations of hospitality. Note that Lk calls this a parable. Does he mean that it is a comparison with the way in which the Pharisees consider themselves invited as by right to the chief places in the wedding-feast of eternal life with God in his Kingdom ? Such a disposition secures exclusion rather than admittance. Cf. Prov 25:6-7 which perhaps inspires the parable and gives an allegorical turn to it.

15-24 Parable of the Great Supper—The similar **f** parable of Mt 22:1-10 is substantially the same though with differences of detail which add to the allegorical significance, e.g. the King makes a marriage for his Son (the Incarnation), he sends his servants (the Prophets) to call men to the feast ; they reject the invitation and kill the messengers (cf. 11:47-51), etc. Lk's parable cannot be so treated ; its plain application is that God wills good to men and his benevolent design will be accomplished whatever obstacles wicked men put in the way. It is obviously related to the Kingdom of God about which our Lord has lately been speaking, 12:31 ; 13:18, and it repeats the teaching of these chapters about the importance of allowing nothing to interfere with the soul's salvation. But the possibilities of allegorical interpretation, for the Pharisees who heard it and for us who read it, are clear : those first invited are the religious leaders who consider themselves as the rightful heirs of the Kingdom, or else the nation which prided itself on being God's Chosen People ; the poor and wretched of the city brought in to take the place of these could represent the ' accursed multitude that knoweth not the Law,' Jn 7:48-49, with the publicans and sinners ; while the outcasts from the highways and hedges might be the Gentiles. By the more gentle rebukes Jesus had addressed to the Pharisees gathered with him at table, 7-14, he had prepared them for the severe warning of this parable, viz. that they were in a fair way to lose their places at the great feast of the Kingdom of God through the contemptuous way in which they had received the invitation of God's chief ambassador, who is now telling them for the last time that the feast is ready.

25-35 The Disciples of Jesus must count the Cost— 760a The logical link between this and the parable is found in the reprobation of those who rejected the invitation through self-love ; he who wishes to imitate Jesus in his devotion to the Kingdom of God must have that detachment which grows out of complete self-surrender. There is a parallel in Mt 10:37-38, but Lk expresses the warning more bluntly with that severity which is one of the marks of the Journey Narrative. Note how this warning is addressed not merely to the intimate disciples but to ' great multitudes '. In 13:17 Lk shows us great enthusiasm among the people after the healing of the infirm woman ; doubtless an enthusiasm rising from Messianic expectations of the traditional sort. Our Lord appears to turn on them and say : ' If you wish to follow me, this is what I expect from you ; now follow if you dare '. If anyone allows wealth, family affection, even love of life to interfere with the claims of discipleship, then such a one is not fit to be a disciple. Even the prospect of seeing oneself marching in a file of condemned men must not make the true disciple hesitate. The two parables that follow, 28-33, proper to Lk, are meant to illustrate this lesson : count the

760a cost before undertaking the duties of discipleship. They also contain the following implied contrast : in worldly affairs, like building and going to war, money and goods are essential to success ; the opposite is true in the great affair of the world to come. 'Every one of you that doth not renounce all that he possesseth cannot be my disciple', surely a divine claim to make. The sense of these parables is not that long consideration is required before a man makes up his mind to be a Christian, but rather that a resolution is demanded fit for every eventuality ; and the eventualities may be severe. Even the parable of salt, 34–35, used by Mt 5:13a to show the duty of a disciple to serve as a purifying and enlightening principle for his fellowmen, is here used only in the sense of the warning in Mt 5:13b. Failure to stick to one's resolution as a loyal disciple is severely condemned, and the favourite formula of 35b is used to draw serious attention to the point. On 'hating' father and mother, cf. § 693d.

b XV 1-32 God's Joy in pardoning the Sinner—The prospect and the tone here change ; there is no longer a note of severity and renunciation but one of confidence in the astonishing kindness of God towards frail human nature, 'a mercy that even anticipates the repentance of the sinner and pursues him in order to render him worthy of pardon' (Lagr., GJC II 62). But there is more than that, for the Pharisees were familiar enough with the Bible's insistence on the mercies of God ; what is revealed here by the Son is the joy that overflows from the Father's heart when he wins back one of his children by repentance. Here is the true meaning of that μετανοία or 'penance' which the Gospel so often insists on. There is little need to explain the three parables in which this truth is illustrated ; a truth that is one of the mysteries of the Kingdom of God revealed not only to the disciples but also to them that are without (cf. 8:10). In view of the stern teaching on renunciation just recorded it is a remarkable contrast to find the publicans and sinners drawing near to Jesus to hear him ; a clear proof that he could speak with such apparent severity without ceasing to show himself the kind and loving person Lk has presented to us in his earlier chapters. It is only the Scribes and Pharisees whose bitter opposition prejudices them against him however he speaks, and here they are still faithful to the role they have always adopted. These parables are spoken in answer to their complaints against the familiar friendliness our Lord insists on showing to sinners.

c 4-7 Parable of the Lost Sheep—A parallel is found in Mt 18:11–14 but in a different context, the warning against scandal. Mt restricts himself to the bare terms of the comparison ; all the details of Lk's version seem so exaggerated that we almost expect the audience to protest that no human shepherd would act in so extraordinary a way : leaving ninety-nine sheep, when the flock is collected at night in the sheep-fold, in order to return to the dark hillside to look for a strayed one ; when it is found, carrying the heavy sheep down the hill on his shoulders with joy ; rousing his fellow shepherds to share his joy. But that is the precise point of the parable ; our Lord's answer to the objection is : 'I agree : no human shepherd would act thus. But that is the way the Divine Shepherd behaves over one of his lost children'. The OT presents God so often in the guise of a Good Shepherd that every Jew must have seen the application ; cf. Is 40:11 ; 49:22 ; 60:4 ; 66:12, etc. There is no lack of consideration for the just in 7, nor is there any ironical reference here to the Pharisees (cf. 18:9). It is merely that the just have not been the occasion for such joy as God and the whole heavenly court feel over the conversion of a sinner. The same conclusion in different words is in 31–32.

d 8-10 The Lost Drachma—Proper to Lk and repeating the same theme, as though to add further emphasis. The Greek drachma is roughly equal to the Roman denarius or penny, reckoned a day's pay for a workman. The situation seems to grow in tragedy ; before it was one lost out of a hundred, now it is one of ten. Hence

there is no improbability in the woman's going to such trouble to find the lost coin, but there is the same improbable invitation to the neighbours to rejoice over the find. The joy of the angels recalls 2:10–14 and contrasts strongly with the grumbling discontent of the Pharisees who, by inference, are not God's friends and neighbours since they do not rejoice with him.

11-32 The Prodigal Son—Nothing parallel to this wonderful parable in any of the other gospels. Lagrange notes that the traditional title is too restricted ; it has been well said that a better title would be The Prodigal Father, who was as reckless in loving as the son was in spending. In this parable, which no mortal would have dared to invent, our Lord reveals the very heart of God in order to inspire the sinner with confidence to approach him. It is not now a question of one out of a hundred, or even out of ten, but one of two, and these two the only sons of a loving father. **12-16.** The contrasts are striking : the younger son and spoilt child, little sensible of the father's love, almost impatient for the father's death so that he may receive the inheritance, departing as soon as he has got his desire. The following details are masterly : loss of money, a great famine, absolute want, a Jewish hireling under a Gentile master in 'a far country', a feeder of swine. A Jew in a pig-sty with his head almost in the pig-trough ! In the allegorization of the parable these details provide a powerful picture of the sad state to which the sinner is reduced when he departs from his heavenly Father. **17-20.** At last his eyes are opened to realize his situation ; as the Gospel insists, the true basis of penance or repentance (μετανοία) is the sincere admission of sinfulness with a determination to destroy sin by returning to God ; cf. 3:3 ff. The suggestion of the parable is clear : all the time that the son has forgotten his father, the father has not forgotten his son, but has looked out daily for his return with longing ; hence he sees him 'when he was yet a great way off'. Unlike the Pharisees, he is waiting with love and compassion to make the first move towards reconciliation. **21-24.** The erring son is not allowed to finish the confession he has prepared ; there can be no question of his being taken back as a hireling : he is restored immediately to the dignity of a son. And lest he be disgraced before the household by his rags and destitution, the father quickly orders a robe of the first quality, a ring for his finger, shoes for his feet ; to complete all and bring us back to the thought of the Messianic Great Supper, a feast of the best is prepared with music and singing. This echoes the joy of God and the angels in 7 and 10. **25-30.** With sudden contrast here now appears over against the loving enthusiasm of the father, the unfeeling coldness of the other son ; we return to the Pharisaic complaint in 2. **31-32.** Here is the true description of God's regard for the just : 'Son, thou art always with me and all I have is thine'. The conclusion in 32 is essentially the same as that of the two former parables. It was long the fashion to regard this parable as an allegory of the Jews (the elder son) and the Gentile sinners ; but the younger son does not represent the sinner : he is the sinner. Some again regard the elder son as representing the real just, others as the hypocritical just, i.e. the Pharisees. In the former case it might be said that the parable shows how even the friends of God do not always realize the unplumbed depths of God's mercy. But it would be false to the parable to see the Pharisees in the elder brother ; our Lord was far from admitting that they had served God faithfully. See Lagr., GJC II 62–7 for an excellent treatment of this chapter.

XVI 1-31 Advice on the Right Attitude to Earthly Goods—All this chapter is proper to Lk save for scattered parallels of 13, 16–18 in Mt. The parables of ch 15 about God's kindness towards the sinner do not alter in any way the fundamental truth that he must be loyally served no matter what the cost ; Lk here returns to the duty of renunciation but adds a positive aspect of that renunciation which is full of

a encouragement. What is to be done with the goods of which a disciple of Christ strips himself ? Jesus reminds him that the poor are always with us ; therefore let him use his goods to make friends with these special friends of God and so secure a welcome for himself in the world to come.

b 1-13 The Unjust Steward—Many find difficulties in the interpretation of this parable, but the meaning is clear enough especially if an emended reading be given to 9. There is question of a steward who manages the estate of a rich man : the steward is a *villicus* or farm-bailiff. Accused of bad management (and with good reason, as the parable hints) he is dismissed. How is he to live ? Afraid to work, ashamed to beg, he is not ashamed to steal. Therefore he calls up the tenants who pay their rent in kind and with them he falsifies their contracts and so cheats the master further. By this piece of trickery the bailiff thinks to make friends and patrons for himself who will welcome him after his dismissal. The lord's commendation of ' *the steward of unrighteousness* ', this dishonest bailiff, is the great difficulty. Which lord ? Surely not the cheated master ! But how could our Lord praise such a piece of swindling so contrary to all his spirit and teaching ? The answer is, as Lagrange points out, that both master and bailiff are ' children of this world ' ; the former learns how he has been swindled in a way that will be difficult to prove : ' he prudently decides to treat it as a joke and makes the comment anyone would make in the circumstances : " A rascal, but a clever rascal ! " ' Our Lord commends neither master nor bailiff. The parable does not say that the bailiff had acted ' wisely ' but ' shrewdly ', *i.e.* with a prudence that belongs to the ideals of this world ; this is what our Lord (not the master here) means in 8*b*, where he compares ' the children of this world ' with ' the children of light ', Hebraisms which denote those who live by the ideals of this world or of the world to come ; *cf.* Eph 5:8 ; 1 Thess 5:5. If only those who have the light to live with a view to their eternal advantage would show the keenness and sagacity of those who live for temporal

c advantage ! 9. An example of how the children of light might imitate the shrewdness of the steward : ' Make *for yourselves* [as he made for himself] friends *through the means of* the mammon of *unrighteousness, in order* that when *it shall be no more with you* they may *welcome* you into everlasting dwellings '. ' Mammon ', an Aramaic word (lit. ' something confided ' or ' deposited '), used under the form of ' Mammon of unrighteousness ' as we speak of ' filthy lucre '. Our Lord does not condemn the possession of wealth absolutely, but demands that in this as in all else a man should regard himself as a steward for God. The day will come when that stewardship shall cease by death ; Vg and DV follow the reading ' when you shall fail ', but ' when it [*i.e.* mammon] shall fail you ' is the preferable reading ; both come to the same meaning. Therefore prepare for that day by giving alms. It is not necessary to conclude that it is the poor, whom we thus secure as friends, who shall themselves welcome us to heaven where they are at home ; ' they ' may be impersonal as in 12:20. But there is an echo here of 6:20 and 16:22. 10-13. The parable is followed by advice about the unrighteous mammon with which is compared something that is true (not the true mammon as the grammatical construction shows) ; but it is evidently a contrast between false riches and genuine riches. The contrast between ' that which is another's ' and ' that which is your own ' may mean the wealth confided to our stewardship by God on the one hand, and our own soul's welfare on the other. Almost verbal parallel between 13 and Mt 6:24.

d 14-18 Denunciation of the Pharisees—The introductory verse is special to Lk, the rest finds parallels in Mt 11:12-13 ; 5:18, 32. The Pharisaic opposition to Christ's teaching on wealth arises not only from their love of money (φιλάργυροι) but from that traditional Jewish attitude which looked on worldly prosperity as a sign of God's favour. But Jesus insists

that God's standards are far otherwise : ' that which **761d** *among men is lifted up* is an abomination before God ', lit. stinks in God's face. For 15*a* see 18:9. The sudden introduction of the ideas in 16-18 may be explained by the supposition that the Pharisees quoted the Law in favour of the traditional attitude. But this is no time, replies our Lord, to look on earthly prosperity as a sign of God's favour, even if the Law did promise it to Israel in return for faithful service. ' The Law had been upheld by the Prophets, of whom John was the last, but from now onwards the Kingdom of God was to be preached ' (Lagr., GJC II 71). In what way does ' everyone use violence towards ' the Kingdom of God ? The Greek says ' everyone advances violently into it '. In view of the demand for stern renunciation it must be concluded that here our Lord means that it is no longer a question of prosperity being a sign of God's favour, but of depriving oneself of *everything* for the Kingdom of God. In 17, perhaps in answer to an unspoken objection, he adds that what he has said is not against the Law ; the Kingdom of God is the beginning of a new order in which the Law finds its fulfilment, for everything in the Law that is necessarily good and true is good and true because it forms part of God's Eternal Law. The remark in 18 seems utterly discordant unless it be taken as a cited example of the way in which Jesus means his teaching about the fulfilment of the Law to be understood. In Mt 19:8-10 he declares that repudiation (remarriage is not included) was against the mind of Moses ; he may well claim here then that the Law is brought to its perfection by his teaching on marriage.

19-31 Dives and Lazarus—The parable logically **e** follows : the fact of being rich is no assurance that a man is God's favourite, despite what was asserted to be the contrary teaching of the Law. Here is added the authority of Abraham to show what was the true mind of Moses, for Moses cannot be put in opposition to Abraham. An ancient opinion took this story as real history, and it is true that our Lord does not elsewhere give names to the actors in his parables. But the general opinion is that we have here a true parable. Note the contrasts again : a rich man, finely clothed and sumptuously fed each day ; a poor beggar, lying at the gate, famished, diseased, reduced to the extremity of being abandoned by all but the despised curs of the street who also wait to be fed with the crumbs of the rich man's table. Omit ' and no one gave him ' with the Greek MSS. The reverse of the medal is shown in 22-24 ; the beggar sitting close to Abraham in the great feast of God's Kingdom, the rich man in hell tortured by fire and parched with thirst. The situation is thus changed : the beggar is rich and the rich man now begs through the good offices of Lazarus. The request is refused : the change of situation is now irrevocably fixed, and there is no means of bridging the gulf of separation. If it is not said, it is at any rate supposed that Lazarus is not only poor but righteous, the rich man not only rich but living for the things of this world ; this is implicit in 27-30. Lk is not here teaching that the poor are necessarily the friends of God and the rich his enemies. **22b-23.** ' *And the rich man also died and was buried ; and* **f** *in hell lifting up his eyes . . .* '. **25.** ' Son, remember that thou didst receive *thy* good things in thy life-time ', *i.e.* the goods thy heart was set upon ; 25*b* supposes the opposite for Lazarus. **27-28.** The rich man confesses that he and his brethren have not understood what it is that wins companionship with Abraham, the ideal friend of God ; but the excuse is inadmissible because the Law and the Prophets teach precisely that, and what could be more authoritative than the Law and the Prophets in the eyes of a Jew ? Thus the parable teaches that Jesus is in full accord with the Law regarding both the significance of wealth and the duty of charity ; *cf.* Deut 26:13 ; Is 58:5-8 ; Amos 6:4-6 ; 8:4-6.

XVII 1-10 Teaching on Scandal, Forgiveness, Faith 762a and Humility—(Mt 18:6-7, 15, 21-22 ; 17:19 ; Mk

762a 9:41). Here Lk begins a new theme. He softens down the inevitability of scandal in Mt 18:7 by saying ' it is impossible that scandals should not come ', *i.e.* it is impossible to avoid them altogether. **1-6** correspond in general terms with the parallels in Mk and Mt, but Lk alone records the Apostles' demand for faith ; this is their sole appearance under that title in the Journey Narrative. It is not a request for theological faith but, as the context proves, for that confidence in God which is requisite for the working of miracles. Some have supposed that the petition had its motive in the great demands just made by Jesus on the subject of forgiveness. But the answer of our Lord is connected by Mt and Mk with the Apostles' failure to heal the epileptic boy and with the withered fig-tree ; Mt 17:19 ; 21:21 ; Mk 11:22-23. In v 3 the words ' against thee ' (*Vg* in te) are not in the Greek. **7-10.** Proper to Lk. Perhaps our Lord's recognition of the Apostles' ability to do miracles calls for this exhortation to the humble recognition on their part of their uselessness ; not that God cares nothing for their services, but they are not to preen themselves on what they do.

b 11-19 Healing of the Ten Lepers—Proper to Lk. The incident occurs while Jesus is still on the way to Jerusalem ; a rare indication of place and a peculiar one, ' *between* Samaria and Galilee '. It is suggested that he had gone north, east of Jordan, crossed the river near Bethshan (Beisan), and now descends west of Jordan towards Jericho where we shall next find him. **12.** The lepers stand afar off as the Law prescribed and Jesus gives them the command that the Law enjoins, Lev 13:49 ; 14:2-4 ; the Samaritan is included in the command because his compatriots follow the Pentateuch. It is not said that the other nine were Jews, but Lk indicates this ; thus the incident serves a double purpose : it shows how the Gospel blessings extend beyond the confines of Israel, and it attacks the unjustifiable confidence of the Jews. The plain suggestion is that the Jewish lepers took their cure as a matter of course, as though God's Messianic blessings were theirs by right of birth. The Samaritan, on the other hand, showed the right attitude : faith, diffidence in his own merits, and consequent gratitude ; God was intervening through Jesus on his behalf, though as a hated Samaritan ' foreigner ' (rather than ' stranger ') he could lay no claim to share in the benefits of Israel. **19b.** The incident concludes with a repetition of the formula ' thy faith *hath saved thee* ' (*cf.* 7:50 ; 8:48 ; 18:42).

c 20-37 The Coming of God's Kingdom and of the Son of Man—This instruction is joined by Mt to the discourse on the ruin of Jerusalem, 24:26-28, 37-41, but with a slightly different arrangement. In his usual manner Lk introduces it by means of a question put by a member of the audience, a question quite in keeping with traditional Messianic views which looked for a catastrophic divine manifestation in favour of Israel. This was not in accordance with realities, as Jesus here shows. No need to be on the lookout for the Kingdom of God as one looked out for a new star ; ' the Kingdom of God is within [or, among] you '. Whatever be the right word here the meaning is clear ; the Kingdom of God was already there, and if the Pharisees did not see it that was because they were looking for something entirely different (*cf.* 11:20). The patristic interpretation favours *in vobis*, in your souls ; but our Lord would hardly have said that of the Pharisees, though as the *Pater* teaches, the Kingdom of God is certainly within those who do the will of God. Such a meaning is naturally favoured by Protestants since it supports, as they think, the thesis of an invisible Church. Our Lord is merely answering the question of 20 : the Kingdom will not *come*, because it is already *here*. Therefore it would not come with a glorious Messianic manifestation. Doubtless this surprised his disciples who had witnessed his miracles and the Transfiguration. In 22-31 he puts an end once and for all to these idle dreams ; ' his disciples must resemble neither worldlings whose minds are set on their own temporal interests and pleasures, nor those visionaries who go no further than to look for signs of salvation ; they must live like men whose hopes are set on eternity. But at the same time, knowing that the Son of Man will not come till his hour has arrived and when he comes he will come unexpectedly, they must work in constant readiness for the time when he will call them to rejoin him ' (Lagr., GJC II 79). **22-24.** A reminder **d** perhaps of a previous warning, that he is destined to leave them and this world in a shocking manner ; repeated in 25. In those days to come they will long for his glorious return, a prediction fulfilled as the Epistles of the NT show. But they must not let their longing desire lead them into the error of thinking he has come and, like the Jews, go running after a pseudo-Messias ; it is useless to go looking for his coming, as fruitless as it would be to look for where the lightning will fall next. In the parallel of Mt 24:26-28 there is mention of the Parousia, the ' presence ', ' coming ' or ' arrival ' of the Son of Man ; Lk avoids the term though it is a favourite with St Paul. He prefers the expression ' the Son of Man in his day ', not the ' one day ' of 22 but the great final Messianic Day when he shall be manifested in his glory ; *cf.* Dan 7:13-14. **26-35.** As that coming will be so sudden, let them **e** neither waste their time in seeking for it nor show that indifference to the judgements of God which was manifested in the examples cited in 26-29 ; many will be taken by surprise and found unprepared in spite of all his efforts (*cf.* Mt 24:37-41 ; 10:39). With the example of Lot's wife our Lord returns to the lesson of complete detachment in affection from the things of this world, even from life itself, where the soul's good is at stake. He does not forbid due preoccupation with the ordinary needs of life ; it is not the mere possession and use of earthly goods that will determine God's judgements, but the soul's attitude towards these goods ; *cf.* 1 Cor 7:26-35. So two persons may be occupied about the same thing, and it will not appear outwardly why God has accepted the one and rejected the other, 34-35. The ' day of the Lord here ' changes to ' in that night ', not so much perhaps because the first example is taken from sleep as that there is now a prospect of judgement, calamity and darkness ; *cf.* 12:20, 35-36 ; 1 Thess 5:2 ; 2 Pet 3:10. **35b.** Omitted in the best MSS ; probably added here from Mt 24:40. **36-37.** Various interpretations are put upon the **f** disciples' question, *e.g.* where will be the place of judgement ? The sense of the question is to be sought in the answer, the literal meaning of which is plain : when one sees birds of prey (vultures rather than eagles) gathering in one direction, the presence of a dead body may be presumed and found by following them. In Mt 24:28 the parable is used by Jesus to indicate that his chosen ones will flock to him as swiftly and surely as vultures smell out their prey ; he is warning his hearers not to be led astray by false rumours, as in 23 above. The difficulty of interpretation in Lk arises from the fact that 37 is separated from that context which it has in Mt. Some interpret it here as meaning : there the judgment will be where sin has been.

XVIII 1-14 Further Instructions on Prayer—Proper to **7** Lk. The last instructions contain a note of impending disaster along with an assurance that the Kingdom of God will be realized in spite of every opposition. Lagrange therefore sees in the first of these parables a word of comfort for the disciples. The warning about the need of being ready to forsake life itself recalls memories of our Lord's predictions of the bitter persecutions they will have to suffer for the name of Christ. But let them never forget that they have a Father in heaven who watches over them, who will hear their cry and even revenge them ; *cf.* 6-22 ; 12:11, 22-32. They had to be warned against the temptation of asking in the days to come why God in his power did not immediately intervene on behalf of his servants : a common complaint at all times with those who suffer persecution from evil men. Hence they must go on

3a praying and not lose heart, advice Jesus illustrates with a parable.

b **2-8 The Wicked Judge and the Widow**—The application of the parable (allegorization would be unfitting here for it would identify God, ' the father of orphans and judge of widows ', Ps 67:6, with this ' judge of unrighteousness ') is that if even a wicked man eventually heard the suppliant widow, will not an infinitely just God do justice to his chosen ones ? **5b.** Insistence here, as in the parable of 11:5-8, on the necessity of importuning till one's prayer is granted. **7b.** Much dispute about the interpretation of these words. Are they a question or an affirmative statement ? Who are those to whom God will (or will not) show himself patient ? Lagrange takes it as a question : ' Will he (God) have patience in regard to them (the persecutors of the elect) ? ' In other words, if God seems slow to revenge his elect, we must not complain that he seems so long-suffering as to abandon his elect. There follows the answer to the question in 8a ; let them go on praying, confident that evil will not finally prevail. The sad prognostication of 8b seems to indicate that although the final victory for God's justice is assured, yet some of the followers of Jesus will not have the resolution and faith to persevere until the end ; paralleled in Mt 24:12. The faith in question is the faith already seen in Lk, a conviction that the presence of Jesus in the world signifies the loving intervention of God for man's salvation. Such a faith is supremely necessary in times of persecution, and it is then that confident prayer must be kept up.

c **9-14 The Pharisee and the Publican**—Josephus describes the Pharisees as ' a sect of the Jews who esteemed themselves more religious than others and thought their interpretation of the Law more accurate ' (BJ 1, 5, 2). Their very name *Perushim*, ' the separated ones ', owed its origin to the fact that they were a class apart, and was originally bestowed on them for their real piety. The typical Pharisee revealed to us in the Gospels and contemporary Jewish writings separated himself from his fellow-men by such a firm conviction of his own righteousness as made him contemptuous of all whom he regarded as incapable of being pleasing to God, *e.g.* those Jews who showed indifference to the minutiae of traditional observance (*cf.* Jn 7:48-49), and of course those of Gentile birth. This, as our Lord said, 16:15, was what made the Pharisees abominable to God. **11.** The prayer is quite in the spirit of one of the Jewish Benedictions prescribed for daily prayer : ' Blessed art thou . . . that thou hast not made me a Gentile . . . a servant . . . a woman ' ; very different from the prayer prescribed by our Lord for his disciples, a prayer making no comparisons but springing from a sense of deep-felt need. The Pharisee in his prayer, as in his life, gives the impression of self-sufficiency, the national vice attacked by St Paul in his description of the very purpose of the Mosaic Law, Gal 3:21-25 ;

d Rom 3:20 ; 5:20. **12.** His prayer completed, he recalls ' the chief points of righteousness which he has accomplished, considerably exceeding the standard prescribed by the Law. . . . Even the Lord himself could hardly demand more, though he might very well desire a little less vain complacency ' (Lagr., GJC II 84). **13.** With the marked contrast characteristic of Lk, the Publican is presented beating his breast repeatedly (ἔτυπτεν impf.), not reciting a list of God's debts to him but declaring himself to be in dire need of divine mercy. The conclusion of 14 is all the stronger from the fact that it omits formal condemnation of the Pharisee, though the word ' justified ', *i.e.* right with God, responds to the ' trusted in themselves as just ' of 9. The parable is the justification of our Lord's attitude to sinners (*cf.* 15:1) and it ends with a repetition of the warning uttered when he twitted the Pharisees with their itch for precedence, 14:11, a warning which cannot fail to remind us of the spirit of the Magnificat, 1:47-54, and the Beatitudes, 6:20-22.

e **15-30 Right Dispositions for Entry into the Kingdom of God**—Some commentators see the end of the Journey Narrative in 18:14, for here Lk resumes the thread of Mt and Mk ; moreover there is now a distinct change of tone. Lagrange prefers to continue it to 18:30 where Lk puts another prediction of the Passion and the commencement of the definitive move towards Jerusalem for the final tragedy. The two incidents narrated here are placed by Mt and Mk also at the beginning of the ascent to Jerusalem from Peraea, but they first describe the discussion with the Pharisees about marriage and repudiation omitted by Lk ; *cf.* Mt 19:1-12 ; Mk 10:1-12. Lk's omission makes the incident of 15-17 appear abruptly, while it falls very well into place in Mt and Mk after the discussion on marriage.

763e

15-17 Jesus and the Children—(Mt 19:13-16 ; Mk 10:13-16). Lk follows Mk with characteristic changes : no mention of the indignation of our Lord against the disciples, Mk 10:14, or of his embracing the children whom he makes ' infants ', βρέφη. The meaning is very clear ; entry into the Kingdom demands the frankness, simplicity and innocence which we love to see in children.

18-30 The Rich Ruler—(Mt 19:16-30 ; Mk 10:17-31) **f** Each of the Synoptists has special details about this man, but Mk's account is the most natural and vivid. In Lk he is a rich ruler, ἄρχων, therefore belonging to the Jewish aristocracy ; Mt adds that he is a young man, a detail implicit in Mk's story too where the man shows that youthful enthusiasm which appears so fittingly after the advice of 15-17 ; he runs up to Jesus and throws himself on the ground. It is tempting to think that it was Mark himself, *cf.* the young man of Mk 14:51-52 ; in both cases the man shows the dispositions of the Mark we know from Acts. It will be noted that Mk alone adds the touching detail of Mk 10:21. The man's question and his whole manner betray his excellent dispositions ; he was concerned about that which Jesus has insisted is the only thing of real importance. But he has not yet reconciled himself to the condition of absolute renunciation on which our Lord has also insisted. **19.** The reply is essentially the same as that made to the Scribe in 10:26, better expressed in Mt 19:17. ' Do you ask me, a man, about a thing that concerns God alone ? What has God himself told you ? ' **20.** It is remark- **g** able that only those commandments are recalled which concern the second of the two great precepts of the Law. **21.** The young man makes a young man's reply with the candour and confidence just recommended by our Lord. Whether he was taking a too optimistic view of himself or not, his disposition and enthusiasm earn for him an invitation to become a disciple, *i.e.* to make the great renunciation demanded by true discipleship. ' Yet one thing is wanting to thee ' ; note Mt's ' if thou wilt be perfect '. The sudden change from spirited enthusiasm to sad despondency, again so characteristic of the young, calls forth our Lord's warning against the danger of wealth, 24-30, after the young man had departed according to Mk and Mt, a detail neglected by Lk. This teaching is given by Lk as in Mk, save for the omission of the disciples' mystification and Mk's repeated warning ' Children, how hard it is to enter the kingdom of God ' (preferable reading of Mk 10:24b). **25.** There **h** is no need to suggest the usual far-fetched interpretations of ' camel ' and ' needle's eye ' in order to tone down the severity of our Lord's warning ; the words mean what they say and so give occasion to the disciples' conclusion that no one can be saved. Our Lord's answer, better put in Lk than in Mt and Mk confirms their conclusion but adds that God himself will save those who adopt the dispositions Jesus has recommended. Riches in themselves are neither good nor bad ; it is undue attachment to riches leading to their abuse that keeps men out of the Kingdom. God can save the rich man by inspiring him to give away his wealth, or he can save him without such renunciation, which the Law indeed does not demand, provided he acts like a good steward in the sense of the

763h parable of 16:1-9. All the same a great reward is promised to those who, rich or poor, renounce all ties of family or possessions ' for the sake of the kingdom of God ' (in Mt 19:29*b* ' for the sake of my name ', in Mk 10:29*b* ' for my sake and the gospel's sake '). Here as elsewhere Lk substitutes Kingdom of God for gospel in Mk, a word that surprisingly he never uses.

XVIII 31-XXIII 56 Arrival at Jerusalem and Passion —This section is grouped into four distinct parts : (1) The arrival at Jerusalem ; (2) Disputes with the Jewish leaders ; (3) The great sermon on the destruction of Jerusalem and the Last Judgement ; (4) The Passion. In a general way Lk follows the narrative of Mk with some omissions and the following notable additions : the incident of Zachaeus, 19:1 ff. ; Jesus weeping over Jerusalem, 19:41 ff. ; prayer for infallibility and primacy of Peter, 22:31 ff. ; Jesus before Herod, 23:6 ff.

764a XVIII 31-4 Further Prediction of the Passion— (Mt 20:17-19 ; Mk 10:32-34). This is Lk's fourth prediction, if we take 17:25 into account. He here omits Mk's note of surprise and fear shown by the disciples, but adds the often repeated remark that what is to happen at Jerusalem is in accordance with the Prophets ; this, taken with the conclusion, 34, should be compared with 24:25-27, 45-46. Jesus is now moving up from the Jordan through Jericho ; he takes only the Twelve, leaving the general crowd of his followers.

b **35-43 Healing of the Blind Man at Jericho**—(Mt 20:29-34 ; Mk 10:46-52). Omitting the request of the Sons of Zebedee, here inserted by Mk and Mt, an incident which would have made a good commentary on 34 (no parallel in Mk and Mt), Lk joins them in narrating this miracle. There are differences which raise difficulties, *e.g.* the incident is at our Lord's entry into Jericho while Mk and Mt put it at his departure. With Mk he speaks of one blind man only (name omitted by Lk) while Mt has two. Various suggestions have been made : *e.g.* the unlikely explanation that Lk tells the story of one of Mt's blind men while Mk deals with the other. Lk's incident seems to be the same as Mk's ; but some, in order to safeguard the truth of Scripture, have held that they are describing two completely different occasions. Others have suggested that there is no greater contradiction of the truth of Scripture here than there is in the different order of temptations in Lk 4:1-13 and Mt 4:1-11. Note that 35 merely says ' when he was near to Jericho ', *ἐν τῷ ἐγγίζειν*, which would do either for coming in or going out ; Lk is generally careless of topographical details. It is true that later we read ' entering in he walked through Jericho ', 19:1, but that is a new incident which need not have occurred on the same occasion, for it is possible that there was a stay of some days in the neighbourhood (*cf.* 19:5). Some hold there is question of two Jerichos, the old and deserted, and the new. In 42 we have the final repetition of the accustomed formula ' thy faith *hath saved* thee ', given here by Mk also. Lk's conclusion, noting the glorifying of God and the praise of God by the people, is also frequent in Lk and peculiar to him.

c XIX 1-10 Zachaeus the Publican—It is worth noting that while Lk has omitted to mention the name of the blind man (if his miracle is the same as Mk's) he is careful to record the name of Zachaeus. Some think that this is because Zachaeus represents the call of the Gentiles. But was he a Gentile ? Jews were willing enough to undertake these posts in the Customs Department, though their fellow Jews called them renegades and hated them as the ancient world hated all publicans and their collaborators. Zachaeus has a Jewish name and a Jewish character. Jericho on account of its situation was an important customs office and would furnish him with good opportunities of profit, if he was none too scrupulous like his colleagues. **3-4.** Were it not for the trouble taken by him to see what sort of person Jesus looked like, we might think him moved merely by idle curiosity, **764c** stirred perhaps by the rumour of miracles. But the sequel contradicts this ; a wealthy man of position will hesitate to risk his dignity in that fashion unless moved by something deeper than curiosity. **5.** Perhaps a preliminary confirmation of Zachaeus' suspicions about Jesus, who thus shows awareness of where he is and what is his name. In 6 Zachaeus proves that he is a brother of the publicans of 15:1 ; there is no doubt about his good dispositions, while the universal complaint of 7 shows what was the common opinion of him. **8.** He immediately begins to put into practice our Lord's teaching on the proper use of wealth ; it does not appear to be restitution of ill-gotten wealth, for he does not admit that he has certainly defrauded anyone by ' sycophancy ', *ἐσυκοφάντησα*, *i.e.* by false denunciation in his office as tax-collector ; see the same word in 3:14 where John the Baptist gives advice to the publicans and their police. *If* he has been guilty of injustice, then he is ready to restore as the Law commands, Num 5:6-7, and even to restore fourfold. That his conduct has not been all it should be, however, may be gathered from 10. Thus Jesus is provided with his reply to the grumblers : Zachaeus, sinner and renegade Jew though he be, has not forfeited his right to the promise made to Abraham ; and in receiving Jesus into his house, he has welcomed the one in whom the promise to Abraham is fulfilled.

11-27 Parable of the Pounds—In spite of the many **d** differences between this and the Parable of the Talents in Mt 25:14-30, many commentators identify them. Maldonatus, for example, admits the identity and attributes the divergences to the evangelists ; it would be safer, according to Lagrange, to say that the differences are due to the handing down of the parable by oral tradition under different forms. In both a master is shown putting his servants to the test ; the faithful are rewarded splendidly, the rest punished severely. The conclusion is the same in both. Lk alone, 11, gives the occasion of the parable : Jesus is ascending to Jerusalem and some of his followers still think in spite of all that there is to be a glorious Messianic manifestation. Perhaps there is a hint of the question of the Sons of Zebedee, Mt 20:20-28 ; Mk 10:35-45, which Lk has omitted. The parable contradicts such hopes ; Jesus is not going to act as a political Messias and start a revolution in order to seat himself on the throne of Israel. He *is* the King, but he is going on a long journey in order to receive royal investiture from his Father. His true disciples will be loyal to him during his absence. He will return : let them be ready for that event. **12.** The **e** comparison is very apt, for everyone knew how the Herodian princes visited Rome in order to receive their kingdoms at the hands of Caesar. What Lk adds in 14 (not in Mt) is precisely what happened when Archelaus went to Rome in 4 B.C. to receive the kingdom inherited from his father, Herod the Great ; the Jews sent an embassy to oppose his claim. The Jewish leaders are now acting in just the same manner towards Jesus, though manifestly the allegory must not be pressed too closely. **17.** Here Mt's allegorization is stronger ; he adds to the reward bestowed the words ' enter thou into the joy of thy Lord '. **20-26.** In Lk the idle servant is dealt with in the same manner as in Mt save for small details ; he is condemned because he has not watched, *i.e.* he has not been active and lively in the interests of his master. He defends himself by attributing evil dispositions to his master, an accusation proved untrue by 17, 19 and 24. The remark added in Lk's account, 25, is not intended to reflect jealousy ; it is a literary manner of bringing out the generosity of the master which has just been called into question. **27.** Another addition in Lk made necessary by his addition in 14. It contains a formidable lesson for the Jewish leaders.

28-40 Triumphal Entry into Jerusalem—(Mt 21:1-9 ; **f** Mk 11:1-10 ; *cf.* Jn 12:12-19). Apart from the short dialogue with the Pharisees, 39-40, Lk's narrative is

5a a close parallel of Mk's. The following points are to be noted in Lk, where the stage is now set for the final unravelling of the plot : Jesus has received acknowledgement from on high at his Nativity, Baptism, Transfiguration ; from his disciples ; from the crowd who have recognized in him one through whose ministrations God is visiting his people. He has shown a clear consciousness of his Divine Sonship, and in virtue of that has made such demands of self-surrender on his followers as none but God could make. In the foregoing parable he has indicated clearly that he is the Messianic King ; he is about to make a fitting entry into his royal city. It is the last sign of his dignity until he shall have attained the glory of his Resurrection ; but that, as we have been repeatedly warned by Lk, is in God's design to be reached only through the humiliation of the Passion.

b 28. A parallel of Mk 10:32a, omitted previously by Lk. **37.** A common custom for the residents of Jerusalem to go out and meet the incoming pilgrims with music and singing. In Lk it is ' all the multitude of his disciples' who praise God ' for all the miracles, δυνάμεις, they had seen '. 'Multitude' ; πλῆθος means a great number ; cf. Ac 1:15. The numbers and the style of their salutation give reason for the complaint of 39. **38.** Omitting the Hebrew *Hosanna* of Mk and Mt, Lk records the salutation as ' Blessed be he-that-cometh, the king, in the name of the Lord ', which recalls the ὁ ἐρχόμενος of John the Baptist, 3:16 ; 7:19. Finally he omits their concluding ' *Hosanna* in the highest' and inserts ' peace in heaven and glory on high ', which recalls the song of the angels, 2:14 ; the angelic prediction is near fulfilment. Lk alone records the objection of the Pharisees in this place, 39, though Mt 21:15–16 places a similar incident later in the temple. Lk here reflects the objection of the citizens in the parable, 19:14 ; the Pharisees are obdurate in their refusal to welcome the Kingdom of God of which Jesus is not merely the representative but the King. It may be noted that only now, at the end of his career, does he allow any public acknowledgement of himself as the Messias-King ; there is no further need of past injunctions about the Messianic Secret. And even now he admits acknowledgement only as a means of testifying to the goodness of God manifested through the miracles, 37 ; see his answer in 40 and cf. Hab 2:11.

c 41–44 Jesus weeps over Jerusalem—Proper to Lk and coming well after the last incident ; the Pharisees fittingly represent the dispositions of Jerusalem. Another of Lk's striking contrasts : the enthusiastic joy of the disciples, the tears of the Master ; their song of peace and glory, his vision of war and desolation, ' the vision of a people delivered over to madness, factions on every side, divisions healed for a time by a despairing rage against a determined enemy who is tightening his toils about the city' (Lagr., GJC II 124). The prediction is so true to life that rationalist critics feel bound to maintain that Lk wrote it after the destruction of Jerusalem in A.D. 70. **42.** If Jerusalem, the city of peace [so the name was interpreted], had recognized the things to her peace *today*, the evils of that *other day* would not have come upon her. The thought of peace is recalled by 38 (cf. also 14:32). **44.** The details of destruction are an echo of Mic 3:12, the prophet's conclusion of a long denunciation of Israel for her sins ; cf. Jer 6:3, 6. All through Lk we are reminded that the Messianic Day is a time of God's beneficent visitation of his people ; 1:68, 78 ; 4:18–21 ; 7:16, 21–23, etc. For the horrors of the siege of Jerusalem see Jos. BJ Books 5 and 6.

d 45–6 Cleansing of the Temple—(Mt 21:12–13 ; Mk 11:15–17 ; Jn 2:14–16). Omitting the incident of the withered fig-tree, placed by Mt after and by Mk before the cleansing of the temple, Lk gives Mk's account of this in shortened form. Jn puts it at the beginning of the ministry, while all three Synoptists ' have put the expulsion of the traders from the Temple during the Pasch immediately preceding the Passion,

and this seems to be demanded by their plan, for they **765d** mention but one Pasch ' (Lagr., GJC I 98), and the Pasch was the reason for the presence of the traders in the temple. Jn gives three Paschs and connects the incident with the first. This is in all probability the correct place, chronologically speaking. See comments on Mt 21:12 ; Mk 11:15 ; Jn 2:13 for further discussion. Lk omits the words ' to all nations ' from Mk's quotation of Is 56:7, at which Plummer is surprised in view of Lk's universalizing tendency ; but it would have been more surprising if he had included them after the recent prediction of the destruction of Jerusalem, with all that it entailed for the liberation of the early Church from the bonds of Judaism. See Edersheim I, 370 ff., for an account of the abuses practised in the temple markets.

47–48 Ministry in Jerusalem—(Mk 11:18–19). **e** Omitting after his manner the details of Mt and Mk concerning the comings and goings from the city, Lk sums up the situation briefly by describing the action of Jesus and its diverse effect on the people and their leaders. Here appear the three categories of the latter which are to be responsible for his death : chief priests, Scribes, and ' the first of the people ', i.e. the aristocracy —the three groups making up the Sanhedrin. One of their chief motives is the fear of his growing influence : all the people are hanging on his lips ; cf. Jn 12:19.

XX–XXI The Last Teachings of Jesus—The hour of **766a** sacrifice drawing near, it is fitting that the whole life of Jesus should now be turned towards the place of sacrifice, the temple. ' Miracles are now done with. All his teaching indicates the clear view he has of what is to come, the fate awaiting him, the punishment about to fall upon the Temple and the people. He manifests a personality far higher than that of the Jewish conception of the Messias, Son of David. The impression is given that he is in command of the shape of events ; death is his own free choice. But he prepares his disciples to carry on his work after he has gone ' (Lagr., S. Luc 505).

XX 1-8 Question of Jesus' Authority—(Mt 21:23–27 ; **b** Mk 11:27–33). Close following of Mk here. Our Lord perseveres in ' *announcing the good tidings* ' ; the desire of Jesus to seek the people's good up to the last moment contrasts with the opposite attitude of his opponents towards him. **2.** The reason of the inquiry made by the representatives of the Sanhedrin need not be his cleansing of the temple ; indeed many of the Pharisees would have sympathized with that in principle, since it was their Sadducean opponents who were responsible for the abuses. As all three Synoptists agree, their chief fear was our Lord's growing popularity. They had not forgotten John the Baptist's ascendancy over the people ; cf. 6b. Their efforts are therefore concentrated on the attempt to ruin the reputation of Jesus with the crowd by taxing him with embarrassing questions ; there follow several such questions. In this instance he completely disconcerts them by associating himself with the popular enthusiasm for John. If they, the self-constituted guides of Israel, are not able to make up their minds about such a person as John, then he denies their right to ask for the source of *his* authority.

9-19 Parable of the Wicked Husbandmen—(Mt **c** 21:33–46 ; Mk 12:1–12). As in Mk save for literary changes and the addition of the threat in 18. Lk omits the details concerning the preparation of the vineyard but adds the interjection of 16b ' God forbid ! ' lit. ' May it not be ! '. Such a detail would appeal to him since it is called forth by the suggestion of 16a that God will choose for himself another people who will prove more faithful than the Chosen Race. The whole parable is so pointed in its allegorical significance, ' a parable of Jewish history ', that liberal critics deny its authenticity ; they maintain that our Lord always used pure parables and that allegorical touches are due to additions made in the light of later events. In the parable (the application of which no one could fail to see) the servants were evidently those whom God

766c had sent to his people : God's last hope comes in the person of his beloved Son, clearly his only Son. The killing of that Son is the final crime, and after the last crime comes punishment. Here Jesus claims that he possesses the title of Son of God in a unique sense, thus providing his enemies with just the pretext they wanted for destroying him.

d 20-26 Question of the Tribute—(Mt 22:15–22 ; Mk 12:13–17). The Jewish leaders are under no misapprehension about the meaning of the parable, 19, but they find it necessary to go warily for fear of the crowd ; hence they set spies to find some pretext for handing Jesus over to the Roman authorities (Lk alone). Lk omits to specify the emissaries (Pharisees and Herodians in Mk and Mt) but identifies them sufficiently by the phrase ' who feign themselves just ' (20, cf. 16:15 ; 18:9). Using subterfuge themselves, they appeal to his well-known straightforwardness and fearless speaking of the truth. It was known to all that neither Pharisees nor Herodians offered opposition to Roman domination : the latter because they depended on it, the former having even asked for incorporation into the empire on the death of Herod the Great (Jos. Ant. 17, 11, 2). But it should be recalled that twenty years before this very question of tribute to Caesar had caused a rebellion which the Romans had put down severely, crucifying 2,000 Jews (Ant. 17, 10, 10). Hence Jesus' answer might have grave consequences with the crowd or with the police. 26. Lk points out that the opponents are completely disconcerted again ; there is nothing in his answer they can seize on to discredit Jesus either with the Roman authorities or with the people.

e 27-40 Question about the Resurrection of the Dead—(Mt 22:23–33 ; Mk 12:18–27). The third question, curiously enough, is one about which Pharisees and Sadducees were at loggerheads (cf. Ac 23:8 ; Ant. 17, 1, 4 ; Lagr., GJC II 142 ff.). Perhaps the explanation is found in the satisfaction of the Sadducees at Jesus' answer to the previous question, for they gave unequivocal support to Rome. Lk runs in accord with Mk and Mt while insisting more emphatically on the theological character of the question. 34-36. Note the Lucan additions ' children of this world ', ' children of God ', ' children of the resurrection ' ; cf. 16:8. These are Hebraistic idioms signifying those who have the characteristics of mortal or immortal life. 37. The Sadducees are disappointed by the answer while their opponents are gratified, 39. A further interesting addition of Lk is 38b, ' for all live to him (God) ', a Pauline expression ; cf. Rom 6:10 ; Gal 2:19.

f 41-44 Question of the Davidic Sonship of the Messias—(Mt 22:41–46 ; Mk 12:35–37). Though Lk agrees with Mk in recording the gratification of the Scribes, he omits the question of one of them now given by Mk which fits in well with the narrative ; but he has already narrated this or a similar incident in 10:25–28. Here he confines himself to the captious questions of the adversaries, so that all may be ' in order '. On this occasion it is Jesus who takes the initiative, perhaps to turn the tables on them. They are seeking to discredit him with the crowd. Having put them to shame with the crowd by making them confess that they can give no satisfactory answer about John the Baptist, he now puts them in a much more serious difficulty by asking them about the Messias's Davidic origin. Whatever disagreements there were about the Messias's character, all agreed that he was to be the Son of David. Thus, as Lk has said in 40, he closes their mouths even in the matter of their boasted ability to interpret the Scriptures. At the same time he provides positive teaching about himself ; for if David himself in the Psalms, of which he was the accredited author (cf. Mt 22:43 ; Mk 12:36), shows the Messias seated at God's right hand, then it follows that the Messias ranks higher than all the servants of God and is consequently much more than a mere Son of David. Who but the Son of God would be invited to sit at God's right hand ? It is at the conclusion of this incident that Mt has placed the remark that from this time no one

dared to pose any more questions, much better here **766f** than where Lk has put it in 40.

45-47 Warning against the Scribes—(Mt 23:1–36 ; **g** Mk 12:37b–40). The attack is carried further into the enemy's camp. Note how Mk concludes the last incident by reminding us of the pleasure of the crowd at Jesus' words, and it seems to be the crowd that he warns against the Scribes ; in Lk the warning is reserved for the disciples. Mt expands the theme, including much of what Lk has already said in 11:37–54. Here Lk agrees closely with Mk ; both conclude with the formidable words of 47b.

XXI 1-4 The Widow's Mite—(Mk 12:41–44). Lk **767a** abbreviates. The connexion with the foregoing is clear : Jesus has just denounced the Scribes (and the Pharisees, cf. 11:43, 14:7), one of the chief censures being that they ' devour the houses of widows ', the biblical type of the poor and forsaken. The Pharisees are φιλάργυροι, ' lovers of silver ', 16:14. The two types are contrasted here : the rich man, evidently one of those just denounced, ostentatiously casting his offering into the trumpet-shaped collecting box of the temple ; the poor widow humbly approaching to put in her two mites, the smallest coin in circulation. The lesson is plain ; they have given ' out of their superfluity ' ; ' she out of her deficiency hath cast in all the livelihood that she had '. She is an excellent example of that complete self-surrender which Jesus demands of his followers.

5-36 The Ruin of the Temple and the Coming of the b Son of Man—In the eschatological discourse (τὰ ἔσχατα, the last things) with which the ministry of Jesus closes, Lk's general plan is the same as Mk's. But he shows greater precision in describing the details of the ruin of Jerusalem, a fact which leads rationalist critics to conclude that his Gospel was written after that event. Mt's eschatological discourse is paralleled by Mk and by what Lk contains on the same subject in 17:20–37, material that Mt and Lk are supposed to have drawn from a common source, such as the hypothetical document Q. Lk shows more care in distinguishing the two themes, the ruin of Jerusalem and the Parousia being confused in Mk. Some have suggested that the Synoptists have blocked together two completely different discourses spoken on different occasions ; it seems unlikely. Hostile critics maintain that in the mind of Jesus the ruin of the temple was the sure sign of the end of the world, and that he consequently was a victim of deception. But it is clear from the Gospels that he distinguished the two events, even if he treated of both at once. The first was to be the sign for the **c** flight of his disciples ; the second was to be a catastrophe from which flight was impossible. The first was predicted as near ; the disciples should see it. As for the second, Jesus refrains from predicting the time ; that was his Father's secret. But why did he deal with both subjects together and thus lead to the possibility of error ? But the error that the end of the temple would be the end of the world was not suggested to men's minds by his words ; every true Israelite was convinced of this already, just as the idea of a world without the city of Rome was unthinkable for the people of the empire. The complete and final destruction of Jerusalem and the temple and the consequent collapse of Judaism and the Mosaic Law ! How could the world go on after that ? Besides, Jewish Messianism, if it meant anything at that time, meant the triumph of Israel and the everlasting supremacy of the Mosaic Law. That is sufficiently clear from the Jewish apocryphal writings. It was therefore necessary for Jesus once more and in an unmistakable manner to disabuse his own disciples of all such notions. He was not that kind of Messias. (But see the commentary on Mt in loc. for a very different view ; cf. also § 417g.)

5-7 The Coming Ruin of the Temple—(Mt 24:1–3 ; **d** Mk 13:1–4). This prediction is admirably introduced in Mt by our Lord's apostrophe of Jerusalem, including the words ' behold your house shall be left desolate ', which Lk has put much earlier ; 13:34–35. Jesus and

7d his disciples were probably on the slopes of Olivet (*cf.* Mk 13:3) whence they looked down upon the temple. Lk in his fashion omits such details. The disciples call their Master's attention to the mighty buildings and ' the offerings ', perhaps the great brazen gates leading into the inner courts which had been given by an Alexandrine Jew; *cf.* Jos. *Ant.* 15, 11. But the temple, built for eternity, will soon be no more than a heap of stones, 19:44 ; Mic 3:12.

e **8-24 Signs of the Coming Catastrophe**—(Mt 24:4-20 ; Mk 13:5-18). The horrible prediction had called forth the startled question of the disciples in 7*b*. **8-11.** The appearance of false Christs, wars, etc. is not to lead them into the error of thinking that the day of destruction is at hand ; Lk omits the concluding apt remark of Mt and Mk, ' these are (but) the beginning of the birth-pangs '. **12-19.** The ruin of the city will be preceded by persecution for Christ's sake ; by omitting Mk 13:10 ' unto all nations the Gospel must first be preached ' Lk avoids the possibility of confusing the time of the two great events. What does **13** mean ? Either that persecution will provide the disciples with an opportunity for witnessing to the truth, as **14** seems to indicate, or else that the persecutions will provide that sort of witness, μαρτύριον, which is borne by martyrdom ; this had already been verified when Lk wrote by the deaths of James, Stephen and others ; *cf.* 16*b*. **15.** Jesus promises to do for his disciples what God himself had promised to Moses, Ex 4:11-12 ; in Mk it is the Holy Ghost who is made the source of inspiration. **18.** This seems either out of place or contradictory of 16*b*, unless it be taken as a proverbial expression (*cf.* 12:7 ; Ac 27:34 ; 1 Kg 14:45 ; 2 Kg 14:11 ; 3 Kg 1:52) signifying that God has control of all in such a way that nothing will happen without his will, and his will towards the disciples is all for their good ; if they lose their life it will be for the good of their soul (*cf.* 12:4-7). Hence the conclusion, ' *by your endurance win* your souls ' ; *cf.* Mk 13:13*b*, ' he who endures unto the end shall be saved '.

f **20-24 The Ruin of Jerusalem**—(Mt 24:15-20 ; Mk 13:14-18). ' Lk here puts in clear terms what Mk has wrapped up in symbolical language such as Gentile readers could with difficulty have understood ' (Lagrange). The ' abomination of desolation standing where it ought not ' is missing, though he retains the word ' desolation ' ἐρήμωσις and applies it to Jerusalem. ἐρήμωσις is an active word meaning ' laying waste '. Jerusalem besieged by armies inevitably recalled to a Jewish mind the thought of Nabuchodonosor's siege and its result, 4 Kg 25:1 ff. That will be the sign for the disciples to flee from the city, for (22 proper to Lk) this is the punishment decreed by God and it cannot be escaped. **24.** Here Lk neglects the Marcan narrative and describes in great detail the fate of the inhabitants of the city, concluding with the prediction ' Jerusalem shall be trodden under foot by [*i.e.* shall be under the heel of] the Gentiles until the times of the *Gentiles* be fulfilled ' ; *cf.* Dan 8:13 ; Apoc. 11:2. The Gentiles are to take the place of the Jews in the divine plan (*cf.* 20:16 and Rom 11:25).

g **25-27 The Coming of the Son of Man**—(Mt 24:29-31; Mk 13:24-27). The mention of the ' times of the Gentiles ' provides an introduction to this theme ; Lk's perspective is now carried beyond the ruin of Jerusalem into the future. Omitting the warnings in Mk and Mt about false rumours concerning the second coming of Christ (already dealt with in 17:23-24) he joins them in describing the signs in the heavens and on earth that shall precede the Parousia. In his context the time of the appearance of these signs is indefinite ; moreover the fear and distress caused by them are not confined to Jerusalem but spread over the world. **27.** The appearance of the Son of Man is described almost in the words of Mk ; but instead of Mk's consolatory words about the gathering together of the elect Lk adds the encouragement of **28.** Since, however, there is no promise that the disciples are to see the Parousia, it seems that **28** must be referred to the signs that shall precede the ruin of Jerusalem ; but **767g** Knabenbauer, Schanz and Plummer refer 28 to the coming of the Son of Man. Our Lord always insists that there shall be no warning signs of his second coming. He will come suddenly, when least expected, like a thief in the night ; 17:24 and 21:34-36.

28-33 Signs of the Approach of the Kingdom of God h —(Mt 24:32-35 ; Mk 13:28-31). Here, as in 17:20 ff., Jesus distinguishes between the Parousia and the coming of the Kingdom of God, which in some way is already ' in you' or ' among you ', 17:21. Note also the distinction between ' then *they* shall see ' of 27 and ' look *you* up and lift up *your* heads ' of 28 ; there is a break in thought. The ' redemption ' in 28 may be taken as the liberation of the disciples from the restraining bonds of Judaism which are not only the persecutions proceeding from the Synagogue, but also the hindrances arising from the Judaizers among the convert Jews of which Lk will write in Ac. The destruction of Jerusalem and the temple solved both of these problems, and provided the occasion for the spread of the Kingdom of God throughout the world, the thing foreseen by the Prophets ; Is 2:2 ff. ; 65:1 ff. ; 66:19 ff. ; Mal 1:11. **30.** ' When they *already* shoot forth [with leaves, not fruit] you know *by looking at them* that summer is *already* nigh ; so you also . . .'. Consequently it is not a question of the Parousia but of something the disciples (some of them at least) will live to see, something the date of which can be roughly fixed ; therefore the ruin of the city.

34-36 Be Ready for the Coming of the Son of Man— i (Mt 24:42 ; Mk 13:33-37 ; *cf.* Lk 12:41-48). Nowhere in Lk do we find the words of Mk and Mt about the ignorance of the Son concerning the last day ; he omits them here ; *cf.* Mk 13:32. There is a distinct change of tone in Lk ; no more talk of encouragement as in 28, but a warning beginning with the admonitory formula, ' take heed to yourselves ' (*cf.* 17:3) which takes the place of Mk's parable. We are back in the situation of 17:26 ff., watching for the coming of the Son of Man. Here, as there, that coming will be a day of judgement and sifting. ' As a snare ' (or trap) should probably be attached to 34 rather than commence a new sentence in 35 ; ' that day will come upon you like a snare ' ; a snare is useless unless laid where least expected ; *cf.* 1 Thess 5:2. Hence, instead of looking out for signs, be always ready. **36.** Lk adds the advice to be constant at prayer ' at every time '.

XXII-XXIII The Passion—Like his fellow evangelists **768a** Lk attaches primary importance to the story of the Passion ; these two chapters account for one ninth part of his Gospel. Here he does not bear such a similarity to Mk as in the preceding part, but shows a clear dependence on some source which is neither Mt nor Mk. His story is composed in order : the plot, the betrayal, the institution of the Eucharist followed by the final discourse, the capture at Gethsemani, the appearance of Jesus before the Sanhedrin, the delivery to Pilate for execution, the crucifixion. There are some changes of order, omissions and additions which distinguish Lk from Mt and Mk. Very notable is the omission of the anointing at Bethany ; but that is sufficiently explained by the inclusion of a similar story early in his Gospel and his dislike of repetitions. **XXII 1-23 The Last Supper**—(Mt 26:1-29 ; Mk **b** 14:1-25 ; *cf.* Jn 13:21-38). **1-6.** Much as in Mk, but abbreviated, save for the addition that Judas acts at the instigation of Satan, *cf.* 4:13 and Jn 13:2, 27. The ' magistrates ' referred to in 4 are merely στρατηγοί, officers of the temple police and therefore Jews ; Lk alone mentions them. **7-14.** Lk alone mentions the identity of the two disciples sent to prepare the Pasch. He is in conformity here with Mt and Mk about the day of the paschal supper, *apparently* against Jn who makes the Jews eat the Pasch after the crucifixion, Jn 18:28. Orthodox scholars are divided as to whether the Synoptists intend us to understand that Jesus and his disciples ate the Jewish Pasch ; according to some Jesus anticipated the Judaean date by one day,

768b following the calendar of the Galilean Jews. See Lagr., *S. Marc* (1911) 330 ff. Beyond doubt according to Lk Jesus celebrates the Jewish Pasch as is evident from 15-18. ' This Pasch ' is clearly the paschal lamb which lies before him as he speaks (*cf.* 7) ; the thought of the immolation of the lamb reminds him of his own sacrifice : ' before *I* suffer '. It is his final celebration of the Pasch with his disciples, the beginning of the new Pasch of the Kingdom of God in the celebration of which he will be always present with them. Thus he does not destroy but fulfils the ancient rite, as he had **c** promised ; *cf.* 16:17 and Mt 5:17-18. **17-18.** In the Jewish rite of the paschal supper there were four separate ceremonial draughts of wine, and this was apparently one of them ; but Mt and Mk place words similar to 18 after the consecration of the chalice ; Mt 26:29 ; Mk 14:25. Why the change of order ? All three Synoptists here envisage the heavenly feast of the world to come rather than the celebration of Mass. **19-20.** The remarkable fact that each synoptist gives a different version of the actual words of consecration furnishes a useful example of the manner in which the evangelists deal with common incidents, which each records after his own manner. It might have been thought that they all would have been scrupulous to observe identical phrasing in such a matter. Lk's version comes nearest, as might be expected, to that of St Paul ; 1 Cor 11:24 ff. Note the following changes and additions : in **19** ' giving thanks ', εὐχαριστήσας, which provides the name Eucharist, instead of Mk's and Mt's ' blessing ' εὐλογήσας (*cf.* Mt 15:36 ; Mk 8:6 with Mt 14:19 ; Mk 6:41 ; Lk 9:16) ; ' which is given for you ' is added after the consecration of the bread, indicating that our Lord has already offered his body to be immolated like the lamb, and that the sacrifice of himself is now an accomplished fact ; ' do this for a commemoration of me ' is added as in 1 Cor 11:24. **20.** ' This chalice *is the new covenant* in my blood, shed for you '. DV following Vg says ' shall be shed ' without authority in the Greek, but ' shed ' seems to be parallel with ' given ' in 19, indicating a sacrifice already offered. For ' the new covenant ' see Ex 24:7-8 ; Jer 31:31 ff. **21-23.** It is only now that Lk makes that reference to the treason of Judas which precedes the institution of the Eucharist in Mk and Mt, as if they wish to remove the traitor from the scene before the solemn moment ; *cf.* Jn 13:21-30. But in Lk it looks as if the giving of his body and blood by our Lord is deliberately contrasted with the contrary action of the traitorous disciple ; note the force of ' but yet behold ' in 21. In 22 Lk expresses with more pronounced emphasis than Mt and Mk the divine preordination of events, though 22*b* insists that the crime of Judas is contrary to the will of God.

d 24-38 Last Discourse to the Apostles—It begins with a dispute among the followers of Jesus (strangely shocking in such circumstances) which Mk and Mt have given much earlier, Mk 10:41-45 ; Mt 20:24-28, after the request of the Sons of Zebedee, where it seems in place. But it is not impossible that such a dispute occurred now, stirred up perhaps by our Lord's recent reference to the Kingdom of God. **25.** ' They that have *authority* over them [the Gentiles] are called ' beneficent ', εὐεργέται. The final word gives a strong touch of reality to the scene ; εὐεργέτης was a title assumed by more than one of the ancient rulers, including the Roman Emperors ; particularly Ptolemy Euergetes (145-117 B.C.) was infamous for his cruel despotism in Egypt. **28-32.** Proper to Lk save for 30*b* which is found in Mt 19:28. Here Jesus renews his accustomed teaching which re-echoes the note of the Magnificat and the Beatitudes. His disciples, by their faithful adherence to him right up to the end, have shared his lowly condition and the trials of his life, such as the enmity of the Jewish leaders, rejection by the heads of the nation, poverty, etc (*cf.* 9:57-62). Therefore they shall share his **e** reign, βασιλεία, kingship. To Peter a special pro-

mise of sharing the prerogatives of his Master is **768e** now given, a promise that appears with all the more significance in that it is joined to a prediction about his fall ; the weak one is to serve as the buttress of his brethren, not through his own native power but through that which is bestowed on him by Christ. It is of importance to note the different number (sing. and pl.) in the use of the second personal pronouns of 31-32. **31.** ' Satan hath *demanded* ', recalling Job 1:11-12. The action of ' sifting ' is not here meant as a means of distinguishing the good from the bad, but rather as a violent shaking and disturbance such as is used when wheat is sifted from the chaff. It is the overthrow and ruin of the Apostles that Satan seeks. If our Lord prays specially for Peter, we need not conclude that he is weaker than the others (despite his later fall) ; it is because more is to depend upon him, as the head, than upon the rest, *viz.* the solid faith of his brethren. He is to serve as the rock of strength for others in his office as head. Clearly the passage, proper to Lk, supposes what Mt has recorded in 16:17-19, omitted by Lk. The faith of Peter is such as Lk has already described in 5:20 ; 7:9 ; 8:25, etc. namely, that Jesus is the Messias, the Son of God ; nor was this denied by Peter later in 57-60. **32b.** ' And thou, *having then* [in the future] *returned*, make firm thy brethren ' ; for the notion of returning in the biblical sense, *i.e.* to God, *cf.* 1:16, 17 (Mal 4:4) ; Ac 9:35 ; 11:21 ; 14:15, etc. **33-34.** All four **f** evangelists record this ; Lk agrees with Jn as to its place, but Mk and Mt put it on the way to Gethsemani. **35-38.** Proper to Lk. The apparent contradiction of our Lord's former and later teaching (10:4 ff. ; 22:49-51, *cf.* Mt 26:52) must be explained in this way : he now wishes to impress upon them that although the principles of his teaching have not altered, nevertheless the times have changed. They are about to enter on a situation of the utmost gravity and danger. Compare the advice concerning the way they are to act in 17:22 ff. ; 21:8 ff. When he first sent them out it was with the counsel to depend on the goodwill of their hearers for their needs ; now there will be no longer goodwill but hatred for his sake. In fact they will be Ishmaels, like men who have no friends and can obtain even the bare necessities of life only by violence ; that is the meaning of ' he that hath not (a sword) let him sell his coat and buy one ', a proverbial expression, not that he recommends such a measure to his disciples (*cf.* 12:22). This furnishes the meaning of his answer to their simplicity in 38 : ' It is enough '. He does not mean that two swords are enough for their protection, but, seeing that they have not understood him, he says with a smile, ' That would be enough for what I meant '. Some think, less probably, that he answers abruptly to change the subject which they have misunderstood : ' Enough of that '. **37.** In confirmation of the advice in 36 ; the quotation is from Is 53 which deals with the Suffering Servant of Yahweh. Jesus envisages his speedy death : ' the things *that have to do with me are coming to their completion* '. He has frequently warned his disciples that the servant must not expect to fare better than the master.

39-46 The Agony at Gethsemani—(Mt 26:30, 36-46 ; **76** Mk 14:26, 32-42). After commencing like Mt and Mk, Lk omits their account of the scandal and flight of the Apostles ; he omits also our Lord's promise of a future meeting in Galilee. In the latter omission he is consistent with his plan of dealing only with the apparitions at Jerusalem. The protestations of fidelity made by Peter and the prediction of his fall have already been mentioned, 33-34 ; Lk does not return to the subject. He abbreviates as usual, omitting to mention the choice of Peter, James and John, the name of the garden, the threefold repetition of Christ's prayers and the failure of the Apostles to keep awake. If he passes over Mk's vivid description of the signs of human weakness in our Lord, Mk 14:33*b*-35, he emphasizes the agony and its material

a effects. Characteristically he draws attention to the earnestness of the prayer : ἐκτενέστερον signifies rather strained effort than prolongation as in DV. **b** **43.** The angelic apparition is proper to Lk ; he omitted the angelic apparitions found in Mk and Mt at the end of the former temptation in the desert ; 4:13 ; Mk 1:13 ; Mt 4:11. Lk alone mentions the agony and sweat of blood, 44. The agony, *i.e.* contest, striving, mental anguish, was evidently the struggle (or its effect) between the sensitive appetite in our Lord which naturally shrank from suffering and death, and the superior will which voluntarily accepted the divine decree : a struggle which is expressed in the prayer of 42. ' His sweat became like *clots* of blood *falling* upon the ground '. Lk says ' like clots of blood ', but an actual sweat of blood seems indicated. A similar phenomenon, betraying extremes of pain and mental anguish, is not unknown in the annals of medicine (Hobart, *Medical Language of St Luke*, 83). The authenticity of 43-44 is much attacked because of its omission in many MSS. But there is good MS evidence for authenticity (א and D, all uncial and cursive MSS and anc. Lat.), the style is Lucan, and none of the Fathers expressed doubts. The omission, particularly in MSS of the Egyptian family, points to suppression on account of theological scruples. The text was commonly used in the 2nd cent. against the Docetists and in the 4th by those who denied the divinity of Christ. **46.** The reproach is addressed to all, not to Peter alone as in Mk and Mt.

c **47-53 The Arrest of Jesus**—Abbreviated account of Mk 14:43-52 ; Mt 26:47-56 ; *cf*. Jn 18:2-11. One or two additions : the protest against the traitorous kiss, 48, which is very characteristic ; the disciples' question about the use of the swords already mentioned, 49 ; the healing of the man's ear, 53 ; the description of the enemy, ' high-priests, *temple-police* (στρατηγοί) and *seniors* ', indicating a delegation from the Sanhedrin, 52 ; the characteristic conclusion in 53*b* ; *cf*. 22:3, 31, 37 ; Col 1:13. The flight of the Apostles is passed over in silence. **51a.** Several opinions : either meaning ' Go no further ' or ' Let them take me ', the latter being the more probable. There is a further suggestion that our Lord is asking the bystanders to give way so that he may heal the injured man : ' Let me get at him ' ; and still another that the remark is addressed to the enemy asking them to excuse the hasty action of the offending disciple.

d **54-71 The Trial of Jesus by the Jews**—Again as in Mk 14:53-72 ; Mt 26:57-75 (*cf*. Jn 18:13-27) with changes of order, omissions and additions. The Jewish leaders wish to procure a condemnation on the ground of revolutionary Messianic claims which will provide a reason for handing Jesus over to the Roman governor for execution. Mk and Mt give two meetings of the Sanhedrin, one in the night, the other on the morning of Friday ; Lk mentions only the second, as usual simplifying and omitting details not necessary to his main purpose. He is concerned to show how Jesus still dominates the whole situation in spite of all appearances to the contrary ; *cf*. 48, 51, 53*b*, 61, 69. God's design is being worked out with the complete agreement of our Lord, a thing that puts the prayer and agony at Gethsemani into proper perspective. **54.** Agreeing with Mk in describing the arrest and Peter's following Jesus, Lk here repeats to complete the story of the Apostle and thus anticipates the order of Mk (*cf*. 3:19 ff.). It will be observed that he spares Peter as far as is reconcilable with the truth. The differences of the four evangelists in recording the denials are not of sufficient weight to alter the tradition of a triple denial ; it may easily be supposed that Peter uttered several denials to each of his three questioners. Lagr., *S. Marc* (1911) 380 ff. **e** **61a.** This touching and significant detail is recorded by Lk alone. **70.** The Sanhedrin, in accordance with their plan, demand if Jesus be the Christ (66 ; but note the additions to the question in Mk 14:61*b* and Mt 26:63*b*) ; he refuses to discuss the point with them

(67–68, proper to Lk) but tells them more than they **769e** ask for by his quotation from the Scriptures ; *cf*. Ps 109:1, and Dan 7:13. This they seize on immediately in the question of 70, to which our Lord replies openly. They now have evidence to condemn him for blasphemy, but they have not secured the condemnation which would be more useful for handing Jesus over to the governor as a Messianic revolutionary. Lk has thus brought things to the conclusion he desires, with a clear affirmation from our Lord of his Divine Sonship resulting in his condemnation by the Jewish authorities. The condemnation he leaves the reader to infer, unless it be said that he wishes to be historically accurate and so abstains from crediting the Sanhedrin with something they had no real power to do : only the Roman governor had the power of life and death.

XXIII 1-5 Jesus is handed over to Pilate—(Mt 27:2 ; **770a** Mk 15:1-5 ; *cf*. Jn 18:28-38). Lk omits the long account in Mt and Mk of the evidence brought by the false witnesses. In the remainder of the Passion narrative he shows more signs of having drawn on sources of his own. His omissions are accounted for by the reasons already mentioned : avoidance of details difficult for a non-Jewish reader, *e.g.* the Aramaic cry from the cross which caused the hearers to think Jesus was calling on Elias ; the custom of demanding the release of a prisoner at the Pasch ; the mockery concerning the destruction of the temple, about which Lk has been silent during the trial. Apart from such details he gives all that Mk contains, and none of Mt's additions to Mk, such as the fate of Judas, Pilate's wife, the earthquake and resurrection of the dead. His most important additions are : the sending of Jesus to Herod, Pilate's protest before the Jews, 13–16, the lamentations of the women of Jerusalem, the prayers of Jesus in 34 and 46, the incident of the Good Thief. His insistence on Pilate's assertions of our Lord's innocence leads some to conclude that Lk tries as much as possible to exculpate the Roman authorities and thus prepares for his description of their accommodating attitude towards the Church in Ac ; but note the callousness of Pilate recorded in 16 and 22. Lk goes to no trouble, however, to spare the Jewish leaders ; the accusation they bring against Jesus, 2, after the conclusion of the trial in 22:71 pillories them as men without scruple.

6-16 Jesus before Herod—The Herod in question is **b** Herod Antipas (son of Herod the Great by Malthace the Samaritan) tetrarch of Galilee since 4 B.C. As the Herod family passed as Jews, doubtless Antipas was in Jerusalem for the paschal feast. This incident, proper to Lk, agrees with what he alone records of Herod in 9:7 ; *cf*. 23:8. We gather the impression here that Pilate, something like Gallio in Ac 18:12 ff., merely sees an opportunity of freeing himself from an embarrassing situation ; let Herod deal with the man since he belongs to Herod's jurisdiction. **9.** Jesus refuses to answer ; ' truth is of no profit to those who are not sincere ' (Lagrange) ; he had already called Herod a fox ; 13:31-32. **11.** Herod's answer is to treat our Lord as a fool of no account : ' with his *band of soldiers* he set him at nought and mocked him, putting on him a *fine* garment ' ; λαμπρός means rather ' shining ' and ' splendid ' than white (*cf*. 16:19). It was all part of the effort to show up Jesus' alleged claim to royalty as something not worth serious consideration, like the similar incident in Pilate's hall omitted by Lk.

17-25 Release of Barabbas—(Mt 27:15-23 ; Mk **c** 15:6-15). It is generally agreed that 17 is a gloss added from Mt 27:15 to explain the sudden introduction of Barabbas in 18. Lk explains who Barabbas is in 25 with proper comments of his own showing the contrast between Barabbas and Jesus ; *cf*. Ac 3:14-15. Barabbas was probably in prison for the very offence of which our Lord was accused by the Jews in 2, *i.e.* revolt against Roman authority.

26-32 The Way of the Cross—Omitting all reference **d** to the scourging and mockery by Pilate's guard, Lk

770d joins Mk and Mt in relating the incident of Simon of Cyrene. Grammatically he makes the Jews lead Jesus out for execution, a fact that leads to the suggestion that he seeks to exculpate the Romans in order to render his Gospel more acceptable to Gentile readers ; but the suggestion takes no account of 26 and 47. The women of Jerusalem may be those charitable Jewish ladies who undertook the duty of attending to the last needs of condemned criminals, a thing that would naturally appeal to the heart of our Lord. The Talmud (*cf.* B. Sanhedrin 43*a*) tells us that one of the cares of these pious women was to provide spiced wine for the dying men ; *cf.* Mk 15:23. In 28–29 there is strong reminiscence of the predictions of 21:23. **30.** Here as in 29 the words of our Lord echo the thoughts of the Prophets in whose language he so often spoke ; *cf.* Is 54:1 ; Os 10:8 ; 9:14. The perspective is still that of the ruin of Jerusalem, God's punishment of the city for the crime it is about to commit. **31.** A parable picturing a man so set on kindling a fire that instead of seeking dry sticks he uses green and damp wood ; its application is to the present circumstances : seeing that to all appearances divine justice now falls on an innocent person, how will it be when the turn of the guilty comes ? Perhaps there is recollection of Ez 20:47. *Cf.* Prov 12:31 ; 1 Pet 4:17–18.

771a 33–38 The Crucifixion—(Mt 27:33–38 ; Mk 15:22–27 ; *cf.* Jn 19:17–27). **33.** 'When they were come to the place called *Cranium*' (Κρανίον, skull). Lk omits the Aramaic *Golgotha* given as Γολγοθά by Mt and Mk. DV has followed Vg which has turned Κρανίον into the Latin equivalent *Calvarium*. The place of public execution was a rocky eminence ; such places are still given the name *ras* or head by the Arabs. **34a.** Proper to Lk ; its authenticity is disputed on account of omission by many good MSS, but the weight of probability is in its favour ; *cf.* Ac 7:59. Of whom is Jesus thinking ? The Romans ? The soldiers, who are Gentiles ? The Jews ? If the Jews, it would seem that the leaders of the people could not be included, in view of 35 where Lk clearly distinguishes ' the people ' and ' the rulers ' (omit ' with them ' after rulers). The people stand beholding ; the rulers stand mocking. Lk here omits the detailed insults relative to the temple, having omitted all reference to accusations about the destruction of the temple during the trial. He joins Mt and Mk in recording the mocking invitation to our Lord to save himself ' if he be the Christ, the *chosen one* of God ' ; in Mk ' the Christ, the King of Israel ' ; in Mt ' King of Israel '. **36.** The drink offered to our Lord by the soldiers in their rude mockery, vinegar in DV, is ὄξος, the sour wine that was the common drink of the poorer classes ; in Mk this is not given until near the end, 15:36, while Mk earlier mentions the offering of spiced wine, 15:23. This is merely another example of Lk's manner of abbreviating and need create no difficulties for a reasonable exegesis. A further example of his manner is in 38 which he has left till now (before the crucifixion in Mk) where it explains the mocking remark of 37.

b 39–43 The Two Thieves—(*Cf.* Mt 27:44 ; Mk 15:32*b*). Lk alone distinguishes the thieves ; according to Mk and Mt both join in insulting Jesus. St Chrysostom reconciles the two accounts by supposing that the Good Thief began by insults and was later converted ; Augustine prefers the more likely solution that Mk and Mt are speaking in general terms as Lk does when he says that ' the soldiers ' offered Jesus sour wine to drink. **39*b*.** ' Thou art the Christ, *art thou not* ? (Then) save thyself and us (too) ' ; not a confession of faith, but a further example of mockery. **40.** What does the Good Thief wish to say ? According to some, ' Dost thou not even fear God seeing that thou art under the same sentence (as we, *i.e.* the Good Thief and Christ) and wilt shortly appear before him ? ' Or better, ' Thou hast not even the fear of God (in thus allowing thyself to attack him in this fashion) seeing that thou art under the same sentence. But thou and I (suffer) justly, for we are only receiving what we have earned,

while this man has done nothing out of place (ἄτοπον) '. **771** The Good Thief associates himself and his companion with Jesus in the same ' judgement ', κρίμα. It is possible that the two thieves along with Barabbas had belonged to one of those bands of Jewish brigands (their attitude proves they were Jews) which flourished at this period, and whose real motive was rebellion against Roman domination ; *cf.* Jos., *Ant.* 17, 10, 8 ; 18, 1, 1. This was the crime of which our Lord was accused, 23:2 ; *cf.* 23:19 for Barabbas and his crime of sedition. Perhaps that is the reason why they are all executed together, the two thieves being hurried to their death through the sudden climax in the plot against Jesus, when they doubtless had hoped for the good fortune Barabbas had met with, Lk 23:42–43. Far from demanding the miracle of an immediate descent from the Cross, the Good Thief asks no more than that Jesus will not forget him when he comes as Messias in the glory of his kingdom. Jesus rewards his act of faith and hope by the promise that he will that very day make him to be with him in perfect bliss. In the apocryphal gospels the Good Thief is called Dismas. [' Paradise ' (LXX rendering of ' Garden ' in Eden, Gen 2:18) signified for the Jews the abode of the blessed. Here, if taken literally in its context, it signifies primarily the limbo of the just, to which Christ's soul was presently to descend.—J.B.O.]

44–49 Death of Jesus—(Mt 27:45–56 ; Mk 15:33–41). **772** Note the following additions in Lk to the narrative of Mk and Mt which he has abbreviated : the failing of the sun, 45, the prayer with which Jesus gives up the ghost, 46, and the emotion of the crowd, 48. The cry of dereliction from the cross is passed over, also the opening of the tombs (proper to Mt) and the enumeration of the Holy Women given by Mk and Mt. He anticipates the rending of the veil of the temple, but that is characteristic of his fashion of grouping together events of a like nature. His omission of the cry of dereliction may well be due to consideration for the susceptibility of the Gentile convert, who will not immediately understand that our Lord is praying very fittingly with all the thoughts of Ps 21 and not merely those of the opening words. For this cry Lk substitutes other words from Ps 30:6 ; ' Into thy hands I *commit* my spirit ', which would leave a very different impression on the mind of a raw Gentile convert. παρατίθεσθαι (commend) means ' to deposit, give into the care of, bring forward ' ; *cf.* Jn 10:17–18. **47.** Lk **b** differs from Mk and Mt in recording the words of the centurion in charge of the execution squad ; he makes the centurion call Jesus ' a just man ', not ' a son of God '. Augustine says they both mean the same thing, taking ' son of God ' in its wide sense. Possibly Lk, realizing how equivocal the phrase ' son of God ' could be in the mouth of a pagan, deliberately avoided its use. **48.** ' Lk has shown us the crowd first enthusiastic for the death of Jesus, then aghast, 35. Such goodness, such self-forgetfulness in the midst of pain, joined with his readiness to forgive and his piety, nature herself suffering in sympathy with his Passion—the whole spectacle brings about a complete change in the volatile crowd. It is a piece of subtle psychological description ' (Lagr., *S. Luc* 593).

50–56 Burial of Jesus—(Mt 27:57–61 ; Mk 15:42–47 ; **c** *cf.* Jn 19:38–42). Lk's more lengthy description of Joseph recalls the pious group with which he opens his Gospel : a morally good man, a faithful observer of the Law, one of those who look for the redemption of Israel in the true spirit of the Scriptures. The attention here to topographical detail is surprising until we remember 1:1–4 ; Mt adds that Joseph was a disciple of Jesus. He was also a member of the Sanhedrin and had voted against the condemnation of Jesus, or at least had absented himself from the session. Jn 19:38–39 associates him with Nicodemus, another Sanhedrite, Jn 7:50. **53.** Lk insists, with the aid of three negatives in Greek, that the tomb had never been defiled by the presence of another corpse, as though wishing to contrast the reverence of the disciples with the opposite attitude

e of our Lord's enemies. **54b.** 'The Sabbath *began to dawn*', ἐπέφωσκεν 'was shining'; a curious phrase because it was still the Parasceve, which did not end until sunset on the Friday when according to Jewish reckoning the Sabbath commenced. It is suggested that Lk is referring to the common Jewish custom, well-known among their Gentile neighbours, of lighting lamps as soon as the Sabbath began.

a XXIV 1-53 The Resurrection and Ascension—'Each of the four evangelists relates in his own way how the tomb of Jesus was found empty, to the great astonishment of Christ's friends. Mt and Mk are the most alike. Lk is usually closer to Mk. As for Jn, he goes his own way but is in agreement with Mk concerning the search made by St Peter. The difficulty of harmonizing the four accounts has been greatly exaggerated. Nothing is more simple provided we do not stick at unimportant details, provided also we pay attention to the way in which each Gospel was composed'. (Lagr., GJC II 283). The main difference between Lk and the other Synoptists is that he omits the appearances of Jesus in Galilee, confining himself to those in the neighbourhood of Jerusalem; but it is unbelievable that he was ignorant of the former, recorded by Mt, Lk and Jn. We have to recall once more what was Lk's aim, remembering that he differs greatly from Mt and Mk in showing that the ministry of Jesus was by no means confined to Galilee. Throughout his Gospel it is clear that Lk has his eyes fixed on Jerusalem, whither the ministry inevitably leads by the design of Providence and according to the prediction of Scripture, 13:33. In his 'second treatise' he will show how the Gospel message spreads from Jerusalem throughout the Roman world until it finally reaches Rome, the centre of the Gentile world. With this in view, there was no special need for his purpose to add details about the appearances in Galilee once he had demonstrated the truth of the Resurrection by means of the appearances at Jerusalem. He has a thesis, and we have seen how much he dislikes multiplying details and incidents of a similar character once his object is attained.

1-12 The Empty Tomb—(Mt 28:1-10; Mk 16:1-8; *cf.* Jn 20 1-18). The general lines of Mk's story are followed with the differences to be noted. The chapter-division here breaks into the sequence of the narrative; this section should begin at 23:55. We have seen that Lk omits to join Mk and Mt in the enumeration of the Holy Women; with his usual foresight he leaves that until the moment when they are to give their testimony of the Resurrection to the Apostles and the disciples, (9-10), when he substitutes the name of Joanna (*cf.* 8:3) for that of Salome in Mk 15:40. He is not interested in the problem of rolling back the heavy stone; it is sufficient for his purpose to say that it was found removed; he adds that on entering the women saw the body of Jesus was gone. That is the main fact which Mt and Mk leave to be understood while they concentrate on the angelic apparition. Instead of Mk's 'young man' and Mt's 'angel of Yahweh', two men appear suddenly, ἐπέστησαν (*cf.* 2:9; Ac 12:7; 23:11 for similar description of supernatural apparitions) who both speak. **3.** 'The Lord Jesus'; first and only appearance of this title in the Gospels, of common use in Acts and Epistles. **6.** Galilee is introduced, as in Mk, but with a different purpose; here it serves merely as a stepping-stone to Jerusalem, from now the centre **e** of the Gospel. **9.** Difficult to reconcile this with Mk 16:8 where the women flee in terror without saying a word of the incident, contrary to Mt 28:8. The explanation may well lie in the fact that there is a clear break in Mk 16:8 (the sentence is not complete) and we are so far ignorant of how the original Mk continued. In view of what is known from the other Gospels, we may surmise that the women recovered from their natural fright in time to hand on the message in the way that Lk describes. **10.** The lack of agreement about the number and the names of the women is a difficulty only for those who wish the Gospel to be a full and exact account of all the details; but human **773c** documents are not written in that way. Here as elsewhere, the thing to be noted is the remarkable independence shown by Lk where he could have copied Mk slavishly had he wished. The discrepancies, far from casting doubt on the reality of the facts, are on the contrary strong arguments in their favour (*cf.* Lagr., GJC I xi ff.). **12.** Some critics wish to eliminate this as a gloss from Jn 20:3–10; there are verbal resemblances with Jn 20:5 and the verse is wanting in certain of the ancient versions. But MS authority guarantees its authenticity; moreover it comes well in Lk after 11, serving to distinguish Peter from the incredulous attitude of the rest. Peter's conclusion from the situation of the grave-clothes is that the body has not been stolen. Thieves would not have stayed to unwrap the corpse. A more complete description in Jn 20:6-7.

13-35 Apparition on the Way to Emmaus—Proper to **774a** Lk except for a brief summary in Mk 16:12. Lk alone records the share taken by a larger group of disciples in the ministry of Jesus; here the same group plays its part in the important task of witnessing to the Resurrection (*cf.* Ac 1:21–22). These two are of those mentioned in 9 but not Apostles; *cf.* 33. They are not obeying the instruction to go to Galilee, Mk 16:7; Mt 28:7, and there meet the risen Jesus; they are going in the totally different direction of Emmaus, lying W. of Jerusalem, and the sequel leads to the conclusion that their faith is shattered. The site of Emmaus is a matter of much dispute on account of the division of the MSS between the readings 60 or 160 furlongs σταδίοι; *cf.* § 82c. Nearly a dozen places have been suggested, but only the following three are now considered: the modern Amwas, lying about 20 m. W. of Jerusalem, which still retains the ancient name though it was called Nicopolis during the 3rd cent. A.D.; Koliniyeh, about 5 m. west, claimed to be the Emmaus mentioned by Josephus, *B.J.* 7, 6, 6; El Kubeibeh, about 7 m. west. The first is the traditional site, though the majority of MSS give 60 σταδίοι and the longer distance seems difficult to reconcile with the Gospel story of the quick return of the two disciples. El Kubeibeh is almost exactly 60 σταδίοι, but its claim to be the site cannot be traced back beyond the time of the Crusades. **16.** Failure to **b** recognize Jesus may have been due to divine intervention, or possibly because of the characteristics of the glorified body; *cf.* Mk 16:12; Jn 20:14; 21:4. **18.** Another, or possibly the same Cleophas, written Κλωπᾶς in Jn 19:25. Much speculation about the other disciple; Origen says he was Simon Peter (*cf.* 34), while some have thought it was Lk himself, perhaps because of the old and improbable tradition that he was one of the Seventy-Two. **19-21.** An excellent summary of the effects of Jesus's ministry on the different classes: the people, the Jewish leaders, the disciples. **21b.** This and the following verse give the impression that they had waited till the third day to see whether Jesus would fulfil his promise of resurrection, and were disappointed. The argument of 22–24 seems to be this: If the women saw the angels, why did not the men-folk see them, the Apostles being so much the more important than the women? And if Jesus had really risen why had he not shown himself? **25.** The reproach is directed against their want of intelligence; ἀνόητοι, *cf.* Gal 3:1. They are like the Jews who have read in the Prophets only the pleasant and glorious things about the Messias; but they must believe 'all', the pleasant and the unpleasant. Our Lord proceeds to give them a lesson in exegesis from 'Moses and all the Prophets', reminding us of the presence of Moses and Elias at the Transfiguration and the subject of their talk with Jesus; 9:30-31. The important thing is to welcome the Messias preordained by divine decree, not the Messias of their grandiose dreams. **29.** 'Far spent' is too strong; the day **c** (*i.e.* the sun) begins to decline from midday. **30.** Augustine interprets the action of Jesus as the celebration of the Eucharist and many follow him; but

774c modern Catholic exegesis tends to favour the contrary opinion. The key seems to be in 35. ' The breaking of bread ' seems to have been an accepted term for the Eucharist : Ac 2:42 ; 20:7 ; 1 Cor 10:16. Some hold that it is the miracles of the multiplication of bread that are envisaged here (*cf.* 9:16) especially as Lk does not make our Lord celebrate the Eucharist with his Apostles at his later appearance the same evening, when, 41–43, it is an ordinary meal that he partakes with them ; but it must be observed that the later eating is intended for a very different purpose. Another opinion is that the disciples recognized Jesus merely from his characteristic way of breaking bread while eating, perhaps with a blessing. Or did they now notice the marks of the nails ? **33.** In Jn 20:24 only ten of the Apostles were present at this first appearance ; but ' the Eleven ' had become a general term, like ' the Twelve ' previously. **34.** ' Saying ' ; grammatically agreeing with the Eleven and the rest, though another reading (with little authority) makes it agree with ' they ', *i.e.* the two disciples ; hence Origen's opinion that the companion of Cleophas was Simon Peter. Confirmation of 34 in 1 Cor 15:5.

d 36-43 Appearance at Jerusalem—*Cf.* Jn 20:19–23. ' It is I : fear not ' is a gloss ; perhaps also ' Peace be to you ' has been added from Jn 20:19, 21, though there is good MS authority for the latter. **37.** This may seem strange after the foregoing, but Lk always insists on the natural fear that results from a supernatural manifestation, 1:12 ; 2:9 ; 4:36 ; 5:10, etc. **42.** ' and a honeycomb ', probably a gloss. Our Lord retained the imprint of the five wounds in his glorified body as a proof of his identity and also as a sign of his triumph over death. His glorified body retained all its physical reality, including its tangibility and its normal organs, as is shown by his eating the proferred food. On the qualities of the risen body, *cf.* 1 Cor 15 *passim.*

775a 44-49 Last Instructions—These last words of Jesus, proper to Lk, demonstrate the consistency of the writer and justify the claim with which he began, that he would set down all things ' in order ' : not a chronological, but a logical order which would show the enchainment of the events described. From the beginning he insists on the fulfilment of the divine plan in the life of Jesus ; he ends on that note. Hence these final instructions weld together the past, *i.e.* the Scriptures, with the future, *i.e.* the mission of the Apostles, in the person of Jesus. The sending out of the Apostles is put by Mt at the post-Resurrection reunion in Galilee

(in Jerusalem apparently by Jn 20:21) ; but these **775** concluding verses of Lk furnish us with a final example of his manner of composition : he arranges his material with more concern about the sequence of ideas than about time and place. But for that we might imagine that this instruction and the Resurrection, and even the Ascension, all took place on the same day. It is to be borne in mind also that Lk, careful writer as he is, already knew what he was to write in his further treatise ; there these events are put into their proper perspective, Ac 1:1–10. **44.** ' Words ' means here **b** events rather than the things about to be spoken of, *i.e.* ' fulfilled words '. What follows is a repetition of the instruction given to the disciples at Emmaus, 19–27. ' Here Christ reveals the meaning of Scripture (*cf.* Rom 10:4) : first with regard to Christ himself, secondly with respect to the work to be accomplished in his name by others. . . . It is Christ's part to suffer, but as the Christ he must rise again. . . . The victorious Christ to whom God had promised the nations for his inheritance almost disappears from the scene of this world ; but if the nations are to be invited to repentance in his name, it is because they are to obtain pardon through his sufferings ' (Lagr., *S. Luc* 614). **47.** With the mention of ' penance *unto* the remission of sins ' Lk has very fittingly brought us back to the beginning of his Gospel ; *cf.* 1:17, 77 ; 3:3. **49.** Written with a view to Ac 2:1–4 ; *cf.* Ac 1:4 ; 2:33. ' Power from on high ' recalls ' the power of the most high ' in 1:35 ; God himself is the chief operating agent in either case, for all has to do with the same object.

50-53 The Ascension—*Cf.* Mk 16:19–20. The way **c** in which Lk here abbreviates the history of the forty days after the Resurrection is characteristic, and perhaps an indication of the fact that he intends to return to the subject. **50.** ' He led them out *towards* Bethany ' ; in Ac 1:12 he led them a Sabbath day's journey ; Bethany is twice that distance ; *cf.* Jn 11:18. Hands lifted up to bless in the traditional fashion, Lev 9:22 ; *cf.* Gen 48:14. **51.** ' And was carried up to heaven ' ; words of doubtful authenticity, perhaps added from Ac ; but there is not the slightest doubt about Lk's meaning. He has now carried his Gospel to the point indicated in 9:51. **53.** Omit ' praising ' as a rejected reading of the Gk. The Gospel ends as it began, in the temple. There are still many things to happen before the disciples are forced by circumstances to understand that the paths of the Church and Synagogue lie in different directions.

THE GOSPEL OF JESUS CHRIST ACCORDING TO
ST JOHN

By W. LEONARD

a Bibliography—(*a*) **Introduction :** L. Baunard[7] (1907) ; L. Fillion (1908) ; C. Fouard[5] (1908) ; L. Pirot (1923) ; C. Martindale (2 vols., 1920–3) ; A. Camerlynck, *De IV Evangelii auctore* (1899) ; M. Lepin, *L'origine du quatrième Evangile* (1907) ; *id.*, *La valeur historique du quatrième Evangile* (2 vols., 1910) ; E. Jacquier[6], Tome 4, *Les Ecrits Johanniques* (1928) ; J. Huby, *L'Evangile et les Evangiles* (1929) ; E. B. Allo, art. *Jean* (*Evangile de Saint*) DBV(S) 815–43; G. Bardy, art. *Jean le Presbytre*, DBV(S) 843–7 ; J. Chapman, *John the Presbyter and the Fourth Gospel* (1911) ; J. Donovan, *The Authorship of the Fourth Gospel* (1935) ; *W. Sanday, *Authorship and Historical Character* (1872), *id.*, *The Criticism of the Fourth Gospel* (1905) ; *T. Zahn, *Einleitung in das N.T.* (Vol. 3, 1899) ; *W. Temple, *Readings in St John's Gospel* ; *E. F. Scott, *The Fourth Gospel* (1910) ; *C. F. Burney, *The Aramaic Origin* (1922) ; *V. H. Stanton, *The Gospels as Historical Documents*, 1920 ; F.R. Hoare, *The Original Order and Chapters of St John's Gospel*, 1944 ; E. Ruckstuhl, *Die Literarische Einheit des Johannesevangeliums*, Fribourg 1951. (*b*) **Commentaries :** Origen (extant only in part, PG 14, 21–829) ; Chrysostom (PG 59, 23–482) ; Cyr. Alex. (PG 73 and 74, 9–756) ; Augustine, 124 *Tractatus* (PL 35, 1379–1976) ; Bede (PL 92, 635–938) ; Aquinas, Vol. 2, Marietti ed. of Gospel Commentaries (1912) ; Bonaventure (ed. Quaracchi, Vol. 6) ; F. Toletus (1588) ; J. Maldonatus (1595) ; F. X. Patrizi (1857) ; V. Corluy (1889) ; J. Knabenbauer[2] (CSS, 1906) ; J. MacRory[3] (1908) ; J. Calmes (1905) ; M.-J. Lagrange (EB 1924) ; A. Durand (VS 1927) ; F. Tillmann[4] (BB 1931) ; W. S. Reilly (WV 1929) ; F. M. Braun[2] (Sainte Bible 1946) ; Vosté, *Studia Joannea* (1930) ; J.-B. Bossuet, *Méditations . . . La Cène* ; V. Huby, *Discours après la Cène* (1932) ; *R. H. Strachan, *The Fourth Gospel, its Significance and Environment*, 1947[3] ; *B. F. Westcott (1908) ; *J. H. Bernard (ICC, 1928) ; *A. Plummer[10] (1913) ; *F. Büchsel in *Das N.T. Deutsch*, 1937[3]. (*c*) **Theology :** There is no systematic Theology of St John by a Catholic author (small fragments of P. Prat's contemplated work are given in monograph by Calès, 1942), but Johannine doctrine is set forth by J. Tixeront, *Théologie Antenicéenne*[7] (1915), J. Lebreton, *Dogme de la Trinité*[8] (1927), and Huby-Rousselot in *Christus* (Manuel d'histoire des religions, 1044–54). Systematic presentation will be found in several non-Catholic ' Theologies of the N.T. ', *e.g.* *G. B. Stevens (1901). For fuller bibliographies, see Höpfl-Gut, *Introductio in N.T.* (1938), and Steinmueller (*Companion to Scripture Studies*, Vol. 3, 1943) ; and for recent works only, Menoud, *L'Evangile de Jean d'après les recherches récentes*, Neuchâtel-Paris 1943.

b Introduction—The Fourth Gospel has always been regarded as touching the highest peak of Christian revelation, and for this reason John the Apostle, its traditional author, is described as 'the divine' and is designated by the eagle that soars high into the heavens. St Jerome wrote that John ' filled to the full with revelation, indited the heaven-sent preface " In the beginning was the Word. . . ." ', *Prol.* to *Comm. in Mt.* Indeed it was the unique sublimity of the ' prologue ' to St John's Gospel, 1:1–14, that eventually gained it a permanent place in the Mass as ' Last Gospel '. Though it has always been regarded

as canonical (see § 776*c*) nevertheless the startling **776b** character of its teaching and style has raised doubts in modern times as to its historical reliability, on which see §§ 779*b*–780*g*.

Canonicity—That Jn has always been regarded as **c** inspired and canonical Scripture hardly requires proof. It is to be found in the best Greek uncial codices of the 4th to 6th cent. (B, S, A, D, C, W) and considerable portions of it appear in many other uncials. The great mass (over 600) of cursives have it. The Egerton Papyrus (early 2nd cent.) contains parts of it mixed with synoptic texts for popular use, showing that at that early date it was already well known and placed on the same level as the Synoptics ; *cf.* M.-J. Lagrange RB 44 (1935) 343. The Chester Beatty papyrus codex of the early 3rd cent. contains portions of it. Jn is likewise found in all ancient NT versions. Allusions to it and quotations from it are found in many 2nd cent. writings, the *Epistles* of St Ignatius (†115), the *Shepherd of Hermas*, Justin Martyr, the *Odes of Solomon* (early 2nd cent.), perhaps also Polycarp in his letter to the Philippians, *c* A.D. 115. Some presbyters mentioned by Irenaeus (†A.D. 202) explained the ' many mansions,' Jn 14:2. Tatian embodied the Gospel in his *Diatessaron* (A.D. 175). The Montanists made much of the Paraclete passages, Marcion incorporating pieces in his own arbitrary gospel ; Gnostics like Valentine and Ptolemy used it and especially Heracleon who seems to have been the first to write a commentary on this gospel. We may also mention here the fragment of papyrus (*recto* Jn 18:31–32—*verso* Jn 18:37–38) in the Rylands collection Manchester (P 52 Rylands 457) discovered in Egypt and dated about A.D. 130, apparently showing that the Gospel may well have been circulating at that date in that country.

Authorship—If we except the views of the Alogi, **d** obscure 2nd cent. heretics who denied the Johannine authorship, not on historical but on doctrinal grounds, there was never any doubt until modern times, that John, the son of Zebedee and one of the twelve Apostles, wrote the Fourth Gospel. The remarkable differences that exist between the Syn. on the one hand and Jn on the other (see § 778*h*) are claimed by many moderns as militating against the ascription of the latter to one of Christ's disciples. These differences, however, were equally well known to the ancients and nevertheless they regarded the son of Zebedee as author. It is difficult to resist the conclusion that a cogent reason for the modern denial is, or at least was, the clear and even startling portrayal in Jn of the divine sonship of Christ. If it could be shown that the gospel was not in fact written by one of our Lord's immediate followers, but by a Christian of later date, the force of the historical evidence would be weakened, thus making it easier to deny its claims. It was felt that time must be allowed for the growth of so clear a belief in Christ's divinity as we see illustrated in Jn, and the Tübingen School, for example, assigned to it the date A.D. 160–70. Today, of course, in the light of recent research and manuscript discoveries (*cf.* § 77*b*), it is not possible to date it later than the first quarter of the 2nd cent., and since the traditional date for the gospel is A.D. 100, this motive for denying the Johannine authorship has largely disappeared.

John the Son of Zebedee—John and his elder brother **e**

776e James were sons of Zebedee and Salome. Zebedee, living near the Lake of Genesareth (perhaps at Bethsaida), was a prosperous fisherman, who employed paid helpers. Whether we regard Salome as a sister (cousin) of the Mother of Jesus depends on the way we read Jn 19:26 and combine the text with Mt 27:56 and Mk 15:40. In any case, Salome was one of the Galilean women who followed Jesus with their ministrations. She was present at the crucifixion.

John was probably still in his teens when he placed himself with Andrew in the school of the Precursor. From the friend of the Bridegroom he passed to the company of the Divine Bridegroom himself. Then, as Andrew brought Simon his brother to Jesus, so, it seems, John brought James. In those earliest days of discipleship he saw the miracle of the marriage feast of Cana and remained with Jesus till after the first Pasch of the public life. Later he and James were called from their father's boat to join Peter and Andrew as future fishers of men.

After twelve of the disciples had been chosen as Apostles, the two brothers together with Peter formed a privileged group. Mk notes (from the mouth of Peter) that Christ called the two ' Boanerges ' or ' Sons of thunder ', to mark their ardent temperament, Mk 3:17. The warmth of their personal attachment, no doubt, prompted the ambitious petition which they made one day through their mother for the places of honour beside Christ in his future kingdom, Mt 20:20 ff. ; Mk 10:35 ff. On an earlier occasion it was chiefly John who, through zeal for his Master's honour, forbade a Jewish exorcist to use the name of Jesus in driving out a devil, Mk 9:38, and again he wanted Jesus to call down fire from heaven on an inhospitable Samaritan village, Lk 9:54. The privileged three, Peter, James and John, were the only ones chosen to be witnesses of the raising of the daughter of Jairus, of the Transfiguration, and of the Agony in Gethsemani.

f There is no serious reason to doubt that the anonymous companion of Andrew mentioned in Jn 1:40 was John himself. Likewise it seems certain that the same Apostle is covered by the appellation ' the disciple whom Jesus loved ', otherwise ' this Apostle would remain without mention in the Gospel, an inconceivable omission ', Strachan. ' The disciple whom Jesus loved ' figures at the Supper, which Peter and he had prepared, as reclining on the breast of Jesus and inquiring who was the traitor, as standing by the cross and receiving the guardianship of the Blessed Virgin, as running with Peter to the tomb on the Sunday of the resurrection, as recognizing the Lord from the boat the morning he appeared on the shore of Lake Tiberias. He is the one whose destiny Peter tried to learn, when he had been told of his own future martyrdom.

All things considered, and in spite of Ac 4:13, it seems difficult not to identify John with that disciple known to the high-priest, who, after our Lord's arrest, secured Peter's admission to the court of the pontifical residence, Jn 18:15. John's continued association with Peter is emphasized in the early chh of Ac. In fact, the list of Apostles there given shows interestingly how in the Apostolic College the ' Juda ' chosen for primacy and the ' Benjamin ' chosen for special predilection by Jesus were brought together. While Mt and Lk have the order : Peter, Andrew, James, John, Mk the disciple of Peter has Peter, James, John (the sons of thunder) and Andrew. Finally Ac has the arrangement : Peter, John, James, Andrew.

g Peter and John were together at the Beautiful Gate, Ac 3:1, before the Sanhedrin, 4:13, and visited Samaria together, 8:14. Between A.D. 42 and 44 James was put to death at Jerusalem, and Peter, but not John, was arrested. We do not meet John again till A.D. 49, when he was present at the Council of Jerusalem, to which perhaps Paul refers when he mentions John amongst ' the pillars ', Gal 2:9.

As Paul and his disciple Timothy took care of the Church of proconsular Asia till the last years of Paul's **7** life (66-7), it does not seem that John came to Ephesus before A.D. 68. Polycarp who was his disciple (perhaps from the beginning) became a Christian in 69. The tradition recorded by Irenaeus and Polycrates of Ephesus (c 190) supposes that the Apostle spent many years in Asia ; that he was relegated by Domitian to Patmos, where he wrote the Apocalypse, that thence he returned to Ephesus under Nerva (96-8), and (if we trust the Syrian chronographer Elias Bar Sinaja) he died in 104, the seventh year of Trajan (98-117).

Various other things concerning John are narrated by ancient writers : his flight from the bath-house because Cerinthus the heretic was within (Irenaeus), his immersion at Rome in a cauldron of boiling oil (Tertullian), his reclamation of a young brigand (Clem. Al.), his repetition in old age of the precept : ' My little children, love one another ' (Jerome). One anecdote actually furnished a symbol of the Apostle, namely, the serpent escaping from the poisoned cup. ' Chosen by Christ as a virgin John remained a virgin for ever ', a fitting guardian of the Virgin Mother.

External Evidence—The Johannine authorship was in **7** pacific possession until the end of the 18th cent., when the attack was started by the English deist Evanson (1792) and continued by the German rationalist Bretschneider (1820). The traditional authorship has however found many modern supporters among non-Catholics, as for example Westcott, Zahn, Stanton, Drummond, Sanday, Feine and Büchsel. Catholic exegetes are unanimous in affirming the apostolic authorship.

We have only to move backwards from the 4th cent. along the links of the chain of testimony, to realize the strength of the Johannine claim. Eusebius of Caesarea (HE 3, 24) writing perhaps as early as 312 and not later than 323 says summarily : ' Let us indicate the undoubted writings of this Apostle [John]. Surely this Gospel which is read by all the churches under heaven must be the first to receive recognition '. Three-quarters of a century earlier Origen, commenting on Jn, was full of the reverence due to a recognized writing of John, who reclined on the breast of Jesus and received Mary as his mother, apud Euseb. HE 6, 25. And Origen's Master, Clement of Alexandria, in an exegetical work entitled *Hypotyposeis*, cited by Eusebius (HE 6, 14), joins to an account of the origin of Mk the following important testimony : ' But John, last of all, being conscious that the exterior facts (τὰ σωματικά) had been set forth in the (other) Gospels, after he had been urged by his friends and divinely moved by the Spirit, composed a spiritual Gospel (πνευματικὸν . . . εὐαγγέλιον). About the same time (c 200) Tertullian at Carthage urges the authority of all four Evangelists by name against Marcion (Adv. Marc. 4, 2.5).

Passing backwards to the 2nd cent. and to the chief **b** churches of the East and West we have Theophilus, a Mesopotamian by birth and sixth Bishop of Syrian Antioch, naming John as author of our Gospel and numbering him amongst the *pneumatophoroi* or divinely inspired. This was about A.D. 179. A decade later, Polycrates, Bishop of Ephesus, defending the Quartodecimans in a letter to Pope Victor, appeals to the authority of Philip the Apostle and of John the Apostle, whom they follow in the date of the Pasch ' according to the Gospel ' (Eus., HE 3, 31). He certainly refers to the written Gospel of John which seven of his own kinsmen, who were bishops in Asia before him, had also followed. In speaking of John as ' reclining on the breast ' of our Lord, Polycrates clearly refers to Jn 13:23 and identifies the Apostle with the Beloved Disciple.

From the same Asiatic circle and from the school of the venerable Polycarp, Bishop of Smyrna and a disciple of John himself, comes Irenaeus, the Asiatic Bishop of Lyons. Polycarp is the immediate link between Irenaeus and John. Now Irenaeus wrote his famous work *Adversus Haereses* in the pontificate of St Eleutherus (175-89). In this work, at the beginning

b of that very third book which gives the list of Popes down to Eleutherus, Irenaeus adds to his account of Mt, Mk, Lk the following : ' Then John, the disciple of the Lord, who had even rested on his breast, himself also published the Gospel, while he was living at Ephesus in Asia '. The Muratorian fragment (*c* A.D. 170) shows that Rome at the same time also held the Johannine authorship ; see § 17*g*.

c It seems, however, that we can invoke even more ancient explicit testimony, though scarcely more authoritative than that of Irenaeus. According to two Prologues prior to the so-called *Monarchian Prologues*, and found in several Latin MSS of the Bible, notably in *Vat. Reginensis* 14 and *Toletanus*, Papias of Hierapolis is a disciple of John the Apostle, and bears witness to the Johannine authorship, saying that ' the Apostle John wrote it against heretics at the request of many bishops '. The value of this is that it quotes Papias, writing *c* A.D. 130. Papias would be nothing less than an immediate witness since he knew the Apostle himself.

The evidence invoked in favour of its canonicity may also be cited as evidence for the Johannine authorship, for even when John is not mentioned by name, there is never any question of any other than the Apostle who is moreover so clearly indicated as such in the Gospel itself.

Internal Evidence—Jn is not at all an anonymous writing in the same sense as its predecessors, and bears distinctive marks of its authorship. Though it is written in correct Greek, and there seems to be no sufficient evidence for Burney's theory of an Aramaic original, the thought, the rhythm of the sentences and sometimes the grammatical constructions are obviously the product of a Semitic mind. Belief in the Hebrew Scriptures is everywhere manifest whether in the words put into the mouths of others or in the Evangelist's own comments. As examples of the latter, more significant for our purpose, we may cite the numerous texts in which the author sees the fulfilment of OT prophecy, the cleansing of the temple, 2:17, Christ's entry into Jerusalem, 12:14, 15, the unbelief of the Jews, 12:38, the distribution of Christ's garments and the casting of lots for his tunic, 19:24, the piercing of Christ's side, 19:36 f. The author's familiarity with Jewish customs is equally manifest. He understands the importance of ritual purifications, 2:6, 11:55, the Jews' dread of contacts with Gentiles, 18:28, the widespread impression that physical misfortune was the result of sin, 9:2. The Semitic style of the narrative is unmistakable, *e.g.* in 3:16–21, 31–36. The author prefers to string together sentences by the use of ' and ' rather than to use subordinate clauses. Though not unknown in Greek, this is far more common in Aramaic and Hebrew, and suggests a knowledge of these languages. There is a distinct tendency, too, to record Aramaic names of persons and places and to interpret them for Greek readers, *e.g.* Messias, 1:41 ; 4:25, Cephas, 1:42, Rabbi, 1:38, Rabboni, 20:16, Golgotha, 19:17.

The writer's familiarity with the country is even more striking. He is familiar in detail with the topography of Jerusalem. He knows that Solomon's Porch is part of the temple, 10:23, that by the Praetorium there is the Pavement called Gabbatha, 19:13, that the Pool of Bethzatha has five porches and is by the Sheep Gate, 5:2. When mentioning places elsewhere he shows detailed knowledge. Cana of Galilee, 2:1, 21:2, Bethany beyond Jordan, 1:28 (to distinguish it from the other Bethany), Aenon near Salim, 3:23. These and many other examples lead inevitably to the conclusion that we have here the record of one who was familiar at first hand with the country and its people.

An equal familiarity and direct acquaintanceship is shown with the actual events. Precise references to time, place, distance, remarks and reactions of persons are scattered profusely throughout the Gospel, often for no other discernible reason than that the writer

knew that it so happened. Thus at the beginning of **777e** the Gospel the author gives us a day by day account and even the very hour of events, 1:29, 35, 39, 43 ; 2:1. He often mentions the name of the speaker even when the remark is unimportant, 6:7, 8 ; 11:16. He observes also that Malchus was the name of the highpriest's servant whose ear Peter cut off, a fact perhaps of importance only to one who was himself known to the high-priest, 18:15. We are told that the five loaves, 6:9, were of barley and that there was much grass at the place of the miracle, 6:10. Lightfoot has moreover noted that the author mentally crosses the Lake of Tiberias as he writes, now speaking of the eastern side, 6:1, 22, and now of the western side, 6:17, 25, as ' across the lake '. The first-hand information is equally evident in such vivid and detailed narratives as that of the scene at Jacob's Well, ch 4, and the healing of the man born blind, ch 9. The cumulative effect of these and other details is to induce us to conclude that we owe the narrative not merely to an eye-witness of the events but to one who was particularly receptive of impressions and of specially retentive memory.

It is not difficult moreover to identify this witness **f** in the narrative itself. He speaks not infrequently as from the intimate circle of Christ's immediate followers: *e.g.* in ch 1, when our Lord calls his first disciples, and, even more strikingly, at the Last Supper, chh 12 ff., when, it is certain, there were none present but the twelve Apostles. Moreover he constantly shows himself acquainted with our Lord's inmost thoughts and feelings, 2:21, 24 ; 11:13, 33, 38. The conclusion is forced upon us that the witness is an Apostle. Which of the Twelve is he ? We note the rather singular omission from the Gospel of all mention of the sons of Zebedee by name, whereas in the Synoptics they are frequently so mentioned. Indeed with Peter they are the most favoured disciples of our Lord, *cf.* § 776*e*. It is difficult to suggest a reason for this silence in Jn, except that one of them is recording the history, and since James was put to death by Herod Agrippa I in A.D. 42 we are left with his brother John as the author.

We may briefly deal here with a pretended discovery **g** that John was martyred together with James by Herod Agrippa, and therefore was dead before Jn was written. Mk's vivid reproduction of Christ's word promising the two ambitious brothers his cup and his baptism is argued to be a ' prophecy after the event ', and should be taken to affirm their common martyrdom in A.D. 44. A fragment of Papias cited by Philip of Side, 430, and Georgios Hamartolos, *c* 867, is produced as confirming this supposition. It says that ' John the Theologian and James were killed by the Jews '. Furthermore a Syriac Martyrology of 411 assigns to James and John a common feast on December 27th.

Our first remark is that this assertion demands an impossible Pauline chronology, since it necessitates the dating of the persecutor's conversion between A.D. 27 and 30. Secondly, with regard to Christ's prophecy, the assumption that it refers to an event (apart from the implied denial of real prophecy) gratuitously supposes that the chalice must mean *violent* death for both brothers, and that their martyrdom is to be regarded as simultaneous. Thirdly, in this hypothesis the silence of Ac 12 regarding John's death would be inexplicable. Fourthly, the title ' the Theologian ' is an anachronism, as attributed to Papias, for this title dates from the 4th cent. Such an inaccuracy in citing Papias leads us to the reasonable conjecture that the Bishop of Hierapolis most probably coupled the names of John the Baptist and James the Apostle, both killed by the Jews, one by Herod Antipas and the other by Herod Agrippa. Fifthly, the common feast of James and John does not suppose a common martyrdom. At Carthage, according to a Martyrology of 505, it was the Baptist and James who were celebrated on 27 Dec. In the Syriac Martyrology there is an evident preoccupation with the title of Apostle (Dec. 26 :

973

777g Stephen the Apostle (!) ; Dec 27 : John and James Apostles ; Dec. 28 : Paul the Apostle and Simon Peter chief of the Apostles) which could easily have occasioned the substitution of John the Apostle for John the Precursor. Papias, therefore, and the Syriac Martyrology furnish no solid evidence against the tradition that John drank the chalice without shedding his blood and died a natural death at Ephesus in extreme old age ; *cf.* Jn 21:23.

778a Recent Non-Catholic Criticism—As stated above it is no longer possible to assign a late 2nd cent. date to the Fourth Gospel and it is now generally recognized to have been written more or less at the time allotted to it by tradition. If the Gospel were written about the end of the 1st cent. and if John the Apostle did indeed survive till then, it might be thought to make little difference to the accuracy of the narrative, whether it was written by him personally or by a contemporary. Nevertheless, though the Apostle is now generally allowed to have had a large part in providing the material of the Gospel, it is still denied by many moderns that he actually wrote it. It is suggested for example that the Gospel clearly distinguishes between the writer and the eyewitness in 19:35 and 21:24. It is allowed that in those passages the eyewitness is the Beloved Disciple, John the son of Zebedee. In 19:35, it is argued, the writer of the Gospel is testifying to the truth of the Beloved Disciple's witness, ' *his* witness is true '. ' He knoweth that he saith true ' is a statement by the writer that the Apostle, now very old, is fully conscious of the truth of his witness (Bernard, *in loc.*). This interpretation is by no means obvious. Why should one who was *ex hypothesi* not an eyewitness testify to the truth of the witness of one who was ? It would surely be more natural to invoke the eyewitness in corroboration of the writer's own statement.

b As for Bernard's interpretation of the following statement (' He [ἐκεῖνος] knoweth that he saith true '), he has to admit that it is quite natural to interpret ἐκεῖνος as the actual writer of the Gospel (*cf.* Jn 9:37 where Christ uses ἐκεῖνος of himself). But if it does so refer, then we are more or less obliged to identify witness with writer, for otherwise we should have a needless repetition of the preceding sentence. Why should it be thought unlikely that the writer should refer to himself in the third person ? After all, St Paul does so in 2 Cor 12:2–5. At the very least Jn 19:35 may equally well be taken in this way and since tradition has in fact always so taken it, we conclude this is the right interpretation. As for Jn 21:24, even if it be conceded that others wrote the verse, so far from weakening the Johannine claim, it is an explicit affirmation that the actual writer is the Beloved Disciple who, we have seen, must be identified with Jn the Apostle.

c It is asked further how we are to account for the strange reticence of the Evangelist regarding the actual name of the Beloved Disciple—Strachan notes the traditional theory that the author, the son of Zebedee, here refers to himself, but that as author, he keeps himself in the background (p 82). ' Yet ', he says, ' the terms of such a reference can scarcely be called modest. It is a much simpler interpretation to suppose that the author of the Gospel is referring to someone other than himself. Then the epithet, " whom Jesus loved " becomes intelligible '.

But surely Strachan has smoothed out one difficulty only to raise a greater—for while it is easy to understand why the son of Zebedee does not name himself if he is indeed the author of the Gospel, it is by no means easy to see why the son of Zebedee is not mentioned by name if the Gospel were written by someone else. Moreover, is the title ' the disciple whom Jesus loved ' in the mouth of that disciple such an offence against modesty ? Given that Jesus had in fact a special predilection for the youngest of the Apostles, John would naturally be struck by the wonder of it and might explain it simply on the ground of his being the Benjamin of Christ's immediate followers and not because of any special merits he might **7** possess.

It is then, it seems, on such grounds as these that **d** we are asked to distinguish between the witness to whom we owe practically all the information in the Gospel and the writer who records it for us, while at the same time rejecting a constant tradition which identifies the two. ' Speaking generally ', says Dr Bernard, ' one cannot distinguish by any features of internal evidence, those parts of the Gospel narrative which plainly rest upon the report of an eyewitness, and those which may be referred to the Evangelist ', p lxxviii. One should go further. Even if the evidence of the Gospel were compatible with the theory that the writer, not himself an eyewitness, gathered his information from one who was, it is clearly more intelligible on the assumption that the eyewitness wrote it himself. There are whole pages of the Gospel where it is unthinkable that anyone but the witness wrote them—or at least dictated them word for word, which comes to the same thing, *cf.* Jn 13–17. Indeed Dr Bernard at times seems to allow to the ' writer ' of the Gospel a role hardly greater than that of scribe. But no Catholic would object to the suggestion that John, like Paul, Rom 16:22, used a scribe to write down his compositions.

It is further pointed out that the Apocalypse, admitted to be by John the Apostle, has no reticence like the Gospel on this point, but gives the name of John openly and repeatedly—why then not the Gospel also, if indeed the Apostle wrote it ? Without pretending to solve every difficulty it may be observed that the Apoc is very different from the Gospel. It is a book of prophecy in which the identity of the prophet has considerable relevance. The Gospel on the other hand is a record of the deeds and words of Jesus Christ in which there is much less need to name the author. Indeed, one may note again (*cf.* § 777*d*) that Jn is less anonymous than the other Gospels.

The critics have gone further and attempted to **e** identify the writer of the Gospel as distinct from the witness. It is noted that the author of the Gospel also wrote the Johannine epistles. Now 2 and 3 Jn each starts by naming the writer as ὁ πρεσβύτερος, the Presbyter or Elder. This term, it is argued, is used in Ac 15:4, 22 to distinguish the disciples of the Apostles from the Apostles themselves and this is the sense in which Irenaeus uses the term οἱ πρεσβύτεροι τῶν ἀποστόλων μαθηταί, *Adv. Haer.* 5, 5, 1 ; 5, 33, 3 ; 5, 6, 2. There is no example in 2nd cent. literature, they say, of the term ' Presbyter ' being used for an Apostle, *cf.* Bernard, p xlvii. Who is this ' Presbyter ' who wrote the Gospel and epistles ? The critics refer us to a statement of Papias who, while describing the sources of his information, says he tried to find out all that the ' presbyters ' reported as being said by Andrew, Peter, Philip, Thomas, James, John, Matthew, or any other of the disciples of our Lord—and also what Aristion and the presbyter John say. It seems clear that two Johns are indicated here and this is the view of Eusebius himself, HE III, 39 ; *cf.* Bardy, DBV(S) 845. Eusebius mentions the fact that there are two tombs at Ephesus bearing the name of John, and suggests that perhaps the John, not the Apostle, wrote the Apocalypse. No one in tradition ever suggested he wrote the Gospel. Yet this is the individual brought in to fill the role of πρεσβύτερος in 2 and 3 Jn, and claim authorship of the 4th Gospel, as well as the epistles. Bernard, adopting substantially the view of Harnack, sums up : ' John the presbyter was the writer and editor of the 4th Gospel, although he derived his narrative material from John the son of Zebedee ', p lxiv.

On what grounds is based the assertion that the term πρεσβύτερος is never used of an Apostle ? It is necessary of course to exclude, beforehand, its use in 2 and 3 Jn and to interpret Papias' use of the word as ' disciple of an Apostle ' though many think he uses it also of Apostles. Moreover the total number

8f of references to ' presbyter ' in the literature of the first two centuries is not so large as to warrant any categoric assertion of the kind. Further, the appellation ὁ πρεσβύτερος at the head of 2 and 3 Jn surely singles the author out in a very special way, far too special a way, one might think, for a mere disciple of an Apostle, otherwise practically unknown. Yet on the assumption that it is the Apostle himself, how suitable a name ! John, the last survivor of the Twelve, and now no doubt far older than all those he lived with, is surely *the* Elder *par excellence* ; *cf.* Bardy, 846, and 1 Pet 5:1.

One further question arises. If the critics are correct, then the composition of Jn was closely similar to that of Mk. As Mk was the follower of Peter and recorded his memories in Peter's old age, so John the Presbyter, a disciple of the son of Zebedee, would have recorded *his* memoirs in the Apostle's old age.

But if this be so, how can one account for the startling difference in tradition ? Whereas the part played by Mk has always been plain in the record of tradition, and the Gospel is under his name, not Peter's, nothing similar is to be found in the tradition of the Fourth Gospel, *cf.* ' The Replies of the Biblical Commission ', § 51*c–e*.

g Purpose and Plan—The Evangelist himself declares his aim, ' These things are written that you may believe that Jesus is the Christ the Son of God and that believing you may have life in his name ', 20:31. He wrote, not so much to convert as to confirm the belief of those who already believed ' that you may keep *believing* ' (πιστεύητε). The Gospel was mainly meant for Christians. These were not Jewish Christians, otherwise it would not have interpreted simple Jewish terms such as Messias and Rabbi. The Jews John has in mind are not readers, but the hostile mass of the Jewish nation who rejected the Messias.

It seems clear too that the Evangelist, without expressly saying so, wrote against those who are called Antichrist in 1 and 2 Jn. These are the Docetists, who held that the divine Christ did not really have a human nature, and the Ebionites, who claimed that the Word of God dwelt only for a time in the man Jesus, from his baptism to his Passion. Jn demonstrates the reality of Christ's human nature and likewise shows that the Word was made Flesh at the moment of the Annunciation. Finally, Jn's insistence on the Baptist's subordination to Christ (' He was not the light ') might be taken as an answer to those followers of the Baptist who were reluctant to transfer their allegiance, 3:25-30.

h That the Evangelist also wrote to supplement the Synoptics appears from a comparison with them. Indeed the explanation of many difficulties in Jn lies in the fact that the author presupposes a knowledge of the Synoptics. ' Thus he omits many things which would have served his purpose, for no other reason apparently than because they were already well known from the earlier Gospels ', MacRory, p xlv. He makes no mention, *e.g.*, of the Transfiguration, or of Christ's confession of divinity before Caiaphas. Again Jn's remark ' For John was not yet cast into prison ', 3:24, surely refers to the mention of this event in the Synoptics as indicating the start of the Galilean ministry ; and its purpose is to inform the reader that Christ's Judaean Ministry took place before the Galilean. Further, there is no account of the Institution of the Eucharist in Jn. In view of the elaborate Eucharistic discourse of Jn 6 and the whole tone of the account of the Last Supper which presupposes the Sacrament of Love, it is clear that John omits the description of its institution for no other reason than that four accounts of it existed already (Mt, Mk, Lk and 1 Cor).

We see then how an examination of the Gospel corroborates the testimony of early writers. Eusebius says Jn expressly records the events before the Baptist's imprisonment, which had been left out by the Synoptics (HE 3, 24) ; Irenaeus notes that John had in mind

' the error sown by Cerinthus and earlier still by those **778h** called Nicolaites ', *Adv. Haer.* 3, 1.

The Gospel seems to fall into the following divisions : **779a**

1:1–18 **Prologue**

1:19–6:72 **The Public Ministry, Part I**

1:19–2:12 The Messias prepares for his Mission
2:13–3:36 First Judaean Ministry
4:1–54 Through Samaria to Galilee
5:1–47 A Feast at Jerusalem
6:1–72 The Bread of Life

7:1–12:50 **The Public Ministry, Part II**

7:1–52 The Breach widens
7:53–9:41 The Light of the World
10:1–11:56 The Good Shepherd
12:1–50 End of the Public Ministry

13:1–17:26 **The Last Supper**

13:1–38 Events in the Supper Room
14:1–31 Consolation
15:1–16:33 Exhortation and Encouragement
17:1–26 Christ's Sacerdotal Prayer for Unity

18:1–21:25 **The Passion and Resurrection**

18:1–19:42 The Passion
20:1–21:25 The Risen Saviour

Characteristics—The Fourth Gospel is **an historical b book** with a dogmatic purpose—things as reconcilable with one another as the earthly life of Jesus of Nazareth is with the stupendous truth of his Godhead. To show that Jesus is the Messias and Son of God, John did not try to write a complete biography—he knew that was impossible, 21:25. His method was to select some of the acts which particularly revealed the divine glory of Jesus, and some of the words in which he revealed himself. The Prologue stands like a divine vestibule exhibiting a synthesis of all that the interior palace of selected history reveals. From beginning to end John sees the glory of the Only-Begotten—the glory of his life, the glory of his passion, the glory of his resurrection, a glory all full of grace and truth. Augustine constantly has recourse to two key-sentences : ' In the beginning was the Word . . . and the Word was made flesh '. Without this key Jn is an enigma.

Since the portrait of Christ in Jn differs apparently from that in the Syn. (on account of notable differences in the discourses and the Evangelist's elaborate use of symbolism) there have been constant attempts to maintain that Jn is in fact not a work of history at all but largely an allegorical composition designed to portray Christ, not as he actually was in life but as he was believed to be at the beginning of the 2nd cent. ' Such a view ', notes MacRory, ' reduces the claim to divinity made by our Lord himself in the discourses of the Gospel to claims set up on his behalf by the Evangelist 70 years or more after his death ', p xlix.

Before dealing with the difficulties it is well to note **c** first that the Gospel presents itself as a record of fact. This is stated categorically in 20:30-31. The text of the Gospel bears this out. We find the same historical persons, the Apostles, the holy women, mentioned individually by name, Caiaphas, Pilate, Joseph of Arimathea. The events, too, generally speaking are the same, the Baptist's testimony, Christ's many miracles, the feeding of the 5,000 and above all the details of the Passion. That Jn relates many events not in the Syn. (and *vice versa*) is accounted for by his intention of supplementing, not repeating their account in detail, *cf.* above § 778*h*.

John wrote a spiritual Gospel, as Clement of Alexandria noted, but its historical guarantees are as concrete as the most critical investigator would wish. The whole is chronologically arranged according to Jewish festivals—at least three Paschs or a period of two full

779c years, Jn 2:13 ; 6:4 ; 12:1, the feast of Tabernacles (15–22 Tishri), and the feast of the Dedication (25 Casleu). Days and hours are noted precisely, lengths of time are marked exactly, 4:40 ; 11:9 ; 12:1 ; 20:26, or approximately, 2:12. The geographical framework is equally solid, in fact there is more Palestinian geography and topography in the Fourth Gospel than in the other three together, *cf.* § 777*e*.

d Events are described not vaguely but with attention to details and with a picturesque realism which falls little short of Mk. Many things omitted by the Synoptics are supplied. Without Jn we should not know of the part played by Philip and Andrew on the day of the first multiplication of bread ; neither should we know of the appearance of Christ before Annas, nor the steps that led Pilate to surrender to the enemies of Jesus, nor the part of Nicodemus in the burial of the Lord. Similar things could be said of the dialogue and incidental details in such scenes as that of Jacob's Well and the washing of the feet.

Of miracles circumstantially described there are seven, two associated with Cana, the cure of the cripple at Bethzatha, the multiplication of bread, the walking on the water, the cure of the man born blind, the resurrection of Lazarus—to which we might add the miraculous catch of 153 fishes after the resurrection. All are regarded as signs, the first two being related to the faith which they increased or provoked, and the second pair being closely connected with the Eucharistic discourse. The symbolism of three others is declared by Jesus himself. He cures on the Sabbath to show that he is one with the Father in a coequal continuity of operation ; he gives sight to the blind, to show that he is the light of the world ; he raises Lazarus, after declaring that he is the resurrection and the life.

e The symbolism of the Fourth Gospel is pronounced and apparently intentional. Nevertheless caution should be used in its investigation lest far more be read into the mind of the Evangelist than was actually there. The opening words of the Gospel ' In the beginning . . .', the reference to the Word as the Light of men, the bringing of new life to men and even the exact arrangement of events into seven days from the Baptist's testimony to the miracle of Cana, reminds us forcibly of the details of Gen ch 1, and can hardly be anything but intentional ; *cf.* Allo, 833. Authors have sought the perfect number seven in many other places in Jn, for example the 7 miracles, but it does not seem that any special significance attaches to it.

We find that Jn gives great prominence to the ideas of Light and Life, and these appear to be constantly represented by the symbols of water and blood respectively. The Life was the Light of men, died on the Cross and from his side pierced by the lance there flowed blood and water, in which many have seen figured the Eucharist and Baptism. One should compare this with the water and blood of 1 Jn 5:5 ff. Allo thinks one may discern a series of 8 events in which these two main ideas are illustrated. Thus : (1) Marriage feast of Cana, water and wine (blood). (2 and 3) Nicodemus and the Samaritan woman, faith symbolized by water, proposed to a Jew and a non-Jew. (4) Healing of ruler's son, 4:46 ff. (5) Paralytic at Pool of Bethzatha. (6) Miracle of loaves (Eucharist) implying wine (blood). (7) Man born blind. (8) Raising of Lazarus. Thus 2, 3, 5, 7 refer to Light, and 4, 6, 8 to Life, while 1 refers to both.

f Granted some symbolism, to a greater or lesser degree, we have now to ask whether this is compatible with an historical work ? It should be observed first that we are not here considering parables which are fictitious narratives designed to convey spiritual teaching. The symbolical or typological method is quite distinct and consists in selecting an actual historical event or fact or person and seeing in it or him a spiritual meaning ; *cf.* § 40. Thus Paul in referring to an episode in the life of Abraham in this way, Gal 4:24, does not imply it did not happen but that it symbolizes a spiritual lesson. As Bernard says, ' It is one thing to spiritualize history : it is quite another to put forth as history a narrative which is not based on fact ', p lxxxvi. There cannot be the slightest doubt that it was John's express purpose and intention to record fact. At the same time he does undertake to interpret the facts, as is shown not only by his comments (*e.g.* 2:21 ; 4:2 ; 20:9) but also by his arrangement and selection of material, so as to present his thesis, 20:30, in the most effective way.

Different Subject Matter—If we had only the Synoptic **g** Gospels we should conclude that Jesus spent almost all his public life preaching in Galilee—and, on the other hand, Jn concentrates mainly on the events in Judaea and Jerusalem. Yet, as said above, the reference to the Baptist's imprisonment in Jn 3:24 indicates that the account is meant to supplement the Synoptics. Again, the Syn. accounts suggest a one-year ministry ; yet in Jn, at least three Paschs are referred to, *cf.* § 791*b*, implying at least two years. But this need cause no special difficulty, because, as Temple has pointed out, ' the Synoptists provide no chronology of the ministry at all until the last week ', p xi. The impression of a one-year ministry is due rather to an absence of chronological indications. Jn, on the other hand, is careful to give many notes of time, *cf.* § 779*c*. On the apparent difference concerning the day of the Crucifixion, see § 802*b*.

The Fourth Gospel indeed, far from being incompatible with the Syn., is rather their necessary complement, see § 778*h*. That our Lord should have ignored Jerusalem and Judaea and preached exclusively in Galilee and that he should then have journeyed to Jerusalem, where he was at once put to death, is hardly intelligible. For, seeing that Christ, on his own admission, was not come but to save the lost sheep of the House of Israel, Mt 15:24, he must surely have offered salvation officially and directly to the leaders of the people and to the inhabitants of the Holy City. Indeed how else can we explain his cry of sorrow over Jerusalem (not just Israel), ' How often would I have gathered thy children ? . . .', Mt 23:37. The explanation is surely given us in Jn. Moreover Jesus, as an orthodox Jew, would be bound by law to visit Jerusalem at the great feasts, and one can hardly believe he would not take such opportunities to preach to the people.

The Discourses—A special feature of the Fourth Gospel **h** is the length of our Lord's discourses. But even more remarkable is the difference between them and those recorded in the Syn. No one can fail to notice, for example, the difference between the Sermon on the Mount or the parables by the lake shore on the one hand, and the discourses of Jesus in the temple on the other. In the former we have elevated moral instruction, homely illustrations from everyday life, an almost complete absence of polemics. In the latter one finds a preoccupation with our Lord's Person and Mission expressed often in difficult language and in a tone of open hostility. The matter and the language are those of crisis—the supreme crisis of acceptance or rejection of his claims. Moreover there seems to be a remarkable similarity in phraseology between what is put into our Lord's mouth and the wording of the rest of the Gospel, so that at times it is not easy to say precisely whether it is our Lord or the Evangelist who speaks, *e.g.* 3:16 ff. All this has led many to ask whether we have not here the Evangelist's developments of what our Lord originally said, rather than an exact historical record of his utterances.

To deal with the last point first. One recognizes **i** of course that our Lord's Aramaic has been put into Greek and that in the translation personal characteristics of the Evangelist appear. It must also be admitted that the discourses are not usually reported *verbatim* in any gospel, as may be seen by the differences in the records of so solemn an utterance as the Words of Institution of the Eucharist. Again, not all that Christ said on any given occasion is necessarily recorded.

b It may be no more than a summary. Finally the later date of Jn's Gospel would give further scope for the personal characteristics of the Evangelist to appear : though one might reasonably ask whether it might not rather be a case of John's having absorbed his Master's modes of thought and expression after so many years of profound meditation on them, to a greater extent than the other Evangelists.

c As regards the different subject-matter—in the first place there is a different audience. In Galilee Jesus was speaking to the simple, unsophisticated fishermen and peasants, who had no vested interests and no malice in their hearts. In Jerusalem it was otherwise. There he came up against the leaders at once, and they from the beginning took their stand against him, Jn 2:18. This being so, the polemical note could not fail to appear in his dealings with them. Moreover, being learned in the law, the Pharisees would expect to discuss deeper matters than those set before the Galileans. Jesus met and overcame them with their own weapons. It is moreover significant that in the Synoptic Gospels the polemical note is equally prominent when our Lord is speaking directly with the Pharisees ; *cf.* Mt 23.

d It is argued further that the ' self-assertiveness ' of Jesus in the Johannine discourses is unlike what we should expect of him, indeed unworthy of him. But surely all depends on whether it is true. That Christ speaks of himself is inevitable if his task is to offer himself for acceptance by the leaders. If his claims were false there would of course be intolerable pride.

It is often conceded that Jn has entered more deeply into the mind of Christ than the other Evangelists, and that his over-all portrait of the Master may give a truer picture than that of the others. But it is maintained that Jn's account is less historical in detail. 'We may sometimes feel sure that this saying or that was uttered by our Lord as it is recorded ; but it would be a mistake to look for original and authentic utterances as each the nucleus of a discourse ', Temple, p xvii.

e It is true of course that Jn does interpret as well as record. He interprets the significance of events, 19:34-37, and also of sayings, 2:21-22. Might he not also expand our Lord's discourses in a similar way ? Some think, *e.g.*, that in 3:16-21 we have the reflexions of the Evangelist, though there is no obvious break after our Lord's words in the preceding verses. So also in 3:31-36 we may have Jn's comments on the Baptist's preceding words. But it is surely destructive of the historical character of the Gospel, so well established as the record of an eyewitness, to maintain that, in effect, we cannot be sure that Christ actually pronounced any of the discourses as recorded in Jn. To those who so readily stress John's supposed inability in his old age to distinguish between what our Lord actually said, and what might be deduced (admittedly under the guidance of the Holy Spirit) from those sayings, we must point out that such a viewpoint does not well agree with the other evidence of the Gospel. If there is one thing which stands out more than another, it is surely the Evangelist's minute attention to details of time, place and persons (see § 777*d–e*). Is it likely that the man who remembered what was said by the Baptist, Andrew, Philip and Nathanael, ch 1, and on another occasion by Andrew, Philip and Peter, ch 6, that the narrator of the vivid and circumstantial story of ch 9 or ch 12 (*cf.* esp. 12:12) would be unable to distinguish between his Master's words and his own reflexions? Moreover, even if for the sake of argument, this were conceded as a possi-**f** bility, we have other factors to reckon with. The readers of the Gospel were not meeting this teaching for the first time. The Gospel was in fact merely the written record of the Tradition which they had cherished continuously over the years. All the evidence shows that this Tradition was jealously guarded and any deviation would be noticed at once. There was indeed theological development almost from the beginning, as

one may see from the epistles, but it was not set down **780f** as the utterances of our Lord. St Paul for example makes it perfectly clear when he is quoting the Lord directly and when he is issuing instructions on his own authority. Speaking of the Eucharistic Assemblies he says, ' For I have received from the Lord that which also I delivered unto you ', 1 Cor 11:23. But ' Concerning virgins I have no precept from the Lord ', 1 Cor 7:25 ; and again, ' But for the rest, I speak, not the Lord ', 1 Cor 7:12. Is it reasonable to suppose that Jn who was more historically minded than Paul should have been so vague as to set down his own reflexions as his Master's sayings ? It may of course be granted that in reporting the discourses Jn had in mind contemporary needs and selected and arranged his material in order to provide an answer to heretics. We have already seen that this consideration must have been in his mind when arranging the Gospel as a whole.

Strachan, in attempting an explanation of the **g** Johannine discourses, suggests a parallel with the OT prophets. ' When a Hebrew prophet used the expression " Thus saith the Lord ", he did not usually mean that the actual words were heard by him with the outward ear, although he may have had " auditions ". He meant that he spoke with certainty and authority the mind of God on a particular situation. . . . The Fourth Evangelist feels himself to be in the same relation of communion in the Spirit with the exalted Christ as the OT prophet experienced with God ', p 17. It is difficult, however, to see any parallel such as Strachan suggests. The OT prophet is generally concerned with communicating to man the mind of God here and now on a particular situation. He is the προφήτης, the speaker on behalf of God, the mouthpiece of God. But it remains clear, generally speaking, that it *is* the prophet who speaks. He is used by God to communicate the message, but the people know the man through whom the message comes. His personality is not hidden as is so often the case with that of the inspired writer. When the prophet says, ' Thus saith the Lord ' all know that the Lord is then and there speaking through him. The Evangelist is in a very different role. His task is to record what the greatest of prophets actually said in definite historical circumstances. Our Lord, the Incarnate Word, was himself the mouthpiece of God. If Jn puts into his mouth what was in fact communicated to the Evangelist at a later date we have a totally different situation. Jn was indeed also a prophet and we have his book of prophecy, the Apocalypse, where it is clear from the beginning that Jn speaks as the mouthpiece of the Risen Lord.

Doctrinal Contents—The present slight sketch can **781a** only be a rough map to guide explorers on their way of discovery in the really inexhaustible riches of the Fourth Gospel. We give little more than a catalogue of the principal points.

Jesus, Messias and Son of God—with the emphasis on the Divine Person—is the theme of John. That Jesus of Nazareth is the Israelite Messias and very God is shown throughout the Gospel in an historical record of Messianic and divine self-revelation consisting of word and work, but all that truth is synthesized in the Prologue. The Prologue presents the Logos as eternal, as distinct from the Father, as himself God, and becoming man to walk amongst men as Jesus of Nazareth. This mystery of the Incarnation is the central message of the Gospel.

The divine Person is called the *Logos*, a term which in this sense is exclusively Johannine, being given to the conquering, bloodstained, royal Rider of the Apocalypse, 19:13, to the visible, audible, tangible ' Word of life ' at the beginning of 1 Jn, and to him who is described as life and light in the Prologue, and appears (without the term *Logos*) as life and light in the pages that follow.

There is no doubt that John, in presenting Jesus as **b** the *Logos*, satisfied an age-old groping of the Hellenic

781b mind. As a philosophical term, *Logos* had first sounded about 500 B.C. at Ephesus on the obscure tongue of Heraclitus. In general it was a principle of organization, order and harmony, and something generically similar occurs in the *Nous* of Anaxagoras and in the prototype ideas of Plato. Before the Christian era Stoicism had taken the Heraclitean *Logos*, regarding it as a productive and governing principle in a pantheistic universe. Under the influence of Platonism, but through the Stoic system, the term was 'in the air' of the Hellenic world into which Christianity came. It was associated with whatever men call 'serious, reasonable, beautiful, well-ordered, fitting, lawful, musical, harmonious'. It was *Logos* that was conceived as making everything just what it should be. But it was neither Stoic thought nor even Judeo-Alexandrian Philonism that directly influenced St John. Between the non-Messianic intermediary abstraction which Philo called *Logos* and the *Logos* of St John there is no relationship.

c The personification of God's creative wisdom in the sapiential books of the OT is the real source of the doctrine of the Logos ; *cf.* Prov 8 ; Wis 7. It was under the influence of these passages that St Paul had already called Christ 'the wisdom of God', I Cor 1:24, 'the image of the invisible God', Col 1:15, 'the effulgence of his glory and the imprint of his substance', Heb 1:3. Through his 'wisdom' God created everything, but he also created and conserves and governs everything through his 'word', Ps 32:6. Thus 'wisdom' and 'word' are interchangeable, and St John chose the second—a happy appellation for the Christ who is the divine light of human intelligences and the divine life of human lives. The term *Logos*, analytically equivalent to supernatural life and light—grace and truth—is a reminder that in Jesus is the fountain of life, and that in his light we shall see light. The 'Word Incarnate' satisfies the Hellenic and human desire for a force which will act on human minds and wills and make the world what it should be.

d The Christology of John presents the **Messiahship** of Jesus in the colours of royalty—King of Israel, 1:50 ; 12:13, coming as Zachary predicted, 12:15, King of the Jews, 18:33 ff. ; 19:19. But his kingship is not of this world ; it is a spiritual kingship, to rule those who will become disciples of that truth to which he bore witness, 18:33-37. Jesus professed his Messiahship to the Samaritan woman, 4:26. Repeatedly he affirmed his mission to the Jews, referred them to the testimony of John the Baptist, 5:33 ff., and of Moses, 5:46 f., and especially to the seal with which the Father sealed him, 6:27. But *cf.* §§ 618*d*, 627*a*, 790*f*.

The title 'son of man' occurs a dozen times, but the Gospel shows abundantly that the 'son of man' is also the 'Son of God', the Only-begotten, 1:14, 18 ; 3:16, 18, who has come down from heaven, who claims unity of operation with the Father, who 'is' before Abraham came to be, who had glory with the Father before the world existed, who even says : 'I and the Father are one'. This transcendence however belongs to a man who on occasion was thirsty and tired, who wept at the tomb of a friend and knew disturbance of soul.

His relation to the Father is also frequently mentioned. His task on earth is to glorify the Father, from whom he has divine life, divine knowledge, and—as man—his command to give his life and take it up again for the sheep which the Father has given him. The programme of his life—his food—is to do the Father's will. His one intent is to promote his Father's glory, and therewith is associated his unassailable sanctity. 'Which of you can convict me of sin?'

e Towards men Jesus is **the Saviour,** to whom he presents himself as the bread of life, as the light, as the door of the sheepfold, as the Good Shepherd, as the way and the truth and the resurrection and the life, as the true vine, a Saviour in every way, not come to judge but to save, and nevertheless appointed by God to judge men finally, because he is the son of man.

The grace of faith given by the Father must draw men to Jesus, to be united to him and live by him. That drawing is very prominent in Jn, the divine attraction being exercised at its utmost by the redeeming sacrifice. 'And I, if I be lifted up from the earth shall draw all men to myself'.

It is, however, the Holy Spirit who is to realize and continue the work of Jesus in souls. The fullest theology of **the Holy Ghost** and therefore the greatest revelation of the mystery of the Blessed Trinity is given by John, especially in recording our Lord's last words in the Supper-room, which promise another Paraclete, the Spirit of truth, proceeding from the Father, sent by Jesus, and therefore proceeding from both Father and Son. This spirit is to be the perpetual Guide of the Apostolic Church into all truth.

The Church also is strongly outlined by Jn. The **f** 'Spiritual Gospel' does indeed insist on the interior working of grace in the individual soul, but it clearly postulates incorporation into a hierarchical organism. It is only necessary to recall the allegory of the flock and the Good Shepherd, the privileges of the Apostolic College of twelve, the primacy conferred on Simon Peter to prove that Jn proclaims a hierarchical Church.

St John is also—and this is quite in keeping with the doctrine of the Incarnation—a great sacramentalist. The sacraments of baptismal regeneration, of the bread of life, of the remission of sins are vividly set before us, and even apart from these institutionally effective sacraments, the most obvious things of the material world—light, water, wind, the shepherd, the flock, the vine—are all signs of things that belong to the supernatural order of grace, *cf.* § 779*e*.

Eschatology is not a marked feature of the Fourth **g** Gospel. The final judgement and the resurrection of the dead are indeed there, but the judgement that discerns the good from the bad is rather represented as taking place here through the attitude which men take towards the truth. In Jn truth is imperious. There can be no neutrality towards it ; one is either for or against, and this attitude decides whether a man is a child of light or a child of the devil, the father of lying. The final judgement will only manifest the response which men have given to the voice of Christ.

The moral teaching of Jn is centred in the inculcation of the precept of charity. Its whole code could be summed up in the Pauline phrase : 'Doing the truth in charity'. In all respects the Evangelist is true to his beloved Master, utterly intransigent in regard to the truth of God and with a heart full of pity towards human misery—shedding tears at the tomb of Lazarus.

The two stories told by St Irenaeus and St Jerome sum up St John admirably : his horror of Cerinthus 'the enemy of truth', and his insistence on the precept 'My little children, love one another'—because this is the precept of the Lord.

Integrity—There are only three passages of the Gospel **h** which need discussion under this heading, but it has been considered preferable to deal sufficiently with two of them (5:3*b*, 4, and ch 20) in the commentary. The passage of the Adulteress, 7:53–8:11, remains. Is it by St John?

The case is briefly as follows. Most important MSS and versions omit this passage from Jn. They are B, S, A, C, W, Θ, etc., many minuscules, the Syriac, Sahidic and Armenian versions, many Latin MSS prior to St Jerome. The Greek Fathers do not comment on it, and it seems to have been unknown to Tertullian and Cyprian. Many MSS note it with an asterisk or insert it after Jn 21:24 or Lk 21:38 (Ferrar Group). Moreover, it seems strangely thrown in between our Lord's discourses and has features of vocabulary and style more like the Synoptics.

On the other hand D and six other uncials have it as well as the great majority of cursives, about 100 Evangeliaria, the Egyptian Bohairic, several Old Latin texts and Vg. It was known to many Greek writers who did not comment on it, even, it seems, to Papias (Eus., HE III 39). The Latin Fathers Ambrose, Jerome and Augustine give it full recognition. Jerome says ' in multis graecis et latinis codicibus invenitur de adultera ' (*Adv. Pelag.* ii. 19), and Augustine supposes it was omitted from some texts because Christ's conduct seemed too lenient (*De Conj. Adult.* ii. 6). It is mentioned in the *Apostolic Constitutions*, ii. 24 (4th cent.).

The difference of style is not conclusive against its Johannine origin, for it is permissible to any writer when dealing with an unusual subject to use words he does not employ elsewhere. Renan even maintained that there is nothing in the passage at variance with the style of the Fourth Gospel. It seems however impossible to prove the point one way or the other.

Is the passage a genuine part of the Gospel tradition ? On the assumption that it is not, no adequate reason can be found to account for its insertion in so many texts, which show that it was widely current at least by the 3rd cent. and known in the 2nd (Papias). But in an age when sins of the flesh were punished with severity by the Christian church, as a reaction against pagan licence, the pericope may well have caused surprise and even scandal (as Augustine suggests), and then have been omitted from many texts. With the milder discipline of the 4th cent. the passage would gradually have re-established itself as authentic. The decree of the Council of Trent declaring the Books of the Bible *with all their parts* as found in the Latin Vulgate, to be inspired and canonical is always regarded as including this passage.

Time and Place of Composition—It is clear from Jn 21:23 that the last chapter was written when the Apostle was very old ; and presumably chh 1–20 were not very much prior to it. St Peter was dead, and the old Jewish world was no more. The Gospel must in fact have been written a long time after the destruction of Jerusalem, as the old Prologue already mentioned, § 777*c*, and also the *Monarchian Prologues* (3rd or 4th cent.) assign priority of date to the Apocalypse, and as Irenaeus seems decisive on the place of writing, namely, Ephesus, we should conclude that the Gospel was written some time after 96, the year of John's return from Patmos. It seems also posterior to the first Johannine Epistle.

Suggested Dislocations of the Text—Many modern writers have pointed out that a number of difficulties are to be observed in the text of chh 4–7, which however disappear if chapters 5 and 6 are transposed. The opening words of ch 6 ' after these things Jesus went away to the *other* side of the sea ' are oddly chosen if a journey from Jerusalem is meant, which must be so if ch 6 follows ch 5. Which side in this case would be the ' other ' ? But if ch 6 follows ch 4 there is no difficulty, for Jesus is at Capharnaum, on the west shore at the end of that ch, and amongst the signs referred to is the one recorded in ch 4. Again the words that begin ch 7 ' After these things Jesus walked in Galilee ' etc, do not seem to follow naturally on ch 6 for throughout the whole of ch 6 Jesus *is* in Galilee. Nor is there any suggestion in ch 6 that the Jews sought to kill him. But if ch 7 follows ch 5 the retirement from Jerusalem to Galilee in 7:1 fits in perfectly after the hostility shown Christ in Jerusalem in ch 5. Thus we have a smooth succession of events if we adopt the order 4, 6, 5, 7. Further, the order of chapters has an important bearing on the identity of the unnamed feast in 5:1 (see commentary).

In view of the harmonious sequence effected by the arrangement chh 4, 6, 5, 7, it is surprising that there is no textual evidence whatever that this was in fact the original order, with the exception of Tatian's *Diatessaron* which can hardly be regarded as proving more than that he also found the story ran more smoothly in the order chh 4, 6, 5, 7.

The transposition was also adopted by Ludolph of Saxony in the 14th cent.

Since the second decade of the present century it has rallied scholars like Meinertz, Lagrange, Olivieri, Joüon, Prat, Grandmaison, Lebreton, Bernard, Braun, Sutcliffe. Others however retain the order attested by all the MSS.

Further discussion of the matter may be found in Sutcliffe, *A Two-Year Public Ministry* and in a review of this work in DR 57 (1939) 308–39.

Attractive as the re-arrangement may be, it cannot, in the absence of any external evidence, be regarded as more than a possibility.

Other re-arrangements of the text are suggested by various scholars (*cf.* Bernard, p xix ff.), but these have less to commend them.

I 1-18 PROLOGUE

I 1-18—On the doctrinal importance of the Prologue **782a** and on the concept and term *Logos*, see § 781 *a, b, c.* The most convenient division seems to be : The Word as God and Creator, 1–5 ; the role of the Baptist and the Advent of the Word, 6–13 ; the Word Incarnate, whose glory, as fount of grace and truth, is witnessed by the Apostles, by the Church, 14–18. **1, 2.** The phrase ' In the beginning ' brings us up to the anterior verge of time from which creation descends, Gen 1:1 ; when the genesis of things began, the Word already *was.* This substantive verb *was* denotes existence and, in the context, pre-existence, self-existence. The Word is, therefore, eternal ; and its name denotes that it is a Wisdom-Being, the Offspring of intelligence. The chain-linking of subjects and predicates in 1*a, b, c* should be noted ; *Logos* links with *Logos* and *Theos* with *Theos*, the order of words in Gk being Predicate-Subject, SP, PS. The Challoner revision of DV had (almost perforce) partially to abandon this order which had been stubbornly retained by the original Rhemish translators. In 1*b* the preposition ' with ' (πρός) marks the Word as distinct from Another called God, but here *God* has the Gk definite article, to show that the relation is that of person to person. The preposition πρός is actually the one chosen by Aristotle to express the category of relation ; it means ' towardness ', but in several passages of the NT it is used with the accusative in the same sense as with the dative, namely, of being or dwelling together but perhaps denotes greater intimacy, Mt 13:56. ' The Word was *with* God ' means *two* not one ; but the unity of the divine essence is safe ; for ' the Word was *God* ', *Theos* here (without the Gk article) being a predicate and a noun of essence. This first verse of the Prologue, therefore, attributes to the Word eternity, distinct personality, Godhead. **2.** The emphatic Rhemish ' this ', changed to ' the **b** same ' by Challoner, stands for the *Logos* of the last stichos, that is, the *Logos-Theos*—' He was in the beginning with God ' is a résumé of his Divinity, his Eternity, and his Personal distinction from him who in vv 14 and 18 is called the Father. The term ' Son ', which pervades the whole subsequent Gospel, does not occur in the best Gk MSS of the Prologue except equivalently, for the Word is called ' Only-Begotten ', 14, and even ' Only-begotten God ', 18. **3-5.** The relation of the Word to all creation in general and to mankind in particular is the theme of these three verses. We pass at once from one pivotal verb, that of *being* to another pivotal verb, that of *coming to be* or *becoming* (εἶναι and γίνεσθαι). **3.** ' All things '— πάντα without the article meaning all and each— ' *through* him came to be '. Our translation uses *by*, to exclude the suggestion of instrumental agency conveyed by *through*. The context, however, sufficiently excludes it, for the Word, being God, cannot be an instrument. Besides, ' Coming to be ' here means creation, and creation is an act immediately divine in which no secondary agent can be a partner. The same preposition is used of God the Creator elsewhere (Rom 11:36 ; *cf.* 1 Cor 8:6 ; Col 1:16). The Word is not an instrument of creation, but since the Word

782b is the Wisdom-Person in the Godhead, the quasi-instrumental expression 'through him' is quite
c appropriate. The next group of words brings us to a problem of punctuation. The absolute universality of the creative action of the Word is emphasized by negative repetition in Semitic fashion : 'Without him nothing *came to be*'. Many ancient authorities placed a full stop here and began the next sentence : 'What has come to be in him was life'. This reading is traceable from the 2nd cent. through the early Gnostics and their adversary Irenaeus, through most of the Alexandrian, Syrian, Palestinian and Latin writers, in very authoritative uncial codices (except B and S which show no punctuation). In ancient versions and in the MS transmission of Vg. St Augustine, to whom its Platonic touch undoubtedly appealed, seems to have made its fortune in the Latin Church. The Clementine edition of Vg remains indecisive (using a comma only between 3 and 4), but the Roman Missal and Ritual are clearly in favour of beginning the new sentence with the words : 'In him was life'. Mainly through St John Chrysostom (it seems) this latter mode of dividing became almost universal in the Greek Church and in later Gk MSS. It had the support of St Jerome amongst Latins, and is adopted by the vast majority of NT editors and commentators. We translate, therefore (noting the change of tense in the verb γέγονεν from aorist to perfect and also the emphasis secured by resolving into its components a Gk negative substantive—'not-one-thing' instead of 'nothing') : '*Without him came to be not-one-thing that has come to be*'. The reading : 'Whatever has come to be, in him was life', though orthodox and beautiful, seems alien to the Evangelist's mind and possibly has its origin in a construe of St John's words by Gnostic commentators. This is a text-critical case in which the authority of the most ancient MS testimony does not
d prevail against other criteria. **4.** The Evangelist next descends from creatures in general to man in particular. 'In him (the Word) was life'. The term life is, of course, to be taken causatively in the sense of Ps 35(36):10—'With thee is the fountain of life, and in thy light we shall see light'. St John is certainly not thinking of plants and beasts, but of man only. Whether 'life' here has the specialized meaning 'spiritual or supernatural life' which it has throughout the whole Gospel (see Bi I [1920] 38–58, 213–39) has been doubted, because of the absence of the article. In any case grace does not supplant, but elevates nature, and consequently spiritual life diffused by the Word as a supernatural gift supposes the life of intelligence and free will. However, the rule of context and the opposition between light and darkness seem decisive in favour of supernatural life. Precisely because man is an intelligent creature, supernatural life for him is primarily light illuminating his mind. Hence baptism was called *photismos* or *illumina-*
e *tion*. **5.** The present tense 'shineth' denotes habitual efficacy extending to past, present and future. The light is there, powerful to illuminate at all times. The metaphor 'darkness' has a moral meaning in St John. It is not merely privation of light but opposition to it (*cf*. 3:19). 'The darkness did not *take* it'. 'Comprehend' is a good translation, in as much as it conveys the ambiguity of the Gk compound verb κατέλαβεν. The Greek Fathers (Cyril of Alexandria excepted) understood this verb in the sense of 'hostile seizure and *suppression*' (*cf*. Mk 9:17). Still, although it is true that the darkness did not overcome the light, this idea does not seem to belong to the sequence of the Evangelist's thought. Therefore, we understand the verb as parallel to the verbs in 10*c*, 11*b*, 12*a*—ἔγνω, παρέλαβον, ἔλαβον in the sense of 'take, receive, welcome'. The darkness was unreceptive (*cf*. Phil. 3:12 f.).
f **6-8.** To what extent St John has the pre-Christian activity of the illuminative Word in mind, is very difficult to assess. Although indeed the mystery of the

Incarnation is first announced in 14, all that runs from 6 to 12 seems nevertheless to refer primarily to the historical appearance of the Word in human form. This is apparently the reason why the Precursor is introduced here, before a series of verses, 9–13, which at first sight seem to refer to the pre-Incarnation manifestations of the Word—to his prophetic advent, as we should say. It is true that from the time of the first promise in Eden the attitude of mankind towards God's plan is implicitly or explicitly an attitude towards the mystery of the Word Incarnate, so that all rejections of the Light in earlier days were only anticipations of the rejection of the Word made flesh. The Precursor is described as a man who appeared on the historical scene ('There *came*' rather than 'There was'). That he was 'sent from God' marks his prophetic mission ; his name denoted the gracious purpose of God, and his whole office was that of a witness to the Light—an office virtually as universal as that of Christ—in order that all might be brought to belief. The negative sentence, 8, emphasizes the role of witness, recapitulates and prepares what follows—John was a lamp, not the Light (*cf*. 5:35). **9-13.** In spite of a strongly seductive temptation (on grounds of apparent ease and of rhythm) to make 'cometh' refer back to 'light' we stand for the Vg interpretation of 9, with all the older interpreters, Greek and Latin (except Theodore of Mopsuestia), and against most moderns (except Knabenbauer, Médebielle, Lebreton). Challoner supplies the demonstrative 'That'. It is perhaps too much like popular speech to translate : '*There it was—the very Light which enlightens every man coming into the world*', but this is really the effect of the emphatic 'was' at the head of the sentence. The redundant adjectival phrase *coming into the world*, found nowhere else in the NT, is a hebraic pleonasm common in rabbinical writings. The 'shining' of the Word (5) is here 'illumination', but the verb in the habitual present must be understood, as above, of the power to illuminate. The word *kosmos* means the created universe. **10.** It (the light) was in the world and the world came to exist through him (through the *Logos-phôs*), but the world (here with its moral nuance, meaning corrupt mankind) did not recognize him. The tragic note is stronger in chh 9 and 10 than in 5, and recurs frequently in chh 1–12. With the reservation already made concerning the central place of the Incarnation in the Evangelist's thought, it is difficult not to see pre-Incarnation rejection of the Light in these words. **11.** 'He came into his own (domain) —Israel, his specially chosen people—and his own did not receive him'. Here we may still admit some implied reference to continued Jewish rejection of the Christ of prophecy throughout the ages of preparation, but there seems no doubt that St John already presents the historical advent of the Incarnate Word, and the great refusal of the Jewish people to receive him. It has been remarked that the stylistic motion of the Prologue is peculiarly 'tidal' and difficult of analysis, but it seems that full tide comes here in 11. The deep tragedy of the Prologue also ends here, 12 being introduced by an adversative δέ, a comparatively rare particle in this Gospel. Here begin the glories of the Incarnation. **12.** The power given to those who received the *Logos-phôs*, whereby they were enabled to become children of God, is the grace of faith. Reception of the Word is itself an act of faith, and faith is the means of appropriating the dignity of divine sonship. Faith is not itself filiation, but the foundation and root of filiation. Hence the phrase (explanatory of the act of voluntary acceptance) : 'to them that believe in his name'—that is, adhere to him and all that his name (Messias and Son of God) signifies. **13.** These 'sons', τέκνα ('offspring' in a very real sense), were not generated from material elements—the blood-products of man and woman—nor from that will of the flesh which is the concupiscence of human sexual life—nor from the deliberate will of man (ἀνδρός, a human father) rationally desiring human propagation, but *were born* from God. The reading ' *was born* ', referring to Christ, though found in Tertullian, St Irenaeus and (possibly) St Justin has only negligible authority from MSS (Latin and Syriac) and is defended only by a few non-Catholic critics. The supernatural birth of Children of God is a very Johannine idea (*cf.* 3:3–6 ; 1 Jn 2:29 ; 3:9 ; 5:4, 18).

14–18. The manifestation of the Word now shows itself in all its *splendid* historical fullness. The term *Logos*, 1, appears again (and also for the last time in the Gospel) in a sentence that means more for mankind than any sentence ever written by a human pen : ' And the Word *became* flesh and dwelt amongst us '. The enunciation seems to come with a sudden shock, but the implied connexion between 13 and 14 is unmistakable. Men can become children of God, because the Word became man and entered our family. Borrowing a thought from St Augustine, we may say, that the wonder of 13 merges into the greater wonder of 14. It belongs to theology to explain the depth of these eight words. The exegetical facts are that the Eternal Divine Person, very God of very God, here called the Word, became, at an historical moment, a man amongst men, sharing (apart from sin) the whole frailty of mortal nature signified by the word ' flesh '. Thus he took up his dwelling amongst us, the Gk word literally meaning : ' He fixed his tent amongst us ', with allusion to the presence of God amongst his people, this being manifested in their Sanctuary by the symbol of a white cloud. St John could not have been insensible to the similarity of sound (especially perceptible to a Semitic ear) between the word ἐσκήνωσεν (' he tented ') and the *Shekinah* which is the Hebrew term for the dwelling of God in the Israelite sanctuary. This ancient manifestation of the glory of God's Majesty is also before his mind, as he proceeds to tell of the glory of the Word made man. **14c.** Using the first person plural and a verb of ocular vision he places himself amongst those who saw with their eyes (*cf.* 1 Jn 1:1) the glory of the Word Incarnate—that is, the external evidences of his divine majesty in words, miracles, Transfiguration, Resurrection—a glory such as belongs to an Only-begotten (who came) from the Father. The Gk ὡς (Lat. *quasi*) simply designates the quality or status (of Only-begotten)—the glory which he has *as being* the Only-begotten. ' *From* the Father ' may be construed with glory or with Only-begotten, but the latter seems more natural, *cf.* 16:27. ' Full of grace and truth ', as far as the adjective goes (for it is indeclinable in the *Koiné*) may be attached to ' glory ' or to ' Only-begotten ', but Vg and commentators generally read the second distich as a parenthesis and make ' full ' an epithet of the *Logos* dwelling Incarnate amongst us. Ps 84(85):11 speaks of ' mercy and fidelity meeting each other '. This OT phrase is here found in surpassing fullness, but St John has taken the expression beyond its OT meaning. ' Grace ' (a word which only occurs in the Prologue) means something more interior and unlimited than *ḥesed* (*cf.* 16, 17), and ' truth ' is not merely the faithful fulfilment of all God's promises but the new revelation of God's majesty and mysterious purpose formerly hidden in the inaccessible light of his divinity. ' Truth ' especially stands in contrast to the umbratic revelation and regime of the Old Dispensation. It is a capital concept in St John's Gospel (*cf.* particularly 4:23 ; 8:32–46 ; 17:17 ; 18:37).

15 seems a surprising insertion, for 16 is the logical continuation of 14, but the Precursor's testimony is of paramount importance in the mind of the Evangelist. As the *fact* of the Baptist's testimony has been already announced in 6–8, its *content* is given here. Note the solemnity of the introduction ; the perfect form of the Gk verb with present meaning renders, as it were, the permanent proclamation of the great herald's voice : ' This *is* he of whom I said : He *who comes* after me [by reason of the time of his ministry] *has taken rank*

before me [in dignity], for he was before me ' [by reason of his eternal pre-existence]. **16** adds a third testimony from the experience of the Christian community (' we ' standing for Christians, not merely for Apostles as in 14). The grace residing in the Word Incarnate was a plenitude, and not merely a derived but an essential plenitude springing from the fountain of the Word. Of that fullness ' we have all received, *that is*, grace for grace ' (' and ' is epexegetic). This phrase, according to a common meaning of the Greek ἀντί, means a succession of graces, and has been variously interpreted—Gospel succeeding Law (St Chrysostom, but improbable, for Law was not grace) —Christian life succeeding faith—better, a continuous succession of graces showing their cumulative abundance. **17.** The reason of this abundance is that a new **f** economy has begun. The Law was given as an external ordinance through Moses, grace and truth have come through Jesus Christ. The interior and real has taken the place of the exterior and the figurative. The proper name of the *Saviour Messias* occurs here for the first time, and thereby the Logos, 1, and the Incarnate, 14, is identified with Jesus of Nazareth, the Christ promised to Israel. ' Truth ' means the revelation of God's intimate secrets. **18.** No man could have brought such a revelation, for no man has ever seen God (except *mediately*, like Abraham, Moses and some of the Prophets). ' The Only-Begotten God '—this reading of codices B, S, C, L, the Sahidic, Bohairic, Peshitta versions, and several Greek Fathers is preferred by most modern editors to the reading ' Only-begotten Son ' of other Gk codices, some Greek Fathers, the Vg and the Latin Fathers generally— that Only-begotten who is in the bosom of the Father, conscious of all divine secrets with the consciousness of consubstantiality, he (ἐκεῖνος) has revealed (lit. *told* [*it*] *forth*, declared [the true nature of God]). Thus ends this sublime prologue. We now descend to historical narrative and follow almost a whole week of events, which, if the marriage of Cana took place on Wednesday (*cf.* § 786*a*), may be plausibly arranged between a Friday and a Wednesday in late February or early March. If we read πρωΐ for πρῶτον in 41, we should have a full week—from Thursday to Wednesday. It is the ' Holy Week ' of the dawn of salvation.

1:19–6:72 THE PUBLIC MINISTRY, PART I

I 19–2:12 The Messiah prepares for his Mission— **784a** In Jn official Israel is called ' the Jews ' ; these form a hostile body from the beginning. The movement of the whole Gospel is manifest in these early pages : an opposition developing into national apostasy, chh 1–12, a few faithful who will ultimately gather round Jesus to hear the last secrets of his heart in the Supper-room, chh 13–17, and after the momentary consternation of the Passion, chh 18–19, will rally again around the victorious Master whom they have not ceased to love, chh 20–21.

I 19–34 The Precursor's Testimony before the Jews— Points to remember are : Jn supposes the synoptic gospels and their account of Christ's baptism ; when he wrote, Judaism had fully declared over a period of sixty years and more its hostility to Jesus of Nazareth and his Church. Of the two testimonies here given before Judaism by the Precursor, one, 19–28, is spoken to a delegation from Jerusalem in the absence of Jesus, the other, 29–34, to a crowd [which also included the Delegation—Gen. Ed.] while the Precursor's index finger points to Jesus actually present on the scene.

19–28. We know that the Jerusalemite attitude to **b** John was superficial, 5:35, and quickly unsympathetic, Mt 3:7 ; 11:18 ; 21:24–26. Some evidence of hostility may be gathered from the present section, but it is mainly a record of John's answer to an inquisitorial commission. The delegation is a highly official one, coming from Jerusalem, the centre of religious government, and composed of Priests and

784b Levites—the former competent religious experts, the latter probably a sort of escort of temple police. **20.** The Delegates refrain from asking the pointed question: 'Art thou the Messias?' but John answers the general question: 'Who art thou?' very pointedly, and with an emphasis and solemnity which is set in evidence by an introductory formula first solemnly positive, then solemnly negative, and once again solemnly positive, saying: 'I am not the Christ'—a categoric negative

c which provoked another question. **21.** Words of Malachias, 4:5 [3:23], and Ben Sira, Ecclus 48:10 f., had given rise to the popular persuasion that Elias should come to anoint the Messias and manifest him (Justin, *Dial.* 8, 4). The Baptist partly fulfilled the prophecy of Malachias (*cf.* Christ's words, Mt 17:10 ff.; Mk 9:11 ff.), for he was Elias in spirit, but to the question of the Jews: 'Art thou Elias?' John answered even more briefly than before: 'I am not'. The question may not have been very serious, for John, in spite of his long stay in the desert, and in spite of his resemblance to Elias in garb and manner of life and fiery zeal, must have been publicly known as the son of Zachary and Elizabeth. Still we cannot be very positive regarding the forgetfulness which a lapse of 30 years can cause. There is, of course, no contradiction between Truth and the Prophet of Truth, for although John was the spiritual Elias of the first advent, he only denied that he was Elias in person. Another

d question remained. The Jews vaguely believed that some prophet, Enoch or Jeremias, would reappear as Precursor of the Messias, and they especially built on an imperfect interpretation of Deut 11:15: 'The Lord thy God shall raise up for thee from the midst of thee, from amongst thy brethren, a Prophet like to me: him you shall hear'. Moses' words were a prophecy of prophetism in Israel culminating in the Messias himself (*cf.* Ac 3:22; 7:37); the Jews, however, thought confusedly that Moses foretold one whom they called 'the prophet', 6:14, whoever he might be, generally making him a Samuel or an Isaias or some other prophet *redivivus*. John's answer was categoric: 'No'. St Gregory and other Fathers have admired the Precursor's solid and curt adherence to the humility which is truth. **22.** Pressed for a positive answer, the Baptist—never so styled, however, in Jn —applied to himself the words of Isaias, 40:3, concerning the herald of Israel's deliverance from Babylonian captivity. God's return at the head of a redeemed people was a figure of Messianic redemption, and the Precursor is the herald who calls for the preparation of a highway of penance. Coming from the mouth of the Baptist there is a very touching solemnity in the words: 'I am the voice of one crying in the wilderness . . .'. The voice sounds and vanishes, and John realized his role to be just that (*cf.* 3:30)—to fade before One greater than himself.

e **24.** Some of those sent (ἀπεσταλμένοι most probably without the article) were Pharisees and were particularly interested in ritual ablutions. **25.** They asked why he baptized. **26.** John explained. His was a simple baptism of water, with no inherent spiritual efficacy beyond its symbolic power of exciting repentance. Hereupon the Baptist turns the minds of his hearers from his own preparatory baptism to the One whose advent he was preparing, and who was already in the midst of Israel, unknown to Israel. **27.** He was coming after his Precursor, but as the Perfect after the imperfect, as the Lord after the servant. In the matter of menial service John declares that he is not worthy to perform the lowliest office towards him, even that of loosing the strap of his sandals. It is noteworthy that John speaking to the delegates from Jerusalem does not mention the baptism of the Holy Spirit, but only draws their attention to the

f *Person* who is already in their midst. **28.** The place is indicated, but Bethania (Bethany) beyond the Jordan has not been identified with certainty. It is, of course, to be distinguished from Bethany on Mount Olivet, less than two miles from Jerusalem. The name

of this Trans-Jordanic Bethania seems to have disappeared before the 3rd cent., for when Origen visited the sacred places *c* A.D. 215 he found only a Bethabara, which, owing to his influence, but rather against his text-critical judgement, supplanted Bethania in some codices. The two places may have been near each other, for the etymological difference between Bethania and Bethabara is that between Ship-ham and Ford-ham. The place was probably near a ford or ferry of the Jordan and (we should surmise) not very far from the eastern head of the present Allenby Bridge. **29-34.**—On the morrow Jesus appeared while John was surrounded by a number of disciples; *cf.* Orchard, *The Rejection of Christ*, DR 56 (1938) 410–26. Recently returned from his fast in the wilderness and probably staying for the time being in some hut near the Jordan, the Saviour *comes* to John to receive testimony. The Matins hymn of St John's Nativity (24 June), the Liturgy, as well as Catholic devotion, and Christian art have emphasized the importance of this scene of 'the pointing finger'. John's words designate Jesus as a Lamb belonging to God and therefore evidently sent by God and to be disposed of according to God's will. The lamb is a symbol of innocence, but whether John at this early stage of manifestation directly indicates that Jesus is a victim cannot be so easily decided—'a sinless Lamb taking away the sin of the world' may be the surface meaning of this word to the crowd, but the fullness of its meaning must include victimhood, for only thus did Jesus actually take away sin. There is an allusion to Is 53:7, but whether John had the paschal lamb or the lamb of daily sacrifice in mind is disputable. 'Sin' is generic and includes all sin original or personal. The next verse, 30, marking Jesus as later than the Baptist in time, but prior in dignity, because of the priority of pre-existence, has already been explained. [It is also the answer to the delegation's question.—Gen. Ed.] **31.** John's statement that he did not know Jesus before the day he baptized him is easily understood of a knowledge of visual recognition. John had been in the wilderness for about 20 years. **32 f.** Though by divine inspiration he recognized Jesus before he baptized him. Mt 3:14, the definite divinely-revealed sign by which he knew him, so as to manifest him to Israel, was the dove, for thus only the giver of the baptism of water recognized the One who should baptize with fire—the reference here being not only to the thorough purification symbolized by fire, but also (prophetically) to Pentecost. **34.** The sentence: 'This is the Son of God', has its plenary sense in the mouth of the Baptist: 'not revealed to him by flesh and blood' but by the voice at the Jordan and the illumination that went with his office of Precursor.

35-51 First Disciples—That this 'morrow', **35,** is the first great day in the autobiography of John the Evangelist is unmistakable. It was also the day on which the Church began to find its Saviour. The solemnity and grace of the simple narrative are equal to the occasion: John the Baptist standing, two disciples near by, a loving look cast by the Precursor on Jesus walking by, the repetition of the great words: 'Behold the Lamb of God. . .'. **37.** The two disciples followed Jesus. The heavenly attraction of which Jesus was to speak later, 6:44; 12:32, had begun to exercise its mysterious power. **38.** Everything is vivid. Jesus turned and gazed on the two men following him. '*What is it you seek?*' is perhaps a better rendering of the tone of Jesus' question, which is memorable as being the first word from the lips of the Saviour in Jn. The disciples' answer shows some embarrassment, but it beautifully and delicately expresses respect (Rabbi) and the desire to spend a while 'at home' with the new-found Master. **39.** 'Come and you *shall see*' is the form which Jesus' gracious invitation has in the best MSS. The writer's precision is to be noted: 'They came, they saw . . . they stayed . . .' from about the tenth hour—from 4 p.m. till dark and (according to the laws of oriental

a hospitality) that night also. St Augustine's comment cannot be omitted : ' They wished to see where he stayed and to do what is written : " The threshold of his door let thy foot wear : rise and come to him assiduously, and be instructed by his precepts ". He showed them where he stayed : They came and they were with him. What a happy day they spent, what a happy night ! Let us also build in our heart and make a house for him to visit. Let him teach us, let him converse with us ' (Tract. in Joann. in loc.).

b 40-42. Andrew (etymologically *Manly*) was one of the two ; the other is not named, but the narrative is too intimate not to reveal him as the disciple whom Jesus loved ; *cf.* chh 13-21. 41. The remark that Andrew *first* found his own brother Simon seems to suggest that John *later* found *his* own brother James ; an implied reference to Philip and Nathanael, 45, seems improbable. The joy of an ancient sage made *Heurēka* an enchanting word, but Andrew's assurance : ' We have found the Messias ' was a more momentous *heurēkamen* than any cry of a scientific discoverer. Messias is, of course, a Grecized Hebrew word meaning ' The Anointed (King of Israel) '. 42. John alone records the original circumstances of the change of Simon's name to Kêpha, which is Aramaic for *Rock*. Jesus looked fixedly upon him and, as it were, penetrated his soul, Ps 138, before giving him the name, which designated him as foundation-elect of the Church, Mt 16:18.

c 43-51. The fourth day of Jn's chronological sequence marks the beginning of Jesus' return journey to Galilee. The allusion to Jacob's Ladder in 51 justifies the conjecture that the route was westwards to Bethel and then along the chief northern highway through Samaria. 43. Philip (' lover of horses '), Greeknamed like his friend Andrew, 6:5, 8 ; 12:22, was, like him, from Bethsaida, a much Hellenized town on the east bank of the Jordan not far from its junction with the Lake of Genesareth. 44. He was probably predisposed by what he heard from his fellow-townsmen, but, in any case, he promptly followed a single word of invitation from Jesus, and communicated his enthusiasm to Nathanael. 45. This Nathanael (the name being equivalent to *Theodore-Deusdedit*) is now commonly identified with the Bar-Tolmai or Bartholomew who is closely associated with Philip in the synoptic lists of Apostles. He was from Cana, 21:2, 4 miles NE. of Nazareth. The wording of Philip's announcement to Nathanael would seem to indicate that the latter was a man of some scriptural learning, if not a scribe. Philip's description of Jesus from his putative father, Joseph, is not surprising, and its retention by St John is a guarantee of the historical fidelity of an Evangelist who knew Jesus to be the

d Son of God. 46. The uncomplimentary reference to Nazareth is almost proverbial. St Matthew saw verified, 2:23, the prophetic description of a lowly, despised Messias, when Jesus became a Nazarene. What we know of Nazareth from the Gospels, Lk 4:29 ; Mt 13:54-58, does not give us a high opinion of its people. The sceptical question of Nathanael may, however, have had some local jealousy in it, but he loyally adopted the good method proposed by Philip : ' Come and see '. 47. ' Truly an Israelite ' was a eulogy that had religious sacredness in it (since God himself had given the name ' Israel ' to Jacob), and the compliment of guilelessness asserted Nathanael's sincerity. Jesus struck the very point of the newcomer's character as a religious man splendidly sincere. 48. There was no lack of humility in the question : ' *Whence comes thy knowledge of me ?* ' What Jesus then revealed about a crisis of thought or feeling experienced by Nathanael was clearly an example of the reading of hearts (*cf.* Ac 1:24). It seems the event referred to was not recent, for, as we are some weeks from the Pasch (*cf.* 2:13), fig-trees were not yet in foliage. 49. In calling Jesus ' Son of God ', Nathanael may indeed have vaguely confessed his divine origin, but our Lord's subsequent words show that he could not

have realized its full import. He certainly confessed **785d** his Messiahship, for St John regards ' King of Israel ' (*cf.* 12:13, 15) as a Messianic title. 50. Nathanael's **e** act of faith was based on the manifestation of divine knowledge by Jesus. 51. The Master assured him that he should see greater things. The double *Amen* of solemn asseveration occurs here for the first of two dozen times in Jn. Jesus also used the single *Amen*, which the Synoptists retained throughout. The vision of heaven open and angels ascending and descending does not refer specially to any definite apparitions of angels between the end of Christ's desert fast (which was gone by) and the day of the Ascension. It alludes to Jacob's dream-vision, Gen 28:12, of a ladder at Bethel (near which place our Lord probably was at the moment), and asserts that the Son of Man in his earthly ministry shall be the centre of communications between heaven and earth —these communications being conceived as angelic goings and comings. The order : ' ascent and descent ' is not that of angelic motion but of a ladder the primary purpose of which is ascent. In this sentence the title ' Son of Man ' occurs for the first time on the lips of Jesus (31 times in Mt, 13 in Jn). Here it is only necessary to repeat : (*a*) that the name carried a suggestion of human lowliness and poetic rareness ; (*b*) that in our Lord's time it was not in use either as a substitute for the first singular personal pronoun nor as a Messianic name ; (*c*) that (notwithstanding) it carried a thinking mind to the Messianic vision of Dan 7:13.; (*d*) that Jesus used it of himself with a variety of pointedness which was very suggestive (most often before his disciples, less often before Pharisees and scribes, seldom before the people, and most solemnly of all at his trial before the Sanhedrin) ; (*e*) that it had the fascination of mystery ; (*f*) and lastly that being a humble title of the Messias, it did not continue to be used in the Church, being found only once in Ac, 7:55, on the lips of St Stephen, but in this case with deliberate allusion to Christ's solemn answer, when adjured by Caiphas to say who he was.

No one who meditates these 33 verses (which follow the sublime Prologue) can remain insensible to the exquisite charm of the narrative. The voice of the great humble Precursor does its work, and the rally of these early disciples to a greater Master than John is the beautiful introduction to the history of Christianity.

II 1-11 The Marriage Feast at Cana—1. The third **786a** day should be reckoned from the beginning of the Galilean journey which covered a distance of some 70 or 80 miles. It may have been a Wednesday, the usual day for the marriage of a maiden. The bridegroom and bride are unknown, and the identifications : Simon the Zealot, John the Evangelist, Susanna, etc., are mere romancing. Cana is not Qāna 8 miles from Tyre, probably not Kirbet Qāna near Sepphoris, but rather Kefr Kenna four miles NE. of Nazareth, for which there is a reasonably solid tradition. If, as is likely, Mary was present as a relative, the invitation to Jesus and his disciples would have been on her account, although Nathanael may have had something to do with it. St Joseph evidently was dead. **2.** Nuptial festivities lasted a week and were called in Aramaic *miṣtîṭâ* (drink-festival) with which accords the rabbinical dictum : ' Where there is no wine, there is no joy '. **3.** As wine supplies (especially when the family was poor) partly depended on gifts from those invited, the advent of Jesus and five disciples may well have contributed to the imminent (or already complete, Codex S) shortage, quickly noted by the charitable eye of the Blessed Virgin. Her brief announcement of the situation to Jesus is meant as a petition. **4.** His answer has created three difficulties : **b** (1) The term of address sounds severe, if not belittling ; (2) the answer seems a refusal ; (3) the reason given admits more than one interpretation. As regards the first : ' Woman ' both in Gk and Semitic is a title not

786b indeed of domestic intimacy (our Lord would not have used it at Nazareth) but of solemn honour. This honorific solemnity of the word on the lips of Jesus himself may be tested in Jn 4:21 ; 20:15, but most of all in 19:26, when he addressed his mother from the cross. Concerning the second : the Master's question which literally reads : ' *What to me and to thee ?* ' has to be understood from biblical and not modern usage. Therefore it does not mean : 'What concern is it of ours ?' or 'There is no need for you to tell me'. In all the biblical passages where it occurs, Jg 11:12 ; 2 Kg 16:10, 19:22 ; 4 Kg 3:13 ; 2 Par 35:21 ; Mt 8:29 ; Mk 1:24, the phrase signifies, according to circumstances, a great or lesser divergence of viewpoint between the two parties concerned. In 2 Kg 16:10 it means total dissent ; in Jg 11:12 it voices a complaint against an invader. In our passage, also, divergence must be admitted. In a sense our Lord's answer is a refusal, but not an absolute refusal, rather a refusal *ad mentem*, as a Roman Congregation would say, and the Blessed Virgin understood her Son's mind from the tone of his voice. His first public miracle belonged to the divine programme of his Messianic mission into which flesh and blood could not enter. His answer is therefore an assertion of independence of his Mother, similar to the word he spoke in the temple about his Father's business. The Blessed Virgin's subsequent action shows that the tone of our Lord's protest on this occasion was neither a curt nor an unqualified refusal. On the third point, namely the sentence : ' My hour is not yet come ', it is obvious that we cannot read the words as a question : ' *Is not My hour already come ?* ' Although the view has the support of Tatian, St Gregory of Nyssa and Knabenbauer, neither the context nor the Gk seem to admit interrogation. ' My hour ' has been variously understood as the hour of my Passion when I shall recognize the mother of my mortality (St Aug), or (more probably) the hour fixed for my public manifestation **c** through the working of miracles. **5.** Mary, understanding perfectly that our Lord's action would not be a family business, but would nevertheless follow the course of charity, gave orders to the servants with all confidence. **6.** The water-pots (perhaps mostly borrowed) were large, for water had to be taken from them and poured on hands and vessels according to the rules of Jewish purification. Stone and not earthenware was proof against legal defilement. Six pots, containing 2 or 3 attic *metretae* each, would give a total capacity between $6 \times 2 \times 8\frac{1}{2} = 102$ and $6 \times 3 \times 8\frac{1}{2} = 153$ gallons. **7.** ' Filled . . . to the brim ' shows the water, as it were, peeping out of the vessels and, no doubt, suggested Crashaw's beautiful pentameter : ' *Nympha pudica Deum vidit et erubuit*—the bashful maiden water saw its God and blushed '. **8.** The *architrichlinus*, to whom the servants were ordered to bring the wine in a smaller vessel, probably in a cup, was to be the first witness of the unexpected provision. He would have been a local expert in convivial arrangements, not a symposiarch of the classic type (*cf.* Ecclus **d** 32:1). **9.** He did not know whence the wine was. **10.** But once he had testified to its excellence, the servants could tell the facts. The custom : ' Good wine to fresh palates, and less good afterwards ' is not otherwise known from contemporary writings, but we cannot deny its local authenticity—possibly it reflects Galilean parsimony—and it is certainly an outspoken testimony that would have called attention to the miracle, so that this would very soon have become known to all present. **11.** This first of Christ's miracles is, like all others, a sign of his divine power showing the ' glory of the Only-begotten '. His disciples had already believed in him, but now they believed more strongly. Catholic piety finds almost inexhaustible riches in these 11 verses (Gospel of 2nd Sunday after Epiphany). The passage shows the sanctity of marriage, the Wisdom of God approving domestic joy, the power of the Blessed Virgin's intercession, and even the law of her mediation. Besides, it suggests the thought that

Christ's own nuptials with his Church have begun, **7** the water of the old dispensation is becoming the good wine of the new, and an image is offered of the Eucharistic wine which is to gladden the heart of man. **12 Descent to Capharnaum**—Not long after the **e** marriage at Cana Jesus went to Capharnaum—a descent of some 1,550 feet, from 870 above Mediterranean level to 680 below, in a distance of less than 20 miles. Not now but later he made Capharnaum his own city, Mt 9:1, by adopting it as the centre of his Galilean ministry. The more probable and common identification is Tell Hum, but the site of Capharnaum has also been sought at 'Ain Tabigha, Kirbet Minyeh and even Kheraze—all of which are within a radius of a few miles. Capharnaum was a very Jewish city, and Peter and Andrew had a house there. It was a natural rendezvous for pilgrims forming into caravans for the Paschal journey to Jerusalem.

The present stay, being for this purpose, lasted ' not many days '. ' His brethren ' were the cousins or other relatives of our Lord, and were certainly neither full nor half-brothers or sisters (*cf.* art. ' Brethren of the Lord ' for discussion of the evidence).

2:13-3:36 First Judean Ministry. **7**
13-22 Cleansing of the Temple—This cleansing is probably to be distinguished from that which took place on Monday before the Passion, Mt 21:12 f. That such a vindication by Jesus of the majesty of his Father's house occurred twice—at the beginning and at the end of the public life—is not improbable ; the differences of detail are not favourable to identification ; moreover, Jn and the Synoptists show enough chronological intention in the matter to exclude the hypothesis of one and the same event. [There are however weighty arguments for holding that there was only one Cleansing of the Temple and that it did indeed occur at the beginning of the public life of our Lord where Jn places it. The reason why the synoptic gospels place it at the end may be that Mk and Lk in general follow the arrangement of Mt which is logical rather than chronological, and which accordingly groups all incidents connected with Jerusalem under the last Jerusalem visit.—Gen. Ed.] **13.** The ' Pasch of the Jews ' marks the feast as belonging to the old order. ' Ascent ' was almost a technical term for the festal pilgrimage. **14.** The sale of sacrificial animals (oxen, sheep, doves) and the setting up of tables of exchange in the court of the Gentiles, within the sacred enclosure (ἱερόν) meant not only unbecoming noise and movement, Mk 11:16, but also avarice in which not the salesmen and changers only but the temple authorities also had their share. Foreign money had to be changed into the ancient half-shekel (called *Tyrian*, approximately 1s 6d) payable as annual capitation tax to the temple by every Israelite over twenty (*cf.* Mt 17:24). **15.** Cords were easily picked **b** up in what had really become a market. Christ made a scourge (' as it were ' is not represented in the best MSS). The text does not say clearly whether the scourge was used on both men and animals ; presumably so, in keeping with the drastic action of spilling the coins (κέρμα) and overturning the tables of the bankers. **16.** Though they sold the offerings of the poor, there is no sufficient reason for supposing that the dove-sellers were less guilty than the others. Christ's action stopped short of dispossessing the culprits, and birds in cages could not be driven out. Moreover, the word addressed to the dove-sellers is really addressed to all. ' My Father's house ' involves the claim of divine Sonship. **17.** This assertion of authority was so striking that the disciples thought of a verse from a Messianic Psalm, 68:10—quoted from LXX with its verb in the future. The verse is not merely accommodated, for in the Psalm the Just One is eaten up by his own zeal, not by the jealousy of persecutors. **18.** Although the uneasy authorities had already received the witness of John the Baptist they now demanded further sign to authenticate

Jesus' personal authority to act thus. **19.** The answer is like that given later to similar demands made in bad faith (*cf.* Mt 16:4): 'Destroy this Temple'—rather 'sanctuary' (*vaós*)—'and in three days I will raise it up'. The sign is the Resurrection. Consequently, our Lord's words refer in no sense to the material inner sanctuary of the Zorobabelian-Herodian temple. The concessive imperative 'Destroy' is prophetic, and shows clearly enough that the Jewish hostility which was to kill Jesus had begun that day. Such a saying from a Master, whose majestic zeal had just vindicated his Father's house, should have provoked attentive thought, and the history of our Lord's trial and crucifixion shows how it impressed itself; but actually it was now turned to ridicule. **20.** A sanctuary 46 years in building to be destroyed and rebuilt in 3 days!—this is the sarcasm, which will be repeated on Calvary. The reference cannot be to the original Zorobabelian temple finished in 516 B.C. and not begun much earlier than 536. The Herodian reconstruction of Zorobabel's edifice is meant. This had begun in the 18th year of Herod's reign (20–19 B.C.) and is generally considered to have been finished only in A.D. 64. If the total includes the 18th year of Herod and counts 46 complete years up to the present Pasch (the aorist οἰκοδομήθη with vaós not ἱερόν as subject, raises a doubt) we can fix with some confidence of probability the spring of A.D. 27 as the date of this event. [On the other hand Fr Sutcliffe (in *A Two Year Public Ministry*) has verified the contention of Fr Power Bi 9 (1928) 257 ff. that v 20 is to be rendered: '*This sanctuary has been built* forty-six years', *i.e.* was completed 46 years before, in 19 B.C.—Gen. Ed.] **21.** Jesus spoke, however, about the sanctuary of his body, the most holy of all temples. **22.** After the resurrection the disciples entered fully into the resurrection texts of the Scripture and this word of Jesus.

23-25 Imperfect Converts—The feast lasted 8 days, during which time many believed on account of the miracles worked by Jesus. Miracles are strong arguments of credibility. They prepare the mind for faith, but faith and especially deep faith is not the mere impression of miracles. These new adherents of Jesus at Jerusalem ' believed in his name '—accepted him as a divinely-sent Master. **24.** St John's double use of the verb πιστεύω cannot easily be rendered in English. Those men trusted Jesus as a Master accredited by heaven, but Jesus did not trust himself to them. **25.** The reason is that he had immediate and intimate knowledge of their dispositions—the 'searcher of hearts,' had no need to be told what depth of faith these believers had. He did not communicate himself entirely to them. St Augustine's application to Catechumens is well known, but is only an accommodated sense.

III 1-21 Nicodemus—The name is Greek (*victorious people*), but the Talmud also attests its Jewish adoption. Pharisee and Sanhedrist of the order of scribes (*cf.* 10) were the religious titles of Nicodemus. **2.** His nocturnal visit shows timidity but not cowardice (*cf.* 7:51; 19:39), and he was also probably moved by a desire to have a quiet talk with Jesus. His approach is respectful (Rabbi) and shows a certain conviction, based on the miracles, regarding the divine mission of Jesus. Nicodemus associates himself with others (probably Pharisees or even Sanhedrists—*cf.* 12:42, though the Pharisees as a body were hostile). **3.** The question of the kingdom of God is what is in the visitor's mind, and it is to this that the solemn answer of Jesus refers: 'Amen, amen, I say to thee, unless a man be born again, he cannot see the kingdom of God '. With the possible exception of Gal 4:9, NT and even Johannine usage stand for ' from above ' rather than ' again ' as a rendering of ἄνωθεν. So also the Greek Fathers and many moderns. However, unless there is a similarly ambiguous word in Aramaic, our Lord, as interpreted by Nicodemus himself, spoke of second birth, other than one's first natural birth. This justifies our ' again ', which represents not only the Latin

version but also the Coptic, Syriac, Armenian, Ethiopic **788a** and Georgian. Without this second birth (which in any case must be ' from above ') a man cannot belong to the kingdom of God (' see ' has the sense of *experience, enjoy*). Kingdom of God occurs only here, 3, 5, in Jn. This term, familiar from the Synoptics, is broadly equivalent to *life* in Jn and to *justice* in St Paul. There is no real distinction between *seeing the kingdom of God* and *seeing life*, 3:36. **4.** Nicodemus, probably **b** an old man himself, reduces our Lord's words to the absurdity of an elder entering his mother's womb to be born again. **5.** The answer of Jesus seems to attach itself closely to the impossibility thus crudely imagined. Water is like the material element giving the new birth, the fecundating power being the Spirit (many MSS of Vg have *Holy* Spirit). This concept is beautifully expressed in the Roman Rite of blessing the Baptismal Font; ' From the immaculate womb of the divine font comes forth a heavenly offspring, born as a new creature '. Water, as the Council of Trent defined (Sess. 7, can. 2), is not to be understood in the metaphorical sense. There is no difference (except one of aspect) between *seeing* the Kingdom of God, 3, and *entering into* it, 5. Like begets like. **6.** ' What is born of the flesh is flesh '—in the physical (not Pauline-moral) sense of the term—' What is born of the Spirit is spirit ', that is, a spiritual being. **7.** Jesus forestalls a second expression of wonder from Nicodemus on the subject of re-birth. It is mysterious, but one must not deny its reality because one does not know the whence, and the how and the whither of it. **8.** The wind is taken as an analogy or parable. It comes apparently as it wills, and its whisper or growl or howl is heard, but one cannot say where it rises or where it dies away. So, the man born of the Spirit shows effects that are perceptible, but the vital processes of the Spirit are invisible. St Augustine supposes that the Holy Spirit is the subject throughout. If so, there may be a reference to the phenomena of Pentecost. **9.** Nicodemus is still puzzled. **10.** In view of **c** Scriptural passages like Ez 36:25 f.; Is 44:3, Jesus points to the anomaly of the ignorance of one who (of the two speaking) is the ' master of Israel ', *i.e.* teacher and interpreter of the Law and Tradition. **11.** Then to ' the master of Israel ' and all like him Jesus asserts his own competence as a divine teacher. Ranging himself for a moment with all competent witnesses in any sphere—or using the plural of majesty (?) —he says : ' Amen, amen, I say to thee, that we speak what we know and we testify what we have seen, and you receive not our testimony '. **12.** Then, resuming the first singular, he refers to the incredulity provoked by his revelations on things (like regeneration) actualized here on earth, and argues (*a minori ad maius*) that the revelation of heavenly things—the mysteries of the divine being—will encounter still greater incredulity. **13.** The Word Incarnate—for he is the real subject of this sentence—is the only witness of heavenly things. No one has ascended to heaven, so as to be there and know the things of heaven, but he that descended from heaven. Coming to be visibly on earth in human flesh—this is the metaphor of descent —he who is the Son of Man has not ceased to be in heaven. As the last phrase : ' Who is in heaven ' is absent from some of the best MSS, including SB, it may be a gloss, but it is an excellent one, giving splendid prominence to the *communicatio idiomatum*, or interchange of divine and human predicates. ' Above ' and ' below ' are spoken of the one Person ; the Son of God was on earth, the Son of Man was in Heaven. This last sentence, 13, really refers to the Incarnation rather than to the beatific vision, which Christ's soul possessed. **14 f.** With the Incarnation the thought of **d** Redemption is closely connected. Faith in the Word Incarnate must also be faith in the Redeemer. **14.** ' Necessity ' is a dominant idea in the whole passage, 7, 14. Here it is the necessity of Christ's redeeming death that is proclaimed. ' Exaltation ' is crucifixion, 8:28 ; 12:32, 34. The brazen serpent raised by Moses

788d as a divine remedy for poisonous serpent bite, Num 21:4 9 ; Wis 16:6 f., was a figure of salvation through Christ crucified. The non-poisonous likeness of a serpent looked upon with faith healed poisoned wounds and preserved temporal life : the sinless Saviour in the likeness of sinful flesh heals the poison wounds of sin and gives life everlasting. **15.** The negative side of salvation, namely, escape from perdition, is not mentioned in the best MSS, and probably comes from 16.

e 16-21. The arguments for regarding these lines not as words spoken to Nicodemus but as reflexions of the Evangelist, seem strong enough to establish a serious probability. It is pointed out that dialogue ceases, the verbs are in the past tense, several expressions occur which are Johannine but are not heard elsewhere from the lips of Jesus (*e.g.* ' Only-begotten ', ' believe in the name ', ' do the truth '). The last of these arguments is impressive, but on the other hand the language is extremely like that of the Johannine discourses of Jesus ; no clear notice of a change of speaker is given ; and the things said are very closely connected with the ideas of Incarnation and Redemption, to the consideration of which Jesus had led Nicodemus. **16.** The motive and fount of salvation is God's love for the world—that is, for mankind. Love made God give and deliver to death his Son (co-equal with himself), his Only-begotten (infinitely beloved), with a view to the salvation of every believer from perdition into eternal life. **17.** Salvation not judgement is the direct purpose of the mission of the **f** Son of God. **18.** Men make their own judgement by their attitude to him, 3:36 ; 5:24 ; 12:48. He who believes incurs no damnation. The unbeliever is already in the state of damnation (κέκριται), for he has established himself as an unbeliever (perfect tense) in the name—that is, in the mission and Godhead—of the Only-begotten Son of God. Note again the insistence on this double title of love and dignity, the order of words being the inverse of 16. The making of one's individual judgement in this actual terrestrial present is powerfully put in terms of light and darkness. The working of grace is supposed, but the accent is on the dispositions of men in regard to the light. St Augustine's application is justly celebrated : ' Many loved their sins, and many confessed their sins. He who confesses and accuses his sins is already on God's side. God (that is the light) accuses your sins : and if you also accuse, you are joined to God. There are, as it were, two things : the man and the sinner. God made man, and man made himself a sinner. Destroy what you made, that God may save what he made. You must hate your own work in you, and love God's work in you. When that which you made begins to displease you, then your good works are beginning, in as much as you are accusing your bad works. The beginning of good works is the confession of bad works. You do truth, and you come to the light. What is it—to do truth ? You do not fondle yourself, you do not caress yourself, you do not flatter yourself, do not say : I am just, when you are really not—then you are beginning to do truth ', *Tr. 12 in Jn.* The same saint said : ' Sore eyes hate the light, which healthy eyes love '.

g 21. ' He who does the truth ', that is, he who has the disposition that co-operates with truth, ' comes to the light, that his works may be made manifest *as being* done in God ', that is, according to God's pleasure. ' In God ', ' with God ', Gen 6:9, ' according to God ', Rom 8:27, scarcely differ in meaning. The words of 19 ff., as this phrase indicates, are more general than St Augustine's comment and refer to the consciousness of general rectitude of life, which is co-operation with God, rather than to the acknowledgement of sin, which, however, is part of the rectitude or honesty of fallen man, *cf.* 1 Jn 1:8. Good will or a right heart prepares a man to welcome truth.

h 22-36 Last Testimony of the Precursor—No close student of Jn will escape the inclination to join the many modern commentators who regard 31-36 of this section as reflexions of the Evangelist. Still, there is not the slightest external indication of a change of speaker ; the thoughts in 31-36 do not go beyond the Precursor's understanding of the mystery of Christ (although we may admit that the Evangelist gives them something of his own personal style) ; the phrase ' wrath of God ' at the end recalls the stern character of the synoptic accounts of the Precursor's preaching.

22-26. The time is loosely marked as after the visit of Nicodemus—presumably soon after the Paschal Octave, for after the departure of the pilgrims hostility to Jesus would have made itself more felt in Jerusalem. The text shows us the Divine Master in some country part of Judaea—a place of springs or streams, or perhaps near the Jordan. He stayed a considerable time there with his disciples, whom he commissioned (*cf.* 4:2) to exercise a ministry of baptism, more probably not that baptism which was to give the Spirit, 7:39, but rather a preparatory rite like that of John. **22.** The Precursor had come to the west of the Jordan and moved north. Aenon (*Ainon*, exactly our English *Wells*) or Salim nearby is situated 8 Roman miles south of Scythopolis (Beisan) by the *Onomasticon* of Eusebius, by St Jerome (*Ep.* 73) and Aetheria. There are still five or seven wells within a small radius in this district. Salim 1¼ miles nearer the Jordan seems to have left its name in the modern Tell es-Sarem. **24.** The indication : ' John not yet imprisoned ' is a precious explanatory reference to the Synoptics, who could easily give the impression that Jesus began his work only after the imprisonment of John. **25.** The dispute of some disciples of John with *a Jew* (S corrected, B, L, A) or *Jews* (S, Vg) about purificatory rites excited in the former a jealousy or group-selfishness towards Jesus which was indeed a *felix culpa*, for it occasioned the Precursor's very striking testimony. (Or was their jealousy really due to the fact that Jesus was now drawing larger crowds than their own master ?) **26.** The popularity of Jesus was evidently rising, and that of John falling in proportion. This was intimated in the disciples' report to John. **27-30.** No wonder the Catholic Church has always given the Precursor a signal place of honour, due not only to his office but to the high dignity of his humility. These words of his are amongst the greatest and most beautiful ever pronounced by human lips. Their gravity, humility, grandeur, and exquisite beauty need to be ' relished interiorly '. **27.** John's mission was from heaven, Mt 21:25 ; Mk 11:30 f.; Lk 20:4 f., to pretend to more than *was given* him would be usurpation. **28.** He was not the Christ, but his Precursor. **29.** Comparing himself to the chief friend attached to a bridegroom, he says that his role and his joy are just like those of such a sincere friend. When the wedding is being celebrated (Christ was already gathering the bridal body of his disciples ; *cf.* Mt 9:15), the 'best man' can only rejoice at the joyful voice of the bridegroom already happy in the possession of his bride. In this sense John's joy is full. **30.** Jesus must increase in the esteem of a multitude of disciples, John must decrease. Let us recall the quaint but fascinating comment which we read in the Breviary (Aug. 29) : ' John dwindled by decapitation, Christ grew on the cross '.

31-36. There seems to be no really cogent reason why we should not attribute these words to the Precursor. All other mortals and all other Prophets including John himself are compared to Christ. **31.** The One whose origin is absolutely from above is over everybody. Terrestrial and celestial (*cf.* 1 Cor 15:47) are terms of immense distinction. The earthly has the limitations of earth, the heavenly is supreme. **32.** As a witness of the things of God, he who comes from heaven has the authority of One who has seen and heard. No one, however (hyperbole for ' very few '), receives his testimony. **33.** To receive his testimony is equivalent to declaring under one's own hand and seal that God speaks the truth. **34.** The Divine Envoy's words are the words of God. The total definitive revelation of God is delivered by him, for God does not give the Spirit in limited measure to the Word Incarnate. **35.** To the Beloved Son, 'in whom he is well-pleased', God must give and does give the plenitude of all authority. Surrender to him by faith brings life everlasting (begun here, consummated hereafter) ; on the other hand, unbelief towards the Son means the forfeiture of life and permanence in the state of wrath.

IV 1-54 Through Samaria to Galilee—It is only at the beginning of this section that Jn first joins the Synoptists, Mt 4:12 ; Mk 1:4 ; Lk 4:14, who begin the public life of Christ in Galilee. The short mission of two days in Samaria, 4:43, is an episode registered only by Jn. Lke Christ's brief stay in the territory of Tyre and Sidon at a later date, Mt 15:21 ff. ; Mk 7:24 ff., it was intended to show that salvation was not for ' the lost sheep of the House of Israel ' only.

1-4 Motive of Journey—The Baptist was already in prison, Mt 4:12 ; Mk 1:14. **1.** ' When *the Lord* therefore understood . . .' (B, C, A, L against S, D Vg). The Master's ordinary human knowledge of providential events usually determined his actions. At this point he knew that the Pharisees (the chief focus of hostility) were aware of the growing movement towards him and his baptism. **2.** The remark that he did not himself baptize may be perhaps a further indication that no sacrament was yet administered. **3.** Judaea was henceforth dangerous, and so the Messianic light was to rise in Galilee, Is 9:1 f. **4.** Some ' necessity ' which Jn does not explain compelled Jesus to go through Samaria. If he was in the Jordan valley (and so it seems) the direct way would have been due north, but the Lord seems to have followed a western road, possibly the less frequented, difficult and fatiguing Wady path that passed by modern Dejân. We may conjecture that the ' necessity ' of journeying through Samaria was in the providential decree, for later ' Jerusalem, Judaea, Samaria and to the ends of the earth ' was to be the Apostolic programme.

5-30 Meeting with the Samaritan Woman—The narrative is a little sketch of divine pedagogy. It not only shows Jesus thirsting and seeking a soul but reveals his method. **5.** The place named Sichar (Sychar) was scarcely the ancient Sichem, replaced since Seleucid days by the city which Titus later rebuilt as Flavia Neapolis (*Nablus*, nearly a mile WNW. of Sichem). Though excavations of 1914 and 1926-8 have revealed that Sichem was still inhabited in the reign of Tiberius, nevertheless the name Sychar, the Onomasticon, the Madaba Map and many Itineraries rather favour the modern village of El 'Askar. This place, at the foot of Ebal to the south-east, is three-quarters of a mile to the north of Jacob's Well, which is close to the foot of Garizim. Joseph's tomb, Jos 24:32, in Joseph's field, Gen 48:22, is popularly located about half-way. **6.** The ' fountain ' of Jacob was really a well supplied from a deep spring. It will be noted that Jesus and the Evangelist keep to the notion of spring (*pēgē*), while the Samaritan woman calls it a well (*phrear*). Tired from the journey—*quaerens me sedisti lassus*—Jesus sat beside or on the margin of the well. There are two significant details : Jesus sat thus—just as he was in his fatigue (Chrys.) just as a tired man sits—and ' it was the sixth hour ', that is, noon, ' the hour of thirst ' (Nonnus). **7.** A woman of Samaria, not the city founded by Omri, but of the land of Samaria, came with her pitcher and rope to procure water. If she came from the township of Sychar, the distance was fairly considerable, and the hour was not the ordinary time (either morning or evening) for drawing water. And as Sychar ('Askar) has a copious spring of its own, the woman most probably came from the fields, and we may be sure

that a special Providence arranged the details of that **789d** day. There is no reason to believe that the woman was known in Samaria by the symbolic name Photina (*Lightsome* like Latin Lucina) given to her in the Greek Menaea (Feb. 26) and the Roman Martyrology (March 20). Without any preliminary address, Jesus asked for a drink. St Augustine notes his double thirst, physical and spiritual, for he really thirsted for the faith of a human soul. **8.** They were alone, for the disciples—a half-dozen perhaps—had gone in a body to buy food from Samaritans who could prove hostile. **9.** The woman recognizing a Jew by his speech or by his dress, Num 15:37 f., called attention to the national hatred between Jews and Samaritans. The descendants of Sargon's and Esarhaddon's colonists from Cutha and other eastern cities were regarded as mixed pagans and schismatics. They had been rejected from partnership in the temple of Zorobabel in the 6th cent. marked as defiant schismatics when the apostate Jewish priest, Manasses, erected a temple on Garizim about 400 B.C., ranked with the hated Edomites and Philistines by Ben Sira, Ecclus 50:28 ; and their reciprocal animosities had survived the destruction of the Samaritan temple by John Hyrcanus in 129 B.C. Josephus (*Ant.* 8, 11 and 20, 6) joins the Gospels, Lk 9:53 ; Jn 8:48, in showing that in our Lord's time friendly relations were not to be expected between Jews and Samaritans. **10.** From the thought **e** of national hatreds, however, and from regarding him simply as a Jew, Jesus raises the mind of the woman to God's love and to the gift from heaven which his own presence is to her. He has asked for a drink, but he can give her ' living water '—the symbol being that of a beverage like bubbling water from a spring (not dormant water from a cistern) figuring by its freshness a living and life-giving energy. **11 f.** The woman now shows the impression made on her fundamentally good heart, for she addresses Jesus as *Kyrie* (Sir), but shifts the theme to the difficulty of a man with no hauling apparatus getting water from a well 100 ft deep (this being a fair average from the recorded soundings), and also to the unlikely supposition that the stranger is greater than the Patriarch Jacob. She thought : either he means he can get water from this well—but how could he without a bucket, 11, or else he means he can get it from some other well or spring better than this ; in which case he evidently thinks himself superior to Jacob, who made this well. No doubt, she suspects that he might be, after all. **13 f.** Jesus turns the comparison of himself and Jacob to a comparison of the two waters. The water of Jacob's well relieves thirst only for a time, the water that Jesus gives is itself a perpetual spring, efficacious for life everlasting. The theological name for it is ' sanctifying grace '. Jesus certainly did not set the physical law of water seeking its own level before the Samaritan woman, but this illustration proposed by Menochius is a good one. **15.** The woman is deeply impressed. Her answer should not be regarded as sarcastic, but as expressing the naïveté of imperfect understanding. She wants the water, for she now vaguely believes that Jesus is a worker of wonders. **16 f.** There is an obstacle, and Jesus reveals it in the **f** moral disorder of this woman's life. ' Call your husband ' would have seemed a very natural remark, for a long public colloquy with a woman was not according to custom. The woman's denial that she had a husband was evasive, equivocal, and perhaps a lie, and it concealed ugly facts which Jesus with merciless mercy unmasked, asserting that her words were literally true. **18.** The woman's record of five husbands in the past followed by the state of unlawful concubinage in the present would imply that she had contracted five *lawful* marriages (beginning probably from her fifteenth year), though we cannot tell for certain. It is possible that she may have been divorced by more than one husband. In any case, she is at present an adulteress. **19 f.** In acknowledging Jesus to be a prophet she implicitly admits it, and is already

789f sympathetically meeting the light of truth. She raises the question of the true religion in terms of the rival **g** claims of Garizim and Jerusalem. **21-24.** Jesus' answer, introduced by a solemn 'Believe me' and a respectful title of address 'Woman', says that the time of particularist cults and local sanctuaries is nearing its end. For the first time in the Gospel record Jesus calls God 'Father', to be adored as such even by the Samaritans. These, heretofore accepting as inspired only the Pentateuch which they often misinterpreted as well, have adored 'what (they) know not' (*i.e.* know very imperfectly) ; but the Jews, being the people destined to give the world Messianic salvation have been progressively enlightened by Prophets and Psalmists and adore what they know. Worship in spirit and in truth is interior worship (not excluding bodily acts and ceremonies) carried out in the light of a full revelation. The hour of that spiritual, Catholic, perfect worship has come, for the Revealer is present. Such worship 'in spirit and truth' is the only worship proportioned to the pure spirituality of God. **25.** The woman remarks that clarification on these points must come from the Messias, known by the Samaritans from the Pentateuch and called *Tabeh* ('the Returned' or 'the Converter'). **26.** Thereupon Jesus pronounces the first great 'I am' of Jn. The Christ is sitting beside Jacob's Well and is revealing himself to a Samaritan woman. The One vaguely apprehended as a miracle-worker, 15, acknowledged as a Prophet, 19, is really the promised Messias. Such a revelation could be made in Samaria where Messianism was not contaminated with nationalistic and political aspirations.

790a **27-30.** Jewish custom was strict in regard to a man conversing with a woman in public. **27.** Hence the surprise of the disciples, who concluded that some necessity had occasioned the conversation, but out of respect for their Master they asked no question. Meanwhile the woman (in a state of excitement, for she leaves the pitcher behind) has gone to the city. **29.** Forthwith she becomes an apostle. Either Jesus had told her other things from her past life, or the expression 'all I ever did' is very natural feminine hyperbole. She does not doubt that Jesus is the Messias, but she invites the inhabitants of Sychar to test it for themselves. Her persuasive tone easily moves a people naturally curious and not indisposed to spend an hour on something new.

b **31-42 Results—31-34.** The disciples expected Jesus to eat. He had been hungry as well as thirsty but had undergone the well-known psychological experience of hunger vanishing before a deeper desire, that of converting a soul. This is the satisfying food that his disciples did not know. They thought that he had received something to eat. He explained that the doing of his Father's will and the accomplishment of his Father's work was the supreme satisfaction of all his desires—it was 'his food'.

c **35-38.** The Father's work, which is Christ's work, is to be also the work of the disciples. It results in the gathering of a spiritual harvest. A remark recently made by the disciples, perhaps at the very moment that they came in view of the Plain of Machneh and the fertile valley between Ebal and Garizim, is taken by Jesus as his introductory sentence ; moreover, a sufficient sprinkling of white in the garments of the approaching Samaritans would justify the verb of ocular vision. **35.** 'Do not you say', etc. : this remark cited from the mouth of the disciples marks a date—January A.D. 29, four months from the wheat harvest. The suggestion that it is a proverb meaning that 'everything takes time' is not likely, and seems excluded by the assignment of a minimum space of four months between sowing and reaping instead of the ordinary or maximum, namely five or six. Besides, the opposition is between four months hence and this moment ; see Bover Bi 3 (1922) 442-4. The golden or yellowing harvest of the British Isles is a white harvest under the Palestine sun. From the

harvest already in view and represented by the troop of Samaritans Jesus passes to the reapers. **36-38.** Let the apostolic reapers have the joy of their work and of their reward, but let them humbly remember the proverb, 'The sower is not always the one who reaps'. The disciples will reap a harvest which Moses and the Prophets and Jesus himself have sown, as laborious tillers of the soil. This thought, while bringing humility in apostolic success, also brings consolation to those who expend apparently sterile labour in what seems an unpromising apostolic field. *Cf.* 1 Cor 3:6-9.

39. The first-fruits of the harvest from that city were those who were convinced by the woman's faith in the 'Searcher of hearts'. **40.** Contact with the Master excited the charity of hospitality in them. Christ accepted, but as his mission was to the House of Israel, stayed only two days—St Augustine's 'two days on account of the two precepts of charity' is perhaps not exegesis but is worth recording. **41.** No miracles are mentioned ; but many more converts surrendered to the power of truth in Jesus' words. Genuine faith —better than the weak miracle-produced conviction of those in Jerusalem, 2:23—seems like the supernaturalization of an innate sympathy for truth. **42.** Besides the human touch in the remark to the woman, note the oecumenical title given to the Saviour in keeping with that worship which belongs particularly neither to Garizim nor to Jerusalem. 'Saviour of the world' occurs only here, as the fruit of Samaritan lips and under John's own pen, 1 Jn 4:14 ; but *cf.* Gen 41:45, where the phrase is used of Joseph. For the pagan use of this title, *cf.* Deissmann, *Light from the Ancient East*, p 369. Philip the Deacon was the next preacher in Samaria, Ac 8:5 ff.

43-45 Return to Galilee—It is only by the unlikely supposition that Jn is tacitly alluding to the hostility of Nazareth, Lk 4:24, that our Lord's saying in this context about a prophet in his own country can be referred to any country except his birthplace Judaea, where the proverb had just been verified. Jesus applied the same proverb later to Nazareth, the place of His boyhood, adolescence and hidden life. **45.** The enthusiastic welcome of the Galileans is explained by what pilgrims from there had seen Jesus do in Jerusalem—nearly ten months earlier according to our chronology (or two months ago according to those who date these verses June A.D. 28).

46-54 Cure of Officer's Son—46. In Johannine geography Cana of Galilee is the place where Jesus made the water wine. The name naturally became music to St John the Apostle, the guardian of the Blessed Virgin Mary. The man, whose son was sick at Capharnaum, was not a ruler (βασιλίσκος of the group of MSS to which D belongs, represented by Vg *regulus*) but a royal officer (βασιλικός), an official of Herod Antipas, conjectured by some (with fair plausibility) to be the procurator Chusa, husband of Johanna, Lk 8:3. **47.** Hearing of Jesus' arrival from Judaea, it seems that he came expressly from Capharnaum, seven hours' journey on foot, though as a royal official he would ride. He must have pressed Jesus to go down to Capharnaum (1,500 feet of descent) that very day, for the boy was dying. **48.** Not only did Jesus use reserve towards faith which was mainly the emotional impression produced by miracles, 2:23 f., but he warned against losing the divine significance of miracles by accepting them as merely useful, 6:26, or as feeding the appetite for wonder. Mere wonder-miracles he never worked, Lk 23:8. Hence Jesus combined 'signs and wonders (prodigies)' in the remark addressed in the plural number to the official and meant for others besides him. His faith was, in any case, far below that of the centurion of Capharnaum, Mt 8:8 f., for he considered that Jesus had to be present to work a miracle. **49.** The repeated pleading of the father is respectful and touching, especially when we consider that the best Gk MSS have 'my little boy' instead of 'my son'. **50.** Note the brevity of the assurance of Jesus, the fewness of whose words in working miracles (*cf.* Mt 8:3 ; Mk 5:41 ; Lk 7:14 ; Jn 11:43) reminds us of the *Fiat* of creation. The text can be taken to imply that the believing father set out on the homeward journey at once, but it would have been more in accord with oriental behaviour for him to have spent the night at Cana and to have begun the descent the following day. **51 f.** His servants came up to meet him and reported the cure as having happened yesterday at the seventh hour, between 1 and 2 p.m. **53.** The father could thus note the synchronism of the cure at Capharnaum and the words pronounced by Jesus twenty miles away at Cana of Galilee. Not only the official became a believing disciple but his whole household, like the household of Cornelius converted in later days by St Peter at Caesarea and the household of Lydia by St Paul at Philippi. **54.** St John, with the obvious intention of supplementing the synoptic gospels, here emphasizes two journeys of Jesus from Judaea into Galilee since the events of the Jordan—each arrival being marked by a miracle, one worked at Cana, the other from Cana.

a V 1-47 A Feast at Jerusalem—Geographical and also exegetical reasons have led many to suspect that the original order of Jn was chh 4, 6, 5, 7, on which see § 781*k, l.* Ch 5 shows the opposition of the Jews definitely marshalled—that is, the leaders of the nation at Jerusalem, especially Pharisees. If the time is a Paschal festival, we have the striking sequence that similar opposition asserts itself vigorously in Galilee a little later, and on the same sabbatarian grounds, Mk 2:23 ff. ; Lk 6:1 ff. ; Mt 12:1 ff. In Jn, however, which concentrates on the opposition at Jerusalem, the charge against Jesus, though connected with an alleged case of Sabbath-breaking, soon centres on his claim to equality with God—the real reason for their compassing his death.

b 1-9 Miracle at the Pool of Bezatha—**1.** In writing ' a festival of the Jews ' the Rheims translators assumed the non-authenticity of the Gk definite article before ' festival '. Certainly MSS and versions, numbered and weighed, leave a strong critical doubt. Editors generally vote for the omission of the article, but in this case we here meet the sole instance of Jn speaking vaguely of a festival and the sole instance in his Gospel of the absence of the article before this particular word. The reading has a bearing but not a necessary bearing on chronological calculation. Without prejudice to the very respectable probability of a public evangelical ministry of only two years and some months, we follow the system suggested by our interpretation of 4:35, and give preference to a ministry of three full years and four Paschs of which this festival would be the 2nd. Of those who transpose ch 5 some hold the festival of 5:1 to be the Pasch mentioned as near in 6:4 (Joüon, Braun, Sutcliffe), others hold for Pentecost (Lagrange), while other supporters of a two-year ministry make it a lesser feast—that of Trumpets (Durand) or Purim (Prat). However unlikely it might seem, we cannot, of course, say *a priori* that Jesus would not have gone up to Jerusalem for what was New Year's Day or even for the very much secularized feast of Purim or ' Lots '. [If Purim be the feast in question, then a two-year Ministry is likely. **c** —Gen. Ed.] **2.** The original Rheims version adhered over-literally to the pre-Clementine designation of the Pool, translating ' upon Probatic '. Neither should it be translated ' a Pool (called) Probatic ', as the present Vg text has it, but a swimming pond (κολυμβήθρα) near ' the sheep-gate ', that is, at the NE. corner of the Temple Area. The place-name is probably Bezatha (S, Bethzatha), meaning ' (Quarter of) the (Rock) Cutting ' rather than Bethsaida (B, W, Vg) or Bethesda (A) which last some have favoured with perhaps not sufficient critical detachment from its beautiful symbolic meaning : ' House of mercy '. Excavations made less than 40 yards NW. of the

Crusaders' Church of St Anne have brought to light **791c** this *natatoria*, a great oblong with four lateral porches and a fifth central dividing porch. **3b.** Here the sick lay ' waiting for the moving of the water '. Critically the participial phrase is very doubtful, being absent from S, B, C, L, A and the doubt is even greater for 4. The Decree of Trent (Sess. iv) does not forbid us to regard the words as a gloss, since the form of 4 varies very much even in the Vg MSS. Neither does the Church in her Liturgy intend to decide the question, when she assigns Jn 5:1-4 to the feast of the Archangel, St Raphael, precisely on account of this 4th verse. [Since v 7 refers to a moving of the water it would seem that a glossator felt it necessary to insert this explanation of the phenomenon.—Gen. Ed.] **5.** Every priest knows St Augustine's ingenious **d** tropological accommodation of the 38 years of infirmity, according to which perfection symbolized by the number 40, when diminished by 2 symbolizing the two precepts of charity, becomes imperfection and infirmity—it should not, however, be presented as exegesis ! **6.** In reply to Jesus' question the man expressed his desire to be cured, especially because his malady was connected with personal sin, 14*b*. **7.** The man, who seems to have been a paralytic, was powerless to reach the source of health without a helper. **8.** The thaumaturgical words of Jesus are like those spoken to the paralytic of Capharnaum, Mt 9:2 *f. Krabattos* (Lat. grabatus) is a Macedonian word denoting a rudimentary bed, generally a simple mat. **9.** The cure was immediate.

10-16 Sabbatarian Grievance—**10.** There are more **e** than twenty, perhaps as many as forty, sabbatarian carrying prohibitions in the Mishnaic treatise *Shabbath*, the carrying of an empty bier or bed being included by implication—in fact, carrying any material burden in the usual way was regarded as forbidden. **11.** The logic of the restored man's answer is that a miracle-worker will be ready to answer for himself. **12.** The Jews ignore the miracle and concentrate on the violation of the Sabbath. **13.** As Jesus had withdrawn, before a demonstration should take place in such a crowded spot (*cf.* Mt 12:16-21), the man did not know who had healed him. **14.** The good spiritual effect of the miracle is probably to be recognized in the man's visit to the temple. The warning given by Jesus shows that in this case there was personal sin behind the infirmity. It is not always so, 9:1-3, and here we cannot say whether sin was the direct physical cause of the malady or the moral cause of such a particular form of penal retribution (*cf.* 1 Cor 11:30). **15.** The man's report to the Jews was not a denunciation but a solemn attestation of the identity of his benefactor.

16. [Both verbs are in the imperfect tense in Gk, and could signify : ' Therefore the Jews *began to* persecute Jesus because he *began to* do these things on the sabbath '. Jn would then be noting the first employment of a new technique of persecution subsequently used with effect in Galilee.—Gen. Ed.] The Jewish persecution on account of this cure evidently took the form of a direct reproach.

17-30 Claim to Divine Sonship—**17.** Jesus' answer, **792a** in which he claims identity of activity with his Father, is the key to 19-30. It reads : ' *My Father is working (even) till now, and I (too) am working* '. **18.** As St Augustine acutely remarked : The Jews understood what the Arians did not understand. The Arians denied the equality of the Son with the Father, which those blind Jews, those murderers of Christ understood from the words of Christ himself. **19-30.** The subject of these difficult verses is not the Word simply but the Incarnate in his consubstantial oneness with the Father and his authority towards men as the giver of divine life and the judge of those who refuse to believe. There is unity of activity between the Father and the Son and also co-equality of dignity and honour. The Son (and he Incarnate) works miracles and gives life, because his Father works (through the

792a one divine nature) the identical works ; it is likewise the Son Incarnate who judges the living and the dead, and precisely because he is man he does so by the final visible judgement which permanently fixes men's voluntary attitude towards him. It is well to keep the concrete circumstances of the discourse in mind, for all the deep theology which this short passage yields is not the immediate object of exegesis, which simply explains the text.

b **19.** When Jesus implied that his action in curing the man was no more Sabbath-breaking than the incessant action of God in the world, the Jews rightly inferred that he made himself equal to God. Jesus does not deny this, but affirms it more strongly. The equality is ineffably real, because it means oneness of action. Jesus is evidently speaking of divine works such as the miracle just wrought. Action depends on knowledge, and there is a perfect communion of knowledge between the Father and the Son, so that the Son cannot do anything except what he 'consubstantially' sees the Father doing. 'To see', says St Thomas, 'is to receive the divine knowledge'; St Augustine had already said that both *to hear* from the Father and *to see* was *to be* from the Father, *Deus ex Deo*. Following a suggestion of St Cyril of Alexandria we might crystallize the thought in Greek terminology by saying that the *homognosis* from which the common action comes is really *homoousia*. There is no divine work that the Son does not do together with the Father, and not merely after the manner that human brain and hand work together in writing, doing the same thing but differently. The Son does every work 'in like manner', that is equally. There is no question

c of the Son just imitating the Father. **20.** The metaphor of ' showing ' on the part of the Father corresponds to the metaphor of ' seeing ' on the part of the Son, and, as St Thomas points out, the love of the Father for the Son is rather the sign than the cause of this community of knowledge and operation. Greater and more astonishing works of divine power are yet to come from the Word Incarnate. **21.** Jesus turns to the idea of life—by which, with St Augustine, we understand supernatural life, which is primarily the life of the soul but also includes the resurrection of the body on the last day. Consequently, the dead whom the Father raises and makes to live are sinners. Of these the Son is equally the free *Resuscitator* and *Vivificator*. **22.** When it is said that *the Father does not judge any man, but has given all judgement to the Son*, it seems that, in accordance with the constant signification of κρίσις in Jn, we must understand not a judgement of discussion but of condemnation, *viz.* exclusion from eternal life. **23.** This communication from Father to Son demands that all men give the Son co-equal honour. In fact, refusal to honour the Son is refusal to honour the Father who sent him. **24.** Acceptance of the word of Jesus and belief in his divine mission infallibly gives eternal life (*i.e.* grace destined to be consummated in glory). The true believer does not incur damnation, but by the act of belief (informed by charity) has definitely passed from the death of sin to the life of

d supernatural grace. **25.** The world is an immense necropolis, but the hour is coming, yea rather *now* is, when those spiritually dead shall hear the voice of the Son of God calling them to life, and those who hear with the virtue of faith shall have life. **26.** The Son's power of giving life comes from his having it. To have life in himself essentially, not participatively, is his prerogative as much as it is the prerogative of the Father. **27.** Moreover, the Father has given him power to exercise judgement, for the visible giver of life (Son of Man) must visibly exclude the unworthy. **28 f.** This visible function at the termination of human history evokes the thought of the general resurrection. To remember that he is the One who shall call all men from their tombs to different destinies according to their works will make what he has said appear less amazing. It is quite clear in this statement that not faith alone but works rooted in faith shall decide

the resurrection of men to life rather than to the judgement of condemnation reserved for those who have done evil things. **30.** Using the first person and a device of speech known as inclusion, Jesus applies the word of his exordium, 19, to his office of judge. In this as in other divine works he can do nothing from himself. Note that while he used the verb ' to see ' when speaking of himself as operator, he uses the verb ' to hear ' when speaking of himself as judge, but when there is question of a condemnation which, as involving executive authority, is particularly a decree of the will, the justice of it is referred to the conformity of Christ's human will with the divine will. Let us remark in conclusion that no one may say that he has understood these 12 verses perfectly, for they are full of the mystery of the Incarnation.

31-47 Jewish Incredulity—All this is both believable and to be believed, and the Jews have ample testimony of it. This Jesus proceeds to show, appealing by condescension to the testimony of the Precursor, 33–35, but chiefly to the testimony of the Father, given in the works that Jesus does, 36–38, and given also in the Scriptures, 39 f., 45–47. He shows at the same time that the cause of the Jews' infidelity was their self-seeking vanity, 41–44.

31. Jesus could and did, 8:14, testify to himself, but here he makes a concession to the legal axiom that no one is to be believed when testifying in his own favour. **32.** The true testimony that Jesus can evoke is that of his Father, although he does not yet clearly say so. **33.** Meanwhile, *ad abundantiam iuris*, he refers to the recent and true testimony of one commonly regarded as a Prophet, recalling the declaration made by the Precursor to the solemn delegation sent from Jerusalem. Quite evidently John declared the truth. **34.** Not that Jesus needs human testimony, but he will use the impressiveness of John's emphatic words to help the Jews to salvation. **35.** Unfortunately they have behaved like children. Before that burning and shining lamp (not yet, it seems, extinguished but hidden behind the walls of Machaerus) they were delighted for a time, but soon turned away on the facile pretext that John was a demoniac, Lk 7:33. **36.** His divine works are the greater testimony to which Jesus can appeal. Of the two exceedingly difficult verses, 37, 38, which follow, the best interpretation seems to be that which supposes an allusion to Deut 18:15-19. It is substantially this : The Father has left testimony (whom your fathers at Sinai asked neither to see nor hear any more save through Moses) ; and what is more, the word of God you have not abiding in you, because you do not believe the *Prophet*, Deut 18:15, whom he has sent. From this Jesus passes to the testimony of the Scriptures. **39 f.** The absence of any other exhortatory imperative and the implied contradiction between seeking life in the Scriptures and rejecting the Giver of life, seem to commend the indicative : ' You search ' rather than the imperative ' Search '. In writings that contain the words of life and show the Messias the Jews seek what suits their own ideas and consequently they do not come to Jesus, in order to have life. **41 f.** Jesus says this, not because he seeks glory from their coming to him, but because he knows that it is through want of genuine love of God that they have gone astray in their quest. **43.** The Envoy of God they will not accept, but a pretender they are always ready to receive—a truth only too well demonstrated in the later history of Judaism, which, it is said, records 64 false Messias, 25 of whom are known by name. **44.** The real obstacle is what we should call hypocritical respectability—the fundamentally wrong disposition called human respect. The seekers of self and human praise are far from faith, access to which is in the humble desire to please God alone. **45-47.** The accuser of the Jews shall not be Jesus but Moses in whom they have set their hope, but whom notwithstanding they refuse to believe. If they believed Moses, they would believe the Christ of whom Moses wrote, when he recorded the words on the Seed of the woman, Gen 3:15, the blessing of Abraham, 12:3, the heir of the sceptre of Juda, 49:10, the Star arising out of Jacob, Num 24:17, the great Prophet, Deut 18:15. How can disciples of Moses, 9:28, who pride themselves on their knowledge of the written word, 7:49, and yet do not really believe it, have faith in the mere spoken words of Jesus? Let us remember that Jewish Scribes and Pharisees were worshippers of the letter, 2 Cor 3.

VI 1-72 The Bread of Life—The time interval between chh 5 and 6, according to the chronological system here adopted, is almost a full year [but only two months if Purim is the 'feast' of ch 5.—Gen. Ed.], which may be filled up by a synoptic harmony based on Mk 2:23-6:29. This episode—the longest Galilean piece in Jn—includes (1) the two miracles of the first multiplication of bread, 1-15, and of Christ walking on the water, 16-21, (2) the Eucharistic discourse at Capharnaum, 26-59-60, with an introductory prologue giving a composition of circumstances, 22-25, and an epilogue showing 'the discernment of spirits' on the theme of the Bread of Life, 60-61-71-72. The miracles that precede the Promise prepare the way for belief in it, for he who fed more than 5,000 miraculously can feed the world eucharistically, and he who walked on water as on solid ground can command and suspend other conditions of matter, in order to be sacramentally present to feed the souls of men.

1-13 First Multiplication of Bread—The miracle is the only one narrated by all four evangelists, the most vividly picturesque description being that of Mk, to which however Jn adds some precise details, such as the question addressed to Philip individually and the discovery made by Andrew.

1-4. Jn's opening indication of time denotes only sequence, without any chronological precision. What direction the journey across the Lake took is not stated but, unless the context decided otherwise, it should be as obvious as *trans Tiberim* was to a Roman. The crossing was from the western shore, on the northern curve of which stood Capharnaum, the missionary city of Jesus, to the eastern side dominated on the north by Bethsaida Julias. The Sea of Galilee, also called the Lake of Genesareth, Lk 5:1, is named by Jn only (*cf.* 21:1) from the city built on its western shore by Herod Antipas, between A.D. 26 and 28, and named Tiberias after the reigning Emperor. This name of the Lake had established itself when Jn was written. The occasion of the journey is gathered from the Synoptics. Mt 14:12 f. connects it with the Precursor's murder, and thus it may be interpreted as a temporary withdrawal from the murderer's territory to that of Herod Philip. Mk and Lk 9:10 date it after the return of the Apostles from a mission; and the former specifies that the Master wanted to give the Twelve a rest from the exhausting work that followed their return, Mk 6:31. **2.** Popular enthusiasm had been running very high; and while Herod imagined that the Miracle-worker of Galilee was John returned to life, others were ready to regard him as Elias or the Prophet, Deut 18:15. The miracles worked on the sick made the crowds (augmented by Paschal pilgrims) observe the departure of Jesus and also urged them to follow him. They flocked to the same destination *on foot*, Mk 6:33. **3.** The mountain on which Jesus sat with his disciples looked out on the Plain now called *El Bateha*. There is an indefinable solemnity in this simple session. **4.** The proximity of the Passover is doubtless marked for a special reason. Twelve months hence the festival of the Jews will give place to 'the new Pasch of the new Law'.

5-9 5. Till the afternoon, Lk, and the approach of evening, Mt, Mk, Jesus taught the crowds, Mk, Lk, and healed their sick, Lk. Mk notes his pity for their abandonment and his care for their hunger, which latter Jn epitomizes in the gesture of Jesus surveying the crowd with his eyes and in his question to Philip on the possibility of buying bread to feed them. A dismissal of the crowd, who could scatter and find **793d** food in the surrounding villages had already been suggested by the Apostles. **6.** The question addressed to Philip was a test put to one who seems to have been a business man. Jesus himself knew what he would do. **7.** The contemporary local price of bread is unknown to us, but Philip estimated that the wages of a labourer working six days a week for eight months would not suffice to procure a little for each of the many gathered there. **8 f.** Andrew, who like Philip was from Bethsaida, found a boy with five barley loaves (the food of the poor) and two little fishes salted perhaps at Taricheae, the 'Salt Fish City', at the SW. corner of the Lake. As three of those small flat Palestinian loaves were required to give one man a fairly abundant meal, Lk 11:5, the supply discovered would have made a picnic for only two or three, or at most five persons. Hence Andrew's question: What are these among so many?

10-13 10. Mt, Mk and Jn note the grassy verdure **e** of the place where the 'Lord prepared a table in the wilderness'. The grass also marks the springtime. Five thousand men, as well as women and children (not estimated but presumably in inferior numbers) sat down or reclined in companies of 50 or 100, Mk 6:40. Mk's description is exquisitely graphic. They looked like flower-beds on the green. **11.** Jesus took the loaves. Jn does not note the gesture of looking to heaven, which owing to the analogy of the situations has passed from Mt, Mk, Lk to the *Qui pridie* narrative in the Latin Mass, but Jn does use εὐχαριστήσας instead of the εὐλογήσας of the synoptists. This verb deliberately repeated in 23 should be regarded as a distinct allusion to the Eucharistic significance of the miracle. The distribution was made by the Apostles, Mt, Mk, Lk, the bread being multiplied either antecedently, or when passing from the hands of Jesus, or (most probably) in the hands of the Apostles. From the loaves and likewise from the fishes each received not the 'little bit' envisaged by Philip but a full meal. **12.** The gathering up of the fragments was an act of reverential economy towards the gift of God. **13.** The place of the Twelve is put in evidence by the 12 baskets—Jewish travelling baskets were almost proverbial (Juvenal, *Sat.* III, 15; Martial, *Epig.* V, 17). Let us take St Augustine's advice and not merely look at the outside of the miracle, like a man who admires calligraphy which he cannot read. Mental comprehension, not mere ocular or imaginative apprehension, should be our endeavour, when we read this miracle on *Laetare* Sunday. The same Word, 'by whom are all things', feeds the world from a few grains of corn, and the same also multiplies himself Incarnate on thousands of altars.

14-15 Effect of the Miracle—14. Though the scribes **f** distinguished, the crowds often identified the Prophet of Deut 18:15 with the Messias. The recent death of the Baptist, the growing fame of Jesus, the national fervour of the time shortly before the Pasch worked together with the miracle to precipitate a popular conclusion. In identifying Jesus with the Prophet the crowds also echo the great festal Psalm: 'Blessed is *he that cometh*', etc. **15.** The rising ferment that would have seized Jesus and set him on the throne of David could have been known by our Lord in an ordinary human way, as Jn's aorist participle suggests. He fled again into the mountain himself alone. No doubt his prayer was like that of the night before he chose the Apostles, Lk 6:12, for the great Eucharistic crisis was at hand.

16-21 Christ walks on the Water—16. The embarka- **g** tion of the Apostles, as darkness was setting in, was not spontaneous. Jesus, wishing to prevent the contagion of popular Messianism from catching even the *compelled* them to depart, Mk, Mt. **17.** The journey to Capharnaum was only some 4 miles almost due west, but Mk indicates, 6:45, that they first turned north-west towards Bethsaida (then much nearer the shore of the Lake than the modern Et-Tell which

798g occupies its site). Some scholars hold without sufficient grounds that there were two Bethsaidas, an eastern and a western. Supposing only one, the Apostles would have expected Jesus to join them there. When he did not do so, they would have turned the boat towards Capharnaum. **18.** The adverse wind which stirred the sea against them as they rowed was evidently a north-westerly, strong but not tempestuous. **19.** As the *stadion* is nearly an English furlong, they had only proceeded between three and four miles at the fourth watch, *i.e.* about 3 a.m., Mt, Lk. Then Jesus appeared walking on the water, drawing near the boat, Jn,

h but moving as if to pass it by, Mk 6:48. **20.** He revealed himself. ' It is I ; be not afraid ' is given by Mt, Mk and Jn. Mt alone records the incident of St Peter and the growing perception of divine sonship. ' Truly thou art the Son of God '. Jn had no need of recording these, but certainly they prepared St Peter for the magnificent act of steadfast faith that was to come, Jn 6:69 f. **21.** As the verb translated : ' they were willing ', is one of desire *fulfilled*, it means that the Apostles did actually take Jesus into the boat, Mt, Mk. The wind ceased, Mt, Mk, but we cannot say with certainty whether Jn indicates a further miracle (one of velocity) when he tells that ' *immediately*' the boat reached land. The landing-point broadly indicated by Mt and Mk as being at *Gennesaret* may have been as far south as Dalmanutha (some place north of Magdala). This and the miracles demanded by local people would explain how Jesus reached Capharnaum only in the evening, when the Sabbath had begun.

794a 22-25 Narrative Introduction to Eucharistic Discourse —**22.** Jn describes the situation on the east coast next day. The crowd that still remained, having bivouacked at El-Bateha, knew that the only boat had left the evening before, and Jesus had not gone in it. **23.** In the course of the morning other boats from Tiberias came near where the miracle preceded by ' the Lord's thanksgiving ' (*eucharist*) had taken place. **24.** As Jesus had not appeared and was nowhere to be found, as many as could made the westward journey to Capharnaum on the available boats, seeking Jesus. **25.** They found him. Jn does not say when or where, but clearly that same day, and probably in the evening, at the synagogue of Capharnaum, 59–60. In asking when Jesus had come they certainly also wanted to know *how* he had come.

b 26-60 The Eucharistic Discourse—The numbering of verses is according to Vg. It is sufficient to note here once for all that 51 of Gk text makes 51, 52 of Vg and DV, and so the latter's 52–72 correspond to 51–71 in Gk text. The Eucharistic character of this discourse is supported by cogent arguments and can claim patristic favour dating most probably from Ignatius of Antioch. Justin and especially Irenaeus can also be cited. The Antiochene Chrysostom, St Gregory of Nyssa, the two Cyrils of Jerusalem and Alexandria not only stand for the Eucharistic interpretation but are pronounced ' realists '. Not merely on account of the allegorism of Origen but for other reasons also, the metaphorical interpretation (eating Christ by faith), which amounts to ' spiritual communion ', has had its vogue in the Church. Though St Augustine can be shown to have understood the discourse eucharistically, later theologians failed to understand sacramental realism owing to his strong emphasis of two points, namely, (*a*) that we must eschew anything like Capharnaite carnalism, and (*b*) that we must look for the fruits described in Jn 6:26–58 in the ecclesiastical unity of the mystic body of Christ ; *cf.* de Lubac, *Corpus Mysticum*, 296.

c The second emphasis was undoubtedly due to his anti-Donatist preoccupations. His treatment of the matter greatly influenced the Latin Middle Age ; and, moreover, 14th and 15th cent. polemics against Greeks giving the Eucharist to infants and against Bohemian utraquists strengthened the ' spiritual ' interpretation. In 1551 (Oct. 11) the Council of Trent used 6:58 as

a Eucharistic text, but, in view of a controversy that took place and continued during the Council, Session XXI (16 July 1562) expressly left the rival interpretations of Jn 6 untouched. Today, however, Catholic unanimity on the Eucharistic interpretation of 6:51–59 is almost absolute, and very few non-catholic interpreters now deny it. It is another case of a tradition being obscured and reasserting itself. If the discourse is not a Promise of the Eucharist, the silence of John the Beloved on the Sacrament of love would be a positive enigma ; the bread of the future to be given not by the Father but by the Son of Man, 27, the clear impression made on the crowds and the disciples, the strongly emphatic comparison with manna, the insistence *à outrance* on Flesh and Blood as food and drink—*very* food and *very* drink—all these things in the non-eucharistic hypothesis would be unintelligible.

Some commentators have held that 26–58 are two or three discourses united together, and Westcott finds not only distinct themes but also distinct audiences at 26 (*crowds*), 41 (Jews) and 51 (where the words begin which scandalize *disciples*). A close examination will, however, show that our Lord from 27 and therefore from the beginning intends to promise the Eucharist. Subsequently his words have the unity of a discourse which is partly a dialogue. Having introduced the subject of a spiritual bread, 27, he identifies it with himself, the One come down from heaven, 35, who can satisfy hunger and thirst, but in believers only. Here unbelief asserts itself in whispered murmuring, and the unbelievers are called by the name ' Jews ', which Jn habitually uses for the hostile crowds. Having explained the necessity of faith, 44–47, Jesus resumes the ' manna ' comparison (32 parallel to 49), and by using the verb ' to eat ' for the first time shows that 48–59 have reference to a food really or physically eaten. There is gradation of parts, not splicing of pieces.

26-34 Material Bread and the Bread of Life——This piece of dialogue marks the great distinction between the bread of physical sustenance (whether it be that of El-Bateha or the manna of the wilderness) and the Bread that nourishes eternal life. **26.** Jesus does not answer a merely curious question, but touches at once the great fundamental fault in the enthusiasm that surrounds him. In the bread of El-Bateha they only saw the temporal blessing of good food, not the spiritual meaning of the miracle. **27.** With the same method as that used at the Samaritan Well, Jesus tells them to labour for, that is, to strive to acquire another food, not a perishable food but a food having usefulness for life everlasting. The Son of Man *will give* this food, empowered as he is to do so by the seal or mark of authentication and approval which the Father—namely God himself—has set upon him. **28.** The crowd like true Mosaists interpret the verb ' labour ' or ' work ' of *many works* commanded by God. **29.** Jesus tells them that the one basic work which God requires of them is belief in himself whom God has sent. **30 f.** The Samaritan woman had said : ' Art thou greater than Jacob ? '—here also the crowd understand that Jesus claims to be greater than Moses, and they demand a miracle greater than the manna that fed the children of Israel in the desert for forty years. They quote in free form Ps 77(78):24 characterizing the manna as bread from heaven. **32.** Again Jesus follows the same line of thought as at the Well of Samaria. Bread from heaven ! Yes, but not *the* bread from the very heaven of God. Moses did not give that bread but the Father (now) is giving the bread from heaven, that is truly such, or really worthy of the name. **33.** The giving is the Incarnation which is for the life not of one people but of the whole world—the life being supernatural life. **34.** The reaction of the crowds hearing of this Bread of God . . . coming down from heaven is just like that of the Samaritan woman : ' Sir, give us always this bread '.

35-40 Jesus the Bread of Life for those who believe f —Here there is a difference, but the parallelism is not

41 entirely broken. The first great 'I am' came later in the conversation with the Samaritan. At this point Jesus pronounces at once his second great 'I am': 'I am the bread of life'. In Samaria he touched a moral impediment in the life of the woman; here at Capharnaum, the hindrance is a lack of faith. The act of coming to Jesus which attains the satisfaction of hunger is the same as the faith which remedies thirst for ever. **36.** Jesus states the tragic fact that the crowds have seen him and still see him (perfect) and yet do not believe. **37.** The fault is theirs not his, but Jesus explains the situation in terms of what we now call efficacious grace. They come who are given to him by the Father and Jesus cannot but welcome all that the Father gives. The use of a global neuter certainly insinuates that the faithful come to Christ in the social unity of a body. **38.** It is towards this body that Jesus must carry out the salvific will of his father, which is the programme of his life. **39.** That programme or will of his Father is described as Jesus' task, namely, to lose nothing of the 'entrusted all', but to save completely even to the resurrection on the last day. **40.** Human liberty, which has not been expressly envisaged in this 'giving' by the Father, is clearly indicated when the salvific will is declared to be this: 'That every one (individually) who seeth the Son and believeth in him may have life everlasting and I will raise him up in the last day'. Belief is a free act. Jesus' work is to save and resurrect; faith leads to eternal life and final resurrection. The language of these verses is remarkable. The Father gives us socially—for we are saved socially—in his Christ, but we come individually. It belongs to Christ the Envoy to lose nothing of what the Sender gives him (cf. 17:12) but to save completely. On our part we have to believe individually in the Son, in order to have the life everlasting and glorious resurrection which the Father wills for us.

g 41-47 Necessity and Nature of Faith—41 f. Descent from heaven, so emphatically asserted, clearly meant divine origin. Hence the murmur of a hostile group called 'Jews' when such a claim was made by one whom probably they usually called Jesus Bar Joseph (cf. 1:45) and who is elsewhere referred to as 'the carpenter, the son of Mary', Mk 6:3. **43 f.** The murmur reveals unbelief and rejection of the gift of God. Faith is again spoken of as an act of 'coming' and the cause of this salutary motion is the Father drawing. Faith works as a divine attraction but not a compulsion destroying human liberty. St Augustine's famous comment, which may be read in *Tr. 26 in Joannem* or in the Breviary (*Feria IV infr. Oct. Pent.*) is a most beautiful passage. Whosoever is thus efficaciously attracted, Jesus will raise him up on the last day. **44.** Faith is due to the interior action of God mentioned by the Prophets, notably Is 54:13 and Jer 31:33 f. It is this interior hearing and learning from the Father that brings a soul to Jesus. Hearing is perception and learning reception, but neither implies immediate vision of the Father. **46.** This belongs exclusively to him who is from God. He has seen the Father. **47.** Solemnly concluding this part, Jesus says: 'Amen, amen, I say to you: He that believeth (in me) hath everlasting life'.

a 48-60 The Bread of Life is the Flesh of Jesus—What has preceded has been on the mystery of the Incarnation, but now he promises the institution of the Blessed Sacrament. So far Jesus has not used the verb *to eat*, although he has spoken of hunger and thirst satisfied by the Bread of life. His hearers only have spoken of the manna *eaten* by the fathers in the wilderness, 31. This reference to the Mosaic miracle he now takes up and sets the promise of the Eucharist, in a form which is really the starkest realism, over against the manna. **48.** He repeats: 'I am the bread of life'. **49 f.** Those who ate the manna as a physical food died. **b 50-52.** This bread from heaven is one that man may eat and not die. The spiritual life which the food confers is eternal, and will not cease because of any limited efficacy in the food. It can only cease through **795b** spiritual suicide. He who eats this bread of life has spiritually that *posse non mori* conferred by the fruit of the tree of life. This is said negatively, but in the next verse the bread of life is emphatically called living bread, and the effect of eating it is declared to be that the participant shall live for ever. To this is added the startling assertion: 'The bread that I will give is my flesh for the life of the world'. This is the *future giving* by the Son of Man for which 27 has prepared us. It is not immediately the Father's gift as the Son Incarnate is in 32. The Bread is given to be eaten, but it is identified with the flesh of Jesus —his human body—given for the life of the whole world of mankind. The sacrificial character of the phrase seems almost certain and has been admitted even by non-catholic scholars. For centuries the old *textus receptus* made this sacrificial sense unmistakable by inserting the phrase 'which I will give' after flesh and defining not bread but flesh (*cf*. Lk 22:19; 1 Cor 11:24).

53. Not merely a murmur but the articulate sound of **c** controversy and dissent made itself heard amongst the Jews, but Jesus only becomes more emphatic, and, if we may say so, more shocking to Jewish feeling. The expressions only grow in solemnity and explicitness and realism. **54.** To the eating of flesh, as a condition of life, is added the drinking of blood, which might have been conceived as positively horrible in view of the Noachic, Gen 9:4, and Levitical blood-prohibitions, Lev 7:26; 17:14. **55.** The negative assertion of 54 is now emphasized by a positive pronouncement which sums up the whole strength of the discourse: 'He that eateth My flesh, and drinketh My blood, hath everlasting life: and I will raise him up on the last day'—here eternal life and resurrection are both mentioned for the third time. No better comment could be sought than the words of Ignatius of Antioch who wrote some ten years after St John. He called the Eucharist: 'the medicine of immortality, an antidote that we should not die, but live for ever in Christ Jesus', Eph 20.

56. The word for eating used in 55, namely τρώγω, **d** is even more surprisingly physical than before. Though it cannot be translated by the crude words 'munch' or 'crunch', it really has some of their realistic strength. Jesus therefore says: 'My flesh is *true* food, and my blood is *true* drink'. *True* or *very* represent the best attested Gk reading preferable to *truly* or *indeed*. **57.** The effect of eating Christ's flesh and drinking his blood is mutual vital immanence by the mixing of vital give and take. It is the sacrament of fellowship in the divine nature and of actual charity. St Cyril of Alexandria's illustration from two pieces of wax melted together is classical, and St Thérèse of Lisieux gave us a living commentary on this verse when she described her first communion not as a meeting with Jesus but a *fusion*. **58.** It seems that it is the flow of life from Christ in the proportional analogy of the communication of life from Father to Son that is guaranteed in the words: 'he who eats me shall also live *by me*', although the translation *for me* is possible and is modelled on Jesus' fidelity as an ambassador of God.

59. The discourse ends in a repetition (figure called **e** 'inclusion') of the comparison with manna: 'This is the bread that came down from heaven. Not as (your) fathers did eat manna and *died*. He that eateth (τρώγων for the fourth time—*cf*. Gk text 54, 56, 57 = Vg 55, 57, 58) this bread shall live for ever'.

A supplementary word must be said on the necessity of the Eucharist as enunciated in the *nisi* pronouncement addressed directly to the sceptical Jews in 54. That necessity is absolute, in the sense that without the 'thing' or grace of the Eucharist there is no salvation, for the Eucharist signifies, effects, and perfects the unity of Christ's mystic body, outside of which no one can be saved. Total deliberate refusal to eat the flesh of Christ would exclude from super-

795e natural life and entail damnation. But the grace of union can be obtained by desire—personal desire, in the case of adults, and the maternal desire of the Church in the case of baptized infants. For infants the sacrament of faith, which is baptism, is necessary in every way, since the actual sacrament is for them, who cannot yet have desire, the only gate to salvation, but the Church incorporating them baptismally thereby desires the Eucharist for them, and, if we may use figurative language, the baptized infant immediately opens his little mouth for the Bread of life—in other words, the recipient of the sacrament of faith is already hungry for the sacrament of charity, which is the Eucharist. The Church has never regarded sacramental communion as necessary for infants ; yet the Council of Trent (Sess. 21) did not condemn 'antiquity' for giving the Eucharist to infants, the custom being local and justified by some circumstances of the times, under the approval of holy bishops. The same Session of Trent also declared that no argument to establish a general precept of communion in both kinds can be drawn from this chapter 'however it be understood according to the various interpretations of holy Fathers and Doctors '

f 60. ' These things (Jesus) said, teaching in the synagogue in Capharnaum '. Codex D as well as Aug and several codices of Vg add ' on a Sabbath '. Most probably the Eucharistic Promise was made in a Sabbath discourse, delivered on Friday evening or Saturday morning. If so, the multiplication of bread took place on Thursday—another link with the Eucharistic institution. The place was probably the synagogue built by the centurion, Lk 7:5, whose words of humility we use before Holy Communion. The ruins of a synagogue of later date, built possibly on the same site, now stand splendidly restored at Tell Hum A lintel of the edifice represents a pot of manna surrounded by vine-leaves and grapes. Surely a providential reminder from Jewish hands !

g 61-67 Effect on Disciples—The Jews, who had never believed, doubtless remained in their unbelief. The discourse proved a test for the faith of certain disciples. **61.** Interpreting our Lord's words like *Capharnaites*— a name coined by exegetes for those who misunderstand through materialistic or even a cannibalistic imagining—many of his disciples declared the promise *hard*, that is, offensive and unbearable. **62.** Their comments were only whispered, but Jesus knew *in himself* what they were, and said : ' *Is this a stumbling-block to you ?* ' **63.** He knows the scandal caused by his words, but he neither revokes nor dilutes anything of what he has said. The elliptic question : ' If then you see the Son of Man ascending where he was before . . . ? ' is intended, not as Maldonatus thought, to increase the scandal, but to rectify what was simply a cannibalistic interpretation. The ascension will perhaps surprise the recalcitrants more, but it will eliminate their chief difficulty about eating the flesh of One who in celestial glory takes his place where he **h** was from eternity. **64.** The words which follow are variously understood. St Cyril of Alexandria, one of the greatest of all expositors of this chapter, has rallied many. He equates ' the spirit that quickeneth ' with the divinity of Christ, and ' the flesh that profiteth nothing ' with the *mere* human nature of Christ. It is, however, an interpretation which a rigorous application of the law of context would seem to exclude. Taken with what goes before and comes after, the words rather refer to the unspiritual, carnal-minded disciples. It is the spiritual view given by faith which gives life ; carnal understanding is profitless. The words spoken by Jesus are the object of spiritual understanding, and in this way only are life-giving ; *cf.* 8:15. **65.** Hence Jesus shows his knowledge of their unbelieving minds, a thing he knew from the beginning as he also knew the one who was to betray him. **66.** That, he explained, was the reason why he had insisted that no man can come to him unless it be given to him from the Father. In humility of

Spirit we may recall the words of St Augustine : **79** *Nondum traheris ? Ora ut traharis.* Pray that the Father may draw you to his Son. **67.** Here another tragic word of the Evangelist sounds over the first schism. The Eucharistic bond of unity divided many disciples from Jesus. ' They walked no more with him '. The fault was not in Jesus ; it is not in the Bread of life. So it happened also in the 16th cent. **68-72. Attitude of the Twelve**—God will not compel **i** human freedom. Free choice must rule the life of man. In that day of defections the test question is put to the Twelve, **68,** ' Will you also go away ? ' **69.** We must be perpetually devoted to Simon Peter for the magnificence of his answer : ' *Go away, to whom ?* ' Jesus could do without them, but they cannot do without him who has the words of eternal life—words that lead to everlasting life and give it. **70.** Peter's profession of faith is certainly less full of heavenly inspiration than that made later near Caesarea Philippi, but scarcely less full of human emotion : ' We have believed (faith comes first) and we have known (intelligence follows belief) that thou art the Christ, *the Holy One of God* '. Copyists conformed the last phrase to the confession of Caesarea Philippi, but the better MSS are decisive. **71.** Peter spoke for the Twelve, but Jesus announced that of the Twelve whom he had chosen one was a devil. It was a lesson of fear and humility for the whole company, who did not then know who the secret apostate was. **72.** St John names him here, interpreting the word of Jesus in the light of events. He was the only Judaean in the apostolic college : Judas, the son of a certain Simon of Qerioth, a place which is, perhaps, to be identified with Carioth Hesron, Jos 15:25, the modern Khirbet-el-Qureitein, 13 m. S. of Hebron.

VII-XII THE PUBLIC MINISTRY, PART II

In the Fourth Gospel, which is the history of light **7** and darkness engaged in a tremendous duel, chh 7–12 form a distinct block. They tell of the supreme combat which Jesus joined with the hostile leaders of his nation at Jerusalem in revealing himself as the Envoy and very Son of God. The two great dominant ideas of light and life partition this section between them. After ch 7, which is a first general sketch of the conflict, Jesus reveals himself as the Light of the World, 8:1–9:41 This revelation takes place at the joyful festival of Tabernacles and is illustrated by the cure of a man born blind. With the parable—allegory of the Good Shepherd—Jesus comes forward more particularly as the Giver of Life. This revelation of the Good Shepherd, giving his life that his sheep may live, continues through the festival of the Dedication and the raising of Lazarus and closes with the decision to put him to death, 10:1–11:56. What remains, 12:1–12:50, tells of the approach of the Paschal festival and the coming of Jesus to meet the hour of which he had so often spoken, the hour appointed by his Father, an hour not of defeat but triumph. He enters Bethany and Jerusalem. The favourite ideas of life and light (in the reverse order to that of the Prologue) occur again at the end of this section, where also figure some reflexions of St John on the tragic blindness of the Jewish people.

7:1-52 The Breach widens. b

7:1-13 Circumstances of the Ascent to Jerusalem— **1.** In refusing to transpose ch 5 (*cf.* § 781*l*) into what seems illuminating proximity to ch 7, and in following the probability that the time of the miracle of Bezatha was a Paschal feast, we committed ourselves to a gap of nearly 12 months between the first declaration of deadly hostility to Jesus at Jerusalem and the Eucharistic crisis close to another Pasch which marked the decline of his popularity in Galilee. Then six months separated the proximity of this spring festival of the Jews, 6:4, from the approach of the autumnal festival of Tabernacles, 7:2. [This gap of 18 months is of course a serious objection to the view that the

5b feast of Jn 5 was the second Passover of the public life, for Jn 7:11–24 makes it clear that the miracle of 5:8 was still fresh in the minds of the Jews. The difficulty disappears if we can assume that the feast in question was the feast of Purim. It would also disappear if the original order of the chapters was chh 4, 6, 5, 7, the present order being the result of a dislocation occurring probably before the publication of the Gospel.—Gen. Ed.] Jn seems to insinuate (in spite of 7:11) that Jesus did not go to Jerusalem for the second last Pasch of his life. He went from place to place in Galilee, because of the set design **c** on his life on the part of the Jews in Judea. Chh 15–18 of Mt with their parallels help to fill the void. It was a time of withdrawal from the synagogue and concentration on the training of the Apostles, important events being a circuit which brought Jesus into Phoenicia and then eastwards into Decapolis ; then from the eastern side of the Lake to Dalmanutha ; thence north for the famous day of Caesarea Philippi, after which occurred the Transfiguration on Thabor and what seems to have been the last visit to his missionary city of Capharnaum. The sentence, 7:1, in which Jn notes these journeys in Galilee (and about it) also marks the end of the Galilean ministry. Events described in Lk 9:51–19:28 are connected by that Evangelist with journeyings towards Jerusalem (9:51 ; 13:22 ; 17:11, *cf.* 19:28), but it seems almost impossible to assign them a convincing chronological order.

d **2.** The feast of Tabernacles (*Sukkoth*, more properly *booths* or *huts*) was a harvest festival celebrated at the middle of the seventh month (determined by the moon of the autumnal equinox and therefore often coinciding with the beginning of the Roman October). The feast lasted a week (15–21 *Tishri*) to which a supplementary day of high festival was added, Lev 23:34 ff. Its characteristics were vintage joy, the joy of living in improvised huts of leafy branches erected everywhere in and around Jerusalem in memory of Israel's pilgrimage in the wilderness, waving of branches (*lulab* of palm, willow, myrtle, and *ethrog* of citron), many sacrifices, sounding of trumpets, *illuminations* in the court of the women, *libations* of water from Siloe mixed with wine. The ceremonies underlined seem to have special bearing on Christ's reference to the outpouring of the Spirit, 37 ff., and to himself as the light of the world, 8:12. **3.** The ' brethren ' of Jesus—his cousins—were those who had once tried to restrain him when he seemed over-zealous, Mk 3:21. Now they want him to appear more in public by passing to Judaea—an apparent indication that he had not been to Jerusalem for the last Pasch, nor perhaps for 9 months (Dedication feast) or 12 (Tabernacles of last year) or even 18 (the Pasch of Bezatha). **4.** The brethren emphasize the apparent contradiction of working miracles and thereby wishing to be a public personage in obscure Galilee. They want him to show himself to the great **e** world in the centre of Judaism. **5.** They had but an imperfect idea of his Messianic mission, since he was bringing no worldly glory to himself and them. **6.** Christ's answer means that the right time for a public ascent to Jerusalem involving a triumphant manifestation had not yet come—there were yet six months to Palm Sunday. The right time for the brethren is any time. **7.** They have the peace of the worldly with the world ; not so Jesus who has the hatred of the world for condemning its badness. **8.** Although the text-critical balance between the reading οὐ, ' not,' and οὔπω, ' not yet ', is rather even, it seems that Jesus really said he was ' not ' going up to this festival, meaning that he was not going with his brethren in the public manner they desired. A scribal change from οὐ to οὔπω, in order to avoid the appearance of dissimulation, is more probable than the reverse. The reason given is the same as before. The appointed time for the public encounter with the full hatred of Jewry has not come. **9.** When the caravan set out, Jesus remained in Galilee. **10.** Not more than

4 or 5 days later he set out for Jerusalem, but as an **796e** unknown pilgrim—probably even without the company of the Twelve. **11.** The enemies in Jerusalem were on the look-out. **12.** There was much whispered talk in the groups that gathered in the city. Those who considered his way of life said he was good, those ruled by human respect agreed with the hostile verdict that he was an impostor (*cf.* Mt 27:63, on which Aug. makes the touching comment : ' This name was given to our Lord Jesus Christ, for the consolation of his servants '). **13.** The friends were not brave enough to speak openly ' for fear of the Jews '.

14–24 Jesus teaching in the Temple—14. Mid-festival **f** would be the fourth day. Jesus teaches in the temple for the first time. **15.** The Jews who, in this context, would be chiefly Pharisee scribes, could not deny his knowledge of Scripture, whereas they knew for certain that he had never frequented a rabbinical school. Hence their outspoken surprise. **16.** Jesus' learning is not that of a self-taught man. What he teaches (as man) has a higher source, namely the One who sent him. St Augustine's beautiful comment which is read in the Breviary (Tuesday after 4th Sunday of Lent) referring the words to eternal generation rather than temporal mission is true theological interpretation rather than literal exposition. It amounts to this : His doctrine is himself and he is the Word of the Father—his own personal self and yet not his own. In this place, however, it is rather as an Envoy that Jesus speaks. **17.** Discernment of the divine origin of the teaching belongs to those who have the sympathy of an obedient will towards God and his truth. **18.** Another test—a moral one—is in the conduct of the Speaker. To seek only the glory of Another who has sent him is not the conduct of a self-constituted philosopher, but of One whose very disinterestedness commends him as truthful and free from the injustice (impiety) that is opposed to truth. **19.** As hostility to Jesus parades under the mantle of Mosaism, he takes up the charge of the event at Bezatha and unmasks the pretended loyalty to the Law of Moses which masqueraded as its justification. To all whose intentions towards him were murderous Jesus can say : ' None of you keepeth the law '. **20.** ' Why seek you to kill me ? ' The crowd, part of which at least may not have been aware of the real situation, set this down as persecution mania. ' Thou hast a demon ' was a common expression for, ' Thou art mad '. **21 ff. g** Jesus, ignoring the remark, turns to the case which occasioned the murderous intention of the Jews. The cure of Bezatha was no violation of the Law of Moses. The introductory ' therefore ', 22, seems to cover the whole process of reasoning but belongs logically to the conclusion, namely, that the Law of Moses was higher and more human than mere sabbatarianism. The law of circumcision on the eighth day—really pre-Mosaic or patriarchal, as the parenthesis says—was such as to include those infants whose eighth day from birth was a Sabbath. So plain was it, that these were to be circumcised and cared for on the Sabbath, that the rabbis formulated the maxim : ' Circumcision ousts the sabbath '. One of them (about A.D. 100) even argued that since allowance was made for circumcision which affected only one of the 248 members of the body, much more consideration should be had for the whole body. Our Lord's argument is rather this : If a beneficial operation like circumcision carried out on the Sabbath only fulfils the law of Moses, why be angry with One who healed a whole man (perhaps both body and soul are meant) on the Sabbath ? **24.** Just judgement according to properly legal and impartial weights and measures must be deeper than superficial appearances.

25–30 Jewish Comment on Christ's Origin—25. The **h** miscellaneous and changing character of the crowds or of prominent elements in them throughout these vivid chapters should be kept well in mind. In the last section Jesus had addressed a hostile group, probably Pharisees, mixed with pilgrims or others who

796h knew nothing of a set design to kill him ; here a more indifferent group of Jerusalemites appear amidst a crowd somewhat favourably disposed. **26.** These Jerusalemites think that the apparent explanation of our Lord's freedom of speech is a change in the national leaders. Have they turned from homicidal enmity to recognition that he is really the Christ ? **27.** But like Trypho about A.D. 130 (Justin, *Dial.* 8) they hold that a man known to be from Galilee does not fulfil the common Jewish conception of a Messias who should be of unknown or mysterious origin. **28 f.** Jesus fixed on this matter of origin. ' *Crying out* '— which means not shouting but taking a higher and more solemn tone—he told them that he who came from Nazareth (as they thought) was not a self-appointed Prophet but an Envoy sent by One who was a true Sender. The adjective ' true ' (ἀληθινός) does not mean ' veracious ' but ' really such '. The Sender is not known to them, but the Envoy does know the One from whom he has his embassy. **30.** Thereupon a move was made in the crowd to arrest him but the arrest did not take place. The immediate reason is not given, but Jn indicates the higher providential reason : ' His hour was not yet come '.

i 31-36 Believers and Emissaries of the Sanhedrin—31. The many who believed under the impression of this word of Jesus were persons who had heard of the many miracles worked in Galilee. The text affords no evidence that Jesus had recently worked many miracles in Jerusalem. **32.** On the hostile side, the Pharisees are the prime movers. Here we have the first official measure taken against Jesus by two Orders of the Sanhedrin. ' The *chief priests* (now mentioned for the first time in Jn) and the Pharisees (scribes) sent *guards* (Levitical police officers) to *arrest* him '. No doubt, the guards were instructed to act with caution, for the crowd was divided in its sympathies. **33-36.** Jesus, knowing that there could be no arrest, till his hour was come, warns his audience that the time is short. Of the three things that he declares, namely, the shortness of his stay, his speedy return to him who sent him, the subsequent frustration of Jewish desire to find him or come to where he is— of these three they seize only on the last. With a disdain which Palestinian Jews commonly nourished, they thought of him as going to the Diaspora or Jews dispersed amongst Greeks, especially in such places as Alexandria and Rome, and even as teaching the Greeks themselves. The repetition in 36 shows that they were particularly puzzled by the words : ' You shall seek me and shall not find me : and where I am, you cannot come '. The words are best understood of Jewry's continually frustrated quest for a true Messias, ever since Jesus of Nazareth, whom they rejected and continue to reject, ascended into heaven. The teaching of Jesus has really gone to the Gentiles, and the irony of their remark, 35, has fallen on the Jews themselves.

j 37-39 Promise of Living Water—37f. It seems that the last great day of the festivity was not the supplementary eighth day (22 *Tišri*) but the seventh—a day of processions, hosannas and special libations. The water of Siloe poured from a golden vessel may have been the occasion of our Lord's words, pronounced by him standing and with the solemnity of a proclamation. Two variant punctuations involve variety of interpretation. Irenaeus, Cyprian, and some other ancient authorities read : ' If any one thirst, let him come to me. And let him who believes in me drink. As the Scripture says : *From within him rivers of living water shall flow* '. In this case, the source of living water indicated by the Scripture would be Christ himself symbolized by the Rock, of which special mention was made in the liturgical chant of Ps 104(105):41 accompanying the libations : ' He rent the rock and water flowed—it ran in the wilderness like a river '. This interpretation, depending on what is really the earliest known punctuation, has in its favour that there is reference to a particular Scripture ;

it supposes that Christ, already symbolized in Jn by **79** the Temple, the Brazen Serpent, the Manna, now appears as the Spiritual Rock from which believers must drink the profusion of the Holy Spirit ; *cf.* 1 Cor 10:4. Nevertheless, however desirous we might be to adopt this grammatically defensible interpretation, which would make the words of Christ an echo of the beautiful promise of Isaias : ' You shall draw waters in joy from the fountains of salvation ', 12:3, and which would also supply a theological argument for the *Filioque*, the natural and obvious connexion of the whole passage seems to favour the punctuation commonly received, and adopted by DV. In this case, it is from the heart of the *believer* that the rivers of living water shall flow. The scriptural reference would be to many passages of the OT, for instance, the effusion of water (and spirit) in Is 44:3 (*cf.* 55:1 ; 58:11), the pure water of Ez 36:25 and especially the water from the temple in 47:1-12, the irrigating fountain of Jl 3:18, the open fountain and living waters of Zach 13:1 ; 14:8. It is not one river but many rivers that shall flow, for the gifts of the Spirit are various, 1 Cor 12. **39.** Jn explains that the water did signify the Spirit. The realization of this promise came at Pentecost. Jn says in language commonly employed when comparing the very little to the very great, that the Spirit was not yet given. Its effusion in such abundance, as a widely distributed gift, and with such every-day frequency was to be consequent on the glorification of Jesus ; *cf.* 16:7.

40-44 For and Against—The effect on the crowd **k** takes four different forms. Some declare Jesus to be the Prophet of Deut 18:15 ; others say he is the Christ ; others object that he came from Galilee and was, as they thought, neither a descendent of David nor a Bethlehemite by birth—both scriptural marks of the Messias, Ps 131(132):11 ; Is 11:1 ; Jer 23:5 ; Mich 5:2 ; others wished to end the matter by arresting him, but again no one laid hands on him.

45-52 Sanhedrin Scene—45 f. Amongst those most **l** favourably impressed were the guards who returned to the Chief Priests and Pharisees empty-handed. They could not arrest One who ' spoke as no man ever spoke '. **47 ff.** The Pharisees dub them as victims of imposture, try to confound them with the example of the religious and intellectual aristocracy, and pour their scorn on the crowd whose ignorance of the law makes them nothing less than a ' cursed crew '. The words were pronounced in anger, but the habitual contempt of the Pharisees for the common people was very great. **50 f.** The brave stand of Nicodemus— for it was really such—showed that a Sanhedrite, a Pharisee, and a distinguished doctor of the law shared in the sympathy of the benighted guards towards Jesus. Nicodemus simply insisted in the name of the Law, Deut 1:16 ff., that no man should be condemned ' unheard '. **52.** They abuse Nicodemus as if he were a Galilean—which to Judaeans ordinarily meant *stupid*, as *Boeotian* did to Athenians. ' Search (*the Scriptures* is a gloss even in Vg) and see that out of Galilee a prophet riseth not '. They forgot that Jonas was from Gethhepher and that Isaias had foretold the rising of a great light in Galilee.

7:53-9:41 The Light of the World. **79**

VII 53-VIII 11 Forgiveness of an Adulteress—This pericope is certainly canonical Scripture. If it is also part of Jn (see § 781h, i, Integrity) its place here is easily understood. The ' most joyful feast ' of Tabernacles with its circumstances of camping out and crowding was not always exempt from moral disorder. **1.** The Mount of Olives from which Jesus came to the temple at dawn is not elsewhere so named by Jn ; *cf.* 18:1. **2.** The people came early (*cf.* Lk 21:38 ; Ac 5:21) and Jesus sitting—as in Galilee—began to teach them. **3.** Scribes and Pharisees—there is no other example of the combination in Jn—*i.e.* lawyers and legal zealots, bring a woman taken in adultery and set her well in view. **4.** There is no need of an inquiry, for they attest that she was taken *flagrante delicto*. **5 f.** The

a Law, as they combine its statutes, appointed the death penalty for adultery, Lev 20:10, and stoning was specified for the infidelity of a betrothed woman, Deut 22:24. The question : ' What sayest thou ? ' was meant to destroy the ascendancy of Jesus over the people. What the party expected was a sentence of mercy which would publicly brand Jesus as one who flouted the Law of Moses. Even a rigorous sentence would make him lose in the eyes of the crowds. To embroil him with the Roman authorities is not an intention that clearly manifests itself yet. Most probably Jesus, in writing with his finger on the ground, wrote neither the sins nor the names, Jer 17:13, of those spiritual adulterers who were seeking to embarrass him. It was simply the gesture of a man not attending to their captious question but absorbed in

b something else. 7. In his divine response to their persistence Jesus carries the matter into the secret tribunal of their own consciences : ' He that is without sin among you, let him first cast a stone at her '. Jesus did not thereby announce a principle that sinful persons may not judge or punish a criminal, but he gave the accusers the discomfort of feeling their hypocrisy. 8 f. As he turned again to the silence of writing (that is meditatively making figures on the ground) they retired one by one, the oldest first, because quicker to take in the situation, and on account of their dignity more fearful of further possible embarrassment before the people. All accusers gone, there was only Jesus and the woman standing before him in the midst of the crowd. 10. Looking up he said, ' Woman, where are they . . . ? Has no man condemned thee ? ' 11. Her simple, respectful answer shows that she felt in some way that she had found not a Judge but a Saviour. The absolution given by ' him who had power on earth to forgive sins ' is here negative in form : ' *Neither do I condemn thee* ' (present rather than future). He does, of course, condemn the sin which he remits. Hence the admonition : ' Go and (*from*) now sin no more '.

c 12-20 Discourse at the Treasury—The place is the *gazophylacium* or place of the collection boxes within the court of the women, where stood the great candelabra for the illuminations of the feast of Tabernacles, now perhaps already terminated but fresh in the memory of everybody. The light recalled the pillar of fire which had guided the Israelites through the wilderness. This is the third great ' I am '. 12. As the Word of God and universal Revealer of heavenly truth Jesus is the light not of one nation but of the world. The image is probably from the column of fire, but God, Ps 26(27):1, and the Messias, Is 49:6, are called light in the OT. To ' follow ' the light means discipleship consisting in active faith, which delivers from the darkness of human ignorance, error, and sin. ' The light of life ' is light coming from the living God (the Word 1:4) and leading to life everlasting. 13. The Jewish objection is : Self-testimony is legally worthless—presumed not true, as not being

d receivable. 14 f. Jesus who condescendingly had let this axiom pass after Bezatha, 5:31, does not do so now, when the light of his self-revelation has grown stronger. Thorough knowledge is a guarantee of testimony, and Jesus knows himself thoroughly—is fully conscious of his origin and his destiny. Hence his testimony has inherent value. The Jews, ignorant both of his origin and his destiny, condemn with a prejudice based on mere appearances, or fleshly, human views, such, for instance, as would exclude a Nazarene carpenter without a moment's consideration. With such a superficial condemnatory judgement Jesus judges no one. 16. As there is now question of judgement not testimony, Jesus seems to say here : If I judge (when the time comes) my judgement is all that a judgement should be ($\dot{a}\lambda\eta\theta\iota\nu\acute{o}\varsigma$), ' for I am not alone, but I and the Father that sent me '. He reminds them that, although he has come to save, he will be their judge one day ' since the Father has given all judgement to the Son ', 5:22. Then he

passes to the twofold testimony which fulfils all legal 797d requirements. 17. Deut. 19:15 was constantly quoted to show the legal sufficiency of the testimony of two witnesses. 18. Here the condition is fulfilled, for Jesus e witnesses by his words and the Father by miraculous works and the prophetic Scriptures. 19. The question : ' Where is thy Father ? ' is not a reference to Joseph of whom the thought could not occur in this context ; rather it is the sneer of unbelievers at appeal to the testimony of one who dwells in light inaccessible— calling a witness from the clouds, as it were. Hence the answer : ' Neither me do you know, nor my Father ; if you did know me, you would *also* know my Father '. ' Perhaps ' derives from *forsitan*, a misleading Latin rendering of the Greek particle $\check{a}\nu$. 20. The place of this discourse is given as indicated above. It is because the arrest of Jesus was sought at every moment, that Jn notes so often that it did not take place, ' because his hour was not yet come '.

21-30 Christ's approaching Departure and Passion— f This discourse repeats the warning that the time for decision is short ; it strongly asserts that Jesus is the divine Envoy he claims to be ; and it declares that his claim will be recognized in the light of the cross.

21. Since this first word is repeated, with an insertion, from a former occasion, 7:34, and is again referred to at the Last Supper, 13:33, it is clear that Jesus meant it to be very solemn. After he shall have gone (six months from now) the Jews shall seek him—that is, shall seek the Messias that he is, although their unbelief rejected him—and they shall die in their sin of unbelief. Their responsibility, therefore, is personal and so great as to lead to obduracy. ' Whither I go, you cannot come '. 22. With more odious mockery than before, 7:35, they think of Jesus committing suicide and thus signalizing himself as one of the great failures of the world. 23. ' From beneath ' and ' from above ' as also ' of this world ' and ' not of this world ' are descriptions that mark the Jews and Jesus as belonging to different spheres. The natural man who lives by his five senses and has his heart fixed in the earth cannot receive the spiritual things that are apprehended by faith. 24. On account of their terrestrial blindness, Jesus says twice that the Jews shall die not only in their sin of unbelief but in all the sins (Gk text) from which faith justifies. To the phrase : ' Unless you believe that I am '—supply ' *what I claim to be* ' (*cf.* 28 ; 13:19). 25. They ask g the question : ' Who art thou ? ' as if he had not been telling them. The first words of our Lord's answer are difficult and have received many interpretations. DV ' The beginning, who also speak to you ' is as clear as Vg seems to be, but what St Jerome left to the Latin Church was not *qui et loquitur* but *quia et loquitur*, which is anything but clear. It is to the Gk and to the Greek Fathers that we must turn. The words $\tau\grave{\eta}\nu$ $\dot{a}\rho\chi\grave{\eta}\nu$ $\ddot{o}$ $\tau\iota$ (or $\ddot{o}\tau\iota$) $\kappa\alpha\grave{\iota}$ $\lambda\alpha\lambda\hat{\omega}$ $\dot{\nu}\mu\hat{\iota}\nu$ may be translated : ' *At the beginning* [*i.e. absolutely*] *what I say to you* '. The meaning will then substantially be : ' (I am) *just what I say I am* '. Considering, however, the depth of incomprehension which the Jewish question supposed, it seems better to follow the exposition, wholly or partly given by the Greek interpreters and most satisfactorily worded by St Chrysostom and his school : ' *Indeed, why do I continue to speak to you at all ?* ' Such a rebuke, similar to Mk 9:18, is not alien to the context, and it has the advantage of doing justice to the verb $\lambda\alpha\lambda\hat{\omega}$ and to the particle $\kappa\alpha\acute{\iota}$. 26. The sequence of thought seems to be : rather than say more about myself as you expect me, ' many things I have to speak and to judge of you '. But (I content myself with affirming once more that I speak the truth), he that sent me is true and *I speak nothing in the world except the things I heard from him* '. 27. ' And they understood not that *he spoke to them of the Father* '. We must, therefore, suppose a different audience from that at the gazophylacium, 18 f. 28. When they shall have crucified the Son of Man h —*lifting up* is a veiled but sufficiently intelligible

797h expression for crucifixion probably quite as clear in Aramaic as our 'swing' for 'hanging' but more dignified, 3:14; 12:32—then they shall know, to their loss and pain and not to their gain, that he was what he said, and that he had only acted and taught as an Envoy of the Father. **29.** There is perpetual unity of action between the two, for the whole programme of Jesus is the will of the Father—' I do always the things that please him'. **30.** Many began to believe at this first mention of the mystery of the cross—*intelligite gloriam crucis ipsius*—genuinely, indeed, but not with full freedom from the trammels of human respect, 12:42.

i 31-47 Matters of Spiritual Paternity—31 f. Initially the words are addressed to the convinced believers (πεπιστευκότας), but the strong mixture of hostility in the audience soon appears. Perseverance is the mark of true discipleship, and the truth of Christ known and practised is the great emancipative power. **33.** The perverted pride of Abrahamite blood (race-religion) was conspicuous in the Jews and had been denounced from the beginning by the Precursor, Mt 3:9. It asserts itself here. Children of Abraham were never slaves (at least by voluntary submission to an alien yoke), they said, and therefore needed no emancipation. **34.** Jesus solemnly points to the spiritual slavery of sin. **35.** Whereas the slave has no permanent rights in a house, the son has. **36.** Therefore emancipation by the Son will be true emancipation. Thus far, on the question of freedom from slavery. **37.** With regard to their Abrahamitic dignity, it does not show itself in practice. 'You seek to kill me, because my word *takes no hold, does not root itself* in you'. **38.** Knowledge in terms of 'seeing' is reserved to Jesus in Jn. He speaks what he has seen with (*i.e.* in the bosom of) his Father; the Jews do what they have heard from their father.

j 39. They indignantly raise the cry of their Abrahamite paternity. Jesus tells them that their works show them to be no true children of Abraham. **40.** Homicidal intentions and voluntary resistance to heavenly truth is not the mark of Abraham. **41.** There is another father whom they imitate—neither God nor Abraham. They understand this at once (in terms of their Scriptures, *e.g.* Jer 2:20) as meaning that they are the children of a people that has spiritually prostituted itself to the service of a false divinity. 'We *were* not born of fornication, we have one Father, God' (original Rheims Tr.). **42.** Their conduct gives them the lie, for they do not love the Son and the Envoy of God. **43.** They do not know his language, because their dispositions make them incapable of understanding his word. **44.** Then comes the fearful sentence: 'You are of your father the devil, and the desires of your father you will do. He was a murderer and an enemy of truth from the beginning'. His original pride was untruth, so that the truth is not in him; by lying deceit, Gen 3, he brought death into the world, Wis 2:24. In this place Christ does not mention the envy of the devil which, however, belonged to his murderous hatred of mankind. That he is a liar and the father of lying has special prominence. False-**k** hood has, as it were, become his second nature. **45.** Hence the Jews, in resisting the truth spoken by Jesus, have ranged themselves in the family of the devil. In the words of Apoc 2:9 ' they are the synagogue of Satan'. **46.** Jesus is supremely worthy of credence, for no one can convict him of sin: 'If I (the unassailably holy) speak the truth, why do you not believe me?' **47.** He concludes with a declaration meaning the same as his solemn assertion before Pilate, 18:37, but here the form of words is: 'He that is of God heareth the words of God. Therefore you hear them not, because you are not of God'. It is to be remarked that Jesus, at a moment when he is convicting the Jews and their father, the devil, of sin, openly challenges them to convict himself of any sin whatever. True, they accused him of breaking the Sabbath, of associating with sinners, of drinking wine,

but these were charges launched by hypocrisy. They **7** do not hear him because by moral disposition they are of the devil; their lives are not dominated by the spirit of obedience to God.

48-59 Insult and a Great Climax—In this series of **l** discourses the great climax occurs in 58: 'Amen, Amen, I say to you, before Abraham was made, I am'. No thoughtful Israelite could hear such a saying without thinking of the words: 'I am who am', Ex 3:14, spoken from the burning bush by him who called himself the God of Abraham, the God of Isaac, and the God of Jacob (*ibid.* 15). The gentle and strong Saviour brings this climax out of an atrocious affront.

48. Those whom truth exasperates easily turn to insult. 'Samaritan' was as opprobrious as *apostate* (*cf.* Ecclus 50:28), and 'thou hast a devil' meant in this context 'impious madman'. **49.** Jesus, who had found faith in Samaria and who was later to speak the parable of the Good Samaritan, Lk 10:30 ff., and to praise the grateful Samaritan, Lk 17:18, took no notice of this national term of insult. **49.** The sons of the devil who treated him as demoniacally insane he answered with a simple denial, adding: '(Rather) I honour my Father, and you *dishonour me*'. **50.** It belongs not to Jesus himself but to the Father to vindicate his Son's honour, which he does by a judgement of condemnation—an allusion to the vengeance that was to fall in A.D. 70. **51.** Turning doubtless once more to the group of believers he said: 'Amen, amen, I say to you, if any man keep my word, he shall not see death for ever'. He meant spiritual death, which primarily strikes the soul but also excludes the body from a glorious resurrection. **52 f.** The Jews, **m** with the malice inherent in their unbelief, twist the words to mean escape from corporal death, experience of which was not so much 'seeing' as bitterly 'tasting'. Jesus was thus making himself greater than all the great dead, including Abraham and the Prophets. That was the utmost arrogance of self-glorification. **54.** Again Jesus remits his glory to the care of the Father whom the Jews called their God. **55.** In reality they did not know God. They lied in pretending they did, but on the contrary, if Jesus should say he did not know him, he would be like the Jews themselves—a liar. To know is to obey, for truth is lived in charity, Eph 4:15. **56.** What follows is stupendous. 'Abra-**n** ham your father rejoiced (*in the hope and desire*) *of seeing* my day: he saw it and was glad'. The day is the whole time of the Incarnation rather than any single day. Abraham could only have seen it by supernatural vision, either by prophetic light in the revelation concerning his seed, Gen 12-3, or in the theophany of Gen 15:8 f., or in the theophanies which many Fathers held to be apparitions, of the Logos, Gen 18:2, or in the joy and divine consolations of the birth of Isaac, the child of promise, Gen 21:1-5. The last of these seems the most probable. That day was Abraham's Christmas. The hypothesis of the Patriarch's spirit seeing the actual day of Christ from Limbo may be considered less tenable. **57 f.** The Jews, inverting our Lord's words, proclaim the absurdity of a man under 50 claiming to have seen Abraham. Jesus was probably between 35 and 40 at the time. St Irenaeus thought he was near 50 (*Haer.* II, 22, 5 f.). We need not suppose that he looked older than his age. The Jews used the round number of a half-century—hundreds and fifties being common reckonings even then, Mk 6-40. **58.** The solemnity of the words: 'Before Abraham *came to exist*, I am' defies comment. **59.** In the ears of the Jews it was horrible blasphemy. They wished to stone him then and there. Jesus hid (by calmly mixing in the crowd) and left the temple.

IX 1-41 Sight is given to the Man born Blind—Much **79** comment would only serve to blunt the fine edge of this graphic, animated and fascinating page. It is the finest description of varying attitudes and reactions in the Gospels. Closely connected with the foregoing revelation of Jesus as the Light of the World, it tells

a of a miracle of physical illumination, 1–7, its public confirmation, 8:12, its victorious emergence from a triple inquiry, 13–18, 19–23, 24–34, its sequel in the spiritual illumination of the healed man, 35–38, its significance as indicated by Jesus himself, 39–41. The following points are to be noted. **1.** Some time probably elapsed between the attempt to stone Jesus and this miracle. **2-4.** The question of the disciples (first mention since 6:68) does not suppose belief in metempsychosis but a popular unphilosophic notion of disease being a punishment of prenatal or parental sin. The providential purpose of this man's congenital blindness was really a manifestation of Jesus through one of the works which he must work till the day of his mortality ends in the night of death. **5.** As long as ever he is in the world, he must visibly be the ' light of the world '. It is to emphasize this that he works **b** the miracle. **6-7.** The dust moistened with spittle may be reminiscent of the creation of Adam, or symbolic of the Word made flesh, but the washing in the pool of Siloam (SE. of Jerusalem) etymologically denoting the water *sent* from Gihon through the tunnel of Ezechias more clearly symbolizes the baptism by which the divine Envoy illuminates. The man went home from the pool with sight restored. **8-12.** The discussion raised amongst neighbours and others who had known the blind beggar results in evidence which has the vigorous brevity of three very positive verbs : *I went, I washed, I* (looked and) *saw.* **13-17.** The fine matter-of-fact positiveness of the healed man appears also in the first inquiry, for while the Pharisees dispute on the case of a Sabbath-breaking miracle-worker, he affirms his belief that the man is a Prophet. **18-23.** The fear of the parents to involve themselves in a statement that could be construed as a confession that Jesus was the Messias is easily understood, for any Jews, especially poor people like these would quail before the threat of excommunication—not apparently the *nezipha* (or one week's ostracism under reprimand), nor the *niddui* (like a Lent of public penance) but the *herem* (a major ban which made its subject a pariah). **c** **24-34.** The second citation of the healed man or rather attempt to bully him into false testimony under adjuration—' give glory to God ' meant : ' *Tell the truth* ', Jos 7:19—leads to a fine duel between hypocrisy and simple truth. The native humour of the brave respondent gives his answers a caustic turn. Abuse —the arm of the defeated—becomes the resource of the Pharisees. Against their ' we know that God spoke to Moses ; but as to this man : we know not whence he is ', the man speaks a ' we know ' of common sense justified in every particular by the concrete circumstances of the case. The Pharisees proceed to a final fury of arrogant abuse and excommunicate him for the crime of being miraculously cured on the Sabbath. **35-38.** Jesus (sought and) found the outcast. Now he only saw the light of day, but, by his courageous confession that his benefactor must be from God, was also coming to the light of truth. That further spiritual illumination Jesus also gave him ' Dost thou believe in the *Son of Man* ? ' is the better attested reading. The man certainly believed there and then that Jesus was the Messias, and probably in the full divine sense of the term, for adoration in Jn seems to mean *latria* only. Certainly the synagogue that had cast him out was already the blindfolded institution which we see represented by St Paul, 2 Cor 3:15, and by medieval art. The city of Saint-Paul-Trois-Châteaux in the valley of the Rhône claims that its first bishop St Restitutus was the man born blind. Whatever the historical verdict may be, the claim deserves to be mentioned. Provence also boasts that he succeeded St Maximin as Bishop of Aix. **39-41.** The judgement of discrimination which Jesus came to exercise in the world is shown by this narrative (*cf.* Lk 2:34). The little ones, with no pretence to be learned or *seers*, come to see, and those who have ' the key of knowledge ' become blind (*cf.* Mt 11:25 ; 23:16 ff.). When the Pharisees ask if they also are

blind, Jesus answers that theirs is not the blindness **798c** which takes away responsibility.

X 1-XI 56 The Good Shepherd. **799a**

X 1-21 The Parable of the Door and the Good Shepherd —This piece is often called an allegory. It is really not such, but a parable, which our Lord applies to himself according to two terms of comparison, namely, the Door of the sheepfold and the Shepherd of the flock. As the application itself is allegory or extended metaphor, the whole may be called a parable-allegory. We can find in it a rather complete definition of the Church charmingly conveyed through a description taken from Palestinian pastoral life. It is no wonder, then, that the fulfilment of the promise made to Simon Peter, Mt 16:18, is expressed in the same language as this, parable, Jn 21:15-17. The parable is connected with the foregoing by a certain association of ideas. A sheep (the man born blind) expelled from the synagogue by the false shepherds of Israel is received by the Good Shepherd. In those who heard the parable, it also evokes that miracle of illumination, 21. Nevertheless, it is the beginning of a new series, and is connected by a common basic idea with the revelations of the Feast of Dedication, 26. It is clear that Jesus, the Light of the World, here shows himself as the Giver of life—a qualification which is sealed, some weeks after the Dedication, by the resuscitation of Lazarus at Bethany, less than two miles from the gates of Jerusalem. This event occasioned that fateful conciliar pronouncement of Joseph Caiphas, 11:50, in which Jn sees a divinely-ordained prophecy that Christ will realize his own parable of the Good Shepherd, 52.

1-6. The picture of the sheep-pen contains all the **b** necessary elements of the instruction to be conveyed —the walled or palisaded enclosure protecting the sheep brought back from their pastures for the night, the door which is open to shepherds but not to thieves who enter in some other way, the scene of the morning, when the shepherd comes from his home or his camp to lead out his sheep to pasture, the pastoral call and its recognition by his own sheep, the familiar solicitude which shows itself in calling the sheep individually by name, the docility with which the flock, ready to fly from a stranger, throng on the heels of their true shepherd. Though the picture was evidently a ' proverb ' from everyday life (which is St John's word for the Hebrew *māšāl*, which the Synoptists call a parable or similitude) the audience did not understand its purpose. **7-10.** Jesus therefore makes the **c** first application and explains : ' I am the door of the sheep ' (and of the shepherds). **8.** ' All others as many as *came before me* (πρὸ ἐμοῦ probably authentic) are thieves and robbers '. St Chrysostom and many commentators have thought that false Messiahs like Judas the Galilean or Theudas, Ac 5:36 f., are chiefly meant, but the verb ' are ' in the present tense seems to refer it to those immediate false shepherds who are the scribes and Pharisees. The sheep did not hear them ; *cf.* Mt 9:36 ; Mk 6:34. In the prophecies of Ezechiel, 34:1-24, God had manifested his intention of taking over the shepherding of his people from self-seeking shepherds and handing it to a Davidic Prince. **9.** When Jesus declares himself the door of safety for all who enter by him, he means primarily shepherds, but thereby he is also the door of the sheep who through him enter to safety and go out to wholesome pastures. **10.** Whereas the thief's intention is destructive, the purpose of Jesus is life-giving. He came that his sheep may have life and have an abundance (of it)—grace, glory, resurrection from the dead.

11-18. In the application of the idea of shepherd, the **d** contrast is not with thieves but with hirelings, and anyone who is presumed not to have an owner's devotedness towards his own sheep. The allegorical description of that devotedness is carried to hyperbole, in order to fit the reality in Jesus. No shepherd could reasonably make a voluntary sacrifice of his life, that

799d his sheep might be safe, but the Good Shepherd has actually done this.

11. The single sentence ' I am the good shepherd ' has a whole world of biblical and ecclesiastical souvenirs clustering around it (Ps 22(23) and 79(80) ; Is 40 ; Jer 23 ; Ez 34 ; Zach 13 ; Lk 15 ; the shepherd of Hermas, the inscription of Abercius, the famous sculptured type of the Roman catacombs). Here. Jesus says at once that the excellence of ' the (great) shepherd of the sheep ', Heb 13:20, is to be found in his self-immolation on behalf of his sheep. **12 f.** The hireling, whose interest is salary, has no such devotedness. We can easily find an interpretation of the ' wolf ', although it belongs to the literary plenitude rather than to the essence of the parable. **14 f.** He repeats ' I am the good shepherd ' *ad incrementum orationis*, and in order to introduce a new trait, that of intimate mutual knowledge of affection between Shepherd and sheep, and also in order to affirm that he fulfils the sublime ideal of pastoral self-devotedness by giving his life for his sheep. The reciprocal knowledge of charity between Shepherd and sheep is proportionately analogous to that between the Father and the Son. The Gk word translated ' lay down ' (my life) may represent either the metaphor of total giving, or of depositing a price, or of putting off life (like **e** a garment). **16.** The sheep of the Good Shepherd are not all to be found within the enclosure of Israel hitherto the only pen established by God himself— but other sheep Jesus must bring from outside, and they shall hear the voice of the Good Shepherd, and there shall be one *flock* (not ' fold ', which, however, is no real distortion of the sense) and one shepherd (*cf.* Eph 2:13–16). [There is no doubt that ποίμνη (grex) ' flock ' is the correct reading in 16*b*, though ' Fold ' (ovile) appears in the Vg and thenceforth universally in mediaeval Latin writers. ' This fold '— the contrast is not between a fold of the Jews and a fold of the Gentiles, but between the fold of the Jewish Church which excluded the Gentiles, and the ' flock ' of the Christian Church which was to include them. ' Other sheep '—here signify simply the Gentiles. MacRory (*op. cit.* 7th ed) comments : ' We have three very important declarations in this verse. (1) The faith was to be preached to the Gentiles ; (2) Christ was to have but one flock, composed alike of Jews and Gentiles ; (3) That one flock was to have one supreme visible head '.—Gen. Ed.] **17.** Jesus returns to the idea of self-immolation. For the reason (because he is obedient unto death) the Father loves the Word Incarnate, laying down his life on the cross, in order to take it up again in the resurrection of the third day. **18.** His is an entirely free oblation of his life ' No man taketh it away from me '—if we read *took* (with S, B and papyrus 45) there would be reference to the attempts to stone or arrest him—' but I lay it down of myself '. It is as God that he says this, and adds moreover ' I have power to lay it down, and I have power to take it up again '. But it is as man that the Word Incarnate received a command from the Father— according to NT usage a *precept* not a mere intimation of good-pleasure usually called a *beneplacitum*.

f **19-21.** Once again the result in the audience was disagreement. Some said these were the words of a demoniac and a madman ; others said that neither those noble words nor the miracle on the man born blind could come from a demoniac. As the parable of the Good Shepherd is a Sunday Gospel (2nd after Easter) it will be useful to sum up the **doctrine of this whole section** very briefly. The sheep come from the Jewish and the Gentile world. Unity is maintained by pastoral authority and care, that of the one Shepherd Christ and of the shepherds that rule in his name—those that come in by the door. There is union of mind and heart between sheep and shepherd. The flock feeds on the wholesome pastures of truth, the sheep individually are consoled by the compassionate solicitude of the Shepherd and they follow him with affectionate docility. The whole flock finds life in the death of the

Shepherd and his resurrection. That great sacrifice **7** willed by the Father, freely offered by Jesus, crowned with life after three days, centres the love of the Father on the Shepherd—and, let us add, should centre the love of the sheep on their Good Shepherd. Gratitude, one of the greatest human motive powers, should grow out of the consciousness that he came that we may have life and an abundance of it.

22-39 The Great Discussion at the Dedication Festival g —This festival called in Hebrew *ḥanukkah* was instituted by Judas Maccabeus, 1 Mac 4:52 ; 2 Mac 10:5, as an eight-day solemnity beginning on 25 Casleu (Kislev), the ninth month of the Jewish year —therefore opening approximately about the third week of December. As commemorating the renewal of worship in the temple in 165 B.C., after the profanations of Antiochus Ephiphanes, it held an important place in the festal calendar. Having presumably occupied the time between Tabernacles and Dedication in the Judaean and Transjordanian ministry which Lk 9:15–11:13 probably records in the main, Jesus came to Jerusalem for this feast. **22 f.** The occasion is marked in a short historical introduction. The season (winter) is mentioned for the sake of Greek readers and to explain why Jesus walked in Solomon's Porch, the eastern side of the temple running along the western verge of Cedron and sheltered from desert winds. St Augustine could not resist referring the words to the human atmosphere : ' It was winter, and they were frigid '. **24.** They gathered around **h** him and pressed him to declare himself. Their question is really a demand that he should finish this suspense of uncertainty for them and say plainly whether he was the Christ. Hitherto Jesus had proved that he was, but had not expressly said so. **25.** He had said so sufficiently, however, and they did not believe, but now as before it is to the proofs, namely the works he has been doing in the name of his Father, that he refers them. His words are going to take them higher than his Messianic title up to his dignity of Son of God, consubstantial with the Father. **26.** In terms of the Good Shepherd parable he tells them the reason of their unbelief. Because of their bad dispositions they are not of his sheep—the Father does not draw them, 6:44. As St Augustine is strongly predestinationist in commenting on this verse, it should be emphasized that the Jews do not receive the grace of faith, because they are voluntarily as blind as a man who shuts his eyes and refuses to open them. That they are not ' of his sheep ' is their own fault. **27.** The description of the sheep as those who hear the Shepherd's voice, those whom Jesus knows, those who follow him, reproduces the thought of the parable, 3 f., 14. **28.** ' Everlasting life ' which occurs just a **i** dozen times in chh 3–6 recurs here, Jesus gives it to his sheep and they shall (as long as they are his sheep) never fall to destruction. No one (either with the stealth of the thief or the violence of the robber) shall snatch them from his hand. It is the power exercised by the violent that is particularly envisaged, and this notion of the Shepherd's unconquerable power to keep his sheep from every adverse force is the point of connexion with the difficult verse that follows. **29.** DV gives the reading of Vg which has the support of the Greek B (Vaticanus) and the Latin Fathers. Translated literally (with the original Rheims) this form of the text says : ' My Father, that which he hath given me, is greater than all '. Both the relative pronoun (ὅ) and the comparative adjective (μεῖζον) are neuter gender. The rival reading followed by the Greek Fathers Basil, Chrysostom, Cyril, makes both words masculine and says : ' *My Father*, who *gave to me is* greater *than all* '. There is no need to refer to the mixture of the two readings in many MSS. The second reading, asserting that the Father *who* gives the sheep to Jesus is *greater* (in power) than all makes an easy sense, but for that very reason may be suspect. The grammatically neuter reading is more difficult. The *thing given* has been understood by St Augustine and St Thomas of the divine nature (and power) given in eternal generation by the Father to the Son ; others understand the *thing given* as the sheep, not simply as sheep but as something given by an omnipotent giver to an omnipotent keeper, as the context demands. The words that follow will fit any of these three senses : 'No one can snatch them out of the hand of my Father'. It is evident that the hand of Jesus is equally omnipotent, for no one can snatch the sheep out of his hand. **30.** 'I and the Father are one'. St Cyril who follows the easier reading of 29*a* crystallizes his interpretation of these few words in the two adjectives *homoousios*, *homodynamos*—consubstantial, com-potent. Similar language is used by Basil and Chrysostom. Because the Arians said that union of will was meant —unanimity or concord of the Father and Christ— the champions of orthodoxy interpreted this text repeatedly (Athanasius about 50 times). Two brief citations will suffice as a summary of patristic thought. ' *Unum* ad naturam referimus, *sumus* ad personarum distinctionem ', Jer. ' *Quod dico, unum*, audiat arianus ; quod dico, *sumus* audiat sabellianus. Non dividat arianus *unum* ; non deleat sabellianus *sumus* ', Aug.

31-39. The Jews understood the magnitude of the claim and again threatened stoning—*bringing* the stones, rather than finding them near in the Porch of Solomon. **32.** Jesus does not withdraw this time (*cf.* 8:59), but asks them to state their motive. Of the many good works he had shown them from his Father, for which particular good work did they want to stone him ? **33.** They answer : ' Not for a good work '—whatever it might be—' but for blasphemy '. The accusation is quite formal : ' Thou, being a man, makest thyself God '. **34.** Jesus does not deny the charge, nor mitigate what he has said, but leads them to reason upward from a Scripture text, according to the favourite rabbinical process of *qal waḥōmer*—from the less to the greater. Ps 81(82):6 (a text of the Law in the wider sense of the term) introduces God addressing the judges of Israel in the solemn words : ' I said : " You are gods " '. **35.** The appellation is God's own and registered in an inviolable Scripture. **36.** Therefore, *a fortiori*, it is not blasphemy to apply it to one of higher dignity. That one is Jesus whom the Father has consecrated and sent into the world, as his anointed, holy Envoy. It is not blasphemy for him to say : ' I am the Son of God ', this being the equivalent of what he had said above. If ' god ' is a metaphor in Ps 81:6, it does not follow that ' Son of God ' is a metaphor here. **37.** It is a higher dignity proved by works which Jesus does as works of his Father. If his word is not sufficient—although it is—at least they should believe those works, so as to recognize and know that ' the Father is in me, and I in the Father '. This mutual *in-being* is a unity of being and nature and signifies an identity such as Jesus later impressed on his Apostle Philip in the same words, 14:10. Therefore, the discourse returns to the earlier assertion of consubstantiality : ' I and the Father are one '. **39.** The Jews did not think that he had retracted, for they wished to seize him, but ' he escaped out of their hands '.

40-42 Departure to Peraea—Jesus returned across the Jordan to the place where he gathered his first disciples —the place where the Precursor was first baptizing. Away from the hostile environment of Jerusalem, many believed in him ; and the memory of John became a motive of belief. Whereas the Precursor had worked no miracles, all he had said of Jesus was true.

XI 1-44 Lazarus called from the Tomb—This is the supreme miracle of the public life, the one which manifests ' the glory of God ' most signally on account of its circumstances ; it is also most decisive in its results, for it led the Sanhedrin to decree Jesus's death. It invites meditation rather than annotations. The narrative divides itself thus : (*a*) the Saviour's journey to Bethany, 1–16 ; (*b*) the meeting with Martha and Mary, 17–32 ; (*c*) the miracle, 33–44 ;

(*d*) the reactions, 45–53 ; (*e*) the retreat of Jesus to **800a** Ephrem under virtual sentence of death, 54–56.

1-16 Bethany (the name being variously interpreted **b** by scientific and popular etymologists as House of poverty, of affliction, of Ananias, of obedience) was situated on the eastern slope of the southern shoulder of Olivet, less than 2 miles (3,000 yards) ESE. from Jerusalem. The village where Martha and Mary lived was mentioned without name in Lk 10:38, but is here named by Jn and described as the village of Mary and Martha her sister. **2.** Mary is named as the anointer with reference probably to Lk 7:37 rather than to Jn 12:3. Although the matter is likely to remain a disputed question, there is a sufficiency of indications in the Gospels to give reasonable assurance to those who, with St Gregory the Great and the Latin Liturgy identify Mary of Bethany with the sinner of Lk 7:37 and Mary Magdalene ; *cf.* §§ 739*b*, 753*g*. The sickness of Lazarus (Grecized from Eliezer) is set at the head of the narrative. His sisters, knowing the danger to the life of Jesus in Judaea decided to inform him only at the last moment. Lazarus died while the messenger was on the way to Transjordania, *i.e.* to some place not far from that other Bethany, 1:28. **3.** In the circumstances no request is conveyed but a simple intimation : ' Behold, he whom thou lovest is sick '. Aug. says beautifully : ' It is enough that thou know ; for thou dost not love and leave it at that '. **4.** In the ordinances of God's providence the sickness was not unto death but, through the raising of Lazarus, for the glory of God, who thereby glorifies his Son, the worker of the miracle. Note especially that Christ foretells this miracle / no less than four times, 4, 15, 41, 42. **6.** Jesus, therefore, though he loved the family at Bethany, waited two days. **7.** His subsequent ' Let us go into Judaea again ' alarmed the disciples. **9-10.** With the little parable of the **c** day and the night Jesus tells them that nothing can happen till the evening of the Passion comes. **11.** Then he announces the sleep of Lazarus his friend which the Evangelist renders by a Gk verb from which we get our word ' cemetery ', to signify the ' dormitory ' of the dead. **12-14.** As the disciples take him to mean ordinary sleep (a good sign in a sick man) he then says plainly that Lazarus is dead. **15-16.** Being absent he did not intervene to cure him—a subject of joy, because of the salutary effect which his greater intervention will have on the faith of his disciples. When Jesus repeats : ' Let us go ', Thomas speaks a word of decision—the decision of a generous pessimist. **17-32.** The death and burial of Lazarus took place probably within a few hours of the departure of the messenger. So four days had elapsed when Jesus came to Bethany. **19.** The mourners (called Jews without the usual hostile meaning) were many, on account of the nearness of Jerusalem, and mourning was maintained with gradation of rigour for 3, 7, and 30 days—compare our Catholic 3rd, 7th and 30th day. Mary was the more celebrated of the sisters, 11:1, but Martha was the mistress of the house. **20.** Hence she went to meet Jesus. The dialogue is magnificent. Note the feminine delicacy and vaguely conceived hope of Martha's first word. **23-24.** In **d** answer to our Lord's assurance : ' Your brother shall rise again ', she makes profession of her faith in the final resurrection, a religious tenet of Judaism that had been growing in clearness since the Maccabean persecutions (*cf.* 2 Mac 12:43 f.). No doubt she had a latent desire of something more immediately consoling. **25-26.** Jesus demanded an act of faith in himself as ' the resurrection and the life ', in the sense of his being their cause or giver, *cf.* 6:39, 40, 44, 54. **27.** Martha's response was magnificent. Though she did not think clearly of the miracle that was to be, she must have felt that the words portended something unusual. **28-32.** She called Mary, who came and, with more emotion, repeated Martha's original words.

33-44. Deeply moved by sympathy (ἐμβριμᾶσθαι) **e** Jesus asked to be led to the tomb. **35.** The sentence

800e ' And Jesus wept ' loses some of its original force by the addition of ' and ' to Jn's asyndetic manner, and loses something in accuracy by use of the same verb as that which denotes the *weeping* or *crying* of Mary and the Jews. The Gk word (ἐδάκρυσεν) means that Jesus broke into silent tears. **36-37.** This sign of friendship moved some, and excited criticism in others, who asked if Jesus could not have prevented his friend's death. **39.** Again giving expression to his feelings of compassion (the verb seems to suggest that Jesus felt angry with Death or the Prince of Death), he ordered the tomb to be opened. Martha only thought of the decaying body of her brother and had to be reminded that she must only have faith in him who will presently

f show her the glory of God. **41-42.** As man Jesus had already made the submission of prayer to his Father and now publicly thanks him for the answer to it already granted and just about to be realized. Jesus wished to make the raising of Lazarus a clear proof of his divinity by calling God to witness to the miracle before it had been wrought. They took the stone from what seems to have been a subterranean cavern without an antechamber and closed not with a round stone running in a level groove but with a horizontal stone. **43.** From this cavern Jesus calls the dead man. Jn has three Gk words for what were probably only two Aramaic words spoken by Jesus with the solemnity of a loud voice. **44.** Lazarus came forth, bandaged as he was and with hands and feet and eyes impeded by the attire of the grave. In order to bring the astonishment of the bystanders to the concrete matter of fact before them, Jesus said simply : ' Loose him and let him go '. From the 4th cent. the tomb of Lazarus was shown where stands the present village of El-'Azariyah (from Byzantine Lazarion).

g 45-53 The Pharisees resolve to kill Jesus—The miracle had the usual opposite effects. Some believed ; others blinded by the light denounced the matter to the enemies of Jesus among the Pharisees. A miracle was no crime, but the growing popularity of the wonder-worker was a danger to the worldly hopes of Judaism. **47.** The chief priests and Pharisees (scribes) gathered in council. The whole discussion centred on the influence which these undoubted miracles were gaining for Jesus. If things go on thus, all will believe in him, and that will mean the end of the temple of Jerusalem and of the Jewish nation. **49.** The gruff counsel of Caiphas was interposed to cut the debate short. **50.** He insisted ' that one man should die for the people and that the whole nation perish not '. **51.** In the sense of the speaker it was merely a political utterance, but God, as Jn remarks, gave the words of the Pontiff of the year (such Caiphas was from A.D. 18–37) a higher prophetic meaning. **52.** Jesus was to die, in order to gather the scattered children of God into one as ' the Israel of God ', Gal 6:16. **53.** From this moment the death of the Son of God is decreed by the chief Council of the Jews. They will choose a suitable time and make show of legal forms, but the matter is decided.

h 54-56 Jesus retires—His hour was not to sound till the Pasch of which he was to be the Lamb. He therefore retired from Jerusalem to spend the remaining weeks away from hostile manoeuvres. The city of Ephrem to which he went is probably the present village of Eṭ-Ṭayibeh, about 12 miles NE. of Jerusalem on the edge of the wilderness of Bethaven. Early pilgrims to the Pasch were already beginning to move. There was much talk about Jesus, especially because the chief priests and Pharisees had given orders that his whereabouts should be reported in view of having him arrested.

801a XII 1-50 End of the Public Ministry—The last journey of Jesus from Ephrem to Jerusalem was a circuit, for we are certain that he passed through Jericho. It is probable that the events and words given by Lk between 17:12 and 19:28 belong to those few days. On this hypothesis Jesus would have touched Galilee once more (at Jenin ?), then passed into Peraea,

and finally made the journey to Jerusalem via Jericho **8** from near the place where his public ministry began. Jn's account of the days which preceded the intimate farewell of Holy Thursday groups itself in six sections which naturally arrange themselves in pairs. The supper at Bethany, 1–11, and the triumph of Palm Sunday, 12–19, are closely associated by the Evangelist with the miracle of Lazarus ; the words occasioned by the petition of some Greeks form two discourses—both under the sign of the cross—namely, that of the grain of wheat, 20–26, and that connected with the Saviour's first prayer of trepidation at the approach of his Passion, 27–36 ; what remains consists of two solemn summaries, one from the Evangelist, 37–43, and the other from the lips of the Divine Master himself, 44–50.

1-11 The Supper at Bethany—Mt, Mk, Jn tell of the **b** anointing at Bethany. Jn marks the date. ' Six days before the pasch ', probably on the Friday evening that began the Sabbath of 8th Nisan, Jesus came to Bethany. Since his return from the grave, it is Lazarus that gives prominence to Bethany. **2.** The supper was on the evening of the Sabbath. Simon the (ex-)leper, probably a friend rather than the father of Lazarus, was the host, Mt 26:6, and Lazarus one of those reclining at table with Jesus ; Martha was serving. It was Mary's magnificent gesture which made that supper memorable wherever the Gospel is preached. Anointing the head of a distinguished guest with perfumed oil was quite a common courtesy, Lk 7:46, and it is this act that is given prominence on this occasion even by Mk, who emphasises the profusion of unguent involved in the woman's act of breaking the neck of the alabaster which contained it. **3.** Jn on the other hand draws attention to the anointing of the Saviour's feet and the extraordinary act of the woman in wiping the ointment off his feet with her hair. Since towels would obviously have been available this incident becomes readily intelligible only on the assumption of the identity of this Mary with the sinner of Lk 7 ; and thus her act is also a recalling of the events of her conversion. *Nard pistic* (genuine) *precious*, probably the Indian product from the nardostachys Jatamansi of the Himalayas, had a penetrating aroma, and Jn (probably with conscious thought of the symbolism) notes that the whole house was filled with the odour. **4-8.** Mt and Mk, if they **c** do not use a plural of category, show that several disciples joined in criticism of the apparently wasteful gesture, but Jn points to Judas Iscariot as the leading and vocal objector. To say that his estimate of the price of the unguent meant so many French francs, or English pounds is mere mathematical equivalence, for 300 *denarii* actually represented the salary of a whole lunar year earned by an ordinary workman working six days a week. **6.** ' *took* the things. . . .' Jn tells that the pretended solicitude of Judas for the poor was really the avarice of a thief who had been appropriating contributions to the money-box (γλωσσόκομον originally a musician's ' tongue-box ') which he administered. **7.** Mt and Mk show that the Divine Master's defence of Mary's action drew attention to its character of anticipated embalmment. The words in Jn mean the same, but we must supply an ellipsis : ' Let her alone (she did not sell it) that she *might* keep it against the day of my burial '. **8.** The proximity of the Saviour's death is also brought out in the words : ' the poor you have always with you, but me you have not always '. **9.** Unmixed spiritual motive is rare in human crowds. The attraction of Jesus and curiosity as regards Lazarus brought a great throng of Jews to Bethany, of whom many believed. **10.** The decision of the chief priests to kill Lazarus as well as involved in the fearful logic of their purpose to destroy the influence of Jesus. But Aug. asks : ' Could he who raised a dead man not raise a murdered man ? '

12-19 Triumphal Entry into Jerusalem—The Johan- **d** nine description of the triumph of Palm Sunday joins that of the Synoptists, but Jn alone mentions palm branches. **13.** In the acclamations of the crowd, taken in the main from the great festal Ps 117(118), he gives prominence to the Messianic title *King of Israel*; *cf.* 1:50. Since he supposes the synoptic narrative, he omits many details such as the presence of its mother with the colt that served as a mount for Jesus, but he joins Mt in pointing to the fulfilment of Zach 9:9, which reads 'Rejoice exceedingly, daughter of Sion', etc. Jn quotes the text freely from memory, and substitutes 'Fear not' for 'rejoice exceedingly'. **16.** It is again recorded that, as on the occasion of the purification of the temple, the fulfilment of Scriptural prophecy in the events of the day did not come home to the disciples till later, 'when Jesus was glorified'. **17.** The enthusiasm of the crowd is connected with the raising of Lazarus, of which some had been eye-witnesses, while others knew from reliable informants that Jesus 'had done this miracle'. **19.** The Pharisees who were the prime haters and deadliest enemies of the 'King of Israel' expressèd their envy in many ways that day (*cf.* Mt, Lk). Jn records their sense of frustration and their admission that 'the (whole) world is gone after him'. Characteristic of St Augustine's tractates on Jn is the question : 'Why are you jealous, blind crowd, because the world has gone after him, by whom the world was made ? '

20-26 The Gentile Visitors—Some men, Greek in language and non-Jewish in race, had come to Jerusalem to worship the one true God whom they (like the centurion of Capharnaum and Cornelius of Caesarea) had learned to know through the influence of the synagogue. The legend of Abgar connects the origin of the Syrian Church of Edessa with these pilgrims. **21.** Wishing to have a private talk with Jesus of whom everyone was speaking, they approached Philip, the Apostle from Bethsaida Julias. His name was Greek and he probably spoke Greek. **22.** Philip consulted Andrew his fellow-townsman, his senior in the school of Christ, and his helper in embarrassment, 6:5-9. Together they told Jesus. **23.** It seems clear enough that Jesus did not say yes. These men were moved by the triumph of Palm Sunday which was not the real triumph of Jesus. His name was to be great amongst the Gentiles in another way. That is what his answer—the parable of the grain of wheat—shows. The hour of the glorification of the Son of Man, which is now so near as to have already come, is the hour of the Passion—to be followed, of course, by the resurrection, ascension and sending of the Holy Spirit. **24-25.** Thereupon he enuntiates that immolation is the condition of spiritual fructification. The grain of wheat is an example. It has the germ of life in it, but that germ does not germinate into the production of other living grains, unless it is subjected to a process of death and burial in the earth. The interests of spiritual, supernatural life must take priority over everything. To love the lower natural life more is to lose the higher ; to hate (which means to love less and subordinately) what is life in this world is the means of self-preservation unto life everlasting. This is the law of self-denial so often proclaimed by the Saviour, of which the highest act is martyrdom. **26.** It is the law of all the ministers or servants of Christ to follow their Master. To be with Jesus in glory—'where I am' by the anticipation of proximate realization—it is necessary to follow after him in the way of the cross. Such servants the Father will honour and crown.

27-36 Agony of Spirit—Jn alone relates this Agony as the Synoptists alone relate the Agony in the garden. The cross frightens us, but it also frightened Jesus, who clearly showed us that he has known every experience of human weakness (apart from sin) that would fit him to be a compassionate priest. **27.** The vivid image of a cruel death brought to Jesus a tremor, freely permitted, of fear. The first Gk words of Jn's version of the Saviour's utterance are an echo of a verse of the *Judica*, Ps 42(43):6, which is also echoed in the *Tristis est anima mea* of Gethsemane. The parallelism

with the agony in the garden is striking : 'My soul **801g** is troubled'—'my soul is sorrowful unto death'; 'what shall I say ?'—'he fell on his face *praying*'...; 'Father, save me from this hour'—'Father... take away this chalice'; 'but for this cause I came unto this hour. Father, glorify thy Son'—'not my will but thine be done'. **28.** The voice from heaven is, however, not like the angel of the Lord strengthening him in Gethsemane. It will be remembered that the voice of his Father was heard at his baptism and his transfiguration. On those occasions it came to accredit the Divine Messias. Now, before the Passion, the voice of God tells that the name of his Father has been glorified in the life of Jesus and shall be glorified in his death. Like the voice addressed to Saul on the road to Damascus, this voice was not understood by all the bystanders. **30.** While they disagreed, some **h** saying it was thunder, others an angel speaking, Jesus told them that the voice had not come to assure him but to assure them. He explains to them how God will be glorified in him. **31.** The judgement which is to fall on the world is a judgement of condemnation, for κρίσις has its usual meaning in the mouth of Christ. The world is the hostile mass of men and its Prince is Satan, who is now about to be cast out of his dominion. In this sense Christ immolating himself is, as Simeon foretold, set for the ruin of many. But Christ is the Saviour. **32.** Lifted up on the cross he shall draw 'all men' rather than 'all things' (Vg but not so strongly attested by Gk MSS and Fathers) to himself. The 'all' is not numerical but excludes every distinction of race or people. **34.** As exaltation meant crucifixion, the crowd fell into a discussion about the contradiction between the idea of a Messias reigning for ever, Ps 109(110) ; Is 9 ; Dan 7, and a Son of Man who was to die. **35.** Without entering into the discussion, Jesus renews his warning that the light is before them and the time short. **36.** Jn says that after these words he hid himself, because he did not stay in Jerusalem but retired to Bethany at night.

37-43 The Reflexions of the Evangelist—In the **i** following reflexions the tragic note of this Gospel sounds again. So many miracles encountering so much unbelief ! What is to be thought of it ? That 'he came to his own and his own received him not' is from a human point of view the great 'scandal of Jesus'. But there is no scandal. **37.** The want of success of Jesus amongst the lost sheep of the House of Israel was due to a perverse disposition foretold in the prophetic Scriptures. **38.** It is from what has been called the Passion of Christ according to Isaias, 53:1 ff., that Jn takes the first oracle describing Israelite unbelief. **40.** The more difficult text cited freely from Is 6:9 f. had been used by Christ himself, Mt 13:14 f., and by St Paul, Ac 28:26 f., of the same kind of incredulous obstinacy. The difficulty is in Jn saying that the Jews could not believe, because Isaias had foretold that they would not, and the text itself attributes their blindness and hardness to God blinding and hardening them. What is predicted in Scripture belongs to God's foreknowledge which is infallible. Therefore the Scripture must be fulfilled in the obstinacy of the Jews as well as in the treason of Judas, 17:12, but clearly that does not necessitate the action of the culprits any more than visual knowledge in the eyewitness of a murder necessitates the murder. In the blinding and hardening we have the mystery of the distribution of grace and its efficaciousness or non-efficaciousness. **41.** Isaias said these things *because* (rather than 'when') he saw his glory, so that the Evangelist identifies Jesus with Yahweh of the famous Isaian vision. Hence Jesus knew how his work amongst the Jews was to turn out. **42-43.** Like Paul later, St John notes that the infidelity of the Jews was not absolutely universal. Many, even amongst the Sanhedrites, believed, but through fear of the Pharisees and of expulsion from the synagogue—human glory hindering zeal for the glory of God—they did not publicly profess their belief.

44-50 Recapitulation of Jesus' teaching—In the last **j**

801j summary the Evangelist recapitulates from the lips of Jesus the main ideas of the various discourses. Jesus had demanded faith in himself as an Envoy of God. **46.** He had repeated that he came into the world as the Light of the World. **47.** He had said that he was a Saviour to save, not a Judge to condemn. **48.** Nevertheless, by their attitude to his word men condemn themselves and by that same word they shall be condemned on the last day. Practically the first and the last word of this part of the Gospel, 1:4 and 12:50, is 'life'. **49-50.** Jesus came into the world with his Father's command to execute and that command is life everlasting—its whole purpose is to give eternal life to those who receive Jesus and keep his words. 'The things, therefore, that I speak, even as the Father said unto me, so do I speak'. 'See', says Chrys., 'how everywhere he shows himself united with him who begot him and that there is no separation'. To see Jesus is to see the Father, to hear Jesus is to hear the words which the Father gave him to speak.

XIII-XVII THE LAST SUPPER

802a The earthly ministry of the Christ to his own nation is finished. Through their leaders and as a people 'the children of the kingdom' are standing in the darkness outside, when Jesus retires with his twelve apostles to eat the Paschal supper. That he did eat a Paschal supper with them is all but certain from the synoptics, but there is nothing explicit in Jn either about such a celebration or about the institution of the Eucharist. While the Synoptists narrate the things done at the Last Supper, Jn magnificently supplements them with a narrative which is mainly a report of the Saviour's words. The whole comprises three great sections : (1) ch 13, an historical prelude (washing of the feet, separation from Judas, and a touching preamble about the Passion, the new commandment, Peter's denial) ; (2) 14-16, the great discourse divided by a gesture of movement into 14 and 15-16 ; (3) 17, the sacerdotal prayer for unity.

b **XIII 1-38 Events in the Supper Room.**
XIII 1-17 Washing of the Feet—Jn has not a word to indicate or describe the place of the Last Supper, but he gives a precious date. Both here and in 18:28 he clearly indicates that the Sanhedrists were not themselves eating the Paschal supper, while Jesus was gathered with his own in the supper room (cenacle). Unless we suppose an improbable official transference of the Pasch of that year to 16 Nisan, the dates must be as follows : Jesus celebrated the Pasch on the evening which began 14 Nisan on the official calendar ; he was crucified about noon 14 Nisan ; the Jewish paschal supper began an hour or two after the Saviour's burial. It is disputed whether Jesus anticipated the date of the Pasch by his own authority (Fouard, Le Camus), or adhered to a Pharisaic rather than a priestly (Sadducee) dating (Vosté, Prat), or followed a different (Galilean) observation of the moon (Lagrange, Braun). Let it suffice to say here that recent studies seem to have given very strong probability to the opinion that Jesus ate the Pasch and instituted the Holy Eucharist after the sundown that closed Thursday 13 Nisan, died on a Friday which was 14 Nisan—a combination which gives very considerable probability to April 7, A.D. 30 as the date of the Redemption. (Nevertheless April 3, A.D. 33, still has its patrons, and their arguments are not negligible ; *cf.* § 676b.)

c **1.** St John loves prologues. They always sound the note of solemnity. Here ' his hour ', so often mentioned before, is defined (with an allusion to the Passover) as the hour of his passage from this world to the Father. The proofs of love which he had given to his own had been many. Now he gave his final proof of that love (unto death, says Aug.) ; or as the Gk phrase ' to the end ' may also signify, he gave them *supreme* proof of his love (Chrys., Cyr.). **2.** What follows brings a terrible shock of contrast. The supper was in progress (δείπνου γινομένου, rather than 'when supper was done '), but the devil had sown treachery in the heart of one of the company, who is now named ' Judas Iscariot, the son of Simon '. Jn had named Judas with similar emphasis when chronicling the day of the Eucharistic promise, Jn 6:72. **3.** There is another antithetic step from the baseness of Judas, to the sublime dignity which Jesus knew was his—universal sovereignty, divine origin, approaching glorification. **4 f.** And we follow yet another step of contrast as Jesus fully conscious of this greatness rises from table to preform a menial act for all his apostles, including Judas, while they reclined at table (their feet outwards). A lesson in humility is, in this context, the obvious intention of Jesus, and as such he himself explains it, 12-17. The customary ceremonial required a washing of hands, but Jesus added the washing of their feet. It is really humility doing a service of charity, this latter virtue being the one which has chief prominence in the magnificent commentary provided by the liturgical texts of Maundy Thursday. The further purpose of symbolic purification, though popularly assumed since Orig. and Aug., does not clearly result from the text. Jn notes every detail of the Saviour's actions, as if the wonder with which he then viewed the Lord thus serving his servants, still transpired through his pen. **6.** Jesus began with Simon Peter, for we cannot conceive the impetuous apostle holding his protest, while the Lord washed the feet of one, or two, or eleven others. **7 f.** English word-order blunts the force of St Peter's protest, as it sounds both in Greek and Latin. The contrast between ' thou ' and ' my ' in the apostle's words implies loving adoration expressing itself with utmost emphasis and vehemence. The amazed tone of the refusal comes from him who had declared Jesus ' the Christ, the Son of the living God '. Even when Jesus asks for acquiescence, adding a promise of explanation in the future, 12-16, Peter remains obstinate. ' Never ', he said. As the refusal proceeded from love, but not according to knowledge, Jesus overcame it by the proper weapon : ' if I wash thee not, thou shalt have no part with me '. In this threat with which Jesus subdues Peter's love, it cannot well be loss of sanctifying grace, or loss of partnership in the Eucharist or in the priesthood or the apostolate that is meant—all interpretations proposed by different commentators—but rather dissociation of mind from the humiliation of the Passion (*cf.* Mt 16:23). **9.** The fear of any sort of separation from Jesus drives the ardent apostle to the other extreme of offering his hands and head also to be washed. **10 f.** One who has taken a bath needs no subsequent partial washing, for total cleanness excludes the necessity of partial cleansing. This seems the most satisfactory interpretation, as the words ' but ' and ' his feet ' are absent from many of the best Gk and Vg MSS. It is in order to show his knowledge of the treason of Judas that Jesus passes to the moral sense saying : ' You are clean, but not all '. **12-17.** Resuming full attire and his place at table, Jesus explained the lesson. The disciples called him *the* Master and *the* Lord, and such he really was. Humble service of one another (washing of feet being a type of all humble services) is what they must learn from this unique Master and Lord. The Church, while keeping the washing of feet in the liturgy of Holy Thursday, has not regarded it as a permanent sacramental, much less a sacrament. It is a generic example given by the Saviour ; and the solemn sentence under double *Amen* emphasizes that the servant being less than his Lord and the apostle being less than his Sender must not be above doing such things. It is not the knowledge, but the practice of such an example that brings the happiness of true discipleship.

18-30 Elimination of the Traitor—It is from such **f** happiness of true discipleship that Jesus passes to indicate the presence of a miserable apostate, without, however, revealing the person to the company. The happiness mentioned did not belong to all the twelve. **18.** Knowing everything, Jesus had chosen them all as members of his apostolic college (*cf.* 6:71), but that one should, by his own fault, betray the confidence shown him was foreseen in the prophetic Scriptures. The text of Ps 40(41):10 is cited according to the Hebrew. The brutal treason of Achitophel, table-companion and intimate counsellor of David, is described as the backward kick of a horse against his Master. Achitophel was the type of Judas. **19.** Jesus is careful to make this known beforehand, ' that, when it shall come to pass, you may believe that I am '—the suppressed predicate being ' what I revealed myself to be ', namely, the Messias, the Son of God. The undetermined ' I am ' on the lips of Jesus is particularly reminiscent of the majesty of ' I am who am '. **20.** This grandeur of Jesus, Messias and Son of God, supplies, it seems, the connecting link between 19 and 20, which latter verse derives the dignity of the faithful apostles from the dignity of the Messias and the dignity of the Father who sent him. It is conceivable that the thought of this divinely high apostolic dignity brought on the disturbance which Jesus freely allowed to arise in his spirit, as he turned his mind to the traitor apostle. Though he had twice touched the subject of uncleanness, 11, and treachery, 18, in the apostolic group, he had not yet spoken directly. **21.** Now, however, he solemnly attests with emotion, ' Amen, amen I say to you, one of you shall betray me '. Only one knew it was himself, but the eleven were in consternation and in doubt, each about himself (as the synoptics show) and each vaguely about everyone else. St Peter, as usual, wished to cut an intolerable situation short. Placed possibly at the right-hand curve of a horse-shoe arrangement of cushions round a more or less circular table which was probably only slightly above the level of the floor, Peter was near enough to communicate with the disciple in front of Jesus, who was reclining with his head about the level of his Master's breast. Here the Evangelist for the first time covers his anonymity with the beautiful and distinctive title ' the disciple whom Jesus loved '. With a gesture of the hand and in a whisper Peter said to John : ' Who is it ? ' The familiarity with which John leaned his head back to get the information is charmingly expressed in Gk by the adverb ' thus ' (*cf.* 4:6), that is, just as a bosom friend would do. **26.** The sign, a dipped morsel, shows that the supper was not yet finished—an indication that the Eucharist had not yet been instituted. The morsel was not the Eucharist, and was probably a cake of unleavened bread, dipped in the special sauce called *charoseth*. This sign, of which the whispered significance was known only to John, was a gesture of friendship towards Judas, but it finally hardened him. **27.** ' After the morsel Satan went into him ' to clench the decision of betraying Jesus. By the words : ' that which thou dost, do quickly ' Jesus separates himself from one who had already completely gone over to the enemy. So well had the reputation of Judas been guarded that the company understood the Master's words of a commission to the bursar regarding some festal expenses or almsgiving to the poor. **30.** Judas went out immediately. ' And it was night '. To adapt a phrase of Aug., night went out into the night ; Judas was going to the Prince of Darkness, separating himself from the Light of the World for ever. There seems to be a growing tendency to rally to the probability (though it is only a probability) that Judas had not received the body of the Lord and was not a priest. [It would be certain if the Eucharist was instituted between the second and third cups of wine and water, as Judas seems to have gone out before the second ; *cf.* § 720*a*.—Gen. Ed.]

31-33 The Glorification of Jesus—Separated from the traitor and thereby set on the way to his Passion the *man* Christ regards his glorification, soon to be accomplished on the cross, as virtually realized. **32.** Since he is to glorify God by his Passion, God will glorify **803a** him ; ' in himself ' may refer to the glorified or to the glorifier. The resurrection and ascension, forming a unity with the Passion, are regarded as immediately imminent. It is after this verse that many harmonizers insert the institution of the Blessed Eucharist. If so, the term of endearment : ' Little children ' (of which this is the only recorded instance from the lips of Jesus) represents the glow of the heart which we now venerate as the Eucharistic Heart. In any case, it introduces a touching adieu, for the Master announces at once his proximate departure and visible withdrawal from his own, in such wise that they cannot accompany him.

34-35 The New Commandment—Jesus gives the old **b** commandment of Lev 19:18 as a new commandment. Mutual fraternal love, as promulgated by the Saviour, is *new* because of the entirely new standard ' as I have loved you '. The first ' that ' introduces the commandment ; ' as ' fixes the standard ; the second ' that ' manifests the deliberate placing of that standard—in other words, Jesus' intention in loving us was that we should love similarly—unselfishly (Cyr.), gratuitously (Chrys.), efficaciously, rightly (Aquin.). **35.** Charity is the badge of true disciples of Christ. Tertullian (*Apol.* 30) sets it down as a note which pagans recognized in the Christian community. 1 Jn is full of the exegesis of this commandment. We should also recall the precious information transmitted by St Jerome (*in Gal.*) that St John in extreme old age could preach nothing else but ' My little children, love one another '. Aug. has the beautiful thought : As Christ the Saviour loved us to save us, so charity should be a thirst for the spiritual salvation of our neighbours, all of whom God wills to be saved. It is primarily amongst disciples in the Christian community, but extends to others without exception, that they also may be disciples.

36-38 Peter's Love and Presumption—St Peter was **c** totally absorbed in the departure of Jesus and fixed in the thought that wherever the Master went he should follow. When Jesus said ' not now ' but *later*, Peter made the bold profession of love and presumption which brought from Jesus the terrible reminder, in the form of a prophecy of the Apostle's triple denial, that fervour does not avail without the consciousness of personal weakness and a correlative dependence on divine grace. Recall the touching prayer of St Philip Neri : ' Lord keep thy hand upon Philip, or Philip will betray thee '. The cockcrow mentioned is the second of Mk—that of the third or fourth watch—before which Peter shall have thrice denied the Master (the *life*, says Aug.) for whom he thought himself *ready to die*.

XIV 1-31 Consolation—The whole discourse, chh **d** 14-16, constitutes a farewell address. Consolation predominates in 14, while the developments of the two succeeding chapters are more exhortatory. The said consolation comes very opportunely to allay the consternation with which the prediction of Peter's denial must have filled the eleven. All that is said is meant to reinforce the consolatory word : ' Let not your heart be troubled '—a phrase occurring in 14:1 and 27. The burden of the thoughts is that the departure of Jesus is not abandonment. The Apostles shall have the assurance of his being their Precursor to paradise, of his future return to take them, and of his permanent interest in them, 1-14, they shall have the assurance of his Paraclete present with them, 15-17, the assurance of Jesus' own interior and living presence, 18-24, the guidance of his Paraclete, 25, 26, and finally the peace with which he bids them farewell as well as the joy that his triumph shall bring them, 27-31.

1-14 The Way to the Father—The movement of this **e** first section is towards the Father in heaven, to whom Jesus is the way, and with whom he is one God. **1.** The remedy for troubled hearts is faith in God and in the Christ. Whether we read a double imperative : ' *believe* . . . believe ' (Chrys., Cyr., Hil.), or (with Vg

803e an indicative ' you believe ' and an imperative ' believe ', God and Jesus are on a level of equality. **2.** ' Many mansions ' mean that a multitude. shall come to the bliss of the Father's house. Diversity of merits (Aug.) is true theology, but not the plain meaning of ' many mansions ' in this context. If it were otherwise—if there were only a few mansions—Jesus would have said so, because his departure was really for the purpose of preparing a place for his own. We must not conceive this preparation in a quasi-material sense of fixing places, but rather understand it of the Saviour's work as intercessor, sender of the Holy Spirit, helper of his combatant soldiers. Thus by preparing the occupants, he prepares the place which they shall occupy. **3.** His return to take them is at the hour of death for each individual (personal, *Veni, Domine Jesu*) and for the whole Church at the Parousia, Apoc 22:20. **4.** They knew vaguely that he was going to God by the way of obedience. So he told them that they knew both the goal and the road. **5.** Thomas, a man of slow, critical mind, objects that they did not

f even know the goal or destination. **6.** Thereupon Jesus gives both the goal and the way their full clear meaning. The Mediator is the way (to be followed by faith and obedience), inasmuch as he is the truth showing the heavenward path, and the living force that causes movement towards the goal, which is an unending vision of truth and an unending possession of life. Coming to the Father is necessarily a supernatural filial motion realized through the Son. There is only one Son in whom we are sons, only one Mediator who is our *way* to the Father. On earth we are wayfarers (*viatores*). **7.** The orientation towards the Father which Jesus gives is perfect. To know him is to know the Father in the unity of the one divine nature. To see him with the eyes of faith is to see the Father. **8.** This mention of seeing the Father raised in the mind of Philip the idea of a theophany, such as was granted to Moses, Ex 33:18, to the 70 elders, Ex 24:9 ff., or to Isaias, 6:1 ff. Hence the apostle who had said to Nathanael, ' Come and see ', now says ' Lord, show us the Father, and it is enough for us '. **9.** Jesus pointed out, in a tone of gentle reproof, that even in more than two or three years Philip had not penetrated his Master's identity with God. **10.** He therefore repeats the teaching of that famous day of the dedication feast, 10:25–38, when he had said, ' I and the Father are one '. The statement of 10:38 is here reiterated in inverse order : ' I am in the Father and the Father in me '. Identity of nature means that the words of Jesus are the words of the Father. *In-being* and *immanence* express the in-

g effable union of the Father and the Son. **11.** Jesus spoke with an authority that commanded belief ; *cf.* Mt 7:29. His word was enough to elicit belief when he said ' I am in the Father and the Father in me '. He is now speaking not to Philip only but to all the Apostles. **12.** If they hesitated with regard to his mere word, they should believe in his divinity because of his divine works. From the mention of these works he proceeds to tell them solemnly (' Amen, amen ') that hereafter anyone believing in him shall do the same works (works of the same kind) and even greater ones. The meaning is not precisely that Peter's shadow was to cure the sick, whereas Jesus only cured them with a word or a touch. No apostolic miracle that we know surpassed the raising of Lazarus and many others of Jesus' miracles ; but the results to be achieved by the Apostles and the Church were to be greater, for example, the conversion of the world, the interior transformation of souls through the communication of the Holy Spirit, the admirable development of the little mustard-seed which the Saviour

h cast into the earth in the days of his mortality. **13.** The power to perform such stupendous works shall not be from the Apostles themselves but from Jesus raised to glory with the Father. He makes it clear that *he* will do the work, even when the apostolic prayer is addressed to the Father ' in his name '. For the Father is to be glorified in the Son. **14.** Similarly **8** when Apostles pray to himself and ask something ' in his name ', he will do it. Jesus is, of course, not speaking of the twelve only, but of the apostolic efficacy of the prayer of the Church at all times. Petition ' in the name ' of Jesus means not merely the use of the formula : *in nomine Christi* or *per Dominum nostrum Jesum Christum*, but intimate apostolic union of mind and heart and intention with the Saviour. We have explained the Rheims text, but it should be noted that in 13 the Gk MSS and the best critical text of Vg read : ' whatsoever you shall ask in my name ', the words ' the Father ' being omitted. The addition, however, gives the true sense of the verse.

15-17 The Paraclete, the Spirit of Truth—' Love in **8** deed and in truth ', that is, love shown by keeping the commandments is the condition of the action of Jesus in the world. On behalf of the *Church loving* his petition to the Father is efficacious. The Father ' will give another Paraclete '. This purely Gk word used by Jn four times of the Holy Spirit, 14:16, 26 ; 15:26 ; 16:7, and once of ' Jesus Christ the advocate of sinners ', 1 Jn 2:1, means literally ' one called in ', as helper, pleader, defender, patron, advocate (especially in a lawsuit). Its active meaning is the usual one. In this discourse the Gk word is either retained (Syr., Copt., Vg, Aeth., Goth.) or translated as ' Consoler ' (Syr.-Pal., Arm., Georg., Slav.) or as ' advocate ' (Vg in Ep). *Consoler* is quite a good rendering, if we understand it to include assistance, advice, protection, intercession, everything, in fact, which is required to sustain and strengthen spiritually. The Paraclete shall remain not a short time only with his recipients, but for ever. **17.** He is the spirit of truth, communicating truth and therefore irreceivable by the world placed under the dominion of the Father of lies. The antipathy of the corrupt world and of the merely natural man to spiritual teaching is like congenital blindness. Reception of the Spirit is itself vision and knowledge of the Spirit. Such vision is possessed by the Apostles (and the apostolic Church) because of the presence of the Spirit, which presence and its interior character is expressed by the two prepositions ' with ' and ' in '.

18-24 Presence of Jesus and the Father—The advent **1** of the Spirit is really the advent of the whole Trinity. Jesus in heaven is not like a departed parent leaving orphaned children. Invisible to corporal eyes (*i.e.* to the world) he shall be visible to the eyes of faith, which faith is a contact between the living Church and its living Saviour. The day of Jesus' coming is Pentecost and every day in which he manifests his spiritual presence. **20.** ' In that day ' there will be the recognition of faith that the Christ is in the Father (with whom as Son he is one God), that the disciples are in him as living members, and that he is in them by infusion of the life they possess owing to their incorporation into him. **21.** Again the condition of love is formally stated. Active love of the Son draws down the Father's love and also the Son's responsive love, which is an intimate manifestation perceived by faith and even sometimes experimentally felt. **22.** Judas (more commonly called Jude, not the Iscariot) expressed his surprise. His surprise was just like the former surprise of the brethren of the Lord to whose number Jude belonged, 7:4, that Jesus should have mentioned no manifestation of himself to the world. **23.** Jesus answered by continuing on the same line of thought. Practical love of Jesus calls down the Father's love and brings a joint visitation of Father and Son, not passing but abiding. **24.** The non-observance of Christ's word is non-observance of the Father's word. Hence such conduct excludes from the divine visitation and manifestation, which is really love meeting love.

25-26 The Paraclete as Teacher and Guide—The connexion between 25 and 26 shows that the function of the Paraclete as Teacher and Mentor will be to give full understanding of the teaching of Jesus. **26** is a Trinitarian verse, for the Father sends the Spirit in the name of Christ. The Holy Spirit is always active in the Church furthering the full development of the truth delivered by Christ.

27-31 Farewell—The conclusion shows an example of Semitic inclusion. The discourse ends as it began in words of encouragement, with a slightly enlarged repetition of one phrase : ' Let not your heart be troubled, nor let it be afraid '. It has often been noted that Latins greeted by wishing *health*, Greeks by wishing *joy*, Semites by wishing *peace*. **27.** The peace (a real tranquillity of order within the human soul) which Jesus wishes is a legacy and a gift, not a mere formula such as the world uses. The peace of Christ excludes both disturbance and pusillanimity. As at the beginning, the Master couples the thought of his departure with that of his coming (his constant coming). As a matter of fact, his departure, instead of being a cause of sorrow, should be a cause of unselfish joy proceeding from the love of benevolence, ' because I go to the Father : for the Father is greater than I '. The greatness of the Father over the Son was conceived by some early Fathers as the relation of giver of the divine nature to him who received it by generation. Though theologically justifiable in the sense of priority of relationship, this conception is not exegesis. Jesus is speaking as the Word Incarnate and as one going to the Father by the glorification of his humanity. The Word as Son was equal to the Father ; the Word Incarnate as man was less than the Father. **29.** As the departure was to be by the scandal of the Passion, Jesus notes that he is telling all this to his Apostles beforehand, in order to keep their faith from succumbing to the shock of events. **30.** Little time is left. The prince of the wicked world—the inspirer of Judas and Jewish hatred—is coming, but against Christ the sinless he has no power. **31.** If Jesus delivers himself to the Prince of Darkness, it is to show the world that he loves his Father and carries out his Father's command. After the signal ' Arise, let us go hence ', he must at least have left the table and gone to another part of the house. It is difficult to suppose that he spoke chh 15–17 on the way to Gethsemani. Some suppose that we have in chh 15–16 a supplementary collection of paralipomena spoken earlier in the supper and closely connected with 13:31–35 ; others think that 27–31 are dislocated and should conclude ch 17.

XV-XVI Exhortation and Encouragement—These two words characterize what is most characteristic in this piece. It builds up the unity of the body of Christ by insistence on vital adhesion to the Saviour and on the cohesive bond of mutual charity, 15:1–17. This fellowship conceived as a living vine and a fruitful fraternity shall have to face the perpetual hostility which the world showed towards Jesus himself, 15:18–25 ; it shall, however, stand and bear its witness to the Saviour in the strength of the Paraclete, 15:26–16:15. The rest is an epilogue of leave-taking which assures the Apostles that they shall have a perpetual source of joy in him and an invincible confidence that his victory over the world shall be theirs, 16:16–35.

XV 1-8 The Vine and the Branches—This is almost a pure allegory, the parabolic element in it being very small. The metaphor of the vine and the vineyard signifying the house of Israel is frequent in the OT. It is found in a beautiful canticle, Is 5:1–7, in Jeremias' divine pleas against Israel, Jer 2:21, in a passage of Ezechiel most closely akin on the negative side to our present allegory, Ez 15:2–8, in the Philo-Ephraimite poet of Ps 79(80)—as also in Jacob's prophetic image of Joseph, Gen 49:22. **1.** ' I am the bread of life, I am the light of the world, I am the door, I am the good Shepherd, I am the resurrection and the life, I am the way, the truth and the life '—to these six great assertions this seventh and last ' I am ' is now added, as the Saviour's own image of the Church which is the extension of himself, the total Christ, the mystic body of Pauline and Catholic theology. The

allegory may have some relation to the Eucharistic **804g** wine which the Apostles had drunk, but in any case ' true vine ' is the man Christ hypostatically planted in the Godhead and realizing the fecundity and excellent fruitage of the vine-image. The cultivation of it is attributed to the Father. **2.** A fruitless branch is lopped off like Judas ; the fruit-bearing branch is pruned by the pruning-knife of trials, and thus relieved of noxious excrescence becomes more fruitful. **3.** The **h** pruning ' clean ' of the Apostles is the result of the word Jesus has spoken to them not only that night but during his whole ministry. **4.** Vital *immanence*—the Eucharistic word of 6:57—is what the disciples must maintain by faith and charity—really by sanctifying grace which is inseparable from the virtues of faith and charity. The branches do not give but take the sap of life from the vine ; therefore there is no fruit without immanent adhesion. **5.** In indicating the meaning of the metaphor ' I am the vine, you the branches ', Jesus says that union secures abundant fructification, ' without me you can do nothing '— a sentence which according to patristic interpretation and the authoritative declaration of the 2nd Council of Orange shows the necessity not only of habitual but of actual grace. These six words exclude every sort of Pelagianism. **6.** A separated vine-branch is proverbially useless, destined only to be cast out, to wither, to burn in fire. Nothing could be stronger than St Augustine's comment : *Aut vitis aut ignis*— either the vine or the fire (of gehenna). **7.** Mutual union of vine and branch means also efficacious prayer, which is the indispensable means of fruitful life. **8.** Fruitfulness and discipleship, which is union of mind and heart with Christ, go together, and in them the Father has received glory, the moment they exist.

9-17 Union of Charity—**9.** The greatness of Christ's **i** love for his disciples is seen in the comparison : ' As the Father loved me '. They must make sure that his love for them continues. **10.** The observance of his commandments, which is the real proof of that union of wills which is called love, will ensure the permanence of Christ's good pleasure towards them, just as in Jesus' own obedience the Father always acknowledged his beloved Son. **11.** These words Jesus has spoken, in order that he may have the joy of the vine in its branches, and that the branches may have the full joy of abundant and precious fruit. **12.** He reduces his commands to *one* which includes all : ' that you love one another, as I have loved you '. **13.** The standard is Jesus' own love, and the measure is that ' greater ' and greatest measure of generosity which will make one ready to sacrifice life itself on behalf of one's ' friends ', who in this context also include one's enemies, who do not return one's love. **14.** Again the proof of friendship with him who is Lord and Master, is conformity of will in obedience—*idem velle, idem nolle, ea demum firma amicitia est*, to will the same, to nill the same, is really firm friendship '. **15.** Servants receive orders but are not given reasons, friends are treated as intimates and admitted to the master's secrets. So Christ made known to his disciples all that he heard, as man and teacher, from his Father. **16.** Most striking characteristic of all, his love was totally gratuitous. He chose them, not they him. This choice is brought back once more to the allegory of the vine : ' I have appointed you that you should go and bring forth fruit, and your fruit should remain '. In the wonderfully bold metaphors of Ps 79(80), the apostolic tendrils of the true vine were to propagate the growth of salvation to the sea and to the Euphrates and to the ends of the earth. Such fecundity is not the result of natural activity but of prayer drawing everything from the Father in the name of his Christ. **17.** All these things that Jesus enjoins have one purpose, ' that you love one another '.

18-XVI 4 Hatred on the part of the World—The **805a** external response of the world to this apparition of divine charity in its midst will, strange to say, be

805a hatred. Persecution is really a mark of the true Church. A Christian will never be surprised at it; rather will he expect it. Christ has forewarned us. **18.** He tells us: 'It (fixedly) hated me before you' (μεμίσηκεν). **19.** The reason of the hostility is found in the fact that the aspirations of disciples of Christ are clearly and categorically opposed to the aspirations of the world. A dissimilarity which is a perpetual reproof must be disliked and hated. 'Not of the world', rather 'chosen out of the world', are the qualifications that make the disciples of Christ a sign of contradiction. **20.** Servants cannot look for better treatment than their Master received. Persecution from many, submissive love from some will be their lot, as it was his. **21.** The name of Christ is the real sign of contradiction, and hatred is heavily charged and intermixed with culpable ignorance: 'they know not him that sent me'. Jesus is speaking of the Jewish world. **22.** The advent of Jesus, their Christ, and his message to them has deprived them of all excuse for their unbelief. **23.** Hatred of Jesus is simply hatred **b** of God the Father. **24.** His works—unique works such as no one ever did—leave them without any plea to excuse them from sin. They have seen him and they have (fixedly) hated him and his Father, whose words the words of Jesus were, and whose works were his works. **25.** So it was predicted in their law (*i.e.* their Scriptures), for a Psalmist said in a Messianic Psalm, 68(69):5: 'They hated me without cause'; *cf.* Ps 34(35):19. The connexion between 25 and 26 seems to be that the inexcusability of the unbelieving Jewish world will continue, but testimony to Jesus will also continue through the Holy Spirit and the Apostles who were with him from the beginning. Thus Jesus seems to refer chiefly, if not exclusively, to the years of active Jewish persecution and to the time which had its horizon in the fall of Jerusalem. **26.** In a sentence, from which a little compendium of the theology of the Holy Spirit might be extracted, the Master now points to the Paraclete as a witness of himself. The Paraclete's relation of origin or procession from the Son is *implicit* in the fact that the Son sends him. He shall equally come from the Father (in this temporal mission), but the eternal procession of the Holy Ghost from the Father is commonly held to be *explicity* stated by the use of the present tense, 'who proceeds from the Father'. That the Spirit is a person appears clearly, for although the 'Spirit of truth' is neuter in Gk, this name is immediately followed by the masculine personal pronoun 'he' (ἐκεῖνος). The Apostles are witnesses of Christ, as having been with him from the beginning (*cf.* Ac 1:21 f.: 10:37 ff.); their testimony is distinguished from, but also united to, the testimony of the Holy Ghost (*cf.* Ac 5:32; 15:28). **XVI 1-4.** These premonitions are a shield against such terrible shocks as might well make them stagger—excommunication from the synagogue, persecution to death which is actually considered by the persecutors (such as Saul was) as an act of homage to God. Culpable ignorance shall be behind it all, but for the persecuted to be forewarned is to be forearmed.

c XVI 5-15 The Work of the Holy Spirit—5. In this precise way Jesus had not yet told of the future stubbornness, fury and fanaticism of Jewish persecution. He does so now because he is going, and they know where he is going, since they have ceased to question him. **6.** From their own (not really disinterested) point of view they see only the sorrowful aspect of his departure. **7.** He therefore tells them of its utility to them. It is the necessary condition of the sending and advent of the Spirit. The benefits of this advent may be summed up as three, (*a*) the evidences of the divinity of the Holy Ghost, (*b*) the abundance of his outpourings of grace, (*c*) the spiritualization of the Apostles' love of Jesus. **8-11.** The Spirit will impeach the world and put it in the wrong on three points: sin, justice, judgement. The world thought Jesus to be guilty and itself guiltless; the world thought that justice was on its side; the world thought that it had no condemnation to incur. The Spirit will show all these suppositions to be false. In the first place, the Spirit will give clear evidence that Jesus was the Messias, and in doing so will lay their sin at the door of the Jews as being a sin of unbelief, a sin against the light. Three thousand in Jerusalem made that admission on Pentecost Sunday, Ac 2:37-41, and every conversion of an enemy of Christ will involve the same confession. Secondly, the Spirit will attest that it is not a culprit who ascended into heaven and sits at the right hand of God. As the Apostles preach, as *charismata* abound, as the Church grows, it will be clear that justice and sanctity belonged to Jesus and not to the Jews who killed him as a malefactor. Thirdly, it will appear that in the battle between Christ and the Prince of this world, it is not the Christ who has succumbed to adverse judgement. Satan has been struck with a sentence of condemnation (κέκριται) and has been cast out of his dominion; *cf.* 12:31. The destruction of idolatry and the expulsion of demons from the possessed were to be amongst the proofs of this, Ac 8:7; 16:18; 19:12.

12-15. Whereas towards the world the Spirit is an accuser from whom there is no escape, towards the Apostles he is Christ's great substitute to guide them into all religious truth. **12.** To render his teaching explicit and clear in detail, Jesus still needed to speak many words, too many for his hearers to take in that evening. He will, therefore, complete their instruction through that other Paraclete. For the fourth time the advent of the Spirit is promised to them, and for the third time he is called 'the Spirit of truth' (14:17; 15:26; 16:13; 'Holy Spirit' in 14:26, *cf.* 20:22). **13.** 'But when he, the Spirit of truth, is come he shall *lead you into* all truth'. This may mean the revelation of new truths left unrevealed by the Christ, but the view that the Spirit is an internal *illuminator* rather than a *revealer* seems more in keeping with the context of this discourse, 14:26, and of the whole Fourth Gospel (1:16-18; *cf.* 1 Jn 2:20-27). In the person of Jesus and his manifestation of himself up to the day of his ascension, Ac 1:3, and sometimes to individual Apostles after the ascension, Ac 9:4; Apoc 1:1, we would seem to have the full final revelation, in the *explicit* understanding of which the Church shall ever grow through the illuminating action of the Paraclete. Thus the Spirit of God (substantial love) would be the fecundating principle to secure the Church's living penetration of the deposit given by the 'Image of the invisible God', Col 1:15, in *implicit fullness*. In Jesus 'all the treasures of wisdom and knowledge are hidden', Col 2:3. The Spirit is not an independent speaker. 'Whatsoever he shall *hear* (BWD Vg against 'hears' of SL) he shall speak'. By particular prophecies and still more by full confidence in the Christian economy (as voiced, for instance, in Apoc) 'the things which are to come he shall show you'. **14 f.** As Jesus glorified the Father, the Paraclete shall glorify Jesus, receiving and showing what is common to the Father and the Son. This statement implies the procession of the Holy Ghost from the Father and the Son as from a co-principle.

16-24 Jesus' Departure and Return—Jesus puzzled the Apostles by telling them that in 'a little while they should not see him' and again in 'a little while they should see him'. The addition 'because I go to the Father' is not authentic in 16, but is added by the Apostles in 17, from what they had already heard, 16:10. Thus they make the subject of their inquiry, 'the little while' and 'the little while', even more enigmatic. The enigma has received many explanations. Aug. terminates the first 'little while' at the ascension, and extends the second to the judgement and the final bliss of heaven. In this explanation the second 'little while' is by no means little, but it is urged that the ages of time, however many, are short, a thousand years being like a day in comparison with eternity. Another interpretation, approved by Aug.

and followed by Aquinas, has the favour of the majority of modern commentators (Maldonatus, however, being a very notable exception). The first *modicum* extends to the crucifixion and burial of Jesus, the second terminates with his resurrection. Thus the 'little whiles' are respectively less than 20 and 40 hours in round numbers. After his resurrection they *saw* him and *rejoiced* with a joy which no one could ever again take from them. **20 ff.** The two states of sorrow and joy are illustrated by the Saviour's parable of a woman in childbirth. **23 f.** It is objected that whereas he says that in that day they will ask no further questions, after the resurrection the Apostles still asked some questions, Jn 21:21 ; Ac 1:6. But Christ evidently means that his resurrection will put his disciples in a permanent condition of certitude about the meaning of what he has said to them. That certitude brought by the resurrection is crowned at Pentecost. Jn himself notes more than once that, when Jesus was glorified, they understood many things that had for formerly been impervious to them, 2:22 ; 12:16. Then they shall also understand the impetratory power given them in the Saviour's mediation—a thing they had not thought of while he was with them in his mortality. ' If you ask the Father anything in my name, he will give it you '. Aug. emphasizes the last word, and argues that only prayer for one's own needs is certainly infallible. It seems difficult to say that Christ intended to affirm this. The order of words in Gk would rather put the emphasis on ' in my name '.

25-32 Conclusion—Even with the tragic note of human weakness sounding so clearly in them, no words could be more comforting than these few verses. **25-27.** ' These things I have spoken to you in *allegories* '. What Jesus had said in the language of symbol and allegory was obscure, but the hour of full light is coming, when ' I will show you plainly of the Father ' ; *cf.* 14:26. That hour shall begin with the resurrection and the mission of the Holy Spirit. Then petition shall be made in the name of Christ—the Apostles and the Church after them shall pray *per Dominum nostrum Jesum Christum*—and although the living intercession of the Saviour on behalf of his own shall go on perpetually, 1 Jn 2:1-3 ; Heb 7:25, the very fidelity of the Apostles' love for Jesus will draw the benevolence of the Father upon them, for they have believed that he came forth from God. **28-30.** With a clearness which, at that moment, seemed new to the eleven he said : ' I came forth from the Father and am come into the world : again I leave the world and I go to the Father '. No one can miss perceiving not only the clarity but the majestic grandeur of this word— a veritable compendium of the Fourth Gospel. The Apostles felt that it answered all the questions they wanted to ask about that enigmatic ' little while '. Not only do they recognize plain speaking (' thou speakest no *allegory* '), but they feel that Jesus has been reading the secrets of their hearts. ' By this ', they say, ' we believe that thou camest forth from God '. **31 f.** He does not doubt the sincerity of their faith, but he speaks a prophecy of human tragedy and divine grandeur. The faith of the Apostles is not solid enough to stand the storm of crisis that is to break that very night. The picture is : His intimates dispersed, Jesus alone—but not alone, for the Father is with him. **33.** To comment on the final word of eternal encouragement would be to spoil it : ' These things I have spoken to you, that in me you may have peace. In the world you shall have distress, but have confidence, I have overcome the world ($\nu\epsilon\nu\iota\kappa\eta\kappa\alpha$) '. It is equivalent to saying : My victory over the powers of evil will be yours. St John remembered it when he wrote to the Churches of Asia : ' This is the victory which vanquished the world, your faith ', 1 Jn 5:4. Jesus has not conquered without conquering in his body which is the Church. Aug. writes : ' They had confidence and they conquered. In whom but in him ? For he would not have conquered the world

if the world conquered his members. Hence the **805h** Apostle says : " Thanks be to God who gives us victory ", 1 Cor 15:57, and he added immediately, " through our Lord Jesus Christ " '.

XVII 1-26 Christ's Sacerdotal Prayer for Unity— 806a The sacerdotal or pontifical character of this majestic prayer of the Saviour is noted more than once by Cyr. Alex. in the course of the ten long chapters which he dedicates to its exposition. It is, of course, v 19 that sounds the specifically sacerdotal note. But the pontifical tone of the whole and the fact that the prayer is a sort of preface to the Passion justifies the title of ' sacerdotal prayer '. However, the theme of it is the unity of the Church through the glorification of the Saviour. The exordium of that great sacrificial prayer, the canon of the Roman Mass, shows some affinities, of which an emphatic supplication for unity is not the least. Christ, as we saw, had probably left the supper-room, 14:31. That he was in the open air (possibly on the flat roof of the house) is suggested but not postulated by the gesture of raising his eyes to heaven. Certainly such a gesture, carefully noted by Jn, would have had more external solemnity, if made under the stars and in the light of the Paschal moon. The prayer is patently tripartite, for Jesus first prays for himself, 1-5, secondly for his Apostles, 6-19, thirdly for the whole Church to be won by the preaching of the Apostles, 20-23. The final epilogue of petition is addressed in two parts to the Father for the reunion of all in glory with Jesus, 24, and for the Church militant as set apart from the world in union with Jesus, who is the revealer of the Father and the total object of the Father's love, for he is the beloved Son gathering the Church through the grace of adoption into intimate unity with himself, 25 f.

1-5 Jesus prays for Himself—The vocative address **b** ' Father ' opens the prayer and also opens the special petition of each part, 5, 11, 21, and furthermore opens the two parts of the epilogue, 24, and 25. Let it be remembered that the prayer follows on a series of words which had begun with the announcement : ' Now the Son of Man is glorified . . .', 13:31, and ended with the encouragement : ' Have confidence, I have conquered the world '. For the third time, 6:5 ; 11:41, Jn contemplates Jesus lifting his eyes to heaven. ' The hour has come ' means that the Passion is about to begin. It is that Passion which will win for Jesus the glory which as man he now asks at the right hand of his Father. **2.** ' *Even as* thou hast given him power over all flesh, *in order* that . . .' The lordship of Christ over all flesh, *i.e.* over the whole human race, is realized by this glorification, given in view of a further glorification of the Father by the Son. The whole function of him who is ' Lord and Christ ' is to give eternal life to those who will receive it by living and abiding faith. **3.** Therefore the Saviour defines in **c** what eternal life consists. It is faith here and vision hereafter, neither of which is arid knowledge but knowledge glowing with charity. The object of such knowledge is the one true God, as distinct from polytheistic idols, and of God's Envoy Jesus Christ. This is perfect Monotheism in the Trinitarian Messianism of the Incarnation. A difficulty has been raised regarding the use of the appellation ' Jesus Christ '. Nowhere else does the Saviour call himself thus. It may be a redactional addition of the Evangelist (Lagrange, Huby, Braun). As usual in our Lord's words (*cf.* 5:24) eternal life possessed by the knowledge of faith here is in the forefront, the knowledge of vision being implicit or in the full perspective. **4 f.** The ' work ', by the fulfilment of which Jesus has glorified the Father, is the Passion already regarded as consummated. It is to the Passion that the glorification of the Redeemer is constantly referred (*cf.* Phil 2:9 ff.). In praying for the glory which was his with the Father, before the world was, Jesus asks that the full glory of the Word should show itself in the Word Incarnate —that he might be set in enjoyment of the glory of

806c which he emptied himself in taking the form of a servant (Cyr.).

d **6-19 Jesus prays for the Apostles**—Petition for the Apostles begins at 9, the preceding words being an introductory preface in which Jesus enumerates the claims which they have to the benevolence of his Father. **6 ff.** Given to him out of the world as out of a mass of corruption, he has made known the Father's name to them. This election is the first fact which entitles them to special consideration. Secondly, they belonged to the Father by the goodness of their dispositions under the guidance of his loving providence. Thirdly, he gave them to Jesus by that interior attractive force of faith which drew them to him (*cf.* 6:37, 39, 44, 66). Fourthly, they had surrendered mind and will to the teaching they had received from Jesus, recognizing that all he had was from the Father, accepting his words, acknowledging his divine origin, and believing in his heavenly mission. **9.** Jesus who prayed for his crucifiers does not absolutely exclude the world from his prayer ; he is interested in the conversion of the world, 23 ; but here he is specially praying for the Apostles. In any case, he could not pray for the world as the world—except for its conversion—because the unspiritual world is hostile to God (*cf.* 8:43 ; Jas 4:4). His prayer for the Apostles is founded on three reasons, which have reference to the present

e moment. **9b-11a.** They belong to the Father as being his Son's very own. Indeed, the Father and the Son have all in common—' all my things are thine and thine are mine ' (*cf.* Lk 15:31 for half the phrase spoken by a father to a son). Moreover, Jesus has been and *is* glorified in them, for they have persevered in their faith, even when others fell away, 6:68 f. Besides, at his departure, they are now about to be left alone in the world. **11b.** It is here that the direct petition for them begins. It is a petition for holiness —for apostolic consecration to the service of God and of truth in the midst of a corrupt world which serves ' the father of lies '. Hence Jesus places the epithet ' holy ' before ' Father '. One recalls the great vision of Is 6 in which the Prophet learned the great distance between God and human corruption so vividly that he constantly calls God ' the Holy One of Israel '. ' Holy Father, keep them in thy name (that divine name) *which* thou hast given to me '. *Which* not *whom* is the reading of the best MSS (BSCLAW etc.). The ' name ' is the divine essence manifesting itself in its attributes of power and wisdom—these together with the divine nature having been communicated from the Father to the Son. The petition is that the Apostles should be kept united in mind and will and heart, realizing a unity modelled on the ineffable pattern in which all is one in a distinction of persons.

f **12-14.** Up to the present, Jesus has kept them, so that none of them fell into such temptation as brought permanent rejection (*cf.* 18:9), except ' the son of perdition '—a Semitism of metaphorical relation denoting destiny, like ' son of gehenna ', ' son of death '. Judas was destined to perish, but by his own fault. The Scripture had foretold it, Ps 40(41):8. The treason of Judas, foreseen as the result of the traitor's own malice, was an element in the plan of redemption. This prayer spoken by Jesus in the world is to secure for the Apostles a full participation in the serene joy which he himself had in the accomplishment of his Father's will. The professors of heavenly doctrine will surely be hated by that world which holds to an earthly philosophy. **15.** Jesus does not ask that they should be taken out of the dangerous environment— this would be the end of their apostolate—but that they be kept from contagion—' evil ' here seems to be the sum of evil influences rather than the personal evil one, although Johannine usage in his first epistle favours the latter. **16.** ' They are not of the world, as I am not of the world '. To keep them from evil, however, is only the negative side of what Jesus desires

g for his faithful ones. **17 ff.** The culmination of his prayer for them is : ' Sanctify them in the truth, thy

word is truth '. What is asked is that God should consecrate them for the priestly office of preaching the truth, for what St Paul calls the ' hierurgy of the Gospel ', Rom 15:16. Their mission is the continuation of the mission of Jesus. **19.** ' And for them do I sanctify myself, that they also may be sanctified in truth '. A word of the same generic signification will vary its sense according to the subject. Jesus *consecrates* himself. That consecration is not the hypostatic union, nor the ' unction ' of his humanity by the Holy Spirit, but the priestly consecration of himself as a victim on the cross. The sacrifice of Christ gives the Apostles a sacrificial *consecration* for their work in a true sense (' in truth ' without the article). It is obviously not an external consecration such as that operated by the sacrifices of the Old Law. It is a sanctification of a kind corresponding to the sacrifice that makes it, and is therefore an internal sanctification ; *cf.* Heb 9:13.

20-23 Jesus prays for the Church—**20.** The prayer passes to the generations to come, to all believers whose faith is founded on the Apostolic teaching. **21.** What Jesus asks for them is unity—a unity of souls, imitative of the Divine Trinity (and, no doubt, a social unity of bodies in which St Cyril sees the effect of the Holy Eucharist)—a unity which will be a proof to the world that God is here. **22.** The glory which Jesus received and which he has given to his Church—to all faithful disciples of the Apostles—is not so much the glory of miracles and wondrous concord (Chrys.), or the glory of Christ's humanity resplendent in the Church (Aug., Thom.), but rather the fundamental glory of divine filiation (Ambrose, *cf.* 1:18). Adoptive sonship includes everything else and especially that unity like to the union of the Father and Son, which is the central petition of this prayer. **23.** ' I in them, and thou in me, that they may be made perfect in one : and that the world may know that thou hast sent me, and hast loved them *even* as thou hast loved me '. Again we have a clear echo of the grace of the Eucharist, 6:57 f. SS Cyril and Hilary and many commentators after them were not wrong in thinking that it is through the Eucharist that this prayer of Jesus is realized. It is through the ' concorporating ' sacrament that the Church is enabled to show the world that the Father loves the Church as he loves his own Son. It is really one love, for the Church is Christ.

24-26 Epilogue—The final petition is that all this magnificence may be fulfilled in the vision of heavenly glory. The glory of the Word shining in his humanity, which we now see through the dark medium of faith, is the final reward. Let us note the strong *Volo* with which Jesus prays for this : ' I will that where I am, they may be with me, that they may see my glory '. This glory is the glory of the Godhead in the Word Incarnate. Such glory, communicated to the sacred humanity in accordance with a divine decree of predestination, manifests the eternal love with which the Father has loved his Son. We may also say—and it is well for us to feel and relish it interiorly—that this strong *Volo* of the Saviour shows magnificently how ' he loved his own who were in the world and loved them unto the end '. He wants his apostolic Church with him in the glory of heaven. The petition ends here, for the remaining verses, **25 f.**, opening with the title : ' Just Father ' separate the Church—as the Lady Electa (to use a Johannine phrase)—from the deliberately blind world. **25.** The recognition in deed and in truth of the mission of Jesus is what saves men ' from the perverse generation ', Ac 2:40, or world, which St Augustine calls by the fearful name of *massa damnata*. To the word ' know ' (recognize) in 25 corresponds the word ' make known ' in 26 : ' I have made known thy name to them '—to the Apostles as foundations of the Church—' and will make it known ' —after the resurrection myself, and after Pentecost by my Spirit—' that the love wherewith thou hast loved me may be in them '—as proved by the gifts of grace —' and I in them '—by the immanence which gives

6i them life in abundance. The profundity of these concluding words did not escape Aug. : ' How ', he asks, ' comes it that the love with which the Father loved his Son is in us also, except for the reason that we are his members, and *in him* we are loved when he, the whole Christ, is loved by the Father—that is, the head and the body ? ' (Tract. 111).

XVIII-XXI THE PASSION AND RESURRECTION

7a XVIII-XIX The Passion—In recording the events of the night and the day that began in Gethsemane and ended at the rock tomb beside the place of crucifixion, Jn only narrates incidents omitted by the Synoptists or, if he rejoins them, otherwise supplements their narratives. The chief headings of the Passion according to Jn are : the arrest of Jesus, 18:1-12, his appearance before Annas and Caiphas synchronizing with the triple denial of St Peter, 13–27, the first interrogation before Pilate, 28–38*a*, the second interrogation—*Ecce homo* and condemnation to the cross, 19:1–16, the crucifixion, 17–22, the division of garments, 23 f., the last words and death of Jesus, 25–30, the piercing of the sacred side, 31–37, his burial, 38–42.

b XVIII 1-12 Arrest—**1.** The journey with which this chapter opens began at the house of the Cenacle (Supper Room) in the SW. quarter of Jerusalem and possibly followed an old Jewish or Maccabean road discovered in recent years by the Assumptionist Fathers. The Water Gate near the Pool of Siloe would be the most probable exit from the city. Turning to the left or north, Jesus and the eleven would have skirted the eastern slope of the old Jebusite site of the city of David and of the temple esplanade, outside the Porch of Solomon. The crossing of ' the brook *of* Cedron '—literally meaning ' the winter stream of turbid (water) '—is mentioned only by Jn, probably with some reminiscence of the pathetic crossing of the same torrent by David, as he fled from Absalom, 2 Kg 15:23. The garden to which Jesus went is named Gethsemane (Oil-press) by the Synoptists. The property evidently belonged to a friend. **2.** Judas knew that place on Olivet, because it was a favourite retreat of Jesus ;
c *cf.* Lk 21:37 ; 22:39. **3.** The arresting party, to which Judas acted as guide, Ac 1:16, was composed of Roman soldiers and Jewish guards. The former, described as a *cohort* commanded by a *tribune*, 12, would in strict parlance number 600 men—or at least 200, this being the strength of a maniple often denoted by the same Gk word (σπεῖρα). Thus the whole party was an armed band of soldiers, Levitical police and lackeys of the chief priests, 10. The lanterns and torches on a night when the moon was full, would have been largely a matter of military routine. **4.** Jn, who omits the kiss of Judas, is careful to note the full foreknowledge and sovereign freedom with which the Saviour gave himself into the hands of his enemies. The little dialogue, 4–8, with its accompanying circumstances is most awe-inspiring. **5.** The band, with which Judas stood, answered the question : ' Whom seek ye ? ' by using the ordinary designation of the Master : ' Jesus of Nazareth ' ; *cf.* Mk 10:47 ; Lk 18:37. The words, ' I am he ', uttered by him who could say : ' I am who am ', caused what Jn undoubtedly attributes to miraculous power, namely, a backward stampede, involving an impressive fall to the ground of many, **d** at least, of the arresting party. **7-8.** The same question having been asked again and answered, Jesus demanded free departure for his companions—not calling them disciples, in order to save them more surely from arrest. **9.** A word of Jesus, 17:12, had guaranteed the eleven against their *moral* destruction (which could have happened if they had been arrested), and so Jn does not seem to extend the word unduly to preservation from *physical* destruction. **10.** In describing the apostolic act of violence which ensued, Jn alone names Simon Peter as the one who struck the blow, joins Lk in specifying the right ear, but is the sole recorder of

the name Malchus, said to be a Nabataean name **807d** (Heb. *Melek*) equivalent to our Rex or Roy—these being used in English both as baptismal and family names. Malchus was a servant of the high-priest, not one of the temple police. **11.** In reprimanding Simon Peter, Jesus made a clear reference to the words of his agony in the garden, otherwise omitted by Jn : ' Chalice ', of course, means the portion assigned to one (in a banquet), not what comes to him by the chance of a lottery *cup*. **12.** In arresting Jesus they bound him, for the traitor had said : ' Lay hold on him and lead him away carefully ', Mk 14:44.

13-27 Before Annas and Caiphas—This narrative **e** raises a difficulty which must be treated briefly here. 24 suggests that Peter's first denial, 15–18, and the first examination of Jesus, 19–23, took place in the house of Annas, who in this hypothesis, is called high-priest in 15, 16, 19, whereas in 13 and 24 the title is given (as elsewhere in Jn 11:49) to Caiphas. As the Synoptists place Peter's denials in the house of Caiphas, one part of the difficulty has been met by supposing that Annas lived in the same pontifical palace as his son-in-law, the Pontiff of the year. Hence the courtyard of Caiphas was also the courtyard of Annas. As there is no trace of a topographical tradition marking a distinct palace of Annas before the 14th cent., this supposition is tenable ; but what of the title ' high-priest ' being given to Annas ? Lk 3:2 and Ac 4:6 are appealed to, but the appeal does not clear the Johannine narrative of confusion. A transposition of 18:24 after 18:13 rectifies the situation. This transposition is not purely arbitrary, for it has the support of the Syro-Sinaitic MS, of Cyril of Alexandria, and (it is said) of a minuscule codex 226, which, however, puts 24 in the *middle* of 13. Certain reasons of internal criticism drawn from the omission or fluctuation of a particle (δέ or οὖν) at the beginning of 24 are also alleged. However, the transposition, though not devoid of probability, does not seem to stand before the united voice of the MSS and versions. The difficulty can be satisfactorily met (even without **f** supposing *one* palace), by understanding ' high-priest ' of Caiphas only and taking 24 as introductory to a resumption of the history of Peter's denials. The whole passage is so evidently a series of reminiscences, that 24 (though seeming to be out of its logical place) is quite characteristic of the evangelist's style. Jn alone mentions that Jesus was brought to Annas first. It was an act of courtesy, for the old man was a *political* power and notoriously shrewd in managing business affairs. Called Hananus (Hananya = the Lord is merciful) by Josephus, he had attained the highpriesthood through Quirinius in 6 B.C., was deposed by Valerius Gratus in A.D. 15, but still succeeded in having five of his sons (Eleazar, Jonathan, Theophilus, Matthias, Ananus the Younger) elevated to the highpriesthood. Lk 3:2 sets him before Caiphas (the actual high-priest) in marking the pontifical year, and in Ac 4:6 he is also named him. Jn gives as reason for this present act of deference to Annas that ' he was the father-in-law of Caiphas, the high-priest of that year '. **14.** Caiphas, whose personal name was Joseph, was altogether 17 years high-priest, 18–36, and was also, as Jn 11:50 reveals him, a politician rather than a priest. Jn here cites the Pontiff's decision of some weeks earlier, to show that the case of Jesus was prejudged. **15 f.** Two disciples, Simon Peter and another, followed Jesus. The studious anonymity as well as the association with Peter indicates the evangelist himself. Some have thought of the young man who had fled in Gethsemane, Mk 14:51 f. How the son of Zebedee came to be known to the high-priest has not been explained, but is not thereby made incredible. A word from him to the portress obtained admission for Peter. **17.** Her question to the Apostle (expecting however a negative answer) shows that she knew his companion was a disciple. Peter denied discipleship. **18.** April nights can be cold at Jerusalem. Hence the brazier in the courtyard, to which Peter drew

807f near, as much to keep up appearances as to warm himself.

g **19-23.** The palace of Caiphas in which this first interrogatory was held, as well as the two judicial sessions of the night, Mt 26:57-68, and of the morning, Mt 27:1, Lk 22:66-71, is traditionally located (since the pilgrim of Bordeaux 333, it seems) near the Cenacle, south of the Sion Gate, now called Neby Dâûd. The claims of the Armenian Monastery of Mount Sion are still upheld, but since 1927 the sanctuary brought to light by the Assumptionists and named Saint Peter in Gallicantu has found strong defenders (Marchet, Power). **19.** The questions of Caiphas have reference to two points—*disciples* whereon a political charge might be grafted, and *teaching*, in view of religious consequences. **20.** Jesus, taking full responsibility, says nothing about the former, and in regard to the latter refers the Pontiff to the public witnesses of his quite open teaching—given in synagogues and in the temple. **22.** This just and dignified answer earned him a blow with the open palm from a guard, who pretended zeal for the honour of the Pontiff. **23.** Jesus, whose teaching on turning the other cheek, Mt 5:39, is most often to be observed by a peaceful interior attitude of soul, calmly reminded the striker that one under accusation can demand proper justice and the proper forms of justice—testimony against him, if he speaks ill, respect for his person, when he speaks well.

h **24.** The short sentence or note which says that Annas sent Jesus bound to Caiphas is inserted here as something which the Evangelist recalls for the purpose of continuing the account of Peter's denials. **25-27.** Nine denials of his Master by Peter can be counted in the Gospels, if variations of persons, circumstances, and verbal forms are taken into account. But all insist that the denials were *three*. Three distinct times, when called to answer by one or more persons at once, Peter denied our Lord. The first denial had no variety of circumstance ; the second and third had. Hence they are variously reported according to the particular circumstance or set of circumstances apprehended by the witness. Jn sets these last two denials in relation to queries from bystanders at the brazier, and from a relative of Malchus. The (second) cockcrow, as we said, 13:38, may have been as close to daybreak as the beginning of the 4th watch, 3-6 a.m.

808a **28-38a First Interrogation before Pilate—28.** The praetorium to which Jesus was brought from Caiphas was the residence of the governor. The procurators of Judaea, who were subordinate to the imperial Legate of Syria, resided habitually at Caesaraea, but came to Jerusalem for the great festivals or whenever a concourse or other circumstances endangered public tranquility. About Pilate's place of residence at Jerusalem there has been a difference of opinion. The Herodian palace near the present Jaffa Gate would seem to be naturally indicated as the Jerusalem residence of the supreme Roman magistrate, and we know from Josephus (BJ 2, 14, 8 ; 15, 5) that a quarter of a century later the governor Gessius Florus lodged there. Pilate also by the famous incident of the shields would have signified his intention of doing so. On the other hand, the *arx Antonia* or vast fortress-palace built by Herod at the NW. angle of the temple area was undoubtedly the most central and best post of vigilance. Especially, when the air was electric, it would be the proper place for the Governor to lodge. Since the 13th cent. the *Via Dolorosa* has begun from there, and excavations made between 1927 and 1932 in the property of the Sisters of Sion seem to have given reasonable grounds for connecting this place with the *Lithostrotos* of Jn 19:13. Probabilities in favour of the Antonia have therefore decidedly grown in recent years. The time was morning, probably as early as 6 a.m. by our clocks. The Sanhedrists did not enter the pagan residence to avoid legal defilement which would prevent them from taking part in the Paschal rites that evening. Meanwhile they were defiling their

consciences with murder. Jesus, we may suppose, was **80** conducted at once to a judgement hall within, entering, perhaps, by the northern long side of the great quadrangular fortress. **29.** Pilate is now mentioned **b** for the first time. Procurator of Judaea since A.D. 26 he is known to us not only from the Gospels but also from Philo and Josephus. His haughty and imprudent contempt of Jewish religious susceptibility is shown by two desecrations of the city, first with ensigns bearing the image of Caesar, and secondly with shields similarly adorned which he set up in the Herodian palace. He also offended Jewish feeling by the appropriation of temple monies for the building of an aqueduct. He was often cruel ; *cf.* Lk 13:1. It was an act of cruelty against Samaritans that led finally in 36 to his deposition by the Syrian Legate Vitellius. The Gospels, however, show that he had something of a Roman sense of justice, was at once sceptical and superstitious, but above all weak as an upholder of right, when his position was thereby threatened. He feared above all things the frown of Tiberius Caesar. Jesus seems to have impressed him from the beginning. So, when he went out (on to a balcony ?) to the Jews, he demanded very categorically the formulation of their charge. **30.** Having come only for the ratification of a capital sentence, which they could not carry out themselves, they were taken aback. They retorted that they would not have delivered up a fellow Jew to Pilate, if he had not done wrong. **31.** Before this vagueness, Pilate pretends to understand the matter as a minor (non-capital) charge, to be judged by themselves according to Jewish law. Thereupon they make it clear that they want the death penalty, admitting that they have not the *ius gladii* or power of execution. **32.** Thus Jesus, as he had foretold, Mt 20.19 ; Jn 3:14 ; 8:28 ; 12:32, was to die by the Roman provincial penalty of crucifixion.

33. Pilate proceeds to an interrogation in the hall **c** within. Of the three charges given by Lk 23:2, namely sedition, anti-fiscal agitation, pretending to royal sovereignty, the governor takes only the last which was *laesa maiestas* or treason in a very definite sense. ' (So) *thou art* the king of the Jews ', is, as the context shows, an assertion uttered with something of an interrogatory tone. Pilate would have expected a negative answer. **34.** Jesus distinguished : Did that statement come from Pilate (a Roman) or from others (namely Jews) ? If king meant a rival of Tiberius, *No* ; if it meant the Israelite Messias, *Yes*. This was what was implied in the question of Jesus to Pilate. **35.** The latter, having signified that the affair against Jesus was all a Jewish matter, asked definitely : ' What hast thou done ? ' **36.** Jesus does not answer this question, except by clearly defining what his kingship is. It is not of terrestrial origin. If it were, his guards— the military force which in that hypothesis he would have had—would have striven against his arrest. Consequently his kingship is not ' from hence '— terrestrial—and therefore he is no Palestinian rival of the majesty of Roman Tiberius. **37.** Pilate, surprised at an avowal of kingship of any kind, asked : ' Art thou a king then ? ' The answer given by Jesus is *Yes*. He is a Teacher-King, born and present in the world to proclaim the royal authority of truth. ' Every one who is of the truth (joined to it by the filial sympathy of true goodness, *cf.* 3:21) heareth my voice ', *i.e.* obeys me. **38a.** Pilate showed the scepticism of his soul by the question : ' What is truth ? ' but went no further. It is at this point that Pilate sent Jesus off to Herod ; *cf.* Lk 23:6-12.

38b. When Jesus was brought back from Herod's **d** court, Pilate, convinced that he had only to deal with a philosopher or a dreamer, went out and again informed the Jews : ' I find no cause in him '. Up to this Pilate has done his duty as a Roman magistrate, but he did not follow out the course of justice by immediately releasing the prisoner. The sending of Jesus to Herod, Lk 23:6-12, was the beginning of compromise ; the proposal of the minor penalty of

d flogging, Lk 23:16, was a further step on the way of weakness. **39 f.** Jn only mentions as a first subterfuge the proposed preference of Jesus to Barabbas (Son of Abba—rather ' Masterson ' than ' Fatherson ' in our English style of names). This suggestion of amnesty likewise violated the innocence of Jesus. Jn tells briefly that the preference was given by the Jews to Barabbas, and ends with one of those characteristically tragic sentences : ' Now Barabbas was a robber '.

a XIX 1-7 Scourging and Ecce Homo—1. Pilate ordered the scourging. Generally a preliminary of crucifixion, it was administered with the *horribile flagellum* made of thongs or the still more horrible *flagrum* armed with bone or metal. The mode of executing the penalty is described elsewhere, § 721*h*. **2 f.** The soldiers themselves took the initiative in the mockery of the crown of thorns. Jn mentions the crown, the purple garment, the mock-imperial salute (imitation of *Ave Caesar imperator*), the blows with the open hand ; he omits the reed, the genuflexions, the spittings. **4.** Pilate seizes on what he considers a new opportunity of saving Jesus. Disfigured by the wounds and blood caused by scourges and thorns, and wearing a crown and a robe that made him look much more pathetic than any tinselled pretender to royalty could possibly be, Jesus was led out. ' Behold the man ' was intended to excite pity or (in the more brutal) such a kind of laughter as would wish to push tragedy **b** no further. **6.** In the chief priests (here mentioned for the first time as a group directing hostilities before the praetorium) and in the Levitical guards in only excited more emphatic hatred. The cry ' Crucify, crucify ', recorded for the first time by Jn and with the stark brevity of verb without object (attested by the best Gk and Lat. MSS) represents a frenzy of hatred. Pilate stiffens before it. There is both sarcasm and strong contempt in the words : ' Take him you and crucify him : for I find no cause in him '. For the third time in Jn (4th in the harmonized narrative) Pilate says, ' I find no cause '. **7.** The Sanhedrists being stung by the scoff at their dependence on Rome to carry out a capital sentence, their fury turns back, in spite of their plans, to the religious charge. For a capital crime against Roman law they substitute a crime against Jewish law—blasphemy, punishable by the Jewish code with stoning or (failing the power to stone) by execution in the Roman way, *i.e.* by substituting the Roman penalty of crucifixion. The words : ' He made himself the Son of God ' can have nothing but their full sense. Otherwise the blasphemy statute of Lev 24:16 could not be invoked.

c 8-16 Last Interrogation and Sentence—8. Pilate must have already felt, at least vaguely, that no man ever faced jealous hatred like this man. Hence his scepticism could not prevent him, on hearing of Jesus' claim to be ' Son of God ', from suspecting that the prisoner might be more than human. **9.** It was, however, superstitious fear and curiosity rather than love of truth that prompted his question : ' Whence art thou ? ' Jesus did not answer. **10.** Pilate's remark in the face of this silence shows that he conceived himself as supreme arbiter of the prisoner's liberty and life. **11.** The answer of Jesus refers to the present situation—to the power of the death-sentence towards which Pilate was drifting. ' The power given from above ' does not refer to Pilate's civil jurisdiction. Pilate has the power to crucify by a permissive decree of God not authorizing the crime but permitting the event in view of the redemption of the world. ' Therefore he that hath delivered me to thee, *hath greater sin* '. The one who has greater sin is Caiphas rather than Judas. The latter's treason was indeed blackest of all, but is not presumed known to Pilate, who had moreover already said : ' Thy own nation and the chief priests have delivered thee up to me '. The ' therefore ' is exceedingly difficult to interpret. The logical connexion implied in it would seem to be conveyed most satisfactorily by the following paraphrase : ' You, Pilate, a pagan and under God's **809c** permissive providence an instrument in this crime, partly unwilling, though sufficiently responsible to be a sinner, have sin indeed, but for the very reason of *your* lesser and *his* greater responsibility, the spiritual ruler of Israel who handed Israel's Messias over to you has greater sin '.

12-16. As Pilate is now seeking to release Jesus it is **d** clear that the religious charge has failed ; and since the political charge has also failed, there is only one thing left, to play on Pilate's fears for his own security. The Sanhedrists now play their last desperate card and wrest the death-sentence from Pilate by intimidation. **12.** After the last word of Jesus—' And from *this* ' is both temporal and logical—Pilate tried to release him. He is deterred by the threat of denunciation to the emperor. Not to be ' a friend of Caesar ' was a serious matter, when the Caesar was Tiberius who, as Suetonius informs us, was atrociously severe where there were suspicions or charges of treason— ' judicia maiestatis atrocissime exercuit ' (*Vita Tiberii*, 58). ' If thou release this man, thou art not Caesar's friend. For whosoever maketh himself a king *declares against* Caesar '—this was decisive. **13.** Pilate had Jesus brought out and set up his tribunal—the folding curule chair of a Roman magistrate—' in the place . . . called Lithostrotos ' (from the remarkable pavement), but also known by the Hebrew (Aramaic) name of Gabbatha, meaning a *height* or *eminence* rather than a bare front (also etymologically possible). **14. e** Jn also carefully notes the time. Parasceve (preparation) had become synonymous with Friday, but here it probably means the preparation day before the Pasch. It was actually Friday, Mk 15:42. The hour was approximately the sixth (probably about 11 a.m., *cf*. Mk 15:20 ' the third hour '). Defeated but haughty towards those forcing his hand, Pilate said : ' Behold your king '. **15.** Another frenzied cry for the crucifixion of their victim—and Pilate responded with the deliberate question : ' *Am I to* crucify your king ? ' To which the leaders of the theocratic people said : ' We have no king but Caesar '. **16.** According to legal form the sentence had to be read—as being irrevocable. A usual form of sentence was *Ibis ad crucem*—' Thou shalt go to the cross '. All that Jn says however is that Pilate delivered him to the Jews that he might be crucified (by an execution squad of four Roman soldiers under the command of a centurion).

16*b*-22 The Crucifixion—Jn is very brief regarding **810a** the *via dolorosa*. He does not repeat what Mt, Mk, Lk had recorded of Simon the Cyrenean, nor the sympathy shown by some women of Jerusalem, Lk. It was of course the soldiers, not the Jews, that took Jesus (and led him out). **17.** The cross which he carried would, on the basis of probabilities established by ancient references to crucifixion, be the *patibulum* or cross-beam only. The upright, which the Gk word σταυρός more properly indicates, would in this case have been already erected at the place of execution. Nevertheless, all the narratives suggest that Jesus carried a heavier weight than a mere cross-beam ; the use of one and the same word by Jn identifies the instrument which Jesus carried with that beside which his mother stood ; Tertullian who knew the facts of crucifixion, writing against Jews (*Adv. Jud*, 10), says very confidently : ' Jesus carried his cross on his *shoulder* '—note singular number, for the *patibulum* was lashed over both shoulders. Jesus, therefore, probably carried the whole cross, which was a *crux immissa* (not *decussata* or *commissa*), having an upright above the cross-beam, to which an inscription could be affixed ; *cf*. § 722*b*. The place of crucifixion was called Golgotha (Aram. *Gulgulta*), meaning *skull*, not because the skull of Adam was unearthed there to receive the flow of Christ's blood—a beautiful conception still often represented on crucifixes—nor because it was like a head in the imaginary topographic skeleton of Jerusalem, but simply because it was a hill promontory

810a such as Arabs in Jerusalem still call *râs* (head). As the Calvary under the roof of the Church of the Holy Sepulchre is most probably the true site, we can calculate the length of the *via dolorosa*—from Antonia to Golgotha—as something over one-third of a mile.

b **18.** Jn repeats, in a different form of words, what the Synoptists recorded of the crucifixion of Jesus *between* two thieves (Is 53:12—but the citation in Mk 15:28 is possibly a gloss imported from Lk 22:37). **19.** The form of the title of the cross, given substantially by Mt, Mk, Lk, is most probably reproduced with verbal accuracy by Jn. As Pilate had to' *write* the sentence of crucifixion, the words ' Jesus of Nazareth King of the Jews ' would be excerpted from some such formula as : *Jesum Nazarenum Regem Judaeorum crucis supplicio animadverti placet.* With the same evident unwillingness the proconsul Galerius Maximus pronounced a similarly worded sentence of decapitation on St Cyprian. **20.** Pilate would have written *Jesus Nazarenus Rex Judaeorum* with his own hand in Latin (the language of administration) and then ordered the same to be written in Greek (the language of lettered people and of pilgrims) and in Hebrew (Aramaic, the spoken language of Palestine). **21 f.** His firmness in refusing to change the title of the cross was a magistrate's insistence on the irrevocability of a Roman sentence, mixed with a desire to have this revenge on the Jews ; but, in God's providence, Pilate's inscription stands as a perpetual monument of the Kingship of Jesus of Nazareth.

c **23-24 Division of Garments**—Here Jn adds notable clarifying details. None of the evangelists say that Jesus was crucified in absolute nakedness, but that was undoubtedly the rule, and the Fathers and commentators have supposed that there was no departure from the rule in this case. Judging from passages in the Talmud, Jewish feeling was against total nudity even in capital executions. The blasphemous (2nd cent. ?) graffito of the crucifixion from the Paedagogium of the Palatine at Rome cannot indeed be adduced as evidence on this point, but it is worth noting that it shows a loin-cloth. Four pieces of the clothing in which Jesus went to Calvary fell to the four soldiers of the execution squad. These (cloak, cincture, sandals and head-dress ?) were divided. The completely woven unsewn tunic was too valuable to tear into pieces. They cast lots for it, and thus literally fulfilled the prophecy of Ps 21(22):19 here cited by Jn, but of doubtful authenticity in Mt. This seamless coat or tunic (which Trier and Argenteuil claim to possess) has, at least from the time of St Cyprian, been regarded as a symbol of the unity of the Church.

d **25-27 Jesus and His Mother**—Jn draws a marked contrast, difficult to render in translation, between the soldiers who did these things and the little group that stood beside the cross. **25.** The balance of the opening phrase (even as estimated by the maker of the Syriac Peshitta) leads us to distinguish not three but four women beside the cross of Jesus. The disputed point is whether ' his mother's sister ' is ' Mary of Cleophas ' or another cousin of our Lady. The general love of anonymity and reticence shown by Jn would suggest that if she is the latter we must identify her with Salome, his own mother, who was certainly on Calvary that day, Mk 15:40. As Mary Cleophas is identifiable with ' Mary the Mother of James the less, and of Joseph ', Mk 15:40, Jn most probably mentions the same three women as Mk, but Jn alone names the Saviour's mother, § 673*b*. The incomparable comment of St Ambrose at the end of a letter to the clergy of Vercellae (Vercelli) should be read in PL 16, 1218. Part of this eloquent page is found in the Breviary

e (Sept 15). **26 f.** The literal or immediate sense of Jesus' words : ' Woman, behold thy son ' (addressed to his mother) and ' Behold thy mother ' (addressed to Jn) is a last touching fulfilment of the fourth commandment. Jesus provides for his mother, and the privileged legatee of this precious trust is ' the disciple whom Jesus loved '. **27***b* indicates this clearly : ' From

that hour (comparable in many ways to the 10th **81** hour of that wonderful first day 1:39) the disciple took her to his *home* '. The further spiritual meaning (which attaches a declaration of the universal spiritual maternity of Mary to these words) is barely suggested by Origen in the 3rd cent., and is not clearly enunciated (except rhetorically by George of Nicomedia, friend of Photius) either in the east or the west, till it finds its theologian in Rupert of Deutz (1070-1129). The position of this interpretation in the Church today scarcely permits us to regard it as an accommodated sense. Jn is mystically the representative of the human race called to be spiritual children of the Mother of Jesus. This motherhood of Mary was, latently at least, the mind of the Church from the earliest times— ' hoc perpetuo sensit Ecclesia ' (Leo XIII, Sept. 5, 1895—*cf*. Pius XI, *Rerum Ecclesiæ*, Feb. 28, 1927).

28-30 Last Words and Death of Jesus—Of the first **f** three words of petition, pardon, and piety spoken by Jesus on the cross, Jn has only the third just dealt with ; of the last four words of desolation (moral suffering), thirst (physical suffering), consummation, and voluntary surrender, he has two : ' I thirst ' and ' it is consummated '. **28.** He fulfilled Ps 68(69):22 (*cf*. Ps 21(22):19) when he said the former of these. The soldiers had sour wine with them—a mixture of acid wine and water called *posca*. A sponge, which served for some purpose or other, formed part of their apparatus. This they dipped in the vessel and fixing it on sprigs of hyssop they offered it to him by means of a reed or cane, as Mt and Mk had already narrated. Jn added the detail of the hyssop. To read ὑσσῷ on a javelin instead of ὑσσώπῳ, as many now do, is not only an unreasonable preference of one codex (476 London) against all other MSS and the ancient versions, but also supposes what, on consideration, is an unlikely scribal lapse. Moreover, it supposes the improbability that ' reed ' or *cane* in Mt, Mk stands for the shaft of a javelin. **30.** ' It is consummated ' means that the work of redemption is accomplished. So it really is at the moment that Jesus, after the seventh word recorded by Luke, bows his head and dies.

31-37 The Transfixion—This passage is the biblical **81** and historical basis of devotion to the Sacred Heart. Its devotional riches may be gathered from the 8 homilies assigned for that Feast and its Octave in the Breviary. Here only the main points of the history are noted. **31.** It was very much the concern of the Jews that the bodies should be removed before sundown of that Parasceve or Friday. Deut 21:23 ordered this removal of an ' accursed one ' (*cf*. Gal 3:14) executed on a tree, and in this case the sacred Sabbath just about to begin was also the Paschal solemnity. Hence the request to Pilate for *crurifragium* (breaking of legs with a hammer or club to bring about immediate death from muscular cramp or shock) and removal. **32.** Soldiers (apparently not the execution squad) came to carry out the order. The legs of the two robbers were broken. Jn mentions a ' first ', but we do not know which it was. **33 f.** The soldiers (two at least) **b** took timely notice that Jesus was dead. One, however, wishing to make assurance doubly sure, *struck* the side of Jesus with a lance (a broad-headed spear) intending, no doubt, to pierce the heart. The word for ' struck ' or ' pierced ' (ἔνυξεν) had become ' opened ' (ἤνοιξεν) in the codices from which the Latin version was made. Hence Augustine's famous reference to the evangelist's ' watchful word '—not really a blunder, however, because Jn's verb means ' to pierce ', which is equivalent to opening. The soldier has been named in hagiographic legend, Longinus (or Spearman). ' Immediately there came out blood and water '. As Jesus had been dead some time, the phenomenon was extraordinary, as the eyewitness Jn certainly recognized. Many attempts have been made to give a physiological explanation, but none of them seems adequately to explain the impression which Jn registers here and in his first epistle,

5:6. Many hold that the water was *serum* which owing to Jesus' intense sufferings collected in the *pericardium*; cf. **IER**. March 1951. But whether the double flow was miraculous or whether it can be explained on natural grounds, as many physiologists claim, is immaterial. There is no doubt about its reality. The Fathers have therefore rightly taken the two liquids as symbols of Baptism and the Eucharist, and, in consequence, see in these regenerating and life-giving streams the graces which produce a second Eve (the Church) from the side of the second Adam sleeping on the cross. **35.** That Jn invokes the knowledge of Jesus to corroborate his own testimony is suggested by the word ἐκεῖνος (Lat. *ille*), but perhaps the pronoun has not its full classical Greek force here. In any case, the testimony is very solemn. **36 f.** Two Scriptures were fulfilled in what happened : the typal precept not to break the bones of the Paschal lamb, Ex 12:46 ; Num 9:12, and a word of Zacharias 12:10, taken from a passage which undoubtedly refers to Messianic times and to the Messias himself. Jn only changes the accusative pronoun from first to third : 'They shall look on *him* whom they pierced '; cf. Apoc 1:7.

38-42 Burial of Jesus—Jn here supplements the synoptics. Joseph of Arimathea (which is Ramathaim-Sophim, the birthplace of Samuel, now Rentis, 8 miles NE. of Lydda) is described as a disciple by Mt, and by Jn as a *secret* disciple. His fear of the Jews vanished at the great hour, for he went boldly to Pilate to ask for the body, Mk. Nicodemus figures in Jn's narrative only. The quantity of aromatic mixture, which he brought, was very considerable (72 lbs avoirdupois of myrrh, a dried Arabian gum, and of aloes, an odoriferous wood crushed fine or powdered). The intention was not embalmment, and there was no anointing ; the women intended doing that later, Lk, Mk. The spices would have been strewn on the shroud, but principally on the funeral bench and within the sepulchral chamber. Jn mentions only smaller bands of linen used for tying. These are to be distinguished from the *sindon* or shroud, Mt, Mk, Lk, and the napkin over the face, Jn 20:7. The shrouding was according to Jewish custom but hurriedly done, and we should say (in view of the intention of the women) that it was provisional ; cf. Barnes, *The Holy Shroud of Turin*, London 1934. Jn alone tells us that the new tomb was in a garden. Finally, it is not unfair to say that DV failed to render the solemn cadences which 19:42 has both in Gk and Latin.

XX 1-XXI 25 The Risen Saviour—That, on the Sunday following the crucifixion and burial of Jesus, the tomb in which he had lain was empty, and that he showed himself alive from the dead many times that day and during forty days are the best certified facts of human history. For thirty years and more eyewitnesses were proclaiming these facts to the world, and shaking the world with their proclamation. The fragmentary written record of their evidence which we possess in the four Gospels is unassailable, but, like all evidence of the kind, it presents difficulties of harmonization. This work of distinguishing persons and moments and other circumstances, so as to eliminate apparent contradictions, belongs mainly to commentators on the Synoptists. Jn concentrates on the empty tomb, on the first appearance to Mary Magdalene, and on three appearances to the Apostles as a body or in representative numbers. His narrative touches the synoptic narrative at four points only. These will be noted as they occur. Jn unites both Judaean and Galilean appearances, for after the three appearances at Jerusalem he records a fourth on the shore of the Sea of Tiberias. This makes the Gospel end serenely, on an April or May morning, beside the waters where the Apostles were formerly called to be fishers of men. The last page dedicates its final words to Simon Peter, the Supreme Shepherd of the Lord's sheep, and to the disciple whom Jesus loved. Chapter

XXI without its epilogue is really the record of an **812a** apparition marked by a miracle, 1-14, to which are attached the conferring of the primacy on Peter, 15-17, the prediction of his martyrdom, 18-19, and the rectification of a misunderstanding about Jn 20-23.

XX 1-10 The Empty Tomb—The Johannine wit- **b** nesses of the empty tomb are first Mary Magdalene and then the two Apostles Peter and John. **1.** After the Sabbath, Mt, Mk on the first day of the week —our Sunday, Lk, Jn—Mary Magdalene came to the tomb (not alone, but with other women). Jn agrees with Lk on the early hour, 'while it was yet dark ', but seems to differ from Mk who says that the sun had risen. As it seems likely that the women had been staying over in Bethany, the difficulty is solved by distinguishing the moment of setting out from the moment of arrival. Whereas in Mk the three women saw the stone already removed, Jn only records the presence and action of her on whom the impression of the empty tomb was most rapid and vivid. **2.** He does not say that Mary looked into the tomb, but the sequel supposes it. She ran back at once to tell the Apostles. The repetition of prepositions seems to indicate that she found Peter and John in different places. Her report is rapid : 'They have taken away the Lord out of the sepulchre, and we know not where they have laid him'. The use of the first person plural shows that she had not gone unaccompanied. **3 f.** Peter and John ran to the tomb. John's youth **c** is sufficient reason for his outrunning Peter. **5.** Bending down to the low opening, he saw the bandages but did not go in—retained possibly by some strong emotion or more probably by respect for Peter. **6 f.** The latter entered and found complete evidence that the body had not been *removed* ; for bodysnatchers would surely never have carefully divested the body of its linen bands before taking it away. The bandages were not in a confused heap, but were 'lying' on the ledge (in the shape of the body and not folded up?). And the napkin that had been over his head was lying apart and carefully rolled up. **8 f.** John perceived the truth at once, and with the light of his faith saw the meaning of some Scriptural prophecy of the resurrection (probably Ps 15(16)). **10.** Each went his way, but Lk shows Peter 'wondering in himself'.

11-18 Appearance to Mary Magdalene—As Aug. says **d** so beautifully : 'When the men went away, a stronger affection kept the weaker sex fixed in the same place '. **11 f.** Mary was so completely absorbed in the grief of her loss, that she only just noticed the two white-robed figures within. **13.** To the question of the angels she has only one answer, 'they have taken away my Lord, and I know not where they have laid him '. **14.** She turned back, possibly because, while she was answering, the angel at the foot of the funeral bench was fixing his eyes on someone outside. Jesus was standing there, but either because he did not show the appearance which he had known, or because of tears in her eyes, or because of her state of soul she did not recognize him. **15.** His double question was identical with that of the angels. With her fixed idea regarding the removal of the body, Mary grasped at what seemed some hope of finding it. This man (whom she thought to be the gardener) could tell her. In her request to the stranger she names no name, only *him, him, him*, as if the whole world should know who *he* was. In saying : 'I will take him away ', it is ' the audacious Mary Magdalene ', as St Thérèse called her, who speaks. **16.** Jesus spoke then. In the sound **e** of the name *Mariam* from the lips of the Saviour we should meditate the voice of the Good Shepherd calling his sheep by name. In calling him *Rabboni* Mary used a form of address which had more solemnity and respect in it than Rabbi. **17.** A gloss in some MSS says : 'She ran forward to touch him '. Most probably she did take hold of his feet, for the words ' Touch me not ', representing a Gk present imperative, mean ' *Do not cling* to me '. The reason of the pro-

812e hibition is that just now she must be a messenger, *apostolorum apostola*. The content of the message is that he is risen and is still with his brethren, till he ascends to his Father—not immediately. There are many interpretations of these difficult words, but the above seems the simplest. **18.** Jn records that Mary delivered her message ; Mk registers the incredulity of the disciples, 16:11.

f **19-23 Appearance to Ten Apostles**—Lk places this apparition after the return of the two disciples from Emmaus. The Apostles had reassembled during the day. The collegiate term ' eleven ' is used by Lk for those gathered, but there were actually only ten. Jn seems to consider the Apostles only, though some others were present, Lk 24:33. Faith in the resurrection had already established itself, for Jesus had appeared to Peter during the day. Nevertheless, Mk tells that the pilgrims from Emmaus were not believed. The joy of the resurrection, it seems, did not exclude the feeling expressed in the popular phrase that some things are too good to be true. The place of reunion is probably the Cenacle. **19.** The news of the empty tomb and the calumny that the body had been stolen by disciples of Jesus, Mt 28:13, was no doubt already circulating in Jerusalem. Hence the fear which made the disciples hide behind closed doors. Jesus, whose glorified body needed no open door to enter by, suddenly stood in their midst. The salute ' Peace be to you ' must have sounded like a general pardon.

g **20.** Proof beyond all doubt of the identity of the Lord was given by the wounded hands and side which he showed them. **21.** The exhibition of these signs of redemption was a fitting introduction to a repetition of ' Peace be to you '. The words that follow conferred on the Apostles the same mission which the Word Incarnate had from the Father, to be exercised in the name and with the authority of Jesus himself. **22 f.** By the symbolic gesture of breathing upon them he signified that he was communicating the Holy Spirit —a partial anticipation of the gift of Pentecost. The words : ' Receive ye the Holy Ghost ' made the meaning quite clear. The power of remitting and retaining sins, clearly supposes judicial authority exercised over sins in a tribunal. Accordingly the Church has perpetually understood this act of the Saviour as the institution of the sacrament of Penance (Trent, Sess. 14). Thus the sacrament of pardon was instituted under a double sign of the Saviour's peace, on the most joyful day of the world's history. It should be noted that in the intention of Christ who gave this power to the members of an apostolic college, Thomas, who was absent, also received it.

h **24-29 Appearance to the Eleven**—The case of Thomas, in whom Jn took a special interest, 11:16 ; 14:5, is very important because, as St Gregory remarks, the slow surrender of Thomas is of more advantage to strengthen our faith than the more ready faith of all the believing Apostles. Besides, the act of faith made by the believing Thomas is the fullest and most explicit of all the confessions of faith recorded in the Gospels. **24.** For the third time Jn mentions Thomas, and for the second time interprets his name, which means ' Twin '. A blend of scepticism and pessimism goes with a melancholic temperament, such as seems to have been that of Thomas. He had probably lost heart more than the others during the Passion, and his absence from the reunion on Easter Sunday may have been due to a hard-headed attitude towards such wishful imagining as he would have thought Mary Magdalene's message to be. However, this is partly conjecture. **25.** The fact is that he met the joyful announcement of the Apostles ' We have seen the Lord ' with a most exacting demand for proof. He required every sort of experimental test, before he would believe that the Crucified was risen. **26.** And he remained in this stubbornness a full week, till Jesus appeared in the same circumstances to all the Apostles, including

i himself. Again our Lord gave his peace, **27,** invited Thomas to apply his tests, and added : ' *Do not become*

an unbeliever but a believer '. This is the force of the Gk words, which indicate that Thomas had not lost the virtue of faith, but was on the way to losing it. **28.** The Apostle, we may feel certain, did not approach to touch Jesus in the way he had demanded, but immediately made his sublime act of faith. The words he spoke do not seem to be either an exclamation nor a vocative, but an elliptic proposition : ' *Thou art my Lord and my God* '. Rather than a confession of the Messianic character and divinity of Jesus, it is a double confession of his divinity. **29.** If we read the words of Christ, which follow, as an assertion, we must understand them thus : ' *Because thou hast seen me (risen), thou hast believed (me to be God)* '. It is better, however, to read them as a question : ' *Is it because thou hast seen me, thou hast believed ?* ' No, because believing does not require seeing. Hence the beatitude (the last evangelical beatitude) of believing without seeing. The more faith is an interior supernatural light—the more it is independent of the support of merely human arguments, the better it is.

30-31 First Epilogue—There are two tenable explanations of this first epilogue. Either the Gospel originally ended here and Jn later added ch 21 with another epilogue, or this first epilogue was originally at the end of 21 and migrated here, when presbyters of Ephesus, gathered around Jn and under divine inspiration, added the final epilogue. The first epilogue sums up the whole purpose of the Fourth Gospel. This writing was not intended as an exhaustive record of the signs wrought by Jesus. The evangelist made a choice of a certain number of facts and discourses, in order to confirm disciples in their faith regarding Jesus as Messias and Son of God, so that believing they may have life in his name—the life meant being everlasting life.

XXI 1-14 Manifestation at the Lake—**1.** After the Paschal octave, the Apostles returned to Galilee. The homes of many of them were near the sea of Tiberias. **2.** Seven of their number were to be witnesses of a second miraculous catch of fishes. Simon Peter was the chief, and with him were Thomas, whose name is again interpreted, Nathanael (Bartholomew) designated here as a native of Cana, the (two) sons of Zebedee, and two whose identity we have no means of establishing. Some commentators, appealing to Jn's habitual reticence about himself and his, regard ' the sons of Zebedee ' as a gloss, but the MSS should be decisive. **3.** Six disciples therefore went with Peter (probably from Capharnaum) and spent a fruitless night fishing on the lake. **4.** As morning was coming (rather than ' when morning was come '), a figure appeared standing on the shore, a hundred yards away. He was not recognized as Jesus, presumably because of the distance and the obscurity of early dawn, and perhaps also because Jesus did not himself wish to be recognized immediately. **5.** To draw attention to the miracle about to take place Jesus asked them : ' *Young men*, have you any *fish* ? ' The word of address is one of familiarity, and the Gk substantive, which means *something-to-eat-with-bread*, is in the circumstances a polite synonym of ' fish '. The unwillingness with which fishermen admit that they have caught nothing is probably reflected in the curt ' No ' that came over the water. **6.** As the boat was probably moving south close to the western shore, the order to put the net out on the right side meant putting it out where fish were less likely to be. Nevertheless the catch was enormous. **7.** John was the first to recognize the Master—*ubi amor, ibi oculus* : love gives eyesight. But if John was a better contemplative, Peter was more prompt in action. His undress meant that he was clothed only in a sort of overall (without tunic) which he quickly girded to come to Jesus directly, more by wading than swimming through the water. **8.** The others followed in the boat, dragging the net. **9.** The breakfast prepared by Jesus on the shore is a touching instance of his solicitude for hungry

3b men—a fire of coals, a fish roasting, bread ready.
c **10 f.** His order to bring some of the catch was only intended to provoke the count. The number 153 has been given many symbolic meanings, mostly in the sense of the catholicity of the Church (Jerome's 153 species of fishes) or the total number of the elect. St Augustine discovered—one can hardly guess how —that 10 (the commandments) and 7 (the gifts of the Holy Ghost) in the addition of the whole series 1, 2, 3 . . . 17 give exactly 153. That the net was not rent suggests the unity and integrity of the Church. The net was used by Christ himself for a parable of the kingdom of heaven. **12-14.** The kindly invitation, the respect of the disciples, who knew who he was and in a sense did not know, and yet did not question him, the charity of the risen Lord ministering—these show that the intimate contact of friendship with Jesus is always the same, yesterday, today, and for ever. **14b.** Jn numbers this as the third manifestation to the disciples in a body.

d **15-17 The Primacy of Peter**—After the meal Jesus proceeded to an act which was of the utmost importance for the future of his Church. From the first day Jesus had called Simon son of John Kêphâ, 1:42, and had declared many months ago that on ' this rock ' he would build his Church, Mt 16:18. Weak as the Rock was during the Passion, the prayer of Jesus for the future confirmer of his brethren, Lk 22:32, was necessarily efficacious. Therefore the Rock is restored to its proper strength in a triple profession of love intended to undo the triple denial. The questions and the answers show that the devoted but presumptuous Peter has found the strength of his devotedness in humility. The whole admirable drama, in which Peter's love of his Master is turned to care of his Master's sheep, is founded on the parable of the Good Shepherd. The first question of Christ, with its term of comparison ' Lovest thou me more than these ? ' was evidently set against the Apostle's boast ' Although all shall be scandalized in thee, I will never be scandalized ', Mt 26:33. Peter does not now dare to say that he loves more than the others, but he does assert that he loves, and appeals to Jesus' knowledge of his heart. The emotion of his third answer, under the sadness of being asked three times, is most touching. To each response the same commission corresponds, expressed in a variety of terms which give it emphasis. ' Feed my lambs—*shepherd* my *sheep*—feed my sheep ' mean the same thing, for there is no reason for the supposition that sheep and lambs mean pastors and people. The whole flock (all the sheep of the Good Shepherd) are committed to Peter's care. To understand this commission as anything less than a primacy of authority over the universal church is to falsify the text. The passage has been dogmatically interpreted in this traditional sense by the Vatican Council, Dz 1822.

e **18-19 Prediction of Peter's Martyrdom**—A vision of Peter's future destiny is annexed to the supreme commission with the solemnity of a double ' Amen '. **813e** The chief shepherd will follow the Good Shepherd even in the manner of his death. The words have some of the mysterious obscurity of prophecy. Against the liberty of Peter's younger days (girding *himself* and walking where he pleased) is set this mysterious future event of his old age. If the counterpart contains only two terms, namely, girding by another, as an old man is helped to dress himself, and being led to a place not naturally desired (a place of execution), the prophecy envisages a violent death only, not the mode of death by crucifixion. The extension of the hands must therefore be the term specifically corresponding to crucifixion, but as the extension of hands is set before girding and being led away, it is difficult to discern how it must be conceived. If the order is part of the prophecy, we must suppose the prisoner lashed to the *patibulum* before being girded and led out to execution. Jn writing after Peter's death notes that Jesus said this ' signifying by what death he should glorify God '. The words ' Follow me ' which Jesus spoke immediately afterwards to Peter are so general as to include imitation, ' even to the death of the cross '.

20-23 Rectification concerning John's Future—The **f** Prince of the Apostles there and then did turn his footsteps to go with Jesus, but seeing John walking just behind, he was seized with a friend's interest in the beloved disciple. Affection and curiosity moved him to ask the question, ' Lord, and this man what ? ' (as the original Rheims translates). The change of *si* to *sic* in many Vg MSS and the adoption of that reading in the Clementine edition has given us the present Vg translation. But read : ' *If* I will have him to remain till I come, what is it to thee ? *do thou* follow me '. This answer really means : Even if I should let him remain till my second coming, what concern is it of thine ? Follow me and leave the destinies of others in my hands. In view of a current rumour making Jesus say that the beloved disciple would not die—a rumour which spread on account of his longevity —Jn here draws attention to the exact form of the word of Jesus concerning him.

24-25 Second Epilogue—The mixture of first plural **g** with first singular in these final words seems to justify the view that St John dictated them surrounded by the presbyters of Ephesus, but *cf.* 1 Jn 1–2. These, according to the Muratorian canon had requested him to write the Gospel, and are now giving testimony of its veracity together with him : ' This is that disciple who giveth testimony of these things, and hath written these things : and we know that his testimony is true. But there are also many ·other things which Jesus did : which if they were written every one, the world itself, I think, would not be able to contain the books that should be written '. Semitic hyperbole, no doubt, like comparing a people to the stars of heaven in multitude or to the sand at the lip of the sea, but how amply justified by the multitude and the magnitude of the things which Jesus did !

THE ACTS OF THE APOSTLES

By C. S. DESSAIN

814a Bibliography—St John Chrysostom, *55 Homilies on Acts*, PG 60, 13 ff. ; St Bede, *In Actus Apostolorum Expositio, in Actus Apostolorum Retractatio*, PL 92 ; *Sir William Ramsay's works, especially *St Paul the Traveller and the Roman Citizen*, 1895 ; J. Knabenbauer, S.J., in CSS, 1899 ; *R. B. Rackham, *The Acts of the Apostles*, 1901, 12 Ed., 1939 ; A. Steinmann, *Die Apostelgeschichte*, BB, 1913, 4th Ed., 1934 ; C. J. Callan, O.P., *The Acts of the Apostles*, 1919 ; *F. J. Foakes-Jackson and *Kirsopp Lake, *The Beginnings of Christianity*, 5 Vol., 1920–1933 ; A. Wikenhauser, *Die Apostelgeschichte und ihr Geschichtswert*, 1921, and *Die Apostelgeschichte übersetzt und erklärt*, 1938 ; *W. L. Knox, *St Paul and the Church of Jerusalem*, 1922, *St Paul and the Church of the Gentiles*, 1939, *The Acts of the Apostles*, 1948 ; J. A. Van Steenkiste, *Commentarius in Actus Apostolorum*, Ed 7, emend. et aucta opera A. Camerlynck et A. Vander Heeren, 1923 ; *A. W. F. Blunt, *The Acts of the Apostles*, 1923 ; E. Jacquier, *Les Actes des Apôtres*, 1926 ; (this is the most complete Catholic commentary). A. Boudou, S.J., *Actes des Apôtres*, 1933 ; Pirot, *Actes des Apôtres*, DBVS, 1 Vol., 42–86 ; F. Prat, S.J., *The Theology of St Paul*, London 1945 ; *Wilson, *The Acts of the Apostles* (tr. from Codex Bezae), S.P.C.K., 1924 ; *A. C. Clark, *The Acts of the Apostles*, 1933 ; C. Lattey, S.J., *The Acts of the Apostles* WV, 1936 ; J. Renié, *Actes des Apôtres*, Bible de Pirot, 1949 ; L. Cerfaux, *La Communauté Apostolique*, 1943 (more illuminating than many larger works, and includes a list of articles on Acts, by the author, chiefly in ETL.) ; G. Ricciotti, *Paolo Apostolo*, 1946. (To Jacquier, Ricciotti and above all, Cerfaux, what follows is greatly indebted.) For a summary of the latest views see J. Dupont, O.S.B., *Les Problèmes du Livre des Actes d'après les travaux récents*, Louvain, 1950.

b Authorship—Ancient tradition and the internal evidence agree in assigning Ac to Luke the Physician, the author of the Third Gospel. (1) *External Evidence.* The Muratorian Canon (*c* 170) makes this attribution, and adds that St Luke was present at events he relates. Irenaeus, *Adv. Haer.*, III, 14, 1, is equally clear, quotes from Ac as Scripture, and emphasizes its trustworthiness. The 2nd cent. ancient Latin and other Prologues of the Gospels, after mentioning St Luke as author of the Third Gospel, add that he also wrote Ac. In the 3rd cent., Clement of Alexandria, *Stromata*, V, 12, and Origen, *C. Celsum*, Bk VI, 11, are both explicit. Tertullian defends the book against Marcion and others, and in *De Jejunio* 10, names St Luke as its author. Eusebius, *Hist. Eccles.* III, 4, confirms these early witnesses from Rome, Asia Minor and Gaul, Egypt and Africa. Even earlier still, Ac is cited by Clement of Rome, *cf. Ep.* 2 and Ac 20:35, and *Ep.* 59 and 26:18, by Ignatius, *Magn.*, V, 1, and *Smyrn.*, III, 3, and by Polycarp, *Phil.* 1 and 2. The sole exception to the witness of antiquity is a homily falsely attributed to St John Chrysostom, *Hom. II in Ascensionem*, PG 52, 780, which declares that the authorship of Ac is variously assigned to Clement of Rome, Barnabas and Luke. The Homilist seems to have confused Ac with Heb, which ancient writers give to Clement or Barnabas.

(2) *Internal Evidence.* Luke is nowhere mentioned, but Ac purports to be a continuation of the Third Gospel. In 1:1 there is a reference to the First Book, which described the ' things which Jesus began to do

and to teach '. That book had been written so that **81** Theophilus might understand the instruction he had ' already received, in all its certainty ', Lk 1:4. Its author now writes for him this second book to describe the spread of the Faith after the death of Jesus. Style, grammar and the words used confirm that the two books are from the same pen.

More cogent still, the second part of Ac, describing **c** the journeys of St Paul, contains a *travel journal* by one of his companions, written in the first person. E. Norden, *Agnostos Theos* (1913) 318, has shown from Cicero and from reports of magistrates to the Senate, that it was usual in ancient times to incorporate eye-witness accounts or diaries, in the first person, when a writer could vouch personally for what he related. Just such a document, in the first person plural, the ' We Sections ', is found in 16:10–17 ; 20:5–15 ; 21:1–18 ; 27:1–28:16. The Travel Journal is interrupted, and the first person ceases to be used, whenever its author is no longer present. If we work out from Ac and the Epistles who were St Paul's companions during the periods covered by the ' We Sections ', St Luke is the only one who was always present, and moreover, unlike the rest, he is never present when the ordinary third person is used. The vivid diary of the eyewitness must clearly be his work.

The way in which St Luke inserts his journal in the **d** narrative implies that he is the author of the whole of Ac, and this is fully borne out by vocabulary, grammar and style. These have been examined minutely, both in the Travel Journal, in the rest of Acts, and in the Gospel, *cf.* Jacquier, LX, Hawkins, *Horae Synopticae* (1909) 174, Harnack, *Luke the Physician* (1907) 26. Even in the account of the sea voyages and the shipwreck, where a number of nautical terms are used which are not found elsewhere, the style and vocabulary remain that of the rest of Ac and the Gospel. St Luke was a man of letters, he knew the value of sources, and wished it to be known when he had been an eyewitness of the facts he related.

The characteristic traits of the Third Gospel can nearly all be paralleled in Ac ; *cf.* Introd. to St Luke. The hand of Luke the Physician, Col 1:14, can be seen in the technical accounts of the healing of the lame man, 3:7, of Publius, 28:8, and elsewhere. St Luke's tenderness shows itself, *e.g.* 20:37 ; 21:13, and his emphasis on the part played by women, *e.g.* Tabitha, Lydia. There is the same love of the poor, and of those not attached to riches, the same universalism, *cf.* § 817*e*, and the same insistence on prayer, *cf.* § 820*f*.

Date of the Book—Although there is no tradition, **e** since the time of St Jerome at least the conclusion has been drawn from Ac itself that it was written during or at the end of St Paul's first captivity, in A.D. 63 or 64. There is never a hint of the fall of Jerusalem, and yet that event so affected the relations of Christians and Jews, and the controversy within the Church concerning the Mosaic Law, that it could hardly have failed to leave some trace. A little earlier, in 64 A.D., the Persecution of Nero began, yet in Ac there is no suggestion of trouble brewing. On the contrary, the empire is shown as friendly, and when the narrative closes, St Paul is found in the capital of the Roman world, preaching freely, and with converts in Caesar's household. *Cf.* § 843*a*. There is never an allusion to

815a St Paul's martyrdom, though his sufferings are fore-told. His own prediction that he would not return to Ephesus, 20:35, is given, although it proved false in the event, as St Luke could hardly have failed to note, if he had been writing after St Paul had returned to Asia. Ac ends suddenly, without our being told how the trial which had brought St Paul to **b** Rome, ended. The obvious deduction from this has always been that St Luke concluded his narrative because he had no more to say. Perhaps St Paul was still a prisoner. More probably he had just been released, because his Jewish accusers had failed to appear. St Luke tells us that he remained a prisoner for 'two whole years', and to his readers this seems to have conveyed that he had fulfilled the statutory period during which an accused must wait for his accusers to appear ; cf. *H. J. Cadbury in *Beginnings*, 5, 326 ff. Thus St Luke would be telling us how and why St Paul was released, but he does not insist on it, because the result of the trial was negative, and did not add to the vindication he had already received from the imperial authorities. It has been argued that the sudden ending was due to St. Luke's intention of composing a third volume, and that when he called the Gospel his 'first' volume, Ac 1:1, and not 'former' he implied as much. However πρῶτος is often used of the first of two in 1st cent. Greek, e.g. Lk 2:2, and an historian does not break off his narrative like a serial novelist, if he can avoid it. It might be added that the 'primitive' tone of the earlier chapters, and St Luke's unfamiliarity with the Epistles of St Paul also help to rule out a late date for Ac. We may safely conclude that it was written in Rome, before the great fire of July 64, which let loose the Neronian Persecution, and which was perhaps the immediate cause of the hurried ending of the book, cf. § 843i.

c St Luke's Sources—A doctor, from Syrian Antioch, who joined St Paul on his Second Journey, and returned to Jerusalem with him at the end of his Third, remaining for years his constant companion, St Luke was able to obtain the most direct information, cf. § 744b. A doctor was a man of importance, familiar with the great, and practising a liberal art. Such a one knew how to collect the materials for a history, and in the case in hand, how to combine his own notes and memories, with the documents he had copied, into an artistic whole. Indeed St Luke in the introduction to his Gospel, 1:2, explains how carefully he collected his information from eyewitnesses, and his treatment of St Mark reveals how faithfully he used his sources.

For the sources of Ac 13–28 there is no need to look beyond St Paul himself, his companions, and St Luke's own observation. Written documents were also used. e.g. the Travel Journal, a copy of the Apostolic Decree, the letter of Claudius Lysias, etc. As to chh 1–12, the vividness of so many of the accounts suggests strongly that they are the work of eyewitnesses, whom it was so easy for St Luke to consult, whether at Antioch, or during the two years A.D. 58–60, of St Paul's captivity at Caesarea, the home of Philip the Evangelist, 21:8. At Antioch and Jerusalem he must have met the chief figures, and he betrays the interest that 'old disciples' have for him, 13:1 ; 21:16. At Rome he certainly met St Mark, Col 4:10 and 14 ; Philem 24. It has even been argued that in these chapters St Luke was following a Marcan source, as he had for his Gospel, cf. RB 29 (1920) 555, and 30 (1921) 86. The strongly Semitic colouring of these early chapters has also suggested their dependence on an Aramaic original ; but this is difficult to prove ; nor should it be forgotten that the first community at Jerusalem was bilingual, and that at the election of the seven Deacons the Greek-speaking Christians were in a considerable majority. Owing to the faithful way in which St Luke copied out his sources, and (since he was writing a history) arranged them in more or less chronological order, it is still possible to dissect them. This has been done very convincingly by L. Cerfaux, *La Composition de la première partie du Livre des Actes*, ETL, 13 (1936), 667–91.

Thus the narrative from the Ascension till the end of **815d** the day of Pentecost must come from the Twelve, and 2:41 to the end of ch 5, where the horizon is limited to the Temple and Jerusalem from the Jewish Christians of the Holy City. The account of the Deacons and St Stephen in 6 and 7 gives the story of some of the Hellenist Christians, and reveals their more universalist point of view. Then follow Acts of Philip, 8, the Conversion of Saul, and Acts of Peter the Missionary, 9:31–11:18, all perhaps preserved at Caesarea. From Antioch comes the account of the beginnings of the church in that city. Careful study has revealed the fullness of St Luke's documentation, and the faithfulness with which he reproduced it.

Historical Value—What has been said as to the author- **816a** ship, date and sources of Ac proves, putting aside Inspiration, how reliable it is. The extraordinary accuracy of St Luke has also been demonstrated by the recent discoveries of archaeology. The story of the 'conversion' of Sir William Ramsay, who had been brought up to regard Ac as a 2nd cent. forgery is well known, and the archaeological evidence can be found in his books. 'Every incident described in the Acts is just what might be expected in ancient surroundings. The officials with whom Paul and his companions were brought into contact are those who would be there. Every person is found just where he ought to be : pro-consuls in senatorial provinces, Asiarchs in Ephesus, *strategoi* in Philippi, politarchs in Thessalonica, magicians and soothsayers everywhere. . . . The magistrates take action against them in a strictly managed Roman colony like Pisidian Antioch or Philippi, where legality and order reigned : riotous crowds try to take the law into their own hands in the less strictly governed Hellenistic cities like Iconium and Ephesus and Thessalonica ', *The Bearing of Recent Discovery on the Trustworthiness of the NT* (1915) 96. Cf. also *E. J. Bicknell in *A New Commentary*, 1928, ' On all sorts of little points connected with the names both of persons and places the author has used a most careful discrimination. . . . Nowhere can he be convicted of a mistake. On many points on which he used to be supposed to be in error he has now been proved to be correct '. Cf. too, Jacquier, ccxxv ; DAFC, ' Epigraphie ', 1428, and *S. L. Caiger, *Archaeology and the NT*, 1939.

There are eighteen **speeches in Ac**, which occupy **b** about one-fifth of the book. It has often been suggested that these are literary inventions, and that St Luke was following the recognized practice of Greek historians, in thus enlivening his history. However Polybius at least took a stricter view, and there is every reason to suppose that St Luke shared it. We know how careful he was over our Lord's discourses in his Gospel, in accordance with the promise of his prologue, Lk 1:4, and the evidential aim of his ' second book ' made the same fidelity no less necessary there also. It is a gratuitous supposition that accuracy in detail and fidelity to sources stopped short at the speeches. Those that we have are, of course, only summaries. Shorthand notes would have been taken at the time, or the substance of a speech written down from memory. The speeches themselves bear strong marks of their authenticity. Thus those of St Peter contain both words and ideas found in 1 Pet, and not found elsewhere in Lk. The Descent into Hell is found in NT only in 2:24 and 1 Pet 3:19. Gamaliel speaks like the liberal Rabbi he was. St Stephen's speech is full of Aramaisms, follows the Jewish method of argumentation, and is far less respectful to Jewish religion than St Luke ordinarily shows himself, On parallels between St James' speech and his Epistle see J. Chaine, *Epître de St Jacques*, lxxxiii. The resemblances between St Paul's speeches in Ac, and his Epistles are particularly striking. Numerous Pauline expressions can be pointed to, OT texts are cited in the same way, and there are many doctrinal points of contact. Justification by faith and the impotence of the Law are insisted on, in the ' programme speech ' to the Jews of Pisidian Antioch. Cf. F. Prat, *op. cit.* I (1945) 54 ff., and Jacquier, cclxvii.

816c The difficulty of reconciling the accounts given in Gal and Ac of the controversy over the Mosaic Law has been brought forward against the historicity of St Luke. The two versions can be sufficiently harmonized, once the difference is realized between St Paul writing in the heat of conflict, to preserve the liberty of his converts, and St Luke, the sober historian, who reduces the controversy to its proper proportions, and is anxious to bring out the fundamental unity of the Church. Indeed one more confirmation of the accuracy of St Luke can be derived from the Epistles of St Paul. St Luke certainly did not use them among his sources, and, as the 'We Sections' prove, he was absent when they were written, or, in the case of the Captivity Epistles, they did not come within the framework of Ac. Many events referred to in the Epistles find no place in Ac, yet the correspondence between them is considerable, and all the more valuable for being indirect and accidental : *e.g.* the great apostolate at Ephesus, Ac 19:10 and 1 Cor 16:9, St Paul's intention of going to Rome, 19:10 and Rom 15:23, the accounts of the evangelization of Thessalonica or Corinth, the collection for the poor at Jerusalem. Ac and the Epistles supplement each other, and once their differing viewpoints are recognized, can be harmonized without difficulty.

d Purpose and Theme—The analysis of Ac reveals that it is not a complete history of the first years of the Church. We are told nothing of the founding of the Church in Rome, nor of the later history of St Peter. This was partly perhaps because St Luke writes only what he can vouch for, but many episodes that he knew about are similarly omitted, *e.g.* much of the history of St Paul, and the later history of the churches he founded, and the development of the organization of the Church. Gospel and Ac form a whole. Both are written to strengthen and enlighten faith. After the history of the visible Christ comes the history of Christ working invisibly through his instruments. The Apostles are to 'preach unto all nations, beginning at Jerusalem', and to be the witnesses of Jesus, Lk 24:47-48. For this purpose they will 'receive the power of the Holy Ghost coming upon' them, and will 'be witnesses unto' Jesus 'in Jerusalem and in all Judaea and Samaria, and even to the uttermost parts of the earth', Ac 1:8. The theme of Acts is the fulfilment of this last command of Our Lord. The book is written to demonstrate the wonderful expansion of Christianity through the world, begun and carried on by the power of the Holy Spirit. We see the Church gradually breaking through the Judaism in which it was born, and spreading to the Greek and Roman world. This universal preaching involves a tragic struggle with the narrow spirit of Jewish religion. Owing to the force and enlightenment of the Holy Spirit, the work of Jesus is accomplished. After the Acts of Jesus in the Gospel come the Acts of the Holy Spirit. Hence the aim of St Luke is not to give a systematic history of the Church, but to describe the Holy Spirit at work founding it, and enabling it to break in upon the pagan world, although it was rejected by the Jews.

817a Doctrinal Content—Being a historical work, by one who had no great interest in theology, it might be expected that little doctrine could be found in Ac. But the Christian Faith is essentially a piece of history, that of God's intervention in the affairs of mankind ; and Ac is the only history we possess of the Coming of the Holy Spirit, and his guidance of the Church during the first momentous thirty years. The four Gospels describe the Incarnation and work of Jesus Christ, and this is the fifth Gospel, that of the Holy Spirit, a unique gospel, and so especially precious.

The doctrine to be found in chh 13–28 is most naturally studied in the context of the theology of St Paul. Hence in what follows attention will be concentrated chiefly on the first twelve chapters, and the insight they afford into the faith and teaching of the Church in Palestine, between A.D. 30 and 45. Indeed a full study would require a subdivision of these twelve

chapters, and the separate consideration of the teaching **81** to be found, and the advance made in the sources as outlined above, § 815*d*. Only thus can be seen, for instance, the step forward taken by St Stephen and the deacons, or the progress made when the pagans were preached to at Antioch. But see on 6:1, 8 and 11:19–26. One further distinction must be made in considering the doctrine of Ac, namely, that between the apologetic discourses of the Apostles, destined for those outside, and the fuller teaching to be gleaned from the lives and prayers of the Christians themselves. Jews and Gentiles had to be led on step by step, and told only the mysteries they could grasp. This helps to explain the archaic character of the earlier discourses, and is one more proof of the accuracy with which St Luke reproduced his sources. The narrative of the life of the first disciples is most valuable in that it brings out incidentally the primitive Christian teaching and faith. Here we find the divinity of our Lord continually affirmed implicitly, and eventually explicitly, and the activity of the Holy Spirit making his own Person known. We see too, the Church, in which alone the Spirit is given, united in love, under the authority of St Peter and the Apostles, its members living a 'new life' of joyful union with God, whose Holy Spirit they have received.

God the Father—The revelation of the Blessed Trinity **b** in the NT was made by showing gradually, and through actions more often than through words, that two other Persons besides the heavenly Father, are the One God of Israel. Hence the concept of the Father in Ac, is that of the true God already to be found in the OT. He is the Creator, everywhere present, 4:24, 14:14, 17:24–28. He reads all hearts, 15:8, and governs all things by his Providence, 1:7, 2:23. Further, he raised Jesus from the tomb, 2:24, he promised the Holy Spirit, 1:4, and from him Jesus received the Promise, 2:33, which was poured out at Pentecost, Through the Holy Spirit the Father works in the Church.

Jesus Christ—In the apologetic preaching, the Apostles **c** generally speak in a veiled way of the divinity of our Lord. They begin by showing that he is the Messias. This is the triumphant conclusion of St Peter's discourse at Pentecost, that Jesus is 'both Lord and Christ', *i.e.* Messias, 2:16–36. His Messianic character is proved from prophecy, miracles, and especially the Resurrection. In the next section, 2:40–5:42, our Lord is referred to by Messianic titles found here only in the NT. He is παῖς θεοῦ, 3:13 (see comm.) the Suffering Servant. But the title has also the sense of 'Son' of God, and that seems to be its meaning when it is used within the new community, 4:30. St Paul preached without any reserve that Jesus is the Son of God, 9:20 ; 13:33. Another Messianic title used in this section only, and presumably discarded as veiled teaching became unnecessary, is the 'Just One', 3:14. At all events, the greatness of the Messias is revealed by his powers. He sends the Holy Spirit, he forgives sins, he is the author of life, 3:15, he is the one saviour of all men, whose name is powerful like that of Yahweh, 4:10 ff., he is to be obeyed like God, 4:19, he sits on the right hand of God, and is the judge of all men.

Jesus is also 'Lord', *Kyrios* ; see on 2:36. In the **d** early discourses, this title implies that the Messias has the royal powers of God. Through learning the functions of the Messias, the Jews were led on to realize his Nature. In 10:36 he is the 'Lord of all men', a much stronger phrase ; *cf.* Phil 2:11 and Apoc 19:16.

The attitude to our Lord within the Church gives, as has been said, a far clearer insight. There the title 'Lord' has become a divine name. *Kyrios*, the LXX translation of Yahweh, is the Gk word chosen to describe the name and being of God, and it is now applied to Jesus, as indeed it was in the Gospel, 4:33 ; 7:58–59 ; 9:1. He is the 'Lord who knows all hearts', 1:24, like his Father. Many other phrases refer to Jesus by this divine name, and it is not always easy

817d to decide whether he or his Father is meant. We may note especially ' faith in the Lord ', *i.e.* Jesus, 5:14 ; 11:17, and 14:22.. Even more revealing are the relations between Jesus and his first followers. Just as God was invoked in the OT, so, and among Jews the fact has an extraordinary significance, Jesus is invoked now. Those who call on the name of the Lord will be saved, Jl 2:32, and Ac 2:21, and Christians are those who call on the name of Jesus, his saints, 9:13-4, 21. They pray to him, 1:24, and turn to him in the moment of trial like St Stephen, and he comes to their aid. They are one with him, 9:4, and in his name they are baptised. Indeed it is a privilege to suffer or die for this name. 5:41 ; 9:16 ; 20:24 ; 21:13. He appears himself from time to time, when guidance is needed, to Ananias, to Peter, to Paul. Paul especially, receives his mandate from Jesus, 26:16, and is encouraged in his missionary labours by such visions, 18:9 ; 23:11. Lastly, Jesus is with his followers through the Holy Spirit he has sent, the Spirit of Jesus, 16:7. On the very explicit 20:28, ' church of God which he has purchased with his own blood ', see comm. Even apart from these later texts, how little separates this faith in practice of the first disciples from the teaching of St Paul and St John ! St Luke had no doubt that it was the same faith all through.

e Salvation the Work of Jesus—There is no salvation in any other name, 4:12, *cf.* 3:16. Through this saviour men obtain remission of sins, 5:31. He is the cause of our salvation, 3:19, 26 ; 10:42-43 ; 15:11. Thus St Peter ; and St Paul teaches the same, 13:38-39 ; 16:31. This salvation is connected with the death of Jesus. He is the ' Suffering Servant ', and his pains have redemptive value, 8:32-35 ; *cf.* 3:13, 18. The discourses of St Peter, St Stephen and St Paul develop the identical theme : the crime of the Jews in killing the innocent Messias, and thus, as had been foretold, fulfilling the plan of God, for the salvation of the human race. Our Lord is the saviour of all men, Gentiles as well as Jews, ' whomsoever the Lord our God shall call ', 2:21 and 39, and he is to be preached to the uttermost parts of the earth, 1:8. This universalism is never in doubt, the only hesitation is over the extent to which Jewish observances are still necessary.

As to the earthly life of our Lord, Ac refers to nearly all the chief events. He comes from Nazareth, and is of the house of David, born of Mary. John the Baptist prepared the way for him, 13:24-25. Beginning in Galilee, he preached, and worked miracles, and appointed Apostles, 10:41-42. After his death and resurrection, his appearances are described, 1:3 ; 10:40-41 ; 13:31, and his Ascension. He sits on the right hand of God, and will come to judge the living and the dead, 3:20 ; 10:42 ; 17:31, all of whom, just and unjust, will rise again, 24:15, 25.

818a The Holy Spirit—To explain the miracle of Pentecost St Peter refers to the Spirit promised in Joel, the Spirit or Power of God, spoken of in the prophetic and sapiential books. Ac is concerned, more than any other book of the NT, with the activity of this Holy Spirit of God, called now ' the Spirit ' (9 times), now ' Holy Spirit ' (18 times), now ' the Holy Spirit ' (24 times), twice ' the Spirit of the Lord ', and once ' the Spirit of Jesus '. The divinity of the Spirit is not in question. Jewish tradition affirmed it. The Spirit of God is divine, as the spirit of man is human, and, as we now learn, to lie to the Holy Spirit is to lie to God, 5:3. The works attributed to the Spirit, inspiring prophets and sanctifying believers, are divine works. And so in Ac too, we find that God spoke by the mouth of the prophets, 3:18, 21, and the Holy Spirit also, 1:16 ; 4:25 ; 28:25. What has to be shown is that the first disciples saw here a Person distinct from the Father and Jesus.

b The Holy Spirit manifests himself especially through his gifts and his activity, and it is through these that we are led to realize that he is a distinct Person. Our Lord promised the Apostles power, ' when the Holy Spirit shall come upon you '. He comes, and **818b** they speak ' according as the Holy Spirit gave them to speak '. He spoke through the ancient prophets, and he also speaks through the NT ones, 11:28 ; 21:11. Much more, it is he who continually guides the Church and the Apostles. He is a ' witness ' along with them, 5:32. He gives instructions to Philip, 8:29, and to St Peter, 10:19, and the great decisions are made by him in conjunction with human persons, ' it hath seemed to the Holy Ghost and to us ', 15:28. The missionaries go out under his orders, 13:2-4. He guides them, 20:23, sometimes holds them back, 16:6-7, and appoints bishops, 20:28. He consoles, 9:31, works miracles, 10:46, 19:6. Sin against him is terribly punished. At every crisis he intervenes, 7:55 ; 11:28 ; 20:23. Finally, he is the object of a special teaching. Those who are ignorant of him, though they may know of the Father and Jesus, are not yet true disciples, 19:1-7. If as yet there are no prayers to the Holy Spirit, this is due to the way in which the economy of salvation was revealed to us.

The Blessed Trinity—In Ac we see the three Persons, **c** but the mystery of the Blessed Trinity, in this historical work, is nowhere didactically set forth. It is none the less presupposed. In 1:4 the Holy Spirit is promised by the Father, and in 2:33 Jesus sends down this Promise, whom he has received from his Father. In 2:38-39, we see God calling men, who are then baptised in the name of Jesus, and receive the Holy Spirit. Then the Spirit of the Lord, 8:39, is also the Spirit of Jesus, 16:7 ; *cf.* J. Lebreton, S.J., *Histoire du Dogme de la Trinité*, 1 (1927[7]) 342-78.

The Gift of the Spirit—The Holy Spirit is the principle **d** of life, who animates the new community. His work of spreading the Gospel, and enabling the disciples to bear witness has already been described. Sometimes he works by the charismata, gifts of tongues, etc., or by strong inspirations enabling their recipients to benefit others. Thus we are told more than twenty times that the disciples or their hearers were filled with the Holy Spirit. This is true especially of the key figures, whose activity and witness are so important for others, Peter 4:8, Stephen, Barnabas, for the vital work at Antioch, where Paul must come, 11:24, and Paul himself, 13:4, 9.

Besides the transient work of the Holy Spirit, Ac speaks of his permanent presence, the Gift hidden in the hearts of the faithful, after Baptism, 2:38 ; 5:32. This Presence sometimes reveals itself externally, 6:3-15, for the Holy Spirit gradually transforms and makes holy those in whom he dwells. The new life of the Spirit begins to spread through the world, and thus Ac shows us the fulfilment of our Lord's promises in Jn 14-16. St Luke's favourite name for the disciples is ' those of the way ', those following the new way of life, 9:2. Of this new life Christ is the author, 3:15, the Apostles are to preach it boldly, 5:20, the Gentiles share it, 11:18 ; 13:48, and failure to preach it is to be the cause of death to others, 20:26.

Common Life—St Luke loves to depict the fervour **819a** and holiness of the first disciples, and the joyful union and charity between them, all effects of the Gift of the Spirit, 2:42-47 ; 4:24-35 ; 13:52. The force of his description is weakened in translation. All persevere ' with one mind ', ' together ', even before Pentecost, when they were ' all together in one place '. Later they were ' in communion ', ' had all things in common ', ' continued daily with one accord ', and increased daily together. They prayed ' with one accord ', ' had but one heart and soul ', and ' all things were common unto them '. There were shadows, from the first, as Ac tells us, but the Apostles did their best to teach and reproduce the life they had led with Jesus. So their followers gave themselves up to the Spirit. They sold their possessions to buy the treasure of the Kingdom. They lived and prayed together, thus becoming the model of all in the future who would wish to lead a religious life. Mutual charity persevered. Tabitha, 9:36, is one example. The

819a churches send alms to the poor at Jerusalem. St Paul's speech to the Presbyters of Ephesus tells the same tale, as do his farewell on the beach at Tyre, 21:5, and the welcome he received from the Christians of Rome.

b **The Church**—From the first, the new life is lived in a community, and one that is autonomous. The outpouring at Pentecost brings it to life, and within it alone is the Spirit given. It is called the Church in the earliest documents, 5:11, *cf.* L. Cerfaux, *La Théologie de l'Eglise suivant St Paul*, Paris 1948², esp. pp 87 and 144. Its leaders realize that they have a mission to the whole world, and that when necessary they must obey God rather than the highest authorities in Judaism, 5:29. The breach with the Synagogue becomes formal once Gentiles are admitted into the Church without circumcision. This proved that the Church could no longer be considered a Jewish sect. It was the new Israel, the new chosen people, 15:14. It was necessary to reaffirm the principle at the Council of Jerusalem, and there St Peter implied that the Jewish law no longer bound even Christian Jews. It was still generally observed by them, however, and only after the fall of Jerusalem was the breach with the Synagogue complete.

c **An Organized Society : the Apostles**—Our Lord in the Gospel gave the Apostles their authority, and fixed their number, which, after the death of Judas, had to be made up. Ac shows them to be (1) Witnesses to the life and Resurrection of Jesus, which are the basis of the new faith, 2:32 ; 4:20 ; 5:30–32 ; 10:39 ; 13:31. (2) Teachers, for Christians must obey the teaching of Jesus, be 'disciples', and have faith in him, if they are to enter the new society. They must accept the 'didache', 'the doctrine of the Apostles', 2:42 ; 10:36–43, 'the things that are of Jesus', 18:25 ; 28:31, *i.e.* the Gospel, our Lord's life and teaching. This the Apostles had received from their 'one Master', and its content fuller than what the NT has preserved for us, is represented in part by the discourses in Mt. (3) Rulers guided by the Holy Spirit, who was promised to them in a special way. Hence, their momentous decisions are also those of the Holy Spirit, and men who lie to them, are said to be lying to him. Much more, the Gift of the Spirit depends on them, for God only gives the Holy Spirit to those 'that obey him', 5:32, that are incorporated in the Church by baptism. The one exception is the Descent of the Holy Spirit on Cornelius and his household, even before they had been baptized. But here a direct divine intervention was necessary, to ensure the admission of Gentiles into the Church without conditions. Yet, in spite of their high Gift, they have to submit at once to authority, and be baptized. 10:44–48. Normally none can receive the Spirit of Christ, who have not entered the body of Christ. The Apostles have their powers from the first. There is no development. They admit the first converts, men give them their property as to God, they can delegate their powers, and are able to pronounce the severest punishment on those who threaten the good name and discipline of the Church. Their prerogatives include the working of miracles, prophesying and the understanding of the Scriptures.

d **The Primacy of St Peter**—If in the Apostles we can see the beginnings of an authoritative hierarchy, even more in St Peter can we trace the first lineaments of the Papacy. St Luke knew that our Lord had made him the leader, *cf.* Lk 22:31–32, and the chief witness, Lk 24:34, *cf.* 1 Cor 15:5, and shows Him to us, performing his functions at once after the Ascension. He arranges for the election of St Matthias. He is the spokesman at Pentecost and afterwards, the chief teacher. He works the first miracle, and remains the principal thaumaturge, 5:15 ; *cf.* 9:38. He wields the authority in the case of Ananias and Sapphira. In the early persecutions by the Sanhedrin, he is the ringleader, and he is the one Herod must arrest. When he is in prison, the special prayer of the Church shows the esteem in which he is held, 12:5, 12, 14.

During the first period, the church at Jerusalem was **819** the whole church of God, and possessed the essential elements of its organization, Apostles, and St Peter at the head. As new districts are evangelized, St Peter is seen to be responsible for them also. After the Gospel has been preached in Samaria, St Peter and St John are delegated to link up the new converts with the mother church, 8:14. 'The word "delegation" must not deceive us, any more than the demeanour, democratic in the old sense of the word, of the primitive community. Authority does not abdicate because it is willing to listen to the Church, and Peter, the delegate of the Church of Jerusalem and of the Apostolic Body—they are one and the same thing—remains the head. There are shades of meaning there which we western people misconstrue. But also, and above all, the same Spirit that gave Peter the first place, and made him the head, inspired the Church and the Twelve to put back into his hands the responsibility for decisions. Whether it is a question of his own initiative, or whether he gets himself delegated, Peter always enjoys full powers', Cerfaux, *La Communauté Apostolique* (1943) 71. The Church is extended to Samaria. St Peter's responsibilities increase, and he makes a pastoral visitation of the Church in Judaea and Samaria, 9:31–32.

The most momentous decision made in apostolic **e** times was that of admitting Gentiles to share in the new Messianic blessings, without having to observe circumcision and the Mosaic Law. This made clear the independence of the new religion. It was St Peter alone, specially enlightened, who made this decision, and it was of great importance for St Luke's story, to show from whom it had emanated. With the growth of the large Gentile church at Antioch, a further development is seen. The Church at Jerusalem, with its love for the temple and the law, becomes archaic. But St Peter has left for Antioch and then Rome. 'As the ship enters the sea of the Gentiles, Peter is at the helm', L. Cerfaux, *ibid.* However, the growth of the Gentile churches leads to an attempt to undo St Peter's decision in the Cornelius case. Later on at the Council of Jerusalem, he reaffirms it, and St James himself explains how God chose him out specially to receive the first Gentiles. St Peter appears above the debate, with the matter already settled in his mind, and his authoritative utterance on the main point at issue is accepted. All are led by the Spirit, St Paul the defender of liberty, St James of the Law, and St Peter, the true shepherd, reconciling them. On 15:19 see comm. The quarrel at Antioch, since it had no lasting effects, St Luke omits out of respect, as we may safely guess, for the Prince of the Apostles, the visible sign of that unity in the Church which St Luke loved so well.

The Sacraments : Baptism—Our Lord's teaching **820** about faith, repentance and baptism is put into practice at once. All who wish to be saved must be baptised with water, 8:36 ; 10:47. Then their sins are remitted, 2:38, 22:16, they belong to the Church, and are able to receive the Spirit, 8:12 ; 9:18 ; 16:33. They become the followers of Jesus, united to him, and are said to be baptised 'in his name', *cf.* comm. on 2:38. By the formula almost certainly used, they are consecrated to the Holy Trinity. Only after this mystery has been taught is baptism conferred, 19:1–7. Concerning the baptism of infants see note on 21:5–6.

Confirmation—Closely associated with baptism, is the **b** laying on of hands to give the Holy Spirit, the 'Baptism of the Spirit', 1:5 ; 11:16. St Peter mentions the effects of the two rites in the same verse, 'be baptised for the remission of your sins, and you shall receive the gift of the Holy Ghost', 2:38 ; and after Pentecost, and for long, in the Church, the two were normally administered together. However, in Ac we learn more about the separate sacrament of Confirmation than anywhere else in the NT. In the account of the Samaritans, 8:15–17, and of the disciples of John, 19:5–6, the laying on of hands comes as something distinct from baptism, and it can only be performed by those holding special authority, Apostles. On the case of Ananias see comm. on 9:17. The Eunuch too, 8:38, seems only to have been baptised, and on the other hand, the Apostles, who had long since repented of their sins, received at Pentecost the Spirit who could not be given till our Lord was glorified, 2:33 ; *cf.* Jn 7:39. The gift was permanent, and, as at Pentecost and with the Samaritans, was often accompanied by the granting of charismata. It seems especially to fit disciples to be witnesses of Jesus, and to enable them to preach with courage and confidence, *cf.* 4:33 and 5:32.

c The Holy Eucharist—St Luke uses the term ' the Breaking of Bread ' for a rite which the disciples practised from the first. A comparison with Lk 22:19 and 1 Cor 10:16 shows that the reference is to the Holy Eucharist, and the action which symbolized the death of Christ, *cf.* comm. on 2:42 and 46. St Paul celebrates the Breaking of Bread, on the Sunday, at Troas, 20:7, 11, and perhaps too, on board ship, 27:35. There may also be a reference to the Holy Eucharist in 1:4.

d Holy Order—The laying on of hands is used not only to give the Holy Spirit, but also to confer authority and spiritual powers, within the Church, in the case of the Seven Deacons, and Paul and Barnabas, 6:1–6 ; 13:3 ; *cf.* comm. *in loc.*

In 11:30 St Luke mentions ' presbyters ' in the church at Jerusalem. They collect alms for the poor, and so have a ministry similar to that of the deacons, but higher, as their title and their place immediately after the Apostles suggest. They are found joined with the Apostles at the Council of Jerusalem, 15:4 ; 16:4, and later, 21:18. They evidently form a sort of college, presided over by St James. St Paul also establishes presbyters in the communities he founds, 14:22. In his farewell to those at Ephesus, he calls them ' bishops ' and says they have been appointed by the Holy Spirit, to feed the church of God, to act as unselfish shepherds, and as teachers, 20:28–35. There are also ' prophets ' and ' doctors ', such as we find in St Paul's epistles, possessing charismatic gifts. Their presence in the church at Antioch, shows the approval of the Holy Spirit, as it had done at Jerusalem, 11:27 ; 13:1. *cf.* also § 659.

e Liturgy and Prayer—The Breaking of Bread is surrounded by prayer, the beginnings of the Mass, whilst the rites of ordination, 6:6 ; 13:2–3 ; 14:22, and confirmation, 8:15, are already part of a liturgy. For long too, the Apostles join in the temple liturgy, 2:46 ; 3:1, and so does St Paul, 21:26 ; 22:17, and in prayer in synagogues as well, 16:13–16. Although our Lord had announced the ruin of the temple, it was also the house of his Father. Only gradually was it realized that new wine could not be put into old bottles. The establishment of the church in such places as Antioch, meant that the splendour of the temple could not longer eclipse the Christian assembly for the Breaking of Bread, prayer and praise held in private houses. Even then much of the Jewish liturgy was taken over, and with it the custom of praying at the Third, Sixth and Ninth hour, and at the hour of the evening sacrifice.

f As in his gospel, St Luke is constantly drawing attention to **prayer**. Our Lord had prayed before the Holy Spirit descended on him, Lk 3:21, and the disciples do the same before the Descent at Pentecost. Prayer and the inspiration of the Holy Spirit go hand-in-hand, 4:31. Cornelius, ' always praying to God ', receives the grace of being the first-fruits of the Gentiles ; and St Peter is praying when he has the vision which compels him to take his momentous step, 10:9. St Luke gives us the first recorded prayer of the community, that preceding the election of St Matthias, and one of thanksgiving after the release of St Peter and St John, 4:24–30. The Church prays ' without ceasing ' for St Peter imprisoned by Herod and is answered by his miraculous escape. St Peter and St Paul pray before working miracles, 9:40 ; 28:8. In the gaol of Philippi at midnight, after their scourging, St Paul and Silas praise God, ' and all they that were

in prison heard them ', 16:25. St Paul exhorts the **820f** presbyters at Ephesus, in their care for others, not to neglect their own souls, and then he prays with them, 20:28, 36, as he does with the Christians of Tyre, 21:5. Common prayer is the sign of union. During the great storm, St Paul's prayer saves all those on the ship, and for the welcome accorded to him by the Church at Rome St Paul gives thanks to God, 28:15.

Angels—In the Gospel of the Holy Spirit we are not **g** allowed to forget the spirits that surround God's throne. How often an ' angel of the Lord ' or ' of God ' guides and protects. Two are present after the Ascension. Twice St Peter is rescued from prison by an angel. Philip is sent to the Ethiopian by one, and another sends Cornelius to St Peter. An angel assures St Paul that all on his ship will escape with their lives. When they appear it is in white apparel and shining, so that the face of St Stephen in the presence of the Sanhedrin looks as if it were the face of an angel. The Jewish doctrine about angels, denied only by the Sadducees, 23:8–9, continues in the Church. This is true as well of guardian angels, who appear in the OT, and who were thought to be able to take on the likeness and the voice of their charges. All this is confirmed in the reference to St Peter's guardian angel, 12:15.

The Text—This has come down to us in two forms, **821a** (1) The ' Alexandrian ' Text, that of the great uncial MSS, B, Sin. A. (2) The ' Western ' Text, represented chiefly by D. This latter has many additions, often of vivid details, *cf.* note on 19:9. A number of these additions are found very early, attested even by the papyri. Hence the theory was put forward by F. Blass in 1895 that St Luke brought out two editions of his work, one in Rome, the ' Western ' Text, and a more concise revision for Theophilus. This theory has not won acceptance. A minute examination of each of the divergent passages seems to show that the great majority of the changes in the Western Text are made in the interests of clarity or piety. It is a corrected text. The classical example of this occurs in the Apostolic Decree, 15:20, 29 ; 21:25. The Western Text reduces the four prohibitions to three, ' to abstain from meat sacrificed to idols, from blood, and from fornication ' and adds the golden rule. Thus prohibitions, chiefly concerned with ritual matters in particular circumstances, have become a moral code of universal application, forbidding, as some of these MSS have it, ' idolatry, homicide and fornication '. The most recent research seems to show that the ' Alexandrian ' text has also been corrected, but rather in the interests of accuracy, and the papyri on the whole favour it. It is a safe text, one to be followed for practical purposes, and on it Vg and DV are based, *cf.* Lagrange, *Critique Textuelle, II. La Critique Rationnelle, Livre II, Les Actes des Apôtres*, 387–463, for an exhaustive discussion ; *cf.* also §§ 581–3.

Chronology—[The reader should take note that Fr **b** Dessain's system of chronology in Ac differs at certain points from the views taken elsewhere by other contributors. Chronological indications should therefore be checked against the Chart in §§ 674–6, and also with other articles such as the commentaries on St Luke's Gospel and on Galatians.—Gen. Ed.].

The Title—though probably not due to St Luke, is very early, being found in St Irenaeus and the Muratorian Canon. Its best attested form is ' Acts of Apostles ' (Sin, B and D), which well describes this history of some of the acts of some of the Apostles.

I–XII The Preaching of the Gospel in Palestine and 822a Syria, St Peter (A.D. 30–44).
I 1–26 Introductory—1–5 The Prologue—1. St Luke begins by linking up Ac with his Gospel. In Lk 1:1 he had already presented his credentials, which make it unnecessary to repeat them. ' The *first* treatise ', *i.e.* the Gospel. The use of ' first ' rather than ' former ' does not, in the Greek, imply that St Luke planned a third volume, *cf.* § 815*b*. The story, only sketched in the Gospel, of the events between the Resurrection and the

822a Ascension, is now filled in, and the impression left by Lk 24:50 ff., that the one followed immediately on the other, is removed, *cf.* v 3. There is still no reference to the appearances in Galilee, but these did not concern St Luke's theme, the spread of the Church from Jerusalem. For Theophilus see Lk 1:3. **2.** Jesus, guided by the Holy Spirit, gave the Apostles their last great commandments, especially that to preach to all nations. It was important to emphasize the part played by the Holy Spirit in this order. St Luke refers elsewhere to our Lord's guidance by the Spirit, Lk 3:22 ; 4:1, 14, 18. **3.** Ac begins and ends with the preaching of the Kingdom of God, *cf.* 28:23 and 31, and the Kingdom is always that on earth, the Church, even, as the context shows, in 14:21. **4.** ' Eating together ' is the translation of all ancient versions and commentators, including Chrysostom in five separate places. This is a rare sense of the Greek word, and the weak but more common sense of ' gathering ' is sometimes preferred. The meal in common was a further proof of the Resurrection, a sign of the union of Jesus and his Apostles, and may even have included the Eucharist. They were to await in the Holy City the Promise of the Father, as in Lk 24:49, the Holy Spirit, promised in the OT, and also by our Lord, Jn 14:16 ; 16:7. **5.** The distinction between the baptism of John and that of the Holy Spirit was made in Lk 3:16. The outpouring of the Holy Spirit is called a ' baptism ', or cleansing, as in Jl 2:28 and Is 44:3, but the sacrament of Baptism is not meant. This we may presume, with St Augustine and St Chrysostom, the Apostles had already received. Leaving aside the case of Cornelius, Christian baptism always preceded the baptism with the Spirit, as is clearly asserted in 2:38.

b **6-12 The Ascension—6.** The Apostles, ' *who had* come together ', *i.e.* for the meal, or perhaps, ' *who had come with him* ', *i.e.* on the road to Bethany, asked. Their question shows that they still hoped for the immediate reign of the Messias, with themselves as his ministers, *cf.* Lk 19:11. They connected the outpouring of the Holy Spirit not merely with Messianic times, but with the Second Coming, and the Final Kingdom. They are reminded that this will only be set up when the whole world has been preached to, *cf.* Mt 24:14. ' Lord ' is a divine title ; *cf.* note on 2:36. **7.** Only the Father knows the times, ' *which he hath fixed by his own authority* ', *cf.* Mk 13:32. **8.** ' But you shall receive *power, when the Holy Spirit shall come upon you* ' ; ' power ' has no article, and is followed by a genitive absolute. Though the timing of God's plan is not revealed, the Apostles will receive the strength their mission requires, and are told its extension. Unlike that in Mt 10:5, it is to the whole world, as in Lk 24:47, *cf.* Mt 28:19, Mk 16:15. Ac will describe the first fulfilment of this programme, in the power of the Spirit. **9.** The Ascension is described elsewhere only in Mk 16:19 and Lk 24 :51 ; *cf.* Art. by P. Benoit in RB (1949) 161 ff. Christ seated on the right hand of God was realized to be so close still, through his Spirit, that the Ascension was not greatly emphasized. The cloud is the veil that hides God in the OT, and also at our Lord's baptism and transfiguration. **10.** The Apostles ' *strained their eyes towards heaven* ', KNT. **11.** The angels bring the Apostles back to earth, and console them in their disappointment at our Lord's answer as to the Second Coming. He will come again in the clouds, *cf.* Mt 26:64. This was not a promise that the Apostles would witness the Second Coming, and when they began to die, none thought the promise vain. **12.** This verse can be reconciled with Lk 24:50 if we suppose that our Lord led the Apostles along the road to Bethany, as far as Mount Olivet. Six furlongs was a Sabbath walk, the distance of the first slopes from Jerusalem.

c **13-14 The Apostles wait in Jerusalem—13.** The Upper Room was more than probably the Cenacle, and the scene of the Descent of the Holy Spirit. This, the first Christian Church, seems to have been the house of St Mark's mother, *cf.* 12:12, and F. Prat, *Jésus-Christ*, II, 521. On the apostolic list see Lk 6:15. **14.** This is the

last mention of our Lady, and she is with the infant church. St Luke, as so often, emphasizes the part played by women, and prayer the bond of union, *cf.* 2:42 ; 20:36, etc.

15-26 The choosing of an Apostle—St Luke was greatly interested in the filling up of the apostolic college, since the only other addition was St Paul. Apostles are those marked out personally by Christ, *cf.* Gal 1:1, and P. Batiffol, *Eglise Naissante*, 52. St Luke always uses the word in this technical sense in Ac, except 14:4 and 13, where Barnabas is included ; and with St Paul who seems to have spread the use of it, he prefers it to the ' disciples ' of the Gospels. **15.** St Peter is the leader in this important matter, the powers conferred in the Gospels already active. **16.** St Peter's faith as to the inspiration of Scripture is here revealed. **18-19.** These verses seem to be St Luke's own account. They interrupt the speech of St Peter, who would hardly have described the event so realistically, nor referred to the language of the inhabitants of Jerusalem as ' their tongue '. St Irenaeus omits them, *Adv. Haer.*, III, xii, 1. Presumably the rope broke, or the branch to which it was tied, and Judas fell forward, *cf.* Mt 27:5-8. There the name of the field is derived from its price, that of the blood of our Lord. St Luke seems to derive it from the blood of Judas. Perhaps both etymologies were current. **20.** Ps 68:26 referred to the enemies of David, the type of the Messias. ' His *office* let another take ', Ps 108:8, formed part of David's curse of Doeg, the prototype of Judas. **21-22.** An apostle is a witness, *cf.* § 819*c* and 1:8 ; 10:37-43 ; 1 Cor 9:1 ; 15:7-8. **23.** Nothing certain is known of Joseph or Matthias. **24.** The first recorded prayer of the community is addressed to Jesus, for ' Lord ' must refer to him, as in 21. He had chosen the Twelve, and must complete the number. He ' knew what was in man ', Jn 2:25. **25.** ' His own place ', the place he had chosen for himself. The Aramaic phrase of which this seems to be a translation is simply a euphemism for ' he died '. **26.** Christ must choose the new Apostle, especially as his Spirit had not yet come, to give St Peter full authority. Recourse was had to lots, in the OT, and for filling the temple offices. There is no mention of imposing hands on Matthias.

II 1-42 The Day of Pentecost—1-4 The Descent of **8** **the Holy Spirit—1.** ' *When the day of Pentecost arrived* '. Originally a thanksgiving for the harvest, Pentecost later celebrated also the giving of the Law on Sinai ; *cf.* § 113*h*. If the Crucifixion was on 14th Nisan, Pentecost fell on a Sunday, the traditional day, and, if in A.D. 30, on May 28th. The scene and actors are the same as in 1:13-15, and their unity is again emphasized. **2.** The coming of the Holy Spirit was made known, first by sound, the wind that could be heard in the City, v 6. The wind was a symbol of the Holy Spirit, *cf.* Jn 3:8, who would soon disperse the little community to the whole world. **3.** The second sign was for sight, tongues of fire. ' And there appeared to them tongues, as it were of fire, *which parted and rested on each one of them* '. ' Observe how it is always " as it were ", and rightly : that you may have no gross sensible notions of the Spirit '. Chrys., *Hom. in Act.* 4 PG 60, 40. Fire symbolized the power and presence of God, Ex 3:2 ; Mal 3:2-3. *Cf.* the prophecy that our Lord would baptize with the Holy Spirit and fire, 1:5 ; Lk 3:16 and 12:49-50. The tongues were first united, a sign of unity, and then parted, so that there was one over each person present, to show that they were to preach to all the ' nations dispersed ', for this was what the tongues symbolized, as the next verse shows. **4.** All were filled with the Holy **h** Spirit, although the Apostles had already received him, Jn 20:22. ' *And they began to speak in other languages, according as the Spirit gave them utterance* '. Their word was to reach all nations who would understand each in his own tongue. A new spiritual language was to be spoken to the whole world. The Spirit has now been given, Jn 7:39, as the rest of Acts exemplifies. All receive the Spirit, and all must share in the apostolic

3b work. The Holy Spirit brings the Church to life and begins to form the members of a new universal kingdom. The Apostles especially are inspired. St Peter can now preach boldly and interpret prophecy. The external gifts of the Spirit are designed to manifest his internal mission. The Spirit of the adoption of sons is poured out in abundance. Many of the Fathers go further than this and see in Pentecost the first giving of the divine adoption and indwelling. Thus they make a distinction between the grace of the OT, and the giving of the Spirit there only foretold, Is 32:15 ; Jer 31:33 ; Ez 11:19 ; 36:26 ; Zach 12:10 ; Jl 2:28 ; *cf.* G. Philips, *La Grâce des Justes de l'Ancien Testament*, ETL 23 (1947) 521 ff. There is a parallel too between Sinai and the Upper Room, *cf.* Ex 20:18. On the feast of the Law, a new Law is given, but for all nations.

c 5-13 The Miracle of Pentecost—5. Many Jews from the Dispersion must have been in Jerusalem for the feast, though the text seems to suggest that those present were permanent dwellers there, *e.g.* for study, like St Paul, but who had been born abroad. Yet these too would be bilingual. *Cf.* R. A. Knox, *Epistles and Gospels*, 151. **6.** ' *And at this sound the multitude came together, and they were bewildered, because each one heard them speaking in his own language* '. The sound of the wind drew the crowds towards the Upper Room. All would have understood Greek sufficiently, but the miracle taught that the preaching was to go to the Gentiles, ' to every nation under heaven '. **7-8.** As the disciples moved into the street and, no doubt, towards the temple to give thanks, the different national groups each heard one who spoke their language. The miracle was one of speaking, not of hearing. **9-10.** The list goes roughly from east to west. **11.** ' Both Jews and proselytes ' perhaps qualifies only the visitors from Rome, but the presence of proselytes further stresses universality. The Fathers draw the parallel between Babel, when God, because of their spirit of pride, dispersed men by confusing their tongues, and Pentecost when the Spirit of God brought all to unity again, in the Church. Chrys. *ibid*, St Aug. *in Ps. 50*, PL 36, 636. **12-13.** To those who could only understand one or two of the languages the scene must have resembled that in 1 Cor 14:23, except that the ordinary gift of tongues could be understood by none of the audience. Gk ' *sweet wine* '. It was too early for the new.

4a 14-36 St Peter's Speech—The change in the disciple who had denied his Master constitutes psychological evidence of the Resurrection. Still more, in the clear explanations St Peter gives of his faith, here and subsequently, we see the Holy Spirit working in the way our Lord had promised during his last discourse, *e.g.* Jn 14:26 ; 16:7-14. St Luke explains, v 40, that he has only given a summary of this tactful speech, which begins with an apologia for the disciples, and then shows, chiefly because of his Resurrection, that Jesus is the Messias.

b 14-21 The Miracle Explained—14. On the leadership of St Peter, see § 819*d, e*. The solemn exordium reveals his new confidence. **15.** The day was divided from daybreak into twelve hours, making the third about 9 a.m. **16.** Jl 2:28-32, quoted from LXX, has been fulfilled. This described the outpouring of the Spirit which was to herald the establishment of the kingdom of the Messias. v 22 ff. will prove that the Messias has come. **17.** To interpret the prophecy, St Peter adds ' in the last days ', *i.e.* the last age, Messianic times, *cf.* Is 2:2. ' All flesh ' will receive the Spirit, and no longer only prophets. Old and young, all mankind is to be saved, *cf.* 21. **19-20.** *Cf.* art. on the Second Coming, § 671*q*. **21.** The Lord in Jl is Yahweh, but St Peter seems to refer to our Lord, whose kingdom must be entered by those to be saved.

c 22-24 Although he died, Jesus rose again, and is therefore the Messias—22. St Luke faithfully reproduces the archaic guarded phrases, so necessary if these fiercely monotheistic Jews were to be led to the truth,

but so unlike Mt 16:16, and so unnecessary in A.D. 63. **824c** **23.** St Peter removes the difficulty that had once been his, Mt 16:21-22, how one crucified could be the Messias. All was by God's plan and foreknowledge, so too St Paul, 13:27-29. Jesus, submitting to the will of his Father was delivered up by him, *cf.* Rom 8:32. Jews killed our Lord, ' wicked men ', Gentiles were only instruments. **24.** Gk, ' *The Sorrows* [*Heb.* ' Bonds '] *of death, because it was not possible for it* [*death*] *to hold him* '.

25-31 A Scripture Proof of the Resurrection—This is **d** based on Ps 15(16):8-11. David spoke, in view of the Messias, words which were only fulfilled in his case, and not in David's. So too St Paul, 13:36. Jews set great store by such proofs. **25.** ' *I saw the Lord always before me* ', at my right, as my defender. **26.** The joy is because his body will live on. **27.** Hell or Hades, not in the modern sense, but Sheol the abode of the dead, is a synonym for death, ' *the place of death* ', *cf.* 1 Pet 3:19. **28.** The speaker will see God. **29.** The triumphant conclusion : the psalm cannot apply to David, whose tomb is mentioned by Josephus, and was known to St Jerome. **30.** Yet David was a prophet, and knew that one of his descendants would be Messias, Ps 102(103):2. **31.** So it must apply to the Resurrection, which he foresaw. The Jews interpreted Ps 15 of the Messias, not David, Ez 34:23 ; 37:24. For explanation of the prophecy see E. F. Sutcliffe, *The OT and the Future Life* (1946) 79.

32-36 The Apostles' Witness to the Resurrection : e Conclusion—32. Fifty days afterwards, St Peter can proclaim without fear of contradiction, that our Lord rose, and that his tomb was empty, *cf.* note on 1:22. **33.** After his Ascension, Christ does what was attributed to God in 17, and sends the Promise, see note on 1:4. Thus the Spirit is on earth, because Christ is in heaven, Jn 16:7. **34-35.** One more psalm, 109:1, in which David speaks either of himself or the Messias, shows that Jesus is the Messias. St Peter learned this from our Lord, Mt 22:43, as also his other applications of psalms, Lk 24:44. Jesus receives the divine name ' Lord ', and ' sit on my right ' means ' have the same power as I '. **36.** The texts converge to the final ' Jesus is Lord, (Kyrios), and Messias '. The two words are roughly synonymous here. Jesus is the Messianic King, he exercises the sovereign powers of God, following his exaltation (v 33). See L. Cerfaux, *Le Titre Kyrios*. RSPT 12 (1923) 137-8, where the purely Jewish and OT origin of the title is proved. On how the Resurrection manifested our Lord's sovereignty, and allowed his divine power to shine out, see M. de la Taille, *Mysterium Fidei*, 171 and 286.

37-40 The Effect of St Peter's Speech—37. Many **f** realize that they have crucified their Messias. **38.** ' *Repent* '. The Baptist and our Lord had begun thus, Mt 3:2 ; 4:17, and the Apostles had been told to continue, Lk 24:47. To Semites the name is the person. ' Baptism in the name ' means ' to be, by the fact of baptism, consecrated, dedicated, subjected to someone ', F. Prat, *op cit*, II (1945) 466 ; § 650*a-o*. Jesus has been shown to be the Messias. To join his community, to belong to him, his baptism must be received. Thus ' baptism in the name of Jesus ' is not a liturgical formula, but distinguishes Christian baptism from *e.g.* that of John the Baptist, 19:5, or that given to proselytes. Mt 28:19 and St Paul's question in 19:3 show that knowledge of the Holy Trinity was necessary, and each Person is mentioned here in 38-39. Forgiveness of sins, a divine prerogative, comes through Jesus. The gift of the Holy Spirit included the divine Indwelling, Sanctifying Grace and Confirmation. **39.** Salvation is first for the Jews, but also for those ' far off ', not Jews of the Dispersion, who were already called, but Gentiles. The Prophets had taught that the reign of the Messias would be universal, *cf.* 2:17, and there were our Lord's express commands. The enlightenment St Peter still required was as to the *way* men were to be admitted to the Church. See note on 10:1.

824f 40. The perverse generation are the Jews who have rejected the Messias, cf. Mt 12:39.

825a 41-42 The Life led by the Newly Baptized—41. Most would already have been familiar with our Lord's life and teaching. All were perhaps not baptized that day ; and see Jn 4:1. **42.** ' *In the teaching of the apostles and in fellowship, in the breaking of bread, and in prayers* '. Vg and DV reduce to three these ' four marks '. There is authoritative teaching from the first, cf. § 819c, and obviously a much fuller doctrine than that to be found in the apologetic discourses of the Apostles. The whole group, Apostles, old disciples and converts form a ' communion ', united with each other and with Jesus. Chrysostom and many non-Catholics see in the ' breaking of bread ' a reference only to common meals, which are mentioned in 46. It is true that this breaking was originally a Jewish rite of thanksgiving for food, but it soon became the earliest technical term for the Eucharist, which at first was celebrated at a meal. It is used of the Eucharist in 20:7, 11, and very probably in 46, and perhaps 27:35 and Lk 24:35. All the accounts of the Institution say that our Lord ' broke bread '. In 1 Cor 10:16 St Paul uses the phrase, and emphasizes how the Eucharist symbolizes and causes the union mentioned in 42. His teaching came from the Twelve, 1 Cor 15:3, 11. The prayers are those surrounding the Eucharist, the beginnings of the Christian liturgy, held in private assemblies, rather than prayers in the temple.

b II 43-V 42 The Heroic Primitive Days at Jerusalem. II 43-47 The Life of the First Christians—The whole section which St Luke must have derived from an eyewitness in the church at Jerusalem, is broken by three summaries, vv 42–47, 4:32–35, 5:12–16, describing the state of the community, and the impression it made externally. **43.** These vv even more than the miracle of Pentecost, reveal the Power that had come to dwell in the Church. Awe was caused by miracles, cf. Lk 5:26, etc., but also by the union and love shown, and it was felt by those outside. **44-45.** St Luke in the Gospel stressed our Lord's teaching on voluntary poverty more than the other evangelists, Lk 12:32–34 ; 16:19 ; 6:20. Here he shows the Apostles teaching the life they had learned and lived with Jesus. The kingdom is sought first, hence the simplicity and joy, but the sharing of goods, though an effect of detachment, is also the especial proof of mutual love and unity, and attracts those who do not believe, cf. Jn 13:35. See on 4:32–35 for the *voluntary* character of this ' communism ', inspired by faith and love, and respecting individual rights, which is still practised by the Religious Orders. **46.** Besides common goods, there are common prayers in the temple, and a common table. All give themselves up to the Spirit. For centuries in the Church, this was the model for a ' religious life '. Parallel with the temple liturgy, the Eucharist (for the technical term can hardly have a different meaning from that in 42) was celebrated in private houses, as in 1 Cor 16:19 ; Col 4:15, etc. **47.** ' *And the Lord added daily to the company of those who were being saved* '. There is a parallel with our Lord, Lk 2:52. Men ' were being saved ', thanks to joining the community, cf. 1 Cor 1:18 ; 2 Cor 2:15.

c III 1-11 The Cure of the Lame Man—1. The evening sacrifice was at the ninth hour, about 3 p.m. SS. Peter and John are together here, 8:14, and in the Gospels, e.g. Lk 5:10 ; Jn 1:35. **2.** The Gate was probably that to the court of the women, and a good post for a beggar, since all entering the temple used it. **4.** The beggar must witness the miracle as plainly as possible. **6.** St Peter has obeyed the counsel of poverty. The name represents the Person whose power effects the cure. Our Lord worked miracles in his own Name, the Apostles invoke his authority. **7.** ' His feet and *ankles* '. The man had been born lame, had to be carried everywhere, and was 40 years old, 4:22. **11.** Solomon's porch, at the east of the temple. was used by those who wished to teach, 5:12 ; Jn 10:23.

12-26 St Peter's Speech—This has the same argument **82** as the first discourse. The lesson of the miracle is driven home, Jesus is shown to be the Messias, and there is a concluding exhortation to repentance. The same main themes will be found in every speech of St Peter, and in that of St Paul, ch 13, for all aimed at setting forth the new faith to the Jews.

12-16 The Miracle is the Work of Jesus Risen—12. e ' *Why do you fasten your eyes upon us, as though by a power or piety of our own we had made him walk ?* ' **13.** God is mentioned in a way that would win Jewish hearts. Jesus is his παῖς, as in 26 and 4:27, 30, translated in Vg and DV ' son ' or ' child '. It probably has this sense in ch 4, when used among the faithful, but it also means ' servant '. Here in his speech to Jews, St Peter aims primarily at showing that our Lord is the Messias, the Servant, familiar to his audience, whose sufferings are described in Is 53. He wishes to prove once more, that Jesus, in spite of his crucifixion, is the Messias. The title ' servant ' is reserved for our Lord. The Apostles call themselves the ' slaves ' δοῦλοι of God. **14.** The Holy One, and the Just are in the OT Messianic titles, cf. Is 53:11, and also especially attributes of God. Our Lord is called the Just One in 7:52 and 22:14, also in speeches to Jews. In this title and that of ' servant ', St Luke preserves the names under which our Lord's divinity was partly veiled, for those not yet able to receive it, cf. § 817a and c. St Peter emphasizes Jewish guilt more than in 2:23. **15.** Our Lord is the author, not of physical life, for the Jews could hardly yet be told that they had killed their Creator, but of the supernatural life of grace, as in Jn 10:10, 28 ; 17:2, etc. **16** is awkward and may be tr. ' *The name of Jesus, thanks to faith in it, has made this man strong, whom you see and know : and the faith which comes from Jesus has given him this perfect health in the presence of you all* '. Thus the power of Jesus is the chief cause of the miracle, and the faith in his power and name, which Jesus gave to St Peter, its instrumental cause.

17-18 The Jews in Ignorance fulfilled the Prophecies f concerning the Suffering Messias—Again since the scandal of the cross must be removed by showing that all was foretold, Is 53, Ps 21, as our Lord had taught, Lk 24: 26–27. On the ignorance, cf. 1 Cor 2:8 ; Lk 23:34 ; Ac 13:27.

19-26 Exhortation to Repentance—19. ' Repent ', cf. 2:38. **20-21.** ' *In order that times of refreshing may come from the presence of the Lord, and that he may send the Christ appointed to you, Jesus . . . .* ' The conversion of the Jews is a necessary preliminary of the Second Coming, Rom 11:25-26, and this is described not as a judgement, but as the restoration of all things, cf. 2 Pet 3:11–13 ; Is 65:17. **22-23.** Deut 18:15-19 quoted freely. **24.** The appeal to the prophets is extended beyond the Second Coming to all Christ's work and the events since Pentecost. **25.** The promise to Abraham included all races. **26.** ' To you first God *has sent his servant, whom he has raised up, to bring you a blessing, by turning every one of you from your wickedness* '. God raised up, *i.e.* sent into the world, his Messias, to save all men, but the Jews first, as in 13:46 ; Rom 10:11-13. The last phrase is perhaps correctly tr. in DV, with its emphasis on freewill.

IV 1-4 Arrest of St Peter and St John—1-2. The **8** priests, better the high-priests, objected to being accused of murder in crucifying our Lord, the temple police to the crowd in Solomon's Porch, and the Sadducees to the preaching of a resurrection, which implied a general resurrection they denied, 23:8. The Officer, cf. 5:24 and 26, was a priest and like the high-priests, one of the Sadducees, who were always more antagonistic than the Pharisees at this time.

5-7 The Meeting of the Sanhedrin—Annas had been deposed in A.D. 15, but St Luke regards him as associated with his son-in-law Caiaphas, who was high-priest, A.D. 18–36 ; cf. Lk 3:2. He ruled through his son-in-law, and later through his sons.

8-12 St Peter's Speech before the Sanhedrin—8. He **b**

who had trembled before the servant-maid, is fearless before the high-priest, through a grace of the Holy Spirit, as our Lord had promised, Mt 10:19 ; Lk 21:14. He rather preaches the new Faith than defends himself. **9.** ' A good deed done to a cripple, *by what means this man has been healed* '. He was present, *cf.* 14. **10.** *Cf.* note on 3:6. **11.** Another prophetic text is quoted, to prove the Resurrection, used by our Lord, Lk 20:17, and repeated in 1 Pet 2:7. The Messias is the corner-stone of the New House of Israel. **12.** Salvation comes through the Person of our Lord, all mention of the law being conspicuously absent, and it is perhaps implied that the saving name of Yahweh has been superseded by the Holy Name.
13-18 The Deliberation of the Sanhedrin—13. ' *Unlearned, ordinary* men '. SS Peter and John were ordinary citizens and unlearned in the teaching of the Rabbis. Their scriptural knowledge aroused astonishment. **17.** The Person of Jesus was not to be the basis of their teaching.
19-22 The Reply of Peter and John—19. God must be obeyed, even against the supreme authority in Israel, and it was from Jesus that the order to preach came, 1:8 ; Lk 24:47. **21.** ' For all men glorified *God for what had happened* '.
23-31 Thanksgiving Prayer of the Church—24. The first recorded prayer after 1:24, begs for grace and miracles to spread the faith. Gk ' *Sovereign* Lord '. *Cf.* Ps 145:6. **25.** Ps 2:1. **27.** The same word παῖς is used as in 3:13, here and in 30. Within the Church it seems best translated ' Son ', especially in the context of the Ps, in which God calls the Messias his Son. He is the Christ, proclaimed to be Son, at his baptism, Ps 2:2, 7. Only St Luke describes Herod's part in the Passion. **28.** *Cf.* 2:23 and 1 Pet 1:20. **29.** The prayer is not for enemies to be confounded, but for the spread of the Gospel. **31.** God shows that the prayer is answered, and a further outpouring of the Spirit enables the Gospel to be preached boldly.
32-35 Summary Description of the Life of the Community—Charity and miracles are the work of the Spirit, *cf.* 2:43-47. These vv prepare for the accounts of Barnabas and Ananias. **32.** Sharing of goods is due to the unity produced by the Holy Spirit, the soul of the Church, *cf.* Encyclical *Mystici Corporis*, 55 (CTS). **33.** The Apostles gave ' *their witness to the Resurrection* ', now confirmed by miracles. **34-35.** The Gk participles here, and the imperfect tense in 2:45 show that property was sold, from time to time, by the owners of it, according as the Church's need dictated. **The sharing of goods was always voluntary.** ' All things ' in Lucan parlance has no absolute sense, and in 32 a general picture is being given. The story of Ananias and Saphira, *cf.* 5:4, makes it clear that they were not bound to sell, and that after they had, the price was still theirs. When Barnabas gave all his property, such exceptional generosity was chronicled. There are examples of houses held privately at Jerusalem, 12:12 ; 21:16. St James, in his Epistle, reveals the existence of rich and poor there. The community of goods does not seem to have been very successful, 6:1, and other churches had continually to send alms, *voluntarily*, ' each man according to his ability ', to Jerusalem, 11:29.
36-37 The Generosity of Barnabas—He sold all his property, and later, like St Paul, worked rather than ' live by the gospel ', 1 Cor 9:6. St Luke loved this lover of poverty, who wanted to give himself up to the Spirit, and found himself caught in the labours and quarrels of a missionary. He must often have met the Apostles at the Eucharist, in the house of the mother of his cousin St Mark, 12:12, Col 4:10, and enjoyed their confidence. He was a large-minded man, and introduced his fellow Hellenist St Paul to them, 9:27. Later they sent him on the delicate mission to the Gentile church at Antioch. Being ' full of the Holy Ghost ', he approved of what had been done, fetched St Paul to help, and together they gave Christianity its orientation 11:22-26. They went on the relief mission to Jerusalem, and returned with St Mark, 12:25. For

the later history of Barnabas see 13-15, and note on **826e** 15:39.
V 1-11 Ananias and Saphira—Here and by the mur- **f** murings, 6:1, we learn that there were shadows, even in the Golden Age. **2.** Through avarice part of the price was retained, through vanity it was pretended that all had been given. **3.** ' Why hath Satan *filled thy heart* ? ' The evil spirit led them to attempt to deceive the Holy Spirit, who filled and possessed the Church and the Apostles, and hence whose spokesman St Peter was. **4.** ' While it remained *unsold* did it not remain to thee ? and after it was sold was it not *at thy disposal* ? ' There was no compulsion to give up the whole price. These verses reveal the personality and divinity of the Holy Spirit. **6.** ' And the young men rising, *wrapped him up* . . .' Both circumstances and climate made quick burial advisable. **8.** St Peter wished to enable Saphira to repent and be truthful, *cf.* Chrysostom, *Hom.* XII. **9.** He does not call down death on her, but announces the judgement of God. **10.** The grave punishment was exemplary, to show the respect due to the Church, and preserve discipline, both so necessary for the persecuted infant community. Ananias and Saphira had received the Holy Spirit and many graces, ' yet it is to be believed that after this life God spared them, for his mercy is great '. St Aug. *Serm.* 148. 1 Cor 11:32 also suggests that death may have a merciful purpose. **11.** ' Church ' used by our Lord in Mt 16:18 now first occurs in Ac as the name of the community at Jerusalem.
12-16 Miracles and Growth, the Third Summary—12. **g** As our Lord had promised, Jn 14:12, miracles come in answer to the prayer of 4:30. **13.** ' The rest ' seem to be those with a certain standing, held back by fear of the Sanhedrin, as contrasted with the people, *cf.* 4:21 and Jn 7:48-49. **15.** ' Beds and *pallets* ', *i.e.* rich and poor were brought out. What warrant this verse and 19:12 provide for attitudes regarded as typically Catholic ! Small examples of that preservation of type, which is the ' first note of a genuine development '. **16.** ' And there came also together *a multitude from the towns around Jerusalem* '. The church had begun to spread in Judaea.
17-42 The Second Persecution of the Apostles : 17-21a **827a** **Arrest and Release—17.** ' The party ' of the Sadducees was alarmed in 4:2, by the teaching, now rather, by the popularity of the Apostles. **19.** The angel led the Apostles out, in such a way that the sentries who were at their posts could not see them, 23. **20.** In Jn 6:69 St Peter says ' Thou hast the words of eternal life ', *cf.* 13:26, the new life of union with God, *cf.* § 818d. **21a.** The day's work begins early in the East.
21b-28 The Apostles re-arrested and brought before **b** **the Sanhedrin—21.** ' The council, even all *the senate of the Jewish people* '. **28.** ' *We laid a strict command on you* '. The high-priest does not refer to the miraculous escape, but accuses the Apostles of disobeying the command of 4:18, and secondly of stirring up the people to seek the lives of the authorities who condemned Jesus, *cf.* Mt 27:25. Clearly the Christians were already a numerous body.
29-32 The Answer of the Apostles—29. St Peter is the leader. Our Lord's command to preach has the authority of God, *cf.* 4:19. **30.** The main facts are once more outlined. Jesus was raised up from the dead. **31.** ' Prince ' is a Messianic title, the deliverer. Saviour completes the idea. Jesus is the leader who saves, the ' author of our salvation ', 3:15 ; Heb 2:10. **32.** The Holy Spirit witnesses to Jesus by outward signs, by inspiring the Apostles' preaching, and by moving mens' hearts to accept it. On this witness of the Holy Spirit see Jn 15:26-27 ; Rom 8:16. The Gift of the Spirit is not for the Apostles only, but for all who obey God.
33-39a The Advice of Gamaliel—33-34. The violent **c** reaction of the Council was calmed by Gamaliel the Elder. He was probably the grandson of Hillel, the founder of the liberal party among the Pharisees. According to the rabbinical writings, he was held in

827c great esteem, and given the title of Rabban. It was said that when he died ' the Law ceased to be held in honour '. He was renowned for his tolerant views, exemplified here, and was the master of St Paul, 22:3. **36.** *Gk* Theudas. Jos. *Ant.* XX. 5, 1. mentions a Messianic movement with a leader of this name, which was put down in A.D. 45. Then a large multitude was involved, and it was with difficulty that they were suppressed. Theudas is a common contraction for many names, and so there must have been a much earlier rebellion, of the kind that was then frequent, to which St Luke here refers. **37.** Judas of Galilee, several times mentioned by Josephus, led a rebellion against the census of A.D. 6–7. This was to have been used for taxation purposes ; and to pay taxes to foreigners was considered a violation of fidelity to Yahweh. **39a.** Gamaliel's advice is in keeping with his character. His prophetic words have lost none of their force. There was a legend that Gamaliel later became a Christian, but his advice was dictated by prudence rather than sympathy, as the comparisons he employs show. And as he is always held in honour in the Talmud, the story of his conversion can hardly be true. St Paul disregarded the prudent advice of his master.

39b–42 The Release of the Apostles—40. The Apostles were scourged, presumably with forty stripes save one, for disregarding the prohibition to preach. **41.** They rejoiced to suffer in the interests of Jesus, as he had told them to, Mt 5:11–12. **42.** ' To teach and preach *Jesus as the Christ* ', *i.e.* Messias.

828a **VI 1–VIII 3 The Deacons and St Stephen. A.D. 36 (?)** —This section describes the advance made by the Hellenist Christians, and St Luke must have derived it from sources preserved by them, perhaps at Antioch, after persecution had driven them from Jerusalem. The transitoriness of the temple and Law are proclaimed, and hence the autonomy of Christianity.

VI 1–7 The Seven Deacons—1. ' *As* the disciples were increasing in number, *the Hellenists murmured* against the Hebrews '. Some time had evidently elapsed since the events in ch 5. The Hellenists were the Greek-speaking Jews of the Dispersion (not Hellenes, Gentile Greeks, *cf.* 11:20), and the Hebrews were Aramaic-speaking Jews of Palestine. The charm of the idyllic years is broken, and the first disagreement, though immediately remedied, has great effects. The care for widows, *cf.* 9:39, and the reference to the daughters of Philip, 21:9, reveal the esteem in which chastity was held. [An interesting addition in Codex Bezae—'in the ministry of the Hebrews' contains a hint that the Hebrews may already have had deacons of their own —Gen. Ed.] **2–3.** The Apostles were teachers, § 819*c cf.* 1 Cor 1:17, and must pray continually, v 4, not only privately, but publicly, and at the Eucharist. They were above petty quarrels, and could not undertake the service of tables. **5.** All the names are Gk, and Nicholas was not even a Jew by birth. Most probably all were Hellenists, Hebrews forming a small minority. **6.** The Seven were chosen by all, and accepted by the Apostles, who by the qualifications they required, v 3, by prayer and the laying on of hands, showed that they were conferring a spiritual power, and making sacred ministers. The deacons not only supervised the distribution of meals, but from the first were chiefly concerned with spiritual affairs ; Stephen and Philip preach, and Philip too baptises, *cf.* DTC Art. *Ordre*, XI, 1239. Though never called *deacons* in Ac, the Seven perform the same functions as the deacons of St Paul's Epistles, and St Luke knew he was describing the origin of the office. **7.** It seems to be implied that the increase (note especially the numerous conversions among the priests) was due to the preaching of the deacons.

b **8–15 The Preaching, Miracles and Arrest of St Stephen** —St Peter and the Twelve had shown that our Lord was the Messias, but like their Master, they still kept the whole Jewish Law. St Stephen now develops the teaching as to the temporary nature of the Law, which the New Covenant was to fulfil and replace, Mt 5:17 ; 19:7–8, and of which Jesus was the Master, Mt 5:22 ; 12:8, and the prophecies as to the destruction of the temple, to be superseded by the spiritual temple of Christ's Body, and by adorers in spirit and truth, Jn 4:23–24. Thus St Stephen proclaims the independence of Christianity, he is the father of the Gentile Church, the precursor of Barnabas and St Paul, and for that he is martyred. **8.** ' Full of grace and *power* '. Deacons share the apostolic power of miracles. **9.** ' The Synagogue *of the Freedmen, as it is called* ', composed originally of descendants of Jews taken to Rome as slaves, by Pompey, in 63 B.C., who perhaps shared a synagogue with the Jews from Africa. Among the Jews from Cilicia was St Paul. The Hellenist Jews reacted violently to the preaching of their former colleague, and later we find St Paul ' disputing ' with them, 9:29. **10.** ' They were not able to resist the wisdom and *the Spirit, with which he spoke* '. Here, and still more in the speech in ch 7, Jesus was keeping the promise of Lk 21:12–15, for this true witness of his. **11–12.** The Hellenists resort to false accusers, and stir up the until then friendly people. **13–14.** St Stephen's teaching is travestied ; *cf.* Mk 14:58. **15.** How often when filled with the Holy Spirit, have saints and mystics had their faces thus transfigured !

VII 1–53 The Speech of St Stephen before the Sanhedrin —He only indirectly answers his accusers by the reverent way he speaks of God's care of Israel, by his praise of Moses, and by showing he speaks of the temple as the prophets had done. His speech is most skilful. He outlines the whole history of the People of God, and, before his Jewish audience, only thus could he obtain a hearing for his thesis that theirs was a transitory dispensation, to be succeeded by adoration in spirit and truth. The speech is so ' alive ' that it leads to the murder of its author. He is not on the defensive, but trying to convince others, a witness, a ' martyr '. St Paul heard the speech, and many of its ideas can be paralleled in his epistles. St Stephen speaks as a Jew to Jews, and uses the allegorical exegetical methods of the Rabbis, whence the closeness of the parallels with Heb. There are also traces of Alexandrinisms, and it is thought that St Stephen had studied in the Jewish schools there.

2–16 Abraham and the Patriarchs—God dealt with them outside the Promised Land, and the Promise and Covenant of Circumcision was made long before the Mosaic Law, which could, it was implied, be followed by a more spiritual regime, *cf.* Gal 3:17 ; Mt 19:8. **2.** Anxious to win over his hearers, St Stephen begins by addressing them with respect and friendliness. ' The God of *the Glory* '. ' Glory ' refers to the cloud (Shekinah), which made known God's presence. St Stephen recalls that God had appeared outside the Holy Land, and before the temple was built. Gen 12 says Abraham received his command in Harran. Possibly he was twice commanded, *cf.* Gen 15:7. In any case, here, and in other divergences from the Heb. text in his speech, St Stephen was following LXX, or the current Jewish traditions, and the inspired writer has reported him accurately. The divergences do not affect the argument. **4.** Gen 11:26 and 32 imply that when God removed Abraham into Canaan his father was still living. **9.** There is implied the comparison between Joseph's treatment by his brothers, and that of Jesus by the Jews. **16.** Gen 23:17 and 33:19 say Jacob bought the field from the children of Hemor, and Abraham a tomb at Mambre.

17–43 The Age of Moses—It was the Jews who rejected Moses as they had Joseph. In his conclusion St Stephen returns to this continual rejection by the Jews of their prophets, 51–53. **22** is used by the Fathers to justify the study of pagan literature. **25.** The parallel is plain between Moses and Jesus. **30.** Holy ground and a revelation of God exist elsewhere than in the temple. An angel appeared, but it was God who spoke. An angel represented God, here and on Mount Sinai, 38 and 53, as we also learn from Gal 3:19 and Heb 2:2.

37. *Cf.* 3:22. Moses had prophesied Jesus, and in rejecting him, it is the Jews who despise Moses. **42.** God turned from his faithless people, and gave them up, *i.e.* in Heb. parlance, withheld graces, and permitted them to indulge in idolatrous worship of the stars ; *cf.* Ez 20:13. **43.** Am 5:25–27. The Israelites even went so far as to carry a tent for Moloch, and the star of the God Rempha, Saturn. St Stephen changed the original ' Damascus ' to ' Babylon ', interpreting prophecy in the light of history, as was the Rabbis' custom. See also commentary on Am 5:25.

44–50 From Moses to Solomon, the Tabernacle was before the Temple—Thus God can again ordain that he should be worshipped elsewhere than in the temple and at Jerusalem, Jn 4:21–24. **44–45.** KNT gives the sense, ' In the wilderness our fathers had the tabernacle with them, to remind them of God's covenant : he who spoke to Moses bade him fashion it after the model which had been shown him. And when God dispossessed the Gentiles, to make room for our fathers' coming, our fathers under Josue brought this tabernacle, as an heirloom, into the land which they conquered '. **46.** David, so favoured by God, had no temple. **48.** This is the climax, God ' dwelleth not in houses made with hands '. Solomon had affirmed as much at the dedication of the temple, 3 Kg 8:27. **49.** Is 66:1 had taught the spiritual adoration of Yahweh, before the legalistic exaltation of the temple.

51–53 Conclusion of the Speech—The history of the Jews is finished, and St Stephen is about to lead up to the supreme infidelity. Meanwhile the anger of his audience shows the uselessness of pursuing the argument. ' Uncircumcised ', no better than pagans, hearts hardened and ears closed to the spiritual meaning of their religion. **52.** *Cf.* Mt 5:12 ; Lk 13:34. The speech has led up to our Lord, only now mentioned. ' The Just One ', see note on 3:14. **53.** The mention of angels emphasizes the sacredness of the Law ; *cf.* v 30. Our Lord had often made this final accusation, Mt 23:3.

54–59 The Martyrdom of St Stephen—**54.** The rage of the Jews, accused of not keeping the Law, and hearing Jesus described as Messias, interrupts the speech. **55.** Everywhere else in the NT Jesus is ' seated ' on the right of God, as in Ps 109:1, but now he ' stands ', ready to aid. Only our Lord calls himself the Son of Man, and only before his resurrection. St Stephen uses the title in the sense that our Lord had at his trial, claiming that he was the Messias of Dan 7:13. **57.** The stoning is outside the city, Lev 24:14. The trial was over, the witnesses had been heard. Perhaps there was not a formal sentence by the Sanhedrin, but a general riot. The date may be A.D. 36 (*cf.* Gal 2:1, but see § 676*f, g*), during the interregnum between the sudden recall of Pilate and the appointment of his successor. In A.D. 62, during a similar vacancy, after the death of Festus, the Sanhedrin ordered the stoning of St James, bishop of Jerusalem. **58–59.** As Jesus had given up his spirit to his Father, so Stephen gives his to Jesus, thus revealing his faith in our Lord's divinity, and completing the intentionally incomplete doctrine of his speech. The parallels between our Lord, and the first witness to imitate him unto death, are many : false witnesses, outside the city, the accusations, the reference to Daniel arousing fury, the commending prayer, and the prayer for persecutors. St Luke is fond of such parallels. He brings them out too in the case of St Paul, see on 20:22 ; 21:12. Saul is mentioned for the first time ; *cf.* 22:20. ' If Stephen had not prayed, the Church would not have gained Paul ', Aug. *Sermo* 315.

VIII 1–3 The Persecution after the Martyrdom—**1.** A general persecution was now begun by the Sanhedrin, with Saul as their chief instrument, 22:5. The new governor, Marcellus, only arrived after some months, and was himself superseded a year later. Persecution developed the Church, (1) because it separated Christians off, (2) because the Gospel began to be preached as far as Syria. The Apostles, as ' Hebrews ', and strict

observers of the Law, were not threatened like the **830a** Hellenist Christians with their wider horizon ; 8:14 shows there was no question of divergence. **2.** The devout men were perhaps Jews, as in 2:5, since most Christians had fled. **3.** *Cf.* 22:4 ; 26:10.

4–40 Acts of Philip the Deacon—**4–9a He preaches in b Samaria**—**4.** The Apostles remaining in Jerusalem, the deacons evangelize. St Luke collected his information from Philip personally at Caesarea. **5.** ' A city of Samaria '. If Sebaste, its capital, is meant, half the inhabitants were pagans. In any event, preaching to Samaritans was a further step towards universality. **6.** *Cf.* our Lord's reception, Jn 4:39–42.

9b–13 Simon Magus—Gnostic legend gave him great c importance, but this ch is all that the NT tells about him. **10.** Simon gave himself out as the representative of God, and his very title is probably a magical formula. This was the first encounter of the Church with the magic that flourished in the pagan world ; *cf.* 13:8 ; 16:16 ; 19:19. **12.** Philip preached about ' the kingdom of God, *and* the name of Jesus Christ '. **13.** Our Lord did not rate highly faith based on miracles, Jn 4:48 ; 14:12, and for this magician they were a temptation, 18.

14–17 SS Peter and John sent from Jerusalem—**14.** On St Peter's position, see § 819*d*. **15–17.** The deacon could not confirm, see § 820*b*. The giving of the Holy Spirit was accompanied by manifestations like those at Pentecost.

18–25 The Sin of Simon—**18–19.** He regarded the d external charismata as the magical effects of the laying on of hands. **20.** St Peter is not cursing Simon, whose conversion he desired, but expressing horror at the traffic proposed, hence ' Simony '. **22.** ' *Repent of this wickedness of thine, and pray to the Lord that if possible the thought of thy heart be forgiven thee* '. The doubt is due to Simon's wrong disposition, 23. **24.** He does not yet repent, but fears a magical efficacy in St Peter's words. **25.** The Apostles extend the Church, and preach ' to many *villages* of the Samaritans '.

26–25 Philip baptizes the Ethiopian—Deut 23:1 for- e bidding admission to Judaism of eunuchs, was not strictly applied, and the word may be used here merely in the sense of ' minister '. Hence many think the pious minister who had come ' to adore ' was a Jew, or at least a proselyte who accepted the whole Law, including circumcision, *cf.* Boudou, *op. cit.* 174. Others consider he was simply one who ' feared God ', see 10:2. In that case Philip, inhibited by none of St Peter's scruples, anticipated the decisive action of the latter, ch 10, but only with an isolated individual, and it was evidently not his usual practise ; *cf.* v 40, and 10:1. However St Luke seems to wish us to understand that the Ethiopian was a real eunuch, for his ministerial office is described separately, ' of great authority ', and that after baptizing Samaritans, Philip took a further step in the direction of universality by baptizing one for whom circumcision was a physical impossibility. **26.** ' This is desert ' is not part of the angel's speech, but is a Lucan parenthesis to explain that ' old ' Gaza, a deserted ruin, some little distance from the inhabited city, is meant. **27.** Candace was the generic name of the queens of Ethiopia, the modern Sudan. **29.** For the interior work of conversion, the guidance of the Spirit is necessary. **32–33.** Is 53:7–8, in LXX. ' *In his humiliation justice was denied him. Who can describe the wickedness of his generation, which has taken his life* ', gives perhaps the meaning. **35.** Philip uses the same argument as his Master, Lk 24:26. **37**, though known to St Irenaeus, is not in the best MSS, and perhaps began as an early gloss to fulfil the need of some confession of faith. **38.** *Cf.* DAC, Art. *Immersion*, VII, 305. **39.** Philip was miraculously removed. Tradition, as far back as St Irenaeus, makes the eunuch the apostle of his country. **40.** Azotus was predominantly Jewish, but Caesarea, 50 m. N., was a pagan city, though it contained many Jews. It was the political capital, and the Procurator's residence. Herod the Great had rebuilt it on a lavish scale, and made the harbour safe

830e in all weathers. It was, or now became, Philip's home, 21·8

831a **IX 1-30 The Conversion of St Paul**—See also §§ 664, 676*f*, *g*.—**1-9 On the Road to Damascus, A.D. 36 (?)** The persecution after the martyrdom of St Stephen, not only spread the Church, but led to the conversion of the man who was to be its chief Apostle in the pagan world. Besides this narrative, St Luke gives two, more oratorical, accounts by St Paul, that to the Jewish mob, 22:6, and the speech before the pagan Festus, 26:12. The slight differences in the accounts reflect their varying audiences and are a guarantee of their historicity. We are meant to understand that here was an event of epoch-making importance, effected, not by the Holy Spirit, but by our Lord in Person, and constituting the new convert an Apostle, on a level with those who had seen him after the Resurrection. **1.** The history is carried on from 8:3. After persecuting with all his might in Jerusalem, Saul turns his attention to the Christian centre next in importance, and the date is still soon after the death of St Stephen. **2.** From 22:5 we learn that the Sanhedrin as well as the high-priest authorized Saul. The Sanhedrin theoretically had jurisdiction over the Jews of the Dispersion, Deut 17:8 ff., and Josephus tells us that the empire had acknowledged this right, *Ant.* XIV, 10 and Jos. *B.J.* I. 24.2. Damascus, 180 m. from Jerusalem, and occupied by the Romans since 65 B.C., was a Hellenistic city with a large Jewish population. The first Christians dwelling there were, no doubt, converts from Pentecost, and were still attending the synagogue. 'Belonging to the way', *i.e.* way of life; *cf.* Gen 18:19; Ps 5:9; 17:31. This was a regular term for the new faith, 18:25-26; 19:9,23; 22:4; 24:14, 22, *cf.* 16:17, and Jn 14:6. To those outside, Christianity appeared essentially as a new **b** way of life. **3.** The place was near enough to Damascus for the journey to be completed on foot, 8. The time was midday, 22:6, and the light that flashed, brighter than the sun. **4.** Saul and his companions fell to the ground, and Saul heard a voice that spoke in Aramaic, adding, at the end of this verse, 'it is hard for thee to kick against the goad, 26:14, *i.e.* the prong used for oxen; *cf.* too, Eccl 12:11. The phrase seems to have been a proverb, and is applied to the external circumstances of the conversion of Saul, who always insisted that he had acted in good faith as a persecutor, and ascribed his conversion to the overpowering grace of God; *cf.* 23:1; 24:16; 1 Cor 15:9-10; 1 Tim 1:12-16. The rationalist attempt to explain the vision away, on psychological grounds, as the resolution of a conflict in Saul's mind, has no basis in the known facts. In persecuting his followers Saul was persecuting Jesus. 'Caput pro membris clamabat'; *cf.* Mt 10:25; Lk 10:16. The Pauline doctrine is here in germ, salvation by faith, *cf.* 26:18, and by the grace of God, and Jesus one with his **c** followers. **5-7a.** Realizing that here is a divine intervention, Saul asks who speaks, prepared at once to obey *cf.* 26:19. His life is changed in an instant. '*I am Jesus whom thou persecutest. But arise, go into the city, and there shall it be told thee what thou must do*'. The intervening words are not found in the Gk MSS, nor in many of Vg. **7b.** Saul's companions fell down at the first shock, but had by now risen to their feet. They heard the voice speak, but they did not understand what was said, as is clear from 22:9, which says, 'they heard not the voice'. The word 'hear' in the later passage is used in the sense of 'understand', as in 1 Cor 14:2. The word for 'voice' in 7 is in the genitive, suggesting the sound, but in 22:9 it is in the accusative, suggesting intellectual perception. 'An old and well-known distinction between the acc. and gen. with ἀκούω saves the author of 9:7 and 22:9 from a patent self-contradiction. . . .' J. H. Moulton, *A Grammar of NT Gk* (1908³) 66. For a parallel of the fact, see Jn 12:28-29. All saw the light, 22:9, only Saul saw Jesus. The vision is attested independently by Ananias, 9:17; 22:14. **8.** *Cf.* 22:11. Saul is led

captive, to learn the faith he had attacked, and later to open the eyes of others, 26:18.

10-19a Saul's Baptism—10. Ananias was a Christian, but also ' a man according to the Law ', 22:12. Jesus receives from his followers the divine title of ' Lord '. **11.** This famous street, once divided in three by a double row of columns, still runs through Damascus from East to West. Nothing is known of Judas. **12.** '*Saul is praying, and he has seen, in a vision, a man named Ananias come in and put his hands upon him to give him sight* '. Ananias is reassured, his visit will be expected. *Cf.* the double vision in the case of Cornelius. Vg and DV take 12 as a parenthesis by St Luke. [It might also be a gloss.—Gen. Ed.] **13.** The Church in Jerusalem obtained the name of the ' Saints ', derived from the OT, owing to the impression produced by the outpouring of the Holy Spirit. Its members were those chosen by God as the kernel of the new Messianic kingdom. They were saints because the Holy Spirit had come to them visibly, and dwelt in them. St Paul was to take over the word and the idea, adding that of ' Noblesse oblige '. *Cf.* 9:32, and L. Cerfaux, ETL 2 (1925) 510. In calling them the saints of Jesus Ananias reveals that for him, Jesus is God. **14.** As much is implied by invoking his name, *i.e.* in the language of the OT, adoring Jesus, *cf.* 21. This ' invocation ' separated Christians from Jews, *cf.* 4:17; 5:28. **15.** The Gk can also be translated ' *a chosen instrument* ', and this metaphor fits better than that of the potter's vessel. The Gentiles are mentioned first because Saul will be their apostle, *cf.* 22:21; Gal 1:15-16; 2:7. From 22:15 and 26:16 we see that Saul is to be a ' minister and witness ' like the other Apostles; *cf.* 1:21; 1 Cor 15:5-11; 9:1; Rom 1:5. He was to appear before proconsuls, governors, Herod and perhaps Nero himself. **16.** Saul will also obtain the blessings promised to those persecuted for Jesus' sake, Mt 5:11, and will learn his sufferings by experiencing them, rather than by revelation, *cf.* rest of Ac, and 2 Cor 11:23-33. **17.** In 22:13-16 St Paul gives more fully the message of Ananias. See too on 26:16. Ananias had the grace of healing, and it may be that the exercise of this and no more, is implied by Saul's being filled with the Holy Spirit. The text, however, leaves it open to us to hold that the outpouring of the Holy Spirit followed the baptism, as always, except in the special case of Cornelius. Then we should say that Ananias, as head of the Christian community at Damascus, had the power to lay on hands for the conferring of the Holy Spirit. **18.** A crust had evidently formed over Saul's eyes. The way Luke the physician describes the miracle, rules out the idea that ' as it were scales ' should be taken metaphorically.

19b-25 Saul preaches at Damascus—19b. Baptism brings Saul into communication with the disciples. **20.** Gal 1:17 says that Saul went to Arabia, and then returned to Damascus, going to Jerusalem three years after his conversion. St Luke omits all reference to this retreat in Arabia. His point of view is that of the external development of the Church, while St Paul was proving that he did not visit Jerusalem for three years. The retreat can be placed at once after 19, or after 22, after a period of preaching in Damascus. The former is perhaps the more likely, if the retreat was sufficiently short to suit the ' immediately ' of 20 and if by Arabia is meant the desert near Damascus. St Luke tells us that Saul was only a few days at Damascus, 19, and yet later, ' when many days were passed ', he is there again, all of which implies an absence. He preached that Jesus is the Son of God, the only occurrence of the phrase in Ac. In view of St Paul's usage, he was already teaching the Jews that Jesus was God like his Father. **22.** Not affirming but ' *proving* ' from Scripture that Jesus was the Messias. **23.** The Jewish plot to slay him (as being an apostate from Judaism) was three years after the conversion. Gal 1:18 (*c* A.D. 39 ?). This date is confirmed by the mention of the Ethnarch of Aretas,

f 2 Cor 11:32, who seems to have ruled in Damascus *c* A.D. 38–40. **24.** In 2 Cor the Jews are not mentioned. They were very influential, and had evidently secured the Ethnarch's support. **25.** '*But his own disciples*'. Saul already had a following. There are still houses built against the walls of Damascus, with windows overlooking.

g 26–30 Saul's Visit to Jerusalem—26. Gal 1:18–19 gives the motive—'to see Peter'. The difficulty in accepting the conversion of Saul may have been increased by lack of information, caused by his retreat in Arabia and by the war between Aretas and Herod Antipas, which interrupted communications. **27.** Barnabas was well qualified to act as intermediary ; see note on 4:36. **29.** Gk has, '*He spoke and disputed with the Hellenists*'. The Hellenists here are Jews, not Christians as in 6:1. The differing use of the term is probably due to St Luke's different sources. Saul the Hellenist takes up the work of St Stephen, and arouses the same fury, *cf.* 22:18. **30.** Saul's stay was cut short and lasted only 15 days unless it was St Peter who left after that period ; and of the Apostles he saw only Peter and James the brother of the Lord, Gal 1:18. During it he was given the vision in the temple and the command to go to the Gentiles, which also speeded his departure, 22:17–21. Perhaps too, as 31 suggests, the Church in Jerusalem was anxious to avoid another persecution like that following the preaching of St Stephen. Saul returned to his home in Tarsus, till fetched by Barnabas, four years later, *c* A.D. 43. Tarsus was a commercial and cultured Hellenized city, on the trade route to Mesopotamia.

a IX 31–XI 18 Acts of St Peter the Missionary—31 A Summary—During A.D. 39–40 the Jews were resisting Caligula's attempt to have his statue set in the temple, so the Church had peace, and was ' built up ', spiritually, as in St Paul's epistles, rather than externally. The description of external growth follows : '*And grew in numbers through the consolation of the Holy Spirit*'. The word ' Paraclesis ' is used for the consolation imparted by the Paraclete.

b 32–35 St Peter at Lydda—32. St Peter makes a visitation of the churches. Lydda was a small town at the southern end of the plain of Sharon.

36–43 St Peter raises Tabitha to Life—36. Joppe was on the coast, 10 m. from Lydda. Tabitha is Aramaic, Dorcas Gk for ' gazelle '. **40.** '*But Peter put them all outside, and knelt down and prayed*' ; *cf.* Mk 5:40, where our Lord had no need to pray. **43.** A tanner was unclean, since he must touch dead bodies, Lev 11:39. St Peter was beginning to ignore Jewish prejudices, and this prepares for the sequel.

c X 1–XI 18 The Conversion of Cornelius—This is the climax of Ac. St Luke leaves no doubt as to its significance, recounting it, like the conversion of St Paul, three times. The Gospel preaching had made it clear that the new kingdom was for all men, and Ac 1–2 ; 3:26, etc., bear this out. Yet a decade after the Ascension, Christians were still observing circumcision and the Mosaic Law, as indeed had our Lord himself. Jews despised pagans, and were hated in return, and Christians were still more or less observant Jews. Only when the Law was seen to be abrogated, could the Gentiles enter the Church in numbers. The teaching of St Stephen, and the preaching of Philip to the Samaritans and the Ethiopian, had prepared the way, and now thanks to visions, and finally the descent of the Holy Spirit on the uncircumcised Cornelius and his friends, the last hesitations of St Peter were removed. It was reserved for him to take the greatest decision the Apostles ever made, and to hold the Church to it in spite of strong opposition. The breach with Judaism was irrevocable. Christianity was seen to be an independent religion. The Messianic blessings could be obtained without circumcision. Jew and Gentile could sit together at the feast of the Kingdom. Our Lord's teaching was fulfilled.

d St Peter's Decision gave the Gentiles their Freedom and made possible the developments at Antioch, **832d** 11:20, and, still more, the work of St Paul. Logically also it freed the Jewish Christians. St Peter was the link between the ' Saints in Jerusalem ' and the new church of the Gentiles. At Jerusalem his decision was accepted, and when later the believing Pharisees disputed it, St James, the bishop of their church, reaffirmed at the Apostolic Council that God had chosen Simon to receive the Gentiles. Although St Peter required so much divine guidance before breaking with the prejudices of his nation, our Lord had taught him, not only that his Church was for all men, but also that the Law was abrogated, Mk 7:2–5, 15 ; 2:21 ff. ; Lk 5:30. This St Peter grasped, at least implicitly. Salvation comes through Jesus, and in Gal 2:11–21 St Paul appeals to a conviction in St Peter dating from before the story of Cornelius ; he was disobeying ' the truth of the Gospel ', and this is borne out by his words and actions in Ac 2:39 ; 4:12 ; 9:43. Still, for him to draw the consequences of his faith, and overcome his repugnance, the divine interventions in ch 10 were needed. The faith was clarified for him first, as in Mt 16:16, and he was able to confirm that of his brethren.

X 1–8 The Vision of Cornelius—1. His name and **e** office show he was a Roman, a Gentile, the descendant of a freedman of a great patrician family, and in rank the equivalent of a non-commissioned officer. Inscriptions reveal the presence of an ' Italian cohort ' at Caesarea in A.D. 69, and it may well have been the same one which with four others, constituted the garrison 30 years earlier. **2.** ' Fearing God ' was the usual term for uncircumcised proselytes, who accepted the Jewish faith, and often many of its practices also. Cornelius had won over his household, and gave alms to the People of God. **3.** He was rewarded by an objective vision at 3 p.m., the time for evening prayer.

9–16 St Peter's Vision—At noon the next day, on the **f** flat housetop, where it was common for Jews to pray. **10.** Ecstasy suggests a mental vision. **11–12.** *Cf.* Lev 11 ; ' vessel '=object. **14.** St Peter answers with his usual impetuosity, in spite of Mk 7:15. **15.** The Voice dealt only with foods, but the application was much wider, 28 ; 11:5 ff.

17–23a Arrival of the Messengers of Cornelius—19–20. The Holy Spirit still has to persuade St Peter to receive Gentiles into his house.

23b–33 The Meeting of St Peter and Cornelius—25–26. g Cornelius showed great veneration for God's messenger, but, being a believer, can hardly have ' adored ' as the Lycaonians did, 14:12, and as St Peter, amazed at such a salutation from a Roman, thought. **28.** *Cf.* Jn 4:9 ; 18:28, etc. **30.** Three days by modern reckoning. **33.** ' We are all present *in the sight of God* ', is the better reading. Cornelius waits to hear what God will speak through St Peter.

34–43 St Peter's Speech—The first recorded address **h** to Gentiles is no longer so greatly preoccupied with the OT, and describes our Lord's life more fully. St Peter must have spoken in Gk, and this is borne out by the involved style, as of one using an unfamiliar language. **34–35 The Principle laid down**—*cf.* Deut 10:17 ; Rom 2:11. God chooses his elect no matter what their nationality. All are acceptable, *i.e.* capable of receiving the gifts of God, and justification, if they are in the right dispositions, irrespective of the observance of the Law.

36–39 Our Lord's Public Ministry—36. The Gk is difficult and the text uncertain, but v 36 seems to introduce our Lord's teaching. God sent the Gospel message to the Jews first, announcing peace with God, through Jesus Christ ; *cf.* Rom 5:1. ' He is lord of all *men* ', and so can give this peace also to Gentiles. On the affirmation of our Lord's Godhead, see § 817*d*. **37.** Cornelius and the company know ' *the story, a story which ran through the whole of Judaea* (KNT) ; *cf.* 1:22. **38.** ' *Concerning* Jesus '. God ' anointed ' his human nature with the graces of the Holy Spirit, *viz.* those he received at his baptism for his work as Messias,

832h Is 61:1. His was the Messianic title Emmanuel, *cf.* Mt 1:23.

i 40-43 Our Lord rose again, and is the Judge who forgives the Sins of all Men—41. Cornelius may be ignorant of the Resurrection, since Christ appeared only to pre-ordained witnesses, but these were qualified ; *cf.* 1:3. **42.** St Peter only mentions the command to preach to the Jewish people, but the whole tenour of his speech (esp. 43) shows that the Gentiles were included, as in 1:8. Jesus will judge those who are alive at his Coming, as well as the dead, *cf.* 1 Pet 4:5. **43.** Is 49:6 ; Mal 1:11 ; Jon and Ps speak of this remission of sins for all men. Faith in Jesus is alone required, 4:12 ; Rom 3:22. The joy of the audience is reflected in 46.

j 44-48 The Pentecost of the Gentiles—44. The Descent took place while St Peter was speaking. He points the parallel with the first Pentecost (47); *cf.* 11:15 ; 15:8. Circumcision and the Mosaic Law were clearly super-seded if Gentiles received the Spirit. **46.** Evidently only the Gentiles received the charismata, which were rather those of 19:6 and 1 Cor 14, than different languages. **47.** This is the only case of the reception of the Holy Spirit before baptism, see § 819c. **48.** The Apostles seem to have left baptizing to others, 1 Cor 1:14.

k XI 1-18 St Peter justifies Himself at Jerusalem—2. ' They of the circumcision ' is not used in the deprecia-tive sense of later controversy, Gal 2:12 ; Rom 4:12, and seems to mean rather those especially attached to legal observances, than the whole church of Jerusalem. **3.** *Cf.* 10:28. Indirectly St Peter's whole action is questioned. His defence is that in this turning point he was guided by God at every step. **12.** He defends the brethren equally guilty of a breach of the Law. **15.** There is no mention of the wind or tongues of fire at this Descent. **16.** Our Lord's words apply also to the Gentiles. **17.** Cornelius and his friends, though sharing only the Apostles' faith in our Lord and not their Jewish observances, had received ' the same *Gift* ' as they at Pentecost. Thus, not to have baptized them would have been to disobey God. **18.** St Peter's decision is accepted. The Gentiles too, have been given that repentance that leads to the new life in God's King-dom, eternal life begun already on earth ; *cf.* 3:15 ; 5:20.

833a XI 19-XII 25 The Growth of the Church in Antioch, and the Decline of that in Jerusalem—Hellenists from Cyprus and Cyrene now began to evangelize Gentiles at Antioch, and for the first time, groups of converted pagans were found in the same church with Jewish Christians. Many Gentiles were converted, and so Barnabas was sent from Jerusalem to investigate ; see on 4:36. After he had approved and had obtained the aid of St Paul, the converts became so numerous as to make their fellow Gentiles realize that theirs was a religion distinct from that of the Jews, whose Law they did not observe, and for whom a name must be invented. This expansion not only had a profound effect on the internal development of the Church (see on 11:26), but provided a centre far more suitable than Jerusalem for the evangelization of the Greco-Roman world. In a Judaea ruled by Procurators, the Church at Jerusalem had been more or less protected, but it suffered severely from Herod's persecution. The Apostles were killed or scattered, St Peter went elsewhere, and the Church grew more Jewish in outlook, and ceased to be mis-sionary. Antioch thus became, for a time, the capital of the Church and its missionary centre. There is a tradition, supported by Gal 2:11, that St Peter ruled there, *cf.* J. Lebreton, *L'Eglise Primitive*, 154. St Luke seems to have come from Antioch, and his information to have been preserved in the church there, which was proud of those who had prepared its path and built it up, St Stephen, the evangelists from Cyprus and Cyrene, and above all Barnabas and St Paul.

b 19-26 The Preaching to the Gentiles at Antioch— ' The Queen of the East ', the capital of Syria, with over half a million inhabitants, Antioch was the third city of the empire, after Rome and Alexandria. It was famous for its Hellenist culture and philosophers, for **83** its monuments, and for its licentiousness. Jews and proselytes were numerous, and had their own ethnarch, and other privileges. **19.** Persecution spread the Church. There were many Jews in Phoenicia, and in Tyre and Sidon its chief towns. The Christians there are mentioned in 21:4, 7 ; 27:3. There were too a number of Jewish colonies in Cyprus, 13:5. **20.** As a result of the news of the Cornelius decision, a new wave of preaching began, this time to ' Hellenes ', Gentiles. This would not have been possible, at least as a general practice, before that decision, nor could the delegate of the Church at Jerusalem possibly have approved of it. St Peter expressly stated later, 15:7, that he was the first to admit Gentiles, and St Luke implies as much by the order of his narrative. Dates bear it out, the conversion of Cornelius, *c* 40 (*cf.* 9:31 note), the mission of Barnabas, *c* 42, allowing 43 for the preaching of v 25, since in 44 Barnabas was back in Jerusalem, 11:30 ; 12:1. For the names of the evangelists from Cyprus and Cyrene, see 13:1. Codex B and other MSS have for those to whom they preached ' Hellenists ', instead of ' Hellenes ', Greeks, as though the new preaching were still only to Hellenist Jews. This reading is so obviously opposed to the context as to be almost uni-versally rejected. To Jews the preachers would have shown that Jesus was the Messias, here they preach that he is Lord, God. **21.** Miracles showed that the new **c** departure was blessed, *cf.* 4:30. **22.** *Cf.* on 4:36. Him-self a Hellenist from Cyprus, and enjoying the con-fidence of the Apostles, the warm-hearted Barnabas was the ideal emissary from the Church at Jerusalem, ready now to admit the uncircumcised into the Church. **23-24.** When he saw the work of the Holy Spirit in the changed lives of these pagans and in their charismata, being himself so full of the Spirit, he exhorted them to cling steadfastly to our Lord, and not to Jewish observances. Guided by God he judged the situation correctly. **25.** Workers were needed for the harvest. Saul was known to be free from Jewish prejudices, and to have a mission to the Gentiles, 9:15 ; 22:21. He had been preaching for several years in Cilicia (see on 9:30) and seemingly to Gentiles, 15:23. **26.** ' Christians ' ; the great number of converts who were free of the Law, attracted to themselves a definite name, confined probably at first to those who had been pagans. It was derived, perhaps in derision, from him who was the centre of their new lives, *cf.* 26:28, and 1 Pet 4:16, the only other NT refs. Tacitus speaks of it as a common designation. St Luke's names for Christians are ' saints ', 9:13 ; ' disciples ', ' brethren ', ' those of the way ', ' those who invoke the name ', 9:14 ; ' believers '. **The Formation of a Gentile Church hastened Develop- d ment**—The change wrought in pagan converts was striking. Also Christianity was seen to be the whole of religion. There was no magnificent temple liturgy to overshadow the breaking of bread. The new liturgy was clearly the centre of the community ; *cf.* 13:2. The Christian life was not lived more intensely than in Jerusalem, but it was lived *alone*. ' The Christians of Antioch seemed, from certain points of view, *more authentic* than those of Jerusalem ', L. Cerfaux, *La Communauté Apostolique*, 85. The Holy Spirit showed his approval by inspiring prophets, and several of them, though not Apostles, had been companions of Jesus, 13:1. The church at Antioch had the authentic mark of charity, and its missionary zeal was soon to make it supersede Jerusalem as the Church's capital.

27-30 The Church at Antioch sends Alms to Jerusalem e —**27.** Following the good reports sent back by Barna-bas, some from Jerusalem who had the charisma of prophecy, came to visit the daughter church. This is the first mention of the NT prophets, *cf.* 13:1, 15:32 and 1 Cor 12 and 14. **28.** Codex D has this as the first ' we-section ', which shows at least that an ancient tradition held St Luke to be at Antioch, and a Christian at this time. On Agabus see 21:10. There were various famines under Claudius, A.D. 41-54, Judaea suffering in A.D. 46-8. **29.** Community of goods may have e helped to impoverish the church at Jerusalem, for which St Paul later so often collected alms. From the first this was a sign of the unity and charity which linked the Gentile churches to their mother, *cf.* note on 21:17–20, and E. B. Allo, O.P., *La Portée de la collecte pour Jérusalem*, RB 45 (1936), 529–37. **30.** The relief was given ' *to the presbyters* ', see § 820*d*. Barnabas and Saul arrived in Jerusalem, after Herod's persecution had broken out, 12:1, and returned after the latter's death, 12:25. Evidently the Apostles were either in prison or scattered. This is borne out by the 2nd cent. tradition that the Apostles dispersed twelve years after the Ascension. It is not easy therefore to identify this journey of St Paul's with that in Gal 2:1–10, see note on 15:1. (See however comm. on Gal, § 893*d*, in favour of this identification.)

f XII 1-25 The Persecution of Herod Agrippa—1-5 St Peter Imprisoned, A.D. 44—1. ' Now *about that* time ', *i.e.* presumably before the arrival of Barnabas and Saul, who found only presbyters at large, and before the spring of 44, when St Peter was arrested. Herod Agrippa I was the grandson of Herod the Great, who put his father Aristobulus to death in 7 B.C. He was then at the age of three, sent to Rome with his mother Berenice, and brought up at the Court. He led a disorderly life, and shortly before the death of Tiberius in A.D. 37, he was thrown into prison. Caligula, his companion in debauchery, released him, and gave him some of the territories of his grandfather. Claudius added Judaea and Samaria in 41, thus completing the restoration. He courted not only the great but also his subjects, and his persecution was intended as a proof of his zeal for the Law. At Jerusalem he kept the Law, and offered the prescribed sacrifices, but in his palace at Caesarea he put up statues to his daughters, and eventually allowed himself to be called a god, v 23. The persecution, undertaken to please the Sanhedrin, differed from that after the death of St Stephen in that it struck at the Apostles, whose acceptance of Gentiles had no doubt alienated popular support. **2.** St James (*cf.* Mk 10:39) was presumably accused of a political crime, since the penalty of blasphemy was stoning. This is the last ref. to St John in Ac, though see Gal 2:9. As to his alleged martyrdom at this time see §§ 607*k* and 777*g*. **3.** During the week following the Passover no leaven was eaten. Crowds of pilgrims thronged the city, and these too Herod hoped to please. **4.** ' Four *groups of four soldiers* '. In the Roman army each group was on duty for one of the four watches of day and night. Two soldiers remained in the cell, with the prisoner chained to them, and the other two were stationed, one at the door of the cell and one at the outer door. These precautions were in view of St Peter's escapes. He was to be condemned after the Pasch, which must not be desecrated by a public execution. Our Lord's death just prior to the Feast had been at the hands of the Romans. Sentence was to be passed publicly, to please the people ; *cf.* Jn 19:13.

g 6-11 St Peter's Release—6. The night before his trial St Peter lay guarded as usual, 4. **7.** The angel ' *awoke* ' him. **8.** The girdle which held up the flowing tunic had to be put on, then the sandals and the cloak. St Peter was to be in no hurry. **10.** The two guards, 4, were passed, and the outer door opened of itself. The prison was probably the Fortress Antonia ; see on 21:31. **11.** The street reached, the angel's work was done, and St Peter realized the miracle.

12-17 St Peter leaves Jerusalem—12. ' *Becoming aware of what had happened* ' he decided it would be unwise to return to his own home. On the house of St Mark's mother see on 1:13. On St Mark, probably the source of this vivid account, see comm. on Mk §§ 724–5. **14.** With persecution raging, the door was locked. **15.** The disciples anticipated the scepticism of later critics. On the guardian angel see § 820*g*. **17.** On St James see on 15:13. St Luke deliberately omits to say where St Peter went, perhaps because, as tradition preserved by Eusebius and others maintains, it was to

Rome. In A.D. 63 it may well have been unwise to **833g** mention St Peter's visit to the capital, in which he then lived or to which he would soon return. If not Rome, then Antioch, which he certainly visited at some time, Gal 2:11. He was back in Jerusalem for the Council in A.D. 49, and that is the last time he appears in Ac.

18-25 The Death of Herod—19. The soldiers seem to **h** have suffered the usual punishment ; *cf.* 16:27 ; 27:42. Herod perhaps hoped to put the blame on them. **20-21.** St Luke and Josephus give independent accounts. According to *Ant.* XIX, 8, 2. Herod was celebrating games, probably in thanksgiving for Claudius's return from his expedition to Britain. He appeared in the amphitheatre in a robe of silver. When the morning rays of the sun lit it up, the flatterers cried out that he was a god. The king gave no reprimand, and as he raised his eyes, saw an owl, the bird of ill omen. He was then seized with sudden internal pains, and died in agony five days later. St Luke gives us the precise nature of the illness and its profound cause. As to the embassy from the Tyrians and Sidonians, ' because their *country depended on the King's country for food* ', there seems to have been trade rivalry between them and Herod's port at Caesarea. They depended on Judaea for corn. **22.** The people were pagans ; see on 8:40. **23.** Contrast 10:26 and 14:14. Herod died the death of the impious, 2 Mac 9:5 ; Is 66:24, in the summer of A.D. 44, and his kingdom was once more ruled by procurators. His children appear in 24:24 and 25:13. **24.** With the persecutor dead, and for the next four years strife between the Jews and the new procurators, the Gospel could once more spread in Judaea. This is the end of the history of the Church of Jerusalem in Ac. It only appears again incidentally, and with the Apostles gone, and the church of the Gentiles growing, it declines in importance ; see on 15:1. **25.** Some MSS including B and Sin. have ' returned *to* Jerusalem ', presumably after distributing relief in Judaea. However, we may safely read, with the great majority of exegetes, as in DV. Barnabas and Saul were planning to continue the preaching to the Gentiles, and saw how valuable the former's cousin would prove, with his personal witness to our Lord's life, and also his knowledge of Gk. The return to Antioch must have been during the second half of A.D. 44.

XIII-XXVIII The Spread of the Gospel throughout the 834a Gentile World. The Preaching and Journeys of St Paul, A.D. 45-63.
XIII-XIV The First Missionary Journey, A.D. 45-9— St Paul now becomes the central figure. The first twelve chapters have prepared the way. He was chosen like the other Apostles by our Lord himself and given a special mission to the Gentiles, 9:15 note. He is still constantly guided by him and by the Holy Spirit. The great vision of 2 Cor. 12:1–6 occurred at this period. The conquest of the Roman world begins, and this first journey leads to the foundation of Gentile churches in Cyprus and S. Galatia.

XIII 1-3 The Sending of Barnabas and Saul—1. On **b** the church at Antioch see § 833*a*, *d*. ' God has set in the church, first apostles, secondly prophets, thirdly doctors ', 1 Cor 12:28. There were no Apostles, since they were founders of churches, and were itinerant. The first three names seem, according to the Gk, to be those of the prophets, the last two, those of the teachers of the faith. Manahen, probably a courtier of Herod Antipas, must have been one of our Lord's disciples, Lk 8:3. The church at Antioch had its own hierarchy. **2.** ' And while they were *worshipping* the Lord '. The Gk is the word from which ' liturgy ' is derived ; the Holy Spirit spoke through the prophets in the assembly. The community was filled with a zeal which the Holy Spirit now directed to the momentous work of converting the Gentile world. **3.** The fasting was to obtain the light of the Holy Spirit. Was the laying on of hands episcopal consecration ? Barnabas and Saul, though called apostles for the first time, 14:4, 13, already had full powers, 11:22, 25, and were

834b members of the body which is claimed to have consecrated them. It seems preferable to regard the rite as a mandate from the Church for the new mission, and it is described in 14:25 as such a commending to the grace of God.

c 4-12 Barnabas and Saul in Cyprus—4. They sail from the port of Antioch. On St Paul's plan of campaign, see F. Prat, *St Paul*, ch 2. Cyprus lay on the route to Asia and the Roman world, converts had already been made there, 11:19, and Barnabas was going to his homeland. **5.** Salamis was the eastern and Paphos the western port. At the synagogues, besides Jews, there would be proselytes, glad to receive the Gospel, without having to observe the Law or circumcision. ' And they had John (Mark) *to help them* '. He had not been sent by the Spirit, 4, as events would show. **6.** It must have taken many months, allowing for the preaching, to reach Paphos. Elymas was not a mere charlatan, as his presence at the court of such a man as this proconsul shows. **7.** But being a ' false prophet ' he evidently practised the occult sciences, *cf.* 8:9. **7.** As a senatorial province, Cyprus was governed by a proconsul. An inscription of Sergius Paulus has been found in the island. ' An *intelligent* man ', with a desire to reach the truth, as is gathered too from Pliny the Elder, *cf.* J. B. Lightfoot, *Essays on Supernatural Religion*, 294, London, 1889. **8.** Bar-jesu had taken the name of Elymas, which is translated ' magician '. As a Jew he would be familiar with many of Saul's arguments. **9.** This is the last use of ' Saul ', and the first of ' Paul '. Like many Jews he had a Jewish and a Roman name. He was Saulus Paulus. He uses the Roman name, on entering into relations with the Gentile world, where, as a Roman citizen by birth, he was a man of position, and could exert an influence not open to a Jew. The use of it may not be unconnected with his meeting Sergius Paulus. Much more important, he is filled with the Holy Spirit, the real source of his influence, and of the miraculous powers he now exercises. **10.** Elymas ' *twists the straight* ways of the Lord ', by trying to poison the proconsul's mind. **11.** His punishment was sent to induce him to cease sinning against the light. **12.** The proconsul was astonished at the truth so miraculously established. St Luke implies that he became a Christian.

d 13-15 To Pisidian Antioch—13. The phrasing shows that St Paul now becomes the leader of the party, for the apostolate of the Gentiles is beginning in earnest, and he takes precedence of Barnabas except during the Council at Jerusalem, 15:12. In Asia Minor, now divided into Roman provinces, Gk was everywhere understood, even among nations which preserved their own language. At Perge, the capital of Pamphylia, St Paul made clear his decision to cross the Taurus range, and preach in Phrygia and Lycaonia, regions incorporated in the southern part of the province of Galatia. John Mark did not feel bound to face the perils involved ; see on 15:38-39. **14.** The 100-mile mountain journey was made along a mule track infested by brigands (*cf.* 2 Cor 11:26) to Pisidian Antioch. It and Lystra belonged to a group of colonies peopled under Augustus by veterans, and intended as a bulwark of the Roman power. Jews had lived and traded here since the time of the Seleucids. St Paul, as always, went first to the Jews. **15.** St Luke describes the synagogue service, at which it was the custom to invite distinguished visitors to speak ; *cf.* Lk 4:16.

e 16-41 St Paul's Speech in the Synagogue—This is given as the type of St Paul's exposition to Jews. To Gentiles he gives elementary theodicy, 14:14. Here he outlines the history of Salvation, and shows the conformity of the new teaching with the Scriptures. The three parts of the great discourse are clearly marked by the apostrophe ' Men brethren ', 16, 26, 38. The first part runs parallel to the speech of St Stephen, the second and third to the early speeches of St Peter, but the whole is thoroughly Pauline in doctrine and style, *cf.* § 816*b*. The conclusion is that justification comes through Jesus.

16-25 The Preparation for the Messias—16. St Paul **f** addresses not only the Jews, but the many proselytes present ' that fear God ' ; *cf.* 10:2. **17.** He begins in a way that can only please his audience. ' With an *uplifted* arm ', a Hebrew metaphor for the power of God. **19-20.** ' *Whose lands he gave them for an inheritance, for about 450 years* ', *i.e.* from the time Canaan was promised to the Patriarchs till Josue. **22.** God can reject those he has chosen. Ps 88:21 and 1 Kg 13:14 are quoted. **23.** Eventually God sent the Messias, according to his promise, *i.e.* as the prophecies generally had foretold ; *cf.* Gal 3:29. **24-25.** St Paul comes on to the last of the prophets, held in honour among Jews, including those of the Dispersion, 18:25 ; 19:3. The Baptist preached before our Lord's ' coming ' or Public Ministry. As he was ' *finishing his life*'s course ' he explained about the Messias, Lk 3:16.

26-37 Jesus is the Messias—For he died and rose again, **g** according to the Scriptures. **26.** The better reading is ' To *us* the word . . . is sent ', not to unbelieving Jews, but to Christians, and Jews and proselytes of the Dispersion ; *cf.* Eph 1:13. **27.** The Jews of Jerusalem and their rulers ' *because they did not recognize him, nor the words of the prophets* . . . have fulfilled them '. The prophecies of the Suffering Servant, etc., should have been clear enough, 3:17. **28.** ' *Although* they found no cause of death in him, they asked Pilate *to have him killed* '. **29.** *Cf.* Lk 18:31 ; 22:37. **32-33** St Paul and Barnabas make known the good news of the promise, to the fathers ' *which God has fulfilled to us their children* '. This promise was made in various texts, now quoted. Many of the Fathers take 33 as referring to the Incarnation, like 3:22, 26, and 7:37, and 34 to the Resurrection, but even if the whole passage is referred to the latter, it is quite clear from St Paul's epistles that he never thought our Lord became Son of God only at the Resurrection. That was the great manifestation of his Sonship, Rom 1:4. **34-35.** St Paul, as always, uses the OT, ' with the respectful freedom of the son of the house, master of the inheritance of his ancestors ' (J. Bonsirven, EREP, 338). His very condensed argument is : God, acc. to Is 55:3, will grant the holy privileges he has promised to David. One of these, as God says in Ps 15:10, is that he will be preserved from corruption. **36.** ' *But* David, *after* he had served the will of God in his *own* generation ' died and saw corruption. **37.** Whereas he whom God raised from the dead, saw no corruption. The argument is that of St Peter, 2:27-31.

38-41 The Necessity of Faith in Jesus—38-39. Through **h** him now shown to be the Messias, ' forgiveness of sins is *proclaimed* to you '. He is the source of forgiveness and justification, an implicit assertion of his Godhead. St Paul's doctrine of justification for all, by faith in Christ without the works of the Law, is thus early stated. *Cf.* ' The word of his *grace* ', 14:3. **40-41.** Hab 1:5. The Israelites were threatened with the invasion of the Chaldeans, but turned a deaf ear to the prophet. Jerusalem was captured, and the Jews punished with exile. The parallel is clear, and St Paul brings it forward when he sees the resistance to his doctrine.

42-43 Effect of the Speech—The people wished to have **i** the teaching repeated. ' Many Jews and *worshipping proselytes* followed Paul '. These proselytes seem to be the same as those who fear God, 16 ; *cf.* note on 5. All these became disciples, without waiting till the following Sabbath, and received the ' grace ' of God. This is the first use of the word in its Pauline sense of a gift of God for our justification.

44-48 The Apostles turn to the Gentiles—44. During the week, the Gentiles had come to hear of the new doctrine of salvation for all, without the Law. **45.** The Jews were furious at seeing the synagogue filled with Gentiles, offered equal terms with them. They blasphemed our Lord. **46.** In God's plan, the Gospel was to be preached to the Jews, Mt 10:6 ; Ac 2:39 ; 10:42 ; Rom 1:16, and chh 9-11. St Paul's universalism always aroused their bitter hostility, and the scene in the synagogue was often re-enacted, *cf.* 18:6. **47.**

The call of the Gentiles is in accord with the prophecy which foretold that the Servant would be their light and salvation, Is 49:6. Jesus is that Servant, and the preachers of the Gospel are the instruments by which the prophecy is fulfilled ; *cf.* 9:15 ; Lk 2:32. **48.** Gentiles are converted in large numbers, and thus a church comes into being, which is composed from the start predominantly of pagan converts. The Gentiles were ordained by God for eternal life, but not the Jews, who refused to believe ; *cf.* Rom 8:29 ; Eph 1:5. The context and the Gk show that it was because they accepted the new teaching, that the Gentiles were put in the ranks of those enjoying eternal life. This is the ' life ' of sanctifying grace, eternal life already begun, for grace is the beginning of glory, but a ' life ' which can still be forfeited.

49-52 End of the Stay at Pisidian Antioch—49. St Luke does not say how long the Apostles remained. It must have taken some months to preach through the region. **50.** The Jews stirred up ' *women of position, who were worshippers* ', *i.e.* proselytes, on whom they had influence, and the magistrates, who were perhaps their husbands. **51.** *Cf.* Lk 9:5. **52.** The church that had been founded at Antioch was full of joy, due to the Holy Spirit present in souls by grace and manifesting his presence by charismata ; *cf.* Gal 5:22.

XIV 1-6 At Iconium—1. This city, the modern Konieh, was a Phrygian town, 80 m. E. of Pisidian Antioch in fertile country at the foot of the Taurus. It lay on the road through the Cilician Gates to the Euphrates, and its trade had attracted a Jewish colony. Now, besides Jews, many Greeks (Hellenes, *i.e.* Gentiles) were converted, but not, for the narrative is very condensed, all at one meeting. **2.** Animosity was aroused against the new church. **3.** Yet charismata confirmed the preaching, and leading to divided opinions, 4, helped to avert immediate persecution. Perhaps a year, A.D. 47-8, was spent at Iconium. **5-6.** The meaning seems to be that a stoning was plotted by the Gentile mob, and by the Jews with the rulers of their synagogue, but that it was prevented by the flight of the Apostles, who visited Lystra, and then Derbe, and the country round them. This was Lycaonia, which had its own language, different from the Phrygian of Iconium.

7-17 At Lystra—One of the colonies of veterans established by Augustus in 6 B.C., 20 m. S. of Iconium, and seemingly too small to have a synagogue for Jews. **8.** St Paul noticed this attentive man. He listened to the account of Jesus the Saviour, and his miracles of healing, believed in him, and had sufficient faith to be healed, Mt 9:28. **9.** The crowd could not fail to realize the greatness of the miracle. **10-11.** The people in their excitement spoke their native Lycaonian. They were perhaps led to think of Jupiter (Zeus) and Mercury (Hermes) because of the legend that these two had been entertained, unawares, in Phrygia, Ovid, *Metamorph.* 8, 611 ff. Hermes was the spokesman of the gods. **12-13.** ' The priest of *the temple of Jupiter that was in front of the city* ', was about to offer sacrifice, at the city gate. When the Apostles heard what was happening beside the city, they ' leapt out into the crowd ' to express their horror and prevent the sacrifice.

14-16 The Speech of the Apostles—All things to all men, they adapt the truths of natural religion, the argument of 17:24-30 and Rom 1-2, to the simple audience. **14.** *Cf.* 1 Thess 1:9. **15-16.** These verses deal with God's apparent abandonment of men. It was only temporary and partial ; *cf.* 17:30 and Rom 3:26. The wickedness of man, following his own will, is gently touched on compared with Rom 1:18 ff. The Gentiles had their graces, and God never left man without the means of reaching the truth. In 17:27 and Rom 2:15 the argument from conscience is brought forward ; here to these nature-worshippers, the arguments from order and causality. The participles are subordinate. God does good by giving rain, thus filling our hearts with gladness.

18-19 Persecution at Lystra—Since they made a number of disciples St Paul and Barnabas were some

time at Lystra, before the Jews, hearing of their success, **835d** came even from Antioch, 100 m. away. Stoning was a Jewish punishment, and the Jews, to hide their crime, brought St Paul out of the city, where the vultures would remove all trace of his body. Whether he died or not, St Luke regards his recovery as a miracle, since he could walk back and leave next day, *cf.* 2 Tim 3:11 ; 2 Cor 11:25. The converts came out in the evening, and surrounded him, and he regained consciousness or life. Among the disciples were Eunice and Timothy, 16:1 ; *cf.* 2 Tim 1:5.

20-27 Derbe and the Return Journey—20. Derbe was **e** the frontier town, 30 m. from Lystra on the road east. Here ' *they made many disciples* ' ; *cf.* 20:4. **21.** The shortest route to Syrian Antioch was through the Cilician Gates, but St Paul wished to revisit the new communities, to exhort them to persevere in their faith in Jesus. St Luke then quotes directly ; *cf.* Lk 24:26 ; Rom 8:17. The context suggests that the kingdom is that on earth, the Church. **22.** In spite of the animosities that had been aroused, the return journey seems to have been entirely devoted to the organization of the new churches. The apostles ' *appointed* ' a college of presbyters in each community, see § 820*d*. They laid hands on them at the liturgical assembly after fasting and prayer, and then commended the faithful to the Lord, Jesus, in whom they now believed. **23.** They did not stop to preach in mountainous Pisidia. **24.** There had been no preaching at Perge before, 13:13. Attalia was its port, 16 m. away. **25.** *Cf.* 13:2-3. **26.** The missionaries are only instruments, *cf.* 1 Cor 3:7-9. A door had been opened not by the works of the Law, but by faith in Jesus. For the metaphor, *cf.* 1 Cor 16:9 ; 2 Cor 2:12. This most successful mission evoked the enthusiasm of the Church at Antioch, which was reached by the winter of A.D. 48-9.

XV 1-35 The Judaizers and the Council of Jerusalem, 836a A.D. 49—St Paul in Gal condemns the Judaizing party ; and the question of how best to reconcile his account with that of Luke in Ac has become very complicated. The view here taken is that Gal 2:1-10 refers to St Paul's third visit to Jerusalem, Ac 15.

[According to the South Galatian Theory St Paul wrote Gal just before the Council of Jerusalem to still the repercussions of the Judaizing controversy among his recent South Galatian converts. If this be so, then Gal 2:1-10 can only refer to an earlier visit, *viz.* Ac 11:30. Nevertheless Gal gives us a wonderful picture of St Paul's mind at the time of this Council, *cf.* § 893*c-d*.—Gen. Ed.]

XV 1-3 The Question of the Observance of the Law b raised at Antioch—1. St Peter's action in the case of Cornelius had been decisive, and made possible the Gentile church at Antioch, and the missions of Barnabas and Saul. The church at Jerusalem, though so devoted to the temple and the Law, had accepted that decision, 11:18, and the initiatives of its delegate, Barnabas. Some of its members were now becoming a little obscurantist, with the Apostles gone , and St James emerging as its first bishop, *cf.* 21:18-26. The reliance it placed on Jewish observances would eventually lead some of its members into heresy ; *cf.* Heb and the history of the Ebionites. Already a party, led by believing Pharisees, 5, and unable to grasp the preparatory and transitory nature of the Law, took alarm at the successful mission of chh 13-14 and the enormous influx of Gentiles into the Church. The Law was a great bulwark of morality, and there was excuse for wondering whether pagans could keep its moral precepts, without observing it entirely. So this party, which did not represent the church at Jerusalem, 13 ff., came to Antioch and insisted that circumcision and the Law were necessary for those who wished to enter the Messianic kingdom on earth, and be saved. **2.** A serious controversy arose, and ' Paul and Barnabas and some *of the others* ' went up to Jerusalem, *cf.* Gal 2:1. It was decided to appeal to the Apostles and presbyters, § 820*d*, at the mother church, whence the objectors

836b had come. **3.** The Judaizing party had evidently little following outside Jerusalem ; *cf.* 20:38 ; 21:5.

c 4-5 The Welcome at Jerusalem — **4.** ' They were *welcomed* by the church and by the Apostles and Presbyters ', *i.e.* with solemnity. St Luke wishes us to realize that the church as a whole did not share the views of the Judaizers. The question had already been decided ; *cf.* 7-11.

d 6-12 The Council. St Peter's Intervention—**6.** This, the first Council, was composed of the church at Jerusalem only, and so was hardly oecumenical. It re-affirmed the decision accepted a decade earlier, that justification came through faith in Jesus, not through the Law, and promulgated a practical measure, to deal with a particular situation. The affair turned out to be much less grave than appeared at first. **7.** Perhaps 6 describes a private meeting, during which ' there had been much *debate* ', and now St Peter announces the result to the multitude. Be that as it may, he speaks with an authority that all accept, and by re-stating his decision in the case of Cornelius, implies that the question should not have been re-opened. **8.** God knows hearts, 1:24, and does not respect persons, 10:34. *Cf.* 10:44. **9.** The hearts of the Gentiles were made pure by Faith, not by circumcision and the Law, Rom 3:24-25. **10.** In view of the Pentecost of the Gentiles, the Judaizers are tempting God, either because they wish for further miraculous proof of his Will, or better, because they doubt the saving power of faith in Christ. They are trying to re-impose an unbearable yoke, *cf.* 7:53. **11.** We might paraphrase : ' We Jews will be saved, not by the Law, but just like the Gentiles, by the grace of Jesus '. St Paul himself could not have said more. For Jews, too, the Law is unnecessary. **12.** Silence shows approval. The objectors hold their peace. But Barnabas and Paul are not silent, they give further evidence that God approves what has been decided by St Peter who exercises a Primacy that none contest, and pronounces authoritatively on the question of doctrine, *cf.* § 819*e*.

e 13-21 The Speech of St James—Traditionally and more probably an Apostle as well as the ' brother of the Lord ', *cf.* comm. on James. He was renowned for his devotion to the Law, and seems to have been the first Apostle to become a local bishop ; *cf.* 12:17. His reply to the Judaizers was thus doubly important. **14.** He refers again to the case of Cornelius, which shows that God is forming a Chosen People from the Gentiles. **15-17.** This is borne out by the prophet Amos, 9:11-12, quoted from LXX. The Heb. promises that the nations once subject to David will be restored to Israel in Messianic times, but this can be understood typically in the same sense as LXX. The kingdom will be restored, so that the rest of men may seek the Lord, and all nations receive a call to enter it. **18.** The better reading is ' *Saith the Lord, who hath made these things known from the beginning* '. **19.** From St James' ' I judge ' it has been argued that he and not St Peter had the first position, but a word cannot prevail against the context, so favourable, here, as in the rest of Ac, to the Petrine primacy. The phrase bears a very different interpretation. ' For which cause ', in view of Simon's action in the case of Cornelius, and of the prophecy, ' I ', without wishing to engage others, ' judge ', am of opinion, a usual sense of the Gk κρίνω, and one found often in Ac, ' that the Gentile converts are not to be disquieted '. St James shows why he adheres to the decision which has already been given by Peter on the point at issue. He then puts forward a practical suggestion, which so far from being a decree of his own, is expressly attributed to the Apostles and presbyters who adopted it, 15:28 ; 16:4. **20.** The freedom of the Gentiles is recognized, but four practices which Jews found particularly heinous in pagans must be forbidden. Thus Gentile converts will not appear so scandalous to Jewish Christians, and relations between the two will be facilitated. On the ' Western ' text of the prohibitions, which is to be rejected, see § 821*a*.

f The Apostolic Decree is given three times, here, 28-29

and 21:25. ' Pollution of idols ' is food offered to idols, 29. Rom and 1 Cor show what difficult questions of conscience this provoked. ' Fornication ' finding a place among ritual matters has led exegetes to explain it as the prohibition of marriage within degrees forbidden by the Mosaic Law. The word must be taken literally. There is enough evidence of pagan licence to show how necessary this clause of the Decree was ; *cf.* the warnings found in St Paul's epistles. Pagan and Jewish standards contrasted sharply in this. ' Things strangled ', *i.e.* animals whose blood was still in them, Lev 17, Deut 12. ' Blood ', this too was forbidden by the Mosaic Law, *ibid.* Neither the blood of animals nor meat with the blood in it were to be eaten.

[The correspondence between the four apostolic prohibitions and those of Lev 17:8, 10, 13 ; 18:5-26, where four prohibitions are laid down as the minimum observance required of Gentiles living in Jewish territory, is too striking to be overlooked. James would therefore appear to be invoking an old legal practice and adapting it to the similar situation of Gentile Christians living in the midst of Christian Jewish communities. The observance of these four prohibitions would provide the Mosaic legal basis for ' intercommunion ' between Christians of Jewish and Gentile origin wherever the Jews predominated, *cf.* CR 20 (1941) 283-94 Art. *Except it be for fornication*, by R. Dyson, S.J., and B. Leeming, S.J.—Gen. Ed.]

21. The most satisfactory explanation of the bearing of this verse on the argument is that here is a matter of charity and expediency, for these things are forbidden in the Law of Moses, esp. Lev 17-18. This is read each week in the synagogues, and Jewish Christians, or Jews too, will be scandalized if Gentile Christians do not observe them. On the other hand the meaning could be that it is not necessary to announce these prohibitions to Jewish Christians, who know them already.

22-29 The Letter sent to Antioch—**22.** After St Peter's speech and St James' plea a unanimity is reached which includes even the Pharisees of 5. Though all were present, the letter was sent by the Apostles and presbyters. Two delegates were chosen to accompany Paul and Barnabas. Nothing is known of Judas. Silas became the companion of St Paul. He was a prophet, 32, and besides being a leading member of the church at Jerusalem, a Hellenist and a Roman citizen, 16:37 ; 2 Cor 1:19. **23.** The letter must in the nature of the case have been carefully preserved. As to **the Scope of the Decree**, the letter is addressed only to Syria and Cilicia, where the dispute had arisen. It held for any churches that could be said to depend on Jerusalem, 21:25. St Paul communicated it to the cities of S. Galatia, which had been evangelized from Antioch. The essential part of the Decree applied universally, and here St Paul's victory was complete. The four prohibitions must have applied only in the churches mentioned above, where Jewish Christians were numerous ; there may be a reference to them in 1 Cor 8:13 and 10:28, but there is none in Gal. They are found observed long afterwards in other parts, but perhaps after they had begun to be transformed into a moral code, as in the ' Western ' text. The decision only applied directly to Gentile Christians, but the disagreement at Antioch, Gal 2:11 ff., shows SS Peter and Paul agreeing that it affected Jewish Christians too, which followed from the principle invoked in 11. **24.** The Judaizers are strongly disowned. The words ' going out ' should be omitted, *i.e.* ' Some members of our community, but without a mandate '. **25.** The Gk emphasizes the complete unity of purpose. The praise heaped on Paul and Barnabas suggests the bitterness of the opposition they had encountered. **26.** They staked their lives continually ; *cf.* 9:23 ; 13:50 ; 14:18. **28.** The Apostles have decided under the infallible guidance of the Holy Spirit. The phrase with which the verse begins is still used by the Church in her conciliar decisions. **29.** The four prohibitions (in the same order as Lev 17-18) are ' necessary ' to avoid scandal and facilitate relations between the two kinds of Christians; *cf.* 20. The Holy Spirit had guided the church of Jerusalem. If its role was now finished, and its horizon was to grow more and more limited and Jewish, at least it had witnessed faithfully to our Lord's command to teach all nations.

30-35 The Decree promulgated at Antioch—30-31. The whole church was assembled, and rejoiced at the news that there was no question of imposing the Law, and that the Judaizers had had no official status. As to the extent to which the Law still bound *Jewish* Christians, see 21:21. **33.** The emissaries having fulfilled their mission receive the kiss of peace. **34.** There is little authority for this verse, which seems to have been inserted to explain the presence of Silas, 40.

XV 36-XVIII 22 The Second Missionary Journey, A.D. 50-2—With the door of faith opened to the Gentiles, the work of preaching must be resumed. This journey brings St Paul, guided as always by the Holy Spirit, 16:6-7, 9; 18:9, to Greece, with Corinth as his main centre.

XV 36-41 The Separation of Paul and Barnabas—36. After a short while, in the spring of 50 when travel became possible again, St Paul's solicitude for his converts, so evident in his epistles, made itself felt. **37.** *Cf.* 12:12. **38.** He considered that St Mark's inconstancy disqualified him, and he was unfamiliar with the churches that were to be revisited. **39.** 'And there arose a *sharp* dissension'. The conciliatory Barnabas wanted his cousin to repair his fault, and so took him to the field where both had laboured previously. Always a peacemaker, he had introduced Saul to the Twelve, welcomed the first Gentile converts at Antioch, and recently the desire to conciliate the Jewish Christians there had led him to dissimulation, in the company of St Peter, Gal 2:13. Indeed it has been suspected that the difference in that matter was not without its effect on the dissension here described. Nevertheless Barnabas remains the standing refutation of all the theories which try to oppose St Peter and St Paul. He was always in St Peter's confidence, with St Mark as a further link, and he was a wholehearted collaborator with St Paul, during the momentous period between the first preaching to the Gentiles at Antioch and the Council of Jerusalem. St Paul refers to him with obvious friendliness in Gal 2:9 and 1 Cor 9:6, and that is all that the NT tells us. Perhaps he did not live long, as we may infer from the presence of St Mark in Rome without his cousin at the time of St Paul's first captivity, Col 4:10. St Mark ended by becoming once again the fellow-labourer of St Paul, Phm 24; 2 Tim 4:11. **40.** Silas (*cf.* 22) must have returned from Jerusalem. He took the place of Barnabas as fellow apostle. St Paul and he were '*recommended* to the grace of *the Lord*' as before. No doubt the same happened to Barnabas and St Mark, but St Luke is no longer recounting their history. **41.** St Paul revisits the scene of his earlier labours, 9:30. The second half of the verse is to be omitted. Probably Silas and Judas had already published the Decree in Cilicia.

XVI 1-5 St Paul in S. Galatia—1. Crossing the Taurus through the Cilician Gates the party reached Derbe and then Lystra. Timothy's mother had instructed him in the Scriptures, 2 Tim 3:15, and St Paul had made him a Christian, 1 Tim 1:2. **2.** His reputation fitted him for the office for which St Paul destined him, though he was still very young, Tim 4:12. **3.** Being the son of a Jewess he would, if uncircumcised, have been considered an apostate, and all relations with Jews would have been impossible. It was well known that he had not been circumcised, his father being a Gentile, *cf.* 1 Cor 9:20. In the very different case of Titus, Gal 2:3, both his parents were Gentiles, and circumcision was demanded as though necessary for salvation. **4.** *Cf.* 15:23.

6-10 From S. Galatia to Macedonia—6. '*And they passed through the Phrygian and Galatian country, having*

been forbidden by the Holy Spirit to preach the word **837c** in Asia'. St Paul's obvious plan was to go to the great coastal towns of the province of Asia, but he was guided due north, through Phrygia to N. Galatia, and (if one accepts the North Galatian Theory) evangelized the North or real Galatians, descendants of 3rd cent. Gallic invaders.

[According to the South Galatian Theory (*cf.* § 893c–d there is no need to postulate a visit to Northern Galatia, and the phrase a 'Phrygo-Galatic region' (and the corresponding passage in 18:23) would then be taken to refer to the districts evangelized on the First Missionary Journey, which were historically both Phrygian and Galatian.—Gen. Ed.]

7-8. 'And when they *had come as far as* Mysia', the Holy Spirit guided them away from Bithynia, and right through Mysia to Troas. It was not yet time for the Gospel to be preached in the rich Gk colonies of Asia Minor. Troas was the usual port for Macedonia. The Holy Spirit proceeds also from the Son who works through him, *cf.* Phil 1:19; Rom 8:9; 1 Pet 1:11; Jn 14:26; 16:7. **9.** At length St Paul is directed positively, and into Europe. The man of Macedonia was probably recognizable by his dress. **10.** The first 'We section' beginning here shows that St Luke now joined St Paul. He seems to have remained at Philippi, where the section ends, 17, for six years, till 20:6.

11-12 At Philippi, A.D. 51—11. They made a direct **d** crossing, stopping for the night off Samothrace. A later crossing took five days, 20:6. Neapolis was the port of Philippi, 10 m. inland, to which it was linked by the Egnatian Way. **12.** Augustus had recently refounded Philippi, in gratitude for his victory there over Brutus and Cassius. He colonized it with veterans and conferred on it the *Jus Italicum*. It was '*the first city encountered*' or '*the leading city of that* part of Macedonia, and *a Roman* colony'; *cf.* 19-21.

13-15 The Conversion of Lydia—13. The Apostles **e** went by the river side, '*where we thought there would be a place of prayer*', perhaps open to the air, there not being enough Jews for a synagogue. Women were held in greater respect in Macedonia than in Greece; *cf.* 17:4, 12. **14.** Lydia was a proselyte from Thyatira in Lydia, which was renowned for its stuffs dyed in purple. **15.** *Cf.* note on 21:5-6 : Though a woman of position she says humbly, 'if [not 'since'] you have judged me faithful'. Her house no doubt became the centre of the church of Philippi, and the home of St Luke. He omits further details of the founding of the church, and relates how the Apostles had to leave.

16-18 The Possessed Slave Girl—16. She was possessed by a 'spirit *of divination*'. The legend ran that a python had uttered the oracles at Delphi until Apollo killed it and took its place. Hence a pythonical spirit was one that foretold the future. **17.** Either the devil was under some compulsion to bear witness, or wished to discredit the Apostles by his praise. **18.** Our Lord acted in his own name; *cf.* Mk. 16:17.

19-24 Arrest of St Paul and Silas—19. As in ch 19, **f** loss of revenue leads to persecution. The magistrates at the Law Courts in the Forum were the Duumvirs of a Roman colony, who had the courtesy title of 'stratēgoi', as in 20. **20-21.** The owners of the girl appeal to anti-semitism, *cf.* 18:2, 17. The law forbade Jewish propaganda among Romans. **22.** *Cf.* 1 Thess 2:2; 2 Cor 11:25. St Paul perhaps claimed Roman citizenship but was disregarded in the tumult. Cicero, *In Verrem* II, v, 62, describes such a happening. **23-24.** By law imprisonment followed flagellation. This was the first persecution by the Roman authorities and the first for which Jews were not responsible.

25-34 In the Prison at Philippi—25. 'Paul and Silas **g** *were in prayer, and singing hymns to* God', no doubt psalms, and remembering Lk 6:23. **26.** The earthquake and its effects were miraculous; *cf.* 4:31. **28.** Suicide was frequent among the Romans. **29-30.** The gaoler knew something of the preaching of the Apostles. Reassured as to his bodily safety, he is aroused by the miracle to consider the safety of his

837g soul. **32.** Paul and Silas instruct him and his family, even before their wounds are dressed. **33.** The former are washed of their wounds, the latter of their sins, cf. note on 21:5-6. **34.** The gaoler rejoiced ' *at having found faith in God* '.

h **35-40 Release and Departure**—**35-36.** In view of the events of the night the strategoi send the lictors to free the prisoners. **37.** The church would have suffered if the preachers of Christianity had escaped like criminals. By the *Lex Porcia* a Roman citizen could not be scourged, and he could only be beaten with rods after he had been condemned to death. Here there had not even been a trial. The magistrates and the whole colony were in danger. In A.D. 44 Claudius had deprived the Rhodians of their privileges for crucifying Roman citizens. His citizenship often protected St Paul, 22:25 ff. A false claim to it was punishable with death. **39.** The magistrates now came personally. **40.** On St Paul's love for the church at Philippi, see comm. on Phil.

838a **XVII 1-9 At Thessalonica**—**1.** The modern Salonica, 100 m. along the Egnatian Way, was a large port with a mixed population, which included a large Jewish colony. **3.** See on 3:18, and for the Resurrection, 26:23 ; 1 Cor 15:3. ' And that this *Jesus whom I preach to you is the Christ* '. **4.** A few Jews were converted and many proselytes and Gentiles, cf. 1 Thess 1-2. **5.** See 1 Thess 2:14-16. Jason must have been well known since his name is introduced without explanation ; cf. Rom 16:21. ' The people ' is probably the Demos or Assembly of the free city. **6.** St Luke calls the rulers by their correct but unusual title of ' Politarchs ', which various inscriptions confirm. ' *These men who have turned the world upside down are here also* '. The MSS of Vg read ' urbem ' instead of ' orbem ' ; cf. 26:26. **7.** Cf. the accusations against our Lord. St Paul had spoken about the spiritual Messianic Kingdom. **8.** ' *The crowd and the Politarchs were disturbed when they heard this* '. **9.** The Politarchs realized that the Jewish accusations were unfounded, and were content to take security for the good behaviour of the Christians. St Paul departs, anxious to avoid difficulties for the church and his host Jason.

b **10-15 At Beroea**—**10.** Then a large town, 50 m. S. of Thessalonica, near Mt Olympus, and with a large Jewish population. **14.** Silas and Timothy remained with the newly founded church. St Paul went by sea. The land route took much longer. It seems that he had intended to follow the Egnatian Way to Dyrrachium and Rome, but was deflected by the persecutions, Rom 15:19, 22. **15.** Silas and Timothy rejoined St Paul at Corinth, 18:5, yet Timothy was with St Paul at Athens, 1 Thess 3:1, 2. Probably both rejoined St Paul at Athens, only to be sent at once to strengthen the new churches in Macedonia, whence they proceeded later to Corinth.

c **16-21 St Paul at Athens**—**16.** Athens which had been pillaged by Sulla in 86 B.C. and was no longer even a provincial capital, preserved most of its statues and temples intact. It was still one of the intellectual and artistic capitals of the world. Its combination of idolatry and intellectual pride was peculiarly repellent to St Paul, who entered the city from Piraeus, along a road on which stood idols and shrines, cf. 1 Cor 8:4 ; 10:19, 20. **17.** In the market or Agora the Athenians indulged their passion for argument, 21. In it stood the portico, the *Stoa Poikile*, which gave the Stoics their name. **18.** St Luke mentions the two rival schools, the Stoics, pantheistic materialists with a high idea of duty, aiming at a life in accord with reason, as a protection against the ills of life, and the Epicureans, also materialists and making the prudent seeking of pleasure the end of life. St Paul was not a stranger to philosophy, for which Tarsus was noted, the Stoic Athenodoras flourishing there early in the 1st cent. ' Wordsower ', lit. a magpie, collector of seeds, hence ' picker up of gossip ', and so contemptuously, a babbler. Some commentators think that the Athenians seem to have taken ' the Resur-

rection ' for a goddess's name ! **19-20.** The Areopagus, the highest judicial court, so-called because it met on the Hill of Ares, took cognizance of religious matters, and possessed enormous influence and prestige. Nothing in the context or in St Paul's attitude suggests that he is on trial. This has led some to see in ' Areopagus ' merely a name for the Hill of Ares, just below the Acropolis. **21.** All the details in these verses can be corroborated from pagan sources.

22-31 St Paul's Discourse to the Athenians—All things to all men, St Paul adapts himself to his frivolous intellectual audience. He quotes the Gk poets, not the OT. **22-25 (1) The true God is the Creator of all things.** —**22.** St Paul addresses the Athenians by the same title as Demosthenes. The word tr. ' superstitious ' means ' fearer of the gods ' and can have a good or bad sense. St Paul wishes to win them and calls them ' *extremely religious* '. **23.** Pausanias and others record that there were several altars to unknown gods in Athens. The altar was erected to whatever god it might be who needed thanking or placating. St Paul takes the title in a mystical sense, and defends himself from the charge of setting forth new gods, 18. **24.** Even Plato and Aristotle had not quite arrived at the truth of an absolute Creator. The Epicureans attributed the world to chance, and the Stoics held matter to be eternal ; cf. Is 42:5. **25.** Gifts and food were offered for the use of the gods.

26-29 (2) He made Man to His Own Image and for Himself—**26.** God ' from one *man* ' caused every nation to dwell on the earth. The argument is from the unity of the human race. Each nation had its separate god from whom it claimed to originate. Since the human race originates from one man made by God, there is only one God. He has not merely arranged seasons, as in 14:16, and geographical boundaries. His Providence in history fixes the times of prosperity and the territorial limits of the nations ; cf. Job 12:23. **27.** Man who was made to seek after God, is like one feeling his way in the dark ; cf. 1 Cor 13:12. Because of this and of the nearness of God, the pagan is without excuse : cf. Rom 1:20. **28.** We depend utterly on God. After what St Paul had said of God the Creator his words could have no pantheistic meaning. The poets are Aratus, Cleanthes and Epimenides, speaking of Zeus.

30-31 (3) They are called to repent because they will be judged by One who rose from the Dead—**30.** This kind of ignorance does not excuse, but lessens, guilt, cf. Rom 1:20. From 14:16 we see that God has never left himself without witness. Now all men in all places must ' *repent* '. The Epicureans held that God did not occupy himself with man, and the Stoics that man was sufficient for himself. Neither saw the need to turn to God and repent. **31.** St Paul omits the Holy Name for which the Athenians were not prepared. God has given faith, or rather a motive for faith, to all by raising Christ from the dead. Or perhaps the Resurrection is given as a proof of the General Resurrection as in 1 Cor 15:12 ff. Hebrew thought did not separate body and soul in the way we do. For all to be judged all must be raised from the dead.

32-34 Effect of the Discourse—**32.** St Paul was listened to only while he spoke of the nature of God and Providence. His teaching about our Lord was cut short. Epicureans and Stoics, unlike Plato, denied the soul's immortality, but all alike thought the resurrection of the body an absurdity. St Paul was coldly dismissed. **33-34.** Here alone in his preaching does St Paul seems to have met with little success. Pride of intellect was more impervious to the Gospel than pagan licentiousness ; cf. 1 Cor 1:18-25. Denis became the first bishop of Athens, Eus., HE III, 4.

XVIII 1-4 At Corinth in the Synagogue, A.D. 51— The capital of Achaia and a large city and port was a byword even in antiquity for immorality. (But see on 1 Cor, § 864d.) **2.** Aquila and Priscilla were almost certainly Christians. St Luke tells us they were Jews to explain their expulsion from Rome, presumably that referred to by Suetonius, *Claudius* 25, after the riots ' impulsore Chresto ', A.D. 49.

The Jewish colony in Rome was large, and a few years later Aquila and Priscilla were back in Rome, Rom 16:3. **3.** They left Corinth with St Paul, 18 and 26. Their house was the church's centre not only at Corinth but at Ephesus, 1 Cor 16:19, and Rome, Rom 16:4-5. **4.** The words ' bringing in the name ', etc., have little MSS authority.

5-11 The Preaching to the Gentiles at Corinth—5. *Cf.* 17:15 note. Silas and Timothy probably brought alms from Macedonia, which made tent-making less necessary, see 2 Cor 11:8-9. *Cf.* also 2 Cor 1:19 ; 1 Thess 1:1 ; 2 Thess 1:1. **6.** *Cf.* 13:45. St Paul disclaims responsibility. 1 and 2 Thess were written from Corinth, and mention the persecution, 1 Thess 2:15 ; 3:7. **7.** ' *Titius* Justus ' was a proselyte, and his house now became the centre of the church. **8.** *Cf.* 1 Cor 1:14-16. For St Paul's account see 1 Cor 2:1-5. **9.** After the Jewish opposition St Paul is again encouraged and guided by Jesus. He often speaks of his discouragement in 2 Cor. **10.** Even in that wicked city many will listen to the call of God ; *cf.* 1 Cor 1:26 ; 6:9-11. **11.** Converts were also made in the province, 2 Cor 1:1. For further details of the building up of the Church in Corinth see § 864*h*. St Paul left in his own time, when he saw that the new community was solidly established and his work crowned with success.

12-17 St Paul before Gallio, A.D. 52—12. From an inscription at Delphi we gather that Gallio arrived to take up office, in 51 or 52, *cf.* *Foakes-Jackson and K. Lake, op. cit.* v, 460 f. He was Seneca's brother, and a weak but agreeable man, faithful to his relatives and friends. **13.** The Jews took advantage of the arrival of a new proconsul to accuse St Paul of breaches of their Law. **14-16.** Gallio seems to have shared his brother's contempt for the Jews. **17.** Sosthenes was probably the author of the accusation against St Paul.
18-22 The Return to Antioch—18. St Luke is anxious to hurry on to tell of the evangelization of the next great centre Ephesus. Cenchreae was the eastern port of Corinth ; *cf.* Rom 16:1. Perhaps during his perils at Corinth St Paul had taken the Nazirite vow that he would not cut his hair, for a period, or till out of danger, Num 6:2 ff. See 21:21. **19-21.** It seems that the ship only stayed long enough for one Sabbath. **22.** ' The church ' is used in its primitive sense, *i.e.* the community at Jerusalem, as in 5:11. This is the last mention of Antioch in Ac.

XVIII 23-XXI 14 Third Missionary Journey, A.D. 53-8—Ephesus was to be the centre of this journey, but first, after passing the Cilician Gates, St Paul spent most of the year in Phrygia and Galatia ; see 16:6.
XVIII 24-8 Apollos at Ephesus—24. Apollos, with whom 1 Cor 1:12-3:22 is concerned, is mentioned to explain the beginning of St Paul's apostolate at Ephesus. **25.** On ' the way ' see 9:2. Apollos taught ' *accurately* ', but not completely. **27.** At Corinth ' he helped them much who had believed, *through the grace* ' he had received from God. *Cf.* 1 Cor 3:6, and for the letter, 2 Cor 3:1.
XIX 1-7 St Paul and the Disciples of John at Ephesus—**1.** St Paul ' passed through the upper *country* ', the high inland plateau of Asia Minor. Ephesus, the capital of the province of Asia, which abounded in flourishing cities, was the richest and most magnificent of them all, with a population of a third of a million. See too on 24. It was the meeting place of traders from east and west, and Seneca describes it as one of the most beautiful cities of the world. **2.** St Paul assumes that these disciples have been baptized and wishes to make sure that they have also received the Holy Spirit, as in the case of the Samaritans, 8:14. They either did not know all John's teaching, or perhaps meant ' We have not heard that the Holy Spirit is now given '. **3.** They seem, like Apollos, to have been disciples of Jews who had left Palestine after hearing only the preaching of John. They had evidently not been instructed by

Apollos, before his departure for Corinth. Jn 1:6 and **839f** 15 ff. and 3:23 ff. suggest the existence in Ephesus at the end of the century, of followers of the Baptist, more or less opposed to Christians. **4.** *Cf.* Jn 1:26 ff. **5-6.** See 2:38. See § 820*b*. For an almost contemporary description of the speaking with tongues (Glossolalia), see 1 Cor 14.
8-12 The Preaching and Miracles at Ephesus—8. The **g** account of the 18 months devoted to the successful founding of the church at Corinth was compressed into a few lines, and now the long apostolate at Ephesus A.D. 54 to 57 is even more briefly related, and even more successful. **9.** On ' the way ' see 9:2. The multitude is the assembly in the Synagogue. Tyrannus was perhaps a Rhetor who gave lessons in eloquence or a philosopher. D adds at the end, ' from the fifth to the tenth hour ', from 10 am.. to 4 p.m., which was certainly the time when the Hall would be free for St Paul to use. **10** is a pregnant summary of St Paul's activity during the three years, 20:31, that he spent at Ephesus ; *cf.* too 20:18-21. Besides earning his living and preaching in the school of Tyrannus, there were the continual relations with the other cities of the province. There were also letters to be written, *e.g.* to Galatia where Judaizers were causing havoc, and to Corinth, including 1 Cor which gives an idea of his labours. At Ephesus ' a great door was opened and many adversaries ', 1 Cor 16:8-9. See also 4:9-13 ; 15:30-33. Apoc 1-3 throws light on these flourishing churches. The burning of the books, the account of the riot, *e.g.* 26, and the friendship of the Asiarchs reveal the extent and depth of St Paul's work. He founded the church in Asia, Aquila and Priscilla only passed through, Rom 16:5. **11-12.** Miracles played their part, as the next verses show. On the warrant for the cult of relics *cf.* 5:15.
13-17 The Jewish Exorcists—13. Lk 11:19. **16.** The **h** Gk word tr. ' both ' can also have the sense of ' all '. See too KNT note. **17** describes the effect on unbelievers, **18** that on the faithful.
18-20 The Burning of the Books—18. Magic was so ingrained that even many Christians had not given it up. **19.** They had practised ' *magical* arts '. The treatises were no doubt sufficiently rare to be of great value. Ephesus was one of the centres that produced them. Livy records a similar burning of magical books, XL, 29.
21-22 St Paul's Plans—After two years and more he **i** proposed to leave Ephesus. The immediate cause of his departure was the riot some months later. One purpose of the visit to Macedonia and Achaia was to collect alms for Jerusalem, 1 Cor 16. Judging the Church to be now firmly established around the Aegean, St Paul wished to go to Rome, but not to remain there, Rom 1:11-15 ; 15:20, 23. In all such matters he was guided by the Holy Spirit, although ' purposed in spirit ' could be taken of his own mind. On the voyages to Corinth see § 866*g-h*. Timothy was sent to Corinth, 1 Cor 4:17. This was perhaps a second errand. On Erastus see Rom 16:23 ; 2 Tim 4:20.
23-40 The Riot of the Silversmiths—An eyewitness's **j** account enlivened by humour. **24.** Ephesus was the sacred city of the fertility goddess Diana. Her temple was about two-thirds of the size of St Peter's, Rome, and contained 127 pillars, 60 feet high. Demetrius and the corporation of silversmiths made miniature copies of the temple containing a statue of the goddess. **28.** If Demetrius had been speaking in the forum, the shouts would soon attract attention. **29.** The theatre is the largest known, and could hold 25,000 people. **30.** St Paul wished to save his friends. Aristarchus accompanied him to Rome, 27:2. **31.** The Asiarchs were the priests responsible for the cult of the emperor. They were very exalted magistrates. They can hardly have been Christians, but it is clear that St Paul had friends in the highest places. **33.** Alexander perhaps wished to disclaim Jewish responsibility. **35.** The town clerk was ' the Scribe of the People ', who presided over the Assembly and ruled the city. His importance is

839j attested by inscriptions, and he was the city's link with the imperial authorities. His able speech saved the situation. He too was evidently a friend of St Paul. ' The city of the Ephesians is *the temple keeper* of the great Diana and *of the statue that fell from heaven* '. Such was the legend, due perhaps to an aerolith. **37.** St Paul had attacked idolatry, but his arguments were adapted to the mentality of his hearers, and he avoided offensive words. **40.** An unauthorized assembly, *a fortiori* a riot, might lead to the loss of the privileges of a free city, since only the Roman authorities could sanction a ' city ' assembly of this kind.

840a XX 1-6 Travels in Macedonia and Greece, A.D. 57-8—1. Note the liturgical farewell, as always, *e.g.* 14:22 ; 16:40. In Macedonia St Paul wrote 2 Cor, and mentioned his trials, 1:8–10 ; 11:23 ff. St Luke does not refer to the troubles in Corinth, which the two Epistles reveal. **2.** St Paul now preached ' as far as unto Illyricum ', Rom 15:19. **3.** The three winter months were spent at Corinth, 1 Cor 16:5-6. Rom was then being written to prepare for the projected visit, 19:21. The plot was to kill St Paul at the port or at sea. **5-6.** Some of the party went ahead to Troas. Another ' we-section '. The first person shows that St Luke joined St Paul at Philippi where Easter was celebrated ; see on 16:10.

b 7-12 The Eucharist at Troas—7. It is clear from 1 Cor 16:2 that Sunday had already become the day for the Christian Assembly and Eucharist. By the Jewish reckoning the night would be that of Saturday. On the Breaking of Bread see 2:42. The verb used for ' assembling ' has for its noun ' Synaxis ', the Gk for Eucharist. **8.** The accident was not due to the darkness. **9.** St Luke means us to understand that Eutychus was dead, 12. **10.** St Paul announces the miracle. **11.** The gathering had been for the Breaking of Bread and the ' tasting ' of Holy Communion. This is now done, with St Paul presiding. He again speaks long, never expecting to return, 25.

13-16 From Troas to Miletus—13. The ship seems to have been at the disposal of St Paul's party till 21:2. He may have taken the short cut by land so as to have more time with the disciples. **14-15.** The details are given to show how no call was made at Ephesus. Miletus was 30 m. S of Ephesus, a port at the mouth of the Meander. **16.** St Luke now gives the reason for the route taken.

c 17-38 The Discourse to the Presbyters of Ephesus— On presbyters see § 820*d*. Only here in Ac does St Paul address his own converts, and his words have much to teach Christian pastors. The speech is thoroughly Pauline in style and subject and in the zeal for souls it reveals. Nearly every sentence can be paralleled in the Epistles. He lays bare his soul, his tender memories, his fears for the future, his love for his own.

18-24 St Paul will go up to Jerusalem in spite of the Dangers—18. Asia is the proconsular province. **19.** *Cf.* 19:9 ; 20:3. **20.** *Cf.* 2 Cor 4:2. St Paul did not teach only in the School of Tyrannus. **22.** He is forced on by the Holy Spirit. He goes resolutely forward in obedience, like his Master who steadfastly set his face to go to Jerusalem, Lk 9:51. He is enlightened both interiorly and exteriorly, 21:4, 11. **24** should probably begin, ' *But I do not hold my life of any account, nor as precious to myself, so long as I may finish my course* '. St Paul's gospel was that of the free gift of God, without the works of the Law.

d 25-31 Pastoral Exhortation and Warning—25. St Paul's statement is a presentiment based on the dangers which threaten him, Rom 15:31, and his plan of going to Spain, *ibid.* v 28. We learn from the Pastoral Epistles that St Paul did in fact revisit Ephesus. St Luke's report of these words shows that he writes before those Epistles, and before St Paul returned to the Aegean. **26.** This is a solemn declaration that he has done his duty. He is innocent of blood, in the matter of pastoral responsibility. The shepherd who does not preach the kingdom is guilty of the spiritual death of his flock. **27.** St Paul has declared to them ' the *whole* counsel of God ' ; *cf.* Eph 1:11. Eph. is the best comm.

on 27. **28.** The presbyters must not neglect their own salvation, 1 Cor 9:27, nor that of the flock over which the Holy Spirit has appointed them, 1 Cor 12:28, ' to *feed* the Church '. The pastoral metaphor, so frequent in the Gospels is kept up. ' The Church of God which he has purchased with his own blood ' (as in DV) is the best supported reading, Sin, B, etc. D and other MSS have ' Church of the Lord ', to avoid the unusual phrase ' the blood of God '. Even this, in view of the reference to Ps 73(74):2 which guarantees the meaning of ' Lord ', affirms the divinity of Christ. However the reading as in DV is to be retained, as the more difficult and so probably the original one. ' The Church of God ' appears eleven times in the Pauline Epistles, and ' The Church of the Lord ' nowhere in the NT. The expression ' the blood of God ' is used by St Ignatius, *Eph.* 1:1, and by other early writers, *cf.* Lightfoot, *Apostolic Fathers*, *Clement of Rome*, II, 13–16, but later became suspected of Apollinarism. It is straining the Gk to translate ' with the blood of his Own ' and supply the word ' Son '. Often in the NT it is said that Jesus purchased us with his blood. **29.** The Pastoral Epistles and the history of St John at Ephesus (*cf.* Apoc. 2:2) show the fulfilment of these predictions. **31.** *Cf.* on 19:10. St Paul gives himself as an example and shows his care for his churches, all as in his Epistles.

32-35 He commends the Presbyters to God—32. The word, God's gracious promises in the Gospel, works powerfully in us ; *cf.* 1 Thess 2:13. God will strengthen and instruct the presbyters by means of the truths of Faith at work in them. **33.** Clothes formed a large part of riches ; *cf.* Mt 6:19. St Paul's disinterestedness often comes out in his Epistles ; *cf.* 18:3. **35.** The presbyters must work so as to support the needy (*cf.* Eph 4:28) and so that none may say they preach the Gospel for the sake of gain, but *cf.* 1 Cor 9:14. The saying of our Lord is not found in the Gospels, though nothing could be closer to their spirit.

36-38 The Farewell to the Presbyters from Ephesus —37. St Paul's gift of sympathy showed itself in tears, 19 ; 2 Cor 2:4 ; Rom 12:15. Often in the Epistles he exhorts the faithful to salute each other with a kiss ; *cf.* the kiss of peace. **38.** The harbour was some distance from the town where the meeting had been held, and all accompanied St Paul, as in 15:3 and 21:5.

XXI 1-6 From Miletus to Tyre—1-2. St Luke is still with the party but of the list in 20:4 only Trophimus and Aristarchus are mentioned again (21:29 and 27:2), and it seems that only these three went on with St Paul. The ship was a coastal vessel, so at Patara in Lycia another ship was taken, going direct to Tyre. **4.** The church at Tyre was founded by Hellenists after the death of St Stephen, 11:19 ; *cf.* 15:3. St Paul, so anxious to reach Jerusalem, must have been forced to wait till the ship sailed. The Holy Spirit was leading him there in spite of the trials which he knew awaited him. It was not through the Spirit that the disciples tried to dissuade him from continuing his journey. The Spirit made known the trials, and their devotion made them try to prevent him from going further as in 10-12. **5-6.** All went down the long sandy strand of the narrow peninsula on which Tyre stood. The conversions of whole families, 16:15 and 33, and this the only mention in Ac of children among the faithful are evidence for the practice of infant baptism.

7-14 From Tyre to Caesarea—7. Ptolemais is the modern Acre. The journey seems to have been continued by sea ; see 15. **8.** For Caesarea see on 8:40. An evangelist was an apostle of the second rank, Eph 4:11. **9.** The daughters of Philip were filled with the Holy Spirit like their father. Their spiritual gifts were closely related to their virginity, which they had chosen as a permanent state ; *cf.* 1 Cor 7, especially v 34. **10-11.** St Luke seems to have forgotten that he had already spoken of Agabus, 11:28. The OT prophets often acted symbolically, Is 20:1-4 ; Jer chh 27, 28, and also our Lord, Jn 13:4. **12-13.** Again St Luke suggests the parallel with our Lord, *cf.* 20:22. *Cf.* also St Peter's words, Mt 16:22, and our Lord's, Lk 12:50.

h 14. It is the will of the Lord Jesus, 13, that must be done. He governs all things ; he is God.

a XXI 15-XXIII 35 St Paul at Jerusalem, A.D. 58—The atmosphere in the city was tense, and made more so by the crowds of pilgrims for the feast of Pentecost. The cruelties of Felix (see 23:24) and the fanaticism of the Zealots were preparing the way for the tragedy of A.D. 70. As for St Paul, from now until his release in Rome, his activity was to be limited by a long captivity. Although he would have many visitors both at Caesarea and Rome, 24:23 ; 28:30-31, the energetic apostolic labours were for the time being at an end.

15-16 The Arrival at Jerusalem—15. The ' preparation ' involved finding pack-horses for the party and their, perhaps bulky, offerings, now that the sea journey was over. **16.** ' Bringing *us to the house of* Mnason '. In the house of this Hellenist any Gentile Christians with St Paul would feel more at ease than among Jewish Christians.

b 17-20 St Paul and the Church at Jerusalem—The opposition of the Judaizers to St Paul's preaching, of which we learn from Gal and Rom, did not enter into the theme of Ac, § 816d. St Luke does not mention them except for the warnings of 20:29-30 and the account of the Council of Jerusalem in ch 15. Like St Paul, Rom 15:1-12, he is anxious to show the unity of Jewish and Gentile Christians. The church at Jerusalem had long since agreed not to impose the Law on Gentile Christians, and now it was prepared to welcome the great enemy of the Judaizers. Misrepresentations of which he had been the object would be the occasion for demonstrating unity and charity. **18.** After a private welcome, 17, there is an official reception by the presbyters and St James ; *cf.* 15:13. The alms which St Paul had collected as a sign of union, Rom 15:25-31, were probably presented, 24:17, but perhaps the gesture was not as effective as had been hoped. The ' We-section ' ends here to begin again with the journey to Rome, 27:2. **19-20.** The news of the conversion of the Gentiles is received with joy (*cf.* 15:12) and St Paul is addressed as ' brother ' by these zealous Jews, now very numerous.

c 21 St Paul's Attitude to the Law—In view of the false accusations against him St Paul was bold indeed to come to Jerusalem. He had taught that the Law does not justify, which would eventually lead to its abandonment even by Jewish Christians. The Jews rightly concluded that he denied an absolute value to Circumcision, the Law and the temple, 28. On the other hand as long as Jewish Christians acknowledged that salvation came through faith in Christ, he had never forbidden them to observe the Law. It became for them something in the nature of a work of supererogation. The breach with the Synagogue was gradual. It is generally held that after A.D. 70 it was complete, and that then all participation in Jewish rites became unlawful. Thus when St Paul now acceded to the request of St James, he did not go against his principles. He was hardly the man to do that. He acknowledged a relative value in the Law, and he seems generally to have observed it himself ; *cf.* 16:3 ; 18:18. He claimed to be a strict Pharisee, 23:6 ; 26:4-5. He protested that he had not offended in anything against the Law or the temple, in which he had come ' to adore ', 24:11 ; 25:8 ; 28:17. These things were not incompatible with the preaching of the new faith. They prepared the way for it, and found in it their fulfilment, 24:14 ; 26:22-23, *cf.* Rom 9-11, 1 Cor 7:18-20.

d 22-26 The Nazirite Vow—22. ' *What then is to be done ? They will certainly hear that you have come* '. St Paul must clear himself of the charges that are reported against him. **23.** The four men had taken the Nazirite vow ; see 18:18. They could not cut their hair until the period of their vow was over, and they had made their offering in the temple. **24.** St Paul must pay the offerings of these four Jewish Christians, whose vow had still seven days to go, 27. He will thus sanctify himself by sharing in their vow, and it will

be seen that he ' walks in the observance of the Law '. **341d** St James meant St Paul to show that he observed the Law, and to refute the report about his attitude, which implied that he despised it. **25.** He is reminded that his vow will not prejudice the case of the Gentile Christians, whose liberty the Apostles and presbyters had recognized at the Council of Jerusalem. Thus his action will not have the effect of that for which he blamed St Peter in the mixed church of Antioch, Gal 2:11 ff. **26.** Being all things to all men, St Paul agrees, goes to the temple, and arranges for the day on which the sacrifice is to be offered. He seems to have had ample funds at his disposal at this period, Ramsay, *St Paul the Traveller*, 310 ff. ' Being purified ' : *cf.* Lev 15:13 ; ' the days of purification ' : *cf.* Num 6:5.

27-30 The Riot in the Temple—27. On the Jews of **e** Asia, see 20:19. **28.** *Cf.* the accusations against St Stephen, 6:14. Passing beyond the boundary stones of the Court of the Gentiles was punishable by death for any Gentile, even for a Roman citizen. One of the temple notices giving this warning in Gk and Latin has been found. **30.** The Levites shut the gates to prevent a profanation of the temple, as they often did in the stormy years before A.D. 70.

31-36 The Arrest of St Paul—31. The Tribune, Claudius Lysias, 22:28, commanded the cohort which garrisoned Jerusalem. It was stationed in the Fortress Antonia, which stood at the NW. angle of the Temple, overlooking it. The whereabouts of ' the steps ' is uncertain. **32.** Riots were frequent, especially at the feasts, hence troops were on the alert. **33.** St Paul is taken, as the cause of the uproar. **34-35.** It being impossible to discover the nature of his crime, he is dragged up the steps to the Fortress whence our Lord had set out for Calvary. **36.** *Cf.* Lk 23:18.

37-40 He obtains Permission to address the Crowd—38. Josephus gives two accounts of this incident, Jos. Ant, 20, 8, 6 ; Jos. BJ 2, 13, 5. The Murderers or Sicarii, so called from the short dagger each kept under his cloak, were the extreme nationalist party. **39.** St Paul has barely escaped with his life from the Jews, and yet all he thinks of is to save their souls. **40.** He speaks in Aramaic and with his hands chained.

XXII 1-21 The Speech to the Jews of Jerusalem— **f** St Paul tries to calm and win over his audience by showing his devotion to the Law before his conversion, his good relations with the Jews after it, and how wishing to preach to them, he only turned to the Gentiles after a vision. The speech is a masterpiece of apostolic tact, but the mention of Gentiles is too much for his audience.

1-16 Persecution and Conversion—1. The address is respectful like St Stephen's, 7:2. ' Hear the *defence* '. **3.** St Paul is a Hebrew of the Hebrews ; see 21:21, Phil 3:3-6 ; Gal 1:13-14 ; ' zealous for God ', a trait which unites him with his hearers, Rom 10:2. On Gamaliel see 5:33. **5.** See 9:2. **6.** The conversion is described to show that St Paul was only obeying the call of God. **9.** See 9:7. **12.** The devotion of Ananias to the Law is emphasized. **14.** On ' the Just One ' see 3:14. **16.** The internal effect of baptism follows, once the external sign has been performed. It is accompanied by a profession of faith, the invocation of the name of the Just One ; see 9:14.

17-21 The Call to the Gentiles—17. St Paul em- **g** phasizes how he was praying in the temple (on his first visit as a Christian, *cf.* 9:30 *supra*), and seems to avoid mentioning our Lord's name. **19-20.** He wished to preach to and save his own people, and thought his former zeal would convince them of his sincerity. **21.** See note 9:15. *Cf.* 2:39.

22-29 The Roman Citizen and the Tribune—22. The **h** idea that the Gentiles without becoming Jews could share their privileges aroused fury. **24.** St Paul was taken into the Fortress for safety, and the Tribune, who had not understood the Aramaic speech, proposed to resort to the usual method of discovering the cause of the trouble. **25.** St Paul draws attention to the twofold injustice. See 16:37. **28.** Claudius

841h Lysias was probably a Greek who had obtained his citizenship under Claudius and taken that emperor's name. Claudius' empress Messalina made a fortune out of the sale of this privilege, Dio Cassius, 60, 17. It was rare at this period for a Jew to be born a citizen. St Paul's family must have had some importance. **29.** St Paul had been bound in order to be scourged, contrary to the *Lex Porcia*, and it had been proposed to torture him before trial, which was forbidden by a law of Augustus. He remained chained ; *cf.* 30 and note on 24:23.

i **XXII 30-XXIII 10 St Paul before the Sanhedrin—30.** Since the accusations deal with religion, in order to discover what they are the Tribune summons the Sanhedrin, which, so that he can be present, must meet outside the temple. **XXIII 1.** In preaching the Gospel St Paul has been obeying God. ' In all good conscience ' is found twenty times in the Epistles. **2.** The high-priest is exasperated at the appeal from his judges to the invisible Judge. Ananias, high-priest from A.D. 47 till he was deposed in 59, was a violent, rapacious man. He was murdered by the Sicarii extremists in A.D. 66, and the prophetical words of 3 were fulfilled. **3.** St Paul spoke not to curse but to assert, ' God will punish you '. There is an allusion to Mt 23:27 ; *cf.* Ez 13:10. Ananias was proposing an illegal outrage, very offensive from one Jew to another. St Paul's cause would suffer if he, a Roman citizen, allowed himself to be so treated before the Tribune. *Cf.* Jn 18:23, our Lord's more wonderful conduct. **5.** St Paul who may have been looking round the Sanhedrin to see whom he could recognize, heard the high-priest's order, without knowing from whom it had come. **6.** St Luke only records a part of the speech. 9 shows that St Paul again recounted his conversion, and our Lord's appearance to him, which proved that Jesus had risen. This led on to the General Resurrection. Perhaps St Paul noticed the different reception the account of our Lord's Resurrection received from the two parties, and hoped to win over the Pharisees, of whom he was one himself ; *cf.* 22:3 ; 26:5. Our Lord had supported the Pharisees on this very question. The ' hope ' is the Messianic hope that God's Kingdom would be set up, of which the resurrection of the dead is a corollary ; *cf.* 26:6-8. Accused of attacking the Law, 21:28, St Paul defends himself by claiming to preach that spiritual kingdom and its consequences, wherein lies the true fulfilment of the Law ; *cf.* 26:22-23. **8.** The Sadducees deny a Resurrection, the existence of angels and the immortality of the soul, ' but the Pharisees confess *all* of them ' (' both ' meaning ' all ' as in 19:16). **9.** Some Pharisees admit that an angel spoke to St Paul in 22:7, 18.

j **11. The Vision of Our Lord**—As amid the trials of Corinth, 18:9, so amid those of Jerusalem, Jesus reassures St Paul, with praise for the past and light for the future. He is to preach in Rome, see on 19:21, and with that climax St Luke's history will end. ' Be constant ', the same word often on our Lord's lips in the Gospels is there tr. ' Be of good heart ', Mt 9:2 ; Jn 16:33.

k **12-22 The Jewish Plot—12.** There are other examples of such oaths under a curse. On the general insecurity see 21:15 and 38, and note the precautions in 23. **16.** Nothing further is known of this nephew. **20.** The better reading makes it the Tribune who was ' to inquire something more certain '.

l **23-30 The Letter of Claudius Lysias—23.** Glad to rid himself of responsibility, the Tribune acted at once and ordered a large escort, perhaps a third of the garrison. The spearmen were probably light infantry. The third hour was about 9 p.m., when in the dark they would attract less attention. **24.** Felix the Procurator of Judaea from A.D. 52 to 60, was a freedman of the imperial household. His brother Pallas was the favourite of Agrippina wife of Claudius and mother of Nero. Strong in this protection, the government of Felix was venal and rapacious, and his cruelties during these critical years paved the way for the

final tragedy. Tacitus says of him that ' indulging in **8** every kind of barbarity and lust, he exercised the power of a king in the spirit of a slave ', *Hist.* V, 9. He delighted to marry into royal families, and Suetonius describes him as ' the husband of three queens ' ; *cf.* 24:24. **25.** The part in brackets is an interpolation. Lysias sends the Elogium or letter to his superior magistrate explaining the matter that is being referred to him. St Luke probably obtained a copy while waiting at Caesarea. **26.** ' Excellency ' was the title of a procurator. **27.** Lysias alters the facts to his advantage. He did not find out that St Paul was a Roman citizen till he was about to scourge him. **28-29.** He writes contemptuously of the Jewish Law. **31-35 St Paul is taken to Caesarea—31.** Antipatris, a **m** pleasure resort in the foothills of Judaea, 30 m. from Jerusalem, was reached by a forced march. **32.** On the plain of Sharon the danger of an attack by conspirators was remote. The 400 infantry being badly needed returned to Jerusalem. **35.** ' Herod's *Palace* ' was built by Herod the Great ; see 8:40. It was used by the Procurators as a residence and prison, hence Lk's reference to it as the ' praetorium '.

XXIV 1-XXVI 32 St Paul at Caesarea, A.D. 58-60. **8** **XXIV 1-9 The Accusation before Felix—1.** The high-priest hired ' Tertullus an *advocate*, and these *laid their plea* against Paul before the Governor '. **2.** As to the praise of Felix for maintaining peace and because ' *reforms are introduced through thy foresight on behalf of this nation* ', see on 23:24. From his reference to ' this nation ' Tertullus seems not to have been a Jew. **5.** The political accusation will appeal to Felix. ' Author ' should be ' *Ringleader* '. **6-8.** Much is omitted in the best MSS. ' *He also tried to profane the temple, but we apprehended him. By examining him thyself thou canst learn from him about all these things of which we accuse him* '.

10-21 St Paul's Defence—10. In Judaea the Procurator **b** could not take up the attitude of Gallio, 18:15. St Paul appeals to him confidently. He had ruled Judaea since A.D. 52, and Samaria before that, hence he was conversant with Jewish problems. **14.** The Way is not a heresy, for in it St Paul serves ' the God *of our Fathers*, believing all that *is according to* the Law, and *written* in the Prophets ', namely the Messianic hope ; see on 21:21 and *cf.* Rom 3:31 ; 10:4. **15.** He also shares the Jewish hope of a resurrection. The Sadducees who denied it, were a small minority. This seems to be the only reference in St Paul to the resurrection of the unjust ; *cf.* F. Prat, *The Theology of St Paul*, II (1945) 360. **16.** ' And hence ', in view of the belief just stated. **17.** . . . ' to *offer* alms to my nation and *sacrifices* '. The alms for the church. Omit ' and vows '. **21.** See 23:6.

22-23 The Case adjourned—22. In view of Lysias' **c** letter, the hearing just concluded, and his knowledge of the Way, Felix ought to have released St Paul. But he was anxious not to offend the Sanhedrin, and since it was impossible to hand over to them an innocent Roman citizen, he fell back on the expedient of an adjournment. **23.** St Paul was under *Custodia Militaris*. The prisoner was chained to a soldier, but not in a public prison, and sometimes even in a private house, as in 28:16. At Caesarea he remained in Herod's Palace.

24-27 The Interview with Felix and Drusilla—24. **d** Drusilla was the youngest daughter of Herod Agrippa I. She was married at the age of 14, but abandoned her husband after two months and became the third wife of Felix, who was a pagan. **25.** St Paul like the Baptist speaks of the virtues the couple flagrantly rejected. Not only his Jewish wife, but Felix too was familiar with the new faith, 22, long peacefully established at Caesarea. **26.** *Cf.* 21:26. **27.** The change of Procurators took place about the middle of A.D. 60. Felix was recalled to answer Jewish complaints of his misrule, hence his anxiety to please them.

XXV 1-5 Festus and the Jews—1. Josephus (BJ, 2, **e** 14, 1) describes Portius Festus as an energetic magistrate who dealt promptly with disorder. He was in every way superior to Felix. He only remained one full day at Caesarea before visiting the storm centre. **4-5.** He appeals to the law. The case has been brought before the court at Caesarea and must be dealt with there. 'Let those among you that *have authority* go down'.

6-12 St Paul appeals to Caesar—7. Festus acted so promptly that there was no time to suborn witnesses. *Cf.* 21:28. **10.** It would have been fatal for St Paul to admit the competence of the Sanhedrin, even though Festus were present. It would have condemned him to death, with his rights as a Roman citizen abandoned. **11.** Thus the weakness of Festus forced him to pronounce the words which suspended all intermediary jurisdiction. Neither condemnation nor acquittal were now possible; *cf.* 26:32. **12.** If there were no adequate grounds, an appeal could be refused, hence the consultation, in this case a formality. Festus makes a statement, '*Thou hast . . . appealed*'. According to Lattey, *op. cit.* 293, 'Strictly speaking it is not an appeal at all, but an ousting of jurisdiction'.

13-22 Festus lays the case before Agrippa—13. Herod Agrippa II was born and educated at Rome. He was only 17 at his father's death in A.D. 44 (see 12:1) and did not succeed him. He was given the tetrarchies of Philip and Lysanias in A.D. 53, and parts of Galilee and Peraea later. He remained loyal to the Romans during the Jewish War. He was cultured, the patron of Josephus, and interested in all that concerned the Jewish religion; *cf.* 26:3, 28. He was, however, living incestuously with his sister Bernice. Her conduct was censured by Juvenal, *Satires,* VI, 156. The Ptolemies imitated the Pharaohs before them in marrying their sisters. Bernice like her brother tried to counsel moderation to the Jews during the War. Later she became the mistress of Vespasian and then of Titus. **14.** Festus consults Agrippa who besides being an instructed Jew, had inherited the protectorate of the temple in A.D. 50. **16.** Gk has '*hand over*' instead of 'condemn'. **18.** 'His accusers *standing around him*', 7. **19.** See 23:6. No political charges could be sustained against St Paul. **21.** Augustus: the emperor Nero. The title 'Augustus' (Sebastos) was regularly used as an imperial title from Augustus himself onwards.

23-27 Festus introduces St Paul to Agrippa—23. The setting for the last discourse in Ac is one of great splendour. **24.** *Cf.* 22:22. **26.** An Elogium (see 23:25) had to be sent to Rome, and Festus now admits that he has no definite charge, 19. The divine title 'lord' was first used of the emperor under Caligula, and became common under Nero.

XXVI 1-23 St Paul's Speech before Agrippa—His defence resembles that before the Jewish mob, ch 22, but adapted to the cultured audience. It too was interrupted. St Paul shows how the Gospel is the fulfilment of the OT, and that he had acted as a loyal Jew in becoming an apostle.

2-11 St Paul's Jewish Faith—3. The Rabbis praised Agrippa for his knowledge of the Law. **4-5.** See 21:21 and 22:3. St Paul's youth was spent in Jerusalem, 'living according to the *strictest party*'. **6.** See 23:6. **8.** His preaching was that the hope had been realized in Jesus, whose Resurrection proved that he was the Messias. 'Why should it be thought incredible *among you*' who believe in the resurrection of the body, 'that God should rise the dead?' **10.** On the saints see 9:13. '*I cast my vote against them*'; *cf.* 7:59. **11.** 'Often have I tried to force them into blasphemy', KNT. It was Jesus they were to blaspheme. St Paul wishes to show how utterly he was changed by his vision.

12-18 His Conversion and Mandate—See 9:1-18. **16.** The message which came through Ananias is attributed direct to its author, as so often in the OT. To mention Ananias served no purpose with this audience; the point to be made was that there had been a revelation from God. **17.** How often Jesus delivered him from his own people and from the

Gentiles! 18. *Cf.* Is 42:7, and Col 1:12-14. Justification by faith was learnt at once; see 9:4. **821i**

19-23 His Missionary Work, preaching what the Prophets foretold—19. 'I was not *disobedient* to the heavenly vision'. **20.** Gal 1:22 shows that the preaching in Judaea must have been on the second visit, 11:30. The Gentiles were to 'repent' and do works worthy of 'repentance'. **21.** The Jews attacked St Paul because he preached salvation to the Gentiles on the same terms as themselves. **22-23.** His preaching is the fulfilment of the old Law which foretold our Lord's sufferings (*cf.* Ac 3:18), his Resurrection (*cf.* 17:3) and that he would be the light, 13:47. Thus he is the Messias. **j**

24-32 The Discussion with Festus and Agrippa—24. The references to the Resurrection and to light for the Gentiles seemed absurd to Festus; *cf.* 17:32. St Paul's learning appeared in his quotations of the prophets, and perhaps Festus had noticed him reading constantly. **25.** St Paul answered courteously. **26.** The speech was meant for Agrippa, who would understand. Our Lord's life, etc. were well known in Judaea, and elsewhere too, *cf.* 17:6. **27.** Believing in the prophets, Agrippa must feel the force of St Paul's proofs. **28.** 'Thou persuadest me to be a Christian *in a short time*' or '*with small effort*' Agrippa is the polite sceptic. Yet the sentence could be tr. 'Thou persuadest me to be a Christian in a short exposition', as though Agrippa had really been moved. **29.** '*In short or long time*' or '*with small or great effort*'. **32.** *Cf.* 25:11. **k**

XXVII 1-XXVIII 31 The Journey to Rome and Captivity there, A.D. 60-3—The preceding chapters, especially 22-26, have formed a kind of defence of St Paul in face of the empire. Again and again his innocence is recognized. St Luke's aim seems to have been to defend not only St Paul but Christians generally, and to show how much they differed from the Jews, who were becoming every day more bitterly opposed to the empire. Instances of the respect of the imperial authorities for St Paul, which contrast with the hostility he encounters from the Jews, continue till the end of the book and his arrival in Rome. At that point the capital of the world having been reached, the church of the Gentiles is fully established. The Apostle of the circumcision had come to Rome, and now the Apostle of the uncircumcision is the only other Apostle to live there. **843a**

XXVII 1-12 From Caesarea to Crete, A.D. 60—1. The last 'we-section' begins. St Luke's eyewitness account is the chief authority for the art of navigation in antiquity. The minute scrutiny of sailors and other experts has confirmed his accuracy and observation; *cf.* J. Smith, *Voyage and Shipwreck of St Paul* (1886). The other prisoners were probably criminals condemned to appear in the arena at Rome. St Paul the Roman citizen who might have been set at liberty was accompanied by St Luke and Aristarchus. They perhaps counted as the two slaves allowed to attend an imprisoned Roman citizen; *cf.* Col 4:10, 'the band Augusta', the Augustan cohort (cohors I Augusta) then apparently stationed near Caesarea. **2.** Adramyttium was a flourishing port near Troas. **3.** On Sidon, 20 m. from Tyre, see 21:4. Julius treated St Paul with great respect throughout the journey. He visited the church '*to be cared for*'. **4.** The NW. wind forced them to sail 'under *the lee* of Cyprus', east of the island. **5-6.** For Lystra read '*Myra*'. It was the port of call for grain ships from Egypt to Italy when the prevailing NW. wind prevented a direct crossing. They embarked on one of these, a *navis oneraria* of 300 tons and more. **7.** The unwieldy ship made slow progress against the wind. Cnidus is the promontory N. of Rhodes, and Salmon that at the NE. of Crete, under the lee, *i.e.* along the south of which they sailed. **8.** For Thalassa read 'Lasea'. **9-10.** After the Fast, the Day of Expiation at the end of September, with the equinoctial gales, the sailing season ended. Relying on all his experience 'Paul *advised* them'. **11.** As the senior official on board the centurion was in command **b**

843b of the ship. **12.** Phenice is probably the modern Phineka, and seems to have been protected from SW. and NW. whence came the dangerous winds; 'looking *to south and north of west*'.

c 13-20 The Great Storm—**13.** 'When they had *weighed anchor*, they sailed along Crete *close in*'. Vg. mistakes the Gk for 'close in' for a proper name. **14.** 'There arose *from the land* a tempestuous wind called *the North-Easter*'. This wind blows suddenly from the mountains of Crete, 7,000 feet high. **16.** Under the lee of Cauda the boat was hoisted on board. **17.** 'helps', supports. Ropes were passed under the ship to hold the timbers together. The shifting Syrtis sandbanks to the South were the terror of sailors : 'the sail yard', probably the mainsail, to act as a sea-anchor. **20.** The sun and the stars were the only guides before the invention of the compass. These disappeared for *several days*'.

21-26 St Paul's Vision—**21.** St Paul refers to his neglected advice to ensure that he is listened to now. **23.** God encourages him in his darkest hours, 18:9 ; 23:11, and after a fortnight of tossing and drifting this was certainly one of them. Notice how he assumes the leadership in this crisis.

d 27-38 The Ship approaches Land—**27.** Malta is 600 m. from Crete. The progress was at the rate of just under 2 m. an hour, which is said to be that of a ship driven helpless. Adria, the Adriatic, included the central Mediterranean. **28.** The fathom is about five feet. **30.** The danger that the ship would break up was increased now that it was stationary. **31.** The expert help of the sailors was necessary if all were to be saved. God had revealed that this would be so, but prudent means must be used. The respect that St Paul inspired and also his practical sense are continually in evidence. **33-34.** There had been no proper meals for a fortnight, 21, and there was exhausting work ahead. **35.** The technical 'he broke bread' can mean either an ordinary meal or the Eucharist (see on 2:42) but probably no more is meant here than prayer of thanksgiving for food. **38.** The ship must be brought as near shore as possible.

e 39-44 The Shipwreck—**39.** A bay with a beach was discovered. **40.** '*So they cast off the anchors and left them in the sea, at the same time unloosing the ropes that tied the rudders, and hoisting the foresail to the wind, they made towards the shore*'. The anchors were now superfluous, but the rudders, long oars on either side of the stern were needed to guide the ship, and the sail to drive it onto the beach. **41.** 'Where two seas meet' : St Paul's Bay answers to St Luke's description, and the identification is generally accepted. The ship grounded on the western shore of the bay, a little south of the island of Gzeier, which lies across the western part of the mouth of the bay, in the channel separating the western end of Gzeier from the mainland. **42.** The soldiers were liable to death if the prisoners escaped ; *cf.* 12:19. **43.** *Cf.* 3. **44.** After the swimmers the rest were ordered to come 'on planks and on pieces of the ship'. Omit 'they carried'.

f XXVIII 1-6 The Landing in Malta—**1.** Originally colonized by Phoenicians, Malta now formed part of the province of Sicily. The Maltese are called 'barbarians' because they spoke Phoenician and not Gk or Latin ; *cf.* I Cor 14:11. The island had long been civilized. **2.** It was late autumn, and all were without sufficient food, sleep and clothes. **3.** The viper fastened on St Paul's hand, and therefore bit it ; *cf.* Mk 16:18. There are no poisonous snakes in Malta today. If this was the case in A.D. 60, one may have escaped from some grain ship from Africa. **4.** The Maltese knew that St Paul was a prisoner. '*Justice*' personified should be read in place of 'vengeance'. **6.** *Cf.* 14:10.

7-10 St Paul at Malta—**7.** 'The chief man of the island' was the title of the representative of the Praetor of Sicily, and is found in inscriptions. Publius seems to have found lodging for all those shipwrecked. **8.** Luke the physician noted the diseases 'fever and *dysentery*'.

g 11-16 Malta to Rome, A.D. 61, Spring—**11.** The journey was continued in a grain ship, which had for sign the Dioscuri, the Twin Brothers Castor and Pollux, the patrons of sailors. **12.** Syracuse, the capital of Sicily, was a usual port of call. **13.** Rhegium (Reggio) is opposite Messina. It was necessary to keep inshore to avoid the currents. Puteoli, the modern Pozzuoli, with the harbour still in use, was then a trading port of far greater importance than Naples, and the terminus for ships from the East. **14.** A Jewish colony had long been settled there, and, as in all the great centres by this date, there was a Christian church. The centurion Julius evidently allowed St Paul much liberty. **15.** The week's stay gave time for his arrival to be notified to the church at Rome, 140 m. distant. Appii Forum, the market of Appius, 43 m. from Rome, is described by Horace, *Satires* 1, 5, as a place where travellers were fleeced. It lay on the edge of the Pontine Marshes, which St Paul may have passed by the canal, which here ran parallel to the Appian Way, the road to Rome. Three Taverns lay 10 m. nearer Rome, the first sight of which was obtained as the Appian Way crossed the Alban Hills. St Paul's labours were well known in Rome, and he had many friends there, Rom 16. The church gave him a tender and reverential welcome, which must have greatly encouraged one so responsive to sympathy. **16.** The city was entered by the Porta Capena, corresponding to the Porta di San Sebastiano. After reporting to the Praetorian Prefect Afranius Burrus, a Stoic philosopher, friend of Seneca and former tutor of Nero, St Paul was allowed to dwell in his own hired lodging, 23, 30. This was a modified form of the *Custodia Militaris* ; see 24:23. He remained chained to a succession of soldiers whom he was thus able to evangelize, Phil. 1:12-13 ; 4:22. Even if the *elogium* of Festus had been lost in the shipwreck, Julius would have given a very favourable report. No statement of the Jewish case was forthcoming, 21.

17-22 The Interview with the Leading Jews—**17.** St Paul lost no time, and as always, turned first to the Jews. Unable to go to the synagogue he invited them to his lodging. Their large colony had recovered from the expulsion under Claudius, 18:2, and enjoyed the protection of the emperor. St Paul had done nothing against the custom of his fathers, because he not only observed the Law (see 21:21), but regarded all his new preaching as the fulfilling of it. **18.** *Cf.* 25:25 ; 26:31. **19.** He explains tactfully why he was constrained to appeal, namely, to avoid assassination or judicial murder. **20.** He wishes to speak of the real cause of his imprisonment ; *cf.* 26:6. **21.** With winter putting an end to sailing, letters could hardly have reached Rome from the Sanhedrin till some time after St Paul's arrival.

23-29 St Paul addresses the Jews—**23.** He speaks of the Messianic Kingdom and the Messias, foretold in the Law and the Prophets ; *cf.* 26:22. **24.** It would seem from the sternness of Paul's farewell that few were really convinced. **25.** 'To *your* fathers' is the better reading, and marks St Paul's separation from Judaism. **26-27.** He quotes Is 6:9-10, from LXX, to sum up the attitude of the Jews. Our Lord used the same text ; see Mt 13:14 f. **28.** These are St Paul's final and prophetic words. The work of the Apostle of the Gentiles is assured. **29** is not found in the best MSS.

30-31 Conclusion—**30.** The aorist implies that St Paul's situation changed 'after two whole years'. This seems to have been the legal period of detention during which accusers could bring their charge, see § 815b. **31.** With the cadence worthy of a final sentence St Paul is left at the centre of the Gentile world. St Luke implies that his preaching was very successful even while he was still a prisoner, and this is confirmed by the Captivity Epistles. The Christians are greatly encouraged, Phil 1:14, and numerous, *ibid* 4:22. St Paul's friends gather round him and he looks forward to release, Phil 1:23 ff. ; 2:24, Phm 22. The Church becomes sufficiently known to be Nero's scapegoat in A.D. 64, and a new era opens in which St Paul himself is to die a martyr.

THE EPISTLE TO THE ROMANS

By A. THEISSEN

Bibliography—Origen, *Commentary on the Epistle to the Romans c* 245, Lat. Paraphrase by Rufinus *c* 450, PG 14 ; Chrysostom, *Homilies on the Epistle to the Romans c* 390, PG 60 ; St Thomas Aquinas (d. 1274), *Expositio in omnes S. Pauli epistolas* ; G. Estius, *In omnes B. Pauli ep. commentarii*, Douay, 1614–16 ; *M. Poole, *Synopsis Criticorum*, 1684–6, vol. 5 ; *Joh. Jak. Wetstein, *Novum Test. Graecum*, 1751 f. ; *H. A. W. Meyer, *Der Brief an die Römer*, 1836, 1899⁹, Engl. Tr. 1876 ; Bernh. a Piconio, *Epist. B. Pauli triplex expositio*, 1838, Engl. Tr. 1889 ; *E. H. Gifford, *Romans*, 1881 ; *C. J. Vaughan, *St Paul's Epistle to the Romans*, 1890 ; J. McEvilly, *An Exposition of the Epistles of St Paul*, 1891 ; R. Cornely, *Ep. ad Romanos*, CSS, 1896, 1927² ; *H. P. Liddon, *Explanatory Analysis of St Paul's Epistle to the Romans*, 1897 ; J. Rickaby, *Notes on St Paul : Cor. Gal, Rom*, 1898 ; *Ch. Gore, *St Paul's Epistle to the Romans*, 1899 ; *A. Jülicher, *Der Brief an die Römer*, 1905, 1929⁴ ; *W. Sanday and *A. C. Headlam, *A Critical and Exegetical Commentary on the Ep. to the Romans*, ICC, 1907 (abbr. SH) ; *H. Lietzmann, *An die Römer*, 1910, 1933⁴ ; *Th. Zahn, *Der Brief des Paulus an die Römer*, 1910, 1925³ ; M.-J. Lagrange, *Epître aux Romains*, 1916, 1931⁴ (the ref. in this com. are to the 1st ed.) ; *K. Barth, *Der Römerbrief*, 1919, 1928⁶, Engl. Tr. 1933 ; C. Lattey, *The Epistle of St Paul to the Romans*, WV, 1921, 1927² ; *N. P. Williams, *The Epistle to the Romans*, SPCK Commentary, 1928 ; *C. H. Dodd, *The Epistle to the Romans*, The Moffatt NT Commentary, 1932 ; P. Boylan, *St Paul's Epistle to the Romans*, 1934 ; J. L. Lilly, *The Epistle to the Romans*, CNT, 1942 ; R. Eaton, *St Paul's Epistle to the Romans*, CTS, nd.

F. Prat, *La Théol. de S. Paul* I, 1908, 1934²³ ; II, 1912, 1933²⁰, Engl. Tr.) ; B. Gut, *Introductio specialis in NT*, 1938 (372–84 good modern bibliogr. references) ; K. Vaughan, *The Divine Armory* (rev. by N. Thompson), 1943 ; A. Tanquerey, *Synopsis Theol. Dogmaticae*, vols I–III, 1943–5²⁵.

Theme—The Christian doctrine of justification (= salvation) is generally regarded as the main doctrinal subject of Rom. The text which best expresses this predominant idea is 1:16 f. ' *The Gospel . . . is a power of God bringing salvation to everyone who believes, to the Jew first but no less to the Greek. For therein a δικαιοσύνη θεοῦ is revealed out of faith* '. The translations of the characteristic δικαιοσύνη θεοῦ differ : the justice of God, DV ; the justness of God, WV ; God's way of justifying us, KNT ; the righteousness of God, AV ; a righteousness of God, RV ; *cf.* § 846*e*. There is a simpler statement of this theme or doctrine by St Augustine, PL 35, 2087 f. : ' Hoc ergo docere intendit, omnibus venisse gratiam Evangelii Domini nostri Jesu Christi ' = he (Paul) intended to teach that the grace of the Gospel of Jesus Christ had come for all. It is true, that St Augustine by speaking of grace instead of justice (= justness) changed St Paul's terminology. But it is equally true, that justifying grace (= sanctifying grace) has become the Catholic term for what is the predominant idea of Rom. Hence it may simplify the understanding of Rom for a Catholic reader if he keeps to the term with which he is familiar. The part of Rom which deals directly with this main theme of salvation or justifying grace is 1:18–8:39 ; *cf.* § 846*b*.

In addition to this main doctrinal theme of Rom **844b** there is a second major doctrinal topic : the defence of the new Christian doctrine of salvation against the objections from Israel, the chosen people of old (= the church of old) which rejected that doctrine as an innovation contradictory to the Established Torah (= the Law of Moses). This secondary theme of Rom is, however, so closely connected with the first that it may well be called a corollary to it. It is dealt with mainly in chh 9–11. But there are many passing references to it in the earlier parts of the epistle, *e.g.* 7:1–6 ; *cf.* Lagrange XXXIX ff. In any case, it would be a mistake to regard Rom as a treatise of one or two doctrines. As in all his letters so in Rom Paul touches upon many topics.

Plan—There is a plan of Rom in every commentary **c** and in every manual of NT introduction ; *e.g.* *M. E. Bengel, *Gnomon NT*, 1862, 494 (on 1:16) ; *J. B. Lightfoot, *Notes on the Epistles of S. Paul*, 1895, 239–43 ; SH XLVII–L ; Prat I 482–9 ; Boylan XXIII–XXXI ; Gut 375–8. To understand the differences in the various plans it must be remembered that a letter is not meant to be a well ordered treatise. The sequence of thought in a letter is determined by the momentary associations of ideas rather than by the strict rules of logic or rhetoric. Hence the allocation of details in the analysis of a longer letter is often bound to be subjective. The main divisions in Rom are, however, clearly marked.

A. 1:1–17 INTRODUCTION.
B. 1:18–11:36 THE DOCTRINAL SECTION.
   I. 1:18–3:20 The need for the salvation of the Gospel.
   II. 3:21–4:25 The way to this salvation.
   III. 5:1–8:39 Effects of this salvation :
     (1) 5:1–21 Hope of eternal glorification,
     (2) 6:1–23 A complete break with sin,
     (3) 7:1–25 Christ the New Law,
     (4) 8:1–39 The indwelling of the Holy Spirit.
   IV. 9:1–11:36 The present exclusion of Israel from this salvation :
     (1) 9:1–29 The divine attributes of faithfulness and justice are defended,
     (2) 9:30–10:21 Israel's fault is exposed,
     (3) 11:1–36 Several other aspects of the problem of Israel's present exclusion from the salvation of the Gospel are mentioned.
C. 12:1–15:13 THE MORAL SECTION.
   I. 13:1–13:14 General exhortations.
   II. 14:1–15:13 Exhortations to the Weak and the Strong in Rome.
D. 15:14–16:27 CONCLUSION.

Authenticity—According to 1:1–7 Paul, the Apostle of **d** the Gentiles, is the author of this epistle. The literal truth of this statement is beyond any reasonable doubt. On the external evidence see SH LXXIV–LXXXIV ; Lusseau-Collomb, *Manuel d'Etudes bibliques* V 1 (1938) 523 f. The internal evidence for the authenticity argues from the agreement of Rom with the genuine Pauline epistles in contents and form. Here the agreement with Gal is to be stressed in particular. On objections against the authenticity of Rom see Lagrange LXI f. ; Gut 378, 1.

844d In connexion with the authenticity of Rom the question has been raised, how much of the wording of the letter may be due to Tertius, who in 16:22 signs as the Apostle's amanuensis. This question is incapable of a conclusive answer. But it would seem safe to argue that the theological depth of the epistle, the agreement with Gal, and the numerous unfinished sentences speak decisively against any considerable share of Tertius in the composition of Rom; *cf.* *O. Roller, *Das Formular der Paul. Briefe*, 1933, 22.

e Purpose—The first purpose of the Apostle must have been to expound in form of instructions and exhortations the theme which has been explained above. The second object of the Apostle in writing this letter evidently was his intention to prepare for a visit to Rome on his journey to Spain, *cf.* 1:10–15 ; 15:22–33 ; Ac 19:21.

But what was St Paul's purpose in going to Rome ? He says himself in 15:20 f. and 2 Cor 10:13–16 that it is against his principles to build upon another man's foundation. According to this principle there was no work for him to do at Rome. For as his own letter proves, Rome already had a flourishing Christian community. Hence St Paul's visit to Rome cannot be said to have been necessary for the expansion of Christianity. The most natural answer would seem to be that it was Rome, the capital of the Empire, which attracted Paul, the Roman citizen, *cf.* *E. L. Hicks, *Studia Biblica* IV (1896) 11. Another plausible explanation is that it was to visit his many personal friends among the Christians of Rome, *cf.* ch 16.

f Much more difficult is the question, why did St Paul write such an elaborate letter to Rome ? Surely there was no need for 7,101 words to prepare for a fortnight's stay with his friends at Rome on his journey to Spain ; *cf.* § 863*a–b*. *F. Godet, *Com. on Romans*, Engl. Tr. I (1890) 80–99, discusses at length the numerous answers that have been given to this question. The explanation which recommends itself as the most natural is that which points out two reasons for the extraordinary length and depth of this epistle : (1) the practical importance of the subject of justification (= salvation) by faith in Jesus Christ at the time, see Gal and note the absence of other fundamental Christian doctrines ; (2) the importance of the church of Rome ; *cf.* the privileged position of the church of Jerusalem, Gal 1:18 f. ; 2:1–10 ; 2 Cor 8:1–9:15 ; Ac 9:26–28 ; 11:27–30 ; 15:1–35 ; 18:22 ; 20:16 ; 21:13. Why St Paul should have considered the church of Rome as especially important is a question which has been answered differently. The answer that the church of Rome enjoyed a privileged position through being St Peter's special field of activity is as reasonable a conjecture as any other that has been put forward, *cf.* Gal 1:18 ; 2:1–10 ; Ac 15:7 ; Boylan IX f.

g Date—Rom was probably written in the first three months of A.D. 58. To begin with it seems certain from 15:25–28 that Rom was written in the winter months preceding the collection journey referred to in 1 Cor 16:1–4 ; 2 Cor 8 ; 9 ; Ac 19:21–21:19 ; 24:17. There is less certainty as regards the year. It depends on the year assigned to St Paul's imprisonment at Caesarea, Ac 23:23–35 ; 24:1–26 which was two years before the recall of Felix and the arrival of Porcius Festus as procurator of Judaea, Ac 24:27. The year of this political event however is disputed ; various calculations have led to A.D. 54, 55, 56, 58, 60, the last being the date most commonly held, *cf.* Prat I 401–404 ; *Schürer I (1901) 577 ff. For a different method of dating Rom see Lagrange XIX. In any case Rom cannot be dated later than A.D. 58 or 59. The religious importance of this date lies in the theological depth and thoroughness here displayed so soon after our Lord's Ascension.

h Place of Composition—Corinth is generally regarded as the place where Rom was written. There is no explicit statement in the epistle to that effect. But apart from the date, the recommendation of Phoebe (16:1 f.) points to Corinth ; and so does the sub-

scription in many MSS, *cf.* *Tischendorf, *NT* II (1872[8]) 457.

The Addressees—That this epistle was addressed to the Christians of Rome in accordance with 1:6 is generally admitted. What is most disputed with regard to the addressees is the question whether the convertsf rom Judaism or from paganism were in the majority. Either possibility has been defended. The result of the controversy which began with *F. C. Baur (d. 1860) seems to be a compromise. In the church of Rome Israelite and Gentile met as in most early Christian communities outside Palestine. There were differences and difficulties between them and dangers of local disturbances, but they were such as must have existed everywhere under similar circumstances at that time. How serious such local disturbances could become Paul knew from what had happened in Galatia, *cf.* Gal. This may have caused him to take up the question of the Mosaic Law so thoroughly in Rom. But even Gal apart, the Christian attitude to the Mosaic Law (= the OT) is a fundamental question of Christian doctrine and that not only for Israelitish Christians but also for Gentile Christians. It deserves therefore at all times such a thorough treatment as we have in Rom quite irrespective of any immediate controversial issues.

A further point that may be mentioned concerning the addressees of Rom is their social status. There is no direct evidence on this question. But the more the poverty of the early Christians of Rome is stressed in accordance with the conditions of the majority of the Jews at Rome (*cf.* SH XXIV) and in analogy with what we know from other early Christian communities (*cf.* 1 Cor 1:26) the more amazing is the theological interest and understanding which St Paul showed that he expected from them by writing such a letter.

Who was the Founder of the Church of Rome ?—That Paul was not the founder of the Church of Rome follows clearly from 1:13 ; 15:19. But so far it is impossible to answer this question positively, because the necessary historical evidence is missing. There are however two conjectures which can claim some probability. (1) The beginning of Christianity at Rome need not be the work of one founder. Rome was a general meeting-place for all nationalities and creeds in the Roman empire, and so it is quite likely that very soon Christians also met there and began to spread the Gospel. That they were Jewish Christians is possible but not necessary ; it has been inferred from the well-known custom that the early Christian missionaries began preaching the Gospel in the Synagogue wherever this opportunity existed. The common reference to Ac 2:10 in support of this conjecture, however, is not to the point, because this reference speaks of Jews from Rome who were then living at Jerusalem, *cf.* Ac 2:5. (2) It may be that St Peter was the founder of the church of Rome. But the available historical evidence only proves Peter's activity and death at Rome, *cf.* U. Holzmeister, *Com. in Epistulas SS Petri et Iudae*, CSS, 1937, 40–71. At all events Peter was not at Rome when Paul wrote this letter. Otherwise there would be some reference to him in ch 16. Such a temporary absence of Peter from one of his foundations or special fields of activity is no more difficult to understand than the absence of Paul from the Pauline churches, *e.g.* Corinth or Ephesus.

The Text—For a good introduction to the critical problems of the text see Lietzmann 1–18. The standard edition of the Greek text is *H. v. Soden, *Die Schriften des NT, Text und Apparat*, 1913. This has been used for the present commentary. For a select list of textual variants see *Westcott-Hort, *The NT* II (1882) 108–14. The standard edition of the Vg text is *J. Wordsworth and *H. J. White, *Novum Testamentum . . .* II 1, Oxford, 1913. The variants of the Vg from the Greek text are noted in the commentaries of Cornely, Lagrange, and Boylan.

Integrity—If allowance be made for accidental textual variants, such as we find in the MSS of every ancient text, only the conclusion of Rom is beset by somewhat more serious difficulties. No less than six different conclusions can be traced in the MSS. They are :

(1) 14:23 om. 15:1–16:27 ;
(2) 14:23 ; 16:20*b* = 16:24 om. 15:1–16:27 ;
(3) 14:23 ; 16:25–27 om. 15:1–16:27 ;
(4) 14:23 ; 16:25–27 ; 15:1–16:24 ;
(5) 14:23 ; 15:1–16:27 ;
(6) 14:23 ; 16:25–27 ; 15:1–16:24 ; 16:25–27.

The respective MS evidence can be found in the critical editions of the text and in the larger comment-aries ; see § 863*l*. On the whole the case seems to be far from clear. But there is agreement on the following points : (1) The best attested text is nr 5 = Rom 14:23 ; 15:1–16:27 ; so ℵ BC etc. ; bo, sah ; vet lat, Vg ; pesh. (2) Marcion was the first to omit 15:1–16:27, partly because the contents contradicted his doctrine, 15:1–13 ; partly because they were of no doctrinal interest, 15:14–16:27. (3) The omission of 15:1–16:27 in some MSS may be due partly to the influence of Marcion, partly to the influence of church lectionaries. The contents of 15:14-16:27 were evi-dently not suitable for reading in church. (4) The theory that Rom 16 is a fragment of a letter addressed not to Rome but to Ephesus can quote no external evidence in its favour. On the internal evidence alleged *cf.* § 863*g*. On the whole question see SH LXXXIX–XCVIII ; R. Schumacher, *Die beiden letzten Kapitel des Röm*, NtAbh, 14, 4 (1929) ; Lietzmann 130 f.

I 1-7 The Opening Salutation—also called super-scription, inscription, prescript. St Paul begins his letter according to contemporary Jewish, Greek and Roman custom with the threefold statement of sender, addressee and greetings. Examples which illustrate this convention of ancient letter-writing are plentiful. A very similar formula is still used in many papal and episcopal encyclicals. For a different opening of a letter see the seven letters in Apoc 2–3.

The most obvious characteristic of the salutation in Rom 1:1–7 is its length and periodic style. The con-ventional superscription was short and formal ; see Jas 1:1 which of all letters in the NT best preserves the stereotyped formula of an ancient letter. St Paul was the first as far as we know to break away from the traditional formula by expanding it and filling it with Christian ideas ; *cf.* the beginning of Gal ; 1 Cor ; Philm ; Tit. But Rom 1:1–7 is the longest and most elaborate of all. Its structure is as follows :

I. Paul, a servant of Jesus Christ, called to be an apostle, set apart for a GOSPEL FROM GOD :
(1) which he had promised before through his prophets in Holy Writ,
(2) which is concerning HIS SON, Jesus Christ, our Lord :
   (*a*) who was born from the family of David according to the flesh,
   (*b*) who was manifested as ' Son of God in Power ' according to his holy Spirit from the time of his resurrection from the dead,
   (*c*) through whom we have received the GRACE OF THE APOSTOLATE,
   (*a*) that for the glory of his name we should win all nations unto obedience of faith,
   (*β*) among whom are ye also, being the called of Jesus Christ :
II. to all who are in Rome, beloved of God, Saints by his call,
III. grace to you and peace from God, our father, and from the Lord Jesus Christ.

For a more elaborate analysis see Prat II 425.

The practical importance of Rom 1:1–7 lies in its doctrinal content. Nearly all the prominent articles of the early Christian faith are gathered together here in one sentence : (1) the Gospel as the fulfilment of the OT, 2 ; (2) the descent of the Messias from the family of David, 3 ; (3) the glorification of Christ, 4 ; (4) the origin, purpose and range of Paul's apostolate, 1, 5, 6. On the theological terminology in this paragraph see SH 17 f.

1. δοῦλος I. X. = ' *slave* of Jesus Christ ' : contains **845c** an important confession of Christian faith. The phrase is not found in the Gospels (contrast Jn 15:15) but occurs frequently in the Pauline and Catholic epistles. All agree that it expresses the Apostle's allegiance to Christ. But opinions differ concerning the definition of this allegiance. The main explanations are : (1) = slave or bondman of Jesus Christ, *cf.* 1 Cor 7:22 ; *i.e.* Paul who claimed his rights as a Roman citizen before the Roman authorities, Ac 16:37 ; 22:25 ; 25:10, regarded himself as a slave of Christ. Many commentators insist with great earnestness on this literal translation. (2) = servant or minister of Jesus. This interpretation avoids the idea of slavery by ex-plaining the phrase as an hyperbole. As such it would be in accordance with the oriental convention of calling even high officials ' slaves ' with reference to their higher authorities, esp. the king ; *cf.* 4 Kg 5:6 ; Cowley, Aram. Pap. 1923, nr 17, 30, 31, 37, 38, 39, 54. This explanation would come very near the idea expressed in Jn 15:15 and could be supported by the stress which St Paul lays on his apostolic authority in this context. Δοῦλος would become synonymous in the NT with διάκονος, θεράπων, οἰκόνομος, ὑπηρέτης which are all different words for servant or minister. (3) = wor- **d** shipper of Jesus Christ. This meaning is based on the OT usage in which ' servant of God ' is commonly used for those whose life is dedicated to the worship and service of God ; *e.g.* Abraham, Ps 104:6, 42 ; Moses, Jos 14:7 ; 3 Kg 8:53 ; 4 Kg 18:12 ; Neh 9:14 ; Ps 104:26 ; Apoc 15:3 ; Josue, Jos 24:29 ; Jud 2:8 ; Job, Job 1:8 ; 2:3 ; 42:8 ; David, Jer 33:21 ff .; Ez 34:23 ; 37:24 ; Ps 17:1 ; 35:1 ; 77:70 ; 88:4, 21 ; Eliacim, Is 22:20 ; Zorobabel, Ag 2:24 ; Daniel, Dan 6:20 ; the OT prophets, Am 3:7 ; Dan 9:6, 10 ; Jer 7:25 ; Esd 9:11 ; the just = saints of the OT, Pss 33:23 ; 68:37 ; 101:15 ; 115:16 ; 118:125 ; 122:2 ; 142:2, 12 ; *cf.* also Lk 1:38 ; 2:29. The doctrinal significance of this ex-planation lies in the implicit confession of our Lord's divinity. As the OT saints were called ' servants of *God* ' so Paul deliberately called himself ' servant of *Jesus Christ*.' (4) = freedman of Jesus Christ. This explanation is derived from the Hellenistic custom of manumission. A slave was freed in a temple by a legal transaction by which his former master transferred his right over him to the God of the temple, a price of redemption being paid symbolically by the God to the former master. Thereafter the former slave was a freedman. In view of this custom Paul could call him-self the slave of Christ to signify that he had been bought free (= redeemed) through Jesus Christ from his former master Sin or Satan ; *cf.* *A. Deissmann, *Licht vom Osten*, 1923⁴, Engl. Tr. 1927, 319–30. This ex-planation draws out Paul's belief in the divinity of Christ even more forcibly than the previous one ; and it would also help to explain the NT term for ' redemp-tion '. Of these four explanations the third is the most common.

2-4 describe in a parenthesis the Gospel the preaching **e** of which St Paul has just proclaimed to be his vocation. First, it is a Gospel promised in the Bible long ago, 2 ; secondly, its central figure is Jesus Christ, 3–4. What is said of Christ in 3–4 can be summarized under two points : (1) Jesus Christ, the son of David ; (2) Jesus Christ, the son of God. **3.** ' from the family of David according to the flesh ' : for the descent of the Messias from the house of David see 2 Sam 7:12–16 ; Ps 88:36 f.; Is 9:6 f. ; Jer 23:5 f. ; 33:15–17, 26 ; Am 9:11 ; Ps of Salom 17:23. For the importance of this doctrine in in the NT *cf.* Mt 1:1, 6, 20 ; 9:27 ; 12:23 ; 15:22 ; 20:30 f. ; 21:9, 15 ; 22:41–46 ; Lk 1:27, 32, 69 ; 2:4, 11 ; Jn 7:42 ; Ac 13:23 ; Rom 9:5 ; 15:8 ; 2 Tim 2:8. Paul however does not enter into a dis-cussion of the question how our Lord's origin from the house of David can be proved ; whether it is to be traced through the family tree of our Lady, or of St Joseph or of both. He evidently takes the fact for certain and is unaware of anybody questioning it. **4** is an important proof-text for the divinity of Christ. But

845e there is no agreement as to the structure of the sentence. The main possible interpretations are : (1) Jesus Christ was manifested (*i.e.* before men) as Son of God by his miraculous power, his infinite sanctity, and by his resurrection ; *cf.* footnote in DV ; (2) Jesus Christ was manifested as 'Son of God in Power' in accordance with his holy spirit (his sanctity = his divine nature) from the time of (or by means of) his resurrection. This latter explanation is recommended by the threefold parallelism between v 3 and v 4 : made . . . son . . . according to. For details see larger commentaries, *e.g.* Cornely 38–46 ; differently Boylan 2–4.

f Τοῦ ὁρισθέντος υἱοῦ τοῦ θεοῦ ἐν δυνάμει = qui praedestinatus est Filius Dei in virtute, Vg ; who was predestinated the Son of God in power, DV ; by an act of power . . . marked out Son of God, WV. The text of Vg followed by DV is unfortunate in that it adds to the verb the preposition 'prae': 'prae-destinatus, pre-destinated. The most natural explanation of this Latin addition is to assume with St Jerome on Eph 1:5 (PL 26, 478) that the Latin usage of the time made no clear distinction between destinare and praedestinare, *cf.* Lagrange, Zahn. Be this as it may, St Augustine, *De praedestinatione sanctorum* 15, 31 (PL 44, 982) seized on this text ; and mediaeval theology on the strength of it developed a discussion ' de praedestinatione Jesu Christi ', *cf.* Aquin., ST III q 24 a 1.2. To assess the theological value of this discussion belongs to dogma. The historical exegesis of Rom 1:4 must keep to the Greek text which can be translated : established, set up, constituted, declared, marked out, manifested, or shown as the Son of God in Power. The choice between these possibilities is difficult. What must be avoided is Adoptianism saying that Christ became Son of God through the resurrection.

g ' Son of God in Power ' : after describing in 3 the Son of God ' in weakness ', Phil 2:6 f., St Paul now raises his eyes to Jesus Christ in glory, power and majesty, seated at the right hand of the Father ; *cf.* Mt 24:30 = Mk 13:26 = Lk 21:27 ; Mt 26:64 = Lk 22:69 ; Mt 28:18 ; Mk 9:1–7 ; 12:36 ; 16:19 ; Ac 2:33 ; 7:55 f. ; Rom 8:34 ; 1 Cor 15:43 ; 2 Cor 5:16 ; Eph 1:20 ; Col 3:1 ; 1 Tim 3:16 ; Heb 1:3 ; 8:1 ; 10:12 ; 12:2 ; 1 Pet 3:22 ; Apoc 3:21 ; 5:12. So among modern Catholic commentators Cornely, Lagrange ; for a list of others see Cornely 39 ; *cf.* also commentaries to Mk 16:19 and to the 6th article of the Apostles' Creed. According to another possible translation of the text ' in power ' is to be connected with the verb : Jesus Christ was shown to be Son of God ' by power ' = by his miracles. These miracles then can be the miracles worked by him and recorded in the four Gospels ; or the miracles worked in his name by the Apostles after his resurrection and recorded in Acts ; or the one great miracle of his resurrection, so WV, Boylan.

h Κατὰ πνεῦμα ἁγιωσύνης = secundum spiritum sanctificationis, Vg ; according to the spirit of sanctification, DV ; in accordance with the holiness of his spirit, WV. This phrase is difficult being unique in the NT and peculiar in itself. The simplest explanation seems to be to understand it of Christ's spiritual being in deliberate contrast to his physical being in 3. According to his physical being = ' according to the flesh ', Christ was the son of David, 3 ; according to his spiritual being = ' according to his spirit distinguished by holiness ', Christ has been shown to be the Son of God in Power from the day of his resurrection (or by the one great sign of his resurrection) ; *cf.* Jn 3:34 ; 8:46 ; Rom 8:11 ; Heb 2:17 ; 4:15 ; 1 Pet 2:22 ; 3:18. So Cornely 29 ff. Influenced by the more developed doctrine of later cent. we today may feel inclined to substitute for Paul's distinction of ' flesh and spirit ' a phrase referring to Christ's ' human and divine nature '. But this would be reading later definitions into the text of St Paul. For an altogether different interpretation see Boylan.

i 5. ' *Unto obedience of faith* ': can mean (1) obedience to the doctrines of the Christian faith, (2) obedience

to God by faith. **7a.** ' Called to be saints ' = saints **8** by his call, WV. The Apostle is not implying that the Christians of Rome were saints because of extraordinary virtue. What he has in mind is that God has called (= chosen) them to be set apart for him in a special way, *cf.* ' called to be an Apostle ' in v 1. They were called by God not because they were saints in their lives already, but they were saints = consecrated to God, since they had been called by him (Augustine). In this sense ' saints ' is a common name for the Christians in St Paul's epistles, Rom 8:27 ; 12:13 ; 15:25, 31 ; 16:2, 15 ; 1 Cor 1:2 ; 6:1 f. ; 14:33 ; 16:1, 15 ; 2 Cor 1:1 ; 8:4 ; 9:1, 12 ; 13:12 ; Eph 1:1 ; 2:19, etc. The origin of this idea is to be found in the OT usage in which ' saints ' refers to Israel as God's *chosen* people, *cf.* Ex 22:31 ; Lev 11:44 ; 19:2 ; 20:7 ; Deut 7:6 ; 14:21 ; 16:19 ; 28:9, etc. **7b** ends the prescript with greetings as was customary. But in the wording of his greetings Paul keeps neither to the Jewish nor to the Greek custom. The Jewish form was šālôm = peace (*cf.* SB I 380–5), the Greek χαίρειν (*cf.* Jas 1:1). Paul instead used the formula χάρις καὶ εἰρήνη except in 1 and 2 Tim. As to the meaning of this formula there are two main interpretations. (1) It can be taken as uniting the Jewish and the Greek formulas. Then it has to be translated ' greetings and peace (= happiness) ' = all best wishes ; (2) The two nouns can be taken in their specific Christian sense, in which case the translation would be ' the grace of God and Christ (*cf.* Rom 3:24 ; Eph 2:5) and the peace of God and Christ (*cf.* Jn 14:27 ; Rom 5:1) be with you '. This second explanation is more in the spirit of St Paul. See Estius.

8-17 Introduction—In accordance with the usage of **8** ancient letter-writing the salutation is followed by an introductory paragraph enlarging on the Apostle's interest in those to whom he is writing. He praises the good repute of their faith, 8 ; he assures them of his prayers, 9 ; and finally expresses his desire to visit them and the hope that his visit will be for their mutual edification and for the benefit of the Gospel. The whole paragraph may well be called a *captatio benevolentiae*. The only letters of St Paul in which a similar introduction is wanting are Gal ; 1 Tim ; Tit ; *cf.* *P. Wendland, Die urchristl. Literaturformen* 1912, 413 f.

St Paul's intention to visit the flourishing mission in Rome raises the question, how this present plan can be reconciled with his principle not to build on another Apostle's foundations, but to preach the Gospel only where Christ was still unknown, Rom 15:20 f. ; 2 Cor 10:15 f. ; *cf.* § 844*e*.

16-17 The Theme of the Epistle—From the literary **b** point of view these two verses clearly belong to the introduction, 8–17, since they explain Paul's statement in the previous sentence, 15, 16*a*, that the delay of his visit to Rome is not due either to fear or to shame. On the other hand, 16 f. are commonly set apart as a special paragraph because they contain the main thesis of the epistle. The points of this thesis are : (1) in the Christian Gospel God offers to men a real salvation ; (2) this salvation is to be obtained by means of faith ; (3) this salvation through faith is offered to all men without any of the traditional distinctions between races and cultures ; (4) this salvation is not an innovation that contradicts but is in full agreement with what is written in the OT. It is impossible to sound the depth of these thoughts in one reading or in a short explanation. A brief exposition of the principal terms and phrases, however, may be useful.

16. ' The Gospel a power of God for salvation ' : **c** σωτηρία = salvation is one of the most comprehensive terms used in the NT to describe the whole purpose of the Incarnation, or to cover the whole range of Christ's mission on earth. Its wide meaning may be gathered from the following list of synonymous or similar terms in the NT : ἁγιασμός sanctification ; ἀνακαίνωσις renovation, renewal ; ἀνακεφαλαιοῦν to re-establish, to bring to a head (in Christ) ; ἀπολύτρωσις redemption ; ἀφθαρσία incorruption ; βασιλεία τῶν οὐρανῶν, τοῦ θεοῦ kingdom of heaven, of God ; δικαιοσύνη justice, justness, righteousness ; δόξα glory ; εἶναι ἐν Χριστῷ to be in Christ = union with Christ ; εἰρήνη peace ; ζωή (αἰώνιος) life (everlasting) ; ἱλαστήριον propitiation ; καταλλαγή reconciliation ; παλιγγενεσία regeneration ; χάρις grace. Every attempt to define salvation has to start from the root-meaning : deliverance, safety, security, well-being. This deliverance can be of a temporal as well as of a spiritual character. Here Paul is evidently thinking of deliverance in the religious or spiritual sense. But this can again be understood negatively, as deliverance from the death of sin ; or positively, as the imparting of a new spiritual life. In either case the deliverance can be past, present or future. Thus, we have been saved through the Incarnation, Tit 3:4 f. ; Eph 2:8 ; we are being saved through Christ in us, 1 Cor 1:18 ; we hope that we shall be saved at the resurrection from the dead on the Last Day, Rom 10:1 ; 13:11 ; 1 Thess 5:8 f. ; Phil 1:19 ; 2:12. The appeal which the word salvation had for Paul's readers can be gathered from its frequency in the OT and in the Graeco-Roman usage of the time. Among the many synonyms for deliverance in the OT (cf. HRCS II 1328 ; HDB IV 357) σωτηρία had become more and more a technical term for the salvation expected from the Messias, so that Messias and Saviour could be used interchangeably, cf. Mt 1:21. In the Graeco-Roman world ' the cry for salvation was loud, persistent, and universal '. Heroes and kings as well as gods were given the title Saviour and the mystery religions developed elaborate theories and rituals of salvation under the patronage of several oriental deities ; cf. *S. Angus, *The Mystery Religions and Christianity*, 1925, 225–30. To bring out the main differences between the Christian doctrine of salvation and that of the pagan cults, stress is to be laid (1) on the historical character of Christ the Redeemer, and (2) on the moral obligations of the Christian faith, cf. Prat II 385–90.

d ' To everyone that believeth ' : the emphasis seems to lie on the verb, because of the parallelism with 17*b*. Faith is the one condition which man has to fulfil, if he wants to obtain the salvation of the Gospel. Without faith neither the privileges of Israel nor the wisdom of the Greeks are of any avail ; cf. 1:17*b* ; 5:1 ; Gal 3:8 ; Jn 3:36 ; 7:38 ; Council of Trent, sess VI cap 8 (Dz 801) ' fides est humanae salutis initium, fundamentum et radix omnis iustificationis, sine qua impossibile est placere Deo (Heb 11:6) et ad filiorum eius consortium pervenire ' = Faith is the beginning of man's salvation, the foundation and root of all justification ; without which (*sc.* faith) it is impossible to please God and to obtain fellowship with his sons. On the fundamental necessity of faith for salvation, here clearly stated by St Paul, all Christian theology agrees. The differences of opinion begin with the definition of this faith. A comprehensive Catholic definition of faith was given by the Vatican Council, sess III cap 3 (Dz 1789) ' Fidem . . . virtutem esse supernaturalem, qua, Dei aspirante et adiuvante gratia, ab eo revelata vera esse credimus, non propter intrinsecam rerum veritatem naturali rationis lumine perspectam sed propter auctoritatem ipsius Dei revelantis, qui nec falli nec fallere potest ' = Faith . . . is the supernatural virtue by which . . . we believe that what has been revealed by God is true, because . . . of the authority of God himself, who revealed it . . .'. Faith then is man's assent to truths revealed. This faith is called theological or dogmatic faith. All definitions of faith in the original Protestant sense are based on the translation of πίστις as confidence, trust. And the confidence is understood as trust in God's mercy on account of Christ's redemption. Trust and you will be saved. This faith is commonly referred to as *fides fiducialis*. For its modification by the Council of Trent see Dz 802, 822. The absence of any reference to sacraments and good works in Paul's thesis in 16 f. has often been noticed. The omission causes no difficulty if faith be understood in the sense of dogmatic

faith, which accepts all the doctrines of the Gospel as **846d** true and obeys all its precepts as divine commandments. For in this faith sacraments and good works are included, cf. Prat II 254–74 ; 311–51.

17a. δικαιοσύνη θεοῦ = iustitia Dei, Vg ; the justice **e** of God, DV, Boylan ; the righteousness of God, AV ; a righteousness of God, RV ; the justness of God, WV ; God's way of justifying us, KNT. The meaning of the term ' justice of God ' here used by St Paul is ambiguous. Taken by itself it can mean (1) an attribute of God : the justice which is in God, the justice which God possesses and practises as judge, commonly called the distributive or vindictive justice of God ; (2) an attribute of man : the justice which is in man but from God, *i.e.* the justice, goodness or perfection which man possesses as a gift from God. This is the same quality which we generally call justifying or sanctifying grace. Generally speaking the first of these two meanings is grammatically the more common and the more natural, but the second is possible too, and the context can make its acceptance necessary, cf. Mt 6:33 ; Rom 10:3 ; 2 Cor 5:21 ; Phil 3:9. The meaning of ' justice of God ' here is still disputed, cf. Prat II 459 f. To understand it of the justice which is in God, is so natural an explanation from the philological point of view, and so strongly supported by the corresponding ' wrath of God ' in 18, that it will probably always have its defenders. Thus Origen-Rufinus, Wetstein, etc., saw here the distributive justice by which God does not exclude anyone from salvation. Ambrosiaster and St Thomas Aq. knew of an explanation which thought of the justice (= fidelity) by which God is sure to fulfil his (Messianic) promises, cf. Rom 3:3 f. Theodoretus of Cyrus in very much the same way included a reference to the vindictive justice of God in Christ's vicarious passion and death. Zahn (1910, 82–84) identified it with Christ himself, who is the incarnation of God's justice revealed in the Gospel, cf. 1 Cor 1:30. More opinions have been collected by *M. Stewart, *Com. on Rom*, 1838, 63 f. ; Cornely, 68 ; Lagrange, RB 11 (1914) 321–31. Nevertheless it remains true that the more common opinion explains the ' justice of God ' in 1:17 as the justice which comes from God to man, *i.e.* justifying grace. So among others, Chrysostom, Augustine, Glossa Ordinaria, Estius, Cornely, Lagrange, Prat I 192 f. ; Boylan. To express this explanation the WV introduced the noun ' justness ', cf. C. Lattey, WV, NT, III (1927) 243. Protestant exegesis prefers the term ' righteousness ' to convey the same explanation that here the ' justice of God ' is a quality of man.

The controversy between Catholic and Protestant **f** exegesis from the time of the Reformation concerns the character of this justice—justness—righteousness. According to Catholic doctrine God not only declares man just but by that act also makes him just ; cf. Council of Trent, sess VI cap 7 (Dz 799) ' The one formal cause (of our justification) is the justice of God, not that by which he himself is just, but that by which he makes us just, that namely, with which we being endowed by him, are renewed in the spirit of our mind, and we are not only reputed, but are truly called and are just ' (J. Waterworth, *The Canons and Decrees of the Council of Trent*, Engl. Tr. 1848). Protestant exegesis on the other hand argues that δικαιοῦν is to be translated ' to declare just ', cf. SH 30 f., 34–9. As in court a judge pronounces a man free or guilty according to the law without intending to affect the real state of his soul, so in the process of justification God merely declares a man just, without affecting his inner state. Man's ' righteousness ', therefore, is merely imputed and not imparted, a fiction rather than a reality. The ensuing paradox that under this supposition man's sinful state remains, though he is declared and treated as just by God, and is expected to act accordingly, is admitted by Protestant theologians, cf. SH 36 ; *J. H. Holtzmann, *NT Theol.* II (1911) 137. The old Protestant position has been abandoned in modern times by Jülicher, Zahn, Lietzmann and others, cf. Lagrange, RB 11 (1914) 325 f. For the rejection of

846f the Protestant explanation and doctrine by the Council of Trent see Dz 821.

g ' From faith to faith ' : seems parallel to ' everyone that believeth ' in 16. Salvation by faith, v 16 = justness by faith, v 17. Repeating himself Paul changed salvation to justice (= justness), but he had no other word for faith. That the justness of the Gospel is to be obtained by faith, therefore, is clearly the general sense. The exact meaning of the phrase ' from faith to faith ' is, however, uncertain. One explanation understands it as a formula which could be translated ' faith all the way ', ' faith first and last '. In support of this interpretation one can quote the similar formulas in Ps 83:8 from strength to strength ; 2 Cor 2:16 from death to death ; 3:18 from glory to glory ; 4:17 beyond all measure ; cf. Jn 1:16. The emphasis then lies on the unique and necessary position of faith in the process of Christian salvation. This would seem to suit the context best, on the supposition that 15 f. are meant to be a summary statement. A second explanation insists on the literal translation ' from faith to faith ', which suggests various degrees of faith in the process of salvation. The faith of the Gospel, then, is here described as a living faith, a faith which grows wider and stronger from day to day, cf. Cornely 71 f. A third explanation understands the phrase as meaning ' justice or justness on the basis of faith unto believers ', cf. 3:22 ; Gal 3:22. So Boylan. This third explanation does not differ essentially from the first in meaning, but it would seem difficult to prove that the second ' faith ' here means all who believe.

h **17b.** ' The just man *will live* by faith ' : Another possible translation is ' He that is just through faith will live ' ; so Lietzmann, Boylan. This quotation from Hab 2:4 can be taken as a third variation on the theme of the epistle, or as a third attempt as it were, to find a striking headline, 17a being the second as parallel to 16. As the shortest of the three 17b is the one most commonly remembered. St Paul's first intention in adding it was evidently to support his thesis with a text from the Bible. For similar texts which he could have quoted cf. Gen 15:6 ; Is 7:9 (MT, Vg, not LXX) ; Mk 16:16. But Hab 2:4 seems to have been a favourite proof-text as it is also quoted in Gal 3:11 ; Heb 10:38. In each of these quotations, however, the prophet's words are interpreted in a typical or spiritual sense, the literal meaning being ' by faithfulness to God the just man will save his (natural) life ', *scil.* from death in the Babylonian captivity. ' He will live ' is the one new idea in this third summary of Paul's thesis. In view of his line of argument in the context there can be no doubt that he is thinking of the supernatural or spiritual life of the Christian soul, as defined in Gal 2:20 ; 5:25 ; cf. Rom 6:11, 13 ; 8:13 ; 14:8.

Summary. The theme of Rom 1:16–17 then can be summed up as salvation—justness of God—life on the one hand, and on the other faith each time. For the same doctrine cf. Jn 6:29 ; Gal 2:16 ; Eph 2:8 f.

847a **I 18–III 20 All Men need the Salvation revealed in the Gospel,** because all have sinned (3:23) and therefore live under the shadow of the wrath of God—This is true of the highly civilized Greeks = Gentiles, 1:18–32, as well as of Israel, God's chosen people, 2:1–3:20. To prove this universal need for the Christian salvation by convicting all of sin is the Apostle's first point in the section 1:18–11:36, which is generally called the dogmatic part of the epistle.

St Paul's way of opening the discussion by showing in the first place the need for the salvation revealed in the Gospel, 1:18–3:20, leaving the nature of that salvation to be explained later, 3:21–8:39, is throughout logical, once it is understood that such is the line of argument intended. This intention, however, a reader may easily fail to see because the Apostle commences his first point in 1:18 without any introduction or transition in our sense of these terms. His γάρ, ' for ' is too weak a particle, for our ears at all events, to be recognized as the beginning of a major section. If this absence of a formal transition is to be explained,

one may think of an interval between the dictation of 1:8–17 and 1:18 ff. But the reason can also be found in the style of St Paul who nowhere shows great concern to obey the rules of rhetoric.

The Apostle's actual proof of the universal need for the Christian salvation in 1:18–3:20 is based on the thesis that all men have been caught in the net of sin. But it is impossible to convince every man individually of sin. Hence the Apostle was bound to generalize, and generally speaking, the proof of all men being under the dominion of sin was not difficult. Biblical as well as pagan literature provided plenty of evidence. For similar biblical texts see Gen 6:5 ; Ps 13:1–3 ; 52:3 ; Eccl 7:21 ; 9:3 ; Is 6:5 ; 64:6 ; Wis 14:23–27 ; 1 Jn 1:8 ; 5:19. Similar texts from non-biblical literature can be found in Lietzmann 33, 35 f. ; Deissmann (§ 845d) 315 ff.

Plan. It is customary to distinguish two major steps **b** in the argument : (1) 1:18–32 dealing with the case of the Gentiles ; (2) 2:1–3:20 dealing with the case of the Israelites. Another arrangement is : (1) 1:18–23 the case of those guilty of gross idolatry ; (2) 1:24–32 the case of those guilty of obvious immorality ; (3) 2:1–3:20 the case of those who condemn both idolatry and immorality and yet are guilty themselves. Of these two the former analysis is undoubtedly in closer agreement with the whole trend of the Apostle's argument. In the world of St Paul there was a clearly marked distinction between Gentiles and Israelites, and every Israelite, worthy of the name, was proud of it. It must, however, be admitted that St Paul passes from the one to the other in 2:1 without any of the literary devices commonly used to indicate the beginning of a new topic. Moreover, it seems he deliberately avoided referring directly by name to the Gentiles in 1:18–32, and to the Israelites in 2:1–3:20. The result is a certain vagueness as the different commentaries show. But if this indefiniteness is intended for the purpose of ensuring a better hearing in both groups, it cannot be used as an argument against the former analysis, which is followed in this commentary.

I 18–32 The Gentiles' Need for the Salvation of the c Gospel—To show the need of the pagan world for the salvation of the Gospel Paul enlarges (1) in 18–23 on the folly of pagan idolatry ; (2) in 24–32 on the moral corruption of pagan life. For a more detailed analysis see *A. E. Garvie, CBi 96.

18–23 The Gentiles' Need for the Salvation of the Gospel in view of their Idolatry—The Gentiles know God, yet they do not honour him accordingly. Their worship is not religion but idolatry. Such folly, however, cannot possibly lead to the blessing of peace which every soul expects from God. On the contrary, their whole religion is patently stamped with the indelible marks of God's curse and wrath.

The term idolatry, not actually used in the text, is here understood in its primary theological meaning, in which it stands for all misinterpretations and misrepresentations of God's attributes, *i.e.* for faulty natural theology in general, cf. 1:23, 25. Only in this wide meaning can idolatry be said to be the beginning of the false and broad way that makes men sink inevitably lower and lower in their morality. And this is evidently the point which St Paul wants to make here. Further, idolatry in the restricted sense, in which it refers to various superstitions practised in connexion with actual idols, would not deserve the first place in this arraignment. For hideous and harmful as many of those superstitious practices may have been, they were hardly as hideous as the perversities referred to in 1:24–27. See also the list of sins in Gal 5:20 where fornication ranks first and idolatry fourth. Similar attacks on pagan idolatry are frequent in the OT, especially in the prophetical and sapiential literature ; cf. Ex 20:2–6 = Dt 5:6–10 (the first of the Ten Commandments) ; Is 44:9–20 ; Jer 10:3 ff. ; Bar 6:3, 72 ; Wis 13–15 ; Pss 95:5 ; 113B:4–8 = 134:5–18. For a list of patristic references see Zorell, *Com. in Is*, 1923, 181, note after Is 44, 23. That according to

c 1:18-23 the pagans' failure to attain salvation was due in the first instance to their false religion or idolatry is a point worth emphasizing in view of so many attempts in all ages to find the root of all trouble in other spheres of human life, *e.g.* in material or intellectual wants.

d 18. 'The wrath of God is revealed' = is being revealed, is revealing itself. The revelation of the wrath of God is considered as being in progress. This follows from the present tense and the context, 1:24, 26, 28. It is God's wrath working itself out in human history by turning the paths which men choose to get away from God into paths of depravity, degeneration and decay. The evidence in this case is the manifest folly of idolatry on the one hand, 1:22 f. ; and the moral corruption of pagan life on the other, 1:24-32. 'Men that detain the truth in injustice' : can mean (1) those who hold down (= hold back) the truth through their immorality ; 'such as in wickedness are repressing the truth ', WV ; 'men whose wrongdoing denies his truth its full scope' KNT ; (2) those who hold fast or possess the truth but with immorality ; *cf.* 1:32. In either case the Apostle clearly says that the religious failure of the Gentiles is due not to insufficient knowledge of God but to inefficient moral principles. The truth of which the Apostle speaks is the true knowledge of God, such as is accessible to human reason, *cf.* 1:19-23. 19. 'That which is known' : can also be translated, that which is knowable of God = all that which man can know about God by applying his natural faculties. 'Manifest in them' = clear to them, in their mind and conscience. Another possible translation is, mani-

e fest among them. 20. 'The invisible things of him' = his invisible attributes, two of which are mentioned in the same verse : his eternal power and divinity. 'Are clearly seen, being understood *by means of the things created*' : that from the visible things man by means of his intellectual faculties can and ought to come to know God, their creator, is common biblical doctrine, *cf.* Pss 8:3 f. ; 18:2 ; 142:5 ff. ; Is 42:5 ; 45:18 ; Job 12:9 ; 36:24 ff. ; Wis 13:1, 5 ; 14:22. The same was defined as dogma by the Vatican Council, sess III, April 24th, 1870 (Dz 1785) : '. . . Ecclesia tenet et docet, Deum rerum omnium principium et finem, naturali humanae rationis lumine e rebus creatis certo cognosci posse ; invisibilia enim ipsius, a creatura mundi per ea quae facta sunt, intellecta, conspiciuntur'. For a long list of references to the same idea in Greek philosophy *cf.* Lietzmann. 23. 'The glory of the incorruptible God ' = of the immortal God, WV ; of the imperishable God, KNT. 'Into the likeness of the image of . . . man . . . birds . . . beasts . . . reptiles ' = into images representing these creatures. Idols in human form are found in all ancient religions. The other three examples of idolatry can easily be illustrated from the religion of the Egyptians who worshipped hawk and ibis ; bull and cat ; and crocodile.

f 24-32 The Gentiles' Need for the Salvation of the Gospel proved from the Immorality of Pagan Life— From the Gentiles' idolatry Paul passes on to their immorality. Immorality must here be taken in the general sense of sins against the second part of the decalogue as distinguished from the sins forbidden in the first three of the Ten Commandments. The Apostle verifies his accusation of general immorality in pagan life with a list of 23 vices. They are arranged in three groups : 24 f., impurity ; 26 f., unnatural vice ; 28-32, a catalogue of twenty-one miscellaneous sins. Each of these groups is marked as such be the same introductory formula παρέδωκεν = tradidit, Vg = God gave them up to, DV in 24 = God delivered them up to, DV in 26, 28.

g 24, 26, 28. 'God *handed them over* to sin ' : the meaning of this phrase has been differently explained, *cf.* Poole 26 f. On the one hand, some Greek Fathers (Chrysostom, Theodoret) explained that God merely permitted men to follow their own free will which, however, when weakened by sin will invariably follow the inclination to evil. On the other hand, St Augustine

coined the paraphrase, *non cogendo sed deserendo* = not by **847g** forcing but by abandoning them, *i.e.* by withholding actual grace as their deserved punishment, *cf.* Aquin. ST II 1 q 79 a 3 ; II 2 q 94 a 3 ad 3. a 4 ad 1. With all respect for either attempt to explain *how* this is possible it would seem necessary to emphasize the greater importance of the *fact* that here St Paul clearly treats immorality as a regular consequence of idolatry, and that in this sequence he sees a divine arrangement or divine law. According to this text it is God's order that the first commandment is the cornerstone of all religious and moral life. Without it the other commandments are a building that has no foundation. This implication is clearly stated in 28 'inasmuch as they did not think it necessary to have (true) knowledge of God, God gave them up to a reprobate mind ; and in Wis 14:27 ' the worship of abominable idols is the cause and the beginning and end of all evil '. To explain *how* this divine order is reconcilable with the absolute goodness of God is part of the general problem of evil rather than of the exegesis of Rom 1:24. For a special note on the relation between idolatry and immorality see Lagrange 36-41. 24 f. 'Uncleanness' **h** = impurity. This can refer generally speaking to any sin as staining man's character. But the context of 24 f. makes it necessary to think here of sins against the sixth commandment = fornication. For the use of the word impurity in this sense *cf.* 6:19 ; 2 Cor 12:21 ; Gal 5:19 ; Eph 4:19 ; 5:3, and contrast the Christian reverence for the body in 1 Cor 6:12-20. 26 f. single out from the sins against the sixth commandment two particularly humiliating types, namely, unnatural vice among both sexes = shameful affections, DV = shameful passions, WV. 27c. 'Receiving in themselves the retribution due to their error ' : refers to the vices of 26, 27ab which are here considered not so much as sins in themselves but as punishment for the sin of idolatry (= error, DV) described in 18-23. 28. '*God gave them up to a worthless mentality* ' = a reprobate mind, WV. *Cf.* Tit 1:15 ' to them that are defiled and to unbelievers, nothing is clean, but both their mind and their conscience is defiled '.

29-32. This is a summary charge of general im- **i** morality in form of a list of 21 (23 Vg) common sins. Similar lists by St Paul can be found in Rom 13:13 ; 1 Cor 5:10 f. ; 6:9 f. ; 2 Cor 12:20 f. ; Gal 5:19-21 ; Eph 4:31 ; 5:3-4 ; Col 3:5, 8 ; 1 Tim 1:9 f. ; 2 Tim 3:2-5 ; *cf.* also Mk 7:21. These lists may have their model in the OT, *e.g.* Ex 20 ; 21:1-23:19 ; 34:14-26 ; Lev 19 ; Dt 27:15-26 ; Os 4:1 f. ; Wis 14:25 f. For a number of references to similar catalogues in classical (stoic) and patristic literature see Lietzmann 35. All attempts to discover a systematic order in Paul's enumeration have failed. The later Greek MSS and Vg have two additions which are probably not genuine : ' fornication ' in 29 ; and ' without fidelity ' in 31. On the whole subject see Lagrange RB 8 (1911) 534 ff. 29. ' Whisperers ' = tale-bearers. 32. ' *And they knowing quite well God's sentence, that all who practise such things deserve death, yet not only practise these things themselves but also applaud those who practise them* ' : in one respect this is but another sin to be added to the previous list, *viz.* the sin of applauding and encouraging wrong-doing. On the other hand, St Paul has obviously set it apart and marked it as the climax of all the depravity mentioned before. This is no exaggeration. For to abet and to applaud evil is doing the devil's own work. The Latin text is uncertain ; Vg and WV differ substantially.

II 1-III 20 Israel's Need for the Salvation of the Gospel **848a** —Continuing his evidence of the universal need for the salvation revealed in the Gospel St Paul here takes up the case of Israel, the Chosen People. But there is no indication in the text of this change of subject. To make such an abrupt transition intelligible, commentators refer to Nathan's conviction of David in 2 Sam 12:1-9. As David whole-heartedly condemned the man of Nathan's parable, 2 Sam 12:1-5, so every Israelite would whole-heartedly join in Paul's condemnation of paganism in 18-32. But there follows in each case

848a the unexpected 'thou art the man' 2 Sam 12:7 = Rom 2:1–3:20.

The progress of thought in 2:1–3:20 is not easy to follow. The sub-divisions proposed in the various commentaries differ widely. The difficulty arises mainly from the various objections with which the Apostle repeatedly interrupts the course of his argument. In addition, the actual objections are not stated in the text, but must be inferred from his answers. The objector is, of course, imaginary, *cf.* SH 69 f., on 3:1 ff.

b II 1-2 **A General Statement introducing Israel's Case with regard to the Salvation of the Gospel**—Without mentioning a name St Paul here introduces the case of a man who condemns the idolatry and immorality depicted in 1:18–32 but is nevertheless guilty himself. Self-complacent he sits in judgement over the religious and moral life of others, but in reality he needs the salvation of the Gospel as much as they.

1a. 'Thou . . . O man, whosoever thou art, that judgest': of whom is St Paul thinking? So far he has addressed himself clearly to all those who were guilty of gross idolatry, 1:18–23, and immorality, 1:24–32. But these apart, there evidently remained a large group of men who condemned idolatry and immorality as much as St Paul did, *e.g.* the followers of stoic philosophy and, much more numerous and outspoken than they, the whole of Israel. Hence the question, did St Paul here think only of Israelites or did he include also the so-called good pagans? Both possibilities are defended by different commentators. The opinion that Paul thought exclusively of Israelites has in its favour that in 2:17 he actually mentions 'the Jew' by name, which he seems to have deliberately avoided before, in order to obtain a better hearing. Moreover, the whole description is said to fit the typical Israelite of the time who was proud of his higher religious and moral standards, *cf.* 2:17–20; Lk 18:9–14. On the other hand there is much to be said in favour of the opinion that here at the beginning Paul is still speaking generally, and includes everybody who fits the description, no matter whether Jew or Gentile. This opinion presents the wider view in every respect. After all, there were good pagans, then as now, and they could not reasonably be said to fall under the accusation of 1:18–32. Hence if they are not included in 2:1–3:20 they escape the Apostle's argument for the universal need of the salvation revealed in the Gospel. This may not be impossible, but there can be little doubt that with 2:1–3:20 he intended to close the ring of his evidence so as to let no one escape from the accusation of being under sin and therefore in need of the salvation of the Gospel.

c **1bc.** 'For wherein thou judgest another thou condemnest thyself. For thou doest the same, *thou who judgest*': this is Paul's summary reply to those who would claim exemption from the previous charges of idolatry and immorality. As can be seen from his later explanations, he does not mean to say that those who belong to this second category are, in spite of their protest, guilty of all the sins enumerated in 1:18–32. But as far as the dominion of sin is concerned they are in the same position as those whom they condemn. For in principle they act in the same way, *i.e.* they, too, do not live according to their knowledge of God; and that is where their sin begins. Their guilt may be less evident owing to their higher knowledge of God, or because their religious and moral life is more refined, but this does not exempt them from the dominion of sin. They are caught in the net of sin like all the rest. This is no doubt a hard argument and one can well understand that the Apostle takes a long time over explaining it, 2:2–3:20. But, in all he says, nowhere does he go back on his word. Again and again he repeats it : all are under sin. There is no exception. Those who judge others, thereby speak their own judgement, *cf.* Jn 8:7 ; 1 Jn 1:10. The practical conclusion which the Apostle wants to be drawn from it all evidently is : living in sin 'you will also die in your sin', Jn 8:21, unless you accept the salvation offered in the Gospel.

3-10 A First Objection—Do not God's kindness, for-**8** bearance and patience give a sufficient guarantee that the threatened punishment of men's sins will be averted, 3–4? To this St Paul sternly replies that such a hope is foolish. On the day of God's judgment his justice alone will rule, giving everybody his due according to his works, *cf.* Ps 61:12 f. ; Prov 24:12. On that day God's goodness will certainly not declare sinners to be saints.

11-24 A Second Objection—Will the Torah, the Law of Sinai, not protect Israel from the wrath of God? Paul's reply is substantially the same as before. On the day of God's judgement it is not God's law that will be weighed in the balance but men's works. On that day sin will be punished as sin, without any respect of persons, no matter whether it was sin against God's will as read in the Torah or as voiced in man's conscience, 11–16. **16.** Some connexion with 15 must be inserted, *e.g.* [as will be evident to all] on the day when God judges. The whole sentence seems to have been added here by St. Paul to answer the excuse that the voice or law of man's conscience is something which it is difficult to prove as it is hidden and secret and that it therefore should not be used in a discussion of this nature. Paul replies : this may be true for the present, but it will not be so on the day of God's judgement. Then all will have to confess that they had God's law written in their hearts.

17-24. The Apostle follows up his first answer with an **e** *argumentum ad hominem*. After a solemn introduction in 17–20 which enumerates all the alleged prerogatives of Israel (but is left without a proper apodosis) he instances in 21–23 the 7th, 6th and 1st commandments against his objector : 'doest thou steal? . . . doest thou commit adultery? . . . doest thou plunder temples?' With reference to these three accusations it would no doubt be an exaggeration to think that Paul regarded every Israelite as a thief, an adulterer, or a temple-robber. His point is rather that these sins were committed by Israelites, though they were expressly forbidden in the Torah, *cf.* SB III 108–15. The Law, therefore, has not saved Israel from sin in the past nor will it save Israel from the wrath of God on the day of judgement. 'Thou that boastest of the law, dishonourest God by breaking the law', 2:23, *cf.* Mt 23:3. 'But we know that the judgement of God is according to truth against those who do such things', 2:2. **22.** 'Dost thou plunder temples', WV. This is commonly understood of pagan temples, *cf.* Dt 7:5 ; Ac 19:37 ; Fl. Jos. *Ant.* IV 8, 10. The incentive to such theft seems to have been the great wealth stored up in many pagan temples. Others understand the phrase of defrauding the revenues due to the temple in Jerusalem. In this case 'dost thou commit sacrilege?' is the better translation.

25-29 A Third Objection—Is not circumcision, **f** Israel's first sacrament, a sufficient guarantee for her salvation? St Paul's answer is that circumcision does not make a man a saint before God, if he does not keep the law of God ; *cf.* Dt 10:16 ; 30:6 ; Jer 4:4 ; 9:26 ; Ez 44:7. And Israel has not kept the law.

III 1-2 A Fourth Objection—If the Law and Circumcision cannot save Israel what then remains of Israel's so highly-praised privileges? Paul's reply begins as if he intended to answer with a long description of Israel's privileged position as in 9:4. In fact, however, he does not get beyond the first point, that she has been entrusted with the Scriptures. **2.** 'The words of God' : can mean (1) the whole OT ; (2) the Messianic promises in the OT, because of v 3.

3-4 A Fifth Objection—What is the use of the Scriptures, since according to Paul's own argument God is no longer bound to his promises after Israel has broken the covenant by unfaithfulness to her obligations? Paul answers as in 2 Tim 2:13 'even if we are unfaithful (= untrue to our trust) God remains faithful (= true to his promises) for he cannot disown himself', *cf.* also Rom 9:6 ; Jer 31 (38 LXX):32. True as it is that God's relation to his people is a bilateral covenant, yet this

f is not all. God's truthfulness and faithfulness to himself are above any changes which man may introduce. Man's untruthfulness and unfaithfulness only serve to bring out the opposite attributes of God all the more clearly. **3.** ' If some have " not believed ", *will their " unbelief " not render ineffective the faithfulness of God ? '* The words in double inverted commas have been understood (1) of Israel's ' unbelief ' in Jesus of Nazareth as the Messias ; (2) of Israel's ' unfaithfulness ' to the covenant of Sinai referred to in 2:11–24, 25–29. The second explanation is recomended by the contrast with God's ' faithfulness ' in the context and by the same thought in 2 Tim 2:13. But see SH and Lagrange.

g 5–8 A Sixth Objection—If our unjustness (= sinfulness) serves to make God's justness (= justice) stand out the more clearly, why are we still threatened with his wrath, and urged to seek justification ? Is God not unjust in punishing such sinfulness ? Paul's reply in 6–8 is difficult to follow. It seems to consist of three points, each meant to lead the objector *ad absurdum*. (1) According to such reasoning God could not judge the world at all, and yet we know that he will judge every-one, and that his judgements will be true, *cf.* 2:2, 6–8 ; Ps 118:137, 142 ; Job 34:10–12, etc. (2) According to such reasoning the Jews could not condemn me (Paul) as a sinner = an apostate, but should rather acquiesce in my apostasy as a means of manifesting and glorifying God's truth in the possession of Israel. Yet the objector, being a Jew, must know very well how harshly Paul is judged by his former coreligionists, 7. So Jülicher. (3) According to such reasoning it would be right to teach as some maintain that I (Paul) do : ' let us do evil that good may come '. Yet, such a doctrine is evidently abhorred by all, 8. **7** is taken by most commentators as a further objection, in which case it is but a weakened repetition of v 5. **8.** ' Let us do evil that good may come ' : is a malicious mis-interpretation of St Paul's doctrine of justification by faith and not by works, *cf.* 6:1, 15.

h 9–20 Concluding Statement of Israel's Need for the Salvation of the Gospel—The Apostle returns from the various digressions in 2:3–3:8 to the principal question of 2:1–2, is he who claims exemption from the charge of idolatry and immorality in 1:18–32 (esp. Israel) en-titled to regard himself as ' just ' before God, or in such a privileged position that he does not need the Christian justification ? St Paul's concluding answer is an un-compromising No. The Jews as well as the Greeks, *i.e.* Israel, the Chosen People (= the Church of old), as well as the pagan world, all are in the bondage of sin, as the Scriptures prove. The Apostle's proof from the Scriptures in 10–18 is a free combination of the following texts from the LXX : Rom 3:10–12 = Ps 13:1–3 = Ps 52:2–4 ; Rom 3:13*a–b* = Ps 5:10 ; Rom 3:13*c* = Ps 139:4 ; Rom 3:14 = Ps 9:28 ; Rom 3:15–17 = Is 59:7 f. ; Rom 3:18 = Ps 35:2. **9.** προεχόμεθα = ' Do we excel them ' = have we Israelites then still any advantage over the Gentiles ? According to this trans-lation the Greek middle is here used for the active, *cf.* Lagrange, Boylan. If the Greek form is taken as passive, the translation is ' are we excelled ' = are we Israelites then in a worse position than the Gentiles ? So SH and WV. ' No, not so ' = (1) not altogether, (2) not at all. In either case, Paul does not deny that Israel has privileges, but she has none as regards the need for the salvation of the Gospel which is the point here under discussion. **20.** Law convinces man of sin (*cf.* 7:7–12) but does not produce justness or salvation, *cf.* Jn 1:17.

i Application of I:18–III:20—St Paul's argument for the universal need of the salvation revealed in the Gospel is still practical and convincing. For laws are still insufficient to make men saints, no matter whether we consider the laws of conscience, or the laws of the various systems of moral philosophy, or the laws of Christian moral theology. All these systems agree in showing the ideal more or less clearly, but they do not produce the longed-for justness—righteousness—salva-tion, because in practice no one lives in complete

accordance with all these laws. ' If we say that we **848i** have no sin, we deceive ourselves, and the truth is not in us ', 1 Jn 1:8. Because of sin men needed the salva-tion of the Gospel in the days of St Paul, and because of sin they still need it today. The need for that salvation is the result not of religious speculations but of hard realities.

III 21–IV 25 The Way to the Salvation of the Gospel 849a —In this second part of the dogmatic section of his letter Paul sets out to describe the means by which the salvation of the Gospel is obtained. The logical con-nexion with the previous discussion, proving man's need for it, is self-evident. The two sections belong together as man's need and God's answer. At the same time it is easy to notice a gap in the argument. Between man's need for salvation and the way to the salvation of the Gospel one expects a discussion on the nature of this salvation. According to the dogmatic textbooks of today such a discussion would have to deal first with Christ's work of redemption, then with the negative side of salvation = justification = remission of sins, and finally with its positive side = sanctification = in-fusion of sanctifying grace. St Paul in his exposition of the way to salvation, 3:21–4:25, and of the effects of salvation, 5:1–8:39, does cover the ground of such a modern discussion on the nature of Christian salva-tion, but in a way that is not systematic according to our standards ; *cf.* Prat I 171 ; II 250–53 ; textbooks of dogma, treatises on Christ's work of Redemption and on Sanctifying Grace, *e.g.* Tanquerey II 749–84 ; III 34–102.

Plan.—According to the most common opinion **b** 3:21–4:25 can be subdivided as follows : (1) 3:21–30 the way to the Christian salvation is faith in Christ ; (2) 3:31–4:25 the Scriptural evidence in favour of this doctrine. Another arrangement is : (1) 3:21–26 the way to the Christian salvation ; (2) 3:27–31 some practical conclusions ; (3) 4:1–25 the case of Abraham as proof from Scripture for the Christian doctrine of salvation by faith.

21–26 The Way to the Christian Salvation is Justifica- c tion by Faith in Christ—In a picture which is very different from that in 1:18–3:20 St Paul here gives a summary description of the new salvation which he is preaching and defending. Unfortunately for us, the description is so brief, compact and sententious that it becomes difficult to understand. The negative picture in 1:18–3:20 is much fuller and easier to analyse. The outstanding importance of the passage, however, is generally recognized. It has been called ' one of the key passages ' of Paul's epistles, ' the epitome and mother idea of Paul's theology ', *cf.* Prat I 205. The characteristics of the Christian salvation singled out in this description by St Paul are : (1) it is a justification which does not come by way of any law, 21 ; (2) it is obtained by faith in Christ, 22*a* ; (3) hence it is open to all, without distinction, 22*b*, 23 ; (4) it has its ultimate origin in the propitiatory death of Christ, 24–26. See the similar description in 1:16 f. ; and the detailed analysis in Prat I 204–6.

21. ' *A justice (justness) of God without law* ' = inde- **d** pendent of, apart from all existing law or legal systems. The law in its various forms (be it conscience, or moral philosophy, or OT Scriptures) offers salvation to all who abide by this law and keep it in every point. From this system of justification the salvation of the Gospel must be clearly distinguished. They are worlds apart. Man's failure in the one is God's opportunity in the other. Another possible explanation translates Law as Mosaic Law, *e.g.* WV, Boylan. **22.** ' *A justice (justness) of God through faith in Jesus Christ* ' : the justness which the Gospel promises is obtained by way of faith in Jesus Christ. The law-fulness of the former system of salva-tion has been replaced by faith-fulness ; *cf.* Council of Trent, sess VI cap 8 (Dz 801), quoted § 846*d*. On the suitability of faith for playing such an important part in the process of salvation see Prat I 172 f. ; Gifford 89. **23.** ' *All . . . have fallen short of the glory of God* ' = the perfection of God, *cf.* 1:23 = the justice of God. In

849d this context it is evidently the justice of God as it was meant to be shared by men, therefore = justness = sanctifying grace ; *cf.* C. Lattey, WV III 245. Others explain δόξα (= glory) here as high opinion, honour, praise, favour from God, which leads to the same idea. All have sinned and thereby lost God's good opinion of them = his favour = his grace. Cornely understands it of eternal life as in 2:7 ; 8:18, 21.

e **24-25.** ' Justified freely by his grace through the redemption . . . in Christ Jesus, whom God hath *set up as* a propitiation . . . in his own blood ' : the Christian justification derives its existence ultimately from the propitiatory death of Christ, which the Council of Trent, sess VI cap 7-8 (Dz 799, 801) called ' the meritorious cause of our justification '. That this central thesis of all Christian doctrine of salvation—justification—sanctification (soteriology) is clearly expressed in our passage is beyond any doubt, and the differences of opinion which exist on the exact meaning of this or that term here employed by St Paul should not be allowed to obscure this fundamental doctrine of the passage ; *cf.* Prat II 181, 184 ; I 380-4 ; SH 91-4, note after 3:26. For a dogmatic treatment see textbooks of dogma, Christology ; *e.g.* Tanquerey II 731-8 (736 !) ; 750-4 ; 776-80. Commentators differ mainly in the explanation of ' redemption ', 24, and ' propitiation ', 25. **24.** ἀπολύτρωσις = redemption. Does this term imply the idea of a ransom being paid, the ransom being the blood of Christ ? This question cannot be decided for certain. The word ἀπολύτρωσις, redemption, taken by itself, need not carry the idea of a ransom. For LXX uses it for the ' deliverance ' from Egypt ; and the NT uses it in the same general sense of ' deliverance ' six times out of ten : Lk 21:28 ; Rom 8:23 ; I Cor 1:30 ; Eph 1:14 ; 4:30 ; Heb 11:35. On the other hand it has the meaning of ' ransom ' in Col 1:14 ; Eph 1:7 ; Heb 9:15. To these references we must add the passages in the NT in which the idea is clearly expressed that the Christians have been ' bought for a price ', 1 Cor 6:20 ; 7:23 ; Gal 3:13 ; 2 Pet 2:1 ; Apoc 5:9 ; *cf.* also Mt 20:28 ; Mk 10:45 ; Ac 20:28 ; 1 Pet 1:18 f. ; Prat II 181. The last two groups of texts provide strong evidence in favour of the idea of a ransom being implied

f also in Rom 3, 24 f. **25.** ἱλαστήριον = propitiation. There can be no doubt that this term describes our Lord's death as propitiation = expiation of our sins. But does it define our Lord's death as a propitiatory *sacrifice ?* The doctrine that Christ's death was a sacrifice for men's sins = a propitiatory sacrifice, follows clearly from such texts as Mt 26:28 and parallels ; 1 Cor 11:24 f. ; 15:3 ; Eph 1:7 ; 5:2 ; Col 1:20 ; Heb 10:12-14 ; 1 Pet 1:18 f. ; 3:18, etc. The question whether this doctrine is also expressed in Rom 3:25 must be left open. For the word ἱλαστήριον (= propitiation) taken by itself cannot be shown to have had the meaning ' propitiatory sacrifice '. According to etymology it signifies ' something connected with reconciliation, propitiation or expiation '. LXX uses it 25 times for ' the lid of the Ark of the Covenant ' = the mercy-seat or propitiatory ; *cf.* Ex 25:17. So also Heb 9:5. The only other text in the NT where it occurs is here, where its exact meaning is consequently largely a matter of conjecture. The main explanations that have been put forward are : (1) a means of propitiation = a propitiatory = a mercy-seat ; (2) a propitiator (taking the adjective as masculine which is possible in the Greek) ; (3) a propitiatory sacrifice. The last of these explanations is favoured in our context by the phrase ' in his own blood ', 25. *Cf.* Prat I 429 f. ; II 180-8 ; SH 91-4.

g **25-26.** The structure of this sentence is : God set up Jesus Christ as a propitiation . . . 25a : (1) *with the intention* of showing his justice, 25b ; (2) *the reason being* his having passed by the sins of the past in patience, 25c, 26a ; (3) *with the intention* of showing his justice in the present time, 26b ; (4) *with the intention* that he may be found just himself and justifying those who believe in Jesus, 26c. Nr 1.3.4 form a clear and

continuous line of thought. But how are we to fit in **8** nr 2 ? It is evidently closely connected with nr 1 and at the same time there is a contrast with nr 3. Accordingly there are two explanations. (1) If the connexion with nr 1 is stressed then it seems inserted to explain why God manifested his justice with such severity in the death of Christ, 25a, 26c. The Apostle warns against interpreting God's forbearance with man's sins in the past as a proof that God's punitive justice had fallen into abeyance for ever. The cross is the true measure of the rigour of God's justice in punishing sin. (2) If the contrast between nr 2 and nr 3 is stressed, *i.e.* the contrast between past and present, then nr 2 seems intended to show that God in the past merely passed by sin but did not justify = sanctify = save the sinner, as he has decided to do in the present time. The choice between these two possibilities depends on the interpretation given to ' the justice of God ' in this paragraph ; *cf.* note on 25b. **25b = 26b.** ' For the shewing of his **h** justice ' : WV translates in both cases ' the justness of God ' = his communicated justice, as in 3:21. This explanation has the advantage of consistency and simplicity. It does away with the necessity of remembering the distinction between justice of God as it is in God and as it is in man ; and it concentrates on the main idea of the whole section 3:21-4:25 which is man's justification according to the Gospel. From the practical point of view, therefore, this explanation is certainly the easiest to follow. But it must be admitted that this is not the only possible explanation. In view of the respective contexts many commentators maintain that Paul's usage of the term ' justice of God ' is not consistent in this paragraph. The different meanings are (1) = God's justice in man = communicated justice = justness, in 21 ; (2) = justice in God, in 25 ; and that with the emphasis on the special meaning of justice as punitive justice, the reference being to God's punitive justice as revealed in the terrible death of Christ for man's sins ; (3) = the justice in God, in 26 ; but with the emphasis on the general meaning of justice = the whole moral perfection of God, as revealed in Christ's propitiation and in the justification of man. See Rickaby, Boylan. **25c, 26a.** ' For the **i** remission of former sins. Through the forbearance of God ', DV = ' because of God passing by former sins in his patience ', so according to the best editions of the Greek text, πάρεσις meaning praeter-mission rather than re-mission. There are two explanations of the idea here expressed. (*a*) In the past God only passed by man's sins in his patience (*cf.* Ac 14:15) but there was no real justification of man, as this was reserved for the present time. Such must be the thought if the justice of God in 25b is = justness. (*b*) God showed his justice so severely in the death of Christ, 25ab, because of his having apparently overlooked man's sins in the past by showing patience. To avoid this patience being misinterpreted as indifference to sin on God's part is one purpose of the terrible death of Christ for man's sins. This must be the idea if the justice of God in 25b is the punitive justice of God. **26b.** ' *That he may be found just himself and justifying him who believes in Jesus* ' : this text makes it very clear that St Paul uses the one term ' justice of God ' in two different meanings : (1) the justice of God as God's attribute ; and (2) the justice of God as communicated and imparted to us.

27-31 Three Practical Conclusions from the Christian j Doctrine of Justification by Faith—These verses throw further light on the way to salvation by means of three conclusions from its previous description in 21-26. (1) The Christian doctrine of justification by faith excludes all that boastful self-sufficiency and self-complacency which the various claims to superiority in law and lawfulness had spread and always will spread among men. In the Christian doctrine of salvation, law and lawfulness have been dethroned from the first place in the process of man's salvation, and their place of honour has been given to faith in Jesus Christ, 27 f. (2) The Christian doctrine of

j justification by faith supersedes the old distinction between Israelites and Gentiles based on circumcision. All attempts to retain that distinction in the question of salvation are in vain. For faith in Jesus Christ cannot be made dependent on circumcision or descent from Abraham. And it is this faith which is henceforward the one only condition for salvation required on the part of man, 29 f. (3) The Christian doctrine of justification by faith is in complete agreement with the Scriptures = the Law of Moses = the Pentateuch, 31. The proof of this follows in ch 4.

k 28. ' Justified by faith without *works of a law* ' : Christian justification is obtained by faith ; no one can earn it by works according to this or that system of law, whatever the name or character of that law may be : be it the law of Israel, or the law of the Gentiles ; be it natural, moral or ceremonial law ; *cf.* 3:20–22 ; Dz 801, 1793 ; Prat I 180 f. Already Origen uttered a warning against the false conclusion that according to this verse works *after* justification are of no account. To draw such a conclusion would be to overlook two important points : (1) Paul is here concerned not with the Christian life after justification, but with the way of obtaining justification. ' Initial justification ' = the beginning of justification, is his point. (2) When Paul does speak of the life after justification has been obtained he leaves no doubt that works are necessary to retain the justification obtained by faith. The evidence is to be found in his many exhortations, *e.g.* Rom 12–14. Among the more popular references to the same effect are Mt 25:34 ff. ; 1 Cor 3:8 ; 2 Cor 11:15 ; Gal 5:6 ; Jas 2:14, 17, 24–26. But St Paul would call these works ' works of faith ' and not ' works of law '. Thus there is no contradiction. Faith leads to virtue, but virtue need not lead to faith (St Gregory the Great, *Hom. 19 in Ez, cf.* Estius). The necessity and meritorious character of good works after justification had to be defended by the Council of Trent, sess VI cap 7, 10 ; Dz 800, 803, 834, 842.

l Another conclusion from 28 that had to be rejected by the Council of Trent is, that *before* justification only faith is necessary as a preparation and no other works. To prove such a conclusion it would be necessary to show that Paul considered here not only the immediate preparation for justification which is admittedly faith, but also the possibilities of a more remote preparation and deliberately excluded any such steps before the decisive act of faith. Such a proof is impossible and other texts show that we must leave room for such a more remote preparation. The Council of Trent, sess VI cap 6 (Dz 798, 819), mentions : fear of God's punishment of sin, Ecclus 1:28 ; Heb 11:6 ; hope of his forgiveness for Christ's sake, Mt 9:2 ; Mk 2:5 ; love of God = hatred of sin, 1 Jn 3:14 ; repentance, Lk 13:3 ; Ac 3:19 ; the resolution to receive the Sacrament of baptism and to keep the commandments, Mt 28:19 ; Ac 2:38 ; *cf.* Tanquerey III 54–8, esp. nr 54.

m Verse 28 has also become famous through Luther's translation ' by faith alone ' = *sola fide*. The adjective ' alone ' was not in the text from which Luther translated, since no MS or edition has it. He may have added it for the purpose of bringing out the sense of the passage more clearly. In fact, however, the addition has led to the false conclusion that—faith excepted—all other works both before and after justification are of no account according to St Paul's doctrine of salvation. This so-called *sola-fides* doctrine was rejected by the Council of Trent, Dz 819, 798, 803 f. 30. ' by faith . . . through faith ' : stylistic variation seems to be the most natural explanation of the difference in the preposition ; so Boylan, differently SH.

n IV 1-25 The Justification of Abraham as a Scripture Proof for the Christian Doctrine of Justification by Faith—The purpose of this digression into OT history is to illustrate and prove the three previous conclusions, 3:27–31, esp. the last, 3:31, that in teaching justification by faith and not by the observance of the Law, the Gospel asserts a doctrine which is not against but

in complete agreement with the Scriptures = OT, esp. **849n** Pentateuch. The argument consists of the following 5 points : (1) 1–8. ' Abraham believed God and that was counted to him as justice ', Gen 15:6 LXX, Vg : this is the proof-text. It has a positive and a negative side. The former is the emphasis on Abraham's faith, the latter consists in the omission of any reference to his works. Both aspects must be taken together to make Abraham a suitable type of the justification of the Gospel by faith without works, 3:27 f. (2) 9–12. Abraham's justification by faith, Gen 15:6, took place *before* his circumcision, Gen 17:9–14, 23–27. The typical significance of this justification of Abraham, therefore, must not be limited to the children of the circumcision (= Israel) only. It is a lesson and example for all. Abraham is first of all ' the father of the faithful ', and that is an older and wider title than ' the father of the circumcision ', 3:29 f. (3) 13–17 **o** continue the proof of the last point : the typical universality of Abraham's justification by faith. The new turn of the argument is the use made of the promise given to Abraham, that he will be the father of many nations, 13, 17. Abraham received this promise, Gen 12:3 ; 15:5 ; 18:18 ; 22:17 f., in view of his faith and not in connexion with any law or commandment. The children of Abraham according to this promise, therefore, are those who are Abraham's children by sharing his faith. Thus, from the very beginning the promise given to Abraham was founded on faith and grace, and this can indeed be regarded as a secure basis of justification. Had it been otherwise, had the promise given to Abraham been made dependent on the observance of a law, there would today be no plea for the fulfilment of the blessing promised to Abraham, because the Law had admittedly been broken, *cf.* Deut 11:26–28. (4) 18–22 are not essential to the argument ; but to pass them by would mean losing one of the best descriptions of faith in general, and of Abraham's faith in particular. The phrase that believing in God Abraham ' hoped against hope ', 18, has rightly become famous. From the earliest times commentators have sought for an adequate paraphrase ; *e.g.* Chrysostom : ' past hope of man, in hope of God ' ; Theodoret : ' past hope according to nature, but in hope of the promise of God ' ; Severianus : ' past hope of his own nature, in hope of the power of him that promised ' (Gifford). (5) 23–25 apply Abraham's justification by faith as a scriptural type of the justification by faith according to the Gospel and so bring this ' proof from Scripture ', 4:1–25, to a close.

13-17. The argument that the promise given to **p** Abraham ranks higher than the Law is repeated in Gal 3:15–18. There is this remarkable difference however, that in Gal the superiority of the promise is based on the simple fact of its being 430 years older than the Law. 23-25. There is admittedly a difference between the object of the faith of Abraham and the faith of a Christian. Abraham had to believe that God would give him a son ; the Christian has to believe that God grants redemption and justification through the death and the resurrection of Jesus Christ. The difference is no doubt substantial. But this difference is not St Paul's point. His point is rather that in either case it is faith and not works on which man is found to be just = justified. Differently, N. P. Williams 460 f.

V 1-VIII 39 Some Immediate Effects of Christian **850a** Salvation, or the Fruits of Christian Justification— After the description of the means by which salvation according to the Gospel is obtained (Christ's redeeming death and man's faith, 3:21–4:25) Paul now recommends this salvation by praising some of its immediate effects, its present blessings. The same subject is treated in modern textbooks of dogma under the title : the formal effects of sanctifying grace, or sanctification. As such fruits we normally enumerate : (1) the forgiveness of sin, unless this be considered rather as the essence of justification ; (2) divine adoption, 1 Jn 3:1 ;

850a (3) the indwelling of the Holy Ghost, 1 Cor 3:16 f.; (4) the gifts of the Holy Ghost; (5) the implanting (infusion) of supernatural virtues, esp. of the three theological virtues: faith, hope and charity; *cf.* Tanquerey III 50 f.

Plan. St Paul's method of treating the effects that follow in the soul upon the acceptance of the salvation offered in the Gospel in 5:1–8:39 is neither systematic nor complete. But the present chapter-division is generally acknowledged to separate the main points: (1) 5:1–21 he who is justified in the sense of the Gospel enjoys a triumphant hope of heavenly glory; (2) 6:1–23 he has ceased to live under the dominion of sin; (3) 7:1–25 he is free from the Law; (4) 8:1–39 he possesses the life and rights of an adoptive son of God. This last chapter can also be taken as a summary presentation of the blessings and principles of the Christian life; *cf.* Cornely.

b V 1-21 The Salvation of the Gospel gives Hope of Final Salvation = eternal glorification—That Paul in this chapter no longer speaks of faith leading to justification, but of sanctifying grace working in the justified, is beyond any doubt. But it is not so easy to see how many effects of this sanctifying grace (= initial salvation) he meant to single out for his description. Boylan distinguishes no less than eight: (1) peace with God, 1; (2) the hope of glory, 2; (3) gladness in tribulation, 3; (4) constancy and tested virtue, 4; (5) God's love for us, 5*a*; (6) indwelling of the Holy Spirit and abundance of infused virtue, 5*b*; (7) imputation of Christ's merits, 6–8; (8) confident hope of salvation and boasting in God, 9–11. Piconio counts four: (1) peace of conscience, 1; (2) the hope and joy of eternal glorification, 2; (3) joy in tribulation, 3–5; (4) joy in God our Father and in Christ our Saviour, 11–21. On the whole it would seem that the argument centres on 'the hope of heaven' as the main point of the passage.

Many commentators prefer to call ch 5 a discussion of *the certainty* of the Christian hope of final salvation, because this particular aspect of the Christian hope of heaven is given by far the greatest space and prominence in 5–21. Others for the same reason go a step further and treat ch 5 as a section by itself and separate it from 6:1–8:39.

Plan. If the hope of heaven is taken as the main point, then the argument has three parts: (1) 1–4 the hope of heaven as the first fruit of salvation; (2) 5–11 the certainty of this hope proved from God's love for us as revealed in the redemption through Christ; (3) 12–21 a second proof for the certainty of this hope of heaven: Christ the anti-type of Adam.

c 1-4 A First Fruit of the Salvation revealed in the Gospel: the hope of final salvation = of eternal glory in heaven—Paul begins his praise and recommendation of the salvation which he preaches by dwelling on the triumphant hope of final salvation hereafter as the consequence of initial salvation here. Initial salvation is the same as justification = sanctification = the obtaining of sanctifying grace = reconciliation with God. Strictly speaking, the first fruit of salvation here enumerated by St Paul is 'peace with God', 1. But as this is only touched upon here, its full explanation can be left to other passages, *e.g.* 2 Cor 5:18–21; Eph 2:11–22; see also Rom 5:10 f.; 8:6; 15:33; 16:20; 1 Cor 14:33; Col 1:20; 3:15; 2 Thess 3:16; Lk 1:79; 2:14, 29, etc.

1. '*We have* peace with God': So Cornely, Sickenberger, Lietzmann, Boylan. The indicative can be defended on external and internal evidence. **2a.** '*Through whom by faith we obtained also our introduction into this grace . . .*': is a relative clause to be connected with 1. Its purpose is to remind us that our peace with God which is the first effect of salvation according to v 1 is no more our own doing than our 'introduction to the faith' (= to Christianity). Both are the work of Christ. It should be noticed that the sentence does not introduce **d** a new fruit of salvation. **2b.** '*and [through whom] we also rejoice in the hope of the glory of God*': unlike those

without hope, Eph 2:12; 1 Thess 4:13, the justified **g** can rejoice, looking forward to the glory to come. It is the hope which we usually call the second theological virtue. Its main, though not only, object is final salvation = everlasting happiness = eternal life = beatific vision. St Paul calls it 'glory of God'. Fuller descriptions of it can be derived from 3:23; 8:18; 1 Cor 2:9; 15:43; 2 Cor 4:17 f.; Phil 3:21; Col 3:4; 2 Tim 2:10. From the grammatical point of view 2*b* is the second part of the relative clause begun in 2*a* from which it cannot be separated without doing violence to the text; *cf.* KNT. But the unfortunate result of this grammatical connexion need not be denied. It is not in accordance with the rules of clear writing to introduce in a second relative clause the point which finally turns out to be the centre of the whole passage. **3-4** is a parenthesis like 2*a*. It forestalls the common objection that the Christian hope of heaven is a sign of weakness leading to inactivity and indifference here on earth. According to 3–4 the Christian hope of heaven has the opposite effect: it makes men strong in tribulation which is the time when this hope is being tested and tried, *cf.* Mt 5:4; Rom 8:37; 2 Cor 1:3–11; Jas 1:3 f. **3.** 'And not only so': a difficult ellipsis. Probably = We do not rejoice in the hope of the future glory only, but we rejoice also in the present tribulations, knowing that these tribulations strengthen that hope. Boylan treats this gladness in tribulation as a third fruit of sanctification.

5-21 The Certainty of the Christian's Hope of Final e Salvation in the Glory of Heaven—In this paragraph St Paul dwells on one characteristic of our hope of heaven, its certainty. This he bases on two foundations: (1) on God's love for us as shown in his Son's death for us, 5–11; (2) on a comparison between the effects of Adam's sin and Christ's redemption, 12–21. In both cases the argument takes a form which follows the first of Hillel's seven rules for the interpretation of Scripture, usually translated as the conclusion from the minor to the major = the conclusion from the less important to the more important; *cf.* 5:9, 10, 15; SB ad Rom 5:9 f. The certainty of such a conclusion must not be identified with that of a categorical syllogism in logic. Its value is rather like that of an emphatic assertion based on an objective similarity and a subjective intuition. Such an assertion has the authority of the speaker, and that is in the case of St Paul the authority of his inspiration. The originality of St Paul in both arguments can be seen from a comparison with the treatment of hope in the OT and in modern theology. The OT keeps repeating that he who puts his trust (hope) in God will not be put to shame (*cf.* Pss 21:6; 24:20; Is 28:16, etc.), and it is a general theologoumenon today, that the certainty of our hope rests on God's faithfulness to his promises. Such statements are so frequent that they have become commonplace. But how daring is their application by St Paul to the greatest problem of all, the reaching of heaven; *cf.* Prat I 237–49.

The doctrine of the Church on the question of in- **f** dividual certainty of final salvation was briefly stated by the Council of Trent, Dz 805, 825, 826. According to Catholic doctrine no one while on earth can be certain of his final salvation without a special divine revelation. In comparing this doctrine with Rom 5:5–21; 8:28–30 it should be remembered that the Council of Trent had to check exaggerations whilst St Paul had to encourage beginnings. All the same, Paul's teaching on the certainty of final salvation in 5–21 needs a corrective, and this corrective follows in ch 6 with its emphatic warnings against sin. This addition by the Apostle himself proves beyond any doubt that the certainty of final salvation stressed in ch 5 is not an unconditional certainty that follows irrevocably on baptism or conversion. Even in Rom there is a condition attached to it, and this condition according to ch 6 is that the Christian convert must live the life demanded by the Gospel.

5-11 God's Love for us as the First Proof for the g Certainty of our Hope of Final Salvation—The

g Christian's hope of eternal glory is no illusion. It is firmly based on God's love for men as revealed in the fact that his Son died for us though we were then still sinners, and therefore ' children of enmity or wrath ', *cf.* 1 Jn 4:10. Starting from this as an acknowledged fact, Paul arrives at his conclusion—the certainty of the Christian hope of final salvation—as follows : If when still sinners (= at enmity with God) we received the grace of initial justification from God's love in view of Christ's death on the cross, how much more can we not now as his friends (= justified by responding in faith to his first love) expect to receive the grace of final salvation from his love in view of Christ's life in heaven ? The whole passage is difficult, the main thought being obscured by too many details. It can be reduced to this : If God's love justified us on the day of our conversion though we then stood before him as sinners, how much more will not the same love save us on the day of the last judgement when we shall stand before him as saints = such as have been justified and redeemed by his Son.

h **5b** is a stray thought as regards the main argument. Before enlarging on the objective evidence of God's love for us in Christ's death (6-8), the Apostle inserts in 5*b* a subjective proof to the same effect by appealing to the readers' personal experience and realization of that divine love in the voice and witness of the indwelling Holy Ghost. **6.** ' For why . . . ? ' : the interrogative sentence of Vg and DV is better read as a categorical statement in accordance with many Greek MSS, *cf.* Boylan. ' According to *a* time ' = in due season, WV. This has been explained in two ways : (1) Christ died for us when we were not only sinners but also remained such for a time, *i.e.* during the time between Christ's death and the readers' conversion. (2) Christ offered himself for us at that time in history which had been appointed by the Father ; *cf.* Rom 3:26 ; 2 Cor 6:2 ; Gal 4:4 ; Eph 1:10 ; 1 Tim 2:6 ; 6:15 ; Tit 1:3. The second is the more common interpretation, but the first is more in harmony with the context, 8 ; *cf.* Cornely. **11.** ' And not only so ' : is an ellipsis, *cf.* 5:3 ; 8:23 ; 9:10 ; 2 Cor 8:19. It can be completed in different ways, *cf.* Boylan 81. The most probable completion would seem to read : we shall not only be saved on the day of the last judgement, but even now, at this present hour with all its afflictions, we glory in God through Jesus Christ, rejoicing in his love for us ; *cf.* 5:3.

i **12-21 Adam understood as a Type of Christ,** another proof for the certainty of the Christian hope of Final Salvation = Eternal Glory in Heaven—' As in Adam all die, so in Christ all shall be made to live ', 1 Cor 15:22 WV, might well serve as a motto for this passage. Our physical connexion with Adam brings us sin and death with undeniable certainty ; in a similar way and with a similar certainty our spiritual connexion with Christ brings us justification and final salvation. In other words, Adam's fall is the beginning and cause of our sin and death ; Christ's redemption is the beginning and cause of our justification and final salvation in heaven. The comparison could also be arranged in this way : Adam——→Sin——→Death ; Christ——→Grace (= justification)——→Eternal Life. For further details see Prat I 438 ff. ; II 171-9.

j This parallel between Adam and Christ and the description of the consequence of Adam's fall as typical of the fruits of Christ's redemption is in biblical theology peculiar to St Paul. Before Rom he had already used it in 1 Cor 15:22, 45-49. But there as here he puts it before his readers without any proof whatever, taking it evidently for granted that they would follow and accept his argument. Thus the idea is not likely to have been entirely unknown to his contemporaries. For attempts to trace it in rabbinical theology see Prat II 171 ; SB III 477 f. (on 1 Cor 15:45). At all events, the whole argument of 12-21 stands or falls with the existence of this parallel between Adam and Christ. If Christ were not the anti-type of Adam in God's economy of salvation then Paul's second argument for

the Christian confidence of reaching eternal glory in **850j** 12-21 would collapse.

What then is the proof value of this parallel between Adam and Christ ? Reason alone, excluding the doctrine of inspiration from the argument, cannot prove that St Paul's typical interpretation of the story of Adam is necessary from the OT point of view. But once it is pointed out—and in this St Paul seems to be original—reason cannot deny that this parallel between Adam and Christ is full of meaning and beauty. Ultimately, however, our acceptance of the Apostle's argument as a true doctrine must be based on our belief in NT (Pauline) inspiration, *cf.* §§ 850*e*, 856*d*.

In most commentaries on 12-21 much space is given **k** to the discussion of the evidence for the Christian doctrine of original sin in this passage. That the idea of original sin is presupposed in the argument of 12-21 can safely be taken as certain ; but it is only one of several side issues. This probably accounts for much of the obscurity of the passage in this particular respect, as the controversies on original sin constantly point out, *cf.* note on 5:12*d* ; Lagrange's special note at the end of ch 5 ; Prat I 213-19, 440 ff., II 57-9.

To translate *guilt* (*guilty*) instead of *sin* in 12-21, seven times, is a special feature of KNT. This translation, though possible according to the dictionary (*cf.* Liddell and Scott I 77*b*) would seem a precarious deviation from the traditional terminology touching original sin in this paragraph.

Plan. The passage can be sub-divided as follows : (1) 12-14 the consequences of Adam's fall ; (2) 15-17 the benefits of Christ's redemption contrasted with Adam's fall ; (3) 18-21 a recapitulation. For a detailed analysis see Prat I 438 f.

12-14 is an anacoluthon. The thought is continued **l** in 18*b* and 21*b* : ' As sin and death through Adam, so redemption and eternal life through Christ ', *cf.* 1 Cor 15:22. **12d.** ἐφ' ᾧ πάντες ἥμαρτον : is ambiguous and has been differently translated. (1) = in quo omnes peccaverunt, Vg ; = in whom all have sinned, DV. Death spread to all men through Adam, ' in whom all sinned '. This is the customary explanation of the Latin text. It clearly understands the clause of original sin = the inherited consequences of Adam's sin in the individual soul. In this sense the Latin text is quoted in the decree of the Council of Trent on original sin, sess. V, Dz 789. (2) Another translation is : ' *because* all sinned '. This is the common rendering of the Greek text, *cf.* note in WV. From Adam's fall death spread to all men, because ever since all men sinned or had sin. Taken by itself this translation could no doubt be understood of every one's personal sin and not of his original sin. It would mean that universal sin (*cf.* 1:18-3:20) was followed by universal death. The main argument against this last explanation is the fact that it does not harmonize with the context. If all die because of their personal sin then the parallelism between Adam and Christ, on which the argument of the whole passage rests, is destroyed. The parallel : Adam-sin-death ; Christ-justness-eternal life is interrupted in its middle part ' sin and justness ' which become the work of individual man. According to St Paul's argument, however, justness is clearly the achievement not of the individual but of Christ. Moreover, in the two sentences, 13-14, which follow upon 12, Paul introduces the case of millions whose death he evidently does not understand as the punishment of their personal sins. It is the case of all those who died before Moses when there was as yet no statutory divine law threatening sin with death. Nevertheless they died, sharing Adam's death ; but then they must have had a share in Adam's sin also, if the principle that through one man's sin death came into the world, 12, is to be true. A simpler illustration to the same effect is the case of those who die before they are capable of sin. The practical result of the whole discussion would seem to be, that those who insist in 12 on the translation ' *because* all sinned ', add from the context : ' because all sinned *in Adam* ' = had original sin. The Latin text obtained the same **m**

850m result less circuitously. **19.** ' Many shall be made just ' : MSS as well as commentators have tried to turn this future into a past tense. To do so is necessary if the whole passage, 12–21, is understood of Christ's justification as it works itself out in the Christian life on earth, *i.e.* before the Last Judgement. But if the whole passage (as in this commentary) is understood as referring to the Christian's final justification in the Last Judgement, then the future tense causes no difficulty. The adjective ' just ' has a meaning wide enough to be used also for the state of ' final ' salvation.

851a VI 1-23 A Second Effect of Justification : the Christian's break with sin—There is no shortage of striking headings for this important chapter ; *e.g.* the Christian sanctification of life ; the new life in Christ ; the Christian's practical holiness ; the Christian and sin ; the Christian's emancipation from the dominion of sin ; no place for sin in the life of the justified ; Christian justification implies an irretrievable rejection of sin and the beginning of a new and holy life.

Subject. Whatever heading may be preferred Paul here passes on to another immediate and major effect of Christian justification : the complete break with sin in and after obtaining justification = sanctifying grace. With us today, it is rather the forgiveness of sins that comes to our mind when the effects of justifying grace as regards sin are to be enumerated. But the forgiveness of sins is not St Paul's subject here. All the weight of the passage is concentrated on the Christian's break with sin. The ensuing victory over sin is discussed in 8:1–8.

b Object. The connexion of ch 6 with the previous ch and the precise object of the Apostle in discussing this subject here are disputed. Was his intention to continue the enumeration of the effects of Christian justification begun in 5:1 ? Or was his purpose to refute lax conclusions from his doctrine, esp. from 5:20 f. ? Or did he intend to insert here, as the spirit moved him, a pressing exhortation to a holy life ? Each of these possibilities has been and can be defended. Those who regard Rom 6 as the description of another effect of justifying grace can quote in their favour, besides simplicity, a long exegetical tradition. It is an explanation which gives the chapter a place in the whole epistle that can easily be remembered. The second opinion which treats 1–23 as a refutation of morally lax (= antinomian) conclusions falsely drawn from St Paul's teaching is supported by the two introductory questions, 1, 15, and by the fact that such false conclusions have actually been drawn from his doctrine. He himself refers to them in 3:7 f. (*cf.* Gal 5:13), and the Nicolaitans are accused of similar ideas in Apoc 2:15 ; *cf.* the Spirituals in post-reformation days. The third opinion treating 1–23 as an exhortation can appeal to the admonitory and exhortatory tone which runs through the whole chapter, *cf.* 2, 3, 11, 12–14, 19. The obvious objection is that Paul clearly begins his exhortations proper with ch 12. It is difficult to choose between these possibilities. Perhaps the true solution lies in the combination of all three. The context demands doctrine ; the subject matter could hardly be expressed without exhortation ; and to think here of a kind of self-defence on the part of St Paul is taking account of what we know from the history of this doctrine.

c Characteristic. St Paul's way of arguing in 1–23 has often been criticized as difficult and complicated, as concealing the real issue under too many words and metaphors and as lacking clear progress of thought. That from a literary point of view these objections are not without some foundation need not be denied. But it must also be remembered that one cause of the difficulty at all events lies in the subject, the problem of sin in life. For it is self-evident that the only straightforward solution of the problem of sin in life is *sinlessness*. But to be henceforward without sin is not among the effects of Christian justification. Sanctifying grace is a gift but also a task. The task it sets is the sanctification of daily life ; and with regard to this task Christians

can fail, and do fail. That is so today and that was so **85** in the days of St Paul. But he believed, as we believe, that the fact of justifying grace makes a great difference to the power of sin. To describe, illustrate, and engrave upon the memory of everyone this new Christian counter-power to sin was the Apostle's first object. In judging his style and diction we should not forget that he lacked all the refinements of later theological terminology. But leaving terminology and style alone, can we today really quote any stronger counter-forces to sin than the two here singled out by St Paul : the mystical union with Christ, 1–11 ; and the hope of eternal reward after a life in the service of Christian holiness, 15–23 ?

Plan. To prove his thesis that Christian justification brings liberation from the dominion of sin St Paul employs two arguments : (1) 1–14 the Christian's break with sin in the sacrament of baptism ; (2) 15–23 the Christian's break with sin because of the punishment of sin on the one hand, and because of the reward of holiness according to Christian doctrine on the other.

1-14 The Christian's Break with Sin in the Sacrament d of Baptism—That in baptism every Christian renounces the devil and all his works is a custom handed down from earliest times. Nevertheless Paul, arguing in 1–14 that there is no more room for sin in a Christian life, does not appeal to these baptismal vows of his readers. He goes much deeper and bases his argument on the (mystical) union with Christ which is the primary purpose of baptism. In baptism the Christian is created, as it were, by being united with Christ. Henceforward, therefore, the Christian's attitude to sin must be the same as that of Christ himself. He must die to sin, as Christ died to sin ; he must be holy as Christ was holy.

This is the substance of the argument in 1–11 and St Paul could well have left it at that. But to drive his point home, he proceeds to demonstrate or prove the existence and the nature of this union with Christ from the two baptismal ceremonies of immersion and emersion. According to St Paul's own exposition the former of these two ceremonies represents the Christian's death and burial with Christ, the latter his resurrection with Christ. When in baptism the catechumen is *immersed* beneath the water, he is thereby, as it were, buried with Christ, sharing his being dead to sin ; and when the Christian *emerges* from beneath the water he thereby rises, as it were, with Christ from the tomb, sharing the new life of the Risen Lord. The theological principles underlying this way of arguing in 1–14 are three : (1) the symbolical meaning of the ceremonies used at baptism ; (2) the sacramental efficacy of baptism ; (3) a real (mystical) union, incorporation, identification of the Christian with Christ as an effect of the sacrament of baptism.

What makes the argument somewhat complicated is **e** the fact that two lines of thought are constantly crossing each other : (1) baptism as dying to sin ; (2) baptism as the beginning of a new life. In a systematic treatment the two aspects would be kept separate and discussed as the negative and the positive effects of baptism. The real difficulty of St Paul's argument, however, is the character of the new life instilled in baptism. For in reality this new life remains far behind its ideal, the life of the risen Christ. With this difficulty St Paul wrestles in 5–9. On the one hand he insists on the fact of this new life being instilled in baptism ; otherwise his whole argument would fall to the ground. On the other hand, he changes from the past to the future tense in describing the transformation worked in the Christian by the infusion of this new life in baptism : ' we *shall* also be in likeness of his resurrection ', 5 ; ' we *shall* also live with him ', 8. Contrast Col 2:12 ; Eph 2:5. The result is that this new life is represented as a life which begins in baptism, 4, but is to be completed in the future, reaching its fullness after death in heaven, 5, 8. This way of presenting the case which is undoubtedly the true one may be compared with ' prophetical compenetration '. But a satisfactory grammatical explanation of these future tenses does not seem to exist.

Plan. There are two clearly marked paragraphs : 1–11 doctrine ; 12–14 corresponding exhortation.

1. Paul introduces his new point, the banishment of sin from Christian life, with an objection suggested by what he had said on sin and grace in the previous sentence 5:20 f., or by the false conclusions which he knew had been drawn from his doctrine ; *cf.* 3:8 ; Gal 5:13 ; 1 Pet 2:16 ; Jas *passim*. If in the past man's sin provided the opportunity for God's grace, why not continue in sin to provide further opportunities for God's grace ? The same objection is repeated in 15. **2.** ' *We who have died* to sin ' : is a metaphor for complete separation from sin. In a more detailed explanation account must be taken of the application of the same metaphor to our Lord in 10. In either case there is agreement that ' to sin ' is dative and not ablative. The dative is then explained as a ' dative of reference ', so that one could paraphrase Paul's thought as follows : as far as sin is concerned we have died ; we have done with sin, we have finished with it. The comparison with death in this metaphor would seem to lie in the complete change and absolute separation from all that was before.

3a. ' We who *were* baptized *into* Christ Jesus ' : introduces the sacrament of baptism into the discussion, and thereby the Apostle's first proof for his thesis that there is no longer any room for sin in the life of a Christian, 2. But how far can baptism be said to have this effect ? This is briefly explained in 4–5 and then further developed in 6–10. As these explanations show, Paul speaking of baptism into Christ Jesus was here thinking not of the formula of baptism—whether it should be Christological or Trinitarian—but of baptism as ' immersion ' into Christ. To combine the idea of baptism and immersion is strange to us, but was natural to Paul and his readers for two reasons : (*a*) the Greek verb βαπτίζειν means to immerse into, to dip into, to plunge into ; (*b*) in the early Christians this idea was kept alive through the ceremony of immersion in their baptism. **3b.** ' We *were* baptized *into* his death ' : if baptism is immersion into Christ, 3*a*, it must include immersion into his death as much as into any other work of his redemption, *e.g.* resurrection, ascension, etc. Why then does St Paul here single out the death of Christ ; and which is the particular aspect of Christ's death that he has in mind ? The answer is given in 10 : Christ's death was his final settlement with all that concerned sin, and baptism is meant to be the same for every Christian.

4. ' As Christ *was raised* from the dead . . . so we also *should* walk in newness of life ' : so far Paul has insisted on the negative aspect of our ' dying to sin ' symbolically represented in the baptismal ceremony of immersion reminiscent of Christ's death and burial ; now he turns from the negative to the positive aspect, the beginning of a new life, symbolically represented by the baptismal ceremony of emersion, which is reminiscent of Christ's rising from the tomb. The new Christian life, therefore, should be a life concerned only with heavenly things, like the life of the Risen Christ ; *cf.* Col 3:2 ; Phil 3:20. **10.** ' *The death he died to sin once and for all* ' : that Christ died to atone *for* men's sins is the general Christian doctrine of the Cross. But this aspect of the death of Christ does not fit into St Paul's argument here, where Christ's dying to sin is quoted as the model of our dying to sin. If the meaning of the metaphor ' dying to sin ' from v 3 is to be kept then Paul must here be thinking of the Cross as Christ's final settlement with regard to all that concerned sin in his life. On Calvary sin's claims were settled once and for all ; henceforward God's claim alone was of practical importance to him. Death to sin on Calvary is followed by a life for God alone beginning with the resurrection. The application to the Christian life is easy. As Christ settled his account with sin on Calvary so does the Christian in baptism, 11. That Christ's account with sin was of a very different character from ours does not affect the argument. **12–14.** Paul passes from doctrine to exhortation.

15–23 The Christian's Break with Sin once more— The Apostle returns to the question of sin in the life of a Christian raised in 6:1 and shows once more that there is no longer any room for sin in a Christian life. The subject is no doubt important enough to bear such a repetition. The content of the passage can be summarized as follows : the Christian is bound to avoid sin and pursue holiness in his life in view of their respective wages according to Christian doctrine, death being the wages in the service of sin, eternal life the wages in the service of holiness. The connexion with 1–14 is disputed. Some would connect it with ch 7 which discusses the liberation from the Mosaic Law and regard it as a third effect of Christian justification ; *cf.* SH. The wording of the introductory question in 15 can rightly be quoted in favour of this view, but the trend of the argument speaks against it.

16–22 develops the parable that man is a servant = slave either under the rule of sin or under the rule of holiness. **16b.** ' Servants . . . of obedience unto *justness* ' : what one expects in the antithesis is : servants of justice (or of the Gospel, or of God) unto life. This conclusion actually follows in 22 f. From the strictly logical point of view therefore 16*b*–21 forms a digression. Its object is to impress the necessity of obedience = of being a servant or slave. The simplest proof is the vocabulary : obedience, 16 (twice) ; to obey, 16, 17 ; slave, 16, 17, 20 ; to be enslaved, 18, 22. It is, however, possible that in 16*b* obedience is but a synonym for Gospel, *cf.* 1:5 ; 15:18. **17.** ' *The form of teaching unto which you were handed over* ' : the normal phrase would be, the form of teaching that has been delivered unto you. In any case it is clear that the phrase presupposes a set of dogmas in early Christianity. On the question what these principal doctrines were, *cf.* Prat II 28–35. **19.** ' *I speak in human terms* ' WV = I express myself in terms which you are certain to understand, *cf.* Gal 3:15 ; Rom 3:5. Paul apologizes for using the obedience of a servant or slave to illustrate the Christian's obedience in the service of God. For in other respects to be a Christian is to have found true freedom, *cf.* Gal 5:1, 13 ; 1 Cor 9:19 ; 2 Cor 3:17 ; Rom 8:15, 21. But see also Mt 11:29 ; 1 Cor 7:22 ; Rom 1:1 ; 7:25 ; 14:18 ; Eph 6:6 ; Phil 1:1 ; 2:22. **20–22.** The life of ' the servant of sin ' (= slave to sin) and of ' the servant of God ' (= slave of God) are compared once more. **20b.** ' You were free *as regards justness* ', WV = you were without it. **21.** The interpunctuation is uncertain. Many commentators translate : ' What fruit did you reap then ? Such as you are now ashamed of . . . death '. **22.** ' Now . . . you have your fruit unto sanctification ' : a difficult phrase because the common meaning of ἁγιασμός = sanctification, does not fit easily into the context. If this meaning is kept, the Apostle's thought is : now you have your fruit in such things (virtues, *cf.* Gal 5:22 f.) as lead immediately to sanctification and thereby finally to life everlasting. But does the structure of the sentence bear such an interpretation ? Many commentators prefer to translate : ' now you have your fruit *in* justness '. And this is what one expects in the context : now you have your fruit (= reward) in the possession of justness (= sanctifying grace) for the present, and in the hope of eternal life for the future. **23.** ' The wages of sin is death, *the gift of God eternal life* ' : sums up the whole passage 15–23. Both the death and the life of which Paul speaks are eternal, *cf.* Mt 10:28 ; Gal 6:7 f. ; 2 Cor 5:10 ; Apoc 20:14 ; but it would be a mistake to think that therefore they do not begin till after the grave, *cf.* 6:4 ; Col 2:12 ; Eph 2:5 ; Jn 17:3.

VII 1–25 A Third Effect of the Justification revealed in the Gospel : Christ the new principle of life in the place of the Old Law ; or the Christian's New Law— There is no conversion without obvious changes in essential religious convictions, and there can be no such changes without the need of defending them against the charges from former friends of disloyalty or apostasy.

852a These are the two general truths which form the background of this chapter. The Christians addressed in Rom were baptized converts and the change defended in ch 7 is their new attitude to the Old Law. Our Lord touches on the same problem in Mt 5:17-48 : . . . it was said . . . but I tell you. Paul takes it up both in Gal and Rom 7. For us today the main points in such a discussion are the fact that the Christian convert was taught a new attitude to the Old Law, and the content of that teaching. In this respect, however, Rom 7 is no great help, because St Paul takes the new Christian attitude to the Old Law for granted, and all his labour goes into defending it, just as the fact and doctrine of baptism is taken for granted in ch 6 ; *cf.* the similar method in modern apologetic treatises.

b Natural as this apologetic method no doubt was in the days of St Paul, it makes his argument in Rom 7 difficult for us unless we begin, as his first readers did, with a real and true conception of that new Christian attitude to the Old Law according to the mind of the Apostle. This new Christian attitude to the Old Law, therefore, may here be briefly stated. For the Christian the Old Law is no longer the first ruling principle in life. This first place of honour and importance the Old Law must yield to Jesus Christ who for our salvation (which is to be obtained in union with him) descended to earth and after his death and resurrection ascended again to heaven. This doctrine is the Christian's first ruling principle in life, and since two cannot be first the Old Law must give way. In other words the centre of Christianity is Christ, not Law ; Christianity is Christo-centric not nomo-centric.

c The point in this doctrine which needs explanation is the term ' Old Law '. We are accustomed to make clear distinctions between the natural moral law and the Mosaic Law ; and again between the moral and the ceremonial law of the OT. Which of these laws then was St Paul thinking of when writing Rom 7 ? This question draws attention to a serious difficulty in the explanation of this ch. The ultimate cause of the difficulty is the ambiguity of the term ' law ' used by St Paul. Taken by itself ' law ' can have any of the four meanings quoted above, and commentators do not agree in their choice. At first it seems clear from ch 7 that the Apostle was thinking of the Mosaic Law. But if the whole epistle, addressed to Gentile as well as Jewish Christians, is taken into account, it appears that it would be oversimplifying his teaching in ch 7 if we limited it to the discussion of the abrogation of the ceremonial law of the OT. For what reason is there to think that Paul did not apply the principles of Rom 7 also to the natural moral law of the Gentiles, which if codified would have all the advantages and the disadvantages of the Mosaic Law pointed out in this chapter : the law is good but man does not keep the law. In view of the whole epistle therefore it seems better to accept the wider interpretation of ' law ' in Rom 7, *i.e.* the Apostle was thinking first of the Mosaic Law = the Torah, but as representative of and including all other law. The sum total of the argument, then, is that for Paul the Christian's union with Christ superseded all that philosophy or theology had ever taught ; he excepted nothing, not even the Torah of Moses, much less any other law.

Plan. Ch 7 falls into three paragraphs : (1) 1-6 for the Christian the law is no longer the first guide in life ; (2) 7-12 the refutation of a first misinterpretation ; (3) 13-25 the refutation of a second misinterpretation.

d **1-6 For a Christian the Old Law is no longer the First Rule in Life**, or ' the transition from Law to Grace ', SH—It is no superficial objection against Christianity from the OT or rabbinical point of view to argue that speaking of a New Testament Law is as precarious as speaking of a new natural law. What was ' divine law for ever ' in the days of God's revelation at Sinai must remain so till the end of this world. And yet it is clear Christian doctrine that there is a New Testament = a New Law. ' *Nova sunt omnia* '. How is this possible, and what are the practical consequences ?

Plan. Paul bases his argument on the legal principle that the binding force of law ceases for the individual at death, 1. This principle is first illustrated by an example from marriage law, 2-3 ; and then applied to the Christian attitude to the Old Law in 4-6.

1. No one will question St Paul's premise that death makes law irrelevant. It is a commonplace truth. What gives colour to its quotation here is the fact that it was used in rabbinical theology to denote a unique privilege of the Mosaic Law. According to rabbinical theology only death could set the Israelite free from the laws of the Torah. With regard to the Torah there was neither dispensation nor abrogation ; *cf.* Targum to Ps 88:6 ; Wetstein and SB on Rom 7:3. Paul keeps the principle but turns it against the Torah by introducing the Christian's sacramental death in baptism. **2-3** make a digression. Instead of at once applying the principle of 1 to the point under discussion, the Christian's liberation from the Old Law, the Apostle goes out of his way, first to illustrate his principle with an example taken from the law of marriage. A married woman bound to her husband under the penalty of adultery becomes free to re-marry after his death. Here then is a clear case in which death cancels law, *cf.* Ruth 1:9. As long as 2-3 are taken as no more than an illustration of this principle generally stated in 1, the argument is simple and clear. The difficulties begin when these two verses are understood further as an allegory applied in 4-6. To quote 2-3 as direct NT evidence for the doctrine of the indissolubility of marriage (because of the omission of any reference to the possibility of divorce according to Deut 24:1 ff.) is perhaps basing too much on an *argumentum ex silentio* ; *cf.* Lagrange.

4-6 contain (*a*) the application of the principle of 1 ; (*b*) the application of the illustration of that principle in 2-3 ; (*c*) the positive description of the New Law = the new dispensation.

(*a*) The application of 1 in 4-6 is clear. The Christian having died with Christ in baptism, 6:1-11, has in this mystical death the charter which sets him free not only from the dominion of sin but also from every allegiance to the Old Law. The result is that he can enter into the new union with Christ without feeling guilty of any disloyalty or apostasy since ' death ' frees man from old obligations. The point which deserves special attention in this argument is the reality of the union with Christ through baptism presupposed in this application. How deeply conscious must the early Christians have been of their union with Christ to accept such an argument ! To a student of rabbinical theology it cannot have meant anything. To him it must have been sheer hair-splitting folly to dispose of the Torah by a ceremonial-sacramental death in baptism. And so it must still appear today to any system of thought which does not accept the Catholic doctrine of the sacraments. The sacramental effects of baptism behind the argument of 4-6, therefore, cannot be stressed too much.

(*b*) The explanation of 4-6 becomes much more complicated as soon as these verses are understood as an application not only of the principle of v 1 but also of the illustration of that principle in 2-3. The main difficulty is that the example, 2-3, speaks of two persons where the application, 4-6, has only one. In the example it is the husband who dies whilst the law ceases for the widow so that she is free to re-marry. According to the application, 4-6, however, it ought to be one and the same person, for it is one and the same individual who dies in baptism and is then free to enter into a new union with Christ. Now to make two persons = one, or one = two, is evidently not in accordance with the rules of grammar or logic ; and the history of the exegesis of the passage shows that this difficulty has never been convincingly solved, *cf.* Cornely 349 f. A summary of present-day exegesis would seem to be : (1) To acknowledge that 7:2-3 is both an illustration of v 1 and at the same time a parable or allegory applied in 4-6. (2) To admit a

g certain amount of inconsistency in detail between parable and application which no one explanation can dispel. (3) To limit the interpretation of the parable to what is essential in St Paul's own application, *i.e.* (a) death sets aside law, and so does the death undergone in the sacrament of baptism, (β) once this death has taken place the Christian is free to transfer his loyalty to Christ in the same way as a widow is free to marry again.

h (c) The description of the New Dispensation = the New Law in 4–6 must be the third point in every explanation of this passage. And it is the most important point for us, since for us the liberation from the Old Law (esp. in the sense of the Mosaic Law) is no longer a practical question. But even in the days of St Paul nothing could possibly be gained merely by an abrogation of the OT Law. All depended, then as now, on what was to take its place, or what use was to be made of the freedom obtained. The answer in 4–6 is very clear. The law is not so much abrogated as superseded. The freedom obtained in baptism is intended to make room for a new guide or principle or master, *viz.* union with Christ risen from the dead ; *cf.* Gal 2:19.

i **4.** This union with Christ as the new guiding principle of life instead of the Old Law is first described as marriage with Christ, risen from the dead, *cf.* 2 Cor 11:2 ; Eph 5:25, 29. The metaphor is in agreement with the illustration used in 2–3. But it may be true that it should not be pressed. Cornely denies that it is continued in 4c and 6. In any case, what St Paul stresses most, is that it must be a union which bears fruit, and thereby proves its superiority over the former state. ' By their fruits you shall know them ', Mt 7:16 f. ; Gal 5:22. **5.** The fruits of the pre-Christian time are then reviewed by way of contrast. That was the time of the ' old man ' = the man in sin, or in the flesh, the man under the law, the man ruled by passions stirred up only to greater heat when encountering the law in the way, *cf.* 6:6 ; 7:7–12 ; 8:13 ; Gal 2:19 ; 5:17 ; Eph 2:3 ; 4:22 ; Col 2:11 ; 3:9. **6.** But all this has passed in the death with Christ ; and in the mystical-sacramental union with him, risen from the dead, there is the ' new man ' = the inward man, the man in the Spirit, the man ' born again out of water and the Holy Ghost '. In him all is new, and his works must bear it out ; *cf.* 7:22 ; Eph 4:24 ; Col 3:10 ; Gal 5:25.

a **7-12 The Refutation of a First Misinterpretation—** The new Christian attitude to the Old Law must not be misinterpreted as if the Old Law were identified with sin. The doctrine that the Christian is no longer under the Old Law, 1–6, has always been liable to misunderstandings. Already in the days of St Paul there were misinterpretations which he had to correct. Here he takes up one of them. Instead of quoting the actual misinterpretation, however, he puts it in the form of a question : ' is then the law sin ? '. To explain the problem in Paul's mind the following paraphrase may be helpful : If on the one hand it is so important for a Christian to get away from the Old Law as is suggested in 1–6 and if, on the other hand, the Law is so closely connected with sin as is maintained in 5:13, 20 ; 7:5, then the logical conclusion would seem to be that the law itself is sin. This conclusion is evidently absurd. But it was drawn by St Paul's opponents to discredit the whole of his doctrine of justification. The objection does not go very deep, and St Paul's refutation is easy to follow. If the law applauded sin it would indeed have to be identified with sin. But, in fact, as everybody knows the law clearly forbids sin, so that there can be no disputing that the law is good and holy, 12. But at the same time, there can be no question of withdrawing the former statement, 5:13, 20 ; 7:5, that there is a close connexion between sin and law. True as it is that the law forbids and exposes sin, it is equally true that in doing so the law at the same time stimulates man's attraction (concupiscence) to sin. This may be strange but the fact cannot be denied.

The proof is to be found in the experience of temptation, **853a** 7–11.

For the purpose of tracing some of the details of **b** Paul's analysis of temptation in 7–11 it may be helpful to treat his description as a scene with four actors : (1) the Law 7, 8, 12 = the Commandment 8, 9, 10, 11, 12. (2) Sin 7, 8, 11. (3) Ego or Self 7, 8, 9, 10, 11. (4) Concupiscence 7, 8. The central figure is Self whose service both Law and Sin are equally anxious to win. The discussion is opened by Law = Commandment, exposing sin as sin so that Self is left in no doubt as to the character of the next speaker, Sin. Nevertheless, the Law loses its suit, thwarted by Concupiscence in man. The result is that Self enters the service of Sin, which means he loses the life promised by the Law, Ez 18:5–9, to earn the wages of Sin, which are misery and death, Rom 6:23 ; Ecclus 21:11. The main questions of theological interest in this paragraph are : (1) Who is the Ego or Self ? (2) What law is St Paul referring to ? (3) What does he mean by Sin ? (4) What is meant by Concupiscence ?

(1) Who is the Ego or Self ? It is characteristic of **c** this and the following paragraph, 13–25, that St Paul argues in the first person. The natural conclusion is that he relates his own experience. On the other hand, to argue from a purely individual experience is out of place in such a general discussion as is developed in Rom. This forces upon us the further conclusion that Paul regarded his own experience in this case as typical. And since he speaks in the past, obviously referring to the time before baptism, it can be further described as typical of the pre-Christian time. Then the question arises whether it is to be considered as a typical experience of Israelites and Gentiles alike or only of the former. The answers differ. All who limit the theme of Rom 7 to a discussion on the Mosaic Law must limit the typical value of Paul's experience accordingly because it is the basis of the whole argument. On the other hand, Rom is addressed to a Christian community consisting of former Israelites as well as of former Gentiles (*cf.* 1:18–3, 20) and there is no evidence that in our chapter Paul is speaking to the former Israelites only. In view of the addressees, therefore, it seems more natural to think that he looked upon his own experience in the matter as generally typical of the time before becoming a Christian without distinguishing between former Israelites and Gentiles.

(2) The law of which St Paul speaks here has been **d** identified with the natural moral law, the Mosaic Law, and both together. The last is the most satisfactory answer. That he foremost had the Mosaic Law in mind follows from the fact that he speaks in the first person. At the same time he must have included the natural moral law because of the former Gentiles among his readers. The simplest solution therefore is to take the law here as the Mosaic Law but as typical of the natural moral law in the same sense as the first person in this description is meant to be typical of man in general, Israelite and Gentile alike. This wider interpretation of ' law ' is not contradicted by the commandment ' Thou shalt not covet ', 7. No doubt this is a quotation from the Decalogue. But the quotation is so free (*cf.* Ex 20:17 ; Deut 5:21) that it fits the natural moral law as well. Nor can it be urged against this explanation that it entails the abrogation of the natural law which is clearly against Christian doctrine. The point of the whole chapter is not the abrogation of the law, but ' who is to be given first place ', Christ or—as it has been heretofore—the law ?

(3) The sin which takes the leading part in this **e** section is not a specified sin against such or such a commandment, but sin in general or sin personified. At the same time it is sin resident in the speaker, 9, 18 ; and that, before it is shown up as such by the law. ' When the commandment came sin re-vived ' ἀνέζησεν, 9. All this combines to describe it as ' original sin personified ' resident in the speaker, *i.e.* in St Paul as in everybody else. If so, it must be remembered that Paul is analysing the pre-Christian state of the soul and

853e that we have here the fact of original sin rather than a definition. To find an unassailable definition of original sin was left to later centuries.

f (4) As to the concupiscense of 7, 8 Paul is evidently using the term ἐπιθυμία not in its widest sense of desire in general, but of evil desires or inclinations towards the forbidden. Moreover, he seems to be thinking of concupiscense at that state in which it becomes or already has become sinful. 'I did not recognize covetousness (*scil.* as such, *i.e.* as forbidden and sinful covetousness) if the law did not say : Thou shalt not covet ', 7. Our moral theology calls this *concupiscentia consequens* = the evil desire approved of and upheld by the will against the law, *cf.* A. Lehmkuhl, *Theol. Moralis* I (1898) 25 ; M. Prümmer, *Manuale Theol. Mor.* I (1923) 53.

g 13-25 The Refutation of a Second Misinterpretation— The new Christian attitude to the Old Law must not be misinterpreted as blaming the law for the consequence of its transgressions = death. According to 7-12 there would be no death without sin, and no sin without law. The logical conclusion would seem to be, that according to such doctrine it is after all the law which causes all the trouble, including death. The purpose of this conclusion is again (as in 7) to lead the Apostle's doctrine to absurdity. This second objection does not go any deeper than the first in 7. Paul's reply in 13-25 is substantially the same as in 7-12. The law is good, 14-16 ; the villain of the piece is sin which frustrates the good intentions of the law, 13, 23. The proof is again taken from the experience of temptation. The description of temptation in 13-23, however, is much more detailed than that in 7-12. In this more detailed analysis of temptation lies the importance of the passage.

h For a closer study of St Paul's analysis of temptation in 13-25 it may again be helpful to treat it as a scene with four speakers : (1) Sin 13, 14, 17, 20 = the other law in 23 = the law of sin 23, 25. (2) The carnal Self 14, sold under sin 14 = the flesh 18, 25 = the body 24. (3) The Law 13, 14, 16 = the law of God 22, 25 = the law of my mind 23. (4) The better Self 15, 19, 21 = the inner man 22 = the mind 25. The conflict takes place between 1 and 2 on the one hand and 3 and 4 on the other, with the result that 3 and 4 are defeated. This result is deplorable : first because it means the death of the better Self = the inner man who has all our sympathy ; and secondly because it establishes the rule and sovereignty of Sin and its satellite, the carnal Self. Thus the analysis of temptation and sin necessarily leads to the vital question : whence is man to expect help and deliverance from this unhappy state ? Paul answers : not through the Law but ' through Christ, our Lord ', 24 f. This is the point he wants to drive home, and the practical conclusion to which the whole discussion is meant to lead.

The peculiar and most noteworthy features of St Paul's analysis of temptation in 13-25 can be studied under the following four questions : (1) What is the origin of the idea of ' the divided Self ' (= the carnal Self *versus* the better Self) which is the most striking addition to 7-12 in 13-25 ? (2) Is Paul here speaking of the time before or after his conversion ? (3) Is his description of the combat between Sin and Law = between the carnal Self and the better Self, historically true ? (4) Is not his picture of man's inability to resist Sin in 13-25 so gloomy that it almost appears as if man were possessed by Sin, so that he is no longer responsible for his actions ?

i (1) ' The divided Self ' can be described as the carnal Self, always on the side of Sin, on the one hand ; and the better Self, the inward man, well meaning but weak and overruled by the carnal Self, on the other. ' For the good which I will, I do not ; but the evil which I will not, that I do ' 19 ; and ' I am delighted with the law of God according to the inward man : but I see another law in my members, fighting against the law of my mind . . .', 23. What suggested this picture to St Paul we do not know There are rab-

binical as well as Greek and Latin parallels ; *cf.* SB III **8** 238-40 ; IV 1, 466-83 excursus on *yēṣer hārā'* ; Wetstein ad 7:15. On the other hand literary dependence on the part of St Paul on any of these sources cannot be proved, and the experience seems too general to call for such an explanation. Moreover in this context the divided Self might be but a development of the ἐπιθυμία, concupiscence in 7, 8, to which St Paul strangely does not refer again in 13-15 under that name.

(2) Modern commentators agree that both context **j** and contents point decisively to the time before conversion. It is the characteristic experience of the soul before conversion to the Christian faith to be ' sold under sin ', 14, and to be unable to carry out its higher aspirations, 15, 18, 23, 25b. To regard this experience as remaining after conversion is against the whole line of the argument, *cf.* 6:6, 9, 12-14, 17, 22 ; 7:6 ; 8 ; and also against all the moral exhortations in St Paul's epistle. Nor is it necessary to understand the picture as a reflexion of the Apostle's own state of soul when writing because he uses the present tense. There is no reason against taking this as an historic or graphic present to denote what is past, so that there is no real change of tense between 7-12 and 13-25. However, the Latin commentators of earlier centuries did commonly refer 13-25 to the time after conversion and baptism. This was due to the influence of St Augustine who used this passage in the Pelagian controversies as an illustration and proof-text for the Christian struggle towards perfection. Details in Cornely 373-6.

(3) Was the power of sin really so overwhelming **k** and was the law really so unable to make men carry out its commandments before Christian faith and grace came to their help ? To begin with, history can rightly object that the natural moral law as well as the Mosaic Law, the Roman law as well as the law of any other state have prevented millions of sins and crimes long before Christianity and that they still do so today. And as regards the Mosaic Law in particular it is a well-known fact, that the Bible is full of praise for it (*cf.* Pss 18 ; 118) and that the Pharisees have never been worried very much about the failures of the *Law*. Against these objections St Paul can be defended by pointing to the other millions of sins which all those laws taken together did not prevent, *cf.* 1:18-3:20. Nor does St Paul's description stand alone. There is confirmatory evidence from Israelites as well as Gentiles. The Israelites read pictures just as dark in the Prophets and the Pss ; *cf.* Is 1:2 f. ; Jer 17, 1, etc. ; Pss 13 = 52 ; 50 ; 94, 10b, etc. ; *cf.* further the rabbinical sayings on the *yēṣer hārā'*, the evil impulse, SB III 238-40 ; IV 1, 466-83 ; Lietzmann, 75 ff. The confirmatory evidence from Greek and Latin literature, too, is plentiful, *e.g.* Ovid, *Metamorph.* VII 19 ff. ; Epictetus, *Enchiridion* II 26, 4 ; see Wetstein ad 7:15. Finally it must be remembered that St Paul would necessarily view life under the law from the glorious height of his newly gained Christian ideals and that as an outstanding saint. This, too, will help in comparing his view of the weakness of human nature with the more optimistic pagan view.

(4) There is no denying that the picture of man's **l** weakness in 13-25 is dark. But St Paul's object in using such dark colours was to show the insufficiency of the law. He wanted to show that the law had proved a failure in the real issue of life which is not merely to forbid sin, but to prevent and overcome sin. And in this respect he argues, sin has ruled up to now in spite of the law ; and all he expects from his readers is to admit this failure of the law as an historical fact. Bent on scoring this point Paul could and did abstract from the question of free will. The failure of the law to overcome sin is either admitted or not. Man's responsibility as the result of his free will will has its place in other discussions. And if we want to find the Apostle's ideas on free will and man's full responsibility for sins committed against the law we must consult

those other passages, *e.g.* 1:18, 20, 21 ; 2:1, 9. There is plenty of evidence that St Paul did hold the sinner responsible for his sins. For further details on these four points see larger commentaries.

VIII 1-39 More Effects of Justification = Sanctifying Grace, or the indwelling of the Holy Spirit—Other common headings of this chapter are : the Christian life ; the life of grace ; the life in the spirit of Christ ; union with Christ ; the principles, blessings and fullness of the Christian, the spiritual, the supernatural life. Of these titles ' the spiritual life ' is probably the most common today. But when used to summarize the contents of ch 8, it must not be limited to special groups or vocations in the Church. Paul speaks of the spiritual life of every Christian. In this general sense it can safely be asserted that ' blessings of the spiritual life ' expresses the topic of Rom 8, though Paul himself does not use those words. His own descriptions of what we usually call the spiritual life vary almost from sentence to sentence. To be in Christ Jesus, 1 ; the law of the spirit of life in Christ, 2 ; to walk according to the spirit, 4 ; to mind the things of the spirit, 5 ; to be in the spirit, 9 ; the indwelling of the spirit, 9, 11 ; to have the spirit of Christ, 9 ; the indwelling of Christ, 10 ; to be guided by the spirit of God, 14 ; to be sons of God, 14 ; to be heirs of God, 17 ; to be joint-heirs with Christ, 14. All these must be taken together whenever we think of the spiritual life in the sense of St Paul, and even then we must add the contrast to the natural life which is there like a cross-current all the time. On the different meanings of ' spirit, spiritual ', etc., in Paul's letters see Prat II 405–7 ; on the union with Christ in the spiritual life, *cf.* P. de Jaegher, *One with Jesus*, 1937.

A general characteristic of the effects of justification or sanctifying grace enumerated in this chapter is the *positive* presentation of the doctrine of redemption ; whereas all that St Paul has said so far on the benefits resulting from redemption was expressed in a form which may be called negative. In ch 5 it was redemption or deliverance from the wrath of God ; in ch 6 from the rule of sin ; in ch 7 from the rule of the law. In ch 8, however, it is the life and power and triumph of the indwelling Holy Spirit. The doctrine of the indwelling Holy Spirit which is generally recognized as another characteristic feature of ch 8 should not be studied without bearing in mind the place which it holds in Paul's theology as a whole ; *cf.* 5:5 ; 8:9, 11 ; 1 Cor 3:16 ; 6:19 ; 2 Cor 1:22 ; 6:16 ; Eph 1:13 ; 4:30 ; also Jn 14:17, etc. and Prat II 406 f. Dogma deals with the same doctrine under the effects of sanctifying grace.

Connexion. It was a fortunate choice to begin a new chapter with 8:1. For the connexion with what precedes, esp. with 7:24, 25*a*, is so close that otherwise the transition to a new point would easily be missed.

The plan followed here traces the spiritual life or the work of the indwelling Holy Spirit, (1) before death 1–8 ; (2) in death 9–11 ; (3) after death 12–17 ; (4) in the present longing for heaven 18–30. (5) A concluding summary : God's love for us in Christ 31–39.

1-8 The Victory of the Indwelling Holy Spirit over the Flesh—' The ruler of this world cometh but in me he has nothing ' is one way in which our Lord describes his triumph over Satan and sin ; and to his disciples returning from their first missionary journey he said, ' I saw Satan like lightning falling from heaven. Behold I have given you power to tread upon serpents and scorpions and upon all the power of the enemy ; and nothing shall hurt you ', Lk 10:18 f. ; *cf.* Mk 16:17 f. ; Jn 14:2 f., 12, 21. Here Paul, too, speaks of victory over Satan and sin, but his approach to the question and his manner of discussing it are different. Paul is looking at the conflict between the spirit of Christ and the spirit of sin or of Satan in every man's own heart. Hence it is the internal victory over Satan and sin rather than the external results on which 1–8 throw light. It becomes a victory over the flesh or the carnal Self.

The force from which this victory over the flesh first **854c** came and still comes according to 1–8 is Christ. To begin with, it was the very purpose of the Incarnation to conquer sin, to break its until then unbroken rule. What was not only unheard of but impossible before Christ has since come to be a fact. Sin has been overcome and it was Christ who set the first example. But not only that, it is part of God's economy of salvation that Christ's victory over sin should continue by means of that same spirit of Christ dwelling in men's hearts. Hence all who have that spirit of Christ can be sure of their victory over the flesh. They will not be spared the conflict between the spirit of Christ and the spirit of Satan in their own souls, but the victory of the spirit of Christ is as certain for the future as it is proved for the past, for the spirit of Christ is neither dead nor changeable.

A special feature of this passage is the contrast **d** between σάρξ and πνεῦμα, the flesh and the spirit. In this Paul may have been influenced by the rabbinical discussions on the *yēṣer ṭōb* and the *yēṣer hārā'* = the good and the bad instinct (impulse), *cf.* SB IV 1, 466–83.

A practical difficulty in this passage is the certainty with which St Paul speaks of the victory of the spirit over the flesh. Did he not know our Lord's warning, ' the spirit is willing but the flesh is weak ', Mt 26:41 ? and does the Apostle not speak here as if in a Christian the inclination to sin (*fomes peccati*) had been extinguished by the grace of justification ? Such conclusions could indeed be drawn, if 1–8 stood alone. But there is plenty of evidence in other parts of Paul's epistles that he, too, was kept well aware of the fact that the victory of the spirit over the flesh can by no means be taken as a matter of course in Christian life, *cf.* 1 Cor 5:1–6:20. His many exhortations show the stress which he laid on co-operation with the spirit of Christ dwelling in us. But in 1–8 Paul is not concerned with the duty of co-operation with grace but with the actual victory of those who are in fact guided by that spirit of Christ. Here, his point is, that the spirit of Christ is by its very nature a spirit of victory over the flesh ; *cf.* Council of Trent, sess V *decretum de pecc. orig.* (Dz 792).

Plan. There is no agreement among commentators **e** as to the divisions to be made in 1–11. Many regard 1–11 as one paragraph combining the victory over the flesh and over death, *cf.* v 2. Others separate 1–4(5) and 5(6)–11. *Cf.* § 854*b* (plan), *e* (on v 2), *h* (connexion).

Style. The exact sequence of thought in detail is difficult to ascertain, *cf.* the use of the connecting particles : γάρ 2, 3, 5, 6, 7 ; δέ 8, 9, 9, 10, 11.

1. ' Now therefore ' : has been explained (*a*) as introducing a summary of chh 5–7 ; (*b*) as indicating the connexion with 7:24, 25*a* ; (*c*) as taking up 7:6 ; (*d*) as referring back to 5:11. ' Condemnation ' : has been taken (*a*) as a sentence of condemnation, *cf.* Council of Trent, sess V (Dz 792) ; (*b*) as the punishment inflicted in the sentence of condemnation ; (*c*) as the consciousness of being under condemnation. This last meaning, if it could be proved, would suit the context best. ' To be in Christ ' : is a phrase which is essential for the study of Pauline mysticism. On its use and meaning see Prat II 391–5, note M. Other figures of speech used in the NT to express the same idea of union with Christ are : the vine and its branches ; the head and the members of the body ; the marriage between Christ and the Church ; to be baptized into Christ ; foundation and building. **2** states the theme developed in 1–13. ' The law of **f** the spirit of life in Christ Jesus ' : is one phrase. It is important but difficult to find a suitable rendering. Equivalents that have been suggested are : the law of the life of grace, the spiritual principle of life, the order of the spiritual life, the Christian life, the supernatural life, the spiritual life. **3** states necessity, mode and fruit of the Incarnation (Thomas Aq.). The sentence can be explained (*a*) as an anacoluthon : what the law could not effect, God [carried out ; and] sending . . .

854f he condemned . . ., *cf.* WV ; (*b*) as an apposition in the nominative or accusative : God condemned sin in the flesh, which the law could not do. ' His own son ' : perhaps chosen deliberately instead of Jesus or Christ, to distinguish him from the adopted sons in 15 f. ' *In* the likeness of sinful flesh ' : so the Greek text against Vg, DV, *cf.* Lagrange ; notice the bearing of the text on the pre-existence of Christ. περὶ ἁμαρτίας, ' of sin ' DV = (*a*) on behalf of sin ; (*b*) as sin offering. ' Condemned ' : according to the context = God made sin stand condemned in the life of Christ, *cf.* Jn 12:31 f **4.** ' That *the demands* of the law may be fulfilled ', WV. The purpose of the Incarnation is to make obedience to the law of God possible for those whose life is spiritual. **5.** ' The things . . . of the flesh . . . of the spirit ' : *cf.* Gal 5:15–25.

g **9-11 The Victory of the Indwelling Holy Spirit over Death,** or the indwelling Holy Spirit as the pledge of the resurrection of the body—From the victory of the spirit of Christ over the flesh in the present life Paul passes on to the victory of the same spirit over death, in the resurrection of the dead body. The pledge of our participation in that resurrection is the indwelling spirit of Christ. This step from the victory of the indwelling Holy Spirit over the living body, 1–8, to the victory of the same Spirit over the dead body, 9–11, which the Apostle's argument here implies is tremendous, and the wide gulf that separates the two should not be overlooked because Paul takes it in his stride. For a fuller treatment of the question of the resurrection of the body see 1 Cor 15 and commentaries.

h The characteristic of 9–11 lies in the precise wording of the doctrine of the resurrection of the body with the special emphasis on the indwelling of the spirit of Christ as the bond of our union with Christ. The body that has been the temple of the spirit of Christ will be raised from the dead by God as he raised Christ from the dead ; *cf.* 1 Cor 6:14 ; 15:20, 23 ; 2 Cor 4:14 ; Phil 3:21 ; 1 Thess 4:14. The value of this argument from the resurrection of Christ to the resurrection of every Christian must be judged not by the rules of logic but by the specific Christian and Pauline doctrine of every Christian's mystical-sacramental union with Christ, the living head of the living Church. Unless this union is believed and understood St Paul's argument has neither force nor meaning.

Connexion. The beginning of a new paragraph with 9 must appear arbitrary from the literary point of view. But it has the advantage of a clear distinction between the two victories of the Spirit (*a*) in life, (*b*) in death, *cf.* v 2.

10. ' Dead ' = mortal, *cf.* v 11. ' The spirit liveth ' = the soul in the state of sanctifying grace, *cf.* Lagrange. **11.** The text is uncertain. It can be : *through* or *because* of his spirit dwelling in you, *i.e.* the indwelling spirit is either efficient or meritorious cause of the resurrection.

855a **12-17 The Victory of the Indwelling Holy Spirit for all Eternity,** or the indwelling Holy Spirit as the pledge of a glorious inheritance in heaven—With reference to his faithful servant's life after death our Lord said, ' because thou hast been faithful over a few things I will place thee over many things. Enter thou into the joy of thy lord ', Mt 25:23. What Paul says in 12–17 is substantially the same. A life on earth according to the spirit of Christ will be followed after death by a life of eternal happiness and glory with Christ glorified.

The first distinctive feature of St Paul's argument is that he calls those who have the spirit of Christ not servants or slaves but sons of God, 14, or children of God, 16 f. The proof which he quotes is the very nature of the spirit received, and its utterance in prayer. The Christian who acts according to the spirit of his baptism knows from experience that he has the spirit of the true children of God, 14 ; *cf.* Jn 7:17 ; 8:31 f. against Jn 8:44. And again when the Christian prays it is to God as his Father. No matter how much stress others may lay on God's absolute omnipotence or terrifying justice, the Christian owing to the spirit of

Christ dwelling in his heart cannot but call out to God, **8** first and above all, as his Father, 15 ; *cf.* Gal 4:1–7.

The second characteristic feature of Paul's argument **b** is that he calls the Christian's eternal glorification not his reward but his inheritance, 17. This follows logically from the former characteristic. For the servant's reward is his pay, but the child's remuneration its inheritance. The Christian as the child of God becomes the heir of God his Father, and the joint heir with Christ his brother. God does not do things by halves. Adoption into the royal family of God implies more than a new name. With the title it also gives the right to share in the possessions of the kingdom ; and the one possession here singled out and put before us is the glory of Christ, that glory into which he entered as his inheritance on the days of his resurrection and ascension. That adoption is followed by heirship is nothing out of the ordinary in the natural order. What must astonish, however, is St Paul's conclusion that the one will follow the other also in the supernatural order. This conclusion, or better application, again defies all logical explanations. As in the question of the resurrection of the body the whole argument presupposes a union between every Christian and Christ which is above and different from any even spiritual union known to us in time and space. Its existence and character must simply be accepted as one of the mysteries of God revealed in the Gospel. But however incomprehensible this mystery may be, without a firm hold on its meaning, no reader can follow St Paul's argument. For the same idea *cf.* Gal 4:6–7 ; Tit 3:7 ; 1 Pet 3:22 ; Apoc 3:21.

12-13 can be taken as conclusion to 11 or as intro- **c** duction to 14 ff. The sense is not affected. **14.** ' Sons of God ' : is a title used in the Bible (*a*) for the angels, Job 1:6 ; 2:1 ; 38:7, etc. ; (*b*) for the Israelites, Ex 4:22 f. ; Dt 14:1 f. ; 32:6–10 ; Os 11:1–4 ; Is 1:4 ; 30:9, etc. ; (*c*) for the just, Ecclus 23:1–4 ; 51:10 (MT) ; Wis 2:13–18 ; 5:5 ; (*d*) for the Christians, 2 Cor 6:16 ff. ; Gal 3:26 ; 4:6 ; Phil 2:15 ; Jn 1:12 f. ; 1 Jn 3:1 f. ; 5:1, 4 f. From these metaphorical usages (the meaning of which differs only in degrees) must be distinguished the metaphysical use implying pre-existence and divinity which the name has when applied to Christ in such passages as 8:3, 32 ; Gal 4:4 ; *cf.* Prat II 140–2 ; Tanquerey II 662 f., III 50 f. **15b** ' Spirit of sonship ' = state of sanctifying grace, *cf.* Dz 796.

15c. ' Abba ! Father ! ' : The repetition has been **d** explained (*a*) as a Greek translation of the Aramaic Abba = father, *cf.* Gal 4:6 ; Mk 14:36 ; (*b*) as a figure of speech (anadiplosis) for the purpose of emphasis ; (*c*) as a relic of an ancient bilingual liturgical (Aramaic-Greek) prayer or ejaculation. The meaning of the phrase cannot be that to pray to God as Father was a Christian innovation or privilege. To think and speak of God as Father is a custom that can be found also in non-Christian religions. For the OT see Ex 4:22 ; Deut 32:6 ; Is 1:2 ; 63:16 ; 64:8 ; Jer 31:9, 20 ; Os 1:10 ; 11:1 ; Mal 1:6 ; 2:10 ; Ecclus 23:1, 4 ; 51:10 (MT) ; Wis 2:16 ; 11:10 (11 Vg) ; 14:3 ; 18:13 (LXX) ; Tob 13:4 (LXX) ; Ps 67:6. Here add the OT proper names compounded with ' Ab ' = father, of which *G. B. Gray, Studies in Hebr. Proper Names*, 1896, counts 31. For the same idea in the OT apocrypha see Jubilees 1:24 f., 28 ; 19:29 ; 3 Macc 5:7 ; *cf.* 7:6 ; 6:3, 8 ; Test. Jud. 24. For the same usage in rabbinical literature, including the ' Shemone Esre ' in which two petitions are addressed to God as Father, see SB I 393–6, on Mt 6:4 ; but here it should be remembered that Abba about this time became also a title of the Rabbis, *cf.* JE I 29–35. Apart from Israel, the idea of God as Father was known also in other Semitic religions, *cf.* Lagrange, ERS 110–18. For the same usage in the religion of primitive races see W. Schmidt, *The Religion of Earliest Man* (CTS Studies in Comparative Religion, no 2) 17. Against false conclusions from the study of comparative religion, however, it is worth pointing out, that to speak of God as Father is much more common in the NT than anywhere else. No less than 263 references in the NT are tabulated by *J. Drummond, *Via, Veritas et Vita*, 1894, 175. At all events the full meaning of the phrase 'Abba! Father!' in 8:13 is not to be found by insisting on the form (which is common to many religions) but must be derived from the spirit in which it is used in Christianity. This spirit is new and sufficiently explained by the context, 14–16.

18-30 The Indwelling Holy Spirit and the Present Longing for Glorification = Perfect Happiness, or the certainty that the Christian life will lead to the glory of heaven—From the height of his contemplation of the Christian's inheritance in heaven, 12–17, Paul is forced back to earth by the contrast between those things to come and things present. In spite of all that he has said in praise of the salvation revealed in the Gospel the present life seems a life of tears everywhere. Nature, animate and inanimate, groans under a law of corruption and longs for the time of its freedom from pain and its full measure of happiness, 19–22 ; and the very same feelings and longings still linger in the Christian soul, in spite of all that the grace of justification may have changed, 23–25(27).

To avoid misunderstandings it is necessary before going further to limit the discussion to the kind of suffering which Paul here has in mind. He is not speaking of this or that suffering in particular, this or that physical pain, this or that social or political evil. He is thinking of the general suffering which may be described as the absence of full happiness, or the universal want of glory, the general longing for glorification or the universal hope and desire for greater things one day to come. But if Christianity does not remove even this 'spiritual suffering' what then is the immediate use or benefit of the indwelling Holy Spirit, or for that matter of the salvation of the Gospel in general? The simplest and today most common Christian answer is the general rule, that suffering is the path to glory. The best proof is the life of our Lord, *cf.* Lk 24:26, 46 ; Ac 17:3 ; 26:23 ; Heb 2:9 f. For the same rule in the life of the Christian *cf.* Mt 10:38 ; 16:24 ; 20:22 f. ; Mk 8:34 f. ;. 10:38 ; Jn 12:24–26 ; Rom 8:17*c* ; 1 Cor 12:26 ; 2 Cor 1:5 ; 4:10 ; 13:4 ; Gal 6:17 ; Phil 1:29 ; 3:10 ; Col 1:24 ; 2 Tim 2:12 ; 1 Pet 1:6, 11 ; 2:21 ; 3:14, 17, 18 ; 4:13 ; 5:1.

The points to be noted in St Paul's reply to this universal cry of suffering rising from the earth are the following three : (*a*) He makes no attempt to deny the existence of this suffering or to belittle its painfulness. (*b*) He answers that this spiritual suffering is not against the indwelling Holy Spirit, but rather its very own voice and expression, 26 f. The reason is that the present indwelling of the Holy Spirit is not the end but only the beginning of the Christian life, 23 ; it is not the fullness but only the pledge of the complete glory to come, *cf.* 2 Cor 1:22 ; 5:5 ; Eph 1:14. It is by its very nature a spirit of hope, 23 f. Those as yet unfulfilled longings in nature as well as in the Christian soul, therefore, are like the pains foreboding and preceding the world's new birth = the final and general glorification of the sons of God, 21 f. In the meantime, *i.e.* in the present time of want and suffering, nature as well as men must and can hold out in this hope of final glorification supported by the indwelling Holy Spirit. (*c*) The Apostle anticipates the objection : is not this hope of unseen glory to come just one more empty promise to the harrassed souls of men ? Far from it ! It is the hope that God will carry out to the end his work of redemption. True enough it is hope, and that means for us waiting. But it is a hope, that is as certain as any hope can be, inasmuch as God is certain to complete the work he has begun, 28–30.

For a deeper appreciation of 18–30 it would be useful to pursue the question, in what does the 'glory to come' here discussed consist ? St Paul himself does not develop this question, the answer can be found in the explanations of 'eternal life', in the last article of the Apostles' Creed, or in the dogmatic treatises on the 'last things'. The relevant Bible texts are collected **855g** in K. Vaughan, 95–104, 427–36.

Object. The explanations of the Apostle's object in 18–30 differ considerably. Some maintain that his purpose was to enlarge on the greatness of the Christian justification by adding a further triumph of the indwelling Holy Spirit over a practical difficulty in life : the universal want of happiness. This explanation has the advantage of showing progress of thought in accordance with the main argument in ch 8. But others see in 18–30 a new discussion on the certainty of the Christian hope of glorification, *cf.* ch 5. In this case 18–30 becomes a kind of scholion or digression to the heavenly inheritance discussed in 12–17. The former explanation is followed in this commentary.

Plan. The commentators who take the certainty of **h** the Christian hope of eternal glory as the keynote of 18–30 gain an easy division of the passage into four paragraphs according to the four proofs for this certainty. They are the witness (1) of creation, 19–22 ; (2) of the Christian soul, 23–25 ; (3) of the Holy Ghost, 26–27 ; (4) of God's economy of salvation, 28–30. If ' the victory and triumph of the indwelling Holy Spirit' is taken as the keynote the following plan may be followed : (1) the victory of the Spirit over the suffering (longing) of irrational nature, 19–22 ; (2) the victory of the Spirit over the suffering (longing) of the Christian soul, 23–25(27) ; (3) the certainty of this victory, 28–30. The difficulty of this plan lies in placing 26 f.

19-22 The Longing of Irrational Nature for Glorifica- i tion and the Holy Spirit dwelling in the Christian Soul —It is unusual for St Paul to give his attention to irrational nature. But when in 19–22 he voices its agony under the burden of its age-long curse we need not think of a sudden flight into poetry. The ideas here expressed are Biblical throughout. That irrational nature was affected by man's (first) sin is clearly stated in Gen 3:17 f. ; and its share in man's redemption follows no less clearly from such messianic prophecies as Is 65:17–25 ; 66:22. For the same idea in the NT see Mt 19:28 ; Ac 3:21 ; 2 Pet 3:13 ; Apoc 21:1. Rabbinical parallels are collected in SB III 840–7, on Apoc 21:1. There remains however something original and unique in the way in which St Paul here personifies these two Biblical doctrines and argues from them to the greatness of the Christian glorification as that ' divine event to which the whole creation moves '.

What is the burden from which irrational creation **j** longs to be redeemed ? St Paul calls it her enforced submission to ματαιότης = purposelessness, senselessness, vanity, 20. This has been understood (*a*) as its physical mutability, transitoriness ; (*b*) as its physical corruption, decay, death ; (*c*) as its moral abuse by sinful man ; (*d*) as the disturbance of the harmony of creation, or rather the absence of fullness of harmony and order = the absence of something that should be there ; *i.e.* in Biblical language = the curse of Gen 3:17 ; in theological terminology = the consequences of original sin. Of these explanations the last seems the most satisfactory, because the third is too narrow, and the first two raise points of natural science which were hardly in the mind of St Paul. For there is nothing in his letters to support the idea that he regarded nature as free from mutability and death before man's fall.

What will the glory to come bring for irrational **k** nature ? Paul answers with ' the glory of the children of God ', 21. Instead one might have expected him to speak of the renovation of nature in the sense of Apoc 21:1, *cf.* WV note. But Paul's wording is negative and may be compared with the negative definition of our redemption = freedom from the curse of sin. Hence, the various speculations on the way in which nature will eventually obtain her freedom from the curse of Gen 3:17 cannot claim the authority of St Paul. It is one of the mysteries not revealed to us, *cf.* Pesch, *Prael. Dogm.* III propos. 54.

What has the longing of irrational nature for glorification, 19–22, to do with the Holy Spirit dwelling

855k in the Christian soul, 23–27? The two voices agree in the longing they express, and thus become supplementary to each other. But if 19–22 were left out the argument would hardly be affected.

856a **23–27 The Longing of the Christian Soul for Glorification and the Indwelling Holy Spirit**—' I desire to be dissolved and to be with Christ ' in heaven (Phil 1:23) would be a good summary of the contents of this passage. In spite of all that St Paul has said in praise of the effects of justifying = sanctifying grace from 5:1 onward, and esp. in ch 8, there still remains a big gap to be filled in the soul. However highly the praises of justification or sanctification on earth may be sung, experience teaches that the soul longs for greater things still. It is with this that St Paul is dealing in 23–27. The commonly accepted term for the object of this desire of the Christian soul is glorification or heaven. Neither term is used in 23–27, but see 18, 21. The terms used in 23–27 are (the full) adoption of the sons of God, and the redemption of our body, 23. For practical purposes, however, it simplifies matters to keep to the established distinction between sanctification and glorification, or between sanctifying grace and glorifying grace. But it must be remembered that the latter distinction is not a distinction in essence but only in time and degree, *i.e.* sanctifying grace is the beginning of glorifying grace, 23; *cf.* 2 Cor 1:22; 5:5; Eph 1:14.

b An important point in the explanation of 23–27 concerns the distinction between the voice of the Christian soul, which has the Holy Spirit, 23–25, and the voice of the Holy Spirit in the Christian soul, 26 f. In either case it is evidently the voice of the indwelling Holy Spirit, *i.e.* of the Holy Spirit dwelling in the soul through sanctifying grace. The difference then seems to be but a difference of intensity in prayer. In 26 f. most commentators think of the charisma of tongues or glossolalia, a form of ecstasy frequently quoted in early Christian literature, *e.g.* Mk 16:17; Ac 10:46; 1 Cor 14:1–23. But this may be too narrow or too exact an interpretation. Ecstatic prayer in general satisfies the text.

Plan. Two points can be distinguished: (1) the voice of the Christian soul, 23–25; (2) the voice of the Holy Spirit, 26 f.

c **23.** ' *Awaiting* adoption ' = the fullness of the blessings conferred on us as sons of God. The context and the comparison with 14–17 make it necessary to insert some noun like: fullness, manifestation, realization, consummation. **24.** ' By hope ': cannot be *dativus instrumenti*, because it is by faith that we are saved and not by hope. Hence it is commonly taken as *dativus modi* = with hope, *i.e.* we are saved with the hope (of glorification) as a part in the present state of justification = sanctification, but *cf.* SH. **26.** ' Infirmity ': *i.e.* of our prayer. ' As we ought to ': can be connected with either verb : (a) we know not . . . ; (b) we should pray. The former is the better connexion, because the context leaves no doubt as to what we ought to pray for—our final glorification. But we are far from knowing the form, contents, etc., of this glorification as we might wish or ought to know.

d **28–30 The Christian's Longing for Glorification is certain to be fulfilled**—The longing for glorification described in 19–22, 23–27 implies not only a vision of still greater things to come but also an element of hope, 23 f. Now hope always needs encouragement to prevent the inevitable thought of possible disappointment from weakening it. The normal form of such encouragement is a reassurance that the object hoped for will materialize. Such a reassurance of the Christian hope of glorification in heaven is the subject of 28–30. The reason on which St Paul bases this reassurance is ' the chain of Providential care with which God does accompany the course of his chosen ', SH 214. Providence has started our Christian life on earth ; Providence will also lead it to perfection in heaven, *cf.* Phil 1:6. Partly different reasons are given in ch 5.

The first point in St Paul's argument is the design of Providence exhibited in the Christian life here and now. Paul enumerates four turning points in this life which bear evident traces of this divine Providence, 29 f. : (a) God foreknew us ; (b) he predestinated us ; (c) he called us ; (d) he justified us. The second point in the argument is the conclusion that these four steps are but four steps before a fifth, which is to be the last and final step, *i.e.* our glorification in heaven. ' Whom God has justified (= sanctified) he will also glorify ', 30. What is the logical value of this conclusion ? St Paul's conclusion in 30 that there must be this fifth step after the previous four is not meant to be a logical deduction. The Apostle presents it as faith based on the works of Providence in the past, 29 f., and on the nature of God who is love, 28. For us it is, in addition to these two motives, belief in the inspiration of St Paul, *cf.* § 850*j*.

Does St Paul teach in 28–30 that every Christian can be certain to reach his final salvation and glorification in heaven ? The question can and must be answered in the affirmative for every true Christian, *i.e.* every Christian who lives up to St Paul's idea of the Christian life. This is, no doubt, introducing a very important condition. But the Apostle himself clearly made this condition in the numerous and urgent exhortations that fill his letters. Once this condition of a true Christian life, however, is accepted the *uncertainty* of final salvation for the individual follows as an inevitable practical consequence, *cf.* 5:5–21 ; Dz 825.

28a. ' All things work together unto good ' = God worketh all things together unto good, WV. The translation depends on what is considered to be the subject of the verb. The form of the text allows (a) θεός, God ; (b) πάντα, all things ; (c) πνεῦμα, the spirit, from 26. In any case the content is a general theological principle, *cf.* Ps 45:2–3 ; 2 Tim 4:8 ; Jas 1:12, etc. Four parallels from Greek literature are quoted by Wetstein ; for rabbinical stories to the same effect *cf.* Wetstein and SB. **28b.** ' *Those who are called according to a plan* ' (design or decree *scil.* of God) = those who love God in 28*a*, *cf.* Eph 1:11 ; 3:11 ; 2 Tim 1:9. It connects the general statement in 28*a* with the application in 29 f. Discussions on absolute predestination ought never to have been built on such an *obiter dictum*. On the history of its exegesis see Cornely and SH. ' To be saints ' : not in the Greek text.

29–30 give a summary description of the process of salvation, apparently in the order of time, *cf.* Eph 1:3–14 ; 2 Thess 2:13 f. **29.** ' Foreknew ' : *cf.* 1 Cor 8:3. As a rendering of the OT *yāda'* it may also have the meaning of the verbs : to elect, prefer, choose, favour, fore-approve of, etc. At all events Paul puts it down as the first stage in man's salvation. The distinction between *ante* and *post praevisa merita* belongs to later theology. ' Predestinated to be made conformable to the image of his Son ' : at the general resurrection, *cf.* 8:17 ; Phil 3:21 ; 1 Cor 15:49 ; WV note on Rom 8:29.. **30.** ' Called ' : refers to the moment of becoming a Christian, *cf.* Jn 6:44. ' Them he also justified ' : *cf.* 1:17 ; 3:21–30. This fourth stage in the process of man's salvation coincides temporally with the previous ' call '. ' Them he also glorified ' : refers to the future glory in heaven. The past tense is a prophetic perfect (aorist).

31–39 A Concluding Paragraph summarizing the blessings of the spiritual life in the assurance of God's love for us in Christ—Coming to the end of his exposition of the Christian life Paul seems to have felt that his explanation (like all later ones) must leave a great number of doubts and difficulties unanswered or untouched. For it lies in the nature of human life that no doctrine can in advance dispose of all difficulties that may arise in practice. But in so far as these difficulties belong to the religious sphere, the Christian life has one general answer which can never fail. All these personal difficulties become insignificant as soon as our eyes turn away from them to contemplate that one great act of the love of God in which he did not spare his own Son for our salvation, *cf.* Jn 3:16. No one

g who believes and considers this truth can doubt that God wills his best under all circumstances. It is true that there will be an examination after death of which we are all afraid, but sanctified by God, 30, we need fear no accusation, 33. There will be a judgement, but redeemed and defended by Christ we need fear no condemnation from his lips, 34. Before that there may be sufferings and violence, but the love of Christ for us will remain unaffected as the sun remains unchanged by the clouds that may hide it for a while. Christ will not forsake us, 35. It may even come for us to a choice between life and death; to a struggle with the evil spirits and devilish powers; to battles with enemies known or still unknown, from above the earth or below the earth, yet all combined they will not be able to wipe out or mar in our souls the picture and reassurance of the love which God has shown us in Christ. However dark the earth may turn, God's love for us in Christ will remain undisturbed and continue to reign above like the spirit of God above the turbulent seas, Gen 1:2. And in his love we are eternally secure, 38 f.

h Connexion. The opening question 'what then shall we say', 31, does not here introduce an objection as in 3:5; 6:1; 7:7; 9:14, but a summary, cf. 9:30. God has given his elect the victory over sin and death, 1–8, 9–11; he has adopted them as sons and heirs, 12–17; he will fulfil their longing for glorification in heaven, 18–30: what more can be said? Paul has come to the end of his argument and looks for a fitting conclusion. The thoughts which occur to him centre round God's love for us in Christ. Thus the passage becomes a summary of ch 8, and at the same time the description of another and last blessing of the spiritual life. This explanation of the connexion between 31–39 and 1–30 is not accepted by all commentators. Some see in 31–39 merely the continuation of 28–30 and therefore treat it as a further, i.e. a fifth reason for the certainty of final salvation. Others regard it as the summary of the whole doctrinal part as the beginning of which they quote 1:16 or 3:21 or 5:1. The truth probably lies in the combination of these opinions. Here as so often Paul shows very little concern to follow the rules of classical composition.

i Characteristic. In any case, it must be remembered that when Paul concluded the first part of his letter with praise of the love which God has shown us in Christ, he did not intend to give a comprehensive or systematic treatment of the subject, cf. 1 Cor 13. His object in writing so far had been to recommend and preach the Christian life by presenting to his readers its greatness, benefits and glory. To crown these praises with a hymn on God's love for us in Christ was a fortunate choice. He could hardly have concluded on a higher or more suitable theme.

Plan. The progress of thought in 31–39 is clearly marked by the four ascending rhetorical questions (Lagrange speaks of four stanzas): (a) 31 f. Who shall be against us, if God is for us? (b) 33 Who shall accuse us? (c) 34 Who shall condemn us? (d) 35–39 Who shall separate us from the love which Christ bears us?

j 32. 'All things': all the Christian needs to obtain, the glory of heaven. 33, 34a. The interpunctuation is uncertain. Consequently the translations vary: (a) Who shall accuse the elect of God? God who justifieth them? [Answer: certainly not.]—Who shall condemn them? Christ Jesus who died for them? [Answer: certainly not.] Cf. Boylan. (b) Who shall accuse the elect of God, when it is God himself who acquits them? Who shall condemn them, when it is Christ Jesus who died for them . . .? Cf. C. J. Vaughan, KNT. (c) Who shall accuse the elect of God? When it is God who justifieth, who will condemn? [Certainly not] Christ . . . who died for them? Of these translations b is the most symmetrical, but c has the support of Is 50:8, a passage which may well have been here in the Apostle's mind. The sense of the argument is not affected. 35. 'From the love of Christ': has been understood (a) as an objective

genitive = our love for Christ; (b) as a subjective **856j** genitive = the love which Christ bears us. The context which discusses the certainty of the glory to come decides in favour of b; cf. 37, 39; Rickaby combines the two meanings. 'Tribulation', etc.: for similar lists of temptations in stoic literature cf. Lagrange. 38. 'Nor angels nor principalities' can mean: (a) good spirits, Gal 1:8, and bad, Eph 6:12; Col 2:15; 1 Pet 3:22, or (b) evil spirits of two different kinds; or (c) spiritual and temporal powers = earthly authorities. δυνάμεις = fortitudo, Vg; might, DV; powers, WV: position peculiar and disputed, often after principalities.

IX 1–XI 36 The Present Exclusion of Israel from the **857a** **Salvation revealed in the Gospel,** or the present separation of Israel from the Church of God—The problem which St Paul sets himself in these three chapters is the failure of the Gospel to convince Israel. How can the Gospel be the true fulfilment of the Messianic promises, when its central doctrine declaring Jesus of Nazareth to be the Messias is rejected by the very Israel to whom God had promised the Messias. With reference to St Paul's answer to this problem it must first be noticed that the Apostle discusses the exclusion of Israel as a whole from the salvation of the Messias and that only here and now, i.e. in the Church on earth. It would lead to grave misunderstandings to think that his subject is Israel's exclusion from heaven at the Last Judgement, which judgement, needless to say, is not collective but individual; cf. Prat I 250; A. Charue, L'Incrédulité des Juifs dans le NT, 1929, 283 ff. and 343–52 where an extensive bibliography on the whole subject can be found.

The connexion of the subject with the preceding parts of the epistle is not stated in the text. Probably its importance at the time was responsible for its place here, cf. Gal. Of the commentators who look for definite points of connexion some go back as far as 1:16, 'the Gospel is a power of salvation . . . for the Jew first', cf. 2:9; others point to 3:1 f., the privileges of Israel; and others to 8:30, divine election.

Importance. In the days of St Paul the theological **b** problems raised by the separation of the Church from Israel and vice versa were probably the subject of daily conversations among Christians as much as other doctrinal differences in the days of later heresies or as social problems are today; cf. Ac; Gal; Charue VII f. Compared with Israel the Christians were but a small minority, with all the external advantages (power, organization, scholarship, tradition, money) on the other side. In this situation Paul more than anyone else, as far as we know, set himself to defend the Christian cause in a scientific theological way; and Rom 9–11 is his most complete effort in this respect that has been preserved. The primary importance of these chapters, therefore, is that they present the first scientific vindication of the Christian cause in combat with the well-equipped theology of the synagogue. They are the first chapters of early Christian apologetics. The terms 'scientific' and 'theological' must, of course, be taken here not in their modern western sense, but in accordance with the methods used at the time in the world of St Paul, cf. Philo and rabbinical theology. Apart from this apologetic aspect of the question which was no doubt foremost in Paul's mind these chapters remain important for theology also because of the principles employed by the Apostle, especially those concerning the problem of evil and divine election or pre-destination to salvation within the Church. Why are the Gentiles in the Church and Israel is not? Why B and not A?

Plan. Chh 9–11 can be divided as follows: (a) 9:1–5, introduction; (b) 9:6–29, the vindication of God's justice and faithfulness in the present exclusion of Israel from the salvation revealed in the Gospel; (c) 9:30–10:21, this exclusion is Israel's own fault; (d) 11:1–36, other points of view from which light can be thrown on the problems raised by Israel's present unbelief and rejection.

857c IX 1-5 Introduction of the New Subject, Israel's exclusion from the salvation of the Messias—This paragraph is evidently meant to be the introduction to a new topic. It has even been taken as the preface of an entirely separate letter. Nevertheless it does not state in one clear sentence what this new topic is. As so often in St Paul's letters the real problem becomes apparent only as the argument proceeds. In this case it is the problem created by the exclusion of Israel, the chosen people of old, from the blessings of the Gospel.

Connexion. There is none according to the rules of literary composition, but *cf.* § 857a. Instead of connecting the new topic with what precedes the Apostle begins by expressing his deep sorrow over the fact that Israel as a whole has not accepted Christ and his Gospel of salvation. Thus 1-5 becomes a kind of *captatio benevolentiae.*

d The first characteristic feature of this passage is the list of Israel's privileges, 4 f. This list is without a biblical parallel, though the Bible is full of references to this or that prerogative of Israel in particular. The purpose which the list fulfills in the context is twofold. ' It explains the Apostle's grief, and reveals the importance of the problem before us ' (SH). The prerogatives of Israel enumerated in 4 f. are : (1) the name ' Israel '—a title of honour and divine favour, *cf.* Gen 32:28 ; Ps 113:2 ; Ecclus 17:15 ; Gal 6:16 ; Eph 2:12. (2) ' Adoption, as sons of God '—*cf.* Ex 4:22 ; Deut 14:1 ; 32:6 ; Jer 31:9 ; Os 11:1. (This adoption is different from that of Rom 8:15 f.) (3) ' The glory '—of God manifested in his special presence at Sinai, Ex 16:10 ; 24:16-18 ; in the tabernacle, Ex 40:32, 34 ; in the first temple of Jerusalem, 3 Kg 8:11. (4) ' The divine covenants '—made with the Patriarchs, Gen 15:18 ; Ex 2:24, etc. ; at Sinai, Ex 19:5 ; 24:7 f., etc. ; with Phinees, Num 25:12 f. ; by Josue, Jos 24:25 ; with David, Ps 88:4, 29, etc. ; by Joiada, 4 Kg 11:17 ; by Ezechias, 2 Par 29:10 ; by Josias, 4 Kg 23:3 ; by Esdras, Esd 10:3. (5) ' The law '—of Moses or the Pentateuch. (6) ' The service of God '—the liturgy according to the law of Moses in the tabernacle and later in the temple of Jerusalem. (7) ' The promises ' concerning the Messias. (8) ' The fathers '—the Patriarchs Abraham, Isaac and Jacob, Ac 3:13, etc. (9) ' The Messias '—who is of their race.

e A second characteristic feature of this paragraph is the statement of the divinity of Christ in 5. This text is discussed at length in every commentary. The different opinions as to its historical meaning are shown in the different punctuations of the text, *cf.* SH 233-8. The first explanation punctuates : ' Christ according to the flesh, who is over all things, God blessed for ever, Amen ', DV. In this form the meaning of the passage is clear and the sequence of thought natural. Besides being the most natural this explanation has also the support of Christian antiquity, *cf.* J. B. Franzelin, *De verbo incarnato*, 1874, 71-82 ; A. Durand, RB 12 (1903) 550-70. In dogma v 5 holds an established place among the Scripture proofs for the divinity of Christ, *cf.* Tanquerey II 634. For other doxologies addressed to Christ, *cf.* 16:27 ; 2 Tim 4:18 ; 1 Tim 3:16 ; Eph 5:14, 19 ; Prat II 130. The second explanation argues that the explicit use of the name ' God ' for Christ is without a parallel in St Paul's letters and that this makes it necessary to avoid such a usage here if that is at all grammatically possible. Those who accept this argument find a corresponding interpretation by inserting a full stop after ' flesh ' or after ' all things '. The remainder of the sentence (5c) then becomes a praise (doxology) not of Christ but of God : ' God, who is above all, be blessed for ever ' ; or ' God blessed for ever, Amen '. This is the exegesis among others of Wetstein, Tischendorf (1869), Jülicher, Lietzmann, *cf.* also RV margin. Its main weakness is its artificiality which betrays itself in the far-fetched arguments necessary to make it appear plausible. More specific reasons which can be urged against it are : (a) 5c has not the recognized form of a Biblical doxology which is : ' Blessed (be) God ', and not ' God (be) blessed ',

cf. Lk 1:68 ; 2 Cor 1:3 ; Eph 1:3. (b) It is against 8‖ Pauline usage to begin a doxology with a new sentence ; *cf.* 1:25 ; 2 Cor 11:31 ; Gal 1:5 ; 2 Tim 4:18, etc. ; Lagrange. (c) What is ultimately gained by this exegesis is less than the extent of the controversy suggests. For the first explanation remains at least equally possible and the doctrine of the divinity of Christ remains unimpaired because it is clear from other texts of St Paul, *cf.* Phil 2:5-11 ; Col 2:9, etc. ; Cornely ; Prat II 124-31.

1. For similar assurances of sincerity *cf.* 2 Cor 1:23 ; f 2:17 ; 11:31 ; 12:19 ; Gal 1:20 ; Mt 5:37 ; Jas 5:12. **3.** ηὐχόμην = (1) I wish, DV ; (2) I could wish, WV . Either translation is possible, *cf.* S. G. Green, *Handbook to the Grammar of the Greek NT*, 1904, 300 ; Blass-Debrunner, *Grammatik*, 1931, § 359, 2. On the moral character of this wish *cf.* Clem. Rom. I 53 ; Rickaby, *ad loc* ; A. Piscetta and A. Gennaro, *Elementa Theol. Moralis* II (1938) 134 ; Lietzmann quotes ' the heroic act ' as an analogy.

6-29 The Vindication of the Divine Attributes of g **Faithfulness and Justice in the Present Exclusion of Israel from the Salvation of the Gospel**—The argument in this section is apologetic. The difficulties to be solved are objections against God's faithfulness, 6-13, and justice, 14-29, in the case of Israel and the Gospel. The practical purpose of these objections—evidently coming from orthodox Israelites—is to prove the Gospel wrong. God has promised Israel the Messianic blessings. If they have now come with no share for Israel then God has broken his solemn promises. This being impossible, the only alternative is that the Messias has not yet come and that the salvation offered in the Christian Gospel is a heresy which Israel rightly rejects.

Characteristic. The passage 6-29 is generally known as difficult. But the difficulties are doctrinal—dogmatical, not textual or exegetical. They centre round the terms : election and predestination ; grace and free will. For history of exegesis see SH 269-75.

6-13 The Vindication of God's Faithfulness in the h **Present Exclusion of Israel from the Salvation of the Gospel**—The objection here to be rejected tries to refute Christianity by arguing that if the Gospel were true, then God would not have kept his Messianic promises to Israel. In his reply Paul tacitly admits that since the Messianic promises were given to Israel their fulfilment also must have come to Israel. Nevertheless there is a fallacy in the objection. The mistake lies in the popular definition of the Israel to whom the divine promises were given. The objecting Synagogue takes it for granted that this Israel is the race of Abraham. Paul rejects this definition. The divine promises were not given to all the lineal descendants of Abraham. From the very beginning the Scriptures insist on the additional principle of God's free election as the examples of Ismael, 6-9, and of Esau, 10-13, prove. Both were descendants of Abraham and yet both were excluded from the blessings of Abraham their father, and of Isaac and Jacob their younger brothers. And these two cases cannot be set aside as exceptions, for they are typical of the Messianic times like the whole of the OT, *cf.* Gal 4:23 ff. As in the case of Abraham's and Isaac's children so also in the history of the Chosen People, it is God's election that constitutes the true Israel of the Scriptures. ' Jacob I have loved and Esau I have hated ', 13 ; Mal 1:2.

Besides this main argument, 6-9, Paul finds in the i case of Esau and Jacob a further illustration of his thesis that God acted freely in electing whom he wished to the membership of Israel. According to Gen 25:23 Jacob was chosen and Esau rejected before either was born. If the election of the one and the rejection of the other had taken place later in their lives their moral conduct might have been made responsible for the distinction. As it is, the lesson which that Bible record wants to drive home can be none other than the freedom of God's election irrespective of descent from Abraham and also irrespective of works, 10-12.

71 The final conclusion then to be drawn from St Paul's reply to the Synagogue is : with regard to Israel to whom the Messianic promises were given we must distinguish between the Israelites who are Abraham's children only by physical descent and the Israelites who are Abraham's children by God's special election, like Isaac and Jacob. Only the latter, irrespective of their number, constitute the true Israel. Hence the self-exclusion of the majority of national Israel from Christianity does not put the Gospel into contradiction to the divine and unchangeable promises of the OT.

j A false interpretation. St Paul's argument in 6–13 has been wrongly quoted as scriptural evidence in favour of absolute predestination in the sense that each individual's eternal destiny is predetermined by an unalterable divine decree. Against such a false conclusion it must be remembered : (1) the two Scripture texts quoted in 13 f. are concerned not with the eternal salvation of Esau and Jacob but with their earthly life ; and again Paul himself is discussing the election to the Messianic promises of Israel, not the election to heaven or hell ; (2) the expression ' I have hated ' in 13 is not to be pressed since it is part of a quotation. And further, when contrasted with ' I have loved ' it may be taken as a Hebrew idiom and translated ' I have loved less ' = I have not chosen, *cf.* Gen 29:30 f. ; Lk 14:26 ; Deut 21:15–17 ; Jg 14:16 ; Prov 14:20 ; so Cornely.

k A slightly different form of the same misinterpretation uses St Paul's subsidiary argument in 10–12 to prove a false doctrine of predestination to heaven or hell in the specific sense of predestination ' independently of works ', *i.e.* independently of merits or demerits, because Esau was rejected before there could be any works against him. Some commentators have tried to meet this difficulty by introducing the idea of God's foreknowledge of Jacob's and Esau's later sins and virtues. The distinction between predestination before and after the prevision of merit (*ante vel post praevisa merita*) is no doubt right and helpful, but was it in the mind of St Paul when writing 10–12 ? It seems simpler and more in accordance with what the text actually says, to disown all theological speculations in 6–13 as regards predestination to heaven or hell because they are outside the scope of the argument. Paul is disputing Israel's claims to the Messianic promises as a nation ; and he does not carry the discussion beyond the limits set to it by this immediate object. The exclusion of (Ismael and) Esau from the Messianic promises proves these claims false and that is all the Apostle wants to prove. St Paul did not intend to prove that Esau could not save his soul because he did not belong to the Chosen People. And there is no evidence to that effect anywhere else in the Scriptures.

6. For a similar distinction within Israel *cf.* 1 Cor 10:18 ; Gal 6:16 ; **10.** ' At once ' = from one.

l **14–29 The Vindication of God's Justice in the Present Exclusion of Israel from the Salvation of the Gospel**— The objection to be refuted in this paragraph is based on Paul's reply to the first. It argues : if Christianity appeals to divine grace as the one and all important condition for belonging to the Elect = the Church, then a terrible injustice is done to all those who are left standing outside. Such a doctrine of grace in the fundamental questions of belonging to the Church is a doctrine of divine favouritism which contradicts God's justice.

Plan. This objection raises a serious theological difficulty and the Apostle argues the point at some length. The following four points may be distinguished in his reply : (1) 14–18, an answer from God's sovereignty ; (2) 19–21, the answer from God's sovereignty repeated ; (3) 22–24, another possible explanation ; (4) 25–29, the answer of the Scriptures.

(1) An answer from God's sovereignty, 14–18. The objector has appealed to the divine attribute of justice ; Paul replies with God's omnipotence, or sovereignty. The two Scripture texts which he quotes as his evidence are, if possible, even more ' predestinarian ' than those used before in 12 f. The one, Ex 33:19, is taken from the history of Moses ; the other, Ex 9:16, from the **8571** history of Pharaoh. God is the sovereign Lord, and as such can choose for his elect whom he likes. ' God hath mercy on whom he will and he hardeneth whom he will ', 18.

(2) The answer from God's sovereignty repeated, **m** 19–21. The dispute with the objector continues. Paul has referred him to the Scriptures and to the Scriptures he goes. If the sovereignty of God's omnipotent will is to be stressed to such an extent, why then does God still accuse and punish men for their unbelief, disobedience and sinfulness ? The Scriptures are full of such accusations and punishments. Surely God cannot be called just and yet, as in the case of Pharaoh, punish men for doing what is nothing but his own omnipotent will. In his reply (20 f.) Paul repeats his previous argument : God is the Sovereign and as such can treat man like the potter his clay. By using this well-known scriptural simile (*cf.* Is 29:16 ; 45:9 f. ; Jer 18:2–6 ; Wis 15:7 ; Ecclus 33:13) the Apostle goes beyond his first answer, 14–18, in that he specifies the sovereignty of God as that of the creator, and man's dependence as that of the creature. The evident conclusion is that man as God's creature has no more right than clay to question his maker's designs, plan or actions.

(3) Another possible explanation, 22–24. Paul's **n** answers so far have been more suppressing than solving the difficulty. Now he introduces the idea of God's mercy mitigating his sovereignty. Unfortunately the sentence remains unfinished. Most commentators complete it in the form of a rhetorical question : ' But [what would you say] if God with such patience endured vessels prepared (= due) for destruction, intending [on the one hand] to express his wrath and display his power, and [intending on the other hand] to make known the wealth of his glory in vessels of mercy which he had made for glory, among whom he called also us both from Jews and Gentiles ? ' The answer which the Apostle expects would then seem to be, that God's long suffering and forbearance, giving time for repentance, can of course set everything right. But then obviously the same divine mercy must be applied also to Israel. And this application indeed follows in ch 11.

(4) The answer of the Scriptures, 25–29. The divine **o** forbearance with vessels of wrath mentioned in 22 is as so often with St Paul no more than a thought thrown in but not followed up. Without even finishing the sentence, 22–23, he seizes on another point in 25–29. However serious the intellectual difficulty from the point of view of justice may be, it is at all events definite scriptural doctrine that the members of the Church in the Messianic time are to come (*a*) from all the Gentiles, and (*b*) only from a remnant of Israel. Hence whatever the Synagogue may say, the Church as she is with but few converts from Israel, is in full agreement with the Scriptures. Things have come to pass as they were foretold. The failure of the Gospel to convince the majority of Israel is no argument against Christianity. Thus the argument is brought back to the point from which it started in 6. The Scripture texts which St Paul quotes are : (*a*) for the conversion of the Gentiles, Os 2:23 ; 1:10 (LXX ed. Swete) = 2:25,1 (LXX ed. Rahlfs) ; (*b*) for only a small number of converts from Israel, Is 10:22 f. ; 1:9. All these texts are used by St Paul in a typical sense. For details see larger commentaries.

18. ' He hardeneth ' : for a full discussion see the **p** dogmatic treatise on grace. There are two opinions. The Thomist school explains it by means of the distinction between sufficient and efficacious grace. God's grace in such a case is sufficient but not efficacious. Because of bad disposition God does not add what would be necessary to make this grace efficacious (*non apponendo gratiam*). According to the Molinists the grace God gives is sufficient, but man does not co-operate. According to man's reception this grace is either efficacious or merely sufficient. In either case the real problem remains, *viz.* the beginning of evil. *Cf.* 3 Kg 18:37 ;

857p 22:21 f.; Is 6:10. **22.** 'If God . . . endured with much patience vessels of wrath': is the one clause in Paul's argument which explicitly refutes the false conclusion of an 'arbitrary' omnipotence. To bring out the importance of the clause it may be helpful to separate it from its adjuncts which are: (1) 'to show his wrath . . .' (a first subordinate final clause); (2) 'to show the riches of his glory . . .' (a second subordinate final clause); (3) to give time for repentance (a third clause added by commentators to complete the thought of St Paul). 'Fitted for destruction' = (a) made for; (b) prepared for by themselves (Chrys. Cornely); (c) due for, ready for (Lagrange). **25.** 'Not-my-people' = *Lo-'ammi*, which was the symbolical name of a son of Osee, cf. Os 1:9. 'Her-that-had-not-obtained-mercy' = *Lo-ruhamah* = no mercy, which was the symbolical name of a daughter of Osee, cf. Os 1:6. **27.** 'Remnant': cf. Is 1:9; 6:13; 10:20-22; 11:11-16; 37:4, 31 f.; 46:3; Jer 6:9; 23:3; 31:7; 40:11, 15; 42:2, 15, 19; 43:5; Ez 5:10; 6:8; 14:22, etc. See § 859b.

858a **IX 30-X 21 The Present Exclusion from the Salvation of the Messias is Israel's Own Fault**—Paul continues his debate upon Israel's exclusion from the salvation of the Messias begun in 9:1 but from another point of view. If the blame for Israel's present position outside the Church cannot be laid on God, 6-29, it is natural to raise the question, who then is to blame. This is the question now taken up and the blame is put on Israel herself. Thus Israel, hitherto the plaintiff in the discussion, now becomes the accused.

Plan. The argument proceeds by three steps: (1) 9:30-33 contains the summary statement of the accusation of Israel; (2) 10:1-13 gives the main proof; (3) 10:14-21 refutes various objections.

IX 30-33 Summary Statement of Israel's Fault—Israel's fault is her mistaken idea of 'justness' = sanctification. Trying to attain to justness by fulfilling the law, Israel finds herself with no room for Jesus, the Messias, who demands faith. As a result the Messias has become for her a stone of stumbling rather than a rock of salvation, as foretold in the Scriptures. **30.** 'Follow . . . attain': metaphors taken from the race course, cf. 9:16; 1 Cor 9:24; Phil 3:12; 1 Tim 6:11 f. **33.** '*A stone to stumble at and a rock to trip over*', WV. The phrase is taken from Is 8:14; the rest of 33 is a free quotation from Is 28:16. The same two texts from Is appear together in 1 Pet 2:6-8. Since Rom 9:33 and 1 Pet 2:6-8 agree in textual variants against LXX a common source has been suggested in the form of an early Christian anthology similar to the testimonies of Cyprian, cf. SH 281 f. 'The stone' refers (1) to YAHWEH in Is 8:14; (2) to Christ in Rom 9:33; 1 Pet 2:8; cf. Ps 117:22; Mt 21:42; Ac 4:11.

b **X 1-13 Israel's Fault is Explained**—The argument is not carried further, for Paul merely enlarges on the mistaken idea of 'justness' already stated in 9:31 f. as the cause of Israel's stumbling. The main line of thought presents no difficulty. In the introduction, 1 f., the Apostle shows once more (cf. 9:1-5) how anxious he is to avoid the impression that his argument is coloured by prejudice or antagonism. In 10:3 f. he repeats 9:31 f., i.e. the point which he wants to prove: Israel strives after justness in her own way, but her way is not the way of God, who makes justness dependent on faith before works. In 5-13 the two ways of striving after justness are further contrasted. The first, v 5 = Lev 18:5, is that of the law, discussed at length in 1:18-3:21. The second, 6-13, is that of faith, fully explained in 3:21-4:25, but here once more summarized in a series of free quotations from Deut 30:11-14; Is 28:16; Joel 2:32 Vg = 3:5 MT, LXX. The main purpose of the OT quotations in 6-13 must in this context be to show that justness according to the Scriptures is to be obtained by faith, cf. 9, 10, 11, 13. At the same time they evidently have the further object of impressing upon the reader that the new way of faith is superior to the old (1) because less difficult, 6-11, and (2) because open to all, 12 f. The vivid

language used to express this second object easily obscures the first and main point, that Israel's guilt is her neglect of the theological principle of faith.

A question of general interest on which commentators disagree is the use of the OT in 6-8, where Paul quotes Moses against his own law. The simplest solution of this difficulty is that the Apostle here uses Deut 30:11-14 not as scriptural evidence for his thesis but that he has no further intention by this quotation than to clothe his own thoughts in scriptural language. This solution is based on the Greek text in which there is no change of subject at the beginning of v 8 (against Vg, DV) so that personified justness is speaking throughout 6-8. If this explanation be accepted then we have here an example of what is called in Hermeneutics 'the accommodated sense', cf. Bar 3:29. So Cornely. For the opinion that Paul uses these texts in a 'typical sense' see Lagrange, Boylan; cf. also SH 302-7.

Another question of general interest in 1-13 is the meaning of the title Lord given to Jesus in 9: ἐὰν ὁμολογήσῃς. . . κύριον Ἰησοῦν = if thou confess . . . the Lord Jesus, DV; Jesus for Lord, WV; that Jesus is Lord, Boylan; cf. 1 Cor 12:3; Ac 11:20; Phil 2:11; 1 Jn 4:2. In general Boylan explains well: 'The title Lord includes all that was preached and believed concerning Jesus—His divinity, Incarnation, Work of Redemption, Resurrection and Glorification'. For a more detailed exegesis the following main interpretations may be mentioned. 'Lord' when used as a title of Jesus Christ by St Paul has been taken: (1) for Hebrew YAHWEH, because LXX often translated the tetragammaton in the OT with *kyrios*, cf. HRCS II 800; and because Paul often applied such texts to Christ, cf. note on 13. So Lattey, *Paul*, 1939, 54. (2) For Aramaic *mari*=my Lord; *maran(a)*=our Lord, found in early Christian prayers to Christ, cf. 1 Cor 16:22; Apoc 22:20; *Didache* 10:5; G. Dalman, *Worte Jesu*, 1898, 276; Boylan 169. (3) In opposition to *kyrios, kyria* in the contemporary cults of hellenistic-oriental syncretism; so *W. Bousset, *Kyrios Christos*, 1913, 113-25; Deissmann, *Licht vom Osten*, 1923, 298 f. (4) In opposition to kyrios in the Roman Caesar cult, cf. *Martyrol. Polycarpi* 8:2. Of these four explanations the first two seem preferable because more in agreement with the continuity of apostolic doctrine. But it may well be granted that according to circumstances the other connotations were stressed; e.g. the divine king against the Roman emperor cult; the one Lord of all, of Israelites as well as Gentiles, against the pagan cults of the time, cf. Rom 10:12; 1 Cor 8:5. In any case it is generally admitted that St Paul's usage of the title Lord for Jesus clearly implies the divinity of Christ and so does everyone of the above four explanations if logically thought out. On the whole question cf. Prat II 117-24; 437 f.; L. de Grandmaison, *Jésus-Christ*, Engl. Tr. III (1934) 379-83; BGDW, s.v. Kyrios; Lietzmann 97-101 on Rom 10:9; *H. J. Cadbury, *Beginnings of Christianity* V (1933) 360-62.

1. 'Paul would not have prayed if he had considered Israel to be irrevocably rejected' (Bengel). **2.** 'Zeal but not according to knowledge': cf. Jn 16:2; Ac 22:3; Gal 1:14; Phil 3:6; 1 Tim 1:13; see also Lightfoot on Col 1:9. **3.** 'The justice of God' = justness, justification, cf. 1:17; 3:5, 21 ff.; 9:31 f.; Phil 3:9; 2 Cor 5:21. **4.** τέλος νόμου = the end of law: can mean (a) the fulfilment of the law, cf. Mt 5:17; Gal 3:24; (b) the abolition of the law, cf. 6:14; Eph 2:15; Col 2:14. 'The law': has here been understood (a) of law in general = all legal systems; (b) of the Mosaic Law. The latter is more in keeping with the context, cf. 9:31 f.; 10:3 f. **6 f.** 'Who shall ascend into heaven . . . or descend into the deep': is used in Deut 30:13 f. as a metaphor for something impossible. Paul's application of the second part to the resurrection of Christ, 7, contains a noteworthy reference to Christ's descent into limbo, cf. Ac 2:27; 1 Pet 3:19; 4:6. **8.** 'But what saith it': scil. the justice = justness of v 6 f. **9.** 'If thou confess with thy mouth . . . and believe in thy heart': develops the metaphor for something near and easy quoted in 8 from Deut 30:14. The sequence 'mouth-heart' is therefore not to be pressed. In the process of justification faith comes before outward profession, *cf.* 10. **10.** A clear text against any theory that faith of the heart alone is sufficient. The profession of faith here demanded is the practice of faith in everyday life. There is no reason for limiting it to times of persecution. 'Justness . . . salvation': appear to be parallel. **12.** 'The same is Lord over all' = Christ, not YAHWEH; because of context, *cf.* 9 ff.; Mt 28:18; Ac 10:36; Eph 3:14 ff.; Phil 2:11. **13.** 'Lord': here refers to Christ, but in Joel 3:5 (= 2, 32 Vg) it refers to YAHWEH. Similar examples of YAHWEH texts applied to Christ are 1 Cor 1:31 = 2 Cor 10:17 = Jer 9:23 f.; 1 Cor 2:16 = Is 40:13; 1 Cor 10:21 = Mal 1:7; 2 Cor 3:16 = Ex 34:34; = Is 45:24.

14-21 Israel's Fault is further Explained—There is no change of subject here. The discussion of Israel's guilt continues. The Apostle's object, however, is no longer merely to show the fact of Israel's fault as in 1–13, but rather to prove that she is also fully responsible for that fault. She is culpable; she has no excuse.

The four excuses that might be made, 14–15*a*, 16*a*, 18*a*, 19*a*, are not convincing. First excuse, 14–15*a*: Where, in the case of the Gospel, is the authority which all preaching needs to make faith reasonable? How can Israel believe the Christian missionaries, without their having proper credentials? Answer, 15*b*: The principle of authority here invoked is perfectly true. But to question the Christian missionaries' authority is forgetting Is 52:7 where the authority of the evangelists (εὐαγγελιζομένων = messengers of the good news) is clearly foretold. Second excuse, 16*a*: If so, the authority of these evangelists must be considered insufficient because they have been unable to convince and convert Israel. Answer, 16*b*, 17: 'That complaint is as old as Isaiah's time' (C. J. Vaughan) and therefore no more disproves the authority of the Apostles than that of Isaias himself, Is 53:1. Third excuse, 18*a*: But has Israel really heard the Gospel? Answer, 18*b*: All the world has heard of it. Fourth excuse, 19*a*: But is Israel aware of what is at stake? Does Israel understand the Gospel? Answer, 19–21: Surely Israel can understand what the Gentiles can understand. The true explanation is not lack of understanding, but that principle of rebellion which underlies all the history of Israel. As in the days of Moses and Isaias, so now; it is disobedience and contradiction in spite of all that God has done for Israel. This explanation of 14–21 follows St Chrysostom; *cf.* Lagrange. Its advantage is that it brings out clearly what is generally considered to be Paul's main line of thought. But it must be admitted that it strains the text. To explain the OT quotations in 15*b* and 16*b* as answers is a possible but at the same time a harsh construction. For a similar construction, however, see 11:8. For two other arrangements of the text see Cornely, v. Soden, Jülicher.

The style of 14–21 has been described as obscure by such careful philological scholars as Jowett and SH. The obscurity arises from the method employed in this argument. St Paul answers various objections with Scripture texts, but does not explain the relation of these quotations to the points under discussion. The reason for this is easy to see. When the Apostle dictated the text his intonation would leave no doubt whether, *e.g.* 15*b* was meant as a question or as an answer. But to read such a compressed dialogue is a very different matter.

A point of special interest in 14–21 is the meaning of the four questions in 14, 15*a*. They are, of course, not four real difficulties but four rhetorical questions, arranged according to the figures of speech called climax. It is also clear that these four questions express only one objection: Israel cannot be expected to call upon the name of Christ, 13, without accredited preachers or teachers = apostles. But the amazing feature is the solemnity with which this objection is

expressed, arguing 'back from effect to cause through **858h** the series of Prayer, Faith, Hearing, Preaching, Sending' (Gifford). Why so elaborate and solemn? The best explanation would seem to be that 'apostolic (= sent) authority and continuity' were points of general interest and great importance in the Church at that time, *cf.* 1:1, 5; 1 Cor 12:28; 2 Cor 5:20; Gal 1:1; 1:18–2:9; Eph 1:1; 2:20; 4:11; Col 1:1; 1 Tim 1:1; 2:7; 3:1 ff.; 2 Tim 1:11; Tit 1:1, 5. **14.** '*Whom* they have not heard', WV. **15** quotes freely Is 52:7. The original text speaks of the messenger (singular!) that brings to Jerusalem the good news of the return from the Babylonian Exile. The LXX by using the verb εὐαγγελίζεσθαι = to evangelize, favoured St Paul's application of the text to the Christian missionaries = apostles. **17.** '*Through* the word of Christ' = (1) the commandment of Christ, *cf.* Lk 5:5; so Cornely, Eaton; or (2) the Gospel, the message of salvation as in 8; so Lagrange. Boylan seems to combine the two meanings.

XI 1-36 Further Points bearing on the Problem of the 859a Present Exclusion of Israel from the Salvation of the Messias—The main theological issues raised by the present exclusion of Israel from the salvation of the Messias in the Church have been decided in chh 9 and 10: God is free in his spiritual government of the world in spite of the election of Abraham and Israel, ch 9; and Israel is responsible for having missed the way in spite of the primary importance of grace in the process of salvation, ch 10. Here St Paul could have left the subject. But in ch 11 he pursues the discussion by viewing the problem from other points of view which he thinks might help to simplify the evident difficulties in the existing situation.

Plan. The whole chapter can be divided into five paragraphs. Israel's rejection: (1) is not complete, 1–6; (2) is not without purpose, 7–12; (3) should give no occasion for contempt of Israel, 13–24; (4) will not last for ever, 25–32; (5) epilogue, 33–36. For another arrangement see SH, Cornely, Lagrange; and Lietzmann, Sickenberger, Boylan.

1-6 The Present Exclusion of Israel from the Salvation b of the Messias must not be Exaggerated, it must not be regarded as complete. The popular use of the phrase 'the rejection of Israel' can easily cause exaggerations. It is not true that the whole of Israel is excluded from the salvation revealed in the Gospel. There are many examples to the contrary. The Apostle himself is one (*cf.* 1:1, 5; Gal 1:1) and there are many more. In fact the situation may well be compared with the days of Elias, when in spite of all appearances to the contrary, 3 Kg 19:14, God reserved for himself no less than 7,000 out of Israel, 3 Kg 19:18. As in those days so now, there is a 'Remnant' of Israel that has been elected by God to become the nucleus of the new Church.

The idea of a remnant or nucleus had already been touched on in 9:27–29. Here it is further developed but not so elaborately as later in 13–24. Still, there is one important addition in 1–6. Anxious to prevent any misunderstanding or weakening of his former doctrine of justification not by works but by faith the Apostle in 6 goes out of his way to stress that this remnant has not been selected because they had been more punctual in the observance of the law. Their election is due to God's grace not to their own works. Grace—faith—works: this is the sequence in the process of salvation. In 1–6 Paul is concerned only with the first of these three.

1a. Another rhetorical question continuing 10:18 f. **3.** 'What the Scripture saith *in the chapter* (= paragraph) of Elias': an ancient way of quoting the OT; *cf.* Mk 12:26 ('in the bush'). **5.** 'Remnant': a noun from the verb translated 'I have left', in 4; only here in NT. *Cf.* § 857*p*.

7-12 The Present Exclusion of the Majority of Israel c from the salvation of the Messias must not be represented as a rejection that is arbitrary or meaningless —From the chosen remnant, 1–6, Paul turns to the

859c majority of Israelites now outside the Church. Their exclusion from the salvation of the Messias is admittedly a fact and a problem. But there are also answers which simplify at least parts of the problem. One such answer, 8–10, recalls that the spiritual blindness or hard-heartedness to which their present unbelief in the Messias is due is a divine punishment foretold in the Scriptures. The texts which St Paul quotes as his proofs are : (1) Deut 29:4 (plus ' a spirit of stupor ', WV, from Is 29:10) and (2) Ps 68:23 f. LXX. A further answer, 11 f., to the problem is that which takes into account the good effects of this punishment. They are two : (1) Owing to the unbelief of Israel the doors of the Church were at once thrown open to the Gentiles, *cf*. Ac 13:46 ; 14:1 ; 18:4 ff. ; 19:9 ; 28:28. (2) The conversion of the Gentiles is meant to rouse the jealousy of Israel and thereby bring her back in due time to the one true Church of God on earth.

d 7–10 is in many commentaries connected with 1–6 under the heading : Israel's rejection is only partial. **8–10.** The final clauses in these OT texts are treated as consecutive clauses by some commentators, *cf*. Mk 4:12 ; Lk 8:10. **9.** ' Table ' : a metaphor for Israel's blessings. **10.** ' Bow down ', Ps 68:24 LXX = ' make their loins shake ', MT : is a metaphor for weakness, here for spiritual blindness, contrast Lk 13:11. **11–24** appears as a new paragraph in many commentaries under the heading : the rejection of Israel is only temporary. **11a.** ' That they should fall ' : The context makes it necessary to add : for ever or irrevocably. **12.** An argument *a fortiori*. ' Offence ' = failure to embrace the faith, is left without its antithesis. ' Diminution ' : either quantitative = in number ; or qualitative = in their position in the Church. ' Fullness ' : antithesis to ' diminution ' ; therefore again either quantitative = referring to the numerical completeness of their final conversion ; or qualitative, referring to the fulfilment (= consummation) of their mission in their final conversion.

e **13–24 The Present Rejection of the Greater Part of Israel** must not be made an occasion for contempt of Israel or for spiritual pride on the part of the converted Gentiles—From the unbelieving Israelites, 7–12, the Apostle turns his attention to the Gentiles who have taken their place in the Church. This time, however, his purpose is not to defend their rights as in Gal but to exhort them to humility.

To begin with, 13–16, Paul stresses a third time (*cf*. 9:1–5 ; 11:1–2) that his missionary work among the Gentiles is in no way meant to be a reflexion on Israel's privileges, *cf*. 1 Cor 9:20. His being pro-Gentile is not equal to being anti-Israel. He is no renegade, and Israel in spite of all has not lost the holiness which she has inherited from the Patriarchs who are, as it were, both her ' firstfruit ' and her ' roots '. This means, that the holiness of the Patriarchs sanctifies the whole of Israel in the same way, as that small first portion (= firstfruit) of dough which according to the law, Num 15:17–21, was set apart for the temple consecrated the whole dough. And again, Israel is holy because she is sanctified by the Patriarchs in the same way as the branches receive their life from the roots of the tree. Boylan compares the objective holiness or ' consecration ' of the children of Christian parents, *cf*. 1 Cor 7:14.

f After this introductory defence of Israel Paul enlarges in 17–24 on the second metaphor of 16 in which he had compared Israel to a tree whose branches must be as holy as its roots (= the Patriarchs). No sooner had he used the phrase than it occurred to him that the Gentile Christians might use it in their favour by arguing that genuine branches of this tree were lopped off, to engraft ' gentile branches '. Hence they might claim now to be alone the living tree and despise Israel as dry wood. The object of 17–24 is to condemn such an attitude towards Israel on the part of the converted Gentiles, and to recommend humility instead.

First, 17 f., the Gentile Christians should remember that before their conversion they belonged but to a ' wild ' olive tree compared with Israel. Therefore when they were engrafted on Israel's ancient stem, it was done contrary to all human standards. They brought nothing to the old tree ; they were engrafted only out of mercy to obtain new life from the ancient stem. Hence all the debt of gratitude and duty of humility is on their side. For another explanation of the simile developed in 17 f. see W. Ramsay, *Pauline Studies*, 1908, 223 f. ; S. Linder, *Palästina Jahrbuch* 26 (1930) 40–3.

In 19–24 Paul derives further motives for humility from the simile of the olive tree in 16, 17–18. He evidently has reason to think that the Gentile Christians may feel inclined to insist on the fact that whatever their origin may have been, at present they are the living branches of the Church while almost all the old branches have been cut off and thrown away on the heap of dry wood. This fact is undoubtedly true. But what the Gentile Christians should learn from it is : (1) fear of God's severity, since he did not spare even his own chosen people, 21, 22a ; (2) gratitude for the grace of their own faith, 22 ; (3) respect for God's omnipotence, 23. The wonderful way in which God, contrary to all that could be expected, has engrafted the Gentiles into the ancient stem of Israel should be a constant reminder to them that he can do the same at any time with those branches that are at present rejected. To belong to the Church is a grace of God ; the one condition on men's part is faith. Gentiles have been received into the Church because they believed, and Israelites have been excluded because they refused to believe.

13 f. are taken as a parenthesis by those commentators who regard 13–24 as a development of 11 f., in which case the new paragraph begins with 11. So Cornely, SH, Lagrange, Jülicher. **15.** ' Loss ' = rejection, WV. ' Receiving ' = restoration to favour, Boylan. ' Life from the dead ' : can be taken (1) metaphorically = an increase of the spiritual life in the whole church on earth so great that it could be compared to a resurrection from the dead, *cf*. Ez 37:3 ff. ; Lk 15:24, 32 ; or (2) literally = the new life after the general resurrection from the dead, *i.e.* the last and perfect stage in the history of the kingdom of God, inaugurated by the conversion of Israel, *cf*. 1 Thess 4:17 ; 1 Cor 15:52. The latter explanation seems more likely because ' the life ' of nr 1 is essential to the Church of all ages. For a history of exegesis *cf*. Cornely. **16.** ' Holy ' : refers to Israel's objective holiness, *i.e.* her being set apart for God = her election, *cf*. 11:28. It must not be identified with the personal sanctification by grace and faith in the Christian sense. **17–24.** Olive tree : a metaphor for Israel in Jer 11:16 ; Os 14:7 ; *cf*. also the vine in Is 5:7 ; Ps 79:9 ; and the fig-tree of Lk 13:6 ff. In 17–24, however, it is no longer the symbol of the church of the OT only, but of the Church in general, *i.e.* the church of the OT continued in the church of Christ, in which Gentile branches are grafted on the old tree, and not planted as new trees. **22.** ' *If thou abide in [his] goodness* ' = kindness of God towards thee.

25–32 The Present Exclusion of Israel from the Salvation of the Messias must not be regarded as Final —From the present, 1–24, St Paul turns his attention to the future. The time will come when the present problem of Israel's exclusion from the salvation of the Messias will cease to exist because of her conversion, which will follow upon the conversion of the Gentiles.

The final conversion of Israel could not be known to St Paul from any natural source. He himself calls it a mystery, 25, *cf*. Mt 13:11 ; 1 Cor 2:7 ; Eph 3:3 f. Nevertheless he does not claim a special revelation as the authority for his statement but argues the point. The reasons which he advances are taken (1) from the Scriptures, (2) from Israel's history, (3) from the divine plan of salvation (= *oeconomia salutis* = soteriology). (1) The evidence from Scripture, 26 f., is the prophecy of Israel's restoration in Is 59:20 f., plus the concluding clause ' when I shall take away their sins ' from Is 27:9.

See also Jer 31 (38):31–34. (2) The reason from Israel's history, 28 f., is the election of the Patriarchs. This is a dogmatic-historical fact which cannot be undone. The promises made to the Patriarchs must one day be fulfilled in every respect, because God is unchangeable, *cf.* Deut 4:31. (3) The reason from the divine plan of redemption, 30–32, is taken from the doctrine so often repeated in Rom that salvation is the gift of God's mercy (= grace = pardon) after man's failure to obtain ' justness ' (= holiness) by his own efforts. In this divine plan, therefore man's failure becomes Mercy's opportunity. So it has been in the case of the Gentile Christians to whom Paul is speaking, so it will be in the case of the now disobedient (= unbelieving) Israelites. ' God has abandoned all to their rebellion (= disobedience, WV = unbelief, DV) only to include them all in his pardon ', 31, KNT, *cf.* 10:12.

25. ' Mystery ' : Lagrange, *Ev. selon S. Luc,* 1927, 396, on Lk 13:35 finds this mystery already revealed by our Lord himself. ' Fulness of the Gentiles ' : need not be pressed so as to mean every individual, nor, **26,** ' all Israel '. **31.** ' For your mercy ' : is dative in the Greek, and as such can be explained : (1) as causal dative to ' they have not obeyed ', *i.e.* the salvation of the Gentiles has become the cause of Israel's unbelief ; (2) as instrumental dative, to ' that they may obtain mercy ', *i.e.* when roused to jealousy through mercy shown to the Gentiles. Nr 2 yields a clear sense but strains the structure of the sentence ; nr 1 follows the natural structure of the sentence but yields a sense which many reject because it would be contradicted by the fact that Israel disobeyed the Gospel before the conversion of any Gentiles. This contradiction, however, need not be pressed. When Paul wrote Rom the mercy shown to the Gentiles *was* a cause that stiffened the resistance of Israel.

33–36 Epilogue—The long list of arguments collected by St Paul in chh 9–11 to explain God's dealing with Israel in past and present has come to an end ; and he ' concludes on a note of baffled wonder and prostrate homage ', WV. It is true, election as well as rejection are facts in Israel's history, and one may call either predestination. But nevertheless and in spite of all the difficulties that remain unsolved Israel's election as well as her present rejection are both part of a wonderful plan, designed by God's mercy, wisdom, understanding, and omnipotence for the purpose of the salvation of all. God is free and can do as he chooses, ch 9 ; Israel is responsible for her failure, ch 10 ; the salvation °of Gentiles and Israelites alike is God's ultimate aim in all his ways, ch 11.

33–36 develop v 32, *cf.* the similar conclusion in 8:35 f. **33.** ' O the depth of the riches, *and* of the wisdom, *and* of the knowledge of God ' : three co-ordinated genitives. ' The riches ' : *scil.* of his mercy, *cf.* 10:12. ' Judgements ' : passed on Jews and Gentiles in the course of history to bring them to a realization of their misery and their need of divine assistance, Boylan. **35** is taken from Job 41:3 MT. The sense is : no one can earn the grace of salvation, so that he can claim it as his right. That Paul is not thinking here of meritorious works and their reward follows from the context and from such passages as 2:5 f. ; 1 Cor 3:8 ; 2 Cor 11:5 ; Gal 6:7 f. ; 2 Tim 4:8, etc. **36a.** ' *From him, through him, and for him is everything* ' : God is the efficient, sustaining and final cause of all ; *cf.* Rickaby. The appropriation of the first to the Father, of the second to the Son, and of the third to the Holy Ghost, is not stated in the text but common in the commentaries of the Latin Fathers after St Augustine, *cf.* Cornely 633 f. Alleged parallels in stoic literature are collected by Lietzmann 107, *e.g.* M. Aurelius IV 23.

XII 1–XV 12 The Moral Section of the Epistle = Exhortations—The purpose of these chapters evidently is to conclude the epistle with counsel and advice for the Christians of Rome in their daily life.

Plan. None of the various plans that have been drawn up to present the contents of these chapters in the form of a logical scheme has found general consent.

The reason seems to be that the Apostle passes from one **860a** point to the next as he pleases without following any prearranged plan. It may, however, be convenient, to distinguish : A. 12:1–13:13, general exhortations ; B. 14:1–15:13, exhortations to the Strong and the Weak at Rome.

XII 1–XIII 14 General Exhortations—These two **b** chapters contain a series of exhortations which cannot be brought under one heading. But it is customary to treat them together as a separate group because of what follows, 14:1–15:13. This long discussion of the relation between the Strong and the Weak evidently stands out as a section by itself.

Plan. No more than a separation of the main exhortations can be attempted. The arrangement followed in this commentary is : (1) 12:1–2, the Christian's service of God ; (2) 12:3–8, the various functions in the Church ; (3) 12:9–16, various precepts ; (4) 12:17–21, love your enemies ; (5) 13:1–7, the Christian and the State ; (6) 13:8–10, charity ; (7) 13:11–14, vigilance.

XII 1–2 The Christian's Service of God, or consecration of body and soul to the service of God—The Apostle begins with an exhortation which many commentators would like to treat as Paul's one basic moral principle. Moral theologians reject this claim as exaggerated. Yet it helps to bring out the importance of these two verses and to explain the extraordinary length of the commentaries.

The main idea is, no doubt, the consecration of body and soul to the service of God. This idea is not new, *cf.* 6:12–23 ; 8:12–17. Its expression in 1–2, however, is of special interest because of the liturgical language employed in 1. Serving God with one's body (and soul ?) is here described as the Christian's sacrifice and worship. This worship is then further recommended as one that is ' reasonable ' and the sacrifice as one that is ' living, holy and well-pleasing to God '. To look at our moral duties in this way has always been found striking, helpful and worthy of the highest praise. See Chrysostom's explanation showing how our eyes, tongue, ears, hands and feet can and should take their share in this sacrifice and worship. On the other hand, this liturgical presentation of our moral duties must not be exaggerated so that it becomes the one and only true Christian sacrifice and worship ; *cf.* A. Keogh, *The Ministry in the Apostolic Church,* WV III 224–42. It must be remembered that this liturgical language is metaphorical as in Phil 2:17 ; 4:18 ; 2 Cor 2:14, 16 ; Rom 15:16. A mere dictionary interpretation easily reads too much into the text.

1. The meaning of this verse is often limited to the **c** body exclusively, so that it becomes a warning against sins forbidden by the 6th Commandment and an exhortation to purity, like 1 Cor 6:12–20 ; 1 Thess 4:3–5. This interpretation is unnecessarily narrow ; *cf.* the use of ' body ' in 6:12–23 ; 7:4–6 ; 8:11 f. To be a sacrifice that is ' living, holy and pleasing to God ', all spheres of life must be included. λογικήν = reasonable, DV ; spiritual, WV ; *cf.* 1:9, Deut 11:13 ; Jn 4:24. The exact meaning depends on the contrast intended. This contrast some would find in the forms of worship observed by Israel according to the OT. But these forms cannot be called *un*-reasonable. Others, therefore, see the contrast in the forms of worship observed by the pagans of the time. This explanation implies that St Paul regarded the pagan liturgy as *un*-reasonable, which is quite plausible. In any case, the mistake to be avoided is to regard this verse as presenting the one and only ' reasonable ' Christian worship. For history of exegesis see Cornely and Lietzmann. **2.** If the wider interpretation of v 1 be accepted then 2 becomes parallel to it. **2c.** ' *That you may discern what is the will of God, i.e. that which is good, and well pleasing, and perfect* ' : The three adjectives seem to be in apposition.

3–8 Let Everybody be Content with his Function in d the Mystical Body of Christ, *i.e.* the Church—Every Christian must be content with that position, function

860d or work that has been assigned to him in the Church through his 'measure of faith', the special grace, charisma or talent, given to him by God. All who argue differently lack sobriety—moderation, temperance and humility. They forget that the Church is a community and as such like a human body in which the perfect service of every part, small and great is necessary for the welfare of the others. The allotment of the different functions (= charismata) in the Church is the work of God. The Christian's duty is to fulfil his task as best he can, no matter whether his task is (1) prophecy or (2) some other service such as (3) teaching, (4) preaching, (5) almsgiving, (6) organizing, (7) performing works of mercy.

Connexion. The reason for this exhortation may have been Paul's vivid recollection of the recent disturbances in the church of Corinth dealt with in 1 Cor 12:1–14:40. At all events these three chapters of 1 Cor are the best commentary on 3–8.

Plan. The sequence of thought can be made easier by distinguishing (1) 3–5, the Mystical Body of Christ as the principle on which all community spirit in the Church is to be based ; (2) 6–8, the application of this principle to seven different activities in the Church.

The doctrinal importance of the passage is its bearing (1) on the charismata = *gratiae gratis datae*, and (2) on the unity of the Church. The larger commentaries discuss here also (3) the relationship between the charismata of 6–8 and the regular early Christian Ministry, *e.g.* SH 358–60.

e **5.** '*Even so we many are one body in Christ and members each of the other*', WV. The human body is frequently used by St Paul as an image of the Christian community = Church, *cf.* 1 Cor 12:12–14, 27 ; Eph 4:15, Col 1:18. **6-8** contain the application of the principle of the Mystical Body laid down in 3–5 ; *cf.* 1 Cor 12:27–30 as the application of 1 Cor 12:12–26. The same idea also in 1 Pet 4:9–11. The structure is difficult because of a double anacoluthon. Hence the additions to the text in the translations : . . . [to be used] according to . . . v 6, DV ; . . . [then let it be] in ministering, v 7, Boylan. KNT divides ' the one sentence into four. **6.** κατὰ τὴν ἀναλογίαν τῆς πίστεως = secundum rationem fidei, Vg ; *in conformity with the faith* : is a very much discussed phrase. There are two main interpretations : (1) = according to the rule of faith, DV. Then the meaning is, let prophecy be checked by what is established Christian doctrine (= *fides quae creditur*) and there will be no room or occasion for such subjectivism, extravagances or exaggerations as bring the charisma of prophecy into disrepute. (2) = as far as the measure of his faith will let him (*scil.* the prophet), KNT ; *cf.* also WV note on 12:3. Then the meaning is, let every prophet keep to the measure of the faith (charisma) assigned to him by God (= *fides qua creditur*), and say nothing except what his charisma of faith prompts him to say. If the prophets are honest, then there will be no abuse. Both explanations agree that Paul's object is to encourage the right use of the gift of prophecy and to check abuses. The first explanation suits this purpose better, because the rule of faith, the doctrine or contents of the faith, offers an objective means for checking any extravagant prophecy, *cf.* Gal 1:8 ; 1 Cor 14:29 ; 1 Thess 5:21.

f **9-16 Further Precepts of Christian Morals**—It is a common and tempting suggestion to regard this paragraph, in view of its beginning in 9, 10a, as a treatment of the commandment of charity. But the precepts which follow this beginning vary so much that they cannot easily be brought under any one heading ; and the commandment of charity is more fully treated in 13:8–10.

The style of 9–16 is aphoristic and elliptic. The free transition from participles to imperatives, to infinitives and then to imperatives again is not in accordance with the rules of syntax.

11c. On the inferior reading ' serving the time ', *cf.* H. A. W. Meyer and Lietzmann. **13.** On the virtue of hospitality, *cf.* Tit 1:8 ; Heb 13:2 ; 2 Jn 10 f. ;

K. Vaughan 171 ; Hasting's *Dictionary of the Apost. Church* I (1915) 586. **14** cannot be a quotation of Lk 6:28, but it may be a reminiscence of our Lord's words, *cf.* 13:9 f. ; Mt 5:44 ; 1 Cor 4:12 ; Lietzmann. **17-21 Conduct towards Enemies**—From duties towards neighbours in general, 9–16, St Paul passes on to conduct towards unfriendly neighbours in particular. Whether the enemies whom the Apostle has here in mind were Christians or non-Christians cannot be decided for certain, nor would it seem necessary to make this distinction. The rules of 17–21 apply in either case.

Similar views on conduct towards enemies. The topics of anger, envy, strife, contention, hatred, enmity, punishment, revenge, war, etc., figure largely in all parts of the Bible. For a collection of references see K. Vaughan 177–81. The main parallels to the Christian teaching in the OT are Ex 23:4 f. ; Prov 25:21. See also the literature on the imprecatory Pss and on Mt 5:38–48. Every Christian discussion of the subject must start from the relevant passage in the Sermon on the Mount, Mt 5:38–48. To this St Paul's short treatment here adds nothing new, except his proofs from the OT, Deut 32:35 ; Prov 25:21 f. The rabbinical theology of NT times does not seem to have had a clear and authoritative teaching on the subject ' love thy enemy ', *cf.* SB I 368 ff. on Mt 5:44 ; III 301 f. on Rom 12:20. A parallel from classical literature that may be quoted is Plato, *Rep.* I 335, where Socrates rejects the popular maxim ' do good to thy friend, and harm to thy enemy ' (Gifford). For more but doubtful parallels see *C. T. Ramage, Scripture Parallels* 1878, 280–3. Our textbooks of moral theology treat the various aspects of the commandment ' love thy enemy ' under the sins against charity, under the 5th commandment and under the capital sins of anger and envy. To avoid wrong conclusions from 17–21 it must be remembered generally that Paul is concerned with the Christian's private conduct towards his enemies. The right and duty of the State to punish and control what is evil, is not in his mind. With this he deals in the next passage, 13:1–7.

20. ' Coals of fire ' : have been understood as a metaphor (1) for the feelings of shame and remorse, (2) for God's judgments.

XIII 1-7 The Duty of Obedience to the Authority of the State—The Apostle passes on to summarize the Christian's duties towards the State. He first insists on the duty of submission and obedience to the ruling government as a divine law. Leaving all questions of the natural law aside he proves this divine law from the fact that no government could obtain or retain power without God's will. Every citizen therefore is bound to render submission and obedience to the *de facto* government because disobeying would be disobeying a divinely appointed authority, a sin which would not be left unpunished, 1–2. In 3–4 the Apostle gives a brief description of the government as it should be, its main function being to support all good and suppress all evil. After this the way is clear for the conclusion which follows in 5. The submission and obedience due to such a government is a matter of conscience, *i.e.* the Christian is to obey for God's sake, and not for fear of being found out and punished. The laws of such a government are not merely penal laws but moral laws. The law of taxation, 6, serves as an example. Finally, in 7 the Apostle concludes with a summary which is reminiscent of the words of our Lord in Mt 22:21 ' Render to Caesar the things that are Caesar's '.

Some of the questions and objections to which **b** St Paul's statements in 1–7 have given rise may here be reviewed. But they must be regarded as belonging more to the history of the exegesis of the paragraph than to its literal interpretation. Most of them are read into the text.

(1) Can a Christian honestly regard and respect as divinely appointed every *de facto* government even when it is resented as usurping, illegitimate, enforced, foreign, tyrannical, pagan, anti-religious, or anti-

b Christian, 1–2 ? Yes, in view of God's justice and providence ; *cf.* Ex 9:16 ; Rom 9:17 (Pharaoh) ; Jer 21:7 ; 29:4–14 ; 51:24 (Babylonian captivity) ; Mt 22:15–22 ; Jn 19:11 (Roman rule in Palestine) ; see also Origen-Rufinus, on Rom 13:1 ; Augustine, *De civ. Dei* 5, 21 ; St Thomas, *Sum. theol.* I q 19 a 9 ; reference from sub-apostolic literature are collected by SH 371 f. For a different answer see Chrysostom and St Thomas *ad loc.*

(2) Can v 2 be quoted to show that a Christian must acquiesce in such a state of affairs as described under nr 1 and regard such a government as established for ever ? No, to wait for and co-operate with God's opportunities by using all legitimate means to bring about improvements in such a government or even to replace it by a better, would seem to be every citizen's right by natural law. At all events every one by natural law has the right to resist injustice even when this injustice is done in the name of a government. In either case, however, the means employed must be in accordance with the moral law ; and here in many cases conscience will have to be the final arbiter for the individual ; *cf.* Boylan, on 13:2 ; SH 372 (on passive obedience) ; Lehmkuhl, *Theol. Moralis*, I (1898) 472 ; Génicot, *Theol. Moralis*, I (1922) 287 f.

c (3) Can v 2 be quoted to show that a Christian is bound to obey government orders also when they are against the divine law ? No, the scriptural guidance in such a situation, however, must be taken from such passages as Mt 22:21 ; Ac 5:29, etc., not from our passage which presupposes normal conditions, *cf.* 3–4.

(4) Can v 2 be used in favour of the State when in conflict with the Church ? No, according to the same principle as under nr 3. See DV (1582) note on 13:4 ; Gore II 124.

(5) Can 1–2 be used to prove that monarchy, the actual form of government at the time, in Rome is the one form of government approved of by St Paul against any other ? No, the terms here used are general. The contrast intended (if any) is not monarchy as against democracy or any other form of government, but government, law and order on the one side, against anarchy, the ruin of every state, on the other.

(6) Can the political conditions under which St Paul wrote Rom be regarded as normal, 3–4 ? Opinions differ. For a favourable description of the Roman government at that time see SH XIII–XVIII. The evidence to the contrary comes mostly from the administration of the provinces, *cf.* CAH XII 712 f. In any case, Paul is here not discussing the grievances of Roman subjects, but stating every citizen's duty of obedience to the state in general. What kind of government, however, he has in mind can be seen from 3–4.

d (7) What does St Paul teach in 3–4 about the duties of a Christian government ? Nothing directly. He is concerned with the duties of subjects to their government. But from 3–4 one may rightly conclude that if the pagan government is to be ' power on the side of good ', how much more must a Christian government live up to this first of all its duties.

(8) Did St Paul himself and the early Church uphold the same principle of obedience to the government even during and after persecution in the Roman empire ? Yes, Paul had suffered injustice at the hands of government authorities before he wrote 1–7 ; *cf.* Ac 16:37 ; 2 Cor 11:25, 32. That his attitude remained the same later can be seen from 1 Tim 2:1–7 ; Tit 3:1. The early Church remained true to the same principle also during the time of persecution, *cf.* 1 Pet 2:13–17 and the numerous references from the sub-apostolic literature collected by SH 371 f. The government of Rome is judged from a different point of view in Apoc 17:6 ; 18:24 ; *cf.* 2:13 ; 6:9 f., but this does not contradict St Paul's principles in 1–7.

(9) Can v 5 be quoted to prove that *all* state laws bind a Christian in conscience ? No, Paul is concerned with obedience to state law in general, not with the questions whether this or that state law might be unjust and therefore not binding in conscience, *cf.* nr 3. **861d**

(10) Can v 6 be used to prove that not paying *all* the taxes imposed by the Government is necessarily sinful ? No, Paul is again speaking of taxes in general not of this or that tax in particular which can quite well be unjust. *Cf.* Catechism of the Council of Trent pt 3 ch 8 qu 10 ; Génicot, *Theol. Moralis* I (1922) 497–501 ; H. Davis, *Moral Theol.* II (1935) 308 f.

(11) Is the exhortation to the Christians of Rome in 1–7 nothing but the prudent advice of an opportunist, arguing that resistance to the Roman government would only do harm, *cf.* Jn 11:48 ? No, the duty of obedience to the government is clearly stated to be a duty imposed by God, 1, 2, 5, and as such is a precept of the moral law, whilst opportunism is ruled by circumstances and selfishness ; against Renan, *cf.* Gifford 211.

8–10 Exhortation to Charity—From loyalty to the **e** government, 1–7, St Paul passes to charity towards one's neighbour. The way in which he treats of charity here is short and precise. For the many different aspects under which he could have considered this characteristically Christian duty *cf.* 1 Jn *passim* ; 1 Cor 13 ; Jas 2:8–10 ; K. Vaughan 160–88 ; textbooks of moral theology, *e.g.* Noldin II (1921) 85–147.

The special feature of 8–10 is the stress laid on the place charity ought to be given among the commandments. The Apostle puts it first. His reason is that he who loves his neighbour will be anxious not to wrong him, *cf.* Mt 7:12. Where there is charity, the 6th, 5th, 7th, 9th and 10th as well as all other commandments will be kept as a matter of course. The objection arises that our Lord in Mt 22:39 clearly puts love of one's neighbour second and not first. Some commentators in defence of St Paul refer to 1 Jn 4:20 and Gal 5:14 arguing that in practice the love of one's neighbour implies the love of God, *cf.* Cornely 683 f. A simpler solution is that Paul called charity the first of the commandments ruling our conduct towards men. This means abstracting from the love of God as not finding a place in the argument : (1) because the context deals with man's duties towards man and not with those towards God ; (2) because the examples of 9 are all taken from the second table of the decalogue and not from the first ; (3) because our Lord's words in Mt 22:39 are so clear and, if not actually quoted here, yet seem to have been in the Apostle's mind.

11–14 Exhortation to Vigilance and Sanctity—It is **f** difficult to find one name for the Christian ideal described in this short paragraph. St Thomas calls it ' honestas ', honourableness, sense of honour, purity of life. It is described both negatively and positively by a series of metaphors mainly taken from time. On the one hand we have sleep, night, and the works of darkness : feasting and drinking, fornication and lewdness (wantonness), wranglings and jealousies ; all these are to be shunned and cast off. On the other hand, there are the marks of a Christian life : vigilance, the light of day, and—one would expect—the *works* of light. But the metaphor is changed to ' the *armour* of light ' which the Christian is to put on.

Connection. Some commentators do not regard 11–14 as a paragraph by itself but as an afterthought to 8–10. Then the meaning of the passage is : let the thought of the coming day of judgement be a further motive to fulfil all the demands of charity set out in 8–10 ; *cf.* Cornely.

The metaphors of 11–14. On their understanding **g** depends the appreciation of the passage. But the exact meaning of some is difficult to ascertain. (1) The sleep from which the Roman Christians are to rise, 11, must be the state of their spiritual life at the time. We may think of sleep then in the sense in which even the five prudent virgins ' slumbered and slept ' before the bridegroom arrived, Mt 25:6 (Gifford). Perhaps we are allowed to go further and think of that carelessness, lukewarmness or indifference which often follows when the first fervour has spent itself, Apoc 2:4 f. ; 3:15 f. ; so Cornely who speaks of ' *socordia, ignavia, tepiditas* '. But it would certainly be exaggerating to interpret this

861g sleep as the soul's sleep of death or state of mortal sin ; *cf.* Apoc 3:1 ff. (against Estius). (2) The vigilance to which Paul exhorts in 11 is the same as that of Mt 24:42 ; 25:13 ; Lk 21:36 ; 1 Cor 16:13 ; Eph 6:18 ; Col 4:2 ; 1 Thess 5:6 ; 2 Tim 4:5 ; 1 Pet 4:7 ; 5:8 ; Apoc 3:2 f. ; 16:15. (3) The night that is far gone, 12, has been explained (*a*) as the whole period of human history before the day of the Last Judgement, (*b*) as the readers' life on earth looked upon as the night that precedes the day of their glorification in heaven, (*c*) as the ' dark ages ' of pagan morals, so Lagrange. (4) The day that is near, 12, has been interpreted (*a*) as the day of the Last Judgement (Parousia), (*b*) as the day of the readers' glorification, (*c*) as the period of Christianity (Christian morals) enlightening the darkness of heathendom. (5) The works of darkness, 12 = all manner of sin. (6) The armour of light, 12, which the Christian is to wear is amply illustrated in the list of Christian virtues in 1 Thess 5:8 ; Eph 6:10–17.

h The nearness of the Parousia or the Second Coming of our Lord, 11. This point is discussed at great length in all modern commentaries. Paul refers to it in 11*c* when reminding his readers that the day of their final salvation is nearer now than when they were baptized. The purpose of the reminder is evidently exhortation to vigilance, *cf.* Lk 12:37 ; 1 Cor 7:29 ; Hebr 10:25, 37 ; 1 Pet 4:7. The modern discussions, however, turn round the question whether this text proves that St Paul regarded the Parousia as imminent. For a full answer to this problem see the commentaries on 1 Thess 4:17. All that need be said here is that inspiration covers no more than what the sacred author actually wrote and with this limitation 11*c* offers no difficulty. The case seems well put by SH 378 ' The language is that befitting those who expect the actual coming of Christ almost immediately, but it will fit the circumstances of any Christian for whom death brings the day '.

11. ' Our salvation ' : the Greek text can also be translated ' now the salvation is nearer to us than when . . .'. What the Apostle means is the final salvation or glorification = the revelation of the children of God in 8:19 = the redemption of the body in 8:23 = the restitution of all things in Ac 3:21. ' When we believed ' : Aorist = when we became believers, or Christians, *cf.* C. J. Vaughan. **14.** ' Put on Christ ' : here in the moral sense, *cf.* Eph 4:24 ; Col 3:12. The same phrase is used in Gal 3:27 in a dogmatic sense for the sacramental effects of baptism.

862a XIV 1–XV 13 Exhortations to the Weak and the Strong in the Church of Rome—Peace and unity in the church of Rome are the subject of this long exhortation. But this time, as distinct from the previous exhortations to the same effect, 12:3–8, 9–16, 17–21 ; 13:8–10, it is peace and unity in one particular point. St Paul has heard of Christians at Rome who abstain from meat, 14:2, and wine, 14:21, and have fixed days set apart for special religious purposes, 14:5. On the other hand he knows that there are others who regard these formalities as having been made unnecessary by the Christian doctrine of salvation, and who therefore judge those who continue to set a great value on their observance as weak in the faith. The Apostle fearing that their differences of opinion might grow into serious disturbances of peace and harmony uses the opportunity of exhorting to unity and mutual tolerance. For the want of exact modern equivalents, the two parties may conveniently be called the Weak and the Strong. On the whole subject *cf.* M. Rauer, *Die Schwachen in Korinth und Rom nach den Paulusbriefen*, BS 21 (1929).

Connexion. Most commentators see the connexion in the contrast with 13:13. It is equally possible that the Apostle left this exhortation last on purpose. The general exhortations in 12:1–13:13 are well suited to prepare the way for the discussion of what was evidently a delicate problem.

b Plan. The whole section can be divided into three parts : (1) 14:1–12, avoid mutual criticism ; (2) 14:13–23, avoid giving scandal; (3) 15:1–13, avoid selfishness.

Difficulties. The general outlines of the situation which the Apostle has in mind are clear. But as soon **8** as attempts are made to reconstruct the argument in detail commentators begin to differ widely. The main controversies centre round these questions : (1) Who were the Weak ? (2) What is meant by the observance of special days ? (3) Why does St Paul not treat the Weak in Rom in the same way as the Weak in Gal ?

(1) Who were the Weak of Rom 14:1–15:13 ? Six answers have been given : (*a*) Converts from the Synagogue who in these matters continued to live according to the Mosaic Law and Jewish custom, *cf.* Col 2:16. (*b*) Converts from Essenism, a Jewish religious body with very severe rules of abstinence, *cf.* Philo, *De vita contemplativa* ed. Mangey II 477. (*c*) Another type of the Weak in 1 Cor 8, who refused to eat meat that had been offered to idols. The Weak of Rom then are understood to have gone a step further and abstained from meat and wine altogether to avoid every possibility of taking meat of this kind, *cf.* Cornely 692 ff. (*d*) Converts from some form of Orphic-Pythagorean Mystery-religion, in which these practices were in vogue at the time ; *cf.* Lietzmann 114 f. (*e*) Christian ascetics, who for various reasons regarded such mortification as the sign of a good Christian life ; *cf.* Lagrange 335. (*f*) Christians of ' excessive scrupulousness '. The complete abstinence from meat and wine, and the observance of special days are in this case no more than illustrations ; *cf.* SH 401 f. Each **c** of these six answers assumes a particular type of religious practice at Rome in the days of St Paul. But none of them can be shown by independent historical evidence to have existed in the Christian community of Rome in those days, and it is easy to raise objections against each of them. (*a*) Complete abstinence from meat and wine was never enjoined in the synagogue. (*b*) The existence of Essene communities outside Palestine cannot be proved, Schürer II (1907) 656 ; nor can abstinence from meat and wine be shown to be characteristic of Essenism, Schürer II 664. (*c*) The situation in 1 Cor 8 is clear and Paul's exhortation essentially the same as in Rom 14:1–15:13. But all this does not explain the ' exaggeration ' in Rome and the observance of special days. (*d*) Orphic-Pythagorean influence is possible but difficult to prove in this particular case. (*e*) Strong ascetical tendencies no doubt existed in early Christianity, *cf.* Ac 4:32–5:11 ; 1 Tim 5:23 ; Col 2:16 ; *Didache* 8 ; *cf.* also the later Encratites, Irenaeus, *Adv. haer.* 28 ; and the Ebionites, Epiphanius, *Haer.* 30:15, 3. But the question is, whence this unusual type of asceticism among the Christians of Rome ? (*f*) Scrupulousness is a common spiritual disease, the existence of which at Rome as anywhere else in the times of St Paul can readily be admitted. But can complete abstinence from meat and wine and the observance of special days be reasonably regarded as typical examples of what we call scrupulousness ? They may have been such under the circumstances, but then they are more than mere illustrations, *cf.* 1 Cor 8. Further, the concessions which St Paul makes to the Weak of Rome cannot be applied to the scrupulous in general. In view of so much uncertainty most modern commentators refuse to decide in favour of one of the above six explanations. Instead they prefer to speak vaguely of a combination of various influences and tendencies known to have existed at the time. Briefly, as far as we know, Jewish as well as pagan current tendencies, pre-Christian as well as Christian thought, may have contributed to the complicated situation presupposed in Rom 14:1–15:13 ; *cf.* SH 399–403 ; Lagrange 335–40 ; Boylan 211 f.

(2) What is meant by the observance of special days **d** in 14:1–15:13 ? The only reference to this practice of the Weak is 14:5. But it may be implied in 14:21*c*. St Paul's description is so vague that one can only discuss the possibilities. (*a*) The special days observed by the Weak may have been holy days = feast-days. In this case the holy days of the OT calendar (Sabbath, New Moon, etc.) would seem to be meant, *cf.* Gal 4:10 f. ; Col 2:16 f. This opinion is naturally held by

all who regard the Weak as converts from the Synagogue, *cf.* Cornely 702. But if they were holy days, one can also think of Christian holy days, *e.g.* Sunday, Apoc 1:10. (*b*) The special days of the Weak more probably were fast days. This explanation is based on the context in which abstinence is the predominant feature. So Lagrange, Boylan. In this case the practice of the Weak may be compared with the early Christian custom of fasting Wednesdays and Fridays, *Didache* 8, or later every Wednesday and Saturday in Rome. The two extreme possibilities which the text theoretically allows, that the Weak fasted every day, and the Strong never, can safely be neglected.

(3) Why does St Paul not treat the Weak in Rom in the same harsh way as the Weak in Gal ? The difference in St Paul's attitude to very much the same question is beyond any doubt. In Gal the Weak stand clearly condemned as being in the wrong ; in Rom Paul pleads for sympathy and understanding. The difference cannot be explained as a change in the Apostle's doctrine, because the doctrine of justification by faith and not by observance of law is essential to his teaching and to Rom in particular, *cf.* 3:21 ; 4:3 f. ; 5:1. The true explanation then can only be found in the different circumstances. And in fact it can be shown from the texts that the two cases were fundamentally different in spite of external similarities. The Weak of Gal tried to enforce circumcision with all its subsequent observances as a sacrament necessary for salvation. Thus the observance or non-observance of the Mosaic Law became a matter of dogma, heresy and excommunication. On the other hand, though the Weak of Rom also had a high opinion of their observances, there is no indication that they regarded them as necessary for salvation. For them as well as for their opponents these observances were a matter of opinion and practice, comparable with pious customs of today. That they preferred to associate with those who shared their views and mode of life was only natural. Nor is it difficult to understand how this preference could become a matter of conscience. ' The stricter the rule, the holier the life ', sums up a very common experience. At all events the Apostle's positive teaching with regard to this point in 14:1–15:13 does not go beyond the conclusion that whenever this or that rule of life comes to be considered as the more perfect, its acceptance or non-acceptance becomes a matter to be decided by the conscience of the individual in question. But that does not make it a matter of dogma, heresy or excommunication in the Church at large. In brief, there is no contradiction between Gal and Rom 14:1–15:13. For similar concessions on the part of St Paul see 1 Cor 8 ; Ac 16:3 ; 21:20–26.

f   XIV 1–12 Let the Strong and the Weak avoid criticizing each other—The Apostle admonishes to mutual tolerance but does not deny the existing difference between the Weak and the Strong. The reasons which impose the self-restraint necessary for this mutual tolerance are : (1) 4–9, the Weak as well as the Strong are Christians and as such belong to Christ. As long as this bond of allegiance to Christ as the one Lord of all exists, no Christian can without trespassing on his Master's rights take it upon himself to condemn a fellow-servant who belongs to Christ as much as he himself. (2) 5*c*, *cf.* 22*c*, 23, it ought to be remembered that besides dogma there is in Christian life also a large province in which it must be left to each Christian to make sure of his own conviction and to follow his own conscience. (3) 10–12, one day each man's conduct will be judged before the tribunal of God ; then each will have to give an account of himself, not of his fellow-Christian. (4) Condemning each other in matters of practice and conscience endangers peace and unity. This fourth reason is derived from the trend of the whole exhortation.

1. ' Weak in faith ' : has been explained (1) as weak in the theological virtue of faith ; (2) as weak in the comprehending of the Christian doctrine of faith ; (3) as weak in applying that faith ; (4) as weak in

conscience ; (5) ' him who is weak receive in faith ', **862f** Sahidic version. Of these nr 4 is the simplest and perhaps the most practical, but nr 3 philologically the more accurate. For whatever the context, faith is wider than conscience. **5***c*. ' *Let each be fully assured in his own mind* ', WV. For if he acted against his own conviction, he would commit sin, *cf.* 14:23. The phrase must not be understood as being satisfied with one's own mind. **7 f.** is a Christian principle of fundamental importance, *cf.* 2 Cor 5:15 ; Gal 2:20 ; Eph 1:21 ; Phil 1:21 ; 2:9, 11 ; 1 Thess 5:10.

13–23 Let the Strong avoid scandalizing the Weak— **g** Having warned both parties against mutual criticism St Paul passes on to the positive duty of mutual edification. This exhortation he addresses to the Strong, excepting perhaps 20, 22 f. In brief : sympathy is Paul's way of meeting the scrupulosity of Christians who are still so weak in their faith that they cannot forget their inherited pious customs through which the kind of food they eat has become part of their religious life, *cf.* 1 Cor 8:7–13.

Plan. The Apostle's thoughts flow backwards and forwards. But studying the reasons with which he tries to persuade the Strong to sacrifice their rights for the benefit of the Weak will help to trace the main sequence of thought. These reasons are : (1) 15*b*, 20–23, the commandment of charity which forbids giving scandal = endangering anyone's supernatural life. (2) 15*c*, 20*a*, the disproportion between the gain of a dish of food and the loss of a soul for which Christ has died. (3) 16, 18, the good reputation of the Christian faith. (4) 17 f., the spiritual character of the kingdom of God, which lies not in the freedom from this or that ceremonial law, but in its supernatural graces and virtues—holiness, peace and joy. (5) 19*a*, the duty of preserving peace and unity in the Church. (6) 19*b*, the duty of mutual edification.

13*b*. ' Stumbling-block or scandal ' : of these two **h** synonyms the latter has been adopted in the CTS Catechism q 206 and 208. Its earliest occurrence in the Greek Bible is Lev 19:14 LXX ; in the Latin Bible Ex 10:7 Vg. The main passage in the NT to be consulted is Mt 18:7 ; *cf.* also St Thomas, *Sum. theol.* II 2 q 43 a 1. **14** is important in the discussion whether and why the Mosaic Law of clean and unclean foods in Lev 11 has been abrogated. As Paul here clearly says, the authority for this abrogation is ' in Christ ', *cf.* Mt 15:10 f., 15–20 ; Mk 7:14 f., 17–23 ; Ac 10:9–16. This verse has also been quoted in defence of indecent art, literature and amusement, *cf.* 1 Tim 4:4. These are said here to be sanctioned for those who resemble the Strong in faith of 14:1–15:13. But this argument, if it were serious, would overlook the evident fact that 14:1–15:13 is concerned with the importance of pious customs not with border cases of immorality. And further, even where pious customs are concerned, in 14:14–23 the Strong are clearly admonished not to insist on their opinion. **19.** ' *Thus we pursue peace and mutual edification* ' : the metaphor ' to build up, to edify ' is frequently used by St Paul for the growth and progress of Christian life, *cf.* 1 Cor 3:9 f., 16 ; 8:10 ; 14:26 ; 2 Cor 6:16 ; 10:8 ; Eph 2:21 ; 1 Thess 5:11. There were occasions when St Paul ' pursued peace ' along different lines, *cf.* Ac 15:1 f. ; Gal 2:3 f. **22***b*. **i** ' He that ' : can be (1) the Strong, whose conscience must condemn him if he chooses to go his own way regardless of the scandal to others ; (2) the Weak, who is advised to follow his own conscience in this matter of foods regardless of the stronger faith of others ; (3) anyone without a scrupulous conscience. **23***b*. ' *Because his eating is not the outcome of faith* ', WV = he acts in bad conscience, KNT. It is generally acknowledged that faith here does not mean abstract dogmatic faith, but applied faith, personal conviction, conscience. **23***c*. The doctrine of this sentence can be expressed in the form of two possible translations. (1) ' All that is done in bad conscience is sin ', *cf.* KNT. In this form the verse states a principle which is true for all men, Christians as well as pagans. (2) ' All that is not the

862i outcome of faith is sin', WV. In this form the principle is true only of Christians. For whatever a Christian does must be in accordance with his faith. To let every action be the outcome of his faith is the Christian's ideal of sanctity according to St Paul, *cf.* 1 Cor 10:31 ; 2 Cor 10:5 ; Col 3:17. This second explanation is to be preferred because of the context, which is concerned with Christians only, and not with pagans. This verse therefore should never have been applied by later theology to the actions of pagans. 23 *fin.* is followed by 16:25–27 (doxology) in some MSS, *cf.* § 863*l.*

j **XV 1–13 Let the Strong in their Relations with the Weak imitate Christ's Example of Unselfishness**—St Paul continues his exhortation to the Strong, 1, 8–12 ; but there are sentences in this paragraph which can be applied also to the Weak, 7*a*, 2 ? 4–6 ? The ambiguity arises from the main object of this exhortation which is to impress the duty of preserving peace and unity in the Church, 5, 6, 7*a*, 13 ; *cf.* 14:19. Enlarging and insisting on this duty, the Apostle could hardly exclude the Weak, but there can be no doubt that he puts the main burden on the shoulders of the Strong.

In addition to the reasons given in 14:13–23 let the Strong remember the example of Christ's humility during his earthly life in general, 1–6. He, our Lord, did not follow the principle of pleasing himself, but submitted for our salvation to all kinds of humiliations —well described in Ps 68:10. Now if Christ acted thus to save and help us, though we were infinitely inferior to him, we too ought to do the same to help those who are weaker than ourselves. No doubt, it is humiliating for the Strong to humble themselves and live like the Weak. But it is equally true that this kind of humiliation is hallowed by Christ's example, 3, approved of by the Scriptures, 4, and deserves to be blest in prayer, 5 f.

k In particular, 7–12, let the Strong bear in mind the unselfishness of Christ in submitting to circumcision and all it implied, 8*a*, though his mission was not only for Israel, 8*b*, but also for the Gentiles as the Scriptures abundantly prove, 9–12. Christ submitted to circumcision and lived according to the law of Moses in order to work for the greater glory of God among the Israelites as well as among the Gentiles—among the Israelites by making them see the faithfulness of God to his promises ; among the Gentiles by causing them to acknowledge and praise the mercy of God. Thus, by aiming at the greater glory of God in everything rather than by thinking of his own ease and pleasure, Christ overcame the difference between Israelites and Gentiles, a difference much greater than the difference between the Strong and the Weak in Rome. If the Strong follow this example and go the humbler way, making the honour of God their rule as Christ did, then the present trouble between the two parties at Rome will soon pass. In brief : as in Phil 2:5–11 our Lord is described as the model of obedience so in Rom 15:1–13 as the model of all peace-making by unselfishness and charity to the greater glory of God.

l The connexion with what precedes is so close that the beginning of a new paragraph at first must seem more disturbing than helpful. On the other hand, 1–13 could stand by itself without 14:13–23. What binds the passage 1–13 together is—and this explains why it is generally treated as a new paragraph—the new motive on which Paul dwells in this exhortation to peace and unity, *viz.* the example of Christ's unselfishness.

One of the more important points on which commentators disagree in this paragraph concerns the place which the difference between Israelites and Gentiles in 8–12 holds in the main argument. Some assign to it a central place in the discussion by taking Israelites and Gentiles as the true name for the Weak and the Strong in the whole section 14:1–15:13. Others treat it as no more than an illustration of the argument for peace and unity beginning with 15:1.

m 3. Why does St Paul quote a text from OT prophecy rather than facts from NT history to illustrate Christ's self-sacrificing charity ? For a refutation of the answer which sees the reason in Paul's ignorance of or indifference to the historical Christ see Prat II 22 f. ; 154 ff. The true explanation seems to be : (1) the OT text recommended itself as a suitable summary of all the relevant historical facts in our Lord's life ; (2) since a Christian cannot be expected to imitate Christ in everything St Paul by quoting the OT gained the scriptural proof that imitating Christ in this matter is an indisputable duty of every Christian. **5.** ' According to Jesus Christ ' : has been explained as in accordance with Christ's (1) will or precept, (2) Gospel or doctrine, (3) spirit, character or example, (4) union with us. Nr 3 suits the context best, *cf.* 15:3, 7. **7.** ' Wherefore ' = (1) because of the principle stated in 15:1 f. and explained in 3–6 ; or (2) in view of the example of Christ, last mentioned in 5, *cf.* 7*b* ; or (3) for the sake of unity in the Church, stressed in 6. **8 f.** The simplest construction of this difficult sentence is : Christ submitted to circumcision (1) that he might confirm the promises of the fathers, (2) that the Gentiles might glorify God for his mercy. **9–12.** The purpose of the four quotations is to prove the statement of 9*a* from the Scriptures. Though Christ lived like an Israelite, he aimed at and achieved the glory of God among the Gentiles.

XV 14–XVI 27 Conclusion—In the matter of greetings, **863** 16:3–16, 21–24, the conclusion of Rom follows the custom of the time. The rest is peculiar to this epistle. Its chief interest lies in what it tells us about St Paul personally.

Plan. (1) 15:14–21, Explanatory comments to avoid misunderstandings. (2) 15:22–33, The immediate purpose of this letter. (3) 16:1–2, Recommendation of Phoebe. (4) 16:3–16, Greetings. (5) 16:17–20, Warning against heresies. (6) 16:21–24, Greetings. (7) 16:25–27, Concluding sentence.

XV 14–21 A Retrospect with Apologies and Explanations—Paul has come to the end of his letter and he begins the customary conclusion by looking back on what he has written, and to whom he has written. As for the contents : the letter before him has grown far beyond the size of an ordinary letter, and much in it may sound bold and daring when read at Rome. As for his readers : why should he have put all this into a letter to Rome, a place where he had never preached ? Why did he not leave the care of the Romans to the Apostle(s) of Rome ?

Plan. Distinguishing the explanations which St Paul **b** here gives for writing such a letter to Rome will help to analyse the sequence of thought. (1) 14 : This long letter does not imply any criticism of the Christians at Rome. On the contrary, Paul shares the widespread admiration of their strong faith and their exemplary Christian life, *cf.* 1:8. (2) 15 : Bold though the language of this letter may be in parts (*e.g.* 6:12–21 ; 8:9 ; 11:17 ff. ; 13:3 ff., 13 f. ; 14:1–15:13) Paul makes no claim to have said anything new. His intention does not go beyond ' refreshing their memories ' on essential points of Christian doctrine, which is the intention of every Christian preacher. (3) 16 : What he has written he has written as the Apostle and ' the priest ' of the Gentiles in accordance with his particular mission in the Church. (4) 17–19 : Apart from the grace of his office as the Apostle of the Gentiles, however, there is still another reason which he could use to defend the authority assumed in writing such a letter to Rome. But to avoid any impression of self-conceit he will mention this other reason only in passing. It is based on the works he can boast of, his achievements in setting up new missions from Jerusalem to the Adriatic coast (Illyria). (5) 20 f. : What follows in these two verses is not a new point, but merely describes in scriptural language the character of Paul's missionary activity. If looking back on his achievements he speaks with more than usual confidence, it is at all events not the empty boasting of one who had the good fortune of reaping what others had sown. In preaching the Gospel it has been one of his constant principles to go where the name

b of Christ had not as yet been heard of. The numerous missions he can quote to his credit are new foundations.

c **16** is remarkable because of its liturgical (sacrificial) language in three terms : (1) ' that I should be a *priest* of Christ Jesus unto the Gentiles, (2) that I should *sacrifice* in the service of God's gospel, (3) and that *my offering* of the Gentiles should be acceptable, being sanctified in the Holy Spirit ', WV ; *cf.* DV and KNT. The essential point in every explanation is to realize that the sacrificial terms used here are metaphorical, and that therefore this verse cannot be quoted against the existence of a specially consecrated priesthood in the Church when Paul wrote, *cf.* Prat I 342 ff. The difficulties lie in the analysis of the metaphors. How can the conversion of the Gentiles become St Paul's sacrifice ? Cornely works out a solution by introducing the idea of baptism in which every convert dies with Christ and thus may be said to participate in Christ's sacrificial death. Most commentators rightly maintain that the exact method or manner of Paul's offering the Gentiles as his sacrifice is not contemplated in the metaphor of v 16. To bring the Gentile world as a worthy sacrifice to the altar of God is probably all that Paul meant to say. For the same idea *cf.* Is 66:19 f. For an interesting application to the foreign missions see Gore II 180.

17-19 is an involved sentence owing to two intentions in the Apostle's mind : (*a*) to defend his authority, for which purpose he appeals to all he has achieved in spreading the Gospel ; (*b*) to avoid the impression of vainglory for which purpose he transfers all the honour of his achievements to Christ. The main difficulty is the connection of the second negative in 18 ; *cf.* WV against KNT. That appealing to his labours and achievements for the Church is not out of keeping with St Paul's character can be seen from the similar passages, 1 Cor 15:10 ; 2 Cor 11:1-12:18 ; Gal 6:17.

d **22-33 St Paul's Programme for the Immediate Future :** Journey to Jerusalem-Rome-Spain—It is not before he comes to the end of his letter that the Apostle states the special occasion which caused him to write. His work east of the Adriatic Sea is done and he is preparing his long desired missionary journey to Spain. Now, on this journey he hopes to call at Rome. The immediate occasion of this letter, therefore, is Paul's wish to prepare for this visit, 22-24. There has to be, however, a delay on account of a collection from the churches in Macedonia and Greece for the church in Jerusalem. For Paul is determined to be personally present at Jerusalem when this token of communion, goodwill, and gratitude on the part of the Gentiles is handed over to the mother-church in the Holy City, 25-29. At the same time he is under no misapprehension of the dangers such a visit implies. For the majority of the inhabitants of Jerusalem his return will mean the return of an apostate of a particularly dangerous kind, and for many of his own brethren in the faith he is still suspect on account of his battles and victories for the rights of the Gentiles in the church. Nevertheless Paul is determined to go to Jerusalem, but realizing the dangers he asks for prayers at Rome, 30-33.

The special points discussed in larger commentaries on this paragraph are : (1) the Christian community of Rome not St Paul's foundation, *cf.* 20, 24, 28 ; (2) his collection journey to Jerusalem, *cf.* 25-29 ; Act 24:17 ; 1 Cor 16:1-4 ; 2 Cor 8-9 ; Gal 2:10.

e **23 f.** is an anacoluthon which can be remedied with the *textus receptus* by adding the apodosis here given in brackets : ' and having been intent on coming to you for many years [I will now do so] when I make my journey to Spain. For I hope, as I pass . . .' Differently in WV. **24.** ' Spain ' : *cf.* 28 ; the earliest references in Christian literature to St Paul's actual visit to Spain are Clement of Rome, *Cor* 5:6 f. ; *Muratorian Fragment*, l. 35-9. **26** is important for fixing the date when Rom was written. It must have been after 2 Cor 8-9 when the collection for Jerusalem was still in full progress (A.D. 57) and shortly before his journey to Jerusalem, Ac 20:1-21:16. **28.** ' Having

consigned ' = having sealed, which is a metaphor that **863e** can mean many things : *e.g.* (*a*) authenticated = declared genuine, (*b*) completed, (*c*) safely delivered ; *cf.* Lagrange, Boylan. **30-33.** Paul asks for prayers at Rome. For similar requests *cf.* 2 Cor 1:11 ; Eph 6:18 ; Phil 1:19 ; 1 Thess 5:25 ; 2 Thess 3:1 ; Phm 22. **32b.** ' *And with you may have a rest* '.

XVI 1-2 A Note of Introduction for Phoebe—About **f** to finish his letter with greetings to his friends at Rome and from his friends in Greece (Corinth or Cenchreae) Paul remembers first from among the latter a Christian lady named Phoebe. He gives her what may be called a note of introduction. Its purpose is to secure for her the welcome and the help of the Christians at Rome on her arrival. Phoebe too must, therefore, have been preparing for a journey to the capital. About the date and purpose of her journey Paul says nothing. But it is an ancient conjecture that he intended to use her journey as an opportunity for sending his letter by a personal carrier ; *cf.* the subscription in many MSS, Tischendorf, *NT* II (1872) 457.

Phoebe is described by St Paul (*a*) as διάκονος, deaconess or helper in the church of Cenchreae ; and (*b*) as προστάτις, patroness or benefactress of many Christians, Paul himself included. The exact meaning of both titles is disputed. On the one hand, it is certain that the corresponding masculine nouns are official titles—the first signifying the office of deacon in the church, *cf.* Ac 6:1-6 ; and the second signifying the office of a president, patron, or legal representative in Jewish as well as Greek and Roman religious organisations, *cf.* BGDW. On the other hand, the feminine use of these titles is found nowhere else in the NT. Further, the second remains unknown in the organization of the Christian Church during the following centuries. And as for deaconesses the four earliest references that can be quoted are : (*a*) Pliny the Younger, *Epist.* X 96, 8, written *c* A.D. 112 ; (*b*) Didascalia, chh 9 and 16 ed. R. H. Connolly (1929) 88, 146-48 = Apost. Constitutions, ed. Funk II 26, III 12, written *c* 3rd cent. ; (*c*) Apost. Constitutions VIII 28, written *c* 4th cent. ; (*d*) Ps-Ignatius, *Letter to Antioch*, 12:2, written *c* 4th cent. Under these circumstances the less technical interpretation of either description remains at least possible if not more probable, *cf.* Vg, DV, WV, KNT. Phoebe is mentioned in the Roman Martyrology on Sept. 3rd and her praises are sung in a sermon of Chrysostom, *opp.* ed. Montfaucon XII (1735) 352.

3-16 Greetings—Having recommended Phoebe especi- **g** ally, St Paul sends greetings to no less than 26 individual Christians and two households at Rome. The following alphabetical list is meant to simplify the various discussions connected with this paragraph. (1) Ampliatus 8, (2) Andronicus 7, (3) Apelles 10, (4) Aquila 3, (5) Aristobulus (the household of) 10, (6) Asyncritus 14, (7) Epaenetus 5, (8) Hermas 14, (9) Hermes 14, (10) Herodion 11, (11) Julia 15, (12) Junia(s) 7, (13) Mary 6, (14) Narcissus (the household of) 11, (15) Nereus 15, (16) Olympias 15, (17) Patrobas 14, (18) Persis 12, (19) Philologus 15, (20) Phlegon 14, (21) Prisca 3, (22) Rufus 13, (23) Stachys 9, (24) Tryphena 12, (25) Tryphosa 12, (26) Urbanus 9, (27) Mother of Rufus 13, (28) Sister of Nereus 15.

Many of these names are well known from Greek literature : *e.g.* 2.3.5.7 ; others are Latin : 1.4.11.12 (13 ?) 21.22.26 ; the only Hebrew name is 10 and possibly 13. Names that are considered rare are 6.16.17.18. It is not necessary to think that Paul knew personally all those to whom he sends special greetings. The names and importance of some can have been known to him from hearsay : *e.g.* (1?) 3.5.6.8.9.10.14. 15.16.17.20 (23 ?) 24.25 (26 ?). The number of women in this list has often been commented on. They are eight or nine apart from those that may be included in the two households 5.14 : *viz.* 11 (12 ?) 13.18.21. 24.25.27.28. Commentators differ as to the number of groups = house-churches, that can be distinguished in this list. Some distinguish three : (1) the house-church of Prisca and Aquila, 3-5*a*, with its members

863g in 5*b*–13 ; (2) the house-church of Asyncritus, etc. 14 ; and (3) that of Philologus, etc. 15. Sickenberger distinguishes four groups : 3–5*a*, 5*b*–13, 14, 15. These house-churches are regarded as the beginning of the Christian parish-organization, *cf.* Ac 12:12 ; Col 4:15 ; Phm 2. The religious interest of this list does not lie in the identification of the persons on which most modern commentaries concentrate but in the indisputable evidence which they give of the personal and human side in St Paul's missionary activity. The mention of so many names in a town which Paul had never visited proves an extraordinary interest in personal contacts. The later history of these names in Christian literature can be traced by means of dictionaries to the NT, dictionaries of Saints, indices to the NT apocrypha, and the Roman Martyrology. Cornely 775 gives as mentioned in the Roman Martyrology 1.5.6.8.10.14.17.19.20.22.23.24.25.26. In addition to these the Greek Menology commemorates 2.3.7.12.15.

h The attempts of archaeologists to identify the names of 3–15 concentrate on the inscriptions of the Roman columbaria from the 1st cent. Nearly all have been found there. But the discovery of a name in a sepulchral inscription does not reveal the identity of the person. The Ampliatus whose name is inscribed over a cell in the Domitilla Catacomb need not be the Ampliatus of Rom 16:8. Whether there is a historical connexion between the house of Prisca, 3, and the Church of Sta Prisca on the Aventine, between Nereus, 15, and the Church SS Nereo ed Achille is disputed. The same uncertainty surrounds the conjectures of Lightfoot (on Phil 4:22, ed. 1888, 171–8) concerning the identification of Aristobulus, 10, with the grandson of Herod the Great, the brother of Agrippa I ; and the identification of Narcissus, 11, with the secretary of the emperor Claudius. Still archaeology has contributed to the study of this chapter by proving the occurrence of these names at Rome in that time.

Is Rom 16:3–15 part of a letter to Ephesus ? The theory that it was so originally is based mainly on the following argument. Paul lived at Ephesus for more than two years, Ac 19:8–10. Writing to Ephesus, therefore, one may well expect him to remember a great number of Christians personally, whilst it is difficult to imagine how he could know so many at Rome where he had never been. *Cf.* B. Gut 380 ff. ; Lagrange 370 ff. ; N.P. Williams 447 f. ; Boylan XVIII–XXII.

i 17–20 Warning against Heresies—This is a digression which may have been caused by the reference to ' all the churches ' in 16. If so, this mere reference to ' all the churches ' was enough to call to Paul's mind the persistent attempts to distort the true doctrine of the Gospel which he had everywhere to fight, *cf.* 2 Tim 3.

What heretics the Apostle had in mind the text does not say. The charges are quite general. Paul accuses them (1) of battening on doctrinal novelties, 17, (2) of material self-interest, 18*a*, and (3) of deceitful oratory, 18*b*. Commentators think of Judaism as in Gal 3:1 or of Antinomianism as in Rom 3:8 ; 6:1 ; Phil 3:17–21. Whether these false teachers were already at work in Rome or are here considered merely as a possible future danger is another question on which commentators differ, *cf.* SH and Lagrange. On the whole it does not seem likely that Paul would leave the treatment of an immediate danger to a parenthesis in the conclusion of his letter, *cf.* 16:19.

j 21–24 Greetings from Corinth—These greetings from Paul's companions continue the greetings from ' all the churches ' in 16. These companions listed in alphabetical order are : (1) Erastus 23, (2) Gaius 23, (3) Jason 21, (4) Lucius 21, (5) Quartus 23, (6) Sosipater 21, (7) Tertius 22, (8) Timothy 21.

All these names with the exception of 5 and 7 occur in Ac or elsewhere in the Pauline epistles. Two or possible three, 2 (6 ?) 8, are mentioned in Ac 20:4 as Paul's companions on his collection journey from Corinth to Troas *via* Macedonia. But the same name need not mean identity of person. The only exception

is Timothy 21. All are agreed that he is the Timothy whose history we can follow from his joining St Paul at Lystra, *c* A.D. 50 (Ac 16:1) to his episcopacy at Ephesus, *c* A.D. 65 (1 Tim 1:3 ; 2 Tim 4:21).

25–27 Concluding Sentence—Paul finishes not as is his custom with good wishes but with a doxology similar to 11:33–36 ; Gal 1:5 ; Eph 3:21 ; Phil 4:20 ; 1 Tim 1:17 ; *cf.* also Heb 13:20 f. ; Jude 24 f. ; Clem. Rom., *Cor* 65:2 ; *Martyrdom of Polycarp* 22:3. Of all these doxologies, however, 25–27 is the most elaborate. Nearly all the main points of the whole letter seem to be gathered here in one powerful finale : the power of God unto salvation ; the revelation of God's plan of salvation in the Gospel ; salvation by faith in Jesus Christ ; the Christian salvation offered to all ; the Apostle's divine mission ; the continuity with the OT. As the Greek text stands in the modern critical editions (with ᾧ in 27) the whole epistle ends in an untranslatable anacoluthon. The effect in the Greek text, however, is a threefold doxology : (*a*) to God the Almighty, 25 f. ; (*b*) to God the All-Wise, 27*a* ; (*c*) to Jesus Christ, 27*b*. Differently WV.

The following analysis may be helpful in tracing the somewhat complicated sequence of thought.

Glory be to God

(I) Who is able to strengthen you [so as to persevere] 25 :
    (1) in accordance with my Gospel
    (2) which is the same as the preaching of Christ,
    (3) which in turn is the same as the revelation of a (divine) mystery.

(II) This mystery is [God's plan of man's salvation] :
    (4) which was veiled in silence for eternal ages 25,
    (5) which however has now become manifest [through the Incarnation] 26,
    (6) and which has [already] been promulgated by the Apostles 26.

(III) This promulgation means 26 :
    (7) that it has been preached to the Gentiles
    (8) for the purpose of making them obedient to the faith = Gospel
    (9) in accordance with a command from God the Eternal,
    (10) with the help of [the evidence from] the prophetical writings [of the OT].

The order of (7)–(10) is slightly different from that in the text, 26. Points (1)–(3) can be taken as synonymous, each explained by that which follows ; (4)–(6) mark the three main stages in the history of salvation ; (7)–(10) stress four major features in the last and present state of that history, *i.e.* the promulgation of God's salvation. These four features are : (7) its universality, (8) salvation by faith in Jesus Christ, (9) the Apostle's mission from God, (10) its connexion with the OT. Vg = DV create two unnecessary difficulties (i) by putting 26 in brackets, and (ii) by obscuring the coordination of the three relative clauses in 25 f., (4)–(6) : the mystery (*a*) which was kept secret, (*b*) but which has now been made manifest, (*c*) and which has been made known.

The genuineness and textual history of 25–27 have been the subject of much dispute. The difficulty arises from the differences in the MSS. A few omit the passage completely : D* (Claromontanus) F*gr* (Augiensis), G (Boernerianus). A number of MSS have the passage after 14:23 : *c* 200 minuscules, mainly von Soden's K = Antiochian recension of Lucianus. The oldest MSS as well as our modern critical editions place it after 16:23 : ℵ (Sinaiticus) B (Vaticanus) C (Ephraemi rescriptus), etc. A few have it twice, after 14:23 and after 16:23 : A (Alexandrinus) P (Porphyrianus), etc. The confusion is nowadays generally traced back to the influence of Marcion who according to Origen-Rufinus X 43 interfered with the text of Rom 15–16 as early as the 2nd cent. ; *cf.* Lagrange 380–6 ; Boylan 256–61 ; Lietzmann 131 ; § 844*m*.

1 and 2 CORINTHIANS

By W. REES

a Bibliography for 1 and 2 Corinthians—Among earlier commentaries the best are those of St John Chrysostom (English trans. in Oxford Library of the Fathers) and St Thomas Aquinas (no English translation). Both are still most valuable for their profound insight into St Paul's meaning. Among modern Catholic commentaries the recent French ones on both epistles by Allo (1934 and 1937) are the fullest and best, a monument of up-to-date learning. There is a very good shorter French commentary by Huby. In English the best is that of Cardinal MacRory, both epistles in one volume 1935³. Among non-Catholic commentaries the fullest and ablest are those in the ICC: Ep I by Robertson and Plummer 1911 and Ep II by Plummer 1915. Menzies has a good commentary on the Second Epistle, 1912, and Goudge has commentaries on 1 and 2 Cor (1899).

b In connexion with the special problems of the Second Epistle the best defences of the 'Kennedy theory' are J. H. Kennedy's own book *The Second and Third Epistles of St Paul to the Corinthians* (1900) and Kirsopp Lake's *Earlier Epistles of St Paul* (1911) pp 112–227. Plummer adopts the theory in its fullest form. Allo, Goudge and Menzies accept it in a moderate form, while MacRory rejects it altogether.

c Of more general works we may mention F. Prat: *The Theology of St Paul* [Eng. trans. 1926–7] above all. Other works will be found in the list given in the article 'The Life of St Paul', § 663a.

1 CORINTHIANS

INTRODUCTION

d A. The City of Corinth—Corinth occupied the site of an old Greek city, famous for its commerce, its pottery and fine bronze work, and notorious for its luxury and immorality. But this city had been destroyed and after a century of desolation a new Roman city had been founded there. It was a 'colonia' deliberately planted by the Roman government to serve as an outpost of Roman influence. It was not till the following century that its people began to regard themselves as the heirs of the Greek city. In Paul's time they still thought of themselves as Romans. **e** Corinth was not a settlement of veteran soldiers like Philippi and Lystra, but of civilians, and a considerable proportion of them are said to have been emancipated slaves or their sons, mainly of Italian origin. The descendants of these men now formed the core of the population, a civic aristocracy, proud of the name of Romans, and still largely imbued with Italian tradition and sentiment. Only Roman citizens could be citizens of Corinth, and the official language was Latin. No doubt a number of Greeks and Asiatics had settled at Corinth by Paul's time, but these for the most part would be outside the citizen-body, and in an inferior position in many ways. The Roman element was still dominant, and although the non-citizens might include some very immoral sections, Corinth was probably one of the more wholesome of the cities in which Paul preached, certainly superior in this respect to Antioch, and very likely to Tarsus and Ephesus also. We have no right to identify Roman Corinth with the vanished Greek city. There is no evidence whatever that the **864e** Roman colonists had revived the gross immorality formerly connected with the worship of Aphrodite at Corinth.

The prosperity of Corinth depended on its control of **f** the Isthmus, across which merchandise and even small ships were frequently being transported. The city profited also by the Isthmian Games, held every two years, which attracted a greater concourse than even Olympia. The city was now the capital of the province of Achaia, the seat of the Roman governor. Corinth was not actually on the Isthmus but a few miles southwest of it, finely situated on a terraced slope two miles from the Corinthian Gulf, and overshadowed by the steep rocky summit of Acrocorinthus (1,880 feet) on which its citadel had once stood. The great central square of the city and some newly planned straight streets had now been adorned with colonnades. A basilica or city hall had been built near the square, as its foundations show—it was probably the place where Paul had appeared before Gallio (Ac 18:12). The great temple of Apollo, of which some pillars are still standing, was five or six centuries old when Paul saw it.

There seems to have been a fair number of Jews living **g** at Corinth. An inscription which stood over the entrance to a synagogue is so rudely lettered that it points to a poor and ignorant community, but perhaps this was not the only synagogue. In any case most of the Jews would not be citizens of Corinth and seem to have been unpopular, as we should expect in a city of Roman traditions. Corinth was the first place west of Antioch where the Jews tried and failed to interrupt Paul's work.

B. The Corinthian Church: Foundation, Crisis, h Pacification—Our only sources of knowledge are Ac 18; 19:21; 20:1–3; Rom 15:23–26; 16:1–2, 21–23, and the two epistles. Paul first arrived at Corinth in A.D. 50 or possibly in 49, § 676f. He spent at least eighteen months there, and for most of the time Silas and Timothy were with him. He gained converts first among Jews and half-proselytes and later among the pagans. In general they seem to have been non-citizens and of humble position, although one name (Titius Justus) suggests a few citizens too. The Jews were very hostile but they had not sufficient influence either with the city council or with the populace to raise effective obstacles. Their appeal to the proconsul Gallio was a failure, Ac 18:12 ff. Paul departed probably towards the end of 51 and perhaps did not see Corinth again for something like four years, but he may have paid a short visit in the intervening time, which he spent chiefly at Ephesus, not very far away by sea.

Within a year of his departure Apollos arrived at **i** Corinth, Ac 18:27. He not only kept Paul's converts together but, having been brought up in Alexandria, where he had received a more thoroughly Greek education than Paul, he gained new converts, both Jewish and pagan, from among men of similar education. After perhaps a year at Corinth, Apollos joined Paul at Ephesus. Later some close associates of St Peter came and made some converts at Corinth. Possibly Peter himself paid a short visit. During the next year

864i or two Corinth received a much longer visit from some Jewish Christians from Palestine who had once been zealous missionaries but had now deteriorated. Paul calls them 'false apostles' (2 Cor 11:13) and it will be convenient to adopt this name for them. Boasting of a close connexion with the original Twelve Apostles, they made it their chief aim to undermine Paul's influence. They seem to have also tolerated a dangerous laxity in the relation of Christians to paganism, and the force of their example would naturally encourage other sections of the church to self-assertion and extravagance. Their influence lowered the whole spiritual level of a promising church. Disturbing rumours about Corinth reached Paul at Ephesus, and at last (in the spring of some year which may be anything from 54 to 57) three leading Corinthian Christians crossed the sea to him. They brought a letter from the loyal Corinthians, which asked for advice on several subjects including the relations of Christians to pagans. The visitors gave Paul a full account of the False Apostles and they probably urged him to come to Corinth at once.

j Paul however seems to have decided to postpone a direct clash with the False Apostles till he had secured the loyalty of a number of doubtful and wavering Christians who must be given some time for reflexion. He therefore wrote our First Epistle : he answers the questions in their letter, severely rebukes several sections of Christians for various faults, and exerts all his eloquence and tenderness to win back the hesitating, but the persons who were the main cause of the troubles are mentioned only twice and then in a reserved manner. At Corinth this letter was backed up by Paul's tried assistant Titus. It was successful. Many who had been confused by the False Apostles returned to their allegiance to Paul. But a minority remained defiant. On hearing the result of his letter, Paul, knowing that he now had the support of the majority, decided that the time had come to speak more plainly. He therefore wrote our Second Epistle, in which he first expressed his joy at the reconciliation, revealing the distress which the crisis had caused him, and then clearly denounced and condemned the False Apostles, and gave a last warning to their followers. Some time later he arrived at Corinth and spent three months there. He may have had to excommunicate some rebellious members, but on the whole the church was restored to peace and order.

This seems to be the most probable account of the crisis at Corinth. Different views are held by many modern scholars, and these will be considered later.

865a C. The False Apostles : (1) Who and what they were —The False Apostles and their party are the main subject of the last chapters of the Second Epistle. It seems practically certain however that they had been active at Corinth for some time before the First Epistle was written. This is the view of Goudge, Plummer, and others, Briefly the evidence for it is : 1. The interval between the epistles (probably well under six months) seems too short for a new trouble of so serious a kind to have arisen. 2. The hostile party mentioned in Ep 1 chh 4 and 9 have many points in common with that of Ep 2. Both deny Paul's equality with the Twelve (1 Cor 9:1–3 ; 2 Cor 11:5 ; 12:11–12) and both claim a superior kind of eloquence or style (1 Cor 4:19 ; 2 Cor 10:10 ; 11:6). 3. The bitter and sarcastic tone in which Paul refers to his opponents in Ep 1 is very like that used in Ep 2 (see Comm. on 1 Cor 4:1 ; 9:1). 4. If the party of 1 Cor 4 and 9 is not identical with that of 2 Cor 10–13, who are they? Can we believe that they suddenly disappeared and that another party, strongly resembling them, as suddenly arose?

b We therefore conclude that the enemies whom Paul speaks of in 1 Cor 4 and 9 are none other than the False Apostles of Ep 2. The tone of these two chapters shows how seriously he thought of them, and they must have been in his thoughts all through Ep 1. Therefore

this is the best place to give a sketch of them, based on **86** indications given in both epistles.

They were Jews and claimed to be of the purest Jewish **c** stock, Palestinians and probably Aramaic-speakers (2 Cor 11:22). They may have been among the early converts at Jerusalem, and at one time they had done some work as Christian missionaries (2 Cor 11:23) and had suffered for their faith. Very likely they were personally known to some of the Twelve, may once have been highly esteemed by these, and may have received letters of recommendation from them (2 Cor 3:1). But in the course of fifteen or twenty years they had greatly deteriorated. Fervour and even honesty had gone, and they were now little better than adventurers, trading on their former reputation.

It has often been thought that they were Judaizers, but **d** there seems to be no good ground for this view. It is true they boasted of their Jewish descent, but so did St Paul. If they were Judaizers, we should have expected the chief points at issue between Paul and the Judaizers (circumcision, ceremonial purity, etc.) to be much more plainly referred to. But they are hardly given a passing allusion (*e.g.* 1 Cor 7:19 ; 9:20) and in a matter-of-fact tone. One longish passage might be equally well directed against Judaizers or Jews, 2 Cor 3:6–18. There is no hint that Paul had the False Apostles in mind when he wrote it, and the calmness of its tone is not favourable to that idea.

Others have suggested that they were 'liberal' Jews, **e** men who had gone too far in seeking compromise with paganism. (See *e.g.* Lake : *Early Epistles*, p 226.) Their probable laxity towards pagan rites and even immorality (see below) fits in with such a view, although such Jews indeed are more commonly found among the Dispersion, whereas the False Apostles seem to have come from Palestine [2 Cor 11:22.] While there are few signs of any tangible false doctrine, yet the use of certain catchwords : 'knowledge', 'liberty' and the phrase : 'All things are lawful' harmonizes with the pretension to a false liberalism which was doubtless a matter of practice rather than theory. Such a practical 'liberalism', based on pure self-interest, must have been common among Jews connected with the Herodian princes and their courts (A. H. M. Jones : *The Herods of Judaea*, p 212).

Paul does not explicitly accuse them of encouraging **f** laxity, but there are strong arguments for connecting them with this fault : (1) There are only two evils which are mentioned at some length in *both* epistles : (*a*) The intrigues of the False Apostles, (*b*) The danger rising from too close association with pagans (1 Cor 8 and 10, and 2 Cor 6:14–7:1). This implies some connexion between the two evils. The association between pagan rites and immorality, though not specially close at Corinth, was always a fact (1 Cor 5:11 ; 10:8). (2) In the First Epistle the ninth **g** chapter, which certainly refers to the False Apostles, is abruptly inserted in the middle of the section on the dangers of intercourse with pagans, an insertion which appears much less surprising if we suppose a connexion between the two subject-matters.

Many believe that the party formed by the False Apostles at Corinth called itself the 'Christ Party'. This view is based on certain interpretations of 1 Cor 1:12 and 2 Cor 10:7. But it is very doubtful if there existed any party calling itself the Christ party (see last note on 1 Cor 1:12), and even if there was one, its identification with that of the False Apostles would be very far from proved by 2 Cor 10:7 which can be quite naturally interpreted without reference to such a party.

It is very unlikely that the False Apostles headed the party which over-rated spiritual gifts, 1 Cor chh 12–14. Paul's tone to this party lacks the bitterness of his references to the False Apostles.

(2) Their Intrigues at Corinth—We may suppose that **h** these persons on their arrival received an enthusiastic welcome owing to what was known about their early missionary work and their connexion with the Twelve

h (from some of whom they may have produced old letters of recommendation), and that they established themselves as honoured visitors without at first showing any ill-feeling towards Paul. But before long they began to form a party of their own, using the double method of self-praise and disparagement of St Paul. They boasted of their acquaintance with the Twelve, dating perhaps from a time before Paul's conversion, and of their labours and sufferings for the gospel. In all this there may have been a considerable amount of truth. On the strength of these merits they assumed an imperious and arrogant manner very different from

i Paul's. As they found that Paul had refused to be supported by the Christians, they thought it wise to pretend to do the same (2 Cor 11:12 note) but they managed to extract contributions from the Corinthians on some excuse or other (*ibid.* 20). They claimed the title of apostles (*ibid.* 13) but not in the full sense in which it was given to the Twelve. They said that they themselves and also Paul, Barnabas, etc., belonged to an inferior class of apostles ; that only the Twelve were entitled to live at the cost of the Church (1 Cor 9:6), and Paul, by refusing to do so, admitted that he was not on an equality with the Twelve (2 Cor 11:5 ; 12:11). This device by which they turned Paul's self-denial into a weapon against him is a good specimen of their mean cunning. They said that Paul had nevertheless contrived to make money from the Corinthians (2 Cor 12:16–18) by getting his assistants to take presents. They said Paul had no dignity, and they ridiculed his delivery and perhaps his language also (2 Cor 10:10). They very likely called him ignorant, and perhaps they even said he was crazy (2 Cor 5:13). Although they did not want to see Paul at Corinth, yet they may have made the postponement of his visit an occasion to accuse him of apathy (1 Cor 4:19) as they on a further postponement accused him of fickleness (2 Cor 1:17).

a Many of these slanders were no doubt put out stealthily so that it was difficult to trace their authors. The simpler Corinthians, remembering the past record of the visitors, might long fail to penetrate their true character and designs. They would become uneasy and perplexed, and probably their anxious desire that Paul should in future accept maintenance from the Church (2 Cor 11:7 f. ; 12:14) was due to the calumnies about his inferiority. If the False Apostles did, as seems likely, countenance an easier intercourse with pagans, they would soon gain many followers among those Christians who for prudential or social reasons were loth to cut themselves off entirely from paganism (see Comm. on 1 Cor 8:1).

b The Corinthian Church was now grievously divided, but the serious division was into two parties only—the followers of the False Apostles and those who were at heart loyal to Paul. A large number of scholars (probably a majority) including those who believe that the False Apostles were Judaizers, are agreed on this point. Few think that the parties of Apollos and Peter were a grave danger to unity, nor was the hypothetical 'Christ party' *unless* this party was identical with that of the False Apostles. Between the two important parties there seem to have been many wavering and confused Christians.

c Perhaps the False Apostles directly encouraged some smaller groups who feared Paul's disapproval. But even without such encouragement, all sorts of unwholesome tendencies would naturally gather momentum as soon as it was realized that Paul's authority and that of the presbyters he had appointed were being undermined. Of this kind were the misuse of the gift of tongues, and the erroneous teaching about the Resurrection and about marriage. The same atmosphere would cause an increase of offences against chastity.

d **D. Other Troubles at Corinth**—Though eclipsed by the plots of the False Apostles, the other troubles were no doubt grave in themselves, as St Paul's language

proves. The danger of compromising Christian truth **866d** by some sort of tolerance of pagan religious rites (whether or not it was aggravated by the action of the visitors) was an urgent one, owing to the worldly advantages which tolerance would secure (see Comm. on 1 Cor 8). The increase of unchastity was another serious matter. Paul opens this subject by speaking of the incestuous marriage and the failure of the church authorities to pronounce excommunication (5, 1). Other passages (1 Cor 5:10–13 ; 6:9–20 ; 10:8 ; 2 Cor 7:1 ; 12:21) indicate that the evil was widespread and obstinate. It was terribly easy for men who had once been pagans and still lived among pagans to fall away from the higher Christian standard after the bonds of discipline had once been relaxed. (See Comm. on 6:12–20 and 7:1.)

The bad example set by the visitors had probably **e** given an impetus to party-spirit in many forms. It is seen not only among the parties expressly mentioned by Paul (1:12) but in a still more odious shape at the very gatherings which preceded the Mass, when the congregation was split up into a number of exclusive circles, the plainest sign of the ruin of Christian charity. (See Comm. on 1:12 and 11:21.)

Corinth had received an abundance of those extraordinary spiritual gifts which God bestowed on the earliest Christians to enable them to gain converts and to weld them together into one body. A number of Corinthian Christians had been particularly fascinated by the miraculous power of speaking new languages, and had made it a regular and disproportionate part of Christian worship (a use for which it was never intended), till it had become a burden and a nuisance to the general body of Christians. (See introd. to ch 12 and ch 14.)

False ideas about the Resurrection had appeared, **f** based probably on Greek popular or learned notions about matter and the body, and leading to denial of the resurrection of the body, and apparently opening the door, in the case of some minds, to doubts about immortality itself. (See introd. to ch 15.)

E. Sequence of Events leading up to the First Epistle g —The epistle was written in March or April (1 Cor 16:8). Perhaps as far back as the summer before, Paul had very likely promised to visit Corinth and all his churches in Greece for the sake of the collection for the Jerusalem Christians.

Some time during the autumn or winter he sent Timothy and Erastus to Macedonia probably in connexion with this collection, Ac 19:21–22.

About the same time or a little later he wrote to the **h** Corinthians a letter which has not been preserved, 1 Cor 5:9. In it he asked them to help in the collection and made known a definite plan for his visit : in the spring he would sail directly across to Corinth, then visit Macedonia and return to Corinth (2 Cor 1:15-16). He had heard of Corinthian Christians lapsing into grave sins, and asked the faithful to break off association with these, 1 Cor 5:9-11.

Probably towards the end of winter he had news of **i** Corinth from 'Chloe's people' (1 Cor 1:11) either by letter or word of mouth. He now heard of the serious division caused by the intrigues of the False Apostles, and of other signs of party-spirit. He seems to have taken no immediate action—perhaps the news was confused or incomplete.

At the beginning of spring, as it seems, the three visitors from Corinth arrived at Ephesus to see him (1 Cor 16:17), sent by the loyal Corinthians who had now reached a state of great distress and alarm. They brought a letter from the church, but for some good reason the chief matter which they wished to lay before him (the mischief which the False Apostles were doing) was communicated to Paul by word of mouth.

Other grave matters raised orally by the visitors were : **867a** (*a*) The failure of the church authorities to deal firmly with the case of incestuous marriage, 5:1–8 ;

1 CORINTHIANS

867a (*b*) uncharitable conduct of some group or groups at the Lord's Supper, 11:17–34 ; (*c*) false teaching about the Resurrection, ch 15.

b We can make a plausible guess at some of the contents of the letter which the visitors brought, for in seven passages in the First Epistle Paul's expressions seem to show that he was replying to questions raised in that letter. Two of these subjects are treated at great length : (*a*) the question of eating food which had been offered to pagan gods—this involved the whole topic of social intercourse between Christian and pagan (chh 8–10) ; (*b*) the right use of extraordinary spiritual gifts, especially the gift of speaking strange languages **c** (chh 12–14). The five other points receive less space. (*c*) They asked for clearer directions about intercourse with notorious sinners (5:9–13) and they asked four questions connected with marriage : (*d*) about some false notion that marriage was sinful (7:1–7) ; (*e*) about the best conduct for converts whose wives or husbands remained pagans (7:8–16) ; (*f*) whether a father should choose marriage or celibacy for his daughters (7:25–38) ; (*g*) whether widows were free to marry again (7:39–40). Finally the letter seems to have asked him to send Apollos over to Corinth (16:12) —no doubt as an alternative to an immediate visit from Paul himself.

d F. The Composition of the First Epistle—St Paul had now before him a full and reliable picture of conditions at Corinth. The problems he had to deal with fell into three groups : (1) The plot of the False Apostles, whose activities have been described (C 1.) This was by far the worst problem. (2) The other troubles laid before him orally by the visitors : the incest, the disorders at the Lord's Supper, and the errors about the Resurrection. (3). The matters contained in the letter from Corinth, especially intercourse with pagans and the use of the ' gift of tongues ', etc.

e To us it may well seem that the natural course would have been to denounce the False Apostles plainly and immediately, either at Corinth or by letter. But Paul decided otherwise. He again postponed his visit (1 Cor 16:5–6 ; 2 Cor 1:15 ff., see notes). He did indeed write at once (our First Epistle) and sent Titus to Corinth, but the letter makes little direct mention of the False Apostles—his plain denunciation was postponed to the Second Epistle, written perhaps three months later. We must believe that Paul had strong reasons for this mode of action. Two possible reasons may be suggested : (1) Perhaps the False Apostles were such accomplished hypocrites that even now Paul was not convinced that the disaffection was due chiefly to them. He was not a suspicious or jealous man—his cordial acceptance of Apollos's work at Corinth is itself a proof of that, and *cf.* Phil 1:15–18. He may have decided to wait for Titus's report before **f** believing the worst about these men (2) It is more likely however that he was aware of their true character, and that his delaying policy was due to that almost limitless patience which was as much a part of him as his fiery energy. He suspected that many Corinthians had erred from thoughtlessness and ignorance and were still loyal to himself at heart. It would be dangerous to force them at once to decide on the purely personal issue. It would be wiser to test their obedience on some matters of principle first, and to do this by letter in order to give time for reflexion and thus to lead them back quietly to their former attachment to himself. (See notes on 2 Cor 1:23 ; 7:12 ; 13:10.)

g The First Epistle therefore deals frankly with all the subjects of the second and third groups, but is reserved about the first. The points raised in the letter from Corinth are treated in the middle portion, while the first and last portions are about the subjects reported by the three visitors. Like the Epistle to the Galatians, it is essentially a letter of reprimand. On at least eight topics he condemns the Corinthians or certain sections of them. His tone is that of an offended father, often stern, sometimes bitter or sarcastic. But **86** he intersperses sentences of tenderness and humility, and several passages of his most moving eloquence. His purpose was not only to test their obedience but also to bring back before them the living image of himself which had been blurred by long absence and calumny ; he wanted both to regain his authority and to re-awaken their dormant affection and devotion ; he desired, as he expressed it later, ' that your zeal for me might be made manifest *to yourselves* ' (2 Cor 7:12, see note). In two passages only it is clear that he refers to the False Apostles (chh 4 and 9). Did these vehement words burst from him in spite of himself contrary to his intention ? We cannot tell, but we can well believe that they were written ' out of much affliction and anguish of heart . . . with many tears ' (2 Cor 2:4).

As Apollos was unable to go to Corinth, his first idea **h** was to ask Timothy, who was then in Macedonia, to go on there (4:17 ; 16:10), but Titus, an older and more experienced assistant, seems to have arrived at Ephesus unexpectedly after the letter was finished, and it was he who actually went as Paul's deputy, either with the three Corinthians or soon after them. Timothy, as far as we know, never came to Corinth till he accompanied Paul there later in the year.

G. Value of the Epistle—Certain passages in the **86** epistle, above all chh 13 and 15, are probably, to the average man, the most familiar things in all St Paul's writings, and well-known phrases meet us everywhere. For its *variety* of precious matter it is surely unequalled among all the letters, because besides its doctrinal and spiritual value it is a most important historical document.

As regards **doctrine,** it contains St Paul's fullest ex- **b** position of the organic unity of Christ's church as his mystical body (ch 12), a subject which appears under other aspects in many places. It also has his fullest passages on the Resurrection (ch 15), on the Holy Eucharist (11:17–34) and on Christian chastity (chh 6 and 7). The supernatural character of the whole Christian religion, founded and maintained by superior Divine wisdom and strength, is insisted on at the beginning (1:18–3:2).

To the ordinary Catholic reader the letter holds out **c** **spiritual** and devotional treasures of the highest kind. First of all, there are the grand outstanding passages— on the wisdom of the Cross (1:18–2:8), Apostolic renunciation (4:9–14), the foundation of chastity (6:15–20), detachment from the world (7:29–32), consideration for weaker Christians (8:11–13 and 9:19–22), charity (13) the resurrection (15:35–58). Although Paul wrote to meet temporary emergencies which are only half understood by us, he dealt with them in the light of eternal principles, so that his words outlast their occasion. He solves every passing problem by looking to Christ and considering the union of the soul to him. Besides these longer passages, **d** nearly all sections of the letter frequently contain weighty and profound sentences, *e.g.* to take a page at random : ' All things are yours ' (3:21), ' he that judgeth me is the Lord ' (4:4), ' What hast thou that thou hast not received " (4:7), etc. A great part of the spiritual value of the epistle comes from its revelation of the author's personality, his wonderful union of tenderness and indomitable courage, of practical sense and high speculation. In this epistle there is one outstanding passage (9:14–27) and some others of note (2:1–6 ; 3:3–8 ; 4:14–21 ; 14:17–19 ; 16:15–18). But every chapter and every section of it bears the mark of its writer—those trumpet-notes, as St John Chrysostom calls them—down to the very last sentences, than which nothing is more characteristic.

As a **historical** document it is more valuable than any **e** other epistle in the New Testament, for none of the others give us so much material for forming a picture of a Christian church in the Apostolic age, at a time of crisis, it is true, but such crises could not have been

3e uncommon. We see here not only the difficulties which we hear of elsewhere (internal rivalries, external temptations, invasions of false doctrine, etc.) but better than anywhere else we see the more prosaic troubles—correction of refractory members, social intercourse with pagans, marriage problems, irreverence at services, questions of dress, control of thoughtless devotees, etc. The view of this unmanageable material is in itself a proof of the superhuman power which the Apostles wielded.

f **H. Short Synopsis—1:1-9** Salutation and Thanksgiving. **1:10-4:21.** The evil of party-division. This includes the description of the true and false wisdom (1:18–3:4), a section on the true function of Christian teachers (3:5–23) and a direct complaint about the False Apostles (ch 4). **Chh 5-7.** Matters connected with the relations of the sexes. This begins with his complaint about the case of incest (ch 5), followed by a digression on litigation among Christians (6:1–11). Then 6:12-20 gives the basic teaching on chastity. Ch 7 deals with three questions about marriage: its lawfulness (1–7), relations between a convert and a pagan wife or husband (8–24), and the marriage of daughters (25–40).

g **Chh 8-11:1.** The problem of social intercourse between Christians and pagans, arising from the question of the lawfulness of eating food offered to pagan gods. Ch 8 shows how this must be solved in the light of the Christian law of charity. This is illustrated by reference to Paul's own example (ch 9); then the danger of presumption is illustrated from Old Testament history (10:1–13). Detailed instruction for conduct, based on these two considerations, are then given (10:14–11:1). **11:2-16.** Women are to veil their heads at prayers. **11:17-34.** He condemns the selfishness, party-spirit and irreverence shown at the suppers preceding the Mass.

h **Chh 12-14.** The over-estimation of certain spiritual gifts, especially the gift of languages. Ch 12 teaches that all the gifts are from God and each one has its place, but only a limited place, in the church. Charity is superior to the rest for it is eternal (ch 13). Ch 14 condemns the way in which the Corinthians have misused the gift of languages and lays down rules for its public use.

Ch 15. The resurrection of the body. He gives the evidence for Christ's resurrection (1–11) and the proof of the resurrection of Christians drawn from it (12–34). He then draws some conclusions about the nature of the resurrection body (35–58).

Ch 16. Brief directions about several matters, especially the collection for Jerusalem (1–4), his coming visit to Corinth (5–9) and the three visitors from Corinth (15–18). Then come his last greetings.

COMMENTARY

89a **I 1-3 Salutation—1.** 'Called', etc.: lit. 'a called apostle'—an apostle appointed by Christ. Elsewhere the phrase occurs only in Rom 1:1. But *cf.* Gal 1:1. He insists on the Divine commission which placed him on a level with the Twelve (*cf.* 2 Cor 11:5; 12:11) not in the same class as Barnabas, etc., still less in the same class as the False Apostles at Corinth. 'Sosthenes': he is inscribed here as nominal joint author of the letter, as Timothy is in the Second Epistle. A Corinthian Jew named Sosthenes had once been one of Paul's chief enemies at Corinth (Ac 18:17). He may have been converted and followed Paul to Ephesus, but we cannot tell: the name was common. **2.** 'Called to be saints': lit. 'holy men called (by God)'. Paul's usual term for Christians is 'holy men' for *Christians* was not yet accepted. The *call* means conversion. See note on v 24. 'That invoke, etc.': *'That invoke in any place the name of our Lord Jesus Christ, their Lord and ours'*.

b **4-9 Thanksgiving for God's Favours to the Corinthians**

—He begins with a few cheerful words, so as not **869b** to start the letter with fault-finding. These words seem to show that he had good hopes of regaining the loyalty of a large proportion of the Corinthians—God's rich blessings to Corinth would surely not be in vain. **4.** 'For you', probably means 'about you'. 'Utterance', *i.e.* power of expression, eloquence. **6-7.** All that had been said to them about Christ (by Paul and others) had been proved true among them by various miraculous signs, such as those spoken of in ch 12—these are the 'graces' mentioned here. **7.** 'Manifestation': the Second Coming of Christ (see 7:26). The thought that this *might* happen very soon was vividly present to the minds of early Christians. **8.** 'Confirm', etc.: '*Make you steadfast unceasingly so as to stand faultless in the day, etc.*' **9.** 'Fellowship', etc.: '*To share the society of his Son*' or '*into union with his Son*'.

I 10-IV 21 The Party Divisions at Corinth— **c** This is the first large section of the letter, setting forth Paul's first complaint against the Corinthians. Although he names several parties, and does not expressly name that of the False Apostles, this last seems to have been in his mind throughout, for ch 4 is directly aimed at it, and seems to be the climax to which the rest leads up. The chief sub-divisions are: (1) The False Wisdom and the True Wisdom (1:18–3:4). (2) The true place and function of the Christian teacher (3:5–23). (3) Paul's reply to his critics and rivals (ch 4). (See Introd. § 867d.)

I:10-17 Paul states his Accusations in general terms— **d** **10.** 'Speak' etc.: '*Agree together*', have no disputes. 'Schisms': '*Divisions*'. **11.** 'The house of Chloe': '*Chloe's people*'. A vague expression: it may mean relatives, servants, or even friends. We know nothing of Chloe, not even whether she herself was a Christian. He evidently means he had *first* heard of these divisions from Chloe's people, but the three visitors would no doubt have told him more. **12.** 'This I say': '*This is what I mean*'. 'Of Paul': '*I follow Paul*', am one of Paul's party. These would be the first converts at Corinth, and would very likely for that reason feel somewhat superior to the later comers. 'Apollo', **e** more correctly '*Apollos*'. He was the Alexandrian Jew who had been converted by Aquila and his wife, had made converts at Corinth since Paul's departure from there, and was now with Paul. (See notes on Ac 18:24–28.) Luke there calls him an eloquent man —he probably had a command of that rhetorical style which was popular in the Greek-speaking provinces: thus he would appeal to a rather more educated class at Corinth. His converts therefore tended to form a group which felt some cultural superiority to Paul's. (See note on 2:4.) 'Cephas': *i.e.* St Peter. Our Lord **f** had said, speaking in Aramaic: 'Thou art a rock (kepha) and on this rock I will build my church'. His original name, Simon, had in course of time been supplanted by Rock, either in its Aramaic form Kephas, or in its Greek translation Petros. Paul uses both names. In view of this verse and 9:5, several scholars have concluded that Peter had paid a short visit to Corinth just before this. This is quite possible but cannot be proved. The 'party of Peter' at Corinth may well have grown up round some friends or converts of Peter's, even if Peter had never been there. Owing to Peter's long association with Christ and his unique position among the Apostles, such a party might feel a little superiority to both Paul's converts and Apollos's. There would probably be a strong Jewish element among them but it is most unlikely that they were Judaizers for (1) It would be the height of impudence for Judaizers to shelter themselves behind Peter's name. (2) We have no evidence that there **g** were any Judaizers at Corinth. (See Introd. § 865d.) Nor is it likely that this is the party of the False Apostles: St Paul seems to admit (see esp. 3:22) that they had a right to use Peter's name, whereas he would have flatly denied such a right to the False Apostles. 'Of Christ': many have thought that Paul here

869g names a fourth party, who denied that the other parties were true Christians, and some have held that this 'Christ party' is to be identified with those who over-estimated spiritual gifts (chh 12–14) or with the party of the False Apostles or with both. But there is no other hint in this part of the letter that there was a Christ party, and no evidence that either of the two groups referred to laid claim to any such title. (Introd. C I.) It seems best therefore to suppose that these words are spoken by Paul in his own person, as a protest against the use of party names : 'But I (Paul) am a follower of Christ.' This fits in well with the next sentence.

870a 13. ' Is Christ divided ? ' A division in his mystical body, the Church, is as monstrous as a division in Christ himself, in his real body or his person. 14. ' Crispus ' : the synagogue-governor whom Paul had converted (Ac 18:8). Caius, more correctly Gaius, was his host during his next visit to Corinth (Rom 16:23). Most converts were baptized by his helpers, Silas, Timothy, etc. 15. ' That you ', etc. : accusing him, not of using another formula, but of intending the converts to be Paulists rather than Christians. A slander of the Judaizers perhaps. 16. ' Stephanas ' was one of the three Corinthians now visiting Paul (16:17, Introd. E). Perhaps he heard Paul dictating this, and reminded him of his baptism. 17. ' Made void ' : ' *Deprived of its power* '. Same thought in vv 18, 22–24 and 2:5.

b I 18-III 4 **The Lower Wisdom and the Higher Wisdom** —Paul does not content himself with particular criticism. He writes two passages of much wider scope, as he loves to do. The first is a magnificent contrast between the inferior wisdom of Judaism and Paganism and the higher wisdom of God as revealed in Christ. Its application to the present case is deferred till its close. **1:18-31 The Lower Wisdom**—Human wisdom in itself is an excellent thing, yet in fact many of its possessors have overlooked truths or fallen into great errors. Knowledge has its special temptations as riches and power have. 18. ' Word ' : ' *Announcement* ', ' *preaching* ', ' that perish ', *i.e.* have rejected the gospel. 19. From Is 29:14. 20. ' Where ', etc. : based on Job 12:17. ' Scribe ', *i.e.* scholar, learned man. 21. God in *his* wisdom permitted the human wisdom of the world to become so distorted that it was no longer **c** able to know him. 22. ' Both ' : ' *The Jews on the one hand . . . on the other* '. ' Signs ' : *i.e.* miracles. The Jews wanted chiefly superhuman *power* in the Messiah, power proved by stupendous miracles. They wanted an emperor mightier than the Roman emperor. A suffering and dying Messiah was a stumbling-block to them, *i.e.* they would not accept him. But the Greeks wanted a teaching which *completely* satisfied the intellect. They were impatient of anything unexplained or mysterious. They hated to accept any great truth on another person's authority. Faith was not in their line. Moreover the idea that suffering could do more than wisdom would appear nonsense to them. 24. ' Called ' : *i.e.* Christians. Our Lord said : ' Many are called but few are chosen '. But the Apostles usually confine the word ' called ' to believers, and use ' called ' and ' chosen ' as identical in meaning. (See 1:2.) 25. ' The foolishness of God ' —God's ways which the world considers foolish. **d** 26. ' Vocation ' : ' *Consider your call* ', *i.e.* your conversion. The converts were nearly all of humble station. ' Flesh '. A word of many shades of meaning in the New Testament : 1. The body. 2. Mankind. 3. Human nature. 4. Human nature in its fallen state, without grace or Christian truth. This is the meaning here. Practically synonymous with ' the world '. 27. ' The foolish things ', etc. : *i.e.* things which the world calls foolish. 28. ' Base ' : *i.e.* ' common ' not high-born or refined. ' Contemptible ' : ' *despised* '. ' That are not ' : Those whose very existence the world ignores, or perhaps those yet unborn but known to God. 29. ' Flesh ' : *i.e.* man—the second meaning

given at v 26. ' Glory ' : ' *boast* ', ' *feel pride* '. 30. ' *But* **87** *it is from Him that you have your being, through Christ* '. Their (spiritual) existence, the life of their souls, is from God ; they are his children, born by grace. 31. ' *So that . . . let him glory* ', etc. Not a quotation but a summary of a long sentence in Jer 9:23–4.

II 1-III 4*a* **The Higher Wisdom**—The spiritual man, **e** *i.e.* the true Christian, derives from God not only a higher wisdom but power and eloquence superior to those which the world admires. In proof of this Paul confidently appeals to their own experience of his preaching at Corinth. 1. ' of Christ ' : better ' *of God* ' —*i.e.* the message about God's love. 2. Better : ' *I decided not to know anything* ', etc. 3. He came after sufferings and anxiety in Macedonia, and disappointment at Athens, and may have been actually ill, *cf.* Ac 18:1–10. Yet St Paul's letters contain many passages which are marvellously eloquent. (See ch 13.) His preaching surely displayed the same gift, and we **f** can hardly believe that he was unaware of it. The eloquence that he here disclaims must be the more or less artificial Atticising style, which was then popular and usually taught in the schools of rhetoric, the style of Wis, of 2 Mac, and of the Jewish writer Philo. Very likely both the False Apostles and Apollos could preach in this style. (See 2 Cor 10:10.) Paul's eloquence is more natural and direct. If he had any model, it was the popular philosophers, whose language is preserved in Epictetus's discourses (§ 602*c*). ' In showing ', etc. : ' *With clear evidence of the Spirit and of the Power* ', *i.e.* the power of God. He probably includes miracles, and also the power to read, enlighten, and move the heart. 6. ' We speak ', etc. : our words are seen to be wise by perfect men, men fully under the influence of grace. The Greek word τέλειος (complete) can mean both *perfect* and *full-grown, adult,* and Paul likes to keep the double meaning in sight. (See 3:1–3 ; 14:20.) Here the word means the same as ' spiritual ' further on. ' Princes ' ' *Great men* ' of all kinds. 7. ' *We speak the wisdom of God, the secret wisdom* **g** *which has been hidden* ', etc., *i.e.* the gospel truth, once only faintly revealed even to prophets, but now open to all who are willing to accept it. 8. ' The Lord of glory ' : either ' the glorious Lord ' or ' the master of all renown and eminence '. 9. To be attached to the *first* half of 7. ' That eye ', etc. : ' *Things which eye,* etc. . . . *all that God has* ', etc. Paul is freely combining two verses of Is (64:4 ; 65:17) and describing not so much the wonders of Paradise as the wonders of the new truth revealed in Christ. 11-12. An argument from human nature, to show that the Holy Spirit can communicate (to all those in whom he dwells by grace) truths inaccessible to ordinary man. (Note that later theologians usually speak of ' grace ' or ' sanctifying grace ' where Paul would commonly have spoken of the indwelling of the Holy Spirit—different aspects of the same thing.) 11. ' *For among men, who knows a man's thoughts ? Only* **h** *the man's spirit, which is in him, knows them. In the same way nobody except God's Spirit knows God's thoughts* '. 12. ' The spirit of this world ' : the false wisdom condemned in ch 1. ' The things ', etc. : the new truths in all their meaning. 13. ' *Not in words taught by human wisdom but in words taught by the Spirit, joining spiritual things to spiritual* ' (Or : ' *interpreting spiritual things in spiritual words* '). In either case the last words mean that the words are as spiritual, as devoid of human artifice, as the Divine truths themselves. II 14-III 1—The terms change : the spiritual man **87** on one side and the ' natural man ' the ' man of flesh ' on the other. 14. ' Sensual ' : ' *Natural* ', *i.e.* worldly-minded. ' Examined ' : *i.e.* only a mind purified by grace can scrutinize, discern, and appreciate it. 15. ' Judgeth . . . judged ' : better : ' *Examines . . . examined* '. Same Greek word as in 14. Not that the spiritual man is subject to no authority, but that he must not bow to the verdict of the worldly-minded, the rulings of public opinion or of false science. 16. The first part is from Is 40:13 ; Who knows God's thoughts that he may lay down the law to Him ? (as

a false human wisdom is constantly doing). 'We', etc. : the spiritually-minded know the thoughts of Christ, which, as he clearly means, are identical with God's. The Divinity of Christ is taken as acknowledged by all. **III 1.** 'Could not': when he was among them. 'Carnal': '*fleshly*', with the same meaning of 'flesh' as in 1:26. Even after their conversion they were only infants in the spiritual life, weak in faith, spiritual insight, and also in charity, as appears later. Only moderate demands could be made on them. This is what he means by 'milk'. **2.** 'Meat': '*Food*', solid food of any kind. See Heb 5:12–14, where the same metaphor is fuller and clearer. **3.** 'Envying': '*Rivalry*'. 'According to man': In man's way, as distinct from God's way. A fourth term, meaning precisely the same as *worldly, natural,* and *fleshly.*

b **III 4*b*–IV 21**—Paul has given a profound and grandly-worded description of the two wisdoms. He now applies this to the Corinthians : their devotion to this or that teacher is a foolish human feeling ; the spiritual man must see in every teacher a mere instrument of God. But the passage goes on to speak of the value and place of teachers in general. Although Paul never names anybody except the three already mentioned, there are now signs that he is thinking of other teachers at Corinth, men of pernicious influence whose party is hostile to himself. These can hardly be other than the False Apostles. See Introd. C, D and F for the evidence for this, and the explanation of his reserve.

c **4*b*–9 Over-estimation of Teachers—5.** '*Servants (of God) by means of whom you have believed (in Christ) and each has done only what the Lord gave him power to do*'. **8.** 'Are one': *i.e.* in the same class. Both are mere instruments, one is as good as the other. 'And every man', etc. : '*Though each (teacher) will receive*', etc. They keep their own personalities, even as instruments. **9.** 'Coadjutors': '*Fellow-workers with God*'. 'Husbandry': '*cultivation*'. The meaning hovers between 'farming' and 'farm'. So also with 'building'—the same double meaning as in English.

d **10–17 The Parable of the Building**—Like all St Paul's parables, it melts and changes. The builders are the teachers, but the building seems to be first the doctrine, then (16–17) the Christian community. **10.** 'Architect': '*Master-builder.*' 'Another': perhaps loosely used for 'others'. The next sentence seems the first hint that some teachers at Corinth have been blameworthy. **12.** 'Precious stones': or perhaps 'costly stone'—marble, etc. The first three materials stand for sound instruction, the others for useless or unsound. 'Stubble': '*Straw*'. The building may turn out to be either a palace or a thatched hut.

e **13.** The best texts omit 'of the Lord'. '*For the Day will show it, for it (i.e. the Day) will be revealed amidst fire*'. The Day of Judgement is sometimes called simply 'the Day' or 'that Day' both by Christ and Paul. If the house still stands for doctrine, the fire means God's judgement on it. **15.** '*If any man's work is burnt down, he will be a loser, though he himself will be saved, but only like something which has been through fire*'. He will be like one pulled out of a burning house, scorched but alive. The unworthy teacher will not lose his soul (he is not therefore guilty of mortal sin) but will lose his work and his special reward. The last words clearly imply some penal suffering, and as Paul connects it so closely with God's judgement, it can hardly be confined to suffering in this world, but seems to include the idea of purificatory suffering after this life, *i.e.* in purgatory.

f **16–17.** The new turn in the parable is accompanied by a sterner tone. Not useless but pernicious teaching, grave sin, and eternal punishment are now the subject. It is most natural to suppose that he was referring to the men whom he later called the servants of Satan 'whose end shall be in accordance with their works' (2 Cor 11:15). **17.** '*If any man is destroying*', etc.—same Greek verb twice. 'Which': '*Which temple*', etc.

g **18–23 Continuation of the Warning of vv 4–9**—The first words take us back to the Two Wisdoms. **871g** Note that the first three verses *may* be addressed to the unnamed teachers as well as to their followers. **18** 'Seems': '*Imagines he is wise*'. **19.** The quotation is from Job 5:13 : '*He who grips*', etc. ; Paul substitutes a more picturesque word for the Hebrew 'catches'. **20.** From Ps 93:13, which however has *men*, not *the wise*. **21.** 'Glory': '*take pride in*', by giving their whole devotion to some human leader. If they gave their first thoughts to God, all men and all creation, being God's, would be theirs too.

IV The Apostolic Office and the Hostile Party—The **h** chapter strongly resembles 2 Cor ; there is irony, severity, strong emotion, evidence of unfriendly criticism, and a statement of the strange contradictions of the apostolic life. The simplest explanation is that the False Apostles were already active at Corinth, but Paul felt the time had not yet come for a pitched battle : these words were forced from him almost involuntarily by his bitter anxiety. Hence the obscurity of some sentences. See ch 9 and Introd. C (1) and F.

IV 1–8*a* The Apostles are answerable to God only— **i** (*cf.* 2 Cor 5:9–11 ; 12:19). He condemns the presumption of persons at Corinth who have adopted a superior and judicial attitude towards him. **1.** 'Ministers': '*Servants*'. 'Dispensers', etc. : '*Stewards of God's secrets*', *i.e.* of the new truths hitherto hidden. A steward was usually a slave administering his master's property under orders. **2.** 'Faithful': it is his master's will that matters, not the opinions of strangers. **3.** 'Judged': *called to account.* 'Man's day': a curious unexplained phrase. The least improbable view is that Christians were so used to 'the Day of the Lord' (*i.e.* of Judgement) that Paul could coin the phrase 'day of man' (judgement of men or of the world) as an antithesis to it. For the malicious things said by the party of the False Apostles about Paul, see Introd. C 2 (§865*h*). 'My own self': only a great saint can confidently leave his own imperfections to God. 'I live now not myself but Christ lives in me' (Gal 2:20). **4.** '*I have no sense of* **j** *guilt*', *i.e.* for unfaithfulness in his apostolic work. **5.** 'Hidden', etc. : '*Things hidden in darkness*': the secrets, good or bad, of each soul. 'From God' (emphatic)—not from man. **6.** '*I have diverted* (or *adapted*) *these words to Apollos and myself*': *i.e.* 'I have made us two the ostensible or nominal theme of my words.' (By *these words* he probably means the entire passage on party divisions.) This is the interpretation of Chrysostom, Lightfoot and Plummer. He means therefore that his own party and Apollos's (probably Peter's also) were not causes of serious trouble, and that the authors of the grave division were persons whom he does not choose to name—evidently the False Apostles. 'That in us', etc. : '*That you may learn* **872a** *from our case the rule* "*Keep to what is written*" *that you may not grow conceited for one man or another in opposition to somebody else*'. The maxim 'Keep', etc., is otherwise unknown, and there is probably some allusion which escapes us. It may however have been used by Jews to mean 'Keep to essentials or to certainties' and may here be a warning against dangerous liberalism of doctrine, or the calumnies spread by the False Apostles against Paul. **7–8.** Usually thought to be addressed to *members* of parties, but may include the unnamed leaders too. The sudden use of the singular in 7 may or may not be significant : such changes were common both in the Old Testament and in the discourses of popular philosophers. **7.** '*Who has made you a better man than your neighbours ?* ' **8.** Here and in 10 the bitter irony is comparable to that of 2 Cor 11:19–20 ; 12:13. 'Full': *i.e.* full-fed : they want nothing Paul can give. 'Reign': '*You are like kings, and that without help from us*'.

8*b*–13 The Heroic Patience required from the Apostles **b** —This passionate outburst resembles two great passages in 2 Cor (4:7–13 ; 6:3–10). It was no doubt

872b provoked by the effrontery and spite of the False Apostles' party. The moderate partisanship of the other groups would never have stung so sharply. **9.** '*For God, I think, has kept us the apostles to the end of the show, as they do with men sentenced to death*'. In the hideous sports of the amphitheatre a group of criminals was often the last item : they killed one another or were massacred. **10.** *i.e.* you care too much for the respect of this world (of pagans and Jews). See § 865*f* (also 10:14–22 ; 2 Cor 6:14–18) for evidence that the False Apostles allowed a compromise with paganism. **13.** '*We are slandered and we answer with persuasion . . . the off-scouring of mankind* '.

c 14–21 An Appeal to the Misguided and a Threat to the Stubborn—This mixture of tenderness and sternness ends the tempestuous episode. These sentences let us see Paul's mind as he wrote—there were many at Corinth whom he hoped to reclaim, but there were others of whom he hoped little. Compare the last chapter of 2 Cor. **15.** 'Instructors ': the Greek word usually means a trustworthy *slave* whom a father employed to look after his son at school or university. ' Not many ' : ' *Not several fathers* ' (there can be only one) . . . *it is I who have begotten you* ', *i.e.* by founding the church at Corinth. **17.** Timothy had probably left Ephesus for Macedonia a little time before this letter was written, Ac 19:22. Apparently Paul had written to him asking him to go on to Corinth, where he was well known, for he had been Paul's helper there, Ac 18 ; 2 Cor 1:19. ' Have I sent ' : ' *I am sending* '. **18.** ' *Some, thinking* (or *declaring*) *that I am not coming to you, have become arrogant, conceited* '. Perhaps Paul had already once postponed his visit (Introd. E) and the hostile party had become bolder and may **d** have made the delay a ground for slander. **19.** ' Power ' : see on 2:4. Note the strong resemblance of this passage to 2 Cor 13:2–4, where ' power ' is also used. **20.** ' Kingdom of God ' : here (as in Rom 14:17) it means ' the spiritual life of Christians '. Usually in St Paul it means Paradise (as 6:10). In the Gospels it usually means the Church, on earth or in heaven or both. **21.** ' *Which do you want ?* ' *i.e.* unless they repent and change, he will have to punish them. *Cf.* 2 Cor 13:2. ' If I come again, I will not spare '. In both places he seems to be addressing the same party.

e V 1–VII 40 Christian Chastity—The three chapters on the relations of the sexes form the second big division of the letter. The arrangement of parts is rather complicated (see Outline § 868*f*) and there are some short digressions. The subject is abruptly introduced, as if Paul were afraid of saying more about the last one, but for a chapter and a half his tone is still sharp. This is far the fullest treatment of the subject in all St Paul's letters and indeed in all the NT. The heart of the matter is in 6:12–20, where the basis of Christian chastity is profoundly and magnificently stated. Pagans and Jews alike would think St Paul's standard fantastically high, *cf.* §§ 601, 596*a* f. Briefly stated, the Christian revolution consisted in this, that the highest standard of chastity ever demanded from women was now made obligatory on men also : the sexes were placed on a moral equality.

f 1–8 Laxity in handling a Case of Incest—Very likely Paul had just heard of this from the three visitors. The weight of his censure falls not on the sinner but on the church authorities, *i.e.* the priests or some of them. The position of this section, and the continuance of a stern tone, points to some connexion of thought with ch 4. It is possible that the slackness of the priests was due to the influence of the False Apostles. **1.** As regards the incest, we cannot tell whether the woman's husband was alive or dead, nor whether the stepson and stepmother were legally married or not, nor whether, if married, they had been married before his conversion. Such a marriage was prohibited by Roman law (which was the law of Corinth) and by the law of most Greek cities, but might well be permitted in some communities in Asia or Egypt, from

which these two may have come. There had been **8** such marriages in Greek royal families, *e.g.* Antiochus I and Stratonice. **2.** ' that he ' : *i.e.* till he should be removed. A question-mark should probably be placed at the end. **4–5.** This is the sentence mentioned in v 3—excommunication. We may be sure that Paul knew that gentler methods were useless. **4.** This v should end with a comma, and ' in the name ', etc., should be taken closely with ' to deliver '. ' My **g** spirit ' : he joins his authority to their act. ' With the power ', etc. : the Church has power to act in His name. Excommunication was well known among the Jews, Jn 9:22. Its purpose always is to bring the sinner to penitence. **5.** ' To Satan ' : the man's *soul*, deprived of grace by his sin, was already to that extent in Satan's power. He was now *visibly* expelled from God's kingdom. But Satan is probably here referred to as the author (by God's permission) of *bodily* ailments (as in Lk 13:16) which the apostles had power to inflict as punishment, Ac 13:11. ' Flesh ' seems to partake of both the first and fourth meaning noted under 1:26, and ' destruction ' will mean something short of death. **6.** ' Leaven ' (yeast) stands for sin spreading from this sinner through the community, like yeast in dough. **7.** Just before the Pasch every good Jew carefully removed all leaven from his house and for eight days only unleavened bread was eaten. For the Christian the Crucifixion is a Pasch which has inaugurated a period of unleavened bread (*i.e.* sinless life) which must continue for ever. ' Christ ', etc. : ' *our pasch has been sacrificed—it is Christ* '.

9–13 No Association with notoriously Sinful Christians 87 of any Sort—Some Corinthians had misunderstood a recent letter of Paul's. The three visitors had probably asked for further explanation. **9.** ' *the epistle* ' (not ' an ') : no doubt many letters, now lost, had been written by him to Corinth during his three years at Ephesus, § 866*h*. **10.** ' Of this world ' : *i.e.* pagan fornicators, or ' *fornicators in general* '. ' Covetous ' : unscrupulous money-makers who stop short of crime. ' Extortioners ' : *thieves and swindlers*. ' Otherwise ', etc. : therefore in a country nominally Christian one must sometimes associate with scandalous Christians. **11.** ' *But now I write* ', *i.e.* in this present passage. ' Brother ' : *i.e.* Christian. ' Idols ' : this implies that some Corinthians did still take part in pagan worship. See 8:1. ' Railer ' : one who reviles a man *to his face* ; occurs again in 6:10. Both are lists of *mortal* sins. Perhaps some of the hostile party had been outrageous in their abuse of those faithful to Paul. **12.** ' Without ' : outside the Church. **13.** ' Put away ', etc. Here the emphasis lies on the last words.

VI 1–11 Litigation before Heathen Courts—This is **b** a digression, inserted *here* apparently because the word ' judge ' in the preceding verses has reminded Paul of it. Note the continuation of the severe tone— *e.g.* the phrase ' Do you not know . . . ? ' occurs six times in this chapter. This present fault is a failure in charity. **1.** ' Unjust ' : *i.e.* pagans. ' Saints ' : Christians, *cf.* 1:2. **2.** The redeemed will be judged, but will also be judges with God, Mt 19:28. **3.** ' Angels ' : *i.e.* fallen angels. ' Of this world ' : secular questions, about property, etc. **4.** ' Despised ' : if the Christians were all that they ought to be, the most insignificant would be sufficiently upright and wise to arbitrate in disputes. But as things are at Corinth, the sentence is hardly meant to be taken literally, as the next words show. **5.** ' Is it ', etc. : ' *Are you so unprovided with a single wise man* ', etc. **7.** ' *That you have lawsuits . . . is in itself a defeat for you* '. **c** A play on words : The very existence of disputes is a defeat for charity, you have lost your case even before you go to court. **8.** He turns suddenly from the injured party in disputes to those who, by sinful rapacity, provoke the disputes. And this leads him back to the thought of the grave sinners in general at Corinth, as at the end of ch 5. **9.** ' Kingdom ' : *i.e.* Paradise. Therefore the sins that follow are mortal. ' Err ' : ' *be deceived* '. Implies that lax

c *teaching* on this matter was current at Corinth and that many were slipping, if not already fallen. Nearly half the sins are sexual, and the placing of ' idolaters ' in the midst of these seems a sign that the two temptations were closely connected in their thoughts at least. The work of the False Apostles seems to have contributed to this relaxation of Christian discipline, § 865h. **11.** ' Washed ' : *i.e.* baptised, and the two next words describe the grace of the sacrament.

d **12-20 The Foundation of Christian Chastity**—The first three verses are answers to false teaching. **12.** ' All . . . me ' : probably a saying of Paul's, which had been perverted at Corinth to justify immorality. (Quoted again 10:23.) In Paul's mouth it meant *either* ' everything not wrong in itself ' (*i.e.* including things prohibited in the Jewish ceremonial law, etc.) *or* ' everything which the perfectly spiritual man wishes to do ' for he never wishes to do evil and has no thwarted desires, *cf.* Gal 5:23 ; 1 Tim 1:9. ' Expedient ' : in the widest sense, including the spiritual good of fellow-Christians. ' I will ', etc. : ' *I refuse to be dominated by anything* '. Difficult, but probably refers to his teaching that sin is slavery and grace freedom, fully set forth in Rom 6, especially 13–16. *Cf.* Gal 5:1, 13. **13.** He quotes the poor quibble with which the impure of every age stifle their conscience : ' God has given us stomachs and it is right and natural to eat. In the same way it is natural and right to satisfy unchaste desires '. Reason alone will demolish this fallacy, but Paul prefers to appeal to revealed truth : eating will cease but the body itself will live in God's presence for ever. Therefore the body made for God must not be debased for present pleasure. ' Meat ' : ' *Food* '. ' Destroy ' : a forcible way of saying that eating will cease. ' For the body ', etc : an extraordinary expression—Christ subordinates himself, as it were, to our salvation. *Cf.* Imitation of Christ, 3, 10, 3 : ' The parts are reversed : Thou servest me rather than I Thee ' and St Thomas Aquinas's tremendous stanza, never adequately translated : ' Se nascens dedit socium ', etc. **14.** Proof that

e the body is eternal and should be respected. Vv 15–20 are crucial : chastity is bound up with the mutual love between the Christian and Christ, and unchastity is unfaithfulness to his claims on us. Christian teaching here is as revolutionary as on charity, *cf.* §602. **15.** ' Members ' : ' *Limbs* '. Christ animates the Church by grace as the soul animates the human body. Paul says ' your bodies ' to contradict those who would confine religion to the soul. **16.** Quotation from Gen 2:24, ' The two shall become one flesh '. **17.** ' One spirit ' : it is chiefly through our spirit, the highest part of us, that we are united to God, but the whole man, body and soul, is elevated by the union. **18.** ' Without (*i.e.* outside) the body ' : a natural exaggeration ; the body is *more deeply* involved in sexual sins than in any others, even *e.g.* gluttony and drunkenness. **19.** ' Your own ' : ' *Your own property* ' ; they are Christ's slaves, bought with his blood. **20.** Good texts omit ' great ' and ' bear ' : ' *Come then, glorify God with your bodies* '. A splendid final hammer-blow to the false Greek ' spiritualization'.

f VII is almost wholly devoted to matters connected with marriage. There is none of the sharpness of the last three chapters. The tone is rather matter-of-fact except for two somewhat digressive passages (vv 17–24, 29–32) which are more animated. For Paul's most impressive utterance on marriage we have to look elsewhere (Eph 5:22–33). But this is his longest passage and a most important one.

g **1-7 Marriage is Right and Natural**—He answers a question in their recent letter, § 867b, c. Vv 1, 28 and 36 seem to show that some Corinthians were inclined to think marriage sinful, a false doctrine taught by many later heretics and usually connected with the oriental idea that matter is essentially evil. The Jewish Essenes seem to have held this view about marriage.

1. ' It is good ', etc. Paul's words, not a quotation from **873g** the letter. **2.** Permission, not command. ' For fear ', etc. : ' *In consideration of the prevailing immorality* '. **4.** ' *The wife has not absolute power . . . but her husband* (*shares her power*) '. **5.** ' For your incontinency : ' *On account of your want of self-control* '. **6.** ' This ' : probably means all the last four verses. **7.** ' Gift ' : The word (charisma) means a special grace to carry out a good work, to consecrate to God a married life no less than a celibate life. See 12:1.

8-16 Separation, Divorce, and the Pauline Privilege— **h** —He begins with a restatement of vv 1–2. **9.** ' *If they have not control over themselves* '. ' To be burnt ' : ' *To be on fire* '. Refers to unlawful desire and the torturing struggle to resist it, not to hell, *cf.* 2 Cor 11:29. **10-11.** First he speaks of separation, which is discouraged, but allowed for grave reasons (adultery, cruelty, drunkenness, etc.), then makes it clear that the marriage cannot be dissolved. **11.** ' *If she does depart* '. ' Put away ' : *i.e.* divorce. He does not explicitly treat of cases where a husband desires separation. **12-16.** A married pagan who becomes a Christian has the option of divorcing the other partner who still remains pagan, and will not live peaceably with the Christian. It only applies to unbaptized persons, and of course is useless if it clashes with civil law, as it would in many modern countries. (In ancient countries civil divorce was much easier than among us.) Although a divorce (not separation), it does not dissolve a sacramental marriage, for unbaptized persons cannot receive as acrament. **12.** Omit ' for '. ' The rest ', *i.e.* those not included **i** under 8 and 10, ' I say, not the Lord ' : Paul had not heard of any pronouncement of Christ on this subject. It does not mean that the rule which follows is only a private opinion of Paul's. He speaks as an apostle, authorized to decide in Christ's name. **14.** ' Sanctified by ' (better ' through ') : a strong expression, for there can be no question of sanctifying grace ; it can only mean that the unbeliever's tolerance brings a blessing which will make his conversion easier. ' Should ' : ' *Would be* '. Evidently the pagan partner allows the children to be brought up as Christians. **15.** ' In peace ' : ' *It is to peace that God has called us* ' ; *i.e.* the purpose of our conversion is to increase peace and harmony not to disturb it. ' Call ' : same sense as in 1:2, 26, etc. **16.** An equally probable translation is : ' *How knowest thou, O wife ?—thou mayest save thy husband* ' —to be taken closely with what precedes.

17-24 Conversion should cause only Necessary Changes, 874a no more—Few passages show Paul's solid common-sense so well. It is he who calls conversion a new birth, etc. The *inevitable* change caused by it was enormous, suppression of life-long habits and pursuit of an ideal unimagined before. But once that was secured, tolerance was to be shown to everything that was not wrong in itself, though perhaps liable to abuse. Therefore war, slavery, taxation, property, etc., are tolerated. Where sin is in question, Christianity brings ' not peace, but a sword '. But in all else ' it is to peace that God has called us '. Hence Christianity is at once revolutionary and conservative, and has been both praised and reviled under either name. **18.** ' Called ' : *i.e.* converted. ' Procure ', etc. Some Jews who wished to mix freely in pagan society (athletics, etc.) disguised their circumcision by a surgical operation—practically a denial of their religion. **19.** ' Nothing ' : an emphatic statement that the Jewish ceremonial laws had been abolished. ' *But the observance . . . is everything* ' : he means all the commandments in force under Christianity. **20.** ' Calling ' : (note the **b** double sense of ' call ') ' *in the same state of life in which he was converted* '. **21.** ' Care not ' : for a slave can be a perfect Christian. ' But if . . . ' : best taken as a parenthesis ' (*Yet, if you can obtain your freedom, choose that rather*) '. Others think that Paul advises him to remain a slave even if he might be free. This seems an unreasonable demand : man's desire for freedom is natural, and slavery *might* be a great obstacle to religion. **22.** ' Freeman ' : ' *Freedman* ' ; emancipated

874b slave. **23.** 'Bought . . .': same words as 6:20. Christ has now a greater right over the slaves than their masters have ; therefore they must serve these masters *chiefly* for Christ's sake : in this way they will not be 'slaves of men'. Paul's great passages on masters and slaves are in Eph 6:5 f. and Col 3:22 f. **24.** 'With God' : ' *In God's sight* '.

c 25-40 For the Sake of God's Service Celibacy is Preferable to Marriage—This is the main theme, but 29–32*a* have a wider scope and 36–38 deal with a special application, advice to a father about his daughters' marriage.

25-28 Main Theme—25. 'Virgins': *i.e.* probably *unmarried girls*. The Corinthians had asked for directions on this subject in their letter, § 867*c*, and Paul eventually gives them in 36–38. But he decides to use this opportunity to deal with the whole subject of celibacy and marriage. 'No commandment . . .': see note on v 12 above. 'Faithful': probably *worthy of trust, i.e.* ' as one whom God in his mercy has deemed worthy of trust '. The trust is the Apostolic office. *Cf.* 1 Thess 2:4. **26.** '*Because of the present distress* ': for the meaning see v 29. 'So to be' : *i.e.* to be unmarried. 'Loosed from . . .': rather awkward expression for ' without a wife ', *i.e.* bachelor or widower. This and 33 show that he has both sexes in view. **28.** 'Tribulation': see 29. 'I spare you': The 'I' is emphatic. '*But I, for my part, would spare you (this tribulation)* '; they would escape it if they took his advice.

d 29-32a The Need of Detachment from the World— Three reasons for this need seem to be in Paul's mind : (1) The growing hostility of the pagan world. Hitherto only the Jews had been consistently hostile, but Paul probably foresaw bitter opposition from pagan masses and their governors. This is most likely the distress (26) and tribulation (28) already spoken of. An unmarried person is better able to bear persecution, private or public. (2) The possibility of an early Second Coming of Christ. Many non-Catholics believe that Paul was *convinced* that Christ would come in the next few years—a rash inference from passages like this one. He knew no more than we do, but whereas we unreasonably ignore the possibility, it was always vividly present to him. See his warning against too confident expectation of it (2 Thess 2:1 f.) written **e** some years before this. (3) The shortness and precariousness of human life. **29-31.** Not a plea for neglecting earthly concerns, but for concentration on God's service and for treating other things as of secondary (but real) interest. **29.** '*This is what I mean* '. **30.** ' weep . . . rejoice': *i.e.* men must take earthly sorrows and joys more lightly than they once did. **31.** '*Like men who do not use it up* ' (not like men who owned it and could never be deprived of it). 'Fashion': *splendour, pomp.* **32a.** 'Solicitude': the same word as Mt 6:25, ' Be not solicitous for your life . . .'.

f 32b-35 Continuation of the Main Theme—He now applies the ideas of the last few verses to the question of marriage. **32.** ' Is solicitous', etc. : *i.e.* if he so desires. It is this desire *alone* that places celibacy above marriage. Without it celibacy has every chance of being on a lower level than married life, more self-centred and self-indulgent, and many do in fact choose it for this reason. Motive is everything. 32–34 are the core of this half-chapter. **33.** ' Is solicitous': *i.e.* is liable to be so. 'Divided': finds it difficult to put God's service first. **35.** 'Snare' : lit. noose or halter. Probably he means that his words are a counsel and must not be taken as a precept (*cf.* v 2), he does not wish to create unnecessary difficulties for them. 'Impediment' : ' *distraction* '.

g 36-38 Advice to Fathers of Unmarried Daughters— It was the universal custom, even among the Romans, that the parents chose husbands for their daughters. Christianity tolerated this custom (which is contrary to natural human right) for the sake of peace, just as it accepted slavery, etc. (see 17–24 *supra* and § 602*a*), and Paul therefore recognizes the father's right also to keep his daughter unmarried for her spiritual good.

Great efforts have been made to prove that the man here concerned is not her father but her fiancé or else a ' spiritual husband ', but there is no respectable evidence *for* this, and the use of γαμίζω (give in marriage) in 38 seems decisive *against* it. **36.** '*If a man thinks he is treating his unmarried daughter unhandsomely* (or *unfairly*) '. ' Above the age ': probably means ' *of marriageable age* '. ' If she marry ' : '*Let them marry* '. **37.** ' Necessity . . . power ', etc. : probably mean that he is not compelled to give her in marriage by inability to make provision for her otherwise.

39-40 Conclusion of the Main Theme—39. The words ' by the law ' have crept in erroneously from Rom 7:2. ' Die ' : ' *Falls asleep* '. ' In the Lord ' : *i.e.* she must marry a Christian. The whole verse of course is equally applicable to men. **40.** ' *I too think that I have . . .* ' : *i.e.* ' I as well as others have authority to speak in Christ's name '. It seems an ironical understatement, aimed at some persons at Corinth who falsely claimed such authority—very likely the False Apostles.

VIII 1-XI 1 Social Intercourse with Pagans— This is the real scope of the third large section of the letter, though it deals primarily only with the question : May a Christian eat food which has been offered to pagan gods ? Paul's answer is : Yes, *provided* it can be done without injury to two Christian duties : (1) The duty of consideration for over-scrupulous Christians (8:7–9:22). (2) The duty of vigilant avoidance of any participation in pagan *worship* (9:23–10:13). Paul ends by giving some detailed directions (10:14–11:1). The primary question itself is of no practical importance to us, but the principles invoked by Paul are eternal and living. Passion, sternness, and irony appear again, and we hear of Christians hostile to himself (9:3)—signs, as it seems, that the party of the False Apostles is involved, § 865 and note on 8:1–6.

It was a question of great importance to the Corinthian Christians. Sacrificial meat would be served at all public dinners and at many, perhaps most, private dinner-parties given by pagans (see §600*h*). A Christian slave in a pagan household would often be offered such meat, and holders of public offices would be expected on certain ceremonial occasions not only to eat it but to take part in the sacrifice. Were Christians absolutely bound to abstention, which might often involve refusing a friend's invitation, angering a master, etc. ? Were they bound to avoid butchers who dealt in sacrificial meat ? (See 10:25.)

VIII 1-6 The Argument for Complete Freedom to eat —It seems clear that this question had been put to St Paul in the letter from Corinth, and backed with this argument. We gather that there were many at Corinth who prided themselves on their enlightened and rational attitude towards paganism, their freedom from superstitious scruples. They used ' knowledge ' as a catchword, and probably also ' liberty ' and ' power '. Paul accepts their argument in itself, but shows that in applying it they offend against charity. It seems likely that the argument was put forth or encouraged by the False Apostles, and that they were pushing it very far, using it to justify participation in pagan worship. This seems to be hinted at in 10:7–8, 14–21. **1.** ' Knowledge ': used with some irony throughout the chapter, most clear in vv 10–11. ' Edifieth ' : ' *builds up* ', *i.e.* strengthens and enlarges our spiritual life. An OT expression often used by Paul, connected with the idea that the soul and the whole Church are God's temple, *cf.* 3:9, 16. The contrast between knowledge and charity is finely set forth in 13:8–12. **3.** ' Known by him ' (God) : in OT language, to be known by God means to be approved by him, *e.g.* Nah 1:7—the knowledge that chiefly matters is God's knowledge of us. **4.** ' *There is no idol in the world* ' : ' Idol ' had come to be a synonym for ' heathen god ', therefore : ' No heathen god exists '. **5.** ' *For although there are so-called gods both in the sky* (sun and moon, adored by pagans) *and on the* *earth* (*i.e.* the idols) '. **6.** ' Unto him ' : he is our goal, destination. ' By him ' : probably refers to their regeneration by grace, *cf.* 2 Cor 5:17, ' If any man is in Christ, he is a new creation '. Such is the argument. Its obvious conclusion, not stated here, is that the eating of sacrificial food is perfectly allowable. As heathen worship is all empty mummery, the food is just like any other food.

7-13 St Paul's Objection and Contrary Decision—He allows the force of the above reasoning, but objects that they have overlooked Christ's teaching about stumbling-blocks (*skandala*) : that an act lawful in itself may become even a mortal sin if it is foreseen that it will place difficulties or temptations in the way of a weaker Christian. This springs from the new and higher law of charity taught by Christ, *cf.* Rom 14:1–15:6, written a few months after this. **7.** According to the best texts : *For some even now, from long habitation to the false god, eat it as a thing consecrated to him.* They cannot shake off their ingrained awe of the god, they feel like men taking part in pagan worship and sinning against Christ. **8.** ' Meat ' : *Food.* ' have the more . . . less ' : ' *gain anything . . . lose anything* '. He means that all *ordinary* food is morally indifferent—obviously he would exclude Holy Communion (11, 27–29). **9.** ' Liberty ' : ' *power* ', probably another catchword, *cf.* 9:12. **10.** ' *If a man sees you, who have knowledge, reclining at table in an idol-house* ' : *i.e.* at a dinner-party given after a sacrifice. ' Emboldened ' : ' *edified* ', see 1. Intense irony, for the weak Christian will in fact be undermined, not built up : he will be encouraged to act against his (erroneous) conscience, and all acts against conscience are sinful. **11.** ' *Yes, and so, thanks to your knowledge, the weak man is lost, a brother for whom Christ died* '. **13.** ' Scandalize ' : *i.e.* impel to sin. He is willing to become a vegetarian in order to smooth the way for weaker Christians.

IX 1-22 Illustrations from St Paul's Own Practice—He wished to show that he had often abstained from lawful actions for the sake of the salvation of others. In the sequel he mentions many kinds of forbearance (19–22) but the first-named one (his refusal to live at the expense of the Corinthians) eclipses all the rest and is spoken of with such abruptness and vehemence that the passage seems at first sight to be a digression, which it is not. Somebody—in all probability the False Apostles—had denied Paul's right to maintenance (3–6) on the ground that he was not an apostle in the same sense as the Twelve. (See § 865*h, i* and 2 Cor 11:5–15.) Here then for the second time the strength of his feelings makes him depart from his plan of postponing a direct clash with this party (see ch 4). Hence also some of the ' boasting ' which we have in the Second Epistle, appears here also. Nevertheless the passage breathes the spirit of heroic charity, which for God's sake and the salvation of souls thinks nothing too hard.

1-14 Proof of his Right to Maintenance—**1.** ' Free ' : *i.e.* from the Jewish Law and from irrational scruples. See its use in verse 19. Perhaps it was also a catchword. ' Seen Christ ' : his meeting with Christ on the Damascus road is mentioned as proof of his Apostolic vocation, Gal 1:15–18. **2.** ' Seal ' : their conversion proved his vocation, as the seal on an article would prove it to be genuine or somebody's property. **3.** ' Examine ' : *call to account* : same word as in 4:3, where the same people probably are in view. ' This ' : *i.e.* the following verses. **4.** ' We ' : in view of the singular in vv 3 and 15, it is clear that throughout this passage ' we ' means Paul alone. ' Eat ', etc. : *i.e.* to receive food and shelter from the faithful. **5.** ' To carry about ' : to bring with him, and expect the same hospitality for her. ' A woman a sister ' : the first word can mean either *woman* or *wife*, the second is taken by nearly everybody to mean *Christian* here. Two interpretations therefore are possible : 1. A Christian woman. 2. A Christian wife. Although some of the Twelve Apostles (including Cephas, *i.e.* Peter) had wives, Catholic commentators have generally preferred the

first version, taking the words to refer to devout women **875i** such as those who assisted our Lord with their money and service (Lk 8:3). Only here is it implied that our Lord's brethren (*i.e.* cousins) had travelled outside Palestine. Peter may have visited Corinth—see 1:12. St Paul's critics evidently maintained that only the Twelve had a right to maintenance. Paul says that *all* missionaries have it, and therefore does not here labour to prove his equality to the Twelve (Introd. C 2 and 2 Cor 1:5–15). **6.** ' *Or is it only myself and Barnabas* **j** *who have no right to cease from working (for our living) ?* ' Barnabas may have visited Corinth. In any case his name must have been well known at Corinth and he seems to have been disparaged by the False Apostles. Paul and Barnabas had not met, as far as we know, since their disagreement at Antioch five or six years before, Ac 15:37–9. **8.** ' According to man ' : as a private opinion. **9.** Quotation from Deut 25:4 ; see note there. ' Treadeth out ' : ' *threshes* '. The text of course had its literal sense, but the principle, here confirmed by God, applied a fortiori to men. **10.** ' For ', etc. ' *Yes, it was written for our sake* '. ' Receive fruit ' : ' *receive his share* '. **11.** ' Carnal ' : ' *earthly, material things* '. Only necessaries are in question. **12.** ' Others ' probably means some true missionaries, perhaps St Peter, etc., not the False Apostles who seem to have prided themselves on disclaiming the right to maintenance (see § 856*h, i* and 2 Cor 11:12). But the meaning may be : Others, *i.e.* all Christians, possess the same ' power ' as you do (same sense as in 8:9)—power to do anything not wrong in *itself*. **13.** Refers to Jewish priests, who were largely supported by the use of the meat, bread, etc., of the offerings. ' Who work ', etc. : ' *Who carry out sacred rites* '. **14.** ' The Lord ordained ', etc. : clearest in Lk 10:7, where he tells the Seventy to live on the charity of those they visit, and adds ' The labourer has a right to his wages '.

15-18 St Paul's Renunciation of this Right—St Paul's **876a** chief reason was the one given in 12—to prevent the Jews and others from being able to say that he profited by the gospel. In Corinth and Ephesus he insisted on earning his bread, but accepted gifts from the Christians of Philippi (2 Cor 11:8–9 ; Phil 4:15) perhaps because there were few Jews at Philippi to calumniate him. **15b** ' *Neither do I write these (present) words in order that* (I may receive free hospitality) '. ' For ', etc. : ' *For I would rather die than—Nobody shall rob me of my boast* '. The first sentence is broken off and left unfinished. **16.** ' A necessity ', etc. : *i.e.* I **b** have no choice. The compelling force was twofold, love of Christ and fear of being held responsible for the loss of souls. **17-18.** St Paul's thought *as a whole* is clear, but there are difficulties about single words, and our text may be corrupt somewhere. This is a paraphrase rather than a translation : ' If I did this (preaching the gospel) by my own free choice, I should deserve a reward. But if I have no choice about preaching the gospel, then I am like a slave carrying out a commission entrusted to him (and deserving no credit for doing so). How then am I to merit any reward ? Only if I preach the gospel for nothing and do not make full use of the power that a missionary has '. By *reward* he means God's special approval.

19-22 His Renunciation of Other Rights—Putting **c** aside the thought of his critics at Corinth, he takes a wider scope and in a serener tone shows how he had habitually assumed burdens which he was not bound to carry, for the sake of making converts or of smoothing the path of Christians. **19.** ' Free ', etc. : ' *Subject to no master* '. **20.** When living among Jews, he observed the Law in his *actions* so as not to shock them, *cf.* Ac 21:21–24. He did not mislead them into thinking he was no more than an ordinary Jew. **21b** ' *To men who have no law I became like a man without law* '. To pagans he made it clear that he was not bound by the Jewish ceremonial law (which repelled them) and moreover he tried to meet them on some common ground—a bare belief in some Divine power—or he

876c appealed to something already familiar to them, *e.g.* the altar to the unknown god. See his speech at Athens, Ac 17:16 f. **22.** ' Weak ' : Christians burdened with scruples and doubts (as in 8:9). For their sake he *acted* as if he shared their scruples. **22b.** ' *That by any and every means I might save men* '.

d 23-27 The 'Unfading Wreath' is worth the Uttermost Effort—This is really a bridge to the next section —the subject is no longer the salvation of others but our own. **23.** ' Partaker ' : *i.e.* that I too may (with those for whom I work) share in its blessings. **24.** Short parable from Greek athletic contests which were extremely popular throughout the eastern provinces. The *only* moral is : a man may be a Christian and yet not be saved, just as a man may run and not win. There is no exact parallelism, and we must not press the comparison. **25.** ' *Everyone who enters for a contest practises the utmost self-denial* ', in diet, etc. ' Corruptible crown ' : *a perishable wreath* (or *garland*).' A garland was the usual prize given to athletes. At the Isthmian Games, celebrated every two years close to Corinth, the garlands were of pine · foliage. **26.** ' at an uncertainty ' : ' *aimlessly* '. ' Fight ' : ' *box* '. **27.** Probably : ' *I hammer at my body and make it my slave* ' : he is speaking, it seems, of mortifications over and above the great inevitable hardships of his life. His picture is of a boxing-match between his soul and his body, in which the body gets the worst of it : ' a castaway ' : *i.e.* rejected by God.

877a X 1-13 The Need of Vigilance and the Danger of Presumption—This is illustrated from the ancient history of Israel. The section grown naturally out of the preceding : ' I myself do not feel secure about my salvation : neither must you. The ancient Israelites received great privileges, yet many fell into grave sins, including pagan worship and pagan vices. You are even now in danger of the same sins, and must not presume foolishly on your strength and rush into temptations '. **1.** ' Fathers ' : Christians are the spiritual descendants of the ancient Israelites. ' All ' : Emphatic, and therefore repeated four times. **2.** ' In Moses ' : *For* or *into Moses*, so as to belong to Moses. By the crossing of the Red Sea and by the presence of the Pillar of Cloud they were bound to Moses (*i.e.* became his followers) as Christians by baptism are (in a higher way) united to Christ. **3.** ' Spiritual food ' : the manna, which was ' spiritual ' as being miraculous and as a foreshadowing of Holy Communion. We **b** might say ' mystical food '. **4.** ' Spiritual rock ' : he means that Christ (as God) accompanied them in their journey. God is often called a rock in the OT. Later Jewish writings have a story about a miraculous rocky spring which followed the Israelites, but Paul can hardly be referring to that. **5.** All enjoyed the blessings, yet many were lost. **6.** ' In a figure of us ' : *As foreshadowings* (or *types*) *of us*. The past events had an inner meaning which looked forward to Christianity, *cf.* §§ 101*e*, 102, 383*a, c*. But another translation is possible : ' *as examples for us* ' (for our imitation or avoidance). ' Coveted,' probably refers to **c** their desire to return to Egypt, Num 11:4. **7-10.** Very serious warnings, showing how unstable many Corinthians were, and (probably) how pernicious the influence of the False Apostles had been. **7b.** From Ex 32:6, just before the worship of the golden calf. Evidently hints that the dinners mentioned in 8:10 might become a step towards paganism. **8.** Refers to Num 25, where the Israelites join in the idolatry and unchastity of the Moabites. **9.** ' Tempt Christ ' : ' *Tempt the Lord* '. The serpents were sent (Num 21:5) after the people had grumbled about the manna. ' To tempt God ' often describes an *unreasonable* demand for miracles. **10.** ' Destroyer ' : probably refers to the plague of Num 14:37 which Paul ascribes to a destroying angel. **11.** ' In a figure ' : or perhaps ' by way of example ', *cf.* v 6. ' Upon whom ', etc. : probably : ' *to whom the fulfilments of past ages have come* ',

i.e. what was dimly foreshadowed in past events has now become a · reality. Christ has come and has founded his kingdom. **13.** According to the best texts : ' *No trial has yet come upon you except what is human* ' (*i.e.* ordinary, moderate). To be joined closely to v 12. They have no ground for self-complacency as they have never endured severe trials. ' And God ', etc. : ' *But God . . .* ' A kind of parenthesis of comfort inserted in the midst of warnings, as if he feared to depress them too much. ' Issue ' : ' *will provide a way of escape* ' (or perhaps : ' *will appoint the outcome of it* ', implying that resistance will be possible).

X 14-XI 1—Having put forward his two guiding thoughts (see beginning of ch 8) St Paul applies them to the question of sacrificial food. Both thoughts are in his mind during the rest of the chapter.
14-22a There can be no Intermixture or Compromise between Christianity and Paganism—Here the second principle is more prominent. The Mass is set in sharp opposition to pagan sacrifices. Holy Communion unites the faithful to Christ and to one another (obliging each to consider the other's welfare) and separates them utterly from everything outside the Christian religion, every god or worship. It is on this separation that Paul here insists. The Real Presence is clearly asserted in v 16 and the comparison of the two worships implies the sacrificial character of the Mass. **14.** ' Wherefore ' : looks back to 12 and 13*a*, not to the last words. **16.** ' Chalice of benediction ' : perhaps two ideas : ' Blessed (by God) and the source of blessings '. ' We bless ' : *i.e.* consecrate. ' Break ' : in Ac 2:46 ; 20:11, etc., the Mass is regularly called the ' breaking of bread '. The Host is still broken at every Mass, but in early times one large loaf was used for the whole congregation, instead of separate particles, *cf.* next verse. **17.** Probably : ' *As the loaf is one, we, though many, are one body, for we all share in one loaf* '. **18.** ' Israel ', etc. : *i.e.* the unconverted Jews. ' Partakers ', etc. : they are united to the altar and therefore to the God whose altar it is. He wishes to establish the general truth that a worshipper is united to the power (good or bad) which he worships. **19-20a.** ' *What then do I mean ? That what . . . is anything (different from ordinary food) ? Or that a false god is anything real ?* (*i.e.* has any existence apart from the image). *No. But that the things* ', etc. 20*a* is from Deut 32:17. He does not mean that each god was to be identified with a particular devil (this would contradict v 19 and 8:4) but that devils encouraged paganism in general, as it kept men in error and sin. In so far as paganism contained good elements, it was under God's influence. **20b-21.** This means that they must not go to a dinner if it involves their attendance at pagan rites. Such attendance destroys the union of the soul to Christ, and unites it instead to something evil. It is substantially the same as his reason against unchastity, 6:13*b*–20. **21.** ' The Lord's table ' : the altar of Mass may properly be called a table. So could the altars of pagans and Jews, Mal 1:7. **22a.** ' *Or are we going to provoke God to anger ?* ' An echo of the same passage (Deut 32:21.). ' Are we ', etc. : *i.e.* we shall not escape punishment.
22b-33. Rules about Sacrificial Food—Here the first principle (regard for scrupulous Christians) is dominant. Paul's solution may be called a compromise : Eat the food as long as you do not offend another's conscience. **22b.** ' All things . . . me ' : this maxim which had been used to justify unchastity (6:12 note) had also been used to defend unlimited freedom about sacrificial food. **23.** ' Edify ' : see 8:1 note. **24.** ' *Nobody must aim at his own good only but must consider that of others as well* '. **25.** ' Shambles ' : ' *Provision-market* '. Some temples would sell their surplus offerings to butchers, etc. ' Asking ', etc. : ' *Asking no conscientious (i.e. scrupulous) questions* '. **26.** ' For " to the Lord belongs the earth and all it contains " ' ', (Ps 23(24) 1, *i.e.* though consecrated to some heathen god, the

food was still God's creation and good. **27.** '*Asking no conscientious questions*'. **28.** 'This', etc.: '*this is sacrificial* (or *consecrated*)'; The best texts omit 'to idols'. The speaker uses the respectful term customary among *pagans*, betraying the strength of his old pagan associations. **29-30.** With bewildering suddenness he turns round and gives a sharp rap to some of the 'weaker brethren' who had presumed to condemn all eating of sacrificial food as sinful in itself. Such uncharitable judgements by scrupulous Christians are more fully criticized in Rom 14:3-4, 6, 10, 13. The scrupulous are not entitled to impose their scruples on others. 'Liberty' to eat sacrificial food. 'Judged': '*condemned*'. 'Partake' of the food. 'Give thanks' to God for the food. *Cf.* Rom 14:6, 'The eater eats in honour of the Lord, for he gives thanks: and the abstainer abstains in honour of the Lord'. Tolerance and kindness must be mutual. **32.** 'Jews ... Gentiles': '*Jews ... Greeks*'; apparently means non-Christians in both cases, for they also must be considered, *cf.* 1 Thess 4:11. **33.** 'Please': '*Try to please*, *cf.* 9:19-23. **11:1.** 'Followers'—imitators in his charitable self-denial.

XI 2-34 We now have two very strongly worded sections about order and decency at Christian worship. **2-16 Women are not to be bare-headed at Worship**——St Paul affirms two things: 1. That the male sex has a certain right to precedence. 2. That *therefore* it is improper for women to be bare-headed at worship. To us this seems very illogical, but no doubt it was the general custom in the eastern provinces that women should always have the head covered in the presence of men, except men of their own family, and it was Paul's rule that established customs, if not sinful, should be scrupulously observed. Hence the heat and bluntness of his language. Modern custom is less strict, and St Paul would no doubt have written differently today. He was certainly no woman-hater, *cf.* Rom 16:12-13; Phil 4:3. If we call him unchivalrous, we must at least remember that he was the first to break the soil from which chivalry sprang. Paul here speaks of women as praying and prophesying, but in 14:34 he says: '*Let women keep silence in the assemblies*. . . .' This has driven some commentators to believe that in this present chapter he is speaking of devotions confined to one household (family and servants). They point out that 'church' (*i.e.* assembly) is not mentioned in this section, as it is in 14:34. This view is certainly difficult, but other explanations of the seeming contradiction (*e.g.* that Paul had changed his mind by ch 14, but forgot to strike out this earlier paragraph) appear to be at least no better.
4. 'Prophesying': speaking by special inspiration, not necessarily about the future, *cf.* 12:10; 14:3. **5.** The most common headgear of women was a portion of the outer garment, the *himation*, drawn up from behind over the head, § 603*a*. It was easily and quickly done. It could be made to cover the face too, but that was not usual. **6.** 'Shorn': '*Let her cut her hair short*'. 'Made bald': '*Have her head shaved*'. **8-9.** Referring to the creation of Eve, Gen 2:18, 21. **10.** 'Because of the angels': these words are a puzzle. All proposed explanations are very improbable. *e.g.* Plummer says: 'If a woman thinks lightly of shocking men, she must remember she will also be shocking the angels, who of course are present at public worship'. Can the angels be so sensitive about human conventions? Others consider the words a marginal note which has slipped into the text. This would solve the difficulty if only some positive evidence for it were found, but there is none. **11.** '*Neither man nor woman can be independent of the other* . . . *for as woman was created from man, so man is born of woman. But all the creation is from God*'. **14.** '*If he lets his hair grow long*'. It was the universal custom among Jews, Greeks and Romans for men to wear the hair short. **16.** He silences any possible objectors

by appealing to Christian custom: '*If any man chooses to be contentious, (then I say that) we have no such custom (of letting women pray bare-headed) neither have the churches of God*'.

17-34 Disorders at Mass—In the Apostolic age the Mass was usually celebrated on Sunday evening, as it seems. The small congregation ate supper together before the Mass, in memory of the Last Supper and of the suppers at which the risen Christ had appeared to the Apostles. The food was provided by the richer Christians and the supper was called 'the Charity' (*Agapé*). There was therefore as yet no fast before Communion. The change to Sunday morning Mass and fasting Communion was made some time before A.D. 112, and may have taken place in the lifetime of the Apostles. On this subject and the Eucharistic doctrine underlying this passage see §§637*b*, 644*h*, 652*f*. By the term 'the Lord's supper' Paul here seems to denote supper and Mass *together*.
17-22 The Supper—**17.** Probably: '*After giving you these directions, I do not praise you for the fact that you come together*', etc. The words 'do not praise' look back to v 2. **18.** 'The church': '*an assembly* or *congregation*'. In the New Testament the word never means a building. Mass was usually in a private house then and for long after. 'Schisms': '*Divisions*'. Members of some of the various parties (including, no doubt, that of the False Apostles) gathered into exclusive circles at the supper, and did not share their food with outsiders. **19.** '*Even factions*' or '*cliques*'. The word *haeresis* still had usually a neutral sense (group or party, Ac 5:17; 15:5, etc.) but Paul always uses it in a bad sense. 'Approved', *i.e.* by God. Party-divisions, though an evil, help to sift the true Christians from the bad. **20.** '*It is not possible to eat* . . .': the meal no longer deserves to be called the Lord's supper. **21.** Two faults are condemned: 1. Each little group began supper as soon as their own members were assembled, without waiting till the whole congregation had come. 2. The food was not evenly shared out. Latecomers and the poorer members who belonged to no party would not receive enough. 'Every one . . .': '*Individuals eat their supper before the others*'. Loose use of 'every' as in 7:2, etc. 'Drunk': Perhaps some natural exaggeration, caused by his disgust at their selfishness. **22.** 'Have not': probably refers especially to slaves, who had no houses of their own. 'Do I . . .': '*Am I to praise you?*' 'Praise you not': ironical understatement, again referring back to v 2.
23-34 Reminder of the Meaning of Mass—To convince them that this unchristian supper is no right preparation for Mass, he formally recalls to them the foundation of the Mass and its meaning. **23.** 'Of the Lord': no doubt indirectly through the other apostles. **24.** 'My body . . .': the best texts read (literally): 'This is my body which is on your behalf'. Doubtless we may supply *given* or *offered* to make the meaning clearer. **25.** 'chalice': the Greek word is the ordinary one for 'cup'. 'The new testament . . .': the Greek word is translated sometimes *covenant* and sometimes *testament*. In either case the meaning is *contract* or *agreement*. The first contract between God and Israel was made through Moses and ratified by a sacrifice—it was the Mosaic Law, the Jewish religion. The new contract is the Christian religion and is ratified by the sacrifice of Calvary. Therefore 'in my blood' means *ratified with my blood*. 'Drink': *i.e.* drink this. We have four accounts of the institution of the Mass (in Mt, Mk, Lk and here), with slight differences in wording. Luke closely resembles Paul, but the other two have: 'This is my blood of the covenant'. The form in the Roman Missal is nearer to the latter though not identical: 'This is the cup of my blood of the new and eternal covenant'. **26.** 'You shall shew': '*You proclaim*'. Paul writes this to remind them of the close connexion of the Mass with Calvary. **27.** 'Guilty . . .': the phrase seems to hover between two meanings: (1) Guilty of the blood (*i.e.* death) of Christ. (2) A sinner

878g against the body and blood, etc. Both are true : in Heb 6:6 *every* mortal sin of a Christian is called a re-crucifixion of Christ. Paul does not labour to prove to the Corinthians that the bread and wine become Christ's body and blood : he treats it as an accepted fact, both here and in 10:16 above. **28.** ' Prove ' : *i.e.* make sure that he is worthy, examine *and approve* himself, *cf.* 16:3 ; 1 Thess 2:4. **29.** The best texts omit ' of the Lord '. ' Not discerning ' : ' *not distinguishing* ' —making no distinction *in act* between the Body and ordinary bread. Their sin was not unbelief but irreverence. **30.** ' Sleep ' : *i.e.* are dead. The verse describes the penalties (' judgements ') sent for their good, as he says in 32. The word ' sleep ' implies a strong hope of their salvation. **31.** ' Judge . . .' : ' *form a right judgement on ourselves* '. **32.** ' Whilst . . .' : ' *by being judged* ', *i.e.* visited with sickness, etc. **33-34.** He returns to the subject of supper. ' Wherefore ' : *i.e.* because the supper is a mere preliminary to the Mass.

h **XII-XIV**—The general subject of these chapters is the right estimation and use of special spiritual favours (charismata), but the main fault which Paul has in view, the abuse of the gift of languages, is not set forth at the beginning, but postponed to ch 14. We first have two chapters on general principles.

St Paul groups together a very large number of things, apparently every Divine help over and above what was *necessary* for salvation : this may be seen by reading the four lists, 12:8–11 ; 12:28 ; Rom 12:6–8 ; Eph 4:11–12. We may make three rough divisions : (1) Graces for those holding authority, whether perma-nent (Apostles and all in Holy Orders) or occasional (teachers, evangelists and recognized prophets). (2) The strikingly miraculous powers (miracles of healing etc., prophecy, speaking in new languages, etc.). (3) Powers to enable ordinary virtues or duties to be exercised in a more perfect way (faith, works of charity, almsgiving, prayer, etc.) : to these we may add the graces to enable men to be good husbands (7:7), good fathers, sons, masters, etc.

i Some of these gifts are visibly miraculous, others are not. Some are closely bound up with sanctifying grace (the third group especially), others may exist without it. Some (especially the second group) were much more common in the first few generations of Christianity than they have been since, and seem to have been temporary helps given to the infancy of the Church. The gifts of this second group were being dispropor-tionately valued at Corinth and against this St Paul makes a threefold protest : (1) *All* special favours (not this class only) are Divine, 12:1–11. (2) All are equally necessary for the good of the Church, 12:12–31*a*. (3) Without charity all gifts are vain, 12:31*b*–13:13. (See § 639).

879a **XII 1-11 All Special Favours are equally from God**— —The Corinthians had asked him some question on this subject, *cf.* 7:1, 25. Introd. E. **1.** ' Things ' : ' *Gifts* '. **2.** ' Went ' : ' *You were led away* (or *astray*) '. **3.** The idols were dumb, but they now have to deal with spiritual powers, both holy and *unholy* also, which *speak* through their human lips, and they need a rule to distinguish good from bad. ' Anathema . . .' ' *May Jesus be accursed* '. A Christian uttering such words when he felt himself gripped by some force beyond his control must be considered as under dia-bolical influence. Baxter says that Puritan fanatics used to utter ' most hideous words of blasphemy ' in moments of supposed inspiration. **4.** ' Graces ' : here Paul has ' charismata ' (plural of charisma, ordinary Greek word meaning ' favour ') as an all-

b embracing word for these graces. **5.** ' Ministries ' : *i.e.* modes of serving, duties. *All the charismata are given for the service of the one Master, Christ.* **6.** ' *Who operates always in all men* ', *i.e.* in all those endowed with the charismata. The doctrine of the Holy Trinity clearly underlies vv 4–6 for ' Lord ' surely

means Christ. **7.** ' *To this or that man however the manifesta-tion of the Spirit is given for the highest good* ' : *i.e.* God's mode of distribution is not haphazard but planned for the widest spiritual good. **8.** ' Word ' : ' *words* ', ' *utterance* '. The first gift is probably higher than the second, but the exact distinction is uncertain. **9.** ' Faith ' must mean some exceptional kind or degree of faith, the faith that could work miracles perhaps, as in 13:2 below. **10.** ' Discerning of spirits ' : power to distinguish good inspiration from bad or pretended inspiration, in cases where such easy rules as that of v 3 were not applicable. ' Tongues ' : ' *languages* ', *cf.* 14:1. ' Speeches ' : ' *languages* ', the same Greek word as before. **11.** ' Dividing ' : ' *distributing* '.

12-26 Parallel between the Church and the Human Body—It is Paul's longest allegory and remarkably consistent, *cf.* 3:10 f. and 2 Cor 3:1–3. Compare our Lord's allegory of the Vine, on a closely similar subject, Jn 15:1–8. The comparison of a society to the human body was familiar to Greeks and Romans. Here the spiritual meaning is present *throughout*. A threefold lesson : 1. Those who are without the more showy gifts must not be depressed or discontented, 15–16. 2. The most richly endowed are useless except as parts of the Christian society, 17–20. 3. The plainer graces are equally needed and nobody must despise them, 21. **13.** ' Members ' : *i.e.* parts or organs. ' Christ ' : logically we should expect ' the Church ', but Paul wishes to insist on the oneness of Christ and his church, as our Lord himself had done in his first words to him : ' Saul, Saul, why persecutest thou me ? ' *cf.* Mt 25:40 ; Jn 15:1, etc.). **13.** ' Baptized into . . .' : ' *made into one body by baptism* '. ' In one Spirit . . .' : probably : ' *We have all had one Spirit poured out upon us* ', *cf.* Is 29:10, ' The Lord has poured out upon you the spirit of drowsiness ', where LXX uses the same Greek verb ; Ac 2:17 ; Tit 3:6. But many prefer : ' We have all been given one Spirit to drink '. **15-17..** To console those who had not received the popular and spectacular charismata. **15.** ' Not of the body ' : *i.e.* not part of the body. **22.** ' More feeble ' : the choice of this word may well be meant to recall the ' weak brethren ' of ch 8, the ignorant and scrupulous Christians. **23.** ' Honour . . . comeliness ' : probably refers to clothing. **24.** ' tempered ' : ' *subtly compounded* or *proportioned* . . . *giving all the more honour to that which lacked it* '. **25.** ' Schism ' : ' *division* '. **26.** ' glory ' : ' *is honoured* '. The human body as a whole feels the pleasure or pain of any part. It ought to be so in the Church.

27-31a Application of the Allegory—**27.** ' Members . . .' : probably : ' *and individually you are parts (organs)* '. **28.** ' Doctors ' : ' *teachers* '. ' Helps . . .' : ' *Gifts of assistance, of government* '. Probably refers to the local Christian office-holders, the deacons and priests, for these also had received charismata through ordination (note on 12:1, *cf.* 1 Tim 4:14). The priests are called ' presidents ' in Rom 12:8 and ' shepherds ' in Eph 4:11. In Ac and the Pastoral Epistles they are called Seniors (presbyteroi) and that was the name that lasted. No doubt some of the prophets and teachers were priests or deacons too. The honourable place assigned to prophets, etc., in these lists has led to the unfounded theory that there were unordained or ' charismatic ' priests. (§§ 657–9). **31a.** ' Better ' : or ' *best, greatest* '. He puts the gift of languages last but one in both lists here, and it is clear from 14:5 that the higher gifts were those that ' built up ', *i.e.* had a greater *social* value (*e.g.* prophecy, teaching).

XII 31b-XIII 13 The Perfect Way—Charity—Charity is necessary for all, as a condition of salvation, but in a higher degree it may be a charisma. Both as virtue and as charisma it stands first in its class, for 1. Without it all the rest are vain. 2. It outlasts all other charismata. This is certainly one of the grandest passages written by Paul : an extraordinary combina-tion of close reasoning and poetic language. The poetic form owes little either to Hebrew or to Greek models, but is free and unartificial, the natural dress assumed by the exalted thought. The exact scope of Love is not directly stated, but it must be understood throughout in its full sense—love of God and of man for God's sake. Outside the Gospels the other great passage on this subject is 1 Jn 4:7–21, which in its very different way is as fine as this.

31b-XIII 3 Virtues and Charismata are Vain without Love—He takes five or six charismata in turn, the miraculous gift of languages being naturally placed first, as it had been especially over-prized. **31b.** '*And moreover I can show you a perfect way*'. **XIII 1.** ' Charity': the Greek word has much the same range of meaning as ' love ' in English. ' Brass ': *i.e.* trumpet or gong. ' Tinkling ' ; ' *Clashing* '. He seems to choose instruments which cannot play a *tune*. **2.** ' Mysteries ': secret unrevealed spiritual knowledge. Perhaps this charisma is ' the utterance of wisdom ' in 12:8. ' Faith ': see note on 12:9. **3.** ' Distribute . . .': almsgiving is among the charismata in Rom 12:8. It must mean almsgiving on a heroic scale. ' To be burned ': he is probably thinking of the fiery furnace in Dan ch 3 or of the Maccabean martyrs (2 Mac 7) for we do not know that any Christian martyrs were burned till A.D. 64, some years after this. But the two best Greek manuscripts read : ' If I lay down my life *for vainglory* and have no love . . . .'

4-7 Description of the Beauty of Christian Love—4. ' Dealeth not perversely ' ; probably : ' *is not ostentatious* '. **5.** ' Is not ambitious ', ' *does nothing dishonourable* '. **7.** ' Rejoiceth with the truth ' : *i.e.* shares in the joy which God and all good men receive from goodness and holiness. Truth here means practically goodness, *cf.* 2 Cor 13:8 ; Jn 3:21 ; 1 Jn 1:6.

8-13 Other Charismata are Transitory, Love is Eternal —The other charismata are bound up with the weakness and imperfection of our present state, and become superfluous hereafter. It now becomes clear that God, not our neighbour, is the first object of love. **8.** ' Falleth away ' ; ' *Is never done with, never becomes obsolete,* ' *cf.* Lk 16:17. ' Prophecies ' : *i.e.* various instances of the prophetic charisma. ' Made void . . . destroyed ' : ' *superseded* '. The Greek word is the same in both cases and also at the end of v 10. **9.** ' In part ' : or ' *imperfectly* '. The knowledge that he speaks of is knowledge of God, *cf.* 12 f. In this world our knowledge of God is indirect and imperfect, based on comparisons and contrasts to things which come within our experience. This dim picture will be abandoned when we know Him directly, ' face to face '. So also the prophet's shadowy foreknowledge is superseded by the reality, and the gift of languages is clearly useless after this life. **10.** ' When . . . ' : *i.e.* in the future life. **11.** Our present life is compared to childhood. **12.** ' See ' : *i.e.* see God. ' Glass ' : ' *mirror* ', *i.e.* indirectly, by a reflexion, which in ancient mirrors (they were only polished metal) would generally be rather dim. ' In a dark manner '. The Greek word *ainigma* (riddle) is used in the OT sense of parable or comparison or figurative language. Therefore ' *by means of (earthly) imagery* '. ' Am known ' : or perhaps ' *have been known* ', and there may be the incidental thought that God's knowledge means God's approval (8:3) though this is unessential to the argument. The conclusion of all this reasoning (8-12) had already been stated at its commencement, and is not repeated. Charity on earth and in heaven is essentially the same, differing only in degree, and is therefore an eternal virtue. **13.** ' And now ' seems to mean ' *For the present* ' or ' *meanwhile* ', for Paul himself intimates elsewhere that faith and hope are only for this life, 2 Cor 5:7 ; Rom 8:24 : they naturally cease when we see what we have believed in, and attain to what we have hoped for.

XIV 1-25 Comparison between two Charismata— Prophecy and Languages—The term *prophecy* seems to have a wide sense, including a miraculous insight into doctrine, morality, and perhaps the thoughts of other men. Ancient Jewish prophets had the same

powers. As regards the charisma of ' tongues ' (*i.e.* languages—one word for both in Greek) by far the best view is that it was the same gift as the Apostles received at Pentecost : the miraculous power of speaking languages not previously learnt. Its purpose, as Paul says in v 22, was the conversion of unbelievers, and to make it a frequent part of Christian worship, as had been done at Corinth, was an abuse. This is, in brief, the complaint that Paul makes. There are two other views about the gift : (1) That it was the sort of unintelligible utterance which we hear of in certain sects, Christian and otherwise, caused by unwholesome religious excitement—in fact, gibberish. In that case Paul would not merely have restricted it, but would very certainly have banned it. (2) That it was the **c** use of *unusual* words (obsolete, poetical, dialectical, etc.) to give an impression of a lofty 'style. Objections : (*a*) We cannot believe God would inspire eccentricity and affectation ; (*b*) It would not be unintelligible— its *drift* at least would be understood ; (*c*) It would be entirely different from the gift of Pentecost, yet Paul uses precisely the same term as is used in Ac.

1-6 Prophecy is Superior because it benefits Others— 1. ' Rather ' : ' *especially* '. **2.** ' Heareth ' : ' *understands* '. ' By the Spirit ' : *i.e.* by inspiration. The word *spirit* in this chapter seems sometimes to mean ' spiritual gift ' or ' inspiration ' especially in v 12. **3.** ' Edification ' : *cf.* 8:1. ' Exhortation ' : ' *encouragement* '. **6.** ' Unless . . .' : compressed, according to Greek idiom. In full : ' I shall profit you only if I speak . . . in revelation . . .'. ' Doctrine ' : ' *teaching* '. Revelation and prophecy seem to mean the same thing, and so with knowledge and teaching. He seems to be thinking of the gifts of the prophet and the teacher, *cf.* 12:28.

7-13 Sounds are Useless unless their Meaning is d understood—He argues from music and ordinary speech. **7.** ' Distinction . . .' Or perhaps ' *a definite arrangement of notes* '. ' How . . . ' : *i.e.* how can the tune be known or recognized ? **9.** ' Tongue ' here probably means the organ itself. ' Speaking . . . ' : *i.e.* wasting your breath. **10.** Probably ' *There are, I suppose, so many kinds of speech in the world, and nothing is speechless* ', *i.e.* no race (or perhaps : no living creature) is without its language or utterance. **11.** ' Power ' : ' *meaning* '. ' *I shall be a barbarian to him who speaks* '. ' Barbarian ' : rather a contemptuous word applied by Greek-speakers to all who did not speak Greek, *cf.* Ac 28:2 ; Rom 1:14. **12.** ' Spirits ' : *i.e.* spiritual gifts, *cf.* note v 2. ' *To abound in them but in such a way that the church may be built up* ' (knit together, strengthened)—for which purpose the gift of languages is useless. **13.** ' Pray . . . interpret '. From this and 5 it seems that sometimes the speaker in a language could not translate what he said.

14-20 Among Christians themselves (whether in pray- e ing or preaching) all Incomprehensible Speech is out of place—His argument is that as the human intellect is not exercised, the benefit cannot be communicated. **14.** ' My spirit ' : either ' *the inspiration within me* ' or ' *the innermost part of my soul* '. ' Without fruit ' : *unfruitful*, *i.e.* unprofitable to others. A truth may be *grasped* by some sort of intuition, but cannot be *communicated* without intellectual activity. **15.** ' *What is the conclusion ?* ' or ' *What is to be done then ?* ' ' I will pray . . . ' : *i.e.* he will welcome every divine inspiration in his (public) prayer, but by the exercise of his intellect he will put his prayer into ordinary Greek words. ' I will sing ' : *Compose songs or hymns* (probably), *cf.* 26. **16.** ' *Otherwise, if you pronounce a blessing in the spirit only* (*i.e.* in an unknown language) *how are those who fill the place of ordinary members to say Amen to your thanksgiving ?* ' The ' ordinary member ' is the Christian who has no charisma or who does not understand the language used. The words *blessing* and *thanksgiving* were often used of the consecration at Mass (10:16) and may mean that here, but may also refer to the grace said at the preceding supper. **18.** ' *I thank God that I can speak (strange) languages better than any of you* '. **19.** ' In the church ', *i.e.* in a gathering

880e of Christians. **20.** ' In sense ' : ' *in mind* '. The gross misuse of ' tongues ' argued a silliness worthy of children. ' perfect ' : ' *grown-up* '.

f 21-25 The Gift of Languages is ' a Sign to Unbelievers ' —**21.** ' The law ' : often used loosely for the *whole* OT, *cf.* Jn 10:34. ' In other tongues . . .' : ' *through men of foreign language and through the mouths of foreigners I will speak to this people, and even so they will not listen to me* '. A paraphrase of Is 28:11 : as the Jews had refused to listen to Isaias, God says he will send the foreign-speaking Assyrians to attack them—the strange language will be, as it were, a Divine voice calling them to repentance. God has given the charisma of languages for a similar purpose. **23-25.** He now seems to go a step further and to argue that even for unbelievers the prophetic gift is more beneficial than that of languages. **23.** ' Unlearned ', *i.e.* ungifted, *cf.* v 16. **24 f.** ' Convinced . . .' : ' *he is convicted by all . . . examined by all* '. The prophetic gift enables them to penetrate into his thoughts and to awaken his conscience without necessarily betraying his secrets to others.

g 26-40 Rules for Orderly Services—We should naturally suppose that he is referring to Mass, and therefore to the first part of it, devoted to Scripture reading, exposition and exhortation, but some think another service had been meant. Evidently great liberty of action had been allowed to members endowed with charismata, but we must remember that some of these were priests or deacons. Paul suppresses four abuses : (1) Too many gifted members had spoken at one service. (2) Members had spoken in strange languages without any interpretation given. (3) Several gifted members had spoken simultaneously on the ground that inspiration could not or should be checked. (4) Women endowed with charismata had been allowed to speak. **26.** ' How . . .' : the same phrase as in v 15. ' Every one ', *i.e.* each of the specially gifted ones, or perhaps : ' individuals ', *cf.* 11:21 ; 12:7. ' Psalm ', which he had been inspired to compose, see v 15. ' Doctrine ' : ' *something to teach* ' : he had the teacher's charisma. ' Revelation ' : the prophetic charisma, *cf.* v 30. **27.** ' Two or . . . three ' : at any one service. **h** ' In course ' : ' *In turn* '. ' One ' : ' *someone* '. **28.** ' Him ' : the member who wishes to speak in a strange language. ' Hold his peace ' : a drastic change in Corinthian practice. **29.** ' Two or three ' in turn at any one service : this is obvious from v 27. ' The rest ' seems to refer loosely to all who had the gift of ' discrimination of spirits ', 12:10. **30.** ' The first ', *i.e.* the prophet who is at the moment speaking. **31.** ' All prophesy ' : seems to contemplate the *possibility* that the majority might possess the prophetic charisma. **32.** ' The spirits ' : ' *the inspiration is under the control of the prophet* '. Therefore there was no need for him to insist on speaking here and now. The same could be said about the gift of languages. For this meaning of ' spirit ', see vv 2, 12. **33.** ' Dissension ' : ' *disorder* '. The best texts omit ' also I teach '. ' Saints ', *i.e.* Christians, as in 1:2, etc. **34-35.** This seems to be inconsistent with 11:2-16, where we hear of women praying and prophesying. See note there. Either ch 11 refers to more private devotions, or ' speak ' here means preaching or instructing and does not include prayer and inspired utterances at the meetings. **34.**
881a ' Churches ' : ' *assemblies, meetings* '. ' Subject ' : ' *in subjection* '. Women are not to exercise any authority in the church. Among men some authority, formal or informal, seems often to have been connected with certain charismata. (See 12:28.) ' The law ' : perhaps refers to Gen 3:16. **35.** ' *It is disgraceful in a woman . . .* ' **36-38.** These stern words refer to all the regulations just given in 26-35. They are aimed at possible objectors and opponents. **36.** The Corinthian church has no right to set itself up as a pattern in opposition to other churches. ' *Did the gospel originate with you ?* (*i.e.* were you the first Christian church ?) *Or are you the only ones who have received it ?* ' **37.** ' Whoever

claims to be a prophet, or to have any spiritual gift, let him recognize that what I write to you is the commandment of the Lord* '. If he disputes that, his claim to inspiration is false. **38.** ' Know not ' : that Paul's words are the commandments of Christ. ' Shall . . .' : better ' *Is* not known '—by God, *cf.* 8:3. **39.** Prophecy is encouraged, but the *public* use of languages is only tolerated.

XV The Immortality of Body and Soul—This is the last big topic of the letter, and Paul's last complaint. Some persons at Corinth were spreading erroneous views on the subject, about which his three visitors had probably told him. Two opinions are possible about the nature of the false teaching :

(1) That only the soul is immortal—the body perishes after death and is never raised up or restored. Such belief in immortality as existed among pagans of the Greek tradition was of this kind. They regarded the idea of bodily immortality as ridiculous, Ac 17:30-33. Such a doctrine among Christians would therefore very likely have a pagan origin.

(2) That only those Christians who are alive at Christ's second coming will receive immortality—those who die before that perish altogether. This opinion, though uncommon, seems to have been taught in some Jewish apocalyptic tracts (not included in Scripture) and some such view was circulating among the Christians of Thessalonica about five years before this, 1 Thess 4:13-16.

The first view best fits the chapter as a whole, and is much the more widely held. Yet some passages seem to imply that the immortality even of the soul had been denied, vv. 19, 29-32, and it appears that the false teachers had not all denied the bodily resurrection of Christ, as we should have expected if they all held the first error only. It is possible that both kinds of error were taught at Corinth, and in that case Paul first directs his words at the two (vv 12-34) and afterwards at the first one. For the history of pre-Christian beliefs about immortality, see §§ 595*a*, 598*l*, and E. F. Sutcliffe's *The Old Testament and the Future Life*.

1-11 Evidence of Christ's Resurrection—This is a summary of what he had previously taught them. **1.** ' Make known ' : for ' remind '—perhaps a sign of impatience. **2.** ' If you hold . . .' : most scholars prefer a different order : (' I wish to remind you) *in what words I preached to you, if you hold them fast . . .* ' **3.** ' Received ' : from the other apostles. **3-4.** ' Scriptures ' : refer to the OT prophecies, not to the Gospels, most of which were not yet written. **5-8.** He mentions six appearances of the risen Lord, chosen no doubt because there were still living and well-known witnesses of them all, and omits others (*e.g.* to Mary Magdalen) probably because the witnesses were dead or unknown. **5.** ' Cephas ' : Christ's appearance to St Peter on the day of his resurrection is nowhere described but is alluded to in Lk 24:34. ' The eleven ' : the best texts say ' *the twelve* '—a round number, for it must refer to the supper on the day of resurrection, when both Judas and Thomas were absent. **6.** Either some occasion not mentioned in the Gospels, or the meeting on a mountain in Galilee described in Mt 28:16-18. **7.** ' James ' : not John's brother, who had been dead many years, but James the Less, the cousin of our Lord, who was still alive and was seen by Paul about a year after this, Ac 21:18 f. This appearance of our Lord is mentioned nowhere else in the NT. **8.** ' Born ', *i.e.* his conversion with his call to the Apostolate was a violent and sudden change comparable to a premature birth. **10.** *i.e.* it is the grace of God that has made me what I am. ' More abundantly ' : he means that he has gained more converts. **11.** ' I . . . they ' : something like ' laboured more fruitfully ' must be understood.

12-28 If there is no Resurrection, Christ has neither risen nor conquered Death—The erroneous teachers admitted that Christ had risen—Paul argues in 12-19

f that if they were consistent, they would deny it, and thereby deny all his work of redemption. It is in this portion (12–34) that the second type of error *seems* at times to be in Paul's mind. **13.** *i.e.* any argument which they used to show the impossibility of a resurrection would tell equally against Christ's. **14.** The resurrection was the proof of the atoning power of the Passion : without it we must believe that Jesus was merely a good man who had sacrificed himself in vain. (See v 17.) **15.** 'Against God' : '*About God*'. **17.** 'in your sins' : their baptism was an empty ceremony if Christ's work had been a failure. **18-19.** His opponents seem to teach that even the souls of dead Christians no longer exist. **19.** 'This life' : this present world. Its good things often have to be renounced for the sake of fidelity to God. But the verse may perhaps mean : 'If in this (new) life in Christ we possess nothing but hopes (*i.e.* empty hopes)

g we are . . .' **20-28.** If the dead do not rise, Christ has not fully undone the evil wrought by the Fall, nor has he been made king of all created things. **20.** 'Firstfruits', *i.e.* first instalment or earnest. Originally the word meant the consecration of the first sheaf, but was now used much like ἀρραβών, *cf.* Eph 1:14. **21-22.** The comparison between Christ and Adam is often in Paul's mind (see vv 45-49 below, and above all Rom 5:12-21). 'In Adam' : owing to Adam's sin. 'All . . . alive', seems to refer primarily to the *spiritual* life, and therefore to the redeemed only, the resurrection of sinners being ignored for the moment. **23.** '*But every one (will rise) in his own rank (or class)* : . . . *next they that are Christ's (will rise) at his coming*'. The last-mentioned are the faithful who had died before Christ's second coming—this seems clear from 1 Thess 4:15-16. He again omits the resurrection of sinners as irrelevant. **24.** 'Kingdom' : '*His royal power*'. This seems to mean our Lord's office of redeemer and Messiah, which ceases when all the redeemed are gathered. A mediator is no longer needed : v 28 seems to have the same meaning. God the Son of course retains his human nature for

h ever. 'Virtue', *i.e.* power. The three words refer to hostile powers, human or diabolical. **25.** '*He (Christ) must reign (as Messiah) until he (God the Father) has, etc.*' Adaptation of Ps 109(110):1, 'Sit thou at my right hand until I make thy enemies thy footstool'. **26.** '*After all other enemies death himself shall be destroyed, for he (God the Father) has placed ALL things under his (Christ's) feet*''. The last words are from Ps 8:8. Paul means that, if there were no resurrection, this prophecy would remain unfulfilled. **26c-28.** Perhaps the best way to take these difficult words is : '*When he (Christ) shall say that all things are subject to himself (with the exception, of course, of him (i.e. the Father) who has made all things subject to him)—when, I say, all things are subjected to him, then the Son himself will become subject* . . .' In this way the first words of 28 are taken as a repetition of the last words of 26. 'All in all' : everything in all creation, *i.e.* in all the redeemed creation there will no longer be anything alien or opposed to God.

i **29-34 Other Arguments for the Resurrection—29.** *For what good will they do* . . .' The meaning is very doubtful. Perhaps some persons at Corinth had desired to become Christians but had been overtaken by death before they could be baptised and some Christian friends had been allowed to undergo a (purely symbolical) baptism for them to show that the dead were counted as Christians. If so, the practice was soon dropped for fear of misunderstanding. Here again and in 30-32 Paul seems to be dealing with a teaching that dead Christians had perished. **30.** Why do we (the Apostles) risk death, if our only hope of immortality is to remain alive till Christ comes ? **31.** Apparently when Paul was at Corinth, in frequent danger and bodily weakness, some Corinthians had said of him : 'He dies daily'. Paul now reminds them of these admiring words. '*I die daily—I call to witness your own boast, which I have to my credit, thanks to Christ*

Jesus'. *Cf.* 2 Cor 4:11-12. **32.** The phrase 'fight **881j** with wild beasts' apparently meant 'lead a hunted, insecure life'. '*If I have lived a hunted life (as the world would call it) at Ephesus, what have I gained by it ?* He was still at or near Ephesus. The dangers he refers to seem to have been owing to Jewish plots (Ac 20:19), not the great riot which came after this date. (Ac 19:23-40). It seems best to join the next two sentences. '*If the dead* . . . *let us*', etc. The last words are from Is 22:13. **33.** 'Evil . . .' : a line from a comedy of the Greek poet Menander, but it had probably become a proverb. '*Bad company is the ruin of a good character*'. It is here a warning against the authors of the false ideas on immortality. **34.** *Come to your senses, as you ought to do, . . . it is an ignorance (not a knowledge) of God that some of you have*'. There seems to be another scornful reference to the word *knowledge* as in ch 8, *cf.* Christ's words to the Sadducees on the same subject : 'You err, not knowing . . . the power of God', Mt 22:29.

35-58 Bodily Resurrection is not contrary to Reason— k The doctrine of a bodily resurrection is a part of revealed truth, an article of Catholic faith. Paul does not attempt to give here a proof of it, but only to remove some difficulties and objections. On the question how far the risen body will be materially identical with the body that dies, theologians differ : the majority teach that some particles at least will be common to both, but others (*e.g.* Billot) hold that this is not necessary.

This passage is an equally good answer to either of the two possible errors (see Introd. to chapter). Next to ch 13 it is the most eloquent passage in the letter, and shows the same wonderful originality of poetic writing used as a vehicle of close argument. It may conveniently be taken in three parts.

35-41 Some Parallels in Nature—First, the history **l** of a seed shows resemblances to both death and transformation. **36.** 'Quickened' : '*Brought back to life*'. **37.** 'Bare grain', *i.e.* without stalk, blade, husk, etc., yet all these will appear again as the plant grows. **38.** 'As he will' : '*As he has decreed*', *i.e.* in fixing the laws of nature. **39-41.** He shows that in the visible universe the words 'body' and 'flesh' are applicable to a vast diversity of forms, suggesting that there may be other and even more marvellous 'bodies' as yet unknown to us. **40.** 'Bodies celestial'—the sun, stars, etc. named in 41. Though not alive, each has its own unity and a certain independence. 'Glory', *i.e.* excellence, perfection. **41.** 'For star . . .' The 'for' may indicate that he is quoting a familiar saying or proverb.

42-50 The Risen Body far excels the Natural Body— 882a This is inferred both from the preceding facts and from the resurrection of Christ. **42.** 'It '—the body. 'Is sown'—dies and is buried. **44.** 'Natural body'. endowed with that natural life which we share with all men (good and bad). 'Spiritual body': not a body made of spirit, an immaterial body (which would be a contradiction), but a material body perfectly fitted to be the instrument of a soul elevated and transfigured by union with God, in short, a body like our Lord's body after his resurrection. 'If . . .' : '*As surely as there is* . . .' **45.** He begins a comparison between Adam and Christ, Adam being considered as type of the 'natural' *i.e.* unregenerate men. 'Living soul' : (Gen 2:7) *animate being*. 'Quickening' : '*Life-giving*'. 'Spirit' : the word implies *super*natural life. **46.** '*It* **b** *was not the spiritual (life) that came first*'. **47.** '*The first man was from the earth, made of dust. The second man was from heaven*'. So run the best texts. **48.** *Such as the man of dust was, such are the men of dust* (in general)— meaning men in this present life, especially the non-Christians. 'They . . .': the redeemed after their resurrection. They will resemble the risen Christ, the 'heavenly man'. **49.** 'Let us bear', etc. Logically we should expect : 'We shall bear', etc. (the natural conclusion of his reasoning) and one of our best texts in fact reads thus and may well be right. The Douay

882b text must mean : Let us live so that we may bear, etc. **50.** 'Flesh and blood' : human nature in its present frail state. There must be a change, to make this material body everlasting.

c 51-58 The Last Change and the Triumph over Death—51. 'Mystery' : '*A secret*' : a newly revealed truth. The best texts read : ' We shall not all sleep (*i.e.* die) but we shall all be changed ', *i.e.* those who are living at our Lord's appearance will undergo an immediate transformation (see end of 52). **52.** Fuller description in 1 Thess 4:13–17. ' And we . . .', *i.e.* the living. The use of ' we ' does not mean that Paul was certain that he would himself be alive, *cf.* §914*g*–*l*. **54.** 'Death . . .' From Is 25:8, where the meaning of the Hebrew text, as Paul knew very well, is : ' He has swallowed up death *for ever* '. The Hebrew of ' for ever ' could be literally translated ' in victory ' and Paul here chooses to use the literal sense so as to join it with the first words of 55 which are an adaptation of Os 13:14. **56.** Death derives its power from sin, for it came into the world as a punishment for sin, and sin would not be recognized as sin if the Law did not denounce it. The two thoughts are fully set forth in Rom chh 5 and 7. **58.** 'Knowing. . . .' Their glorious future is secure even if they die before Christ's coming.

d XVI 1-18 Directions about the Immediate Future— In twelve verses he deals rapidly with four practical matters, the collection for Jerusalem Christians, his coming visit to Corinth, Timothy's visit, and Apollos' plans.

1-4 The Collection—At this time Paul was organizing a collection to be made in all the churches he had founded (in four provinces : Achaea, Macedonia, Asia and Galatia) for the mother-church at Jerusalem. (See Introd. E and §889*a* ff.) Besides relieving their needs, it was to be a practical proof of his own loyalty and that of his converts to the teaching of Christ, and an answer to the slanders of Judaizers. It had evidently been spoken of in some previous communication. A good deal more is said about it later in 2 Cor 8 and 9. **1.** ' Galatia ' : we do not know when these instructions were sent. **2.** ' First day ', *i.e.* Sunday. ' With himself ' : by him, in his own keeping. It was not therefore to be handed in at Mass, apparently. ' *Laying up what he can afford* '. **3.** More likely : ' *I will send them with letters* (from myself) *to carry your gift* '. **4.** ' That I . . . go '. He did in fact accompany them, Ac 20.

e 5-9 His Coming Visit—His promised visit had apparently been already postponed : see 4:18 and Introd. E. He now announces a further delay, caused partly by a postponement of his departure from Ephesus and partly by a change, as it seems, in his route—he was going through Macedonia instead of crossing directly by sea. This delay (which in fact amounted to some months) was a deliberate act, in order to give the Corinthians time to decide whether they would be loyal to him, 2 Cor 1:23–2:3 : see Introd. F. **5.** ' When . . .': best interpreted as *a change* of route, the same change as is referred to in 2 Cor 1:15–17, which his enemies used against him (§§883*b*, 885*ef*). **5-6.** ' For I . . . abide ' : ' *for I am (only) passing through Macedonia, but with you I shall stay some time perhaps* '. **6.** ' That you . . .' : the ' you ' is emphasized. ' Bring me . . .' : probably included the idea of helping him with necessaries for his journey. If he did not go to Jerusalem, he meant to go to Italy and Spain, Rom 15:23–24. **7.** ' Not . . . now . . by the way '. These words might imply that he had once already ' seen them by the way ', *i.e.* paid them a short visit since his long stay with them. Such a short visit may have taken place—see 2 Cor Introd. D 3. But ' not . . . now ' may have another sense, *e.g.* ' not as I originally intended ' or ' not now, whatever may happen in future ' (for he perhaps regarded this as his last visit— **f** see Ac 20:25). ' Some time ' : he spent three months in Achaea, most of it at Corinth no doubt, Ac 20:3. **8.** ' Until Pentecost '. This implies that he was writing some time in March or April, for Pentecost is generally

about the end of May. **9.** ' *A great and effective door* ', *i.e.* opportunity (for spreading the Gospel). ' Door ' is a Jewish expression. ' *And there are many adversaries* '. The riot stirred up by the pagan shrine-makers at Ephesus probably took place in May of that year, and Paul no doubt could already see signs of coming trouble, Ac 19:23–40.

10-11 Timothy's Visit to Corinth—This proposed visit has been mentioned in 4:17. ' If Timothy come '. Probably : ' *Whenever Timothy comes* '. ' Without fear . . . despise him '. Five years before this, when Timothy first came to Corinth with Paul, he would have been hardly more than a boy. Paul feared they would still treat him as a boy. **11.** ' Conduct him . . .' : same term as *bring* in v 6. ' The brethren '. Erastus was one of Timothy's companions, Ac 19:22.

12 Apollos's Plans—Probably the loyal Corinthians had asked for Apollos, if Paul could not come. St Paul's desire that Apollos should go over to Corinth is a clear proof of his confidence in this friend. He knew that Apollos was not supporting the ' party of Apollos ' at Corinth and that he was the best man to restore harmony there. ' The brethren ', *i.e.* the three visitors from Corinth, see v 17. ' Not his will ' : Or perhaps : ' *Not God's will* '.

13-18 Last Messages—These relate largely to the three visitors, whose presence has not hitherto been mentioned, though one of them, Stephanas, was named in 1:16. About the purpose of their visit see Introd. E. Stephanas was probably a priest, and the other two may have been. **13.** ' Watch ' : ' *Keep awake* '. ' Be strengthened ' : summon all your energy, pull yourselves together. **14.** ' Things ' : ' *Actions* '. **15.** The best texts have only the name of Stephanas here. The other two have slipped in by mistake from v 17. ' The house ' may include not only relatives but also freedmen and slaves. ' Firstfruits of Achaea ' (*cf.* 15:20). They were among the first converts made in the province, not necessarily the very first, for these seem to have been Athenians, Ac 17:34. Perhaps they were the first at Corinth. **16.** This probably means that Stephanas and one or two members of his household were priests. *Cf.* similar language in 1 Thess 5:12. **17.** Fortunatus and Achaicus may or may not have been members of Stephanas's household. ' Because . . .' : *i.e.* they have brought messages of loyalty (and perhaps gifts) which ought to have come sooner. This seems however an ungracious thing to say at the end of a letter, and another meaning is possible : ' They have satisfied the need which you felt '—the desire felt by the better Corinthians to send their good wishes and perhaps gifts to Paul. **18.** ' *They have cheered my heart and yours* ', *i.e.* the faithful at Corinth have derived as much happiness from sending the messengers as Paul has had from receiving them, a kind and affectionate thought. ' Know . . . ' : ' *Therefore pay them all respect* '.

19-24 Conclusion—19. ' Asia ' : the Roman province called Asia, the western part of Asia Minor. Aquila and Prisca (as Paul always calls her) were well-known at Corinth, for they had been there with Paul, Ac 18: 2–3. They had lived at Ephesus during Paul's long stay there. ' With whom . . .' : Erroneous addition, not in the Greek. **22.** ' Kiss ' : common salutation among friends in ancient times, Mt 27:49. Here it perhaps refers to the solemn kiss given at Mass, of which the Pax is a relic. **21-24.** He writes the last few lines with his own hand, after dictating the rest. He had adopted this practice as a proof of the genuineness of the letters, as he explains in 2 Thess 3:17. ' Anathema ' : *i.e.* accursed, *cf.* 12:3. There should be a full stop after this. ' Maran atha ' : an Aramaic sentence : ' The Lord is coming '. Paul gives the same thing in Greek in Phil 4:5. Evidently it was one of those short Hebrew and Aramaic expressions which had become familiar even to converts from paganism, like Amen, Alleluia, Pascha. **24.** Either ' *My love is with you all* ', or ' *May my love be with you all* '. The second would be a wish that even the most hostile of the Corinthians should be reconciled to him.

2 CORINTHIANS

INTRODUCTION

Bibliography—See § 864*a*

A. Events between the Two Epistles—The troubles which occasioned the First Epistle are described in the Introduction to it. The letter was written at the height of these troubles, in the spring of some year between A.D. 54 and 57. The Second Epistle was written a few months later. St Paul's assistant Titus was sent to Corinth as Paul's envoy with, or shortly after, the First Epistle, armed with special powers for dealing with the crisis. The effect of the letter, backed by Titus's words, was profound. Many well-meaning Corinthians had been dazzled and confused by the specious language of the False Apostles (see 1 Cor Introd. C), and Paul's long absence had dimmed the impression made by his former visit. But now the stern warnings of the letter, joined to its marvellous eloquence, brought them back, as it were, into his very presence. Their old loyalty and reverence were re-kindled. His enemies were not silent however, for it is probably now that three offensive statements of theirs were heard: (1) 'His letters indeed are impressive and vigorous but his appearance is undignified and he is contemptible as a speaker' (2 Cor 10:10). (2) From the words in 2 Cor 1:12–14 (see notes) we gather that they said something like this: ' Paul writes about every subject except the one which he has most at heart—his desire to turn you against us and to destroy our influence. It is a shifty and dishonest letter.' There was a grain of truth in the first part of this, which made it dangerous (1 Cor Introd. F). (3) They called Paul fickle and irresponsible (2 Cor 1:17) because he had again postponed his visit to Corinth and was going to Macedonia first.

But the time for intrigue and slander had gone by. A considerable number (probably a majority) had been brought to their senses by Paul and Titus, and refused to listen to Paul's enemies. They promised to correct all the abuses of which he had written. The man who had contracted the unlawful marriage was excommunicated. Titus was received with the greatest respect and humility, and was able to start the collection for the Palestinian Christians (2 Cor 8:6). He then set out for Asia by way of Macedonia. But a section of the Corinthians remained hostile to Paul, friends of the False Apostles, and men who would not give up the dangerous compromise with paganism, which the False Apostles had at least connived at. While Paul was at Ephesus in great suspense about the result of the letter, new troubles had broken out at Ephesus itself (2 Cor 1:8–10). This must be the pagan outbreak described in Ac 19:23–40, caused by Demetrius's agitation among the shrine-makers, and culminating during the great feast of Artemis (Diana) in May of the same year. Perhaps an attack of his chronic malady occurred also. After the disorders, he left Ephesus to await Titus at Troas (2 Cor 2:12). But anxiety and perhaps illness so oppressed him that he left a half-founded church there and crossed to Mace-donia. Here, probably at Philippi, he caught Titus on his way and heard the good news. His joy was immense (2 Cor 7). Assured of the substantial loyalty of the Corinthians, he now felt able to deal plainly with the rebels there, and soon afterwards wrote the Second Epistle in order to carry the re-conquest of Corinth a step further.

B. Structure and Composition—Although the language throughout the letter shows signs of careful choice and deliberation, the structure is certainly odd, and this oddness is by no means confined to chh 10–13, as is sometimes said. Paul must have had two distinct objects in the letter: (1) To seal his reconciliation with the majority of the Corinthians, who had now re-affirmed their loyalty to him. (2) To make an out-spoken attack on the defiant minority, to denounce

their leaders, and by threats or appeals to win over as **883d** many of this party as possible. We may briefly call these two purposes Reconciliation and Controversy.

But St Paul's recent experience (intense misery and **e** triumphant use of it for good) had stamped on his mind a new and overwhelming impression of the mean-ing of the Cross for the Christian and the Apostle, the paradox of power in and through suffering, and this thought is so dominant throughout the epistle that his two immediate purposes are not only seen in its light, but are sometimes eclipsed by it. We may call this the Paradox.

He had decided that his controversial purpose must involve something resembling self-laudation, and this was no doubt one reason why he shrank from it and postponed the main controversial passage to the end, although in several earlier passages he seems to be on the point of embarking on it (1:12–20; 4:1–6; and above all 6:11–7:3).

Two feelings therefore, the mighty impression of recent events and distaste for the task of self-assertion, have so much interfered with the plan which he no doubt had in his mind, that this letter is the most confused of all the Pauline epistles. The postponement of the great denunciatory passage to the end is only one instance of this: the long digression in the story of his meeting with Titus (2:14 to 7:4) is at least equally extraordinary, so is the abrupt passage 6:11–7:3 which many radical critics want to cut out as spurious or misplaced. Indeed the first six chapters are the least **f** orderly in the letter, much less so than chh 10–13. In some places the disorder is our gain: the great digression in the first half contains some of the grandest passages in the epistle.

The distribution of the three chief subjects may be seen from this list: Reconciliation: 1:23–2:13; 7:4–16. Controversy: 1:12–22; 2:17–3:3; 4:1–6; 5:11–13; 6:11–7:3; 10:1–11:29; 12:11–13:10. Paradox: 1:3–11; 2:14–16; 4:7–15; 6:3–10; 11:30–12:10. The paradox, as it figures prominently in both parts of the letter, gives it a real measure of unity, and also gives it its chief spiritual value.

C. Other Views about Intermediate Events—A new **g** theory which arose during the last century was first made widely known in England by J. H. Kennedy's book in 1900 (§ 864*b*). For brevity's sake we may call it Kennedy's theory. It has been accepted wholly or partly by many scholars, both Catholic and Pro-testant. In Section B above I have noted and tried to account for Paul's postponement of his denunciation of the False Apostles to the end of the letter. The comparative calm of the first nine chapters is suc-ceeded by four chapters of reproaches, irony, threats, and appeals. It is something unique in Paul's letters. Kennedy offers a different explanation, namely, that the Second Epistle is not one letter but two, which by mistake have been joined together in the *wrong order*: chh 10–13 are a severe letter which has lost its begin-ning, and chh 1–9 are a ' letter of reconciliation ' written *after* the severe letter. We therefore have three letters to Corinth: (*a*) Our First Epistle, (*b*) chh 10–13 of our Second Epistle, (*c*) chh 1–9 of our Second Epistle.

Further arguments for this theory are: (1) If 2 Cor 1–9 **h** belong to a third letter, then the letter referred to in 2 Cor 2:4 and 7:8–12 is not the First Epistle but the severe letter (*i.e.* 2 Cor 10–13). It is argued that the First Epistle is not nearly severe enough to fit the terms used in these two places. (2) An individual offender is mentioned in 2 Cor 2:5–11 and 7:12. It is said that the language used is inappropriate for the incestuous man of 1 Cor 5:1–5 (to whom it is traditionally applied) and must mean somebody who had been guilty of a *personal* offence or insult to Paul, and that this further implies that important events had taken place since the First Epistle. (3) This suggestion of intermediate events seems to be corroborated by five passages in the Second Epistle (mostly in chh 10–13) which seem to indicate that Paul had paid a recent visit to Corinth

883h and had met with opposition and disappointment there. This visit would be between the First Epistle and the severe letter, and the offender mentioned in 2 Cor chh 2 and 7 may well be somebody whom he had then met at Corinth.

i Therefore, according to Kennedy's theory, the intermediate events may be summarized thus : ' About the time when the First Epistle was written, a party opposed to Paul (whoever they were) was gaining influence at Corinth, encouraged by some visiting missionaries. When this Epistle was read at Corinth, the opposition became open rebellion, in which a large proportion of the church was involved. Paul, on hearing of this, sailed from Ephesus to Corinth. He failed to quell the rebels, and one of them distinguished himself by some offensive act or words. After a short and stormy visit, Paul returned to Asia, and wrote a stern letter, the bulk of which is preserved in 2 Cor chh 10–13. He condemned the chief offender (this passage is now lost), denounced the visitors, and said he would shortly return and would excommunicate all who had not submitted. On hearing this letter, which was brought by Titus, the majority returned to their allegiance to Paul, and the offender was excommunicated. The visitors departed, if they had not gone already, and Titus was able to re-start the collection, which had been dropped. On hearing this news, Paul wrote a letter to Corinth, consisting of 2 Cor chh 1–9 '.

884a This theory has three main items : (1) Paul wrote an intermediate letter. (2) Our 2 Cor is divisible, and chh 10–13 are the intermediate letter. (3) Paul paid an intermediate visit to Corinth.

The theory contains nothing which is irreconcilable with Catholic doctrine. It offers a simple and complete solution to one vexatious question (the character of 2 Cor chh 10–13) and on that ground one could wish to see it proved. But it raises serious new difficulties, as will be seen. Fifty years ago, however, there seemed a fair hope that further investigation might both increase the evidence for it and reduce the difficulties in its way. This hope has been disappointed. Painstaking investigation by many scholars has failed to add anything noteworthy to the case as stated by Kennedy, while the objections to it appear, after mature consideration, stronger than ever. It is now unlikely that any more evidence will be found. Kennedy's theory seems destined to remain an unproved hypothesis for ever. It has had half a century to establish itself and has failed to do so. It seems best to reject it in favour of a view which is at least *equally* arguable and has the support of tradition. Several scholars (especially Allo among Catholics, and Goudge, Menzies, etc., among non-Catholics) accept the first and third points of the theory, but not the second. But these two parts are at least as difficult to prove as the second, and in fact the whole theory is a unity and is essentially an attempt to explain the difficulty of 2 Cor chh 10–13—the second point is its chief attraction, without which it would never have gained such wide support. Without this, the raison d'être of the theory is gone. It seems best to reject it as a whole. We will briefly examine each part.

b The Question of an Intermediate Severe Letter—Cannot the letter referred to in Epistle II be Epistle I ? Catholic tradition till this century has held that it can be, and this view is upheld by some very eminent non-Catholic scholars such as B. Weiss and Zahn. But all supporters of Kennedy's theory deny it :

(1) From 2 Cor 2:4 we learn that the letter was written ' in much tribulation and anguish of heart . . . with many tears '. It is said that this is hardly applicable to our Epistle I. But there are two passages (chh 4 and 9) which may well have been written in anguish and tears. St Paul wept more readily than northerners do—see Phil 3:18 and Ac 20:19, 31.

(2) From 2 Cor 7:8–11 we gather that the earlier letter was a stern and sharp-toned one. It is absurd to say that the First Epistle cannot be described as sharp and severe. On at least eight distinct subjects,

beginning at the first chapter and ending with the fifteenth, Paul reprimands and censures his readers. Some of his expressions may almost be called ferocious. What modern bishop would venture to use language like 4:21 ; 5:2 ; 11:5–6 ; 14:23 ? If this is not severity, it is hard to say what is. It is true there are quiet passages like chh 7 and 12, and the two great poetical ones which have a perfect serenity (chh 13 and 15 : 35–58) but half the letter has the note of reproof.

(3) In 2 Cor 2:5–11 an individual wrongdoer is mentioned immediately after the ' severe letter ', and in 7:12 an individual seems to be mentioned as having been the partial cause of the letter. It is said that both passages clearly mean somebody who had wronged Paul personally, and therefore cannot refer to the incestuous person of 1 Cor 5:1–9, who is the only *individual* plainly mentioned in Epistle I. But (a) It is not clear that both passages of Epistle II refer to the same person. (b) The second may well refer to one of Paul's slanderers—see note on 2 Cor 7:12. (c) In the first passage Paul protests that they must not regard the offence as particularly directed against himself, and to take his denial as a proof that it *was* so directed seems highly precarious reasoning. There seems no good reason why the case of 1 Cor 5 should not be the one referred to. (See notes on 2 Cor 2:5–11.)

It seems therefore permissible to believe that the letter alluded to in Epistle II is none other than Epistle I.

D 2. Is the Second Epistle one letter or two ?—The objections against dividing the letter may be briefly stated thus :

(1) There is no external evidence whatever in favour of dividing the letter. There is no sign in any manuscript or in any early writer that the two portions had ever existed in separation from one another. From its very first publication therefore the letter was in its present form.

(2) There is a real though not obvious unity of theme. It is the thought of the conjunction of grandeur and suffering in the apostolic office. This thought is explicit enough in the first part, but it is with us all through the last chapters also and emerges clearly in 11:30–12:10 (see B supra).

(3) Although the idea of peace and reconciliation is no doubt prominent in the first half, the sky is by no means unclouded : there are repeated signs that the trouble is not over, that there are still things to be set right. They occur in nearly every chapter. (See the notes on 1:12–2:3 ; 2:17–3:3 ; 4:2–5 ; 5:11–12 ; 5:20–6:2 ; 6:11–7:3 ; 8:20–21.) In particular 6:11–7:3 is noteworthy. These passages do form a preparation for chh 10–13. They are rumblings of a coming storm.

(4) St Clement of Rome, writing about A.D. 96, shows himself familiar with the First Epistle, but unacquainted with the Second. It seems likely therefore that the First Epistle was in circulation about A.D. 80 or earlier, while the Second was published many years later. The delay could only have been due to some fear that misunderstanding or discredit might arise from chh 10–13. But there could have been no possible objection to the publication of chh 1–9 if it was a separate letter. Must we conclude that the two letters were already mutilated and attached well before A.D. 80 ? That is not easy to believe.

(5) If the offender of 2 Cor 2:4–11 is not the incestuous man of 1 Cor 5, he must be somebody mentioned in the lost portion of the ' severe letter '. Again, if the change of route mentioned in 2 Cor 1:15–16 is not the same as that of 1 Cor 16:5, this change must also have been mentioned in the lost first portion of the ' severe letter '. But these reasons would lead us to believe that whole passages, not merely a few lines, had been lost—a difficult view when we consider the probability that these letters were frequently read to the church.

(6) The *accidental* combination of two documents

generally leaves much more tangible clues than we have here. But if we once admit the possibility of editorial changes in order to harmonize the two parts, then the authenticity of every passage in the epistle is brought under suspicion.

(7) From 2 Cor 7:14 we gather that Titus's recent visit to Corinth was either his first visit or his first one as Paul's envoy. But 12:18 refers to some visit of Titus as Paul's envoy. If 12:18 belongs to an earlier letter than 7:14 it contradicts the plain meaning of 7:14.

(8) Several small peculiarities of language are more common in *each* of the two portions of this epistle than they are in the epistles of St Paul in general, *e.g.* the phrase ἐν παντὶ.

(9) It is not necessary to suppose that the last four chapters are *addressed to* the rebellious minority. They are *aimed at* this minority, and this is made sufficiently clear at the beginning (in 10:2, see note). After that the 'you' would naturally be taken as meaning more particularly those who were still defiant, though it is not apparently *confined* to these till near the end of ch 12—perhaps because a much larger number had once erred.

D 3. The Question of an Intermediate Visit—Did Paul ever visit Corinth between his first long stay and the writing of Epistle II, and if so, when? No such visit is mentioned in *Acts*, but *Acts* is not an exhaustive history. The two questions must be considered separately. (1) Was there an intermediate visit? The answer to this depends on the interpretation of seven sentences in the two epistles. No less than five of these (1 Cor 16:7; 2 Cor 2:1; 12:14; 12:21; 13:1) are more or less ambiguous, and can be interpreted either as implying or as not implying such a visit. See the commentary on these verses. Of the remaining two passages, one (2 Cor 1:15-16) seems definitely against the visit, and the other (2 Cor 13:2) seems just as definitely in favour of it (see commentary). Evidence could hardly be more equally balanced. Either view seems possible, but if there was a visit, several of the above passages would show that it was connected with painful memories of some sort. (2) If we assume a visit, was it before or after Epistle I? If we place it before, there is no great difficulty, but if after Ep. I, then we are practically forced, it seems to me, to accept the account given of it by Kennedy (883*i*) which is improbable in the highest degree. How can we believe: (1) That Paul was defied to his face, not by a party but by the whole Corinthian church. (2) That Paul ran away from his rebellious converts or at least gave all the appearance of doing so. (3) That having retreated from Corinth he wrote a letter on the lines of chh 10-13, full of threats about his next visit. (4) That this letter subdued those whom his audible words had failed to move. (5) That Titus succeeded where Paul had failed. We conclude that if there was an intermediate visit, it took place some time before Epistle I (the view of Lightfoot, Sanday, and Zahn), perhaps a year or two before it, and was occasioned by some temporary trouble which was quickly and completely settled and has left no record in the New Testament. There must have been many such unchronicled troubles.

E. Value of the Epistle—Its doctrinal value is much smaller than that of the First Epistle. It is however of great historical interest, its spiritual teaching is immensely valuable, and for the biography of St Paul it is perhaps the most important of all his epistles. As to **doctrine**, the theme of the union of the church to Christ is here modified by the additional thought of the relation of the Christian minister (especially the apostle) to both, his authority and the conditions for its fruitful exercise. We may again recall St Thomas's words that the letter is about the Christian ministry, good and bad. There are important passages too on the purpose and meaning of the Mosaic Law and on the resurrection. Chapters 7 to 9 are of considerable **historical** value, but for the history of Paul

himself the whole epistle is most interesting. Not only **885a** does it contain many facts about the Corinthian crisis, but also about his previous life (11:16–12:19). In addition, the lively feeling which here is given free and ready expression endows the letter with a pictorial or dramatic quality beyond any other epistle (*e.g.* 1:23 f.; 3:1; 6:11; 7:2; 10:10; 11:1; 11:11; 12:11). Unfortunately we have not the key to all the **b** allusions and this uncertainty often repels the casual reader. As a **spiritual** work the epistle is surpassed by none. Its insistent theme is the efficacy of suffering in union with Christ. It is true that Paul is speaking more particularly of the sufferings of an apostle, but the principle is in fact the foundation of *all* Christian sanctity. This theme appears at the beginning (1:5) and remains with us to the end (13:4). Coming from the apostle's deepest conviction it retains an indestructible freshness. Two passages are of outstanding eloquence (4:7–12 and 6:3–10), but perhaps the most impressive of all is the autobiographical statement (12:7–10). We must also mention the magnificent passage on the hope of immortality (4:16–5:9) and the tender affection of the two reconciliation passages (1:23–2:11; 7:5–16).

F. Short Synopsis—1:1–11. Salutation, and the **c** lesson of recent events.

1:12–22. Answer to two recent calumnies.

1:23–2:13. The previous letter and the repentant sinner.

2:14–3:3. Affirmation of Paul's Apostolic commission.

3:4–6:10. A picture of the True Apostle. The Apostolic office is superior to the ministry of the Mosaic Law (3:4–18). The Apostles are outspoken and fearless by God's power, though weak and afflicted (4:1–15). They can look confidently beyond death (4:16–5:10). Paul again protests his sincerity and the greatness of the Apostolic mission (5:11–6:2) and concludes with a splendid passage on the strength-in-weakness manifested in the Apostles (6:3–10).

6:11–7:3. Urgent appeal to the disobedient members.

7:4–16. Titus's report and St Paul's joy at the reconciliation.

8 and 9. Arrangements for the collection for Jerusalem.

10 to end of letter, Paul vindicates himself against the False Apostles and gives a last warning to the rebellious. After defending himself against some mean slanders (10:1–11) he asserts that his opponents are braggarts and intruders and roundly denounces them as 'false apostles' (10:12–11:15). He then makes his 'boast' about his sufferings for Christ (11:16–29) and mentions his visions and his infirmity (11:30–12:10). He speaks of his coming visit, makes a last appeal to obstinate sinners, and threatens severe measures against those who will not listen to it (12:11–13:10).

13:11–13. Conclusion.

I 1–III 3 Recent Events and St Paul's Comments— **886a** It is not the events themselves but their inner meaning, the eternal truths behind them, that fill St Paul's mind, and above all, the truth that God's power operates through human weakness and suffering: this appears in every Christian life but most startlingly in that of the apostles. This is the grand law of strength-in-weakness, the theme which dominates the whole epistle, *cf.* § 883*e* and the notes on 1:3–7; 4:7–15; 6:2–10; 12:9–10.

I 1–2 Salutation—1. 'Timothy'. His name is joined to Paul's in the salutation of five other letters. He was well known at Corinth for, when little more than a boy, he had been with Paul during his long stay there.

3–11 Thoughts suggested by his Recent Agony— **b** 3. 'Comfort'. The same Greek root-word (παρακαλέω, etc.) is unfortunately translated by three different words (consolation, comfort, exhortation) in the next

886b verses. Better to keep *consolation* and *console* throughout. The word is far more common in this epistle than in any other. Here at the very beginning (3-7) he sets forth the law of victorious suffering forcibly and clearly, joined with that of the union of the faithful to Christ. Christ, the apostles, and all the faithful, share the same sufferings, which by this union become a means of consolation and power, not only to the sufferer but also to others. **4.** 'Us'. In this passage the 'we' seems to mean all the apostles. In the epistle as a whole 'we' very often means Paul only. **5.** 'Our comfort' probably means both the consolation he felt and that which he could impart. **6.** 'Whether . . . whether'. Not successive but simultaneous, two aspects of the same thing. It is the *joy in suffering* that is the secret of his power. 'Consolation': omit clause beginning : 'or whether we be exhorted' which has crept in by mistake and read : 'it is for your consolation which operates in endurance', etc. He implies that they too have sufferings. We do not know what these were. Compare 1 Cor 10:13. **7.** 'That our hope', etc. : '*And our hope for you is steadfast*'. He is now looking farther, to the supreme consolation of heaven. 'The sufferings' : Christ's and Paul's. **8.** It is only now that he mentions the terrible experience which had occasioned his previous words. The riot at Ephesus, when he and his friends were in danger of death from a furious mob, must be **c** a part of the ordeal, Ac 19, and § 883*e*. 'Strength' of man, not of God, as we see in a moment. 'were weary' : *despaired of life*. **9.** '*But we received* (or perhaps *passed*) *sentence of death on ourselves* (*i.e.* he felt convinced that life was over, and bowed to God's will), *that we might not rest our confidence in ourselves*', etc. The words *confident* and *confidence* are unusually common in this epistle. **11.** 'Withal' : *also*. 'this gift' : '*the blessing* or *mercy*'. He is thinking chiefly of future mercies of God, which he knows he will need (at his visit to Jerusalem perhaps). 'Many . . . many' : the prayers of a multitude, being answered, end in a multitude of thanksgivings.

12-22. He now answers two recent calumnies, which were probably put forward by his enemies at Corinth when the First Epistle was read there, § 883*b*.

d 12-14 That his Letters were not straightforward—
12. 'Glory' : '*pride*' or '*proud boast*'. 'Simplicity' : '*with God-given honesty and sincerity*'. 'Carnal wisdom' : '*worldly wisdom*'. 'In the grace', etc. : '*trusting only in God's mercy*'. 'Conversed' : '*lived*'. **13-14.** '*For we write nothing to you except what you acknowledge as true, and I hope you will acknowledge it always, as you have practically acknowledged in regard to us that we are your pride, as you yourselves will be our pride in the day of the Lord Jesus*'. It seems likely that in regard to 1 Cor Paul's enemies had said that he cared little about the faults which he explicitly condemned in it, and that its main purpose was to undermine their own power—a terribly plausible lie because it contained an element of truth. 'In part' : '*more or less*'. 'In the day' : *i.e.* at His second coming.

e 15-22 That Paul had been fickle and inconsiderate—
—Great and natural disappointment was felt by the Corinthians when they found on reading 1 Cor 16:5 that he had delayed his visit again and was going to Macedonia first. (Note on 1 Cor 16:5, 4:18, and § 867*e*.) His enemies said that this change of plan (which may well be the *second* change) showed that he was both fickle and careless of the feelings of the Corinthians. **15.** 'Before' : *i.e.* originally, some time before 1 Cor was written. 'A second grace' : *a second blessing*—which the apostle's presence would be certain to bring. The natural meaning of these words would be that Paul had never been to Corinth since his first long visit. We cannot possibly attach these words to the proposed visit on his return from Macedonia (see next verse) for in that case their right place is in the middle of v 16, after ' come to you '. Nor can ' second ' mean 'double' either in Greek or in English, § 884*g*.
f 16. ' Pass by you ' : ' *to take you on my way to Macedonia* ' :

he meant to cross by sea from Ephesus to Corinth, then go overland to Macedonia. ' Brought on my way ' : they would escort him to the port and provide him with some necessaries, *cf.* the same phrase in 1 Cor 16:6, 11. **17.** ' Use lightness ' : act in a capricious, fickle manner. ' According to the flesh ', *i.e.* to suit his own comfort or vanity. ' That there ', etc. : ' *So that with me it is " Yes, Yes and No, No " '*, *i.e.* so that I am the sort of man who says ' Yes ' today and ' No ' tomorrow. In the next few verses also it is best to substitute *Yes* for *It is* and *No* for *It is not*. **18.** So ' *As surely as God is faithful, our language to you was not Yes-and-No* '. It is a kind of oath : as truly as God is faithful to his promises, so Paul also does not promise lightly, or change his plan without strong reason. **19.** ' *For the son of God . . . was not Yes-and-No, but in him there has been only Yes* ', *i.e.* the gospel which Paul had preached was as unchangeable as Christ himself. ' Sylvanus ' : the full form of the name Silas. Silas had been with Paul at Corinth, Ac 18. **20.** ' *For he is the Yes to all the promises of God* '. God's promises (of a Saviour, etc.) are all fulfilled in Christ. ' Therefore ', etc. : ' *Therefore it is in Him* (in virtue of his redemptive act) *that the Amen is pronounced by us to the glory of God* '. It was already the custom to end a prayer with some words of praise followed by Amen, *cf.* Apoc 3:14. **21.** The thought is enlarged : as the apostles reflect God's own constancy, so the faithful also are God's and partake in his steadfast strength. ' Confirmeth ' : ' *keeps us steadfast* '. ' Anointed ' : very likely he is thinking of baptism. **22.** ' Sealed '. The seal was used to mark something as a man's property : God has marked the faithful as his own. He may refer to baptism or to confirmation. ' The pledge of the Spirit ', *i.e.* the pledge consisting of the Holy Spirit. The presence of the Spirit (what we usually call sanctifying grace) is the pledge (*i.e.* the first instalment) of eternal life, *cf.* Eph 1:14, ' the Holy Spirit . . . who is the pledge of our inheritance '.

23-II 4 The True Reason for his Change of Plan— His delay in coming was not a selfish whim, but due to a desire to win more of them back to repentance and loyalty, that he might find fewer to punish when he came. **23.** *i.e.* I call God to look into my soul and to bear me witness that, etc. ' To spare you ' : he was determined to excommunicate those whom he found still defiant, *cf.* 13:2. ' I came not ' : ' *I gave up the thought of coming* '. ' Not because . . . stand ' : the last words mean that their faith was sound (*cf.* 8:7), and therefore did not need *correction* but could be strengthened and made into ' joy and peace in believing ' (Rom 15:13) ; and for this purpose he offers himself as their helper, not their master.

II 1. ' Not to come ', etc., may either mean ' not to pay another sorrowful visit ' or ' not to pay another visit if it was going to be sorrowful '. Only the first interpretation would indicate that there had been already one sorrowful visit, §884*g*. **2.** It would grieve him to punish beloved friends who should be his joy and delight. 2 and 3 are a grand expression of true spiritual love, wounded by its own severity, like our Lord weeping over Jerusalem. **3.** ' *For this very reason I wrote to you* ', *i.e.* wrote the First Epistle. ' That my joy ', etc. : a touching appeal to the undutiful to repent in order to spare *him*. **4.** ' Affliction ' : now that the letter has done its work, he admits the anguish it cost him to write so many harsh words. ' That you might know ', etc. : one of his marvellous unexpected endings. We should have expected : ' that you might repent ', but he boldly says that they would *understand* that his severity was a proof of love.

5-11 Reconciliation of the Incestuous Man—The man who had married his stepmother (1 Cor 5:1-5 notes) had at once been excommunicated as Paul had directed. He had quickly repented and separated from her, but the sentence had been allowed to stand till St Paul could be consulted, and therefore the sinner had been excluded from the church for weeks.

Paul protests that not he but they are the party chiefly injured, and begs them to receive him back at once. Many modern scholars however think that this passage refers to another person, §884*c*. **5.** ' *Whoever has caused sorrow has not caused it to me* (only) *but to all of you to some extent—that I may not be too hard* '. The last part is difficult and uncertain. **6.** ' Rebuke ' : ' *penalty* ', *i.e.* the excommunication. ' Many ' : ' *the many.*'—the Corinthian church in general. **7.** ' swallowed up ', etc. : he might despair of pardon and relapse into the same sin or worse. **8.** ' Confirm ', etc. : ' *give him an assurance of your love* '. He evidently means that they were to welcome him back to the church. The sole object of the sentence (his penitence) had been attained. **9.** ' Know ', etc. : ' *put you to the test* '. In 7:8–12 the same statement is made about the same letter. Obviously it cannot mean that he was indifferent to the particular faults condemned in it, but that they were overshadowed by the question : Would the Corinthians in a body desert him when they read his severe criticisms and his many demands on them, and attach themselves altogether to the False Apostles ? **10.** ' *The one whom you pardon, I also pardon* '. ' In the person ', etc. : or perhaps ' *in the presence of Christ* ', *cf.* 1 Cor 5:4, where he tells them to excommunicate the man ' in the name of the Lord Jesus . . . with the power of the Lord Jesus Christ '. **11.** ' Satan ' : another echo of 1 Cor 5 ' to hand such a man over to Satan ' ; see note. He must no longer be left in Satan's power, *i.e.* cut off from the Sacraments.

12–13 The Journey to meet Titus—first part—The subject changes abruptly. He begins to tell how Titus brought him the good news that the majority of Corinthians had remained loyal to him. **12.** ' Troas ', the port near the entrance to the Dardanelles. He travelled there from Ephesus, and apparently he had arranged to meet Titus there. ' For the gospel ' : ' *To preach the gospel* '. ' Door ', *i.e.* an opportunity, *cf.* 1 Cor 16:9. He means that he was gaining many converts. **13.** He was in such suspense about events at Corinth that he sailed to Europe, probably to Philippi, knowing that Titus would travel that way.

14–17 God's Power as seen in his Apostles—Just when we expect to hear of his meeting Titus, he breaks off, and we have to wait till 7:5 (nearly four chapters) for the continuation. Nothing could show better that Paul's mode of writing is unique : he is a law unto himself, and it is dangerous to argue about him from the analogy of other writers. He again praises God for manifesting his power through such weak instruments as himself, *cf.* 1:8–10 ; 7:5–7. **14.** ' Maketh us to triumph ' : more likely : ' *Leads us* (as captives) *in his triumphal procession* ' ; a daring image : God's conquering love seems almost to overstretch human capacity and to drag his apostle after him. ' The odour ', etc. : ' *The perfume of the knowledge of Himself* ', *i.e.* the Gospel. **15.** ' *In the nostrils of those who are saved and of those who are lost we are a sweet perfume of Christ rising up to God* '. The next verse makes the meaning clearer. The image in his mind seems to be that of the incense smoke which accompanied the daily sacrifice in the Temple. The saved are those who have accepted the Gospel and are in a state of grace. **16.** ' *To some* (we are) *a perfume* (which operates) *from death to death*, *i.e.* becomes more and more deadly, *cf.* 3:18 ; Rom 1:17. Christ often says the same, *e.g.* ' To him that hath shall be given ', etc. Nobody who hears the Gospel can remain where he was. He is either better or worse, and so on progressively. ' These things ' : *i.e.* this task (of an apostle). It requires an extraordinary grace. Paul knows he has received it, but says ' Our sufficiency is from God ' (3:5). Omit the ' so ' in DV. **17.** ' adulterating ' : or perhaps : ' *Making a trade of* '— using the Gospel to gain profit or influence (an allusion to the False Apostles at Corinth). ' From God ' : ' *inspired by God* '. ' In Christ ' : ' *In union with Christ* '.

III 1–3 Paul needs no Letter of Recommendation— The allusion to the False Apostles brings him back for a moment to current events. **1.** ' again ' : perhaps his **887a** enemies had accused him of self-praise in 1 Cor chh 4 and 9. ' Epistles ', etc. : the False Apostles had either brought such letters to Corinth or obtained some from the Corinthians. **2.** His work at Corinth is a ' letter of introduction ' which will prove to all the world what sort of apostle he is. ' Our hearts ' : We should have expected *your*, but he suddenly decides to bring in the additional thought that their names were written in *his* heart, as he expressly says in 7:3. **3.** His letter (*i.e.* work) is Christ's, and Paul is only a secretary (minister). ' Stone ' : His work is now compared, not to a letter, but to an inscription on stone, in fact to the Two Tables of the Law. It is all an excellent example of Paul's elusive imagery. *Cf.* 1 Cor 3:10.

III 4–VI 10 A Picture of the True Apostle—This **b** is the second large division of the letter. Though it comes in almost like a digression, it is the most important passage except chh 10–13, for which it is a preparation, § 883*d*. There are three predominant ideas : (1) The apostles are the ministers of a revelation far greater than that of Moses (3:4–18). (2) Yet in themselves they are nothing : it is God who works through them (4:7–15 ; 6:3–10). (3) Though surrounded by misery they have a serene confidence which can look beyond death (4:16–5:11). Much of what he says of the apostles has an application to all Christian sanctity, and the plainest and richest spiritual treasures of the epistle lie in this portion. Intermingled with these sublime thoughts are verses which show that Paul never forgot present circumstances for a moment. In him the mystic and man of action were always united (4:1–6 ; 5:11–14 ; 6:1–2).

III 4–18 As Christianity is greater than Judaism, so c are its Ministers endowed with Greater Power— **4–5.** He takes up the thought of 2:14–16, as appears from ' sufficient ' in 5. ' Of ourselves ' : ' *From ourselves, by our own strength* '. **6.** ' Testament ' : the Greek word is regularly used to describe the covenant (*i.e.* contract) made between God and Israel on Sinai. The *new* covenant therefore means practically the religion of Christ. ' In the letter ' : ' *Ministers not of the letter* ', etc. '. By ' letter ' he means the whole Jewish religion, based on the written Law of Moses, and by ' spirit ' the religion of Christ. The first was essentially a body of regulations bringing knowledge of God's will, but not in itself giving the supernatural strength to carry it out : Christ did give that strength. The one therefore kills, because its only direct result is a deeper sense of sin and guilt. This thought is fully set forth in Rom 7. ' Quickeneth ' : ' *gives life* '. **7.** ' Glory ' : the unbearable radiance of Moses' face when he returned from his meeting with God is described Ex 34:29. ' Is made void ' : ' *was transitory, destined to fade* ', as indeed the Mosaic Law itself was. **8.** ' Rather **d** in glory ' : ' *More glorious* '. **9.** ' Ministration of justice ' : ' *The* (apostolic) *office which guides men to holiness* '. **10.** ' *For even that which was glorious* (i.e. the Mosaic Law) *has become inglorious* (has been outshone) *in this respect by reason of the superior glory* ' of the Gospel. **11.** ' That which remaineth ' : *i.e.* the Gospel, which is eternal. **12–18.** He is arrested by another thought suggested by Moses' veil—the obscurity of the earlier revelation, and the failure of the Jews to penetrate to the hidden truth within it, which was Christ. The Gospel reveals clearly what had been dimly foreshadowed in the Law. **12.** ' Confidence ' : the Greek word means especially boldness of *speech*. **13.** ' On the face ', etc. : *On the termination of that which was passing away*, *i.e.* the disappearance of the radiance. Or perhaps : *On the fulfilment of that which*, etc., *i.e.* on Christ who was the fulfilment of the Law. Unlike Moses, the preacher of the Gospel uses no veil, no reserve, but can put forth the whole truth. **14. e** ' Senses ' : ' *Minds* '. ' Old testament '. The term is not yet used in our sense, but means the first five books (Genesis to Deuteronomy), called the ' Law ', a portion of which was read every Sabbath in the synagogue.

887e ' Because ', etc. : ' *Because it is only in Christ* (at the coming of Christ) *that it is removed* '. **15.** ' Heart ' : In Jewish diction the heart was the seat of intelligence. **16.** ' *But when a man turns to the Lord, the veil is taken away* '. When a Jew accepts the Gospel, he sees the real meaning of the Law. **17.** ' A spirit ' : ' *The spirit* '. This verse is a parenthesis to explain 16. Paraphrase : ' When I say " the Lord " I mean " the spirit " ' (*i.e.* the Gospel and the grace it leads to, see 6) and where this Divine grace is, it brings liberty from that slavery which is the condition of those who are under the Mosaic Law—slavery to ignorance and sin '. **18.** ' *But we all, with face uncovered, beholding* ', etc.' Two ideas are compressed together : (1) The Christian, having known the wonderful revelation of God in Christ (' the glory of the Lord ') proclaims it fearlessly without reserve (' with face uncovered '). (2) By gazing on Christ, he at once begins to acquire something of Christ-like splendour which grows brighter till it is made perfect in heaven. ' From glory to glory ' : *i.e.* to greater and greater glory.

f IV 1-6 The Openness of True Apostles and the Shiftiness of False Ones—The passage is suggested by the recent verses, but turns definitely to the doings of his enemies at Corinth. **1** ' Mercy ' probably means both his conversion and his call to the apostleship. ' Faint not ' : ' *Remain undaunted* '. **2.** A protest against the underhand methods of the False Apostles. ' Hidden ', etc. : ' *All shameful subterfuges* '. ' Conscience ' : *i.e.* he is not content to captivate the ear or the emotions. **3.** ' *But if our gospel is hidden* ', *i.e.* if it does remain obscure or meaningless to anybody. It was, and 'is, impossible so to present Christian truth that it carries conviction to *everybody*. What impedes the act of faith is often some affection to sin, as he explains in 4. The verse may be an answer to some complaint or slander. **4.** ' The god ', etc.—Satan, whom our Lord calls ' the prince of this world ' (Jn 16:11). The power which he wields is usurped but real ; worldly men do choose him as their god. ' The minds of unbelievers ' practically means : ' He (Satan) has blinded their minds so as to prevent them from believing '. **5-6.** The apostle's greatness comes from God, not from himself. **5.** ' Preach not ourselves ' : his message is not something he has invented, and he does not preach it **g** to gain power or applause for himself. **6.** The revelation which had burst upon him on the Damascus road was as much God's act as the first creation of light. ' The face of Christ ' : it was no vision, but his bodily presence, as Paul says in 1 Cor 15:8.

7-15 Divine Power and its Weak Instruments—A more forcible re-statement of that paradox with which the epistle began (1:3-11). **7.** ' We ' : *the apostles*. ' Treasure ' : the light of the Gospel, and also no doubt the apostolic grace. These gifts are entrusted to men who have no great learning or polish or impressive appearance, like gold hidden in an earthenware jar, not displayed as an ornament. The jar denotes not only the apostle's body but his whole human equipment. ' Excellency ' : ' *pre-eminence, distinction* '. ' May be ', etc., *i.e.* that everybody, especially the apostle himself, may *see* that his eloquence, miracles, success, etc., are due to the Divine power in him, not to himself. **8.** ' We are oppressed but not crushed, perplexed but not in despair '. **9.** ' Cast down ' : ' *Struck to the earth* ', like men on a battlefield. In their agonizing **h** trials they are spared nothing except defeat. **10.** ' Mortification ' : ' *execution, death* '. The Crucifixion is reproduced in the apostles, and their suffering, borne for Christ's sake, is merged in his. ' Saul, why persecutest thou me ? ' ' Life ' means in the first place the marvellous grace of apostleship. This sentence shows that their sufferings were actually a means towards their work. Perhaps there is also a glance forward towards final glory, as in 14. **11.** A restatement of 10. ' Delivered unto death ' : ' *we are at death's door* ', from whatever cause (prosecution, plots, riots, sickness, etc.). ' Mortal flesh ', *i.e.* even in this world they become superhuman agents. **12.** Sums

up the last four verses. **13-15.** These verses form. a **88** bridge to the next subject, Apostolic Confidence. **13.** ' *Having that spirit of faith which is expressed by the words of Scripture* ' : ' I believed ', etc. ' Spirit of faith ' : divine inspiration to believe, God-given faith. ' *I believed* ', etc. : quoted from Ps 115:1 (116), in LXX. **14.** Faith and hope (confidence) go together and they will not allow him to be silent. ' Place us ' : ' *Present us* (alive before him) *and you also* '. **15.** ' Everything (my preaching and suffering) *is for your sakes* '. Or perhaps : ' *I would do anything for you* ' : almost the same words come in 12:19. ' That the grace ', etc., *i.e.* that God's grace may be spread wider by being received into more souls, and may thereby multiply the words of thanksgiving which rise to God's glory, *cf.* 1:11.

IV 16-V 10 The Apostle's Confidence—St Paul gives **i** the deepest reasons which nerve an apostle to unceasing effort : the firm hope of a glorious life with God, and the thought of the account he must give for the extraordinary gifts bestowed on him. There are few finer passages in his writings. The impressive preface in the Mass for the Dead is based on it. On the same subject *cf.* 1 Cor 15:47-58 ; Rom 8:11-23. **16.** ' We faint not ' : he goes back to the thought and words of 4:1. ' Though ', etc. : ' *Though our outward self* (the body) *is wearing out, yet the inward self* (the soul, transformed by grace) *gains new strength daily* '. **17.** ' *Our temporary and light tribulation wins for us* ', etc. It is made ' light ' by faith and hope—viewed by ordinary standards it is a ' death ' (12). ' Weight of glory '. He compares eternal life to a mass of treasure, as our Lord often did, Mt 6:20 ; 13:44, etc.

V 1. ' If ', etc. : ' *When this poor hut, our earthly home,* **j** *falls to pieces, we have . . .* ' : *i.e.* it is as certain as if the glorified body were already made and waiting for us. **2.** ' In this '—the earthly body. Omit ' also '. ' Clothed upon with our habitation ' : a mixture of images, not uncommon in Paul, *cf.* 1 Tim 6:19 (' Storing away a good foundation '). **3.** Probably : ' Because when once we *have* put it on, we shall not find ourselves naked '. The thought seems to be the same as in 4, where it is clearer. **4.** ' Tabernacle '—the poor hut, our body. ' Groan ' : there are two pains, present suffering and the longing for the glorious life with Christ. But relief from the first *alone* is worthless to him. He states this in homely language : ' *We wish not to put off our clothing* (the misery of bodily life) *but to put on more clothing* '. Immortality is pictured as a cloak enveloping the whole man, body and soul. **5.** ' Maketh us ' : ' *Has prepared us* '—perhaps a new image of ourselves as a field tilled and sown by God. ' The pledge ', etc., see 1:22. **6-9.** The thought of a glorious home concentrates itself into a desire for that Person without whom heaven itself would be nothing. Of this ' pain of exile ' Paul speaks some years later in Phil 1:21-25. **8.** Omit ' but '. The sentence is a continuation of v 6. **9.** ' We labour ' : ' *We do our utmost* '. He reminds himself that his present business is to do Christ's will *here*, and therefore goes on to mention the Judgement. This smooth return from heaven to earth is as fine as anything. Paul was no visionary though he had visions. **10.** ' The proper things ', etc. : ' *The due reward of his earthly life* '.

11-14a Protest of his Honest Intentions—Difficult **k** sentences : he is evidently defending his own apostleship against the False Apostles. **11.** ' Persuasion ' may refer both to winning converts and to keeping them faithful, as he is now doing in the case of the Corinthians. He has to use ' persuasion ' (*i.e.* coaxing and tact), but his fundamental honesty is clear to God and ought to be clear to the Corinthians. **12.** ' To glory ' —to speak with pride. ' Who glory in face ' : ' *Who boast of their external advantages and are without goodness of heart* '. These advantages were Jewish birth, early acquaintance with the Twelve, etc. **13.** Apparently : ' If we are mad, we are mad for God's sake ; if we are sane, we are sane for your sake '. Perhaps they had accused him of craziness. **14.** ' *Christ's love holds us in its grip* ' : the memory of Christ's great love for men dominates all his actions.

14b-17 New Life—He dwells on the superhuman power of Christianity, which has made a new world. Resembles the thought of ch 3. **14b.** ' Were dead ' : ' *Have died*'. All Christians have (in baptism) died to their old sinful selves and risen to a new life of grace, lived for Christ. More fully in Rom 5:3–14. **15.** ' All : '. The colon following ' all ' should be a comma. **16.** ' We know . . .' : we no longer look at men according to the world's standards, but as God sees them. ' And if . . .' : ' *Even if we knew Christ* . . .' : probably means : Even if some of us (the Twelve, etc.) knew Christ as neighbour, relative, etc., this is nothing in comparison with the knowledge of him as Saviour. A reply perhaps to his enemies' interested praise of the Twelve. **17.** ' *Whoever is in Christ is a new creation* '— such is the effect of grace on the soul.

V 18-VI 2 The Apostles as God's Ambassadors—18. ' To us '—the Apostles. ' Ministry ' : ' *Service* or *work* '. **19.** It is almost a re-statement of 18. ' The *message* of reconciliation ', the Gospel. **20.** His appeal is addressed to the world, not to the Corinthians, but is no doubt meant to remind the defiant Corinthians that they are still unreconciled to God. ' God, as it were . . .' : ' *For God appeals through us* '. Omit ' you '. **21.** ' Hath made sin ' : *i.e.* ' Has made Christ to be sin ', a saying deliberately meant to be startling. God allowed Christ to suffer a punishment fit only for sinners, and in that sense made him a sinner. There may be some further meaning. ' Justice . . .', *i.e.* men endowed with supernatural justice (holiness). **VI 1.** ' Helping '—sharing in God's action. This verse seems to be more particularly addressed to the rebellious Corinthians. **2.** A kind of parenthesis. The quoted words are spoken by God in Is 49:8. ' Accepted ' —opportune.

b 3-10 Final Statement of the Apostolic Paradox—This is the most eloquent of the three passages, *cf.* 1 Cor 4:9–13 ; 2 Cor 4:7–12. He describes first the apostles' sufferings, then God's gifts to them, then the incomprehensible figure which they presented to the world's eye. **3.** ' Offence '—anything that discourages the weaker Christians, see 1 Cor 8:7. **4.** ' Let us . . .' : ' *Winning a good name for ourselves* '. **5.** ' stripes ' : he had been flogged eight times, as he tells us in 11:24. ' Seditions ' : ' *Riots* '—when insulted or beaten by angry mobs. ' Watchings ' : ' *Sleeplessness* '. ' Fastings ' : probably means hunger owing to poverty, travel, or pressure of missionary work, for he seems to omit all deliberate mortifications here, *cf.* 11:27. **6.** ' Chastity ' : ' *Innocence* or *purity of intention* ' (including both chastity and uprightness). ' Knowledge ', *i.e.* theological insight, a grasp of the intellectual side of Christianity. ' Sweetness ', *i.e.* kindness, gentleness. ' The Holy Ghost ' : the Spirit is of course the giver of *all* the gifts mentioned in 6 and 7, but here he seems to be named as the source of the extraordinary and miraculous powers such as prophecy, healing, strange languages, etc., powers which Paul certainly possessed but which nowhere else appear in this list, see 1 Cor 12. **c 7.** ' The word of truth '—the plain and faithful preaching of the gospel. ' The power of God ' which made his preaching powerful to move and convince. ' *Bearing the arms proper to goodness* on the right, etc.'—the sword in the right hand and the shield on the left arm. So the whole means ' a fully armed soldier of goodness ', *cf.* Eph 6:13–17. **8.** ' *Amidst honour and dishonour* (or *disgrace*) *amidst good report* ' : there now come seven pairs of terms : the second always gives the perfect truth, the first term states a falsehood or half-truth. ' Known ' : ' *well-known* '. **9.** ' Dying ' refers perhaps to both bodily frailty and danger. ' Chastised ' : perhaps ' flogged but not executed '. In Roman practice the one often preceded the other. **10.** ' needy ' : ' *poor* '. The whole verse forms the pinnacle of the first half of this letter, just as 12:9 perhaps maybe called the pinnacle of the second half.

VI 11-VII 3 Urgent Appeal for Reconciliation and 888d Reform—Those who wish to divide the letter (*cf.* § 884*d*) find this passage such an insuperable difficulty to their theory that many of them consider it an interpolation, for they hold that a complete reconciliation has already taken place. But there is no evidence against its genuineness. It is found in every manuscript, and its last sentences lead on naturally to the following passage, see 7:4. In all the first nine chapters this passage is the clearest proof that Paul still had much to set right at Corinth. It may be that he actually began here his direct attack on the False Apostles but changed his mind and postponed it in order first to demonstrate clearly his reconciliation with the majority. See Introd. B and D, 2(3). In these verses he complains of two things : a want of friendliness to himself and a grave laxity in their dealings with pagans and paganism. Such laxity, we may believe, had been allowed or encouraged by the False Apostles. (Introd. 1 Cor C.)

11. *i.e.* I have opened my heart to you, to show you **e** all my thoughts and to welcome your confidence in return. **12.** ' Straitened in us ' : ' *Faced with a barrier on my side : the barrier stands in your own hearts* '. **13.** ' *Give me a just recompense* (*i.e.* friendship for friendship) *and throw open your own hearts* '. **14.** Here begin six verses of warning against contamination with paganism, see parallel in 1 Cor 10:14–21. Marriage between Christians and pagans is certainly *included*, but the warning has a far wider sweep than that. ' Yoke ' : the metaphor is taken from the two plough-oxen, joined together by the wooden bar (yoke) which rested on their necks. ' Do not be harnessed to the plough with an unbeliever '. Then five sharp questions, all condemning such dangerous associations. **15.** Belial in the New Testament seems to be practically another name for Satan. **16.** The quotation, from here to the end of 18, is a patchwork (as St Paul's long quotations often are) based chiefly on Lev 26:12 and Is 52:11 with echoes and adaptations of other passages, all chosen to show that the union of the faithful to God involves a separation from false religion.

VII 1. A milder tone. But the *content* of the verse is **f** very serious for ' defilement of flesh and spirit ' seems clearly to imply that some Christians, after conversion, had been guilty of both pagan worship and pagan unchastity. **2.** He now returns to the subject of mutual confidence. ' Receive us ' : ' *Make room for us* ' (in your hearts), do not, shut the door against us, *cf.* 6:12. ' We have injured . . .' : three sentences which either deny false accusations or denounce the False Apostles or perhaps both. **3.** ' We have said before ' seems to refer to 3:2 above.

4-16 Titus's Report on his Visit to Corinth, and St g Paul's Joy—He now takes up the narrative of recent events just where he had dropped it at 2:13 (*q.v.*) and then puts aside, for the moment, every thought except that of his immense happiness because the majority of the Corinthians had proved loyal to him in the hour of crisis. It is the tender joy of the prodigal's father, or of the shepherd, a joy that *seems* almost to make light of the sin. **4.** Probably : ' I speak with great frankness *to* you, I speak with great pride *about* you . . . *after* all our tribulation '. Note the ease with which ' I ' becomes ' we ' and vice versa throughout the epistle. **5.** Continuation from 2:13. There he spoke of his spirit, here of his flesh, but in these passages both words seem to mean the whole man, though they often are opposed terms. ' Combats ' : we do not know what troubles this refers to. **6.** ' the humble ' : ' *the miserable* or *helpless* '. **7.** ' Relating ' : meaning practically ' *for he related* your desire ' to see Paul and to please him. ' Your mourning ' : their sorrow for their transgressions.

8-9. Another picture of severity inspired by true **h** charity, as in 2:2. ' If I did repent . . .', *i.e.* when Titus first related their bitter contrition, Paul feared he had been too severe in the First Epistle, but later he felt that the good accomplished was well worth the pain.

888h 'For a time': God does not desire the pain of contrition to last after it has served its purpose. 'Unto penance': '*in a way that led to repentance*'. 'According to God': '*In God's way*', the spiritual, supernatural way, not 'according to man' or 'according to the flesh'—Paul's regular expressions for life lived on the natural or worldly level. 'Damage': that they might be gainers, not losers, by his severity. But it may mean 'that we may not need to inflict punishment on you'. **10.** 'Penance steadfast unto salvation': a slight play on words 'Repentance not to be regretted and leading to salvation'. But possibly it means: 'a better mind leading to a salvation which cannot be bettered'. 'The sorrow of the world', *e.g.* the torture of jealousy, offended pride, disappointed i ambition, etc. **11.** 'Carefulness': '*What keen zeal* (or *energy*) *it has inspired in you*'. 'Defence': *i.e.* pleas in defence of their conduct as far as it was innocent. 'Indignation' against the guilty ones among them, and probably in particular against the False Apostles. 'Fear' of Paul's anger, 'Desire' to see him. 'Revenge': '*retribution, infliction of punishment*' on notorious offenders, such as the incestuous man. 'To be undefiled': he cannot mean that they have proved that they never were to blame, but either that they were rid of the fault *now* or that a large number of them had been guilty of apathy and thoughtlessness rather than malice. **12.** 'For his sake . . .' It is not likely, on the whole, that this refers to the incestuous marriage. The one who suffered wrong is very likely Paul himself, as the victim of slander, and the author of the wrong will then be some outstanding person among the False Apostles' party. Or the singular is used for a class or group of persons: 'the wrongdoers'. In any case the *not* is best taken as *not so much*, for the correction of individuals certainly *was* one object of his letter. He must mean that his chief purpose was to j regain the majority. 'Our carefulness'. This gives an easy meaning, but some of the best manuscripts read: 'in order that your devotion to us might be made apparent to yourselves in God's sight', *i.e.* petty human considerations had misled them, but his letter forced them to search their consciences, to look at the matter from God's standpoint, to choose between Paul and his enemies: they *discovered* that they must side with Paul. **13.** 'Therefore:' '*That is why we are consoled*'. 'In our consolation:' Perhaps '*over and above our own consolation*'. The 'all' here and in v 15 must not be pressed, in view of 6:11–7:3. It is what he wishes and appeals for, rather than a present fact. **14.** '*Whatever words of praise I spoke* to him of you'. The natural conclusion from this is that Titus had not previously been to Corinth. 'As we have spoken . . .': Very condensed: 'The kind words which I spoke to Titus about you have proved true in spite of my own fears. Believe then that there is equal truth (*i.e.* honesty and faithfulness) in every word I have ever said to you (in spite of my severity and other men's slander)'. **15.** 'Bowels': '*his kindness* or *sympathy*'.

889a **VIII–IX The Collection for Jerusalem**—The space given to this proves what importance Paul attached to it. There may well have been desperate poverty among the Christians at Jerusalem, but this gift meant much more than material relief: it was a visible proof that Paul's converts were loyal to the apostolic body and regarded themselves as one with the Jewish Christians, not as a separate Pauline church, as Judaizers no doubt said they did. Hence the collection was made in all the four provinces where Paul had last worked, and the chief cities were asked to send delegates to carry it. Seven or eight delegates did assemble in the following spring and accompanied Paul to Jerusalem, Ac 20:4.
b **VIII 1–15 He urges them to keep up their Contributions**—See § 866g. Paul had given instructions in 1 Cor 16:2 about the mode of collection, and it appears from the present passage that this plan had now been

set in operation under Titus's direction. Paul himself was at present encouraging the collection in Macedonia and several times half-playfully fans the spirit of emulation between the two provinces. **1.** 'The grace': the power of giving gladly. **2.** This verse explains what the grace was: '*That under the heavy ordeal of distress their overflowing joy and their deep poverty have made more abundant the riches of their generosity*', *i.e.* their hardships had made them more liberal, not less so. **3.** 'Were willing' is not in the Gk, but some such verb has to be understood. Perhaps '*they are giving*' would be better. **4.** 'The grace . . .': '*the favour of a share in the service . . .*' 'The Saints:' the Christians of Jerusalem. **5.** '*Going beyond all our hopes*, they gave': Paul had hoped for gifts from them, but they placed themselves and all they had at his service, *subject only to God's will* (as the last words mean). **6.** 'grace'—work of charity. Titus had started, or accelerated, the work of collection and would now return to speed it to its conclusion. **7.** It is best to supply mentally some word like 'I appeal to you' at the beginning and to change the colon to a comma. 'Word': '*eloquence*'. Their knowledge and eloquence are mentioned at the very beginning of the first letter (1 Cor 1:5) and it is sometimes implied that they thought too highly of both. 'Carefulness': '*Zeal, fervour*'. 'Charity', *i.e.* love. 'This grace', the power to give unstintingly. **8b.** '*testing the genuineness of your charity by means of the zeal of others*': a half-confession of his little manoeuvre. **9.** This appeal to Christ's example and to the very act of incarnation, is very like Paul. 'grace': '*kindness, mercy*'. **10.** 'advice', as distinct from a command—*cf.* v 8. 'Is profitable', or perhaps '*is becoming, proper*'. 'To do . . .': As the text stands it seems to imply that the wish is greater than the deed. Have the two words been transposed by a slip of the tongue or pen? But some solve the problem by taking 'have begun' as 'were the first to . . .' 'A year ago': '*last year, as far back as last year*'. We do not known whether he refers to the civil year which began some time in October, or to the Jewish religious year which began usually in March. The former would be more natural in writing to so many non-Jews and would indicate the previous autumn, but the latter would fit the circumstances better, giving a date about February, § 866g. **11.** 'to perform *according to your means*'. **12.** '*For if the goodwill is there. . . .*' **13.** 'By an equality': probably a current phrase which could stand by itself without verb, like 'share and share alike'. The sharing of course is voluntary. **14.** 'Their abundance' may either mean that a time may come when Corinth may be glad of money from Jerusalem, or may refer to the next world where the Corinthians will reap the benefits of the spiritual gifts (the Gospel) which came to them from Jerusalem. **15.** Quotation from Ex 16:17, about the gathering of manna. Better: 'He that had *gathered* much . . . that had *gathered* little. . . .'
16–24 The Return of Titus with two Companions— Titus's arrival at Corinth would precede Paul's coming by perhaps a few weeks. There can be little doubt that he was to carry this letter with him. His visit therefore had the double purpose of hastening the collection and of bringing Paul's last warning (chh 10–13) to the still defiant party at Corinth. **16.** 'the same carefulness' (*i.e.* eagerness) probably means an enthusiasm equal to Paul's own, which fits in well with 7:13–16. **17.** 'Accepted': *Has accepted*. 'Exhortation': the request to re-visit Corinth. 'More careful': *more eager* than one who went merely to please Paul. 'Went': '*Is going*'. This verb, together with 'have sent' in 18 and 22, are probably epistolary past tenses (common in Greek and Latin letters) and mean the same as an English present. **18.** 'Have sent': '*Are sending*'. 'The brother, *who has won praise through all the churches by his preaching of the gospel*'. Neither of Titus's two companions is named, though both (especially the first) were men of some note. It is almost incredible that Paul omitted

these names. The name is vital in a recommendation of this sort. It seems therefore likely that these two afterwards apostatized or otherwise disgraced themselves, and that the names were omitted from the letter in later public reading, to avoid painful memories or misunderstanding, and thus had been lost before its publication, which was about forty years after this. The first man was one of the delegates to Jerusalem and his name may be in the list in Ac 20:4. It has been widely believed however that the first-mentioned is Luke, but it is hard to see why Luke's name should ever have been expunged. **19.** 'Ordained' : '*Appointed*'. 'Travels', *i.e.* the journey to Jerusalem. 'Grace' : '*Charity* or *kindness*'—the collection. 'Our . . . will' : '*To prove our own zeal*'. **20-21.** A parenthesis. Paul had asked them (1 Cor 16:3) to send the money by their own delegates (and was sending this delegate with Titus) in order to put himself above any suspicion of having profited by the collection. **20.** 'Avoiding', etc. '*For we wish to safeguard ourselves against any blame in connexion with this large sum* . . .' **21.** 'Forecast' : '*Plan, arrange*'—disarming even unreasonable suspicion, as far as possible. An echo of Prov 3:4. **22.** 'Have sent' : '*Are sending*'. This second brother is not apparently a delegate. 'Proved' : '*Found by experience*'. 'Confidence' seems to indicate that this brother had been at Corinth before. **23.** '*As for Titus, he is* . . . *and as for our brethren, they are the apostles*', etc. Both had at some time acted as delegates or envoys for churches—not 'delegates of *Christ*', which is the usual meaning of *apostle* in the New Testament. 'Glory of Christ' : either 'men whose lives commend the name of Christ to mankind' or 'men in whom Christ delights'. **24.** 'Show . . .' by hastening on the collection, which would be heard of in other provinces.

IX 1-5 Paul will be Disgraced if they are Backward —He appeals to their affection towards himself as well as to their emulation. Too frank and jocular to be called diplomatic. The *whole* paragraph is an explanation of 'boasting' in 8:24, hence the 'for'. **1.** 'Ministry' : '*Assistance*' (the collection). **2.** 'Forward mind' : '*Eagerness*'. Achaea of course includes Corinth, its capital. Omit 'also'. '*Has been ready since last year*' ; *cf.* 8:10. Paul seems to have assured the Macedonians that the Corinthians made very short work of anything they had begun. '*Your zeal has roused to action very many*.' **3.** '*I am sending*' : see note on 'went' in 8:17. St Paul evidently wished the Corinthian collection to be complete or nearly so *before* his arrival, although he intended to make a long stay at Corinth. 'In this behalf :' '*In this point*'. **4.** 'the Macedonians' : probably the three first men named in Ac 20:4, 'me . . . we' : both singular and plural seem to mean only Paul. He can assume that his reputation is as dear to them as their own—he must have already felt very sure of the majority among them. 'Matter' : the Greek word can also mean expectation or confidence. Same doubt exists in 11:17. **5.** 'blessing . . . covetousness' : '*an act of charity, not a scheme of exploitation*'.

6-15 The Blessings of Open-handed Charity—6. 'in blessings' : '*with an eye to* (gaining) *blessings*', *i.e.* gives material goods, confident of a reward from God. **7.** 'Every one' : a verb such as 'ought to give' must be supplied. 'sadness', *i.e.* a sullen, grudging spirit. 'of necessity'—with a feeling of compulsion. 'For God', etc. : *cf.* LXX (but not the Hebrew) text of Prov 22:8. 'God blesses a cheerful man and a ready giver'. **8.** 'to make *every blessing abound for you*', *i.e.* to reward their charity by spiritual and also temporal blessings. **9.** From Ps 111(112):9 (one of the Sunday Vespers psalms). 'He' is the good man. 'Dispersed': '*scattered*' (his gifts). 'His justice', etc., *i.e.* his deeds of charity will always be remembered by God, here and hereafter. **10.** The subject now is God. 'bread . . . seed', *i.e.* both enough for themselves and to give in charity, which, like the sown corn, will again produce a fruitful harvest. 'justice': '*goodness*'. **11.** '*generosity* which worketh', etc. Here a new thought enters,

which fills the rest of the chapter—the gratitude of the **889j** Palestinian Christians, both to God and to their bene-factors, and the friendly interest and understanding which the gift would promote between Jewish and Gentile Christians. To Paul this moral result meant more than anything else. 'Through us', *i.e.* Paul (or Paul and his assistants) as organizer of the collection. **12** 'administration . . . office' : he must surely intend to include the givers, therefore : '*the assistance* (or *relief*) *given by this act of charity*'. **13.** Another case of a loosely attached participle ('glorifying') : '*On seeing the evidence furnished by this relief, they will glorify God for your humble assent to the gospel of Christ and for your open-handed charity to themselves and to all men*'. **14.** There may be some fault in the Greek, but the general meaning seems to be : (1) The brethren at Jerusalem will pray for you. (2) They will feel a strong affection towards you because of this proof that the same Spirit is exerting his mighty influence at Corinth and at Jerusalem. It is this fellow-feeling between such diverse Christians that Paul calls an 'unspeakable gift' in v 15.

X-XIII St Paul vindicates Himself against the False **890a** **Apostles and gives a Last Warning to their Friends**— The tone of persuasive appeal in ch 9 suddenly changes to a very stern one, which prevails to the end of the letter. The main problems of this section have been dealt with in the Introduction. We need only repeat here the conclusions arrived at there : (1) One main purpose of the whole letter is to deal squarely and firmly with the party of False Apostles. This is done in these chapters, and much of the first seven chapters are a preparation for them. (2) Although he does not speak directly *to* this party, except apparently in most of ch 13, yet it would become clear from 10:2 that the whole of this part of the letter is directed *at* them. (Introd. D 2 [9].) (3) On the postponement of this subject see what is said in § 883*d* and note on 6:11.

X 1-11 Denial of some Mean Slanders—The slanders **b** call up a very ugly picture of their authors, men of vulgar spite and base cunning. **1.** 'I Paul myself'. Perhaps he wishes here to speak strictly in his own person, excluding Timothy the joint author, *cf.* 1 Thess 2:18 ; Col 1:23. 'Who', etc. : this description is obviously false and must be an ironical repetition of a sneer of his enemies. 'Lowly' : '*Insignificant*'. **2.** 'Wherewith', etc. : more likely : '*Wherein I consider myself able to take strong action against some* who reckon', etc. This would be readily understood as a reference to the False Apostles and thus would introduce them clearly as the subject of this part of the letter. 'According to the flesh' : in a wordly manner. Ambition, avarice, etc., are probably meant. 'In the flesh' : in the body and subject to its infirmities, including his chronic disorder, *cf.* 11:30 ; 12:7. 'War' : we should have expected 'walk', but it is very like him to introduce this new idea which fills the next three verses. **4.** 'Carnal' of human make and strength. 'mighty in or *through* God'. **4-5.** 'destroying', etc. : loosely **c** joined participle—see 9:13. '*We destroy reasonings and every towering structure that is erected against the knowledge of God*'. Probably refers not so much to heretical doctrine as to unseasonable reasoning such as is noticed in 1 Cor 8:1-6. (See 11:4 below.) **5.** 'Bringing', etc. : *i.e.* we bring, etc. **6.** *We shall be ready to punish all disobedience, as soon as your obedience has reached its height*'— the highest point to which it can be brought by persuasion and warning. Those who were still rebellious after receiving this letter would be excommunicated as he says more clearly in ch 13. **7.** 'See', etc. Uncertain, but probably 'Look at what is before your eyes', *i.e.* at the plain facts. 'Whoever trusts . . .' : this refers to the False Apostles. Paul admits that they are, or were, 'ministers of Christ' (11:23). Others have taken these words to refer to the 'Christ party' (1 Cor 1:12 last note). **8.** 'More', *i.e.* more than **d** the modest claim he had made in v 7. 'Edification' : lit. 'building up' of a Christian community, as of a spiritual temple to God. 'Not . . . ashamed'—his

890d boast could be made good. **10.** ' Say they ' : more likely : ' says he '—a quotation from *one* of his enemies whose name he does not think worth giving us. ' Bodily presence . . . speech ' : the False Apostles themselves may well have approached much nearer than Paul did to that rather theatrical figure which was already becoming fashionable in Greece, the popular orator-philosopher, like Euphrates with his ' tall stature, noble features, waving hair, and immense white beard ' (Pliny Ep 1, 10). Paul, it seems, was without these charms. He was also without the artificial eloquence which was then in vogue and was possessed by many Jews, such as Philo. Paul had a finer but less fashionable eloquence, and certainly made a deep impression on many, even on educated and unsympathetic persons like Felix and Agrippa II.

e **12-18 The False Apostles are Braggarts and Intruders** —St Paul drops his defensive tone and becomes aggressive. This continues till it reaches a climax at 11:15. Paul had done with hints and skirmishing, and was resolved on battle. **12a.** ' Match ' : ' *Put ourselves on a level with* '. **12b.** The more probable Greek text means : ' *They foolishly measure themselves by themselves and compare themselves with themselves* ', i.e. they make themselves the pattern of perfection. **13.** ' beyond our measure ' : ' *inordinately. But (we will glory) in accordance with the size of that portion which God has given us as our share, a size large enough to reach as far as you* '. **14.** ' For (in order to touch and include Corinth) *we do not stretch our hands unduly as if* ', etc. ' For we ', etc., more likely : ' *We were the first to come preaching to you the gospel of Christ* '. It was this *prior* arrival of his which made Corinth his domain, and made his enemies intruders

f and busybodies. **15.** ' having hope ', etc. From here to the end of 16 the DV is very confused. Read : ' *having hopes that with the increase of your faith we may so prosper within our allotted sphere as to overflow it and preach in still more distant regions—instead of entering another's territory and bragging about gains which have cost us nothing* '. This complaint about intrusion had already been made in a gentler form in 1 Cor 4:15. He refers here to his desire to preach in the west. He was thinking chiefly of Spain, but he wished to visit Rome on his way there. (Rom 15:19-28.) **17.** Summary of Jer 9:23-24, cf. 1 Cor 1:31. **18.** ' Is approved ' : ' *passes the test* ', when judged by the true (i.e. divine) standard. God's ' commendation ' then must be the various forms of grace given for sanctification and effective influence.

g **XI 1-15 He prepares for Self-assertion, and roundly denounces the False Apostles**—**1.** ' My folly ' : ' *a little folly from me* '. The folly is the self-praise which begins in 22. This is the first hint that it is coming, but he digresses again as if he shrank from the painful necessity. **2.** ' Jealous *for* you ' with God's own jealousy, a divine jealousy. He uses language familiar from the OT. God was the bridegroom of his people, his church, and Paul was the bridegroom's friend, vigilant against rival suitors and lovers. It is clearly implied that the false teachers are enemies of God. **3.** ' Subtilty ' : ' *craftiness* '. ' From the *purity and innocence that are due to Christ* '. **4.** ' He that cometh ' : ' *the newcomer, the visitor* '. It seems to denote some one of the False Apostles, or else is a collective term for them all. The best interpretation is : If the new teachers had brought a religion which surpassed what the Corinthians had already received from Paul, there would be some reason for honouring them. But instead of the word ' honour ' Paul characteristically substitutes ' endure ' for they had been haughty and exacting (see v 20). This sentence therefore implies that their *doctrinal* teaching was not unsound. (1 Cor Introd. C.) **5.** ' *I consider that I have not in any way been inferior to the greatest apostles* ', i.e. to the Twelve. Many scholars think that Paul meant the False Apostles here, calling them ironically ' the great apostles ', but it is incredible that Paul should have honoured these adventurers by calling himself their equal, when his apostleship was in fact incomparably superior to theirs. **6.** ' Rude ' : untrained (in the professional

orator's art), see 10:10. ' Knowledge '—of God, as in 10:5. ' But . . . you '. The Greek may be corrupt, but the general sense probably is : ' But we have revealed (the truth) fully to you '. **7-11.** These verses are an answer to the malicious lie that Paul by working for his living had admitted his inferiority to the Twelve. The False Apostles said that only the Twelve had a right to maintenance. Paul had already denied this in 1 Cor 9:1-15, and claimed the right for *all* missionaries. In order to be consistent and to outface Paul, the False Apostles had to make a pretence of earning their living (cf. v 12 and § 865i). **7.** ' Humbling myself ' refers to manual work, more despised by pagans than by Jews. ' Exalted ' : raised to the dignity of Christians. ' Freely ' : without payment or cost. **8.** ' Taken from ' : *plundered other churches* '—a natural exaggeration (see 9), but it does mean that the poorer Macedonians had felt the sacrifice ' For your ministry :' ' *in order to serve you* '. **9.** Probably refers to his first visit to Corinth. He seems to have been ill and depressed, and perhaps not able to earn enough, but Silas and Timothy arrived with gifts of money from Thessalonica and Philippi, Ac 18:5 ; Phil 4:15 ; 1 Thess 3:1-8. ' Wanted ' : ' *was in need* '. **10.** ' *As surely as the truth of Christ is in me, this boast shall not be denied me in Achaea* '. He observed the same rule in Asia and Macedonia. **11.** He had given them his reasons, partly at least, in 1 Cor 9:15-18. Some loyal Corinthians had evidently been hurt at his refusal of help, and thought him cold and unfriendly. Other friends may have wished to support him in order to vindicate his equality to the Twelve. ' God knows ' : implies that the preceding words are absurd. **12.** ' That I ', etc. *That I may not give any handle to those who are looking for a handle : that in their boasted mode of life they may be seen to stand just where I do.* They had paraded their self-denial in refusing support : if Paul had accepted support, they would have used this as a handle, and redoubled their accusations of usurpation and rapacity, cf. 12:16. Some critics, relying on v 20, believe that the False Apostles did accept maintenance (cf. 1 Cor 9:12), and that Paul continued to refuse it so that they could not say they stood on an equal footing with him in this matter. But v 20 need only mean that their self-support was a pretence and that they extorted gifts, etc. **13-15.** The most downright attack in the epistle. Paul at last feels able to speak plainly. **13.** ' *For such men are false apostles, dishonest workmen* '. These last words may *include* a sarcasm about their pretence of working for their living : ' *disguising themselves as* '. ' Transform ' has the same sense in vv 14 and 15. **14.** ' Of light ' : belonging to God's glorious realm, cf. ' sons of light '. **15.** ' Therefore it is *nothing remarkable* if his *servants . . .* ' ' Justice ', i.e. of divine goodness. Their reward will be what their deeds have deserved.

XI 16-29 St Paul indulges in the Foolishness of Boasting—Paul at last embarks fairly on the disagreeable task which he seems long to have been nerving himself for, and frankly compares his own service of Christ with that of the False Apostles. He does not here seek to prove his equality to the Twelve by appealing to Christ's direct commission, as he does in Gal, chh 1-2. This for some good reason he considers unnecessary here. Many ideas and phrases in this passage carry us back to chh 1-6, especially to the picture of the true apostle (3:4-6:10). One passage supplements and completes the other. There we have the ideal, here the embodiment of it.

16. When he began the sentence, he intended apparently to repeat v 1 : ' Again I say, bear with a little folly from me ', but he breaks off and makes a new beginning : ' Again I say . . . Let no man think ', etc. The brackets therefore are misleading. ' Take me ' : accept me, indulge me, as a fool. **17.** ' According to God . . . flesh '. The same meanings as in 5:16 and 7:9. He is going to *appear* to imitate the worldly-wise, not the saints. ' This matter '. Or perhaps ' this confidence ' or ' purpose '. The same doubt as in 9:4. **19-20.** Ironical praise referring to the *past* conduct of the great number who had once been imposed upon by the False Apostles. Indignation and pity, smothered for months, and only half-revealed in the First Epistle, now find a free outlet when he feels sure of their loyalty. 'Devour you'. As the Pharisees 'devoured widows' houses'. 'Take from you': the Greek word probably means 'take you in, victimize you', as in 12:16—deceit as well as rapacity. 'Lifted up': 'Is arrogant'. 'Strike you': '*treat you as dirt, trample on you*'. **21.** '*I confess with shame that I myself have indeed "cut a poor figure"*'. It is practically a quotation of his enemies' description of him in 10:10. He apologises for being such a poor bully. 'Wherein', etc.: '*But wherever boldness is shown . . . I am bold too*'. **22.** The three terms (Hebrews, Israelites, seed of Abraham) all seem to mean precisely the same, and the repetition is only for emphasis. But perhaps the first may include the capacity to speak Aramaic. **23.** 'Ministers': '*servants*'—a vague word which might mean any active help in spreading the gospel. 'I speak *madly*: I am a *better one*'. 'Stripes': *blows*. 'Deaths': *i.e.* dangers of death. **24-27.** His heroic sufferings for Christ since his conversion, which had taken place seventeen to twenty-five years before. It is clear that the tale of endurance told by St Luke in the Acts falls far short of completeness—Luke's omissions probably belong mostly to the earlier years of Paul's work. Of the eight floggings which Paul mentions, only one is recorded by Luke (Ac 16:22). 'Forty . . . save one'. When flogging was imposed as a penalty by Jewish law, forty lashes was the maximum, and it was customary to make it thirty-nine for fear of a miscount, Deut 25:1-3. The Jews' power to inflict such penalties outside Palestine must have been confined to those large cities where the Jewish communities were autonomous, § 587a. Therefore Damascus, Tarsus, and Antioch at an early date in Paul's career are the most likely scenes of these sufferings. **25.** 'With rods', *i.e.* on the order of some *Roman* official. We know of only one case, the illegal flogging at Philippi (Ac 16:22). Only the higher provincial governors could order a Roman citizen to be flogged, and therefore the two other floggings were probably ordered by the governor of Syria on some accusation of causing disorder. 'Stoned': this was at Lystra by a mob incited by Jews, eight or ten years before this (Ac 14:18). 'Thrice . . . shipwreck'. The shipwreck in Ac 27 was still to come, therefore these three disasters were probably in early voyages which are omitted in Ac. 'Depth of the sea': '*on the open sea*', *i.e.* far from land, on a raft or wreckage. **26.** 'Waters': '*dangers from rivers*'—flooded rivers which had to be crossed by fords or boats. 'Wilderness': waste uninhabited areas through which some of the roads of Asia passed, *e.g.* the high passes over the Taurus. 'False brethren': men nominally Christians, who hated him and were unscrupulous in their opposition. He gives this name to Judaizers in Gal 2:4, but there were many other shades of opposition—the unsound mystics and rigorists, to say nothing of mere impostors. **27.** 'Watchings': '*loss of sleep*'. Paul chose to do two men's work, to be a missionary and a manual worker, and therefore often had to encroach deeply on the night. Moreover the Christians often could only meet for services at night or before daybreak (Ac 20:7-11). 'Fastings': most likely to be loss of meals owing to poverty, journeys, etc., *cf.* 6:5. **28.** 'Without', *i.e.* external things, bodily trials and dangers. He goes on to speak of mental trials. 'Instance': '*care, anxiety*'. There are several doubtful points however in this verse. **29.** He gives one example of his anxieties. '*Who is weak without my sharing his weakness?*' Paul regularly uses the word 'weak' about Christians who were over-scrupulous especially in regard to food, holy days, etc., and insists that others are bound to make things easier for them even at the cost of inconvenience to themselves, see 1 Cor 8:9-13; Rom 14. 'On fire' may mean both indignation and anxiety.

XI 30-XII 10 St Paul's Ecstasy and his Chronic In- 891c firmity—This difficult passage has three parts: (1) The escape from Damascus. (2) The ecstasy. (3) The infirmity. The words 'weakness' (infirmity) and 'to be weak' mark both its beginning and end, and come six times in all. This word certainly means his bodily infirmity or disease in 12:9. It seems best therefore to take 'infirmity' *throughout* the passage as referring to this. Vv 30-33 are therefore a preparation for the definite mention of it in 12:7, but right in the middle of the passage he puts his ecstasy, no doubt because he considered that the best setting for it. If we assume that his infirmity was some sort of nervous trouble (a widely held view), it seems quite possible that it was caused or aggravated by the manner of his escape from Damascus, and this would explain (what is otherwise incomprehensible) the special emphasis on that event here. He does not expressly connect the two, but that might be unnecessary in writing to anybody who knew the exact form of his disorder. The famous story about Pascal's carriage-accident, if it is true, would be a parallel. Many scholars however think that 'weakness' at the beginning and end of this passage refers back to the heroic sufferings of 24-27, while admitting that in 12:9 the word means his disorder. But in that case the word changes its meaning *twice* in the 14 verses. Moreover the sufferings of 24-27 are proofs of strength not weakness; they are glorious, not humiliating. And why should Paul apologise for mentioning them if he thought they were signs of weakness?

31. Referring to the connexion between his escape **d** and the infirmity. **32.** The event occurred two or three years after his conversion, at least 15 years before this letter. 'Governor': '*the ethnarch* of King Aretas'. Aretas was king of the Nabataeans, whose territory, called 'Arabia', stretched along the east and south of Palestine. Damascus seems to have been added to it about A.D. 38. The ethnarch would be the local governor appointed by Aretas. The event is described in Ac 9:23-5. **33.** 'Basket'. The Greek word means a large flexible basket, used to carry hay and sometimes corn.

XII 1. The 'if' is omitted in the best MSS. Para- **e** phrase: 'Boasting is the order of the day. It is true that it is not for our good, but at any rate I will proceed, and speak of my visions . . .' It is of only one vision that he does speak. We get the impression that he had never mentioned this before, that it was different from other visions and that he had approached as nearly as a living man can to the direct contemplation of God. He had already told the Corinthians about the one on the road to Damascus (1 Cor 9:1; 15:8). Four others are mentioned in Ac (16:9; 18:9; 22:18; 27:23). But here all the signs, especially the strangely ambiguous language, show that he was claiming something far beyond the other visions, an overwhelming experience. **2.** 'A man': there can be no doubt that he means himself. 'In Christ': Either 'in the Church' (as Rom 16:7) or 'rapt by the power of Christ'. Omit 'above'. The date (*thirteen* years past, according to our expression) would be A.D. 41 to 44, not long after the escape from Damascus. 'Whether', etc. This doubt does not seem to arise in most visions, and helps to mark this one out—an ecstasy. 'Third heaven': he is using the language of some astronomical system which he had heard of (there were many). He certainly means the highest (or farthest) sphere, regarded as the place where God dwells. **3.** Doubtless the same vision. **4.** 'Paradise': **f** evidently means the same thing as 'third heaven'. The word meant a park, but it had now come to denote the place where the souls of the good awaited the resurrection (Lk 23:43). 'Secret'. Or perhaps '*unutterable*'. 'Not granted' probably means that they are of their nature incommunicable. **5.** 'For', *i.e.* 'about'. **6.** 'Shall . . . will'. More natural to say *should* and *would*. '*That nobody may impute to me*

891f *something more than he sees . . . or hears . . .*' This seems to mean that he was afraid that, if he said more, some of his converts from paganism might regard him as semi-divine. Such ideas were common, *cf.* §598*q*. **7.** The Greek is very strange. It seems likely that Paul began a sentence and left it unfinished, *cf.* 11:16. ' *And owing to the grandeur of the revelations—Therefore that I might not become proud. . . .*' He at last discloses

g that he has been speaking of himself. ' Sting ' : ' *a thorn for the flesh*'. The image is that of a thorn or splinter embedded in the body. But ' flesh ' may be wide enough in meaning to cover both body and mind, the natural man. St Paul's ailment is expressly mentioned only here and Gal 4:13–14, where we gather that it was a severe trial to those around him. Nervous disorder, ophthalmia, and malaria, are the best suggestions, and the first has the largest support and the special advantage that it might explain the reference to Damascus (see on 11:30). ' *Messenger of Satan* ', *i.e.* something sent by him, for all disorder is ultimately traceable to him. **8.** ' Thrice ' : perhaps during the three first attacks. **9.** Christ's answer might be taken as a summary of the whole epistle. Man's weakness is, in his present circumstances, often the best condition for God to achieve great things through him ; see 1:5 ; 4:10. **10.** ' I please myself ' : ' *I gladly accept* '. ' Infirmities ', etc., *i.e.* the ' thorn ', whatever it was. He here adds it to a summary list of the sufferings enumerated before. ' In *outrages* (the word means always insult and generally violence), in *hardships*, in *persecutions*, in *the last extremities*. ' For when ', etc. Another summary of the deepest thoughts of the epistle.

h **XII 11–XIII 13 Last Protests and Last Warnings—XII 11–18 Last Protests**—These eight verses are a kind of appendix to the whole self-assertive passage. The question of maintenance again comes in. **11.** ' Foolish . . .' echoes 11:16 and refers to the intervening passage. ' No way ', etc. : practically a repetition of 11:5. ' Nothing ' : *cf.* 1 Cor 15:9 (' I am the least of the apostles ') and 1 Tim 1:15 (' . . . sinners of whom I am the chief '). We should set these words against the unwilling self-praise of this letter. **12.** Omit ' yet '. ' *The marks (proofs) of an apostle have been produced before you in the form of patience under all kinds of sufferings and of signs* ', etc. The three words ' signs . . . deeds ' all mean miracles. He ranks his patient endurance above miracles, but he can and does confidently appeal to miracles done by himself at Corinth. **13.** He means apparently that the marks of apostolic grace have been as plain at Corinth as in any church founded by another apostle. ' *For in which respect have you been less favoured than the rest of the churches, except that I indeed* (as compared with other apostles in their churches) *was not burden-*

i *some to you ?* ' **14.** The first sentence can mean either : ' For the third time I have made ready to pay this visit ', or : ' I am now ready to pay my third visit '. The second, which fits the context somewhat better, would imply that there had been an intermediate visit, §884*g*. ' The things ' : *i.e.* their money. ' Lay up ' : ' *to save money* '—to make provision for their children's education. Later the grown-up children of course might be bound to support their parents, but this later stage does not come into St Paul's picture : they are his *little* children and cannot be expected to do anything for him. **15.** ' Although ', etc. : the better Greek texts read : ' If I love you more, am I loved less in return ? ' *i.e.* does every new sign of my love cause a diminution

j of yours ? **16.** He abruptly cites and rebuts one of the false accusations of his enemies : ' *Granted—I myself was not a burden to you, but, like the rascal I am, I played a trick on you, I suppose ?* ' The accusation, as the next verse shows, was that his assistants had taken presents at his suggestion and for his use. **17.** ' Overreach ', *i.e.* make some profit out of them. **18.** Probably epistolary tenses as in 8:17, 18, 22 ; ' *I have asked Titus* (to visit you) *and I am sending the brother* '. It is the same visit as arranged in ch 8 and is referred to almost in the

same words—strong evidence that ch 8 was written before this. The ' brother ' is probably the first of the two mentioned in ch 8. § 884*f*. Titus is the only one who has been to Corinth already, so the following question is only about him. The 'we' means Paul and Titus. **XII 19–XIII 10 Last Warnings and Appeals**—The stern chapters have hitherto been addressed to the majority of the Corinthians, for many now repentant had allowed themselves to be misled. But the remainder is addressed to the still rebellious members—this becomes clearer in 13:2. Many tender expressions are mingled with the sternness. But it is an ultimatum : those who have not repented and submitted before his arrival will be excommunicated.

XII 19–XIII 6 Last Warnings—19. ' *Have you been thinking all this time that we have been on our defence before you ?* ' He has in fact been defending himself, but he says he did so freely at his own choice, he is not answerable to them, but to God. ' We speak . . . Christ ' : exactly the same words as in 2:17, see note. ' But all things ', etc. : meaning : ' But I would do anything for the good of your souls, my dearly loved ones ', *i.e.* he will not stand on his dignity when it is a question of winning them back. The verse which begins so roughly ends in marvellous gentleness. **20.** ' I shall be found ', etc., *i.e.* be forced to act as a stern judge : ' dissensions ', etc. : ' *party-divisions, backbiting, malicious whispers, conceit, confusion, should still persist among you* '. This verse and the next enumerate the chief faults condemned in 1 Cor with one great exception (laxity towards paganism). Paul seems to fear that the party of the False Apostles had become a rallying point for all kinds of bad Christians at Corinth. **21.** The beginning is ambiguous in the Greek, and can be translated either as in the DV or ' Lest, when I come again, God should humble me '. The DV implies that he had already undergone one humiliation at Corinth, *i.e.* that there had been a ' painful intermediate visit '. The other translation does not imply this, *cf.* §884*g*. ' And I mourn ' : *i.e.* ' *And lest I should mourn . . .* ' He calls their sin his humiliation, such was his charity. ' Done penance ' : ' *repented* '. ' Lasciviousness ' : ' *licentiousness* '—a wide word. Who are these ' former sinners ' who have never repented of unchastity ? Probably Gentile converts who have never given up the immorality which they practised as pagans. Perhaps they have also continued to participate in pagan rites. In that case they may be the persons addressed in 6:10–7:3. The omission of any express mention of pagan practices here seems to make this more likely. The same persons are again meant in 13:2 onwards. **XIII 1.** The first words are again ambiguous, and mean either ' This is my third visit ', or ' For the third time I am on the point of setting out to visit you '. In the latter case the point would be : I have not been hasty in coming : the sinners have had time to reflect, *cf.* 1:23 (' It was to spare you that I put off my visit to Corinth '), §884*g*. ' *Every charge must be proved by the evidence of two or three witnesses* '. This was the rule of Jewish criminal procedure, and is quoted from Deut 19:15. Here St Paul means that he is going to use the same fair procedure in deciding which of the Corinthians deserve excommunication, *cf.* 1 Tim 5:19. **2.** ' *To former sinners and to all the rest I gave notice and I give it now, as present the second time so now while absent, that when I come again I shall not spare* ' (*i.e.* shall act severely). An involved sentence, but it seems to indicate that he had already paid them a second visit, and during the recent troubles. It therefore appears to contradict 1:15 (see note there) and is the strongest evidence for such a visit, *cf.* §884*g*. The Greek may be corrupt. If there was no recent visit, the words ' I gave notice ' would probably refer to what he has said in 1:23 or 10:2. For ' former sinners ', see note on 12:21. **3.** ' *For you seek a proof . . .* ' ' In you ', *i.e.* among you. He says he must be severe with the defiant members because they have asked for evidence that Christ speaks through Paul, *i.e.* they have denied that he is an apostle in the full sense, as the

Twelve are. How will his severity prove that they are wrong? It seems clear that it must be severity wielding a *miraculous* power of punishment, such as Paul had used when he inflicted temporary blindness on the sorcerer Elymas (Ac 13:8–11). Only the Apostles seem to have had such powers. From 1 Cor 5:3–5 we gather that physical suffering (intended only to bring repentance) was a frequent consequence of excommunication. If Paul's excommunication of these rebellious Corinthians were immediately followed by some bodily affliction, he would have furnished all the 'proof' that they could have desired. **4.** 'Weakness', *i.e.* the weak nature and humble condition which he assumed at his incarnation, *cf.* Heb 2:14–18; 5:2. 'Weak in him': weak with and for Christ, in union with Christ, joining our infirmities to his and accepting ours for his sake. The verse again recalls that thought of strength-in-weakness which underlies the whole epistle. By his own weakness Paul here meant everything that would make the world despise him, as a poor Jewish worker, unpolished and physically afflicted. 'We shall live . . . towards you'—yet by the same union he would give evidence of divine life and power in his dealings with the rebels. **5.** He asks them to search their consciences which will at once tell them that they are in the wrong: 'Test your own selves to see if you are sound in your religion (*i.e.* in a state of grace)'. For 'faith' must be taken in a wide sense here. He has twice commended their faith in the strict sense (1:23; 8:7) and can hardly be casting doubt on that now. Another translation is possible: 'If you are sound in faith (as you are), test your own selves', etc. 'That Christ', etc., *i.e.* that you are in the state of grace. The opposite to this is meant by 'reprobate' (lit.: rejected by God)—in a state of mortal sin. Their self-examination would in fact show them that they were reprobate and lead to their repentance. In all other passages of St Paul the word ἀδόκιμος has this sense of 'rejected by God' and therefore it seems very unlikely that it has any other sense here. But most commentators prefer in these three verses (5–7) to interpret it as 'failing to give the proof'—the visible proof of divine power mentioned in 3. This gives a good meaning but seems a hazardous departure from

Paul's regular use. **6.** *Either* their self-examination *or* (failing that) his divinely enforced sentence would prove to them that God was on his side.

7-10 Last Appeal—The menacing tone changes to one of touching appeal. He protests that to win them back to Christ would be worth almost any sacrifice of personal honour or reputation. **7.** 'do no evil', *i.e.* cease from doing wrong. For the moment he ignores past wrongdoing. It is just possible however that he said: 'Would to God that you had done no evil'. 'Not that . . .' *i.e.* 'My prayer and desire is, not that we may be clearly vindicated (by God's evident act) but that you may do right even at the cost of our appearing no better than reprobates (*i.e.* sinners)', *cf.* Rom 9:3 ('I could wish that I myself were accursed and cast away from Christ for the sake of my brethren (the Jews)'). **8.** 'The truth': he means either the Gospel (the *whole* Christian revelation) or the rules of truth and justice as far as they applied to the case now before him. **9.** 'For we rejoice' that we should count for little (should be despised) provided you are great (*i.e.* in holiness). 'This also', etc: '*this is our very prayer* (the very desire of our hearts)'. **10.** Omit 'more'. The last half of the verse is repeated exactly from 10:8.

11-13 Conclusion—Probably written with his own hand. **11.** 'For the rest': '*In conclusion*'. 'Take *comfort* (or *courage*)': very natural after this stormy letter. 'Have peace': '*live in peace*'. **12.** 'Holy kiss': as in several other letters, always probably refers to the kiss of peace at Mass. 'The saints', *i.e.* the Christians at the Macedonian city from which he wrote, *cf.* §883*c*. **13.** This benediction is unique. There is no other *short* passage in St Paul where the doctrine of the Holy Trinity is so clearly indicated. 'Grace': the root-meaning is mercy or favour. 'the charity of God': '*God's love*' (for men). This seems to be the regular meaning of 'love of God' in St Paul. 'Communication of the Holy Ghost'. Many shades of meaning are suggested. Perhaps the most probable are: (1) Participation in the Holy Ghost, parallel to 1 Cor 10:16 ('partaking of the body of the Lord'). (2) Union with the Holy Ghost, parallel to 1 Cor 1:9 ('fellowship of his son Jesus Christ').

GALATIANS

By Dom B. ORCHARD

893a Bibliography—F. Amiot, *Epître aux Galates*, Paris, 1946[1] (Verbum Salutis XIV) ; Dom J. Chapman, *St Paul and the Revelation to St Peter, Mt 16 : 17*, RBn 29 (1912) 133-47 ; Cornely, *Commentarius in epist. ad Galatas*, Paris, 1892 ; *De Witt-Burton, *A critical and exegetical Commentary on the Epistle to the Galatians* (ICC), Edinburgh, 1921 ; *W. L. Knox, *St Paul and the Church of Jerusalem*, Cambridge, 1925[1] ; M.-J. Lagrange, O.P., *Epître aux Galates*, Paris, 1918 (Etudes Bibliques) ; *Kirsopp Lake, *The Earlier Epistles of St Paul*, London, 1930[2] ; *J. B. Lightfoot, *Saint Paul's Epistle to the Galatians*, London, 1884[8] ; John MacEvilly, *An Exposition of the Epistles of St Paul*, vol. 1, London, 1855 ; Dom B. Orchard, *A New Solution of the Galatians Problem*, JRB 28 (1944) 154-74 ; B. à Piconio, *Epistle of St Paul to the Galatians* (Exposition of the Epistles of St Paul, vol. II, tr. Prichard, London, 1890) ; *W. M. Ramsay, *A Historical Commentary on St Paul's Epistle to the Galatians*, London, 1900[2] ; F. Prat, S.J., *La Théologie de Saint Paul*, Paris, 1920[8] ; Steinmann, *Der Brief an die Galater*, Bonn, 1935 ; E. Tobac, *Galates (Epître aux)*, DTC.

b Authenticity and Genuineness—Suffice it to say that the Epistle itself and its attribution to St Paul have been accepted by all the ancient ecclesiastical writers and by all modern critics, save certain radical members of the discredited Dutch School of Bauer and his associates, and by Loisy in his later years. Our Epistle is certainly quoted by St Ignatius of Antioch, St Polycarp and St Justin ; it is explicitly attributed to St Paul by St Irenaeus and his contemporaries, and is already found in the Muratorian Canon and in all the catalogues drawn up by the earliest Councils. Moreover the internal evidence reveals in every line the unique hand and personality of St Paul, as every serious reader will agree.

c Date and Destination—The researches of Professor Sir William Ramsay (*cf. op. cit.*) have proved that in the time of St Paul the Roman Province of Galatia straddled Asia Minor from north to south and embraced not only the basin of the R. Halys (Galatia strictly so-called) but also the territory of the ancient countries of Lycaonia and Pisidia, as well as a great deal of the ancient kingdom of Phrygia. At the end of the 3rd cent. the Province of Galatia was divided by Diocletian, only the northern portion retaining the name of Galatia. It was probably ignorance of this fact that led St Jerome and other 4th cent. writers to believe that the letter was addressed to the Galatians of North Galatia. It is certain from the itinerary of Ac 13-14 that Paul did not visit northern Galatia on his first journey, and the later narrative of Ac (16:6-8 ; 18:23) does not suggest that he ever did so during his second or third journeys. If Galatians can also mean the *south* Galatians, evangelized on the first missionary journey, and if the internal evidence of Gal can be harmonized with the data of Ac, then there is an overwhelming case for accepting the modern view that it was written after the first missionary journey but before the Council of Jerusalem (A.D. 49). For the epistle is so obviously concerned with the circumcision question debated and settled at the Council of Jerusalem, Ac 15, that it is most embarrassingly difficult to date it after this event.

Moreover all the internal evidence of the Epistle **d** favours the view that it is dealing with that same controversy—all, that is, except Gal 2:3-5, which seem to constitute an obvious reference to St Paul's third visit to Jerusalem at the time of the Council. If we admit this reference then, of course, we are bound to date the letter after the Council (with all the attendant difficulties of explaining why there is no reference to the decrees of the Council in the Epistle, and so on). If, however, we take Gal 2:1-10 as an account of events that occurred during St Paul's second visit to Jerusalem (recorded in Ac 11:29-30), *with a couple of parentheses and a reference to 'false brethren' inserted in view of the controversy raging when he wrote the epistle*, then there is no longer any serious objection to accepting the early date of Gal. Full discussion of this important point is impossible within the scope of the present commentary, but the outline of the exegetical argument will be found below in the comments on 2:1-10. The view adopted here, therefore, is that Gal was addressed to the converts of St Paul's first missionary journey, being despatched probably whilst on his way up to Jerusalem for the Council in A.D. 49, *cf.* Ac 15:3. (For details see my article in JRB (1944) 154-74.) Gal is thus the earliest of St Paul's epistles, and throws most valuable light on Ac 13-16.

Occasion and Object—The occasion of the Epistle **e** was the news that his Galatian converts (mostly Gentiles, as it would appear from Ac 13-14 ; Gal 4:8) were being won over by certain 'false brethren' to the doctrine that circumcision and the Mosaic Law were as necessary to salvation as faith in Christ, 2:16 ; 5:2. Acceptance of this doctrine would logically result in the conclusion that faith in Christ, and therefore the redemption on the Cross, was insufficient to justify a man without adherence to the Law of Moses ; in other words, all converts to Christianity were bound to Judaize, *i.e.* live as Jews. This would have been a mortal blow at the universality of the Church and clean contrary to the teaching of Christ and the subsequent instruction to St Peter, Ac 10-11.

These Judaizers, Ac 15:1, 5, 24, had gone down to Antioch and there, it seems, had wrongly alleged the authority of the Apostles for their doctrine. Not content with causing mischief at Antioch, some of them had secretly, 2:4, gone into southern Galatia to attempt to win over Paul's converts to their way of thinking.

Their chief arguments were the agreed fact that the **f** Law of Moses was divinely instituted and that Christ had said he came 'not to destroy but to fulfil the Law', Mt 5:17. To overcome any scruples of the Galatians they declared that their teaching had the support of the Twelve whose authority was in any event superior to that of Paul, who (they claimed) was probably also in agreement in his heart of hearts. Paul's reaction was swift and violent. Stirred to his depths and quivering with just indignation he at once dictated this passionate vindication of his apostolic authority and crushing denunciation of their wicked error and of all who followed or favoured it. He put the true issue to the Galatians with unmistakable force and clarity : 'If you be circumcised, Christ shall profit you nothing', 5:2. We know that in the main his appeal succeeded because not only did the Council of Jerusalem fully endorse Paul's policy and action but there is also no hint of any dissidence when a short time afterwards he again passed through the southern Galatian region ' delivering unto them the decrees for to keep that were decreed by the apostles and ancients that were at Jerusalem ', Ac 16:4.

Doctrine—Like all the letters of Paul, Gal is embarrassingly rich in dogmatic content not only directly but also by way of countless allusions to doctrines which he presupposes his readers to know thoroughly. Thus we have an allusion to the peculiar and pre-eminent position of St Peter, whose example is sufficient even to detach Barnabas from his allegiance to St Paul, 2:13, his assumption of the existence of one authoritative Church, universal in extent, entered by baptism, one in doctrine, and ruled with infallible and absolute authority by the Apostles, Gal 1:9, 2:9 ; 3:27, 28 ; 6:16. There are also invaluable references to the doctrine of the Blessed Trinity (1:3 ; 3:2, 5, 14 ; 4:6) and to that of personal union with Christ, and of our union with one another in Christ, 2:20 ; 3:27, 28 ; 4:19 ; 6:15. But its main teaching concerns the general economy of salvation for all, Jew and Gentile, based on faith in God's promises, and the relation of the Law of Moses to it.

It has been well said that the starting point of this epistle as of St Paul's theology is his vision of the glorified Christ on the road to Damascus, 1:16. In the splendour of that vision he knew Christ to be the only begotten Son of God who became man to redeem the world and who by his sacrificial death on the Cross and resurrection from the dead compensated in his own person for the sins of the whole world and merited pardon for sin, sanctifying grace and the promise of eternal life for all who believe and obey him, without distinction of race, class or sex, 1:4, 3:20, 28 ; 4:5.

The Judaizers, however, insisted that in order to participate in the benefits of the redemption every catechumen must observe the Law of Moses, including the rite of circumcision, and asserted that salvation was impossible without it. Now these Christian Pharisees were affected by the strongest school of thought in contemporary Judaism, the school that esteemed the Law of Moses as eternal and immutable, even, it would seem, identifying it with the divine wisdom and regarding it as the source of grace and life, of joy and peace (J. Bonsirven, *Le Judaïsme Palestinien*, Paris, 1934, I, 302–3). But though he admitted the Law to be divinely given, 3:19, St Paul refused to allow it any redemptive power or power to justify, for that would be to put it in the place of the unique and utterly sufficing sacrifice of Christ on the Cross, 3:21. The error was fundamental and had to be instantly crushed, for compromise was impossible without nullifying the Cross of Christ, 2:21. So in this Epistle, while showing that for all men for all time salvation has been, is, and always will be based on belief in Christ and his justifying grace, he devotes more space to showing the Galatians why the Law cannot justify and what its true place in the economy of salvation is.

For St Paul there are three stages in the religious life of the world from the time of Abraham, the founder of the Jewish race and the greatest hero and saint of ancient Israel : (1) from Abraham to Moses : during which justification came through faith in God's promises, without any positive law properly so-called (circumcision being only the sign of God's covenant with Abraham, Gen 17:11) ; (2) from Moses to Christ : during which justification came through faith in the promises, but with the obligation besides of keeping the Law positively given on Sinai (faith, not Law, justifying) ; (3) since Christ : justification by faith in him and at the same time by the keeping of the Law of the Gospel (which is much more than a new and improved edition of Judaism).

Christianity is not so much an addition to and a completion of the imperfect OT regime as a positive religion of pardon, justification, salvation and life **894b** through Christ and in Christ, prolonging beyond the interlude of the Law of Moses the covenant concluded by God with Abraham and his posterity. In this Epistle the extrinsic, adventitious and transitory character of the Mosaic Law clearly appears. It is emphasized by the fact that the Law was promulgated by the mediation of angels and of Moses and under the form of a bilateral contract which the apostasies of the Jewish people could render inoperative. The promises, on the contrary, were made to Abraham directly and *unilaterally* ; they are by way of favour, are without any condition (circumcision was only imposed later as a sign and seal of the covenant) and concern all the peoples of the world. For St Paul the essential thing for every human being is the establishment and promotion of the divine life in the soul through union with Jesus—which *cannot* be done by adherence to the Law, 3:20, 21. This divine life Abraham received by faith in God's promises independently of the works of the Law and by a pure favour of God, 3:6–9. Justification (δικαιοσύνη), which **c** means for St Paul the passage from the state of enmity with God resulting from original and actual sin to the state of sonship in which we possess the divine life of Christ in ourselves, is always the free gift of God to us in virtue of the gift of faith. Christians, whether Jew or Gentile, are now the true sons of Abraham and heirs of the promises because they too have received justification by faith in the Son of God, likewise entirely out of God's liberality. Christ by dying on the Cross as the representative of the whole human race satisfied for the sins of the whole human race whether committed explicitly against the Law of Moses or against the natural law. Like Christ the Christian must die to the Law through the Law so that he may live to God, 2:19. This mystical death to all the impulses of his lower nature which the Christian undergoes in baptism makes him live on a new plane in which he ' walks in the Spirit,' 5:25 f., and so is no longer under the Law, 5:18. This liberty of the sons of God comes from the doing to death of the vices and concupiscences of the flesh ; he is a new creature, 6:15, whose life, being the life of Christ, of whom he is a member and also of whom he is a temple, 2:20 ; 3:6 ; 1 Cor 6:15, 19, shows forth the fruits of the Spirit, 5:22–23, against which there is no law, the life of faith that worketh by charity, 5:6.

The True Nature of the Law of Moses—Since justifica- **d** tion has never at any time in the religious history of mankind come through the observance of the Law but only through faith in the promises, what is the position of the Law in the history of the Jews ?

The Law imposed a curse on all who were subject to it, yet failed to keep it, but did not supply the means to keep it ; it merely provided a standard or code by which the Jews were judged and by which their transgressions were revealed (and even increased because of their failures to keep the Law), 3:19. The Law was like a prison, for it revealed the unhappy servitude of the human race and itself offered no means of escape, 3:22 ; but it did at the same time perform the useful function of isolating the Jews from pagan vice and idolatry, did in fact keep them together and directed them towards the future Messias, 3:22. In this sense before the coming of Christ, mankind was a minor and a pupil, and the Law was his pedagogue and tutor, 3:24. Now that Christ has come the task of the pedagogue has ended ; the Jews are no longer under his authority but have entered into full sonship and inheritance, 4:5–6. Thus the part of the Law in the history of the Jews was that of a provisional and transitory dispensation suitable for the adolescence of the human race and destined to pass away when the coming of Christ inaugurated its full maturity. There is now in consequence no distinction between Jew and Gentile, 3:28.

St Paul gives the following **proofs of the abrogation of e the Law of Moses** and of its powerlessness to justify,

894e 2:16–21: (1) The Apostles and faithful have always acted on the assumption of its powerlessness; (2) Scripture itself declares it, Ps 142(143):2; (3) the abandonment of the Law on the strength of the sufficiency of the redemption would, if the Law still retained its obligatory character, be sin, the blame for which we should have to place upon Christ—which would be blasphemous: whilst on the contrary those who are putting themselves again under the yoke of the Law must admit the sin of having abandoned it in the first place; (4) the Christian, being mystically crucified, has died to the Law with Christ; (5) since the death of Christ, which is the source of all graces, has infinite value, to set up another means of arriving at perfect justice is to deny the redemptive power of the Cross of Christ (*cf.* Prat, *op. cit.*, I, 198–9); (6) the characteristics of the regime of Law are incompatible with those of the Promise; for whereas the Promise is the source of freely given spiritual goods, the Law always offers a *quid pro quo*, a measured recompense for a measured service, 3:12; (7) Christ by his death on the Cross, in which ' he became a curse for us ', 3:13, redeemed us from the curse of the Law by fulfilling in his Person all the requirements of the Law perfectly and at the same time making complete and perfect satisfaction for all the transgressions of the Jews (and mankind in general) against the Law. The Law thus satisfied has no further claims on him nor on the rest of the human race in so far as they are united to him by baptism. The Law therefore has no further power over him or over us and hence Paul can say, ' For I, through the Law am dead to the Law, that I may live to God: with Christ I am nailed to the Cross ', 2:19.

f (8) To conclude his argument St Paul gives the famous allegory of Agar and Sara, representing the two testaments. Agar the slave represents the synagogue; Sara, the free-woman, symbolizes the Church. Their respective sons take after the condition of their mothers. Therefore those who wish to Judaize rank themselves with Ismael, the son according to the flesh, and renounce the patrimony given to Isaac, the son of the promise, which is also that of Christians who are the true spiritual heirs of Abraham. The point of the comparison is that the lesser and imperfect testament must give place to the new and perfect one, for the two are incompatible, and cannot co-exist: ' Cast out the bondwoman and her son: for the son of the bondwoman shall not be heir with the son of the free woman ', 4:30; Gen 21:9–13.

This is one of the best examples of the use of the spiritual sense of Scripture to prove a thesis, *cf.* Amiot, *op. cit.* 202, Note 1; J. Bonsirven, *Exégèse Rabbinique*, 275, 309–10, Prat, *op. cit.* I, 221–2; Lagrange, *op. cit.* 118–22.

For further treatment of the Law and Justification *cf.* commentaries on Rom and Heb, and art. ' Christianity in Apostolic Times '.

g **I 1–II 21 Vindication of his Apostolic Authority**— The haste in which this Epistle was composed is shown by the abruptness of the beginning and the deferment of any greeting to his correspondents till v 3.

I 1–5 Introduction—1. From the first word Paul claims the fullness of the apostolic authority, for his, too, is from God (unlike that of false apostles which is ' of men ') ; and like the Twelve he has been commissioned not by the mediation of men (' by man ') but directly by Jesus Christ, (Ac 9:3 f., and so by God the Father, who thus constituted Paul a true witness of the Resurrection. 2. ' All the brethren who are with me ' probably refers to his small band of companions ' The churches of Galatia ' refer to the local churches founded during the first missionary journey, Ac 13:14 f.; the omission of all commendation of them is pointed. 3. These words of greeting are found in all the epistles of St Paul save Hebrews, and they clearly show that the Galatians believed without question Paul's teaching of the complete equality of the Son with the Father.

Κύριος (Lord) is always a divine title with St Paul (*cf.* J. Lebreton, *Histoire du Dogme de la Trinité*, 1927[7], I, 368, and 1 Cor 8:6). 4. Paul will later show them that their readiness to accept circumcision demonstrated their failure properly to value the atoning death of Christ. 5. Doxology. The everlasting character of God's Kingdom is contrasted with the present evil age. **6-10 A Stern Rebuke for their Apostasy**—6. According to the view of the date and occasion of the Epistle taken in § 893c–d no more than a few months had elapsed since Paul had left them; *cf.* Ac 14:22 f. Lightfoot notes that this is the sole instance in which St Paul omits to express his thankfulness for their faith in addressing any Church, substituting for it this indignant expression of surprise. ' I wonder that you are so soon *in process of abandoning* him (God) . . . *for* another gospel—which is not another'. 7. There can be no other gospel: it is merely a matter of certain men (Judaizers) presenting a false teaching utterly incompatible with the true gospel. 8. Any such teacher should be regarded as given over to destruction, utterly excluded from the Kingdom of God (anathema), and hence by inference excommunicated also. The Church in its Councils has taken over the use of this same formula. 9. His solemn anathema clearly shows that he regards himself as infallible, and Christianity as a religion of authority. 10. Clearly his Judaizing opponents had falsely accused him of compromising and of lack of consistency in the past; *cf.* 5:11.

I 11-II 21 The Mission of St Paul by God the Father himself—The Judaizers of Galatia maintained that *their* gospel came from Christ through the Twelve Apostles, but Paul declares that the Gospel of Jesus Christ was directly revealed to him by God the Father in the same way that St Peter himself received it, Mt 16:16 f., Gal 1:16 (*cf.* Chapman, RBn 29 (1912) 133–47); hence his gospel is as authoritative as that of Peter and identical with it. 11-12. His gospel is not a man-made doctrine, nor has it been transmitted through a man but it came, as Chapman says, ' by a revelation of Jesus Christ, which taught me who He is ' (rather than Lightfoot's subjective genitive, ' by a revelation from Jesus Christ '). 13 f. He begins explaining in detail how his Gospel teaching has always been independent of, though fully in accord with, that of the Twelve. 13. ' Conversation ': *i.e.* manner of life. ' Beyond measure ': far more than the other Jews. 14. Cf. Phil 3:5–6. He advanced more quickly in knowledge and authority than any of his contemporaries, because of his greater zeal for the traditions (added to the Law by the Pharisees); *cf.* Mt 23 *passim.* 15. There is perhaps here a play on the meaning of the word ' Pharisee '. Paul, already ' a Separated One ' from his birth, had been in a more profound sense ' separated ' or pre-destined before his birth (*cf.* Jer 1:5) to his Christian vocation. 16. The reference here is primarily to his conversion, Ac 9:3 f. ' Immediately I *conferred not with* flesh and blood ': this revelation of the Son to him by the Father was so all-sufficing that he had no need to seek further enlightenment even from the Twelve, including St Peter. 17-24. He now gives a list of his movements in subsequent years to prove that his few contacts with the Twelve had not been for the purpose of obtaining doctrinal information.

17. ' The apostles who were before me ', *i.e.* the Twelve, chosen in point of time before him. ' Arabia ' probably means the country south of Damascus, the kingdom of the Nabataeans, rather than the district of Sinai. We have no record of what happened during these three years, but while the opinion of the Fathers is that he immediately started preaching, many now prefer to think that he devoted himself to a life of prayer and meditation similar to that of St Benedict at Subiaco. 18. ' After three years ', *i.e.* three years from his conversion according to the Jewish mode of reckoning; *cf.* Mt 16:21. On the date of St Paul's conversion, *cf.* § 895c. ' to see ' (ἱστορῆσαι): to make the direct official acquaintance of Peter, *cf.* Ac 9:26–30.

19-20. Paul declares on oath that of the Twelve he saw only Peter and James on this visit. ' James ' is most probably James the Less, the first bishop of Jerusalem, a cousin of our Lord ; cf. §§ 672-3. **21.** Paul now evangelized the regions near his native city of Tarsus in Cilicia and around Antioch in Syria ; cf. Ac 9:30 : 11:25. **22-24.** Outside Jerusalem he was not known in Judaea at that time save by reputation, though he was to become much better known to the Churches of Judaea during his next visit, the Famine Relief visit, Ac 11:29-30.

II 1-10—The complicated question of the identification of this visit to Jerusalem with the corresponding visit in Ac has been briefly discussed in § 893c–d. The visit recorded here is therefore taken to be identical with the famine relief visit of Ac 11:29-30 ; cf. also Chrys. Hom. in Ac 25:2, PG 60, 193. **1.** ' After fourteen years ' : St Paul is still pursuing the same line of argument as in the latter part of the preceding chapter ; he means ' fourteen years ' from his conversion according to Jewish reckoning, cf. § 124g, i.e. anything between say 12¼-14 full years after his conversion. The date of this visit could not have been later than the winter of A.D. 46-7, when the famine was at its height ; cf. Ac 11:29-30 for further details. According to the view taken here St Paul's conversion must have occurred between A.D. 31-4 ; but cf. §831a for a different view. ' Titus ' was one of St Paul's early Gentile converts. His name is not mentioned in Ac, but several times in 2 Cor. St Paul wrote to him the Pastoral Epistle of the same name. **2.** Paul's going up to Jerusalem in obedience to ' a revelation ' is quite compatible with his other purpose of taking the famine relief. Indeed, it is not forcing the text to make it mean that he went up in response to the ' revelation ' made to Agabus (Ac 11:18). But if we take it as a special revelation made to himself, then in this revelation he was instructed to compare his teaching with that of the Twelve not for the purpose of reaching an agreement (which already existed), but for mutually confirming their complete doctrinal harmony and in order to forestall future possible sources of disagreement over matters of practical policy. ' Communicated to them . . . ' : instructed by his revelation Paul thought it prudent and necessary, not to ask for approbation but privately to compare his teaching with that of the Twelve and to secure recognition of their complete harmony and agreement lest there should be any misunderstanding or threat of rupture between him and Peter, James and John, i.e. lest he had, or should, ' run in vain ' ; ' but privately before the authorities ' ; τοῖς δοκοῦσιν is a term of honour, not of depreciation. This action of Paul was therefore taken to safeguard unity, and in view of the storm that arose in Ac 15 it was well to have secured in advance the full trust of, and complete accord with, the Apostles. **3-5** form a parenthesis that interrupts Paul's account of his private conference with Peter, James and John ; what happened at their conference and what resulted from it is told in 6-10. **3.** We have seen that on this visit Paul brought with him the Jew Barnabas and the Greek Titus, both his friends and helpers. This verse begins a parenthesis as Paul suddenly introduces a new consideration, viz. that in tacitly approving of his having Titus as a collaborator, uncircumcised Gentile though he was, the Apostles showed that they were already committed in principle to the admission of uncircumcised Gentiles into the Christian fellowship. The question of circumcising Titus never arose at all ; the question, St Paul means, was not raised on that occasion, though it would have been, if the Apostles had ever accepted the views of the Judaizers. **4.** ' But (your liberty is now in danger) because of false brethren . . . ' : the words in brackets, or some clause such as ' I only mention Titus here ', are required to complete the sense, both subject and verb being wanting in the Gk ; cf. Orchard, art. cit. supra. These ' false brethren ' are the persons mentioned in Ac 15:1-2. ' into servitude ', viz. by

insisting on the necessity of circumcision and the **895e** observance of the Mosaic Law by all Gentile converts. **5** sums up the resistance described in Ac 15:2 f., and concludes the parenthesis. **6** resumes the description **f** of Paul's private conference. The authorities, i.e. the three Apostles, imparted no fresh knowledge to him, saw nothing defective or incorrect in his teaching, but on the contrary heartily recognized his mission as being directly from God. ' But of these who are looked up to as authorities ' : St Paul is depreciating not the Twelve themselves, but the extravagant and exclusive claims set up for them by the Judaizers, viz. the fact that the Twelve knew Jesus in the flesh before his Resurrection did not give them any special advantage over him, for God does not judge according to this. Both he and they are Apostles in the fullest sense and God does not regard the difference between him and them in the circumstances of their call. While admitting fully their Apostolic Authority his own is not dependent on their approbation. **7.** ' . . . in the same way as to Peter was that of the circumcision ' : the revelation made to Paul in Ac 9:3 f. is comparable only with that made to Peter in Mt 16:16 f. ; cf. Chapman, art. cit. supra. **8.** ' He who wrought for Peter ', by **g** making his apostolate fruitful among the Jews, ' wrought for me also among the gentiles '. ' The gospel of the uncircumcision ' means ' the uncircumcised Gentiles as the object of the apostolate ' (Lagrange). This mission of Paul to the Gentiles must not be understood in any exclusive or monopolistic sense, but he himself had been called in the designs of God primarily for work among the Gentiles. Peter as the Chief of the Apostles and the centre of unity had the responsibility of welding the Jewish and Gentile elements in the Church into one whole and because of his closer contact with the mother-church of Jerusalem and of his pre-eminence among the Apostles (cf. Roiron, RSR [1913] 501-4) he personifies for Paul the principal agent in the conversion of the Jews, at this particular time at any rate. Of course St Paul never renounced, nor did St Peter ever confine himself to, the evangelization of the Jews ; cf. Ac 10-11 ; 1 and 2 Pet passim. **9.** ' the grace ', i.e. of the Gentile apostolate ; cf. Rom 1:5. ' James and Cephas and John '. Lightfoot (in loc.) remarks that when St Paul is speaking of the missionary office of the Church at large, St Peter holds the foremost place, 7, 8 : when he refers to a special act of the Church of Jerusalem, St James is mentioned first, as here ; cf. Ac 12:17 ; 15:13 ; 21:18. On St Paul's relative use of Cephas and Peter, see Chapman, art. cit. 143. ' Who are regarded as pillars ', a statement without any touch of irony or depreciation. The accord here made between the Three Pillars and Paul on the latter's second visit to Jerusalem was to be renewed on his third visit to the Holy City, Ac 15 passim. In all probability they agreed on a territorial delimitation of their spheres, the Pillars retaining the evangelization of Palestine, whilst St Paul kept to the westward ; cf. also Rom 15:20. **10.** ' Only (they would) that we should be mindful of the poor ; which was the very thing I had also been careful to do '. The aorist ἐσπούδασα can bear here a pluperfect sense. The reference is clearly to the famine relief collection, Ac 11:29-30. St Paul's constant solicitude for the welfare of the mother-Church in Jerusalem is also seen in 1 Cor 16:1-4 ; 2 Cor 8-9 ; Rom 15:26-27 ; Ac 24:17 ; also § 637a.

11-21 The Incident at Antioch—It would appear **h** that the incident at Antioch took place either immediately before or immediately after the first missionary journey of Paul. **11.** Cf. also 14 infra. This statement implies that St Paul both recognized and venerated the authority of St Peter as being superior to his own (Lagrange) ; there is no ground for the assumption that Paul considered himself superior to Peter. The use of the title Κηφᾶς and its contrast with Πέτρος, 7-8, show that he was fully aware of Peter's position as The Rock ; cf. McNabb, New Testament Witness to St Peter, London, 1928, 43-6. **12.** St Peter was

895h scandalizing Gentile Christians. It is clear from this verse and from Ac 10:5-10 that Peter now made no distinction between clean and unclean foods. It is also clear from Ac 15:24 that the emissaries from Jerusalem must either have exceeded their powers or abused them. It was presumably for the sake of peace and to avoid serious friction that Peter ' *withdrew gradually* ' from taking meals with the Gentile converts in Antioch. Peter's authority led the rest of the Jewish Christians and even Paul's own lieutenant, Barnabas, to follow his example. **13.** Though Peter's attitude was negative, it was nevertheless ' hypocritical ' in the sense that his action was not in conformity with his convictions, and the truth of the Gospel and the liberty of the Gentiles (not to mention the Jews as well) from the Mosaic Law would very soon have been endangered.

i **14-21** sum up St Paul's speech on this occasion to Peter and to the faithful of Antioch. **14a.** ' the truth of the Gospel ', *i.e.* liberty of conscience with respect to the ritualistic prescriptions of the Mosaic Law. Paul reproached Peter not with a doctrinal error, but with not holding firm in the principle which he recognizes, ' conversationis vitium, non praedicationis ' (Tert., *De praescript.* 23). ' before them all ', *i.e.* before a formal gathering of Jewish and Gentile Christians. **14b.** Peter is accused of exerting a moral pressure in favour of Judaizing since the Gentile Christians would feel themselves bound to submit in order not to be separated from the chief of the Apostles. *N.B.*—For the local compromise agreed on for the storm-centre areas of Syria, Cilicia and Galatia, see Ac 15:28-29. No word is said there about Jewish Christians and the Mosaic ritual, but Gentile Christians are to observe four prohibitions, which seem to be identical with those formerly imposed in the OT upon Gentile minorities in Jewish territory, for the sake of peaceful living, *cf.* Lev 17:8, 10, 13 ; 18:26. **15.** Said perhaps with a slight touch of irony, but the verse emphasizes the special privileges of Israel as a race possessing a rule of conduct vastly superior to anything found among Gentile nations, whom they therefore referred to as sinners. **16** gives the essence of Paul's position. *Cf.* Ac 15:11. ' Justification ' in St Paul means an interior purification by which a man's sins are utterly blotted out and he is made acceptable to God in virtue of faith with charity, and good works, *cf.* § 894c, and Rom 2-5. The last part of the verse is a free quotation of Ps 142(143):2 ; no one under the Old Dispensation was justified, not even by the works of the Law, save by the foreseen merits of Christ, and through faith in God's promise of Redemption. It would seem that Paul is in fact using this text in an accommodated sense, *cf.* RB (1938) 503-4.

896a **17.** A difficult verse, which seems to mean : seeing that in order to be justified in Christ it was necessary to abandon our old ground of legal righteousness and to become ' sinners ' (*i.e.* to put ourselves in the position of heathen), may it not be argued that Christ is thus made a minister of sin ? (Lightfoot). ' Heaven forbid that anyone should teach that justification by faith without the Law makes a man a sinner ; for Christ would be responsible '. **18.** But to put oneself back again under the Law after having abandoned it would indeed be ' to make oneself a *transgressor* of it '. This verse seems to hint at the possible consequence of Peter's action. Renunciation of the Law is then absolutely imperative. If the Jew who abandons it apparently makes himself a ' sinner ', he does it in reality in order to be at once justified in a marvellous participation of the life of Christ. He will have gained infinitely more than he has lost.

b **19.** ' For I died to the *Law* through (the) law . . . ' : he died to the Mosaic Law through a mystic death realized through faith and baptism, by which a Christian puts on Christ and is united to his death ; *cf.* Gal 3:29 ; Rom 6:3. ' Through (the) law ' is a difficult phrase, and is easier, perhaps, to understand as ' through the law of faith ', *cf.* 6:2, than ' through the Law of Moses ', which, in causing as

it were the death and Resurrection of Christ, does the same for us in virtue of our solidarity with him. Being freed from the bondage of the Law by this mystic death, the Christian now lives with the life of God and in union with him. ' With Christ I *was and am concrucified* ' : the perfect tense of the Greek verb indicates that the state acquired by a man on the day of his justification by baptism still endures. For further development of the idea of concrucifixion, *cf.* Gal 5:24 ; 6:14 ; Rom 6:6. **20.** ' *And it is no longer I that live*, but Christ liveth in me '. These words have inspired a great mystical literature which has attempted to draw out their meaning. ' Walking in the spirit ' (5:25) the Christian is ' another Christ ' in virtue of his mystical union with him. His present physical life since his conversion is a life elevated and animated by faith in Christ. **21.** To return to the practice of the Law of Moses would be to spurn this incomparable gift of divine life. If justification could be gained through the Law then the Redemption was unnecessary and a mockery.

We are not told the effect of these words on Peter, but obviously Paul would not have related the incident unless the issue had been favourable to him and Peter had seen his mistake. At the subsequent Council of Jerusalem, Ac 15:6 f., the conditions laid down for the fraternization of Gentile Christians with the rest of the Church (in which Peter concurred) marked a complete victory for St Paul on all the essential points.

III 1-V 12 The Gospel of Paul agrees with the Promises of the Old Testament—Paul, having established fully the independence and authority of his teaching and its full acceptance by the other Apostles, including Peter, now demonstrates its full harmony and continuity with the doctrine of the OT. The Judaizers had misunderstood the relation between Christianity and the OT, so he sets out the doctrinal basis of his doctrine of the liberty of the Gentiles from the Mosaic Law, by showing that they are the heirs of the promises and of the blessing given to Abraham before the Law and before Circumcision. The New Dispensation is not merely superimposed on the Old Dispensation, nor an enriched edition of it. But the two are incompatible, the New driving out the Old.

3:1. Omit ' that you should not obey the truth '. ' Before whose eyes *Jesus Christ crucified has been exhibited* ': these words show the important place held by the Passion in the preaching of Paul. **2-5.** He tells them to recall to mind that it was the wonderful and beneficent activity of the Holy Spirit among them that had transformed their lives, and not adhesion to the Mosaic Law ; *cf.* Ac 13-14. **2.** ' The hearing of faith ' here and in 5 means ' faith which has come through hearing '. **4.** ' Suffered ' : the Greek could also equally well mean ' experienced ' ; in which case the reference would be to the magnitude of their supernatural experiences. **6.** The answer to the question put in 5, *viz.* ' By faith of course ' is omitted by St Paul as being too obvious to require statement. ' It is written ' is not in Gk, but the sense is ' And so it was with Abraham who believed . . . '; *cf.* Gen 15:1-6. Abraham was justified because of his faith in God who had just promised him a numerous posterity (and ultimately the Messias) at a time when humanly speaking it was impossible for him or Sara to have a son. The comparison between Abraham and the Christian rests on the fact that in either case it is faith in God's promises and not the works of the Law that makes them pleasing to God. **7.** The only true sons of Abraham are those who imitate his faith. The virtue of faith brings the Gentiles closer to Abraham than carnal descent brought the Jews. **8.** ' *evangelized* Abraham *in anticipation* ', *i.e.* gave him the good news in advance. The Scripture blessed the Gentiles in and with Abraham because it foresaw that faith would play the same part in their salvation and bring them the same blessings. Abraham was justified by faith fifteen years before ever the law of circumcision was imposed ; *cf.* Ramsay, *op. cit.*

896e § xxxi. **9.** Those who rely on faith in Jesus Christ for their justification shall be blessed with the faithful
f Abraham. **10.** But everyone who is under, or who puts himself under, the Law is morally obliged to keep it in its entirety under pain of malediction, Deut 27:26. It is true that before Christ for a Jew faith also required the faithful observance of the Law. **11.** But this is no longer so ; since Christ abrogated the Law, faith in Christ alone suffices. The quotation from Hab 2:4 refers in its original context to the faith of the Jewish exiles in the accomplishment of God's promise regarding the return from the Babylonian captivity ; it may be translated either ' the just man *shall* live by faith ', *i.e.* in virtue of faith, or ' he who is just by faith shall live '. **12.** The Law, as such, has not faith for its principle. The quotation from Lev 18:5 proves that the Law is concerned solely with works and with nothing else. St Paul means that the vivifying principle even in OT observance of the Law was faith. **13.** But now redemption through Christ has taken away all value from legal observances. The Law could only reveal the deficiencies of human conduct ; it could not cure them or atone for them. This Christ himself did in redeeming us by the sacrifice of the Cross. As regards Deut 21:23 it is clear that in the case of Christ the curse is only apparent and in the common estimation of men. But he took upon himself all the penalties due to the human race for its transgressions of God's Law, and atoned for them by his death, thus completely negating the curse. **14.** And because Christ is God as well as man, ' the blessing of Abraham ' (which is justification by participation in the life of God through the Holy Spirit, the Spirit of Jesus) is given alike to Jew and Gentile through his death and resurrection.

g **15-29 The Blessings of Abraham are Inherited solely through an Indefectible Promise**—**15.** He institutes a comparison from human affairs. ' A man's *will*, if it be *valid*, no man *annuls* or *adds fresh clauses to it* '. **16.** *Cf.* Gen 13:14–17 ; 17:5–8 ; 22:15–18. St Paul, with the Jewish Rabbis, takes the promise of the possession of the land of Canaan symbolically of the glorious and eternal Messianic Kingdom. ' Thy seed ' is Christ, considered as the principle of unity of the human race, and through whom the promises were fulfilled. **17-18.** The Law coming 430 years later did not in any way modify the testament of the inheritance by God's free promise. Paul follows the LXX ; *cf.* Ex 12:40 and §§ 124–5. **19.** ' because of transgressions ', *i.e.* to reveal sins. Jewish tradition held that the Law was given to Moses as mediator by means of angels. **20.** Though this verse might mean that the Law is inferior to the Promise because it comes from God indirectly whilst the Promise comes without intermediary, St Paul probably means that the Mosaic covenant was a bilateral alliance involving a mediator (Moses) and the possibility of the covenant failing through the transgression of the Jews, whereas God's Promise was *unilateral*, unconditional, indefectible, and could not be modified by the Law. **21.** The Law could only be against the promises if it could give life. **22.** ' hath *shut up* all under sin ' as in a prison—the Scripture is here represented as doing that which it declares to be done ; *cf.* Deut 27:26. **23.** ' were *guarded* ', *i.e.* protected, by being shut up. **24.** The pedagogue was a superior slave entrusted with taking a boy through the streets to his schoolmaster. **26.** The coming of the faith means the fulfilment of the Promise, and all who believe become sons of God. **27.** Baptism is the consequence of the act of faith, and the newly baptised are as it were clothed with Christ, nay more (**28**) they are one *person* with him. A magnificent proclamation of the unity and spiritual equality of all human beings. **29.** The Christian is the true seed of Abraham and true heir to the Promise ; Christians are the true ' Israel of God ' ; *cf.* 6:16.

h **IV:1-11 At Christ's coming the Period of Tutelage gives place to that of Full Worship of God**—**3.** ' elements of the world ' probably signify those imperfect rules of conduct which held humanity in a kind of **896h** slavery—for the Jews their legal observances, for the Gentiles their pagan rites and customs. **4.** A very important verse from which we learn of the pre-existence of the Son, of his taking flesh from a Woman, *cf.* Apoc 12:1–2, at a time predetermined by God, and of his further condescension in his submission to the Law, *cf.* Lk 2:21. ' Fulness of the time ', the time fixed by God for the ending of the minority of the human race, *cf.* Eph 1:10, also Heb 1:1. ' born of a woman ' : the only direct mention of the Blessed Virgin in the Pauline writings ; the Gk γενόμενον, ' made ', is practically synonymous with γεννώμενον, ' born ', and so we render with WV and RV. ' born under the law ' : subject to the Mosaic Law. **5.** The two-fold object of the divine plan, to redeem the Jews from the Law and to confer divine sonship on all. **6.** The Holy Ghost, the Spirit of Jesus, gives the Christian this sonship and the intimate conviction thereof. **7.** Sonship gives inheritance of God's kingdom. **8-10.** ' by nature ', *i.e.* in reality. These verses imply that most of the Galatian converts were Gentiles ; nevertheless they have already started to observe the Jewish calendar. **11.** He fears lest his work among them may have utterly failed.

12-20 A Digression revealing his Anxiety concerning i their Lapse—**12.** A plea for unity. **13-14.** This ' infirmity ' or weakness of health, though a ' *trial* ' to them, did not diminish their welcome. **15.** *sc.* What has now become of your rejoicing ? Some think this verse hints at St Paul's having some disease of the eyes. **17.** ' They pay court to you *for bad motives* ; and they would *hatch* you *out* ' (in order to exploit you, *cf.* JTS 40 (1939) 149–51), so that you in turn may pay court to them '. **18.** ' *But it is always good to be courted for a good motive* ', *i.e.* by Paul himself. **19.** Owing to their lapse he has again to go through the labour of begetting them in Christ. **20.** ' Change my voice ', *i.e.* modify my severe tone, ' because I am *perplexed about* you '.

21-31 The Allegory of the Two Covenants—On **897a** rabbinic exegesis, *cf.* Bonsirven, *Exégèse Rabbinique*, 275, 309–10. Paul assumes the existence of the mystical sense (*cf.* § 40) in Scripture, in which events and figures of the OT are types of the NT. Taking yet another illustration from the history of Abraham, he shows that those who rely on the Law instead of faith in the Promise are to be excluded from the inheritance ; *cf.* Prat, *op. cit.*, I, 221. **22.** *Cf.* Gen 16:15 ; 17:15–21 ; 21:2, 9. **23.** ' According to the flesh ' : on the one side all happened according to nature ; but on the other, according to a divine promise, miraculously realized. **24.** ' Which things are allegorically interpreted ' as follows. **25.** ' (For Sinai is a mountain in Arabia) ' : a supplementary confirmation of his interpretation inserted in parenthesis ; for Ismael is connected with Arabia through being the ancestor of the chief Arab tribe. Arabia then denoted all the land S. and E. of Palestine. ' *She corresponds* to that Jerusalem. . . .' **26.** *i.e.* the Church. **27.** *Cf.* Is 54:1, with which the Rabbis connected Is 51:2. **28.** ' . . . children of *a* promise '. **29.** The hostility of the Ismaelites to the Israelites was a commonplace in rabbinic writings, *cf.* also 1 Par 5:10, 19 ; Ps 82(83):6–8. **30.** *Cf.* Gen 21:10. **31b.** [V:1a]. A variant reading gives the sense : ' Christ freed us in order that we should be free, not slaves '. **V:1** [V:1b]. Having escaped the **b** slavery of paganism, they are exhorted not to fall again into slavery—of Judaism this time. **2.** The Judaizers must have told the Galatians that circumcision was necessary for salvation (*cf.* Ac 15:1). **4.** ' made void *from* Christ ', *i.e.* made nothing and separated from him. **5.** ' in spirit ', *viz.* acting by the Holy Spirit. ' The hope of justice ', *i.e.* the good things received through justification. **6.** Faith working through charity is all-sufficing.

7-12 An Attack on the Judaizers—**9.** Though few in number they are capable of ruining the Church.

897b **11.** *Cf.* 1:10. It appears from this verse that the Judaizers claimed St Paul as at least a secret supporter of circumcision for Gentiles. His reply is that if he were such, (1) he would not be persecuted as he is, and (2) then also what is for them the 'scandal of the cross' would—*per impossibile*—be set aside. **12.** ' *Let them* who trouble you *castrate themselves !* ' A strong sarcasm. If these Judaizers are so interested in the question let them go one better than circumcision !

c **V:13-VI:10 Christian Liberty is not Licence and requires Good Works done in Charity**—The danger that freedom from legal observances may lead Christians into excesses of other kinds can only be guarded against by the practice of Christian charity. **14.** *Cf.* Lev 19:18. **17-18** form a slight digression. **17.** By ' the spirit ', St Paul means the intelligence and will of a man when guided by the Holy Ghost ; by ' the flesh ', the same powers divorced from the guidance of the Holy Spirit and so leading to evil. **18.** ' But if you are led by the Spirit, you are not under the Law of Moses '. **19-23** contrast the works of the flesh with the fruits of the Spirit. **19.** ' fornication ' : πορνεία signifies rather sexual irregularity in general. ' Luxury ' is not in Gk. **20.** ' Emulations ', *i.e.* jealousies. **21.** ' Revellings ', *i.e.* sacred orgies. **22-23.** DV following Vg makes the number of ' fruits ' up to twelve, by adding ' longanimity, modesty, chastity '. **23.** *Cf.* 18. The Law was largely negative ; there is now no limit to the practice of virtue under the influence of the Spirit. **24.** The Christian by his baptism has died to all ' the works of the flesh '. **25.** Yet the complete victory over ourselves is not yet ours, but will be if we *follow the Spirit*.

26-VI:10 Injunctions regarding our Neighbour—VI:1. **897** ' If any man be *caught out* . . .' **2.** ' Burdens ' : *i.e.* both spiritual trials and the moral weaknesses of ourselves and others which we must help to carry. **4.** Let each man examine his own conscience, and thus find his ground for boasting in himself and not by comparison with others. **6.** ' And let him that is instructed in the Word (*i.e.* the Gospel) share with his teacher all his (temporal) goods '. **9.** ' . . . let us not lose heart '.

11-18 Autograph Epilogue—It was St Paul's custom **e** to dictate his epistles to an amanuensis and only to write the last paragraph in his own handwriting as a proof of genuineness ; *cf.* Rom 16:22 ; 1 Cor 16:21, etc. **11.** ' See *with what large letters* . . .', *i.e.* in a large hand. **12.** ' . . . as desire to *make a fair show* in the flesh . . . that they may not *be persecuted for the cross of Christ* '. Fear of persecution by the synagogue was therefore a leading motive in the Galatian movement towards circumcision. **14.** ' . . . *through which* the world is crucified. . . .' **15.** All that matters now is to be ' a new creature ' transformed by baptism into a Son of God, being made one with Christ by the seal of the Holy Spirit. **16.** ' The Israel of God ', *i.e.* the Church in general. **17.** St Paul orders that there be no further disputes on these matters. ' The marks of the Lord Jesus ' are almost certainly the marks of the ill-treatment he had already received in Galatia during his first missionary journey ; *cf.* Ac 14 *passim*.

18. sums up the teaching of the epistle : it is by ' grace ' that we are saved and not by the Law ; *cf.* Ac 15:11.

THE EPISTLE TO THE EPHESIANS

By D. J. LEAHY

Bibliography—*T. K. Abbott, *Ephesians and Colossians*, ICC, 1897 ; R. P. Benoit, *L'Horizon Paulinien de l'Epître aux Éphésiens*, RB 46 (1937) 342–61 ; H. Coppieters, *Les Récentes Attaques contre l'Epître aux Éphésiens*, RB 9 (1912) 361–90 ; St Chrysostom PG 62 (tr. *Library of the Fathers*, vol 6) ; G. S. Hitchcock, *The Epistle to the Ephesians*, London, 1913 ; P. Ketter, Eph, Phil, Col, Phm in vol. 15 of *Die h. Schrift für das Leben erklärt*, Freiburg i. B., 1937 ; I. Knabenbauer, S.J., CSS, 1912 ; R. P. Médebielle, *Epître aux Éphésiens* (vol. 6 of *La Sainte Bible*, ed. Pirot), Paris, 1938 ; R. P. Médebielle, DBVS, vol. II, 638 ff., art. *Eglise* ; J. Rickaby, S.J., *Further Notes on St Paul*, London, 1911 ; *J. Armitage Robinson, *St Paul's Epistle to the Ephesians*, London, 1914[2] ; S. Thomae Aquinatis, *In Omnes S. Pauli Ep.*, vol. II, Turin, 1929 ; J.-M. Vosté, O.P., *Commentarius in Epistulam ad Ephesios*, Rome, 1932[2] ; *B. F. Westcott, *St Paul's Epistle to the Ephesians*, London, 1906.

Place of Origin and Date—Eph is one of the four *Captivity Epistles*, all written whilst St Paul was a prisoner, as he mentions in each. According to Ac the Apostle was imprisoned for two years at Caesarea, and he was also imprisoned at Rome. For eighteen centuries nobody suggested that these epistles were written at any other place than Rome, but in modern times Caesarea and Ephesus have been suggested in its stead. Neither has more than a little support from internal evidence, and none at all from tradition. We can safely assume that the epistles were written in Rome. Tychicus (6:21) is the messenger who carries Eph to its destination. The same man, with Onesimus, is the bearer of Col and Phm (Col 4:7–9). Now in Phm (22) St Paul says that he expects to be released shortly, since he asks for a lodging to be prepared for him. Hence, we can place the Captivity Epistles towards the end of the Apostle's first captivity in Rome, in A.D. 63. This is the opinion of practically all Catholics and of the majority of non-Catholic writers of note. There is no clear indication whether Col preceded Eph, but most writers think it did (*cf*. F. Prat, *The Theology of St Paul*, vol. I, 280). Eph and Col are companion epistles ; on their relation, *cf*. Introduction to Col, § 909i.

Destination—On one point nearly all modern commentators are agreed, *viz*. that Eph was not written exclusively to the church at Ephesus, the only writer of note who maintains the contrary being Fr Cornely, S.J. The chief reason for this agreement is the impersonal character of the epistle. Paul had lived for nearly three years at Ephesus and had many friends and co-workers there (*cf*. Ac 20:17 ff.). In view of this fact the omission from the epistle of all allusion to his experiences there is disconcerting for anyone claiming that the epistle is addressed to the Ephesians alone. Phil, written about the same time, abounds in personal allusions. Moreover, Timothy is at the Apostle's side, and he is well known to the Ephesians (*cf*. Ac 19:22), yet there is no mention of him in the greeting of this epistle, though he is mentioned in all the other Captivity epistles. Admittedly, this point decides nothing by itself : Rom abounds in salutations, although the Apostle had not visited Rome at the time of writing. Similarly, 1:15 is not relevant : the verse

does not imply that Paul knew only from hearsay 898c of his readers' conversion ; it refers to the spiritual progress which had been reported to him.

Nearly all commentators, then, are agreed that Eph d was not written to Ephesus exclusively. Beyond this point agreement ends. There are two main opinions on the precise destination : (1) Eph is a *circular* (*encyclical*) *epistle*. This view, first suggested tentatively by *Theodore Beza (1598) and developed by *James Ussher (1722), is the more popular among commentators today, Catholic and Protestant. Among Catholics we may mention Fouard, Belser, Lagrange (*cf*, RB 38 [1929] 290–3), Prat, Merk, Lusseau-Collomb, J. Schmid (BS 22 [1928]), Hitchcock, Médebielle. This theory explains why the epistle is impersonal ; it has still to explain why the title *in Ephesus* appears in the greeting according to most MSS. Here the supporters of the encyclical theory divide among themselves. Ussher and many others claim that the words *in Ephesus* are not authentic. They are absent from the important *Vaticanus* and *Sinaiticus* codices, from the Chester-Beatty papyrus (P 46) which dates from about 200, and from the important cursives codex 1739 of Mt Athos (10th or 11th cent.) and codex 424 of Vienna (11th cent.). Ussher suggested that in the autograph a blank space occurred at this point, to be filled in by the names of several churches in Asia Minor, as occasion offered itself. The difficulty against this theory is that no other names occur in the MSS. Indeed, the words *in Ephesus* are found in all the MSS (including the important codices A and D) other than those mentioned above.

M.-J. Lagrange (RB 38 [1929] 292) is more plausible e in retaining the words *in Ephesus*. The epistle is an encyclical addressed first to the Ephesians, who were then to pass it on to the churches of Asia Minor. It is very probably the letter which Paul mentions, Col 4:16. The words *in Ephesus* could easily have disappeared from certain copies, either by design (as ' in Rome ', Rom 1:7, 15, missing in codex G), or accidentally.

(2) Eph *was written to the church at Laodicaea*. This f theory, too, explains the impersonal character of the epistle ; for Paul had not personally evangelized Laodicaea. Moreover, it provides an answer to the question : Why, if Eph is an encyclical intended for several churches, did Paul not mention them (*cf*. 2 Cor 1:1 ; Gal 1:1–2) ? Thirdly, it regards Col 4:16 as a reference to this epistle. Lastly, there is the testimony of Marcion. We learn from Tertullian (*Adv. Marcion*. 5, 11, 17, PL 2, 532–4) that Marcion read ' in Laodicaea ' in place of *in Ephesus*. Since there is no doctrinal reason why Marcion should change *in Ephesus* for ' in Laodicaea ' many writers, Protestant and Catholic (among the latter are Knabenbauer, Delatte, Simon-Prado, Vosté, Huby) think the epistle was written to the Laodicaeans.

The great difficulty in this theory is to explain why the name Laodicaea disappeared from the MSS to give way to Ephesus. Most of the supporters suggest a reason drawn from Apoc 3:14–19, where the angel of Laodicaea severely reprimands the city. Copyists thought they ought to erase the name of a city which no longer merited the name of holy and faithful. But

898f the reproach levelled at Laodicaea was the outcome of love (Apoc 3:18) ; the threats were conditional ; and in fact the Laodicaeans repented later on. But by that time, says Vosté, it was too late : the name *Laodicaea* had already disappeared from the copies. But why had *Ephesus* been substituted ? There is no extant MS with the title *in Laodicaea* ; on the contrary, patristic tradition, beginning with St Irenaeus, is for an original *in Ephesus.*

g Authenticity—The first doubts on the authenticity were expressed by De Wette (19th cent.). But the standard work against the authenticity was written by *H. Holtzmann (*Kritik der Epheser u. Kolosserbriefe,* 1872). In England the common view among non-Catholic writers is to admit the authenticity (Lightfoot, Hort, Westcott, Salmond, Abbott, Robinson, Murray, Lock, etc.). There are still a few who follow Holtzmann's lead, though they discard or modify several of his arguments. Thus *J. Moffat (*An Introduction to the Literature of the NT,* Edinburgh, 1911) ; *E. J. Goodspeed (*The Meaning of Ephesians,* Chicago, 1937), both of whom suggest that the epistle was the work of a disciple of St Paul's. Goodspeed suggests that Paul's letters were first collected when attention was drawn to his life by the publication of Acts. The collector of the letters wrote Eph (on the basis of Col and other letters) as a kind of covering letter, or summary, for the collection.

h The arguments used by writers who deny the authenticity are exclusively internal. The chief argument of Holtzmann's is the literary resemblance between Eph and Col. The latter is said to be genuine, but Eph is said to be merely a general doctrinal essay written later on the basis of the particular letter to the Colossians. Coppieters in 1912 and Benoit in 1917 dealt satisfactorily with this objection to the authenticity. They explained the undoubted literary resemblance on the basis of the traditional view that St Paul was the writer of both epistles.

Other arguments used by those who deny the authenticity are based on the vocabulary and style of Eph. The *hapax legomena* in Eph, however, number only 43 ; they are roughly equal to the number found in the undoubtedly genuine Gal, and a dozen are found in the description of the Christian's armour (6:10–17).

The argument based on different doctrines in the two epistles is no longer used. There is no contradiction, but a development easily explained by the traditional teaching that the two epistles were written by St Paul about the same time.

i Contents—In captivity at Rome the Apostle's thoughts turn to the empire founded by Christ, our Redeemer in Heaven. The epistle is a non-controversial exposition of how mankind is one in Christ, and of God's purpose for the world through the Church. He sees the redeemed, Jews and Gentiles, bound together in one body ascending from earth to Heaven, to the body's head, Christ. In short, the doctrinal part of the epistle is a theological treatise on the Church.

P. Benoit describes the horizon of Eph as a diptych. In one picture we see Christ triumphant in Heaven (1:20). From Heaven he, as Head of the Church (1:22 ; 4:15 ; 5:23), distributes the vital force to the body which enables it to grow (4:16) ; he builds the house, of which he is the chief corner-stone (2:20). Moreover, he loves the Church, as a husband loves his wife (5:28), since at the time of the marriage he gave himself up for her (5:25) and saved her (5:23) by washing away all stain at baptism (5:26 f.).

In the other picture we see the Church saved and won by Christ, thanks to his atoning sacrifice, a new man (2:15), one body (2:16) subject to him, as wife is to husband (5:24) ; yet at the same time growing —developing as a body which keeps receiving nourishment from its head (4:16). The Church is like a building (2:20 ff.), the growth and construction of which are pointing to the goal of ' a perfect man ' (4:13) ; of ' a holy temple ' ; of ' a dwelling of God '

(2:21 f.). There at its goal the Church will have achieved its role of complement to Christ the Redeemer (1-23)—will have reached ' the full measure of maturity ' (4:13).

The Church—Three metaphors indicate the nature and the characteristics of the Church. It is *one* ; for ' to one single head belongs one body ; otherwise we have a monstrosity. As there is only one natural Christ, it is impossible that there should be more than one mystical Christ ' (Prat, *The Theology of St Paul,* II, 279 ; *cf.* commentary on 4:3–6). It is *holy* : its members are *in Christ* (a characteristic expression of the epistle), and in him they are made holy (1:13–14, 23 ; 3:16, etc.) and are saved (1:4–5, 7, 15, 18, etc.). It is *universal* : the despised Gentiles without hope are now with the Jews ' fellow-citizens of the saints and the household of God ' (2:19 ; *cf.* Col 3:11). It is *apostolic* : to Christ the Apostles and Prophets are joined as the foundations on which the temple of the Holy Spirit, which is the Church, is raised up (2:20). Finally, the Church is a *visible society.* It was to a Church that must teach and rule that Christ gave Apostles, Prophets, Evangelists, Shepherds and Teachers (4:11). In this epistle, however, St Paul supposes, rather than diligently expounds, the visible nature of the Church, and this chiefly because his main theme here is the mystical union between Christ and the Faithful in the Church. (*Cf.* Prat, *loc. cit.,* 275–83 ; Vosté, 42–58.)

In the Captivity epistles especially (and nowhere more deeply than in Eph) St Paul leads us into the inner nature and working of the Church. The Apostle sees the history of humanity under two heads, Adam and Christ. By Adam's sin all men were lost ; by the merits of Christ all members of his body, the Church, are saved (*cf.* Rom 5:12, 19 ; 1 Cor 15:22). And the influence of Christ as head reaches deeper and wider than that of Adam's sin (Rom 5:12–21). In the ' Great Epistles ' St Paul used the teaching of the ' Whole Christ ', the Mystical Body, mainly for exhortatory purposes ; he was concerned with the union of members among themselves in Christ, rather than with their union with Christ himself. But in the Captivity epistles the theme of the Mystical Body is no longer incidental ; it is the central teaching. More precisely, St Paul concentrates on the active role of the head, Christ. Pius XII wrote : ' Christ is in us through His Holy Spirit, Whom He imparts to us and through Whom He acts within us so that any divine effect operated in our souls by the Holy Spirit must be said to be operated in us also by Christ. . . . It is due also to this communication of the Spirit of Christ that all gifts, virtues and miraculous powers which are found so eminently, most abundantly and in their source in the Head, stream into all the members of the Church and in them are perfected daily according to the place of each in the Mystical Body of Jesus Christ, and that, consequently, the Church becomes as it were the fulness and completion of the Redeemer, Christ in the Church being brought to a complete achievement . . . Christ, Head and Body, is the whole Christ ' (MCC, 76, CTS ed. 1944).

St Paul may well have learned his physiology from the ' beloved physician ', St Luke (Col 4:14). It is that of the Greek medical writers, and may now be out of date. No matter. It serves only as a vehicle to convey the teaching, an envelope to deliver the message that although Christ is in every respect superior to the whole organism, he is nevertheless present everywhere in the Church. All the life of the members, all the force, perfection and merit comes from the vital and continuous flow of grace from the head. Christ is the Head and Saviour of the Body (5:23). The Body is the Church, a living organism, growing in charity (4:16), the chief agent of its development, the bond uniting and consolidating the whole organism. Christ, then, is in the Christian ; the Christian is in Christ. It is only in and by the Church that men can live in Christ. And without the Church Christ would

m be incomplete (1:23). In Eph we see that the Church is Christ, always living, always doing the work of Christ, adoring, thanking and praising the Blessed Trinity, leading men to God to save and sanctify them. ' It is not enough to represent the Church as a society endowed with legislative power, custodian of a sacred teaching and rite conveying holiness, like a wonderful bureaucracy in charge of a factory founded by God himself. That would be seeing only the external architecture, the Church from the outside. In its inner nature, and in its essence, it is Christ himself, always visible, always living, unfolding in her and by her all the riches and the magnificence of divine life ' (Médebielle, DBV(S) II 668).

n Analysis—Introduction 1:1–14.
1. *Greeting*, 1:1–2.
2. *Prologue*, The Mystery of God's will decreed in eternity, 1:3–14.

Part I. Doctrine. 1:15–3:21.
1. God's power shown in raising Christ to be Head of the Church, 1:15–23.
2. God's power shown in raising us to salvation in Christ, whether we are Jews or Gentiles, 2:1–10.
3. Hence, Jews and Gentiles alike are fused into One New Unique Man. The ' Mystery ', then, fulfilled in the Church, 2:11–22.
4. How the ' Mystery ' was promulgated to the Gentiles, 3:1–21.

Part II. Moral. The Christian Life. 4:1–6:20.
1. General Injunctions, 4:1–5:21.
2. Family Life, 5:22–6:9.
3. Epilogue, The Christian Warfare, 6:10–22.
4. Conclusion, 6:23–24.

9a I 1-2 The words **at Ephesus** are absent from the most important MSS. This raises the interesting question of the destination of the epistle ; on which see § 898c.
3-14 Prologue—The Apostle is overwhelmed by feelings of gratitude as from his prison cell in the centre of the Roman Empire he contemplates God's love for mankind. In this ' Magnificat ' (one unbroken sentence in the original) he is not content merely to praise God's *bounty* ; he qualifies the word with *rich*.
3-6 God's eternal purpose—Paul contemplates God the Father's loving plan in eternity to choose us out and to heap on us blessings that are both spiritual and supernatural by reason of our being in Christ. The goal of that eternal election is that we be holy (4b), *i.e.* separated from the world and consecrated to God ; unspotted in his sight : so that our charity can withstand the penetrating gaze of God. **5.** How can such holiness be possible ? It is made possible by God's *fore-ordaining* us to be his adopted children in Christ. The notion of the adoption of children is frequent in St Paul (*e.g.* Rom 8:15–23 ; Gal 4:5) and except for Rom 9:4 always denotes the interior dignity of those who are in Christ. At our rebirth (Baptism) God infuses into us his own nature, and at once our relation to God is that of child to father. In his beloved son (6c) God loves us and makes us lovable only in so far as we are one in and with Christ.
b 7-13a Realized in Christ—The Redemption and the Mystery—7-8. Paul descends to speak of the greatest proof of God's love for us : our redemption in Christ. This means that we are loosed from the shackles of sin and from God's anger, the price being the sacrifice of Christ's blood (*cf.* Heb 9:22). Secondly, we are engulfed by the treasure of God's grace. Equipped in this way we are able to understand things in the light of eternal truth—such is the meaning of *wisdom* (*cf.* 1 Cor 2:7)—and to conduct our lives accordingly (*prudence*). **9.** But if the benefits of the Redemption are to wield an influence in our lives, the Redemption itself must be made known to us. That is why the Apostle attaches the greatest importance to the revelation of what he calls ' the mystery of his (God's) will '. The expression *mystery* is characteristic of Eph and Col. Its general meaning is an idea or work of God which is out of reach of man's natural knowledge,

and which having been held secret by God for a long **899b** time is at length revealed. In these two epistles, however, it has a particular sense ; it refers to God's redemptive plan for all mankind (*cf.* 10c), long a secret, now revealed in Christ (*cf.* Col 1:26).
Having mentioned the secret (9a) the Apostle describes **c** its unfolding. First, it is centred in Christ (*in him*, 9c). Secondly (**10**), it is executed and revealed in the fullness of times (10a), *i.e.* in the Messianic age. Before the Incarnation there was a succession of periods ; but they were incomplete, without harmony, unless they were seen as preparing the way for a period which would make them an harmonious whole (*cf.* Gal 4:4). Hence the Divine secret was a ' dispensation ' (10a), *i.e.* a systematic arrangement.
10b The Contents of the Mystery : all things are **d** gathered up into one under their head, Christ. DV ' re-establish ' and Vg ' instaurare ' express only part of what St Paul says. The verb ἀνακεφαλαιώσασθαι is derived not from κεφαλή ' a head ' but from κεφαλάιον ' a sum total ' ; a ' recapitulation '. And the preposition ἀνά means not repetition (as in Vg), but ' together '. It refers back to elements that had been scattered, and which now are together again. The etymological sense, then, of this compound verb is ' to present as one whole ' (*cf.* Vosté). St Paul uses the same verb in this sense (Rom 13:9), and many writers think that its meaning here is only what the etymology allows. But the same writers observe that in the sequel the Apostle shows that the work of unity is in fact brought about by Christ being the head of the body. It seems best to interpret the word in the context. The context is about the ' Head ' of the body. May we not see already in this word not only the bringing together of all things in Christ, but also the way in which he makes them all one in him, *viz.* by becoming the head of the body (*cf.* §898k–l). E. Leen ('The True Vine and its Branches', 34) writes : ' The idea . . . is not merely that Christ restored order in creation out of the chaos created by the Fall. Nor is it that Jesus summarizes or synthesizes all creation in Himself. His thought is much more profound. It is that God, in order to reward Christ for having laid down His life to expiate the sins of humanity, made Him to be a new Head for Humanity. Humanity supernaturally slain, or, to use a metaphor, decapitated by the disobedience of Adam, is " re-capitated " or " re-headed " by the obedience of Christ ' (*cf.* E. Mersch-Kelly, The Whole Christ, Part II, ch 2, ' St Irenaeus and the " Recapitulation " ').
The Apostle goes on to say what things must be gathered under the head, Christ : ' all things . . . that are in heaven and on earth '. Under Christ as head, then, the whole universe must be gathered together and presented as one. Previously it had been scattered by sin, *cf.* Col 1:20.
11-13a. In the verses that follow the Apostle descends **e** from the universal aspect of the Redemption to contemplate its effect on the two classes of humanity, the Jews converted to Christ (11–12) and the Gentile converts who are also in Christ.
13a-14 God's eternal purpose perfected by the Holy Spirit—Two metaphors characterize the mission and function of the Holy Spirit. He is the *seal* stamped on our souls at Baptism as the mark of ownership ; he is the *pledge* (the word denotes an actual portion of a whole) of the blessed life paid in full in Heaven. The refrain, *unto the praise of his glory*, sung for the third time brings the hymn to its conclusion, and shows that the whole expansion of the mystery of salvation, in time and in eternity, by the work of the Three Persons, reaches its final goal in exalting the glory of God.
15-23 Christ ascended to glory, head of the Church f —From the hymn of triumph St Paul turns to the prayer which introduces the doctrinal part of the epistle (which ends at 3:21). **15-17.** First, after thanking God for his readers' faith and charity, the Apostle begs God, the source of all glory, to develop

899f in them the gift of wisdom (*i.e.* a firm grasp of supernatural truths) and revelation (which lays bare truths once hidden) ; that thus equipped they may possess a deeper understanding of God, *unto the full knowledge of himself*. **18-19a**. In other words, he asks God to bestow the gift of burning faith and love enabling them to appreciate both the blessings which God has in store for the elect, and the mighty power of God at work in the lives *of us who believe*.

g **19b-23**. They can measure the working of God's almighty power by the Resurrection and Exaltation of Christ. **20**. The Apostle fixes his eyes on Christ, risen, ascended, glorified and made Head of the Church—no need then for them to be despondent when they reflect on their human frailty. **22**. The sequence of the glory and exaltation conferred on Christ by God has a remarkable crescendo up to the climax, he is 'head over all the Church'. This, in the mind of St Paul, is a greater dignity than that of being sovereign over all the angels and all things. The Church is raised to the hypostatic order. 'Look again whither he hath raised the Church ! As though he were lifting it up by some engine, he hath raised it up to a vast height, and set it on yonder throne ; for where the Head is, there is the body also. There is no interval of separation between the Head and the body ; for were there a separation, then were the one no longer a body, then were the other no longer a head' (Chrysostom). Between the head and the body there is a common nature ; hence Christ is bound more intimately with the faithful than with the Angels. *Cf.* § 898*k-l*.

900a **23 The fullness of him**—'perhaps the most remarkable expression in the whole epistle' (Robinson). A head without a body is incomplete. Every body gives completion, fullness, to its head, and it is clear that the Church, the body, is the fullness, or completion, of Christ, the head. But the Church is no ordinary group of persons, and Christ is no ordinary head. 'Comparing the Mystical Body with a moral body we must also notice between these a difference which is by no means slight. . . . But in the Mystical Body there is in addition to this common aspiration another internal principle, really existing and operative both in the whole structure and in each of its parts, and this principle is of such excellence that by itself it immeasurably transcends all bonds of unity by which any physical or moral body is knit together' (Pius XII, MCC, 60). The Church continues Christ ; it is united with him like an organism with the life that quickens it. The Church expresses Christ ; without her Christ would be incomplete ; with her he has completion, 'fulness'. Of course the body adds nothing new to Christ ; for the body has all its growth, all its life from him, the head. 'It is from him that grace and strength descend upon the whole Church, and God sees us and blesses us only for His sake, in Him and through Him. But He had to have this supernatural expansion, in order that the eyes of all might contemplate the plenitude that was not manifest in His individual existence' (Mersch-Kelly, 121).

b At Col 1:24 St Paul uses this conception when speaking of his sufferings on behalf of the Colossians. He can rejoice in them ; for the sufferings of the members of the Church and the sufferings of Christ are one. Christ goes on suffering in the sufferings of the Church. 'Just as Christ receives the complement, the *pleroma*, of His own life in their lives, so in their sufferings He receives the consummation and the pleroma of His Passion' (Mersch-Kelly, 132). We give fullness, completion to Christ largely through our sufferings. 'Christ's satisfaction works its effect in us inasmuch as we are incorporated with Him, as the members with their head. Now the members must be conformed to their head. Consequently, as Christ first had grace in His soul with bodily passibility, and through His Passion attained to the glory of immortality, so we likewise, who are His members are freed by His Passion from all debt of punishment, yet so

that we first receive in our souls the "spirit of adoption **90** of sons", whereby our names are written down for the inheritance of immortal glory, while we yet have a passible and mortal body : but afterwards "being made conformable" to the sufferings and death of Christ, we are brought into immortal glory, according to the saying of the Apostle (Rom 8:17), "And if sons, heirs also . . . yet so if we suffer with Him, that we may be also glorified with Him"' (Aquin., III, 49, 3 ad 3). 'The daily passion of the Christian, **c** who is united to Christ by faith and charity, wears to God the aspect of the Passion of His only Begotten Son. This consoling thought sheds a new light on the baffling problem of human pain. The holy souls who recognize Christ suffering in, and through, themselves, learn to attach positive value to what human nature shrinks from as a great evil. The heroic souls who, rising above the patient endurance of pain, positively look for it, in order that their assimilation to Christ may be made more perfect, do more than sanctify themselves by their sufferings. They take an effective part in redeeming the human race. They co-operate subordinately to Christ, in the work of redemption' (Leen, *op. cit.*, 76). 'The Church is the fullness of Christ, because it completes and perfects him in the plan of redemption, the nourishment of grace being able to go from the Head to the members only through the medium of the body' (Prat, *op. cit.*, I, 299). We have given an *active* sense to the word *fullness*. This is the common view, and it fits in well with the context and with St Paul's thought (*cf.* Col 1:24). Nevertheless, certain writers regard the word as passive, the sense then being that the Church is the fullness of Christ, because it is the receptacle filled by him with all supernatural blessings. Among those sharing this view are Knabenbauer, Lightfoot, Schmid, Huby.

The expression, 'who is filled all in all', is patient **d** of two or three senses in the Greek. The main point to decide is whether the verb is in the middle (with active meaning) or passive voice. We follow Vg in regarding it as a passive (thus conforming to the passive sense found in 87 other instances in the NT). The Church, then, completes Christ, who is himself completed (filled) only by all his members.

In Eph St Paul speaks of the fullness *of* Christ, Christ being the centre of the perfection which he gives to and receives from the Church. In Col he speaks of the fullness *in* Christ, Christ being the centre of that perfection which he possesses in himself absolutely. *Cf.* VD 14 (1934) 49-55.

II 1-10 Convert Jews and Gentiles : What they were, e and what they are (*viz.* members of the same Body of which Christ is the Head)—They can measure God's power by contemplating their deliverance from Satan (whom the Jews regarded as wielding power from the air). **3**. The Jews were in the same state of guilt (*cf.* 5) : 'by nature children of wrath, even as the rest'. The context does not refer directly to original sin, and St Paul here by the expression 'by nature' seems to mean simply 'by natural impulse'. This is the sense understood by the Greek Fathers and by St Jerome. St Augustine, however, took the sense to be 'by birth', and he pointed to this text as a direct reference to original sin, when he was writing against the Pelagians. **5**. 'Dead in sins' : convert Jews and Gentiles alike are quickened together, not merely along with Christ, but *in him*—in the Body of which Christ is the head and they the members, *cf.* Col 2:13. **8**. This great privilege issues from a twofold gift : grace on the part of God, faith on the part of man—faith being the instrument for grace to act. This gift is wholly from God, and the Council of Orange (529) used this text to prove that the *beginnings* of faith are a gift of grace (Dz 199). **10**. The reason why all this issues from God and not from ourselves is that we are his workmanship created in Christ Jesus—a new creation just as surely as our entry into natural life was a creation.

00f 11-22 Christ's Atonement—The Apostle's readers were converts from paganism. **12.** They were outside the *society* (DV ' conversation ') of Israel, despised by the Jews, immersed in the terrestrial order, without Christ . . . without God in this world ; for before their conversion they had no clear idea of God. **13-14.** How was the distance between privileged and unprivileged bridged ? How did peace in Christ come about ? St Paul explains that the barrier between Jew and Gentile (symbolized by the barrier in front of the Court of Israel in the Temple) was broken down by the blood of Christ, by the cross (16*a*). **15.** This expiatory sacrifice of Christ ' in his flesh ' (14*c*) abrogated the Law consisting of peremptory commands enforced by the decrees of Rabbis. Rickaby translates the last word well as ' comminations ', *i.e.* curses on transgressors. The first result of the abrogation of the Law is that Jews and Gentiles are not merely fused into one people : they are made one in one man. **17.** Christ, the author of our peace, brought the thrilling news (DV ' preached ') in person for the Gentiles, who were afar off, and for the Jews, who were nigh. **18.** By his merits and propitiatory sacrifice (' by him ') we are both introduced into the presence of (' access ') the Father in One Holy Spirit. The bond of love and peace which joins the Father to the Son is also the bond of union for the members of the g Church. **19-22.** To explain the full enfranchisement of the Gentiles, St Paul uses metaphors, because ' the union of the Faithful with Christ is closer than words can tell ' (Rickaby). The convert Gentiles are fellow-citizens of God's own household. The second metaphor : they are stones in the building which is the Church. This edifice has for foundations the Apostles and the NT Prophets (*cf.* 4:11 ; Ac 11:27 ; 13:1 ; 1 Cor 12:28, etc.). And Christ himself is the corner-stone ' which binds together both the walls and the foundations ' (Chrysostom). The third metaphor (21) is complex. We have to picture the holiest part of the Temple in process of being built. At the same time this Temple is a living organism, the life and growth of which comes from Christ. In this holy-of-holies, which is also an organism, the Gentiles are living stones. *Cf.* the hymn ' Caelestis urbs Ierusalem ' sung at the feast of a Dedication of a church :

' Thou heavenly, new Jerusalem,
Vision of peace in prophet's dream,
With living stones built up on high
And rising to yon starry sky '.

(M. Britt, O.S.B., *The Hymns of the Breviary and Missal*, London, 1925.)

The Apostle has set forth the vocation of the Gentiles to the One Church of Christ. He now proceeds to describe how Christ is the Revealer of this mystery, and how Paul himself is the herald.

01a III 1-21 How the mystery was promulgated to the Gentiles—**1.** He begins a prayer to conclude what he has been saying in ch 2, but mention of the Gentiles sets him off on a digression (2-13), and it is only in 14 that the idea of 1 is taken up again.

In this digression he writes of his God-given work on behalf of the Gentiles. He is the herald of the mystery. In a few words he describes the contents of the mystery. **6.** The Gentiles are blessed equally with the Jews ; for they are fellow-heirs in the same Messianic inheritance, members of the body of Christ (WV ' concorporate '). In a word, they have ' the same benefits, the same body and the same spirit ' (Médebielle). **7-8.** His gratitude is deep : he is *less than the least of the faithful*, yet his mission is no less than to enlighten all men on the *inexhaustible riches of Christ*. **10-11.** Even the angels will come to know the merciful, manifold, and eternal wisdom of God, as they watch the Church continuing Christ's mission on earth. No room, then, for craven fear ; in Christ we are led to the Father.

b So far the Apostle has been thinking of his mission, but now ' he hears, as it were, the clink of his chain, and remembers where he is and why he is there '

(Robinson). His readers must not lose heart : im- **901b** prisonment does not spell the end of his mission (*cf.* Col 1:24). **14-15.** When he returns to utter the prayer begun at 1, he turns directly to the Father . . . ' of whom all paternity in heaven and earth is named '. This seems best understood as follows : Just as a family (πατριά) comes from a father (πατήρ), so every family, every society, every group among angels and men has God for Creator and Father. The point is that God is the prototype of all Fatherhood ; human fatherhood is the copy and derivative of the divine, *cf.* §§ 640*a*, *f*, 649*b*. **16.** He prays that the Holy Spirit will make their souls supernaturally strong, (**17**) that Christ will take up his permanent abode (κατοικεῖν is distinct from παροικεῖν ' to take a lodging ') in their hearts. It is by faith, living by charity, that Christ comes to take possession of our hearts. From faith St Paul passes on to charity. By a twofold metaphor he points to a very strong charity (' rooted ' ; ' founded ') which he prays will be the working principles of their lives. **18.** Ultimately, the prayer is for light to know. **c** To know what ? The Greek Fathers (followed among modern writers by Vosté, Huby, Robinson) suggested it was *the mystery* described above. It seems better, however, to regard 19 as explanatory of 18, with the result that Paul is here praying that they will be given light to grasp how great is the love of Christ. Of course, that love was shown forth in the mystery ; so the two opinions are not in conflict. Christ's love is described by four words grouped under one article— an arrangement that conveys the idea of the vastness of that love. **19.** In fact, the love of Christ can never be fully comprehended.

20-21 The Doxology—The doxology, which concludes the prayer and the doctrinal part of the epistle, invokes, first, the boundless generosity of God, and then, the twofold instrument of God's glory : Christ and the Church.

The Christian Life—The last three chapters of the **902a** epistle apply the teaching of the first three to the Christian's life, as a member of the Church and of society, and to his individual life. This is called the **moral part of the epistle.** It has two sections, the first (4:1-5:21) consisting of General Injunctions, the second (5:22-6:9) concentrating on Family Life. There follows an Epilogue (6:10-22) and the Conclusion (6:23-24).

IV 1-3 Eagerness to preserve Unity in Love—Their privileges in Christ are great ; their practical daily life must reflect their vocation—*noblesse oblige*. **2.** The first of four duties that St Paul calls for are those which Christ described as characteristic of his heart (Mt 11:29), humility and meekness ; (**3**) but the main concern here is an appeal for *a positive eagerness* (DV ' careful ') to keep intact the unity of the spirit —regarded as already existing. There is one body, and hence one spirit, regarded as distinguishable from (though of course dependent on) the Holy Spirit. The ' unity of the spirit ', then, means the mutual harmony among the members of the body. ' In the bond of peace ' : there can be no union without some bond. Here the bond joining the minds together is peace (the genitive of apposition). Peace shrinks from any wilful break of union. *Cf.* Jn 14:27. Robinson (pp 92-3) : ' At any rate no separation of " body " or " spirit " is contemplated : and the notion that there could be several " bodies " with a " unity of spirit " is entirely alien to the thoughts of St Paul. It is especially out of place here, as the next words show '.

4-6 The sevenfold Unity of the Church—The seven **b** elements of this unity are arranged under three main considerations. **4.** The first consideration is that we are members of **one body**, *i.e.* one visible society. This key-word implies that just as in any body there is only one principle of life and unity, so all the members of the Church should be animated by one and the same supernatural spirit, which issues from the Holy Spirit (*cf.* 2:22). Moreover, by reason of God's call-

1123

902b ing, we have **one and the same hope**—eternal life. So we ought to journey to the same goal hand in hand. **5.** The second main consideration has for its operative word, **One Lord,** *i.e.* Christ. We all have the same Lord and Master. This implies that we are all united to him by the same interior faith, and that we have the same baptism into Christ, conferred once and for all. **6.** The third consideration concerns God the Father. St Paul indicates three perfections which serve unity. He is 'above all' (no place, then, in us for pride, the source of discord); he is *throughout all*—in the sense that he makes us his instruments for good (no place, then, for contempt of one's neighbour, another potent factor of discord); he is 'in all'; *cf.* 2:22; Rom 8:11; 1 Cor 6:19, etc.

c 7-16 Unity not uniformity—**7.** Grace here does not mean sanctifying grace, but the spiritual gifts given to every one of us in view of the common good of the Church (*cf.* 13, 16; Rom 12:3; 1 Cor 12; 2 Cor 10:13). **8.** To emphasize the fact that all these gifts are from God alone, the Apostle points to Christ victorious in Heaven distributing freely the gifts after his triumph on earth. He uses the LXX version of Ps 67:19, and dwells especially on the words 'he ascended' and 'he gave'. The psalm in its literal sense describes a triumphal procession. A rich booty is offered to Yahweh, who *receives* it. But the Targum on this psalm regards God as receiving presents to be given to men; hence effectively giving presents to men. So St Paul's change from the MT and LXX 'he received' to 'he gave' was probably a common interpretation. In any case the Apostle uses the psalm in a *typical* sense. God's distributing gifts to men typifies Christ after the Ascension enriching members of his Church with spiritual gifts. The rest of the citation is incidental. He led captivity (abstract for concrete) captive is equivalent to 'He has triumphed like a victorious king'. As St Paul mentions this only, as it were, in passing, there is no need for us to try **d** to identify the captives. **11-13.** The point he makes in his list of gifts given to members of the Church is that their aim is to enlarge the range of the unity of the Church, and to develop its intensity, until *we all* (as one man) *attain to the unity of the faith and of the full knowledge of the Son of God* (13a WV). Then, all of us together will become a perfect man, God's new man, grown to manhood, *to the measure of the stature which belongs to the body of Christ* (13b Médebielle). *Cf.* 1:23. **14-16.** The corollary of this is that the Christian must put into practice Christ's teaching, especially Charity; for Christ is at once the head and the pattern of a Christian's development. **16.** Christ's body (the Church) owes all its growth to the head (Christ). Hence (*a*) the solidity of the whole organism; (*b*) mutual dependence of the parts—each joint contributes to the working of the whole; (*c*) the perfection of each member—according to the function of each limb; (*d*) the growth—by reason of the union with Christ. The final phrase 'in charity' marks the principle by which the holy shrine grows.

e 17-24 Put off the Old Man, put on the New—**22.** The old man is that corruption of heart and mind which concupiscent nature, bereft of grace, brings on man; it is the 'natural' man as opposed to the 'spiritual', Rom 1:18-32; 6:6; 1 Cor 2:14, 15. **23.** Baptized people must be constantly at work to keep fresh and new their inmost thoughts—that is the meaning of 'the spirit of your mind'. The old man was stripped off at Baptism, but the new state then created has to be carefully watched (renewed)—like the permanent way on the railway. **24.** St Paul gives the chief reason for the remarks in 22-23: Baptism is a new creation (*cf.* 2 Cor 5:17; Gal 6:15).

f 25-31 Examples—The sins here mentioned are against fraternal charity. **26a.** 'Be angry: and sin not' is a quotation of Ps 4:5 according to LXX. The first clause is concessive: if we feel anger rising within us (even when the anger is righteous) we must refuse to let it master us; we must combat it externally by showing a readiness to forgive. **26b.** 'Let not the **90** sun go down upon your anger' is a figure denoting quick pardon. **27.** 'Give not place to the devil' is perhaps a metaphor borrowed from the boxing ring. **31.** Five nouns here mark the progressively strong feelings and acts of the 'old man' when irritated. First, bitterness, *i.e.* sullen resentment, then anger, which is the outburst of passion; then indignation, the settled feeling of passion. Finally, *abusive language* (DV 'blasphemy').

32-V2 We must copy Christ—St Paul has shown **90** that we must co-operate with divine grace first, negatively, by putting off the old man. He now declares that we should exercise the virtues that belong to one who is baptized into Christ. **1.** We are most dear children of God in Christ. A father likes to find his image in his child. **2.** Christ gave his life on our behalf; his death was a voluntary expiation. The words oblation and a sacrifice are borrowed from the OT sacrifices for sin, and they are applied to the sacrifice on the Cross. 'For an odour of sweetness' is a common biblical metaphor suggested by the smoke of incense rising to heaven. The metaphor, then, refers to a victim pleasing to God. Prat (2, p 185) says: 'It is, therefore, probable that, having in view the general idea of sacrifice, of which Jesus is the perfect antitype, he denotes by "victim" (θυσία) the bloody sacrifice of Calvary, and by "oblation" (προσφορά) the voluntary and loving offering which Christ makes of himself to his Father. The two notions of priest and victim would, therefore, be associated here; and, as in the epistle to the Hebrews, be reunited in the person of Jesus'.

V 3-14 Purity—**5.** 'No fornicator . . . hath inherit- **b** ance in the kingdom of Christ.' The verb is in the present tense. The sinner deprives himself of the spiritual blessings of the Church on earth, and loses all right to eternal reward. **10.** 'Proving what is well pleasing to God', *i.e.* searching out carefully 'like a money-changer who is not content with a glance at a coin, but who weighs and sounds it' (St Jerome). **14.** The quotation here is from some Christian baptismal hymn.

15-21 Life in prayer—**15.** The phrase 'redeeming **c** the time' is a metaphor from the market place. Food is short; you must seize the opportunity to buy. In God's intention each moment of our lives is given to us in view of our eternal destiny in Heaven. We redeem time whenever we use it in doing a good work. The effort is all the more urgent, since the days are evil (*cf.* Phil 2:15).

22-33 Family Life : man and wife—Down to this **d** point in the *moral* part of his epistle St Paul has been giving general injunctions on how we must live the Christian life. Now he gives special consideration to the family, and first of all to husband and wife. **22.** 'As to the Lord' provides the key to the thoughts here expressed. Baptism confers equality on all individuals from the point of view of religion, but in society (of which the family is at once the smallest and most important unit) there is a natural hierarchy. The husband is the head; the wife is subject to him. By Baptism this order is not broken; it is ennobled. St Paul compares it with the love of the Church for Christ, the head. There should, then, be no room for either despotism or craven fear. Pius XI ('Casti connubii', 31 Dec. 1930): 'If the husband is the head, the wife is the heart'.

25. In using his authority the husband must take as **e** his model Christ's love for the Church. 'Thou hast seen the measure of obedience, hear also the measure of love. Wouldst thou have thy wife obedient to thee, as the Church is to Christ? Take then thyself the same provident care for her, as Christ takes for the Church. Yea, even if it shall be needful for thee to give thy life for her . . . refuse it not' (Chrysostom). Christ's love for the Church was perfect: he delivered himself up for it. **26.** And this supreme act of love had for its goal and its effect a baptism of the Church, whereby at once it is made holy. 'The laver of water' is a metaphor based on the bath of water solemnly presented by Greeks to a bride on the eve of her marriage. This Greek custom had a purificatory and religious significance. ' In the word ' is best read in connexion with what immediately precedes (i.e. the laver of water). The sense, then, is that the purification-sanctification conferred on the Church by the death of Christ is a baptism of water accompanied, or conditioned by, a sacramental formula. **28.** That men should love their wives as their own bodies suggests in the context not a carnal love, but generous love. Moreover, it must be a love ennobled by the fact that it reflects the supernatural love of Christ for the Church, the body of Christ, of which (30) we are members.

f **31.** In consideration of the unique union between husband and wife ('for this cause') 'a man shall leave . . . and shall cleave to his wife '. In citing Gen 2:24 here St Paul implies that marriage connotes complete unity, and this by its very nature as instituted by God in the time of our first parents. **32a.** ' This is a great sacrament.' As in 1:9 and 3:3, 9 Vg translates the Greek μυστήριον by ' sacramentum ', which in turn has become DV ' sacrament ', in the sense of having a hidden meaning. The union of man and wife as described in Genesis has a hidden meaning besides the obvious giving and receiving of each party. This hidden meaning is great, not in the sense that it is hard to understand, but that it is important, far-reaching ; (*32b*) *I mean in reference to Christ and to the Church* (WV). There is no doubt about the general sense here : in uniting husband and wife God created a type of the future union between Christ and the Church.

g Some theologians (Palmieri, Perrone, etc.) demanded that the type (marriage) and the anti-type (union between Christ and the Church) must correspond exactly. Marriage must, then, imply not only unity and indissolubility, but holiness as well. In other words, the unity in marriage would be a bond of supernatural grace. If that is so, then St Paul must have had in mind here *Christian* marriage as a *sacrament* in the strict sense of that term. The Council of Trent was not so explicit. It used this text not as proof of the sacrament, but as providing a suggestion of the sacrament ('Innuit', Dz 969). Moreover, none of the Greek or Latin Fathers claimed that this text of itself *proved* that Christian marriage is one of the seven sacraments. Most theologians now take the view that once we know from Tradition that matrimony is one of the seven sacraments, we can use this text to show how Christian marriage is the living expression and realization of the union (and all that this union implies) between Christ and the Church. In the context St Paul is looking at matrimony only in so far as it is a sign of unity, and he has in mind matrimony of all time, from Adam through all ages. He does not say that this unity is an outward sign conferring a special grace on man and wife *ex opere operato*. Yet, these reservations made, it is clear that if any lawful union between man and wife can be referred to Christ's union with the Church, surely that is true in a fuller sense of the union between Christians, when the bond not only signifies, but effects the union of God with man. That union is by sanctifying grace. The *origin* of this ' mystery ' can be traced through the OT (Ps 44(45) ; Cant, Ez 16:1–63, etc.) to the teaching of Christ in the NT (Mk 2:19–20 ; *cf.* Jn 3:29 ; Mt 22:1–14). **33.** Nevertheless St Paul returns to the practical : Supposing you have not quite grasped the symbolism latent in the union of matrimony, at least let every one of you . . . fear, *i.e.* reverence.

04a VI 1–4 Children and Parents—**1.** The expression ' in the Lord ' at once points to the right motive and to the limits of the obedience of children to parents. **2.** In the decalogue the fourth commandment is the first (and only) one carrying with it an explicit promise. **3.** The Jews understood the promise to refer to temporal blessings, but in the Christian dispensation it is transferred to the region of spiritual favours. **4.** Fathers must be firm and kind ; they must bring up their children in the Christian way.

5–9 Slaves and Masters—The civilization of the day b was built on slavery. As in Col 3:22–25, St Paul does not openly denounce the system ; he is content with instilling principles which prepare the way for its abolition. He regards the slave as a person depending on Christ, possessing, then, the key to eternal happiness in Heaven. **9.** And masters must reciprocate with kindness based on the same religious viewpoint. God is the master of masters.

10–22 Epilogue : The Christian Warfare—The c Apostle's thought at the close is that if all is well within, there is still a foe outside for every Christian to face.

10–13 A Call to Arms—St Paul describes the Christian armed for the spiritual struggle in terms borrowed from the equipment of the Roman soldiers. We have to be clothed from head to foot, if (13*b*) we are to stand in all things perfect, *i.e.* if having fought, we are to stand upright, victorious. **12b.** Without the armour of God we stand powerless against the deceits of the rulers of the world of this darkness, *i.e.* men enmeshed by the darkness arising from sin ; against the spirits of wickedness in the high places, *i.e.* evil spirits whose wills are fixed in wickedness, and who envelop and besiege us from all sides (*cf.* 2:2).

14–17 The Divine Panoply—The seven weapons, d defensive and offensive, are described by metaphors drawn from both the armour of the Roman soldier on active service and from the description of the weapons borne by the divine Warrior (Messias) in Is 59:14, 17 (*cf.* Is 11:5 ; 52:7 ; Wis 5:17–20). The chief pieces of the Christian's armour are : breast-plate, shield, helmet, and sword. **14b.** ' The breast-plate of justice ' undoubtedly refers to sanctifying grace guarding the virtues, just as the soldier's breast-plate guarded the heart. In 1 Thess 5:8 the breast-plate is faith and charity. **15.** ' Your feet shod with the preparation of the gospel of peace ' seems to have the sense : zealous to carry with speed the glad tidings which effect peace, *cf.* Is 52:7–9 ; Rom 1:15. **16.** ' The shield of faith ' refers to the door-like shield rounded to the shape of the body. The Christian's protection and inspiration is in the principles of faith, in which the flaming missiles of the most wicked one are put out. **17a.** ' The helmet of salvation '. The helmet guards the head and inspires confidence amid danger. According to 1 Thess 5:8 (*cf.* Is 59:17) it is the hope of salvation. **17b.** ' The sword of the spirit '. The sword was a double-edged weapon. The spiritual sword is provided by the Holy Spirit and is endowed with his power. It is the word of God, not specifically the Gospel (λόγος), but every message from God (ῥῆμα Θεοῦ). Since, however, the divine utterances have culminated in the Gospel message, we may in fact regard the sword as the Gospel teaching, *cf.* Heb 4:12 f.

18–20 Prayer—The victorious use of the weapons e described is bound by one condition, prayer. **18.** The Apostle here recommends the different kinds of prayer : of adoration and of petition, vocal and silent (' in the spirit '). And he tells his readers what qualities earnest prayer should have. **19–20.** He asks them to place him, an ambassador in a chain, in the forefront of their prayers (*cf.* 1 Cor 9:16) ; for he needs grace to preach boldly, assuredly and persuasively.

21–22 Mission of Tychicus—These two verses are f found substantially the same in Col 4:7 f., and they constitute the only personal words of the whole epistle. In Col we do not find the words ' that you also may know . . . what I am doing ', and many writers see an indication here that Col had already been written, the ' you also ' implying that the Colossians (and possibly others) would already know. Tychicus is mentioned in Ac 20:4 together with Trophimus as a native of proconsular Asia, perhaps of Ephesus

904f (2 Tim 4:12). He met St Paul at Troas when the Apostle was on his way to Jerusalem in the third missionary journey. He may well have gone with Trophimus (Ac 21:29) on that occasion to Jerusalem. He appears again as bearer of this epistle and of Col, towards the end of the Apostle's first Roman captivity. Some five years later we find him again with St Paul, who speaks of sending him to visit Titus in Crete (Tit 3:12), and who not long afterwards sent him to Ephesus (2 Tim 4:12). He merited by long service the title of ' my dearest brother and faithful minister in the Lord '. **22a.** ' Whom I have sent ' is the past tense (aorist) used in letters. It does not mean that at the time of writing Tychicus was already in the readers' midst. When he arrives, he will tell them of the position of St Paul and his companions in prison, and he will console them. This may well mean that while the Apostle's friends thought he would die in prison (*cf.* 3:13), he himself was hoping for an early release.

23-24 The Concluding Salutation—This is remarkable in its solemn, impersonal and indirect tone, *cf.* § 898*c*. The Apostle asks God to give his readers peace, *i.e.* the tranquil possession of spiritual favours ; then charity with faith (*cf.* 1:15 f.), finally grace, *i.e.* God's love which is given to all who love Christ, and which equips them for immortality and incorruptibility (St Jerome).

PHILIPPIANS

By C. LATTEY, S.J.

5a Bibliography—Chrysostom (PG 62) ; J. Knaben-bauer, S.J. (CSS 1912) ; Cornelius a Lapide, S.J. (Rome 1908) ; A. Goodier, S.J. (WV 3, 1939³) ; F. Prat, S.J., *Theology of St Paul* (London 1938) ; J. Huby, S.J., *Les Épîtres de la Captivité* (Paris 1935) ; DTC 12, 1414–34 ; 8, 2339–49 ; CBQ 1 (1939) 296 ; *J. Lightfoot, *Philippians* (London 1903) ; *R. Vincent, *Philippians and Philemon* (ICC 1902) ; *H. Moule (CSCB 1918) ; *H. Alford, *Greek Testament* (London 1880) ; *J. Michael, *Philippians* in Moffatt Commentary (London 1943) ; *G. Duncan, *St Paul's Ephesian Ministry* (London 1939) ; *F. Badcock, *Pauline Epistles* (S.P.C.K 1937) ; *Moffatt, *Introduction to the Literature of the New Testament* (Edinburgh 1912² ; with full bibliographies) ; *Ramsay, *St Paul the Traveller* (London 1895, and other works and articles) ; C. Lattey, S.J., *Theses Paulinae* (Rome 1926) ; C. Lattey, S.J. (ed.), *The Incarnation* (CSSL Cambridge 1926) ; *Moulton and Milligan, *The Vocabulary of the Greek Testament illustrated from the Papyri and other non-literary Sources* (London 1930).

b Authenticity and Canonicity—The evidence for these is so strong that it does not appear worth while to draw out the proofs at any length. Already St Polycarp, early in the 2nd cent., mentions in his epistle to the Philippians that St Paul wrote them letters, ch 3, probably grouping with the Philippian epistle those to the neighbouring church of Thessalonica (so Moffatt, 174). And it is fairly obvious that ch 2 sect. 1 of his epistle is drawing on Phil 3:21 ; 2:10, and ch 9 sect. 2 on Phil 2:16 (Gal 2:2 is not so likely) and most clearly of all ch 12 sect. 3 on Phil 3:18. In the *Martyrdom of Polycarp* (ch 1 sect. 2), written probably soon after the middle of the 2nd cent., there is a reference to Phil 2:4. A little earlier than this Marcion accepted it, and about A.D. 200 the Muratorian Fragment also names it among St Paul's epistles. Irenaeus (*post* A.D. 150: PG 7, 1026 ; 1158), Tertullian (2nd–3rd cent. : PL 2, 826 ; 863), Clement of Alexandria (do., PG 8, 312 ; 408 ; 557) all quote the epistle as Paul's. There has been practically no variation in the Catholic tradition. Text and commentary should make it clear that no attention need be paid to the not very plausible attempts to prove the epistle a composite work.

c Philippi—Philip II of Macedon (359–336 B.C.) founded (or more strictly, re-founded) Philippi in 356 B.C., naming it after himself ; it had formerly been called Krenides ('little fountains'), from the many springs in the mountains to the N. of it. It became part of eastern Macedonia, very near Thrace, and on the edge of a great plain which stretches inland to the N. and NW. It had easy access across Mt Pangaeum to the fine harbour of Neapolis, Ac 16:11, and the gold mines in the neighbourhood were of enormous value to Philip, furnishing him with the sinews of war and diplomacy. Rome conquered Macedon in 168 B.C. ; but there was a great development in the position in 42 B.C., when Antony and Octavian (later Augustus) defeated Brutus and Cassius, and founded a Roman colony there, the *Colonia Iulia Augusta Philippensium*, in honour of the victory. The word *Iulia* signifies the triumph of the cause of Julius Caesar. Eleven years later Augustus strengthened the city with a

second foundation. The city thus acquired the **905c** *Ius Italicum*, with the right of proprietorship according to Roman law, and exemption from poll-tax and land-tax ; it would have its own *duumviri* (supreme magistrates), the ' praetors ' of Ac 16:20, 35–39. Cicero (*De Leg. Agr.* 2:34) speaks with amusement of such claims to be called praetors ; and we may note the touch of pride also in ' us Romans ', Ac 16:21.

Christian Beginnings at Philippi—The story may be **d** said to begin at Ac 16:1, when St Paul chooses Timothy to accompany him, for the Apostle associates Timothy with himself in the opening address of the epistle, as one already well known to the Philippians, and proposes to send him to them, Phil 2:19–24, for his own further information about them, adding at the same time a warm commendation of one who was doubtless his most beloved disciple. But Silas was his chief helper at this time, Ac 15:40 ; 16:19, 25, 29. After having visited the churches already evangelized, they were directed by the Holy Ghost and the vision of a Macedonian into Macedonia, sailed to Neapolis and thence proceeded to Philippi, Ac 16:12. From the fact that there is no mention of a synagogue but only of a place of prayer, 16:13, we may infer that Jews were not numerous there, nor indeed should we expect them to be so in a Roman colony. Still, as usual, they attended the Jewish meeting-place, evidently with some fruit, and Lydia, a seller of purple from the city of Thyatira, a proselyte, Ac 16:14, was baptized with her household, and they took up their abode with her, 16:13–15. But St Paul's exorcism of the girl with a divining spirit caused her masters to lose their profit from her, and they dragged Paul and Silas before the magistrates, who beat and cast them into prison, whence a miracle caused the chief gaoler to take them into his house and tend them, so that in the end he and his household were baptized, 16:33. It is gratuitous in such cases as those of Lydia and the gaoler to suppose that the baptizing stopped short at the babies : it is against the texts, and supposes a prejudice at variance with St Paul's teaching of new life in Christ. The magistrates came to realize their own injustice, and were content to release the prisoners ; but St Paul protested that they were Roman citizens, and bade the magistrates come themselves and do so. Hearing that they were Roman citizens, the magistrates accordingly came in some trepidation and excused themselves, for they might have been brought into serious trouble ; and they asked Paul and Silas to leave the city, which they did, 16:40.

The fact that St Luke ceases to write in the first person from the time that St Paul's party crosses over to Macedonia, Ac 16:10, to the time when they had just left Philippi on their way to Jerusalem towards the end of the third missionary journey, Ac 20:5, makes if fairly clear that he was left behind there to organize and develop the local church. From Phil itself we gather that the Apostle had planted and Luke had watered with much success, and that ' the beloved physician ', Col 4:14, had infused into them some of his own love and care for Paul.

The Epistle—The Pauline epistles divide into definite **e** groups with marked similarities in each group, though each epistle also has its own characteristic features. 1–2 Thess obviously belong to each other and stand

1127

905e apart. Gal and Rom deal with the same fundamental theme of justification by faith, the former as an intensely practical question, the latter a more dogmatic exposition to a non-Pauline church. 2 Cor has something of the fire of Gal and of the highly personal character of 1 Cor. In the same way the epistles of the captivity (Eph Col Phil Phm) are usually shorter, and more Christocentric. Eph and Col are especially similar, the former more concerned with Christ in the Church and the latter with Christ in himself. Phil has the finest passage of all upon the person of Christ, and something of the delicate charity of which Phm is full. The Pastoral Epistles obviously have a character all their own ; Heb alone stands out as the address of a rabbi trained at the feet of Gamaliel to the church which would understand best such a manner of exegesis.

Thus we are led naturally to envisage the epistles of the captivity as a group by themselves, in which Phil takes its place : a group which we accordingly suppose to have been written about the same time, and under the same circumstances. All of them show St Paul a prisoner, Eph 3:1 ; 4:1 ; 6:20 ; Col 4:3, 10 ; Phm 9, 23 ; Phil 1:7, 13, 14, 17. The unanimous witness of tradition points to Rome as the place of his imprisonment, and this is confirmed with especial force in the case of Phil, because of the mention of the praetorian guard in 1:13 ; the soldiers would naturally relieve each other in the custody of Paul. See *e.g.* Vincent's note on the passage, 51–52, confirming Lightfoot's view. The mention of Caesar's household in Phil 4:22 is another strong argument.

The date of the epistles would thus fall in the year of the first Roman captivity, *c* A.D. 59–61 ; from the second captivity there was to be no deliverance ; contrast Phil 1:25–26 with 2 Tim 4:6–8 The main reason why Paul wrote Phil seems to have been the outburst of gratitude and affection at their renewed alms and their solicitude for his welfare (see especially Phil 4:10–20), in which we can hardly be wrong in seeing the hand and heart of St Luke.

Hence there seems to be no single strong dogmatic or moral purpose underlying the epistle. Incidentally, however, two doctrines are touched upon in a manner that deserves special attention, though a detailed explanation of the texts is left to the commentary.

f **Doctrine**—The passage on the divinity of Christ, 2:5–11, the most striking treatment of the subject in the Pauline epistles, first deserves attention. It should be noticed that St Paul has no intention of teaching his readers anything new, but presupposes the doctrine as already known, in order to draw from it a lesson of humility. In the same way in Rom 9:5 the emphatic statement of the same truth is merely to show that he is fully aware of the privileges of the Jews, their supreme privilege being that God himself took flesh as one of them. Similarly in 1 Cor 11:17–34 the Apostle presupposes the Real Presence as already believed, in order to draw from it the lesson of greater reverence in the celebration of the Eucharist. Humility is to lead to greater harmony, especially among the women, 4:2–3, who held a better position in Macedonia than elsewhere, a fact illustrated to some extent by Lydia, Ac 16:14–15, 40, with whom St Luke probably took up his abode.

The subject of justification is treated fully elsewhere, but some light is thrown upon it in this epistle. Justness (or righteousness) is not merely the favour of God, but comes *from* God, 3:9, being therefore something in the soul itself, springing from faith, which itself is a gift of God, not being the reward of merit strictly so called, 1:29. This justness means unity with Christ in his passion and death, so that from being crucified with him we partake also in the newness of his risen life, 3:10–11, 20–21, a theme expounded with fuller emphasis in the other epistles of the captivity, Eph 2:1–10 ; 3:14–19 ; 4:15–16, 22–23 ; Col 2:6–13 ; 3:3–11. The Christians are to ' work out your salvation with fear and trembling ', Phil 2:12, a strong expression for awe and reverence, not to be taken too

literally, as we see from Ps 2:11 ; Eph 6:5–8 ; 2 Cor **90** 7:15. It is not to hinder the joy to which he exhorts them in 3:1 ; 4:4.

I 1–2 Greeting—St Paul, after his gracious manner, **9**(associates Timothy with himself in the greeting, since he was well known to the Philippians and had worked among them ; he may well have talked over the epistle with Timothy, but the latter is not really a joint author. The epistle is much too personal to be anything but exclusively Paul's own. In the opening greeting of 1 Cor even Sosthenes finds a place. ' Christ ' (Anointed, Messias) gradually came to be used as a proper name, but as yet might either precede or follow ' Jesus '. ' saints ', holy as members of the Church, and as possessed personally of sanctifying grace, which Paul usually presupposes in his Christians in general ; *cf.* Eph 2 etc. ' bishops ', as yet equivalent, it would seem, to ' presbyters ' : compare ' presbyters ' (DV ' ancients ') in Ac 20:17 with ' bishops ' in Ac 20:28 ; and so elsewhere. The churches were still ruled by colleges of priests, visited at intervals by the Apostles, or by delegates with episcopal powers, such as Timothy and Titus. The college of diocesan bishops was to succeed the college of Apostles, but was not to be appointed by the latter at once.

2. Paul's fairly frequent custom of putting Christ in this way on an equality with God the Father is one sign of his belief in Christ's divinity, though of course not so explicit as 2:5–11.

3–8 Thanksgiving—**5–7.** ' communication ' or ' fellow- **b** ship ', probably alluding to their alms and sympathy ; *cf.* 4:10–18. **8.** ' bowels ', where we should say ' heart '. But in Holy Scripture the latter word has a more intellectual implication.

9–11 Intercession—**10.** ' approve the better things ', the more perfect way ; similarly in Rom 2:18. **11.** ' the fruit of justice ' or righteousness which cometh through Jesus Christ, the whole supernatural state etc.

12–14 The Furtherance of the Gospel—**13.** ' so that my bonds ', what I have said and done while in bonds, ' have become manifest in Christ ', through his power and grace working in me, ' *throughout the whole praetorian guard* ', the soldiers of which would relieve each other in guarding me, ' *and to everybody else besides* ', the many visitors coming to see me. **14.** ' the greater number of the brethren in the Lord ', in Christ's Church and in his grace, ' confident by reason of my bonds ', what I have said and done in bonds.

15–20 Though with Various Motives—There are **c** jealousies and strife, perhaps among some disciples of St Peter (*cf.* 1 Cor 1:11–12 ; 3:3–4) or among some Jews or Judaizers (*cf.* 3:2–9) ; but the whole tone of the letter forbids us to suppose that St Paul was seriously alarmed at the Judaizing, as he was in the case of the Galatians. **17.** ' thinking to embitter my bondage '. **18.** ' by all means, *whether for motives false or true* '. Evidently there was no danger of grave errors. **19.** Quoting Job 13:16 (LXX). ' the Spirit of Jesus ', as in Rom 8:9 ; *cf.* Jn 15:26. The Holy Ghost proceeds from the Father and the Son as one.

21–26 The Apostle's Own Mind—**21.** *Cf.* Gal 2:20. This unity with Christ is both individual and corporate, through his Mystical Body. **22.** ' *fruitful labour* ', implied again in 24. **23.** ' a desire to *set forth* ' : the Greek word is both a nautical and military term, to ' weigh anchor ' or ' strike camp '. It cannot mean ' to be dissolved ', as in Vg. **25.** ' And this I *know confidently*, that I shall remain, and remain close beside you all, unto your *progress* and joy in the faith '. **26.** ' that you may have abundant ground in me for *boasting* in Christ Jesus ', owing to my fruitful labour ; *cf.* 22, 24. ' Boasting ' is a favourite term of St Paul's, but it must be ' in the Lord ' (1 Cor 1:31 ; 2 Cor 10:17 ; *cf.* Jer 9:23–24), all glory being ascribed to God for what he has accomplished in or through oneself. The Magnificat is a supreme example of this spirit.

27–30 His Care for the Philippians—**27.** ' let your *conduct* '. ' one spirit . . . one mind ' : St Paul was

c afraid of dissensions among them ; *cf.* 2:2–4 ; 4:2–3.
28. 'adversaries', such as the Apostle's own, 30,
whether pagans, as at Philippi itself, Ac 16:19–34,
or Jews, Phil 3. In itself such conduct was a sufficient
token of perdition to those acting in bad faith and
malice ; but Paul himself longed eagerly to convert
both Jew (*cf.* Rom 9:1–5) and Gentile, *cf.* Rom 1:13–16.
29. An important statement that faith itself is not the
reward of merit strictly so called. **30.** '*and now hear
to be mine*' still.

a **II 1–11 Humility, after Christ's Example**—This passage
is treated at some length in *The Incarnation* (*op. cit.*).
1. 'any consolation' etc. on your part towards me ;
this appears reasonably certain from the final imperative corresponding to the if's, 'fill up my joy '.
'any encouragement through charity, any fellowship
in the Spirit ', in the Holy Ghost ; see on 1:19, also
Eph 4:3–4. '*any affection and compassion*'. **2.** 'Fill up
my joy by thinking alike . . . the same (*i.e.* mutual)
charity . . . *with one soul and one mind*'. **3.** 'better
than themselves '. Such a precept, if taken quite
literally, could only lead to false conclusions ; but
human nature so inclines all to think too well of
themselves that effort must be put forward in a contrary direction. **4.** 'each looking not merely to his
own interests, but *also* to those of others '. ' *also* ' is
in the Gk, though not in Vg, and thus makes it necessary
to insert ' *merely* ' to bring out the sense ; Paul does
not mean that one is not to attend to one's own affairs.
5. We must aim at the same dispositions that were
Christ's in his Incarnation. He humbled himself by
becoming man at all, and still further by his crucifixion.
Paul presupposes Christ's Godhead as already believed ;
no readiness to lower oneself can compare with his.
6. 'in the form of God '. This word ($\mu o \rho \phi \dot{\eta}$) is the
regular technical term in Aristotelian philosophy for
' form ' as opposed to ' matter ' ; but we must beware
of interpreting it too strictly along these lines, for
St Paul was no peripatetic or scholastic. The Greek
Fathers take the word as equivalent to ' nature ', in
the rough and ready language of popular philosophy,
and in full accord with St Paul's meaning ; still, it
is very difficult to believe that the word had entirely
lost any implication of visible appearance, and it is
more easy to suppose that he slightly stretched the
meaning of the word, in order to contrast with it
' the form of a slave ' in 7. Such is the opinion expressed by Père Prat (*Théologie de S. Paul*, 1st ed.
Paris 1908, p 442), though he seems to have withdrawn it afterwards. In any case there can be no
doubt of St Paul's meaning.

b 'Who, **being in the form of God** '. The Greek
word, $\dot{\upsilon} \pi \dot{\alpha} \rho \chi \omega \nu$, here translated ' being ', probably
means more than that, and is best taken to express
previous existence ; however, as examples can be
produced to the contrary, it is wiser not to press the
point, and merely to insist that the mere meaning
of ' being ', taken in this particular context, must in
any case signify such previous existence : ' being in
the form of God, he took the form of a slave '.
' thought it not robbery ' : this word ' robbery '
translates Vg *rapinam*, but not the rather difficult
Greek word $\dot{\alpha} \rho \pi \alpha \gamma \mu \acute{o} \nu$, a noun with a masculine
termination giving the object of the verb, whereas
a neuter termination (in this case $\ddot{\alpha} \rho \pi \alpha \gamma \mu \alpha$) would
be a more usual way to express the action of the verb.
' He counted it not a prize to be on an equality with
God ' (RV) seems the best English rendering ; but
' prize ' needs explanation. The Gk means something to be grasped and held fast, a *festzuhaltendes Gut*,
as the Germans say. He did not insist on being God
and nothing but God, *but* took the form cf a slave.
This interpretation has been expounded and proved
by Lightfoot at considerable length. It is also the
earliest Christian interpretation, for the letter of the
churches of Lyons and Vienne (*c* A.D. 178), quoted in
Eusebius' Church History, in referring to the humility
of Christ, stops at the words just quoted, as already
sufficiently indicating that humility, and do not add

the words, ' but he emptied himself ' etc. (*Eus.*, HE **907b**
5, 2, 2). This is the natural flow of sense and sentence :
' He did not count it a prize . . . *but* emptied himself ' ; if the text meant ' He did not count it robbery,
usurpation etc.' then it would have to continue, but
nevertheless he emptied himself '. There would be **a**
strong contrast implied, whereas Paul (as often) is
merely using parallel expressions to bring out his full
meaning. ' to be equal to God ' : so Vg *aequalem*,
somewhat simplifying the Gk, which is really an
adverbial expression, which we might render roughly,
' to be as good as God ' ; but the sense is the same.

7–9 ' **emptied himself** ' : such is the literal mean- **c**
ing of the verb, but of course it is used metaphorically,
as always in NT (5 times, always by St Paul himself),
' to make of no account (as here), futile, meaningless ',
etc. Similarly the corresponding adjective (' empty ')
is used 18 times in NT, but likewise always metaphorically, ' empty-handed, useless ', etc. Christ
evidently could not empty himself of his Godhead,
even in part ; but outside the Church this expression,
' he emptied himself ' has been misinterpreted to imply
something like this. Such are called ' kenotic ' theories,
from the Greek words in question, $\kappa \epsilon \nu \acute{o} \varsigma$ ' empty ' and
$\kappa \epsilon \nu \acute{o} \omega$ ' I empty '. Mgr R. A. Knox has explained this
matter in an excellent lecture on ' Kenotic Theories '
in *The Incarnation* ; *cf.* § 905*a*.

What St Paul himself stresses, indeed, is Christ's
Divinity, and that so strongly that if we had not the
guidance of a multitude of other passages (Rom 5:15
etc.), we might think that his Humanity was something
unreal. Here, for example, we have ' the form of a
slave ', ' in the likeness of men ', ' in habit found as
man ' (rather, ' in *outward form* ' or shape). But these
expressions are preparing the way for the tremendous
emphasis on Christ's Godhead which follows ; Christ's
Person is divine, and it was the Divine Person that
assumed human nature. **8.** ' He humbled himself ' :
the whole emphasis is here, the example for the
Philippians to follow. **9.** ' hath exalted him ', a very
strong word, lit. ' super-exalted ' : WV ' exalted him
above the highest '. ' the name ', **the name Jesus,** as
is clear from the following verse. ' Lord ' in itself is
not a name at all, but a very common word, used
even by slaves to their masters ; nor was it ' given ' in
the obvious sense to Christ, like the name Jesus, as
narrated by St Paul's follower St Luke (Lk 1:31).

10–11. ' *at* the name '. There is a reference to Is **d**
45:23 : ' to me every knee shall bow, every tongue
shall swear ', where we should say in English, ' by
me every tongue shall swear '. Absolute Godhead
is asserted in Isaias, and is here ascribed to Christ.
But for ' swear ' Paul substitutes ' confess ', and goes
on to give what is to be the subject of that confession.
As Christ has suffered in his sacred humanity, so he
is to be glorified for ever in that humanity, which is
to receive divine adoration in virtue of the Divine
Person who has assumed it. Every tongue is to ' confess that Jesus Christ is Lord, to the glory of God the
Father '. Possibly we should translate with Vg ' in
the glory ', for it seems to make rather better sense
of the special allusion to God the Father, and there
is no doubt that the preposition $\epsilon \dot{\imath} \varsigma$ with the accusative
(as in the Gk here) could at this period bear this
sense. See, for example, Milligan, *Selections from the
Greek Papyri* (Cambridge 1912), no. 13 (= P. Oxy.
294), *ad init.*, where $\dot{\epsilon} \nu$ with the dative is used in the
sense of ' place to ', and $\epsilon \dot{\imath} \varsigma$ with the accusative in
the sense of ' place at '. Every tongue is to confess
that ' Jesus Christ is Lord ', which is the confession
of Christ's Godhead, since the Jews did not use the
proper name of God, Yahweh, but spoke and read
' the Lord ' in its place, a practice followed by Vg
and all except some modern versions. St Paul's usual
practice is not to use ' Lord ' for God the Father or
the Holy Ghost, nor yet for God as such (the Blessed
Trinity), except where he is quoting the OT. The
fact that he uses ' Lord ' for God in OT passages
would compel him to explain that he did not mean

907d it in this sense when he applies it to Christ ; but on the contrary he lays stress on the confession that 'Jesus is Lord', here and in Rom 10:9 and 1 Cor 12:3. And indeed, even apart from all this, there is ample proof that he taught that Christ is God.

e **12-30 12.** '**with fear and trembling**', a phrase implying reverence and awe, as again in 2 Cor 7:15 ; Eph 6:5. Vincent here well calls it ' a filial dread of offending God '. The English words are apt to give an exaggerated idea of the ' fear ' involved, which is not incompatible with joy ; *cf.* Phil 3:1 ; 4:4 ; Ps 2:11. **13.** ' We can do no good work of ourselves towards our salvation ; we need the help of God's grace ' (Catechism Q. 138). **15.** *Cf.* Deut 32:5. **17.** ' Even if I am to be *poured out* ' as a libation (drink-offering) ' over the *solemn* ' or ceremonial, ministerial, liturgical, or even priestly ' offering of your faith '. ' sacrifice of your faith '. In this metaphor the Philippians are the priests, offering their own faith, *i.e.* their whole life of faith. Rom 12:1 is somewhat similar. St Paul again compares the shedding of his blood to a libation in 2 Tim 4:6 ; there it is impending, here it is as yet a mere possibility. The figure seems to suit the pagan sacrifices rather better than the Jewish, in which latter the libations were poured around and not on the altar, and were less prominent. ' and *share the joy* of all of you '. **18.** ' and *share my joy* '. **21** has always been a puzzle, for St Paul usually speaks highly of his fellow-workers, *e.g.* of Epaphroditus, 25-30. Perhaps he found Timothy the readiest to serve him without excuse. Of Epaphroditus we only know for certain what we find here and in 4:18 ; it hardly seems likely that he is the Epaphras of Phm 23 ; Col 1:7 ; 4:12 (which last verse makes him a native of Colossae). **25.** ' your messenger ', sent on a special commission : the Greek word is ' apostle ', which bears also this meaning. **30.** ' *hazarding* his life ', a word taken from gambling, like κυβία (lit. ' dicing ') in Eph 4:14 (DV ' wickedness '). ' that which on your part was wanting ' : perhaps with a slight hint that St Paul had not expected any neglect on their part ; *cf.* 4:10.

f **III 1-21**—Practically the whole of this chapter is directed against the **Jews and Judaizers,** but for the most part rather in the calm spirit of Rom than in the heat of Gal ; the danger of Judaizing does not seem to be a pressing one, nor do the Jews seem to have been numerous at Philippi. ' Their numbers at Philippi appear to have been very scanty ' (Lightfoot, 52). **1.** Paul himself is joyful, 4:10, and is eager that the Philippians should be so likewise, 4:4. Very likely he had written to them before, and with the same exhortation. **2.** ' Look at those dogs ' : a term of contempt. ' evil workers ', more especially as practising and inculcating circumcision. ' concision ', a play on the word ' circumcision ', with the implication that it has now become mere mutilation. **3.** The true circumcision is now of heart and soul ; *cf.* Ac 7:51. **4.** Even from their own point of view there is more to be said for Paul than for them. **5.** ' a Hebrew *born of* Hebrews, *in observance of* the Law a Pharisee, **6,** *in zeal a persecutor* of the Church. **8.** ' *by reason of the excellence of the knowledge* of Christ Jesus ', *i.e.* in comparison with such knowledge. **9-10.** For this unity and utter fulfilment of the Christian in Christ, and of Christ in the Christian, see Eph and Col ; for justness, not from the Law, but from God, based upon faith, see Rom and Gal. **12.** ' *Not that I have already secured this, or am already made perfect ; rather I press on, in the hope that I may lay hold of that for which Christ Jesus hath laid hold of me* '. **14.** ' *to gain the reward of God's heavenly call, i.e.* held out by the call.

g **15.** ' as are *mature* ' in the faith, understanding its implications etc. ; *cf.* 1 Cor 2:6 (' among the *mature* '). **16.** ' Nevertheless whereunto we are come, *by that same let us walk* ', *i.e.* whatever truth we have attained, let us order our lives by that. What is added in Vg does not belong to the original text. **17.** ' *Unite in* imitating me '. **18.** ' many ', *i.e.* Jews and Judaizers ;

but the general impression one gets is that relatively **90** they are not very numerous or important at Philippi itself, though always a dangerous element for the Christian communities. ' enemies of the cross of Christ ' in several ways, not understanding that thereby Christ had taken wholly upon himself the curse attaching to the non-observance of the Law by Jews, Gal 3:13, as well as atoning for all the sins of mankind etc. **19.** ' whose God is their belly ' : this has nothing to do with greediness, but refers to their insisting on the distinction between clean and unclean foods, now obsolete ; *cf.* Rom 14:14 ; 16:18. ' whose glory is in their shame ', *i.e.* in their shameful parts, their circumcision, also now obsolete. **20.** ' our citizenship ' or ' *country* ', for which, **21,** our Saviour will glorify our bodies, making them like to his own glorious Body ; *cf.* 1 Cor 15.

IV 1-9 The Dissensions—**1.** A touching verse, but **90** the Latin superlatives are not in the Gk : ' *beloved . . . desired . . . beloved* '. ' so ', as set forth above ; but the Apostle immediately goes on, **2,** to press his exhortation to concord (*cf.* 2:1-7) on the two ladies whose squabbles were presumably the chief cause of trouble. He even goes on, **3,** to urge his ' loyal yoke-fellow ' or comrade to ' assist them ', evidently to compose their differences, ' *seeing that* [such is the force of the particular Greek relative pronoun used here] they have toiled with me in the gospel, as have also Clement ' etc. Some (*e.g.* Knabenbauer and Vincent) think that ' Synzygus ' (here translated ' yoke-fellow ') is a proper name, and that instead of ' loyal ' we should translate ' rightly so named ', *i.e.* genuine. But such a name does not occur in the NT nor (so far as is known) out of it, and it would be surprising that Paul should not have mentioned elsewhere one whose worthy claim to the name he should so emphatically assert. Such an emphasis on the name, however, would not in itself be strange ; *cf.* Phm 10, 11, 20. To the present writer it seems likely that Silas may be meant ; he may have been at Philippi about this time, and so prominent a companion of Paul, who had first evangelized Philippi along with him, would not need to be named. The prominence of the two ladies as a source of trouble illustrates the greater importance of women in Macedonia, of which the position of Lydia, Ac 16:14-15, 40, is another example ; *cf.* § 905*f.* ' Clement ' was early identified with Clement of Rome (*e.g.* by Origen in Ioann. 1:29 ; PG 14, 293), generally admitted to be responsible for the well-known letter to the Corinthians. The ' Clement ' here in question was a prominent fellow-worker of St Paul, and there is no serious chronological difficulty ; still, the name was common, and the identification must remain uncertain. **4.** *Cf.* 3:1. **5.** ' your modesty ' or general forbearance. This exhortation doubtless has some connexion with what has preceded ; and so of the next two verses. ' The Lord is nigh '. There are certainly passages in St Paul which create a difficulty because he seems to speak of the end of the world as imminent ; but this need not be considered one of them. There is nothing in the context about the end of the world ; the Christians are to live in joy, gentleness, freedom from care, trustful and thankful prayer, peace in Christ. And on the other hand the notion of the Lord being nigh would be familiar from Ps 118 (119) 151 ; 144(145) 18. And it is reinforced here by 7 ; *cf.* 1:21 ; 3:9 ; etc. **7.** ' *will guard* your hearts '. **8.** ' modest ' in a general sense, seemly, dignified. ' lovely ', rather ' *lovable* '. ' *whatever is virtuous and praiseworthy* ' ; omit ' of discipline '.

10-21. An affectionate ending—**10.** ' *Indeed in this* **b** *matter you were thinking* (about me all along), *but you lacked opportunity* '. Paul lovingly excuses them. **11.** ' *Not that I speak because I was in want* ' ; *lit.* ' according to want '. He does not deny the want, but it is not his motive in speaking ; he was hardened to that. ' *I have learnt to be self-sufficing in whatever circumstances I am* '. **12.** ' *I have been initiated in everything* and in

8b all things, both to plenty and to hunger'. 'initiated' is a term taken from the pagan mysteries, the verb of which our word 'mystery' itself is a noun. St Ignatius of Antioch (martyred early 2nd cent.) in his letter to the Ephesians, ch 12, calls them 'fellow-initiates of Paul'. **14.** 'You have done well in sharing with my affliction', *i.e.* with me in my affliction. **15.** 'when I departed from Macedonia (*cf.* Ac 17:1–15) no church entered into relation of giving and receiving with me', *i.e.* 'opened a debit and credit account with me'; the terms are financial, as again in 17, 'accumulating to your account'. St Paul is referring to the return of temporal gifts for spiritual, but not of course as a strict bargain ; *cf.* 1 Cor 9:11–14 ; Rom 15:27. **17.** 'the fruit' could likewise probably bear the sense of 'interest' on an investment, meaning here the recompense for the charitable deed, and, **18,** 'I have' (or, as one might render it in this sense, 'I have received') is a technical expression in drawing up a receipt, found also in the Sermon on the Mount, Mt 6:2, 5, 16. They have received full payment, the transaction is finished, they must be content to sign the receipt and expect nothing more. For these various terms *cf.* Moulton-Milligan, *Vocabulary.* 'an **908b** odour of sweetness ' : *cf.* Ex 29:18, and often in OT for the sweet savour of an acceptable sacrifice, here in a metaphorical sense. **19.** 'from his riches my God will in Christ Jesus satisfy with glory *your every need*'. 'glory', as often in Paul (Col 1:11 ; Eph 3:16 ; Rom 3:23) for grace, which is here chiefly in question.

22–23. 22. The imperial household was enormous, **c** containing men and women of every status, and even slaves might hold high and confidential positions. Paul may have come to know some of them through the praetorian guard, and may be paying tribute to their importance and help. His salutations in Rom 16, sent even before his arrival in Rome, are also significant, as is likewise the epistle of St Ignatius of Antioch to the Romans, in which he expresses a fear that their influence may deliver him from the martyrdom for which he longs. **23.** St Paul probably writes this verse with his own hand, after dictating the rest ; this was a custom of the time, a kind of signature and a guarantee of genuineness ; *cf.* 2 Thess 2:2 ; 3:17 ; 1 Cor 16:21 ; Gal 6:11 ; Col 4:18.

THE EPISTLE TO THE COLOSSIANS

By D. J. LEAHY

909a Bibliography—*T. K. Abbott, *Epistle to the Colossians*, ICC nd ; St John Chrysostom, PG 62 (tr. *Library of the Fathers*, vol. 14) ; J. Huby, S.J., *Les Epîtres de la Captivité* (*Verbum Salutis* series), Paris, 1935 ; P. Ketter, *Die Heilige Schrift für das Leben erklärt*, vol. 15, Freiburg in B., 1937 ; J. Knabenbauer, S.J., *Commentarius in S. Pauli Epistolas* (CSS), Paris, 1912 ; *J. B. Lightfoot, *St Paul's Epistle to the Colossians*, London, 1890⁹ ; R. P. Médebielle, *Epître aux Colossiens* (in *La Sainte Bible*, ed. Pirot), Paris, 1938 ; F. Prat, S.J., *The Theology of Saint Paul*, London, 1942⁴ ; *L. B. Radford, *The Epistle to the Colossians* (Westminster Commentaries), London, 1931 ; J. Rickaby, S.J., *Further Notes on St Paul*, London, 1911 ; S. Thomae Aquinatis, *In Omnes S. Pauli Epistulas*, vol. II, Turin, 1929.

b The Church at Colossae—The origin of the town's name is unknown ; it has nothing to do with ' Colossus ' or 'Colosseum' ; it is probably an adaptation of the name of Lake Koloe, not far distant. The town lay in the south-western corner of Phrygia. The traveller setting out eastwards to the Euphrates from the seat of Government, Ephesus, would take the great trade road through the Meander Valley for about one hundred miles to Laodicea. Eleven miles farther on he would come to Colossae ; or six miles northwards he would come to Hierapolis. These cities lay in the Valley of the Lycus, a tributary of the Meander. Colossae itself was situated among mountains which marked the upper reaches of the valley and the point of entry into the tableland of central Asia Minor. Today the district is desolate, but in ancient times it was prosperous. Xerxes halted there on his famous march against the Greeks in 481 B.C., and later Cyrus stayed there for seven days (Xenophon, *Anabasis*, 1, 2, 6). Josephus (Ant 12, 3, 4) relates that Antiochus III, the Great (223–187 B.C.) transferred two thousand Jewish families from Babylonia and Mesopotamia into Lydia and Phrygia. These were allowed to use their own laws and were well treated. Some of them must surely have settled in Colossae. St Paul's epistle supposes that there is a Jewish element among the people there.

In the first cent. of the Christian era the town was already in a state of decay. It had been outstripped by nearby Laodicea, founded in the third cent. B.C. and renowned for its trade in black wool and medicine. Indeed, as J. Huby (p 1) declares, if St Paul had not written this epistle, the name, Colossae, would be known only to specialists in ancient history.

c St Paul did not found the churches in the Lycus Valley personally ; they are not included in the description of the Apostle's journeys in Acts, and in this epistle he writes of the Christians gathered together at Colossae and Laodicea in terms which suggest that he had never seen them face to face (Col 1:7 ; 2:1). Nevertheless, the Church at Colossae was closely bound to the Apostle, and he hoped to visit it personally after writing to Philemon (Phm 22). *Hearing your faith* (1:4) does not mean that the Apostle was only then for the first time becoming acquainted with the Christians at Colossae. How the Church at Colossae came to be founded was probably in the following way : St Paul spent over two years at Ephesus, and after he had been thrust out of the synagogue there and was preaching daily in the school lent by, or rented

from, Tyrannus (Ac 19:9), ' all who dwelt in Asia **90** heard the word of the Lord, both Jews and Greeks ' (Ac 19:26). Among those who came from the Lycus Valley were the Colossians, Epaphras (4:12) and Philemon (4:9 ; the slave, Onesimus, was from Colossae ; hence also his master, Philemon). Epaphras acted as a missionary in his native valley, founding churches at Hierapolis and Laodicea (Col 4:13) as well as in Colossae itself (Col 1:7 ; 4:12–13). He was assisted by Philemon, who provided accommodation for a church in his house (Phm 1–2). It is likely that both of them were Gentiles, since Paul mentions specially Jesus Justus as a Jew (Col 4:11). Indeed, the majority of the Christians at Colossae appear to have been Gentile converts ; *cf.* 1:21, 27 ; 2:13, etc. But that there was a Judaic element is, as we have seen, *a priori* probable, and it is confirmed by several allusions in the epistle (2:11, 14, 16 ; 3:11, etc.).

Date, Occasion and Purpose—This epistle is one of **d** the four *Captivity Epistles*, all written whilst St Paul was in prison and all within a short time of one another. The captivity was the Apostle's imprisonment in Rome (61–63, *cf.* § 898b).

St Paul intended this epistle for all the Lycus Valley churches (*cf.* 4:16), but that does not imply that it is a circular letter, like Eph. The people in the Lycus Valley were closely bound together ; they shared the dangerous tendencies which were the direct occasion for the writing of the epistle. It was doubtless the affair of Onesimus and the letter to Philemon which led Paul to direct the epistle in the first instance to Colossae. Whilst in prison in Rome, the Apostle received a visit from Epaphras, who told him of the growing faith and charity of the people at Colossae (1:7 ; 2:5 ; 4:13). This news was good ; but there was something disturbing in the report too. There were false teachers there. In brief, they were saying that Christians should worship spiritual beings who were alleged to be intermediaries between God and man. The effect of this false teaching was to rob Christ's person and work of their unique and supreme importance. To combat these errors St Paul wrote this epistle, which, then, can be described as a polemical treatise. His method was to make clear the supremacy of Christ's person and work—to exalt both above intermediate beings.

In detail, the **Errors** were essentially Judaistic **e** (*cf.* P. Benoit RB 54 [1947] 624), though they were shot through with a *false asceticism* and *false speculation* which came from Hellenistic syncretism (*cf.* Abbott, xlix). The Apostle supposes that his (Jewish) readers see a close relation between the Law of Moses and the angels. This idea was not new : there are traces elsewhere in the NT (Ac 7:38, 53 ; Gal 3:19 ; Heb 2:2), and it was taken for granted by many Jews in rabbinical circles which regarded the Torah as a supernatural being, the real value of which was judged not in its creation, but in its promulgation through angels (*cf.* J. Bonsirven, S.J., *Le Judaïsme Palestinien*, Paris, 1934, I, 250). The angels were regarded as guardians of the Torah, and they would destroy those who refused to accept it (J. Bonsirven, *loc. cit.*, I, 232 ; *cf.* SB III, 554–6). At Colossae, then, the Judaizers wanted the Old Law to stand ; they wanted divine worship to be given to those celestial beings and all they stood for. J. B. Lightfoot (p 71) : ' Even the

1132

9e enforcement of the initiatory rite of Judaism may be inferred from the contrast implied in St Paul's recommendation of the spiritual circumcision (2:2) '.

f At the same time there was a tendency which Lightfoot (*ibid.*) describes as ' an element of theosophic speculation, which is alien to the spirit of Judaism proper . . . a shadowy mysticism which loses itself in the contemplation of the unseen world '. It was a tendency later to develop into Gnosticism (*cf.* Lightfoot, 74–111). Meanwhile, it appeared as a claim to an exclusive and profound knowledge of celestial beings (*cf.* 2:18).

The two bad tendencies had one common root : matter was evil and therefore hateful to God. Between God and man, between infinite and finite, yawned a chasm that could not be bridged. In their bewilderment the false teachers, yearning to approach God, turned to angelic beings as instruments of communication between God and man, and as objects of worship.

In his refutation St Paul shows that it was only Christ who filled that chasm ; his Person—the Word Incarnate—was their solution ; the celestial beings, the alleged intermediaries, to whom St Paul gives the name *angels* (2:18), or *thrones, dominations, principalities, powers* (1:16 ; 2:10, 15) are not divine, are not mediators. They are not closer to man than Christ is ; they are subordinate to Christ, the Divine Mediator.

g The **Doctrinal Teaching** is in perfect harmony with the rest of St Paul's teaching—salvation by union with and in Christ ; deliverance from the old man of the flesh and from the Law ; entry into the new man by possession of eternal life, already acquired by Baptism but awaiting development in Heaven.

But ' The distinctive feature of this epistle is its Christology. The doctrine of the Person of Christ is here stated with greater precision and fulness than in any other of St Paul's epistles '. (Lightfoot, 120.) Positively, the Apostle here lays great emphasis on the Divinity and Manhood of Christ. He is pre-existent and is supreme over all creation ; he has a function in the creation and government of the world ; he has a function as Redeemer of the world ; he is Head of the Church, the mystical body.

h **Authenticity**—Abbott (*op. cit.* p L) ' About its early and uncontroverted reception as the work of St Paul, there is no doubt '. There are probable allusions to the epistle in Clement of Rome (1 Cor 49, 2 ; Col 3:14) ; in Barnabas (12, 7 ; Col 1:16) ; St Ignatius (Eph 10, 3 ; Col 1:23). St Irenaeus quotes from every chapter and attributes the epistle explicitly to St Paul (*Adv. Haer.* 3, 14, 1). Similarly, there is no doubt about its authenticity in the works of Tertullian, Clement of Alexandria, Origen. In the Muratorian Canon the epistle occupies the same position as in our MSS. The Chester-Beatty papyrus (P 46), which dates from the first half of the third cent., reproduces it, and Eusebius mentions it as one of the uncontested epistles. Even the heretics, Marcion and the Valentinians, quote it as the word of God.

Attacks on the authenticity have been based on purely internal or subjective reasons. Thus Mayerhoff (*Der Brief an die Kolosser*, Berlin, 1838) excited interest by declaring that the epistle was a treatise against Gnostics, and since the earliest Gnostic writer known is Cerinthus, the epistle could not have been written until two centuries after the date of St Paul's death. At the same time Mayerhoff viewed with suspicion the connexion between St Paul and the Christology of the epistle. Though Mayerhoff attracted a few critics to his view, the fact is that today the vast majority of non-Catholic commentators admit that the epistle is from the hand of St Paul.

i **Relation between Col and Eph**—These two are called companion epistles, first because they were written about the same time, and especially because of their striking literary likeness. Abbott (p xxiii) quotes a list of parallel passages compiled by De Wette. It comprises some fifty verses of each epistle. It is noticeable that the parallels occur mostly in the moral section of each epistle, and this is not surprising, since once St Paul had formulated precepts for domestic behaviour, for example, he would naturally frame the same instructions in similar language in a second epistle written at the same time (possibly on the same day) to churches which he had not known personally. The contexts, the doctrinal ideas, are not the same in each epistle. **909i**

The principal idea of Col is the pre-eminent dignity **j** of Christ's person, whether considered in his eternal life or in his relations with the world—' in all things holding the primacy ' (1:18*c*). The moral teaching develops from this. The principle of man's perfection is not something external (3:21–22) ; it is within him, for it is Christ dwelling in his soul (3:17). It is in virtue of his union with Christ that man achieves merit : man's perfection is not so much a fleeing from sin, as a continual progress up to God by and in Christ.

The principal idea of Eph is the Church, the union of the faithful with and in Christ, as members of the body of which he is the head. This theme occupies the first three chapters, but corresponding to this Col has only ch 1. Indeed, the whole of Col 2 has no parallel in Eph. The moral teaching of Eph is an exhortation to lead the Christian life in view of the doctrine expounded in the first three chapters. The Apostle insists especially on *unity* in and with Christ, the head of the body : internal unity with him by faith, hope and charity ; external by professing the same Christianity, all doing their part to build up the whole Christ. The striking passage on charity in unity (4:1–16) has no parallel in Col. ' It must be recognized that nowadays those who deny the authenticity of Eph are abandoning the argument drawn from the literary likeness between that epistle and Col. Nobody now speaks of a servile reproduction, or of an imitation without any show of originality.' (Coppieters RB 9 [1912] 371.)

I 1–3*a* **The Greeting**—**1.** It is noteworthy that St **910a** Paul uses his title ' apostle of Jesus Christ ' even to a church which he had not personally founded (*cf.* § 909*c*). What he is going to write in this epistle is authoritative ; that is why he begins by quoting his credentials (*cf.* 1 Cor 1:1 ; 2 Cor 1:1 ; Eph 1:1, etc.). With his own name he associates that of Timothy, a brother in affection, who ministered to the Apostle in captivity (*cf.* Phil 2:19–23), and who is mentioned in all the Captivity Epistles, except Eph. Indeed, Timothy appears to have written out this epistle at the Apostle's dictation (4:18). **2.** Those who are addressed are the Christians at Colossa (the orthography of the town's name varied), and, as in all his later epistles beginning with Rom, St Paul describes them as ' the saints ', *i.e.* the new Israel consecrated to God by Baptism in Christ ; they are also ' the faithful brethren ', *i.e.* whose faith in Christ is firm (*cf.* Ac 10:45 ; Eph 1:1 ; 2 Tim 4:3, 12, etc.). **3***a.* The ' grace ' is the supernatural bounty of God and Christ ; it is the foundation on which ' peace ' or union with God, is built. As in Eph, Paul raises the common Greek and Hebrew salutations to the supernatural order.

3*b***–8 Thanksgiving**—St Paul has heard from Epaphras **b** (7) of the state of their faith, hope and charity ; for this he gives thanks always. **5.** The dominant note here is hope of the good things awaiting them in Heaven. Radford : ' The future glory casts a new light on the present struggle '. We may infer at once that it is perfectly lawful for Christians to practise their religion with a view to eternal recompense (*cf.* Eph 6:6–9 ; 1 Pet 1:3–22 ; Apoc 14:13). The Council of Trent (Sess. 6, cap. 16) has stated the Catholic doctrine of merit : every good work done in the state of Grace is rewarded by God with a title to an increase of eternal bliss. The Church has condemned the proposition attributed to Fénelon, ' There is an habitual state of love of God without admixture of any motive of self-interest, and this is perfect charity '

910b (Dz 1327). The important word in this quotation is, of course, 'habitual'. **6.** The Apostle's view of the Gospel territory is 'the whole world'. Already the Gospel had been preached in most provinces of the Roman Empire (*cf.* Rom 1:8), and it is probable that the Apostles had already evangelized Africa, Egypt and Gaul. The Gospel came to the Colossians as part of the world-wide movement.

c 9-14 Prayer for their spiritual progress—9.—'Therefore' sums up what he has written of the good they possess. Chrysostom : 'For as in the games we cheer on those most who are near upon gaining the victory, so truly does Paul also most exhort those who have achieved the greater part'. The Apostle is thinking of the false teachers, with their speculations, their claim to know (*gnosis*). He prays daily that his readers will be equipped intellectually with the perfection of knowledge (*epignosis*, DV 'the knowledge')—the deepest understanding—of God's will (*cf.* Lightfoot, 248–54). Further, he prays that this intellectual conviction be accompanied by 'all wisdom' (whereby a man sees all things with reference to God) and 'spiritual understanding' (whereby he clearly discerns between right and wrong). **10.** Thus equipped by God the Christian's life should show four qualities : (i) Zeal to please God (this being the probable sense of 'in all things pleasing') ; (ii) 'fruitfulness', like a tree, 'in every good work', accompanied by a deepening knowledge of God ; (iii) **11.** Determination to carry out God's will patiently, without wrath (DV 'longsuffering') and joyfully ; (iv) **12.** A spirit of thanksgiving for the whole favour of salvation through Christ's redemption (*cf.* Eph 1:6–7 ; Ac 26:18).

More precisely, this thanksgiving embraces three effects of the Redemption. First, the Father '*hath fitted us for our portion of the inheritance of the saints in light*' (WV). All the supernatural benefits and God himself, their source, are described by the figure of light (*cf.* Ac 9:3 ; Eph 5:7–13, etc.). **13.** Second, we have been snatched from being slaves to the power of darkness— 'from an arbitrary tyranny' (Lightfoot)—to the well ordered '*kingdom of his beloved Son*' (WV). **14.** Third, we have 'redemption', *i.e.* liberation from a state of guilt, forgiveness of former sins (*cf.* Eph 1:7).

d 15a Christ and God the Father—St Paul here begins the doctrinal part of the epistle ; he continues it down to 2:7. Christ is the 'image of the invisible God'. 'Image' (εἰκών), says St Thomas (*op. cit.*) connotes three qualities at the same time : (*a*) it must have a likeness with the original prototype, (*b*) it must be derived from the prototype, (*c*) it must belong to the same species as the prototype. Hence, mere likeness alone would not be enough. A photograph is a likeness ; it is not an image in the sense used here. But a son is the image of his father (but not *vice versa*). By 'God' here, of whom Christ is the image, the Apostle means God the Father (as in 2 Cor 4:4). To him St Paul gives the title 'invisible'. Prat (I, 288) : 'Invisibility belongs especially to him, considered either as God (and then it is common to him and to the Son, his perfect image) or considered as the Father, as St Paul seems to hint, and as a great number of the ancient ecclesiastical writers have thought ; in this case it would designate the personal and incommunicable attribute, by virtue of which the Father, source and principle of the Godhead, sends the other Persons, but is not sent by them'. Christ, then, is the image of the Father, because he manifests him to mankind. *Lightfoot : 'the underlying idea of the εἰκών, and indeed of the λόγος generally, is the manifestation of the hidden'. Hence, there is no need to follow St Thomas here (and other writers, *e.g.* St Chrysostom) saying 'he is the image not only of the invisible God, but is himself as invisible as the Father'.

In itself 'image' does not demand *equality* with the archetype ; but in fact we know that Christ, the image, is 'identical with the Father in every particular, differing from him only by the fact of being begotten' (St John Damascene, quoted Prat *ibid*). *Cf.* v 19.

15b-17 Christ and the Universe—He has absolute **91** supremacy over all natural creation, because he is 'the firstborn of every creature'. 'Firstborn' here (as Rom 8:29 ; Col 1:18) is used in the metaphorical sense of pre-existence before creation. *Radford (p 174) : 'It implies more than priority ; it implies a relationship to God which cannot be predicated even of angels or men, much less of other creatures'. (*Cf.* Prat I, 289 f. ; C. F. Burney, JTS 27 [1926] 160 f.) Christ, then, being eternal, is supreme ; yet he is the final revelation of God (**16**). 'For' indicates the reasons. 'In him were all things created.' In particular, he is the Creator of celestial beings, some of whom the Apostle here names (*cf.* Eph 1:21)— perhaps those to whom the false teachers paid most respect. The three prepositions, *in* him, *by* him, *unto* him, indicate how the act of creation occurred, and at the same time provide a summary of the relations of the Son to the universe. 'In him' : he was the centre of unity, of harmony and cohesion, when the act of creation took place. All creatures, past, present and future, are suspended ontologically from the Christ, and cannot be fully understood if their relation with him is broken. St Thomas (*op. cit.*) : 'A worker **f** constructs an object by making it take on his mental ideal ("forma"). He clothes, as it were, his ideal with external matter, as a man builds a house according to the plan which he has worked out in his mind. And thus God is said to do everything by his wisdom, because the wisdom of God is to created things what the art of the builder is to the house. The mental ideal ("forma") and wisdom is the Word, and hence all things are created in him, as in a certain exemplar'. 'By him' : he is the efficient cause of all things. 'Unto him' : all things are pointed towards him as their final goal and meaning (*cf.* Apoc 22:13). It is noteworthy that the verb here (ἔκτισται) is perfect, indicating that there is a continuous, ever present, relation between all created things and Christ, who is their efficient cause and goal. The Apostle makes this thought even clearer in the next verse. **17.** All things were not only created by the Son ; they 'consist' in him. St Thomas (*op. cit.*) : 'If God were to withdraw his power from us, all things would fall apart.' As Lightfoot observes, 'the action of gravitation which keeps in their place things fixed, and regulates the motion of things moving is an expression of his mind'.

The implied conclusion of this section is clear enough : Christ has absolute sovereignty over the whole created universe. Between him and celestial beings no comparison is possible ; they are creatures, he the divine Creator ; they are finite, he is infinite.

18-19 Christ and the Church—Christ is also absolute **91** sovereign in the Church. **18a.** 'And he' is emphatic : the same Person who is Creator, Conserver and Final Cause of all things—and not some angelic deputy—is also 'Head of the body' (*cf.* Eph 1:22b). The head is distinct from the body (*cf.* 1:24 ; Eph 1:23 ; 5:23) ; yet it is united to the body, as the next words show : he is 'the beginning', *i.e.* the origin, the cause of all the supernatural growth of the members. Thus the figure of Christ as head of the body serves Paul's purpose of insisting both on Christ's sovereignty over the members and on his nearness to them. Radford : 'He is supreme over creation, but supreme in the Church, distinct from creation, but identified with the Church'. **18b.** 'The firstborn from the dead', *i.e.* the first to rise from the dead to a new life, and the cause of the resurrection of those associated with him in his triumph (*cf.* 1 Cor 15:20 ; Apoc 1:5). The expression 'has nothing in common with "firstborn of every creature"' (Prat, I, 290). **18c.** 'that in all things he may hold the primacy'. All these prerogatives place him (and not some creature) supreme in the natural and religious realms. **19.** 'For in him it hath pleased the Father that all the fulness should dwell' (WV). The usual sense of *fulness* is totality. Here it may denote all existence (P. Benoit, O.P., RB 54 [1947] 625), or—and this is the commoner view

a —it may denote ' the combined sum of the perfections which constitute the divine essence : in other words, divinity itself'. (Prat I, 295). *Cf.* 2:9. Moreover, Christ possesses this fullness in permanent fashion (κατοικεῖν, DV ' dwell '). This verse provides the ultimate reason for Christ's sovereignty over all things.

b 20-23 Christ's Work : Reconciliation—St Paul has described the Person of Christ : he is the image of the invisible God (1:15), Creator (1:16–17) ; sovereign over the universe and supreme in the work of Redemption (1:18–20). He now draws the consequence of this, that through Christ alone must reconciliation be effected. **20.** The reconciliation affects ' all things . . . both as to the things that are on earth and the things that are in heaven '. There is no difficulty in understanding that all things on earth (*i.e.* primarily the human race) are reconciled to God through Christ (*cf.* Rom 8:20–22) ; but how explain the reconciliation of the things in heaven? Knabenbauer (pp 303–5) refers to a variety of suggestions made, and since his time other opinions have been added (*e.g.* Huby, 47). The most probable interpretation is that Paul is referring to angels. The false teachers regarded the angels as intermediate beings, guardians of the Law of Moses, and holding in their hands the list of punishments due to transgressors (*cf.* 2:14). Now Christ has brought peace and reconciliation to all through the Cross. *Cf.* B. N. Wambacq RB 55 (1948) 35–42. The participle ' making peace ' having the same subject as the main verb emphasizes that the first step comes from the Father. The peace is effected ' through the blood of his cross '. The sacrifice on Calvary is the effective mediation ; it bears peace between heaven and earth (*cf.* Eph 4:1–6). Chrysostom : ' Earth became heaven, since heaven was about to receive

c what came of earth.' **22a.** For his sacrifice of reconciliation Christ, the Mediator, chose a body that could feel the sting of pain and death. **22b.** What is the effect for the Colossians ? From being what they have become ' holy, unspotted, blameless ', a three-fold description of the state of Grace based on a metaphor drawn from the qualities required for an OT sacrificial victim (*cf.* Eph 1:21 ; 1 Thess 2:10). **23.** It is a firm state, not to be upset by false teaching. What the Apostle says is no mere fancy of his own devising—he is an ambassador of Christ.

d 24 The Work of Christ and the sufferings of the Apostle—(I) ' now rejoice in my sufferings for you '. The ' now ' is noteworthy : Paul is ' an ambassador in chains ' (Eph 6:20). ' And fill up ' : Vg ' adimpleo ', DV ' fill up ' disregards the two prepositions which appear before the simple verb in the Greek. With the first preposition (ἀντί) the verb indicates a want being met by two complementary operations (*cf.* Lk 14:12). The second preposition (ἀνά) means ' up to the top ' (like filling a cup to the brim). The whole word shows the Apostle by reason of his sufferings on behalf of the Colossians supplying something not supplied by Christ, and the result of the combined operation between Christ and the Apostle is to satisfy the want fully. ' Those things that are wanting of the sufferings of Christ ' : he does not say that the suffering of Christ is not completed, but that certain aspects of those sufferings (*cf.* plural) need to be made perfect. ' In my flesh ' denotes the whole man, body and soul.

e What are the sufferings, or afflictions, of Christ to which Paul brings (along with the operation of Christ) completeness ? Are they those endured by Christ ; or are they those suffered by the members of Christ's Mystical Body, other than St Paul ? There are two opinions, each of which has Catholic supporters. First, the afflictions are those endured by Christ. The Passion is complete, infinite in its atoning or satisfactory power. To this power neither St Paul nor anyone else could add anything. But the application of the merits of Christ's Passion to individual souls involves a toll of suffering, especially on the part of those chosen by Christ as his ministers (*cf.* 1 Cor 3:9). The Apostle looks down at his prison bonds. His sufferings are in union with those of Christ. They are the vehicle for **911e** conveying the Passion to the hearts and souls of men, and in this way they bring completeness to the Passion in an external way. That he should call his own sufferings in the service of Christ the afflictions of Christ in his flesh is in accordance with similar expressions, 2 Cor 1:5 ; 4:10 ; Phil 3:10.

The other opinion regards the sufferings of Christ as **f** those of the mystical body (*cf.* Ac 9:14). St Augustine (*Enarr.* in Ps 62, 4) : ' Thou [member of Christ's Body] sufferest so much as was to be contributed out of thy sufferings to the whole sufferings of Christ, that hath suffered in our Head, and doth suffer in his members, that is, in our own selves '. The Passion of Christ, then, is continued in the members of his Body, the Church. This fits in with the truth that the Church is in a real though mystical sense Christ himself. (*Cf.* R. H. Benson, *Christ in the Church*, esp. Parts I and IV.)

Though the exegete here ' can advance only with caution ' (Prat), the first opinion seems preferable ; it gives the ordinary sense of the phrase ' the sufferings of Christ '. In either opinion we are presented with an important lesson : suffering can be, not a terrifying enigma in our eyes, but something very precious, since it is the instrument God chose to redeem us, and we can make our sufferings serve in the cause of Christ's Passion. *Cf.* Rom 8:18, 28 ; *cf.* §900b. J. Rickaby, S.J. (' An Old Man's Jottings ', 231) : ' Suffering, merely as such, does not sanctify. It did not sanctify the Bad Thief. The wicked in hell suffer, but are not made holy. The only suffering that sanctifies is suffering patiently borne for God, suffering accepted in obedience to God's will, suffering hallowed by the obedience of Him who was " made obedient even to the death of the Cross " (Phil 2:8). . . . The obedience of comfort is good, but the obedience of suffering is heroic. And God requires it, sooner or later, of everyone. You may be gold, but you must be stamped with the cross to pass as current coin for heaven.'

25-29 The Work of Christ continued in St Paul's g Apostolate—**25.** The purpose of his ministry is ' to utter the full word of God ' (WV). **26.** This he further defines as ' the mystery '. Here, as at Eph 3:1–3 (*cf.* Rom 16:25 f.), the Apostle has in mind the comprehensive truth, once hidden, now revealed by Christ, which embraces all others. It is the whole plan of man's redemption, timeless, yet revealed and enacted by the Incarnation and Death of Our Saviour. One phase of the mystery is that it is world-wide in its benefit. St Paul often insists on this phase. **27b.** The one-time pagans of Colossae now have ' Christ in you ' (the punctuation of the DV is better omitted here).

II 1-7 St Paul's care for all, especially for the Colos- h sians—**3.** It is in Christ, then, and not in some coterie of false teachers, that all the ' treasures of wisdom and knowledge ' are hidden. **5b.** ' Beholding your order '— a metaphor based on the ranks (τάξιν) and strong united force of soldiers (στερέωμα). He is not dismayed. He has the report from Ephaphras, and he sees them as a disciplined body presenting a bold front to adversaries. **6-7.** He ends the doctrinal part with an appeal for loyalty to Christ : the root of their religious life, the principle of their cohesion and progress in Christ.

8-III 4 Polemical. False Wisdom and the True—8. 912a Erroneous Teaching. The time has come to confront the false teaching. Though it goes by the name of *philosophy* (the only mention of the word in the Bible), it is really a kind of bait for error—' an empty deceit ' —based on ' the traditions of men ' (contrast 6a), closely allied to the ' elements of the world '. This last expression seems to denote observance of days, months and years (16b). In other words, the elements are connected with the sun and moon, or with cosmic forces generally. Chrysostom, ' By *elements of the world* he means the sun and moon '. The Greek word στοιχεῖον meant the first step in anything ; hence the cosmic forces of nature, or the A B C of knowledge (*cf.* KNT Gal 4:3 : ' the schoolroom tasks ').

912b **9-10 True Wisdom Life in Christ**—9. 'For in him dwelleth all the fulness of the Godhead corporeally.' On 'fulness', see on 1:19. 'Godhead' translates a Greek word (θεότης) which is a *hapax legomenon* in the Bible. It denotes the Divine Nature itself (*cf.* Prat II, 152). And the significance of 'all' before 'the fulness' is to denote each and all of the divine perfections in their highest degree (infinity). The complete Divine Nature, then, abides permanently (κατοικεῖ) in Christ; it also abides 'corporeally'. This last expression means 'in a body, in the form of a body'. The text teaches that the Divinity and Humanity are united in the one person of Christ—as the soul by dwelling in the body constitutes with it one single principle. Prat: 'Your pretended philosophy, said St Paul, is only a vain deceit; you will linger in elementary, childish doctrines; you ask for the protectors and mediators of a chimerical world of the imagination, and you neglect him in whom, in a visible and tangible form, free from error and illusion, dwelleth all the fulness of the Godhead bodily. As he possesses this absolute plenitude permanently, he will cause it to flow out upon you in spiritual graces, and you can therefore dispense with all other intercessors.' **10a**. 'And you are filled in him'; by reason of their incorporation in Christ they are filled with all his fulness (*cf.* Eph 1:23). *Cf.* § 646c

c **11-15 Baptism and its Effects**—11. With Circumcision he constrasts the spiritual circumcision instituted by Christ—Baptism. 12. In describing the effects of Baptism the Apostle uses again the symbolism of Rom 6:3 ff. 13. He dwells on the note of forgiveness. 14. He uses a metaphor drawn from 'the handwriting with its decree that was against us'. The 'handwriting', lit. something written out by hand; hence usually an indenture of debt. See 1:20. On the Cross God swept away the Mosaic Law and all its demands. 15. It follows that God despoiled the 'principalities and powers'. At this point the Apostle uses a metaphor taken from a Roman triumph. Having stripped the angels God exposes them '*in public*' (DV 'confidently') in the triumphal procession.

d **16-23 Erroneous Practices**—16. Between the bodily asceticism (concerning meat and drink) and the observance of Jewish festival days the bond of connexion seems to have been observance of the Jewish Law. 17. But all this was useful and good only in so far as it was a 'shadow' of the future salvation; salvation through Christ is '*the reality*' (DV 'body'), *cf.* Heb. 10:1. 18. '*Let no one cheat you of your prize, delighting in self-abasement and worship of angels and "taking his stand" on what he hath seen, foolishly swollen with his fleshy conceit*' (WV). This reading omits with the most important Greek MSS the negative before 'seen'. 19. No need for an external Jewish practice, or even for an angel to come between a Christian and Christ. From the Head the whole Body receives its life, cohesion and growth. The description is almost the same as Eph 4:16, with the difference that there the Apostle emphasizes the union of the members between themselves, while here his thought is of their dependence on the Head.

913a **III 1-4 True Perfection, Life in Christ**—1. At Baptism they died a mystical death when they went down into the cleansing water, but they died only to be raised to a new life in Christ (*cf.* Rom 6:4; Eph 2:4 ff. etc.). 2. But to live means to think, to love, to act. Their life should be one long *sursum corda*, until the members of his Body will be joined with their Head in manifest glory. *Cf.* Prayer for Ascension Day. **5-9 Vices to be kept Dead**—St Paul here begins the moral part of the epistle—the application of the doctrine to their daily lives. 5. Though a Christian is dead to the lower passions, they can rebel (*cf.* 1:28; Eph 4:13). They must be '*kept dead*' (DV 'mortify') by refusing to let them guide conduct. The sins mentioned are those to which the readers are especially tempted. But they can all be grouped under three heads, impurity, avarice and pride (*cf.* 1 Jn 2:16). On

'covetousness which is the service of idols' many **9** commentators observe that the phrase can be best understood in the light of Mt 6:24, and is then seen to refer to men who make wealth their god. It is possible however, that Paul here condemns love of gain acquired by associating with some pagan practice; *cf.* VD 12 (1932) 370.

10-17 Virtues to be practised—9b-10. 'The stripping **b** of the old man with his deeds' and the 'putting on of the new', first accomplished at Baptism, are tasks that have to be constantly renewed. A good gardener constantly weeds; the permanent way needs constant supervision. In 1 Cor 2:6 Paul regards some Christians as already perfect in the sense that they have a proved capacity and desire for truth (*cf.* Phil 3:15). But here (as also 1:28; Eph 4:13) he sees perfection as a continual renewal. **11b**. 'Christ is all and in all': he is the complete gift; in him all distinction is obliterated—the Christian, whatever his social standing (11a) possesses Christ. **14b**. 'Charity . . . the bond of perfection.' Chrysostom: 'The Apostle says not "charity is the crown", but something greater, "the bond", the latter being more necessary than the former; for a crown is a heightening of perfection, but a bond is a holding together of the component parts of perfection'. **15**. 'The peace of Christ' should '*stand as umpire*' (DV 'rejoice') in Christian hearts (*cf.* Eph 4:3). Chrysostom: 'He sets up an arena in our hearts, and games, and a wrestling match, and an umpire'. **16**. 'The word of Christ' is his teaching; it must be theirs 'abundantly', *i.e.* to the point of overflowing into (i) 'teaching and admonishing' one another and (ii) praise of God rising up from their hearts '*in thanksgiving*' (DV 'in grace') to God. The 'psalms' here are generally regarded as Christian hymns after the model of the Psalms of David. It is difficult to distinguish precisely between *psalms, hymns* and *canticles* (*cf.* Eph 5:19).

III 18-IV 1 Duties in the Home—As in Eph 5:21-6:9 **c** Paul shows that the Christian spirit must permeate everyday duties. The same logical order is observed here (wife, husband, children, parents, slaves and masters). But here the counsels are briefer. There are only two additions. **25**. First, with regard to slaves—to the sanction of reward for good is added that of punishment for injustice on the part of the slave. **1**. Second, with regard to masters—to the duty of justice is added that of '*fairness*' (DV 'equal').

IV 2-6 General Counsels—2. 'Instant in prayer' means perseverance. Prayer here (*cf.* Eph 6:18) refers to continued awareness of the presence of God. It implies '*vigilance*' (DV 'watching'). **5b**. 'Redeeming the time.' The expression occurs (Eph 5:16) where the context concerns general progress. Here the context is the apostolate. We must make the most of every opportunity to propagate the faith. **6**. Their 'speech' must be 'always in grace', *i.e.* courteous, and 'seasoned with salt', *i.e.* marked with supernatural flavour (*cf.* Mk 9:49).

7-18 Epilogue: Personal Salutations—8. The **d** Apostle in prison (18) is sending Tychicus, the bearer of the epistle and of that to the Ephesians (Eph 6:21), '*that ye may know our condition*' (WV). 9. With Tychicus goes Onesimus. There is no word here about his being a slave—we learn that from Phm—and Paul singles him out for praise. Then come salutations from six companions in captivity. 10. It is only here that we learn that Mark, the writer of the Second Gospel, was cousin to Barnabas, and we do not know whether he reached the Colossians (10b). 12. Again Paul praises Epaphras who is '*wrestling by his prayer*' on behalf of his fellow-Colossians. 14. Luke, 'the most dear physician', was the companion of St Paul and writer of the Third Gospel and Acts. Demas later abandoned the Apostle (2 Tim 4:9). 18. The final verse was written by St Paul himself (he had dictated up to this point). *Cf.* 2 Thess 3:17; 1 Cor 16:21; Gal 6:11. He is a prisoner for Christ's sake, for the Gospel, for them. 'Grace be with you.'

1 and 2 THESSALONIANS

By Dom B. ORCHARD

a **Bibliography**—St John Chrysostom, PG 62 ; St John Damascene PG 95 ; Knabenbauer, *In Epistolas ad Thessalonicenses*, CSS, Paris, 1913 ; Vosté, *Commentarius in Epistolas ad Thessalonicenses*, Rome, 1917 ; Lattey, *I & II Thessalonians*, WV, 1927²; Steinmann, *Die Briefe an die Thessalonicher*, BB, Bonn, 1935 ; Eaton, *Epistles of St Paul to the Thessalonians*, London, 1939 ; Costello, *I & II Thessalonians*, CNT, 1942 ; Amiot, *Epîtres aux Thessaloniciens*, Verbum Salutis XIV, Paris, 1946 ; *Lightfoot, *I & II Thessalonians* in *Notes on the Epistles of St Paul*, London, 1895 ; *Findlay, *I & II Thessalonians*, CBSC, 1891 ; *Milligan, *St Paul's Epistles to the Thessalonians*, London, 1908 ; *Frame, *Thessalonians*, ICC, Edinburgh, 1912 ; *Plummer, *A Commentary on St Paul's First Epistle to the Thessalonians*, London, 1918 ; *Plummer, *A Commentary on St Paul's Second Epistle to the Thessalonians*, London, 1918 ; *Bicknell, *I & II Thessalonians*, London, 1932 ; S. Obiols, *Epistoles de Sant Pau als Thessalonicenses* (La Biblia, Monestir de Montserrat) 1930 ; D. Buzy, *Epîtres aux Thessaloniciens* (La Sainte Bible [Pirot] tom. XII) 1936, pp 129–90 ; art. *Thessaloniciens (Epîtres aux)* and *Eschatologie* (D. Buzy and A. Brundt) DTC. The present commentary is especially indebted to Vosté, Amiot, Frame, Milligan and Plummer.

b **Thessalonica**—Thessalonica, the modern Salonika, was founded by Cassander in 315 B.C. and was named after his wife, the step-sister of Alexander the Great. The city became the chief naval station of the Macedonian kings, and the advantages of its situation for commerce and naval warfare secured it a rapid and increasing prosperity. It was perhaps the most important city of the Roman Province of Macedonia and became the place of residence of the proconsul and virtually its capital. Its situation on the Via Egnatia, the highway connecting Rome with her eastern provinces, added enormously to its importance. In the Second Roman Civil War the city took the side of Octavius and Antony, and in reward was made a free city, ruled by its own assembly and magistrates, who were called politarchs (Ac 17:5–6). In the time of St Paul, therefore, the city was important, populous, and a strategic centre for the spread of the Faith in Macedonia. Its population was chiefly Greek, but on account of its commercial advantages many other nations were represented, especially the Jews, who formed a large and powerful community possessing a synagogue. Save for the Jews, its inhabitants were idolaters, and as licentious as any other seaport population of those days.

c **The Church in Thessalonica** at the time of the Epistles consisted of a few Jewish converts and a large number of convert pagan Greeks (Ac 17:4 ; 1 Thess 1:9). Though the account of Paul's visit in Ac would lead us to assume that he only spent three weeks there on his second missionary journey, most commentators agree that the flourishing state of the Thessalonian Church at the time of the Epistles presupposes a total length of residence of some three to six months, during which he converted a great number of Gentiles and set up a system of Church government (1 Thess 5:12–14). It was in fact his great success with the Gentiles that roused the envy of the Jews (Ac 17:5) and led to a riot. Though they failed to find Paul, the situation was sufficiently menacing to **914c** cause the brethren to send him and Silas away by night to Beroea. From there the relentless persecution of the Jews of Thessalonica drove him down to Athens (Ac 17:15), where Timothy rejoined him. Being most anxious to know how his recent Thessalonian converts were facing up to the bitter persecution of the Jews, he despatched Timothy to find out and report back to him (1 Thess 3:2).

Occasion—The First Epistle to the Thessalonians is the **d** result of the favourable report brought back by Timothy to Paul who in the interval had moved on to Corinth (Ac 18:5). Along with the good news of their spiritual progress and of their patient endurance of persecution, Timothy also, it seems, informed Paul that the Jews were trying to discredit the authority of the three missionaries. He also brought two questions, possibly in writing, that required immediate answer as they were disturbing the minds of some in the Thessalonian Church, one concerning the date of the Parousia or Second Coming, and the other the fate of those of their brethren who, by their premature death, could not possibly be witnesses of the Parousia. The Apostle's answer to the latter question satisfied them, but his clear statement of his own and every one else's ignorance of the date of the Second Coming of Christ did not convince some of the Thessalonians and necessitated the Second Epistle in which he reaffirmed the total ignorance of all mankind of the date of the Parousia and calmed their apprehensions of the possibility of its immediate approach by enumerating certain things that must happen beforehand.

Date, place and genuineness—It seems certain that **e** both Epistles were composed at Corinth in the early part of his stay during the second missionary journey at a time when Silas and Timothy were with him (1 Thess 2:17). As Gallio seems to have been resident in Corinth as proconsul during the latter part of St Paul's stay (Ac 18:11, 18) in the spring of A.D. 51 or 52, the date of the First Epistle may be fixed as between the autumn of 50 and the spring of 52. The Second Epistle seems from internal evidence to have been written from two to six months after the First.

That both Epistles are genuine writings of St Paul is beyond all doubt, and there is no need to rehearse the arguments here. It may be noted, however, as a point of interest, that both Epistles are written throughout in the first person *plural* (except for the final salutation) on account of the part played by both Silas and Timothy in the conversion of Thessalonica.

Doctrinal Content—These epistles are especially **f** remarkable for the glimpse they give us of the personality of Paul and of his love of the brethren and friendship for his converts. Many times does he thank God for their good progress in the Christian way of life and praise them for having become a pattern to all in the province of Macedonia (1 Thess 1:3–8). The Thessalonians are his 'brothers' for whom his love is so intense that he would gladly communicate to them not only the Gospel but his very soul, thoughts and feelings, indeed, his life, 'because you are become most dear to us' (1 Thess 2:8). Though they are only friends and brethren of a few months' standing he cannot continue without news of their progress even for a short time, and he 'lives again'

914f when he learns not only that they are doing well but that they are as desirous to see him again as he to see them (1 Thess 3:6–8).

The fundamental Pauline teaching on our Union with God in Christ, the Son of God, and his full divinity and equality with God the Father is made clear in the first salutation of both epistles. All the main Doctrines found in the other epistles, *e.g.* the redemptive work of Christ, sanctification through the Holy Spirit, grace, the laws of Christian morality, are taken for granted in many passing allusions. The chief subject is, however, the Second Coming, or Parousia, of Christ, to which the next section is devoted. There is also an interesting reference to a group of rulers of the Church in 1 Thess 5:12–14, and though they are given no name we may assume that they are similar to the clergy ordained previously in South Galatia (Ac 14:22). It is also interesting to note that the controversy over the value of circumcision and the Mosaic Law, which was still barely a couple of years past and which had produced the Epistle to the Galatians (*cf. in loc.*), finds no echo in Thessalonica.

g The most important teaching in the Epistles is, however, usually held to be his teaching on **The Second Coming, or Parousia,** and this section will therefore attempt to summarize their Eschatology. The Apostle teaches that the whole spiritual life of every man must be directed towards preparing for the Parousia ' that your whole spirit and soul and body may be preserved blameless in the coming of our Lord Jesus Christ ' (1 Thess 5:23, *cf.* Ac 17:31). It was, however, their misapprehension of the bearing of this doctrine on their everyday life that led him to reiterate the necessity of continuing steadily with the humdrum business of earning their daily bread by hard work instead of standing about gossiping waiting for the Parousia, as some were doing. The scope of the following remarks is limited to showing that his teaching on the Parousia is consistent with itself, consistent with the teaching of Christ in the Gospels, and identical with the teaching of the Church today.

h His doctrine may be schematized under the following heads : (1) There is at present a withholding power (ὁ κατέχων, τὸ κατέχον) that prevents the Lawless One (the Antichrist), the emissary of Satan, from manifesting himself fully (2 Thess 2:6) ; (2) When, however, this force is removed the Antichrist will deceive and destroy many (2 Thess 2:8–11, *cf.* Mt 24:21–24) ; (3) The Second Coming, or appearance, of Christ, properly so called (1 Thess 4:16 ; 2 Thess 1:7–8 ; *cf.* 1 Cor 15:52 ; Mt 24:29–31) ; (4) His victory over Antichrist (2 Thess 2:8) ; (5) The gathering together of the dead raised to life again and of the living newly transformed to be judged by Christ (1 Thess 4:15–17, *cf.* 1 Cor 15:51–53 ; 2 Thess 1:8–10 ; Rom 2:5–16, 14:10 ; 1 Cor 3:13 ; 2 Cor 5:10 ; 1 Tim 5:24 ; 2 Tim 4:1 ; Heb 6:2, 9:27, 10:27, *cf.* also Mt 25:31 f., Ac 17:31) ; (6) The reunion with Jesus and the consummation of the reign of Christ (1 Thess 4:17 ; 1 Cor 15:24, 28).

i The first point to grasp is that St Paul's teaching on this subject is firmly based on the words of our Lord in the Gospels and especially Mt 24—indeed, the writer believes that our present Greek Matthew was the principal source of the eschatological teaching of these epistles—(*cf.* Orchard, *Thessalonians and the Synoptic Gospels*, Bi 19 [1938], 19 ff.). In no respect is St Paul's teaching an innovation, save in the particular point of the lot of those who die before the Parousia (1 Thess 4:13 f.), where he expressly claims a personal divine revelation. The same is true of his doctrine of the Antichrist (2 Thess 2:1–11) all of which he has drawn, according to the instruction of our Lord in Mt 24:15, from Daniel 9–12 (*cf.* Orchard, *St. Paul and the Book of Daniel*, Bi 20 [1939], 172–9). There is, therefore, no need to look for its sources in the Apocryphal writings.

j In the second place we have the Apostle's repeated declaration of his own complete ignorance of the time

and date of the Second Coming (1 Thess 5:1, 10). **9** Now ignorance of the date meant that so far as he, Paul, knew, it was just as likely to come the next day as a thousand years later, provided that the signs that were to precede its coming had already been verified. The first sign was the destruction of Jerusalem (which in fact took place in A.D. 70, some years after the Apostle's death) ; for according to Mt 24 the end cannot come before the fulfilment of the prophecy of the destruction of Jerusalem, which was promised before ' this generation shall pass away ' (Mt 24:34). (How much time was then to elapse between this event and the Second Coming Mt does not make clear.) St Paul, therefore, knew that as his generation would witness the destruction of Jerusalem he might quite possibly live to see it himself, and even live on into the years beyond it when the Parousia might come at any moment, provided that in the meantime the other signs preceding it had also been fulfilled. Being in this state of uncertainty he could quite **k** justifiably identify himself either with those who would be alive at the Parousia (1 Thess 4:13 ; 1 Cor 15:51–53) or with those dead in Christ who would then rise first (1 Thess 4:14 ; 1 Cor 6:14). Nor must we forget that Thessalonians was written at a time when only twenty years of the forty that constitutes a biblical ' generation ' had already passed away and that the Apostle himself was still in the prime of life. But naturally as old age approached, he must have realized that his own chance of being alive at the Parousia became correspondingly more and more remote. And thus when he wrote 2 Tim in his old age he knew he would not live to see the Parousia and was ready and eager for death (2 Tim 4:6). A careful study of these and the other epistles confirms the tradition of the Church that while the Apostle's views on the Parousia were consistent from first to last, the passage of time gradually led him to modify their personal application to himself.

Nor is there any real difficulty in such passages as **l** 1 Thess 3:12–13, 5:23, which may be taken as typical of most Pauline warnings to be prepared for the Second Coming ; for they remind his readers and hearers that they will all be judged in that day whether they are then alive or whether they are dead and then raised up. Again, a passage such as 1 Thess 1:10 shows that he encouraged his converts to look forward as eagerly as he himself to the Parousia, without worrying whether they died before it or not. For as he taught in 1 Thess 4:13 f. ' the dead in Christ ', of whom there were already not a few, would be at no disadvantage with the living at the Parousia. It was the privilege and joy as well as the duty of all Christians to look forward to that glorious coming in order ' that whether we watch or sleep we may live together with him ' (1 Thess 5:10). The Biblical Commission was therefore fully justified when in June 1915 it laid down that St Paul never said or taught, in public or in private, anything that was not perfectly compatible with his own ignorance of the time of the Parousia ; *cf.* § 52*e*.

1 THESSALONIANS

I 1 Greeting—Although the Epistle was entirely his **9** own composition St Paul associates Sylvanus (the Silas of Ac) and Timothy, his two chief assistants on his second missionary journey, with his greetings and message throughout. This verse shows that he had taught the Thessalonians the equality of Jesus Christ, the Second Person of the Blessed Trinity, with God the Father. Omit the second ' in '.

2-10 Thanksgiving for their Conversion—**3.** Render **b** ' labour *of* charity '. Basing all their hope on Christ, they had fruitfully exercised the three Theological Virtues. **4.** In this behaviour he sees their active response to God's gratuitous gift of Faith by which they were chosen (elected) members of Christ's

Kingdom. Omit stop after v 3. **5.** God's favour to them was shown by the efficacy and fullness of St Paul's preaching amongst them on the one hand, and by the sincerity and depth of their conversion on the other.— ' our gospel ' : the ' glad-tidings ' of salvation through Christ as proclaimed by St Paul.—' in power ' : either ' by miracles ' or ' efficaciously '.—' followers ' : *cf.* I Cor 4:16 ; Phil 3:17. **7-8.** These verses favour a residence of some months in Thessalonica, during which, and afterwards, the praise of their life *sounded forth* in all directions. **9.** ' they themselves ' : the inhabitants of Macedonia and Achaia.—' from idols ' : implying that the majority had formerly been pagans, not Jews. **10.** St Paul urges them to order their life towards the Second Coming and to look forward to it ; he does not imply that they will live to see it— *cf.* §914*j*.—' the wrath to come ' : the judgement of condemnation on the wicked at the Parousia, *cf.* 5:9 ; 2 Thess 1:8.

c II 1-12 A Defence of his Conduct amongst them— The apologetic character of this description of his preaching is apparent in the praise of his own work and life among them. **1.** ' not in vain ' : neither hollow nor lacking in sincerity. **2.** *Cf.* Ac 16:19 f. which relates their scourging and imprisonment.—' in much carefulness ' : in much *striving*. **3.** His motives for preaching were entirely pure and disinterested. He taught neither error nor indulgence of sexual passion nor did he use guile or deceit to attract converts.—' exhortation ' : practically equals *instruction*. **5.** ' occasion ' : pretext, *i.e.* a pretended disinterestedness regarding money. **7.** ' been burdensome ' : they might have claimed either ' special honour ' or ' the expenses ' of their board and lodging, *cf.* the proverb ' honos propter onus '.—' little ones ' : the balance of textual evidence is slightly in favour of the Vg ' little ones ' (*νήπιοι*) as against ' gentle ' (*ἤπιοι*). Because of the sudden change of metaphor, by which St Paul first describes himself as a babe and then in the next line as a nursing-mother, many would prefer ' gentle '. But the change of metaphor is Pauline and our present text should stand.—' a nurse ' : he loves them like a mother and teaches them like a father (v 11). The true punctuation of 7-8 is uncertain.—**9** : *cf.* Ac 18:3 ; Phil 4:15 f. **12.** *cf.* Gal 5:21 ; I Cor 6:9 ; 15:24,50 ; 2 Thess 1:5.—' kingdom ' : the Kingdom of the Messias whose ' glory ' will be revealed at the end of the world. This Kingdom consists in an invisible sharing of the divine nature on earth, a sharing that will become visible and glorious in the definitive and eternal phase of God's Kingdom.

d 13-16 Praise of their Behaviour : Condemnation of the Jews—13. ' which worketh ', *viz.* the Word of God. **14.** ' *imitators* ' of the Christian Churches in Judaea ; by suffering persecution from their fellow-citizens and countrymen in Thessalonica ; it was indeed an honour for them to suffer in such good company. The Judaean persecutions in question are probably those referred to in Ac 8:1 f. ; 9:1-2 ; 12:1. **15-16.** This outburst of St Paul's against the Jews is not paralleled elsewhere and seems to have been evoked by their opposition to his work at Corinth as formerly at Thessalonica and Beroea.—' the prophets ' : *cf.* Mt 5:12 ; 23:34.—' adversaries to all men ' : precisely because they do all in their power to prevent St Paul preaching to the pagan world. Nothing was so repugnant to them as the proclamation that they no longer had a monopoly of the Messianic Kingdom. ' to fill up ' : *cf.* Mt 23:32. When the pre-ordained measure of their sins has been filled to capacity (the process has been long drawn out) then retribution will fall suddenly. Whilst the time God allows to all men is a time for acquiring their measure of grace to those who repent, for the stiff-necked it is by their own fault a time for filling up the measure of their sins.—' the wrath of God ' is either the Day of Judgement, or the destruction of Jerusalem and the public rejection of the Jewish race, as foretold by Christ (Mt 24). The latter is more likely.—' is come upon them to the end ' :

the verb is proleptic, *i.e.* St Paul is so sure of the **915d** terrible penalty awaiting the Jews that he speaks as if it has already come upon them ' *to the uttermost* '.

17-III 10 St Paul's anxiety about them until re- **e** lieved by Timothy's return. **17.** ' have *been anxious beyond measure* to see your face '. **18.** ' us ' : here, Paul himself. **19.** ' Coming ' : the Parousia, the technical word used to signify the glorious coming of Christ at the end of the world ; *cf.* Mt 24:3 f.

III 2. ' *deacon* of God ' : another reading, ' *fellow-worker* of God ', is also well attested ; *cf.* I Cor 3:9. **3-4.** *cf.* Ac 14:21. **5.** ' The Tempter ' is Satan ; *cf.* Mt 4:3. **6-10.** Timothy's favourable report filled him with joy and gave him fresh life. **10.** ' accomplish those things that are wanting ' : to complete their catechetical instruction so abruptly broken off, *cf.* Ac 17:5.

11-13 A Prayer for the Thessalonians—He prays God not only to bring him to them but to enlarge their charity and keep them in readiness for the coming (Parousia) of Christ. **11.** ' direct ' : this verb is singular in the Greek, thus showing that the two Persons, Father and Son, share the same divine nature. **13.** Christians are to direct all their attention to preparation for the Last Judgement, of which the Particular Judgement at the hour of death is in a sense merely the anticipation.—' the saints ' : probably the angels, *cf.* Zach 14:5 ; Mt 25:31 ; the souls of the just do not seem to be included under the term here. The ' Amen ' is possibly a liturgical addition.

IV 1-11 Exhortations to Purity (1-8), Love of the f Brethren (9-10) and Honest Work (11)—St Paul here reaffirms certain precepts of the Christian moral code that he had already explained at Thessalonica. **3.** The first principle of this code is that God expects all Christians to be holy, *i.e.* ' separated from sin ', and in the first place to preserve their holiness or sanctity (*ἁγιασμός*) by abstention from every form of sexual vice (*πορνεία*). But among the ancient heathen, as with the modern pagan, the commonest and greatest obstacle to a holy way of life was extra-marital sexual indulgence, which was regarded as practically inevitable and was treated almost as a matter of course like eating and drinking. Hence the necessity of giving stringent charges against it to Gentile converts. **4.** Commentators, both ancient and modern, are about equally divided between taking *σκεῦος κτᾶσθαι* to mean either (1) to acquire or gain possession (control) of his own body, or (2) to acquire (*i.e.* marry) his own wife. The former explanation would lay emphasis on personal chastity, and the latter on chastity in marriage. **6a.** ' And that no one should *sin against* or *take advantage of* his brother *in this matter*.' **6b-8.** The reasons for these prohibitions. The appeal to the indwelling of the Holy Spirit is his supreme argument in his exhortations to purity ; *cf.* I Cor 6:19. **11.** Apparently certain weaker-minded brethren, obsessed by a belief in a speedy return of Christ gave up earning their living, thus drawing the ridicule of non-Christians (' them that are without ') to whom they had not been ' *behaving fittingly* ', and becoming a charge upon the community (' and that you *need* nothing of any man's '), *cf.* 2 Thess 3:10 f.

IV 12-V 11 The Second Coming—This passage is **916a** remarkable for the large number of reminiscences of the First Gospel, which indicate that St Paul was familiar with the Greek text of Mt 24. He here answers two questions conveyed to him through Timothy concerning—

(A) 12-18 The Lot of those who die before the Parousia—12. *cf.* Mt 27:52 ; Jn 11:11. The Thessalonians knew their dead would rise again but apparently feared that they would not find them in Christ's retinue at the time of his glorious return. **13.** St Paul assures them that their dead will indeed be there ; ' slept through Jesus ', a unique phrase, equivalent to ' the dead who are in Christ ' of 15, *cf.* Rom 14:7-8. **14.** ' In (the) word of the Lord ' must either mean ' on the direct authority of a personal revelation of Christ

916a to St Paul himself ', or it must refer to some saying or teaching of our Lord's not recorded in the Bible, since nowhere in the Gospels did He touch on this precise point. ' we who are alive . . .' : this much discussed phrase is either (1) a quotation from the words of the question put by the Thessalonians, or (2) a literary device, common in St Paul, by which he puts himself into the place and state of mind of his correspondents, and ranks himself among those, whether now living or yet unborn, whom the Lord will find alive at his return. As it is clear from his answer to their second question (5:1–12) that neither he nor anyone else knows the time of the Second Coming, there can be no question here of his either teaching or hinting at the imminence of the Parousia, as many moderns have thought. His utilization of Mt 24 is conclusive of his conformity with Christ's own teaching on the Parousia, cf. § 914i.

b **15.** ' with a *shout of command,* [*viz.*] with an archangel's voice and with God's trumpet ', cf. Mt 24:31 ; 1 Cor 15:52. This act will re-establish the holy dead in full equality with those living at the last day. **16.** Then will take place both for those newly raised from the dead and for those who are alive the mysterious transformation that will make their bodies incorruptible and immortal and enable them to enjoy the beatific vision and union. There is no indication here or elsewhere of an interval for a millenary terrestrial reign of Christ before his heavenly reign begins, as Schweitzer thought. **17.** Since those who have already died in Christ will therefore be at no disadvantage in the Resurrection of the Just, there is no ground for anxiety, but only for consolation.

c **(B) V 1–11 The Uncertainty of the Time of the Parousia**—Having explained the identity of the lot of the living and of the dead at the moment of the Parousia, St Paul now deals with the second question : Is the Parousia close at hand ? **1–2.** Neither the time in general nor the particular date can be known ; cf. Mt 24:43. The Parousia is the supreme ' day of the Lord '. **3.** It is abundantly clear that St Paul had the thought of Mt 24:36–51 before his mind when he wrote this answer. The Parousia will be as catastrophic as the Deluge and as unheralded and as sudden as the visit of the thief in the night. **4–8.** No one can escape the visitation, but it is possible to be ready for it whenever it comes, and to live in a state of watchfulness. As Christians belong to the light and to the day and not to the darkness of sin they will confidently await ' the day of the Lord ', provided they have been ever watchful and sober and have put on the armour of the three theological virtues. **9.** ' but unto the *acquisition* of salvation ', to which God predestines all believers. **10.** In any case whether alive or dead when he comes matters nothing in comparison with living with Jesus (in heaven) afterwards.

d **12–14 Exhortations to Laity and Clergy**—**12–13.** The laity are invited to respect and love the hierarchy set by St Paul to work among, rule over, and advise them. **14.** ' rebuke the *disorderly* ' : cf. 2 Thess 3:6. The Greek ἄτακτος literally refers to a soldier who breaks ranks. The hierarchy in Thessalonica, probably as yet only priests and deacons, are to be conscientious, patient and universally charitable.

15–18. Four general directions, summarizing the Christian life, for the practice of charity, joy, prayer and thanksgiving.

19–21. Brief advice on the treatment of charismata at liturgical assemblies, cf. 1 Cor 12 and 14, where he treats of ' prophesying ' and the ' speaking with tongues ', etc., at much greater length. ' Extinguish not the Spirit ' : '*do not suppress*' such manifestations of the Holy Spirit.

e **23–28 Final Prayers and Requests**—**23.** ' that your entire spirit and soul and body may be preserved *free from all defect* . . .' This passage does not prove that St Paul believed in a trichotomy or threefold division of the human being, as opposed to the dichotomy or twofold division he follows elsewhere, cf. Prat, *La Théologie de Saint Paul*, 1925[12], II, 61, 173–4 490–2. For him σῶμα is the material body, ψυχή the soul, the principle of the sensible life and seat of the passions. πνεῦμα on the other hand, is the most elevated part of the soul by which it resembles God, *i.e.* the reason informed by grace. **26** : cf. Rom 16:16, 1 Cor 16:20, doubtless, the origin of the liturgical kiss of peace. **27.** He demands that the epistle be publicly read so that it may reach the ears of all in the Thessalonian church.

2 THESSALONIANS

I 1–2 Greeting—Cf. 1 Thess 1:1.

3–12 Thanksgiving and Encouragement—This thanksgiving and warm appreciation of their spiritual progress is intended to prepare them for the rebuke in the next chapter. **4.** They have well understood and faithfully carried out the principal teachings of St Paul, especially in their endurance of external and internal trials. **5.** ' For a *pledge* ' : lit. proof ; their present suffering is a sure sign of their future reward. **6–10.** A digression on the rewards and punishments to be meted out respectively to the just and to sinners at the Parousia, by a complete reversal of the fortunes of persecutors and persecuted. **8.** Two classes of wicked : (1) those who have failed to keep the natural law of God, (2) those who have heard the Gospel and rejected it. **9.** ' who shall suffer *just judgement,* eternal destruction [separation] from the face of the Lord ' *i.e.* the pain of loss of God ; whereas for the just there will be the beatitude of eternal union. **10.** ' in that day ' : the day of the Parousia. This phrase is to be taken with ' when he shall come '. **11b.** *i.e.* make fully efficacious every delight [of yours] in goodness and activity inspired by faith. **12.** The ' name ' of Christ is put for the Person according to the usual biblical manner of expression.

II 1–12 The Parousia and the Antichrist—This pericope contains much matter the interpretation of which still remains obscure. Paul not only borrows words and phrases from the apocalyptic passages of the OT and NT but speaks elliptically as well. He develops further the teaching of 1 Thess 4:13 ff. The basis of his teaching is, however, to be found in Mt 24 and Daniel 11 ; cf. § 914i.

1. ' And *as regards* the coming of our Lord . . . we beseech you ' ; cf. Mt 24:31, Mk 13:27. The Apostle proceeds to answer two questions that have been put to him on the coming of the Lord and on the gathering together of the faithful to Christ. **2.** ' . . . nor be *troubled*, neither by spirit nor by *discourse* nor by *epistle*, as *though* from us, as if the day of the Lord *was here* '. It appears that some had not only ignored the Apostle's previous letter (1 Thess) but had actually falsely invoked his authority for spreading a rumour that the Day of the Parousia was actually ' dawning '. **3.** They are not to be deceived ; the Parousia is not imminent. ' For [*the Day of the Lord will not come*] unless there come the revolt first ' against Christ (which itself presupposes the conversion of a large part of the world) and there be revealed ' the man of *lawlessness*, the son of perdition ', *i.e.* the man who is not only destined to perdition but brings perdition (as Christ brings salvation). **4.** The phraseology is apocalyptic and need not be taken literally : the meaning is that the opposer (whom we may justly equate with the Antichrist of Jn 17:12, 1 Jn 2:18, etc.) will endeavour to substitute himself for the true God and to obtain full divine honours from men. **5.** It is clear that when St Paul was personally instructing them he had expounded carefully and at length (cf. 1 Thess 5:2) the apocalyptic teaching of Mt 24 and Dan 7:25 ff., 11:36 ff., cf. § 914i. **6.** The meaning seems to be : And now you have yourselves had experience of the working of the withholding or restraining power which keeps the Man of Lawlessness in check until his appointed time. The revelation of the Man of Lawlessness is dependent on the removal of a mysterious obstacle that is described in 6 as τὸ κατέχον (what withholdeth) and in 7 as ὁ κατέχων (he who withholdeth). Among the many suggestions as to the nature of this obstacle, the following seem to be the most plausible ; (a) Tertullian's view that it is the Roman Empire seen as ' a restraining power of law and order ' ; (b) the view (proposed by Buzy and followed by Amiot) that it is the collectivity constituted by the sum total of the preachers of the Gospel ; and (c) the view of Prat that it is the Archangel St Michael who appears as the champion against the forces of evil in Dan 12:1 and Apoc 12:7-9 ; 20:1-3, 7, where the angel binds and looses Satan. There is no tradition of the Church on this point to **d** assist us to decide. **7.** ' Mystery ' here means ' a secret to be revealed '.—' the mystery of *lawlessness* ' probably denotes the present secret and partially ineffective activity of the Man of Lawlessness ; *cf.* Buzy, RSR (1934) 404 f. This verse confirms the statement of 6. The lawlessness is at present working secretly on account of the check imposed, but ' *only until he who now withholds be taken out of the way* '. **8.** ' Then shall *the Lawless One* be revealed ', only to find himself destroyed by the mere breath of the Lord's mouth, imagery borrowed from Is 11:4. **9-11.** A description of the Parousia of the Antichrist, the Man of Lawlessness. The removal of the withholding or restraining power will permit the Parousia of the Antichrist, a lying counterpart of the true Parousia of Christ that will follow it and immediately destroy the Lawless One. **9.** ' in all *lying* power and signs and wonders '. **10.** ' The love of the truth ' may be taken objectively as the love the truth has for men, or subjectively as the love of men for the truth. ' To believe *the Lie*.' **11.** ' have consented to *unrighteousness* '. For further discussion of the nature of this apostasy, see art. *Eschatologie, op. cit.*

e **The Character of the Antichrist**—Is the Antichrist to be an individual or a collectivity ? Most modern commentators consider him to be a mere personification of the evil forces that will, it seems, get the upper hand at the end of the world. According to St Paul the activity of the Man of Lawlessness is already taking place, although he is not yet revealed. He certainly cannot be Satan himself as he receives his powers from him. As this activity has been going on for nineteen

centuries, the Antichrist would seem to be an apocalyptic **917e** personification of the powers of evil let loose. Moreover in the Gospels (esp. Mt 24) our Lord nowhere speaks of one Antichrist but of many false Christs and false prophets. With this agrees St John's teaching in his Epistles, whilst in the Apocalypse he symbolizes the sum total of persecuting political powers and false prophets by the two beasts who are the emissaries of Satan. On the other hand, the teaching of St Paul on the Antichrist is quite compatible with his being a single person, and the manner in which all the Sacred Books from Daniel to Apocalypse speak of him, as a man incarnating all the forces of evil and as the false counterpart of Christ himself in the last days of the world, does not permit us to lay aside as improbable the view that the Antichrist is indeed an individual ; *cf.* Rigaux, *L'Antéchrist*, Paris, 1932.

12-III 5 Further Encouragement and Exhortation— f 12. ' firstfruits ' : another reading in the Greek which gives the meaning ' from the beginning ' has slightly more MS support. ' of the spirit ', *i.e.* the Holy Spirit. **13.** ' unto the *acquisition* of ' the glory of the Lord when he returns at the Parousia. **14.** Revealed truth is transmitted both by oral and written tradition, as the Church has always taught. **15.** ' in [*his*] grace '. The traditional character of St Paul's own teaching in the matter of the Parousia is discussed in § 914*g-l*. **III:2.** ' *for not to all does the faith belong* '. **3.** ' from *the evil one* ' ; there seems to be a reminiscence of the Our Father in this and the preceding verse.

III 6-15 A Special Exhortation to work—*Cf.* I Thess 5:14. All are bidden to act in accord with the Apostle's teaching and to get on quietly with their daily work, and to avoid vain idling in view of the supposed imminence of the Parousia. **11b.** The play of words in the Greek is preserved in the well-known rendering ' doing no business but being busybodies '. **13-15.** A special word to the main body of loyal followers of the Apostle. The offender is to be subject to a minor excommunication to bring him to a more reasonable frame of mind. **13.** ' . . . *do not fail* in well doing '.

16-18 Conclusion—16. ' *peace at all times and in every way* '. **17.** As a sign of authenticity (in view of 2 Thess 2:2) St Paul here pointedly directs the attention of his correspondents to his custom of autographing the final salutation in every epistle of his.

THE PASTORAL EPISTLES
1 and 2 TIMOTHY, TITUS

By R. J. FOSTER

918a Bibliography—*H. Alford, *The Greek Testament*, III, Cambridge, 1894 ; R. G. Bandas, *The Master Idea of St Paul's Epistles or the Redemption*, Bruges, 1925 ; G. Bardy, *Epîtres Pastorales*, Paris, 1938 (*La Sainte Bible*, Pirot, XII) ; P. Delatte, O.S.B., *Les Epîtres de Saint Paul*, Louvain, 1928 ; *P. N. Harrison, *The Problem of the Pastoral Epistles*, Oxford, 1921 ; *A. E. Humphreys, *The Epistles to Timothy and Titus*, Cambridge, 1925 ; J. Knabenbauer, CSS, 1923 ; *W. Lock, *The Pastoral Epistles*, Edinburgh, 1924 (ICC) ; J. McEvilly, *An Exposition of the Epistles of St Paul*, Dublin, 1875 ; *R. St J. Parry, *The Pastoral Epistles*, Cambridge, 1920 ; F. Prat, *The Theology of St Paul*, Eng. Trans., London, 1926 ; C. Spicq, O.P., *Les Epîtres Pastorales*, Paris, 1947 ; CNT ; WV ; SCSS ; E. Valton, *Evêques*, DTC ; A. Michiels, *Evêques*, DAFC ; L. Marchal, *Evêques*, DBVS ; H. Dieckmann, *De Ecclesia*, Freiburg, 1924.

b The Name—These three epistles are usually grouped together under the title *Pastoral Epistles*, a name which fittingly describes their character, since they are not addressed to any church or individual in his private capacity, but to Timothy and Titus *as pastors* for their guidance in ruling the communities committed to their care. The use of the word *pastoral* in connexion with them goes back at least to the time of Thomas Aquinas (*cf*. Prol. to 2 Tim), but the modern practice of referring to them as the Pastorals may be traced to the course of lectures given at Halle University by Paul Anton in 1726–7, *cf*. Harrison, 13 ; Spicq, xxi.

c The Occasion and Date of the Epistles—In the course of a general tour of the East, probably in the year A.D. 66, as St Paul was making his way up the coast of Asia Minor towards Macedonia he left Timothy at Ephesus to deal with a dangerous situation brought about by the activities of false teachers. 1 Tim was written during this journey, maybe in Macedonia itself. No doubt St Paul was anxious because of the grave responsibilities resting on Timothy's youthful shoulders, and so wished to renew his counsels and warning in writing. At this time too he wrote the epistle to Titus who was confronted in Crete with a situation very similar to that at Ephesus. 2 Tim was written shortly after the Apostle had been re-arrested, and taken back to Rome, while he was awaiting his final trial. Knowing that death was imminent he summoned Timothy to Rome by letter and at the same time renewed his warnings and counsels, urging him to courage in the faithful fulfilment of his pastoral charge. The Pastoral Epistles, therefore, help us to fill in the gap between the end of Acts and Paul's death.

d Timothy—Timothy, who belonged to Lystra in Lycaonia, was the son of a Jewish mother and a Gentile father. He was probably converted to the Christian faith along with Eunice, his mother, and Lois, his grandmother, during St Paul's first missionary journey. When the latter revisited Lystra he resolved to make Timothy his companion in future missionary work. On account of the Jews Paul was careful to have his disciple circumcised in order to facilitate his work amongst the members of the Chosen Race with whom they were so frequently to make contact. From that time onwards he became the Apostle's constant companion. As is shown by the frequent references to him

in the epistles and by the important missions he accomplished (*cf*. 1 Thess 3:2 ; 1 Cor 4:17 ; 16:10), he enjoyed St Paul's complete confidence : ' For I have no man so of the same mind, who with sincere affection is solicitous for you', Phil 2:20. During the first Roman imprisonment he was with his master and afterwards accompanied him as far as Ephesus on the last missionary journey. There he was left to take charge of the local church, *cf*. 1 Tim 1:3. In 2 Tim he is bidden to go to Rome before the winter, 4:21. Little is known of his later life as bishop of Ephesus.

Titus—Titus who was a Gentile was probably con- **e** verted to the faith by St Paul who addresses him as his ' beloved son ', 1:4. He accompanied Paul and Barnabas on their journey to Jerusalem and, although the Judaizers demanded that he be circumcised, Paul resisted them ; *cf*. Gal 2:1 ff. During the third missionary journey Titus was twice sent on urgent missions to Corinth and succeeded in restoring harmony between that Church and its Apostle, 2 Cor 7:13-15 ; 8:16-24. We lose sight of him after this until the time of the epistle addressed to him. This found him in Crete, where he had been entrusted with the organization of the Church, Tit 1:5. Later he was summoned to meet Paul at Nicopolis in Epirus and eventually during the final imprisonment he was sent to Dalmatia, 2 Tim 4:10.

The Authenticity of the Pastoral Epistles—Their **f** authenticity is not universally admitted today, *cf*. for example, *A. M. Farrer, *The Ministry in the NT*, in *The Apostolic Ministry*, ed. K. E. Kirk, Oxford, 1946, p 160 : ' Of course the Pastorals affect antiquity and apostolic authorship, and it is conceivable that in Titus the writer becomes suddenly conscious of the pose and puts in an equation between elders and bishops which he believes to have once obtained '. The arguments brought against their authenticity have been ably summarized by Harrison, whose thesis is that the ' epistles received their present shape at the hands, not of Paul, but of a Paulinist living in the early years of the second century ', p v. Briefly the difficulties may be grouped together under three headings : (i) The views attacked in the Pastorals are Gnostic in character and belong to a period later than St Paul. (ii) The Church organization implied is too advanced. (iii) The style and more especially the *vocabulary* are not the Apostle's. On these points one may suggest the **g** following considerations. (i) The historical background of the Pastorals does not require the developed Gnostic environment of the 2nd century. As indicated § 919*d*, the teachers mentioned in the epistles were for the most part Jews, and errors similar to theirs may be found described in Col, the authenticity of which is generally accepted, *cf*. Col 2:4, 8, 16, 23. Points of similarity between their teaching and that of the later Gnostics may be admitted. (ii) Church organization found in the Pastorals, far from being too advanced, is exactly what would be expected at the period when they purport to have been written, *i.e*. at the end of Paul's life. His authority is as clear and decisive as ever, he gives commands and guidance to his representatives. What we should expect and what we actually find is the new position in which these representatives now find themselves. Since Paul is near the end of his life they are made to feel that for the future the responsi-

8g bility which he had borne so long is to be theirs. They are to succeed him and carry his burden. Such is the setting into which the Pastorals fit. Also the absence of a clearly defined hierarchy in the Pastorals, such as certainly existed in the 2nd cent, is another indication

h that they were written in the 1st century. (iii) **The Style of the Pastorals**—The Apostle's style varies, the earlier epistles differing in style from the Captivity epistles, and it has been remarked that it would not be easy to prove that 1 Thess, Col and 1 Cor all come from the same pen. The Pastorals, although possessing traits common to Phil have a style of their own, simpler, clearer, more rhythmic and balanced than the other Paulines and they lack those long difficult periods. The language is more technical and shows a wider Hellenistic vocabulary.

However, if we take account of the time when they were written, of their purpose and of their recipients, we should expect a change from Paul's other writings and precisely that change in style actually found in the Pastorals. Here, for instance, we have a man advanced in years, who recalls the past, as older men like to do (1 Tim 1:12-17 ; 2 Tim 1:3, 6 ; 2:2 ; 3:10-12 ; Tit 1:5) and, mellowed by age, thinks of the future, by love, advice, and counsel urging his younger disciples to continue his work. He is no longer writing under the stress of everyday events and publicly solving the problems of harassed churches, but is advising trusted disciples about safeguarding the Church of the future. He is not now concerned to argue and to prove with his earlier impetuosity, but rather to exhort and to guide. His style is therefore more measured and calm, without declamation or rhetorical argument and in consequence the syntax, too, shows a change,

i e.g. the absence of particles, ἄρα, οὖν, (absent also from Col and Phil but present in Gal) also ἴδε, ἰδού, ποῦ, cf. Spicq cxv. It would be a matter for surprise if a man of dynamic character like Paul, capable of the differing style of Phil and Gal, and of adapting himself to such contrasted situations as those found at Athens and Ephesus (Ac 17:22-31 ; 20:18-35) a man, moreover of long and varied ministry and one who had spent the previous four or five years in the new environment of Rome, did not show some changes in his later writings, the Pastorals. Plato whose literary evolution in old age is even greater than that of Paul, shows a similar tendency to a more uniform style and a newer and wider vocabulary. In some respects the same has been shown to be the case with Schiller, Goethe, and Shakespeare. St Paul in thus adapting himself to his new milieu and using his wider acquaintance with the Hellenistic world in presenting the Gospel message—as for instance using the pagan Hellenistic words γυμνασία and εὐσέβεια in 1 Tim 4:8 —sets us an example of turning current language and usage to good account in conveying Christian truth ; cf. further Spicq, loc. cit. But though there is this natural change, the usual Pauline characteristics are there : the anacolutha and parentheses (1 Tim 1:3-5 ; 10-12 ; Tit 1:1), the same love of compound words (cf. Spicq cviii, n. 3), the same lists and maxims (1 Tim 2:1-2 ; 3:2-4 ; 4:1-3 ; 5:12 f. ; 6:4 f. ; 2 Tim 3:1-5 ; 4:7 ; Tit 1:8-10), the same antitheses (2 Tim 1:7, 12), the Hebraisms and metaphors from military life and sport and the same formulae of salutation.

19a The argument based on difference of vocabulary is more forceful. Harrison points out that the ' Pastorals consist of some 902 words of which 54 are proper names. Of the remaining 848, 306 or 36 per cent are not found in any of the ten Paulines ', 20. Further the vocabulary bears a striking resemblance to that of the Apostolic Fathers and Latin writers of the early 2nd cent., and hence, it is argued, would point to a 2nd cent. date. The list of Pauline hapax legomena is impressive, but it must not be used too forcefully, otherwise it might prove three separate authors for the three epistles ! The list includes words which occur in LXX and would therefore have been known to Paul ; there are cognates to words used elsewhere by him and words

which must have been current at that time but which **919a** he had no occasion to use previously, e.g. terms dealing with Church organization and erroneous doctrines. That new subject-matter does give occasion for new vocabulary is clear, for example, from 1 Cor where 200 of the 310 hapax legomena occur in sections treating of new subjects. Parry gives the number of hapax legomena in the Pastorals connected with new subjects as 286. In fact, of the 306 Pastoral hapax legomena 131 occur elsewhere in the NT (125 of these also occur in writings before A.D. 50) and of the remaining 175 at least 153 can be quoted before A.D. 50. The probability is then that the few remaining words are previous to and not later than that date since words may be long current in daily use before they appear in literary works, cf. F. R. Montgomery Hitchcock, ' Tests for the **b** Pastorals ', JTS 30 (1929) 279. Spicq notes that only 18 words have not been found in writers before A.D. 100 (p cx). Difference in expression and width of vocabulary are also to be expected from the Apostle's contact with Latin idiom and Roman Greek, thus εὐχαριστῶ gives place to χάριν ἔχω (gratiam habeo), διό to δι' ἣν αἰτίαν (quam ob causam) and the frequent πιστὸς ὁ λόγος corresponds to the Latin proverb, ' verum illud verbum ', cf. Spicq, cxiv. This Latin influence would also account for the similarity to the pagan Latin writers and the Apostolic Fathers, since Clement, Hermas, and Justin were Christians of Rome and therefore subject to the same influences as Paul. Nor should one neglect the similarities between the vocabularies of the Pastorals and earlier Epistles for, of the 612 words they all have in common, 38 are proper to Paul and are not found elsewhere in the NT. In addition many favourite expressions of St Paul are to be found throughout the Pastorals, e.g. οἴδαμεν δὲ ὅτι, εἰ δέ τις and see the full list in Spicq cxvii. There remains, lastly, the possibility that Paul used a secretary; Luke has been suggested since he was in close contact with him at this time and so may have been responsible for the more ordered and Hellenistic style.

Finally it is impossible to explain how these epistles **c** came to be assigned to St Paul if they did not actually belong to him. The **external evidence** for their Pauline character is overwhelming : there are the **explicit statements** of Irenaeus, Adv. Haer., I, 1, Prol. ; III, 3 ; 4 ; 14, PG 7, 438 ; 755 ; 854 ; 914 ; the Muratorian Fragment, lines 60 ff.; Clement of Alexandria, Strom., 1:1 ; 14 ; II, 11, PG 8, 690 ; 758 ; 990 ; Tertullian, C. Marc., V, 21 ; De Praescr., 25 ; De Pudic., 13, PL 2, 20 ; 43 ; 44 ; 556 ; 1057 ; Eusebius, Hist. Eccl., III ; 3:5, PG 20, 218 ; 270. **Implicit testimony** comes from earlier times. In fact Spicq argues that there is a reference in 2 Pet 3:15 to 1 Tim 1:16. 2 Pet alludes to a passage of Paul's regarding Christ's long-suffering with sinners. Although a number of texts from various epistles have been suggested as apposite, none is more suitable than 1 Tim 1:16 where the Apostle sets forth his own case as the classic example of our Lord's long-suffering, cf. Spicq xcv. But much will depend upon the date assigned to 2 Pet, cf. J. Chaine, Les Épîtres Catholiques (Paris, 1939) 28 ff. In Clement of Rome's Epistle to the Corinthians there are more than 25 passages which show close correspondence with the Pastorals ; Ignatius of Antioch, obviously with 1 Tim 1:4 in mind, writes : ' Be not deceived with strange doctrines nor with old fables which are unprofitable ', Magn., 8:1, cf. also Smyrn., 10, 2 and 2 Tim 1:16 ; Polycarp not only shows his acquaintance with the Pastorals, but also presupposes that his readers are familiar with them, cf. Phil., 4:1 and 1 Tim 6:7, 10. The force of tradition regarding the Pauline authorship of the Epistles is so strong that in view of it the Biblical Commission has laid it down that they are to be held as Pauline. It also states that this opinion is not weakened by the difficulties commonly advanced from differences of style and language, cf. § 51l-o ; SCSS 3, 352 f.

The Doctrine of the Pastorals. **d**
The Preservation of True Doctrine—At Ephesus and

919d Crete, where Timothy and Titus exercised their episcopal ministry, false teachers, for the most part of Jewish origin, were spreading error of a pernicious character. Their teaching was not markedly heretical, but in the nature of misleading conjecture or vain quibbling in the Jewish rabbinical style : ' From which things some going astray, are turned aside unto vain babbling, desiring to be teachers of the law ', 1 Tim 1:6-7. The consequences, however, were grave ; strife and contention were engendered and threatened the unity and harmony of the communities, *cf.* 2 Tim 2:23 ; faith became enfeebled so that some of the faithful began to fall away, and already there appear traces of the erroneous practices characteristic of the later Gnostics and Manicheans ; *cf.* 1 Tim 4:3. The position was aggravated by the motive actuating the false teachers, which was ' filthy lucre ', Tit 1:10 f. To counteract this evil the Apostle relied upon a zealous, carefully chosen ministry jealously guarding the ' deposit of faith ' and handing on ' sound doctrine '

e to communities of well-ordered life. The **sound doctrine** of which St Paul stresses the need is that received from the Apostles : ' Hold the form of sound words *which thou hast heard of me* ', 2 Tim 1:13 f. It is ' sound ', *i.e. health-giving* (ὑγιαινοῦσα) in contrast to the ' canker ' of error, 2 Tim 2:17. Such is its importance for the well-being of the community that Timothy was urged to grasp it firmly and retain it, to preach it carefully and publicly without fear or favour, to select diligently fellow workers who in their turn would transmit it faithfully, *cf.* 1 Tim 4:11, 13, 16 ; 5:22 ; 6:3 ; 2 Tim 2:2 ; 4:2 ; Tit 2:1 f. St Paul was anxious to secure this faithful transmission of the Truth because of the dangers which he knew to lie ahead and against which he uttered repeated warnings, *cf.* 2 Tim 3:1 ff. ; 4:3. In a striking passage illustrative of his inspiring faith he described the Church herself as the ' pillar and ground of truth ', 1 Tim 3:15. She is a witness, she safeguards the truth, explains its hidden mysteries and preserves the moral life which is necessarily based upon it. Nevertheless, although the Church is a fortress against error, much depends upon the life and character of her ministers, and so he stresses the need for them to maintain high ideals, preserve good morals, and preach sound doctrine, 1 Tim 3:1 ff. ; Tit 1:5 ff. With impressive urgency he concludes, 1 Tim : ' O Timothy, keep that which is committed to thy trust, avoiding the profane novelties of words and oppositions of knowledge falsely so called, which some *professing* have erred concerning the faith '. In our modern way of speech St Paul is teaching that Christ's doctrine must be handed on and will be guaranteed by an infallible Church guided by the Spirit of God, which now as ever has need of apostolic and worthy priests.

f Bishop and Presbyter—While dealing with the organization of the communities St Paul makes mention of the *presbyters* and of the office and qualities of a bishop, *episcopos*. What light do the Pastorals throw upon the difficult Episcopos-Presbyter question and what distinction do they make in their use of these terms ? Whatever view is taken of the identity of presbyters and episcopoi in the NT, the *existence* of bishops in the modern sense in Apostolic times is in no way in doubt. For example, there is no doubt that Timothy and Titus themselves were bishops since they ordain, 1 Tim 5:19-22 ; Tit 1:5-7 ; 1 Tim 3:8-10 ; they are responsible for sound doctrine and judge the presbyters, 1 Tim 1:3 ; 3:1-15 ; 4:11 ; 5:19 ; 6:2 ; 2 Tim 4:2-5. It is likely that in the beginning the Apostles kept in their own hands the control of the churches they founded, sending their fellow missionaries who possessed episcopal authority, *legati a latere* as it were, to represent them, and the *presbyter-episcopoi* would assist in their work under their direction in the localities to which they were appointed.

g First of all it can be admitted that from the beginning of the 2nd cent., in Asia Minor at least, the title *episcopos* was reserved to the ecclesiastical superior now known as bishop, *cf.* Ignatius of Antioch, *Phil* 1:1 ; *Eph* 2 ; *Magn* 2, and that *presbyter* corresponded with the modern use of priest. But it cannot be shown that this usage held in the 1st cent., and different interpretations are given of the passages in the NT where these terms occur. Catholic opinions may be reduced to five classes : (i) The two words correspond to the modern use of bishop and priest. (ii) The two words were used indiscriminately to include bishops and priests. (iii) That all, whether *episcopoi* or presbyters, were bishops. (iv) That the words were synonymous and indicated *simple priests only*. In favour **h** of this view it has been pointed out that nowhere in the NT do we find the expression ' bishops and priests ' (or its equivalent) as representing two distinct orders or classes. On the contrary the names are closely connected and refer to the same ministers. This would explain the omission of presbyters in Phil 1:1 ; 1 Tim 3. In Ac 20:17 ff. Paul addresses the presbyters of Ephesus as *episcopoi*, though they were not bishops, since he later left Timothy there to exercise episcopal duties. The reason for the title on this occasion would be that these presbyters exercised an ' episcopacy ', *i.e.* the function or duty of ' supervising ' or ' shepherding ' the local community. Similarly in 1 Pet 5:1 f. the presbyters are urged to fulfil their office of *episcopoi*. The Apostle orders Titus (1:5) to set up presbyters in each city, and in speaking of their necessary virtues and character lays down what is demanded of an *episcopos*, a way of reasoning which shows that the *episcopos* is a presbyter. The parallelism of Tit 1:6 and 1 Tim 3:1 ff. and the lists of qualities there given show the close connexion between the *episcopos* of Timothy and the presbyter of Titus. (Both passages are referred to in the ordination of a priest and the consecration of a bishop, and both are used in the first nocturn of a Confessor Bishop.) (v) The latest view, that of **92** Spicq, 84 ff., is a modification of iv. In his opinion the words were at one time used one for the other, but there had been a gradual adaptation of names corresponding with the progressive evolution of the hierarchy. The word ἐπισκέπτομαι, for instance, at first denoted one aspect of an Apostle's ministry, namely the periodic visitation and vigilant supervision of the various communities ; *cf.* Ac 15:36. Then the name *episcopos* was employed gradually for priests who exercised the pastoral ministry in the local churches ; *cf.* Ac 20:28 and Phil 1:1. By the time of the Pastorals the name *episcopos* had become a technical term for a *special kind of presbyter*, namely a *presiding* one, who fulfilled a special function, the episcopacy, whose duty it was to preside and in whom special qualities were sought. Thus the way was prepared for the still later use of the word *episcopos* to denote the rulers of the Church, the successors of the Apostles, *i.e.* bishops in the modern sense of the word. For an interesting contribution to the discussion by an Anglican theologian, see G. Dix, *The Apostolic Ministry*, 1946.

Evidence for this view is found by Spicq in the Pas- **b** torals. Thus in 1 Tim 3:4-5 ; Tit 1:7, the principal function of the *episcopos* is to preside or exercise rule (προιστάμενος), like the father of a family or the administrator of a household, and so a candidate for this office must show signs of an aptitude for exercising authority. It is moreover the first time that the case of an *episcopos* is dealt with explicitly and not merely by way of passing allusion. He is now the holder of an office sufficiently well defined to be the object of a definite desire, an office expressed by the abstract term ἐπισκοπή, 1 Tim 3:1. This use of the word has no parallel in the NT, except in Ac 1:20 where, however, it means the apostolic office. It is also the first time that *episcopos*, immediately related to the office, is used in the singular and that the person receives his appointment by one of Paul's representatives after due examination of his suitability. In other words *episcopos* has become a technical term indicating one who holds a specific office and exercises a particular function. But it is not used with the precise meaning

b which it had in the 2nd cent., *i.e.* to denote the monarchical episcopate, since there is no indication of any
c subordination of presbyters to the *episcopos*. ' In fact it would appear ', says Spicq, ' that the *episcopos* is a presbyter, although every presbyter is no longer an *episcopos* in the new meaning of the term. In other words the presbyter-episcopos has no quality essentially different from that of all other presbyters, nor even, in all likelihood, a privileged dignity—and that is why the desire (ὄρεξις) must be stimulated. But he does exercise a special function'. 93. Thus the office of ἐπισκοπή, common to all presbyters earlier at Ephesus and Philippi, is now reserved to one person specially qualified and, although all priests retain the authority previously exercised, there is but one who presides. His dignity is no greater than that of his fellow priests, but the duty he undertakes is more important, more extensive and charged with greater responsibility than that of the priests as a whole. This function of presiding is as yet vague, but from the analogy with profane literature, the LXX and the context of 1 Tim 3, we might conjecture that the holder of this office would preside at assemblies, direct prayers and take the chief part in worship. In a word, by the time of the Pastorals the word *episcopos* would indicate a priest who was ' primus inter pares '.

d **Christ's Mediatorship**—Although it is true that the Apostle is concerned in these epistles with foiling the attempts made to undo his work, he does, as indeed he must, touch upon those essentials of the Christian faith which occur so frequently in his other epistles. In 1 Tim 2:5 ff. he speaks of Christ's mediatorship showing how he exercises an efficacious mission because, on the one hand he was sent by God and, on the other, is man's representative ; in the hypostatic union two natures are united in one person through whom God and man are brought together in reconciliation : ' For there is one God and one mediator of God and men, the man Jesus Christ, who gave himself a redemption for all '. The word ' gave ' emphasizes Christ's love and obedience, the voluntariness of the act by which he gave his life a ransom to secure our freedom from Satan's thraldom. This idea is developed in Tit 2:14, where the concept of ransom is carried further still to its ultimate effects in us : ' that he might redeem us from all iniquity, and might cleanse to himself a people acceptable, a pursuer of good works ' ; *cf.* 1 Tim 1:15. Another important aspect of the Redemption stressed in the Pastorals is **God's will to save all men.** Since man after the Fall could not of himself regain his lost status, God had to come to his aid. This he did and extended succour to all who responded to his
e call, *cf.* 1 Tim 4:10 ; 1:15 ; 2:4 ; 3:16. **Other important points of doctrine** may be briefly mentioned, we must offer prayers for all (2:1) ; for the living and the dead (2 Tim 1:18) ; the qualities necessary in candidates for orders (Tit 1:5 ff. ; 1 Tim 3:1 ff.) ; the apostolate of good example (1 Tim 4:12) ; the dangers of the active life if divorced from the interior life and without due regard for spiritual perfection : ' Our Lord demands in explicit fashion from all those whom he associates with his apostolate, that not only do they *maintain* their virtue, but that they *make progress* in it. The proof exists in every page of the Epistles of St Paul to Timothy and Titus, and in the appeals of the Apocalypse to the Bishops of Asia ', Dom Chautard, O.C.R., *The Soul of the Apostolate* (Dublin, 1937) 63.

THE FIRST EPISTLE TO TIMOTHY

a **I 1-2 Greeting.**
3-20 The Safeguarding of True Doctrine—Immediately the Apostle presses forward to express the thoughts uppermost in his mind which concern, first and foremost, the urgent need of restraining false teachers and so preventing the spread of false doctrine and practice. **3.** Characteristically he begins with

an unfinished sentence ; in his anxiety to deal with 921a the repression of errors he leaves aside the directions to be given to Timothy to which he returns in ch 2 ; *cf.* 2:1 ' I desire therefore. . . .' **4. Fables and Endless Genealogies**—*Cf.* 4:7 ; 6:20 ; 2 Tim 2:16, 23 ; Tit 3:9. Some think that these were part of some teaching similar to that of the later Gnostics, a sort of pre-Gnosticism, referring to successive generations of aeons or angelic beings from the creator of the material universe. More probably Paul has in mind Jewish speculations which added legends and spurious pedigrees to the OT narrative. The apocryphal *Book of Jubilees* is an excellent example of the futile speculation he is attacking. He is obviously not concerned here with formal heresies which would have been denounced in sterner tones, but rather with vain and idle questions, quibbling about the Law, all of which was either misleading or to no purpose. **5.** ' The b Commandment '—This is either the charge given to Timothy or the Divine Law, the Christian Dispensation itself. ' Unfeigned Faith '—a sincere faith free from any surreptitious compromising with Jewish doctrines and practices. **6.** It appears that these false teachers at Ephesus concerned themselves with the Mosaic Law and the part it should play in Christian life. Their knowledge of the law and their attempts to apply it were at fault. **9.** ' The law is not made for the just man '—St Paul turns aside to discuss the true role of the law, which is to restrain sinners by making them conscious of and giving them a true knowledge of their sins. **10.** ' Who defile themselves with mankind '—who sin against nature. ' Men stealers '—slave-dealers or kidnappers. ' Sound doctrine '—Note St Paul's insistence on a body of truths to be accepted and guarded, *cf.* 1 Thess 4:1 ; 2 Thess 2:14 ; 1 Cor 15:1 ff.
12-17 Personal Digression—The mention of the Gospel c leads him to consider what he owes to God who has made him a minister of the New Covenant. He recalls how he, a sinner and persecutor, has been considered trustworthy and appointed to Christ's ministry. Thoughts such as these were intended to encourage Timothy and all his followers, to spur them on to greater efforts so as not to disappoint him who had placed such trust in them. Paul's vocation was the supreme example of God's long-suffering and lovingkindness. Who but the Apostle himself could have been responsible for this extremely personal message ? It is in itself a guarantee of the authenticity of the passage. **14.** The change wrought in him was complete ; his life was flooded with divine grace, along with faith and love abundantly bestowed. **15.** ' A faithful saying '—This phrase, which occurs several times in the Pastorals, serves to confirm the truth or reliability of a statement : ' It is a true saying '. The saying in this instance is some familiar aphorism which stresses our Lord's work of salvation while at the same time indicating his pre-existence and Incarnation. **16.** ' For the information of them that believe '—The lesson or moral to be drawn is that after the mercy shown to the Apostle none should despair. Paul should serve as a *typical instance* or *pattern* of the way Christ would deal with others. **18.** ' This precept '— the charge given to Timothy. ' The prophecies going before on thee '—probably revelations made either to the Apostle himself or through Christian prophets (*cf.* Ac 13:1 ff.) regarding Timothy's zeal and fitness for the ministry. St Paul recalls the prophecies to inspire him with confidence. **20.** ' Hymenaeus ', whose name occurs again in 2 Tim 2:17, was responsible for the spread of false doctrine, particularly concerning the resurrection. ' Alexander ' may be the coppersmith of 2 Tim 4:14 who grievously wronged the Apostle. ' Delivered up to Satan '—some form of excommunication, *cf.* 1 Cor 5:4 f. ' That they may learn not to blaspheme '—That they may be taught (by correction) not to blaspheme.
II 1-15 Public Worship—**1.** ' For all men '—for all d without exception, not for fellow Christians only.

921d 2. 'For kings and for all that are in high station'—
These are given special mention because their attitude
is fraught with grave consequences for the well-being
of the Church and the individual. The command
gains force when we bear in mind that the ruler then
in power was Nero. The injunction to pray for those
responsible for the guidance of the state is more urgent
today than ever, since society is now so highly organized
and controlled that the individual is liable to be at the
mercy of some form of totalitarian control. 2.
'Chastity'—*gravity*, referring to the serious thought of
our duty towards God and our neighbour. The idea
of the Apostle is this: freedom from anxiety and
uncertainty regarding the intentions of those in charge
of the destiny of the state would enable individuals to
pursue their duty towards God and society and at the
same time enable the Church to continue her apostolate.
e 4. 'Who will have all men to be saved'—'The
clearest anti-Calvinistic text in the NT', *A New Commentary*. Here we have a doctrine of the highest
importance and consolation for each one of us, since
there is no indication in the text of anyone at all being
excluded. On the contrary the discourse is emphatic
and the universality of God's will to save is reinforced
by the fourfold repetition of the word *all* in the first
few verses; *cf.* Prat, II, 78, 'It is vain to object that
the divine wish to save is necessarily limited by the
addition " that all may come to the knowledge of the
truth "; for, we are assured, since this second proposition cannot be absolutely and universally true,
the first one cannot be true either. The reply is easy:
all human beings have not the use of reason, but all,
without a single exception, are capable of eternal
salvation; thus, while the phrase referring to the
knowledge of the truth limits itself naturally to men
who are capable of knowing it, the other is limited by
nothing and should, according to the rules of sound
f exegesis, retain its full significance.' 5. 'One
Mediator'—a confirmation of the universality of
salvation. As man, Jesus represented the whole
human race. Since in him the two natures of God and
of man were united he was able to atone for the sin of
mankind and secure a return of its lost inheritance.
Through him alone we have regained access to the
Father. This passage is not contrary to the Catholic
practice of invoking the aid of the saints, for the
Apostle in speaking of *Christ as Mediator of our redemption*,
says nothing against our invoking the saints as *intercessors*. In fact St Paul himself in asking the prayers of
others, as he frequently does, stresses the need for intercessors that we may more surely make use of the redemption gained for us by the mediation of Christ.
6. 'Redemption'—*cf.* Mt 20:28. 'A testimony in due
times'—At the time appointed by his heavenly Father,
Jesus bore witness to God's will that all should be
saved, and in his turn St Paul, fully conscious of his
special mission to proclaim the universality of the
Gospel, recalls his commission as the Apostle of the
Gentiles. 8. 'Lifting up pure hands'—The customary attitude for prayer was standing erect with
arms outstretched. 'Without anger and contention'
g —fitly disposed for prayer. 9. 'In like manner'—
Women are urged, in the same way as men, to pray
and join in the apostolate of prayer. 'In decent
apparel'—Worship is not the time for display of
fashion; on the contrary, women are to dress with
becoming modesty, making virtuous acts and good
works their glory. On St Paul's teaching regarding
women see an interesting explanation of this passage in
Enjoying the NT by Margaret T. Monro (London, 1945)
153 f. 11. It is the duty of men, not women, to rule
and give instruction in the public assembly; the
reasons for this St Paul adduces from Genesis where it
is shown that man was first created and that woman
was the occasion of his fall. 15. For their part women
are to manifest their own womanly virtues, and St Paul
stresses in particular the sanctifying effect of motherhood, which is one of the means (not the only one,
cf. 1 Cor 7:25 ff.), by which they will be saved.

III 1-13 The Character and Qualifications of 92
Ministers—Following the directions about public
worship the Apostle outlines the character and
qualifications which should be found in priests and
deacons, the Church's ministers. It is Timothy's duty
to safeguard the well-being of Church organization at
Ephesus. 1. 'The office of a bishop'—*cf.* § 919*f*.
'Desireth a good work'—*noble, distinguished* work. The
phrase draws attention to the labour and service
involved in ecclesiastical administration and apostolate.
Those who desire to participate desire something which
is noble and praiseworthy. Spicq suggests another
interpretation. He thinks that at Ephesus there may
have been those who set too great store by extraordinary
charismata to the consequent detriment of those men
daily administering church affairs. Such a mentality
is illustrated in *Didache* 15, 1: 'Now appoint for yourselves bishops and deacons worthy of the Lord, men
meek and not avaricious, upright and proved; for
they, too, render you the service of the prophets and
teachers. Despise them not, therefore, for they are
the ones who are honoured of you together with the
prophets and teachers'. St Paul may, then, have been
recalling here that the episcopacy was a noble function
in itself quite apart from its dignity in relation to other
gifts. Men were needed to undertake it and those
who offered themselves as candidates—this is the
meaning of ὀρέγω rather than 'desire'—were to be
encouraged and congratulated; Spicq 77. 2. Blame- **i**
less'—irreproachable in conduct because of his dignity
as God's representative. 'Husband of one wife'—
Those are not to be accepted who have married again
after the death of their first wife lest this should prove
an occasion for criticism; *cf.* 1 Tim 3:12; 5:9.
Celibacy as a law for the clergy is of later ecclesiastical
institution, although as a counsel it was urged by St Paul
himself, 1 Cor 7:8 ff. 3. 'No striker'—Not given to
violence or brawling, not contentious or aggressive.
4. 'In subjection with all chastity'—*with all respect*.
Must keep his children in order by gaining their
respect. 6. 'Not a neophyte'—not a person newly
converted to the faith for fear lest, becoming proud and
conceited, he may share the fate of Lucifer. 7. 'Snare
of the devil'—the meaning is either that a Christian
whose past life was open to suspicion might bring
discredit upon the Church through the scandal which
the devil might attach to his name, or that a person,
whose former conduct was not beyond reproach,
might, when reminded of those earlier failings, lapse
into despair and so become ensnared by Satan and lose
the faith. 9. 'Mystery of faith'—The truths revealed
by Christ, the Christian Gospel. 11. 'The women'
—It is suggested that deaconesses are intended, namely
those who helped in ministering to women and relieving
the needs of the poor. 13. 'A good degree'—*position,
standing*. Some maintain that it refers to the promotion
of a deacon to the office of priest; others apply it to
a deacon's reward in the next life.
III 14-IV 16. False Teaching—15. *cf.* § 919*e*. 16. **922**
'Mystery of Godliness'—Our Lord himself. 'Which
was manifested in the flesh, was justified in the spirit'
—probably part of an early Christian hymn. The
relative 'which' is masculine in the Greek and therefore refers to our Lord. 'Manifested in the flesh'—
appeared in the flesh, *i.e.* the Incarnation. 'Justified
in the spirit'—vindicated during his life by his miracles
wrought by the power of the Holy Spirit or after his
death by his Resurrection; *cf.* Rom 1:4. **IV: 1.** 'The
Spirit saith'—What follows (1-3) was made known
by the Holy Spirit through one of the early Christian
prophets. 'In the last times'—*in later times, i.e.* in
the future, in this Messianic era. 2. 'Having their
conscience seared'—grown callous in conscience like
flesh seared with a hot iron. Though fully conscious
of bearing guilty marks they persist in misleading
others. 3. 'Forbidding others to marry'—behind
these prohibitions there may lie the dualistic principles
which were already apparent in Asia Minor when this
epistle was written and which were part of the Gnostic

2a heresy. St Paul objects to these prohibitions when they are the outcome of false principles which would regard marriage and certain foods as impure, but he has no objection to abstaining from marriage or to fasting when properly understood and based on sound principles; *cf.* 1 Cor 7:8 ff.; 2 Cor 6:5; 11:27; 1 Cor 9:27. When the Church bids us fast and abstain she does so, not because she regards certain foods as evil, but to help us to mortify our appetites, to conquer self and so to make spiritual progress. **4.** *Cf.* Gen 1:31.
b 5. ' Sanctified by the word of God '— blessed by a blessing scriptural in form, a scriptural grace. **7.** *Cf.* 1:4. **8.** ' Bodily exercise '—Mere training of the body profits but little. ' Profitable to all things '—Holiness is all availing, *i.e.* for this life and the next. **9.** ' A faithful saying '—This assertion regarding the good effects of true piety is worthy of full and unqualified acceptance. **12.** ' Let no man despise thy youth '— At the time Timothy was between thirty and forty, and so comparatively young for his position, especially in comparison with Paul and the presbyters. Personal virtue and edifying conduct had to supply lack of years. ' In conversation '—*behaviour.* **13.** ' Attend unto reading '—public reading and instruction. **14.** ' Grace '—charisma; here it refers to the sacramental grace of the priesthood bestowed on Timothy. ' Given thee by prophecy '—the phrase διὰ προφητείας is ambiguous. It may be an accusative plural, *on account of prophecies* made by those faithful present at the ordination of Timothy who were endowed with the gift of prophecy, *cf.* 1 Tim 1:18. Alternatively it is genitive singular, in which case the prophetic utterance is regarded as the cause of the promotion of Timothy. A further suggestion is that the phrase may refer to some form of prophetic prayer uttered by the Apostle over Timothy; a sort of *form* of ordination. ' With the imposition of the hands of the priesthood '—*cf.* 2 Tim 1:6, whence it appears that both Paul and the local presbyters imposed hands upon Timothy, the former bestowing the sacrament, the latter accompanying or co-operating thus making the ceremony a common liturgical act. ' The use of the preposition μετά (used here) instead of διά (2 Tim 1:6) leads us not to attribute to the imposition of hands on the part of the presbyterate the same value as to the laying on of Paul's hands; the latter is active and produces the effect (διά), while the former is only concomitant (μετά); one is essential to the rite, the other enhances its brilliancy ', Prat II, 270.
c V 1–VI 2 Precepts for Various Classes—Older people are to be treated with reverence, and the younger as equals in the family of Christ. **3.** ' Honour '—Here the word means the granting of material help, *cf.* 17; Mt 15:4–6. ' Widows indeed '—Those who have no relatives to support them; the question therefore concerns those widows who need relief from the public funds of the Church; *cf.* Ac 6:1. **4.** ' Let *these* learn first '—let the children and grandchildren learn first . . . *i.e.* these relatives are to learn that their first duty according to their religion is towards their own household so that they should make every effort to support their parents. **6.** ' Is dead while she is living '—a true widow is faithful to her religious duties, avoiding that dissipation which is spiritual death. **8.** A further confirmation of what has been said in 4. It is a general affirmation that anyone who neglects the care of his dependents, has ' denied the faith and is worse than the infidel ', because pagans normally **d** respond to their natural feelings and instincts. **9.** In order to qualify for support from the Church the widow must be sixty, married not more than once and known to be of good character, exercising such good works as those listed in 10. **10.** ' Received to harbour '— ' been hospitable '. It is difficult to avoid the conclusion from the whole of this passage that ' the widows ' are some sort of primitive inchoate but recognized religious order or institution within the Church, living a life of devotion under some kind of rule and vow, *cf.* Polycarp *Phil.* 4, Ignatius *Smyrn.* 13; *cf.* also Spicq, xlviii–l. **11.** Younger widows are not to be placed

upon the list of those to receive support because they **922d** might prove unstable and then, yielding to their desires to remarry, might break their pledges to Christ. ' When they have grown wanton *against* Christ they *want to* marry '. They yield to their ' desires ' and reject their subjection to Christ. **12.** ' Their first faith ' —the pledges made to Christ. **13.** ' Withal being idle ' —Their living on public funds would expose them through consequent idleness to the evils mentioned here. **17.** ' Double honour '—*Cf.* 3. Those fulfilling **e** their duties, especially that of preaching the word, are worthy of more liberal support. **18.** *Cf.* 1 Cor 9:9 where he explains the application of Deut 25:4. The saying of our Lord here quoted is found in Lk 10:7. Is not this an example of the quoting of OT and NT together as Scripture? **19.** Timothy is urged to use the judicial power which he possesses as a bishop, without prejudging a case and without partiality or bias. **22.** A warning against ordaining priests without due inquiry into their character and fitness for the office. By ordaining the unworthy he would make himself responsible for the sins which they committed as ministers of Christ and for the harm which would befall the Church in consequence. Some writers, however, apply the verse to the sacrament of penance, seeing here a warning against precipitately bestowing absolution from sin or censure on those not rightly disposed. **23.** ' Keep thyself chaste '—holy, undefiled, free from fault. ' Use a little wine for thy stomach's sake '—For some reason, perhaps as a means of pre- serving chastity, Timothy completely abstained from wine. St Paul cautions him against excessive austerity which might impair his health. The Apostle realized the demands of the active ministry and so urged his disciple to take the means necessary to enable himself to fulfil his arduous duties. **24** refers either to the question of not ordaining the unworthy or, as some suggest, to the judgement of priests.
VI 1–2—Speaking of the conduct of slaves, St Paul **f** lays down that they are to fulfil their duties towards their masters, whether Christian or not, in such a way that they bring credit, and not ill repute, to the Christian name. Greater loyalty and service should be given to a Christian master on account of the common bond of the faith. There is no direct legis- lation against slavery, but Christ's doctrine stressing the equality of all in God's sight eventually created an atmosphere in which slavery could not survive; *cf.* Eph 6:5 ff.
VI 3–10 Final Warnings—St Paul returns to his **g** warnings against those proud-minded, ignorant teachers who bring about their own ruin by idle controversies and speculations from which the evils mentioned in 4 spring. Religion is thought of by them merely in terms of monetary profit. To counteract this the Apostle wishes to foster a spirit of disinterestedness in preachers of the Gospel, pointing out the dangers attendant on avarice and the futility of amassing wealth which must be left behind at death. **10.** ' The desire of money is the root of all evils '—avarice stifles love of higher things and so leaves the road open to all forms of sin. **13.** ' Who gave testimony under Pontius Pilate '—The word used is μαρτυρήσαντος whence our word ' martyr '. Here however the reference is not to our Lord's passion and death but to his *bearing witness* before Pilate that he was the Messias, Jn 18:36 f. It was only later that the word μαρτυρέω came to have the technical meaning of bearing witness by *shedding one's blood. Cf.* J. Donovan, S.J., *The Authorship of St John's Gospel* (London, 1936) 75 f.
17–19. ' Warning to the Rich '—This remarkable **h** passage stresses our absolute need of the life of grace, that ' new creation ' which uplifts and ennobles us and so enables us to see God who lives in light inaccessible. Note the paradox that we are to *see* God whom *no man can see* (*cf.* 1 Jn 3:1–2) which brings out the need for the life of grace. **20.** ' that which is committed ' —The *deposit* of faith. Timothy is warned to guard the treasure of sound doctrine which, as a sacred trust, has

922h been committed to his keeping. He must shun those travesties of true teaching which led others to fall away from the faith. ' Faith's doctrines which God has revealed are not put before us as some philosophical discovery to be developed by human ingenuity but as a divine trust (depositum) handed over to the Spouse of Christ for her faithful safeguarding and infallible exposition ', The Vatican Council, Dz 1800.

THE SECOND EPISTLE TO TIMOTHY

923a **I 1-2 Greeting—1.** ' According to the promise of life ' —The purpose of his apostleship was to announce the promise of eternal life.

3-5 Declaration of Love and Anxiety to see Timothy —3. ' From my forefathers '—His own service of God, learnt from his forefathers, had at all times been conscientious and single-minded, even in those days when, following the way he thought to be right, he had persecuted the Church of Christ. ' That without ceasing '—*as without ceasing*. The meaning is : I give thanks to God whenever I make mention of you, as I do continually, in my prayers night and day. **4.** ' Mindful of thy tears '—probably those shed at their parting, a sign that their love was reciprocal. **5.** ' Eunice '—a Christian Jewess ; *cf.* Ac 16:1.

b 6-II 13. He appeals to Timothy to show Courage— This appeal to Timothy to be courageous in the exercise of his ministry is based upon the nature of the grace given to him (6) ; Christ's love as shown by the Redemption (9 f.) ; the example of Paul himself (12) ; the defection of false friends (15) ; the zeal of Onesiphorus (16). **6.** ' Grace ' (χάρισμα) is here a permanent gift which one can draw upon and revive. It is not a gift which is withdrawn by the Holy Spirit nor is it the character or power of order which has no need of being revived and is incapable of diminution or decline. It is the supernatural fitness received for the worthy exercise of the 'sacred ministry. ' Something like what we call the grace of a calling—that is to say, the totality of spiritual gifts and the right to the actual graces which the duties of the episcopate require. Although associated with the character and power of Holy Order, it is nevertheless distinct from them. While the character is indelible and the power inalienable, this *charisma* may become enfeebled through a want of effort or of vigilance ; if it does not reach the point of extinction, it needs at least to be rekindled. St Paul indicates very plainly the nature of this *charisma*, when he adds " For God hath not given us the spirit of fear, but of power and of love and of sobriety " ', Prat II, 271. To carry out his mission successfully Timothy had only to draw upon the treasures of ordination graces always at his disposal—a reminder for us not to neglect **c** those we have received. St Thomas suggests that Timothy had been remiss in the discharge of some of his duties, particularly that of preaching. ' Imposition of my hands '—The external rite by which Timothy was raised to the episcopate. Prat shows how this passage together with 1 Tim 4:14 illustrates the three principal elements of a sacrament ; the external rite ; a permanent grace, which can be revived for all spiritual needs of the ministry ; and as shewn, a special sanctifying grace symbolized and given in the actual sacramental rite. **7.** The spirit bestowed by God at ordination is not one of timidity, but of fortitude, love, self-discipline. Timothy should therefore press forward in his ministry without fear or misgiving. **9.** St Paul gives a brief but telling summary of his doctrine of divine election, showing how we have been delivered by Christ's blood, freely chosen out by God from all eternity to be members of the mystical body of Christ, and that, not because of any merits of ours but solely on account of God's goodness ; *cf.* Eph 1:3-14. God's love as made known by the Redemption is a further motive for **d** zealous service. **12.** St Paul sets before Timothy his

own example of suffering. ' These things '—his chains. **9** ' Whom I have believed '—to whose safe-keeping I have entrusted myself. ' That which I have committed '—The pronoun ' μου ' may indicate either the deposit which *I* have entrusted to God or that which God has entrusted *to me*. In the former case the ' deposit ' will refer to the merits won in particular by his sufferings which Paul had deposited with God until the great day of final recompense ; in the latter it may refer either to the apostolic office committed by God to Paul and regarded by Paul as a stewardship, or to the Gospel itself, the sound doctrine of the following verse. ' That day '—the day of judgement. **14.** ' The good *deposit* '—again the same word as in 12. Here it is either the doctrine committed to his care or his episcopal ministry. **15.** The Apostle emphasizes his appeal by recounting his disappointments in the past. In Asia certain Christians had lacked the courage to appear as his friends. Of Phigellus and Hermogenes we know nothing further. However the loyalty of Onesiphorus' household stood out in sharp contrast as a noble exception. **16-18.** These verses seem to imply Onesiphorus' death, and, since he prays God to have mercy upon his soul, show that prayers are profitable not only to the living, but also to the dead. They are an early illustration of Christian prayer for the dead.

II. The exhortation to courage in adversity is con- **e** tinued, reinforced by illustrations from the lives of the soldier, the athlete and the farmer. **2.** ' By many witnesses '—The meaning of the phrase is not clear. Some suggest ' in the presence of many witnesses ', but this hardly represents διά. A more likely suggestion is that Paul is referring to what Timothy had learnt from him directly and from witnesses who attested facts of which the Apostle himself-had no personal experience. ' The same commend '—St Paul, now a prisoner, still strives his utmost to ensure the faithful transmission of the Gospel. In a passage such as this we see the important part which oral teaching and tradition played and still must play in instructing the faithful and accurately handing down the teaching of Christ. **3.** ' Labour ' **f** —*Take thy share of suffering*. The cross of suffering precedes the crown of glory. **4.** ' With secular business '—Like a true soldier Timothy must give himself over fully to his duty. Taken in conjunction with 6 this verse seems to suggest that Timothy was imitating St Paul by earning his own livelihood, but was thus distracted by secular business. But, as the Apostle points out, the first share of the harvest belongs to the husbandman, and in the same way Timothy has a right to his maintenance. The material support so received from the faithful will be amply repaid by the zealous energy of an apostle untrammelled by secular worries ; *cf.* 1 Tim 5:17 f. ; 1 Cor 9:1-12. Timothy's true duty lies in the work of his ministry. **8.** The example of our Lord. He became man, passed through the same trials as we do, and then entered into his glory. But the emphasis is upon *risen from the dead* ; it is this thought that he sets before Timothy to inspire him to follow the example of Christ and also of Paul himself in undergoing suffering so as to reach glory. **9.** ' Not bound '—despite the imprisonment of the Apostle as though an evildoer the Gospel would continue to spread. God's power is not limited to one instrument. **11-13.** Possibly an extract from an early hymn. ' If we be dead with him '—With Christ we must be crucified, *i.e.* our flesh must be crucified with its passions ; with Christ we must be buried, and with Christ we arise from beneath the waters of baptism as from the grave, in the glory of a new and risen life. **12.** *Cf.* Mt 10:33 ; Lk 12:9.

14-18 Timothy's Conduct in facing his Task — **g** Timothy finds himself confronted by a difficult situation, aggravated by the activities of false teachers. Careful but effective handling of the situation is necessary. By his conduct Timothy must strive to win God's approval and the respect of the faithful ; wordy disputes, detrimental to those concerned and

3g to the spread of the Gospel, are to be avoided. **14.** Charging them *to avoid controversy*. **17-18.** Hymenaeus and Philetus, *cf.* 1 Tim 1:20, probably understood the Resurrection in a purely spiritual fashion, perhaps misunderstanding and misrepresenting the Apostle's doctrine of our spiritual resurrection with Christ in baptism ; *cf.* Rom 6:3 ff.

h **19-26 The Endurance of the Church**—Notwithstanding the propagation of false doctrine, the body of the faithful will remain firm, its faith indestructible ; *cf.* 1 Tim 3:15 ; Heb 12:28 ; Mt 7:24-27. 'No matter what heresies arise the faith of the Church can never be destroyed. But firmness in the faith on the part of the individual members of the Church depends on two factors : predestination and free will ; ' God knoweth who are his ', yet his elect will be saved through their free will, ' let everyone depart '. We have always to bear in mind St Augustine's words, ' Why he draws this man and not that man seek not to discover unless you would fall into error ', *Tract. in Joann.*, 26, 2. **20.** The metaphor changes. Christians are compared to the various vessels used in a house ; *cf.* Rom 9:19-24.

4a **III 1-9 Future Dangers**—**1.** ' In the last days '—In this Messianic era in which we live. He is speaking of false doctrines already spread about, since Timothy is cautioned against those who propagate them. As the Apostle looks still further into the future he sees dangers increasing since the flood of false teaching will inevitably bring with it a corresponding corruption of morals. **8.** Jannes and Mambres (Jambres) are the names given by Jewish tradition to the magicians who opposed Moses before Pharaoh ; *cf.* Ex 7:11.

b **10-17 Further Encouragement**—Once more St Paul sets before Timothy his own example and reminds him of the time when he undertook his ministry and of the persecutions suffered by Paul at that time in Timothy's own country. Timothy is urged not to forget all this now, but rather to draw present comfort from the way in which God came to Paul's assistance and rescued him ; *cf.* Ac 13-14. **14.** ' Of whom ' —plural, therefore including besides Paul Timothy's mother and grandmother ; *cf.* 1:5. **15.** ' Scriptures ' —means at least the OT. This verse and 16 demonstrate the value of the Scriptures, both for one's own perfection and for the instruction of others. **16.** A most important passage regarding the inspiration of Scripture, *cf.* A. Bea, *De Inspiratione* (Rome, 1933), 33-5. The verse may be translated either *Every Scripture is inspired of God and is profitable for teaching* or *Every Scripture inspired of God is profitable for teaching*, but in either case the inspiration of Scripture is assumed, the writer being content to indicate its various uses. **17.** ' Man of God '—minister of Christ ; *cf.* 1 Tim 6:11. ' Furnished to every good work '—made proficient for his duties by study of the Scriptures. These rightly used give life and unction to preaching. Study of the Scriptures is an obligation upon pastors if they are to carry out their duties effectively and fruitfully.

c **IV Final Exhortation to Timothy**—**1.** ' Living and the dead '—*cf.* 1 Thess 4:16. The phrase in the creeds that Christ will come to judge the living and the dead is taken from this passage. The ' living ' are those who will be alive when Christ comes on the last day ; *cf.* 1 Cor 15:51 f. ' At once a difficulty arises about the just who are alive at the last day. St Paul meets it by telling of a ' mystery ' ; these just it is true will not die, but none the less their bodies will have to be glorified—*all* the just, the living and the dead will be *changed*. When the *dead* rise incorruptible *we*, the living shall be *changed* ; our corruptible bodies will put on incorruption. After that supreme moment death will have lost all power over us ', WV, 3, 222. **2.** ' In season—out of season '—Timothy must be persistent, ready to instruct or reprove at all times, whether acceptable to the hearers or not. The errors spread by false teachers are to be defeated by Timothy's own persevering patience, sound preaching, and

faithful fulfilment of duty in face of hardship. Paul's 924c pleading is the more urgent since he is aware that his own death is not far distant.

6-8 The Apostle's Reward—As he reflects upon his d approaching death he takes occasion to look back over his long strenuous career with all its trials and sufferings and then goes on to tell how he awaits from the just judge the crown, the reward he has earned by faithful service. **8.** The ' crown ' is at once the sign and reward of a good life ; it is the vision of God ; *cf.* 1 Cor 13:9-12 ; 1 Jn 3:1-2. There is, however, in addition, the aureola due to particular merit, for instance to the martyr, virgin, doctor. ' Of justice '—hence justly merited ; eternal life is at once the reward of merit and a ' grace ' or ' free gift ' of God, because without God's grace there can be no merit. St Augustine expresses it : ' In crowning our merits, God only crowns his own gifts '. ' Just judge . . . render '—These words are a further important witness to the doctrine of merit. ' In that day '—the day of judgement. There may be here a reference to the particular judgement, since the supposition is that the judgement and reward are to follow closely upon death.

9-18 Paul's Lonely Imprisonment—Paul's associates, e with the exception of Luke, have left him on various missions so that the Apostle summons Timothy to visit him. **9.** Demas is mentioned only in Col 4:14 ; Phm 24. Crescens is otherwise unknown ; his departure is not defection, nor is it censured. Mark was obviously reconciled to St Paul after the events of Ac 13:13 ; 15:38. ' Cloak '—Some think that this may refer to some book-wrap for the book-rolls mentioned here. It is, however, probably a winter cloak which he needed during his imprisonment. Alexander may be the person mentioned in 1 Tim 1:20. He is obviously known to Timothy. He may have followed the Apostle to Rome and become an accuser or he may possibly have taken part in the events leading to the Apostle's final arrest. However he must have returned to Ephesus since Timothy is warned against him.

16-18 Paul's Trial—' At my first answer '—This refers f to the preliminaries of the trial, the first hearing of the case. No one came forward to witness on his behalf. For his part, Paul was able to seize the occasion of self-defence to preach the Gospel. ' I was delivered '— probably means, secured a remand. While he cannot feel assured of the final acquittal, he does feel assured of his eternal salvation. ' Mouth of the lion '—danger. **18.** Note how the doxology is applied to Christ. It is from him that grace, deliverance and salvation come, and to him thanks and honour are paid ; *cf.* Prat II, 122.

19-21 Final Greetings—Erastus, mentioned in Rom 16:23, was the city treasurer of Corinth. Trophimus was an Ephesian of pagan origin. Linus—according to Irenaeus the successor of Peter as Bishop of Rome.

THE EPISTLE TO TITUS

I 1-4 Greeting—The rather formal nature of the 925a greeting may be explained by the official character of the letter, and by its purpose, which was to emphasize the authority of Paul's emissary and to impress the false teachers in Crete. **1.** ' According to the faith of the elect '—The purpose of Paul's apostolate is to make still more secure in Crete that faith and knowledge which promotes right living and true worship of God. **2.** ' Who lieth not '—A unique phrase intended as a contrast to the absence of truth to be found amongst the Cretan teachers, *cf.* 12. **3.** ' In due times '—God's promise of eternal life, though hidden away from eternity, had been made known at the appointed time and spread abroad by the preaching of the Apostles including Paul himself. **4.** ' Common faith '—Titus himself was an uncircumcised Gentile (Gal 2:3) and there may be here a hint of his gentile origin since the ' common ' faith would be that belong-

925a ing to both Jew and Gentile. Otherwise the phrase means simply ' in communion of faith '.

b **5-16 The Mission of Titus**—Titus had been left at Crete to stem the progress of error and evil practice by appointing faithful and trustworthy ministers to preserve the true Christian tradition and way of life. **5.** ' Priests '—The word used here is ' presbyters '; note however that the word ' episcopos ' is substituted in 7 for ' presbyter '. Regarding the question of ' priest ' and ' bishop ' in the Pastorals, *cf.* §§ 919*f*–920*c*. **5 ff.** *Cf.* 1 Tim 3:1-7. The qualities which are demanded of Christ's ministers are particularly necessary in this instance on account of the many false teachers, mainly Jewish, who for the sake of gain were trying to undermine Christian doctrine and practice. These false teachers are spoken of in much the same terms as those at Ephesus, *cf.* § 921*i*. **7.** ' Bishop '—Episcopos, *cf.* §§ 919-20. This name, which means overseer, inspector, superintendent, describes the ' function ' better than presbyter. **12.** ' The Cretans are always liars '—quotation from the Minos of Epimenides, a Cretan poet (*c* 600 B.C.). Callimachus (*c* 300-240 B.C.) quotes the first half of it in his Hymn to Zeus, applying it to the Cretan legend that the tomb of Zeus was on the island. The phrase was no doubt familiar and cannot be used to prove that the Apostle possessed a wide knowledge of the classics. **14.** Titus is urged to act firmly against them in order to preserve the faith. **15.** ' All things are clean '—In addition to their doctrinal errors these false teachers retained the distinction between clean and unclean foods. This distinction, St Paul points out, no longer obtains ; what matters is the internal disposition with which we regard things, all things are clean to those who are clean of heart, while the unclean contaminate everything with which they come into contact, *cf.* 1 Cor 6:12 ; 10:23 ; Mt 15:11 ; Lk 11:41. **16.** Their conduct belies their profession that they possess the true knowledge of God ; *cf.* Mt 7:16 ff.

c **II 1-10 The Christian Ideal for the Various Classes**— Titus is called upon to remedy the disorder brought about by the fraudulent missionaries and that he may be successful in this the Apostle sets before him the duties of various classes of people with the ideals at which they are to aim. He is especially insistent on good family life, which had been disrupted by those pseudo-guides ; *cf.* 1:11. **4.** A tradition of wholesome family life is to be established and handed on from women of maturer years to those younger. **6.** ' Sober ' —self-controlled—Youth must practise self-control in all things ; there must be no yielding to youthful impulsiveness. **7.** Titus himself is to set the example. **8.** ' That he who is on the contrary part '—so that our adversaries may be put to shame, having no opportunity for speaking ill of us. **9-10.** Slaves are again (*cf.* 1 Tim 6:1) urged to be submissive to their masters and indeed to give such good service that they bring credit upon the Christian religion.

d **11-15** form the Epistle read at the first Mass on Christmas Day. St Paul sets before his readers the reasons why they should respond to the call to reach the Christian ideal, namely because of God's graciousness—this is the meaning of ' grace ' here, rather than sanctifying grace—towards *all men*, revealed in the Incarnation and the preaching of the Gospel. ' To all men '—On this account the Apostle makes his appeal to all classes of people in 1–10 above. All are, in fact, affected by Christ's advent, the benefits of the Incarnation are not limited to any particular privileged body, but are meant to be shared by all. The effect of our Lord's coming is now made known. **12.** ' Instructing us '—*Training us*, guiding us continuously to regulate our lives by practising piety, justice, self-restraint, *i.e.* by performing our duties to God (godly), to our neighbour (justly) and to ourselves (soberly). This passage is aptly chosen for Christmastide, recalling as it does, the practical bearing of the Incarnation on our conduct. ' The blessed hope '—*i.e.* the object of

hope ; the hope to which correspondence with the **92** blessings of the Incarnation will lead us, the glory of the second coming of Christ. **13.** ' The great God and **e** our Saviour Jesus Christ '—The liturgy in using these words at Christmas focuses our attention upon the divine Nature of the Child who is born for us. He is our Great God and Saviour. Both nouns refer to Jesus Christ : ' It is consoling to see the exegetes of our day coming back more and more to the traditional interpretation. If it were a question of the Father, the Apostle would not add to God the epithet of ' great ' which naturally is the principle of divinity. Moreover the *Parousia* is always the glorious manifestation of the Son coming to judge the world, never that of the Father. Finally—and this argument is decisive—the two titles ' great God ' and ' Saviour ' being included in Greek under the same article, must refer to the same person ; to be able to isolate them and to connect the second only to Jesus Christ, this latter name would have to be placed between the two ', Prat, II, 127 ; *cf.* also WV and Bandas *op. cit.* 187. **14.** ' Who gave himself for us '—Christ's love, as manifested in his passion and death is a further reason for diligence in the pursuance of Christian ideals. Christ loved us and gave himself for us ; in return, then, the Christian redeemed by Christ's blood must spend himself in Christ's service ; *cf.* Gal 2:20. **14.** ' A people acceptable '—a reference to God's choice of Israel in the OT, *cf.* Deut 7:6 ; 14:2 ; 26:18 ; Ex 19:5 ; 1 Pet 2:9. ' Good works '—those already pointed out above, 2:1-10. **15.** Titus is urged to exercise the *authority* which he possesses as the Apostle's delegate and as a minister of Christ. He has the right to command and guide.

III 1-3 Christian Citizenship—The Apostle calls **f** upon them to fulfil their duties as members of society, civic and municipal. Far from weakening loyalty to the State, faith in Christ is rather a guarantee of its strength, because the nation as such is derived from God, *cf.* Eph 3:15, and in consequence must be loyally served by the Christian as a matter of duty ; *cf.* CR 22 (Aug. 1942) 337 ff., art. *Patriotism*, by Rev. L. L. McReavy. **2.** In relation to his fellow citizens the Christian must show himself to be understanding, tolerant, forbearing, careful to avoid injuring his neighbour's character by evil talk. **3.** ' For we ourselves '—As an added incentive to considerate treatment of those not enlightened by the Christian faith, St Paul reminds them of their own past, *cf.* Eph 4:17 ff. ; Rom 1:18 ff. The lesson he wishes them to draw is patience with the failings of others. He then reminds them that their own calling was not due to themselves, but solely to God's goodness.

4-7 Baptism and Justification—The Epistle of the **g** Second Mass on Christmas day. ' Not by the works of justice '—not because of any works of ours done before justification whether according to the natural or Mosaic Law : those works did not constitute the motive for God's bestowing the grace of justification —the motive was solely God's mercy. ' By the laver of regeneration '—This laver or *bath* of regeneration is Baptism, by which we are delivered from that slavery of sin into which we were born (our first birth) and become sons of God (our regeneration or second birth), *cf.* Jn 3:3 ff. ' Renovation of the Holy Ghost ' —expresses another aspect of our regeneration ; it is a *renewal* effected by the Holy Spirit, the production of a new ' being ' by which we are restored to divine sonship, it is the ' new creation ' spoken of in 2 Cor 5:17 ; Gal 6:15 ; Eph 4:24. Sin, actual and original, is remitted by the infusion of a new life which takes the place of spiritual death. Bandas, 181, notes here the reference to the Holy Trinity : ' Again, the Apostle says that our baptismal regeneration is due to the Father who, without any regard to merits which we neither possessed nor were capable of acquiring, had mercy on us ; it is due also to Jesus Christ who is our Saviour and Mediator ; and finally it is due to the Holy Spirit, the Common Envoy of the Father and the

TITUS III

5g Son, our Sanctifier, who is liberally poured out upon us'. **7.** The life of grace 'justifies' or renders a man 'just' in the sight of God; hence springs up hope of eternal life seeing that he is now a son of God and co-heir with Christ. In a word, baptism is the beginning of a life which is eternal. 4–7 gives us a summary of the process of justification (*cf.* Prat I, 331*n*–332; II, 259–60) and point to the effects of Christ's coming

h as we celebrate his nativity. **9.** 'Foolish questions and genealogies'—*cf.* 1 Tim 1:4. **10.** 'Heretic'—αἱρετικόν whence our word heretic. Here it rather refers to a person who is a centre of dissension and strife, a 'factious person'. Such an individual is to be admonished and if still obdurate is to be regarded as excluded from the Church. **11.** 'Condemned by his own judgement'—*self-condemned*; by his stubborn refusal to submit to the Church's authority he puts 925h himself outside the Church, *i.e.* is excommunicated; *cf.* 1 Cor 5:5. **12-15 Final Instructions**—Artemas—not otherwise known in NT, but acc. to tradition one of the Seventy and Bp of Lystra. Tychicus—*cf.* 2 Tim 4:12. Nicopolis—in Epirus. It has been suggested that Paul intended to make it a centre for the evangelization of Epirus and may have been arrested there. Zenas the Lawyer—not mentioned elsewhere in NT, but by tradition Bp of Diospolis and author of apocryphal Acts of Titus. He was probably a 'lawyer' in the Jewish sense. 'Necessary uses'—such as the needs of Zenas and Apollos. Christians should earn an honest living and so be able to meet all the expenses demanded of the congregation, such as those mentioned in the preceding verse.

THE EPISTLE OF ST PAUL TO
PHILEMON

By S. SHEARER, C.P

926a Bibliography—F. Prat, *The Theology of St Paul*, London, 1933², I, pp 275-9 ; C. Toussaint, art. 'Philemon', DBV ; E. Robin, art. 'Philemon', DTC ; *A. T. Robertson, 'Philemon and Onesimus, master and slave', Exp. VIII 19 (1920), 29-48 ; M. Roberti, *La lettera di S Paolo a Filemone e la condizione giuridica dello schiavo fuggitivo*, Milan, 1933 ; J. Dutilleul, art. 'Esclavage', DTC ; P. Allard, art 'Esclavage', DAFC.

b Introduction—This short Epistle must surely rank as a perfect example of the letter-writer's art. Its object is simple enough—to seek forgiveness for the bearer, a runaway slave ; yet in it the Holy Ghost has used all the skill, grace and warmth of style that St Paul's cultured mind and generous heart could command.

It was written at the same time and in the same circumstances of captivity as the Epistle to the Colossians. While still a prisoner Paul had met and converted Onesimus, a slave who had run away from his master, Philemon, after having perhaps first robbed him (v 18). He has now persuaded Onesimus to return, overcoming his well-founded fears of punishment by writing these few conciliatory lines for him to take back with him to his master.

c The authenticity and canonicity of the Epistle are beyond question. Its preservation is probably due to the veneration of Philemon's family for anything connected with one to whom they owed their Christian faith (v 19). Philemon is not mentioned elsewhere in the New Testament, but we may gather from the Epistle that he was the wealthy, eminent and charitable owner of a house-church in one of the early Christian communities. That this community was at Colossae seems clear enough from a comparison with the Epistle to the Colossians. Onesimus himself was from Colossae (Col 4:9). Epaphras, who was a native of Colossae and had evangelized it, and Luke, Mark, Aristarchus and Demas send special greetings through Paul to Philemon, as they had done to the Colossians in general (Col 4:10-14). Archippus, who is generally regarded as Philemon's son (as Appia is generally taken to be his wife) is also spoken of in Col 4:17 as exercising an important office at Colossae.

d Doctrinal Content—Noteworthy is the prudent restraint without compromise of principle that marks St Paul's attitude towards slavery. He respects the legal rights of Philemon and abstains from open condemnation of the system (to proclaim its immediate abolition in the world of his time would have been to precipitate civil war and worse social evils). But he is careful to inculcate the principle that will soften the harshness of slavery and cause the gradual disappearance of the system in the future—the principle of the brotherhood of all men in Christ.

e 1-7 Introduction—In the opening salutations to Philemon and his household, Paul is joined by Timothy, the companion of his captivity (1-2).

There follows a graceful eulogy of Philemon's charity and practical faith. The thought of the help that these have afforded his fellow Christians has been the source of great happiness and comfort to Paul (7) and has called forth from him particular thanks to God, with a special remembrance of Philemon in his prayers

(4-5). V 6 in the Vg seems to mean that Paul prays there may be due recognition of Philemon's generosity and the good works among the Christian community to which it has given rise ; the Greek reads : 'May (their ?) participation in thy faith become effective in the clear knowledge of all the good that is in us, unto Christ.''

8-21 Body of the Epistle—The way has now been f delicately prepared for the main portion of the Epistle—the plea for mercy for Onesimus ; this too is treated with consummate skill.

Paul is so anxious to save Onesimus from the terrible punishments (including even crucifixion) to which he is legally liable that he gives Philemon a gentle reminder that he has the undoubted right as an Apostle to issue a definite command in the matter ; though, as he tactfully adds, his knowledge of Philemon's character leads him rather to appeal to his charity. In the name of charity, therefore, and further, in the name of his grey hairs and now of the chains of imprisonment that Christ's service has brought him, Paul makes his request on behalf of the child whom he has brought forth into the light of the Christian faith during his captivity (8-10) : let Philemon receive him back as though Paul had sent him his own heart (12). True, in the past Onesimus has belied the name he bears, but now he can show both Philemon and Paul how well it suits him (11) (the Greek name Onesimus means ' profitable '). Indeed, if he were to stay on to minister to Paul's needs he could at the same time be acting as the representative of Philemon : but dearly as Paul would like this, he leaves it to Philemon's free choice (13-14).

Perhaps, as an added motive for forgiveness, there is g for Philemon in this matter a divine plan of ' loss and gain '—perhaps his temporary loss of Onesimus as slave was purposely designed to bring him everlasting gain of Onesimus as brother ; if he is a beloved brother especially to Paul, how much more must he be so to Philemon, both naturally, as a result of his forgiveness, and supernaturally, because of his new relationship with him through their common faith in Christ (15-16). Again, does not Philemon regard Paul as friend and fellow ? Let him therefore welcome Paul's ' other self.' And let him not be deterred by the remembrance of any wrongs or losses he has suffered from Onesimus—let him charge these to Paul ; though ' if they were to settle their accounts, it would be Philemon who would remain the debtor ' (Prat)—to the extent of his whole spiritual being (18-19). Paul wittily suggests that Philemon should discharge this debt by, as it were, becoming an Onesimus to him (the play on words in the Greek is difficult to reproduce in English)—that is, granting his request, and so bringing him Christian comfort. In v 21 Paul may be hinting that Philemon's forgiveness should even extend as far as granting Onesimus his complete freedom.

22-25 Conclusion—The Epistle ends with the incidental information that Paul expects to be released (through Philemon's prayers, he adds typically) and would like to have accommodation ready for him at Philemon's house. The final salutations are from companions of Paul who would be especially well known to Philemon.

1152

THE EPISTLE TO THE
HEBREWS

By W. LEONARD, D.S.S.

a **Bibliography**—(*a*) *Introductory :* The recent General Manuals of Merk, Renié, Lusseau-Collomb, Höpfl-Gut, Gächter, Gutjahr, Meinertz, Steinmueller, and the following special studies : B. Heigl, *Verfasser u. Adresse des Briefes an die Hebräer* (1905) ; J. Quental, *Destinataires de l'Epître aux Hébreux*, RB (1912) ; J. Nikel, *Der Hebräerbrief*, BZ (1914) ; L. Méchineau, *L'Epistola agli Ebrei secondo le risposte della Commissione Biblica* (1917) ; *K. Bornhäuser, *Empfänger u. Verfasser des Briefes an die Hebräer* (1932) ; A. Vitti, *Introductio in S. Paulum* (1934) ; id. *L'Ambiente vero della Lettera agli Ebrei* in *Miscellanea Biblica* (1935) ; id. *Le Bellezze stilistiche della Lettera agli Ebrei*, Biblica (1936) ; L. Pirot, *Hébreux* (*l'Epître aux*) DBV(S) (1938) ; W. Leonard, *Authorship of the Epistle to the Hebrews* (1939) ; A. Dubarle, *Rédacteur et destinataires de l'Epître aux Hébreux* RB (1939).

(*b*) *Commentaries :* Chrysostom, Theodoretus, Primasius (Haymo), Aquinas, à Lapide, L. Zill (1879) ; A. Schäfer (1893) ; A. Padovani (1896) ; C. Huyghe (1901) ; J. Graf (1918) ; P. Boylan WV (1924) ; Rohr, BB (1932) ; A. Médebielle, Sainte Bible (1938) ; J. Bonsirven, VS, Paris 1943⁵ ; *F. Bleek (1840) ; *B. F. Westcott (1928)³ ; *J. Moffatt ICC (1924) ; *A. Nairne CBSC (1917).

(*c*) *Theological :* F. Prat, *Théologie de Saint Paul* I²³ (1934) II²⁰ (1933) ; C. Perrella, *De iustificatione secundum Epistolam ad Hebraeos*, Bi (1933) ; L. G. da Fonseca, *Foedus an Testamentum ?*, Bi (1927–8) ; E. Dimmler, *Melchisedech-Gedanken über das Hohepriestertum Christi nach dem Hebräerbrief* (1921) ; V. Padolskis, *L'idée du sacrifice de la Croix dans l'Epître aux Hébreux* (1935) ; M. A. Mathis, *The Pauline Pistis-Hypostasis according to Heb 11:1* (1920) ; J. Bonsirven, *Le Sacrifice et le Sacerdoce de J.-C. d'après l'Epître aux Hébreux* NRT (1939) ; *E. Riehm, *Lehrbegriff des Hebräerbriefes* (1867) ; *H. L. MacNeill, *The Christology of the Epistle to the Hebrews* (1914) ; *Büchsel, F. *Die Christologie des Hebräerbriefs* (1922) ; *A. Nairne, *The Epistle of Priesthood*² (1915).

INTRODUCTION

b **Contents and Characteristics**—The writing placed in our Bibles between the thirteen Pauline Epistles and the seven Catholic Epistles is itself a letter. The author calls it so, 13:22, but he also calls it in the same sentence a ' word of exhortation '. Written to a community which was in serious difficulties and dangers, it comes very close to the form of a homily. While the author really writes a great treatise in the brief form of a letter, he never forgets that he is warning and exhorting.

A ' headless ' letter, without salutation or exordium or preliminary communications, it belongs to what Roller (*Das Formular der Paulinischen Briefe*, 1933) has described as a ' fore-asiatic ' or Levantine type. It opens abruptly with a magnificent Prologue. It closes, however, with an Epilogue which is quite personal and epistolary.

The author's concern is a great contrast. He wishes to set the revelation or religion, which has been recently brought by the Son of God, against the revelation or religion formerly taught by God to the Hebrew Fathers through the Prophets. The superiority of the New over the Old is really the one lesson of our Epistle, and it is taught by insisting on the super-excellence of Christ **927b** from every point of view. This includes simultaneous insistence on the inferiority of the Old Dispensation in all respects. Its imperfection and insufficiency to remit sin and give confident access to God are amply shown in such terms as make the letter a great impeachment, *cf.* 8:7, 8.

The Prologue, 1:1–4, is practically a synthesis of **c** everything, for it sets the Person of the Son and his work and his victory in most splendid prominence, making special mention of the ' cleansing of sin ', which he *alone* wrought (ποιησάμενος), before he passed to his throne on the right hand of Majesty on high.

Christ's superiority over the Angel Ministers of the Old Covenant, 1:5–14, is just allowed to stand out in an Old Testament anthology—mostly Psalm texts. A warning, 2:1–4, flows from that superiority and from the mention of Christian salvation of which the Angels are helpers. Then it is shown that the salvation was won by the self-abasement of the Son below the angelic state of immortality. His sovereignty—a universal sovereignty of glory and honour—is actually the reward of a death endured on behalf of men who were held in slavery by sin and death. As his death was a sacrificial death, Christ thereby wrought our atonement through the trials of mortality and suffering, entering simultaneously into such full experience of human weakness as fitted him to be a compassionate or sympathetic High Priest, 2:6–18. The sacerdotal thesis of the Epistle, already insinuated in the Prologue, 1:3, here comes into clear view and is to dominate the rest of the letter. Heb is above all the Epistle of the Priesthood of Christ.

Christ ' Apostle and Pontiff ' is meanwhile shown to be superior to Moses, the legislative mediator of the Old Alliance, 3:1–6*a* ; and a long warning is also based on this vindication of Christ's higher position in the House of God, 3:6*b*–4:13. Very aptly the warning and exhortation are made to gravitate towards the divine rest which was lost (in type) by the unbelieving generation that Moses led.

Our author now returns to the Pontiff — the **d** thoroughly sympathetic Pontiff—of our religion and in an atmosphere of confidence we stand prepared to contemplate his High Priesthood, 4:14–16.

Human weakness and divine vocation are two conditions of High Priesthood, for the Priest must have the sympathy with men which belongs to a fellow-sufferer and the confidence of access to God which comes from a heavenly authorization. Jesus here figures both as Son and as Melchisedechian Pontiff. When he has been set before us in the robes of priestly sympathy—praying as a sufferer, and then glorified, and the Cause of our salvation—we salute him as High Priest according to the order of Melchisedech and await developments, 5:1–10.

Those developments do not come until a warning of great severity, but mercifully tempered with words of confidence and encouragement, has prepared dull ears for hearing, 5:11–6:20. Thereupon, Melchisedech is dialectically made to assert his superiority over Aaron. Christ, typified by him, is seen receiving homage from Abraham and blessing him—annulling Mosaism together with its priesthood—holding his own priesthood

927d on a title of everlasting life—being confirmed by divine oath as the guarantor of a better covenant—and remaining as an all-sufficient Priest for ever, 7:1–25. A sort of intermedial epilogue is inserted here, 7:26–28.

The long section 8:1–10:18 which ends and crowns the dogmatic part of the letter is concerned with Christ as the Minister of a better sanctuary, 8:1–5, as the Mediator of a better Covenant, 8:6–13, as the, Offerer of a better Sacrifice than that of Expiation day and in fact as the Abolisher by his one all-sufficient sacrifice of the whole weak and insufficient multiplicity of Mosaic sacrifices, 9:1–10:18.

The moral part or last exhortation of this 'word of exhortation', 10:19–13:17, can be summed up in the one word : 'Perseverance'. It is a fine combination of heart-shaking severity, well-motived comfort, inspired encouragement, and strong exhortation to persevere to the end. The epilogue has been mentioned already, 13, 18–25.

e Taking up Heb after a careful reading of the thirteen epistles of St Paul, we shall be struck with the differences. The author seems a calm, placid man compared with that divine volcano whom we venerate as the Apostle of the Gentiles. His expository and argumentative order is so remarkable that St Thomas Aquinas said with admirable felicity : 'No other Scripture moves with such fine order of words and sentences.' A very careful study of the letter will reveal a most perfect system of joinings—a very noteworthy thing in a writing which so constantly combines dogmatic exposition with exhortation. One might easily guess that this writing was not dictated to an amanuensis, as St Paul's letters were. In fact it has been said that the great Apostle 'speaks' in his letters, while this man 'writes'. Although the author constructs periods of the classical type quite as rarely as St Paul, yet he balances his thoughts very skilfully, and frequently uses paronomasia, alliteration and other stylistic elegances. He appears to pay much attention to rhythm. At times his vocabulary sounds learned, for he uses words like αἰσθητήριον, μετριοπαθεῖν, δημιουργός. These are only a few of the obvious things which a reader of the Greek text will notice. Critical readers will say, like Origen, that this is a more 'Greek thing' and more a work of art than Paul's letters are.

928a Canonicity and Authenticity—It is of Catholic faith that Hebrews is an inspired Scripture belonging to the canon of divine books which the Church received from the Apostles. The final verdict in the matter was given by the Council of Trent (Session IV, Apr. 8, 1546). By placing Heb in its list as one of fourteen Paulines the Council favoured the Pauline authenticity of our letter but did not directly define it.

Outside of Catholic circles denial of Pauline authorship became almost universal during the 19th cent. The early obscurity in which the Epistle was involved throughout western Christendom was used to discount eastern unanimity, and the first clear assertion of Pauline paternity at Alexandria was regarded as a guess or an exegetical conclusion. Against this current of denial the Biblical Commission raised a bank on June 24, 1914. The first of three queries set before the Commission reads as follows : 'Doubts concerning the divine inspiration and Pauline origin of the Epistle to the Hebrews, doubts which were chiefly caused by abuse on the part of heretics, were current in the early centuries and held the minds of some Christians in the west. It is, therefore, asked whether in spite of the perpetual, unanimous, constant, assertion of the Oriental Fathers, with which the whole Western Church entered into complete agreement after the 4th cent. —whether in spite of this and in spite of the action of Supreme Pontiffs and sacred Councils, especially that of Trent—in spite also of the perpetual use of the universal Church, such force is to be attributed to the said doubts as to justify hesitation in receiving this letter not only amongst the canonical writings—which is defined as of faith—but also as a letter to be certainly placed amongst the genuine writings of St Paul ? The

answer was negative, that is : No such force is to be **9?** attributed to those early doubts (EB 429).

The human authorship of a writing is primarily an **b** historical matter and must be settled by consulting historical testimonies. Now historical testimony is available here, and in spite of some obscurities is cogent. History says that Paul is the author of the Epistle to the Hebrews. These are briefly the facts. The letter was certainly used and held sacred by Pope Clement of Rome about A.D. 95. St Polycarp of Smyrna probably alludes to it. Fifteen or twenty years later, St Justin representing Palestine, Asia Minor and Rome, is also a probable witness for the first half of the 2nd cent. Later, in the West some unexplainable obscurity covered it, beginning apparently in the second half of that century. St Irenaeus of Lyons writing in the last quarter of the century used it as sacred, but only seldom, and not under the name of Paul. The Muratorian Canon in its mutilated state excludes it. About A.D. 200 the Roman presbyter Caius rejected it. Hippolytus of Rome, who lived into the thirties of the 3rd cent., used it as sacred, but (if we trust two notes in the *Bibliotheca* of Photius) denied that it was Paul's. In Africa Tertullian cites it about 220 not as Scripture but as a writing of Barnabas having some authority. St Cyprian neither uses it nor includes it in his collection of Pauline Letters to Seven Churches. If the so-called *Tractatus Origenis* edited by Battifol and Wilmart in 1900 are really a western work of A.D. 300 or later, the name of Barnabas was associated with our letter at the beginning of the 4th cent. The African canon of 359 called after Mommsen mentions only thirteen letters of St Paul. That is as far as documents allow us to follow western opinion, for no argument can be drawn from the omission by oversight of Phil, Thess, Heb from the 4th cent (?) canon of the Codex Claromontanus. The Ambrosiaster who wrote under Pope Damasus (366–384) is also a doubtful witness.

In the East things are quite otherwise. The facts **c** must be given very compendiously. At Alexandria, shortly after 150 we find the presbyters (amongst whom Pantaenus must have taken his place well before 180), handing down our letter as a Pauline writing. Clement, a disciple of Pantaenus since 180 and his successor as head of the Didaskaleion about 200, noticed the great difference of style, but did not think of receding from the Alexandrian tradition of Pauline authorship. He supposed—or perhaps the suggestion had been made earlier—that the letter was written in Aramaic and translated into Greek by Luke. The great critic Origen also held fast to the assertion of the Ancients regarding Paulinity, but explained the un-Pauline elegance of the letter by assuming that a *scholiographos* (a writer working on notes), Luke or Clement of Rome or rather *God-knows-who* would be responsible for the phrasing and composition of the letter.

Origen's critical opinion did not obtain a following in his own Greek-speaking East. Although there is not a single dissenting voice heard either in Alexandria or any other Oriental Church on the question of the Pauline origin of our letter, such writers as consider the literary question adopt the hypothesis of an Aramaic original, ably written and skilfully translated. Clement's and not Origen's view also dominated in the West, when doubts about the letter had vanished.

The Arian controversy increased interchange of **d** relations between East and West. From the time that St Athanasius was in Rome and Trier, from the time of St Hilary's return from exile in Asia Minor, the epistle to the Hebrews had come into its own in the West also. St Augustine declared that the authority of the Oriental Churches was decisive with him, and the Councils of Hippo and Carthage (EB 11–15) renewed the sacred and Pauline credit of Heb in Africa, just as the action of Pope Innocent (405) did in Rome and throughout the other Western lands.

Dissenting voices were not heard again until the days of Humanism. Catholics, with one or two exceptions, then as before held to Pauline authorship, but Origen's

8d hypothesis mostly displaced that of Clement as an explanation of the stylistic excellence of the letter. Protestants, with a few notable exceptions attributed Heb to some other writer besides St Paul, and in the 19th cent. the negation of Pauline authorship became altogether prevalent amongst non-Catholic scholars. Apollos was regarded as the author by Luther and by many after him ; Silas was the choice of others ; Philip the Deacon of Sir W. Ramsay ; Barnabas has had the suffrages of Renan, Zahn, Salmon and recently Bornhäuser ; Aquila and Priscilla (joint authors) were favoured by Harnack. Others, like Westcott, content themselves with the assumption of an Alexandrian Jew, while for others, like Moffatt, he is a great unknown, ' a voice and nothing more '.

Many of the literary difficulties against Pauline origin have already been mentioned as characteristics of the letter—the absence of name, exordium, opening salutation—the purity of its Greek together with the elegance and perfection of diction and style. To these add the peculiar mode of citing the Old Testament and arguing from it—furthermore the difference of doctrinal viewpoint between this letter and the Paulines. The Biblical Commission was asked in 1914 whether the arguments drawn from these differences were such as to weaken belief in Pauline authorship ; or whether on the contrary the perfect harmony of doctrine and doctrinal assertions, the similarity of the admonitions and exhortations, the frequent coincidences of phrase and vocabulary rather favour and confirm Pauline origin. The Commission answered *No* to the first ; *Yes* to the second. The Pauline authorship stands (EB 430).

e We have to confine ourselves here to brief statements that might seem too dictatorial, but they have been well weighed and considered. The thought of the letter is indubitably Pauline, and there is no real difference of viewpoint beyond that required for the treatment of a new subject not entirely absent from the Paulines but never treated *ex professo* — namely the Priesthood and sacrifice of Christ. The mode of citing Scriptures as God's utterances or under a formula of indefinite anonymity is peculiar, but not entirely foreign to St Paul, and perhaps adopted as more suited to a Hebrew circle of addressees. The literary argument remains. Even the most painstaking comparison leaves a considerable residue of stylistic features that seem un-Pauline. There are, however, very notable ' concords ' and the ' discords ' are found to be reducible in a measure that would surprise some of the bolder impressionist critics.

This brings us to the third query set before the Biblical Commission : ' Whether Paul the Apostle is to be regarded as the author of this epistle in such a sense that it must necessarily be asserted that he not only conceived and expressed the whole of it under the inspiration of the Holy Ghost, but that he also gave it that form in which it has come to us ? ' The answer was *No*, with due reservation regarding any further judgement of the Church (EB 431).

f Therefore, on the question of the Epistle's form, which includes everything that belongs to arrangement, composition and adornment, the Commission allows wide freedom. Actually modern scholarship has made the hypothesis of a translation from an Aramaic original untenable, but Origen's view of ' Pauline thoughts composed and phrased by a redactor ' is widely held by Catholic writers. Personally we can only state the conviction produced by a long and minute study of the matter. St Paul does not seem to have dictated the letter. Either he wrote it with his own hand or he used a collaborator. In the latter case, however, the collaborator's part must be reduced to rather small proportions, if the indubitable Pauline origin of the letter is to stand. The development of ideas and the internal cohesion of thought go so much with the language, that Paul must be regarded as the dominant cause of everything, except perhaps the smoothing of transitions, the filling of phrases or the final polishing of

the whole. A genius—such as St Paul most certainly **928f** was—is always capable of doing surprising things, and experience has shown that comparatively little retouching (especially at the joints) can sometimes work in a writing a great literary transfiguration. The identity of the secondary hand will probably have to be left in the future as in the past to the divine omniscience.

Purpose and Addressees—The purpose of this ' word **929a** of exhortation ' is clear. The fibre of the community to which it was directed had been weakened, and defections were to be feared. The author wishes to give them a magnificent tonic, so as to strengthen them against the danger of falling away. He wishes to bring them back to the fervour of their first days and to a worthy emulation of the faith of leaders whose lives had been crowned with a glorious end.

This purpose is closely bound up with the identity of the Addressees. The title ' To the Hebrews ' is itself a highly authoritative indication, for it stands in all the MSS and is mentioned early in the 3rd cent. by Clement of Alexandria and by Tertullian. The letter was certainly sent to a circle well versed in the Old Testament and acquainted with the rites and terminology of Jewish worship. They had heard the Gospel from the disciples of Jesus ; had gone through persecution early, but had not seen a great number of martyrdoms. All these things point to a Jewish community, and furthermore, the community was of such a kind as is difficult to find outside of Jerusalem. This is the traditional view. The Addressees were the whole Hebraeo-Christian community of the Holy City. Recently Bornhäuser has added a plausible but not fully established precision. The author would have had chiefly in mind converts from the ranks of the Levitical Priesthood such as those mentioned in Ac 6:7.

Time and Place—There is only one exact chronological **b** indication in the letter itself, namely, the fact of Timothy's release, but unfortunately we know nothing about the time or circumstances of such an occurrence.

On the assumption that the letter was addressed to the Judaeo-Christian community of Jerusalem, we can gather from the text other indications which serve to fix an approximate date. The temple and its worship had evidently not ceased. Therefore Heb must be placed before the fateful year A.D. 70. Moreover, there is no indication that the Jewish war had broken out. Seeing that St Paul hoped to see the Hebrews soon, 13:23, he could not have written the letter after the autumn of 66, when the attempt of the Legate Cestius Gallus on Jerusalem had ended hopes of peace. In fact it is difficult to suppose that Heb could have been written after the news of the provocatory doings of Gessius Florus had reached Italy in midsummer 66.

Therefore, most probably St Paul wrote before the summer of that year. This is the late extreme. As an earlier extreme—an *annus ante quem non*—we may place 62. In that year or the following James, the brother of the Lord and Bishop of Jerusalem, was martyred, and some others, also probably Christians, were stoned to death. Trouble developed after the death of James through the ambition of a certain Thebutis, and during the years which followed till the revolt of 66, Jewish nationalism under the patronage of Herod Agrippa II was exceedingly vigorous. Such national enthusiasm would naturally emphasize the cult of the magnificent temple.

The beginning of 63 seems unlikely, for Paul was apparently not a prisoner when he wrote our Epistle. As his eyes were turned to the East, we may suppose that he had finished his intended journey to Spain. Hence he did not write before the year 64, and if the imprisonment of Timothy resulted from the Neronian persecution, the beginning of 65 seems to possess a maximum of probability.

With regard to place, we are in a better position to decide. The ' brethren from Italy ' who send greetings, 13:24, are most naturally understood to be Italians and in Italy. Therefore, the letter was written from Italy, perhaps from Rome.

929c Theological Doctrine—The Epistle to the Hebrews is of very great theological importance. So much was this felt in some Egyptian circles that it was placed immediately after Rom. This is the place it holds in the Chester Beatty Papyrus Codex (P⁴⁶) of the early 3rd cent. Its Christological doctrine, in particular, crowns the Christology of St Paul and advances to the very threshold of Johannine heights. In the following brief summary the teaching of our Epistle will be treated under the headings : (a) God and His Salvific Providence ; (b) Christology ; (c) Soteriology ; (d) Human Justification, Sanctification and Salvation ; (e) the Holy Spirit ; (f) the Church ; (g) Eschatology.

(a) God, in the Epistle to the Hebrews, is in the first place ' the living God ' of Hebrew religion, the God who was not ashamed to call himself the God of Abraham and Isaac and Jacob. It is chiefly as the Revealer *speaking* formerly through the Prophets and last of all through his Son that he pervades the Epistle. When God is mentioned, the first Person of the Blessed Trinity is undoubtedly meant, but he is nowhere called the Father of our Lord Jesus Christ as in other Paulines. In fact, it is only through the citation of two prophetic texts, 1 Kg 7:14 and Ps 2:7, that he directly and indirectly receives his Trinitarian name of Father, which, however, is implied in the name of Son given nine times to Christ. The teaching of the Epistle is undoubtedly Trinitarian, and all the three Persons are actually mentioned in one brief context, where it is said that *God* bore witness to the doctrine first spoken through the *Lord*, vouchsafing distributions of the *Holy Spirit* according to his will, 2:3, 4.

d God is the Creator and End of all things, 2:10. The Creator is specially called ' the Father of spirits ' which in the context means ' human souls ', 12:9. The paternity of God as the adopting Father of a human family is mentioned not only in the text in which the divine scheme of salvation is outlined, 2:10, but also in the passage where God appears disciplining his children to holiness, 12:5–10.

Of the attributes of God his severe justice is perhaps most prominent, for his punitive wrath appears in the just retribution of disobedience, 2:2, in his punishment of the rebellious generation of the Exodus, 3:16–19, in his severity towards apostates, 6:8, 10:31. His terrific majesty appeared on Sinai, 12:18–21, and he is described as a ' consuming fire ', 12:29. But while the note of God's severity is kept up throughout the letter, he also appears as the God ' who does not forget good deeds ', 6:10,' and as ' the God of peace ', 13:20. His goodness is the reason of his severity, for his gifts are so great that contempt of them is an outrage of incalculable magnitude. He wishes ' to bring many children to glory ', 2:10, destining them to participate in the happiness of his own Sabbath rest, 4:3–10. In fact, his condescension towards man is astounding. The angels are the ministering helpers of human salvation, 1:14 ; man through the Incarnation is destined for a glory and honour not granted to those superior spirits, 2:5–16 ; for man, if he wills, God's throne is a throne of grace, 4:16.

e Man appears in the Epistle as a weak creature needing God's help very much. Sin and death are his sad heritage. But God's scheme of salvation was precisely a scheme to bring strength out of weakness and life out of death. Christ's mortal humanity fitted him to be a Propitiator and a sympathetic High Priest. Next after Rom there is no Epistle which so effectively teaches us, as Heb does, to say that we are sinners and do need the cleansing grace of God. But it insists magnificently on the sinlessness of Jesus. In approaching God, sinners, as our Epistle teaches, can feel that they stand behind a sympathetic Pontiff who attracts them by the cords of fellowship in suffering, and inspires their confidence by his sinlessness and all-sufficient atonement. Besides the ' weakness of flesh and blood ' (which is man), there is very little ' anthropology ' in Heb—nothing, for instance, like the psychology of Rom 7.

Although there is mention of the holiness of the **9**primitive Patriarchs, Abel and Enoch and Noe, God's plan of salvation is regarded as the realization of the promise made to Abraham. No doubt the Hebrew destination of the letter had some part in determining the prominence given to the great Patriarch, but the salvific Providence of God as conceived by our author is so much centred in the ' seed of Abraham ' that the proposition : ' In no wise is it to the help of angels that (Christ) comes, but he comes to the help of Abraham's seed ' contains nothing that does not belong to the whole web of this letter.

(b) Christ is the centre of our Epistle, as he is the **9**centre of all Pauline theology. He is the *Saviour*, spoken of under his saving name of ' Jesus ' ten times ; he is *the Christ* or *Christ* six and three times respectively ; the double name *Jesus Christ* occurs in three very solemn places, 10:10, 13:8,21. Above all, Jesus is *the Son of God*. It is Jesus the Son of God who has passed as our great High Priest into heaven, 4:14 ; to him Melchisedech has been typically assimilated, 7:3 ; him apostates crucify again, 6:6, and trample under foot, 10:29. The most characteristic usage of the Epistle is that of the anarthrous υἱός used to qualify the *Son* as Supreme Revealer, 1:2, as Supreme Ruler of the House of God, 3:6, as exhibiting the contrast of that divine dignity and an obedience learned in the school of suffering, 5:8, as the High Priest established by oath and perfected for ever, 7:28. His Lordship is recognised in the title ' Our Lord ' prefixed once to the name Jesus, 13:20 ; and the titles ' the Lord ', 2:3, and ' our Lord ', 7:14, also occur unattached. Special titles of the Saviour such as are found in the same precise form nowhere else in the New Testament are : ' Author of salvation, 2:10, Apostle and High Priest of our religion, 3:1, great Priest, 10:21, Author and Finisher of faith, 12:2, and the Great Shepherd of the Sheep ', 13:20.

In fixing the plenary divine sense of the appellation **b** ' Son of God ' and in presenting Christ as true God and true man our Epistle stands excelled only by the Johannine writings. The Son is a distinct divine Person through whom the Almighty created the world. ' Light of Light, and Imprint of the Divine Substance ', he is a distinct but consubstantial Person proceeding by generation from the Father, 1:3, 5. He is the omnipotent sustainer of the universe, 1:3. His supereminence over the angels belongs essentially to his Godhead, though its manifestation in the sacred humanity belongs to the exaltation of that humanity. Similarly his universal heirship is derived from his Sonship, though actualized in his glorification.

The **Incarnation** is set forth in an extraordinarily rich **c** and specifically sacerdotal manner. If the Son were not Man, he would not be a priest. Just as in Ps 109, which in a true sense is the greatest OT fountain of our Epistle, priesthood is inseparably bound up with the Messianic kingship. However, it is a Psalm of man's destined grandeur as Sovereign of creation and of the infra-angelic littleness of his mortality that is used to show the Priest-Victim in whom Manhood attains its unlimited kingship over the universe. Man who had lost immortality by disobedience had to attain the predestined glory of his adoptive sonship by treading the way of painful obedience. Hence ' the grace of God ' was that the Man who recapitulates humanity ' should taste death for all ', 2:9. As the Author of human salvation the Son, according to a plan of solidarity with our condition, was to attain his own glory, the perfection of his Saviourship and the sympathy of his priestly quality by undergoing sufferings and death. He could not, of course, give up his natural Sonship and become an adopted Son, but he could and did become the brother of those called by God into participation in his Sonship. In the Incarnation he finds fellowship of flesh and blood with men, makes his own their attitude of filial creature-confidence towards God, and submits to all the physical debt of human guilt, even to death. Thus the devil's empire of death was

0c broken and the black slavery of mortality undone. Man was weak, and the Saviour became weak ; man was subject to pain, and the Saviour submitted to pain ; man was liable to mental anguish, and the Saviour experienced anguish. By the Incarnation therefore he bound himself to us in a full programme of *sympathy*. The knowledge that he sinlessly experienced all the painful trials of sinful flesh gives sinners every confidence in this faithful High Priest.

d One who has meditated Heb 2:5-18 will be in possession of the main points of its teaching on the humanity of Christ. We learn elsewhere of his prayer, 5:7, that he endured the cross and its shame and suffered contradictions from sinners, 12:2, 3. Opprobrium was his lot, 13:13 ; *cf.* 11:26. He shed his blood, 9:12, was numbered amongst the dead, and was raised from death, 13:20. He passed through the heavens, 4:14 f., and sat down at God's right hand, 1:3. He shall come again to gather his own to final salvation, 9:28. Furthermore, such circumstantial details are mentioned as his descent from Abraham, 2:16, and from the tribe of Juda, 7:14. He preached just over a generation before the Epistle was written, 2:3. His crucifixion was a public spectacle, 6:6, which took place outside the gate of Jerusalem, 13:12. There is no mention either of his manifestation of himself after the resurrection or of his visible ascension into heaven.

e (c) The **Soteriology** of Heb is the very core of its sacerdotal theology. Actually, apart from the use of the name *Jesus*, Christ is nowhere called Saviour, but he is represented as having brought salvation and proclaimed it, 2:3 ; he is the appointed Author of human salvation, 2:10, the Cause of eternal salvation for all who obey him, 5:9, and the final Giver of salvation at his second coming, 9:28. His work, conceived in its sacerdotal aspect, is essentially that of saving the people from their sins. He made a cleansing of sins, 1:3, and established a covenant whose special fruit is the remission of sin in the interior domain of conscience, 8:12 ; 9:14 ; 10:18. The remission accorded is a positive renewal of the human soul, for Christ is the *sanctifier*, 2:11. Sin is destroyed even in its most terrible consequence, for Christ's work ends the empire of death by which the devil held men in the servitude of hopeless fear, 2:14, 15. There is no such fullness regarding the causal mode of the salvific work as we find in Rom and other Paulines. However, the meritoriousness of Christ's death is implied in his obedience, 5:8 ; 10:9, and its value as redemption or ransom is explicitly mentioned twice, 9:12, 15. Our Epistle concentrates on the sacrificial character of Christ's death, and his blood is regarded as sprinkled to cleanse, rather than shed to purchase. This ritual point of view, however, does not exclude the juridical concept, for Christ's sacrifice effects an expiatory propitiation, 2:17, and releases men from a servitude, 2:15. At the same time it is true that the sacerdotal conception of salvation, precisely because it is worked out liturgically in relation to the high-priestly ministry of Expiation Day, is notably, though not fundamentally, different from the soteriological elements found in other Paulines. In all the Pauline writings, the death and glorification of Christ puts salvation within the reach of mankind, but whereas the author of the Epistles to the Gentile Churches emphasizes the *resurrection* of Christ, the author of the Epistle to the Hebrews emphasizes the Saviour's Τελείωσις as an entry into the heavenly sanctuary. In other words, St Paul in the other epistles fixes his gaze more particularly on the first moment of the Saviour's ' perfection ' or glorification, while in Heb he fixes it on the last. Nevertheless he has shown explicitly in one place, 13:20, that the resurrection is no more extraneous to his soteriology here than the session at the right hand of the Father is to the soteriology of Rom and the Captivity Letters. In Eph and Col the ' Christ above ' does become exceedingly important because of his headship of the mystical body. This is an approach to the thought of Heb, though not to be identified with its characteristic-

ally sacerdotal outlook. Such a professedly sacerdotal **930e** soteriology is certainly a signal addition to the Pauline theology. It can only be outlined very briefly here.

It is, of course, theologically certain that the hypostatic **f** union was a sacerdotal anointing, but it may be doubted whether our author regarded the words : *Thou art my Son*, as a specific call to priesthood. That call or vocation is, however, certainly conveyed by the great sacerdotal Psalm-oracle : ' Thou art a Priest for ever according to the order of Melchisedech ', Ps 109:4 ; Heb 5:6. The justice and peace that belong to Melchisedech's name and title, his unlimited life and freedom from fleshly limitations, the superiority he exercises over Abraham by tithing and blessing him, are all supremely fulfilled in Christ. The qualities of Christ the Priest were such that he needed nothing but to do his priestly work and have it crowned with perfection, so that the beneficiaries of his Priesthood might recognize that they have as High Priest ' a Son perfected for ever ', 7:28.

The priestly work of Christ is in terms of the liturgy of Expiation Day. He offered sacrifice for the sins of the people, 7:27 ; by the sprinkling of his sacrificial blood he cleanses our conscience from dead works, to serve the living God, 9:14 ; his one sacrifice was so efficacious that nothing remains except to gather finally those who expect salvation from him, 9:28 ; it is as limitless as the human generations for whom it is intended, for ' by one oblation he has perfected for ever those who are undergoing sanctification ', 10:12-14.

His sacrifice was a work of obedience to the will of **g** God decreeing that *we* should be sanctified by the offering of the body of Christ once for all, 10:10. The main points in this regime of sanctification are that it belongs to a sphere which is not merely terrestrial ; it realizes a Covenant which is primarily one of interior enlightenment together with real remission of sin within the human conscience ; it supplants the inefficacious sacrificial system of the Old Covenant. The fact that Christ the testator died to establish the New Covenant gives the Covenant itself a testamentary character, 9:15-17. In reading the highly liturgical presentation of all these truths, it is necessary to remember that everything is dependent on the mystery of the Cross. It is in his blood that Christ attains his ' perfection ', entering the Holy of Holies ; it is in his blood that we have remission of sins ; it is in his blood that we have confidence regarding the efficacy of the entrance-way provided for us into the heavenly sanctuary ; in approaching him we approach the Mediator of the New Covenant and a blood of sprinkling that speaks better than Abel ; it is by his blood that he sanctifies the people. But Christ shed his blood once for all ; we must beware of taking the Epistle to mean that he performs a sacrificial liturgy in heaven. Other details will be found in the commentary.

(d) **Subjective salvation** which is individual justifica- **931a** tion and sanctification occupies a minor place in Heb. As St Thomas Aquinas noted, ' the excellence of Christ is the theme of this Epistle ', and consequently his Person and his work in their objective greatness is what chiefly matters. The scattered elements of the Epistle's psychological soteriology can, however, be gathered and systematized.

Christ's sacrifice established a ' better ' Covenant between God and mankind. Its Mediator was solemnly appointed by a sworn oracle, 7:22. To that superior solemnity belongs a superior efficacy. It was not in the power of the Old Covenant to bring about a spiritual approach of the soul to God ; but in the better hope now introduced we really do draw near to him, 7:19. The effects of the Mosaic Dispensation were external and its promises temporal ; the effects of the New Dispensation are internal and its promises eternal. The New Covenant is, however, not an ordinance of divine unilateral graciousness. In purifying the conscience, it obliges or binds the conscience. In other words, the grace of God requires co-operation. Christ is the cause of salvation for those who *obey* him, 5:9.

931a His gift is interior light, and interior remission, and devotion to God's law—all characteristics of the New Covenant in the Jeremian oracle. Those who obey him enter the ranks of the many sons whom God will bring to glory, 2:10. They are called partakers of a heavenly vocation, 3:1, partakers of Christ, 3:14, partakers of the Holy Ghost, 6:4. This life of participation with Christ and with the Holy Spirit gives a very strong confidence which is called the ' boast of hope ', 3:6. But hope supposes faith, and must not be separated from charity, and actually the great triad of virtues is mentioned twice, 6:9-12 ; 10:19-25. Divine life must be strengthened by grace not Jewish meats, 13:10, and all must ' pursue holiness without which no one can see the Lord ', 12:14. We thus come to the truth that the life in question is really the effect of grace—obviously what theologians call habitual grace. Those who totally fall away from Christian life ' outrage the Spirit of grace ', 10:29, and those who neglect their salvation ' fall short of the grace of God ', 12:15. In the sentence : ' Let us have grace whereby we may serve God acceptably (well-pleasingly) with reverence and godly fear ', 12:28, *grace* must be an interior endowment of the soul. Actual grace is also mentioned, for what else can *grace* for seasonable aid be ? 4:16.

b How does this life originate ? Supernaturally of course, for nothing is greater than its own cause. When we observe that the state of friendship with God is expressed in Heb by the two verbs προσέρχεσθαι (to approach) and εὐαρεστῆσαι (to please), we can see that the beginning of Christian life must be the act of faith, because ' without faith it is impossible to *please*, for he who *approaches* God must believe that he exists, and that for those who seek him, he is a remunerator ', 11:6.

The Council of Trent (VI, 8) uses this text in defining the Catholic doctrine that ' faith is the beginning of human salvation, the foundation and root of all justification '. Faith in our Epistle occupies a place not at all below that of Rom, but the special character of Heb is the reason why faith appears so much dyed in the colours of hope. The promises are chiefly its object. Charity in Heb retains its Pauline queenship. It is something that God does not forget, 6:10, and on which he particularly smiles, 13:16. The moral virtues recommended must be noted in the text and commentary. Final salvation is attained after death in the vision of God. The heroes of the Great Martyrology, 11, have had to wait for it, but now possess it together with those Christians who have trodden the way of faith. With these they form the company of ' spirits of the just made perfect ', 12:23. The final resurrection is an article of the elementary Catechesis of 6:1-2, and some of the heroes of faith are declared not to have accepted deliverance from death ' that they might obtain a better resurrection ', 11:35, but in the thesis proper of our Epistle it is only the gathering of the elect with Christ that is mentioned as the final act of human salvation, 9:28.

c (*e*) The Epistle's teaching on **the Holy Ghost** can be dealt with very briefly. He is called ' the Spirit of grace ' as being the Giver of grace, and is a *Person* whom apostasy outrages, 10:29. That he is the third Person of the Blessed Trinity may be lawfully inferred from 2:3-4. He is called the Holy Spirit and the eternal Spirit, 2:4, etc. ; 9:14. There is no clear assertion of the appropriation of the Incarnation to the operation of the Holy Ghost, and the same is true of the other Paulines. In the seven relevant texts of our Epistle four functions are attributed to the Spirit : (1) the inspiration of Scriptures, (2) the sanctification of Christ's soul, (3) the distribution of charismata, and (4) the sanctification of the faithful.

Twice words of David, Ps 94, and once words of Jeremias, 31:33, are set down as words of the Holy Ghost. Similarly, he is the designer of the typological arrangements of Israelite worship, 9:8 ; Christ offered his sacrifice through the eternal Spirit, 9:14 ; God

has confirmed the Gospel delivered by his Son through **931** the distributions made by the Holy Ghost, 2:4 ; and the faithful are not only partakers of Christ, but partakers of the Holy Spirit, 6:4. Those who dishonour the blood of the Covenant in which they were sanctified also insult the Holy Spirit, 10:29. Compare St Paul's : ' Do not sadden the Holy Spirit of God in whom you were sealed for the day of redemption ', Eph 4:30. Briefly, then, the Holy Ghost inspired the written word which proclaims Christ, sanctified the soul of Christ and co-operated in his work, confirm Christ's spoken word, and sanctifies Christ's faithful.

(*f*) When closely examined Heb reveals an im- **93?** portant **ecclesiology.** In the first place there is every indication that the New Regime—' the world to come ' of which Christ is the sovereign administrator, 2:5—is no less organic than the Old. In fact the House in which Moses ministered is replaced by the House over which the Son has been placed, and ' his house we are ', 3:6. We have a common heavenly calling, 3:1, recognize the same Lord, Apostle and Pontiff, and hold the same Confession of faith, 3:2. It is, however, not a matter of individual adhesion to Christ. The bond of brotherhood and the unity of aspiration towards the heavenly rest must be socially maintained. The faithful must consider each other in order to stir up charity and good works, 10:24, and aloofness from the community is to be avoided, 10:25. Obedience to superiors is a sacred duty, 13:17. In the last chapter *hegoumenoi* (superiors or prelates) are mentioned no less than three times.

It is true that the House of God also figures as a city **b** and a kingdom and that in this two-fold imagery emphasis is on the future. We seek the city which is to come, 13:14, and we receive an unshakable kingdom, 12:28. But from the Epistle's point of view on the mountains of Israel, the future city and the unshakable kingdom is also the Church of the present time. Our fellowship with heaven is a fellowship realized in good measure here on earth. This is shown especially in the contrast between the Hebrew Sinai and the Christian Sion, 12:22-24. The Christian Sion is ' both here and beyond '. If the myriads of angels—a festive assembly—and God the Judge of all, and the spirits of just men made perfect belong especially to the heavenly consummation, on the other hand, Mount Sion and the City of the Living God and the Celestial Jerusalem can designate the whole Church ; while the approach to an assembly of firstborn enrolled in heaven and to the Mediator of a New Covenant and to a blood of sprinkling which speaks better than Abel's refers without ambiguity to those who are still on the *way* to the final attainment of the promises.

(*g*) Of the Pauline Epistles Heb could claim to be **c** the one—not even excepting the specially eschatological letters to the Thessalonians—which sets our face most steadily and continually towards the heavenly city. The expectation of the Old Testament is perfected in the aspiration of the New, for Christ at the right hand of God is the goal of our τελείωσις, and our confident hope is that we shall enter the Sanctuary in the blood of Jesus, 10:19. The presentation of eternal happiness as a sabbatic rest, 4:9, is only very slightly paralleled in the Paulines (2 Thess 1:7—ἄνεσις, Vg *requies*), but figures in the second (or third) beatitude and, with still closer approximation to the language of Heb, is proclaimed by a voice from heaven in Apoc 14:13. There is great coherence in the way the pilgrim conception of life pervades our Epistle. The Gospel remains an ἐπαγγελία or ' promise ' and the writer goes back to the old tabernacle of Israel's wanderings for the prefigurative material of his exposition of Christ's work. The movement out of the camp of Judaism towards the lasting city, 13:13, does not end in the Church Militant, and the unshakable kingdom which we receive, 12:28, is not so much the Messianic era of time as the Messianic stability of unchanging eternity.

The ' last things ' in our Epistle may be summed up **d** as follows : The pilgrimage of human life ends with

932d death, 9:27. Death is followed by judgement—whether particular or general being left undetermined, although the context favours the latter, 9:27. Judgement here and hereafter is made by the searching light of God's word, 4:12, 13, and the final sentence is eternal, 6:2. In order of time this final discernment is preceded by the coming of Christ, who however does not appear as a Judge but a Saviour, 9:28. Judgement is attributed to God, 10:30 ; 12:23. The wrath of fire, 10:27, or eternal rest, 4:11, stand at the end of the way. The prophetic and Pauline conception of the great final ' day ' is not absent, 10:25, and perhaps the end of Jerusalem is here included in this expression as in our Lord's eschatological discourse.

It seems that the accompaniments of Christ's coming are touched upon in the citation, 1:6, that invites all the angels to adore him. A word from the Prophet Aggeus (2:6) tells of ' a movement of heaven and earth ' which is to usher in an unchanging kingdom, 12:28. The final consummation shall, according to our author, set all things in subjection to Christ, 2:8, and make his enemies the footstool of his feet, 10:13.

COMMENTARY

933a **Prologue I 1-4**—The absence of the writer's name, of personal greeting to the addressees, of any specific epistolary exordium are things which have attracted attention from early times. Reasons suggested for the omission of Paul's name are : reverence for Christ the Apostle of the Hebrews, Paul's consciousness that he himself was the special Apostle of the Gentiles, unwillingness to antagonize Hebrews by setting the name of an ' anti-legalist ' at the head of the letter, consideration of the position of the Mother Church at Jerusalem. The omission of the writer's name almost necessarily entailed absence of greeting and of such compliments or good wishes as were usual in Pauline epistles. Moreover, although a letter, this writing—subsequently to be described as ' a word of exhortation ', 13:22—comes close to the form of a homily. A NT parallel is found in the abrupt beginning of 1 Jn, and many similar examples occur in the papyrus letters of the 1st and 2nd cent., and still more abundantly in the 4th.

Since the central theme of Heb is the superiority of the New Dispensation over the Old, the whole matter is majestically summarized in a preface full of stately grandeur. We should note the weighty dignity of its thoughts, its very remarkable stylistic balance, and the special graces of paronomasia and rhythm. It is, as it were, a nutshell presentation of what is to follow, set in terms of the greatness of Christ. A seven-point portrait of the Incarnate Son very skilfully glides, 4, into the special statement of his superiority over the Angel administrators of the Sinaitic Covenant.

b **1-2a The Two Revelations**—' God speaking ' is the central idea, the past being contrasted with the present under three aspects. A progressive series of (1) piecemeal and modally diversified revelations, (2) spoken to the Hebrew fathers, (3) through the prophets, has given place (1) in this definitive age, to a revelation (2) spoken to us, (3) through ONE who is SON. The Vg actually gives fuller balance than is usually ascribed to the Greek words by making ' last of all ' the counterpart of ' at sundry times and in divers manners ', while the phrase : ' in these days ' balances ' in times past '. The ' divers manners ' probably refers to different modes of communication : oracles spoken to the ear, mental illuminations, visions received through the internal or external senses, and not so much to the formal distinctions of prophecy, instruction, commination, legislation, etc. Note, however, that one and the same God speaks in the Old and the New Age.

c **2b-3 The Characteristics of the Son**—This Epistle uses the word SON without the article almost as a proper name of Christ, cf. 3:6 ; 5:8 ; 7:28. In the septenary list of his descriptives (numbering them by the letters a–g) the distribution of these descriptives between the divine pre-existent Person and him incarnate is as **933c** singularly skilful as the arrangement is remarkable. The first two descriptives (a, b) form a pair referring respectively to Christ's Manhood and his Godhead ; the third and fourth (c, d) form another pair describing, in metaphors of light and image, his divine personality, and to this double description the Greek ' adjunctive ' particle τε closely annexes the prerogative of universal and omnipotent Conservatorship (e). This last of a ' divine four ' (b–e) corresponds to the first, namely, to the Creatorship which has figured as the first predicate of his divinity (b). The basic heirship of the hypostatic union (a) is then supplemented by reference to the work of redemption (f)—here called ' a cleansing ' in forecast of future sacerdotal developments—and lastly by the crowning glorification of enthronement in heaven (g). Thus the Incarnation, announced with fourfold emphasis on the Godhead of the Son, is completed by the Passion and Glorification of the Man Christ, cf. Phil 2:5-11.

(a) To be ' appointed heir of all things ' connotes **d** sonship and denotes that the one *appointed* is man. Heirship includes no notion of succession, but only the assured possession promised in Ps 2:8. It belongs to sonship, Gal 4:7 ; Mt 21:38, and therefore follows from the hypostatic union. In the divine economy of redemption, however, the actual exercise of ' all power in heaven and earth ' belongs to the ' Christ enthroned '.

(b) ' By whom he made the world ' : since the act of creation is incommunicably divine, there can be no question of instrumental agency. As in Jn 1:3, ' by ' or ' through ' only signifies that the one divine power is exercised by the Father, who has it unoriginate, and by the Son who receives it with the divine nature from the Father. The world (in Greek αἰῶνες) is either the successive ages of time and the things that exist in them, or more probably (cf. 11:3) the whole universe of created things.

(c) The Son is ' the brightness of ' the Father's ' glory '. The Gk present participle is significant after the two aorists : ' whom he "*appointed*" . . . through whom he "*made*" . . . who *being the Radiance*'. The term ἀπαύγασμα is, no doubt, borrowed from the one OT passage in which it occurs, Wis 7:26. There Divine Wisdom figures as ' the radiance of light, the mirror of activity, the image of goodness '. This association of radiance with mirror and image, joined to the fact that the ending -μα denotes a result rather than an action, goes to show that the ἀπαύγασμα is not merely brightness-adherent but brightness issuing and having issued, in other words, radiance or effulgence reflected as an image of the luminous fountain. Since ' glory ' means the divine nature in the perfection that manifests itself, ' radiance of his glory ' is equivalent to the *lumen de lumine* of our Nicene Creed.

(d) The radiation metaphor might seem to fall short **e** in signifying distinction of person ; therefore it is supplemented by the description : ' figure of his substance '. Again the Gk χαρακτήρ is more expressive than ' figure '. It means an imprinted, ingraven *image* expressly reproducing the traits of that from which it is made. A statue which was the likeness of its prototype is described in a Gk inscription of Antiochus I of Commagene as χαρακτὴρ μορφῆς ἐμῆς, but the stamp of a seal or signet is the most obvious source of the metaphor—the express reproduction of an impress. An image (cf. 2 Cor 4:4 ; Col 1:15) which thus originates from and expresses the divine substance, nature, or essence, must be consubstantial, so that the *homoousios* emerges very distinctly from the combined descriptions of ' radiance ' and ' express image '. That there is question of the pre-existent Christ is evident from the close connexion with the following present participial phrase :

(e) ' Upholding (*carrying*) all things by the word of his power ' : the universe is at the order of his imperial will. The Son is, therefore, the Conservator of creation (' all things ', 2:8, 10) the universal, all-provident, all-sustaining Governor. Col. 1:15-17 should be read.

933e The passage combines with this to form a splendid Christological diptych.

(*f*) The expiatory work of Christ is briefly summed up as a '*cleansing* of sins', in anticipation of the 'liturgical' section of the Epistle, 8:1–10:18.

(*g*) The triumphantly enthroned Christ crowns the septenary. The elevation of the Priest to the place of honour beside the throne of God's 'Majesty on high', that is, in heaven, is a keynote of this sacerdotal epistle, *cf*. 6:1 ; 10:18 ; 12:8. The thought is simply that of Ps 109, as solemnly interpreted by Christ himself, Mt 22:44 ; 26:64.

f 4 Statement of Christ's Superiority over Angels—It is to the elevation of Christ 'in the glory which was his before the world was' that his superiority above the Angel ministers of Mosaic revelation is attached. Hence the participle γενόμενος : '*having been* made '. The distance of his superiority is seen in ' the *better* name' which he 'has inherited', for he is now established in possession of the glory of his Sonship, *cf*. Phil 2:11, where ' the name' is not *Son* but *Kyrios*, that is, Yahweh—with no real difference of sense, however.

934a 5–14 Scriptural Proofs—It is important to remember that the Apostle does not intend to prove that Christ is the Son of God and very God. That is supposed as a basic dogma. He simply wishes to give to the dignity of divine Sonship the weight of biblical texts, so as to show its immense superiority over the dignity of angelic ministers. The application is not equally compelling in the case of every citation, but the whole series is an imposing array. The Apostle chooses seven passages, beginning with an oracle from the Psalm of Christ's sovereign heirship or kingship and ending with the Psalm of his exaltation in glory. Therefore, as in the series of descriptives above, the two poles are Incarnation and Glorification. Only the middle text, that is, the fourth, is concerned exclusively with angels. The following remarks will sufficiently illustrate the series. **5.** The first citation (never addressed to any angel) is from Ps 2:7—a directly Messianic prophecy of Christ's kingship founded on his divine filiation. 'My Son', as determined by the words 'I have begotten Thee', is an address never used by God in the singular number to any single individual except Christ. That reservation is important, for angels are called 'sons of God' in the plural, Job 1:7 ; 2:1 ; Pss 28:1 ; 88:7 ; the collective Israel is called God's first-born, Ex 4:22 ; and Israelites as a body are called sons in the plural number, Deut 32:19. The metaphorical sense is thus kept distinct from the proper sense of divine filiation and generation. 'To-day' is understood of the day of the Incarnation or any undetermined subsequent particular day. The 'begetting' is real not adoptive, and the Gk perfect of LXX well expresses its perfect and permanent reality.

The second text literally refers to Solomon, but typally to Christ, for whom ' the throne of David his father' is ultimately destined, and who is also God's Son **b** in the plenary sense of the term. **6.** Whether the second 'again' merely serves to introduce a third citation or should be attached to the verb is doubtful. The adversative particle δέ at the head of the sentence seems to favour the latter view. The provenance of the text is also doubtful. In verbal form it is nearest to Deut 32:43 (LXX)—a known source of Pauline citation, Rom 15:10—but the claims of Ps 96:7 are strong, although the LXX rendering ' angels' covers '*Elohim*', considered by some to mean pagan divinities. Whichever may be its source, the text literally refers to a judgement Theophany and may apply typally to the Son to whom ' the Father has given all judgement'. The second coming of Christ seems to be what is in the Apostle's mind, *cf*. 9:28. The Son is called πρωτότοκος rather in the human sense of Rom 8:29 and Col 1:18 than in the divine pre-existential sense of Col 1:15. He receives the adoration of Angels (*Elohim* in Ps 96:7, Heb). **7.** The fourth—the sole text referring exclusively to the Angels—is from Ps 103:4. There seems no doubt that St Paul and the LXX read ' spirits ' or

' winds ' as a predicate of the verbal object ' Angels '. **934b** So did the Targum of the Psalms. Syntactic probability would seem to require this translation, but the context of the Psalm strophe is naturally taken to demand the rendering 'Who makes the winds his angels', a sense which nearly all modern scholars support. In this case, the Apostle's argument could stand, but is less natural. However, in spite of the *apparent* Psalm context, the possibility of a sudden transition from elemental forces to angels is really not unnatural in a Hebrew poet, and there is a fair parallel in Ps 17:10. We have to reckon very often with rapid changes in the psychological context of oriental poetry. **8.** The Apostle then contrasts the Son with those ministering spirits. The contrasting Son is supplied by the nuptial Psalm of a royal Prince who is certainly the Messias and most probably the Messias directly and exclusively. It seems that an historical royal wedding cannot have been more than the occasion of the Psalm. The royalty of the Prince is in the forefront, but he is also actually addressed as God : ' Thy throne, O God, is for ever and ever ', Ps 44:7. **10–12.** To this divine **c** Person is also applied a Psalm text which addresses Yahweh Himself, the Almighty Restorer of Sion. Cited from LXX, Ps 101:26–28, with two unimportant variations, the text strongly pictures the eternal unchangeableness of God. **13.** Lastly, in a quotation introduced interrogatively, like the first, and with the perfect tense of the verb ' to say ' the Son is shown enthroned ' at the right hand of majesty on high ', and the final word is said on the inferiority of Angels : ' Are they not all ministering spirits sent to minister *on behalf of* them who shall receive the inheritance of salvation ? ' The angels are essentially servants, at the order of God, ' public ministers ' deputed to particular ' service ' on behalf of those on the way of salvation, and thus, in a sense, ' servants of servants '. The doctrine of Guardian Angels in general is implied in this text, but not necessarily the doctrine of a single Guardian Angel for each single Christian. That is a precision derived from other sources.

II 1–4 Exhortation to Steadfastness—Being ' a word of **d** exhortation ', Heb mixes admonition very continuously with dogmatic considerations. These warning are all directed against the danger of apostasy, 2:1–4 ; 3:7–4:13 ; 5:11–6:20 ; also the long final exhortation, 10:19–12:29. Here, with the usual joining skill of the writer, the exhortation is attached to the word ' salvation ', 1:14, and rests on the incomparable superiority of Christ over the Angels.

1. The first sentence is somewhat weakened in Vg. Render : ' *Therefore it is necessary that we pay a greater surplus of attention to the things heard* (the truths once delivered), *lest perhaps we should miss the port* (of salvation) '. A final catastrophe is what is to be feared. **2–3.** The sanctions of the Old Law, which was promulgated by angels (*cf*. Ac 7:53 ; Gal 3:19) showed how strongly God willed it ratified against transgression and disobedience ; *a fortiori* ' how shall we escape, if we neglect so great a salvation ? ', *cf*. 1 Cor 10:1–11. Its imperative firmness is the very greatest, having been first spoken (*by God*, as in the whole Epistle) through the Lord, having been delivered with irrefutable authority by witnesses who had heard Christ, having been authenticated (**4**) by signs (wrought expressly for proof), by prodigies astounding, by various showings of power, and by charismatic distributions of the Holy Spirit according to God's will. St Paul says : ' confirmed *unto us* by them that heard ', either by *enallage* (the first person plural so often used by a preacher identifying himself with his audience), or because he refers to the earthly ministry of Christ. This sentence does not exclude Pauline authorship, and in fact it occurs in a short paragraph which, in spite of five unique expressions, is overwhelmingly Pauline in thought and language. It splendidly illustrates the fallaciousness of verbal statistics.

5–18 Christ Head of the Messianic Regime—This **e** section asserts the Messianic sovereignty of Christ, 5–9,

e and show how the Incarnation and Passion belong to its divinely ordered fitness, 10–18. **5-9.** The Messianic kingdom, as being the kingdom of heaven, having its final phase beyond this world, is called 'the world to come'—the rabbinical '*ôlām habbā*'. God did not subject it to Angels but to man, or more exactly to 'a Man'. This is shown from a Scripture text introduced in a special way. In the seven texts of ch 1 God spoke ; here the formula is : 'Someone, as you know, in a certain place gave solemn testimony, saying : What is man, etc.'. Only once in this whole Epistle, 4:7, is a biblical quotation given under the name of its human author. This peculiarity has been represented as un-Pauline, but it would be natural enough in a letter to Hebrews, whose rabbis often used this method of indefinite quoting, the same being also followed by the Hellenistic Jew, Philo of Alexandria.

f **6-8.** Ps 8 is a canticle of the greatness of God and of the littleness and greatness of man. In the three verses cited (5–7 with the omission, in the critical Greek text, of the stichos 7*a*) three ideas are marked for emphasis : (1) man's diminution, so as to be something short of angels, (2) his exaltation to glory and honour, (3) the subjection of all things to him. The key to St Paul's use of the Psalm here, as in 1 Cor 15:27, and Eph 1:22, is its Messianic character. Applied to mankind in general the Psalm has a certain universality of meaning founded on the universal sovereignty indicated in Gen 1:27, but the absoluteness of the sovereignty it describes belongs to the Messias. The Psalmist sees man's inferiority to Angels (Heb. *Elōhîm* 'divine dignitaries' rather than 'God') in his mortality. **8.** But that same mortality in the Messias is the cause of man's exaltation to glory and honour—a glory and honour only partially realized in man's present lordship over creation, but entirely realized in the glorified Christ, although the sovereignty to which it belongs has not yet actually extended itself to 'everything'. The temporal sense of 'a little' (*i.e.* 'a little while') is tempting, but is foreign to the psalm and not really postulated by the connexion of St Paul's thought. **9.** The glory of Christ, which is the reward for 'the suffering of death', manifests the gracious intention of God that he should die for each and every one. It is insinuated here but not asserted, as in 1 Cor 15:26, 27, that the destruction of death will complete the full sovereignty of Christ.

5a **10-18 Congruity of the Passion**—Man's mortality—here marked as his *infra*-angelic condition—is in actual historical fact a penal appendage of the guilt of sin. Hence the fitness of an expiation by way of suffering and death. **10.** Not necessity nor moral obligation but the beauty of an harmonious fitness drew God, the final and efficient Cause of all things, to choose this means to an end fixed by his goodness. The end was that of 'bringing many *sons* to glory'. The Gk participle ἀγαγόντα translated 'who had brought' does not mark priority of time over the principal verb, and therefore the interpretation '*qui adduxerat = qui adducendos praeordinaverat*' is not necessary. The whole verse should be translated : '*It befitted him, for whom are all things and by whom are all things, because he set himself to bring many sons to glory—it befitted him to perfect the Author of their salvation through sufferings*'. The prepositional description of God (for whom—by whom) is very Pauline, *cf.* Rom 11:26 ; 1 Cor 8:6 ; Col 1:16, 20. In 'bringing many'—an indefinitely great number—as *sons* to the glory of his bliss, he fittingly chose to bring the Author of their salvation to the goal (τελειῶσαι) by the way of sufferings. '*Leader* of their salvation' would harmonize with the idea of God 'leading or bringing', but 'Author' is favoured by Heb 5:9 ; 12:2. The concept in the verb τελειοῦν, namely, 'to perfect, consummate, bring to final attainment' is very characteristic of this Epistle ; *cf.* for verb, 5:9 ; 7:19, 28 ; 9:9 ; 10:1, 14, 11:40 ; 12:23—for abstract noun τελειότης 6:1—for verbal noun τελείωσις 7:11—for nomen agentis τελειωτής 12:2. Really the notion of 'consummation' sums up the whole theology of the *better* revelation and the *better* priesthood and the *better* covenant and the *better*

sacrifice, and these sum up Hebrews. **11.** The reason **935b** of this brotherhood in pain is found in the principle of family solidarity. SON and sons—Sanctifier and sanctified—claim, at least analogically, one heavenly father, 'the One from whom they are' being God and not Adam (following Chrysostom, Theodoret, Aquinas, Westcott, Vitti against Estius, à Lapide, Bisping, Médebielle). This divine family association is fittingly joined to human association. **12-13.** That Christ calls men his brethren is emphasized by citing three texts, Ps 21:23 ; Is 8:17*b*, 18*a*. The first places the Messias amongst his brethren, the second in the human fellowship of confidence towards God, the third sets him at the head of a family group of which Isaias and his two sons are types. In the last text for 'children' read 'brethren'. **14-18.** Such solidarity was the reason that **c** the Son shared human weakness ('blood and flesh' being the Gk order of words here), through which (*a*) he broke the empire of death, (*b*) delivered men from sin, (*c*) fitted himself with sacerdotal sympathy.

14-15. (*a*) He became mortal, in order that by dying he might destroy the power of the Prince of death, namely, the devil, who caused man's spiritual death and corporal death, Gen 3:15 ; Wis 2:24, and wished to bring him to eternal death. Hence the freedom from the slavery of fear gained by those who now say : 'For me to live is Christ and to die is gain', Phil. 1:21.

16-17. (*b*) Christ did not come to help immortal angels but mortal men—and firstly the race of Abraham to which he belonged and to which the divine promises were made. Note this probable indication that the letter is addressed to Hebrews. The verb rendered 'take hold' and sometimes unduly pressed to mean 'taking the nature of men and not of angels', simply signifies 'to help'. As helper of mortals, he had to resemble his brethren in every possible way (in all things) so as to become merciful by partnership in misery, and so as to be a faithful High Priest towards God—joined at once to the miserable and to the Merciful—so as to expiate the sins of the people. The title of 'Priest' is first given to Christ here, 2:17. All the changes of a rich sacerdotal theology shall be rung on it in the subsequent chapters (except 11 and 12).

18. (*c*) Experience of suffering and of trial is the best school of compassion. Knowing pain and trial, Christ is a competent Helper for those who are being tried. Compare the words of Virgil's Sidonian Dido : 'Non ignara mali miseris succurrere disco', Aen I, 630.

III 1—IV 13 Christ's Superiority over Moses—Again, **d** a transition is effected with admirable naturalness and skill, the comparison with Moses being grafted on the word 'faithful', 2:17, and subsequent comparison with Aaron being distantly prepared by setting the two titles : 'Apostle' (like Moses) and 'High Priest' (like Aaron) side by side as belonging to Jesus. The superiority of Christ over Moses was a tremendous truth for a Hebrew circle and is here made the basis of a very long exhortation, 3:7-4:13.

III 1-6 Christ and Moses—1. 'Holy brethren' is singularly honorific and only very doubtfully paralleled in 1 Thess 5:27. 'Brethren' is really a title derived from the efficacious call given from the Father in heaven and leading to heaven. The Hebrews are asked to consider the 'Legate' who called, and the 'High Priest' who sanctified, namely, Jesus. **2.** His fidelity likens him to Moses as eulogised by God in Num 12:7 ; but the circumstances of that fidelity set him immeasurably above Moses. **3-5.** As Man, Jesus was faithful to his Maker 'in the whole house' or people of God. The points of Christ's superiority are : (1) He himself '*made*' the house of Israel, since he is God ; (2) Moses was faithful in that house as an honourable servant (θεράπων) to speak things as they were to be said in God's name (τῶν λαληθησομένων), but Christ stands as SON (without the article) 'over' (not 'in') his own house. **6.** This statement leads to the long exhortation ; for Christ's house we are, provided we keep to the end our 'bold confidence and *the boast of our* hope'—very

935d Pauline expressions (the second exclusively Pauline) for the assurance of the theological virtue of hope.

e III 7-IV 13 Exhortation to Fidelity—Under Moses an unfaithful generation was fearfully punished by exclusion from the temporal rest of Chanaan ; much more must Christians fear the apostasy which would exclude them from eternal rest. **7-9.** This is the substance of the solemn commination extracted from the two warning strophes of the invitatory Psalm, Ps 94. Its words are referred to the Holy Spirit, the Author of Scripture. It is cited, 94:8-11, from LXX, with its etymological renderings of the local names *Meribah* (quarrel) and *Massah* (temptation). The constantly recurring waywardness of Hebrew hearts in the desert consisted in doubting that the all-provident God was with them. They sulked when God seemed to leave them in the lurch, and they demanded tests of his fidelity and power. **10.** Almost every day they forgot the miracles of yesterday. St Paul heightens the picture of Hebrew rebellion by making the forty years a constant repetition of *Meribah* and *Massah*, ' where your fathers tempted me, proved and saw my works forty years '. Here he inserts a ' for which cause ' to show that God was just in his anger and in his decree to exclude the rebellious generation from Chanaan. There is no falsification of the text and no departure from historical truth. **11.** ' If they shall enter ' means : ' They shall not enter '—an elliptic form of oath : ' (May I cease to be God) if they shall enter '. The rest or repose of Chanaan is typal (*cf.* 3rd, otherwise 2nd, beatitude)—a figure of eternal rest. The application here presents close affinities with 1 Cor 10:1-13, but we must not commit the exaggeration of asserting that every one of the generation of the Exodus was eternally lost !

f 12-15. The admonition of the Psalmist applies to later generations of Israelites and to Christians as well. It is a warning against badness of heart consisting in unbelief and reaching the point of departure from the living God. **12.** The ' living God ' is powerful to fulfil both his promises and his threats, *cf.* 10:31. **13.** Corporate self-encouragement or mutual social exhortation is needed as long as the ' To-day ' of each day of life lasts. ' Hardening by the deceit of sin ' is a striking expression on which Estius remarks : ' The heart softened by the pleasure of sin little by little grows hard towards the precepts of God '. Sin is seductive, *cf.* Rom 7:8-11. **14.** The participation in Christ which we have, though very intimate (like his participation in our humanity, 2:14), will not last, unless we keep ' the beginning of his substance '—that is, *faith* which is the beginning, root, and foundation of Christian life (Chrys., Theodoret)—firm to the end. ' Beginning of his substance ', however, may simply mean ' our first hope in him ', *cf.* 10:32.

16-19. No one is exempted from fear, as the rhetorical questions based on the Psalm show. The punishment of their provocation of God fell on *all* the privileged ones of the Exodus, on *all* whom sin condemned to leave their corpses in the desert, on *all* the unbelieving Hebrews excluded from the rest of the Promised Land. Note well that 16 should read : ' *Who were they who heard and rebelled ? Was it not all those who came out of Egypt under Moses ?* ' Rebellion against God, death in the desert, exclusion from Palestine, all attach themselves to the sin of unbelief (ἀπιστία) against which the warning is being given.

936a IV 1-10 Rest of Heaven promised to the Faithful—The antitypal rest promised to the Hebrews remains. Warning changes to exhortation. **1.** Note the use of the first person plural : ' Let us fear '. If we are unfaithful we have everything to fear ; if we are faithful, the rest or repose which Chanaan prefigured lies open before us. The generation of the Exodus missed the promised repose through their own fault and if we miss, it will also be through our own fault. **2.** The word which they heard did not profit the Israelites *either* because *it* did not mix by faith with the persons who heard it (συγκεκερασμένος), *or* because *they* did not mix by faith with those who like Josue and Caleb (rightly) heard it (συγκεκερασμένους). The two readings are almost equally attested. The DV follows a Vg reading (later adopted in the Clementine edition) which gives a confused sense. Read therefore : ' But the word of hearing did not profit them *since it was not united with faith in those who heard* '. Lack of faith frustrated the word of hearing. **3-5.** These verses say in effect that God's rest on the seventh day, Gen 2:2, is the image not only of the weekly Sabbath, but of the temporal rest of Chanaan, and especially of the eternal rest to which men are invited after the labours of life. Unbelief excludes from it. **6-8.** Therefore, since God's rest is open to men, and the generation of the Exodus missed it through unbelief, God fixes (limiteth) a day, which in David he calls ' To-day ', so long after the conquest of Chanaan. Whether St Paul wishes to quote David himself in citing Ps 94 or merely designates the Davidic collection by the name ' David ' may be doubtful, but certainly he dates the Psalm as Davidic or post-Davidic, for his purpose is to show that the rest of Chanaan is not the rest which God promised in an inspired poem composed *such a long time* after the conquest of Chanaan by Josue (Grecized *Jesus*, 8). **9.** Therefore, he concludes ' a *sabbatismos* remains for the people of God '. The Gk *sabbatismos* is found nowhere else in the whole Greek Bible. It means not merely rest but the observance or enjoyment of rest. **10.** It is ceasing from work like the Creator, and the Apostle at least implies that it is the reward of works (*cf.* Apoc 14:13, so familiar from the Daily Requiem epistle), and that it is participation in God's happiness.

11-13 Conclusion—This little finale really deserves to **b** be called a peroration. It eloquently insists that every effort must be made to enter into that rest, which is equivalent to saying that every means must be taken to avoid the fate of the incredulous Israelites. They fell by resisting the word of God. We may fall in the same way. The qualities of the word of God, 12, 13, are such that there is no escape from its imperious authority, no hope of shirking our responsibility towards it. The word or *logos* is so boldly personified that some commentators have even identified it with the personal *Logos*. The context is against this view, but the word of God's revelation is so authoritative as to be ultimately interchangeable with God who speaks it. ' Living ' stands at the head of the list of its attributes, that is, the word of God is full of power to act with living force ; it is effectual in attaining its purpose ; more trenchant than any two-edged sword—as the short double-edged *machaera* is a cutting rather than a stabbing instrument, our equivalent phrase would be ' as keen as a razor cutting fine and deep '. The subtle thoroughness of its dissection is expressed by saying that it reaches as far as dividing sensitive soul from thinking spirit (μερισμός, active verbal), and no closely knit joint, no hidden marrow of the bones is left untouched by it. This elaborate metaphor reveals in God's word an all-searching power which becomes even more ' personal ' when the word is presented as a ' discerner ' (κριτικός) of thoughts and intentions of the heart, a veritable judge of how one thinks and how one is minded, how one stands in regard to thought and feeling. The ' heart ' is sometimes regarded as the seat of thought, but more often of man's moral life, *cf.* Mt 15:17-20. **13.** Here the word finally identifies itself with God's all-seeing knowledge, or rather he takes the place of his word : Nothing created is invisible to him, *cf.* Ps 138 ; all things discover themselves and stand bare (τετραχηλισμένα) before his eyes. It seems that the second metaphor is taken from the bending back and baring of the necks of animals for the sacrificial stroke of the knife. The literal meaning of τραχηλίζειν is to act with or on the neck—hence various usages of the term in the language of horse-riding, wrestling and sacrifice. All the ancient versions, like the Vg, make the participle a reinforcing synonym of the preceding adjective γυμνά, ' naked '. Hence, ' all things are naked and open to his eyes ' is quite good. The final phrase ' To whom our speech (λόγος) is ' may be rendered ' about whom we are

6b speaking ', but clearly it means : ' To whom our *account is* ', *i.e.* to whom we must render an account of ourselves '.

c IV 14-VII 28 The Superiority of Christ's Priesthood—Up to this the comparison between Christ and the angels and also between Christ and Moses has been personal. From this forward the comparison will be one of priesthood and priestly ministries, as between the Aaronic and Christian priesthood. Here, therefore, the sacerdotal theology of Heb begins.
IV 14-V 10 Christ's High Priesthood—**14-16.** A characteristic introduction (*cf.* 10:19 ; also 2 Cor 3:12) leads us to the thesis. It is a brief and gripping exhortation to confidence. The three basic ideas of the exhortation are : We have a Pontiff who has gone through to the place of repose, thoroughly sympathetic with our weaknesses, permanently established as a Mediator beside the throne of grace. Note the following : ' Great high-priest ' (*cf.* ' great priest ', 10:21)—this is a title of double grandeur once given to Simon Machabeus, 1 Mac 13:42. ' Passed into the heavens ' links on to the *sabbatismos* and suggests future developments regarding the Holy of Holies. Jesus, whose divine sonship has already appeared five times unequivocally, is here called straight out and emphatically ' the Son of God '. The religion which has such a priest, in such a sanctuary—the very Son of God—is a religion to which we must hold on. The difficulties must not discourage us. **15.** He is greatly capable of compassionating our infirmities, for, remaining sinless, he has nevertheless gone through every generic experience of human suffering We should note that the sinlessness which sets him apart from us does not diminish his fellow-feeling for us, but makes it greater and purer, because absolutely free from all egoism. **16.** Again we meet a key-word ' Let us go ' (approach). This movement of access to God in worship pervades our Epistle, *cf.* 7:25 ; 10:1, 22 ; 11:6 ; 12:18, 22. In a very elegant phrase we are assured that at the throne of God's grace we shall find mercy and obtain grace (an elegant *chiasmus* in Greek) in the form of help suited to each time and circumstance.

7a V 1-4 Description of a High Priest—Description rather than definition, although the mediatorial function of priesthood between God and mankind, which is of the essence of priesthood, is very clearly in the forefront. **1.** A man ' *from amongst* men and *on behalf of* men accredited *to* (approach) God '—that is a priest. **2-3.** As a representative of mankind he must be compassionate with the ignorant and erring, being endowed with a compassion flowing from his own sense or experience of human weakness. Hence he offers—so it was with the OT priesthood—for his own sins as well as for the people's. Note that the verb which is used for ' compassionate ' (μετριοπαθεῖν) is remarkable (found only here in the Greek Bible). It means measured or, as we should say, intelligent sympathy. ' Compassed with infirmity ' is also a striking phrase partially paralleled by the ' besetting, ever-ready, pressing sin ' of 12:1. **4.** Being accredited to God, a priest is not self-constituted. He does not take the honour ' *of his own proper motion* ', but is called by God immediately, or mediately like Aaron.

b V 5-10 Application of the Description to Christ—The description is applied in inverse order : Christ's vocation first, 5, 6, and fellowship in human suffering second, 7-10.
5-6 Vocation—It was not Christ who glorified or honoured himself with the dignity of priesthood. It was the One who spoke to him the oracle of Ps 2. This whole phrase, including the citation, is probably only a periphrasis for ' His Father '. There is no specific sacerdotal appointment in the words : ' Thou art My Son ' (although in reality divine Sonship confers every dignity on the humanity of Jesus), but in the wonderful interlacing of thought discernible in this Epistle the oracle of the super-angelic Son, 1:5, is here, 5:5, joined to the great sacerdotal oracle of Ps 109. Besides, the royal Ps 2 and the royal Sacerdotal Ps 109 are twin

poems of David's highest inspiration. The divine **937b** declaration : ' Thou art a priest ' is only cited here to show Christ's divine appointment, but in ch 7 all the riches of its theology will be set forth.
7-10 The Suffering Priest—Gethsemani rather than **c** Calvary is the scene here, some words of which, 7, appropriately figure on the façade of the Church of the Agony on Mount Olivet. Christ is presented in his *weakness*, and St Paul realized, better than John Maldonatus (who makes the remark) could ever realize, that nowhere was Jesus more evidently one of our weak human selves than in Gethsemani. Being innocent, he could not offer sacrifice for his own sins, like the Aaronic High Priest, but he could pray (for himself and for us) out of the anguish of the mortal weakness which he deigned to take for our salvation.
7. Note that ' the days of his flesh ' are the days of his mortality, and that ' prayers and supplications '— petitions and entreaties—aptly describe the words uttered under the olive trees. The Gospels do not mention tears and loud prayer, but these go together with the ' sadness unto death ' and with the audibility of Christ's words ' a stone-throw ' away. St Paul does not say that Christ prayed to be saved from death, but that he prayed to ' him who was able to save him from death '. The interpretation ' he was heard (by being released) from his fear ', though adopted by many commentators, is scarcely probable ; the Vg rendering ' heard for his reverence ' being more in keeping with the usual NT meaning of εὐλάβεια, 12:28, εὐλαβέομαι, 11:7, and εὐλαβής, Lk 25 ; Ac 2:5 ; 8:2 ; 22:12. **8.** Although ' Son ' (without addition or article in Gk), ' he learned obedience by the things which he suffered '. Christ acquired experimental knowledge in the school of experience. The hardness of obedience he learned by obeying through most difficult sufferings even to the acceptance of a death involving the utmost pain and shame. The thought of Heb here joins the great Pauline text of Phil 2:8. The paronomasia ἔμαθεν ἀφ' ὧν ἔπαθεν was a familiar Gk commonplace (πάθει μάθος [Aeschylus], παθήματα μαθήματα [Herodotus]). **9.** This verse carries us back to the declaration of 2:10. Christ eternally glorified with the merit of his suffering— ' consummated '—became (at that moment) for all who obey him a cause of eternal salvation. Thus the eternally efficient Saviour of all men, who call themselves and are his disciples by obedience, is the One called by God ' the high priest according to the order of Melchisedech '.
V 11-VI 20 Admonition of Reproach and Encourage- d ment—The admonition is a trumpet-call to attention before the exposition of a great theme. It begins with reproach addressed to backward pupils, 5:11-14 ; warns them with terrifying severity of the danger of apostasy, 6:1-8 ; raises their spirits by reminding them of the promise attaching to their good deeds in the past and the present, 9-12 ; and inspires confidence by holding up the example of Abraham, 13-20.
V 11-14 Hebrew Backwardness—**11.** On the Melchisedechian priesthood of Christ the Apostle has much to say that is difficult of exposition especially to a circle of dull hearers like the Hebrews. Their dullness is described as being ' hard of ears or hearing ', but the Apostle clearly refers to their slow, sluggish, heavy dullness of spirit. It is a moral fault due to their lack of zeal for progress. **12.** Scholars brought to the school of Christ so many years ago should now be masters, but alas ! they still need to get lessons in the very elements or A B C of Christian doctrine. The ' elements (στοιχεῖα) of the beginning of the words of God ' are the rudimentary truths contained in the catechesis or catechism of first instruction. The Apostle calls these rudiments ' milk ' or ' baby food ' in contrast to the solid instruction imparted to those spiritually grown up, *cf.* 1 Cor 3:1 ff. ; but note that in 1 Pet 2:2 milk stands rather for a pure wholesome food. **13.** He who belongs to the milk category is ' unskilful in the word of justice ', not proficient in the practice of Christian life. Actually he is a babe in the matter of moral progress. **14.** Solid

937d food is for the perfect who have reached the development of their age as Christians, this development being the result of habitual exercise of their faculties of moral perception (αἰσθητήρια) for the discernment of good and evil. Both ἕξις, which is permanent facility acquired by exercise, and αἰσθητήρια with the generic meaning of 'senses' are *hapax legomena* in NT, but St Paul uses αἴσθησις, Phil 1:10, to denote ripe judgement in moral things.

e VI 1-8 Forward! and beware of falling backward into Apostasy—This section forms a unity which produces a powerful impression. It is like a general saying to his troops 'Forward! . . . but there must be no cowards'. It says in effect: 'Let us go on, if God permits . . . but one can do nothing with renegades'.
1-2. Note the usual enallage of exhortation : ' Let *us* ' (since progress is a duty) ' go on to perfection ' (in the exposition of higher doctrine, as the context shows). ' Leaving *the rudiments* ' means leaving the simple basic truths of the catechetic outlines. Six catechetic articles forming closely connected pairs are mentioned : (1) ' Repentance from dead works ' : twice in this epistle (*cf.* 9:14) the expression ' dead works ' is used for the state of sin which, being spiritual death, can only produce dead deeds, deprived of divine life. ' Do penance ' is the first word of an apostle, *cf.* Mk 1:15 ; Ac 2:38 ; 3:19 ; 17 ; 30 ; 20:21 ; 26:20 ; (2) ' faith towards God ', the positive side of the movement of conversion ; (3) ' the doctrine of baptisms ' include the necessary distinction of Christian baptism from the baptism of John and Jewish ritual washings ; (4) ' imposition of hands ' is closely connected with the foregoing and primarily to be understood of confirmation, *cf.* Ac 19:6 ; (5) ' resurrection of the dead ', as we know from St Paul, 1 Cor 15, was included together with the resurrection of Christ in the oral catechesis of all the Apostles ; (6) ' eternal judgement ' is the general judgement after the resurrection of the body, which fixes the destiny of each one for ever and is therefore called ' eternal '.

938a **3.** To the little phrase ' if God permit ' is attached the tremendous warning against apostasy which is the chief passage amongst a half-dozen marking Heb as a severe epistle. **4.** The Apostle virtually says : We can go on to higher teaching, but it would be wasted on apostates (or apostatizers), for it is impossible to convert an apostate. The adjective ' impossible ' is made as emphatic as it can be, standing like a fearful red-letter sign at the head of the sentence, but we must note that the impossibility is placed not in God who can work any miracle of grace, but primarily in the apostolic minister of reconciliation who has no fulcrum for the work of renewing a renegade. The latter in fact has incapacitated himself for the reception of ministrations by the paralysing ingratitude of his rejection of Christian riches and by his complete break away from all contact with the source of salvation. **4-5.** Let us first see what apostates have deliberately thrown away : They were once brought from darkness to light through the illumination of faith and of baptism, and ' they *fell away* '—they also tasted the heavenly gift by intimate participation in the distributions made by the Holy Spirit (ordinarily after imposition of hands ; *cf.* Ac 8:17 ; 19:6), an experience which is described by St Paul as ' being given to drink ', 1 Cor 12:13, of the waters of life (*cf.* Is 12:3 ; Jer 2:13 ; Jn 4:14 ; 7:37), ' *and they fell away* '—they also became partakers of the charismata by which the presence of the Holy Ghost was palpably felt in the community, ' *and they fell away* ' —moreover, they recognized by taste or delightful experience how good the word of God is and the manifestation of God's power in the miracles of the Messianic era, ' *and they fell away* '—these four or five : the light of truth, the joy of grace (including perhaps the Holy Eucharist ?), the charismata of the Holy Spirit, the experience of God's sweet word and of his miraculous evidences they rejected. More precise identification than this we cannot attempt. The illumination seems to include the sacrament of baptism which in later times came to be called *phôtismos* ; the **93** heavenly gift seems to have been tasted in confirmation and in the liturgical assemblies where the Eucharist was celebrated ; the participation of the Holy Spirit may refer more particularly to the varieties of *gratiae gratis datae* ; the participle γευσαμένους construed with the accusative in the fourth member would seem to indicate recognition of God's work as good and of his miracles as being the signs of the final age. From all these things ' they fell away ', a thought expressed in the text by the single aorist participle παραπεσόντας, but repeated four times in the above explanation to bring out its impressive power. It is impossible ' *to renew* ' (ἀνακαινίζειν) —inaccurately rendered ' renovari ', *i.e.* ' to be renewed '—such as these to penance for they are re-crucifying by their own personal doing (lit. for themselves) the Son of God and holding him up to mockery. These are fearful words. Every apostate stages in his own life a deliberate repetition of the apostasy and deicide committed by the Jews on Good Friday. *While* they act thus, wilfully rejecting the only Saviour, it is impossible to renew them to penance and conversion.

What is the nature of the impossibility ? The **b** Novatian heretics and the Montanist Tertullian (citing these words, under the name of Barnabas) used the text to prove that some sins are irremissible and that the Church has no power to absolve from them. But the text regards not pardon but repentance.

Briefly, some have taken it to mean simply that there can be no second baptism, no second baptismal *concrucifixion* with the Saviour (' re-crucifying ' and ' holding up to mockery ' being taken in a good sense). True as this is in itself, it is clearly not the meaning of the text. Others insist most emphatically on the active infinitive ' to renew ' and take the words to mean that it is impossible for men, but it always remains possible for God. However, the severity of the passage makes this distinction more than unlikely. The text as expounded above shows that the impossibility is connected with the moral dispositions of persons who have committed such a hardening sin and who are continuing their break-away from the Saviour. The subjoined parable, 7, 8, ending in plain allegory, 8*b*, shows this. **7-8.** They are not the ground that drinks the rain with any thirst for justice, so as to be productive and give evidence of God's blessing. They are like the ground cursed in Gen 3:17, for they only produce thorns and thistles ; they are under reprobation, near to the final curse ; their end is for burning, *cf.* Lk 8:4-8.

9-12 Encouragement—The tone changes ; the Christian **c** ministry is not a ministry of discouragement but of encouragement. Note the tender title : ' Dearly beloved '. **9.** The Apostle has better hopes for the Hebrews ; he has confidence of things more favourable to their salvation. **10.** Past services done in the name of God, past and present ministrations of *charity* to fellow-Christians are things of which the justice of God will take account. It is the Catholic doctrine of the meritoriousness of good works done in the state of grace. They deserve a continuance of God's favour. **11.** The Apostle's ardent desire is that there should be no relaxation, but zeal for the full realization of *hope* to the very end. **12.** Thus they shall escape that dull sluggishness and imitate those who through *faith* and patience inherit (present participle) the promise. Note the mention of all three theological virtues and the special mention of patience, which is the moral strength of hope.

13-20 Confidence in the Certitude of Hope—Mention **d** of the inheritors of the promise brings up the example of Abraham, *cf.* Rom 4:13-21. **13.** The promise of Messianic blessing which God made to Abraham is of capital importance, as St Paul shows so fully in Rom and Gal, and as the Church proclaims so beautifully when she speaks of the *lux sancta quam olim Abrahae promisisti et semini eius.* It was a sworn promise and thus rested on two sovereign guarantees, the unbreakable word of God and his inviolable oath. Thus did he assure us of the immutability of his promise. **13-15.** To

8d Abraham God swore by himself, for he had no one greater to swear by, and Abraham who received the promise of blessing and posterity attained the promise by patience. **16.** The oath was a guarantee suited to human habits, for a sworn declaration or promise is commonly regarded as incontrovertible, because of the sanctity of a higher Guarantor. **17-18.** In those circumstances or on this account (ἐν ᾧ D.V. 'Wherein') God gave us the double security of his word and his oath, in order that we who took refuge in God from the perils of salvation (οἱ καταφυγόντες, not to be construed with κρατῆσαι) may have a strong exhortation (motive, we should say) to hold on to the hope set before us. **19.** That hope is like an anchor for the soul, reliable and strong enough to keep us safely moored in the severest storms. Recall the anchor as a symbol of hope in the paintings of the Roman catacombs. It would seem that it is hope itself and not the metaphorical anchor that is regarded as going behind the veil. This extension of the metaphor seems too extraordinary. It would be like an anchor biting the shore and mooring the ship to it rather than biting the bottom of the sea and immobilizing the vessel. Immovable constancy is given by hope, and hope has its object behind the veil of the antitypal sanctuary, which is heaven itself, symbolized by the sacred cube of the Holy of holies. **20.** Thither, as a Precursor, Jesus has entered on our behalf, that is, not for himself only but also for us, and always in the quality of what he has become, namely, a '*high priest for ever according to the order of Melchisedech*'.

e VII 1-28 Superiority of Melchisedechian Priesthood—
The excellence of the Priest according to the order of Melchisedech is shown from the details of the typal Melchisedech's biblical record, 1-3; his superiority over the Levitical or Aaronic priesthood is shown from the relation of Melchisedech to Abraham, 4-10; the perfection of the new priesthood is shown to be an abrogation of the old priesthood and of the regime to which it belonged, 11-28.

1-3. Extra-biblical speculation on the mysterious figure of Melchisedech need not detain us. Was he a Semite, a Japhetite, or, being a Chanaanite king, did he belong to the cursed seed of Cham? Various fancies clustered around his name and different brands of pseudo-Christian Melchisedechian heretics venerated him as a manifestation of the Logos, of the Holy Ghost, or even as a divine priestly power superior to Christ himself. St Paul argues entirely from the positive and negative details of the biblical notice, which he summarizes from Gen 14, with close adherence to LXX. Every single point of the summary is utilized. The personal name means 'King of justice'; the place of his royalty Salem (Jerusalem) designates him as 'King of peace'; but the royal titles are only incidental to the Apostle's theme; it is as a 'Priest of God Most High' that Melchisedech is here envisaged. No mention is made of the kind of sacrifice he offered, for the Eucharistic significance of Melchisedech does not belong to our Epistle. He met the victorious but still childless Abraham (*cf.* 10), blessed him, and received from him the honour of a tithe of the booty. **2.** The Priest Melchisedech thus blessing and receiving tithe from the Patriarch of the promise, Gen. 14, and the future great grandfather of the twelve tribes, supplies the two essential positive points. But the divinely intended omissions of the sacred text are also significant.

f 3. On Melchisedech's origin there is complete silence —no mention of father or mother or ancestral line— and he is without certificate of birth or of death. The inspired page presents him in this negative manner as a living Priest, and so, being assimilated to the Son of God in the quality of a type, he remains a priest in perpetuity. Note that the three adjectives : 'without father, without mother, without recorded descent' should be taken together. St Paul did not think of Christ having no temporal father, having no eternal mother, and having no priestly genealogy, though he had a royal one. It is simply as possessing a divinely given negative certificate of life that Melchisedech is a type

of the Eternal Priest. Whether St Paul knew certain **938f** facts now revealed by the Tell el Amarna tablets about the kings of Jerusalem claiming kingship not by succession but by divine appointment must remain doubtful and, in any case, contributes nothing to the exegesis of this passage.

4-10 Superiority of Melchisedech over Abraham and 939a Levi—The argument here is easily grasped. **4.** That Abraham the Patriarch was great was simply a Hebrew axiom. Yet he gave tithes to Melchisedech from the choicest of the spoils (lit. ' the top things of the heap ') and received blessing from him. **5-6.** Levitical priests had the right to receive tithes from their brethren, though these also had the dignity of children of Abraham, but in the person of Melchisedech one who was no Levite laid Abraham himself under tithe. Melchisedech also blessed the very Patriarch in whom the promise of future blessing was vested. **7.** And undoubtedly the bestowal of authoritative priestly blessing is the act of a superior. **8.** Moreover, the Levitical priests, being priests in a line of succession, had death written on them even while they gathered tithes, but Melchisedech lives on without a successor, having that negative diploma of life mentioned above. **9-10.** To put the matter almost paradoxically (ὡς ἔπος εἰπεῖν), Levi the tither was tithed by Melchisedech, for Levi was then included in the still potential fatherhood of the childless Abraham. The word 'loins,' 5, 10, is a Hebraism for virility or generative power. Aquinas raises the objection : ' But Christ also was in the loins of Abraham when Melchisedech tithed and blessed him ! ' He answers : Seminally, *no* ; as to the bodily substance taken from the Blessed Virgin, *yes*. The virginal conception of Christ makes the difference.

11-28 Imperfect and Perfect Priesthood—The appoint- **b** ment of a Priest according to the order of Melchisedech marks the Aaronic priesthood as transitory, 11-14; (*a*) **9-12.** Perfection is the end of every divine arrangement, and if perfection was to come through the Levitical priesthood—this priesthood being the basis of the whole cultural system of the Mosaic Law—why should another —a different (ἕτερος)—Priest arise according to the order of Melchisedech and not be called according to the order of Aaron? **12.** A theocratic law lapses totally when its priesthood lapses. Now the Aaronic priesthood does lapse with the introduction of the Melchisedechian priesthood, and with it lapses the law which has no provision for any other but a Levitical priesthood. **13.** It is historically evident that ' Our Lord '—note the title—of whom the oracle of priesthood according to the order of Melchisedech was spoken, has come from the tribe of Juda, no member of which tribe ever had access to the altar to perform priestly functions, and moreover, the Law of Moses has no inkling of any connexion between priesthood and that same tribe of Juda.

(*b*) **15-17.** This is still more evident from the mode of duration of the priesthoods. The Priesthood which arises according to the order of Melchisedech is a lasting personal priesthood, not a priesthood transmitted from father to son according to a law of carnal succession. **16.** The Melchisedechian Priest holds his priesthood ' according to the power of an indissoluble (or unending) life ', for the oracle says : ' Thou art a Priest for ever according to the order of Melchisedech '.

(*c*) **18-19.** Thus, to come back to the idea of τελείωσις **c** or perfection, the former regime is set aside because of its weakness and unprofitableness. Really the law brought nothing to perfection, for of itself it conferred no interior sanctity and it gave no power to do the good which it commanded. With the setting aside of the law we hail the introduction of a better hope—note the word ' better ' three times in this ch and ten times elsewhere in Heb—and through this better hope we draw near to God in the confidence which arises from pardon and the spirit of adoption and the assurance of glory. The τελείωσις realized by the priesthood of Christ is all these things : forgiveness and grace and glory.

(*d*) **20-22.** Another circumstance which marks the

939c superiority of the priesthood of Christ is the solemnity of the oath which ratifies it and confirms its irrevocable finality. The priests of the House of Aaron were inaugurated without any divine oath, but Christ with an oath never to be repented of. In this respect Jesus stands as the sponsor (or surety, or mediatorial guarantor) of a better covenant. Covenant or covenant-testament appears here for the first time and will appear sixteen times in the sequel in eleven changes of context. This sentence, 20a, 22, with its parenthesis, 20b, 21, has an indescribable majesty in our author's Greek.

(e) **23-25.** As unending life was contrasted with fleshly succession in 15-17, the oneness and permanence of Christ's priesthood is finally set against the multiplicity of priests whom death prevented from remaining. **23.** They were many, for no one of them, all being mortal, could remain, but he, because he remains for ever, has a priesthood which does not pass away (ἀπαράβατον). **24.** The DV here does not represent the full force of the Gk which means : ' He, because he remains for ever, holds his priesthood as a priesthood *untransmissible*, everlasting '. **25.** Hence he is also a perpetual Saviour, a perpetual Mediator, an everliving Advocate, ' able to save perfectly—or perpetually (Vg, Coptic, Syriac)—those who come to God through him, always living to make intercession for them ' (*cf.* Rom 8:34, the tones of which are here echoed). At the end of the sentence Vg substitutes ' us ' for ' them '. The presence of Christ's sacred humanity in heaven is itself a perpetual pleading, our names are better written in his sacred wounds than the names of the twelve tribes on the gems of Aaron's pectoral, and his heart's desire for our salvation is before God always.

d 26-28 Conclusion—26. Such indeed was the High Priest whom in all fitness we should have—utterly holy and exalted and effective. He is all piety towards God (ὅσιος), without any tinge of harmful malice (ἄκακος) which would diminish our confidence in him, without any defilement to dim the lustre of his holiness—hence separated from sinners with a transcendence which has raised him above the heavens. **27.** His work is absolutely efficacious, for he has no need day by day, like the high priests—that is, *toties quoties* on Expiation Day —to offer sacrifices for his own sins, then for those of the people. For the people alone he came to offer, and this he did once for all, offering himself. **28.** In fine— and the sentence sounds like a triumphal chant—the law sets up men as high priests—men having weakness, that is, sin and mortality, but the word of the oath announced through the mouth of David, long after the law, sets up One who is Son (again without the article) and whose perfection is consummated for ever in priestly achievement and in glory.

N.B.—27a creates a difficulty. It was only on Expiation Day (Lev 16) and not ' daily ' that the high priest was bound to offer sacrifice first for himself and then for the people. Some commentators answer that St Paul is referring to the actual practice of the high priest, who offered the double sacrifice every day ; but such practice is not otherwise attested. The most satisfactory answer is that St Paul's gaze here is entirely on the high priest and Expiation day. He mentions the daily sacrifices of ' every priest ' for the first time specifically in 10:11, and in a new context. In the present context, which is entirely high-priestly, καθ'ἡμέραν, meaning ' day by day ', refers to each Expiation day as it came round once a year.

e VIII 1-X 18 Superiority of Christ's Sacrifice—The kernel of Heb being the priesthood of Christ, it remains to show in detail the superior efficacy of his priestly work. St Paul shows this superiority in relation to the old sanctuary, the old covenant, the annual and daily sacrifices of the old dispensation.

VIII 1-5 Superiority of Christ's Sanctuary—At first sight this section seems to be simply a matter of contrasting heaven with the Mosaic tabernacle, but it will be found that a purely local interpretation of it is difficult to maintain. The contrast is certainly between celestial and terrestrial, and place considerations are included, but it cannot simply be worked out in terms of ' above the sky and on this earth below '. The **93** celestial has to be conceived socially as the Church, which is the kingdom of heaven. The interpretation here followed is that of St Cyril of Alexandria (*De adoratione in spiritu et veritate*, Bk 9, PG 68, 590–631).

1. ' *A principal or main point in the subject under discussion* is **f** (the following) : Such is the High Priest that we have (*cf.* 7:26)—a High Priest who has taken his seat at the right hand of the throne of majesty (*cf.* 1:4) in heaven (*cf.* 4:14 ; 6:20) '. **2.** The enthroned Christ does not offer sacrifice in heaven, for sitting is not the posture of a ministering Priest ; yet ' having made a cleansing of sins ', 1:4, he *is* a minister of the sanctuary. What is this ' Sancta ' or Sanctuary ? It is generally taken to mean the place of God's special manifestation which we call Heaven ; but Christ *reigns* in heaven, he does not minister. It seems, therefore, that the Sanctuary must be the whole Church Militant and Triumphant, which is the extension of that Tabernacle of God which is Christ himself, Jn 2:19, 21, which St Paul calls by the local name of ' the Jerusalem above ', Gal 4:26, and which St John heard described to him as ' the tabernacle of God with men ', Apoc 21:3. This is the perfect (ἀληθινή) tabernacle or tent which the Lord (ὁ κύριος here meaning God) pitched, not man. **3.** Christ must have offered a sacrifice belonging to and bringing him into that celestial sphere. Sacrifice is the correlative of priesthood, for every high priest is appointed to offer gifts and sacrifices (*i.e.* oblations of all kinds as in 5:1). Christ could not be a priest without having a victim to offer. **4.** ' *Yea rather*, if he were on earth, he would *not* be a priest, because the legal victims were being offered by priests of a tribe to which he did not belong '. His sacrifice had therefore to be offered and consummated outside of the terrestrial sphere of Mosaism. **5.** The Levitical priests do not belong to the heavenly sphere, for they serve a sanctuary which is only an image and shadow of the heavenly realities. This is intimated in the history of the institution of the tabernacle itself, Ex 40, for the oracle addressed to Moses said : ' See that thou make all things according to the pattern shown to thee on the mount ' The rabbis imagined a design in fire or light shown to Moses in vision and visually representing the tabernacle as it was to be set up. The Epistle, however, indicates that Moses received some revelation of the Messianic and heavenly realities which his Hebrew tabernacle was to foreshadow. **6.** A verse of conclusion and transition **g** states that Christ has obtained a more excellent ministry (λειτουργία) inasmuch as he is the mediator of a better covenant established on better promises. The word ' Mediator ' occurs here in Heb for the first of three times, also 9:15 ; 12:24. It is always a title of Jesus and related to ' covenant '. It occurs also thrice in the other Paulines, in two different contexts, Gal 3:19, 20 ; 1 Tim 2:5, once of Moses in relation to the old Covenant and once of Christ in relation to redemption. As the redemptive character of Christ's sacrifice is here implied (*cf.* 9:12), the Mediator combines in a higher way the sacerdotal and ambassadorial offices of Aaron and Moses. The ' better ' covenant is the alliance based on the redemption-transaction to which our author will later attribute the special character of testament, 9:16, 17. The ' better promises ' are chiefly pardon, grace and glory.

7-13 Superiority of the New Covenant—7. On the **940** principle that God does not lay aside a perfect ordinance for a less perfect one (beginning high and ending low —*cf.* Gal 3:3), his introduction of a second covenant must imply censure of the former one. **8.** Actually that censure is spoken by God himself through the prophet Jeremias, 31:31–34 (Heb). The censure indeed falls first on the Israelites, but it also embraces the regime which could not change the nation's ' heart of stone into a heart of flesh ', Ez 11:19. The text is taken from an impressive group of Restoration oracles Jer 30–33) in which the Messianic future looms large. Christ our Lord had alluded to the same text

a in the institution of the Eucharist, Lk 22:20 ; 1 Cor 11:25, and it is also the background of 2 Cor 3. Cited from the LXX 38:31–34 with interesting but merely accidental variations, it announces a *new* covenant different from that of the Exodus which the people did not keep. **9.** Note that whereas DV has 'And I regarded them not', Jer 31:32c has : 'I gave up caring for them', which is probably the true sense (*cf.* Gesenius-Buhl *sub voce* II ; also Peshitta). God's rejection of the old Israel was very clearly forecast at the Babylonian **b** captivity. **10.** This verse describes the new covenant as an interior law under which knowledge and obedience will be a matter of inner light and love rather than external teaching and the discipline of a code. **12.** It states that the remission of sins is a special characteristic of the New Covenant, *cf.* 10:15–18. It is, however, on the word 'new' that the Apostle's present argument rests. **13.** To describe the second covenant as 'new' is to declare the former one old, senescent, and near its demise—ἀφανισμός is very frequent in Jer (LXX) in the sense of 'destruction'. Jer 30–33 should be read as a whole ; they are the finest pages of a great prophet.

c **IX 1–28 Superiority of Christ's Sacrifice**—Christ was a sacrificing Priest, Minister of a sanctuary and Mediator of a new Covenant, but what is of supreme importance in this Covenant is the sacrifice on which it is based, for there is no religious regime without sacrifice. Hence the logical development of the Apostle's argument leads him to consider the sacrificial ritual of the old alliance and that of the new. He proceeds to do so in terms of the Israelite sanctuary and with supreme emphasis on the greatest sacrificial ceremony of the Jewish year, that of *Yôm hakkippūrîm*—Expiation Day or Day of Atonement (10 Tišri).

IX 1–10 The Tabernacle and Day of Atonement—**1.** '*Of course* (this is often the best English equivalent of μὲν οὖν) the former (Covenant) also had *ordinances of worship* and a sanctuary *of this world*', *i.e.* a terrestrial sanctuary, and not in the sense of an ecumenical or universal one. **2.** The Apostle describes not the Zorobabelian-Herodian temple but the tabernacle as set up by Moses. There is great argumentative prudence and subtle suggestiveness in thus taking a Pentateuchal basis and in going back to the days when the Ark was still in the midst of Israel. **2–5.** The description of the tabernacle and its appurtenances is summary but not wanting in splendour. The first oblong tent which was set up by Moses is mentioned, in which is noted the seven-branched ' lampstand ' (DV ' candlesticks ') placed to the south or left, and the table (covered with gold) on which stand the twelve loaves of shew-bread, this being on the north or right side. This oblong, called the Holy, is seen to terminate west in a *second* veil or curtain, thus distinguished from the first or entrance veil. **3.** Behind this second veil stands the tent or sacred cube called the Holy of Holies or Most Holy, having as its appurtenances a golden ' altar of incense ' (DV ' censer ') placed outside the veil, and then, within the veil, the Ark of the Covenant covered completely with gold. In the Ark mention is made of an urn having or containing manna, of the rod of Aaron that blossomed, of the tables of the Covenant. **5.** Over the Ark stand Cherubim of glory—that is, throne-bearers of God's glorious Majesty—covering with their wings the ' propitiatory ' or golden cover of the Ark which is called in Heb. *Kappōreṭ*, to which Luther gave the happy name of *Gnadenstuhl*, a reminiscence of Heb 4:16—the 'mercy-seat' of AV. The Gk ἱλαστήριον and Lat. *propitiatorium* designate it as an instrument of expiation or atonement.

d In the above exposition care has been taken to bring out a literary quality of the text which is generally lost sight of. Apart from saying that the first tent ' was set up ', there is no past tense in the paragraph, only verbless phrases and present participles. The Apostle evidently wishes the tabernacle to stand before the Hebrews in the ' legal present ', for the Messianic age is ' the world to come '. *Cf.* ' the Jerusalem which now is ', Gal 4:25.

Two objections must be briefly deal with. (1) The **940e** ' altar of incense ' (*thymiaterion*) is placed within the Holy of Holies, instead of outside it. The answer is that the verb used, namely, ' having ' not ' containing ', expresses the close relation of the altar of incense with the inner sanctuary. In 3 Kg 6:22 this altar is called ' the altar belonging to the *d'bîr* or inner sanctuary ' while Ex 40:5 calls it ' the altar of incense before the Ark '. Moreover, according to the letter reproduced in 2 Mac 2:5 Jeremias hid the altar of incense together with the Ark and Tabernacle, for they went together. (2) The assertion that in the Ark were manna, and Aaron's rod, and the tables of the Covenant seems to contradict 3 Kg 8:9 which says that the Ark contained only the tables. A possible answer would be that the author of 3 Kg and the author of Heb speak of different times, but we have no positive information on the point. A satisfactory reply is that the urn of manna and the sacerdotal rod which were *beside* the Ark are comprehended or lumped together with the stone tables which were *within* the Ark.

6–7 Day of Atonement—The Apostle does not intend to **f** go into details about liturgical symbolism, but he wishes to note one important thing. **6–7.** Officiating priests enter the Holy at all times—twice a day for the offering of incense, and at other times to perform blood-ritual, to see to the lamps, to change the shew-bread on the Sabbath ; but into the second tent or Holy of Holies entrance is allowed only once a year (actually four times in the performance of one liturgy), the only privileged person being the high priest, who enters not without blood but for the purpose of sprinkling the propitiatory and sanctuary with the blood of the bull which he has offered for his own sinful ignorances and also with the blood of the goat which he has offered for the sins or ignorances of the people. **8.** The intention of the Holy Spirit in arranging Israelite worship in such wise that the outer sanctuary should retain its position (στάσις) as the usual place of priestly access to God, and that the inner sanctuary should be an annual high-priestly reserve is to show that the way to the antitypal Holy of Holies of heaven has not yet been opened. **9.** The outer sanctuary is really a parable-image of the present pre-Messianic (not Messianic) time—a parable according to which such oblations and sacrifices of every kind are offered as are powerless to purify the conscience and interiorly perfect the worshipper. **9–10.** These oblations and victims are really nothing more than part and parcel of the system which included food distinctions and drink prohibitions and various ritual washings, and, just like these, are really only fleshly regulations (DV ' Justices of the flesh ' : read δικαιώματα in apposition to ' gifts and sacrifices ', omitting ' and ' before ' justices '). These fleshly regulations are merely temporary, imposed until the time of Messianic reform or betterment, διόρθωσις.

11–28 The Day of Eternal Atonement—Firstly, the work **g** of Christ the High Priest is described in a magnificent synthesis, 11–14 ; secondly, in relation to the Covenant which his blood sealed, 15–22 ; thirdly, in its absolute efficacy and finality, 23–28.

11–14 Synthesis—This passage which, with the addition of two verses from the next paragraph, is the Epistle for Passion Sunday and the Feast of the Precious Blood, continues in the symbolic language of the Tabernacle and Day of Atonement. Its chief difficulty—a very considerable difficulty—is to determine what is the tabernacle through which Christ passed. **11.** The Apostle says in a tone of majestic contrast : ' Christ having come into the world in the quality of High Priest of the spiritual and eternal good things of the Messianic future, passed through *the* greater and more perfect tabernacle not made with hands, and entered . . . the sanctuary '. The sanctuary is everlasting glory, or, in the simpler language of place, heaven ; but what is the tabernacle ' through which ' he entered ? As the entrance was made through the Passion, the only satisfactory answer seems to be : his own mortal Body, *cf.* ' the veil, which is his flesh ', 10:20. This would

940g explain why the Apostle not only says 'not made with hands' but adds the words : 'that is, not of this creation', for the Body of Christ was formed as a temple of God by the Holy Ghost. It is, of course, impossible to deny that the writer is thinking of the two localized poles, earth and heaven ; but he evidently does not regard the blue curtain of the sky as the veil of a sanctuary. Christ passed from the condition of mortality to glory. Thus the glorified Christ, finding of course his proper habitation in heaven, constitutes the interior sanctuary. 'The flesh is a veil', says Chrysostom, ' as concealing the Godhead ; and likewise a tabernacle as holding the Godhead'. There is no express reference in the Epistle to the Ascension of Christ. He, as it were, enters heaven from the Cross in the sprinkling of his blood, and at the end of the Epistle it is in the Blood of the New Testament that God brings him forth from the dead, 13:20. Not that our author was unaware of the three days (some thirty-five hours) of entombment and the forty days of glory on earth, but he is thinking in the juridical terms of Atonement Day. Christ expiating sin on the Cross and sacerdotally sprinkled with his own blood *de jure* enters eternal glory at the moment that the veil of his mortality is broken ; and at the same moment the veil of the temple —surely the inner veil—is rent, with a synchronism which seems to find its tremendous explanation in Christ's sixth word : ' It is consummated ' (τετέλεσται). With all the prophecies about the Messianic redemption now fulfilled, the Old Covenant and the Ritual of Lev 16 have come **h** to an end. **12.** ' Not by the blood of goats nor of calves but by his own blood (Christ) entered once into the holies, having obtained eternal redemption'. The heavenly sanctuary is opened once for all and for ever, for the blood of expiation is an eternal ransom, that is, the infinite price of eternal freedom. **13.** The cleansing efficacy of blood belongs to two different spheres, that of outer purification and that of interior purification. The sprinkled blood of sacrificial goats and calves and the lustral water made from the ashes of a red heifer offered in sacrifice, Num 20, cleanse those who have contracted legal defilement of one kind or another, that is, cleanse them externally in view of externally unimpeded communion with God's people. These sprinklings have limited but real legal efficacy in the sphere to which they belong. **14.** But how much more shall not the blood of Christ be efficacious in the interior sphere of conscience ? ' By the Holy Ghost (Gk, ' eternal spirit ', probably meaning the Holy Ghost ; otherwise ' his own eternal Godhead ') he offered himself unspotted unto God'. He was Priest and Victim—a Victim utterly without blemish (*cf.* 1 Pet 1:19). ' Cleansing ' (*cf.* 1:3 ; Eph 5:20 ; Tit 2:14) is wrought within the conscience so that the beneficiary receives new life to serve the living God. The impressive phrase ' Living God ' occurs four times in our Epistle, and five times in the other Paulines. It reminds us that the God of Abraham and Isaac and Jacob, the God of the Hebrew Fathers and of the Apostles was no idol and no mere philosophical abstraction.

941a 15-22 Covenant Significance—The Redeemer is a Mediator, and what he mediates is the new covenant of friendship between God and mankind. **15.** With language partly similar to that of the great redemption passage of Rom 3:21-26 the Apostle insists that the New Covenant is enacted by a death that redeemed the transgressions which were without atonement under the former Covenant, so that those who have been called may receive the promise of eternal inheritance made to the Patriarchs. Christ, the Mediator, dying to establish a Covenant, is evidently a testator and the Covenant is a Testament receiving its validity through death. There seems to be no doubt that in 16 and 17 διαθήκη is not simply the equivalent of the Hebrew *bᵉrîṭ* meaning pact or alliance, but that it has its most usual Greek signification of ' last will or testament '. **16.** ' Where there is a testament, the death of the testator must *receive public attestation* ' (φέρεσθαι). **17.** For a testament is effective only after death (ἐπὶ νεκροῖς)—it has no legal

force while the testator lives. **18-20.** It was in view of **941a** this testamentary character of the Messianic Covenant that the inauguration of the Sinaitic Covenant and the dedication of its sanctuary and its holy things were accompanied by the death of victims of sacrifice and the sprinkling of blood. The actions of Moses are described and the words of Ex 24:8 (alluded to in the consecration of the chalice at the Last Supper) are textually cited. Many ceremonial details mentioned are not found in Exodus, but are gathered from analogous ceremonies elsewhere described in the Pentateuch, Lev 14 ; 4, 5 ; 16:15 ; Num 19:9. **21.** An anointing of the tabernacle and its utensils is all that is mentioned in the sacred page, Ex 40:9 ; Lev 8:10, but on the analogy of the consecration of Aaron and his sons, aspersion of blood is presumed for all great consecrations. **22.** Very few purifications and those minor ones were carried out without blood, and even such a permission as that of a sin-offering of meal for the poor, Lev 5:11, did not alter the general principle enunciated here and also current as a rabbinical *Mashal* : ' Without shedding of blood there is no remission '.

23-28 Finality of Christ's Sacrifice—Four chief ideas **b** are conveyed in these lines : (*a*) **23.** The purifications of the Old Law were shadows and affected shadow-types of heavenly things only, and yet animal blood was required ; but the heavenly things themselves (τὰ ἐπουράνια) must be purified by better sacrifices (plural of category really meaning only one sacrifice applied in many ways). As purifications fall only on the Church militant that must be the primary meaning of ἐπουράνια (Chrys. Theodoret.). These things of the Church combatant are ' heavenly things ', for they are of heavenly origin, belong to the sphere of eternal life and end in heaven. **24.** It really was no hand-made sanctuary that Christ entered but heaven itself, to appear now before God on our behalf. Entering here has opened the road for ever. (*b*) **25-26a.** He does not offer himself again and again to effect a periodical expiation like the annual expiation made by the Israelite high priest. If that were so, he should have suffered many times over, since the beginning of the world. (*c*) **26b.** But now *once* and once only, in the last age of the world, he has appeared for the abolition of sin through his sacrifice. (*d*) **27-28.** As far as Christ's work is concerned nothing remains but the consummation. Just as death comes to men once and is not repeated—only judgement next—so also Christ offered himself once ' to take away the sins of many ' (any number Is 53:12), and at his second coming shall make his appearance in order to gather in those who expect him as Saviour, Phil 3:20, 21.

X 1-18 Superior Efficacy of Christ's One Sacrifice c Abolishes Legal Sacrifices—Here the Apostle's gaze is still more on the Church militant, as it undergoes sanctification for heaven. Christ's sacrifice is compared once again with the yearly liturgy of atonement and subsequently with the perpetual daily round of Israelite sacrifices. Here also four points seem to sum up the text : (1) Sacrifices incessantly repeated show their powerlessness by their very repetition, 1-4 ; (2) Christ's one obedience, as the Scriptures show, replaced them all, 5-10 ; (3) the daily liturgy of simple Levitical priests is as powerless as that of Atonement Day and even more palpably powerless, 11 ; (4) the sacrifice of Christ is the consummation of everything, for it really remits sins, 12-18.

1-4 Legal Sacrifices Powerless—The best way of conceiving the Apostle's terminology (*shadow, image, things*) seems to be this. **1.** The Law had only mere shadow signs, the new economy of the Church militant has the image (the object itself, the reality) in the institutional means of grace, while the good things to come embrace both grace and glory. The impotence of the yearly expiation, shown by its constant repetition, was its inability to give interior perfection (τελειῶσαι) or effect pardon of sin. **2.** The sacrificial ritual was really only a yearly amnesty, not a purification of consciences once for all. **3.** In fact the amnesty included a yearly

1c anamnesis or commemoration of sins. **4.** It was, of course, impossible that the blood of calves and goats should take away guilt.

d 5-10 Christ's Obedience—Christ himself in a programmatic Psalm-text, 39:7-9a, announces the abolition of legal sacrifices of every sort and their replacement by his own obedience—which obedience actually was sacrificial obedience unto death. **5.** Coming into the world he speaks the words of this Psalm which may well be directly Messianic as most of the ancients and also post-Tridentine commentators of note, like Agellius and Bellarmine, held. It is at the very least typally Messianic. In this latter case, David must have been in such a situation that God wanted no sort of material sacrifice from him. The language used is, it seems, the most absolute rejection of legal sacrifice in any OT passage, *cf*. Pss 49:8 ; 50:18 ; 68:32. The verses are cited according to LXX, which differs from the Heb. mainly which reads ' Ears thou hast opened for me ', instead of Paul's ' a body thou hast fitted to me '. In spite of the high editorial authority of Rahlfs, this seems to be the original Alexandrian Gk reading. The sense of the verse is not substantially changed, for the obedience of Christ (open-eared promptness) was exercised by offering his body. Hence St Paul can lawfully emphasize the word ' body ' from the LXX. **5-10.** The Psalm text, as expounded here is a five-point oracle : (1) ' Thou wouldst not ', 5, removes legal sacrifices ; (2) ' Behold, I come ', 7, marks a new era, but, of course, not an era without sacrifice ; (3) the sacrifice of the Messias, though instinct with obedience, is not metaphorical but real, 8–9 ; (4) it is the sacrifice of his body, 10 ; (5) it is the will of God, 10, that this obedience unto death be our sanctifying sacrifice offered once for all (ἐφάπαξ used since 7:27 for the third and last time with a thud of emphasis).

e 11-18 The Daily Liturgy and the One Eternal Sacrifice —**11.** Repetition, repetition, repetition—that is the law of the daily sacrifices of Mosaism, for they can *never* take away sin. Christ's sacrifice for sins is, on the contrary, *one* and unrepeatable. **12-13.** Having offered it, he sits for ever at the right hand of God, awaiting the full actualization of his sovereignty in the subjection of all his enemies. **14.** For by one offering he has perfected (τετελείωκεν) for ever those who are undergoing sanctification. **15.** Once again, under the name of the Holy Ghost the Inspirer, part of the oracle of Jeremias is quoted in inverted order, to show that the New Covenant brings the remission of sins. **18.** Then the Apostle concludes : ' Where there is remission of these, an oblation for sin *finds no place any longer* '. What then of all our Masses ? one may ask. The answer is that they are only the one Sacrifice of Christ perpetually commemorated, re-presented, applied to our daily needs, individual and social. The unity of Christ's sacrifice is a tremendous truth, and nowhere is it so tremendously driven home as in the Epistle to the Hebrews.

PARAENETIC PART, X 19-XIII 17

2a This moral part is an exhortation to perseverance in the faith. Its first section, 10:19–39, opens with an encouraging ' we-exhortation ' to faith, hope and charity, 19–25, continues with a severe warning against apostasy, 26–31, and terminates in a direct and comforting appeal based on past good deeds, 32–39. Each of the three subdivisions ends in the thought of judgement. The second section (ch 11) opening with a practical definition of faith, 1–3, is a Martyrology of heroic examples of faith from the primitive age, 4–7, the patriarchal age, 8–22, the days of the Exodus, and Conquest, 23–31, followed by more miscellaneous examples out of the long period from Judges to Machabees, 32–38. The Martyrology is crowned by the remark that all those heroes of faith attained the perfection of glory (τελειοῦσθαι) only in *our* Christian age, 39. The third section (ch 12) resumes exhortation especially to patience, firstly, with a ' we-appeal '

centring in the example of Christ, 1, 2—this continues **942a** in the second person plural with consolatory remarks on God's paternal discipline, 3–13 ; then, in a special admonition to peace, holiness and fidelity which ends in a grandiose characterization of the Mosaic Sinai and the Christian Sion, 14–24. There follows a final warning, 25–29, in which, as it were, the sound of the last trumpet itself accompanies the proclamation that there can be no refusal of this final revelation of God now spoken in the Messianic end of time. The Epistle, in a sense, ends here ; 13:1–17 is of the nature of an appendix and contains a set of precepts loosely strung together but skilfully attached to the main theme of the Epistle.

X 19-26 Steadfastness—' Unwavering confidence **b** rooted in faith and working in charity ' is the watchword. **20.** Christ is the inaugurator of the newly opened way to the Sanctuary through the veil of his flesh, and since he is also High Priest over the House of God, he inspires the boldness of our confidence. **22-24.** Sincerity, fullness of faith, the sprinkling and washing that come from repentance and baptism give the conscience freedom of access. ' Let us approach . . . let us hold fast . . . let us consider each other ' are the three exhortatives which urge the practice of the three divine virtues. Hope particularly is founded on the fidelity of God to his promises, and charity must be social. **25.** The necessity of ' provoking ' charity, of frequenting liturgical gatherings, of mutual exhortation is all the greater ' as you see the day approaching '. The Parousia is meant, but the judgement on Jerusalem (five years hence) is probably included.

26-31 Apostasy—**26-29.** The sin contemplated is **c** deliberate and persistent rejection of the truth once sufficiently received. For such sinners, on account of their moral condition, no sacrifice is operative and there is no prospect but the wrath of God. Much worse than the capital crime of blasphemy, mercilessly punished with death under the old legislation, is the sin of him who has trampled on the Son of God, treated the sanctifying blood of the Covenant as a common thing-of-nothing, and outraged the Spirit of grace. **30.** The vengeance text from Deut 32:35 verbally differs from both Heb. and LXX but agrees with St Paul's citation in Rom 12:19. The judgement text as uttered by Moses, Deut 32:36, really refers to judgement *in favour* of God's people, but every such judgement entails punishment of enemies. **31.** The Apostle ends with one of the three terrible dicta of Heb, *cf*. 6:8 ; 12:29.

32-39 Old Memories—Remembrance of days of fervour **d** is a most powerful antidote against relaxation. The Hebrews had ' endured a great contest of sufferings ' and proved themselves good spiritual athletes. Pain, shame, active sympathy with persecuted fellow-Christians, and spoliation fell to their lot—in the days of Stephen, for example. **35.** This courage of confidence must not be thrown away, and patience is necessary in order to keep doing God's will and thus secure salvation. **36-39.** Prefaced by the words : ' a little while, a very little while ', Is 26:20, the well-known text of Hab 2:3c, 4a, 4b is cited in the order 3c, 4b, 4a. Thus an eschatological warning is made to end in the chiasmus : *faith* gives life, *withdrawal* displeasure to God—' but we are not persons of *withdrawal* to our perdition, rather of *faith* to the saving of our souls '. The homiletic ' we ' concludes this direct appeal.

XI 1-3 Nature of Faith—**1.** Faith is not theologically **943a** defined but rather described in reference to things not yet possessed and not yet seen. Hence its voluntative and intellectual sides are considered. For the human will faith is a basic support (ὑπόστασις) as it holds to a revealed but absent end ; for the intellect it is the argument or proof (ἔλεγχος) giving conviction of what is not evident to senses or intellect. This is one of many explanations of this difficult sentence. **2.** It is by faith the ancient saints (οἱ πρεσβύτεροι) earned their testimony of praise. **3.** By faith we know that the world was created by God's word of command, so that the visible came out of invisible nothingness. Literally the text

943a says : ' *so that it was not from things that appear that the visible (universe) came to be* '.

b 4-7 Primitive Age—4. Abel's faith is attested by his better sacrifice (choice firstlings), by its acceptance through some heavenly sign, by the cry of his innocent blood when dead. **5-6.** Enoch was exempted from death, because he pleased God, which is impossible without faith in God as Beginning and End—Creator and Remunerator. **7.** Faith in a future chastisement—one hundred years distant—showed the heroism of Noe who thereby condemned the world (with a condemnation of comparison) and became the heir of the justice which is by faith.

c 8-22 The Patriarchs—8-10. Abraham when called at Ur obeyed blindly and left for Charran (Haran), where he first learned that his destination was Canaan. He lived in the land of promise as a stranger with no fixed abode—a *tent*-dweller—continuing to do so even with his co-heirs Isaac and Jacob. His hope was in a still unseen but firmly founded city whose architect and builder is God. **11.** Abraham's faith brought a blessing also on Sara for the founding of a posterity, because he believed the promise of God, in spite of his wife's barrenness and old age and his own centenarian years. **12.** Therefore from a man as good as dead sprang a race (both carnal and spiritual) as numerous as the stars and innumerable as the sand at the lip of the sea. **13-15.** The faith of these men was fundamentally a longing for the heavenly fatherland. For its sake they left home, professed themselves pilgrims, and continued their exile when they could have returned to their original fatherland—and all that stands to their credit, while they could only give a distant salute to the glorious things of the promises which they died without attaining. **16.** They certainly looked for a better country than Ur, namely, a heavenly one. The desire was, it seems, implicit, for there was as yet no explicit revelation about heaven. Therefore, God is not ashamed to be called ' the God of Abraham, the God of Isaac, the God of Jacob ', *cf.* Christ's use of this appellative, Ex 3:6 ; Mt 22:32. **17-19.** In the offering of Isaac Abraham's faith did not spare an only son who was actually the sole heir of the promises, for he believed that God could find a way of realizing his promise even by raising Isaac from the dead. **19b.** Hence he received him as a type of Christ sacrificed and brought back from death. **20.** Faith kept Isaac from revoking the spiritual blessing given to Jacob and the merely temporal blessing given to Esau. **21.** By faith Jacob blessed Ephraim and Manasses, consciously crossing his hands irrespective of their ages, Gen 48:15 ; and earlier, Gen 47:31, he honoured Joseph's posterity by bowing to the top of Joseph's rod (not apparently ' to the top of his bed ', or ' resting on the top of his staff '). **22.** Faith in the future Exodus and destiny of Israel made Joseph give orders for the burial of his bones in Canaan.

d 23-31 Exodus and Conquest—23-26. Moses' parents who saw in the beauty of their infant son a sign of divine destiny, 23, and Moses himself, refusing the life of an Egyptian Prince, in order to suffer with Israel and thus share the reproach of Christ, showed faith in a divine reward. **27.** When leaving Egypt in the face of Pharaoh's wrath, Ex 12:37, Moses attended to the Unseen as if he saw It. **28-31.** The Paschal blood, the passage of the Red Sea, the fall of the walls of Jericho, the preservation of Rahab are so many further eulogies of faith.

e 32-38 Miscellaneous Examples—32. Impossible in a letter to continue the enumeration. Hence six names and a category (the Prophets) are mentioned only, and the eulogies reduced to the compendious form of a series of events in which faith shone forth. The peculiar order of the six names is to be noted—three pairs in the chronological order of their succession, but the second name of each pair is historically his companion's predecessor. **33-35a.** Conquest of kingdoms and doing of justice belong to many judges and kings, and very many persons obtained promises. Escape from lions

(Daniel), from fire (three young men), from the sword **94** (David, etc.) are prodigies of preservation rewarding faith. Recovery from sickness (Ezechias), strength in war (Judges), destruction of alien camps (Judges), resurrections from death (sons of the widow of Sarepta and of the Sunamite) are all attributable to faith. **35b-37a.** Heroic endurance likewise : on the rack (Machabean Martyrs) ; by refusal of life in view of a better resurrection (Eleazar) ; through scoffings (Eliseus), scourgings and imprisonment (Jeremias) ; under stoning (Zacharias), under trials (or burning ?) under the saw (Isaias ?), under the sword (many prophets). **37b-38.** At mention of those in sheepskins and goatskins one thinks of men like Elias—men going about in want, distress, affliction, ' of whom the world ' that maltreated them ' was not worthy '—a really lyrical phrase in this context. **38b.** We know of fifty prophets who lived in caverns to escape the fury of Jezabel. **39-40.** Yet all these men and women had to await *our* age—the fullness of time—before they could receive the promises and come to the perfection of glory which by faith they merited. Such is the greatness of Messianic privilege which apostates would throw away.

XII 1, 2 All Eyes on Christ—The foregoing Roll of **94** Honour summons a dense cloud of witnesses who tell of the victories of faith. Therefore—and the ' therefore ' is most unusually emphatic—let us do our part. Our part is conceived athletically, *cf.* 1 Cor 9:24 f. ; Gal 5:7 ; Phil 3:14 ; 2 Tim 4:7. Let us, free from every weight and every sin that besets us and stands only too ready to lay hold of us (εὐπερίστατος)—let us with patience run the race (ἀγών ' contest ') lying before us, looking away (from ephemeral things) and fixing our eyes on Jesus the Author (rather than Leader) and the Finisher of our faith—who first brought it to us and will give it the final perfection of vision. He is a perfect Model, for in view of (rather than instead of) the joy set before him, he endured the cross, thinking nothing of the shame and ignominy of it, and he has taken his seat (*for ever*, as the perfect tense denotes) at the right hand of the throne of God.

3-13. That ' Sign of contradiction ', which is Jesus, **b** well considered is a remedy for all faint-heartedness, 3. There had been few martyrdoms amongst this Hebrew-Christian community, and the ordinary discipline of hard-knocks is only what children must expect. Prov 3:11 is cited as showing that chastisement is a sign of God's love. **4-8.** To be under discipline therefore is a cause of joy, for it makes those who partake of it feel that they belong to the family. **9.** Submission to the chastising hand of an earthly father of our flesh has been a matter of filial reverence. Are we then to demur when the heavenly Father of spirits uses a chastening hand to lead us to eternal life ? **10.** Human discipline fits us for a fleeting life, and it may at times be arbitrary or wrong, but God's educational regime is always profitable and sanctifying. **11.** Not the present but the future is the proper test. Chastisement here and now is painful, but later it produces the peaceful fruit of justice. **12-13.** Therefore, no slackness ! The limping limb must not be allowed to get dislocated but rather set on the way of recovery.

14-24 Peace, Holiness, Fidelity : Sinai and Sion—14. **c** Peace belongs to the children of God ; and striving after the purity of holiness is the necessary road to the vision of God. **15.** Charity has an ' episcopal ' eye ; its overseership must ensure that no one defaults from the grace of God, and that no bitter root of poisonous influence causes disturbance resulting in the defilement of the many. **16-17.** The spirit of fornication and profane low-mindedness—the latter (and perhaps both) exemplified in Esau—is not to be tolerated. The dangers of a mentality steeped in earth are very real. Esau sold his rights of primogeniture for one mess of pottage, and later when he sought, even with tears, a return of the paternal blessing—which in the Providence of God his profanity had sold to Jacob—he was rejected by his father Isaac who refused to repent of his decision. Opportunities can be irreparably lost by the low-

4c minded, *cf.* §§ 938*a*, *b*, 942*c*. **18.** Sion demands greater fidelity and sweeter obedience than Sinai. This is powerfully shown in a two-panelled picture. **19-21.** Sinai was a material mountain, blazing with terrible fire, surrounded by such darkness as precedes a storm, and the murkiness of heaped-up clouds, disturbed even by the fury of tempestuous wind. The long-drawn sound of a trumpet and the angelic voice representing God so dreadful that the people asked that they should be spared those terrors of God's Majesty. Even a beast that touched the Mountain, while God legislated from it, had to be stoned. Moses himself showed the awe which he felt for he said ' I am utterly terrified and trembling '—words substantially spoken by him on account of the apostasy of the Golden Calf, Deut 9:19, but psychologically representing his terror at the whole scene of God's majesty manifested on the Mountain. **22-24.** On the other hand, Christians have come to a Mountain which is Sion, to a City which is the city of the Living God, to a Jerusalem which is heavenly—to myriads of angels, a truly festive assembly (πανηγύρει) —to a Church of first-born enrolled in heaven (all enjoying the privileges of primogeniture : blessing and double portion—and enrolled in God's book of heavenly citizens), to God the Judge of all, and to those favourably judged by him, namely, the spirits of the just who have come to perfection in the beatific vision already attained—to the Mediator of the New Covenant Jesus (of whom much has been said)—and to a blood of sprinkling crying for pardon more loudly than the blood of Abel cried for vengeance. The Rest and Peace of Sion are in this diptych set in strong contrast to the terrors of Sinai.

d **25-29 Last Warning**—When God speaks, the earth shakes. He spoke from Sinai and the people made an act of refusal. He speaks now from heaven and this time his voice produces a shaking of earth and heaven, that is, of all creation—a shaking predicted by Aggeus, 2:6-8, and ending in an unchangeable kingdom. Therefore, we who have received that kingdom must have grace and serve God with a great desire to please him—always with pious reverence and deep fear, for our God is a consuming fire, Deut 4:24 ; 9:3.

e **XIII 1-17 Appendix—1-6.** Various admonitions. Charity, purity, detachment are the first triad. Charity must be constantly fraternal, given to hospitality (in the exercise of which Abraham and Lot received Angels, Gen 18:3), and compassionate (nourished by the remembrance of our fellowship in misery). Marriage must be surrounded with great respect in all that belongs to it. God, the great Defender of undefiled nuptial unions, will not fail to punish fornicators and adulterers. Detachment from money goes with trust in Providence, which trust is inspired by the freely adapted words of God to the Israelites in general, Deut 31:6, and to Josue in particular, Deut 31:6 ; Jos 1:5. The Psalm text, 117:6, is an act of confidence from the Hymn of the Cornerstone.

Loyalty, 7, 8, religious fidelity, 9-16, obedience to **944e** superiors, 17, sum up the rest. Devoted remembrance of dead leaders (like Stephen, James the son of Zebedee, James the son of Alpheus) is a reminder that the ' Faith of our Fathers ' is the faith of today and of tomorrow—' Jesus Christ yesterday and today and the same (he remains) for ever ', 8. **9.** An unchangeable faith is necessary. Therefore every doctrinal drift has to be guarded against, and the heart fed with grace rather than the superstition of unprofitable food regulations. **10-14.** It is very controverted whether the **f** Eucharistic Altar is the altar from which the servants of the tabernacle cannot eat. The trend of this very difficult passage seems to be : Jesus Crucified is our altar. He was an Expiatory Victim for sin. Now the flesh of Jewish victims on the day of Annual Expiation was not eaten, the bodies being burned outside the camp. Jesus realized this prophetic detail of expiation ritual, for he suffered outside the gate of Jerusalem. Those, therefore, who belong to Jesus must go outside the camp of Judaism to him, even at the cost of carrying his reproach. This is really the programme of all those who decide to leave the Jewish world (and, extensively, every merely terrestrial camp) behind them, in their resolution to journey to the lasting City of Heaven. The author does not say that the body of Jesus is not eaten, and, of course, it was not burned. He says that we have an altar and implies that we eat from it. Knowing the Eucharistic history of the Jerusalem community as we do, Ac 2:42, it seems solidly probable that the Eucharist was in the mind of St Paul as he wrote these words. **15-16.** To the great real victim, he adds metaphorical victims of praise ('fruit of lips'), and also the well-pleasing victims of beneficence and generously helpful communication in the needs of others. **17.** Submission to superiors is urged from the beautiful motive of sympathy with their watchful solicitude. They have to give an account. That it should be a sad one is our loss rather than theirs.

XIII 18-25 Epilogue—18-19. The Apostle asks the **g** prayers of the Hebrews, in the consciousness of his own devotedness, and in the hope of returning to them sooner. **20-21.** In turn, he prays for them in the remembrance of Christ's resurrection through the blood of an eternal testament, asking that God, who thus brought back from the dead the Great Shepherd of the sheep, might, through him their Mediator, fit the Hebrews for the doing of every good in the well-pleasing accomplishment of the will of God. The doxology goes to our Lord Jesus Christ. **22-25.** Concluding, he begs that the word of consolation written with epistolary brevity be well received, 22, and announces that Timothy has been released (from a captivity otherwise unknown). The final salutations are to the ' Superiors and all the Saints '. Those ' from Italy ' are presumably in Italy, from where (probably Rome) the letter was written : ' Grace be with you all. Amen '.

THE CATHOLIC EPISTLE OF
ST JAMES THE APOSTLE

By H. WILLMERING, S.J.

945a Bibliography—G. Estius, *In Omnes D. Pauli Epistolas et Catholicas Commentarii*, ed. L. Vivès, t. 3, Paris, 1891 ; A. Camerlynck, *Commentarius in Epistolas Catholicas*, Bruges, 1909[5] ; *J. H. Ropes, *Epistle of St James*, ICC, Edinburgh, 1916 ; J. Chaine, *L'Epître de Saint Jacques*, Paris, 1927 ; J. Charue, *Les Epîtres Catholiques*, La Sainte Bible, ed. Pirot, Tome XII, Paris, 1938 ; J. Bonsirven, art. *Epître de Saint Jacques*, DBVS, Paris, 1948, 783–95 ; M. Meinertz, *Der Jakobusbrief*, BB, Bonn, 1932[4].

b The Author—'James the servant of God and of our Lord Jesus Christ', this is all the direct information which the author of this Epistle gives about himself. Is it to be considered an authentic work of apostolic times, or ' as probably the pseudonymous production of a Christian of Jewish origin, living in Palestine in the last quarter of the 1st cent. or in the first quarter of the second ' as Ropes conjectures (p 1) ? Catholic tradition solidly favours authenticity, and many non-Catholic authors concur with this tradition. Those who hold that the Epistle is pseudonymous point out : its pure Greek style, its silence on many questions which were agitating the Church of the first generation, and its uncertain position in the NT canon. Yet the following facts strongly favour authenticity. A forger would have identified himself with James the Apostle, or the Lord's brother, by inserting the title in the inscription. Likewise the authoritative tone adopted by the author seems to indicate that he held an official position which would be recognized by Jewish converts. Lastly, the Epistle has many points of contact with the First Gospel, and ' there is every appearance that the writer had been a personal follower of the Lord ', *G. Salmon, *Introduction to the NT*, London, 1904[9], 454.

c Assuming, therefore, that the author belonged to NT times, can we identify him with one of the Apostles of Christ, or with the Lord's brother, the Bishop of Jerusalem ? The majority of the Fathers of the Western Church identify the writer with James the Apostle, the son of Alphaeus, whereas in the Eastern Church the opinion of Eusebius, *Hist. Eccl.* 2, 23, 4, led some to distinguish between the son of Alpheus and the Lord's brother, who was Bishop of Jerusalem. For a discussion of the question ' The Brethren of the Lord ' *cf.* §§ 672–3. There are, however, solid arguments for the view that James the Apostle is identical with James the Lord's brother. In Gal 1:19 St Paul writes : ' But other of the Apostles I saw none, save James the brother of the Lord ' ; and 2:9 he says : ' James and Cephas and John, who seemed to be pillars, gave to me and Barnabas the right hand of fellowship ', where James is put on a par with Peter and John, two Apostles. Ac 1:13 names all the Apostles, and among them the name of ' James ' appears twice. Later, 12:2 we read : ' And he (Herod Agrippa) killed James the brother of John with the sword '. In the same chapter, 12:17, Peter, who had just been miraculously delivered from prison, says : ' Tell these things to James and the brethren '. Here ' James ' is used without any distinguishing epithet, and we logically think of the only other James mentioned earlier in Acts, namely, James the son of Alpheus. Ac 15:13, James again appears at the side of Peter, and speaks with apostolic authority to Paul and Barnabas and the whole Christian church. Ac 21:18 tells how this same James receives an account

from Paul of his missionary labours, an evident indica- **9** tion that he held an official position in the Jerusalem community.

Canonicity—Until the middle of the 3rd cent. the **d** inspired character of Jas was questioned by some churches and accepted by others ; and a century later Eusebius, *Hist. Eccl.* 3:25, lists Jas among the ' antilegomena ' or disputed books of the NT. St Jerome, *De Vir. Illust.* 2, writes : ' Some hold it was actually written by another under his name, though in the course of time it gradually was accepted as authentic '. It is omitted from the canonical list contained in the Muratorian Fragment, but finds a place on other canonical lists of NT books, *e.g.* of Athanasius, PG 26, 1176 ; Origen, PG 12, 857 ; Cyril of Jerusalem, PG 33, 500 ; Third Council of Carthage, Dz 92 ; Pope Damasus, Dz 84 ; Innocent I, Dz 96. Commentaries on Jas were written by Clement of Alexandria and SS Cyril of Jerusalem and John Chrysostom, PG 64, 1039 ff. Finally, Jas is quoted as Scripture by SS Ephraem, Hilary, Jerome, Ambrose, Augustine and others. Hence we can claim that this Epistle found almost universal acceptance in the Church from the 4th to the 16th cent., when Erasmus, Cajetan and Luther revived the doubt about its authenticity and canonicity. Both were settled for Catholics at the fourth session of the Council of Trent, Dz 784.

Destination and Purpose—The Epistle was addressed **e** to Christians, 1:18 ; 2:1 ; converts from Judaism, 1:1 ; exposed to trials of many kinds, 1:2, 12 ; 5:7, 10 ; poor in material goods, 2:5 ; and oppressed by the rich, 2:6. Amid such hardships they sometimes manifested a lack of ' the wisdom from above ' ; *e.g.* they sought too eagerly for material richs, 4:1 f, catered for the rich and snubbed the poor in their community, 2:1–3 ; neglected the corporal works of mercy, 2:14–17 ; failed to control the tongue, 3:14 ; and quarrelled among themselves, 4:1 f. Such faults were common to all Jewish communities, and cannot be used to identify any particular community to which this Epistle was sent. The purpose of the author was to correct these faults and to encourage the faithful to be patient, constant in faith, cheerful, charitable, sincere, and to seek the peace and wisdom that descends from above, 3:17 f.

Date and Place of Composition—There is considerable **f** uncertainty about the time when this Epistle was written. Scholars who admit the authenticity are nearly equally divided in claiming an early or a late date. The former group call attention to the primitive character of the teaching embodied in this Epistle, to the absence of any trace of the decision adopted by the Council of Jerusalem, Ac 15:28 f., or of the controversy which occasioned it. The allusions to hunger, poverty and persecution are said to indicate the date of composition as A.D. 45, when the famine foretold by Agabus, Ac 11:28–30, and the persecution inflicted on the Church by Herod Agrippa, Ac 12:1 ff., were raging, *cf.* CE 8, 276. The other group consider these arguments less cogent than the following, which postulate a later date : the teaching of St Paul regarding justification by faith seems to have called forth some of the statements made in Jas 2:14–26. Likewise the conditions mentioned in the Epistle, namely, a certain laxity in the performance of Christian obligations,

f 2:14 ff. ; lack of charity, 1:27 ff., mercy, 2:13 ff., moderation, 3:1 ff., temperance, 4:1–5, humility, 4:6–10 and justice 5:1–6, seem very much out of place in the earliest Christian period. Since the date assigned to St James' death is about A.D. 62, the probable date of composition might be A.D. 61, and the probable place Jerusalem, where James was bishop, *cf.* Chaine, LXXXVII ff.

g Theme and Analysis of the Epistle—Many different topics are treated, and often the transition is abrupt. What St James chiefly wished to correct was the tendency among converts from Judaism to follow the ways of worldly instead of heavenly wisdom. After a brief salutation, he alludes to various trials and bids his readers to bear them with joy and patience, 1:2–4, for which wisdom is needed that must be secured by confident prayer, 5–8 ; help may also be found in a correct estimate of the existing conditions of life, 9–11. Happy are they who remain steadfast under trial, for their reward will be an eternal crown, 12. Not all will be constant, but if any are overcome let them not blame God for their sin, who tempts no man to evil, 13–18. It avails naught to be a mere hearer of the law, 19 ; so let them curb a tendency to anger and malice, practise charity and purity, 20–27. Directly opposed to Christian justice and charity is the practice of catering for the rich and despising the poor ; for God chose many of the latter to the faith, and the rich as a class are enemies of Christ and his followers. Christians must observe the whole law, and so speak and act as the Gospel requires, for according to its precepts they will be judged, 2:1–13.

Faith without works is a contradiction, and charity that limits itself to kind words, without manifesting itself in works of mercy, is an anomaly. A mere theoretical faith in God differs little from the belief of the devils. Abraham's and Rahab's faith revealed itself in works, which shows that faith without works is dead, 14–25.

h No one should be over-anxious to assume the responsibility of a teacher, and all should exercise great care in restraining the tongue, a powerful instrument for good or evil. He who controls his tongue has perfect self-command. How inconsistent and unnatural to use the same instrument to praise God and curse the neighbour, 3:1–12. Gentleness and moderation are products of true wisdom, whereas envy, contention and falsehood spring from earthly wisdom, 13–18. Wars and contentions grow out of unrestrained desires. By becoming too attached to this world, men are alienated from God. Only humble submission, purity of heart, and true repentance can draw down God's favour and grace, 4:1–10. Detraction and rash judgment should be carefully avoided, 11–13*a*. Man is ever dependent on God for life and everything else ; hence when he acts and speaks as if he were his own master, he violates God's rights, 13*b*–17. Terrible will be the judgement of God on the rich, who glory in riches accumulated through injustice and used for purposes of self-indulgence and oppression of the just, 5:1–6. Then follow words of comfort for the oppressed, who are exhorted to be patient and trust in God, as did Job. Let them avoid swearing, and have frequent recourse to prayer, particularly in times of sadness, joy, sickness of body or soul ; for God willingly hears the prayers of the just, as is proved by the example of Elias, 7–18. Finally, they are told to work for the conversion of their erring brethren, 19–20.

a Doctrinal Content—Being pre-eminently a practical message, the Epistle does not expound the distinctive teachings of Christianity, but rather supposes them ; *e.g.* we shall find no reference to the redemption through the passion and death of Christ, to his resurrection or the coming of the Holy Spirit. Yet the exhortations are Christian in tone, and there are many allusions to Christ's teachings, particularly as found in the Sermon on the Mount. Like his Divine Master, St James stresses the blessedness of poverty and purity of heart ; he would have us bear our trials with joy and pray with

confidence ; he warns against yielding to anger, form- **946a** ing rash judgements, indulging in oaths, courting the friendship of the world ; he shows the uselessness of faith without works. But all these are practical, not doctrinal matters.

It has sometimes been rashly asserted that St James **b** contradicts the teaching of St Paul on *justification by faith.* In Rom 3:20 and Gal 2:16, the latter states that man is justified not by the works of the law, but by faith ; St James, on the contrary, insists that faith without works is dead and of no avail for salvation, 2:14–26. The explanation of this apparent discrepancy is to be found in the different approach of each writer to the subject. St James is explaining the nature of faith which justifies, namely, that it cannot remain purely theoretical, but must issue in good works. St Paul, however, is arguing against certain Judaizers, who wish to make salvation dependent on the observance of the Mosaic Law. His point is that Christians are freed from the yoke of the Mosaic Law and not bound by its precepts. The Christian law has superseded the old law , hence the works of the old law are worthless for salvation, whereas faith in Christ is absolutely necessary for it. But St Paul does require good works to accompany faith and to spring from its teachings. In Gal 5:6 he speaks of ' faith that worketh by charity ' ; Rom 2:6, ' God will render to every man according to his works ' ; Eph 2:10 says that we are created to perform good works ; and every Epistle has its exhortations to practise Christian virtues, *e.g.* Rom 12–14 ; Eph 4–6. It is the teaching of the Council of Trent, session 14, **c** *De Extrema Unctione*, canons 1–4, Dz 926–9, that Jas 5:14 refers to the **Sacrament of Extreme Unction.** There is question in this passage of a Christian who is seriously ill. He is to summon the priests of the church, who should do two things for the sufferer : ' pray over him ', *i.e.* apply certain prayers with perhaps an imposition of hands, and ' anoint him with oil in the name of the Lord ', *i.e.* by commission and with the authority of Christ. This latter phrase applies to both the prayer and the action. Accordingly the anointing is to be regarded as a religious rite and not as a medicinal remedy, which seems to follow also from the effects described in verse 15 : God will save the sick man, raise him up, and forgive him his sins. The first two phrases, independently of the context, might refer to a restoration of bodily health ; but the third phrase expresses an undoubted spiritual effect, which includes a bestowal of sanctifying grace. ' To save ' is used five times in this Epistle, 1:21 ; 2:14 ; 4:12 ; 5:20 and in this context 5:15. In the first four instances it refers to *saving the soul* ; hence it is very probable that it has the same meaning here. Without excluding a restoration of bodily health, we claim that ' saving the soul of the sick man ' is a legitimate interpretation of the phrase in its context. The purpose, therefore, of the prayer of faith and the anointing with oil is to heal the soul and wipe out the remains of sins of the sick man. Restoration to health through the Sacrament of Extreme Unction is a secondary effect which does not always happen. *Cf.* C. Pickar, O.S.A. art. *Is Anyone Sick among You?* CBQ 7 (1945) 165–74.

Text and Style—Variant readings in the Greek text **d** of this Epistle are few and of little importance. Vg differs from the Greek text about eight times, as indicated in the commentary. The style of Jas is individual and striking, unlike that of any other book of the NT. It somewhat resembles that of Prov and Wis, and occasionally rivals the oratory of the prophets. The Greek is fluent and accurate, the vocabulary extensive, the expression vivid and colourful. It abounds in apt and impressive illustrations frequently drawn from nature. Some of the warnings and rebukes are severe and cutting, being prompted by true zeal and sincerity of purpose.

I-1 The Greeting—The short and simple form of this **e** greeting corresponds to the ordinary type of address of a Greek letter, Ac 23:26. James, like Moses, is a servant of God ; and like Peter, a slave of Jesus Christ,

946e 2 Pet 1:1. His words of spiritual counsel and encouragement are addressed to the Christian Israel in all parts of the world. On 'the dispersion' *cf.* I Pet 1:1.

2-4 Value of Trials—This opening paragraph shows the anxiety of the writer for the faithful under trial. **2.** Aware that their faith is being put to the test by manifold afflictions, he bids them to look upon themselves as blessed when they suffer persecution for justice's sake. **3.** For the time of trial is a training school in which lessons of endurance, constancy, and solid virtue are effectively taught. Men of strong faith will stand firm in times of affliction when weaker brethren falter and give way. **4.** Patient endurance tends to purify the soul, to sanctify and perfect it. A soul is perfected by the removal of everything contrary to the love of God, *cf.* Aquin. ST II, 2, Q. clxxxiv, Art. 2.

f 5-8 Plea for Heavenly Wisdom—Usually men see only the pain and difficulty connected with afflictions, and far from bearing them with joyful resignation they complain bitterly and even rebel against them. **5.** Human nature, left to its own resources and guided only by natural reason, is incapable of regarding the hardships of life as sources of joy. Only God-given wisdom can cause men to look upon tribulations as messengers of Divine Providence. **6.** This wisdom is bestowed upon those who ask for it with confidence. God is always ready to grant it with fatherly affection, setting no limits to his generosity and administering no reproaches. But the prayer must be made with faith, *i.e.* with entire confidence, never doubting God's goodness and bounty. **8.** He who hesitates will not be heard because he is 'double-minded', *i.e.* when he prays, his mind fluctuates between hope and fear, doubt and desire; and his whole conduct is fickle and inconsistent. Is it surprising that such a petitioner should receive nothing from God?

g 9-11 Practical Application—**9.** The poor man, through the patient endurance of poverty, will resemble his Divine Lord, who promised eternal life to the poor in spirit, Mt 5:3. Thus is he exalted through his low condition. **10.** The rich man, under the influence of divine wisdom, should humble himself before God, and recognize the worthlessness and transient nature of his wealth. Two other possible interpretations of this verse are : the rich man is to rejoice when he is brought low by adversity; and, taking the phrase ironically, the rich man rejoices in what is worthless in God's sight, hence by glorying in perishable wealth he is actually degrading himself, because he does not live up to Christian standards. The first meaning seems best in the context. **12.** The climax to this section on the value of trials is reached in the reward promised to the man who remains steadfast. With character matured, virtue perfected, and the love of God fully tested by trials patiently endured, the victor's crown of eternal glory will be his according to God's promise.

h 13-18 The Source of Temptation to Evil—Unfortunately not all Christians remain steadfast and many are overcome by temptation. They are warned not to throw the blame for their failure on God. Temptations may be considered as external trials or internal solicitations to sin. Previously St James was speaking about tests of character or of virtue; now he refers to influences that allure to sin. In themselves temptations are not sins, and when resisted they are the occasions for exercising virtue. When not resisted, the voluntary yielding to the temptation is what constitutes the sin. **13.** Weak men are so apt to try to shift the blame for their inconstancy on God, who put them in such circumstances, gave them so yielding a disposition, and allowed them to meet with such evil companions. But God himself ' *is untempted by evil* ', and everything sinful is utterly foreign to his nature. He cannot desire evil, nor solicit man to commit evil. **14.** Temptation to evil has its source in the individual. The bait that draws and allures him is concupiscence, the unruly passions and disorderly appetites. Sensuality or pride is aroused by some inducement to self-indulgence:

anger or jealousy is stirred up by someone crossing his **946b** path, or standing in the way of his ambitions. When passion is aroused, it acts like a lustful woman on the will of man; it seeks to induce the will to enter into an unlawful alliance. **15.** If the will consents, the first sin is committed through the evil desires that fill the heart, whereby concupiscence is said to conceive. The desires may lead to acts, and graver sin results. Finally, the sinful state may persist and grow to a sinful habit. Thus completed, sin begets death, eternal death, which stands in contrast to the ' crown of life ' held out to him who resists temptation.

17. Good gifts come from God, because he is Goodness **i** itself. Unlike the luminous bodies which he created by an act which entitles him to be called ' the Father of lights ', he is unchangeable in his eternal purpose, which is never obscured or altered. No need to find here ' echoes of Zoroastrian cult ' or ' astrological speculation '. The beauty of the oriental heaven by day and night deeply impressed the Psalmist, Ps 18:1 ff., and might readily suggest to a naive observer that the Creator of such bright, spotless, heavenly bodies could not will anything evil; also, to the fact that the mutations and revolutions of the heavenly bodies indicate dependence on a Creator, *cf.* Meinertz, 24. **18.** God's most perfect and absolutely free gift to us is our regeneration through the word of truth, the Gospel, whereby he willed to make us ' *a kind of first-fruits of his creatures* '. Under the old dispensation, the first-fruits of the harvest were offered to the Lord as an acknowledgement that the entire harvest came from him and belonged to him. Under the new dispensation, those regenerated through faith and baptism are the first-fruits of the human race. They belong to God, and are a reminder that all men belong to their Creator, and have duties towards him.

19-21 Curbing Anger and Malice—Dedication to the **947** service of God puts the regenerated under special obligations, expressed in a proverb similar to sayings in the OT; Prov 13:3; 17:27; Ecclus 5:13 f.; 20 passim. **19.** A certain eagerness in hearing, and reticence in speech, and slowness to take offence is recommended. Men are often sorry for having said too much, or having spoken out of anger; but they seldom regret that they listened first and held their angry feelings under control. **20.** Outbursts of anger are not conducive to holiness, and God's cause may suffer much through untimely and intemperate zeal. **21.** Another hindrance to holiness is uncleanness, *i.e.* every kind of sinful defilement, and ' *excess of malice* ', which is opposed to meekness. These hindrances are like weeds that encumber the ground and prevent the growth of the seed, the implanted word, Mt 13:22; but when the word of God is free and unencumbered, it is able to save men's soul.

22-27 Doers and Hearers of the Word—**22.** The **b** Gospel requires the co-operation of man's will to make it effective for salvation. It is not enough to listen to it and approve it; it must be taken to heart and reduced to action. Apparently some of the readers had not been making sufficient efforts to live in strict conformity with Gospel principles; yet these must regulate their lives, not merely in general but in every phase of it. Whoever is satisfied with knowing what is required, without making the necessary effort to act according to this knowledge, is deceiving himself by thinking that he is on the road to salvation. **24.** The comparison to a man, who idly gazes into a mirror without having any definite purpose in mind while doing so, illustrates the fallacy by which the ' hearer ' is deceiving himself. The reflexion of the mirror will not remove the stains and blemishes it discloses. **25.** Now the Gospel is a mirror of the soul, which shows one's conformity or lack of it to the requirements of Christian conduct. Looking into it calls for a spiritual change; and if this does not follow, no benefit has been received. Compared to the old law, the Gospel is ' the perfect law of liberty ', being founded on love and not on fear, Rom 8:15. One who continually lives according to its principles leads **a**

7b blessed life. He is at peace with God and his neighbour. **26.** As illustrations of what must be done and what should be avoided, St James cites three urgent duties : restraint of the tongue, a practical interest in the needs of orphans and widows, and an avoidance of the vices of the pagan world.

c **II:1-13 No Snobbery**—If the true Christian spirit demands an active benevolence towards the poor and afflicted, then a display of partiality towards the rich in Christian assemblies is entirely out of place and in direct contradiction to the principles of the Gospel. Hence the opening admonition : ' My brethren, have not the faith ', *i.e.* do not try to reconcile the faith, ' *of our glorious Lord Jesus Christ* with respect of persons '. **2.** The church is for the poor as well as for the rich, and to make a show of servility towards a well-dressed and obviously wealthy person by offering him a place of honour, while ushering a poorly clad man into a corner, is to be snobbish and unjust in judgement. **4.** Such conduct is based solely on external appearances, which often enough belie the interior character. **5.** It also contradicts the judgement of God, who shows more favour to the poor. The majority of the first converts belonged to that class, which is indicative of God's favour, because he thus makes them heirs of eternal life instead of bestowing upon them material riches.

d **6.** The rich, as a class, are enemies of Christ and of his followers. They oppress Christians and drag them before the law courts, and worst of all they blaspheme the holy name of Christ. **8.** The ' royal law ' of fraternal charity forbids snobbery. It is called the ' royal law ' because it is a fundamental principle of the kingdom of Christ, which together with ' the first and greatest commandment ' forms the ground-work on which ' dependeth the whole law and the prophets ', Mt 22:40. **10.** On account of the unity and internal cohesion of the law, a man who violates one precept, is guilty of transgressing the law as a whole. **11.** Not all sins are equal ; but every serious sin (and there is question here of grave matter) indicates contempt for the authority of the Lawgiver. **12.** The words and deeds of Christians should always conform to the law of Christ, which is ' the law of liberty ' because, through the spirit of adoption, the baptized are set free from the spirit of bondage attached to the old law, Rom 8:15 ; and by this law of liberty all Christians will be judged. **13.** There is a law of divine retribution ; but at times mercy triumphs over severity.

e **14-26 Faith and Works**—Faith is lifeless if nothing issues from it. Faith without works will not obtain mercy for us at the judgement. **14.** A believer, who contents himself with kind words and wishes but does not practise works of mercy towards a fellow Christian reduced to extreme necessity, boasts of a faith that lacks an essential quality to make it effective for eternal salvation. Hence, faith without works is worthless and unprofitable to the possessor. **18.** If faith really exists, it is interior, and cannot be shown to others ; whereas, if it issues in good works, these may be offered as proofs of one's faith. **19.** To demonstrate the worthlessness of a mere theoretical faith, an example is furnished by the belief in the unity of God. Even the devils assent to this doctrine ; furthermore, it causes them to tremble ; but this shows that such assent is valueless for eternal life. **20.** The kind of faith that is necessary for salvation is like Abraham's, who was justified by works, because his faith issued in unhesitating obedience to God's order to sacrifice his son Isaac. By this his faith was perfected. **25.** Rahab gave shelter to the spies of Josue, and saved their lives, because she firmly believed in the God of Israel, Jos 2:11 ; thus furnishing another example of faith productive of works.

f **III 1-12 Control of the Tongue—1.** The next admonition is : ' *Be ye not many teachers* ', since not everyone is qualified to teach, and he who poses as an instructor without the requisite qualifications is liable to a severe judgement. **2.** The office of teaching then suggests the manner of controlling the tongue. In many ways faults may be committed, but in none more readily than in too

great freedom of speech. The man who has perfect **947f** control of his tongue may have his faults, but compared with him who continually offends by speech he is a perfect man. The self-control implied in properly guarding the tongue will manifest itself in one's whole conduct.

3-5. Two similes are used to illustrate the possibility of **g** control and the smallness of the instrument involved. **6.** The destructive power of the tongue is likened to that of fire. Sometimes a tiny spark may kindle an entire forest. There is such possibility of evil in uncontrolled speech, that the tongue is called ' a world of iniquity '. By it defiling passions may be kindled, fostered and gratified. Thus it may set on fire and destroy the whole course of life, because the source from which the tongue derives its destructive power is the devil. The great difficulty of curbing the tongue requires prayer for grace and constant watchfulness. ' Inflameth the wheel of our nativity ', *i.e.* life is likened to a wheel which is in continuous motion from birth till death, and throughout this period the tongue may give trouble. **9.** How inconsistent some men are, when they first use the tongue to praise God, and then turn upon their fellowmen with curses and slanders. This inconsistency is also pointed out by two illustrations from nature. Some of the similes used by St James are likewise found in classical authors ; *e.g.* man's control of natural forces and brute animals is contrasted with his lack of self-control in Sophocles, *Antigone*, 332-50 ; 475 f. A tiny spark kindling a great forest is used by Homer, *Iliad*, II, 455, and Virgil, *Georg.*, II, 303 ; but it is more likely that St James adopted this figure from Prov 16:27 or Ecclus 28:12.

13-18 True and False Wisdom—Sins of the tongue are **h** often prompted by an affectation of being endued with more knowledge than others, and perfect control of it indicates a truly wise man. Wisdom may always be recognized by its works : purity, tranquillity, modesty, docility, equity, mercy and piety.

IV:1-10 Sources of Discord—A serious lack of control **948a** of the tongue, and an absence of true wisdom, are manifested by party strifes and individual quarrels, that originate from innate concupiscence and selfish desires. Concupiscence has its seat in our bodily members, and uses them as instruments to self-gratification which, far from leading to true happiness, engenders hatred and envy of others. Necessary favours should be sought from God through prayer. But when one asks for worldly things for the purpose of self-gratification, how can God grant the request ? **4.** The attachment to worldly riches or pleasures is a species of spiritual adultery. God and the world stand opposed to each other as rivals, and we cannot serve two opposing masters, Mt 6:24. **5.** In many places the inspired writings state that the Spirit who dwells in man is a jealous God, Ex 20:5 ; Deut 5:9 ; Os 1-3 ; Zach 8:2. **6.** If God craves the undivided love of man, it is because he bestows blessings incomparably greater than the world can offer. **7.** In order to obtain this more **b** abundant grace, we must first be humble and submissive to his will, resist the devil and put him to flight, and then draw near to God and live in his presence. The hands, typical of exterior actions, and the heart, seat of our affections, must be cleansed from sin by sincere contrition and purpose of amendment, and from attachment to worldly honours and pleasures ; otherwise we remain ' double-minded ', *i.e.* divided in our allegiance, wishing to follow God and the world simultaneously. **9.** When St James urges his readers to ' be afflicted, and mourn, and weep ', he does not ask them to suppress all moderate laughter, and forego all innocent joy ; but he is pointing out to the worldly-minded what they must do to regain God's favour and grace.

11-12 Detraction—Further cautions are given against **c** sinful judging and censuring one's neighbour, which have their origin in resentment and envy. To depreciate the character of a fellow-man, is to depreciate the law. A detractor steps out of his province and invades

948c that of Almighty God, who alone is the supreme and universal Lawgiver and Judge.

13-17 Presumption—Who will dare boast his independence of God and display an arrogant self-reliance in temporal matters ? Our Lord's parable of the Rich Fool, Lk 12:19 f., should be a sound warning against drawing up far-reaching plans for the future. **17.** Whoever is aware of his duty of dependence on God and deliberately ignores it, cannot be free from sin.

d V:1-6 Woe to the Rich—We have here a prophetic denunciation of the rich as a class, beginning with a call to attention : ' *See here now, ye rich* '. The warning is given, probably not to wealthy Christians, but to such men as make the quest of riches their chief aim in life. They may seem prosperous and happy to the casual observer, but in reality their lot is such as will make them weep and howl. **2.** The riches they accumulated with so much toil and care, and from which they promised themselves so much, will soon perish through the most insignificant agencies of nature. **3.** They will lose what they treasured so highly, and a pain as severe as fire will be the remorse brought on by the guilt incurred in accumulating their wealth. On the day of judgement they will perish with their wealth. **4-6.** Three reasons are indicated for this severe judgement : first, injustice was practised in acquiring riches, *e.g.* wages were withheld from labourers ; secondly, wealth was abused in the pursuit of pleasures and luxury. With a threat of judgement hanging over their heads, they lived like senseless cattle, that continue to graze peacefully till the hour of slaughter. Thirdly, they condemned and put to death inoffensive men, who offered no resistance. Not our Lord, but his persecuted followers, are the objects of this injustice.

e 7-11 Comfort for the Oppressed—The victims of the rich, and all who suffer the trials of life, are now exhorted to wait with trustful patience and submission the arrival of the day of deliverance, termed ' the day of the coming of the Lord '. The reference seems to be to the coming of the Son of Man about which the disciples asked Christ on Mount Olivet, Mt 24:1-42. The prophecy uttered on that occasion was partly fulfilled when the Romans captured Jerusalem and destroyed the Jewish temple. This happened so short a time after this letter was written, that the Apostle could say : ' the coming of the Lord is at hand '. The complete fulfilment must await the day of final judgement, when all wrong will be righted, all patient endurance rewarded, *cf.* §§ 670-1. **9.** ' *Murmur not, brethren, one against another* ' : that would be yielding to impatience and irritability, and might lead to recriminations and rash judgements, to merit a severe sentence from the righteous Judge, who is so near that he seems to be standing at the door. **10-11.** Seek encouragement from the example of the OT prophets and Job, who endured so much in the proper spirit, and were liberally rewarded for their conduct.

f 12 Avoid Swearing—Oaths are not forbidden in court, or on other solemn occasions ; but swearing in common conversation, or for trifling matters, is sinful, and must be avoided by Christians, whose simple word should be enough to vouch for the truth of what is said.

g 13-18 Occasions for Prayer—Many are the vicissitudes of life. Prayer is the first and best remedy for any person suffering from sadness and desolation. It is not **94** easy to pray at such times, but to do so furnishes speedy relief. If, on the contrary, one is in a happy mood, let him praise God in song. Just as prayer saves a man from despair in time of desolation, so prayer will rescue him from pride in time of consolation. **14.** When a serious bodily ailment confines one to bed, ' let him call the priests of the church ', says the Apostle. ' They are to pray over the sick man, and anoint him with oil in the name of the Lord '. That there is question here of the religious rite of Extreme Unction, and not a corporal remedy only, may be gathered from the fact that ' the priests of the church ', and not a physician, are called ; that the anointing is carried out ' in the name of the Lord ', *i.e.* with the power and the authority conferred by the Lord ; that it is intimately related to ' the prayer of faith ', *i.e.* the prayer said by the priests in the name of the Church, not the prayer of the sick man. **15.** As a result of the prayer and the anointing, God ' shall save the sick man, and raise him up ; and if he be in sins, they shall be forgiven him '. What is the meaning of these three phrases ? ' Save ' occurs 1:21 ; 2:14 ; 4:12 and 5:20 in the sense of acquiring eternal salvation ; hence, we may rightly infer that it has that meaning here. ' To raise up ' means that, in addition to spiritual succour, God will restore the sick man to health, if he sees fit. Forgiveness of sins, the third effect mentioned, seems to indicate that the spiritual result to be obtained is the main purpose for administering the rite. For a further explanation *cf.* § 946c.

There is considerable difference of opinion about the **h** meaning of **16.** ' Therefore ' which is found in the oldest MSS seems to join this admonition to the preceding one ; yet it is hard to see what connexion a mutual confession of sins has with the anointing of the sick. Perhaps ' therefore ' has reference to the next clause, ' pray for one another ' as Camerlynck, 72, suggests. Then the sense would be : If the prayer of faith over the sick, together with the anointing, is able to save the sick man ; and ' if he be in sins, they shall be forgiven him ', then it is expedient to ' pray one for another that you may be saved ', *i.e.* eternally. For the purpose of convincing one another of the need of mutual prayer, a mutual confession of sin is recommended. Older interpreters, like St Thomas, *S. T. Suppl.* q. 6, a. 6, and St Robert Bellarmine, *De Poenit.* lib. 3, c. 4 ; regard this passage as an exhortation to sacramental confession, thereby assigning a very restricted meaning to the phrase, ' confess your sins one to another ', namely, confession of sins to a delegated priest. Interpreters, who defend this restricted meaning, cite as examples, Rom 15:7 ; 1 Thes 5:11 ; Eph 5:21. In these passages, they claim, the restricted meaning of ' one another ' is borne out by the context. But only the last instance allows such a meaning, and it is doubtful whether it may be applied in the present context.

17. In order to encourage the practice of mutual **i** prayer, St James calls attention to the efficacy of a just man's prayer, and cites as an outstanding example the results obtained by the prophet Elias, 3 Kg 17 and 18. **19-20 Conclusion**—The Epistle ends with a final recommendation to work for the conversion of the erring brethren, promising as a reward for such zeal a full remission of sins and final salvation.

THE FIRST EPISTLE OF
ST PETER

By H. WILLMERING, S.J.

9a Bibliography—G. Estius, *cf.* 945*a* ; A. Camerlynck, *cf.* 945*a* ; *C. Bigg, *Epistles of SS Peter and Jude*, ICC, Edinburgh, 1922 ; W. Vrede, *Der erste Petrusbrief*, BB 9, Bonn, 1932⁴ ; U. Holzmeister, S.J., *Epistula Prima S. Petri*, CSS, Paris, 1937 ; *E. G. Selwyn, *The First Epistle of St Peter*, London, 1947 ; *F. W. Beare, *The First Epistle of St Peter*, Oxford, 1947 ; G. Thils, *L'Enseignement de Saint Pierre*, Paris, 1943 ; J. Daniélou, *Déluge, Baptême, Jugement*, Dieu vivant, 8 (1947), 97–112. A. Charue, *cf.* § 945*a*.

b Authorship—The authorship of St Peter, the Apostle, was universally accepted until recently. In the early Church 1 Pet was known and utilized by SS Clement of Rome, Ignatius, Papias, Polycarp, and by the authors of the *Epistle of Barnabas* and the *Shepherd of Hermas*. It is quoted as St Peter's by St Irenaeus, Clement of Alexandria, Origen, Tertullian, St Cyprian, etc., and Eusebius lists it among the uncontroverted sacred writings, *Hist. Eccl.* 3, 2, 52. It is found in all canonical lists of NT books, except in the Muratorian Fragment, which omission in this case is insignificant. It likewise had its place in the Old Latin and Syriac versions.

c Modern non-Catholic scholarship commonly objects to the Petrine authorship for three reasons. (1) The epistle implies that Christianity is proscribed, and its adherents are being persecuted by Roman officials ; but such a general persecution did not occur until the time of Trajan (A.D. 98–117). (2) There is a dependence on the Pauline Epistles, especially Rom and Eph, and it is very unlikely that St Peter would borrow from his rival, St Paul. (3) The style is far removed from the colloquial Greek which a Galilean fisherman would use. We answer : (1) The persecution implied in 2:12 ; 3:9–16 ; 4:4–16 came from the pagan crowds (Gentiles), not from the Roman officials. It consisted of slanders, outrages, false accusations of crime, reproaches for the name of Christ. Such forms of persecution Christians were exposed to from the beginning, *cf.* Suetonius, *Nero* 16 ; Tacitus, *Annales* 1, 44. (2) We admit that the author was acquainted with Rom and Eph, but deny that SS Peter and Paul were rivals, who differed in their teaching of Christianity. (3) It is very probable that St Peter made use of Silvanus, 5:12, as his secretary, and that, as St Jerome remarks, *Ep. ad Hedib.* 120, 11, PL 22, 1002, we may attribute the correct style to him.

d Destination and Purpose—The epistle was sent to the churches of Pontus, Galatia, Cappadocia, Asia and Bithynia, 1:1, five provinces which comprised nearly the whole of Asia Minor. Because it is addressed ' to the elect, who are sojourners in the dispersion ', some think that converts from Judaism are primarily addressed ; but such expressions as ' former desires of ignorance ', 1:14, ' called out of darkness ', 2:9, ' who in time past were not a people, but are now a people of God ', 2:10, and the vices mentioned in 4:2–4, seem to indicate that the Apostle had Gentile converts chiefly in mind. It is best to consider the churches addressed as composed of converts from both classes, and there is nothing in the epistle which supposes that St Peter was personally known to his readers.

The Christians in these provinces were suffering trials of various kinds, 1:6, ' for justice's sake ', 3:14. They were reproached for the name of Christ, and

slandered as criminals, 4:14 f. Slaves suffered at the **949d** hands of their masters, 2:19, and wives from husbands, 3:1. The persecution was severe and widespread, but unofficial and spasmodic. It cannot be identified with the Neronian or later persecutions. To these sufferers the Apostle offers words of consolation and encouragement. Since they were in danger of yielding under the strain of calumny and violence, the example of the suffering Christ is set before them, 2:21, by whose precious blood they were ransomed, 1:19, by whose resurrection God regenerated them, and destined them for eternal glory, 1:3 f. Accordingly they are urged to bear their sufferings patiently, 2:18 ; 3:14 ; 4:13 ; to practise every Christian virtue : submission to authority, charity, watchfulness, humility, 4:7 f. ; 5:5 f.

Date and Place of Composition—For St Peter's residence **e** and death in Rome there is solid evidence that goes back to the end of the 1st cent. This is admitted by A. Harnack, *Chronologie der altchristl. Literatur*, I, 240–3, 703–10 ; H. Lietzmann, *Petrus und Paulus in Rom*, Berlin, 1927, 226–38 ; F. J. Jackson, *Evidence for the Martyrdom of Peter and Paul in Rome*, JBL 46 (1927) 74–8 ; *cf.* Holzmeister, 37–71. Hence, when the Apostle concludes with : ' The church that is in Babylon . . . saluteth you ', 5:13, we may reasonably presume that ' Babylon ' here, as in Apoc 14:8 ; 16:19 ; 17:5 ; 18:2, 10, 21, refers to Rome as the place of composition. This was held by Papias and Clement of Alexandria, according to Eusebius, *Hist. Eccl.* 2, 15 ; *cf.* also St Jerome, De Vir. Illust. 8, PL 23, 622.

The Apostle seems to have known Eph, because he outlines the same duties for slaves, for wives, for husbands, as in Eph 5:22–33 ; 6:5–8 ; *cf.* also 1 Pet 3:22 and Eph 1:21. Since Eph was written during St Paul's first Roman captivity, which terminated A.D. 62, and in the absence of any clear evidence in 1 Pet of an official Roman persecution of Christians, such as was inaugurated by Nero in August 64, we may date 1 Pet somewhere between A.D. 62 and 64.

Theme and Analysis—The unifying thought in 1 Pet **f** is that God calls Christians to a new and higher life, which leads to an eternal inheritance. This fact should stimulate the faith and hope of the readers, and cause them to bear all trials patiently, live a holy life, and remain steadfast in faith and charity.

The salutation is similar to that used by St Paul. The Apostle addresses the scattered members of the Christian churches of Asia Minor, 1:1f., and blesses God for his great mercy in calling them to a new life of hope, based on the resurrection of Christ, 3. The prospect of an eternal inheritance and the joy of salvation should outweigh all present trials and sufferings, 4–9. Ages ago the prophets sought to share these Messianic blessings, and even the angels longed to behold them, 10–12. Let them lead a holy life, as befits the children of a holy Father, 13–17, ransomed with the precious blood of Jesus Christ, 18–21, and in particular, let them practice charity, 22–25.

Progress in holiness must be based on Christ as the **g** foundation-stone, 2:1–9. As members of a royal priesthood and of God's people, they must edify their pagan neighbours by refraining from sins of the flesh, and by obedience to authority, 11–17. Slaves should submit to masters with Christ-like patience, 18–25 ; wives should obey their husbands, and influence them for

949g good by proper conduct ; husbands should treat their wives as co-heirs of eternal life, 3:1-7. All Christians should be compassionate, humble, forgiving, and patient, so as to merit God's protection, 8-12. They should courageously confess their faith before men, be blameless in conduct, full of Christ-like zeal, that they may win a share in Christ's glory, 13-22. His sufferings should cause them to abhor sin and check unruly passions, 4:1-6. The thought of death and judgement should prompt them to pray, practise charity, and work for God's glory, 7-11. He is glorified by suffering resulting from an adherence to Christian principles, and not by such as are caused by evil conduct, 17-19.

The presbyters are to watch over their flocks with tender care, 5:1-4. Obedience, humility, and vigilance are recommended to the laity, whom the devil seeks to destroy, but who are under God's protection, 5-11. Conclusion : greetings from Rome, and final blessing, 12-14.

h Doctrinal Content—The epistle is chiefly hortatory, yet it contains a rich stratum of doctrinal matter. In keeping with his purpose, the author frequently stresses the Christian's relationship with God the Father and the Son. **The Father** called him to the faith, 1:15 ; regenerated him, 1:3 ; has care of him, 5:7 ; will perfect him through suffering, and strengthen him in it, and then reward him with eternal glory, 5:10. The Christian's duties to the Father include : fidelity, faith and trust, 1:21 ; praise, 5:11 ; service, 2:16 ; fear, 2:17. **God the Son** is the Model of innocence and virtue, 2:21-23 ; he is the chief shepherd, 5:4 ; the shepherd and bishop of his flock, 2:25 ; who died for man, 3:18 ; thus ransoming him with his blood, 1:2, 19 ; who will come again, 1:7, 13 ; to judge mankind, 4:5 ; he is now at the right hand of the Father, 3:22. The Christian's duties to Christ are : to love him, and believe in him whom they have not seen, 1:8 ; to imitate his patience, 1:23 ; share his sufferings, 3:18 ; 4:13 f. **The Holy Spirit** is mentioned as the source of the means of sanctification, 1:2 ; as the inspirer of those who instruct the faithful, 1:12 ; and as the helper of those who are reproached unjustly, 4:14.

i Text and Style—Comparatively few MSS contain the Catholic Epistles ; hence, in 1 Pet, as in the others, there are few variant readings in the Greek text. Vg follows the Greek text closely and seldom differs from it.

The style is clear, simple, individual and grammatically correct. The vocabulary is large, and contains many words not used elsewhere in the NT. There is a striking arrangement of words in the sentences. Although the author is indebted to many passages of both OT and NT, he does not quote or borrow them as such, but weaves them into his own thought, using them to prove a point or strengthen an exhortation.

950a I 1-2 Salutation—St Peter is the only author of the Catholic Epistles to make use of his apostolic title. Writing to a community outside of Palestine, he uses the Greek form of the name which Christ bestowed upon him, Jo 1:42 ; Mt 16:18 ; and because the readers probably did not know him personally, he mentions his position as ' an Apostle of Jesus Christ ' to indicate his official claim to their regard and obedience. The letter is addressed ' *to the elect who are sojourners in the dispersion*' of Pontus, etc., *i.e.* to Christians, who are exiled from their real fatherland and are scattered among the inhabitants of the districts of Asia Minor. For further details, *cf.* § 949*d*. **2.** They are called to the faith ' according to the foreknowledge of God the Father ', *cf.* Rom 8:28 ff., who decreed to give them all the means of salvation and sanctification through the Holy Spirit, which goal is achieved by obedience to Jesus Christ. Ex 24:3-8 tells how God made a covenant with the Israelites, when Moses sprinkled the people with the blood of calves as ' the blood of the covenant ', and pledged their obedience to God's law. At the Last Supper, Christ inaugurated a new covenant in his own blood with his followers, whereby they contracted to obey and follow him. Thus

they became the new people of God by the ' sprinkling **9** of the blood of Jesus Christ '.

3-5 Thanksgiving for God's Mercy—Such a prayer, **b** as the Apostle formulates here, the Jews often used, and St Paul opens 2 Cor and Eph in a similar way. God is blessed for bestowing upon Christians a new life of hope, the basis of which is the resurrection of Jesus Christ ; its goal is an inheritance, imperishable and secure, which is still in the future, but is already prepared, and only waits for the proper time to be revealed. That time is the day of the second coming of Christ.

6-12 Joy in Time of Trial—**6.** In the assurance which faith gives them of securing eternal salvation, they should be able to bear with joy the various trials to which Divine Providence subjects them. **8.** Unlike human love, which depends upon personal contact for its existence, their love is for one whom they have not seen, or rather for one whom they have only seen with the eyes of faith. By believing in him, they have a foretaste of the unspeakable joy of the glorified. **10-12.** Due to their interest in the Messianic salvation, the OT prophets tried to fathom the meaning of future events made known to them. They were particularly anxious to know the time when the sufferings and glorifications of the Messias were to take place, but were informed that their prophecies would not be fulfilled during their life time. How fortunate, therefore, are those for whom the prophets predicted such mysteries of grace, which were explained to them by men, who spoke by the Holy Spirit sent from heaven. And not only the prophets, but even the angels longed for a chance to witness and understand the mystery of salvation.

13-16 Exhortation to Holiness—Holiness is a demand **c** put upon them by their new faith. **13.** As the Israelites at the time of the Exodus, girded their loins to be ready for a hasty departure, so must Christians be ready for the long journey to eternity. Accordingly, they must not let their thoughts be preoccupied with the interests and pleasures of this life, but ' be sober ', *i.e.* vigilant, so as to attain that blessed grace, which will have its fulfilment on the day of the revelation of Christ. **16.** If in the OT the chosen people were to imitate the All-holy God by cultivating purity of heart and blameless conduct, nothing less than this is demanded of Christians, *cf.* Lev 11:44 ; 19:2 ; 20:7.

17-21 Exhortation to Reverence—**17.** While invoking God as a Father, let them ' converse in fear ', *i.e.* stand in awe of him, and conduct themselves as dutiful children, since he is an impartial judge. **18.** A second reason for reverence is the redemption from ' your vain conversation ', *i.e.* the useless manner of life of their forefathers. **20.** The plan of redemption was ' foreknown ', *i.e.* decreed from eternity ; but the fulfilment was reserved for ' the last times ', *i.e.* the Messianic age. **21.** ' *For your sakes, who through him believe in God* '. Gratitude, therefore, should prompt them to reverence God, who glorified Jesus to sustain their hope.

22-25 Exhortation to Charity—St Peter supposes that the Gospel has already had such good effect on his readers as to purify their souls from selfish and sordid motives in their obedience, and that it has produced in them a sincere love for the brethren. This affection is grounded on the supernatural regeneration which they have in common ; hence, it proceeds not from corruptible seed, as happens in man's natural birth, but is had ' by the word of God ', *i.e.* the Gospel.

II 1-10 Exhortation to Progress—Christians are called **d** to a new and higher life, free from malice, deceit, hypocrisy, envy and detraction. Lately born anew, they must develop an appetite for the milk of God's word, and by continually feeding on it grow to maturity in the faith. **2.** ' the rational milk without guile ', *i.e.* unadulterated, without any admixture of falsehood. **3.** A further inducement to progress are the sweet consolations, which the Lord brings when he takes possession of a soul, *cf.* Ps 33:9. **4-5.** They are to become ' a spiritual house ', built up on Christ as the corner-stone. Christ is ' a living stone ', *i.e.* one capable of growth and expansion, capable also of imparting life to others. They are to share in and reproduce this **d** quality by becoming ' as living stones built up ' into a temple of God by progress in holiness. But they not only compose the temple, they also minister in it. They constitute a new priesthood that is holy, *i.e.* they are consecrated to God's service, to offer up spiritual sacrifices of prayer and good works, which are acceptable to God because they are offered through Christ as Mediator. **6.** God Himself laid this corner-stone, and he promised salvation to those who believe in Christ, **e** Is 28:16. **7.** The Jewish nation, through their leaders, rejected Christ, as was foretold by the Psalmist, 117:22. **8.** For those who will not believe in him, Christ is a stone over which they stumble to their eternal ruin, ' whereunto also they are set ', *i.e.* as God has decreed for their punishment, *cf.* § 698*d*, *e*. **9.** The Apostle now applies to his readers all the attractive titles of the Israelites, which belong to Christians in a fuller and truer sense. **10.** Then wishing to make them realize what their conversion meant, he bids them compare their former with their present state, which he does by paraphrasing Os 2:23 f.

11-12 Exhortation to edify Others—They dwell as strangers in a pagan world ; hence, their moral conduct must be faultless, lest they scandalize the Gentiles. Even though many ' speak against you as evil-doers ', *i.e.* slander your conduct, yet if it be faultless, it will bring the Gentiles to praise God ' in the day of visitation ', *i.e.* when God makes the truth known to them.

13-16 Obedience to Civil Authorities—Christians are **f** to accept the established forms of government and to submit to those in authority ' *for the sake of the Lord* ', *i.e.* Christ, in order not to bring discredit upon his teaching and Church. ' The king as excelling ', *i.e.* as supreme ruler. **13.** ' The governors ' or administrators of the provinces, the deputies of the supreme ruler. **15.** Submission to their authority is indirectly obedience to God, the source of all authority. It has a very practical side, since it silences those who through ignorance or malice slander the Christian way of life. **16.** By obeying the laws, Christians do not ' make liberty a cloak of malice ', as calumniators said they did ; but they make the will of God the standard of their conduct. **17.** This is a brief and clear statement of Christian duties towards God and man.

18-25 Obedience of Slaves to their Masters—In a **g** society where slaves outnumbered the free, and the treatment of slaves was not always humane and just, it called for great discretion on the part of the Apostles to handle this delicate question. They did not try to overthrow the existing order and make freemen out of slaves, but without in the least approving slavery as an institution, they did try to make good slaves out of bad ones. Here St Peter insists that slaves give respectful obedience to their masters, whatever their disposition might be. Should they be treated with cruelty and injustice, they should not complain, but bear their harsh treatment with patience, thus gaining the approval of God, and imitating the example of their Lord and Master Jesus Christ, who did not complain when he was treated unjustly, as was predicted by Is 53:4-9. There are no less than seven quotations from Isaias in this chapter : vv 6, 8, 9, 12, 22, 24, 25.

III 1-7 Duties of Husbands and Wives—Among all **h** the nations of the 1st cent., after marriage a wife passed under the dominion of her husband and was subject to him. Here again the apostolic teaching did not interfere with the existing social order. **1.** St Peter admonishes Christian wives to render due obedience to their husbands in everything that the law of God permits. Thus unbelieving husbands, who could not be won over to Christianity by argument, might be influenced by the ' conversation ', *i.e.* good example of their wives, when they reflected on their modest and respectful conduct towards themselves. **3.** The Apostle stresses the need of modesty in dress and ornamentation, and points out that such outward adornment is insignificant, whereas inner beauty of character, such as is manifested by an unassuming and quiet disposition,

is an enduring attraction to both God and man. **5.** To **950h** prove how greatly God values such a disposition, he cites the example of the holy women of the OT. **6.** Sara calls Abraham ' my lord ', Gen 18:12. Let Christian wives do what is right, and with a calm spirit, and they will resemble Sara. **7.** But the duties are not one-sided. Husbands are to dwell with their wives, and their association with them in the home is to be ' according to knowledge ', *i.e.* with a just recognition of the relative positions of husband and wife. They should make allowance for the natural physical weakness of women, and give them the regard which is due to them as ' co-heirs of the grace of life ', *i.e.* equally destined to share eternal life. Such an attitude will help a man at prayer ; when wives are unjustly treated, husbands may expect their prayers to go unheeded.

8-12 Mutual Duties of Christians—8. ' In fine ' **i** indicates that the instructions which follow are applicable to all Christians. They are to be ' all of one mind ', *i.e.* adopt a similar viewpoint, and ' have compassion ', *i.e.* share one another's sorrows and joys, and love one another with more than ordinary natural affection. Fraternal charity is the bond for both unity and sympathy, and will make them ' merciful ', *i.e.* tender-hearted and ' humble ', *i.e.* humble-minded in their dealings with one another. **9.** Towards their pagan neighbours, who view them with suspicion and hostility, they must adopt an attitude of non-resistance, bear evil patiently without retaliating, even returning good for evil, and blessings for curses. **10-12.** The quotation, Ps 33:13-17, means that God will not overlook the man who controls his speech and does what is right, but will grant him a peaceful and happy life, and will answer all his prayers.

13-22 Suffering with Christ—Those who do good may **951a** look to God for protection, and whatever he allows them to suffer for the faith will be richly rewarded, Mt 5:10-12. No reason, therefore, to be alarmed. Nothing can so well serve as an answer to the enemies of the Christian name as the holy lives of those who bear it. **16.** When a vindication of their faith and hope is demanded, it is to be made with gentleness and respect, not in an overbearing manner, but fully conscious of speaking the truth. Thus will the accusers be ashamed when they recognize their upright conduct. **18.** Christ's passion and death offers encouragement, who, though innocent, died for the sins of mankind, that he might lead men to God. Physically he died, but his soul lived on. **19.** ' In which ', *i.e.* state, while the soul was separated from the body, ' he preached ', *i.e.* announced salvation—κηρύσσειν without a qualifier in the NT refers to good news ; and there is no instance in the NT where it implies bad news, Holzmeister, 300. ' To the spirits ', who cannot be the angels who sinned, 2 Pet 2:4 ; nor the souls of the lost, who are beyond the reach of salvation ; but the souls of the just. ' In prison ', *i.e.* the place where the just souls were detained till heaven was open to them. **20.** These souls ' had been sometime incredulous, *when the patience of God waited* ', *i.e.* for their conversion. This happened ' in the days of Noe, when the ark was a building '. During this period they persisted in their sinful state, but we must suppose that when the deluge came they repented. These persons perished in the waters of the deluge, but Noe and his family, totalling eight persons, were saved by entering the ark, not only ' from the water ', but ' by water ', *i.e.* the water carried the ark aloft. **21.** **b** Thus the water of the deluge is the type of the water of baptism, which saves you. Baptism, however, is not a washing of dirt from the body, but is ' *the requirement of a good conscience towards God* ', *i.e.* a conscience ready to do God's will. This effect it has ' through the resurrection of Jesus Christ ', with whom Christians were buried in baptism and have risen to a new life, Rom 6:4. Another interpretation, which supposes that the author had in mind passages from the *Book of Enoch*, identifies the ' spirits ' with the progeny of the angels whose sin is supposed to be described in Gen 6:1-4. Christ proclaimed to these evil spirits their defeat by his

951b resurrection from, and victory over death. The rest of the passage contains a symbolism that found great favour among the early Christian writers. The figure eight is the type of the new creation, ushering in a new world. Noe, as the type of Christ, is the father of a new race. The flood was a type of baptism, because this sacrament accomplishes a judgement—judging, destroying the ' body of sin ', as the deluge destroyed the old sinful world (*cf.* Daniélou, 97–112). **22.** The words ' swallowing . . . life everlasting ' are wanting in all Greek MSS and in many of Vg. The angels in heaven are subject to Christ, *cf.* Heb 1:4, 6, 13 f.

c IV 1-6 Risen with Christ to a New Life—**1.** Christ accepted suffering ; so must the good Christian. If he suffers for, and with Christ, he is armed against sin. This demands a continual practice of virtue, which strengthens the will, and makes it able to resist temptation and avoid sin. **2.** Such a sufferer will not live ' after the desires of men ' ; being united with Christ in his sufferings, he lives ' according to the will of God '. **3.** St Peter's readers had in time past ' fulfilled the will of the Gentiles ' by taking part in their licentiousness and idolatry. **4.** But now that they have kept away from such sinful habits, they are subjected to scornful criticism. **5.** Why should they mind this, since they know that these critics are subject to the judgement of him, ' who is ready to judge the living and the dead ', *cf.* Ac 10:42 ; 2 Tim 4:1. **6.** Because all men are to undergo judgement, ' the gospel was preached also to the dead '. This may refer back to 3:19 f., where sinners who paid for their unbelief by suffering temporal death in the deluge were ' judged according to men in the flesh ', but the purpose of that judgement was to save them from eternal condemnation, that they ' may live according to God, in the spirit '. To these souls Christ appeared, and announced to them the good news of their salvation. St Augustine has a different explanation : ' Nothing forces us to understand that the Gospel was preached in the other world ; but in this life the Gospel was preached to the dead, that is, to infidels and sinners, that when they believe ' they might be judged indeed according to men in the flesh ', that is, might be subjected to various trials in the flesh, and even to death, ' but may live according to God, in the spirit ', *Ep.* 164, 7, 21 ; PL 33, 717 f.

d 7-11 The Duty of Charity—The thought of judgement should never be far from a Christian's mind. For the NT teaching on the second coming *cf.* §§ 670–1, 914*g–e*. Its wholesome influence should help them to be circumspect and sober so as to be disposed for prayer. **8.** Fraternal charity should never be wanting, and such ' charity covereth a multitude of sins ', *i.e.* if they have true love for their neighbour, they will be willing to cover their sins in silence, not speak about them, forget them, *cf.* Prov 10:12 ; Jas 5:20. Moreover, a strong and active love will blot out their own sins as well. **9.** ' Using hospitality ' which would be exercised chiefly towards fellow Christians, and missionaries coming from abroad. It might also have reference to ' housechurches ' as Selwyn suggests, *i.e.* ' to the ordinary social life of Christian communities ', 218. Let them dispense this hospitality cheerfully, ' without murmuring '. **10.** Whatever ' grace ', χάρισμα, any Christian has should be used for the good of others. **11.** Two kinds of charisms are mentioned, speaking and ministering. A fuller list occurs in Rom 12:6–8 ; 1 Cor 12–14. The doxology here refers to God, not to Christ.

e 12-19 The Duty of Suffering for Christ—The severe trial, which threatened to affect them, should not cause surprise, but joy, since it will associate them more closely with Christ. **12.** ' The burning heat ' is the symbol of the afflictions and persecutions that await them. This may perhaps refer to the calumnies, annoyances and petty persecutions which the first Christians had to put up with everywhere ; or it may refer to something more definite. Persecutions are not something new for Christians to experience. **13.** They are to rejoice in proportion as they share in the sufferings of Christ, for this shall redound to their joy ' when his

glory shall be revealed '. **14.** Reproaches endured for the name of Christ brings the Holy Spirit upon them. **15.** Whereas it would be most shameful to suffer just punishment for crimes committed, **16,** to suffer as a Christian is no disgrace ; by bearing the name they glorify God. The name ' Christian ' was first given to the followers of Christ at Antioch, Ac 11:26, and was later used by King Agrippa, Ac 26:28, with a touch of irony. **17.** These sufferings are the beginning of God's judgement in his own household. They will sift the virtuous from the lax Christian. And if this is thought severe, what will happen to those who disregard the Gospel? **18.** Owing to the severity of the trials and sufferings, even a just man may be saved with difficulty. What then of the godless sinners? **91.** But God will faithfully support those who ' suffer according to his will '.

V 1-4 Pastoral Duties—' The ancients ', πρεσβύτεροι, officials of the local church, who govern the flock of Christ, Ac 20:28 ; 1 Tim 5:17 ; Tit 1:5 ; instruct the faithful, 1 Tim 5:17 ; Tit 1:9 ; and administer the sacraments, Jas 5:14. In Ac 20:28 those previously addressed as πρεσβύτεροι, are here called ἐπίσκοποι, ' bishops ' ; and in the Pastoral Epistles the qualifications outlined for one class are equally those for the other, *cf.* 1 Tim 3 ; Tit 1:5–7 ; accordingly the two terms may be regarded as convertible in the NT. St Peter says : ' I beseech, who am myself also an ancient ', συμπρεσβύτερος, *i.e.* one belonging to your rank, ' and a witness of the sufferings of Christ ' ; this is probably stressed, because of the admonitions to the faithful that preceded, to suffer for, and with Christ ; ' as also a partaker of that glory which is to be revealed ' ; this statement may recall the fact that St Peter witnessed Christ's transfiguration, Mt 17:1–9 ; 2 Pet 1:16–18. **2.** ' Feed the flock of God which is among you ' ; he is inviting them to share locally the office entrusted to himself by the risen Christ over the entire flock of God, Jn 21:15–17. He demands three conditions for doing this : (1) it must not be shared reluctantly ; (2) nor used avariciously ; (3) nor exercised domineeringly. Such traits would disedify, whereas they must be patterns of virtue, and that sincerely, ' from the heart '. **4.** Their model, ' the prince of pastors ', a title used only here, and most likely suggested by ' I am the good shepherd ', Jn 10:14. By feeding their flock they ' shall receive a never failing crown of glory '. The crown here symbolizes their eternal reward for merit.

5-11 General Christian Duties—' Ye young men ' : some understand here the junior officials of the church, others the general class of young men. ' *And be ye all closely associated with one another in humility* ', *i.e.* practise it as fostering union. The quotation is from Prov 3:34. **6.** Humble yourself and God will exalt you, Jas 4:10. **7.** A quotation from Ps 54:23. **8.** Vigilance is necessary in order to escape the snares of the devil, **9,** whose attacks are to be combated with the principles of faith. But there is another adversary to Christians, an ally of the devil, namely, the world, ready to afflict the brethren. **10.** God's grace should give them assurance, and the reward of eternal glory should spur them on to suffer a little in order to be made perfect.

12-14 Conclusion—Silvanus, who in all probability is the same as Silas, St Paul's companion on his second missionary journey, Ac 15:22, 32, 40 ; and the Silvanus of 1 Thess 1:1 ; 2 Cor 1:19 ; may have been both the bearer and the secretary of this letter, *cf.* § 949*c*. ' That this ', *i.e.* the Christian faith, ' is the true grace of God '. **13.** ' In Babylon ', *i.e.* Rome, so-called in Apoc 14:8 ; 16:19 ; 17:5 ; 18:2, 10 ; also in *Orac. Sybil.* 5, 159 f. ; *4 Esdr.* 3:1 ; *Apoc. Baruch*, vis. ii, 1. ' My son, Mark ' : he is the son of Mary, to whose house St Peter went after his release from prison, Ac 12:12 ; who was with St Paul in Rome during his captivity, Col 4:10 ; who had been his companion with Barnabas, when they preached the Gospel in Cyprus, Ac 13:5 ; who wrote the second Gospel, Eusebius, HE 3, 29, 15 ; ' my son ' is a term of affection for his disciple. Perhaps St Peter baptized him. **14** ' Salute one another with *the kiss of charity* ', a sign of Christian brotherhood.

THE SECOND EPISTLE OF
ST PETER

By H. WILLMERING, S.J.

a Bibliography—G. Estius, *cf.* § 945*a* ; A. Camerlynck, *cf.* § 945*a* ; *C. Bigg, *cf.* § 949*a* ; W. Vrede, *Der zweite Petrusbrief*, BB, Bonn, 1932⁴ ; J. Chaine, *Les Epîtres Catholiques*, Paris, 1939 ; A Charue, *cf.* § 945*a* ; J. Daniélou, *cf.* § 945*a*.

b Authenticity and Canonicity—The authenticity of 2 Pet is more disputed today than any other book of the NT. Most non-Catholic scholars class it as pseudonymous, chiefly for two reasons : (*a*) lack of external evidence in the early centuries ; (*b*) difference of style from 1 Pet (*cf.* § 952*j*). Catholic exegetes, and some prominent non-Catholics, defend its authenticity. It may be admitted that the evidence of early recognition of 2 Pet is weaker than for any other NT writing. There are no undisputed quotations from it before the time of Origen (A.D. 230), but as Bigg says : ' The shortness of the Epistle, its subject-matter of limited interest, and containing few quotable phrases, may account for the fact that it was not quoted then, as it is probably very seldom quoted even in the present day ; yet its attestation is strong ', 210 f. There is good evidence for its canonicity, even if its Petrine authorship is not so well attested. It is of course included in the Tridentine Canon.

c Let us list **the external evidence** for both authenticity and canonicity that is undisputed. Origen records the controversy (*cf.* Eusebius, HE 6, 2, 58), but places the Epistle in his canon of Holy Scripture, PG 12, 857, and quotes from it six different times in his writings, sometimes naming St Peter as the author. Bishop Firmilian, a contemporary of Origen, mentions in a letter to St Cyprian, that St Peter wrote an epistle against the heretics, which can only refer to 2 Pet, *Ep.* 75, 6. St Athanasius quotes it twice, *De Trin.* dial. 1 ; *Contra Arian.* or. 3 ; Bishop Methodius of Olympus, *Frag. de Resur.* ; Theophilus of Antioch, *Ad Autol.* 2:9, 13 ; St Basil, *Adv. Eun.* 5. Clement of Alexandria, according to Eusebius, HE 6, 14, 1, wrote a commentary on all seven Catholic Epistles, a work which has not come down to us. 2 Pet is listed as one of the inspired books of the NT in the canons of SS Athanasius, PG 26, 1176 ; and Cyril of Jerusalem, PG 33, 500 ; of Codex Claromontanus, and Codex Mommsen ; of the Councils of Laodicea, and of Carthage, Dz 92 ; of Popes SS Damasus, Dz 84, and Innocent I, Dz 96. Although Eusebius places it on his list of disputed books, HE 3, 25, 3, and expresses doubt about its authenticity, HE 3, 3, 1, yet St Jerome acknowledges all seven Catholic Epistles as Scripture, *Ep. ad Paulin.* 53, 9 ; but mentions the controversy about authenticity, *De Vir. Illustr.* 3, 1. Didymus of Alexandria wrote a commentary on 2 Pet, which has survived in a Latin translation. The statement in a postscript, that the Epistle is not authentic, is probably by the translator.

d **The internal evidence** favours authenticity (in the writer's opinion) despite the difficulties raised by (*a*) its more original vocabulary and style, (*b*) its quotation of, and dependence on, ' lesser ' authorities, such as Jude and the Pauline Epistles. Neither difficulty is insuperable. As regards the latter, it is clear that the author of 2 Pet regarded the writings of St Paul as inspired scripture, and there is no reason to think that he regarded Jude in any other light. As regards the former, St Jerome (Ep 120 *ad* Hedibiam, 11)

considered that the difference was due to the employ- **952d** ment of different secretaries, and this may be the true explanation. Nevertheless, these differences are often exaggerated, and it has been said (by B. Weiss, quoted in Jacquier, *Histoire des Livres du N.T.*, III, 300–1) that no book of the New Testament is so like 1 Pet as 2 Pet ! There is undoubtedly a deep underlying parallelism and connexion of thought between the two epistles, which does not seem to be the result of slavish imitation by some pseudepigrapher, but which is rather the result of references to, or drawings upon the same stock of ideas, as might be expected from two products of the same brain ; *e.g.* in both epistles we find the same approach to such topics as Noah and the Flood, the Last Days, the New Creation, the Transfiguration of Christ, the Galilean appearance to Peter, the influence of the Pauline Epistles, the Parousia and the virtues of patience, vigilance and sobriety. Moreover, the writer claims to be ' Simon Peter, servant and Apostle of Jesus Christ ', 1:1 ; and mentions that he was present at Christ's transfiguration, 1:16–18. He calls St Paul ' our most dear brother Paul ', 3:15 ; says that he had a prediction from Christ regarding his sudden death, 1:14 ; and identifies himself with the author of 1 Pet, 3:1. This last circumstance indicates that he knew this Epistle. But would a forger have been so careless about imitating the manner of address, style and vocabulary of 1 Pet ? If a studied and conscious imitation of 1 Pet are lacking, are there perhaps subtle similarities of thought and expression in both epistles ? Yes, the ardent temperament, which is so noticeable a characteristic of St Peter in the Gospels, betrays itself in 2 Pet every now and then, in the way that he comes quickly to the point, 1:3–5 ; 2:1 ; in the use of vigorous language against the false teachers, 2:3, 9–13 ; in the tender and affectionate manner of addressing his readers, 3:1, 11–14.

Destination and Purpose—In 3:1 the author says : **e** ' Behold this second epistle I write to you ', thus indicating that it is addressed to the same group of readers to whom 1 Pet was sent. This was inscribed ' to the elect, who are sojourners in the dispersion of Pontus, Galatia, Cappadocia, Asia and Bithynia ', 1 Pet 1:1, five provinces of Asia Minor, where the Christian congregations consisted of both Jewish and pagan converts.

The occasion and purpose must be gathered from the epistle itself. Certain false teachers, of low morals and covetous disposition, were threatening to corrupt the faith and conduct of these Christian communities, 2:1–3. They denied that Jesus Christ was the Redeemer, 2:1, spoke disparagingly of holy things, particularly about the angels, 2:10, taught licentiousness by word and deed, 2:2, 10, 13 f., ridiculed the second coming of Christ and the judgement, 3:3 ff. Accordingly the Apostle exhorts his readers to have a high regard for their Christian calling, to grow in knowledge of the truth and in holiness, and avoid sin most carefully, that they may be found worthy of admission into the everlasting kingdom of Jesus Christ, 3:4–11. He also warns them against those who are trying to seduce them by immoral practices and ruin their faith, 2:1–3, 12–19 ; 3:11–18.

Time and Place of Composition—This letter was **f**

952f probably written a short time before the Apostle's death, 1:12–15. According to an ancient tradition, St Peter died in Rome during the persecution of Nero, A.D. 66 or 67. So we may tentatively date the epistle, A.D. 65 or 66, and give as its probable place of origin the city of Rome.

g Theme and Analysis—Because of the certainty of Christ's return and the judgement which follows it, it is important for all followers of Jesus Christ to grow in the knowledge of the truth, and in the practice of Christian virtues. Let the readers beware of certain false teachers, who are seeking to deceive and destroy them.

After the introductory address and greeting, the Apostle exhorts his readers to progress in knowledge and every Christian virtue, in order to show themselves grateful to God, who called them to be partakers of the divine nature here and hereafter, 1:3–11. Communicating to them that Christ had predicted his sudden death, St Peter states his purpose in writing this letter, 12–15. As a solid basis for his exhortation and warning, he adduces the transfiguration of Christ as a proof of the credibility of the Apostles, who preached to them the return of Christ, which event had been foretold long ago by the prophets, 16–21. There follows a stern denunciation of certain false teachers, whom God will punish severely for their impiety, 2:1–11. He describes their immorality, avarice and duplicity, 12–19, and warns the Christians of the grave danger of relapsing into pagan vice, 2–22. Then he takes issue with the claims and assertions of the heretics, and answers all their difficulties against the fact of Christ's return, 3:1–6. He describes the destruction of the present world by fire, 7–10, and concludes with an exhortation to watchfulness, 11–18a. He ends with a doxology to Christ, 18b.

h Doctrinal Content—2 Pet is a strong appeal for a good Christian life, and in order to persuade his readers to embrace it more earnestly, St Peter exhibits ' our Lord and Saviour Jesus Christ ' in the most fascinating light. **Jesus Christ** is God, 1:11, and God is the Father of Jesus Christ, 1:17. If as man he is subordinate to the Father, yet he has received from God the Father honour and glory, 1:17. The occasion was the transfiguration of Christ on the holy mount, which the writer himself witnessed, 1:18. Divine power and majesty are his, 1:16, and ' as all things of his divine power, which appertain to life and godliness are given to us ', 1:3, and ' as he has called us by his own proper glory and virtue ', 1:3, he has a claim on our gratitude and loyalty, 1:4 ; 3:14. Christ is the giver of grace and of knowledge, 3:18. Five times the title of ' Saviour ' is applied to him, usually in combination with some other divine title, such as ' God ', or ' Lord ' ; and his kingdom, which we are called to enter, is everlasting, 1:11. His precepts we must obey, 3:2. The OT prophets foretold, and the Apostles preached his second coming, 3:2, which every Christian should look for, and even hasten by leading a holy life, 3:12, 14.

i Thus the chief attention is centred on Christ, and the Father and Holy Spirit are mentioned in relation to Christ. Yet the patience and long-suffering of the Father, who desires the repentance of sinners, 3:9, is contrasted with his treatment of the rebel angels, whom he punished according to strict justice, 2:4. The Holy Spirit inspired the holy men, *i.e.* the prophets of the OT.

The nature of **sanctifying grace** is described by mentioning its most startling effect, namely, that by it we are made *partakers of the divine nature*. The true notion of biblical inspiration is given in 1:21, where St Peter says that the OT prophets did not speak their prophecies on their own initiative, but were God-inspired, *i.e.* the source of their utterances was the Holy Spirit. He illumined their minds, and moved their wills to speak or write only what God willed, and he guided them in the process of speech or composition in such a way that they uttered nothing contrary to the truth.

j Text and Style—Variant readings of the Greek text are of minor importance. The Vg text has several **9** minor additions in 1:2, 7, 8, 10 ; 2:4 and 3:4. Sometimes the same Greek word is translated by several Latin words, and 2:10 seems to be a mistranslation, *cf.* commentary *in loc.*.

To explain the difference of style of the two Epistles of St Peter, St Jerome suggested that two different secretaries were used by the Apostle, *Ep. ad Hedib.* 120. Bigg lists the vocabulary peculiar to both Epistles of St Peter, and draws the following conclusion : ' The vocabulary of 1 Pet is dignified ; that of 2 Pet inclines to the grandiose ', 225. He notes the fondness of the writer of both epistles for the plural of abstract nouns, the similarities in the use of the article, the habit of repeating words. ' A curious feature of 2 Pet ', he says, ' is the tendency to fall into iambic rhythm ' ; yet he attaches little value to this feature. His conclusion is : (1) the style of the two epistles is different, but not openly incompatible in expression, and in the formal use of Scripture ; (2) the favourite phrases of one epistle are not those of the other ', 238.

I:1-2 Salutation—The writer makes use of his double **9** name, ' Simon Peter ', and of a twofold title, ' servant and Apostle of Jesus Christ '. The readers, probably the same to whom 1 Pet was sent, 3:1, are designated here in general terms, ' to them that have obtained equal faith with us '. We might conclude from this that many readers were converts from paganism. That God called them to the same faith with the Apostles was a purely gratuitous favour, bestowed ' in the justice of our God and Saviour Jesus Christ ', *i.e.* impartially on all who desired it, whether Jew or Gentile. To them the Apostle wishes an abundance of grace and peace, and states the condition on which an increase of these blessings may be obtained, namely, a fuller knowledge of God and of Jesus Christ, our Lord.

3-11 Exhortation to Spiritual Progress—Calling atten- **b** tion to the very great blessings which they received through faith, he points out that earnest co-operation is required to correspond with such a gift. **3.** Christ, by his divine power, gives his followers all the graces that are necessary for a supernatural life of holiness. He it was who brought them the knowledge of God through which they are to achieve salvation, and by manifesting in his own person divine attributes of glory and virtue, he drew them to the faith. **4.** Through these same attributes he gave ' most great and precious promises ', namely, that those who abide in him, like a branch on a fruitful vine, will bear much fruit for eternal life, Jn 15:1–8. By abiding in Christ, they ' may be made partakers of the divine nature ', because like the sap that flows from the vine through the branches, enabling them to bear fruit, so from Christ there issues a new, supernatural force, which is shared by all who are united with him by faith and love. This intimate union of Christ with his followers, also unites them with God the Father, Jn 14:20–23 ; 17:21–23, and with the Holy Ghost, Jn 14:16 f. By enjoying such intimate fellowship with the Blessed Trinity, 1 Jn 1:3, a Christian is in an analogous sense a partaker of the divine nature in the measure that is possible to a creature.

To share this extraordinary favour, it is necessary to **c** avoid ' the corruption of that concupiscence which is in the world, *cf.* 1 Jn 2:16, because it leads men to live alienated from God. So the first step towards union with God is freedom from sin. Christians should be ' dead to sin ', Rom 6:2, ' but alive unto God, in Christ Jesus our Lord ', Rom 6:11. **5.** hence ' employing all care, minister in your faith, virtue ', *i.e.* let your faith lead you to a life of virtue. The principles of faith point out what is right, and supply the motives for virtuous action. ' In virtue, knowledge ', *i.e.* he who practises virtue has a knowledge of God's will and follows it. **6.** This calls for ' abstinence ', *i.e.* self-control, and ' patience ', *i.e.* endurance of trials and sufferings with resignation, and one who has reached this stage of perfection is endowed with ' godliness ', *i.e.* perfect conformity to God's will. **7.** His will is, that we love

3c our brethren, 1 Jn 4:7, and practise charity towards all men.

d **8.** Where these virtues flourish, the knowledge of Christ is practical and productive of good works ; **9,** where they are lacking, blindness and short-sightedness have brought on a forgetfulness of having been cleansed from former sins. The sins referred to are those of the pagan past, which were washed away by the waters of baptism. This sacrament should have produced a marked change in their lives. When, however, no such change occurs, and no growth in holiness results, it is a sign that they have lost sight of their higher goal, the cause for which is culpable forgetfulness. **10-11.** Therefore, let them strive earnestly to acquire solid virtue, in order to be worthy of their calling. The effort required for this will help to keep them from committing sin, and will entitle them ' to enter into the joys of their Lord ', Mt 25:23.

e **12-15 Purpose of the Epistle**—The Apostle thinks it necessary to remind them of these truths, because he knows that his departure from this earthly tabernacle is at hand. This the Lord Jesus made known to him ; but we cannot be certain whether it was by a special revelation not recorded, or whether he is referring to the prophecy made by the risen Lord on the shores of the Sea of Galilee, Jn 21:18 f. **15.** He promises to leave behind him a memorial of his teachings. Is the present Epistle such a memorial, as many think ; or are we to look upon the Second Gospel, sometimes called ' the Memoirs of St Peter ', as the record ' whereby you may keep a memory of these things ' ?

f **16-21 Certainty of Christ's Return—16.** Changing now from the first person singular to the plural, perhaps to indicate that the return of Christ with power and majesty was considered a topic of prime importance by all the Apostles, he insists that this truth differs greatly from the artificial fables of the false teachers, who contradict the apostolic teachings. **17.** The transfiguration of Christ, Mt 17:1-9, is cited as a proof of the singular glory, which belongs to him ; and St Peter vouches for its reality, because he was an eye-witness of the scene, and heard the Father proclaim Christ, ' My well-beloved Son, in whom I am well pleased '. **19.** After witnessing his glory, the prophecies regarding Christ's return take on a fuller and clearer meaning for the author, and he urges the readers to attend well to them, because they are ' as a light that shineth in a dark place, until the day dawn ', i.e. these prophecies should serve the faithful as a guide during the present dark times, until the time of fulfilment comes, when the ' day-star ', i.e. Christ himself, will illumine them. A less probable interpretation of this passage is : Whereas the Apostle's testimony about the transfiguration is a definite proof of Christ's return, yet prophecy affords a more conclusive one to refute the false teachers, or to convince his readers, because the OT prophecies concerning Christ are a light to illumine the path of faith until the day of their fulfilment. Some had already been fulfilled ; hence the certainty they may hold **g** regarding those still awaiting fulfilment. **20.** It is of prime importance to know that prophecy of Scripture is not subject to private interpretation by every individual, as the false teachers assume it is, because prophecy is from God, and is not like mere human conjectures of future possibilities. Scriptural prophecy is divine revelation, and concerns future events known to God alone. Christ, and those appointed by him to teach in his name, have the authority to interpret God's revelations. Another interpretation of this passage is : No prophecy of Scripture is made by private interpretation, i.e. prophets do not make up their own prophecies, but receive them from God, cf. §§ 35a, 952i.

h **II:1-3 Warning against False Teachers**—The severe denunciation contained in this chapter is similar to the one in Jude 4-16 not only in thought and imagery, but is presented in almost the same order and often in identical language. Since Jude is more spontaneous and less reflective, it is usually considered to be the original (cf. § 960d). The Apostle puts his Christian readers on guard against certain deceitful teachers, **953h** who by their evil lives and their spirit of avarice are luring some to destruction. **1.** ' False prophets among the people ', i.e. of the OT, cf. Jer 5:31 ; 14:14 ; 27:9 f. ; Ez 13:3, 6-9 ; Zach 13:1-5. ' Among you lying teachers ', cf. 1 Tim 4:1-3 ; 2 Tim 3:1-8. ' Sects of perdition ', i.e. factions leading to the ruin of the Christian way of life. **2.** ' Their riotousnesses ', i.e. lustful excesses. ' The way of truth shall be spoken evil of ', i.e. they bring Christian truth into bad repute. **3.** Through covetousness they exploit the faithful for gain, but their punishment will not be long delayed.

4-9 Examples of Divine Vengeance—Three instances **i** of God's punishment are given : (1) the rebel angels ; (2) the wicked antediluvians ; (3) the inhabitants of Sodom and Gomorrha. From the fate of these three classes one may conjecture what God will do to the false teachers. **4.** ' The angels that sinned ' are the same that are mentioned in Jude 6. ' *Thrusting them down into hell, he delivered them to pits of darkness* ' ; this is the reading of the best MSS. ' To be reserved unto judgement ', i.e. although they were punished immediately after committing sin, their solemn condemnation before the whole world awaits the day of general judgement. **5.** ' And spared not the *ancient* world ', i.e. the antediluvian race mentioned in Gen 6:5 ff. ' Noe, the eighth person ', i.e. Noe's wife, his three sons and their wives were with him in the ark. On the prominence of Noe as a type of Christ in early Christian literature, cf. Daniélou, 98-103. Noe is called a ' preacher of justice ' ; Gen makes no mention of this, but Jewish tradition does, cf. SB 3, 769. **6.** The destruction of Sodom and Gomorrha, Gen 19:24 ff. **9.** ' The Lord knoweth how to deliver the godly from *trial* ', i.e. as is shown by the rescue of Noe and Lot from their wicked surroundings.

10-22 The Wickedness of the False Teachers—10. **954a** Such summary punishment in the past should be a warning to those who disregard the moral law and legitimate authority. But the false teachers are ' audacious, self-willed, and fear not *to revile majesty* ' ; in all probability the divine Majesty is meant, and sacred things directly connected with God, but cf. § 961c. **11.** ' A railing judgement ' most likely refers to the example given by Jude 9. **12.** ' But these men . . . *reviling what they do not understand* ', i.e. being carnal minded, they cannot understand or appreciate spiritual things. **13.** They live for the pleasures of the day, and such is their conduct, that they are ' stains and spots, *indulging in their deceits while they feast with you* ', i.e. using their power of deception to further their own plans even on those whose guests they were. Another reading is : ' Using their love-feasts as an opportunity for indulgence even while they feast with you '. The former reading is supported by the best MSS ; cf. § 961d. **14.** ' Having eyes full of adultery and of sin that ceaseth not ', i.e. whatever they see stirs up their passions and leads them to commit more and graver sins, particularly by enticing weaker souls to sin. Nor is this their only habitual vice ; they are equally skilled in the ways of gaining wealth. For these reasons they are a curse to themselves and others. **15.** Because of their avarice they have ' followed the way of Balaam of Bosor '. According to Num 22:6 Balaam was the son of Beor, who was misled by avarice to disregard the command of God, and who narrowly escaped destruction when he was reprimanded by ' the dumb beast used to the yoke ', cf. Num 22:21-33.

17. The shallow-mindedness and deceit of the false **b** teachers furnish the Apostle with a number of withering metaphors. **18.** Their levity appears in the boastful and exaggerated claims they make to higher wisdom ; their trickery lures with the bait of sensuality those who are least fit to resist, namely, those who were recently converted from paganism, and who had not yet fully conquered their former errors and bad habits. **19.** ' Promising them liberty ' ; not the freedom from sin that a Christian should strive to preserve, but the

954b worst type of slavery to human passions, from which baptism had set them free ; but what else could be expected from ' slaves of corruption '. **20.** Through Christian teachings they had been liberated from ' the pollution of the world ' ; yet should they become ' again entangled in them and overcome ', they are worse off than before. **21.** They have not the excuse of ignorance, **22,** and their conduct is no better than the disgusting habits of senseless beasts.

c **III:1-10 A Refutation of the False Teachers**—The Apostle warns the readers against the sceptics, who deny the second coming of Christ ; he exhorts them to constant expectation of that coming. **1.** ' This second epistle '; the first is probably our 1 Pet ; ' sincere mind ', *i.e.* not contaminated by false teachings. **3.** ' In the last days ', *i.e.* the time subsequent to the coming of the Messias. **4.** ' Where is his promise or his coming ? ' *i.e.* where is the fulfilment of the promised return of Christ ? An entire generation of believers passed away without witnessing it, and all things continue, etc., *i.e.* the continuity of nature has not been interrupted by such a catastrophe as Christ predicted would happen before his return, Mk 13:19. The inference is : nothing has happened yet ; hence nothing is likely to happen in the future.

d **5.** St Peter replies : Heaven and earth were created by God, and after a long period of apparent sameness in the course of nature, his word effected a sudden change in the condition of the world and its inhabitants by the waters of the deluge. God can, and will, effect another change in the heavens and the earth as they now exist, and that will be effected by fire. It will immediately precede the second coming of Christ ; ' that the heavens were *of old*, and the earth *was formed by God's word out of water and by means of water* ', *i.e.* as is narrated in Gen 1:9, when God spoke the waters were gathered into one place, and dry land appeared. **6.** ' perished ', *i.e.* through the waters of the deluge, Gen 7:21-23. **7.** The parallel between the deluge and the end of the present world is drawn by our Lord himself, Mt 24:37-39 ; Lk 17:26 f. That fire will accompany the judgement of God is stated in Pss 49:3 ; 96:3 ; Is 66:15 ; Soph 1:18 ; 3:8 ; 1 Cor 3:13 ; 2 Thess 1:8 ; that the present inhabited world will perish by fire was a late Jewish tradition, SB 3, 775.

e **8-9.** The reason for the delay of Christ's return. With God there is no time element ; everything is present to his mind, and such distinctions of time as we make have no meaning in the divine plans. Whatever delay there may be, is a proof of God's patience. He wills that no one shall perish, but that all be brought to repentance, *cf.* 1 Tim 2:4. **10.** Yet we must guard against presumption, and not put off repentance till it is too late. ' The day of the Lord shall come as a thief ', *i.e.* suddenly and unexpectedly, *cf.* Mt 24:43 f. ; 1 Thess 5:2. ' The heavens shall pass away *with a crackling sound* ', like that of a conflagration, ' and the elements ', probably the sun, moon and stars, as in Mt 24:29, ' shall be melted with heat ', *i.e.* dissolved, ' and the earth and the works that are in it ', *i.e.* all human constructions, ' shall be burnt up '.

11-18 Exhortation to Watchfulness—In view of this **f** great catastrophe, let them live ' in holy conversation and godliness ', *i.e.* in unworldliness and piety, and look forward to the day of the Lord's coming. **12.** Another interpretation of this verse is : By distinguishing themselves as true followers of Christ, they will fill up the number of the elect, and thus hasten the time of the Lord's coming. **13.** ' New heavens and a new earth according to his promises ', *cf.* Is 65:17 ; 66:22. It is not likely that the Apostle means that the earth, after its destruction, will be restored as the dwelling-place of the just. The new heavens and earth are more probably a figurative representation of the abode of the blessed in eternal bliss. **14.** Earnestly strive to live without sin, without blame, without contention. **15.** The patience of the Lord gives you time to make sure your salvation. About this St Paul wrote in Rom 2:4, and about the preparation to be made for the second coming in both 1 and 2 Thess and 1 Cor 3:13 ; 4:5 ; 15:51-54 ; *cf.* § 919*c*. **16.** ' As also in all his epistles ' **g** may simply mean all the epistles with which St Peter was acquainted, and not that a collection of all St Paul's Epistles was in existence when 2 Pet was written. ' In which are certain things hard to be understood, which the unlearned and the unstable wrest . . . to their destruction '—may refer to 2 Thess 2:3 f. ; 1 Cor 15:44 ; 3 Cor 5:1-4, etc., or to his teachings about Christian liberty, justification by faith independent of the Mosaic Law, equality of all before Christ, etc. ; such doctrines those who were poorly instructed in the faith, or not firmly grounded in Christian morality would distort so as to pervert the Apostle's meaning, thereby harming themselves and others spiritually. ' The other scriptures '—here St Peter classes St Paul's Epistles with the other inspired writings of the OT, showing how greatly he esteemed St Paul's writings. Perhaps it also indicates that at this early date the Pauline Epistles were read at the Christian gatherings together with the OT. It is the earliest reference we have to the canon of the NT. It might also have a bearing on the date of 2 Pet. **17.** Being forewarned, let the readers guard against being misled by false and unwise interpretations of apostolic teachings. Rather may they adhere firmly to what they believed in the past, **18,** and increase in grace, and in the knowledge of Christ, to whom the Apostle pays devout homage in a concluding doxology.

THE EPISTLES OF
ST JOHN

By H. WILLMERING, S.J.

955a **Bibliography**—G. Estius, *cf.* § 945*a* ; *B. F. Westcott, *The Epistles of St John*, London, 1892³ ; A. Camerlynck, *cf.* § 945*a* ; *A. E. Brooke, *The Johannine Epistles*, ICC, Edinburgh, 1928 ; W. Vrede, *Der erste, zweite und dritte Johannesbrief*, BB, Bonn, 1932⁴ ; J. Bonsirven, S.J., *Epîtres de Saint Jean*, Paris, 1935² ; J. Chaine, *Les Epîtres Catholiques*, Paris, 1939² ; R. Leconte, art. *Epîtres de Saint Jean*, DBV(S) 797–815.

THE FIRST EPISTLE OF ST JOHN

b **Author**—This Epistle, like the Fourth Gospel is anonymous ; but an early and constant tradition assigns both works to the Apostle St John. The testimony, according to Eusebius, HE 3, 39, 17, begins with Papias, a disciple of St John. Explicit reference to 1 Jn is found in the writings of St Irenaeus, PG 7:925 ; 927 ; Clement of Alexandria, PG 8, 661 ; 1004 ; Tertullian, PL 2, 147 ; 173 ; Origen, *cf.* Eusebius, HE 6, 25, 8 ; and St Cyprian, PL 3, 1138 ; 4, 289 ; 628 ; who name St John the Apostle as the author. The evidence of quotation may be drawn from the *Didache, Epistle of Barnabas*, Polycarp, *Shepherd of Hermas, Epistle of Diognetus.*

The internal evidence, that this Epistle has the same author as the Fourth Gospel, is equally abundant and convincing. Style, structure of sentences, repetition of certain words and phrases, lack of particles, vocabulary —all are very similar to what we find in the Fourth Gospel. Compare 1:1, 5 f. with the Prologue, particularly Jn 1:1, 4 f. ; or 2:3–5 with Jn 14:21, 23 f. ; 2:7 f. with Jn 13:34 f. ; 15:12 f., etc. Chaine lists thirty passages that are common to both, 106 f. ; Westcott has a similar list, xli ff. The proof that the Fourth Gospel was written by St John the Apostle is given in §§ 776*d*–778*f*.

c **Canonicity**—This Epistle is listed in the Muratorian Fragment and in all subsequent canonical lists of NT books. Eusebius, HE 3, 25, classes it among the sacred writings which were universally accepted as inspired. St Jerome, *De Vir Illust.* 9, 18, explicitly mentions that it was universally accepted in the church ; St Augustine, *Tract, 7:5 in 1 Jn*, mentions it by name as canonical.

d **Destination and Purpose**—The prevailing opinion of scholars is that the First Epistle is closely associated with the Fourth Gospel both in time and purpose. Some call it a ' preface ', the majority prefer to consider it a ' postscript ' to the Gospel. Both writings have the same double purpose : to prove that Christ is God and eternal life, and that in Christ we have eternal life and are united with God.

Since 1 Jn lacks the customary form of a letter, *e.g.* salutation and conclusion, special greetings and message to a definite church, it is commonly considered to be an encyclical letter, addressed to a number of churches. The writer is aware of the condition of his readers, whom he affectionately calls : ' children, little children, and beloved ', and repeatedly addresses in the second person. Three times he says : ' I write to you ', and thrice ' I wrote to you '. Since the Epistle presupposes the facts of Christ's life and teaching, and draws practical lessons from them, it is preferable to consider 1 Jn to have been written shortly after the Gospel, probably in one of the last years of

the 1st cent. A very reliable tradition states that the **955d** beloved disciple spent his last years at Ephesus, where he is said to have composed the Gospel, St Irenaeus, *Adv. Haer.* 3, 1, 1. It is very probable, therefore, that this Epistle was likewise sent from Ephesus to the churches of Asia Minor, to which St John sent the seven letters included in the Apocalypse, 1:4–3:22.

Theme and Analysis—St John is disturbed by the **e** appearance of false teachers, who made a distinction between the human Jesus and Christ the Son of God, and also by the worldly spirit, which was undermining the moral character of the Asiatic Christians. To assure eternal life to his readers, the Apostle stresses the need of union with the Father and the Son, which is realized practically by obedience to the commandments, particularly to the precept of brotherly love.

The Apostle begins by claiming to be an eye-witness of the activity of the Word. He says that he has a message from Christ for his readers, which will assure them life everlasting and fellowship with the Father and his Son, 1:1–4. God is light and perfection ; union with him is impossible for those who walk in darkness, 5–7. To walk in the light means to keep free from sin and observe the commandments, 1:8–2:6 ; particularly the precept of brother love, 7–11. After commending them for their sincerity, 12–14, he urges them not to be misled by an inordinate love of the world, 15–17, and carefully to avoid false teachers, who separate Jesus from the Christ and, therefore, deny both Father and Son, 18–26.

Let them hold fast to what they were taught from the beginning, 27–29, and prove that they are children of God by avoiding sin, 3:1–10. What distinguishes the children of God from those of the devil is the practice of fraternal charity after the manner of Christ, 11–18, whom they must firmly acknowledge as God's Son, 19–24.

There follows another warning about distinguishing **f** between truth and error, 4:1–6. A proof of the connexion between the precept of fraternal charity and faith in Jesus as the Son of God is indicated by God's love for mankind. He so loved the world that he sent his only-begotten Son into the world, 7–11. This should prompt Christians to practise true charity towards one another, because charity is the bond between man and the invisible God, 12–21. Love of the neighbour is rooted in faith in the divinity of Christ. In that belief is victory over the world and fellowship with Christ, 5:1–5. We have a threefold witness to this important truth, 6–12. Faith in Christ's divinity begets the greatest confidence, which manifests itself in prayer, 13–17. Then the Apostle concludes with a summary : children of God do not sin, Christians are children of God, and they know God through his Son, 18–21.

Doctrinal Content—The First Epistle may be called a **g** summary of St John's theology. This must not be understood in the sense that it is a development of one or more theses, nor is it an exposition of various doctrinal truths. The Apostle contents himself with the simple statement of a number of fundamental truths, which serve him as a basis for moral instruction. God is light, 1:5 ; we must walk in the light if we would have fellowship with him, 1:6. God is holiness, 2:29 ; to be children of God we must avoid sin and be holy,

955g 3:2 f. God is love, 4:7 ; to share God's love we must love the brethren, 4:7.

Of **Christ** we learn : that he is the Word, 1:1 ; hence, we must learn to know him, who manifested himself to us, 2:22 f. ; He is the Son of God, 1:2 f. ; the only-begotten Son, 4:9. To deny this is to have the spirit of Antichrist, not that of God, 4:9. He was sent into the world by the Father, that he might show his love for mankind, 4:9. This should teach us to love one another, 4:7. Christ laid down his life for us, 3:16 ; cleansed us from sin with his blood, 1:7, and became our propitiation for sin, 2:2, to bring us into closer fellowship with one another. Christ is also our advocate with the Father, so that if we sin we may obtain forgiveness, 2:1. In him is eternal life, and if we have the Son, *i.e.* are united to him by grace, we too shall have eternal life, 5:11.

h A few words must be said here about the heresy against which St John warns his readers. It is probably the false teaching of **Cerinthus** and his followers which is here condemned. According to St Irenaeus, *Adv. Haer.* 1, 26, 1, Cerinthus claimed that Jesus was nothing more than a man, born of Mary and Joseph. At the time of his baptism by St John, the aeon, Christ, descended upon him in the form of a dove, and remained united with him till the passion, when he again left him. Hence, Cerinthus ' denieth that Jesus is the Christ ', 2:22 ; he ' dissolveth Jesus ', 4:3, by separating the man Jesus from the aeon Christ ; he ' believeth not that Jesus is the Son of God ', 5:5. Since by these false statements he deceived men, and set himself against Christ, he is called ' the liar ', 2:22, and ' the Antichrist ', 4:3. The same authority, who was a pupil of St Polycarp, who in turn sat at the feet of the beloved disciple, mentions that the Fourth Gospel was written to offset the errors of Cerinthus, *Adv. Haer.* 3, 2, 1 ; but M. Bardy, *Cérinthe*, RB (1921) 349, questions the correctness of this assertion.

i In 1 Jn another series of instructions centres around the **new life** of a Christian. He is born of God, 2:29 ; 4:7 ; 5:1, and this creates a new relationship with God. Christians are children of God, 3:1 f., who at present enjoy a close union with God, so that he is said to be in them and to abide in them, 2:5 f. ; and after this life they ' shall be like to him, because they shall see him as he is ', 3:2. There are, however, very definite obligations incurred by Christians, who must not commit sin, 3:6, but keep the commandments, 2:29, particularly the precept of fraternal charity, 3:23. This precept is called a new commandment, 2:7, without which we walk in darkness, 2:9 ff., and are not children of God, 3:10. It must fill the soul and not be restricted to words, but should manifest itself in deeds, 3:17 f. We cannot truly claim to love God unless we also love our brethren, 4:20. We forfeit union with God if we love the world, 2:15 ; or deny that Christ is the Son of God, 2:23.

j Style and Text—In one way the style is extremely simple, in another it is very complicated. The sentence structure is simplicity itself, and individually each sentence is easy to understand ; but the connexion of one sentence with the next is often difficult to grasp. There is usually no logical sequence of thought ; yet there is development. A certain solemnity and unction are apparent, which make the Apostle's admonitions very impressive.

The Greek text offers few textual problems, but the Latin text, from which the DV is made, has a passage, 5:7*b*, *c*–8*a*, which is lacking in all Greek MSS, except very late ones ; in all ancient versions, except the Latin ; in about fifty Vg MSS, including the best ; likewise in the majority of Greek and Latin Fathers. According to some authorities, the passage was first quoted by Priscillian, who died in 380, and was first introduced into the Spanish Vg MSS, *cf.* A. Merk, S.J., *Compendium Introductionis in SS*, 1929, 779. Others hold that Tertullian, St Cyprian, and the whole African Church showed an acquaintance with this text, *cf.* CSAB 4, 326–31. It is now generally held that this passage, called the *Comma Johanneum*, is a gloss that **955j** crept into the text of the Old Latin and Vg at an early date, but found its way into the Greek text only in the 15th and 16th cent.

I:1-4 Introduction—Beginning without address or **956a** salutation, and even omitting his name and title, the author asserts his character as witness to the actual manifestation of the Word of life, Jesus Christ. The Word, who was with the Father from all eternity, Jn 1:1, assumed human nature in order to procure eternal life for the human race. He became man that he might be the life of men. This great mystery the Apostle now reveals to his readers. But he reports nothing on insufficient proof ; he records what he himself has seen, pondered, and touched. **3-4.** The revelation is made for two reasons : first, that the readers may share ' fellowship ' with the Apostles, *i.e.* may partake of the union that joins all in Christ, and through Christ with God. Secondly, by realizing more fully this fellowship with the Father and the Son they will continually increase in joy. On John's use of the first person singular and plural, *cf.* Jn 21:24, 25.

5-7 God is Light—**5.** The Apostle has a message from **b** Christ which relates to the nature of God. He is the absolutely pure, spiritual, perfect being, who can best be represented to men by light. In him there is neither defect nor imperfection, nothing inconsistent with absolute excellence. Our Lord said repeatedly during his public ministry : ' I am the light of the world ', Jn 8:12 ; 9:5 ; 12:35 f. ; *i.e.* the source of all truth and moral goodness. Since Father and Son are one, and have the same nature, what is true of the Son is true of the Father. ' Darkness ', in St John's terminology, means the absence of truth and moral goodness, the prevalence of error and sin, *cf.* 2:8, 9, 11 ; Jn 1:5 ; 8:12. **6.** Since God is so perfect a being, no one who leads a sinful life can claim fellowship with him, because union with God and a life of sin are incompatible states. **7.** We ' walk in the light ' if we lead good and holy lives. Holiness binds all Christians with God and with one another, and makes one a partaker of the graces merited by the blood of Jesus Christ.

I:8-II:2 Sin and Its Remedy—Certain members of **c** the Church, misled by pride and self-deception, maintained that they committed no sins. To this group the Apostle declares that whosoever dares to make such a claim is not guided by the truth, but is a victim of self-deception. **9.** Moreover, it is not sufficient to acknowledge ourselves to be sinners interiorly, we must ' confess our sins ', *i.e.* make an exterior acknowledgement of them. It is not stated here to whom they must be confessed in order that they may be forgiven. Christ commissioned the Apostles to absolve contrite sinners upon their confession of sins, Jn 20:23, and God who ' is faithful and just ' will ' forgive us our sins ' as he promised, *e.g.* Ps 102:3 ; Mic 7 :18 f. **10.** St John points out that even sincere Christians fall into sin. Should anyone dare to say the contrary, he makes God a liar, because he said explicitly that all men are sinners, Ps 13:3 ; Prov 20:9 ; Eccl. 7:21. **2:1.** The Apostle urges his readers to be very careful to avoid sin ; yet he knows the weakness of human nature, and holds out the hope of pardon to the sinner, because ' we have an advocate with the Father ', *i.e.* one who intercedes for us and for the whole world. **2.** Christ exercises this office of advocate for sinners by continually offering the merits of his passion and death on their behalf ; thus ' he is the propitiation for our sins ', *cf.* Heb 9:24, 26.

3-6 Fidelity to the Old Commandments—True and **d** solid knowledge of God is not just theoretical, but practical. True knowledge of God leads to love of God, which manifests itself in a constant effort to carry out the divine will expressed in the commandments. Christ must serve him as Model in this respect.

7-11 And to the New—Because of its practical character, the precept of fraternal charity calls for special consideration. At first the Apostle calls it ' an old

956d commandment', because God implanted it in the human heart from the beginning, and he expressly enjoined it on the Chosen People, Lev 19:18. For Christians it received its full significance in the teachings of Christ, Mt 6:2 ff. ; Lk 10:29 ff. ; Jn 15:12 f. In so far as this commandment was fully carried out, first by Christ and then by his followers, it may be called a new commandment. As Christians, their situation was quite different from what it had been in the time of darkness, when they lived like the Gentiles around them. They were now united by a new bond of faith, and their charity to one another, though virtually comprised in the old commandment, was new in regard to its practice, motives and obligations. **9.** To fail in charity is to fail in the principal obligation imposed by Christian faith. He who hates his brother shows that he is not swayed by motives of faith, but by selfishness, like those who still live in pagan darkness. **10.** Christianity emphasizes the reasonableness of universal charity, and by following its teachings we give no occasion of scandal to others. **11.** Hatred is a sign of spiritual blindness, and he who allows himself to be swayed by this blind passion knows not where it may lead him.

e **12-14 An Appeal**—In this section the readers are twice addressed as 'little children ', which probably includes the whole community ; then as 'fathers ', specifying the more mature ; finally as 'young men ' or the immature. Corresponding to the twofold series of addresses is a change of tense of the verb, from the present 'I write ' to the aorist 'I wrote '. Many think that the present form refers to what is contained in the Epistle, and the past form indicates what had been written in the Gospel. Others, with greater probability, maintain that the present tense indicates the author's viewpoint, the past that of the readers. A third difficulty arises from the Greek particle ὅτι, to which most scholars assign a causal significance ; others prefer a declarative sense, i.e. 'that ', which in my opinion is preferable here.

f **12.** Accordingly, to the community as a whole the Apostle declares : ' Your sins *have been* forgiven you for his name's sake '. Jesus Christ, your Redeemer, obtained for you this great grace, removing the obstacle that would hinder your union with God. **13.** Then addressing the 'fathers ', he commends them for their mature knowledge of the faith. The 'young men ' are praised for gaining a victory over the devil, probably by curbing their passions and forming good habits. **14.** In the second series he says : ' *I wrote to you, little children, that* you have known the Father ', and have given proof of this by keeping the commandments. The next clause is missing in Vg, but is found in the Greek text. It is a repetition of 13*a*, except for the change of tense : ' I wrote to you, fathers, that you have known him, who is from the beginning '. The second appeal to the 'young men ' is based on their spiritual strength, on their perseverance in faith, and their victory over Satan.

g **15-17 A Warning**—Directly opposed to God's will are the inordinate desires or concupiscences that centre around self. The 'world ' in St John's terminology stands for men who are hostile to God and opposed to Christ's teachings. A worldling is a typically selfish creature, who craves for the gratification of his animal nature. A man, who becomes inordinately attached to what worldlings seek, alienates himself from the love of God. **16.** Three things in particular draw the heart away from God. They are : ' the concupiscence of the flesh ', i.e. an inordinate love for pleasure, a craving to gratify the lower animal passions, a yielding to the vices of gluttony, drunkenness, impurity, luxury ; ' the concupiscence of the eyes ', i.e. a passionate attachment to riches and material possessions, a yielding to the vice of avarice ; ' and the pride of life ', i.e. an uncontrolled desire for honours, esteem, rank, pomp and show, a yielding to the vices of pride, ambition, vanity and self-exaltation. It is evident that such passions do not have their origin in God, and do not belong to the

life which is from God. **17.** They spring from a corrupt **956g** world, and, like the world, they are even now in the process of passing away. Being of short duration, they cannot satisfy the human heart. God alone can satisfy it, and only obedience to his will can bring man full satisfaction and unending joy.

18-27 Warning against Antichrist—Three evil forces **957a** are leagued against the Father, and against the Son there are also many opponents, called ' antichrists '. St John is the only NT writer to use the name ' Antichrist '. Every opposing teacher, who strives to rob the faithful of their belief and love of Christ, is deserving of the name, although the Apostle admits St Paul's prophecy of one chief opponent, ' the man of sin ', 2 Thess 2:3. In harmony with our Lord's prediction, Mt 24:24, St John declares that many antichrists have arisen even now. From this fact we are to conclude ' that it is the last hour '. This phrase is not to be taken literally as the time immediately before the judgement, but can refer to the entire period of the Christian dispensation. Thus rabbinic tradition calls the whole period following the advent of the Messias ' the future world '—' *Olam habba* ', cf. SB 4, 816-44 ; and St Peter refers to the apostolic age as ' the last time ', 1 Pet 1:5, 20. During this period truth and error concerning the person of Jesus Christ will be disseminated, the former by authorized apostles, the latter by false teachers.

19. It is a cause of great distress to the beloved disciple **b** that these teachers of error were once members of the Church. **20.** In contrast to these apostates are those ' who have the unction from the Holy One ', i.e. from Christ, whose name signifies ' the Anointed One ', and who in baptism anointed them with sanctifying grace and the gifts of the Holy Spirit, and enlightened them. The oldest MSS, e.g. B, S, P, read ' even as you all know ' ; Vg agrees with the majority of MSS, ' and you know all things '. **22.** ' Who is *the* liar '. The falsehood of Antichrist is the denial that Jesus is the Messias, i.e. the Anointed One, and that he is the Son of God. **23.** Anyone who denies the eternal generation of the Son from the Father, ' hath not the Father ', i.e. has no fellowship with him. **26-29.** There is reason for warning them against false seducers. Not that they need explicit instruction in the matter. They have received the unction of the Holy Spirit who will enlighten them concerning what they must know. His teachings are the truth, without any admixture of falsehood. Let them hold fast, therefore, to the faith which he imparted to them. Thus they will be able to meet their Judge with confidence ; for he judges justly and approves those who lead good lives.

III:1-10 Conduct of the Children of God—**1.** Because **c** God has adopted the faithful into his family, the world, which is inimical to God, hates them. **2.** But adoption entitles them to a future state of glory, like that of God himself. The true nature of that glorification is not yet clear ; but after this life faith will give way to the intuitive vision of God, in which they will reflect his glory and nature. **3.** Whosoever wishes to see God, the very Source of purity and holiness, must strive to be holy and keep himself free from all taint of sin. **4.** ' Whosoever committeth sin, committeth *transgression of the law* ; and sin is *lawlessness* ' ; hence, of its very nature it separates the soul from God. **5.** Sin also renders futile the merits of Christ. **6.** Therefore, every Christian is obliged to avoid sin that he may remain united with Christ. Wilfully and knowingly to transgress the law of God indicates a lack of proper knowledge of Christ. He who has seen Christ with the eyes of faith, and has recognized ' that he appeared to take away our sins and in him there is no sin ' strives to become like him, free from all deliberate sin. **7-8.** A just man observes the law of God, and he who sets it at naught imitates the devil. Satan is the author of sin ; Christ is his mighty opponent. **9.** Sin is also at variance with the divine adoption. When St John says that one who is born of God cannot sin, he does not mean that every baptized person is confirmed in

957c grace and cannot fall from that state, but that sin is entirely incompatible with a true child of God, *cf.* Rom 6:6, 11 f., 14. **10.** Hence, only they who avoid sin deserve to be called ' the children of God '; they who do not, are ' the children of the devil '.

d **11-24 Fraternal Charity the Characteristic Mark of God's Children**—To ascertain the spiritual state of any Christian, and to determine his relationship with God, we need but observe how he reacts to the essential precept of fraternal charity. Children of God manifest an active and disinterested love for the neighbour ; the children of the devil are characterized by sullen and envious hatred. **14.** We follow the way of life when we love the brethren. **15.** To cherish hatred for anyone is to develop the disposition of a murderer and forfeit eternal life. **16.** Christ, who laid down his life for us, is the perfect example of charity. We should be ready to make a similar sacrifice if called upon to do so. **17.** This being the ideal, how radically wanting in charity is he, who sees his brother in dire need, yet does nothing to help him. The reason for such heartless conduct is the absence of love of God. Love of God and of the neighbour are inseparable. **18.** In practising either, we must not rest satisfied with expressions of devotion and good will. **19.** Only when charity is active does conscience assure us that we are leading sincere Christian lives. **20.** And should it accuse us of faults, God, who knows us better than we know ourselves, will understand the sincerity of our love. **21-22.** If a good conscience finds nothing reprehensible, we may confidently expect that God will grant a favourable answer to our petitions. **23.** Two things sum up what is most pleasing to him ; faith in the divine personality of Jesus Christ, and brotherly love according to Christ's instructions. **24.** Observance of the commandments is indispensable for union with God. The presence of the Holy Spirit gives us moral assurance of this union, who manifests his presence by the spirit of charity.

958a **IV:1-6 The Discernment of Spirits—1.** Besides those impulses which have their origin in ourselves, there are two other kinds of spiritual activity, which come from without. God can enlighten the mind and move the will of man, either immediately or through the agency of others. On the other hand, the evil spirit tries to perplex and disquiet the faithful with false teachings, and he can imitate the appearance of good in order to deceive men. Hence, the Apostle warns his readers not to trust every spirit, but to put the revelation they receive, or the teaching they hear to a test, to see whether it is from God or from the devil. **2-3.** Teachers, who are animated by the divine Spirit, defend the incarnation of the Son of God. Those who make a distinction between Jesus, a mere man, and Christ, the Son of God, are not of God, but of Antichrist. **4.** The Apostle is grateful that his ' little children ' have not been deceived by such false teachers, because God, who dwells in them, has helped them to persevere in the truth.

b **7-21 God and Charity**—After showing this distinction between the children of God and those of the world, St John next proves that love of God and of the neighbour are so closely related that the one cannot exist without the other. **7.** Those who love their Christian brethren are united to God and know him, *i.e.* are able to distinguish his revelation from the false teachings of men. **9-10.** When God in his infinite mercy determined to restore fallen mankind to its original supernatural state, his love knew no bounds. He sent his only-begotten Son into the world to be a sacrifice of propitiation for our sins. **11.** This was an act of purest love. For we were his enemies, deserving punishment. Yet he chose this method to teach us to love our brethren. **12-14.** When we love one another, the invisible God dwells in us, because by this act we resemble God, whose love in sending his Son to be the Saviour of the world we freely admit and confess. **15-17.** By faith and love we are united to God and to one another, and if we perfect ourselves in love, we need not fear the day of judgement. **18.** Just as love **958b** unites two persons, so fear separates them. There is a servile fear of God that is incompatible with perfect charity. This looks only to the punishment, and he who is influenced solely by it fears to approach a just God. He fears the punishment more than the fact of offending God. Such ' fear is not in charity '. There is also a filial fear of God, which considers only that sin is an offence against God. Such fear springs from love and is wholesome. **20-21.** Because it is easier for us to love what we see than what we do not see, therefore, he who hates his brother cannot truthfully claim that he loves God, particularly since God himself has commanded us to love our brother.

V:1-5 Love rooted in Faith—1. Further proof that **c** faith and love unite us to God and to one another is this : belief in Jesus as the promised Messias must precede baptism. Through this sacrament we are ' born of God ' and become children of God. It also gives us the Holy Ghost, the Spirit of love, and thus begets in us a love of God ' who begot ' together with a love of others who are ' born of him '. **2.** Three inseparable dispositions are : to love the children of God, to love God, and to keep his commandments. **4.** What is it that gives the Christian the power of overcoming the world hostile to God ? The Apostle says it is faith, which not only furnishes the motives, but the help of divine grace.

6-12 Threefold Witness to Christ's Divinity—6. Jesus **d** Christ ' came by water and blood '. Water and blood are symbols and refer, the one to the baptism of Christ, the other to his death. At his baptism, the Father proclaimed him his beloved Son, Mt 3:17. At his death, ' the centurion and they that were with him watching Jesus . . . said : " This was indeed the Son of God " ', Mt. 27:54. ' Not by water alone ' may have been added to refute the error of Cerinthus, who taught that he who died on the cross was not the Son of God, but the man Jesus ; for the teaching of Cerinthus, *cf.* § 955*h*. Here St John insists that, even amid the humiliations and sufferings of the passion, Jesus Christ was the Son of God. A third witness is added, namely, the Holy Spirit, who speaks through the Apostles and proclaims the divinity of Christ to the whole world.

7. According to the Clementine Vg, the three Persons **e** of the Blessed Trinity are the heavenly witnesses to Christ's divinity, corresponding to the threefold witness on earth. The Father gave testimony at the baptism, and the transfiguration, Mt 17:5 and in the temple court, Jn 12:28 ; the Word repeatedly gave testimony to his divinity by his words and works during his public ministry ; the Holy Spirit likewise testified at the baptism, on the day of Pentecost, and later through the Apostles. ' And these three are one ', have one identical nature. Concerning the authenticity of this text, *cf.* § 955*j*. **8.** The Jewish law required the agreement of two or three witnesses for satisfactory evidence, Deut 19:15. That is why St John produces the threefold witness, and adds : ' and these three are one ', *i.e.* they all proclaim the divinity of Jesus Christ. **9.** If a threefold human witness is accepted to confirm the truth of a matter, how can any one dare to set aside a threefold divine testimony, and practically make God a liar ?

13-21 Conclusion—13. The purpose of the Epistle, **f** like that of the Gospel. is to awaken in its readers a realization that a firm hope of attaining eternal life is theirs, because they believe in the divinity of Jesus Christ. **14.** A second result of their sincere faith is the assurance that any petition, that conforms to God's will, will be granted. **16.** This confidence in prayer extends to all the members of the church, and should encourage the faithful to pray for those who have fallen into sin. The Apostle distinguishes a ' sin unto death ', which from the context seems to mean deliberate apostasy from the faith, a denial that Jesus is the Son of God. Since such sinners cut themselves off from their brethren, St John does not ask his readers to pray for them,

958f though he does not expressly forbid such prayers, nor does he say that the fate of the apostate is sealed.

g **18-21.** The main purpose of the Epistle is then summarized by a threefold repetition of 'we know': God's children do not commit sin, *i.e.* they receive abundant grace to avoid deliberate sin, and their love for their heavenly Father prompts them to use this grace. Secondly, we are born of God and are out of reach of the wicked world. Thirdly, we know God through faith in his Son, who became man that we might be incorporated in his Mystical Body. This Son is true God, and is our hope for eternal life. Let them be on their guard against any form of idol worship.

THE SECOND AND THIRD EPISTLES OF ST JOHN

959a **Bibliography**—*cf.* § 955*a*.

Author—The writer of both epistles calls himself 'the ancient' or 'the presbyter', the name whereby he was well known to his readers. A tradition, but not nearly as strong as for the First Epistle, assigns these two short letters to St John the Apostle. Since he wrote them in his old age, and since St Peter calls himself a 'presbyter', 1 Pet 5:1, St John, also, could appropriately use such a title.

b As regards **external evidence,** St Irenaeus twice quotes 2 Jn as the work of the Lord's disciple, PG 7, 633, 927. By calling 1 Jn 'the longer epistle', Clement of Alexandria seems to know of other epistles which St John wrote, PG 8, 1004. Origen concedes that St John wrote a second and a third epistle, according to Eusebius, HE 6, 25, who also quotes St Dionysius of Alexandria as evidence for the authenticity of these two short letters. Eusebius himself thinks they are genuine, *Demonstr. Evang.* 3, 5, PG 22, 216; yet admits that 'not all consider these epistles to be genuine, HE 6, 25. St Jerome remarks that some attributed these letters to the Presbyter John, a different person from St John the Apostle, *De Vir. Illustr.* 9, 18; his own opinion, however, was that St John the Apostle wrote them, *Ad Theod.* 75, 3; *Ad Paulin. Ep.* 53, 8; *Ad Ageruch.* 123, 12. St Cyril of Jerusalem, *Catech.* 4, 36; and St Augustine, *De Doctr. Christ.* 2, 8; admit them as genuine.

c The **internal evidence** is strongly in favour of authenticity. Both writings have the same characteristics of style and language that mark the First Epistle and the Fourth Gospel. We find repeated in these letters such expressions as 'knowing the truth', 2 Jn 1; 'the truth which abides in us', 2; 'walking in the truth', 4; 'walk according to the commandments', 6; 'the commandment of charity', 6; 'to abide in the doctrine of Christ', 9; 'follow not what is evil', 3 Jn 11; 'to bear witness', 12: all of which are genuine Johannine phrases.

Canonicity—Reference to one, and perhaps to both epistles is made in the Muratorian Fragment. They are definitely accepted as inspired writings by the Councils of Hippo (A.D. 393) and Carthage (A.D. 397), and subsequently were recognized universally as part of the canon of the NT.

d **Destination and Purpose**—The Second Epistle is inscribed: 'To the lady Elect and her children', 1:1. This inscription has puzzled exegetes from the earliest times. Is it addressed to a mother and her family or to a particular church, symbolically called 'a lady Elect'? The reasons for preferring the latter interpretation are chiefly, the salutation of 13, 'of thy sister Elect', and the assurance in 1 that her children are loved by 'all that have known the truth'. While not apodictic arguments, these two phrases do seem more applicable to a local church than to a private family.

2 Jn is an earnest exhortation to practical charity, and a warning against false teachers. After a rather lengthy salutation, St John expresses his joy that the persons addressed live according to the true faith, and **959d** he beseeches them earnestly to love one another. By so doing they will keep the commandments. Let them be on guard against seducers, who deny the incarnation of Jesus Christ, and have the spirit of Antichrist. Let them continue to hold the doctrine of Christ, and refuse to communicate with heretics. Further instructions will be imparted by word of mouth when he comes to them.

3 Jn is addressed to a definite individual, 'to the **e** dearly beloved Gaius', and differs from 2 Jn by its personal tone. In this letter the Apostle mentions that for unworthy reasons certain missionaries have been refused hospitality by Diotrephes, who is presumably the bishop of the local church. For this the Apostle rebukes him, while praising Gaius for his faith and charity. May he continue to show hospitality to visiting brethren. Demetrius also comes in for a word of praise. Finally, St John expresses the hope of seeing Gaius shortly.

The Second Epistle

1-3 Salutation—The writer does not mention his name; **f** merely assumes the title 'the ancient' or 'the presbyter'. For the meaning of 'presbyter' as a church official, *cf.* 1 Pet 5:1. In view of his great age and singular authority, St John the Apostle could justly call himself 'the ancient', by which title he probably was known to his contemporaries. The recipients of the letter are 'a lady Elect and her children', *cf.* § 959*d*. The Apostle expresses high regard and love for the persons addressed, which sentiments, he remarks, are shared by all the faithful. He wishes them 'grace . . . mercy and peace'.

4-6 Exhortation to Fraternal Charity—The writer opens on a note of joy, the cause of which is the faith and charity '*of some* of thy children'. He praises what he can, before pointing out what needs correction. The 'commandment from the Father' is to walk in truth, *i.e.* live according to Christian principles. **5.** There must have been some dissension in this community, or there would be no reason for insisting on the precept of charity. **6.** Seven of the ten precepts directly concern the neighbour; hence, 'if we walk according to his commandments', we practise charity; and the motive for keeping them all must be divine love.

7-11 Warning against False Teachers—A firm faith **g** in the divinity and in the incarnation of Jesus Christ is needed to preserve true Christian charity. Many seducers are seeking to undermine this faith. These men should be avoided, because they have the spirit of the Antichrist, and may cause them to lose the full reward for their past good deeds. **9.** They profess to advance beyond the teachings of Christ, as if our Lord had not taught the full truth. Now, whosoever follows their teaching, cuts himself off from God. **10.** In order to prevent this threatening danger to the faith, the Apostle enjoins that the customary hospitality is not to be extended to teachers of false doctrines. **11.** These men ought not even to receive the usual greeting, lest this be interpreted as a sign of recognition and approval.

12-13 Conclusion—St John hopes soon to visit this community, and to impart further instruction by word of mouth. He concludes with a greeting from 'thy sister Elect', *i.e.* from the church where he is staying.

The Third Epistle

1-2 Salutation—As in the preceding letter, so here, St **h** John calls himself 'the ancient' in addressing a short message to Gaius, a person about whom nothing definite is known. Whether Gaius was a layman or a presbyter, is not clear from the context of the letter. The Apostle's salutation consists of a prayer that Gaius may prosper both materially and spiritually.

959h **3-8 Praise of Gaius**—The writer expresses great satisfaction with the reports he has heard about the character and activity of Gaius. **4.** He says : ' I have *no greater joy* than this, to hear that my children walk in truth '. Besides commending the solid faith of Gaius, he lauds his sincere charity towards the brethren, who are strangers. These men were the itinerant missionaries, who praised the hospitality extended to them before the whole church. **6.** St John asks him to lend them further assistance, because they depended entirely on finding support in the different churches they visited, ' taking nothing of the Gentiles '. He intimates that by rendering them this help, he himself was spreading the truth.

i **9-10 Censure of Diotrephes**—Explaining, perhaps, why such assistance was not rendered by the bishop or pastor of the church, the Apostle remarks : ' *I wrote indeed to the church* ', presumably the one to which Gaius belonged, and of which Diotrephes perhaps was bishop. There is nothing definitely known about Diotrephes ; only what is stated here. It seems that this man refused

to entertain such itinerant missionaries, even those sent **959i** out by St John himself ; nay, more, he even dared to forbid anyone to show them hospitality, and excommunicated those, who like Gaius, disregarded his prohibition. So we have here an ambitious and selfish pastor, who set himself in opposition to the aged Apostle, who threatens to give him a public reprimand, should he come to this place.

11-12 Approval of Demetrius—The spirit and conduct of Diotrephes is not ' of God ', and his example is not to be imitated. Highly commendable, however, has been the conduct of Demetrius, as everyone testifies, and as his truly Christian behaviour indicates. Again we are in ignorance about this individual, merely knowing that he was a true and loyal servant of God, as St John testifies.

13-14 Conclusion—A fuller explanation is not necessary because the Apostle hopes to see Gaius in the near future, when they can discuss details at greater length. He sends greetings from those who are with him, and wishes to be remembered individually to all his friends.

THE EPISTLE OF
ST JUDE

By H. WILLMERING, S.J.

960a Bibliography—G. Estius, *cf.* § 945*a* ; A. Camerlynck, *cf.* § 945*a* ; *C. Bigg, *cf.* § 949*a* ; W. Vrede, Der Judasbrief, BB, Bonn, 1932 ; J. Chaine, *cf.* § 952*a*.

b The Author—In the inscription of this short epistle we read : ' Jude, the servant of Jesus Christ and brother of James '. There is no further indication in the letter to identify the writer. In the list of the Apostles two are named Judas, *cf.* Mt 10:3 ; Mk 3:18 ; Lk 6:16 ; Ac 1:13 ; one is Judas the Iscariot, who betrayed the Lord, the other is called ' Thaddaeus ' or ' Lebbaeus ' or ' of James ', which according to Catholic interpreters means ' the brother of James '. Non-Catholic writers are loath to identify the Apostle with the author of the epistle ; hence they claim that ' son ' is to be supplied. The fact that the author mentions James indicates that the latter was well known and highly respected by the recipients of the letter. Catholics justify their interpretation of ' brother ' by citing Mk 6:3, where James and Jude are mentioned together as ' brothers of Christ '. The position of James the brother of the Lord in the church of Jerusalem is indicated in Ac 15:13 where with St Peter he settles the dispute about the circumcision of Gentile converts ; and in Ac 21:18–25, where he acts as head of the church in Jerusalem, and welcomes St Paul after his third missionary journey. He is called an ' Apostle ' by St Paul in Gal 1:19. An early tradition says that Bishop James was a life-long Nazarite and celibate (Hegesippus, quoted by Eusebius, HE 2, 23, 4). But if Jude is an Apostle and a brother of the Lord, why does he not make use of these titles in the letter ? The reason is probably the same that prompted James to omit both titles, namely, humility. On the ' Brethren of the Lord ', *cf.* §§ 672–3.

c Canonicity—This epistle is placed on his list of disputed books by Eusebius, HE 3, 25, 3. St Jerome gives the reason why not all accepted it as an inspired writing : ' Jude has left us a short epistle, which is one of the seven Catholic Epistles ; but since he quotes the apocryphal Book of Henoch it is rejected by many. Yet it deserves a place in Holy Scripture because of its antiquity and the use that is made of it ' (*De Vir. Illust.* 4). Early Christian writers of the 3rd cent. who defend its authenticity and quote it as Scripture, are : Clement of Alexandria, *Paedag.* 3, 8 ; *Strom.* 3, 2 ; Origen, *Com. in Mt* 10, 17 and 17, 30 ; *In Ep. ad Rom* 3, 6 ; 5, 1 ; Tertullian, *De Cultu Femin.* 1, 3. It is found in the canons of the Muratorian Fragment (A.D. 160) of SS Athanasius, PG 26, 1176 ; Cyril of Jerusalem, PG 33, 500 ; Damasus, Dz 84 ; Innocent I, Dz 96 ; of the Councils of Hippo, Laodicea and Carthage III, Dz 92.

d The Relation between Jude and 2 Pet—Both letters were written to warn certain Christian communities of a grave danger to faith and morals propagated by false teachers. There is, however, a closer connexion between the two epistles that arises from a common purpose. There is great similarity of thought and language, as may be seen by comparing Jude 3-18 with 2 Pet 1:5 ; 2:1-18. Which letter was written first ? There is no agreement on the answer, but the priority of Jude has a slightly better claim. The style of Jude is more fluent, and certain obscure expressions that occur in Jude 9, 11, 12 are clarified in 2 Pet 2:10 ; 2:15 and 2:13 respectively. Others,

however, hold that 2 Pet 2 shows direct dependence **960d** on Jude.

The Relation between Jude and the Book of Henoch e —There is great probability, as St Jerome asserts above, § 960*c*, that Jude made use of the apocryphal Book of Henoch. This does not prove that Jude considered the contents of Henoch as inspired ; nor does it indicate that he approved of every statement contained therein. Henoch was held in high esteem in the early Church, and it may have contained some genuine Jewish traditions.

Destination and Purpose—The letter is addressed ' to **f** them that are beloved in God the Father, and preserved in Jesus Christ, and called ', 1, which address might apply to any Christian community. From the tone of the letter it seems to be directed to a definite church or group of churches in a definite locality. The arguments drawn from the OT and Jewish tradition would have greater weight with converts from Judaism, and the fact that the writer calls himself ' the brother of James ' implies that he is writing to Christians who had a high regard for James. Such communities must be sought in Palestine, Syria and Mesopotamia, where the majority of the converts were from Judaism ; and tradition assigns these very countries to St Jude as the field of his apostolic labours. We may legitimately suppose, therefore, that this epistle was addressed to the churches in these regions.

The epistle was occasioned by the spread of a dangerous heresy, which threatened to undermine Christian life and belief. A band of godless men, who denied God's sovereignty and led immoral lives, were deceiving many and leading them astray. St Jude earnestly warns his readers against such deceivers, and urges them to hold fast to the true faith and persevere in the love of God.

Time and Place of Composition—Nothing definite is **g** known about either. The date usually given by those who admit the authenticity is somewhere between 62 and 67, the dates assigned to the deaths of SS James and Peter.

Analysis—After the greeting the Apostle begs his readers to contend earnestly for the faith, preached to them by the Apostles, against the ungodly men who are advocating lawlessness and immorality, 3 f. He calls their attention to the punishments which God had inflicted on unbelievers, rebels and profligates in the past, 5-7. Despite such warning examples, these seducers defile the flesh, despise authority and speak evil of those who exercise it, 8-10. Their sin is like that of Cain, of Balaam and of Core, 11-13. Henoch foretold their condemnation, 14-15. May the readers be forewarned, and use the safeguards provided by faith, namely, prayer, love of God and hope in Christ, 17-21. Let them encourage the wavering, bring back the fallen, but avoid the profligates, 22 f. God can preserve them from sin. May they give him glory and honour now and forever, 24 f.

Text and Style—The Greek text varies only in two or three places, and the variants are of little importance. Vg follows the Greek closely. The style is impassioned, somewhat vague, picturesque and vigorous.

1-2 Salutation—Although the writer was a relative of **961a** our Lord, he does not mention the fact, but humbly

961a refers to himself as a ' bond-servant' of Jesus Christ, and gives his relationship with James, Bishop of Jerusalem, who was everywhere well known to converts from Judaism. He addressed those whom God in his love called to the faith and whom he preserved in it by uniting them to his Son Jesus Christ. **2.** The Apostle wishes them a threefold divine blessing in fullest measure : mercy from God, peace with him, and charity towards their fellowmen.

3-4 Purpose of the Letter—It seems probable that the Apostle planned to write a general letter about what is most necessary for salvation ; but a sudden danger immediately caused him to send in writing a warning plea, urging the faithful to preserve unchanged the deposit of the faith which had been transmitted to them by the Apostles. **4.** Ravenous wolves have entered the Christian flock to destroy it. Long ago did Christ indicate such deceivers as constituting a real menace to the church, Jn 10:1. Two charges are brought against these particular seducers : they abused the grace of God by indulging in licentiousness, and by their immoral conduct they denied in practice the authority of God and of Jesus Christ.

b **5-7 Warning Examples**—**5.** The Apostle calls attention to several instances, already well known to them, in which God inflicted severe punishment for sin. The first is taken from Num 14:1–36. The lesson inculcated by the destruction of the unbelieving Israelites is that no Christian may presume on his privileges, since those who were brought out of Egypt by a series of astounding miracles nevertheless died in the wilderness because of their unbelief. There are three variant readings for 5*b* : the oldest Greek MSS and Vg have ' Jesus'; others have ' the Lord'; and a few have ' God'. Here, as in 1 Cor 10:4, 9, Christ is said to have accompanied the Israelites in their wanderings through the wilderness. **6.** The second example is the fall of the angels. ' Kept not their principality', *i.e.* the state in which God created them ; ' forsook their own habitation', *i.e.* they forgot their proper rank by aspiring to equality with God their Creator ; ' unto the judgement of the great day', *i.e.* the day of general judgement, referred to in Ac 2:20 ; Apoc 6:17, when the rebel angels will receive their final sentence. **7.** The third instance is recorded in Gen 19:25 ; ' suffering the punishment of eternal fire', *i.e.* the effects of the fire which destroyed these sinners are depicted as permanent, *cf.* Wis 10:7.

c **8-13 The Nefarious Conduct of the Seducers**—**8.** Now follows the application of the preceding examples to the false teachers. ' In like manner *these in their dreams*', *i.e.* dreaming in the sleep of sin, ' defiled the flesh', by giving themselves over to immorality, like the Sodomites ; ' and despise dominion', *i.e.* scorn authority, like the disgruntled Israelites ; ' *and revile majesty*', speak ill of those who exercise authority. Some interpret ' δόξαι' as angels, *i.e.* beings in whom the divine Majesty is reflected. **9.** In contrast to their outrageous conduct is the restraint used by St Michael in his dispute with Satan over the body of Moses. This incident is not mentioned in Scripture, but may have been a Jewish oral tradition, which is well known to the readers of this epistle. According to Clement of Alexandria, *Adumbrat. in Ep. Jud.* and Origen, *De Princ.* 3, 2, 1, St Jude is quoting an apocryphal work, *The Assumption of Moses.* In the fragment of the work that has come down to us, this story is not found. The passage claims that the Archangel Michael passed no hasty judgement on the arch-enemy, but left his condemnation in God's hands. **10.** ' Blaspheme', *i.e.* revile, speak abusively of; ' things they know not' are spiritual things ; ' things they naturally know, like dumb beasts', sensual passions, natural cravings.

d **11.** Next the Apostle likens the false teachers to three

notorious sinners mentioned in OT : Cain, Balaam **961** and Core. Throughout the epistle the author has a liking for triads ; *e.g.* 1, 2, 4, 5–7, 11. By not curbing their passions, in contempt of God's warning, Gen 4:7, they resemble Cain. Balaam allowed selfish avarice to stifle conscience, and disregarded the threats of divine punishment, Num 31:8. Core rebelled against the authority of Moses, Num 16:1–36. **12.** Using a series of metaphors to describe their shameless conduct, St Jude says : ' *These are spots in your love-feasts, when they feast with you without fear*', *i.e.* at the liturgical banquets, ' ἀγάπαι', when Christians gathered to share with one another the food they brought as a sign of union and mutual love, and which was followed by ' the Lord's supper' (*cf.* 1 Cor 11:20 f.) ; these deceivers were blots, misfits, or as some texts read, ' rocks' or hidden reefs to wreck the faith of those assembled. ' Fear' refers to the fear of God. Their boastfulness, which produced nothing, is likened to clouds that promise rain but are driven before the wind. Their lack of virtuous deeds causes them to resemble trees in autumn, that should be loaded down with fruit but are barren. This proves that they are utterly dead, and deserve nothing better than to be uprooted. **13.** Their boisterous and obscene conduct is illustrated by the turbulent waves of the sea that wash ashore filth and slime. Their departure from sound doctrine and morality is similar to the course of a wandering star that disappears in the darkness forever.

14-16 Henoch's Prophecy of Judgement—**14.** The **e** prophecy of Henoch is not contained in Scripture, but is found almost verbatim in the apocryphal *Book of Henoch*, 1, 9. By quoting this passage, St Jude does not approve of everything contained in this strange work. He merely vouches for the fact that the prophecy is recorded that the Lord will execute judgement upon all ungodly sinners, such as the men in question. **16.** Enlarging further on the character of the false teachers, he calls them ' murmurers full of complaints', *i.e.* men who are discontented with their lot, who do as they please, whose speech is boastful and vain for the most part, but who will stoop to flattery when this is advantageous to them.

17-19 Warning of the Apostles—That false teachers **f** and seducers will appear ' in the last days', and will resemble in character the men here characterized as ' mockers walking according to their own desires in ungodliness', is stated by St Paul, 1 Tim 4:1 ; 2 Tim 3:1, and less clearly by our Lord, Mt 24:11. Similar prophecies, no doubt, were uttered by all the Apostles of Christ in their instructions to the people, but their words have not been recorded.

20-23 Final Exhortation—**20.** Whereas the heretics **g** are pulling down the church of Christ stone by stone, St Jude desires his readers to build up their character firmly ' upon your most holy faith', *i.e.* according to its holy teachings and after the example of its holy Founder. This can only be accomplished with the help of the Holy Ghost, whose assistance must be sought through prayer. **21.** Love of God, and the mercy of Jesus Christ will bring them ' unto life everlasting'. **22-23.** The Greek text is rather uncertain. In some MSS there are two clauses, in others three. Most textual critics prefer the reading in which three classes of offenders are mentioned. The first class seem to be wavering ; they are to be taught the truth by instruction and argument. The second class seem to have yielded, but can still be rescued. The third class are utterly depraved and their condition is hopeless. They should judge them mercifully, but hold them in fear and keep them at a safe distance, as they would a contaminated garment.

24-25. The epistle concludes with a solemn doxology.

THE APOCALYPSE

By C. C. MARTINDALE, S.J.

62a Bibliography—Fr E. B. Allo, O.P., *Apocalypse*, Paris, 1921 ; *H. B. Swete, *The Apocalypse of St John*, London, 1906 ; F. Ribera, S.J., *In sacr. Apocalysim Commentarii*, Lyons, 1592 ; B. Viegas, S.J., *Commentarii Exegetici in Apoc*, Paris, 1606 ; W. H. Simcox, *The Revelation of St John the Divine* (CBSC), Cambridge, 1902 ; J. J. L. Ratton, *The Apocalypse of St John*, London, 1915 ; *R. H. Charles, *The Revelation of St John*, 2 vols (ICC), Edinburgh, 1920 ; R. Eaton, *The Apocalypse of St John*, London, 1930 ; O. Karrer, *Die Geheime Offenbarung*, Einsiedeln-Köln, 1940 ; E. Burrows, S.J., *The Pearl in the Apocalypse* (JTS), 43, 1942 ; R. J. Loenertz, O.P., *The Apocalypse of St John* (tr. by Hilary Carpenter, O.P.), London, 1947.

b The Apocalypse and its Author—The last book of the NT is entitled : Apocalypse of (*i.e.* written by) John. Who was this John ? But for certain doctrinal objections, ancient tradition would have been unanimous— he was John the Apostle, the son of Zebedee. In the 2nd cent. the 'Apocalypse' was known throughout the Church, regarded as inspired by God, and written by a John whom St Justin (*c* 140 : *Dial.*, 81, 4) calls 'one of the apostles of Christ' : Justin knew Ephesus well. Polycarp, John's disciple (martyred at Smyrna, 155-6), quotes the Apocalypse complete with grammatical abnormalities : the Muratorian Fragment (Rome : 155-200) mentions the Apocalypse as John's, manifestly meaning the Apostle : Irenaeus (177-8) familiar with Gaul, Rome and the East ; *cf.* the Letter from Lyons, doubtless drawn up by him ; and *Adv. Haer.*, ii, 22, 5 ; iv, 21, 11 ; v, 26, 1) is certain that it is by John, disciple of the Lord. Tertullian (*c* 205-10 : *Adv. Marc.*, iii, 14, 24 ; iv, 5 : and *De resurr. carnis*, 27) is no less clear. The list were easily amplified. But a certain Roman priest Caius (*c* 205) startlingly assigned the book to John's great adversary Cerinthus who, under the pseudonym ' a great apostle ', declared that it taught a terrestrial 'kingdom of Christ' lasting 1,000 years of nuptial festivity. The Montanists, passionately believing in personal mystical inspiration, fostered a reaction against the Johannine writings and objected to symbolism *as such* : ' What use to me is John's Apocalypse when it talks of Seven Angels or Seven Trumpets ? ' But they acknowledge that the ruck of Christians ascribe the book to the Apostle : thus they witness to the tradition while deriding it.

c But about 250 Dionysius bishop of Alexandria, disliking the book's symbolism and 'millenarianism', 'guessed' that its author was different from that of the Gospel : 'Many men are called John, and they say that there are two tombs in Ephesus, each called John's ! ' His reasoning, then, is purely personal not traditional : no one so far had heard of this 'other John '. Eusebius however (HE iv, 13, 8) says that either the book must be ranked as among the undisputed NT books or rejected as apocryphal, and suggests that its author 'might be' John the Presbyter mentioned by Papias : this 'other John' might account for the story of the 'two tombs'. So for slightly over a century there was a partial eclipse of the Apocalypse : it was accepted in the West, doubted or rejected in the East : but soon the entire Church accepted it—there was no rival tradition, and the doubts had been raised **962c** on impressionist or doctrinal grounds. Towards the end of the 19th cent., it was argued that neither Gospel nor Apocalypse was written by the Apostle, or that only the latter was : but a reaction set in, and it is very generally admitted that both documents are by one author : since we hold that the Fourth Gospel was written by John the son of Zebedee (see §§ 776d–778f), we regard the Apocalypse too as having been written by him.

Impossible, here, to do more than indicate lines of **d** argument for or against identity of authors. Verbally, the Apocalypse is more akin to the Johannine Gospel and Epistles than to the rest of the NT. Grammatically and syntactically the differences are startling, but the coincidences far more subtle, so that those who believe in different authors sometimes postulate a sort of ' Asia Minor ' dialect due, maybe, to 'John of Ephesus', which influenced all the Johannine writings. Doctrinally, Jn is said to present a 'human' Christ : the Apocalypse, a tremendous heavenly Judge and King —as to this, see the Commentary : enough to note here that only in the Gospel and the Apocalypse is our Lord called the 'Logos' ; nowhere could His divinity be more strongly stressed than in the former ; throughout the Gospels κρίσις, judgement, is a keyword ; Christ's role as Judge at the End is, if anything, less emphasized in the Apocalypse. In short, the latter seems to be more closely allied with Jn than with the Synoptists. Then we are told that the spirit and method controlling the two documents differ profoundly. But, first, each is built up out of contrasts—Light, Dark ; Truth, Lie ; Life, Death—and Lamb, Wild Beast ; Bride, World-Wanton ; Jerusalem, Babylon ; Michael, Dragon (see Commentary). Again, the historical events in Jn are chosen for their spiritual significance—John uses the material fact as symbol for a spiritual truth : in the Apocalypse he chooses a spiritual truth and devises a symbol for it. Again, the Apocalypse is put into carefully articulated groups of ' seven ' : in the Gospel, John selects seven significant miracles (many other 'septuples' are to be found there ; see Abbott, *Johannine Grammar*, 2624–7) : this is the more remarkable since certain expressions (*e.g.* ' these things have I spoken to you ') could hardly have been observed as used seven times save by a student *looking* for such a system : they do not construct a pattern as ' sevens ' do in the Apocalypse—though it too contains various ' *latent* sevens '. Another habit of John's, specially noticeable in the Apocalypse, is that having all that he proposes to say already in his mind he will provide a self-contained picture into which, none the less, some element of what he will say *next* enters : his sections are separate, yet 'dove-tailed'. His mounting tide rolls forward and the wave crashes : it retreats, carrying back some shingle : forward it sweeps again, covering a new reach of shore, and so on, till it reaches its appointed limit.

The Pattern of the Apocalypse—The book consists **e** of a Prologue ; the 'book' itself, and an Epilogue. The Prologue is (*a*) general and (*b*) particular. (*a*) 1:1–8 Title ; author ; sanction ; salutation of recipients ; ascription of praise to Christ. (*b*) 1:9–3:22. Christ commands John to write to the Asiatic

962e communities, telling them 'things present and to come'. John obeys, writing a sevenfold 'covering letter', insisting chiefly on 'things present'. The Epilogue (22:6–21) corresponds closely with Prologue (*a*), amplifying it by many expressions used in the bulk of the book.

This falls into two substantial parts : A (4:1–11:18) and B (11:19–22:5) :

A (I) A DOUBLE PREPARATORY VISION (remaining as an unchanged background to all that follows)

(*a*) The everlasting worship of God by all Creation (ch 4).
(*b*) The universal role of God incarnate, suffering and triumphant (ch 5).

THE BREAKING OF SEVEN SEALS

(*a*) A group of 4 Seals : Four Horsemen (6:1–6).
(*b*) A group of 2 Seals : the cry of the Martyrs and the answer to it (7–17).
(*c*) A double vision interposed (ch 7).
(*d*) The Seventh Seal (8:1).

A (II) A DOUBLE PREPARATORY VISION

(*a*) The Prayer of the Martyrs in Heaven (8:2–4).
(*b*) Its effects on earth, seen generally (8:5).

THE SOUNDING OF SEVEN TRUMPETS

(*a*) A group of 4 Trumpets : the woes of inanimate Nature (8:6–13).
(*b*) A group of 2 Trumpets : a double war of spirits and of men (ch 9).
(*c*) A double vision interposed (10–11:14).
(*d*) The Seventh Trumpet (11:15–18).

(Prefatory Vision to Part B : The Apparition of the Ark of God ; 11:19.)

B (I) A DOUBLE PREPARATORY VISION

(*a*) The Woman, Mother of Christ (12:1–6).
(*b*) The Dragon, would-be conqueror of Christ (7–12).

SEVEN GREAT 'MYSTERIES'

(*a*) A group of 4 Mysteries—the Dragon ; the Wild Beast from the Sea ; the Wild Beast from the Land ; the Lamb (12:13–14:5).
(*b*) A group of 2 Mysteries (14:6–13).
(*c*) A double vision interposed (14:14–20).
(*d*) The Seventh Mystery (15:1–4).

B (II) A DOUBLE PREPARATORY VISION (15:5–8)

THE OUTPOURING OF SEVEN PLAGUES

(*a*) A group of 4 Plagues (16:1–9).
(*b*) A group of 2 Plagues (10–12).
(*c*) A double vision interposed (13–16).
(*d*) The Seventh Plague (17–21).

f There follows what could be called Part C, or Part B (III). The structure here may be less distinct, perhaps owing to a new *kind* of symbolism used ; possibly because of the ever-increasing emotion under which John writes.

(A Prefatory Vision : 17:1–2.)

A DOUBLE PREPARATORY VISION

(*a*) The World Wanton (17:3–6).
(*b*) Explanation of this 'Mystery' (7–18).

SEVEN VISIONS

(*a*) A group of 4 Visions—The Doom pronounced on Rome (18:1–8) : Dirge over Rome (9–20) : the Destruction of Rome (21–24) : the Triumph of the New Jerusalem (19:1–10).
(*b*) A group of two Visions—Christ's Advent as

Conqueror (19:11–16) : the Destruction of the Beast (17–21). **962**

(*c*) A double vision interposed—The Binding of the Dragon and the Reign of the Saints for 1,000 years (20:1–6) : The Destruction of the Dragon (7–10).
(*d*) The Seventh Vision : Judgement and Consummation (11–15).

A Double Vision of God proclaiming the New Jerusalem (21:1–8) and of the New Jerusalem itself (21:9–22:5) corresponds to the Double Vision of God and of the Lamb prefixed to the central part of the book. (Epilogue : 22:6–21.)

Prophecy : Prediction : 'Apocalypse'—The book **g** therefore belongs to a certain class of prophetic writing, *i.e.* 'Apocalypse', and is traditional. But it is also original. The word 'apocalypse', un-veiling', is frequent in both Testaments. St Paul speaks of the unveiling of God's Judgements, of Christ, of the 'sons of God', and says that he has had personal unveilings (*cf.* Rom 2:5 ; 8:19 ; 16:25 ; 1 Cor 1:7 ; 2 Cor 12:7 ; Gal 1:12). Prophecy can include 'prediction', and Apocalypse can include actual comment and practical advice ; yet we might say that the former begins from earth and rises to heaven, while the latter begins from heaven and descends to interpret human life in the light of eternity. Now if St Paul heard 'words that transcend all words'—'words that no man may utter' (2 Cor 12:4), should he have wished to relate that experience he must perforce have done so in symbols. So too would any other ecstatic. Hence an 'apocalyptic dialect' grew up, especially when the Ending of the World was being dealt with. Nor was this disdained by our Lord himself. The message might be new ; but the diction, inherited. John's message was new—it was concerned a Messias not only promised, but arrived. So he could not but *use* and *adapt* the ancestral symbolism. He would have adapted it in any case, being a true artist : thus he simplifies Ezechiel's vision of God and quite 'de-humanises' it : he accepts many a suggestion from his own environment : he will use various symbols for one thing, or allow one symbol to float from one meaning to another. Some of his symbolism may remain inexplicable for us, not only because we cannot fully share the knowledge of his Asiatic readers, but because he wrote at times 'in cipher' what he had already explained or would explain later and could not risk writing openly, *e.g.* about the Emperors ; *cf.* St Paul : 2 Thess 2. We may, then, say that a Prophet can have five planes of consciousness within himself, all interpenetrating—he might see something concrete, actual or imminent ; a city, or an invasion, and, he might allude to this directly, or under some symbol—a strong king attacks a weak one ; a lion devours a gazelle. Or, he might see a persecution as 'typical', **h** a summing-up of the world-enduring conflict between Right and Wrong—thus the End of the World could be seen *in* the sack of Jerusalem, when *a* 'world' undoubtedly did end, as another did when Christendom broke up, or, may be, in 1945. Again, he could see all this as having its counterpart in man's soul : or, yet again shifting his perspective, he could contemplate a world of spiritual prototypes, more 'real' than transitory events. Finally, he might 'see God', so far as that is granted to man. Delicate indeed the task of judging upon which plane the Apocalyptist's eye is focused, for, while seeing more than one, he will *focus* especially upon one. Our suggestions therefore are but tentative, nor do we forget that John was inspired to write as he did, so that his words have God for Author.

It is clear that *one man* must have arranged the component elements of the book into their strange mosaic—'7', *i.e.* '4'; 2 ; (2) ; 1 '. So we need not suppose that John 'saw' all these visions 'on end' : they may have been 'lights in prayer' granted at different times in his life, remembered by him (as

62h Mary ' kept all these things ', reflecting on them, inter-connecting them : Lk 2:19, 51) and finally arranged by him as we have them. If this be so, the question of ' when ' the visions were granted, lapses, though we still can ask when the book was composed. But more. It becomes evident that the episodes (starting with the Seals) cannot represent a sequence in time—century by century, era by era. Commentators used to struggle to show that they do : probably no one attempts this now. John's eye is fixed throughout on one subject—Christ's Triumph in a hostile world. True, we shall see that he focuses more and more on contemporary events ; but in reality the consumma-tion is reached at the end of each group of seven, though, foreseeing (as we said) what he will write down next, he causes the theme of, or some item in, the following group of visions to be anticipated in the previous one.

63a I hold, then, that the book is a complex whole constructed by one man, who does not, for example, incorporate earlier (hypothetical) apocalypses ; who modifies the traditional dialect to suit his genius and environment ; that its doctrine is identical with that of the Fourth Gospel and that its diction and style are nearer to that than to the Synoptists. Is this paradoxical in view of the differences on grammar, vocabulary and style which have been a main reason for the denial of identity of authorship, or at least for assigning the purer Greek of the Gospel to ' disciple-secretaries ' used by the aged John ? (See on the Pentateuch, § 48b, and on Hebrews, § 52c.) But (a) the style of the Fourth Gospel hardly suggests to me an adapting hand, let alone mind ; and (b) it is absurd to say that a man cannot write in very different styles, especially when both his material and his mood are different. John, receiving shock after shock of ecstasy and struggling to write down sym-bolically and traditionally what could not really be written down at all, cannot but have written in a quite special way. Had we Aquinas's Summa only, we would not have expected his hymns : having the hymns we are not surprised by the Summa. Had we only St John of the Cross's lyrics, would we have expected his prose works (or vice versa) ? Having both, we see—once he explains his symbolism—how truly, yet surprisingly, they harmonize. John was steeped in the apocalyptic passages of the Prophets, especially Daniel, Ezechiel and Zacharias : he may have read earlier or contemporary apocalypses—Enoch (166-164 B.C.) ; The Secrets of Enoch (A.D. 1-50) ; especially Baruch (contemporary ?) : but he does not quote, and the non-canonical documents are altogether beneath him artistically and spiritually : we need not mention anything that followed him. One cannot precisely prove that the book was written by the son of Zebedee or at any definite date : the only reason for asserting that parts of it could not have been written before a late date (94-6 : see § 970k, l) would be the assumption that prediction is impossible.

b **The Recipients of the Apocalypse : Emperor-Worship : Gnosticism**—John sent his Apocalypse into a world where two main dangers were manifest. One was Emperor-worship, due at its lowest to the immemorial oriental wish to flatter its princes, flattery welcomed at any rate by unbalanced emperors like Nero, Caligula or Domitian. It was due, too, to a far-sighted policy, especially when linked with the Goddess Rome. Emperor-worship alone held together the heteroge-neous cultures that formed the Empire, and this worship insinuated itself into every part of life—military, social, bureaucratic, commercial : every reunion involved some Emperor-worship ; to avoid it, a man must practically ostracize and ruin himself. But even the hard-headed Roman felt that ' Rome ' existed ' not without the gods ' and was herself ' divine ' : so in proportion as the Emperor incarnated ' Rome ', he too became divine. Finally, the prevalent Stoic philosophy regarded the Logos—the departmental ' expression ' of ' God '—as socially made visible in the

system of Empire. Thus he who dissociated himself **963b** from this was not only disloyal, but an enemy of civilization, animated by a ' hatred for the (civilized) human race ' and must be got rid of.

Secondly, a vaguely religious philosophy was every- **c** where taking many fluid forms later to be known, collectively, as ' Gnosticism '. It tended to regard all ' matter ' as bad, so that God could never come into contact with it : contact was made through an enormous series of existences each less spiritual than the preceding one. Somewhere in this series was the ' Logos '. Those then who did not wish to exclude Christianity held that our Lord's body was unreal, an ' appearance ' only : or, that a divine Power laid hold of a human body and used it like a marionette between, e.g. the Temptation and the Agony (or the Death). You could either get rid of this evil matter by extreme asceticism—no marriage ! no eating of flesh-meat ! ; or, you could regard your body as so definitely not your Self that it did not matter what it did : the divine spark, ultimately to be reunited with God, remained inviolate though in prison. Thus all religions were relatively ' true ', being but expres-sions of the Inexpressible Super-Reality and useful for the common herd who did not know the ' depths ' of this doctrine as true Gnostics (Know-ers) did (see § 965a).

This was but on its way to systematization when the Apocalypse was written ; but St Paul's letters to the Ephesians and Colossians and indeed St John's first Epistle often refer to its embryo. Both Christian ' intellectuals ' and the average Christian were hard pressed. The latter could so easily be persuaded that Emperor-worship was a mere social formality : the former, that Gnosticism was just ' broad-mindedness '. The intransigence of St John will be seen hurling itself against both these misconceptions and imple-ments its decisions about actual problems by its vision of eternal Truth.

The Title : ' The Revelation of (i.e. given by, through) 964a John' I 1-3 The Scope of the Book—' The Revelation of Jesus Christ, which God gave to him to show to his servants—what must soon take place—which he showed —sending it by his Angel—to his servant John—who witnessed to the Word of God and the witness of Jesus Christ—all that he saw.'

1. The Revelation of Jesus Christ. Is he the Revealer or the Revealed ? Both. He revealed himself to St Paul (2 Thess 1:7 ; Gal 1:16, etc.). God entrusts what he reveals, to his Son that he in his turn may reveal it to the world by means of his pro-phets—in this case, John (cf. Jn 17:8 ; 14:10). **2.** Christ receives, transmits, and is God's Word and John witnesses to that to which Christ witnesses (cf. Jn 5:32, 32, 37). The whole of Jn is concerned with the Utterance of God and the witnesses to it—miracles ; the Baptist ; the Evangelist ; the Holy Spirit. But this revelation is also a prediction of what must ' soon' happen : ' the moment is near '. **3.** Blessings on those who ' read the prophecy aloud ' and on those who listen and who ' keep ' what is written, remembering, reflecting (like Mary, Lk 2:19, 51). Since Christ evidently is speaking himself, who is the ' Angel '? Our Lord himself alludes to his Angel (22:6) and as a rule it is an angel who addresses or summons John. Probably John, under the spell of the OT, felt that he must not suggest that he saw God with his eyes or heard him with his ears, and gravitated towards the OT expression ' The Angel of Yahweh ', i.e. God precisely as revealing his invisible Self.

4-6. Salutation to the Readers, i.e. the ' seven churches ' **b** in ' Asia ', and ascription of glory and power to the Eternal, to Christ, slain, risen, Redeemer and Uni-versal King. **4.** The ' seven Churches '; see § 964f. ' From him that is, and was, and is to come ' : literally, ' from the Existing, the Was, and the Coming ' (moreover, the preposition ἀπό, ' from ', which governs the genitive, is here followed by the nominative :

964b but the words are an immutable title, outside grammatical construction. So too (5) 'from Jesus Christ' (genitive) is followed by 'the Witness' (etc.) in the nominative. But these titles too are exclamatory and detached. 'Who *is*' occurs five times in the Apoc, though twice without 'the Coming' : God's essential Being is an eternal Now. The future participle ἐσόμενος would be less meaningful for John than a word implying not only futurity but Arrival (the Last Day). Humanity can express eternity only by such words as 'He who was, is, and will be'. The 'Seven Spirits that are before the Throne of God'. Who are these ? Either John omits the Holy Spirit, or these are He—but if so, why so strangely spoken of ? Or, if not he, who are these Spirits ? John's word πνεύματα seldom means 'angels', else we might think of the (apocryphal) 'Angels of the Face', supremely mighty spirits who may represent an endeavour to express the totality of God's action 'outwards'. Here I think they represent the Holy Spirit thus—they are the totality of God's activity especially in regard of his Son (*cf.* Is 11:2, where the Spirit reposing on the Messias is, it is true, six-fold in Hebrew but made sevenfold in the LXX : *cf.* too the Seven Eyes of Yahweh and those of the Lamb which rove throughout the world : Zach 4:10 ; Apoc 5:6). Since the Apoc knows the Holy Spirit (*e.g.* 22:17) and that the Son is co-equal with his Father, it seems impossible that John should join seven created spirits with Father and Son as givers of grace and peace, especially as he places them *between* the Father and the Son. Therefore the Seven Spirits are the Holy Spirit whose 'totality' is seen as seven-fold (disconcertingly, maybe, to us but not to one under the spell of the OT) and acting on the Son of God as made flesh—the Witness wholly to be trusted ('faithful'), first-born from the dead (*cf.* Col 1:18 ; *infra*, 19:16, etc.), the Ruler over the kings of the earth (a warning note : the Apoc will have much to say of Christ triumphant over Caesar-anti-God).

c 5. 'To him who loves us (present, not past participle) and loosed us (λύσαντι, not λούσαντι, 'washed') from our sins (*i.e.* by means of) his blood.' 6. He has made us 'a kingdom (*i.e.* a royal race) and priests' (*cf.* Ex 19:6 ; 'a priestly kingdom' ; 1 Pet 2:5, 9 ; 'a holy kingly priesthood'). Our redemption is not only negative—we are no more 'unclean' : it is not only *from*, but *to* ; to incorporation into the Living Christ, and so, to a sharing in his prerogatives. 7. A characteristic cry of exultant vision. 'Bewail themselves' should be 'shall beat (their breasts)' (*cf.* Zach 12:10 ; Jn 19:37). 'With the clouds', *cf.* Dan 7:13 ; Mat 24:30. Might not 'Yes ! Amen !' be joined to 8, as part of the solemn seal set by God on the Prophet's words ? The combination of Greek with Hebrew was significantly emphatic : *cf.* 'Abba ! Father !', Mk 14:36 ; Rom 8:15 ; Gal 4:6. 'Alpha and Omega', first and last letters of the Greek alphabet, *i.e.* that Alphabet from which all words are made (*cf.* Is 41:4 ; 44:6, etc.). This title, proper to God, Eternal, All-Ruler, is given to Christ in 22:13. These eight verses, then, include the whole doctrine of the Trinity, Incarnation, Redemption, the Church, the Judgement of the World (in every age) by Christ. What Un-Veiling can show more than that ?

d 9-20 The Mandatory Vision—John, exiled in the quarry-island Patmos and rapt in ecstasy, is told to write to the Churches of Asia : he turns, and sees the Living Christ moving about among those Communities and receives his Mandate so to write. 9. John in exile is sharing in the perseverance during that persecution which does not prevent Christians from being a Kingdom. He 'found himself' there 'because of the Word of God and the Witness of Jesus' (*i.e.* the witness given by, or to, Jesus, or both). 10. He was 'in the spirit', seized by the spirit of 'prophecy' (*cf.* 1 Cor 14:1, 32 ; Apoc 22:6, etc.). 'The Lord's Day' : Sunday.—Why 'behind me' ? In Homer, the future comes up from behind a man—he does not

foresee it. Or, nothing that John had been seeing or **964c** hearing 'led up to' his 'revelation' (*cf.* Ez 3:12). 11. The Voice tells him to write to the Seven Churches in Asia. 12. He turns to 'look at the Voice'. The Vision, the Hearing, are expressed in terms recalling Daniel (esp. ch 7) and later apocalyptic writings, *e.g.* Enoch 46:14 ff., where the Seer beholds : 'One who had a head of days (*i.e.* was aged ; *i.e.* here, eternal) and his head was white like wool. With him was one whose face was like a man. This is the Son of Man who reveals all the treasures of that which is hidden, because the Lord has chosen him and he will arouse the Kings and the Mighty from their couches and the strong from their thrones. Before the sun and the constellations were created . . . his Name was named before the Lord of Spirits' (48:3 ff.). John uses OT symbols proper to God alone, transferring them to Christ, pre-existing and everlasting. The Figure is definitely human (Dan 7:17 ; and our Lord's use of the expression 'Son of Man' : see § 621h) : in long priestly robe (Ex 28:4 ; *cf.* Zach 3:4) and royal golden girdle (Dan 10:5) : for the flaming eyes his piercing gaze, reading the heart's secrets, *cf.* of an angel (Dan 10:6, 14). 15. The feet of purified bronze (?), firm **e** and indomitable, unlike the clay-and-iron feet of Nabuchodonosor's image (Dan 2:23, 34) : the 'voice of many waters' (*cf.* Ps 92:4, 5), sonorous, even thunderous, yet not harsh. 16. The Word of God, 'more piercing than any two-edged sword, reaching to the division of the soul and the spirit, of the very joints and marrow, disentangling the inmost thought and intentions of the heart' (Heb 4:12). On the Seven Stars, held by Christ, and the Seven Lampstands among which he moves, see on 20. 17. John falls prostrate (*cf.* 19:10 ; 21:8 ; Is 6:5 ; Dan often). The Vision uses our Lord's remembered words, 'Fear not ! ' 'I am the First and the Last' (human history, from end to end, is unintelligible apart from the Incarnation : see § 966d) : 'the Living One (essentially a divine title in OT), and dead did I become ; and see ! I am living for ever and ever !' St John's Gospel and his Apocalypse are built up around the idea of Life (*cf.* Ac 3:15 ; 'Chieftain of Life'). 'The Keys of Death and of Hades' : Christ is Lord also of the Dead (Death and Hell are here 'places', the world of the bodily-dead : *cf.* 6:8 for personification). He who holds the keys of city, house, treasury, controls what is in them (*cf.* Is 22:22. In Mt 16:19, the Messias inherits the Keys of the Kingdom of Heaven and hands them over to Peter). 20. Defines the nature of this book—it is to contain 'things that are', and 'what shall be after these'. Present, and Future. But as a 'mystery', as having an inner meaning, symbolized. A hint is at once given of how to approach the apocalyptic symbols—Christ moves among seven lampstands : these are the Communities to which John must write : and the 'stars' that Christ holds are the 'angels' of those communities.

II 1-III 22 The 'Covering Letter to the Seven f Church of Asia'—1. Asia is the proconsular province. True, it contained many Christian centres besides those here named, *e.g.* Hierapolis, Colossae, Magnesia. But 'seven', as always, means 'totality'. But why choose *these* seven towns ? Ramsay (*Letters*, ch 14) thinks they were situated on a 'circular road' by which Rome linked up the most important parts of the province. John would naturally send his letter first to Ephesus ; his courier would then go north to Smyrna and Pergamum ; then, south-east, and then back by the central part of the road to Ephesus. But, why choose unimportant towns like Philadelphia rather than *e.g.* Cyzicus ? Ramsay conjectures that 'Asia' was divided into seven 'postal' areas within which letters might be distributed from a centre commercially or otherwise important. But other towns might be *Christian-wise* more important. What are the 'Angels' of the Churches ? Elsewhere in Apoc 'angel' means, as usual, a personal spirit acting as messenger. Does it here mean simply the messenger who carried the

964f letters ? No : why write *to* messengers ? Nor do the symbolic stars suit them. Are they the bishops of the various communities ? The Latin Fathers incline to this view. But it were too severe to make a bishop responsible for the faults of an entire community ! The Greek Fathers tend to think of Guardian Angels. Still, such angels can hardly be *blamed*, though Daniel (10:13 and 12:1) equips nations and rivers with ' princes ' who are angels and actually opposed to one another. The extremes are clear—Christ, the Sun (16) ; and the Churches—the Lamps. In between are the Stars, the angels. Three ' planes of reality ', with appropriate symbols. Not that John was borrowing from Plato that intermediate world of ' ideas ', realities higher than their poor concrete version, the ' things ' that surround us. The Jews already had a floating belief in a more ' real ' because a ' heavenly ' Ark, Book of the Law, Temple furniture and so forth. In this document, we see John's mind hovering, so to say, between heaven and earth. He is sending a heavenly message in a heavenly way to groups of men who should themselves be heavenly. He sees, as with Christ's eyes, the perfect Community ; conscious that the earthly fact by no means corresponds with that, he calls the ' ideal ' an ' angel ' : what other word could he dispose of ? With his eye, first, on the ideal, he writes to it, and sends it with a message to the ' real ', soon enough forgetting the ' ideal ' and its symbol and focusing on the real, but always reverting to Christ, that Sun from which alone comes the fire that sets the lamps alight.

g **1-7 The Letter to Ephesus**—Ephesus, by far the most important city of ' Asia ' as governmental centre, ' gate between Rome and Orient ', rich international market, home of general and philosophical education and magic arts (*Ephesia grammata* ; *cf.* Ac 19:19) ; famed above all for the immemorial cult and temple of the Asiatic goddess whom the Greeks called Artemis and the Romans Diana (columns from a temple 500 years older than what John saw are in the British Museum). Its vast precinct was an asylum for criminals, a home of prostitutes, and contained a shrine of Augustus and, later, three associate Caesar-temples. **1.** Christ moves around among the Lampstands : in this central city he is seen as it were *in* all the churches of ' Asia '. **2.** Unsanctioned itinerant preachers come there (*cf.* 2 Tim 3:5-6) : but the Ephesian Christians would not tolerate heterodoxy (and *cf.* 6), though (**4**) they had grown slack in good works. **5.** Let them repent, else, ' I am coming at thee ! ' Christ would remove the lamp of Ephesus ! **7.** But the persevering and victorious should eat of the Tree of Life in the eternal Paradise (contrast the veto in Gen 3:22). Are there allusions here to the frequent shifting of the Ephesian population owing to the constant silting up of the harbour ? And to the sacred Artemisian tree on early Ephesian coins ? This will not seem far-fetched when we see, below, how John nearly always gives a side-glance to something local and familiar. On the Nicolaitans ; see below, 15.

h **8-11 Smyrna**—The ' beauty-spot ', the ' idol ' (ἄγαλμα) of Asia. Its palaces on the eastward hills were known as its ' wreath ' or coronet. Almost from 200 B.C. it was devoted to the imperial cult and even under Antiochus Epiphanes opened a temple to the Goddess Rome. Its loyalty earned it the title ' Faithful '. Its Jewish community was savagely hostile to Christians : it would be Jews who egged on the populace to demand the death of its bishop St Polycarp (A.D. 156) during the imperial games. **8.** Christ, First, but also Last, slain, but now alive, (**9**) knows their poverty—' but thou art rich ! '—and the blasphemies of the Jews— ' Jews ' ? A misnomer ! A ' synagogue ' ? Yes ! but of Satan ! *Cf.* 24. **10.** The Smyrniots shall suffer persecution—sharp, including martyrdoms, but short (' 10 days ' : on John's use of numbers, see § 969g). Let them be ' faithful '—to death ! Christ would give them a wreath of Life, nor (**11**) would they be hurt by the ' second death ', that of the soul.

12-17 Pergamum—Whence ' parchment ', there **965a** fabricated. A colossal altar of Zeus dominated both city and plain. Caesar-worship developed as from 29 B.C. A centre for the cult of the healer-hero Asklepios : sick pilgrims slept in his temple : Aelius Aristides (2nd cent.) having done so received a new name, Theodorus, and was given a sacred emblem that he carried about as pious consolation. If this practice was normal, 17 may allude to it. **13.** This concentration of paganism may explain ' the Throne of Satan : where Satan dwells '. The local Christians had held firm, even in the days of Antipas (a protomartyr ? otherwise unknown). **14-16.** Still, they contain men who ' hold the teaching of Balaam who taught Balak (Num 31:16) to ensnare the Israelites—to eat idols' food and commit fornication. So thou too hast, even thou, men who similarly hold the teachings of the Nicolaitans '. (No reason for connecting this name with the deacon of Ac 6:5.) St Paul, writing to the Ephesians and Colossians shows that fore-runners of the Gnostics (see § 963c and below, 20 and 24) existed who encouraged ' laxism ' sharing in feasts where food coming from temple-sacrifices was eaten (not illegitimate in itself, but suggesting that the banqueters joined too in the actual worship ; see 1 Cor 8), and where immorality often resulted from such orgies. The ' laxists ' said : ' These meals are merely social, not religious : no risk of sin ! ' John rejects this : Christ will ' come at ' the guilty with his sword sharper than any such casuistry, or than the persecutor's. **17.** The Victor would be given, not *that* food, but the ' hidden manna ', and a white token, medallion, engraved with a ' new name ' known to none but the recipient. The Manna, ' bread from heaven ', had been hidden in the Ark (Ex 16:23 ; *cf.* Heb 9:4) : tradition said that it should be restored at the time of the Messias (*cf.* Jn 6) : in the catacombs the Eucharist was symbolized by a manna-jar. Again, it was widely believed that each thing had an ' inner self ', to which a secret name corresponded. He who knew that name had power over the essence of the thing. This ' secret ' name was sometimes engraved in magic characters on a token of ivory or stone, to be worn round the neck or as a ring. Christ by his union with the soul gives it a new ' self ' known only to him and to his Christian. The Promises increasingly concern this supernatural, indeed Eucharistic, union.

18-29 Thyatira—Commercially very active, with **b** guilds of bakers, dyers, tanners, potters, wool-workers, linen, leather, bronze, etc. Life was practically impossible save in a trade-guild which meant joining in its feasts. **19 ff.** John praises the Thyatirans : but, they tolerate a ' modern Jezebel ' (see 3 Kg 16-21 ; 4 Kg 9), who like the ' modern Balaam ' (14), seduces them into laxity—infidelity to the One God who had espoused Israel was immemorially called adultery (**22**). He whose flaming eyes penetrate all specious excuses and read men's hearts bids them break off this adulterous alliance—she shall indeed be placed in a bed, but one of torment : The Victorious shall share in Christ's own victory (27 ff.), and he will give them that Morning Star which is himself (*cf.* 22:16 ; 2 Pet 1:19) —the Prophets were lamps ; Christ, the Dawn-Star rising in men's hearts. (Why not the Sun ? full daylight ? Because while we live by faith, we exist at best but in a twilight.) Thyatira had a female Sibyl who ' prophesied ' there : later, the Montanists had heretic ' prophetesses ' there : so this ' Jezebel ' may have been no mere collectivity, but an actual woman, claiming to reveal ' deep things '—the ' Depth ' was afterwards a technical Gnostic word. ' Deep things ? ' cries John. ' May be ! But the " deep things " of Satan ! ' (*cf.* 9). ' I lay on you no other burden ', *i.e.* no fresh obligations : John remembers the decree in Ac 15:28 : ' (We) . . . lay on you no further burden, save to abstain from things sacrificed to idols . . .' John had joined in making that decree : the recurrence of the subject-matter revives the formula.

965c III 1-6 Sardis—Built on a hill that looked impregnable but was fissured mud, not rock, it had twice been surprised and taken, by the Persian Cyrus and by Antiochus the Great. Its special cult was the Nature-Goddess of Asia, Cybele (Artemis, etc.) but also that of the Emperor. Had the local Christians succumbed to these? **1-3.** 'I know thy works'—hitherto a formula of praise : here, stern rebuke. If the Sardians do not repent, Christ will come ' like a thief ', just when unexpected (cf. 16:15, certainly an echo of Mt 24:42 ff.; Lk 12:36 ff.). **4 f.** 'Names ', i.e. persons. 'White' robes. In the Graeco-Roman world white symbolized not only purity but also joy and especially triumph.

d 7-13 Philadelphia—A small earthquake-racked town : for long, its people had hardly dared to live within its walls. The Christians here were few, but faithful. **7.** Christ, the Holy One (in the Apoc, always a divine title), the True One (i.e. authentic : no false Messias : used ten times in the Apoc, nine in John's Gospel, once in the First Epistle : otherwise, only four times in Heb and once in 1 Thess—a thoroughly Johannine word), opens with his divinely authoritative Keys (cf. Is 22:22) **(8)** a door for the Philadelphians' influence. **9.** Persecution was to reach them from Jews rather than from pagans—' men from the synagogue of Satan—who say they are Jews but are not—they lie ! '—yet even they shall recognize that ' I have loved thee '. **10.** But a persecution is about to break out ' everywhere '. If the Philadelphians hold good ' and shall have preserved the doctrine of Christ's endurance ' (i.e. the teaching that the Christian must persevere as Christ did, and for him) they shall be kept safe here and for ever. **12.** Christ will make the Conqueror a column in God's Temple and never shall he leave it : Christ will engrave on it the Name of God, that of the New Jerusalem, and, ' my own new Name '. Our incorporation into Christ. The columns are not the temple, yet without them it cannot stand (cf. St Paul : without the head, the body dies : but without the body, the head is meaningless : see Col 1:18). On columns and tiles of temples was often engraved the name of the god to whom they were sacred : here, the Christian has on him the consecrating name of God, but also that of the supernatural Jerusalem, the Church (cf. Gal 4:26 ; Heb 12:22) : and also, Christ's own ' New Name ' (above, 2:17) : he gives a new name, a new self, to the Christian : here, he receives a New Name owing to the Christian's incorporation into him : the Mystical Christ-Jesus and his Christians co-corporate is always growing. See Col 1:24 ; 2:19.

e 14-21 Laodikia—A proud self-sufficient city famed for banks and gold-traffic ; for its glossy black wool ; its eye-salve (collyrium) exported throughout the Empire, and opposite the hot springs of Hierapolis, nausea-provoking when tepid. **14.** Christ, proclaiming his absolute paramountcy, says (15 f.) that the tepidity of the Laodikeans will make him vomit them out of his mouth. **17.** They say : ' I am rich ! I have made my money ! I am in need of nothing ! '—' and dost not know that thou art the pitiable one—poor, blind and naked '. **19.** Terrible rebuke, but due precisely to Christ's loving them, and followed by words of tenderest intimacy. **20.** ' See, I am standing at the door and am knocking. If a man opens to me, I will come in to him, and sup with him, and he with me.' The Communion of ' one with One ', even in this life, but looking forward to the final call when the victorious soul shall share Christ's throne even as Christ shares God's. (3:14 is almost verbally what St Paul wrote in Col 1:15. He meant that letter to be read by neighbouring Laodikia too.)

These letters vividly portray the life of Asiatic Christians—mostly humble folks ; poor, and the poorer because of the demands of their Faith, and tempted to compromise with prosperous paganism—to yield to the suggestion that a pagan-Christian mysticism was conceivable ; to be beaten down, if not by the insane worship of the Nature-Goddess,

then by the overwhelming dominance of imperial **965e** Rome. And vivid is the personality of John—inflexible, still the ' son of the thunderbolt ', yet intimately aware of each detail of his readers' environment—his symbolism is never haphazard : his heart is as tender as Paul's. Complete and authoritative is his theology of Christ, eternal Son of God, all-wise, all-powerful, yet ' moving around ' among his Christians, knocking till they open, building them into himself, giving them that Manna, that Dawn-Star which are himself ; giving, and receiving, the New Name proper to the New Self—Christ and Christian co-corporate.

PART A

The Apocalypse of the Future : (IV:1-XI:17). **966a**
A (I) A Double Preparatory Vision (remaining as an unchanged background to all that follows).
(a) Ch 4. The everlasting worship of God by all Creation—**1-11.** John sees the Throne of God, and the Universe from heaven's point of view. **1.** ' I saw ' (aorist) ' a door lying wide open ' (perfect). The fact is always there ; but only those whose eyes are ' enlightened ' see it. John hears the first voice and sees the door (already a spiritual communication), but forthwith ' became in the Spirit ' (a yet deeper ecstasy). **2.** ' A Throne was set '—built ; decked. The Enthroned is not, as in Ezechiel, human-wise described or even named. **3.** He is ' like the jasper and sardius to look upon ' and surrounded by a rainbow ' like an emerald '. (John emphasizes ' like ', ' as it were ' : he can find no better translation of what he sees.) The stones are probably green and red : but why a rainbow ? and why ' emerald ' ? A symbol, since the flood, of enduring covenanted mercy : ' upon us is established his mercy : The loyalty of the Lord endureth for ever ' (Ps 116:2). Andrew of Caesarea (6th–7th cent.?) says : ' The divine Nature is ever green and flowering '—σμαραγδίζουσα—participle : a tremulous play of green. **4.** The Throne is surrounded by 24 Elders, also enthroned : a spiritual court or senate (cf. Is 24:23 ; Dan 7:10). Why 24 ? Not a normal symbolical number. But surely, no reference to the 24 courses of priests (1 Par 24:7 ff.) ; still less, to the 24 Babylonian gods north and south of the Zodiac ! Surely, the ' Church ', the Elect, from ' beginning to end '—the 12 Patriarchs and the 12 Apostles—the ideal Church, as in God's mind. It were over-logical to ask how John can bow down to Apostles of whom he is one ; or how he sees the Church before the Book is opened which relates its history (ch 5). These 24 are triumphant (white robes, royal and priestly crowns, cf. 4:10 ; 5:11). **5.** ' Thunders, voices and lightnings ' : traditional in Theophanies. The Seven Lamps, the Seven Spirits of God (see above 1:4) : the Holy Spirit, symbolized, as often, by the multiplicity-totality of his gifts or energizing : septiformis munere. **6a.** The **b** crystal Sea ' in front of ', i.e. all round the Throne. The Hebrew visualized the earth as flat, with waters ' under ' it ; and above it, the solid vault of the ' firmament ' supporting the ' upper waters ' on which rested the Throne of God (cf. Gen 1 ; Ex 24:10). But since John never uses any detail as merely decorative but always as symbolic, this Sea may well figure the absolute inaccessibility, the ' otherness ', of the Enthroned. **6b.** ' In the midst of the Throne and around the Throne, 4 Beings—how translate ζῷα ? Not ' animals ' merely. ' Creatures ? ' Inadequate ; half contemptuous to our ears. ' Living Beings ? ' Accurate, but clumsy. We resign ourselves to ' Beings '. They are either at the four corners of the Throne if it is square ; or at the ends of its diameters if it is visualized as circular. I think one ' Being ' fronted John ; one was seen from behind ; the other two, in profile. But did John visualize details ? How, for example, could he see (8) that these Beings were interiorly ' full of eyes ' ? **7b.** Tradition (Ez 1-15 ff. and many apocryphal books) placed four mysterious Beings usually under God's chariot or throne. Ezechiel

66b derived his plastic imagery from the composite Babylonian figures (originally astronomical figures), and equipped each Being with all four faces, human, lion, bull, eagle. John simplifies Ezechiel's Cherubs but joins to them the six-winged Seraphs of Isaias (ch 6) and also their triple *Sanctus* : and possibly the 'Watchers' (the eyes) of apocryphal tradition. But what *are* these Beings? Irenaeus (*Adv. Haer.*, iii, 11, 8) is the first we know to have applied them to the 4 Evangelists—simply because they *are* 4 : there are 4 regions of the earth ; 4 main winds ; and the Maker of the World gives us his Gospel accordingly as fourfold. But their innumerable 'eyes' signify consciousness—unsleeping, universal. It is in accord with traditional symbolism to see in them the whole of Nature which, even if inanimate, is, 'after its kind', giving glory to God. Thus the whole of Creation— pure spirits ; supernaturalized mankind ; Nature *as God knows it*—joins in giving him that praise which is the true end of its existence. **9.** 'When' should be 'whensoever', and the following verbs in the future. John, aware of what his document will contain, foresees a whole series of such acclamations.

c **(b) 5:1-14**—A scroll is seen in God's hand, covered with writing but so closely sealed that no one can read it. John laments this, but hears that the Lion of the Tribe of Judah has conquered and can open it. Forthwith he sees between the Throne and those who surround it a Lamb that had been slain and yet is standing upright. The Lamb advances and takes the scroll and all Creation acclaims him as worthy to open it since his Blood has ransomed men throughout the world, and made them kings and priests before God. The whole spiritual world and then all Creation repeat and amplify this acclaim. **1-5.** The Sealed Scroll (*cf.* Is 29:11 and especially Ez 2:9) is an ὀπισθόγραφος, *i.e.* written on both sides, but so tightly sealed (*seven* seals) that it cannot be unrolled and read by any created thing. But the Lion of Judah, of the stock of David (*i.e.* the Messianic King) has conquered, and so, can do so. This scroll is the world's history, an enigma *apart from* the Incarnation, Saving Death and **d** Resurrection of the Son of God. **6-9.** The Lamb, slain yet alive (*cf.* 1:18), stands ' between ' the Throne and Creation—a Mediator. His ' 7 horns ' are the plenitude of Power ; the ' 7 eyes ', the plenitude of Wisdom (see 1:4 ; 4:5 ; Zach 3:9-10 ; 4:10—says the Seven Eyes of Yahweh). This plenitude is in God, and in the Lamb, and is sent by him throughout the world. The symbols are not disconnected, but indicate the Trinity. **7.** When the Lamb ' takes ' the scroll, **(9)** Nature sings a ' new ' song. ' Newness ' is a key-word in the Apoc : ' behold, I make all things new ' (21:5 and often). A ' new song ' often in OT, as fit for solemn occasions (Ps 32:3, etc.). Nature is not to be abolished, but made new (*cf.* 2:17 ; 3:12 ; 21:1). Nature, then, offers praise and prayer (incense, already symbolical in OT) : the Lamb prophesied in Is 53:7 as future, *has* now been sacrificed and effected a universal ransom : *he* is worthy to explain the Book—in fact, *is* its Explanation. (The Martyrs, by union with him, share in this worthiness : *cf.* 6:9.) **9-12.** After this whole group of sub-angelic Nature, innumerable spirits (*cf.* Dan 7:10) utter their sevenfold shout of praise. **13.** Then the whole of Creation unites in worship before the One Throne belonging alike to God and to the Lamb. ' Heaven, earth, and under-earth ' is merely part of Hebrew literary tradition : ' all that is '. Upon this praise, Nature and Church alike set their ' Amen ', seal of absolute agreement. (In 12, Greek MSS have ' riches ' ; the Latin ' Godhead ' is wrong, for Godhead is not one among several attributes belonging to the Lamb on the same plane as the others.)

e **VI 1-VIII 1 The Breaking of Seven Seals**—John cannot use his imagery quite consistently, for so long as the scroll remains fastened by even one seal it cannot be unrolled. But he is offering a gradual exhibition of great principles, or energies at work, discernible in

life by the keen-sighted. One of the ' Beings ' calls **966e** ' Come ! '—not to John, but to the ensuing Apparition, which does not emerge from the scroll, but passes across the Seer's field of vision. There follows **(a) the breaking of a group of 4 seals—1.** The First Seal. A Horseman appears (*cf.* Zach 1:8-11 ; 6:1-7). He rides a white horse and receives a bow and a crown and goes forth to conquer and again to conquer. Nothing will persuade me that this horseman is the same as the ' Word of God ' in ch 19 simply because each rides on a conqueror's white horse and is crowned. The remaining 3 horsemen are all disasters ; each is summoned in the same way ; they are all on one plane of thought and imagery. John introduces at once a *main theme* of his book—what we should call ' aggressive imperialism ' in the widest sense : later, it will be seen as Roman imperialism in particular. Why a ' bow ' ? Possibly because of the haunting contemporary threat to Rome, the archer Parthians (ch 9). **3-4.** The Second Seal. A Red Horse. Its rider creates War. No imperialism possible without it. **5-6.** The Third Seal. A Black Horse. Its rider holds scales : ' A measure of wheat for a denarius (a day's wage) : three measures of barley (coarser grain) for the same—but do not injure oil or wine (olives and vines) '. The inevitable result of even victorious war : it reduces the very victors to penury—a whole day's wage is demanded for the minimum needed for existence. **7-8.** The Fourth Seal. A ' Wan ' Horse— **f** the colour of decay is meant. His rider is Death ; his escort Hell—the same thing. War is followed by famine and pestilence : this trio often occurs in OT and in our experience. (LXX often translates Hebrew ' death ' by pestilence which suits this context. Idle to say that Death is allowed to kill by means of death.) The ' wild beasts ' may be meant literally. Civilization collapses and men are too weak to restrain them. Or, men revert to ' jungle law '.—In Zach 1:8 ; 6:1-8 the 4 Horses are the 4 Winds (often symbolizing God's messengers or instruments of judgement.—Ps 103:4 ; Jer 49:36 ; Dan 7:24, and below, ch 8). All the more reason for seeing here 4 objects of the same *sort* under cavalry symbols. This, then, is the series : Extension of Godless Power : this involves war : this creates terrible decline in ' standard of life ' which unless arrested brings about famine and epidemic. John, however, intending to write more, says (8) that only a quarter of the earth was destroyed. **(b) 9-17 A group of Two Seals**—The Prayers of the **g** Martyrs in heaven (9-11) and their effect on earth (12-17). **9 f.** ' Under the altar.' ' The ', not ' an ' : John has pictured all the heavenly ' furniture ' though he has not yet thought of mentioning it. ' Under ' : ' at the foot of ' the altar of Holocaust, where the sacrificial blood was shed. The ' life ' is in the blood. The immediate perspective is formed by the Martyrs under Nero (A.D. 64) asking when justice shall triumph and being told to wait for the martyrdoms under Domitian (A.D. 96) : but beyond these are all the martyrdoms of history. **11.** The ' white robe ' shows that *these* Martyrs have already triumphed. ' How long ? ', a dramatic enquiry : *cf.* 18, 20 ; 19:2 ; and especially Esdras 4:35-37 where the souls of the righteous dead ask when their reward shall come. An archangel says : ' When the number of your compeers shall be complete.'

VI 12-VII 17 The Sixth Seal—A vision displaying pre- **h** liminaries to the ending of the world and the salvation of the elect. **12-17.** Earthquake : sun blackened : moon like blood ; the sky itself like a scroll torn in the middle and rolling up to its two ends. ' Apocalyptic and eschatological dialect '. See Agg 2:6 ; Nah 1:6 ; Mal 3:2 and Lk 21:36 ; Jl 2:30-31, quoted by St Peter, Ac 2:39 ; Is 34:4 ; used by our Lord in Mt 24:29 ; Mk 13:24 ; Lk 21:35. The ' dialect ' persisted for centuries, *e.g.* to describe the death of some important Jew. The cosmic catastrophes represent (as often in OT, especially earthquakes) social upheavals : these always precede, on a grand scale, the break-up, or

967a end, of a ' world ' or social order.—(c) **VII 1-17 A double vision interposed**—The vision of the actual consummation is ' held up ' while (a) the Elect from the Twelve Tribes are sealed with God's sign ; and (b) those from all the rest of the world. Why did John construct the Apoc on this curious plan ? His Gospel certainly looks back to *Genesis*—' In the beginning ' : the ' water and the Spirit ' : *cf.* too his use of the ' tree of life '. Does he so look back here too, in his account of the creation of a *new* heaven and earth ? I think it possible that John, building his whole book on a system of 7's, like the 7 days of the First Creation, saw a distinction in kind between the ' work ' of the first four days, that of the fifth and sixth, and the unique consummatory ' rest ' of the 7th. But why does he throughout insert a double vision between the 6th and 7th of each ' group ' ? Perhaps simply because here, in ch 7, he wished to allude to the salvation of the elect under the two dispensations, and then, having done this once, liked to preserve the same numerical construction throughout. John sees, therefore, a ' check ' imposed upon the destroying winds till the ' servants of God ' in Israel, and then throughout the world, be signed for exemption upon their foreheads (1:8 ; 9:17). In Apoc and later Jewish literature angels are held to control the elements. The 4 winds, if let **b** loose, would destroy the earth. **2-3.** Therefore an Angel from the sunrise—source of light and rescue— forbids this till the Elect be ' sealed ' on their foreheads See Ez 9 : an angel marks those exempt from the destruction carried out by 4 others. *Cf.* the marking of the Israelites' doorposts in Ex before the passing of the Destroying Angel. Soldiers too and slaves were branded thus as belonging to a legion or a master. ' Seal ' was a very early Christian name for baptism (and confirmation) : *cf.* too 2 Cor 1:22 ; Eph 1:13, and the caricature, the Mark of the Beast, below. *This* seal, then, has nothing to do with the Seven Seals : those sealed up the scroll ; these stamp a mark on the forehead identifying the person as ' exempt '. **4-8.** ' 144,000 ' : this vast figure—100 times 12 times 12— means an enormous multitude : John, like Paul, foresees a great conversion of Israel to Christ. Why is Dan omitted from the list of tribes ? Because John distinguishes ' Joseph ', *i.e.* his own Ephraim, from Manasses, so that one tribe had to be left out to preserve the number 12 ? Still, why *Dan* ? Because tradition said that ' Antichrist should come from Dan ', **c** so that that tribe was treated as reprobate ? **9-12.** Then John sees the innumerable host of the Saved from throughout the world : heaven joins in their 7-fold cry of Glory. **15-17** display the present and future beatitude of the Saved, in exquisite form and rhythm. Note the paradoxes—the Blood that washes white (14) : the Lamb who is a Shepherd (17). The fountains of living water : *cf.* Jn 4:10, etc. ; 7:38 ff. ; Apoc 21:6, etc. Compare Ps 22:15, ' shall spread his tent over them ' : the word is found only here and John 1:14. ' Day and night ', *i.e.* always, with unconscious memory of the continuous Temple-worship. But in 21:22, 25 ; 22:5, no more Temple exists, nor night. The ' great ' tribulation may indeed be the final persecution ; or that which endures throughout the Church's history ; or Domitian's, or all three, according to John's ' focus ' : but with it endures her triumph. **VIII 1 (d). The Seventh Seal**—Silence in Heaven ' as though for half an hour '. Not merely because this series of visions ends, and with a ' sabbath-rest ', but because the Consummation is ineffable. The vision outstrips words, symbols, and thought itself. One of the most overwhelming ' revelations ' of this Book.

d A. (II) VIII 2-XI 18.

A Double Preparatory Vision (a) 8:2-4—The prayer of the Martyrs in heaven. **2.** The ' Seven Angels '. Tradition placed 7, 6, 4 or 3 specially ' great ' Angels before God's Face (*cf.* Tob 12:15). To each is here given a trumpet. Throughout the OT and *cf.* Mt

24:31 and 1 Cor 15:52, trumpets symbolize the summons **96** of God, especially to Judgement, but also, the promulgation of feasts and disasters. Another angel takes his stand on (the steps of ?) the altar of burnt-sacrifice whence he brings burning coal to put it in a censer full of incense (the prayers of the Saints : *cf.* 3:4 ; 6:9-11). (b) **5.** Then the burning coal with clouds of incense rising from it is thrown down to the earth, *cf.* Lk 12:42. These Prayers have a double effect— they obtain mercy save when it is refused ; but even when mercy is rejected and they provoke chastisement, it is chastisement that can be curative. This prepares for the actual sounding of the Trumpets. This new series of visions stands in no time-relation to what has preceded them, though their symbolism begins to look forward to what John will use in the second Part of the Book. The literary background is on the whole the Plaguing of Egypt.

The Sounding of Seven Trumpets (a) 7-12 A group of e 4 Trumpets—A third of the earth and its vegetation is destroyed : then, a third of the sea and what is on or in it : then, a third of the fresh waters : then, a third of the heavenly bodies. These occurrences are not consecutive nor to be taken literally. (How visualize the destruction of a ' third ' of seas and rivers ? or the darkening of a third of the night ? And the Sixth Seal showed us the stars as already fallen.) This new set of visions shows us the *same* thing under *different* (more concrete) symbols. Conceivably John has seen an Aegean thunderstorm, and rain reddened by Sahara-dust, or a volcanic eruption, or a meteor ; but, more probably, his imagination is stimulated by the plagues of Egypt. **11.** ' Wormwood ' traditionally signified perversion of justice, or the fruits of idolatry, or divine chastisements (Am 5:7 ; 6:13 ; Deut 29:12 ; Jer 9:14, 15). The waters are not embittered because the star is made of wormwood ; but because they are corrupted, the star is so named. Possibly the Eagle announcing further disasters is introduced because of the different character of those woes—they concern men and spirits, not inanimate nature, and even of that, only part, not even half, was destroyed.

(b) IX 1-21 A group of Two Trumpets—The literary **f** and psychological inspiration of the strange imagery of the following passage is clear ; but lack of space may make the attempted explanation seem over-dogmatic. Briefly, John sees a host of evil spirits, and a host of invading Parthians. He symbolizes the spirits by ' locusts '. But, having *all* that he proposes to say already in his mind, the imagery proper to each part infuses itself into the other : he equips the locusts with features suited to the Parthian cavalry, and the Parthian horsemen, with features proper to the diabolic locusts. **1.** The Star that has *already* fallen from heaven (perfect tense : *cf.* Lk 18:18) is the Angel of the Abyss : in Hebrew, Abaddon ; in Greek, Apolluon. Abaddon, ' Destruction ', meant Sheol (Hades), the pit into which souls went, but it could be personified, as here (*cf.* Job 26:6 ; 28:22). The Pit is pictured as having a shaft up to the earth, with a padlocked lid. The Destroying Spirit receives its key (*cf.* 1:18 ; the Keys of Death and Hades ; and 20:1). **2 ff.** He unlocks it : a column of smoke **g** arises whence issue evil spirits dense as a plague of locusts. But they are scorpion-locusts, able to sting with their tails (3, 10), and are like battle-horses (7), making a noise like a cavalry charge (9) ; they wear gold crowns, have human faces and hair like women's, and wear iron breastplates. They are not allowed to injure vegetation (as locusts do) but to hurt men (as scorpions do) yet not to kill them. This plague lasts five months. For plagues of locusts, see Ex 10:12-15, but especially Jl 1:4, and ch 2 where a real plague of locusts is *idealized* as an invading army—in Apoc the invading army is *symbolized* as diabolic locusts. Locusts have often (apart from the whirr, indeed roar, of their onset) suggested a horse-like resemblance (German : ' Heupferd '. Italian : ' cavaletta '. An

67g Arab saying is that they are, as to their head, like horses ; their chest, like lions ; their feet, like camels ; their body, like snakes ; their antennae, like virgins) : but John's locusts have tails ' like scorpions '. Why ? (a) Nearer-East art was full of composite figures— men-scorpions, men-horses, men-ants often having one or more scorpion-tails. A similar sort of figure represented the zodiac sign ' Sagittarius, ' the Archer ' : the Greek Apollo was an archer whose arrows inflicted pestilence : the *kind* of image was, therefore, familiar in John's environment. (b) But why does he here select, precisely, scorpions ? We shall see this when we reach the 6th Trumpet—enough to say, now, that the Parthians were eminently horsemen, *and* archers, and able to shoot back over their shoulders, as scorpions strike with their tails back over their body. So the devil-locusts are seen also as devil-scorpions. **13 ff.** A voice from one of the ' horns ' (i.e. at one of the corners) of the Altar bids the 4 angels who are ' bound ' by the Euphrates to be loosed so that the winds may destroy one third of mankind (i.e. of the civilized world). These are not ' bad ' angels, but simply in charge of winds and hitherto forbidden to let them blow. The Book of the Ethiopic Enoch (56:5) speaks of the Parthians as sent against the Holy Land and the Syriac version of 4 Esdras says : 'Let these 4 kings (cf. Daniel's ' princes '?) be loosed, that are bound by the great river Euphrates, who shall destroy one third of mankind '. This alludes to the Parthians, invasion by whom was anxiously feared by the Roman

h Empire. **16.** The Parthians are essentially horsemen —John hears that their forces are 200 millions. Here the material fact begins to take on features proper to the spiritual symbol, the locusts, just as they had taken on features proper to the Parthians. **17.** These horsemen have breastplates the colour of fire, hyacinth and brimstone, the horses have heads like lions snorting flame, smoke and sulphur ; their tails were like serpents with heads—with *these* they do their harm. Thus the picture of the scorpions ' colours ' that of the cavalry just as the long-haired backward-shooting Parthian provided the scorpion-element in the description of locusts with antennae like floating female hair. The two visions shoot details back and forth into one another : the devils are ' Parthianized ', the Parthians become half Satanic. But both the details, and the method, so strange to us, would have seemed almost common-place to John's contemporaries. Of course the Parthians stand but as symbol of all world-enduring onslaughts upon God's elect : Satan keeps stirring up wicked men who become the very instruments of hell : indeed, the Parthians as such remain hardly a moment in the forefront of John's consciousness. **20-21.** Despite these woes, men do not repent of their idolatries—their sinful worship of whatsoever they *prefer to God.*

968a (c) **X:1-XI:14 A Double Vision interposed. An Angel with the ' Little Book ': the Two Witnesses**—Ch 10 describes a strong radiant Angel, holding a *small* book. Seven thunder-claps resound, but John is told not to write down what they say. He is then ordered to ' eat ' this bitter-sweet book and to prophesy to many races, nations and kings. Ch 11:1-14 describes how he is then bidden to measure the Temple, excluding the Outer Court which like the City itself is abandoned to pagan desecration for 42 months. Two Witnesses prophesy for 1,260 days—they are the two olive-trees, the two lamps burning before the Lord ; during their prophetic period they can take vengeance on men and on inanimate nature alike. Then ' the Beast from the Abyss ' shall conquer and slay them : they lie exposed for 3½ days and are then assumed into heaven. An earthquake : many perish, but the rest give glory to God. **10:1.** The Angel (cf. the announcing Angel of 5:2) : he is a resplendent blaze of light—no need to visualize details as e.g. Dürer did. He holds a ' small ' book, open—the visions will be narrower and will concern the Roman and the Asiatic world as such, displayed to all eyes. Since the unrolling

of the first great scroll there are no more secrets (yet **968a** see 3 and 4). He strikes from sea to land—I think, from Rome (overseas, for John) to Asia. The vision is an ' intermediate ' ecstasy : John is not now in that heaven to which he was told to ' come up ' (4:1). **3-4.** ' *The* Seven Thunders ' : there is still **b** something that John must not tell : is it some closer definition of the Consummation ? **5b.** But the Angel swears solemnly that ' there shall be no more delay ' (not ' time ' : 6) : not indeed that the Parousia is imminent—it awaits the Seventh Trumpet : but the world-age in which John was living *was* rapidly reaching its end : ' No more delay ! ' cf. 6:11 ; 2 Pet 3:3 ff. **7 ff.** The 7th Trumpet will denote the ' consummation of the Mystery of God ', ' the joyous news that he has given to his servants the Prophets to proclaim ', that is, the accomplishments of the whole of the divine plan. **11.** But before that, John ' must ' prophesy what more exactly concerns Imperial Rome as such.—The ' eating ' of the book (assimilation of its contents)— from Ez 3:1-3. It contains God's words—therefore, sweetness : but, his terrible judgements—therefore, John *adds* bitterness.

XI:1 ff. **The ' measuring ' of the Temple, its Altar** **c** **and Worshippers**—**1.** Modelled on Ez 40 ; 43:13-17, and Zach 2 where the ' new ' all-holy Jerusalem is measured for preservation and purification. **2a.** The ' outer court ' and the City at large are to be given up to pagan desecration. (The essential Church shall not perish even during world-persecution.) **2b.** This desecration lasts, in apocalyptic language, ' a time, times and half a time ' (see Dan 7:25, etc.), i.e. 3½ years, 42 months, or 1,260 days—' persecution-time ', stereotyped since the original 3½ years (June 168- Dec. 165 B.C.) during which the Jews were subjugated by the would-be imperialist paganizer Antiochus Epiphanes. **3.** But God keeps two penitentially garbed Witnesses there. Why two ? First, because two witnesses were the necessary minimum in Jewish law for witness to be valid. Then, John's recollection of Zacharias's ' measuring ' makes him think also of that prophet's figure of the People as the ' lamp ' fed by the oil from two olive-trees, doubtless Josue and Zorobabel, heads of the priesthood and of the royal house. **4.** Here the remaining witnesses are both lamp *and* oil ; 5, 6 ; finally, because of the firm expectation of at least one pre-Messianic witness— always Elias (cf. Mal 3:1-3 ; 4:5 ; and Mt 11:10) ; or indeed two witnesses, Elias and e.g. Enoch, Moses or Esdras who should arrive before the End. Elias could ' shut up the heavens ' (3 Kg 17:1 ; in Lk 4:25 that drought lasts 3½ years), and Moses brought plagues on Egypt. **7.** What is ' the ' Wild Beast from **d** the Abyss who fights and slays them ? He was not mentioned in ch 9 ! John's mind is already haunted by his next section where the Beast is a protagonist : there is a dawning of that vision within this one. **8-10.** Their corpses lie exposed 3½ days—brief triumph-hour for their enemies who had been tortured (10) by their preaching for 3½ years. This occurs in the ' great city ', ' symbolically called ' Sodom ' and ' Egypt ', where their Lord, too, was crucified ' (8). But if Rome, actual or mystical, is the focus of persecution, as the forthcoming sections make clear, why not use here ' Babylon ', the recognized cipher-name for Rome ? Because the ' measurement ' visions had inevitably ' set the scene ', so far, in Jerusalem : because Jerusalem was, for John, the Great *Apostate* : and because the sack of the city (A.D. 70) was vivid in his memory. **11-13.** But the Witnesses are resuscitated, assumed into heaven, and their enemies are either converted, or perish. This is the end of the ' interlude vision ' but not of John's prophecy. So far, he has seen the world, which should have been all Holy-City, Holy-Land, turned into the wickedest of cities, Sodom, and of lands, Egypt—nay, into one vast Calvary ; and the Church shrinking till she seems to have no more even a minimum witness-voice (but she preserves her Altar) : yet her witnesses revive, as

968d they always will; are glorified, and—await the recurrence of even fiercer persecution. But first, John

e closes this scheme of visions by the **(d) 15-18 Sounding of the Seventh Trumpet**—All Nature and Super-Nature acclaim—whom ? 'The Art, the Wast': but 'who is to come' is omitted, for he *is* come : the consummation is complete : John sees no new vision (*cf.* the Seventh Seal), but does, this time, hear the final Triumph-cry.

f Summary of Part A—So far the Apoc has taught us nothing new. But it has reinforced in dramatic imagery the lesson inculcated ever since *Genesis*—that God exists, is the paramount Lord, Eternal and All-Perfect, of all the world—that world in which are men. And that men, by sin, have tried to make chaos of that cosmos—and what *is* sin, and what has it always been ? The desire of man to 'be as God', self-sufficient ; to create man's own kingdom here on earth. 'I will not serve.' Hence wars ; hence every evil peace. But always there have been 'servants of God', and always God has spoken to them through his prophets, and supremely and definitely through his Son. Those who believe and obey shall be everlastingly saved : those who are obdurate in rebellion shall be for ever lost. These general truths have been several times repeated, yet not· *merely* repeated : the waves retreat, only to crash farther forward ; and now they will fall full on to the times of John himself, and the world in which those to whom he is immediately writing have to live.

PART B

g B (I) XI:19-XV:4.
XI:19 A Prefatory Vision to Part B—As Heaven was opened to John before the first part of his visions, so it is here too, but with a specially 'incarnational' colouring : the Ark of God is no longer hidden, but displayed and actually opened : ' the Word spread his tent amongst us ' : the Shekinah (true to its significance) *dwells* amongst us. Only here and in his Gospel (1:14) does John use the word ἐσκήνωσεν, though see Apoc 21:3 ; 13:6 ; God's ' tent ', ' tabernacle '. *Cf.* ' The Doctrine of the Shekinah and the Theology of the Incarnation ' in *The Gospel of the Infancy and other Essays*, by E. Burrows, S.J.

h XII 1-16 A Double Prefatory Vision (a) 1-16 A great ' symbol ' in the sky—1, 2. A Woman, radiant with sun, moon and stars, crying aloud in her birth-pangs. **3, 4.** Another symbol in the sky : a fiery-red Dragon, with 7 heads royally crowned and 10 horns : his tail sweeps to earth one third of the stars. **4.** He watches for the Birth that he may devour the Child. **5.** But the Man-Child, when born, is carried up to God's throne to shepherd the nations with the Messianic rod. **6.** The Woman flees to an ' appointed place ', in the desert, ' that they may nourish her there ' 1,260 days (persecution-time). **(b) 7-16 War in the sky—7.** Michael and his angels against the Dragon and his own. **8, 9.** Michael conquers and the Dragon is cast down to earth. **10-12.** A paean over this real yet unfinished victory : the Martyrs have conquered, but the Devil has come down to the Earth, furious, aware that his time is short. **13, 14.** The Dragon in fact pursues the Woman who flies with eagle's wings to the desert for her ' time, times and half a time ' (see above, 1,260 days). **16.** The Serpent tries to engulf her with a flood cast from his mouth : but the Earth opens *her* mouth and swallows the water up. **17.** So the Dragon, in anger against the Woman, goes to make war upon ' the rest of her offspring '—those faithful to the commandments of God, who hold fast to the witness to Jesus.—This verse really belongs to the next section but may be usefully mentioned here as helpful for the explanation of the Woman.

i Explanation of 1-17 supra. Begin with what is clearest. The Child (5) is the Messias : Ps 2:9 is certainly alluded to (see 9, 14, 15 ; Gn 3:1). ' The Dragon is the primeval Serpent ; he who is called

' Devil ' and ' Satan ' (9)—the Adversary, the **96** Slanderer, ' who sets all the nations astray ' (*ib.* ; *cf.* Zach 3:1 ff. ; esp. Job 1:6 ff. ; 2:2 ff. : ' to wander ' as opposed to ' walk ' is a thoroughly Johannine contrast : often in his Gospel) : the Accuser (10 ; see esp. Job 1:9 ff.). It is at least appropriate that the Serpent should cast forth the water-flood (15), because of the vague but traditional association of the sea-monster Tiamat (Tehom : the watery abyss) with water and chaos : *cf.* Ez 29:3 ; 32:2 ; Ps 74:14 ; and, I think, Job 7:12. But this was a very faded imagery, important only if we saw Babylonian astronomical imagery consciously used throughout this section (which we do not). Michael was Protector (opposed here to Adversary, Accuser) of Israel (Dan 10:1, 13, 21, etc.) : here, of the New Israel. The Fall of Satan : Lk 10:18. The war between Michael and good angels and evil angels is highly elaborated in apocryphal literature.—For the crowned heads and the horns, see §970*k*, sqq.—The **j** Woman. Her celestial array : *cf.* Ps 103:2 ; Can 6:10. In the *Testaments of the XII Patriarchs* Levi is like the sun, and Judah was ' brilliant as the moon and beneath his feet were 12 stars ', which suffices, I think, to show that the adornment is not significant in detail, but traditional, and doubtless in origin astronomical. Who is this Woman ? Clearly, the Mother of the Messias (2, 5), but also of a vast posterity (17) which endures to the end of time. She is, then, as symbolic as the Dragon, and indeed John says so (1, 3), and is comparable with the ' Jerusalem on high, the Mother of us all ' (Gal 4:26) : Jerusalem, whether terrestrial or ideal, especially as representing the whole people of God, the Bride of God (see also below, 19:7 ; 21:10), was constantly figured as a woman, mother of the Holy People from whom, in OT times, the Messias was to come. The mass of tradition sees in the Woman *both* the Synagogue and the Church : there is no break, in God's eyes, between them. Hippolytus († after 235) : ' Never shall the Church cease from producing from her heart the Word that in the world is persecuted by the unbelieving '. Victorinus († *c* 303), the first Latin commentator on Apoc : ' She is the ancient Church of the Patriarchs and Prophets and the Saints and the Apostles. The groanings and the torments of her yearnings were upon her until she should see that Christ, the fruit of her people according to the flesh, had from that very race taken up a body.' Augustine (on Ps 42) : ' This Woman is the ancient City of God.' Bede († 735) : ' Ever the Church, though the Dragon fight against her, is bearing Christ.' Beatus († 776) : ' Ever was this Woman, before the Lord's advent, in travail.' This does not exclude John's having seen our Lady **k** in this Woman—how could he *not* ? Having spent so long in her company, he *could* not have written of the Mother of the Messias without being conscious of her, any more than he could have written about ' eating the flesh and drinking the blood ' of Christ without thinking of the Eucharist. And the moment he thinks of the ' primeval serpent ' he *must* have remembered Eve ; so the Woman becomes the Second Eve, and we have the series—the ' Mother of the Messias ' : the Universal Eve : Jerusalem and the People : the Church and Mary. The *immediate* appearance of Mary as the Second Eve in patristic literature must surely be due in part to this passage. Notice that the Enthroned remains immobile. It is Michael—' Who is like to God ? '—who wages war on the Dragon—' I will not serve ' (and below : ' Who is like to the Beast ? '). John has by now introduced almost every symbol he will use later.

XII:13-XV:4 Seven Great Mysteries. **969**
XII:13-XIV:5 (a) A group of 4 Mysteries—13-17. The Dragon. He, prevented from injuring the Church *as such* (the Woman), for she is enabled to escape him and is nourished in the ' wilderness ' for ' persecution-time ', turns to make war on ' the rest of her offspring ', *i.e.* Christians throughout their history. **14.** The

969a 'eagle's wings' indicate directly only that the Woman's flight is swift enough to save her from the Dragon, though *cf.* Ex 19:4; Deut 32:11; Ez 17:3—the 'great' eagle, 'the great-winged, the wide in his out-stretching'. In one sense, the Church is always in flight, in exile, in the desert, nourished on desert-food, the Manna, or the bread that gave Elias strength for 40 days, in short, the Eucharist. **16 f.** The Earth swallows the Dragon-flood; a pictorial detail possibly suggested by the Asiatic streams that vanish into the fissured soil. Still, the very earth is on the side of heaven, not of hell! The 'ideal' allegoric vision is now closed, though the transition to actual history (related, of course, symbolically) has been gradual—a melting-into, rather than a dove-tailing.

b **XII:18–XIII 10 The Wild Beast from the Sea**—The Dragon stands on the seashore 18: 'he stood' is a better reading than 'I stood'), and from overseas appears a Wild Beast with 7 heads and 10 crowned horns engraved with blasphemous names. It is like a leopard, a bear, and a lion. To this Wild Beast from overseas the Dragon delegates his throne and authority and great power. One head had been wounded to death but had been cured. The world went gaping after the Beast and adored the Dragon, saying: 'Who is like to the Beast?' And the Beast made war on the Saints for 42 months, and all save the Elect adored it. **13:1 f.** For the heads, horns and crowns, see below, §§ 970*j*, sqq. For the head 'slain but restored to life', see § 970*k*. The whole is modelled on Daniel ch 7, though for once, John *combines* symbols —his Beast is swift as leopard, trampling as bear, fierce as lion (2). In Daniel, 4 beasts were 4 empires. We have here the Roman Empire seen collectively (for the heads, or horns, are emperors who will reign successively). **2b.** Satan hands this Empire to his delegate—irony of the Dragon 'cast down' yet giving his throne to the Beast: but recall his offer to our Lord: 'To thee will I give all this power and the glory thereof, for to me they are handed over, and to whom I will, I give them' (Lk 4:6). One would say that this Fallen Angel had indeed been originally entrusted with the 'princedom' of this our world, and that his perverted intelligence makes him imagine that it still is his—and indeed, he exercises great **c** power within it. **5 f.** 'Blasphemous titles': certain emperors (*e.g.* Domitian) called themselves 'Lord God'; all were treated as divine: Rome was a goddess (*Dea Roma: cf.* 2 Thess 2:4 ff.). The parody of Michael, 'who is like to God?' by the cry: 'Who is like to the Beast?', is obvious (the parody of the Lamb, slain yet alive again (5:6; see 8, and 13:14; 17:11) will become more precise later on. The Beast was 'allowed to act' for the stereotyped 42 months: its victory would appear complete (*cf.* the Two Witnesses above) save (8) for the Elect whose names are written, from the beginning of the world, in the Book of Life belonging to the Slain Lamb. **10.** A parenthetic verse: 'Shall we not resist?' 'No! If prison be your destiny, go to prison. If you take the sword, by the sword you shall perish. Herein, O Saints, is the sphere of your faithful endurance.'

d **11-18 The Wild Beast from the Land**—A second Beast, coming from the land. Its two horns are lamb's horns, but its voice is the Dragon's. It acts as representative of the first Beast, authoritatively. **13.** It works miracles and brings down fire from heaven. **15.** It causes an image of the Beast to be made and to speak: and all who refuse to worship it shall be killed. **17.** And all without exception must be marked with the mark of the Beast, nor can they even buy or sell unless they bear that mark. 'If you have the wits—work it out! It is the number of a (definite) **e** man. It is 666!' **Explanation of Second Beast**—This Beast, then, is the delegate of the first Beast, even as he was of the Dragon. It came from the mainland, *i.e.* for John, the province of Asia. In Asia, an 'Asiarch' was high-priest of emperor-worship in each city, but also president of the league or 'commune'

of that cult in the whole of 'Asia'. But delinquent **969e** Christians would be brought for actual trial and punishment to the proconsul and his subordinate magistrates. This second Beast may well then be a collectivity like the first—the civil and religious authority in the province, speaking (so far) mildly, though to the same effect as the Dragon—its horns were lamb's horns, and since he will be named (19:20) the False Prophet we can recall our Lord's warning about 'false prophets who come to you in sheep's clothing but inwardly are ravening wolves' (Mt 7:15). (For a quite different but plausible interpretation, see below, §971*c*.) The whole Emperor-cult revolved around the image of the Emperor, homage paid to which was the ultimate test of loyalty. Pliny (A.D. 112) in the north of the province, a mild and meticulous man, would produce the imperial statue with those of the gods: if Christians would sacrifice to it with wine and incense they were freed. **13-15.** 'Miracles'? **f** Fire? Speaking statues? Were actual conjuring-tricks used? Quite possibly. Mithraic statues exist having tubes making possible the emission of flames such as are sculptured on bas-reliefs of the same figure: ventriloquism was doubtless used in some cults: the 'legend' of Alexander Abonoteichos (an Asiatic contemporary of St John) tells of his huge snake which wore a mask that he made to talk 'ventriloquially'. Christians, though not yet being martyred on any general scale, were boycotted (17), and 'marked men'. **16.** Were they literally 'branded'? Ptolemy I (217 B.C.) branded Jews who submitted to registration with the 'stamp' of the god Dionysos. Soldiers, slaves, certain devotees, were appropriately marked. Probably the 'mark of the Beast' is another travesty—that of the 'seal' of Baptism (*e.g.* 7:3). **18.** *Cf.* the challenge in 9: 'Here is a riddle, but a **g** place for acuteness of wit! Let him who *can*, reckon up the **Number of the Beast.** For it is the number of a (real) *man*. It is 666.' All interpretations are conjectural, but I think that all may be discarded save the following. The letters of the Greek and Hebrew alphabets stood for numbers—*alpha* and *aleph*—for 1; *beta*, *beth* for 2, and so on. Therefore a name could be stated as the sum of its letters—scrawled on a wall at Pompeii is read: 'I love her whose number is 545'. (Awkward, because names of different letters could add up into the same sum!) The Sibylline Oracles (1:324-331) say: 'Then shall come the Son of the Great God . . . having four vowels; the consonant in him is doubled. But I will tell you the full number: eight units; as many tens, and 8 hundreds —that is what the name shall reveal to the friends of unbelief; but do thou think upon the immortal and most high Son of God, the Christ.' The name of IESOUS, therefore, in Greek, amounted to 888. I return to this below. What then was '666'? Irenaeus has a variant reading, 616. Idle to look elsewhere than to imperial Rome for the bearer of this name. And the name and title of 'Neron Caesar' written in Hebrew characters add up to 666, or, if the final *n* of *Neron* be dropped (as in Latin) to 616. There are objections to this which seem to me slight in view of further considerations. A variety of this 'game' of number-names was this: Certain numbers had an esoteric value attached to them; so if a name added up into a number which for other reasons had such a value, the person bearing it was felt himself to have that value. But 777 was a perfect number: 888, transcending it throughout by one, was the Messianic number; 666, injured throughout by one, was easily seen to be 'Antichrist's number'; if then Neron Caesar added up to 666, and 666 independently meant Antichrist, Nero *was* Antichrist. Finally, if (as we shall see) Domitian, reigning presumably when John composed his Apocalypse, and an eminent persecutor, was known as 'Nero come to life again', 666 will naturally have stood for him too, or the collectivity of persecutors, imperial, or *any* Antichrist who will endure so long as this world does. But we cannot

969g even summarize the other arguments surrounding this topic.

h XIV:1-5 The Lamb upon Mount Sion with his Retinue—After the Dragon and his two Wild Beasts, the Lamb, and a throng of followers having his Name, and God's, upon their foreheads ; they stand upon Mount Sion and sing a hymn that none can learn but they : they are virgins, first-fruits for God and for the Lamb. **1.** Mount Sion, where the Lamb is standing, contrasted with the shifting sands where the Dragon stands (12:18), indicates security. 144,000 is a ' perfect number '. The Seal of God on their forehead is contrasted with the Mark of the Beast, above. **2, 3.** The song, and the music like thunderous waters, seems to be sung first by the inhabitants of heaven, but is learnt and repeated by the multitude. **4, 5.** Tradition takes their virginity in the strict sense : else, the fact that they have never been faithless but follow the Lamb everywhere might suggest that they have never been false to their spiritual wedlock with the True God (immemorial metaphor) by idolatry, which indeed fits the context better.

i (b) 6-13 A group of Two Mysteries—Three angels proclaim the approach of God's judgement upon the world ; (8) the fall of the great City, ' Babylon ' ; and 9-11, the punishment of those who have accepted the Mark of the Beast. **6 f.** ' Another Angel ' : perhaps in contrast with the Eagle of 8:13, but probably just ' yet another angel '. He has an ' eternal gospel ', or message, to proclaim. Medieval mystics, and, later, reformation heretics, saw, in this, some new enduring revelation opposed to, or supplementing, what had hitherto been transitorily or inadequately revealed. It simply means the ultimate and everlasting triumph of the One God Creator of all that is : let all therefore worship him and him alone. **8.** The second Angel proclaims in prophetic anticipation the fall of the pagan city ' Babylon ', the Wanton, source of world-corruption—titles to be worked out later. This is modelled closely on, e.g. Is 21:9 ; Jer 50:2, etc. Persecuting forces like Niniveh, Babylon, Tyre and now Rome have given the maddening cup of spiritual **j** as well as bodily harlotry to their subjects. **9-11.** But the third Angel declares that God will give them *his* Cup—his Cup of Wrath ; see the same fierce contrast in Os 7:5. This wine is ' mixed ', yet ' unmixed '—not diluted as normally with water, but mingled with worse intoxicating drugs. Twice John insists that they who worship the Beast and receive his Mark are those to whom he refers (11) : they have no rest ' day or night ' in their torment : contrast those who worship God, day and night, in their gladness of salvation (7:15 ; and 4:8). Does **12**—' Here is the endurance of the Saints ! '—belong to what precedes or to what follows ? If to the former—the Faithful must show that endurance in the imperial persecution : if to the latter, they will find the reward of their endurance in what John is about to say. **13.** A Voice from Heaven declares that those who die in the Lord are forthwith blessed—their good works follow them into heaven. What Voice ? God's own ? or rather the Holy Spirit's (13*b*) speaking through the Prophet ?—To die, or rest, in the Lord : *cf.* 1 Cor, 15:18 ; 1 Thess 4:16. Vg punctuates wrongly and substitutes *iam* for the emphatic *vaí* : ' Blessed are the dead . . . from now on ! Forthwith !' ' *Yes* ', says the Spirit, ' they shall rest from their troubles, for their good works follow along with them.'

970a (c) 14-20 A Double Vision interposed—**14-16.** The Son of Man, crowned, throned on a white cloud, holds a sickle which an Angel bids him reap with, for the harvest is ripe. He does so. **17-10.** An Angel is then bidden to perform earth's vintage, for the grapes too are ripe. They are cast into the winepress outside the city, and trodden. Blood foams up ' to the bridles of the horses ' and deluges the land. What is this *double* ' Judgement ' ? He who is seated upon the cloud is, like the Enthroned, not named, but, being ' like a Son of Man ' is certainly the Messias (*cf.*

Dan 7 :13–14 ; Mt 24:30) coming for judgement : an **970a** Angel can well call to him,. as we ourselves do at Advent and Pentecost. But why a Harvester *and* a Vintager ? Is Christ's harvesting incomplete ? does he gather only the Elect ? (so P. Allo.) I incline to think that John, for his systematic arrangement, had to introduce *two* Visions and used the very ancient symbols of harvest and vintage for these, and then possibly assigned the harvesting to Christ (though in Mt 13:39 the reapers are the angels), and the vintaging, seen in terms of blood and therefore of punishment, to subordinates. Certainly the ' white ' cloud—unlike a thunder-cloud—suggests benevolence, not wrath : and the Angel having power ' over *the* fire ' (18. He **b** came from the altar—of holocaust ?) may allude to hell-fire : but that Christ should save with his own hand and entrust damnation to others seems to me unusual, inaccurate and displeasing. **19.** ' Cast ' does not mean ' hurl ', but ' set it to work '. Mt 10:34 has the same word for ' sending ' peace upon earth. The winepress was ' outside the city ', presumably Jerusalem (Jl 3:12 ; Zach 14:4). Very likely [*ib.* 10] the royal winepress was actually on the Mount of Olives). **20.** ' 1,600 furlongs ' can but mean a vast extent : nothing material or (here) mystical corresponds to it, though it *may* mean the whole world *other than* the Holy City. (*Ib.*) Blood ' up to the bridles ' unfortunately must mean a flood, not a splashing spray, *if* the image is traditional (it is elaborated in Enoch 1:8 ff.) : if it is, one must suppose that John took two symbols of the final judgement and re-used them as his double vision.—What are these ' horses ' abruptly introduced ? Perhaps since the Last Day was traditionally expressed as a treading of a winepress, *and* as a battle, the mention of the winepress inevitably suggested battle-imagery, just as battle-imagery in ch 19 evokes the mention of a winepress. (The Hebrews had, so to say, various ' dialects ' : an idolatry-dialect—' that have eyes and see not, ears and hear not, etc.' : a ' Last Day ' dialect—' stars falling from heaven ', etc. ; a battle-dialect, which used certain phrases almost automatically though they were not meant to be taken literally—*e.g.* washing one's hands in an enemy's blood.)

(d) XV 1-4 The Seventh Mystery—John sees, as the **c** closing vision of this series, the lake of crystal ' mingled with fire ' on which stand the conquerors in the battle with the Beast. They hold the ' harps of God ' and sing the ' Song of Moses and of the Lamb '. St John does indeed put on their lips the ' song of Moses ' (*cf.* Ex 15:1–21, and several Psalms). But as for the Song of the Lamb, he neither does nor can tell it, any more than he could say, *e.g.* what the Seventh Seal revealed.

B (II) XV:5-XVI:21 The Seven Bowls containing d Plagues.

XV 5-8 A Double Preparatory Vision.

(a) 15:5-7 The ' Temple of the Tent of the Witness' in heaven is opened—The Seven Angels, to whom are given the Bowls containing the Plagues—the ' last plagues ', for ' in them is consummated the wrath of God '—come forth. They are dressed as priests (Ez 9:2) about to carry out a ' liturgy ' to God's honour.

(b) 7-16:1 One of the Four Living Beings gives the Bowls to the Angels—The Temple was filled with smoke and no one could enter it till the outpouring was completed. A great Voice from the Temple bids the Angels fulfil their mission.—The 7 Bowls are equivalent to the Cup of God's Wrath (14:10). Why is it one of those Four who gives the Bowls ? If they indeed are ' Nature ', it is intelligible that human nature supplies to God, by its own actions, the material for his judgements : God cannot but act ' appropriately ' to the behaviour of mankind (see the mysterious verses in Ps 17:25, 26). **8.** The Sanctuary becomes inaccessible even to intercession. The wicked have sealed their doom. Do the above, and what follows, indicate a *hasty* composition due to John's strong emotion and desire to reach the end ? In 15:1

970d John *sees* the Angels who 'have' the Plagues: in 16:5 the temple is opened and the Angels appear; in 7, the Living Being *gives* the Plagues to the Angels. Moreover, we expect these 'consummatory' events to be worked out in some detail: but they are hardly more than alluded to, and the 'scheme' of composition, though adhered to, is but sketched.

e (a) **16:1-9 A group of 4 Plagues**—Plagues of the mystical Egypt. A murrain strikes men who have the mark of the Beast: it gangrenes their flesh; the very soil is corrupted. Then the sea: it becomes blood. Then the fountains of fresh water; they too become blood, and the 'Angel of the Waters' cries that the judgement is just—the Adversary had poured out Christian blood like water—blood shall he drink! The Altar acknowledges the same. Then the sun is made to scorch mankind, but they blaspheme and are not converted. See Ex 7–9. **5.** 'Who is to come' is omitted, *cf.* 11:17. *Cf.* 7:1; 14:18 for the Angels in charge of the waters. **8.** The heat of the sun is intensified: contrast 8:12 where it is darkened.

(b) **10-12 A group of 2 Plagues**—The fifth Bowl is poured out on the Throne of the Beast: men chew their tongues in anguish—to prevent themselves from crying out? or perverted rage against self? They remain unconverted.—The sixth Bowl dries up the Euphrates—to allow free passage for the Parthians to attack Rome? or are the Easterns going to side with the Beast against the Lamb?

f (c) **13-16 A Double Vision interposed**—Foul spirits like frogs emerge from the mouths of Dragon, Beast and False Prophet—miracle-working demons going to summon the kings of the earth to the final battle. (Christ is coming suddenly!)—They do in fact assemble at 'Harmagedon'. **13.** The False Prophet is the Second Beast: *cf.* 13:14; 19:20. Why 'frogs'? The Egyptian plague of frogs, not utilized so far, suffices to suggest them. Perhaps the frogs suggest the pettiness, the futile croaking of God's enemies, in contrast with the songs of his friends. **15.** Christ intervenes for a moment to re-assure the Faithful; they will not be disgraced.

16. 'Harmagedon' (RV, AV, Armageddon): the 'mountain of Megiddo': Megiddo was in the plain of Esdraelon, but partly overlooked by hills where troops would gather to descend for cavalry action below. Sion is the citadel of the Lamb. This plain was the 'cockpit' of Syria—a fatally central position on the N.–S. road between Egypt and Mesopotamia: of all the battles fought there no Jew would ever forget that in which the Egyptians overthrew Josias (4 Kg 23:29; *cf.* Zach 2:1; Ez who places the final conflict with God on the mountains of Israel (38:8, 21) may already be in John's mind: *cf.* 20:7 ff. below.

g (d) **17-21 The Seventh Plague**—A Voice says: 'It is consummated'. Catastrophes of all nature follow—never so great an earthquake! Babylon falls into three parts—every island fled—no more mountains! Smashing hail falls upon men but they blaspheme the more because of it. **17.** Yet men survive? Either, this series of plagues, as such, is completed; or, John when first composing it meant to stop there: but, in his final scheme of the Apoc, much remained to be written. **19.** The 'Great City' is broken in three: its power is reduced to very little: the capitals of the provinces or allied kingdoms fall: the 'islands' (ancient image for realms overseas) disappear: the earthquake lays the mountains low.

h B (III) **XVII:1-XXII:5.**
XVII 1-2 The Prefatory Vision—An Angel tells John to come and he will show him the judgement of the great Harlot, seated over many waters, with whom the kings of the world committed wantonness, for she has made the world drunk with the wine of her lustfulness. **1.** 'Seated on': as we say that a town is 'on' the Thames, etc. **2.** This 'fornication' means that the world's Powers, whatever their regime, have joined in the worship of the Goddess Rome and allied themselves to her essential paganism. **3a.** A deeper ecstasy.

3-18 The Double Preparatory Vision. **970i**
(a) **3b-6.** A Woman, seated on a scarlet Beast covered with blasphemous names and having 7 heads and 10 horns. She is dressed in purple and scarlet, gilded, bedizened with precious stones and pearls. In her hand is a gold cup filled with her abominable harlotry. On her forehead, a significant name: 'Babylon the Great, Mother of Harlots and of the filth of the earth'. John stood appalled, seeing her drunk with the blood of the martyrs. The Angel proceeds to explain this.
(b) **7-18.** The Beast he had seen was, and is not, but is about to ascend from the abyss and go to destruction. All, who were not from the origin in the Book of Life, shall go marvelling after the Beast when they see that it Was, and Is not, and Shall be. ('Here is the meaning, thou that understandest!') The Seven Heads are Seven Hills, where she is enthroned. But they are *also* seven Kings: 5 are fallen; the 6th is now; the 7th is not yet come; but once come, he can remain but for a brief while. As for the Beast that was and is not—why! it is an 8th, and yet is one of the 7, and goes to perdition. The 10 Horns are 10 kings—well, they are not yet *kings*, but they take their authority along with the Beast, for an hour. They have but one mind; and as for their authority, they hand it over to the Beast. These shall war with the Lamb and he shall conquer them . . . (He adds): The Waters that the Woman sits above are races and nations and languages. These Horns and the Beast shall hate the Wanton and strip and burn and devour her. This Wanton is the City, the Great City, that has royal rule over the kings of the earth.
Further explanation of XVII 1 ff.—The Harlot is **j** the City Rome (18): the Beast is the Empire on which the City is seated (3*b* ff.): the 'waters' (15) the medley of nations composing it. The 7 Heads are the 7 Hills of Rome (9); the *domini colles* ('Hence', *i.e.* from the Janiculum, 'may you see the seven lordly hills—Hence may you reckon up the whole of Rome': Martial): purple and scarlet (4), its flamboyant ostentation, contrasted with the 'white' of the Bride of the Lamb, below and *passim*: 'gilded'; bedizened with gold, or possibly alluding to prostitutes who actually gilded themselves. 'Pearls': contemporary Roman women were quite mad about them: 'The name on her forehead (5)': perhaps not merely symbolical; prostitutes used to write their names over their doors. **10 ff.** But the 7 heads are *also* 7 kings: John explicitly states that a symbol may have more than one meaning. Of these, one as it were incarnated the Beast itself. 'It *was*, and *is* not, and is to have its advent' (11). Supreme parody of the Lamb! Can we be more explicit? Not with absolute certainty. The Beast undoubtedly represents **k** the total Roman Empire and indeed the world-enduring succession of such Powers as would be self-sufficient. The temporal expression of the enduring Power seems stricken to death, but only to revive. The chaotic year following the enforced suicide of Nero must have looked like the end of the Empire. But with the Flavian dynasty it came to life again. Thus Assyria, Egypt, Babylonia, Persia had come to an end: Rome would do so too, but something would replace it. We, nearly 2,000 years later, have seen similar phenomena: the Beast may even now be re-emerging from its abyss, ravening for world-domination and the extermination of Christ and of his Church. But John, picking up afresh the symbolism of the 7 Heads, is clearly pointing to individuals. The system I prefer is this—Starting with the first Emperor, Augustus, you then have Tiberius, Gaius, Claudius and Nero. These five, says John, are dead. The chaotic year of Galba, Otho and Vitellius followed who can hardly have seemed real emperors to anyone, certainly not to one living, like John, in Asia, and under the Flavian dynasty of which Vespasian was the Emperor, the 6th, therefore, in the list. Then is to come one who reigns only for a very brief space—Titus, in fact, who ruled for scarcely a year—a brief

970k flash of extreme popularity destined not to survive (10). Such are the 7. Domitian followed (11), 'an eighth, who is yet one of the seven'. How so? The people had had a morbid affection for the mad genius Nero. Impossible to believe that he was dead! (Compare the belief about Barbarossa, and even Lord Kitchener, and many others.) He was alive—he was in Parthia—at least he would come to life again. Men spoke of 'Nero redux': 'Nero redivivus'. The myth reached Jewish and even Christian circles: the Sibylline Books keep speaking of a Nero who should return as devil incarnate, rival of God, from across the Euphrates. And even pagan Rome had nicknamed the horrible Domitian 'Nero': this **l** prevailed as late as Tertullian. The Beast, therefore, was *a man* (see §969*d*): he seemed identifiable with Nero: but Domitian was Nero-restored-to-life—he was, then, the 8th, yet one of the 7, and, incarnated the Beast. But he too was 'on his way to perdition'. The 10 Horns (12). In Dan 7:7 there are 10 horns on the head of his 4th Beast, kings who coalesce into an empire. In Apoc too the 'horns' are kingdoms, incorporated into the Roman Empire and unanimously working its will against the Church but ultimately turning against the Empire and destroying it, the Beast itself helping them. These kingdoms are to receive a very brief authority along with the Beast (12); but after the fall of Rome they will turn also against the Beast, and the Empire itself was indeed to break up into mutually warring parts: then, it is authoritatively declared, they too shall be defeated by the Lamb (14). And indeed, how swiftly vanishing, how uncreative, were the Huns, the Vandals, the Visigoths and Ostrogoths and the rest! Still, to the end, there will be the attempt to create *some* anti-God omnipotent State: the battle lasts till the end of time, ever-renewed.

971a (*a*) **18:1 19:10 A Group of Four Visions**—1–8 An Angel proclaims the Doom of Rome. This and the following passages are very simple but superb rhetoric, based firmly on prophetic model, *e.g.* Is 13:19 ff.; Jer 15 and 51, etc., but to my mind far surpassing them in grandeur and passion. **5.** 'Her sins are welded together' (into a solid mass). **9–20.** The Dirge over Rome. *Cf.* Ez 26:16–18, etc. John cannot but feel a *horrified admiration* for the flamboyant magnificence over which he chants his dirge. **21–24.** The Destruction of Rome. **19:1–10.** The exultation of the Saints. Heaven and earth exult over this Judgement. The hour for the Marriage of the Lamb is come, and his Bride is ready in 'linen white and shining'—the righteous actions of the Saints—contrasted with the purple and scarlet silks of the Harlot. **10.** 'The spirit of prophecy is the witness given by—and to—Jesus.'

b (*b*) **19:11–21 A Group of Two Visions**—11–16. The Destruction of the Beast and of the False Prophet is accomplished by One who rides on a white horse, 'Faithful and True', the Judge. His sword is his Word: he wears many crowns of victory; he holds the Messianic iron-shod club; on cloak and thigh is engraved his Name—'the Word of God'—and yet, no one knows it but himself—and further: 'King of kings and Lord of lords'. A throng of white-robed fellow-conquerors escorts him. **11.** The Lord is 'faithful', keeping his promises to his followers. **12.** The 'many crowns' correspond to the conquered kingdoms: but the crowns of the Dragon (12:3) and of the Beast (13:1) are upon *many* heads. He to whom they now belong is One. **16.** The name that all can read—'King of kings', etc., is on his cloak and thigh: *scl.*, where the folds of the cloak lie smooth: equestrian statues were sometimes thus engraved. The 'real name', the 'Word of God', is himself (*cf.* Jn 1:1): no one—not even we Christians here ourselves—can exhaust its meaning.

c **17–21.** An Angel calls from the sun to 'all birds that fly' to come and devour the flesh of all God's enemies. The Beast assembles his armies: they and the False Prophet are seized and thrown into the lake burning

with brimstone, and the Divine Word destroys the **971c** rest. *Cf.* Ez 39:4, 17–20: and Mt 24:28. The birds and their feast are as symbolical as the 'Sword' which is the Word (Eph 6:17). Here (20) the Beast and Prophet are as symbolical as (20:14) Death and Hades which also are cast into the burning lake. (All 'brimstone' allusions look back, presumably, to the destruction of the Cities of the Plain which left an indelible impression on the Hebrew mind.) But if the Beast, indeed, symbolizes the recurring attempt of the civil power to set itself up against God, to what can the False Prophet correspond in the successive centuries? After his first appearance the Second Beast, or False Prophet, plays no personal role. He has become a stock figure. But Fr Allo has suggested that he represented, rather than the Asiarch, that vague solvent 'toleration' which was then going to become Gnosticism (§965*a*) and which ended by mating with the Emperor cult seeing that all religions were in reality forms of the ultimate inexpressible One, itself best symbolized, in the sky, by the Sun, on earth, by the Emperor. The lazy flattering notion that all creeds are finally much of a muchness (except the Catholic Faith, consciously and admittedly unique and exclusive) is indeed as modern as it was prevalent in ancient but decadent days. There could then be two 'foci' of anti-Christianity—the openly persecuting State, and the vague subservient 'religion' which the State could patronize without damage to itself. Its role is as disastrous and more subtle. (I myself incline to think that the Second Beast was, at first, the Asiarch, but by now has become 'generalized' and stands for all who wield authority delegated from imperial Rome—all official representatives of the Beast—and has in fact lost all separate personality.)

(*c*) **XX 1–10 A Double Vision interposed**—(1–6) The **d** Binding of the Dragon and the Reign of the Saints. (7–10) The Destruction of the Dragon.

1–3. An Angel chains and imprisons the Dragon for 1,000 years: the Saints and Martyrs are enthroned and reign with Christ for the same time: this is the First Resurrection. **4–6.** Over these the Second Death has no power.—John had shown, first, the Dragon: then, the Beasts: then, the City Rome. He now shows their destruction in the inverse order—Rome; the Beasts; the Dragon. But first, the Dragon is 'chained' only for a while, the direct consequence of his defeat by Michael. These visions do not show events following one another in time: the 'events' are simultaneous *spiritually*: it is the Seer whose eye is looking ever *deeper*.—The Abyss, Satan, the Serpent: see 9:11, etc. **4.** 'Thrones of Judgement.' *Cf.* Mt 19:28; Lk 22:30; 1 Cor 6:3. The Faithful and especially the Martyrs are associated with Christ in passing verdict on the world. **2, 4, 5.** The 'thousand years' and the 'first resurrection' have been a crux for commentators, but almost wholly because these have struggled to make the events of the visions successive. Yet the destruction of the Beast (the sum-total of human anti-Christian forces) cannot but take place at the end of the world and so must synchronize with that of the Dragon. Therefore the 'millennium' coincides with the preceding period, persecutions included. The Apparition of Christ, his 'Parousia', *is* the End, already related under varying images several times, and nothing new can follow it. In the OT (*cf.* esp. Is 54 and 60; **e** Ez 40–47) we see the disasters of the People followed by a triumphant rebuilding of Jerusalem and a Messianic, but earthly, period of well-being indefinite in duration. Towards the Christian era this notion was more spiritualized, but (on the whole) involved the reign of the Messias on earth for a considerable time (the number of years varies), followed (sometimes accompanied) by the bodily resuscitation of good Jews and the beginning of eternity. John was certainly aware of these floating ideas (see below on Gog and Magog), but all critics would agree that he adapts his symbols to his own purpose: we disregard, then, the theory of a 'Jewish millennium'. Some Christian

THE APOCALYPSE XXII

71e writers (Papias—not a prudent authority: Irenaeus, far more serious: Tertullian, heretic: a few others, but second-rate) were *influenced* by the Jewish notions prevalent especially after the sack of Jerusalem (A.D. 70), but do not speak with one voice and seldom with conviction. St Augustine (*Civ. Dei*, 20, 7-13, etc.) retracts his earlier inclination to believe in a millennium *after* the final Judgement, and the break with any earlier interpretations was definite: the Council of Ephesus already spoke of 'aberrations' and 'fabulous doctrines'. Augustine and Jerome are to be followed: they regard the chaining of Satan and the reign of the Saints as the whole period subsequent to the Incarnation. The power of Evil *is* in fact broken: Christians in whom Grace *are* in fact 'kings and priests' however they be harassed. These, then, are not only the martyrs or 'confessors' already in heaven, but all who do not 'worship the Beast', even though yet unborn: *cf.* ch 7; 15:2-4; esp. 14:1-5.

f The *number* '1,000' *may* be suggested by the Jewish notion that the world existed 7,000 years, corresponding to the 7 'days' of creation, of which the last (year or day) was one of 'rest': after this, an 8th 'millennium' was to be created—eternity. But in Apoc it means the grace-age in which the Faithful are living, whether on this earth or forthwith after bodily death in heaven (Apoc 14:13). There is, then, a First Death (Sin) and a Second (Damnation), and parallel to this, a First Resurrection, by grace: *cf.* Eph 5:14; Col 3:1, and all St Paul's treatment of the effects of baptism, and Jn 5:25 where not only those who *shall* hear Christ's word *shall* live, but (24) 'he that heareth *hath* "eternal life"'.

Yet St John himself makes it clear that Satan has been no more than crippled, for he still has power over the souls numerous as the 'sands of the sea' who compose the hostile troops of the next little section.— After the 1,000 years, Satan is unbound and comes forth to deceive the nations of all the world. 'Gog and Magog.' They besiege the 'camp of the Saints' and the 'beloved city'. But fire descends and devours them, and the Devil is cast into the fiery lake to rejoin the Beast and his Prophet. 'Gog and Magog': see Ez 38-39. They summed up, and afterwards symbolized, the 'enemies of God' especially at the Last Day. Useless to dwell on their original signification, *i.e.* northern peoples, the Scythians in particular. For John, they come from everywhere and invest the Church but are decisively defeated. The spiritual Tempter himself, after a final explosion of iniquity, is destroyed, as the 7th Vision will show.

g (d) XX 11-15 The Seventh Vision—'A great white Throne': from before him who was enthroned there, 'heaven and earth fled away'. All the Dead stood before it; books were opened, and 'another book', that of Life. The Sea and the Grave gave up their dead and all were judged according to their works written in the books. And Death and the Grave and all not written in the Book of Life were thrown into the fiery lake—this is the Second Death. **11.** The 'white' throne? because of the purity of this Judgement? of the divine triumph? Here too the Judge is not named; *cf.* 4:2. Heaven and earth 'fled'— as it were, cowered back, conscious that nothing is 'pure in thy sight' (Job 25:5): but the whole universe, in fact, remains present or becomes so. **12.** The books are the history of each, and, the Register of the Saved. **13.** Death and the Grave (identical) are personified. All, whether they had died on land or sea, are judged: after that, there is no more death, temporal or spiritual.

h A Double Vision (XXI-XXII:5) corresponding to the double vision of God and of the Lamb prefixed to the central part of the book which is now being concluded. **21:1-3 The Proclamation of the New Jerusalem.** A new heaven and a new earth. No more sea. The New Jerusalem descends from God dressed like a bride. A Voice cries that God's dwelling is with men: he shall be called 'God-with-them'. There shall be no

more sorrow—the 'first things' have passed away. **971h** Then he who is enthroned tells John to write, for all is accomplished—all is made new. He himself is the Origin and End: to the thirsty he will give the Water of Life: the Conqueror shall be his son. But evil-doers shall be cast out into the Second Death. **1.** A 'new' heaven and earth: see below. No more sea—the Jews disliked the sea, symbol of agitation and chaos, as, to the Greeks, of barrenness. **2.** Heaven descends and *penetrates* the earth—nature is supernaturalized. *Cf.* Heb 3:2; 9:11. Ez 37:27; Jer 31:33. **3.** The Shekinah (*cf.* § 968g) becomes permanent. 'God-with-us', Emmanuel: Is 7:14, 8:8, 10. The notion of the Holy Land or the Holy City, as a bride wedded to Yahweh was immemorial: *cf.* the Messianic role, Mt 22:1; 25:1; Jn 3:29 and the doctrine of St Paul about the union of the Church and of each soul with Christ, *e.g.* 2 Cor 11:2; Eph 5:25. **6 f.** Alpha and Omega: of the Father, 1:8; of the Son, 22:13. The symbolism returns to that of the beginning of the book. **8.** The Cowards, contrasted with the Victorious. The 'defiled' probably refers to perverted vices. 'Sorcerers', *i.e.* poisoners: poisoning was then a prevalent crime and connected with witchcraft.

9-XXII 5 Vision of the New Jerusalem—John is **972a** summoned to see the Bride herself, Spouse of the Lamb. A walled city with 12 gates, 3 on each side of her quadrilateral: her height, breadth and depth are equal: her gates are engraved with the names of the 12 tribes of Israel; her foundation-stones with those of the Apostles. All these glowed with precious stones; the gates were each 'one pearl'; the city itself and her streets, 'transparent gold'. No temple there, nor light of sun nor moon: God and the Lamb themselves are light and temple. That light will attract all nations—the doors will never be shut day or night—but there will *be* no night! Yet nothing impure can enter into her. A river of life flows from the Throne—the Grove of Life around it constantly providing fruit and leafage for the healing of the nations.—The City, then (16) is four square, of vast size (see Ez 48:30-35): its height is identical with its sides. If we visualize this, we must see a pyramid, not a cube! And what use would be a wall 144 cubits high round a cube of 12,000 furlongs? Anyhow the numbers merely symbolize vastness and perfection. The Church is universal, and 'invests' the 'mountain' of the whole earth. John is probably adapting the shape of a Babylonian *ziqqurat*, composed of vast superimposed 'platforms' each smaller than the lower one and having no doubt a shrine on the topmost. **14.** The foundations will then be the supporting **b** walls of 12 towering 'storeys', and not juxtaposed; and the precious stones, an incrustation lending a colour-scheme to the whole uprising mountain-city. (The 'storeys' of ziqqurats were apparently of different colours, like the concentric Persian city-walls.) The gates (12) are named after the tribes of the spiritual Israel; for the sentinel angels, *cf.* Is 62:6. The foundations are the Apostles (*cf.* Eph 2:20: 'built up on the foundations of the Apostles and Prophets). 'Jasper crystal-clear' (κρυσταλλίζοντι; *cf.* above, σμαραγδίζουσα) transparent, with light rippling through it? In 4:6, the sea is 'crystalline', and the river in 22:1; and the gold of the streets (21:21) is as clear as glass. Does John want to avoid too hard and metallic a vision? One may compare French colour-verbs ending in -oyer. What is *rougeoyant*, *verdoyant* is softer, more mobile, more subtle than what is merely red or green: and John's 'transparent gold' must have been like a mist illuminated by the sunrise from within. The City is 'like jasper' (11) but 'having the glory of God' himself 'like jasper' in 4:3. The colours of the precious stones appear to be a deep soft green: a very deep blue-green: green like a peacock's tail or the shifting tints of a pigeon's throat: then, pure emerald: in the sardonyx white mingles with transparent rose: then comes deep crimson: the next **3**

1207

972b stones re-introduce the softest yellows and gold-green : finally you have the glorious sapphire melting into **c** violet amethyst. The City therefore ascends, terrace by terrace, with translucent golden paths mounting through the Grove of Life, leafy because of the River of Life which comes cascading down from the Throne of God and of the Lamb : it is the Grace-giving Spirit, *vivificans*. For the jewels, *cf.* not so much the high-priest's breastplate (Ex 27:17-28) as Is 54:11.—' God and the Lamb (on an equality as in 7:9 ff. ; 14:4, etc.) *are* the Temple (perhaps *cf.* Jn 2:21) and the Light (21:23). The previous *mise en scène* of the heavenly temple and its ' furniture ' can now lapse. This Throne is at the summit of the pyramidal mountain-city. Strictly speaking, the ' kings and peoples ' (24-27) need not ' come ' as though there were a world outside the City. The point is that they *are there* and in that Light (*cf.* esp. Ps 86 (Vg) : ' I will make mention of Rahab (Egypt) and Babylon as among those that know me : See the Philistines, the Tyrians, the Ethiopic folk—all these were " born there " ! ' (That is, find their true selves, lives and citizenship in the ultimate Sion.) **25.** Nothing hinders their entry, and whatever good there was among them, they bring with them as to its proper place and source. *De tuis donis ac datis.* God-created Nature is now fully super-naturalized and better than re-united with him.

d XXII 6-21 Epilogue—An Angel assures John that what he has said is trustworthy (and Christ interpolates that he is coming quickly). John, overwhelmed, falls prostrate before the Angel but is checked by him. Our Lord bids John ' publish ' his book : let the sinner sin even worse—the righteous become still holier —nothing can alter the accomplishment of the divine plan. Jesus, Origin and End, Root and Race of David, the bright morning Star, has sent his Angel to bring this testimony. Nothing must be added to this book or subtracted from it.—John attempts to end the book ; but the divine and angelic voices, and the voice of the Spirit and of the Bride herself, keep breaking through. Still shaken by his ecstasy, John pronounces the last invocation and the last blessing.—The Epilogue corresponds duly with the opening of the book. **6.** The Speaker is presumably the Angel of 21:9. The ' Lord of the spirits of the prophets ' is He who controls their inspiration. **7.** ' I come quickly ' is the voice of Christ breaking through. **8.** ' Yes ! It is I, John, who heard, etc. ' : all this concluding part of Apoc has always impressed the present writer as though John were with difficulty coming back to normal consciousness as his ecstasy leaves him. Fragmentary voices, so to say, divine, angelic and human, beat upon one another. **9.** The Angel is a fellow-servant : the prophets are John's brothers. Different **e** in nature, they all serve each in his way. **10.** The Book is for the public at large—therefore, not unintelligible. **11 ff.** Let men proceed as they will—farther from God or nearer to him—God's response cannot be impeded. **13.** Christ applies God's name to himself : *cf.* 1:8, 17 ; 21:6. **14** contains the *seventh* blessing thus uttered in Apoc.—The Tree of Life, forbidden in ' Genesis ' is here offered to all who choose to enter by the divine doors into a better-than-Paradise. A full circle. **16.** So too the divine history (David-Christ) reaches its consummation.—The Morning Star shines during this life : the full Sun, hereafter. **17.** The cry of the Spirit (*cf.* Rom 8:26, 27) is uttered from the heart of the Church even on earth (for she

prays : ' Come ! ') : but this Bride *is* the New **972** Jerusalem ; therefore that City is the *whole* Church, as in heaven, so on earth. Already she drinks the Living Water. **18-19** show John's sense of the plenitude of his authority and sanction. **20.** Christ approves this—' Yes ! I come quickly ! '—the 7th time these words are used. Which of us would notice these ' latent ' uses of the number 7, were we not *expecting* John to pursue his scheme into its last recesses ? The sentence certainly alludes to the Coming of Christ, and not to an imminent return of and visit from the Apostle. **21.** Serenity and dignity of this conclusion ! John goes back to the work and suffering of each day, but is not separated from the reality and glory of which he had received so transcendent an intimation.

The ' theology ' of the book is complete and clear— **f** God, transcendent yet omnipresent, remains immutable and invisible throughout : the Enthroned is Paramount yet never named. But there are, too, the Word of God, and His Spirit. There is the Incarnation ; there are the saving Death and Resurrection ; there are the Church and the incorporation of Christian into Christ and that union of which sacramental marriage is St Paul's chosen symbol : there are Baptism (the ' seal ') and the Eucharist : there is Mary, the mystical Second Eve. But though the Incarnation, the Church, Mary, the Sacraments as it were plunge God into human history (after all, St John says ' as if ', ' like ', and so forth so often that we may be forgiven our ' as it were '), St John, starting (as Apocalypists do) from God, tapers down through great enduring principles into the events of his own day, and thereafter rises up once more into what is everlasting—the only true ' society ', the New, the Real Jerusalem. For, into the divine plan Sin has inserted itself : first, the angelic sin—pride in some mysterious form. ' I will not *serve* ! ' This has seeped down into our poor human race, so that men have ever since wished to be self-sufficient and the Son of God incarnate had to say : ' I am among you as one who *serves* '. Hence John is more **g** occupied, if I may say so, with the condition of Christians in any period of their existence than with abstract principles. Without the principles, life becomes mere chaos, at the mercy of any tyrant who is strong enough and unscrupulous enough to impose himself upon it. No call, on the one hand, to force any one sentence of the Apocalypse into a materially exact prediction of what is happening in our own day ; but every reason for seeing the great truths that John proclaims as operative now. Looking back, I am not sorry that he is so steeped in OT imagery, because not only *we* have the right to see the OT looking forward to Christ—*Christus cogitabatur*—but John enables us to hear Christ's voice singing itself back into all that ancient God-guided history. We live in what is neither merely past, nor present, nor future. Life has become, for us, Christo-centric. We live by no mere abstract philosophy of God and of human nature : nor yet, by any mere system of Ethics detached from doctrine. Christ is our radiating centre : in Him we must live ; with him die ; with him rise into our immortality. ' Per ipsum, et cum ipso, et in ipso ' : by means of him ; in company with him ; incorporated into him—thus alone do we become what God calls us to be. No need to visualize that, or to try to state it in adequate human terms : when the Seventh Seal was broken, there was silence in heaven.

INDEX

*All references are to the **section numbers** in the margin*

The index records not only those passages where the principal treatment of a subject is to be found (indicated in heavy type), but all others in which it is dealt with or which have an important bearing on it.
Proper names, on the whole, are listed in their Douay form. The familiar English spelling is, however, generally booked in addition as a cross-reference.

(DEUTERONOMY) consistency with rest of Pentateuch 210e, 211abc, 212bc, 213a, 219c

Josiah's reforms and 135bdoq, 211a, 280gi

law code 135pq, 215–19e

law of one sanctuary 132g, 135de, **211cd,** 215a–dg, 216c, 217e, 219f, 280g

Mosaic authenticity 48d, 135bdeq, 211ab, 222a, 280g

(the) name 210b

papyrus fragments 77ac

post-Mosaic additions **135pq,** 211b, 213ad, 214ce, 215eg, 216ac, 217cd, 218bdjk, 219dg, 220bc, 222af

Priests and Levites and 217e

refers to rest of Pentateuch 130ef

threatens exile 212g, 220b, 280g

DEUTERONOMIST WRITINGS 44df, 135o, 265e, 270 l, 278f

DEVELOPMENT OF DOCTRINE 12d, **18f,** 39 lm, 40g, **84e,** 86g,102d, 104c, 137def, 211g, 397m, 400b, 780f, 805d

DEVILS, Demons 92j, 137e, 144ad, 540t, 593a, 643f, 653c, 718h, 856j, 904c (see also Exorcism, Fall, Satan)

Asmodeus 302c, 304e, 305j

Azazel 191fij

Babylonian demonology 593a

Beelzebub (q.v.) 729cd

Belial 272h, 593a

blind to Christ's divinity 730h, 750ij

Christ's Messiahship recognized by 727fg, 728h, 730h

disease and 88b, 705d, **757f,** 759a, 872g, 891g

driving away 179f (see also Exorcism)

dwelling in deserts 306c, 429f, 475e, 683c, **697f,** 750i, 757g

idols, pagan gods as 393d, 475b, 637b, 653c, 693b, 877h

limited powers of 302c

miracles of 91a

personal names of 593a

returning sevenfold 757g

satyrs, wild animals 429f, 475e

theoretical faith of 947e

torments 730h

unleashed for a while 690c, 730h

DEVOTION TO DEATH, Destruction 211g, 272g, 273n (see also Ban)

DEW 56e

D'HULST 6a

DIADOCHI, see Successors

DIANA OF THE EPHESIANS 81f, 839j, 883c, 964q, 965c

sacristan of 81f

temple of 81f, **600f, 839j, 964g**

the great θεά, θεός 81f

DIARIES 814c

DIASPORA, see Dispersion

DIATESSARON, Tatian's **25d-g,** 26ad, 81a, 607i (see also Arabic)

DIBELIUS M. 609a–c

DIBLAH, see Riblah

DIBON 57i, 80j, 233f, 273 l, 430dei, 435i

DICHOTOMY OF MAN 916e

DICTATION 37c, 77f, 581c, 661h, 844d, 870a, 927e (see also Pauline Epistles)

of Scriptures by God 34e, 413c

DIDACHE, The 14d, 17hj, 639c

DIDACTICISM OF SCRIPTURE 223e–g, 301bfi, 308fj

Didaskaleion of Alexandria, The 3e, 5a

Didascalia, The 93i

DIDRACHMA, The 705fg

DIDYMUS THE BLIND 3e

DIES, see Jemima

Dies Irae 92o, 541d, 542e

DIGGING THROUGH WALLS 328f

DIMON, see Dibon

DINAH 59h, 155e, 158b, 309j

DIOCLETIAN 8b, 309c

Edict of 17h

DIODORUS OF TARSUS 3e

DIONYSIA, The 576c

DIONYSIUS, Denis, the Areopagite 838g

DIONYSIUS EXIGUUS 617c, **674b**

DIONYSOS 969f

DIOS 267m

DIOTREPHES 658d, 959ei

DISCERNING OF SPIRITS 879ab, 958a

DISCIPLES, The 657d, 756c, 760a, 765b, 774a, 833d, 834b (see also Apostles, Seventy-two)

(the) beloved disciple 776f (see also John)

false Messianic ideas among 754g, 762de, 764d, 767c, 774b (see also Apostles)

flock of Christ 758d

friends of Christ 720e, 758c

(the) holy women 710b, 742g, 754a, 757ab, 772a, 773b

Pharisee disciples 742h, 772c

pluck corn on Sabbath 218o, 696a, 728e

would-be disciples 690a

DISCIPLESHIP, Christian 685gi, 704g, 730b, 752g–i, 756b, 797i, 813ef, 818bd, 819c, 826f

cost, demands of 690a, 733b, 734ad, 735df, 760a, 763gh, 767e

reward of 735f

kindred of Christ 697g,

self-surrender of 752h, 760a, 765a, 767a

DISCIPLINE, Church 689d 699f, 706f, 781i, 819c, 886j (see also Excommunication)

DISCORD 948ab (see also Corinthian Church)

DISCRETION, Years of, see Age

DISCRIMINATION 404e

DISCUS THROWING 575e

DISEASE **190a-q,** 397h, 402e (see also Destroyer, Lepers)

bubonic plague 168b, 279i

devils and **88b,** 705d, **757f,** 759a, 872g, 891g

cattle 168a

Job's 317b, 320h

psoriasis 190bc

scab 168b, 190b

sin and disease 690e (see also Death)

skin diseases 689b

DISINTERESTEDNESS 660m, 840f

DISMAS 771b

DISOBEDIENCE **145a,** 238m, 272g, 470f

DISPENSATIONS, Eras, Aeons 715b, 899b

the Christian 77h, 674b, 709e, 720g, 852fg, 957a, 971ef

from the Law 696ab, 752d, 852e

the old and the new 36a, 101b–d, 102p, 366g, 462h, 642b, 653k, 671bc, 678a, 685bh–686e, 693df, 699e, 700d, 705a, 715b, 717a, 733cd, 736f, 737d, 738c, 746b, 747bd, 783def, 786d, 894b, 896d, 927ab, 931a, 932a, 933ab, 944c

DISPERSION, Diaspora, The Jewish 8a, 12b, 13ac, 71e, **75,** 122m, 388bc, 389g, 398a, 403cd, 404acd, 428o, 442c, 444g, 445e, 448i, 450clp, 451s, 453c, 470a, 523j, 545p, 550o, 584bd, **588e-g,** 589ac, 682g, 796i, 823c, 828ab, 833b, 835a (see also Septuagint)

autonomous communities of 588f

city centres of 68a, 588e

commerce and 75a, 588ef

influence of Hellenism on 589g

Jerusalem, the Sanhedrin, and 587ab, 588f, 831a

language of 588e, 589c

relations with Gentiles 584ce, 588g, 590b

spread of Christianity and 14c, 737g, 909b, 914b, 949d

writings of 589g

DISPERSION OF HUMAN RACE 32 l, 147e

DISPOSITIONS, Importance of Interior 79h, **114 l, 115h,** 146a, 183j, 184bc, 187d, 192d, 285s, 325i, 348e, 349a, 370d, 371g, 378d, 397cd, **404c,** 423be, 437i, 449cdf, 451n, 457a, 478j, 514n, 517h, 518e, 519c, 523e, 536e, **545ef,**

549f, 642e, 685k, 691b, 729gh, 730a, 731b, 732h, 737kn, 752i, 758b, 762e, 925b

DITTOGRAPHY 283e, 285j, 286hh, 287t, 480f, 486x, 489d, 492k, 493fh, 581b

DIVES AND LAZARUS 327j, 584k, 761ef

DIVIDER, see Bastard

DIVINATION, among the Philistines 423j

Babylonian 79h, 443p

by a pythonical spirit 837e, 905d

by dreams (q.v.) 550m

by ephod 238g, 242 l, 245a–c, 247j, 252 l, 255d

by lots 231b, 236h, 252d, 370j, 532b (see also Urim and Thummim)

by magic 192s, 193c, 217f

by Scriptures 563e

by stars 443p

by teraphim **106h,** 154m, 155f, 254c

Greco-Roman 600ij

with a cup 157k

DIVINITY OF CHRIST 3b, 40h, 271j, 604f, 620bcg, 622a–f, 628c, 640o, **641a-j,** 662c, 680j, 681af, 682b, 688c, 690g, 693h, 695b–d, 696b, 699g, 701f, 704ab, 705de, 717bc, 718f, 726cd, **727c,** 728bfh, 730f, 733df, 736f, 738ef, 740h, 742fg, 743g, 746cd, 748ej, 749e, **750bi,** 751i, 753abh, 754f, 760ae, 763f, 765a, 766cf, 769e, 776d, **781a-e, 782a-d, 783,** 791a, **792,** 793h, 795i, 817acd, 829j, 831f, 832h, 833b, 834gh, 840eh, 845deh, 857e, 858de, 871a, **905ef, 907a-c, 911a,** 912b, 915a, 920d, 925e, 927c, **930a-c,** 933c–934b, 936c, 955d, **957b,** 958de, 959d, **964cd,** 965d, **972ce** (see also Christology, Incarnation)

and the Resurrection 881f

'Christ' for 'Yahweh' in NT 641fh, 694e, 746c, 749e, 801i, 817d, 824b, 826b, 831d, 840h, **858e,** 877bc, **907d,** 933f, 934b, 951d, 952i, 953i

evidenced by miracles 730f, 732g, 733f, 751e

foretold or implied in OT 14b, 339a, 340b, 347d, 352d, 421d, 427i

hidden from devils 728h, 730h, 750ij

lumen de lumine 933d

manifested at Transfiguration 733d

primitive preaching economic **817c,** 824c, **825e,** 829f

proclaimed at his Baptism **727c,** 750c

Divino Afflante spiritu, see Pius XII

DIVISION OF NORTH FROM SOUTH, see Schism

DIVORCE 38e, 42e, 100b, 110h, 219a, 403e, 680i, 686b, **708b-d, 735b,** 761d, 763e, 873hi

bad cooking as grounds for 596b

evils of 400b

Hillel and Shammai 686b, 708bcd

Jewish grounds for 596b, 735b

(a) Jewish male privilege 596b, 686b, 735b

mixed marriages and 289k, 294e–i

(the) Matthean exception 708b–d, 735b

Our Lord and 42e, 100b, 110h, 143i, **686b, 708b-d, 735b,** 761d, 763e

Moses and 686b, 708c

paganism and 602b, 874b

Pauline privilege 654i, 660f, 873hi

remarriage after 219a, 761d

Roman law and 735b

separation a mensa et toro 654g, 708e, 761d, 873hi

DJEBEL QARANTAL 683e

DJEMET-NASR CULTURE 117ab

DOCETISM 769b, 778g

and sex relations 145a

DOCILITY 660kl, 735c

DOCTORS, MEDICAL, see Physicians

DOCTORS OF THE LAW 85k, 586d, 617g, 672d, 750a

DOCTRINE, see Dogma

DODANIM 149h

DODO, Dodai, the Ahohite 243f, 284de

(MASS) (the) fraction, breaking of bread (*q.v.*) 774c, 820ce, **825a**, 833d, 843d, **877f**
(the) heavenly liturgy, offering 939e–g
heretics dispense with wine 94i, 652h
incense to be used at 556d
inculcates the Scriptures 10b
institution of 100b, 624a, 644f–j, **652b–eg**, **653f**, 657f, **717f–720c**, **739gh**, **768c**, 825a, 878f
(the) kiss of peace 882c, 892f, 916e, 951h
(the) last Gospel 776b
(the) *Lavabo* 344c
(a) memorial 642a, 652i, 653ae, 657f
of requiem 936a, 938d
(the) Offertory ceremony 186k
one with sacrifice of cross **653fj**, 878f
order of Epistles at 661e
preparation for 878fg
' *qui pridie* . . .' 793e
said in private houses 637c, 652g, 878e
symbolism of the two kinds 657h
thanksgiving, eucharist 652g, 880e (*see also* Blessings)
unde et memores 653a
MASSACRES 211g, 218d (*see also* Ban)
MASSAH 171h, 375a, 683d, 935e (*see also* Meribah)
MASSEBAH, *see* Pillars
MASSORETES, The 21j, **22b–d**, 540e
confuse ' to ' and ' against ' 280o
different schools 22cd
Massora parva, magna, finalis 22c–e
originate vowels points 22bd
targum Massora 24f
MASTEMA, The 593a
MASTURBATION 402f
MATERIALISM IN GREEK PHILOSOPHY 599e
MATERNAL AFFECTION 305f
MATHAN, Matthan 750h
MATHANIAS, Mattaniah 66d, 281a, 477f (*see also* Sedecias)
MATHATHIAS, Mattathias 68d, 559d, 561c, **562f–i**
MATHUSALA, Methuselah 138b
MATTATHIAS, *see* Antigonus, Mathathias
MATTHEW, Gospel of St 41e, 677–723 (*see also* Synoptic)
agreements with Luke as opposed to Mark 610cdfi, 611ac, 679a
alleged dependence on Luke 679f, 745e
and Epistle of St James 945bg, 947ad, 948ae
and the fall of Jerusalem 678abg, 715–17
aramaic original 606bd, 607fg, 614b, 615a, 677c–f, 678ab, 679ade, 687e, 689d, 697b, 700e, 703e, 704c, 714i, 722c, 745de
aramaisms, Semitic flavour 614b, 679de, 686eghi, 687ab, 691c, 694b, 695c, 696cf, 697bd, 698b, 699ag, 702aef, 703c, 706d, 708d, 714df
authorship, authenticity 677b–e, 678bf
Biblical Commission on 50a–g, 51ab, 678b, 679a
Christology 680j, 681af, 682b, 688c, 690g, 693h, 694e, 695b–d, 696b, 697a, 699fg, 701f, 704ab, 705de, 717bc, 718f, 751a
date of 606g, 677a, 678a
discourses in 678c, 679def
ecclesiastical, gospel of the Church 678g
elements dependent on Mark 679e
historicity 699f, 701d, 703a, 704e, 705g, 717b, 722d (*see also* Gospels)
infancy narrative 614d, 617e, 678d, 680–82d
inspiration of 35a, 37de, 679g
Jeremias for Zacharias in 27:9 37e, **721de**
Jewish, Palestinian traits of 607g, 614d

(MATTHEW, Gospel of St) (the) Logia **607f**, 677d, 678b
matter peculiar to 678d, 679a, 699b, 700a–d, 701e, 702e, 703a, 704b, 705fg, 706fg, 707bc, 708de, 709eg–i, 710h, 711bf, 712ad, 718fgh, 721g
on marriage of Joseph and Mary 680h–j, 748d
order, scheme, style of 132d, **607c**, **678cg**, **679de**, 685a, 688d, 689af, 690b, 694b, 697g, 708a, 719a, 720c, 723b, 724d
OT citation on **677f**, 678d, 681ag, 689g, 696d, 698d, 699e, 710g, 711b, 721d
our Greek version of 677ef, 678ab, 679a–g, 703a, 704c, 713c
Papias on 677df
parallels with Mark 610c–f, 679e
priority defended 9c, 50bl, **607b–g**, 610*g*i, **611c–615**, 679a–f
reference to Wisdom 388d, 389e
sacred number seven in 680f, 697f, 703de, 707a, 712d
St Paul and **615a**, **661j**, 678ag, 704g, 708ef, 709e, 710c, 714j, **715bd**, 716cg, 720ab, **914c**, 915de, **916a–c**, 917bc
theme purpose of 678d–g, 752h
MATTHEW, St 689a, 690e, 691ab, 692e, 698b, 728c, 751c, 752b (*see also* Levi)
his name 691a
the publican, taxgatherer 584n, 691a, 692e, 751i
MATTHIAS, St 639g, 657ac, 709f, 724f, 752f, 819d, 820f, **822d**
MATURITY, Christian 907g
MAUNDY THURSDAY 802bcde
MAURICE, F. D. 606f
MAZZALOTH 280j
MAZZAROTH **333d**
McGINLEY, L. J. 609d
MEALS 602h, 652fg (*see also* Manners, Messianic)
grace at 363e, 596f, 774c, 880e
reclining at 311c, 400c, 433b, 526m, 602h, 719f, 739f, 761e
ruler of the feast 769j
sacrificial meals 215c (*see also* Idolothyta, Peace-offering)
sanctity, religious nature of 652i
use of common dish 719f, **739f**
women's place at 602h
MEASURES, *see* Weights and Measures
line, reed 492c, 546d
MECCA 269d
MEDABA, Medeba, *see* Madaba
MEDES, Media 121 l, 122d, 149h, 280 l, 283m, 287aa, **289c**, 309a, 429ae, 432a, 459n, 467
Cyrus conquers 420e, 429e
seven counsellors of 307c, 311c
MEDIATION, of Angels 645n, 934b
of Mary 40j, 786d
of Moses, Aaron 442i, 645n, 646c, 896g
of priests 936c
of the suffering servant 441 l
MEDIATOR, CHRIST THE ONE **640f**, 642j, 645e, 646c, 671u, 803f, 881g, 909f, 911bc, 912b, **920d**, 930g, 932b, 939cg, 941a, 944c, 950d, 966d (*see also* Covenant, New)
and the invocation of Saints 921f
the Colossian heresy 909df, 912bd
MEDITERRANEAN SEA 54j, 235a, 554c
MEDIUMSHIP 192s, 256f, 280a, 879a (*see also* Necromancy)
MEEKNESS COUNSELLED 129j, 374f, 380f, 398c, 685e
MEGABYSUS 122h (*see also* Artaxerxes I)
MEGALITHIC CULTURE 57d
MEGASTHENES 500j
MEGIDDO 55b, 57g, 58c, 59g, 66c, 117b, 119e, 228d, 240de, 241i, 275i, 276c, 280o, 287cfaa, 477d, 552d, **970f** (*see also* Armageddon, Josias, Nechao)
plain of 55b

(MEGIDDO) stables of Solomon 63j, 80f, 267ik, 269gi
stele of Sheshonkh I at 64e, 78a, 120m
MEGILLOTH (scrolls) 246b, 382e, 469ab
MEHUNIM, Meunim, *see* Maon
MELCHI 750h
MELCHIZEDECH 120o, **151ab**, 232d, 339a, **360d**, 462h–r, 547c, 548d, 642g, 653f, 927d, **930af**, **938e–939b**
MELCHOM, *see* Milcom
MELITO OF SARDIS 14e, 94f
MELKART, the Tyrian Baal **64gh**, 65c, 114c, 226gh, 265c, 270h, **271fgkl**, 273k, **276e**, 287e, 418g, 460d, **514i**, 575e, 579e (*see also* Jehu, Jezebel, Jonadab)
Jehu exterminates cult of **276e**, 460d
Lord of the Dance, Baal Marqod 271 l
prophets of 273abm, **416a**, **418g**, 459i, 553b
sky-god, Hadad 271gkl
worshipped in Jerusalem 275ef, 276di
MELKITES, The 25c
MELLO, *see* Millo
MELOTHUS 309c
Memento Mori 381d–f
MEMORY AND ORAL TRADITION 135a, 139a, 679b
MEMPHIS (Noph) 118c, 309b, 432d, **456e**, 488f
MEMRA, The 388g, 607 l, 592c
MENAHEM, Manahem 65b, 266gi, 277hi, 749h
pays tribute to Assyria 64c, 65b, **79d**, 121e, 124d, 277hi, 425i
MENANDER 226g, 267m, 271fg, 881j
MENDICANCY 660 l
MENELAUS, the high-priest 68b, 551h, 560b, 562g, 575f, 576a, 580a
MENI 451k
MENINGITIS 689d
MENSTRUATION 191a, 192j, 691f, 730j
MENTAL SUFFERING, of Christ 769b
of Job 317dek, 320k, 325j
MEPHIBOSHETH, *see* Merib-Baal
MERARI, The sons of 236h, 283pr, 285fgi
MERCENARIES 267ch, 465bc, 559e, 577b
of David 63h, 259i, 261f, 264a, 267c
of Herod 71e
MERCURY 373f, 835b
MERCY 110f, 208f, 211g, 545efh, 548a, 549dfg, 685e, 707b (*see also* God)
misplaced 272g
vessels of 857n
MERCY SEAT, Propitiatory 111ag, **177b**, 191g, 285q, 849f, 940c
MERENPTAH, *see* Mernephtah
MERIBAH 134b, 171h, 196e, 354e, 357f, 359b, 935e, 938a
MERIBATH-KADESH 493i
MERIB-BAAL, Miphiboseth 258ab, 260a, 261eg, 262f, 263b, 283bb
MERIT, Doctrine of **642fg**, 643c, 856f, 859 l, **910b**, 923d, **924d**, 938c (*see also* Rewards)
grace and merit 546a, 643c, 924d
human frailty and 397i
imputed merit 850b
merits of Christ **84h**, 422f, 426ae, 427c, 642g, 850b, 894e, 895i, 930e
merits of patriarchs, saints, martyrs 34c, 214b, 271a, 484j, **642f**, 859e, 966d
predestination and 857k
prevision of merit **84h**, 422f, 426ae, 427c, 856f, 857k, 895i
source of merit 643c, 909i
MERK'S EDITION OF NT 583h
MERNEPHTAH 120e, 125c
and the sea peoples 120f
Pharaoh of the Exodus 60de, 62d, 78a, 119h, **163a–d**, 228b
stele of 62a, 78a, 125c, 163d
MERODACH-BALADAN II 66a, **121h**, 269c, **279 1**, 420d, 433a
MEROM 57i, 233cd
MEROZ **241j**, 245e

(Parousia) like the flood 717bc
like the lightning 670iln, 671c, 716d
like the sprouting fig 671d, 717a
many parousias 625e, 671ey, 717de, 733c, 737deg, 738ac
Maran atha 641f, **858d**, 882i
modern heterodoxy concerning 670bc
near, imminent 38c, 626c, 655b, 660ap, 670m, **671dnop**, 693a, 704g, 737b, 756c, 758g, 882i, 908a
precursor of 671k, 733e
revealing of secrets at 730k
Our Lord's ambiguity concerning 670f–j, 671f–l, 715ab (*see also* Economy)
signs of the times 737af, 738b–d (*see also* Signs of the times)
will faith survive to 763b
PARTHENON, The 600f
PARTHIA, Parthians 70eh, 71bc, **122 l**, 563d, 571df, **598i**, **966e**, 967f–h, 970e
PARTRIDGE 244j
PARVAIM, Parwayim 286g
PASAGARDAE, The 289c
PASCAL 891c
PASCH 287p (*see also* Passover)
PASCHAL LAMB 40ah, 102, 103a, 113g, 169e, 216c, 287opz, 417g (*see also* Lamb of God, Passover)
at Last Supper 720a, 722e, 768b
not a bone broken 811c
type of Christ 40a, 163h, 169di, 644h, 649d, 768b, 811c
PASSION, The 42d, **102n**, 338b, 388k, 419g, 422cdf, **441i–m, 444h–l, 445h–k, 446**, 689g, **719–22, 739–42, 768–72, 807–11**, 896d, 920d, 925e, 929e, 930d, 933c, 934ef, 937c, 940g (*see also* Cross, Crucifixion, Death, Gethsemane)
according to the Scriptures 740bc, 764a, 774b, 775b
beatific vision uninterrupted in 722e
(the) blood and water 649e, 779e
Christ smitten before high-priest 686d, 721h
complete, yet completed by us 42e, 899bc, **900bc**, 911df
congruent 935a–c
(the) crown of thorns 722a, 741f, 809a
drama of 620g
ecce homo 721h, 741f
effects of 746f, **900bc**, 949g, 950g, 951a
exemplary 925e, 949g, 950g, 951a
for the Church 898il
foretold by Christ 619f, 620ace, 621h, 670g, 691c, 704e, 705ce, 710a, 719ab, 720ab, 733ae, 734a, 735f, 739g–i, 752a, 754g, 755ad, 762d, 764ab, 765a, 768bcf
Herod Antipas and 754e, 770b
Our Lady and 85k, 86dk, 742g
mob's behaviour 721h, 741c, 772b
Our Lord's prayer during 343d, 345b, 722d, 742d, 772a
primary importance of 768a
(the) sacred wounds 547i, **552d**, 553b, 939c
(the) scarlet robe 538h, 722a, 741f
(the) scourging and mocking 721h, 445i, 721h, 722a, 741df, 770b, 808d, **809a**
(the) youth who fled naked 725b, 740d, 763f, 807e
PASSOVER, Pasch 103a, **169**, 175j, 199f, 216cd, 303c, 360g, 362g, 395a, 714g, 719a, 732h, 758e (*see also* Paschal Lamb)
and Azymes 113gf, **169ab**, 719d
and the Last Supper, Passion 83e, 113g, 719d, 739de, 768bc, 802b, 823a, 833f, 872g
bitter herbs 169e, 719f
blood on the doorposts 169dg, 642c, 967b
Chalice of Benediction 720a (*see also* Blessing)
Christ our Passover 40a, 169i, 644h,

649d, 768b, 793c (*see also* Lamb of God)
(Passover) cups of wine at 720ab, 739d
date of 83g, 768b
development of rite 169a–c, 216c, 292i, 360gi, 362g, 493c
exclusion of uncircumcised, etc. **106f**, 169i
Galilean date of 719d, 768b
Hallel hymn 362g, 720c, 739di
hour of sacrifice contested 169e
in NT times 169e, 360gi, 362g, 719e, 720a
linked with Pentecost 193t
loins girt for journey 758e, 950c
name of feast **113f**, 169d, 287p
paschal amnesty 741c
paschal sauce 739d, 802h
paschal sheaf **113h**, 193s
some historic OT passovers 113g, 280m, 287p
standing at 739f
temple traders at 765d, 766b
type of Calvary and Mass 163h, 169di, 768b
whited sepulchres at 714g
wine ceremonies at 768c
PASTORAL EPISTLES 641 l, 661b–d, 905e, **918–20** (*see also* Timothy, Titus)
Apostolic Fathers and 919c
authenticity 51 l–o, **918f–919c**, 921c
date 51 l–o, 661f, 918c
(the) ministry in 919f–920c, 951f
style, vocabulary of 918h–919b
PATERNAL ADVICE 305c
PATERNITY, acknowledgment of 154hi, 320 l
legal paternity, *see* Joseph
spiritual paternity 797i–k
PATHROS, *see* Phatures
PATIBULUM, The 722b, 813e, 910a
PATIENCE 42a, 317b–k, 398c, 680j, 938c, 942d, 946eg, 948e, 949dg, 950i, 953c, 969cj (*see also* God, Job)
PATMOS 776g, 781j
PATRIARCHS, The 59, 60a, 125d–g, 484 l, 857d
ages, longevity of 32 l, 125d, 134c, **140b–f**, 149p, 152j
altar prayers of 106a
altars raised by 106ac
antediluvian 138bcd, 140be, 146g, 148c, 283a
customary laws of 59h, 139g, 150c, 151g, 152j, 153e, 156kl
daughter's rights 79k
historicity of 45gh, **59hi**, 79jk, 104d, 105a, 135 lm, **139–40**
husbandry of 139d, 318c
idolatry and 59d, 106h
importance of 104g
in heaven 759b
laws of 128
merits, prayers of 642f
monotheists 105a–c
morality of 106d
names of 59h
polygamy of 110h
primogeniture, birth-right 218g
religion of 104–6, 113f, 150a, 151i, 154b, 213d
ritual of 106a
sacrifices of **106a–c**, 146a, 147b, 151a, 154o, 318c, 320c
sanctify Israel 859ef
sanctuaries of 318c
semi-nomadic **59g**, 113f, 139d, 152k, 153hn, 156i
sins of 106h, 139b
status of wives of 79k
times of 45gh, **59**, 139cd
tribal interpretation of 59i
twelve 159a
vows 318c
weaknesses and virtues of 106h
PATRIOTISM, Christian 857d, 925f
PATRISTICS 5e, 6cd (*see also* Fathers)
PATROBAS 863g

PATROS, Phatures 428o, 464f, 488df
PAUL, Apocalypse of 94j
PAUL, St 631e, **663-9**, 776g, 818d, 823c, 829f, 868d, 929c, 930aef (*see also* Christology)
and Agrippa II **842g-j**, 890d
and Apollos 839e (*see also* Apollos)
and Felix 842a–d
and Festus 831a, **842e-j**, 890d
and Gallio 81ce, 839c
and Our Lady 896h
and Roman Government 660t, 843a, 861cd
and St Barnabas 831g, 833a–e, 834b–835, 836b, **837a**, 893g, 918e
and St James 841bcd, 895bfg, 946b, 960b
and St John 653i, 895e–g
and St Luke **667fg**, 744c–e, 745ij, 746ef, 747f, 748b, 751bc, 757ad, 759b, 761b, 762e, 763d, 766e
and St Mark 725ab, 834cd, 837a, 924e
and St Peter 606ab, 657op, 831g, **832d**, 836g, **837a**, 893g, **895abe-h**, 896c
and St Stephen 828b, 829a, 834d, 841ef
and the Sanhedrin 841i
and Silas 837a, 908a (*see also* Silas)
and the Twelve **641c**, 662e, **667de**, **831g**, 836, 837a, 841bcd, **895a-g**
and Timothy (*q.v.*) 659e, 905d
(the) apologist 40i, 633c, 648f, 834e, 835c, 838d, 839j, 857b
apostle of the Gentiles 115g, 633b, 636f, **669ab**, 831aeg, 833c, 834a, 841g, 843a, 859e, **863b**, **895fg**, 901ab, 914c, **921f**
apostolic call, commission 656e, 657c, **664f**, 831cg, 834a, 869a, 894g, 895a
apostolic life and work 656e, 871h–872b, **876b**, 887b–l, 888a–d
apostolic status of 831a, 863c, 865ahi, 866a, 869a, 873i, 874c, 875g–j, 881a, 890g–k, 893f, 894g, 895abf, 918g
appeals to Caesar 660t, 744ef, **842f**, 843h
at Antioch in Pisidia 3c, 834d–k, 895bh
at Antioch on the Orontes 631e, 833a–eh, 835e, 836abg, 839c
at Athens 40i, 633c, **838b-g**, 876c, 882g, 914c
at Beroea 838b
at Caesarea 815c, 840h, 841am, 842, 844g, 898b
at Corinth 81ce, 633d, 676g, 816c, 838b, 839a–c, 840a, 844h, 864gh, 870a, 876a, 882e, 890i, 914de
at Damascus 676fg, 831ef, 891d
at Derbe 835e
at Ephesus 81f, 632a, 816c, 819a, 820d, 839c–j, **840c-f**, 863h, 864hi, 867h, 876a, 881j, 882f, 883c, 898c, 909c, 918c, 919h
at Iconium 835a
at Jerusalem 657p, **676fg**, 725a, 831g, 833e, **836**, 841a–l, 842i, 893d, 895bc–g, 981e (*see also* Councils)
at Lystra 835a–d, 891a
at Perga, Perge 835e
at Philippi 81e, 816a, 820f, 837d–h, 876a, 905cd, 915c
at Rome 774cf, 815a, 819a, 820f, 841aj, 843ag–i, 882 l, 898b, 899a, 905e, 909d, 918ci, 919b, 949e
at Tarsus 831g, 833c, 837a, 838c
at Thessalonica 81e, 816c, 838a, 914c, 915b
at Troas **652fg**, 820c, **837c**, 840b, 904f
at Tyre 819a, 820f, 840gh
attitude to death 840c, 887ij, 906c, 914k, 924d
baptism and confirmation of 650g, 831e, 841f
birth, birthplace 94j, **663b**, 828b, 831g, 895b (*see also* Tarsus)
boasting 656e, 849j, 875g, 876a, 883e, 890g–891, 906c
bonds, imprisonment 661f, **666d-j**, **667b**, 744ef, 815a–c, 837fg, **841-3**, 844g, 898b, 901b, 904ef, 905de, 906b,

(SACRIFICE OF CHRIST) sufficient, final, irrepeatable 893eh, 894cq, **941bce**
the heavenly offering, liturgy **939cf**
SACRILEGE 65d, 250g, 259b, 273f, 687e, 716a, 736c, 737h, 848f (*see also* Core, Holiness)
of Antiochus IV 562ce, 576c
of Crassus 70h
of Heliodorus 68b, 575b, 576b
of Pompey 70e, 561b
SADISM, Pagan 601k
SADNESS 403f
SADDUCEES, The 70b, 113i, 169e, 376e, 379d, **588ab**, 592a, 620f, 625b, 682gh, 703fg, 711b–i, 713ab, **736h**, 766b, 827a, 881j
accept the Pentateuch only 713b, 736hi
and Hellenism 588a, 589f, 736h
and Pentecost 113i
and Rome 736h, 766e
denial of angels 736h, 820g, 841i, 842b
denial of Providence 713a
denial of survival and resurrection 115d, 339e, 579e, **588a**, **713a**, 736i, 766e, 820a, 841i, 842b, 881j
denial of spirit, immortality 115d, 736h, 841i, 842b
extinction of 588b
political opportunism of 588b, 736h
reject oral obligations 588a
scribes of 751i
worldliness of 588a
SADLIER, Printer 30k
SADOC, Zadok 179a, 249k, 259j, 261e, 262i, 267fg, 283n, 284hln, 285t, 286a
SADOCITES 492n
SAFE DEPOSITS 585b
SA-GAZ, The 119 l, 120a
SAGES, The 267 l, 283b, 484j, 487q
SAGITTARIUS 967g
SAHIDIC BIBLE 4b, 781h, 783f
ST GALL, monastery 4c
ST PETER'S BASILICA 338a
SAINTS, The 34c, 503jkl, 504e, 931b, 942ab
merits of 214b, 271a, **642f**, 859e, 966d
OT and Christian, compared 102g
Pauline term for Christians 656a, 845i, 869a, 906a, 910a
prayers of 334fg, **642f**, 948i, 966dg, **967d**
SAKKALA, The 228a
SAKKUTH 278i, 527i
SALADIN 567d
SALAMANU, King of Moab 519p
SALAMIS, Battle of 289c, 311e, 543c, 545k
in Cyprus 834c
SALATHIEL, Shealtiel 283e, 291a, **543fg**, 680e, 750g
SALCAH, Salecha 57j, 233g
SALEBIM 239d
SALEM *for* JERUSALEM 151b, 335c, 360d, 938e
SALIC LAW 173f
SALIM 788i
SALMAN 519p
SALMANA 242j
SALMANASAR, *see* Shalmaneser
SALMON, Mt 351c
SALOME (*see also* Alexandra Salome)
daughter of Herodias 701b, 731f
mother of Hyrcanus 70d
wife of Zebedee 710b, 722g, 773b, 776e, 810d
SALT 734e (*see also* Covenant)
and nomad hospitality 184e
given to new-born children 484 l
losing its savour 685g, 734e
Lot's wife 152d, 392f
of Dead Sea 56a, 152c
sacrificial 184de, **492 l**, 734d
sowing with 243e
spiritual 913c
symbol of friendship 734e
valley of 277b

SALT-WORT, *see* Purslane
SALUTATIONS 640o (*see also* Greetings, Pauline Epistles)
SALVATION 448ac, 449dej, 450k, 593c, 641 l, 643e, **645g**, 648 l, 688a, 693a, 733b, 759b, 844bf, **846bcg**, 848g, **849**, 850a, 856df, 859i, 927cd, 929e, 930ce, 931a, 950e (*see also* Jesus, Justification, Redemption)
bible-study and 2a, 10b–d
certainty and uncertainty of 640m, 645g, **794f**, 850**bef**, 854c, 855eh, 856d–f, 905f, 907e
charity needed for 879f
demands effort 688a
faith and 643k, **648 l–o** (*see also* Justification)
for converting others 948i
God's initiative in 648o
Greco-Roman concept of 846c
individual and collective 388i, 392c–h, 394–5
initial and final 625d, 850bfm, 861h, 931b
in, through Christ, its author 547f, 550g, 749h, 751a, 817ce, 826b, 827b, 832d, 834eh, 836d, 842i, 930ace, **935a, 937c**
in, through the Church 657m, 795e, 824b, 825b, **857jk**
man's supreme need 704f, 758cd, 759f, 764f
ordinary, extraordinary means 147f
OT concept of **846c**, 849j
perseverance (*q.v.*) and 715d
riches and 763gh
sacerdotal aspect of 930e
(the) saved 688a, 712d, 759b, 886 l, 935a (*see also* Elect)
social and individual 794f
subjective salvation 931ab
through motherhood 654f, 660d, 921g
universally needed 847–48i
universally offered 448b, 646c, 688c, 735i, 739h, 743e, 746f, 824bf, 834j, 846be, 849c, 859k, 863 l, **921ef**, 925d
worked out with fear and trembling 640m, 645g, 905f, 907e
SAMAL, Hittite State of 275a
SAMARIA 57g, **58ch**, **64bef**, 79d, 80de, 228d, **271e**, 274j, 287x, 309e, 386b, 410e, 412f, 413f, 420b, 437a–c, 439h, 478c, 527b, 534e, 692f, 693d
besieged by Benhadad III 274m
church of 819d, 820b, 832e
deportees from 278e
fall of 65b, **79d**, **121fg**, 135oq, 265e, **278de**, 279b, 303bd, **318r**, **420bc**, 425p, 432a, 456e, 462d, 514h, 519cdk
Herod's city, Sebaste 58h, 271e
Hill of 274j
Hyrcanus destroys 70b
palaces of Omri, Ahab 64g, 80de, 273c
plantation of 121fij, 124c, 275h, **278ghi**, 291ei, 304a, 322b, 538m
population of 584gh
seat of Persian Governor 67e, 289g
temple of Melkart in 276e
three regions of 569a
SAMARITAN OSTRACA, The 19k, 80e
SAMARITAN PENTATEUCH 12b, 67h, 232a, 789g
ages of patriarchs in 140e, 150a
date of 21h
Phoenician script of 21h
textual peculiarities **21 l**, 77a, 125e
SAMARITANS, The 58cd, 67c, 121f, 169e, 218k, **278g**, 291ei, 406i, 756g, 789d
and Antiochus IV 562d, 563q, 576b
conversion of 651e, 776g, 820b
hated by Jews 58h, 756f, 789d
hostility to Nehemias 295e, 296a–chi
Maccabaean conquest of 58e
Messianic hope among 789g
our Lord and 55c, 114e, 584n, 756afg, 757a, **789c–790d**
returned exiles and 67c, 281j, 288c, 291e, 295h, 543c, 544a

(SAMARITANS) schism 299f, 584eg
syncretism among 278hi
the good Samaritan 41b, 114e, 584n, 756fg, 757a
the grateful Leper 762b
the woman at Sychar 40h, 55c, 58h, 643c, 649d, 670e, 757a, 779e, **789c–790d**, 794e
SAMARITAN TEMPLE 67h, 70b, 299f, **789df**
the appeal to Deuteronomy 21 l
SAMGAR, Shamgar 238e, **239j**
SAMMAEL 718h
SAMMURAMAT 121d (*see also* Semiramis)
SAMSON 57e, 63d, 238dei, **244**, 313b, 360d
cunning of 160c
his strength supernatural 242f, 244aegjk
Nazarite dedication of 244ae
popular hero 244a
solar mythology and 244bc
SAMUEL 63c–e, 276o, 406d, 711d
Agag slain by **38e**, 206n, **253a**
and sacrifice 114 l
ancestors and sons of 283p
apparition at Endor 256f
attitude to monarchy 251cd, 252h
Books of, *see* Kings I and II
character 252h
childhood 177j, **249a–250a**
death of 255k
(an) ' Ephraimite ' Levite 283pq
gospel of the Infancy and 103a, 249h, 748g
growth of 249i
name 249e
prayer of 251b
prophetical call 250a
prophetic communities and 63d, 252d, 254i, 410c–e
reformer, judge 63cd, 251ab
regulation of Levites 283ee
Saul and 252a–k, 253ab, 254i, 256f, 409f, 411a, 414i, 418f
writings of 11f, **224d**, 282w, 285t
SANBALLAT, the Horonite 67eh, 289gj, **295e**, 296ah, 299f
SANCTIFICATION 1g, 2, 635b, 846c, 850abc, 851a–ik, 858bc, 929cd, 930g, 931ae, 949gh, 950d, 953a–d (*see also* Holiness)
and suffering 388i, 389g, 457g, 853f, 911ef, 946eg
Christ the sanctifier 930e
of the people 929f
through the Holy Spirit 914f
SANCTUARY 174d, **178d**, 218a, 267c, 964g (*see also* Centralization, Holy Place, Refuge)
SANCTUARY LAMP 250a (*see also* Lampstand)
Sanctus, The 425 l, 966b
SANDAL-WOOD 269i, 286d
SANDALS 731c
SANDAY, W. 607ahj
SANDSTORM, *see* Khamsin
SANHEDRIN, The 70ad, 74cde, 289s, 308eh, 310h, 570a, 587ab, 620df, 681e, 682g, 685j, 719a, 720f, 721ab, 722h, 736cef, 739a–c, 740ce–j, 741a, 754g, 766ab, 769de, 772c, 796il
apostles before 776g, 826abg, 827bc, 831a, 841i
Judicial procedure of 587b
meeting-place of 721a, 740g
origin of 70f
Rome and 70f, 74cd, 587b
triple division of **681e**, 754g, 765e
SANITARY PRESCRIPTIONS 109g, 183 l, 189b, 190ir–q, 191a, 218 l
SANTES PAGNINI 581e
SAPHAN, *see* Shaphan
SAPHON 243 l
SAPIENTIAL, *see* Wisdom
SAPPHIRA 636e, 654b (*see also* Ananias)
SARA OF ECBATANA 302bc, 304–7
SARAA 244aegj
SARACENS 487f

List of Maps

Index of Names in Maps

MAP 2

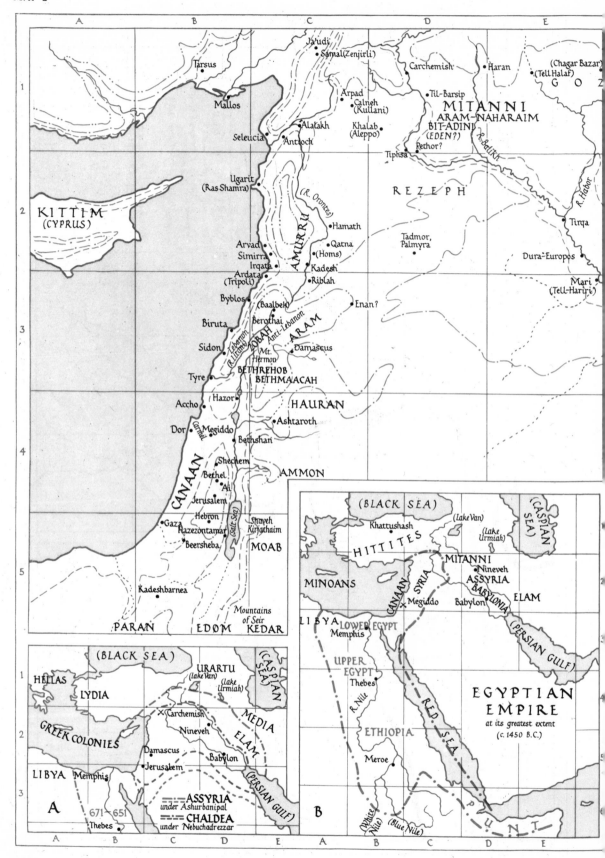

THOMAS NELSON & SONS LTD

Parkside Works Edinburgh 9
3 Henrietta Street London WC2
312 Flinders Street Melbourne C1
5 Parker's Buildings Burg Street Cape Town

THOMAS NELSON & SONS (CANADA) LTD
91-93 Wellington Street West Toronto 1

THOMAS NELSON & SONS
19 East 47th Street New York 17

SOCIÉTÉ FRANÇAISE D'ÉDITIONS NELSON
25 rue Henri Barbusse Paris Vᵉ

First published February 1953
Copyright 1953 by THOMAS NELSON & SONS

L-2-58

MAP 1

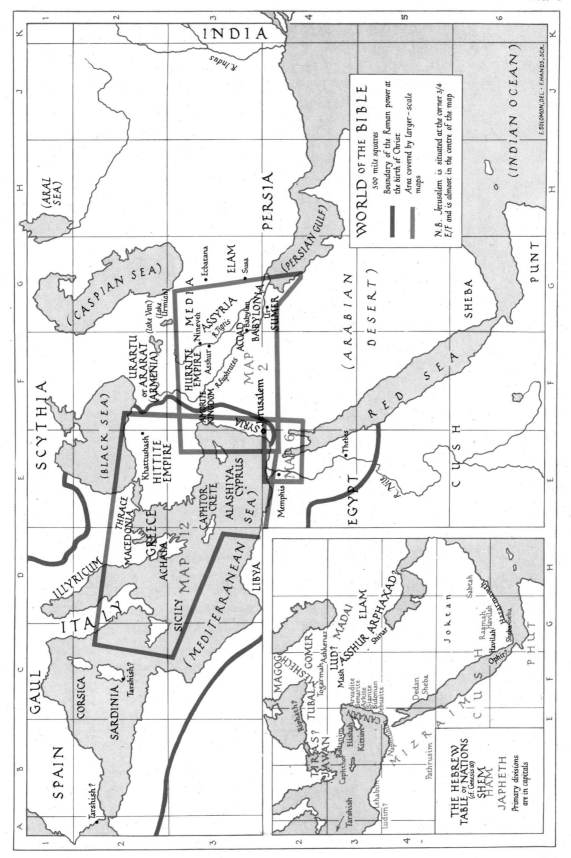

WORLD of the BIBLE

500 mile squares

Boundary of the Roman power at
the birth of Christ

Area covered by larger-scale
maps

N.B. Jerusalem is situated at the corner 3/4
E/F and is almost in the centre of the map

E.SOLOMON.DEL.· F.HANDS.SCR.

(INDIAN OCEAN)

INDIA

R.Indus

(ARAL
SEA)

PERSIA

(CASPIAN SEA)

(Lake Van)
(Lake Urmiah)

MEDIA
·Ecbatana
ELAM
·Susa

(PERSIAN GULF)

URARTU
or ARARAT
(ARMENIA)

HURRITE
EMPIRE ·Nineveh
Asshur· ·ASSYRIA
R.Tigris
R.Euphrates ACCAD
Babylon· ·SUMER
·BABYLONIA Ur·

AMORITE
KINGDOM
Jerusalem·
·SYRIA

(ARABIAN

DESERT)

MAP 2

MAP 6

SHEBA

PUNT

SCYTHIA

(BLACK SEA)

Khattushash·
HITTITE
EMPIRE

THRACE
MACEDONIA

GREECE

ACHAIA

CAPHTOR,
CRETE

ALASHIYA,
CYPRUS

(AEGEAN
SEA)

·Thebes

RED SEA

CUSH

EGYPT
·Memphis
R.Nile

GAUL

SPAIN

CORSICA
Tarshish?
SARDINIA

ILLYRICUM

ITALY

SICILY MAP 12

LIBYA

(MEDITERRANEAN)

Tarshish?

Tarshish?

THE HEBREW
TABLE of NATIONS
(cf. Genesis 10)
SHEM
HAM
JAPHETH
Primary divisions
are in capitals

MAGOG

TUBAL
MESHECH
GOMER
Togarmah Ashkenaz

LUD?
Mash MADAI
ASSHUR ARPHAXAD?
ELAM

Shinar

TIRAS?
JAVAN
Caphtor Rodanim
Elishah Kittim
Kittim

CANAAN
Arvadite
Gemarite
Arkite
Sinite
Sidonian
Jebusite

MIZRAIM
Naphtuhim
Pathrusim

Lehabim

Ludim?
Tarshish
Dodanim?
Riphath?

Dedan
Sheba

Joktan
Sabtah
Raamah
Havilah Hazarmaveth
Ophir? Sheba

CUSH

PHUT

1297

MAP 2

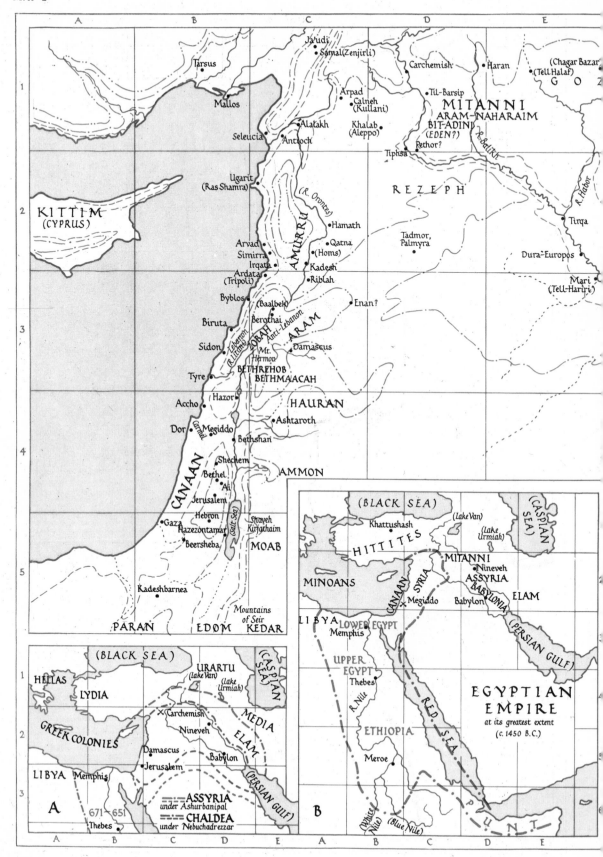

KITTIM
(CYPRUS)

Tarsus

Mallos

Seleucia

Antioch

Ja'udi
Samal (Zenjirli)

Arpad
Calneh
(Kullani)

Alalakh

Khalab
(Aleppo)

Carchemish

Haran

(Chagar Bazar)
(Tell Halaf)

G O Z

MITANNI
ARAM–NAHARAIM
BIT-ADINI
(EDEN?)

Til-Barsip

Pethor?

Tiphsa

R E Z E P H

Tirqa

R. Habor

Ugarit
(Ras Shamra)

(R. Orontes)

A M U R R U

Hamath

Arvad
Simirra
Irqata
Ardata
(Tripoli)

Qatna
(Homs)

Kadesh
Riblah

Tadmor,
Palmyra

Dura-Europos

Mari
(Tell-Hariri)

Byblos

(Baalbek)

Berothai

Enan?

Biruta

Sidon

Tyre

Lebanon
(R. Litani)
Mt.
Hermon

OBAH
Anti-Lebanon

A R A M

Damascus

BETHREHOB
BETHMAACAH

Accho

Dor

Hazor

Megiddo
Carmel

Bethshan

HAURAN

Ashtaroth

C A N A A N

Shechem

Bethel

Ai

Jerusalem

Hebron

Gaza

Hazezontamar

Beersheba

(Salt Sea)

Shaveh
Kirjathaim

MOAB

AMMON

Kadeshbarnea

PARAN

EDOM

Mountains
of Seir

KEDAR

Inset A

(BLACK SEA)

HELLAS

LYDIA

GREEK COLONIES

LIBYA   Memphis

URARTU
(Lake Van)
(Lake
Urmiah)

(CASPIAN
SEA)

×Carchemish

Nineveh

Damascus

Jerusalem

Babylon

MEDIA

ELAM

(PERSIAN GULF)

671–651

ASSYRIA
under Ashurbanipal
CHALDEA
under Nebuchadrezzar

Thebes

A

Inset B

(BLACK SEA)

Khattushash

(Lake Van)

(Lake
Urmiah)

(CASPIAN
SEA)

HITTITES

MINOANS

CANAAN
×SYRIA
×Megiddo

MITANNI
Nineveh
ASSYRIA
BABYLONIA
Babylon

ELAM

LIBYA
LOWER EGYPT
Memphis

UPPER
EGYPT
Thebes

R. Nile

(PERSIAN GULF)

EGYPTIAN
EMPIRE
at its greatest extent
(c. 1450 B.C.)

ETHIOPIA

Meroe

RED SEA

(White Nile)   (Blue Nile)

P U N T

B

MAP 2

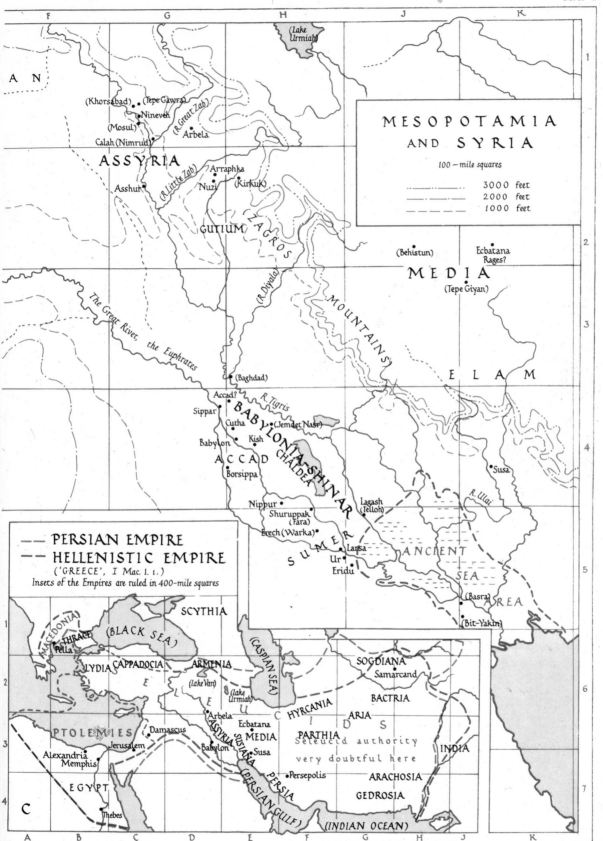

MESOPOTAMIA
AND SYRIA

100 — mile squares

	3000 feet
	2000 feet
	1000 feet

(Lake Urmiah)

AN

(Khorsabad) (Tepe Gawra)
•Nineveh
(Mosul)
Calah (Nimrud)
Arbela
ASSYRIA

(R. Great Zab)

(R. Little Zab)

Arrapkha
Asshur
Nuzi (Kirkuk)

GUTIUM

ZAGROS

(R. Diyala)

(Behistun)
Ecbatana
Rages?
MEDIA
(Tepe Giyan)

MOUNTAINS

ELAM

The Great River, the Euphrates

(Baghdad)
Accad?
Sippar
Cutha
Babylon Kish (Jemdet Nasr)
ACCAD
Borsippa

R. Tigris

BABYLONIA–SHINAR

CHALDEA

Nippur
Shuruppak (Fara)
Erech (Warka)
SUMER
Larsa
Ur
Eridu

Lagash (Telloh)

R. Ulai

•Susa

ANCIENT

SEA

AREA

(Basra)

(Bit-Yakin)

PERSIAN EMPIRE
HELLENISTIC EMPIRE
('GREECE', I Mac. l. 1.)
Insets of the Empires are ruled in 400-mile squares

SCYTHIA

MACEDONIA
THRACE (BLACK SEA)
Pella
LYDIA CAPPADOCIA ARMENIA
(Lake Van)
(Lake Urmiah)
(CASPIAN SEA)

SOGDIANA
Samarcand

BACTRIA

ARIA

HYRCANIA

PARTHIA
Seleucid authority
very doubtful here
INDIA

PTOLEMIES
Damascus
Jerusalem
Alexandria
Memphis
EGYPT
Thebes
C

Arbela
Ecbatana
ASSYRIA
MEDIA
Babylon
SUSIANA Susa
PERSIA
Persepolis
(PERSIAN GULF)
(INDIAN OCEAN)

ARACHOSIA
GEDROSIA

INDIA

MAP 3

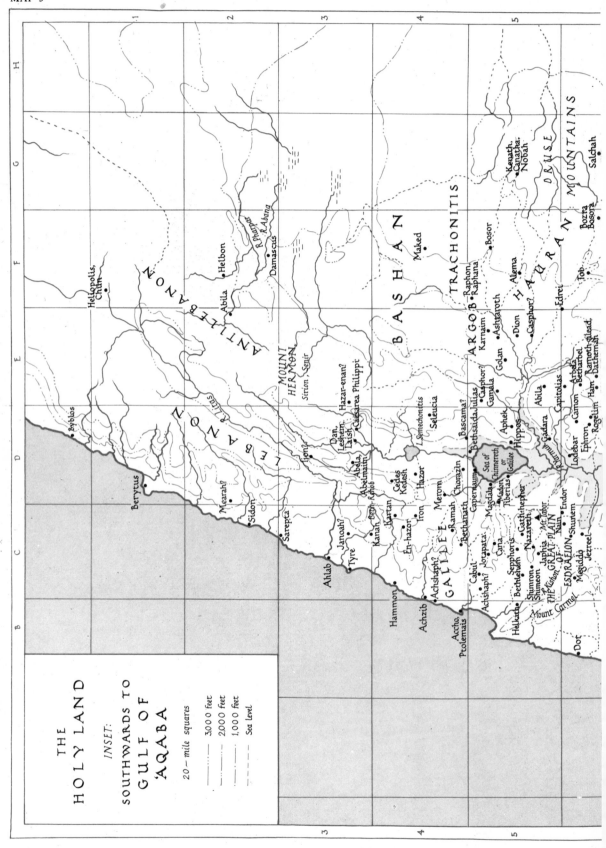

THE
HOLY LAND

INSET:
SOUTHWARDS TO
GULF OF
'AQABA

20 – mile squares

———— 3000 feet
———— 2000 feet
———— 1000 feet
– – – – Sea Level

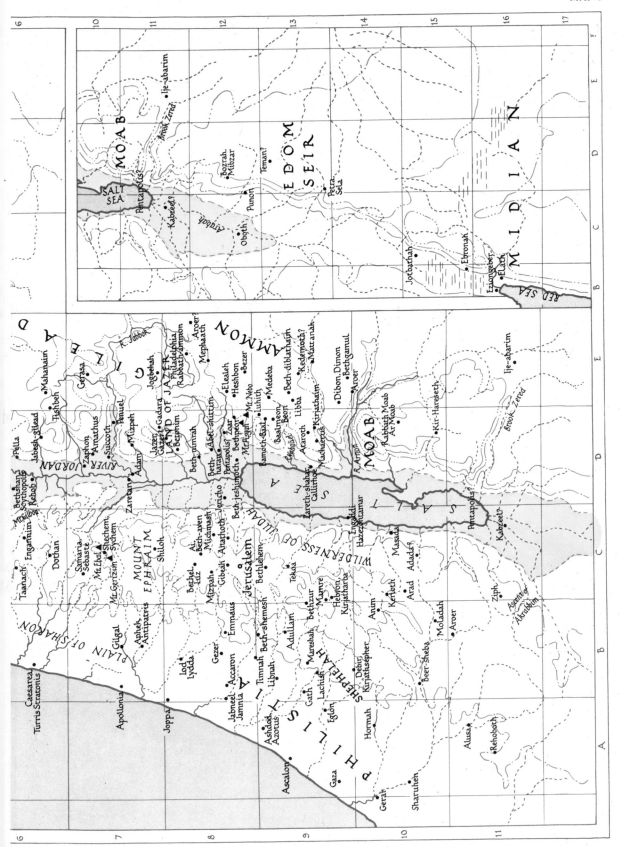

MAP 3

MAP 4

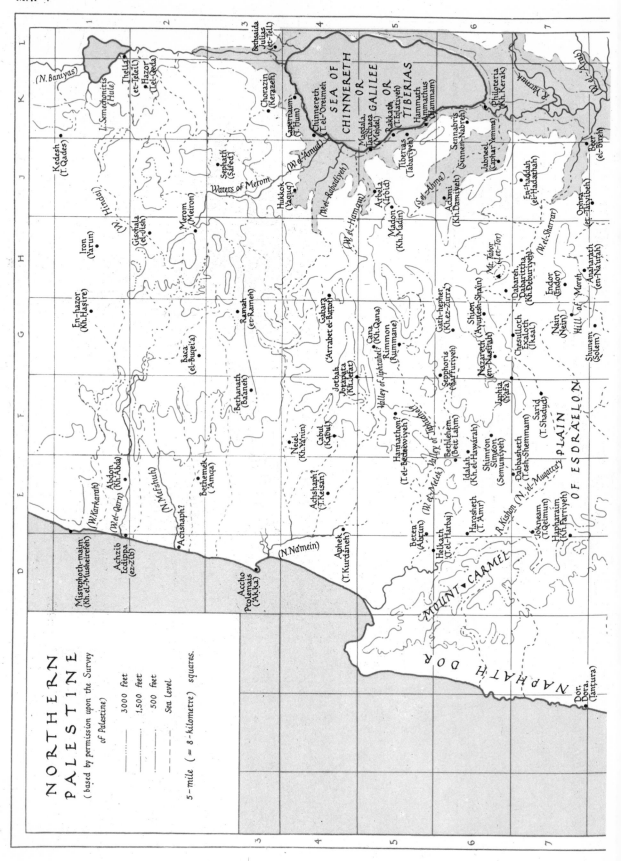

NORTHERN
PALESTINE
(based by permission upon the Survey
of Palestine)

.... 3000 feet
--------- 1,500 feet
--------- 500 feet
--------- Sea level

5-mile (= 8-kilometre) squares.

(N. Baniyas)

L. Semechonitis
(Hule)

Kedesh
(T. Qades)

Thella
(et-Teleil)

Hazor
(Tel-Qeda)

Chorazin
(Kerazeh)

Bethsaida
Julias (et-Tell)

SEA OF
CHINNERETH
OR
GALILEE
OR
TIBERIAS

Capernaum
(T. Hum)

Chinnereth
(T. el-'Oreimeh)

Magdala,
Taricheae
(Mejdel)

Rakkath
(T. Eqlatiyeh)

Hammath
(Hammam)

Philoteria
(Kh. Kerak)

R. Yarmuk

(W. el-'Amud)

Sephath
(Safed)

Hukkok
(Yaquq?)

Waters of Merom

(W. el-Rabadiyeh)

(W. el-Hamam)

Tiberias
(Tabariyeh)

Sennabris
(Sinnen-Nabreh)

Jabneel
(Caphar Yamma)

En-haddah
(el-Hadathah)

Beer
(el-Bireh)

(W. el-'Arab)

Merom
(Meiron)

Gischala
(el-Jish)

(W. Hindaj)

Iron
(Yarun)

Arbela
(Irbid)

Madon
(Kh. Madin)

(S. el-Ahna)

Adami
(Kh. Damiyeh)

Ophra
(et-Taiyibeh)

En-hazor
(Kh. Hasire)

Ramah
(er-Rameh)

Gabara
('Arrabet el-Buttof)

Mt. Tabor
(et-Tor)

Dabareh,
Dabaritcha
(Kh. Deburiyeh)

Endor
(Endur)

Anaharath
(en-Na'urah)

Baca
(el-Buqei'a)

Cana
(Kh. Qana)

Rimmon
(Rummane)

Gath-hepher
(Kh. ez-Zurra)

Shion
(Ayun esh-Sha'in)

Hill of Moreh

Bethanath
(Ba'aneh)

Jotbah
Jotapata
(Kh. Jefat)

Valley of Jiphtahel?

Nain
(Nein)

Shunem
(Solem)

Abdon
(Kh. Abda)

Bethemek
('Amqa)

Neiel
(Kh. Ya'nin)

Cabul
(Kabul)

Hanhathon?
(T. el-Bedeiwiyeh)

Nazareth
(en-Nasirah)

Sepphoris
(Saffuriyeh)

Chesulloch
Exaloch
(Iksal)

PLAIN

Misrephoth-maim
(Kh. el-Musheirefeh)

(W. Kurkarah)

(W. el-Qarn)

Achzib
Ecdippa
(ez-Zib)

(N. Mefshuh)

Achshaph?

Achshaph?
(T. Keisan)

Aphek
(T. Kurdaneh)

Bethlehem
(Beit Lahm)

Valley of Jiphthahel

Idalah
(Kh. el-Hawarah)

Shimron
Simeon
(Semuniyeh)

Dabbusheth
(T. esh-Shemmam)

Japhia
(Yafa)

Sarid
(T. Shaduch)

OF ESDRAELON

Accho
Ptolemais
(Akka)

(N. Na'mein)

(W. el-Malek)

Beten
(Abtun)

Helkath
(T. el-Harbaj)

Harosheth
(T. 'Amr)

R. Kishon (N. el-Muqatta')

Jokneam
(T. Qeimun)

Hapharaim
(Kh. Farriyeh)

MOUNT CARMEL

NAPHATH DOR

Dor,
Dora
(Tantura)

MAP 4

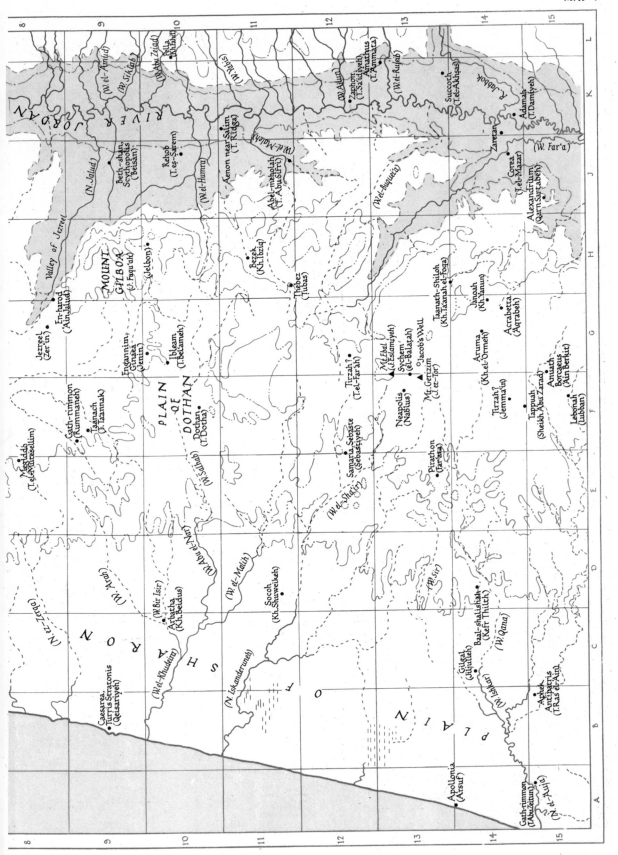

MAP 5

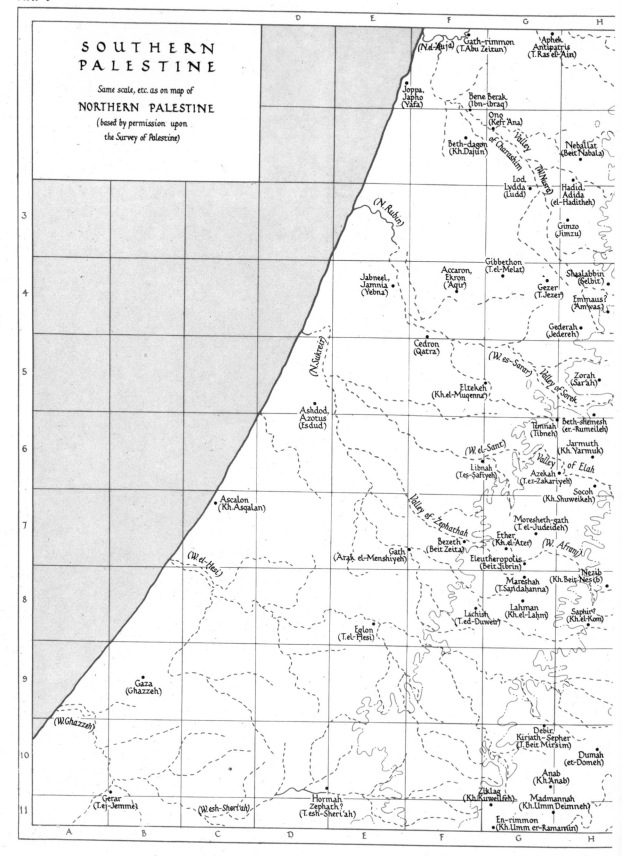

SOUTHERN
PALESTINE

Same scale, etc. as on map of

NORTHERN PALESTINE

(based by permission upon
the Survey of Palestine)

MAP 5

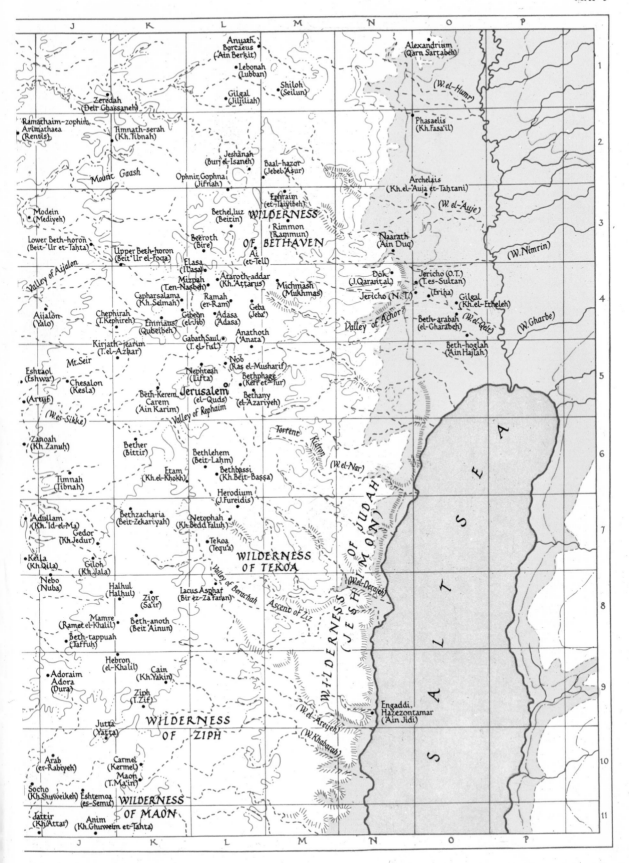

MAP 6

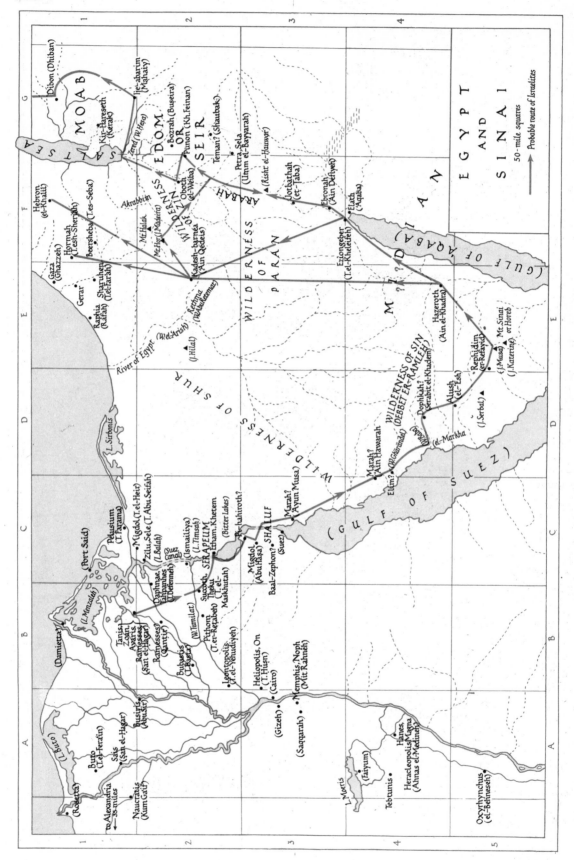

MAP 7

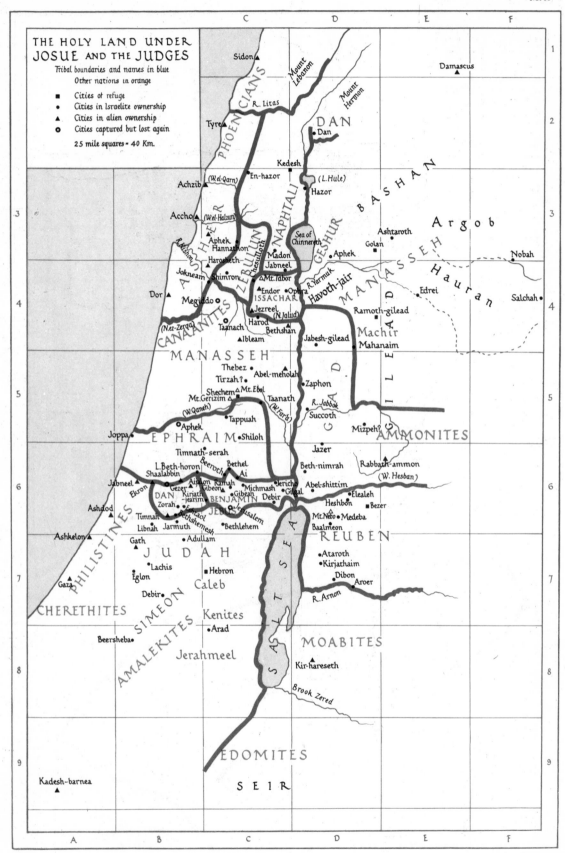

THE HOLY LAND UNDER
JOSUE AND THE JUDGES

Tribal boundaries and names in blue
Other nations in orange

■ Cities of refuge
• Cities in Israelite ownership
▲ Cities in alien ownership
○ Cities captured but lost again

25 mile squares = 40 Km.

Sidon

Damascus

Mount Lebanon

R. Litas

Mount Hermon

DAN

Tyre

PHOENICIANS

Dan

Kedesh

En-hazor

(L. Hule)

BASHAN

Achzib

(W. el-Qarn)

Hazor

NAPHTALI

Argob

Accho

(W. el-Halzun)

Ashtaroth

Nobah

Aphek

Hannathon

Golan

Aphek

Hauran

Harosheth

GESHUR

MANASSEH

Jokneam

Shimron

Madon

Jabneel

Edrei

Salchah

Dor

Megiddo

CHESULLOTH

ZEBULUN

Mt. Tabor

R. Yarmuk

Havoth-jair

(N. ez-Zerqa)

Endor

Ophra

ISSACHAR

Ramoth-gilead

CANAANITES

Jezreel

(N. Jalud)

Machir

Taanach

Harod

Bethshan

Jabesh-gilead

Ibleam

Mahanaim

MANASSEH

Thebez

Abel-meholah

Zaphon

G I L E A D

Tirzah?

Shechem

Mt. Ebal

Taanath

R. Jabbok

Mt. Gerizim

(W. Farh)

Succoth

Mizpeh?

(W. Qaneh)

Joppa

Tappuah

AMMONITES

EPHRAIM

Shiloh

Jazer

Timnath-serah

Beth-nimrah

L. Beth-horon

Beeroth

Bethel

Rabbath-ammon

Shaalabbin

Ai

(W. Hesban)

Jabneel

Ajalon

Ramah

Ekron

Gezer

Gibeon

Michmash

Jericho

Kiriath

DAN

-jearim

Gibeah

Gilgal

Abel-shittim

Zorah

BENJAMIN

Debir

Ashdod

Timnah

JEBUS

Heshbon

Elealeh

Bezer

Eshtaol

Jerusalem

Mt. Nebo

Medeba

Libnah

Jarmuth

Bethshemesh

Baalmeon

Ashkelon

Gath

Bethlehem

REUBEN

Adullam

PHILISTINES

JUDAH

Ataroth

Lachis

Hebron

Kirjathaim

CHERETHITES

Eglon

Dibon

Gaza

Debir

Caleb

Aroer

SIMEON

R. Arnon

Kenites

Arad

MOABITES

Beersheba

Jerahmeel

Kir-hareseth

AMALEKITES

Brook Zered

SALT SEA

EDOMITES

Kadesh-barnea

SEIR

MAP 8

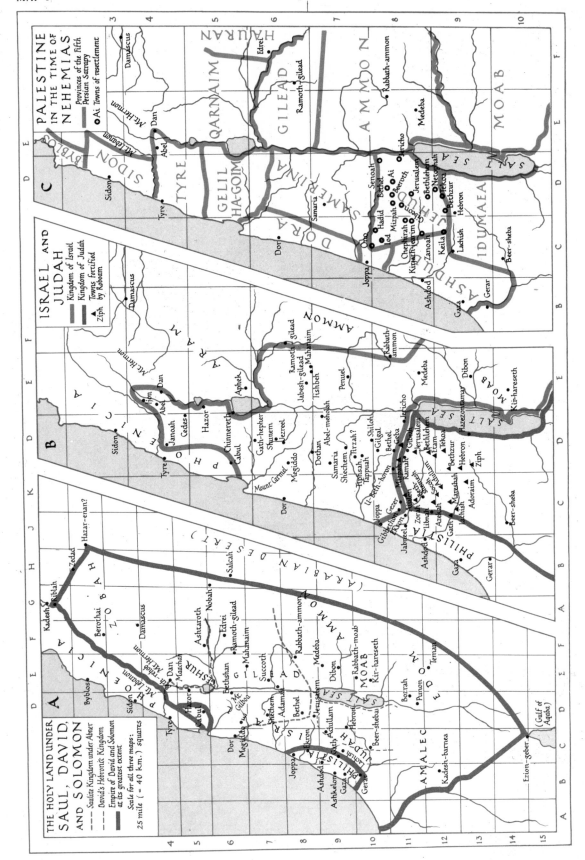

MAP 9

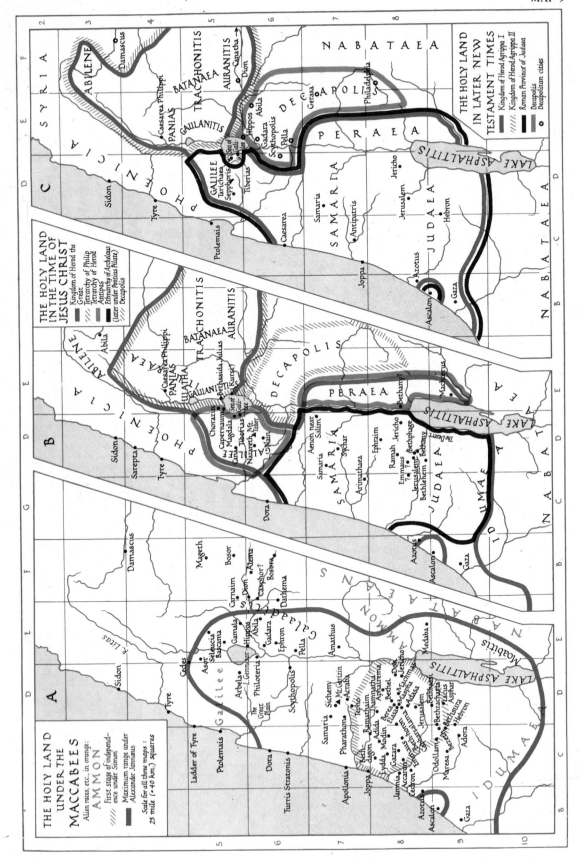

THE HOLY LAND UNDER THE MACCABEES

Alien races, etc., in orange: AMMON

First stage of independence under Simon

Maximum range under Alexander Jannaeus

Scale for all three maps: 25 mile (=40 km.) squares

THE HOLY LAND IN THE TIME OF JESUS CHRIST

Kingdom of Herod the Great
Tetrarchy of Philip
Tetrarchy of Herod Antipas
Ethnarchy of Archelaus (later under Pontius Pilate)
Decapolis

THE HOLY LAND IN LATER NEW TESTAMENT TIMES

Kingdom of Herod Agrippa I
Kingdom of Herod Agrippa II
Roman Province of Judaea
Decapolis
Decapolitan cities

MAP 10

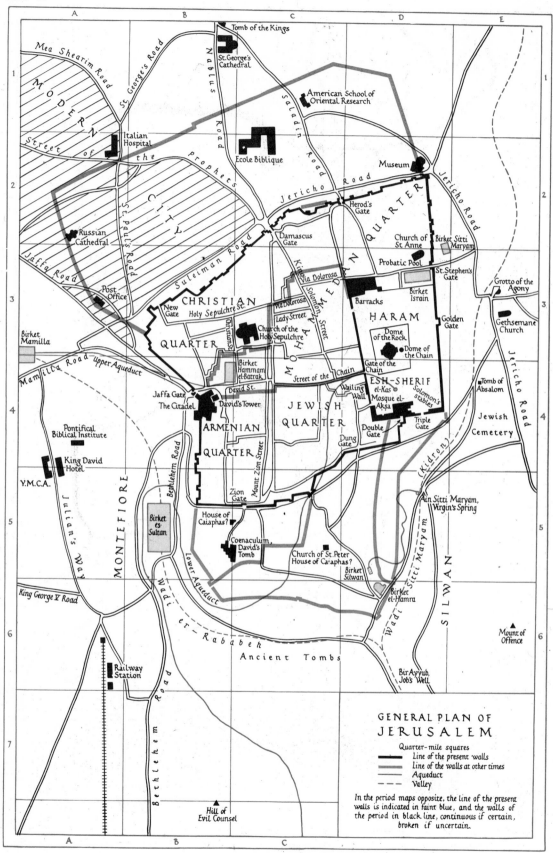

GENERAL PLAN OF
JERUSALEM

Quarter-mile squares

Line of the present walls

Line of the walls at other times

Aqueduct

Valley

In the period maps opposite, the line of the present
walls is indicated in faint blue, and the walls
of the period in black line, continuous if certain,
broken if uncertain.

MAP 11

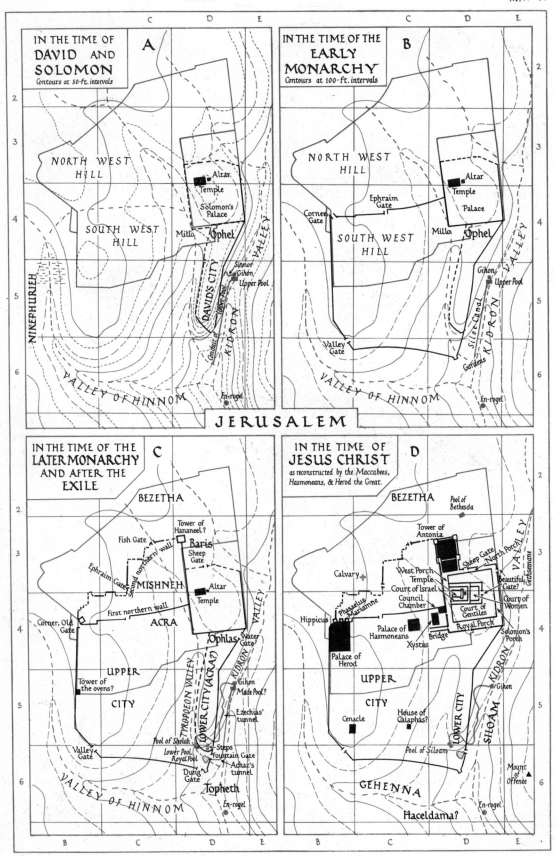

IN THE TIME OF DAVID AND SOLOMON
Contours at 50-ft. intervals

A

NORTH WEST HILL

SOUTH WEST HILL

NIKEPHURIEH

Altar
Temple
Solomon's Palace
Millo
Ophel
DAVID'S CITY
Sinnor
Gihon
Upper Pool
Conduit of Upper Pool
KIDRON VALLEY

VALLEY OF HINNOM

En-rogel

IN THE TIME OF THE EARLY MONARCHY
Contours at 100-ft. intervals

B

NORTH WEST HILL

SOUTH WEST HILL

Altar
Temple
Palace
Ephraim Gate
Corner Gate
Millo
Ophel
Gihon
Upper Pool
Siloe Canal
Valley Gate
Gardens
KIDRON VALLEY

VALLEY OF HINNOM

En-rogel

JERUSALEM

IN THE TIME OF THE LATER MONARCHY AND AFTER THE EXILE

C

BEZETHA

Fish Gate
Tower of Hananeel?
Baris
Sheep Gate
Ephraim Gate
Second northern wall
MISHNEH
Altar
Temple
First northern wall
Corner, Old Gate
ACRA
Ophlas
Water Gate
UPPER CITY
Tower of the ovens?
TYROPOEON VALLEY
LOWER CITY (ACRA)
KIDRON VALLEY
Gihon
Made Pool?
Ezechias' tunnel
Valley Gate
Pool of Shelah
Steps
Lower Pool, Royal Pool
Fountain Gate
Dung Gate
Achaz's tunnel
Topheth

VALLEY OF HINNOM

En-rogel

IN THE TIME OF JESUS CHRIST
as reconstructed by the Maccabees, Hasmoneans, & Herod the Great.

D

BEZETHA

Pool of Bethesda

Tower of Antonia
Calvary
Sheep Gate
North Porch
West Porch Temple
Court of Israel
Council Chamber
Court of Gentiles
Beautiful Gate?
Court of Women
Gethsemane
KIDRON VALLEY
Phasaelus
Hippicus
Mariamne
Palace of Hasmoneans
Xystus
Bridge
Royal Porch
Solomon's Porch
Palace of Herod
UPPER CITY
Cenacle
House of Caiaphas?
LOWER CITY
SILOAM
Gihon
KIDRON
Pool of Siloam
Mount of Offence

GEHENNA

Haceldama?

En-rogel

MAP 12

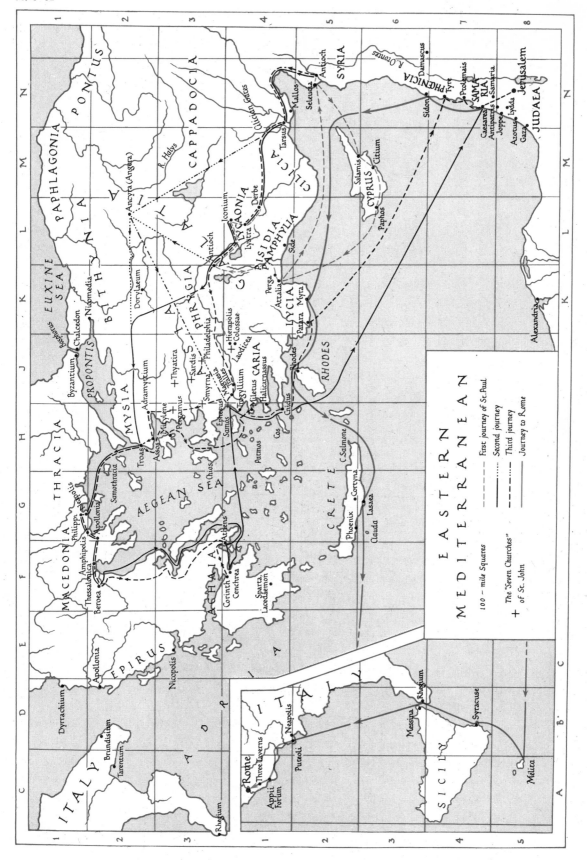

E A S T E R N
M E D I T E R R A N E A N

100 – mile Squares

The "Seven Churches"

✝ of St. John

First journey of St. Paul
Second journey
Third journey
Journey to Rome